Le Dictionnaire Hachette-Oxford Concise

Concise Oxford-Hachette French Dictionary

Concise
Oxford-Hachette
French Dictionary

French ·····⟩ English
English ·····⟩ French

Edited by
Marie-Hélène Corréard · Valerie Grundy

Third edition edited by
Jean-Benoit Ormal-Grenon · Natalie Pomier

Le Dictionnaire
Hachette-Oxford
Concise

français ----> anglais

anglais ----> français

Sous la direction éditoriale de

Marie-Hélène Corréard · Valerie Grundy

Nouvelle édition sous la direction éditoriale de

Jean-Benoit Ormal-Grenon · Natalie Pomier

OXFORD
UNIVERSITY PRESS

Great Clarendon Street, Oxford OX2 6DP

Oxford University Press is a department of the University of Oxford.
It furthers the University's objective of excellence in research, scholarship,
and education by publishing worldwide in

Oxford New York

Auckland Cape Town Dar es Salaam Hong Kong Karachi Kuala Lumpur
Madrid Melbourne Mexico City Nairobi New Delhi Shanghai Taipei Toronto

With offices in

Argentina Austria Brazil Chile Czech Republic France Greece
Guatemala Hungary Italy Japan South Korea Poland Portugal
Singapore Switzerland Thailand Turkey Ukraine Vietnam

Oxford is a registered trade mark of Oxford University Press
in the UK and in certain other countries

Published in the United States
by Oxford University Press Inc., New York

© Oxford University Press 1995, 1998, 2004

First edition published 1995
Second edition published 1998
This edition published 2004

British Library Cataloguing in Publication Data

Data available

Library of Congress Cataloging in Publication Data

Data available

OUP ISBN 978-0-19-860975-9
Hachette Livre ISBN: 2.01.280565.5
EAN : 9782012805651

© Oxford University Press 2000.

Adapté à la nomenclature du *Dictionnaire Hachette Oxford Concise* par les Éditions Hachette.

43, Quai de Grenelle, 75905 Paris Cedex 15

www.hachette-education.com

10 9 8 7 6 5 4 3
Typeset in Swift, Arial and Meta
by Intractive Sciences Ltd., Gloucester
Printed in Germany by Clausen & Bosse

Préface
Preface

La langue évolue en permanence. Les domaines d'activité ne cessent de se multiplier.

Au début du troisième millénaire, il nous a semblé nécessaire de rendre compte de ces mutations. Cette édition du *Dictionnaire Hachette Oxford Concise* a été établie à partir de la nouvelle édition du *Grand Dictionnaire Hachette Oxford* et des recherches menées au quotidien par les équipes éditoriales de Hachette et de Oxford University Press. Elle s'est enrichie de milliers de mots, acceptions et exemples nouveaux, apparus dans les langues française et anglaise au cours des dernières années.

Cet ouvrage comprend également des notes culturelles, au fil du texte, qui abordent des points spécifiques de la civilisation de la France et des pays anglophones. Sa nouvelle maquette et sa présentation en couleur permettront à l'utilisateur d'accéder rapidement à l'information recherchée.

Enfin, convaincus qu'un dictionnaire bilingue se doit d'être le reflet de son époque tant du point de vue de sa nomenclature que des outils d'aide à la communication qu'il propose, nous avons réorganisé et développé la partie "communication mode d'emploi", au centre de l'ouvrage, pour offrir à l'utilisateur une image plus complète des réalités linguistiques et culturelles de nos sociétés.

Direction
Ghislaine Stora

Responsable d'édition
Jean-Benoit Ormal-Grenon

Language is in a state of permanent evolution as the fields of human activity develop and proliferate. These changes cannot be ignored. This new edition of the *Concise Oxford-Hachette French Dictionary* has been compiled from the latest edition of the *Oxford-Hachette French Dictionary* and the on-going research undertaken by the editorial teams of Hachette Livre and Oxford University Press. It reflects the thousands of new words, meanings, and expressions which have come into French and English in the last few years.

In addition, this edition introduces cultural notes on aspects of life in English- and French-speaking countries and now has a completely redesigned colour layout to enhance the appearance and user-friendliness of the text. The popular "Guide to effective communication" has also been revised and the dictionary now provides the user with a comprehensive overview of the linguistic and cultural reality of the French- and English-speaking worlds.

Publishing Manager
Vivian Marr

Chief Editor
Natalie Pomier

Le Dictionnaire Hachette-Oxford Concise
Concise Oxford-Hachette French Dictionary

Nouvelle Édition/Third Edition

Direction éditoriale/Chief editors
Jean-Benoit Ormal-Grenon
Natalie Pomier

Deuxième Édition/Second Edition
Marie-Hélène Corréard
Valerie Grundy

Communication mode d'emploi/
Guide to effective communication
Marianne Chalmers
Élodie Vialleton

Notes culturelles/Cultural notes
Martine Bouiller
Mary O'Neill
Annie Sussel

Correctrices/Proofreaders
Elspeth Anderson
Isabelle Stables

Conseiller en lexicographie/
Lexicographical Adviser
Beryl Atkins

Français d'ailleurs/French outside France
Liliam Hurst
Dominique Péladeau

Notes d'usage lexicales et correspondence/
Lexical usage notes and correspondence
Hénri Béjoint
Richard Wakely

Assistés par
Ghislaine Ansieau
Lucy Atkins
Agnès Sauzet

Phonetique/Phonetics
Jane Stuart-Smith
Isabelle Vodoz

Consultants en terminologie/
Specialist terminology consultants
Centre de Recherche en Traduction et Terminologie
Université Lumière-Lyon II
Philippe Thoiron
Malcolm Harvey

University of Brighton
Tony Hartley
Malcolm Slater
Dimity Castellano

Anglo-américain/North American English
Charles Lynn Clark
Kristin Clayton

Table des matières
Contents

Dictionnaire français–anglais 1   **French–English dictionary 1**

Communication mode d'emploi   **Guide to effective communication**

Dictionnaire anglais–français 637   **English–French dictionary 637**

Appendices   **Appendices**

Remerciements
Acknowledgements

Nous tenons à remercier ici un certain nombre de personnes et d'organismes qui n'ont pas été mentionnés dans la liste des collaborateurs du projet, en particulier Beth Levin, de Northwestern University, qui nous a permis d'utiliser son travail sur la classification des verbes anglais.

Nous remercions également tous ceux qui nous ont aidés à constituer le corpus de français contemporain qui, avec le corpus d'anglais moderne d'Oxford, a joué un rôle linguistique important dans l'élaboration de ce dictionnaire. Nous remercions également tous ceux qui ont collaboré au grand *Dictionnaire Hachette–Oxford* et dont le travail a rendu possible le présent ouvrage.

Nous adressons nos remerciements à tous ceux qui nous ont apporté leur aide et fait bénéficier de leur savoir tout au long de notre entreprise.

The editors would like to extend their warmest thanks to a certain number of people and organizations not mentioned in the list of contributors, particularly Beth Levin of Northwestern University, who allowed us to make use of her work on English verb classification.

We are also indebted to all those who made it possible for us to build the corpus of contemporary French, which, with the Oxford Corpus of Modern English, has been the cornerstone of this dictionary. We thank too all the people who contributed to the unabridged *Oxford–Hachette French Dictionary* on which the present volume is based.

Finally we would like to thank all those people, too numerous to mention here, who have contributed their support and the benefit of their knowledge to the writing of this dictionary.

Les marques déposées

Les mots qui, à notre connaissance, sont considérés comme des marques ou des noms déposés sont signalés dans cet ouvrage par ®. La présence ou l'absence de cette mention ne peut pas être considérée comme ayant valeur juridique.

Note on proprietary status

This dictionary includes some words which have, or are asserted to have, proprietary status as trade marks or otherwise. Their inclusion does not imply that they have acquired for legal purposes a non-proprietary or general significance, nor any other judgement concerning their legal status. In cases where the editorial staff have some evidence that a word has proprietary status this is indicated in the entry for that word by the symbol ®, but no judgement concerning the legal status of such words is made or implied thereby.

Introduction

Le *Dictionnaire Hachette-Oxford Concise* a été rédigé à partir du grand *Dictionnaire Hachette-Oxford*. Nous en avons repris les principes et les avons adaptés pour des utilisateurs moins expérimentés ou plus jeunes.

Le choix des traductions a fait l'objet d'un soin particulier. En règle générale, à chaque acception d'un mot correspond une seule traduction. Cette traduction a été vérifiée dans les très nombreux exemples de langue réelle tirés de nos corpus électroniques (voir p. xiii). On ne trouvera deux ou plusieurs traductions équivalentes que dans les rares cas où elles sont vraiment interchangeables. Les mots sont accompagnés de leurs structures grammaticales usuelles et de la traduction de ces structures.

Divers éléments (indicateurs de contexte et/ou indicateurs de collocations, décrits en détail dans *Comment se servir du dictionnaire?*, p. xxi) distinguent une acception et ses différentes nuances. Il est ainsi facile de choisir la traduction la plus appropriée.

Pour faciliter l'accès à l'information, les mots composés anglais et les mots composés français avec trait d'union figurent à leur place, dans l'ordre alphabétique.

La presentation des verbes à particule anglais met en évidence la position du complément.

La nomenclature anglaise accorde une large place à l'anglo-américain et les usages purement britanniques ou anglo-américains sont spécifiés comme tels. La nomenclature française prend en compte le français des pays francophones autres que la France. Dans la partie français-anglais, nous offrons en traduction les variantes graphiques ou lexicales de l'anglo-américain chaque fois que cela s'impose.

Pour répondre plus complètement aux besoins de l'utilisateur, nous lui proposons, pour aborder la langue qu'il apprend, des outils supplémentaires sous forme de notes d'usage sur le lexique et sur les mots grammaticaux, des modèles de correspondance, des tableaux de conjugaison, des organigrammes, etc.

On trouvera au fil du dictionnaire ces notes d'usage dont l'objectif est d'aider l'utilisateur qui apprend une langue étrangère. Elles présentent les particularités d'expression de l'une et l'autre langue. Elles sont rédigées en français dans la partie français-anglais et en anglais dans la partie anglais-français pour permettre à l'utilisateur de s'exprimer dans une langue qui n'est pas la sienne.

Notes d'usage lexicales

Elles apparaissent en encadré dans le corps du dictionnaire. Elles donnent sous une entrée générique (pays, langue, couleur, jour de la semaine, âge, date, etc.), l'essentiel des exemples de constructions qu'on ne peut, faute de place, faire figurer sons chacun des mots spécifiques qui constituent cet ensemble générique. La liste de ces notes lexicales se trouve p. 1355.

Notes culturelles

Les notes culturelles apparaissent au fil du texte dans l'ordre alphabétique. Elles abordent des points spécifiques de la civilisation et des institutions de la France, du Royaume-Uni et des États-Unis

Notes d'usage grammaticales

Elles mettent en évidence la façon dont les mots lexicaux s'articulent autour des mots grammaticaux pour donner un sens aux phrases. Elles rassemblent des éléments essentiels d'usage et de structure. Les notes courtes figurent au début de l'article, les plus longues apparaissent en encadré à proximité de celui-ci.

Communication mode d'emploi

Les modèles de lettres sont classés par grands thèmes qui couvrent la correspondance privée, la correspondance commerciale, le voyage et l'emploi. Les lettres anglaises et les lettres françaises portant sur un même sujet sont placées sur des pages en vis-à-vis afin de pouvoir les comparer facilement.

Mots et expressions de liaison

Cette section propose une sélection de mots et expressions de liaison afin de mieux structurer les productions écrites.

Courrier électronique et Internet

Nous présentons le vocabulaire de base du courrier électronique et de l'Internet illustré d'exemples de messages électroniques et de pages web.

Petites annonces

La profusion des abréviations rend souvent les petites annonces difficiles à lire et à comprendre pour le lecteur non-averti. Nous proposons des exemples d'annonces et un lexique bilingue des abréviations courantes.

Introduction

This dictionary is based on the *Oxford–Hachette French Dictionary*. The editorial principles are similar to those applied in the larger dictionary and we have taken an equal degree of care to safeguard the interests of the various types of user. The entries have been simplified in order to make the dictionary more accessible to less experienced language learners.

Particular care has been taken in the selection of the translations. As a general rule, only one translation will be given for each sense of the headword. Each translation has been checked using our electronic corpora (see p. xi), which give us a wealth of examples of words in use in real, everyday circumstances. Where appropriate, other translations which have been found to work in more restricted contexts, will be shown in examples. The grammatical information necessary for using a translation is given wherever necessary.

Where nuances of meaning within a sense of the headword are translated in different ways, these nuances are pinpointed by semantic indicators and/or typical collocates. For a step-by-step guide to using this information to arrive at the most suitable translation, see the section *Using this Dictionary* on pp. xv–xx.

Headwords, compounds, and phrasal verbs stand out clearly on the page. For easy reference, English compounds and French hyphenated compounds are placed within the overall alphabetical order of headwords. Phrasal verbs are presented unambiguously and, for French users, clearly show the position of the noun object.

The dictionary has a wide coverage of North American as well as British English, and exclusively British or North American usage is marked. The French headword list includes vocabulary of French outside France.

For users working in a language not their own, access to the language is not confined to the individual dictionary entry. Leafing through the dictionary, they will find lexical usage notes, notes on function words, model letters, documents, advertisements, and verb tables.

Lexical usage notes

These are boxed notes which give the user facts about certain words that behave alike, for example names of countries, languages, colour terms, and days of the week and provide ways of discussing topics such as age dates, time and measurement.

Cross-references to the notes are given at all the relevant entries.

Cultural notes

Cultural notes are provided throughout the dictionary. They explain cultural and institutional aspects of life in France, the United Kingdom and the United States.

Notes on function words

The notes within or near function word entries are again intended for use by people seeking to work in a foreign language. They provide basic translation information on such grammatical words as pronouns, prepositions, and modal verbs.

The function word notes are readily identifiable in the dictionary. In cases where the information can be presented fairly briefly, the note will be found at the top of the entry, immediately under the headword. In cases where the necessary information is more lengthy and complex, the notes are boxed and clearly visible, appearing as close as possible to the headword concerned.

Guide to effective communication

A comprehensive set of model letters and documents, designed to help users to express themselves in a foreign language, is to be found in the centre of the dictionary. A list of the types of letters and documents is given on p. xxx.

French link words and expressions

This section provides a selection of words and expressions which contribute to well-structured writing.

French advertisements

These allow the user to make use of small ads in a foreign newspaper, which are often made incomprehensible by their extensive use of abbreviations. The sample advertisements, with accompanying guides to understanding them, are to be found on pp. xxx in the centre of the dictionary.

Using email and the Internet

This section provides a review of the basic language of email together with screen illustrations.

A corpus-based dictionary

The dictionary was written using two electronic databases or 'corpora', one French and one English.

A corpus is a database containing extracts from the text of books, newspapers, magazine articles, etc as well as transcripts of a variety of recordings of spoken language. In a matter of seconds, the computer finds and displays all the occurrences of a particular word in the corpus. The corpus contains some 1,500 concordance lines for the word *measure*, two samples of which are given below. The computer displays the various forms of a word along with those which come before and after it in the sentence. Fig. 1 shows the lines ordered alphabetically according to the words after *measure* and Fig. 3 according to those that come immediately before it. Displaying the word in context like this allows us to focus on important constructions and their relative frequency.

For an English–French entry, the English-speaking editor scanned the corpus for an overview of the various meanings of the word, for constructions that had to be included, for examples of usage, and for common collocations that should not be missed. The French-speaking editor also studied the English corpus in order to get a clear idea of the scope and range of meaning of the word. The French corpus offered the chance of checking exactly how a French word or phrase was used and comparing this with the way the headword was used in the English corpus. Was it safe to give a particular French word as a

measure /ˈmeʒə(r)/ ▶ p. 977, p. 1240, p. 723, p. 1311, p. 1323, p. 1191

A n **1** (unit) unité *f* de mesure; **weights and** ∼**s** les poids *mpl* et mesures *fpl*; **liquid** ∼ mesure *f* de capacité pour les liquides; **it's made to** ∼ (garment) c'est fait sur mesure, c'est du sur mesure; **2** (of alcohol) mesure *f*; **he gave me short** ∼ il a triché sur la quantité; **3** (device for measuring) instrument *m* de mesure; **4** (qualified amount, extent) **a** ∼ **of success** un certain succès; **a small** ∼ **of support** un soutien limité; **a good** *ou* **wide** ∼ **of autonomy** une grande autonomie; **in large** ∼ dans une large mesure; **in full** ∼ [*feel, possess, contribute*] pleinement; **5** (way of estimating) (of price rises) mesure *f*; (of success, anger) mesure *f*, indication *f*; (of efficiency, performance) critère *m*; **to be the** ∼ **of** donner la mesure de; **to give some** ∼ **of** donner une idée de [*delight, talent*]; **to use sth as a** ∼ **of** utiliser qch pour mesurer [*effects, impact*]; **this is a** ∼ **of how dangerous it is** ceci montre à quel point c'est dangereux; **beyond** ∼ [*change*] énormément; [*beautiful*] extrêmement; **it has improved beyond** ∼ il y a eu d'énormes progrès; **to take the** ∼ **of sb** jauger qn; **I have the** ∼ **of them** je sais ce qu'ils valent; **6** (action, step) mesure *f*; **to take** ∼**s** prendre des mesures; **safety** ∼ mesure de sécurité; **as a precautionary** ∼ par mesure de précaution; **as a preventive** ∼ à titre préventif; **as a temporary** ∼ provisoirement

B vtr **1** (assess size) mesurer [*length, rate, person*]; **to** ∼ **sth in** mesurer qch en [*metres*]; **to get oneself** ∼**d for** faire prendre ses mesures pour; **2** (have measurement of) mesurer; **to** ∼ **four by five metres** mesurer quatre mètres sur cinq; **a tremor measuring 5.2 on the Richter scale** une secousse de 5,2 sur l'échelle de Richter; **3** (assess) mesurer [*performance, ability*] (**against** à); **4** (compare) **to** ∼ **sth against** comparer qch à [*achievement*]

(Idioms) **for good** ∼ pour faire bonne mesure; **to do things by half-**∼**s** se contenter de demi-mesures

(Phrasal verbs)

■ **measure off**: ▶ ∼ **off [sth]** mesurer [*fabric*]
■ **measure out**: ▶ ∼ **out [sth]** mesurer [*land, flour, liquid*]; doser [*medicine*]; compter [*drops*]
■ **measure up**: ▶ ∼ **up** [person] avoir les qualités requises; **to** ∼ **up to** être à la hauteur de [*expectations*]; soutenir la comparaison avec [*achievement*]; ▶ ∼ **up [sth]** mesurer [*room etc*]

Fig 2

```
077989  takeovers between 1922 and 1988 . .PP The study 's main measure of an acquisition 's success
166340  ians from the land of Prester John . But the price was a measure of autonomy granted to what w
288665  r drink ? I 'm starving ! " .PP As Taff poured me a good measure of cider and handed me a boil
052886  e South-east , the CSO said they should not be used as a measure of comparative living standar
211311  cution of many millions of calculations . .PP The common measure of computer performance , MIP
@52886  that Matthaus can be both stagehand and leading man is a measure of his impact . Schillaci 's
402323   gendarmes have been introduced to an Oxford school is a measure of how seriously schools in O
177775  would make the APR more than 5,000 per cent _ at least a measure of how very little use follow
244999  enses all practically at the last . I think Gode has the measure of most men or women , at lea
009912  s , but mainly will just to allow the two men to get the measure of one another . <sect> Forei
220797  aluminium company whose arrival in Banbury had brought a measure of prosperity to the town in
037783  sks . ` For me at any rate , ` I reply . There will be a measure of relief even in Anna 's sor
009912  e Lambeth , they do not see a low registration rate as a measure of success . .PP Lambeth 's f
052886  at kind of cash . " Money was important to him only as a measure of success , ` to prove that
287166  wn . The oil companies , whose business depends in large measure on those cars , spend similar
052886  continuing refusal by BR to set targets against which to measure performance . A 24 per cent i
224156  ox have chosen . This move has been promoted as a safety measure , permitting slip when the to
009912  ast take advantage of its new opportunities and the West measure up to its new responsibilitie
009912  r of clubs in the Football League whose press facilities measure up to UEFA 's minimum standar
104055  ive , rather than an intellectual knowing . It cannot be measured by scientific instruments _
```

Fig 1

```
000790 jan in the Toscanini/Koussevitsky tradition , adding for good measure the name of Charles Mue
200317 ut . But he 'd done neither ! She silently swore and for good measure swore again . Then she
227590 r in the cream and stir well . Give one last beating for good measure . .PP Turn your mixture
155798 New Europe , with a sprinking of gardening thrown in for good measure , is Weidenfeld and Nic
320079 tic red , white , and blue bands with grey thrown in for good measure . The PTEs sport their
111836 ith Harold Lloyd and Fatty Arbuckle trivia thrown in for good measure ) , revealing that Keat
212161 ps Durham , Bristol , Edinburgh and Exeter thrown in for good measure . .PP A third explanati
009912 nd the soaps , are figuratively thrown into the ring for good measure . There is the daunting
006992 k to find some greenery and space for Flush and then for good measure he took a pencil and dr
```

Fig 3

translation of the English headword, or to translate an English phrase or idiom in a particular way? Were the English word and its French equivalent used in the same type of contexts? Did one have informal or technical overtones that the other did not have? We shall look at some real examples of what the corpus contributed to the dictionary in the case of the word *measure*.

A study of the corpus throws up many instances of as a [ADJECTIVE] *measure*—a construction so common that many users will be looking for it in the dictionary. Sense 6 (Fig. 2) therefore offers several examples of it, all of them taken directly from the corpus.

Ordering the concordance lines according to the word before the headword ('sorting on left context') highlighted other phrases and idioms, enabling the editors to see, for example, that the phrase *for good measure* was extremely common (Fig. 3 shows some of the 22 examples). The French editor's instinct was to translate it simply by *pour faire bonne mesure*, but even in such apparently straight-forward cases the editors

carry out routine checks. The translation offered must be adequate for all the contexts in which the English phrase is found and the editors must satisfy themselves that the French equivalent phrase appears in very similar contexts, i.e. that it does not have a much wider scope, or a much narrower one, than the phrase it is being used to translate. Here again, the French corpus was consulted: there were many examples of *pour faire bonne mesure*. In every case, the match between the two phrases was perfect, and the simple equivalence was recorded in the IDIOMS section of the dictionary entry.

The corpus formed the dictionary entries, shaping them to meet the needs of today's users, highlighting important constructions, exemplifying difficult meanings, focusing attention on common usages, leading the editors to subtle variations of meaning in English and French parallel constructions, helping them to pick out the best and safest translations for the headwords in all their many and varied uses.

B. T. S. Atkins

Un dictionnaire à partir de corpus

Le dictionnaire a été rédigé à partir de deux corpus électroniques, l'un français, l'autre anglais.

Un corpus est une base de données réunissant des textes imprimés et des transcriptions d'enregistrements d'origine et de nature très diverses. En quelques secondes l'ordinateur recense et affiche toutes les occurrences dans le corpus d'un mot donné. Le corpus contient quelque 1500 lignes de concordance du mot *measure* dont deux échantillons figurent ci-dessous. Les exemples sont présentés soit par ordre alphabétique des formes du mot recherché et des mots qui suivent (fig. 1), soit par ordre alphabétique des mots qui précèdent (fig. 3). Cette présentation du mot en contexte permet de repérer les constructions importantes et leur fréquence.

Pour chaque entrée de la partie anglais-français, le rédacteur anglophone a parcouru le corpus anglais pour avoir une vue d'ensemble des sens d'un mot, relever les constructions à inclure, trouver des exemples d'emplois particuliers et des collocations courantes à ne pas manquer. Le rédacteur francophone a également étudié le corpus anglais pour se faire une idée claire du domaine et des sens couverts par le mot en question. Ensuite, il a vérifié dans le corpus français l'emploi exact des mots ou expressions français afin de pouvoir établir une comparaison avec l'emploi de l'entrée dans le corpus anglais. Est-il bien prudent de donner tel mot français comme traduction de l'entrée anglaise, ou de

measure /ˈmeʒə(r)/ ► p. 977, p. 1240, p. 723, p. 1311, p. 1323, p. 1191

A n **1** (unit) unité f de mesure; **weights and ~s** les poids mpl et mesures fpl; **liquid ~** mesure f de capacité pour les liquides; **it's made to ~** (garment) c'est fait sur mesure, c'est du sur mesure; **2** (of alcohol) mesure f; **he gave me short ~** il a triché sur la quantité; **3** (device for measuring) instrument m de mesure; **4** (qualified amount, extent) **a ~ of success** un certain succès; **a small ~ of support** un soutien limité; **a good** ou **wide ~ of autonomy** une grande autonomie; **in large ~** dans une large mesure; **in full ~** [feel, possess, contribute] pleinement; **5** (way of estimating) (of price rises) mesure f; (of success, anger) mesure f, indication f; (of efficiency, performance) critère m; **to be the ~ of** donner la mesure de; **to give some ~ of** donner une idée de [delight, talent]; **to use sth as a ~ of** utiliser qch pour mesurer [effects, impact]; **this is a ~ of how dangerous it is** ceci montre à quel point c'est dangereux; **beyond ~** [change] énormément; [beautiful] extrêmement; **it has improved beyond ~** il y a eu d'énormes progrès; **to take the ~ of sb** jauger qn; **I have the ~ of them** je sais ce qu'ils valent; **6** (action, step) mesure f; **to take ~s** prendre des mesures; **safety ~** mesure f de sécurité; **as a precautionary ~** par mesure de précaution; **as a preventive ~** à titre préventif; **as a temporary ~** provisoirement

B vtr **1** (assess size) mesurer [length, rate, person]; **to ~ sth in** mesurer qch en [metres]; **to get oneself ~d for** faire prendre ses mesures pour; **2** (have measurement of) mesurer; **to ~ four by five metres** mesurer quatre mètres sur cinq; **a tremor measuring 5.2 on the Richter scale** une secousse de 5,2 sur l'échelle de Richter; **3** (assess) mesurer [performance, ability] (against à); **4** (compare) **to ~ sth against** comparer qch à [achievement]

⟨Idioms⟩ **for good ~** pour faire bonne mesure; **to do things by half-~s** se contenter de demi-mesures

⟨Phrasal verbs⟩

■ **measure off**: ► **~ off [sth]** mesurer [fabric]
■ **measure out**: ► **~ out [sth]** mesurer [land, flour, liquid]; doser [medicine]; compter [drops]
■ **measure up**: ► **~ up** [person] avoir les qualités requises; **to ~ up to** être à la hauteur de [expectations]; soutenir la comparaison avec [achievement]; ► **~ up [sth]** mesurer [room etc]

Fig 2

```
077989  takeovers between 1922 and 1988 . .PP The study 's main measure of an acquisition 's success
166340  ians from the land of Prester John . But the price was a measure of autonomy granted to what w
288665  r drink ? I 'm starving ! " .PP As Taff poured me a good measure of cider and handed me a boil
052886  e South-east , the CSO said they should not be used as a measure of comparative living standar
211311  cution of many millions of calculations . .PP The common measure of computer performance , MIP
@52886  that Matthaus can be both stagehand and leading man is a measure of his impact . Schillaci 's
402323  gendarmes have been introduced to an Oxford school is a measure of how seriously schools in O
177775  would make the APR more than 5,000 per cent _ at least a measure of how very little use follow
244999  enses all practically at the last . I think Gode has the measure of most men or women , at lea
009912  s , but mainly will just to allow the two men to get the measure of one another . <sect> Forei
220797  aluminium company whose arrival in Banbury had brought a measure of prosperity to the town in
037783  sks . ` For me at any rate , ` I reply . There will be a measure of relief even in Anna 's sor
009912  e Lambeth , they do not see a low registration rate as a measure of success . .PP Lambeth 's f
052886  at kind of cash . " Money was important to him only as a measure of success , ` to prove that
287166  wn . The oil companies , whose business depends in large measure on those cars , spend similar
052886  continuing refusal by BR to set targets against which to measure performance . A 24 per cent i
224156  ox have chosen . This move has been promoted as a safety measure , permitting slip when the to
009912  ast take advantage of its new opportunities and the West measure up to its new responsibilitie
009912  r of clubs in the Football League whose press facilities measure up to UEFA 's minimum standar
104055  ive , rather than an intellectual knowing . It cannot be measured by scientific instruments _
```

Fig 1

```
000790 jan in the Toscanini/Koussevitsky tradition , adding for good measure the name of Charles Mue
200317 ut . But he 'd done neither ! She silently swore and for good measure swore again . Then she
227590 r in the cream and stir well . Give one last beating for good measure . .PP Turn your mixture
155798 New Europe , with a sprinking of gardening thrown in for good measure , is Weidenfeld and Nic
320079 tic red , white , and blue bands with grey thrown in for good measure . The PTEs sport their
111836 ith Harold Lloyd and Fatty Arbuckle trivia thrown in for good measure ) , revealing that Keat
212161 ps Durham , Bristol , Edinburgh and Exeter thrown in for good measure . .PP A third explanati
009912 nd the soaps , are figuratively thrown into the ring for good measure . There is the daunting
006992 k to find some greenery and space for Flush and then for good measure he took a pencil and dr
```

Fig 3

traduire une expression de telle ou telle manière? Les termes anglais et français sont-ils utilisés dans le même genre de contextes? L'un d'eux a-t-il des nuances familières ou techniques que ne possède pas l'autre? Voyons, à partir d'exemples précis, en quoi, pour l'entrée *measure*, le corpus a contribué au dictionnaire.

L'étude du corpus fait ressortir plusieurs fois la structure *as a* [ADJECTIF] *measure*, dont la fréquence suggère que de nombreux lecteurs la chercheront dans le dictionnaire. La catégorie 6 (fig. 2) en donne donc plusieurs exemples, tous extraits du corpus.

En classant les lignes de concordance selon l'ordre alphabétique des mots qui se trouvent avant le terme choisi (classement dit 'selon le contexte gauche'), les rédacteurs se sont rendu compte que la locution *for good measure* était fréquemment employée (extraits tirés de 22 exemples en fig. 3). La première réaction du rédacteur français a été de la traduire par *pour faire bonne mesure*; mais même dans des cas apparemment aussi simples, les rédacteurs ont procédé aux vérifications d'usage. Une traduction donnée doit en effet s'adapter à tous les contextes

où apparaît la locution anglaise, et les rédacteurs doivent s'assurer que l'équivalent français apparaît dans des contextes très semblables, c'est-à-dire, qu'il n'a pas une portée plus large ni plus limitée que celle de l'expression qu'il traduit. Là encore, le corpus français a été consulté, et a offert de nombreux exemples de *pour faire bonne mesure*. Les deux versions étant parfaitement adaptées dans chaque cas, cette simple équivalence a été retenue dans la section IDIOMS de l'article.

Le corpus a servi à mettre en forme les articles de façon à ce qu'ils répondent aux besoins des utilisateurs d'aujourd'hui, en faisant ressortir les constructions importantes, en illustrant les acceptions difficiles, en attirant l'attention sur les emplois les plus fréquents, en amenant les rédacteurs à établir de subtiles nuances entre des constructions anglaises et françaises apparemment parallèles et en les aidant à choisir les traductions les mieux adaptées et les plus sûres pour les diverses acceptions de chaque entrée.

B. T. S. Atkins

Using this dictionary

Each entry in the dictionary is organized hierarchically, by grammatical category, then sense category. Grammatical categories are always in the same order. In the English–French part of the dictionary, the rule is that if the word has a use as an irregular inflected form, like the entry *left* for example, this will come first. Next will come the noun category, if there is one, then the adjective, then the adverb. Verbs, idioms, and phrasal verbs come last, in that order. The way the entry *kindly* is constructed is shown in the diagram below. To translate *he thought kindly of her*, you would go through the steps shown on the right. The section that follows gives other examples of how to get the best out of the dictionary for various kinds of translation task.

As a general rule, all meanings of a word are to be found in one single entry, provided they are pronounced in the same way, exclusive of stress shifts. English compounds have their own place in the alphabetical order of the dictionary, either as separate entries or, where several fall

together in the alphabet, grouped together under the first element.

The French–English entries follow a similar sequence, but adjectives precede nouns and non-hyphenated compounds appear together in a separate category at the end of the entry. French hyphenated compounds are given separate-entry status. On both sides of the dictionary, the order of sense categories reflects frequency of use, the most commonly used coming first. Within sense categories, distinctions between alternative translations are shown by means of sense indicators in round brackets and/or collocates giving typical context, which appear in square brackets.

❶ kindly /ˈkaɪndlɪ/
❷ A *adj* [*person, nature*] gentil/-ille; [*smile, interest*] bienveillant; **❸** [*face*] sympathique **❹**
B *adv* ① (in a kind way) avec gentillesse; **to speak ~ of sb** avoir un mot gentil pour qn; ② (*obligingly*) gentiment; **would you ~ do/refrain from doing** auriez-vous l'amabilité de faire/de ne pas faire; ③ (*favourably*) **to look ~ on** approuver [*activity*]; **to think ~ of** avoir une bonne opinion de; **to take ~ to** apprécier

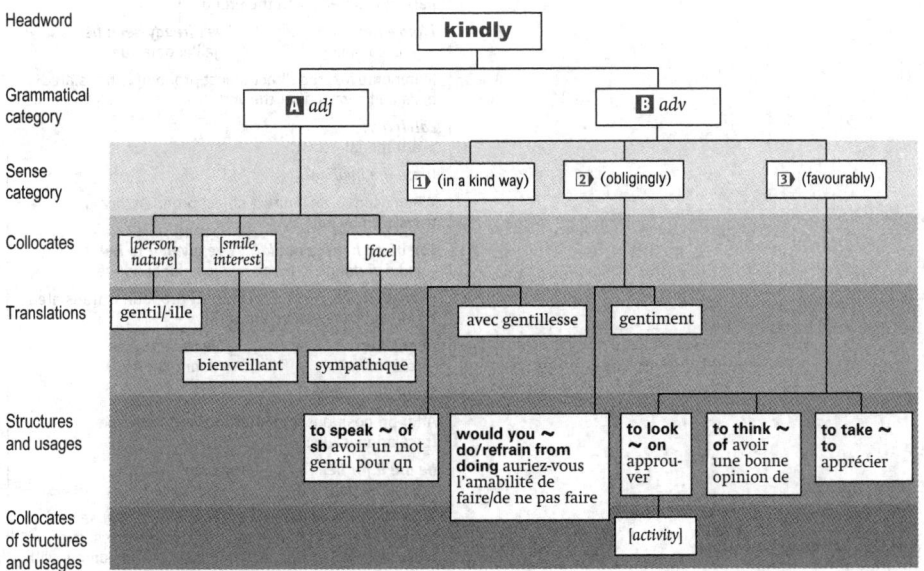

Headword		**kindly**
Grammatical category	**A** *adj*	**B** *adv*
Sense category		① (in a kind way) ② (obligingly) ③ (favourably)
Collocates	[*person, nature*] [*smile, interest*] [*face*]	
Translations	gentil/-ille	avec gentillesse gentiment
	bienveillant sympathique	
Structures and usages	**to speak ~ of sb** avoir un mot gentil pour qn	**would you ~ do/refrain from doing** auriez-vous l'amabilité de faire/de ne pas faire	**to look ~ on** approuver	**to think ~ of** avoir une bonne opinion de	**to take ~ to** apprécier
Collocates of structures and usages		[*activity*]

Using this dictionary

Goal 1	Translate	**he treated her kindly**

Process **1** Identify the problem word or phrase.

> **kindly**

---

2 Look up *kindly* and choose the appropriate grammatical category.

> **B** *adv*

kindly /'kaındlı/
A *adj* [*person, nature*] gentil/-ille; [*smile, interest*] bienveillant; [*face*] sympathique
B *adv* ① (in a kind way) avec gentillesse; **to speak** ∼ **of sb** avoir un mot gentil pour qn; ② (obligingly) gentiment; **would you** ∼ **do/refrain from doing** auriez-vous l'amabilité de faire/de ne pas faire; ③ (favourably) **to look** ∼ **on** approuver [*activity*]; **to think** ∼ **of** avoir une bonne opinion de; **to take** ∼ **to** apprécier

---

3 Choose the appropriate sense category.

> ① (in a kind way)

kindly /'kaındlı/
A *adj* [*person, nature*] gentil/-ille; [*smile, interest*] bienveillant; [*face*] sympathique
B *adv* ① (in a kind way) avec gentillesse; **to speak** ∼ **of sb** avoir un mot gentil pour qn; ② (obligingly) gentiment; **would you** ∼ **do/refrain from doing** auriez-vous l'amabilité de faire/de ne pas faire; ③ (favourably) **to look** ∼ **on** approuver [*activity*]; **to think** ∼ **of** avoir une bonne opinion de; **to take** ∼ **to** apprécier

---

4 Note the translation.

> avec gentillesse

kindly /'kaındlı/
A *adj* [*person, nature*] gentil/-ille; [*smile, interest*] bienveillant; [*face*] sympathique
B *adv* ① (in a kind way) avec gentillesse; **to speak** ∼ **of sb** avoir un mot gentil pour qn; ② (obligingly) gentiment; **would you** ∼ **do/refrain from doing** auriez-vous l'amabilité de faire/de ne pas faire; ③ (favourably) **to look** ∼ **on** approuver [*activity*]; **to think** ∼ **of** avoir une bonne opinion de; **to take** ∼ **to** apprécier

---

5 If necessary look up *treat* in the same way and *her* in the special grammatical note box, near the normal entry for *her*.

her

When used as a direct object pronoun, *her* is translated by *la* (*l'* before a vowel). Note that the object pronoun normally comes before the verb in French and that, in compound tenses like perfect and past perfect, the past participle agrees with the pronoun:

I know her	*I've already seen her*
= je la connais	= je l'ai déjà vue

In imperatives, the direct object pronoun is translated by *la* and comes after the verb:

catch her!
= attrape-la!

(*note the hyphen*)

When used as an indirect object pronoun, *her* is translated by *lui*:

I've given her the book	*I've given it to her*
= je lui ai donné le livre	= je le lui ai donné

In imperatives, the indirect object pronoun is translated by *lui* and comes after the verb:

phone her	*give them to her*
= téléphone-lui	= donne-les-lui

(*note the hyphens*)

After prepositions and after the verb *to be* the translation is *elle*:

he did it for her	*it's her*
= il l'a fait pour elle	= c'est elle

When translating *her* as a determiner (*her house* etc.) remember that in French possessive adjectives, like most other adjectives, agree in gender and number with the noun they qualify; *her* is translated by *son* +

Note the information on agreement.

Result	The translation	**il l'a traitée avec gentillesse**

| Goal 2 | Translate *a sophisticated nightclub* in the phrase | **they spent the rest of the evening in a sophisticated nightclub in Mayfair** |

Process	1 Look up *nightclub*. English compounds appear in alphabetical order in the wordlist. `nightclub`	**nightcap** /'naɪtkæp/ n 1▸ (hat) bonnet *m* de nuit; 2▸ (drink) **to have a** ~ boire quelque chose (avant d'aller se coucher) **nightclub** n boîte *f* de nuit **nightclubbing** n **to go** ~ aller en boîte○ **nightdress** n chemise *f* de nuit **nightie**○ /'naɪtɪ/ n chemise *f* de nuit **nightingale** /'naɪtɪŋɡeɪl, US -tng-/ n rossignol *m* **night**: ~**life** /'naɪtlaɪf/ n vie *f* nocturne; ~**-light** n veilleuse *f* **nightly** /'naɪtlɪ/ *adj* gén de tous les soirs; [*revels, visitor, disturbance*] littér nocturne
	2 Note the translation. `boîte f de nuit` Note the usage information in italics. *'f'* indicates feminine gender.	**nightclub** n boîte *f* de nuit
	3 Look up *sophisticated* and select the most appropriate numbered sense category. `1▸ (smart)`	**sophisticated** /sə'fɪstɪkeɪtɪd/ *adj* 1▸ (smart) [*person*] (cultured) raffiné, sophistiqué pej; (elegant) chic *inv*; [*clothes, fashion*] recherché; [*restaurant, resort*] chic *inv*; [*magazine*] sophistiqué; 2▸ (discriminating) [*mind, taste*] raffiné; [*audience, public*] averti; [*civilization*] évolué; 3▸ (elaborate, complex) [*equipment, technology*] sophistiqué; [*argument, joke*] subtil; [*style*] recherché
	4 Look for the noun collocate, in square brackets, which is closest to your context. `restaurant`	**sophisticated** /sə'fɪstɪkeɪtɪd/ *adj* 1▸ (smart) [*person*] (cultured) raffiné, sophistiqué pej; (elegant) chic *inv*; [*clothes, fashion*] recherché; [*restaurant, resort*] chic *inv*; [*magazine*]
	5 Note the translation. `chic`	**sophisticated** /sə'fɪstɪkeɪtɪd/ *adj* 1▸ (smart) [*person*] (cultured) raffiné, sophistiqué pej; (elegant) chic *inv*; [*clothes, fashion*] recherché; [*restaurant, resort*] **chic** *inv*; [*magazine*] sophistiqué; 2▸ (discriminating) [*mind, taste*] raffiné; [*audi-*
	6 Note the usage information in italics. `inv` This means that the form of the adjective *chic* does not change in the feminine or the plural.	**sophisticated** /sə'fɪstɪkeɪtɪd/ *adj* 1▸ (smart) [*person*] (cultured) raffiné, sophistiqué pej; (elegant) chic *inv*; [*clothes, fashion*] recherché; [*restaurant, resort*] chic *inv*; [*magazine*] sophistiqué; 2▸ (discriminating) [*mind, taste*] raffiné; [*audience, public*] averti; [*civilization*] évolué; 3▸ (elaborate, complex) [*equipment, technology*] sophistiqué; [*argument, joke*] subtil; [*style*] recherché

| **Result** | The translation of the whole sentence | **ils ont fini la soirée dans une boîte de nuit chic de Mayfair** |

· ·

Goal 3   Translate   **I've forgotten to bring my umbrella**

Process **1** Look up *forget* and choose the appropriate grammatical category.

        A *vtr*

forget /fə'get/ (*p prés* **-tt-**; *prét* **-got**; *pp* **-gotten**)
A *vtr* **1**) (not remember) oublier (**that** que; **to do** de faire; **how** comment); ~ **it!** (no way) n'y compte pas!; (drop the subject) laisse tomber!; (think nothing of it) ce n'est rien!; **2**) (put aside) oublier; **she'll never let me** ~ **it** elle n'est pas près de me le faire oublier; **3**) lit, fig (leave behind) oublier
B *vi* oublier
(Phrasal verb)
  ■ **forget about:** ► ~ **about [sth/sb]** (overlook) oublier

2 Choose the most appropriate numbered sense category.

       1) (not remember)

forget /fə'get/ (*p prés* **-tt-**; *prét* **-got**; *pp* **-gotten**)
A *vtr* **1**) **(not remember)** oublier (**that** que; **to do** de faire; **how** comment); ~ **it!** (no way) n'y compte pas!; (drop the subject) laisse tomber!; (think nothing of it) ce n'est rien!; **2**) **(put aside)** oublier; **she'll never let me** ~ **it** elle n'est pas près de me le faire oublier; **3**) lit, fig **(leave behind)** oublier
B *vi* oublier
(Phrasal verb)
  ■ **forget about:** ► ~ **about [sth/sb]** (overlook) oublier

3 Note the translation.

       oublier

forget /fə'get/ (*p prés* **-tt-**; *prét* **-got**; *pp* **-gotten**)
A *vtr* **1**) (not remember) **oublier** (**that** que; **to do** de faire; **how** comment); ~ **it!** (no way) n'y compte pas!; (drop the subject) laisse tomber!; (think nothing of it) ce n'est rien!; **2**) (put aside) oublier; **she'll never let me** ~ **it** elle n'est pas près de me le faire oublier; **3**) lit, fig (leave behind) oublier
B *vi* oublier
(Phrasal verb)
  ■ **forget about:** ► ~ **about [sth/sb]** (overlook) oublier

4 Look for the basic structure you need.

       to do

forget /fə'get/ (*p prés* **-tt-**; *prét* **-got**; *pp* **-gotten**)
A *vtr* **1**) (not remember) oublier (**that** que; **to do** de faire; **how** comment); ~ **it!** (no way) n'y compte pas!; (drop the subject) laisse tomber!; (think nothing of it) ce n'est rien!; **2**) (put aside) oublier; **she'll never let me** ~ **it** elle n'est pas près de me le faire oublier; **3**) lit, fig (leave behind) oublier
B *vi* oublier
(Phrasal verb)
  ■ **forget about:** ► ~ **about [sth/sb]** (overlook) oublier

5 Note the translation.

       de faire

forget /fə'get/ (*p prés* **-tt-**; *prét* **-got**; *pp* **-gotten**)
A *vtr* **1**) (not remember) oublier (**that** que; **to do de faire**; **how** comment); ~ **it!** (no way) n'y compte pas!; (drop the subject) laisse tomber!; (think nothing of it) ce n'est rien!; **2**) (put aside) oublier; **she'll never let me** ~ **it** elle n'est pas près de me le faire oublier; **3**) lit, fig (leave behind) oublier
B *vi* oublier
(Phrasal verb)
  ■ **forget about:** ► ~ **about [sth/sb]** (overlook) oublier

6 Use the translation of the basic structure to translate your sentence looking up at the appropriate place in the dictionary any other words you don't know how to translate.

Result   The translation   **j'ai oublié d'apporter mon parapluie**

Goal 4 Translate   **the police have sealed off the street**

Process **1** *Seal off* is a phrasal verb, so go to the end of the entry *seal* where you will find the phrasal verbs listed in alphabetical order, each verb clearly signalled by a square bullet.

■ seal off

seal /siːl/

A n ① Zool phoque m; ② Jur, gen (insignia) sceau m; **to set one's ~ on** lit apposer son cachet sur; fig conclure; **to set the ~ on** sceller [*friendship*]; confirmer [*trend, regime*]; **to give sth one's ~ of approval** approuver qch; **look for our ~ of quality** exigez le label de qualité; ③ (to keep intact) (on container) plomb m; (on package, letter) cachet m; (on door) scellés mpl; ④ (closure) fermeture f

B vtr ① cacheter [*letter*]; ② (close) sceller [*oil well, pipe*]; boucher [*gap*]; ③ (make airtight, watertight) fermer [qch] hermétiquement [*jar, tin*]; ④ fig sceller [*alliance*] (**with** par); conclure [*deal*] (**with** par); **to ~ sb's fate** décider du sort de qn

C sealed pp adj [*envelope*] cacheté; [*door*] scellé; [*orders*] sous pli cacheté; [*jar*] fermé hermétiquement

(Phrasal verbs)

■ **seal in** conserver [*flavour*]
■ **seal off**: ► ~ **[sth] off, ~ off [sth]** ① (isolate) isoler; ② (cordon off) gen boucler; barrer [*street*]
■ **seal up**: ► ~ **[sth] up, ~ up [sth]** fermer [qch] hermétiquement [*jar*]; boucher [*gap*]

---

2 Look for the appropriate phrasal verb pattern.

~ [sth] off, ~ off [sth]

■ seal off: ► ~ **[sth] off, ~ off [sth]** ① (isolate) isoler; ② (cordon off) gen boucler; barrer [*street*]

---

3 Select the appropriate sense category of the phrasal verb pattern.

② (cordon off)

■ seal off: ► ~ [sth] off, ~ off [sth] ① (isolate) isoler; ② (cordon off) gen boucler; barrer [*street*]

---

4 Select the appropriate collocate showing context for the translation, in this case typical objects of the verb translations.

street

■ seal off: ► ~ [sth] off, ~ off [sth] ① (isolate) isoler; ② (cordon off) gen boucler; barrer [*street*]

---

5 Identify the appropriate translation.

barrer

■ seal off: ► ~ [sth] off, ~ off [sth] ① (isolate) isoler; ② (cordon off) gen boucler; **barrer** [*street*]

---

6 Now construct the translation of the sentence, putting the verb in the correct tense and person.

Result The translation   **la police a barré la rue**

Using this dictionary

Goal 5	Translate	**chat échaudé craint l'eau froide**

| Process | 1 | Look up all the words you do not know and find a literal translation. If this does not make sense in your context, ask yourself whether the phrase could be an idiom, saying, or proverb. The answer is yes, because you can see immediately that cats and cold water have no relation to the wider context. | |

| | 2 | Select the word or words that you are least familiar with.

échaudé | |

| | 3 | Will this word appear in this form in the dictionary? No, *échaudé* is part of a verb. Look up the infinitive form.

échauder | **échauder** /eʃode/ [1] *vtr* ①(décourager) to put [sb] off; ②(ébouillanter) to scald
(Idiome) **chat échaudé craint l'eau froide** Prov once bitten, twice shy Prov |

| | 4 | Look for the phrase in the IDIOMS category.

(Idiome) **chat échaudé craint l'eau froide** | **échauder** /eʃode/ [1] *vtr* ①(décourager) to put [sb] off; ②(ébouillanter) to scald
(Idiome) **chat échaudé craint l'eau froide** Prov once bitten, twice shy Prov |

| | 5 | Note the information PROV which tells you that the expression is a proverb in French as its translation is in English.

Prov | **échauder** /eʃode/ [1] *vtr* ①(décourager) to put [sb] off; ②(ébouillanter) to scald
(Idiome) **chat échaudé craint l'eau froide** Prov once bitten, twice shy Prov |

| Result | The translation | **once bitten, twice shy** |

| Goal 6 | Understand the meaning of the acronym *SMIC* in the phrase | **ils sont payés au SMIC** |

| Process | 1 | Look up *SMIC* and follow the indication provided by the arrowed cross-reference. | **SMIC** /smik/ *nm*: *abbr* ► **salaire** |

| | 2 | Look up *salaire*. | |

| | 3 | Scan the entry for *SMIC*. Abbreviations and acronyms will always be in the compound block at the end of the entry.

SMIC | **salaire** /salɛʀ/ *nm* ① (paie) salary; (à la journée, à l'heure, à la semaine) (taux) wage; (somme) wages (*pl*); ~ **annuel/mensuel** annual/monthly salary; ~ **brut/net** gross/take-home pay; ~ **de misère** or **famine** starvation wage; ② fig (récompense) reward (**de** for); (châtiment) punishment (**de** for)
(Composés) ~ **de base** basic salary GB, base pay US; ~ **d'embauche** starting salary; ~ **minimum interprofessionnel de croissance**, **SMIC** guaranteed minimum wage; ~ **unique** single income |

| | 4 | Note the full form of the acronym.

salaire minimum interprofessionnel de croissance | (Composés) ~ **de base** basic salary GB, base pay US; ~ **d'embauche** starting salary; ~ **minimum interprofessionnel de croissance**, **SMIC** guaranteed minimum wage; ~ **unique** single income |

| Result | The explanation or, as in this case, the equivalent | **guaranteed minimum wage** |

Comment se servir du dictionnaire?

Les articles du dictionnaire ont une structure hiérarchisée; ils sont subdivisés en catégories grammaticales (introduites par des majuscules sur fond bleu et présentées dans un ordre fixe) qui sont elles-mêmes subdivisées en catégories sémantiques (introduites par des chiffres arabes). Les catégories sémantiques et les nuances de sens sont différenciées par des indicateurs sémantiques et/ou des indicateurs de collocations et apparaissent selon un ordre qui donne la priorité aux sens les plus fréquents. Pour traduire *tiède* dans la phrase *boire tiède* la démarche à suivre est indiquée par les numéros dans la figure ci-contre. La structure hiérarchisée est illustrée ci-dessous avec l'arborescence de l'entrée *tiède*.

En règle générale, les homographes homophones ont été regroupés sous la même entrée sans tenir compte de l'étymologie; dans les autres cas, l'entrée est répétée et on lui a attribué un numéro d'homographe. Locutions idiomatiques et proverbes sont regroupés en fin d'article.

> **❶tiède** /tjɛd/
> **A** *adj* **①** lit (désagréablement) [*café, soupe*] lukewarm; [*bain*] tepid; (agréablement) [*eau, air, nuit*] warm; [*saison, température*] mild; **②** fig (sans enthousiasme) lukewarm
> **B** *nmf* (membre d'un parti, groupe) pej lukewarm *ou* half-hearted
> **❷** supporter; **❸** pej half-hearted believer
> **C** *adv* **servez ~** serve slightly warm; **dépêche-toi ou tu vas manger ~** hurry up or your food will get cold; **il fait ~** (dehors) it's mild; (dedans) it's nice and warm

Certaines caractéristiques liées à la structure de la langue sont particulières à un côté du dictionnaire. Ainsi dans la partie français-anglais, les mots composés sans trait d'union sont regroupés alphabétiquement en fin d'article.

Dans la partie anglais-français les verbes à particule apparaissent toujours en fin d'article, dans l'ordre alphabétique. Les mots composés sont à leur place dans la nomenclature. On trouvera dans les pages suivantes quelques exemples d'utilisation du dictionnaire tant pour la compréhension que pour la traduction en anglais.

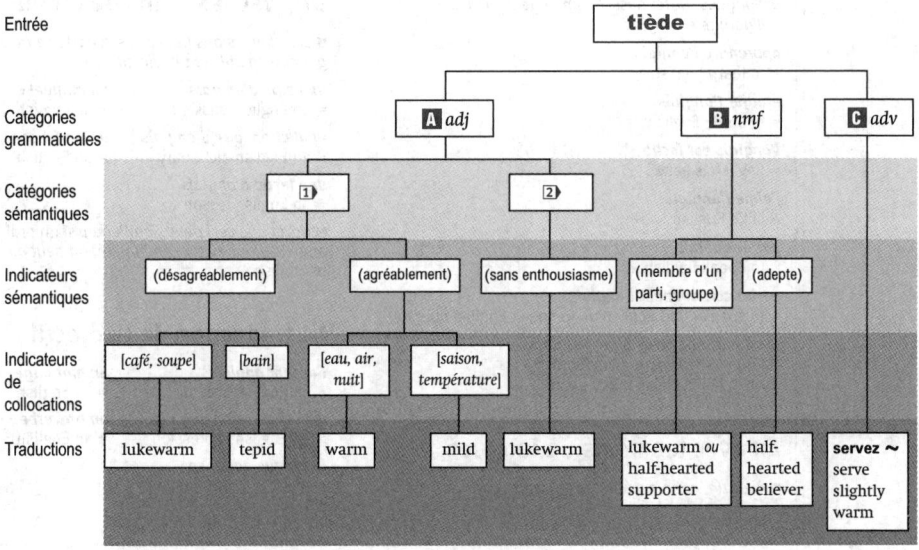

Entrée								tiède		
Catégories grammaticales					**A** *adj*				**B** *nmf*	**C** *adv*
Catégories sémantiques				**①**			**②**			
Indicateurs sémantiques		(désagréablement)		(agréablement)		(sans enthousiasme)		(membre d'un parti, groupe)	(adepte)	
Indicateurs de collocations	[*café, soupe*]	[*bain*]	[*eau, air, nuit*]	[*saison, température*]					
Traductions	lukewarm	tepid	warm	mild	lukewarm	lukewarm *ou* half-hearted supporter	half-hearted believer	**servez ~** serve slightly warm

. . . .

Objectif 1 Traduire | **j'apprends le finnois**

Méthode 1 Rechercher les mots inconnus en anglais. La traduction du substantif est

Finnish

finnois, ~**e** /finwa, az/ ▶ p. 336
A *adj* Finnish
B *nm* Ling Finnish

---

2 Noter le renvoi à une note d'usage lexicale, ici la note sur les langues.

▶ p. 336

finnois, ~**e** /finwa, az/ ▶ p. 336
A *adj* Finnish
B *nm* Ling Finnish

---

3 Toutes les informations nécessaires à la traduction sont fournies dans le premier exemple, il est inutile de faire d'autres recherches.

Penser à utiliser la forme progressive pour rendre l'idée de processus (être en train de).

Les langues

■ *Les adjectifs comme* anglais *peuvent aussi qualifier des personnes:* un touriste anglais (▶ p. 561) *et des choses:* la cuisine anglaise (▶ p. 333). *Dans les expressions suivantes,* English *est pris comme exemple; les autres noms de langues s'utilisent de la même façon.*

Les noms de langues

■ *L'anglais n'utilise pas l'article défini devant les noms de langues. Noter aussi l'emploi de la majuscule, obligatoire en anglais.*

apprendre l'anglais
= to learn English

étudier l'anglais
= to study English

l'anglais est facile
= English is easy

j'aime l'anglais
= I like English

parler anglais
= to speak English

parler couramment l'anglais
= to speak good English *ou* to speak English fluently

je ne parle pas très bien l'anglais
= I don't speak very good English
  ou my English isn't very good

En *avec les noms de langues*

■ *Avec un verbe,* en ang~~~ se traduit par in ~

une émission en anglais
= an English-language broadcast

* *Noter que* an English book *est ambigu, t~~~* un livre français, *qui peut signifier un liv~~~ ou un livre qui vient de France.*

Mais attention:

traduire en anglais
= to translate into English

De *avec les noms de langu~~~*

■ *Les expressions françaises avec de se tr~~~ général en utilisant l'adjectif.*

un cours d'anglais   **un manuel ~~~**
= an English class   = an English~~~

un dictionnaire d'anglais   **un professe~~~**
= an English dictionary   = an English~~~

une leçon d'anglais
= an English lesson

■ *Noter que ceci peut signifier aussi* un pro~~~ anglais. *Pour éviter l'ambiguïté, on peut di~~~* of English.

La traduction de l'adjectif ~~~

l'accent anglais   **un mot ang~~~**
= an English accent   = an English~~~

une expression anglaise   **un proverbe~~~**
= an English expression   = an English~~~

la langue anglaise
= the ~~~ language

Résultat Traduction | **I'm learning Finnish**

Comment se servir du dictionnaire?

Objectif 2 Traduire **il neigeait à notre départ de Moscou**

Méthode 1 Rechercher l'entrée *neiger* dans la nomenclature. L'exemple et sa traduction sont au présent et la phrase à traduire est à l'imparfait, il suffit de changer le temps.

> it was snowing

neiger /nɛʒe/ [13] *v impers* to snow; **il neige** it's snowing

2 Rechercher l'entrée *départ* dans la nomenclature et choisir la catégorie sémantique adéquate. La première convient exactement. Une traduction générale est fournie.

> departure

départ /depaʀ/ *nm* ⓵ (d'un lieu) departure; ∼ **des grandes lignes**/**des lignes de banlieue** Rail (platforms for) main line/suburban departures; **téléphone avant ton** ∼ phone before you leave; **se donner rendez-vous au** ∼ **du car** (au lieu) to arrange to meet at the bus; **vols quotidiens au** ∼ **de Nice** daily flights from Nice; **le train a pris du retard au**

3 Mais un des exemples donnés plus bas a des points communs avec la phrase à traduire.

> **téléphone avant ton** ∼
> phone before you leave

Le groupe nominal *ton départ* est traduit par la tournure verbale *you leave*.

départ /depaʀ/ *nm* ⓵ (d'un lieu) departure; ∼ **des grandes lignes**/**des lignes de banlieue** Rail (platforms for) main line/suburban departures; **téléphone avant ton** ∼ phone before you leave; **se donner rendez-vous au** ∼ **du car** (au lieu) to arrange to meet at the bus; **vols quotidiens au** ∼ **de Nice** daily flights from Nice; **le train a pris du retard au** ∼ **de Lyon** the train was late leaving Lyons; **être sur le** ∼ to be about to leave; **il n'y a qu'un** ∼ **du courrier par jour** the post GB *ou* mail US only goes once a day; ⓶ (exode) exodus (**vers** to); ⓷ (d'une fonction, organisation) departure; (démission) resignation; **le** ∼ **en retraite** retirement; ⓸ Sport start; ∼ **arrêté**/**décalé**/**lancé** standing/staggered/flying start; **prendre le** ∼ (d'une course) to be among the starters; **prendre un nouveau** ∼ fig to make a fresh start; ⓹ (début) start; **au** ∼ (d'abord) at first; (au début) at the outset; **langue de** ∼ source language; **salaire de** ∼ starting salary; **capital de** ∼ start-up capital

4 Pour trouver la construction qui nous intéresse il faut consulter l'entrée *leave* toujours en employant la même méthode: rechercher dans la nomenclature, choisir la catégorie grammaticale qui convient et la parcourir en détail.

Un exemple peut servir utilement de modèle car il contient la tournure verbale *he left* suivie de l'indication du lieu *home*.

leave /liːv/
Ⓐ *n* ⓵ (also ∼ **of absence**) (time off) gen congé *m*; Mil permission *f*; **to take three days'** ∼ prendre trois jours de congé; ⓶ (permission) autorisation *f*; **to give sb** ∼ **to do** donner à qn l'autorisation de faire; **by** *ou* **with your** ∼ avec votre permission; ⓷ (departure) **to take** ∼ **of sb** prendre congé de qn; **he took his** ∼ il a pris congé
Ⓑ *vtr* (*prét*, *pp* **left**) ⓵ (depart from) gen partir de [*house, station etc*]; (more permanently) quitter [*country, city etc*]; (by going out) sortir de [*room, building*]; **he left home early** il est parti tôt de chez lui; **to** ∼ **school** (permanently) quitter l'école; **to** ∼ **the road**/**table** quitter la route/table; **to** ∼ **the track** [*train*] dérailler; **to** ∼ **the ground** [*plane*] décoller; **to** ∼ **one's seat** se lever; **I left him cleaning his car** quand je suis parti, il nettoyait sa voiture; **the smile left her face** fig

5 Il ne reste plus qu'à trouver la traduction de *Moscou*.

Moscou /mɔsku/ ► p. 621 *npr* Moscow

Résultat La traduction n'est pas strictement parallèle au texte français mais elle est exacte et naturelle en anglais.

it was snowing when we left Moscow

Comment se servir du dictionnaire?

Objectif 3 Traduire *to advertise* dans la phrase | **there's no need to advertise our weak points**

Méthode **1** Rechercher *advertise* et choisir la catégorie grammaticale pertinente.

    A *vtr*

advertise /ˈædvətaɪz/
A *vtr* ❶ (for publicity) faire de la publicité pour {*product, service*}; annoncer {*price, rate*}; ❷ (for sale) mettre *or* passer une annonce pour {*car, house*}; ❸ mettre *or* passer une annonce pour {*job, vacancy*}; ❹ (make known) signaler {*presence*}; afficher {*weakness*}; **I wouldn't ~ the fact** à votre place, je n'en ferais pas état
B *vi* ❶ (for sales, publicity) faire de la publicité; ❷ (for staff) passer une annonce

2 Passer en revue toutes les traductions principales données dans cette catégorie grammaticale et choisir celle qui se rapproche du contexte.

    afficher [*weakness*]

advertise /ˈædvətaɪz/
A *vtr* ❶ (for publicity) faire de la publicité pour {*product, service*}; annoncer {*price, rate*}; ❷ (for sale) mettre *or* passer une annonce pour {*car, house*}; ❸ mettre *or* passer une annonce pour {*job, vacancy*}; ❹ (make known) signaler {*presence*}; afficher {*weakness*}; **I wouldn't ~ the fact** à votre place, je n'en ferais pas état
B *vi* ❶ (for sales, publicity) faire de la publicité; ❷ (for staff) passer une annonce

---

Résultat Traduction | **il est inutile d'afficher nos points faibles**

Objectif 4 Traduire *make out* dans la phrase | **I couldn't make out what he was saying**

Méthode **1** Rechercher l'entrée *make*. Rechercher les verbes à particule clairement signalés à la fin de l'article.

■ **make for**: ▶ ~ **for [sth]** ❶ (head for) se diriger vers; ❷ (help create) permettre, assurer; ▶ ~ **for [sb]** ❶ (attack) se jeter sur; ❷ (approach) se diriger vers
■ **make good**: ▶ ~ **good** réussir; ▶ ~ **good [sth]** ❶ réparer {*damage, omission*}; rattraper {*lost time*}; combler {*deficit*}; ❷ tenir {*promise*}
■ **make off** filerᴼ; **to ~ off with** se tirerᴼ avec
■ **make out**: ▶ ~ **out** ❶ (manage) s'en tirerᴼ; ❷ ᴼUS

2 Rechercher *make out* dans les verbes à particule présentés alphabétiquement.

3 Rechercher la structure qui se rapproche le plus de celle à traduire c'est-à-dire la forme transitive présentée de la façon suivante.

    ▶ ~ **out [sth], ~ [sth] out**

■ **make out**: ▶ ~ **out** ❶ (manage) s'en tirerᴼ; ❷ ᴼUS (grope) se peloterᴼ; ❸ (claim) affirmer (**that** que); ▶ ~ **out [sth], ~ [sth] out** ❶ (see, distinguish) distinguer; ❷ (claim) to ~ **sth out to be** prétendre que qch est; ❸ (understand, work out) comprendre (**if** si); **I can't ~ him out** je n'arrive pas à le comprendre; ❹ (write out) faire, rédiger; **to ~ out a cheque to sb** faire un chèque à qn; **it is made out to X** il est à l'ordre de X; ❺ (expound) **to ~ out a case for** argumenter en faveur de; ▶ ~ **oneself out to be** prétendre être {*rich, brilliant*}; faire semblant d'être {*stupid, incompetent*}

4 Examiner les traductions fournies.

Choisir celle qui convient au contexte.

    comprendre

■ **make out**: ▶ ~ **out** ❶ (manage) s'en tirerᴼ; ❷ ᴼUS (grope) se peloterᴼ; ❸ (claim) affirmer (**that** que); ▶ ~ **out [sth], ~ [sth] out** ❶ (see, distinguish) distinguer; ❷ (claim) to ~ **sth out to be** prétendre que qch est; ❸ (understand, work out) comprendre (**if** si); **I can't ~ him out** je n'arrive pas à le comprendre; ❹ (write out) faire, rédiger; **to ~ out a cheque to sb** faire un chèque à qn; **it is made out to X** il est à l'ordre de X; ❺ (expound) **to ~ out a case for** argumenter en faveur de; ▶ ~ **oneself out to be** prétendre être {*rich, brilliant*}; faire semblant d'être {*stupid, incompetent*}

Résultat Traduction | **je n'arrivais pas à comprendre ce qu'il disait**

Objectif 5   Comprendre *AGM* dans la phrase

the Chamber of Commerce is holding its AGM on Wednesday

Méthode   **1**   Rechercher l'entrée dans la nomenclature. *AGM* est une abréviation dont la traduction est fournie à la forme développée comme l'indique un renvoi.

AGM *n: abrév* ► **Annual General Meeting**

> ► **Annual General Meeting**

2   L'entrée *Annual General Meeting* se trouve dans la nomenclature et elle est suivie de l'abréviation qui est répétée.

Annual General Meeting, AGM *n* assemblée *f* générale annuelle

> **AGM**

Noter que l'emploi des majuscules diffère entre les deux langues.

Résultat   Glose explicative ou, dans le cas présent, traduction de *AGM*.

assemblée générale annuelle

Objectif 6   Traduire

green about the gills

Méthode   **1**   Le mot qui pose un problème de compréhension est *gills*. En supposant qu'il s'agit d'un substantif au pluriel, l'entrée recherchée sera *gill*.

2   Le mot figure sous deux entrées repérées par un numéro d'homographe en raison d'une différence de prononciation.

gill¹ /gɪl/ *n* (of fish) branchie *f*
⟨Idiom⟩ green about the **~s**○ blanc/blanche comme un linge
gill² /dʒɪl/ ► p. 723 *n* (measure) quart *m* de pinte

Pour chaque entrée une traduction est fournie mais l'expression *green about the gills* reste difficile à comprendre.

3   S'agit-il d'une locution figée? Si oui, elle figurera en fin d'article sous la rubrique ɪᴅɪᴏᴍꜱ.

gill¹ /gɪl/ *n* (of fish) branchie *f*
⟨Idiom⟩ green about the **~s**○ blanc/blanche comme un linge

> ⟨Idiome⟩

L'article *gill¹* comporte une telle rubrique et l'expression recherchée y figure.

Résultat   La traduction rend le sens de l'expression, pas celui des mots qui la composent.

blanc comme un linge

The structure of French-English entries

headword ——— **bagage** /bagaʒ/ ——————————————— IPA pronunciation

    A *nm* ① (effets) luggage; (de soldat) kit; ② (sac, valise) piece of
    luggage; ③ *fig* (connaissances) knowledge; (diplômes) qualifi-
    cations (*pl*); (expérience) credentials (*pl*)

part of speech plus gender ——— **B bagages** *nmpl* luggage ¢; **faire/défaire ses** ∼**s** to pack/
    unpack (one's suitcases)

compounds in block at end ——— (Composé) ∼ **à main** hand luggage, carry-on baggage US
of entry   (Idiomes) **plier** ∼○ to pack up and go; **partir avec armes et** ——— idioms in block at end of
    ∼**s** to up sticks and leave; **passer à l'ennemi avec armes**   entry
    et ∼**s** to defect

    bagarre /bagaʀ/ *nf* ① (empoignade) fight (**entre** between);
    ∼**s avec la police** clashes with the police; ∼ **générale** ——— examples
    free-for-all; ② *fig* (lutte) fight, struggle; (dispute) clash, con- ——— figurative use
    frontation; **entrer dans la** ∼ to join the fray

register symbol ——— **bagarrer**○; **se bagarrer** /bagaʀe/ [1] *vpr* to fight (**pour** ——— number of verb group,
    informal ○   for)   referring to the French verb
    very informal ❶   tables at the end of the
    vulgar or taboo ●   dictionary

feminine form of headword ——— **bagarreur**○, **-euse** /bagaʀœʀ, øz/
    A *adj* (agressif) aggressive; (combatif) **être** ∼ to like to pick a
    fight

plural form ——— **boyau**, *pl* ∼**x** /bwajo/
    A *nm* ① (intestin) gut; ② (pour raquette, violon) catgut; ③ (pour
    saucisse) casing; ④ (pneu) tubeless tyre GB *ou* tire US; ⑤ (pas- ——— grammatical category
    sage) back alley; ⑥ (tuyau flexible) hose   ——— Arabic sense number
    B ○**boyaux** *nmpl* (intestins) insides○

abbreviation ——— **BP** *written abbr* ► **boîte**   ——— cross-reference

The structure of English-French entries

headword — **mash** /mæʃ/
grammatical category — **A** n ⟨1⟩ Agric pâtée f; ⟨2⟩ (in brewing) trempe f; ⟨3⟩ ◦GB Culin purée f (de pommes de terre)
B vtr ⟨1⟩ (also ~ **up**) écraser [fruit]; **to ~ potatoes** faire de la — Arabic sense numbers
purée; ⟨2⟩ (in brewing) brasser

acronym — **MASH** /mæʃ/ n US (abrév = **mobile army surgical hos-** — part of speech
pital) unité f médicale de campagne — translation

IPA pronunciation showing — **mask** /mɑːsk, US **mæsk**/
North American variation **A** n gen masque m; (for eyes only) loup m
B vtr masquer [face]; dissimuler [truth, emotions]; masquer — typical object collocates
[taste, drug]

compounds in alphabetical — **mask**: **~ed ball** n bal m masqué; **~ing tape** n ruban
order m adhésif

mason /'meɪsn/ ► **p. 1181** n ⟨1⟩ Constr maçon m; ⟨2⟩ **Mason** — page number cross-
(also **Free~**) franc-maçon m reference to a lexical usage
note

abbreviation — **ME** n ⟨1⟩ Med abrév ► **myalgic encephalomyelitis**; ⟨2⟩ US — cross-reference to full form
Post abrév écrite = **Maine**; ⟨3⟩ Ling abrév ► **Middle English**;
North American usage ⟨4⟩ US Med abrév ► **medical examiner**

meadow /'medəʊ/ n ⟨1⟩ (field) pré m; ⟨2⟩ ¢ (also **~land**) — sense indicator
prés mpl, prairies fpl; ⟨3⟩ (also **water ~**) prairie f inondable

translation — **meadowsweet** n reine-des-prés f — gender of translation

North American variant — **meagre** GB, **meager** US /'miːgə(r)/ adj [income, sum,
spelling meal] maigre (before n); [living] chiche; [response, returns]
piètre (before n)

meal /miːl/ n ⟨1⟩ (food) repas m; **to enjoy one's ~** bien — example
manger; **to go out for a ~** aller (manger) au restaurant; — swung dash as substitute for
⟨2⟩ (from grain) farine f headword in examples
idioms in block at end of ⟨Idiom⟩ **don't make a ~ of it**◦! n'en fais pas tout un plat◦! — register symbol
entry **meal ticket** n ⟨1⟩ (voucher) ticket-repas m; ⟨2⟩ ◦fig (quality, ◦ informal
◑ very informal
separate entry for complex — **meal ticket** n ⟨1⟩ (voucher) ticket-repas m; ⟨2⟩ ◦fig (quality, ● vulgar or taboo
compound qualification) gagne-pain m inv; (person) **I'm just a ~ for you!**
pour toi je ne suis qu'un portefeuille!

Structure du texte français-anglais

entrée — **paillette** /pajɛt/ *nf* ⓵ (disque brillant) sequin, spangle US; **robe à ~s** a sequined *ou* spangled US dress; ⓶ (poudre brillante) glitter ¢; ⓷ (de roche) splinter; **savon en ~s** soap — information grammaticale sur la langue cible (mot non dénombrable)
flakes (*pl*)

transcription phonétique — **panier** /panje/ *nm* ⓵ (en osier, rotin, etc) basket; (corbeille à papier) wastepaper basket; (dans un lave-vaisselle) rack; **mettre** — exemple
or **jeter au ~** lit to throw [sth] out; fig to get rid of; ⓶ Sport (au basket-ball) basket; **marquer un ~** to score a basket; ⓷ (de jupe, robe) pannier; **robe à ~s** dress with panniers
(Composé) **~ à salade** (ustensile) salad shaker; (fourgon de police)○ Black Maria GB, paddy wagon US

(Idiomes) **être un ~ percé**○ to spend money like water; **ils** — idiomes regroupés en fin **sont tous à mettre dans le même ~**○ they are all much of d'article
a muchness GB, they are all about the same; **mettre tous ses œufs dans le même ~**○ to put all one's eggs in one basket; **le haut** *or* **dessus du ~**○ the pick of the bunch

sigle/acronyme — **PAO** /peao/ *nf* ⓵ *abbr* ► **production**; ⓶ *abbr* — renvoi à une entrée ► **publication**

forme du féminin — **parcheminé**, **~e** /paʁʃəmine/ *adj* ⓵ [*papier*] with a parchment finish (*épith*); ⓶ [*peau*] papery; ⓷ [*visage,* information sur l'existence *main*] shrivelled^{GB}
d'une variante
orthographique nord-
américaine (donnée sous **pare-brise** /paʁbʁiz/ *nm inv* windscreen GB, wind- — partie du discours l'entrée du côté shield US
anglais/français)

pare-chocs /paʁʃɔk/ *nm inv* bumper — mot composé avec trait d'union ayant valeur d'entrée à part entière

traduction avec sa variante **parking** /paʁkiŋ/ *nm* ⓵ (parc de stationnement) car park GB, nord-américaine parking lot US; (place de stationnement) parking space; ⓶ (stationnement) controv parking; **~ interdit** no parking

forme du pluriel — **passereau**, *pl* **~x** /pasʁo/ *nm* ⓵ gén passerine; ⓶ † (moineau) sparrow

patron, **-onne** /patʁɔ̃, ɔn/
catégorie grammaticale — **A** *nm,f* (directeur, gérant) manager, boss○; (propriétaire) owner, — indicateurs de niveau de boss○; **être son propre ~** to be one's own boss○ langue
B *nm* ⓵ (en couture) pattern; ⓶ (taille) large; **grand ~** extra-large
mots composés sans trait (Composés) **~ d'industrie** captain of industry; **~ de** d'union regroupés **pêche** skipper, master
alphabétiquement
peste /pɛst/ *nf* ⓵ ► p. 195 Méd plague; ⓶ ○(personne — renvoi à une note d'usage insupportable) pest○ lexicale
(Idiome) **je me méfie de lui comme de la ~**○ I don't trust him an inch

domaines — **poulet** /pulɛ/ *nm* ⓵ Zool, Culin chicken; ⓶ ○(terme d'affection) **mon ~** my pet○, honey US symbole indiquant un
(Composés) **~ d'élevage** ≈ battery chicken; **~ fermier** — équivalent dans la langue ≈ free-range chicken cible

numéros de catégorie — **preuve** /pʁœv/ *nf* ⓵ (argument) proof ¢; **une ~** a piece of sémantique en chiffres evidence; **donner la ~ que** to prove that; **faire ses ~s** arabes [*personne*] to prove oneself; [*chose*] to prove itself; **jusqu'à** — indicateurs de collocation **~ du contraire** until proved otherwise; **il doit être malade, la ~, c'est qu'il n'a pas mangé** he must be ill, the fact that he has not eaten proves it; ⓶ (expression) demonstration; **~ d'amour** demonstration of love; **faire ~ de** to show; **~ de bonne volonté (de la part de)** goodwill gesture (from)

numéro de conjugaison — **proscrire** /pʁɔskʁiʁ/ [67] *vtr* (interdire) to ban; (bannir) to — indicateurs sémantiques banish

Structure du texte anglais-français

entrée	**mail** /meɪl/
	A *n* ① (postal service) poste *f*; **by** ~ par la poste; ② (correspond-
indicateur sémantique	ence) courrier *m*; ③ Mil Hist **a coat of** ~ une cotte de
	mailles; ④ (emails) **to check one's** ~ vérifier sa boîte à
mot composé ayant valeur d'entrée à part entière	**main line**
	A /ˌmeɪn ˈlaɪn/ *n* Rail grande ligne *f*
	B /ˈmeɪnˌlaɪn/ *noun modifier* [station, terminus, train] de
indicateur de niveau de langue	grande ligne
	C ○**mainline** /ˈmeɪnlaɪn/ *vi* argot des drogués se piquer
transcription phonétique	**mainly** /ˈmeɪnlɪ/ *adv* surtout, essentiellement
groupe de mots composés	**main**: ~ **man**○ *n* US copain *m*, pote○ *m*; ~**mast** *n*
	grand mât *m*; ~ **memory** *n* Comput mémoire *f* centrale;
	~ **office** *n* (of company, organization, newspaper) siège *m*
	(social); ~ **road** *n* (country) route *f* principale; (in town)
	grande rue *f*; ~**sail** *n* grand-voile *f*
partie du discours	**map** /mæp/
	A *n* (of region) carte *f* (**of** de); (of town, underground) plan *m* (**of** de);
	weather ~ carte météo(rologique); **street** ~ plan des rues;	tiret ondulé remplaçant l'entrée dans les exemples
	the political ~ **of Europe** fig le paysage politique de l'Eu-
	rope
	B *vtr* ① faire la carte de [region, planet]; faire le plan de
	[town]; ② Comput faire une projection de
	(Idiom) **to put sb/sth on the** ~ mettre qn/qch en vedette
verbe à particule	(Phrasal verb)
	■ **map out**: ▶ ~ **out** [sth], ~ [sth] **out** élaborer, mettre	construction d'un verbe à particule
	[qch] au point [plans, strategy]; planifier [schedule]; tracer
	[sb's future]
catégorie grammaticale	**material** /məˈtɪərɪəl/
	A *n* ① (data) documentation *f*, documents *mpl*; **teaching** ~	numéro de catégorie sémantique en chiffres arabes
	matériel *m* pédagogique; **reference** ~ ouvrages *mpl* de
	référence; ② (subject matter) contenu *m*; ③ Theat, TV (script)
	texte *m*; (show) spectacle *m*; **she writes all her own** ~ elle
	écrit ses textes elle-même; Mus elle est auteur-
	compositeur; ④ (substance) gen matière *f*, substance *f*; Constr,	domaines
	Tech matériau *m*; **packing** ~ matériaux *mpl* d'emballage;
	waste ~ déchets *mpl*; ⑤ (fabric) tissu *m*, étoffe *f*; ⑥ (person-
	al potential) étoffe *f*; **she is star** ~ elle a l'étoffe d'une
	vedette; **to be university** ~ être capable d'entreprendre
	des études universitaires
	B **materials** *npl* (equipment) matériel *m*; **art** ~**s**, **artist's** ~**s**	exemple
	fournitures *fpl* de dessin; **cleaning** ~**s** produits *mpl* d'en-
	tretien
	C *adj* ① (significant, relevant) [assistance, benefit, change, damage,
	evidence] matériel/-ielle; [question] important; [fact] perti-
	nent; **to be** ~ **to sth** se rapporter à qch; ② (concrete) [com-
	fort, gains, possessions, success] matériel/-ielle; **in** ~ **terms** sur	traduction
	le plan matériel; **to do sth for** ~ **gain** faire qch par
	intérêt
	matron /ˈmeɪtrən/ *n* ① GB (nurse) (in hospital) infirmière *f* en
	chef; (in school) infirmière *f* (*chargée également de l'intendan-*	glose explicative
	ce); ② (of nursing home) directrice *f*; ③ US (warder) gardienne
	f; ④ (woman) péj matrone *f* péj
	matronly /ˈmeɪtrənlɪ/ *adj* [duties, manner] de mère de	indicateurs de collocation
	famille, de matrone; [figure] fort, corpulent
transcription phonétique de la prononciation nord-américaine	**minute²** /maɪˈnjuːt, US -ˈnuːt/ *adj* [particle] minuscule;
	[quantity] infime; [risk, variation] minime
variante orthographique nord-américaine	**mouldy** GB, **moldy** US /ˈməʊldɪ/ *adj* moisi; **to go** ~
	moisir
	mown /məʊn/ *pp* ▶ **mow**	renvoi à une entrée
sigles/acronymes	**MP** *n* ① GB (*abrév* = **Member of Parliament**) député *m*;
	② *abrév* ▶ **military policeman**
	mpg *n* (*abrév* = **miles per gallon**) miles *mpl* au gallon

The pronunciation of French

The symbols used in this dictionary for the pronunciation of French are those of the IPA (International Phonetic Alphabet). Certain differences in pronunciation are shown in the phonetic transcription, although many speakers do not observe them—e.g. the long 'a' /ɑ/ in *pâte* and the short 'a' /a/ in *patte*, or the difference between the nasal vowels 'un' /œ̃/ as in *brun* and 'in'/ɛ̃/ as in *brin*.

Transcription

Each entry is followed by its phonetic transcription between slashes, with the following exceptions:
• written abbreviations (*bd*, *ha*, etc.)
• cross-references from an inflected to a base form (*yeux*, *fol*)
• cross-references from a variant spelling to the preferred form (*clef*/*clé*, *peinard*/*pénard*).

Alternative pronunciations

Where the speaker has a choice of pronunciations, these are shown in one of the following two ways:
• by the use of brackets e.g. *syllabe* /sil(l)ab/, *déficit* /defisi(t)/
• in full, separated by a comma e.g. *revenir* /ʀəvniʀ, ʀvəniʀ/.

Morphological variations

The phonetic transcription of the plural and feminine forms of certain nouns and adjectives does not repeat the root, but shows only the change in ending. Therefore, in certain cases, the presentation of the entry does not correspond to that of the phonetic transcription e.g. électricien, -ienne /elɛktʀisjɛ̃, ɛn/.

Phrases

Full phonetic transcription is given for adverbial or prepositional phrases which are shown in alphabetical order within the main headword e.g. *emblée*, *d'emblée* /dɑ̃ble/, *plain-pied*, *de plain-pied* /d(ə)plɛ̃pje/.

Consonants

Aspiration of 'h'
Where it is impossible to make a liaison this is indicated by /'/ immediately after the slash e.g. *haine* /'ɛn/.

Assimilation
A voiced consonant can become unvoiced when it is followed by an unvoiced consonant within a word e.g. *absorber* /apsɔʀbe/.

Vowels

Open 'e' and closed 'e'
A clear distinction is made at the end of a word between a closed 'e' and an open 'e' e.g. *pré* /pʀe/ and *près* /pʀɛ/, *complet* /kɔ̃plɛ/ and *combler* /kɔ̃ble/. Within a word the following rules apply:
• 'e' is always open in a syllable followed by a syllable containing a mute 'e' e.g. *règle* /ʀɛgl/, *réglementaire* /ʀɛgləmɑ̃tɛʀ/
• in careful speech 'e' is pronounced as a closed 'e' when it is followed by a syllable containing a closed vowel (*y, i, e*) e.g. *pressé* /pʀese/
• 'e' is pronounced as an open 'e' when it is followed by a syllable containing an open vowel e.g. *pressant* /pʀɛsɑ̃/.

Mute 'e'
The pronunciation of mute 'e' varies considerably depending on the level of language used and on the region from which the speaker originates. As a general rule it is only pronounced at the end of a word in the South of France or in poetry and it is, therefore, not shown. In an isolated word the mute 'e' preceded by a single consonant is dropped e.g. *parfaitement* /paʀfɛtmɑ̃/, but *probablement* /pʀɔbabləmɑ̃/.

In many cases the pronunciation of the mute 'e' depends on the surrounding context. Thus one would say *une reconnaissance de dette* /ynʀəkɔnɛsɑ̃sdədɛt/, but, *ma reconnaissance est éternelle* /maʀkɔnɛsɑ̃sɛtetɛʀnɛl/. The mute 'e' is shown in brackets in order to account for this phenomenon.

Open 'o' and closed 'o'
The difference between open 'o' and closed 'o' is not clear and speakers may hesitate, particularly in the pronunciation of compound words whose first element ends in 'o' e.g. *socioprofessionnel* etc. It is not possible to opt for one or the other to apply to all cases. Where the word seems to function more like a single word the 'o' tends to be pronounced as an open 'o'. Where the two elements of the compound retain a degree of autonomy, as is often the case when they are

hyphenated, the 'o' tends to be pronounced as a closed 'o' e.g. *psychothérapie* /psikoteʀɑpi/, but *psychologie* /psikɔlɔʒi/.

Stress

There is no real stress as such in French. In normal unemphasized speech a slight stress falls on the final syllable of a word or group of words, provided that it does not contain a mute 'e'. This is not shown in the phonetic transcription of individual entries. *I. V.*

Vowels

	as in				*as in*		
a		patte	/pat/	o	*as in*	gros	/gʀo/
ɑ		pâte	/pɑt/	ɔ		corps	/kɔʀ/
ɑ̃		clan	/klɑ̃/	ɔ̃		long	/lɔ̃/
e		dé	/de/	œ		leur	/lœʀ/
ɛ		belle	/bɛl/	œ̃		brun	/bʀœ̃/
ɛ̃		lin	/lɛ̃/	ø		deux	/dø/
ə		demain	/dəmɛ̃/	u		fou	/fu/
i		gris	/gʀi/	y		pur	/pyʀ/

Consonants

	as in				*as in*		
b	*as in*	bal	/bal/	ŋ	*as in*	dancing	/dɑ̃siŋ/
d		dent	/dɑ̃/	p		porte	/pɔʀt/
f		foire	/fwar/	ʀ		rire	/ʀiʀ/
g		gomme	/gɔm/	s		sang	/sɑ̃/
k		clé	/kle/	ʃ		chien	/ʃjɛ̃/
l		lien	/ljɛ̃/	t		train	/tʀɛ̃/
m		mer	/mɛʀ/	v		voile	/vwal/
n		nage	/naʒ/	z		zèbre	/zɛbʀ/
ɲ		gnon	/ɲɔ̃/	ʒ		jeune	/ʒœn/

Semi-vowels

	as in		
j	*as in*	fille	/fij/
ɥ		huit	/ɥit/
w		oui	/wi/

Prononciation de l'anglais

Les sons et leur transcription

Alphabet phonétique

La prononciation de chaque entrée est donnée en notation phonétique entre des barres obliques //. On trouvera le tableau des signes utilisés à la page xxxiv. A la différence de l'écriture orthographique de l'anglais dans laquelle la même lettre peut prendre des valeurs différentes, par exemple le *c* dans *cat* (/kæt/) et *city* (/ˈsɪtɪ/), dans l'alphabet phonétique, chaque signe représente un seul son.

Anglais britannique

La prononciation standard de l'anglais britannique suit immédiatement le mot-vedette. Cette prononciation correspond à la Received Pronunciation (RP) qui est la forme d'anglais britannique la plus répandue.

Prononciation du /r/

En anglais britannique, le *r* ou *re* à la fin d'un mot ne se prononce que si le mot qui suit commence par une voyelle. C'est pourquoi, dans la transcription phonétique, ces sons sont indiqués entre parenthèses, par exemple *hair* /heə(r)/, *hire* /haɪ(r)/.

L'accent

Accent d'intensité

Les mots anglais polysyllabiques comportent une syllabe plus fortement accentuée que les autres. L'accent d'intensité est indiqué au moyen du signe /ˈ/ placé devant la syllabe qu'il affecte, par exemple *city* /ˈsɪtɪ/. Certains mots longs ont deux accents d'intensité, l'un plus fort, appelé accent primaire et également noté /ˈ/, l'autre plus faible, appelé accent secondaire et noté /ˌ/: *pronunciation* /prəˌnʌnsɪˈeɪʃn/.

Déplacement de l'accent d'intensité

En général on évite d'avoir à prononcer deux accents d'intensité dans des syllabes adjacentes. Ainsi dans la phrase *Lisa is thirteen*, on prononcera /ˌθɜːˈtiːn/, mais dans *Lisa has thirteen bicycles*, on dira /ˌθɜːtiːn ˈbaɪsɪkls/. On notera que le déplacement de l'accent d'intensité est valable pour toutes les catégories de mots et que tout mot ayant un accent secondaire suivi d'un accent primair peut perdre ce dernier lorsqu'il est suivi par un mot dont la première syllabe porte l'accent d'intensité primaire.

Variantes dans la prononciation

Variantes britanniques

Il arrive pour de nombreux mots que plusieurs prononciations soient acceptées. Dans ce cas les variantes sont données, la prononciation la plus courante étant placée en premier, par exemple *economic* /ˌiːkəˈnɒmɪk, ˌekəˈnɒmɪk/.

Formes fortes et formes faibles

Certains mots courants tels que *a*, *the*, *and*, *but*, *for*, *me*, *them*, *can*, *have*, etc. peuvent se prononcer de deux (ou plus) façons différentes: une forme forte et une (ou plus) forme faible. Des deux, la forme faible est la plus fréquente: c'est celle qui se rencontre dans la chaîne parlée.

La forme forte s'utilise pour un mot isolé, ou encore pour souligner le mot dans une phrase. On trouvera la prononciation des deux formes dans le dictionnaire, la forme forte étant donnée la première, par exemple *and* /ænd, ənd/.

Dans la chaîne parlée, les formes faibles de *be* et *have* suivent souvent un pronom personnel. On notera que pronom et verbe sont généralement combinés en une forme contractée qui est une forme faible, par exemple *you're* /jɔː(r)/, *I'm* /aɪm/.

Contractions

Dans la langue écrite, les contractions se font par omission d'une ou deux lettres auxquelles on substitue une apostrophe ('), par exemple *can't*. Dans la langue parlée, il y a contraction quand une syllabe disparaît et que la syllabe restante comporte une voyelle autre que /ə/. La contraction est très fréquente pour certains verbes auxiliaires suivis de *not*, par exemple *don't* /dəʊnt/. (Ces formes ne sont pas des formes faibles et peuvent être accentuées.)

Mots étrangers

L'anglais possède un certain nombre de mots et expressions d'origine étrangère qui se sont intégrés à la langue et ont acquis une prononciation anglaise, par exemple *coffee* /ˈkɒfiː/, *bungalow* /ˈbʌngələʊ/.

D'autres, bien que d'emploi courant, continuent à être perçus comme étrangers, d'où de grandes variations dans la manière dont ils sont prononcés. Beaucoup de ces mots sont français et de ce fait contiennent des voyelles nasales qui n'existent pas on anglais, par exemple *salon, en route*. La prononciation de ces sons est complexe pour les locuteurs de l'anglais et l'on peut entendre des sons totalement transformés aussi bien qu'une prononciation française correcte. La prononciation adoptée dans ce dictionnaire est la forme anglicisée des mots étrangers et l'on trouvera /'sælɒn/, /ˌɒn 'ruːt/.

Prononciation de l'anglais d'Amérique du Nord

Celle-ci est indiquée après la prononciation RP chaque fois qu'il y a une différence marquée entre les deux, ainsi pour le mot *graph* /grɑːf, US græf/.

La prononciation de l'anglais d'Amérique du Nord donnée ici est celle du General American.

Bien que les symboles utilisés soient les mêmes que pour la RP, on notera que certains sons, en particulier los voyelles, ont une valeur différente. On notera également que /r/ se prononce toujours en anglais d'Amérique du Nord, ce qui n'est pas le cas en anglais britannique: *car, start*. Dans la transcription phonétique, la prononciation donnée sera celle de l'anglais britannique /kɑː(r)/, /stɑːt/.

Dérivés et composés

Dérivés

Les dérivés apparaissant généralement comme des entrées à part entière dans le dictionnaire, leur prononciation sera indiquée systématiquement.

Mots composés

En anglais, les mots composés s'écrivent soit en un seul mot ('closed compounds'), soit en deux mots parfois reliés par un trait d'union. Pour économiser de la place, la prononciation n'est pas toujours donnée, mais il suffira de consulter la prononciation des deux éléments du mot.

Au cours de l'articulation d'un mot composé il se produit souvent des changements phonétiques. Sous l'influence du phonème qui le suit, un son peut changer de valeur, comme dans *boatman* où le *t* devient un *p* /'bəʊpmən/, ou disparaître complètement, comme dans *windscreen* qui se prononce /'wɪnskriːn/. Ce phénomène d'assimilation, plus ou moins marqué selon la rapidité d'élocution, se rencontre constamment dans la chaine parlée. Toutofois, c'est toujours la forme complète qui est donnée dans le dictionnaire.

Voyelles et diphtongues

iː	*de* see	/siː/	ɜː	*de* fur	/fɜː(r)/				
ɪ	sit	/sɪt/	ə	ago	/ə'gəʊ/				
e	ten	/ten/	eɪ	page	/peɪdʒ/				
æ	hat	/hæt/	əʊ	home	/həʊm/				
ɑː	arm	/ɑːm/	aɪ	five	/faɪv/				
ɒ	got	/gɒt/	aʊ	now	/naʊ/				
ɔː	saw	/sɔː/	ɔɪ	join	/dʒɔɪn/				
ʊ	put	/pʊt/	ɪə	near	/nɪə(r)/				
uː	too	/tuː/	eə	hair	/heə(r)/				
ʌ	cup	/kʌp/	ʊə	pure	/pjʊə(r)/				

Consonnes

p	*de* pen	/pen/	s	*de* so	/səʊ/
b	bad	/bæd/	z	zoo	/zuː/
t	tea	/tiː/	ʃ	she	/ʃiː/
d	did	/dɪd/	ʒ	vision	/'vɪʒn/
k	cat	/kæt/	h	how	/haʊ/
g	got	/gɒt/	m	man	/mæn/
tʃ	chin	/tʃɪn/	n	no	/nəʊ/
dʒ	June	/dʒuːn/	ŋ	sing	/sɪŋ/
f	fall	/fɔːl/	l	leg	/leg/
v	voice	/vɔɪs/	r	red	/red/
θ	thin	/θɪn/	j	yes	/jes/
ð	then	/ðen/	w	wet	/wet/

Aa

a, A /a, ɑ/
A nm inv (lettre) a, A; **vitamine A** vitamin A; **de A à Z** from A to Z; **le bricolage de A à Z** the A to Z of DIY; **démontrer qch à qn par A plus B** to demonstrate sth conclusively to sb
B A nf (abbr = **autoroute**) motorway GB, freeway US

à /a/ prép

⚠ La préposition à se traduit de multiples façons. Les expressions courantes du genre machine à écrire, difficile à faire etc sont traitées respectivement sous **machine, difficile** etc.
Les emplois de à avec les verbes avoir, être, aller, penser, etc. sont traités sous les verbes.
Pour trouver la traduction correcte de à on aura intérêt à se reporter aux mots qui précèdent la préposition ainsi qu'aux notes d'usage répertoriées ▸ p. 1411.
On trouvera ci-dessous quelques exemples typiques de traductions de à.

[1] (avec un verbe de mouvement) **se rendre au travail** to go to work; **aller de Paris ∼ Nevers** to go from Paris to Nevers; [2] (pour indiquer le lieu où l'on se trouve) **∼ la maison** at home; **∼ Paris** in Paris; [3] (dans le temps) **∼ 10 ans** at the age of 10; **au printemps** in (the) spring; [4] (dans une description) with; **le garçon aux cheveux bruns** the boy with dark hair; [5] (employé avec le verbe être) **il est ∼ plaindre** he's to be pitied; **je suis ∼ vous tout de suite** I'll be with you in a minute; **c'est ∼ qui de jouer?** whose turn is it?; **c'est ∼ toi** it's your turn; **(c'est) ∼ lui de décider** it's up to him to decide; [6] (marquant l'appartenance) **∼ qui est cette montre?** whose is this watch?; **elle est ∼ elle** it's hers; **c'est ∼ vous cette voiture?** is this your car?; **une amie ∼ moi** a friend of mine; **encore une idée ∼ elle** another of her ideas; [7] (employé avec un nombre) **nous avons fait le travail ∼ deux** two of us did the work; **(en s'y mettant) ∼ dix on devrait y arriver** ten of us should be able to manage; **∼ nous tous on devrait y arriver** between all of us we should be able to manage; **∼ trois on est serrés** with three people it's crowded; **mener 3 ∼ 2** to lead 3 (to) 2; **∼ 100 kilomètres-heure** at 100 kilometres^GB per ou an hour; **au 74 de la rue Bossuet** at 74 rue Bossuet; **∼ quatre kilomètres d'ici** four kilometres^GB from here; **∼ 3 euros le kilo** at 3 euros a kilo; **un timbre ∼ soixante centimes** a sixty-cent stamp; **(de) huit ∼ dix heures par jour** between eight and ten hours a day; [8] (marquant une hypothèse) **∼ ce qu'il paraît** apparently; **∼ ce qu'il me semble** as far as I can see; **∼ vous entendre** to hear you talk; [9] (dans phrases exclamatives) **∼ nous!** (en levant son verre) (here's) to us!; **∼ ta santé, ∼ la tienne!** cheers!; **∼ tes souhaits** bless you!; **∼ vous l'honneur!** (de couper le gâteau) you do the honours!; (après vous) after you!; **∼ nous (deux)!** (avant un règlement de compte) let's sort this out between us; **∼ demain** see you tomorrow; **∼ la prochaine** see you next time!; [10] (dans une dédicace) '**∼ ma mère**' (dans un livre) 'to my mother'; (sur une tombe) 'in memory of my mother'

abaissement /abɛsmã/ nm [1] (diminution) (de prix, taux) cut (**de** in); (de seuil, niveau) lowering; [2] (avilissement) (de soi-même) self-abasement; (d'autrui) debasement

abaisser /abese/ [1]
A vtr [1] (en valeur) to reduce [prix] (**à** to; **de** by); to lower [niveau] (**à** to; **de** by); [2] (en hauteur) to lower [mur] (**de** by); [3] (faire descendre) to pull down [manette]
B s'abaisser vpr [1] (descendre) [rideau de scène] to fall; [2] (s'avilir) to demean oneself; **s'∼ à faire qch** to stoop to doing sth

abandon /abɑ̃dɔ̃/ nm [1] (état) state of neglect; **état d'∼** neglected state; **être à l'∼** [maison, domaine] to be abandoned; [enfant] to be running wild; [jardin] to be neglected; **laisser à l'∼** to allow [sth] to fall into decay [maison]; to allow [sth] to become overgrown [terres]; [2] (de projet, méthode) abandonment; (de droit, privilège) relinquishment; [3] (de cours, d'épreuve) withdrawal (**de** from); (de fonctions) giving up (**de** of); **contraint à l'∼** forced to withdraw; **vainqueur par ∼** winner by default; [4] (attitude détendue) relaxed attitude

⟮Composés⟯ **∼ du domicile conjugal** desertion of the marital home; **∼ d'enfant** abandonment of a child; **∼ de poste** desertion (of one's post)

abandonné, ∼e /abɑ̃dɔne/
A pp ▸ **abandonner**
B pp adj [1] (délaissé) [épouse, ami, cause] deserted; [véhicule, maison, nation] abandoned; [2] (désaffecté) [chemin, usine] disused; [3] (qui n'a plus cours) [méthode] discarded; [modèle] discontinued

abandonner /abɑ̃dɔne/ [1]
A vtr [1] (renoncer à) gén to give up; (à l'école) to drop [matière]; **∼ les recherches** to give up the search; **je peignais, mais j'ai abandonné** I used to paint, but I gave it up; **∼ la partie** or **lutte** lit, fig to throw in the towel; [2] (céder) to give [bien] (**à qn** to sb); to hand [sth] over [gestion] (**à qn** to sb); (se retirer de) to give up [fonction, études]; Sport (avant l'épreuve) to withdraw; (pendant l'épreuve) to retire; **∼ la course** to withdraw from the race; [4] (quitter) to leave [personne, lieu]; to abandon [véhicule, objet, navire]; **∼ Paris pour Nice** to leave Paris for Nice; [5] (délaisser) to abandon [enfant, famille, animal]; to desert [foyer, épouse, poste, cause]; [6] (livrer) **∼ qch à** to leave ou abandon sth to; **∼ qn à son sort** to leave ou abandon sb to his/her fate; [7] (faire défaut) [courage, chance] to desert [personne]; **mes forces m'abandonnent** my strength is failing me; [8] (lâcher) to let go of [outil, rênes]; [9] Ordinat to abort
B s'abandonner vpr [1] (se confier) to let oneself go; [2] (se détendre) to let oneself go; **s'∼ dans les bras de qn** to sink into sb's arms; [3] (se laisser aller) **s'∼ au désespoir** to give in to despair

abasourdir /abazuʀdiʀ/ [3] vtr (stupéfier) to stun

abat-jour /abaʒuʀ/ nm inv lampshade

abats /aba/ nmpl (bœuf, porc, mouton) offal ℂ; (de volaille) giblets

abattage /abataʒ/ nm [1] (d'arbre) felling ℂ; [2] (d'animal de boucherie) slaughter ℂ

abattant /abatã/ nm (de bureau) (drop) leaf; (de WC) lid

abattement /abatmã/ nm [1] (dépressif) despondency; [2] (réduction) gén reduction; (pour impôt) allowance

⟮Composé⟯ **∼ fiscal** tax allowance GB ou deduction US

abattis /abati/ nmpl Culin giblets

abattoir /abatwaʀ/ nm slaughterhouse

abattre /abatʀ/ [61]
A vtr [1] (tuer) to slaughter [animal de boucherie]; to destroy [animal dangereux]; (avec une arme à feu) to shoot [sb] down [personne]; to shoot [animal]; **l'homme à ∼** the prime target; fig the one to beat; [2] (faire tomber) to pull down [bâtiment]; to knock down [mur]; to bring down [statue]; to shoot down [avion]; [personne] to fell [arbre]; [tempête] to bring down [arbre, pylône]; [3] (découvrir) to show [carte, jeu]; **∼ ses cartes** or **son jeu** lit, fig to put one's cards on the table; [4] (accabler) (physiquement) to wear [sb] out; (moralement) to demoralize; **on ne va pas se laisser ∼!** we're not going

to let things get us down!; **5** (accomplir) to get through [travail]

B **s'abattre** vpr **s'~ sur** [orage] to beat down on; [oiseau] to swoop down on; [malheur] to descend upon

abbatiale /abasjal/ nf abbey church

abbaye /abei/ nf abbey

abbé /abe/ nm **1** (supérieur d'une abbaye) abbot; **2** (prêtre) priest; **monsieur l'~** Father; **l'~ Pop** Father Pop

abbesse /abɛs/ nf abbess

abc /abese/ nm ABC, rudiments

abcès /apsɛ/ nm inv abscess; **~ dentaire** (dental) abscess; **crever** or **vider l'~** fig to resolve a crisis

abdication /abdikasjɔ̃/ nf lit, fig abdication

abdiquer /abdike/ [1] vi [souverain] to abdicate (**en faveur de** in favour^{GB} of); (renoncer) to surrender (**devant qn/qch** to sb/sth)

abdomen /abdɔmɛn/ nm abdomen, stomach

abdominal, **~e**, mpl **-aux** /abdɔminal, o/
A adj abdominal
B **abdominaux** nmpl **1** Anat abdominal muscles; **2** Sport stomach exercises

abdos○ /abdo/ nmpl **1** (muscles) abs○; **2** (exercices) abdominal exercises

abeille /abɛj/ nf bee

aberrant, **~e** /abɛʀɑ̃, ɑ̃t/ adj (absurde) absurd; (anormal) aberrant

aberration /abɛʀasjɔ̃/ nf aberration

abêtir /abetiʀ/ [3]
A vtr to turn [sb] into a moron○
B **s'abêtir** vpr to become stupid

abêtissant, **~e** /abetisɑ̃, ɑ̃t/ adj mindless

abîme /abim/ nm **1** (précipice) abyss; **2** (écart) gulf (**entre** between); **un ~ nous sépare** there is a gulf between us; **3** (ruine) ruin; **toucher le fond de l'~** gén to hit rock bottom; (moralement) to be at one's lowest ebb

abîmer /abime/ [1]
A vtr to damage; **très abîmé** badly damaged; **il a eu le nez abîmé dans la bagarre** his nose was injured in the fight
B **s'abîmer** vpr (se détériorer) [objet] to get damaged; [fruit] to spoil; **s'~ la vue** to ruin one's eyesight

abject, **~e** /abʒɛkt/ adj despicable, abject; **de façon ~e** despicably

abjection /abʒɛksjɔ̃/ nf abjectness

abjurer /abʒyʀe/ [1]
A vtr to abjure sout [religion]
B vi Relig to recant

ablatif /ablatif/ nm Ling ablative

ablation /ablasjɔ̃/ nf excision, removal; **subir une ~ de la rate** to have one's spleen removed

abnégation /abnegasjɔ̃/ nf self-sacrifice; **faire preuve d'~** to act selflessly

aboiement /abwamɑ̃/ nm (de chien) barking **¢**

abois /abwa/ nmpl **aux ~** lit at bay; fig in desperate straits

abolir /abɔliʀ/ [3] vtr to abolish

abolition /abɔlisjɔ̃/ nf abolition

abominable /abɔminabl/ adj abominable

abomination /abɔminasjɔ̃/ nf abomination

abondamment /abɔ̃damɑ̃/ adv [boire, illustrer] copiously; [pleuvoir] heavily; [évoquer, souligner] at length; **l'événement fut ~ commenté** the event was commented on at considerable length; **~ documenté** [livre] extremely well-researched; **rincer ~ à l'eau** rinse thoroughly with water

abondance /abɔ̃dɑ̃s/ nf **1** (de produits, renseignements) wealth; (de récolte, ressources) abundance; (de main-d'œuvre) abundant supply; **en ~** in abundance; **il y a ~ de** there's plenty of; **2** (aisance) affluence; **vivre dans l'~** to live in affluence

(Idiome) **~ de biens ne nuit pas** Prov wealth does no harm

abondant, **~e** /abɔ̃dɑ̃, ɑ̃t/ adj **1** (en quantité) [nourriture, récolte] plentiful; [source] lit, fig abundant; [remarques, illustrations] numerous; **une main-d'œuvre ~e** an abundant supply of labour; **un courrier ~** a large number of letters; **2** (riche) fml [style] rich; **être ~ en** to be rich in [découvertes, surprises]; **3** (fourni) [chevelure] [végétation] lush

abonder /abɔ̃de/ [1] vi **1** (être en quantité) [fruits, produits, exemples] to abound; [gibier, poisson] to be plentiful; **2** (avoir en quantité) **~ en** to be full of

(Idiome) **~ dans le sens de qn** to agree wholeheartedly with sb

abonné, **~e** /abɔne/ nm,f (lecteur, téléspectateur) subscriber; (voyageur, spectateur) season ticket holder; **~ au gaz** gas consumer

abonnement /abɔnmɑ̃/ nm **1** (de périodique, télévision) subscription (**à** to); **souscrire un ~** to take out a subscription (**à** to); **2** (de transport, théâtre) (**carte d'**)**~** season ticket (**à** for); **3** (au téléphone) rental system charge; (au gaz, à l'électricité) standing charge

abonner /abɔne/ [1]
A vtr **~ qn à qch** (à un périodique) to take out a subscription to sth for sb; (au théâtre, concert) to buy sb a season ticket for sth
B **s'abonner** vpr (à un périodique, la télévision) to subscribe (**à** to); (à un moyen de transport, au théâtre) to buy a season ticket (**à** for)

abord /abɔʀ/
A nm **1** (comportement) manner; **être d'un ~ aimable** to have a pleasant manner; **sous des ~s grincheux c'est un tendre** his gruff exterior hides a kind heart; **2** (approche) access; **être d'un ~ aisé** to be accessible; **à l'~ de** on approaching; **3** (contact) **au premier ~** at first sight
B **d'abord** loc adv **1** (avant autre chose) first; **va d'~ te laver les mains** go and wash your hands first; **2** (contrairement à la suite) at first; **j'ai d'~ cru à une mauvaise plaisanterie** at first I thought it was a bad joke; **3** (primo) firstly, first; **4** (en priorité) first (of all); **les femmes et les enfants d'~** women and children first; **tout d'~** first of all; **5** (avant tout) for a start; **d'~ je refuse de lui parler** for a start I refuse to speak to him
C **abords** nmpl area (sg) around; **aux ~s de qch** in the area around sth

abordable /abɔʀdabl/ adj **1** [produit, prix] affordable; **à des prix très ~s** very reasonably priced; **2** [texte] accessible; **3** [personne] approachable

abordage /abɔʀdaʒ/ nm (collision) collision; (attaque) boarding; **à l'~!** stand by to board!

aborder /abɔʀde/ [1]
A vtr **1** (commencer à traiter) to tackle [problème, sujet]; **vous n'abordez pas le problème comme il faut** you're not going about the problem the right way; **2** (approcher) to approach [personne, obstacle]; **avant d'~ le virage** on the approach to the bend; **3** (entamer) to enter; **4** [voyageur, navire] to reach [lieu, rive]
B vi [voyageur, navire] to land

aborigène /abɔʀiʒɛn/
A adj (d'Australie) Aboriginal
B nmf (d'Australie) Aborigine

abortif, **-ive** /abɔʀtif, iv/ adj abortifacient

aboutir /abutiʀ/ [3]
A **aboutir à** vtr ind **1** lit **~ à** [rue, escalier] to lead to; [personne] to end up in [village, place, rue]; to end up at [fontaine, église]; **2** fig **~ à** to lead to [accord, résultat, rupture]
B vi [négociations, projet] to succeed; **ne pas ~** not to come off

aboutissants /abutisɑ̃/ nmpl **les tenants et les ~ de qch** the ins and outs of sth

aboutissement /abutismɑ̃/ nm (de carrière, rêve, d'évolution, effort) culmination; (de conférence, parcours) outcome

aboyer /abwaje/ [23]
A ○vtr [personne] to bark [ordres] (**à** at); to shout [injures] (**à** at)
B vi [chien] to bark (**après**, **contre** at); [personne] to shout (**après**, **contre** at)

abracadabrant, **~e** /abrakadabrɑ̃, ɑ̃t/ adj bizarre

abrasif, **-ive** /abrazif, iv/
A adj abrasive
B nm abrasive

abrégé /abreʒe/ nm **1** (de texte) summary; **faire l'~ de** to summarize; **en ~** [mot, expression] in abbreviated form; [texte, discours] in summarized form; **2** (ouvrage) concise handbook

abréger /abreʒe/ [15] vtr **1** (rendre court) to shorten [mot, expression]; to summarize [texte, discours]; **~ 'télévision' en 'télé'** to shorten 'television' to 'TV'; **version abrégée de qch** abridged version of sth; **2** (rendre bref) to cut short [*visite, carrière*]; **abrège**○**!** keep it short!; ∼ **les souffrances de qn** to put an end to sb's suffering; **disons, pour ∼, qu'ils se séparent** to cut GB *ou* make US a long story short, let's just say they are separating

abreuver /abʀøve/ [1]
A *vtr* to water [*animal*]; ∼ **qn d'injures** to heap abuse on sb
B **s'abreuver** *vpr* liter [*animal*] to drink

abreuvoir /abʀøvwaʀ/ *nm* (lieu) watering place

abréviation /abʀevjɑsjɔ̃/ *nf* abbreviation

abri /abʀi/ *nm* gén shelter; (pour voiture) carport; (cabane) shed; **se servir de qch comme ∼** (en se mettant derrière) to shelter behind sth; (en se mettant dessous) to shelter under sth; **trouver un ∼ provisoire sous/dans** to take shelter temporarily under/in; **à l'∼** (à couvert) under cover; (en lieu sûr) safe; **être à l'∼** to be sheltered; **être à l'∼ de** (d'un mur) to be sheltered by; (du vent) to be sheltered from; **courir se mettre à l'∼** to run for shelter; **personne n'est à l'∼ d'un accident** accidents can happen to anybody; **personne n'est à l'∼ d'une erreur** everybody makes mistakes; **à l'∼ de l'humidité** in a dry place

⸨Composés⸩ ∼ **antiaérien** air raid shelter; ∼ **antiatomique** nuclear shelter; ∼ **souterrain** underground shelter *ou* bunker

abricot /abʀiko/ ▸ p. 140
A *adj inv* (couleur) apricot
B *nm* **1** (fruit) apricot; **confiture d'∼s** apricot jam; **à l'∼** [*yaourt, tarte*] apricot (épith); **2** (couleur) apricot

abricotier /abʀikɔtje/ *nm* apricot tree

abriter /abʀite/ [1]
A *vtr* **1** [*bâtiment*] to shelter [*personnes, animaux*]; to house [*organisation, objets*]; to host [*activité, réunion*]; **2** [*pays*] to provide a base for [*activité*]; to provide a home for [*personnes*]
B **s'abriter** *vpr* (des intempéries) to take shelter (**de** from); (des balles, du feu) to take cover (**de** from); **s'∼ derrière le secret professionnel** to shelter *ou* hide behind professional confidentiality

abrogation /abʀɔgɑsjɔ̃/ *nf* repeal

abroger /abʀɔʒe/ [13] *vtr* to repeal

abrupt, ∼**e** /abʀypt/ *adj* **1** [*colline, chemin*] steep; [*paroi*] sheer; **2** [*personne, ton*] abrupt

abruptement /abʀyptəmɑ̃/ *adv* (en pente) steeply; (soudainement) suddenly; (de manière brusque) abruptly

abruti, ∼**e** /abʀyti/
A *adj* (idiot) stupid
B *nm,f* offensive moron○

abrutir /abʀytiʀ/ [3]
A *vtr* **1** (rendre passif) [*bruit*] to deafen; [*chaleur*] to wear [sb] out; [*alcool, médicament, fatigue*] to have a numbing effect on; [*coup*] to stun; **abruti par les médicaments** dopey with medicine; **2** (rendre idiot) [*alcool, tâche*] to stultify; **3** (accabler) ∼ **qn de travail** to overwhelm sb with work
B **s'abrutir** *vpr* **1** (devenir stupide) to become dull-witted; **2** (s'accabler) **s'∼ de travail** to wear oneself out with work

abrutissant, ∼**e** /abʀytisɑ̃, ɑ̃t/ *adj* [*vacarme*] deafening; [*chaleur*] exhausting; [*tâche*] mind-numbing

abscons, ∼**e** /apskɔ̃, ɔ̃s/ *adj* fml abstruse

absence /apsɑ̃s/ *nf* **1** (disparition temporaire, inexistence) absence; **'en cas d'∼ adressez-vous à côté'** 'if out please enquire next door'; **on a téléphoné pendant votre ∼** somebody phoned while you were out; **nous avons regretté votre ∼ à la réunion** we were sorry (that) you didn't attend the meeting; **briller par son ∼** to be conspicuous by *ou* in US one's absence hum; **2** (défaut) lack; **l'∼ de pluie** the lack of rain; **3** (perte de mémoire) **il a des ∼s** *ou* **des moments d'∼** at times his mind goes blank

absent, ∼**e** /apsɑ̃, ɑ̃t/
A *adj* **1** (éloigné longtemps) away (*jamais épith*) (**de** from); (éloigné brièvement) out (*jamais épith*) (**de** of); **2** (qui ne s'est pas présenté, ne participe pas) [*élève, employé*] absent (**de** from); **3** (inexistant) absent (**de** from); **4** (absorbé) absent-minded; **d'une voix ∼e** absent-mindedly
B *nm,f* absentee; **'∼s excusés...'** 'apologies for absence...'; **Leconte était le grand ∼ du tournoi** Leconte was notably absent from the tournament

⸨Idiome⸩ **les ∼s ont toujours tort** Prov those who are absent always get the blame

absentéisme /apsɑ̃teism/ *nm* absenteeism

absenter: **s'absenter** /apsɑ̃te/ [1] *vpr* (longtemps) to go away; (brièvement) to go out; **ne vous absentez pas trop longtemps** don't be gone for long; **s'∼ de** to go out of, to leave

abside /apsid/ *nf* apse

absolu, ∼**e** /apsɔly/
A *adj* gén absolute; [*règle*] hard and fast; [*tempérament*] uncompromising; **sauf en cas d'∼e nécessité** only if absolutely necessary; **défense ∼e d'ouvrir cette porte** it is absolutely forbidden to open this door; **le secret le plus ∼ sur** the utmost secrecy about; **un repos ∼** complete rest
B *nm* absolute

absolument /apsɔlymɑ̃/ *adv* absolutely; **'êtes-vous d'accord?'—'∼ pas!'** 'do you agree?'—'absolutely not!'; **tenir à faire qch** to insist (up)on doing sth; **il veut ∼ réussir** he's determined to succeed; **il faut ∼ que tu ailles à Rome** you really must go to Rome

absolution /apsɔlysjɔ̃/ *nf* Relig absolution

absolutisme /apsɔlytism/ *nm* absolutism

absorbant, ∼**e** /apsɔʀbɑ̃, ɑ̃t/ *adj* **1** [*substance*] absorbent; **à grand pouvoir ∼** highly absorbent; **2** [*travail*] absorbing

absorber /apsɔʀbe/ [1] *vtr* **1** (s'imbiber) [*matériau*] to absorb; **2** (consommer) to take [*nourriture, médicament*]; **3** (retenir) [*organisme, plante*] to absorb; **4** (nécessiter) to absorb [*argent*]; to occupy [*esprit*]; **absorbé par qch** absorbed in sth; **absorbé dans ses pensées** lost in one's thoughts; **5** (intégrer) [*entreprise*] to take over; [*parti, région, secteur*] to absorb

absorption /apsɔʀpsjɔ̃/ *nf* **1** (de nourriture, médicament) taking; **l'∼ de ce médicament est déconseillée aux femmes enceintes** pregnant women are advised not to take this medicine; **2** (de liquide, soleil, choc, d'oxygène) absorption; **3** (d'entreprise) takeover

absoudre /apsudʀ/ [75] *vtr* Relig to absolve

abstenir: **s'abstenir** /apstəniʀ/ [36] *vpr* **1** (ne pas voter) to abstain; **2** (éviter) **s'∼ de qch/de faire** to refrain from sth/from doing; **s'∼ de tout commentaire** to refrain from any comment; **abstenez-vous de café** keep off coffee; **'pas sérieux s'∼'** 'no time-wasters'

⸨Idiome⸩ **dans le doute, abstiens-toi** Prov when in doubt, do nowt Prov

abstention /apstɑ̃sjɔ̃/ *nf* abstention; **il y a eu 10% d'∼** 10% abstained

abstinence /apstinɑ̃s/ *nf* abstinence

abstraction /apstʀaksjɔ̃/ *nf* abstraction; **faire ∼ de** to forget [*douleur, goût, différence*]

abstrait, ∼**e** /apstʀɛ, ɛt/
A *adj* abstract
B *nm* **1** (opposé à concret) abstract; **dans l'∼** in the abstract; **2** (art) abstract art

absurde /apsyʀd/
A *adj* absurd
B *nm* absurd; **démontrer qch par l'∼** to prove sth by contradiction

absurdité /apsyʀdite/ *nf* **1** (caractère) absurdity; **l'∼ de ses déclarations** the absurdity of his/her statements; **2** (acte, parole) nonsense ¢; **tu dis des ∼s** you're talking nonsense

abus /aby/ *nm inv* abuse; **l'∼ d'alcool** alcohol abuse; **'∼ dangereux'** 'can seriously damage your health'; **il y a de l'∼!**○ that's a bit much○!

⸨Composés⸩ ∼ **de confiance** breach of trust; ∼ **de langage** misuse of language; ∼ **de pouvoir** abuse of power

abuser /abyze/ [1]
A *vtr* liter to fool; **se laisser ∼** to be taken in
B **abuser de** *vtr ind* **1** (faire un usage excessif de) ∼ **de l'alcool** to drink to excess; ∼ **des sucreries** to overindulge in sweet things; **2** (profiter de) ∼ **de la situation** to exploit the situation; ∼ **de la patience de qn** to take advantage of sb's patience; **je ne voudrais pas ∼** (de votre gentillesse) I don't want to impose (on your kindness); ∼ **de sa force** to abuse one's strength; **3** (violenter) ∼ **de qn** to sexually abuse sb
C *vi* (exagérer) to go too far; **je suis patient mais il ne faut pas ∼** I may be patient but don't push me too far

⸨Idiome⸩ **si je ne m'abuse** if I'm not mistaken

a

abuseur /abyzœʀ/ nm molester

(Composé) ~ **d'enfants** child abuser

abusif, -ive /abyzif, iv/ adj **[1]** (exagéré) excessive; **faire un usage** ~ **de qch** to use sth excessively; **[2]** (injuste) gén unfair; [détention] wrongful; **[3]** (impropre) improper; **emploi** ~ **d'un terme** improper use of a term; **donner une interprétation abusive de qch** to misrepresent sth; **[4]** (possessif) [mère] over-possessive

abusivement /abyzivmã/ adv **[1]** (exagérément) excessively; **[2]** (injustement) wrongly; **[3]** (improprement) misguidedly; **terme employé** ~ term improperly used

abyme /abim/ nm **structure** or **composition en** ~ (de pièce) play-within-a-play; (de tableau) image repeated to infinity; (de roman) 'Chinese boxes' structure

acabit /akabi/ nm pej **de cet** or **du même** ~ of that sort; **les gens de ton** ~ people like you

acacia /akasja/ nm **[1]** (d'Europe) **(faux)** ~ locust tree, false acacia; **miel d'**~ acacia honey; **[2]** (de régions chaudes) acacia

académicien, -ienne /akademisjɛ̃, ɛn/ nm,f gén academician; (de l'Académie française) member of the Académie française

académie /akademi/ nf **[1]** (école) school; ~ **de peinture** or **de dessin** art academy; **[2]** Scol, Univ ≈ local education authority GB, school district US

> ℹ **Académie française** A scholarly body composed of 40 life members selected on the basis of their contribution to scholarship or literature. It is primarily known nowadays for its role in monitoring developments in the French language and for its rulings on French usage which are encoded in the *Dictionnaire de l'Académie française* but which are not always taken seriously by the public at large.

académique /akademik/ adj **[1]** gén academic; (de l'Académie française) of the Académie française; **[2]** Scol, Univ ≈ of the local education authority GB ou school district US; **[3]** (en art) academic

académisme /akademism/ nm academicism

acajou /akaʒu/

A adj inv **[1]** ▸ p. 140 (couleur) mahogany; **[2]** (qui imite) **table** ~ imitation mahogany table

B nm (arbre) mahogany tree; (bois) mahogany; **table en** ~ mahogany table

acariâtre /akaʀjɑtʀ/ adj gén cantankerous

acarien /akaʀjɛ̃/ nm dust mite

accablant, ~e /akablã, ãt/ adj [chaleur, silence] oppressive; [tristesse] overwhelming; [fait] damning

accablement /akabləmã/ nm depression

accabler /akable/ [1] vtr **[1]** (écraser) [chaleur, mauvaise nouvelle] to devastate; **être accablé de soucis** to be overwhelmed with worries; ~ **qn de** to overburden sb with [impôts]; ~ **qn d'injures** to heap insults on sb; **[2]** (condamner) [témoignage, enquête, personne] to condemn

accalmie /akalmi/ nf (de temps) lull; fig (de lutte, crise) lull; (d'activité) slack period

accaparant, ~e /akaparã, ãt/ adj very demanding

accaparer /akapaʀe/ [1] vtr to hoard [marchandises]; to corner [marché]; to monopolize [personne, pouvoir]; to pre-occupy [esprit]

accédant, ~e /aksedã, ãt/ nm,f ~ **à la propriété** home-buyer

accéder /aksede/ [14] vtr ind **[1]** (atteindre) ~ **à** to reach [lieu]; **[2]** (obtenir) ~ **à** to achieve [gloire]; to obtain [poste]; to reach [fonctions]; ~ **à la propriété** to become a home-owner; ~ **au pouvoir** to come to power; **[3]** fml (satisfaire à) ~ **à** to grant [prière]

accélérateur, -trice /akseleratœr, tris/ nm Aut accelerator; **appuyer sur l'**~ to step on the accelerator; **donner un coup d'**~ **à qch** fig to give sth a boost

(Composé) ~ **de particules** particle accelerator

accélération /akselerasjõ/ nf (de vitesse) acceleration (de of); (de consommation) sharp increase (de in)

accéléré, ~e /akselere/ adj accelerated; **à un rythme** ~ at an increasingly fast rate; **stage de formation** ~e intensive course

accélérer /akselere/ [14]

A vtr (hâter) to speed up [rythme, mouvement]; to accelerate

[processus, réaction]; ~ **le pas** to quicken one's step

B vi **[1]** [conducteur] to accelerate; **accélère!** speed up! **[2]** (se dépêcher)○ fig to get a move on○

C s'accélérer vpr **[1]** (aller plus vite) [pouls, mouvement] to quicken; **les événements s'accélèrent** the pace of events is quickening; **[2]** (s'intensifier) [phénomène, tendance] to accelerate

accent /aksã/ nm **[1]** (façon de parler) accent; **avoir l'**~ **bordelais** to have a Bordeaux accent; **[2]** (sur une lettre) accent; **prendre un** ~ [mot, lettre] to have an accent; (sur une syllabe) ~ **tonique** stress; ~ **de hauteur** pitch; **mettre l'**~ **sur qch** fig to put the emphasis on sth; **[4]** (nuance, note) overtone; ~ **de sincérité** hint of sincerity; ~ **de vérité** ring of truth

accentuation /aksãtɥasjõ/ nf **[1]** (de crise) escalation; (d'inégalités) heightening; (de phénomène) worsening; (de tendance) increase; **[2]** (de syllabe) stress; (en poésie) accentuation; **[3]** (de lettres) accents (pl)

accentuer /aksãtɥe/ [1]

A vtr **[1]** (rendre plus évident) [situation] to accentuate [inégalités]; to heighten [tensions]; to increase [tendance]; **[2]** (tenter de faire ressortir) [personne] to highlight [trait de caractère]; to emphasize [aspect]; **[3]** (rendre tonique) to stress; (en poésie) to accentuate [syllabe]; **[4]** (écrire) to put an accent on [lettre]; **lettre accentuée** accented letter

B s'accentuer vpr to become more marked

acceptable /akseptabl/ adj **[1]** (tolérable) [seuil, norme, condition] acceptable; **rendre qch** ~ to make sth acceptable (à to); **[2]** (passable) [travail, qualité] passable; [résultat] satisfactory

acceptation /akseptasjõ/ nf acceptance; **sous réserve d'**~ subject to acceptance

accepter /aksepte/ [1] vtr to accept [invitation, personne, défi, excuse]; to agree to [condition, contrat]; ~ **qch de qn** to accept sth from sb; ~ **de faire qch** to agree to do sth; **s'il te plaît, accepte!** please say yes!; **faire** ~ **qch** to get sth accepted

acception /aksepsjõ/ nf sense; **dans toute l'**~ **du terme** or **mot** in every sense of the word

accès /aksε/ nm inv **[1]** (moyen, possibilité d'atteindre) access; **moyens d'**~ means of access; **d'un** ~ **facile** easy to get to; [personne] approachable/unapproachable; **l'**~ **au village** (possibilité d'atteindre) access to the village; (moyen d'atteindre) the way into the village; **cela donne** ~ **à** (mener) it leads to; **toutes les voies d'**~ **sont barrées** (routes) all approach roads are closed off; '~ **aux quais'** 'to the trains'; **[2]** (moyen d'entrer) **l'**~ **à** access to; **les** ~ **du bâtiment** the entrances to the building; **les** ~ **de la ville** the approach roads to the town; **[3]** (droit d'entrée) **ne pas avoir** ~ **à** not to be admitted to; **interdire l'**~ **aux enfants** not to admit children; '~ **interdit'** 'no entry'; '~ **interdit aux chiens'** 'no dogs (allowed)'; **[4]** (possibilité d'obtenir, utiliser) access; **avoir** ~ **à** to have access to; **[5]** (possibilité de participer à) **l'**~ **à** access to [profession, cours]; admission to [club, école]; **[6]** (possibilité de comprendre) **d'un** ~ **facile** accessible; **d'un** ~ **difficile** not very accessible; **[7]** (crise) **l'**~ **de colère** fit of anger; ~ **de fièvre** bout of fever; **par** ~ by fits and starts; **[8]** Ordinat access

accessible /aksesibl/ adj **[1]** [lieu, ouvrage] accessible (à to); **langage** ~ **à tous** a language which can be understood by everyone; **[2]** [emploi] ~ **à** open to; **[3]** [prix, tarif] affordable (à qn to sb); **[4]** (qu'on peut approcher) [personne] approachable

accession /aksesjõ/ nf ~ **à** accession to [trône, pouvoir]; attainment of [indépendance]; ~ **à la propriété** home-buying

accessit /aksesit/ nm honourable○GB mention

accessoire /akseswaʀ/

A adj [problème] incidental

B nm **[1]** (d'auto, de vêtement) accessory; (d'appareil) attachment; ~**s de salle de bains** bathroom accessories; ~**s de toilette** toilet requisites; **[2]** Cin, Théât ~**s** props

(Idiome) **ranger au magasin des** ~**s** to shelve

accessoirement /akseswarmã/ adv (en plus) incidentally, as it happens; (le cas échéant) if desired

accessoiriste /akseswarist/ ▸ p. 372 nmf props man/woman

accident /aksidã/ nm **[1]** (dommage) accident; ~ **grave** serious accident; **l'**~ **a fait deux morts** two died as a result of the accident; **un** ~ **est si vite arrivé!** accidents can easily happen!; **il y a 10 000 morts par** ~ **chaque année** 10,000 people die in accidents every year; [2] (problème) hitch; (événement inhabituel) one off○; hum accident; ~ **de parcours**○ hitch; hum accident; **une découverte faite par** ~ (par hasard) a chance discovery; [3] Méd accident; ~ **cardiaque** cardiac event; [4] (inégalité) ~ **de terrain** irregularity in the landscape, accident spéc

Composés) ~ **d'avion** plane crash; ~ **corporel** accident involving injury; ~ **ferroviaire** rail accident; ~ **de montagne** climbing accident; ~ **de la route** road accident; ~ **du travail** industrial accident

accidenté, ~**e** /aksidɑ̃te/
A adj [1] [personne] injured; [véhicule] involved in an accident (après n); [2] [chemin, terrain] uneven
B nm,f accident victim; **les** ~**s de la route** road accident victims; **les** ~**s du travail** people injured at work

accidentel, **-elle** /aksidɑ̃tεl/ adj accidental

accidentellement /aksidɑ̃tεlma/ adv [1] (dans un accident) accidentally; [2] (par hasard) by accident

accidenter /aksidɑ̃te/ [1] vtr to bump [véhicule]

acclamation /aklamasjɔ̃/ nf cheering ¢; **sous les** ~**s de** to the cheering of

acclamer /aklame/ [1] vtr to cheer, to acclaim

acclimater /aklimate/ [1]
A vtr to acclimatize
B s'**acclimater** vpr [plante, animal] to become acclimatized; [personne] to adapt

accointances /akwɛ̃tɑ̃s/ nfpl contacts

accolade /akɔlad/ nf [1] (embrassade) embrace; **donner l'**~ **à qn** to embrace sb; [2] (signe) brace

accoler /akɔle/ [1] vtr ~ **une étiquette à** to attach a label to

accommodant, ~**e** /akɔmɔdɑ̃, ɑ̃t/ adj [personne] accommodating

accommoder /akɔmɔde/ [1]
A vtr [1] to prepare [aliment, plat]; **l'art d'**~ **les restes** the art of using up leftovers; [2] (adapter) to adapt
B vi [œil] to focus
C s'**accommoder** vpr s'~ **de qch** (positif) to make the best of sth; (plus résigné) to put up with sth; s'~ **à** to adapt to

accompagnateur, **-trice** /akɔ̃paɲatœr, tris/ ▸ p. 372 nm,f [1] Mus accompanist; [2] (d'enfants) accompanying adult; (de groupe touristique) courier; **vingt athlètes et** ~**s** twenty athletes and accompanying personnel

accompagnement /akɔ̃paɲmɑ̃/ nm [1] Mus accompaniment; **sans** ~ unaccompanied; ~ **musical** musical arrangement; [2] Culin accompaniment; [3] (de malade) caring (**de** for); (de touristes) accompanying; **mesures d'**~ attendant measures

accompagner /akɔ̃paɲe/ [1]
A vtr [1] (se déplacer avec) to accompany; (conduire) to take (**à** to); **tu m'accompagnes à la gare?** will you come to the station with me?; **je vais vous (y)** ~ (en voiture) I'll take you (there); (à pied) I'll come with you; ~ **un enfant à l'école** to take a child to school; **20% de réduction à la personne qui vous accompagne** 20 % reduction for any person travelling○ with you; **ces personnes vous accompagnent?** are these people with you?; **accompagné/non accompagné** [bagage, enfant] accompanied/unaccompanied; [2] (aller de pair avec) to accompany; **une cassette accompagne le livre** there's a cassette with the book; **CV accompagné de deux photos** CV ou resumé US together with two photographs; **l'inflation et les problèmes qui l'accompagnent** inflation and its attendant problems; [3] (soutenir) to back; [4] Mus to accompany (**à** on); [5] (être servi avec) **vin pour** ~ **un plat** wine to accompany a dish
B s'**accompagner** vpr Mus to accompany oneself (**à** on); (s'associer à) to be accompanied (**de** by)

accomplir /akɔ̃plir/ [3]
A vtr [1] (s'acquitter de) to accomplish [tâche, mission]; to fulfil○ [obligation]; to do [service militaire]; to serve [peine de prison]; ~ **de grandes choses** to achieve great things
B s'**accomplir** vpr [vœu, prévisions] to be fulfilled○

accomplissement /akɔ̃plismɑ̃/ nm (d'activité, de mission) accomplishment; (réalisation) achievement

accord /akɔr/ nm [1] (consentement) agreement (**à** to); **donner son** ~ **à qch** to agree to sth; **donner son** ~ **pour faire** to authorize sb to do; **d'un commun** ~ by mutual agreement; [2] (pacte) agreement (**portant sur** on);

(non formel) understanding; ~ **de cessez-le-feu** ceasefire agreement; **conclure un** ~ to enter into an agreement; ~**s de commerce** trade agreements; [3] (avis partagé, entente) agreement (**sur** on); **en** ou **d'**~ **avec qn** in agreement with sb; **être d'**~ **(que)** to agree (that); **je ne suis pas d'**~ **avec toi là-dessus** I disagree with you on this; **Pierre est d'**~ **pour faire** Pierre has agreed to do; **je suis/je ne suis pas d'**~ **pour payer** I am/I am not willing to pay; **je ne suis pas d'**~ **pour que nous fassions** I am not in favour○ of our doing; **se mettre** ou **tomber d'**~ to come to an agreement; **mettre tout le monde d'**~ (du même avis) to bring everybody round○ to the same way of thinking; (mettre fin aux querelles) to put an end to the argument; **tu es d'**~ **pour la plage**○**?** are you on for the beach○?; **'on signe?'—'d'**~**'**○ 'shall we sign?'—'OK○, all right'; [4] (entre personnes, couleurs, styles) harmony; **être en** ~ **avec** (avec écrit, tradition, promesse) to be in keeping ou consistent with; **agir en** ~ **avec le règlement** to act in accordance with the rules; [5] Ling agreement; [6] Mus (notes) chord

Composés) ~ **à l'amiable** informal agreement; ~ **de gré à gré** mutual agreement; ~ **de principe** agreement in principle; ~ **salarial** wage settlement

accordéon /akɔrdeɔ̃/ ▸ p. 389
A nm accordion; **en** ~ fig [chaussettes] wrinkled; [voiture] wrecked; **plier qch en** ~ to fold sth into pleats; **plié en** ~ folded into a concertina
B (-)**accordéon** (in compounds) **porte** ~ folding door

accordéoniste /akɔrdeɔnist/ ▸ p. 372, p. 389 nmf accordion-player

accorder /akɔrde/ [1]
A vtr [1] (octroyer) ~ **qch à qn** to grant sth to sb, to grant sb sth [faveur, prêt, entretien, permission, droit]; to give ou award sth to sb, to give ou award sb sth [indemnité, bourse]; to give sth to sb, to give sb sth [réduction, chance, interview]; ~ **une aide financière à qn** to give sb financial assistance; **peux-tu m'**~ **quelques instants?** can you spare me a few moments?; ~ **sa confiance à qn** to put one's trust in sb; [2] (prêter) to attach [importance, valeur] (**à** to); to pay [attention]; [3] (concéder) ~ **à qn que** to admit to sb that; **il n'a pas entièrement tort, je te l'accorde** he's not entirely wrong, I'll give you that; [4] (harmoniser) to match [coloris] (**avec** with); [5] Mus to tune [instrument]; [6] Ling to make [sth] agree [mot] (**avec** with)
B s'**accorder** vpr [1] (s'octroyer) to give oneself [repos, congé]; [2] (être ou se mettre d'accord) to agree (**sur** about, on); **ils s'accordent à dire** (tous les deux) they both say; (eux tous) they all say; [3] (s'entendre) [personnes] to get on together; [4] (s'harmoniser) [couleurs] to go (together) well; **leurs caractères s'accordent** they are well matched; [5] [adjectif, verbe] to agree (**avec** with); [6] Mus to tune up

accordeur /akɔrdœr/ ▸ p. 372 nm tuner

accostage /akɔstaʒ/ nm docking

accoster /akɔste/ [1]
A vtr [1] Naut to come alongside [quai, navire]; [2] (aborder) to accost [personne]
B vi Naut to dock

accotement /akɔtmɑ̃/ nm verge; ~ **meuble** or **non stabilisé** soft verge GB, soft shoulder

accouchement /akuʃmɑ̃/ nm delivery; ~ **à terme/avant terme** or **prématuré** full-term/premature birth; **préparation à l'**~ preparation for birth

Composés) ~ **provoqué** induced delivery; ~ **sans douleur** natural childbirth; ~ **par le siège** breech birth

accoucher /akuʃe/ [1]
A vtr to deliver
B accoucher de vtr ind ~ **de** to give birth to [enfant]; (produire)○ ~ **de** to produce [œuvre, idée]
C vi to give birth

accoucheur /akuʃœr/ ▸ p. 372 nm **médecin** ~ obstetrician

accoucheuse /akuʃøz/ ▸ p. 372 nf midwife

accouder : s'accouder /akude/ [1] vpr to lean on one's elbows (**à, sur** on)

accoudoir /akudwar/ nm arm-rest

accouplement /akuplɑ̃mɑ̃/ nm [1] (pour reproduction) mating; [2] Tech coupling

accoupler /akuple/ [1]
A vtr [1] (pour reproduction) to mate (**à** with); [2] Tech to couple
B s'**accoupler** vpr to mate

accourir /akuRiR/ [26] *vi* to run up; **~ au secours de qn/pour faire** to rush to sb's aid/to do; **les candidats sont accourus de toute la région** candidates came running from all over the area

accoutrement /akutRəmɑ̃/ *nm* pej get-up○

accoutrer /akutRe/ [1]
A *vtr* pej **~ qn de qch** to rig sb out in sth
B s'accoutrer *vpr* to get oneself up (**de** in); **il s'accoutre vraiment n'importe comment!** he dresses any old how!

accoutumance /akutymɑ̃s/ *nf* [1] gén familiarization; **une période d'~** an acclimatization period; [2] (à un médicament) addiction (**à** to)

accoutumé, **~e** /akutyme/
A *adj* (habituel) customary
B comme à l'accoutumée *loc adv* as usual

accoutumer /akutyme/ [1]
A *vtr* fml to accustom
B s'accoutumer *vpr* **s'~ à (faire) qch** to grow accustomed to (doing) sth; **être accoutumé à (faire) qch** to be used *ou* accustomed to (doing) sth

accrédité, **~e** /akRedite/ *adj* [représentant] accredited (**auprès de** to); [fournisseur] authorized

accréditer /akRedite/ [1] *vtr* [1] (rendre crédible) to give credence to [opinion, rumeur]; to lend weight to [idée, théorie]; [2] (faire reconnaître) to accredit [ambassade]

accroc /akRo/ *nm* (déchirure) tear (**à** in); **faire un ~ à qch** to tear sth; **sans ~(s)** fig without a hitch

accrochage /akRoʃaʒ/ *nm* (affrontement) clash (**entre** between); (légère collision) bump (**avec** with)

accroche-cœur, *pl* **~s** /akRoʃkœR/ *nm* kiss curl

accrocher /akRoʃe/ [1]
A *vtr* [1] (suspendre) to hang (**à** from); [2] (attacher) to hook [sth] on (**à** to); **la chaîne était mal accrochée** the chain wasn't hooked on properly; [3] (faire un accroc à) to catch [bas, pull] (**à** on); [4] (heurter) to bump into; [5] (attirer) to catch [regard, attention]
B *vi* [1] (coincer) [fermeture] to stick; [2] (attirer) [titre, image, publicité] to catch on
C s'accrocher *vpr* [1] (se suspendre) lit (à une corniche) to hang on; (à un poteau) to cling (on) (**à** to); **accroche-toi à la branche** hang on to the branch; [2] (s'attacher) lit, fig [personne] to cling (**à** to); **s'~ au bras de qn** to cling to sb's arm; **l'hameçon s'est accroché à ma veste** the hook got caught on my jacket; [3] ○(tenir bon) **s'~ pour faire** to try hard to do; **accroche-toi!** (sur une moto) hang on to your hat!; (avant histoire, film) brace yourself!; [4] (se disputer) **s'~ avec qn** to have a brush with sb

(Idiome) **avoir le cœur** *or* **l'estomac bien accroché** to have a strong stomach

accrocheur, **-euse** /akRoʃœR, øz/ *adj* (attrayant) [chanson, air] catchy; [image, titre] eye-catching

accroissement /akRwasmɑ̃/ *nm* growth, increase

accroître /akRwatR/ [72] *vtr*, **s'accroître** *vpr* to increase

accroupi, **~e** /akRupi/ *adj* gén squatting (down); (pour se cacher) crouching

accroupir: s'accroupir /akRupiR/ [3] *vpr* gén to squat (down); (pour se cacher) to crouch (down)

accru, **~e** /akRy/ *pp* ▸ accroître

accueil /akœj/ *nm* (manière) welcome, reception; **~ froid** cool reception; **il a reçu le meilleur ~** he received the warmest of welcomes; (service) reception

accueillant, **~e** /akœjɑ̃, ɑ̃t/ *adj* [1] [personne] hospitable *ou* welcoming (**à l'égard de** to); [2] [maison] homely GB, homey US; [ville, campagne] friendly, welcoming; [appartement, chambre] inviting

accueillir /akœjiR/ [27] *vtr* [1] (souhaiter la bienvenue) to welcome; [2] (recevoir) to receive [personne, livre, décision]; **bien/mal ~ qn/qch** to give sb/sth a good/bad reception; **j'ai été bien accueilli** (à l'arrivée) I was given a warm welcome; (pendant le séjour) I was made to feel very welcome; **ils ont été accueillis par des acclamations** they were greeted with cheers; [3] (contenir) to accommodate [personnes]; [4] (prendre en charge) [organisme, hôpital] to cater for

acculer /akyle/ [1] *vtr* (dans une situation) **~ qn à (faire) qch** to force sb into (doing) sth; **~ qn à la ruine/au désespoir** to drive sb to ruin/to despair

accumulateur /akymylatœR/ *nm* accumulator GB, storage battery; **~ de chaleur** storage heater; **~ de froid** freeze pack

accumulation /akymylasjɔ̃/ *nf* [1] (action, résultat) accumulation; **une ~ de preuves** a mass of evidence; [2] (emmagasinage) storage; **radiateur à ~** storage heater

accumuler /akymyle/ [1]
A *vtr* (entasser) store (up) [objets]; (amasser) to accumulate [biens, capital]; (répéter) to make a succession of [erreurs]; to have a string of [succès]; (emmagasiner) to store (up) [énergie, chaleur]
B s'accumuler *vpr* (s'entasser) [neige, commandes] to pile up; (s'accroître) [stocks, dettes] to accrue

accusateur, **-trice** /akyzatœR, tRis/
A *adj* [silence, doigt] accusing (épith); [présence, discours] accusatory
B *nm,f* accuser; **~ public** Hist public prosecutor

accusatif /akyzatif/ *nm* Ling accusative

accusation /akyzasjɔ̃/ *nf* [1] (reproche grave) accusation; Jur (formulation) charge; **mettre qn en ~** Jur to indict sb; [2] (ministère public) **l'~** the prosecution

accusé, **~e** /akyze/
A *adj* (accentué) [traits] strong; [ride] deep; [relief] marked
B *nm,f* defendant; **les ~s** the accused

(Composé) **~ de réception** acknowledgement of receipt

accuser /akyze/ [1]
A *vtr* [1] [plaignant] to accuse (**de** of); [juge] to charge (**de** with); **accusé du meurtre de sa femme** (par le plaignant, un témoin) accused of murdering his wife; (à l'issue du procès) charged with murdering his wife; [2] (rendre coupable) [personne] to accuse [personne] (**de (faire)** of (doing)); to blame [sort]; [fait] to point to [personne]; **accusé d'espionnage** accused of spying; **les photos qui l'accusent** the incriminating photos; **~ qn/qch de tous les maux** to put all the blame on sb/sth; [3] (rendre évident) to show [baisse, déficit]; **~ une hausse** to show an increase; [4] (confirmer) **~ réception** to acknowledge receipt (**de** of)
B s'accuser *vpr* [1] (soi-même) to take the blame (**de qch** for sth; **d'avoir fait** for doing); [2] (l'un l'autre) to accuse each other (**de (faire)** of (doing)); [3] (s'aggraver) to become more marked

(Idiome) **~ le coup** to be visibly shaken

acerbe /asɛRb/ *adj* acerbic

acéré, **~e** /asere/ *adj* lit [objet] sharp

acétique /asetik/ *adj* acetic

achalandé, **~e** /aʃalɑ̃de/ *adj* controv (approvisionné) **bien/mal ~** well-/poorly-stocked

acharné, **~e** /aʃaRne/
A *pp* ▸ acharner
B *pp adj* [partisan] passionate; [fumeur, séducteur] incorrigible; [travail] unremitting; [lutte, discussion] fierce; **c'est un travailleur ~** he works relentlessly

acharnement /aʃaRnəmɑ̃/ *nm* (énergie) furious energy; **l'~ de qn à faire** sb's determination to do; **son ~ au travail** the fact that he/she works so relentlessly; **lutter avec ~** to fight tooth and nail

acharner: s'acharner /aʃaRne/ [1] *vpr* [1] (s'obstiner) to persevere; **s'~ à faire** to try desperately to do; **à force de s'~** by persevering; **s'~ contre** to fight against [projet]; [2] (continuer des violences) **s'~ sur** [personne, animal] to keep going at [victime, proie]; fig [personne] to hound [enfant, collaborateur]; **la fatalité s'acharne sur eux** they're dogged by bad luck

achat /aʃa/ *nm* [1] (action) **l'~ de qch** buying sth, the purchase of sth; **un ~** a purchase; **c'est plus cher à l'~** it's more expensive to buy; **25% à l'~** 25% of the total at the time of purchase; **l'~ sur catalogue** buying by mail order; **faire des ~s** to do some shopping; **l'~ par téléphone** telephone shopping; [2] (objet acheté) purchase

acheminement /aʃ(ə)minmɑ̃/ *nm* [1] (de personnes, vivres) transportation (**vers** to); **des retards dans l'~ du courrier** postal delays; [2] fig **l'~ du pays vers la ruine** the country's march toward(s) ruin

acheminer /aʃ(ə)mine/ [1]
A *vtr* (transporter) to transport [personne, vivres] (**vers** to); **~ le courrier** to handle the mail
B s'acheminer *vpr* [1] [personne, troupe] to make one's way (**vers** to *ou* toward(s)); [2] fig **s'~ vers** [négociations] to move toward(s); [pays, économie] (aboutissement fâcheux) to head for *ou* toward(s); (aboutissement positif) to move toward(s)

acheter /aʃte/ [18]

A vtr ① to buy; ~ **qch sur catalogue** to buy sth from a catalogueᴳᴮ; ~ **qch à qn** (pour lui) to buy sth for sb; (chez lui) to buy sth from sb; ~ **pour 2 euros de qch** to buy 2 euros worth of sth; ~ **qch 2 euros** to buy sth for 2 euros; ~ **français** to buy French products; ② (soudoyer) to buy

B **s'acheter** vpr ① (pour soi) **s'~ qch** to buy oneself sth; ② (être disponible à l'achat) **cela s'achète où?** where can you get it?

acheteur, -euse /aʃtœʀ, øz/

A adj [pays] importing

B nm,f ① (client) buyer, purchaser; **je vends ma voiture, es-tu ~?** I'm selling my car, would you like to buy it?; **à ce prix-là je ne suis pas ~** at that price, I'm not interested; ② ▸ p. 372 (professionnel) buyer

achevé, ~e /aʃve/ adj liter [œuvre, technique] accomplished; [exemple, forme, modèle] perfect

achèvement /aʃevmã/ nm (de travaux, projet, roman) completion; (de discussions) conclusion

achever /aʃve/ [16]

A vtr ① (terminer) to finish [travail]; to conclude [discussions]; to complete [projet, visite, enquête, service militaire]; to end [vie]; ~ **de faire** to finish doing; ② (réussir) **ta démonstration a achevé de me convaincre** the proof you gave me finally convinced me; ③ (tuer) to destroy [animal]; to finish off [personne]; ④ ᐤ(épuiser) [personne, effort] to wear [sb] out, to finishᐤ; ⑤ ᐤ(terrasser) [scandale, ruine] to finish [sb] off

B **s'achever** vpr to end (**par** with; **sur** on); **le jour s'achève** the day is drawing to a close

achoppement /aʃɔpmã/ nm **pierre d'~** stumbling block

acide /asid/

A adj ① (pas assez sucré) [goût] acid, sour; (agréablement) [goût] sharp; (comme propriété naturelle) [aliment] acidic; ② [odeur] acrid; ③ Chimie acid, acidic

B nm ① Chimie acid; ~ **gras** fatty acid; ② ᐤ(drogue) acidᐤ

(Composé) ~ **aminé** amino acid

acidité /asidite/ nf (désagréable) gén acidity; (agréable) tartness, sharpness; Chimie acidity

acidulé, ~e /asidyle/ adj ① [goût] slightly acid; ② [parfum] tangy; [jaune, vert] acid

acier /asje/

A ▸ p. 140 adj inv steel(y)

B nm ① (alliage) steel; **d'~** [cuve] steel (épith); [muscle, nerf] of steel; **avoir un moral d'~** to be made of stern stuff; ② (industrie) steel industry

aciérie /asjeʀi/ nf steelworks (+ v sg ou pl)

acné /akne/ nf acne; ~ **juvénile** teenage acne

acnéique /akneik/ adj [peau] acned

acolyte /akɔlit/ nmf (complice) pej henchman, acolyte

acompte /akɔ̃t/ nm ① (premier versement) down payment; (arrhes) deposit; (versement partiel) part payment; ~ **sur salaire** advance on salary

(Composé) ~ **provisionnel** (pour impôt) ≈ first instalmentᴳᴮ

acoquiner: s'acoquiner /akɔkine/ [1] vpr **s'~ avec qn** to get thickᐤ with sb

Açores /asɔʀ/ ▸ p. 303 nprfpl **les ~** the Azores

à-côté, pl **~s** /akote/ nm ① (avantages) perk; (gains) **se faire de petits ~s** to make a bit on the sideᐤ; ② (dépenses) extra

à-coup, pl **~s** /aku/ nm (secousse) jolt; **les ~s du moteur** the coughs and splutters of the engine; **par ~s** lit, fig by ou in fits and starts

acoustique /akustik/

A adj acoustic

B nf Phys acoustics (+ v sg); (d'un lieu) acoustics (pl)

acquéreur /akeʀœʀ/ nm buyer, purchaser; **elle est ~** she's interested; **se porter ~ de** to state one's intention to buy; **se rendre ~ de** to purchase

acquérir /akeʀiʀ/ [35]

A vtr ① (devenir propriétaire de) to acquire; (en achetant) to purchase; ② (arriver à avoir) to acquire; ~ **une formation** to undergo training; ~ **la certitude que** to become convinced that; ~ **de la valeur** to gain in value; **il est acquis à notre cause** we have his support; **il est acquis que** it is accepted that

B **s'acquérir** vpr ① (s'obtenir) **s'~ facilement** to be easy to acquire; ② (s'apprendre) **quelque chose qui s'acquiert** something you acquire; **l'expérience s'acquiert avec l'âge** experience comes with age

acquiescement /akjɛsmã/ fml nm **donner son ~ à** to acquiesce to

acquiescer /akjese/ [12] vi to acquiesce; ~ **d'un signe de tête** to nod in agreement; **et sa fille d'~** and the daughter agrees

acquis, ~e /aki, iz/

A pp ▸ **acquérir**

B pp adj ① (obtenu, en psychologie) acquired; ② (reconnu) [principe, droit] accepted, established; **les avantages ~** the gains; **tenir qch pour ~** to take sth for granted

C nm inv ① (connaissances) knowledge; ② (avantage obtenu) ~ **syndicaux** union gains; ~ **sociaux** social benefits; **c'est un ~** that is one thing gained; ③ (en psychologie) **l'~** acquired knowledge

(Idiome) **bien mal ~ ne profite jamais** Prov ill-gotten gains never prosper

acquisition /akizisjɔ̃/ nf ① (achat) purchase; **prix d'~** purchase price; ② Ordinat data capture; ③ (de musée, bibliothèque) acquisition; ④ (processus) acquisition

acquit /aki/ nm Comm receipt; **pour ~** received

(Idiome) **par ~ de conscience** to put one's mind at rest

acquittement /akitmã/ nm Jur acquittal

acquitter /akite/ [1]

A vtr ① Jur to acquit [personne]; **faire ~ qn** to get sb acquitted; ② (payer) to pay

B **s'acquitter** vpr **s'~ de son devoir** to discharge one's duty; **s'~ d'une dette** lit to pay off a debt; fig to repay a debt of gratitude

âcre /akʀ/ adj [goût, fruit] sharp; [fumée, odeur] acrid

acrimonie /akʀimɔni/ nf liter acrimony littér

acrobate /akʀɔbat/ ▸ p. 372 nmf lit, fig acrobat

acrobatie /akʀɔbasi/ nf ① (mouvement) **faire des ~s** Sport to do ou perform acrobatics; fig to jump through all sorts of hoops. ② (activité) **l'~** acrobatics (+ v sg); ~ **aérienne** aerobatics (+ v sg)

acronyme /akʀɔnim/ nm acronym

acrylique /akʀilik/ adj, nm acrylic

acte /akt/

A nm ① (action) act; **mes/tes ~s** my/your actions; **être libre de ses ~s** to do as one wishes; **faire ~ de candidature** to put oneself forward as a candidate; **faire ~ de présence** to put in an appearance; **j'en prends ~** I'll bear it in mind; ③ Théât act; ④ Philos actual

B **actes** nmpl (de congrès, réunion) proceedings; Relig acts

(Composés) ~ **d'accusation** bill of indictment; ~ **de décès** death certificate; ~ **de foi** act of faith; ~ **gratuit** gratuitous act; ~ **manqué** Freudian slip; ~ **de mariage** marriage certificate; ~ **de naissance** birth certificate; ~ **sexuel** sexual act; ~ **de vente** bill of sale; **l'Acte unique européen** Single European Act

acteur, -trice /aktœʀ, tʀis/ nm,f ① ▸ p. 372 Cin, Théât actor/actress; ~ **de cinéma/théâtre** film/stage actor; ② (participant) **~s de la scène politique** actors on the political stage; **les ~s d'un drame** the protagonists of a tragedy; ③ (agent) agent (**de** of)

actif, -ive /aktif, iv/

A adj ① (occupé) active; **les femmes actives** working women; **la vie active** working life; ② (pas passif) [participation] active; **un rôle ~ dans qch** an active part in sth; **une part active à qch** an active part in sth; ③ (plein d'énergie) gén active; [marché, secteur] buoyant; ④ (agissant) [substance, principe] active; ⑤ Ling [forme, voix] active

B nm ① Fin **l'~** the assets (pl); **à mettre à l'~ de qn** fig a point in sb's favourᴳᴮ; ② Ling active (voice)

C actifs nmpl Écon working population (sg)

action /aksjɔ̃/ nf ① (fait d'agir) action; **il serait temps de passer à l'~** gén it's time to act; (combattre) it's time for action; **entrer en ~** Mil to go into action; **un homme d'~** a man of action; **en ~** [personne] in action; [mécanisme] in operation; **mettre qch en ~** to put sth into operation; ② (façon d'agir) action; **programme d'~** plan of action; **moyens d'~** courses of action; **l'~ du temps** the effects of time; **sous l'~ de qch** under the effect of sth; **l'~ de qn sur qch/qn** sb's influence on sth/sb; ④ (bonne, mauvaise) action; act; **une ~ stupide** a stupid act; **des ~s criminelles** criminal acts; **bonne/mauvaise ~** good/bad deed; ⑤ (initiative) initiative; Mil, Jur action; **intenter une**

a

~ **en justice à qn** to take legal action against sb; ⑥ (histoire) action; **l'~ se situe à Venise** the action takes place in Venice; **un film d'~** an action film; **un roman d'~** an adventure novel; ⑦ (en finance) share; **~s et obligations** securities; **une société par ~s** a joint stock company; ~ **nominative** registered share

actionnaire /aksjɔnɛʀ/ *nmf* shareholder, stockholder US; ~ **majoritaire** majority shareholder

actionner /aksjɔne/ [1] *vtr* (mettre en marche) to activate [*sirène, mécanisme*]; (faire fonctionner) to operate

activement /aktivmã/ *adv* actively; **participer ~ à** to take an active part in

activer /aktive/ [1]
A *vtr* ① (hâter) to speed up [*travail, préparatifs*]; to stimulate [*digestion*]; ② (intensifier) [*vent*] to stir up [*flamme*]; [*personne*] to stoke [*feu*]; ③ Chimie to activate
B **s'activer** *vpr* (s'affairer) to be very busy (**pour faire** doing); (se dépêcher)○ to hurry up

activiste /aktivist/ *adj*, *nmf* activist

activité /aktivite/ *nf* ① (occupation) activity; ~ **professionnelle** occupation; **c'est une ~ manuelle** it's manual work; **exercer une ~ rémunérée** to be gainfully employed; **cesser ses ~s** [*entreprise, commerçant*] to stop trading; [*avocat, médecin*] to stop working; **reprendre ses ~s** [*entreprise, commerçant*] to start trading again; [*malade, vacancier*] to go back to work; ② (fonctionnement) activity; **l'~ de la rue** the bustle of the street; **être en pleine ~** [*atelier*] to be in full production; [*rue*] to be bustling with activity; [*personne*] to be very busy; **en ~** [*volcan*] active; [*usine*] in operation; [*travailleur*] working; [*militaire*] in active service GB ou on active duty US; ③ (énergie) (de personne) energy; **d'une ~ débordante** brimming with energy

actrice *nf* ▸ **acteur**

actualisation /aktualizasjɔ̃/ *nf* (mise à jour) (processus) updating ℂ; (résultat) update

actualiser /aktualize/ [1] *vtr* (mettre à jour) to update, to bring [sth] up to date

actualité /aktualite/
A *nf* ① (événements) current affairs (*pl*); **l'~ culturelle** cultural events (*pl*); **être à la une de l'~** to be in the headlines; ② (d'idées, de débat, livre) topicality; (de réflexion) relevance; **sujets d'une brûlante ~** burning issues; **d'~** [*thème, question*] topical; **toujours d'~** still relevant today (*jamais épith*); **plus d'~** no longer at issue
B **actualités** *nfpl* (à la télévision, radio) news; (au cinéma) newsreel (*sg*)

actuel, -elle /aktuɛl/ *adj* ① (présent) present, current; **en l'état ~ de l'enquête** at the current stage of the enquiryᴳᴮ; **en l'état ~ des connaissances** in the present state of our knowledge; **à l'époque actuelle** in the present day; **dans le monde ~** in today's world; **l'~ territoire de la Pologne** the territory of present-day Poland; ② (d'actualité) [*œuvre, débat*] topical

actuellement /aktuɛlmã/ *adv* (en ce moment précis) at the moment, at present; (à notre époque) currently

acuité /akuite/ *nf* (d'intelligence, de perception) acuteness; (de son) shrillness; (de douleur) intensity

acupuncteur, -trice /akypɔ̃ktœʀ, tʀis/ ▸ p. 372 *nm,f* acupuncturist

acupuncture /akypɔ̃ktyʀ/ *nf* acupuncture

adage /adaʒ/ *nm* saying, adage

adaptable /adaptabl/ *adj* ① (souple) adaptable (à to); ② (réglable) adjustable; ~ **à toutes les circonstances** or **tous les besoins** all-purpose (*épith*)

adaptateur, -trice /adaptatœʀ, tʀis/
A ▸ p. 372 *nm,f* Cin, Théât adapter
B *nm* Tech adapter

adaptation /adaptasjɔ̃/ *nf* ① (réajustement) adaptation; **faculté d'~** capacity for adaptation; ~ **à** adjustment to; **problèmes d'~** difficulty in adapting; ② Cin, Mus, Théât adaptation; ~ **libre** loose adaptation

adapté, ~e /adapte/ *adj* ① (approprié) suitable (à for); ~ **à la situation** suited to the circumstances; ② (inséré) [*personne*] adjusted (à to); ③ Cin, Théât adapted (à, **pour** for; **de** from)

adapter /adapte/ [1]
A *vtr* ① (poser) to fit (à to); ② (modifier) to adapt [*équipement*]; ③ (rendre conforme) to adapt [*loi, formation*] (à to); ④ Cin, Théât [*personne*] to adapt [*roman*] (à, **pour** for)

B **s'adapter** *vpr* ① Tech (s'insérer) [*outil, pièce*] to fit (**dans** into); ② (s'habituer) [*personne*] to adapt (**à** to)

additif, -ive /aditif, iv/
A *adj* Math additive
B *nm* (substance) additive; (article, clause) rider (**à** to)

addition /adisjɔ̃/ *nf* ① Math addition ℂ; **il sait déjà faire les ~s** he can already do addition; **faire une erreur d'~** to make a mistake in the addition; **vérifier des ~s** to check sums; **ton ~ est fausse** your sum is wrong; **l'~ des voix** the counting of the votes; ② (ajout de produit) addition; ③ (dans un restaurant) bill, check US; **payer l'~** lit to foot the bill; fig to pay for it

additionner /adisjɔne/ [1]
A *vtr* to add
B **s'additionner** *vpr* (s'accumuler) to add up

adduction /adyksjɔ̃/ *nf* adduction; ~ **d'eau** water conveyance

adepte /adɛpt/ *nmf* (de secte) follower; (de doctrine) supporter; (de personne) disciple; (d'activité) enthusiast

adéquat, ~e /adekwa, at/ *adj* ① (approprié) [*réponse, environnement, choix*] appropriate; [*outil*] suitable; ② (suffisant) [*niveau, formation, soins*] adequate

adéquation /adekwasjɔ̃/ *nf* ① (conformité) appropriateness (**à, avec** to); ② (de modèle) adequacy (**à** to)

adhérence /adeʀɑ̃s/ *nf* (de colle, papier) adhesion (**à** to); (de pneu, semelle) grip; Méd adhesion

adhérent, ~e /adeʀɑ̃, ɑ̃t/
A *adj* [*matière*] which adheres (**à** to) (*après n*)
B *nm,f* (membre) member

adhérer /adeʀe/ [14] *vtr ind* ① (coller) ~ **à** *gén* to stick to; **le pneu adhère à la route** the tyre GB ou tire US grips the road; ② (s'inscrire) ~ **à** to join [*parti, association*]; to become a member of [*organisme*]; (être membre) to be a member of; ③ (se rallier) ~ **à** to subscribe to [*doctrine, politique*]

adhésif, -ive /adezif, iv/
A *adj* adhesive
B *nm* adhesive

adhésion /adezjɔ̃/ *nf* ① (appartenance) membership (**à** of GB, in US); ② (inscription) **l'~ est gratuite** membership is free; **l'~ d'un pays à l'UE** the entry of a country into the EU; **le club vient d'enregistrer dix nouvelles ~s** the club has just enrolled ten new members; ③ (soutien) support (**à** for)

adieu, *pl* ~**x** /adjø/ *nm* goodbye, farewell sout; **se dire ~** to say goodbye (to each other); **dire ~ à qn**, **faire ses ~x à qn** to say goodbye to sb; **un discours d'~** a farewell speech; ~ **le ski** it's goodbye to skiing

adipeux, -euse /adipø, øz/ *adj* [*tissu, cellule*] fatty; [*visage*] podgy

adjacent, ~e /adʒasɑ̃, ɑ̃t/ *adj* adjacent (**à** to)

adjectif, -ive /adʒɛktif, iv/
A *adj* adjectival
B *nm* adjective; ~ **déterminatif** determiner

adjoindre /adʒwɛ̃dʀ/ [56]
A *vtr* **on m'a adjoint un assistant** I've been assigned an assistant; ~ **une pièce au dossier** to attach a document to the file
B **s'adjoindre** *vpr* to take on [*collaborateur, équipe*]

adjoint, ~e /adʒwɛ̃, ɛ̃t/ *nm,f* assistant
〔Composé〕 ~ **au maire** deputy mayor

adjonction /adʒɔ̃ksjɔ̃/ *nf* addition (**à** to)

adjudant /adʒydɑ̃/ ▸ p. 283 *nm* Mil (terre) ≈ warrant officer class II GB, ≈ warrant officer US; (air) *intermediate rank between flight sergeant and warrant officer* GB, ≈ warrant officer US; **oui, mon ~** lit yes, sir; fig, hum yes, sergeant

adjudant-chef, *pl* **adjudants-chefs** /adʒydɑ̃ʃɛf/ ▸ p. 283 *nm* ≈ warrant officer class I GB, ≈ chief warrant officer US

adjudication /adʒydikasjɔ̃/ *nf* (de biens) auction; ~ **judiciaire** sale by order of the court

adjuger /adʒyʒe/ [13]
A *vtr* (vendre aux enchères) to auction; **adjugé 500 euros** auctioned for 500 euros; **une fois, deux fois, adjugé!** going, going, gone!
B **s'adjuger** *vpr* to grant oneself [*part*]; to take [*coupe, titre*]

adjuration /adʒyʀasjɔ̃/ *nf* plea

adjurer /adʒyʀe/ [1] *vtr* to implore (**de faire** to do)

adjuvant /adʒyvɑ̃/ *nm* Chimie additive

ADM /adɛɛm/ *nf* (*abbr* = **arme de destruction massive**) WMD

admettre /admɛtR/ [60] *vtr* ① (reconnaître) to accept, to admit [*fait, hypothèse*]; to admit [*tort, échec, erreur*]; **il faut (bien) ~ que la situation est difficile** it has to be admitted that the situation is difficult; **tout en admettant qu'ils ne l'aient pas fait exprès** whilst accepting that they didn't do it deliberately; ② (accepter) to admit [*personne*] (**dans** to); **elle n'a pas réussi à se faire ~ comme déléguée** she didn't get accepted as a delegate; **je n'admets pas que l'on soit en retard** I won't tolerate people being late; **nous n'admettrons aucune exception** no exceptions will be made; **je n'admets pas qu'on me traite de cette façon** I won't be treated in this way; ③ (supposer) ~ **que** to suppose (that); **'suppose que je gagne!'—'bon, admettons'** 'suppose I win!'—'all right then, suppose you do'; ④ Scol, Univ (accepter) to admit (**en** to); **il n'a pas été admis à se présenter à l'examen** he wasn't allowed to take the exam; **les enfants admis à l'école** children admitted to school; **être admis à l'oral** to get through to the oral; **elle a été admise au concours** she passed the exam; ⑤ (recevoir) to admit (**à** to); **nos salles de classe ne peuvent ~ que 20 élèves** our classrooms can only admit 20 pupils; **être admis à l'hôpital** to be admitted to hospital

administrateur, -trice /administRatœR, tRis/ ▸ p. 372 *nm,f* ① (de bibliothèque, théâtre) administrator; ② (membre du conseil d'administration) director; ③ (de fondation, succession) trustee; ④ (gestionnaire) administrator

(Composé) ~ **de biens** property manager

administratif, -ive /administRatif, iv/ *adj* ① (relatif à l'administration) [*bâtiment, personnel, réforme*] administrative; ② (émis par l'administration) [*rapport*] official

administration /administRasjɔ̃/ *nf* ① Admin, Pol (appareil) administration; ~ **centrale** central administration; ② (fonction publique) civil service; **entrer dans l'~** to go into the civil service; ③ (contrôle) administration; ~ **d'une ville** administration of a city; **sous ~ militaire** under military rule; ④ (gestion) management; ~ **des entreprises** business management; ⑤ (de médicament, sacrement) administration

(Composés) ~ **douanière** customs service; ~ **fiscale** Inland Revenue GB, Internal Revenue US; ~ **judiciaire** Jur receivership; ~ **pénitentiaire** prison service

administré, ~e /administRe/ *nm,f* constituent

administrer /administRe/ [1] *vtr* ① (gérer) to administer [*projet, fonds*]; to run [*économie, pays, compagnie*]; ② (donner) to administer [*médicament, sacrement*] (**à** to); to produce [*preuve*]; to give [*correction, gifle*] (**à** to)

admirable /admiRabl/ *adj* admirable; **être ~ de dévouement** to show admirable devotion

admirablement /admiRabləmɑ̃/ *adv* [*faire*] admirably; [*fait*] superbly

admirateur, -trice /admiRatœR, tRis/ *nm,f* admirer

admiratif, -ive /admiRatif, iv/ *adj* admiring (*épith*)

admiration /admiRasjɔ̃/ *nf* admiration (**pour** for); **avec ~** in admiration; **être en ~ devant qn/qch** to be lost in admiration for sb/sth; **avoir de l'~ pour qn** to admire sb; **digne d'~** admirable

admirer /admiRe/ [1] *vtr* to admire; **très admiré** much admired; ~ **qn de faire** to admire sb for doing

admis, ~e /admi, iz/
Ⓐ *pp* ▸ **admettre**
Ⓑ *pp adj* (reconnu) [*opinion, pratique, théorie*] accepted
Ⓒ *nm,f* Scol, Univ successful candidate

admissibilité /admisibilite/ *nf* ① (d'étudiant) eligibility (*to take oral after written examination*); ② (de preuve, témoignage) admissibility; ③ (d'hypothèse) acceptability

admissible /admisibl/ *adj* ① [*dose, seuil, comportement, argument*] acceptable; [*preuve, témoignage*] admissible; ② [*étudiant*] eligible (*to take oral after written examination*)

admission /admisjɔ̃/ *nf* ① (accueil) admission (**à, en** to); ~ **en maison de retraite** admission to a retirement home; **faire une demande d'~** to fill in an application form; **bureau** *or* **service des ~s** reception; ② (droit) ~ **à** eligibility for; ③ (reconnaissance) admission (**de la part de** by; **que** that); ④ Tech intake

admonester /admɔnɛste/ [1] *vtr* to admonish

ADN /adeɛn/ *nm* (*abbr* = **acide désoxyribonucléique**) DNA

ado○ /ado/ *nmf* teenager

adolescence /adɔlesɑ̃s/ *nf* adolescence

adolescent, ~e /adɔlesɑ̃, ɑ̃t/
Ⓐ *adj* adolescent, teenage (*épith*)
Ⓑ *nm,f* teenager, adolescent

adonner: s'adonner /adone/ [1] *vpr* **s'~ à** to devote oneself to [*travail, sport, art*]; **s'~ au plaisir** to live a debauched life; **il s'adonne à la boisson** he drinks too much

adopter /adɔpte/ [1] *vtr* gén to adopt; to pass [*loi*]

adoptif, -ive /adɔptif, iv/ *adj* [*enfant, pays*] adopted; [*parent*] adoptive

adoption /adɔpsjɔ̃/ *nf* gén, Jur adoption; (de loi) passing; **pays d'~** adopted country; **Anglais d'~** English by adoption

adorable /adɔRabl/ *adj* adorable

adorablement /adɔRabləmɑ̃/ *adv* [*vêtu*] delightfully; [*naïf*] charmingly

adorateur, -trice /adɔRatœR, tRis/ *nm,f* worshipperGB

adoration /adɔRasjɔ̃/ *nf* worship, adoration; **être en ~ devant qn/qch** to worship sb/sth

adorer /adɔRe/ [1] *vtr* to adore

(Idiome) **brûler ce qu'on a adoré** to turn against what one used to hold dear

adosser /adose/ [1]
Ⓐ *vtr* ① (appuyer) to lean (**à** on; **contre** against); ~ **un meuble contre un mur** (verticalement) to stand a piece of furniture against a wall; (un peu incliné) to lean a piece of furniture against a wall; **être adossé à qch** [*personne*] to be leaning against sth; ② (placer à côté) ~ **une maison contre qch** to build a house backing on to sth
Ⓑ **s'adosser** *vpr* ① [*personne*] **s'~ à/contre qch** to lean back on/against sth; ② [*maison, village*] **s'~ à qch** to back onto sth

adoucir /adusiR/ [3]
Ⓐ *vtr* to soften [*peau, eau, éclairage, expression*]; to soothe [*gorge*]; to moderate [*son, voix*]; to sweeten [*boisson, mets*]; to alleviate [*misère*]; to ease [*sort, chagrin*]; to mitigate [*rigueur, régime*]
Ⓑ **s'adoucir** *vpr* [*température*] to become milder; [*lumière, voix*] to become softer; [*pente*] to become more gentle; [*chagrin*] to be soothed; [*conditions*] to be alleviated

adoucissant, ~e /adusisɑ̃, ɑ̃t/
Ⓐ *adj* [*lotion*] soothing
Ⓑ *nm* (pour la lessive) softener

adoucissement /adusismɑ̃/ *nm* (de température) improvement (**de** in); (de conditions) alleviation; (de voix) softening

adrénaline /adRenalin/ *nf* adrenalin

adresse /adRɛs/ *nf* ① (domicile) address; **c'est une bonne ~** it's a good place; **se tromper d'~** fig (de personne) to pick the wrong person; (de lieu) to pick the wrong place; **remarque lancée à l'~ de qn** remark directed at sb; **à l'~ des participants** for the benefit of the participants; ② (habileté physique) dexterity; ③ (habileté intellectuelle) skill; **avec ~** skilfullyGB; ④ (allocution) address; ⑤ (en lexicographie) headword; (en sociolinguistique) **forme** *or* **formule d'~** form of address; ⑥ Ordinat address

(Composé) ~ **électronique** Ordinat email address, e-mail address

adresser /adRese/ [1]
Ⓐ *vtr* ① (destiner) to direct [*critique, menace*] (**à** at); to put [*demande, question*] (**à** to); to make [*déclaration*]; to deliver [*ultimatum, message*] (**à** to); to present [*recommandation, pétition*] (**à** to); to put out [*appel*] (**à** to); to aim [*coup*] (**à** at); ~ **la parole à qn** to speak to sb; ~ **un sourire à qn** to smile at sb; ~ **des éloges à qn** to praise sb; ② (expédier) to send [*lettre*]; ③ (écrire l'adresse) to address [*lettre*]; ④ (diriger) to refer [*personne*] (**à qn** to sb)
Ⓑ **s'adresser** *vpr* ① (parler) **s'~ à qn** to speak to sb; ② (contacter) **s'~ à** to contact [*ministère, ambassade*]; **s'~ à une firme japonaise** to go to a Japanese firm; **adresse-toi à ton père** ask your father; **pour les visas, adressez-vous au consulat** apply to the consulate for visas; ③ (être destiné) **s'~ à** [*mesure, invention*] to be aimed at; (toucher) **s'~ à** [*instinct, conscience*] to appeal to; ④ (échanger) to exchange [*salut, lettres*]; **s'~ la parole** to speak to each other

adroit, ~e /adRwa, at/ *adj* [*personne*] skilfulGB; [*réponse, discours*] clever; **geste ~** deft move; **être ~ de ses mains** to be good with one's hands

adroitement /adRwatmɑ̃/ *adv* skilfullyGB

ADSL /adeɛsɛl/ nm (abbr = **asymetrical digital subscriber line**) ADSL

aduler /adyle/ [1] vtr to worship, to adulate

adulte /adylt/

A adj [personne, relation] adult, grown-up; [nation] mature; [animal, plante] full-grown

B nmf adult, grown-up

adultère /adyltɛʀ/

A adj adulterous

B nm adultery

adultérin, ~**e** /adylteʀɛ̃, in/ adj **enfant** ~ child born of adultery

advenir /advəniʀ/ [36] v impers fml (survenir) to happen; **advienne que pourra** come what may; (devenir) ~ **de** to become of

adverbe /advɛʀb/ nm adverb

adversaire /advɛʀsɛʀ/ nmf gén opponent; Mil adversary

adverse /advɛʀs/ adj [équipe] opposing; [thèse] opposite; [attaque, manœuvre] from the opposite camp; **partie** or **camp** ~ opposite camp

adversité /advɛʀsite/ nf adversity

aération /aeʀasjɔ̃/ nf (en ouvrant une fenêtre) airing; (avec un appareil) ventilation; **conduit d'**~ airduct

aérer /aeʀe/ [14]

A vtr **1** to air [pièce, draps]; **pièce aérée** airy ou well-ventilated room; **2** to space out [texte]

B s'**aérer** vpr [personne] to get some fresh air; **s'**~ **l'esprit** to think about something different for a change

aérien, **-ienne** /aeʀjɛ̃, ɛn/ adj **1** Aviat [transport, désastre, base, attaque, carte] air (épith); [photographie] aerial; **2** Météo [courant, phénomène] air (épith); **3** (en l'air) [câble, circuit] overhead; [racine, plante] aerial; **métro** ~ elevated section of the underground GB ou subway US; **4** (léger) [démarche] floating; [grâce] exquisite; [musique] ethereal

aéro-club, pl ~**s** /aeʀoklœb/ nm flying club

aérodrome /aeʀodʀom/ nm (small) airfield

aérodynamique /aeʀodinamik/

A adj aerodynamic

B nf aerodynamics (+ v sg)

aérodynamisme /aeʀodinamism/ nm aerodynamic properties

aérofrein /aeʀofʀɛ̃/ nm air brake

aérogare /aeʀogaʀ/ nf (air) terminal

aéroglisseur /aeʀoglisœʀ/ nm hovercraft

aérogramme /aeʀogʀam/ nm aerogram, air letter

aéronautique /aeʀonotik/

A adj [industrie] aeronautics; [ingénieur] aeronautical

B nf aeronautics (+ v sg)

aéronaval, ~**e**[1], mpl ~**s** /aeʀonaval/ adj air and sea

aéronavale[2] /aeʀonaval/ nf Fleet Air Arm GB, Naval Aviation US

aérophagie /aeʀofaʒi/ ▸ p. 195 nf wind, aerophagia

aéroport /aeʀopɔʀ/ nm airport

aéroporté, ~**e** /aeʀopɔʀte/ adj [troupes] airborne; [matériel] transported by air

aéroportuaire /aeʀopɔʀtɥeʀ/ adj airport (épith)

aérosol /aeʀosɔl/ nm aerosol

aérospatial, ~**e**[1], mpl **-iaux** /aeʀospasjal, o/ adj [industrie] aerospace (épith); [véhicule, lanceur] space (épith)

aérospatiale[2] /aeʀospasjal/ nf aerospace industry

aérostatique /aeʀostatik/

A adj aerostatic

B nf aerostatics (+ v sg)

affable /afabl/ adj affable

affabulation /afabylasjɔ̃/ nf (invention) fabrication ¢; **c'est de l'**~ that's pure fabrication

affabuler /afabyle/ [1] vi to tell tall stories

affadir /afadiʀ/ [3]

A vtr lit to make [sth] tasteless [sauce]; fig to make [sth] dull [texte, personnage]

B s'**affadir** vpr **1** lit [plat] to lose its flavour[GB]; **2** fig [intérêt] to fade; [argument] to lose impact

affaiblir /afeblir/ [3]

A vtr to weaken

B s'**affaiblir** vpr [autorité, gouvernement, économie] to be weakened; [personne, voix, vue, détermination, volonté] to get

weaker; [santé, mémoire] to deteriorate; [bruit] to grow fainter; [monnaie] to be weakening (**face à** against); **le sens du mot s'est affaibli** the meaning of the word has weakened; **sortir affaibli d'une maladie** to be drained by an illness

affaiblissement /afɛblismɑ̃/ nm **1** (de personne, pays, monnaie, sens) (processus) weakening; (état) weakened state; **2** (de bruit, vue, santé) fading; **3** (de volonté, courage, détermination) diminishing; **4** (de volume, quantité) reduction (**de** in)

affaire /afɛʀ/

A nf **1** (ensemble de faits) gén affair; (à caractère politique, militaire) crisis, affair; (à caractère délictueux, scandaleux) (d'ordre général) scandal; (de cas unique) affair; (soumis à la justice) case; **l'**~ **de Suez** the Suez crisis; **une** ~ **de corruption** a corruption scandal; **condamné pour une** ~ **de drogue** convicted in a drug case; **2** (histoire, aventure) affair; **une** ~ **délicate** a delicate matter; **j'ignore tout de cette** ~ I don't know anything about the matter; **une sale** ~ a nasty business; **quelle** ~! what a business!; **c'est une** ~ **d'argent** there's money involved; **et voilà toute l'**~ and that's that; **3** (occupation, chose à faire) matter, business; **il est parti pour une** ~ **urgente** he's gone off on some urgent business; **c'est toute une** ~ it's quite a business; **c'est une (tout) autre** ~ that's another matter (entirely); **ce n'est pas une petite** ~ it's no small matter; **c'est mon** ~, **pas la vôtre** that's my business, not yours; **ça ne change rien à l'**~ that doesn't change a thing; **l'**~ **se présente bien** things are looking good; **j'en fais mon** ~ I'll deal with it; **4** (spécialité) **il connaît bien son** ~ he knows his job; **c'est une** ~ **de femmes** it's women's business; **la mécanique, c'est leur** ~ mechanics is their thing; **c'est une** ~ **de spécialistes** it's a case for the specialists; **5** (transaction) deal; **une bonne/mauvaise** ~ a good/bad deal; **faire** ~ **avec qn** to do a deal with sb; **la belle** ~°! big deal°!; **6** (achat avantageux) bargain; **j'ai fait une** ~ I got a bargain; **7** (entreprise) business, concern; ~ **industrielle** industrial concern; **c'est elle qui fait marcher l'**~ lit she runs the whole business; fig she runs the whole show; **8** (question, problème) **c'est une** ~ **de temps/goût** it's a matter of time/ taste; **c'est l'**~ **de quelques jours** it'll only take a few days; **en faire toute une** ~° to make a big deal° of it; **on ne va pas en faire une** ~ **d'État!** let's not make a big issue out of it!; **c'est une** ~ **de famille** it's a family affair; **9** (difficulté, péril) **être hors** or **tiré d'**~ [malade] to be in the clear; **se tirer d'**~ to get out of trouble; **on n'est pas encore sortis** or **tirés d'**~ we're not out of the woods yet; **10** (relation) **avoir** ~ **à** to be dealing with; **tu auras** ~ **à moi!** you'll have me to contend with!

B affaires nfpl **1** (activités lucratives) gén business ¢; (d'une seule personne) business affairs; **être dans les** ~s to be in business; **faire des** ~s **avec** to do business with; **il gère les** ~s **de son oncle** he runs his uncle's business affairs; **voir qn pour** ~s to see sb on business; **le monde des** ~s the business world; **2** (problèmes personnels) business ¢; **ça, c'est mes** ~s°! that's my business!; **occupe-toi de tes** ~s°! mind your own business!; **mettre de l'ordre dans ses** ~s to put one's affairs in order; **parler de ses** ~s **à tout le monde** to tell everybody one's business; **3** (effets personnels) things, belongings; **mes** ~s **de sport** my sports things; **4** Admin, Pol affairs; ~s **publiques** public affairs

(Composé) **les** ~s **courantes** daily business (sg)

(Idiomes) **être** ~ ~ to be in one's element; **il/ça fera l'**~ he/that'll do; **ça a très bien fait l'**~ it was just the job; **elle fait** or **fera notre** ~ she's just the person we need; **ça fera leur** ~ (convenir) that's just what they need; (être avantageux) it'll suit them

affairer: s'**affairer** /afeʀe/ [1] vpr to bustle about (**à faire** doing); s'~ **auprès de qn** to fuss over sb

affairisme /afeʀism/ nm pej wheeling and dealing°

affairiste /afeʀist/ nmf pej wheeler-dealer°

affaisser: s'**affaisser** /afese/ [1] vpr **1** [route, terrain] to subside; [visage, épaules, pont] to sag; **toit affaissé** sagging roof; **2** (s'effondrer) [personne] to collapse (**sur** on; **dans** into); [tête] to droop; **3** (se tasser) **un vieillard qui s'affaisse avec l'âge** an old man who is shrinking with age; **4** [ventes, bénéfices] to decline

affaler: s'**affaler** /afale/ [1] vpr (tomber) (de fatigue) to collapse; (par accident) to fall; **affalé sur le lit** slumped on the bed

affamé, ~**e** /afame/

A pp ▸ **affamer**

B pp adj **1** lit starving; **2** fig ~ **de** hungry for
C nm,f lit **les** ~s the starving
(Idiome) **ventre** ~ **n'a pas d'oreilles** Prov ≈ a hungry man is
an angry man

affamer /afame/ [1] vtr to starve [personne, pays]

affectation /afɛktasjɔ̃/ nf **1** (de bâtiment, d'argent) allocation (**à** to); **2** (nomination) (à un emploi, une fonction) appointment (**à** to); (dans un lieu) posting (**à** to); **3** (comportement)
affectation; **avec** ~ in an affected way

affecter /afɛkte/ [1] vtr **1** (feindre) to feign, to affect [senti-
ment, émotion]; to affect [genre, comportement]; to take on
[forme]; **gaieté affectée** feigned cheerfulness; ~ **d'être** to
pretend to be; **il affecte la gaieté** he's putting on a show of
cheerfulness; ~ **de grands airs** to put on airs; **2** (allouer)
to allocate [matériel, lieu, argent] (**à** to); **3** (nommer) (à une
activité, un poste) to appoint (**à** to); (dans un lieu, un pays) to post
(**à, en** to); **4** (toucher, affliger) to affect [pays, marché, autorité,
personne]; **affecté d'une légère surdité** slightly deaf

affectif, -ive /afɛktif, iv/ adj gén emotional; Psych
affective

affection /afɛksjɔ̃/ nf **1** (tendresse) affection (**pour** for);
prendre qn en ~ to become fond of sb; **2** Méd complaint

affectionner /afɛksjɔne/ [1] vtr to be particularly fond
of [chose, activité]; to be very fond of [personne]

affectivité /afɛktivite/ nf feelings (pl), affectivity

affectueusement /afɛktɥøzmɑ̃/ adv affectionately

affectueux, -euse /afɛktɥø, øz/ adj affectionate

affermir /afɛʀmiʀ/ [3]
A vtr **1** (consolider) to strengthen [autorité, conviction, volonté,
voix]; to consolidate [pouvoir, position]; to firm up [muscle,
chair]; **2** (rendre plus défini) to sharpen up [style, écriture]
B s'affermir vpr **1** [autorité, pouvoir, croissance] to be consolidated; [voix] to become stronger; [muscle, chair] to firm
up; [terrain] to become firmer; [santé] to become better;
2 [style, écriture] to become sharper

affermissement /afɛʀmismɑ̃/ nm (de pouvoir, reprise) consolidation; (de volonté, muscles, voix) strengthening; (d'économie)
improvement (**de** in)

affichage /afiʃaʒ/ nm **1** (publicitaire, électoral) billsticking,
billposting; **communiqué par voie d'**~ [résultat] posted
(up); **campagne d'**~ poster campaign; **à** ~ **numérique**
[réveil] with digital display; **2** Ordinat display; **3** (de connaissances, savoir) display
(Composé) ~ **à cristaux liquides** liquid crystal display, LCD

affiche /afiʃ/ nf (publicitaire, électorale) poster; (administrative, judiciaire) notice; **à l'**~ Cin now showing; Théât on; **tenir l'**~ **pendant deux ans** [pièce] to run for two years; **quitter l'**~ to
come off

affiché, ~e /afiʃe/
A pp ▸ **afficher**
B pp adj **1** Écon [hausse, résultat] published; [bénéfice]
declared; **2** [optimisme, volonté, dédain, objectif, opinion]
declared; **3** Ordinat [donnée, texte] displayed

afficher /afiʃe/ [1]
A vtr **1** (coller) to put up [affiche]; **'défense d'**~**'** 'no flyposting'; **2** (faire connaître par voie d'affiche) to display [prix]; to
post (up) [décret, résultat]; ~ **complet** Cin, Théât to be sold
out; [hôtel] to be fully booked; [parking] to be full;
3 Comm, Fin [Bourse, marché, entreprise] to show [hausse,
résultat]; **4** fig (montrer) to show [admiration, confiance,
détermination]; to declare [ambitions]; to display [mépris,
autorité]; to flaunt péj [opinions, liaison, vie privée]; ~ **le sourire** lit to have a big smile; (feindre) to put on a big smile;
5 Ordinat to display
B s'afficher vpr [personne] to flaunt oneself; [sourire, joie] to
appear (**sur** on)

afficheur /afiʃœʀ/ nm (employé) poster GB ou billboard US
sticker

affichiste /afiʃist/ ▸ p. 372 nmf poster artist

affilé, ~e¹ /afile/ adj [lame] sharpened

affilée², d'affilée /dafile/ loc adv in a row; **pendant deux
semaines d'**~ for two weeks in a row; **parler trois heures
d'**~ [amis] to talk nonstop for three hours; [politiciens,
directeur] to talk for three hours without a break

affiler /afile/ [1] vtr to sharpen

affilier /afilje/ [2]
A vtr to affiliate (**à** to)

B s'affilier vpr to become affiliated (**à** to)

affiner /afine/ [1]
A vtr to refine [métal]; to fine [verre]; to refine [stratégie, style,
jugement]; to have a slimming effect on [taille, silhouette]
B s'affiner vpr [jugement] to become keener; [style, goût] to
become (more) refined; [taille] to slim down

affinité /afinite/ nf affinity

affirmatif, -ive¹ /afiʀmatif, iv/
A adj [réponse, signe] affirmative; [personne, ton] assertive; **faire
un signe de tête** ~ to nod agreement
B nm Ling affirmative; **à l'**~ in the affirmative

affirmation /afiʀmasjɔ̃/ nf **1** gén assertion; (de sentiment,
religion) affirmation; **l'**~ **de soi** assertiveness; **2** Ling
assertion

affirmative² /afiʀmativ/
A adj ▸ **affirmatif**
B nf affirmative; **répondre par l'**~ to reply in the affirma-
tive; **dans l'**~ if the answer is yes

affirmer /afiʀme/ [1]
A vtr **1** (soutenir) to maintain [vérité, contraire]; **'je n'ai pas
l'intention de démissionner', affirma-t-il** 'I have no intention of resigning,' he declared; ~ **faire** to claim to do;
~ **que** to maintain ou claim (that); **pouvez-vous l'**~**?** can
you be sure about it?; **la police ne peut encore rien** ~ the
police are not yet able to make any positive statement; **je
vous l'affirme** I can assure you (of it); **2** (prouver) to assert
[talent, personnalité, autorité]; **3** (proclamer) to declare, to
affirm [volonté, désir] (**à** to)
B s'affirmer vpr [progrès, tendance] to become apparent;
[personnalité, style] to assert itself; **s'**~ **comme** to establish
oneself/itself etc as

affleurer /aflœʀe/ [1] vi **1** lit [récif] to show on the surface; ~ **au niveau du sol** [eau, pétrole] to come up to
ground level; [roche, minerai] to come through the soil;
2 fig [thème, sentiment] to surface, to crop up

affliction /afliksjɔ̃/ nf fml affliction; **jeter** or **plonger qn
dans l'**~ to afflict sb deeply; **être dans l'**~ to be in a state
of distress

affligeant, ~e /afliʒɑ̃, ɑ̃t/ adj **1** (attristant) distressing;
2 (consternant) pathetic, depressing

affliger /afliʒe/ [13]
A vtr **1** (frapper) [destin] to afflict (**de** with); **2** (peiner) to
distress
B s'affliger vpr to be distressed (**de qch** about sth)

affluence /aflyɑ̃s/ nf (de personnes) crowd(s); (d'objets)
abundance

affluent /aflyɑ̃/ nm Géog tributary

affluer /aflye/ [1] vi [personnes] to flock (**à, vers** to); [eau, air,
sang] to rush (**à, vers** to); [argent] to flow (**à, vers** to); [plain-
tes, lettres] to pour in

afflux /afly/ nm inv (de sang) rush; (de personnes) flood; (de
capitaux, produits) influx

affolant, ~e /afɔlɑ̃, ɑ̃t/ adj (effrayant) frightening, disturbing; **il fume trois paquets par jour, c'est** ~**!** he smokes
three packets a day, it's awful!

affolement /afɔlmɑ̃/ nm panic; **être en proie à l'**~ to be
in a state of panic; **pas d'**~**!** don't panic!

affoler /afɔle/ [1]
A vtr to terrify, to throw [sb] into a panic [personne]; **être
affolé** to be panic-stricken
B s'affoler vpr [personne, animal] to panic; [aiguille de bous-
sole] to spin

affranchi, ~e /afʀɑ̃ʃi/ nm,f emancipated slave

affranchir /afʀɑ̃ʃiʀ/ [3]
A vtr **1** (en collant des timbres) to stamp [lettre]; (avec une machine)
to frank; **2** (libérer) lit, fig to free (**de** from)
B s'affranchir vpr to free oneself (**de** from)

affranchissement /afʀɑ̃ʃismɑ̃/ nm **1** (de lettre) (avec des
timbres) stamping; (avec une machine) franking; (coût) postage;
2 (libération) (de peuple, pays) liberation; (de serf, d'esclave) freeing; (de minorité) emancipation

affres /afʀ/ nfpl littér agony (sg); (de douleur) agony (sg); (de faim)
pangs; (de jalousie) throes; **les** ~ **de la mort** death throes

affréter /afʀete/ [14] vtr to charter [avion, bateau]

affréteur /afʀetœʀ/ nm charter company

affreusement /afʀøzmɑ̃/ adv [se conduire, parler] abominably; [laid, blessé] horribly; [malade] terribly; **parler** ~ **mal** to
speak appallingly badly

affreux, -euse /afʀø, øz/ *adj* (laid) hideous; (abominable) dreadful; (désagréable) [*temps, route, vacances*] awful; **c'est ~ le monde qu'il y a** it really is terribly busy

affriolant, ~e /afʀiɔlɑ̃, ɑ̃t/ *adj* [*femme*] alluring; [*vêtement*] titillating; [*idée*] tempting

affront /afʀɔ̃/ *nm* affront (**à** to); **il m'a fait l'~ de refuser** he insulted me by refusing

affrontement /afʀɔ̃tmɑ̃/ *nm* confrontation, clash (**avec** with; **entre** between)

affronter /afʀɔ̃te/ [1]
A *vtr* to face, to confront [*adversaire, situation*]; to brave [*montagne, froid*]
B **s'affronter** *vpr* [*adversaires*] to confront one another; [*idées*] to clash

affublement /afyblǝmɑ̃/ *nm* attire†

affubler /afyble/ [1]
A *vtr* pej ~ **qn de** to deck sb out in [*vêtement, ornement*]; to saddle sb with [*prénom*]
B **s'affubler** *vpr* **s'~ de** to deck oneself out in [*vêtement, ornement*]; to take on [*nom*]

affût /afy/ *nm* **1** Mil ~ (**de canon**) (gun) carriage; **2** (à la chasse) hide (blind US; **chasser à l'~** to hunt game from a hide GB *ou* blind US; **se tenir à l'~** lit to lie in wait; fig to be on the lookout (**de** for)

affûter /afyte/ [1] *vtr* to sharpen; (avec une meule) to grind

afghan, ~e /afgɑ̃, an/ ▸ p. 392, p. 336
A *adj* Afghan
B *nm* Ling Afghan

afin /afɛ̃/
A **afin de** *loc prép* ~ **de faire** in order to do, so as to do; ~ **de ne pas faire** so as not to do
B **afin que** *loc conj* so that; ~ **que les jeunes trouvent du travail** so that young people might find work; ~ **qu'il ne se sente pas abandonné** so that he won't feel neglected

AFNOR /afnɔʀ/ *nf* (abbr = **Association française de normalisation**) AFNOR (*French standards authority*)

AFP /aɛfpe/ *nf* (abbr = **Agence France-Presse**) AFP (*French news agency*)

africain, ~e /afʀikɛ̃, ɛn/ *adj* African

Afrique /afʀik/ ▸ p. 230 *nprf* Africa; **République d'~ du Sud** Republic of South Africa

Afrique-Équatoriale /afʀikekwatɔʀjal/ *nprf* Hist ~ **française** French Equatorial Africa

Afrique-Occidentale /afʀikɔksidɑ̃tal/ *nprf* Hist ~ **française** French West Africa

afro- /afʀo/ *préf* ~**-brésilien** Afro-Brazilian; ~**centrisme** afrocentrism; ~**-jazz** African Jazz

afro-américain, ~e, *mpl* ~**s** /afʀoameʀikɛ̃, ɛn/ *adj* Afro-American, African American

Afro-américain, ~e, *mpl* ~**s** /afʀoameʀikɛ̃, ɛn/ *nm,f* Afro-American, African American

AG /aʒe/ *nf*: abbr ▸ **assemblée**

agaçant, ~e /agasɑ̃, ɑ̃t/ *adj* annoying, irritating

agacement /agasmɑ̃/ *nm* irritation

agacer /agase/ [12] *vtr* **1** (excéder) to annoy, to irritate; **tu commences à m'~ avec tes cris** your shouting is starting to annoy me; **2** (lanciner) to set [sth] on edge [*dent*]; to grate on [*nerf*]

agapes /agap/ *nfpl* feast (*sg*), banquet (*sg*)

agate /agat/ *nf* **1** (minéral) agate; **d'~** (couleur) agate-coloured^{GB}; **2** (bille) marble

âge /ɑʒ/ *nm* **1** (nombre d'années) age; **ils sont du même ~** they are the same age; **faire son ~** to look one's age; **paraître plus/moins que son ~** to look older/younger than one's years; **bien porter son ~** to be good for one's age; **sans ~** ageless; **un homme d'un certain ~** a middle-aged man; **une personne d'un ~** **avancé** an elderly person; **avancé, grand ~** great age; **avoir l'~** *or* **être en ~ de faire** to be old enough to do; **il est mort à 95 ans, c'est un bel** ~ he died at 95, a fine old age; **30 ans, c'est le bel ~** 30 is a good age; **2** (vieillesse) (old) age; **s'assagir avec l'~** to calm down as one gets older; **vieux avant l'~** to be old before one's time; **prendre de l'~** to grow old; **3** (période de la vie) age; **à tout ~, à tous les ~s** at any age; **être entre deux ~s** to be middle-aged; **avoir passé l'~ de faire** to be past the age when one does; **être encore/ne plus être en ~ de faire** to be still young enough/to be too old to do; **va t'amuser, c'est de ton ~!** go and have fun,

you're young!; **4** (époque) age; **à travers les ~s** through the ages

⬭(Composés) **l'~ adulte** adulthood; ~ **du bronze** Bronze age; ~ **du fer** Iron age; **l'~ d'homme** manhood; **l'~ ingrat** the awkward *ou* difficult age; **d'~ mûr** mature; **l'~ mûr** maturity; ~ **d'or** golden age; ~ **de la pierre** Stone age; **l'~ de la retraite** retirement age; **l'~ scolaire** school age; **l'~ tendre** youth

âgé, ~e /ɑʒe/ *adj* [*personne*] old, elderly; ~ **de 12 ans** 12 years old; **les personnes ~es de 15 à 35 ans** people aged between 15 and 35

agence /aʒɑ̃s/ *nf* **1** Comm agency; **2** Admin agency, bureau; **3** (de banque) branch

⬭(Composés) ~ **immobilière** estate agents (*pl*) GB, real-estate agency US; ~ **matrimoniale** marriage bureau; ~ **de placement** employment agency; ~ **de presse** news agency; ~ **publicitaire** advertising agency; ~ **de voyage** travel agency, travel agents (*pl*) GB; **Agence nationale pour l'emploi, ANPE** *French national employment agency*

agencement /aʒɑ̃smɑ̃/ *nm* (de pièces) layout; (de mots, phrases) arrangement; (de couleurs, motifs) setting out

agencer /aʒɑ̃se/ [12] *vtr* **1** (disposer) to lay out [*pièce*]; to put together [*éléments, couleurs*]; **2** (structurer) to construct [*intrigue, scénario*]

agenda /aʒɛ̃da/ *nm* **1** (carnet prédaté) diary; **2** (programme) agenda

⬭(Composé) ~ **électronique** electronic personal organizer

agenouiller: s'agenouiller /aʒnuje/ [1] *vpr* **1** lit to kneel (down); **être agenouillé** to be kneeling; **2** fig **s'~ devant** to bow to [*pouvoir*]; to kowtow to [*personne*]

agent /aʒɑ̃/ ▸ p. 372 *nm* **1** (de l'État) Admin officer, official; Pol agent; ~ **du gouvernement** government official; ~ **secret/double** secret/double agent; **2** Comm agent; **3** (employé) employee; ~**s contractuels** contract staff; **4** Chimie, Ling agent

⬭(Composés) ~ **artistique** Théât theatrical agent; ~ **d'assurances** insurance broker; (vendeur) insurance salesman; ~ **de change** stockbroker; ~ **de la circulation** traffic policeman; ~ **commercial** sales representative; ~ **comptable** accountant; ~ **hospitalier** nursing auxiliary GB, nurse's aide US; ~ **de liaison** liaison officer; ~ **maritime** shipping agent; ~ **de police** policeman; ~ **provocateur** agent provocateur; ~ **technique** technician

agglomération /aglɔmeʀasjɔ̃/ *nf* **1** (ville) town; (village) village; **l'~ lyonnaise** Lyons and its suburbs; **vitesse maximum en ~** Aut maximum speed in built-up areas; **2** Tech agglomeration (**de** of)

aggloméré /aglɔmeʀe/ *nm* chipboard

agglomérer /aglɔmeʀe/ [14]
A *vtr* to agglomerate
B **s'agglomérer** *vpr* [*personnes*] to gather together; [*habitations*] to be grouped together

agglutiner: s'agglutiner /aglytine/ [1] *vpr* [*badauds*] to crowd together (**à** at); [*mouches*] to cluster together; **s'~ autour de** [*curieux*] to crowd around; [*maisons*] to be clustered around

aggravant, ~e /agʀavɑ̃, ɑ̃t/ *adj* Jur aggravating

aggravation /agʀavasjɔ̃/ *nf* (de situation, maladie) worsening; (de chômage, dette, déficit) increase (**de** in)

⬭(Composé) ~ **de peine** Jur increase in sentence

aggraver /agʀave/ [1]
A *vtr* **1** (rendre pire) to aggravate, to make [sth] worse; ~ **son cas** to make things worse; **voi aggravé** aggravated robbery; **2** (accroître) to increase
B **s'aggraver** *vpr* (devenir pire) to get worse, to deteriorate; (en augmentant) to increase

agile /aʒil/ *adj* [*personne, animal*] agile; [*doigts, pas, esprit*] nimble

agilement /aʒilmɑ̃/ *adv* nimbly, with agility

agilité /aʒilite/ *nf* agility

agios /aʒjo/ *nmpl* bank charges

agir /aʒiʀ/ [3]
A *vi* **1** (accomplir une action) to act; **il a agi sous le coup de la colère** he acted in anger; **il parle beaucoup mais agit peu** he's all talk and no action; ~ **avec prudence** to proceed with caution; **2** (se comporter) to behave, to act; **bien/mal**

L'âge

Quel âge avez-vous?

■ *L'anglais n'emploie pas le verbe* to have (avoir) *pour exprimer l'âge, mais le verbe* to be (être).

quel âge a-t-il?
= how old is he? *ou* what age is he?

■ *Les deux mots* years old *peuvent être omis pour les personnes, mais pas pour les choses.*

elle a trente ans
= she is thirty years old *ou* she is thirty

il a quatre-vingts ans
= he is eighty *ou* he is eighty years old

la maison a cent ans
= the house is a hundred years old

atteindre soixante ans
= to reach sixty

Nick est plus âgé qu'Isabelle
= Nick is older than Isabelle

Isabelle est plus jeune que Nick
= Isabelle is younger than Nick

Nick a deux ans de plus qu'Isabelle
= Nick is two years older than Isabelle

Isabelle a deux ans de moins que Nick
= Isabelle is two years younger than Nick

Louis a le même âge que Mary
= Mary is the same age as Louis

Louis et Mary ont le même âge
= Louis and Mary are the same age

on te donnerait seize ans
= you look sixteen

j'ai l'impression d'avoir seize ans
= I feel sixteen

on lui donnerait dix ans de moins
= he looks ten years younger

Âgé de

il est âgé de quarante ans
= he is forty years of age

un homme de soixante ans
= a man of sixty

un enfant de huit ans et demi
= a child of eight and a half

une femme âgée de quarante ans
= a woman aged forty

M. Stein, âgé de quarante ans
= Mr Stein, aged forty

à l'âge de cinquante ans
= at fifty *ou* at the age of fifty (*GB*), at age fifty (*US*)

il est mort à vingt-sept ans
= he died at twenty-seven *ou* at the age of twenty-seven

un homme âgé de soixante ans
= a sixty-year-old man

■ *Noter l'utilisation du trait d'union. Noter aussi que* year, *qui fait partie de l'adjectif, ne prend pas la marque du pluriel.*

■ *Lorsque l'on parle d'êtres humains ou d'animaux, le mot qui suit* old *peut être sous-entendu. Ainsi, a* three-year-old *peut être un enfant ou un animal (souvent un cheval).*

un enfant de cinq ans et demi
= a five-and-a-half-year-old

une course pour les trois ans
= a race for three-year-olds

Mais:

un vin de soixante ans d'âge
= a sixty-year-old wine

L'âge approximatif

■ *L'anglais emploie indifféremment* about *et* around *dans ce cas.*

elle a dans les trente ans
= she's about thirty *ou* around thirty

elle a une cinquantaine d'années
= she's about fifty *ou* around fifty

il n'a pas encore dix-huit ans
= he's not yet eighteen

il vient d'avoir quarante ans
= he's just over forty
  ou (*plus familier*) he's just turned forty

il aura bientôt cinquante ans
= he's just under fifty

elle a entre trente et quarante ans
= she's in her thirties

elle a dans les quarante-cinq ans
= she's in her mid-forties

elle va sur ses soixante-dix ans
= she's in her late sixties *ou* she's nearly seventy

elle va avoir vingt ans
= she's in her late teens *ou* she's almost twenty

il a tout juste dix ans
= he's just ten

il a à peine douze ans
= he's barely twelve

Les personnes âgées de X ans

les plus de quatre-vingts ans
= the over eighties

les moins de dix-huit ans
= the under eighteens

■ *Les mots anglais en* -arian *sont des noms:*

ce sont des septuagénaires
= they're septuagenarians

elle est octogénaire
= she's an octogenarian

∼ to behave well/badly (**envers, avec** toward(s)); ∼ **en lâche** to act like a coward; ③ (avoir un effet) [*substance, médicament*] to take effect, to work; ∼ **sur qch/qn** to have an effect on sth/sb; ∼ **sur le marché** Fin to influence the market; ④ (intervenir) ∼ **auprès de qn** to approach sb
B **s'agir de** *vpr impers* ① **de quoi s'agit-il?** (question) what is it about?; (problème) what's the matter?; **mais il ne s'agit pas de ça!** but that's not the point!; **il s'agit de ta santé!** it's your health that's at stake (here)!; **il s'agit de votre** mari it's about your husband, it's to do with your husband; **on connaît maintenant les gagnants: il s'agit de messieurs X et Y** we now know who the winners are: they're Mr X and Mr Y; **d'après les experts il s'agirait d'un attentat** according to the experts, it would appear to be an act of terrorism; **quand il s'agit d'argent/de faire le ménage** when it comes to money/to doing the housework; **s'agissant de qch/qn** as regards sth/sb; **il s'agit bien de partir en vacances maintenant que je suis au chômage!**

iron now that I'm unemployed it's hardly the (right) time to talk about going on vacation!; ② (il est nécessaire de) **il s'agit de faire vite** we/you etc must act quickly; **il s'agit de savoir ce que tu veux!** make up your mind!; **il s'agit pour le gouvernement de relancer l'économie** what the government must do now is boost the economy; **il s'agirait de se mettre d'accord** we'd better get it straight

agissements /aʒismɑ̃/ nmpl pej activities, doings

agitateur, -trice /aʒitatœʀ, tʀis/
A nm,f Pol agitator
B nm (dispositif) agitator; (baguette) stirring rod

agitation /aʒitasjɔ̃/ nf ① (de mer) choppiness; (d'air) turbulence; (de branche) swaying; (de malade, d'impatient) restlessness; ② (de maison, rue) bustle (**de** in); (de marché) activity; ③ (nervosité) agitation; ④ (malaise social) unrest

agité, ~e /aʒite/
A adj [mer] rough; (moins fort) choppy; [malade] agitated; [rue] bustling; [vie] hectic; [esprit, sommeil] troubled; [période] turbulent; [nuit] restless
B nm,f ① Méd **les ~s** the mentally disturbed; ② (indiscipliné) troublemaker, disruptive element

agiter /aʒite/ [1]
A vtr ① (remuer) to wave [main, mouchoir]; to shake [boîte]; to shake up [liquide]; to wag [queue]; to flap [aile]; **le vent agite les feuilles** the wind is rustling the leaves; **voile agitée par le vent** sail flapping in the wind; **barque agitée par les vagues** boat tossed by the waves; **un tremblement agitait mon corps** my whole body was shaking; ② (brandir) to raise [menace, spectre]; ③ (troubler) to trouble; ④ (débattre) to debate, to discuss [problème]
B s'agiter vpr ① (remuer) [personne] gén to fidget; (au lit) to toss and turn; [branche] to sway (in the wind); ② (s'affairer) to bustle about; ③ (perdre son calme) [esprit, peuple] to become agitated ou restless

agneau, pl ~x /aɲo/ nm ① Zool, Culin lamb; ② (cuir) lambskin

agnelle /aɲɛl/ nf ewe lamb

agonie /agɔni/ nf death throes (pl); **être à l'~** [personne] to be dying; [régime] to be in its death throes; **son ~ a été longue** he/she died a slow death

agonir /agɔniʀ/ [3] vtr **~ qn d'injures** to hurl insults at sb; **en rentrant, il s'est fait ~** when he got home he was told off soundly

agonisant, ~e /agɔnizɑ̃, ɑ̃t/ adj dying

agoniser /agɔnize/ [1] vi lit, fig to be dying

agrafe /agʀaf/ nf ① (pour vêtements) hook; ② (pour papiers) staple; ③ Méd skin clip

agrafer /agʀafe/ [1] vtr to fasten [vêtement]; to staple (together) [papiers]

agrafeuse /agʀaføz/ nf stapler

agraire /agʀɛʀ/ adj [société] agrarian; [réforme] land (épith)

agrandir /agʀɑ̃diʀ/ [3]
A vtr ① (en dimensions) to enlarge [ville, photo, trou]; to extend [pièce, maison]; to widen [tunnel, marge]; **les yeux agrandis par la peur** his/their etc eyes wide with fear; **la peinture blanche agrandit la pièce** white paint makes the room look bigger ou larger; ② (en importance) to extend [famille]; to expand [entreprise, parti]
B s'agrandir vpr [trou] to get bigger; [ville, famille, entreprise] to expand; [marge, yeux] to widen

agrandissement /agʀɑ̃dismɑ̃/ nm ① Phot enlargement; ② (de maison, pièce) extension; (d'ouverture) enlargement; (d'entreprise) expansion; **faire des travaux d'~** (dans une maison) to build an extension

agrandisseur /agʀɑ̃disœʀ/ nm enlarger

agréable /agʀeabl/ adj nice, pleasant; **avoir un physique ~** to be good-looking; **~ à l'œil/au toucher** pleasing to the eye/to the touch; **~ à vivre** [personne] pleasant to be with; ▸ utile

agréer /agʀee/ [11] vtr ① (accepter) to agree to [demande]; **veuillez ~ mes salutations distinguées** (personne non nommée) yours faithfully; (personne nommée) yours sincerely; ② (reconnaître officiellement) to recognize [sb] officially [diplomate]; to authorize [concessionnaire]; to register [taxi, nourrice, médecin]; to approve [matériel, association, établissement]; **agent agréé** Comm authorized dealer

agrégat /agʀega/ nm ① Biol, Constr, Écon aggregate; ② fig jumble (**de** of)

agrégation /agʀegasjɔ̃/ nf ① Univ high-level competitive examination for recruitment of teachers; ② (de particules) aggregation

agrégé, ~e /agʀeʒe/ nm,f: holder of the agrégation

agréger: **s'agréger** /agʀeʒe/ [15] vpr ① (se coller) [particules] to aggregate; ② (se joindre) **s'~ à** [personne, groupe] to join

agrément /agʀemɑ̃/ nm ① (validation officielle) approval; **retirer son ~ à une école** to withdraw a school's accreditation; ② (accord) agreement; ③ (charme) (d'activité) pleasure; (de personne, lieu, chose) charm; **plein d'~** [séjour] very pleasant; [lieu] full of charm (après n); **sans ~** [existence] dull; [visage, maison] unattractive; [décor, pièce] cheerless; **voyage d'~** pleasure trip

agrémenter /agʀemɑ̃te/ [1] vtr to liven up [texte, histoire] (**de** with); to cheer up [réunion] (**de** with); to brighten up [jardin, existence] (**de** with); to supplement [repas, plat] (**de** with); **un ensemble immobilier agrémenté de nombreux services** a property development offering many facilities

agrès /agʀɛ/ nmpl ① Sport apparatus ¢; ② Naut tackle

agresser /agʀese/ [1] vtr ① (physiquement) to attack [personne, pays]; (pour voler) to mug [personne]; ② (moralement) [personne] to be aggressive with [personne]; **se sentir agressé** to feel threatened (**par** by); **les images télévisées nous agressent** we are bombarded by pictures on television; ③ (être trop fort) [shampooing] to be too harsh; [fumée] to attack

agresseur /agʀesœʀ/ nm (individu) attacker; (groupe, peuple) aggressor

agressif, -ive /agʀesif, iv/ adj ① [personne, animal] aggressive (**avec qn** with sb; **envers qn** toward(s) sb); [tempérament, ton, environnement, publicité] aggressive; **d'un ton ~** aggressively; ② [couleur] violent; [son] ear-splitting; [images] threatening

agression /agʀesjɔ̃/ nf ① (par une personne) attack; (pour voler) mugging; (par un pays) act of aggression; **~ à main armée** armed assault; **les ~s de la vie urbaine** the stresses and strains of city life; ② Psych aggression

agressivité /agʀesivite/ nf aggressiveness

agricole /agʀikɔl/ adj [produit, ouvrier] farm; [coopérative] farming; [problème] agricultural; [syndicat] farm workers'

agriculteur, -trice /agʀikyltœʀ, tʀis/ ▸ p. 372 nm,f farmer; **une famille d'~s** a farming family

agriculture /agʀikyltyʀ/ nf farming, agriculture spéc
(Composé) **~ biologique** organic farming

agripper /agʀipe/ [1]
A vtr to grab
B s'agripper vpr **s'~ à** to cling to

agro-alimentaire, pl ~s /agʀoalimɑ̃tɛʀ/
A adj [industrie, filière, complexe] food processing; **la recherche ~** food research
B nm food processing industry; **un géant de l'~** a food giant

agrochimie /agʀoʃimi/ nf agro-chemistry

agro-industrie /agʀoɛ̃dystʀi/ nf agro-industry

agronome /agʀonɔm/ ▸ p. 372 nmf **(ingénieur) ~** agronomist

agronomie /agʀonɔmi/ nf agronomy

agrume /agʀym/ nm citrus fruit

aguerrir /ageʀiʀ/ [3]
A vtr [expérience] to harden [personne] (**à qch** to sth); **~ des troupes au combat** to toughen soldiers for battle; **soldats aguerris** (au combat) seasoned soldiers
B s'aguerrir vpr to become hardened ou inured sout (**à**, **contre** to)

aguets: aux aguets /ozagɛ/ loc adv **être aux ~** (à l'affût) to lie in wait; (se méfier) to be on one's guard; (surveiller de près) to be watching like a hawk

aguicher /agiʃe/ [1] vtr (sexuellement) to lead [sb] on; (pour vendre) to attract [client]

aguicheur, -euse¹ /agiʃœʀ, øz/ adj alluring

aguicheuse² /agiʃøz/ nf pej tease péj

ah /a/
A nm inv (d'étonnement, admiration) gasp; (de soulagement, satisfaction) sigh
B excl oh!; **~ non alors!** certainly not!; **~, tu vois!** see!; **~ bon?** really?; **~ ~ ~!** (rire) ha ha ha!

ahaner /aane/ [1] *vi* (grogner) to grunt with effort; (peiner) to strain

ahuri, **~e** /ayʀi/
A *adj* (hébété) dazed; (étonné) stunned
B *nm,f* pej halfwit péj

ahurir /ayʀiʀ/ [3] *vtr* to stun

ahurissant, **~e** /ayʀisɑ̃, ɑ̃t/ *adj* [*nouvelle, bruit*] incredible; [*personne, force*] incredible; [*chiffre*] staggering; **c'est ~!** it's absolutely incredible!

ahurissement /ayʀismɑ̃/ *nm* amazement

aide¹ /ɛd/ ▸ p. 372
A *nmf* (dans un travail) assistant
B aide- (in *compounds*) **~-bibliothécaire/-cuisinier** assistant librarian/cook; **~-électricien/-mécanicien** electrician's/ mechanic's mate GB *ou* helper US; **~-soignant** nursing auxiliary GB, nurse's aide US
(Composé) **~ de camp** aide-de-camp

aide² /ɛd/ *nf* **1** (secours) (d'individu, de groupe) help, assistance; (d'État, organisme) assistance; **appeler à l'~** to call for help; **à l'~ de** with the help *ou* aid of; **apporter son ~ à qn** to help sb; **venir à l'~ de qn** to come to sb's aid *ou* assistance; **2** (en argent) aid **¢**; **recevoir des ~s de** to receive financial aid from
(Composés) **~ au développement** foreign aid; **~ à domicile** home help GB, home helper US; **~ familiale** mother's help GB, mother's helper US; **~ judiciaire** legal aid; **~ sociale** social security benefits GB, welfare benefits US

aide-éducateur, **-trice**, *pl* **aides-éducateurs**, **aides-éducatrices** /ɛdedykatœʀ, tʀis/ ▸ p. 372 *nm,f*: classroom assistant

aide-mémoire /ɛdmemwaʀ/ *nm inv* aide-mémoire sout; **c'est mon ~** I use it to jog my memory

aider /ede/ [1]
A *vtr* **1** (prêter son concours à) to help (**à faire** to do); **en quoi puis-je vous ~?** how can I help you?; **se faire ~ par qn** to get help from sb; **~ qn de ses conseils** to give sb helpful advice; **le vin aidant** wine playing its part; **2** (subventionner) to aid [*industrie, désherités*]; to give aid to [*pays pauvre*]
B aider à *vtr ind* **à** to help toward(s) [*compréhension, financement*]; **~ à faire** to help in doing
C s'aider *vpr* **1** (soi-même) **s'~ de** to use [*dictionnaire, outil*]; **en s'aidant de** with the help of; **2** (les uns les autres) to help each other

aïe /aj/ *excl* (de douleur) ouch!; (d'inquiétude) **~ (~ ~)**, **que se passe-t-il?** oh dear, what's going on?; (d'anticipation) **~ ~ ~!... oh NO!...**

aïeul, **~e** /ajœl/ *nm,f* grandfather/grandmother

aïeux /ajø/ *nmpl* liter ancestors

aigle /ɛgl/ *nm* Zool eagle

aiglefin /ɛgləfɛ̃/ *nm* haddock

aiglon /ɛglɔ̃/ *nm* eaglet

aigre /ɛgʀ/ *adj* **1** lit (au goût, à l'odorat) [*odeur*] sour; **2** fig [*paroles*] sharp; [*caractère*] sour; **d'un ton ~** sharply; **tourner** *or* **virer à l'~** [*plaisanterie*] to turn sour

aigre-doux, **-douce**, *pl* **aigres-doux**, **aigres-douces** /ɛgʀədu, dus/ *adj* **1** Culin [*fruit, goût*] bittersweet; [*cuisine, sauce*] sweet and sour; **2** fig [*propos, communiqué*] barbed

aigrefin /ɛgʀəfɛ̃/ *nm* swindler

aigrelet, **-ette** /ɛgʀəlɛ, ɛt/ *adj* [*goût, fruit*] rather sour; [*voix*] shrill; **un petit vin ~** a sharpish wine

aigrette /ɛgʀɛt/ *nf* Zool (oiseau) egret; (plumes) crest

aigreur /ɛgʀœʀ/ *nf* **1** gén (de lait, fruit) sourness; (de vin) sharpness; **2** Méd **des ~s d'estomac** heartburn **¢**; **3** fig bitterness

aigrir /egʀiʀ/ [3]
A *vtr* to embitter [*personne*]
B s'aigrir *vpr* **1** [*personne*] to become embittered; **2** [*vin, aliment*] to turn sour

aigu, **-uë** /egy/
A *adj* **1** [*son, voix, note*] high-pitched; **2** [*douleur, symptôme, problème*] acute; [*phase*] critical; **3** [*perception, sens*] keen
B *nm* (de chaîne stéréo) treble; (de voix) high notes (*pl*)

aigue-marine, *pl* **aigues-marines** /ɛgmaʀin/ *nf* aquamarine

aiguillage /eguijaʒ/ *nm* (appareil) points (*pl*) GB, switch US; (manœuvre) switching to another line; **une erreur d'~** a

signalling^GB error; fig a mix-up

aiguille /eguij/ *nf* **1** (en couture, médecine, botanique, génie nucléaire) needle; **~ à coudre/à tricoter** sewing/knitting needle; **2** (de montre, chronomètre) hand; (de jauge, d'altimètre) needle; (de balance) pointer; **dans le sens/le sens inverse des ~s d'une montre** clockwise/anticlockwise; **3** Géog peak; **4** Zool garfish

aiguiller /eguije/ [1] *vtr* **1** (vers un endroit) to direct [*personne*] (**vers** toward(s)); to send [*courrier, dossier*] (**vers** to); to steer [*conversation*] (**sur** toward(s)); **c'est ce qui nous a aiguillés dans nos recherches** that's what put us on the right track in our research; **2** Rail **~ un train** to switch a train to a new line

aiguilleur /eguijœʀ/ ▸ p. 372 *nm* Rail pointsman GB, switchman US
(Composé) **~ du ciel** air traffic controller

aiguillon /eguijɔ̃/ *nm* **1** Zool sting; **2** (stimulant) incentive; **3** (bâton) goad; **4** Bot thorn

aiguillonner /eguijone/ [1] *vtr* **1** (stimuler) to spur [*personne*]; to stimulate [*ambition*]; **la faim m'aiguillonnant...** driven by hunger...; **2** lit to goad [*bœuf*]

aiguiser /egize/ [1] *vtr* **1** lit to sharpen [*lame, griffes, crocs*]; **2** fig to whet [*appétit*]; to arouse [*curiosité*]; to heighten [*sentiment*]; to stimulate [*concurrence*]; to sharpen [*intelligence*]; to hone [*style*]

aiguiseur /egizœʀ/ ▸ p. 372 *nm* knife grinder

ail, *pl* **~s** *ou* **aulx** /aj, o/ *nm* garlic

aile /ɛl/ *nf* (en vol); (de moulin) sail; (de voiture) wing GB, fender US; (d'armée) flank
(Composés) **~ de corbeau** (noir) raven black; **~ delta** Aviat delta wing; Sport hang-glider; **~ du nez** Anat wing of the nose
(Idiomes) **battre de l'~**, **ne battre que d'une ~** [*croissance*] to have fallen off; [*économie, entreprise*] to be struggling; **se sentir pousser des ~s** to feel exhilarated; **rogner les ~s de qn** to clip sb's wings; **prendre un coup dans l'~** to suffer a setback; **avoir un coup dans l'~°** to be the worse for drink; **voler de ses propres ~s** to stand on one's own two feet

ailé, **~e** /ele/ *adj* winged

aileron /ɛlʀɔ̃/ *nm* **1** (d'oiseau) wing tip; (de requin) fin; **2** (d'avion) aileron; **3** (de coque) fin; **4** (de planche de surf) skeg; **5** (de voiture de course) aerofoil GB, airfoil US

ailier /elje/ *nm* **1** (au football) winger; **~ gauche** left winger GB *ou* wing US; **2** (au rugby) wing three-quarter

ailleurs /ajœʀ/
A *adv* elsewhere; **ici comme ~** here as elsewhere; **des artistes venus d'~** artists from other places; **nulle part ~** nowhere else; **partout ~** everywhere else; **ici ou ~, ça m'est égal** here or somewhere else, it's all the same to me
B d'ailleurs *loc adv* besides, moreover, what's more; **d'~, je n'étais pas là** besides, I wasn't there; **il a fait des tentatives, d'~ fort timides** he made some rather feeble attempts; **l'excuse de mon mal de tête, d'~ bien réel,...** the excuse of having a headache, which I might add was true,...
C par ailleurs *loc adv* **par ~, l'inflation a atteint un taux record** in addition, inflation has reached a record level; **par ~, je n'ai pas encore reçu les marchandises** may I also add that I have not yet received the goods; **des efforts pour comprendre un problème par ~ complexe** efforts to understand a problem which is in some respects complex
(Idiomes) **être ~, avoir l'esprit ~** to be miles away

aimable /ɛmabl/ *adj* **1** (gentil) [*personne*] pleasant; [*mot*] kind; **c'est très ~ à vous** it's very kind of you; **nous informons notre ~ clientèle que** we wish to inform our customers that; **2** (poli) [*propos, façon*] polite
(Idiome) **être ~ comme une porte de prison** to be a miserable so-and-so

aimablement /ɛmabləmɑ̃/ *adv* (avec politesse) politely; (avec gentillesse) kindly

aimant, **~e** /ɛmɑ̃, ɑ̃t/
A *adj* affectionate, loving
B *nm* magnet; **~ naturel** magnetite

aimanter /ɛmɑ̃te/ [1] *vtr* to magnetize

aimer /eme/ [1]

A vtr **1** (d'amour) to love [*personne*]; ~ **qn à la folie** to adore sb; **2** (apprécier) to like, to be fond of [*personne, chose*]; **il t'aime bien/beaucoup** he's fond/very fond of you; **j'aime bien l'opéra** I like opera; ~ **la chasse** to like hunting; ~ **faire**, ~ **à faire** liter to like doing; **j'aime à croire que** I like to think that; **cette plante aime l'ombre** this plant likes shade; **je n'aime pas qu'on me dise ce que j'ai à faire** I don't like being told what to do; **j'aimerais autant rester à la maison ce soir** I'd rather stay at home tonight; **j'aime autant te dire qu'il n'était pas content!** I may as well tell you that he wasn't very pleased!; **j'aime mieux nager que courir** I prefer swimming to running; **j'aimerais mieux que tu ne le leur dises pas** I'd rather you didn't tell them; **il n'a rien de cassé? j'aime mieux ça!** nothing's broken? thank goodness!; **vous acceptez de me rembourser? j'aime mieux ça!** (ton menaçant) you agree to pay me back? that's more like it!

B **s'aimer** vpr **1** (d'amour) to love each other; **aimez-vous les uns les autres** love one another; **2** (s'apprécier) **elles s'aiment bien** they like each other

aine /ɛn/ nf groin

aîné, ~**e** /ene/

A adj (de deux) elder; (de plus de deux) eldest

B nm,f **1** (enfant) (premier de deux) elder son/daughter, elder child; (premier de plus de deux) eldest son/daughter, eldest child; **2** (frère, sœur) elder ou older brother/sister; **3** (personne plus âgée) elder; (personne la plus âgée) oldest; **c'est mon** ~ he's older than me; **il est de vingt ans mon** ~ he's twenty years older than me; **les** ~**s de la tribu** the elders of the tribe

aînesse /enɛs/ nf **droit d'**~ law of primogeniture

ainsi /ɛ̃si/

A adv **1** (de cette manière) **c'est** ~ **que l'on faisait le beurre** that's how ou the way they used to make butter; **le mélange** ~ **obtenu** the mixture obtained in this way; **je t'imaginais** ~ that's how I imagined you; **le monde est** ~ **fait que** the world is made in such a way that; **elle est** ~ that's how ou the way she is; **c'est la vie** such is life, that's the way it goes; **c'est** ~ **qu'on m'appelait** that's what they used to call me; ~ **parlait le prophète** thus spoke the prophet; **le jury se compose** ~ the panel is made up as follows; ~ **fut fait** that's what was done; ~ **soit-il** Relig amen; **2** (introduisant une conclusion) thus liter, so; ~, **depuis 1989...** thus, since 1989...; ~ **tu nous quittes?** so you're leaving us then?

B **ainsi que** loc conj **1** (de même que) as well as; **les employés** ~ **que leurs conjoints sont invités** employees together with their partners are invited; **l'Italie** ~ **que quatre autres pays d'Europe** Italy, along with four other European countries; **2** (comme) as; ~ **que nous en avions convenu** as we had agreed; ~ **qu'un automate** like a robot

aïoli /ajɔli/ nm: provençal garlic mayonnaise

air /ɛR/

A nm **1** (que l'on respire) air; **le bon** ~ clean air; **renouveler l'**~ **d'une pièce** to let some air circulate in a room; **à l'**~ **libre** outside, outdoors; **concert en plein** ~ open-air concert; **activités de plein** ~ outdoor activities; **la vie au grand** ~ outdoor life; **on manque d'**~ **ici** it's stuffy in here; **de l'**~[○]! (va-t'en) get lost[○]!; **prendre l'**~ to go out and get some fresh air; **2** (brise, vent) **il n'y a pas d'**~ there's no wind; **un déplacement d'**~ a rush of air; **un courant d'**~ a draught GB ou draft US; **ça fait de l'**~ there's a draught GB ou draft US; **3** (autour de la terre) air; **jeter qch en l'**~ to throw sth into the air; **les bras en l'**~ one's arms (up) in the air; **planer dans les** ~ to glide into the air; **par** ~ by air; **regarder en l'**~ to look up; **avoir le nez en l'**~ to daydream; **dans l'**~ fig [*réforme, idée*] in the air; **il y a un virus dans l'**~ there's a virus going around; **en l'**~ [*menace, paroles*] empty; [*projet, idée*] vague; **parler en l'**~ to speculate; **envoyer** or **flanquer qch en l'**~[○] to send sth flying; **tout mettre en l'**~[○] (mettre en désordre) to make a dreadful mess; (faire échouer) to ruin everything; **4** (manière d'être) manner; (expression) expression; **avec un** ~ **résolu** in a resolute manner; **avoir un drôle d'**~ to look odd ou funny; **avoir un** or **l'**~ **distingué** to look distinguished; **d'un** ~ **triste** with a sad expression; **d'un** ~ **fâché/désolé** angrily/helplessly; **il y a un** ~ **de famille entre vous deux** you two share a family likeness; **elle a eu l'**~ **fin(e)**[○]! she looked a fool!; **la maison a l'**~ **d'un taudis** the house looks like a slum; **cela m'en a tout l'**~ it seems ou looks like it to

me; **j'aurais l'**~ **de quoi?** I'd look a right idiot!; **cela n'a l'**~ **de rien mais** it may not look it, but; **il n'a pas l'**~ **de comprendre** he doesn't seem to understand; **cela a l'**~ **d'être solide** it looks strong; **cela a l'**~ **d'être une usine** it looks like a factory; **il a l'**~ **de vouloir faire beau** it looks as if it's going to be fine; **5** (ambiance) **un** ~ **d'abandon** an air of neglect; **un** ~ **de fête** a carnival atmosphere; **6** (mélodie) tune; **un** ~ **d'opéra** an aria; **jouer toujours le même** ~ lit to play the same tune over and over again; fig to come out with the same old story

B **air-** (in compounds) ~**-mer** air-to-sea

(Composé) ~ **conditionné** (système) air-conditioning; (que l'on respire) conditioned air

(Idiomes) **il ne manque pas d'**~[○]! he's got a nerve!; **brasser** or **remuer de l'**~[○] to give the impression of being busy; **prendre** or **se donner de grands** ~**s** to put on airs; **j'ai besoin de changer d'**~ (d'environnement) I need a change of scene; (par agacement) I need to go and do something else

airain† /eRɛ̃/ nm bronze

aire /ɛR/ nf **1** (domaine) sphere; ~ **d'activité** sphere of activity; **2** (surface) area; **3** (nid) eyrie

(Composés) ~ **d'atterrissage** (pour avion) landing strip; (pour hélicoptère) landing pad; ~ **de chargement** loading bay; ~ **de jeu** playground; ~ **de lancement** launching pad; ~ **de loisirs** recreation area; ~ **de repos** rest area; ~ **de services** services (pl) GB, motorway GB ou freeway US service station; ~ **de stationnement** parking area

airelle /ɛRɛl/ nf (myrtille) bilberry; (baie rouge) cranberry

aisance /ɛzɑ̃s/ nf **1** (facilité) ease; **l'**~ **de ta démarche** the ease with which you walk; **l'**~ **de ton style** your flowing style; **avec** ~ with ease; **2** (opulence) comfort, affluence; **vivre dans l'**~ to live comfortably

aise /ɛz/

A adj liter pleased; **j'en suis fort** ~ hum I'm very pleased about it

B nf liter (contentement) pleasure; **d'**~ [*sourire, ronronner*] with pleasure

C **aises** nfpl **tenir à** or **aimer ses** ~**s** to like one's creature comforts; **il prenait ses** ~**s sur le canapé** he was stretched out on the sofa

D **à l'aise** loc **être à l'**~ or **à son** ~ (physiquement) to be comfortable; (financièrement) to be comfortably off; (psychologiquement) to be at ease, to feel comfortable (**avec qn** with sb); **mettre qn à l'**~ to put sb at his/her ease; **mettre qn mal à l'**~ to make sb feel ill at ease ou uncomfortable; **mets-toi à l'**~ make yourself comfortable; **en prendre à son** ~ **avec qch/qn** to make free with sth/sb; **à votre** ~! as you wish ou like!

aisé, ~**e** /eze/ adj **1** (simple) easy; **2** (cossu) wealthy; **être** ~ to be well-off; **les classes** ~**es** the well-off; **3** (sans contrainte) [*manières*] easy; [*style*] flowing

aisément /ezemɑ̃/ adv easily

aisselle /ɛsɛl/ nf armpit

Aix-la-Chapelle /ɛkslaʃapɛl/ ▸ p. 621 npr Aachen

ajonc /aʒɔ̃/ nm gorse bush

ajouré, ~**e** /aʒuRe/ adj **1** [*napperon*] (entièrement) open-work (épith); (bord) hemstitched; **2** [*clocher, balcon*] with ornamental apertures

ajournement /aʒuRnəmɑ̃/ nm (de voyage, décision) postponement; (de débat, procès) adjournment; ~ **de peine** Jur non-imposition of a sentence

ajourner /aʒuRne/ [1] vtr to postpone, to put off [*voyage, projet, décision*]; to adjourn [*débat, procès*]

ajout /aʒu/ nm addition; **faire des** ~**s** to make additions (à to)

ajouter /aʒute/ [1]

A vtr to add (à to); ~**/ne pas** ~ **foi à qch** fml to put faith/no faith in sth; **la chaleur ajoutée à la pollution fait que...** the heat on top of all the pollution means that...

B **ajouter à** vtr ind ~ **à** to add to [*confusion, chagrin*]

C **s'ajouter** vpr **s'**~ **à** to be added to; **à cela s'ajoute...** to that may be added...; **les désordres sociaux viennent s'**~ **aux difficultés économiques** on top of the economic difficulties there is also social unrest

ajustage /aʒystaʒ/ nm fitting

ajustement /aʒystəmɑ̃/ nm **1** Tech fit; **2** (adaptation) adjustment; ~ **des prix** price adjustment

ajuster /aʒyste/ [1] vtr **1** (régler) to adjust [*bretelle, prix, horaire*]; to alter [*robe, chemise*] (à to); to calibrate [*balance*]];

to shorten [*rênes*]; ~ **qch à** or **sur qch** lit to make sth fit sth; **corsage ajusté** close-fitting bodice; **2** (arranger) to arrange [*coiffure*]; **3** (viser) to take aim at [*lapin*]; ~ **son tir** or **coup** lit to adjust one's aim; fig to fix a more precise target

ajusteur /aʒystœʀ/ ▸ p. 372 *nm* fitter

alacrité /alakʀite/ *nf* alacrity littér

alaise = **alèse**

alambic /alɑ̃bik/ *nm* Chimie still

alambiqué, ~e /alɑ̃bike/ *adj* [*expression, style*] convoluted; [*explication*] tortuous

alanguir /alɑ̃giʀ/ fml **3** *vtr* [*amour, musique*] to make [sb] languid; [*chaleur*] to make [sb] listless; **geste alangui** languid gesture

alarmant, ~e /alaʀmɑ̃, ɑ̃t/ *adj* alarming

alarme /alaʀm/ *nf* alarm; **donner l'~** to raise the alarm; **c'est ce qui a donné l'~** that was what made us/them realize something was wrong

alarmer /alaʀme/ **1**
A *vtr* to alarm
B s'alarmer *vpr* to become alarmed (**de qch** about sth); **vous n'avez aucune raison de vous ~** there's no cause for alarm

alarmisme /alaʀmism/ *nm* alarmism

albanais, ~e /albanɛ, ɛz/
A ▸ p. 392 *adj* Albanian
B ▸ p. 336 *nm* Ling Albanian

albâtre /albɑtʀ/ *nm* alabaster

albatros /albatʀos/ *nm inv* albatross

albigeois, ~e /albiʒwa, az/ *adj* Albigensian

albinos /albinos/ *adj inv, nmf inv* albino

album /albɔm/ *nm* **1** (livre illustré) illustrated book; ~ **de bandes dessinées** comic strip book; **2** (pour timbres, cartes etc) album; **3** (disque) album

(Composé) ~ **à colorier** colouring^GB book

albumine /albymin/ *nf* albumin

alcali /alkali/ *nm* alkali

alcalin, ~e /alkalɛ̃, in/ *adj* alkaline

alchimie /alʃimi/ *nf* alchemy

alcool /alkɔl/ *nm* **1** (boisson) alcohol; **vous prendrez bien un petit ~?** will you have a little drop of something?; ~ **de poire** pear brandy; **sans ~** [*cocktail*] non-alcoholic; [*bière*] alcohol-free; **il ne boit que des ~ s forts** he only drinks spirits; **2** (alcoolisme) **s'adonner à** or **sombrer dans l'~** to take to drink; **3** (substance) alcohol; **boire de l'~** to drink alcohol; **forte teneur en ~** high alcohol content

(Composés) ~ **à brûler** methylated spirits, meths^O GB; ~ **à 90°** ≈ surgical spirit GB, rubbing alcohol US; ~ **de menthe** mentholated alcohol

alcoolique /alkɔlik/ *adj, nmf* alcoholic

alcoolisé, ~e /alkɔlize/ *adj* alcoholic; **une boisson peu/ non ~e** a low-alcohol/non-alcoholic drink

alcoolisme /alkɔlism/ *nm* alcoholism

alcootest /alkɔtɛst/ *nm* **1** (appareil) Breathalyzer®; **2** (contrôle) breath test

alcôve /alkov/ *nf* alcove; **d'~** [*histoires, secrets*] of the boudoir

aléa /alea/ *nm* (de temps, nature, marché) vagary; (économique, financier) hazard; **les ~s du métier** occupational hazards

aléatoire /aleatwaʀ/ *adj* **1** [*événements, succès, résultat*] unpredictable; [*profession*] insecure, risky; **le caractère ~ de** the unpredictability of [*résultat*]; the unstable nature of [*emploi*]; **2** Math, Ordinat random; **3** Jur [*acte*] aleatory

alémanique /alemanik/ ▸ p. 336 *adj, nm* Alemannic

alène /alɛn/ *nf* awl

alentour /alɑ̃tuʀ/
A *adv* surrounding; **visite de la ville et de la région ~** visit of the town and surrounding area; **les maisons d'~** the surrounding houses
B alentours *nmpl* (environs) surrounding area (*sg*); **les ~s de la ferme** the area around the farm
C aux alentours de *loc prép* (de lieu) around; (de chiffre, date) about, around

alerte /alɛʀt/
A *adj* (vif) [*personne, esprit*] alert; [*démarche*] brisk; [*style, jeu, interprétation*] lively
B *nf* alert; **être en état d'~** lit to be in a state of alert; fig to be

on the alert; **donner l'~** to raise the alarm; **donner l'~ à qn** to alert sb; ~ **générale** full alert

(Composés) ~ **aérienne** air raid warning; ~ **à la bombe** bomb scare

alerter /alɛʀte/ **1** *vtr* **1** (donner l'alerte) to alert; **2** (informer) to alert (**sur qch** to sth)

alèse /alɛz/ *nf* undersheet, mattress protector

alevin /alvɛ̃/ *nm* young fish

alexandrin /alɛksɑ̃dʀɛ̃/ *adj m, nm* alexandrine

alezan, ~e /alzɑ̃, an/ *adj* [*cheval*] chestnut

alfa /alfa/ *nm* (herbe) esparto grass; (fibre) esparto; (papier) esparto paper, alfa paper

algèbre /alʒɛbʀ/ *nf* algebra

algébrique /alʒebʀik/ *adj* algebraic

Alger /alʒe/ ▸ p. 621 *npr* Algiers

Algérie /alʒeʀi/ ▸ p. 230 *nprf* Algeria

algérien, -ienne /alʒeʀjɛ̃, ɛn/ ▸ p. 392 *adj* Algerian

algérois, ~e /alʒeʀwa, az/ ▸ p. 621 *adj* of Algiers

algie /alʒi/ *nf* pain; ~ **dentaire** toothache

algue /alg/ *nf* (d'eau douce) alga; (marine) seaweed **C**; **des ~s** (d'eau douce) algae; (marines) seaweed

alias /aljas/
A *nm* Ordinat alias
B *adv* alias

Ali Baba /alibaba/ *npr* ~ **et les quarante voleurs** Ali Baba and the forty thieves; **une vraie caverne d'~** a real Aladdin's cave

alibi /alibi/ *nm* **1** Jur alibi; **fournir un ~ très solide** to give a watertight alibi; **2** (prétexte) excuse; **il a invoqué l'~ d'une importante réunion de travail** he gave an important business meeting as his excuse

alicament /alikamɑ̃/ *nm* nutraceutical, functional food

aliénation /aljenasjɔ̃/ *nf* gén alienation; Méd ~ **(mentale)†** insanity

aliéné, ~e /aljene/ *nm,f* Méd insane person

aliéner /aljene/ **14**
A *vtr* **1** (détourner) ~ **qn à qn** to alienate sb from sb; **ces mesures lui ont aliéné une partie du vote socialiste** these measures have lost him/her a section of the socialist vote; **2** Philos, Sociol to alienate [*personne*]
B s'aliéner *vpr* (détourner) to alienate [*confrères, électorat, opinion publique*]; **tu t'es aliéné leur estime** you have lost their esteem

aligné, ~e /aliɲe/ *adj* Pol [*pays*] aligned; **non ~** non-aligned

alignement /aliɲ(ə)mɑ̃/ *nm* **1** (rang) row, line; **2** (mise côte à côte) alignment; **3** (pour la conformité) alignment; ~ **de qch sur qch** alignment of sth with sth; **l'~ de sa conduite sur celle de qn d'autre** bringing one's behaviour^GB into line with sb else's; **4** (de voie publique) alignment

aligner /aliɲe/ **1**
A *vtr* **1** (mettre côte à côte) to put [sth] in a line, to line [sth] up; (mettre en ligne droite) to line [sth] up, to align [*objets, points*]; **2** (rendre conforme à) ~ **qch sur qch** to bring sth into line with sth; **3** (énumérer) to give a list of [*arguments, chiffres*]; (accumuler) to line up [*somme*]; to notch up^O [*kilomètres, bons résultats*]; ~ **les fautes** to make one mistake after another ou the other; **4** (présenter) to line up [*équipe*]
B s'aligner *vpr* **1** (être côte à côte) to be in a line; **2** (se mettre en file) to line up; (en formation militaire) to fall into line; **3** **s'~ sur** to align oneself with [*pays, parti*]; **s'~ sur le règlement** to conform with the rules

aliment /alimɑ̃/ *nm* **1** (pour êtres humains, animaux) food; (pour animaux d'élevage) feed; (pour plantes) nutrient; **2** fig **fournir un ~ à qch** to feed sth

alimentaire /alimɑ̃tɛʀ/ *adj* lit [*besoins, comportement*] dietary; [*ration, industrie, pénurie*] food; **produits** or **denrées ~s** foodstuffs; **régime ~** diet; **trouble du comportement ~** eating disorder

alimentation /alimɑ̃tasjɔ̃/ *nf* **1** (manière de se nourrir) diet; ~ **saine** healthy diet; **une ~ riche en** a diet rich in; **2** (action de se nourrir) feeding; **3** Comm (produits alimentaires) food; (industrie) food industry; (commerce) food retailing; **magasin d'~** food shop, grocery store; **4** (approvisionnement) (en papier, oxygène) feeding (**de** of); **l'~ en eau** the water supply; **l'~ d'une arme à feu** loading a firearm

a

alimenter /alimɑ̃te/ [1]
A *vtr* ⓵ to feed [*personne, animal*]; ⓶ (approvisionner) [*torrent, eau*] to feed [*lac, turbine*]; [*tuyau, système*] to feed [*chaudière*]; ~ **qch en** to feed sth with [*papier, données*]; **la centrale alimente toute la ville** the power station supplies the whole town with electricity; ~ **un budget** to fund a budget; ⓷ fig to fuel [*conversation, feu*]
B **s'alimenter** *vpr* ⓵ [*personne*] to eat; [*animal*] to feed; **s'~ de** [*personne*] to live on; [*animal*] to feed on; ⓶ (en eau, gaz, électricité) [*ville*] **s'~ en** to be supplied with; ⓷ [*conversation, haine*] **s'~ de** to thrive on

alinéa /alinea/ *nm* (rentré) indentation; (ligne rentrée) indented line; (paragraphe) paragraph

alitement /alitmɑ̃/ *nm* bed rest

aliter, s'aliter /alite/ [1] *vpr* to take to one's bed; **être/rester alité** to be/to remain confined to bed

alizé /alize/ *adj m, nm* (**vent**) ~ trade wind

allaitement /alɛtmɑ̃/ *nm* (humain) feeding 匚; (animal) suckling 匚

allaiter /alete/ [1] *vtr* [*femme*] to breast-feed; [*animal*] to suckle; ~ **au biberon** to bottle-feed

allant, ~e /alɑ̃, ɑ̃t/
A *adj* active, lively
B *nm* drive, bounce; **avoir de l'~, être plein d'~** to have plenty of drive, to be full of bounce; **perdre son ~** to run out of steam

allécher /aleʃe/ [14] *vtr* to tempt (**avec** with); ~ **qn avec des promesses** to tempt sb with promises

allée /ale/
A *nf* ⓵ (chemin) (de jardin, bois) path; (de parc) gén path; (plus large) avenue; (de château, maison) (carrossable) drive; (de ville) avenue; **une ~ de peupliers** an avenue of poplars; **les ~s du pouvoir** fig the corridors of power; ⓶ (entre des rangées de sièges) aisle
B **allées** *nfpl* ~**s et venues** comings and goings; **surveiller les ~s et venues de qn** to watch sb's movements; **faire des ~s et venues entre les bureaux** to go back and forth between offices
(Composés) ~ **cavalière** bridleway, bridle path; ~ **forestière** forest trail

allégation /alegasjɔ̃/ *nf* allegation; ~**s mensongères** false allegations

allégé, ~e /aleʒe/
A *pp* ▸ **alléger**
B *pp adj* [*aliment*] (en graisses) low-fat; (en sucre) diet (*épith*)

allégeance /aleʒɑ̃s/ *nf* allegiance

allégement /aleʒmɑ̃/ *nm* ⓵ (en poids) lightening; ⓶ (réduction) (de charges) reduction; (de contrôles) relaxing; (de structures) simplification; ~ **fiscal** tax relief; ⓷ (de conditions de détention) improvement

alléger /aleʒe/ [15]
A *vtr* ⓵ (rendre moins lourd) to lighten; ⓶ (rendre moins important) to reduce [*dette*] (**de** by); to cut [*impôt*]; to simplify [*dispositif, procédure*]; to relax [*contrôle*]; ~ **les horaires scolaires** to reduce the school day; ⓷ (rendre moins pénible) to improve [*conditions de détention*]; to alleviate [*souffrances*]
B **s'alléger** *vpr* ⓵ (devenir moins lourd) to get lighter; ⓶ (devenir moins important) [*dette, impôt*] to be reduced; [*dispositif, procédure*] to be simplified; [*embargo*] to be relaxed; ⓷ (devenir moins pénible) to be improved

allégorie /alegɔʀi/ *nf* allegory

allègre /alɛgʀ/ *adj* [*texte, style*] light; [*récit, ton*] lighthearted; [*pas, humeur*] buoyant

allégrement /alegʀəmɑ̃/ *adv* ⓵ (avec allégresse) joyfully; ⓶ (sans souci) iron blithely; **mettre ~ qn en prison** to throw sb in jail without a second thought

allégresse /alegʀɛs/ *nf* joy; **dans l'~** in joyful mood; **participer à l'~ générale** to share in the general rejoicing

alléguer /alege/ [14] *vtr* (invoquer) to invoke; (prétexter) to allege

Allemagne /alman/ ▸ p. 230 *nprf* Germany; **la République fédérale d'~** the Federal Republic of Germany; **l'~ unie** unified Germany

allemand, ~e /almɑ̃, ɑ̃d/
A ▸ p. 392 *adj* German
B ▸ p. 336 *nm* Ling German

aller¹ /ale/ [9]
A *v aux* ⓵ (marque le futur) **je vais rentrer chez moi** I'm going home; **j'allais partir** I was just leaving; **j'allais partir quand**

---

aller¹

Lorsque *aller* fait partie d'une expression figée comme *aller dans le sens de, aller de pair avec* etc., l'expression est traitée sous l'entrée **sens, pair** etc.

On notera les différentes traductions de *aller* verbe de mouvement indiquant:

un déplacement unique dans le temps:

je vais au théâtre ce soir
= I'm going to the theatre this evening *ou* une habitude:

je vais au théâtre tous les lundis
= I go to the theatre every Monday

....

aller + infinitif

La traduction dépend du temps:

je vais apprendre l'italien
= I'm going to learn Italian

il est allé voir l'exposition
= he went to see the exhibition

j'allais me marier quand la guerre a éclaté
= I was going to get married when the war broke out

va voir
= go and see

va leur parler
= go and speak to them

j'irai voir l'exposition demain
= I'll go and see the exhibition tomorrow

je vais souvent m'asseoir au bord de la rivière
= I often go and sit by the river

il ne va jamais voir une exposition
= he never goes to see exhibitions

On notera que pour les activités sportives on peut avoir:

aller nager
= to go swimming *ou* to go for a swim

aller faire du vélo
= to go cycling *ou* to go on a bike ride

On trouvera ci-dessous des exemples et des exceptions illustrant *aller* dans ses différentes fonctions verbales.

---

il est arrivé I was about to leave when he arrived; **l'homme qui allait inventer la bombe atomique** the man who was to invent the atomic bomb; **il va le regretter** he'll regret it; **ça va ~ mal**○ there'll be trouble; **tu vas me laisser tranquille?** will you please leave me alone!; ⓶ (marque le futur programmé) **je vais leur dire ce que je pense** I'm going to tell them what I think; ⓷ (marque le mouvement) ~ **rouler de l'autre côté de la rue** to go rolling across the street; ~ **atterrir**○ **sur mon bureau** to end up on my desk; ⓸ (marque l'inclination) **va savoir!** who knows?; **qu'es-tu allé te mettre en tête?** where did you pick up that idea?; **qui irait le soupçonner?** who would suspect him?; **pourquoi es-tu allé faire ça?** why did you have to go and do that?; **allez-y comprendre quelque chose!** just try and work that out!; ⓹ (marque l'évolution) **la situation va (en) se compliquant** the situation is getting more and more complicated; ~ **(en) s'améliorant** to be improving; **la tristesse ira (en) s'atténuant** the grief will diminish
B *vi* ⓵ (se porter, se dérouler, fonctionner) **comment vas-tu, comment ça va?** how are you?; **ça va (bien)** I'm fine; **les enfants vont bien?** are the children all right?; **comment va la santé?** how are you keeping?; ~ **beaucoup mieux** to be much better; **bois ça, ça ira mieux** drink this, you'll feel better; **tout va bien?** is everything going all right?; **vous êtes sûr que ça va?** are you sure you're all right?; **les affaires vont bien** business is good; **ça va l'école?** how are things at school?; **ça ne va pas très fort** (ma santé) I'm not feeling very well; (la vie) things aren't too good; (le moral) I'm feeling a bit low; **ça va mal entre eux** things

aren't too good between them; **qu'est-ce qui ne va pas?** what's the matter?; **la voiture a quelque chose qui ne va pas** there's something wrong with the car; **tout est allé si vite!** it all happened so quickly!; **ne pas ~ sans peine** *or* **mal** not to be easy; **ça va de soi** *or* **sans dire** it goes without saying; **l'amour ne va jamais de soi** love is never straightforward; **ça va tout seul** (c'est facile) it's a doddle○ GB, it's easy as pie; **les choses vont très vite** things are moving fast; **on fait ~○** struggling on○; **ça peut ~○**, **ça ira○** could be worse○; **ça va, non○** *or* **la tête○?** are you mad○ GB *ou* crazy○?; ⟨**2**⟩ (se déplacer) to go; **allez tout droit** go straight ahead; **~ et venir** (dans une pièce) to pace up and down; (d'un lieu à l'autre) to run in and out; **la liberté d'~ et venir** the freedom to come and go at will; **les nouvelles vont vite** news travels fast; **où vas-tu?** where are you going?, where are you off to?; **en Pologne/au marché** to go to Poland/to the market; **je suis allé de Bruxelles à Anvers** I went from Brussels to Antwerp; **allons-y!** let's go!; **je l'ai rencontré en allant au marché** I met him on the way to the market; **~ sur** *or* **vers Paris** to head for Paris; **~ vers le nord** to head north; **va-t-on vers une nouvelle guerre?** are we heading for another war?; **j'y vais** (je m'en occupe) I'll get it; (je pars○) I'm going, I'm off○; **où va-t-il?** where is he off to○?; **où va-t-on?**, **où allons-nous○?** fig what are things coming to?, what's the world coming to?; ⟨**3**⟩ (pour se livrer à une activité) **~ au travail** to go to work; **~ à la chasse** to go hunting; **~ au pain○** to go and get the bread; **~ aux courses○** *or* **commissions○** to go shopping; **~ aux nouvelles** to go and see if there's any news; ⟨**4**⟩ (s'étendre dans l'espace) **la route va au village** the road leads to the village; **la rue va de la gare à l'église** the street goes from the station to the church; ⟨**5**⟩ (convenir) **ma robe, ça va?** is my dress all right?; **ça va, ça peut aller○** (en quantité) that'll do; (en qualité) it'll do; **ça va comme ça** it's all right as it is; **ça ne va pas du tout** that's no good at all; **la traduction n'allait pas** the translation was no good; **une soupe, ça (te) va?** how about some soup?; **va pour une soupe○** soup is okay○; **ça va si je porte un jean?** can I wear jeans?; **si le contrat ne te va pas, ne le signe pas** don't sign the contract if you're not happy with it; **si ça va pour toi, ça va pour moi○** if it's okay by you, it's okay by me○; **ma scie ne va pas pour le métal** my saw is no good for metal; **ça te va bien de faire la morale○** iron you're hardly the person to preach; ⟨**6**⟩ (être de la bonne taille, de la bonne forme) **~ à qn** to fit sb; ⟨**7**⟩ (flatter, mettre en valeur) **~ à qn** to suit sb; **ta cravate ne va pas avec ta chemise** your tie doesn't go with your shirt; **les meubles vont bien ensemble** the furniture all matches; **je trouve que ta sœur et son petit ami vont très bien ensemble** I think your sister and her boyfriend are ideally suited; ⟨**8**⟩ (se ranger) to go; **les assiettes vont dans le placard** the plates go in the cupboard; ⟨**9**⟩ (faculté) **pouvoir ~ dans l'eau** to be waterproof; **le plat ne va pas au four** the dish is not ovenproof; ⟨**10**⟩ (dans une évaluation) **la voiture peut ~ jusqu'à 200 km/h** the car can do up to 200 kph; **certains modèles peuvent ~ jusqu'à 1 000 francs** some models can cost up to 1,000 francs; ⟨**11**⟩ (en arriver à) **~ jusqu'au président** to take it right up to the president; **~ jusqu'à tuer** to go as far as to kill; **leur amour est allé jusqu'à la folie** their love bordered on madness; ⟨**12**⟩ (dans le temps) **~ jusqu'en 1914** to go up to 1914; **la période qui va de 1918 à 1939** the period between 1918 and 1939; **le contrat allait jusqu'en 1997** the contract ran until 1997; **~ sur ses 17 ans** to be going on 17; ⟨**13**⟩ (agir, raisonner) **vas-y doucement, le tissu est fragile** careful, the fabric is delicate; **tu vas trop vite** you're going too fast; **vas-y, demande-leur!** (incitation) go on, ask them!; **vas-y, dis-le!** (provocation) come on, out with it!; **allons, allez!** (pour encourager, inciter) come on!; **si tu vas par là, rien n'est entièrement vrai** if you take that line, nothing is entirely true; ⟨**14**⟩ (contribuer) **y ~ de sa petite larme** to shed a little tear; **y ~ de son petit discours** to do one's party piece; **y ~ de ses économies** to dip into one's savings; **y ~ de sa personne** to pitch in; ⟨**15**⟩ (se succéder) **ça y va la vodka avec lui** he certainly gets through the vodka; **ça y allait les coups** the fur was flying○; ⟨**16**⟩ (servir) **l'argent ira à la réparation de l'église** the money will go toward(s) repairing the church; **l'argent est allé dans leurs poches** they pocketed the money; ⟨**17**⟩ (enfreindre) **~ contre la loi** [personne] to break the law; [acte] to be against the law; **je ne peux pas ~ contre ce qu'il a décidé** I can't go against his decision

C **s'en aller** vpr ⟨**1**⟩ (partir, se rendre) **il faut que je m'en aille** I must go *ou* leave; **va-t'en!** go away!; **s'en ~ au travail** to go

off to work; ⟨**2**⟩ (disparaître) **les nuages vont s'en ~** the clouds will clear away; **la tache ne s'en va pas** the stain won't come out; **avec le temps, tout s'en va** everything fades with time; ⟨**3**⟩ fml (mourir) to pass away; ⟨**4**⟩ (avoir l'intention de, essayer) **je m'en vais leur dire ce que je pense** I'm going to tell them what I think; **va-t'en savoir!** who knows?

D v impers ⟨**1**⟩ (être en jeu) **il y va de ta santé** your health is at stake; ⟨**2**⟩ (se passer) **il en va souvent ainsi** that's often what happens; **il en va de même pour toi** that goes for you too; **il en va autrement en Corée** things are different in Korea; ⟨**3**⟩ Math **40 divisé par 12 il y va 3 fois et il reste 4** 12 into 40 goes 3 times with 4 left over

aller² /ale/ nm ⟨**1**⟩ (trajet) **j'ai fait une escale à l'~** I made a stopover on the way out; **j'ai pris le bus à l'~** (en allant là) I took the bus there; (en venant ici) I took the bus here; **l'~ a pris trois heures** the journey there took three hours; **il n'arrête pas de faire des ~s et retours entre chez lui et son bureau** he keeps running to and fro from his house to the office; **billet ~** gén single ticket GB, one-way ticket US; (d'avion) one-way ticket; **billet ~ (et) retour** return ticket GB, round trip (ticket) US; **match ~** first leg; ⟨**2**⟩ (ticket) **~ (simple)** single (ticket) GB, one-way ticket (pour to); **~ (et) retour** return ticket

allergie /alɛʁʒi/ nf Méd allergy; **avoir une ~ à** Méd to have an allergy to; fig to be allergic to

allergique /alɛʁʒik/ adj Méd, fig allergic (à to)

allergisant, **~e** /alɛʁʒizɑ̃, ɑ̃t/ adj Méd [produit] allergenic; **un produit qui a une action ~e** a product which causes allergic reactions

allergologue /alɛʁɡɔlɔɡ/ ▸ p. 372 nmf allergist

alliage /aljaʒ/ nm ⟨**1**⟩ (produit) alloy; **en ~** (épith); ⟨**2**⟩ (association) combination

alliance /aljɑ̃s/ nf ⟨**1**⟩ (bague) wedding ring; ⟨**2**⟩ (entente) alliance; **faire ~ avec** to form an alliance with; ⟨**3**⟩ Relig Covenant; ⟨**4**⟩ (mariage) fml union sout, marriage; ⟨**5**⟩ (combinaison) fml combination

⟨Composé⟩ **l'~ atlantique** the Atlantic Alliance

allié, **~e** /alje/
A pp ▸ **allier**
B pp adj (uni) related by marriage (à qn to sb); (par un traité) [nation] allied; **le débarquement ~** the Allied landings
C nm,f (proche) ally; (parent) relative; **les ~s** Mil Hist the Allies

allier /alje/ [2]
A vtr ⟨**1**⟩ Tech to alloy [métaux] (à, avec with); ⟨**2**⟩ (combiner) to combine (et, à with); ⟨**3**⟩ (par un mariage) to unite [sth] by marriage [familles]
B s'allier vpr ⟨**1**⟩ Pol, Mil (s'unir) to form an alliance (avec, à with); ⟨**2**⟩ (s'harmoniser) [sons, couleurs] to go (well) together

alligator /aligatɔʁ/ nm alligator

allitération /al(l)iteʁasjɔ̃/ nf alliteration ¢

allô /alo/ excl hello!, hallo!

allocation /al(l)ɔkasjɔ̃/ nf ⟨**1**⟩ (action) granting; ⟨**2**⟩ (somme) benefit, benefits (pl) US; **une ~ de 5 000 euros** 5,000 euros in benefit *ou* benefits US

⟨Composés⟩ **~ chômage** unemployment benefit *ou* benefits US; **~ logement** housing benefit *ou* benefits US; **~ vieillesse** discretionary retirement pension; **~s familiales** family allowance (sg)

> ⓘ **Allocations familiales** Known colloquially as *les allocs*, they cover both maternity benefits and child benefit generally. For a first child, a working mother is entitled to sixteen weeks of paid maternity leave financed by the state. After the birth of a second child, child benefit is payable monthly.

allocs /alɔk/ nfpl family allowance

allocution /al(l)ɔkysjɔ̃/ nf address

allonge /alɔ̃ʒ/ nf ⟨**1**⟩ (de table) leaf; ⟨**2**⟩ (de boxeur) reach

allongé, **~e** /alɔ̃ʒe/ adj ⟨**1**⟩ (longiforme) elongated; ⟨**2**⟩ [trot, galop] extended

allongement /alɔ̃ʒmɑ̃/ nm ⟨**1**⟩ (de liste, procédure, délais) lengthening; (de vacances) extension; ⟨**2**⟩ (de voyelle) lengthening; ⟨**3**⟩ (de ressort) extension

allonger /alɔ̃ʒe/ [13]
A vtr ⟨**1**⟩ (coucher) to lay [sb] down; ⟨**2**⟩ (agrandir) to lengthen [robe, rideau] (de by); to extend [liste, vacances] (de by); to prolong [espérance de vie] (de by); **~ le visage de qn** to

make sb's face look longer; ∼ **le pas** to quicken one's step; ③ (étirer) to stretch [sth] out [bras]; ④ (diluer) to water [sth] down [café, vin]; **allongé d'eau** watered down; ⑤ ○(dans un combat) to floor○ [adversaire]

B vi [jours] to lengthen

C **s'allonger** vpr ① (pour se reposer) to lie down; (s'étirer) to stretch out; **allongé sur le dos** lying on his back; ② (s'agrandir) to get longer; **ta silhouette s'allonge** you look slimmer

allouer /alwe/ [1] vtr ① (donner) to allocate [somme] (à qn to sb; à qch for sth); ② (accorder) to grant [prêt, indemnité] (à qn to sb; à qch for sth); to allot, to allow [temps] (à qn to sb; à qch for sth)

allumage /alymaʒ/ nm ① Aut ignition; ② (de lampe, chauffage) switching on; **l'∼ est automatique** it switches on automatically

allumé○, **∼e** /alyme/

A adj ① (fou) mad○; ② (ivre) tipsy○; **être bien ∼** to be well oiled○

B nm,f (fou) **c'est un ∼** he's mad○

allume-cigare(s) /alymsigaʀ/ nm inv cigar lighter

allume-gaz /alymgaz/ nm inv gas lighter

allumer /alyme/ [1]

A vtr ① (par la flamme) to light [bougie, gaz]; to strike [allumette]; to start [incendie]; **le feu ne va pas rester allumé** the fire is not going to stay alight GB, lighted US; ② (électriquement) to switch [sth] on, to turn [sth] on; **le couloir est allumé** the light is on in the corridor; **laisser ses phares allumés** to leave one's headlights on; **allume!** switch on the light!; ③ (exciter) to stir [imagination]; to arouse [désir]; to turn [sb] on○ [personne]

B **s'allumer** vpr ① (électriquement) [lampe, radio, chauffage] to switch on; ② fig [regard] to light up

allumette /alymɛt/ nf match

allumeur, -euse /alymœʀ, øz/ ▸ p. 372

A nm,f ① **∼ de réverbères** lamplighter; ② ○(qui séduit) tease

B nm Aut distributor

allure /alyʀ/ nf ① (de marcheur) pace; (de véhicule) speed; **à vive ∼** at high speed; **modérer** or **ralentir son ∼** to slow down; **à toute ∼** [conduire] at top speed; [marcher, réciter, manger] really fast; **à cette ∼** at this rate; ② (apparence) (de personne) appearance; (de vêtement) look; (d'événement) aspect; **avoir des ∼s de** to look like; **il a une drôle d'∼** he's a funny-looking chap; **prendre l'∼** or **des ∼s de** [changement, révolte] to begin to look like; ③ (distinction) style; **elle a beaucoup d'∼** she's got a lot of style; **avoir fière ∼** to cut a fine figure

allusif, -ive /alyzif, iv/ adj ① (qui contient une allusion) allusive; ② (qui parle par allusions) indirect; **elle est restée très allusive** she spoke very indirectly

allusion /alyzjɔ̃/ nf (sous-entendu) allusion (à to); **faire ∼ à** to allude to; **∼ perfide** innuendo

alluvial, ∼e, mpl -iaux /alyvjal, o/ adj alluvial

alluvion /alyvjɔ̃/ nf alluvium; **des ∼s** alluvia

almanach /almana(k)/ nm almanac

aloès /alɔɛs/ nm inv aloe

aloi /alwa/ nm **un succès de bon ∼** a well-deserved success; **une plaisanterie de mauvais ∼** a tasteless joke; **une gaieté de bon ∼** a simple cheerfulness

alors /alɔʀ/

A adv ① (à ce moment-là) then; **c'est ∼ qu'il prit la parole** it was then that he started to speak; **il avait ∼ 18 ans** he was 18 at the time; **∼ seulement** only then; **le pays, ∼ sorti de la crise, pourra** the country which by then will be out of recession, will be able to; **la mode d'∼** the fashion in those days; **le premier ministre britannique d'∼** the British Prime Minister at the time; **mes romans d'∼** my novels of the time; **jusqu'∼** until then; ② (dans ce cas-là) then; **je m'en vais** I'm going then; **(mais) ∼ cela change tout!** but that changes everything!; **et ∼?** so what?; **∼? que faisons-nous?** so? what shall we do?; ③ (de ce fait) so; **il était tard, ∼ j'ai pris un taxi** it was late so I took a taxi; ④ (pour résumer) then; **on se voit demain ∼?** we'll see each other tomorrow then?; ⑤ (ou bien) or; **ou else; je serai dans la cuisine ou ∼ dans le jardin** I'll be in the kitchen or in the garden; ⑥ ○(dans un récit) so; **∼ il me dit...** so he said to me...; ⑦ (pour renforcer une exclamation) **non mais ∼!** honestly!; **ça ∼!** (étonnement) good grief!; **∼ ça!** (indignation) that's not on!

B **alors que** loc conj ① (pendant que) while; ② (tandis que) when; **tu lui souris ∼ que tu le détestes** you smile at him while (in fact) you hate him

C **alors même que** loc conj even though

alouette /alwɛt/ nf lark

alourdir /aluʀdiʀ/ [3]

A vtr [fardeau] to weigh [sb] down [personne]; [problème] to make [sth] tense [atmosphère]; **le subjonctif alourdit la phrase** the subjunctive weighs the sentence down; **manteau alourdi par la pluie** coat heavy with rain; **le dernier témoignage a alourdi les accusations** the statement by the last witness weighed heavily against the accused

B **s'alourdir** vpr [paupières] to grow heavy; [air] to get heavy; [dépenses] to increase; **le bilan de victimes s'est alourdi** the death toll has risen

alourdissement /aluʀdismɑ̃/ nm (de l'impôt, de prélèvement) increase (**de** in)

alpaga /alpaga/ nm (animal, laine) alpaca

alpage /alpaʒ/ nm mountain pasture

alpestre /alpɛstʀ/ adj alpine

alphabet /alfabɛ/ nm ① (signes) alphabet; ② (manuel) ABC (book)

alphabétique /alfabetik/ adj alphabetical

alphabétisation /alfabetizasjɔ̃/ nf (enseignement de l'écriture) literacy tuition

alphabétiser /alfabetize/ [1] vtr (enseigner) to teach [sb] to read and write [personne]; to promote literacy in [pays]

alphanumérique /alfanymeʀik/ adj alphanumeric

alpin, ∼e /alpɛ̃, in/ adj alpine

alpinisme /alpinism/ ▸ p. 000 nm mountaineering

alpiniste /alpinist/ nmf mountaineer, climber

alsacien, -ienne /alzasjɛ̃, ɛn/

A ▸ p. 504 adj [personne] from Alsace; [cuisine, population] of Alsace

B ▸ p. 336 nm Ling Alsatian

altération /alteʀasjɔ̃/ nf (détérioration) (de facultés) impairment (**de** of); (de denrée) spoiling (**de** of); (d'environnement) deterioration (**de** in); (de sentiment, couleur) change (**de** in)

altercation /altɛʀkasjɔ̃/ nf altercation

altérer /alteʀe/ [14]

A vtr ① (détériorer) to affect [saveur, relation, santé]; to spoil [denrée]; to mar [joie]; to alter [sentiment]; to change [expression]; to fade [couleur]; ② (falsifier) to distort [fait]; to adulterate [substance]; ③ **être altéré de sang/de pouvoir** to thirst for blood/power

B **s'altérer** vpr [santé, saveur] to become impaired; [denrée] to spoil; [voix] to falter; [sentiment] to change

altermondialiste /altɛʀmɔ̃djalist/ adj, nmf alterglobalist

alternance /altɛʀnɑ̃s/ nf ① gén alternation; **en ∼ avec** alternately with; **'l'Avare' se joue en ∼** 'l'Avare' is on every other night; ② Pol **choisir l'∼** [électorat, pays] to opt for a change in power

alternateur /altɛʀnatœʀ/ nm alternator

alternatif, -ive¹ /altɛʀnatif, iv/ adj ① gén alternate; ② Électrotech alternating; ③ Sociol alternative

alternative² /altɛʀnativ/ nf alternative

alternativement /altɛʀnativmɑ̃/ adv alternately

alterné, ∼e /altɛʀne/ adj alternating

alterner /altɛʀne/ [1]

A vtr gén to alternate; **∼ les cultures** to rotate crops

B vi ① (se succéder) to alternate (**avec** with); ② (se relayer) **∼ avec qn pour faire qch** to take turns with sb (at) doing sth

altesse /altɛs/ nf ① (titre) **son Altesse royale** His/Her Royal Highness; ② (personne) prince/princess

altier, -ière /altje, ɛʀ/ adj haughty

altimètre /altimɛtʀ/ nm altimeter

altitude /altityd/ nf ① (hauteur) altitude; **prendre de l'∼** [avion, ballon] to gain altitude or height; **à basse/haute ∼** [neiger, voler] at low/high altitude; **quelle est l'∼ du mont Blanc?** how high is Mont Blanc?; **des sommets de plus de 6 000 mètres d'∼** peaks more than 6,000 metres^GB high; **avoir une faible ∼** to be close to sea-level; ② (haute montagne) **en ∼** [pousser, neiger] high up (in the mountains); **station d'∼** mountain resort

alto /alto/

A adj [saxophone, clarinette] alto

B *nm* [1] ▸ p. 389 (instrument) viola; [2] ▸ p. 372 (musicien) viola player GB, violin US; [3] (voix) alto

altruiste /altʀɥist/
A *adj* altruistic
B *nmf* altruist

aluminium /alyminjɔm/ *nm* aluminium GB, aluminum US; **en ~** aluminium (*épith*) GB, aluminum (*épith*) US

alvéole /alveɔl/ *nf* [1] (de ruche) alveolus; [2] (de poumon) alveolus; (de dent) tooth socket; [3] (de roche) cavity

alvéolé, ~e /alveɔle/ *adj* honeycombed

amabilité /amabilite/
A *nf* [1] (gentillesse) kindness; **avec ~** kindly; **quelle ~!** iron charming!; [2] (politesse) courtesy; **avec ~** politely
B amabilités *nfpl* (prévenances) **faire des ~s à qn** to be polite to sb; **se dire des ~s** lit to exchange pleasantries; iron to exchange insults

amadouer /amadwe/ [1]
A *vtr* to coax, to cajole [*personne, animal*]; **~ qn pour qu'il fasse qch** to cajole sb into doing sth
B s'amadouer *vpr* [*personne*] to soften

amaigrir /amegʀiʀ/ [3] *vtr* [*maladie, régime*] to make [sb] thinner [*personne*]; **je l'ai trouvée très amaigrie** I found her much thinner; **un visage amaigri par la maladie** a face made thin by illness

amaigrissant, ~e /amegʀisɑ̃, ɑ̃t/ *adj* slimming

amaigrissement /amegʀismɑ̃/ *nm* weight loss, loss of weight

amalgame /amalgam/ *nm* [1] gén mixture; (d'idées) pej hotchpotch GB, hodgepodge US; [2] (pour les dents, en chimie) amalgam

amalgamer /amalgame/ [1] *vtr* [1] (associer) pej to lump together [*problèmes*]; [2] (mélanger) to blend, to amalgamate [*ingrédients*]

amande /amɑ̃d/ *nf* Bot [1] (fruit) almond; **yeux en ~** almond(-shaped) eyes; [2] (dans un noyau) kernel

amandier /amɑ̃dje/ *nm* almond tree

amanite /amanit/ *nf* amanita; **~ phalloïde** death cap

amant /amɑ̃/ *nm* lover

amarante /amaʀɑ̃t/
A ▸ p. 140 *adj inv* amaranthine
B *nf* (plante, colorant) amaranth

amarrage /amaʀaʒ/ *nm* [1] (de bateau) mooring; [2] (fixation) tying, fastening; [3] Astronaut docking

amarre /amaʀ/ *nf* (cordage) rope; **les ~s** moorings; **rompre les ~s** to break its moorings; **larguer les ~s** lit to cast off; fig to set off

amarrer /amaʀe/ [1] *vtr* [1] Naut to moor; **~ à** to moor alongside [*quai*]; to moor to [*anneau, piquet*]; [2] (attacher) to tie (**à, sur** to)

amas /ama/ *nm inv* [1] (d'objets, de sable, neige) pile; (de tôle, ruines) heap; Méd (de sang, graisse) accumulation; [2] (en astronomie) cluster; [3] (en géologie) mass

amasser /amase/ [1]
A *vtr* to amass, to accumulate [*fortune, livres, papiers*]; to lay in [*provisions*]; to acquire [*connaissances*]; to amass [*preuves*]; to collect [*témoignages*]
B s'amasser *vpr* [*objets, neige*] to pile up; [*preuves*] to build up

amateur /amatœʀ/
A *adj inv* amateur; **radio ~** radio ham○
B *nm* [1] (connaisseur) (en sport, photographie) enthusiast; (en vin) connoisseur; **~ de jazz** jazz lover; **c'est un grand ~ de cigares** he's a great lover of cigars; **pour les ~s de sensations fortes** for thrill-seekers; **~ de catch** wrestling fan; [2] (collectionneur) **~ d'antiquités** antiques collector; [3] (non-professionnel) amateur

amazone /amazon/ *nf* (cavalière) horsewoman; **monter en ~** to ride sidesaddle

Amazone /amazon/
A *nf* Mythol Amazon
B ▸ p. 259 *nprm* Géog **l'~** the Amazon (river)

Amazonie /amazɔni/ ▸ p. 504 *nprf* Amazon

ambages: **sans ambages** /sɑ̃zɑ̃baʒ/ *loc adv* without beating around the bush

ambassade /ɑ̃basad/ *nf* [1] (lieu, service) embassy; [2] (employés) embassy staff; (diplomates) embassy officials

ambassadeur, -drice /ɑ̃basadœʀ, dʀis/ *nm* ambassador; **l'~ de France au Chili** the French ambassador to Chile

ambassadrice /ɑ̃basadʀis/ *nf* (épouse d'ambassadeur) ambassador's wife

ambiance /ɑ̃bjɑ̃s/ *nf* [1] (atmosphère) atmosphere, ambiance; [2] (gaieté) lively atmosphere; **tu peux compter sur lui pour mettre de l'~** you can count on him to liven things up; **ça manque d'~ ici**○ it's not exactly lively here

ambiant, ~e /ɑ̃bjɑ̃, ɑ̃t/ *adj* [1] [*air*] surrounding; **à température ~e** at room temperature; [2] fig [*pessimisme*] pervading; [*état d'esprit*] prevailing

ambigu, -uë /ɑ̃bigy/ *adj* [*réponse, mot, situation*] ambiguous; [*personnage*] multifaceted; [*sentiment, attitude*] ambivalent

ambiguïté /ɑ̃biɡɥite/ *nf* [1] (de mot, situation) ambiguity; **sans ~** [*question*] unambiguous; [*situation*] clear-cut; [*définir, dire*] unambiguously; [2] (de personnage) enigmatic nature; (de sentiment) ambivalence

ambitieux, -ieuse /ɑ̃bisjø, øz/
A *adj* ambitious
B *nm,f* ambitious person; **les ~** ambitious people

ambition /ɑ̃bisjɔ̃/ *nf* ambition; **avoir de l'~** to be ambitious; **un homme sans ~** a man with no ambition; **avoir l'~ de faire qch** to have an ambition to do sth; **je n'ai pas l'~ de réformer le système en un mois** I don't aim to change the system in a month

ambitionner /ɑ̃bisjɔne/ [1] *vtr* to aspire to [*poste, place*]; to aim for [*médaille, titre sportif*]; **~ de faire** to aim to do

ambivalence /ɑ̃bivalɑ̃s/ *nf* ambivalence

ambre /ɑ̃bʀ/ *nm* (résine) **~ (jaune)** amber; **couleur d'~** amber; **collier d'~** amber necklace

ambré, ~e /ɑ̃bʀe/ *adj* [1] ▸ p. 140 (couleur d'ambre) amber; [2] (à senteur d'ambre) perfumed with ambergris

ambroisie /ɑ̃bʀwazi/ *nf* Mythol ambrosia

ambulance /ɑ̃bylɑ̃s/ *nf* ambulance

ambulancier, -ière /ɑ̃bylɑ̃sje, ɛʀ/ ▸ p. 372 *nm,f* ambulance driver

ambulant, ~e /ɑ̃bylɑ̃, ɑ̃t/ *adj* [*artiste*] itinerant; [*marchand*] mobile; [*cirque*] travelling GB; **théâtre ~** itinerant players (*pl*); **service de restauration ~e** train buffet trolley; **vendeur ~** (dans une gare) snack trolley man; **c'est un cadavre ~**○ he's/she's a walking skeleton○

âme /ɑm/ *nf* [1] Philos, Relig soul; **(que) Dieu ait son ~** (may) God rest his/her soul; [2] (nature profonde) soul, spirit; **avoir une ~ de poète** to have the soul of a poet *ou* a poetic soul; **avoir l'~ d'un chef** to have the spirit of a leader; [3] (siège de la pensée et des émotions) soul; **avoir l'~ sensible** to be a sensitive soul; **interprétation sans ~** soulless interpretation; **socialiste dans l'~** a socialist to the core; [4] (conscience morale) soul; **paix de l'~** spiritual peace; **en mon ~ et conscience** in all honesty; [5] (personne, habitant) soul; **c'est une ~ généreuse** he/she has great generosity of spirit; **pas ~ qui vive** not a (living *ou* single) soul; [6] (de nation, parti) soul (**de** of); (de complot) moving spirit (**de** in)

(**Composés**) **~ damnée** partner in crime; **~ en peine** soul in torment; **errer comme une ~ en peine** to wander around like a lost soul; **~ sœur** soul mate

amélioration /ameljɔʀasjɔ̃/ *nf* improvement

améliorer /ameljɔʀe/ [1]
A *vtr* to improve [*résultat*]; to increase [*production*]; **un pique-nique amélioré** hum a superior picnic
B s'améliorer *vpr* to improve; **ça ne va pas en s'améliorant**○ things aren't getting any better

amen /amɛn/ *nm inv* Relig amen; **dire ~ à tout** fig to agree to everything

aménagé, ~e /amenaʒe/ *adj* [1] (transformé) converted; [2] (équipé) equipped; **l'appartement est mal ~** the apartment is not very well appointed

aménagement /amenaʒmɑ̃/ *nm* [1] (de région, ville) development; **l'~ du territoire** ≈ town and country planning; [2] (de port de plaisance, routes) construction; (d'espaces verts) creation; (de parc, terrain de sport) laying out; [3] (de fermette, grenier) (en transformant) conversion; (en améliorant) improvement; [4] (en équipant) (de cuisine) equipping; (de magasin) fitting; [5] (de maison, bateau) fitting; [6] (par rapport à un règlement, une loi) adjustment; **l'~ du temps de travail** flexible working hours (*pl*)

aménager /amenaʒe/ [13] *vtr* 1 (en transformant) to convert; (en améliorant) to do up; 2 (en équipant) to equip [*cuisine*]; to develop [*région*]; to fit out [*magasin*]; 3 (créer) to create [*espaces verts*]; to build [*route*]; to make [*coin-repas*]; to lay out [*jardin*]; 4 (en adaptant) to arrange [*emploi du temps*]; to adjust [*règlement*]

amende /amɑ̃d/ *nf* fine; **être condamné à une** ∼ to be fined; **'défense d'afficher sous peine d'**∼' 'billstickers will be prosecuted'

Idiome faire ∼ **honorable** to make amends

amendement /amɑ̃dmɑ̃/ *nm* 1 Jur amendment (**à** to; **sur** on); 2 Agric (opération) enrichment

amender /amɑ̃de/ [1]
A *vtr* 1 Jur to amend [*loi*]; 2 Agric to enrich [*sol*]
B **s'amender** *vpr* to mend one's ways; **un criminel amendé** a reformed criminal

amène /amɛn/ *adj* liter affable

amener /amne/ [16]
A *vtr* 1 (mener) ∼ **qn quelque part** [*personne, train*] to take sb somewhere; 2 (venir avec) ∼ **qn (quelque part)** to bring sb (somewhere); **quel bon vent vous amène?** what brings you here?; 3 (apporter) controv ∼ **qch (à qn)** to bring (sb) sth; 4 (convoyer) [*personne, organisme*] to bring [*eau, marchandises*]; 5 (provoquer) to cause [*problèmes, maladie*]; to bring [*pluie, gloire*]; to bring about [*renouveau*]; 6 (aborder) to bring up, to introduce [*sujet, question*]; ∼ **qch sur le tapis**○ to bring sth up; **être bien amené** [*conclusion*] to be well-presented; [*phrase, remarque*] to be well-timed; 7 (conduire) fig ∼ **qn à** to lead sb to [*conclusion*]; to bring sb to [*question*]; ∼ **qn à faire** to lead sb to do; **nous serons amenés à nous revoir** we shall doubtless meet again; ∼ **un liquide à la bonne température** to bring a liquid to the right temperature; 8 (tirer vers soi) [*pêcheur*] to pull in [*filet*]; [*navigateur*] to strike [*voile*]
B **s'amener**○ *vpr* (venir) to come; (arriver) to turn up○ (**avec** with); **amène-toi!** come here!

amenuiser /amənɥize/ [1]
A *vtr* 1 gén to reduce [*chance, risque*]; 2 Tech to plane down [*planche*]
B **s'amenuiser** *vpr* [*réserves, espoir, chance, clientèle*] to dwindle; [*risque*] to lessen; [*temps*] to slip by

amer, -ère /amɛr/ *adj* lit, fig bitter

américain, ∼e /amerikɛ̃, ɛn/
A ▸ p. 392 *adj* American
B *nm* Ling American English

américaniser /amerikanize/ [1]
A *vtr* to Americanize
B **s'américaniser** *vpr* to become Americanized

amérindien, -ienne /amerɛ̃djɛ̃, ɛn/ *adj* Amerindian

Amérindien, -ienne /amerɛ̃djɛ̃, ɛn/ ▸ p. 392 *nm,f* Amerindian, American Indian

Amérique /amerik/ ▸ p. 230 *nprf* America; ∼ **centrale/latine** Central/Latin America; ∼ **du Nord/du Sud** North/South America

amerrir /amerir/ [3] *vi* [*hydravion*] to land (on water); [*vaisseau spatial*] to splash down

amertume /amɛrtym/ *nf* lit, fig bitterness

ameublement /amœblǝmɑ̃/ *nm* (meubles) furniture; (secteur d'activité) furniture trade *ou* business

ameublir /amœblir/ [3] *vtr* to break up [*sol*]

ameuter /amøte/ [1]
A *vtr* 1 (alerter) [*personne, bruit*] to bring [sb] out; 2 (attrouper à des fins hostiles) to stir [sb] up (**contre** against); 3 (pour la chasse) to whip [sth] in [*chiens*]
B **s'ameuter** *vpr* [*foule, passants*] to mass, to gather

ami, ∼e /ami/
A *adj* **nous sommes très** ∼**s** we are very good friends
B *nm,f* friend; **se faire des** ∼**s** to make friends; **je m'en suis fait une** ∼**e** I made a friend of her; **un** ∼ **de toujours** a lifelong friend; **'un** ∼ **qui vous veut du bien'** 'a well-wisher'; **en** ∼ as a friend; **un** ∼ **des bêtes** an animal lover; **l'association des** ∼**s de Pouchkine** the friends of Pushkin; ▸ **faux**¹

Idiomes **les bons comptes font les bons** ∼**s** Prov a debt paid is a friend kept; **c'est dans le besoin** *or* **malheur qu'on connaît ses** ∼**s** Prov a friend in need is a friend indeed

amiable: à l'amiable /alamjabl/ *loc* [*se séparer*] on friendly terms; [*séparation*] amicable; [*adoption*] by private agreement; [*divorce*] by mutual consent; **s'arranger à l'**∼ to come to an amicable agreement

amiante /amjɑ̃t/ *nm* asbestos

amibe /amib/ *nf* Zool, Méd amoeba

amical, ∼e¹, *pl* **-aux** /amikal, o/ *adj* friendly

amicale² /amikal/ *nf* association

amicalement /amikalmɑ̃/ *adv* 1 (gentiment) [*aider*] kindly; [*accueillir*] warmly; [*concourir*] in a friendly way; **bavarder** ∼ to chat (away) happily; 2 (en fin de lettre) **(bien)** ∼ best wishes

amidon /amidɔ̃/ *nm* starch

amidonner /amidɔne/ [1] *vtr* to starch [*linge*]

amincir /amɛ̃sir/ [3]
A *vtr* 1 (faire paraître mince) [*vêtement*] to make [sb] look slimmer; 2 (avec un outil) to plane down [*planche*]
B **s'amincir** *vpr* 1 [*personne, visage*] to get slimmer; 2 [*planche, couche*] to get thinner

amincissement /amɛ̃sismɑ̃/ *nm* 1 (de personne) slimming; 2 (de couche de glace) thinning (down)

aminé, ∼e /amine/ *adj* **acide** ∼ amino acid

amiral, ∼e, *mpl* **-aux** /amiral, o/
A *adj* **vaisseau** ∼ flagship
B ▸ p. 283 *nm* admiral

amirauté /amirote/ *nf* 1 (grade) admiralship; 2 (corps des amiraux) admiralty; (résidence) Admiralty House

amitié /amitje/
A *nf* friendship (**pour** for); **par** ∼ out of friendship; **entretenir l'**∼ to keep friendship alive; **en toute** ∼ as a friend; **éprouver de l'**∼ **pour qn** to have friendly feelings toward(s) sb; **se prendre d'**∼ **pour qn** to take a liking to sb; **faire à qn l'**∼ **de faire** to be kind enough to do; **se lier d'**∼ **avec qn** to strike up a friendship with sb; **être fidèle en** ∼ to be a faithful friend
B **amitiés** *nfpl* (en fin de lettre) kindest regards

ammoniac /amɔnjak/ *nm* (gaz) ammonia

ammoniaque /amɔnjak/ *nf* ammonia

amnésie /amnezi/ *nf* amnesia

amnésique /amnezik/
A *adj* amnesic
B *nmf* amnesiac

amniotique /amnjɔtik/ *adj* amniotic

amnistie /amnisti/ *nf* amnesty (**en faveur de** for)

amnistier /amnistje/ [2] *vtr* to grant an amnesty to [*délinquent*]; to grant an amnesty for [*délit*]

amocher○ /amɔʃe/ [1]
A *vtr* to bash○ [sb/sth] up [*personne, voiture*]
B **s'amocher** *vpr* to bash oneself up○; **s'**∼ **le nez** to bash up○ one's nose

amoindrir /amwɛ̃drir/ [3]
A *vtr* to reduce [*résistance*]; to weaken [*autorité, personne*]; **il est sorti très amoindri de cette épreuve** he came out of that ordeal a lesser man
B **s'amoindrir** *vpr* [*forces*] to diminish; [*différences*] to grow less

amoindrissement /amwɛ̃drismɑ̃/ *nm* (de pouvoir, forces, facultés) weakening; (de ressources) reduction

amollir: s'amollir /amɔlir/ [3] *vpr* 1 (devenir mou) to soften, to go *ou* become soft; 2 (s'affaiblir) to grow weak

amonceler /amɔ̃sle/ [19]
A *vtr* to pile up
B **s'amonceler** *vpr* [*nuages, sable, neige*] to build up; [*preuves, soucis, ennuis*] to pile up, to accumulate

amoncellement /amɔ̃sɛlmɑ̃/ *nm* (processus) (de sable, terre) piling up; (résultat) (de sable, neige) pile; (de richesses) mass

amont /amɔ̃/
A *adj inv* [*ski*] uphill
B *nm* Géog (de cours d'eau) upper reaches (*pl*); **en** ∼ lit upstream (**de** from); fig upstream (**de** of); **naviguer d'**∼ **en aval** to sail downstream

amoral, ∼e, *mpl* **-aux** /amɔral, o/ *adj* amoral

amorçage /amɔrsaʒ/ *nm* (d'obus, de pompe) priming; (de discussions, négociations) initiating; **l'**∼ **de la reprise économique paraît difficile** getting economic recovery underway seems difficult

amorce /amɔrs/ *nf* 1 (de processus, discussion) initiation; (de route, voie ferrée) initial section; (de pellicule) leader, tongue;

a

l'**∼ d'un sourire** the hint of a smile; **2** (pour la pêche) bait; **3** (détonateur) (d'arme) cap, primer; (de pétard) cap; **pistolet à ∼s** cap gun

amorcer /amɔʀse/ [12]
A vtr **1** (commencer) to begin; [véhicule] to go into [virage]; **il amorça un geste pour ouvrir la fenêtre** he made as if to open the window; **2** (appâter) to bait; **3** Tech (mettre en route) to prime [pompe]; to arm, to activate [arme à feu]; **4** Ordinat to boot
B s'amorcer vpr to begin, to get under way

amorphe /amɔʀf/ adj **1** (apathique) apathetic; **2** Chimie amorphous

amortir /amɔʀtiʀ/ [3] vtr **1** (atténuer) to deaden [bruit]; to absorb [choc]; to break [chute]; **2** (rentabiliser) **j'ai amorti mon ordinateur en quelques mois** my computer paid for itself in a few months; **3** Sport (au tennis) to kill [balle]; (au football) to trap [ballon]

amortissement /amɔʀtismã/ nm **1** (de bruit) deadening; (de choc) absorption; (de chute) cushioning; **2** (de dette) redemption; (d'emprunt) paying off; **3** (en comptabilité) depreciation

amortisseur /amɔʀtisœʀ/ nm Tech shock absorber; Phys damper

amour /amuʀ/
A nm **1** (affection) love; **l'∼ filial** filial love; **c'est le grand ∼ entre eux** they are passionately in love; **lettre d'∼** love letter; **par ∼ pour qn/qch** out of love for sb/sth, for the love of sb/sth; **mourir d'∼** to die of a broken heart; **l'∼ de la liberté** the love of liberty; **pour l'∼ de l'art** for the sake of art; **pour l'∼ de Dieu** lit for the love of God; fig for heaven's sake; **2** (personne aimée) gén love; (forme d'adresse) darling; **c'était un ∼ de jeunesse** it was a youthful romance; **3** ○(relations sexuelles) love; **faire l'∼○ avec** to make love with; **les plaisirs de l'∼** the pleasures of love-making; **4** ○(charmant) **∼ de** adorable
B amours nmpl ou nfpl **1** Zool **saison des ∼s** mating season; **2** (aventures) love affairs; **les ∼s de** the amorous adventures of; **à tes ∼s!** (quand on éternue) bless you!
(Composés) **∼ courtois** Hist courtly love; **∼ d'enfance** childhood sweetheart
(Idiomes) **vivre d'∼ et d'eau fraîche** to live on love alone; **revenir à ses premières ∼s** to return to one's first love

amouracher: **s'amouracher** /amuʀaʃe/ [1] vpr **s'∼ de** to become infatuated with

amourette /amuʀɛt/ nf passing infatuation

amoureux, -euse /amuʀø, øz/
A adj **1** (de quelqu'un) **être/tomber ∼** to be/to fall in love (de with); **2** (passionné) **être ∼ de peinture** to be a lover of painting; **3** (qui dénote de l'amour) [relation, regard] loving; [élan, comportement] of love; **vie amoureuse** love life
B nm,f lover; **un ∼ de musique** a music-lover

amour-propre /amuʀpʀɔpʀ/ nm self-esteem; **il est blessé dans son ∼** his pride is hurt

amovible /amɔvibl/ adj [capuchon, housse, doublure] detachable; [étagère, siège, cloison] removable

ampère /ãpɛʀ/ nm Phys amp, ampère

amphibie /ãfibi/ adj Zool, Aut amphibious

amphithéâtre /ãfiteatʀ/ nm **1** (naturel, antique) amphitheatreGB; **2** Univ lecture theatreGB ou hall

amphore /ãfɔʀ/ nf amphora

ample /ãpl/ adj **1** (large) [manteau, robe] loose-fitting; [jupe, manche] full; [geste] sweeping; **2** (abondant) [quantité] ample; [récolte] abundant; [détails] full; **je me tiens à votre disposition pour de plus ∼s renseignements** I would be pleased to provide you with any further information; **3** (puissant) [style, phrase] rich; [voix] sonorous

amplement /ãpləmã/ adv fully; **c'est ∼ suffisant** that's more than enough

ampleur /ãplœʀ/ nf (de problème) size, extent; (de projet, sujet, d'étude) scope; (d'événement, de catastrophe, tâche) scale; (de dégâts, réactions) extent; **prendre de l'∼** [épidémie, rumeur] to spread; [manifestations, parti] to grow in size; **le mouvement prend de plus en plus d'∼** the movement is becoming more and more extensive; **de (très) grande ∼** on a large ou vast scale

amplificateur, -trice /ãplifikatœʀ, tʀis/
A adj [effet, force] magnifying
B nm amplifier

amplification /ãplifikasjõ/ nf **1** Phys amplification; **2** (extension) (de relations, d'échanges) development; (de grève, revendications) escalation; (de débat) expansion

amplifier /ãplifje/ [2]
A vtr to amplify [son, courant]; to magnify [geste, rumeur]; to expand [grève, échanges]
B s'amplifier vpr [son] to grow; [échanges] to grow; [grève] to intensify; [tendance] to gain momentum

amplitude /ãplityd/ nf amplitude

ampoule /ãpul/ nf **1** Électrotech **∼ (électrique)** (light) bulb; **une ∼ de 100 watts** a 100-watt bulb; **2** (de médicament) (buvable) phial; (injectable) ampoule; **3** (sur la peau) blister
(Composé) **∼ de flash** flash bulb

ampoulé, ∼e /ãpule/ adj pej bombastic

amputation /ãpytasjõ/ nf amputation; fig drastic cut (de in)

amputer /ãpyte/ [1] vtr **1** Méd to amputate [membre]; to perform an amputation on [personne]; **il a été amputé du bras droit** he had his right arm amputated; **2** (réduire) to cut [sth] drastically [texte, crédits, discours]; **∼ qch de qch** to cut sth from sth

amulette /amylɛt/ nf amulet

amusant, ∼e /amyzã, ãt/ adj **1** (distrayant) entertaining; **trouver ∼ de faire** to find it entertaining to do; **2** (drôle) funny, amusing; **le plus ∼ c'est que** the funniest thing is that; **3** (surprenant) funny

amusé, ∼e /amyze/ adj [sourire, regard, air] amused, of amusement (après n); **elle a eu un sourire ∼** she smiled in amusement

amuse-gueule /amyzgœl/ nm inv (chose à grignoter) cock-tail snack GB, munchies (pl) US

amusement /amyzmã/ nm entertainment; **regarder qn avec ∼** to enjoy watching sb

amuser /amyze/ [1]
A vtr (divertir) to entertain; (plaire) to amuse [personne]; **laisse-le, si ça l'amuse!** let him be, if that's what makes him happy; **ce qui m'amuse c'est que** what I find amusing is that; **ça les amuse de faire** they enjoy doing
B s'amuser vpr **1** (jouer) [enfant, animal] to play (avec with); **pour s'∼** for fun; **dépêche-toi, je n'ai pas le temps de m'∼** hurry up, I haven't got time to mess about○; **ne t'amuse pas à ce petit jeu avec moi** don't play that little game with me; **2** (passer du bon temps) [enfant, adulte] to have a good time; **s'∼ comme des fous○** to have a great time ou a ball○; **amuse-toi bien!** enjoy yourself; **3** (s'aviser de) **ne t'amuse pas à faire cela** don't go about doing that; **4** (se moquer) liter **s'∼ de qch/qn** to make fun of sth/sb

amuseur, -euse /amyzœʀ, øz/ nm,f entertainer

amygdale /ami(g)dal/ nf tonsil; **se faire opérer des ∼s** to have one's tonsils taken out

an /ã/ ▸ p. 13, p. 155, p. 582 nm **1** (durée) year; **une fois par ∼** once a year; **2** (de date) year; **en l'∼ deux mille** in the year two thousand; **en l'∼ de grâce 1616** in the year of Our Lord 1616; **l'∼ 55 avant J.-C./après J.-C.** 55 BC/AD; **3** (pour exprimer l'âge) **avoir huit ∼s** to be eight (years old); **les moins de dix-huit ∼s** the under-eighteens; **il est mort à 25 ∼s** he died at the age of 25; **une fille de 7 ∼s** a 7-year-old girl; **whisky de douze ∼s d'âge** twelve-year-old whisky
(Idiome) **bon ∼, mal ∼** year in, year out

anabolisant, ∼e /anabolizã, ãt/
A adj anabolic
B nm anabolic steroid

anachronique /anakʀɔnik/ adj anachronistic

anachronisme /anakʀɔnism/ nm anachronism

anagramme /anagʀam/ nf anagram

anal, ∼e, mpl **-aux** /anal, o/ adj anal

analgésie /analʒezi/ nf analgesia

analogie /analɔʒi/ nf analogy

analogique /analɔʒik/ adj analogical

analogue /analɔg/ adj similar (à to), analogous sout (à to)

analphabète /analfabɛt/ adj, nmf illiterate

analphabétisme /analfabetism/ nm illiteracy

analyse /analiz/ nf **1** gén (examen) analysis; **faire l'∼ de qch** to analyseGB sth; **en dernière ∼** in the final analysis; **avoir l'esprit d'∼** to have an analytical mind; **2** Méd test;

③ Math (discipline) calculus; ④ Psych psychoanalysis; **faire une ~, être en ~** [patient] to be in analysis

(Composés) **~ grammaticale** parsing; **faire l'~ grammaticale d'une phrase** to parse a sentence; **~ logique** clause analysis; **~ de sang** blood test; **~ d'urine** urine test

analyser /analize/ [1] vtr ① gén to analyse^GB [problème, substance, texte]; ② Méd to test [sang, urine]; ③ Psych to psychoanalyse^GB; **se faire ~** to be in analysis

analyste /analist/ ▸ p. 372 nmf analyst

analyste-programmeur, -euse, mpl **analystes-programmeurs** /analistprɔgramœr/ ▸ p. 372 nm,f analyst-programmer

analytique /analitik/ adj ① gén, Philos analytical; ② Psych analytic

ananas /anana(s)/ nm inv pineapple

anarchie /anarʃi/ nf lit, fig anarchy

anarchique /anarʃik/ adj lit, fig anarchic

anarchisme /anarʃism/ nm anarchism

anarchiste /anarʃist/
A adj anarchistic
B nmf anarchist

anathème /anatɛm/ nm anathema

anatomie /anatɔmi/ nf ① (science, structure) anatomy; ② ^O(silhouette) figure; **elle a une belle ~** she's got a good figure; ③ (analyse) analysis

(Composé) **~ artistique** (spécialité) life drawing; (œuvre) life study

anatomique /anatɔmik/ adj [étude, planche, dessin] anatomical; [forme, objet] anatomically designed

ancestral, ~e, mpl **-aux** /ãsɛstral, o/ adj ancestral

ancêtre /ãsɛtR/ nmf ① (aïeul) ancestor; ② ^O(personne âgée) old man/woman; ③ (forme ancienne) ancestor; (précurseur) father, forerunner

anche /ãʃ/ nf Mus reed

anchois /ãʃwa/ nm inv anchovy

ancien, -ienne¹ /ãsjɛ̃, ɛn/
A adj ① (d'autrefois) former; **mon ancienne école** my old school; ② (vieux) old; **dans l'~ temps** in the old days; ③ [histoire, langue] ancient; **la Grèce ancienne** ancient Greece; **l'~ français** Old French; ④ Art, Comm [style, monnaie, tableau] old; [voiture] vintage; [meuble] antique; [livre] old, antiquarian; ⑤ (dans une profession) senior
B nm ① (vétéran) (de congrégation, tribu) elder; (d'entreprise) senior member; **les ~s du village** the village elders; **les ~s** (les personnes âgées) the older people; ② (qui a été membre) (d'entreprise) old member; (de grande école) graduate; ③ (immobilier) **l'~** older property; ④ Comm (vieilles choses) antiques (pl); ⑤ (pour distinguer des générations) elder; **Caton l'~** Cato the Elder
C anciens nmpl ancients

(Composés) **~ combattant** veteran; **~ élève** Scol old boy; Univ graduate; **l'Ancien Régime** the Ancien Régime; **l'Ancien Testament** the Old Testament

ancienne²: à l'ancienne /alãsjɛn/ loc [confiture, meuble] traditional; [fabriqué] in the traditional way

anciennement /ãsjɛnmã/ adv formerly

ancienneté /ãsjɛnte/ nf ① (de personne) seniority (dans in); **promotion à l'~** promotion based on seniority; **trois mois/ans d'~** three months'/years' service; ② (de tradition, relique) antiquity; ③ (âge) age

ancrage /ãkraʒ/ nm Naut (action d'ancrer) anchoring; (mouillage) anchorage

ancre /ãkR/ nf Naut anchor; **jeter l'~** lit to cast anchor; fig to settle down; **lever l'~** lit to weigh anchor; fig^O to get a move on^O

ancrer /ãkRe/ [1]
A vtr ① Naut to anchor [navire]; ② (fixer) to fix [idée]; to establish [parti, coutume]; **~ qch dans la réalité** to anchor sth to reality
B s'ancrer vpr ① Naut to anchor, to cast anchor; ② fig [idée] to become fixed (dans in); [parti, coutume] to become established; **société trop ancrée dans ses habitudes** society which is too set in its ways

andouille /ãduj/ nf ① Culin andouille; ② ^Ofool

androgyne /ãdRɔʒin/
A adj androgynous
B nm androgyne

androïde /ãdRɔid/ nm android

andropause /ãdRɔpoz/ nf male menopause

âne /ɑn/ nm ① Zool donkey, ass; ② ^O(personne stupide) dimwit^O; Scol dunce

anéantir /aneãtiR/ [3]
A vtr ① (détruire) to ruin [récoltes]; to lay waste to [ville]; to wipe out [peuple]; to shatter [espoir]; ② (abattre) [nouvelle] to crush; [fatigue] to exhaust; [chaleur] to overwhelm
B s'anéantir vpr [espoir, rêve] to be shattered

anéantissement /aneãtismã/ nm ① (de ville) destruction; (de peuple) annihilation; (de récolte) devastation; ② (d'espoir) shattering; (d'une personne) total collapse

anecdote /anɛkdɔt/ nf anecdote; **un auteur qui se perd dans l'~** an author who digresses on trivial topics; **pour l'~** as a matter of interest

anecdotique /anɛgdɔtik, anɛkdɔtik/ adj anecdotal

anémie /anemi/ nf ① ▸ p. 195 Méd anaemia; ② fig weakness

anémier /anemje/ [2]
A vtr ① Méd to make [sb] anaemic [personne]; ② fig to weaken
B s'anémier vpr ① Méd to become anaemic; ② fig to grow feeble

anémique /anemik/ adj ① Méd anaemic; ② fig weak, anaemic

anémone /anemɔn/ nf anemone

ânerie /anRi/ nf (parole) silly remark; (action) silly blunder; **dire des ~s** to talk rubbish^O ou nonsense; **faire des ~s** to do silly things

ânesse /anɛs/ nf she-ass, female donkey; **lait d'~** asses' milk

anesthésie /anɛstezi/ nf ① Méd anaesthesia; **faire une ~ locale** to give sb a local anaesthetic; **sous ~ générale** under general anaesthetic; ② fig (de l'opinion publique) anaesthetizing

anesthésier /anɛstezje/ [2] vtr to anaesthetize

anesthésique /anɛstezik/ adj, nm anaesthetic

anesthésiste /anɛstezist/ ▸ p. 372 nmf anaesthetist GB, anesthesiologist US

aneth /anɛt/ nm dill

anévrisme /anevRism/ nm aneurysm

anfractuosité /ãfRaktɥozite/ nf crevice

ange /ãʒ/ nm ① Relig angel; **être un ~ de patience** to be patience itself; ② (terme d'affection) angel, darling

(Composés) **~ déchu** fallen angel; **~ exterminateur** avenging angel; **~ gardien** guardian angel

(Idiomes) **être aux ~s** to be in seventh heaven, to be walking on air; **'un ~ passe!** 'somebody's walked over my grave!'; **un ~ passa** there was a lull in the conversation; **discuter du sexe des ~s** to count how many angels can dance on the head of a pin

angélique /ãʒelik/
A adj angelic
B nf Bot, Culin angelica

angelot /ãʒlo/ nm cherub

angélus /ãʒelys/ nm inv Relig angelus

angevin, ~e /ãʒvɛ̃, in/ ▸ p. 621 adj Angevin (épith), of Anjou (après n)

angine /ãʒin/ ▸ p. 195 nf Méd throat infection

(Composés) **~ diphtérique** angina diphtherica; **~ de poitrine** angina pectoris; **~ rouge** tonsillitis

angiogenèse /ãʒjoʒənɛz/ nf angiogenesis

angiome /ãʒjom/ ▸ p. 195 nm angioma

anglais, ~e¹ /ãglɛ, ɛz/
A adj English
B ▸ p. 336 nm Ling English

(Idiome) **filer à l'~e** to take French leave

Anglais, ~e /ãglɛ, ɛz/ nm,f Englishman/Englishwoman; **les ~** the English

anglaise² /ãglɛz/
A adj ▸ anglais
B nf ① (boucle) ringlet; ② (écriture) slanted script

angle /ãgl/ nm ① Math angle; ② (coin) corner; **être à** or **faire l'~ de deux rues** to be at the corner of two streets; **le bâtiment qui fait l'~** the building on the corner; **bibliothèque d'~** corner bookcase; **faire un ~** [rue] to bend;

3) (point de vue) angle; **vu sous cet ~** viewed from this angle

(Composés) **~ droit** Math right angle; **faire un ~ droit avec qch** to make a right angle with sth; **se couper à ~ droit** to intersect at right angles; **~ mort** Aut, Aviat blind spot; Mil dead angle

Angleterre /ɑ̃glətɛʀ/ ▸ p. 504 *nprf* Géog England

anglican, **~e** /ɑ̃glikɑ̃, an/ *adj, nm,f* Anglican

angliciser /ɑ̃glisize/ [1]
A *vtr* to anglicize
B **s'angliciser** *vpr* to become anglicized

angliciste /ɑ̃glisist/ *nmf* (spécialiste) Anglicist; (étudiant) student of English

anglo-américain, **~e**, *mpl* **~s** /ɑ̃gloameʀikɛ̃, ɛn/
A *adj* gén Anglo-American; Ling American English (*épith*)
B ▸ p. 336 *nm* Ling American English

Anglo-Normande /ɑ̃glonɔʀmɑ̃d/ ▸ p. 303 *adj f* **les îles ~s** the Channel Islands

anglophone /ɑ̃glɔfɔn/
A *adj* English-speaking; **littérature ~** literature of the English-speaking countries; **civilisations ~s** the English-speaking world
B *nmf* gén English speaker; (au Canada) Anglophone

anglo-saxon, **-onne**, *mpl* **~s** /ɑ̃glosaksɔ̃, ɔn/ *adj*
1) Hist, Ling Anglo-Saxon; **2)** (d'Angleterre et des États-Unis) Anglo-Saxon, British and American

angoissant, **~e** /ɑ̃gwasɑ̃, ɑ̃t/ *adj* (alarmant) alarming; (effrayant) frightening

angoisse /ɑ̃gwas/ *nf* **1)** gén, Psych anxiety (**devant, de** about); **dans l'~ de faire** for fear of doing; **2)** (crise d'anxiété) anxiety; **3)** Philos anguish, angst

angoissé, **~e** /ɑ̃gwase/ *adj* [*voix, visage, personne*] anxious

angoisser /ɑ̃gwase/ [1]
A *vtr* to worry [*personne*]
B *vi* to be anxious *ou* nervous

angolais, **~e** /ɑ̃gɔlɛ, ɛz/ ▸ p. 392 *adj* Angolan

angora /ɑ̃gɔʀa/ *adj, nm* angora

anguille /ɑ̃gij/ *nf* Zool, Culin eel

(Idiome) **il y a ~ sous roche** there's something going on

angulaire /ɑ̃gylɛʀ/ *adj* Math, Phys angular

anguleux, **-euse** /ɑ̃gylø, øz/ *adj* [*visage, traits*] bony; [*aspect, contours*] jagged; [*personne*] prickly

anicroche /anikʀɔʃ/ *nf* hitch; **sans ~(s)** without a hitch

animal, **~e**, *mpl* **-aux** /animal, o/
A *adj* **1)** Biol animal (*épith*); **2)** (digne de l'animal) [*foule*] savage; [*comportement*] brutish
B *nm* animal

(Composés) **~ de compagnie** pet; **~ domestique** domestic animal; **~ nuisible** pest; **~ sauvage** wild animal

animalerie /animalʀi/ *nf* **1)** (dans un laboratoire) animal house; **2)** ▸ p. 000 (magasin) pet shop GB, pet store US

animalier, **-ière** /animalje, ɛʀ/
A *adj* wildlife (*épith*)
B *nm,f* ▸ p. 372 (dans un laboratoire) animal keeper
C *nm* ▸ p. 372 Art wildlife artist

animateur, **-trice** /animatœʀ, tʀis/ ▸ p. 372 *nm,f* **1)** (de club) coordinator; (de groupe d'études, d'association) leader; (de projet, congrès, festival) organizer; **2)** (présentateur) presenter; **3)** Cin (technicien) animator

animation /animasjɔ̃/ *nf* **1)** (de groupe, d'émission, exposition) organization; (de ventes, service commercial) coordination; (de festival, cérémonie) orchestration; **elle a été chargée de l'~ du stand** she's in charge of running the stand; **~ culturelle** promotion of cultural activities; **2)** (entrain) life, vitality; **mettre de l'~ dans une réception** to liven up a reception; **ville qui manque d'~** town that lacks vitality; **une soirée sans ~** a lacklustre^GB party; **3)** (de rue, marché, lieu de travail) hustle and bustle; (de personnes) excitement; **4)** (activité dirigée) organized activity; **5)** Cin animation

animé, **~e** /anime/ *adj* **1)** (vivant) [*débat, soirée, orateur, période*] lively; [*rue*] bustling; Fin [*marché*] brisk; **2)** (inspiré) **~ de bonnes intentions** spurred on by good intentions; **3)** Ling, Philos animate

animer /anime/ [1]
A *vtr* **1)** (diriger) to lead [*débat, groupe*]; to run [*stage, revue*]; to

present [*émission, spectacle*]; **animé par** [*groupe, spectacle*] organized by; [*mouvement*] led by; [*émission*] presented by; **2)** (rendre vivant) to liven up [*ville, récit, réunion*]; **3)** (inspirer) [*sentiment*] to drive (on) [*personne*]; **4)** (rendre brillant) to put a sparkle into [*regard*]; **une lueur d'intérêt anima son visage** his/her face brightened with interest; **5)** (insuffler la vie) lit [*âme, vie*] to animate [*corps, matière*]; fig [*artiste, lumière*] to bring [sth] to life [*œuvre*]

B **s'animer** *vpr* **1)** (devenir vif) [*conversation, débat*] to become lively; [*réunion, jeu*] to liven up; [*visage, expression*] to light up; [*orateur, participant*] to become animated; **2)** (s'agiter) [*lieu public, auditoire*] to come to life; **3)** (prendre vie) to come to life

animosité /animozite/ *nf* animosity (**envers** toward(s); **entre** between)

anis /ani/ *nm inv* **1)** Bot (plante) anise; (graine) aniseed; **à l'~** [*biscuit, bonbon*] aniseed (*épith*); [*boisson*] aniseed-flavoured^GB; **2)** (bonbon) aniseed drop

ankyloser: **s'ankyloser** /ɑ̃kiloze/ [1] *vpr* [*personne, jambes, bras*] to get stiff; **j'ai les jambes ankylosées** my legs are stiff

annales /anal/ *nfpl* **1)** (de pays, période) annals; **ça restera** *or* **c'est à inscrire dans les ~** fig that will go down in history; **2)** (d'un examen) book of past papers

anneau, *pl* **~x** /ano/
A *nm* **1)** (bague, attache) ring; **2)** (de planète, ver de terre) ring; **3)** (de champignon) annulus
B **anneaux** *nmpl* Sport rings

année /ane/ ▸ p. 582 *nf* year; **l'~ en cours** this year; **en quelle ~ le disque est-il sorti?** what year was the album released?; **avec les ~s** over the years; **d'~ en ~** year by year; **d'une ~ à l'autre** from one year to the next; **l'~ 1962** the year 1962; **l'~ Mozart** the Mozart year; **ces dix dernières ~s** over the last ten years; **il a fait une ~ de droit** he has done one year of law; **souhaiter la bonne ~ à qn** to wish sb a happy new year; **tout le long de l'~** throughout the year; **en quelques ~s** within the space of a few years; **dans quelques ~s** in a few years; **en début/fin d'~** early/late in the year; **(dans) les ~s 80** (in) the eighties; **location à l'~** annual rent

(Composés) **~ bissextile** leap year; **~ civile** calendar year; **~ fiscale** tax year; **~ de référence** base year; **~ sabbatique** sabbatical year; **~ universitaire** academic year; **les Années folles** the Roaring Twenties

année-lumière, *pl* **années-lumière** /anelymjɛʀ/ *nf* light-year

annelé, **~e** /anle/ *adj* **1)** Zool ringed; **2)** Archit annulated

annexe /anɛks/
A *adj* **1)** (contigu) [*local, salle*] adjoining; **2)** (complémentaire) [*questions*] additional; [*dossier*] attached
B *nf* **1)** (bâtiment) annexe GB, annex US; **2)** (document complémentaire) appendix

annexer /anɛkse/ [1]
A *vtr* **1)** Pol [*État, pays*] to annex [*territoire, pays*]; **2)** (joindre) to append (**à** to)
B **s'annexer** *vpr* (s'approprier) to appropriate

annexion /anɛksjɔ̃/ *nf* Pol annexation (**par** by)

annihilation /aniilasjɔ̃/ *nf* **1)** gén (d'espoirs) death; (d'efforts) destruction; **2)** (destruction) annihilation

annihiler /aniile/ [1] *vtr* to destroy [*efforts, espoirs*]; to cancel out [*effet, résultats*]

anniversaire /anivɛʀsɛʀ/
A *adj* date *or* jour **~ de** anniversary of
B *nm* **1)** (de personne, d'entreprise) birthday; **bon ~ !** happy birthday!; **2)** (d'événement) anniversary

annonce /anɔ̃s/ *nf* **1)** (action) announcement; **à l'~ du déficit** when the deficit was announced; **2)** (message) advertisement, advert^○ GB, ad^○; **~ publicitaire** advert^○; **faire passer une ~** to place an advertisement (**dans** in); ▸ **petit**; **3)** Jeux declaration; **faire une ~** (au bridge) to bid; **4)** (indice) sign

(Composé) **~ immobilière** property ad^○

annoncer /anɔ̃se/ [12]
A *vtr* **1)** (faire savoir) to announce [*nouvelle, décision*] (**à** to); **elle nous a annoncé son départ** she informed us that she was leaving; **ils nous ont annoncé la nouvelle** gén they told us the news; (mauvaise nouvelle) they broke the news to us; **2)** (signaler l'arrivée de) to announce; **qui dois-je ~?** what

a

name shall I give?; ③ (prédire) to forecast [*phénomène, événement*]; ④ (être l'indice de) [*événement, signal*] to herald [*événement*]; **n'~ rien de bon** to be a bad sign; ⑤ (au bridge) to bid; **~ la couleur** (aux cartes) to call trumps; fig to lay one's cards on the table

B s'annoncer *vpr* ① (se manifester) [*crise, tempête*] to be brewing; ② (se présenter) **la saison s'annonce bien** the season is off to a good start; **l'été s'annonce chaud** the summer looks like being a hot one; **la récolte 92 s'annonce excellente** the '92 harvest promises to be very good; **la semaine s'annonce difficile** it looks as if this week is going to be difficult; ③ (prévenir de sa venue) **Oncle Paul s'est annoncé** Uncle Paul said he was coming

annonciateur, -trice /anɔ̃sjatœʁ, tʁis/ *adj* [*ange*] herald (*épith*); [*signe, signal*] warning (*épith*) (**de** of)

Annonciation /anɔ̃sjasjɔ̃/ *nf* Annunciation

annotation /anɔtasjɔ̃/ *nf* annotation

annoter /anɔte/ [1] *vtr* to annotate [*ouvrage*]; to write notes on [*copie, devoir*]

annuaire /anɥɛʁ/ *nm* ① (d'adresses, du téléphone) directory; **ne pas être dans l'~** not to be in the phone book GB, to have an unlisted number; ② (recueil) yearbook

(Composés) ~ **électronique** electronic directory; ~ **téléphonique** telephone directory, phone book GB

annuel, -elle /anɥɛl/ *adj* ① (de chaque année) annual, yearly; ② (qui dure un an) [*abonnement*] annual, one-year (*épith*); [*contrat*] one-year (*épith*)

annulaire /anɥlɛʁ/ *nm* Anat ring finger

annulation /anylasjɔ̃/ *nf* ① gén (de mesure) abolition; (de sanction, loi) repeal; (d'événement) cancellation^GB; **proposer l'~ de la dette du tiers monde** to suggest writing off Third World debts; ② Jur (de procédure) quashing; (d'élection) cancellation^GB; (de traité) revocation; (de mariage) annulment

annuler /anyle/ [1]

A *vtr* ① (supprimer) to cancel [*rendez-vous, voyage*]; to write off [*dette*]; to discount [*résultat sportif*]; ② to declare [sth] void [*élection*]; to revoke [*testament*]; to quash [*procédure*]; to repeal [*loi*]; **~ le permis de conduire de qn** to remove sb's driving licence^GB

B s'annuler *vpr* to cancel each other out

anoblir /anɔbliʁ/ [3] *vtr* to ennoble

anodin, -e /anɔdɛ̃, in/ *adj* (insignifiant) [*personne*] insignificant; (sans risques) [*substance*] harmless; [*remède*] mild; [*sujet*] safe, neutral; [*question*] innocent

anomalie /anɔmali/ *nf* gén anomaly; Biol abnormality; Tech fault

ânon /anɔ̃/ *nm* ① (petit de l'âne) donkey foal; ② (petit âne) little donkey

ânonner /anɔne/ [1] *vtr* ① (en hésitant) to stumble through [*texte, leçon*]; ② (sans expression) (lire) to read [sth] in a drone; (réciter) to recite [sth] in a drone

anonymat /anɔnima/ *nm* gén anonymity; (discrétion) confidentiality; **sortir de l'~** (dire son nom) to reveal one's identity; (devenir célèbre) to emerge from obscurity

anonyme /anɔnim/

A *adj* ① (sans nom) [*auteur, lettre, don*] anonymous; ② (neutre) [*décor, style*] impersonal

B *nmf* unknown man/woman; **les ~s** anonymous people

anorak /anɔʁak/ *nm* anorak

anorexie /anɔʁɛksi/ *nf* anorexia

anormal, -e, *mpl* -aux /anɔʁmal, o/ *adj* ① (inhabituel) [*taux*] abnormal; [*événement*] unusual; ② (injuste) unfair; ③ ○(déficient) [*enfant*] abnormal

anormalité /anɔʁmalite/ *nf* abnormality

ANPE /aɛnpeœ/ *nf* (*abbr* = **Agence nationale pour l'emploi**) *French national employment agency*

> ℹ️ **ANPE** The national agency providing services for the unemployed as well as for employers seeking manpower. Job seekers must agree to take training offered by the *ANPE* in order to qualify for unemployment benefits. Benefits, paid by the ASSEDIC, are calculated according to the last salary earned by the job seeker and the duration of his/her period of unemployment. In the initial period of unemployment, a job seeker receives a high percentage of his/her last salary. This figure is gradually reduced to the point where the job seeker no longer qualifies for benefits and is known as a *chômeur/-euse en fin de droits*.

anse /ɑ̃s/ *nf* ① (de tasse, panier) handle; ② Géog cove

antagonisme /ɑ̃tagonism/ *nm* antagonism

antagoniste /ɑ̃tagonist/

A *adj* ① [*groupes, forces*] opposing; [*méthodes, intérêts*] conflicting; ② Anat [*muscles*] antagonist

B *nmf* antagonist

antalgique /ɑ̃talʒik/ *adj, nm* analgesic

antan: d'antan /dɑ̃tɑ̃/ *loc adj* littér [*guerres, fêtes*] of old (*après n*); [*prestige*] former; **les métiers d'~** the old trades; **le Lyon d'~** the Lyons of yesteryear littér

antarctique /ɑ̃taʁktik/ *adj* Antarctic

Antarctique /ɑ̃taʁktik/ *nprm* ① ▸ p. 230 (continent et eaux) Antarctic; (continent seul) Antarctica; ② ▸ p. 406 (océan) **océan ~** Antarctic Ocean

antécédent, ~e /ɑ̃tesedɑ̃, ɑ̃t/ *nm* ① (fait du passé) past history; **un ~ judiciaire** a criminal record; ② Méd medical history; **y a-t-il des ~s d'allergie dans votre famille?** do you have a family history of allergy?; ③ Ling, Math antecedent

antéchrist /ɑ̃tekʁist/ *nm* Antichrist

antédiluvien, -ienne /ɑ̃tedilyvjɛ̃, ɛn/ *adj* antediluvian

antenne /ɑ̃tɛn/ *nf* ① (de radio, télévision) aerial; (de radar, satellite) antenna; **~ parabolique** satellite dish; **~ télescopique** telescopic aerial; ② (liaison) **être sur** *ou* **à l'~** to be on the air; **passer à l'~** to go on the air; **l'~ est à vous** over to you; ③ (poste détaché) branch; **~s commerciales** commercial outlets; **~ médicale** medical unit; ④ (d'insecte, de crustacé) antenna; **avoir des ~s** fig to have a sixth sense

antérieur, ~e /ɑ̃teʁjœʁ/ *adj* ① (précédent) [*salaire, situation, œuvre*] previous; **le texte est ~ à 1986** the text was written prior to 1986; ② (placé devant) [*partie, face*] front; [*membre, ligament*] anterior; ③ [*voyelle*] front (*épith*)

antérieurement /ɑ̃teʁjœʁmɑ̃/ *adv* previously; **~ à** prior to

antériorité /ɑ̃teʁjɔʁite/ *nf* anteriority

anthologie /ɑ̃tɔlɔʒi/ *nf* anthology

anthracite /ɑ̃tʁasit/

A ▸ p. 140 *adj inv* (couleur) charcoal grey GB *ou* gray US

B *nm* anthracite

anthrax /ɑ̃tʁaks/ *nm inv* Méd carbuncle

anthropologie /ɑ̃tʁɔpɔlɔʒi/ *nf* anthropology

anthropologiste /ɑ̃tʁɔpɔlɔʒist/, **anthropologue** /ɑ̃tʁɔpɔlɔɡ/ ▸ p. 372 *nmf* anthropologist

anthropophage /ɑ̃tʁɔpɔfaʒ/

A *adj* cannibalistic

B *nmf* cannibal

anthropophagie /ɑ̃tʁɔpɔfaʒi/ *nf* cannibalism

antiacarien, -ienne /ɑ̃tiakaʁjɛ̃, ɛn/ *adj* anti-dust mite

antiadhésif, -ive /ɑ̃tiadezif, iv/ *adj* nonstick

antiaérien, -ienne /ɑ̃tiaeʁjɛ̃, ɛn/ *adj* antiaircraft (*épith*)

antialcoolique /ɑ̃tialkɔlik/ *adj* **mesure/campagne ~** anti-alcohol measure/campaign; **centre de cure ~** detoxification centre^GB

antiatomique /ɑ̃tiatomik/ *adj* [*vêtement*] (anti-)radiation (*épith*); **abri ~** nuclear shelter

antibiotique /ɑ̃tibjɔtik/ *adj, nm* antibiotic; **aux ~s** with antibiotics; **sous ~s** on antibiotics

antiblocage /ɑ̃tiblɔkaʒ/ *adj inv* **système ~ des roues** anti-lock braking system, ABS

antibrouillard /ɑ̃tibʁujaʁ/ *adj inv* Aut **phare ~** fog light

antibruit /ɑ̃tibʁɥi/ *adj inv* soundproof

antibuée /ɑ̃tibɥe/ *adj inv* **dispositif ~** demister

anticalcaire /ɑ̃tikalkɛʁ/ *adj* **agent** *or* **produit ~** water softener

anticancéreux, -euse /ɑ̃tikɑ̃seʁø, øz/ *adj* [*traitement*] cancer (*épith*); [*médicament*] anti-cancer (*épith*)

antichambre /ɑ̃tiʃɑ̃bʁ/ *nf* lit, fig anteroom; **l'~ de la gloire** fig the way to stardom

antichar /ɑ̃tiʃaʁ/ *adj inv* antitank (*épith*)

antichoc /ɑ̃tiʃɔk/ *adj inv* ① (protecteur) **casque ~** crash helmet; ② (incassable) [*montre*] shockproof

anticipation /ɑ̃tisipasjɔ̃/ *nf* (prévision) anticipation; **film/ roman d'~** science fiction film/novel

anticipé, ~e /ɑ̃tisipe/ *adj* [*départ, élection, libération*] early; **avec mes remerciements ~s** thanking you in advance

anticiper /ãtisipe/ [1]

A vtr ① (prévoir) to anticipate [réaction, coup, changement]; to foresee [invention]; ~ **qch de trois mois** to anticipate sth by three months; **n'anticipons pas!** let's not get ahead of ourselves!; ② (effectuer à l'avance) to bring [sth] forward [paiement]

B **anticiper sur** vtr ind to anticipate [événements]

C vi (au tennis, aux échecs) to think ahead

anticonceptionnel, -elle /ãtikõsɛpsjɔnɛl/ adj contraceptive

anticoncurrentiel, -ielle /ãtikõkyʀãsjɛl/ adj anticompetitive

anticonformiste /ãtikõfɔʀmist/ adj, nmf nonconformist

anticonstitutionnel, -elle /ãtikõstitysjɔnɛl/ adj unconstitutional

anticorps /ãtikɔʀ/ nm inv antibody

anticorrosion /ãtikɔʀɔʒjõ/ adj inv rustproof

anti-crevaison /ãtikʀəvɛzõ/ adj inv **bombe** ~ Aut puncture sealant spray

antidater /ãtidate/ [1] vtr to antedate

antidémarrage /ãtidemaʀaʒ/ nm immobilizer; ~ **électronique** electronic immobilizer

antidémocratique /ãtidemɔkʀatik/ adj undemocratic

antidépresseur /ãtidepʀɛsœʀ/ nm antidepressant

antidérapant, ~e /ãtideʀapã, ãt/ adj [pneu, chaussée] nonskid; [semelle] nonslip

antidopage /ãtidɔpaʒ/ adj [contrôle, test] dope; [mesure, lutte] against doping (après n); **subir un contrôle** ~ to be dope-tested

antidote /ãtidɔt/ nm lit, fig antidote (**contre** against; **à, de** for)

antiémeute /ãtiemøt/ adj inv **police/véhicule** ~ riot police/vehicle

antifasciste /ãtifaʃist/ adj, nmf antifascist

antifatigue /ãtifatig/ adj inv [bas, collant] support (épith)

antigang /ãtigãg/ adj inv **brigade** ~ crime squad

antigel /ãtiʒɛl/ adj inv, nm antifreeze

antigouvernemental, ~e, mpl -aux /ãtiguvɛʀnmãtal, o/ adj anti-government

antihéros /ãtieʀo/ nm inv anti-hero

anti-inflammatoire, pl ~s /ãtiɛ̃flamatwaʀ/ adj, nm anti-inflammatory

anti-inflation /ãtiɛ̃flasjõ/ adj inv anti-inflation

antijeu /ãtiʒø/ nm ₵ unsporting behaviour

antillais, ~e /ãtijɛ, ɛz/ adj West Indian

Antilles /ãtij/ ▸ p. 504 nprfpl **les** ~ the West Indies; **les** ~ **françaises** the French West Indies; **les Petites/Grandes** ~ the Lesser/Greater Antilles

(Composé) ~ **néerlandaises** Netherlands Antilles

antilope /ãtilɔp/ nf antelope

antimilitarisme /ãtimilitaʀism/ nm antimilitarism

antimite /ãtimit/ adj, nm moth-repellent

antimondialisation /ãtimõdjalizsjõ/ nf antiglobalization

antimondialisme /ãtimõdjalism/ nm anti-globalization

antinomie /ãtinɔmi/ nf antinomy

antinomique /ãtinɔmik/ adj [lois, éléments] antinomic; [idées, concepts] paradoxical

antiparasite /ãtipaʀazit/ adj inv **dispositif** ~ suppressor

antipathie /ãtipati/ nf antipathy (**pour** toward(s), to; **entre** between); **j'éprouve de l'**~ **pour eux** I dislike them

antipathique /ãtipatik/ adj [personne, défaut] unpleasant; **il m'est** ~ I dislike him

antipelliculaire /ãtipelikylɛʀ/ adj [shampooing] antidandruff (épith)

antiphrase /ãtifʀɑz/ nf antiphrasis; **par** ~ ironically

antipode /ãtipɔd/

A nm Géog antipodes (pl); **être l'**~ **de** to be the antipodes of; **être aux** ~**s de** lit to be the antipodes of; fig to be the exact opposite of

B **antipodes** nmpl (pays lointain) **les** ~**s** the other side of the world

antipoison /ãtipwazõ/ adj inv **centre** ~ poisons unit

antipollution /ãtipɔlysjõ/ adj inv **la lutte** ~ the fight against pollution; **barrage** ~ oil-trapping boom; **impôt** ~ pollution tax

antiquaire /ãtikɛʀ/ nmf ▸ p. 372 antique dealer

antique /ãtik/ adj ① (de l'Antiquité) [cité, théâtre, période] ancient; **la Rome/la Grèce** ~ ancient Rome/Greece; ② (ancien) [croyance, demeure] age-old (épith); ③ (démodé) [véhicule] antiquated; [costume] old-fashioned

antiquité /ãtikite/

A nf ① (objet) antique; **un magasin d'**~**s** an antique shop; **les** ~**s** antiques; ② (de coutume) ancientness

B **antiquités** nfpl Art antiquities

Antiquité /ãtikite/ nf antiquity; **dans l'**~ in antiquity

antireflet /ãtiʀəflɛ/ adj inv [surface, verre] nonreflective; Phot antiglare

antirides /ãtiʀid/ adj inv anti-wrinkle (épith)

antirouille /ãtiʀuj/

A adj inv (pour protéger) rust-proofing (épith); (pour enlever) rust-removing (épith)

B nm (pour protéger) rust inhibitor; (pour enlever) rust remover

antiroulis /ãtiʀuli/ adj inv [dispositif] roll-damping

antisèche○ /ãtisɛʃ/ nf students' slang crib○

antisémite /ãtisemit/

A adj anti-Semitic

B nmf anti-Semite

antisémitisme /ãtisemitism/ nm anti-Semitism

antiseptique /ãtisɛptik/ adj, nm antiseptic

antisismique /ãtisismik/ adj anti-seismic

antisocial, ~e, mpl -iaux /ãtisɔsjal, o/ adj antisocial

antistatique /ãtistatik/ adj antistatic

antistress /ãtistʀɛs/ adj inv [voyage, séjour] stress-free; [médicament, traitement] stress-relieving

antitabac /ãtitaba/ adj inv antismoking

antitache /ãtitaʃ/ adj inv **traité** ~ stain-resistant

antiterroriste /ãtiteʀɔʀist/ adj **lutte** ~ fight against terrorism

antithèse /ãtitɛz/ nf antithesis; **elle est l'**~ **de son frère** fig she's the exact opposite of her brother

antituberculeux, -euse /ãtitybɛʀkylø, øz/ adj [vaccin] tuberculosis (épith)

antivenimeux, -euse /ãtivənimø, øz/ adj **produit/sérum** ~ antivenin product/serum

antivirus /ãtiviʀys/ nm inv Ordinat antivirus software

antivol /ãtivɔl/

A adj inv **dispositif** ~ antitheft device

B nm (de vélo, moto) lock; (de voiture) steering lock, anti-theft device

antonyme /ãtɔnim/ nm antonym

antre /ãtʀ/ nm ① (d'animal) den; ② fig den

anus /anys/ ▸ p. 136 nm inv anus

Anvers /ãvɛʀ/ ▸ p. 621, p. 504 npr Antwerp

anxiété /ãksjete/ nf anxiety; **état d'**~ anxiety state; **crise d'**~ panic attack; **avec** ~ anxiously

anxieusement /ãksjøzmã/ adv anxiously

anxieux, -ieuse /ãksjø, øz/

A adj [personne, voix, attente] anxious; [attitude] concerned; ~ **de savoir** anxious to know

B nm,f worrier

aorte /aɔʀt/ nf aorta

août /u(t)/ ▸ p. 380 nm August

apaisant, ~e /apɛzã, ãt/ adj [paroles, voix, personne, lotion, crème] soothing; [influence] calming; [déclaration] conciliatory

apaisement /apɛzmã/ nm **geste/mesure d'**~ calming gesture/measure; **politique d'**~ policy of appeasement; **tentative d'**~ attempt to appease

apaiser /apeze/ [1]

A vtr (calmer) to pacify [personne]; to ease [conflit]; to calm [colère, inquiétude]; to satisfy [faim, soif, désir]; to soothe [brûlure, douleur]; ~ **les esprits** to ease people's minds; **il est revenu, l'esprit apaisé** he came back, his mind at rest

B **s'apaiser** vpr [vent, colère] to die down; [débat] to calm down; [curiosité, faim, douleur] to subside

apanage /apanaʒ/ nm **être l'**~ **de qch/qn** to be the prerogative of sth/sb

aparté /apaʀte/ *nm* **en** ~ gén in private; Théât in an aside

apathie /apati/ *nf* (personnelle, politique) apathy; (économique) stagnation

apathique /apatik/ *adj* apathetic

apatride /apatʀid/
A *adj* stateless
B *nmf* stateless person; **les** ~**s** stateless people

APD /apede/ *nm* (*abbr* = **appel de préparation à la défense**) compulsory Ministry of Defence workshop for 16-18 year-olds

apercevoir /apɛʀsəvwaʀ/ [5]
A *vtr* ① (voir avec peine) to make out; ② (voir brièvement) to catch sight of; ③ (prévoir) to see [*difficultés, possibilités*]
B **s'apercevoir** *vpr* ① (se rendre compte) **s'**~ **que** to notice that, to realize that; **s'**~ **de** to notice [*erreur, supercherie*]; **sans s'en** ~ without realizing; ② (se voir) (sans se parler) to catch sight of each other; (en se parlant) to meet briefly

aperçu /apɛʀsy/ *nm* ① (échantillon) (de talent, caractère) glimpse (**de** of); (de situation, situation) outline (**de** of); ② (point de vue) insight (**sur** into)

apéritif /apeʀitif/ *nm* aperitif GB, drink

apesanteur /apəzɑ̃tœʀ/ *nf* weightlessness

à-peu-près /apøpʀɛ/ *nm inv* vague approximation, (rough) guess

apeuré, ~e /apœʀe/ *adj* (effrayé) frightened; (craintif) timid

aphasie /afazi/ *nf* aphasia

aphone /afɔn/ *adj* **être** ~ to have lost one's voice

aphorisme /afɔʀism/ *nm* aphorism

aphrodisiaque /afʀodizjak/ *adj, nm* aphrodisiac

aphte /aft/ *nm* mouth ulcer

aphteuse /aftøz/ ▸ p. 195 *adj f* **fièvre** ~ foot-and-mouth disease

api: d'api /dapi/ *loc adj* **pomme d'**~ small apple

à-pic /apik/ *nm inv* sheer drop

apiculteur, -trice /apikyltœʀ, tʀis/ ▸ p. 372 *nm,f* beekeeper

apiculture /apikyltyʀ/ *nf* beekeeping

apitoiement /apitwamɑ̃/ *nm* pity (**sur** for)

apitoyer /apitwaje/ [23]
A *vtr* to move [*sb*] to pity [*personne*]; **n'essaie pas de m'**~ don't try to get my sympathy
B **s'apitoyer** *vpr* **s'**~ **sur (le sort de) qn** to feel sorry for sb

aplanir /aplaniʀ/ [3]
A *vtr* to level [*terrain, chemin*]; to iron out [*difficultés, problèmes*]; to ease [*tensions*]
B **s'aplanir** *vpr* [*difficultés*] to be ironed out; [*tensions*] to ease

aplati, ~e /aplati/ *adj* [*sphère, forme*] oblate; [*fruit, tuyau*] flattened; [*nez*] flat

aplatir /aplatiʀ/ [3]
A *vtr* to flatten [*carton, tôle*]; to smooth out [*coussin, oreiller*]; to smooth down [*cheveux*]; to press [*coutures, plis*]; **mon chapeau est tout aplati!** my hat is all squashed!
B **s'aplatir**° *vpr* (être servile) **s'**~ **devant qn** to grovel in front of sb

aplomb /aplɔ̃/
A *nm* ① (confiance en soi) confidence; (équilibre) balance; **manquer d'**~ to lack confidence; **avoir de l'**~ to be confident; **avec** ~ confidently, with aplomb; **vous ne manquez pas d'**~! you've got a nerve!; ② (direction) **à l'**~ **de** directly below
B **d'aplomb** *loc adv* ① (en équilibre) [*étagère, armoire*] straight; [*personne*] steady; ② °(en bonne santé) **tu te sens d'**~? do you feel well?; **ça va te remettre d'**~ it will put you back on your feet

apnée /apne/ *nf* apn(o)ea; **plonger en** ~ to dive without an aqualung

apocalypse /apɔkalips/ *nf* apocalypse; **vision/paysage d'**~ apocalyptic vision/landscape

apocalyptique /apɔkaliptik/ *adj* apocalyptic

apocryphe /apɔkʀif/
A *adj* apocryphal
B *nm* **les** ~**s** the Apocrypha

apogée /apɔʒe/ *nm* ① (paroxysme) peak (**de** of); **atteindre** or **connaître son** ~ to peak; ② (d'une période, orbite) apogee

apolitique /apɔlitik/ *adj* apolitical

apologétique /apɔlɔʒetik/ *adj* ① (qui loue) laudatory; (qui justifie) justificatory; ② Relig apologetic

apologie /apɔlɔʒi/ *nf* (pour louer) panegyric (**de** of); (pour justifier) apologia (**de** for); **faire l'**~ **de qch** (justifier) to justify sth; (louer) to applaud sth; **faire l'**~ **de qn** (louer) to praise sb

apoplexie /apɔpleksi/ *nf* apoplexy; **crise d'**~ lit, fig apoplectic fit; **elle était au bord de l'**~ fig she was on the verge of having an apoplectic fit

a posteriori /apɔsteʀjɔʀi/
A *loc adj inv* [*connaissances*] inductive
B *loc adv* [*se justifier, décider*] after the event; ~, **il semblerait que** with hindsight, it would appear that

apostolat /apɔstɔla/ *nm* ① Relig apostolate; ② (activité désintéressée) apostolic mission

apostrophe /apɔstʀɔf/ *nf* ① Ling apostrophe; ② (remarque) remark

apostropher /apɔstʀofe/ [1] *vtr* to heckle

apothéose /apɔteoz/ *nf* (moment fort) (de spectacle) high point; (d'événement) grand finale; (d'œuvre) supreme achievement; (de carrière) culmination; **finir** or **s'achever en** ~ [*spectacle*] to end in a blaze of glory; **l'arrivée de ma belle-mère a été l'**~! iron my mother-in-law's arrival was the last straw!

apothicaire /apɔtikɛʀ/ *nm* **comptes d'**~ complicated calculations

apôtre /apotʀ/ *nm* lit, fig apostle

apparaître /apaʀɛtʀ/ [73]
A *vi* ① (devenir visible) [*personne, spectre, bouton, problèmes, produit*] to appear; [*lune, soleil*] to come out; ~ **à la télévision/en public** to appear on television/in public; **laisser** ~ to reveal; ② (se révéler) to become apparent; **laisser** ~ [*analyse, rapport*] to show; **faire** ~ (montrer) to show; (révéler) to reveal; ~ **comme une victime** to be seen as a victim; ③ (sembler) to appear (to be); ~ **à qn** to appear to sb to be; ~ **(à qn) comme** to appear (to sb) to be; ~ **comme un gâchis** to seem a waste
B *v impers* **il apparaît que** it appears that

apparat /apaʀa/ *nm* (faste) grandeur; **d'**~ ceremonial; **en grand** ~ [*fêter*] with pomp and ceremony; [*être habillé*] in ceremonial regalia

appareil /apaʀɛj/ *nm* ① (machine, instrument) device; (pour la maison) appliance; ~ **de mesure** measuring device; ~ **de contrôle** control; ~ **de radio/télévision** radio/television set; ~ **de projection** projector; ~ **photographique** or **photo** camera; ~ **photo numérique** Phot digital camera; ~ **électroménager** household appliance; ~ **(dentaire)** (dentier) dentures (*pl*); (tige métallique) brace GB, braces (*pl*) US; ~ **auditif** hearing aid; ~ **orthopédique** orthopaedic appliance; ② (téléphone) telephone; **qui est à l'**~? who's calling please?; **on te demande à l'**~ you're wanted on the phone; **passe-moi l'**~ give me the phone; **Vladimir à l'**~ (this is) Vladimir speaking; ③ (avion) plane; ④ Anat system; **l'**~ **digestif** the digestive system; ⑤ (système) apparatus; **l'**~ **d'État/du parti** the state/party apparatus; ⑥ (ensemble de notes) ~ **critique** critical apparatus

(Idiome) **être dans le plus simple** ~ to be in one's birthday suit

appareillage /apaʀɛjaʒ/ *nm* ① Naut (départ) **prêt pour l'**~! ready to cast off!; ② (appareils) equipment

appareiller /apaʀeje/ [1] *vi* [*bateau*] to cast off

apparemment /apaʀamɑ̃/ *adv* ① (selon toute apparence) apparently; ~ **pas!** apparently not!; ② (en apparence seulement) seemingly

apparence /apaʀɑ̃s/ *nf* appearance; **ne jugez pas sur les** ~**s** don't judge by appearances; **ne vous fiez pas aux** ~**s** appearances are deceptive; **pour sauver les** ~**s** to keep up appearances; **contre toute** ~ despite every indication to the contrary; **il est jeune d'**~ he looks young; **homme d'**~ **jeune** young-looking man; **elle n'est calme qu'en** ~ she only seems calm; **en** ~ seemingly; **sous l'**~ **de la bonté** under the guise of kindness; **'ils sont d'accord?'** **—'selon toute** ~' 'they agree?'—'it would seem so'; **'ils sont d'accord'—'en** ~ **(seulement)** 'they agree'—'only on the surface'; **des personnes en** ~ **si différentes** people outwardly so different

apparent, ~e /apaʀɑ̃, ɑ̃t/ *adj* ① (visible) [*signe, partie, bouton, couture*] visible; [*trouble, fragilité*] apparent; **sans raison** ~**e** for no apparent reason; ② (trompeur) [*facilité, indulgence*] seeming

apparenté, ~e /apaʀɑ̃te/ adj [personne, famille] related (à to); [entreprise] allied; ~ **socialiste** allied to the socialist party

apparenter: s'apparenter /apaʀɑ̃te/ [1] vpr **s'~ à** to resemble

appariteur /apaʀitœʀ/ nm ① Univ (gardien) ≈ porter GB, college staff member who handles mail and reception duties; (surveillant d'examen) invigilator GB, proctor US; ② (de laboratoire) laboratory technician

apparition /apaʀisjɔ̃/ nf (de personne, bouton, problème, planète, produit) appearance; (de spectre) apparition (**à qn** to sb); (de mouvement, science) emergence; (d'invention) advent; **refaire son** ~ to reappear

appartement /apaʀtəmɑ̃/ nm flat GB, apartment; **plante d'**~ houseplant; **se retirer dans ses** ~**s** to retire to one's chamber liter

(Composé) ~ **témoin** show flat GB, show apartment US

appartenance /apaʀtənɑ̃s/ nf affiliation; **il ne dissimule pas son** ~ **au mouvement** he is openly affiliated to the movement; **condamné pour** ~ **à un groupe terroriste** condemned for being a member of a terrorist organization

appartenir /apaʀtəniʀ/ [36]

Ⓐ **appartenir à** vtr ind ① (être la propriété) ~ **à** [objet, propriété, capital] to belong to; ② (revenir) ~ **à** [victoire] to belong to; **la décision t'appartient** the decision is yours; ③ (faire partie) ~ **à** [personne] to be a member of; ~ **à un club** to be a member of a club

Ⓑ v impers (être du ressort de) **il appartient à qn de faire** it is up to sb to do

appât /apɑ/ nm bait Ⓒ; **attirer avec un** ~ to lure with bait; **mettre un** ~ **à l'hameçon** to bait the hook; **l'**~ **du gain** the lure of profit

appâter /apɑte/ [1] vtr to lure [poisson, gibier]; to bait [hameçon, piège]; to lure [personne] (**par, avec** with)

appauvrir /apovʀiʀ/ [3]

Ⓐ vtr lit, fig to impoverish

Ⓑ **s'appauvrir** vpr to become impoverished

appauvrissement /apovʀismɑ̃/ nm impoverishment

appeau, pl ~**x** /apo/ nm decoy

appel /apɛl/ nm ① (invitation pressante) call; **'dernier** ~ **pour Tokyo'** 'last call for Tokyo'; ~ **au secours** lit call for help; fig cry for help; **à l'**~ **de leur mère** when they heard their mother calling; ② (supplique) appeal; **lancer un** ~ to make an appeal; **lancer un** ~ **à la radio** to put out an appeal on the radio; ③ (incitation) ~ **à** call for [solidarité]; appeal for [calme]; call to [armes]; plea for [clémence]; ~ **à la grève** strike call; **lancer un** ~ **à** to call for [solidarité, grève]; to appeal for [calme]; ~ **au meurtre** death threat; **lancer un** ~ **au meurtre contre qn** to call for sb's assassination; ④ Télécom call; **tél éphonique/radio** phone/radio call; ⑤ (recours) ~ **à** appeal to [personne, bon sens]; **faire** ~ **à** [personne] to call [pompiers, police, spécialiste]; to bring in [artiste]; to call up [capitaux]; [gouvernement] to call in [armée, police, puissance étrangère]; [tâche] to call for [connaissances]; **faire** ~ **à la justice** to go to court; ⑥ (vérification) gén roll call; Scol registration; **faire l'**~ gén to take the roll call; Scol to take the register; **manquer à l'**~ gén to be absent at the roll call; Scol to be absent at registration; ⑦ Mil (convocation) call up GB, draft US; ⑧ (attirance) **l'**~ **de** the call of [large, forêt]; ⑨ Jur appeal; **faire** ~ to appeal; **faire** ~ **d'un jugement** to appeal against a decision; **perdre en** ~ to lose an appeal; **juger en** ~ to hear an appeal; **sans** ~ lit without further right of appeal; **une décision sans** ~ fig a final decision; **condamner sans** ~ fig to condemn out of hand; ⑩ Sport take off; **prendre son** ~ to take off; ⑪ Jeux (aux cartes) signal; **faire un** ~ to signal for a card; ⑫ Ordinat call; **d'**~ [programme, station, séquence] calling (épith); [demande, indicatif, mot] call (épith)

(Composés) **l'**~ **du 18 juin** Hist General de Gaulle's appeal of 18 June 1940; ~ **d'air** draught GB ou draft US; ~ **d'offres** invitation to tender; ~ **de phares** flash of headlights GB ou high beams US; ~ **du pied**° veiled invitation, discreet appeal

appelé, ~e /aple/ nm Mil conscript, draftee US; **les** ~**s du contingent** the conscripts

appeler /aple/ [19]

Ⓐ vtr ① (dénommer) to call [personne, chose]; **comment ont-ils appelé leur fille?** what did they call their daughter?; **comme appelles-tu cet arbre?** what's this tree called?;

j'appelle ça du vol I call that robbery; **il se fait** ~ **Robert** (pour son plaisir) he likes to be called Robert; (par sécurité) he goes by the name of Robert; ② (téléphoner) to phone GB, to call; **je t'appelle demain** I'll phone you tomorrow; ~ **qn par l'interphone** to call sb on the intercom; ③ (faire venir) to call [docteur, ambulance, pompier, taxi, ascenseur]; to send for [employé, élève]; **le devoir m'appelle** duty calls; ~ **qn sous les drapeaux** to call sb up; ~ **qn en justice** to summon sb to appear in court; ④ (inciter) ~ **qn à** to incite sb to [révolte]; ~ **qn à faire** to call on sb to do; ⑤ (destiner) ~ **qn à** to assign sb to [charge, fonction]; to appoint sb to [poste]; **il a été appelé à de hautes fonctions** he was called to high office; **mon travail m'appelle à beaucoup voyager** my work involves a lot of travel; ⑥ (exiger, entraîner) [crime, comportement] to call for [sanction]; ~ **l'attention de qn sur qch** to draw sb's attention to sth; **la violence appelle la violence** violence begets violence

Ⓑ **en appeler à** vtr ind to appeal to [générosité, bon sens, population]

Ⓒ vi (crier) [personne] to call; **en cas de besoin, appelez** if you need anything, just call; ~ **à l'aide** to call for help; ~ **à la grève** to call for strike action

Ⓓ **s'appeler** vpr **comment s'appelle cette fleur en latin?** what is this flower called in Latin?; **comment t'appelles-tu?** what's your name?; **je m'appelle Paul** my name's Paul; **voilà ce qui s'appelle une belle voiture!** now, that's what you call a nice car!; **nous nous appelons par nos prénoms** we call each other by our first names; **on s'appelle!** we'll be in touch!

(Idiomes) **ça s'appelle reviens**° ! don't forget to give it back!; ~ **les choses par leur nom** or **un chat un chat** to call a spade a spade

appellation /apɛlasjɔ̃/ nf name, appellation sout; ~ **d'origine (de produit)** indication of country of origin

(Composés) ~ **d'origine contrôlée**, **AOC** Vin appellation contrôlée; ~ **d'origine protégée**, **AOP** UE Protected Designation of Origin, PDO

appendice /apɛ̃dis/ nm appendix

appendicite /apɛ̃disit/ ► p. 195 nf appendicitis

appentis /apɑ̃ti/ nm inv (bâtiment) (adossé) lean-to; (non adossé) shed

appesantir /apəzɑ̃tiʀ/ [3]

Ⓐ vtr [âge, froid] to slow down [démarche]; [inactivité] to dull [esprit]

Ⓑ **s'appesantir** vpr (insister) **s'**~ **sur** to dwell on

appétissant, ~e /apetisɑ̃, ɑ̃t/ adj ① [mets] appetizing; **peu** ~ unappetizing; ② °[personne] appealing

appétit /apeti/ nm ① (de mangeur) appetite; **le bon air donne de l'**~ fresh air gives you an appetite; **perdre l'**~ to lose one's appetite; **mettre qn en** ~ lit, fig to whet sb's appetite; **couper l'**~ **de qn** to take sb's appetite away; **avoir un** ~ **d'oiseau** to eat like a bird; **manger avec** ~ to eat heartily; **bon** ~! enjoy your meal!; ② (de plaisirs, culture) appetite (**de** for); (de gloire, pouvoir) hunger (**de** for); **les** ~**s de conquête du pays** the country's expansionist ambitions

applaudir /aplodiʀ/ [3]

Ⓐ vtr lit, fig to applaud; **ils ont été très applaudis par le public** they got a big round of applause from the audience

Ⓑ vi ① lit [personne, foule] to applaud, to clap; ② fig (approuver) to approve; ~ **des deux mains** to applaud ou approve heartily

applaudissement /aplodismɑ̃/ nm ① lit applause Ⓒ; **elle a quitté la salle sous un tonnerre d'**~**s** she left the room to thunderous applause; ② fig (approbation) acclaim Ⓒ; **le livre a reçu l'**~ **de la critique** the book has met with critical acclaim

applicable /aplikabl/ adj [loi, sanction] applicable (**à** to); **facilement** ~ [idée, mesure] easy to implement

applicateur /aplikatœʀ/ nm applicator

application /aplikasjɔ̃/ nf ① (soin) care; **écrire avec** ~ to write with care; ② (de loi, règlement, d'accord) (respect) application; (mise en œuvre) implementation; (de peine) administration; **étendre le champ d'**~ to extend the application; **mettre en** ~ to apply [théorie]; to implement [loi, règlement]; **entrer en** ~ to come into force; **en** ~ **de l'article 5** in accordance with article 5; ③ Ind, Méd, Tech application; ④ Ordinat (programme) application program

applique /aplik/ nf (lampe) wall light

appliqué, ~e /aplike/ adj ① [élève] hardworking; [travail, écriture] careful; ② [science] applied

a

appliquer /aplike/ [1]

A vtr **1** (mettre) to apply [vernis, fond de teint, compresse] (sur to); to put [cachet] (sur on); **2** ○(donner) to give [baiser, sobriquet] (à qn to sb); **3** (mettre en œuvre) to implement; [politique, ordres]; to apply [loi]; ~ **une peine à qn** to administer a sentence on sb; **4** (respecter) to abide by [règlement]; to follow [quotas]; **5** (utiliser) to apply [technique] (à to)

B **s'appliquer** vpr **1** (avec soin) to take great care (**à faire** to do); **elle ne s'applique pas** she doesn't take much care; **s'~ à écrire lisiblement** to take care to write legibly; **2** (concerner) **s'~ à qch/qn** to apply to sth/sb

appoint /apwɛ̃/ nm **1** (somme d'argent) exact change; **faire l'~** to tender GB ou provide US the exact change; **2** (complément) **rôle d'~** supporting role; **salaire d'~** supplementary income; **chauffage d'~** additional heating GB, space heater US

appointements /apwɛtmɑ̃/ nmpl fml salary (sg)

appointement /apɔ̃tmɑ̃/ nm landing stage

apport /apɔʀ/ nm **l'~ de** the provision of [aide financière, solution, modifications]; the bringing-in of [idées nouvelles]; **grâce à l'~ d'eau** thanks to the provision of water; ~ **de capitaux** capital contribution; **les ~s de l'Asie à l'art européen** Asia's contribution to European art; ~ **calorique** caloric intake

(Composé) ~ **quotidien recommandé** recommended daily amount, RDA

apporter /apɔʀte/ [1] vtr **1** (transporter) (en venant) to bring; (en allant) to take; ~ **qch à qn** (en venant) to bring sb sth; (en allant) to take sb sth; **2** (fournir) to give [soutien, explication, sensation]; to bring [savoir-faire, amélioration, nouvelle, gloire, liberté, maladie]; to bring in [fonds, revenus]; to bring about [changement, révolution]; ~ **de l'aide à qn** to help sb; ~ **son concours à qch** to help with sth; ~ **sa contribution à qch** to contribute to sth; ~ **beaucoup de soin à son travail** to do one's work with great care; ~ **la preuve de qch** to bring proof of sth; ~ **des modifications à qch** to modify sth; **les modifications apportées** the modifications made; **ce stage ne m'a rien apporté** I didn't get anything out of this course; **cet homme ne peut rien t'~** this man has nothing to offer you

apposer /apoze/ [1] vtr fml to affix [affiche, signature] (sur on); ~ **un visa** to stamp a visa

apposition /apozisjɔ̃/ nf Ling apposition

appréciable /apresjabl/ adj substantial; **il y avait un nombre ~ de spectateurs** there were a good many spectators; **un grand jardin en ville, c'est ~** it's nice to have a big garden in the centre^GB of town

appréciatif, -ive /apresjatif, iv/ adj (approbateur) [jugement, regard] appreciative

appréciation /apresjasjɔ̃/ nf **1** (de distance, résultat, proposition) estimate; (financière) evaluation; **faire une erreur d'~** to make a misjudgment; **2** (jugement) assessment; **c'est une question d'~** it's a question of taste; **être laissé à l'~ de qn** to be left to sb's discretion; **3** (de monnaie) appreciation

apprécier /apresje/ [2]

A vtr **1** (juger favorablement) to appreciate [art, vin, qualité]; to like [personne]; **elle n'a pas apprécié** iron she wasn't exactly pleased; **un chercheur des plus apprécié** a highly valued researcher; **ce que j'apprécie chez elle** what I like about her; **2** (évaluer) to value [objet]; to estimate [distance, vitesse]; to assess [conséquences, résultat]

B **s'apprécier** vpr **1** (s'aimer) [personnes] to like one another; **2** (augmenter de valeur) [monnaie] to appreciate

appréhender /apreɑ̃de/ [1] vtr **1** (arrêter) [police] to arrest, to apprehend sout; **2** (redouter) to dread (**de faire** doing); **j'appréhende toujours un peu les examens** I'm always a bit apprehensive before exams; **3** (concevoir) fml to comprehend [phénomène]

appréhension /apreɑ̃sjɔ̃/ nf **1** (crainte) apprehension; **avec ~** apprehensively; **2** (conception) apprehension

apprendre /apʀɑ̃dʀ/ [52]

A vtr **1** (étudier) to learn (**à faire** to do); ~ **qch par cœur** to learn sth by heart, to learn sth off by heart GB; **le bonheur d'~** the joy of learning; ~ **l'italien** to learn Italian; **2** (être informé de) to learn [vérité] (**par qn** from sb; **sur qch/qn** about sth/sb); to hear [information] (**par qn** from sb; **sur qch/qn** about sth/sb); to learn of [événement, décision] (**par qn** through sb); ~ **qch par la presse** to see sth in the papers; **3** (enseigner) to teach; ~ **qch à qn** to teach sb sth;

~ **à conduire à qn** to teach sb (how) to drive; **cela t'apprendra!** that'll teach you!; **ce n'est pas à toi que je l'apprendrai** you don't need me to tell you; **4** (faire savoir) [personne, journal] to tell; **tu ne m'apprends rien** you're not telling me anything new

B **s'apprendre** vpr **s'~ facilement/difficilement** to be easy/difficult to learn; **la patience, cela s'apprend** patience is something you can learn

apprenti, ~e /apʀɑ̃ti/

A nm,f gén trainee; (d'artisan) apprentice; **être ~ chez qn** gén to train with sb; (avec un artisan) to serve an apprenticeship with sb; **entrer comme ~ chez qn** to be apprenticed to sb

B **apprenti(-), apprentie(-)** (in compounds) **1** gén trainee; (de métier artisanal) apprentice; ~ **boulanger** baker's apprentice; ~ **serveur** trainee waiter; **2** (sans expérience) ~**-ministre** novice minister

(Composé) ~ **sorcier** sorcerer's apprentice; **jouer les ~s sorciers** to open a Pandora's box

apprentissage /apʀɑ̃tisaʒ/ nm **1** gén training; (de métier artisanal) apprenticeship; (chez un artisan) **faire son ~ de boulanger** to train as a baker; **être en ~** gén to be a trainee; (chez un artisan) to be an apprentice; **2** (étude) learning; **l'~ d'une langue/de la lecture** learning a language/to read; **faire l'~ de la démocratie** to take the first steps toward(s) democracy; **faire l'~ de la vie** to learn about life

apprêt /apʀɛ/ nm **1** (sur mur, plafond) size; (sur bois) primer; **2** (affectation) affectation; **sans ~** unaffected

apprêté, ~e /apʀɛte/ adj [style] affected; [coiffure] fussy

apprêter /apʀɛte/ [1]

A vtr to finish [étoffe]; to size [mur, plafond]; to prime [bois]

B **s'apprêter** vpr **s'~ à faire** to be about to do

apprivoiser /apʀivwaze/ [1] vtr to tame [animal]; to win [sb] over [personne]; **animal apprivoisé** tame animal

approbateur, -trice /apʀɔbatœʀ, tʀis/ adj **sourire/hochement ~** smile/nod of approval

approbation /apʀɔbasjɔ̃/ nf approval (**de** of)

approchable /apʀɔʃabl/ adj **il n'est guère ~** (distant) he's rather unapproachable; (occupé) one never gets to see him

approchant, ~e /apʀɔʃɑ̃, ɑ̃t/ adj [valeur] approximate; **quelque chose d'~** something similar

approche /apʀɔʃ/

A nf **1** (arrivée) approach (**de** of); **il s'est enfui à mon ~** he ran off as I approached; **2** (imminence, proximité) approach (**de** of); **à l'~ or aux ~s de l'hiver** as winter approaches; **à l'~ de la nuit** at dusk; **à l'~ or aux ~s de la trentaine il décida que...** as he neared thirty, he decided that...; **3** (manière d'aborder) approach (**de** to); **d'~ difficile/aisée** [œuvre, auteur] hard/easy to get to grips with; **personne d'~ difficile** unapproachable person; **personne d'~ aisée** friendly person

B **approches** nfpl **aux ~s de la ville** on the outskirts of town; **aux ~s de la côte** near the coast

approcher /apʀɔʃe/ [1]

A vtr **1** (déplacer) **approche ta chaise** pull up your chair; ~ **le verre de ses lèvres** to raise the glass to one's lips; **2** (contacter) to approach; **ne m'approche pas** don't come near me; **on ne peut pas les ~** (occupés) you can never get to see them; (trop distants) they're unapproachable

B **approcher de** vtr ind ~ **de** to be (getting) close to; **nous approchons du but** we're nearly there

C vi to approach; **sentir la mort ~** to feel death drawing near; **l'heure du départ approchait** it was nearly time to leave; **approche** come here; **la nuit approche** it's getting dark; **les examens approchent** the exams are coming up

D **s'approcher** vpr **s'~ de qn/qch** (aller) to go near sb/sth; (venir) to come near sb/sth

approfondi, ~e /apʀɔfɔ̃di/ adj detailed, in-depth (épith); **étudier de façon ~e** to study in detail

approfondir /apʀɔfɔ̃diʀ/ [3]

A vtr **1** fig to go into [sth] in depth [sujet]; **vous auriez pu ~** you could have gone into the subject in greater depth; **inutile d'~** don't go into detail; ~ **ses connaissances** to improve one's knowledge; **2** lit to deepen [canal, trou]

B **s'approfondir** vpr [crevasse, trou] to deepen

approfondissement /apʀɔfɔ̃dismɑ̃/ nm (de connaissances) improvement; (de débat) development; (de relations) consolidation; (de crise) deepening

approprié, **∼e** /apʀɔpʀije/ adj [moyens, technique, régime] appropriate

approprier: s'approprier /apʀɔpʀije/ [2] vpr to take, to appropriate sout [chose, idée]; to seize [pouvoir]

approuver /apʀuve/ [1] vtr **1)** gén to approve of [action, décision, projet]; **je t'approuve totalement** (sur une idée) I quite agree with you; **je t'approuve d'avoir accepté** I think you were right to accept; **2)** Pol [commission, ministres] to approve [texte, projet, budget]; [parlement] to pass [projet de loi, décret]

approvisionnement /apʀɔvizjɔnmɑ̃/ nm supply (en of); **l'∼ de la ville en eau** supplying the town with water

approvisionner /apʀɔvizjɔne/ [1]

A vtr to supply [ville, marché] (en with); to load [arme automatique]; to pay money into [compte en banque]; **une boutique mal approvisionnée** a badly stocked shop; **votre compte n'est plus approvisionné depuis trois mois** your account has not been in credit for three months

B **s'approvisionner** vpr **1)** (faire des provisions) to stock up (en on, with); **2)** (acheter) **la compagnie s'approvisionne en papier auprès de l'usine** the company gets its supplies of paper from the factory

approximatif, -ive /apʀɔksimatif, iv/ adj [devis, coût, croquis, chiffre] rough; [traduction] approximate; **dans un anglais ∼** in broken English

approximation /apʀɔksimasjɔ̃/ nf **1)** (chiffre) rough estimate; (traduction, concept) approximation; **2)** Math approximation

approximativement /apʀɔksimativmɑ̃/ adv approximately

appui /apɥi/ nm **1)** (soutien) lit, fig support; **∼ matériel/moral** material/moral support; **à l'∼ de cette thèse** in support of this theory; **prendre ∼ sur** to lean on; **point d'∼** Phys fulcrum; **2)** Constr **∼ (de fenêtre)** window sill; **3)** Mil support; **∼ aérien** air support; **4)** Mus (de voix) placing

appui-tête, pl **appuis-tête** /apɥitɛt/ nm headrest

appuyé, **∼e** /apɥije/ adj [regard] intent; [plaisanterie] heavy

appuyer /apɥije/ [22]

A vtr **1)** (poser) to rest [tête] (sur on; contre against); to put [main, pied] (sur on; contre against); to lean [coude, objet] (sur on; contre against); **2)** (presser) to press (sur on; contre against); **∼ son doigt** to press one's finger; **3)** (baser) to support, to back up [raisonnement] (sur with); **4)** (soutenir) to back [personne, candidat]; to support [action, projet]; [blindés] to support [offensive]

B vi **1)** (presser) **∼ sur** (avec le doigt) to press; (avec le pied) to put one's foot on; **appuie sur l'accélérateur!** put your foot down!; **∼ sur la détente** to pull ou press the trigger; **2)** (insister) **∼ sur** to stress [syllabe, mot]; to emphasize [aspect, argument]

C **s'appuyer** vpr **1)** (prendre appui) to lean (sur on; contre against); **2)** (se fonder) **s'∼ sur** [personne] to rely on [personne, théorie, auteur]; to draw on [loi, rapport]; [étude] to be based on [connaissance, concept]

âpre /ɑpʀ/ adj **1)** (désagréable) [goût] bitter; [voix] harsh; [froid, vent] bitter; **2)** (acharné) [lutte] fierce; [discussion] bitter; **∼ au gain** grasping

après /apʀɛ/

A adv **1)** (dans le temps) (ensuite) afterwards; (plus tard) later; **tu finiras ∼** you can finish afterwards; **aussitôt** ou **tout de suite ∼** straight after that ou afterwards; **longtemps ∼** a long time after ou afterwards; **et ∼ que s'est-il passé?** and then what happened?, and what happened next?; **peu/bien ∼** shortly/long after(wards); **l'année d'∼** the year after; **pas la semaine prochaine celle d'∼** not next week, the week after next; **la fois d'∼** the next time; **le train d'∼** the next train; **l'instant d'∼** a moment later; **2)** (dans l'espace) **tu vois le croisement, j'habite (juste) ∼ à droite** can you see the crossroads? I live (just) past ou beyond it on the right; **peu ∼ il y a un lac** a bit further on there's a lake; **la page/le chapitre d'∼** the next page/chapter; **3)** (dans une hiérarchie) **les loisirs d'abord, le travail passe ∼** leisure first, work comes after; **4)** (marquant l'agacement) **et ∼?** so what?○

B prép **1)** (dans le temps) after; **passer ∼ qn** to go after sb; **peu ∼ minuit** shortly after midnight; **∼ mon départ** after I left; **∼ quelques années** a few years later; **∼ impôt** after

---

après

après adverbe se traduit généralement par *afterwards* et après préposition par *after*.

Les expressions telles que courir après qn/qch, crier après qn etc. sont traitées respectivement sous **courir**, **crier** etc.

après entre dans la composition de nombreux mots qui s'écrivent avec un trait d'union (*après-demain, après-guerre, après-midi* etc.). Ces mots sont des entrées à part entière et on les trouvera dans la nomenclature du dictionnaire. Utilisé avec un nom, propre ou commun, pour désigner la période suivant un événement ou la disparition d'une personne, il se traduit par *post* et forme alors un groupe adjectival que l'on fait suivre du nom approprié:

l'après-Gorbatchev
= the post-Gorbachev period

l'après-crise
= the post-recession period

l'après-1789
= the post-1789 period

On notera:

l'après-8 mai
= the period following 8 May

la France de l'après-de Gaulle
= post-de Gaulle France

---

tax; **∼ tout** after all; **∼ quoi** after which; **∼ coup** after the event, afterwards; **jour ∼ jour** day after day, day in day out; **∼ tout ce qu'il a fait** after all (that) he's done; **j'irai ∼ avoir fait la sieste** I'll go after I've had a nap; **2)** (dans l'espace) after; **∼ l'église/la sortie de la ville** after the church/you come out of the town; **∼ toi sur la liste** after you on the list; **∼ vous!** (par politesse) after you!; **il est toujours ∼ son fils**○ he's always on at his son; **3)** (dans une hiérarchie) after; **faire passer qn/qch ∼ qn/qch** to put sb/sth after sb/sth

C **d'après** loc prép **1)** (selon) **d'∼ moi** in my opinion; **d'∼ lui** according to him ou in his opinion; **d'∼ la loi** under the law; **d'∼ mes calculs/ma montre** by my calculations/my watch; **d'∼ ce qu'elle a dit** from what she said; **2)** (en imitant) from; **d'∼ un dessin de Gauguin** from a drawing by Gauguin; **3)** (adapté de) based on; **un film d'∼ un roman** a film based on a novel

D **après que** loc conj after; **∼ que je leur ai annoncé la nouvelle** after I told them the news

après-demain /apʀɛdmɛ̃/ adv the day after tomorrow

après-guerre, pl **∼s** /apʀɛɡɛʀ/ nm ou f postwar years (pl); **la génération d'∼** the postwar generation

après-midi /apʀɛmidi/ nm ou f inv afternoon; **en début/fin d'∼** early/late in the afternoon; **j'y vais le samedi ∼** I go there on Saturday afternoons; **2 heures de l'∼** 2 in the afternoon, 2 pm

après-rasage, pl **∼s** /apʀɛʀazaʒ/ adj inv, nm aftershave

après-shampooing, pl **∼s** /apʀɛʃɑ̃pwɛ̃/ nm conditioner

après-ski /apʀɛski/ nm inv (chaussure) snowboot

après-vente /apʀɛvɑ̃t/ adj inv **service ∼** (département) after-sales service department; (activité) after-sales service

âpreté /ɑpʀəte/ nf **1)** (de lutte) fierceness; (de discussion) bitterness; **∼ au gain** greed for gain; **2)** (de fruit) bitterness

a priori /apʀijɔʀi/

A loc adj inv [jugement] a priori

B loc adv **1)** gén **∼, ça ne devrait pas poser de problèmes** on the face of it there shouldn't be any problems; **∼ je ne connais personne qui puisse** offhand I can't think of anybody who could; **∼ je ne peux rien décider** right now I can't make a decision; **rejeter ∼ une proposition** to reject a proposal out of hand; **2)** Philos a priori

C nm inv a priori assumption

a

à-propos /apʀɔpo/ *nm inv* **interrompre avec** ~ to make an apposite interruption; **cette déclaration manque d'**~ this declaration is inapposite; **agir avec** ~ to do the right thing

apte /apt/ *adj* ⓵ (compétent) ~ **à** good at; **c'est l'homme le plus** ~ **à décider** he is the best man to decide; ⓶ (en état) fit; ~ **à l'enseignement/au travail** fit to teach/for work

aptitude /aptityd/ *nf* ⓵ (compétence) aptitude (**à** for; **à faire** for doing); ⓶ ~ **à l'enseignement/au travail/au service** fitness to teach/for work/for active duty

aquarelle /akwaʀɛl/ *nf* ⓵ (procédé) watercolours^{GB} (*pl*); ⓶ (œuvre) watercolour^{GB}

aquarium /akwaʀjɔm/ *nm* aquarium, fish tank

aquatique /akwatik/ *adj* ⓵ [*flore, faune*] aquatic; ⓶ [*jardin, sport*] water (*épith*)

aqueduc /akdyk/ *nm* Constr aqueduct

aqueux, ~euse /akø, øz/ *adj* aqueous

aquifère /akɥifɛʀ/ *adj* water-bearing, aquiferous spéc

aquilin /akilɛ̃/ *adj m* [*nez, profil*] aquiline

aquilon /akilɔ̃/ *nm* liter north wind

aquitain, ~e /akitɛ̃, ɛn/ ► p. 504 *adj* of Aquitaine; **le bassin** ~ the Aquitaine Basin

arabe /aʀab/
A *adj* [*architecture, civilisation*] Arab; [*chiffre, dialecte, écriture*] Arabic
B ► p. 336 *nm* Ling Arabic; ~ **classique** classical Arabic

Arabe /aʀab/ *nmf* Arab

arabesque /aʀabɛsk/ *nf* arabesque

Arabie /aʀabi/ ► p. 230, p. 504 *nprf* Arabia; **désert d'**~ Arabian desert
⟨Composé⟩ ~ **Saoudite** Saudi Arabia

arabique /aʀabik/ *adj* (d'Arabie) Arabian

arable /aʀabl/ *adj* arable

arachide /aʀaʃid/ *nf* peanut, groundnut GB; **huile d'**~ peanut oil

arachnéen, -éenne /aʀaknéɛ̃, ɛn/ *adj* ⓵ lit arachnid-an; ⓶ fig, liter gossamer (*épith*)

araignée /aʀeɲe/ *nf* Zool spider
⟨Composé⟩ ~ **de mer** spider crab
⟨Idiome⟩ **avoir une** ~ **au plafond**[○] to have a screw loose[○]

araméen /aʀaméɛ̃/ *nm* Ling Aramaic

araser /aʀaze/ [1] *vtr* to level off [*mur*]; (en menuiserie) to plane down

aratoire /aʀatwaʀ/ *adj* ploughing GB, plowing US

arbalète /aʀbalɛt/ *nf* crossbow

arbitrage /aʀbitʀaʒ/ *nm* ⓵ Sport (en boxe, football, rugby) refereeing; (en base-ball, cricket, tennis) umpiring; ⓶ (de différend) arbitration

arbitraire /aʀbitʀɛʀ/ *adj* arbitrary

arbitrairement /aʀbitʀɛʀmɑ̃/ *adv* arbitrarily

arbitre /aʀbitʀ/ *nm* ⓵ ► p. 372 Sport (en boxe, football, rugby) referee; (en base-ball, cricket, tennis) umpire; ⓶ fig **être l'**~ **d'une consultation électorale** to hold the balance of power in an election; ⓷ Jur (de différend) arbitrator

arbitrer /aʀbitʀe/ [1]
A *vtr* ⓵ Sport to referee [*match de boxe, football, rugby*]; to umpire [*match de base-ball, cricket, tennis*]; ⓶ (régler) to arbitrate in [*différend*]
B *vi* to arbitrate (**entre** between)

arboré, ~e /aʀbɔʀe/ *adj* [*terrain*] planted with trees (*après n*)

arborer /aʀbɔʀe/ [1] *vtr* ⓵ (porter avec ostentation) [*personne*] to sport [*objet*]; ⓶ (montrer) to wear [*sourire, air*]; to parade [*attitude, idée*]; ⓷ (porter normalement) [*personne, groupe*] to bear [*enseigne, couleur*]; [*navire, avion, bâtiment*] to fly [*pavillon, drapeau*]

arborescent, ~e /aʀbɔʀesɑ̃, ɑ̃t/ *adj* Bot, Ordinat tree (*épith*)

arboriculture /aʀbɔʀikyltyʀ/ *nf* arboriculture

arbouse /aʀbuz/ *nf* arbutus berry

arbre /aʀbʀ/ *nm* ⓵ (végétal) tree; ⓶ (diagramme) tree (diagram); ⓷ Tech shaft; ~ **de transmission** transmission shaft
⟨Composés⟩ ~ **à cames** Aut camshaft; ~ **généalogique** family tree; ~ **de Judée** Judas tree; ~ **de Noël** Christmas tree

arbrisseau, *pl* ~**x** /aʀbʀiso/ *nm* small tree

arbuste /aʀbyst/ *nm* shrub

arc /aʀk/ *nm* ⓵ Sport bow; **tendre** *or* **bander un** ~ to bend a bow back; ⓶ (courbe) curve; **en (forme d')** ~ arched; ⓷ Archit arch
⟨Composés⟩ ~ **brisé** lancet arch; ~ **de cercle** arc of a circle; ~ **électrique** electric arc; ~ **plein cintre** round arch; ~ **de triomphe** triumphal arch

arcade /aʀkad/ *nf* Archit arcade; ~**s** (ensemble) archways
⟨Composé⟩ ~ **sourcilière** arch of the eyebrow

arcanes /aʀkan/ *nmpl* liter mysteries

arc-bouter: s'arc-bouter /aʀkbute/ [1] *vpr* to brace oneself (**contre** against)

arceau, *pl* ~**x** /aʀso/ *nm* ⓵ (de voûte) arch; ⓶ (de tonnelle, croquet) hoop; ⓷ Aut (de voiture) roll bar; ⓸ (de lit) cradle

arc-en-ciel, *pl* **arcs-en-ciel** /aʀkɑ̃sjɛl/ *nm* rainbow

archaïque /aʀkaik/ *adj* archaic

archaïsme /aʀkaism/ *nm* archaism

archange /aʀkɑ̃ʒ/ *nm* archangel

arche /aʀʃ/ *nf* Archit arch
⟨Composés⟩ ~ **d'alliance** Ark of the Covenant; ~ **de Noé** Noah's Ark

archéologie /aʀkeɔlɔʒi/ *nf* archaeology

archéologique /aʀkeɔlɔʒik/ *adj* archaeological

archéologue /aʀkeɔlɔg/ ► p. 372 *nmf* archaeologist

archer /aʀʃe/ *nm* archer

archet /aʀʃɛ/ *nm* Mus bow

archétype /aʀketip/ *nm* archetype; **l'**~ **du héros** the archetypal hero

archevêché /aʀʃəveʃe/ *nm* ⓵ (domaine) archdiocese; ⓶ (siège) archbishop's palace

archevêque /aʀʃəvɛk/ ► p. 590 *nm* archbishop

archi○ /aʀʃi/ *préf* ~**comble**, ~**plein** chock-a-block; ~**connu** really well-known; ~**millionnaire** millionaire several times over

archiduc /aʀʃidyk/ ► p. 590 *nm* archduke

archiduchesse /aʀʃidyʃes/ ► p. 590 *nf* archduchess

archipel /aʀʃipɛl/ *nm* archipelago

architecte /aʀʃitɛkt/ ► p. 372 *nmf* lit, fig architect

architectural, ~e, *mpl* **-aux** /aʀʃitɛktyʀal, o/ *adj* architectural

architecture /aʀʃitɛktyʀ/ *nf* ⓵ lit, Ordinat architecture; ⓶ fig structure

archiver /aʀʃive/ [1] *vtr* to archive

archives /aʀʃiv/ *nfpl* archives, records; **je vais fouiller dans mes** ~ hum I'll go through my (old) papers

archiviste /aʀʃivist/ ► p. 372 *nmf* archivist

arçon /aʀsɔ̃/ *nm* (en équitation) tree; **cheval d'**~**s** pommel horse

arctique /aʀktik/ *adj* arctic

Arctique /aʀktik/ *nprm* ⓵ ► p. 504 (région) Arctic; ⓶ ► p. 406 (océan) **l'océan** ~ the Arctic Ocean

ardemment /aʀdamɑ̃/ *adv* passionately; **être** ~ **républicain** to be an ardent republican

ardent, ~e /aʀdɑ̃, ɑ̃t/ *adj* [*braise*] glowing; [*flamme, soleil*] blazing; [*regard, foi, désir*] burning; [*souhait, piété*] fervent; [*lutte*] fierce; [*zèle, discours*] impassioned; [*partisan*] passionate; [*patriote*] fervent; [*jeunesse*] hot-blooded; **être** ~ **au combat** to fight fiercely; **être** ~ **au travail** to be an enthusiastic worker

ardeur /aʀdœʀ/ *nf* (de personne) ardour^{GB}; (de foi, patriotisme) fervour^{GB}; (de néophyte) keenness GB, enthusiasm; **modérer** *or* **calmer les** ~**s de qn** to cool sb's ardour^{GB}; ~ **révolutionnaire** revolutionary zeal; ~ **au travail** enthusiasm for work; **travailler avec** ~ to work hard; **redoubler d'**~ to try twice as hard

ardoise /aʀdwaz/
A ► p. 140 *adj inv* slate-grey GB, slate-gray US
B *nf* ⓵ (roche) slate; ⓶ (tuile) slate; **toit d'**~**(s)** slate roof; ⓷ (d'écolier) slate; ⓸ ○(dette) debt; **avoir une** ~ **chez un commerçant** to owe a shopkeeper money

ardu, ~e /aʀdy/ *adj* (difficile) [*travail*] arduous; [*négociations, problème*] taxing

are /aʀ/ ► p. 568 *nf* one hundred square metres^{GB}, are

arène /aʁɛn/ *nf* [1] (dans un amphithéâtre) arena; (au cirque) ring; (pour corridas) bullring; *fig* arena; [2] (amphithéâtre) ~s amphitheatre^GB (*sg*)

(Idiome) **descendre dans l'**~ to enter the ring

arête /aʁɛt/ *nf* [1] Zool fishbone; **retirer les** ~s **d'un poisson** to bone a fish; **sans** ~s boned; [2] (de toit, montagne) ridge; (de voûte) groin; (de prisme, roche) edge; (de nez) bridge

argent /aʁʒɑ̃/ ▸ p. 34 *nm* [1] (monnaie) money; **dépenser son** ~ **sans compter** to spend one's money like water^○; **pour de l'**~ for money; **en avoir pour son** ~ to get one's money's worth; [2] (métal) silver; **en** ~, **d'**~ silver (*épith*)

(Composés) ~ **liquide** cash; ~ **de poche** pocket money

(Idiomes) **le temps c'est de l'**~ time is money; **prendre pour** ~ **comptant** to take [sth] at face value

argenté, ~e /aʁʒɑ̃te/
A *pp* ▸ **argenter**
B *pp adj* (plaqué d'argent) silver-plated; **un bougeoir en métal** ~ a silver-plated candlestick
C *adj* [1] (couleur) silvery; [2] ^○(fortuné) loaded^○; **n'être pas très** ~ to be hard up^○

argenter /aʁʒɑ̃te/ [1] *vtr* lit, fig to silver

argenterie /aʁʒɑ̃tʁi/ *nf* silverware, silver

argentier /aʁʒɑ̃tje/ *nm* Hist treasurer

argentin, ~e /aʁʒɑ̃tɛ̃, in/ *adj* [1] (son) silvery; [2] ▸ p. 392 (d'Argentine) Argentinian; **la République** ~e the Argentine Republic

Argentine /aʁʒɑ̃tin/ ▸ p. 230 *nprf* Argentina

argile /aʁʒil/ *nf* clay

argileux, **-euse** /aʁʒilø, øz/ *adj* clayey

argot /aʁgo/ *nm* slang; **un mot d'**~ a slang word

argotique /aʁgɔtik/ *adj* (propre à l'argot) slang (*épith*); (peu raffiné) slangy

arguer /aʁge/ [1]
A *vtr* ~ **que** to claim that
B arguer de *vtr ind* (prétexter) ~ **de** to give [sth] as a reason (**pour faire** for doing); **arguant du fait que** pointing to the fact that

argument /aʁgymɑ̃/ *nm* (raison) argument (**en faveur de** for; **contre** against); ~ **choc** *or* **massue** decisive argument; ~ **décisif** deciding factor; **trouver de bons** ~s **en faveur de**/**contre qch** to make a good case for/against sth

argumentation /aʁgymɑ̃tasjɔ̃/ *nf* line of argument

argumenter /aʁgymɑ̃te/ [1] *vi* to argue (**sur** about; **contre** against); **défense solidement argumentée** soundly argued defence^GB

argus /aʁgys/ *nm inv* Aut used car prices guide

argutie /aʁgysi/ *nf liter* quibble

aride /aʁid/ *adj* [1] (terre, climat) arid; [2] (sujet) dry

aridité /aʁidite/ *nf* [1] (de terre, climat) aridity; [2] (de lecture) dryness

aristocrate /aʁistɔkʁat/ *nmf* aristocrat

aristocratie /aʁistɔkʁasi/ *nf* aristocracy

aristocratique /aʁistɔkʁatik/ *adj* aristocratic

arithmétique /aʁitmetik/
A *adj* arithmetical
B *nf* arithmetic

arlequin /aʁləkɛ̃/ *nm* harlequin

armada /aʁmada/ *nf* [1] (armée) *hum* army; **l'invincible Armada** Hist the Spanish Armada; [2] ^○(grand nombre) (de personnes) avalanche; (de camions) huge fleet

armateur /aʁmatœʁ/ *nm* (propriétaire) shipowner

armature /aʁmatyʁ/ *nf* [1] (de tente, store, d'abat-jour) frame; (de soutien-gorge) underwiring **₵**; (de voûte) arch reinforcement; (de béton armé) reinforcing steel rods (*pl*); **à** ~ (soutien-gorge) underwired; **sans** ~ (soutien-gorge) light control (*épith*); [2] (de région, parti, d'entreprise) infrastructure; [3] (de roman) structure

arme /aʁm/
A *nf* [1] (objet) weapon; **l'**~ **du crime** the murder weapon; **charger une** ~ to load a gun; [2] *fig* (moyen) weapon; **une** ~ **à double tranchant** a double-edged sword; [3] Mil (corps d'armée) branch of the armed services
B armes *nfpl* [1] Mil arms (*pl*); **aux** ~s! to arms!; **reposez** ~s! order arms!; **prendre les** ~s (guerre) to take up arms;

(insurrection) to rise up in arms; **par la force des** ~s by force of arms; **jeter** *or* **rendre les** ~s *fig* to surrender; **en** ~s (peuple, soldats, insurgés) armed; **mourir les** ~s **à la main** to die fighting; **passer qn par les** ~s to execute sb by firing squad; **à** ~s **égales** lit, fig on equal terms; **donner** *or* **fournir des** ~s **contre soi** *fig* to provide ammunition against oneself; **faire ses premières** ~s *fig* to start out; [2] (armoiries) coat (*sg*) of arms

(Composés) ~ **blanche** *weapon with a blade*; ~ **de destruction massive** weapon of mass destruction; ~ **à feu** firearm; ~ **de poing** handgun; ~ **de service** standard issue weapon

armé, ~e¹ /aʁme/
A *pp* ▸ **armer**
B *pp adj* [1] lit (muni d'armes) armed (**de** with); ~ **jusqu'aux dents** armed to the teeth; **vol à main** ~e armed robbery; [2] *fig* (pourvu) equipped (**de** with; **contre** against); ~ **pour faire** (personne) equipped *ou* in a position to do; **il est bien** ~ **pour réussir** he's well equipped to succeed

armée² /aʁme/ *nf* [1] *gén* armed forces (*pl*); (de terre) army; **être dans l'**~ to be in the army; **être à l'**~ to be doing one's military service; [2] (grand nombre) army, bunch *péj*

(Composés) ~ **d'active** regular army; ~ **de l'air** air force; **l'**~ **de réserve** the reserves (*pl*); **l'**~ **de terre** the army

armement /aʁməmɑ̃/ *nm* [1] (moyens armés) *gén* armament; (de personne, troupe) weapons (*pl*); (d'unité mobile) weaponry; ~ **léger**/**lourd** light/heavy armament; [2] (ensemble d'armes) arms (*pl*); **ventes d'**~ arms sales; [3] (mise en état de marche) (d'arme) arming; (d'appareil photo) winding on; [4] (de navire) fitting out

arménien, **-ienne** /aʁmenjɛ̃, ɛn/
A ▸ p. 392 *adj* Armenian
B ▸ p. 336 *nm* Ling Armenian

armer /aʁme/ [1]
A *vtr* [1] (munir d'armes) to arm (**de** with; **contre** against); [2] (renforcer) to reinforce (béton) (**de** with); [3] (prémunir) to arm (**contre** against); [4] (équiper) to fit out (navire); [5] (mettre en ordre de marche) to arm (arme); to wind on (appareil photo); ~ **un fusil** to cock a rifle
B s'armer *vpr* to arm oneself (**de** with); **s'**~ **de patience** to summon up one's patience

armistice /aʁmistis/ *nm* armistice

armoire /aʁmwaʁ/ *nf gén* cupboard; (pour vêtements) wardrobe; ~ **vitrée** glass-fronted cupboard

(Composés) ~ **chauffante** hot cupboard; ~ **électrique** switchgear cubicle; ~ **frigorifique** cold store; ~ **à glace** lit wardrobe with a full length mirror; **c'est une** ~ **à glace**^○ *fig* he/she is built like a tank^○; ~ **à linge** linen cupboard, linen closet US; ~ **métallique** metal locker; ~ **normande** large wardrobe (*in traditional Norman style*); ~ **à pharmacie** medicine cabinet; ~ **de toilette** bathroom cabinet

armoiries /aʁmwaʁi/ *nfpl* arms

armure /aʁmyʁ/ *nf* Hist Mil armour^GB; *fig* form of protection

armurerie /aʁmyʁʁi/ *nf* [1] ▸ p. 372 (magasin, atelier) gunsmith's; [2] Mil gun room

armurier /aʁmyʁje/ ▸ p. 372 *nm* [1] (qui vend, répare) gunsmith; [2] (dans l'armée) armourer^GB

ARN /aɛʁɛn/ *nm* (abbr = **acide ribonucléique**) RNA

arobas(e) /aʁɔbas, aʁɔbaz/ *nm* at sign

aromates /aʁɔmat/ *nmpl* herbs and spices

aromatique /aʁɔmatik/ *adj* aromatic

aromatiser /aʁɔmatize/ [1] *vtr* to flavour^GB; **aromatisé au citron** lemon-flavoured^GB

arôme /aʁom/ *nm* [1] (odeur) aroma; [2] (additif alimentaire) flavouring^GB; **à l'**~ **de fruit** fruit-flavoured^GB

arpège /aʁpɛʒ/ *nm* arpeggio

arpent /aʁpɑ̃/ *nm* Hist arpent; **quelques** ~s *fig* a few acres

arpenter /aʁpɑ̃te/ [1] *vtr* to stride along (rues); to pace up and down (couloirs)

arpenteur /aʁpɑ̃tœʁ/ ▸ p. 372 *nm* (land) surveyor

arqué, ~e /aʁke/ *adj* (sourcils) arched; (nez) hooked; **avoir les jambes** ~es to have bandy *ou* bow legs

L'argent et les monnaies

■ *Pour la prononciation des nombres en anglais* ▸ **p. 398**.

L'argent en Grande-Bretagne

écrire	dire
1p	one p ([pi:]) *ou* one penny *ou* a penny
2p	two p *ou* two pence
5p	five p *ou* five pence
20p	twenty p *ou* twenty pence
£1*	one pound *ou* a pound
£1.03	one pound three pence†
	ou one pound three p‡
£1.20	one pound twenty
	ou one pound twenty pence
	ou one pound twenty p
£1.99	one pound ninety-nine
£10	ten pounds
£200	two hundred pounds
£1,000§	one thousand pounds
	ou a thousand pounds
£1,000,000	one million pounds *ou* a million pounds

L'argent aux États-Unis

écrire	dire
1c	one cent *ou* a cent
2c	two cents
5c	five cents
10c	ten cents
25c	twenty-five cents
$1*	one dollar *ou* a dollar
$1.99	one dollar ninety-nine
$10	ten dollars
$200	two hundred dollars
$1,000	one thousand dollars§
	ou a thousand dollars
$1,000,000	one million dollars¶ *ou* a million dollars

L'argent en France

écrire	dire
0,20 €	twenty cents
1 €	one euro
1,50 €	one euro fifty cents *ou* one euro fifty
2 €	two euros
2,75 €	two euros seventy-five cents
	ou two euros seventy-five
20 €	twenty euros
100 €	one hundred euros *ou* a hundred euros
200 €	two hundred euros
1 000 €	one thousand euros *ou* a thousand euros
2 000 €	two thousand euros
1 000 000 €	one million euros *ou* a million euros
2 000 000 €	two million euros

* *L'anglais place les abréviations £ et $ avant le chiffre, jamais après.*

† *On ne dit jamais* point *pour les sommes d'argent.*

‡ *Si le chiffre des* pence *est inférieur ou égal à 19, on n'omet pas* pence *ou* p: one pound nineteen pence, *mais* one pound twenty.

§ *Noter que l'anglais utilise une virgule là où le français a un espace.*

¶ *Les numéraux français* millier *ou* million, *qui sont des noms, se traduisent en anglais par des adjectifs:* deux millions de francs = two million francs. *Pour plus de détails,* ▸ **p. 398**.

il y a 100 pennies dans une livre
= there are 100 pence in a pound

il y a 100 cents dans un dollar
= there are 100 cents in a dollar

il y a 100 centimes dans un euro
= there are 100 cents in a euro

Les pièces et les billets

■ *Attention:* billet *se dit* note *en anglais britannique, et* bill *en anglais américain.*

■ *Noter l'ordre des mots dans les adjectifs composés anglais, et l'utilisation du trait d'union. Noter aussi que* pound, dollar *etc. qui font partie de l'adjectif composé, ne prennent pas la marque du pluriel:*

un billet de 10 livres
= a ten-pound note (*GB*)

un billet de 50 dollars
= a fifty-dollar bill (*US*)

un billet de 100 €
= a hundred-euro note (*GB*) *ou* a hundred-euro bill (*US*)

une pièce de 20 pennies
= a 20p piece (dire [ə twɛntɪ pi: pi:s])

une pièce de 50 pennies
= a 50p piece

une pièce d'une livre
= a pound coin

■ *Noter que* pièce *se traduit par* coin *pour l'unité monétaire et au-delà, et par* piece *pour toute fraction de l'unité monétaire.*

une pièce de 50 centimes
= a 50-cent piece

une pièce de 1 €
= a one-euro coin

une pièce de 2 €
= a two-euro coin

Mais aux États-Unis:

une pièce de 5 cents
= a nickel

une pièce de 10 cents
= a dime

une pièce de 25 cents
= a quarter

Les prix

combien ça coûte?
= how much does it cost? *ou* how much is it?

ça coûte 200 livres
= it costs £200 *ou* it is £200

le prix de l'appareil photo est de 200 livres
= the price of the camera is £200

à peu près 200 livres
= about £200

presque 200 livres
= almost £200

jusqu'à 20 dollars
= up to $20

15 euros le mètre
= 15 euros a metre

■ *Noter l'absence d'équivalent anglais de la préposition française de avant le chiffre dans les expressions de ce genre.*

☛ Voir page suivante

L'argent et les monnaies *suite*

plus de 200 livres
= over £200 *ou* more than £200

moins de 300 livres
= less than £300

un peu moins de 250 livres
= just under £250

■ *Noter l'ordre des mots dans les adjectifs composés anglais et l'utilisation du trait d'union. Noter aussi que* franc, cent *etc. qui font partie de l'adjectif composé, ne prennent pas la marque du pluriel:*

un timbre à 1 euro
= a one-euro stamp

un timbre à 75 centimes
= a seventy-five-cent stamp

un billet de théâtre à 10 livres
= a £10 theatre ticket (*dire* a ten-pound theatre ticket)

une bourse de deux mille livres
= a £2,000 grant (*dire* a two-thousand-pound grant)

une voiture à 50 000 dollars
= a $50,000 car (*dire* a fifty-thousand-dollar car)

■ *L'anglais considère parfois une somme d'argent comme une unité indissociable, et donc comme un singulier:*

ça coûte dix livres de plus
= it is an extra ten pounds

encore dix livres
= another ten pounds

dix livres, ça fait beaucoup d'argent
= ten pounds is a lot of money

prends tes 20 €, ils sont sur la table
= take your 20 euros, it's on the table

Le maniement de l'argent

payer en livres
= to pay in pounds

faire une transaction en euros
= to make a transaction in euros

50 livres en liquide
= £50 in cash

un chèque de 500 livres
= a £500 cheque

un chèque de voyage en dollars
= a dollar travelers' check

un chèque de voyage en livres
= a sterling travellers' cheque

changer des livres en euros
= to change pounds into euros

le dollar vaut 1,12 euros
= there are 1.12 euros to the dollar

faire la monnaie d'un billet de 100 dollars
= to change a 100-dollar bill

Le système lsd

■ *Le système non-décimal utilisé en Grande-Bretagne jusqu'en 1971 reposait sur la* livre, *le* shilling *et le* penny. *Le* penny (*pluriel* pence) *était abrégé en* d., *à cause du latin* denarius. *Il y avait douze* pence *dans un* shilling *et vingt* shillings *dans une* livre.

---

arquebuse /aʀkəbyz/ *nf* arquebus

arquer /aʀke/ [1]
A *vtr* to bend [*barre*]; **~ le dos** to arch one's back
B **s'arquer** *vpr* [*poutrelle, barre*] to become bowed

arrachage /aʀaʃaʒ/ *nm* (de récolte) picking; (de dent, poteau) pulling out; (de broussailles, souche) digging out; **~ des mauvaises herbes** weeding

arraché /aʀaʃe/ *nm* Sport snatch; **obtenir qch à l'~** *fig* to snatch sth; **vol à l'~** bag snatching

arrache-clou, *pl* **~s** /aʀaʃklu/ *nm* claw hammer

arrache-pied: d'arrache-pied /daʀaʃpje/ *loc adv* **travailler d'~** to work flat out

arracher /aʀaʃe/ [1]
A *vtr* **1** (déraciner) [*personne*] to dig up [*légumes*]; to dig out [*broussailles, souche, poteau*]; to uproot [*arbre*]; [*ouragan*] to uproot [*arbre, poteau*]; **~ les mauvaises herbes** to weed; **2** (détacher vivement) [*personne*] to pull [sth] out [*poil, dent, ongle, clou*] (**de** from); to tear [sth] down [*affiche*]; to rip [sth] out [*page*]; to tear [sth] off [*masque*] (**de** from); [*vent*] to blow [sth] off [*feuilles*]; to rip [sth] off [*toit*] (**de** from); **l'obus lui a arraché le bras** the shell blew his/her arm off; **3** (ôter de force) to snatch [*personne, objet*] (**de, à** from); **~ qch des mains de qn** to snatch sth out of sb's hands; **elle s'est fait ~ son sac** she had her bag snatched; **~ qn à la mort** to snatch sb from the jaws of death; **~ qn à la misère** to rescue sb from poverty; **~ qn à sa famille** to tear sb from the bosom of his/her family; **4** (tirer brutalement) **~ qn à** to rouse sb from [*rêve, torpeur, pensées*]; to drag sb away from [*travail*]; **5** (soutirer) to force [*augmentation, compromis*] (**à qn** out of sb); to extract [*secret, précision, consentement*] (**de, à qn** from sb); to get [*mot, sourire*] (**de, à qn** from sb); **ils leur ont arraché la victoire** they snatched victory from them; **~ un nul** Sport to manage to draw GB *ou* tie; **la douleur lui a arraché un cri** he/she cried out in pain
B **s'arracher** *vpr* **1** (s'ôter) **s'~ les cheveux blancs** to pull out one's grey GB *ou* gray US hairs; **s'~ les poils du nez** to pluck the hairs from one's nose; **2** (se disputer pour) to fight over [*personne, produit*]; **3** (se séparer) **s'~ à** to rouse

oneself from [*pensées, rêverie*]; to tear oneself away from [*travail, étreinte*]

⟨Idiomes⟩ **~ les yeux à** *or* **de qn** to scratch sb's eyes out; **c'est à s'~ les cheveux**○**!** (difficile) it's enough to make you tear your hair out!; **s'~ les yeux** to fight like cat and dog

arracheur /aʀaʃœʀ/ *nm* **~ de dents** quack

⟨Idiome⟩ **mentir comme un ~ de dents** to be a born liar

arraisonner /aʀezɔne/ [1] *vtr* to board and inspect [*navire, avion*]

arrangeant, ~e /aʀɑ̃ʒɑ̃, ɑ̃t/ *adj* obliging

arrangement /aʀɑ̃ʒmɑ̃/ *nm* **1** (accord) agreement; **2** (disposition) arrangement; **3** Math permutation; **4** Mus arrangement

arranger /aʀɑ̃ʒe/ [13]
A *vtr* **1** (organiser) to arrange [*voyage, réunion*]; to organize [*vie*]; **2** (régler) to settle [*conflit*]; to sort out [*malentendu, affaires*]; **cela ne va pas ~ les choses** that won't help matters; **pour ne rien ~, pour tout ~** iron to make matters worse; **le temps arrangera peut-être les choses** perhaps things will improve with time; **3** (disposer) to arrange [*objets, fleurs, pièce*]; **4** (remettre en ordre) to tidy [*cheveux*]; to straighten [*châle, gilet*]; **ton coiffeur t'a bien arrangé!** iron your hairdresser has made a right mess of your hair○!; **5** (modifier) to rearrange [*texte*]; **6** (réparer) to fix; **7** (convenir) **tu dis ça parce que ça t'arrange** you say that because it suits you
B **s'arranger** *vpr* **1** (s'améliorer) to improve; **tout finira par s'~** things will sort themselves out in the end; **2** (se mettre d'accord) **s'~ avec qn** to arrange it with sb; **s'~ à l'amiable** to come to a friendly agreement; **3** (prendre des dispositions) **arrange-toi pour être à l'heure** make sure you're on time; **4** (se débrouiller) **il n'y a que trois lits mais on s'arrangera** there are only three beds but we'll sort something out; **arrange-toi avec ça** try and make do with that; **5** ○(s'habiller) **elle ne sait pas s'~** she doesn't know how to do herself up nicely

arrangeur, -euse /aʀɑ̃ʒœʀ, øz/ *nm,f* Mus arranger

arrérages /aʀeʀaʒ/ *nmpl* arrears

arrestation /aʀɛstasjɔ̃/ *nf* arrest; **être en état d'~** to be under arrest; **procéder à l'~ de** to arrest

arrêt /aʀɛ/ *nm* ① (de véhicule) stopping; (de combats) cessation; (de livraison, transaction) cancellation; (de production, distribution) halt; (de croissance économique) cessation; (halte) stop; **attendez l'~ complet du train/de l'avion** wait until the train/plane has come to a complete stop; **faire un ~ de deux heures** to stop for two hours; **l'~ des hostilités/ essais nucléaires** an end to hostilities/nuclear testing; **décider l'~ de la production** to decide to halt the production; **sans ~** (sans interruption) nonstop, without stopping; (à tout moment) constantly; **ce train est sans ~ jusqu'à Toulouse** this train goes nonstop to Toulouse; **il faut sans ~ répéter la même chose** the same thing has to be repeated over and over again; **à l'~** [*voiture, camion, train*] stationary; [*machine*] (prête à fonctionner) idle; (hors tension) off; **marquer un temps d'~** to pause; **un coup d'~** a halt; **donner un coup d'~ à** to stop *ou* halt; **être en ~** [*chien*] to point; **être aux ~s** Mil to be under arrest; ② (lieu) stop; **un ~ de bus** a bus stop; ③ C (sur un panneau) stop; ④ Jur ruling

(Composés) **~ du cœur** heart failure; **~ sur image** freeze-frame, still; **faire un ~ sur image** to freeze a frame; **~ de jeu** Sport stoppage time; **jouer les ~s de jeu** to play injury time; **~ de mort** death sentence; **~ de travail** (pour grève) stoppage of work; (pour maladie) (événement) sick leave **₵**; (document) sick note; **être en ~ de travail** to be on sick leave

arrêté, ~e /aʀete/

Ⓐ *pp* ▸ **arrêter**

Ⓑ *pp adj* ① (convenu) settled; ② (inébranlable) [*idée, principe*] fixed

Ⓒ *nm* Admin order, decree; **~ ministériel** ministerial decree; **~ d'expulsion** (contre un étranger) expulsion order, deportation order; (contre un locataire) eviction notice *ou* order; **~ municipal** bylaw; **~ préfectoral** bylaw (*issued by a prefecture*)

arrêter /aʀete/ [1]

Ⓐ *vtr* ① (stopper) gén to stop; to switch off [*machine, moteur, appareil*]; to halt [*production*]; to give up [*études, alcool*]; **~ qn** (dans une conversation) to stop sb; **rien ne les arrête** fig (pour faire un voyage, pour s'amuser) there's no stopping them; (pour gagner de l'argent) they'd stop at nothing; **qu'est-ce qui t'arrête?** what's stopping you?; **~ de faire** to stop doing; (renoncer) to give up doing; **arrête de mentir** stop lying; **~ de fumer** to give up smoking; **~ de travailler** (définitivement) to stop work; **le trafic est arrêté sur la ligne B** service has been suspended on the B line; **arrête tes bêtises!** (tais-toi) stop talking nonsense!; (cesse de faire des bêtises) stop fooling around!; **je n'arrête pas en ce moment!** I'm always on the go⚪ these days!; **'tu n'as qu'à travailler!' —'mais je n'arrête pas!'** 'you should work!'—'but that's what I'm doing!'; **être arrêté pour trois semaines** to be given a sick note for three weeks; ② (appréhender) [*police*] to arrest; **arrêtez-la!** stop her!; ③ (déterminer) to fix [*lieu, date*]; to make [*décision*]; to decide on [*plan, principe, mesure*]

Ⓑ *vi* (cesser) [*bruit, cri*] to stop; **le téléphone n'arrête pas** the phone rings all the time; **arrête!** (tu m'ennuies) stop it!; (je ne te crois pas) I don't believe you!

Ⓒ **s'arrêter** *vpr* ① (faire un arrêt) [*personne, train*] to stop; **arrête-toi ici** stop here; **sans s'~** without stopping; **s'~ pour se reposer** to stop for a rest; **s'~ à Grenoble** [*personne*] to stop off in Grenoble; [*train, car*] to stop in Grenoble; ② (cesser de fonctionner) to stop; ③ (cesser) [*hémorragie, pluie, musique*] to stop; **s'~ de faire** to stop doing; **ils ne vont pas s'~ là** fig they won't stop there!; ④ (renoncer à) to give up (**de faire** doing); **s'~ de fumer** to give up smoking; ⑤ (se terminer) [*enquête, histoire, chemin, jardin*] to end; **l'affaire aurait pu s'~ là** that could have been the end of the matter; ⑥ (fixer son attention sur) **s'~ sur** to dwell on [*point*]; **s'~ à** to focus on [*détails, essentiel*] ; **ce dernier point mérite qu'on s'y arrête** this last point merits some attention

arrhes /aʀ/ *nfpl* deposit (sg); **verser des ~** to pay a deposit

arrière /aʀjɛʀ/

Ⓐ *adj inv* [*poche*] back; Mil [*base*] rearguard; Aut [*vitre, roue, feux*] rear; [*banquette*] back; **siège ~** (de voiture) back seat; (de moto) pillion; **la partie ~ du bâtiment** the rear of the building

Ⓑ *nm* ① (partie) (de voiture, bâtiment) back, rear; (de train, d'avion) rear; (de navire) stern; **à l'~** (dans une voiture) in the back; (dans un train, bus) at the back *ou* rear; (au rugby, football) at the back; **le moteur est à l'~** the engine is at the back; **une voiture avec le moteur à l'~** a rear-engine car; **en ~** (direction) gén backward(s); **pencher la tête en ~** to tilt one's head back; **rester en ~** (parmi les spectateurs) to stand back; (après le départ des autres) to stay behind; (par sécurité, crainte) to keep back; (traîner) to lag behind; **regarder en ~** lit, fig to look back; **remonter de deux ans en ~** to go back two years; **revenir en ~** lit to turn back; fig to take a backward step; (sur un enregistrement) to rewind; **se coiffer en ~** to wear one's hair off the face; **en ~ de** (derrière) behind; **vers l'~** backwards; ② Sport (au rugby, hockey) fullback; (au football) defender; (au basket) guard; (au volley) back-line player; **les ~s** (au rugby) the backs; (au football) the defence^{GB}; ③ Mil (territoire) civilian zone; (population) civilian population

Ⓒ **arrières** *nmpl* Mil rear (sg); **surveiller ses ~s** lit, fig to watch one's rear; **assurer ses ~s** fig to cover one's back

arriéré, ~e /aʀjeʀe/

Ⓐ *adj* ① [*idées, pratique*] outdated; [*pays, société*] backward; [*personne*] behind the times (*jamais épith*); ② Psych retarded

Ⓑ *nm* arrears (*pl*)

arrière-boutique, *pl* **~s** /aʀjɛʀbutik/ *nf* back of the shop

arrière-cour, *pl* **~s** /aʀjɛʀkuʀ/ *nf* backyard

arrière-garde, *pl* **~s** /aʀjɛʀgaʀd/ *nf* rearguard

arrière-goût, *pl* **~s** /aʀjɛʀgu/ *nm* aftertaste

arrière-grand-mère, *pl* **arrière-grands-mères** /aʀjɛʀgʀɑ̃mɛʀ/ *nf* great-grandmother

arrière-grand-oncle, *pl* **arrière-grands-oncles** /aʀjɛʀgʀɑ̃tɔ̃kl, *pl* gʀɑ̃zɔ̃kl/ *nm* great-great-uncle

arrière-grand-père, *pl* **arrière-grands-pères** /aʀjɛʀgʀɑ̃pɛʀ/ *nm* great-grandfather

arrière-grands-parents /aʀjɛʀgʀɑ̃paʀɑ̃/ *nmpl* great-grandparents

arrière-grand-tante, *pl* **arrière-grands-tantes** /aʀjɛʀgʀɑ̃tɑ̃t/ *nf* great-great-aunt

arrière-neveu, *pl* **~x** /aʀjɛʀnəvø/ *nm* great-nephew

arrière-nièce, *pl* **~s** /aʀjɛʀnjɛs/ *nf* great-niece

arrière-pays /aʀjɛʀpei/ *nm inv* back country

arrière-pensée, *pl* **~s** /aʀjɛʀpɑ̃se/ *nf* ulterior motive; **sans ~** without reservation

arrière-petite-fille, *pl* **arrière-petites-filles** /aʀjɛʀpətitfij/ *nf* great-granddaughter

arrière-petite-nièce, *pl* **arrière-petites-nièces** /aʀjɛʀpətitnjɛs/ *nf* great-great-niece

arrière-petit-fils, *pl* **arrière-petits-fils** /aʀjɛʀpətifis/ *nm* great-grandson

arrière-petit-neveu, *pl* **arrière-petits-neveux** /aʀjɛʀpətinəvø/ *nm* great-great-nephew

arrière-petits-enfants /aʀjɛʀpətizɑ̃fɑ̃/ *nmpl* great-grandchildren

arrière-plan, *pl* **~s** /aʀjɛʀplɑ̃/ *nm* background

arrière-saison, *pl* **~s** /aʀjɛʀsɛzɔ̃/ ▸ p. 536 *nf* late autumn GB, late fall US

arrière-train, *pl* **~s** /aʀjɛʀtʀɛ̃/ *nm* ① (d'animal) hindquarters (*pl*); ② ⚪(d'humain) behind

arrimage /aʀimaʒ/ *nm* ① Naut stowing; ② Astronaut docking

arrimer /aʀime/ [1] *vtr* ① gén to stow [*sth*] away; **~ qch à** *ou* **sur qch** to fasten sth to sth; ② Astronaut to dock (**à** with)

arrivage /aʀivaʒ/ *nm* Comm delivery

arrivant /aʀivɑ̃, ɑ̃t/ *nm,f* **les premiers ~s** the first to arrive; **nouvel ~** newcomer

arrivé, ~e[1] /aʀive/

Ⓐ *pp* ▸ **arriver**

Ⓑ *pp adj* ① (au but) **le dernier ~** the last person to arrive; ② (socialement) **être ~** to have made it

arrivée[2] /aʀive/ *nf* ① (moment) arrival; **après mon ~** after I arrived; **~ au pouvoir** accession to power; **depuis son ~ au pouvoir** since he/she came to power; **guetter l'~ du courrier** to watch out for the post; **trains à l'~** arrivals; **je t'attendrai à l'~ (du train)** I'll meet you off GB *ou* at US your train; ② (de course) finish; **à l'~** at the finish; ③ Tech inlet; **~ d'air** air inlet

arriver /aʀive/ [1]
A vi **[1]** (parvenir) [*personne, avion, lettre*] to arrive; (s'acheminer) [*personne, pluie*] to come; **je suis arrivée avant toi** I got here before you; **l'eau arrive par ce tuyau** the water comes in through this pipe; **j'arrive!** I'm coming!; **j'arrive de Londres** I've just come from London; **~ en courant** to come running up; **~ en tête** to come first; **~ dans les premiers** (en compétition) to be among the first to finish; (à une soirée) to be among the first to arrive; **[2]** (atteindre) **~ à** to reach [*niveau, âge, accord*]; to find [*solution*]; to achieve [*but, résultat*]; **~ aux chevilles** [*eau*] to come up to one's ankles; [*jupe*] to come down to one's ankles; **~ (jusqu')à qn** [*nouvelle, odeur*] to reach sb; **'qu'en est-il du chômage?' —'j'y arrive'** 'what about unemployment?'—'I'm coming to that'; **[3]** (réussir) (socialement) to succeed; gén **~ à faire** to manage to do; **je n'arrive pas à faire** I can't do; **je n'arrive à rien** I'm getting nowhere; **~ à ses fins** to achieve one's ends; **[4]** (aboutir) **en ~ à** to come to; **on en arrive à des absurdités** you end up with nonsense; **j'en arrive à croire que...** I'm beginning to think that...; **[5]** (survenir) [*accident, catastrophe*] to happen; **ce sont des choses qui arrivent** these things happen, it's just one of those things
B v impers **qu'est-il arrivé?** what happened? (à to); **que t'arrive-t-il?** what's wrong with you?; **il arrive un moment où** there comes a time when; **il arrive que qn fasse** sometimes sb does; **est-ce qu'il t'arrive d'y penser?** do you ever think about it?

arriviste /aʀivist/
A adj ruthlessly ambitious
B nmf upstart, arriviste GB

arrogance /aʀɔɡɑ̃s/ nf arrogance

arrogant, ~e /aʀɔɡɑ̃, ɑ̃t/
A adj arrogant
B nm,f arrogant person

arroger: **s'arroger** /aʀɔʒe/ [13] vpr to appropriate [*titre, prérogatives*]; to assume [*droit, pouvoir, fonction*]; **s'~ le monopole de** to claim a monopoly on

arrondi, ~e /aʀɔ̃di/
A adj **[1]** [*objet*] rounded; [*visage, encolure*] round; **femme aux formes ~es** shapely woman; **[2]** [*voyelle*] rounded
B nm (d'objet, de visage) roundness; (d'épaule) curve; (de jupe, robe) hemline; **l'~ du col** the shape of the neck

arrondir /aʀɔ̃diʀ/ [3]
A vtr **[1]** (rendre rond) to round [sth] off [*objet*]; to round off [*bord*]; to open [sth] wide [*yeux*]; **~ une jupe** to make the hem of a skirt even; **coiffure qui arrondit le visage** hairstyle that makes one's face look round; **[2]** (adoucir) to make [sth] softer [*mouvement*]; to polish [*phrase*]; **[3]** (dans un calcul) to round off [*chiffre*]; **~ à l'euro supérieur/inférieur** to round up/down to the nearest euro; **en arrondissant** in round figures; **[4]** (augmenter) to increase [*fortune, patrimoine*]
B **s'arrondir** vpr **[1]** (devenir rond) [*objet*] to become round(ed); [*personne, visage, ventre*] to fill out; [*yeux*] to widen; **[2]** (augmenter) [*fortune*] to be growing
Idiome **~ les angles** to smooth the rough edges

arrondissement /aʀɔ̃dismɑ̃/ nm **[1]** (de ville) arrondissement; **[2]** (petite région) *administrative division in France, larger than a canton but smaller than a department*

ⓘ Arrondissement A subdivision of a *département*. Each *arrondissement* has a *sous-préfet* representing the state administration at local level. In Paris, Lyons and Marseilles, an *arrondissement* is a sub-division of the commune, and has its own *maire* and local council.

arrosage /aʀozaʒ/ nm **[1]** (de plante, champ) watering; (de sol) spraying; **[2]** Mil (bombardement) bombardment

arroser /aʀoze/ [1]
A vtr **[1]** [*personne*] (avec un arrosoir, un tuyau) to water [*plante, champ*]; (avec un arroseur) to sprinkle [*plante, champ*]; [*personne, arroseuse*] to spray [*rue, trottoir*]; [*pluie, rivière*] to water; **région bien arrosée** region with a lot of rainfall; **~ qch d'essence** to douse sth with petrol GB ou gasoline US; **un orage arrive, on va se faire ~○!** there's a storm coming on, we're going to get soaked!; **[2]** Culin to baste [*rôti*]; to sprinkle [*gâteau*] (**de** with); to lace [*cocktail, café*] (**de** with); **[3]** (avec une boisson) to drink to [*promotion, victoire*]; **~ un repas à la bière** to wash a meal down with beer; **[4]** (avec des balles) to spray; (avec des obus) to bombard; **[5]** ○(corrompre) **~ qn** to grease sb's palm○

B **s'arroser**○ vpr (se fêter) **ça s'arrose** that calls for a drink

arroseur /aʀozœʀ/ nm (appareil) sprinkler

arrosoir /aʀozwaʀ/ nm watering can

arsenal, pl -aux /aʀsənal, o/ nm **[1]** Naut naval shipyard; **[2]** Mil arsenal; **[3]** ○(matériel) gear **𝄡; tout un ~ de** a whole battery of

arsenic /aʀsənik/ nm arsenic

art /aʀ/
A nm **[1]** (création, œuvres) art; **l'~ pour l'~** art for art's sake; **[2]** (savoir-faire) art; (habileté) skill; **c'est tout un ~ de créer un parfum** creating a perfume is an art in itself; **c'est du grand ~** it's a real art; **avoir l'~ et la manière** to have the skill and the style (**de faire** to do); **avec ~** (artistement) artistically; (habilement) skilfully^GB; **[3]** (don) knack (**de faire** of doing); **il a l'~ de parler pour ne rien dire** he's very good at talking without saying anything
B arts nmpl arts
Composés **~ déco** art deco; **~ dramatique** drama; **~ floral** flower arranging; **~ de la guerre** art of war; **~ lyrique** opera; **~ nouveau** art nouveau; **~ oratoire** public speaking; **~ de la table** art of entertaining; **~ de vivre** art of living; **~s appliqués** applied arts; **~s décoratifs** decorative arts; **~s ménagers** home economics; **~s plastiques** plastic arts

Artaban /aʀtabɑ̃/ npr **fier comme ~** proud as a peacock

artère /aʀtɛʀ/ nf **[1]** Anat artery; **[2]** (voie) artery; **grande ~, ~ principale** (rue) main thoroughfare ou street; (route) arterial road

artériel, -ielle /aʀteʀjɛl/ adj arterial

arthrite /aʀtʀit/ ▸ p. 195 nf arthritis

arthrose /aʀtʀoz/ ▸ p. 195 nf osteoarthritis

artichaut /aʀtiʃo/ nm (globe) artichoke

Idiome **avoir un cœur d'~** to be fickle (*in love*)

article /aʀtikl/
A nm **[1]** (de journal) article (**sur** about, on); **[2]** Ling article; **[3]** (de dictionnaire) entry; **[4]** Comm item; **~s de consommation courante** basic consumer items; **faire l'~ à qn** (pour vendre) to give sb the sales pitch; fig to try to win sb over; **[5]** Jur (de loi, traité, convention) article; (de contrat) clause
B articles nmpl Comm goods (pl); **~s de sport** sports equipment; **~s de toilette** toiletries
Composés **~ de fond** feature article; **~ de synthèse** synthesis; **~ de tête** editorial
Idiome **être à l'~ de la mort** to be at death's door

articulation /aʀtikylasjɔ̃/ nf **[1]** Anat (jointure) joint; (mouvement) articulation; **[2]** (d'appareil) mobile joint; **[3]** (de son) articulation; **[4]** (de phrase) linking sentence; (de paragraphe) linking paragraph; **[5]** (d'argumentation) (logical) connection; (de dissertation, discours) structure

articulé, ~e /aʀtikyle/ adj [*autobus, membre*] articulated; [*glace*] adjustable

articuler /aʀtikyle/ [1]
A vtr **[1]** (prononcer) to articulate [*mot, son*]; to utter [*phrase*]; **articule quand tu parles!** speak clearly!; **[2]** (assembler) to connect [*pièce*] (**sur** to); **[3]** (structurer) to structure [*idées, discours*]
B **s'articuler** vpr **[1]** Anat **s'~ à** or **avec** to articulate with; **[2]** (en mécanique) **s'~ à** or **sur** to connect to; **[3]** fig **s'~ autour de** to be based on

artifice /aʀtifis/ nm **[1]** (ruse) gén trick; (de séducteur) ploy; **[2]** (moyen) device; **les ~s du style** stylistic devices; **[3]** (résultat) effect; **~s scéniques** stage effects; **[4]** (attitude) artifice; **sans ~** [*être*] unpretentious; [*agir*] unpretentiously

artificiel, -ielle /aʀtifisjɛl/ adj **[1]** (fabriqué) gén artificial; [*port, lac, colline*] man-made; **[2]** (faux) pej [*besoins*] artificial; [*vie, plaisirs*] superficial; [*gaieté, rire*] forced; [*enthousiasme*] false; **[3]** (arbitraire) gén arbitrary; [*argumentation*] contrived

artificiellement /aʀtifisjɛlmɑ̃/ adv **[1]** [*produire*] by artificial means, artificially; **[2]** [*différencier*] arbitrarily

artificier /aʀtifisje/ ▸ p. 372 nm **[1]** (de feux d'artifice) fireworks manufacturer; (d'explosifs) explosives manufacturer; **[2]** (qui désamorce) bomb disposal expert

artillerie /aʀtijʀi/ nf Mil (matériel, corps) artillery; **~ antiaérienne** anti-aircraft guns (pl)

artilleur /aʀtijœʀ/ nm Mil artilleryman, gunner

artisan /aʀtizɑ̃/ ▸ p. 372 nm **[1]** (travailleur) artisan, (self-employed) craftsman; **[2]** (auteur) architect

artisanal, ~e, *mpl* **-aux** /aʀtizanal, o/ *adj* [*activité, foire*] craft (*épith*); [*méthode*] traditional; **les petites entreprises** ~es cottage industries; **de fabrication** ~e [*objet*] hand-crafted; [*aliments, bombe*] home-made

artisanalement /aʀtizanalmã/ *adv* **fabriqué** ~ [*objet*] hand-crafted; [*aliments*] home-made

artisanat /aʀtizana/ *nm* ① (activité) craft industry, cottage industry; ② (groupe social) artisans (*pl*)

(Composé) ~ **d'art** arts and crafts

artiste /aʀtist/ ▸ p. 372

Ⓐ *adj* (créatif) artistic

Ⓑ *nmf* ① (créateur) artist; ② (chanteur, danseur, musicien) artist performer; (de music-hall) artiste; ~ **de cinéma** film actor; ~ **lyrique** opera singer

(Composé) ~ **peintre** painter

artistement /aʀtistəmã/ *adv* artistically

artistique /aʀtistik/ *adj* artistic

artistiquement /aʀtistikmã/ *adv* artistically

as /ɑs/ *nm inv* ① (aux cartes) ace; (au tiercé) **l'**~ number one; ② ○(champion) ace○; ~ **du volant** ace○ ou crack driver; ~ **du ciel** flying ace; **être un** ~ **en cuisine** to be a brilliant○ cook; ③ Sport (au tennis) ace

(Composé) ~ **de pique** lit ace of spades; fig○ [*croupion*] parson's nose; **être ficelé** or **fagoté comme l'**~ **de pique**○ to look a mess

(Idiomes) **être plein aux** ~○ to be loaded○, to be stinking rich○; **passer à l'**~○ [*somme d'argent*] to be ou to go down the drain; [*projet, augmentation*] to go by the board; [*consommations*] gén to be overlooked; (sur une facture) to be left off the bill

AS /aɛs/ *nf* ① (abbr = **Armée secrète**) Secret Army; ② *abbr* ▸ **association**

ascendance /asãdãs/ *nf* ① (ligne généalogique) descent; ② (ancêtres) ancestry

ascendant, ~e /asãdã, ãt/

Ⓐ *adj* [*courbe, trait*] rising; [*mouvement*] upward; [*astre*] ascending

Ⓑ *nm* ① (ancêtre) ancestor; (parent) ascendant; ② (pouvoir) influence (**sur** over); ③ (en astrologie) ascendant

ascenseur /asãsœʀ/ *nm* lift GB, elevator US

(Idiome) **renvoyer l'**~ to return the favour○GB

ascension /asãsjõ/ *nf* ① (en montagne) ascent; **faire l'**~ **de** to climb; ② (d'avion) ascent; ③ fig rise

Ascension /asãsjõ/

Ⓐ *nf* Ascension

Ⓑ ▸ p. 303 *nprf* Géog **île de l'**~ Ascension Island

ascensionnel, **-elle** /asãsjɔnɛl/ *adj* [*mouvement*] upward; [*vitesse*] climbing

ascète /asɛt/ *nmf* ascetic

ascétisme /asetism/ *nm* asceticism

aseptique /asɛptik/ *adj* aseptic

aseptisation /asɛptizasjõ/ *nf* (de pièce) disinfection; (d'instrument) sterilization

aseptisé, ~e /asɛptize/ *adj* [*musique, art*] sanitized; [*vie, monde*] sterile; [*décor, ambiance*] impersonal

aseptiser /asɛptize/ [1] *vtr* to disinfect [*plaie, pièce*]; to sterilize [*instrument*]

asexué, ~e /asɛksɥe/ *adj* Biol asexual

asiatique /azjatik/ *adj* Asian

Asie /azi/ ▸ p. 230 *nprf* Asia; ~ **Mineure** Asia Minor

asile /azil/ *nm* ① gén refuge; Relig sanctuary; **demander l'**~ **politique** to seek political asylum; ② (établissement) ~ **de vieillards** old people's home; ~ **d'aliénés** lunatic asylum; ~ **de nuit** night shelter; **il est bon pour l'**~○ he should be locked up○

asocial, ~e, *pl* **-iaux** /asɔsjal, o/

Ⓐ *adj* antisocial

Ⓑ *nm,f* social misfit

asparagus /aspaʀagys/ *nm* asparagus fern

aspect /aspɛ/ *nm* ① (perspective) side; **voir qch sous son** ~ **positif** to see the good side of sth; **examiner qch sous tous ses** ~**s** to examine sth from every angle; **je n'avais pas vu la situation sous cet** ~ I hadn't seen the situation in that light; ② (facettes) aspect; **par bien des** ~**s** in many respects; ③ (apparence) appearance; **changer d'**~ to change in appearance; **reprendre son** ~ **normal** to look

normal again; **d'**~ **redoutable** formidable-looking; **d'**~ **engageant** pleasant-looking; **avoir l'**~ **du cuir** to look like leather; **garder l'**~ **du neuf** to stay looking new; ④ Ling aspect

asperge /aspɛʀʒ/ *nf* ① (légume) asparagus; ② ○(personne) pej beanpole○, string bean US

asperger /aspɛʀʒe/ [13]

Ⓐ *vtr* (avec un jet) to spray (**de** with); (accidentellement) to splash (**de** with); (pour humecter) to sprinkle (**de** with)

Ⓑ **s'asperger** *vpr* to splash oneself (**de** with); **il s'est aspergé de champagne** he sprayed champagne all over himself

aspérité /aspeʀite/ *nf* ① (de sol, planche) bump (**de** in); (de paroi rocheuse) protrusion sout (**de** on); ② (de voix, caractère) harshness

aspersion /aspɛʀsjõ/ *nf* ① (avec un tuyau, produit) spraying; ② Relig (avant la messe) asperges (+ *v sg*); (au baptême) aspersion

asphalte /asfalt/ *nm* asphalt

asphyxiant, ~e /asfiksjã, ãt/ *adj* asphyxiating

asphyxie /asfiksi/ *nf* ① Méd death by suffocation, asphyxia; ② fig [*de réseau, d'entreprise*] paralysis

asphyxier /asfiksje/ [2]

Ⓐ *vtr* ① Méd to asphyxiate; **mourir asphyxié** to die of suffocation; ② fig to paralyze

Ⓑ **s'asphyxier** *vpr* ① Méd to suffocate to death; (avec un gaz) to asphyxiate; ② fig [*pays, économie*] to become paralyzed

aspic /aspik/ *nm* ① Zool asp; ② Culin aspic; ~ **de légumes** vegetables in aspic

aspirant, ~e /aspiʀã, ãt/

Ⓐ *adj* [*pompe*] suction; [*ventilateur*] extractor

Ⓑ ▸ p. 283 *nm* Mil (armée de terre, de l'air) ≈ senior officer cadet; (marine) ≈ midshipman cadet

aspirateur /aspiʀatœʀ/ *nm* ① (appareil ménager) vacuum cleaner, hoover® GB; ② Méd aspirator

aspiration /aspiʀasjõ/ *nf* ① (désir) aspiration (**à** for); ② (de poussière) sucking up; (de liquide) drawing up; (d'air) drawing in; ③ (en respirant) inhalation; **pendant l'**~ when inhaling, when breathing in

aspirer /aspiʀe/ [1]

Ⓐ *vtr* ① (inhaler) to breathe in [*air*]; to inhale [*fumée*]; ② (avec une paille, un tuyau) to suck up; (avec un aspirateur) to suck up [*poussière*]; to vacuum [*tapis, pièce*]; (avec une pompe) (pour extraire) to pump [*sth*] up [*liquide*]; (pour vider) to pump [*sth*] out; ③ Ling **consonne aspirée** aspirated consonant

Ⓑ **aspirer à** *vtr ind* to yearn for [*calme, liberté*]; to aspire to [*gloire, fonction*]; ~ **à faire** to desire to do

aspirine® /aspiʀin/ *nf* aspirin

(Idiome) **être blanc comme un cachet d'**~ to be lily white

assagir /asaʒiʀ/ [3]

Ⓐ *vtr* to quieten GB ou quiet US [sb] down

Ⓑ **s'assagir** *vpr* (devenir sage) to quieten down GB, to quiet down US; (se ranger) to settle down

assaillant, ~e /asajã, ãt/ *nm,f* attacker, assailant; **les** ~**s** Mil the attacking forces

assaillir /asajiʀ/ [28] *vtr* ① (attaquer) [*ennemi*] to attack; [*pluie*] to buffet; ② (envahir) [*doute*] to plague; ③ (se précipiter sur) [*mendiant*] to assail; [*journaliste*] to set upon; ~ **de questions** to bombard with questions

assainir /aseniʀ/ [3]

Ⓐ *vtr* to clean up [*maison, rivière, atmosphère, organisation*]; to stabilize [*économie*]; to streamline [*entreprise, gestion*]; ~ **les finances** to make the finances healthier

Ⓑ **s'assainir** *vpr* [*atmosphère, environnement*] to become healthier; [*marché, situation*] to stabilize

assainissement /asenismã/ *nm* ① lit (de logement, rivière, région, d'atmosphère) cleaning up; ② fig (de situation) stabilization; (d'entreprise) streamlining

assaisonnement /asɛzɔnmã/ *nm* (vinaigrette) dressing; (sel, poivre, épices) seasoning

assaisonner /asɛzɔne/ [1] *vtr* (avec du sel, du poivre, des épices) to season (**de** with); (avec de la vinaigrette) to dress (**de** with)

assassin, ~e /asasɛ̃, in/

Ⓐ *adj* [*main, regard*] murderous; [*campagne*] vicious; **remarque** ~**e** poisoned arrow; **faire** or **lancer une remarque** ~**e à qn** to make a scathing remark to sb

Ⓑ *nm* gén murderer; (par idéologie) assassin; **'à l'**~**!'** 'murder!'

assassinat /asasina/ *nm* gén murder; (idéologique, politique) assassination

assassiner /asasine/ [1] *vtr* ⓵ (tuer) gén to murder; (par idéologie) to assassinate; ⓶ (détruire) to destroy; ⓷ ᵒ(critiquer) to slateᵒ

assaut /aso/ *nm* gén attack (**de** on); (de place forte) assault (**de** on); **donner l'~, monter à l'~** to attack; **se lancer** *or* **monter à l'~ de** to launch an attack on; **prendre d'~** to storm; **le buffet a été pris d'~** the buffet was besieged; **à l'~!** attack!; **les ~s du froid** the onslaught of cold weather

assèchement /asɛʃmɑ̃/ *nm* lit (en drainant) draining; (en vidant) emptying; (dû au climat) drying up *ou* out

assécher /aseʃe/ [14]
A *vtr* lit (drainer) to drain; (vider) to empty; (dessécher) to dry up
B **s'assécher** *vpr* [étang, puits] to dry up; [marais, sol] to dry out

ASSEDIC /asedik/ *nf* (abbr = **Association pour l'emploi dans l'industrie et le commerce**) *organization managing unemployment contributions and payments*

assemblage /asɑ̃blaʒ/ *nm* ⓵ (de moteur, meuble) assembly (**de** of); (de feuillets) gathering; (de vêtement) sewing together; **l'~ des pièces par soudure** the welding together of parts; ⓶ (en menuiserie) joint; ⓷ (d'objets, idées, de données) collection, assemblage; (de couleurs, sons) combination; ⓸ Ordinat assembly

assemblée /asɑ̃ble/ *nf* ⓵ (foule) gathering; Relig ~ (**de fidèles**) congregation; ⓶ (réunion convoquée) meeting; ⓷ Pol (groupe élu) assembly

(Composés) ~ **générale**, **AG** general meeting; **l'Assemblée nationale** the French National Assembly

> ℹ️ **Assemblée nationale** The lower house of the French parliament, in which 577 *députés* are elected for a five-year term. A member, who must be at least 23 years old, has to be elected by at least 50% of the votes cast and, if necessary, a second round of voting is held to ensure this. Party affiliation is indicated by a *député*'s allocation to a seat within a left-right gradation in the semi-circular chamber.
> The *Assemblée nationale* passes laws, votes on the Budget, and questions ministers (who cannot be *députés*).

assembler /asɑ̃ble/ [1]
A *vtr* ⓵ (monter) to assemble, to put [sth] together [pièces, moteur]; to make up, to sew [sth] together [vêtement, pull]; ~ **des pièces par collage** to glue pieces together; ⓶ (disposer ensemble) to combine [mots]; [sons]; ⓷ Ordinat to assemble
B **s'assembler** *vpr* [foule] to gather; [conseillers, députés] to assemble

(Idiome) **qui se ressemble s'assemble** Prov birds of a feather stick together Prov

asséner /asene/ [14] *vtr* ⓵ (donner) ~ **un coup à qn/qch** lit, fig to deal sb/sth a blow; ⓶ fig (lancer) to hurl [questions, injures] (**à** at); to fling [remarque]; to fling back [réplique]; **une réplique bien assénée** a well-aimed retort

assentiment /asɑ̃timɑ̃/ *nm* assent, consent

asseoir /aswaʀ/ [41]
A *vtr* ⓵ to sit [sb] up [personne allongée]; **faire ~ qn** (contraindre) to make sb sit down; (convier) to offer a seat to sb; ⓶ Constr to seat, to bed [fondations]; ⓷ to establish [autorité, réputation]; to set up [argument]; ⓸ to base [cotisation, impôt]; ⓹ ᵒto staggerᵒ, to astound
B **s'asseoir** *vpr* ⓵ [personne debout] to sit (down); [personne allongée] to sit up; **s'~ à une** *or* **autour d'une table** lit to sit down at a table; fig to sit down at the negotiating table; ⓶ ᵒ(mépriser) **s'~ sur** not to give a damn aboutᵒ

assermenté, ~e /asɛʀmɑ̃te/ *adj* [témoin, expert] sworn (épith), on oath (*jamais épith*)

assertion /asɛʀsjɔ̃/ *nf* assertion

asservir /asɛʀviʀ/ [3] *vtr* to enslave [peuple, personne]; to subjugate [pays] (**à** to); to control [presse]; **être asservi à** to be a slave to

asservissement /asɛʀvismɑ̃/ *nm* fml ⓵ (de pays) subjugation; (de peuple) enslavement; (de presse) control; ⓶ (état) subjection (**à** to); **maintenir un pays dans l'~** to keep a country enslaved; ⓷ fig (de personne) subservience (**à** to); ⓸ Tech (système) servomechanism

assesseur /asesœʀ/ *nm* Jur magistrate's assistant

assez /ase/ ▸ p. 483 *adv*

> ⚠️ Lorsqu'il signifie 'suffisamment', *assez* se traduit par *enough*: *les pommes ne sont pas assez mûres* = the apples are not ripe enough; *tu ne manges pas assez* = you don't eat enough.
> On notera la place de *enough* avec un adjectif: *assez grand (pour faire)* = tall enough (to do). ▸ 1 ci-dessous.
> Lorsqu'il est utilisé pour atténuer un jugement *assez* se traduit par *quite*: *il est assez grand* = he's quite tall. ▸ 2 ci-dessous.

⓵ (évaluation) enough; ~ **de temps** enough time; **serons-nous ~?** will there be enough of us?; **il ne travaille pas ~** he doesn't work hard enough; **j'en aurai ~ de quatre** four will be quite enough (for me); **en avoir ~**ᵒ to be fed upᵒ (**de** with); **avez-vous ~ mangé?** have you had enough to eat?; ⓶ (jugement) quite; ~ **jeune** quite young; ~ **souvent** quite often, fairly often; **je suis ~ pressé** I'm in rather a hurry; **je suis ~ d'accord** I tend to agree; **je les trouve ~ ennuyeux** I find them rather boring

assidu, ~e /asidy/ *adj* [travail] diligent; [soins] constant; [visites] regular; [élève] diligent, assiduous; [employé, chercheur] hard-working; [amateur de théâtre, lecteur] devoted, assiduous; [amoureux] devoted

assiduité /asidɥite/ *nf* ⓵ (application) diligence; **avec ~** [travailler] diligently; [s'entraîner] assiduously; [lire, regarder] regularly; [courtiser] assiduously; ⓶ (fréquentation régulière) regular attendance
B **assiduités** *nfpl* assiduities

assidûment /asidymɑ̃/ *adv* [travailler] diligently; [fréquenter, s'entraîner] assiduously

assiégeant, ~e /asjeʒɑ̃, ɑ̃t/ *nm,f* besieger

assiéger /asjeʒe/ [15] *vtr* Mil, fig to besiege

assiette /asjɛt/ *nf* ⓵ (vaisselle, contenu) plate; **finis ton ~** finish what's on your plate; **il n'a pas touché à son ~** he hasn't touched his food; ⓶ (à cheval) seat; **perdre son ~** to become unseated; ⓷ (d'imposition) ~ (**fiscale**) tax base; **détermination de l'~ fiscale** tax assessment

(Composés) ~ **anglaise** Culin assorted cold meats (pl); ~ **creuse** soup plate; ~ **à dessert** dessert plate; ~ **plate** dinner plate; ~ **à soupe = ~ creuse**

(Idiome) **ne pas être dans son ~** to be out of sorts

assiettée /asjete/ *nf* plateful

assignation /asiɲasjɔ̃/ *nf* ⓵ (attribution de crédits) allocation; ⓶ Jur ~ (**à comparaître**) (de défendeur) summons (sg); (de témoin) subpoena

(Composés) ~ **en justice** summons to appear before the court; ~ **en référé** urgent summons (*to appear before the court within three days*); ~ **à résidence** house arrest

assigner /asiɲe/ [1]
A *vtr* ⓵ to assign [tâche, rôle] (**à** to); to allocate [crédits] (**à** to); ⓶ to fix [date, limite] (**à** to); to ascribe [valeur] (**à** to); ⓷ Jur ~ **à comparaître** to summons [défendeur]; to subpoena [témoin]; ~ **qn à résidence** to put sb under house arrest
B **s'assigner** *vpr* ~ **un but** to set oneself a goal

assimilable /asimilabl/ *adj* ⓵ (comparable) ~ **à** comparable to; ⓶ Jur (équivalent) ~ **à** [personne] deemed; [avantage, pratique] deemed equivalent to; ⓷ (par l'esprit) **des notions ~s dès l'âge de cinq ans** ideas which can be assimilated from the age of five; ⓸ [population, substance] easily assimilated (**par** by)

assimilation /asimilasjɔ̃/ *nf* ⓵ (comparaison) comparison (**de qch à qch** between sth and sth); ⓶ (de connaissances, population, substance) assimilation

assimilé, ~e /asimile/ *nm* **cadres et ~s** management and those in the same category

assimiler /asimile/ [1]
A *vtr* ⓵ (considérer équivalent) ~ **leur silence à un refus** to consider their silence tantamount to a refusal; ~ **les travailleurs à des machines** to treat workers as machines; ⓶ Jur ~ **une prime à un salaire** to consider a bonus equivalent to a salary; **être assimilé cadre** to have executive status; ⓷ (absorber) to assimilate [population, leçon, substance]; to learn [métier]
B **s'assimiler** *vpr* ⓵ [style, méthode] to be comparable (**à** to); ⓶ [population] to become assimilated; [substances] to be assimilated

assis, ~e¹ /asi, iz/
A *pp* ▸ **asseoir**

B *pp adj* [1] (position) **être** ~ (et non debout) to be sitting down; (et non allongé) to be sitting up; (installé sur un siège) to be sitting down *ou* seated; **j'étais** ~ **à mon bureau** I was sitting at my desk; **rester** ~ **des heures à attendre** to sit about waiting for hours; **reste** ~ (ne te lève pas) don't get up; (ne bouge pas) sit still; ~**!** (à un chien) sit!; **on est mal** ~ **dans cette voiture** the seats in this car are uncomfortable; [2] [*réputation*] well-established (*épith*); [3] °staggered

C *adj* [*personne, position*] seated

assise² /asiz/

A *nf* (fondement) basis, foundation

B assises *nfpl* gén meeting; Pol conference; Jur assizes

assistanat /asistana/ *nm* [1] Univ assistantship; [2] (aide de l'État) *pej* charity

assistance /asistɑ̃s/ *nf* [1] (secours) gén assistance; (à l'étranger) aid; **demander l'**~ **d'un avocat** to ask for legal representation; ~ **médicale** medical care; ~ **judiciaire** legal aid; **porter** *or* **prêter** ~ **à qn** to assist sb; [2] (auditoire) audience; [3] (présence) attendance (**à** at)

(Composés) ~ **respiratoire** artificial respiration; **Assistance publique** ≈ welfare services

assistant, ~**e** /asistɑ̃, ɑ̃t/ ▸ p. 372 *nm,f* gén assistant; Scol (language) assistant; Méd assistant doctor

(Composés) ~ **de production** Cin, TV production assistant; ~ **personnel** Ordinat personal digital assistant, PDA; ~ **réalisateur** Cin, TV assistant director; ~**e maternelle** (nourrice) childminder GB, babysitter US; ~**e sociale** social worker

assisté, ~**e** /asiste/

A *adj* [1] [*personne*] gén assisted (**de** by); (par l'État) receiving benefit GB, on welfare US; [2] Ordinat ~ **par ordinateur** computer-aided (*épith*); [3] Aut [*freins, direction*] power (*épith*)

B *nm,f person receiving benefit* GB *ou welfare* US; **avoir une mentalité d'**~ *pej* to think one can live on government handouts *pej*

assister /asiste/ [1]

A *vtr* [1] (aider) to assist (**de, par** by); **dans** with); [2] (secourir) to aid [*réfugiés, pays*]

B assister à *vtr ind* [1] (être présent) ~ **à** to be at [*mariage, spectacle*]; to be present at [*couronnement*]; to attend [*réunion, cours*]; [2] (observer) ~ **à** to witness

associatif, **-ive** /asɔsjatif, iv/ *adj* [1] Ling, Math, Psych [*rapport, loi, lien*] associative; [2] Jur, Sociol [*personne*] belonging to an association; [*réseau, tissu*] of associations; **les milieux** ~**s** associations; **mouvement** ~ (ensemble) association; (tendance) trend toward(s) the forming of associations; **vie associative** community life

association /asɔsjasjɔ̃/ *nf* [1] gén association; **en** ~ **avec** in association with; [2] (de couleurs, styles, substances) combination

(Composés) ~ **à but non lucratif** non-profitmaking organization GB, non-profit organization US; ~ **de malfaiteurs** Jur criminal conspiracy; ~ **sportive**, **AS** sports association

associé, ~**e** /asɔsje/

A *adj* (after n) [*membre, directeur, professeur*] associate (*épith*); [*entreprises, organismes*] associated (*épith*)

B *nm,f* associate, partner

associer /asɔsje/ [2]

A *vtr* [1] (réunir) to bring together [*personnes*]; [2] (faire partager) ~ **qn/qch à** to include sb/sth in; [3] (combiner) to combine [*objets*] (**à** *or* **et** with); [4] (rapprocher) to associate (**à** with)

B s'associer *vpr* [1] (s'unir) [*personnes, sociétés*] to go into partnership, to link up (**à, avec** with); **s'**~ **pour faire** to join forces to do; [2] (se rallier) **s'**~ **à** to join [*mouvement*]; to join in [*décision, opération*]; [3] (partager) **s'**~ **à la peine de qn** to share in sb's sorrow; [4] (se combiner) (matériellement) to combine, to be combined (**à** with; **pour faire** in order to do); (abstraitement) to be associated (**à** with; **pour faire** to do)

assoiffé, ~**e** /aswafe/ *adj* [1] lit thirsty; [2] fig ~ **de** thirsting *ou* hungry for [*pouvoir, liberté*]; ~ **de sang** bloodthirsty

assombrir /asɔ̃bʀiʀ/ [3]

A *vtr* [1] lit [*arbres, couleur*] to make [sth] dark [*lieu*]; [*nuages*] to darken [*ciel*]; [2] fig [*nouvelle, événement*] to cast a shadow over [*période, soirée*]; [*tristesse*] to cloud [*visage*]

B s'assombrir *vpr* [1] lit [*ciel*] to darken; [2] fig [*visage, perspectives*] to become gloomy

assommant°, ~**e** /asɔmɑ̃, ɑ̃t/ *adj* [1] (ennuyeux) deadly boring°; [2] (agaçant) **tu es** ~ **avec tes questions** you're a real pain° with your questions

assommer /asɔme/ [1] *vtr* [1] (étourdir) to knock [sb] senseless; ~ **qn à coups de massue** to club sb senseless; [2] °(ennuyer) to bore [sb] to tears°; [3] °(agacer) ~ **qn** to get on sb's nerves; [4] °(accabler) [*nouvelle*] to stagger; [*chaleur*] to overcome

Assomption /asɔ̃psjɔ̃/ *nf* Assumption

assorti, ~**e** /asɔʀti/ *adj* [1] [*couleurs, linge*] matching; **bien/mal** ~ well-/ill-matched; **un abat-jour** ~ **aux rideaux** a lampshade that matches the curtains; [2] (varié) [*pâtisseries, bonbons*] assorted

assortiment /asɔʀtimɑ̃/ *nm* [1] (d'outils, de pinceaux) set; (de fromages, charcuterie, légumes) assortment; (de produits de beauté) selection; [2] (de tons, couleurs) match; [3] Comm stock

assortir /asɔʀtiʀ/ [3]

A *vtr* [1] (harmoniser) to match [*couleurs, vêtements*] (**à** to; **avec** with); to match [*convives*]; [2] (compléter) ~ **qch de qch** to add sth to sth; [3] Comm (approvisionner) to stock [*magasin*]

B s'assortir *vpr* [1] [*couleurs, objets, vêtements*] to match; **s'**~ **à** *or* **avec qch** to match sth; [2] (être complété) **s'**~ **de qch** to come with

assoupir /asupiʀ/ [3]

A *vtr* [1] (endormir) to make [sb] drowsy [*personne*]; [2] (atténuer) to dull [*sens*]

B s'assoupir *vpr* [1] lit [*personne*] to doze off; [2] fig [*enthousiasme, passion*] to wane; [*haine*] to abate; [*querelle*] to die down; [*activité économique*] to be in a lull

assoupissement /asupismɑ̃/ *nm* (somnolence) drowsiness; (sommeil) doze

assouplir /asupliʀ/ [3]

A *vtr* [1] (rendre moins rigide) to make [sth] supple [*cuir*]; to soften [sth] up [*chaussures*]; to soften [*linge, lainage*]; to make [sth] more supple [*corps, membres*]; to loosen [*muscles*]; [2] (rendre moins strict) to relax [*règlement, politique, sanctions*]; to make [sth] more flexible [*méthode, système*]; to make [sth] less strict [*régime*]

B s'assouplir *vpr* [1] (devenir moins rigide) [*chaussures, linge, lainage*] to get softer; [*corps, membres, cuir*] to become more supple; fig [*caractère, personne*] to become more accommodating; [2] (devenir moins strict) [*règlement, politique*] to become more relaxed; [*position, attitude, système*] to become more flexible

assouplissant /asuplisɑ̃/ *nm* fabric softener

assouplissement /asuplismɑ̃/ *nm* [1] (de cuir, lainage) softening; (de linge) conditioning; [2] Sport **faire des** ~**s** *or* **des exercices d'**~ to limber up; [3] (de règlement, politique, d'attitude) relaxing

assouplisseur /asuplisœʀ/ *nm* fabric conditioner

assourdir /asuʀdiʀ/ [3]

A *vtr* [1] (rendre sourd) to deafen [*personne*]; [2] (atténuer) to muffle [*bruit*]

B s'assourdir *vpr* [1] [*bruit*] to become muffled; [2] [*phonème*] to become voiceless

assourdissant, ~**e** /asuʀdisɑ̃, ɑ̃t/ *adj* deafening

assourdissement /asuʀdismɑ̃/ *nm* [1] (de personne) (action) deafening; (état) temporary deafness; [2] (de bruit) muffling; [3] (de phonème) devoicing

assouvir /asuviʀ/ [3] *vtr* to satisfy [*faim, désir, curiosité*]; to assuage [*colère, passion*]

assouvissement /asuvismɑ̃/ *nm* [1] (action) (de faim, désir, curiosité) satisfying; (de colère) assuaging; [2] (résultat) satisfaction

assujetti, ~**e** /asyʒeti/

A *adj* ~ **à** liable for [*impôt*]; ~ **à la sécurité sociale** obliged to participate in the French national health and pensions system

B *nm,f* (à un impôt) person liable for tax; (à une cotisation) contributor

assujettir /asyʒetiʀ/ [3]

A *vtr* [1] (astreindre) to subject (**à** to); [2] (soumettre) to subjugate, to subdue [*pays, peuple*]; [3] (fixer) to secure

B s'assujettir *vpr* [*personne*] to submit (**à** to)

assujettissement /asyʒetismɑ̃/ *nm* subjection (**à** to); ~ **à l'impôt** liability to tax

assumer /asyme/ [1]

A *vtr* [1] to take [*responsabilité*]; to hold [*fonctions*]; to meet [*coûts*]; **2**‣ to come to terms with [*condition, identité, passé*]; to accept [*conséquences*]

B **s'assumer** *vpr* **1**‣ to come to terms with oneself; **2**‣ to take responsibility for oneself

assurance /asyʀɑ̃s/ *nf* **1**‣ (aisance, aplomb) (self-)confidence; (maîtrise) assurance; **montrer de l'∼** to be self-confident; **prendre de l'∼** to gain confidence; **regard plein d'∼** confident look; **avec ∼** confidently; **2**‣ (promesse) assurance; (certitude) certainty; **obtenir** *or* **recevoir l'∼ que** to be assured that; **donner à qn l'∼ que** to assure sb that; **3**‣ (garantie) insurance (**contre** against); (contrat) insurance (policy); (compagnie) insurance company; (prime) insurance (premium); **souscrire une ∼ contre l'incendie** to insure against fire; **avoir une bonne ∼** to be well insured; **4**‣ (prestations) benefit **₵** GB, benefits (*pl*) US; **5**‣ (en alpinisme) belaying

⬭Composés⬮ **∼ automobile** car insurance; **∼ chômage** (système) unemployment insurance; (prestations) unemployment benefit GB *ou* benefits (*pl*) US; **∼ incendie** fire insurance; **∼ individuelle accident** personal accident insurance; **∼ maladie** (système) health insurance; (prestations) sickness benefit GB *ou* benefits (*pl*) US; **∼ maternité** maternity benefit GB *ou* benefits (*pl*) US; **∼ mixte** endowment policy *ou* insurance; **∼ multirisque** comprehensive insurance; **∼ multirisque habitation** comprehensive household insurance; **∼ mutuelle** (association) mutual insurance company; **∼ responsabilité civile** third-party insurance; **∼ scolaire** pupil's personal accident insurance; **∼s sociales** social insurance **₵**; **∼ au tiers** third-party insurance; **∼ tous risques** comprehensive insurance; **∼ vieillesse** state pension; **∼ voyage** travel insurance

assurance-crédit, *pl* **assurances-crédit** /asyʀɑ̃skʀedi/ *nf* credit insurance

assurance-vie, *pl* **assurances-vie** /asyʀɑ̃svi/ *nf* life insurance

assuré, ∼e /asyʀe/
A *pp* ▸ **assurer**
B *pp adj* **1**‣ (sûr) sure, certain (**de faire** of doing); **75% des voix leur sont ∼es** they are sure of 75% of the vote; **soyez ∼ de ma reconnaissance** I am very grateful to you; **2**‣ (protégé) insured; **la personne ∼e** the insured party; **non ∼** uninsured
C *adj* **1**‣ [*démarche, air*] confident; [*main*] steady; **dit-il d'une voix ∼e** *or* **d'un ton ∼** he said confidently; **mal ∼** [*pas, main*] unsteady; [*geste, ton*] nervous; [*voix*] unsteady, trembling; **2**‣ [*échec, réussite*] certain; [*situation, succès*] assured; **opération dont la réussite est ∼e** operation which is sure to succeed
D *nmf* insured party

⬭Composé⬮ **∼ social** social insurance contributor

assurément /asyʀemɑ̃/ *adv* gén definitely; (pour autoriser) most certainly; **∼ pas** gén definitely not; (pour refuser) certainly not

assurer /asyʀe/ [1]
A *vtr* **1**‣ (affirmer) **∼ à qn que** to assure sb that; **ce n'est pas drôle, je t'assure** believe me, it's no joke; **qu'est-ce que tu es maladroit, je t'assure⁰**! you really are clumsy!; **2**‣ (faire part à) **∼ qn de** to assure sb of [*affection, soutien*]; **3**‣ (protéger) to insure [*biens*] (**contre** against); **4**‣ (effectuer) to carry out [*maintenance, tâche*]; to provide [*service*]; (prendre en charge) to see to [*livraison*]; **le service ne sera pas assuré demain** there will be no service tomorrow; **∼ la liaison entre** [*train, car*] to run between; [*ferry*] to sail between; [*compagnie*] to operate between; **∼ la gestion de** to manage; **∼ sa propre défense** Jur to conduct one's own defence⁰ᴮ; **∼ les fonctions de directeur** to be director; **5**‣ (garantir) to ensure [*bonheur, gloire*]; to ensure, to secure [*victoire, paix, promotion*]; to give [*monopole, revenu*]; (par des efforts, une intervention) to secure [*droit, poste*] (**à qn** for sb); to assure [*position, avenir*]; to protect [*frontière*]; **il veut leur ∼ une vieillesse paisible** he wants to give them a peaceful old age; **l'exposition devrait ∼ 800 emplois** the exhibition ought to create 800 jobs; **∼ ses vieux jours** to provide for one's old age; **6**‣ (rendre stable) to steady [*escabeau*]; (fixer) to secure [*corde*]; to fasten [*volet*]; **7**‣ (ne pas risquer) **∼ une balle** to play a safe ball; **8**‣ (en alpinisme) to belay [*grimpeur*]
B *vi* **1**‣ ⁰(être à la hauteur) to be up to the mark⁰; **∼ en chimie** to be good at chemistry; **∼ avec les filles** to have a way

with the girls; **2**‣ Sport to play it safe
C **s'assurer** *vpr* **1**‣ (vérifier) **s'∼ de qch** to make sure of sth, to check on sth; **s'∼ que** to make sure that, to check that; **2**‣ (se procurer) to secure [*avantage, aide*]; **s'∼ une bonne retraite** to arrange to get a good pension; **s'∼ une position de repli** to make sure one has a fall-back position; **3**‣ (prendre une assurance) to take out insurance; **s'∼ contre l'incendie/sur la vie** to take out fire/life insurance; **4**‣ (se prémunir) **s'∼ contre** to insure against [*éventualité, risque*]; **5**‣ (en alpinisme) to belay oneself

assureur /asyʀœʀ/ ▸ p. 372 *nm* (contractant) underwriter; (intermédiaire) insurance agent; (compagnie) insurance company

⬭Composé⬮ **∼ conseil** insurance adviser *ou* consultant

astérisque /asteʀisk/ *nm* asterisk

astéroïde /asteʀɔid/ *nm* asteroid

asthmatique /asmatik/ *adj, nmf* asthmatic

asthme /asm/ ▸ p. 195 *nm* asthma

asticot /astiko/ *nm* maggot

asticoter⁰ /astikɔte/ [1] *vtr* to needle⁰

astigmate /astigmat/ *adj* astigmatic

astiquer /astike/ [1] *vtr* to polish

astral, ∼e, *mpl* **-aux** /astʀal, o/ *adj* astral

astre /astʀ/ *nm* star; **l'∼ du jour** liter the sun; **l'∼ de la nuit** liter the moon

astreignant, ∼e /astʀɛɲɑ̃, ɑ̃t/ *adj* [*tâche, horaires*] demanding; [*discipline, mesures*] strict

astreindre /astʀɛ̃dʀ/ [55]
A *vtr* **∼ qn à qch** [*personne*] to force sth upon sb; [*réglementation*] to bind sb to sth; **∼ qn à faire** to compel sb to do
B **s'astreindre** *vpr* **s'∼ à qch** to subject oneself to sth; **s'∼ à faire** to force oneself to do

astreinte /astʀɛ̃t/ *nf* **1**‣ Jur periodic penalty payment; **2**‣ (contrainte) liter constraint

astringent, ∼e /astʀɛ̃ʒɑ̃, ɑ̃t/ *adj* astringent

astrologie /astʀɔlɔʒi/ *nf* astrology

astrologique /astʀɔlɔʒik/ *adj* astrological

astrologue /astʀɔlɔg/ ▸ p. 372 *nmf* astrologer

astronaute /astʀɔnot/ ▸ p. 372 *nmf* astronaut

astronautique /astʀɔnotik/ *nf* astronautics (+ *v sg*)

astronome /astʀɔnɔm/ ▸ p. 372 *nmf* astronomer

astronomie /astʀɔnɔmi/ *nf* astronomy

astronomique /astʀɔnɔmik/ *adj* astronomical

astrophysicien, -ienne /astʀɔfizisjɛ̃, ɛn/ ▸ p. 372 *nm,f* astrophysicist

astrophysique /astʀɔfizik/ *nf* astrophysics (+ *v sg*)

astuce /astys/ *nf* **1**‣ (ingéniosité) gén cleverness; (sagacité) shrewdness, astuteness; **être plein d'∼** [*enfant*] to be very clever; [*adulte*] to be extremely shrewd; **2**‣ (truc) trick; **toute l'∼ consiste à faire** the trick's in doing; **une ∼ juridique** a crafty legal manoeuvreᴳᴮ; **3**‣ (jeu de mots) pun; (plaisanterie) joke

astucieux, -ieuse /astysjø, øz/ *adj* (ingénieux) clever; (sagace) sharp, shrewd

asymétrie /asimetʀi/ *nf* asymmetry

asymétrique /asimetʀik/ *adj* asymmetrical

atchoum /atʃum/ *nm* (also onomat) atishoo

atelier /atəlje/ *nm* **1**‣ (d'artisan, de bricoleur) workshop; (d'artiste) studio; (de couturier) design studio; **2**‣ (dans une usine) shop, workshop; **3**‣ (groupe de travail) working group; (séance de travail) workshop

atermoiement /atɛʀmwamɑ̃/ *nm* procrastination **₵**

atermoyer /atɛʀmwaje/ [23] *vi* to procrastinate

athée /ate/
A *adj* atheistic
B *nmf* atheist

athéisme /ateism/ *nm* atheism

athlète /atlɛt/ *nmf* athlete; **carrure d'∼** athletic build

athlétique /atletik/ *adj* athletic

athlétisme /atletism/ ▸ p. 327 *nm* athletics (+ *v sg*) GB, track and field events; **faire de l'∼** to do athletics

Atlantique /atlɑ̃tik/ ▸ p. 406 *nprm* **l'(océan) ∼** the Atlantic (Ocean)

atlas /atlas/ *nm inv* **1**‣ (livre) atlas; **2**‣ (vertèbre) atlas

atmosphère /atmɔsfɛʀ/ *nf* lit, fig atmosphere; **j'ai besoin de changer d'~** I need a change of air

atmosphérique /atmɔsfeʀik/ *adj* atmospheric

ATNC /ateɛnse/ *nm* (*abbr* = **agent transmissible non conventionnel**) Biol, Méd unconventional transmissible agent, prion

atoll /atɔl/ *nm* atoll

atome /atom/ *nm* atom

(Idiomes) **ne pas avoir un ~ de courage** not to have an ounce of courage; **avoir des ~s crochus**○ **avec qn** to hit it off with sb○

atomique /atɔmik/ *adj* [*énergie, centrale, arme*] nuclear; [*bombe, nombre, structure*] atomic

atomisation /atɔmizasjɔ̃/ *nf* (de pouvoir, parti, société) fragmentation, atomization

atomiser /atɔmize/ [1] *vtr* to fragment [*secteur, parti*]

atomiseur /atɔmizœʀ/ *nm* spray, atomizer

atomiste /atɔmist/

A *adj* [1] [*savant, chercheur*] nuclear; [*structure, théorie*] atomic; [2] Philos atomist

B *nmf* [1] ▸ p. 372 nuclear scientist; [2] Philos atomist

atone /atɔn/ *adj* [1] [*vie, groupe*] apathetic; [*personne*] lifeless; [2] [*mot, syllabe*] unstressed, unaccented

atonie /atɔni/ *nf* (de personne, pouvoir, marché) sluggishness, apathy; (de regard, voix) lifelessness

atonique /atɔnik/ *adj* atonic

atours† /atuʀ/ *nmpl* finery **₵**; **mettre ses plus beaux ~** to deck oneself out in all one's finery

atout /atu/ *nm* [1] Jeux (carte) trump; (couleur) trumps (*pl*); **c'est ~ cœur** hearts are trumps; [2] fig (avantage) asset; (avantage sur les autres) trump card; **jouer son dernier ~** to play one's last card; **~ supplémentaire** additional advantage; **avoir tous les ~s en main** to hold all the aces; **mettre tous les ~s dans son jeu** to leave nothing to chance

âtre /ɑtʀ/ *nm* hearth

atroce /atʀɔs/ *adj* [1] [*blessure, sentiment, nouvelle*] dreadful; [*souffrance, douleur*] atrocious; [*peur*] terrible; [*supplice*] horrific; [*crime, mort*] horrible; [*acte, spectacle*] horrifying; [2] ○[*nourriture, temps, accent*] atrocious, appalling; **tu es ~!** you are dreadful!

atrocement /atʀɔsmɑ̃/ *adv* [1] [*mutiler*] dreadfully; [*souffrir*] horribly, terribly; **j'ai ~ mal** I'm in agony; [2] ○[*ennuyeux, bête*] dreadfully; [*laid*] atrociously

atrocité /atʀɔsite/ *nf* [1] (caractère) atrocity; [2] (crime) atrocity; [3] (calomnie) **dire des ~s sur** to say dreadful things about; [4] ○(chose laide) hideous monstrosity; [5] (laideur) **c'est d'une ~!** it's absolutely hideous!

atrophie /atʀɔfi/ *nf* Méd, fig atrophy

atrophier: s'atrophier /atʀɔfje/ [2] *vpr* [1] Méd to atrophy; **bras atrophié** wasted arm; [2] fig [*facultés*] to atrophy; [*économie, marché*] to decline

attabler: s'attabler /atable/ [1] *vpr* to sit down at (the) table

attachant, ~e /ataʃɑ̃, ɑ̃t/ *adj* [*personne*] charming, engaging; [*caractère*] charming; [*animal*] sweet

attache /ataʃ/ *nf* [1] gén tie; (ficelle) string; (corde) rope; (courroie) strap; [2] Anat (articulation) joint; (de muscle) point of attachment; **avoir des ~s fines** to have delicate ankles and wrists; [3] fig (lien) tie

attaché, ~e /ataʃe/ ▸ p. 372 *nm,f* attaché

(Composé) **~ d'administration** administrative assistant

attachement /ataʃmɑ̃/ *nm* [1] (sentimental) attachment (à to); [2] (de principe) commitment (à to)

attacher /ataʃe/ [1]

A *vtr* [1] (lier) gén to tie [*personne, animal, mains*] (à to); to tether, to fasten [*laisse, corde*] (à to); (avec une chaîne) to chain [*chien*] (à to); to lock [*bicyclette*] (à to); (en entourant) to tie up [*personne, paquet*]; **~ qn à un poteau** to tie sb to a stake; **~ ses lacets** to tie (up) one's laces; **~ ses chaussures** to do up one's shoes; [2] (fermer) to fasten [*ceinture, collier, vêtement*]; [3] (accorder) to attach [*importance, valeur*]; [4] (employer) **~ qn à son service** to take sb into one's service, to employ sb; [5] (associer) **les privilèges attachés à un poste** the privileges attached to a post; **~ son nom à une découverte** to link one's name to a discovery

B *vi* (coller) to stick (à to)

C **s'attacher** *vpr* [1] (se fixer) to fasten, to do up (**par derrière**

at the back); **le lierre s'attache aux pierres** ivy clings to stones; [2] (s'efforcer) **s'~ à démontrer** to set out to demonstrate; [3] (se lier affectivement) **s'~ à qn/qch** to become attached to sb/sth, to grow fond of sb/sth

attaquable /atakabl/ *adj* [1] [*lieu, place*] **facilement ~** easy to attack; [2] [*théorie, position*] shaky; [3] [*testament*] contestable

attaquant, ~e /atakɑ̃, ɑ̃t/ *nm,f* [1] Mil attacker; [2] Sport gén attacker; (au football) striker

attaque /atak/ *nf* [1] Mil attack; **passer à l'~** to move onto the attack; **à l'~!** charge!; [2] (de banque, magasin) raid; (de personne) attack; **~ à main armée** armed raid; [3] fig (critique) attack; **~ en règle** full-scale attack; **pas d'~s personnelles!** no personal comments!; [4] Méd (d'apoplexie) stroke; (cardiaque) attack; [5] Sport (au football, rugby) break; (en course) break; (au tennis, golf) drive; (en alpinisme) attempt; (à la rame) beginning of a stroke; [6] Mus striking up

(Idiomes) **être** *or* **se sentir d'~** to feel on GB *ou* in US form; **être (assez) d'~ pour faire qch** to feel up to doing sth; **je ne me sens pas très d'~**○ **le matin** I don't feel too lively in the morning

attaquer /atake/ [1]

A *vtr* [1] Mil to attack [*troupe, pays*]; **~ sur tous les fronts** to attack on all sides; [2] (agresser) to attack [*personne*]; to raid [*banque, magasin, train*]; [3] (critiquer) to attack; [4] Jur to contest [*contrat, testament*]; **~ qn en justice** to bring an action against sb GB, to lawsuit sb US; [5] [*acide*] to attack; [6] (commencer) to launch into [*discours*]; to make a start on [*lecture, rédaction*]; to get going on [*tâche*]; to attack [*plat*]; to attempt [*escalade*]; [7] to tackle [*problème*]; [8] Mus to strike up [*air*]; to attack [*note*]

B *vi* [1] (au football, rugby) to break; (au tennis) to drive; [2] (commencer à parler) to begin (brusquely)

C **s'attaquer** *vpr* **s'~ à** to attack [*personne, œuvre, politique*]; to make a start on [*tâche*]; to tackle [*problème*]; **tu t'attaques à plus fort que toi** you're taking on somebody who is more than a match for you

attardé, ~e /ataʀde/

A *adj* [1] (en retard) late; **quelques passants ~s** some people out late; [2] (démodé) pej old-fashioned; [3] (mentalement) pej retarded

B *nm,f* (handicapé mental) pej mentally retarded person

attarder: s'attarder /ataʀde/ [1] *vpr* [1] lit (rester) to stay; (traîner) to linger; [2] fig (s'arrêter) to take one's time; **s'~ sur** to dwell on [*point, aspect*]

atteindre /atɛ̃dʀ/ [55]

A *vtr* [1] (arriver à) to reach [*lieu, niveau*]; [*personne, réforme*] to achieve [*but*]; [*projectile*] to reach [*cible*]; **arbre qui peut ~ 40 mètres** tree which can grow up to 40 metres^{GB} high; [2] (frapper) [*projectile, tireur*] to hit; [3] (affecter) [*maladie, malheur*] (de façon durable) to affect; (brusquement) to hit; [*parole blessante*] to affect; **~ qn dans son honneur** to cast a slur on sb's honour^{GB}; [4] (toucher) to reach [*public*]

B **atteindre à** fml *vtr ind* to achieve [*connaissance*]

atteint, ~e¹ /atɛ̃, ɛ̃t/ *adj* [1] (affecté) affected (**de, par** by); **très ~** badly affected; **être ~ de** (de façon durable) to be suffering from [*maladie*]; [2] (frappé) hit (**de, par** by); [3] ○(timbré) **être ~** to be touched○

atteinte² /atɛ̃t/ *nf* **~ à** attack on; **hors d'~** [*personne, paix, poste*] beyond reach; [*cible*] out of range; [*rester, sembler*] out of reach; **porter ~ à** to undermine [*crédit, prestige*]; to damage [*honneur*]; to endanger [*sécurité*]; to infringe [*droit*]; to threaten [*environnement*]; **~ aux droits de l'Homme** infringement of human rights; **~ à l'ordre public** Jur public order offence^{GB}; **~ à la sécurité** *or* **sûreté de l'État** breach of national security; **~ à la vie privée** breach of the right to privacy

attelage /atlaʒ/ *nm* [1] (système) (de cheval) harness; (de bœuf) yoke; (de wagon) coupling; (de remorque) towing attachment; (de fusée) docking *ou* coupling device; [2] (animaux) gén team; (de deux bœufs) yoke; [3] (équipage) horse-drawn carriage; [4] (sport) (carriage) driving; [5] (processus) (de cheval) harnessing; (de bœuf) yoking; (de remorque) hitching up; (de wagon) coupling

atteler /atle/ [19]

A *vtr* (attacher) to harness [*cheval*] (à to); to yoke [*bœuf*]; to hitch up [*remorque*]; to couple [*wagon*] (à to)

B **s'atteler** *vpr* **s'~ à une tâche/à faire** to get down to a job/ to doing

attelle /atɛl/ *nf* Méd splint

attenant, **~e** /atnɑ̃, ɑ̃t/ *adj* **1** (accolé) [*pièce*] adjacent (**à** to); **2** (associé) [*problème*] related (**à** to)

attendre /atɑ̃dʀ/ [6]

A *vtr* **1** gén to wait for [*personne, événement*]; to wait until *ou* till [*date*] (**pour faire** to do); **j'attends qu'il finisse** *or* **ait fini** I'm waiting for him to finish; **il attend impatiemment Noël** he can't wait for Christmas; **aller ~ qn à la gare** to (go and) meet sb at the station; **qu'attends-tu pour répondre?** why don't you answer?; **j'attends de voir pour y croire** I'll believe it when I see it; **se faire ~** to keep people waiting; **le serveur se fait ~** the waiter is taking a long time; **la réaction ne se fit pas ~** the reaction was instantaneous; **~ son jour** *or* **heure** to bide one's time; **reste ici en attendant que la pluie cesse** stay here until the rain stops; **en attendant mieux** until something better turns up; **où étais-tu, on ne t'attendait plus!** where were you? we'd given up on you!; ▸ **ferme¹**; **2** (être prêt, préparé) [*voiture, taxi*] to be waiting for; [*chambre, appartement*] to be ready for; **un délicieux repas m'attendait** a delicious meal awaited me; **3** (être prévu, prévisible) [*succès, aventure*] to await, to be in store for [*personne*]; **quel avenir nous attend?** what does the future hold (in store) for us?; **les élections sont attendues comme un test** the elections are being viewed as a test; **4** (compter sur) **je les attends pour 5 heures** I'm expecting them at five; **elle attend un bébé** *or* **un enfant** she's expecting a baby; **~ de qn qu'il fasse** to expect sb to do; **j'attendais mieux de ce roman** I found the novel rather disappointing

B *vi* to wait; (au téléphone) to hold; **attends un peu!** wait a moment; (menace) just (you) wait!; **faire ~ qn** to keep sb waiting; **sans plus ~** without further delay; **en attendant** (pendant ce temps) in the meantime; (néanmoins) all the same, nonetheless; **tu ne perds rien pour ~**ᵒ! I'll get youᵒ, just you wait!

C **s'attendre** *vpr* **s'~ à qch/à faire** to expect sth/to do; **s'~ à ce que qn fasse/qch se produise** to expect sb to do/sth to happen; **il fallait s'y ~** it was to be expected; **avec lui, il faut s'~ à tout** with him, anything can happen

(Idiome) **tout vient à point pour qui sait ~** Prov everything comes to him who waits Prov

attendrir /atɑ̃dʀiʀ/ [3]

A *vtr* **1** (émouvoir) to touch, to move [*personne*]; to touch [*cœur*]; **se laisser ~** to soften; **tu ne vas pas te laisser ~ par lui!** you're not going to let him soften you up!; **sourire attendri** tender smile; **2** Culin to tenderize [*viande*]

B **s'attendrir** *vpr* (s'émouvoir) [*personne*] to feel moved; **son regard s'attendrit** his/her eyes softened; **s'~ sur qn/soi-même** to feel sorry for sb/oneself; **s'~ sur ses malheurs** to lament one's misfortunes

attendrissant, **~e** /atɑ̃dʀisɑ̃, ɑ̃t/ *adj* [*spectacle, mots*] touching, moving; [*candeur*] endearing; **être ~ de naïveté** to be endearingly naïve

attendrissement /atɑ̃dʀismɑ̃/ *nm* (affectueux) tenderness; (ému) emotion; **avec ~** tenderly

attendrisseur /atɑ̃dʀisœʀ/ *nm* tenderizer

attendu¹ /atɑ̃dy/

A *prép* given, considering

B **attendu que** *loc conj* given *ou* considering that; Jur whereas

attendu², **~e** /atɑ̃dy/

A *adj* **1** (prévu) expected; **2** (souhaité) **le jour (tant) ~** the long-awaited day

B *nm* Jur **~s d'un jugement** grounds for a decision

attentat /atɑ̃ta/ *nm* (contre un individu) assassination attempt (**contre** on); (contre un groupe, bâtiment) attack (**contre** on); **~ à la bombe** bomb attack

(Composé) **~ à la pudeur** indecent assault

attente /atɑ̃t/ *nf* **1** (processus) waiting ¢; (période) wait; **l'~ du verdict** waiting for the verdict; **deux heures d'~** a two-hour wait; **mon ~ a été vaine** I waited for nothing; **dans l'~ de vous lire** looking forward to hearing from you; **en ~** [*passager*] waiting; [*dossier, affaire*] pending (*jamais épith*); Télécom [*appel, demandeur*] on hold (*épith, après n*); **commandes en ~** Comm back orders; **2** (espoir) expectations (*pl*); **répondre à l'~ de qn** to come up to sb's expectations

attenter /atɑ̃te/ [1] *vtr ind* **~ à ses jours** to attempt suicide; **~ à la vie de qn** to make an attempt on sb's life

attentif, **-ive** /atɑ̃tif, iv/ *adj* **1** [*personne*] attentive; **être ~ à** to pay attention to [*propos, détail, évolution*]; to be mindful of [*convenances*]; **sous le regard ~ de leur mère** under the watchful eye of their mother; **prêter une oreille attentive à qn** to listen carefully to sb; **2** [*lecture, travail, description*] careful; [*examen*] close; [*soin*] special; **3** [*soins*] special; **être ~ aux besoins de qn** to be attentive to sb's needs

attention /atɑ̃sjɔ̃/

A *nf* **1** (vigilance) attention; **porter son ~ sur qch/qn** to turn one's attention to sth/sb; **à l'~ de F. Pons** for the attention of F. Pons; **faire ~ à qch** to mind [*voitures, piège, marche*]; to watch out for [*faux billets, verglas*]; to be careful of [*soleil*]; to consider [*conséquences*]; to take care of [*vêtements*]; to watch [*alimentation, santé*]; to pay attention to [*mode, détails*]; **ne faites pas ~ à ce qu'elle dit** don't take any notice of what she says; **fais ~ à ce que tu fais** be careful what you do; **faire ~ à qn** (écouter) to pay attention to sb; (surveiller) to keep an eye on sb; (remarquer) to take notice of sb; **fais ~ aux voleurs!** beware of thieves!; **fais ~ à toi** take care of yourself; **avec ~** carefully; **fais ~, c'est très dangereux** be careful, it's very dangerous; **2** (marque de gentillesse) **j'ai été touché par toutes ces ~s** I was touched by all these kind gestures; **être plein d'~s pour qn** to be very attentive to sb; **il a eu la délicate ~ de faire** he was thoughtful enough to do

B *adv* (cri) look out!, watch out!; (écrit) gén attention!; (en cas de danger) warning!; (panneau routier) caution!; **~ à la marche** mind the step; **~, les dossiers d'inscription doivent être retirés avant lundi** please note that application forms must be collected by Monday; **mais ~, il faut réserver à l'avance** however, you must book GB *ou* reserve in advance; **~, je ne veux pas dire...** don't get me wrong, I don't mean...

attentionné, **~e** /atɑ̃sjone/ *adj* [*personne*] attentive, considerate (**pour, envers** toward(s), to); [*soins*] special

attentisme /atɑ̃tism/ *nm* wait-and-see attitude

attentivement /atɑ̃tivmɑ̃/ *adv* [*écouter, suivre*] attentively; [*examiner, regarder*] carefully

atténuantes /atenɥɑ̃t/ *adj fpl* **circonstances ~** Jur mitigating *ou* extenuating circumstances

atténuation /atenɥasjɔ̃/ *nf* (de douleur, tension) alleviation, relief; (de nuisance) reduction; (d'effet) mitigation; (de rigueur) relaxation

atténuer /atenɥe/ [1]

A *vtr* to ease [*douleur, tension, chagrin*]; to lessen [*désespoir*]; to weaken [*impression, effet*]; to soften [*choc*]; to reduce [*inégalités, gravité*]; to tone down [*reproche*]; to relax [*sévérité*]; to dim [*lumière*]; to tone down [*couleur, éclat*]; to make [sth] less strong [*odeur, goût*]; to mitigate [*faute*]

B **s'atténuer** *vpr* [*douleur*] to ease; [*colère, chagrin*] to subside; [*corruption*] to lessen; [*tendance*] to become less pronounced; [*inégalités*] to be reduced; [*ride, couleur*] to fade; [*tempête, bruit*] to die down

atterrant, **~e** /ateʀɑ̃, ɑ̃t/ *adj* (consternant) [*bêtise*] appalling; [*image, nouvelle*] shattering

atterré, **~e** /atere/ *adj* **1** (consterné) appalled; **d'un air ~ aghast**; **2** (en état de choc) shattered

atterrer /atere/ [1] *vtr* to leave [sb] aghast

atterrir /ateʀiʀ/ [3] *vi* **1** Aviat to land; **~ en catastrophe sur le ventre** to make a crash landing/a belly landing; **2** ᵒ[*dossier, personne*] to land upᵒ

atterrissage /ateʀisaʒ/ *nm* landing; **~ en catastrophe** crash landing

attestation /atɛstasjɔ̃/ *nf* (déclaration) attestation; (sous serment) affidavit; (certificat) certificate

attester /atɛste/ [1] *vtr* **1** (certifier) to vouch for; (témoigner) to testify to; **~ que** to vouch for the fact that; (témoigner) to testify that; **forme attestée/non attestée** Ling attested/unattested form; **2** (être preuve de) to prove, to attest to

attiferᵒ /atife/ [1]

A *vtr* to rig [sb] outᵒ (**de, avec** in)

B **s'attifer** *vpr* to rig oneself outᵒ (**de, avec** in)

attique /atik/

A *adj* Attic

B ▸ p. 336 *nm* Ling Attic dialect

attirail /atiʀaj/ *nm* gear; **~ de pêche** fishing tackle; **l'~ du parfait bricoleur** the well-equipped DIY enthusiast's tool kit

a

attirance /atiʀɑ̃s/ *nf* attraction (**pour** to); **éprouver** *or* **avoir de l'~ pour** to feel drawn toward(s), to be attracted to; **l'~ du vide** the fascination of the abyss

attirant, **~e** /atiʀɑ̃, ɑ̃t/ *adj* attractive

attirer /atiʀe/ [1]

A *vtr* [1] (faire venir) gén, Phys to attract [*foudre, personne, animal, capitaux, convoitises*]; **~ l'attention de qn sur qch** to draw sb's attention to sth; **~ qn à soi** to draw sb to oneself; **le bruit l'attira dans le jardin** the noise drew him to the garden GB *ou* yard US; **~ qn dans un coin** to take sb into a corner; **~ qn dans un piège** to lure sb into a trap; **~ qn par des promesses** to entice sb with promises; [2] (séduire) [*personne, pays*] to attract; [*études, métier*] to appeal to; **les brunes l'attirent** he goes for brunettes; [3] (susciter) to bring [*honte, critique*] (**à, sur** on); **~ des ennuis à qn** to cause sb problems

B **s'attirer** *vpr* **s'~ le soutien de qn** to win sb's support; **s'~ la colère de qn** to incur sb's anger; **des nombreuses critiques** to attract criticism; **s'~ des ennuis** to get into trouble

attiser /atize/ [1] *vtr* to kindle [*sentiment, convoitises*]; to fuel [*discorde*]; to stir up [*haine*]; to fan [*feu*]

attitré, **~e** /atitʀe/ *adj* [1] (officiel) official; **chauffeur ~** official driver; **représentant ~** accredited representative; [2] (habituel) regular; **client ~** regular customer

attitude /atityd/ *nf* [1] (maintien) bearing; (position) attitude, posture; (pose) pose; **~ de soumission** submissive attitude; [2] (conduite) attitude (**envers** to)

attouchement /atuʃmɑ̃/ *nm* [1] (sexuel) (sans consentement) (sexual) interfering ¢, molesting ¢; (avec consentement) fondling ¢; [2] (de guérisseur) laying on ¢ of hands

attraction /atʀaksjɔ̃/ *nf* gén, Ling, Phys attraction; **~ touristique** tourist attraction

(Composés) **~ terrestre** Earth's attraction; **~ universelle** gravitation

attrait /atʀɛ/ *nm* [1] (attirance) appeal, attraction; (de l'interdit) lure; **plein d'~** very attractive; **sans ~** unattractive; **avoir de l'~ pour qn** to appeal to sb; [2] (goût) liking (**pour** for)

attrape-mouches /atʀapmuʃ/ *nm inv* [1] (plante) flytrap; [2] (piège) gén flytrap; (papier collant) flypaper

attrape-nigaud, *pl* **~s** /atʀapnigo/ *nm* con○; **tomber dans un ~** to fall for a con

attraper /atʀape/ [1]

A *vtr* [1] (saisir en mouvement) to catch [*personne, animal, ballon*]; **tiens, attrape!** here, catch!; [2] (capturer) to catch [*malfaiteur, animal*]; **se faire ~** to get caught; **attrapez-le!** stop him!; [3] (prendre) to catch hold of [*corde, jambe*]; **~ une bouteille par le goulot** to pick up a bottle by the neck; **tu peux ~ le livre sur l'étagère?** can you reach and get the book from the shelf?; [4] ○(contracter) [*personne*] to catch [*froid, maladie*]; to get [*coup de soleil, mal de tête*]; to pick up [*manie, accent*]; **tu vas ~ du mal!** you'll catch something!; [5] ○(surprendre) to catch [sb] out; **il a été bien attrapé d'apprendre que** he was really caught out by the news that; **~ qn en train de faire** fig to catch sb doing; [6] ○(réprimander) to tell [sb] off; **se faire ~** to get told off; [7] ○(recevoir) to get [*coup, punition*]

B **s'attraper** *vpr* [*maladie*] to be caught

attrayant, **~e** /atʀɛjɑ̃, ɑ̃t/ *adj* gén attractive; [*lecture*] pleasant; **peu ~** gén unattractive; [*tâche, lecture*] unappealing

attribuable /atʀibɥabl/ *adj* attributable (**à** to)

attribuer /atʀibɥe/ [1]

A *vtr* [1] (donner) to allocate [*numéro, logement, tâche*]; to grant [*droit*]; to award [*prix, bourse*]; to lend [*importance, sens*]; Fin to allot [*actions*]; **~ qch à la fatigue** to put sth down to tiredness; **~ la responsabilité de qch à qn/qch** to hold sb/sth responsible for sth; [2] (reconnaître) **~ à qn** to credit sb with [*invention, qualité*]; to ascribe to sb [*œuvre*]; **on attribue ce tableau à Poussin** this painting is attributed to Poussin

B **s'attribuer** *vpr* **s'~ la meilleure part** to give oneself the largest share; **s'~ tout le mérite** to take all the credit for oneself

attribut /atʀiby/ *nm* [1] (propriété) attribute; (symbole) symbol; [2] Ling **adjectif ~** predicative adjective

attribution /atʀibysjɔ̃/

A *nf* gén allocation (**à** to); (d'avantage) awarding (**à** to); (d'actions) allotment (**à** to); (de nationalité) granting (**à** to); (d'œuvre) attribution (**à** to)

B **attributions** *nfpl* (de personne) remit (*sg*); (de tribunal) competence; **ça n'entre pas dans mes ~s** it doesn't come within my remit

attristant, **~e** /atʀistɑ̃, ɑ̃t/ *adj* [1] (peinant) distressing, upsetting; [2] (consternant) depressing; **d'une bêtise ~e** depressingly stupid

attrister /atʀiste/ [1]

A *vtr* (peiner) to sadden; **j'ai été attristé d'apprendre** I was sorry to hear

B **s'attrister** *vpr* [1] (exprimer sa tristesse) to lament (**de** about); [2] (être peiné) to be saddened (**de** by)

attroupement /atʀupmɑ̃/ *nm* gathering; **~ de manifestants** crowd of demonstrators; **causer un ~** to cause a crowd to gather

attrouper: **s'attrouper** /atʀupe/ [1] *vpr* to gather (**devant** in front of; **autour de** around)

au /o/ *prép* (= **à le**) ▸ **à**

aubade /obad/ *nf* dawn serenade

aubaine /obɛn/ *nf* [1] (chance) godsend; [2] (bonne affaire) bargain

aube /ob/ *nf* [1] (point du jour) dawn; **à l'~** at dawn; [2] (début) dawn; **à l'~ de** at the dawn of; **à l'~ des années 20** in the early twenties; [3] Tech (en bois) paddle; (en métal) blade; **roue à ~s** paddle wheel; [4] Relig (de prêtre) alb; (d'enfant de chœur) cassock; (pour la communion solennelle) alb

aubépine /obepin/ *nf* hawthorn

auberge /obɛʀʒ/ *nf* inn

(Composé) **~ de jeunesse** youth hostel

(Idiome) **tu n'es pas sorti de l'~**○! you're not out of the woods yet!

aubergine /obɛʀʒin/ ▸ p. 140

A *adj inv* aubergine

B *nf* Bot, Culin aubergine, eggplant US

aubergiste /obɛʀʒist/ ▸ p. 372 *nmf* innkeeper

aubier /obje/ *nm* sapwood

aucun, **~e** /okœ̃, yn/

A *adj* [1] (dans une phrase négative) no, not any; **il n'y a plus ~ espoir** there's no hope left; **elle l'a fait sans ~e hésitation** *or* **sans hésitation ~e** she did it without any hesitation; **en ~e façon** in no way; [2] (quelque) liter any; **je l'aime plus qu'~e autre** I love her more than anybody

B *pron* [1] (dans une phrase négative) **je n'ai lu ~ de vos livres** I haven't read any of your books; **~ de ses arguments n'est convaincant** none of his arguments are convincing; **'tu as reçu beaucoup de lettres?'—'~e!'** 'did you receive many letters?'—'not one!'; [2] (quiconque) liter **je doute qu'~ d'entre eux réussisse** I doubt that any of them will succeed; **d'~s** some

aucunement /okynmɑ̃/ *adv* in no way; **je n'avais ~ l'intention de faire** in no way did I mean to; **je ne suis ~ surpris** I'm not surprised in the least, I'm not at all surprised; **il n'a ~ l'intention de l'épouser** he hasn't got the slightest intention of marrying her

audace /odas/ *nf* [1] (hardiesse) boldness; **il manque d'~** he's not very daring; [2] (effronterie) audacity, nerve○; (de geste, propos) impudence; **avoir l'~ de faire qch** to have the audacity *ou* nerve○ to do sth; **il ne manque pas d'~** he's got a nerve○; [3] (innovation) **les ~s des architectes** the daring creations of architects; **~s stylistiques** stylistic daring (*sg*)

audacieux, -ieuse /odasjø, øz/

A *adj* (hardi) audacious, daring; (effronté) bold

B *nm,f* daring *ou* bold person

(Idiome) **la fortune sourit aux ~** Prov fortune favours○GB the brave Prov

au-dedans /odədɑ̃/ *adv* inside

au-dehors /odəɔʀ/ *adv* [1] lit outside; **'ne pas se pencher ~'** 'do not lean out of the window'; [2] fig outwardly

au-delà /od(ə)la/

A *nm* Relig beyond, hereafter

B *adv* beyond; **je veux bien aller jusqu'à 150 euros mais pas ~** I'm quite prepared to go up to 150 euros but no more

C **au-delà de** *loc prép* beyond; **~ des frontières** beyond the borders; **~ de 20%** over 20%

au-dessous /odəsu/

A *adv* [1] (plus bas) below; **l'étagère ~** the shelf below; **tu vois le dictionnaire, mon livre est ~** you see the dictionary, my book is underneath; ②▸ (marquant une infériorité) under; **les enfants de 10 ans et** ~ children of 10 years and under

B au-dessous de *loc prép* ①▸ (plus bas que) below; ~ **du genou** below the knee; ②▸ (inférieur à) ~ **de zéro** below zero; **les enfants** ~ **de 13 ans** children under 13, the under-thirteens; **les chèques** ~ **de 15 euros** cheques GB *ou* checks US for under 15 euros; **être** ~ **de tout**○ (ne pas être à la hauteur) to be absolutely useless; (moralement) to be despicable

au-dessus /odəsy/
A *adv* ①▸ (plus haut) above; **l'étagère** ~ the shelf above; **il habite l'étage** ~ he lives on the next floor up *ou* on the floor above; ②▸ (marquant une supériorité) above; **les enfants de 10 ans et** ~ children of 10 and over, the over-tens; **la taille** ~ the next size up

B au-dessus de *loc prép* ①▸ (plus haut que) above; ~ **des nuages** (up) above the clouds; **deux étages** ~ **de chez moi** two floors up from me; **un pont** ~ **de la rivière** a bridge over the river; **se pencher** ~ **de la table** to lean across the table; ②▸ (supérieur à) above; ~ **de zéro/de la moyenne** above zero/average; **les enfants** ~ **de 3 ans** children over 3 years old; **les chèques** ~ **de 150 euros** cheques GB *ou* checks US for over 150 euros

au-devant: **au-devant de** /odəvãdə/ *loc prép* (à la rencontre) **aller** ~ **de qn** lit to go to meet sb; **aller** ~ **des clients** fig to go out looking for custom; **aller** ~ **des désirs de qn** to anticipate sb's wishes; **aller** ~ **des ennuis** to let oneself in for trouble

audible /odibl/ *adj* audible

audience /odjãs/ *nf* ①▸ Jur hearing; **lever l'**~ to close the hearing; **salle d'**~ courtroom; ②▸ (entretien) audience sout; ③▸ (succès, attention) success; **jouir d'une grande** ~ **auprès des jeunes** to have a lot of success with young people; ④▸ TV, Radio (personnes) audience; (chiffres) audience ratings (*pl*)

audimat® /odimat/ *nm* audience ratings (*pl*)

audio /odjo/ *adj inv* audio

audionumérique /odjonymeʀik/ *adj* **disque** ~ digital audio disc

audiovisuel, -elle /odjovisɥɛl/
A *adj* ①▸ Radio, TV broadcasting; **techniques audiovisuelles** broadcasting technology; ②▸ Ling, Vidéo audiovisual
B *nm* ①▸ Radio, TV broadcasting; ②▸ (équipement) audiovisual equipment; ③▸ (méthodes) audiovisual methods

audit /odit/ *nm* audit

auditeur, -trice /oditœʀ, tʀis/ *nm,f* ①▸ gén, Radio listener; ②▸ Fin auditor; ③▸ Ling hearer
(Composé) ~ **libre** Univ *person following a university course with no obligation to take the exam*

auditif, -ive /oditif, iv/ *adj* [*nerf, conduit*] auditory; [*troubles, appareil*] hearing (épith); [*mémoire*] aural

audition /odisjɔ̃/ *nf* ①▸ (perception, écoute) hearing; ②▸ Cin, Mus, Théât (essai) audition; **passer une** ~ to be auditioned, to go for an audition; **faire passer une** ~ **à qn** to audition sb; ③▸ Jur hearing, examination

auditionner /odisjɔne/ [1] *vtr, vi* to audition

auditoire /oditwaʀ/ *nm* audience

auditorium /oditɔʀjɔm/ *nm* auditorium

auge /oʒ/ *nf* ①▸ (d'animal) trough; ②▸ (de maçon) mortar trough; ③▸ Géog U-shaped valley; ~ **glaciaire** glacial valley

augmentation /ogmɑ̃tasjɔ̃/ *nf* ①▸ (accroissement) increase; ~ **de 3%** 3% increase; ②▸ (majoration) increase; **une** ~ **(de salaire)** a pay rise GB *ou* raise US

augmenter /ogmɑ̃te/ [1]
A *vtr* to raise, to increase [*nombre, salaire, charge, volume*] (**de** by); to increase [*valeur, production*] (**de** by); to extend [*durée*] (**de** by); to increase [*risque*]; ~ **le loyer de qn** to put sb's rent up; ~ **ses revenus** to supplement one's income (**en faisant** by doing); ~ **qn de 200 euros** to give sb a rise GB *ou* raise US of 200 euros
B *vi* (devenir plus élevé) [*prix, revenus, loyer*] to increase (**de** by), to go up (**de** by); [*température*] to rise (**de** by); [*surface, capacité*] to increase (**de** by); **les timbres ont augmenté** stamps have gone up

augure /ogyʀ/ *nm* ①▸ (devin) (dans l'Antiquité) augur; fig, hum soothsayer, oracle; ②▸ (signe) omen; (dans l'Antiquité) augury; **être de bon/mauvais** ~ **pour qch/qn** to be a good/bad omen for sth/sb

augurer /ogyʀe/ [1] *vtr* ①▸ (attendre) **que peut-on** ~ **de cette attitude?** what should we expect from this attitude?; **je n'augure rien de bon de cette rencontre** I can't see any good coming of this meeting; **cela augure mal de l'avenir** it doesn't bode well for the future; **cela laisse** ~ **une difficulté** this suggests we can anticipate a difficulty; **me laissant** ~ **que** giving me to understand that; ②▸ (annoncer) to herald

auguste /ogyst/
A *adj* [*personne*] august; [*geste*] noble
B *nm* (clown) circus clown

aujourd'hui /oʒuʀdɥi/ *adv* ①▸ (ce jour) today; ~ **en huit** a week (from) today; ②▸ (de nos jours) today, nowadays; **la jeunesse d'**~ the youth of today; **la France d'**~ present-day France

aulne /on/ *nm* alder

aumône /omon/ *nf* hand-out, alms† (*pl*); **faire l'**~ **à** to give alms to; **demander l'**~ to ask for charity

aumônerie /omonʀi/ *nf* chaplaincy

aumônier /omonje/ ▸ p. 372 *nm* chaplain

aune[1] /on/ *nm* = aulne

aune[2] /on/ *nf* (mesure) ≈ ell; **à l'**~ **de** by the yardstick of

auparavant /opaʀavɑ̃/ *adv* before

auprès /opʀɛ/
A *adv* liter nearby
B auprès de *loc prép* ①▸ (à côté de) next to, beside; (aux côtés de) with; **reste** ~ **de lui** stay with him; **il s'est rendu** ~ **de sa tante** he went to see his aunt; ②▸ (en comparaison de) compared with; ③▸ (en s'adressant à) **s'excuser** ~ **de qn** to apologize to sb; **renseigne-toi** ~ **de la mairie** ask for information at the town hall; **un sondage effectué** ~ **de 2 000 personnes** a poll carried out among 2,000 people; ④▸ (en relation avec) fml to; **représentant** ~ **de l'ONU** representative to the UN; ⑤▸ (dans l'opinion de) **il passe pour riche** ~ **d'eux** to them he's rich; **il a perdu toute crédibilité** ~ **des électeurs** he has lost all credibility among voters; **l'émission a du succès** ~**du public** the programme^{GB} is a success with the public

auquel ▸ lequel

aura /oʀa/ *nf* aura

auréole /oʀeɔl/ *nf* ①▸ (tache) ring; ②▸ (couronne) halo; ③▸ (prestige) glory

auréoler: **s'auréoler** /oʀeɔle/ [1] *vpr* **s'**~ **de** to take on an aura of; **auréolé de** basking in the glow of

auriculaire /oʀikylɛʀ/
A *adj* auricular
B *nm* little finger, pinkie

aurifère /oʀifɛʀ/ *adj* ①▸ [*minerai*] auriferous; ②▸ Fin **valeurs** ~**s** gold stocks

aurore /oʀɔʀ/ *nf* lit, fig dawn **₵**; **se lever aux** ~**s** to get up with the lark
(Composés) ~ **australe** aurora australis; ~ **boréale** Northern Lights (*pl*), aurora borealis

auscultation /ɔskyltasjɔ̃/ *nf* Méd examination

ausculter /ɔskylte/ [1] *vtr* Méd to examine

auspices /ɔspis/ *nmpl* auspices; **sous les** ~ **de** under the auspices of

aussi /osi/
A *adv* ①▸ (également) too, as well, also; **moi** ~, **j'ai du travail** I have work too; **il sera absent et moi** ~ he'll be away and so will I; ②▸ (dans une comparaison) ~ **âgé que** as old as; ~ **riche soit-elle** (as) rich as she may be; **cette émission concerne les femmes** ~ **bien que les hommes** this programme^{GB} concerns women as well as men; ~ **longtemps que** as long as; **c'est** ~ **bien** it's just as well; ③▸ (si, tellement) so; **je ne savais pas qu'il était** ~ **vieux** I didn't know he was so old; **dans une** ~ **belle maison** in such a nice house
B *conj* ①▸ (en conséquence) so, consequently; **je m'en doutais,** ~ **ne suis-je guère surprise** I suspected it, so I'm not entirely surprised; ②▸ ○(d'ailleurs) **'on lui a volé son sac'**—**'quelle idée** ~ **de le laisser traîner!'** 'her bag was stolen'—'well, it was stupid to leave it lying about!'; **mais** ~, **pourquoi est-ce que tu y es allée?** why on earth did you go there?

aussitôt /osito/
A *adv* ①▸ (immédiatement) immediately, straight away; ~ **après ton départ** straight after you left; ②▸ (juste après) ~ **arrivé** as soon as *ou* the moment he arrived; **elle n'avait pas**

~ **quitté la pièce qu'il entra** no sooner had she left the room than he came in; ~ **dit** ~ **fait** no sooner said than done

B **aussitôt que** *loc conj* as soon as

austère /ɔstɛʀ, ostɛʀ/ *adj* [*personne, éducation, allure, vie, économie*] austere; [*expression, visage*] stern; [*vêtement*] severe; [*monument, lieu*] forbidding; [*livre*] dry

austérité /osteʀite/ *nf* **1** (d'allure, économie, éducation, de lieu, personnne, vie) austerity; **2** (de vêtement, visage) severity; **3** (d'œuvre) dryness

austral, ~e, *mpl* ~s /ostʀal/ *adj* **1** (du sud) austral; **vents** ~s austral winds; **2** (de l'hémisphère Sud) southern; **été** ~ southern summer

Australie /ostʀali/ ▸ p. 230 *nprf* Australia

Australie-Méridionale /ostʀalimeʀidjɔnal/ ▸ p. 504 *nprf* Southern Australia

australien, -ienne /ostʀaljɛ̃, ɛn/ ▸ p. 392 *adj* Australian

Australie-Occidentale /ostʀaliɔksidɑ̃tal/ ▸ p. 504 *nprf* Western Australia

austro-hongrois, ~e, *mpl* ~ /ostʀoɔ̃grwa, az/ *adj* Austro-Hungarian

autant /otɑ̃/

A *adv* **il n'a jamais** ~ **neigé/plu** it has never snowed/rained so much; **je t'aime toujours** ~ I still love you as much; **essaie** *or* **tâche d'en faire** ~ try and do the same; **triste** ~ **que désagréable** as sad as it is unpleasant; ~ **je comprends leur chagrin**, ~ **je déteste leur façon de l'étaler** as much as I understand their grief, I hate the way they parade it; **cela m'agace** ~ **que toi** it annoys me as much as it does you; **je les hais tous** ~ **qu'ils sont** I hate every single one of them; **je me moque de ce que vous pensez tous** ~ **que vous êtes** I don't care what any of you think; **j'aime** ~ **partir tout de suite** I'd rather leave straight away; **j'aime** ~ **te dire qu'il n'était pas content** believe me, he wasn't pleased; ~ **dire que la réunion est annulée** in other words the meeting is cancelled^{GB}; ~ **parler à un mur** you might as well be talking to the wall; ~ **que faire se peut** as far as possible; ~ **que je sache** as far as I know; ~ **que tu peux** (comme tu peux) as much as you can; (aussi longtemps que tu peux) as long as you can

B **autant que** *dét indéf* **1** (avec un nom dénombrable) ~ **de cadeaux/de gens** so many presents/people; **leurs promesses sont** ~ **de mensonges** their promises are just so many lies; ~ **de femmes que d'hommes** as many women as men; **2** (avec un nom non dénombrable) ~ **d'énergie/d'argent** so much energy/money; ~ **de gentillesse** such kindness; **ce sera toujours** ~ **de fait** that'll be done at least; **je n'ai pas eu** ~ **de chance que lui** I haven't had as much luck as he has; **je n'avais jamais vu** ~ **de monde** I'd never seen so many people

C **d'autant** *loc adv* **cela va permettre de réduire d'**~ **les coûts de production** this will allow an equivalent reduction in production costs; **les salaires ont augmenté de 3% mais les prix ont augmenté d'**~ salaries have increased by 3% but prices have increased by just as much; **d'**~ **plus!** all the more reason!; **d'**~ **moins** even less, all the less; **d'**~ **moins contrôlable** even less easy to control; **je le comprends d'**~ **moins** I find it even harder to understand; **d'**~ **que** all the more so as; **d'**~ **plus heureux/grand que** all the happier/bigger as

D **pour autant** *loc adv* gén for all that; **je ne vais pas abandonner pour** ~ I'm not going to give up for all that; **sans pour** ~ **tout modifier** without necessarily changing everything

E **pour autant que** *loc conj* **pour** ~ **que** as far as; **pour** ~ **qu'ils se mettent d'accord** if they agree; **pour** ~ **que je sache** as far as I know

autarcie /otaʀsi/ *nf* autarky; **vivre en** ~ to be self-sufficient

autel /otɛl/ *nm* altar

auteur /otœʀ/ *nm* **1** (qui a écrit) author; **2** (créateur) (de chanson) composer; (d'œuvre artistique) artist; **film d'**~ art film; **3** (de réforme, loi) author; (de découverte) inventor; (de crime) perpetrator; (de coup d'État) leader; **l'**~ **du canular** the hoaxer; **l'**~ **de mes jours** hum (mère) my revered mother; (père) my revered father

(Composé) ~ **dramatique** playwright

auteur-compositeur, *pl* **auteurs-compositeurs** /otœʀkɔ̃pozitœʀ/ *nm* songwriter

authenticité /otɑ̃tisite/ *nf* (de document, fait) authenticity; (de sentiment) genuineness

authentifier /otɑ̃tifje/ [2] *vtr* to authenticate

authentique /otɑ̃tik/ *adj* (vrai) [*fait, récit*] true; [*tableau, document*] authentic; *sentiment*] genuine

autisme /otism/ *nm* autism

autiste /otist/

A *adj* autistic

B *nmf* autistic person

auto /oto/

A *adj inv* **assurance** ~ car *ou* motor insurance GB, automobile insurance US

B *nf* car, automobile US

(Composé) ~ **tamponneuse** bumper car, dodgem

autobiographie /otobjoɡʀafi/ *nf* autobiography

autobiographique /otobjoɡʀafik/ *adj* autobiographical

autobus /otobys/ *nm inv* bus

autocar /otokaʀ/ *nm* coach GB, bus US

autocensurer: s'autocensurer /otosɑ̃syʀe/ [1] *vpr* to practise^{GB} self-censorship

autochtone /otɔkton/

A *adj* **1** (aborigène) native, autochthonous spéc; **2** [*terrain*] autochthonous

B *nmf* native, autochthon spéc

autocollant, ~e /otɔkɔlɑ̃, ɑ̃t/

A *adj* self-adhesive

B *nm* sticker

autocrate /otokʀat/

A *adj* autocratic

B *nmf* autocrat

autocratie /otokʀasi/ *nf* autocracy

autocritique /otokʀitik/ *nf* self-criticism **Ȼ**; **faire son** ~ to go through a process of self-criticism

autocuiseur /otokɥizœʀ/ *nm* pressure cooker

autodafé /otodafe/ *nm* **1** Hist Relig (cérémonie) auto-da-fé; **2** (destruction par le feu) book-burning; **faire un** ~ **de qch** fig to throw sth on the bonfire

autodéfense /otodefɑ̃s/ *nf* gén self-defence; Méd auto-immunity

autodestructeur, -trice /otodɛstʀyktœʀ, tʀis/ *adj* self-destructive

autodestruction /otodɛstʀyksjɔ̃/ *nf* self-destruction

autodétermination /otodetɛʀminasjɔ̃/ *nf* self-determination

autodétruire: s'autodétruire /otodetʀɥiʀ/ [69] *vpr* [*person*] to destroy oneself; [*cassette*] to self-destruct; [*missile*] to autodestruct

autodidacte /otodidakt/

A *adj* gén self-educated; (dans un domaine) self-taught

B *nmf* self-educated person, autodidact sout

autodiscipline /otodisiplin/ *nf* self-discipline

autodrome /otodʀom/ *nm* racetrack

auto-école, *pl* ~s /otoekɔl/ *nf* driving school

autofinancement /otofinɑ̃smɑ̃/ *nm* self-financing

autofocus /otofɔkys/

A *adj inv* autofocus

B *nm inv* (appareil) autofocus camera

autogérer: s'autogérer /otoʒeʀe/ [14] *vpr* [*entreprise*] to be run on a cooperative basis

autogestion /otoʒɛstjɔ̃/ *nf* (d'entreprise) worker management, cooperative management; (de collectivité) collective management

autographe /otoɡʀaf/ *adj, nm* autograph

auto-immunisation, *pl* ~s /otoimynizasjɔ̃/ *nf* auto-immunity

automate /otomat/ *nm* lit, fig robot, automaton; **gestes d'**~ robotic *ou* robot-like movements; **comme un** ~ like a robot

automation /otomasjɔ̃/ *nf* controv automation

automatique /otomatik/

A *adj* automatic

B *nm* **1** Télécom **l'**~ STD, subscriber trunk dialling^{GB}; **2** (revolver) automatic (revolver); **3** Phot automatic camera

automatiquement /otomatikmɑ̃/ *adv* **1** (de façon automatique) automatically; **2** °(inévitablement) inevitably

automatisation /otɔmatizasjɔ̃/ *nf* automation

automatiser /otɔmatize/ [1] *vtr* to automate

automatisme /otɔmatism/ *nm* (de personne, fonction) automatism; (de machine) automatic functioning; **acquérir des** ~**s** to acquire automatic reflexes

automitrailleuse /otomitʀajøz/ *nf* armoured^GB car

automne /otɔn/ ▸ p. 536 *nm* autumn GB, fall US; **en** ~ in autumn GB, in the fall US

automobile /otɔmɔbil/

A *adj* **1** [*industrie, assurance, accessoire, constructeur*] car (*épith*); **2** Sport [*course*] motor (*épith*); [*circuit*] motor racing (*épith*)

B *nf* **1** (voiture) (motor) car, automobile US; **2** (industrie) **l'**~ the car industry GB, the automobile industry US

automobiliste /otɔmɔbilist/ *nmf* motorist

autonome /otɔnɔm/ *adj* **1** Pol [*région, république*] autonomous; **2** (autogéré) [*filiale, gestion*] independent, autonomous; [*syndicat*] nonaffiliated, independent, [*personne*] self-sufficient; **3** Ordinat [*unité*] stand-alone; [*système, équipement*] off-line

autonomie /otɔnɔmi/ *nf* **1** (indépendance) autonomy; **2** (distance) range; ~ **de vol** flight range

autonomiste /otɔnɔmist/ *adj, nmf* separatist

autoportrait /otopɔʀtʀɛ/ *nm* self-portrait

autopsie /otɔpsi/ *nf* postmortem (examination), autopsy

autopsier /otɔpsje/ [2] *vtr* to carry out a postmortem (examination) on, to perform an autopsy on [*cadavre*]

autoradio /otoʀadjo/ *nm* car radio

autorail /otoʀaj/ *nm* rail car

autorisation /otɔʀizasjɔ̃/ *nf* **1** (accord) *gén* permission (**de faire** to do); (officielle) authorization (**de faire** to do); **2** (document) permit

autorisé, ~**e** /otɔʀize/ *adj* **1** (approuvé) [*biographie, édition, agent*] authorized; [*parti*] legal; [*représentant*] Comm accredited; **non** ~ unauthorized; **2** (officiel) [*personne*] authorized; **milieux** ~**s** official circles; **3** (toléré) [*tension, pression*] permitted; **poids maximum en charge** ~ maximum permitted load

autoriser /otɔʀize/ [1]

A *vtr* **1** (donner une permission) [*personne*] to allow [*visite*]; [*autorités*] to authorize [*paiement, visite*]; ~ **qn à faire** to give sb permission to do, to authorize sb to do; **2** (donner un droit) [*événement, loi*] ~ **qn à faire** to entitle sb to do; **ce qui autorise à penser que** which makes it reasonable *ou* legitimate to think that; **rien ne vous autorise à agir ainsi** you have no right to behave like that; **3** (rendre possible) [*situation, conditions*] to make [sth] possible [*réalisation, innovation*]; **la situation n'autorise aucune baisse des prix** the situation doesn't allow of any price reductions; **rien n'autorise ce pessimisme** there are no grounds for such pessimism

B s'autoriser *vpr* **s'**~ **de qch** to use sth as an excuse (**pour faire** to do)

autoritaire /otɔʀitɛʀ/ *adj, nmf* authoritarian

autoritarisme /otɔʀitaʀism/ *nm* authoritarianism

autorité /otɔʀite/ *nf* **1** (domination) authority (**sur** over); **faire qch d'**~ (de façon impérieuse) to do sth decisively; (sans consulter) to take it upon oneself to do sth; **2** (ascendant) authority; **il n'a aucune** ~ **sur ses enfants** he has no control over his children; **faire** ~ [*personne*] to be an authority (**en, en matière de** on); [*ouvrage*] to be authoritative; **3** (spécialiste) authority, expert; **4** Admin (pouvoir établi) authority; (personnel) **les** ~**s** the authorities

autoroute /otoʀut/ *nf* motorway GB, freeway US

autoroutier, **-ière** /otoʀutje, ɛʀ/ *adj* motorway (*épith*) GB, freeway (*épith*) US

auto-stop /otostɔp/ *nm* hitchhiking; **faire de l'**~ to hitchhike

auto-stoppeur, **-euse** *mpl* ~**s** /otostɔpœʀ, øz/ *nm,f* hitchhiker

autour /otuʀ/

A *adv* **un parterre de fleurs avec des pierres** ~ a flowerbed with stones around it; **tout** ~ all around

B *autour de* **1** (marquant le lieu) around, round GB; ~ **de la table/du soleil** around the table/the sun; **2** (marquant une approximation) around, round GB; ~ **de 10 h/200 euros** around 10 o'clock/200 euros; **3** (au sujet de) **un débat/une conférence** ~ **du thème du pouvoir** a debate/a conference on the theme of power; **un débat** ~ **de cinq**

thèmes a debate centred^GB around five themes; **la publicité organisée** ~ **de cet événement** *fig* publicity organized around this event

autre /otʀ/

⚠ Lorsqu'il est adjectif indéfini et employé avec un article défini *autre* se traduit par *other*: *l'autre rue* = the other street.

On notera que *un autre* se traduit par *another* en un seul mot.

Les autres emplois de l'adjectif ainsi que le pronom indéfini sont traités ci-dessous.

Les expressions comme *nul autre, comme dirait l'autre, en voir d'autres, avoir d'autres chats à fouetter* etc se trouvent respectivement sous **nul, dire, voir, fouetter** etc.

En revanche *l'un... l'autre* et ses dérivés sont traités ci-dessous.

A *adj indéf* **1** (indiquant la différence) other; **l'**~ **jour** the other day; **une** ~ **idée** another idea; **un** ~ **jour** some other day; **pas d'**~ **solution** no other solution; **l'effet obtenu est tout** ~ the effect produced is completely different; **quelque chose/rien d'**~ something/nothing else; **quoi d'**~? what else?; **l'actrice principale n'est** ~ **que la fille du metteur en scène** the leading actress is no other than the director's daughter; **2** (supplémentaire) **tu veux un** ~ **bonbon?** do you want another sweet GB *ou* candy US?; **ils ne veulent pas d'**~**s enfants** they don't want any more children; **donnez-moi dix** ~**s timbres** give me another ten stamps; **3** ○(après un pronom personnel) **nous** ~**s/vous** ~**s** we/you

B *pron indéf* **1** (indiquant la différence) **où sont les** ~**s?** (choses) where are the other ones?; (personnes) where are the others?; **je t'ai pris pour un** ~ I mistook you for someone else; **certains estiment que c'est juste, d'**~**s non** some (people) think it's fair, others don't; **elle est pourrie cette pomme, prends-en une** ~ this apple is rotten, have another one; **tu n'en as pas d'**~**s?** haven't you got any others?; **ce que pensent les** ~**s** what other people think; **l'un est souriant l'**~ **est grognon** one is smiling the other one is grumpy; **aussi têtus l'un que l'**~ as stubborn as each other, both equally stubborn; **des récits plus vivants les uns que les** ~**s** stories each more lively than the one before; **ils se respectent les uns les** ~**s** they respect each other; **'aimez-vous les uns les** ~**s'** 'love one another'; **l'un après l'**~, **les uns après les** ~**s** one after the other; **chez lui c'est tout l'un ou tout l'**~ with him it's all or nothing; **à d'**~**s**○! I pull the other one (it's got bells on○)!, go and tell it to the marines○! US; **prends-en un** ~ **si tu aimes ça** have another one if you like them; **si je peux je t'en apporterai d'**~**s** if I can I'll bring you some more; **ils ont deux enfants et n'en veulent pas d'**~**s** they have two children and don't want any more

C *autre part* *loc adv* somewhere else

autrefois /otʀəfwa/ *adv gén* in the past; (précédemment) before, formerly *sout*; (en un temps révolu) in the old days, in days gone by *littér*; **c'est là que je travaillais** ~ that's where I worked before *ou* I used to work; ~, **quand Paris s'appelait Lutèce** long ago, when Paris was called Lutetia; **mes habitudes/ma vie d'**~ my former habits/life; **les coutumes/légendes d'**~ old customs/legends

autrement /otʀəmã/ *adv* **1** (de façon autre) [*faire, voir, agir*] differently, in a different way; [*décider, conclure*] otherwise; [*nommé, appelé*] otherwise; **ça ne s'explique pas** ~ there's no other explanation for it; **un escroc n'aurait pas agi** ~ it's the sort of thing you would expect from a crook; **parlez-moi** ~, **je vous prie** don't talk to me like that, please; **il n'en est pas** ~ **des films** it's no different for films; **il ne peut (pas) en être** ~ that's the way it has to be; **c'est comme ça, et pas** ~ that's just the way it is; **on ne peut pas faire** ~ there's no other way; **comment aurait-elle pu faire** ~? what else could she have done?; **je n'ai pas pu faire** ~ **que de les inviter** I had no alternative but to invite them; **on ne peut y accéder** ~ **que par bateau** you can only get there by boat; **je ne l'ai jamais vue** ~ **qu'en jean** I've never seen her in anything but jeans; **ça s'est passé** ~ **que prévu** it did not turn out as expected; ~ **dit** in other words; **2** (sans quoi) otherwise; ~ **ne compte pas sur moi** otherwise don't count on me; **3** ○(à part cela) otherwise, apart from that; **4** ○(beaucoup plus) ~ **grave** (much) more serious; ~ **aimable** (much) nicer; **c'est**

a

∼ **plus petit qu'ici** it's much smaller than here; **5** ○(spécialement) **il n'était pas** ∼ **impressionné** he wasn't particularly *ou* unduly impressed

Autriche /otʀiʃ/ ▸ p. 230 *nprf* Austria

Autriche-Hongrie /otʀiʃɔ̃gʀi/ *nprf* Hist Austro-Hungary

autrichien, -ienne /otʀiʃjɛ̃, ɛn/ ▸ p. 392 *adj* Austrian

autruche /otʀyʃ/ *nf* ostrich

(Idiome) **pratiquer la politique de l'**∼ to bury one's head in the sand

autrui /otʀɥi/ *pron indéf* others (*pl*), other people (*pl*)

auvent /ovɑ̃/ *nm* (de maison) canopy; (de tente, caravane) awning

aux /o/ *prép* (= **à les**) ▸ **à**

auxiliaire /oksiljɛʀ/
A *adj* **1** Ling auxiliary; **2** (accessoire) [*machine*] auxiliary; [*motor*] back-up (*épith*); [*service*] supplementary; [*moyen*] additional; Ordinat [*mémoire*] additional; **3** ▸ p. 372 (non titulaire) **maître** ∼ assistant teacher; **infirmier** ∼ nursing auxiliary GB, nurse's aide US
B *nmf* assistant, helper
C *nm* Ling auxiliary (verb)

(Composé) ∼ **médical** medical auxiliary GB *ou* aide US

auxquels, auxquelles ▸ **lequel**

avachi, ∼**e** /avaʃi/ *adj* [*valise, chaussure*] which has lost its shape (*épith, après n*); [*fauteuil*] shapeless

avachir: s'avachir /avaʃiʀ/ [3] *vpr* [*fauteuil*] to sag; [*personne*] to let oneself go; **avachi devant la télévision** slumped in front of the television

aval /aval/ *nm* **1** Géog (de cours d'eau) downstream part; **en** ∼ downstream (**de** from); **2** Géog (de pente) lower slopes (*pl*); **en** ∼ lower down (**de** from); **3** (de processus) **en** ∼ downstream (**de** from); **4** Fin (engagement de payer) guarantee; **donner son** ∼ **à** to endorse; **5** (approbation) **vous avez mon** ∼ I'm behind you; **donner son** ∼ **à qn** to give sb one's approval

avalanche /avalɑ̃ʃ/ *nf* **1** (de neige) avalanche; **2** (de critiques, coups) avalanche; (de compliments) shower

avaler /avale/ [1] *vtr* **1** (ingurgiter) to swallow [*aliment, sirop, carte de crédit*]; fig [*entreprise*] to swallow up [*entreprise*]; **'ne pas** ∼**'** Méd 'not to be taken internally'; **j'ai avalé de travers** it went down the wrong way; ∼ **ses mots** to swallow one's words; **2** (inhaler) to inhale [*fumée, vapeur*]; **3** ○(admettre) to swallow [*mensonge*]; **c'est dur à** ∼ it's difficult to swallow

avaleur /avalœʀ/ ▸ p. 372 *nm* ∼ **de sabres** sword swallower

à-valoir /avalwaʀ/ *nm inv* Fin instalment^GB

avance /avɑ̃s/
A *nf* **1** (progression) advance; **2** (avantage) lead; **conserver son** ∼ to keep one's lead; **avoir/prendre de l'**∼ **sur** to be/to pull ahead of; **3** Fin (acompte) advance
B **à l'avance** *loc adv* in advance
C **d'avance** *loc adv* **il a perdu d'**∼ he has already lost; **payer d'**∼ to pay in advance; **d'**∼ **je vous remercie** I thank you in advance; **avoir cinq minutes d'**∼ to be five minutes early
D **en avance** *loc adv* **1** (sur l'heure) early; **arriver en** ∼ to arrive early; **2** (sur les autres) **le Japon est en** ∼ **sur l'Europe** Japan is ahead of Europe; **il est en** ∼ **pour son âge** he's advanced for his age
E **avances** *nfpl* advances; **faire des** ∼**s à qn** to make advances to sb, to come on to sb○ US

avancé, ∼**e**^1 /avɑ̃se/ *adj* **1** (précoce) [*enfant, élève*] advanced; **2** (évolué) [*technique, niveau de vie*] advanced; [*opinion, idée*] progressive; **3** (décomposé) **le poisson a l'air un peu** ∼ the fish looks as if it's going off GB *ou* bad; **4** (loin du début) advanced; **dans un état de décomposition** ∼**e** in an advanced state of decomposition; **être bien** ∼ [*travail, recherche*] to be well advanced; **la saison est bien** ∼**e** it's late in the season; **je ne suis pas plus** ∼ I'm none the wiser; **te voilà bien** ∼**!** iron that's done you a lot of good! iron; **5** Mil [*poste*] advanced

avancée^2 /avɑ̃se/ *nf* **1** (de toit, rocher) overhang; **le belvédère forme une** ∼ **sur le ravin** the belvedere projects over the ravine; **2** (progression) advance (**sur** over); **les sondages confirment l'**∼ **du candidat** the opinion polls confirm the candidate's progress; **l'**∼ **des connaissances en ce domaine** advances made in this field of knowledge

---

avant^1

Lorsque *avant* est adverbe il se traduit par *before* sauf lorsqu'il signifie 'en premier lieu, d'abord'; il se traduit alors par *first*:

si tu prends la route, mange quelque chose avant
= if you're going to drive, have something to eat first

Lorsque *avant* est préposition il se traduit par *before* sauf dans le cas où une limite de temps est précisée; il se traduit alors par *by*:

à retourner avant le 30 mars
= to be returned by 30 March

avant entre dans la composition de nombreux mots qui s'écrivent avec un trait d'union (*avant-hier, avant-guerre, avant-coureur* etc.). Ces mots sont des entrées à part entière et on les trouvera dans la nomenclature du dictionnaire. Utilisé avant un nom pour désigner une période précédant un événement ou l'avènement d'une personne, il se traduit par *pre-* et forme alors un groupe adjectival que l'on fait suivre du nom approprié:

l'avant-1945
= the pre-1945 period

l'avant-Thatcher
= the pre-Thatcher era

l'avant-sommet
= the pre-summit discussions

---

avancement /avɑ̃smɑ̃/ *nm* **1** (dans une carrière) promotion; **2** (dans des travaux, des connaissances) progress; **3** (d'une limite) ∼ **de l'âge de la retraite** lowering of the retirement age

avancer /avɑ̃se/ [12]
A *vtr* **1** (dans l'espace) to move [sth] forward [*objet*]; ∼ **une main timide** to hold one's hand out shyly; ∼ **un siège à qn** to pull *ou* draw up a seat for sb; **la voiture de Monsieur est avancée** your car awaits, sir; **2** (dans le temps) to bring forward [*départ, voyage, réunion*]; **elle avança vers le guichet** (elle alla) she went up to the ticket office; (elle vint) she came up to the ticket office; **2** (progresser) [*personne*] to make progress; [*travail*] to progress; **le travail avance vite** the work is making good progress; **j'ai bien avancé dans mon travail** I've made good progress with my work; **et votre projet? ça avance**○? and your project? how is it coming along?; **faire** ∼ **la science** to further science; **3** (faire progresser) to get ahead with [*travail*]; **classe les fiches, ça m'avancera** sort out the cards, it'll help me get on more quickly; **cela ne nous avance à rien** that doesn't get us anywhere; **4** (prêter) ∼ **de l'argent** [*banque*] to advance money; [*parent, ami*] to lend money; **5** (changer l'heure) ∼ **sa montre de cinq minutes** to put one's watch forward (by) five minutes; **6** (affirmer) to put forward [*accusation, théorie*]; to propose [*chiffre*]; ∼ **que** to suggest that
B *vi* **1** (progresser dans l'espace) [*personne, véhicule*] to move (forward); [*armée*] to advance; ∼ **d'un mètre** to move forward (by) one metre; **elle poussait mon frère pour le faire** ∼ she was pushing my brother forward; **elle avança vers le guichet** (elle alla) she went up to the ticket office; (elle vint) she came up to the ticket office; **2** (progresser) [*personne*] to make progress; [*travail*] to progress; **le travail avance vite** the work is making good progress; **j'ai bien avancé dans mon travail** I've made good progress with my work; **et votre projet? ça avance**○? and your project? how is it coming along?; **faire** ∼ **la science** to further science; **3** (par rapport à l'heure réelle) ∼ **de dix minutes** to be ten minutes fast; **4** (faire saillie) [*menton, dents*] to stick out, to protrude; [*cap, presqu'île*] to jut out (**dans** into); [*balcon, plongeoir*] to jut out, to project (**au-dessus de** over)
C **s'avancer** *vpr* **1** (physiquement) **s'**∼ **vers qch** to move toward(s) sth; **s'**∼ **vers qn** (aller) to go toward(s) sb; (venir) to come up to sb; **ne t'avance pas près du bord** don't go near the edge; **2** (dans une tâche) to get ahead; **3** (faire saillie) to jut out, to protrude (**dans** into; **sur, au-dessus de** over); **4** (se hasarder à) **je me suis un peu avancé en lui promettant le dossier pour demain** I shouldn't have committed myself by promising him I'd have the file ready for tomorrow

avanie /avani/ *nf* liter humiliation **₵**

avant^1 /avɑ̃/
A *adv* **1** (dans le temps) gén before, beforehand; (d'abord) first; **que faisait-il** ∼**?** what was he doing before?; **bien** ∼ long before; **la séance d'**∼ the previous performance; **pas ce**

lundi mais celui d'~ not this Monday but the previous one; **la fois d'~ nous nous étions déjà perdus** we got lost the last time as well; **2** (dans l'espace) before; **tu vois l'église, j'habite (juste)** ~ can you see the church? I live (just) before it; **il l'a mentionné ~ dans l'introduction** he mentioned it earlier in the introduction; **je crois que la dame était** ~ I think this lady was first; **il est inutile de creuser plus** ~ there's no point in digging any further; **refuser de s'engager plus** ~ lit to refuse to go any further; fig to refuse to get any more involved; **3** (dans une hiérarchie) before; **le T vient** ~ T comes before; **mon travail passe** ~ my work comes first

B *prép* **1** (dans le temps) before; ~ **mon départ/retour** before I leave/come back; ~ **la fin** before the end; **peu** ~ **minuit** shortly before midnight; ~ **le 1ᵉʳ juillet** by 1 July; **j'aurai fini** ~ **une semaine** I will have finished within a week; ~ **peu** shortly; **2** (dans l'espace) before; ~ **la poste** before the post office; **3** (dans une hiérarchie) before; **faire passer qn/qch** ~ **qn/qch** to put sb/sth before sb/sth; ~ **tout,** ~ **toute chose** (surtout) above all; (d'abord) first and foremost

C **avant de** *loc prép* ~ **de faire** before doing

D **avant que** *loc conj* ~ **qu'il (ne) fasse** before he does

E **en avant** *loc adv* forward(s); **se pencher/faire un pas en** ~ to lean/to take a step forward(s); **en** ~, **marche!** Mil forward march!; **en** ~ **toute!** Naut, fig full steam ahead!; **en** ~ **la musique**○! off we go!; **mettre qn/qch en** ~ to put sb/sth forward; **mettre en** ~ **le fait que** to point out the fact that

F **en avant de** *loc prép* ahead of [*groupe*]

avant² /avɑ̃/

A *adj inv* [*roue, siège, patte*] front

B *nm* **1** (partie antérieure) **l'**~ the front; **aller de l'**~ to forge ahead; **d'**~ **en arrière** backwards and forwards; **2** Sport forward

avantage /avɑ̃taʒ/ *nm* **1** (point positif, supériorité) advantage (**sur** over); **reprendre l'**~ to regain the advantage (**sur** over); **être à l'**~ **de qn** [*situation, transaction*] to be to sb's advantage; **paraître à son** ~ to look one's best; **2** (profit) advantage; **tirer** ~ **de qch** to take advantage of sth; **retirer un** ~ **de qch** to profit from sth; **avoir** ~ **à faire** to be better off doing; **3** Sport (au tennis) advantage; **4** (mesure favorable) benefit; ~**s sociaux** benefits package (*sg*); ~ **fiscaux** tax benefits

avantager /avɑ̃taʒe/ [13] *vtr* **1** (favoriser) [*personne*] to favourᴳᴮ; [*situation*] to be to the advantage of; ~ **Pierre par rapport à Paul** to favourᴳᴮ Pierre over Paul; **être avantagé par rapport à qn** to be at an advantage compared with sb; **être avantagé dès le départ** [*personne, entreprise*] to have a head start; **2** (mettre en valeur) to show [sb/sth] off to advantage

avantageusement /avɑ̃taʒøzmɑ̃/ *adv* **1** (sous un jour favorable) [*dépeindre*] favourablyᴳᴮ; **2** (honorablement) **tirer** ~ **parti de qch** to use sth to one's advantage; **ce système remplace** ~ **le précédent** this system is an improvement on the previous one

avantageux, -euse /avɑ̃taʒø, øz/ *adj* **1** (intéressant) [*condition, offre, solution, marché*] favourableᴳᴮ, advantageous (**pour qn** to sb); [*taux, prix, placement*] attractive; [*produit*] good value (*jamais épith*); **tirer un parti** ~ **de qch** to use sth to one's advantage; **2** (flatteur) [*opinion, aspect*] favourableᴳᴮ; [*description, termes, vêtement*] flattering; [*physique*] superior; **sous un jour** ~ in a favourableᴳᴮ light; **en termes très** ~ in very flattering terms

avant-bras /avɑ̃bʀa/ *nm inv* forearm

avant-centre, *pl* **avants-centres** /avɑ̃sɑ̃tʀ/ *nm* centreᴳᴮ forward; **jouer** ~ to play centreᴳᴮ forward

avant-coureur, *pl* ~**s** /avɑ̃kuʀœʀ/ *adj m* **signes** ~**s** early warning signs

avant-dernier, -ière, *pl* ~**s** /avɑ̃dɛʀnje, ɛʀ/

A *adj* **l'**~ **jour** the last day but one

B *nm,f* the last but one; **l'**~ **d'une famille de cinq enfants** the second youngest of five children

avant-garde, *pl* ~**s** /avɑ̃gaʀd/ *nf* **1** (mouvement) Art, Littér avant-garde; **cinéma d'**~ avant-garde cinema; **2** (pointe) **à l'**~ in the vanguard; **à l'**~ **de la recherche** in the vanguard of research; **3** Mil vanguard

avant-gardiste, *pl* ~**s** /avɑ̃gaʀdist/ *adj* avant-garde

avant-goût, *pl* ~**s** /avɑ̃gu/ *nm* foretaste

avant-guerre, *pl* ~**s** /avɑ̃gɛʀ/ *nm ou f* **l'**~ the prewar period; **l'Espagne d'**~ prewar Spain

avant-hier /avɑ̃tjɛʀ/ *adv* the day before yesterday

avant-midi /avɑ̃midi/ *nm inv* C (matin) morning

avant-poste, *pl* ~**s** /avɑ̃pɔst/ *nm* **1** Mil outpost; **2** fig **être aux** ~**s** to be in the vanguard

avant-première, *pl* ~**s** /avɑ̃pʀəmjɛʀ/ *nf* preview

avant-propos /avɑ̃pʀɔpo/ *nm inv* foreword

avant-scène, *pl* ~**s** /avɑ̃sɛn/ *nf* **1** (partie de scène) forestage; **2** (loge) box

avant-veille, *pl* ~**s** /avɑ̃vɛj/ *nf* **l'**~ two days before

avare /avaʀ/

A *adj* miserly; ~ **de qch** sparing with; **être** ~ **de paroles** to use words sparingly; **il n'est pas** ~ **de compliments** he's generous with his compliments

B *nmf* miser

avarice /avaʀis/ *nf* meanness GB, miserliness

avarie /avaʀi/ *nf* **1** Naut problem; **2** Comm, Jur (dommage matériel) damage ¢; (dommage de transport maritime) average ¢

avarié, ~e /avaʀje/

A *pp* ▸ **avarier**

B *pp adj* (gâté) [*viande, poisson*] rotten

avarier: **s'avarier** /avaʀje/ [2] *vpr* [*viande, poisson*] to go rotten

avatar /avataʀ/ *nm* **1** (mésaventure) controv mishap; **2** (changement) change; **connaître des** ~**s** to undergo changes; **3** Relig (réincarnation) reincarnation

avec /avɛk/

A ○*adv* **mon chapeau lui a plu, elle est partie** ~ she liked my hat and went off with it

B *prép* with; **viens** ~ **tes amis** bring your friends with you; **une maison** ~ **piscine** a house with a swimming pool; **se marier** ~ **qn** to marry sb, to get married to sb; **et** ~ **cela, que désirez-vous?** what else would you like?; **je fais tout son travail et** ~ **ça il n'est pas content!** I do all his work and he's still not happy!

avenant, ~e /avnɑ̃, ɑ̃t/

A *adj* [*personne*] pleasant

B **à l'avenant** *loc adv* **être à l'**~ to be in keeping

avènement /avɛnmɑ̃/ *nm* **1** (de souverain) accession; (d'homme politique, ère) advent; ~ **au trône** accession to the throne; **2** Relig Advent

avenir /avniʀ/ *nm* future; **à l'**~ in future GB, in the future US; **dans un** ~ **proche/immédiat** in the near/immediate future; **avoir de l'**~ to have a future; **d'**~ [*métier*] with a future; [*technique*] of the future

⸨Idiome⸩ **l'**~ **appartient à ceux qui se lèvent tôt** Prov the early bird catches the worm Prov

aventure /avɑ̃tyʀ/

A *nf* **1** (épopée) adventure; **partir à l'**~ to set off in search of adventure; **2** (péripétie) adventure; **3** (entreprise risquée) venture; **4** (intrigue amoureuse) affair

B **d'aventure** *loc adv* by chance; **si d'**~ **il venait...** if by chance he should come...

⸨Idiome⸩ **dire la bonne** ~ **à qn** to tell sb's fortune

aventurer: **s'aventurer** /avɑ̃tyʀe/ [1] *vpr* lit, fig to venture (**dans** in; **sur** onto; **jusqu'à** to)

aventureux, -euse /avɑ̃tyʀø, øz/ *adj* adventurous

aventurier, -ière /avɑ̃tyʀje, ɛʀ/ *nm,f* gén, péj adventurer/adventuress

avenu, ~e¹ /avny/ *adj* **nul et non** ~ null and void

avenue² /avny/ *nf* lit, fig avenue

avéré, ~e /aveʀe/ *adj* [*fait, goût*] recognized; [*maladie*] confirmed; **il est** ~ **que** it is proven that

avérer: **s'avérer** /aveʀe/ [14] *vpr* **le téléphone s'avère (être) un outil indispensable** the telephone is proving (to be) an indispensable tool; **il s'avère que** it transpires that, it turns out that

averse /avɛʀs/ *nf* lit, fig shower

aversion /avɛʀsjɔ̃/ *nf* aversion (**pour qn/qch** to sb/sth); **avoir qn/qch en** ~ to have a loathing for sb/sth; **prendre qn/qch en** ~ to develop a loathing for sb/sth

averti, ~e /avɛʀti/ *adj* **1** (avisé) [*lecteur, visiteur*] informed; **2** (expérimenté) [*professionnel*] experienced

avertir /avɛʀtiʀ/ [3] *vtr* **1** (informer) to inform; **2** (lancer une menace à) to warn

a

---

avec

La préposition *avec* se traduit presque toujours par *with* quand elle marque:

....

l'accompagnement

danser avec qn
= to dance with sb

du vin blanc avec du cassis
= white wine with blackcurrant

....

la possession

la dame avec le chapeau noir
= the lady with the black hat

une chemise avec un grand col
= a shirt with a large collar

....

la relation

être d'accord avec qn
= to agree with sb

avec lui c'est toujours pareil
= it's always the same with him

....

la simultanéité

se lever avec le soleil
= to get up with the sun

....

l'opposition

se battre avec qn
= to fight with sb

être en concurrence avec qn
= to be in competition with sb

....

l'identité de vue

je suis avec toi
= I'm with you

....

le moyen

avec une fourchette
= with a fork

avec une canne
= with a stick

avec de l'argent
= with money

Quand elle désigne la manière elle se traduit souvent par un adverbe formé à partir du nom qui la suit:

avec attention
= carefully

avec passion
= passionately

On trouvera ces expressions sous **attention, passion** etc.

On notera toutefois que *avec beaucoup d'attention*, *avec une grande passion* se traduisent: with great care, with a lot of passion. Les expressions telles que *avec l'âge/l'expérience/les années* etc. sont traitées respectivement sous **âge, expérience, année** etc.

On trouvera dans l'entrée des exceptions et des exemples supplémentaires.

---

avertissement /avɛʀtismɑ̃/ *nm* [1] gén, Jur, Scol warning; [2] Sport caution; [3] (dans un livre) foreword

avertisseur /avɛʀtisœʀ/
A *adj m* [*panneau*] warning
B *nm* gén alarm; Aut horn

aveu, *pl* ~**x** /avø/ *nm* [1] (de méfait) confession; **faire** ~**x** to make a confession; [2] (de défaut) admission; **de son propre** ~ on his/her own admission

aveuglant, ~**e** /avœglɑ̃, ɑ̃t/ *adj* [*clarté*] blinding

aveugle /avœgl/
A *adj* [1] (sans vue) blind; **devenir** ~ to go blind; [2] (sans lucidité) [*confiance, passion*] blind; (sans discernement) [*violence, tir*] indiscriminate; **la passion le rend** ~ he's blinded by passion
B *nmf* blind person; **les** ~**s** the blind

aveuglement /avœgləmɑ̃/ *nm* (égarement) liter blindness; **faire preuve d'un** ~ **coupable** to be shamefully unaware

aveuglément /avœglemɑ̃/ *adv* blindly

aveugler /avœgle/ [1]
A *vtr* (rendre aveugle) lit, fig to blind; (éblouir) lit, fig to dazzle, to blind
B **s'aveugler** *vpr* to hide the truth from oneself

aveuglette: **à l'aveuglette** /alavœglɛt/ *loc adv* [1] (à tâtons) **avancer à l'**~ to grope one's way along; [2] (au hasard) [*décider, agir*] in an inconsidered way

aviateur, -trice /avjatœʀ, tʀis/ ▸ p. 372 *nm,f* airman/ woman pilot

aviation /avjasjɔ̃/ *nf* [1] (civile) (secteur) aviation; (industrie) aircraft industry; [2] Mil **l'**~ the air force; [3] (activité) **l'**~ flying; **faire de l'**~ to fly

aviatrice *nf* ▸ aviateur

aviculteur, -trice /avikyltœʀ, tʀis/ ▸ p. 372 *nm,f* [1] (de volailles) poultry farmer; [2] (d'oiseaux) aviculturist

aviculture /avikyltyʀ/ *nf* [1] (de volailles) poultry farming; [2] (d'oiseaux) aviculture

avide /avid/ *adj* (vorace) [*yeux*] greedy; [*lecteur*] avid; (cupide) greedy; ~ **de** avid for [*pouvoir*]; eager for [*affection, honneurs*]; ~ **de sang** bloodthirsty

avidement /avidmɑ̃/ *adv* [1] (voracement) [*manger*] greedily; [*lire*] avidly; [2] (avec ardeur) [*chercher*] eagerly

avidité /avidite/ *nf* [1] (cupidité) greed (**de** for); **avec** ~ [*manger*] greedily; [2] (vif désir) eagerness (**de** for); **avec** ~ eagerly

avilir /aviliʀ/ [3]
A *vtr* to demean [*personne*]
B **s'avilir** *vpr* [*personne*] to demean oneself

avilissant, ~**e** /avilisɑ̃, ɑ̃t/ *adj* demeaning

avilissement /avilismɑ̃/ *nm* degradation

aviné, ~**e** /avine/ *adj* liter [*personne*] inebriated littér; [*regard, visage*] drunken

avion /avjɔ̃/ *nm* [1] (appareil) (aero)plane GB, airplane US, aircraft (*inv*); **dans l'**~ on the plane; **aller à Rome en** ~ to go to Rome by air, to fly to Rome; **envoyer qch par** ~ to send sth air mail; [2] (vol) flight; [3] (activité) **l'**~ flying; **je déteste (prendre) l'**~ I hate flying; **il n'a jamais pris l'**~ he's never been on a plane, he's never flown

(Composés) ~ **de chasse** fighter (plane); ~ **de ligne** civil aircraft, liner; ~ **en papier** paper aeroplane GB *ou* airplane US; ~ **à réaction** jet (plane); ~ **de tourisme** light passenger aircraft

avion-taxi, *pl* **avions-taxis** /avjɔ̃taksi/ *nm* air taxi

aviron /aviʀɔ̃/ *nm* [1] ▸ p. 327 Sport rowing; **faire de l'**~ to row; [2] (rame) oar

avoir[1]

Généralités

Dans la plupart des situations exprimant la possession ou la disponibilité, *avoir* sera traduit par *to have* ou *to have got*:

j'ai des livres
= I have (got) books

j'ai des enfants
= I have (got) children

j'ai des employés
= I have (got) employees

je n'ai pas assez de place
= I don't have (*ou* I haven't got) enough room

je n'ai pas assez de temps
= I don't have (*ou* I haven't got) enough time

la maison a l'électricité
= the house has electricity

la maison a cinq pièces
= the house has five rooms

j'aurai mon visa demain
= I'll have my visa tomorrow

ils vont/elle va avoir un bébé en mai
= they're/she's having a baby in May

Les autres sens de *avoir*, verbe transitif simple (obtenir, porter, triompher de etc.), sont traités dans l'entrée.

On notera qu'en règle générale les expressions figées du type *avoir raison, avoir beau, en avoir marre, il y a belle lurette, il y a de quoi* etc. seront traitées respectivement sous **raison, beau, marre, lurette, quoi** etc.

On pourra également consulter les diverses notes d'usage répertoriées ► **p. 1355**, notamment celles consacrées à l'expression de **l'âge**, aux **douleurs et maladies**, à l'expression de **l'heure** etc.

On trouvera ci-dessous les divers emplois de *avoir* pour lesquels une explication est nécessaire.

avoir = verbe auxiliaire

avoir verbe auxiliaire se traduit toujours par *to have* sauf dans le cas du passé composé:

ils avaient révisé les épreuves quand je suis parti
= they had revised the proofs when I left

quand ils eurent (ou ont eu) révisé les épreuves, ils sont partis
= when they had revised the proofs, they left

ils auront fini demain
= they will have finished tomorrow

il aurait (ou eût) aimé parler
= he would have liked to speak

Lorsqu'on a un passé composé en français, il sera traduit soit par le prétérit:

ils ont révisé les épreuves en juin
= they revised the proofs in June

ils ont révisé les épreuves avant ma démission
= they revised the proofs before I resigned

je suis sûr qu'il l'a laissé là en partant
= I'm sure he left it here when he left

soit par le 'present perfect':

ils ont révisé les épreuves plusieurs fois
= they have revised the proofs several times

avoir = verbe semi-auxiliaire

De même, *avoir* semi-auxiliaire dans les tournures attributives du type *avoir le cœur malade/les genoux cagneux*, se traduit de façon variable (*to be* ou *to have*) selon la structure adoptée par l'anglais pour rendre ces tournures; voir, en l'occurrence, les entrées **cœur** et **cagneux**; mais c'est en général sous l'adjectif que ce problème est traité.

Emplois avec à

avoir à + infinitif

Exprimant l'obligation ou la convenance, cette locution verbale se rend généralement par *to have to* suivi de l'infinitif:

j'aurais à ajouter que ...
= I would have to add that ...

tu auras à rendre compte de tes actes
= you'll have to account for your actions

je n'ai pas à vous raconter ma vie
= I don't have to tell you my life-story

vous n'aviez pas à le critiquer
= you didn't have to criticize him

il n'a pas à te parler sur ce ton
= he shouldn't speak to you in that tone of voice

j'ai beaucoup à faire
= I have a lot to do *ou* I've got a lot to do

tu n'as rien à faire?
= don't you have anything to do?
ou haven't you got anything to do?

j'ai à faire un rapport
= I have to write a report *ou* j'ai un rapport à faire
ou I have a report to write

n'avoir qu'à

Quand cette locution équivaut à *suffire*, plusieurs possibilités de traduction se présentent:

tu n'avais qu'à = tu aurais dû

Elle se rend par *should have* suivi du participe passé

tu n'as qu'à leur écrire
= you only have to write to them
ou you've only got to write to them,
ou all you have to do is write to them

tu n'auras que cinq minutes à attendre
= you'll only have to wait five minutes

tu n'avais qu'à faire attention
= you should have paid attention

tu n'avais qu'à me le dire
= you should have told me

tu n'avais qu'à partir plus tôt
= you should have left earlier

Emplois avec en

On trouvera sous **assez, marre** etc. les expressions figées *en avoir assez, en avoir marre* etc. Voir aussi les emplois avec *il y a* plus bas.

Expression du temps: *en avoir pour*

L'anglais distingue généralement entre une tâche précise (*to take*) et une activité ou absence indéterminée (*to be*):

☛ Voir page suivante

avoir[1] *suite*

vous en avez (ou aurez) pour combien de temps?
(à faire ce travail)
= how long will it take you?

(à me faire attendre)
= how long are you going to be?

j'en ai pour cinq minutes (je reviens)
= I'll be five minutes

je n'en ai pas pour longtemps
= I won't be long

j'en ai eu pour deux heures
= it took me two hours

Expression du coût: *en avoir pour*

Se traduit par *to cost* suivi du pronom personnel complément correspondant au pronom sujet français (voir aussi **argent**):

j'en ai eu pour 200 euros
= it cost me 200 euros

nous en aurons pour combien?
= how much will it cost us?

Expression de l'existence

il y a du lait dans le réfrigérateur
= there's some milk in the fridge

il y a des souris au grenier
= there are mice in the attic

il n'y a pas de riz
= there's no rice *ou* there isn't any rice

il n'y a plus de riz
= there's no more rice *ou* there isn't any more rice

il doit y avoir des souris dans le grenier
ou il y aura des souris dans le grenier
= there must be mice in the attic

il n'y a pas eu moins de 50 concurrents
= there were no less than 50 competitors

il y a chapeau et chapeau
= there are hats and hats

il y aura Paul, Marie, ...
= there will be Paul, Marie, ...

et il y aura Paul et Marie!
= and Paul and Marie will be there!

il n'y a pas de raison de faire
= there's no reason to do

il n'y a pas de raison que tu fasses
= there's no reason for you to do

il a dû y avoir quelque chose de grave
= something serious must have happened

qu'est-ce qu'il y a? (*qui ne va pas*)
= what's wrong?

(qui se passe)
= what's going on?

il y a qu'elle m'énerve
= she's getting on my nerves, that's what's wrong

il y a que l'ordinateur est en panne
= the computer has broken down

Attention, un mot singulier en français peut être traduit par un mot fonctionnant comme un pluriel en anglais:

il y a beaucoup de monde
= there are a lot of people

y avait-il du monde?
= were there many people?

Expression du temps

il est venu il y a longtemps
= he came a long time ago

il est venu il y a cinq ans
= he came five years ago

il y a cinq ans que j'habite ici
= I have been living here for five years

il y aura cinq ans demain que j'ai pris ma retraite
= it will be five years tomorrow since I retired

il y aura deux mois mardi que je travaille ici
= I will have been working here for two months on Tuesday

il n'y a que deux mois que je suis ici
= I have only been here for two months

il n'y a que deux mois que je travaille ici
= I have only been working here for two months

il n'y a pas cinq minutes qu'il est parti
= he left less than five minutes ago

il n'y a pas 200 ans que l'espèce est éteinte
= the species has been extinct for no more than 200 years

il y a combien de temps que tu habites ici?
= how long have you lived here?

il y a combien d'années que tu habites ici?
= how many years have you lived here?

il y a combien de temps qu'on ne s'est vus?
= how long is it since we last met?

il y a combien d'années qu'on ne s'est vus?
= how many years has it been since we last met?

Expression de la distance

Elle se fait généralement à l'aide du verbe *to be*:

combien y a-t-il jusqu'à la gare?
= how far is it to the station?

combien y a-t-il d'ici à la gare?
= how far is it to the station from here?

combien y a-t-il encore jusqu'à la gare?
= how much further is it to the station?

il y a 15 kilomètres jusqu'à la gare
= the station is 15 kilometres away

il y a 15 kilomètres d'ici à la gare
= the station is 15 kilometres away from here

il y a au moins 15 kilomètres
= it's at least 15 kilometres away

il y a encore 15 kilomètres
= it's another 15 kilometres

il n'y a pas 200 mètres d'ici à la gare
= it's less than 200 metres from here to the station

il n'y a que 200 mètres d'ici à la gare
= it's only 200 metres from here to the station

il y a à + infinitif

il y a à manger pour quatre
= there's enough food for four

il y a (beaucoup) à faire
= there's a lot to be done
(ceci traduit également *il y a de quoi faire*)

☞ Voir page suivante

avoir¹ *suite*

souligner le danger qu'il y a à faire
= to stress how dangerous it is to do

souligner l'avantage qu'il y a à faire
= to stress how advantageous it is to do

les risques qu'il y avait/aurait à faire
= how risky it was/would be to do

il n'y a pas à hésiter
= there's no need to hesitate

il n'y a pas à s'inquiéter
= there's no need to worry

il n'y a pas à discuter!
= no arguments!

'il n'y a qu'à le repeindre!'
= 'all you have to do is repaint it!'

'y a qu'à, c'est facile à dire!'
= 'just repaint it! easier said than done!'

....

il y en a qui, il y en a pour

L'existence se rend par *there is/are*, le temps par *to take*, et le coût par *to cost* ou *to come to*:

il y en a qui n'ont pas peur du ridicule!
= there are some people who aren't afraid of being laughed at!

il y en a toujours pour se plaindre (*ou qui se plaignent*)
= there's always someone who complains

il y en a (*ou aura*) *pour deux heures*
= it'll take two hours

il y en a eu pour deux heures
= it took two hours

il y en aurait eu pour deux heures
= it would have taken two hours

il n'y en a plus que pour deux heures
= it'll only take another two hours

il y en a encore pour combien de temps?
= how much longer will it take?

il y en a (*ou aura*) *pour 200 euros*
= it'll cost (*ou* come to) 200 euros

il y en a eu pour 200 euros
= it cost (*ou* came to) 200 euros

Noter aussi:

il n'y en a que pour leur chien
= they only think of their dog *ou* their dog comes first

Remarque: certaines formes personnelles du verbe *avoir* sont équivalentes au présentatif *il y a*. En corrélation avec le relatif *qui*, elles ne se traduisent pas; directement suivies de l'objet présenté, elles se traitent comme *il y a*:

j'ai mon stylo qui fuit
= my pen is leaking

elle avait les larmes aux yeux
= there were tears in her eyes

j'ai ma cicatrice qui me fait souffrir
= my scar is hurting

à droite, vous avez une tapisserie d'Aubusson
= on your right, there's an Aubusson tapestry

---

avis /avi/ *nm inv* **①** (opinion) opinion (**sur** on, about); **à mon** ∼ in my opinion; **les** ∼ **sont partagés** opinions differ; **je suis de ton** ∼ I agree with you; **être d'**∼ **que** to be of the opinion that; **de l'**∼ **général** in most people's opinion; **changer d'**∼ to change one's mind; **②** (conseil) advice (**sur** on, about); **sans** ∼ **médical** without consulting your doctor; **sauf** ∼ **contraire** unless otherwise informed sout; **③** (de jury, commission) recommendation; ∼ **favorable/défavorable** favourableᴳᴮ/unfavourableᴳᴮ recommendation; **④** (annonce) notice; ∼ **à la population** (affiche) public notice; (cri) public announcement; **lancer un** ∼ **de recherche** (pour un disparu) to issue a description of a missing person; (pour un malfaiteur) to issue a description of a wanted person

(Composés) ∼ **de coup de vent** gale warning; ∼ **au lecteur** foreword; ∼ **de passage** calling card (*left by meter reader, postman etc*)

(Idiome) **deux** ∼ **valent mieux qu'un** Prov two heads are better than one

avisé, ∼**e** /avize/ *adj* [*personne, conseil*] sensible; **être bien/mal** ∼ to be well-/ill-advised

aviser /avize/ [1]
A *vtr* **①** (prévenir) to notify; **②** †(apercevoir) to catch sight of
B *vi* **nous aviserons plus tard** we'll decide later; **'et s'il n'est pas là?'—'j'aviserai'** 'and if he's not there?'—'I'll see'
C **s'aviser** *vpr* **①** (se rendre compte) **s'**∼ **que** to realize that; **s'**∼ **de qch** to notice sth; **②** (oser) **ne t'avise pas de recommencer** don't do that again

aviver /avive/ [1]
A *vtr* **①** (exciter) to intensify [*chagrin, désir, colère*]; to increase [*intérêt*]; to stir up [*querelle*]; to make [sth] more acute [*douleur physique*]; **②** (rehausser) to liven up [*couleur*]; to brighten up [*teint*]; **③** (attiser) to kindle [*feu*]; **un vent violent avivait l'incendie** a strong wind fanned the flames
B **s'aviver** *vpr* fig [*chagrin*] to deepen; [*désir, intérêt*] to grow stronger; [*douleur*] to become more acute

avocat /avɔka/ ▸ **p. 372** *nm* **①** Jur gén lawyer, solicitor GB, attorney (at law) US; (au barreau) barrister GB, (trial) lawyer US; ∼ **de la défense** counsel for the defence; ∼ **de l'accusation** counsel for the prosecution; **②** fig (d'une idée) advocate (**de** of); (d'une cause, personne) champion (**de** of); **se faire l'**∼ **de** to champion; **③** Bot, Culin avocado (pear)

(Composés) **l'**∼ **du diable** the devil's advocate; **se faire l'**∼ **du diable** to play devil's advocate; ∼ **général** Advocate-General

avocate /avɔkat/ *nf* female lawyer

avoine /avwan/ *nf* oats (*pl*)

avoir¹ /avwaʀ/ [8] *vtr* **①** (obtenir) to get [*objet, rendez-vous*]; to catch [*train, avion*]; **j'ai pu vous** ∼ **votre visa** I managed to get your visa for you; **je n'ai pas eu mon train** I didn't catch my train; **②** (au téléphone) **j'ai réussi à l'**∼ I managed to get through to him/her; **③** (porter) to wear, to have [sth] on; **elle avait une robe bleue à son mariage** she wore a blue dress at her wedding; **④** ◦(triompher) to beat, to get◦, to have; **cette fois-ci, on les aura** this time, we'll get *ou* have them; **⑤** (duper) to have◦; (par malveillance) to con◦; **elle s'est fait** *or* **laissée** ∼ she's been had◦; **⑥** (éprouver moralement) to feel; ∼ **du chagrin/de la haine** to feel sorrow/hate; **qu'est-ce que tu as?** what's wrong *ou* the matter with you?; **qu'est-ce qu'il a à conduire comme ça?** why is he driving like that?; **⑦** (servant à exprimer l'âge, des sensations physiques) **j'ai 20 ans/faim/froid** I am 20 years old/hungry/cold; **la salle a 20 mètres de long** the room is 20 metresᴳᴮ long

avoir² /avwaʀ/ *nm* **①** Comm (somme) credit; (attestation) credit note; **②** (possessions) assets (*pl*), holdings (*pl*)

(Composé) ∼ **fiscal** tax credit

avoisinant, ∼**e** /avwazinɑ̃, ɑ̃t/ *adj* neighbouringᴳᴮ

avoisiner /avwazine/ [1] *vtr* **①** [*somme*] to be close to, to be about; ∼ **(les) 200 euros** to be close to 200 euros; **②** [*ferme, village*] to be near [*forêt, route*]

avortement /avɔʀtəmɑ̃/ *nm* **①** Méd abortion; **②** (échec) collapse (**de** of)

avorter /avɔʀte/ [1] *vi* **①** Méd (par intervention) to have an abortion; (spontanément) to abort, to miscarry; **se faire** ∼ to have an abortion; **faire** ∼ **qn** [*personne*] to carry out an abortion on sb; [*pilule*] to induce abortion in sb; **②** [*projet*] to be aborted

avorton /avɔʀtɔ̃/ *nm* (personne, animal, plante) pej runt

avouable /avwabl/ *adj* [*sentiment*] worthy; [*motif*] respectable; **méthode peu ~** rather dubious method

avoué, ~e /avwe/
A *adj* [*ennemi, revenu*] declared; [*intention*] avowed; [*terroriste*] self-confessed; **le mobile ~ du crime** the motive given for the crime
B ▸ p. 372 *nm* Jur ≈ solicitor GB, attorney(-at-law) US

avouer /avwe/ [1]
A *vtr* to confess [*amour, haine*]; to confess (to) [*crime*]; to admit, to confess [*ignorance, dépit, peur*]; **~ un penchant pour qch** to admit (to) a weakness for sth; **avoue** *or* **tu avoueras que c'est ridicule** you must admit, it's ridiculous
B *vi* [*suspect*] to confess; [*fautif*] to own up
C **s'avouer** *vpr* (se déclarer) **s'~ rassuré** to say one feels reassured; **s'~ battu** to admit defeat

avril /avʀil/ ▸ p. 380 *nm* April

axe /aks/ *nm* **1** gén axis; Tech axle; **2** (route) major road; **l'~ Paris–Metz** the main Paris–Metz road; **3** (prolongement) **dans l'~ du bâtiment** straight along the road from the building; **la cible est dans l'~ du viseur** the target is lined up in the sights; **4** Hist **l'Axe** the Axis

axer /akse/ [1] *vtr* **1** lit to centre^GB [*vis*]; to line up [*pièce*]; **2** fig (baser) to base (**sur** on); (concentrer) to centre^GB (**sur** on); **~ ses recherches sur un thème** to focus one's research on a theme

axiome /aksjom/ *nm* axiom

ayant droit, *pl* **ayants droit** /ɛjɑ̃dʀwa/ *nm* **1** (à une prestation, une allocation) legal claimant, beneficiary; **2** (ayant cause) assign

ayatollah /ajatɔla/ ▸ p. 590 *nm* ayatollah

azalée /azale/ *nf* azalea

azimut /azimyt/ *nm* **1** (en astronomie) azimuth; **2** fig **défense tous ~s** Mil total defence^GB; **négociations/débat tous ~s** wide-ranging negotiations/debate; **arrestations tous ~s** extensive *ou* wholesale arrests; **dans tous les ~s** everywhere, all over the place

azimuté°, ~e /azimyte/ *adj* crazy°

azote /azot/ *nm* nitrogen

aztèque /astɛk/ *adj* Aztec

azur /azyʀ/ *nm* **1** ▸ p. 140 (couleur) azure; **2** (ciel) liter azure, skies (*pl*)

azyme /azim/ *adj* unleavened

b, B /be/ *nm inv* b, B; **le b a ba** the rudiments

BA /bea/ *nf* (*abbr* = **bonne action**) good deed

baba /baba/
A °*adj inv* **en être** *or* **rester** ~ to be flabbergasted°
B *nm* ① Culin ~ **(au rhum)** (rum) baba; ② °(personne) ~ **(cool)** hippie

babil /babil/ *nm* twittering, chattering, babbling

babiller /babije/ [1] *vi* to babble, to chatter

babines /babin/ *nfpl* Zool chops

babiole /babjɔl/ *nf* (objet) trinket; (affaire) trifle

bâbord /babɔʀ/ *nm* port (side); **terre à** ~! land to port!

babouche /babuʃ/ *nf* oriental slipper

babouin /babwɛ̃/ *nm* baboon

baby-blues° *nm inv* baby blues°

baby-foot /babifut/ ▸ p. 327 *nm inv* table football

bac /bak/ *nm* ① °Scol (*abbr* = **baccalauréat**) baccalaur-eate; ② (bateau) ferry; ③ (cuve) gén tub; Ind vat; Phot tray; **évier à deux** ~**s** double sink

(Composés) ~ **blanc** Scol mock baccalaureate; ~ **à fleurs** plant tub; ~ **à glace** ice tray; ~ **à légumes** vegetable compartment (in fridge), crisper US; ~ **professionnel** Scol ≈ GNVQ (*secondary school vocational diploma*); ~ **à sable** sandpit GB, sandbox US

baccalauréat /bakalɔʀea/ *nm* Scol baccalaureate (*school leaving certificate taken at 17–18*)

ℹ Baccalauréat known informally as the *bac*, is an examination sat in the final year of the *lycée* (*la terminale*), so usually at age 17 or 18. Students sit exams in a fairly broad range of subjects in a particular category: the *bac S* places the emphasis on the sciences, for example, whilst the *bac L* has a literary bias. Some categories cater for students specializing in more directly job-based subjects such as agriculture.

bâche /baʃ/ *nf* tarpaulin; **toile de** ~ canvas sheet

bachelier, -ière /baʃəlje, ɛʀ/ *nm,f:* holder of the (French) *baccalaureate*

bâcher /baʃe/ [1] *vtr* to cover [sth] with tarpaulin [*véhicule*]; **un camion bâché** a covered truck

bachotage° /baʃɔtaʒ/ *nm* Scol cramming

bacille /basil/ *nm* bacillus; ~ **de Koch** Koch bacillus

bâcler /bakle/ [1] *vtr* to dash [sth] off [*devoirs, travail*]; to rush through [*cérémonie*]; **c'est du travail bâclé** it's a slap-dash job

bacon /bekɔn/ *nm* smoked back bacon

bactéricide /bakteʀisid/
A *adj* bactericidal
B *nm* bactericide

bactérie /bakteʀi/ *nf* bacterium; **des** ~**s** bacteria

bactérien, -ienne /bakteʀjɛ̃, ɛn/ *adj* bacterial

badaud, -e /bado, od/ *nm,f* (curieux) onlooker

badge /badʒ/ *nm* ① (insigne) badge; ② (identité) badge, name tag; (avec piste magnétique) swipe card

badgeuse /badʒøz/ *nf* time clock

badiane /badjan/ *nf* star anise

badigeonner /badiʒɔne/ [1] *vtr* ① (à la chaux) to white-wash; (en couleur) to paint; ② (barbouiller) to daub (**de** with); ③ Méd to paint [*blessure, gorge*] (**de** with); ④ Culin to brush (**de** with)

badin, ~e¹ /badɛ̃, in/ *adj* [*ton*] bantering; [*humeur*] playful

badinage /badinaʒ/ *nm* ① (attitude) bantering; ② (propos) banter

badine² /badin/
A *adj* ▸ **badin**
B *nf* ① (baguette) switch; ② (canne) cane

badiner /badine/ [1] *vi* to banter, to jest; **il ne badine pas avec le règlement** he doesn't mess about when it comes to rules

baffe° /baf/ *nf* clout, slap

baffle /bafl/ *nm* (enceinte) speaker; (écran acoustique) baffle

bafouer /bafwe/ [1] *vtr* to scorn

bafouille° /bafuj/ *nf* letter

bafouiller /bafuje/ [1]
A *vtr* to mumble [*excuse*]
B *vi* [*personne*] to mumble; [*moteur*] to splutter

bagage /bagaʒ/
A *nm* ① (effets) luggage; (de soldat) kit; ② (sac, valise) piece of luggage; ③ fig (connaissances) knowledge; (diplômes) qualifications (*pl*); (expérience) credentials (*pl*)
B **bagages** *nmpl* luggage ∅; **faire/défaire ses** ~**s** to pack/unpack (one's suitcases)

(Composé) ~ **à main** hand luggage, carry-on baggage US

(Idiomes) **plier** ~° to pack up and go; **partir avec armes et** ~**s** to up sticks and leave; **passer à l'ennemi avec armes et** ~**s** to defect

bagagiste /bagaʒist/ ▸ p. 372 *nm* baggage handler

bagarre /bagaʀ/ *nf* ① (empoignade) fight (**entre** between); ~**s avec la police** clashes with the police; ~ **générale** free-for-all; ② fig (lutte) fight, struggle; (dispute) clash, confrontation; **entrer dans la** ~ to join the fray

bagarrer°: **se bagarrer** /bagaʀe/ [1] *vpr* to fight (**pour** for)

bagarreur°, **-euse** /bagaʀœʀ, øz/
A *adj* (agressif) aggressive; (combatif) **être** ~ to like to pick a fight
B *nm,f* bruiser°, fighter

bagatelle /bagatɛl/ *nf* ① (affaire) triviality; ② (objet) **je lui ai acheté une** ~ I bought him/her a little something; ③ (somme) trifle; ~ **de** iron trifling sum of

bagnard /baɲaʀ/ *nm* convict

bagne /baɲ/ *nm* ① (prison) penal colony; ② (peine) penal servitude

bagnole° /baɲɔl/ *nf* car

bagou(t)° /bagu/ *nm* volubility, glibness péj; **avoir du** ~ to have the gift of the gab

bague /bag/ *nf* (anneau) ring; (de cigare) band; (de tuyau) collar

(Idiomes) **avoir la** ~ **au doigt** to be married; **elle lui a passé la** ~ **au doigt** she got him to the altar

baguer /bage/ [1] *vtr* to ring [*oiseau, arbre*]; Tech to collar [*tuyau*]; **doigts bagués** be-ringed fingers

baguette /bagɛt/ *nf* ① (pain) baguette, French stick; ② (bâton) gén stick; (de tambour) drumstick; (pour manger) chopstick; ~ **d'encens** incense stick; ~ **de chef d'orchestre** conductor's baton; **mener qn à la** ~ fig to rule sb with a rod of iron; ③ (moulure) beading; (pour cacher) casing; ④ (de bas, chaussettes) clock

(Composés) ~ **de fusil** ramrod; ~ **magique** magic wand; ~ **de sourcier** water-divining rod

b

bahut /bay/ *nm* [1] (buffet) sideboard; [2] ○(lycée) students' slang school; [3] ○(camion) truck; [4] (malle) chest

bai, ~e¹ /bɛ/ ▸ p. 140 *adj* bay

baie² /bɛ/ *nf* [1] Géog bay; [2] Bot berry; [3] ~ **(vitrée)** picture window

baignade /bɛɲad/ *nf* [1] (activité) swimming; '~ **interdite**' 'no swimming'; [2] (lieu) bathing spot

baigner /beɲe/ [1]
A *vtr* [1] (donner un bain à) to bath GB, to bathe US, to give [sb] a bath [*enfant, malade*]; [2] (pour soulager) to bathe [*œil, blessure*] (**dans** in; **avec** with); [3] (inonder) **il avait le visage baigné de larmes** his face was bathed with tears
B *vi* ~ **dans l'huile** [*saucisses*] to be swimming in grease; ~ **dans son sang** to be lying in a pool of one's own blood; **ça baigne**○ things are going fine
C **se baigner** *vpr* [1] (dans la mer, une piscine) to have a swim; [2] (dans une baignoire) to have GB *ou* take US a bath

baigneur, -euse /bɛɲœʀ, øz/
A *nm,f* (personne) swimmer, bather†
B *nm* (poupée) baby doll

baignoire /bɛɲwaʀ/ *nf* [1] (pour se laver) bath GB, bathtub; [2] Théât ground-floor box

bail, *pl* **baux** /baj, bo/ *nm* gén lease; (de trois ans ou moins) tenancy agreement; **donner à** ~ to lease out; **prendre à** ~ to lease; **ça fait un** ~ **qu'on ne s'est pas vus**○! we haven't seen each other for ages○!

bâillement /bajmɑ̃/ *nm* yawn; **retenir un** ~ to stifle a yawn

bâiller /baje/ [1] *vi* [1] [*personne, animal*] to yawn (**de** from, out of); [2] [*col, chaussure*] to gape (open); [*porte*] to be ajar

bailleur, bailleresse /bajœʀ, bajʀɛs/ *nm,f* lessor
Composé ~ **de fonds** Comm backer, silent partner

bâillon /bajɔ̃/ *nm* gag; **mettre un** ~ **à** to gag

bâillonner /bajɔne/ [1] *vtr* to gag [*presse*]

bain /bɛ̃/ *nm* [1] (liquide) bath; **prendre un** ~ to have GB *ou* take a bath; **être dans son** ~ to be in the bath GB *ou* bathtub; [2] (baignade) swim; **après le** ~ after a swim; [3] (bassin) **grand** ~ deep end; **petit** ~ children's GB *ou* baby pool
Composés ~ **de bouche** (produit) mouthwash; **faire des** ~**s de bouche** to rinse one's mouth (out); ~ **de boue** mudbath; ~ **bouillonnant** whirlpool bath; ~ **fixateur** fixing bath; ~ **de foule** walkabout; **prendre un** ~ **de foule** [*personnalité*] to go (on a) walkabout GB, to mingle with the crowd US; ~ **de friture** cooking oil; ~ **de jouvence** rejuvenating experience; ~ **de minuit** midnight swim; **faire des** ~**s de pieds** to soak one's feet; ~ **à remous** Jacuzzi®; ~ **révélateur** developing bath; ~ **de sang** bloodbath; ~ **de siège** Méd sitz bath; ~ **de soleil** (corsage) suntop; **prendre un** ~ **de soleil** to sunbathe; ~ **de teinture** (produit) dye; (bac) vat of dye; ~ **turc** Turkish bath; ~ **d'yeux** (produit) eyewash; ~**s de mer** sea bathing **₵**
Idiomes **se remettre dans le** ~ to get back into the swing of things; **mettre qn dans le** ~ to implicate sb

bain-douche, *pl* **bains-douches** /bɛ̃duʃ/ *nm* public baths

bain-marie /bɛ̃maʀi/ *nm* **au** ~ gén in a bain-marie; (crèmes, sauces) in a double boiler

baïonnette /bajɔnɛt/ *nf* Mil bayonet; Électrotech bayonet fitting

baisemain /bɛzmɛ̃/ *nm* hand-kissing **₵**; **faire le** ~ **à qn** to kiss sb's hand

baiser /beze/ *nm* kiss; **bons** ~**s** love (and kisses)

baisse /bɛs/ *nf* [1] gén (de température, pression) fall, drop; (de lumière) fading, dimming; (d'influence, de qualité) decline; **une** ~ **de 10°/de pression** a fall *ou* drop of 10°/in pressure; [2] Écon (décidée) cut; (constatée) fall, drop, decrease; **la** ~ **du dollar** the fall in the value of the dollar; **une** ~ **des loyers de 2%** a 2% drop in rents; **être en** ~ [*taux, actions, valeurs*] to be going down; [*résultats*] to be decreasing; **le marché est à la** ~ (en Bourse) the market is bearish; **revoir des prévisions à la** ~ to revise estimates downward(s); **spéculations à la** ~ bear speculations

baisser /bese/ [1]
A *vtr* [1] (abaisser) to lower [*volet, store*]; to wind [sth] down [*vitre*]; to pull down [*pantalon, visière*]; to turn down [*col*];

~ **la tête** (par précaution) to lower one's head; (vivement) to duck one's head; (par soumission, de honte) to bow; ~ **les yeux (de honte)** to look down (in shame); ~ **les bras** lit to lower one's arms; fig to give up; ~ **le nez** fig to hang one's head; [2] (réduire) to turn down [*son, volume*]; to dim [*lumière*]; [*autorité*] to cut [*prix, taux*]; [*circonstances*] to bring down [*prix, taux*]
B *vi* [1] (diminuer de niveau) gén to go down (**à** to; **de** by); (brusquement) to fall, to drop; [*lumière*] to fade; [*eaux*] to subside; [*qualité, criminalité*] to decline; ~ **dans l'estime de qn** to go down in sb's esteem; ~ **d'un ton**○ [*personne*] fig to calm down; [2] (diminuer de valeur) [*prix, résultat, taux, production*] to fall; [*salaires, actions*] to go down; [*pouvoir d'achat, chômage, emplois*] to decrease; [*productivité, marché*] to decline; [*budget*] to be cut; [*monnaie*] to slide; [3] (diminuer de qualité) [*vue*] to fail; [*ouïe, facultés*] to deteriorate
C **se baisser** *vpr* [*personne*] (pour passer, saisir) to bend down; (pour éviter) to duck; [*levier*] to go down

baissier, -ière /besje, ɛʀ/
A *adj* bearish
B *nm* (en Bourse) bear

bajoue /baʒu/ *nf* [1] Culin (de porc, veau) cheek; [2] ○(joue humaine) jowl, chop

bal /bal/ *nm* (cérémonieux) ball; (simple) dance
Composés ~ **champêtre** village dance; ~ **costumé** fancy-dress ball, costume ball US; ~ **masqué** masked ball; ~ **musette** dance with accordion music

balade /balad/ *nf* (à pied) walk; (à moto, vélo) ride

balader○ /balade/ [1]
A *vtr* [1] (à pied) to take [sb] for a walk; (en voiture) to take [sb] for a drive; [2] (emporter avec soi) to carry [sth] around
B **se balader** *vpr* [1] (faire une balade) (à pied) to go for a walk; (à moto, vélo) to go for a ride; (en voiture) to go for a drive; [2] (voyager) to travel
Idiome **envoyer qn** ~○ to send sb packing○

baladeur, -euse¹ /baladœʀ, øz/
A *adj* [*lampe*] portable
B *nm* walkman®, personal stereo

baladeuse² /baladøz/ *nf* portable lamp

baladin /baladɛ̃/ *nm* strolling player

balafre /balafʀ/ *nf* (marque) scar; (entaille) slash, gash

balai /balɛ/ *nm* [1] (pour le sol) broom; **passer le** ~ to sweep the floor; **du** ~○! go away!; [2] (d'essuie-glace) blade; [3] Électrotech brush; [4] ○(an) **avoir 50** ~**s** to be fifty

balai-brosse, *pl* **balais-brosses** /balɛbʀos/ *nm* stiff broom

balai-éponge, *pl* **balais-éponges** /balɛepɔ̃ʒ/ *nm* squeeze mop

balaise○ = **balèze**

balance /balɑ̃s/ *nf* [1] (pour peser) scales (*pl*); **faire pencher la** ~ fig to tip the scales; [2] (de comptes) balance; [3] (équilibre) balance; [4] Audio balance
Composés ~ **commerciale** balance of trade; ~ **des comptes** = ~ **des paiements**; ~ **de cuisine** kitchen scales; ~ **des paiements** balance of payments; ~ **à plateaux** balance; ~ **de précision** precision balance; ~ **romaine** steelyard

Balance /balɑ̃s/ ▸ p. 635 *nprf* Libra

balancé, -e /balɑ̃se/ *adj* **bien** ~ [*phrase*] well-balanced; [*personne*]○ well-built

balancelle /balɑ̃sɛl/ *nf* swing seat, garden hammock

balancement /balɑ̃smɑ̃/ *nm* (de branches, corps) swaying **₵**; (de bras, jambes, hanches, corde) swinging **₵**; (de tête) lolling **₵**

balancer /balɑ̃se/ [12]
A *vtr* [1] (faire osciller) [*vent*] to sway [*branches*]; to swing [*cordage*]; ~ **les bras** to swing one's arms; [2] ○(jeter) to chuck○, to throw [*projectile, ordures*] (**sur** at); to chuck out○, to throw out [*vieux habits, objets inutiles*]; ~ **une gifle à qn** to whack sb○; [3] ○(dire) (brutalement) to toss off [*phrases, réponse*]; (pêle-mêle) to bandy [sth] about [*chiffres*]; ~ **des statistiques à la figure de qn** to fling statistics at sb; [4] ○(dénoncer) ~ **qn** to squeal on sb○; [5] to balance [*compte*]
B *vi* [1] (osciller) [*branches*] to sway; [*corde, trapèze*] to swing; [*bateau*] to rock; [2] (hésiter) ~ **entre deux personnes** to hesitate *ou* be torn between two people
C **se balancer** *vpr* [1] (se mouvoir) [*personne, animal*] to sway; [*bateau*] to rock; **se** ~ **d'un pied sur l'autre** to shift from

one foot to the other; **se ~ sur sa chaise** to rock on one's chair; [2] ○(se jeter) **se ~ du sixième étage** to fling oneself off the sixth GB ou seventh US floor

balancier /balãsje/ *nm* [1] gén (d'horloge, de métronome) pendulum; **politique de ~** fig seesaw politics; [2] (pour funambule) balancing pole; [3] Zool haltere

balançoire /balãswaʀ/ *nf* (suspendue) swing; (qui bascule) seesaw

balayage /balɛjaʒ/ *nm* [1] (avec un balai) sweeping; [2] (en coiffure) **se faire faire un ~** to have highlights put in; [3] (en électronique) scanning

balayer /baleje/ [21] *vtr* [1] (avec un balai) to sweep (up); [2] (frôler) **~ le sol** [cape, manteau] to brush the ground; [3] [vent] to sweep across [plaine]; to sweep [sth] away [nuages, feuilles]; [faisceau, regard] to sweep; [mitrailleuse] to rake; [4] (faire disparaître) to brush [sth] aside [objections, rumeurs]; to sweep [sth] aside [craintes]; [5] (en électronique) to scan

(Idiome) **~ devant sa porte** to put one's own house in order before criticizing other people

balayette /balɛjɛt/ *nf* (short-handled) brush

balayeur -euse[1] /balɛjœʀ, øz/ ▸ p. 372 *nm,f* (personne) road sweeper

balayeuse[2] /balɛjøz/ *nf* (machine) mechanical road-sweeper GB, mechanical street-sweeper US

balbutiant, ~e /balbysjã, ãt/ *adj* (qui bredouille) stammering; (qui débute) in its infancy

balbutiement /balbysimã/ *nm* lit stammering ₡; fig (début) first step

balbutier /balbysje/ [2]
A *vtr* to stammer
B *vi* (bredouiller) to stammer; (débuter) to be in its infancy

balbuzard /balbyzaʀ/ *nm* osprey

balcon /balkɔ̃/ *nm* [1] Constr balcony; [2] Théât balcony, circle; [3] Naut (rambarde) bow pulpit, stern pulpit; (galerie) Hist stern gallery

baldaquin /baldakɛ̃/ *nm* canopy

Bâle /bɑl/ *npr* [1] ▸ p. 621 (ville) Basel; [2] ▸ p. 504 (région) **le canton de ~** the canton of Basel

Baléares /baleaʀ/ ▸ p. 303 *nprfpl* **les (îles) ~** the Balearic Islands

baleine /balɛn/ *nf* [1] Zool whale; [2] (de corset) whalebone, stay US; (de col) stiffener, stay US

(Composé) **~ de parapluie** umbrella rib

(Idiome) **rire** or **se tordre comme une ~**○ to laugh one's head off○

baleinier, -ière[1] /balɛnje, ɛʀ/
A *adj* [bateau, industrie] whaling
B ▸ p. 372 *nm* (pêcheur) whaler

baleinière[2] /balɛnjɛʀ/ *nf* (bateau) whaleboat

balèze○ /balɛz/ *adj* [1] (grand et fort) hefty○; [2] fig [intellectuel] fantastic○, brilliant GB; [sportif] fantastic○

balisage /balizaʒ/ *nm* (de port, chenal) beaconing; (de piste d'aviation) runway lighting; (de route) signposting; (de sentier) marking; (de texte) tagging

balise /baliz/ *nf* [1] Aviat, Naut beacon; [2] (sur route) signpost; [3] Rail signal; [4] (de sentier, piste de ski) marker; [5] Ordinat tag

baliser /balize/ [1] *vtr* [1] Aviat, Naut to mark [sth] out with beacons; [2] (travaux publics) to signpost [route]; [3] Rail to mark [sth] out with signals [voie ferrée]; [4] Sport to mark out [sentier]; [5] Ordinat to tag [texte]

balistique /balistik/
A *adj* [missile] ballistic
B *nf* ballistics (+ v sg)

baliverne /balivɛʀn/ *nf* nonsense ₡

balkanique /balkanik/ *adj* Balkan (épith)

balkanisation /balkanizasjɔ̃/ *nf* (de territoire) Balkanization; (d'institution) break-up

ballade /balad/ *nf* [1] Mus (instrumentale) ballade; (chanson) ballad; [2] Littérat (forme fixe) ballade; (forme libre) ballad

ballant, ~e /balã, ãt/
A *adj* [bras] dangling; [tête] lolling; [câble, cordage] slack
B *nm* **avoir du ~** [véhicule] to sway around; [cordage] to be slack

ballast /balast/ *nm* Naut, Rail ballast

balle /bal/ *nf* [1] (objet) ball; **renvoyer la ~ (à qn)** lit to throw the ball back (to sb); fig to retort (to sb); **se renvoyer la ~** (discuter) to keep a lively argument going; (se rejeter la responsabilité) to keep passing the buck; ▸ **bond**; [2] (échange, envoi) shot; **~ coupée** sliced shot; **~ de jeu** game point; [3] (d'arme à feu) bullet; [4] ○(franc) franc; [5] (de café, foin) bale; (de papier) ream; [6] Bot husk

(Composé) **~ à blanc** blank (bullet)

ballerine /balʀin/ *nf* [1] ▸ p. 372 (danseuse) ballerina, ballet dancer; [2] (chaussures) (de danse) ballet pump; (de ville) ballerina-style shoe

ballet /balɛ/ *nm* [1] (danse, musique) ballet; [2] (va et vient) **~ diplomatique** diplomatic comings and goings (pl)

(Composé) **~ aquatique** Sport synchronized swimming

ballon /balɔ̃/ *nm* [1] Sport ball; Aviat, Météo balloon; (jouet) balloon; [2] (verre) **(verre) ~** wine glass; [3] Aut **~ (alcootest)** Breathalyzer®; [4] Géog round-topped mountain

(Composés) **~ captif** tethered ou captive balloon; **~ dirigeable** airship GB, blimp US; **~ d'eau chaude** hot water tank; **~ d'essai** lit pilot balloon, trial balloon; **~ ovale** (jeu) rugby; (objet) rugby ball; **~ d'oxygène** lit oxygen bottle; fig life-saver; **~ prisonnier** team game where players hit by the ball become the prisoners of the opposite team; **~ rond** (jeu) soccer; (objet) football GB, soccer ball

ballonnement /balɔnmã/ *nm* bloating

ballonner /balɔne/ [1] *vtr* **~ le ventre** to make one's stomach bloated

ballon-sonde, *pl* **ballons-sondes** /balɔ̃sɔ̃d/ *nm* sounding balloon

ballot /balo/ *nm* [1] (paquet) bundle; [2] ○(sot) nerd○, fool

ballotin /balɔtɛ̃/ *nm* **~ de chocolats** small box of chocolates

ballottage /balɔtaʒ/ *nm* Pol absence of an absolute majority in the first round of an election; **il y a ~** there has to be a runoff (ballot); **être mis en ~** to face a runoff

ballottement /balɔtmã/ *nm* tossing, jolting

ballotter /balɔte/ [1]
A *vtr* [1] [mer] to toss [sb/sth] around [embarcation]; [cahot] to jolt [personne, véhicule]; [2] fig **être ballotté entre sa famille et son travail** to be torn between one's family and one's job
B *vi* [bateau] to be buffeted; [voiture, objet, tête] to jolt

ball-trap, *pl* **~s** /baltʀap/ *nm* (appareil) trap (for clay pigeon shooting); (sport) clay pigeon shooting

balluchon = **baluchon**

balnéaire /balneɛʀ/ *adj* [station] seaside (épith)

balourd, ~e /baluʀ, uʀd/
A *adj* uncouth
B *nm,f* (personne) oaf

balourdise /baluʀdiz/ *nf* [1] (gaucherie) clumsiness; [2] (acte) blunder, faux-pas; (parole) gaffe, faux-pas

balte /balt/ ▸ p. 504 *adj* Baltic

baluchon /balyʃɔ̃/ *nm* bundle

(Idiome) **faire son ~** to pack one's bags (and leave)

balustrade /balystʀad/ *nf* (en ciment, pierre) parapet; (en métal) railing; (avec colonnettes) balustrade

balustre /balystʀ/ *nm* baluster

bambin, ~e /bãbɛ̃, in/ *nm,f* kid○, child

bambou /bãbu/ *nm* [1] lit bamboo; [2] fig **coup de ~** (facture) steep ou hefty bill; **avoir le coup de ~** (être fatigué) to be knackered◑ GB ou bushed○ US

bamboula /bãbula/ *nf* [1] ○(fête) bash○; [2] (danse, musique) bamboula

ban /bã/
A *nm* (applaudissements) round of applause (**pour** for); (roulements de tambour) drum roll; (sonnerie) bugle call; **ouvrir le ~** (de réunion) to start the proceedings
B **bans** *nmpl* banns

(Idiome) **mettre qn au ~ de la société** to ostracize sb from society

banal, ~e /banal, o/ *adj* [1] (mpl **~s**) commonplace, unremarkable, banal; **peu** or **pas ~** rather unusual; [2] (mpl **-aux**) Hist communal

banalisation /banalizasjɔ̃/ *nf* **la ~ de l'informatique** the way in which computing has become part of everyday life

banaliser /banalize/ [1] *vtr* ① (généraliser) to make [sth] commonplace; ② (rendre ordinaire) **voiture banalisée** unmarked car

banalité /banalite/ *nf* ① (d'histoire, de vie) commonplace nature; (de remarque, d'idée) triteness; ② (propos, écrit, manque d'originalité) banality

banane /banan/ *nf* ① Bot banana; ② (coiffure) quiff, French pleat; ③ (sac) bumbag GB, fanny pack US

bananier, -ière /bananje, ɛʀ/
Ⓐ *adj* banana (épith)
Ⓑ *nm* ① Bot banana tree; ② (bateau) banana boat

banc /bɑ̃/ *nm* ① (siège) bench; ~ **public** bench; **sur les ~s de l'école** at school; ② Pol (au Parlement) bench GB, seats (pl) US; ③ (de poissons) shoal; (d'huîtres) bed; ④ (de terrain) layer, bed; ⑤ Tech bench
(Composés) ~ **des accusés** dock; **au ~ des avocats** at the bar; ~ **de brume** patch of mist; ~ **de coraux** coral reef; ~ **d'église** pew; ~ **d'essai** lit test bench; fig testing ground; **au ~ de l'infamie** in the dock; ~ **de nage** thwart; ~ **de sable** sandbank; **au ~ des témoins** in the witness box GB, on the witness stand US

bancaire /bɑ̃kɛʀ/ *adj* ① [activité, secteur, service] banking; ② [carte, compte, chèque, prêt] bank (épith)

bancal, ~e /bɑ̃kal/ *adj* [chaise, table] rickety; [solution, raisonnement] shaky; **la dernière phrase est ~e** the last sentence does not really stand up

banco /bɑ̃ko/ *nm* (au baccara) banco; **faire ~** to go banco; **gagner le ~** fig to make a packet○

bandage /bɑ̃daʒ/ *nm* (de blessure) bandage; (de roue) tyre

bande /bɑ̃d/ *nf* ① (de malfaiteurs) gang; ② (de touristes, d'amis) group, crowd; ~ **de crétins!** you bunch of idiots!; **ils font ~ à part** they don't join in; ③ (d'animaux sauvages) pack; ④ (de tissu, papier, cuir) gén strip; (plus large) band; (pour blessure) bandage; ⑤ (forme allongée) gén strip; (qui orne) (rayure) large stripe; (en bordure) band; ~ **de terre** strip of land; ⑥ (support d'enregistrement) tape; Cin film; ⑦ (au billard) cushion; ⑧ Naut **donner de la ~** to list
(Composés) ~ **d'arrêt d'urgence**, hard shoulder; ~ **banalisée** = ~ **publique**; ~ **dessinée, BD**○ (dans les journaux) comic strip; (livre) comic book; (genre) comic strips (pl); ~ **d'essai** Phot test strip; ~ **de fréquences** waveband; ~ **originale** Cin original soundtrack; ~ **publique** Citizens' band, CB; ~ **de roulement** Aut tread; ~ **rugueuse** Aut rumble strip; ~ **sonore** Cin soundtrack; (d'autoroute) rumble strip; ~ **Velpeau®** crepe bandage GB, Ace bandage® US
(Idiome) **apprendre qch par la ~**○ to hear sth on the grapevine

> ℹ **Bande dessinée** It plays a significant cultural role in France. More than a comic book or entertainment for the youth, it is a form of popular literature known as the *neuvième art* and celebrated annually at the *Festival d'Angoulême*. Cartoon characters such as *Astérix*, *Lucky Luke*, and *Tintin* are household names and older comic books are often collectors' items.

bande-annonce, *pl* **bandes-annonces** /bɑ̃danɔ̃s/ *nf* trailer

bandeau, *pl* ~**x** /bɑ̃do/ *nm* ① (pour ne pas voir) blindfold; (d'œil malade) eye patch; **avoir un ~ sur les yeux** fig to be blind; ② (de coiffure) headband

bandelette /bɑ̃dlɛt/ *nf* ① (pour blessure, momie) bandage; ② (de soie, papier etc) small strip

bander /bɑ̃de/ [1] *vtr* ① (panser) to bandage; ② (avec un bandeau) ~ **les yeux à qn** to blindfold sb; ③ (tendre) to bend [arc]; to stretch [ressort]; to tense [muscles]

banderole /bɑ̃dʀɔl/ *nf* banner

bande-son, *pl* **bandes-son** /bɑ̃dsɔ̃/ *nm* soundtrack

bandit /bɑ̃di/ *nm* ① (malfaiteur) bandit; ② (homme sans scrupules) crook; ③ (enfant) rascal
(Composé) ~ **de grand chemin** highwayman

banditisme /bɑ̃ditism/ *nm* **le ~** crime; **le grand/petit ~** organized/petty crime

bandoulière /bɑ̃duljɛʀ/ *nf* shoulder strap

bang /bɑ̃g/ *nm* (supersonique) sonic boom

banlieue /bɑ̃ljø/ *nf* ① (périphérie) suburbs (pl); **de ~** [ville, hôpital] suburban; ② (quartier) suburb

banlieusard, ~e /bɑ̃ljøzaʀ, aʀd/ *nm,f* person from the suburbs, suburbanite

banni, ~e /bani/ *nm,f* exile

bannière /banjɛʀ/ *nf* (tous contextes) banner
(Composé) **la ~ étoilée** the star-spangled banner, the Stars and Stripes
(Idiome) **c'est la croix et la ~** it's hell

bannir /baniʀ/ [3] *vtr* ① (chasser) to banish [personne] (de from); ② (exclure) to ban [coutume, sujet]

bannissement /banismɑ̃/ *nm* banishment (de from)

banque /bɑ̃k/ *nf* ① (établissement) bank; **mettre un chèque à la ~** to pay in ou deposit a cheque GB ou check US; ② (activité) banking; ③ (de jeu) bank
(Composés) ~ **d'affaires** merchant bank; ~ **de dépôt** deposit bank; ~ **à domicile** home banking; ~ **de données** Ordinat data bank; ~ **d'émission** issuing bank; ~ **d'organes** Méd organ bank; ~ **du sang** Méd blood bank; **Banque mondiale** World Bank

banqueroute /bɑ̃kʀut/ *nf* ① Fin bankruptcy; ② fig (échec) complete failure

banquet /bɑ̃kɛ/ *nm* (cérémonie) banquet; (repas) feast

banqueter /bɑ̃kte/ [23] *vi* to banquet; (faire bonne chère) to feast

banquette /bɑ̃kɛt/ *nf* (de restaurant) wall seat, banquette US; (de train) seat; (de fenêtre) window seat

banquier /bɑ̃kje/ ▸ p. 372 *nm* banker

banquise /bɑ̃kiz/ *nf* ice floe

bantou, ~e /bɑ̃tu/ ▸ p. 336
Ⓐ *adj* Géog Bantu
Ⓑ *nm* Ling Bantu

bantoustan /bɑ̃tustɑ̃/ *nm* homeland

baptême /batɛm/ *nm* ① Relig baptism; **donner le ~ à** to baptize; ② (de bateau) naming GB, christening; (de cloche) blessing; ③ (initiation) baptism
(Composé) ~ **de l'air** first flight

baptiser /batize/ [1] *vtr* ① Relig to baptize; **se faire ~** to be baptized; ② (nommer) to call; (surnommer) to nickname; ③ (inaugurer) to name GB, to christen [navire]; to bless [cloche]

baptismal, ~e, *mpl* **-aux** /batismal, o/ *adj* [eau] baptismal

baptisme /batism/ *nm* Baptist doctrine

baptistère /batistɛʀ/ *nm* baptistry

baquet /bakɛ/ *nm* ① (récipient) tub; ② (siège) bucket-seat

bar /baʀ/ *nm* ① (lieu, comptoir, meuble) bar; ② (poisson) sea bass; ③ Phys bar

baragouiner○ /baʀagwine/ [1]
Ⓐ *vtr* to gabble [propos, phrase]; to speak [sth] badly [langue]
Ⓑ *vi* to witter○ GB, to gibber

baraka○ /baʀaka/ *nf* luck; **avoir la ~** to be lucky

baraque /baʀak/ *nf* ① (construction légère) shack; ② ○(maison) pad○, house; (en mauvais état) dump○
(Composé) ~ **foraine** fairground stall ou stand US
(Idiomes) **casser la ~**○ to be a resounding success; **casser la ~**○ **à** or **de qn** to mess things up for sb○

baraqué○, ~**e** /baʀake/ *adj* hefty, husky US

baraquement /baʀakmɑ̃/ *nm* ① (ensemble) group of huts; ② Mil army camp

baratin○ /baʀatɛ̃/ *nm* (pour vendre) spiel○, sales pitch; (pour séduire) sweet-talk; (pour convaincre) smooth talk○

baratiner○ /baʀatine/ [1]
Ⓐ *vtr* (pour vendre) to give [sb] the spiel; (pour séduire) to chat [sb] up; (pour convaincre) to try to talk [sb] round GB, to try to persuade
Ⓑ *vi* to jabber (on)

baratineur○, -**euse** /baʀatinœʀ, øz/ *nm,f* (beau parleur) smooth talker○; (menteur) liar

baratte /baʀat/ *nf* churn

barbant○, ~**e** /baʀbɑ̃, ɑ̃t/ *adj* boring

barbare /baʀbaʀ/
Ⓐ *adj* ① (féroce, choquant) barbaric; ② Hist barbarian
Ⓑ *nmf* barbarian

barbarie /baʀbaʀi/ *nf* barbarity, barbarism

barbe¹ /baʀb/ *nm* (cheval) barb

barbe² /baʀb/
Ⓐ *nf* ① (d'homme) beard; ~ **naissante** stubble; **une vieille ~**

pej an old fogey○GB; **parler dans sa** ~ fig to mutter into one's beard; **rire dans sa** ~ fig to laugh up one's sleeve; ② Zool (de bouc, chien) beard; (de plume) barb; (de poisson) barbel; ③ Bot (d'épi, de céréale) awn; ④ Tech (de papier) rough edge; (de pièce métallique) burr; ⑤ ○(chose ennuyeuse) **quelle** ~!, **c'est la** ~! what a drag○!

B ○*excl* **la** ~! I've had enough!; **la** ~ **avec leurs consignes!** to hell with their orders○!

(Composés) ~ **de capucin** Bot wild chicory; ~ **à papa** Culin candyfloss GB, cotton candy US

(Idiomes) **à la** ~ **de qn** under sb's nose; **avoir de la** ~ **au menton** to be an adult

barbelé, ~**e** /baʁbəle/
A *adj* [*fil*] barbed
B *nm* barbed wire ¢

barber○ /baʁbe/ [1]
A *vtr* to bore [sb] stiff○
B **se barber** *vpr* to be bored stiff○

Barberousse /baʁbəʁus/ *npr* Barbarossa

barbiche /baʁbiʃ/ *nf* (d'homme) goatee (beard); (de chèvre) (small) beard

barbichette /baʁbiʃɛt/ *nf* (small) goatee (beard)

barbichu, ~**e** /baʁbiʃy/ *adj* with a goatee (beard) (*épith, après n*)

barbier /baʁbje/ ▸ p. 372 *nm* barber

barbillon /baʁbijɔ̃/ *nm* ① (petit barbeau) small barbel, small goatfish US; ② (de poisson) barbel; (de volaille) wattle; (de bétail) barb

barbiturique /baʁbityʁik/
A *adj* barbituric
B *nm* barbiturate

barboter /baʁbɔte/ [1]
A ○*vtr* (voler) to nick○ GB, to filch○ (**à** from)
B *vi* [*canard*] to dabble; [*enfant*] to paddle; **faire** ~ **un gaz** to bubble a gas through a liquid

barboteuse /baʁbɔtøz/ *nf* romper-suit

barbouiller /baʁbuje/ [1]
A *vtr* ① (salir) to smear (**de** with); **il est tout barbouillé** his face is all dirty; ② (couvrir) to daub (**de** with); ③ pej (peindre) ~ **des natures mortes** to do daubs of still lives pej; ~ **du papier** to write drivel pej; ④ (rendre malade) **être** *or* **se sentir barbouillé** to feel queasy
B **se barbouiller** *vpr* (se salir) **se** ~ **le visage de qch** to get one's face all covered in sth

barbu, ~**e**¹ /baʁby/
A *adj* bearded
B *nm* bearded man

barbue² /baʁby/ *nf* Zool brill

barda○ /baʁda/ *nm* baggage, gear○; Mil kit

barde¹ /baʁd/ *nm* (chantre) bard

barde² /baʁd/ *nf* (de lard) bard

bardé, ~**e** /baʁde/
A *pp* ▸ **barder**
B *pp adj* fig (couvert) covered (**de** in)

barder /baʁde/ [1]
A *vtr* Culin to bard [*rôti, volaille*]
B ○*vi* **ça barde chez les voisins!** sparks are flying next door!

barème /baʁɛm/ *nm* (recueil de tableaux) (set of) tables; (méthode de calcul) scale; ~ **d'imposition** tax schedule *ou* scale; ~ **de correction** marking-scheme; ~ **des prix** price list

barge /baʁʒ/ *nf* (embarcation) barge

baril /baʁil/ *nm* ① (récipient) barrel, cask; (pour vin) cask; (pour poudre) keg; ② (unité de capacité) barrel

barillet /baʁijɛ/ *nm* ① Tech (de pistolet, serrure) cylinder; (d'horloge) barrel; ② Anat middle ear

bariolé, ~**e** /baʁjɔle/ *adj* ① (multicolore) [*habits, tissus*] multicoloured○GB; pej gaudy; ② (mélangé) [*foule*] motley

barjaquer /baʁʒake/ [1] *vi* H (bavarder) to chatter

baromètre /baʁɔmɛtʁ/ *nm* barometer

barométrique /baʁɔmetʁik/ *adj* barometric

baron /baʁɔ̃/ *nm* ① ▸ p. 590 (personne) baron; ② Culin ~ **d'agneau** saddle and hind legs of lamb

baronne /baʁɔn/ ▸ p. 590 *nf* baroness

baroque /baʁɔk/
A *adj* ① Art baroque; ② (bizarre) bizarre

B *nm* **le** ~ the baroque

baroud○ /baʁud/ *nm* ~ **d'honneur** last-ditch stand

baroudeur /baʁudœʁ/ *nm* ① (soldat) fighter, warrior; ② (aventurier) adventurer

barouf○ /baʁuf/ *nm* row, racket, fuss

barque /baʁk/ *nf* (small) boat

(Idiomes) **mener la** ~ to be in charge; **bien/mal mener sa** ~ to manage things well/badly

barquette /baʁkɛt/ *nf* (tartelette) (small) tart; (récipient) (pour fruits) punnet GB, basket US; (de margarine) tub; (pour plat cuisiné) container

barrage /baʁaʒ/ *nm* ① (sur l'eau) dam (**sur** on); ② (de police) roadblock; (de manifestants) barricade; **faire** ~ **à qn/qch** fig to block sb/sth

barre /baʁ/ *nf* ① (pièce de métal, bois etc) bar, rod; ② (petite tablette) bar; ~ **de chocolat** chocolate bar GB, candy bar US; ③ Naut tiller, helm; **être à** *or* **tenir la** ~ lit, fig to be at the helm; ④ (bande) band; ⑤ (trait écrit) stroke; **la** ~ **du t** the cross on the t; ⑥ Sport (en football) crossbar; (en saut) bar; ⑦ (pour la danse) barre; ⑧ Jur (des avocats) bar; (des témoins) ≈ witness box GB, witness stand US; ⑨ (seuil) mark; **tu places la** ~ **trop haut** you're expecting too much; ⑩ (dans un estuaire) sandbar; (hautes vagues) tidal wave; ⑪ (en géologie) ridge; ⑫ Mus ~ **de mesure** bar (line)

(Composés) ~ **d'appui** safety rail; ~ **de défilement** Ordinat scroll bar, slider; ~ **d'espacement** space bar; ~ **fixe** horizontal bar; ~ **à mine** jumper; ~ **oblique** slash, stroke; ~ **d'outils** Ordinat toolbar; ~ **de remorquage** tow bar

(Idiomes) **avoir un coup de** ~○ to feel drained all of a sudden; **c'est le coup de** ~ **dans ce restaurant**○ that restaurant is a rip-off○; **c'est de l'or en** ~ it's a golden opportunity

barreau, *pl* ~**x** /baʁo/ *nm* ① (de cage, fenêtre, prison) bar; ② (d'échelle) rung; ③ Jur (dans prétoire) bar; **le** ~ (avocats) the Bar

(Composé) ~ **de chaise** lit rung of a chair; (cigare)○ fat cigar

barrer /baʁe/ [1] *vtr* ① (obstruer) to block [*voie, accès*] (**avec** with); ~ **le passage à qn** lit, fig to stand in sb's way; '**route barrée**' 'road closed'; ② (rayer) to cross out [*mot, mention, paragraphe*]; ~ **un chèque** to cross a cheque; ③ (traverser) **une cicatrice lui barrait le front** he/she had a scar across his/her forehead; ④ Naut (prendre la barre) to take the helm of; (être à la barre) to be at the helm of; (en aviron) to cox

barrette /baʁɛt/ *nf* ① (pour les cheveux) (hair) slide GB, barrette US; ② (bijou) bar brooch; ③ Relig red biretta; **recevoir la** ~ to become a cardinal; ④ (insigne de décoration) ribbon

barreur, -**euse** /baʁœʁ, øz/ *nm,f* gén helmsman; (en aviron) cox; **avec** ~ coxed; **sans** ~ coxless

barricade /baʁikad/ *nf* barricade

barricader /baʁikade/ [1] *vtr* to barricade [*rue*]

barrière /baʁjɛʁ/ *nf* ① (clôture) fence; (porte) gate; (de passage à niveau) level crossing gate GB, grade crossing gate US; ② (obstacle) lit, fig barrier

(Composés) ~ **automatique** Rail automatic barrier; ~ **corallienne** coral reef; ~ **métallique** crowd barrier; ~**s douanières** tariff barriers

barrique /baʁik/ *nf* (tonneau) barrel

barrir /baʁiʁ/ [3] *vi* [*éléphant*] to trumpet; [*rhinocéros*] to bellow

bar-tabac, *pl* **bars-tabac** /baʁtaba/ *nm* café (*where stamps and cigarettes can be purchased*)

baryton /baʁitɔ̃/ ▸ p. 98 *adj, nm* Mus baritone

bas, basse¹ /bɑ, bas/
A *adj* ① [*maison, table, mur*] low; [*salle*] low-ceilinged (*épith*); ② [*nuage*] low; [*côte, terre, vallée*] low-lying (*épith*); **le ciel est** ~ the sky is overcast; ③ [*fréquence, pression, température, prix, salaire, latitude*] low; Mus [*note*] low; [*instrument*] bass; **vendre qch à** ~ **prix** to sell sth cheap; **un enfant en** ~ **âge** a very young child; **de** ~ **niveau** [*produit*] low-grade; [*élève, classe*] at a low level (*après n*); [*style, texte*] low-brow; **les cours sont au plus** ~ (en Bourse) prices have reached rock bottom; ④ [*origine, condition*] low, lowly; **les postes les plus** ~ the lowest-grade jobs; ⑤ [*époque, période*] late; ⑥ [*esprit, vengeance, complaisance*] base; **de** ~ **étage** [*individu*] common; [*plaisanterie*] coarse, vulgar
B *adv* ① (à faible hauteur) low; **comment peut-on tomber si** ~!

b

(dans l'abjection) how can one sink to such a low level!; **loger un étage plus ~** to live one floor below; **plus ~ dans la rue** further down the street; ② (dans un texte) **voir plus ~** see below; ③ (doucement) [*parler*] quietly; **tout ~** [*parler*] in a whisper; [*chanter*] softly; **mettre ~** (abattre) to bring [sb/ sth] down [*dictateur, régime*]; **mettre ~ les armes** lit (se rendre) to lay down one's arms; fig (renoncer) to give up the fight; ▸ **mettre B**; ④ (mal) **être au plus ~** (physiquement) to be extremely weak; (moralement) to be at one's lowest

C nm inv ① (partie inférieure) bottom; **le ~ du visage** the lower part of the face; **les pièces du ~** the downstairs rooms; **vers le ~** [*incliner*] downward(s); ② (vêtement) stocking; ③ Mus ℂ **chanter dans le ~** to sing bass notes (*pl*)

D **en bas** loc (au rez-de-chaussée) downstairs; (en dessous) down below; (sur panneau, page) at the bottom; **en ~ de** at the bottom of [*falaise, page*]; **il habite en ~ de chez moi** he lives below me; **l'odeur vient d'en ~** the smell is coming from below

(Composés) **~ de casse** (en imprimerie) lower case; **le ~ clergé** Relig the lower clergy; **~ de gamme** Ind, Comm adj low-quality (*épith*); nm lower end of the market; **~ de laine** fig nest egg, savings (*pl*); **~ morceaux** Culin cheap cuts; **~ sur pattes** short-legged (*épith*); **le ~ peuple** the lower classes; **les ~ quartiers** the seedy *ou* poor districts (of a town); **basse saison** Tourisme low season; **basses eaux** (de mer) low tide ℂ; (de rivière) low water ℂ

(Idiomes) **avoir des hauts et des ~** to have one's ups and downs; **à ~ les tyrans!** down with tyrants!

basalte /bazalt/ nm basalt

basané, ~e /bazane/ adj (hâlé) sunburned^GB, (sun-) tanned

bas-bleu, pl **~s** /bablø/ nm bluestocking

bas-côté, pl **~s** /bakote/ nm ① (de route) verge GB, shoulder US; ② (d'église) (side) aisle

basculant, ~e /baskylã, ãt/ adj **pont ~** bascule bridge; **camion à benne ~e** tipper lorry GB, dump truck

bascule /baskyl/ nf ① Tech rocker; **fauteuil/cheval à ~** rocking chair/horse; ② (balançoire) seesaw; ③ (pour peser) weighing machine

basculement /baskylmã/ nm ① fig (renversement) swing; ② (sur route) lane deviation

basculer /baskyle/ [1]
A vtr Télécom to transfer [*appel*]
B vi ① (tomber) [*objet, personne*] to topple over; [*benne*] to tip up; **faire ~** to tip up [*benne*]; to tip out [*chargement*]; to knock [sb] off balance [*personne*]; ② fig [*match, vie*] to change radically; **~ à droite** Pol to swing over to the right; **~ dans la guerre** to be plunged into war; **faire ~** to turn [*match, opinion*]

base /baz/ nf ① (partie inférieure) base (**de** of); ② fig (assise de système, théorie) basis (**de** of); (point de départ) basis (**de** for); **sur la ~ de** on the basis of; **servir de ~ à** to serve as a basis for; **à la ~ de qch** at the root *ou* heart of sth; **avoir des ~s en chimie** to have a basic grounding in chemistry; **salaire/formation de ~** basic salary/training; **données de ~** source data; **repartir sur de nouvelles ~s** fig to make a fresh start; ③ (ingrédient essentiel) base (**de** of); **poison à ~ d'arsenic** arsenic-based poison; **le riz forme la ~ de leur alimentation** rice is their staple diet; ④ Chimie base; ⑤ Math base; ⑥ Ling (radical) root; ⑦ (cosmétique) make-up base, foundation; ⑧ Mil base; ⑨ (de parti) **la ~ the rank and file

(Composés) **~ de données** Ordinat data base; **~ d'imposition** tax base; **~ de lancement** launching site

Bas-Empire /bazãpiʀ/ nprm Hist **le ~** the Later Roman Empire

baser /baze/ [1]
A vtr ① (fonder) to base [*théorie, stratégie, économie*] (**sur** on); ② (installer) gén, Mil to base [*unité, missile, société*] (**à, en** in)
B **se baser** vpr **se ~ sur qch** to go by sth [*chiffres, étude*]

bas-fond, pl **~s** /bafɔ̃/
A nm (haut-fond) shoal; (dépression) dip
B **bas-fonds** nmpl (de société) dregs (of society); (de ville) seedy parts

basilic /bazilik/ nm ① (plante) basil; ② (animal) basilisk

basilique /bazilik/ nf basilica

basique /bazik/ adj gén, Chimie basic; (en géologie) basal

basket /baskɛt/ ▸ p. 327 nm ① (sport) basketball; ② (chaussure) trainer

(Idiome) **lâcher les ~s à qn**° to give sb a break°

basketteur, -euse /baskɛtœʀ, øz/ nm,f basketball player

basque /bask/ ▸ p. 336
A adj Basque
B nm Ling Basque

basques /bask/ nfpl basques

(Idiome) **être pendu aux ~ de qn**° to be always hanging on sb's coat-tails

basse² /bas/
A adj ▸ **bas A**
B ▸ p. 98, p. 389 nf Mus (partie, chanteur, instrument) bass; (voix) bass (voice); **~ continue** (bass) continuo

(Composé) **~ de viole** Mus viola da gamba

basse-cour, pl **basses-cours** /baskuʀ/ nf (poulailler) poultry-yard; (volailles) poultry

basse-fosse, pl **basses-fosses** /basfos/ nf dungeon

bassement /basmã/ adv despicably, basely

bassesse /bases/ nf ① (caractère vil) baseness, lowness; **avec ~** [*se comporter, agir*] basely; ② (acte vil) base *ou* despicable act; **prêt à toutes les ~s** prepared to stoop to anything

bassin /basẽ/ nm ① (de parc) ornamental lake; (plus petit) pond; (fontaine) fountain; (de piscine) pool; ② (plat creux) bowl; ③ Géog basin; ④ Anat pelvis; ⑤ Méd bedpan; ⑥ Écon area

(Composés) **~ d'effondrement** fault-basin, rift; **~ d'emploi** labour^GB pool; **~ hydrographique** drainage basin; **~ minier** mineral field *ou* basin

bassine /basin/ nf (récipient) bowl; (contenu) bowlful

(Composé) **~ à confitures** preserving pan

bassinet /basinɛ/ nm (petite bassine) small bowl

(Idiome) **cracher au ~** to cough up°

bassiste /basist/ ▸ p. 372 nmf bass player

basson /basɔ̃/ ▸ p. 389 nm ① (instrument) bassoon; ② (instrumentiste) bassoonist

bastide /bastid/ nf ① (ville fortifiée) (medieval) fortified town; ② (maison) country house (*in Provence*)

bastingage /bastẽgaʒ/ nm (garde-corps) ship's rail

bastonnade /bastɔnad/ nf beating

bas-ventre, pl **~s** /bavãtʀ/ ▸ p. 136 nm lower abdomen; **recevoir un coup dans le ~** lit, fig to be hit below the belt

bât /ba/ nm pack-saddle

(Idiome) **c'est là que le ~ blesse** that's where the shoe pinches

bataille /bataj/
A nf ① Mil battle; **livrer ~ à qn** to give battle to sb; ② (lutte morale) battle, war; **~ du pouvoir** battle for power; **mener la ~ contre qn/qch** to wage war against sb/sth; ③ (lutte physique) fight; ④ (aux cartes) ≈ beggar-my-neighbour^GB
B **en bataille** loc adj [*cheveux*] dishevelled^GB; [*sourcils*] bushy; [*stationnement*] perpendicular

batailler /bataje/ [1] vi (lutter) fig to fight, to battle

batailleur, -euse /batajœʀ, øz/
A adj [*enfant*] aggressive; [*tempérament*] belligerent
B nm,f fighter

bataillon /batajɔ̃/ nm lit, fig battalion; **Dupond? inconnu au ~** hum Dupond? never heard of him

bâtard, ~e /bataʀ, aʀd/
A adj ① fig [*solution, œuvre, style*] hybrid; [*statut*] ill-defined; [*couleur*] indefinite; ② [*chien*] crossbred; ③ offensive [*enfant*] bastard injur
B nm,f ① (chien) mongrel; ② (enfant) offensive bastard injur
C nm (pain) small loaf of bread

bateau, pl **~x** /bato/
A adj inv [*sujet, question*] hackneyed
B nm ① (embarcation) boat; **aller en** *or* **par ~** to go by boat; **faire du ~** gén to go boating; (voile) to go sailing; ② (forme) **encolure ~** boat neck; ② °(plaisanterie) joke; **mener qn en ~** to take sb in; ④ (sur un trottoir) dropped kerb GB *ou* curb US

(Composés) ∼ **amiral** flagship; ∼ **de commerce** cargo boat, merchant ship; ∼ **de guerre** warship; ∼ **de plaisance** pleasure boat; ∼ **pneumatique** rubber dinghy; ∼ **de sauvetage** lifeboat

bateau-école, pl **bateaux-écoles** /batoekɔl/ nm training ship

bateau-mouche, pl **bateaux-mouches** /batomuʃ/ nm: large river boat for sightseeing

bateleur, -euse /batlœr, øz/ nm lit tumbler, juggler

batelier, -ière /batəlje, ɛr/ ▶ p. 372 nm,f boatman/boatwoman

batellerie /batɛlri/ nf inland water shipping

bâti, ∼e /bati/
A pp ▶ **bâtir**
B pp adj ⓵ [maison] built; **terrain** ∼ developed site; ⓶ [histoire] constructed
C nm ⓵ (terrain) developed site; ⓶ (de fenêtre, porte, machine) frame; ⓷ (en couture) tacking

batifoler /batifɔle/ [1] vi (jouer) to romp about; (flirter) to flirt

bâtiment /batimɑ̃/ nm ⓵ (construction) building; ⓶ (métier) building trade; ⓷ (navire) ship

(Composé) ∼ **de guerre** battleship

bâtir /batir/ [3]
A vtr ⓵ to build [édifice]; ⓶ to build [fortune, réputation, avenir]; to base [argumentation, rapport] (**sur** on); ⓷ to tack [ourlet]
B se **bâtir** vpr [personne] to build oneself [maison]; to build up [fortune]; [maison, fortune] to be built

bâtisse /batis/ nf (maison) house; (bâtiment) building

bâtisseur, -euse /batisœr, øz/ nm ⓵ Hist Constr (maçon) master-builder; ⓶ fig (créateur) builder

bâton /batɔ̃/ nm ⓵ (bout de bois) stick; **retour de** ∼ backlash; ⓶ (objet allongé) stick; **un** ∼ **de cire** a stick of wax; ⓷ (trait vertical) vertical stroke; (pour compter) bar; ⓸ ᵒ(dix mille francs) ten thousand francs

(Composés) ∼ **blanc** baton (used for directing traffic); ∼ **de maréchal** lit marshal's baton; fig pinnacle of one's career; ∼ **de rouge (à lèvres)** lipstick

(Idiomes) **être le** ∼ **de vieillesse de qn** to be sb's support in their old age; **discuter à** ∼**s rompus** to talk about this and that; **mettre des** ∼**s dans les roues de qn** to put a spoke in sb's wheel

bâtonnet /batɔnɛ/ nm ⓵ (petit bâton) stick; ⓶ (de rétine) (retinal) rod

(Composés) ∼ **ouaté** cotton bud GB, cotton swab US; ∼ **de poisson** fish finger GB, fish stick US

bâtonnier /batɔnje/ ▶ p. 590 nm ≈ president of the Bar

batracien /batrasjɛ̃/ nm batrachian

battage /bataʒ/ nm ⓵ ᵒpublicity, hypeᵒ; **faire du** ∼ **autour de qch** to hype sthᵒ, to give sth the hard sell; ⓶ (de blé) threshing; (de beurre) churning

battant, ∼e /batɑ̃, ɑ̃t/
A adj ∼ **neuf** brand new; **à deux heures** ∼**es** on the stroke of two; **le cœur** ∼ with a beating heart
B nm,f fighter
C nm ⓵ (de porte, fenêtre) hinged section; (de table, comptoir) leaf; **porte à deux** ∼**s** double door; ⓶ (de cloche) clapper; ⓷ (de drapeau) fly

batte /bat/ nf Sport bat GB, paddle US

battement /batmɑ̃/ nm ⓵ (de cœur, pouls) beating ⓒ, beat; ⓶ (de pluie, tambour) beating ⓒ; ⓷ Mus, Phys beat; ⓸ (d'ailes) flutter; (de cils) fluttering ⓒ; (de paupières) blinking ⓒ; (de danseur) battement; (de nageur) (en crawl) flutter kick ⓒ; (en brasse) frog kick ⓒ; ⓹ (entre deux activités) break; (attente) wait; (période creuse) gap

batterie /batri/ nf ⓵ (de grand orchestre) percussion section; (de jazz, rock) drum kit; ⓶ (artillerie, régiment) battery; **dévoiler ses** ∼**s** fig to show one's hand; ⓷ Aut, Électrotech battery; ⓸ (série) (de caméras, missiles, tests) battery; (de projecteurs) bank; (de satellite) array; (d'avocats, experts) battery

(Composé) ∼ **de cuisine** Culin pots and pans (pl)

batteur /batœr/ ▶ p. 372 nm ⓵ (de grand orchestre) percussionist; (de jazz, rock) drummer; ⓶ (au cricket) batsman; (au baseball) batter; ⓷ Culin whisk

(Composé) ∼ **électrique** hand mixer

batteuse /batøz/ nf (de céréales) threshing machine

battoir /batwar/ nm ⓵ (instrument) beater; ⓶ ᵒ(main) pawᵒ, hand

battre /batr/ [61]
A vtr ⓵ (l'emporter) to beat, to defeat [adversaire]; to break [record]; ∼ **qn au tennis/aux élections** to beat sb at tennis/in the elections; **se faire** ∼ **par 6 à 2** to lose 6-2; ⓶ (frapper) to beat [personne, animal]; ∼ **qn à coups de pied/poing** to kick/punch sb repeatedly; ⓷ (taper sur) to beat [matelas, tapis]; to beat [métal]; to thresh [blé]; ∼ **l'air/l'eau de ses bras** to thrash the air/the water with one's arms; ∼ **monnaie** to mint coins; ⓸ (heurter) [pluie] to beat ou lash against [vitre]; [mer] to pound ou beat against [rocher]; [artillerie] to pound [position]; ⓹ Culin to whisk [œuf]; ⓺ Jeux to shuffle [cartes]; ⓻ Mus ∼ **la mesure** to beat time; ⓼ (parcourir) to scour [pays, forêt]
B battre de vtr ind ⓵ (agiter) to flap its wings; ∼ **des cils** to flutter one's eyelashes; ∼ **des mains** to clap (one's hands); ∼ **des paupières** to blink; ⓶ (jouer) ∼ **du tambour** to beat the drum
C vi ⓵ [cœur, pouls] to beat; **le sang me battait aux tempes** I could feel my temples throbbing; ⓶ [porte, volet] to bang
D se **battre** vpr ⓵ (lutter) to fight (**contre** against; **avec** with); **se** ∼ **pour obtenir qch** fig to fight for sth; **se** ∼ **avec une serrure** hum to struggle with a lock; ⓶ (échanger des coups) to fight; ⓷ (se frapper) **se** ∼ **la poitrine** to beat one's breast

(Idiomes) ∼ **en retraite devant qch/qn** to retreat before sth/sb; ∼ **son plein** to be in full swing; **je m'en bats l'œil**ᵒ I don't give a damnᵒ

battu, ∼e¹ /baty/
A pp ▶ **battre**
B pp adj [enfant, femme] battered; fig [mine, air] tired

battue² /baty/ nf (à la chasse) beat

baudetᵒ /bodɛ/ nm (âne) donkey, ass

(Idiome) **être chargé comme un** ∼ to be loaded down like a mule

baudrier /bodrije/ nm ⓵ (d'uniforme) shoulder strap; ⓶ (d'alpinisme) harness

baudroie /bodrwa/ nf angler fish, monkfish

baudruche /bodryʃ/ nf ⓵ (matière) rubber skin; (ballon) balloon; ⓶ fig, pej wimpᵒ péj

(Idiome) **se dégonfler comme une** ∼ to lose one's nerve

bauge /boʒ/ nf ⓵ (de sanglier) wallow; ⓶ (lieu sale) pigsty; ⓷ (torchis) cob, clay and straw mortar

baume /bom/ nm balm, balsam

(Idiome) **mettre du** ∼ **au cœur de qn** to be a solace to sb

baux /bo/ nmpl ▶ **bail**

bavard, ∼e /bavar, ard/
A adj ⓵ (loquace) talkative; ⓶ (indiscret) **il est trop** ∼ he talks too much; ⓷ pej (prolixe) [roman, film, critique] long-winded péj
B nm,f ⓵ (personne loquace) chatterbox; ⓶ (personne indiscrète) indiscreet person, bigmouthᵒ

bavardage /bavardaʒ/ nm ⓵ (action) chattering; ⓶ (indiscrétions) gossip ⓒ; ⓷ (propos) idle chatter

bavarder /bavarde/ [1] vi ⓵ péj (parler) to talk, to chatter; ⓶ (s'entretenir) to chat (**avec** with); ⓷ (médire) to gossip (**sur** about)

bavarois, ∼e /bavarwa, az/
A adj Bavarian
B nm Culin Bavarian cream, bavarois

bave /bav/ nf (de personne) dribble; (de crapaud) spittle; (d'animal) slaver; (d'escargot, de limace) slime

baver /bave/ [1] vi ⓵ [personne] to dribble; [animal] to slaver; ⓶ (couler) [stylo] to leak; [pinceau] to dribble; [encre, peinture] to run

(Idiome) **en** ∼ to have a hard time

bavette /bavɛt/ nf ⓵ (pour bébé) bib; ⓶ Culin flank; ⓷ Aut mudflap

(Idiome) **tailler une** ∼ᵒ **avec qn** to have a good chat with sb

baveux, -euse /bavø, øz/ adj ⓵ [enfant, bouche] dribbling; ⓶ [omelette] runny

bavoir /bavwar/ nm bib

bavure /bavyr/ nf ⓵ (tache) smudge; ⓶ (erreur) blunder

bayer /baje/ [21] vi ∼ **aux corneilles** to gape

bazar /bazaʀ/ nm ① (magasin) general store, bazaar; ② ○(désordre) mess; ③ ○(affaires) clutter

bazarder○ /bazaʀde/ [1] vi (jeter) to throw out; (vendre) to sell off

bazarette /bazaʀɛt/ nf convenience store

BCBG○ /besebeʒe/ adj (abbr = **bon chic bon genre**) iron chic and conservative

BCG /beseʒe/ nm (abbr = **bacille bilié de Calmette et Guérin**) Méd BCG

bd written abbr = **boulevard** 1

BD○ /bede/ nf: abbr ▸ **bande**

béant, **~e** /beã, ãt/ adj [plaie, trou, sac] gaping

béarnaise /beaʀnɛz/ nf Béarnaise sauce

béat, **~e** /bea, at/ adj [personne] blissfully happy; [sourire, air, expression] blissful, beatific hum; **rester ~ devant qch** to gaze enraptured at sth; **~ d'admiration devant** wide-eyed with admiration for

béatement /beatmã/ adv blissfully, rapturously

beau (**bel** before vowel or mute h), **belle¹**, mpl **~x** /bo, bɛl/
Ⓐ adj ① (esthétiquement) [enfant, femme, visage, yeux, cheveux] beautiful; [homme, garçon] handsome; [jambes] nice; [corps, silhouette] good; [couleur, son, jardin, objet] beautiful; **se faire ~** to do oneself up; **faire qn ~** to smarten sb up; **ce n'est pas (bien) ~ à voir**○! it's not a pretty sight!; ② (qualitativement) [vêtements, machine, spectacle] good; [collection, spécimen] fine; [travail, cadeau] nice; [temps, jour] fine, nice; [journée, promenade] lovely; [discours, projet] fine; [effort, victoire] nice; [geste, sentiment] noble; [carrière] successful; [succès, avenir, optimisme] great; **fais de ~x rêves!** sweet dreams!; **il fait ~** the weather is fine; **il n'est pas ~ de faire** it's not nice to do; **un ~ jour** one fine day; **au ~ milieu de** right in the middle of; **c'est beau ~ tout ça, mais**○ that's all very fine, but; **trop ~ pour être vrai** too good to be true; **ça serait trop ~**○! one should be so lucky○!; **ce ne sont que de belles paroles** it's all talk; ③ (quantitativement) [somme, héritage] tidy; [salaire] very nice; [appétit] big; **belle pagaille** absolute mess; **bel égoïste** awful egoist

Ⓑ nm ① (choses intéressantes) **qu'est-ce que tu as fait de ~?** done anything interesting?; ② Philos (beauté) **le ~** beauty; ③ Météo **le temps est/se met au ~** the weather is/is turning fine

Ⓒ **avoir beau** loc verbale **j'ai ~ essayer, je n'y arrive pas** it's no good my trying, I can't do it; **l'économie a ~ se développer, le chômage progresse** even if the economy does develop, unemployment is still growing; **on a ~ dire, ce n'est pas si simple** no matter what people say, it's not that easy

Ⓓ **bel et bien** loc adv ① (irréversiblement) well and truly; **bel et bien fini** well and truly over; ② (indiscutablement) definitely

(Composés) **~ fixe** Météo fine weather; **être au ~ fixe** [temps, baromètre] to be set fair; [affaire, relation] to be going well; **avoir le moral au ~ fixe**○ to be on a high○; **~ gosse**○ good-looking guy○; **~ parleur** smooth talker; **~ parti** (homme) eligible bachelor; (femme) good match; **épouser un ~ parti** to marry money; **~ sexe** fair sex; **~x jours** (beau temps) fine weather ₵; (belle époque) good days; **bel esprit** bel esprit; **belle page** (en imprimerie) right-hand page; **belle plante**○ gorgeous specimen○; **belles années** happy years

(Idiomes) **faire le ~** [chien] to sit up and beg; [personne] to show off; **c'est du ~**○! iron lovely! iron; **tout ~ (tout ~)!** (pour calmer) easy(, easy)!

beaucoup /boku/ ▸ p. 483
Ⓐ adv ① (modifiant un verbe) a lot; (dans les phrases interrogatives et négatives) much; **aimer ~ qn/qch** to like sb/sth a lot ou a great deal; **la fin du roman surprend ~** the ending of the novel is very surprising; **s'intéresser ~ à qch** to be very interested in sth; **je n'ai pas ~ aimé le concert** I didn't enjoy the concert very much; **il n'écrit plus ~** he doesn't write much any more; **~ à boire** a lot to drink; **c'est ~ dire** that's going a bit far; **c'est déjà ~ qu'elle soit venue** it's already quite something that she came; ② (modifiant un adverbe) much, far; **~ mieux** much ou a lot better; **~ moins/plus d'argent** far ou much less/more money; **~ moins de livres** far fewer books; **~ plus vite** much faster; **~ trop far** too much, much too much; **~ trop grand** far ou much too big; ③ (un grand nombre) **~ de** a lot of [objets, idées]; (dans les phrases interrogatives et négatives) **~ de** a lot of, a

great deal of [argent, eau, bruit]; **il ne reste plus ~ de pain** there isn't much bread left; **il n'y a pas ~ de monde** there aren't many ou a lot of people; ④ (avec valeur pronominale) many; **~ sont retraités** many are pensioners

Ⓑ **de beaucoup** loc adv by far

Ⓒ **pour beaucoup** loc adv **ta réussite est due pour ~ à** your success is largely due to; **être pour ~ dans** to have a lot to do with

beauf○ /bof/ nm ① (abbr = **beau-frère**) brother-in-law; ② (rustre) pej boor○

beau-fils, pl **beaux-fils** /bofis/ nm ① (gendre) son-in-law; ② (fils du conjoint) stepson

beau-frère, pl **beaux-frères** /bofʀɛʀ/ nm brother-in-law

beau-papa, pl **beaux-papas** /bopapa/ nm father-in-law

beau-père, pl **beaux-pères** /bopɛʀ/ nm ① (de conjoint) father-in-law; ② (d'enfant) stepfather

beaupré /bopʀe/ nm (mât de) **~** bowsprit

beauté /bote/ nf beauty; **la ~ idéale** ideal beauty; **la ~ d'un paysage** the beauty of a landscape; **d'une grande ~** very beautiful; **de toute ~** exquisite; **être en ~** to look really good; **avoir la ~ du diable** to be in the bloom of youth; **se faire une ~** to do oneself up; **faire qch pour la ~ du geste** to do sth because it is a nice thing to do; **commencer/finir en ~** to start/to end with a flourish; **elle se prend pour une ~** she thinks she's a great beauty

beaux-arts /bozaʀ/ nmpl fine arts and architecture

beaux-parents /bopaʀã/ nmpl parents-in-law

bébé /bebe/ nm baby; **des cheveux de ~** baby hair; **aliments pour ~s** baby food; **~ phoque** baby seal; **attendre un ~** to be expecting a baby

bec /bɛk/ nm ① (d'oiseau) beak, bill; (de tortue, poisson) beak; (de dauphin) snout; **donner des coups de ~** to peck (**dans** at); **(nez en) ~ d'aigle** hooked nose; ② (de pichet, casserole) lip; (de théière) spout; (d'instrument à vent) mouthpiece; (de stylo) nib; ③ C, H (baiser) kiss

(Composés) **~ Bunsen** Bunsen burner; **~ de gaz** gas street-lamp; **~ verseur** pourer(-spout)

(Idiomes) **clouer le ~ à qn**○ to shut sb up○; **se retrouver le ~ dans l'eau**○ to be stuck, to be left high and dry; **tomber sur un ~**○ to come across a snag

bécane○ /bekan/ nf (deux-roues) bike○

bécarre /bekaʀ/ nm natural; **ré ~** D natural

bécasse /bekas/ nf ① (oiseau) woodcock; ② (sotte) featherbrain○

bécasseau, pl **~x** /bekaso/ nm ① (oiseau de rivage) sandpiper; ② (jeune bécasse) young woodcock

bécassine /bekasin/ nf ① (oiseau) snipe; ② (sotte) silly goose○

bec-de-cane, pl **becs-de-cane** /bɛkdəkan/ nm (serrure) spring lock; (poignée) door handle

bec-de-lièvre, pl **becs-de-lièvre** /bɛkdəljɛvʀ/ nm harelip

bêche /bɛʃ/ nf (à lame pleine) spade; (à dents) garden fork

bêcher /beʃe/ [1] vtr to dig [sth] (with a spade) [jardin]

bêcheur, **-euse** /bɛʃœʀ, øz/ nm,f stuck-up○ person

becquée /beke/ nf beakful; **donner la ~ à** to feed [oisillon]

bedaine○ /bədɛn/ nf paunch

bedeau, pl **~x** /bədo/ nm verger

bédéphile○ /bedefil/ nmf comic strip fan

bedonnant○, **~e** /bədɔnã, ãt/ adj [personne] paunchy

bée /be/ adj f **être bouche ~** to gape (**devant** at); **être bouche ~ de surprise** to be open-mouthed in surprise

beffroi /befʀwa/ nm Archit belfry

bégaiement /begɛmã/ nm (trouble) stammer, stutter

bégayer /begeje/ [21] vtr, vi to stammer

bègue /bɛg/
Ⓐ adj **être ~** to stammer
Ⓑ nmf **c'est un/une ~** he/she has a stammer

bégueule /begœl/ adj prudish

béguin○ /begẽ/ nm **avoir le ~ pour qn** to have a crush on sb

beige /bɛʒ/ ▸ p. 140 adj, nm beige

beignet /bɛɲɛ/ *nm* gén fritter; (à la pâte levée) doughnut, donut○ US; **~ au sucre** doughnut

(Composé) **~s de crevettes** prawn crackers

bel *adj m* ▸ **beau A, D**

bêler /bele/ [1] *vi* to bleat

belette /bəlɛt/ *nf* weasel

belge /bɛlʒ/ ▸ p. 392 *adj* Belgian

belgicisme /bɛlʒisism/ *nm* Belgian French expression

Belgique /bɛlʒik/ ▸ p. 230 *nprf* Belgium

bélier /belje/ *nm* ① Zool ram; ② Hist, Mil battering ram

Bélier /belje/ ▸ p. 635 *nprm* Aries

bellâtre /bɛlɑtʀ/ *nm* handsome hunk

belle² /bɛl/

A *nf* ▸ **beau A**

B *nf* ① (femme) **courtiser les ~s** to go courting the ladies; **ma ~** darling, love○ GB, doll○ US; ② (maîtresse) lady friend; ③ (partie) decider

C **de plus belle** *loc adv* with renewed vigour○ᴳᴮ; **crier de plus ~** to shout louder than ever

D belles○ *nfpl* (paroles) stories

(Composé) **la Belle au Bois dormant** Sleeping Beauty

(Idiomes) **(se) faire la ~**○ (s'évader) to do a bunk○ GB, to take a powder○ US; **en faire voir de ~s à qn** to give sb a hard time

belle-famille, *pl* **belles-familles** /bɛlfamij/ *nf* in-laws (*pl*)

belle-fille, *pl* **belles-filles** /bɛlfij/ *nf* ① (bru) daughter-in-law; ② (fille du conjoint) stepdaughter

belle-mère, *pl* **belles-mères** /bɛlmɛʀ/ *nf* ① (de conjoint) mother-in-law; ② (d'enfant) stepmother

belles-lettres /bɛllɛtʀ/ *nfpl* literature ₵, belles lettres ₵

belle-sœur, *pl* **belles-sœurs** /bɛlsœʀ/ *nf* sister-in-law

belliciste /belisist/ *adj* [*politicien, discours, opinion*] warmongering (épith); [*gouvernement, parti*] hawkish

belligérant, **~e** /beliʒeʀɑ̃, ɑ̃t/

A *adj* [*partie, pays*] warring; [*troupes*] combatant; **États non ~s** nonbelligerent states

B *nm* ① (pays) belligerent, warring party; ② (combattant) combatant

belliqueux, **-euse** /belikø, øz/ *adj* (agressif) aggressive

belote /bəlɔt/ ▸ p. 327 *nf* belote (*card game*)

belvédère /bɛlvedɛʀ/ *nm* (pavillon) belvedere, gazebo

bémol /bemɔl/ *nm* ① Mus flat; **mi ~** E flat; ② (atténuation) damper

bénédictin, **~e** /benediktɛ̃, in/ *adj, nm,f* Benedictine; **travail de ~** fig painstaking task

bénédiction /benediksjɔ̃/ *nf* blessing; **cet emploi est une ~ du ciel** that job is a godsend; **c'est une ~!** it's a miracle!

bénéfice /benefis/ *nm* ① (gain financier) profit; **~ brut/net** gross/net profit; **faire des ~** to make a profit (**sur** on); ② (action bénéfique) benefit; ③ (avantage) advantage; **le ~ de l'âge** the prerogative of age; **tirer ~ de qch** to gain advantage from sth; **il n'en tire aucun ~** he doesn't get anything out of it; **au ~ d'une œuvre caritative** in aid of a charity; **~ du doute** benefit of the doubt

bénéficiaire /benefisjɛʀ/

A *adj* [*affaire*] profitable

B *nmf* beneficiary

bénéficier /benefisje/ [2] *vtr ind* **~ de** to receive [*aide financière, formation, appui*]; to enjoy [*immunité, soutien populaire, avantages*]; to benefit from [*conjoncture favorable*]; to get [*privilège, publicité*]; **faire ~ qn de** to give sb [*tarif réduit, bourse*]

bénéfique /benefik/ *adj* beneficial; **avoir un effet ~** to be beneficial; **être ~ à qn** to do sb good

Bénélux /benelyks/ *nprm* Benelux

benêt /bənɛ/

A *adj m* simple

B *nm* half-wit

bénévolat /benevɔla/ *nm* voluntary work

bénévole /benevɔl/

A *adj* voluntary

B *nmf* voluntary *ou* volunteer worker, volunteer

bénévolement /benevɔlmɑ̃/ *adv* on a voluntary basis

bénigne *adj f* ▸ **bénin**

bénignité /beniɲite/ *nf* ① Méd (de maladie) mildness; (de tumeur) nonmalignancy; ② (de faute) harmlessness; (de critique) mildness

bénin, -igne /benɛ̃, iɲ/ *adj* [*maladie, blessure*] minor; [*tumeur*] benign; [*faute, erreur*] minor

béni-oui-oui○ /beniwiwi/ *nm inv* yes-man

bénir /beniʀ/ [3] *vtr* to bless; **Dieu vous** *or* **te bénisse** God bless you; **béni soit le ciel!** thank God!

bénit, **~e** /beni, it/ *adj* [*cierge*] blessed; [*water*] holy

bénitier /benitje/ *nm* holy water font

benjamin, **~e** /bɛ̃ʒamɛ̃, in/ *nm,f* ① (dans une famille) youngest son/daughter; (dans un groupe) youngest member; ② Sport ≈ junior (*aged 10–11*)

benne /bɛn/ *nf* (de chantier, camion) skip GB, dumpster® US; (de mine) (colliery) wagon; (contenu) wagon(ful); (de téléphérique) car

(Composés) **~ à béton** concrete mixer; **~ à ordures** (camion) waste disposal GB *ou* garbage US truck; (conteneur) skip GB, dumpster® US

béotien, -ienne /beɔsjɛ̃, ɛn/

A *adj* Géog Boeotian

B *nm,f* (ignorant) ignoramus

BEPC /beapese, bɛps/ *nm* (*abbr* = **Brevet d'études du premier cycle**) *former examination at the end of the first stage of secondary education*

béquille /bekij/ *nf* ① Méd crutch; **marcher avec des ~s** to be on crutches; ② Tech (de bicyclette, moto) kickstand

bercail /bɛʀkaj/ *nm* ① Relig fold; ② ○(foyer) home

berçante /bɛʀsɑ̃t/ *nf* C rocking chair

berceau, *pl* **~x** /bɛʀso/ *nm* ① (de bébé) cradle; **dès** *or* **depuis le ~** from the cradle; ② (lieu d'origine) (de personne, famille) birthplace; (de religion, peuple) cradle

bercer /bɛʀse/ [12]

A *vtr* to rock [*enfant*]; **~ un enfant pour l'endormir** to rock *ou* lull a baby to sleep; **~ qn de promesses** to string sb along with promises

B se bercer *vpr* **se ~ d'illusions** *or* **de vains espoirs** to delude oneself

berceuse /bɛʀsøz/ *nf* ① (chanson) lullaby; ② (siège) rocking chair

béret /berɛ/ *nm* beret; **~ basque** Basque beret

bergamote /bɛʀgamɔt/ *nf* ① (poire) bergamot (pear); ② (agrume) bergamot (orange); **thé à la ~** earl grey tea

berge /bɛʀʒ/ *nf* (de rivière, canal) bank; **la ~ du canal** the canal bank; **voie sur ~** quayside road

berger, -ère¹ /bɛʀʒe, ɛʀ/ ▸ p. 372 *nm,f* shepherd/ shepherdess

(Composés) **~ allemand** German shepherd (dog), Alsatian GB; **~ des Pyrénées** Pyrenean mountain dog

bergère² /bɛʀʒɛʀ/ *nf* (fauteuil) wing chair

bergerie /bɛʀʒəʀi/ *nf* (abri) sheep barn

(Idiome) **faire entrer le loup dans la ~** to set the fox to mind the geese

bergeronnette /bɛʀʒəʀɔnɛt/ *nf* wagtail

berk○ /bɛʀk/ *excl* yuk○!

Berlin /bɛʀlɛ̃/ ▸ p. 621 *npr* Berlin

berline /bɛʀlin/ *nf* ① (automobile) four-door saloon GB, sedan US; ② (attelage) berlin

berlingot /bɛʀlɛ̃go/ *nm* (bonbon) twisted hard candy

berlinois, ~e /bɛʀlinwa, az/ ▸ p. 621 *adj* Berlin (épith)

Berlinois, ~e /bɛʀlinwa, az/ ▸ p. 621 *nm,f* Berliner

berlue○ /bɛʀly/ *nf* **avoir la ~** to be seeing things

bermuda /bɛʀmyda/ *nm* bermudas (*pl*)

Bermudes /bɛʀmyd/ ▸ p. 303 *nprfpl* **les ~s** Bermuda (*sg*)

berne /bɛʀn/ *nf* **en ~** [*drapeau*] at half-mast

berner /bɛʀne/ [1] *vtr* to fool, to deceive

besace /bəzas/ *nf* (sac) pouch

besogne /bəzɔɲ/ *nf* job; **une basse ~** a menial chore; **abattre de la ~** to get through a lot of work; **tu vas vite en ~, toi!** you don't waste any time, do you!

besogneux, -euse /bəzɔɲø, øz/ *nm,f* ① (tâcheron) drudge; ② †(pauvre) needy person

besoin /bəzwɛ̃/

A *nm* need (**de** for; **de faire** to do); **répondre à un ~** to meet a need; **si** ~ **est, en cas de** ~ if need be; **avoir** ~ **de qch/qn** to need sth/sb; **j'ai bien** ~ **de ça**! iron that's all I need! iron; **avoir** ~ **de faire** to need to do; **j'ai** ~ **de changer d'air** I need a change of scene; **tu as** ~ **qu'on s'occupe de toi** you need somebody to take care of you; **il n'est pas** ~ **de faire** there is no need to do; **est-il** ~ **que je vienne?** is it necessary for me to come?; **est-il** ~ **de le dire?** need I remind you?; **éprouver le** ~ **de faire** to feel a need to do; **pour les** ~**s de la cause** for the good of the cause; **être dans le** ~ to be in need; **être à l'abri du** ~ to be free from want

B **besoins** nmpl needs; ~**s actuels** today's needs; **subvenir aux** ~**s de qn** to provide for sb; ~**s en eau/personnel** water/staff requirements

(Idiome) **faire ses** ~**s**○ [personne] to relieve oneself; [animal] to do its business

bestial, ~**e**, mpl **-iaux** /bɛstjal, o/ adj brutish

bestialité /bɛstjalite/ nf (caractère bestial) brutality

bestiaux /bɛstjo/ nmpl gén livestock ¢; (bovins) cattle (+ v pl)

bestiole○ /bɛstjɔl/ nf (insecte) bug; (animal) animal

bétail /betaj/ nm gén livestock ¢; (bovins) cattle (+ v pl); **aliments pour le** ~ cattle feed

bête /bɛt/

A adj [personne, air, idée, question] stupid; [problème] simple; [accident] silly; **tu es bien** ~ **d'avoir accepté** it was stupid of you to accept; **il n'est pas** ~ he's no fool; **ce n'est pas** ~ **ça!** that's not a bad idea!; **suis-je** ~! how stupid of me!; ~ **à pleurer** too stupid for words; **je suis restée toute** ~ I was dumbfounded; ~ **et méchant** nasty; **il est** ~ **et discipliné** he just does as he's told; **c'est tout** ~ it's quite simple; **c'est (trop)** ~ **d'en arriver là** it's (such) a shame that things should come to this; **c'est** ~**, je ne peux pas venir** it's a shame I can't come

B nf gén creature; (quadrupède) animal; **nos amis les** ~**s** our four-legged friends; **il a une cinquantaine de** ~**s** he has around 50 head of cattle

(Composés) ~ **à bon Dieu** Zool ladybird GB, ladybug US; ~ **à concours**○ exam fiend○; ~ **à cornes** Zool horned animal; ~ **curieuse** freak; ~ **féroce** Zool ferocious animal; ~ **noire** bête noire GB, pet hate; ~ **sauvage** Zool wild animal; ~ **de somme** Zool beast of burden; ~ **de travail** workaholic

(Idiomes) **il est** ~ **comme ses pieds**○ or **à manger du foin**○ he's (as) thick as two short planks○ GB, he's as dumb as can be; **chercher la petite** ~○ to nit-pick○; **reprendre du poil de la** ~○ to perk up; **travailler comme une** ~○ to work like crazy○

bêtement /bɛtmɑ̃/ adv stupidly; **il suffit (tout)** ~ **de faire** you simply need to do

bêtifiant, ~**e** /bɛtifjɑ̃, ɑ̃t/ adj [ouvrage, paroles, émission] idiotic

bêtise /bɛtiz/ nf **la** ~ stupidity; **il est d'une** ~ **incroyable** he's incredibly stupid; **c'est de la** ~ it's stupid; **faire une** ~ to do something stupid ou a stupid thing; **dire des** ~**s** to talk nonsense; **j'ai fait une** ~ **en acceptant** I was stupid to accept; **surtout pas de** ~**s!** be good now!; **se fâcher pour une** ~ to get angry over nothing

(Composé) ~ **de Cambrai** Culin mint

bêtisier /betizje/ nm collection of howlers○

béton /betɔ̃/ nm concrete; **de** or **en** ~ lit concrete (épith); fig watertight

(Composé) ~ **armé** reinforced concrete

bétonnière /betɔnjɛʀ/ nf concrete mixer

bette /bɛt/ nf Swiss chard

betterave /betʀav/ nf beet; ~ **rouge** beetroot

beuglement /bøgləmɑ̃/ nm [1] (de vache) mooing; (de taureau) bellowing; [2] ○ (de personne) bawling, yelling

beugler /bøgle/ [1]
A vtr to bellow (out) [chanson, ordre, injures]
B vi [1] [vache] to moo; [bœuf, taureau] to bellow; [2] ○ (hurler) [personne] to yell; [télévision] to blare out

beur○ /bœʀ/ nmf second-generation North African (living in France)

beurette○ /bœʀɛt/ nf second-generation North African girl (living in France)

beurre /bœʀ/ nm butter; ~ **doux** unsalted butter; ~ **d'anchois/de saumon** anchovy/salmon paste

(Composés) ~ **blanc** sauce made out of butter, vinegar and shallots; ~ **d'escargot** garlic and parsley butter; ~ **noir** Culin black butter; **œil au** ~ **noir**○ black eye

(Idiomes) **faire son** ~○ to make a packet○; **compter pour du** ~○ to count for nothing; **vouloir le** ~ **et l'argent du** ~○ to want to have one's cake and eat it

beurré○, ~**e** /bœʀe/ adj (soûl) plastered○

beurrer /bœʀe/ [1] vtr to butter [pain, tartine]; to grease [sth] with butter [moule à gâteau]; **une tartine de pain beurré** bread and butter

beurrier /bœʀje/ nm butter dish

beuverie /bœvʀi/ nf drinking session

bévue /bevy/ nf blunder

Beyrouth /beʀut/ ▸ p. 621 nprm Beirut

biais /bjɛ/
A nm inv (moyen) way; **par le** ~ **de qn** through sb; **par le** ~ **de qch** by means of sth
B **de biais, en biais** loc adv **couper une étoffe en** ~ to cut material on the cross; **jeter des regards en** ~ **à qn** to cast sidelong glances at sb

biaiser /bjɛze/ [1] vi to hedge

bibelot /biblo/ nm ornament

biberon /bibʀɔ̃/ nm (baby's) bottle GB, (nursing) bottle US; **nourrir au** ~ to bottle-feed; **c'est l'heure du** ~ it's time for his/her feed

biberonner○ /bibʀɔne/ [1] vi to booze○, to drink

bibine○ /bibin/ nf péj cheap wine, plonk○ GB

bible /bibl/ nf bible; **la Bible** the Bible

bibliographie /biblijɔgʀafi/ nf bibliography

bibliographique /biblijɔgʀafik/ adj bibliographical

bibliothécaire /biblijɔtekɛʀ/ ▸ p. 372 nmf librarian

bibliothèque /biblijɔtɛk/ nf **[1]** (endroit, collection) library; **[2]** (meuble) bookcase

biblique /biblik/ adj biblical

bic® /bik/ nm biro®

bicarbonate /bikaʀbɔnat/ nm Chimie bicarbonate

(Composé) ~ **de soude** sodium bicarbonate

bicentenaire /bisɑ̃tnɛʀ/
A adj two-hundred-year-old (épith); **être** ~ to be two hundred years old
B nm bicentenary GB, bicentennial US

biceps /bisɛps/ nm inv biceps; **avoir des** ~ to have muscular arms; **jouer des** ~○ to flex one's muscles

biche /biʃ/ nf Zool doe; **ma** ~○ my pet GB, honey US

bichlorure /biklɔʀyʀ/ nm dichloride

bichonner○ /biʃɔne/ [1] vtr (dorloter) to pamper

bicolore /bikɔlɔʀ/ adj [drapeau] two-coloured^{GB} (épith); [étoffe] two-tone

bicoque○ /bikɔk/ nf little house, dump○ péj

bicorne /bikɔʀn/ nm (chapeau) cocked hat

bi-cross /bikʀɔs/ ▸ p. 327 nm inv (discipline, vélo) BMX

bicyclette /bisiklɛt/ nf **[1]** (objet) bicycle, bike○; **à** ~ [aller, parcourir] by bike; **un tour à** ~ a bike ride; **aller au travail à** ~ to cycle to work; **faire de la** ~ to cycle; **[2]** (activité) cycling

bidasse○ /bidas/ nm soldier

bide○ /bid/ nm **[1]** (échec) flop; **faire un** ~ to be a flop

bidet /bidɛ/ nm **[1]** (de salle de bains) bidet; **[2]** ○(cheval) nag

bidon /bidɔ̃/
A ○adj inv [compagnie, numéro] bogus; [excuse, histoire] phoney; **chèque** ~ dud cheque
B nm **[1]** (récipient) (portatif) can; (baril) drum; (gourde) flask; ~ **d'essence** (contenant) petrol can GB, gas can US; (contenu) can of petrol GB ou gas US; ~ **de peinture** tin GB ou can of paint; **[2]** ○(ventre) stomach; **[3]** ○(bluff) **c'est du** ~ it is a load of hogwash○

bidonner○: **se bidonner** /bidɔne/ [1] vpr to laugh, to fall about○

bidonville /bidɔ̃vil/ nm shanty town

bidule○ /bidyl/ nm (objet) thingy○ GB, thingamajig○

bief /bjɛf/ nm reach

bielle /bjɛl/ nf connecting rod; **couler une** ~ to run a big end; **j'ai coulé une** ~ the big end has gone

biélorusse /bjelɔʀys/ ▸ p. 392 adj Byelorussian

Biélorussie /bjelɔʀysi/ ▸ p. 230 nprf Byelorussia

bien /bjɛ̃/

A *adj inv* [1] (convenable) être ~ dans un rôle to be good in a part; être ~ de sa personne to be good-looking; **il n'y a rien de ~ ici** there's nothing of interest here; **voilà qui est ~** that's good; **ce n'est pas ~ de mentir** it's not nice to lie; **ce serait ~** it would be nice; **ça fait ~ d'aller à l'opéraᴼ** it's the done thing to go to the opera; **les roses font ~** the roses look nice; [2] (en bonne santé) well; **ne pas se sentir ~** not to feel well; **t'es pas ~ᴼ!** you're out of your mindᴼ!; [3] (à l'aise) **je suis ~ dans ces bottes** these boots are comfortable; **on est ~ au soleil!** isn't it nice in the sun!; **je me trouve ~ ici** I like it here; **nous voilà ~!** iron we're in a fine mess!; [4] ᴼ(de qualité) **un quartier ~** a nice district; **des gens ~** respectable people; **un type ~** a gentleman

B *adv* [1] (correctement) gén well; [*fonctionner*] properly; [*interpréter*] correctly; ~ **payé** well paid; ~ **joué!** fig well done!; **aller ~** [*personne*] to be well; [*affaires*] to go well; **ça s'est ~ passé** it went well; **la voiture ne marche pas ~** the car isn't running properly; **ni ~ ni mal** so-so; **parler (très) ~ le chinois** to speak (very) good Chinese; **il travaille ~** (élève) his work is good; (artisan) he does a good job; **il est ~ remis** (malade) he's made a good recovery; ~ **se tenir à table** to have good table manners; ~ **employer son temps** to make good use of one's time; **j'ai cru ~ faire** I thought I was doing the right thing; **il fait ~ de partir** he's right to leave; **c'est ~ fait pour elle!** it serves her right!; **tu ferais ~ d'y aller** it would be a good idea for you to go there; ~ **m'en a pris de refuser** it's a good thing I refused; [2] (complètement) [*arroser, décongeler, laver, mélanger, propre, cuit*] thoroughly; [*remplir, sécher, sec, fondu*] completely; [*lire, écouter, regarder*] carefully; ~ **à droite** well over to the right; ~ **devant** right at the front; ~ **profiter d'une situation** to exploit a situation to the full; [3] (agréablement) [*présenté, situé*] well; [*s'habiller*] well, smartly; [*décoré, meublé*] tastefully; [*logé, installé, vivre*] comfortably; **femme ~ faite** shapely woman; **aller ~ à qn** [*couleur, style*] to suit sb; **se mettre ~ avec qn** to get on good terms with sb; ~ **prendre une remarque** to take a remark in good part; [4] (hautement) [*aimable, triste*] very; [*apprécier, craindre*] very much; [*simple, vrai, certain, évident*] quite; **il s'est ~ mal comporté** he behaved really badly; **il y a ~ longtemps** a very long time ago; **merci ~** thank you very much; **tu as ~ raison** you're quite right; **c'est ~ dommage** it's a real pity; ~ **rire** to have a good laugh; **c'est ~ promis?** is that a promise?; **c'est ~ compris?** is that clear?; ~ **au contraire** on the contrary; **c'est ~ joli tout ça, mais** that's all very well, but; ~ **mieux/moins/pire** much ou far better/less/worse; ~ **trop laid/tard** much too ugly/late; ~ **plus riche/cher** much ou far richer/more expensive; ~ **plus, il a volé!** not only that, he also takes her money!; ~ **sûr** of course; ~ **entendu** or **évidemment** naturally; ~ **souvent** quite often; [5] (volontiers) **j'irais ~ à Bali** I wouldn't mind going to Bali; **je veux ~ t'aider** I don't mind helping you; **j'aimerais ~ essayer** I would love to try; **je le vois ~ habiter à Paris** I can just imagine him living in Paris; [6] (malgré tout) **il faut ~ le faire** it has to be done; **il faudra ~ s'y habituer** we'll just have to get used to it; **il finira ~ par se calmer** he'll calm down eventually; [7] (pour souligner) **ça prouve/montre ~ que** it just goes to prove/show that; **j'espère ~ que** I do hope that; **je sais/crois ~ que** I know/think that; **insiste ~** make sure you insist; **on verra ~** well, we'll see; **sache ~ que je n'accepterai jamais** let me tell you that I will never accept; **je m'en doutais ~!** I thought as much!; **je t'avais ~ dit de ne pas le manger!** I told you not to eat it!; **il le fait ~ lui, pourquoi pas moi?** if he can do it, why can't I?; **veux-tu ~ faire ce que je te dis!** will you do as I tell you!; **tu peux très ~ le faire toi-même** you can easily do it yourself; **il se pourrait ~ qu'il pleuve** it might well rain; **que peut-il ~ faire à Paris?** what on earth can he be doing in Paris?; [8] (réellement) definitely; **c'est ~ lui/mon sac** it's definitely him/my bag, it's him/ my bag all rightᴼ; **c'est ~ ce qu'il a dit** that's exactly what he said; **il ne s'agit pas d'une erreur, mais ~ de fraude** it's not a mistake, it's fraud; **c'est ~ ici qu'on vend les billets?** this is where you get tickets, isn't it?; **tu as ~ pris les clés?** are you sure you've got the keys?; **est-ce ~ nécessaire?** is it really necessary?; **c'est ~ de lui!** it's just like him!; **voilà ~ la politique!** that's politics for you!; **c'est ~ le moment!** iron great timing!; **c'est ~ le moment de partir!** iron what a time to leave!; [9] (au moins) at least; **elle a ~ 40 ans** she's at least 40, she's a good 40 years old; [10] (beaucoup) **il y a ~ des années** a good many years ago; ~ **des fois** often, many a time; ~ **des gens** lots of people; **il s'est donné ~ du mal** he's gone to a lot or a great deal of trouble; **mon fils me donne ~ du souci** my son is a great worry to me; **avoir ~ de la chance** to be very lucky; **je te souhaite ~ du plaisir!** iron I wish you joy!

C *nm* [1] (avantage) good; **pour le ~ du pays** for the good of the country; **pour le ~ de tous** for the general good; **pour ton ~** for your own good; **ce serait un ~** it would be a good thing; **sacrifier son propre ~ à celui d'autrui** to put others first; **le ~ et le mal** good and evil; **faire le ~** to do good; **ça fait du ~ aux enfants** it's good for the children; **ça leur fait du ~** it does them good; **mon repos m'a fait le plus grand ~** my rest did me a world of good; **grand ~ vous fasse!** iron much good may it do you!; **vouloir le ~ de qn** to have sb's best interests at heart; **vouloir du ~ à qn** to wish sb well; **dire du ~ de qn** to speak well of sb; **on dit le plus grand ~ du musée** people speak very highly of the museum; **on a dit le plus grand ~ de toi** a lot of nice things were said about you; **parler en ~ de qn** to speak favourablyᴳᴮ of sb; [2] (possession) possession; **perdre tous ses ~s dans un incendie** to lose all one's possessions in a fire; **les ~s de ce monde** material possessions; **hériter des ~s paternels** to inherit one's father's estate; **dilapider son ~** to squander one's fortune; **des ~s considérables** substantial assets; **la santé est le plus précieux des ~s** you can't put a price on good health

D *excl* ~**!** good!

E bien que *loc conj* although; ~ **qu'il le sache** although he knows

⬭ Composés ~**s de consommation** consumer goods; ~**s d'équipement** capital goods; ~**s d'équipement ménager** household goods; ~**s fonciers** land ¢; ~**s immobiliers** real estate ¢; ~**s mobiliers** personal property ¢; ~**s personnels** private property ¢; ~**s publics** public property ¢

⬭ Idiome **tout est ~ qui finit ~** Prov all's well that ends well Prov

bien-être /bjɛ̃nɛtʀ/ *nm* [1] (sensation agréable) well-being; [2] (protection sociale) welfare; [3] (situation matérielle satisfaisante) comforts (*pl*)

bienfaisance /bjɛ̃fəzɑ̃s/ *nf* charity; **société de ~** charity; **soirée de ~** charity gala

bienfaisant, ~e /bjɛ̃fəzɑ̃, ɑ̃t/ *adj* [*influence*] beneficial; [*personne*] beneficent

bienfait /bjɛ̃fɛ/ *nm* [1] (acte généreux) kind deed; **c'est un ~ du ciel** it's a godsend; [2] (effet bénéfique) beneficial effect

bienfaiteur, -trice /bjɛ̃fɛtœʀ, tʀis/ *nm,f* benefactor/ benefactress

bien-fondé /bjɛ̃fɔ̃de/ *nm* (d'idée) validity; (de demande) legitimacy

bienheureux, -euse /bjɛ̃nøʀø, øz/
A *adj* blessed
B *nm,f* **les ~** the blessed

bien-pensant, ~e, *mpl* ~**s** /bjɛ̃pɑ̃sɑ̃, ɑ̃t/ *adj* [*personne*] right-thinking; péj self-righteous

bienséance /bjɛ̃seɑ̃s/ *nf* propriety; **les règles de la ~** the rules of polite society

bientôt /bjɛ̃to/ *adv* soon; **je reviens ~** I'll be back soon; **à ~** see you soon; **à ~ le plaisir de vous lire** I look forward to hearing from you soon; **on est ~ arrivés?** are we nearly there?

bienveillance /bjɛ̃vɛjɑ̃s/ *nf* benevolence (**envers** to); **avec ~** [*regarder, parler, sourire*] benevolently; **par ~** out of kindness; **étudier une requête avec ~** to look at a request favourablyᴳᴮ; **je sollicite de votre haute ~** fml may I respectfully request

bienveillant, ~e /bjɛ̃vɛjɑ̃, ɑ̃t/ *adj* benevolent

bienvenu, ~e¹ /bjɛ̃vəny/
A *adj* welcome
B *nm,f* **être le ~** to be welcome; **soyez la ~e** welcome!

bienvenue² /bjɛ̃vəny/ *nf* welcome (**à, dans** to); ~ **dans notre pays** welcome to our country; **souhaiter la ~ à qn** to welcome sb; **en signe de ~** in welcome

bière /bjɛʀ/ *nf* [1] (boisson) beer; **de la ~** beer; **deux ~s** two beers; ~ **(à la) pression** or **en fût** C draught GB ou draft US beer; [2] (cercueil) coffin, casket US; **mettre qn en ~** to lay sb in a coffin

b

Composés ~ **blonde** lager; ~ **brune** ≈ stout; ~ **rousse** brown ale

biffer /bife/ [1] *vtr* to cross out

biffure /bifyʀ/ *nf* crossing-out GB, erasure US

bifteck /biftɛk/ *nm* steak; ~ **haché** extra lean minced beef GB, chopped meat US

Idiomes **gagner son** ~○ to earn a living *ou* crust GB; **défendre son** ~○ to look out for number one○

bifurcation /bifyʀkasjɔ̃/ *nf* (de voie) fork

bifurquer /bifyʀke/ [1] *vi* ① [*route, voie ferrée*] to fork; ② [*automobiliste*] to turn off; ③ (dans ses études, sa carrière) to change tack

bigame /bigam/
A *adj* bigamous
B *nmf* bigamist

bigamie /bigami/ *nf* bigamy

bigarré, ~e /bigaʀe/ *adj* [*tissu*] multicoloured GB; [*foule, société*] colourful GB

bigleux○, -euse /biglø, øz/ *adj* pej poor-sighted; **complètement** ~ as blind as a bat○

bigorneau, *pl* ~**x** /bigɔʀno/ *nm* winkle

bigot, ~e /bigo, ɔt/ *nmf* religious zealot

bigoudi /bigudi/ *nm* roller

bigrement○† /bigʀəmã/ *adv* jolly○ GB, extremely

bijou, *pl* ~**x** /biʒu/ *nm* piece of jewellery GB *ou* jewelry US; (de très grande valeur) jewel; ~**x en or** gold jewellery GB *ou* jewelry US; **leur maison est un vrai** ~ their house is an absolute gem; **un petit** ~ **mécanique** a marvel of engineering

bijouterie /biʒutʀi/ ▸ p. 372 *nf* ① (magasin) jeweller's GB, jewellery shop GB, jewelry store US; ② (art) jewellery GB, jewelry US; ③ (commerce) jewellery GB *ou* jewelry US trade

bijoutier, -ière /biʒutje, ɛʀ/ ▸ p. 372 *nmf* jeweller GB

bilan /bilã/ *nm* ① (financier) balance sheet; **établir un** ~ to draw up a balance sheet; **déposer son** ~ to file a petition in bankruptcy; ② (aboutissement) outcome; ③ (de catastrophe, d'accident) toll; **'accident de voiture, ~: deux morts'** 'two killed in a car accident'; ④ (évaluation) assessment; **faire** *or* **dresser le** ~ **de qch** to assess sth; **quel est le** ~ **de l'année?** how did the year turn out?; ~ **de santé** checkup; ⑤ (compte rendu) report

bilatéral, ~e, *mpl* **-aux** /bilateʀal, o/ *adj* [*négociations, contrat*] bilateral; **stationnement** ~ parking on both sides of the street

bilboquet /bilbɔkɛ/ ▸ p. 327 *nm* cup-and-ball

bile /bil/ *nf* bile

Idiomes **se faire de la** ~○ to worry (**pour qch** about sth); **déverser sa** ~○ to vent one's spleen

biler: se biler○ /bile/ [1] *vpr* to worry (**pour qch** about sth)

bilieux, -ieuse /biljø, øz/ *nmf* (personne colérique) irritable person

bilingue /bilɛ̃g/ *adj* bilingual

bilinguisme /bilɛ̃gɥism/ *nm* bilingualism

billard /bijaʀ/ ▸ p. 327 *nm* (jeu) billiards (+ *v sg*); (table) billiard table

Composés ~ **américain** pool; ~ **anglais** snooker

Idiome **passer sur le** ~○ to have an operation

bille /bij/ *nf* ① ▸ p. 327 (d'enfant) marble; (au billard) ball; ② Tech ball; **déodorant à** ~ roll-on deodorant

Idiomes **reprendre** *or* **retirer ses** ~**s**○ to pull out; **placer ses** ~**s**○ to stake out one's position; **foncer** ~ **en tête**○ to go blindly ahead

billet /bijɛ/ *nm* ① (argent) (bank)note, bill US; ~ **de 20 euros** 20-euro note; **faux** ~ forged bill; ② (de transport, d'admission) ticket

Composés ~ **de banque** banknote, bank bill US; ~ **doux** love letter; ~ **vert**○ dollar, greenback○ US

Idiome **je te fiche mon** ~ **que**○ I bet you anything that

billetterie /bijɛtʀi/ *nf* (de billets de banque) cash dispenser

billettiste /bijɛtist/ ▸ p. 372 *nmf* ① Presse writer of short articles; ② (employé) ticket clerk

billevesées /bilvəze, bijvəze/ *nfpl* nonsense ¢

billion /biljɔ̃/ ▸ p. 398 *nm* (mille milliards) billion GB, trillion US

billot /bijo/ *nm* block

bimbeloterie /bɛ̃blɔtʀi/ *nf* (objets) knick-knacks (*pl*)

bimensuel /bimãsɥɛl/ *nm* (journal) fortnightly magazine GB, semimonthly US

bimoteur /bimɔtœʀ/ *nm* (avion) twin-engined plane

binaire /binɛʀ/ *adj* binary

biner /bine/ [1] *vtr* to hoe

binette /binɛt/ *nf* (outil) hoe

binoclard, ~e○ /binɔklaʀ, aʀd/ *nm,f* pej four-eyes○

binocle /binɔkl/
A *nm* pince-nez
B **binocles**○ *nfpl* specs○, glasses

binôme /binom/ *nm* Math binomial

bio¹ /bjo/ *préf* bio; ~**luminescence** bioluminescence

bio² /bjo/
A *adj inv* (naturel) **aliments** ~ health foods; **produits** ~ organic produce ¢; **avoir des goûts** ~ to be a health food freak; **yaourt** ~ bio yoghurt
B ○*nf* (biographie) biography

biochimie /bjoʃimi/ *nf* biochemistry

biochimique /bjoʃimik/ *adj* biochemical

biochimiste /bjoʃimist/ ▸ p. 372 *nmf* biochemist

biodégradable /bjodegʀadabl/ *adj* biodegradable

biodiversité /bjodivɛʀsite/ *nf* biodiversity

bioénergie /bjoenɛʀʒi/ *nf* bioenergetics (+ *v sg*)

biographe /bjogʀaf/ *nmf* biographer

biographie /bjogʀafi/ *nf* biography

biographique /bjogʀafik/ *adj* biographical

biologie /bjolɔʒi/ *nf* biology

Composés ~ **cellulaire** cell biology; ~ **moléculaire** molecular biology

biologique /bjolɔʒik/ *adj* ① Biol biological; ② [*ferme, produit*] organic.

biologiste /bjolɔʒist/ ▸ p. 372 *nmf* biologist

bionique /bjonik/ *nf* bionics (+ *v sg*)

biophysique /bjofizik/ *nf* biophysics (+ *v sg*)

bioterrorisme /bjotɛʀɔʀism/ *nm* bioterrorism

bip /bip/ *nm* (son) beep; ~ **sonore** tone

bipartisme /bipaʀtism/ *nm* two-party system

bipède /bipɛd/ *nm* biped

biphasé, ~e /bifaze/ *adj* two-phase

biplace /biplas/ *adj, nm* two-seater

biplan /biplã/ *nm* (avion) biplane

bique○ /bik/ *nf* ① (chèvre) nanny goat; ② (femme) pej **une vieille** ~ an old bag○

biquet○ /bikɛ/ *nm* (chevreau) kid; **mon** ~ sweetheart○

biquette○ /bikɛt/ *nf* (jeune chèvre) young female goat; **ma** ~ sweetheart○

biréacteur /biʀeaktœʀ/ *nm* twin-engined jet

birman, ~e /biʀmã, an/ ▸ p. 336, p. 392
A *adj* Burmese
B *nm* Ling Burmese

Birmanie /biʀmani/ ▸ p. 230 *nprf* Burma

bis¹ /bis/
A *adv* ① (dans une adresse) **15** ~ 15 bis; ② Mus (indication) bis
B *nm inv* **l'orchestre a joué trois** ~ the orchestra did three encores

bis², ~e¹ /bi, biz/ ▸ p. 140 *adj* [*couleur*] greyish GB *ou* grayish US brown

bisaïeul, ~e /bizajœl/ *nm,f* great-grandfather/great-grandmother

bisannuel, -elle /bizanɥɛl/ *adj* biennial

biscornu, ~e /biskɔʀny/ *adj* quirky

biscotte /biskɔt/ *nf* continental toast

biscuit /biskɥi/ *nm* (gâteau sec) biscuit GB, cookie US

Composés ~ **à la cuillère** sponge GB *ou* lady US finger; ~ **salé** cracker; ~ **de Savoie** sponge cake

bise² /biz/
A *adj f* ▸ **bis²**
B *nf* ① ○(baiser) kiss; **faire la** ~ **à qn** to kiss sb on the cheeks; ② (vent) North wind

biseau, *pl* ~**x** /bizo/ *nm* ① (bord) bevel (edge); **tailler en** ~ to bevel; **glace en** ~ bevelled GB mirror; ② (outil) bevel; **tailler au** ~ to bevel

biseauter /bizote/ [1] *vtr* to bevel; **cartes biseautées** marked cards

bisexuel, -elle /bisɛksɥɛl/ *adj, nm,f* bisexual

bison /bizõ/ *nm* (d'Europe) bison; (d'Amérique) buffalo

Bison Futé® /bizõfyte/ *nm*: *TV and radio traffic monitoring service*

> ⓘ Bison Futé Symbolized by a little Native American, *Bison Futé* is a creation of the *Centre National d'Information Routière*, the French traffic information service which reports on travel conditions nationwide, particularly during holiday periods when traffic is heaviest, and recommends alternative routes (*les itinéraires 'bis'*) for travellers keen to avoid traffic jams. The *Bison Futé* traffic tips are broadcast across the full range of media (radio, TV, the national press, the internet and minitel) and appear at regular intervals on the road system itself. Information is updated constantly to reflect actual traffic conditions enabling motorists to choose the best time to travel. Allied to *Bison Futé* is a colour-coding system to mark the relative intensity of traffic on the roads at any time (green, red, yellow and black) which is a key factor in staggering holiday traffic on the roads.

bisou○ /bizu/ *nm* kiss

bisquer○ /biske/ [1] *vi* to be furious

bissectrice /bisɛktris/ *nf* bisector

bissextile /bisɛkstil/ *adj* **année** ~ leap year

bistouri /bisturi/ *nm* bistoury

bistre /bistr/ ▸ p. 140 *adj* [*couleur*] yellowish brown; [*peau*] swarthy

bistro(t)○ /bistro/ *nm* bistro, café

bit /bit/ *nm* bit

BIT /beite/ *nm* (*abbr* = **Bureau international du travail**) ILO

bitoniau○ /bitonjo/ *nm* whatsit○

bitume /bitym/ *nm* ① Chimie bitumen; ② (de route) asphalt

bitumer /bityme/ [1] *vtr* to asphalt [*route*]

biunivoque /biynivɔk/ *adj* Math one-to-one

bivouaquer /bivwake/ [1] *vi* to bivouac

bizarre /bizar/ *adj* [*objet, parole, acte*] odd; **comme c'est** ~ how odd; [*personne*] strange

bizarrement /bizarmã/ *adv* strangely

bizarrerie /bizarri/ *nf* ① (caractère étrange) strangeness (**de** of); ② (chose étrange) quirk; **une** ~ **de l'Histoire** a strange turn of history; **une** ~ **de la langue** a peculiarity of the language

bizut(h) /bizy/ *nm* students' slang ① (étudiant) fresher○ GB, freshman US; ② (novice) newcomer, rookie○

bizuter /bizyte/ [1] *vtr* students' slang to rag○, to haze○ US [*étudiant*]; (brimer) to bully [*nouveau*]

blabla○ /blabla/ *nm inv* waffle○ GB, hogwash○ US

black-blanc-beur○ /blakblãbœr/ *adj inv* multiculti○, multicultural

blafard, ~e /blafar, ard/ *adj* pale

blague /blag/ *nf* ① (plaisanterie, histoire) joke; (mensonge) fib○; **c'est pas des** ~**s** I'm not kidding○; **ne me raconte pas de** ~**s** tell me the truth; **sans** ~! no kidding○!; ~ **à part** seriously, joking apart; **faire une** ~ **à qn** to play a trick on sb; ② (farce) trick; ③ (tabatière) ~ **(à tabac)** tobacco pouch

blaguer○ /blage/ [1] *vi* (plaisanter) to joke; **il dit ça pour** ~ he's kidding○

blagueur○, **-euse** /blagœr, øz/ *nm,f* joker

blaireau, pl ~x /blero/ *nm* ① (animal) badger; ② (pour rasage) shaving brush

blâme /blɑm/ *nm* ① (désapprobation) criticism; ② (sanction) official warning

blâmer /blɑme/ [1] *vtr* (désapprouver) to criticize; **on ne peut pas le** ~ you can't blame him

blanc, blanche¹ /blɑ̃, blɑ̃ʃ/ ▸ p. 140
Ⓐ *adj* ① (couleur) white; ~ **cassé** off-white; ~ **crémeux** cream; ~ **laiteux** milk white; ~ **de peur** white with fear; ② (occidental) white; **homme/quartier** ~ white man/district; ③ (innocent) **il n'est pas** ~ **dans l'histoire** he was certainly mixed up in it; **ne pas être** ~ to have a less than

spotless reputation; ④ (vierge) blank; **page/feuille blanche** blank page/sheet

Ⓑ *adv* **il gèle** ~ there's a hoarfrost

Ⓒ *nm* ① (couleur) white; ② (peinture) white paint; **peindre en** ~ to paint [sth] white [*mur, meuble*]; ③ (linge) household linen; ④ (vêtements) white; **être habillé en** ~ to be dressed in white; ⑤ Culin (de volaille) white meat; (de poireau) white part; (d'œuf) white; **un** ~ **de poulet** a chicken breast; ⑥ (vin) white wine; (verre de vin) glass of white wine; ⑦ (espace entre des mots) (volontaire) blank; (involontaire) gap; **laisser en** ~ to leave [sth] blank [*nom, adresse*]; ⑧ (liquide correcteur) correction fluid; ⑨ (temps mort) lull; ⑩ (dans la tête) **j'ai eu un** ~ my mind went blank; ⑪ (en cosmétique) (poudre) white powder; ⑫ Bot (moisissure) powdery mildew; ⑬ Mil **coup à** ~ blank shot; **charger à** ~ to load [sth] with blanks

Ⓓ **blancs** *nmpl* (aux échecs, aux dames) white (*sg*); **je prends les** ~**s** I'll be white

(Composés) ~ **de chaux** whitewash; ~ **de l'œil** white of the eye; ~ **d'œuf** egg white

(Idiomes) **c'est écrit noir sur** ~ it's there in black and white; **quand l'un dit** ~, **l'autre dit noir** they can never agree on anything; **avec lui/elle, c'est (toujours) tout** ~ **ou tout noir** he/she sees everything in black-and-white terms; **se regarder dans le** ~ **des yeux** to gaze into each other's eyes

Blanc, Blanche /blɑ̃, blɑ̃ʃ/ *nm,f* white man/woman

blanc-bec, pl blancs-becs /blɑ̃bɛk/ *nm* pej greenhorn

blanchâtre /blɑ̃ʃatr/ ▸ p. 140 *adj* whitish

blanche² /blɑ̃ʃ/
Ⓐ *adj f* ▸ **blanc** A
Ⓑ *nf* Mus minim GB, half note US

Blanche-Neige /blɑ̃ʃnɛʒ/ *npr* Littérat Snow White

blancheur /blɑ̃ʃœr/ *nf* (couleur) whiteness

blanchiment /blɑ̃ʃimã/ *nm* ① (d'argent) laundering; ② (de tissu, pâte à papier) bleaching

blanchir /blɑ̃ʃir/ [3]
Ⓐ *vtr* ① (rendre blanc) to whiten [*chaussures, surface*]; to light up [*ciel, route*]; to bleach [*textile, pâte à papier, farine*]; to refine [*sucre*]; to blanch [*légumes, viande, amandes*]; ~ **(à la chaux)** to whitewash [*mur, plafond*]; **donner son linge à** ~ to send one's linen to the laundry; ② (disculper) to clear [*accusé, nom*] (**de** of); ③ to launder [*argent sale*]

Ⓑ *vi* [*cheveux*] to turn grey GB ou gray US; [*ciel*] to grow light; ~ **de rage** to go white with rage; **faire** ~ Culin to blanch [*légumes, viande, amandes*]

Ⓒ **se blanchir** *vpr* (se disculper) to clear oneself (**de** of; **auprès de** in the eyes of)

blanchissage /blɑ̃ʃisaʒ/ *nm* **service de** ~ laundry service

blanchissant, ~e /blɑ̃ʃisã, ãt/ *adj* bleaching

blanchisserie /blɑ̃ʃisri/ ▸ p. 372 *nf* laundry

blanchisseur /blɑ̃ʃisœr/ ▸ p. 372 *nm* (personne) laundry worker; (magasin) laundry

blanchisseuse /blɑ̃ʃisøz/ *nf* laundress

blanc-seing, pl blancs-seings /blɑ̃sɛ̃/ *nm* **donner un** ~ **à qn** to give sb carte blanche

blanquette /blɑ̃kɛt/ *nf* ~ **de veau** blanquette of veal

blasé, ~e /blaze/
Ⓐ *adj* blasé; **être** ~ **de qch** to be blasé about sth
Ⓑ *nm,f* blasé person; **jouer les** ~**s**, **faire le** ~ to affect a blasé attitude

blason /blazõ/ *nm* (armoiries) coat of arms, blazon spéc

(Idiome) **redorer son** ~ to restore one's reputation

blasphémateur, -trice /blasfematœr, tris/ *nm,f* blasphemer

blasphématoire /blasfematwar/ *adj* blasphemous

blasphème /blasfɛm/ *nm* blasphemy ℭ

blasphémer /blasfeme/ [1] *vi* to blaspheme

blatte /blat/ *nf* cockroach

blé /ble/ *nm* (céréale) wheat; ~ **en herbe** wheat in the blade

(Composé) ~ **noir** buckwheat

bled○ /blɛd/ *nm* village

blême /blɛm/ *adj* pale

blêmir /blemiʀ/ [3] vi [personne, visage] to pale; ~ **de peur/ rage** to go white with fear/rage

blennorragie /blenɔʀaʒi/ ▸ p. 195 nf gonorrhea

blessant, ~**e** /blesã, ãt/ adj [propos] cutting

blessé, ~**e** /blese/ nm,f (par accident) injured man/woman; (par arme) wounded man/woman; Mil casualty; **les** ~**s** gén the injured; Mil the wounded; **l'explosion a fait 20** ~**s** 20 people were injured in the explosion; **il n'y a pas de** ~**s** nobody has been hurt; Mil there are no casualties

(Composés) ~ **de guerre** person wounded in the war; **les** ~**s de guerre** the war wounded; ~ **de la route** road accident victim

blesser /blese/ [1]

A vtr **1** (par accident) to hurt; (dans un conflit armé) to wound; **il a été blessé à la tête** he sustained head injuries; ~ **qn d'un coup de couteau** to stab sb; ~ **qn d'un coup de revolver** to shoot sb (with a gun); **il a été blessé par balle** he received a bullet wound; **2** (offenser) to hurt [personne, amour-propre]; **il s'est senti blessé** he felt hurt; ~ **qn au vif** to cut sb to the quick

B se blesser vpr **je me suis blessé au bras en tombant** I fell and hurt my arm

blessure /blesyʀ/ nf (lésion) injury; (plaie) wound; ~ **légère/ grave** minor/serious injury ou wound

blet, **blette¹** /blɛ, blɛt/ adj overripe

blette² /blɛt/ nf Swiss chard

bleu, ~**e** /blø/

A adj **1** ▸ p. 140 (couleur) blue; **des yeux** ~**s** blue eyes; ~ **vert** blue-green; ~ **ardoise** slate blue; ~ **canard** peacock blue; ~ **marine** navy blue; ~ **noir** blue-black; ~ **nuit** midnight blue; ~ **outremer** ultramarine; ~ **pétrole** petrol-blue; ~ **roi** royal blue; ~ **turquoise** turquoise blue; ~ **de peur** white with fear; **2** Culin [entrecôte, viande] very rare

B nm **1** ▸ p. 140 (couleur) blue; **2** (ecchymose) bruise; **se faire un** ~ to bruise oneself; **3** (vêtement) ~ **(de travail)** (combinaison) overalls (pl); (veste et pantalon) workman's blue cotton jacket and trousers; **4** (fromage) blue cheese; **5** ○(nouvelle recrue) soldiers' slang rookie○; (débutant) beginner

(Idiome) **avoir une peur** ~**e de qch** to be scared stiff○ of sth

bleuâtre /bløɑtʀ/ ▸ p. 140 adj bluish

bleuet /bløɛ/ nm **1** Bot cornflower; **2** C (myrtille) blueberry, bilberry

bleuir /bløiʀ/ [3]

A vtr to turn [sth] blue

B vi to turn blue

bleuté, ~**e** /bløte/ ▸ p. 140 adj bluish

blindage /blɛ̃daʒ/ nm armour^GB plating, security reinforcement

blindé, ~**e** /blɛ̃de/

A adj **1** [division, unité, corps] armoured^GB; **2** (renforcé) **porte** ~**e** security door

B nm armoured^GB vehicle

blinder /blɛ̃de/ [1] vtr ~ **une porte** to put security fittings on a door; ~ **un véhicule** to armour-plate^GB a vehicle

blinquer /blɛ̃ke/ [1] vi B (briller) to shine; **faire** ~ to polish

blizzard /blizaʀ/ nm blizzard

bloc /blɔk/

A nm **1** (masse solide) block (**de** of); **se retourner tout d'un** ~ to pivot round GB ou around US; **2** (de personnes) group (**de** of); Pol bloc; **faire** ~ to side together; **faire** ~ **contre qn** (s'unir) to unite against sb; (être unis) to be united against sb; **3** (pour écrire) notepad; ~ **de papier à lettres** writing pad; **4** (d'actions, de titres) block; **5** Ordinat block

B à bloc loc adv [serrer, visser, fermer] tightly; [charger, gonfler] fully

C en bloc loc adv (entièrement) outright

(Composés) ~ **de départ** starting block; ~ **opératoire** surgical unit

blocage /blɔkaʒ/ nm (de route, véhicule, marchandise) blocking; ~ **des vins dans le port** blockade of wines in the port; ~ **de la vente des armes** ban on sales of arms; (situation de) ~ deadlock; ~ **des prix/salaires** price/wage freeze; **faire un** ~ **mental** to have a mental block

bloc-note, pl **blocs-notes** /blɔknɔt/ nm notepad

blocus /blɔkys/ nm inv blockade

blond, ~**e¹** /blɔ̃, ɔ̃d/ ▸ p. 140

A adj [cheveux, barbe] fair; [personne] fair-haired; [caramel, épi]

golden; [tabac] light; **cigarette** ~**e** Virginia tobacco cigarette; **nos chères têtes** ~**es** our little darlings

B nm,f (femme) blonde GB, blond US; (homme) blond; ▸ **faux¹**

blonde² /blɔ̃d/

A adj f ▸ **blond A**

B nf **1** (cigarette) Virginia tobacco cigarette; **2** (bière) lager

blondinet, -**ette** /blɔ̃dinɛ, ɛt/ nm,f fair-haired boy/girl

blondir /blɔ̃diʀ/ [3] vi [cheveux, personne] to go blonde ou blond US; [épi, champ] to turn golden; **faire** ~ **qch** Culin to brown [sth] lightly [beurre, caramel]

bloqué, ~**e** /blɔke/

A pp ▸ **bloquer**

B pp adj **1** (obstrué) blocked; **avoir les reins** ~**s** to have a blockage in the kidneys; **2** (immobilisé) [mécanisme, porte] jammed; **elle/la voiture est** ~**e** she/the car is stuck; ~ **par la neige** snowbound; [fonds, compte] frozen; **il a le dos** ~ his back has seized up; **3** fig **être** ~ [activité, carrière, négociations] to be at a standstill; [situation] to be dead-locked; **4** (mentalement) **être** ~ to have a (mental) block (**sur** about)

bloquer /blɔke/ [1]

A vtr **1** (obstruer) to block [route, entrée, porte]; Mil to blockade [ville, port]; ~ **la route** lit to block the road; fig to block the way; **2** (coincer) (accidentellement) to jam [mécanisme, porte]; (volontairement) to lock [volant]; to wedge [porte]; to secure [écrou]; **3** (immobiliser) to stop [véhicule, voyageur, circulation, marchandise]; Sport to catch [ballon]; **4** Écon to freeze [compte, salaires, crédit, dépenses, prix]; to stop [chèque]; ~ **des capitaux** to lock up capital; **5** (enrayer) to stop [projet, contrat]; to prevent [ovulation]; **6** (grouper) to lump [sth] together [heures, jours, personnes]; to bulk [commandes]

B vi **1** **il y a quelque chose qui bloque** something is jamming; **2** ○B students' slang (étudier) to swot○ GB, to bone up○ US

C se bloquer vpr **1** [frein, mécanisme, porte] to jam; [volant, roue] to lock; **2** [personne] to retreat

bloqueur, -**euse** /blɔkœʀ, øz/ nm,f B students' slang (étudiant zélé) swot○ GB, grind○ US

blottir: se blottir /blɔtiʀ/ [3] vpr se ~ **contre qn/qch** (par affection) to snuggle up against sb/sth; (par peur, froid) to huddle up against sb/sth; se ~ **dans les bras de qn** to huddle up in sb's arms; **blotti contre mon épaule** buried in my shoulder; **blotti au pied de la montagne** nestled at the foot of the mountain

blousant, ~**e** /bluzã, ãt/ adj [robe, chemisier] full

blouse /bluz/ nf **1** (tablier) overall; ~ **blanche** white coat; **2** (chemisier) blouse; **3** (de paysan) smock

blouson /bluzɔ̃/ nm blouson

(Composés) ~ **d'aviateur** bomber jacket; ~ **noir** ≈ rocker

blue-jean, pl ~**s** /bludʒin/ nm jeans (pl)

bluet /blyɛ/ nm cornflower

bluffer○ /blœfe/ [1] vtr, vi to bluff

BNF /beɛn/ nf (abbr = **Bibliothèque nationale de France**) national library in Paris

boa /bɔa/ nm (serpent, parure) boa

bob /bɔb/ nm (chapeau) (sailor's) sunhat

bobard○ /bɔbaʀ/ nm fib○, tall story

bobine /bɔbin/ nf **1** (de fil, câble, film) reel; (de métier à tisser) bobbin; (de machine à écrire) spool; **2** Électrotech coil

bobo¹○ /bɔbo/ nm baby talk **1** (douleur physique) pain; **se faire** ~ to hurt oneself; **j'ai** or **ça fait** ~ it hurts; **2** (petite plaie) scratch

bobo² /bɔbo/ adj, nmf (abbr = **bourgeois bohème**) bobo high-achieving professional who combines a wealthy lifestyle with an anti-establishment attitude and a concern for quality of life

bobsleigh /bɔbslɛg/ ▸ p. 327 nm **1** (engin) bobsleigh, bob-sled US; **2** (activité) bobsleighing

bocage /bɔkaʒ/ nm hedged farmland

bocal, pl -**aux** /bɔkal, o/ nm **1** (récipient) jar; **mettre en bocaux** to preserve; **2** (aquarium) (fish)bowl

(Composé) ~ **gradué** measuring jug

bock /bɔk/ nm **1** (chope) beer glass; **2** (bière) glass of beer

bœuf, pl **bœ** nm **1** (animal) (de boucherie) bullock GB, steer US; (de trait) ox; **2** (viande) beef; **3** ○Mus jam (session); **faire un** ~○ lit to have a jam; fig to be a great success

(Composés) ~ **gros sel** boiled beef; ~ **mode** braised beef

(Idiomes) **qui vole un œuf vole un** ~ Prov once a thief, always a thief; **fort comme un** ~○ as strong as an ox; **souffler comme un** ~○ to huff and puff; **faire un effet** ~○ to make a fantastic○ impression

bof○ /bɔf/ *excl* **'tu aimes la soupe?'—'~, pas vraiment!'** 'do you like soup?'—'hmm, not particularly'; **'tu préfères la mer ou la montagne?'—'~!'** 'which do you prefer the sea or the mountains?'—'I don't mind'

bogue /bɔg/ *nf* Ordinat bug

bohème /bɔɛm/
A *adj* [*personne, caractère*] bohemian
B *nf* (milieu artiste) **la** ~ bohemia; **vie de** ~ bohemian lifestyle

bohémien, -ienne /bɔemjɛ̃, ɛn/ *nm,f* ① (tzigane) Bohemian, Romany; ② (vagabond) tramp

boire¹ /bwaʀ/ [70]
A *vtr* ① (consommer) [*personne*] to drink; ~ **dans un verre** to drink out of a glass; **ce vin bon à** ~ this wine is ready to drink; **il m'a fait** ~ he got me drunk; **allons** ~ **un verre** let's go for a drink; **il y a à** ~ **et à manger dans leur théorie** fig there's both good and bad in their theory; ② (absorber) [*plante*] to drink; [*papier, buvard, moquette*] to soak [sth] up [*liquide*]
B se boire *vpr* **ce vin se boit frais** this wine should be drunk chilled; **ce porto se boit bien** this port is very drinkable

(Idiomes) ~ **comme un trou**○ to drink like a fish○; **qui a bu boira** Prov once a drinker, always a drinker

boire² /bwaʀ/ *nm* drink; **le** ~ **et le manger** food and drink; **il en a perdu le** ~ **et le manger** fig it has taken over his whole life

bois /bwa/
A *nm inv* ① (lieu) wood; ② (matière) wood; ~ **de chêne** oak; **c'est en** ~**?** is it made of wood?; ~ **massif** solid wood; **table en** ~ wooden table; **travailler le** ~ to work in wood; ~ **de construction** timber; ▸ **petit**; ③ Art (gravure sur) ~ woodcut
B *nmpl* ① Zool (de cerf) antlers; ② Mus **les** ~ (dans un orchestre) the woodwind section

(Composés) ~ **aggloméré** chipboard; ~ **de chauffage** firewood; ~ **mort** firewood; ~ **de placage** wood veneer; ~ **de rose** rosewood

(Idiomes) **être de** ~ to be insensitive; **ne pas être de** ~ to be only human; **il va voir de quel** ~ **je me chauffe**○ I'll show him; **faire feu** *or* **flèche de tout** ~ to turn anything to good account

boisé, ~e /bwaze/ *adj* [*terrain*] wooded; **dans les régions ~es** in the woodlands

boisement /bwazmɑ̃/ *nm* afforestation

boiser /bwaze/ [1] *vtr* (planter) to plant [sth] with trees [*terrain*]

boiserie /bwazʀi/ *nf* (lambris) ~**(s)** panelling^GB ⊄

boisson /bwasɔ̃/ *nf* drink; ~ **alcoolisée/non alcoolisée** alcoholic/soft drink; **être pris de** ~ to be under the influence

boîte /bwat/ *nf* ① gén box; (en métal) tin; (de conserve) tin GB, can; **petits pois en** ~ tinned peas GB, canned peas; **mettre des fruits en** ~ to can fruit; **mise en** ~ canning ⊄; ② ○(cabaret) nightclub; **aller** *or* **sortir en** ~ (une fois) to go out to a nightclub; (d'habitude) to go clubbing; ③ ○(entreprise) firm; (bureau) office; (école) school

(Composés) ~ **d'allumettes** (pleine) box of matches; (vide) matchbox; ~ **automatique** Aut automatic gearbox GB *ou* transmission; ~ **de conserve** tin GB, can; ~ **de couleurs** Art paint box; ~ **crânienne** Anat cranium; ~ **à gants** Aut glove compartment; ~ **à** *or* **aux lettres** Postes post box GB, mailbox US; fig (personne) go-between; (adresse fictive) accommodation address; ~ **à** *or* **aux lettres électronique** electronic mailbox; ~ **à malice** bag of tricks; ~ **à musique** Mus musical box GB, music box US; ~ **noire** Aviat black box; ~ **de nuit** nightclub; ~ **à ordures** (d'intérieur) rubbish bin GB, garbage can US; ~ **à outils** toolbox; ~ **postale, BP** PO Box; ~ **de raccordement** junction box; ~ **de vitesses (automatique/mécanique)** (automatic/manual) gearbox; ~ **vocale** voice mail box

(Idiome) **mettre qn en** ~○ to tease sb

boiter /bwate/ [1] *vi* [*personne*] to limp; [*meuble*] to wobble; [*raisonnement*] to be shaky; [*phrase*] (incorrecte) to be badly put together; (maladroite) to be clumsy

boiteux, -euse /bwatø, øz/
A *adj* ① [*personne*] lame; [*meuble*] wobbly; ② [*raisonnement, alliance, paix*] shaky; [*vers*] lame
B *nm,f* lame person

boîtier /bwatje/ *nm* gén case; (d'appareil photo) body; (de téléphone) casing

boitiller /bwatije/ [1] *vi* to limp slightly

bol /bɔl/ *nm* ① (récipient, contenu) bowl; **un** ~ **de café** a bowl of coffee; ② ○(chance) luck; **coup de** ~ stroke of luck; **avoir du** ~ to be lucky

(Composé) ~ **d'air** breath of fresh air

bolée /bɔle/ *nf* ~ **de cidre** bowl of cider

bolet /bɔlɛ/ *nm* boletus

bolide /bɔlid/ *nm* (véhicule) high-powered car; **comme un** ~ at high speed; **passer comme un** ~ to shoot past

bolivien, -ienne /bɔlivjɛ̃, ɛn/ ▸ p. 392 *adj* Bolivian

bolle○ /bɔl/ *nf* C (personne intelligente) brain○

bolognaise /bɔlɔɲɛz/ *adj inv* [*spaghetti*] bolognese (*épith, après n*) GB, with meat sauce (*après n*) US

bombage /bɔ̃baʒ/ *nm* ① (action) graffiti spraying; ② (résultat) sprayed graffiti

bombance /bɔ̃bɑ̃s/ *nf* **faire** ~ to have a feast

bombarde /bɔ̃baʀd/ *nf* ① Hist Mil bombard; ② Mus (bois) bombardon; (jeu d'orgue) bombarde

bombardement /bɔ̃baʀdəmɑ̃/ *nm* ① Mil gén bombardment; (avec des bombes) bombing; (d'artillerie) shelling ⊄; ~ **aérien** air raid; ② (jet) (de projectiles) pelting; (de questions, critiques) bombardment; **être soumis à un** ~ **de critiques** to get bombarded with criticism

bombarder /bɔ̃baʀde/ [1] *vtr* ① Mil gén to bombard; (avec des bombes) to bomb; (avec des obus) to shell; ② (harceler) ~ **qn de tomates** to pelt sb with tomatoes; ~ **qn de questions** to bombard sb with questions; ~ **qn de coups de fil/lettres** to inundate sb with phone calls/letters; ③ Phys to bombard; ④ ○(nommer) ~ **qn à un poste** to catapult sb into a job

bombardier /bɔ̃baʀdje/ *nm* ① (avion) bomber; ② (aviateur) bombardier

bombe /bɔ̃b/ *nf* ① Mil bomb; ~ **artisanale** homemade bomb; **attaque/attentat à la** ~ bomb attack; **faire l'effet d'une** ~ to come as a bombshell; ② (atomiseur) ~ **(aérosol)** spray; ~ **de peinture** paint spray; ③ (coiffure) riding hat

(Composés) ~ **A** A-bomb; ~ **atomique** atomic bomb; ~ **à billes** shrapnel bomb; ~ **au cobalt** Méd cobalt therapy unit; ~ **éclairante** flare bomb; ~ **gigogne** cluster bomb; ~ **glacée** Culin bombe (glacée); ~ **guidée** smart bomb; ~ **H** H-bomb; ~ **à hydrogène** hydrogen bomb; ~ **incendiaire** Mil incendiary bomb; (artisanale) incendiary device; ~ **insecticide** insecticide spray; ~ **lacrymogène** Mil teargas grenade; ~ **à neutrons** neutron bomb; ~ **perforante** penetration bomb; ~ **à retardement** time bomb; ~ **soufflante** air-blast bomb

(Idiomes) **arriver/partir à toute** ~○ [*personne*] to rush in/off; **faire la** ~○ (s'amuser) to live it up; (dans l'eau) to dive-bomb

bombé, ~e /bɔ̃be/ *adj* [*front*] domed; [*forme, vase*] rounded; [*lentille*] convex; [*route*] cambered; [*parquet, mur*] bulging

bomber /bɔ̃be/ [1]
A *vtr* ① (gonfler) ~ **le torse** lit to thrust out one's chest; fig to swell with pride; ② ○(peindre) to spray-paint [*inscription, mur*]
B *vi* ① [*planche, mur*] to bulge out; ② ○(rouler vite) to belt along○

bombyx /bɔ̃biks/ *nm inv* bombyx

(Composé) ~ **du mûrier** silk-worm moth

bôme /bom/ *nf* Naut boom

bon, bonne¹ /bɔ̃, bɔn/
A *adj* ① (de qualité, compétent, remarquable, utile) good; **prends un** ~ **pull** take a warm jumper; **il a encore de bonnes jambes** he can still get around; **elle est (bien) bonne, celle-là**○**!** (amusé) that's a good one!; (indigné) I like that!; **ça fait un** ~ **bout de chemin** it's quite a way; **voilà une bonne chose de faite!** that's that out of the way!; **j'ai un** ~ **rhume** I've got a rotten cold; **nous sommes ~s derniers** we're well and truly last; **il n'est pas** ~ **à grand-chose** he's pretty

b

useless; **il serait ~ qu'elle le sache** she ought to know; **à quoi ~?** what's the point?; **tous les moyens leur sont ~s** they'll stop at nothing; [2] (gentil) [*personne, paroles, geste*] kind (**avec, envers** to); [*sourire*] nice; **un homme ~ et généreux** a kind and generous man; **il a une bonne tête** he looks like a nice person; **tu es trop ~ avec lui** you're too good to him; **avoir ~ cœur** to be good-hearted; **il est ~, lui**⊙**!** iron it's all very well for him to say that!; [3] (correct) [*moment, endroit, numéro, réponse, outil*] right; **c'est ~, vous pouvez y aller** it's OK, you can go; **c'est ~ pour les riches** it's all right for the rich; **c'est tout juste ~ pour les chiens!** it's only fit for dogs!; [4] (utilisable) [*billet, bon*] valid; **le lait ne sera plus ~ demain** the milk will have gone off by tomorrow; **tu es ~ pour la vaisselle, ce soir!** you're in line for the dishes tonight!; **me voilà ~ pour une amende** I'm in for a fine⊙; [5] (dans les souhaits) **bonne nuit/chance** good night/luck; **~ anniversaire** happy birthday; **bonne journée/soirée!** have a nice day/evening!

[B] *nm,f* (personne) **les ~s et les méchants** good people and bad people; (au cinéma) the good guys and the bad guys⊙, the goodies and the baddies⊙ GB

[C] *nm* [1] (ce qui est de qualité) **il y a du ~ dans cet article** there are some good things in this article; **la concurrence peut avoir du ~** competition can be a good thing; [2] (sur un emballage) **coupon**; (contremarque) **voucher**; **cadeau gratuit contre 50 ~s** free gift with 50 coupons; **~ à valoir sur l'achat de** voucher valid for the purchase of; [3] Fin bond

[D] *excl* (satisfaction) good; (accord) all right, OK; (intervention, interruption) right, well; **~, on va pouvoir y aller** good, we can go; **~, il faut que je parte** right, I must go now; **~, ~, ça va!** OK, OK!; **allons ~!** oh dear!

[E] *adv* **ça sent ~!** that smells good!; **il fait ~** (à l'extérieur) the weather's mild; **il fait ~ vivre ici** it's nice living here; **il ne fait pas ~ le déranger** it's not a good idea to disturb him

[F] **pour de bon** *loc adv* (vraiment) really; (définitivement) for good; **j'ai cru qu'il allait le faire pour de ~** I thought he'd really do it; **je suis ici pour de ~** I'm here for good; **tu dis ça pour de ~?** are you serious?

(Composés) **~ de commande** order form; **~ de croissance** Fin share option, stock option; **~ enfant** good-natured; **~ d'essence** petrol GB *ou* gas US coupon; **~ de garantie** guarantee slip; **~ garçon** nice chap; **~ marché** cheap; **~ mot** witticism; **~ de réduction** Comm discount voucher; **~ à rien** good-for-nothing; **~ sens** common sense; **~ teint** dyed-in-the-wool (*épith*); **~ à tirer** pass for press; **~ de transport** travel voucher; **~ du Trésor** Treasury bond; **~ usage** good usage; **~ vivant** *adj* jovial; *nm* bon viveur; **bonne action** good deed; **bonne femme**⊙ pej (femme) woman; (épouse) wife; **bonne parole** word of God; **bonne pâte** good sort; **bonne sœur**⊙ nun; **bonnes mœurs** Jur public decency ¢; **~s offices** good offices

(Idiome) **il m'a à la bonne** I'm in his good books

bonasse /bɔnas/ *adj* pej meek

bonbon /bɔ̃bɔ̃/ *nm* sweet GB, candy US; **des ~s** sweets GB, candy US; **~s fourrés** sweets GB *ou* candy US with a soft centre

(Composés) **~ acidulé** acid drop GB, sour ball US; **~ à la menthe** mint

bonbonne /bɔ̃bɔn/ *nf* (en verre) demijohn; (plus grand) carboy; **~ de gaz** gas cylinder;

bonbonnière /bɔ̃bɔnjɛR/ *nf* (boîte) sweet dish GB, candy dish US

bond /bɔ̃/ *nm* [1] lit, gén (de personne, d'animal) leap, bound; fig (dans le temps) jump; **franchir qch d'un ~** to leap across sth; **se lever d'un ~** to leap to one's feet; **~ en avant** to leap forward; [2] fig (progrès) leap; (hausse) (de prix) jump (**de** in); (de bénéfices, d'exportations) leap (**de** in); **~ en avant** leap forward; (découverte) breakthrough; [3] Mil thrust; **progresser par ~s** to progress through a series of thrusts

(Idiomes) **saisir la balle au ~** to seize the opportunity; **faire faux ~ à qn** to let sb down

bonde /bɔ̃d/ *nf* [1] (orifice) (de piscine) outlet; (d'étang) sluice; (de lavabo) plughole; (de tonneau) bunghole; [2] (bouchon) (de piscine) outlet cover; (d'étang) sluicegate; (de lavabo) plug; (de tonneau) bung

bondé, -e /bɔ̃de/ *adj* packed (**de** with)

bondieuserie⊙ /bɔ̃djøzRi/ *nf* pej (objet) religious souvenir

bondir /bɔ̃diR/ [3] *vi* [1] (sauter) [*personne, animal, flamme, torrent*] to leap; **~ de joie** to jump for joy; [2] (s'élancer) **~ sur qn/qch** to pounce on sb/sth; [3] (gambader) [*animal*] to leap about; [4] (s'indigner) to react furiously, to hit the roof⊙

bondissement /bɔ̃dismɑ̃/ *nm* leap, bound

bonheur /bɔnœR/ *nm* [1] (état de plénitude) happiness; **être au comble du ~** to be ecstatic; [2] (moment heureux) pleasure; **faire le ~ de** [*personne, cadeau*] to make [sb] happy [*personne, enfant*]; [*exposition, événement*] to delight [*spectateur, touriste*]; **pour le plus grand ~ de qn** to the great delight of sb; [3] (chance) pleasure; **par ~** fortunately; **au petit ~ (la chance)** [*répondre, décider, chercher*] at random; **tu ne connais pas ton ~!** you don't realize how lucky you are!; [4] fml (réussite) **il manie la métaphore avec ~** he uses metaphor to great effect

(Idiomes) **le malheur des uns fait le ~ des autres** Prov one man's meat is another man's poison Prov; **l'argent ne fait pas le ~** Prov money can't buy happiness; **alors, tu as trouvé ton ~**⊙**?** did you find what you wanted?

bonhomie /bɔnɔmi/ *nf* good-nature

bonhomme /bɔnɔm/ *pl* **~s, bonshommes** /bɔ̃zɔm/
[A] *adj* [*air, propos, gendarme*] good-natured
[B] ⊙*nm* (homme) fellow, chap⊙; (mari) old man⊙; **découper des ~s de carton** to cut out little cardboard people

(Composé) **~ de neige** snowman

(Idiome) **aller** *or* **suivre son petit ~ de chemin** to go peacefully along

bonification /bɔnifikasjɔ̃/ *nf* [1] Sport bonus points; [2] Fin bonus

boniment /bɔnimɑ̃/
[A] *nm* (de camelot) sales patter
[B] **boniments** *nmpl* stories; **raconter des ~s à qn** (mensonges) to give sb some story⊙ (**à propos de qch** about sth); (flatteries) to smooth-talk sb

bonjour /bɔ̃ʒuR/ *nm* gén hello; (le matin) good morning, hello; (l'après-midi) good afternoon, hello; **~ à votre sœur** say hello to your sister for me; **allô, ~!** hello!

(Idiome) **être simple** *or* **facile comme ~**⊙ to be dead easy⊙ GB, to be easy as pie⊙ US

bonne² /bɔn/
[A] *adj f* ▸ **bon A**
[B] ▸ p. 372 *nf* [1] (domestique) maid; **je ne suis pas ta ~!** I'm not the maid!; [2] (plaisanterie) **tu en as de ~s, toi!** you must be joking!; **une bien ~** a good joke

(Composés) **~ d'enfants** nanny; **~ à tout faire** pej skivvy⊙ GB pej, maid

bonne-maman, *pl* **bonnes-mamans** /bɔnmamɑ̃/ *nf* grandma

bonnement /bɔnmɑ̃/ *adv* **tout ~** (quite) simply

bonnet /bɔnɛ/ *nm* [1] (coiffe) hat; (de bébé) bonnet; [2] (de soutien-gorge) cup; [3] Zool reticulum

(Composés) **~ d'âne** Scol dunce's cap; **~ de bain** bathing cap; **~ de nuit** nightcap; fig wet blanket⊙

(Idiomes) **prendre qch sous son ~** to make sth one's concern; **avoir la tête près du ~** to be hot-tempered GB *ou* hotheaded

bonneterie /bɔnɛtRi/ *nf* (activité) **la ~** hosiery; (magasin) hosiery shop

bonnetier, -ière /bɔntje, ɛR/ ▸ p. 372 *nm,f* Comm hosier

bon-papa, *pl* **bons-papas** /bɔ̃papa/ *nm* granddad⊙, grandpapa⊙

bonshommes ▸ **bonhomme**

bonsoir /bɔ̃swaR/ *nm* (à l'arrivée) good evening, hello; (au départ) good night; (avant le coucher) good night

bonté /bɔ̃te/
[A] *nf* (de personne) kindness (**envers** toward(s)); (de Dieu, Ciel) goodness; **c'est mon jour de ~** hum I'm feeling generous today; **voudriez-vous avoir la ~ de faire** fml would you please be kind enough to do; **~ divine!** good heavens!
[B] **bontés** *nfpl* (gentillesses) kindness ¢ (**pour** toward(s))

bonus /bɔnys/ *nm inv* no-claims bonus

bonzerie /bɔ̃zRi/ *nf* buddhist monastery

booléen, -éenne /bɔleɛ̃, ɛn/ *adj* boolean

b

boom /bum/ *nm* ～ **économique** economic boom; **une industrie en plein ～** a booming industry

booster○ /buste/ [1] *vtr* to boost

boqueteau, *pl* ～**x** /bɔkto/ *nm* copse

borborygme /bɔrbɔrigm/ *nm* (bruit) (de faim) rumbling **₵**; (de digestion) gurgling **₵**

bord /bɔr/ *nm* **1** (limite) gén edge; (de route) side; (de cours d'eau) bank; **le ～ de l'assiette** the edge of the plate; **au ～ de** lit on *ou* at the edge of [*chemin, lac, rivière*]; fig on the brink of [*drame*]; on the verge of [*faillite*]; **ils se sont assis au ～ du lac** they sat down by the lake; **au ～ de l'eau** [*restaurant*] waterside (*épith*); [*manger, jouer*] by the waterside; **au ～ de la mer** [*maison, village, terrain*] by the sea (*après n*); [*activité, vacances*] at the seaside (*après n*); **le ～ de la mer** the seaside; **du ～ de mer** [*avenue, village, activité*] seaside (*épith*); **à ～** edge-to-edge; **2** (pourtour) (de tasse, verre, cratère, lunettes) rim; (de chapeau) brim; **à ～s relevés** [*chapeau*] with a turned-up brim; **soucoupe à large ～** wide-rimmed saucer; **3** (dans un véhicule) **à ～** [*être, travailler, dîner, dormir*] on board, aboard; **monter à ～** to go aboard, to board; **à ～ d'un navire/avion** on board a ship/plane; **par-dessus ～** [*tomber, jeter*] overboard; **de ～** [*instrument, personnel*] on board (*après n*); **on fera**○ **avec les moyens du ～** we'll make do with what we've got; **4** fig (tendance) side; **ils sont du même ～** they're on the same side; **de tous ～s** from all sides; **il est un peu anarchiste sur les ～s** he has slightly anarchic tendencies; **5** (côté) side; **d'un ～ à l'autre** from one side to the other; **tirer des ～s** (en bateau) to tack

bordeaux /bɔrdo/
A ▸ p. 140 *adj inv* burgundy
B *nm* Bordeaux; ～ **rouge** claret

bordée /bɔrde/ *nf* **1** Mil (décharge) broadside; (canons) broadside; **tirer une ～** lit to fire a broadside; fig to go on a binge○; **2** Naut (route) tack
(Idiome) **lâcher une ～ d'injures** to let out a volley of abuse

border /bɔrde/ [1] *vtr* **1** (suivre un contour) to line (**de** with); **route bordée d'arbres** road lined with trees; **2** (entourer) [*plage*] to skirt [*côte*]; [*plantes*] to border [*massif, lac*]; **3** (longer) [*chemin, cours d'eau*] to border, to run alongside [*maison, terrain*]; [*marin, navire*] to sail along [*côte*]; **4** (arranger la literie) to tuck [sb] in [*personne*]; **5** (garnir) to edge [*vêtement*] (**de** with); **un mouchoir bordé de dentelle** a lace-trimmed handkerchief; **6** Naut to take up the slack in [*voile*]; to ship [*avirons*]; ～ **un navire** (en bois) to plank; (en metal) to plate

bordereau, *pl* ～**x** /bɔrdəro/ *nm* **1** (feuille) gén form, slip; (de commerce, banque) note; (en informatique) sheet; ～ **de commande** order form; **2** (en Bourse) contract; **3** (de dossier juridique) docket

bordure /bɔrdyr/
A *nf* **1** (de terrain, tapis, vêtement) border; **2** (contour externe) (de route, quai) edge; (de trottoir) kerb GB, curb US; **3** Naut (de voile) foot
B en bordure de *loc prép* **1** (sur le bord) (en un point) next to [*parc, terrain*]; (en entourant) on the edge of [*parc, terrain*]; (en longeant) next to, running alongside [*canal, voie ferrée*]; on the side of [*route, chemin*]; **2** (à proximité) just outside [*village, ville*]

boréal, ～**e**, *mpl* **-aux** /bɔreal, o/ *adj* boreal

borgne /bɔrɲ/
A *adj* **1** [*personne*] one-eyed (*épith*); **il est ～** he has only one eye; **2** (bouché) **fenêtre ～** obstructed window; **3** (mal famé) seedy
B *nmf* one-eyed man/woman

borne /bɔrn/
A *nf* **1** (sur une route) ～ **(kilométrique)** kilometreGB marker; **2** (autour d'une propriété) boundary stone; (autour d'un édifice) post; **3** (pour bloquer le passage) bollard GB, post US; **4** ○(kilomètre) kilometreGB; **5** Électrotech terminal; **6** Math limit; ～ **supérieure/inférieure** upper/lower bound
B bornes *nfpl* fig (limites) limits, boundaries; **une stupidité sans ～** boundless stupidity; **leur ambition est sans ～s** their ambition knows no bounds
(Composés) ～ **d'incendie** fire hydrant; ～ **téléphonique** (sur l'autoroute) emergency telephone; (pour taxis) taxi stand telephone
(Idiome) **dépasser les ～s** to go too far

borné, ～**e** /bɔrne/ *adj* [*personne*] narrow-minded; [*esprit, existence*] narrow; [*intelligence*] limited

borner /bɔrne/ [1]
A *vtr* **1** (marquer la limite de) Jur to mark out the boundaries of [*propriété*]; [*rivière, montagne*] to border [*pays, région*]; **2** (limiter) to limit [*ambition, désirs*] (**à qch** to sth; **à faire** to doing)
B se borner *vpr* **1** (se contenter) **se ～ à faire** [*personne*] to content oneself with doing; **2** (se limiter) **notre rôle se borne à analyser** our role is limited to analysingGB

bosniaque /bɔsnjak/ ▸ p. 392 *adj* Bosnian

bosquet /bɔskɛ/ *nm* grove

bosse /bɔs/ *nf* **1** (difformité) (sur le dos) hump; (sur le nez, un terrain) bump; **2** (après un choc) (sur la tête) bump; **3** (sur un objet) dent
(Idiome) **avoir la ～ de**○ to have a flair for; **rouler sa ～** to knock about

bosseler /bɔsle/ [19] *vtr* gén to dent; (en orfèvrerie) to emboss

bosser○ /bɔse/ [1] *vi* to work

bossoir /bɔswar/ *nm* (d'embarcation) davit; (d'ancre) cathead

bossu, ～**e** /bɔsy/
A *adj* (infirme) hunchbacked; (qui se tient mal) round-shouldered
B *nm,f* hunchback
(Idiome) **rire comme un ～** to laugh like a drain

bot /bo/ *adj m* **pied ～** club foot

botanique /bɔtanik/
A *adj* botanical
B *nf* botany

botaniste /bɔtanist/ ▸ p. 372 *nmf* botanist

botte /bɔt/ *nf* **1** (chaussure) boot; ▸ **plein**; **2** (de fleurs) bunch; (de foin, paille) bale; **3** (en escrime) thrust
(Composés) ～**s de caoutchouc** wellington boots, wellingtons; ～**s de cheval** riding boots; ～**s d'égoutier** waders; ～**s de sept lieues** seven league boots
(Idiome) **être à la ～ de qn** to be under sb's heel

botté, ～**e** /bɔte/
A *pp* ▸ **botter**
B *pp adj* with boots on; ～ **de cuir** leather-booted

botter /bɔte/ [1] *vtr* **1** (chausser de bottes) to put [sb's] boots on; **2** ○(plaire) **ça le botte!** he loves it, he really digs it○; **3** (frapper du pied) to kick; ～ **le derrière**○ **de qn** to boot sb up the backside○

botteur, **-euse** /bɔtœr/ *nm,f* Sport striker

bottier /bɔtje/ *nm* bootmaker

bottillon /bɔtijõ/ *nm* bootee

bottin® /bɔtɛ̃/ *nm* telephone directory, phone book

bottine /bɔtin/ *nf* ankle-boot

bouc /buk/ *nm* (animal) billy goat; (barbe) goatee
(Composé) ～ **émissaire** scapegoat
(Idiome) **sentir le ～** to stink

boucan○ /bukã/ *nm* (bruit) din, racket○

boucaner /bukane/ [1] *vtr* to smoke-dry

boucanier /bukanje/ *nm* **1** (pirate) buccaneer; **2** (chasseur) hunter of wild ox

bouche /buʃ/ *nf* **1** (cavité buccale) mouth; **2** (lèvre) mouth, lips (*pl*); **s'embrasser sur la ～** to kiss on the lips; **3** (organe de la parole) **ouvrir la ～** to speak; **il n'a pas ouvert la ～ de toute la soirée** he hasn't said a word all evening; **il n'a que ce mot à la ～** that word is never off his lips; **dans sa ～, ce n'est pas une insulte** coming from him, that's not an insult; **apprendre qch de la ～ de qn** to hear sth from sb; **se transmettre de ～ à oreille** [*nouvelle*] to be spread by word of mouth; **4** (personne) **avoir trois ～s à nourrir** to have three mouths to feed
(Composés) ～ **d'aération** air vent; ～ **de chaleur** hot-air vent; ～ **d'égout** manhole; ～ **d'incendie** fire hydrant; ～ **de métro** tube entrance GB, subway entrance US
(Idiome) **faire la fine ～ devant qch** to turn one's nose up at sth

bouché, ～**e¹** /buʃe/
A *pp* ▸ **boucher¹**
B *pp adj* **1** fig [*profession, secteur*] oversubscribed; **2** ○pej (stupide) stupid; **3** (en bouteille) [*cidre*] bottled

bouche-à-bouche /buʃabuʃ/ *nm inv* **faire le ～** to give mouth-to-mouth resuscitation (**à qn** to sb)

b

bouche-à-oreille /buʃaɔʀɛj/ nm inv le ~ word of mouth

bouchée² /buʃe/
A pp adj f ▸ **bouché**
B nf (contenu de la bouche) mouthful; **pour une ~ de pain** fig for next to nothing; **ne faire qu'une ~ d'un gâteau** to wolf a cake down; **ne faire qu'une ~ d'un adversaire** fig to make short work of an opponent; **mettre les ~s doubles** fig to double one's efforts
(Composé) ~ **à la reine** vol-au-vent

boucher¹ /buʃe/ [1]
A vtr ① (mettre un bouchon à) to cork; ② (obstruer) to block; (en encrassant) to clog (up); (en comblant) to fill; ~ **les trous** lit to fill the holes; fig to fill the gaps
B se boucher vpr ① (se fermer) **se ~ le nez** lit to hold one's nose; **se ~ les oreilles** lit to put one's fingers in one's ears; ② (s'obstruer) [lavabo] to get blocked; [artères] to get clogged up; [oreilles] to feel blocked; [nez] to get blocked; **tu as les oreilles bouchées ou quoi?** iron are you deaf or what○?; ③ Météo **temps/ciel bouché** overcast weather/sky
(Idiome) **en ~ un coin à qn**○ to amaze sb

boucher²,-ère¹ /buʃe, ɛʀ/ ▸ p. 372 nm,f butcher

bouchère² /buʃɛʀ/ nf (épouse de boucher) butcher's wife

boucherie /buʃʀi/ nf ① ▸ p. 372 (magasin) butcher's shop, butcher's; (commerce) butcher's trade, butchery; ② fig (tuerie) slaughter
(Composé) ~ **chevaline** horsemeat butcher's

bouche-trou, pl ~s /buʃtʀu/ nm stand-in

bouchon /buʃɔ̃/ nm ① (qu'on enfonce) (en liège) cork; (autre) stopper; (de baignoire) plug; ② (qui se visse) (de bidon) cap; (de tube, d'encrier) top, cap; ③ (de cire, cérumen) plug; ④ (de la circulation) traffic jam; ⑤ (pour la pêche) float
(Idiome) **pousser le ~ trop loin** to push it a bit○

bouchonné, ~e /buʃɔne/
A pp ▸ **bouchonner**
B adj [vin] corked

bouchonner /buʃɔne/ [1]
A vtr (frotter) to rub down [cheval]
B ○vi **ça bouchonne partout** there are traffic jams everywhere

bouclage /buklaʒ/ nm ① (de ceinture) fastening; ② (achèvement) completion; ③ (dans la presse) **la nouvelle de sa mort est arrivée après le ~** the news of his death arrived after the newspaper had been put to bed; ④ (encerclement) cordoning off; ⑤ Ordinat wraparound

boucle /bukl/ nf ① (de ceinture, chaussure) buckle; ② (de cheveux) curl; (de lacet, corde) loop; (de lettre) loop; ③ TV, Vidéo **en ~** in a continuous loop; ④ Ordinat loop
(Composé) ~ **d'oreille** earring

bouclé, ~e /bukle/ adj [cheveux, perruque] curly

boucler /bukle/ [1]
A vtr ① (attacher) to fasten [ceinture de sécurité, bagages]; ② ○(fermer) to lock [porte, coffre]; ③ ○(encercler) [police] to cordon off [quartier]; to close [frontière]; ④ (achever) to complete [enquête]; to close [dossier]; to sign [accord]; ⑤ (en finance) to balance [budget]; ~ **les fins de mois** to make ends meet at the end of each month; ⑥ (dans la presse) to put [sth] to bed [journal, édition]; ⑦ ○(mettre en prison) to lock [sb] up; **faire ~ qn** to get sb locked up
B vi [cheveux] to curl
(Idiomes) **la ~** to shut up; ~ **la boucle** to come full circle

bouclette /buklɛt/ nf ① (de cheveux) small curl; ② (tissu) (laine) ~ bouclé (wool)

bouclier /buklije/ nm shield

bouddha /buda/ nm (représentation) buddha

bouddhisme /budism/ nm Buddhism

bouddhiste /budist/ adj, nmf Buddhist

bouder /bude/ [1]
A vtr to avoid [personne]; to stay away from [spectacle]; to steer clear of [marchandise]
B vi to sulk

bouderie /budʀi/ nf (action) sulking

boudeur, -euse /budœʀ, øz/ adj sulky

boudin /budɛ̃/ nm ① Culin ≈ black pudding GB, blood sausage; ② ○pej (femme) lump○
(Idiome) **s'en aller** or **partir** or **finir en eau de ~** to come to nothing

boudiné, ~e /budine/ adj (gros) [doigt, main] podgy

boudiner /budine/ [1] vtr ① Tech to coil [fil de fer]; ② (serrer) **sa robe la boudine** her dress shows every bulge; **être boudiné dans qch** to be squeezed into sth

boudoir /budwaʀ/ nm (salon) boudoir; (biscuit) ladyfinger

boue /bu/ nf ① (terre) mud; (sédiment) silt; ② (scandale) **traîner qn dans la ~** to drag sb's name through the mud

bouée /bwe/ nf ① (gonflable) rubber ring; ② (balise) buoy
(Composé) ~ **de sauvetage** lit lifebelt GB, life preserver US

boueux, -euse /buø, øz/ adj [terrain, chemin] muddy

bouffant, ~e /bufɑ̃, ɑ̃t/ adj [chemisier, pantalon] baggy; [manche] puffed; [coiffure] bouffant

bouffe○ /buf/ nf (activité de manger) eating; (nourriture) food, grub○; (repas) meal

bouffée /bufe/ nf ① (souffle) (d'odeur) whiff; (de tabac, vapeur, vent) puff; **une ~ d'air frais** lit, fig a breath of fresh air; **tirer une ~** to have a puff ou drag○; ② (accès) rush (**de** of); ~ **d'orgueil** surge of pride
(Composé) ~ **de chaleur** Méd hot flush GB, hot flash US

bouffer /bufe/ [1]
A ○vtr ① (manger) to eat; ② (accaparer) **se faire ~** to be taken over (**par** by); ③ (consommer) to guzzle [essence]; to burn [huile]; ④ (dépenser) to throw [sth] away [argent]; ⑤ (utiliser) to take up [espace]
B vi ① ○(manger) to eat; (beaucoup) to eat a lot, to stuff oneself○; ② (gonfler) [vêtement] to billow out
(Idiome) **se ~ le nez**○ to be at each other's throats

bouffi, ~e /bufi/ adj (physiquement) puffy; **il a le visage ~ par l'alcool** his face is puffy with drink

bouffon, -onne /bufɔ̃, ɔn/
A adj farcical
B nm ① (plaisantin) clown; **faire le ~** to clown about ou around; ② Hist (de cour) jester; (de théâtre) buffoon

bouffonnerie /bufɔnʀi/ nf ① (acte) antics (pl); ② (effets comiques) buffoonery; ③ (caractère) ridiculousness; ④ Théât farce

bouge /buʒ/ nm (logement) hovel; (café) dive

bougeoir /buʒwaʀ/ nm candleholder; (haut) candlestick

bougeotte○ /buʒɔt/ nf restlessness; **avoir la ~** to be restless

bouger /buʒe/ [13]
A vtr (tous contextes) to move
B vi ① (faire un mouvement, se déplacer) to move; **ne bougez plus, je prends une photo!** keep still, I'm taking a photo!; **c'est malin, tu m'as fait ~!** that's great, you jogged me!; ② ○(évoluer) [secteur, entreprise, pays] to be on the move; ③ ○(être animé) **ville qui bouge** lively town; ④ ○(réagir) to show signs of unrest; ⑤ ○(varier) [prix, score, prévision] to change; **tu peux le laver à la machine, ça ne bougera pas** you can wash it in the machine, it won't shrink
C se bouger vpr (personne) (se pousser) to get out of the way; (se dépêcher) to get a move on○; (se donner du mal) to put some effort in

bougie /buʒi/ nf ① (de cire) candle; ② Tech sparking plug GB, spark plug

bougon, -onne /bugɔ̃, ɔn/
A adj grumpy
B nm,f grumbler

bougonner /bugɔne/ [1] vi to grumble

bougre○ /bugʀ/ nm (type) bloke○; **bon ~** good sort; **pauvre ~** poor devil; ~ **d'imbécile** you damn○ idiot

bougrement○ /bugʀəmɑ̃/ adv ~ **difficile** damn○ hard

bougresse○ /bugʀɛs/ nf bird○ GB, chick○, woman

bouillabaisse /bujabɛs/ nf bouillabaisse, fish soup

bouillant, ~e /bujɑ̃, ɑ̃t/ adj ① (qui bout) boiling; ② ○(très chaud) boiling (hot)

bouille○ /buj/ nf face

bouillie /buji/ nf Culin gruel; (pour bébés) baby cereal; **en ~** [légumes] pej mushy

bouillir /bujiʀ/ [31] vi ① gén [eau, lait] to boil; **faire ~** to boil; ② fig (s'emporter) [personne] to seethe

bouilloire /bujwaʀ/ nf kettle

bouillon /bujɔ̃/ nm ① (potage) broth; ② (liquide de cuisson, concentré) stock; ③ (de liquide qui bout) bubble; **bouillir à gros ~s** to boil, to bubble

(Composés) ~ **de culture** Biol nutrient broth; fig hotbed (**pour** of); ~ **gras** Culin meat stock

(Idiome) **boire un** ~ (en nageant) to get a mouthful; (en affaires) to come a cropper○, to sustain losses

bouillonnant, ~e /bujɔnɑ̃, ɑ̃t/ adj [eaux] foaming; [personne] lively

bouillonnement /bujɔnmɑ̃/ nm ⊞ (de vagues) foaming; ⊡ fig **le** ~ **du marché** the frentic activity of the market

bouillonner /bujɔne/ [1] vi ⊞ [liquide chaud] to bubble; [eaux] to foam; ⊡ [personne] ~ **d'activité** to be bustling with activity

bouillotte /bujɔt/ nf hot-water bottle

boulanger, -ère[1] /bulɑ̃ʒe, ɛʁ/ ▸ p. 372 nm,f baker

boulangère[2] /bulɑ̃ʒɛʁ/ nf (épouse de boulanger) baker's wife

boulangerie /bulɑ̃ʒʁi/ ▸ p. 372 nf ⊞ (magasin) bakery, baker's; ⊡ (activité) bakery trade

boulangerie-pâtisserie, pl **boulangeries-pâtisseries** /bulɑ̃ʒʁipɑtisʁi/ nf bakery (selling cakes and pastries)

boule /bul/
A nf (de bowling) bowl; (de jeu de boules) boule; (de rampe d'escalier) knob; **mettre qch en** ~ to roll sth up into a ball; **avoir une** ~ **dans la gorge** to have a lump in one's throat
B **boules** ▸ p. 327 nfpl boules

(Composés) ~ **de cristal** crystal ball; ~ **de naphtaline** mothball; ~ **puante** stink bomb; ~ **Quiès**® earplug; ~ **à thé** tea infuser GB, tea ball US

(Idiomes) **avoir la** ~ **à zéro**○ to have no hair left; **perdre la** ~○ to go mad; **mettre qn en** ~○ to make sb furious; **avoir les** ~**s**○ (angoisse) to have butterflies○ (in one's stomach); (colère) to be hopping mad○; **ça me fout les** ~**s**◐ (angoisse) the thought of it makes me sick○; (exaspération) it really gets to me○

bouleau, pl ~**x** /bulo/ nm birch

bouledogue /buldɔg/ nm bulldog

bouler /bule/ [1] vi **envoyer qn** ~○ to send sb packing○

boulet /bulɛ/ nm ⊞ (projectile) ~ **(de canon)** cannonball; ⊡ (de bagnard) ball and chain; ⊟ fig millstone; **être un** ~ **pour qn** to be a millstone around sb's neck; ⊞ (de charbon) coal nut

(Idiome) **tirer à** ~**s rouges sur qn/qch** to launch a fierce attack on sb/sth

boulette /bulɛt/ nf ⊞ (de pain, papier) pellet; ⊡ ○(bourde) blunder

boulevard /bulvaʁ/ nm ⊞ (avenue) boulevard; ⊡ Théât farce; **théâtre de** ~ farce

(Composé) ~ **périphérique** ring road GB, beltway US

bouleversant, ~e /bulvɛʁsɑ̃, ɑ̃t/ adj (émouvant) deeply moving; (pénible) distressing

bouleversement /bulvɛʁsəmɑ̃/ nm upheaval

bouleverser /bulvɛʁse/ [1] vtr ⊞ (émouvoir) to move [sb] deeply; (affliger) to shatter; ⊡ (mettre en désordre) to wreak havoc in [paysage, ville]; to turn [sth] upside down [maison, dossiers]; ⊟ (désorganiser) to disrupt; ⊞ (changer) to change

boulier /bulje/ nm abacus

boulimie /bulimi/ nf Méd bulimia

bouliste /bulist/ nmf boules player

boulodrome /bulɔdʁom/ nm area for playing boules

boulon /bulɔ̃/ nm bolt

boulonnage /bulɔnaʒ/ nm Tech (d'un élément) bolting; (d'éléments entre eux) bolting together

boulonner /bulɔne/ [1]
A vtr to bolt [sth] on [élément]; to bolt together [éléments]
B vi to work, to slave away

boulot, -otte /bulo, ɔt/
A adj tubby
B ○nm ⊞ (tâche) work; **au** ~! (toi) get to work!; (moi, nous) let's get to work!; ⊡ (emploi) job

boulotter○ /bulɔte/ [1] vtr to eat

boum[1] /bum/
A nm ⊞ (bruit) bang; ⊡ ○(développement) **être en plein** ~ [économie, ventes, affaires] to be booming; **faire un** ~ [naissances] to boom
B excl (explosion) bang!

boum[2] /bum/ nf (fête) party

bouquet /bukɛ/ nm ⊞ (floral) ~ **(de fleurs)** bunch of flowers; (composé) bouquet; (petit) posy; ⊡ (de feu d'artifice) final flourish; ~ **final** crowning piece; ⊟ (d'arbres) clump; ⊞ (de fines herbes) bunch; ⊠ (de vin) bouquet

(Composé) ~ **numérique** TV digital channel package

(Idiome) **c'est le** ~! (le comble) that's the limit○!

bouquetin /buktɛ̃/ nm ibex

bouquin○ /bukɛ̃/ nm book

bouquiner○ /bukine/ [1] vtr, vi to read

bouquiniste /bukinist/ ▸ p. 372 nmf secondhand bookseller

bourbeux, -euse /buʁbø, øz/ adj muddy

bourbier /buʁbje/ nm ⊞ lit quagmire; ⊡ fig tangle, quagmire

bourde /buʁd/ nf (bévue) blunder

bourdon /buʁdɔ̃/ nm ⊞ Zool bumblebee; ⊡ (cloche) tenor bell; ⊟ Mus (d'orgue) bourdon

bourdonnement /buʁdɔnmɑ̃/ nm (d'insecte) buzzing **¢**; (de ruche) humming **¢**; (de moteur) hum; (d'hélicoptère, avion) drone

bourdonner /buʁdɔne/ [1] vi [insecte] to buzz; [moteur] to hum; [avion, hélicoptère] to drone; [foule] to murmur

bourg /buʁ/ nm market town

bourgade /buʁgad/ nf small town

bourgeois, -e /buʁʒwa, az/
A adj ⊞ [libéralisme] bourgeois; péj [morale] middle-class; ⊡ (cossu) **quartier** ~ wealthy residential district; ⊟ Jur [habitation] for private use (après n)
B nm,f ⊞ (personne de la classe moyenne) middle-class person, bourgeois péj; ⊡ Hist (sous l'Ancien Régime) bourgeois; (au Moyen Âge) burgher

bourgeoisie /buʁʒwazi/ nf ⊞ (classe moyenne) middle classes (pl); ⊡ Hist, Pol bourgeoisie

bourgeon /buʁʒɔ̃/ nm (en botanique) bud

bourgeonner /buʁʒɔne/ [1] vi (en botanique) to bud, to burgeon

bourgogne /buʁgɔɲ/ nm (vin) Burgundy

Bourgogne /buʁgɔɲ/ ▸ p. 504 nprf **la** ~ Burgundy

bourguignon, -onne /buʁgiɲɔ̃, ɔn/
A adj of Burgundy
B nm Culin beef bourguignon, beef casserole cooked in red wine

bourlinguer○ /buʁlɛ̃ge/ [1] vi (beaucoup naviguer) to sail the seven seas; (beaucoup voyager) to travel around a lot

bourrache /buʁaʃ/ nf borage

bourrade /buʁad/ nf (avec la main, l'épaule) shove; (avec le coude) (sharp) nudge

bourrage /buʁaʒ/ nm (remplissage) (de fauteuil, coussin) stuffing; (de pipe) filling; (de cartouche) wadding

(Composé) ~ **de crâne** brainwashing

bourrasque /buʁask/ nf (de vent) gust; (de neige) flurry

bourratif, -ive /buʁatif, iv/ adj very filling, stodgy

bourre /buʁ/ nf ⊞ (pour remplissage) stuffing; (déchets textiles) flock; (de cartouche) wad; ⊡ (en botanique) down

(Idiome) **être à la** ~○ to be pushed for time

bourré, ~e /buʁe/ adj [train, musée] packed; [valise, sac] bulging (**de** with); ~ **de fric**○ stinking rich○

bourreau, pl ~**x** /buʁo/ nm ⊞ (exécuteur) executioner; ⊡ (criminel) butcher; (persécuteur) tormentor

(Composés) ~ **d'enfant** child beater; ~ **de travail** workaholic

bourrelet /buʁlɛ/ nm ⊞ Tech (d'étanchéité) weather strip; (amortisseur) pad; ⊡ (adiposité) ~ **(de graisse)** roll of fat

bourrelier, -ière /buʁəlje, ɛʁ/ ▸ p. 372 nm,f (sellier) saddler; (maroquinier) leather craftsman/craftswoman

bourrellerie /buʁɛlʁi/ nf ⊞ (sellerie) (fabrication) saddlery; (produits) tack; ⊡ (maroquinerie) (fabrication) making of leather goods; (produits) leather goods (pl)

bourrer /buʁe/ [1]
A vtr ⊞ (remplir) to cram [sth] full [valise, caisse]; to fill [pipe]; to wad [arme à feu]; ~ **qch de** to cram sth with; ⊡ (gaver) ~ **qn de** to stuff sb with [nourriture]; to dose sb up with [médicaments]; ⊟ ○(frapper) ~ **qn de coups** to lay into sb○
B vi (remplir l'estomac)○ [aliment] to be filling
C se **bourrer** vpr (se gaver) se ~ **de** to stuff oneself with

[aliments]; to dose oneself up with *[médicaments]*

bourricot /buʀiko/ *nm* donkey

bourrique /buʀik/ *nf* ① (ânesse) donkey; ② ○(entêté) pig-headed person

bourru, **~e** /buʀy/ *adj* gruff

bourse /buʀs/
A *nf* ① (de soutien financier) grant GB, scholarship US; (pour le mérite) scholarship; (pour un projet particulier) grant; ② (porte-monnaie) purse; ③ fig budget; **pour les petites ~s** for limited budgets; ④ (vente d'objets d'occasion) **~ aux livres** second-hand book sale
B **bourses** *nfpl* Anat scrotum (sg)

(Composé) **~ d'étude** grant

Bourse /buʀs/ *nf* Fin stock exchange; (valeurs cotées) shares (pl); **la ~ de Paris a monté** shares on the Paris Stock Exchange have gone up; **faire son entrée à la ~ de Milan** to be listed on the Milan Stock Exchange for the first time; **une société de ~** a broking GB *ou* brokerage US firm

(Composés) **~ de commerce** commodity exchange; **~ du travail** Ind *local trade union offices*

boursicoter /buʀsikɔte/ [1] *vi* *[personne]* to dabble in stocks and shares

boursier, **-ière** /buʀsje, ɛʀ/
A *adj* (financier) *[cotation, valeur]* stock exchange, stock market (épith); *[semaine, mois]* trading (épith); **le marché ~** share prices
B *nm,f* (bénéficiaire d'une bourse) (pour raisons financières) grant holder GB, scholarship student US; (pour mérite) scholar GB, scholarship student US

boursouflé, **~e** /buʀsufle/ *adj* (enflé) *[peau, surface]* blistered; *[visage, paupière]* puffy; *[corps]* bloated

boursouflure /buʀsuflyʀ/ *nf* (de peau) swelling **C**; (de papier, peinture) blister

bousculade /buskylad/ *nf* ① (choc) (volontaire) jostling; (involontaire) crush; ② (précipitation) rush

bousculer /buskyle/ [1]
A *vtr* ① (heurter) (involontairement) to bump into *[personne]*; (volontairement) to knock about *[personne]*; ② (malmener) to jostle *[équipe]*; ③ (presser) to rush *[personne, programme]*
B **se bousculer** *vpr* ① (se heurter) to bump into each other; ② (être nombreux) to fall over each other (**pour faire** to do)

bouse /buz/ *nf* cow dung **C**; **une ~ (de vache)** a cowpat

bousiller ○/buzije/ [1]
A *vtr* ① (gâcher) to botch *[travail]*; ② (détériorer) to wreck *[appareil, moteur]*; to smash up *[véhicule]*; to bust○ *[mécanisme]*
B **se bousiller** *vpr* **se ~ la santé/la vue** to ruin one's health/eyesight

boussole /busɔl/ *nf* compass

bout¹ /bu/ *nm* ① (dernière partie) (de nez, branche, ficelle, table, rue, processus) end; (pointe) (d'épée, aile, de langue, doigt) tip; (de chaussure) toe; **en ~ de piste** Aviat at the end of the runway; **tout au ~ de la rue** at the very end of the street; **ciseaux à ~s ronds** round-ended scissors; **à ~ carré/rouge** *[bâton, doigt, aile]* square-/red-tipped; **au ~ du jardin/champ** at the bottom of the garden/field; **siège en ~ de rangée** aisle seat; **lire un livre de ~ en ~** to read a book from cover to cover; **parcourir une liste d'un ~ à l'autre** to scour a list; **d'un ~ à l'autre du spectacle/de l'année** throughout the show/the year; **marcher d'un ~ à l'autre de la ville** to walk across the city; **coller ~ à ~** to stick *[sth]* end to end; **être incapable de mettre deux phrases ~ à ~** to be unable to string two sentences together; **rester jusqu'au ~** to stay until the end; **aller jusqu'au ~** to go all the way; **aller (jusqu')au ~ de** to follow through *[idée, exigence]*; **aller au ~ de soi-même** to push oneself to the limit; **écouter qn jusqu'au ~** to hear sb out; **lutter jusqu'au ~** to fight to the last drop of blood; **elle est à ~** she can't take any more; **je suis à ~ de forces** I can do no more; **ne me pousse pas à ~** don't push me; **être à ~ d'arguments** to run out of arguments; **venir à ~ de** to overcome *[problème, difficultés]*; to get through *[tâche, repas]*; **au ~ d'une semaine/d'un certain temps** after a week/a while; **au ~ du compte** ultimately; **à ~ portant** at point-blank range; ② (morceau) (de pain, chiffon, fil, papier) piece; (de terrain) bit; **~ de bois** gén piece of wood; (allongé) stick; **~s de papier/ferraille** scraps of paper/metal; **par petits ~s** *[apprendre, manger]* a bit at a time; *[payer, recevoir]* in dribs

and drabs; *[occuper, progresser]* little by little; **un petit ~ de femme**○ a tiny woman

(Composés) **~ de chou**○ sweet little thing○; **~ d'essai** Cin screen test; **~ filtre** (de cigarette) filter tip

(Idiomes) **tenir le bon ~**○ to be on the right track; **voir le ~ de qch** to get through sth; **ne pas être au ~ de ses peines** *or* **ennuis** not to be out of the woods yet; **ne pas savoir par quel ~ commencer** not to know where to begin; **mettre les ~s**○ to leave, to clear off○ GB, to split○ US

bout² /but/ *nm* Naut rope; **filer par le ~** to slip anchor

boutade /butad/ *nf* (trait d'esprit) witticism

boute-en-train /butɑ̃tʀɛ̃/ *nmf inv* live wire fig

bouteille /butɛj/ *nf* ① (emballage) bottle; **~ de lait** (contenant) milk bottle; (contenu) bottle of milk; **~ de gaz** cylinder *ou* bottle of gas; **mettre le vin en ~s** to bottle wine; **boire à la ~** to drink out of the bottle; ② (produit vinicole) bottle; **une bonne ~** a good bottle of wine; ③ Sport **faire de la plongée avec des ~s** to dive with breathing equipment

(Composé) **~ d'oxygène** oxygen cylinder

(Idiomes) **prendre de la ~**○ (âge) to be getting on; **jeter** *or* **lancer une ~ à la mer** to make a last despairing bid for help

bouteur /butœʀ/ *nm* bulldozer

boutique /butik/ *nf* ① (d'artisan, de commerçant) shop GB, store US; (de prêt-à-porter) boutique; **plier ~** lit, fig to shut up shop; ② ○(maison, entreprise) place

boutiquier, **-ière** /butikje, ɛʀ/
A *adj* pej small-minded
B *nm,f* Comm shopkeeper

boutoir /butwaʀ/ *nm* snout; **coup de ~** attack

bouton /butɔ̃/ *nm* ① (en couture) button; **sans ~s** buttonless; ② Tech (d'appareil) (à tourner) knob; (à presser) button; ③ Méd spot GB, pimple US; ④ (de fleur) bud

(Composés) **~ de fièvre** Méd cold sore; **~ de manchette** cuff link; **~ de porte** doorknob

bouton-d'or, *pl* **boutons-d'or** /butɔ̃dɔʀ/ *nm* buttercup

boutonner /butɔne/ [1]
A *vtr* to button *[vêtement]*; **~ qn** to do up sb's buttons
B **se boutonner** *vpr* *[vêtement]* to button up

boutonneux, **-euse** /butɔnø, øz/ *adj* *[visage]* spotty GB, pimply US

boutonnière /butɔnjɛʀ/ *nf* (de vêtement) buttonhole; **il porte une fleur rouge à la ~** he's wearing a red buttonhole GB *ou* boutonniere US

bouture /butyʀ/ *nf* cutting

bouturer /butyʀe/ [1]
A *vtr* to take a cutting from *[plante]*
B *vi* *[plante]* to propagate from cuttings

bouvier /buvje/ *nm* ① ▸ p. 372 (personne) oxherd; ② (chien) bouvier

bouvreuil /buvʀœj/ *nm* bullfinch

bovidé /bɔvide/ *nm* bovid; **les ~s** the Bovidae

bovin, **~e** /bɔvɛ̃, in/
A *adj* bovine
B *nm* bovine; **des ~s** cattle (+ *v pl*); **150 ~s** 150 head of cattle

box, *pl* **boxes** /bɔks/ *nm* (pour véhicule) lock-up garage; (pour cheval) stall; (dans un bar) alcove; (dans un dortoir, parloir) cubicle; (de travail) section

(Composé) **~ des accusés** Jur dock

boxe /bɔks/ ▸ p. 327 *nf* boxing; **champion de ~** boxing champion; **faire de la ~** to do boxing, to box

(Composé) **~ française** savate

boxer¹ /bɔksɛʀ/ *nm* (chien) boxer

boxer² /bɔkse/ [1]
A ○*vtr* (frapper) to punch
B *vi* ① (pratiquer la boxe) to box; ② (livrer un match de boxe) to have a fight on

boxeur /bɔksœʀ/ ▸ p. 372 *nm* boxer

boyau, *pl* **~x** /bwajo/
A *nm* ① (intestin) gut; ② (pour raquette, violon) catgut; ③ (pour saucisse) casing; ④ (pneu) tubeless tyre GB *ou* tire US; ⑤ (passage) back alley; ⑥ (tuyau flexible) hose

B ○**boyaux** *nmpl* (intestins) insides○
boycotter /bɔjkɔte/ [1] *vtr* to boycott
BP *written abbr* ▸ **boîte**
bracelet /bʀaslɛ/ *nm* (au poignet) gén bracelet; (large) bangle; (souple) wristband; (au bras, à la cheville) bangle
[Composés] ∼ **électronique** electronic tag; ∼ **de montre** watchstrap
bracelet-montre, *pl* **bracelets-montres** /bʀaslɛ-mɔ̃tʀ/ *nm* wristwatch
braconner /bʀakɔne/ [1] *vi* to poach
braconnier /bʀakɔnje/ *nm* poacher
bradé, ∼**e** /bʀade/ *adj* **prix** ∼**s** knockdown prices
brader /bʀade/ [1]
A *vtr* [1] (vendre à bas prix) to sell [sth] cheaply; [2] (liquider) to sell off
B *vi* to slash prices
braderie /bʀadʀi/ *nf* [1] Comm (marché) street market; (magasin) discount store; [2] (vente) clearance sale; (liquidation) selling off
braguette /bʀagɛt/ *nf* flies GB (*pl*), fly US
braillard○, ∼**e** /bʀɑjaʀ, aʀd/
A *adj* (qui crie) yelling (*épith*); (qui pleure) bawling (*épith*)
B *nm,f* loudmouth
braille /bʀɑj/ *nm* Braille; **en** ∼ in Braille
brailler○ /bʀɑje/ [1]
A *vtr* to yell out [*injure*]; to bawl out [*chanson*]
B *vi* (crier) to yell; (chanter fort, pleurer) to bawl
braiment /bʀɛmɑ̃/ *nm* braying ¢
braire /bʀɛʀ/ [58] *vi* to bray
braise /bʀɛz/ *nf* live embers (*pl*)
braiser /bʀeze/ [1] *vtr* Culin to braise
bramer /bʀɑme/ [1] *vi* [*cerf*] to bell
brancard /bʀɑ̃kaʀ/ *nm* (civière) stretcher; (de charrette) shaft
[Idiome] **ruer dans les** ∼**s** to rebel
brancardier /bʀɑ̃kaʀdje/ ▸ p. 372 *nm* stretcher-bearer
branchage /bʀɑ̃ʃaʒ/
A *nm* branches (*pl*)
B **branchages** *nmpl* (branches coupées) cut branches
branche /bʀɑ̃ʃ/ *nf* [1] (d'arbre) branch; ∼ **maîtresse** limb; [2] Culin **céleri en** ∼**s** sticks of celery; **épinards en** ∼**s** spinach on the stalk; [3] (secteur) field; [4] (de famille) branch; [5] (de chandelier) branch; (de lunettes) arm; (d'étoile) point
branché○, ∼**e** /bʀɑ̃ʃe/ *adj* trendy
branchement /bʀɑ̃ʃmɑ̃/ *nm* [1] (à un réseau, à une prise) connection; [2] (conduite d'eau) branch pipe; (ligne électrique) lead GB, cable US
brancher /bʀɑ̃ʃe/ [1]
A *vtr* [1] (avec prise) to plug in [*télévision, téléphone*]; [2] (au réseau) to connect (up) [*eau, gaz, électricité, téléphone*]; to connect [*usager, maison*]; **faire** ∼ **le téléphone** to have the phone connected; [3] (aiguiller) ∼ **qn sur** to get sb onto [*sujet*]; [4] (intéresser) **je vais au cinéma, ça te branche?** I'm going to the cinema, are you interested?
B **se brancher** *vpr* Radio, TV (capter) **se** ∼ **sur** to tune into [*poste, station*]
branchie /bʀɑ̃ʃi/ *nf* gill, branchia spéc
brandade /bʀɑdad/ *nf* ∼ **(de morue)** brandade, dish of flaked salt cod
brandir /bʀɑ̃diʀ/ [3] *vtr* to brandish [*arme, objet*]
brandon /bʀɑ̃dɔ̃/ *nm* firebrand
[Composé] ∼ **de discorde** bone of contention
branlant, -**e** /bʀɑ̃lɑ̃, ɑ̃t/ *adj* [*meuble, construction*] rickety; [*mur, mât*] unstable; [*dent*] loose; [*raisonnement, régime*] shaky
branle /bʀɑ̃l/ *nm* (oscillation) swing; **mettre qch en** ∼ to set [sth] in motion [*mesure, projet, convoi*]; **se mettre en** ∼ [*convoi, personnes*] to get going; [*processus*] to be set in motion
branle-bas /bʀɑ̃lbɑ/ *nm inv* (agitation) commotion
[Composé] ∼ **de combat** Mil, fig action stations
branler /bʀɑ̃le/ [1]
A *vtr* ∼ **la tête** *or* **du chef** to nod one's head
B *vi* (osciller) [*mur*] to wobble; [*escalier, construction, échafaudage, chaise*] to be rickety; [*dent*] to be loose

braquage /bʀakaʒ/ *nm* [1] ○(de supermarché, banque) robbery; [2] Aut (steering) lock, turning circle
braque /bʀak/
A ○*adj* crazy
B *nm* Zool ∼ **allemand** German shorthaired pointer
braquer /bʀake/ [1]
A *vtr* [1] (diriger) to point [*arme, caméra*] (**sur, vers** at); to train [*télescope, projecteur*] (**sur, vers** on); to turn *ou* fix [*yeux*] (**sur, vers** on); **tous les projecteurs sont braqués sur lui** fig he's in the spotlight, the spotlight is on him; **tous les regards sont braqués sur vous** lit, fig all eyes are upon you; [2] Aut to turn [*volant, roues*] (**à gauche/droite** hard left/right); [3] ○(viser) to point a gun at; [4] ○(attaquer) to rob [*banque*]; [5] ○(buter) ∼ **qn contre qch/qn** to turn sb against sth/sb; **ne le braque pas** don't get his back up; **il est braqué** he's dug his heels in
B *vi* Aut [*chauffeur*] to turn the wheel full lock GB *ou* all the way US; [*véhicule*] **bien/mal** ∼ to have a good/poor lock GB, to turn well/badly; **braque à gauche** turn (the wheel) sharply to the left
C **se braquer** *vpr* (viser) **se** ∼ **sur/vers** [*arme, caméra*] to be pointed at; [*télescope, projecteur*] to be trained on; [*yeux*] to be turned on; (se buter) to dig one's heels in; **se** ∼ **contre qn** to turn against sb
braqueur○ /bʀakœʀ/ *nm* robber
bras /bʀɑ/ ▸ p. 136 *nm inv* [1] Anat arm; **prendre qn dans ses** ∼ to take sb in one's arms; **avoir les** ∼ **en croix** to have one's arms outstretched; **par le** ∼ [*tenir, prendre*] by the arm; **au** ∼ **de qn** on sb's arm; ∼ **dessus** ∼ **dessous** lit, fig arm in arm; **porter qch à bout de** ∼ lit to carry sth with one's arms straight out; fig to keep sth afloat; **baisser les** ∼ fig to give up; **en** ∼ **de chemise** in one's shirtsleeves; **rester les** ∼ **croisés** to stand idly; **croiser les** ∼ lit to fold one's arms; fig to twiddle one's thumbs; [2] (main-d'œuvre) manpower, labour[GB]; [3] Géog (de fleuve) branch; [4] Tech (de fauteuil, d'électrophone, ancre) arm; (de brancard) pole; [5] (de mollusque) tentacle
[Composés] ∼ **droit** fig right hand man; ∼ **de fer** (épreuve physique) arm wrestling; (lutte d'influence) trial of strength; ∼ **de mer** sound
[Idiomes] **les** ∼ **m'en tombent** I'm absolutely speechless; **avoir le** ∼ **long** to have a lot of influence
brasier /bʀazje/ *nm* inferno
bras-le-corps:**à bras-le-corps** /abʀalkɔʀ/ *loc adv* [1] lit [*soulever*] bodily; [2] fig head-on
brassage /bʀasaʒ/ *nm* [1] Ind (de bière) brewing; [2] (mélange) (de personnes) intermingling; (d'idées, de cultures) cross-fertilization; (d'air) mixture
brassard /bʀasaʀ/ *nm* [1] gén armband; [2] (d'armure) arm-piece
brasse /bʀas/ *nf* Sport (style) breaststroke; (mouvement) stroke; **à la** ∼ in breaststroke
[Composé] ∼ **papillon** butterfly (stroke)
brassée /bʀase/ *nf* [1] (de fleurs, papier, bois) armful (**de** of); [2] (de chiffres, personnalités) (whole) host (**de** of)
brasser /bʀase/ [1] *vtr* [1] (remuer) [*personne*] to toss [*salade*]; to toss [sth] around [*idées*]; to shuffle [*cartes à jouer*]; to shuffle [sth] around [*papier*]; to gather [sth] up [*feuilles mortes, linge*]; [*vent*] to blow about [*feuilles*]; to intermingle [*population*]; **il brasse des millions** he handles big money; [2] to brew [*bière*]
[Idiome] ∼ **de l'air**○ to talk a lot of hot air○
brasserie /bʀasʀi/ ▸ p. 372 *nf* [1] (café, restaurant) brasserie; [2] (usine) brewery; [3] (secteur) brewing industry
brasseur, -**euse** /bʀasœʀ, øz/ *nm,f* (de bière) brewer
brassière /bʀasjɛʀ/ *nf* [1] (de bébé) (en coton) baby's vest; (en tricot) baby's top; [2] (soutien-gorge) crop top
bravade /bʀavad/ *nf* (attitude) bravado
brave /bʀav/ *adj* (gentil) nice; (courageux) brave
bravement /bʀavmɑ̃/ *adv* [1] (avec courage) bravely; [2] (sans hésiter) boldly
braver /bʀave/ [1] *vtr* to defy [*personne, ordre, tabou*]; to brave [*tempête, danger*]
bravo /bʀavo/
A *nm* **un grand** ∼ **à** a big cheer for GB, let's hear it for
B *excl* (pour applaudir) bravo!; (pour féliciter) well done!
bravoure /bʀavuʀ/ *nf* bravery

break /bʀɛk/ nm ① Aut estate car GB, station wagon US; ② (d'attelage) (shooting) break

brebis /bʀəbi/ nf inv Zool ewe; **les ~** the flock

brèche /bʀɛʃ/ nf ① (trou) (dans un mur) hole; (dans une haie) gap; ② Mil (trouée) breach

(Idiomes) **battre qn/qch en ~** to give sb/sth a pounding; **être sur la ~** to be on the go

bréchet /bʀeʃɛ/ nm wishbone

bredouille /bʀəduj/ adj lit, fig empty-handed

bredouiller /bʀəduje/ [1] vtr, vi to mumble

bref, brève¹ /bʀɛf, bʀɛv/
A adj ① (court) [apparition, séjour] brief; [son] short; **soyez ~** be brief; ② (sec) [ton] curt
B adv (pour résumer) **(en) ~** in short

brelan /bʀəlɑ̃/ nm Jeux three of a kind; **~ de 10** three tens

breloque /bʀəlɔk/ nf (objet) charm

brème /bʀɛm/ nf (poisson) bream

Brésil /bʀezil/ ▸ p. 230 nprm Brazil

brésilien, -ienne /bʀeziljɛ̃, ɛn/ ▸ p. 392 adj ① Géog Brazilian; ② [slip, maillot de bain] high-cut

Bretagne /bʀətaɲ/ ▸ p. 504 nprf **la ~** Brittany

bretelle /bʀətɛl/
A nf ① (de robe, maillot, sac à dos, d'accordéon) strap; ② (de fusil) sling; **porter l'arme à la ~** to carry a weapon slung over one's shoulder; ③ (d'autoroute) slip road GB, ramp US
B **bretelles** nfpl braces

(Idiome) **se faire remonter les ~s○** to get told off○

breton, -onne /bʀətɔ̃, ɔn/
A adj Breton; **être ~** to be from Brittany
B ▸ p. 336 nm Ling Breton

breuvage /bʀœvaʒ/ nm ① (boisson étrange) pej brew; ② C (boisson) beverage

brève² /bʀɛv/
A adj f ▸ bref A
B nf ① (information) news flash; ② (voyelle, syllabe) short

brevet /bʀəvɛ/ nm ① (d'invention) **~ (d'invention)** patent; **après le dépôt du ~** after patenting; ② (diplôme) **~ de secourisme** first aid certificate

(Composés) **~ des collèges** Scol certificate of general education; **~ de pilote** Aviat pilot's licence^GB; **~ de technicien supérieur, BTS** Univ advanced vocational diploma

brevetable /bʀəvtabl/ adj [invention] patentable

breveté, ~e /bʀəvte/
A pp ▸ breveter
B pp adj (diplômé) [pilote] qualified

breveter /bʀəvte/ [20] vtr **(faire) ~** to patent [invention]

bréviaire /bʀevjɛʀ/ nm ① Relig breviary; ② fig bible

bribes /bʀib/ nfpl (de conversation) snatches; (d'histoire) bits and pieces; **par ~** bit by bit

bric; de bric et de broc /dəbʀiked(ə)bʀɔk/ loc adv [s'habiller] any old how; [meublé] with bits and pieces

bricolage /bʀikɔlaʒ/ nm ① (activité) DIY GB, do-it-yourself; ② (travail non professionnel) makeshift job

bricole /bʀikɔl/ nf ① (menu objet) **acheter une ~** to buy a little something; **des ~s** bits and pieces; ② (de harnais) breast harness

bricoler /bʀikɔle/ [1]
A ○ vtr (tenter de réparer) to tinker with [moteur, appareil]; (confectionner) to knock up GB, to throw together [étagère, système]; (truquer) to fiddle GB ou tamper with US [compteur, machine]
B vi (faire du bricolage) to do DIY GB, to fix things US

bricoleur, -euse /bʀikɔlœʀ, øz/
A adj **être ~** to be good with one's hands
B nm,f (personne habile) handyman/handywoman; (personne qui fait du bricolage) DIY enthusiast GB, do-it-yourselfer

bride /bʀid/ nf ① (de cheval) bridle; ② (de boutonnage) button loop

(Idiomes) **partir à ~ abattue** to dash off; **avoir la ~ sur le cou** to have free rein

bridé, ~e /bʀide/ adj **yeux ~s** slanting eyes

brider /bʀide/ [1] vtr ① to bridle [cheval]; ② (contenir) to control [personne]; to curb [élan, liberté, spontanéité]

bridgeur, -euse /bʀidʒœʀ, øz/ nm,f Jeux bridge player

briefer /bʀife/ [1] vtr to brief

brièvement /bʀijɛvmɑ̃/ adv briefly

brièveté /bʀijɛvte/ nf brevity

brigade /bʀigad/ nf ① Mil brigade; **~ d'infanterie** infantry unit; ② (dans la police) squad; ③ Admin (groupe de travailleurs) team

(Composés) **~ de gendarmerie** small unit of gendarmes; **~ de sapeurs-pompiers** fire brigade GB, fire department US

brigadier /bʀigadje/ ▸ p. 283 nm ① Mil (caporal) ≈ corporal (in tank, artillery or transport division); ② (de sapeurs-pompiers) fire chief

brigand /bʀigɑ̃/ nm (bandit) brigand, bandit

brigandage /bʀigɑ̃daʒ/ nm (armed) robbery, banditry†

briguer /bʀige/ [1] vtr to crave [honneur]; to set one's sights on [poste]

brillamment /bʀijamɑ̃/ adv gén brilliantly

brillance /bʀijɑ̃s/ nf (d'astre, de diamant) brilliance; (de tissu, papier) sheen

brillant, ~e /bʀijɑ̃, ɑ̃t/
A adj ① (luisant) [yeux, plumage] bright; [cheveux, surface polie, métal] shiny; [surface mouillée] glistening; **regard ~ de joie** eyes shining with joy; ② (admirable) brilliant; **pas ~** euph [résultat] not brilliant; [situation] quite bad; [santé, affaires] none too good, rather poor
B nm ① (éclat) (de surface polie, cheveux) shine (**de** of); ② (diamant) (cut) diamond, brilliant

briller /bʀije/ [1] vi ① (luire) [soleil, lampe, métal] to shine; [flamme] to burn brightly; [diamant] to sparkle; [surface mouillée, neige, larme] to glisten; [nez] to be shiny; (pétiller) to sparkle; **tout brillait de propreté** everything was sparkling clean; **faire ~ ses chaussures** to shine one's shoes; **shampooing qui fait ~ les cheveux** shampoo which makes your hair shine; **les étoiles brillent** the stars are out; ② (exprimer) [yeux, regard] **~ de** to blaze with [colère]; to burn with [fièvre, désir]; ③ (se distinguer) [mondain, causeur] to shine; [élève] (dans une matière) to be brilliant (**en** at), to shine (**en** in)

brimade /bʀimad/ nf bullying ¢; **être victime de ~s** to be bullied

brimer /bʀime/ [1] vtr ① (maltraiter) to bully [personne]; ② (fruster) **se sentir brimé** to feel picked on

brin /bʀɛ̃/ nm ① (tige) **un ~ de muguet/persil** a sprig of lily-of-the-valley/parsley; **un ~ de paille** a wisp of straw; **un ~ d'herbe** a blade of grass; ② (peu) **un ~ de** a bit of; **faire un ~ de causette** to have a little chat; **un ~ exagéré** a touch exaggerated

brindille /bʀɛ̃dij/ nf twig

bringue○ /bʀɛ̃g/ nf ① (beuverie) drinking party; (fête) rave-up○; ② (fille) **(grande) ~** beanpole

brinquebaler /bʀɛ̃kbale/ [1] vi [chargement] to rattle about; [véhicule] to jolt along; [personne] to be shaken

brio /bʀijo/ nm (talent) brilliance; Mus brio

brioche /bʀijɔʃ/ nf ① Culin brioche, (sweet) bun; ② ○ (ventre) paunch

brioché, ~e /bʀijɔʃe/ adj Culin brioche (épith)

brique /bʀik/ nf ① Constr brick; ② (emballage de lait, jus de fruit) carton

briquer /bʀike/ [1] vtr to polish up; Naut to scrub down

briquet /bʀikɛ/ nm (de fumeur) (cigarette) lighter

briqueterie /bʀiketʀi/ nf (industrie) brickworks (+ v sg ou pl); (usine) brickyard

bris /bʀi/ nm (rupture) gén, Jur (de matériel, scellés) breaking; **la police d'assurance ne couvre pas le ~ de glaces** the insurance policy does not cover broken windows or mirrors

brisant, ~e /bʀizɑ̃, ɑ̃t/
A adj high explosive; **explosif ~** high-explosive charge
B nm (haut-fond) shoal
C brisants nmpl (vagues) breakers

brise /bʀiz/ nf breeze; **légère/bonne ~** light/fresh breeze

brise-bise /bʀizbiz/ nm inv half-curtain

brise-fer /bʀizfɛʀ/ nm inv destructive child

brise-glace /bʀizglas/ nm inv ① (navire) icebreaker; ② (de pont) ice-breaker

brise-jet /bʀizʒɛ/ nm inv (rubber) spout

brise-lames /bʀizlam/ nm inv breakwater

briser /bʀize/ [1]

A vtr **1** (rompre) to break [objet, jambe]; **2** (interrompre) to break [rythme, élan]; to stop [tentative, attaque, ascension]; to break down [résistance]; to crush [révolte]; [travailleur] to break [grève]; [police] to stop [grève]; **3** (mettre fin à) to break [silence, monopole]; to break down [tabou]; to shatter [rêve, idylle]; **4** (détruire) to destroy [pays, structure]; to break [personne]; to wreck [carrière, vie]; to shatter [image]; **l'émotion lui brisait la voix** his/her voice was breaking with emotion; **avoir le cœur brisé** to be broken-hearted; **5** (épuiser) to shatter [personne]

B **se briser** vpr **1** (se rompre) [vitre, os] to break; [vague] to break (**sur, contre** against); **2** (s'interrompre) [rêve] to be shattered; **3** (s'altérer) [voix] to break

brise-tout /bʀiztu/ nm inv (personne) butterfingers (sg)

briseur, -euse /bʀizœʀ, øz/ nm,f wrecker

Composé ~ **de grève** strike breaker

brise-vent /bʀizvã/ nm inv Agric windbreak

bristol /bʀistɔl/ nm (carton) Bristol (board)

brisure /bʀizyʀ/ nf (fêlure) crack; (débris) fragment

britannique /bʀitanik/ ▸ p. 392 adj British

Britannique /bʀitanik/ ▸ p. 392 nmf un/une ~ a British man/woman; **les** ~**s** the British (people)

Britanniques /bʀitanik/ ▸ p. 303 adj fpl **les îles** ~ the British Isles

broc /bʀo/ nm ewer

brocante /bʀokãt/ nf **1** (activité) bric-à-brac trade; **2** (marché) flea market

brocanteur, -euse /bʀokãtœʀ, øz/ ▸ p. 372 nm,f bric-à-brac trader

brocarder /bʀokaʀde/ [1] vtr to ridicule, to gibe at

brocart /bʀokaʀ/ nm (étoffe) brocade

broche /bʀoʃ/ nf **1** (bijou) brooch; **2** Culin spit; **faire cuire qch à la** ~ to spit-roast sth; **3** Méd pin

broché, ~e /bʀoʃe/

A pp ▸ **brocher**

B pp adj [livre] paperback (épith), softcover (épith)

brocher /bʀoʃe/ [1] vtr **1** (en imprimerie) to bind [sth] (with paper) [livre]; **2** (tisser) to brocade

brochet /bʀoʃɛ/ nm Zool pike

brochette /bʀoʃɛt/ nf Culin (tige) skewer; (mets) kebab, brochette

brocheur, -euse¹ /bʀoʃœʀ, øz/ ▸ p. 372 nm,f book binder

brocheuse² /bʀoʃøz/ nf (machine) binder, binding machine

brochure /bʀoʃyʀ/ nf (fascicule) booklet; (de voyage) brochure

brocoli /bʀokɔli/ nm broccoli ¢

brodequin /bʀodkɛ̃/ nm **1** (laced) boot; **2** (autrefois) buskin

broder /bʀode/ [1] vtr, vi to embroider

broderie /bʀodʀi/ nf **1** (art) embroidery; **2** (ouvrage) piece of embroidery, embroidery ¢

brodeuse /bʀodøz/ nf (personne) embroiderer

brome /bʀom/ nm Chimie bromine

bromure /bʀomyʀ/ nm bromide

bronche /bʀɔ̃ʃ/ nf bronchus; **les** ~**s** the bronchial tubes; **avoir les** ~**s fragiles** to have a weak chest

broncher /bʀɔ̃ʃe/ [1] vi [obéir] **sans** ~ without a murmur

bronchite /bʀɔ̃ʃit/ ▸ p. 195 nf bronchitis ¢

bronzage /bʀɔ̃zaʒ/ nm **1** (activité) (sun-)tanning; (hâle) tan; **2** Tech (de matière) bronzing

bronze /bʀɔ̃z/ nm (matière, objet) bronze

bronzé, ~e /bʀɔ̃ze/ adj [personne] (sun-)tanned

bronzer /bʀɔ̃ze/ [1]

A vtr (hâler) to tan [peau]

B vi [personne] to get a tan, to go brown; [peau] to tan

bronzeur /bʀɔ̃zœʀ/ nm (ouvrier) bronze-smelter, bronzer

brossage /bʀosaʒ/ nm (des cheveux, dents) brushing ¢; (du dos) scrubbing ¢

brosse /bʀos/ nf **1** gén brush; **donner un coup de** ~ **à qch** to give sth a brush; **avoir les cheveux (taillés) en** ~ to have a crew cut; **2** B (balai) broom

Composés ~ **à cheveux** hairbrush; ~ **à dents** toothbrush; ~ **à habits** clothesbrush; ~ **à ongles** nailbrush

brosser /bʀose/ [1]

A vtr **1** (frotter) to brush [vêtements, cheveux, dents]; to scrub [dos]; to brush [sb] down [personne]; **2** (peindre) to paint [toile, paysage]; **3** (décrire) to give a quick outline of

B °vi B schoolchildren's slang (s'absenter) to skip school

C **se brosser** vpr to brush oneself down; **se** ~ **les dents/ cheveux** to brush one's teeth/hair

brou /bʀu/ nm (écale) husk

Composé ~ **de noix** walnut stain

broue /bʀu/ nf C **1** (bière) beer; **2** (mousse) (de bière) head; (de lait) froth

brouette /bʀuɛt/ nf (véhicule) wheelbarrow; (contenu) barrowful

brouhaha /bʀuaa/ nm hubbub; **un grand** ~ a loud hubbub

brouillage /bʀujaʒ/ nm **1** Radio, Télécom (provoqué) jamming; (involontaire) interference; **2** fig (de pistes) covering up; (de données) mixing up

brouillard /bʀujaʀ/ nm **1** Météo fog; **il y a du** ~ it's foggy; **un** ~ **à couper au couteau** a pea souper GB, a thick fog; **2** (pulvérisation) spray; **3** Comm (livre) daybook

Composé ~ **givrant** Météo freezing fog

brouillasser /bʀujase/ [1] v impers to drizzle

brouille /bʀuj/ nf (momentanée) quarrel; (durable) rift

brouiller /bʀuje/ [1]

A vtr **1** (rendre trouble) [produit] to make [sth] cloudy [liquide]; [pluie] to blur, to smudge [nom, texte]; [larmes] to blur [vue]; [personne] to cover (over) [empreintes]; ~ **les pistes** or **les cartes** fig to confuse ou cloud the issue; **2** Radio, Télécom [personne] to jam [signaux, émission]; [parasites] to interfere with [émission, réception]

B **se brouiller** vpr **1** (se fâcher) [personnes, groupes] to fall out; **se** ~ **avec qn** to fall out with sb; **être brouillé avec les chiffres** fig to be hopeless with figures; **2** (devenir trouble) [liquide] to become cloudy; [vue] to become blurred; [esprit, souvenirs] to become confused; **avoir le teint brouillé** to look ill; **le temps se brouille** it's clouding over

brouillon, -onne /bʀujɔ̃, ɔn/

A adj **1** (sans soin) [personne, copie] untidy; **2** (désorganisé) [personne] disorganized; [esprit, style, discours] muddled; [émission, conférence] disorganized

B nm **1** (première rédaction) C (de texte, discours, devoir) rough draft; **faire qch au** ~ to do sth in rough; **2** (papier) ¢ **(papier)** ~ rough paper

broussaille /bʀusaj/ nf (dans sous-bois) undergrowth ¢; (sur terrain inculte) scrub ¢; (dans jardin, parc) bushes (pl); **cheveux en** ~ tousled hair

broussailleux, -euse /bʀusajø, øz/ adj **1** [terrain, région] covered with bushes; [jardin] overgrown; **2** [cheveux] tousled

brousse /bʀus/ nf Bot bush

brouter /bʀute/ [1]

A vtr [chèvre] to nibble [herbe, feuilles]; [vache, mouton] ~ **(l'herbe)** to graze

B vi Aut to judder

broutille /bʀutij/ nf trifle

broyer /bʀwaje/ [23] vtr (écraser) to grind [grain, couleurs, aliments]; to crush [pierre, bras, pied]

Idiome ~ **du noir** [personne] to brood

broyeur, -euse /bʀwajœʀ, øz/

A adj grinding, crushing

B nm (machine) crusher, grinder

bru /bʀy/ nf daughter-in-law

brucellose /bʀysɛloz/ nf ▸ p. 195 brucellosis

brugnon /bʀyɲɔ̃/ nm nectarine

brugnonier /bʀyɲɔnje/ nm nectarine tree

bruine /bʀɥin/ nf drizzle

bruiner /bʀɥine/ [1] v impers to drizzle

bruire /bʀɥiʀ/ [3] vi liter [feuille, papier, tissu] to rustle; [ruisseau] to murmur; [insecte] to hum

bruissement /bʀɥismã/ nm liter (de feuille, papier, tissu, vent) rustle ¢, rustling ¢; (de ruisseau) murmur ¢; (d'insecte) humming ¢

bruit /bʀɥi/ nm **1** (son) noise; **on n'entend pas un** ~ you can't hear a sound; ~ **étouffé** thud; **un** ~ **de marteau**

hammering; **un ~ de casseroles/d'assiettes** the clatter of saucepans/of plates; **un ~ de ferraille** a clang; **j'entends un ~ de pas/voix** I can hear footsteps/voices; **on dirait un ~ de moteur** it sounds like an engine; [2] (tapage) noise; **faire du ~** to make a noise, to be noisy; **il y a du ~** it's noisy; **faire un ~ infernal** or **d'enfer** [machine] to make a terrible din; [voisins] to make an awful racket; **sans ~** silently; [3] fig (commotion) **son film a fait beaucoup de ~** his/her film attracted a lot of attention; **beaucoup de ~ pour rien** a lot of fuss about nothing; **une affaire qui a fait du ~** an affair that caused an uproar; [4] (rumeur) rumour^{GB}; **le ~ court que** rumour^{GB} has it that

Composés **~ de couloir** rumour^{GB}; **~ de fond** background noise

bruitage /bʀɥitaʒ/ nm Cin, Théât sound effects (pl)

bruiteur /bʀɥitœʀ/ nm sound effects engineer

brûlant, ~e /bʀylɑ̃, ɑ̃t/ adj [1] (très chaud) [fer à repasser, casserole] hot; [thé, soupe] boiling hot; [vent, sable, asphalte, radiateur] burning hot; [soleil] blazing; [2] (fiévreux) [personne, front] burning hot; **être ~ de fièvre** to be burning with fever; [3] (urgent) [question, thème] burning; [4] (ardent) [passion] burning; [amour] passionate; [regard] blazing

brûlé, ~e /bʀyle/

A nm,f Méd **un grand ~** a third degree burns victim; **service des grands ~s** burns unit

B nm **odeur de ~** smell of burning; **avoir un goût de ~** to taste burned; **ça sent le ~** lit there's a smell of burning; fig things are becoming unpleasant

brûle-parfum(s) /bʀylpaʀfœ̃/ nm inv incense burner

brûle-pourpoint: à brûle-pourpoint /abʀylpuʀpwɛ̃/ loc adv point-blank

brûler /bʀyle/ [1]

A vtr [1] (mettre le feu) to burn [papiers, broussailles, encens]; to set fire to [voiture, maison]; **~ un cierge à** to light a candle to; **~ qn vif** to burn sb alive; [2] (consommer) to burn [combustible, calories]; to use [électricité]; [3] (provoquer une brûlure) [acide, flamme, huile] to burn [personne, peau]; [eau, thé] to scald [peau, corps]; [aliments, alcool] to burn [estomac, gorge]; [soleil] to burn [peau]; to scorch [herbe]; **être brûlé par une explosion** to get burned in an explosion; **être brûlé au visage** to suffer burns to one's face; **attention, ça brûle!** careful, it's very hot!; **être brûlé par le soleil** [personne] to get sunburned; **l'argent te brûle les doigts** fig money burns a hole in your pocket; **j'ai les yeux qui me brûlent** my eyes are stinging; [4] Méd to cauterize [verrue] (à with); [5] [○](ne pas respecter) to ignore [stop, priorité]; **~ un feu (rouge)** to jump[○] the lights

B vi [1] (se consumer) [bois, bougie] to burn; [forêt, maison, ville] to be on fire; **bien/mal ~** [combustible] to burn well/badly; **3 000 hectares de forêt ont brûlé** 3,000 hectares of forest have been destroyed by fire; **faire ~** to burn [papier, pneu]; to burn [sth] down [maison]; [2] Culin [rôti, tarte] to burn; [3] (flamber) [feu] to burn; [4] (désirer) **~ de faire, ~ d'envie de faire** to be longing to do; **~ (d'amour) pour qn** to be consumed with love for sb; [5] Jeux (à cache-tampon) **tu brûles!** you're getting very warm!

C se brûler vpr to burn oneself (avec with; en faisant doing); **se ~ la langue** to burn one's tongue

brûlis /bʀyli/ nm **culture sur ~** slash-and-burn cultivation

brûlure /bʀylyʀ/ nf [1] Méd burn; [2] (marque) burn mark

Composé **~s d'estomac** Méd heartburn **Ⓒ**

brume /bʀym/ nf [1] (brouillard léger) mist; (en mer) (sea) mist; (brouillard épais) fog; [2] (vapeur) (d'aérosol) mist; [3] (état confus) haze

Composé **~ de chaleur** heat haze

brumeux, -euse /bʀymø, øz/ adj [1] Météo (de chaleur) hazy; (de froid) misty, foggy; [2] (peu clair) [esprit, idée] hazy

brun, ~e¹ /bʀœ̃, bʀyn/

A ▸ p. 140 adj [peau, tissu, fourrure] brown, dark; [cheveux, barbe] dark; [yeux] brown; [personne] dark-haired; [tabac] black; **cigarette ~e** black tobacco cigarette; **bière ~e** ≈ stout GB

B nm,f (homme) dark-haired man; (femme) dark-haired woman

C nm (couleur) brown

brunante /bʀynɑ̃t/ nf C (crépuscule) dusk; **à la ~** at dusk

brunâtre /bʀynɑtʀ/ ▸ p. 140 adj brownish

brune² /bʀyn/

A adj f ▸ brun

B nf [1] (cigarette) black tobacco cigarette; [2] (bière) ≈ stout GB

C à la brune loc prép littér at dusk

brunir /bʀyniʀ/ [3]

A vtr (bronzer) [soleil] to tan

B vi [1] [personne, peau] to tan; [cheveux] to get darker; [2] Culin to brown; **faire ~** to brown [sauce, beurre]

brushing /bʀœʃiŋ/ nm blow-dry

brusque /bʀysk/ adj [1] [personne, ton] abrupt (avec qn with sb); [2] (imprévu) [mouvement] sudden; [virage] sharp

brusquement /bʀyskəmɑ̃/ adv [1] [dire, interrompre] abruptly; [2] [ralentir, entrer, mourir] suddenly; [freiner] sharply

brusquer /bʀyske/ [1] vtr [1] (traiter sans ménagement) to be brusque with; [2] (précipiter) to rush

brusquerie /bʀyskəʀi/ nf (rudesse) brusqueness

brut, ~e¹ /bʀyt/

A adj [1] (non traité) [coton, soie, matière] raw; [minerai, pétrole] crude; [pierre précieuse] rough, uncut; [marbre, granit] rough; [laine] untreated; [sucre] unrefined; **à l'état ~** in its natural state; [2] [champagne, vin mousseux] dry, brut; [cidre] dry; [3] [salaire, bénéfice] gross; [4] [poids, charge] gross

B adv gross

C nm (pétrole) crude (oil); (champagne) dry champagne

brutal, ~e mpl **-aux** /bʀytal, o/ adj [1] (brusque) [coup, choc] violent; [douleur, mort] sudden; [hausse, chute] dramatic; [coup de frein] sharp; [2] (violent) [ton, caractère, discours] brutal; [geste] violent; **être ~ avec qn** (physiquement) to be rough with sb; (en paroles) to be brutal with sb; [3] (choquant) [réalité] stark

brutalement /bʀytalmɑ̃/ adv [1] (avec violence) [réprimer, frapper] brutally; [fermer, ouvrir] violently; [2] (brusquement) [changer, baisser] dramatically; [mourir, s'arrêter] suddenly; [freiner, accélérer] sharply

brutaliser /bʀytalize/ [1] vtr to ill-treat [personne, animal]

brutalité /bʀytalite/ nf [1] (violence) brutality; [2] (brusquerie) suddenness; [3] (acte de violence) (act of) brutality **Ⓒ; les ~s policières** police brutality

brute² /bʀyt/

A adj f ▸ **brut A**

B nf [1] (personne violente) brute; [2] (personne sans culture) lout

Idiome **comme une ~** [taper] savagely; [dormir] like a log; [travailler] like a horse

Bruxelles /bʀysɛl/ ▸ p. 621 npr Brussels

bruxellois, ~e /bʀyselwa, az/ ▸ p. 621 adj Brussels (épith)

bruyamment /bʀɥijamɑ̃/ adv [rire, éternuer, protester] loudly; [entrer, sortir] noisily

bruyant, ~e /bʀɥijɑ̃, ɑ̃t/ adj [1] lit [conversation, musique] loud; [enfant, jeu] noisy, boisterous; [pièce, rue] noisy; [2] fig [renommée, succès] resounding

bruyère /bʀyjɛʀ/ nf [1] (plante) heather; (racine) briar; **terre de ~** heath; [2] (lieu) heath

BSR /beesɛʀ/ nm (abbr = **brevet de sécurité routière**) road safety certificate

BTP /betepe/ nm (abbr = **bâtiment et travaux publics**) building and civil engineering

BTS /beteɛs/ nm: abbr ▸ **brevet**

bu, ~e /by/ pp ▸ **boire**

buanderie /bɥɑ̃dʀi/ nf [1] (dans une maison) laundry room; [2] C (laverie automatique) launderette GB, Laundromat® US

buccal, ~e mpl **-aux** /bykal, o/ adj oral

bucco-dentaire /bykodɑ̃tɛʀ/ adj [hygiène] oral

bûche /byʃ/ nf [1] (de bois) log; [2] [○](chute) tumble; **prendre** or **ramasser une ~** to fall (flat on one's face)

Composé **~ de Noël** Culin yule log

bûcher¹[○] /byʃe/ [1] vi to slog away[○]

bûcher² /byʃe/ nm [1] (de condamné) stake; [2] (de mort) (funeral) pyre; [3] (réserve) woodshed

bûcheron /byʃʀɔ̃/ ▸ p. 372 nm lumberjack

bûchette /byʃɛt/ nf [1] (objet) (pour le feu) stick; **des ~s pour allumer le feu** kindling **Ⓒ**; [2] (pour compter) counting rod; [3] Culin individual yule log

bûcheur[○], **-euse** /byʃœʀ, øz/ adj [élève, étudiant] industrious

bucolique /bykɔlik/ adj bucolic, pastoral

budget /bydʒɛ/ nm budget

budgétaire /bydʒetɛR/ adj [prévisions, déficit, excédent] budget (épith); [contrôle] budgetary, budget (épith); [contraintes, restrictions] budgetary; [année] financial GB, fiscal US

budgétiser /bydʒetize/ [1] vtr to include [sth] in the budget [dépense, recette]

buée /bɥe/ nf (de froid) condensation; (d'haleine) steam

buffet /byfɛ/ nm 1 (meuble) (de salle à manger) sideboard; (de cuisine) dresser; 2 (de gare) buffet; 3 (table garnie) buffet

buffle /byfl/ nm buffalo

buis /bɥi/ nm (buisson) box tree; (haie) box hedge; (bois) boxwood

buisson /bɥisɔ̃/ nm (sauvage) bush; (cultivé) shrub

(Composé) ~ ardent Bible burning bush; Bot pyracantha

buissonnière /bɥisɔnjɛR/ adj **faire l'école** ~ to play truant GB, to play hooky○ US

bulbe /bylb/ nm 1 (de plante) bulb; 2 (coupole) onion(-shaped) dome

(Composés) ~ dentaire root of tooth; ~ pileux hair bulb; ~ rachidien medulla oblongata

bulbeux, -euse /bylbø, øz/ adj bulbous

bulgare /bylgaR/ ▸ p. 392, p. 336 adj, nm Bulgarian

bulldozer /byldozœR/ nm bulldozer

bulle¹ /byl/ nm inv **papier** ~ unbleached paper

bulle² /byl/ nf 1 (d'air, de gaz) bubble; **faire des** ~**s** to blow bubbles; 2 (de bande dessinée) speech bubble

bulletin /byltɛ̃/ nm 1 (informations) bulletin, report; ~ **météorologique** weather forecast; ~ **scolaire** ou **de notes** school report GB, report card US; 2 (document) certificate; (d'abonnement, adhésion) form; ~ **de salaire** or **paie** payslip; ~ **de naissance** birth certificate; 3 (bon) ~ **de commande** order form; ~ **de participation** (dans un jeu) entry form; 4 (publication) bulletin; 5 (rubrique de journal) (colonne) column; (page) page; 6 Pol (de vote) ballot ou voting paper; ~ **blanc** blank vote; ~ **nul** spoiled ballot paper

bulletin-réponse, pl **bulletins-réponse** /byltɛRepɔ̃s/ nm reply coupon

bulot /bylo/ nm whelk

buraliste /byRalist/ ▸ p. 372 nmf 1 (de bureau de tabac) (vendant des articles pour fumeurs) tobacconist; (vendant des cigarettes et journaux) newsagent GB, newsdealer US; 2 (de bureau de paiement) clerk

bure /byR/ nf 1 (étoffe) frieze; 2 (vêtement) habit; **porter la** ~ to be a monk

bureau, pl ~**x** /byRo/ nm 1 (meuble) desk; 2 (pièce individuelle) (chez soi) study; (au travail) office; **heures d'ouverture des** ~**x** office hours; 3 (établissement) office; **ouvrir un** ~ **à Londres** to open an office in London; 4 (organe directeur) board; ~ **exécutif** executive board

(Composés) ~ **d'accueil** reception; ~ **de change** bureau de change, foreign exchange office; ~ **d'études** (recherche) research department; (conception) design office; ~ **de poste** post office; ~ **de tabac** (articles pour fumeurs) tobacconist's; (cigarettes, journaux) newsagent GB, news stand US; ~ **de tri** sorting office; ~ **de vote** polling station; **Bureau international du travail**, **BIT** International Labour Office, ILO

bureaucrate /byRokRat/ nmf pej bureaucrat

bureaucratie /byRokRasi/ nf (administration) bureaucracy; (pouvoir des bureaucrates) officialdom

bureautique /byRotik/ nf office automation

burette /byRɛt/ nf 1 (pour l'huile, le vinaigre) cruet; 2 (de messe) cruet; 3 Tech oil applicator; (plus grand) oilcan

burin /byRɛ̃/ nm chisel; **sculpter au** ~ to chisel

buriner /byRine/ [1] vtr 1 (graver) to engrave; 2 (dégrossir) to chisel out [statue, bloc]; 3 (marquer) to furrow [visage, traits]; **avoir les traits burinés** to have a deeply furrowed face

burlesque /byRlɛsk/

A adj [tenue, idée, histoire] ludicrous; [farce, film, scène] farcical

B nm Cin, Littérat **le** ~ the burlesque

burqua /byRka/ nf burk(h)a

bus /bys/ nm inv 1 (véhicule) bus; 2 Ordinat bus

busard /byzaR/ nm harrier

buse /byz/ nf 1 Zool buzzard; 2 ○(idiot) clot○ GB, clod○; **triple** ~! you total ou prize idiot○!; 3 Tech (conduit) pipe, duct; (embout) nozzle

business○ /biznɛs/ nm inv 1 (affaires commerciales) business; 2 (affaires privées) affairs; 3 (situation embrouillée) business, affair; **je ne comprends rien à tout ce** ~ this whole business is a mystery to me

(Composé) ~ **angel** Fin private backer, business angel

busqué, ~e /byske/ adj [nez] hooked

buste /byst/ nm 1 (sculpture) bust; 2 (torse) chest; 3 (seins) bust

bustier /bystje/ nm (sous-vêtement) long-line bra; (vêtement) bustier; **robe** ~ bustier dress

but /by(t)/ nm 1 (objectif) goal; (intention) aim, purpose; (ambition) aim; **atteindre son** ~ to reach one's goal; **marcher sans** ~ to walk aimlessly; **nous touchons au** ~ our goal is in sight; **mon** ~ **dans la vie est de** my aim in life is to; **il s'est fixé pour** ~ **la présidence** he has set his sights on the presidency; **dans quel** ~ **est-il venu?** what was his purpose ou object in coming here?; **dans ce** ~ with this aim in view; **faire qch dans un** ~ **désintéressé** to do sth with no ulterior motive; **aller droit au** ~ to go straight to the point; 2 Sport (au football) goal; (au tir) target

(Idiomes) **demander/déclarer de** ~ **en blanc** to ask/declare point-blank; **annoncer qch de** ~ **en blanc à qn** to spring sth on sb

butane /bytan/ nm Calor gas® GB, butane

buté, ~e¹ /byte/ adj [personne, air] stubborn, obstinate

butée² /byte/ nf 1 Tech stop; ~ **d'une porte** doorstop; 2 Archit buttress

buter /byte/ [1]

A vtr 1 (rendre têtu) to make [sb] even more stubborn; 2 Constr (étayer) to prop up [mur]; 3 ○(tuer) to kill [personne]

B vi 1 [personne] to trip, to stumble; ~ **contre qch** (trébucher) to trip over sth; (se heurter) to bump into sth; ~ **sur** or **contre** to come up against [obstacle, difficulté]

C se buter vpr (s'obstiner) **il va se** ~ he'll be even more stubborn

buteur /bytœR/ nm (au rugby) (place-)kicker; (au football) leading goal scorer

butin /bytɛ̃/ nm 1 (de guerre) spoils (pl); 2 (de vol) haul, loot; 3 (de recherche) fruits (pl)

butiner /bytine/ [1]

A vtr 1 [abeilles] to gather pollen from [fleurs]; 2 fig (glaner) to glean, to pick up [renseignements]

B vi [abeilles] to gather pollen

butoir /bytwaR/ nm 1 Rail buffer; 2 Tech stop; 3 (date limite) **(date)** ~ deadline

butte /byt/ nf mound

(Idiome) **être en** ~ **à** to come up against [difficultés]; to be the butt of [sarcasmes, moquerie]

buvable /byvabl/ adj 1 (à boire) [médicament] to be taken orally (après n); 2 (pas mauvais) drinkable

buvard /byvaR/ nm 1 (matière) **(papier)** ~ blotting paper **C**; 2 (feuille) sheet of blotting paper; 3 (sous-main) blotter

buvette /byvɛt/ nf (de gare, fête) refreshment area

buveur, -euse /byvœR, øz/ nm,f 1 (alcoolique) drinker, alcoholic; 2 (personne qui boit) drinker

byzantin, ~e /bizɑ̃tɛ̃, in/ adj Byzantine; **querelles** ~**es** fig hairsplitting quarrels

BZH (written abbr = **Breizh**) Brittany

Cc

c, C /se/ *nm inv* c, C; **c cédille** c cedilla

c' ▸ ce

CA *written abbr* ▸ **chiffre**

ça /sa/ *pron dém*

⟨Idiomes⟩ **elle est bête et méchante avec** ∼ she's stupid and what's more she's nasty; **et avec** ∼**?** anything else?; **rien que** ∼**!** iron is that all! iron; **c'est** ∼**!** that's right!; **eh bien, c'est** ∼**, ne te gêne pas!** iron oh, carry on GB *ou* keep going, don't mind me! iron; ∼ **va?** (la vie) how are things?; (l'affaire proposée) is that a deal?; ∼ **y est, ∼ recommence!** here we go again!; ∼ **y est, j'ai fini!** that's it, I've finished!; ∼ **y est, il pleut!** here comes the rain!; **'alors, ∼ y est, tu es prêt?'—'non, ∼ n'y est pas!'** 'well, are you ready?'—'no, I'm not!'

çà /sa/ *adv* ∼ **et là** here and there

cabale /kabal/ *nf* ① (intrigue, intrigants) cabal; **monter une ∼ contre qn** to form a cabal against sb; ② Relig cabbala

caban /kabɑ̃/ *nm* sailor's jacket

cabane /kaban/ *nf* ① (habitation) hut; ② (abri) shed; ③ ⁰(prison) nick⁰

cabanon /kabanɔ̃/ *nm* (abri) shed

cabaret /kabaʀɛ/ *nm* cabaret

cabas /kaba/ *nm* shopping bag

cabillaud /kabijo/ *nm* cod; **filet de ∼** cod fillet

cabine /kabin/ *nf* (de bateau, fusée) cabin; (de camion) cab; (de laboratoire de langue) booth; (de piscine) cubicle; (pour se changer) changing room

⟨Composés⟩ ∼ **de douche** shower cubicle; ∼ **d'essayage** fitting room; ∼ **de pilotage** cockpit; ∼ **téléphonique** phone box GB, phone booth

cabinet /kabinɛ/

A *nm* ① (local) office; (de médecin, dentiste) surgery GB, office US; (de juge) chambers (*pl*); ② (affaires et clientèle) practice; (cabinet collectif) firm; (de médecins, dentistes) practice; **ouvrir un ∼** to set up in practice; ③ (agence) agency; ∼ **immobilier** estate agent's; ④ Pol (gouvernement) cabinet; (de ministre, préfet) staff; ∼ **ministériel** minister's personal staff; ⑤ (de musée) exhibition room

B **cabinets** *nmpl* toilet (*sg*), loo⁰ (*sg*) GB, bathroom (*sg*) US

⟨Composés⟩ ∼ **de consultation** surgery GB, office US; ∼ **noir** cubbyhole; ∼ **de toilette** bathroom

cabinet-conseil, *pl* **cabinets-conseil** /kabinɛkɔ̃sɛj/ *nm* firm of consultants

câblage /kablaʒ/ *nm* ① (connexions) wiring; ② (mise en place) wiring; ③ TV cabling; **faire le ∼ d'une ville** to install cable television in a town

câble /kabl/ *nm* (en métal, synthétique) cable; (en fibres végétales) rope; ∼ **porteur** (de pont) suspension cable; (de téléphérique) carrying cable

⟨Composés⟩ ∼ **d'amarrage** mooring rope; ∼ **de remorque** (de navire) towline

câbler /kable/ [1] *vtr* ① (connecter) to wire; ② (télégraphier) to cable

cabochard⁰, ∼**e** /kabɔʃaʀ, aʀd/ *adj* stubborn

caboche⁰ /kabɔʃ/ *nf* (tête) head; **mets-toi ça dans la ∼** get that into your thick skull

cabosser /kabɔse/ [1] *vtr* to dent; **(tout) cabossé** battered

cabot⁰ /kabo/ *nm* (chien) pej dog, mutt⁰ péj

cabotage /kabotaʒ/ *nm* coastal shipping

cabotin, ∼**e** /kabotɛ̃, in/ *adj* **être** ∼ to like playing to the gallery

cabrer /kabʀe/ [1]

A *vtr* to make [sth] rear [cheval]

B **se cabrer** *vpr* ① [cheval] to rear (**devant** at); ② [personne] to jib; ③ Aviat [avion] to zoom

cabri /kabʀi/ *nm* kid; **sauter comme un** ∼ to gambol like a lamb

cabriole /kabʀijɔl/ *nf* ① (de clown, d'enfant, animal) capering **¢**; **faire des** ∼**s** to caper about; ② (de cheval) capriole; ③ (en danse) cabriole

cabriolet /kabʀijɔlɛ/ *nm* Aut convertible, cabriolet; (voiture à cheval) cabriolet

CAC® /kak/ *nm* (*abbr* = **Compagnie des agents de change**) **indice** ∼ **40,** ∼ **40** Paris Stock Exchange index

caca /kaka/ *nm* baby talk poo GB, poop US; **il a fait** ∼ **dans sa culotte** he pooed GB *ou* pooped US in his pants

⟨Composé⟩ ∼ **d'oie** (couleur) greenish yellow

cacahuète /kakawɛt/ *nf* peanut

cacao /kakao/ *nm* (poudre, boisson) cocoa

cacaotier /kakaotje/, **cacaoyer** /kakaɔje/ *nm* cacao tree

cacarder /kakaʀde/ [1] *vi* [oie] to honk

cacatoès /kakatɔɛs/ *nm* cockatoo

cachalot /kaʃalo/ *nm* sperm whale

cache¹ /kaʃ/ *nm* (feuille opaque) mask

cache² /kaʃ/ *nf* hiding place; ∼ **d'armes** arms cache

caché, ∼**e** /kaʃe/

A *pp* ▸ **cacher**

B *pp adj* [trésor, charme, beauté, sens] hidden; [complot, douleur, désir, amour] secret

cache-cache /kaʃkaʃ/ ▸ p. 327 *nm inv* hide and seek; **jouer à** ∼ lit, fig to play hide and seek

cache-col /kaʃkɔl/ *nm inv* scarf

cachemire /kaʃmiʀ/ *nm* cashmere; **de** *or* **en** ∼ cashmere (épith); **motif** ∼ paisley pattern

Cachemire /kaʃmiʀ/ ▸ p. 504 *nprm* **le** ∼ Kashmir

cache-pot /kaʃpo/ *nm inv* flowerpot holder, planter

cacher /kaʃe/ [1]

A *vtr* to hide; ∼ **son visage dans ses mains** to hide *ou* bury one's face in one's hands; ∼ **sa nudité** to cover one's nakedness; ∼ **son jeu** fig to keep one's cards close to one's chest; ∼ **qch à qn** to conceal *ou* hide sth from sb; **il leur a caché la mort de son chien** he didn't tell them his dog had died; **je ne vous cache pas que je suis inquiète** frankly, I'm worried; **pour ne rien vous** ∼ to be quite frank

B **se cacher** *vpr* ① gén to hide; (temporairement) [personne] to go into hiding; [animal] to go to ground; **il ne s'en cache pas** he makes no secret of it; **quelle organisation se cache derrière les émeutes?** which organization is behind these riots?; ② (disparaître) [soleil, objet] to disappear

cachet /kaʃe/ *nm* ① (comprimé) tablet; **un** ∼ **d'aspirine**® an aspirin; ② (à l'encre) stamp; (de cire) seal; ∼ **de la poste** postmark; **'le** ∼ **de la poste faisant foi'** 'as attested by date on postmark'; ③ (chic) style; (marque distinctive) cachet; ④ Cin, Théât (paie) fee

cacheter /kaʃte/ [20] *vtr* to seal

cachette /kaʃɛt/ *nf* hiding place; **sortir de sa** ∼ gén to come out of one's hiding place; [fugitif] to come out of hiding; **en** ∼ on the sly

ça¹

I. *ça* sert à désigner

Pour désigner un objet présent, on utilisera *this* si l'objet est proche, *that* s'il est plus éloigné:

aide-moi à plier ça
= help me fold this

Pour récapituler, reprendre ce dont il s'agit, on utilisera *that*:

à part ça
= apart from that

et tout ça, parce que…
= and all that because …

tu n'en as pas envie, je vois ça
= you don't feel like it, I can see that

où as-tu entendu ça?
= where did you hear that?

me faire/dire ça, à moi!
= fancy doing/saying that to me (of all people)!

c'est pour ça qu'il est parti
= that's why he left

il ne manquait plus que ça!
= that's all we needed!

on dit ça !
= that's what they/you etc. say!

Attention:

sans ça
= otherwise

II. *ça* est sujet du verbe

(Voir également les verbes **aller**, **être**, **faire**, **marcher** ainsi que la note d'usage sur **la mesure du temps** pour l'expression *ça fait un an/deux mois que*)

ça représente un objet:

si ça flotte, ce n'est pas une pierre
= if it floats, it can't be a stone

ça coûte cher?
= is it expensive?

ça représente un fait, une déclaration, une idée déjà mentionnés: si le ton est neutre, on emploiera *it*, mais s'il est emphatique, on utilisera *that*:

ça fait mal
= it hurts

Lorsqu'il s'agit d'une simple constatation, mais quand il exprime la surprise, l'indignation:

ça fait mal
= that hurts!

de même:

ça ne marchera pas
= it won't work (*est une affirmation neutre*)

alors que:

ça ne marchera pas
= that won't work
  (*rejette avec force la solution proposée*)

ça paraît incroyable
= it seems incredible *ou* that seems incredible
  (*selon l'emphase*)

Dans les phrases ci-dessous, nettement emphatiques, *that* est la traduction qui s'impose:

ça suffit, voyons!
= that's enough!

ça t'a étonné, n'est-ce pas?
= that surprised you, didn't it?

ça représente ce qui va être explicité:

ça m'inquiète de la voir dans cet état
= it worries me to see her in that state

ça vaut la peine qu'il y aille
= it's worth his going

ça n'est pas pour me vanter, mais…
= I don't want to boast, but …

On notera cependant:

la rue a ça de bien qu'elle est calme
= one good thing about the street is that it is quiet

ça a une valeur impersonnelle:

ça souffle aujourd' hui!
= it's windy today!

ça chauffe aujourd' hui!
= it's hot today!

ça représente une personne: dans ce cas on utilisera le pronom personnel approprié, *he*, *she* ou *they*:

et ça se croit malin!
= and he/she etc. thinks he's/she's etc. clever!

La nature de *ça* n'est pas définie: on pourra souvent traduire par la tournure impersonnelle *there is/are*, comme dans les exemples suivants:

ça sent le brûlé
= there's a smell of burning

ça tapait de tous les côtés
= there was banging everywhere

ça criait de tous les côtés
= there was shouting everywhere

Lorsque *ça* est sujet de rappel, il ne se traduit pas:

la télévision, ça m'ennuie
= television bores me;

voyager (ou les voyages), ça revient cher
= travelling is expensive

et le jardin, ça pousse?
= how's the (*ou* your) garden doing?

ça a une valeur d'insistance. La tournure est emphatique:

qu'est-ce que c'est que ça?
= what's that?

ça, je m'en moque!
= I couldn't care less about that!

ça, ça ne compte pas!
= that doesn't count!

c'est bizarre, ça ou ça, c'est bizarre
= that's strange

On notera que les gallicismes *c'est ça qui/que* sont traités sous le verbe **être**.

Pour renforcer une interrogation:

pourquoi ça?
= why's that?

'je l'ai vu' 'quand/où ça?'
= 'I saw him' 'when/where was that?'

'tu la connais?' 'qui ça?'
= 'do you know her?' 'who do you mean?'

'je ne veux pas' 'comment ça, tu ne veux pas?'
= 'I don't want to' 'what do you mean, you don't want to?'

'c'est faisable' 'comment ça?'
= 'it can be done' 'how?'

Dans une comparaison (voir également **comme**):

ce n'est pas si facile que ça
= it's not as easy as (all) that *ou* it's not that easy

la dernière fois que je l'ai vu, il n'était pas plus haut que ça!
= last time I saw him, he was only so high!

☛ Voir page suivante

ça¹ *suite*

Attention:

tu te lèves toujours aussi tard que ça? (*l'heure qu'il est*)
= do you always get up this late?
(*l'heure mentionnée*)
= do you always get up that late?

Avec valeur d'interjection:

ça, par exemple! (*indigné*)
= well, honestly!
(*surpris*)
= well I never!

ça, alors! (*surpris*)
= well I never!

ça, oui!
= definitely!

ça, non!
= no way! *ou* absolutely not!

ça, pour se plaindre, il se plaint!
= talk about complain, he does nothing else!

ça, comme bavard, il n'y a pas mieux!
= he can certainly talk all right!

ça, mon vieux, débrouille-toi!
= sort it out for yourself, mate!

---

cachot /kaʃo/ *nm* (de prison moderne) prison cell; (de prison ancienne) dungeon; **faire trois jours de** ~ to be locked up alone for three days

cachotterie /kaʃɔtʀi/ *nf* little secret; **faire des** ~**s à qn** to keep things from sb

cachottier, -ière /kaʃɔtje, ɛʀ/ *adj* secretive

cacophonie /kakɔfɔni/ *nf* cacophony

cactus /kaktys/ *nm inv* cactus

c-à-d (*written abbr* = **c'est-à-dire**) ie

cadastral, ~**e,** *mpl* **-aux** /kadastʀal, o/ *adj* [*plan*] cadastral; [*registre*] land (*épith*)

cadastre /kadastʀ/ *nm* (registre) land register, cadastre^GB; (administration) land registry

cadavérique /kadaveʀik/ *adj* [*pâleur, odeur*] deathly (*épith*); [*teint*] deathly pale

cadavre /kadavʀ/ *nm* ⓵ (de personne) gén corpse; (de victime) body; (d'animal) body, carcass; ~ **ambulant**○ walking skeleton; ⓶ ○(bouteille vide) dead bottle

caddie /kadi/ *nm* ⓵ (au golf) caddie; ⓶ ®(de supermarché) shopping trolley GB, shopping cart US

cadeau, *pl* ~**x** /kado/
A *nm* present, gift; **faire un** ~ **à qn** to give sb a present; **je t'en fais** ~ (je te l'offre) I'm giving it to you; (je ne veux pas d'argent) I'm making you a present of it; (tu peux le garder) you can keep it; **il ne fait pas de** ~**x** (commerçant) he's not exactly cheap; (juge, examinateur) he's very strict; **ils ne se font pas de** ~**x** they don't do each other favours^GB; **se faire un** ~ to treat oneself; **et, en** ~, **un disque** and a record as a free gift; **mon chef c'est pas un** ~○ my boss is a pain○
B (-)**cadeau** (*in compounds*) gift; **papier(-)**~ wrapping paper

(Composé) ~ **empoisonné** poisoned chalice

cadenas /kadna/ *nm* padlock

cadence /kadɑ̃s/ *nf* ⓵ (de mouvements, pas) rhythm; **en** ~ [*marcher*] in step; [*ramer*] rhythmically; ⓶ (de sons, poème) cadence; ⓷ (de travail, production) rate; **relâcher/tenir la** ~ to slacken/to keep up the pace; ⓸ Mil (de tir) rate; ⓹ Mus (enchaînement d'accords) cadence

cadencé, ~**e** /kadɑ̃se/ *adj* **les slogans cadencés des manifestants** the rhythmic chanting of the demonstrators

cadet, -ette /kadɛ, ɛt/
A *adj* (de deux) younger; (de plus de deux) youngest
B *nm,f* ⓵ (enfant) (dernier de deux) younger son/daughter, younger child; (dernier de plus de deux) youngest son/daughter, youngest child; ⓶ (frère, sœur) younger brother/sister; ⓷ (personne plus jeune) junior; (personne la plus jeune) youngest; **un homme de trente ans ton** ~ a man thirty years your junior; ⓸ Sport *athlete between the ages of 15 and 17*; ⓹ Mil cadet

cadrage /kadʀaʒ/ *nm* ⓵ (action) framing; ⓶ (résultat) composition

cadran /kadʀɑ̃/ *nm* (de montre, boussole) face; (de compteur) dial; ~ **solaire** sundial

(Idiome) **faire le tour du** ~○ to sleep round GB *ou* around US the clock

cadre /kadʀ/
A *nm* ⓵ (de tableau, miroir) frame; ⓶ (lieu) setting; (milieu) sur-

roundings (*pl*); ⓷ (domaine délimité) **cela sort du** ~ **de mes fonctions** that's not part of my duties; **sortir du** ~ **de la légalité** to go outside the law; ⓸ (structure) framework; **en dehors du** ~ **scolaire** outside a school context; ⓹ (employé) executive; ~ **moyen/supérieur** middle ranking/senior executive; **les** ~**s moyens/supérieurs** middle/senior management (+ *v pl*); ⓺ (de bicyclette, moto) frame; ⓻ (dans un formulaire) space, box; ⓼ Ordinat frame
B **dans le cadre de** *loc prép* ⓵ (à l'occasion de) on the occasion of; **dans le** ~ **de cette journée particulière** on this special occasion; ⓶ (dans le contexte de) (de lutte, négociations, d'organisation) within the framework of; (de campagne, plan) as part of; **recevoir une formation dans le** ~ **d'une entreprise** to undergo training within a company

(Composé) ~ **de vie** (living) environment

cadrer /kadʀe/ [1]
A *vtr* to centre^GB [*image, scène*]; **la photo est mal cadrée** the photo is off-centre^GB; **photo bien cadrée** well-composed photo
B *vi* to tally, to fit (**avec** with); **ça ne cadre pas** it doesn't fit

cadreur /kadʀœʀ/ ▸ p. 372 *nm* Cin cameraman

caduc, caduque /kadyk/ *adj* ⓵ (dépassé) obsolete; (sans effet) null; **rendre qch** ~ to render sth null and void; ⓶ [*feuille*] deciduous; **arbre à feuilles caduques** deciduous tree

cafard /kafaʀ/ *nm* ⓵ ○(mélancolie) depression; **avoir le** ~ to be down in the dumps○; **un coup de** ~ a fit of depression; **donner le** ~ **à qn** to get sb down○, to make sb depressed○; ⓶ (insecte) cockroach

cafardeux, -euse /kafaʀdø, øz/ *adj* [*personne*] glum; [*nature, tempérament*] gloomy

café /kafe/
A ▸ p. 140 *adj inv* (couleur) dark brown
B *nm* ⓵ (substance, boisson, arôme) coffee; ~ **vert** unroasted coffee; ~ **en grains** coffee beans (+ *v pl*); ~ **soluble** instant coffee; **prendre un** ~ to have a coffee; **glace au** ~ coffee ice cream; ⓶ (établissement) café; ⓷ (fin d'un repas) **au** ~ at the end of the meal

(Composés) ~ **crème** espresso with milk; ~ **au lait** coffee with milk; **peau** ~ **au lait** coffee-coloured^GB skin; ~ **noir** black coffee

café-concert, *pl* **cafés-concerts** /kafekɔ̃sɛʀ/ *nm* café with live music

caféier /kafeje/ *nm* coffee tree

caféine /kafein/ *nf* caffeine

cafétéria /kafeteʀja/ *nf* cafeteria

café-théâtre, *pl* **cafés-théâtres** /kafeteatʀ/ *nm* café with live theatre^GB

cafetière /kaftjɛʀ/ *nf* ⓵ (récipient) coffee pot; (appareil) coffee maker; ⓶ ○(tête) head; **il n'a rien dans la** ~ he's brainless

(Composé) ~ **électrique** coffee machine

cafouillage○ /kafujaʒ/ *nm* (confusion) bungling○ **Ȼ**

cafouiller○ /kafuje/ [1] *vi* [*personne*] to get flustered; [*appareil*] to be on the blink○; **il a fait** ~ **nos projets** he messed up our plans; **ça cafouille** things are in a mess

cage /kaʒ/ nf **1** (pour animaux) cage; **en ~** caged; **mettre en ~** to cage [animal]; to put [sb] behind bars [personne]; **dans une ~ de verre** behind a glass screen; **vivre en ~** fig to be cooped up○; **2** ○Sport goal

⟨Composés⟩ **~ d'ascenseur** lift shaft GB, elevator shaft US; **~ d'escalier** stairwell; **~ à lapins** lit, fig○ rabbit hutch; **~ à oiseaux** birdcage; **~ à poules** lit hen coop; **~ thoracique** rib cage

⟨Idiome⟩ **tourner comme un ours** or **lion en ~** to pace up and down like a caged animal

cageot /kaʒo/ nm crate

cagibi /kaʒibi/ nm store cupboard

cagneux, -euse /kaɲø, øz/ adj **avoir les genoux ~** to be knock-kneed

cagnotte /kaɲɔt/ nf **1** (caisse commune) kitty; **2** (de loterie) jackpot; **3** (économies) (pour plus tard) nest egg; (plus général) **une jolie ~** a nice little sum

cagoule /kagul/ nf gén balaclava; **deux hommes en ~** two hooded men

cahier /kaje/
A nm **1** (carnet) notebook; Scol exercise book; **2** (en imprimerie) section
B **cahiers** nmpl (revue) journal (sg)

⟨Composés⟩ **~ de brouillon** rough book; **~ de devoirs** homework book; **~ d'exercices** exercise book; **~ de textes** homework notebook; **~ de travaux pratiques** lab book, laboratory notebook

cahin-caha○ /kaɛ̃kaa/ adv [marcher, avancer] with difficulty; **les affaires vont ~** business isn't going too well

cahot /kao/ nm jolt; **les ~s** fig the ups and downs

cahotant, ~e /kaɔtɑ̃, ɑ̃t/ adj [route, carrière] bumpy

cahoté, ~e /kaɔte/ adj (secoué) shaken about; (éprouvé) buffeted; **~ par la vie** buffeted by life

cahoter /kaɔte/ [1] vi [véhicule] to bounce along

cahute /kayt/ nf (cabane) hut, shack

caïd /kaid/ nm **1** (gangster) boss; **jouer les ~s** to act tough; **2** ○(personne importante) big shot; (personne supérieure) star; (personne très compétente) wizard

caillasse /kajas/ nf (cailloux) stones (pl)

caille /kaj/ nf Zool quail

cailler /kaje/ [1]
A vtr to curdle
B vi (se figer) [lait] to curdle; [sang] to congeal
C **se cailler** vpr **1** [lait] to curdle; [sang] to congeal; **2** ○(avoir froid) [personne] to be freezing
D ○v impers **ça caille** it's freezing

caillot /kajo/ nm clot

caillou, pl **~x** /kaju/ nm **1** (pierre) pebble; **gros ~** stone; **du ~**○ rock ⊄; **avoir un ~ à la place du cœur** fig to have a heart of stone; **2** ○(tête) **ne plus avoir un poil sur le ~** to be as bald as a coot○; **ne rien avoir dans le ~** to be brainless

caillouteux, -euse /kajutø, øz/ adj [sol, route] stony

caïman /kaimɑ̃/ nm cayman

Caire /kɛʀ/ ▸ p. 621 npr **le ~** Cairo

caisse /kɛs/ nf **1** (boîte) gén crate; (de champagne, vin) case, crate; (bac) planter; **2** (de voiture) shell, body; **3** ○(voiture) car, old banger○; **4** (tambour) drum; **5** (pour l'argent) (tiroir) till; (appareil) cash register; (coffret) cash box; **les ~s de l'État** the Treasury coffers; **tenir la ~** (normalement) to be the cashier; (un moment) to be on the cash desk; fig to hold the purse strings; **6** (guichet) (de magasin) cash desk; (de supermarché) checkout (counter); (de banque) cashier's desk; **7** (capital, organisme) fund; **~ de secours** relief fund

⟨Composés⟩ **~ enregistreuse** cash register; **~ d'épargne** ≈ savings bank; **~ noire** slush fund; **~ à outils** toolbox

⟨Idiome⟩ **à fond la ~**○ [partir, s'en aller] at breakneck speed; [mettre la musique] at full blast

caissette /kɛsɛt/ nf gén small box ou case; (pour fruits) crate

caissier, -ière /kesje, ɛʀ/ ▸ p. 372 nm,f cashier

caisson /kɛsɔ̃/ nm (à bouteilles) crate

⟨Composé⟩ **~ de décompression** decompression chamber

cajoler /kaʒɔle/ [1] vtr (être tendre avec) to make a fuss over; (flatter) to bring [sb] round GB ou around US

cajolerie /kaʒɔlʀi/ nf (caresse) cuddle; (parole) compliment

cajoleur, -euse /kaʒɔlœʀ, øz/ adj (tendre) affectionate

cajou /kaʒu/ nm **noix de ~** cashew nut

cake /kɛk/ nm fruit cake

cal /kal/ nm callus; **des ~s** calluses

calabrais, ~e /kalabʀɛ, ɛz/ ▸ p. 504 adj Calabrian

calamar /kalamaʀ/ nm squid

calaminer: se calaminer /kalamine/ [1] vpr to carbonize, to coke up; **être calaminé** to be coked up

calamité /kalamite/ nf **1** (malheur) disaster, calamity; **2** ○(personne insupportable) pain○; (catastrophe ambulante) walking disaster

calandre /kalɑ̃dʀ/ nf Aut (radiator) grille^GB

calcaire /kalkɛʀ/
A adj [sel] calcium (épith); [eau] hard; [minéral] calcareous; [terrain] chalky; [plateau, roche] limestone (épith)
B nm **1** (roche) limestone; **2** (dépôt blanc) fur GB, sediment US; **enlever le ~ d'une bouilloire** to descale a kettle

calcification /kalsifikasjɔ̃/ nf calcification

calciné, ~e /kalsine/ adj (carbonisé) charred; (soumis à une chaleur intense) scorched

calciner /kalsine/ [1] vtr (carboniser) to char; (au four) to burn [sth] to a crisp; Chimie to calcine

calcium /kalsjɔm/ nm calcium

calcul /kalkyl/
A nm **1** (opération) calculation; **faire des ~s** to make some calculations; **faire le ~ de qch** to calculate sth; **'à combien est-ce que ça va me revenir?'—'attends, il faut que je fasse le ~'** 'how much will it come to?'—'wait, I'll have to work it out'; **2** (matière) arithmetic; **3** (tactique) calculation; **agir par ~** to act out of self-interest; **être un bon ~** to be a good move; **4** Méd stone
B **calculs** nmpl (estimations) calculations

⟨Composés⟩ **~ mental** mental arithmetic; **~ rénal** kidney stone; **~ urinaire** stone in the bladder

calculateur, -trice^1 /kalkylatœʀ, tʀis/
A adj calculating
B nm,f calculating person; **c'est un ~** he's very calculating
C nm Ordinat computer

calculatrice^2 /kalkylatʀis/ nf (pocket) calculator

calculer /kalkyle/ [1]
A vtr **1** (compter) to calculate, to work out; **2** (évaluer) to weigh up [avantages, chances]; to gauge [résultats, effort]; **~ son rythme** Sport to pace oneself; **tout bien calculé** all things considered; **3** (préméditer) **~ son coup** to plan one's move
B vi to calculate

calculette /kalkylɛt/ nf pocket calculator

Caldoche /kaldɔʃ/ nmf European New Caledonian

cale /kal/ nf **1** (pour meuble, porte) wedge; (pour roue) chock; (pour surélever) block; **2** Naut (ship's) hold

calé○, **~e** /kale/ adj **1** (instruit) bright; **~ en qch** brilliant at sth; **2** (complexe) difficult

calebasse /kalbas/ nf **1** Bot calabash, gourd; **2** ○(tête) head

calèche /kalɛʃ/ nf barouche, calash

caleçon /kalsɔ̃/ nm **1** (sous-vêtement masculin) boxer shorts (pl), underpants (pl); **~ long** long johns○ (pl); **2** (vêtement féminin) leggings (pl)

calembour /kalɑ̃buʀ/ nm pun, play on words

calendes /kalɑ̃d/ nfpl calends

⟨Idiomes⟩ **aux ~ grecques** never in a month of Sundays○; **renvoyer qch aux ~ grecques** to postpone sth indefinitely

calendrier /kalɑ̃dʀije/ nm **1** calendar; **~ républicain** French Revolutionary calendar; **2** (programme) schedule; **3** (dates) dates (pl)

calepin /kalpɛ̃/ nm notebook

caler /kale/ [1]
A vtr **1** (stabiliser) to wedge [roue, pied de table]; to steady [meuble]; to support [rangée de livres]; **~ sa tête sur un oreiller** to rest one's head on a pillow; **2** ○(remplir) **petit déjeuner qui cale l'estomac** breakfast that fills you up
B vi **1** (s'arrêter) to stall; **2** (abandonner) to give up; **j'ai calé au dessert** I gave up when it came to the dessert; **~ sur un problème** to get stuck on a problem
C **se caler** vpr (s'installer) to settle (**dans** in)

calfeutrer /kalføtʀe/ [1]

A vtr to stop up [fissure]; to draughtproof [porte, fenêtre]

B se **calfeutrer** vpr to shut oneself away

calibre /kalibʀ/ nm ① (diamètre) (d'arme à feu, de tuyau, balle) calibreᴳᴮ; (de câble) diameter; **arme de gros** ~ large-bore weapon; ② (d'œufs, de fruits, légumes) size; ③ (étalon) gauge; ④ (mesure) template, pattern; ⑤ ○(pistolet) gun; ⑥ (de personne) calibreᴳᴮ

calibrer /kalibʀe/ [1] vtr ① (donner le calibre convenable à) to calibrate; ② (régler) to calibrate; ③ (classer) to size [œufs, fruits, légumes]

calice /kalis/ nm Relig chalice

calife /kalif/ nm caliph

califourchon: **à califourchon** /akalifuʀʃɔ̃/ loc adv astride; **à** ~ **sur une chaise** astride a chair

câlin, ~**e** /kɑlɛ̃, in/

A adj [air, ton] affectionate; [personne] cuddly

B nm cuddle; **faire un** ~ **à qn** to give sb a cuddle

câliner /kaline/ [1] vtr to cuddle

calleux, -**euse** /kalø, øz/ adj calloused, rough-skinned

calligraphie /kaligʀafi/ nf calligraphy

calligraphier /kaligʀafje/ [2] vtr to write [sth] in a decorative hand

callosité /kalozite/ nf callus

calmant, ~**e** /kalmɑ̃, ɑ̃t/

A adj gén [musique, parole] soothing; [médicament] sedative

B nm sedative

calmar /kalmaʀ/ nm squid

calme /kalm/

A adj ① (paisible) [mer, temps] calm; [ciel, nuit] still; [endroit, Bourse, vie, personne] quiet; ② (maître de soi) calm; **restons** ~**s!** let's keep calm!

B nmf (personne tranquille) calm person; **c'est un grand** ~ he is unflappable

C nm ① (environnement paisible) peace (and quiet); **j'ai besoin de** ~ I need peace and quiet; ② (absence d'agitation) calm; (de foule, d'assemblée) calmness; (de mer, nuit, sanctuaire) stillness; **lancer un appel au** ~ to appeal for calm; **c'est le** ~ **avant la tempête** lit, fig it's the calm before the storm; **le** ~ **est revenu** calm has returned; **dans le** ~ peacefully; ③ (maîtrise de soi) composure; **avec le plus grand** ~ with the greatest composure; **garder** or **conserver son** ~ to keep calm; **avec** ~ calmly; **du** ~**!** (reste tranquille) calm down!; (fais moins de bruit) quiet!; ④ (sérénité) inner peace; ⑤ Météo, Naut calm

calmement /kalməmɑ̃/ adv calmly

calmer /kalme/ [1]

A vtr ① (apaiser) to calm [sb/sth] down [personne, animal]; to defuse [situation]; to tone down [discussion]; to subdue [agitation, colère]; to allay [inquiétude]; ~ **le jeu** fig to calm things down; ~ **les esprits** to calm people down; ② (atténuer) to ease [douleur]; to bring down [fièvre]; to dampen [passions, désir]; to take the edge off [faim, soif]

B se **calmer** vpr ① (s'apaiser) [personne, situation] to calm down; [tempête] to abate; [agitation, colère] to die down; [discussion] to quieten ᴳᴮ ou quiet US down; [inquiétude] to subside; [désir] to cool; **calme-toi!** (reste tranquille) calm down!; (fais moins de bruit) quieten ᴳᴮ ou quiet US down!; **les esprits se sont calmés** tempers have cooled; ② (s'atténuer) [douleur] to ease; [fièvre, faim] to die down; [bruit] to subside

calomnie /kalɔmni/ nf slander

calomnier /kalɔmnje/ [2] vtr to slander

calomnieux, -**ieuse** /kalɔmnjø, øz/ adj slanderous

calorie /kalɔʀi/ nf calorie; **régime (à) basses** ~**s** low-calorie diet

calorifère /kalɔʀifɛʀ/ adj heat-conveying

calorifique /kalɔʀifik/ adj calorific

calorique /kalɔʀik/ adj calorie (épith); **ration/valeur** ~ calorie intake/content

calot /kalo/ nm (couvre-chef) Mil forage cap ᴳᴮ, overseas cap US; (pour femme) brimless hat

calotte /kalɔt/ nf ① (couvre-chef) skull cap; ② ○(tape) slap; fig **prendre une bonne** ~ to be given a slap

(Composé) ~ **glaciaire** icecap

calque /kalk/ nm (copie) tracing; (papier) tracing paper; (imitation) replica

calquer /kalke/ [1] vtr ① (imiter) to copy [comportement]; ~ **qch sur qch** to model sth on sth; ② (reproduire) to trace [motif, dessin]

calumet /kalymɛ/ nm calumet; ~ **de la paix** peace pipe; **fumer le** ~ **de la paix avec qn** fig to make (one's) peace with sb

calvados /kalvados/ nm calvados (apple brandy distilled in Normandy)

calvaire /kalvɛʀ/ nm (épreuves) ordeal; Relig (monument) wayside cross; (lieu) Calvary; Art Calvary

calvinisme /kalvinism/ nm Calvinism

calvitie /kalvisi/ nf (affection) baldness; **avoir un début de** ~ to be going bald

camaïeu /kamajø/ nm ① (pierre) cameo; ② Art monochrome (painting); **en** ~ in monochrome; ③ (de tissu) shades (pl); **en** ~ **vert** in green shades

camarade /kamaʀad/ nmf ① gén friend; ~ **d'école** schoolfriend; ~ **d'atelier** workmate; ~ **de régiment** army pal○ ou buddy○; ② Pol comrade; **la** ~ **Markova** Comrade Markova

camaraderie /kamaʀadʀi/ nf comradeship, camaraderie

Cambodge /kɑ̃bɔdʒ/ ▸ p. 230 nprm Cambodia

cambouis /kɑ̃bwi/ nm dirty grease

(Idiome) **mettre les mains dans le** ~ to get one's hands dirty

cambré, ~**e** /kɑ̃bʀe/ adj [dos] arched; [pied, chaussure] with a high instep (épith, après n); **avoir le pied bien** ~ to have a finely arched foot

cambrer /kɑ̃bʀe/ [1]

A vtr to curve [objet]; to arch [chaussure]; ~ **les reins** or **le dos** to arch one's back

B se **cambrer** vpr [personne] to arch one's back

cambriolage /kɑ̃bʀijɔlaʒ/ nm burglary

cambrioler /kɑ̃bʀijɔle/ [1] vtr to burgle ᴳᴮ, to burglarize US; **se faire** ~ to be burgled ᴳᴮ, to be burglarized US

cambrioleur, -**euse** /kɑ̃bʀijɔlœʀ, øz/ nm,f burglar

cambrousse○ /kɑ̃bʀus/ nf **la** ~ the sticks○ (pl), the country; **en pleine** ~ in the middle of nowhere; **n'être jamais sorti de sa** ~ to be a country bumpkin

cambrure /kɑ̃bʀyʀ/ nf (état courbé) bending; (courbe) curve

(Composés) ~ **des pieds** instep; ~ **des reins** small of the back

came /kam/ nf ① (en mécanique) cam; ② ⊕(drogue) drugs (pl)

camé○, ~**e**[1] /kame/

A adj **être** ~ to be on drugs

B nm,f junkie○, drug addict

camée[2] /kame/ nm cameo

caméléon /kameleɔ̃/ nm lit, fig chameleon

camelote○ /kamlɔt/ nf pej junk○, rubbish ᴳᴮ

camembert /kamɑ̃bɛʀ/ nm ① (fromage) Camembert; ② (en statistique) pie chart

camer⊕: **se camer** /kame/ [1] vpr to be on drugs

caméra /kameʀa/ nf (cine-)camera ᴳᴮ, movie camera US

Cameroun /kamʀun/ ▸ p. 230 nprm Cameroon

camerounais, ~**e** /kamʀunɛ, ɛz/ ▸ p. 392 adj Cameroonian

caméscope® /kameskɔp/ nm camcorder

camion /kamjɔ̃/ nm truck, lorry ᴳᴮ

(Composés) ~ **à benne** tipper truck; ~ **de déménagement** removal van; ~ **frigorifique** refrigerated truck ou lorry ᴳᴮ; ~ **militaire** military truck

camion-citerne, pl **camions-citernes** /kamjɔ̃sitɛʀn/ nm tanker

camionnette /kamjɔnɛt/ nf van

camionneur /kamjɔnœʀ/ ▸ p. 372 nm (conducteur) lorry driver ᴳᴮ, truck driver

camisole /kamizɔl/ nf camisole; ~ **de force** straitjacket

camomille /kamɔmij/ nf (plante) camomile; (infusion) camomile tea

camouflage /kamuflaʒ/ nm ① Mil (dispositif) camouflage; **tenue de** ~ camouflage fatigues (pl); ② fig (de la vérité) concealing ₵; (transformation des faits) disguising ₵ (en as)

camoufler /kamufle/ [1]

A vtr ① Mil to camouflage; ② (cacher) to cover up [vérité]; to

conceal [*intention*]; to hide [*argent*]
B **se camoufler** *vpr* to hide; **se ~ le visage** to cover one's face

camp /kɑ̃/ *nm* **1** Mil camp; **~ d'entraînement** training camp; **2** (prison) camp; **~ de prisonniers** prison camp; **~ de détention** *or* **réclusion** detention centre^{GB}; **3** (campement provisoire) camp; **~ de réfugiés** refugee camp; **4** Sport, Pol side; **dans le ~ adverse** on the other side
(Composés) **~ de concentration** concentration camp; **~ d'extermination** extermination camp; **~ de la mort** death camp; **~ de travail** labour^{GB} camp
(Idiomes) **ficher**[○] *or* **foutre**[◐] **le ~** to split[○], to leave; **tout fout le ~**[◐] everything is falling apart

campagnard, ~e /kɑ̃paɲaʀ, aʀd/
A *adj* [*vie, fête*] country (*épith*); [*accent, repas, meuble*] rustic
B *nm,f* country person; **les ~s** country people

campagne /kɑ̃paɲ/ *nf* **1** (régions rurales) country; (paysage) (open) countryside; **habiter (à) la ~** to live in the country; **en pleine ~** in the countryside; **2** (opération) campaign; **~ électorale/publicitaire** election/advertising campaign; **~ de vaccination** vaccination drive; **faire ~** to campaign; **se mettre en ~ pour trouver qch** fig to set about finding sth; **3** (période d'activité) year; **4** Mil campaign; **se mettre en ~ pour trouver qch** fig to set about finding sth
(Idiome) **battre la ~**[○] to be off one's rocker[○]

campagnol /kɑ̃paɲɔl/ *nm* vole

campanule /kɑ̃panyl/ *nf* campanula, bellflower

campement /kɑ̃pmɑ̃/ *nm* (lieu) camp; **établir un ~** to set up camp; **matériel de ~** camping equipment

camper /kɑ̃pe/ [1]
A *vtr* (décrire) to portray [*personnage*]; to depict [*paysage, scène*]
B *vi* to camp; **~ sur ses positions** fig to stand firm
C **se camper** *vpr* **se ~ devant qch/qn** to stand squarely in front of sth/sb

campeur, -euse /kɑ̃pœʀ, øz/ *nm,f* camper

camphre /kɑ̃fʀ/ *nm* camphor

camping /kɑ̃piŋ/ *nm* **1** (activité) camping; **faire du ~** to go camping; **faire du ~ sauvage** to camp rough; **2** (lieu) campsite GB, campground US

camping-gaz® /kɑ̃piŋgaz/ *nm inv* camping stove

campus /kɑ̃pys/ *nm inv* campus; **hors ~** off-campus

Canada /kanada/ ▸ p. 230 *nprm* Canada

Canadair® /kanadɛʀ/ *nm* water bomber, air tanker

canadien, -ienne¹ /kanadjɛ̃, ɛn/ ▸ p. 392 *adj* Canadian

canadienne² /kanadjɛn/ *nf* (veste) sheepskin-lined jacket; (tente) ridge tent

canaille /kanɑj/
A *adj* mischievous
B *nf* (personne) villain; **petite ~** rascal

canal, *pl* **-aux** /kanal, o/ *nm* **1** (voie navigable) canal; **le Grand Canal** the Grand Canal; **2** (moyen) channel; **3** Anat (tube) duct; **4** Télécom (fréquence) channel

canalisation /kanalizasjɔ̃/ *nf* **1** (tuyau) pipe; (réseau) mains (*pl*); **2** (action de diriger) channelling^{GB}

canaliser /kanalize/ [1] *vtr* **1** to canalize [*cours d'eau*]; **2** (diriger) to channel

canapé /kanape/ *nm* **1** (siège) sofa, settee; **~ convertible** sofa bed; **2** Culin canapé

canapé-lit, *pl* **canapés-lits** /kanapeli/ *nm* sofa bed

canaque /kanak/ *adj* Kanak

canard /kanaʀ/ *nm* **1** (animal) duck; **chasse aux ~s** duck shooting; **2** [○](sucre) sugar lump dipped in coffee or brandy; **3** [○](journal) rag[○], newspaper; **4** Mus (fausse note) wrong note; **5** [○](terme d'affection) darling
(Composés) **~ de Barbarie** Muscovy duck; **~ boiteux** fig lame duck; **~ laqué** Peking duck
(Idiome) **ça ne casse pas trois** *or* **quatre pattes à un ~**[○] it's nothing to write home about

canarder[○] /kanaʀde/ [1] *vtr* lit, fig to snipe at [*personne, positions*]

canari /kanaʀi/ *nm* (oiseau) canary

canasson[◐] /kanasɔ̃/ *nm* nag[○], horse

cancan /kɑ̃kɑ̃/ *nm* **1** [○](commérage) gossip **¢**; **faire** *or* **raconter des ~s** to gossip; **2** (danse) (French) ~ cancan

cancaner[○] /kɑ̃kane/ [1] *vi* [*personne*] to gossip

cancanier, -ière /kɑ̃kanje, ɛʀ/ *adj* [*personne*] gossipy (*épith*); **il est (très) ~** he's a (real) gossip

cancer /kɑ̃sɛʀ/ *nm* **1** ▸ p. 195 Méd cancer; **avoir un ~** to have cancer; **un ~ du sein** breast cancer; **~ de l'estomac** cancer of the stomach; **2** fig cancer

Cancer /kɑ̃sɛʀ/ ▸ p. 635 *nprm* Cancer

cancéreux, -euse /kɑ̃seʀø, øz/
A *adj* [*tumeur, cellule*] cancerous; [*personne*] with cancer (*épith*, *après n*)
B *nm,f* gén person with cancer; (sous traitement) cancer patient

cancérigène /kɑ̃seʀiʒɛn/ *adj* carcinogenic

cancérologie /kɑ̃seʀɔlɔʒi/ *nf* cancer research; **service de ~** cancer ward

cancre /kɑ̃kʀ/ *nm* dunce

cancrelat /kɑ̃kʀəla/ *nm* cockroach

candélabre /kɑ̃delabʀ/ *nm* candelabra GB, candelabrum US

candeur /kɑ̃dœʀ/ *nf* ingenuousness

candi /kɑ̃di/ *adj m* **fruit ~** candied fruit; **sucre ~** sugar candy

candidat, ~e /kɑ̃dida, at/ *nm,f* **1** Pol candidate; **être** *or* **se porter ~ aux élections** to stand for election GB, to run for office US; **~ désigné** *or* **officiel** nominee; **2** (à un examen) candidate; **les ~s au permis de conduire** people taking the driving test; **3** (à un poste, statut) applicant (à for); **le ~ retenu** the successful applicant; **être** *or* **se porter ~ (à un poste)** to apply (for a post); **4** Jeux contestant (à in); **5** (aspirant) **il n'est pas ~ au mariage** he's not the marrying type; **pour la vaisselle, il n'y a pas beaucoup de ~s** hum when it comes to doing the dishes, there aren't many takers *ou* volunteers

candidature /kɑ̃didatyʀ/ *nf* **1** (à une élection) candidacy; **retirer sa ~** to stand down GB, to drop out US; **2** (à un poste, statut) application; **~ spontanée** unsolicited application; **faire acte de ~** to apply (à for)

candide /kɑ̃did/ *adj* ingenuous

cane /kan/ *nf* (female) duck

caneton /kantɔ̃/ *nm* duckling

canette /kanɛt/ *nf* **1** (bouteille) **~ (de bière)** (small) bottle of beer; **2** (boîte) **~ de bière** can of beer; **3** (de machine à coudre) spool; **4** Zool (female) duckling

canevas /kanva/ *nm inv* (toile) canvas; (ouvrage) tapestry work; fig framework

caniche /kaniʃ/ *nm* poodle; **~ nain** toy poodle

caniculaire /kanikylɛʀ/ *adj* scorching

canicule /kanikyl/ *nf* **1** (chaleur) **hier, c'était la ~** yesterday was a real scorcher[○]; **sortir en pleine ~** to go out in the scorching heat; **2** (période chaude) dog days (*pl*); (vague de chaleur) heatwave

canif /kanif/ *nm* gén penknife, pocketknife

canin, ~e¹ /kanɛ̃, in/ *adj* [*race*] canine; [*exposition, nourriture*] dog (*épith*)

canine² /kanin/ *nf* (dent) canine (tooth)

caniveau, *pl* **-x** /kanivo/ *nm* (de chaussée) gutter

canne /kan/ *nf* **1** (pour marcher) (walking) stick; **une ~ à pommeau** a stick with a knob; **2** Bot cane; **3** [◐](jambe) pin[○], leg
(Composés) **~ anglaise** (forearm) crutch; **~ à pêche** fishing rod; **~ à sucre** sugar cane

canné, ~e /kane/ *adj* [*fauteuil, chaise*] cane (*épith*)

canneberge /kanbɛʀʒ/ *nf* cranberry

cannelé, ~e /kanle/ *adj* [*colonne, verre*] fluted

cannelle /kanɛl/ *nf* cinnamon

cannelure /kanlyʀ/ *nf* (de colonne) flute; **~s** fluting **¢**

cannette = **canette 1, 2, 3**

cannibale /kanibal/
A *adj* cannibal (*épith*)
B *nmf* cannibal

cannibalisme /kanibalism/ *nm* cannibalism

canoë /kanɔe/ ▸ p. 327 *nm* **1** (embarcation) (Canadian) canoe; **descendre une rivière en ~** to canoe down a river; **2** (sport) canoeing; **faire du ~** to go canoeing

canoë-kayak /kanɔekajak/ ▸ p. 327 *nm* canoeing

canon /kanɔ̃/
A *adj m inv* Jur **droit ~** canon law
B *nm* **1** Mil (arme) (big) gun; (sur un avion) cannon; Hist cannon;

~ de 75 (mm) 75-mm gun; **tirer un coup de ~** to fire a gun; **entendre des coups de ~** to hear cannon fire; **boulet de ~** cannonball; ② Mil (tube d'arme) barrel; **à ~ lisse** smoothbore (épith); **à ~ rayé** rifled; **fusil à ~ double** double-barrelledᴳᴮ shotgun; **fusil à ~ scié** sawn-off GB ou sawed-off US shotgun; ③ Mus canon; **chanter en ~** to sing in a round; ④ (principe) canon; ⑤ Relig canon

Composés ~ **antiaérien** antiaircraft gun; ~ **arroseur** sprinkler; ~ **à eau** water cannon; ~ **mitrailleur** heavy machine gun; ~ **à neige** snow-blower

cañon /kanjɔ̃, kanjɔn/ nm canyon

canonique /kanɔnik/ adj Relig [décret] canonical; **droit ~** canon law; **d'âge ~** hum of a venerable age

canoniser /kanɔnize/ [1] vtr to canonize

canonnière /kanɔnjɛʀ/ nf (navire) gunboat

canot /kano/ nm (small) boat, dinghy; ~ **pneumatique** rubber ou inflatable dinghy; ~ **de sauvetage** Naut lifeboat; Aviat life raft

canotier /kanɔtje/ nm (chapeau) boater

canson® /kɑ̃sɔ̃/ nm drawing paper

cantate /kɑ̃tat/ nf cantata

cantatrice /kɑ̃tatʀis/ ▸ p. 372 nf (d'opéra) opera singer; (de musique classique) (professional) singer

cantine /kɑ̃tin/ nf ① (restaurant) canteen GB, cafeteria; ② (malle) tin trunk

cantique /kɑ̃tik/ nm canticle; **le Cantique des ~s** the Song of Songs

canton /kɑ̃tɔ̃/ nm Admin canton

cantonade: à la cantonade /alakɑ̃tɔnad/ loc adv **parler à la ~** to speak to no-one in particular; Théât to speak off

cantonais, ~e /kɑ̃tɔnɛ, ɛz/ ▸ p. 336, p. 621
Ⓐ adj Cantonese
Ⓑ nm Ling Cantonese

cantonal, ~e¹, mpl -aux /kɑ̃tɔnal, o/ adj cantonal

cantonale² /kɑ̃tɔnal/ nf Pol ~ **(partielle)** by-election; **les ~s** cantonal elections

cantonnement /kɑ̃tɔnmɑ̃/ nm Mil (stationnement) (dans une ville, région) stationing 𝒞; (chez l'habitant) billeting 𝒞; (lieu) gén quarters (pl); (camp) station

cantonner /kɑ̃tɔne/ [1]
Ⓐ vtr ① Mil gén to station; (chez l'habitant) to billet (**chez** with); ② (restreindre) ~ **qn dans un lieu** to confine sb to a place; ~ **qn dans le rôle de** to reduce sb to the role of
Ⓑ **se cantonner** vpr **se ~ dans un rôle** to restrict oneself to a role

cantonnier /kɑ̃tɔnje/ ▸ p. 372 nm road-mender

canular /kanylaʀ/ nm hoax

canyon = cañon

caoutchouc /kautʃu/ nm ① (matière) rubber; **de** or **en ~** rubber (épith); **être en ~** to be made of rubber; ② (plante) rubber plant; ③ (élastique) rubber band

caoutchouteux, -euse /kautʃutø, øz/ adj rubbery

cap /kap/ nm ① Géog (promontoire) cape; **le ~ Horn** Cape Horn; **doubler** or **franchir un ~** to round a cape; ② (obstacle) hurdle; ③ (limite) mark; **passer le ~ de la cinquantaine** to pass the fifty mark; ④ (orientation) course; **changer de ~** to change course; **mettre le ~ sur** to head for; **mettre le ~ au sud** to head south

Cap /kap/ ▸ p. 621 npr **le ~** Capetown

CAP /seape/ nm: abbr ▸ **certificat**

capable /kapabl/ adj capable (**de faire** of doing); **c'est quelqu'un de très ~** he's a very capable person; **il n'est même pas ~ de faire cuire un œuf dur** he can't even boil an egg!; **il est ~ de tout pour garder sa place** he would do anything to keep his job; **ils sont bien ~s de nous dénoncer** I wouldn't put it past them to turn us in; **'bon salaire si ~'** 'good salary for the right person'

capacité /kapasite/ nf ① (aptitude) ability; **un chercheur d'une grande ~** a researcher of great ability; ② (potentiel) capacity; ~ **de 100 mégawatts** 100 megawatt capacity; ~ **de mémoire** Ordinat memory capacity ou size; ~ **d'accueil d'un hôtel** capacity of a hotel; **machine à laver à ~ variable** washing machine with variable load settings

Composé ~ **en droit** Univ, Jur basic legal qualification

cape /kap/ nf cape; **film de ~ et d'épée** swashbuckler

Idiome **rire sous ~** to laugh up one's sleeve

capeline /kaplin/ nf wide-brimmed hat

CAPES /kapɛs/ nm (abbr = **certificat d'aptitude professionnelle à l'enseignement secondaire**) secondary school teaching qualification

capharnaüm /kafaʀnaɔm/ nm shamblesᴼ (+ v sg); **quel ~, ta chambre!** what a shambles your room is!

capillaire /kapilɛʀ/
Ⓐ adj ① (de vaisseau sanguin) capillary; ② (de cheveu) hair (épith); **soins ~s** hair care
Ⓑ nm Anat capillary

capitaine /kapitɛn/ ▸ p. 283 nm ① Mil (dans l'armée de terre, la marine) ≈ captain; (dans l'armée de l'air) ≈ flight lieutenant GB, ≈ captain US; ② Sport captain

Composés ~ **de corvette** ≈ lieutenant commander; ~ **de frégate** ≈ commander; ~ **d'industrie** captain of industry; ~ **au long cours** fully-licensed captain; ~ **des pompiers** fire chief; ~ **de port** harbourᴳᴮ master; ~ **de vaisseau** ≈ captain

capitainerie /kapitɛnʀi/ nf ① (administration) port authority; ② (bâtiment) port authority buildings (pl)

capital, ~e¹, mpl -aux /kapital, o/
Ⓐ adj ① (fondamental) gén key (épith), crucial, [importance] major; **une découverte ~e dans la recherche contre le cancer** a major breakthrough in cancer research; **c'est d'une importance ~e** it's of the utmost importance; **il est ~ de faire** it's essential to do; ② [lettre] capital; ③ (de mort) **peine ~e** capital punishment
Ⓑ nm ① Fin capital; ② Écon capital; **le ~ et le travail** capital and labourᴳᴮ; ③ (ressource) **notre ~ santé** our health; **le ~ humain/industriel** human/industrial resources (pl)

Composé ~ **décès** death benefit

capitale² /kapital/ nf ① (d'un pays) capital (city); ② (centre) capital; **Lyon, ~ des gourmets** Lyon, a paradise for gourmets; ③ (lettre) capital; **en ~s d'imprimerie** in block capitals

capitaliser /kapitalize/ [1] vtr to capitalize

capitalisme /kapitalism/ nm capitalism

capitaliste /kapitalist/ adj, nmf capitalist

capital-risque /kapitalʀisk/ nm inv venture capital

Capitole /kapitɔl/ nprm ① (de Rome) (colline) **(mont) ~** Capitoline; (temple) Capitol; ② (de Washington) Capitol

capitonner /kapitɔne/ [1] vtr to pad

capitulation /kapitylasjɔ̃/ nf capitulation (**devant** to); ~ **sans conditions** unconditional surrender

capituler /kapityle/ [1] vi to capitulate (**devant** to)

caporal, pl -aux /kapɔʀal, o/ ▸ p. 283 nm ① Mil (armée de terre) ≈ corporal; (armée de l'air) ≈ corporal GB, ≈ sergeant US; ② (tabac) caporal

caporal-chef, pl caporaux-chefs /kapɔʀalʃɛf, kapɔʀoʃɛf/ ▸ p. 283 nm (armée de terre) rank between corporal and sergeant; (armée de l'air) rank between corporal and sergeant GB ou staff sergeant US

capot /kapo/ nm Aut bonnet GB, hood US

capotage /kapɔtaʒ/ nm (échec) collapse

capote /kapɔt/ nf ① (manteau) great-coat; ② (de voiture, landau) hood GB, top; ③ ᴼ(préservatif) ~ **(anglaise)** condom, French letterᴼ

capoter /kapɔte/ [1] vi ① (échouer) to collapse; **faire ~** to ruin; ② (se retourner) [voiture] to overturn

câpre /kɑpʀ/ nf caper; **sauce aux ~s** caper sauce

caprice /kapʀis/ nm ① (fantaisie) (de personne) whim; (de temps, marché, nature, voiture) vagaries (pl); **sur un ~** on a whim; **céder aux ~s de qn** to indulge sb's whims; ② (accès de colère) tantrum; **faire un ~** to throw a tantrum

capricieusement /kapʀisjøzmɑ̃/ adv (comme un enfant gâté) capriciously; (avec fantaisie) whimsically

capricieux, -ieuse /kapʀisjø, øz/ adj [personne] capricious; [mécanisme] temperamental; [temps, destin] fickle; [cours d'eau] irregular

capricorne /kapʀikɔʀn/ nm capricorn beetle

Capricorne /kapʀikɔʀn/ ▸ p. 635 nprm Capricorn

câprier /kɑpʀije/ nm caper shrub

La capacité

■ *Pour mesurer les liquides, on utilise traditionnellement les* pints, *les* quarts *(rares aujourd'hui) et les* gallons *en Grande-Bretagne et aux États-Unis. Les liquides comme le vin ou l'essence sont de plus en plus vendus au litre, mais cela n'a pas modifié les habitudes des consommateurs. L'automobiliste anglais ou américain achète donc désormais son essence en litres, mais compte toujours sa consommation en gallons.*

■ *Pour les mesures en* cm^3, dm^3, m^3 *etc. voir* **le volume ▸ p. 628**. *Pour la prononciation des nombres, voir* **les nombres ▸ p. 398**.

Les mesures britanniques: équivalences

				dire	
1 pint	= 0,57l	1 litre* 1l†	=	1.76‡ pt	*pint*
1 quart	= 2 pints = 1,13l			0.88 qt	*quarts*
1 gallon	= 8 pints = 4,54l			0.22 galls	*gallons*

Les mesures américaines: équivalences

				dire	
1 pint	= 0,47l	1 litre* 1l†	=	2.12‡ pts	*pint*
1 quart	= 2 pints = 0,94l			1.06 qt	*quarts*
1 gallon	= 8 pints = 3,78l			0.26 galls	*gallons*

* *Attention: on écrit* litre *en anglais britannique, et* liter *en anglais américain.*

† *L'abréviation de* litre (l) *est la même en anglais qu'en français.*

‡ *Noter que l'anglais utilise un point là où le français a une virgule.*

il y a 1 000 centimètres cubes dans un litre
= there are 1,000 cubic centimetres in a litre

1 000 centimètres cubes font un litre
= 1,000 cubic centimetres make one litre

il y a huit pintes dans un gallon
= there are eight pints in a gallon

quelle est la contenance de la bouteille?
= what is the size of the bottle?
    ou (moins familier) what is the capacity of the bottle?

combien contient-elle?
= what does it hold?

elle contient 2 litres
= it holds two litres

elle a une contenance de 2 litres
= its capacity is two litres

la contenance de la bouteille est de 2 litres
= the capacity of the bottle is two litres

■ *Noter l'absence d'équivalent anglais de la préposition française de* avant *le chiffre dans les deux derniers exemples.*

la bouteille fait 2 litres
= the bottle holds 2 litres

elle fait à peu près 2 litres
= it holds about 2 litres

presque 3 litres
= almost 3 litres

plus de 2 litres
= more than 2 litres

moins de 3 litres
= less than 3 litres

A a une plus grande contenance que B
= A has a greater capacity than B

B a une moins grande contenance que A
= B has a smaller capacity than A

A a la même contenance que B
= A has the same capacity as B

A et B ont la même contenance
= A and B have the same capacity

■ *Noter l'ordre des mots dans les adjectifs composés anglais, et l'utilisation du trait d'union. Noter aussi que* litre, *employé comme adjectif, ne prend pas la marque du pluriel.*

une bouteille de deux litres
= a 2-litre bottle

un réservoir de 200 litres
= a 200-litre tank

■ *Mais on peut également dire* a tank 200 litres in capacity.

deux litres de vin
= two litres of wine

vendu au litre
= sold by the litre

ils utilisent 20 000 litres par jour
= they use 20,000 litres a day

elle fait 8 litres aux 100
= it does 28 miles to the gallon

■ *En anglais, on compte la consommation d'une voiture en mesurant non pas le nombre de litres nécessaires pour parcourir 100 kilomètres, mais la distance parcourue (en miles) avec 4,54 litres (un gallon) de carburant.*

---

capsule /kapsyl/ *nf* ① (de bouteille) (bouchon) cap; (enveloppe du bouchon) capsule; ② (médicament) capsule; ③ (de fusée) capsule; ④ (détonateur) cap

capsuler /kapsyle/ [1] *vtr* to put a cap on [*bouteille*]

capter /kapte/ [1] *vtr* ① (recevoir) to get [*émission, chaîne*]; to pick up; ② (saisir) to capture [*expression, image*]; ③ (attirer) to catch [*attention*]; ④ (absorber) to soak up [*lumière*]; ⑤ (recueillir) to collect [*eaux*]

capteur /kaptœr/ *nm* sensor; ∼ **à infrarouges** infra-red sensor

Composé ∼ **solaire** solar cell

captif, -ive /kaptif, iv/ *adj, nm,f* captive

captivant, ∼e /kaptivɑ̃, ɑ̃t/ *adj* [*livre*] enthralling; [*récit*] gripping; [*moment*] riveting; [*musique*] captivating

captiver /kaptive/ [1] *vtr* [*beauté*] to captivate; [*voix, musique*] to enthral^{GB}; [*histoire, personne*] to fascinate

captivité /kaptivite/ *nf* captivity; **vingt ans de** ∼ twenty years in captivity

capture /kaptyr/ *nf* ① (action d'attraper) capture; ② (ce qui est attrapé) catch; **une belle** ∼ a good catch

capturer /kaptyre/ [1] *vtr* lit, fig to capture

capuche /kapyʃ/ *nf* hood

capuchon /kapyʃɔ̃/ *nm* (de vêtement) hood; (de stylo) cap

capucin /kapysɛ̃/ *nm* (moine) Capuchin friar

capucine /kapysin/ *nf* nasturtium

Cap-Vert /kapvɛr/ ▸ p. 303, p. 230 *nprm* **îles du** ∼ Cape Verde islands

caquet /kakɛ/ *nm* (de bavard) prattle; **rabattre son** ∼[○] to stop crowing[○]; **rabattre le** ∼ **à qn**[○] to put sb in his/her place, to take sb down a peg or two

caqueter /kakte/ [20] *vi* [*poule*] to cackle; [*bavard*] to prattle

car¹ /kaʀ/ *conj* because, for

car² /kaʀ/ *nm* (véhicule) coach GB, bus

(Composés) ~ **de police** police van; ~ **(de ramassage) scolaire** school bus

carabine /kaʀabin/ *nf* [1] (arme) rifle; ~ **22 long rifle** .22 rifle; ~ **à air comprimé** air rifle; ~ **à plombs** shotgun; [2] (jouet) toy gun; ~ **à flèches** pop gun

carabiné, ~**e** /kaʀabine/ *adj* [fièvre] raging; [migraine] ferocious; [rhume] stinking○

carabinier /kaʀabinje/ *nm* [1] (policier italien) carabiniere; **les** ~**s** the carabinieri; [2] Hist carabineer

Carabosse /kaʀabɔs/ *npr* **la fée** ~ the wicked fairy

caracoler /kaʀakɔle/ [1] *vi* [1] (avoir une position favorable) to be well ahead; ~ **en tête** to be well in the lead; [2] [cheval] to prance; [cavalier] to parade

caractère /kaʀaktɛʀ/ *nm* [1] (signe d'écriture) character; ~**s d'imprimerie** (type d'écriture) block capitals; **en gros** ~**s** in large print; **en** ~**s gras** in bold type; [2] (tempérament) nature; **nous n'avons pas le même** ~ we are different characters; **avoir bon** ~ to be good-natured; **avoir mauvais** ~ to be bad-tempered; **être d'un** ~ **facile** to have an easy-going nature; **avoir un sacré**○ ~ (coléreux) to have a foul temper; (difficile) to be absolutely impossible; [3] (forte personnalité) character; **avoir du** ~ to have character; **il n'a aucun** ~ he's got no backbone; [4] (de maison, lieu) character; **'fermette de** ~**'** 'small farm with character'; [5] (type humain) character; **une étude de** ~**s** a study of character types; [6] (marque distinctive) characteristic; [7] (côté, valeur) nature; **avoir un** ~ **politique** to be of a political nature; **ma demande n'a aucun** ~ **définitif** my request has nothing definite about it; **film à** ~ **pornographique** pornographic film

(Idiomes) **avoir un** ~ **de chien** *or* **cochon**○, **avoir un sale** ~ to have a vile temper; **avoir un** ~ **en or** to have a delightful nature

caractériel, **-ielle** /kaʀakteʀjɛl/ *adj* [troubles] emotional; [personne] disturbed

caractériser /kaʀakteʀize/ [1]
A *vtr* to characterize
B se caractériser *vpr* to be characterized (**par** by)

caractéristique /kaʀakteʀistik/
A *adj* characteristic
B *nf* characteristics (*pl*)

carafe /kaʀaf/ *nf* [1] (récipient) carafe; [2] ○(tête) head; **ne rien avoir dans la** ~○ to have nothing upstairs○

carafon /kaʀafɔ̃/ *nm* (récipient) small carafe

caraïbe /kaʀaib/ *adj* Caribbean

Caraïbes /kaʀaib/
A *nmpl* (peuple) Caribs
B *nprfpl* [1] ▸ p. 303 (îles) Caribbean (islands); [2] ▸ p. 406 (mer) **mer des** ~ Caribbean Sea

carambolage /kaʀãbɔlaʒ/ *nm* (de voitures) pile-up

caramboler /kaʀãbɔle/ [1]
A *vtr* to collide with
B se caramboler *vpr* to collide with each other

caramel /kaʀamɛl/ *nm* [1] (liquide) caramel; [2] (bonbon) toffee GB, toffy US; ~ **mou** ≈ fudge

caraméliser /kaʀamelize/ [1]
A *vtr* (transformer) to caramelize; (recouvrir) to coat [sth] with caramel
B se caraméliser *vpr* to caramelize

carapace /kaʀapas/ *nf* (d'animal) shell, carapace; (protection) ~ **de béton** concrete shell; fig armour^GB

carapater○: **se carapater** /kaʀapate/ [1] *vpr* to beat it○

carat /kaʀa/ *nm* carat; **or 18** ~**s** 18-carat gold

(Idiome) **dernier** ~⁰ at the latest

caravane /kaʀavan/ *nf* (véhicule) caravan GB, trailer US; (de désert) caravan; ~ **publicitaire** publicity cars (*pl*)

(Idiome) **les chiens aboient, la** ~ **passe** sticks and stones may break my bones (but words will never hurt me)

caravelle /kaʀavɛl/ *nf* (bateau) caravel

carbonade /kaʀbɔnad/ *nf* (viande grillée) carbonado

carbone /kaʀbɔn/ *nm* carbon; (papier) carbon paper; (feuille) sheet of carbon paper

(Composé) ~ **14** carbon 14; **dater qch au** ~ **14** to carbon-date sth; **datation au** ~ **14** (radio)carbon dating

carbonique /kaʀbɔnik/ *adj* carbonic; **neige** ~ dry ice

carbonisé, ~**e** /kaʀbɔnize/ *adj* [1] [véhicule] burned-out (épith), burned out (jamais épith); [débris, arbre, corps] charred; [2] Culin burned to a cinder (jamais épith), burned

carboniser /kaʀbɔnize/ [1] *vtr* [1] Chimie to carbonize; [2] (brûler complètement) to burn [sb] to death [personne]; to reduce [sth] to ashes [forêt, maison, corps]; to char [objet, arbre, poutre]

carburant /kaʀbyʀã/ *nm* fuel

carburateur /kaʀbyʀatœʀ/ *nm* carburettor GB, carburetor US

carbure /kaʀbyʀ/ *nm* carbide; **les** ~**s** carbides

carburer /kaʀbyʀe/ [1]
A *vtr* Tech to carburize
B *vi* [1] Aut **bien/mal** ~ to be well/badly tuned; [2] ○(fonctionner) **il carbure au vin rouge** hum he runs on red wine; [3] ○(travailler dur) to work flat out

carcan /kaʀkã/ *nm* (entrave) ~ **administratif** administrative constraints (*pl*) *ou* straitjacket; **le** ~ **des institutions** institutional rigidity

carcasse /kaʀkas/ *nf* [1] (squelette d'animal) carcass; [2] ○(corps humain) body; **promener** *or* **traîner sa** ~ to bum around; [3] ○(épave de véhicule) shell; [4] (armature) (de navire) skeleton; (de bâtiment, hangar) frame

carcéral, ~**e**, *mpl* **-aux** /kaʀseʀal, o/ *adj* prison (épith); **le milieu** ~ the prison environment

cardan /kaʀdã/ *nm* universal joint

carder /kaʀde/ [1] *vtr* to card

cardiaque /kaʀdjak/
A *adj* heart (épith); **avoir des ennuis** ~**s** to have heart trouble; **être** ~ to have a heart condition
B *nmf* person with a heart condition

cardinal, ~**e**, *mpl* **-aux** /kaʀdinal, o/
A *adj* cardinal
B *nm* [1] ▸ p. 590 Relig cardinal; **le** ~ **Newman** Cardinal Newman; [2] Ling, Math cardinal number; [3] Zool cardinal (grosbeak), redbird US

cardiologie /kaʀdjɔlɔʒi/ *nf* cardiology

cardiologue /kaʀdjɔlɔg/ ▸ p. 372 *nmf* cardiologist

cardiopathie /kaʀdjɔpati/ *nf* heart disorder

cardon /kaʀdɔ̃/ *nm* cardoon

carême /kaʀɛm/ *nm* **le** ~ Lent; **observer le** ~ to observe *ou* keep Lent

(Idiome) **avoir une face de** ~ to look as miserable as sin

carence /kaʀãs/ *nf* [1] Méd deficiency; [2] (absence) lack; [3] (manquement) shortcomings (*pl*); **les** ~**s de la loi** the shortcomings of the law

carène /kaʀɛn/ *nf* hull (below the waterline)

caressant, ~**e** /kaʀesã, ãt/ *adj* [enfant, geste, regard, parole] affectionate; [vent, rayon] soft

caresse /kaʀɛs/ *nf* (à un animal) stroke; (à une personne) caress, stroke; **couvrir qn de** ~**s** to caress sb all over; **il aime les** ~**s** he likes being stroked; **faire une** ~ *or* **des** ~**s à** to stroke

caresser /kaʀese/ [1]
A *vtr* [1] (de la main) to stroke [animal, joue, cheveux, barbe, objet]; ~ **qn du regard** *or* **des yeux** to look at sb lovingly *ou* fondly; [2] (effleurer) [soleil, vent, lumière] to caress [joue, cheveux]; [3] (avoir en soi) to entertain [rêve, idée]
B se caresser *vpr* to stroke; **se** ~ **la barbe** to stroke one's beard

(Idiomes) ~ **qn dans le sens du poil** to stay on the right side of sb; ~ **la bouteille** to be on the bottle○

cargaison /kaʀgɛzɔ̃/ *nf* [1] (chargement) cargo; [2] ○(grande quantité) load

cargo /kaʀgo/ *nm* Naut freighter, cargo ship; ~ **mixte** passenger-cargo ship

cari /kaʀi/ = curry

caricatural, ~**e**, *mpl* **-aux** /kaʀikatyʀal, o/ *adj* [dessin] (deliberately) grotesque; [récit] caricatural

caricature /kaʀikatyʀ/ *nf* [1] (genre) caricature; [2] (dessin) (d'une personne) caricature; (de plusieurs personnes, situation) cartoon; **faire une** ~ to draw a caricature *ou* cartoon; [3] (représentation déformée) caricature; **dans ses romans il fait une** ~ **de la société** his novels caricature society; [4] (parodie) mockery; ~ **de procès** mockery of a trial

caricaturer /kaʀikatyʀe/ [1] *vtr* to caricature

caricaturiste /kaʀikatyʀist/ ▸ p. 372 *nmf* caricaturist, cartoonist

carie /kaʀi/ *nf* (lésion) decay **ℂ**; (trou) cavity

carié, **~e** /kaʀje/ *adj* decayed

carier /kaʀje/ [2]
A *vtr* to cause [sth] to decay [*dent*]
B **se carier** *vpr* [*dent*] to decay

carillon /kaʀijɔ̃/ *nm* **1** (d'église, de beffroi) (cloches) bells (*pl*); (sonnerie) chimes (*pl*); **2** (pendule) (chiming) clock; (sonnerie) chimes (*pl*); **une horloge à ~** a chiming clock; **3** (de porte) (door) chimes (*pl*)

carillonner /kaʀijɔne/ [1]
A *vtr* **1** [*cloches*] to chime [*heure*]; to chime (out) [*air*]; to ring *ou* peal out for [*événement*]; **2** °(faire savoir) to broadcast
B *vi* **1** [*cloches*] to ring out; (très fort) to peal out; **2** (à une porte) to ring (loudly)

carillonneur /kaʀijɔnœʀ/ *nm* bell-ringer

caritatif, **-ive** /kaʀitatif, iv/ *adj* charitable; **une association** *or* **organisation caritative** a charity

carlingue /kaʀlɛ̃g/ *nf* Aviat cabin; Naut keelson

carme /kaʀm/ *nm* Carmelite, white friar

carmélite /kaʀmelit/ *nf* Carmelite nun

carmin /kaʀmɛ̃/ ▸ p. 140
A *adj inv* carmine
B *nm* (matière) cochineal; (couleur) carmine

carnage /kaʀnaʒ/ *nm* carnage **ℂ**, massacre; **ils ont fait un véritable ~** they massacred everyone

carnassier, **-ière** /kaʀnasje, ɛʀ/
A *adj* carnivorous
B *nm* carnivore

carnaval, *pl* **~s** /kaʀnaval/ *nm* (fête) carnival

carnavalesque /kaʀnavalɛsk/ *adj* (grotesque) grotesque; (de carnaval) carnival (*épith*)

carne⁰ /kaʀn/ *nf* (viande) leathery meat

carné, **~e** /kaʀne/ *adj* meat-based (*épith*)

carnet /kaʀnɛ/ *nm* **1** (calepin) notebook; **2** (groupe de tickets, bons) book; **j'achète mes timbres en ~** I always buy a book of stamps
(Composés) **~ d'adresses** address book; **~ de chèques** chequebook GB, checkbook US; **~ de correspondance** *or* **de notes** Scol mark book; **~ de rendez-vous** appointments diary; **~ de route** travel journal; **~ de santé** health record; **~ à souches** counterfoil book

carnivore /kaʀnivɔʀ/
A *adj* Zool carnivorous
B *nm* carnivore; **les ~s** the carnivores

carotène /kaʀɔtɛn/ *nf* carotene

carotide /kaʀɔtid/ *adj*, *nf* carotid

carotte /kaʀɔt/
A ▸ p. 140 *adj inv* (orange foncé) carrot-coloured^GB; (roux) [*cheveux, poils*] carroty
B *nf* (plante) carrot; **~s râpées** grated carrot **ℂ**
(Idiomes) **les ~s sont cuites°** the game is up°; **manier la ~ et le bâton** to use stick-and-carrot tactics

carpe¹ /kaʀp/ *nm* carpus

carpe² /kaʀp/ *nf* carp
(Idiome) **il est resté muet comme une ~** he never said a word

carpette /kaʀpɛt/ *nf* **1** (tapis) rug; **2** °(personne) pej doormat°
(Idiome) **s'aplatir comme une ~ devant qn** to grovel to sb

carquois /kaʀkwa/ *nm* quiver

carre /kaʀ/ *nf* (de ski, patin) edge

carré, **~e** /kaʀe/
A *adj* **1** gén [*objet, forme*] square; **des chaussures à bout ~** square-toed shoes; **2** (anguleux) [*visage, menton, paume*] square; [*silhouette*] stocky; **~ d'épaules** broad-shouldered; **3** (direct) [*personne*] straightforward; [*réponse*] straight; [*refus*] outright; **4** ▸ p. 568 (mesure) square; **prix du** *or* **au mètre ~** price per square metre^GB
B *nm* **1** (figure) gén square; (de ciel, plantations) patch; (de chocolat) piece; **avoir une coupe au ~** [*femme*] to have one's hair cut in a bob; **je vais lui mettre la tête au ~°** I'll beat the hell out of him/her°; **un lit (fait) au ~** a meticulously made bed; **~ blanc** 'suitable for adults only' sign on French TV;

2 Math square; **le ~ de deux** two squared; **deux au ~ égale quatre** two squared is four; **3** (de viande) **~ d'agneau** rack of lamb; **4** (aux cartes) **avoir un ~ de dix** to have the four tens; **5** C (place) square

carreau, *pl* **~x** /kaʀo/ *nm* **1** (de sol) (floor) tile; (de mur) (wall) tile; **2** (carrelage) tiled floor; **3** (vitre) window-pane; **à petits ~x** with small panes; **faire les ~x** to clean the windows; **regarder à travers les ~x** to look out of the window; **4** (carré) (sur du papier) square; (sur du tissu) check; **papier à ~x** squared paper; **jupe à ~x** check(ed) skirt; **~x bleus et blancs** blue-and-white checked (*épith*); **papier à grands ~x** large-squared paper; **5** ▸ p. 327 Jeux (carte) diamonds (*pl*); **avoir du ~** to be holding diamonds; **6** Hist (marché) market (floor); **7** (de mine) pithead; **8** (d'arbalète) bolt
(Idiomes) **étendre qn sur le ~°** to lay sb out°; **rester sur le ~°** (dans une bagarre) to be killed; (dans une affaire) to be left high and dry°; **se tenir à ~°** to watch one's step

carrefour /kaʀfuʀ/ *nm* **1** (intersection) gén junction; (de deux routes) crossroads (+ *v sg*); **~ ferroviaire** railway junction *ou* intersection; **2** (lieu de passage) crossroads (+ *v sg*); (réseau de communications) transport hub; **~ international** international meeting point; **3** (moment stratégique) crossroads (*sg*); **être à un ~ de qch** to be at a crossroads in sth; **au ~ de la biologie et de la chimie** at the meeting point of biology and chemistry; **4** (forum) debate

carrelage /kaʀlaʒ/ *nm* **1** (sol) tiled floor; **2** (ensemble de carreaux) tiles (*pl*); (pose) tiling

carreler /kaʀle/ [19] *vtr* to tile

carrelet /kaʀlɛ/ *nm* (poisson) plaice

carreleur /kaʀlœʀ/ ▸ p. 372 *nm* tiler

carrément /kaʀemɑ̃/ *adv* **la situation devient ~ inquiétante** the situation is becoming downright worrying; **il vaut ~ mieux les jeter** it would be better just to throw them out; **reprenons ~ depuis le début** let's start again right from the beginning; **elle m'a ~ accusé de mentir** she accused me straight out of lying; **il a ~ démissionné** he went straight ahead and resigned

carrer: **se carrer** /kaʀe/ [1] *vpr* (s'installer) **se ~ dans un fauteuil** to ensconce oneself in an armchair

carrière /kaʀjɛʀ/ *nf* **1** (profession) career; **une ~ d'écrivain** a career as a writer; **militaire de ~** career officer; **faire ~ dans l'armée** to make a career in the army; **2** (lieu d'extraction) quarry; **~ d'ardoise** slate quarry; **~ de sable** sandpit

carriole /kaʀjɔl/ *nf* **1** (charrette) cart; **2** °(voiture) pej jalopy°, car

carrossable /kaʀɔsabl/ *adj* suitable for motor vehicles (*après n*)

carrosse /kaʀɔs/ *nm* (horse-drawn) coach; ▸ **roue**

carrosserie /kaʀɔsʀi/ *nf* (de voiture) bodywork; (conception) coachbuilding; (réparation) body repair work; **atelier de ~** body repair workshop

carrossier /kaʀɔsje/ ▸ p. 372 *nm* (réparateur) coachbuilder

carrousel /kaʀusɛl/ *nm* (pour enfants) merry-go-round, carousel

carrure /kaʀyʀ/ *nf* **1** lit shoulders (*pl*); **avoir une ~ imposante** to have broad shoulders; **2** fig innate qualities (*pl*), calibre^GB; **avoir la ~ d'un président** to have the necessary qualities to be a president

cartable /kaʀtabl/ *nm* (d'écolier) schoolbag; (avec des bretelles) satchel; (d'adulte) briefcase

carte /kaʀt/ *nf* **1** (pour écrire) card; **2** (document) gén card; (laissez-passer) pass; **3** ▸ p. 327 Jeux card; **~ à jouer** playing card; **jouer aux ~s** to play cards; **mettre ~s sur table** fig to put one's cards on the table; **il possède plus d'une ~ dans son jeu** he's got other cards up his sleeve; **4** Géog map; **~ marine/du ciel** sea/astronomical chart; **5** Biol **~ génétique** genetic menu; **6** (au restaurant) menu; **manger à la ~** to eat à la carte, to order from the menu; **horaire à la ~** fig personalized timetable; **activités sportives à la ~** choice (*sg*) of sporting activities
(Composés) **~ d'abonnement** Rail season ticket; **~ d'adhérent** membership card; **~ d'assuré social ≈** national insurance card; **~ bancaire** bank card; **~ bleue®** credit card; **~ de crédit** credit card; **~ d'électeur** polling card GB, voter registration card US; **~ d'étudiant** student card, student ID card; **~ de**

fidélité discount card; ~ **grise** car registration document *ou* (*pl*) papers US; ~ **d'identité** identity card, ID card; ~ **jeunes**® (young persons') railcard; Comm (young people's) discount card; ~ **kiwi**® ≈ family railcard; ~ **de lecteur** library card; ~ **magnétique** gén magnetic card; (pour ouvrir une porte) swipe card; ~ **maîtresse** lit master card; fig trump card; ~ **à mémoire** *or* **à microprocesseur** smart card; ~ **orange**® season ticket (*in the Paris region*); ~ **perforée** punch card; ~ **postale** postcard; ~ **de presse** press pass; ~ **professionnelle** identity card (*showing occupation*); ~ **à puce** smart card; ~ **de réduction** discount card; ~ **routière** roadmap; ~ **de sécurité sociale** = ~ **d'assuré social**; ~ **de séjour** resident's permit; ~ **SIM** Télécom SIM card; ~ **de téléphone** phonecard; ~ **vermeil**® senior citizen's rail pass; ~ **verte**® Aut ≈ certificate of motor insurance; ~ **des vins** wine list; ~ **de visite** gén visiting card; (d'affaires) business card; ~ **vitale** Ordinat social insurance smart card; ~ **de vœux** greetings card

(Idiomes) **donner ~ blanche à qn** to give sb carte blanche *ou* a free hand; **brouiller les ~s** to confuse the issue

ℹ️ Carte d'identité Not to be confused with a passport, this is a proof of identity carried by most French citizens. It is issued free of charge generally by the *préfecture* and is valid for ten years. Though not compulsory, it is often used to guarantee payments by cheque and is accepted as a travel document within EU member states.

cartel /kaʀtɛl/ *nm* [1] Écon cartel; [2] Pol coalition

carter /kaʀtɛʀ/ *nm* (de moteur) crankcase; (de boîte de vitesses) casing

carte-réponse, *pl* **cartes-réponses** /kaʀtʀepɔ̃s/ *nf* reply card

cartésien, -ienne /kaʀtezjɛ̃, ɛn/ *adj*, *nm,f* Cartesian

cartilage /kaʀtilaʒ/ *nm* Anat, Zool cartilage; Culin gristle

cartilagineux, -euse /kaʀtilaʒinø, øz/ *adj* Anat, Zool cartilaginous; Culin gristly

cartomancie /kaʀtɔmɑ̃si/ *nf* fortune-telling

cartomancien, -ienne /kaʀtɔmɑ̃sjɛ̃, ɛn/ ► p. 372 *nm,f* fortune-teller

carton /kaʀtɔ̃/ *nm* [1] (matière) cardboard; **de** *or* **en** ~ cardboard (*épith*); [2] (boîte) (cardboard) box; **c'est resté dans les ~s** lit it's still in the box; fig it didn't get past the drawing-board; [3] (carte) card

(Composés) ~ **à dessin** portfolio; ~ **d'invitation** invitation card; ~ **jaune** Sport yellow card; ~ **ondulé** corrugated cardboard; ~ **rouge** Sport red card

(Idiome) **faire un ~**○ (remporter un succès) to do great○; (tirer sur une cible) to shoot at a target

cartonné, ~e /kaʀtɔne/ *adj* **couverture ~e** (de livre) hard cover

cartonner /kaʀtɔne/ [1]
Ⓐ *vtr* (en reliure) to bind
Ⓑ ○*vi* (marquer) to score

carton-pâte /kaʀtɔ̃pɑt/ *nm inv* pasteboard; **en** *or* **de** ~ lit pasteboard (*épith*); fig cardboard (*épith*)

cartouche¹ /kaʀtuʃ/ *nm* (sur un plan) title block; (sur une carte) legend

cartouche² /kaʀtuʃ/ *nf* [1] (de fusil) cartridge; [2] (de stylo, d'imprimante) cartridge; (de gaz) refill; **une ~ d'encre** an ink cartridge; [3] (emballage) ~ **de cigarettes** carton of cigarettes; [4] Ordinat cartridge

(Composé) ~ **à blanc** Mil blank cartridge

(Idiome) **brûler ses dernières ~s** to play one's last cards

cartoucherie /kaʀtuʃʀi/ *nf* cartridge factory

cartouchière /kaʀtuʃjɛʀ/ *nf* cartridge belt

cas /kɑ/
Ⓐ *nm inv* [1] (circonstance) case; **en pareil ~** in such a case; **auquel ~** in which case; **dans tous les ~** in every case; **au ~ où il viendrait** in case he comes; **prends ta voiture, au ~ où**○ take your car, just in case; **en ~ de besoin** if necessary, if need be; **en ~ d'incendie** in the event of a fire; **savoir être sévère ou pas selon les ~** to know how to be strict or not, as circumstances dictate; **ne pas déranger sauf pour un ~ grave** do not disturb except in an emergency; **le ~ échéant** if need be; **dans le ~ contraire, vous devrez...** should the opposite occur, you will have to...;

dans le meilleur/pire des ~ at best/worst; **c'est un ~ à envisager** it's a possibility we should bear in mind; **en aucun ~** on no account; **elle ne veut en aucun ~ quitter son domicile** she doesn't want to leave her home under any circumstances; **c'est le ~ de le dire!** you can say that again!; [2] (situation particulière) case; **étudier le ~ de qn** to look into sb's case; **le ~ de Sophie est spécial** Sophie's is a special case; **au ~ par ~** case by case; **être dans le même ~ que qn** to be in the same position as sb; **n'aggrave pas ton ~** don't make things worse for yourself; [3] (occurrence) case; **un ~ rare** a rare occurrence; **c'est vraiment un ~ ta sœur!** hum your sister is a real case○; [4] (en grammaire) case; [5] (cause) **c'est un ~ de renvoi** it's grounds for dismissal
Ⓑ **en tout cas, en tous les cas** *loc adv* [1] (assurément) in any case, at any rate; **ce n'est pas moi en tout ~** it's not me at any rate; [2] (du moins) at least

(Composés) ~ **de conscience** moral dilemma; ~ **de figure** scenario; ~ **de force majeure** case of force majeure; ~ **limite** borderline case; ~ **social** socially disadvantaged person; ~ **type** typical case

(Idiome) **il a fait grand ~ de son avancement** he made a big thing of his promotion; **elle n'a fait aucun ~ de mon avancement** she didn't attach much importance to my promotion

casanier, -ière /kazanje, ɛʀ/ *adj* [personne] stay-at-home (*épith*); [existence] unadventurous; **il est très ~** he's a real stay-at-home *ou* homebody US

casaque /kazak/ *nf* (de jockey) jersey, silk

casbah /kazba/ *nf* (citadelle, quartier) kasbah; (maison)○ pad○

cascade /kaskad/ *nf* [1] (chute d'eau) waterfall; [2] Cin stunt; [3] (de rires) roar; (d'incidents, de réactions) series (+ *v sg*); **crises en ~** series of crises

cascadeur, -euse /kaskadœʀ, øz/ *nm,f* ► p. 372 stuntman/stuntwoman

case /kɑz/ *nf* [1] (maison) hut, cabin; [2] (de damier, monopoly®) square; **sauter une ~** to jump a square; **reculer d'une ~** lit to move *ou* go back a square; fig to move backward(s); [3] (sur un formulaire) box

(Composés) ~ **départ** lit start; fig square one; **retour à la ~ départ** back to square one; **repasser par la ~ départ** to pass go; ~ **postale** C, H PO Box

(Idiome) **il lui manque une ~**○ he's/she's got a screw loose○

casemate /kazmat/ *nf* (abri) bunker

caser○ /kaze/ [1]
Ⓐ *vtr* [1] (placer) to put, to stick○; **tu as réussi à ~ ton expression favorite!** you've managed to slip in your favourite^{GB} expression!; [2] (marier) to marry off [enfant]; [3] (loger) to put [sb] up; [4] (trouver un emploi pour) to find a place for
Ⓑ **se caser** *vpr* to tie the knot○, to get married

caserne /kazɛʀn/ *nf* Mil barracks

(Composé) ~ **de sapeurs-pompiers** fire station

casher /kaʃɛʀ/ *adj inv* kosher

casier /kɑzje/ *nm* [1] (meuble) ~ **(de rangement)** rack; ~ **à bouteilles** bottle rack; [2] (pour le courrier) pigeonhole; [3] (de pêche) pot; ~ **à langoustes** lobster pot

(Composé) ~ **judiciaire** police record; **avoir un ~** to have a (police) record; **mon ~ judiciaire est vierge** I don't have any police record

casque /kask/ *nm* [1] (de motard, pilote) crash helmet; (d'ouvrier, de mineur) safety helmet, hard hat; (de cycliste) cycle helmet; [2] Mil helmet; [3] Audio, Mus headphones (*pl*); (sèche-cheveux) hairdrier GB, hairdryer US

(Composés) ~ **de chantier** safety helmet, hard hat; ~ **intégral** full-face crash helmet; ~ **de pompier** fireman's helmet; **Casque bleu** Blue Helmet

casqué, ~e /kaske/ *adj* helmeted

casquer○ /kaske/ [1] *vi* (payer la note) to foot the bill; (être puni) to carry the can○ GB, to take the rap○

casquette /kaskɛt/ *nf* [1] (vêtement) cap; ~ **de base-ball** base-ball cap; [2] (fonction) hat; (étiquette) label

cassant, ~e /kasɑ̃, ɑ̃t/ *adj* [1] [bois, cheveux, métal] brittle; [2] (tranchant) [ton, personne] curt, abrupt

casse¹○ /kɑs/ *nm* break-in, heist○ US

casse² /kɑs/ *nf* [1] (objets cassés) breakage; **payer la ~** to pay for breakage *ou* for the damage; **il y a eu beaucoup de ~ pendant le déménagement** a lot of things got broken during the move; **2** (lieu) breaker's yard, scrap yard; **mettre à la ~** to scrap

cassé, ~e /kase/ adj [voix] hoarse

casse-cou /kasku/
A adj inv [personne] reckless; [lieu] dangerous
B nmf inv (personne) daredevil

casse-croûte /kaskʀut/ nm inv snack

casse-noisettes /kasnwazɛt/, **casse-noix** /kas-nwa/ nm inv nutcrackers (pl)

casse-pieds○ /kaspje/
A adj inv **être ~** [gêneur] to be a pain in the neck○; [raseur] to be a bore; [corvée] to be a drag○ ou bore
B nmf inv (gêneur) pain in the neck○; (raseur) bore

casser /kase/ [1]
A vtr **1** (briser) to break [objet, os]; to crack [noix]; **les vandales ont tout cassé dans la maison** the vandals wrecked the house; **~ les prix** to slash prices; **~ le rythme d'une course** to slow down the pace of a race; **~ la figure**○ ou la **gueule** à qn to beat sb up○; **2** ○(dégrader) to demote [militaire, employé]; **3** (annuler) to quash [jugement]; to annul [arrêt]; **4** ○(humilier) to cut [sb] down to size [personne]
B vi **1** (se briser) to break; **2** (se séparer)○ [couple] to split up
C se casser vpr **1** ○(partir) to go away; **'bon, je me casse!'** 'right, I'm off○!'; **2** (se briser) to break; **la clé s'est cassée net** the key snapped in two; **3** (se blesser) se ~ une ou la jambe to break one's leg; **se ~ la figure**○ (tomber par terre) [piéton] to fall over GB ou down; [cavalier, motard] to take a fall; (avoir un accident) to crash; (échouer) [entreprise, projet] to fail; (se battre) [personnes] to have a scrap○; **il ne s'est pas cassé la tête** he didn't exactly strain himself; **se ~ la tête○ (sur un problème)** to rack one's brain (over a problem); **se ~ la tête○ à faire qch** to go out of one's way to do sth
Idiomes **~ les pieds○ à qn** to annoy sb; **~ la croûte○ ou la graine**○ to eat; **ça casse pas des briques**○ it's nothing to write home about○; **ça te prendra trois heures, à tout ~**○ it'll take you three hours at the very most ou at the outside; **qui casse (les verres) paie** if you cause damage, you pay for it

casserole /kasʀɔl/ nf (récipient) saucepan, pan; **~ émaillée** enamelled^{GB} saucepan ou pan
Idiome **chanter/jouer comme une ~**○ to sing/to play atrociously

casse-tête /kastɛt/ nm inv (problème) headache fig; (jeu, devinette) puzzle; **~ chinois** Chinese puzzle

cassette /kasɛt/ nf **1** (de bande) tape; **~ vierge** blank tape; **2** (petit coffret) casket
Composé **~ vidéo** video (cassette); **en ~ vidéo** on video

casseur /kasœʀ/ nm **1** ▸ p. 372 (ferrailleur) scrap dealer; **2** (manifestant) rioting demonstrator; **3** (cambrioleur)⟩ burglar

cassis /kasis/ nm inv **1** (arbre) blackcurrant (bush); (fruit) blackcurrant; **crème de ~** blackcurrant liqueur; **2** (sur la route) dip

cassolette /kasɔlɛt/ nf (récipient) small ovenproof dish

cassonade /kasɔnad/ nf soft brown sugar

cassoulet /kasulɛ/ nm: meat and (haricot) bean stew

cassure /kasyʀ/ nf **1** (endroit brisé) break; **2** (rupture) split, rupture; **3** (en géologie) fracture

castagne○ /kastaɲ/ nf fight, scrap○; **il va y avoir de la ~** there's going to be a fight ou scrap○

castagnettes /kastaɲɛt/ ▸ p. 389 nfpl castanets; **jouer des ~** to play the castanets

caste /kast/ nf Sociol caste; péj class

castillan, ~e /kastijã, an/ ▸ p. 336
A adj Castilian
B nm Ling Castilian

castor /kastɔʀ/ nm beaver

castrer /kastʀe/ [1] vtr to castrate

castrisme /kastʀism/ nm Castroism

cataclysme /kataklism/ nm lit, fig cataclysm

catacombes /katakɔ̃b/ nfpl catacombs

catadioptre /katadjɔptʀ/ nm reflector

catalan, ~e /katalã, an/ ▸ p. 336
A adj Catalan
B nm Catalan

catalogue /katalɔg/ nm catalogue^{GB}; **~ de l'exposition** exhibition catalogue^{GB}; **acheter qch sur ~** to buy sth by mail order

cataloguer /katalɔge/ [1] vtr **1** (dresser la liste de) to catalogue^{GB}; **2** (juger définitivement) to label

catalyser /katalize/ [1] vtr lit, fig to catalyse^{GB}

catalyseur /katalizœʀ/ nm catalyst (de for, of)

catalytique /katalitik/ adj catalytic

cataplasme /kataplasm/ nm poultice

catapulter /katapylte/ [1] vtr to catapult

cataracte /kataʀakt/ nf cataract

catastrophe /katastʀɔf/ nf disaster; **~ aérienne** air disaster; **tourner à la ~** to end in disaster; **ce n'est pas une ~** it's not the end of the world; **en ~** in a (mad) panic; **atterrissage en ~** crash landing
Composé **~ naturelle** act of God

catastrophé, ~e /katastʀɔfe/ adj devastated

catastrophique /katastʀɔfik/ adj disastrous

catastrophisme /katastʀɔfism/ nm doomwatch

catch /katʃ/ ▸ p. 327 nm wrestling; **faire du ~** to wrestle

catcheur, ~euse /katʃœʀ, øz/ ▸ p. 372 nm,f wrestler; **avoir des épaules de ~** to be built like a wrestler

catéchisme /kateʃism/ nm catechism; **faire le ~ aux enfants** to teach children the catechism

catégorie /kategɔʀi/ nf **1** (type) category; **de première/deuxième ~** top/low-grade; **2** Admin class; **3** Sociol group; **~ socioprofessionnelle** social and occupational group; **4** Sport class; **hors ~** in a class of one's own; **toutes ~s** all-round

catégorique /kategɔʀik/ adj **1** (inébranlable) adamant; **refus ~** adamant ou categoric refusal; **2** (sans ambiguïté) categoric

catelle /katɛl/ nf H (carreau) tile

cathare /kataʀ/ adj, nmf Cathar

cathédrale /katedʀal/ nf cathedral

catherinette /katʀinɛt/ nf: single woman aged 25

cathodique /katɔdik/ adj Phys cathodic; **tube ~** cathode-ray tube

catholicisme /katɔlisism/ nm (Roman) Catholicism

catholique /katɔlik/
A adj (Roman) Catholic; **ce n'est pas très ~**○ hum it's a bit unorthodox; **ne pas avoir l'air très ~**○ to look a bit dubious
B nmf (Roman) Catholic

catimini: en catimini /ɑ̃katimini/ loc adv on the sly

cauchemar /koʃmaʀ/ nm nightmare; **faire un ~** to have a nightmare

cauchemardesque /koʃmaʀdesk/ adj [expérience] nightmare (épith); [scène] nightmarish

causal, ~e, mpl **-aux** /kozal, o/ adj causal

causalité /kozalite/ nf causality

causant○, **~e** /kozɑ̃, ɑ̃t/ adj talkative, chatty○

cause /koz/ nf **1** (origine) cause; **un rapport de ~ à effet** a relation of cause and effect; **il n'y a pas d'effet sans ~** there's no smoke without fire; **2** (raison) reason; **pour une ~ encore indéterminée** for a reason as yet unknown; **il s'est fâché et pour ~** he got angry and with good reason; **sans ~** groundless; **c'est une ~ de licenciement immédiat** it's a ground for immediate dismissal; **pour ~ de maladie** because of illness; **fermé pour ~ de travaux** closed for for renovation; **avoir pour ~ qch** to be caused by sth; **à ~ de** because of; **3** (ensemble d'intérêts) cause; **une ~ perdue** a lost cause; **gagner qn à sa ~** to win sb over to one's cause; **prendre fait et ~ pour qn** to take up the cause of sb; **pour la bonne ~** for a good cause; **4** (affaire) case; **les ~s célèbres** the causes célèbres, the famous cases; **être en ~** [système, fait, organisme] to be at issue; [personne] to be involved; **être hors de ~** to be in the clear; **mettre qn/qch en ~** to implicate sb/sth; **mettre hors de ~** to clear; **remettre en ~** to challenge [principe, hiérarchie, décision]; to cast doubt on [projet, efficacité, signification]; to undermine [efforts, proposition, processus]; **tout est remis en ~** everything has been thrown back into doubt; **se remettre en ~** to pass one's life under review; **remise en ~** (de système) reappraisal; **avoir or obtenir gain de ~** to win one's case; **donner gain de ~ à** to decide in favour^{GB} of

ce

L'adjectif démonstratif:
ce, cet, cette, ces

Lorsque *ce* (parfois renforcé par *-ci*) marque la proximité dans l'espace ou le temps, on le traduira par *this*:

prends ce livre(-ci) plutôt que celui-là
= take this book, not that one

il a plu ce matin
= it rained this morning

ce mois-ci
= this month

un de ces jours
= one of these days

Lorsque *ce* (parfois renforcé par *-là*) marque l'éloignement, on le traduira par *that*:

cet homme(-là)
= that man

cette année-là
= that year

en ces temps lointains
= in those far-off days

Lorsque le nom n'est pas suivi de *-ci* ou *-là*, on prendra en compte le contexte pour choisir la traduction:

dans cette maison
(*celle où l'on se trouve*)
= in this house
(*celle dont on parle*)
= in that house

j'aime ces endroits calmes
(*tels que celui où nous sommes*)
= I like these quiet places

(*tels que celui dont on parle*)
= I like those quiet places

en ces temps difficiles
(*maintenant*)
= in these difficult times
(*autrefois*)
= in those difficult times

On notera que *that* sert aussi à indiquer que le locuteur se distancie d'une chose ou d'une personne, souvent pour marquer sa désapprobation:

tu es ridicule avec ce chapeau!
= you look ridiculous in that hat!

ce garçon m'énerve!
= that boy gets on my nerves!

Attention aux expressions suivantes:

cette nuit
(*passée*)
= last night
(*à venir*)
= tonight

en ce moment
= at the moment
(*précis*)
= at this moment in time

Le pronom démonstratif: *ce, c'*

L'emploi du pronom démonstratif avec le verbe *être* est traité à l'entrée du verbe **être¹**.

Les autres emplois sont traités ci-dessous, voir **B.**

Ⓘ**diomes**) **en toute connaissance de** ～ in full knowledge of the facts; **en tout état de** ～ in any case; **en désespoir de** ～ as a last resort

causer /koze/ [1]
A *vtr* ① (provoquer) to cause; ～ **de la peine à qn** to cause sb grief; ～ **du tort à qn** to wrong sb; **ma santé m'a causé des soucis** my health has given me cause for concern; ② ᴼ(discuter de) to talk; ～ **travail** to talk shop
B causer[○] de *vtr ind* to talk about; ～ **de choses et d'autres** to talk about this and that
C ᴼ*vi* to talk (**avec** to; **à propos de** about); **cause toujours tu m'intéresses**ᴼ! iron fascinating, I'm sure! iron

causerie /kozʀi/ *nf* (entretien organisé) talk; (entretien libre) chat; **une** ～ **au coin du feu** a fireside chat

causetteᴼ /kozɛt/ *nf* chat; **faire la** ～ **avec qn** to have a little chat with sb

causse /kos/ *nm* limestone plateau

caustique /kostik/ *adj* caustic

cautériser /koteʀize/ [1] *vtr* to cauterize

caution /kosjɔ̃/ *nf* ① (garantie financière) Comm deposit; Fin guarantee, security; Jur bail; **libéré sous** ～ released on bail; ② (soutien) support; **apporter sa** ～ **à** to lend one's support to; ③ (garantie morale) guarantee; **sujet à** ～ open to doubt

cautionner /kosjone/ [1] *vtr* ① (soutenir) to give one's support to; **être cautionné par** to have the support of; ② Comm, Fin to stand surety for [*personne, projet*]

cavalcade /kavalkad/ *nf* ① (course bruyante) stampede; ② (défilé de cavaliers) cavalcade

cavaleᴼ /kaval/ *nf* (évasion) escape; **en** ～ on the run

cavalerᴼ /kavale/ [1]
A *vi* (courir) to rush about; ～ **dans** to rush around; ～ **après** to chase after; ～ **après les femmes** to be a womanizer
B se cavaler**ᴼ *vpr* to leg it**ᴼ, to scarper**ᴼ, to run

cavalerie /kavalʀi/ *nf* cavalry

cavaleurᴼ, **-euse** /kavalœʀ, øz/ pej
A *adj* womanizing (*épith*)/man-chasing (*épith*)
B *nm,f* womanizer/man-chaser

cavalier, -ière /kavalje, ɛʀ/
A *adj* ① (impertinent) cavalier; ② (en dessin) **vue cavalière** bird's eye view; **perspective cavalière** isometric projection; ③ (pour cheval) **allée cavalière** bridle path
B *nm,f* ① (en équitation) horseman/horsewoman; (en promenade) horse rider; **être bon** ～ to be a good rider; ② (pour danser) partner
C *nm* ① Mil cavalryman; ② (aux échecs) knight

Ⓘ**diome**) **faire** ～ **seul** [*personne, entreprise*] to go it alone; Sport to be ahead

cavalièrement /kavaljɛʀmɑ̃/ *adv* in a cavalier fashion

cave /kav/ *nf* ① cellar; **de la** ～ **au grenier** high and low; ～ **voûtée** vault; **avoir une bonne** ～ [*individu*] to have a good cellar; [*restaurant*] to have a good winelist; ② (entreprise vinicole) cellar; ③ (magasin) wine merchant

caveau, *pl* ～**x** /kavo/ *nm* vault; ～ **de famille** family vault

caverne /kavɛʀn/ *nf* (grotte) cavern

caviar /kavjaʀ/ *nm* caviar

cavité /kavite/ *nf* cavity; ～ **buccale** oral cavity

Cayenne /kajɛn/ *nf* Géog Cayenne; Hist Cayenne penal settlement

CB /sebe/ *nf* (*abbr* = **Citizens' Band**) bande ～ CB

CCP /sesepe/ *nm: abbr* ▸ **compte**

CD /sede/ *nm* (*abbr* = **compact disc**) CD

CD-I /sedei/ *nm inv* (*abbr* = **compact disc interactif**) CD-I

CD-ROM /sedeʀɔm/ *nm* (*abbr* = **compact disc read only memory**) CD-ROM

ce /sə/ (**c'** /s/ before *e*, **cet** /sɛt/ before vowel or mute *h*), **cette** /sɛt/, *pl* **ces** /se/
A *adj dém* ① ᴼ(avec un sujet redondant) **alors,** ～ **bébé, ça**

pousse? how's the baby doing?; **et ces travaux, ça avance?** how's the work progressing?; **cet entretien, ça s'est bien passé?** how did the interview go?; **2** (de politesse) **et pour ces dames?** what are the ladies having?; **3** (suivi d'une précision) **il n'est pas de ces hommes qui disent** he's not the kind of man to say; **elle a eu cette chance que la corde a tenu** she was lucky in that the rope held; **j'ai un de ces rhumes!** I've got an awful cold!; **je ne pensais pas qu'il aurait cette audace** I never thought he would be so cheeky; **tu as de ces idées!** you've got some funny ideas!

B *pron dém* **1** (utilisé seul) **~ faisant** in so doing; **tout s'est bien passé, et ~, grâce à vos efforts** everything went well, and that was all thanks to you; **sur ~, je vous quitte** with that, I must take my leave; **2** (avec une proposition relative) **fais ~ que tu veux** do what you like; **~ dont tu as besoin** what you need; **il a fait faillite, ~ qui n'est pas surprenant** he's gone bankrupt, which is hardly surprising; **~ qui m'étonne, c'est qu'il ait accepté** what surprises me is that he accepted; **il s'étonne de ~ que tu ne le saches pas** he's surprised (that) you don't know; **il tient à ~ que vous veniez** he's very keen that you should come *ou* for you to come; **~ que c'est grand!** it's so big!; **c'est étonnant ~ qu'il te ressemble!** it's amazing how much he looks like you!; **~ que c'est que d'être vieux!** what it is to be old!; **~ que c'est que les enfants!** that's children for you!; **~ qu'il ne faut pas faire!** the things one has to do!; **~ que** *or* **qu'est-~ que**○ **j'ai faim!** I'm starving!; **~ qu'il**○ **pleut!** it's pouring!

CE /sə/ *nf: abbr* ▸ **cours**

ceci /səsi/ *pron dém* this; **à ~ près** with one slight difference; **à ~ près que** except that; **~ n'empêche pas cela** the one doesn't necessarily exclude the other; **~ compense cela** things balance out; **cet hôtel a ~ de bien que** one good thing about this hotel is that

cécité /sesite/ *nf* blindness; **atteint de ~** blind; **souffrir de ~ partielle** to be partially sighted

céder /sede/ [14]
A *vtr* **1** (laisser) to give up [*tour, siège, part*] (**à qn** to sb); to yield [*pouvoir, droit*] (**à qn** to sb); to make over [*bien*] (**à** to); **~ le passage** *or* **la priorité** to give way (**à** to); **il m'a cédé sa place** he let me have his seat; **~ la place** fig to give way (**à** to); **2** (vendre) to sell (**à qn** to sb); **'cède villa bord de mer'** 'for sale: seaside house'; **3** (être inférieur) **ne le ~ en rien à** to be on a par with
B *céder à vtr ind* **~ à** to give in to, to yield to
C *vi* **1** (fléchir) [*personne*] to give in; **2** (casser) [*poignée, branche*] to give way; (ne plus résister) [*serrure, porte*] to yield; **faire ~ une porte** to force a door

cédérom /sederɔm/ *nm* CD-ROM

cedex /sedɛks/ *nm (abbr = courrier d'entreprise à distribution exceptionnelle) postal code for corporate users*

cédille /sedij/ *nf* cedilla

cèdre /sɛdʀ/ *nm* (arbre) cedar; (bois) cedar(wood)

CEE /seəə/ *nf: abbr* ▸ **communauté**

CEEA /seəəa/ *nf (abbr = Communauté européenne de l'énergie atomique) EAEC*

cégep /seʒɛp/ *nm* C *(abbr = collège d'enseignement général et professionnel) college of further education in Quebec offering two-year courses*

CEI /seəi/ *nf: abbr* ▸ **communauté**

ceindre /sɛ̃dʀ/ [55] *liter*
A *vtr* **1** (entourer) **~ sa taille d'un ruban** to put *ou* tie a ribbon around one's waist; **2** (mettre) to put on [*armure*]; to gird [*épée*]
B *se ceindre vpr* **se ~ d'un pagne** to put a loincloth on; **se ~ la tête d'un bandeau** to put a headband on

ceint, ~e /sɛ̃, sɛ̃t/ ▸ **ceindre**

ceinture /sɛ̃tyʀ/ *nf* **1** (pour tenir) belt; **2** (en couture) waistband; **3** (gaine) girdle; **4** (taille) waist; **avoir de l'eau jusqu'à la ~** to be up to one's waist in water; **coup en dessous de la ~** a blow below the belt; **5** Sport (prise) waist hold; (lien) belt; **être ~ noire** to be a black belt (**de** in); **6** (ce qui entoure) ring; **boulevard de ~** ringroad

(Composés) **~ orthopédique** surgical corset; **~ de sauvetage** lifebelt; **~ de sécurité** safety *ou* seat belt

(Idiomes) **faire ~**○ to go without; **se serrer la ~** to tighten one's belt

ceinturer /sɛ̃tyʀe/ [1] *vtr* **1** (être autour) [*réseau, murailles*] to encircle [*ville, terrain*]; **2** (maîtriser) to collar○ [*malfaiteur*]; Sport to tackle [*adversaire*]

ceinturon /sɛ̃tyʀɔ̃/ *nm* belt

cela /səla/ *pron dém*

⚠ Dans de nombreux emplois, *cela* et *ça* sont équivalents. On se reportera donc à cette entrée

1 gén that; **il y a dix ans de ~** that was ten years ago; **quant à ~** as for that; **~ dit** having said that; **2** (sujet apparent ou réel) it; (emphatique) that; **~ m'inquiète de la voir dans cet état** it worries me to see her in that state; **mais ~ ne vous appartient pas!** but that doesn't belong to you!; **il est coupable, ~ est sûr!** he is guilty, that is certain!

(Idiome) **voyez-vous ~!** did you ever hear of such a thing!

célébration /selebʀasjɔ̃/ *nf* celebration

célèbre /selɛbʀ/ *adj* famous (**pour, par** for); **tristement ~** notorious

célébrer /selebʀe/ [14] *vtr* **1** (fêter) to celebrate [*événement*]; **2** (accomplir) to celebrate [*messe, mariage, culte*]; to perform [*rite*]; **3** (vanter) to praise [*personne*]; to remember [*mort, disparu*]; to extol [*qualité*]

célébrissime /selebʀisim/ *adj* extremely famous

célébrité /selebʀite/ *nf* (gloire) fame; (personnage) celebrity

céleri /selʀi/ *nm* **1** (en branches) celery; **2** (céleri-rave) celeriac; **~ en branches** celery; **~ rémoulade** grated celeriac in a mayonnaise dressing

céleri-rave, *pl* **céleris-raves** /selʀiʀav/ *nm* celeriac

célérité /seleʀite/ *nf* (rapidité) fml promptness; **avec ~** promptly

céleste /selɛst/ *adj* [*corps, phénomène, puissances*] celestial; [*gloire, esprit*] heavenly; [*colère, messager*] divine

célibat /seliba/ *nm* (état) single status; (chasteté) celibacy

célibataire /selibatɛʀ/
A *adj* single; **je suis ~ pour quelques jours** I'm on my own for a few days
B *nmf* (homme) bachelor, single man; (femme) single woman; **mère ~** single mother; **~ endurci** confirmed bachelor

celle ▸ **celui**

celle-ci ▸ **celui-ci**

celle-là ▸ **celui-là**

celles-ci ▸ **celui-ci**

celles-là ▸ **celui-là**

cellier /selje/ *nm* cellar

cellulaire /selylɛʀ/ *adj* **1** (de la cellule) cell (*épith*); (fait de cellules) cellular; **2** [*régime, système*] of solitary confinement

cellule /selyl/ *nf* **1** (en biologie) cell; **~s nerveuses/sanguines** nerve/blood cells; **2** (de prison, monastère, ruche) cell; **3** (en sociologie) unit; **4** (de parti) cell; **5** (en photo, informatique) cell; **6** (d'électrophone) cartridge

(Composé) **~-souche** stem cell

cellulite /selylit/ *nf* (graisse) cellulite; (inflammation) cellulitis

cellulose /selyloz/ *nf* cellulose

celte /sɛlt/ *adj, nm* Celtic

Celte /sɛlt/ *nmf* Celt

celtique /sɛltik/ *adj, nm* Celtic

celui /səlɥi/, **celle** /sɛl/, *mpl* **ceux** /sø/, *fpl* **celles** /sɛl/ *pron dém*

⚠ Voir aussi **celui-ci** et **celui-là**

the one; **ceux, celles** (personnes) those; (choses) those, the ones; **non, ~ qui parlait** no, the one who was talking; **~ des deux qui finira le premier** the first one to finish; **ceux d'entre vous qui veulent partir** those of you who want to leave; **tous ceux qui étaient absents** all those who were absent; **tes yeux sont bleus, ceux de ton frère sont gris** your eyes are blue, your brother's are grey GB *ou* gray US; **faire ~ qui n'entend pas** to pretend not to hear; **heureux ~/ceux qui...** happy is he/are those...

celui-ci /səlɥisi/, **celle-ci** /sɛlsi/, *mpl* **ceux-ci** /søsi/, *fpl* **celles-ci** /sɛlsi/ *pron dém* **1** (désignant ce qui est proche dans l'espace) this one; **ceux-ci, celles-ci** these; **2** (annonçant ce qui suit) **je n'ai qu'une chose à dire et c'est celle-ci** I have only one thing to say and it's this; **3** (ce dernier) **elle**

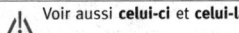

essaya la fenêtre mais celle-ci était coincée she tried the window but it was jammed; **il entra, suivi de son père et de son frère;** ~ **portait un paquet** he came in, followed by his father and his brother, the latter of whom was carrying a parcel; **celle-ci est très serviable mais celui-là est plus efficace** she is very obliging but he's more efficient; [4] (l'un) **ils ont tous apporté quelque chose:** ~ **une bouteille, celui-là un gâteau** they all brought something: one brought a bottle, another a cake

celui-là /səlɥila/, **celle-là** /sɛlla/, mpl **ceux-là** /søla/, fpl **celles-là** /sɛlla/ pron dém

⚠ Pour les sens 1, 3 et 4 voir aussi **celui-ci**

[1] (désignant ce qui est plus éloigné) that one; **ceux-là, celles-là** those (ones); [2] (le suivant) **si je n'ai qu'un conseil à te donner, c'est** ~ if I only have one piece of advice for you, it's this; [3] (le premier des deux) the former; [4] (l'autre) another; [5] (par rapport aux précédents) **il fit une autre proposition, plus réaliste celle-là** he made another proposal, a more realistic one this time; [6] ᵒ(emphatique) **il exagère,** ~**!** that fellowᵒ GB ou guyᵒ is pushing it a bitᵒ!; **celle-là, alors, quelle idiote!** what an idiot that woman is!; ~, **alors!** (admiratif) what a man!; (irrité) that man!; **regardez-moi** ~**: il n'est même pas rasé!** look at him! he hasn't even shaved!; [7] ᵒ**elle est bien bonne, celle-là!** that's a good one!; **je ne m'attendais pas à celle-là** I didn't expect that!; ~ **même** the very one

cendre /sɑ̃dʀ/ nf ash; ~ **de cigarette** cigarette ash; **pommes de terre cuites sous la** ~ potatoes baked in the embers; **réduire en** ~**s** to reduce to ashes

cendré, ~**e** /sɑ̃dʀe/ ▸ p. 140 adj ash (grey); **des cheveux blond** ~ ash blond hair

cendrier /sɑ̃dʀije/ nm ashtray

Cène /sɛn/ nf **la** ~ the Last Supper

censé, ~**e** /sɑ̃se/ adj **être** ~ **faire** to be supposed to do; **nul n'est** ~ **ignorer la loi** ignorance of the law is no excuse

censeur /sɑ̃sœʀ/ nm [1] Scol school official in charge of discipline; [2] (moraliste) **s'ériger en** ~ **de qch** to set oneself up as a critic of sth

censure /sɑ̃syʀ/ nf [1] (interdiction) censorship; **(commission de)** ~ board of censors; **menacé par la** ~ in danger of being censored; [2] Pol censure

censurer /sɑ̃syʀe/ [1] vtr [1] (expurger) to censor; (interdire) to ban; [2] Pol to pass a vote of censure ou no confidence in [gouvernement]

cent¹ /sɑ̃/ ▸ p. 398, p. 155

A adj gén a hundred, one hundred; **deux** ~**s** two hundred; **deux** ~ **trois/vingt-cinq** two hundred and three/twenty-five; ~ **à deux** ~**s personnes** between a hundred and two hundred people

B pron **ils sont venus tous les** ~ all one hundred of them came

C nm hundred; **un** ~ **d'œufs** a ou one hundred eggs; **vendre au** ~ to sell by the hundred

D pour cent loc adj per cent; **un placement à sept pour** ~ an investment at seven per cent; **dix à vingt pour** ~ or **10 à 20% des enseignants** between ten and twenty per cent of teachers; **une jupe** ~ **pour** ~ or **100% coton** a hundred per cent cotton skirt; **je ne suis pas sûr à 100%** I'm not a hundred per cent sure

Idiomes **faire les** ~ **pas** to pace up and down; **être aux** ~ **coups**ᵒ to be worried sickᵒ, to be in a stateᵒ; **faire les quatre** ~**s coups** to be a real tearaway; **attendre** ~ **sept ans**ᵒ to wait for ages; **durer** ~ **sept ans**ᵒ to last for ages ou forever

cent² /sɛnt/ ▸ p. 34 nm (centième de dollar, florin, rand, shilling) cent; Belg (centième d'euro) cent

centaine /sɑ̃tɛn/ nf [1] (cent unités) hundred; **la colonne des** ~**s** the hundreds column; [2] (environ cent) about a hundred; **nous étions une** ~ there were about a hundred of us; **une** ~ **de milliers de manifestants** about a hundred thousand protesters; **des** ~**s de femmes** hundreds of women; **quelques** ~**s de tonnes** a few hundred tons; **les victimes se comptent par** ~**s** there are hundreds of victims; **les lettres arrivent par** ~**s** letters are arriving in hundreds; [3] (âge) **avoir la** ~ to be about a hundred; **approcher de la** ~ to be getting on for a hundred; **dépasser la** ~ to be over a hundred

centenaire /sɑ̃tnɛʀ/

A adj [1] (de cent ans) [arbre, objet] hundred-year-old (épith); **plusieurs fois** ~ several hundred years old; [2] [personne] centenarian; **elle est** ~ she's a hundred years old; [3] (se produisant une fois par siècle) **crue** ~ one-in-a-hundred-years flood

B nmf **c'est une** ~ she's a hundred years old

C nm (anniversaire) centenary GB, centennial US

centième /sɑ̃tjɛm/ ▸ p. 398

A adj hundredth

B nf Théât **la** ~ the hundredth performance

centilitre /sɑ̃tilitʀ/ ▸ p. 87 nm centilitreᴳᴮ

centime /sɑ̃tim/ ▸ p. 34 nm (monnaie) ~ **(d'euro)** cent; Hist (centième de francs) centime; (somme infime) penny, cent US; **pas un** ~ not a penny; **calculer au** ~ **près** to work things out to the last penny; **dépenser jusqu'au dernier** ~ to spend one's last penny

centimètre /sɑ̃timɛtʀ/ nm [1] ▸ p. 347, p. 568, p. 575, p. 624, p. 628 (unité) centimetreᴳᴮ; [2] (distance infime) inch; **ne pas avancer d'un** ~ not to move an inch; [3] (ruban) tape measure

Composés ~ **carré** square centimetreᴳᴮ; ~ **cube** cubic centimetreᴳᴮ

centrafricain, ~**e** /sɑ̃tʀafʀikɛ̃, ɛn/ ▸ p. 392 adj of the Central African Republic; **République** ~**e** Central African Republic

Centrafrique /sɑ̃tʀafʀik/ ▸ p. 230 nprm Central African Republic

central, ~**e¹,** mpl **-aux** /sɑ̃tʀal, o/

A adj [1] (au centre) central; **l'Europe** ~**e** Central Europe; **court** ~ (en tennis) centreᴳᴮ court; **ordinateur** ~ host computer; **chercher quelque chose de plus** ~ to look for something more central; [2] (principal) main

B nm Télécom ~ **(téléphonique)** (telephone) exchange

centrale² /sɑ̃tʀal/ nf [1] (productrice d'énergie) power station; ~ **nucléaire** or **atomique** nuclear power station; ~ **hydraulique** hydroelectric power station; [2] (en politique) ~ **syndicale** or **ouvrière** confederation of trade unions; **les** ~**s syndicales** the trade unions; [3] (prison) prison; [4] Comm ~ **d'achat** (groupement) central purchasing agency

centralisateur, -trice /sɑ̃tʀalizatœʀ, tʀis/ adj centralizing

centraliser /sɑ̃tʀalize/ [1] vtr to centralize; **verrouillage centralisé** central locking

centralisme /sɑ̃tʀalism/ nm centralism

centre /sɑ̃tʀ/ nm [1] (milieu) centreᴳᴮ; **au** ~ **de qch** in the centreᴳᴮ of sth; **habiter dans le** ~ to live in the centre; **le** ~ **(de la France)** central France; [2] (lieu) centreᴳᴮ; **un grand** ~ **industriel** a large industrial centreᴳᴮ; [3] (établissement, organisme) centreᴳᴮ; [4] (point essentiel) centreᴳᴮ; **il se prend pour le** ~ **du monde** he thinks the whole world revolves around him; [5] Pol **le** ~ the centreᴳᴮ; **les partis du** ~ the centre parties; ~ **gauche/droit** centreᴳᴮ left/right; **elle est au** ~ she's in the centreᴳᴮ; [6] Anat centreᴳᴮ; ~ **nerveux** Anat, fig nerve centreᴳᴮ; **les** ~**s vitaux** the vital organs; [7] (passe du ballon) centreᴳᴮ pass

Composés ~ **d'accueil** reception centreᴳᴮ; ~ **aéré** children's outdoor activity centre; ~ **antipoison** poisons unit; ~ **commercial** shopping centreᴳᴮ; ~ **de dépistage** screening unit; ~ **de détention** detention centreᴳᴮ; ~ **de documentation** (dans une école) library; (pour professionnels) resource centreᴳᴮ; ~ **de documentation et d'information, CDI** learning resources centreᴳᴮ; ~ **dramatique** arts centreᴳᴮ for theatre; ~ **équestre** riding school; ~ **d'examens** Scol examination centreᴳᴮ; ~ **de formation** training centreᴳᴮ; ~ **de gériatrie** geriatric hospital; ~ **de gravité** centreᴳᴮ of gravity; ~ **hospitalier** hospital complex; ~ **hospitalier universitaire, CHU** ≈ teaching hospital; ~ **d'inertie** centreᴳᴮ of inertia; ~ **de loisirs** leisure centreᴳᴮ; ~ **médical** health centre; ~ **de recherches** research centreᴳᴮ; ~ **de remise en forme** health farm; ~ **de soins** clinic; ~ **sportif** sports centreᴳᴮ; ~ **de traitement** Ordinat processing centreᴳᴮ; ~ **de transfusion sanguine** blood transfusion centreᴳᴮ; ~ **de tri** (postal) sorting office; ~ **universitaire** university; ~ **de vacances** holiday GB ou vacation US centreᴳᴮ; **Centre d'information et de documentation jeunesse, CIDJ** youth information centreᴳᴮ; **Centre d'information et d'orientation** Scol national careers guidance centreᴳᴮ; **Centre national** d'enseignement à distance, **CNED** national centre^{GB} for distance learning

centrer /sɑ̃tʀe/ [1] *vtr* [1] (fixer par rapport au centre) to centre^{GB}; [2] (diriger) **être centré sur qch** to be centred^{GB} around sth; **école centrée sur l'enseignement de la musique** school which focuses on the teaching of music; [3] Sport to centre^{GB}

centre-ville /sɑ̃tʀəvil/ *nm* **centres-villes** town centre^{GB}; (de grande ville) city centre^{GB}

centrifuge /sɑ̃tʀify3/ *adj* centrifugal

centrifugeur /sɑ̃tʀify3œʀ/ *nm* centrifuge

centrifugeuse /sɑ̃tʀify3øz/ *nf* (en électroménager) juice extractor; (en chimie, mécanique) centrifuge

centriste /sɑ̃tʀist/ *adj*, *nmf* centrist

centuple /sɑ̃typl/
A *adj* **une somme ∼ d'une autre** an amount a hundred times greater than another
B *nm* **dix mille est le ∼ de cent** ten thousand is a hundred times one hundred; **rendre au ∼** fig to repay a hundred times over

cep /sɛp/ *nm* **∼ (de vigne)** vine stock

cépage /sepa3/ *nm* grape variety; **∼ cabernet** Cabernet grape

cèpe /sɛp/ *nm* cep

cependant /səpɑ̃dɑ̃/
A *conj* (pourtant) yet, however; **votre devoir est bon mais il y a ∼ quelques erreurs** your work is good; however, there are a few mistakes; **une ambiguïté subsiste ∼** one ambiguity remains, however
B *cependant que* *loc conj* (tandis que) whereas, while

céphalée /sefale/ *nf* headache

céramique /seʀamik/ *nf* [1] (matière) ceramic; **en ∼** ceramic (épith); [2] (objet) ceramic; [3] (art, industrie, technique) ceramics (+ v sg)

cerbère /sɛʀbɛʀ/ *nm* (garde du corps) minder; (gardien) watchdog

cerceau, *pl* **∼x** /sɛʀso/ *nm* hoop; **pousser un ∼** to bowl a hoop

cerclage /sɛʀkla3/ *nm* [1] (de tonneau) hooping; [2] Méd **faire un ∼ du col de l'utérus** to put in a cervical stitch

cercle /sɛʀkl/ *nm* [1] (figure) circle; **en ∼** in a circle; **entourez le verbe d'un ∼** ring ou circle the verb; **décrire des ∼s** [avion, oiseau] to circle (overhead); **faire ∼ autour de qn** to gather around sb; [2] (groupe) circle; [3] (association) circle, society; Jeux, Sport club; (local) club; [4] (de tonneau) hoop

(Composés) **∼ inscrit** inscribed circle; **∼ polaire** polar circle; **∼ polaire antarctique** Antarctic circle; **∼ polaire arctique** Arctic circle; **∼ vicieux** vicious circle

cercler /sɛʀkle/ [1] *vtr* to hoop [tonneau]; **les noms cerclés de** ou **en rouge** the names circled in red; **lunettes cerclées** rimmed glasses

cercueil /sɛʀkœj/ *nm* coffin

céréale /seʀeal/
A *nf* cereal, grain ¢; **cultiver des ∼s** to grow cereals
B **céréales** *nfpl* Culin cereal ¢; **manger des ∼s** to eat cereal

céréalier, -ière /seʀealje, ɛʀ/ *adj* [production] cereal (épith); [région] cereal-growing (épith)

cérébral, ∼e, *mpl* **-aux** /seʀebʀal, o/
A *adj* Anat, Méd cerebral; (intellectuel) [travail] intellectual; [personne] cerebral
B *nm,f* cerebral type

cérémonial, *pl* **∼s** /seʀemɔnjal/ *nm* ceremonial

cérémonie /seʀemɔni/
A *nf* ceremony; **tenue** ou **habit de ∼** ceremonial dress
B **cérémonies** *nfpl* (politesse exagérée) ceremony ¢; **faire des ∼s** to stand on ceremony; **sans ∼s** [repas, invitation] informal; [recevoir] informally

cérémonieux, -ieuse /seʀemɔnjø, øz/ *adj* ceremonious; **d'un air ∼** ceremoniously

cerf /sɛʀ/ *nm* stag

cerfeuil /sɛʀfœj/ *nm* chervil

cerf-volant, *pl* **cerfs-volants** /sɛʀvɔlɑ̃/ *nm* (jouet) kite; (insecte) stag beetle

cerise /s(ə)ʀiz/
A ▸ p. 140 *adj inv* **(rouge) ∼** cherry-red, cerise

B *nf* cherry

cerisier /s(ə)ʀizje/ *nm* (arbre) cherry (tree); (bois) cherry-wood

cerne /sɛʀn/ *nm* ring

cerné, ∼e /sɛʀne/ *adj* **avoir les yeux ∼s** to have rings under one's eyes

cerneau, *pl* **∼x** /sɛʀno/ *nm* **∼x de noix** walnut halves

cerner /sɛʀne/ [1] *vtr* [1] (encercler) to surround; **vous êtes cernés!** you're surrounded!; [2] (définir) to define [question, problème]; to make [sb] out [personne]; to determine [personnalité, besoins]; [3] (entourer d'un cercle) to outline [figure, dessin] (de with)

certain, ∼e /sɛʀtɛ̃, ɛn/
A *adj* [1] (convaincu) **∼ de** certain ou sure of; **es-tu ∼ d'avoir fermé le gaz?** are your certain ou sure that you turned off the gas?; [2] (indiscutable) certain, sure; **tenir qch pour ∼** to be certain of sth; **c'est sûr et ∼°** it's absolutely certain; **ils vont gagner, c'est ∼!** they're bound to win!; **il est ∼ qu'il n'aurait jamais pu faire ce qu'il a fait sans sa femme** he certainly couldn't have done what he did if it hadn't been for his wife; **ils vont à une mort ∼e** they're heading for certain death; **une influence ∼e** an undeniable ou a definite influence; **un homme d'un âge ∼** a man of advanced years; [3] (fixé) [date, prix] definite
B *adj indéf* (before n) [1] (mal défini) **elle restera un ∼ temps** she'll stay for some time ou for a while; **un ∼ nombre d'erreurs** a (certain) number of mistakes; **une ∼e image de la France** a certain image of France; **dans une ∼e mesure** to a certain ou to some extent; **d'une ∼e manière** in a way; [2] (devant un nom de personne) **un ∼ M. Grovagnard** a (certain) Mr Grovagnard; [3] (intensif) some; **il faut un ∼ culot°** it takes some nerve°; **un homme d'un ∼ âge** a man who's no longer young; **il avait déjà un ∼ âge** he was already getting on in years
C **certains, certaines** *adj indéf pl* some; **à ∼s moments** sometimes, at times
D **certains, certaines** *pron indéf pl* some people; **∼s d'entre eux** some of them

certainement /sɛʀtɛnmɑ̃/ *adv* [1] (sans certitude) most probably; **c'est ∼ quelqu'un de très compétent** he/she must be a very competent person; [2] (avec certitude) certainly; **tu y es ∼ pour quelque chose!** you have certainly got something to do with it!; [3] (pour renforcer) certainly; **mais ∼!** certainly ou of course!; **∼ pas!** certainly not!

certes /sɛʀt/ *adv* (en signe de concession) admittedly; **ce ne sera ∼ pas facile mais...** admittedly it won't be easy but...; **il est séduisant, ∼, mais prétentieux** he is good-looking, certainly, but he is conceited; **∼ non!** certainly not!

certificat /sɛʀtifika/ *nm* [1] (document officiel) certificate; **∼ attestant que** certificate showing that; [2] (document privé) testimonial

(Composés) **∼ d'aptitude professionnelle, CAP** vocational training qualification; **∼ de bonne vie et mœurs** ≈ character reference; **∼ de garantie** certificate of guarantee; **∼ de naissance** birth certificate; **∼ de résidence** proof of residence; **∼ de scolarité** proof of attendance (at school or university); **∼ de travail** document from a previous employer giving dates and nature of employment

certifié, ∼e /sɛʀtifje/ *adj* **professeur ∼** fully qualified teacher

certifier /sɛʀtifje/ [2] *vtr* [1] gén to certify, to authenticate [signature]; **∼ conforme** to authenticate; **copie certifiée conforme** certified copy; [2] (affirmer) **elle m'a certifié que** she assured me that

certitude /sɛʀtityd/ *nf* [1] (caractère indubitable) certainty; **on sait avec ∼ que** we know for certain that; **seule ∼, il est parti à midi** all we know for certain is that he left at noon; [2] (conviction) conviction; **avoir la ∼ que** to be certain that

cérumen /seʀymɛn/ *nm* earwax; **bouchon de ∼** cerumen blockage

cerveau, *pl* **∼x** /sɛʀvo/ *nm* [1] Anat brain; [2] (siège de l'intelligence) mind; [3] (personne intelligente) brain°; **exode** ou **fuite des ∼x** brain drain; **la chasse aux ∼x** talent hunting; **c'est un ∼** he/she has an outstanding mind; [4] (directeur) brains (+ v sg); (centre directeur) nerve centre

(Idiome) **avoir le ∼ fêlé°** ou **dérangé** to be deranged ou cracked°

cervelas /sɛʀvəla/ *nm* saveloy

cervelet /sɛʀvəlɛ/ nm cerebellum

cervelle /sɛʀvɛl/ nf [1] (substance) brains (pl); **se brûler** or **se faire sauter la** ~° to blow one's brains out°; ~ **de veau** Culin calf's brains; [2] °(tête) brain; **il n'a rien dans la** ~ he's brainless; **elle a une** ~ **d'oiseau** she's a bird-brain°

cervical, ~e, mpl **-aux** /sɛʀvikal, o/ adj cervical

cervoise /sɛʀvwaz/ nf (barley) beer

ces ▸ **ce**

CES /seəɛs/ nm [1] abbr ▸ **collège**; [2] abbr ▸ **contrat**

césar /sezaʀ/ nm [1] Cin César (film award); [2] (dictateur) caesar

César /sezaʀ/ npr **Jules** ~ Julius Caesar; **rendons à** ~ **ce qui est à** ~ render unto Caesar that which is Caesar's

ⓘ **Césars** The French equivalent of the Hollywood Oscars. At the annual televised ceremony, prizes are awarded to cinema personalities for achievements in the previous cinema and TV year. The prize was designed by the French sculptor César, hence its name.

césarienne /sezaʀjɛn/ nf caesarian (section)

cessante /sesɑ̃t/ adj f **toute(s) affaire(s)** ~**(s)** fml forthwith sout

cessation /sesasjɔ̃/ nf suspension

(Composé) ~ **d'activité** gén suspension of activities; (retraite) retirement; Comm closing down

cesse /sɛs/ nf **elle n'a de** ~ **de démontrer...** she's forever demonstrating...; **sans** ~ [parler, changer] constantly; **un nombre sans** ~ **grandissant** an ever increasing number; **des machines sans** ~ **plus puissantes** ever more powerful machines

cesser /sese/ [1]
Ⓐ vtr to cease [traitement, livraisons]; to end [soutien, répression]; ~ **de faire** to stop doing; ~ **toute activité** [entreprise] to cease trading; ~ **les combats** to stop fighting; ~ **de fumer/d'espérer** to give up smoking/hope; ~ **d'exister** to cease to exist; ~ **de payer** to cease payment; **les prix ne cessent d'augmenter** prices keep (on) rising
Ⓑ vi [activité] to cease; [vent] to drop; [pluie] to stop; **faire** ~ to put an end to [rumeur]; to put a stop to [combats]; to end [poursuites]

cessez-le-feu /seselfø/ nm inv ceasefire

cession /sesjɔ̃/ nf transfer

c'est-à-dire /setadiʀ/ loc conj [1] (pour préciser) that is (to say); [2] (ce qui signifie) ~ **que** which means (that); **'j'ai presque fini'—'** ~ **que tu viens de commencer'** 'I've nearly finished'—'what you mean is that you've barely started'; **'le travail est trop dur'—'** ~**?'** 'the work is too hard'—'what do you mean?'; [3] (pour rectifier, excuser) ~ **que** well, actually; ~ **qu'il est jeune** well, you know, he's young

césure /sezyʀ/ nf (de vers) caesura; (de fin de ligne) line break

cet ▸ **ce**

CET /seəte/ nm: abbr ▸ **collège**

cette ▸ **ce**

ceux ▸ **celui**

ceux-ci ▸ **celui-ci**

ceux-là ▸ **celui-là**

Ceylan /selɑ̃/ nprm Hist Ceylon; **thé de** ~ Ceylon tea

CFDT /seɛfdete/ nf (abbr = **Confédération française démocratique du travail**) CFDT (French trade union)

CFTC /seɛftese/ nf (abbr = **Confédération française des travailleurs chrétiens**) CFTC (French trade union)

CGC /seʒese/ nf (abbr = **Confédération générale des cadres**) CGC (French trade union)

CGT /seʒete/ nf (abbr = **Confédération générale du travail**) CGT (French trade union)

chacal, pl ~**s** /ʃakal/ nm Zool, fig jackal

chacun, ~e /ʃakœ̃, yn/ pron indéf [1] (chaque élément) each (one); ~ **de** each one of, every one of; ~ **d'entre nous** each (one) of us, every one of us; **ils ont** ~ **sa** or **leur chambre** they each have their own room; **vous avez droit à une boisson** ~ you're each entitled to a drink; **nous avons** ~ **pris notre veste** we all took our jackets; [2] (tout le monde) everyone; **comme** ~ **sait** as everyone knows; ~ **son tour** everyone in turn; ~ **son tour!** wait your turn!; ~ **ses goûts** every man to his own taste; ~ **pour soi (et Dieu**

pour tous) every man for himself (and God for us all); **tout un** ~ everyone; **à** ~ **son métier** every man to his own trade

chagrin, ~e /ʃagʀɛ̃, in/
Ⓐ adj [personne] despondent; **d'humeur** ~**e** despondent
Ⓑ nm (peine) grief; **faire du** ~ **à qn** to cause sb grief; **accablé de** ~ grief-stricken; **avoir du** ~ to be sad; **elle a eu de nombreux** ~**s** she's had many sorrows; **mourir de** ~ to die of a broken heart; **avoir un gros** ~ [enfant] to be very upset; ~ **d'amour** unhappy love affair

chagriner /ʃagʀine/ [1] vtr [1] (peiner) to pain, to grieve; [2] (contrarier) to bother, to worry; **il y a quelque chose qui me chagrine dans cette histoire** there's something about this story which bothers me

chahut /ʃay/ nm racket°; **faire du** ~ [fêtard] to make a racket°; [élève] to play up the teacher

chahuter /ʃayte/ [1]
Ⓐ vtr [élève, classe] to play up; [personne, groupe] to heckle [orateur]; **se faire** ~ **par qn** gén to be heckled by sb
Ⓑ vi to mess around (**avec** with)

chahuteur, -euse /ʃaytœʀ, øz/ adj disruptive

chaîne /ʃɛn/
Ⓐ nf [1] (entrave) chain; **mettre les** ~**s à qn** to put sb in chains; **attacher qn avec des** ~**s** to chain sb up; [2] (de transmission) chain; ~ **de vélo** bicycle chain; [3] Ind assembly line; **travailler à la** ~ to work on the assembly line; **produire (qch) à la** ~ to mass-produce (sth); **on n'est pas à la** ~° fig we're not machines, you know!; **système éducatif à la** ~ conveyor-belt education system; [4] (bijou) chain; ~ **en or** gold chain; [5] (succession) chain; **des catastrophes en** ~ a series of disasters; **réaction en** ~ chain reaction; [6] (organisation) network; ~ **de solidarité** support network; **faire la** ~ to make a chain; [7] Géog chain, range; [8] (de télévision) channel; **deuxième** ~ channel 2; [9] Comm chain; ~ **de magasins** chain of stores; [10] Audio system; ~ **stéréo** stereo system; [11] Chimie chain
Ⓑ **chaînes** nfpl Aut snow chains

(Composés) ~ **de fabrication** production line; ~ **de montage** assembly line; ~ **thématique** special interest channel

chaînette /ʃɛnɛt/ nf [1] (bijou) chain; ~ **en argent** silver chain; [2] (de transmission) small chain

chaînon /ʃɛnɔ̃/ nm link; ~ **manquant** missing link

chair /ʃɛʀ/
Ⓐ ▸ p. 140 adj inv flesh-coloured ᴳᴮ
Ⓑ nf [1] Anat flesh ⓒ; ~**s meurtries** bruised flesh; **bien en** ~ plump, well-padded°; [2] (de fruit, légume, poisson) flesh; (de volaille) meat; ~ **à saucisses** sausage meat; [3] (corps) flesh; **être de** ~ to be only human

(Composés) ~ **à canon**° cannon fodder; ~ **fraîche** young bodies (pl); ~ **de poule** gooseflesh, goose pimples (pl), goosebumps (pl); **donner la** ~ **de poule à qn** [froid] to give sb gooseflesh; [peur] to make sb's flesh creep

(Idiomes) **transformer qn en** ~ **à pâté** or **saucisses**° to make mincemeat of sb°; **l'esprit est ardent mais la** ~ **est faible** Bible the spirit is willing but the flesh is weak Bible

chaire /ʃɛʀ/ nf [1] Relig (tribune) pulpit; (siège) throne; [2] Univ (poste) chair; (tribune) rostrum

chaise /ʃɛz/ nf (siège) chair; ~ **pliante** folding chair

(Composés) ~ **pour bébé** = ~ **haute**; ~ **électrique** electric chair; ~ **haute** high-chair; ~ **longue** deckchair; ~ **percée** commode; ~ **à porteurs** sedan chair; ~ **roulante** wheelchair

(Idiome) **être assis entre deux** ~**s** to be in an awkward position

chaland, ~e /ʃalɑ̃, ɑ̃d/
Ⓐ nm,f (client) regular customer
Ⓑ nm Naut barge

chaldéen, -éenne /kaldeɛ̃, ɛn/
Ⓐ adj Chaldean
Ⓑ nm Ling Chaldean

châle /ʃɑl/ nm shawl

chalet /ʃalɛ/ nm (de montagne) chalet; (maison en bois) chalet-style house

chaleur /ʃalœʀ/
Ⓐ nf [1] (sensation physique) heat; (douce) warmth; **la** ~ **du soleil** the heat of the sun; **vague de** ~ heatwave; **coup de** ~ heat stroke; **il faisait une** ~ **moite** it was muggy; **il fait une de ces** ~**s**°! it's boiling (hot)°!; ~ **animale** body heat;

2▸ (de personne, voix, coloris, d'accueil) warmth; 3▸ Zool (**être**) **en** ～ (to be) on heat; **les** ～**s** the heat **¢**

B chaleurs *nfpl* Météo **les** ～**s** the hot season (*sg*); **les premières** ～**s** the first days of the hot season

chaleureusement /ʃalœʀøzmɑ̃/ *adv* [*applaudir, remercier*] warmly; [*soutenir*] wholeheartedly; **accueillir qn** ～ to give sb a warm welcome

chaleureux, -euse /ʃalœʀø, øz/ *adj* [*personne, accueil, paroles*] warm; [*public, applaudissements*] enthusiastic; [*soutien*] wholehearted; [*atmosphère*] friendly; [*endroit*] welcoming

challenge /ʃalɑ̃ʒ/ *nm* 1▸ (défi) challenge; 2▸ Sport (épreuve) tournament; (trophée) trophy

chaloir† /ʃalwaʀ/ *v impers* **peu me** *or* **m'en chaut** it matters little to me

chaloupe /ʃalup/ *nf* (à rames) rowing boat GB, rowboat US; (à moteur) (motor) launch

chalumeau, *pl* ～**x** /ʃalymo/ *nm* 1▸ (outil) blowtorch; ～ **à souder** welding torch; 2▸ ▸ p. 389 (flûte) pipe; 3▸ (pour boire) straw

chalut /ʃaly/ *nm* trawl; **jeter le** ～ to shoot the trawl; **pêcher (qch) au** ～ to trawl (for sth)

chalutier /ʃalytje/ *nm* ▸ p. 372 (bateau) trawler; (marin) trawlerman

chamade /ʃamad/ *nf* **battre la** ～ to beat wildly

chamailler○: **se chamailler** /ʃamaje/ [1] *vpr* to squabble

chamarré, ～**e** /ʃamaʀe/ *adj* (multicolore) brightly coloured^GB

chambard○ /ʃɑ̃baʀ/ *nm* 1▸ (vacarme, désordre) din, racket○; 2▸ (bouleversement) upheaval

chambardement○ /ʃɑ̃baʀdəmɑ̃/ *nm* (bouleversement) shake-up○; (désordre) mess

chambarder○ /ʃɑ̃baʀde/ [1] *vtr* 1▸ (mettre sens dessus dessous) to turn [sth] upside down; 2▸ (modifier) to upset [*projets, habitudes*]

chambouler○ /ʃɑ̃bule/ [1] *vtr* 1▸ (bouleverser) to upset [*projet*]; to shake up [*vie, établissement*]; ～ **les habitudes de qn** to upset sb's routine; 2▸ (mettre en désordre) to mess [sth] up [*meubles*]; (mélanger) to mix [sth] up [*photos, papiers*]; **ils ont tout chamboulé (dans la maison)** they turned the whole house upside down

chambranle /ʃɑ̃bʀɑ̃l/ *nm* (de porte, fenêtre) frame

chambre /ʃɑ̃bʀ/ *nf* 1▸ (pour dormir) gén room; (chez soi) room, bedroom; ～ **d'hôtel** hotel room; ～ **pour une personne/ pour deux personnes** single/double room; ～ **à deux lits** twin room; **faire** ～ **à part** to sleep in separate rooms; **avez-vous une** ～ **de libre?** have you got any vacancies?; **politicien en** ～ hum armchair politician hum; 2▸ Mus **musique de** ～ chamber music; 3▸ (assemblée parlementaire) house; 4▸ Admin (organe professionnel) chamber; 5▸ Tech (enceinte close) chamber

(Composés) ～ **à air** inner tube; ～ **d'amis** guest room; ～ **basse** Lower House; ～ **de bonne** maid's room; ～ **de commerce (et d'industrie)** chamber of commerce; ～ **à coucher** (pièce) bedroom; (mobilier) bedroom suite; ～ **forte** strong room; ～ **frigorifique** *or* **froide** cold (storage) room; ～ **à gaz** gas chamber; ～ **haute** Upper House; ～ **d'hôte** ≈ room in a guest house; '～**s d'hôte'** 'bed and breakfast'; ～ **d'isolement** Méd isolation room; ～ **noire** Phot (boîte) camera obscura; (local) darkroom; ～ **de torture** torture chamber; **Chambre des communes** House of Commons; **Chambre des députés** Chamber of Deputies; **Chambre des lords** House of Lords

chambrée /ʃɑ̃bʀe/ *nf* Mil (dortoir, soldats) barracks

chambrer /ʃɑ̃bʀe/ [1] *vtr* 1▸ to bring [sth] to room temperature [*vin, bouteille*]; **ce vin rouge se boit chambré** this red wine should be drunk at room temperature; 2▸ ○(se moquer de) to tease

chameau, *pl* ～**x** /ʃamo/ *nm* 1▸ Zool camel; 2▸ ○(personne désagréable) nasty person; **c'est un** ～ he's/she's really nasty

chamelier /ʃaməlje/ ▸ p. 372 *nm* camel driver

chamelle /ʃamɛl/ *nf* she-camel

chamois /ʃamwa/
A ▸ p. 140 *adj inv* (ocre jaune) fawn
B *nm* Zool chamois

champ /ʃɑ̃/
A *nm* 1▸ (terre cultivable) field; **des** ～**s de coton** cotton fields; **prendre à travers** ～**s** to cut across the fields; **aux** ～**s** in the fields; **en pleins** ～**s** in open country; 2▸ (domaine) field; **le** ～ **culturel** the cultural arena; **le** ～ **des investigations** the scope of the investigations; **le** ～ **est libre, on peut y aller** the coast is clear, we can go ahead; **avoir le** ～ **libre** to have a free hand; 3▸ Phot, Cin field; **le** ～ **visuel** the field of vision; **être dans le** ～ to be in shot; **voix hors** ～ offscreen voice; 4▸ Phys, Ling, Math field

B à tout bout de champ○ *loc adv* all the time

(Composés) ～ **de bataille** Mil, fig battlefield; ～ **de courses** racetrack; ～ **de foire** fairground; ～ **de manœuvre** training area; ～ **de mines** minefield; ～ **de tir** (terrain d'exercice) firing range; (portée) range

champagne /ʃɑ̃paɲ/ *nm* champagne; **boire du** ～ to drink champagne; ～ **brut/sec/demi-sec** extra-dry/dry/ medium-dry champagne

champagnisé /ʃɑ̃paɲize/ *adj* **vin champagnisé** sparkling wine

champenois, ～**e** /ʃɑ̃pənwa, az/ *adj* 1▸ ▸ p. 504 Géog of the Champagne region; 2▸ Ind **méthode** ～**e** champagne method

champêtre /ʃɑ̃pɛtʀ/ *adj* [*fête, bal*] village (*épith*); [*scène, paysage*] rural; **déjeuner** ～ lunch in the country

champignon /ʃɑ̃piɲɔ̃/ *nm* 1▸ Culin mushroom; ～ **vénéneux** poisonous mushroom, toadstool; **aller aux** ～**s** to go mushroom picking; 2▸ Bot, Méd fungus; 3▸ (ornement) (dans un jardin) toadstool; 4▸ ○(accélérateur) throttle, accelerator; **appuyer sur le** ～ to put one's foot down GB, to step on the gas US

(Composés) ～ **atomique** mushroom cloud; ～ **hallucinogène** hallucinogenic mushroom, magic mushroom○; ～ **de Paris** button mushroom GB, champignon US

(Idiome) **pousser comme des** ～**s** to pop up like mushrooms

champignonnière /ʃɑ̃piɲɔnjɛʀ/ *nf* mushroom bed

champion, -ionne /ʃɑ̃pjɔ̃, ɔn/ *nm,f* 1▸ Sport champion; 2▸ ○(qui excelle) **être** ～ to be in a class of one's own; ～ **de la gaffe** prize fool; 3▸ ○(leader) **pays** ～ **de la lutte contre la drogue** country which leads the field in the fight against drugs; 4▸ ○(défenseur) champion; **se faire le** ～ **d'une cause** to champion a cause

championnat /ʃɑ̃pjɔna/ *nm* championship

chance /ʃɑ̃s/ *nf* 1▸ (sort favorable) (good) luck; **c'est bien ma** ～**!** iron just my luck!; **pas de** ～**, tu as perdu!** hard luck, you've lost!; **coup de** ～ stroke of luck; **la** ～ **a voulu que je le croise** as luck would have it, I bumped into him; **avoir de la** ～ to be lucky; **ne pas avoir de** ～ to be unlucky; **avoir une** ～ **du tonnerre**○ to have the luck of the devil; **c'est une** ～ **de pouvoir partir** we're lucky to be able to leave; **par** ～ luckily, fortunately; 2▸ (possibilité) chance; **il y a de fortes** ～**s (pour) qu'elle vienne** there's every chance that she will come; **il a ses** ～**s** he stands a good chance; **mettre toutes les** ～**s de son côté** to take no chances; **conserver toutes ses** ～**s** still to have a chance; **'il va pleuvoir?'—'il y a des** ～**s'** 'is it going to rain?'—'probably'; 3▸ (fortune) luck; 4▸ (occasion favorable) chance, opportunity; **la** ～ **de ma vie** the chance *ou* opportunity of a lifetime; **laisser une** ～ **à qn** to give sb a chance; **saisir sa** ～ to seize the opportunity; **c'est la réunion de la dernière** ～ the meeting is the last hope

chancelant, ～**e** /ʃɑ̃slɑ̃, ɑ̃t/ *adj* 1▸ (qui manque d'équilibre) [*démarche*] unsteady; [*objet*] rickety, shaky; [*personne*] staggering; ～ **de fatigue** staggering with tiredness; **avancer d'un pas** ～ to walk unsteadily; 2▸ (fragile) [*courage, pouvoir, foi*] wavering; [*moral*] flagging; [*volonté*] faltering; [*empire, trône*] tottering

chanceler /ʃɑ̃sle/ [19] *vi* 1▸ (perdre l'équilibre) [*personne*] to stagger; [*objet*] to wobble; 2▸ (manquer de fermeté) to waver; 3▸ (être menacé) [*pouvoir, trône*] to totter; [*santé*] to be precarious

chancelier /ʃɑ̃səlje/ *nm* gén chancellor; (d'ambassade) chancery

chancellerie /ʃɑ̃sɛlʀi/ *nf* (en France) Ministry of Justice; (en Allemagne, Autriche) Chancellorship

chanceux, -euse /ʃɑ̃sø, øz/
A *adj* (fortuné) lucky
B *nm,f* ¢ lucky man/woman

Le chant et les chanteurs

Les voix et les chanteurs

soprano	*ténor*
= soprano*	= tenor
mezzo-soprano	*baryton*
= mezzo-soprano	= baritone
contralto	*baryton-basse*
= contralto	= bass-baritone
	([beɪs, 'bærɪˌtəʊn])
haute-contre	*basse*
= counter-tenor	= bass

* *Pour* une soprano, *on dira* a soprano, *et pour parler d'un jeune garçon on précisera* a boy soprano.

■ *Dans les expressions suivantes,* ténor *est pris comme exemple; les autres noms de voix s'utilisent de la même façon.*

il est ténor
= he's a tenor *ou* he sings tenor

■ *Les expressions françaises avec de se traduisent par l'emploi du nom de la voix en position d'adjectif.*

une voix de ténor
= a tenor voice

la tessiture de ténor
= the tenor range

un solo de ténor
= a tenor solo

---

chancre /ʃɑ̃kʀ/ *nm* canker

chandail /ʃɑ̃daj/ *nm* sweater, jumper GB

Chandeleur /ʃɑ̃dlœʀ/ *nf* Relig Candlemas

chandelier /ʃɑ̃dəlje/ *nm* (à une branche) candlestick; (à plusieurs branches) candelabra^{GB}

chandelle /ʃɑ̃dɛl/ *nf* **1** (bougie) candle; **lire à la lueur d'une ~** to read by candlelight; **s'éclairer à la ~** to use candles for lighting; **un dîner aux ~s** a candlelit dinner; **2** Sport **faire la ~** to do a shoulder stand

(Idiomes) **devoir une fière ~**○ **à qn** to be hugely indebted to sb; **faire des économies de bouts de ~s** to make cheeseparing economies; **tenir la ~**○ to play gooseberry○; **brûler la ~ par les deux bouts** to burn the candle at both ends; **le jeu n'en vaut pas la ~** the game isn't worth the candle; ▸ **trente-six**

change /ʃɑ̃ʒ/ *nm* **1** (taux) exchange rate; **2** (opération) (foreign) exchange; **gagner/perdre au ~** lit to make/to lose money on the exchange; **perdre au ~** fig to lose out; **en quittant son emploi précédent il a gagné** *or* **il n'a pas perdu au ~** when he left his previous job it was a change for the better

changeant, ~e /ʃɑ̃ʒɑ̃, ɑ̃t/ *adj* **1** (inconstant) changeable, fickle; **d'humeur ~e** moody; **2** (chatoyant) [*tissu*] shimmering; [*couleur, reflet*] changing, shifting

changement /ʃɑ̃ʒmɑ̃/ *nm* **1** (modification) change (**de** in); **~ de température** change in temperature; **~ en mieux/pire** change for the better/worse; **2** (de train, bus, d'avion) change; **Bordeaux-Bruxelles sans ~** Bordeaux-Brussels straight through

(Composés) **~ d'adresse** change of address; **~ de décor** Théât, Cin scene change; fig change of scene

changer /ʃɑ̃ʒe/ [13]

A *vtr* **1** (échanger) to exchange [*objet*] (**pour, contre** for); to change [*secrétaire, emploi*] (**pour, contre** for); **2** (convertir) to change [*argent*]; **~ des euros en dollars** to change euros into dollars; **3** (remplacer) to change [*objet*] (**par, pour** for); to replace [*personne*] (**par, pour** with); **4** (déplacer) **~ qch de place** to move sth; **~ un livre d'étagère** to move a book to another shelf; **5** (modifier) to change; **cette coiffure te change** you look different with your hair like that; **qu'est-ce que ça change?** what difference does it make?; **tu as changé quelque chose à ta coiffure** you've done something different with your hair; **ça n'a rien changé à mes habitudes** it hasn't changed my habits in any way; **cela ne change rien (à l'affaire)** that doesn't make any difference; **cela ne change rien au fait que** that doesn't alter the fact that; **on ne peut rien y ~** we can't do anything about it; **~ sa voix** to disguise one's voice; **6** (transformer) **~ qch/qn en** to turn sth/sb into; **7** (rompre la monotonie) **cela nous change de la pluie** it makes a change from the rain; **ça va le ~ de sa vie tranquille à la campagne** it'll be a change from his quiet life in the country; **8** (renouveler les vêtements de) to change

B **changer de** *vtr ind* **~ de** to change; **~ de travail** to change jobs; **~ de place** [*personne*] to change seats (**avec** with); [*objet*] to be moved; **nous avons changé de route au retour** we came back by a different route; **~ de rue** to move to another street; **~ d'adresse** to move to a new address; **quand il m'a vu il a changé de trottoir** when he saw me he crossed over to the other side of the road; **elle change de bonne tous les mois** she has a new maid every month; **~ d'opinion** *or* **d'avis** to change one's mind; **changeons de sujet** let's change the subject; **~ de sexe** to have a sex change; ▸ **chemise**

C *vi* **1** (se modifier) [*situation, santé, temps*] to change; **il ne change pas** he never changes; **il a changé en bien/mal** he's changed for the better/worse; **il y a quelque chose de changé dans leur comportement** there's something different about their behaviour^{GB}; **pour ~ nous allons en Espagne cet été** for a change we are going to Spain this summer; **pour ne pas ~** as usual; **2** (être remplacé) [*personne, livre*] to be changed; [*horaire*] to change

D **se changer** *vpr* **1** (mettre d'autres vêtements) to get changed; **2** (se transformer) **se ~ en** to turn *ou* change into

(Idiomes) **~ d'air** to have a change of air; **~ du tout au tout** to change completely

changeur, -euse /ʃɑ̃ʒœʀ, øz/
A ▸ p. 372 *nm,f* Fin money changer
B *nm* **1** Hist money changer; **2** Comm (appareil) change machine

chanoine /ʃanwan/ ▸ p. 590 *nm* canon; **le ~ Kir** Canon Kir

(Idiome) **être gras comme un ~** to be as round as a barrel

chanson /ʃɑ̃sõ/ *nf* **1** (texte chanté) song; **~ folklorique** traditional folk song; **~ paillarde** bawdy song; **2** (genre) song; **la ~ française/pour enfants** French/children's song; **faire carrière dans la ~** to make a career as a singer; **vedette de la ~** singing star; **3** ○(propos) **c'est toujours la même ~** it's always the same old story *ou* song; **je connais la ~** I've heard it all before; **4** Littér song, epic (poem); **la Chanson de Roland** the Chanson de Roland

(Composés) **~ d'amour** love song; **~ à boire** drinking song; **~ de geste** chanson de geste; **~ de marin(s)** sea shanty; **~ à succès** hit (song)

chansonnette /ʃɑ̃sɔnɛt/ *nf* (frivole) light-hearted song

chansonnier, -ière /ʃɑ̃sɔnje, ɛʀ/ ▸ p. 372 *nm,f* cabaret artist

chant /ʃɑ̃/ *nm* **1** (activité) singing; **aimer le ~** (chanter) to like singing; (écouter) to like songs; **leçon de ~** singing lesson; **2** (sons caractéristiques) (d'oiseau, de baleine) song; (de coq) crow(ing); (de grillon) chirp(ing); (de cigale) shrilling; (de vent, ruisseau, d'instrument) sound; **au ~ du coq** at cockcrow; **3** (composition musicale) song; **~ à plusieurs voix** part-song; **~s profanes** profane songs; **4** (poésie) ode; (division) canto; **~ funèbre** funeral lament

(Composés) **~ choral** choral singing; **~ du cygne** swansong; **~ d'église** hymn; **~ grégorien** Gregorian chant; **~ de Noël** Christmas carol

chantage /ʃɑ̃taʒ/ *nm* blackmail; **faire du ~ à qn** to blackmail sb; **il me fait du ~ au suicide** he's using threats of suicide to blackmail me

chantant, ~e /ʃɑ̃tɑ̃, ɑ̃t/ *adj* **1** (mélodieux) [*voix, accent*] singsong (épith), lilting; **2** (qui chante aisément) [*mélodie*] tuneful

chanter /ʃɑ̃te/ [1]
A *vtr* **1** Mus to sing [*air*]; **spectacle chanté et dansé** musical

spectacular; [2] (célébrer) to sing (of), to celebrate [*exploit*, *héros*]; **∼ les louanges de qn** to sing sb's praises; [3] ○(raconter) **qu'est-ce qu'il nous chante?** what's he talking about?; **∼ qch sur tous les tons** to harp on about sth

B chanter à○ *vtr ind* (plaire) **ça te chante d'aller à la campagne?** do you fancy○ going to the country?

C *vi* [1] [*personne*] (juste) **∼ juste/faux** to sing in tune/out of tune; **une voix qui chante** a lilting voice; [2] [*oiseau*] to sing; [*coq*] to crow; [*grillon*] to chirp; [*cigale*] to shrill; [*bouilloire*] to sing; [*vent*] (dans les voiles) to sing; (dans les arbres) to rustle; [*source*] to bubble; [3] (subir du chantage) **faire ∼ qn** to blackmail sb

chanterelle /ʃɑ̃tʀɛl/ *nf* [1] Bot chanterelle; [2] Mus E-string

chanteur, -euse /ʃɑ̃tœʀ, øz/
A *adj* **oiseau ∼** songbird
B ▸ p. 372 *nm,f* singer; (de groupe) vocalist; **∼ de charme** crooner; **∼ des rues** street singer

chantier /ʃɑ̃tje/ *nm* [1] (site) building *ou* construction site; **∼ de démolition** demolition site; **le ∼ a été ouvert l'été dernier** the construction work began last summer; **'∼ interdit au public'** 'no admittance to the public'; **en ∼** [*bâtiment*] under construction; [*loi*, *document*] in the process of being drafted; [*film*] in the process of being made; **notre maison sera en ∼ tout l'hiver** the work on our house will go on all winter; **mettre en ∼** to undertake [*projet*]; **remettre en ∼** to resurrect, to dust [sth] off; [2] (entrepôt) builder's yard; [3] ○(lieu en désordre) mess, shambles○ (*sg*); [4] (de tonneau) gantry; [5] (dans une mine) face
(Composé) **∼ naval** shipyard

chantonner /ʃɑ̃tɔne/ [1]
A *vtr* to hum [sth] to oneself
B *vi* to hum to oneself

chantre /ʃɑ̃tʀ/ *nm* [1] Relig cantor; **voix de ∼** rich and powerful voice; [2] (laudateur) eulogist (**de** of); (poète) bard

chanvre /ʃɑ̃vʀ/ *nm* (plante, fibre) hemp; **toile de ∼** hempen cloth

chaos /kao/ *nm inv* [1] (désordre) chaos; [2] (de rochers) blockfield

chaotique /kaɔtik/ *adj* chaotic

chapardage○ /ʃapaʀdaʒ/ *nm* (action) pilfering; (petit vol) petty theft

chaparder○ /ʃapaʀde/ [1] *vtr* to pinch○

chape /ʃap/ *nf* [1] Constr (surface étanche) screed GB, screed coat; **∼ de béton** concrete screed; [2] (couche) fml **∼ de nuages** blanket of cloud; [3] Aut (de pneu) tread; [4] Relig (manteau) cope

chapeau, *pl* **∼x** /ʃapo/
A *nm* [1] (couvre-chef) hat; [2] (de gâteau) top; (de tuyau de cheminée) hood; [3] (en mécanique) cap; [4] Presse introductory paragraph; [5] (de champignon) cap
B ○*excl* well done!
(Composés) **∼ chinois** (coquillage) limpet; Mus Turkish Crescent; **∼ claque** opera hat; **∼ de gendarme** paper hat; **∼ haut de forme** top hat; **∼ de lampe** lampshade; **∼ melon** bowler (hat) GB, derby (hat) US; **∼ de paille** straw hat; **∼ de plage** sun hat; **∼ de roue** Aut hubcap; **démarrer sur les ∼x de roues**○ [*conducteur, voiture*] to shoot off at top speed; [*film, roman, soirée*] to get off to a good *ou* cracking start
(Idiomes) **porter le ∼**○ to carry the can GB, to take the blame *ou* rap○; **coup de ∼** à hats off to; **tirer son ∼** à to take one's hat off to

chapeauter○ /ʃapote/ [1] *vtr* (contrôler) [*personne*] to head; **le ministère chapeaute notre équipe** our team works under the ministry

chapelet /ʃaplɛ/ *nm* [1] Relig (objet, prières) rosary; [2] (d'oignons, de saucisses, villages) string; (d'îlots) chain; (de jurons) stream; **en ∼** in a string

chapelier, -ière /ʃapəlje, ɛʀ/
A *adj* [*industrie, commerce*] hat (épith)
B ▸ p. 372 *nm,f* hatter

chapelle /ʃapɛl/ *nf* [1] Relig chapel; **la ∼ de la Sainte Vierge** the Lady chapel; [2] (groupe) pej clique, coterie; [3] Mus choir
(Composé) **∼ ardente** temporary mortuary

chapelure /ʃaplyʀ/ *nf* breadcrumbs (*pl*)

chaperon /ʃapʀɔ̃/ *nm* [1] (personne) chaperon(e); [2] †(coiffe) hood; **le Petit Chaperon rouge** Little Red Riding Hood

chaperonner /ʃapʀɔne/ [1] *vtr* to chaperone

chapiteau, *pl* **∼x** /ʃapito/ *nm* [1] (tente) marquee GB, tent; (de cirque) big top; [2] (de colonne) capital

chapitre /ʃapitʀ/ *nm* [1] (division) (de livre) chapter; (de rapport) section; [2] (rubrique) **et au ∼ des faits divers...** and now, other news...; [3] (sujet) subject; **sur ce ∼** on this subject; **au ∼ de** on the issue of; [4] (période) chapter; [5] (d'un budget) section, item; **∼ des recettes** section on revenue; [6] Relig chapter
(Idiome) **avoir voix au ∼** to have a say in the matter

chapka /ʃapka/ *nf* fur hat

chapon /ʃapɔ̃/ *nm* (jeune coq) capon

chaque /ʃak/

⚠ Si l'on veut insister sur ce qui fait l'homogénéité d'un ensemble de phénomènes, d'individus ou d'objets on traduit *chaque* par *every*: *chaque année ils allaient faire du ski* = they used to go skiing every year; si l'on veut mettre l'accent sur les phénomènes ou les individus pris séparément on utilisera plutôt *each* (mais *every* ne serait pas faux pour autant): *la situation se détériore chaque année* = each year the situation gets worse.
On remarquera que *every* ne s'utilise que pour parler de plus de deux personnes, objets ou phénomènes; dans l'exemple suivant, seul *each* est correct: *au volley-ball, chaque équipe est composée de six joueurs* = in volleyball, each team is made up of six players.

A *adj indéf* each, every; **∼ travailleur** (dans l'absolu) every worker; (dans un groupe particulier) each worker; **∼ chose en son temps!** all in good time!; **la situation devient ∼ jour plus compliquée** the situation becomes more and more complicated by the day *ou* each day *ou* every day; **il me dérange à ∼ instant** he's always disturbing me
B ○*pron* (chacun) each; **il revend ses disques (à) 10 euros ∼** he's selling his records for 10 euros each

char /ʃaʀ/ *nm* [1] Mil tank; **∼ léger** light tank; [2] (antique) chariot; [3] Agric cart, wagon; **∼ à foin** haycart, haywagon; [4] (de carnaval) float; [5] ○(bluff) bluff; **arrête ton ∼!** come off it!; [6] ○C (voiture) car
(Composés) **∼ d'assaut** Mil tank; **∼ à bancs** *horse-drawn wagon with benches*; **∼ à bœufs** oxcart; **∼ à voile** Sport (sur roues) sand yacht; (sur patins) ice yacht

charabia○ /ʃaʀabja/ *nm* gobbledygook○, double Dutch

charade /ʃaʀad/ *nf* riddle

charançon /ʃaʀɑ̃sɔ̃/ *nm* weevil

charbon /ʃaʀbɔ̃/ *nm* [1] Ind coal; **faire griller qch sur des ∼s (de bois)** to barbecue sth; [2] (médicament) charcoal; [3] ▸ p. 195 Méd anthrax; [4] Bot smut; [5] Art charcoal; (dessin) charcoal drawing; [6] Électrotech (balai) carbon brush; (électrode) carbon
(Composé) **∼ de bois** charcoal
(Idiomes) **être sur des ∼s ardents** to be like a cat on a hot tin roof; **aller au ∼**○ (aller au travail) to get to work; (effectuer une tâche pénible) to do the menial work

charbonner /ʃaʀbɔne/ [1]
A *vtr* to blacken [*visage, joue, mur*]
B **se charbonner** *vpr* **se ∼ le visage** to blacken one's face

charbonneux, -euse /ʃaʀbɔnø, øz/ *adj* [1] (évoquant le charbon) gén sooty; [*paupière*] black with make-up (*jamais épith*); [2] Méd [*fièvre*] anthracic

charbonnier, -ière /ʃaʀbɔnje, ɛʀ/
A *adj* [*centre*] coalmining (épith); [*production, industrie*] coal (épith)
B ▸ p. 372 *nm,f* (marchand) coalman/coalwoman
C *nm* Naut collier GB, coaler

charcuter○ /ʃaʀkyte/ [1]
A *vtr* [1] (opérer) [*chirurgien*] to hack [sb] about [*malade*]; [2] (découper) to make a mess of carving [*viande*]; [3] (dénaturer) to carve up [*texte*]
B **se charcuter** *vpr* (se couper) to cut oneself badly

charcuterie /ʃaʀkytʀi/ *nf* [1] Culin (produits) cooked pork meats (*pl*); [2] ▸ p. 372 **∼ (traiteur)** (magasin) pork butcher's; (rayon dans un supermarché) delicatessen counter

charcutier, -ière /ʃaʀkytje, ɛʀ/ ▸ p. 372 *nm,f* (commerçant) pork butcher

chardon /ʃaʀdɔ̃/ nm thistle

chardonneret /ʃaʀdɔnʀe/ nm goldfinch

charentais, ~e¹ /ʃaʀɑ̃tɛ, ɛz/ ▸ p. 504 adj [personne] from the Charente region; [melon] Charentais

charentaise² /ʃaʀɑ̃tez/ nf (pantoufle) carpet slipper

charge /ʃaʀʒ/ nf

A **1** (fardeau) lit, fig burden, load; (cargaison) (de véhicule) load; (de navire) cargo, freight; Naut (fait de charger) loading; **prendre qn en ~** [taxi] to take sb as a passenger *ou* fare; **prise en ~** (dans un taxi) minimum fare; **2** Archit, Constr load; **3** (responsabilité) responsibility; **avoir la ~ de qn/qch** to be responsible for sb/sth; **trois enfants à ~** three dependent children; **il s'est bien acquitté de sa ~** he carried out his task well; **prendre en ~** [tuteur] to take charge of [enfant]; [services sociaux] to take [sb] into care [enfant]; [sécurité sociale] to accept financial responsibility for [malade]; to take care of [frais, dépenses]; **prise en ~** (par la sécurité sociale) agreement to bear medical costs; **la prise en ~ des réfugiés/dépenses sera assurée par...** the refugees/expenses will be taken care of *ou* looked after by...; **se prendre en ~** to take care of oneself; **mes neveux sont à ma ~** I support my nephews; **ces frais sont à la ~ du client** these expenses are payable by the customer; **à ~ pour lui de faire** it's up to him to do; **4** Admin (fonction) office; **occuper de hautes ~s** to hold high office; **~ de notaire** notary's office; **5** (preuve) evidence; **il n'y a aucune ~ contre lui** there's no evidence against him; **6** Mil (assaut) charge (**contre** against); (d'explosifs) charge; **7** Électrotech, Phys charge; **~ positive/négative** positive/negative charge; **8** (contenu) **~ émotionnelle** emotional charge; **~ symbolique** symbolic content

B **charges** nfpl gén expenses, costs; (de locataire, copropriétaire) service charge (sg); **les ~s de l'État** government expenditure ₵

(Composés) **~ de travail** workload; **~s fiscales** tax expenses; **~s locatives** maintenance costs (payable by a tenant); **~s patronales** employer's social security contributions; **~s sociales** welfare costs

(Idiomes) **revenir à la ~** to try again; **revenir à la ~ contre qch** to renew one's attack on sth

chargé, ~e /ʃaʀʒe/

A pp ▸ charger

B pp adj [particule] charged; **être ~ de** [branches] to be heavy *ou* laden (down) with [fruits, neige]; [bras] to be covered with [bijoux]; to be full of [nuages, ratures]; **un regard ~ de menaces** a threatening look; **être ~ de famille** to have dependents

C adj [personne, véhicule] loaded; [horaires, style] heavy; [journée] busy; [décorations] over-ornate; [langue] coated; **trop ~** overloaded; **avoir un casier judiciaire ~** to have had several previous convictions

(Composés) **~ d'affaires** Pol chargé d'affaires; **~ de cours** Univ part-time lecturer; **~ de mission** Pol representative

chargement /ʃaʀʒəmɑ̃/ nm **1** (objets transportés) gén load; (marchandises) (par avion, bateau) cargo, load; (par camion) load; **2** (mise à bord) loading; **3** (d'arme, appareil) loading; (de poêle) stoking; (de logiciel) loading; **4** Électrotech (de batterie) charging

(Composé) **~ postal** registered mail ₵

charger /ʃaʀʒe/ [13]

A vtr **1** gén to load [marchandises] (**dans** into; **sur** onto); to load [véhicule, navire, animal] (**de** with); **~ un client** [taxi] to pick up a passenger *ou* fare; **trop ~** to overload sth; **2** (remplir le chargeur) to load [arme, appareil photo]; **3** Ordinat to load [disquette, programme] (**dans** into); **4** Électrotech to charge [batterie, accumulateur]; **5** (outrer) to overdo [description, aspect]; **6** (confier une mission à) **~ qn de qch** to make sb responsible for sth; **~ qn de faire** to give sb the responsibility of doing; **elle m'a chargé de vous transmettre ses amitiés** she asked me to give you her regards; **c'est lui qui est chargé de l'enquête** he is in charge of the investigation; **7** (accabler) to bring evidence against [accusé]; **8** (attaquer) to charge at [foule]

B vi [armée, taureau] to charge

C se charger vpr **1** (s'occuper) **se ~ de** to take responsibility for; **je m'en charge** I'll see to it; **je me charge de le leur dire** I'll tell them; **je me charge de la boisson** I'll take care of the drinks; **2** (prendre des bagages) to weigh oneself down; **3** Mil **se ~ facilement** [arme] to be easy to load

chargeur /ʃaʀʒœʀ/ nm **1** Mil (objet) magazine; (personne) loader; **il a vidé son ~ sur le caissier** he fired a full round of bullets at the cashier; **2** Électrotech charger; **3** Phot cartridge; Cin film magazine; **4** Ordinat loader; **5** (débardeur) loader; **6** (expéditeur) loader, shipper

chariot /ʃaʀjo/ nm **1** (poussé à la main) trolley GB, cart US; **~ de supermarché** supermarket trolley GB, shopping cart US; **2** (motorisé) truck; **3** (tiré par des chevaux) waggon^GB; **4** (de machine à écrire) carriage; **5** Cin (de caméra) dolly

charisme /kaʀism/ nm charisma

charitable /ʃaʀitabl/ adj charitable (**envers** toward(s), to); **tendre une main ~** à fig to lend a helping hand

charitablement /ʃaʀitabləmɑ̃/ adv (avec charité) charitably; (gentiment) kindly

charité /ʃaʀite/ nf **1** (aumône) charity; **appel à la ~ publique** charity appeal; **vente de ~** charity sale; **la ~ s'il vous plaît** spare me some change, please; **2** (bienveillance) kindness; **il a eu la ~ de faire** he was kind enough to do; **3** Relig charity

(Idiome) **~ bien ordonnée commence par soi-même** Prov charity begins at home Prov

charlatan /ʃaʀlatɑ̃/ nm (guérisseur) quack^○; (vendeur) con man; (politicien) fraud

Charles /ʃaʀl/ npr Charles

(Composés) **~ le Bel** Charles the Fair; **~ Quint** Charles the Fifth (of Spain); **~ le Téméraire** Charles the Bold

charlot^○ /ʃaʀlo/ nm clown; **arrête de faire le ~!** stop clowning!

Charlot /ʃaʀlo/ npr Charlie (Chaplin)

charlotte /ʃaʀlɔt/ nf **1** (dessert) charlotte; **2** (bonnet) mobcap

charmant, ~e /ʃaʀmɑ̃, ɑ̃t/ adj **1** (plaisant) [personne, sourire, lieu] charming, delightful; [soirée, enfant] delightful; [objet] lovely; **c'est ~!** iron charming *ou* wonderful! iron; **un ~ bambin** iron a little dear iron; **2** (aimable) very nice (**avec** to)

charme /ʃaʀm/

A nm **1** (de personne, sourire, visage) charm; **une opération de ~** a public relations exercise; **c'est une véritable offensive de ~ pour convaincre les électeurs** they are really trying to woo the electorate; **faire du ~ à qn** to use one's charms on sb; **faire du ~** *or* **son numéro de ~ à qn pour qu'il fasse qch** to try to charm sb into doing sth; **2** (de lieu, musique) charm; **cela a le ~ de la nouveauté** it has (a certain) novelty value; **cela ne manque pas de ~** (mode de vie, roman) it is not without its charms; (proposition) it is not unattractive; **3** (qui envoûte) spell; **tomber sous le ~ de qn** to fall under sb's spell; **4** Bot hornbeam

B **charmes** nmpl euph physical attributes euph

(Idiome) **se porter comme un ~** to be as fit as a fiddle

charmer /ʃaʀme/ [1] vtr to charm; **se laisser ~ par qn** to fall for *ou* succumb to sb's charms

charmeur, -euse /ʃaʀmœʀ, øz/

A adj [sourire] winning, engaging; [attitude] charming, engaging; [regard] engaging

B nm,f charmer

(Composé) **~ de serpents** snake charmer

charnel, -elle /ʃaʀnɛl/ adj [plaisirs, amour] carnal

charnier /ʃaʀnje/ nm gén mass grave; Hist (lieu couvert) charnel house

charnière /ʃaʀnjɛʀ/

A nf **1** (de porte, coquillage) hinge; **2** fig (lien important) bridge (**entre** between); **3** Anat joint

B (-)charnière (in compounds) **époque(-)~** transitional period; **rôle(-)~** pivotal role

charnu, ~e /ʃaʀny/ adj [bras, fruit, poulet] plump; [lèvre] fleshy, thick; [crabe] meaty

charognard /ʃaʀɔɲaʀ/ nm **1** (hyène, chacal) carrion feeder; (vautour) vulture; **2** (profiteur) pej vulture péj

charogne /ʃaʀɔɲ/ nf (d'animal) rotting carcass; (d'humain) rotting corpse

charolais, ~e /ʃaʀɔlɛ, ɛz/ ▸ p. 504 adj Charolais

charpente /ʃaʀpɑ̃t/ nf **1** Constr (de toit) roof structure; (de bâtiment) framework; (de bateau) structure; **bois de ~** timber; **2** Anat (structure interne) framework; (constitution) build; **~ osseuse** skeleton; **3** (de livre, film) structure

charpenté, ~e /ʃaʀpɑ̃te/ adj [vin] robust; **bien ~** [personne] well-built (épith)

charpentier /ʃaʀpɑ̃tje/ ▸ p. 372 nm carpenter

charpie /ʃaʀpi/ nf fig **être en ~** to be in shreds; **réduire** or **mettre qch en ~** to tear sth to shreds

charretée /ʃaʀte/ nf cartload; **par ~s** lit, fig by the cartload

charretier /ʃaʀtje/ ▸ p. 372 nm carter

(Idiome) **jurer comme un ~** to swear like a trooper

charrette /ʃaʀɛt/ nf ① (voiture à deux roues) cart; ② (série) **il a fait partie de la première ~ de licenciés** he went in the first wave ou round of layoffs

(Composés) **~ à bras** handcart, barrow; **~ des condamnés** Hist tumbril

charrier /ʃaʀje/ [2]

Ⓐ vtr ① (avec un chariot, une brouette) to cart; ② (tirer avec effort) to haul [troncs d'arbre, blocs de pierre]; ③ (entraîner) [cours d'eau] to carry [sth] along; ④ ○(se moquer de) to tease [sb] unmercifully

Ⓑ ○vi to go too far; **faut pas ~** that's really pushing it○!

charrue /ʃaʀy/ nf plough, plow US

(Idiome) **mettre la ~ avant les bœufs** to put the cart before the horse

charte /ʃaʀt/ nf charter; **la ~ des droits de l'homme** the Charter of Human Rights

charter /ʃaʀtɛʀ/

Ⓐ adj inv charter (épith)

Ⓑ nm charter plane

chartreux /ʃaʀtʀø/ nm (moine) Carthusian monk

Charybde /kaʀibd/ npr Charybdis

(Idiome) **tomber de ~ en Scylla** to jump out of the frying pan into the fire

chas /ʃa/ nm inv (d'aiguille) eye

chasse /ʃas/ nf ① (activité) gén hunting; (au fusil) shooting; **aller à la ~** to go shooting GB ou hunting US; (à cheval) to go hunting; **~ au lièvre** hare coursing; **la ~ aux papillons** catching butterflies; **~ au trésor** treasure hunt; ② (saison) **la ~ est ouverte/fermée** it's the open/closed season; ③ (gibier) **faire (une) bonne ~** to get a good bag; **se partager la ~** to share the game; ④ (domaine) (pour le petit gibier) shoot; (pour le gros gibier) hunting ground; **~ gardée** lit, fig preserve; ⑤ (poursuite) chase; **donner la ~ à, prendre en ~** to chase; **faire la ~ aux araignées** to wage war on spiders; **faire la ~ aux trafiquants** to hunt down traffickers; ⑥ (recherche) hunting (à for); **~ aux autographes** autograph-hunting; **être à la ~ de** or **à** to be hunting for; ⑦ Mil (avions) **la ~, l'aviation de ~** fighter planes (pl); ⑧ (de WC) **~ (d'eau)** (toilet) flush; **actionner la ~** (manette) to flush the toilet; **tirer la ~** (chaîne) to pull the chain

(Composés) **~ à la baleine** whaling; **~ aux cerveaux** head-hunting; **~ à l'homme** manhunt; **~ aux sorcières** witch-hunt; **~ sous-marine** Sport harpoon fishing, harpooning

(Idiome) **qui va à la ~ perd sa place** Prov leave your place and you lose it

chassé-croisé, pl **chassés-croisés** /ʃasekʀwaze/ nm ① (manœuvres) continual coming and going (**entre** between); **chassés-croisés amoureux** romantic intrigue (sg); ② (en danse) chassé-croisé, (et to partners)

chasse-neige /ʃasnɛʒ/ nm inv snowplough GB, snowplow US; **faire du ~** to snowplough GB, to snowplow US

chasser /ʃase/ [1]

Ⓐ vtr ① [animal] to hunt [proie]; ② [personne] gén to hunt; (au fusil) to shoot GB, to hunt; **~ le renard** to go (fox) hunting; **~ la baleine** to go whaling; ③ (éloigner) [personne] to chase away [animal]; [police] to get rid of [badauds]; [bruit, mauvais temps] to drive away [touristes, client]; (expulser) to drive out [immigrant, ennemi]; (congédier) to fire [domestique]; **~ qn de** (de place, rue, terrain) to drive sb out of ou from; (de lieu fermé) to throw sb out of; **le bruit nous a chassés de chez nous** we were driven out of our home by the noise; **être chassé du pouvoir** to be ousted from power; ④ (disperser) to dispel [fumée, odeur, doute]; **~ une idée de son esprit** to banish a thought from one's mind; ⑤ (faire avancer) to herd [bétail, oies]; ⑥ (déloger) to force [sth] out [eau]; to knock [sth] out [tenon]

Ⓑ vi ① (aller à la chasse) gén to go hunting; (avec un fusil) to go shooting GB ou hunting US; ② (déraper) [voiture, moto] to skid; ③ Naut **le navire chasse sur ses ancres** the ship is dragging her anchor

chasseresse /ʃasʀɛs/ nf liter huntress littér

chasseur, -euse /ʃasœʀ, øz/

Ⓐ nm,f (animal, personne) hunter; **~ de renards** fox hunter; **être un bon ~** (au fusil) to be a good shot; (avec une meute) to be a good huntsman; **un groupe de ~s** (au fusil) a shooting party; (avec une meute) a hunt

Ⓑ nm ① Mil (soldat) chasseur; (régiment) **le 2ᵉ ~** the 2nd (regiment of) chasseurs; ② Mil (avion) fighter (aircraft); (pilote) fighter pilot; ③ (groom) bellboy GB, bellhop US

(Composés) **~ alpin** soldier trained for mountainous terrain; **~ de baleine** whaler; **~ à cheval** light cavalryman; **~ d'images** camera buff; **~ de prime** bounty hunter; **~ à réaction** jet fighter; **~ de sons** recording buff; **~ de têtes** lit, fig head-hunter

châssis /ʃasi/ nm ① (de fenêtre) frame; ② Aut chassis; **~ surbaissé** drop frame chassis; ③ Agric cold frame; ④ Art (pour tapisserie, broderie) frame; (en sculpture) pointing machine; ⑤ Rail underframe

chaste /ʃast/ adj gén chaste; [personne] celibate; [oreilles] innocent

chastement /ʃastəmɑ̃/ adv [aimer] chastely, in a chaste fashion; [s'habiller] modestly, demurely; **vivre ~** to lead a chaste life

chasteté /ʃastəte/ nf chastity

chat /ʃa/ nm ① (animal) gén cat; (mâle) tomcat; ② ▸ p. 327 Jeux **jouer à ~** to play tag ou tig GB; **c'est toi le ~** you're 'it'

(Composés) **~ de gouttière** (tigré) tabby cat; (commun) ordinary cat, alley cat; **~ perché** Jeux off-ground tag ou tig GB; **~ sauvage** wildcat; **le Chat botté** Puss in Boots

(Idiomes) **donner sa langue au ~** to give in; **il n'y a pas un ~○** the place is deserted; **avoir un ~ dans la gorge** to have a frog in one's throat; **il ne faut pas réveiller le ~ qui dort** Prov let sleeping dogs lie Prov; **être** or **s'entendre comme chien et ~** to fight like cat and dog; ▸ **échauder, fouetter, rat, souris**

châtaigne /ʃatɛɲ/ nf ① Bot (sweet) chestnut; ② ○(coup de poing) clout○, punch

châtaignier /ʃatɛɲe/ nm (arbre) (sweet) chestnut (tree); **une table de ~** or **en ~** a chestnut table

châtain /ʃatɛ̃/ ▸ p. 140 adj m [cheveux, barbe] brown; **il est ~** he's got brown hair

château, pl **~x** /ʃato/ nm ① (forteresse) castle; ② (résidence) (royale) palace; (seigneuriale) castle; ③ (grande demeure) manor

(Composés) **~ de cartes** lit, fig house of cards; **~ d'eau** water tower; **~ fort** fortified castle; **~ de sable** sand castle

(Idiome) **mener la vie de ~** to live the life of Riley GB, to live like a prince

châtelain, ~e /ʃatlɛ̃, ɛn/ nm,f ① (propriétaire) owner of a manor; ② Hist lord/lady (of the manor)

chat-huant, pl **chats-huants** /ʃaɥɑ̃/ nm tawny owl

châtier /ʃatje/ [2] vtr liter ① (punir) to punish [fautif, délit]; **~ qn pour son insolence, ~ l'insolence de qn** to punish sb for his/her insolence; ② (soigner) to polish [style]; to refine [langage]

(Idiome) **qui aime bien châtie bien** Prov spare the rod and spoil the child Prov

chatière /ʃatjɛʀ/ nf ① (porte) catflap; ② (en spéléologie) crawl

châtiment /ʃatimɑ̃/ nm punishment

chatoiement /ʃatwamɑ̃/ nm shimmering

chaton /ʃatɔ̃/ nm ① (petit chat) kitten; ② (sur les arbres) catkin; ③ (de bague) (monture) setting; (pierre) gem; ④ ○(flocon de poussière) ball of fluff; ⑤ (terme d'affection) **mon ~** my darling

chatouille○ /ʃatuj/ nf tickle ₵; **faire des ~s à qn** to tickle sb

chatouiller /ʃatuje/ [1] vtr ① lit to tickle; **ça me chatouille dans le dos** my back is tickling; ② (flatter) to titillate [palais]; to tickle [curiosité]; to flatter [orgueil]; ③ ○(énerver) to nettle, to irritate [personne]

(Idiome) **~ les côtes à qn** euph to tan sb's hide

chatouilleux, -euse /ʃatujø, øz/ adj ① (sensible aux chatouilles) ticklish; ② (susceptible) [personne] touchy (**sur** about)

chatoyant, **~e** /ʃatwajɑ̃, ɑ̃t/ *adj* **1** [*mer, couleur*] shimmering; [*plumage*] iridescent; **2** [*style, écriture*] sparkling

chatoyer /ʃatwaje/ [23] *vi* [*couleur, mer*] to shimmer

châtrer /ʃɑtʀe/ [1] *vtr* (castrer) to neuter [*chat*]; to geld [*cheval*]; to castrate [*homme, taureau, chien*]

chatte /ʃat/ *nf* (female) cat

(Idiomes) **être gourmand comme une ~** to be a piggy○; **une ~ n'y retrouverait pas ses petits** it's a real mess

chatter /tʃate/ *vi* to chat

chaud, **~e** /ʃo, ʃod/

A *adj* **1** (à température élevée) hot; (modérément) warm; **à four ~/très ~** in a warm/hot oven; **on nous a servi des croissants tout ~s** we were served piping hot croissants; **2** (qui donne de la chaleur) [*pièce*] (agréablement) warm; (excessivement) hot; **3** (récent) **'ils sont mariés?'—'oui, c'est tout ~'** 'they're married?'—'yes, it's hot news'; **4** (enthousiaste) [*félicitations*] warm; [*partisan*] strong; **être ~ pour faire** to be keen on doing; **5** (agité) [*région, période*] turbulent; [*sujet*] sensitive; [*discussion*] heated; **un des points ~s du globe** one of the flash points of the world; **~e ambiance ce soir chez les voisins!** hum things are getting heated next door tonight!; **6** (attrayant) [*coloris, voix*] warm; **7** ○(de prostitution) euph [*quartier*] red light (*épith*)

B *adv* **il fait ~** (agréablement) it's warm; (excessivement) it's hot; **ça ne me fait ni ~ ni froid** it doesn't matter one way or the other to me; **manger ~** to eat hot foods; **'servir ~'** 'serve hot'

C *nm* (chaleur) heat; **on crève○ de ~ ici!** we're roasting○ in here!; **avoir ~** (modérément) to be warm; (excessivement) to be hot; **nous avons eu ~** lit we were very hot; fig we had a narrow escape; **donner ~ à qn** [*course, aventure*] to make sb sweat; **tenir ~ à qn** to keep sb warm; **ça me tient ~ aux pieds** it keeps my feet warm; **se tenir ~** [*personnes, animaux*] to keep warm; **~ devant○!** watch out!; **prendre un coup de ~** [*plante*] to wilt (in the sun); **tenir ou garder au ~** lit to keep [sb] warm [*personne*]; to keep [sth] hot [*plat, boisson*]; fig (pour parer à une éventualité) to have [sth] on standby [*matériel, projet*]

D **à chaud** *loc adv* **à ~** [*analyser*] on the spot; [*réaction*] immediate; Tech [*étirer*] under heat; **opérer à ~** to do an emergency operation

(Composé) **~ et froid** Méd chill

chaudement /ʃodmɑ̃/ *adv* **1** [*vêtu*] warmly; **2** (vivement) [*féliciter*] warmly; [*recommander*] heartily

chaudière /ʃodjɛʀ/ *nf* boiler

chaudron /ʃodʀɔ̃/ *nm* cauldron

chaudronnerie /ʃodʀɔnʀi/ *nf* (industrie) boilermaking industry; (usine) boilerworks (+ *v sg*); (articles) **grosse ~** industrial boilers (*pl*); **petite ~** pots and pans (*pl*)

chaudronnier, **-ière** /ʃodʀɔnje, ɛʀ/ ▸ p. 372 *nmf* (ouvrier) boilermaker

chauffage /ʃofaʒ/ *nm* **1** (chaleur artificielle) heating; **une chambre sans ~** an unheated bedroom; **mettre le ~** to put the heating on; **le ~ de notre maison coûte très cher** the house is very expensive to heat; **2** (installations) heating; **~ par le sol** underfloor heating; **3** (appareil) heater; **~ d'appoint** extra heater GB, space heater US; **4** (élévation de la température) heating; **après un léger ~** after heating gently

chauffagiste /ʃofaʒist/ ▸ p. 372 *nmf* heating engineer

chauffant, **~e** /ʃofɑ̃, ɑ̃t/ *adj* [*surface*] heating

chauffard○ /ʃofaʀ/ *nm* pej reckless driver, road hog○

chauffe /ʃof/ *nf* Tech **1** (opération) stoking; **2** (lieu) fire chamber

chauffe-eau /ʃofo/ *nm inv* water-heater; **~ à gaz à accumulation** gas storage water-heater

chauffe-plat /ʃofpla/ *nm inv* dish warmer

chauffer /ʃofe/ [1]

A *vtr* to heat [*pièce*]; to heat (up) [*métal, objet, liquide, plat*]; **trop chauffées** overheated; **~ du fer à blanc** to bring iron to a white heat; **~ l'auditoire à blanc** fig to whip the audience into a frenzy; **~ le public** to warm up the audience

B *vi* **1** (devenir chaud) [*plat*] to heat (up); [*moteur*] to warm up; [*four*] to heat up; **faire ~** to heat [*eau, aliment*]; to warm [*assiette, biberon*]; to heat (up) [*four*]; to warm (up) [*moteur*]; **mettre à ~** to put [sth] on to heat [*eau*]; to heat up [*plat*]; to warm [*biberon*]; **2** (devenir trop chaud) [*moteur*] to overheat; **ne**

laissez pas l'appareil ~ toute la nuit don't leave the appliance running all night; **3** (produire de la chaleur) [*radiateur*] to give out heat; **4** ○fig (être animé) **avec ce groupe, ça va ~!** this group's going to liven things up!; **si le patron l'apprend, ça va ~!** if the boss finds out, there'll be big trouble!; **5** Jeux to get warm

C **se chauffer** *vpr* **se ~ au coin du feu** to warm oneself by the fire; **se ~ au soleil** [*personne, animal*] to bask in the sun; **nous nous chauffons au charbon** we have coal-fired heating

chaufferie /ʃofʀi/ *nf* (de bâtiment) boiler room; (de bateau) stokehold

chauffeur /ʃofœʀ/ *nm* **1** ▸ p. 372 Aut gén driver; (de particulier) chauffeur; **voiture avec/sans ~** chauffeur-driven/self-drive car; **faire le ~ pour qn** to chauffeur sb about; **2** (de chaudière) gén stoker; Rail fireman

(Composés) **~ du dimanche** pej Sunday driver; **~ de maître** chauffeur

chauffeuse /ʃoføz/ *nf* (fauteuil) low armless easy chair

chaume /ʃom/ *nm* **1** Agric (tige) stubble **₵**; (champ) stubble field; **2** (pour toiture) thatch

chaumière /ʃomjɛʀ/ *nf* **1** (avec toit de chaume) thatched cottage; **2** (petite maison) liter humble cottage; **faire jaser dans les ~s** hum to cause tongues to wag

chaussant, **~e** /ʃosɑ̃, ɑ̃t/ *adj* well-fitting

chaussée /ʃose/ *nf* **1** (route) road(way) GB, highway; (rue) street; **2** (revêtement) surface; **~ déformée** uneven road surface; **3** (chemin surélevé) causeway; (remblai) embankment

chausse-pied, *pl* **~s** /ʃospje/ *nm* shoehorn

chausser /ʃose/ [1]

A *vtr* to put [sth] on [*chaussures, skis*]; to put [sth] on [*lunettes*]; to take [*étriers*]; **être mal chaussé** to be poorly shod; **elle était chaussée de pantoufles** she was wearing slippers; **se faire ~ sur mesure** to have one's shoes made to measure

B ▸ p. 575 *vi* **je chausse du 41** I take a (size) 41; **ces mocassins chaussent grand** these loafers are large-fitting

C **se chausser** *vpr* **1** (mettre ses chaussures) to put (one's) shoes on; **se ~ de qch** to put on sth; **2** (s'équiper) to get ou buy (one's) shoes

chaussette /ʃosɛt/ *nf* (vêtement) sock

(Idiome) **laisser tomber qn comme une vieille ~○** to cast sb off like an old rag

chausseur /ʃosœʀ/ *nm* **1** ▸ p. 372 (commerçant) shoe shop manager; **2** ▸ p. 372 (fabricant) shoemaker

chausson /ʃosɔ̃/ *nm* **1** (pantoufle) slipper; (de bébé) bootee; (de danse) ballet shoe ou pump; (de sport) pump

(Composé) **~ aux pommes** Culin apple turnover

chaussure /ʃosyʀ/ *nf* **1** (soulier) shoe; (à tige haute) boot; **~ basse** shoe; **~ montante** ankle boot; **~ de tennis** tennis shoe; **~ de ski** ski boot; **rayon ~s** shoe department; **2** (industrie) footwear industry; (commerce) footwear trade

(Idiome) **trouver ~ à son pied** (compagnon) to find the right person

chaut† ▸ **chaloir**

chauve /ʃov/

A *adj* bald; fig, liter bare

B *nm* bald(-headed) man

chauve-souris, *pl* **chauves-souris** /ʃovsuʀi/ *nf* Zool bat

chauvin, **~e** /ʃovɛ̃, in/

A *adj* chauvinistic, jingoistic

B *nm,f* chauvinist, jingoist

chaux /ʃo/ *nf inv* lime; **lait de ~** whitewash; **blanchir** *or* **passer à la ~** to whitewash; **~ vive** quicklime

chavirer /ʃaviʀe/ [1] *vi* [*navire*] to capsize; **faire ~ un navire** to capsize a ship; **faire ~ les cœurs** to be a heartbreaker

chef¹ /ʃɛf/ *nm* **1** (meneur) leader; **qualités de ~** leadership qualities; **2** (supérieur) superior, boss○; Mil (sergent) sergeant; **3** (dirigeant) gén head; Comm (d'un service) manager; **~ de l'Église** head of the Church; **l'exemple doit venir des ~s** the example must come from the top; **architecte en ~** chief architect; **commandant en ~** Mil commander-in-chief; **4** Culin **~ (cuisinier** *or* **de cuisine)** chef; **5** ○(as, champion) ace; **se débrouiller comme un ~** to manage splendidly; **6** †(tête) head; **de mon/leur (propre) ~** on my/their own initiative; **7** (chapitre) **au premier ~** primarily, first and foremost

Composés) **~ d'accusation** Jur count of indictment; **répondre à un ~ d'accusation** to answer a charge; **~ d'atelier** (shop) foreman; **~ de cabinet** principal private secretary; **~ de chantier** works GB ou site foreman; **~ d'équipe** foreman; **~ d'établissement** head teacher; **~ d'État** head of state; **~ d'état-major** Chief of Staff; **~ de fabrication** production manager; **~ de famille** head of the family ou household; **~ de file** gén leader; Pol party leader; **~ de gare** stationmaster; **~ de gouvernement** head of government; **~ d'orchestre** conductor; **~ du personnel** personnel manager; **~ de plateau** Cin, TV floor manager; **~ de projet** project manager; **~ de publicité** (d'agence) account executive; (annonceur) advertising manager; (dans les médias) advertising (sales) manager; **~ de rayon** department supervisor ou manager; **~ de service** Admin section ou department head; Méd clinical director GB, chief physician US; **~ de tribu** headman

chef² /ʃɛf/ nf boss○; **c'est elle la ~** she's the boss○

chef-d'œuvre, pl **chefs-d'œuvre** /ʃɛdœvr/ nm masterpiece

chef-lieu, pl **chefs-lieux** /ʃɛfljø/ nm (ville) administrative centre

cheik(h) /ʃɛk/ nm sheik(h)

chelem /ʃlɛm/ nm **1** (aux cartes) slam; **2** Sport **gagner le grand ~** to win the Grand Slam

chemin /ʃ(ə)mɛ̃/ nm **1** (route) country road; (étroit) lane; (de terre) (pour véhicule) track; (pour piétons) path; **être toujours sur les ~s** to be always on the road; **2** (passage) way; **les obstacles qui sont** or **se trouvent sur mon ~** lit, fig the obstacles which stand in my way; **3** (direction, itinéraire, trajet) way; **se tromper de ~** to go the wrong way; **sur le ~ du retour/de l'école** on the way back/to school; **reprendre le ~ du bureau** to go back to the office ou to work; **le ~ le plus court pour** the quickest way to; **le plus court ~ vers la paix** the shortest path to peace; **on a fait un bout de ~ ensemble** (à pied) we walked along together for a while; (dans la vie) we were together for a while; **~ faisant, en ~** on ou along the way; **faire tout le ~ à pied/en boitant** to walk/to limp all the way; **il a su trouver le ~ de mon cœur** fig he's found the way to my heart; **cette femme fera/a fait du ~** this woman will go/has come a long way; **l'idée fait son ~** the idea is gaining ground; **montrer le ~** (donner l'exemple) to lead the way; **être sur le bon ~** gén to be heading in the right direction; **prendre le ~ de la faillite** to be heading for bankruptcy; **s'arrêter en ~** lit to stop off on the way; fig to stop; **tu ne vas pas t'arrêter en si bon ~!** don't stop when things are going so well!; **le ~ de la gloire** the path of glory; **le ~ de la célébrité/perdition** the road to fame/ruin; **le destin l'a mis sur mon ~** fate threw him in my path; **4** (tapis) (carpet) runner

Composés) **le ~ des écoliers** the long way round GB ou around US; **prendre le ~ des écoliers** to take the long way round GB ou around US; **~ de fer** Rail (infrastructure) railway, railroad US; (mode de transport) rail; **par ~ de fer** by rail; **~ de halage** towpath; **~ de table** (table) runner; **~ de terre** (pour véhicule) dirt track; (pour piétons) path; **~ de traverse** path across ou through the fields; **~ vicinal** country lane

cheminée /ʃ(ə)mine/ nf **1** (de maison) (conduit complet) chimney; (sur le toit) chimney stack; (foyer) fireplace; (manteau) mantelpiece; **2** (d'usine) chimney; **3** (de fosse, cave) shaft; **4** (de bateau, locomotive) funnel, smokestack US; **5** (de mine) chute; **6** (en montagne) chimney

cheminement /ʃ(ə)minmɑ̃/ nm **1** (avance) (slow) progression; **2** (voie suivie) course; **le ~ de sa pensée** his/her train of thought

cheminer /ʃ(ə)mine/ [1] vi **1** (marcher) to walk (along); Mil (avancer à couvert) to advance (under cover); **2** (avancer) **~ à travers/entre** [ruisseau, sentier] to wend its way through/between littér; **3** (progresser) [idée, pensée] to progress, to develop

cheminot /ʃ(ə)mino/ nm railway worker GB, railroader US

chemise /ʃ(ə)miz/ nf **1** (pour hommes) shirt; **2** (lingerie) vest GB, undershirt US; **3** (en papeterie) folder; **4** Tech (intérieure) lining; (extérieure) jacket; **5** Constr facing

Composé) **~ de nuit** (pour femme) nightgown, nightdress GB; (pour homme) nightshirt

Idiomes) **j'y ai laissé ma ~**○ it broke the bank; **je m'en moque comme de ma première ~**○ I don't give two hoots○ GB ou a hoot○ US; **changer d'avis comme de ~**○ to change one's mind at the drop of a hat; **mouiller sa ~**○ to work hard

chemiser /ʃ(ə)mize/ [1] vtr **1** Culin to line [moule]; **2** Tech to jacket [pièce, conduit]

chemiserie /ʃ(ə)mizʀi/ nf (industrie) shirt-making trade; (fabrique) shirt factory; (magasin) shirt shop GB ou store US

chemisier, -ière /ʃ(ə)mizje, ɛʀ/ nm (vêtement) blouse

chenal, pl **-aux** /ʃənal, o/ nm (de fleuve, d'estuaire) channel, fairway; (d'usine) flume; (de moulin) millrace

chenapan /ʃənapɑ̃/ nm hum scallywag○, rascal

chêne /ʃɛn/ nm (arbre) oak (tree); (bois) oak

chenet /ʃənɛ/ nm firedog, andiron

chenil /ʃənil/ nm **1** (niche) kennel; **2** (pension pour chiens) kennels (sg)

chenille /ʃənij/ nf **1** Zool caterpillar; **2** Aut caterpillar; **véhicule à ~s** tracked vehicle; **3** (fil à tricoter) chenille

chenu, -e /ʃəny/ adj liter [vieillard, barbe] hoary; [arbre] leafless

cheptel /ʃɛptɛl/ nm (bétail) livestock; **~ bovin** beef ou dairy herd; **~ ovin/porcin** sheep/pig population

chèque /ʃɛk/ nm cheque GB, check US; **faire un ~** to write a cheque GB ou check US; **à l'ordre de M. Daw** cheque GB ou check US payable to Mr Daw; **les ~s sont acceptés à partir de 15 euros** 'no cheques GB ou checks US under 15 euros'

Composés) **~ bancaire** cheque GB, check US; **~ en blanc** blank cheque GB ou check US; **~ en bois**○ rubber cheque○ GB ou check US; **il m'a fait un ~ en bois** the cheque GB ou check US he wrote me bounced; **~ emploi service** Admin banking money voucher for casual worker which credits their social security records; **~ postal** ≈ giro cheque; **~ sans provision** bad cheque GB ou check US; **~ de voyage** traveller's cheque GB ou traveler's check US; **~s postaux** (service) ≈ National Girobank

chèque-cadeau, pl **chèques-cadeaux** /ʃɛkkado/ nm gift-token

chèque-vacances, pl **chèques-vacances** /ʃɛkvakɑ̃s/ nm: staff holiday discount voucher

chèque-voyage, pl **chèques-voyage** /ʃɛkvwajaʒ/ nm traveller's cheque GB ou check US

chéquier /ʃekje/ nm chequebook GB, checkbook US

cher, chère¹ /ʃɛʀ/

A adj **1** (aimé) [personne] dear; [objet, visage] beloved; **la mort d'un être ~** the death of a loved one; **2** (précieux) ~ à [thème, principe, idée] dear to sb (épith, après n); **selon une formule qui lui est chère** as his/her favourite[GB] saying goes; **un site ~ au poète** a place the poet was fond of; **3** (pour interpeller) dear; **~ ami, vous avez tout à fait raison!** my dear friend, you're absolutely right!; **ah, mais c'est ce ~ Dupont!** well, if it isn't our dear old Dupont!; **4** (dans la correspondance) dear; **~s tous** dear all; **5** (onéreux) expensive, dear; **pas ~** cheap, inexpensive; **pas ~ du tout** reasonably-priced; **la vie est plus chère** the cost of living is higher

B nm,f **mon ~** gén dear; (condescendant, à homme plus jeune) my dear boy; (à homme plus âgé) my dear sir; **ma chère** gén dear; (condescendant, à femme plus jeune) my dear girl; (à femme plus âgée) my dear lady

C adv **1** lit (en argent) a lot (of money); **les vêtements en cuir coûtent ~ à nettoyer** having leather clothes cleaned is expensive ou costly; **coûter plus/moins ~** to cost more/less; **acheter ~** to buy at a high price; **se vendre ~** [objet] to fetch a lot; **je l'ai eu pour moins ~** I got it cheaper; **ils font payer très ~ leur services** they charge an awful lot for their services; **2** fig (en importance) [payer] dearly; **le blocus a coûté ~ à notre économie** our economy paid a high price for the blockade

Idiome) **ne pas donner ~ de qn** or **de la peau de qn**○ not to rate sb's chances (highly)

chercher /ʃɛʀʃe/ [1]

A vtr **1** (essayer de trouver) to look for; **~ un mot dans le dictionnaire** to look up a word in the dictionary; **~ qn du regard dans la foule** to look (about) for sb in the crowd; **'cherchons vendeuses'** 'sales assistants wanted'; **son**

c

regard cherchait celui de sa femme he sought his wife's eye; **elle chercha quelques pièces de monnaie dans sa poche** she felt for some coins in her pocket; ~ **le sommeil** to try to get some sleep; **ne cherchez plus!** look no further!; **2** (s'efforcer) **à faire** to try to do; **3** (prendre) **aller ~ qn/qch** gén to go and get sb/sth; (passer prendre) to pick sb/sth up; **aller ~ qch** [*chien*] to fetch sth; **envoyer qn ~ qch** to send sb to get sth; **4** (r éfléchir à) to try to find [*réponse, idées*]; to look for [*prétexte, excuse*]; (se souvenir de) to try to remember [*nom*]; **je cherche mes mots** I can't find my words; **j'ai beau ~, impossible de m'en souvenir** I've thought and thought and still can't remember it; **pas la peine de ~ bien loin** you don't have to look too far; **5** (imaginer) **où est-il allé ~ cela?** what made him think that?; **6** (atteindre) **ça va ~ dans les 500 euros** it must fetch GB ou get US about 500 euros; **ça doit ~ dans les cinq ans de prison** it would get you about five years in prison; **7** (aller à la rencontre de) to look for [*complications*]; **elle t'a giflé mais tu l'as bien cherché** she slapped you but you asked for it

B se chercher vpr **1** un écrivain qui se cherche (raison d'être) a writer trying to find himself; (style, idées) a writer who is feeling his way; **2** **se ~ des excuses** to try to find excuses for oneself; **3** ○(se provoquer) to be out to get each other○

chercheur, -euse /ʃɛʀʃœʀ, øz/ ▸ p. 372 *nm,f* researcher

(Composé) **~ d'or** gold-digger

chère² /ʃɛʀ/
A adj f ▸ **cher**
B nf fml food, fare; **faire bonne ~** to eat well

chèrement /ʃɛʀmɑ̃/ adv (difficilement) **~ acquis** gained at great cost

chéri, ~e /ʃeʀi/
A adj beloved; **l'enfant ~ de** the darling of
B nm,f **1** (en adresse) darling; **ma ~e** my darling; **2** (favori) darling; **3** ○(amoureux) boyfriend/girlfriend

chérir /ʃeʀiʀ/ [3] vtr liter to cherish [*personne*]; to hold [sth] dear [*principe, idée*]

cherra ▸ choir

chérubin /ʃeʀybɛ̃/ nm **1** Relig **des ~s** cherubim; **2** Art cherub; **3** (enfant) iron little angel ou cherub

chétif, -ive /ʃetif, iv/ adj [*enfant*] puny; [*plante*] scrawny

cheval, pl **-aux** /ʃ(ə)val, o/
A nm **1** Zool horse; **~ sauvage** wild horse; **à (dos de) ~** on horseback; **monter à ~** to ride a horse; **à ~!** mount!; (pro-menade à ~) (horse) ride; **tenue de ~** riding clothes (pl); **remède de ~** strong medicine; **fièvre de ~** raging fever; **miser sur le bon ~** fig to back the right horse; **2** ▸ p. 327 (activité) horse-riding; **3** (viande) horsemeat; **4** (personne) real Trojan; **(vieux) ~ de retour** (homme politique) war horse; (récidiviste) habitual offender, old lag○; **5** ○(femme masculine) pej **c'est un vrai ~** she's built like a horse
B **à cheval sur** loc prép **à ~ sur un mur** astride a wall; **à ~ sur deux pays** spanning two countries; **le domaine est à ~ sur la route** the estate straddles the road; **à ~ sur le rouge et le violet** in between red and purple; **être à ~ sur les principes** to be a stickler for principles

(Composés) **~ d'arçons** pommel horse; **~ à bascule** Jeux rocking horse; **~ de bataille** hobbyhorse; **~ de course** racehorse; **~ fiscal**, unit for car tax assessment; **~ de labour** carthorse GB, drafthorse US; **~ marin** Zool sea horse; **~ de selle** saddle horse; **~ de Troie** Trojan horse; **chevaux de bois** merry-go-round horses

(Idiomes) **ne pas être un mauvais ~** not to be such a bad sort; **monter sur ses grands chevaux** to get on one's high horse

chevaleresque /ʃ(ə)valʀɛsk/ adj **1** Littérat [*littérature, poème*] chevaleresque; **2** (courtois) chivalrous

chevalerie /ʃ(ə)valʀi/ nf chivalry

chevalet /ʃ(ə)valɛ/ nm **1** (de peintre) easel; (de menuisier) trestle, sawhorse; **2** (de violon) bridge

chevalier /ʃ(ə)valje/ nm (tous contextes) knight; **armer qn ~** to knight sb

(Composés) **~ errant** knight errant; **~ noir** Fin black knight; **~ servant** hum devoted admirer

chevalière /ʃ(ə)valjɛʀ/ nf signet ring

chevalin, ~e /ʃ(ə)valɛ̃, in/ adj **1** (ayant rapport au cheval) equine; **boucherie ~e** horse butcher's; **2** (ressemblant au cheval) horsey

cheval-vapeur, pl **chevaux-vapeur** /ʃ(ə)valvapœʀ, ʃ(ə)vovapœʀ/ nm horsepower

chevauchée /ʃ(ə)voʃe/ nf ride

chevaucher /ʃ(ə)voʃe/ [1]
A vtr **1** (être assis sur) to sit astride [*animal, objet*]; **2** (recouvrir en partie) to overlap
B vi **1** (en imprimerie) [*caractères*] to become misaligned; **2** liter to ride
C se chevaucher vpr to overlap

chevêche /ʃəvɛʃ/ nf Zool little owl

chevelu, ~e /ʃəvly/ adj pej [*homme*] long-haired (épith)

chevelure /ʃəvlyʀ/ nf **1** (cheveux) hair **C**; **une abondante ~ bouclée** a mass of curly hair; **2** (de comète) tail

chevet /ʃəvɛ/ nm **1** (de lit) bedhead; **être au ~ de qn** to be at sb's bedside; **2** (meuble) bedside table; **3** Archit (d'église) chevet

cheveu, pl **~x** /ʃəvø/
A nm **1** (poil) hair; **avoir quelques ~x blancs** to have a few grey GB ou gray US hairs; **avoir le ~ rare** to be a bit thin on top; **2** (petite dimension) hair's breadth; **être à un ~ de qch/de faire** to be within a hair's breadth of sth/of doing; **ne tenir qu'à un ~** to hang by a thread
B cheveux nmpl (chevelure) hair **C**; **avoir les ~x longs** to have long hair; **avoir les ~x blancs** to have grey GB ou gray US hair; **se laver les ~x** to wash one's hair; **se faire couper les ~x** to have one's hair cut; **avoir les ~x en bataille** to have tousled hair; **une histoire à vous faire dresser les ~x sur la tête** a story that makes your hair stand on end

(Idiomes) **avoir un ~ sur la langue** to have a lisp; **venir comme un ~ sur la soupe** to come at an awkward moment; **se faire des ~x○ (blancs)** to worry oneself to death (**pour** about); **couper les ~x en quatre** to split hairs; **être tiré par les ~x** to be far-fetched

cheville /ʃ(ə)vij/ ▸ p. 136 nf **1** Anat ankle; **jupe qui arrive à la ~** ankle-length skirt; **on avait de l'eau jusqu'aux ~s** we were ankle-deep in water; **2** Constr (pour vis) rawplug; (pour assemblage) peg; (en bois) dowel; **3** (d'instrument de musique) peg; **~ d'accord** tuning peg; **4** (de boucherie) butcher's hook; **5** (dans un poème) pej padding **C** péj

(Composé) **~ ouvrière** fig kingpin; **être la ~ ouvrière de...** to play a key role in...

(Idiomes) **il n'arrive pas à la ~ de Paul** he can't hold a candle to Paul; **avoir les ~s qui enflent** to get big-headed; **être en ~ avec○** to be in cahoots with○

cheviller /ʃ(ə)vije/ [1] vtr to peg

(Idiome) **avoir l'âme chevillée au corps** to have a tremendous hold on life

chèvre¹ /ʃɛvʀ/ nm (fromage) goat's cheese

chèvre² /ʃɛvʀ/ nf **1** Zool goat; (femelle du bouc) nanny-goat; **2** (peau) goatskin

(Idiomes) **devenir ~○** to go round the bend○ GB, to go nuts○; **ménager la ~ et le chou** to tread the middle ground

chevreau, pl **~x** /ʃəvʀo/ nm kid

chèvrefeuille /ʃɛvʀəfœj/ nm honeysuckle

chevrette /ʃəvʀɛt/ nf **1** Zool (chèvre) young nanny goat; (femelle du chevreuil) (female) roe deer; **2** (trépied) tripod

chevreuil /ʃəvʀœj/ nm **1** Zool roe (deer); (mâle) roebuck; **2** Culin venison

chevron /ʃəvʀɔ̃/ nm **1** (poutre) rafter; **2** (motif) chevron; **les ~s** or **le ~** (petits) herringbone pattern; (grands) chevron design; **3** Archit chevron; **4** Mil (galon) chevron, stripe

chevronné, ~e /ʃəvʀɔne/ adj [*personne*] experienced

chevrotant, ~e /ʃəvʀɔtɑ̃, ɑ̃t/ adj [*voix*] quavering

chevroter /ʃəvʀɔte/ [1] vtr, vi to quaver

chevrotine /ʃəvʀɔtin/ nf buckshot

chez /ʃe/ prép **1** (au domicile de) **~ qn** at sb's place; **~ David** at David's (place); **rentre ~ toi** go home; **je reste ~ moi** I stay at home; **tu peux dormir ~ moi** you can sleep at my place; **je ne veux pas de ça ~ moi!** I'll have none of that in my home!; **fais comme ~ toi** make yourself at home; **derrière ~ eux il y a une immense forêt** there is a huge forest behind their house; **vous habitez ~ vos parents?** do you live with your parents?; **2** ▸ p. 372 (au magasin, cabinet de) **la montre ne vient pas de ~ nous** this watch doesn't come from our shop GB *ou* store US; **en vente ~ tous les dépositaires** on sale at all agents; **va ~ Hallé, c'est un très bon médecin** go to Hallé, he's/she's a very good doctor; **une montre de ~ Lip** a Lip watch; **publié ~ Hachette** published by Hachette; **~ l'épicier du coin** at the local grocer's; **'~ Juliette'** (sur une enseigne) 'Juliette's'; **3** (dans la famille de) **~ moi/vous/eux** in my/your/their family; **comment ça va ~ les Pichon?** how are the Pichons doing?; **ça va bien/mal ~ eux** things are going well/badly for them; **4** (dans le pays, la région de) **~ nous** (d'où je viens) where I come from; (où j'habite) where I live; **~ eux ils appellent ça...** in their part of the world they call this...; **un nom bien de ~ nous** (de France) a good old French name; (de notre région) a good old local name; **5** (parmi) among; **~ l'homme/l'animal** in man/animals; **6** (dans la personnalité de) **ce que j'aime ~ elle, c'est son humour** what I like about her, is her sense of humour^{GB}; **c'est une obsession ~ elle!** it's an obsession with her!; **7** (dans l'œuvre de) in; **~ Cocteau** in Cocteau

chic /ʃik/
A *adj* **1** (élégant) [*personne, vêtement*] smart GB, chic; **2** [○](sophistiqué) [*école, personne, hôtel, quartier*] chic; **3** [○](gentil) nice
B *nm* chic; **avoir le ~ pour faire** to have a knack for doing; **avec ~** with style; **avoir du ~** to have style; **c'est du dernier ~** it's the height of sophistication
C *adv* [*s'habiller*] smartly GB, stylishly

chicane /ʃikan/ *nf* **1** (formée par obstacles) chicane; (tracé de route, piste) double bend; **en ~** on alternate sides; **2** (tracasserie) bickering **⊄**; **3** Jur (point de détail) delaying tactics (*pl*); (procédure) pej legal quibbling *péj*

chicaner /ʃikane/ [1]
A *vtr* (harceler) **~ qn sur qch** to argue with sb about sth
B *vi* (discuter) to squabble (**sur, pour** over); (faire des manières) to fuss (**sur** about)
C se chicaner *vpr* to squabble (**pour** over)

chiche /ʃiʃ/
A *adj* **1** (parcimonieux) mean GB, stingy; **2** [○](capable) **être ~ de faire qch** to be able to do sth
B [○]*excl* **'je vais le faire'—'~!'** 'I'll do it'—'I dare you!'; **~ que je le fais!** bet you I can do it!

chichement /ʃiʃmã/ *adv* [*manger, vivre*] frugally; [*donner*] meanly GB, stingily; [*décorer*] sparsely; [*payer*] poorly

chichi[○] /ʃiʃi/ *nm* sans **⊄**; **ne fais pas de ~s pour moi!** don't go to any trouble!; **sans ~(s)** [*personne*] straightforward; [*réception*] informal

chicon /ʃikɔ̃/ *nm* (endive) chicory

chicorée /ʃikɔʀe/ *nf* **1** Bot chicory; (salade) endive GB, chicory **⊄** US; **2** Culin (poudre) chicory; (boisson) chicory coffee

chicot[○] /ʃiko/ *nm* (dent) stump, snag

chien, chienne¹ /ʃjɛ̃, ʃjɛn/
A [○]*adj* bloody-minded GB, nasty; **~ de temps** wretched weather; **ma chienne de vie** my wretched life
B *nm* **1** (animal) dog; **~ à poil ras/long** short-/long-haired dog; **'~ méchant'** 'beware of the dog'; **2** (fusil) hammer; **3** Naut **coup de ~** fresh gale
C de chien[○] *loc adj* [*métier, temps*] rotten; **vie de ~** dog's life; **avoir un caractère de ~** to have a lousy[○] character; **être d'une humeur de ~** to be in a foul mood; **ça me fait un mal de ~** it hurts like hell[○]; **avoir un mal de ~ à faire** to have an awful time doing
(Composés) **~ d'arrêt** pointer; **~ d'aveugle** guide dog; **~ de berger** sheepdog; **~ de chasse** retriever, gundog; **~ de garde** lit guard dog; fig watchdog; **~ de mer** dogfish; **~ policier** police dog; **~ de race** pedigree dog; **~s écrasés** Presse fillers; **~ de traîneau** sled dog
(Idiomes) **traiter qn comme un ~** to treat sb like a dog *ou* like dirt; **être couché en ~ de fusil** to be curled up; **entre ~ et loup** at dusk; **elle a du ~** she's got what it takes; **ce n'est pas fait pour les ~s**[○] it's there to be used; **garder à qn un ~ de sa chienne** to bear a grudge against sb

chiendent /ʃjɛ̃dã/ *nm* Bot couch grass, scutch grass; **brosse de ~** scrubbing brush
(Idiome) **pousser comme du ~** to grow like a weed

chienlit /ʃjãli/ *nf* havoc, chaos

chien-loup, *pl* **chiens-loups** /ʃjɛ̃lu/ *nm* Alsatian GB, German shepherd

chienne² /ʃjɛn/
A *adj f* ▸ chien
B *nf* (animal) bitch

chiffe /ʃif/ *nf pej* **~ molle** drip, wet blanket

chiffon /ʃifɔ̃/ *nm* **1** (morceau d'étoffe) rag, (piece of) cloth; **une poupée de ~s** a rag doll; **2** (pour nettoyer) duster; **donner** *or* **passer un coup de ~ sur qch** to give sth a quick dust *ou* wipe; **donner** *or* **passer un coup de ~** to do some dusting; **3** (document sans valeur) scrap of paper
(Idiome) **parler** *or* **causer**[○] **~s** to talk (about) clothes

chiffonné, -e /ʃifɔne/ *adj* **1** (fatigué) [*visage*] tired-looking; **2** [○](chagriné) troubled, ruffled

chiffonner /ʃifɔne/ [1]
A *vtr* **1** (froisser) to crumple (up) [*feuille*]; to crease, to crumple [*tissu*]; **2** [○](chagriner) to bother [*personne*]
B se chiffonner *vpr* [*tissu*] to crease, to crumple

chiffonnier, -ière /ʃifɔnje, ɛʀ/
A ▸ p. 372 *nm,f* rag-and-bone man/woman
B *nm* (meuble) chiffonnier
(Idiome) **se battre comme des ~s** to fight like cat and dog

chiffrable /ʃifʀabl/ *adj* [*pertes, dégâts*] calculable; **les pertes ne sont pas ~s** it's impossible to put a figure on the losses

chiffre /ʃifʀ/ *nm* **1** (symbole) figure; (numéro, nombre) number; **écrire le montant en ~s** to write the amount in figures; **un numéro à six ~s** a six-figure *ou* six-digit number; **2** (résultat) figure; **3** (statistique) statistic; **les ~s officiels** the official statistics; **4** (total) total; **~ global** total amount; **5** (code) (de message) code; (de coffre) combination; **le (service du) Chiffre** the cipher room; **6** (monogramme) monogram
(Composés) **~ d'affaires, CA** turnover GB, sales (*pl*) US; **~ arabe** Arabic numeral; **~ romain** Roman numeral; **~ de vente** sales (*pl*)

chiffrer /ʃifʀe/ [1]
A *vtr* **1** (évaluer) to put a figure on, to assess [*coût, pertes*]; to cost [*travaux*]; **~ à** to put *ou* assess [sth] at [*coût, dépenses, pertes*]; to put the cost of [sth] at [*travaux*]; **données chiffrées** figures; **2** (coder) to encode [*message*]; **3** (marquer) to monogram [*linge, vaisselle*]; **4** (numéroter) to number [*pages*]
B [○]*vi* (coûter cher) **ça chiffre vite** it soon adds up
C se chiffrer *vpr* **se ~ à** to amount to, to come to

chignole /ʃiɲɔl/ *nf* **1** (outil) hand drill; **2** [○](voiture) pej banger[○] GB, junker[○] US, car

chignon /ʃiɲɔ̃/ *nm* bun; (plus élégant) chignon; **avoir un ~** to wear one's hair in a bun

chiite /ʃiit/ Relig *adj, nmf* Shiite

chilien, -ienne /ʃiljɛ̃, ɛn/ ▸ p. 392 *adj* Chilean

chimère /ʃimɛʀ/ *nf* **1** (rêve) wild dream, chim(a)era sout; **se complaire dans des ~s** to live in a dream world; **poursuivre des ~s** to chase rainbows; **de folles ~s** crazy fantasies; **2** Mythol Chim(a)era; **3** Biol, Bot chim(a)era; Zool (poisson) chim(a)era

chimérique /ʃimeʀik/ *adj* [*projet, espoir*] wild; [*animal*] fabulous; [*personne, esprit*] fanciful

chimie /ʃimi/ *nf* **1** chemistry; **2** (transformation) liter alchemy

chimiothérapie /ʃimjoteʀapi/ *nf* chemotherapy

chimique /ʃimik/ *adj* **1** [*produit*] chemical; [*fibre*] man-made; **2** péj [*nourriture*] synthetic; [*goût*] chemical

chimiste /ʃimist/ ▸ p. 372 *nmf* chemist; **ingénieur ~** chemical engineer

chimpanzé /ʃɛ̃pãze/ *nm* chimpanzee

Chine /ʃin/ ▸ p. 230 *nprf* China; **~ continentale** mainland China; **République populaire de ~** People's Republic of China

chiner /ʃine/ [1]
A *vtr* to dye the warp threads of [*tissu*]; **tissu chiné** chiné fabric
B [○]*vi* (chercher) to bargain-hunt, to antique US; (vendre) to deal in second-hand goods

chinois, -e /ʃinwa, az/
A *adj* **1** ▸ p. 392 Géog Chinese; **2** [○](tatillon) nitpicking[○]
B *nm* **1** ▸ p. 336 Ling Chinese; **2** Culin conical strainer
(Idiome) **pour moi c'est du ~** it's double-Dutch GB *ou* Greek to me

chiot /ʃjo/ *nm* puppy, pup

chiper○ /ʃipe/ [1] *vtr* to pinch○ (**à** from)

chipie○ /ʃipi/ *nf* pej cow○ péj

chipoter○ /ʃipɔte/ [1] *vi* **①** (faire des difficultés) to quibble (**sur** over); **②** (marchander) to haggle (**sur** over); **③** (pour manger) to pick at one's food

chipoteur, -euse○ /ʃipɔtœʀ, øz/
A *adj* **①** (exigeant) difficult; **②** (sur le prix) **être ~** to haggle over everything; **③** (à table) fussy
B *nm,f* **①** (personne exigeante) nit-picker; **②** (sur le prix) person who haggles over everything; **③** (à table) fussy *ou* picky US eater

chips /ʃips/ *nf inv* crisp GB, potato chip US

chique /ʃik/ *nf* plug *ou* quid GB (of tobacco)
⸂Idiomes⸃ **avaler sa ~**○ to kick the bucket; **couper la ~**○ **à qn** (faire taire) to shut sb up○; (surprendre) to leave sb speechless

chiqué○ /ʃike/ *nm* **①** (bluff) **c'est du ~** it's a put-on *ou* sham○; **②** (affectation) airs (*pl*); **faire du ~** to put on *ou* give oneself airs; **sans ~** without affectation

chiquenaude /ʃiknod/ *nf* flick

chiquer /ʃike/ [1] *vtr* **tabac à ~** chewing tobacco

chiromancie /kiʀɔmɑ̃si/ *nf* palmistry, chiromancy; **faire de la ~** to read palms

chiropracteur /kiʀɔpʀaktœʀ/ ▸ p. 372 *nm* chiropractor

chirurgical, ~e, mpl -aux /ʃiʀyʀʒikal, o/ *adj* surgical

chirurgie /ʃiʀyʀʒi/ *nf* surgery

chirurgien /ʃiʀyʀʒjɛ̃/ ▸ p. 372 *nm* surgeon

chirurgien-dentiste, pl chirurgiens-dentistes /ʃiʀyʀʒjɛ̃dɑ̃tist/ ▸ p. 372 *nm* dental surgeon

chlore /klɔʀ/ *nm* chlorine

chlorer /klɔʀe/ [1] *vtr* to chlorinate

chlorhydrique /klɔʀidʀik/ *adj* hydrochloric

chloroforme /klɔʀɔfɔʀm/ *nm* chloroform

chlorophylle /klɔʀɔfil/ *nf* chlorophyll

chlorure /klɔʀyʀ/ *nm* chloride

choc /ʃɔk/
A *adj inv* **'prix ~!'** 'huge reductions'; **c'est l'argument ~!** there's no answer to that!; **le film ~ de l'année** the most sensational film of the year
B *nm* **①** (rencontre brutale) (d'objets) impact, shock; (de vagues) crash; (de personnes) collision; Aut (collision) crash; (sans gravité) bump; **résister aux ~s** to be shock-resistant; **sous le ~** under the impact; **②** (bruit) (violent) crash, smash; (sourd) thud; (métallique) clang; (de vaisselle) clink; **③** (affrontement) **les troupes ont résisté au premier ~** the troops have weathered the first onslaught; **troupe** *or* **unité de ~** Mil shock troops; **de ~** [journaliste, patron] ace○; **④** (commotion) shock; **être encore sous le ~** (après une nouvelle) to be still in a state of shock; (après un accident) to be still in shock; **tenir le ~** to cope; **traitement de ~** shock treatment
⸂Composés⸃ **~ culturel** culture shock; **~ nerveux** (nervous) shock; **~ opératoire** post-operative shock; **~ pétrolier** oil crisis

chocolat /ʃɔkɔla/
A ▸ p. 140 *adj inv* (couleur) chocolate-brown
B *nm* **①** (substance) chocolate; **gâteau au ~** chocolate cake; **~ à croquer** plain chocolate; **tablette de ~** chocolate bar; **②** (friandise) chocolate; **une boîte de ~s** a box of chocolates; **③** (boisson) chocolate
⸂Composés⸃ **~ à cuire** cooking chocolate; **~ en poudre** drinking chocolate

chocolaterie /ʃɔkɔlatʀi/ *nf* chocolate factory

chocolatier, -ière /ʃɔkɔlatje, ɛʀ/ ▸ p. 372 *nm,f* chocolate maker

chœur /kœʀ/ *nm* **①** (groupe) choir; (d'opéra) chorus; **②** (morceau) chorus; **chanter en ~** to sing in chorus; **'reprenons tous en ~'** 'all together now'; **③** (de théâtre) chorus; **④** Archit chancel, choir; **⑤** fig chorus (**de** of); **le ~ des grévistes** all the strikers (*pl*); **en ~** [dire, affirmer] in unison; [rire, souffrir] all together

choir /ʃwaʀ/ [51] *vi* liter to fall; **la bobinette cherra** the latch will drop

choisi, ~e /ʃwazi/ *adj* **①** (sélectionné) [morceaux, œuvres] selected; **②** (recherché) [expressions, terme] carefully chosen; **③** (sélect) [société, clientèle] select

choisir /ʃwaziʀ/ [3] *vtr* to choose (**entre** between); **~ son camp** fig to choose sides; **~ de faire** to choose to do; **bien/mal ~** to make the right/wrong choice; **~ qn comme ministre** to choose *ou* pick sb as a minister; **c'est à toi de ~** it's up to you

choix /ʃwa/ *nm inv* **①** (option) choice (**entre** between; **parmi** among); **avoir/ne pas avoir le ~** to have a/no choice; **mon ~ est fait** I've made my choice; **faire le ~ de rester** to choose to stay; **je te laisse le ~ du jour** you decide on the date; **fixer** *or* **arrêter** *or* **porter son ~ sur** to settle *ou* decide on; **②** (assortiment) choice; **③** (sélection) selection; **un ~ d'instruments** a selection of instruments; **④** (qualité) **de ~** [produit] choice; [candidat, collaborateur] first-rate; **les places de ~ sont toutes réservées** the best seats are all reserved; **un morceau de ~** (en boucherie) a prime cut; **de second ~** poor quality (*avant n*)

choléra /kɔleʀa/ ▸ p. 195 *nm* cholera

cholestérol /kɔlesteʀɔl/ *nm* cholesterol; **avoir du ~**○ to have a high cholesterol level

chômage /ʃomaʒ/ *nm* unemployment; **être au** *or* **en ~** to be unemployed; **s'inscrire au ~** to register as unemployed; **mettre qn au** *or* **en ~** to make sb redundant GB, to lay sb off
⸂Composés⸃ **~ partiel** short time (working); **~ technique** layoffs (*pl*)

chômé, ~e /ʃome/ *adj* **jour ~** day off; **fête ~e** national holiday

chômer /ʃome/ [1]
A *vtr* not to work on [journée]
B *vi* **①** (être improductif) [personne, machine, capital] to be idle; **nous ne chômons pas en ce moment!** we're not short of work at the moment!; **②** (être sans travail) [employé] to be out of work; [usine, machines] to stand idle; [industrie] to be at a standstill

chômeur, -euse /ʃomœʀ, øz/ *nm,f* unemployed person; **les ~s de longue durée** the long-term unemployed; **~s en fin de droit** unemployed people no longer eligible for benefit

chope /ʃɔp/ *nf* beer mug, tankard

choquant, ~e /ʃɔkɑ̃, ɑ̃t/ *adj* shocking; **~ de franchise** shockingly frank

choquer /ʃɔke/ [1] *vtr* **①** (scandaliser) to shock [personne]; **ça l'a choqué de voir ça** he was shocked to see it; **si le mot choque** if the word is shocking *ou* causes offenceGB; **ça choque** it's shocking; **cela risque de ~** [comportement, film, remarque] it might cause offenceGB; **②** (commotionner) [événement, nouvelle] to shake [personne]; [chute, accident] to shake [sb] (up); **être choqué** Méd to be in shock; **③** (blesser) [vue, sensibilité] to jar on [oreille]; to go against [bon sens]

choral, ~e¹, mpl ~s *or* **-aux** /kɔʀal, o/
A *adj* choral
B (*pl* ~s) *nm* chorale

chorale² /kɔʀal/ *nf* choir

chorégraphe /kɔʀegʀaf/ ▸ p. 372 *nmf* choreographer

chorégraphie /kɔʀegʀafi/ *nf* choreography

choriste /kɔʀist/ *nmf* (d'église) chorister; (d'opéra) member of the chorus; (de chorale) member of the choir

chorus /kɔʀys/ *nm inv* Mus chorus; **faire ~ avec qn** fig to join in with sb

chose /ʃoz/
A ○*adj* **se sentir tout ~** to feel out of sorts
B *nf* **①** (objet) thing; **quelle autre ~ pourrais-je leur acheter?** what else could I buy them?; **'une bière'—'la même ~ (pour moi)'** 'a beer'—'the same for me'; **la même ~ s'il vous plaît** the same again, please; ▸ **quelque C**; **②** (entité) thing; **et, ~ incroyable, il a dit oui** and the incredible thing is that he said yes; **de deux ~s l'une** it's got to be one thing or the other; **c'est toujours la même ~ ici/avec lui** it's always the same here/with him; **même ~ pour ta sœur** the same goes for your sister; **une ~ communément admise** a widely accepted fact; **je pense** *ou* **j'ai pensé à une ~** I've thought of something; **c'est autre ~** that's different; **et si on parlait d'autre ~** let's talk about something else; **voilà autre ~!**○ that's something else!; **③** (affaire, activité, message) thing; **j'ai une ~/deux ou trois ~s à vous dire** I've got something/two or three things to tell you; **(vous direz) bien des ~s à Madame Lemoine** give my regards to Mrs Lemoine; **c'est pas des ~s**○ **à dire** that's the last thing to say; **parler de**

~s et d'autres to talk about one thing and another *ou* this and that; en mettant les ~s au mieux/au pire at best/ at (the) worst; mettre les ~s au point to clear things up; on verra plus tard, chaque ~ en son temps we' ll cross that bridge when we come to it; avant toute ~ (auparavant) before anything else; (surtout) above all else; 'avez-vous déménagé?'—'c'est ~ faite' 'have you moved?'—'it's all done'; voilà *or* c'est une bonne ~ de faite that's one thing out of the way; ④ (ce dont il s'agit) matter; la ~ en question the matter in hand; la ~ dont je vous parle what I'm talking about; il a pris la ~ avec humour he saw the funny side of it; il a bien/mal pris la ~ he took it well/ badly; ⑤ (personne) ce n'est qu'une pauvre ~ he/she is a poor little thing; ⑥ ○(activités sexuelles) être un peu porté sur la ~ to like it○, to be keen on sex; ⑦ ○(nom de substitution) Chose m'a dit qu'il... what's-his-name/what's-her-name *ou* thingummy told me that he...

C choses *nfpl* ① (réalité) les ~s étant ce qu'elles sont things being what they are; ② (domaine) les ~s de l'esprit/de la chair things of the mind/of the flesh; les ~s de la religion religious matters; les ~s de la vie (quotidienne) the little things in life

(Composés) ~ imprimée printed word; ~ publique liter res publica, state

chosifier /ʃozifje/ [2] *vtr* Philos to reify

chou, *pl* ~x /ʃu/ *nm* ① (légume) cabbage; soupe aux ~x cabbage soup; ~ farci stuffed cabbage; ▸ chèvre²; ② (pâtisserie) choux bun GB, pastry shell US; ③ ○(personne aimable) dear; ferme la porte tu seras un ~ be a dear and close the door

(Composés) ~ de Bruxelles Brussels sprout; ~ à la crème cream puff; ~ rave kohlrabi; ~ rouge red cabbage; ~ vert green cabbage

(Idiomes) bête comme ~○ really easy; faire ~ blanc○ to draw a blank; faire ses ~x gras de qch○ to use sth to one's advantage; être dans les ~x○ to bring up the rear; aller planter ses ~x ailleurs to go to pastures new; rentrer dans le ~○ de qn (physiquement) to beat sb up; (oralement) to give sb a piece of one's mind

chouan /ʃwã/ *nm* Chouan (*Royalist insurgent from western France during the Revolution*)

choucas /ʃuka/ *nm* jackdaw

chouchou○ /ʃuʃu/ *nm* ① (du professeur) pet; (du public) darling; ② (pour les cheveux) scrunchie

chouchouter○ /ʃuʃute/ [1] *vtr* to pamper

choucroute /ʃukʀut/ *nf* sauerkraut

chouette /ʃwɛt/
A ○*adj* great○, neat○ US; être ~ avec qn to be really nice to sb
B *nf* Zool owl; vieille ~ fig pej old harridan

chou-fleur, *pl* **choux-fleurs** /ʃuflœʀ/ *nm* cauliflower

chou-rave, *pl* **choux-raves** /ʃuʀav/ *nm* kohlrabi

chourer⁀ /ʃuʀe/ [1] *vtr* to pinch○; se faire ~ qch to have sth pinched

choyer /ʃwaje/ [23] *vtr* to pamper [enfant, client]

chrétien, -ienne /kʀetjɛ̃, ɛn/ *adj*, *nm,f* Christian

chrétienté /kʀetjɛ̃te/ *nf* la ~ Christendom

christ /kʀist/ *nm* Art un ~ (sculpté) a sculpted Christ; (peint) a figure of Christ; (crucifix) a crucifix; un ~ en croix a crucifixion

Christ /kʀist/ *npr* le ~ Christ

christianiser /kʀistjanize/ [1] *vtr* to Christianize

christianisme /kʀistjanism/ *nm* le ~ Christianity

chromatique /kʀɔmatik/ *adj* ① Mus chromatic; ② (relatif aux couleurs) chromatic

chrome /kʀom/ *nm* ① Chimie chromium; ② Aut faire les ~s to polish the chrome

chromer /kʀome/ [1] *vtr* to chrome-plate

chromosome /kʀomozom/ *nm* chromosome

chromosomique /kʀomozomik/ *adj* chromosome (épith)

chronique /kʀonik/
A *adj* (tous contextes) chronic
B *nf* Presse column, page; Radio, TV programme^GB; tenir une ~ Presse to have a column; TV, Radio to have a spot

chroniqueur, -euse /kʀonikœʀ, øz/ ▸ p. 372 *nm,f* Presse columnist, editor; Radio, TV commentator; ~ littéraire book

---

reviewer; ~ dramatique drama critic

chronologie /kʀonoloʒi/ *nf* chronology

chronologique /kʀonoloʒik/ *adj* chronological

chronométrage /kʀonometʀaʒ/ *nm* timing

chronomètre /kʀonometʀ/ *nm* ① (chronographe) stopwatch; ② (montre de précision) chronometer

chronométrer /kʀonometʀe/ [14] *vtr* to time

chrysalide /kʀizalid/ *nf* chrysalis; sortir de sa ~ fig to come out of one's shell

chrysanthème /kʀizɑ̃tɛm/ *nm* chrysanthemum

chu ▸ choir

CHU /seaʃy/ *nm: abbr* ▸ centre

chuchotement /ʃyʃotmã/ *nm* (de personnes) whisper

chuchoter /ʃyʃote/ [1]
A *vtr* to whisper
B *vi* [personne] to whisper; [ruisseau, vent] to murmur

chuintant, ~e /ʃɥɛ̃tã, ãt/ *adj* bruit ~ (sifflement) hissing sound; (frottement) swishing sound

chuintement /ʃɥɛ̃tmã/ *nm* ① (de vapeur) hiss; (de pneus) swish; ② (en prononciation) ≈ lisp, pronunciation of *s* as *sh*

chuinter /ʃɥɛ̃te/ [1] *vi* ① [vapeur] to hiss gently; [pneu] to swish; ② [personne] ≈ to lisp, to pronounce *s* as *sh*; ③ [chouette] to hoot

chum○ /tʃœm/ *nm* C (ami) friend; (petit ami) boyfriend

chut /ʃyt/ *excl* shh!, hush!

chute /ʃyt/ *nf* ① (action de tomber) fall; faire une ~ [personne] to have *ou* take US a fall; [objet] to fall; faire une ~ de moto to fall off a motorbike; faire une ~ de 5 mètres to fall 5 metres^GB; ② (fait de se détacher) (de feuille) fall; ~ des cheveux hair loss; ~s de pierres falling rocks; ③ (cascade) ~ d'eau waterfall; les ~s du Niagara Niagara Falls; ④ Météo fall; fortes ~s de neige heavy snowfall (sg); ⑤ (baisse) drop (de in); (de monnaie) fall; Fin ~ du dollar fall in the price of the dollar; ~ à la Bourse fall on the stock market; ~ de tension Méd sudden drop in blood pressure; ⑥ (de ministre, régime) fall (de of); (d'empire) collapse (de of); Mil (de ville, forteresse) fall (de of); ⑦ Relig la ~ the Fall; ⑧ (fin) (de texte, film) ending; (d'histoire) punch line; ⑨ (de tissu, papier, cuir) offcut

(Composés) ~ des corps Phys gravity; ~ libre free-fall; tomber en ~ libre to fall through the air; économie en ~ libre fig plummeting economy; la ~ des reins the small of the back; ~ du rideau Théât fall of the curtain

chuter /ʃyte/ [1] *vi* (baisser) [température, tension, prix] to fall, to drop; [ventes, production] to fall; [actions] to fall; ~ de/à 10 francs to fall *ou* drop by/to 10 francs; faire ~ les cours to cause prices to fall

Chypre /ʃipʀ/ ▸ p. 303, p. 230 *nprf* Cyprus

chypriote /ʃipʀijot/ ▸ p. 392 *adj* Cypriot

ci /si/
A *dét dém* cette page-~ this page; ces mots-~ these words; ces jours-~ (récemment) these last few days; (bientôt) in the next few days; (en ce moment) at the moment; ces temps-~ (récemment) lately; (à présent) at the moment; à cette heure-~ (de la journée) at this time of day; (de la nuit) at this time of night; il doit être arrivé à cette heure-~ he must have arrived by now; vers cette heure-~ around this time
B *pron dém* this; ~ et ça this and that; ▸ comme

ci-après /siapʀɛ/ *adv* gén below; voir ~ see below

cible /sibl/ *nf* target; prendre qn/qch pour ~ fig to pick on sb/sth; servir de ~ aux moqueries de qn to be the butt of sb's jokes

cibler /sible/ [1] *vtr* Comm to target

ciboulette /sibulɛt/ *nf* Bot chive; Culin chives (pl)

cicatrice /sikatʀis/ *nf* lit, fig scar

cicatrisant, ~e /sikatʀizã, ãt/ *adj* [substance] healing

cicatrisation /sikatʀizasjɔ̃/ *nf* lit, fig healing

cicatriser /sikatʀize/ [1] *vtr*, se cicatriser *vpr* lit, fig to heal

Cicéron /siseʀɔ̃/ *npr* Cicero

ci-contre /sikɔ̃tʀ/ *adv* opposite

ci-dessous /sidəsu/ *adv* below; voir ~ see below, v. infra sout

ci-dessus /sidəsy/ *adv* above; voir ~ see above, v. supra sout

ci-devant /sidəvã/ *adj inv* former

CIDJ /seideʒi/ nm: abbr ▸ **centre**

cidre /sidʀ/ nm cider; ~ **doux/sec** sweet/dry cider

cidrerie /sidʀəʀi/ nf (local) cider-works

CIE /seiə/ nm (abbr = **contrat initiative-emploi**) job creation scheme offering financial incentives to employers

ciel /sjɛl, sjø/ nm ① (pl **ciels**) Météo sky; ~ **clair** or **dégagé** clear sky; **les ~s d'Afrique** African skies; **carte du ~** star chart; ② (pl **cieux**) (firmament) liter sky; **les cieux étoilés** the starry skies; **entre ~ et terre** fig between heaven and earth; **sous des cieux plus cléments** in kinder climes; **à ~ ouvert** [piscine, musée] open-air; [égout] open; [mine] opencast GB, strip US; ③ (pl **cieux**) Relig (paradis) heaven; **être au ~** to be in heaven; **le royaume des cieux** the kingdom of heaven; ④ (providence) liter heaven; **remercier le ~** to thank heaven; **(juste) ~!** (good) heavens!; **c'est le ~ qui t'envoie** you are a godsend

(Idiome) **remuer ~ et terre** to move heaven and earth (**pour faire** to do)

cierge /sjɛʀʒ/ nm (d'église) (church) candle

cieux ▸ **ciel** 2, 3

cigale /sigal/ nf cicada

cigare /sigaʀ/ nm (à fumer) cigar

cigarette /sigaʀɛt/ nf cigarette

(Composé) ~ **(à) bout filtre** filter-tip (cigarette)

ci-gît /siʒi/ loc verbale here lies

cigogne /sigɔɲ/ nf Zool stork

ciguë /sigy/ nf (poison, plante) hemlock

ci-inclus, **~e** /siɛ̃kly, yz/ adj, adv enclosed

ci-joint, **~e** /siʒwɛ̃, ɛ̃t/
A adj enclosed; **la copie ~e** the enclosed copy
B adv enclosed

cil /sil/ nm eyelash

ciller /sije/ [1] vi ~ **(des yeux)** to blink; **sans ~** lit unblinkingly; fig without batting an eyelid

cimaise /simɛz/ nf (de corniche) cyma; (à mi-hauteur) picture rail

cime /sim/ nf top

ciment /simɑ̃/ nm lit, fig cement

cimenter /simɑ̃te/ [1]
A vtr ① Constr to cement [mur, briques]; to concrete [sol, allée]; ② fig to cement [amitié]
B se cimenter vpr [amitié] to grow stronger

cimenterie /simɑ̃tʀi/ nf (usine) cement works

cimeterre /simtɛʀ/ nm scimitar

cimetière /simtjɛʀ/ nm ① lit cemetery, graveyard; (d'église) churchyard, graveyard; ② fig graveyard

(Composé) ~ **de voitures** scrapyard

ciné○ /sine/ nm cinema GB, pictures○ (pl) GB, movies (pl) US

cinéaste /sineast/ ▸ p. 372 nmf film director

ciné-club, pl ~**s** /sineklœb/ nm film club

cinéma /sinema/ nm ① (bâtiment) **(salle de)** ~ cinema GB, movie theater US; **aller au ~** to go to the cinema GB ou movies○ US; ② (art, technique) cinema; (industrie) film industry; **de ~** film (épith) GB, movie (épith) US; **une école de ~** a film school; **faire du ~** to be in films; **adapté pour le ~** adapted for the screen; ③ ○fig **c'est du ~** it's just playacting; **arrête ton ~** (faire semblant) cut out the play-acting; (faire un drame) stop making such a fuss○; **se faire tout un ~** to start imagining things

(Composés) ~ **d'animation** animation; ~ **d'art et d'essai** (salle) cinema showing art films GB, art house US; (genre) art films (pl); **le ~ muet** silent films (pl); **le ~ parlant** the talkies○ (pl)

cinémathèque /sinematek/ nf cinematheque

cinématographique /sinematɔgʀafik/ adj film (épith) GB, movie (épith) US

cinéphile /sinefil/ nmf cinema enthusiast GB ou buff○

cinéraire /sineʀɛʀ/ adj [urne] funerary

cinétique /sinetik/
A adj kinetic
B nf kinetics (+ v sg)

cing(h)alais, **~e** /sɛ̃galɛ, ɛz/ ▸ p. 336
A adj Sinhalese
B nm Ling Sinhalese

cinglant, **~e** /sɛ̃glɑ̃, ɑ̃t/ adj ① lit [vent] biting; [pluie] driving (épith); ② fig [remarque] scathing; [démenti] stinging; [défaite, échec] crushing, ignominious

cinglé○, **~e** /sɛ̃gle/
A adj mad○, crazy○
B nm,f (fou) loony○, nut○; (chauffeur) maniac

cingler /sɛ̃gle/ [1]
A vtr ① [pluie, vent] to sting [visage]; ② (avec un fouet) to lash
B vi Naut ~ **vers** to head for

cinoche○ /sinɔʃ/ nm ① (art) cinema GB, pictures○ (pl) GB, movies (pl) US; ② (salle) cinema GB, movie theater US

cinq /sɛ̃k/ ▸ p. 398, p. 296, p. 155 adj inv, pron, nm inv five

(Idiome) **il a dit les ~ lettres** ≈ he said a naughty word

cinquantaine /sɛ̃kɑ̃tɛn/ nf about fifty; **avoir une ~ d'années** to be about fifty; **la ~ de passagers qui attendaient** the fifty or so passengers who were waiting; **une bonne ~** well over fifty; **nous étions plus d'une ~** there were more than fifty of us

cinquante /sɛ̃kɑ̃t/ ▸ p. 398, p. 155 adj inv, pron fifty

cinquantenaire /sɛ̃kɑ̃tnɛʀ/
A adj fifty-year-old (épith), fifty years old (jamais épith)
B nm fiftieth anniversary

cinquantième /sɛ̃kɑ̃tjɛm/ ▸ p. 398 adj fiftieth

cinquième /sɛ̃kjɛm/ ▸ p. 398, p. 155
A adj, nmf fifth; ▸ **roue**
B nf Scol second year of secondary school, age 12–13

(Composé) **la Cinquième République** Hist the fifth Republic

> ℹ **Cinquième République** As established by the constitution of 1958 and still valid today, the *Cinquième République* refers to the regime founded along the lines laid down by Charles de Gaulle, emphasizing the role of a strong executive and institutions in guaranteeing stability.

cintre /sɛ̃tʀ/
A nm ① (pour vêtement) hanger; ② Archit curve
B cintres nmpl Théât **les ~s** the flies

cintré, **~e** /sɛ̃tʀe/ adj [manteau] waisted; [chemise] tailored

cintrer /sɛ̃tʀe/ [1] vtr ① (en couture) to take [sth] in at the waist [veste]; ② Archit to arch [porte]; to vault [galerie]; ③ Tech to bend [tuyau]

cirage /siʀaʒ/ nm (produit) (shoe) polish; ~ **en crème** shoe cream

(Idiome) **être dans le ~**○ (à demi conscient) to be half-conscious, to be out of it○; (désorienté) to be all at sea

circoncire /siʀkɔ̃siʀ/ [64] vtr to circumcise

circoncision /siʀkɔ̃sizjɔ̃/ nf male circumcision

circonférence /siʀkɔ̃feʀɑ̃s/ nf circumference

circonflexe /siʀkɔ̃flɛks/ adj **accent ~** circumflex (accent)

circonscription /siʀkɔ̃skʀipsjɔ̃/ nf Admin district

(Composé) ~ **électorale** (de député) ≈ electoral constituency GB ou district US; (de conseiller, maire) ≈ electoral ward

circonscrire /siʀkɔ̃skʀiʀ/ [67] vtr ① (limiter) to contain [incendie, épidémie]; to limit [sujet, domaine] (**à** to); ② (délimiter) to define

circonspection /siʀkɔ̃spɛksjɔ̃/ nf caution (**envers qn** toward(s) sb; **envers qch** about sth); **avec ~** cautiously

circonstance /siʀkɔ̃stɑ̃s/
A nf ① (condition) circumstance; **en raison des ~s** under the circumstances; ② (situation) situation; **en toute ~** in any event; **en la ~** in this particular case; **pour la ~** for the occasion; **être à la hauteur des ~s** to be equal to the occasion
B de circonstance loc adj [poème] for the occasion (après n); [blague, programme] topical; [sourire, attitude] artificial; **faire une tête de ~** to assume a fitting expression

(Composé) ~**s atténuantes** Jur extenuating circumstances

circonstanciel, **-ielle** /siʀkɔ̃stɑ̃sjɛl/ adj Ling [complément, proposition] adverbial

circonvolution /siʀkɔ̃vɔlysjɔ̃/ nf convolution; **décrire des ~s** to twist and turn

circuit /siʀkɥi/ *nm* ① Sport circuit; ② (de tourisme) tour; **faire le ~ des châteaux de la Loire** to tour the Châteaux of the Loire; **ne pas suivre les ~s touristiques** to go off the beaten track; ③ (d'activité) circuit; **~ économique** economic process; **être mis hors ~** [*personne*] to be put on the sidelines; **remettre qch dans le ~** to put sth back into circulation; **vivre en ~ fermé** to live in a closed world; ④ Tech circuit

⸢Composés⸣ **~ d'alimentation** feed system; **~ hydraulique** hydraulic system; **~ imprimé** printed circuit; **~ intégré** integrated circuit

circulaire /siʀkylɛʀ/ *adj, nf* circular

circulation /siʀkylasjɔ̃/ *nf* ① (de véhicules) traffic; **rue interdite à la ~** street closed to traffic; **faire la ~** [*agent*] to be on traffic duty; (en cas d'accident) to direct traffic; ② (déplacement, échange) circulation; **la libre ~ des personnes, des marchandises et des capitaux** the free movement of people, goods and capital; **être en ~** [*billets, produit, modèle*] to be in circulation; [*bateau*] to be in operation; [*train*] to be running; **mettre en ~** to put [sth] into circulation [*billets, produit*]; **disparaître de la ~** lit, fig [*personne, produit*] to disappear from circulation; **retirer de la ~** to withdraw [sth] from circulation [*billet, produit*]; ③ (d'air, de gaz, sang) circulation; **avoir une mauvaise ~** to have poor circulation

circulatoire /siʀkylatwaʀ/ *adj* [*troubles*] circulatory

circuler /siʀkyle/ [1] *vi* ① (être en service) [*train, bus*] to run; [*bateau*] to operate; **'ne circule pas le dimanche'** (train, bus) 'does not run on Sundays'; ② (aller d'un lieu à un autre) to get around; (sans but précis) to move about; (être en voiture) to travel; **circulez, il n'y a rien à voir!** move along, there's nothing to see!; ③ (se répandre) [*rumeur, plaisanterie, idée*] to circulate, to go around *ou* about; **faire ~** to circulate [*information, idée*]; to spread, to put about [*rumeur*]; ④ (être distribué) [*marchandises, billets, journal*] to circulate; ⑤ [*sang, air*] to circulate; **faire ~** to circulate

cire /siʀ/ *nf* wax; **en ~** wax (*épith*)

⸢Composés⸣ **~ d'abeilles** beeswax; **~ à cacheter** sealing wax

ciré /siʀe/ *nm* oilskin

cirer /siʀe/ [1] *vtr* to polish [*chaussures, parquet*]

⸢Idiome⸣ **~ les pompes de qn** to suck up to sb○

cireuse¹ /siʀøz/ *nf* (appareil) (floor) polisher

cireux, -euse² /siʀø, øz/ *adj* [*aspect*] waxen; [*consistance*] waxy

cirque /siʀk/ *nm* ① (spectacle) circus; **un numéro de ~ a** circus act; ② ○(chahut) racket○; (désordre) shambles○ (*sg*); **arrête ton ~!** stop your nonsense!; **c'est le ~ pour se garer à Oxford** it's a real performance parking in Oxford; ③ (dans l'Antiquité) **les jeux du ~** circus games

cirrhose /siʀoz/ ▸ p. 195 *nf* cirrhosis

⸢Composé⸣ **~ du foie** cirrhosis of the liver

cisaille /sizaj/ *nf* (de jardinier, d'orfèvre) pair of shears; **~s** shears

cisailler /sizaje/ [1] *vtr* ① (avec une cisaille) to shear [*tôle*]; to cut [*câble*]; ② (par usure) to shear off

ciseau, *pl* **~x** /sizo/

A *nm* ① Tech chisel; ② Sport (saut) scissors jump; (prise de lutte) scissors hold

B ciseaux *nmpl* scissors (*pl*); (gros et robustes) shears; **saut en ~x** scissors jump; **tailler à grands coups de ~x** to cut boldly

ciseler /sizle/ [17] *vtr* Tech to chase [*métal*]; to chisel [*bois, pierre*]

ciselure /sizlyʀ/ *nf* (de métal) chasing; (de pierre, bois) carving

Cisjordanie /sisʒɔʀdani/ ▸ p. 504 *nprf* **la ~** the West Bank (of Jordan)

cistercien, -ienne /sistɛʀsjɛ̃, ɛn/ *adj, nm,f* Cistercian

citadelle /sitadɛl/ *nf* lit, fig citadel

citadin, ~e /sitadɛ̃, in/

A *adj* city (*épith*)

B *nm,f* city-dweller

citation /sitasjɔ̃/ *nf* gén quotation

cité /site/ *nf* ① (ville) city; (plus petite) town; (antique) city; ② (ensemble de logements) housing estate; ▸ **dortoir B**

⸢Composés⸣ **la ~ des Papes** Avignon; **~ universitaire** student halls (*pl*) of residence GB, dormitories (*pl*) US

cité-jardin, *pl* **cités-jardins** /siteʒaʀdɛ̃/ *nf* garden city GB, planned town US

citer /site/ [1] *vtr* ① (rapporter exactement) to quote [*personne, phrase, passage*]; **je cite** I quote; ② (mentionner) to name [*titre, œuvre*]; to cite [*personne, exemple, chiffres*]; ③ Jur to summon [*témoin*]; **être cité en justice** to be issued with a summons

citerne /sitɛʀn/ *nf* tank

cithare /sitaʀ/ ▸ p. 389 *nf* zither

citoyen, -enne /sitwajɛ̃, ɛn/ *nm,f* citizen

citoyenneté /sitwajɛnte/ *nf* citizenship

citron /sitʀɔ̃/

A ▸ p. 140 *adj inv* **(jaune) ~** lemon (yellow)

B *nm* ① Bot, Culin lemon; **goût de ~** lemony taste; ② ○(tête) **il n'a rien dans le ~** he isn't all there○

⸢Composés⸣ **~ givré** lemon sorbet (*served inside a lemon*); **~ vert** lime

⸢Idiomes⸣ **presser qn comme un ~**○ to squeeze sb dry○; **se presser le ~**○ to rack one's brains

citronnade /sitʀɔnad/ *nf* lemon squash GB, lemonade US

citronné, ~e /sitʀɔne/ *adj* [*odeur*] lemony; [*crème*] lemon(-flavoured^GB)

citronnelle /sitʀɔnɛl/ *nf* Bot citronella

citronnier /sitʀɔnje/ *nm* lemon tree

citrouille /sitʀuj/ *nf* ① Bot, Culin pumpkin; ② ○(tête) head

⸢Idiome⸣ **avoir la tête comme une ~**○ to feel as if one's head was going to burst

civet /sivɛ/ *nm* ≈ stew; **~ de lièvre** jugged hare ⦰

civière /sivjɛʀ/ *nf* stretcher

civil, ~e /sivil/

A *adj* (non militaire) civilian; (non religieux) [*mariage*] civil; [*enterrement*] non religious; (non pénal) civil

B *nm* (personne) civilian; **se mettre en ~** [*soldat*] to dress in civilian clothes; [*policier*] to dress in plain clothes; **dans le ~** in civilian life

civilisation /sivilizasjɔ̃/ *nf* civilization

civiliser /sivilize/ [1]

A *vtr* lit, fig to civilize

B **se civiliser** *vpr* to become civilized

civique /sivik/ *adj* civic; **avoir l'esprit ~** to have a sense of civic responsibility; **instruction** *or* **éducation ~** civics (+ *v sg*)

clac /klak/ *nm* (de porte) slam; (de piège) snap; (de fouet) crack

claie /klɛ/ *nf* ① (à fromages, fruits) wicker rack; ② (clôture) hurdle

clair, ~e¹ /klɛʀ/

A *adj* ① (pâle) [*couleur*] light; [*teint*] (rosé) fair; (frais) fresh; **avoir les yeux ~s** (bleus) to have pale blue-grey GB *ou* blue-gray US eyes; ② (lumineux) [*logement, pièce*] light; ③ Météo [*nuit, temps*] clear; **par temps ~** (de jour) on a clear day; ④ (limpide) clear; **à l'eau ~e** [*rincer*] in clear water; ⑤ (intelligible) [*texte, idées*] clear; **suis-je ~?** do I make myself clear?; ⑥ (sans équivoque) [*message, décision*] clear; **il faut que les choses soient (bien) ~es** let's get things straight; **c'est ~ net et précis** it's absolutely clear; **passer le plus ~ de son temps** to spend most of one's time (**à faire** doing; **dans** in); ⑦ (pas touffu) [*forêt, blé*] sparse

B *adv* **il faisait ~** it was already light; **il fait ~ très tôt** it gets light very early; **il fait ~ très tard** it stays light very late; **voir ~** lit to see well; **j'aimerais y voir ~ dans cette histoire** fig I'd like to get to the bottom of this story; **parler ~** fig to speak clearly

C *nm* ① (clarté) light; **en ~** TV unscrambled; Mil, Ordinat in clear; (pour parler clairement) to put it clearly; **mettre ses idées au ~** fig to get one's ideas straight; **tirer une affaire au ~** to get to the bottom of things; ② (couleur) light colours^GB (*pl*)

⸢Composé⸣ **~ de lune** moonlight

⸢Idiome⸣ **c'est ~ comme de l'eau de roche** it's crystal clear

claire² /klɛʀ/ *nf* (bassin) oyster bed; **fine de ~** Culin claire oyster

clairement /klɛʀmã/ *adv* clearly

clairet /klɛʀɛ/ *nm* (vin) light red wine

claire-voie, pl **claires-voies** /klɛʀvwɑ/ nf ~ [volets, porte] openwork

clairière /klɛʀjɛʀ/ nf clearing, glade

clairon /klɛʀɔ̃/ ▸ p. 389 nm ① (instrument) bugle; **sonner du** ~ to sound the bugle; ② (personne) bugler

claironnant, ~e /klɛʀɔnɑ̃, ɑ̃t/ adj [voix] strident

claironner /klɛʀɔne/ [1] vtr to shout [sth] from the roof-tops

clairsemé, ~e /klɛʀsəme/ adj [arbres, maisons] scattered; [cheveux, public, foule] thin

clairvoyance /klɛʀvwajɑ̃s/ nf perceptiveness

clairvoyant, ~e /klɛʀvwajɑ̃, ɑ̃t/ adj fig [personne] perceptive

clamer /klame/ [1] vtr to proclaim (**que** that); ~ **haut et fort son soutien** to loudly proclaim one's support

clameur /klamœʀ/ nf roar

clan /klɑ̃/ nm lit, fig clan; **esprit de** ~ clan mentality, clannishness

clandestin, ~e /klɑ̃dɛstɛ̃, in/ adj [organisation, journal] underground (épith); [immigration, commerce, travail] illegal; [prostitution] clandestine; **passager** ~ stowaway

clandestinement /klɑ̃dɛstinmɑ̃/ adv (illégalement) illegally

clandestinité /klɑ̃dɛstinite/ nf (d'activité, organisation) secret ou clandestine nature; **atmosphère de** ~ atmosphere of secrecy; **dans la** ~ [passer, se réfugier] underground; [vivre] in hiding; [opérer] in secret; **sortir de la** ~ to come out into the open; **travailler dans la** ~ to work illegally

clap /klap/ nm clapperboard

clapet /klapɛ/ nm ① (soupape) valve; ② ○(bouche) mouth, trap○

clapier /klapje/ nm rabbit hutch

clapoter /klapɔte/ [1] vi to lap

clapotis /klapɔti/ nm inv lapping (**de** of)

claquage /klakaʒ/ nm pulled ou strained muscle; **se faire un** ~ to pull a muscle

claque¹ /klak/ nm (chapeau) (**chapeau**) ~ opera hat

claque² /klak/ nf ① (gifle) slap; **donner une** ~ **à qn** to slap sb; **recevoir une** ~ to get a slap; ② ○(humiliation) slap in the face; (échec) beating; **se prendre une** ~ **aux élections** to take a beating at the elections; ③ Théât claque

(Idiome) **en avoir sa** ~○ to be fed up (to the back teeth○ GB)

claqué○, ~e /klake/ adj (épuisé) knackered○ GB, done in○

claquement /klakmɑ̃/ nm (de porte, fenêtre) bang; (de fouet) crack; (de tonnerre) clap; (de langue, talons) click; (répété) (de porte, fenêtre) banging ¢; (de bannière, voile) flapping ¢; **le** ~ **des sabots** (de personne) the clatter(ing) of clogs; (de chevaux) the clip-clop of hooves

claquemurer: se claquemurer /klakmyʀe/ [1] vpr to shut oneself away (**dans** in)

claquer /klake/ [1]
A vtr ① (fermer) to slam [porte]; ~ **la porte au nez de qn** lit, fig to slam the door in sb's face; **partir** or **sortir en claquant la porte** lit to storm out slamming the door behind one; **ils sont partis en claquant la porte** (pendant des négociations) they walked out closing the door on further negotiations; ② ○(épuiser) to exhaust, to wear [sb] out [personne]; ③ ○(dépenser) to blow○ [argent, paie]
B vi ① (avec un bruit) [porte, volet] to bang; [coup de feu] to ring out; [bannière, voile] to flap; (se fermer) [porte] to slam shut; **faire** ~ **la porte** to slam the door; **faire** ~ **son fouet** to crack one's whip; ② (avec une partie du corps) ~ **des doigts** to snap one's fingers; ~ **des talons** Mil to click one's heels; ~ **des mains** to clap (one's hands); **elle claque des dents** her teeth are chattering; **faire** ~ **sa langue** to click one's tongue
C **se claquer** vpr ① (se distendre) **se** ~ **un muscle** to pull ou strain a muscle; ② ○(s'épuiser) to wear oneself out (**à faire** doing)

claquettes /klakɛt/ nfpl tap dancing (sg); **faire des** ~ to tap dance

clarifier /klaʀifje/ [2] vtr ① fig to clarify [position, situation, débat]; ② lit to clarify [mélange, beurre]

clarinette /klaʀinɛt/ ▸ p. 389 nf clarinet

clarinettiste /klaʀinetist/ ▸ p. 372 nmf clarinettist

clarté /klaʀte/ nf ① (lumière) light; ② (de l'eau, du verre) clarity; (de teint) fairness; ③ fig (de style, d'exposé) clarity; **avec** ~ clearly

classe /klas/ nf ① Scol (groupe d'élèves) class, form GB; (niveau) year, form GB, grade US; **redoubler une** ~ to repeat a year; **passer dans la** ~ **supérieure** to go up a year; ② Scol (cours) class, lesson; **les élèves de Mme Dupont n'auront pas** ~ Mrs Dupont's class won't be having any lessons; **après la** ~ after school; ③ Scol (salle) classroom; ④ Sociol, Pol class; **les** ~ **sociales** social classes; **une société sans** ~s a classless society; ⑤ (catégorie) class (**de** of); ⑥ (rang) gén class; Admin grade; **champagne de première** ~ first-class champagne; ⑦ (élégance) class; **avoir de la** ~ to have class; **c'est pas la** ~○! that's not very stylish!; ⑧ Tourisme class; **billet de première/seconde** ~ first-/second-class ou standard GB ticket; **voyager en première** ~ to travel first class; ⑨ Mil **faire ses** ~s lit to do one's basic training; fig to start out; **un cinéaste qui a fait ses** ~s **à la télévision** fig a film director who started out in television

(Composés) ~ **d'adaptation** special needs class; ~ **d'âge** age group; ~ **de mer** educational schooltrip to the seaside; ~ **de neige** educational schooltrip in the mountains including skiing lessons; ~s **préparatoires (aux grandes écoles)** preparatory classes for entrance to Grandes Écoles

classement /klasmɑ̃/ nm ① (en catégories) classification (**de** of); **faire un** ~ **alphabétique** to put into alphabetical order; ② (rangement) filing (**de** of); **faire du** ~ **dans ses papiers** to sort one's papers out; ③ (d'élèves, employés) grading (**de** of); ~ **trimestriel** Scol termly position (in class); **avoir un mauvais** ~ [élève] to be in the bottom half of the class; ④ Sport ranking (**de** of); **prendre la tête du** ~ to get first place; ⑤ (d'hôtel, de restaurant) rating (**de** of); ~ **deux étoiles** two-star rating; ⑥ Jur ~ **d'une affaire** closing of a case

classer /klase/ [1]
A vtr ① (classifier) to classify; ~ **par ordre alphabétique** to classify in alphabetical order; ~ **des nombres en ordre décroissant** to place numbers in descending order; **être classé comme dangereux** to be considered dangerous; ② (ranger) to file (away) [documents] (**dans** in); ③ Jur, Pol to close [dossier, affaire]; **c'est une affaire classée** fig the matter is closed; ④ Admin to list [bâtiment]; ~ **un château monument historique** to list a castle as a historical monument; ⑤ (attribuer un rang à) to class [pays, élèves]; to rank [chanson, joueur] (**parmi** among); **un sportif classé au plan international** a world class sportsman; **un joueur de tennis classé** a ranked ou seeded tennis player; **non classé** unseeded; ⑥ ○(juger) to size [sb] up
B **se classer** vpr to rank (**parmi** among); **se** ~ **comme le pays le plus pauvre** to be listed as the world's poorest country; **se** ~ **deuxième** Sport [personne] to rank second

classeur /klasœʀ/ nm ① (à anneaux) ring binder; (à compartiments) file; ② (meuble de rangement) filing cabinet

classicisme /klasisism/ nm ① Art, Littérat classicism; ② (conformisme) traditionalism, conservatism

classification /klasifikasjɔ̃/ nf classification (**de** of)

classifier /klasifje/ [2] vtr to classify

classique /klasik/
A adj ① (gréco-latin) classical; **la littérature grecque** ~ classical Greek literature; **faire des études** ~s Scol, Univ to do classics; ② Ling [langue] classical; ③ (pour une époque, un genre) classical; **théâtre** ~ **français** French classical theatre; ④ (consacré) [auteur, œuvre] classic; ⑤ (harmonieux, sobre) classic; **de coupe** ~ of classic cut; ⑥ (courant) [exemple, histoire, situation] classic; [traitement, méthode] classic, standard; (habituel) [symptôme, réaction] classic; [conséquence] usual; **c'est** ~○! it's typical!; **c'est le coup** ~○! it's the same old story!; ⑦ (traditionnel) [grammaire] traditional; [arme] conventional
B nm ① (auteur) classical author; ② (œuvre) classic; **un** ~ **du genre** a classic of its kind; **je connais mes** ~s○! I know my classics!

classiquement /klasikmɑ̃/ adv (de façon traditionnelle) traditionally

claudicant, ~e /klodikɑ̃, ɑ̃t/ adj limping

claudiquer /klodike/ [1] vi to limp

clause /kloz/ nf clause (**sur** on)

claustrer /klostʀe/ [1]
A vtr to confine

B **se claustrer** *vpr* to shut oneself away (**dans** in)

claustrophobe /klostʀɔfɔb/ *adj* claustrophobic

claustrophobie /klostʀɔfɔbi/ *nf* claustrophobia

clavecin /klavsɛ̃/ ▸ p. 389 *nm* harpsichord

claveciniste /klavsinist/ ▸ p. 372 *nmf* harpsichordist

clavicule /klavikyl/ *nf* collarbone, clavicle spéc

clavier /klavje/ *nm* (tous contextes) keyboard

(Composé) ∼ **numérique** numeric keypad

claviériste /klavjeʀist/ *nmf* keyboard player

claviste /klavist/ ▸ p. 372 *nmf* **1** (imprimeur) typesetter; **2** Ordinat keyboarder

clé /kle/

A *nf* **1** Tech (de serrure, mécanisme, conserve) key; **la ∼ de ma chambre** the key to my bedroom; **laisser la ∼ sur la porte** to leave the key in the door *ou* lock; **sous ∼** under lock and key; **fermer à ∼** to lock; **projet ∼s en main** turnkey project; **solution ∼s en main** ready-made solution; **prix ∼s en main** Aut on the road price GB, sticker price US; **2** (condition, solution) key (**de** to); **détenir la ∼ du bonheur** to know the secret of true happiness; **la ∼ des songes** the key to the interpretation of dreams; **roman à ∼** roman à clef; **3** (outil) spanner GB, wrench; **4** Mus (de flûte, clarinette) key; (de violon, guitare) peg; (de trompette) valve; (de tambour) tuning screw; (dans une notation) clef; **∼ de fa/de sol/d'ut** bass *ou* F/treble *ou* G/alto *ou* C clef; **5** Sport (prise) armlock; **faire une ∼ à qn** to get sb in an armlock

B **(-)clé** (*in compounds*) **poste/mot/document(-)∼** key post/word/document

C **à la clé** *loc adv* (comme enjeu) at stake; Mus in the key-signature; **avec, à la ∼, une récompense** with a reward thrown in

(Composés) ∼ **d'accès électronique** Télécom digital security coding; ∼ **d'accordeur** Mus tuning key; ∼ **anglaise** = ∼ **à molette**; ∼ **à bougie** Aut plug spanner GB, spark-plug wrench US; ∼ **de contact** Aut ignition key; ∼ **à molette** adjustable spanner GB *ou* wrench US; ∼ **plate** (serrage) open end spanner GB *ou* wrench US; ∼ **à sardines** Culin sardine tin key GB, sardine can key US; ∼ **de sûreté** (de serrure) Yale® key; ∼ **de voûte** Archit, fig keystone

(Idiomes) **prendre la ∼ des champs** to escape; **mettre la ∼ sous la porte** (partir) to leave; (faire faillite) to go bankrupt

clef = **clé**

clémence /klemɑ̃s/ *nf* **1** (indulgence) leniency (**envers** to); **2** (de climat) mildness (**de** of)

clément, ∼**e** /klemɑ̃, ɑ̃t/ *adj* **1** [*juge*] lenient (**envers** to), clement sout (**envers** to); **se montrer ∼** to show clemency (**envers** to); **2** [*température, hiver*] mild, clement sout

clémentine /klemɑ̃tin/ *nf* clementine

cleptomanie /klɛptɔmani/ *nf* kleptomania

clerc /klɛʀ/ ▸ p. 372 *nm* Admin, Jur clerk; ∼ **(de notaire)** notary's clerk; **être (grand) ∼ en la matière** to be an expert on the subject

clergé /klɛʀʒe/ *nm* clergy

clérical, ∼**e**, *mpl* **-aux** /kleʀikal, o/ *adj* **1** [*vie, fonction*] clerical; **2** [*parti, presse*] that supports the Church (*épith, après n*)

cliché /kliʃe/ *nm* **1** Phot (négatif) negative; (photo) snapshot; **prendre un ∼** to take a snap; **2** (lieu commun) cliché; **3** (d'imprimerie) plate

client, ∼**e** /klijɑ̃, ɑ̃t/ *nm,f* (de magasin) customer; (d'avocat, de notaire) client; (d'hôtel) guest, patron; (de taxi) passenger, fare; **être ∼ d'un magasin** to be a regular customer in a shop GB *ou* store US

(Idiome) **c'est à la tête du ∼** it depends whether they like the look of you

clientèle /klijɑ̃tɛl/ *nf* **1** (de magasin, restaurant) customers (*pl*); (d'avocat, de notaire) clients (*pl*); (de médecin) patients (*pl*); **avoir une bonne ∼** [*magasin, restaurant*] to have a lot of customers; [*avocat, médecin*] to have a large practice; **se faire une ∼** to build up a clientele; **ils ont une ∼ d'entreprises** they deal with firms; **2** (habitude d'achat) custom; (à plus grande échelle) business; **je vais lui retirer ma ∼** I'll take my custom elsewhere, I'll take my business elsewhere

clignement /kliɲəmɑ̃/ *nm* ∼ **d'œil** blinking **₵**

cligner /kliɲe/ [1] *vtr ind* ∼ **des yeux** (plisser les yeux) to screw up one's eyes; (battre des paupières) to blink; ∼ **de l'œil** to wink

clignotant, ∼**e** /kliɲɔtɑ̃, ɑ̃t/

A *adj* flashing

B *nm* Aut (pour tourner) indicator GB, turn signal US, blinker US; **mettre son ∼** to indicate GB *ou* signal

clignoter /kliɲɔte/ [1] *vi* [*lumière*] (une fois) to flash; (longtemps) to flash on and off; [*étoile*] to twinkle

climat /klima/ *nm* Météo, Géog, fig climate; **sous d'autres ∼s** liter in other climes

climatique /klimatik/ *adj* climatic

climatisation /klimatizasjɔ̃/ *nf* air-conditioning

climatiser /klimatize/ [1] *vtr* (maintenir la température de) to air-condition [*pièce*]; (équiper) to install air-conditioning in [*maison*]; **hôtel climatisé** air-conditioned hotel

climatiseur /klimatizœʀ/ *nm* air-conditioner

climatologie /klimatɔlɔʒi/ *nf* climatology

clin /klɛ̃/ *nm* ∼ **d'œil** lit wink; fig allusion; **faire un ∼ d'œil à qn** lit to wink at sb; **en un ∼ d'œil** in a flash, in the wink of an eye littér

clinicien, -ienne /klinisjɛ̃, ɛn/ *nm,f* clinician

clinique /klinik/

A *adj* clinical

B *nf* **1** (établissement) private hospital; **2** (médecine) clinical medecine

(Composé) ∼ **vétérinaire** veterinary clinic

clinquant, ∼**e** /klɛ̃kɑ̃, ɑ̃t/ *adj* flashy○

clip /klip/ *nm* **1** (vidéoclip) videoclip; **2** (bijou) (broche) clip brooch; (boucle d'oreille) clip-on

clique /klik/ *nf* (groupe) clique

(Idiome) **prendre ses ∼s et ses claques**○ to pack up and go

cliquer /klike/ [1] *vi* Ordinat to click (**sur** on)

cliqueter /klikte/ [20] *vi* [*clés*] to jingle; [*chaîne*] to rattle; [*mécanisme*] to go clickety-clack; [*aiguilles à tricoter*] to click

cliquetis /klikti/ *nm inv* (d'aiguilles à tricoter) clicking; (d'épée) rattle; (de couverts) clinking

clitoris /klitɔʀis/ *nm inv* clitoris

clivage /klivaʒ/ *nm* gén, Pol (division) divide (**entre** between); **le ∼ Nord-Sud** the North-South divide; ∼ **d'opinion** division of opinion

cloaque /klɔak/ *nm* **1** fig cesspit; **2** Zool cloaca

clochard, ∼**e** /klɔʃaʀ, aʀd/ *nm,f* tramp

clochardiser: **se clochardiser** /klɔʃaʀdize/ [1] *vpr* to be reduced to vagrancy

cloche /klɔʃ/ *nf* **1** (instrument sonore) bell; **on a entendu dix coups de ∼** we heard the bell ring ten times; **en (forme de) ∼** bell-shaped; ▸ **déménager**; **2** (ustensile de jardinage) cloche; **3** ○(imbécile) clot○ GB, clod○, idiot; **4** ○(clochard) tramp; **la ∼** the down-and-outs (*pl*)

(Composé) ∼ **à fromage** cover of cheese dish

(Idiomes) **se taper la ∼**○ to have a good *ou* slap-up GB meal, to pig out○; **entendre plusieurs sons de ∼** to hear several different versions; **sonner les ∼s**○ **à qn** to bawl sb out○; **se faire sonner les ∼s**○ to get bawled out○

cloche-pied: **à cloche-pied** /aklɔʃpje/ *loc adv* **sauter à ∼** to hop

clocher¹ /klɔʃe/ [1] *vi* (être défectueux) [*argumentation*] to be faulty; **il y a quelque chose qui cloche dans** there's something wrong with

clocher² /klɔʃe/ *nm* **1** (d'église) (en pointe) steeple; (tour) church *ou* bell tower; **2** fig (pays natal) home town; **esprit de ∼** parochial *ou* small-town mentality; **querelle de ∼** local quarrel

clocheton /klɔʃtɔ̃/ *nm* **1** (ornement) pinnacle; **2** (petit clocher) little steeple

clochette /klɔʃɛt/ *nf* **1** (petite cloche) (little) bell; **2** (fleur) bell

cloison /klwazɔ̃/ *nf* **1** Constr partition; (mobile de bureau) screen; ∼ **étanche** lit watertight bulkhead; fig watertight compartment; **2** fig (barrière) barrier (**entre** between)

(Composé) ∼ **extensible** folding room-divider

cloisonnement /klwazɔnmɑ̃/ *nm* (d'administration, de services) compartmentalization; **les ∼s entre** the barriers between [*services, groupes*]

cloisonner /klwazɔne/ [1] *vtr* **1** Constr to partition [*pièce*]; to divide up [*espace*]; **2** *fig* to divide up [*société*]; to compartmentalize [*secteurs, administration*]; to erect barriers between [*groupes*]

cloître /klwɑtʀ/ *nm* cloister

cloîtrer /klwatʀe/ [1]
A *vtr* (enfermer) to shut [sb] away
B **se cloîtrer** *vpr* (s'enfermer) to shut oneself away; **se ~ dans le silence** to retreat into silence

clone /klon/ *nm* clone

cloner /klone/ [1] *vtr* to clone

clope○ /klɔp/ *nm ou f* fag○ GB, ciggy○, cigarette

clopin-clopant○ /klɔpɛ̃klɔpɑ̃/ *loc adv* **1** (en boitant) **marcher ~** to hobble along; **partir ~** to hobble off; **2** (mal) **aller ~** [*économie, affaires*] to limp along

clopinettes○ /klɔpinɛt/ *nfpl* **gagner des ~** to earn peanuts○

cloporte /klɔpɔʀt/ *nm* woodlouse; **des ~s** woodlice

⬭Idiome⬭ **vivre comme un ~**○ to live like a hermit

cloque /klɔk/ *nf* (sur la peau, de la peinture) blister

⬭Idiome⬭ **être en ~**⁹ to be up the spout○ GB, to be knocked up⁹, to be pregnant

clore /klɔʀ/ [79]
A *vtr* **1** (mettre fin à) to close [*débat, scrutin, compte*] (**par** with); **2** (être la fin de) to end, to conclude [*congrès*]; to end [*roman*]; **un dîner a clos le congrès** the conference ended with a dinner; **3** (fermer) *liter* to close [*yeux*]; to block, to seal off [*passage*]; to seal [*enveloppe*]; **4** (enclore) to enclose [*terrain*] (**de** with); **5** (conclure) to conclude [*accord*]
B **se clore** *vpr* (se terminer) to end (**par** with)

clos, ~e /klo, oz/
A *adj* (fermé) **monde ~** *fig* self-contained world; **à la nuit ~e** *liter* after nightfall
B *nm inv* (terrain) fenced *ou* enclosed field

clôture /klotyʀ/ *nf* **1** (barrière) (de bois) fence; (de fil de fer) wire fence; (de grillage) chain-link *ou* wire-mesh fence; (grille) railings (*pl*); (haie) hedge; **~ électrique** electric fence; **mur de ~** enclosing wall; **poser une ~ autour d'un terrain** to fence in *ou* enclose a field; **2** (de débat, scrutin) close; (de souscription) closing; (de magasin, bureau) closing; (de saison) close; **discours de ~** closing speech; **~ des inscriptions le 3 mai à midi** closing date for registration, noon on 3 May

clôturer /klotyʀe/ [1]
A *vtr* **1** (enclore) to enclose, to fence in [*terrain*]; **~ avec du fil de fer barbelé** to surround [sth] with barbed wire; **2** (terminer) [*personne*] to close [*débat, liste, compte*]; [*discours, cérémonie*] to end, to bring [sth] to a close [*débat, festival*]
B *vi* Fin **~ à 50 centimes** to close at 50 cents; **~ à la hausse/baisse** to close up/down
C **se clôturer** *vpr* [*congrès*] to end (**par** with)

clou /klu/
A *nm* **1** Tech nail; **ceinture à ~s** studded belt; **2** (attraction) (de spectacle) star attraction; (de soirée) high point; **3** (furoncle) boil; **4** ⁹(mont-de-piété) **mettre qch au ~** to take sth to the pawnshop
B **clous** *nmpl* **1** (passage pour piétons) pedestrian crossing (*sg*) GB, crosswalk (*sg*) US; **2** ⁹(rien) **des ~s!** no way!

⬭Composé⬭ **~ de girofle** Bot, Culin clove

⬭Idiomes⬭ **enfoncer le ~** to drive the point home; **ne pas valoir un ~**○ not to be worth a thing

clouer /klue/ [1] *vtr* **1** (fixer avec de gros clous) to nail down [*caisse*]; to nail up [*pancarte*]; to nail together [*planches*]; **2** (fixer avec de petits clous) to tack [*moquette, affiche*]; **3** (immobiliser) **~ au sol** to pin [sb] down [*adversaire*]; **les avions sont restés cloués au sol** the planes were grounded; **4** (invalider) **~ au lit/chez soi** to confine [sb] to bed/to one's home

clouté, ~e /klute/ *adj* studded (**de** with); **passage ~** pedestrian crossing GB, crosswalk US

clown /klun/ *nm* clown; **quel ~!** *fig* what a comedian!; **faire le ~** to clown about

clownerie /klunʀi/ *nf* **~s** clowning **℣**; **arrête tes ~s** stop clowning about

club /klœb/ *nm* (société, local) club; *fig* (groupe) group

⬭Composé⬭ **~ de vacances** holiday camp

cm (*written abbr* = **centimètre**) cm; **cm²** (centimètre carré) cm²; **cm³** (centimètre cube) *gén* cm³; (moteurs) cc

CM /seɛm/ *nm: abbr* ▸ **cours**

CMU /ceɛmy/ *nf: abbr* ▸ **couverture**

CMV /seɛmve/ *nm* (*abbr* = **cytomégalovirus**) CMV, cytomegalovirus

CNED /knɛd/ *nm: abbr* ▸ **centre**

CNPF /seɛnpeɛf/ *nm* (*abbr* = **Conseil national du patronat français**) Hist *national council of French employers*

CNRS /seɛnɛʀɛs/ *nm* (*abbr* = **Centre national de la recherche scientifique**) *national centre for scientific research*

coaccusé, ~e /koakyze/ *nm,f* codefendant

coactionnaire /koaksjɔnɛʀ/ *nmf* joint shareholder

coagulant, ~e /kɔagylɑ̃, ɑ̃t/
A *adj* coagulative
B *nm* coagulant

coagulation /kɔagylasjɔ̃/ *nf* coagulation

coaguler /kɔagyle/ [1] *vi*, **se coaguler** *vpr* [*sang*] to coagulate; [*lait*] to curdle

coalisé, ~e /kɔalize/ *adj* [*forces, pays, partis*] allied; [*intérêts*] combined

coaliser: se coaliser /kɔalize/ [1] *vpr gén* to unite; Pol to form a coalition; **se ~ contre la misère/pollution** to unite to combat poverty/pollution

coalition /kɔalisjɔ̃/ *nf* coalition

coaltar○ /kɔltaʀ/ *nm* **être dans le ~** to be in a daze

coasser /kɔase/ [1] *vi* to croak

cobalt /kɔbalt/ *nm* cobalt; **bleu ~** cobalt blue

cobaye /kɔbaj/ *nm* lit, fig guinea pig

cobra /kɔbʀa/ *nm* cobra

coca /kɔka/
A *nm* Bot (arbuste) coca
B *nm ou f* (extrait) coca extract

cocagne /kɔkaɲ/ *nf* **mât de ~** ≈ greasy pole; **pays de ~** land of Cockaigne

cocaïne /kɔkain/ *nf* cocaine

cocaïnomane /kɔkainɔman/ *nmf* cocaine addict

cocarde /kɔkaʀd/ *nf* (sur uniforme) cockade; (emblème national) (sur un avion) roundel; (sur un véhicule) official badge; **~ tricolore** Hist revolutionary cockade; (en tissu) rosette

cocasse /kɔkas/ *adj* comical

cocasserie /kɔkasʀi/ *nf* (de propos) comical nature

coccinelle /kɔksinɛl/ *nf* **1** (insecte) ladybird, ladybug US; **2** ○(voiture) beetle○, Volkswagen® car

coccyx /kɔksis/ *nm inv* coccyx

coche /kɔʃ/ *nm* (diligence) (stage)coach

⬭Idiome⬭ **manquer le ~** to miss the boat

cocher¹ /kɔʃe/ [1] *vtr* to tick GB, to check US

cocher² /kɔʃe/ *nm* (de diligence) coachman; (de fiacre) cabman

cochère /kɔʃɛʀ/ *adj f* **porte ~** carriage entrance

cochon, -onne /kɔʃɔ̃, ɔn/
A ○*adj* **1** (pornographique) [*film, magazine*] dirty; [*personne*] dirty-minded; **2** (malpropre) [*personne*] messy, dirty
B ○*nm,f* **1** (personne malpropre) *pej* pig○, slob○; **travail de ~** botched job; **2** (personne lubrique) sex maniac; **espèce de vieux ~!** you dirty old man!; **tu n'es qu'une cochonne** you've got a mind like a sewer
C *nm* **1** Zool pig, hog; ▸ **confiture, perle**; **2** Culin pork

⬭Composés⬭ **~ d'Inde** Zool Guinea pig; **~ de lait** Agric, Culin sucking pig

⬭Idiomes⬭ **travailler comme un ~**○ to make a mess of a job; **il ira loin, si les petits ~s ne le mangent pas** he'll go far, if nothing gets in his way; **un ~ n'y retrouverait pas ses petits** it's like a pigsty, it's a real shambles○

cochonnaille○ /kɔʃɔnaj/ *nf:* products made from pork such as salami, bacon, pâté and ham

cochonnerie○ /kɔʃɔnʀi/ *nf* **1** (chose de mauvaise qualité) junk○ **℣**; **il ne mange que des ~s** he only eats junk food; **c'est de la ~ ce stylo** this pen is crap○ *ou* useless; **2** (saleté) mess **℣**; **faire des ~s** to make a mess; **3** (obscénité) obscenity; **dire des ~s** to say smutty○ *ou* dirty things

cochonnet /kɔʃɔnɛ/ *nm* **1** Zool piglet; **2** (à la pétanque) jack

cocker /kɔkɛʀ/ *nm* (cocker) spaniel

cocktail /kɔktɛl/ nm ① (boisson) cocktail; (plat composé) ~ **de fruits** fruit cocktail; ② fig (mélange) mixture; ③ (réception) cocktail party

(Composé) ~ **Molotov** Molotov cocktail

coco /koko/ nm ① (noix) coconut; **huile de ~** coconut oil; ② ᴼ(terme d'affection) darling; ③ ᴼ(individu) **c'est un drôle de ~ celui-là!** that guy's a bit of an oddball ᴼ; ④ ᴼ(communiste) pej commie ᴼ péj, red ᴼ péj

cocon /kɔkɔ̃/ nm lit, fig cocoon

(Idiome) **s'enfermer dans son ~** to withdraw into one's shell

cocorico /kɔkɔriko/ nm (also onomat) cock-a-doodle-do

cocotier /kɔkɔtje/ nm coconut palm

(Idiome) **secouer le ~** ≈ to clean out the dead wood

cocotte /kɔkɔt/ nf ① ᴼ(poule) baby talk hen; ② ᴼ(terme d'affection) **ma ~** honey; ③ ᴼ† péj (femme) loose woman; ④ Culin (récipient) casserole dish GB, pot; **cuire qch à la ~** to casserole GB ou stew sth

(Composé) ~ **en papier** paper hen (origami style)

cocotte-minute®, pl **cocottes-minute** /kɔkɔtminyt/ nf pressure cooker

cocotterᴼ /kɔkɔte/ [1] vi to stink, to pong ᴼ GB

cocuᴼ, ~**e** /kɔky/ nm,f lit deceived husband/wife; fig dupe

codage /kɔdaʒ/ nm coding, encoding

code /kɔd/

A nm ① (recueil) code; ~ **de déontologie** code of practice; ② (conventions) code; ③ (écriture, message) code; ~ **chiffré** number code; ④ Ordinat code; ~ **de contrôle d'erreur** error-checking code

B **codes** nmpl (phares) dipped GB ou dimmed US (head)lights, low beam (sg); **se mettre en ~s** to dip GB ou dim US one's headlights

(Composés) ~ **(à) barres** Comm bar code; ~ **civil** Jur civil code; ~ **confidentiel (d'identification)** personal identification number, PIN; ~ **génétique** Biol genetic code; ~ **de la nationalité** regulations (pl) as to nationality; ~ **pénal** Jur penal code; ~ **postal** Post code GB, zip code US; ~ **de la route** highway code GB, rules (pl) of the road US; **passer son ~** ᴼ Aut to take the written part of a driving test

coder /kɔde/ [1] vtr to code, to encode

codétenu, ~**e** /kɔdetny/ nm,f fellow prisoner

codifier /kɔdifje/ [2] vtr to codify [lois]; to standardize [langue, usage]

codirecteur, -trice /kɔdiʀɛktœʀ, tʀis/ nm,f (responsable) joint manager; (administrateur) joint director

coefficient /kɔefisjɑ̃/ nm ① (proportion) ratio; ② (pourcentage indétermine) margin; ~ **d'erreur** margin of error; ~ **de sécurité** safety margin; ③ Scol, Univ weighting factor in an exam; **l'anglais a un ~ élevé** English results are heavily weighted; **la chimie est au ~ 4** chemistry results are multiplied by 4; ④ Math coefficient; Phys (d'expansion, absorption) coefficient; (d'élasticité, écrasement) modulus

coentreprise /kɔɑ̃tʀəpʀiz/ nf joint venture

coéquipier, -ière /koekipje, ɛʀ/ nm,f team-mate

coercitif, -ive /kɔɛʀsitif, iv/ adj coercive

coercition /kɔɛʀsisjɔ̃/ nf coercion

cœur /kœʀ/

A nm ① Anat heart; **il a le ~ malade** he has a heart condition; **serrer qn sur ou contre son ~** to hold sb close; **en forme de ~** heart-shaped (épith); **avoir mal au ~** to feel sick GB ou nauseous US; **lever ou soulever le ~ de qn** to make sb feel sick GB ou nauseous US; ▸ **accrocher, joie, loin**; ② Culin heart; ~**s de poulets** chicken hearts; ~ **de palmier** palm heart; ③ fig (de fruit, roche, matière, réacteur) core; (de problème, région, bâtiment) heart; (d'arbre) heartwood; **au ~ de** (de région, ville) in the middle of; (de bâtiment, problème, système) at the heart of; **au ~ de l'été** in the height of summer; **au ~ de l'hiver/la nuit** in the dead of winter/ night; ④ (personne) **un ~ simple** a simple soul; **mon (petit) ~** sweetheart; ⑤ (siège des émotions) heart; **agir selon son ~** to follow one's heart; **écouter son ~** to go by feelings; **aller droit au ~ de qn** [attentions, bienveillance] to touch sb deeply; [attaque, remarque] to cut sb to the quick; **avoir un coup de ~ pour qch** to fall in love with sth; **faire mal au ~** to be heartbreaking; **ça me fait mal au ~ de voir** it makes me sick at heart to see; **ça me fait chaud au ~ de voir** it

does my heart good to see; **mon ~ se serre quand...** I feel a pang when...; **problème de ~** emotional problem; ▸ **gros**; ⑥ (être intime) heart; **venir du ~** to come from the heart; **je suis de tout ~ avec vous** my heart goes out to you; **aimer qn de tout son ~** to love sb dearly; **parler à ~ ouvert** to speak openly; ⑦ (siège de la bonté) **avoir bon ~** to be kind-hearted; **ton bon ~ te perdra** you're too generous; **ne pas avoir de ~** to be heartless; **faire appel au bon ~ de qn** to appeal to sb's better nature; **une personne de ~** a kind-hearted person; ▸ **fortune**; ⑧ (courage) courage; **le ~ m'a manqué** my courage failed me; **redonner du ~ à qn** to give sb new heart; ⑨ (énergie) heart; **mettre tout son ~ dans qch/à faire** to put one's heart into/into doing; ⑩ (envie) mood; **je n'ai pas le ~ à plaisanter** I'm not in the mood for jokes; **je n'ai plus le ~ à rien** I don't feel like doing anything any more; ▸ **ouvrage**; ⑪ Jeux (carte) heart; (couleur) hearts (pl); **jouer (du) ~** to play hearts; **trois/dame de ~** three/Queen of hearts

B **à cœur** loc adv fait ou moelleux à ~ [fromage] fully ripe; **avoir à ~ de faire** to be intent on doing; **prendre qch à ~** (être résolu) to take sth seriously

C **de bon cœur** loc adv willingly; **pas de bon ~** (rather) unwillingly; **'merci!'—'c'est de bon ~'** 'thank you!'—'you're welcome'; **il brossait le sol et y allait de bon ~** he was scrubbing the floor with a will; **rire de bon ~** to laugh heartily

D **par cœur** loc adv by heart; **connaître qn par ~** to know sb inside out

(Idiomes) **avoir du ~ au ventre** ᴼ to be brave; **être beau or joli comme un ~** to be as pretty as a picture; **avoir le ~ sur la main** to be open-handed; **il a un ~ gros or grand comme ça** ᴼ he's very big-hearted; **avoir un ~ de pierre or marbre** to have a heart of stone; **il ne le porte pas dans son ~** he's not his favourite ᴳᴮ person euph; **le ~ n'y est pas** my/your etc heart isn't in it; **si le ~ t'en dit** if you feel like it; **avoir qch sur le ~** to be resentful about sth

coexister /kɔegziste/ [1] vi to coexist

coffrage /kɔfʀaʒ/ nm (habillage) box

coffre /kɔfʀ/ nm ① (meuble) chest; ~ **à jouets** toy box; ② (pour valeurs) gén safe; (individuel dans banque) safety deposit box; **la salle des ~s** the strongroom; ③ Aut boot GB, trunk US

(Idiome) **avoir du ~** ᴼ (avoir une voix puissante) to have a powerful voice

coffre-fort, pl **coffres-forts** /kɔfʀəfɔʀ/ nm safe

coffrer ᴼ /kɔfʀe/ [1] vtr (arrêter) ~ **qn** to put sb inside ᴼ

coffret /kɔfʀɛ/ nm ① (petit coffre) casket; ~ **à bijoux** jewellery GB ou jewelry US box; ② (de disques, cassettes, livres) boxed set

cofondateur, -trice /kɔfɔ̃datœʀ, tʀis/ nm,f co-founder

cogérer /kɔʒeʀe/ [14] vtr to co-manage

cogestion /kɔʒɛstjɔ̃/ nf joint management

cogiter /kɔʒite/ [1] hum

A ᴼ vtr to dream up [plan]

B vi to cogitate, to think (sur about)

cognac /kɔɲak/ nm cognac (brandy from the Cognac area)

cognée /kɔɲe/ nf (woodman's) axe GB ou ax US

(Idiome) **jeter le manche après la ~** to throw in the towel

cogner /kɔɲe/ [1]

A vtr ① (heurter) (accidentellement) to knock (contre against, on); (volontairement) to bang (contre against, on); **tu as dû ~ la tasse** you must have given the cup a knock; ② ᴼ(battre) to beat up

B vi ① (frapper) ~ **contre** [volet] to bang against; [branche] to knock against; [projectile] to hit; **ma tête/la pierre est allée ~ contre la vitre** my head/the stone hit the window; ~ **à la porte** to bang on the door; ② ᴼ(frapper du poing) [boxeur, agresseur] to hit out; ~ **dur or fort** to hit hard; **ça va ~** there's going to be a brawl; ③ ᴼ(être chaud) [soleil] to beat down; **ça cogne sur la plage** it's baking (hot) on the beach; ④ (battre) [cœur, sang] to pound

C **se cogner** vpr ① (se heurter) to bump into something; **se ~ contre** to hit; **se ~ le genou/la tête** to hit ou bump one's knee/head (contre on); **se ~ à la tête/au genou** to get a bump on the head/on the knee; **se ~ le pied contre une pierre** to stub one's toe on a stone; ② ᴼ(se battre) to have a punch-up ᴳᴮ, to have a fistfight

cognitif, -ive /kɔɡnitif, iv/ adj cognitive

cohabitation /kɔabitasjɔ̃/ nf ① living with somebody; ② Pol period when the French president and the government are drawn from opposing parties

ⓘ Cohabitation A period in which the government and the Président de la République come from opposite political camps. The first instance of political cohabitation in the 5th Republic occurred in 1986 when François Mitterrand (PS) was president and Jacques Chirac (RPR) became prime minister ▸ parti

cohabiter /kɔabite/ [1] vi [personnes] to live together; [choses] to coexist

cohérence /kɔerɑ̃s/ nf ① (de discours, raisonnement) (logique) coherence; (homogénéité) consistency; (de programme, d'attitude) consistency; **manquer de** ~ to be inconsistent; ② (de molécules, d'éléments) cohesion

cohérent, ~e /kɔerɑ̃, ɑ̃t/ adj [raisonnement] (logique) coherent; (homogène) consistent; [attitude, programme] consistent

cohésion /kɔezjɔ̃/ nf cohesion

cohorte /kɔɔʀt/ nf ① ○(groupe) crowd; ② Mil cohort

cohue /kɔy/ nf (monde) crowd; (désordre) **c'est la** ~ it's a crush ou scramble

coi, coite /kwa, kwat/ adj (silencieux) **rester** or **se tenir** ~ to remain quiet; **j'en suis resté** ~ it left me speechless

coiffant, ~e /kwafɑ̃, ɑ̃t/ adj gel ~ styling gel

coiffe /kwaf/ nf (couvre-chef) gén headgear; (de religieuse) wimple

coiffer /kwafe/ [1]
Ⓐ vtr ① (arranger les cheveux de) ~ **qn** (mettre en forme) to do sb's hair; (peigner) to comb sb's hair; **il coiffe ses cheveux en arrière** he combs his hair back; **se faire** ~ **par qn** to have one's hair done by sb; **elle est bien coiffée** her hair is nicely done; **elle est mal coiffée** her hair is untidy; **elle est coiffée court** she has short hair; ② (mettre) to put [sth] on [chapeau, casque]; **coiffé d'une casquette** wearing a cap; ③ (chapeauter) [entreprise] to control; [personne] to head

Ⓑ **se coiffer** vpr ① (s'arranger les cheveux) to do one's hair; (se peigner) to comb one' s hair; **tu t'es coiffé avec un clou!** you look as if you' ve been dragged through a hedge backward(s)○!; **les cheveux frisés se coiffent mal** curly hair is difficult to keep tidy; ② (se couvrir la tête) **se** ~ **de qch** to put sth on

(Idiomes) **être né coiffé** to be born with a silver spoon in one's mouth; ~ **qn au poteau** or **sur le fil**○ to beat sb by a whisker

coiffeur, -euse¹ /kwafœʀ, øz/ ▸ p. 372 nm,f hairdresser; **aller chez le** ~ [femme] to go to the hairdresser's, to have one's hair done; [homme] to have one's hair cut

coiffeuse² /kwaføz/ nf (meuble) dressing table

coiffure /kwafyʀ/ nf ① (coupe de cheveux) hairstyle; **faites-moi cette** ~ do my hair like that; ② (profession) hairdressing; ③ (élément de costume) headgear ¢

coin /kwɛ̃/
Ⓐ nm ① (angle) corner; **un** ~ **de table** the corner of a table; **à tous les** ~**s de rue** everywhere, all over the place; **un placard qui fait le** ~ a corner cupboard; **les** ~**s et recoins** the nooks and crannies; **aux quatre** ~**s de la ville** all over the town; **j'ai dû poser mon sac dans un** ~ I must have put my bag down somewhere; **assis au** ~ **du feu** sitting by the fire; **une causerie au** ~ **du feu** a fireside chat; ▸ **petit**; ② (extrémité) (d'œil, de bouche) corner; **regarder qch/qn du** ~ **de l'œil** to watch sth/sb out of the corner of one's eye; **un sourire en** ~ a half-smile; **un regard en** ~ (sournois) a sidelong glance; ③ (morceau) (de terre) plot; (de pelouse) patch; (d'ombre) spot; **un** ~ **ensoleillé** a sunny spot; **un** ~ **de paradis** an idyllic spot; **un** ~ **de ciel bleu** a patch of blue sky; **un** ~ **de verdure** a green bit; **dans un** ~ **de ma mémoire** in my memory; ④ (lieu d'habitation) part; **un** ~ **de France/de l'Ardèche** a part of France/of the Ardèche; **dans le** ~ (ici) around here, in these parts; (là-bas) around there, in those parts; **nous étions dans le même** ~ we were in the same area; **le café du** ~ the local café; **je ne suis pas du** ~ I'm not from around here; **de quel** ~ **est-il?** where does he come from?; **les gens du** ~ the locals; **dans un** ~ **paumé**○ or **perdu** in the middle of nowhere; **dans un** ~ **perdu de la Lozère** in a remote part of the Lozère; **connaître les bons** ~**s pour manger/pour les champignons** to know all the good places to eat/to find mushrooms; ⑤ (en papeterie) (pour photos) corner; (pour classeur) reinforcing corner; ⑥ Tech (pour fendre) wedge

Ⓑ **coin(-)** (in compounds) ~**-repas/-salon** dining/living area; ~**-bureau** work area

(Idiome) **rencontrer qn au** ~ **d'un bois** to meet sb in a dark alley

coincé, ~e /kwɛse/ adj ① (incapable de bouger) stuck; (incapable de sortir) trapped; **rester** ~ **dans des embouteillages** to be stuck in traffic jams; ~ **entre qch et qch** [meuble, maison] wedged between sth and sth; **il n'a pas pu se lever, il était** ~○ he couldn't get up, his back had gone○; ② ○(incapable d'agir) stuck○; **sans mes outils je suis** ~ without my tools I'm stuck; **il était** ~ **entre l'opposition et son propre parti** he was caught between the opposition and his own party; ③ ○(collet monté) uptight○

coincer /kwɛse/ [12]
Ⓐ vtr ① (immobiliser) to wedge [objet]; (pour maintenir ouvert) to wedge [sth] open; (pour maintenir fermé) to wedge [sth] shut; [éboulement, neige] to trap [personne]; **ils m'ont coincé contre le mur** they pinned me (up) against the wall; ② (bloquer) to jam [objet, clé, fermeture]; **j'ai coincé ma fermeture** my zip GB ou zipper US is jammed ou caught; ③ (dans une porte, fermeture) to catch [vêtement, doigt]; ④ ○(retenir) to catch, to corner [personne]; ⑤ ❶(arrêter) [police] to pick [sb] up○, to nick○ GB [criminel]; ⑥ ○(prendre en défaut) to catch [sb] out [personne]

Ⓑ vi ① (résister au mouvement) [fermeture, tiroir] to stick; **la pellicule coince dans l'appareil** the film is sticking; ② ○(créer des problèmes) [relations] to cause problems; **ça coince** there's a problem

Ⓒ **se coincer** vpr ① (se bloquer) [objet] to get stuck ou jammed; ② (se prendre) **se** ~ **les doigts** to get one's fingers caught; **se** ~ **une vertèbre**○ to trap a nerve in one's back

coïncidence /kɔɛsidɑ̃s/ nf (tous contextes) coincidence

coïncider /kɔɛside/ [1] vi (dates, dépositions) to coincide (**avec** with); [goûts] to be similar (**avec** with); **faire** ~ **l'offre et la demande** to make supply and demand match

coin-coin /kwɛ̃kwɛ̃/ nm inv (also onomat) quack; **faire** ~ to go quack quack

coing /kwɛ̃/ nm quince

coït /kɔit/ nm coitus; ~ **interrompu** coitus interruptus

coite ▸ **coi**

coke /kɔk/ nm (charbon) coke

cokéfaction /kɔkefaksjɔ̃/ nf coking

col /kɔl/ nm ① (de vêtement) collar; ~ **de fourrure** fur collar; **sans** ~ collarless; ~ **rond** round neckline; ~ **carré** square neckline; ~ **en V** V neckline; ▸ **faux¹**; ② Géog pass; **le** ~ **du Lautaret** the Lautaret pass; ③ (d'objet, de bouteille, vase) neck; ④ Anat (de vessie, fémur) neck; **il s'est cassé le** ~ **du fémur** he broke his hip(bone); ⑤ †(cou) neck

(Composés) ~ **blanc** Sociol white-collar worker; ~ **bleu** Sociol blue-collar worker; ~ **de l'utérus** cervix

cola /kɔla/ nm Bot cola tree; **noix de** ~ cola nut

colchique /kɔlʃik/ nm autumn crocus

coléoptère /kɔleɔptɛʀ/ nm beetle

colère /kɔlɛʀ/ nf ① (humeur) anger (**contre qch** at sth; **contre qn** with sb), wrath sout; ~ **froide** contained anger; **être rouge de** ~ to be flushed with anger; **avec** ~ in anger; **être en** ~ to be angry (**contre** with), to be mad○ (**contre** at); **se mettre en** ~ to get angry (**contre** with), to get mad○ (**contre** at); **passer sa** ~ **sur qn** to take out ou vent one's anger on sb; **sous le coup de la** ~ in a fit of anger; ② (crise) fit; (caprice) tantrum; **faire** or **piquer**○ **une** ~ (crise) to have a fit; (caprice) to throw a tantrum; **il était dans une** ~ **noire** he was in a rage; ③ (de la mer) fury, wrath sout; (des cieux) wrath sout; (d'un volcan) fury

coléreux, -euse /kɔleʀø, øz/ adj [personne] quick-tempered, irascible; [tempérament] irascible

colibacille /kɔlibasil/ nm E coli, Escherichia coli

colibri /kɔlibʀi/ nm hummingbird

colifichet /kɔlifiʃɛ/ nm (bijou) trinket; (bibelot) knick-knack

colimaçon /kɔlimasɔ̃/ nm snail

(Composé) **escalier en** ~ spiral staircase

colin /kɔlɛ̃/ nm (merlu) hake; (lieu noir) coley

colin-maillard /kɔlɛ̃majaʀ/ ▸ p. 327 nm jouer à ~ to play blind man's buff

colique /kɔlik/ nf ① (diarrhée) diarrhoea; **avoir la** ~ to have diarrhoea; ② (douleur abdominale) stomach pain; (chez le bébé) colic ¢; ~**s néphrétiques** renal colic

colis /kɔli/ *nm* parcel

⬭Composés⬭ ~ **alimentaire** food parcel; ~ **piégé** parcel bomb; ~ **postal** parcel sent by mail; ~ **postaux** (service) parcel post

colistier, -ière /kɔlistje, ɛʀ/ *nm,f* fellow candidate GB, running mate US

colite /kɔlit/ ▸ p. 195 *nf* colitis

collaborateur, -trice /kɔlabɔʀatœʀ, tʀis/ *nm,f* ⬭1⬭ (collègue) colleague; (assistant) assistant; ~ **du ministre** adviser to the minister; ⬭2⬭ (employé) employee; ⬭3⬭ (journaliste) contributor (**de** to); ⬭4⬭ Hist pej collaborator

collaboration /kɔlabɔʀasjɔ̃/ *nf* ⬭1⬭ (à une revue, un journal) contribution (**à** to); (à un ouvrage, un projet) collaboration (**à** on); **en** ~ **avec** in collaboration with; ⬭2⬭ Hist Pol collaboration (**avec** with)

collaborationniste /kɔlabɔʀasjɔnist/ *adj* [*journal, discours*] collaborationist

collaborer /kɔlabɔʀe/ [1] *vi* ⬭1⬭ (participer) ~ **à** to contribute to [*journal, revue*]; to collaborate on [*projet, ouvrage*]; ⬭2⬭ (travailler) to collaborate (**avec** with)

collage /kɔlaʒ/ *nm* ⬭1⬭ Art (technique, œuvre) collage; ~**s photographiques** photo montages; ⬭2⬭ (affichage) **le** ~ **des affiches** billposting GB, putting up posters; ~ **sauvage** flyposting

collagène /kɔlaʒɛn/ *nm* collagen

collant, ~e /kɔlɑ̃, ɑ̃t/
A *adj* ⬭1⬭ (adhésif) [*substance*] sticky; ⬭2⬭ (gluant) [*main, terre, riz, bonbon*] sticky; ⬭3⬭ (moulant) [*robe, pantalon*] skintight, tight-fitting; ⬭4⬭ ○(importun) [*personne*] clinging; [*vendeur*] persistant
B *nm* tights (*pl*) GB, panty hose (+ *v pl*) US; ~ **de danse** dance tights

collatéral, ~e, *mpl* **-aux** /kɔlateʀal, o/ *adj* ⬭1⬭ Anat [*nerf*] collateral; ⬭2⬭ Jur [*succession, ligne*] collateral; ⬭3⬭ (de côté) [*nef, rue*] side (*épith*); ⬭4⬭ fig [*dommages*] collateral

collation /kɔlasjɔ̃/ *nf* (repas) light meal

colle /kɔl/ *nf* ⬭1⬭ (adhésif) gén glue; (pour papier peint) (wallpaper) paste; **mettre de la** ~ **sur qch** to put glue on sth; ~ **forte/à bois** strong/wood glue; ⬭2⬭ ○(question difficile) poser○; **poser une** ~ **à qn** to set sb a poser○; ⬭3⬭ ○(retenue) students' slang detention; **deux heures de** ~ two hours' detention; ⬭4⬭ ○(oral) students' slang oral test

⬭Composé⬭ ~ **blanche** paste

⬭Idiome⬭ **vivre à la** ~○ to live together

collecte /kɔlɛkt/ *nf* (de fonds, vêtements) collection; **faire une** ~ to raise funds (**pour** for)

collecter /kɔlɛkte/ [1] *vtr* to collect

collecteur, -trice /kɔlɛktœʀ, tʀis/
A *adj* **centre** ~ collection point
B *nm,f* (personne) collector

⬭Composés⬭ ~ **de fonds** fundraiser; ~ **d'impôts** tax collector

collectif, -ive /kɔlɛktif, iv/
A *adj* ⬭1⬭ gén [*travail, responsabilités*] collective; [*démissions, licenciements*] mass (*épith*); [*chauffage*] shared; [*billet, assurance*] group (*épith*); **immeuble** ~ block of flats GB, apartment building US; **donner une punition collective à toute la classe** to punish the whole class; **l'équipe pratique un bon jeu** ~ the team plays well together; ⬭2⬭ Ling collective
B *nm* gén collective; (groupe de pression) action group

⬭Composé⬭ ~ **budgétaire** supplementary finance bill

collection /kɔlɛksjɔ̃/ *nf* ⬭1⬭ (de timbres, photos) collection (**de** of); ~ **de timbres/tableaux** stamp/art collection; **c'est un timbre/badge de** ~ this stamp/badge is a collector's item; **j'ai acheté deux timbres de** ~ **pour mon frère** I bought two stamps for my brother's collection; **faire** ~ **de qch** to collect sth; ▸ **pièce**; ⬭2⬭ (ouvrages) (du même genre) series (+ *v sg*); (du même auteur) set; **toute la** ~ **de Tintin®** the whole set of Tintin® books; ⬭3⬭ (en couture, mode) collection

collectionner /kɔlɛksjɔne/ [1] *vtr* to collect [*timbres, papillons*]; ~ **les erreurs/les gaffes** to make one mistake/ blunder after another

collectionneur, -euse /kɔlɛksjɔnœʀ, øz/ *nm,f* collector

collectivement /kɔlɛktivmɑ̃/ *adv* [*gérer, négocier*] collectively; [*démissionner*] en masse, as a body

collectivité /kɔlɛktivite/ *nf* ⬭1⬭ (groupe) group; ~ **professionnelle** professional body; ⬭2⬭ (ensemble des citoyens) community

⬭Composés⬭ ~ **locale** local authority GB, local government US; ~**s publiques** state, regional and local authorities GB, federal, state and local government US; ~ **territoriale** region with a measure of autonomy

collège /kɔlɛʒ/ *nm* ⬭1⬭ (école) ~ **(d'enseignement secondaire), CES** secondary school GB, junior high school US (*up to age 16*); ⬭2⬭ (assemblée) college; ~ **électoral** electoral college

⬭Composés⬭ ~ **d'enseignement technique, CET** technical secondary school in France

collégial, ~e, *mpl* **-iaux** /kɔleʒjal, o/ *adj* [*église*] collegiate; [*assemblée, pouvoir, système*] collegial

collégien, -ienne /kɔleʒjɛ̃, ɛn/ *nm,f* schoolboy/schoolgirl

⬭Idiome⬭ **se faire avoir**○ **comme un** ~ to be completely taken in

collègue /kɔlɛg/ *nmf* colleague; (dans une lettre) **Cher** ~ Dear Sir

coller /kɔle/ [1]
A *vtr* ⬭1⬭ (faire adhérer) to stick, to glue [*bois, papier, carton*]; to paste up [*affiche*]; to hang [*papier peint, tissu mural*]; to stick [sth] on [*étiquette, timbre, rustine®*]; to stick down [*enveloppe*]; to stick [sth] [*feuilles, morceaux*]; Cin to splice [*film, bande magnétique*]; ~ **des affiches** to stick ou post bills; **il avait les cheveux collés par la peinture** his hair was matted with paint; **ta colle ne colle pas bien le carton** your glue isn't very good for sticking card; ⬭2⬭ (appuyer) ~ **qch contre** *or* **à qch** to press sth against sth; **il avait un pistolet collé à la tempe** there was a pistol pressed to his head; **il la colla contre le parapet** he pushed her up against the parapet; ⬭3⬭ ○(mettre) to stick○; **je leur ai collé la facture sous le nez** I stuck○ the bill (right) under their noses; **tu vas te faire** ~ **une amende** you'll get landed○ with a fine; **si tu continues, je te colle une gifle** *or* **je vais t'en** ~ **une** if you keep on, I'm going to slap you; **on lui colle une étiquette de chanteur engagé** he's being labelled○GB as a political singer; ⬭4⬭ ○(dans un examen, un jeu) **je me suis fait** ~ **en physique** I failed *ou* flunked○ physics; ⬭5⬭ ○(donner une retenue à) to give [sb] detention [*élève*]
B *vi* ⬭1⬭ (adhérer) [*colle, timbre, enveloppe*] to stick; [*pâtes*] to stick together; [*boue, substance*] to stick; ~ **à un véhicule** fig to drive close behind a vehicle; ~ **au sujet** to stick to the subject; **mon tee-shirt mouillé me collait à la peau** my wet T-shirt was clinging to my skin; **ton passé te colle à la peau** fig your past never leaves you; ⬭2⬭ ○(être cohérent) **leur analyse ne colle pas à la réalité** their analysis doesn't fit with the facts; **leurs témoignages ne collent pas** their evidence doesn't tally; **tout colle!** it's all falling into place!
C **se coller** *vpr* ⬭1⬭ (s'appuyer) **se** ~ **à** *or* **contre qn/qch** to press oneself against sb/sth; **ils se sont collés au sol** they lay flat on the ground; **l'alpiniste se collait à la paroi** the climber clung to the rockface; ⬭2⬭ ○(pour une activité) **dès qu'il rentre, il se colle devant son ordinateur** as soon as he comes in he's glued○ to his computer

collerette /kɔlʀɛt/ *nf* (grand col) ruffle; (fraise) ruff

collet /kɔlɛ/ *nm* (piège) snare

⬭Idiomes⬭ **être** ~ **monté** to be prim; **mettre la main au** ~ **de qn** [*police*] to collar○ sb; **prendre** *or* **saisir qn par le** ~ to grab sb by the collar

colleur, -euse[1] /kɔlœʀ, øz/ ▸ p. 372 *nm,f* ~ **(d'affiches)** billposter, billsticker

colleuse[2] /kɔløz/ *nf* Cin splicer

collier /kɔlje/ *nm* ⬭1⬭ (bijou) necklace; ~ **de perles** string of pearls; ~ **de fleurs** garland of flowers; ⬭2⬭ (d'animal) collar; ⬭3⬭ (barbe) beard

⬭Idiomes⬭ **reprendre le** ~ to get back into harness; **donner un coup de** ~ (intellectuellement) to get one's head down; (manuellement) to put one's back into it

collimateur /kɔlimatœʀ/ *nm* collimator

⬭Idiome⬭ **avoir qn dans le** ~○ to have it in for sb○

colline /kɔlin/ *nf* hill

collision /kɔlizjɔ̃/ *nf* ⬭1⬭ (choc) collision; **entrer en** ~ **avec** to collide with; ⬭2⬭ (affrontement) clash, conflict

colloque /kɔl(l)ɔk/ *nm* conference, symposium

collusion /kɔlyzjɔ̃/ *nf* collusion (**avec** with)

collyre /kɔliʀ/ *nm* eyedrops (*pl*)

colmater /kɔlmate/ [1] *vtr* ① (*boucher*) to plug, to seal off [*fuite*]; to seal [*fente*]; ② *fig* ~ **les brèches** to fill in the gaps

Colomb /kɔlɔ̃/ *nprm* **Christophe** ~ Christopher Columbus

colombage /kɔlɔ̃baʒ/ *nm* half-timbering; **ferme à** ~**s** half-timbered farmhouse

colombe /kɔlɔ̃b/ *nf* ① (*oiseau*) dove; ② (*partisan de la paix*) dove; ③ (*terme d'affection*) **ma** ~ my little love; ▸ **crapaud**

colombien, -ienne /kɔlɔ̃bjɛ̃, ɛn/ ▸ p. 392 *adj* Colombian

colombier /kɔlɔ̃bje/ *nm* dovecote

colon /kɔlɔ̃/ *nm* ① (*de terres inhabitées*) colonist; ② (*de colonie de vacances*) child (*at children's holiday camp*); ③ ᴼsoldiers' slang colonel

côlon /kolɔ̃, kɔlɔ̃/ *nm* colon

colonel /kɔlɔnɛl/ ▸ p. 283 *nm* Mil (dans l'armée de terre) ≈ colonel; (dans l'armée de l'air) ≈ group captain GB, ≈ colonel US

colonial, -e, *mpl* **-iaux** /kɔlɔnjal, o/ *adj, nm,f* colonial

colonialisme /kɔlɔnjalism/ *nm* colonialism

colonialiste /kɔlɔnjalist/ *adj, nmf* colonialist

colonie /kɔlɔni/ *nf* ① Pol colony; **les** ~**s** the colonies; ② (*groupe*) (d'artistes) colony; (ethnique) community; ③ Zool, Biol colony

⬭Composé⬭ ~ **de vacances** holiday camp (*for children*)

colonisateur, -trice /kɔlɔnizatœr, tris/
Ⓐ *adj* colonizing
Ⓑ *nm,f* colonizer

colonisation /kɔlɔnizasjɔ̃/ *nf* colonization

coloniser /kɔlɔnize/[1] *vtr* to colonize

colonnade /kɔlɔnad/ *nf* colonnade

colonne /kɔlɔn/ *nf* gén column; (de lit) (bed)post; Archit column, pillar; **défiler** ~ **par cinq** to march in fives; **sur cinq** ~**s à la une** Presse splashed across the front page; ~ **d'air** air stream

⬭Composés⬭ ~ **blindée** Mil armoured^GB column; ~ **de direction** Aut steering column; ~ **montante** Constr riser; ~ **vertébrale** Anat spinal column

colonnette /kɔlɔnɛt/ *nf* small column

colorant, -e /kɔlɔʀɑ̃, ɑ̃t/
Ⓐ *adj* colouring^GB
Ⓑ *nm* gén colouring^GB agent; (en teinture) dye; Chimie stain; Culin colouring^GB; (pour cheveux) colourant^GB

coloration /kɔlɔʀasjɔ̃/ *nf* ① (action) colouring^GB; (de textiles) dyeing; (de bois, cellule) staining; (de cheveux) tinting; (permanente) dyeing; ② (couleur) colour^GB; (de peau) colouring^GB; (nuance) shade

coloré, -e /kɔlɔʀe/ *adj* ① (teinté) [*objet*] coloured^GB; [*visage*] (par l'air vif) ruddy; (par l'alcool) florid; ② (pittoresque) [*vie, foule*] colourful^GB; [*style*] lively

colorer /kɔlɔʀe/ [1]
Ⓐ *vtr* ① (teinter) to colour^GB [*liquide, verre*]; to tint [*photo, cheveux*]; to stain [*bois, cellule*]; (teindre) to dye [*textiles, cheveux*]; ~ **qch en vert** to colour^GB sth green; ② (empreindre) [*nostalgie*] to tinge
Ⓑ **se colorer** *vpr* [*visage*] to flush

coloriage /kɔlɔʀjaʒ/ *nm* (action) colouring^GB; (dessin colorié) coloured^GB picture; (dessin à colorier) picture for colouring^GB in

colorier /kɔlɔʀje/ [2] *vtr* to colour in GB, to color US [*dessin*]; ~ **qch en rouge** to colour^GB sth red

coloris /kɔlɔʀi/ *nm inv* gén colour^GB; (nuance) shade

colossal, ~e, *mpl* **-aux** /kɔlɔsal, o/ *adj* colossal, huge

colosse /kɔlɔs/ *nm* giant

colportage /kɔlpɔʀtaʒ/ *nm* hawking

colporter /kɔlpɔʀte/ [1] *vtr* ① (répandre) to spread [*ragots*]; ② (vendre) to peddle [*marchandises*]

colporteur, -euse /kɔlpɔʀtœʀ, øz/ *nm,f* (marchand) pedlar

colt /kɔlt/ *nm* (pistolet) gun, Colt®

coltinerᴼ**: se coltiner** /kɔltine/ [1] *vpr* ① (porter) to lugᴼ [*objet lourd*]; ② (devoir se charger de) to get lumbered with GB, to get stuckᴼ [*corvée, personne*]

col-vert, *pl* **cols-verts, colvert** /kɔlvɛʀ/ *nm* mallard (*inv*)

colza /kɔlza/ *nm* rape; **huile de** ~ rapeseed oil

coma /kɔma/ *nm* coma; **dans le** ~ in a coma

comateux, -euse /kɔmatø, øz/ *adj* comatose

combat /kɔ̃ba/ *nm* ① Mil fighting **☣; les** ~**s ont repris** the fighting has broken out again; ~**s aériens/terrestres** air/land battles; **envoyer au** ~ to send into combat; **mettre hors de** ~ to disable; **partir au** ~ to set off for battle; ② Pol struggle (**contre** against; **pour** for); **mener le** ~ to lead the struggle; **livrer un** ~ to campaign (**contre** against; **pour** for); ③ Sport bout; ~ **de boxe** boxing bout; (**mettre**) **hors de** ~ (to put) out of action

⬭Composés⬭ ~ **de coqs** cock fight; ~ **singulier** single combat

combatif, -ive /kɔ̃batif, iv/ *adj* (déterminé) assertive; (agressif) aggressive; [*boxeur, armée*] full of fighting spirit

combativité /kɔ̃bativite/ *nf* fighting spirit

combattant, -e /kɔ̃batɑ̃, ɑ̃t/
Ⓐ *adj* ① (combatif) [*esprit*] fighting; ② (de combat) [*troupe, unité*] combat
Ⓑ *nm,f* combatant; ▸ **ancien**

combattre /kɔ̃batʀ/ [61]
Ⓐ *vtr* to fight
Ⓑ *vi* to fight (**contre** against; **pour** for)

combien¹ /kɔ̃bjɛ̃/
Ⓐ *adv* ① ▸ p. 347, p. 453, p. 483, p. 575 (dans une interrogation) ~ **coûte une bouteille de vin?** how much *ou* what does a bottle of wine cost?; ~ **mesure le salon?** how big is the lounge?; ~ **êtes-vous/sont-ils?** how many of you/them are there?; ② (modifiant un verbe) **il est triste de voir** ~ **la situation s'est dégradée** it's sad to see how the situation has deteriorated; **il est difficile d'expliquer** ~ **je les apprécie** it's difficult to explain how much I appreciate them; ③ (modifiant un adjectif) **c'est cher mais** ~ **efficace!** it's expensive but so effective!; **il souligne** ~ **est précieuse l'aide de ses collègues** he stresses how valuable his colleagues' help is to him; ④ (modifiant un adverbe) ~ **peu d'idées** how few ideas; ~ **peu d'or** how little gold
Ⓑ **combien de** *dét inter* ① (avec un nom dénombrable) how many; ~ **d'élèves accueillerez-vous en septembre?** how many pupils will you receive in September?; **c'est à** ~ **de kilomètres?** how far away is it?; ~ **de kilomètres y-a-t-il entre les deux villes?** how far apart are the two towns?; ~ **de fois** (nombre de fois) how many times; (fréquence) how often; (avec un nom d'années? in how many years time?; ② (avec un nom non dénombrable) how much; **de** ~ **de pain as-tu besoin?** how much bread do you need?; ~ **de temps faut-il?** how long does it take?

combien² /kɔ̃bjɛ̃/ ▸ p. 575 *nmf inv* ① (ordre) **tu es la** ~ᴼ**?** (dans une queue) how many people are before you?; ② (date) **le** ~ **sommes-nous?, on est le** ~ᴼ**?** what's the date today?; **vous arrivez le** ~**?** what date are you arriving?; ③ (mesure) **tu chausses du** ~**?** what size shoes do you take?; ④ (fréquence) **tu le vois tous les** ~**?** how often do you see him?

combinaison /kɔ̃binɛzɔ̃/ *nf* ① (agencement) (action) combining; (résultat) combination; ② Chimie, Math combination; ③ (de serrure, coffre-fort) combination; ④ (sous-vêtement) (full-length) slip; (tenue de sport) jumpsuit; (d'ouvrier) overalls (*pl*) GB, coveralls (*pl*) US

⬭Composés⬭ ~ **d'aviateur** flying suit; ~ **de plongée** wetsuit

combinardᴼ**, -e** /kɔ̃binaʀ, aʀd/ *pej*
Ⓐ *adj* **il est** ~ (débrouillard) he's a fixerᴼ *ou* wheeler-dealerᴼ; (magouilleur) he's a schemer
Ⓑ *nm,f* (débrouillard) fixerᴼ, wheeler-dealerᴼ; (magouilleur) schemer

combineᴼ /kɔ̃bin/ *nf* (moyen) trickᴼ; (intrigue) scheme; **être de** *or* **marcher dans la** ~ to be in on it

combiné /kɔ̃bine/ *nm* Télécom handset, receiver

combiner /kɔ̃bine/ [1]
Ⓐ *vtr* ① (réunir) to combine (**à, avec** with); ② (calculer) to work out [*horaire, plan*]
Ⓑ **se combiner** *vpr* ① (se mélanger) [*éléments*] to combine (**à, avec** with); ② (s'harmoniser) [*couleurs, saveurs*] to go together

comble /kɔ̃bl/
Ⓐ *adj* [*salle*] packed; **faire salle** ~ (pour une conférence) to have a capacity audience; (un spectacle) to play to packed houses; **la mesure est** ~**, je démissionne!** that's the last straw, I resign!

B *nm* **1** (point extrême) **le ~ de l'injustice** the height of injustice; **c'est le ~ de l'horreur** it's absolutely horrific; **il était au ~ de la joie** he was absolutely delighted; **être à son ~** [*émotion, suspense*] to be at its height; **porter qch à son ~** to take sth to its extreme; **être au ~ du désespoir** to be in the depths of despair; **pour ~ de malchance j'ai raté mon avion!** to crown it all, I missed my plane!; **et, ~ du raffinement, les draps étaient en soie!** and, as the ultimate in refinement, there were silk sheets!; **c'est un** *or* **le ~!**○ that's the limit!; **2** (pallier) roof space; **de fond en ~** [*fouiller, nettoyer*] from top to bottom; [*changer, détruire*] completely

C **combles** *nmpl* attic (*sg*)

combler /kɔ̃ble/ [1] *vtr* **1** (remplir) to fill (in) [*fossé, tranchée*]; **2** (pallier) to fill in [*lacunes*]; to make up [*déficit*]; to make up for [*manque, perte*]; **~ son retard** to make up (for) lost time; **~ son retard technologique** to catch up in the field of technology; **3** (satisfaire) to fulfil^GB, to satisfy [*besoin, désir*]; **la vie m'a comblé** I've had a wonderful life; **~ qn** to fill sb with joy *ou* delight; **~ qn de cadeaux/d'honneurs**^GB to lavish presents/honours^GB on sb; **merci beaucoup, je suis comblé!** thank you very much, I don't know what to say!; **c'est une femme comblée** she has everything she could possibly want

combustible /kɔ̃bystibl/
A *adj* combustible
B *nm* fuel; **~ nucléaire** nuclear fuel

combustion /kɔ̃bystjɔ̃/ *nf* combustion

comédie /kɔmedi/ *nf* **1** Littérat, Théât comedy; **2** (attitude feinte) play-acting; **c'est de la ~** it's just an act; **jouer la ~** to put on an act; **3** ○(caprice) scene; **faire une ~** to make a scene; **4** ○(histoire) **quelle ~ pour avoir un visa** what a palaver○ to get a visa

(Composés) **~ de boulevard** light comedy; **~ musicale** musical

comédien, -ienne /kɔmedjɛ̃, ɛn/
A *adj* **il est (un peu) ~** (simulateur) he puts it on; (hypocrite) he's a sham
B *nm,f* **1** ▸ p. 372 (acteur) actor/actress; (acteur comique) comic actor/actress; **2** fig **c'est un ~** (simulateur) he puts it on; (hypocrite) he's a sham

comestible /kɔmɛstibl/
A *adj* edible
B **comestibles** *nmpl* food **¢**; **marchand de ~s** grocer

comète /kɔmɛt/ *nf* comet

comique /kɔmik/
A *adj* **1** Théât [*genre, personnage*] comic; **2** (amusant) funny
B *nmf* (humoriste) comedian
C *nm* **1** (pitre) clown; **2** (genre) comedy; **3** (drôlerie) **c'est d'un ~!** it's so funny!; **c'est du plus haut ~** it's absolutely hilarious

comité /kɔmite/ *nm* **1** Admin committee; **~ exécutif** executive committee; **~ directeur** executive *ou* management committee; **2** (groupe) **~ restreint** small group; **dîner en petit ~** intimate little dinner

(Composés) **~ central** Pol Central Committee; **~ d'entreprise, CE** works council GB

> **ⓘ** **Comité d'entreprise** A representative body of workers and management, required by law in any business with more than 50 employees, and entitled to an annual report from the owners, and consultation on all proposed changes. The *comité d'entreprise* also organizes social activities and holiday packages and arranges discount prices on selected goods and services.

commandant /kɔmɑ̃dɑ̃/, ▸ p. 283 *nm* (dans l'armée de terre) ≈ major; (dans l'armée de l'air) ≈ squadron leader GB, ≈ major US

(Composés) **~ de bord** Aviat, Naut captain; **~ en second** Mil ≈ second-in-command

commande /kɔmɑ̃d/ *nf* **1** Comm order; **passer une ~ (à qn)** to place an order (with sb); **2** Littérat, Art commission; **passer ~ de qch à qn** to commission sb to do sth; **3** Tech control; **tableau de ~** control panel; **~ à distance** remote control; **à double ~** dual-control; **être aux** *or* **tenir les ~s** lit to be at the controls; fig to be in control; **se mettre aux** *or* **prendre les ~s de** lit to take the controls of; fig to take control of; **4** Ordinat command

commandement /kɔmɑ̃dmɑ̃/ *nm* **1** Mil (direction) command; **avoir le ~ de** to be in command of [*armée*]; **2** Mil

(ordre) order, command; **à mon ~, feu!** at *ou* on my command, fire!; **3** (autorités militaires) command; **4** Relig **les dix ~s** the Ten Commandments

commander /kɔmɑ̃de/ [1]
A *vtr* **1** Comm to order; **~ qch à qn** to order sth from sb; **2** (demander l'exécution de) to commission [*livre, tableau, sondage*]; **3** Mil (être à la direction de) to command, to be in command of [*armée*]; **4** (exercer une autorité sur) **il aime ~ tout le monde** he loves ordering everyone about; **5** (exiger) **les circonstances commandent la prudence** the circumstances call for caution; **6** (actionner) [*dispositif, ordinateur*] to control [*mécanisme*]
B **commander à** *vtr ind* (avoir autorité sur) **~ à** to be in command of
C *vi* [*personne, chef*] to give the orders, to be in command; **c'est moi qui commande!** I'm in charge!
D **se commander** *vpr* (être contrôlable) **la passion, ça ne se commande pas** passion doesn't come to order; **ces choses ne se commandent pas** you can't force these things

commanditaire /kɔmɑ̃ditɛʀ/ *nmf* **1** (bailleur de fonds) sleeping partner GB, silent partner US; **2** (sponsor) backer, sponsor; **3** (d'un crime) **le ~ d'un assassinat** the person behind an assassination

commanditer /kɔmɑ̃dite/ [1] *vtr* to finance [*société*]; to sponsor [*projet*]; to be behind [*crime*]

commando /kɔmɑ̃do/ *nm* commando

comme /kɔm/
A *adv* how; **~ il a raison!** how right he is!
B *conj* **1** (de même que) **ici ~ en Italie** here as in Italy; **ils sont bêtes, lui ~ elle** he's as stupid as she is; **il est paresseux, ~ sa sœur d'ailleurs** he's lazy, just like his sister; **fais ~ moi** do as I do; **~ toujours** as always; **j'y étais allé ~ chaque matin** I'd gone there as I did every morning; **jolie ~ tout** ever so pretty GB, really pretty; **2** (dans une comparaison) **il est grand ~ sa sœur** he's as tall as his sister; **c'est tout ~**○ it comes to the same thing; **elle me traite ~ un enfant** she treats me like a child, she treats me as if I were a child; **je voudrais un manteau ~ le tien** I'd like a coat like yours; **elle a fait un geste ~ pour se protéger** she made a movement as if to protect herself; **3** (dans une explication) **des pays industrialisés ~ les États-Unis et le Japon** industrialized countries such as *ou* like the United States and Japan; **alors ~ ça tu vas travailler à l'étranger?** so you're going to work abroad then?; **puisque c'est ~ ça** if that's the way it is, if that's how it is; **~ si je n'avais que ça à faire!** as if I had nothing better to do!; **~ si j'avais besoin de ça!** that's the last thing I needed!; **4** ○(dans une approximation) **elle a eu ~ un évanouissement** she sort of fainted, she had a kind of fainting fit; **5** (indiquant l'intensité) **avare ~ il est, il ne te donnera rien** he's so mean, he won't give you anything; **6** (indiquant une fonction) **travailler ~ jardinier** to work as a gardener; **7** (puisque) as, since; **~ elle était seule** as *ou* since she was alone; **8** (au moment où) as; **~ il traversait la rue** as he was crossing the road

(Idiomes) **~ quoi!** which just shows!; **~ ci ~ ça**○ so-so○

commémoratif, -ive /kɔmemɔʀatif, iv/ *adj* [*plaque, timbre*] commemorative; [*cérémonie*] memorial

commémoration /kɔmemɔʀasjɔ̃/ *nf* commemoration

commémorer /kɔmemɔʀe/ [1] *vtr* to commemorate

commencement /kɔmɑ̃smɑ̃/
A *nm* (phase initiale) beginning; (point de départ) start; **au ~** at the beginning; **dès le ~** from the start; **du ~ à la fin** from start to finish, from beginning to end; **commencez par le ~** start *ou* begin at the beginning
B **commencements** *nmpl* (premiers moments) beginnings (*pl*); **~s pénibles** difficult beginnings

commencer /kɔmɑ̃se/ [12]
A *vtr* **1** (entreprendre) to start, to begin [*travail, discours*]; **c'est lui qui a commencé!** (la dispute) he started it!; **elle a commencé le piano à six ans** she started playing the piano when she was six; **tu commences bien l'année!** that's a good start to the year!; **le film est commencé** the film has already started; **2** **~ à** *or* **de faire** to begin to do; **je commence à comprendre** I'm beginning to understand; **ça commence à bien faire**○ *or* **à suffire**○**!** it's getting a bit much!
B *vi* [*année, film, rue*] to start, to begin; [*processus*] to begin; **pour ~, c'est trop cher** for a start, it's too expensive; **commence par le plafond** start with the ceiling; **par où** *or* **quoi**

c

comment¹

Lorsqu'il signifie 'de quelle manière', *comment* se traduit généralement par *how*:

comment vas-tu au travail?
= how do you get to work?

comment as-tu fait pour arriver avant moi?
= how did you manage to get here before me?

je ne comprends pas comment tu as pu te perdre
= I don't understand how you managed to get lost

dis-moi comment elle a réagi
= tell me how she reacted

comment résoudre le problème?
= how can this problem be solved?

as-tu compris comment faire?
= do you understand how to do it?

il ne sait même pas comment faire cuire un œuf au plat
= he doesn't even know how to fry an egg

Attention: certains verbes comme *appeler, nommer* etc. ont une construction différente en anglais:

comment appelles-tu cet objet?
= what do you call this object?

On se reportera au verbe.

Lorsqu'il peut être remplacé par 'pourquoi', *comment* se traduit par *why*:

comment ne m'a-t-on pas averti?
= why wasn't I told?

Lorsqu'il sert à exprimer l'indignation ou la surprise, *comment* se traduit par *what*:

comment? il est marié?
= what? he's married?

Lorsqu'il sert à faire répéter une information, *comment* se traduit par *pardon*:

comment? qu'est-ce que tu dis?
= pardon? what did you say?

On trouvera exemples supplémentaires et exceptions ci-dessous.

vais-je ∼? where shall I start?; **par qui vais-je ∼?** who shall I start with?; **commence par obéir!** for a start you can do as you're told!; **∼ comme secrétaire** to start (off) as a secretary
C *v impers* **il commence à pleuvoir/neiger** it's starting *ou* beginning to rain/to snow
comment¹ /kɔmɑ̃/ *adv* ① (de quelle manière) how; **∼ le sais-tu?** how do you know (that)?; **il faut voir ∼ il nous a traités!** you should have seen the way he treated us!; ② (pour faire répéter) **∼, peux-tu répéter?** sorry, could you say that again?; **Paul ∼?** Paul who?; ③ (évaluation) **∼ est leur fils?** what's their son like?; **∼ trouves-tu ma robe?** what do you think of my dress?, how do you like my dress?; ④ (indignation, surprise) **∼ cela?** what do you mean?; **∼ ça se fait°?** how come°?, how is that?; **∼? tu voudrais des excuses?** what? you expect me to apologize?; ⑤ (intensif) **∼ donc!** but of course!; **'c'était bon?'—'et ∼°!'** 'was it nice?'—'it certainly was!'
comment² /kɔmɑ̃/ *nm* **le ∼** the how
commentaire /kɔmɑ̃tɛʀ/ *nm* ① (remarque) comment (**sur** about); ② Radio, TV commentary (**de** on); **∼ en direct** live commentary; ③ Littérat commentary
commentateur, -trice /kɔmɑ̃tatœʀ, tʀis/ ▸ p. 372 *nm,f* commentator
commenter /kɔmɑ̃te/ [1] *vtr* ① (dire son opinion sur) to comment on [*décision, déclaration, événement*]; ② (donner des explications) to give a commentary on [*film, visite*]; **commenté par** with a commentary by; ③ Radio, TV (décrire) to commentate on [*match, événement*]; **commenté par** commentated on by; ④ Littérat, Scol to comment on [*texte*]
commérage /kɔmeʀaʒ/ *nm* gossip **¢**

commerçant, ∼e /kɔmɛʀsɑ̃, ɑ̃t/
A *adj* **rue ∼e** shopping street; **nation très ∼e** great trading nation; **il n'est pas très ∼** he's not interested in pleasing the customer
B ▸ p. 372 *nm,f* shopkeeper, storekeeper US; **petit ∼** small shopkeeper *ou* storekeeper US; **grand** *or* **gros ∼** large retailer; **les ∼s ferment en août** the shops *ou* stores US close in August
commerce /kɔmɛʀs/ *nm* ① (magasin) shop, store US; **dans le ∼** in the shops *ou* stores US; ② (entreprise commerciale) business; ③ (activité) trade; **faire le ∼ de** to trade in; **faire ∼ de** to sell; **faire du ∼** to be in business; ④ (fréquentation) *liter* company; **être d'un ∼ agréable** to be good company
(Composés) **∼ de détail** retail trade; **∼ équitable** fair trade; **∼ extérieur** foreign trade; **∼ de gros** wholesale trade
commercer /kɔmɛʀse/ [12] *vi* to trade (**avec** with)
commercial, ∼e, *mpl* **-iaux** /kɔmɛʀsjal, o/
A *adj* ① Comm commercial; **carrière ∼e** career in sales and marketing; ② Écon trade; **accord ∼** trade agreement
B *nm,f* sales and marketing person
commercialisation /kɔmɛʀsjalizasjɔ̃/ *nf* marketing
commercialiser /kɔmɛʀsjalize/ [1] *vtr* to market
commère /kɔmɛʀ/ *nf pej* gossip; **c'est une vraie ∼!** he/she is a real gossip!
commettre /kɔmɛtʀ/ [60]
A *vtr* ① (faire) to make [*erreur*]; to commit [*crime*]; to carry out [*attentat, massacre*]; ② (préposer) **∼ qn à un emploi** to appoint sb to a post
B **se commettre** *vpr fml* **se ∼ avec des indésirables** to associate with undesirable characters
commis /kɔmi/ ▸ p. 372 *nm inv* (employé) (de ferme) hand; (de bureau) clerk; (de commerce) shop assistant GB, salesclerk US
(Composé) **∼ voyageur** travelling^{GB} salesman
commisération /kɔmizeʀasjɔ̃/ *nf* commiseration
commissaire /kɔmisɛʀ/ ▸ p. 372 *nm* ① (dans la police) **∼ (de police)** ≈ police superintendent; ② (membre d'une commission) commissioner; ③ (surveillant, organisateur) steward
(Composés) **∼ de bord** purser; **∼ de la République** prefect
commissaire-priseur, *pl* **commissaires-priseurs** /kɔmisɛʀpʀizœʀ/ ▸ p. 372 *nm* auctioneer
commissariat /kɔmisaʀja/ *nm* ① (local) **∼ (de police)** police station; ② (commission) commission
commission /kɔmisjɔ̃/
A *nf* ① (groupe de travail) committee; ② Comm, Fin commission; **être payé à la ∼** to be payed on a commission basis; ③ (mission) **faire une ∼ pour qn** to do *ou* run an errand for sb; ④ (message) **faire la ∼ à qn** to give sb the message
B **commissions**° *nfpl* shopping **¢**; **faire les ∼s** to do one's *ou* the shopping
commissionnaire /kɔmisjɔnɛʀ/ ▸ p. 372 *nm* ① Jur, Comm agent, broker; ② (coursier) messenger; **∼ (d'hôtel)** doorman
commissionner /kɔmisjɔne/ [1] *vtr* to commission
commissure /kɔmisyʀ/ *nf* (de lèvres) corner
commode /kɔmɔd/
A *adj* ① (pratique) *gén* convenient; [*instrument, outil*] handy; ② (aisé) easy; **ce serait trop ∼** it would be too easy; ③ **ne pas être ∼** (être strict) to be strict; (être difficile) to be difficult (to deal with)
B *nf* (meuble) chest of drawers
commodément /kɔmɔdemɑ̃/ *adv* [*situé*] conveniently; [*installé*] comfortably; [*se déplacer*] easily
commodité /kɔmɔdite/ *nf* convenience
commotion /kɔmosjɔ̃/ *nf* ① Méd (ébranlement) concussion; **∼ cérébrale** concussion (*of the brain*); ② fig (émotion) shock
commotionner /kɔmosjɔne/ [1] *vtr* ① lit to concuss; ② fig to shake
commuer /kɔmɥe/ [1] *vtr* to commute [*peine*] (**en** to)
commun, ∼e¹ /kɔmœ̃, yn/
A *adj* ① (venant de plusieurs personnes) [*travail, œuvre*] collaborative; [*désir, accord, conception*] common; [*candidat, politique, projet*] joint (*épith*); **d'un ∼ accord** by mutual agreement; ② (appartenant à plusieurs) [*pièce, équipement, souvenirs*] shared; [*langue, passé*] common; [*biens*] joint (*épith*); **nous avons des**

amis ~**s** we have friends in common; **pour le bien** ~ for the common good; **après dix ans de vie** ~**e** after living together for ten years; ③ (semblable) [*intérêts, traits*] common (**à** to); [*ambition, objectifs*] shared; **les événements d'hier sont sans** ~**e mesure avec les précédents** yesterday's events are on an altogether different scale from previous ones; ④ (courant) common; **elle est d'une beauté peu** ~**e** she's uncommonly beautiful; ⑤ (ordinaire) pej [*goût, personne*] common péj; [*visage*] plain; **c'est/il est d'un** ~**!** it's/he's so common!

B *nm* ordinary; **sortir du** ~ to be out of the ordinary; **le** ~ **des mortels** ordinary mortals (*pl*); **hors du** ~ exceptional

C **en commun** *loc adv* [*écrire, produire*] jointly, together; **avoir qch en** ~ to have sth in common; **mettre ses moyens** *or* **ressources en** ~ to pool one's resources; **nous mettons tout en** ~ we share everything

D **communs** *nmpl* (bâtiment) outbuildings (*pl*)

> ⓘ **Commune** The smallest administrative unit, headed by a *maire* and a *conseil municipal*. Each village, town and city is a *commune*, of which there are 36,000 nationwide.

communal, ~**e**, *mpl* **-aux** /kɔmynal, o/ *adj* [*budget*] local council GB, local government US; [*bâtiment*] local council GB, community US; **chemin** ~ ≈ public track; **terrain** ~ common land

communautaire /kɔmynotɛʀ/ *adj* ① Pol [*budget, droit*] Community; [*population*] of the Community (après *n*); ② (d'une collectivité) **la vie** ~ life in a community; **les règles** ~**s** the rules of a community

communautarisme /kɔmynotaʀism/ *nm* communitarianism

communauté /kɔmynote/ ▸ p. 230 *nf* ① (groupe humain) community; ② (collectivité) commune; **vivre en** ~ to live in a commune; ③ Relig community; ④ Jur ~ (**de biens**) joint ownership; ⑤ (identité) community; **une** ~ **d'idées/de valeurs** shared ideas/values

(Composés) **Communauté économique européenne**, **CEE** Hist European Economic Community, EEC; **Communauté des États indépendants**, **CEI** Commonwealth of Independent States, CIS

commune² /kɔmyn/
A *nf* ① (village) village; (ville) town, district; ② Hist **la Commune (de Paris)** the (Paris) Commune
B **communes** *nfpl* Pol **les Communes**, **la Chambre des** ~**s** the (House of) Commons

communément /kɔmynemɑ̃/ *adv* [*admettre, désigner*] generally

communiant, ~**e** /kɔmynjɑ̃, ɑ̃t/ *nm,f* ① (qui communie) communicant; ② (qui fait sa première communion) (**premier**) ~ child taking his/her first communion

communicatif, -ive /kɔmynikatif, iv/ *adj* ① [*personne, nature*] talkative; ② [*gaieté, passion*] infectious

communication /kɔmynikasjɔ̃/ *nf* ① Télécom call; ~ **téléphonique** telephone call; **être en** ~ **avec qn** to be on the line to sb; **mettre qn en** ~ **avec qn** to put sb through to sb; ② (relations sociales) communications (*pl*); **problème de** ~ communications problem; ~ **de masse** mass communications; ③ (transmission) communication; **demander** ~ **d'un dossier à qn** to ask sb for a file; ④ (au conseil des ministres) report; (à une conférence) paper; **faire une** ~ **sur** to give a paper on; ⑤ (relation personnelle) communication **₵**; **être en** ~ **avec qn** to be in communication with sb; **mettre qn en** ~ **avec qn** to put sb in touch with sb; ⑥ (média) communications (*pl*); **groupe de** ~ communications group; ⑦ (liaison) **moyens** *or* **voies de** ~ communications (*pl*)

communier /kɔmynje/ [2] *vi* ① Relig [*personne*] to receive Communion; ② fig to commune (**avec** with); ~ **dans la douleur de qn** to share in sb's grief

communion /kɔmynjɔ̃/ *nf* ① Relig Communion; ② (accord) communion; **se sentir en** ~ **avec qch/qn** to feel in harmony with sth/sb

(Composés) ~ **privée** Relig first communion; ~ **solennelle** Relig solemn declaration of faith made at the age of 11

communiqué /kɔmynike/ *nm* ① (de presse) communiqué, press release; ② (de parti, gouvernement) statement

communiquer /kɔmynike/ [1]
A *vtr* ① (faire connaître) [*journaliste*] to announce [*date, décision*];

[*personne*] to give [*adresse, liste*] (**à** to); [*personne*] to declare [*intention*] (**à** to); ② (transmettre) [*personne*] to pass on [*dossier*] (**à** to); to convey [*sentiment*] (**à** to)
B *vi* ① Ling, Sociol, Télécom to communicate (**avec** with); ② Archit [*pièces*] to be adjoining; ~ **avec** to adjoin [*pièce*]
C **se communiquer** *vpr* ① (se transmettre) [*personnes*] to pass on [sth] to each other [*information*]; ② (se répandre) [*feu, peur*] to spread (**à** to)

communisme /kɔmynism/ *nm* communism

communiste /kɔmynist/ *adj, nmf* communist

commutateur /kɔmytatœʀ/ *nm* switch

commutatif, -ive /kɔmytatif, iv/ *adj* commutative

commutation /kɔmytasjɔ̃/ *nf* ① gén commutation; ② Ordinat message switching

commuter /kɔmyte/ [1] *vtr* to commute

comorien, -ienne /kɔmɔʀjɛ̃, ɛn/ ▸ p. 392 *adj* Comoran

compact, ~**e** /kɔpakt/ *adj* ① (dense) [*brouillard, foule*] dense; [*terre*] compact; ② (peu encombrant) [*meuble*] compact; **sous format** ~ [*livre*] in pocket edition; ③ (solide) [*groupe*] monolithic; [*peloton*] compact

compacter /kɔpakte/ [1] *vtr* ① Ordinat to compress [*données*]; ② Constr, Écol to compact [*sol, ordures*]

compagne /kɔpaɲ/ *nf* ① (amie) (female) companion; ② (femelle) mate

compagnie /kɔpaɲi/ *nf* ① (présence) company; **tenir** ~ **à qn** to keep sb company; **en** ~ **de** together with; ② (groupe) company; **salut la** ~**!** hello everybody!; ③ Comm company; ④ Mil company; ⑤ Théât company; ⑥ (colonie animale) ~ **de perdrix** covey of partridges

(Composés) ~ **aérienne** airline; ~ **d'assurance** insurance company; ~ **pétrolière** oil company

compagnon /kɔpaɲɔ̃/ *nm* ① (ami) companion; ② (amant) partner; ③ (mâle) mate; ④ (artisan) journeyman; ⑤ (franc-maçon) fellow of the craft

(Composés) ~ **d'armes** comrade-in-arms; ~ **d'infortune** companion in misfortune; ~ **de route** fellow traveller^GB; ~ **de voyage** travelling^GB companion

comparable /kɔpaʀabl/ *adj* comparable (**à** to)

comparaison /kɔpaʀɛzɔ̃/ *nf* ① (rapprochement) comparison (**à, avec** with); **c'est sans** ~ **le plus confortable** it's far and away the most comfortable; ② (en rhétorique) simile; ③ Ling comparison; **adjectif/adverbe de** ~ comparative adjective/adverb

comparaître /kɔpaʀɛtʀ/ [73] *vi* Jur to appear (**devant** before); **être appelé à** ~ to be summoned to appear

comparatif, -ive /kɔpaʀatif, iv/
A *adj* comparative
B *nm* Ling comparative

comparé, ~**e** /kɔpaʀe/ *adj* comparative

comparer /kɔpaʀe/ [1]
A *vtr* to compare (**à, avec** with)
B **se comparer** *vpr* (soi-même) **se** ~ **à qn/qch** (pour évaluer) to compare oneself with sb/sth; (s'assimiler) to compare oneself to sb; (être comparable) to be comparable; **ça ne se compare pas** there's no comparison

comparse /kɔpaʀs/ *nmf* ① Théât extra; **rôle de** ~ walk-on part; péj minor part; ② (acolyte) sidekick^○; **on n'a arrêté que les** ~**s** they have only arrested the small fry

compartiment /kɔpaʀtimɑ̃/ *nm* compartment

compartimenter /kɔpaʀtimɑ̃te/ [1] *vtr* ① lit ~ **un coffret** to divide a box into compartments; ~ **un grenier** to divide up a loft with partitions; ② fig to compartmentalize [*administration, science*]

comparution /kɔpaʀysjɔ̃/ *nf* Jur appearance (**devant** before)

compas /kɔpa/ *nm* ① (de géométrie) compass, pair of compasses US; ② Aviat, Naut compass

compassion /kɔpasjɔ̃/ *nf* compassion

compatibilité /kɔpatibilite/ *nf* compatibility

compatible /kɔpatibl/ *adj* compatible (**avec** with)

compatir /kɔpatiʀ/ [3] *vi* to sympathize; **je compatis à votre douleur** fml I feel for you in your sorrow sout

compatissant, ~**e** /kɔpatisɑ̃, ɑ̃t/ *adj* compassionate

compatriote /kɔpatʀiɔt/ *nmf* fellow-countryman/fellow-countrywoman, compatriot

compensation /kɔpɑ̃sasjɔ̃/ *nf* compensation; ~**s financières** financial compensation

compensatoire /kɔ̃pɑ̃satwaʀ/ *adj* compensatory

compensé, ~e /kɔ̃pɑ̃se/ *adj* 1 **semelle** ~e wedge heel; 2 Méd compensated

compenser /kɔ̃pɑ̃se/ [1]
A *vtr* to compensate for [*défaut*]; to make up for [*dommages*]; to offset [*pertes*]
B **se compenser** *vpr* **les gains et pertes se compensent** the profits offset the losses; **ses défauts et ses qualités se compensent** his/her good qualities make up for his/her faults

compère /kɔ̃pɛʀ/ *nm* 1 (partenaire) partner; (dans une tromperie) accomplice; 2 (camarade) mate° GB, buddy° US; 3 (individu) **joyeux/rusé** ~ cheery/crafty fellow°

compétence /kɔ̃petɑ̃s/ *nf* 1 (aptitude) (dans une matière, un domaine) ability; (dans un emploi, une activité) competence, skill; **faire appel aux** ~**s de qn** to call upon sb's expertise; 2 (aptitude légale) competence; **relever de la** ~ **de qn** to fall within the competence of sb; 3 (fonction) domain, sphere; **être** *or* **entrer dans les** ~**s de qn** to be in sb's domain

compétent, ~e /kɔ̃petɑ̃, ɑ̃t/ *adj* 1 (qualifié) competent; 2 (qui a l'autorité) [*autorité*] competent; [*service*] appropriate; **tribunal** ~ court of competent jurisdiction; **le maire est seul** ~ **pour faire** the mayor is the only one with the authority to do; **le tribunal de Rennes n'est pas** ~ **pour juger cette affaire** this case does not come within the jurisdiction of the Rennes court

compétitif, **-ive** /kɔ̃petitif, iv/ *adj* competitive

compétition /kɔ̃petisjɔ̃/ *nf* 1 (concurrence) competition (**entre** between); **être en** ~ **avec** to be competing with; **l'esprit de** ~ the competitive spirit; 2 (activité) competition; **voiture de** ~ competition car; **faire de la** ~ to compete; **sport de** ~ competitive sport; 3 (épreuve) ~ **(sportive)** sporting event; ~ **de natation** swimming event

compétitivité /kɔ̃petitivite/ *nf* competitiveness

compilation /kɔ̃pilasjɔ̃/ *nf* compilation

complainte /kɔ̃plɛ̃t/ *nf* lament

complaire: se complaire /kɔ̃plɛʀ/ [59] *vpr* **se** ~ **à faire** to take pleasure in doing; **se** ~ **dans le malheur** to wallow in misery; **se** ~ **dans son ignorance** to bask in one's own ignorance

complaisamment /kɔ̃plɛzamɑ̃/ *adv* 1 (aimablement) obligingly; 2 (avec trop d'indulgence) indulgently; 3 (avec autosatisfaction) complacently

complaisance /kɔ̃plɛzɑ̃s/ *nf* 1 (volonté de faire plaisir) kindness, readiness to oblige; **pavillon de** ~ flag of convenience; 2 (indulgence excessive) **la** ~ **d'un père à l'égard de ses enfants** a father's indulgence toward(s) his children; **leur** ~ **à l'égard du régime** their soft attitude toward(s) the regime; **décrire la situation sans** ~ to give an objective assessment of the situation; 3 (autosatisfaction) complacency, smugness

complaisant, ~e /kɔ̃plɛzɑ̃, ɑ̃t/ *adj* 1 (prévenant) obliging; 2 (trop indulgent) indulgent (**avec** with); **sa description des faits est trop** ~e he's too uncritical in his account of the facts; **un mari** ~ a husband who turns a blind eye; 3 (autosatisfait) *pej* complacent *péj*, self-satisfied *péj*

complément /kɔ̃plemɑ̃/ *nm* 1 (revenu) ~ **de salaire** extra payment; 2 (de programme, travail, financement) supplement; ~ **de formation** further training; 3 Ling complement; ~ **d'agent** agent; ~ **d'objet direct** direct object

complémentaire /kɔ̃plemɑ̃tɛʀ/ *adj* 1 (supplémentaire) [*formation*] further; [*activité, somme*] supplementary; **pour tous renseignements** ~**s** for further information; 2 (apparié) [*personne, qualité, équipement*] complementary (**de** to); 3 Math complementary

complet, **-ète** /kɔ̃plɛ, ɛt/
A *adj* 1 (total) [*arrêt, silence, révision*] complete; [*échec*] total; 2 (sans manques) [*œuvres*] complete; [*enquête, gamme*] full; **un artiste** ~ an all-round artist; 3 (approfondi) comprehensive; **de façon (très) complète** (very) thoroughly; 4 (plein) [*train, hôtel, salle*] full; '~' (dans un hôtel) 'no vacancies'; (dans un théâtre) 'sold out'; (dans un parking) 'full'; **le gouvernement au** ~ the entire government; **être (réuni) au (grand)** ~ to be all present
B *nm* (costume) suit; ~ **trois pièces** three-piece suit

complètement /kɔ̃plɛtmɑ̃/ *adv* 1 (totalement) completely; **pas** ~ not entirely; **je m'en moque** ~ I couldn't care less; 2 (en entier) **j'ai** ~ **repeint la**

maison I've repainted the whole house; **elle a** ~ **refait son article** she has rewritten her whole article *ou* her article in its entirety

compléter /kɔ̃plete/ [14]
A *vtr* 1 (s'ajouter à) to complete [*collection*]; to top up [*somme*]; to supplement [*connaissances*]; **pour** ~ **le tout** *or* **tableau**° iron to cap it all; 2 (être complémentaire de) to complement [*personne*]; 3 (remplir) [*personne*] to complete [*phrase*]; to complete, to fill in [*questionnaire*]
B **se compléter** *vpr* (l'un l'autre) [*éléments, personnes*] to complement each other

complet-veston†, *pl* **complets-veston** /kɔ̃plɛvɛstɔ̃/ *nm* suit

complexe /kɔ̃plɛks/
A *adj* complex
B *nm* 1 Psych complex; **il n'a pas de** ~ he hasn't got any hang-ups°, he has no inhibitions; 2 (ensemble d'installations) complex; ~ **sportif** sports complex

(Composé) ~ **d'Œdipe** Oedipus complex

complexé, ~e /kɔ̃plekse/ *adj* **il est très** ~ he has a lot of hang-ups°

complexer /kɔ̃plekse/ [1] *vtr* to give [sb] a complex [*personne*]

complexité /kɔ̃pleksite/ *nf* complexity

complication /kɔ̃plikasjɔ̃/ *nf* 1 (embarras) complication; **aimer les** ~**s** to like complicating matters; 2 Méd complication

complice /kɔ̃plis/
A *adj* 1 (qui aide) **être** ~ **de qch** to be a party to sth; 2 (de connivence) [*air, silence*] of complicity (*épith, après n*)
B *nmf* 1 (comparse) accomplice (**de qch** in sth); **se faire le** ~ **de qch** to be a party to sth

complicité /kɔ̃plisite/ *nf* (collaboration) complicity; (entente) bond; **sourire de** ~ smile of complicity

compliment /kɔ̃plimɑ̃/
A *nm* 1 (parole de félicitations) compliment; **faire un** ~ **à qn** to compliment sb (**sur** on); 2 (petit discours) (nice little) speech
B **compliments** *nmpl* 1 (félicitations) compliments; **(tous) mes** ~**s!** congratulations!; **faire des** ~**s à qn** to compliment sb (**sur, pour** on); 2 (formule de politesse) **avec les** ~**s de...** with the compliments of...; **mes** ~**s à votre mère** my regards to your mother

complimenter /kɔ̃plimɑ̃te/ [1] *vtr* to compliment

compliqué, ~e /kɔ̃plike/ *adj* 1 gén complicated; [*esprit*] tortuous; **si tu ne t'arrêtes pas de pleurer, ce n'est pas** ~°, **tu vas au lit!** it's quite simple, if you don't stop crying you'll go straight to bed!; 2 Méd [*fracture*] compound

compliquer /kɔ̃plike/ [1]
A *vtr* to complicate; ~ **la vie** *or* **l'existence de qn** to make life difficult for sb
B **se compliquer** *vpr* 1 (devenir complexe) to get more complicated; 2 (rendre plus complexe) **se** ~ **la vie** *or* **l'existence** to make life difficult for oneself

complot /kɔ̃plo/ *nm* plot

comploter /kɔ̃plɔte/ [1]
A *vtr* to plot [*attentat, ruine*]; to plan [*mauvais coup*]
B *vi* to plot (**contre** against; **de faire** to do)

comportement /kɔ̃pɔʀtəmɑ̃/ *nm* gén behaviour°GB; (de sportif, voiture, Bourse) performance

comporter /kɔ̃pɔʀte/ [1]
A *vtr* 1 (inclure) to include; ~ **une bibliographie** to include a bibliography; 2 (être composé de) to comprise; ~ **trois parties** to comprise three parts; 3 (présenter) to entail [*risque*]
B **se comporter** *vpr* 1 [*personne, animal*] to behave, to act; **se** ~ **en dictateur** to behave like a dictator; 2 (fonctionner) [*sportif, voiture, Bourse*] to perform

composant /kɔ̃pozɑ̃/ *nm* 1 Tech (élément) component; 2 Chimie (élément simple) constituent

composante /kɔ̃pozɑ̃t/ *nf* 1 gén (élément) element; 2 Math, Phys, Ling component

composé, ~e /kɔ̃poze/
A *adj* 1 (fait d'éléments divers) [*bouquet, style*] composite; [*salade*] mixed; 2 (affecté) affected
B *nm* Chimie compound

composer /kɔ̃poze/ [1]
A *vtr* 1 (constituer) [*éléments, personnes*] to make up; **composé de** made up of; **le groupe est** ~ **à 90% de femmes** 90% of

the group are women; **2** (réaliser) [*personne*] to put [sth] together [*menu*]; to select [*équipe*]; to make up [*bouquet*]; **3** Art, Littérat, Mus to compose [*morceau, texte*]; to paint [*tableau*]; **4** to dial [*numéro*]; **~ son code secret** to enter one's pin number; **5** (en imprimerie) to typeset [*page, texte*] **B** *fml vi* (trouver un compromis) to compromise; **~ avec** to come to a compromise with [*personne*]
C se composer *vpr* **1** (être constitué) **se ~ de** to be made up of; **2** (adopter) to assume [*attitude, expression*]

composite /kɔ̃pozit/ *adj* **1** (divers) heterogeneous; **2** Tech [*matériau*] composite; **3** Archit composite

compositeur, -trice /kɔ̃pozitœr, tris/ ▸ p. 372 *nm,f* **1** Mus composer; **2** (typographe) typesetter

composition /kɔ̃pozisjɔ̃/ *nf* **1** (éléments constitutifs) (de gouvernement, délégation) make-up, composition; (d'équipe) line-up, composition; (de produit, d'aliment) ingredients (*pl*); (chimique, pharmaceutique) composition; **2** (mise en place) (de gouvernement) formation; (de comité) setting up; (d'équipe) selection; (de liste, menu) drawing up; (de bouquet) making up; **de ma/leur ~** of my/their invention; **3** Art, Littérat, Mus composition (**de** by); **~ florale** flower arrangement; **4** Cin, Théât (incarnation) performance (**de** as); **5** Scol end-of-term test; **6** (en imprimerie) typesetting; **l'article est à la ~** the article is being typeset
⬭ (Idiome) **être de bonne ~** to be good-natured

composter /kɔ̃pɔste/ [1] *vtr* (au tampon) to (date)stamp; (au poinçon) to punch

compote /kɔ̃pɔt/ *nf* Culin stewed fruit, compote; **~ de pommes** stewed apples (*pl*); **mettre qn en ~⁰** to beat sb black and blue

compréhensible /kɔ̃pʀeɑ̃sibl/ *adj* **1** (concevable) understandable; **2** (intelligible) comprehensible

compréhensif, -ive /kɔ̃pʀeɑ̃sif, iv/ *adj* understanding

compréhension /kɔ̃pʀeɑ̃sjɔ̃/ *nf* **1** (faculté, aptitude) understanding; **2** (de texte, paroles) comprehension; (de langue) understanding, comprehension; **pour aider à la ~** to make it easier to understand; **3** (indulgence) **faire preuve de ~** to show understanding; **attitude pleine de ~** sympathetic attitude

comprendre /kɔ̃pʀɑ̃dʀ/ [52] **A** *vtr* **1** (saisir le sens de) to understand; **si je comprends bien** if I understand correctly; **il m'a dit son nom au téléphone mais je n'ai pas bien compris** he told me his name on the phone but I didn't quite catch it; **ne te mêles pas de cela, tu as compris** *or* **c'est compris!** keep out of it, do you hear *ou* understand?; **il ne comprend rien à rien** he hasn't got a clue; **c'est à n'y rien ~** it's completely baffling; **mal ~ qn/qch** to misunderstand sb/sth; **être compris comme une menace** to be interpreted as a threat; **~ qch de travers⁰** to get sth all wrong; **se faire ~** to make oneself understood; **être lent à ~** to be slow on the uptake; **2** (se rendre compte de) to understand; **ce n'est pas facile, je comprends** it's not easy, I realize that; **je n'ai pas le temps, tu comprends** you see, I haven't got time; **3** (admettre) to understand [*attitude, sentiment*]; (faire preuve de compréhension envers) to understand [*person*]; **je comprends qu'il soit furieux** I can understand his anger; **comme je le comprends!** I understand him exactly; **4** (se faire une idée de) to see [*métier, vie*]; **5** (être totalement constitué de) to consist of, to comprise; **6** (être partiellement constitué de) to include
B se comprendre *vpr* **1** [*personnes*] (l'un l'autre) to understand each other *ou* one another; **2** (soi-même) **je me comprends** I know what I'm trying to say; **3** (être compréhensible) [*attitude, sentiment*] to be understandable; **4** (être compris) **le terme doit se ~ ici dans son sens large** the term is to be understood *ou* taken in its broadest sense

compresse /kɔ̃pʀɛs/ *nf* compress

compresser /kɔ̃pʀese/ [1] *vtr* to compress

compressible /kɔ̃pʀesibl/ *adj* **1** Phys, Chimie compressible; **2** (réductible) reducible

compression /kɔ̃pʀesjɔ̃/ *nf* **1** Tech compression; **2** (action de réduire) reduction; **3** (diminution effective) cut (**de** in); **~s budgétaires** budget cuts

comprimé /kɔ̃pʀime/ *nm* tablet

comprimer /kɔ̃pʀime/ [1] *vtr* **1** (serrer) to constrict [*ventre, buste*]; to squeeze [*pâte*]; **2** Méd (appuyer sur) to compress, to constrict [*objet, organe*]; **3** Tech to compress [*liquide, gaz*]; **air comprimé** compressed air; **4** (réduire) to cut [*dépenses, budget*]

compris, ~e /kɔ̃pʀi, iz/
A *pp* ▸ **comprendre**
B *pp adj* (inclus) including; **loyer de 500 euros charges ~es/non ~es** rent of 500 euros inclusive/exclusive; **service ~** service included; **TVA ~e/non ~e** including/not including VAT
C tout compris *loc adv* in total, all in⁰ GB; **prix tout ~** all-in GB *ou* inclusive price
D y compris *loc adv* including; **y ~ à Paris** in Paris too

compromettant, ~e /kɔ̃pʀɔmetɑ̃, ɑ̃t/ *adj* compromising

compromettre /kɔ̃pʀɔmɛtʀ/ [60]
A *vtr* **1** (mettre en danger) to endanger, to jeopardize [*santé, chances*]; to compromise [*victoire*]; to impair [*efficacité*]; **2** (souiller) to compromise [*personne*]; to damage [*prestige*]
B se compromettre *vpr* (risquer sa réputation) to compromise oneself

compromis, ~e /kɔ̃pʀɔmi, iz/
A *adj* **1** (menacé) [*carrière, projet*] in jeopardy; **2** (souillé) [*personne*] compromised; [*réputation*] damaged; **être ~ dans un scandale** to be involved in a scandal
B *nm* compromise (**entre** between)

compromission /kɔ̃pʀɔmisjɔ̃/ *nf* (entre personnes) deal; (avec sa conscience) compromise of principle

comptabiliser /kɔ̃tabilize/ [1] *vtr* **1** (additionner) to count (the number of) [*erreurs, entrées*]; **2** (en comptabilité) to enter *ou* record [sth] in the books

comptabilité /kɔ̃tabilite/ *nf* **1** (concept, discipline) accountancy; **2** (profession, activité) accounting; **3** (tenue de livres) bookkeeping; **faire sa ~** to do one's accounts; **4** (ensemble des comptes) accounts (*pl*); **5** (service) accounts department

comptable /kɔ̃tabl/
A *adj* **1** (de comptabilité) [*document, année*] accounting; [*service*] accounts; **agent ~** accountant; **2** Ling countable; **non ~** uncountable
B ▸ p. 372 *nmf* (spécialiste) accountant; (personne qui tient les livres) bookkeeper

comptant /kɔ̃tɑ̃/
A *adv* [*payer*] cash; **acheter une maison ~** to pay cash for a house
B au comptant *loc adv* [*vendre*] for cash

compte /kɔ̃t/
A *nm* **1** (calcul) count; **faire le ~ de qch** to work out [*dépenses, recettes*]; to count (up) [*personnes, objets*]; **si je fais le ~ de ce qu'il me doit** if I work out what he owes me; **le ~ est bon** that works out right; **tenir le ~ de qch** to keep count of sth; **comment fais-tu ton ~ pour faire...?** fig how do you manage to do...?; **au bout du ~** (pour constater) in the end; **tout ~ fait** (tout bien considéré) all things considered; (en fait) when all is said and done; **en fin de ~** (pour conclure) at the end of the day; **tout ~ fait** *or* **en fin de ~, c'est lui qui avait raison** when all is said and done, HE was right; **2** (résultat) (d'argent) amount; (d'objets, heures, de personnes) number; **le ~ y est** (en argent) that's the right amount; (en objets, personnes) all present and correct; **le ~ n'y est pas, il n'y a pas le ~** (en argent) that's not the right amount; (en objets, personnes) that's not the right number; **il a son ~⁰** (battu ou tué) he's done for⁰; (ivre) he's had a drop too much; **nous avons eu notre ~ d'ennuis** fig we've had more than our fair share of problems; **à ce ~-là** (dans ces conditions) in that case; **3** (considération) **prendre qch en ~, tenir ~ de qch** to take sth into account; **~ tenu de** considering; **4** (intérêt personnel) **être** *or* **travailler à son ~** to be self-employed; **se mettre** *or* **s'installer** *or* **s'établir à son ~** to set up one's own business; **prendre des jours de congé à son ~** to take a few days off without pay; **pour le ~ de qn** on behalf of sb; **y trouver son ~** to get something out of it; **à ~ d'auteur** at the author's expense; **5** (en comptabilité) account; **tenir les ~s** to keep the accounts; **6** Fin account; **~ bancaire** *or* **en banque** bank account; **7** Comm (ardoise) account; **j'ai un ~ chez un libraire** I have an account with a bookshop GB *ou* bookstore; **mettre qch sur le ~ de qn** lit to charge sth to sb's account; fig to put sth down to sb; **8** (somme à payer) **voilà votre ~** here's your money; **9** (explication, rapport) **rendre ~ de qch à qn** (rapporter) to give an account of sth to sb; (justifier) to account for sth to sb; **rendre des ~s à qn** [*responsable*] to be answerable to sb; **demander des ~s à qn** to ask for an explanation from sb; **10** (notion nette) **se rendre ~ de** (être conscient) to realize; (remarquer) to notice; **11** (sujet) **je ne sais rien sur leur ~** I

don't know anything about them; [12] Sport (en boxe) count

B **à bon compte** loc adv lit (à peu de frais) [acheter] cheap; [acquérir, voyager] cheaply; fig (sans difficulté) the easy way; **s'en tirer à bon ~** to get off lightly

(Composés) **~ chèques** current account GB, checking account US; **~ chèque postal, CCP** post office account; **~ d'épargne** savings account; **~ à rebours** count-down; **le ~ à rebours de la campagne est commencé** fig the run-up to the elections has started; **~s d'apothicaire** complicated calculations

compté, ~e /kɔ̃te/ adj **ses jours sont ~s, ses heures sont ~es** his/her days are numbered; **à pas ~s** lit with measured steps; fig cautiously

compte-gouttes /kɔ̃tgut/ nm inv dropper; **au ~** lit with a dropper; fig (avec parcimonie) sparingly

compter /kɔ̃te/ [1]

A vtr [1] (dénombrer) to count; **on compte deux millions de chômeurs** there is a total of two million unemployed; **on ne compte plus ses victoires** he/she has had countless victories; **je ne compte plus les lettres anonymes que je reçois** I've lost count of the anonymous letters I have received; **il a toujours compté ses sous** he has always watched the pennies; **sans ~** [donner, dépenser] freely; [2] (évaluer) **une bouteille pour trois** to allow a bottle between three people; **il faut ~ environ 100 euros** you should reckon on GB ou count on paying about 100 euros; **je préfère ~ large** I prefer to be on the safe side; [3] (faire payer) **~ qch à qn** to charge sb for sth; **il m'a compté 30 euros de déplacement** he charged a 30 euro call-out fee; [4] (inclure) to count; **je vous ai compté dans le nombre des participants** I've counted you as one of ou among the participants; **sans ~ les primes** not counting bonuses; **sans ~ les soucis** not to mention the worry; **notre club compte des gens célèbres** our club has some well-known people among its members; [5] (projeter) **~ faire** to intend to do; **je compte m'acheter un ordinateur** I'm hoping to buy myself a computer; [6] (s'attendre à) **il comptait que je lui prête de l'argent** he expected me to lend him some money; **'je vais t'aider'—'j'y compte bien'** 'I'll help you'—'I should hope so too'

B vi [1] (dire les nombres) to count; **il ne sait pas ~** he can't count; [2] (calculer) to count, to add up; **il sait très bien ~, il compte très bien** he's very good at counting; [3] (avoir de l'importance) to matter (pour qn to sb); **ce qui compte c'est qu'ils se sont réconciliés** what matters is that they have made it up; **c'est l'intention** or **le geste qui compte** it's the thought that counts; **ça compte beaucoup pour moi** it means a lot to me; **le salaire compte beaucoup dans le choix d'une carrière** pay is an important factor in the choice of a career; [4] (avoir une valeur) to count; **~ double/triple** to count double/triple; [5] (figurer) **~ au nombre de, ~ parmi** to be counted among; [6] **~ avec** (faire face) to reckon with [difficultés, concurrence]; (ne pas oublier) to take [sb/sth] into account [personne, chose]; **il doit ~ avec les syndicats** he has to reckon with the unions; **il faut ~ avec l'opinion publique** one must take public opinion into account [personne, chose]; [7] **~ sans** (négliger) not to take [sb/sth] into account [personne, chose]; **c'était ~ sans le brouillard** that was without allowing for the fog; [8] **~ sur** (attendre) to count on [personne, aide]; (dépendre, faire confiance) to rely on [personne, ressource]; (prévoir) to reckon on [somme, revenu]; **vous pouvez ~ sur moi, je vais m'en occuper** you can rely ou count on me, I'll see to it; **ne compte pas sur moi** (pour venir, participer) count me out; **je vais leur dire ce que j'en pense, tu peux ~ là-dessus** or **sur moi!** I'll tell them what I think, you can be sure of that!; **quand il s'agit de faire des bêtises, on peut ~ sur toi** hum trust you to do something silly!

C se compter vpr **leurs victoires se comptent par douzaines** they have had dozens of victories; **les faillites dans la région ne se comptent plus** there have been countless bankruptcies in the area

D **à compter de** loc prép as from; **pendant 12 mois à ~ de la date de vente** for 12 months with effect from the date of sale

E **sans compter que** loc conj (en outre) and what is more; (d'autant plus que) especially as

compte(-)rendu, pl **comptes(-)rendus** /kɔ̃tʀɑ̃dy/ nm (de débat, travaux, d'événement) report; (d'article, de livre) review

compteur /kɔ̃tœʀ/ nm (de fluide) meter; (de distance) clock; **~ d'eau** water meter; **la voiture a 50 000 km au ~** the car has 50,000 km on the clock

(Composés) **~ kilométrique** ≈ milometer; **~ de vitesse** speedometer

comptine /kɔ̃tin/ nf (pour choisir) counting rhyme; (chansonnette) nursery rhyme

comptoir /kɔ̃twaʀ/ nm [1] (de café) bar; **au ~** at the bar; [2] (de magasin) counter; **~ parfumerie** perfume counter; [3] Hist trading post; [4] Fin branch (of the Banque de France)

(Composé) **~ d'enregistrement** check-in desk

compulser /kɔ̃pylse/ [1] vtr to consult

comte /kɔ̃t/ ▸ p. 590 nm gén count; (titre anglais) earl

comté /kɔ̃te/ nm [1] Admin county; [2] Hist earldom (land)

comtesse /kɔ̃tɛs/ ▸ p. 590 nf countess

comtois, ~e /kɔ̃twa, az/ ▸ p. 504 adj of Franche-Comté

con●, conne /kɔ̃, kon/

A adj [1] (bête) pej fucking● stupid, bloody❶ GB stupid; [2] (facile) dead○ easy

B nm,f offensive bloody❶ idiot GB injur, stupid jerk○ injur; **faire le ~** to mess about, to arse around❶; **idée/voiture à la ~** lousy○ idea/car

concasser /kɔ̃kase/ [1] vtr [1] Culin, Tech to crush; [2] Mus to mix

concave /kɔ̃kav/ adj concave

concavité /kɔ̃kavite/ nf [1] (état) concavity; [2] (partie creuse) hollow

concéder /kɔ̃sede/ [14] vtr [1] Admin, Comm, Écon to grant [monopole, franchise] (à to); to contract out [travaux] (à to); **autoroute concédée** motorway GB ou freeway US (which is) under private management; [2] (admettre) to concede

concentration /kɔ̃sɑ̃tʀasjɔ̃/ nf [1] (attention) concentration; **j'ai besoin de quelques instants de ~** I need to concentrate for a few moments; [2] (accumulation) concentration (de of); **~ de troupes aux frontières du pays** build-up of troops on the country's borders; [3] Chimie concentration; [4] Écon concentration; **~ horizontale/verticale** horizontal/vertical integration

(Composé) **~ urbaine** conurbation

concentré, ~e /kɔ̃sɑ̃tʀe/

A adj [1] (attentif) **un air ~** a look of concentration; [2] (condensé, rassemblé) concentrated

B nm [1] Chimie (solution) concentrated solution; [2] (aliment) concentrate; **~ de tomate** tomato purée GB ou paste US

concentrer /kɔ̃sɑ̃tʀe/ [1]

A vtr **~ ses efforts sur qch** to concentrate one's efforts on sth

B se concentrer vpr [1] (être attentif) to concentrate (sur on); (se préparer mentalement) to gather one's thoughts; [2] (être dirigé) **se ~ sur qch** [efforts, attention] to be concentrated on sth; [3] (être rassemblé) [population, erreurs, usines] to be concentrated; [4] (se rassembler) **les grévistes se sont concentrés devant l'usine** the strikers gathered outside the factory

concentrique /kɔ̃sɑ̃tʀik/ adj concentric

concept /kɔ̃sɛpt/ nm concept

conception /kɔ̃sɛpsjɔ̃/ nf [1] Biol conception; [2] (formulation d'idée) conception; [3] (élaboration de la forme) design; **au stade de la ~** at the design stage; [4] (idée) idea; (façon de voir) conception

conceptualiser /kɔ̃sɛptɥalize/ [1] vtr to conceptualize

concernant /kɔ̃sɛʀnɑ̃/ prép [1] (touchant) concerning; [2] (en ce qui concerne) as regards, with regard to

concerner /kɔ̃sɛʀne/ [1] vtr [1] (viser) to concern; **en ce qui me concerne** as far as I am concerned; **en ce qui concerne le salaire** as regards salary, as far as salary is concerned; **cela ne vous concerne pas** (ne vous vise pas) it does not concern you; (ne vous regarde pas) it's no concern of yours; [2] (toucher) to affect; **cette décision nous concerne tous** this decision affects all of us

concert /kɔ̃sɛʀ/

A nm [1] Mus concert; **~ en plein air** open-air concert; [2] (bruits émis) **~ de klaxons®** a blaring of horns; **~ d'applaudissements** roar of applause; **~ de critiques** barrage of criticism; [3] (entente) **le ~ des nations** the alliance of nations

B de concert *loc adv* ils ont agi de ~ they worked together

concertation /kɔ̃sɛʀtasjɔ̃/ *nf* **①** (discussions) consultation; **agir en ~ avec** to act in consultation with; **②** (fait de travailler de concert) cooperation

concerté, ~e /kɔ̃sɛʀte/ *adj* [*plan, action*] concerted

concerter /kɔ̃sɛʀte/ [1]
A *vtr* to plan
B se concerter *vpr* to consult each other

concertiste /kɔ̃sɛʀtist/ ▸ p. 372 *nmf* concert performer

concerto /kɔ̃sɛʀto/ *nm* concerto

concession /kɔ̃sesjɔ̃/ *nf* **①** (compromis) concession (**à** to; **sur** on); **film sans ~s** uncompromising *ou* forthright film; **②** (attribution) concession; **~ de travaux** works contract; **③** (droit d'exploitation) (de mine, territoire) concession; (de produit) distributorship; Aut dealership; **④** (dans un cimetière) burial plot

concessionnaire /kɔ̃sesjɔnɛʀ/ *nmf* **①** (détenteur d'un droit) gén concessionaire; **②** (commerçant) (pour un produit) distributor; (pour un service) agent; Aut dealer

concevable /kɔ̃s(ə)vabl/ *adj* conceivable

concevoir /kɔ̃s(ə)vwaʀ/ [5]
A *vtr* **①** (élaborer) to design [*produit, projet*]; **bien/mal conçu** well/badly designed; **②** (procréer) to conceive [*enfant*]; **③** (comprendre) to understand; **je conçois très bien que** I fully understand why; **je ne conçois pas de faire** I cannot conceive of *ou* imagine having to do; **④** (considérer) to see (**comme** as); **~ la politique comme un métier** to see politics as a job; **⑤** (ressentir) *fml* to conceive [*haine*]; to have [*doute*]
B se concevoir *vpr* **①** (être imaginable) to be conceivable; **②** (être compréhensible) to be understandable; **③** (s'élaborer) **se ~ sur ordinateur** to be designed on a computer

concierge /kɔ̃sjɛʀʒ/ ▸ p. 372 *nmf* caretaker GB, superintendant US; **c'est une vraie ~** *fig* (bavard) she's a real gossip

concile /kɔ̃sil/ *nm* Relig council

conciliable /kɔ̃siljabl/ *adj* reconcilable

conciliabule /kɔ̃siljabyl/ *nm* consultation, confab○

conciliant, ~e /kɔ̃siljɑ̃, ɑ̃t/ *adj* conciliatory

conciliateur, -trice /kɔ̃siljatœʀ, tʀis/ *nm,f* conciliator

conciliation /kɔ̃siljasjɔ̃/ *nf* conciliation; (d'époux) reconciliation; **commission de ~** arbitration committee

concilier /kɔ̃silje/ [2]
A *vtr* **①** gén to reconcile; **②** (gagner) *fml* **cette loi lui a concilié l'opinion publique** this law won over public opinion to his/her side
B se concilier *vpr* (conquérir) to win [*bienveillance, soutien*]; to win over [*opinion publique, personne*]

concis, ~e /kɔ̃si, iz/ *adj* concise

concision /kɔ̃sizjɔ̃/ *nf* conciseness; **avec ~** concisely

concitoyen, -enne /kɔ̃sitwajɛ̃, ɛn/ *nm,f* fellow-citizen

concluant, ~e /kɔ̃klyɑ̃, ɑ̃t/ *adj* conclusive

conclure /kɔ̃klyʀ/ [78]
A *vtr* **①** (déduire) to conclude (**que** that); **que concluez-vous de ces chiffres?** what conclusion do you draw from these figures?; **il ne faut pas se hâter d'en ~ que** we mustn't jump to the conclusion that; **②** (régler) to conclude [*accord*]; **~ un marché** to close *ou* clinch *ou* strike a deal; **'marché conclu!'** 'it's a deal!'; **③** (mettre à) [*personne*] to conclude [*discours*] (**par** with); **④** (être la fin de) [*concert, match*] to bring [sth] to a close [*festival, journée*]
B conclure à *vtr ind* (décider) **~ à la culpabilité de qn** to conclude that sb is guilty; [*jury*] to return a verdict of guilty
C *vi* Jur **~ en faveur de/contre qn** [*témoignage*] to go in favourᴳᴮ of/against sb; [*juge, jury*] to find in favourᴳᴮ of/against sb

conclusion /kɔ̃klyzjɔ̃/
A *nf* **①** (déduction) conclusion; **en ~** in conclusion; **~, il y a un problème**○ in other words, there's a problem; **~, le dîner a été annulé**○ so, the dinner was cancelledᴳᴮ; **tirer les ~s d'une expérience** to learn from an experience; **ne tire pas de ~s hâtives** don't jump to conclusions; **②** (de traité, marché) conclusion; **③** (dénouement) (de discours, session) close; (d'aventure) outcome
B conclusions *nfpl* **①** (résultats) (d'analyse, autopsie) results; (d'enquête, de rapport) findings; **②** Jur (d'expert) opinion (sg); (de jury) verdict (sg); (de plaignant) pleadings, submissions

concocter○ /kɔ̃kɔkte/ [1] *vtr* to concoct [*dessert, sauce*]; to devise [*réponse, programme*]

concombre /kɔ̃kɔ̃bʀ/ *nm* cucumber

concordance /kɔ̃kɔʀdɑ̃s/ *nf* (similarité) concordance (**de** between); (compatibilité) compatibility; **la parfaite ~ de leurs témoignages** the fact that their accounts agree in every respect; **s'il y a ~ entre les résultats** if the results tally
(Composé) **~ des temps** Ling sequence of tenses

concordant, ~e /kɔ̃kɔʀdɑ̃, ɑ̃t/ *adj* [*faits*] corroborating; [*témoignages, informations*] which are in agreement (*épith, après* n)

concordat /kɔ̃kɔʀda/ *nm* Relig concordat

concorde /kɔ̃kɔʀd/ *nf* *fml* harmony, concord

concorder /kɔ̃kɔʀde/ [1] *vi* [*résultats, descriptions, témoignages*] to tally; [*évaluations*] to agree

concourir /kɔ̃kuʀiʀ/ [26]
A *vi* **①** (participer) [*athlète, candidat*] to compete (**pour** for; **dans** in); [*livre, film*] to be entered (**pour** for); **②** Math (converger) to converge
B concourir à *vtr ind* **①** (collaborer pour) **~ à qch/à faire** [*facteurs*] to combine to bring about sth/to do; [*personnes*] to work together toward(s) sth/to do; **②** (contribuer à) [*facteur, personne*] **~ à qch** to help bring about sth; **~ à faire qch** to help do sth

concours /kɔ̃kuʀ/ *nm inv* **①** (de piano) competition; (agricole) show; **~ d'élégance** *fig* fashion show; **~ de beauté** beauty contest; **être hors ~** to be ineligible to compete; **②** Admin, Scol competitive examination; **③** (aide) help, assistance; (appui) support; (collaboration) cooperation; **avec le ~ de l'orchestre des Jeunes** (participation) with the Youth orchestra; **④** Sport (en athlétisme) field event
(Composés) **~ de circonstances** combination of circumstances; ; **~ hippique** (sport) show jumping; (épreuve) horse show

> ⓘ **Concours** Entry in many areas of the public services, including the teaching profession, as well as the most prestigious institutes of higher education, depends on succeeding in a competitive examination or *concours*. The number of candidates admitted depends on the number of posts or places available in a given year.

concret, -ète /kɔ̃kʀɛ, ɛt/ *adj* **①** (réel) [*mesure, résultat*] concrete; [*présence*] tangible; **②** (pragmatique) [*esprit, personne*] practical

concrètement /kɔ̃kʀɛtmɑ̃/ *adv* (en termes réels) in concrete terms; (en pratique) in practical terms

concrétisation /kɔ̃kʀetizasjɔ̃/ *nf* (d'alliance) concrete expression; (d'espoir) fulfilmentᴳᴮ; (d'ambition) achievement; **quant à la ~ de ce projet** as for turning this project into a reality

concrétiser /kɔ̃kʀetize/ [1]
A *vtr* **①** to make [sth] a reality [*projet*]; to give concrete expression to [*accord*]; to make [sth] concrete [*stratégie*]; **②** Sport (marquer) to score
B se concrétiser *vpr* [*projet*] to become a reality; [*offre*] to materialize; [*espoir*] to be fulfilled

concubin, ~e /kɔ̃kybɛ̃, in/ *nm,f* Jur common law husband/wife

concubinage /kɔ̃kybinaʒ/ *nm* cohabitation; **ils vivent en ~** they live together (as husband and wife), they cohabit Admin

concupiscent, ~e /kɔ̃kypisɑ̃, ɑ̃t/ *adj* lecherous, concupiscent *sout*

concurrence /kɔ̃kyʀɑ̃s/
A *nf* **①** (rivalité) competition; **faire (de la) ~ à qn** to compete with sb; **prix défiant toute ~** unbeatable price; **jeu de la ~** free play of competition; **②** (concurrents) **la ~** competitors (*pl*)
B jusqu'à ~ de *loc prép* up to a limit of

concurrencer /kɔ̃kyʀɑ̃se/ [12] *vtr* [*personne, entreprise*] to compete with; **être rudement concurrencé par** to come up against fierce competition from

concurrent, ~e /kɔ̃kyʀɑ̃, ɑ̃t/
A *adj* rival
B *nm,f* (pour un poste) rival; Comm, Sport competitor

concurrentiel, -ielle /kɔ̃kyʀɑ̃sjɛl/ *adj* competitive

condamnable /kɔ̃danabl/ *adj* reprehensible; **les parents sont ~s** the parents are to blame

condamnation /kɔ̃danasjɔ̃/ *nf* **1** Jur (action) conviction; (peine) sentence; **2** (vive critique) condemnation; **3** Aut (verrouillage) ~ **électronique** *or* **centralisée des portières** central locking

condamné, ~e /kɔ̃dane/
A *adj* **1** (très malade) terminally ill; **2** (fermé) [*porte, fenêtre*] sealed up
B *nm,f* convicted prisoner
(Composé) ~ **à mort** condemned man/woman

condamner /kɔ̃dane/ [1] *vtr* **1** Jur (infliger une peine à) to sentence; ~ **qn à une amende** to fine sb; **il a été condamné à quatre mois de prison avec sursis** he was given a four-month suspended sentence; ~ **qn pour vol** to convict sb of theft; **2** (interdire) [*loi, article*] to punish [*vol, trafic*]; **3** (désapprouver fortement) [*personne, pays*] to condemn [*acte, décision*]; **4** (astreindre à) ~ **qn à** to condemn sb to; **il se voit condamné à un choix difficile** he's being forced to make a difficult choice; ~ **qn à faire** to compel sb to do; **5** (sceller) to seal up [*fenêtre, porte*]; (fermer à clé) to shut up [*pièce*]; to lock [*portières*]; **6** (ruiner) to spell death for [*société, industrie*]; **7** (déclarer incurable) **les médecins l'ont condamné** the doctors have given up hope of saving him

condensateur /kɔ̃dɑ̃satœʀ/ *nm* condenser

condensation /kɔ̃dɑ̃sasjɔ̃/ *nf* condensation

condensé /kɔ̃dɑ̃se/ *nm* (résumé) summary; (recueil) digest

condenser /kɔ̃dɑ̃se/ [1] *vtr*, **se condenser** *vpr* to condense

condescendance /kɔ̃desɑ̃dɑ̃s/ *nf* condescension

condescendre /kɔ̃desɑ̃dʀ/ [6] *vtr ind* ~ **à** to condescend to

condiment /kɔ̃dimɑ̃/ *nm* **1** Culin (à la cuisson) seasoning; (à table) condiment; **2** fig spice

condisciple /kɔ̃disipl/ *nmf* fellow student

condition /kɔ̃disjɔ̃/
A *nf* **1** (circonstance nécessaire) condition; **c'est possible à** ~ **d'avoir le temps** it's possible provided (that) one has the time; **je vous prêterai la somme, mais sous** ~ I'll lend you the money, but on certain conditions; **sous** ~ [*libéré*] conditionally; **achat sous** ~ purchase on approval; **sans** ~**(s)** [*capitulation*] unconditional; [*capituler*] unconditionally; **imposer ses** ~**s** to impose one's own terms; **le talent n'est pas la seule** ~ **du succès** talent is not the only requirement for success; ~ **préalable** precondition; ~**s d'attribution d'une bourse** eligibility for a grant; **2** Jur (clause) term; **3** (forme) condition; **être en mauvaise** ~ **(physique)** to be out of condition *ou* unfit; **mettre qn en** ~ **(physiquement)** to get sb fit; (mentalement) to prepare sb; **4** (situation sociale) condition; **la** ~ **ouvrière** the conditions of working-class life; **la** ~ **féminine** *ou* **des femmes** women's position in society; **il s'intéresse beaucoup à la** ~ **féminine** he's very interested in women's affairs; **5** (niveau social) ~ **(sociale)** social status; **accepter sa** ~ to accept one's lot in life; **un jeune homme de** ~ **modeste** a young man from a humble background; **des personnes de toutes** ~**s** people from all walks of life; **6** Ling conditionality
B **conditions** *nfpl* **1** (ensemble de circonstances) conditions; **dans ces** ~**s** (dans cet environnement) in these conditions; (puisque c'est comme ça) in that case; **2** Comm (modalités) terms; ~**s de financement** methods of financing

conditionnel, -elle /kɔ̃disjɔnɛl/
A *adj* gén, Ling conditional
B *nm* Ling conditional

conditionnement /kɔ̃disjɔnmɑ̃/ *nm* **1** (de personne) conditioning; **2** (emballage) packaging ¢; ~**s** forms of packaging
(Composé) ~ **sous vide** vacuum packing

conditionner /kɔ̃disjɔne/ [1] *vtr* **1** (influencer) to condition [*personne, comportement, animal*]; **2** (déterminer) **votre habileté conditionne votre réussite** your success depends on your skill; **3** (emballer) to package (**en** in); **conditionné sous vide** vacuum-packed

condoléances /kɔ̃doleɑ̃s/ *nfpl* condolences; **toutes mes** ~ please accept my deepest sympathy

condom /kɔ̃dɔm/ *nm* condom

conducteur, -trice /kɔ̃dyktœʀ, tʀis/
A *adj* **1** Phys conductive; **un matériau peu** ~ a poor conductor; **2** (qui guide) [*principe*] guiding
B ▸ p. 372 *nm,f* **1** (de véhicule) driver; **2** (responsable) (de machine) operator; (de travaux) foreman
C *nm* Phys conductor
(Composés) ~ **de bestiaux** drover; ~ **d'engin** ≈ bulldozer driver; ~ **de travaux** foreman

conductibilité /kɔ̃dyktibilite/ *nf* conductivity

conductible /kɔ̃dyktibl/ *adj* conductive

conduire /kɔ̃dɥiʀ/ [69]
A *vtr* **1** (accompagner) to take [*personne*]; (en voiture) to drive [*personne*] (**à** to); **se faire** ~ **à la gare en taxi** to take a taxi to the station; **conduisez monsieur à sa chambre** show the gentleman to his room; **2** (mener à un lieu) **un bus vous conduira à l'hôtel** a bus will take you to the hotel; **le chemin conduit à l'église** the path leads to the church; **la route qui conduit à Oxford** the road that goes to Oxford; **3** (faire aboutir) ~ **à qch** to lead to sth; ~ **qn à la faillite** to make sb bankrupt; ~ **qn à la folie/au désespoir** to drive sb to madness/to despair; **4** (être aux commandes de) to drive [*voiture, train*]; to ride [*moto*]; **5** (guider) to lead [*personne*] (**à** to); **6** (faire évoluer) to conduct [*recherches, négociations*]; to pursue [*politique*]; to carry out [*projet*]; to run [*affaire commerciale*]; **7** (être à la tête de) to lead [*délégation, troupe*]; **la liste conduite par le candidat socialiste** the list headed by the socialist candidate; **8** Phys to conduct [*électricité, chaleur*]
B **se conduire** *vpr* to behave

conduit /kɔ̃dɥi/ *nm* **1** Constr conduit; **2** Anat canal
(Composés) ~ **d'air chaud** hot-air duct; ~ **de fumée** flue; ~ **de ventilation** ventilation shaft

conduite /kɔ̃dɥit/ *nf* **1** (manière d'être) gén behaviour[GB]; (d'écolier) conduct; **zéro de** ~ black mark for bad behaviour[GB]; **avoir une** ~ **bizarre** to behave oddly; **ils n'accepteront pas qu'on leur dicte leur** ~ they will not put up with being told what to do; **2** (d'enquête) conducting; (de travaux) supervision; (d'entreprise) management; (de nation) leadership; **mon père m'a laissé la** ~ **des affaires** my father left me to run the business; **3** (de voiture, train) driving; (de moto) riding; **4** Aut (colonne de direction) **voiture avec** ~ **à gauche** left-hand drive car; **5** ○(examen) driving test; **6** (canalisation) pipe
(Composé) ~ **accompagnée** driving accompanied by a qualified driver

cône /kon/ *nm* cone

confection /kɔ̃fɛksjɔ̃/ *nf* **1** **la** ~ (industrie) the clothing industry; (vêtements) ready-to-wear clothes (*pl*); **2** (élaboration) making

confectionner /kɔ̃fɛksjɔne/ [1] *vtr* to make [*gâteau, vêtement*]; to prepare [*repas*]

confectionneur, -euse /kɔ̃fɛksjɔnœʀ, øz/ ▸ p. 372 *nm,f* manufacturer of ready-to-wear clothing

confédération /kɔ̃federasjɔ̃/ *nf* confederation
(Composé) **la Confédération helvétique** Switzerland

confédéré, ~e /kɔ̃federe/
A *adj* confederate; [*États*] confederate; [*syndicats*] confederated
B **confédérés** *nmpl* Hist **les** ~**s** the confederates

confédérer /kɔ̃federe/ [14] *vtr* to confederate

conférence /kɔ̃feʀɑ̃s/ *nf* **1** (discours, cours) lecture; **2** (congrès) conference; **3** (discussion) debate
(Composés) ~ **de presse** press conference; ~ **au sommet** summit meeting

conférencier, -ière /kɔ̃feʀɑ̃sje, ɛʀ/ ▸ p. 372 *nm,f* gén speaker; Univ lecturer

conférer /kɔ̃feʀe/ [14] *vtr* **1** to confer [*droit, statut*]; to award [*décoration*]; ~ **le baptême à qn** to baptize sb; **2** fml [*fonction, âge*] to give [*droit, privilège*]

confesse○ /kɔ̃fɛs/ *nf* confession

confesser /kɔ̃fese/ [1]
A *vtr* to confess [*péché, ignorance*]; ~ **qn** to hear sb's confession
B **se confesser** *vpr* **1** Relig to go to confession; **se** ~ **de qch** to confess (to) sth; **2** (se confier) **se** ~ **à un ami** to confide in a friend

confesseur /kɔ̃fesœʀ/ *nm* confessor

confession /kɔ̃fesjɔ̃/ *nf* **1** (aveu) confession; **2** Relig confession; **3** (foi) faith
(Idiome) **on te donnerait le bon Dieu sans** ~ you look as if butter wouldn't melt in your mouth

confessionnal, *pl* **-aux** /kɔ̃fesjɔnal, o/ *nm* confessional

confessionnel, -elle /kɔ̃fesjɔnɛl/ *adj* gén denominational; [*école*] denominational GB, parochial US

confetti /kɔ̃feti/ *nm* confetti **¢**; **un ~** a piece of confetti

confiance /kɔ̃fjɑ̃s/ *nf* [1] (foi en l'honnêteté) trust (**en** in); **en toute ~** with complete confidence; **de ~** [*personne*] trustworthy; [*mission*] which requires (the utmost) trust; **avoir ~ en qn, faire ~ à qn** to trust sb; **il va tricher, tu peux lui faire ~!** iron you can rely on him to cheat! iron; **j'ai ~ en l'avenir** I feel confident about the future; [2] (foi en la compétence) confidence (**en** in); **faire ~ à** to have confidence in; [3] (assurance) confidence; **~ en soi** (self-)confidence; **ces champignons ne m'inspirent pas ~** I don't feel altogether happy about these mushrooms; **mettre qn en ~** to put sb at ease; [4] Pol **voter la ~** to pass a vote of confidence

confiant, ~e /kɔ̃fjɑ̃, ɑ̃t/ *adj* [1] (certain) confident; [2] (assuré) (self-)confident; [3] (se fiant aux autres) [*personne, regard*] trusting

confidence /kɔ̃fidɑ̃s/ *nf* secret, confidence; **être dans la ~** to be in on the secret; **faire des ~s à qn sur qch** to confide in sb about sth; **sur le ton de la ~** confidentially

⌜Composé⌝ **~s sur l'oreiller** pillow talk **¢**

confident /kɔ̃fidɑ̃/ *nm* [1] gén, Théât confidant; [2] (fauteuil) tête-à-tête

confidente /kɔ̃fidɑ̃t/ *nf* gén, Théât confidante

confidentialité /kɔ̃fidɑ̃sjalite/ *nf* confidentiality

confidentiel, -ielle /kɔ̃fidɑ̃sjɛl/ *adj* confidential

confier /kɔ̃fje/ [2]
A *vtr* [1] (remettre) **~ qch à qn** to entrust sb with sth [*mission, poste*]; to entrust sth to sb [*argent, valise*]; **~ (la garde d')un enfant à qn** to leave a child in sb's care; **on m'a confié la direction du projet** I have been put in charge of the project; [2] (dire en confidence) **~ qch à qn** to confide [sth] to sb [*peines, intentions*]; **~ un secret à qn** to tell sb a secret
B **se confier** *vpr* to confide (**à** in)

configuration /kɔ̃figyRasjɔ̃/ *nf* [1] lit shape; **la ~ du terrain** the lie of the land; **la ~ des lieux** the layout of the premises; [2] fig (disposition) configuration; (situation) set-up; [3] Ordinat, Phys configuration

confiné, ~e /kɔ̃fine/ *adj* [1] (enfermé) **~ dans une pièce** confined to a room; **esprit ~ dans la routine** mind stuck in a rut; [2] [*atmosphère*] lit, fig stuffy; [*air*] stale; [3] [*espace*] confined, restricted

confiner /kɔ̃fine/ [1]
A *vtr* [1] (enfermer) **~ qn dans une pièce** to confine sb to a room; [2] (restreindre) **~ qn à une tâche** to restrict sb to a task
B **confiner à** *vtr ind* **~ à** to border on
C **se confiner** *vpr* to shut oneself away *ou* up; **se ~ dans un rôle** to restrict oneself to a role

confins /kɔ̃fɛ̃/ *nmpl* (de territoire) boundaries; (de désert) edges; **aux ~ de l'Europe et de l'Asie** on the borders of Europe and Asia; **aux ~ de la psychologie** fig on the borders of psychology

confirmation /kɔ̃fiRmasjɔ̃/ *nf* [1] (ratification) confirmation; **être la ~ de qch, apporter la ~ de qch** to confirm sth; [2] Relig confirmation

confirmer /kɔ̃fiRme/ [1]
A *vtr* [1] to confirm [*commande, fait*]; to uphold [*verdict*]; to bear out [*témoignage*]; **~ qn dans son opinion** to reinforce sb's opinion; [2] Relig to confirm
B **se confirmer** *vpr* [*bruit, nouvelle*] to be confirmed; [*témoignage*] to be corroborated; **il se confirme comme l'un de nos meilleurs acteurs** he has established himself as one of our best actors

confiscation /kɔ̃fiskasjɔ̃/ *nf* confiscation, seizure Jur

confiserie /kɔ̃fizRi/ *nf* [1] ▸ p. 372 (magasin) confectioner's (shop); [2] (fabrication, commerce) confectionery; [3] (produits) confectionery **¢**

confiseur, -euse /kɔ̃fizœR, øz/ ▸ p. 372 *nm,f* confectioner

confisquer /kɔ̃fiske/ [1] *vtr* [1] (prendre) to confiscate [*bien, propriété*]; [2] fig (accaparer) to monopolize [*gestion*]; **~ la direction de** to take control of

confit, ~e /kɔ̃fi, it/
A *adj* Culin [*fruits*] crystallized; [*cornichon*] pickled; [*canard*] preserved
B *nm* confit; **~ de canard** confit of duck

confiture /kɔ̃fityR/ *nf* Culin jam, preserve; (d'agrumes) marmalade

⌜Idiomes⌝ **donner de la ~ aux cochons** to cast pearls before swine; **mettre qch en ~**○ to wreck sth○

confiturier /kɔ̃fityRje/ *nm* (récipient) jam pot (*for serving*)

conflictuel, -elle /kɔ̃fliktɥɛl/ *adj* [*sujet*] controversial; [*tendances*] conflicting; **c'est une situation conflictuelle** it's a (potential) source of conflict

conflit /kɔ̃fli/ *nm* gén conflict; (du travail) dispute; **~ de compétence** demarcation dispute

⌜Composés⌝ **~ de générations** generation gap; **~ social** industrial strife; **~ du travail** industrial dispute

confluent /kɔ̃flyɑ̃/ *nm* confluence

confluer /kɔ̃flye/ [1] *vi* [1] Géog to meet, to join; **~ avec** to flow into; [2] fig [*troupes*] to converge (**vers** on)

confondant, ~e /kɔ̃fɔdɑ̃, ɑ̃t/ *adj* staggering

confondre /kɔ̃fɔdR/ [53]
A *vtr* [1] (ne pas distinguer) to mix up, to confuse; **je l'ai confondu avec son cousin** I mistook him for his cousin; **tous secteurs confondus** all sectors taken together; [2] (mêler) liter to merge; [3] (décontenancer) fml to stagger; **leur ignorance me confondait** I found their ignorance staggering; [4] (démasquer) to expose [*accusé, traître*]
B **se confondre** *vpr* [1] (se mêler) [*formes, couleurs*] to merge; [*événements, faits*] to become confused; [2] (être identique) [*intérêts, espoirs*] to coincide; **notre avenir se confond avec celui de l'Europe** our future is bound up with that of Europe; **ma vie se confond avec mon œuvre** my life and my work are one; [3] (se répandre) fml **il s'est confondu en excuses** he apologized profusely; **il s'est confondu en remerciements** he was effusive in his thanks

conforme /kɔ̃fɔRm/ *adj* [1] (en accord) **être ~ à** to be in keeping with [*loi, tradition*]; to comply with [*règlement*]; [2] (identique) **être ~ à l'original** to conform to the original; **photocopie certifiée ~** Admin certified true copy

conformé, ~e /kɔ̃fɔRme/ *adj* **bien ~** normally formed; **mal ~** malformed

conformément /kɔ̃fɔRmemɑ̃/ *adv* **~ à** in accordance with

conformer /kɔ̃fɔRme/ [1]
A *vtr* [1] (rendre conforme) **il doit ~ sa décision aux directives gouvernementales** his decision should comply with government directives; [2] Tech (donner une forme à) to shape
B **se conformer** *vpr* (à un usage) to conform (**à** to); (à un règlement, une norme) to comply (**à** with)

conformisme /kɔ̃fɔRmism/ *nm* [1] péj conformity, conventionality; **elle est d'un ~!** she's such a conformist!, she's so conventional!; [2] Relig conformity

conformiste /kɔ̃fɔRmist/ *adj, nmf* gén, Relig conformist

conformité /kɔ̃fɔRmite/ *nf* **~ à la loi** compliance with the law; **en ~ avec** [*agir*] in accordance with; **mettre qch en ~ avec** to make sth comply with; **vérifier la ~ de la traduction à l'original** to check that the translation is faithful to the original

confort /kɔ̃fɔR/ *nm* comfort; **le ~ moderne** modern conveniences (*pl*); **maison avec tout le ~, maison tout ~** house with all modern conveniences; **il me faut mon ~** I must have my creature comforts; **ça va déranger ton ~** it'll disturb your cosy GB *ou* cozy US existence; **~ d'écoute** quality of reception; **~ d'utilisation** user-friendliness

confortable /kɔ̃fɔRtabl/ *adj* comfortable; **pas ~** uncomfortable; **peu ~** rather uncomfortable

confortablement /kɔ̃fɔRtabləmɑ̃/ *adv* comfortably

conforter /kɔ̃fɔRte/ [1] *vtr* to consolidate [*position, régime*]; to reinforce [*situation*]; **~ qn dans une opinion** to confirm sb in his/her opinion

confraternel, -elle /kɔ̃fRatɛRnɛl/ *adj* fraternal

confraternellement /kɔ̃fRatɛRnɛlmɑ̃/ *adv* fraternally

confrère /kɔ̃fRɛR/ *nm* (de travail) colleague; (d'association) fellow member; **ses ~s musiciens** his/her fellow musicians; **dans un entretien accordé à un ~ de la presse écrite** in an interview given to a newspaper

confrérie /kɔ̃fReRi/ *nf* brotherhood

confrontation /kɔ̃fRɔ̃tasjɔ̃/ *nf* [1] (de témoins, d'idées) confrontation; (de textes) comparison; [2] (débat) debate; (affrontement) clash

confronter /kɔ̃fRɔ̃te/ [1] *vtr* to confront [*témoins, théories*]; to compare [*expériences, textes*]; **~ qch avec** (pour vérifier) to check sth against

confus, ~e /kɔ̃fy, yz/ *adj* ⓵ (indistinct, obscur) confused; **un mélange ~** a hotchpotch GB, a hodgepodge US; ⓶ (vague) [*sentiment, crainte*] vague; ⓷ (navré) sorry; (gêné) embarrassed

confusément /kɔ̃fyzemɑ̃/ *adv* [*requérir, expliquer*] confusedly; [*sentir*] vaguely

confusion /kɔ̃fyzjɔ̃/ *nf* ⓵ (désordre) confusion; **jeter la ~ dans les esprits** to throw people into confusion; ⓶ (gêne) embarrassment; ⓷ (méprise) mix-up

(Composés) **~ de peines** Jur concurrency of sentences; **~ des pouvoirs** Pol non-separation of powers

congé /kɔ̃ʒe/ *nm* ⓵ (arrêt de travail) leave 𝒞; **prendre quatre jours de ~** to take four days off; **avoir ~ le lundi** to have Mondays off; ⓶ Scol holiday GB, vacation US; **en France les écoles ont ~ le mercredi** in France there is no school on Wednesdays; ⓷ (fin de contrat) notice; **donner (son)** or **signifier son ~ à qn** to give sb notice

(Composés) **~s payés** paid leave 𝒞; **~s scolaires** school holidays GB *ou* vacation US (*sg*)

(Idiome) **prendre ~ de qn** to take leave of sb

congédier /kɔ̃ʒedje/ [2] *vtr* to dismiss

congelable /kɔ̃ʒlabl/ *adj* suitable for home freezing

congélateur /kɔ̃ʒelatœr/ *nm* freezer, deep-freeze; (dans un réfrigérateur) freezer compartment

congélation /kɔ̃ʒelasjɔ̃/ *nf* gén freezing; (d'huile) congelation

congelé, ~e /kɔ̃ʒle/
A *adj* frozen; **produits ~s** frozen foods
B *nm* frozen foods (*pl*)

congeler /kɔ̃ʒle/ [17] *vtr*, **se congeler** *vpr* to freeze

congénère /kɔ̃ʒenɛr/ *nmf* (d'animal) fellow creature; (de personne) **vous et vos ~s** pej you and your like

congénital, ~e, *mpl* **-aux** /kɔ̃ʒenital, o/ *adj* congenital

congère /kɔ̃ʒɛr/ *nf* snowdrift

congestif, -ive /kɔ̃ʒɛstif, iv/ *adj* congestive

congestion /kɔ̃ʒɛstjɔ̃/ *nf* congestion

(Composés) **~ cérébrale** stroke; **~ pulmonaire** congestion of the lungs

congestionner /kɔ̃ʒɛstjɔne/ [1] *vtr* to congest; **il est tout congestionné** he's all flushed

conglomérat /kɔ̃glɔmera/ *nm* ⓵ (d'entreprises, de roches) conglomerate; ⓶ fig (mélange) conglomeration

Congo /kɔ̃go/ ▸ p. 230, p. 259 *nprm* Congo

congolais, ~e /kɔ̃gɔlɛ, ɛz/
A ▸ p. 392 *adj* Congolese
B *nm* Culin (small) coconut cake

congre /kɔ̃gr/ *nm* conger eel

congrégation /kɔ̃gregasjɔ̃/ *nf* ⓵ Relig congregation; ⓶ (assemblée) hum assembly

congrès /kɔ̃grɛ/ *nm inv* conference; **le Congrès** Congress

congressiste /kɔ̃grɛsist/ *nmf* (conference) delegate

congru, ~e /kɔ̃gry/ *adj* Math congruent (**à** with)

conifère /kɔnifɛr/ *nm* conifer

conique /kɔnik/ *adj* Math conical; **de forme ~** cone-shaped

conjecture /kɔ̃ʒɛktyr/ *nf* conjecture 𝒞; **vaines ~s** idle speculation

conjecturer /kɔ̃ʒɛktyre/ [1] *vtr* fml to speculate

conjoint, ~e /kɔ̃ʒwɛ̃, ɛ̃t/
A *adj* [*démarche, déclaration*] joint (*épith*); [*questions, situations*] linked
B *nm,f* spouse; **les ~s** the husband and wife

conjointement /kɔ̃ʒwɛ̃tmɑ̃/ *adv* ⓵ (de concert) jointly; **~ et solidairement** Jur jointly and severally; ⓶ (en même temps) at the same time; **~ avec** together with

conjonctif, -ive /kɔ̃ʒɔ̃ktif, iv/ *adj* ⓵ Anat conjunctival; ⓶ Ling conjunctive

conjonction /kɔ̃ʒɔ̃ksjɔ̃/ *nf* conjunction

conjonctivite /kɔ̃ʒɔ̃ktivit/ ▸ p. 195 *nf* conjunctivitis

conjoncture /kɔ̃ʒɔ̃ktyr/ *nf* situation; **bonne ~** favourable^{GB} conjunction of circumstances

conjoncturel, -elle /kɔ̃ʒɔ̃ktyrɛl/ *adj* [*déficit, politique*] short-term; [*situation, fluctuations*] economic; [*crise*] temporary, cyclical; [*prélèvement*] temporary; **évolution conjoncturelle** current trends

conjugaison /kɔ̃ʒygɛzɔ̃/ *nf* ⓵ Biol, Ling conjugation; ⓶ fig (réunion) combination; **la ~ de leurs efforts** their joint efforts (*pl*)

conjugal, ~e, *mpl* **-aux** /kɔ̃ʒygal, o/ *adj* [*amour, fidélité*] conjugal; [*drame*] marital; [*vie*] married

conjuguer /kɔ̃ʒyge/ [1] *vtr* ⓵ Ling to conjugate [*verbe*]; ⓶ (combiner) to combine, to unite [*efforts*]

conjurateur, -trice /kɔ̃ʒyratœr, tris/ *nm,f* chief conspirator

conjuration /kɔ̃ʒyrasjɔ̃/ *nf* ⓵ (complot) conspiracy; ⓶ (d'influences maléfiques) conjuration

conjuré, ~e /kɔ̃ʒyre/ *nm,f* conspirator

conjurer /kɔ̃ʒyre/ [1] *vtr* ⓵ to avert [*crise, inflation*]; to ward off [*danger, sort*]; to banish [*angoisse, solitude*]; ⓶ **je vous en conjure** I beg you

connaissance /kɔnɛsɑ̃s/
A *nf* ⓵ (savoir) knowledge (**de** of); **avoir ~ de qch** to know something about sth; **il a une profonde ~ de la psychologie humaine** he has a deep understanding of the way the human mind works; **prendre ~ d'un texte** to acquaint oneself with a text; **donner ~ de qch à qn** to inform sb of sth; **porter à la ~ de qn que** fml to advise sb that; **en ~ de cause** with full knowledge of the facts; ⓶ (conscience) consciousness; **rester sans ~** to be unconscious; ⓷ (sur le plan social) acquaintance; **j'ai fait leur ~ hier** I met them yesterday; **faire (plus ample) ~ avec qn** to get to know sb (better); **un visage de ~** a familiar face; **se retrouver en pays de ~** (avec des gens que l'on connaît) to be among familiar faces; (dans un domaine familier) to find oneself on familiar ground
B **connaissances** *nfpl* (théoriques) knowledge 𝒞; (pratiques) experience 𝒞; **'~s en informatique souhaitées'** 'computing experience desirable'

connaisseur, -euse /kɔnɛsœr, øz/
A *adj m* [*air, œil*] expert
B *nm,f* expert, connoisseur; **regarder qch en ~** to look at sth with an expert eye

connaître /kɔnɛtr/ [73]
A *vtr* ⓵ to know [*fait, nom, événement*]; **il ne tient jamais ses promesses, c'est (bien) connu** it is common knowledge that he never keeps his promises; **je ne leur connais aucun vice** I don't know them to have any vices; **tu connais la nouvelle?** have you heard the news?; **ne ~ que son devoir** to think of nothing but one's duty; ⓶ to know, to be acquainted with [*sujet, méthode, auteur*]; **la mécanique, je ne connais que ça** or **ça me connaît!** I know quite a bit about mechanics; ⓷ to know [*faim*]; to experience [*crise*]; to enjoy [*gloire*]; to have [*difficultés*]; **ils ont connu la défaite** they were defeated; **il a connu la prison** he's been to prison before; **les problèmes d'argent, ça me connaît**°! I could tell you a thing or two° about money problems!; **~ des hauts et des bas** to have one's/its ups and downs; **~ une fin tragique** to come to a tragic end; **~ une forte croissance** to show a rapid growth; ⓸ to know [*personne, acteur*]; **c'est bien mal la ~** they/you're misjudging her; **faire ~ qn à qn** to introduce sb to sb; **Bernadette? je ne connais qu'elle!** Bernadette? I know her very well!; **il ne me connaît plus depuis qu'il est passé officier** he ignores me now that he's an officer; ⓹ †(coucher avec) to know†, to have a sexual relationship with; ⓺ Jur **~ de** to have jurisdiction over [*affaire, cause*]; **avoir à ~ de** to judge *ou* hear [*cas*]
B **se connaître** *vpr* ⓵ (soi-même) to know oneself; **'connais-toi toi-même'** 'know thyself'; **il ne se connaissait plus de joie** fml he was beside himself with joy; ⓶ (l'un l'autre) to know each other; ⓷ (être compétent) **s'y ~ en théâtre** to know all about theatre; **c'est le carburateur qui est bouché ou je ne m'y connais pas**° if I know anything about it, it's the carburettor GB *ou* carburetor US that's blocked

(Idiomes) **on connaît la chanson** or **musique!** we've heard it all before!; **~ qch comme sa poche** to know sth like the back of one's hand

conne ▸ **con** A, B

connecter /kɔnɛkte/ [1] *vtr* to connect (**à** to)

connétable /kɔnetabl/ nm Hist supreme commander of the French armies

connexe /kɔnɛks/ adj related (**à** to)

connexion /kɔnɛksjɔ̃/ nf lit, fig connection

connivence /kɔnivɑ̃s/ nf (complicité) connivance ℂ; (accord tacite) tacit agreement; **signe de ~** sign of complicity; **être de ~ avec qn** to connive with sb

connotation /kɔnɔtasjɔ̃/ nf connotation

connoter /kɔnɔte/ [1] vtr to connote

conque /kɔ̃k/ nf Zool, Archit conch

conquérant, ~e /kɔ̃keʀɑ̃, ɑ̃t/
A adj [peuple] conquering; fig [air] triumphant
B nm,f (guerrier) conqueror

conquérir /kɔ̃keʀiʀ/ [35] vtr to conquer [pays, sommet]; to capture [marché]; to gain [pouvoir]; to win [amitié, personne]; to win over [auditoire]; **leur talent a conquis Paris** they captivated Paris with their talent

(Idiome) **se croire en pays** or **terrain conquis** to lord it over everyone

conquête /kɔ̃kɛt/ nf conquest; **faire la ~ d'un pays** to conquer a country; **~s sociales** social victories; **partir à la ~ de** to set out to conquer [pays, sommet, pouvoir]; to set out to capture [marché]; to set out to achieve [bonheur]; **faire la ~ d'une femme** to win the heart of a lady

conquis, ~e /kɔ̃ki, iz/ ▸ **conquérir**

consacré, ~e /kɔ̃sakʀe/ adj **formule** or **expression ~e** time-honoured[GB] expression; **selon la formule ~e** as the expression goes; **artiste ~** recognized artist; **être ~ joueur de l'année** to be designated player of the year

consacrer /kɔ̃sakʀe/ [1]
A vtr **1** to devote [effort, vie, exposition] (**à** to); **2** to sanction [rupture, alliance]; **l'usage a consacré le mot** the word has gained acceptance through use; **3** Relig to consecrate [basilique, évêque]; to ordain [prêtre]; **jour consacré** holy day
B se consacrer vpr **se ~ à** to devote oneself to

consanguin, ~e /kɔ̃sɑ̃gɛ̃, in/ adj **union ~e, mariage ~** marriage between blood relations; **frère ~** half brother (having the same father)

consciemment /kɔ̃sjamɑ̃/ adv consciously

conscience /kɔ̃sjɑ̃s/ nf **1** (morale) conscience; **écouter (la voix de) sa ~** to follow one's conscience; **j'ai ma ~ pour moi** my conscience is clear; **2** (connaissance) awareness; **avoir ~ de** to be aware of; **prise de ~** realization; **~ de soi** self-awareness; **scruter les ~s** to read people's thoughts; **perdre/reprendre ~** to lose/to regain consciousness; **avoir toute sa ~** to be fully lucid

(Composé) **~ professionnelle** conscientiousness

consciencieusement /kɔ̃sjɑ̃sjøzmɑ̃/ adv **1** (avec sérieux) conscientiously; **2** (comme il se doit) dutifully

consciencieux, -ieuse /kɔ̃sjɑ̃sjø, øz/ adj gén conscientious; [enfant, époux] dutiful

conscient, ~e /kɔ̃sjɑ̃, ɑ̃t/
A adj **1** (au fait) aware; **2** (lucide) conscious; **de façon ~e** consciously
B nm conscious

conscription /kɔ̃skʀipsjɔ̃/ nf conscription GB, draft US

conscrit /kɔ̃skʀi/ nm **1** Mil conscript GB, draftee US; **2** ᐤ(de la même année) **c'est mon ~** he was born in the same year as me

consécration /kɔ̃sekʀasjɔ̃/ nf **1** (reconnaissance) recognition; **connaître la ~** to win recognition; **2** Relig (de basilique, d'évêque) consecration; (de prêtre) ordination

consécutif, -ive /kɔ̃sekytif, iv/ adj gén, Ling consecutive; **retards ~s à la modernisation** delays resulting from modernization; **série de procès ~s au scandale** series of court cases following the scandal

consécutivement /kɔ̃sekytivmɑ̃/ adv consecutively

conseil /kɔ̃sɛj/ nm **1** (avis) advice ℂ; **~ d'ami** piece of friendly advice; **quelques ~s de prudence** a few words of caution ou warning; **donner à qn le ~ de faire** to advise sb to do; **il est de bon ~** he always gives good advice; **2** (assemblée) council; **tenir ~** to hold a meeting; **3** (conseiller) consultant; **~ en gestion** management consultant

(Composés) **~ d'administration** board of directors; **~ de classe** staff meeting (for all those teaching a given class); **~ de discipline** disciplinary committee; **~ de famille** Jur Board of Guardians; (non officiel) family meeting ou gathering; **~ général** Pol council of a French department; **~ de guerre** council of war; **~ des ministres** gén council of ministers; (en Grande-Bretagne) Cabinet meeting; **~ de révision** Mil medical board (assessing fitness for military service); **~ de surveillance** supervisory board; **~ d'université** senate; **Conseil d'État** Council of State (advising government on administrative matters); **Conseil supérieur de l'audiovisuel, CSA** Radio, TV body which monitors broadcasting; **Conseil supérieur de la magistrature** High Council for the Judiciary; **~s d'entretien** cleaning ou care instructions

conseillé, ~e /kɔ̃seje/ adj [modèle, activité] recommended; **il est ~ de faire** it is advisable to do

conseiller, -ère /kɔ̃seje, ɛʀ/ [1]
A nm,f **1** (expert) adviser[GB]; consultant; **~ du président** presidential adviser; **~ en communication** communications adviser; **2** (guide) counsellor[GB]
B nm (membre de conseil) councillor[GB]; (diplomate) counsellor[GB]
C vtr **1** (proposer) to recommend [lieu, activité, prudence]; **~ à qn de faire** to advise sb to do; **2** (servir d'expert à) to advise [personne]; **se faire ~ par qn** to seek advice from sb

(Composés) **~ commercial** commercial counsellor[GB]; **~ culturel** cultural counsellor[GB]; **~ (principal) d'éducation** chief supervisor; **~ d'État** member of the Council of State; **~ général** Pol councillor[GB] for a French department; **~ municipal** town councillor[GB]; **~ d'orientation** careers adviser; **~ régional** regional councillor[GB]

consensuel, -elle /kɔ̃sɛ̃sɥɛl/ adj [politique] consensual; [réforme] based on consensus

consensus /kɔ̃sɛ̃sys/ nm inv consensus

consentant, ~e /kɔ̃sɑ̃tɑ̃, ɑ̃t/ adj [personne] willing; Jur consenting; **les parents doivent être ~s** the parents must give their consent; **sourire ~** smile of consent

consentement /kɔ̃sɑ̃tmɑ̃/ nm consent (**à** to); **divorce par ~ mutuel** Jur divorce by consent GB, no-fault divorce US

consentir /kɔ̃sɑ̃tiʀ/ [30]
A vtr to grant [permission, prêt]; to allow [avantage]
B consentir à vtr ind **~ à qch/à faire** to agree to sth/ to do

(Idiome) **qui ne dit mot consent** Prov silence means consent Prov

conséquence /kɔ̃sekɑ̃s/ nf consequence (**pour** for; **sur** to); **être lourd de ~s** to have serious consequences; **tirer les ~s de qch** to learn one's lesson from sth; **ne pas tirer à ~** to be of no consequence; **~ heureuse** happy result; **avoir pour ~ de faire** to have the effect of doing; **avoir pour ~ le chômage** to result in unemployment; **en ~ (de quoi)** as a result (of which); **agir en ~** to act accordingly; **avoir des qualifications et un salaire en ~** to have qualifications and a corresponding salary

conséquent, ~e /kɔ̃sekɑ̃, ɑ̃t/
A adj **1** (important) substantial; **2** (cohérent) consistent; **3** Géog, Ling, Philos consequent
B par conséquent loc adv therefore, as a result

conservateur, -trice /kɔ̃sɛʀvatœʀ, tʀis/
A adj **1** Pol conservative; **2** Chimie preservative
B nm,f **1** Pol conservative; **2** ▸ p. 372 (de musée) curator; (de bibliothèque) chief GB ou head US librarian
C nm Chimie preservative; **'garanti sans ~s'** 'no preservatives'

(Composé) **~ des hypothèques** land registrar

conservation /kɔ̃sɛʀvasjɔ̃/ nf **1** (protection) (d'espèce, de patrimoine) conservation; (de livres, tableaux) preservation; **2** (d'aliment) preservation; **lait longue ~** long-life milk GB; **3** Phys conservation

(Composé) **~ des hypothèques** Admin land registry

conservatisme /kɔ̃sɛʀvatism/ nm conservatism ℂ; **les ~s** conservative attitudes

conservatoire /kɔ̃sɛʀvatwaʀ/
A adj Jur protective
B nm academy; **~ de musique** conservatoire of music

(Composé) **Conservatoire national des arts et métiers** (musée) museum of technology; (centre d'études) institute for engineering studies

conserve /kɔ̃sɛʀv/
A nf **1** Ind canned food; **~s de poissons** canned fish; **fruits**

en ∼ canned fruit; **boîte de** ∼ can; 2 Culin preserve

B **de conserve** loc adv [agir] in concert; [naviguer] in convoy

conserver /kɔ̃sɛʀve/ [1] vtr 1 to keep [brouillon, emploi]; to retain [influence, titre]; ∼ **son calme** to keep calm; ∼ **l'anonymat** to remain anonymous; 2 Culin to preserve [aliment]; ∼ **dans du vinaigre** to pickle; **'à** ∼ **au frais'** 'keep refrigerated'; 3 (maintenir jeune) [sport] to keep [sb] young [personne]; **homme bien conservé** well-preserved man

conserverie /kɔ̃sɛʀvəʀi/ nf 1 (usine) cannery; 2 (secteur) canning industry

considérable /kɔ̃sideʀabl/ adj [fortune, difficulté, retard] considerable; [rôle, événement] significant; **l'enjeu est** ∼ the stakes are high

considérablement /kɔ̃sideʀabləmɑ̃/ adv considerably, significantly

considération /kɔ̃sideʀasjɔ̃/ nf 1 (facteur) consideration; **en** ∼ **de** in view of; **sans** ∼ **de** irrespective of; 2 (respect) consideration; **jouir d'une** ∼ **unanime** to be respected by all; 3 (remarque) reflection

considéré, ∼**e** /kɔ̃sideʀe/ adj (en question) under consideration

considérer /kɔ̃sideʀe/ [14]

A vtr 1 (juger) ∼ **qn/qch comme (étant)** to consider sb/sth to be; ∼ **comme criminels ceux qui polluent l'atmosphère** to regard those who pollute the atmosphere as criminals; **il considère comme acquise sa victoire électorale** he sees himself as having already won the election; 2 (envisager) to regard [personne]; to consider [chose]; **à tout bien** ∼ all things considered; 3 (respecter) to have a high regard for; 4 (examiner) to consider; 5 (regarder attentivement) to look at [personne, spectacle]

B **se considérer** vpr 1 (soi-même) **se** ∼ **(comme)** to consider oneself (to be); 2 (l'un l'autre) **se** ∼ **(comme)** to regard one another as being; (s'étudier) to gaze at each other

consignation /kɔ̃siɲasjɔ̃/ nf 1 Jur, Fin deposit; 2 Comm **en** ∼ on consignment

consigne /kɔ̃siɲ/ nf 1 (ordre) orders (pl), instructions (pl); **donner** ∼ **de faire** to give orders to do; **donner** or **lancer une** ∼ **de grève** to issue strike orders; **passer la** ∼ **à qn** to pass the word on to sb; **'**∼**s à suivre en cas d'incendie'** 'fire regulations'; 2 (pour les bagages) left luggage office GB, baggage checkroom US; 3 (de bouteilles, d'emballages) deposit

(Composé) ∼ **automatique** left luggage lockers (pl) GB, baggage lockers (pl) US

consigné, ∼**e** /kɔ̃siɲe/ adj [bouteille, emballage] returnable; **non** ∼ nonreturnable

consigner /kɔ̃siɲe/ [1] vtr 1 to record, to write [sth] down [fait, souvenir]; 2 Mil to confine [soldat]; Scol to give [sb] detention [élève]; 3 to consign [objet, marchandise]; 4 to charge a deposit on [bouteille]

consistance /kɔ̃sistɑ̃s/ nf 1 (de pâte, sauce, peinture) consistency; **manquer de** ∼ [sauce, peinture] to be too runny; **prendre** ∼ to thicken; 2 (d'argument, de théorie) substance, weight; **sans** ∼ [personne] spineless; [bonheur] with no basis in reality

consistant, ∼**e** /kɔ̃sistɑ̃, ɑ̃t/ adj [repas, investissement] substantial; [plat] nourishing; [sauce, peinture] thick; [livre] with some substance; [argument] solid

consister /kɔ̃siste/ [1] vi 1 (résider) ∼ **en** or **dans** to consist in; **en quoi consiste mon erreur?** where have I gone wrong?; 2 (être fait) ∼ **en** to consist of [éléments, parties]; **en quoi consiste cette aide?** what form does this aid take?

consœur /kɔ̃sœʀ/ nf 1 (d'une personne) female colleague; 2 (d'une banque, organisation) counterpart

consolant, ∼**e** /kɔ̃sɔlɑ̃, ɑ̃t/ adj comforting

consolation /kɔ̃sɔlasjɔ̃/ nf consolation

console /kɔ̃sɔl/ nf console

(Composés) ∼ **de jeu vidéo** games console; ∼ **de mixage** mixing desk

consoler /kɔ̃sɔle/ [1]

A vtr to console [personne] (**de** for); to soothe away [peine]; **cela console de savoir que** it is some consolation to know that; **si ça peut te** ∼ if it is any comfort to you

B **se consoler** vpr 1 (soi-même) **se** ∼ to find consolation; **se** ∼ **de** to get over [échec]; 2 (réciproquement) to console each other

consolidable /kɔ̃sɔlidabl/ adj 1 [dette] fundable; 2 [structure] reinforceable

consolidation /kɔ̃sɔlidasjɔ̃/ nf 1 (de mur) strengthening; (de position) consolidation; 2 (de dette) consolidation, funding; (de chiffre d'affaires, bilan) consolidation; (de monnaie) strengthening; 3 (de fracture) mending

consolider /kɔ̃sɔlide/ [1]

A vtr (renforcer) to strengthen [mur]; to consolidate [position, résultat, bénéfice, dette]; to strengthen [monnaie]; Méd to set [fracture, tissus]

B **se consolider** vpr 1 (se renforcer) gén to grow stronger; [position] to be consolidated; [structure] to be strengthened; 2 (s'affermir) to consolidate; 3 Méd [fracture, tissus] to mend

consommable /kɔ̃sɔmabl/

A adj 1 [aliment] edible; [boisson] drinkable; 2 Tech expendable

B **consommables** nmpl Comm, Ordinat consumables

consommateur, -trice /kɔ̃sɔmatœʀ, tʀis/

A adj consumer (épith); ∼ **de pétrole/d'énergie** oil-/energy-consuming (épith)

B nm,f 1 Écon consumer; **défense des** ∼**s** consumer protection; 2 (de café, bar) customer

consommation /kɔ̃sɔmasjɔ̃/ nf 1 consumption; ∼ **intérieure** domestic consumption; ∼ **des ménages** household consumption; **pour ma** ∼ **personnelle** for my personal use; **faire une grande** or **grosse** ∼ **de** to use a lot of; **limitez la** ∼ **de matières grasses** avoid eating fatty foods; **une réduction de la** ∼ **de sodium** a reduction in sodium intake; 2 (boisson) drink; **régler les** ∼**s** to pay for the drinks; 3 (accomplissement) consummation sout

consommé, ∼**e** /kɔ̃sɔme/

A adj [art, artiste] consummate; **avec un sens** ∼ **du spectacle** with a consummate sense of the theatrical

B nm Culin consommé

consommer /kɔ̃sɔme/ [1]

A vtr 1 (utiliser) to consume; **ma voiture consomme énormément** my car consumes a lot of petrol GB ou gas US; 2 (manger) to eat; (boire) to drink; ∼ **de la drogue** to take drugs; 3 (accomplir) fml to consummate sout [mariage]; to complete [rupture]

B vi 1 Écon to consume; 2 Comm (boire) to drink

C **se consommer** vpr 1 (être mangé) to be eaten; **le gaspacho se consomme froid** gazpacho is eaten cold; 2 (être utilisé) to be consumed

consonance /kɔ̃sɔnɑ̃s/ nf consonance; **un mot aux** ∼**s étrangères** a foreign-sounding word

consonant, ∼**e** /kɔ̃sɔnɑ̃, ɑ̃t/ adj consonant

consonantique /kɔ̃sɔnɑ̃tik/ adj [langue] consonantal; [groupe] consonant (épith)

consonne /kɔ̃sɔn/ nf consonant

consortium /kɔ̃sɔʀsjɔm/ nm consortium

conspirateur, -trice /kɔ̃spiʀatœʀ, tʀis/

A adj conspiratorial

B nm,f conspirator

conspiration /kɔ̃spiʀasjɔ̃/ nf conspiracy

conspirer /kɔ̃spiʀe/ [1]

A vi (comploter) to conspire, to plot (**contre** against)

B **conspirer** à vtr ind ∼ **à** to conspire to bring about [malheur, succès]; ∼ **à faire** to conspire to do

conspuer /kɔ̃spɥe/ [1] vtr to boo

constamment /kɔ̃stamɑ̃/ adv 1 (invariablement) always; 2 (sans interruption) [augmenter] continuously; [maintenir] consistently; 3 (très souvent) [dérangé, malade] constantly

constance /kɔ̃stɑ̃s/ nf 1 (caractère stable) (de sentiment, phénomène) constancy; (d'opinion) consistency; 2 (persévérance) steadfastness; **affirmer avec** ∼ **que...** to hold steadfastly that...; **travailler avec** ∼ to work steadily; 3 °(patience) patience

constant, ∼**e**[1] /kɔ̃stɑ̃, ɑ̃t/ adj 1 gén constant; [personne] (dans ses affections) constant; (dans ses opinions) consistent; 2 (continu) [progression] continuous; [hausse] continual; 3 (persévérant) liter [personne] steadfast; [résolution] firm.

⚠ On utilise continuous pour décrire une action qui ne cesse pas et continual pour décrire une action qui se répète.

constante[2] /kɔ̃stɑ̃t/ nf 1 Math, Phys constant; 2 fig (trait) permanent feature

constat /kɔ̃sta/ *nm* **1** (procès-verbal) certified *ou* official report; **2** (bilan) assessment; **3** (preuve) acknowledgement

⟨Composés⟩ ~ **(à l')** **amiable** accident report drawn up by the parties involved; ~ **d'adultère** Jur record of adultery; ~ **d'échec** fig admission of failure; ~ **d'huissier** Jur bailiff's report

constatable /kɔ̃statabl/ *adj* observable

constatation /kɔ̃statasjɔ̃/
A *nf* **1** (observation) observation; **c'est une simple** ~ it's simply a statement of fact; **2** (enquête) investigation; (rapport d'enquête) report
B **constatations** *nfpl* (conclusions) findings

constater /kɔ̃state/ [1] *vtr* **1** (observer) to notice; ~ **une amélioration** to note an improvement; ~ **(par) soi-même** to see for oneself; **2** (établir) to ascertain, to establish [fait]; (consigner) to record [délit]; ~ **le décès** to certify that death has occurred

constellation /kɔ̃stɛlasjɔ̃/ *nf* **1** (en astronomie) constellation; **2** (groupe) (de partis, villes) cluster; (de firmes) group

constellé, ~**e** /kɔ̃stɛle/ *adj* ~ **de** spangled with [étoiles]; scattered with [fleurs]; riddled with [fautes]; spotted with [taches]; **ciel** ~ **d'étoiles** starry sky

consternant, ~**e** /kɔ̃stɛʀnɑ̃, ɑ̃t/ *adj* [fait] distressing; [bêtise] appalling

consternation /kɔ̃stɛʀnasjɔ̃/ *nf* consternation, dismay

consterner /kɔ̃stɛʀne/ [1] *vtr* to fill [sb] with consternation; **mine consternée** look of dismay

constipation /kɔ̃stipasjɔ̃/ *nf* constipation

constipé, ~**e** /kɔ̃stipe/ *adj* **1** Méd constipated; **2** ᵒfig (contraint) **avoir l'air** ~ to look uptight

constiper /kɔ̃stipe/ [1] *vtr* to make [sb] constipated; **le chocolat constipe** chocolate causes constipation

constituant, ~**e** /kɔ̃stituɑ̃, ɑ̃t/
A *adj* constituent
B *nm* gén, Ling constituent

Constituante /kɔ̃stituɑ̃t/ *nf* Hist, Pol Constituent Assembly

constitué, ~**e** /kɔ̃stitue/ *adj* **1** (physiquement) **personne bien/mal** ~**e** person of sound/unsound constitution; **2** Pol [autorité, société] constituted

constituer /kɔ̃stitue/ [1]
A *vtr* **1** (être) to be, to constitute; **le vol constitue un délit** theft constitutes an offence^{GB}; **2** (mettre en place) to form [équipe, commission]; **3** (composer) to make up [ensemble]; **4** Jur to settle [dot, rente] (**à, pour** on); ~ **qn héritier** to appoint sb as heir
B **se constituer** *vpr* **1** (se mettre en place) [parti, réseau] to be formed; **2** (créer pour soi) to build up [réseau, clientèle, réserve]; to get oneself [alibi]; **3** (se grouper) **se** ~ **en** to form [parti, association]; **se** ~ **(se faire) se** ~ **prisonnier** to give oneself up; **se** ~ **partie civile** to institute a civil action

constitutif, -**ive** /kɔ̃stitytif, iv/ *adj* **1** [élément] constituent; **2** Pol [assemblée] constituent; [congrès] founding; [réunion] inaugural; [texte] constitutional

constitution /kɔ̃stitysjɔ̃/ *nf* **1** (création) ~ **d'une société** setting up of a company; **en voie de** ~ currently being set up; ~ **de capital** capital accumulation; ~ **de stocks** stockpiling; **2** (physique) constitution; **bonne** ~ sound constitution; **3** Jur (de rente, pension) settling ₵; ~ **de partie civile** institution of civil action proceedings

Constitution /kɔ̃stitysjɔ̃/ *nf* constitution

constitutionnel, -**elle** /kɔ̃stitysjɔnɛl/ *adj* constitutional

constructeur, -**trice** /kɔ̃stʀyktœʀ, tʀis/
A *adj* **1** (créateur) constructive; **2** Constr **société constructrice** construction company; **3** Zool **animal** ~ **builder**
B ▸ p. 372 *nm,f* **1** Ind manufacturer; ~ **automobile** or **d'automobiles** car manufacturer; ~ **naval** shipwright; **2** Constr builder

constructible /kɔ̃stʀyktibl/ *adj* building (épith), suitable for development (après n); **terrain** ~ building land

constructif, -**ive** /kɔ̃stʀyktif, iv/ *adj* **1** constructive; **2** Constr building épith; **les normes constructives** building standards

construction /kɔ̃stʀyksjɔ̃/ *nf* **1** gén building; **en (cours de)** ~ under construction; **bâtiment de** ~ **ancienne** old building; **2** Écon (secteur industriel) **la** ~ the construction

industry; **3** Ind manufacture; ~ **de moteurs** engine manufacture; **de** ~ **japonaise** made in Japan; ~ **aéronautique** aircraft manufacturing; ~ **électrique** electrical engineering; ~ **ferroviaire** railway construction; ~ **navale** shipbuilding; **4** Pol, Ling, Math construction; **5** (élaboration) construction; **une pure** ~ **de l'esprit** pure imagination

constructivisme /kɔ̃stʀyktivism/ *nm* constructivism

construire /kɔ̃stʀɥiʀ/ [69]
A *vtr* **1** to build; ~ **des voitures** to manufacture cars; **se faire** ~ **une villa** to have a villa built; **2** fig to build [Europe, avenir]; to shape [personnalité, image]; **3** Ling to construct [phrase, théorie]; **4** Math to construct [triangle]
B **se construire** *vpr* **1** (bâtir pour soi) **se** ~ **une maison** to build a house for oneself; **se** ~ **son identité** fig to shape one's own identity; **2** (être bâti) to be built; **3** Ling to be constructed; **se** ~ **avec le subjonctif** to take the subjunctive

consul /kɔ̃syl/ *nm* consul

consulaire /kɔ̃sylɛʀ/ *adj* consular

consulat /kɔ̃syla/ *nm* **1** Admin consulate; **2** Hist **le Consulat** the Consulate

consultable /kɔ̃syltabl/ *adj* available for consultation (après n)

consultant, ~**e** /kɔ̃syltɑ̃, ɑ̃t/ ▸ p. 372 *nm,f* consultant

consultatif, -**ive** /kɔ̃syltatif, iv/ *adj* consultative

consultation /kɔ̃syltasjɔ̃/ *nf* **1** (heures de réception des malades) surgery hours (pl) GB, office hours (pl) US; ~ **des nourrissons/de planning familial** baby/family planning clinic; **2** (examen médical) consultation; **3** (fait de prendre un avis) consulting; **après** ~ **des experts** after consulting the experts; ~ **électorale** election; ~ **juridique** legal consultation; **4** (délibération) consultation; **5** (de calendrier, livre, document) consultation; **'**~ **sur place'** (dans une bibliothèque) 'for reference use only'; **la** ~ **de l'annuaire n'a rien donné** we/they etc looked in the directory but in vain

consulter /kɔ̃sylte/ [1]
A *vtr* to consult [personne, ouvrage]; ~ **le peuple** to hold a general election
B *vi* Méd (recevoir les patients) to hold surgery GB, to see patients
C **se consulter** *vpr* **1** (échanger des vues) to consult together; **se** ~ **du regard** to exchange glances; **2** (être consultable) **'se consulte sur place'** 'for reference use only'

consumer /kɔ̃syme/ [1]
A *vtr* **1** (brûler) to consume [forêt]; **2** fig, liter **l'amour le consumait** he was consumed with love; **la maladie qui la consume** the illness which is eating away at her; **il a consumé son temps/sa vie en vains plaisirs** he wasted his time/his life in idle pleasures
B **se consumer** *vpr* **1** (brûler) to be burning; **la mèche devrait se** ~ **en quelques minutes** the fuse should burn out in a few minutes; **2** fig, liter to waste away; **se** ~ **d'amour** to be consumed with love (**pour** for); **se** ~ **en vains efforts** to weary oneself in vain efforts

contact /kɔ̃takt/ *nm* **1** (relation) contact ₵; **prendre** ~ **avec** to make contact with; **garder le** ~ to keep in touch; **entrer en** ~ **avec** to get in touch with; **avoir un bon** ~ **avec qn** to get on well with sb; **être d'un** ~ **agréable** to be easy to get on with; **elle est devenue plus sociable à ton** ~ she's become more sociable through spending time with you; **2** (toucher) contact; **3** Électrotech contact; **couper le** ~ Aut to switch off the ignition; ▸ **faux¹**; **4** (personne) contact

contacter /kɔ̃takte/ [1]
A *vtr* to contact
B **se contacter** *vpr* to get in touch with each other

contagieux, -**ieuse** /kɔ̃taʒjø, øz/ *adj* **1** Méd contagious; **2** fig [rire, enthousiasme] infectious, catching (jamais épith)

contagion /kɔ̃taʒjɔ̃/ *nf* **1** Méd contagion; **2** fig infectiousness; **craindre la** ~ **de certaines idées** to fear the spread of certain ideas

contamination /kɔ̃taminasjɔ̃/ *nf* contamination

contaminer /kɔ̃tamine/ [1] *vtr* gén to contaminate; [virus] to infect [personne]; to contaminate [programme]

conte /kɔ̃t/ *nm* **1** Littérat tale, story; ~ **de fées** fairy tale; **2** (racontar) story

contemplatif, -**ive** /kɔ̃tɑ̃platif, iv/ *adj* contemplative

contemplation /kɔ̃tɑ̃plasjɔ̃/ nf contemplation

contempler /kɔ̃tɑ̃ple/ [1]
A vtr **1** (du regard) to survey [spectacle]; to contemplate [paysage]; to look at [photo, vitrine]; **2** (par la pensée) to reflect on [théorie]
B se contempler vpr to gaze at oneself

contemporain, ~e /kɔ̃tɑ̃pɔʀɛ̃, ɛn/
A adj contemporary; **roman** ~ **de** novel contemporaneous with
B nm,f contemporary (**de** of)

contenance /kɔ̃t(ə)nɑ̃s/ nf **1** ▸ p. 87, p. 628 (volume) capacity; **2** (allure) bearing; **essayer de se donner une** ~ to try to appear composed; **perdre** ~ to lose one's composure; **faire bonne** ~ to keep an air of composure

contenant /kɔ̃t(ə)nɑ̃/ nm packaging

conteneur /kɔ̃t(ə)nœʀ/ nm container

contenir /kɔ̃t(ə)niʀ/ [36]
A vtr **1** to contain [substance, erreur]; **2** ▸ p. 87, p. 628 [tonneau] to hold [litre]; [salle] to accommodate [spectateur]; **3** to contain [foule, colère]
B se contenir vpr to contain oneself

content, ~e /kɔ̃tɑ̃, ɑ̃t/
A adj happy, pleased; **je suis** ~e **que tu sois là** I'm glad you're here; **il est toujours** ~ **de lui** he is always so self-satisfied; **non** ~ **de ne rien faire, il s'endette** not content with doing nothing, he is running up debts
B nm **(tout) son** ~ [manger, dormir] to one's heart's content; **avoir son** ~ **de** to have one's fill of

contentement /kɔ̃tɑ̃tmɑ̃/ nm contentment, satisfaction

contenter /kɔ̃tɑ̃te/ [1]
A vtr to satisfy [clientèle, curiosité]; **il est facile à** ~ he is easy to please
B se contenter vpr se ~ **de** to content oneself with; **je me contente de peu** I make do with very little; **il s'est contenté de rire** he just laughed

contentieux, -ieuse /kɔ̃tɑ̃sjø, øz/ Jur
A adj contentious
B nm inv **1** (litige) bone of contention; **2** (service) legal department; (affaires) litigation

contenu, ~e /kɔ̃t(ə)ny/
A adj [sentiment] restrained; [colère] suppressed
B nm **1** (de récipient) contents (pl); **2** (d'œuvre) content

conter /kɔ̃te/ [1] vtr liter to tell [histoire]; to recount [aventure]
(Idiome) **s'en laisser** ~ (une fois) to be taken in; (toujours) to be easily taken in

contestable /kɔ̃tɛstabl/ adj questionable

contestataire /kɔ̃tɛstatɛʀ/
A adj [mouvement, journal] anti-authority, anti-establishment; **étudiant** ~ student protester
B nmf protester

contestation /kɔ̃tɛstasjɔ̃/ nf **1** Pol (de pouvoir) protest (**de** against); (dans une organisation) dissent (**de** from); **2** (de véracité, droit) challenging (**de** of); **être sujet à** ~ to be questionable; **il y a sujet** or **matière à** ~ there are grounds for dispute ou contention; **sans** ~ **possible** beyond dispute

conteste: **sans conteste** /sɑ̃kɔ̃tɛst/ loc adv unquestionably

contesté, ~e /kɔ̃tɛste/ adj controversial

contester /kɔ̃tɛste/ [1]
A vtr to question [authenticité, décision, nécessité]; to contest [droit, testament]; to dispute [chiffre, frontière]; to challenge [impôt, projet]
B vi **1** (ne pas être d'accord) to raise objections; **2** (faire de l'opposition) to protest

conteur, -euse /kɔ̃tœʀ, øz/ nm,f storyteller

contexte /kɔ̃tɛkst/ nm **1** Ling, fig context (**de** of); **2** (conjoncture) situation

contigu, -uë /kɔ̃tigy/ adj [pièces, jardins] adjoining

contiguïté /kɔ̃tiguite/ nf contiguity sout

continence /kɔ̃tinɑ̃s/ nf continence, continency

continent, ~e /kɔ̃tinɑ̃, ɑ̃t/
A adj continent
B nm Géog **1** (partie du monde) continent; **2** (par opposition à une île) mainland

continental, ~e, mpl **-aux** /kɔ̃tinɑ̃tal, o/ adj gén continental; (par opposition à un territoire insulaire) mainland (épith)

contingence /kɔ̃tɛ̃ʒɑ̃s/
A nf Philos contingency
B contingences nfpl (faits imprévus) contingencies; (faits sans importance) trivial circumstances

contingent, ~e /kɔ̃tɛ̃ʒɑ̃, ɑ̃t/
A adj contingent
B nm **1** (groupe) contingent; Mil conscripts (pl), draft US; **soldat du** ~ conscript; **2** Comm, Écon quota; **3** Jur, fig (quote-part) share

contingenter /kɔ̃tɛ̃ʒɑ̃te/ [1] vtr (limiter) to fix a quota for [importations]; (répartir) to distribute [sth] using a quota system [matière première]

continu, ~e /kɔ̃tiny/
A adj continuous; **de façon** ~e continuously
B en continu loc adv [information] nonstop; [fabrication, travail] continuous

continuation /kɔ̃tinɥasjɔ̃/ nf continuation; **bonne** ~! all the best!

continuel, -elle /kɔ̃tinɥɛl/ adj continual

continuellement /kɔ̃tinɥɛlmɑ̃/ adv continually

continuer /kɔ̃tinɥe/ [1]
A vtr to carry on, to continue [combat, conversation]; to continue [études, voyage]
B vi to continue, to go on; **c'est un bon début, continuez!** it's a good start, keep it up!

continuité /kɔ̃tinɥite/ nf continuity

continûment /kɔ̃tinymɑ̃/ adv continuously

contondant, ~e /kɔ̃tɔ̃dɑ̃, ɑ̃t/ adj [arme] blunt

contorsion /kɔ̃tɔʀsjɔ̃/ nf lit, fig contortion

contorsionner: se contorsionner /kɔ̃tɔʀsjone/ [1] vpr [personne] to tie oneself in knots; (pour se dégager) to wriggle and writhe; [serpent] to writhe

contorsionniste /kɔ̃tɔʀsjonist/ ▸ p. 372 nmf contortionist

contour /kɔ̃tuʀ/
A nm (d'objet, de montagne, bouche, dessin) outline; (de corps, visage, paysage) contour; (de meuble) line
B contours nmpl (méandres) twists and turns

contourner /kɔ̃tuʀne/ [1] vtr to by-pass [ville]; to skirt (around) [colline]; to get round [difficulté]

contraceptif, -ive /kɔ̃tʀasɛptif, iv/
A adj contraceptive
B nm contraceptive

contraception /kɔ̃tʀasɛpsjɔ̃/ nf contraception; ~ **orale** (moyen) oral contraception; (pilule) oral contraceptive

contractant, ~e /kɔ̃tʀaktɑ̃, ɑ̃t/
A adj contracting
B nm,f contracting party

contracter /kɔ̃tʀakte/ [1]
A vtr **1** to contract, to tense [muscle]; to tense [visage]; **une grimace contracta sa bouche** or **ses traits** he/she grimaced; **l'émotion lui contracta la gorge** his/her throat tightened with emotion; **2** Ling to contract [forme]; **3** (s'engager dans) to incur [dette]; to conclude [marché]; to take out [emprunt]; to enter into [engagement]; to form [amitié]; **4** Méd to contract [maladie]
B se contracter vpr **1** [muscle] to contract; [visage, personne] to tense up; [gorge] to tighten; **2** Phys [substance] to contract; **3** Ling [forme] (éventuellement) to contract; (obligatoirement) to be contracted

contraction /kɔ̃tʀaksjɔ̃/ nf **1** (état) tenseness; (spasme) contraction; **2** Ling, Phys contraction

contractuel, -elle /kɔ̃tʀaktɥɛl/
A adj **1** Jur [obligation] contractual; **2** Admin [personnel] contract (épith)
B nm,f **1** (employé) contract employee; **2** ▸ p. 372 (contrôlant le stationnement) traffic warden GB, meter reader US

contracture /kɔ̃tʀaktyʀ/ nf **1** (de muscle) contracture, spasm; **2** Archit contracture

contradiction /kɔ̃tʀadiksjɔ̃/ nf contradiction; **être en** ~ **avec** to contradict [personne, principe]; **il ne supporte pas la** ~ he can't bear to be contradicted

contradictoire /kɔ̃tʀadiktwaʀ/ adj [idée, témoignage] contradictory; **être** ~ **à** to be in contradiction to

contraignant, ~e /kɔ̃tʀɛɲɑ̃, ɑ̃t/ adj restrictive

contraindre /kɔ̃tʀɛ̃dʀ/ [54]

A *vtr* **1** (obliger) **être contraint au repos** to be forced *ou* compelled to rest; **je me vois contraint de démissionner** I have no option but to resign; **2** (réprimer) to restrain [*sentiments, désir*]; to curb [*goût*]

B se contraindre *vpr* **1** (se forcer) **se ~ à** to force oneself to; **2** (se contenir) *liter* to exercise self-control

contraint, **~e**[1] /kɔ̃tʀɛ̃, ɛ̃t/ *adj* **1** (obligé) **~ et forcé** *Jur* under duress; **2** (gêné) [*air*] strained; [*sourire*] forced

contrainte[2] /kɔ̃tʀɛ̃t/ *nf* **1** (pression) pressure; (coercition) coercion; **par la ~** forcibly prevented; **sous la ~** under duress; **2** (exigence) constraint; **3** (gêne) strain; **sans ~** without restraint

contraire /kɔ̃tʀɛʀ/

A *adj* **1** [*effet, sens, décision*] opposite; *Naut* [*vent*] contrary; (en conflit) [*avis, intérêts*] conflicting (**à** with); [*forces*] opposite (**à** to); **être ~ aux usages** to be contrary to custom; **dans le cas ~** (should it be) otherwise *sout*; **sauf avis ~** unless otherwise informed; **2** (défavorable) [*destin, force*] adverse; **le sort leur fut ~** fate was against them

B *nm* **le ~** the opposite (**de** of); **je pense (tout) le ~** I take the opposite view; **ne dites pas le ~** don't deny it; **au ~ de tes amis** unlike your friends; **dire tout et son ~** to keep contradicting oneself

contrairement /kɔ̃tʀɛʀmɑ̃/ *adv* **à ce qu'on pourrait penser** contrary to what one might think; **~ à qn/à la France** unlike sb/France

contralto[1] /kɔ̃tʀalto/ ▸ p. 98 *nm* (voix) contralto

contralto[2] ▸ p. 98 *nf* (femme) contralto

contrariant, **~e** /kɔ̃tʀaʀjɑ̃, ɑ̃t/ *adj* **1** [*personne*] contrary (*jamais épith*); **il n'est pas ~** he is accommodating; **2** [*événement*] annoying

contrarier /kɔ̃tʀaʀje/ [2] *vtr* **1** (chagriner) to upset; (fâcher) to annoy; **2** (contrecarrer) to frustrate, to thwart [*projet*]; to hinder [*progression*]; **~ un gaucher** to make a lefthanded person write with his/her right hand

contrariété /kɔ̃tʀaʀjete/ *nf* upset; **éprouver une vive** *or* **grande ~** to feel very upset

contraste /kɔ̃tʀast/

A *nm* contrast; **faire ~ avec** to contrast with

B par contraste *loc adv* in contrast (**avec** with), by way of contrast

contrasté, **~e** /kɔ̃tʀaste/ *adj* **1** [*couleurs, périodes*] contrasting; **2** [*image, photo*] with good contrast (*épith, après n*); [*tableau*] with sharp contrasts (*épith, après n*); **3** *fig* [*résultats*] uneven; [*semaine, année*] of sharp contrasts (*épith, après n*)

contraster /kɔ̃tʀaste/ [1]

A *vtr* to contrast [*couleurs, motifs*]; to give contrast to [*photo*]

B *vi* to contrast (**avec** with)

contrat /kɔ̃tʀa/ *nm* (accord) contract, agreement; *Jur* (document) contract; *fig* (pacte) arrangement, understanding; **s'engager par ~ à** to contract to; **remplir son ~** to fulfil[GB] one's pledge

(Composés) **~ emploi solidarité, CES** *part-time work for the young unemployed*; **~ initiative emploi** *recruitment incentive*

contravention /kɔ̃tʀavɑ̃sjɔ̃/ *nf* **1** (amende) fine; (pour stationnement illicite) parking ticket; (pour excès de vitesse) speeding ticket; **dresser (une) ~ à qn** *gén* to fine sb; (pour stationnement illicite) to issue a parking ticket; **2** *Jur* (infraction) minor offence[GB]; **être en ~ (à la loi)** to be in breach of the law

contre[1] /kɔ̃tʀ/

A *prép* **1** (marquant un contact entre personnes) **viens ~ moi** come to me; **ils étaient couchés l'un ~ l'autre** they were lying close together; **2** (marquant l'opposition) against; **être seul ~ tous** to stand alone against everyone else; **on ne peut rien ~ ce genre de choses** there's nothing one can do about that kind of thing; **dix ~ un** ten to one; **230 voix ~ 110** 230 votes to 110; **Nantes ~ Sochaux** *Sport* Nantes versus Sochaux; **le procès Bedel ~ Caselli** the Bedel versus Caselli case

B *adv* **1** (marquant un contact) **il y a un mur et une échelle appuyée ~** there's a wall and a ladder leaning against it; **2** (marquant l'opposition) **la majorité a voté ~** the majority voted against it

C par contre *loc adv* on the other hand

contre[2] /kɔ̃tʀ/ *nm* **1** (d'opposition) **le pour et le ~** the pros and cons (*pl*); **2** *Sport* counter-attack; **faire un ~ ~** to counter-attack; **3** *Jeux* (au bridge) double

---

contre¹

En général la préposition *contre* se traduit par *against* lorsqu'elle sert à indiquer:

un contact entre des choses:

pousse le fauteuil contre le mur
= to push the armchair (up) against the wall

(Les expressions telles que *joue contre joue*, *pare-chocs contre pare-chocs*, *furieux contre* sont traitées sous l'élément principal, respectivement **joue**, **pare-chocs**, **furieux** etc.)

une opposition:

lutter/réagir/voter contre le racisme
= to fight/react/vote against racism

une défense:

s'assurer contre le vol
= to take out insurance against theft

se protéger contre une attaque
= to protect oneself against an attack

On aura toujours intérêt à consulter l'article de l'élément principal.

Lorsque *contre* sert à indiquer la proximité, il se traduit par *next to*:

leur jardin est contre le mien
= their garden is next to mine

Lorsque *contre* sert à indiquer un échange, il se traduit par *for*:

changer une chemise trop petite contre une plus grande
= to change a shirt which is too small for a larger one

Lorsque *contre* sert à indiquer une comparaison, il se traduit par *as against*:

22% contre 10% le mois dernier
= 22% as against 10% last month

On trouvera ci-dessous d'autres exemples de *contre* dans ses diverses fonctions.

---

contre-accusation, *pl* **~s** /kɔ̃tʀakyzasjɔ̃/ *nf Jur* counter-charge

contre-allée, *pl* **~s** /kɔ̃tʀale/ *nf* (de route) service road; (de parc) side path; (d'église) side aisle

contre-amiral, *pl* **-aux** /kɔ̃tʀamiʀal, o/ ▸ p. 283 *nm* ≈ commodore

contre-attaque, *pl* **~s** /kɔ̃tʀatak/ *nf* counter-attack

contre-autopsie, *pl* **~s** /kɔ̃tʀotɔpsi/ *nf* second autopsy

contrebalancer /kɔ̃tʀəbalɑ̃se/ [12]

A *vtr* **1** (faire équilibre à) to counterbalance [*poids, force*]; **2** (compenser) to offset [*importance, influence*]

B se contrebalancer *vpr* **1** (s'équilibrer) to counterbalance each other; **2** ○(se moquer de) **se ~ de qch** not to give a damn○ about

contrebande /kɔ̃tʀəbɑ̃d/ *nf* **1** (activité) smuggling; **faire de la ~ de vodka** to smuggle vodka; **la ~ d'armes** gunrunning; **sortir qch en ~** (dans un pays) to smuggle sth out of the country; **2** (marchandises) smuggled goods (*pl*)

contrebandier, **-ière** /kɔ̃tʀəbɑ̃dje, ɛʀ/ *nm,f* smuggler

contrebas: **en contrebas** /ɑ̃kɔ̃tʀəba/ *loc adv* (down) below; **en ~ de** (de montagne, hauteur) at the foot of; **la maison est en ~ de la route** the house is at a lower level than the road

contrebasse /kɔ̃tʀəbas/ *nf* **1** ▸ p. 389 (instrument) double bass; upright bass US; **2** ▸ p. 372 (musicien) double bass player

contrebasson /kɔ̃tʀəbasɔ̃/ *nm* **1** ▸ p. 389 (instrument) contrabassoon; **2** ▸ p. 372 (musicien) contrabassoon player

contrecarrer /kɔ̃tʀəkaʀe/ [1] *vtr* to thwart, to foil [*effort, projet*]; to counteract [*influence, décision*]

contrechamp /kɔ̃tʀəʃɑ̃/ nm (prise de vue) reverse angle; (plan) reverse shot

contrecœur: à **contrecœur** /kɔ̃tʀəkœʀ/ loc adv [donner, prêter] grudgingly, reluctantly; [travailler, accepter] reluctantly

contrecoup /kɔ̃tʀəku/ nm (conséquences) effects (pl); **le ~ d'une opération** the after-effects of an operation; **par ~** as a result

contre-courant, pl **~s** /kɔ̃tʀəkuʀɑ̃/ nm counter-current; **nager à ~** to swim against the current; **aller à ~ de la mode** to go against the fashion

contredanse /kɔ̃tʀədɑ̃s/ nf [1] ○parking ticket; [2] (danse) contredanse

contredire /kɔ̃tʀədiʀ/ [65]
A vtr [1] (dire le contraire) to contradict; [2] (démentir) [personne, fait, déclaration] to contradict, to belie [témoignage, thèse]; [document] to belie [témoignage, résultat]
B **se contredire** vpr [1] (soi-même) to contradict oneself; [2] (l'un l'autre) [personnes] to contradict each other; [témoignages] to conflict

contrée /kɔ̃tʀe/ nf [1] (pays) liter land, clime littér; **des ~s lointaines** far-off lands; [2] (région) region

contre-enquête, pl **~s** /kɔ̃tʀɑ̃kɛt/ nf second enquiry GB, second inquiry US

contre-espionnage, pl **~s** /kɔ̃tʀɛspjɔnaʒ/ nm [1] (lutte) counter-intelligence; [2] (organisation) counter-intelligence service

contre-exemple, pl **~s** /kɔ̃tʀɛgzɑ̃pl/ nm exception, counter-example

contre-expertise, pl **~s** /kɔ̃tʀɛkspɛʀtiz/ nf second opinion

contrefaçon /kɔ̃tʀəfasɔ̃/ nf [1] (action) de signature, billet, carte de crédit) forging; (de pièces) counterfeiting; (d'invention, enregistrement) pirating; (de brevet) infringement; [2] (résultat) (signature, billet, gravure) forgery; (pièce, montre) counterfeit; (enregistrement, édition) pirated copy

contrefacteur /kɔ̃tʀəfaktœʀ/ nm (de billets, cartes de crédit, tableau) forger; (de pièces) counterfeiter; (de logiciels, signatures, inventions) pirate

contrefaire /kɔ̃tʀəfɛʀ/ [10] vtr [1] Comm, Jur (falsifier) to forge [signature, billet, carte de crédit]; to counterfeit [pièce, montre]; to pirate [invention, enregistrement]; to infringe [brevet]; [2] (imiter) to imitate [personne, voix]; [3] (déguiser) to disguise [voix, écriture]

contreficher○: **se contreficher** /kɔ̃tʀəfiʃe/ [1] vpr not to give a damn○ (**de** about; **que** it)

contrefort /kɔ̃tʀəfɔʀ/ nm [1] Géog foothills (pl); [2] Archit buttress; [3] (de chaussure) back, counter spéc

contre-indication, pl **~s** /kɔ̃tʀɛ̃dikasjɔ̃/ nf contra-indication

contre-indiqué, **~e**, mpl **~s** /kɔ̃tʀɛ̃dike/ adj [médicament] contraindicated; [activité] inadvisable

contre-interrogatoire, pl **~s** /kɔ̃tʀɛ̃tɛʀɔgatwaʀ/ nm cross-examination

contre-jour, pl **~s** /kɔ̃tʀəʒuʀ/ nm Phot, Cin [1] (effet) backlighting; **à ~** against ou into the light; [2] (photo) contre-jour ou back-lit photograph

contremaître, **-esse** /kɔ̃tʀəmɛtʀ, kɔ̃tʀəmɛtʀɛs/ ▸ p. 372 nm,f foreman/forewoman

contremarque /kɔ̃tʀəmaʀk/ nf [1] Théât, Cin pass (for re-entry into theatre); [2] (dans les transports) voucher showing that the bearer is travellingGB on a group ticket; [3] Admin, Comm counterseal

contre-offensive, pl **~s** /kɔ̃tʀɔfɑ̃siv/ nf counter-offensive

contrepartie /kɔ̃tʀəpaʀti/ nf [1] (équivalent) equivalent (**en** in); [2] (contrepoids) **c'est la ~ de la liberté** it is the price you have to pay for freedom; **mais la ~ est que le salaire est élevé** but this is offset by the high salary; [3] (dédommagement) compensation; **en ~** (en compensation) in compensation (**de** for); (en échange) in return (**de** for)

contrepet /kɔ̃tʀəpɛ/ nm, **contrepèterie** /kɔ̃tʀəpɛtʀi/ nf (deliberate) spoonerism

contre-pied, pl **~s** /kɔ̃tʀəpje/ nm [1] fig **prendre le ~ de ce que dit qn** (en paroles) to say the opposite of what sb says (**de** about, on); [2] Sport **prendre qn à ~** to wrong-foot sb

contreplaqué /kɔ̃tʀəplake/ nm plywood

contre-plongée, pl **~s** /kɔ̃tʀəplɔ̃ʒe/ nf low-angle shot

contrepoids /kɔ̃tʀəpwa/ nm [1] lit, fig counterweight, counterbalance; **faire ~** to act as a counterbalance; **faire ~ à qch** lit, fig to counterbalance sth; [2] (de funambule) balancing pole

contrepoint /kɔ̃tʀəpwɛ̃/ nm counterpoint

contrepoison /kɔ̃tʀəpwazɔ̃/ nm lit, fig antidote

contre-pouvoir, pl **~s** /kɔ̃tʀəpuvwaʀ/ nm forces (pl) of opposition

contre-publicité /kɔ̃tʀəpyblisite/ nf adverse publicity

contrer /kɔ̃tʀe/ [1]
A vtr [1] (se dresser contre) to counter [armée, délinquance]; to fend off [concurrent, opposition]; to combat [agressivité]; to oppose [parti]; to block [initiative]; [2] Sport to block [adversaire]
B vi Jeux (aux cartes) to double

Contre-Réforme /kɔ̃tʀəʀefɔʀm/ nf Counter-Reformation

contre-révolution, pl **~s** /kɔ̃tʀəʀevɔlysjɔ̃/ nf counter-revolution

contrescarpe /kɔ̃tʀɛskaʀp/ nf counterscarp

contresens /kɔ̃tʀəsɑ̃s/ nm [1] (erreur) misinterpretation; (en traduisant) mistranslation; **faire un ~ sur qch** to misinterpret ou misconstrue sth; [traducteur] to mistranslate sth; [2] (absurdité) aberration; [3] (sens contraire) **à ~** [rouler, avancer] in the opposite direction; (dans le mauvais sens) the wrong way; [raboter] against the grain

contretemps /kɔ̃tʀətɑ̃/ nm inv [1] (difficulté) setback, contretemps sout; [2] Mus syncopation; **à ~** lit [jouer] gén on the off-beat; (par erreur) out of time; fig [agir, parler, intervenir] at the wrong moment

contre-terrorisme, pl **~s** /kɔ̃tʀətɛʀɔʀism/ nm counter-terrorism

contre-ut, pl **~(s)** /kɔ̃tʀyt/ nm high C

contre-valeur, pl **~s** /kɔ̃tʀəvalœʀ/ nf Fin exchange value

contrevenir /kɔ̃tʀəvəniʀ/ [36] vtr ind **~ à** to contravene

contre-vérité, pl **~s** /kɔ̃tʀəveʀite/ nf untruth

contre-voie, pl **~s** /kɔ̃tʀəvwɑ/ nf **descendre à ~** to get out on the wrong side of the track

contribuable /kɔ̃tʀibɥabl/ nmf taxpayer

contribuer /kɔ̃tʀibɥe/ [1] vtr ind **~ à** to contribute to; **cela y a beaucoup contribué** it was a major factor; **~ aux dépenses** to pay one's share of the expenses

contribution /kɔ̃tʀibysjɔ̃/
A nf (participation) contribution; **mettre qn à ~** to call upon sb's services
B **contributions** nfpl [1] (impôts) (à l'État) taxes; (à la commune) local taxes; **~ directes** direct taxes; [2] (bureau) tax office (sg)

contrit, **~e** /kɔ̃tʀi, it/ adj contrite, apologetic; **d'un air ~** apologetically

contrôlable /kɔ̃tʀolabl/ adj [1] (maîtrisable) [situation, coût, variable, maladie] controllable; [2] (pouvant être surveillé) which can be monitored (après n); **difficilement ~** difficult to monitor (après n)

contrôle /kɔ̃tʀol/ nm [1] (maîtrise) control (**de** of; **sur** over); **prendre/perdre le ~** to take/lose control; **prendre le ~ de** Fin to take a controlling interest in; **dispositif de ~** control mechanism; [2] Admin check; **~ de police/sécurité** police/security check; **~ des billets** ticket inspection; **~ douanier** customs control; [3] Fin audit; [4] (suivi) monitoring *𝒞*; [5] Scol, Univ test; **~ de géographie** geography test; [6] Méd check-up; **sous ~ médical** under medical supervision

(Composés) **~ antidopage** dope test; **~ des changes** exchange controls (pl); **~ des connaissances** assessment; **~ continu (des connaissances)** continuous assessment; **~ fiscal** tax investigation; **~ d'identité** identity check; **~ judiciaire** legal restrictions (pl) pending trial; **~ des naissances** birth control; **~ des passeports** passport control; **~ sanitaire** health control; **~ de soi** Psych self-control; **~ technique (des véhicules)** Aut MOT (test) GB

contrôler /kɔ̃tʀole/ [1]
A vtr [1] (exercer son autorité sur) to control [pays, organisation]; [2] (maîtriser) to control [prix, tremblement, ballon]; [3] (superviser) to monitor [opération]; [4] (vérifier) [inspecteur] to check [identité, billet]; [douanier] to inspect [bagage];

[comptable] to audit [comptes]; [contrôleur] to inspect [comptes]; [percepteur] to check [déclaration d'impôt]; [employé] to test [produit]; [chercheur] to verify [résultat]; [conducteur] to check [huile]; ~ **que** to make sure that

B **se contrôler** vpr (se maîtriser) to control oneself

contrôleur, -euse /kɔ̃trolœʀ, øz/ ▸ p. 372 nm,f gén inspector; ~ **aérien** air-traffic controller

contrordre /kɔ̃tʀɔʀdʀ/ nm ① gén **une série d'ordres et de** ~**s** a series of conflicting orders; **sauf** ~ unless I/you etc hear to the contrary; ② Mil counter command

controverse /kɔ̃tʀɔvɛʀs/ nf controversy (**sur** about)

controversé, ~e /kɔ̃tʀɔvɛʀse/ adj controversial

contumace /kɔ̃tymas/ nf par ~ in absentia

contusion /kɔ̃tyzjɔ̃/ nf bruise, contusion spéc

contusionner /kɔ̃tyzjɔne/ [1] vtr to bruise

convaincant, ~e /kɔ̃vɛ̃kɑ̃, ɑ̃t/ adj ① (concluant) convincing; ② (persuasif) persuasive; ③ Sport [tactique] impressive

convaincre /kɔ̃vɛ̃kʀ/ [57]
A vtr ① to convince [incrédule] (**de** of; **que** that); to persuade [indécis] (**de faire** to do); **je ne suis pas convaincu** I remain to be convinced; **se laisser** ~ to let oneself be persuaded; (à tort) to allow oneself to be persuaded; ② Jur to prove [sb] guilty (**de** of)
B **se convaincre** vpr to convince oneself (**de** of)

convaincu, ~e /kɔ̃vɛ̃ky/ adj (résolu) [partisan] staunch; **d'un ton** ~ with conviction

convalescence /kɔ̃valesɑ̃s/ nf convalescence; **être en** ~ to be convalescing; **sortir de** ~ to finish convalescing

convalescent, ~e /kɔ̃valesɑ̃, ɑ̃t/ adj, nm,f convalescent

convecteur /kɔ̃vɛktœʀ/ nm convector heater

convenable /kɔ̃vnabl/ adj ① (approprié) suitable; ② (acceptable) [résultat, salaire, travail] reasonable, decent; [vin, repas] acceptable, decent; **tout juste** ~ barely acceptable; ③ (bienséant) [vêtement] decent; [conduite, manières] proper; **pas** ~ [vêtement] inappropriate; ④ (respectable) [gens, famille] respectable

convenablement /kɔ̃vnabləmɑ̃/ adv ① (sans erreur) [fonctionner, s'exprimer] properly; ② (de façon acceptable) [manger, travailler, payer] reasonably well; ③ (de façon appropriée) [vêtu] properly; ④ (sans choquer) [se vêtir] decently; [se conduire] properly

convenance /kɔ̃vnɑ̃s/
A nf **pour** ~ **personnelle** for personal reasons; **lundi ou mardi, à votre** ~ on Monday or Tuesday, at your convenience
B **convenances** nfpl (bienséance) (social) conventions; **respecter les** ~**s** to respect convention ou the conventions; **par souci des** ~**s** for propriety's sake

convenir /kɔ̃vniʀ/ [36]
A vtr ① (concéder) to admit (**que** that); ② (s'entendre) to agree (**que** that)
B **convenir à** vtr ind ▸ **à** to suit [personne, goût]; to be suitable for [circonstance, activité]; **si cela vous convient** if it suits you; **c'est tout à fait ce qui me convient** it's exactly what I need; **de la taille qui convient** of a suitable size; **de la façon qui convient** in the appropriate manner; **l'homme qui convient** the right man
C **convenir de** vtr ind ① (reconnaître) ~ **de** to admit, to acknowledge [faute]; to acknowledge [qualité] ; **j'en conviens** I accept that; ② (s'accorder sur) ~ **de** [personnes] to agree on [date, prix]; ~ **de faire** to agree to do
D **se convenir** vpr [personnes] (être assortis) to be well suited
E v impers ① (il est sage, correct, nécessaire) **il convient de faire** one should do ou ought to do; **il convient que vous fassiez** you should do ou ought to do; ② (il est entendu) fml **il est convenu que** it is agreed that; **ce qu'il est convenu d'appeler le réalisme** what is commonly called realism

convention /kɔ̃vɑ̃sjɔ̃/
A nf ① (accord, contrat) gén agreement; (officiel) covenant; (entre nations) convention; (clause) article, clause; ② (usage admis) convention; **de** ~ conventional; ③ (assemblée) Pol convention
B **conventions** nfpl (convenances) convention **C**

(Composés) ~ **collective** cf collective labour GB agreement; **Convention nationale** Hist National Convention

conventionné, ~e /kɔ̃vɑ̃sjone/ adj [clinique] registered; **médecin** ~ doctor approved by the Department of Health

(whose fees are refunded); **médecin non** ~ private doctor; **les tarifs** ~**s** charges approved by the French Health Department

conventionnel, -elle /kɔ̃vɑ̃sjɔnɛl/ adj ① gén conventional; **armes non conventionnelles** nonconventional weapons; ② Jur [clause] contractual

convenu, ~e /kɔ̃v(ə)ny/
A pp ▸ **convenir**
B pp adj ① (décidé) [date, prix, termes] agreed; ② (conventionnel) [expression, tour] conventional; [sourire] polite, forced

convergence /kɔ̃vɛʀʒɑ̃s/ nf ① (d'idées, intérêts, de politiques) convergence; **la** ~ **des volontés a permis de...** a joint effort of will has made it possible to...; ② (de faisceaux lumineux, lentille) convergence; (de chemins) meeting; ③ Math convergence

convergent, ~e /kɔ̃vɛʀʒɑ̃, ɑ̃t/ adj convergent

converger /kɔ̃vɛʀʒe/ [13] vi ① [chemins, véhicules, personnes] to converge (**vers** on); ② fig **nos réflexions convergent vers les mêmes conclusions** our thoughts are leading us to the same conclusions; **nos opinions convergent** we're of the same opinion; ③ Math, Phys to converge

conversation /kɔ̃vɛʀsasjɔ̃/ nf conversation (**avec** with); **la** ~ **mondaine** or **de salon** polite conversation; **faire les frais de la** ~ (en être l'objet) to be the chief topic ou subject of conversation; (la mener) to do all the talking; **avoir de la** ~ to be a good conversationalist; **anglais de** ~ conversational English; **dans la** ~ **courante** in everyday ou ordinary speech

(Composé) ~ **à trois** Télécom three-way calling

converser /kɔ̃vɛʀse/ [1] vi to converse sout (**avec** with)

conversion /kɔ̃vɛʀsjɔ̃/ nf ① Relig, fig conversion (**à** to); ② (transformation) (d'entreprise) conversion (**en** into); (d'employé) re-training; ③ (de monnaie, dette) conversion (**en** into); ④ (de mesures, poids) conversion (**en** into); converting (**en** into); ⑤ Sport (en ski) kick-turn

converti, ~e /kɔ̃vɛʀti/
A pp ▸ **convertir**
B pp adj converted
C nm,f convert

(Idiome) **prêcher un** ~ to preach to the converted

convertible /kɔ̃vɛʀtibl/ adj ① Fin [devise] convertible (**en** into); ② Math, Ordinat convertible (**en** to); ③ (transformable) **canapé** ~ sofa-bed

convertir /kɔ̃vɛʀtiʀ/ [3]
A vtr ① (faire changer d'idée) to convert [personne, parti, gouvernement] (**à** to); ② (transformer) to convert [industrie, logements] (**en** into); ③ Fin to convert [devise, dette] (**en** into); ④ Math, Ordinat to convert [fractions, texte] (**en** to)
B **se convertir** vpr [personne] to convert, to become a convert (**à** to); [entreprise] to change products; **le pays doit se** ~ **au libéralisme** the country must adopt liberalism

convertisseur /kɔ̃vɛʀtisœʀ/ nm converter

convexe /kɔ̃vɛks/ adj convex

conviction /kɔ̃viksjɔ̃/
A nf ① (certitude) conviction; **avoir la** ~ **que** to be convinced that; ② (fougue, sérieux) conviction
B **convictions** nfpl (opinions) convictions

convier /kɔ̃vje/ [2] vtr ① (inviter) to invite [personne] (**à** to); ② (engager) to invite [personne] (**à faire** to do); to ask [population, entreprise] (**à faire** to do)

convive /kɔ̃viv/ nmf guest

convivial, ~e, mpl **-iaux** /kɔ̃vivjal, o/ adj ① [atmosphère, réunion] friendly; ② Ordinat user-friendly

convivialité /kɔ̃vivjalite/ nf ① (de personne) friendliness; (d'atmosphère, de réunion) warmth, conviviality; ② Ordinat user-friendliness

convocation /kɔ̃vɔkasjɔ̃/ nf ① (appel) (d'assemblée) convening, convocation sout; (d'individu) gén summoning; Mil (de réserviste) calling up; (pour entrevue) invitation; **se rendre à une** ~ gén to attend as instructed; Jur to obey a summons; **se présenter à un bureau sur** ~ Admin to call at an office after being requested to do so; ② (lettre) (ordre) gén notice to attend; Jur summons (+ sg); Mil call-up papers (pl); (invitation) invitation; ~ **aux examens** notification of examination timetables

convoi /kɔ̃vwa/ nm ① (de véhicules, troupes) convoy; '~ **exceptionnel**' Aut 'abnormal load'; ② Rail train; **un** ~ **de marchandises** a goods train

convoiter /kɔ̃vwate/ [1] vtr to covet

convoitise /kɔ̃vwatiz/ *nf* gén desire; (péché) covetousness; (ambition, gourmandise) greed; (concupiscence) lust; (cupidité) lust for money; **regarder qch avec ~** to cast covetous glances at sth; [*enfant*] to look longingly at sth

convoquer /kɔ̃vɔke/ [1] *vtr* ① (appeler à se réunir) to call, to convene [*réunion, assemblée*]; ② (appeler à se présenter) to send for [*élève*]; Jur to summon [*témoin*]; Mil to call [sb] up [*soldat, officier*]; **être convoqué à un examen** to be asked to attend an exam; **être convoqué pour un entretien** to be called for interview

convoyer /kɔ̃vwaje/ [23] *vtr* ① (escorter) to escort [*prisonnier, navires*]; (transporter) to transport [*or, marchandises*]; ② (jusqu'à son lieu d'utilisation) to ferry [*bateau, avion*]

convoyeur, -euse /kɔ̃vwajœʀ/
A ▸ p. 372 *nm,f* (de prisonnier) prison escort; (de marchandise) courier; **~ de fonds** security guard
B *nm* ① Ind conveyor; ② Naut **navire ~** escort ship

convulser /kɔ̃vylse/ [1] *fml vtr* (tordre) [*peur, douleur*] to convulse, to contort [*visage*]; to grip [*estomac*]

convulsif, -ive /kɔ̃vylsif, iv/ *adj* ① [*sanglots, mouvement*] convulsive; [*rire*] nervous; ② Méd [*toux, maladie*] convulsive

convulsion /kɔ̃vylsjɔ̃/ *nf* ① Méd convulsion; **être pris de ~s** to be seized by convulsions; ② Pol (troubles) convulsions (*pl*), turmoil **𝄐**

cool○ /kul/
A *adj inv* cool○, laidback○
B *adv* **s'habiller ~** to dress in a laidback○ way

coopérant /kɔɔpeʀɑ̃/ *nm: young man working abroad in lieu of military service*

coopérateur, -trice /kɔɔpeʀatœʀ, tʀis/
A *adj* cooperating
B *nm,f* ① (associé) collaborator; ② (membre d'une coopérative) member of a cooperative

coopératif, -ive /kɔɔpeʀatif, iv/
A *adj* cooperative
B *nf* (groupement) cooperative; (magasin) co-op

coopération /kɔɔpeʀasjɔ̃/ *nf* ① gén (collaboration) cooperation; **apporter sa ~ à un projet** to cooperate in a project; ② *programme of aid to developing countries*

coopérer /kɔɔpeʀe/ [14]
A **coopérer à** *vtr ind* **~ à** to cooperate (on *ou* in)
B *vi* to cooperate

coopter /kɔɔpte/ [1] *vtr* to co-opt [*personne*]

coordinateur, -trice /kɔɔʀdinatœʀ, tʀis/
A *adj* coordinating
B *nm,f* (personne) coordinator

coordination /kɔɔʀdinasjɔ̃/ *nf* ① gén coordination; ② (groupe) joint committee

coordonné, ~e /kɔɔʀdɔne/
A *adj* ① [*gestes, travail*] coordinated; [*vêtement*] coordinating (*épith*); ② Ling [*proposition*] coordinate
B **coordonnés** *nmpl* (vêtements) coordinates

coordonnées /kɔɔʀdɔne/ *nfpl* ① Géog, Math coordinates; ② (adresse) address and telephone number

coordonner /kɔɔʀdɔne/ [1] *vtr* to coordinate

copain○, **copine** /kɔpɛ̃, in/ *nm,f* (camarade) friend; (acolyte) pej crony; (amoureux) **son ~** her boyfriend; **sa copine** his girlfriend; **on sort en ~s** we go out as friends
(Composés) **~ de classe** school friend; **~ de régiment** old army buddy○
(Idiome) **être ~s comme cochons**○ to be as thick as thieves

coparentalité /kɔpaʀɑ̃talite/ *nf* co-parenting

copeau, *pl* **~x** /kɔpo/ *nm* ① (de bois, métal) shaving; **des ~x de bois** wood shavings; ② Culin **~x de chocolat** chocolate shavings

Copenhague /kɔpɛnag/ *npr* ▸ p. 621 Copenhagen

copie /kɔpi/ *nf* ① (de document, tableau, logiciel, film) copy; **être la ~ conforme de qn** to be the spitting image of sb; ② (duplication) copying **𝄐**; ③ Scol (feuille) sheet of paper; (devoir) paper; **ramasser les ~s** to collect the papers; ④ (en imprimerie) copy
(Composés) **~ certifiée conforme** Jur certified true copy; **~ de sauvegarde** Ordinat back-up copy
(Idiome) **revoir sa ~** to revise one's work

copier /kɔpje/ [2] *vtr* ① (transcrire) to copy [*lettre, texte*]; **vous copierez dix fois...** write out ten times...; ② (reproduire) to

copy [*tableau*]; ③ Scol **~ sur qn** to copy *ou* crib from sb [*voisin*]
(Idiome) **tu me la copieras (celle-là)**○! I'm not likely to forget that in a hurry!

copieur, -ieuse /kɔpjœʀ, øz/
A *nm,f* ① Scol cheat; ② (plagiaire) imitator
B *nm* photocopier

copieusement /kɔpjøzmɑ̃/ *adv* [*manger*] heartily, a lot; [*illustrer*] lavishly; [*annoter*] copiously; **il m'a servi ~** he gave me a generous portion; **un repas ~ arrosé** a meal with lots to drink; **se faire ~ disputer** hum to get well and truly told off

copieux, -ieuse /kɔpjø, øz/ *adj* [*repas*] substantial, hearty; [*portion*] generous; [*notes*] copious; [*rapport*] weighty, substantial

copilote /kɔpilɔt/ *nmf* ① Aviat, Naut co-pilot; ② Aut co-driver

copinage○ /kɔpinaʒ/ *nm* pej cronyism péj

copine ▸ copain

coprésidence /kɔpʀezidɑ̃s/ *nf* (d'association, de club) joint presidency; (de comité) joint chairmanship

coprésident /kɔpʀezidɑ̃/ *nm* (de société, d'association) joint president; (de comité, réunion) co-chair

coprésidente /kɔpʀezidɑ̃t/ *nf* (de société, d'association) joint president, co-president; (de comité, réunion) co-chair, co-chairwoman

coprévenu, ~e /kɔpʀevny/ *nm,f* co-defendant

coproducteur, -trice /kɔpʀɔdyktœʀ, tʀis/ *nm,f* co-producer

coproduction /kɔpʀɔdyksjɔ̃/ *nf* co-production

coproduire /kɔpʀɔdɥiʀ/ [69] *vtr* to co-produce

copropriétaire /kɔpʀɔpʀijetɛʀ/ *nmf* ① (dans un immeuble) owner (*of a flat in a jointly-owned building*); ② (de bien, cheval) joint owner, co-owner

copropriété /kɔpʀɔpʀijete/ *nf* (à deux) joint ownership; (à plus de deux) co-ownership; **posséder qch en ~** (à deux) to be joint owner of sth; (à plus de deux) to be co-owner of sth; **acheter qch en ~** to buy sth jointly with someone; **vendre des appartements en ~** to sell apartments in a block to individual buyers; **un immeuble en ~** a block of individually owned flats GB

copulation /kɔpylasjɔ̃/ *nf* copulation

copuler /kɔpyle/ [1] *vi* to copulate (**avec** with)

coq /kɔk/ *nm* ① (de poulailler) cockerel, rooster US; (oiseau mâle) cock; **au chant du ~** at cockcrow; **rouge comme un ~** [*personne*] bright red in the face; ② Culin cockerel; ③ Archit (de clocher) weathercock; ④ (séducteur) **le ~ du village** the local Casanova
(Composés) **~ de bruyère** grouse; **~ de combat** fighting cock; **~ au vin** coq au vin
(Idiomes) **être comme un ~ en pâte** to be in clover; **sauter du ~ à l'âne** to hop from one subject to another

coquard○, **coquart**○ /kɔkaʀ/ *nm* black eye

coque /kɔk/ *nf* ① Naut hull; ② Aviat (d'hydravion) fuselage; Aut (car) body; ③ Zool (coquillage) cockle; ④ (coquille) shell

coquelet /kɔklɛ/ *nm* young cockerel

coquelicot /kɔkliko/ *nm* poppy

coqueluche /kɔklyʃ/ *nf* ① ▸ p. 195 Méd whooping-cough, pertussis spéc; ② ○fig (chanteur, sportif) idol

coquet, -ette /kɔkɛ, ɛt/ *adj* ① [*personne*] (effet produit) well turned-out; (attitude) **être ~** to be particular about one's appearance; ② (plaisant) pretty; ③ ○[*somme*] tidy○ (*épith*); [*héritage*] substantial

coquetier /kɔktje/ *nm* eggcup

coquettement /kɔkɛtmɑ̃/ *adv* [*regarder*] coquettishly; [*s'habiller*] stylishly; [*meubler*] prettily

coquetterie /kɔkɛtʀi/ *nf* ① (souci de plaire) interest in one's appearance; (excessif) vanity; **s'habiller avec ~** to dress stylishly; **par ~** out of vanity; ② (envers les hommes) coquetry; ③ (maniérisme) affectation; **ses ~s** (minauderies) her coquettish ways
(Idiome) **avoir une ~ dans l'œil**○ to have a cast in one's eye

coquillage /kɔkijaʒ/ *nm* ① (mollusque) shellfish (*inv*); ② (coquille) shell

coquille /kɔkij/ *nf* ① (d'œuf, de noix, mollusque) shell; **poussin à peine sorti de sa ~** newly-hatched chick; ② Culin (ravier) scallop-shaped dish; (mets) **~ de saumon** scalloped salmon GB, salmon served in a shell US; ③ (en imprimerie) misprint; ④ Archit shell; (feston) scallop; ⑤ Sport box GB, cup US; ⑥ (d'épée) guard; ⑦ Méd (plâtre) spinal jacket

(**Composés**) **~ de beurre** butter curl; **~ Saint-Jacques** scallop; (écaille) scallop shell

coquillette /kɔkijɛt/ *nf* Culin small macaroni ¢; **des ~s** (small) macaroni

coquin, ~e /kɔkɛ̃, in/
A *adj* ① (espiègle) [*enfant, air*] mischievous; ② (osé) [*coup d'œil, film*] naughty, saucy
B *nm,f* (enfant) scamp; **petit ~!** you little monkey *ou* scamp!
C *nm* ‡(scélérat) scoundrel, rascal

cor /kɔʀ/ *nm* ① ▸ p. 389 Mus horn; **sonner** *ou* **donner du ~** to blow the horn; ② Méd corn; ③ Zool (de cerf) tine; **(cerf de) 6 ~s** 6-point stag, 6-pointer

(**Composés**) **~ anglais** cor anglais; **~ basset** basset horn; **~ de chasse** hunting horn; **~ d'harmonie** French horn; **~ à pistons** valve horn

(**Idiome**) **réclamer** *or* **demander qch à ~ et à cri** to clamour^GB for sth

corail, *pl* **-aux** /kɔʀaj, o/
A *adj inv* ① (couleur) coral(-pink)
B *nm* ① Zool coral; **une barrière de ~** a coral reef; ② (bijoux) coral; ③ Culin (de crustacé) coral

corallien, -ienne /kɔʀaljɛ̃, ɛn/ *adj* coral (épith)

Coran /kɔʀɑ̃/ *nm* **le ~** the Koran

coranique /kɔʀanik/ *adj* (loi) Koranic; [préceptes] of the Koran

corbeau, *pl* **-x** /kɔʀbo/ *nm* ① Zool crow; **grand ~** raven; **noir ~** raven black; ② ○(auteur de lettres anonymes) poison-pen letter writer; ③ ○(prêtre) offensive priest; ④ Archit corbel

corbeille /kɔʀbɛj/ *nf* ① (en vannerie, plastique) basket; (de bureau) tray; **une ~ en osier** a wicker basket; **une ~ de fleurs** a basket of flowers; ② Théât dress circle; ③ (à la Bourse) trading floor; ④ Archit bell

(**Composé**) **~ à papier** (à l'intérieur) (en osier) wastepaper basket; (en métal, en plastique) wastepaper bin

corbillard /kɔʀbijaʀ/ *nm* hearse

cordage /kɔʀdaʒ/ *nm* ① Naut (corde) rope; **~s** rigging ¢; ② (de raquette) stringing

corde /kɔʀd/ *nf* ① (câble, lien) rope; **à semelles de ~** rope-soled; ② (d'arc, de raquette) string; (pendaison) **la ~** hanging; ④ Sport **être à la ~** [coureur] to be on the inside; [cheval] to be on the rail; **prendre un virage à la ~** to hug a bend; ⑤ Mus (d'instrument) string; ⑥ (fil de chaîne) warp thread

(**Composés**) **~ à linge** clothes line; **~ lisse** Sport climbing rope; **~ à nœuds** Sport knotted (climbing) rope; **~ raide** lit, fig tightrope; **~ de rappel** Sport abseiling rope; **~s vocales** vocal chords

(**Idiomes**) **pleuvoir** *or* **tomber des ~s**○ to rain cats and dogs○; **tirer sur la ~** to push one's luck; **ce n'est pas dans mes ~s**○ it's not my line; **c'est juste dans tes ~s**○ it's just your sort of thing; **faire jouer la ~ sensible** to tug at the heartstrings; **quand la ~ est trop tendue, elle casse** Prov (d'une personne) if you push somebody too far, they'll snap; (d'une situation) if you allow a situation to reach a certain point, something's got to give; ▸ **pendu**

cordée /kɔʀde/ *nf* (en alpinisme) roped party (of climbers); **~ de secours** mountain rescue party; **premier de ~** leader

cordelette /kɔʀdəlɛt/ *nf* thin cord

cordelière /kɔʀdəljɛʀ/ *nf* (corde) cord

corder /kɔʀde/ [1] *vtr* ① Sport to string [raquette]; ② (lier) to tie up [sth] with rope [malle]

cordial, ~e, *mpl* **-iaux** /kɔʀdjal, o/
A *adj* [accueil, relations] cordial; [personne] warm-hearted; [sentiment] warm
B *nm* cordial

cordialement /kɔʀdjalmɑ̃/ *adv* warmly; **détester qn ~** to dislike sb heartily; **~ (vôtre** *or* **à vous)** (dans une lettre) yours sincerely

cordialité /kɔʀdjalite/ *nf* (de relations) warmth; (de personne) friendliness

cordillère /kɔʀdijɛʀ/ *nf* cordillera

(**Composé**) **la Cordillère des Andes** the Andes Cordillera

cordon /kɔʀdɔ̃/ *nm* ① (de rideau) cord; (de tablier, bourse, sac) string; (de chaussure) lace; **tenir les ~s de la bourse** fig to hold the purse-strings; ② (d'appareil électrique) flex GB, cord US; ③ (ligne) (d'agents, de troupes) cordon; (d'arbres) row; ④ Anat cord; ⑤ (décoration) (ruban) ribbon; (écharpe) sash

(**Composé**) **~ ombilical** umbilical cord

cordonnerie /kɔʀdɔnʀi/ ▸ p. 372 *nf* ① (fabrication) shoe-making; ② (réparation) shoe repairing; ③ (boutique) cobbler's

cordonnet /kɔʀdɔnɛ/ *nm* ① (fil solide) buttonhole thread; ② (petit cordon) thin cord

cordonnier /kɔʀdɔnje/ ▸ p. 372 *nm* cobbler

(**Idiome**) **les ~s sont toujours les plus mal chaussés** Prov it's always the baker's children who have no bread Prov

Corée /kɔʀe/ ▸ p. 230 *nprf* Korea; **République démocratique populaire de ~** Democratic People's Republic of Korea

coréen, -éenne /kɔʀeɛ̃, ɛn/ ▸ p. 336, p. 392
A *adj* Korean
B *nm* Ling Korean

coresponsabilité /kɔʀɛspɔ̃sabilite/ *nf* shared responsibility

Corfou /kɔʀfu/ ▸ p. 621 *npr* Corfu

coriace /kɔʀjas/ *adj* tough

coriandre /kɔʀjɑ̃dʀ/ *nf* coriander

Corinthe /kɔʀɛ̃t/ ▸ p. 621 *npr* Corinth; **raisins de ~** currants

corinthien, -ienne /kɔʀɛ̃tjɛ̃, ɛn/
A ▸ p. 621 *adj* Corinthian
B *nm* Archit **le ~** the Corinthian order

corne /kɔʀn/ *nf* ① (de vache, chamois etc, d'escargot) horn; (de cerf) antler; **animal à ~s** horned animal; **donner un coup de ~ à qn** to butt sb; **blesser qn d'un coup de ~** to gore sb; ▸ **taureau**; ② (substance) horn; ③ ▸ p. 389 (instrument) horn; ④ (de chapeau) point; ⑤ ○(peau durcie) **avoir de la ~ aux pieds** to have calluses on one's feet

(**Composés**) **~ d'abondance** horn of plenty, cornucopia; **~ de brume** Naut foghorn

(**Idiomes**) **faire les ~s à qn** to jeer at sb (with a gesture of the hand); **hou les ~s!** (dit par un enfant) you're no good!; hum shame on you!; **avoir** *or* **porter des ~s** to be a cuckold†

cornée /kɔʀne/ *nf* cornea

corneille /kɔʀnɛj/ *nf* crow

cornemuse /kɔʀnəmyz/ ▸ p. 389 *nf* bagpipes (pl)

corner /kɔʀne/ [1]
A *vtr* (plier) to turn down the corner of [page]; **page cornée** dog-eared page
B *vi* ① (conducteur) to hoot GB, to honk; ② (sonneur) to blow a horn

cornet /kɔʀnɛ/ *nm* ① (emballage conique) (paper) cone; **un ~ de dragées** a cornet of sugared almonds; ② Culin (pâtisserie) horn; (pour glace) cone; ③ Mus (d'orgue) cornet stop; (petit cor) post horn

(**Composés**) **~ acoustique** ear trumpet; **~ à dés** dice cup; **~ à pistons** cornet

cornette /kɔʀnɛt/ *nf* (de religieuse) cornet, wimple

cornettiste /kɔʀnɛtist/ ▸ p. 372 *nmf* cornet player, cornetist

corniaud /kɔʀnjo/ *nm* (chien) mongrel

corniche /kɔʀniʃ/ *nf* ① (de bâtiment) cornice; (de meuble) moulding GB, molding US, beading; (de plafond) coving; ② Géog (escarpement) ledge (of rock); **(route en) ~** cliff road

cornichon /kɔʀniʃɔ̃/ *nm* ① Bot, Culin gherkin; ② ○(idiot) nitwit○

cornière /kɔʀnjɛʀ/ *nf* ① (de tuiles) valley; ② (équerre) angle iron

Cornouailles /kɔʀnuaj/ ▸ p. 504 *nprf* Cornwall

cornu, ~e¹ /kɔʀny/ *adj* [animal] horned

cornue² /kɔʀny/ *nf* retort

corollaire /kɔʀɔlɛʀ/ *nm* corollary

corolle /kɔʀɔl/ *nf* Bot corolla; **en ~** [jupe] flared; [vase] flower-shaped

Le corps humain

■ *L'anglais utilise souvent l'adjectif possessif avec les noms des parties du corps, là où le français utilise l'article défini.*

fermer les yeux
= to close one's eyes

je me suis frotté les mains
= I rubbed my hands

il a levé la main
= he put his hand up

elle se tenait la tête
= she was holding her head

il s'est cassé le nez
= he broke his nose

elle lui a cassé le nez
= she broke his nose

────────────────────

Pour décrire les gens

■ *La tournure française avec* avoir (il a le nez long) *peut se traduire en anglais par une tournure avec* to be (his nose is long), *ou par une tournure avec* to have (he has a long nose).

il a les mains sales
= his hands are dirty *ou* he has dirty hands

il a mal aux pieds
= his feet are sore *ou* he has sore feet

il a le nez qui coule
= his nose is running *ou* he has a runny nose

il a les cheveux longs
= his hair is long *ou* he has long hair

elle a les yeux bleus
= she has blue eyes *ou* her eyes are blue

elle a de beaux cheveux
= she has beautiful hair *ou* her hair is beautiful

■ *Noter aussi:*

l'homme avec une jambe cassée
= the man with a broken leg

l'homme à la jambe cassée
= the man with the broken leg

la fille aux yeux bleus
= the girl with blue eyes

■ *Noter enfin que les tournures anglaises suivantes ne peuvent être utilisées que pour décrire des caractéristiques durables:*

la fille aux yeux bleus
= the blue-eyed girl

ceux qui ont de longs cheveux
= long-haired people

■ *Pour la taille des personnes* ▸ **p. 575;** *pour le poids* ▸ **p. 453;** *pour la couleur des yeux, des cheveux* ▸ **p. 140;** *pour les maladies et douleurs* ▸ **p. 195.**

---

coron /kɔrɔ̃/ *nm* miners' terraced houses (*pl*)

coronaire /kɔrɔnɛr/ *adj* [*artère, veine*] coronary

coronarien, -ienne /kɔrɔnarjɛ̃, ɛn/ *adj* coronary

corporatif, -ive /kɔrpɔratif, iv/ *adj* corporate (*épith*)

corporation /kɔrpɔrasjɔ̃/ *nf* [1] gén corporation; [2] Jur corporate body, body corporate; [3] Hist guild

corporatisme /kɔrpɔratism/ *nm* corporatism

corporel, -elle /kɔrpɔrɛl/ *adj* [1] (du corps) [*besoin, fonction*] bodily; [*température, lotion, soin*] body; [*châtiment*] corporal; [2] Jur (matériel) corporeal

corps /kɔr/ *nm inv* [1] Anat body; ~ **humain** human body; **qu'est-ce qu'elle a dans le ~?** fig what has got GB *ou* gotten US into her?; **(combat)** ~ **à** ~ hand-to-hand combat; **lutter (au)** ~ **à** ~ to fight hand to hand; **passer sur le** ~ **de qn** fig to trample sb underfoot; [2] Sociol (groupe) body; (profession) profession; ~ **d'ingénieurs** body of engineers; ~ **enseignant** teaching profession; **le** ~ **électoral** the electorate; **faire** ~ **avec** (avec sa famille, un groupe) to stand solidly behind; (avec la nature) to be at one with; [3] Mil corps; ~ **d'armée** army corps; ~ **expéditionnaire** expeditionary force; [4] (de doctrine, texte) body; [5] Tech (partie principale) (d'instrument, de machine) body; (de meuble) main part; (de bâtiment) (main) body; [6] (consistance) body; **prendre** ~ to take shape; [7] (objet) body; [8] Chimie substance; ~ **gras** fatty substance; [9] (de caractère d'imprimerie) type size; [10] (de vêtement) bodice; (de cuirasse) breastplate

(Composés) ~ **de ballet** corps de ballet; ~ **calleux** corpus callosum; ~ **de chauffe** heater; ~ **composé** compound; ~ **constitué** constituent body; ~ **du délit** Jur corpus delicti; ~ **diplomatique** diplomatic corps; ~ **et biens** Naut with all hands; ~ **de garde** guardroom; ~ **gazeux** gas; ~ **jaune** Anat corpus luteum; ~ **judiciaire** Jur judicature; ~ **simple** element; ~ **strié** corpus striatum

(Idiome) **tenir au** ~ to be nourishing

corps-mort, *pl* ~**s** /kɔrmɔr/ *nm* Naut mooring

corpulence /kɔrpylɑ̃s/ *nf* stoutness, corpulence; **de forte** ~ of stout build

corpulent, ~**e** /kɔrpylɑ̃, ɑ̃t/ *adj* stout, corpulent

corpus /kɔrpys/ *nm inv* corpus

corpuscule /kɔrpyskyl/ *nm* Anat, Phys corpuscle

correct, ~**e** /kɔrɛkt/ *adj* [1] (sans erreur) [*calcul, réponse, interprétation*] correct; [*copie*] accurate; [2] (convenable) [*tenue*] proper; [*conduite*] correct; [*personne*] polite; [3] ○(de qualité suffisante) [*résultat, vin*] reasonable, decent; [*devoir*] adequate, reasonable; [*logement*] adequate; [4] (honnête) [*personne*] fair, correct

correctement /kɔrɛktəmɑ̃/ *adv* [1] (sans erreur) correctly; [2] (convenablement) properly; [3] (raisonnablement) [*manger, loger, traiter*] decently; [*travailler, être payé*] reasonably well

correcteur, -trice /kɔrɛktœr, tris/
A *adj* corrective
B ▸ p. 372 *nm,f* [1] (d'examen) examiner GB, grader US; [2] (d'épreuves) proofreader

(Composés) ~ **d'acidité** Chimie, Ind acidity regulator; ~ **automatique d'orthographe** Ordinat automatic spell-checker

correctif, -ive /kɔrɛktif, iv/ *adj* corrective

correction /kɔrɛksjɔ̃/ *nf* [1] (action de corriger) gén correcting; (de manuscrit) proofreading; **apporter une** ~ à qch to correct sth; [2] (attribution d'une note) (d'examen) marking GB, grading US; [3] (modification) correction; [4] (punition) gén hiding○; (fessée) spanking; [5] (exactitude) accuracy; (justesse) correctness; [6] (convenance) (de tenue, conduite) correctness; (politesse) good manners (*pl*); **manquer de** ~ to have no manners

correctionnel, -elle[1] /kɔrɛksjɔnɛl/ *adj* peine correctionnelle penalty (imposed by court); **tribunal** ~ magistrate's court

correctionnelle[2] /kɔrɛksjɔnɛl/ *nf* magistrate's court

corrélation /kɔrelasjɔ̃/ *nf* correlation (**entre** between); **être en (étroite)** ~ **avec qn** to be (closely) related *ou* connected to sth

correspondance /kɔrɛspɔ̃dɑ̃s/ *nf* [1] (lettres) letters (*pl*); [2] (courrier) mail; (échange de courrier) correspondence (**entre** between); **faire des études par** ~ to do a correspondence course; [3] (pour un journal) correspondence; [4] (lien, ressemblance) correspondence (**entre** between); [5] (dans les transports) connection; **vols en** ~ connecting flights; [6] Math correspondence

correspondant, ~**e** /kɔrɛspɔ̃dɑ̃, ɑ̃t/
A *adj* [*avantage, chiffre, emploi, reçu*] corresponding; [*étiquette, boulon*] matching

B nm,f **1** (par courrier) gén correspondent; (dans le cadre d'un passe-temps) penfriend GB, pen pal; **2** Télécom votre ~ the person you are calling; **3** Admin, Comm correspondent; **4** (pour un journal) correspondent

correspondre /kɔʀɛspɔ̃dʀ/ [6]
A corresponadre à vtr ind **1** (être approprié à) ~ à to match [dimension, contenu, formation, programme]; to suit [goût]; **2** (équivaloir à) ~ à to correspond to; ~ à to correspond to; (coïncider avec) [élément] to correspond to; ~ à la description to match the description; ce qu'il m'en a dit ne correspond pas du tout à la réalité what he told me about it bears no relation to reality; **3** (être lié à) ~ à to correspond to [événement, caractéristique]
B vi **1** (écrire) to correspond (avec with); **2** ~ par téléphone to communicate by phone
C se correspondre vpr [éléments] to correspond

corrida /kɔʀida/ nf bullfight; c'est la ~ pour se garer à Oxford it's a real performance parking in Oxford

corridor /kɔʀidɔʀ/ nm corridor

corrigé /kɔʀiʒe/ nm Scol correct version; recueil d'exercices avec ~s collection of exercises with answers

corriger /kɔʀiʒe/ [13]
A vtr **1** (éliminer les erreurs) gén to correct [texte]; to proofread [manuscrit, texte]; to read [épreuves]; **2** (redresser) to correct [erreur, défaut, jugement]; to redress [situation]; to improve [manières]; to correct [trajectoire, instrument]; (adapter) to adjust [position, chiffre]; to modify [théorie]; ~ le tir Mil to alter one's aim; fig to adjust ou modify one's tactics; **3** Scol to mark GB, to grade US [copie, examen]; **4** (châtier) gén to give [sb] a hiding○; (fesser) to give [sb] a spanking
B se corriger vpr **1** (en parlant) to correct oneself; **2** (s'améliorer) to mend one's ways; se ~ d'un défaut to cure oneself of a fault

corroborer /kɔʀɔbɔʀe/ [1] vtr to corroborate

corroder /kɔʀɔde/ [1] vtr to corrode

corrompre /kɔʀɔ̃pʀ/ [53]
A vtr **1** (soudoyer) to bribe [policier, juge]; **2** (pervertir) to corrupt [jeunesse, mœurs, goût]
B se corrompre vpr [mœurs, jeunesse] to become corrupted

corrompu ~e /kɔʀɔ̃py/ adj [société, juge, gouvernement] corrupt

corrosif, -ive /kɔʀozif, iv/
A adj [substance] corrosive; (mordant) [esprit, remarque] caustic
B nm corrosive

corrosion /kɔʀozjɔ̃/ nf (de métal) corrosion

corrupteur, -trice /kɔʀyptœʀ, tʀis/
A adj corrupting
B nm,f (qui soudoie) briber; (qui déprave) corrupter

corruption /kɔʀypsjɔ̃/ nf **1** (avec de l'argent, des cadeaux) bribery (de of); **2** (état) corruption (de in); **3** (perversion) corruption (de of)

corsage /kɔʀsaʒ/ nm **1** (chemisier) blouse; **2** (de robe) bodice

corsaire /kɔʀsɛʀ/ nm **1** (personne) corsair; **2** (pantalon) pedal pushers (pl)

corse /kɔʀs/
A ▸ p. 504 adj [fromage, accent] Corsican
B ▸ p. 336 nm Ling Corsican

Corse /kɔʀs/ ▸ p. 303 nprf Corsica

corsé, ~e /kɔʀse/ adj **1** Culin [café] strong; [vin] full-bodied; [sauce] spicy; **2** (grivois) racy, spicy; **3** ○(difficile) [problème] tough; **4** ○(élevé) [facture] steep

corser /kɔʀse/ [1]
A vtr **1** (compliquer) to make [sth] more difficult [exercice, problème]; pour ~ l'affaire (just) to complicate matters; **2** (accentuer le goût) to strengthen the flavourGB of [sauce]; (avec des épices) to make [sth] spicier [sauce, plat]
B se corser vpr to get more complicated

corset /kɔʀsɛ/ nm corset

corso /kɔʀso/ nm ~ fleuri procession of floral floats

cortège /kɔʀtɛʒ/ nm **1** (défilé) procession; suivi d'un ~ d'enfants followed by a troop of children; **2** (série) liter la guerre et son ~ de misères war and its trail of misery
(Composé) ~ funèbre (funeral) cortège

cortical, ~e, mpl **-aux** /kɔʀtikal, o/ adj cortical

corvée /kɔʀve/ nf **1** (activité pénible) chore; les ~s ménagères household chores; aller les voir, quelle ~! it's

---

a real bore ou grind○ to have to go and see them; **2** (travail obligatoire) duty; Mil fatigue (duty); tu es de ~ de patates○ it's your turn to peel the potatoes; être de ~ pour faire to have been roped into doing; **3** Hist corvée (peasant's day of unpaid labourGB for feudal lord)

coryza /kɔʀiza/ ▸ p. 195 nm head cold, coryza spéc

cosaque /kɔzak/ nm Cossack

coscénariste /cosenaʀist/ nmf co-writer

cosinus /kɔsinys/ nm inv cosine

cosmétique /kɔsmetik/
A adj lit, fig cosmetic
B nm cosmetic ou beauty product; des ~s cosmetics

cosmique /kɔsmik/ adj cosmic

cosmologie /kɔsmɔlɔʒi/ nf cosmology

cosmonaute /kɔsmɔnot/ ▸ p. 372 nmf cosmonaut

cosmopolite /kɔsmɔpolit/ adj cosmopolitan

cosmos /kɔsmos/ nm cosmos

cossard○, ~e /kɔsaʀ, aʀd/
A adj [personne] lazy, bone idle○
B nm,f idler, loafer○, lazybones○ (+ v sg)

cosse /kɔs/ nf **1** Bot (de fève, pois) pod; (de graine) husk; **2** (en électronique) terminal; **3** ○(paresse) laziness

cossu, ~e /kɔsy/ adj [personne] well-to-do; [intérieur] plush; [existence] comfortable; [maison] smart, posh○

costal, ~e, mpl **-aux** /kɔstal, o/ adj Anat, Zool costal

costard○ /kɔstaʀ/ nm (costume) suit

Costa Rica /kɔsta ʀika/ ▸ p. 230 nprm Costa Rica

costaricien, -ienne /kɔstaʀisjɛ̃, ɛn/ ▸ p. 392 adj Costa Rican

costaud○ /kɔsto/
A adj **1** [personne] (fort) strong; (vigoureux) sturdy; il est assez ~ euph (gros) he's pretty hefty○; tu peux lui dire, elle est ~ (moralement) you can tell her, she can take it; **2** (solide) [chaussures, bicyclette] sturdy; [matériau, assemblage] strong; [mur, maison] sturdily built; [alcool] strong; [aliment] spicy, hot; c'est du ~ ta machine! that's a solid machine you have there!
B nm (homme) sturdily built man

costume /kɔstym/ nm **1** (ensemble veste, pantalon) suit; il est toujours en ~ cravate he always wears a suit and tie; **2** Théât, Cin costume; répéter en ~ to have a dress rehearsal; **3** Hist costume
(Composés) ~ de bain swimming costume; ~ de cérémonie ceremonial dress **C**; ~ marin sailor suit; ~ trois pièces three-piece suit

costumer se costumer /kɔstyme/ [1] vpr to put on fancy dress; soirée costumée fancy-dress party, costume party US

costumier, -ière /kɔstymje, ɛʀ/ ▸ p. 372 nm,f (de troupe) wardrobe master/mistress; (indépendant) costumier

cotation /kɔtasjɔ̃/ nf Fin quotation

cote /kɔt/ nf **1** Fin (valeur en Bourse) quotation; (liste des valeurs) (stock exchange) list; entrée or admission à la ~ stock exchange listing; inscrit or admis à la ~ listed (on the stock exchange); actions hors ~ unlisted shares; **2** (de voiture d'occasion, timbre) quoted value; **3** (aux courses) odds (pl); **4** (de personne, lieu, film) rating; avoir la ~ auprès de qn [célébrité] to be popular with sb; [individu] to be well thought of by sb; ne plus avoir la ~○ to have fallen from grace; **5** (sur un plan) dimension; **6** (sur une carte) spot height; à la ~ plus/moins 20 20 metres above/below sea level; **7** (marque de classement) classification mark; (numéro de livre) pressmark GB, call number US
(Composés) ~ d'alerte flood level; fig danger level; ~ d'amour or de popularité popularity rating

côte /kot/
A nf **1** Géog (littoral) coast; **2** Géog (pente) hill; dans une ~ on a hill; **3** Anat rib; vraie/fausse ~ true/false rib; **4** Culin chop; ~ de bœuf rib roast; **5** (en tricot) rib; col à ~s ribbed collar; tricoter les ~s to do the ribbing; **6** Bot rib
B côte à côte loc adv side by side
(Composé) Côte d'Azur French riviera
(Idiome) se tenir les ~s to split one's sides with laughter

coté, ~e /kote/ adj (prestigieux) être (très) ~ to be (very) well thought of

côté /kote/

A *nm* **1** Anat (flanc) side; **2** (partie latérale) side (**de** of); **de l'autre ~ du mur** over (the other side of) the wall; **changer de ~** (au tennis) to change ends; **3** (direction) way, direction; **de quel ~ allez-vous?** which way are you going?; **ils sont arrivés des deux ~s** they came from both directions; **4** (aspect) side; **prendre** *or* **voir les choses du bon ~** to look on the bright side of things; **par certains ~s** in some respects; **d'un ~** (d'une part) on the one hand; (en un sens) in one respect *ou* way; **d'un autre ~** (d'autre part) on the other hand; (dans un autre sens) in another respect *ou* way; **~ santé, ça va** healthwise *ou* on the health side, it's all right; **5** (branche familiale) side (**de** of); **6** (camp) side; **être du ~ de qn** to be on sb's side

B **à côté** *loc adv* **1** (à proximité) **il habite à ~** he lives nearby *ou* close by; **les voisins d'à ~** the next-door neighbours⁰ᴮ; **2** lit, fig (en dehors) **le ballon est passé à ~** the ball went wide; **répondre à ~** (par erreur) to miss the point; (volontairement) to sidestep the question; **3** (en comparaison) by comparison; **4** (simultanément) **elle est étudiante et travaille à ~** she's a student and she works on the side

C **à côté de** *loc prép* **1** (à proximité de) next to; **2** (en dehors de) **le ballon est passé à ~ du but** lit the ball went wide of the goal; **passer complètement à ~ de la question** fig (par erreur) to miss the point completely; (volontairement) to sidestep the issue; **3** (en comparaison) compared to; **4** (en plus de) besides; **à ~ de ça⁰** (par ailleurs) for all that

D **de côté** *loc adv* **1** (obliquement) **faire un pas de ~** to step aside *ou* to one side; **2** (sur la partie latérale) side (épith); **des places de ~** Théât side seats; **3** (en réserve) aside; **mettre de ~** to put [sth] aside *ou* on one side [argent, livre]; **mettre sa fierté de ~** to swallow one's pride

E **du côté** *loc prép* **1** (vers) **aller du ~ de Dijon** to head for Dijon; **mes parents habitent du ~ de Beaune** my parents live near Beaune; **2** (en ce qui concerne) as for; **le Président, de son ~, a dit...** the President, for his part, said...; **il s'amuse, de ce ~-là, il n'y a rien à craindre** he's having fun, as far as that's concerned, there's nothing to worry about; **indique-t-on du ~ de la Commission** people in the Commission are saying; **il se tourne du ~ des dramaturges américains** he's turning toward(s) the American dramatists; **10 morts du ~ des manifestants** 10 dead among the demonstrators

F **aux côtés de** *loc prép* lit, fig (près de) **aux ~s de qn** [être, rester] beside sb, at sb's side; **aux ~s de qn/qch** [se retrouver] beside *ou* alongside sb/sth; [siéger, s'engager, travailler] alongside sb/sth

G **de tous (les) côtés** *loc adv* (partout) **regarder/courir de tous ~s** to look/to run all over the place; **une ville cernée de tous ~s** a town surrounded on all sides; **ils arrivent de tous ~s** they're coming from all directions

coteau, **~x** /koto/ *nm* **1** (pente) hillside; **à flanc de ~** on the hillside; **2** (colline) hill; **3** (vignoble) (sloping) vineyard

Côte-d'Ivoire /kotdivwaʀ/ ▸ p. 230 *nprf* Ivory Coast

côtelé, **~e** /kotle/ *adj* **velours ~** corduroy, cord

côtelette /kotlɛt/ *nf* Culin chop

coter /kote/ [1]

A *vtr* **1** Fin (admettre à la cotation) to list [titre]; **action cotée en Bourse** share listed on the stock market; **2** (numéroter) to give a pressmark GB *ou* call number US to [livre]; **3** Tech to dimension [dessin industriel]; to put spot heights on [carte]

B *vi* **1** (valoir) **~ 15 euros** [titre] to be quoted at 15 euros; [voiture, œuvre] to be priced at 15 euros; **~ en hausse/en baisse à la clôture à 392** to close up/down at 392; **2** (aux courses) to be quoted at

coterie /kotʀi/ *nf* pej circle, clique péj

cothurne /kotyʀn/ *nm* buskin, cothurnus

côtier, **-ière** /kotje, ɛʀ/ *adj* [ville, navigation, chemin] coastal; [pêche] inshore

cotillon /kotijɔ̃/ *nm* **1** (à la sécurité sociale, une caisse de retraite) cotillion; **2** † petticoat

cotisation /kotizasjɔ̃/ *nf* **1** (à la sécurité sociale, une caisse de retraite) contribution; **~ vieillesse** contribution to a pension fund; **2** (à une association) subscription; (à un syndicat) dues (pl), subscription

cotiser /kotize/ [1]

A *vi* **1** (à un régime de protection) to pay one's contributions; **~ à une caisse de retraite** to pay one's superannuation contribution; **2** (à une association, un syndicat) to pay one's subscription (**à** to)

B **se cotiser** *vpr* to club together GB, to go in together

coton /kotɔ̃/ *nm* **1** (plante, fibre) cotton; **drap de** *or* **en ~** cotton sheet; **2** (ouate) cotton wool GB, cotton US; (morceau d'ouate) piece of cotton wool GB *ou* cotton US

(Composé) **~ hydrophile** cotton wool GB, absorbent cotton US

(Idiomes) **filer un mauvais ~** (être en mauvaise santé) to be in a bad way; **élever un enfant dans du ~** to give a child a very sheltered upbringing; **elle est ~⁰, ta question** it's a tricky question; **j'ai les jambes en ~** (après un choc) my legs have turned to jelly; (après une maladie) I am wobbly on my legs

cotonnade /kotonad/ *nf* cotton fabric

cotonneux, **-euse** /kotonø, øz/ *adj* [brouillard] like cotton-wool (après n); [nuage] fleecy; [ciel] full of fleecy clouds (après n)

cotonnier, **-ière** /kotonje, ɛʀ/

A *adj* cotton

B *nm* Bot cotton plant

côtoyer /kotwaje/ [23]

A *vtr* (être près de) to be next to; (fréquenter) to move in [milieu]; to mix with [personnes]; fig to be in close contact with [mort, danger]

B **se côtoyer** *vpr* [personnes] to mix; [extrêmes] to be side by side

cotte /kɔt/ *nf* (vêtement de travail) overalls (pl)

(Composés) **~ d'armes** Hist surcoat; **~ de mailles** Hist coat of mail

cou /ku/ ▸ p. 136, p. 575 *nm* neck; **embrasser qn dans le ~** to kiss sb's neck; **avoir des ennuis** *or* **problèmes jusqu'au ~⁰** fig to be up to one's neck in problems; **être endetté jusqu'au ~⁰** fig to be up to one's eyes in debt

(Idiomes) **se casser** *or* **rompre le ~** to break one's neck; **se mettre/avoir la corde au ~⁰** to tie/to have tied the knot⁰

couac⁰ /kwak/ *nm* Mus wrong note; fig jarring note

couard, **~e** /kwaʀ, aʀd/ fml

A *adj* cowardly

B *nm,f* coward; **c'est un ~** he's a coward

couchage /kuʃaʒ/ *nm* (organisation) sleeping arrangements (pl); (lit) bed; (matériel pour dormir) bedding; **un studio avec ~ pour six** a studio that sleeps six

couchant /kuʃɑ̃/

A *adj m* **soleil ~** setting sun; **au soleil ~** at sunset

B *nm* **1** (coucher du soleil) sunset; **2** (ouest) liter west

couche /kuʃ/

A *nf* **1** (de vernis, peinture, d'apprêt) coat; (d'aliments, de poussière, neige) layer; **une ~ d'huile** a film of oil; **2** (strate) stratum, layer; **la ~ d'ozone** the ozone layer; **'préserve la ~ d'ozone'** 'ozone-friendly'; **3** Sociol sector; **les ~s laborieuses** the working classes *ou* sectors; **4** (pour bébés) nappy GB, diaper US; **5** (lit) liter bed

B **couches**† *nfpl* (accouchement) childbirth (sg)

couché, **~e** /kuʃe/ *adj* (penché) [écriture] sloping

couche-culotte, *pl* **couches-culottes** /kuʃkylɔt/ *nf* disposable nappy GB *ou* diaper US

coucher¹ /kuʃe/ [1]

A *vtr* **1** (allonger) to put [sb] to bed [malade, enfant]; to lay out [blessé, mort]; **2** (mettre à l'horizontale) to lay [sth] on its side [armoire]; to lay [sth] down [échelle, planche]; **3** (faire pencher) [vent, pluie] to flatten [blés, herbes]; **4** (écrire) liter **~ qch par écrit** to put sth down in writing [idées, phrases]; **~ qn sur son testament** to name *ou* mention sb in one's will

B *vi* **1** (dormir) to sleep; **~ avec qn** to sleep with sb; **2** (passer la nuit) **~ chez qn** to sleep at sb's (house); **~ sous la tente** to sleep in a tent; **~ sous les ponts** fig to sleep rough GB *ou* outdoors

C **se coucher** *vpr* **1** (s'allonger) [personne, animal] to lie (down); **se ~ sur/dans son lit** to lie (down) on/in one's bed; **se ~ sur le dos/côté** to lie on one's back/side; **se ~ sur le ventre** to lie flat on one's stomach; **je dois rester couché** I have to stay in bed; **2** (aller dormir) [personne] to go to bed; **les enfants sont couchés** the children are in bed; **3** (se pencher) [tige, blés] to bend; [voilier] to list; (chavirer) to keel over; **se ~ sur** [motard, cycliste] to lean forward over [guidon]; **4** (disparaître à l'horizon) [soleil] to set, to go down

coucher² /kuʃe/ *nm* bedtime; **à l'heure du ~** at bedtime

(Composé) **~ de soleil** sunset; **au ~ du soleil** at sunset

couchette /kuʃɛt/ nf (de train) couchette, berth; (de bateau) berth; **un train à ~s** a sleeper GB, a Pullman (car) US

couci-couça○ /kusikusa/ adv so-so○

coucou /kuku/
A nm **1** Zool cuckoo; **2** Bot cowslip; **3** ○(avion) (old) crate○; **4** (horloge) cuckoo clock
B ○excl (bonjour) cooee!; (en se cachant) peekaboo!

coude /kud/ ▸ p. 136 nm **1** Anat elbow; **~s au corps** with elbows tucked in; **donner un coup de ~ à qn** (pour attirer l'attention) to nudge sb, give sb a nudge; (en se battant) to jab sb with one's elbow; **jouer des ~s pour atteindre le buffet** to elbow one's way to the buffet; **2** (partie de manche) elbow; (pièce) elbow patch; **3** (de chemin, tuyau) bend; (de fleuve) bend, elbow

(Idiomes) **travailler ~ à ~** to work shoulder to shoulder; **être au ~ à ~** to be neck and neck; **se serrer** or **se tenir les ~s** to stick together; **lever le ~**○ to drink a bit; **garder qch sous le ~** to put sth on the back burner

coudé, ~e¹ /kude/ adj bent at an angle

coudée² /kude/ nf (mesure) cubit

(Idiome) **avoir les ~s franches** to have elbow room

cou-de-pied, pl **cous-de-pied** /kudpje/ nm (dessus du pied) instep; (articulation) ankle joint

couder /kude/ [1] vtr to bend

coudre /kudʀ/ [76]
A vtr (en couture) to sew [ourlet]; (en reliure) to stitch; to sew [sth] on [bouton, pièce]; to stitch [sth] on [semelle]; to stitch (up) [robe, plaie]
B vi to sew

(Idiome) **leur histoire est cousue de fil blanc** you can see through their story

couenne /kwan/ nf Culin (bacon) rind

couette /kwɛt/ nf **1** (couverture) duvet, continental quilt GB, comforter US; **2** (coiffure) **~s** bunches GB, pigtails US; **se faire des ~s** to put one's hair (up) in pigtails

couffin /kufɛ̃/ nm Moses basket GB, bassinet US

couic /kwik/ nm (also onomat) squeak

couinement /kwinmɑ̃/ nm (de souris, chaton, jouet) squeak; (de lapin, porc, freins) squeal; (de porte, ressort) creak; (de chien, d'enfant) whine

couiner /kwine/ [1] vi [souris, chaton, jouet] to squeak; [lapin, porc, freins] to squeal; [ressort, porte] to creak; [chien, enfant] to whine

coulant, ~e /kulɑ̃, ɑ̃t/ adj [camembert] runny; [personne] easy-going; [style] flowing

coulé, ~e¹ /kule/
A adj **1** (souple) [mouvement] fluid, flowing; [graphisme, écriture] flowing; [style] flowing, fluid; **2** Naut [navire] sunken
B nm Mus slide

coulée² /kule/ nf **1** (en métallurgie) casting; **2** (d'une substance) **~ de boue/neige** mudslide/snowslide; **~ de lave** lava flow; **~ de peinture** drip of paint; **3** Sport (en natation) glide

couler /kule/ [1]
A vtr **1** (verser) to cast [métal, verre]; to pour [béton]; **~ une dalle de béton** to make a concrete slab; **2** (fabriquer) to cast [buste, cloche]; **3** (faire sombrer) lit to sink [navire]; fig○ to put [sth] out of business [entreprise, commerce]; **4** ○(faire échouer) [matière, épreuve] to make [sb] fail [élève, étudiant]; **ce sont les maths qui l'ont coulé** it was his maths mark GB ou math grade US that brought him down; **les scandales l'ont coulé** the scandals ruined him○
B vi **1** (se mouvoir) [eau, ruisseau, boue, larmes, sang] to flow; [sève, peinture, colle, maquillage] to run; **la sueur coulait sur mon front** sweat was running down my forehead; **~ de** to run ou flow from [robinet, fontaine, réservoir]; to run ou flow out of [plaie]; **faire ~ qch** to run [eau]; to pour [vin, mazout]; **2** (se fluidifier) [fromage] to go runny; **3** (glisser) [neige] to slide; **faire ~ du sable entre ses doigts** to let some sand run through one's fingers; **4** (fuir) [robinet, stylo] to leak; [nez] to run; **5** (sombrer) [bateau, personne] to sink; **je coule!** I'm drowning!; **6** (passer paisiblement) liter [vie, temps] to slip by; **7** Bot [fleur, fruit] to drop; **8** ○(faire faillite) [entreprise, projet] to go under, to sink; **faire ~ une société** [personne, concurrence] to put a company out of business; **9** (être bien formulé) to flow
C se couler vpr (se glisser) **se ~ dans** to slip into [foule]; to slip between [draps]; **se ~ entre** to slip between [obstacles, gens]

(Idiome) **~ des jours heureux** to lead a happy life

couleur /kulœʀ/
A nf **1** gén colour GB; **(de) quelle ~ est ta voiture?** what colour GB is your car?; **une veste de ~ verte/~ abricot** a green/apricot-coloured GB jacket; **avoir la ~ de qch** to be the colour GB of sth; **faire prendre ~** Culin to brown; **plein de ~** fig [récit, description] vivid, colourful GB; **sans ~** lit, fig colourless; **2** Cin, Phot, TV **photo en ~** colour GB photograph; **3** (substance colorante) colour GB, paint; **boîte de ~s** paintbox; **4** (coloration des joues) colour GB; **tu as pris des ~s!** you've got some colour GB in your cheeks!; **une personne de ~** a coloured GB person; **5** Jeux (aux cartes) suit; **6** (pour les cheveux) haircolour GB; **7** (tendance politique) **~ politique** political colour GB; **8** (aspect) light; **sous des ~s trompeuses** in a false light
B couleurs nfpl **1** (drapeau) colours GB; **2** (marque) colours GB; **un avion aux ~s d'Air France** an aircraft with the Air France livery; **3** (vêtements de couleur) coloureds GB

(Composé) **~ locale** local colour GB

(Idiomes) **ne pas voir la ~**○ **de qch** never to get a sniff of sth○; **il m'en a fait voir de toutes les ~s**○ he really gave me a hard time, he put me through the mill○; **passer par toutes les ~s (de l'arc-en-ciel)**○ to change colour GB

couleuvre /kulœvʀ/ nf grass snake

(Idiome) **avaler des ~s**○ (être humilié) to endure humiliation; (être trompé) to believe anything one is told

coulissant, ~e /kulisɑ̃, ɑ̃t/ adj sliding (épith)

coulisse /kulis/ nf **1** Théât **les ~s, la ~** (côtés) the wings; (loges) the dressing rooms; **en ~, dans les ~s, dans la ~** (arrière-scène, loges) backstage; fig behind the scenes; **2** (rainure) runner; **à ~** [porte, cloison] sliding; **3** (ourlet) casing; (cordon) drawstring

coulissé, ~e /kulise/ adj **points ~s** running stitches; **short ~** or **à la taille ~e** shorts with a drawstring waist

coulisser /kulise/ [1] vi (dans une rainure) to slide; **faire ~ qch** (pour ouvrir/fermer) to slide sth open/shut

couloir /kulwaʀ/ nm **1** (de bâtiment) corridor GB, hallway US; (de train) corridor; (de station de métro) passage; **bruits de ~s** rumours GB; **2** (sur la chaussée) **~ de circulation** ou **réservé** bus (and taxi) lane; **~ aérien** air (traffic) lane; **3** (sur stade, en piscine) lane; (sur court) tramlines (pl) GB, alley US; **4** Géog corridor

coup /ku/ nm

⚠ Les expressions comme **coup de barre**, **coup de maître**, **coup de téléphone** etc seront normalement dans le dictionnaire sous le deuxième élément donc respectivement sous **barre**, **maître**, **téléphone** etc.

1 (choc physique) (neutre) knock; (brutal) blow, whack○; (dur, par accident) bang; (qui entaille) stroke; (d'un mouvement tranchant) chop; (du plat de la main) smack; (sec et rapide) rap; (léger et appuyé) tap; (léger et fouettant) flick; (de la pointe) poke, prod, jab; **~ à la porte** knock at the door; **~ de marteau** hammer blow; **d'un ~ de hache** [couper, tuer] with a single blow from an axe GB ou ax US; **à ~s de hache** [couper, tuer] with an axe GB ou ax US; **casser la porte à (grands) ~s de marteau** to break down the door with a hammer; **à ~s de subventions** by means of subsidies; **fièvre combattue à ~s d'antibiotiques** fever controlled with antibiotics; **sous le ~ d'un embargo** under an embargo; **donner un ~ de qch à qn** gén to hit ou strike sb with sth; **donner un ~ de poing/pied/couteau à qn** to punch/kick/stab sb; **prendre un ~** [personne, voiture] to get a knock; **en avoir pris un ~**○ fig (être très abîmé) to have taken (quite) a punishing; **rendre ~ pour ~** lit to fight back; fig to give tit for tat; **en venir aux ~s** to come to blows (pour over); **les trois ~s** Théât three knocks signalling GB that the curtain is about to rise; **2** (choc moral) gén blow; (plus modéré) knock; **porter un ~ (sévère) à** to deal [sb/sth] a (severe) blow [personne, organisation]; **en cas de ~ dur** (accident) should anything really bad happen; (difficulté) if things get rough; **ça m'a donné un ~ (sacré)** ○○ it gave me an awful shock; **sous le ~ de la colère** in (a fit of) anger; **sous le ~ de la fatigue/peur** out of tiredness/fear; **être sous le ~ d'une forte émotion** to be in a highly emotional state; **tomber sous le ~ d'une condamnation** to be liable to conviction; **3** (bruit) gén knock; (retentissant) bang; (sourd) thump, thud; **au douzième ~ de minuit** on the last stroke of midnight; **sur le ~ de dix heures**○ around ten; **~ de gong** stroke of a gong; **~ de sifflet** whistle blast; **4** (mouvement rapide) **se**

Les couleurs

■ *Attention: certains noms et adjectifs de couleurs français ont plusieurs traductions possibles. Par ex.,* brun *peut être* brown, dark, black *etc. Consulter les articles dans le dictionnaire.*

La couleur des choses

■ *Dans les expressions suivantes,* vert *est pris comme exemple; les autres adjectifs et noms de couleurs s'utilisent de la même façon.*

Les adjectifs

de quelle couleur est-il?
= what colour is it?

il est vert
= it's green

une robe verte
= a green dress

Les noms

■ *En anglais, les noms de couleurs n'ont en général pas d'article défini.*

j'aime le vert
= I like green

je préfère le vert
= I prefer green

le vert me va bien
= green suits me

porter du vert
= to wear green

une gamme de verts
= a range of greens

avez-vous le même modèle en vert?
= have you got the same thing in green?

le même vert
= the same green

en vert
= in green

je t'aime bien en vert
= I like you in green

s'habiller en vert
= to dress in green

habillé de vert
= dressed in green

■ *Avec les verbes* to paint (*peindre*) *et* to dye (*teindre*), *le* en *français n'est pas traduit:*

peindre la porte en vert
= to paint the door green

teindre un chemisier en vert
= to dye a blouse green

Les nuances

très vert
= very green

vert clair
= light green

vert pâle
= pale green

vert profond
= deep green

un chapeau vert foncé
= a dark green hat

un vert plus foncé
= a darker green

la robe était d'un vert plus foncé
= the dress was a darker green

un vert affreux
= a dreadful green

sa robe est d'un joli vert
= her dress is a pretty green

vert foncé
= dark green

vert vif
= bright green

vert pastel
= pastel green

vert soutenu
= strong green

une robe vert clair
= a light green dress

un joli vert
= a pretty green

■ *Noter l'absence d'équivalent du* de *français.*

■ *En anglais comme en français, on peut exprimer une nuance en utilisant le nom d'une chose dont la couleur est typique. Noter que l'adjectif prend un trait d'union* (sky-blue), *mais pas le nom* (sky blue).

bleu ciel
= sky blue

une robe bleu ciel
= a sky-blue dress

une veste vert pomme
= an apple-green jacket

vert pomme
= apple green

vert tilleul
= sage green

■ *De même,* navy-blue (*bleu marine*), midnight-blue (*bleu nuit*), blood-red (*rouge sang*) *etc. En cas de doute, consulter le dictionnaire. En ajoutant* -coloured (*GB*) *ou* -colored (*US*) *à un nom, on obtient un adjectif composé qui correspond au français avec* couleur.

une robe couleur framboise
= a raspberry-coloured dress (*GB*)
  a raspberry-colored dress (*US*)

des collants couleur chair
= flesh-coloured tights (*GB*)

un papier peint couleur crème
= cream-coloured wallpaper (*GB*)

■ *Noter enfin:*

bleu-noir
= blue-black

verdâtre
= greenish

un jaune verdâtre
= a greenish yellow

■ *Attention: ces adjectifs n'existent pas pour toutes les couleurs. En cas de doute, consulter le dictionnaire. On peut toujours utiliser* shade, *comme on utilise* ton *ou* nuance *en français.*

un joli ton de vert
= a pretty shade of green

Les gens ► p. 136

■ *L'anglais n'utilise pas d'article défini dans les expressions suivantes:*

avoir les cheveux blonds
= to have fair hair

avoir les yeux bleus
= to have blue eyes

■ *Noter les adjectifs composés anglais:*

un blond
= a fair-haired man

une brune
= a dark-haired woman

un enfant aux yeux bleus
= a blue-eyed child

■ *Mais on peut aussi dire:* a man with fair hair, a child with blue eyes *etc.*

La couleur des cheveux

■ *Les adjectifs des deux langues ne sont pas exactement équivalents, mais les correspondances suivantes sont utiles. Noter que* hair *est toujours au singulier.*

les cheveux noirs
= black hair

les cheveux bruns
= dark hair

les cheveux châtains
= brown hair

les cheveux blonds
= fair hair (*ou* blond(e): *voir le mot français* blond *dans le dictionnaire*)

☛ Voir page suivante

c

Les couleurs *suite*

les cheveux roux
= red hair

les cheveux gris
= grey (*GB*) *ou* gray (*US*) hair

les cheveux blancs
= white hair

La couleur des yeux

les yeux bleus
= blue eyes

les yeux bleu clair
= light blue eyes

les yeux gris
= grey (*GB*) *ou* gray (*US*) eyes

les yeux verts
= green eyes

les yeux gris-vert
= greyish green (*GB*)
ou grayish green (*US*) eyes (grey-green *et* gray-green
sont aussi possibles)

les yeux marron
= brown eyes

les yeux marron clair
= light brown eyes

les yeux noisette
= hazel eyes

les yeux clairs
= light-coloured (*GB*) *ou* light-colored (*US*) eyes

les yeux noirs
= dark eyes

---

donner un (petit) ∼ de brosse/peigne to give one's hair a (quick) brush/comb GB, to brush/comb one's hair (quickly); **donner un ∼ sur la table** to dust the table; **les volets ont besoin d'un ∼ de peinture** the shutters need a lick of paint; **d'un ∼, d'aile** with a flap of its wings; ⑤ Jeux, Sport (au tennis, golf, cricket) gén stroke; (qu'on juge) shot; (aux échecs, dames) move; (aux dés) throw; (à la boxe) blow, punch; (au karaté) (du poing) punch; (du tranchant) chop; (du pied) kick; **tous les ∼s sont permis** lit, fig no holds barred; **∼ défendu** Jeux, Sport foul; ⑥ (d'arme à feu) (décharge, détonation) shot; (munition) round; **blesser qn d'un ∼ de fusil** *or* **pistolet** to shoot and wound sb; **tuer qn d'un ∼ de fusil** *or* **pistolet** to shoot sb dead; ⑦ ○(action organisée) (opération illégale) job○, racket○; (vilain tour) trick○; (manœuvre) move; **monter un ∼** to plan a job○; **∼ monté!** set-up○!; **mettre qn dans le ∼** to cut sb in on the deal○; **être sur un gros ∼** to be onto something big○; **il a raté son ∼**○ he blew it○; **réussir son ∼** to pull it off; **être dans le ∼** (impliqué) to be in on it; (au courant) to be up to date, to know what's going on; **tu n'es plus dans le ∼!** fig you're behind the times!; **être/rester hors du ∼** (non impliqué) to have/to keep one's nose clean○; ⑧ (fois, moment) **essayer encore un ∼** to have another shot; **du premier ∼** (immédiatement) straight off; (à la première tentative) at the first attempt; **(encore) un ∼ pour rien** no go again○; **à chaque ∼, à tout ∼, à tous les ∼s** every time; **ce ∼-ci/-là** this/ that time; **du ∼**○ as a result; **du même ∼**○ by the same token; **pour le ∼**○ this time; **après ∼** afterwards, in restropect; **au ∼ par ∼** as things come; **∼ sur ∼** in succession; **tout d'un ∼, tout à ∼** suddenly, all of a sudden; **d'un ∼, d'un seul ∼** just like that; **en un seul ∼** in one go○; **sur le ∼** (à ce moment-là) at the time; (immédiatement) instantly, on the spot; **pleure un bon ∼** have a good cry; **respire un grand ∼** take a deep breath; **boire à petits ∼s** to sip; **boire à grands ∼s** to swig; ⑨ ○(boisson) drink; **je te paye un ∼ (à boire)** I'll buy you a drink; **donne-moi encore un petit ∼ de gin** give me another shot○ of gin

⟨Composés⟩ **∼ bas** (en boxe) blow *ou* punch below the belt; **∼s et blessures** Jur assault and battery; **∼ droit** (au tennis) (forehand) drive; **faire un ∼ droit** (au tennis) to drive; **∼ fourré** dirty trick; **∼ franc** (au football) free kick

⟨Idiomes⟩ **tenir le ∼** (résister à l'épreuve) [*personne*] to make it○; [*véhicule, chaussures*] to last out; [*lien, réparation*] to hold; (ne pas abandonner) [*personne*] to hold on; [*armée*] to hold out; (faire face) to cope; **j'ai vu venir le ∼** I could see it coming; **faire ∼ double** to kill two birds with one stone; **en mettre un ∼**○ to give it all one's got○; **être aux cent ∼s**○ to be worried sick○, to be in a state○; **faire les quatre cents ∼s**○ to be up to no good; **attraper le ∼ pour faire qch**○ to get the knack of doing sth; ▶ **pierre**

coupable /kupabl/
A adj ① gén, Jur [*personne, entreprise*] guilty (**de qch** of sth; **d'avoir fait** of doing); **s'être rendu ∼ de qch** to have committed sth; ② (répréhensible) [*pensées*] shameful; [*amour*] illicit
B nmf gén, Jur culprit; (dans un procès) guilty party
coupage /kupaʒ/ nm (de vin) blending

---

coupant, ∼e /kupɑ̃, ɑ̃t/ adj sharp; fig cutting

coup-de-poing, pl **coups-de-poing** /kudpwɛ̃/ nm ∼ **américain** knuckle-duster GB, brass knuckles (pl) US

coupe /kup/ nf ① Sport cup; **la ∼ du Monde** the World Cup; ② (coiffure) haircut; **faire une ∼ à qn** to give sb a haircut; ③ (processus) cutting out; (façon) cut; **cours de ∼ et couture** dressmaking course; ④ (diminution) cut; **annoncer une ∼ de 10% dans le budget** to announce a cut of 10% in the budget; ⑤ (action de couper) cutting (**de** of); **vendu à la ∼** not sold pre-packed; ⑥ (surface d'exploitation) felling area; ⑦ Cin, Littérat, Presse (censure) (action) cutting; (résultat) cut; ⑧ (à fruits, dessert) bowl; (à champagne) glass; ⑨ Biol section; **une (vue en) ∼ de qch** a section of sth; ⑩ (aux cartes) void; ⑪ Ling boundary; **∼ syllabique** syllabic division

⟨Composés⟩ **∼ au bol** pudding GB *ou* dessert US bowl cut; **∼ en brosse** crew cut; **∼ dégradée** layered cut; **∼ réglée** periodic felling

⟨Idiomes⟩ **la ∼ est pleine** enough is enough; **être sous la ∼ de l'État** to be under the control of the State; **vivre sous la ∼ de parents autoritaires** to live under the thumb of authoritarian parents

coupe-cigare, pl **∼s** /kupsigaʀ/ nm cigar cutter

coupe-circuit /kupsiʀkɥi/ nm inv fuse

coupée /kupe/ nf gangway

coupe-faim /kupfɛ̃/ nm inv appetite suppressant

coupe-feu /kupfø/
A adj inv fire-proof; **porte ∼** fire door
B nm inv (en forêt) firebreak

coupe-gorge /kupgɔʀʒ/ nm inv (lieu) rough place; (quartier) rough area

coupe-ongles /kupɔ̃gl/ nm inv nail clippers (pl)

coupe-papier /kuppapje/ nm inv paper knife, letter opener

couper /kupe/ [1]
A vtr ① (sectionner) to cut [*ficelle, papier, fleur*] (**avec** with); to cut down [*arbre*]; to chop [*bois*]; (ôter) to cut [sth] off, to cut off [*frange, branche, membre*]; **∼ un fil avec les dents** to bite a thread off; **∼ la journée** fig to break up the day; **j'ai coupé par le bois** fig I cut through the wood; ② Culin to cut (up), to slice [*pain*]; to carve [*rôti*]; to cut (off) [*tranche*]; to cut, to chop [*légumes*]; **∼ qch en tranches** to slice sth; ③ (en couture) (d'après un patron) to cut out [*vêtement*]; (raccourcir) to shorten; ④ (entamer) [*lanière*] to cut into [*chair*]; [*couteau, ciseaux*] to cut [os, métal]; ⑤ Cin to cut; (pour censurer) to cut (out) [*images*]; ⑥ (croiser) [*route, voie*] to cut across [*route*]; Math [*droite, courbe*] to intersect with [*axe*]; **∼ la route à qn/un véhicule** to cut in on sb/a vehicle; ⑦ (pour faire obstacle) [*barrage, police*] to cut off [*route*]; **une veste qui coupe bien du vent** a jacket that keeps out the wind; ⑧ (interrompre) [*agence*] gén to cut off [*électricité, eau*]; (pour non-paiement) to disconnect [*électricité, eau, téléphone*]; [*usager*] to turn off [*chauffage, eau, gaz*]; to switch off [*électricité, contact*]; **un œuf dur coupe la faim** a hard boiled egg takes

the edge off your hunger; ∼ **les vivres à qn** lit to cut off sb's food supply; fig to stop giving sb money; ∼ **l'appétit à qn** to ruin ou spoil sb's appetite; ∼ **le souffle à qn** lit, fig to take sb's breath away; ∼ **la parole à qn** to interrupt sb; [9] (isoler) ∼ **qn de qn/qch** to cut sb off from sb/sth; [10] (mélanger) to dilute (jus de fruit, vin]; (à la fabrication) to blend [vin]; [11] (au tennis) to slice [balle, revers]; [12] Jeux (pour mélanger) to cut; (avec une carte) to trump; [13] (castrer) to neuter, to castrate [chat, chien]

B vi **attention ça coupe!** be careful, it's sharp ou you'll cut yourself!; **ça coupe beaucoup mieux** it cuts a lot better

C se couper vpr [1] (se blesser) to cut oneself (**avec** with); **il s'est coupé le doigt** (entamé) he cut his finger; (amputé) he cut his finger off; [2] (s'isoler) **se ∼ de qn/qch** to cut oneself off from sb/sth; [3] (se fendre) [cuir] to crack; [étoffe] to tear, to rip; [4] (se tailler) **ça se coupe facilement** it's easy to cut; [5] (se croiser) to cross, to intersect

(Idiome) **tu n'y couperas pas** you won't get out of it; ▸ **main**

couperet /kupRε/ nm (de boucher) cleaver; (de guillotine) blade; **la nouvelle est tombée comme un ∼** the news came as a bolt from the blue

couperose /kupRoz/ nf broken veins (pl)

coupe-vent /kupvɑ̃/ nm inv [1] (anorak) windcheater GB, windbreaker US; [2] (haie) windbreak

couple /kupl/ nm [1] (avec lien amoureux) (personnes) couple; (relation) relationship; (de danseurs) couple, pair; (d'animaux) pair; **le ∼ de marcheurs** the two walkers (pl); [2] Électrotech, Phys couple; [3] Aviat, Naut frame

(Composés) **∼ moteur** engine torque; **∼ résistant** resisting torque

coupler /kuple/ [1] vtr to couple

couplet /kuple/ nm (de chanson) verse; Littérat (deux vers) couplet; **faire son ∼ sur** pej to trot out the same old stuff about

coupole /kupɔl/ nf Archit cupola, dome

coupon /kupɔ̃/ nm [1] (de tissu) remnant; [2] Théât ticket voucher; [3] (de transport) multiuse ticket (in travel pass); [4] Fin coupon

coupure /kupyR/ nf [1] (pause) break; [2] (fossé) gap (**entre** between); [3] (passage censuré ou éliminé) cut; [4] (rupture) break; **une ∼ nette avec le passé** a clean break with the past; [5] (blessure) cut; [6] (d'eau, de gaz) **une ∼ d'électricité** or **de courant** gén a power cut; (pour non-paiement) disconnection of electricity supply; **'∼s d'eau pour travaux'** 'the water will be cut off several times during the repairs'; [7] Fin (billet de banque) (bank)note GB, bill US; **petites ∼s** notes of small denomination

(Composé) **∼ de journal** or **de presse** (newspaper) cutting ou clipping

cour /kuR/ nf [1] (de maison, bâtiment) courtyard; (où l'on joue) playground; (de ferme) yard; **la ∼ des grands** lit the older children's playground; fig the big league; **sur ∼** overlooking the courtyard; [2] (de souverain) court; (de personne en vue) entourage; [3] (à une jeune fille) courtship; **faire la ∼ à** to court; [4] Jur court; **messieurs, la ∼'** 'all rise'

(Composés) **∼ d'appel** Jur court of appeal GB ou appeals US; **∼ d'assises** Jur criminal court; **∼ d'école** schoolyard; **∼ d'honneur** main courtyard; **∼ intérieure** inner courtyard; **∼ martiale** Mil court-martial; **passer en ∼ martiale** to be court-martialled; **∼ des Miracles** Hist area of a city frequented by beggars and thieves; fig den of thieves; **Cour Pénale Internationale** International Criminal Court; **∼ de récréation** playground; **Cour de cassation** court of cassation

(Idiome) **jouer dans la ∼ des grands** to take on the big boys

courage /kuRaʒ/ nm [1] (bravoure) courage, bravery; **avec ∼** bravely, courageously; **avoir du ∼** to be brave ou courageous; **avoir le ∼ de ses opinions** to have the courage of one's convictions; [2] (énergie) energy; **je n'ai même pas le ∼ de me doucher** I don't even have the energy to have a shower; **bon ∼!** good luck!; **perdre ∼** to lose heart; **reprendre ∼** to take fresh heart; [3] (dureté) **je n'ai pas eu le ∼ de dire non** I didn't have the heart to say no

courageusement /kuRaʒøzmɑ̃/ adv [1] (bravement) courageously, bravely; [2] (avec décision) with a will

courageux, -euse /kuRaʒo, øz/ adj (vaillant) courageous, brave; **sois ∼** be brave; **je ne me sens pas très**

∼ **aujourd'hui** I haven't got much energy today

couramment /kuRamɑ̃/ adv [1] (avec aisance) [parler, écrire] fluently; [2] (communément) [admis, utilisé] widely; **cela se fait ∼** it's very common

courant¹ /kuRɑ̃/ prép ∼ **janvier** some time in January

courant², **-e** /kuRɑ̃, ɑ̃t/

A adj [1] (fréquent) [mot, pratique, erreur] common; [2] (ordinaire) [langue] everyday; [procédure, fonctionnement] usual, ordinary; Comm [taille] standard; [3] (avec référence temporelle) [semaine, mois, année, prix] current; **le 15 du mois ∼** the 15th of this month

B nm [1] (mouvement de l'eau, de l'air) current; **il y a beaucoup de ∼** there's a strong current; **contre le ∼** lit against the current; fig against the tide; **suivre le ∼** lit to go with the current, to go downstream; fig to go with the flow; **remonter le ∼** fig to get back on one's feet; [2] Électrotech current; ∼ **électrique** electric current; **il n'y a plus de ∼** the power has gone off; **le ∼ passe bien entre elle et lui** fig they get on very well; [3] (tendance) trend; **un ∼ de pensée** a current of thought; [4] (déplacement) movement; **les ∼s migratoires** migratory; [5] (période) **dans le ∼ de** in the course of

C au courant loc adj [1] (informé) **être au ∼** to know; **je ne suis pas du tout au ∼ de ce qu'il veut faire** I really don't know what he wants to do; **mettre qn au ∼** to put sb in the picture, to fill sb in (**de** about); **tenir qn au ∼** to keep sb posted (**de** about); [2] (au fait) **être très au ∼** to know all about it; **pour les questions techniques demande à Paul, il est très au ∼** for technical questions ask Paul, he knows all about it; **mettre qn au ∼** to bring sb up to date (**de** on); **se tenir au ∼** to keep up to date (**de** on)

(Composé) **∼ d'air** draught GB, draft US; **leur fils est un vrai ∼ d'air** hum their son is never in one place for more than five minutes at a time

courbatu, **-e** /kuRbaty/ adj stiff

courbature /kuRbatyR/ nf ache; **avoir des ∼s** to be stiff; **être plein de ∼s** to be stiff all over

courbaturé, **-e** /kuRbatyRe/ adj (après un effort) stiff; (pendant une grippe) aching

courbe /kuRb/

A adj curved

B nf [1] (représentation graphique) curve; ∼ **ascendante des prix** rising price curve; **la ∼ de popularité du ministre** the minister's popularity rating; [2] (de rivière) bend; (de route) curve, bend; (de sourcil) arch; **faire une ∼** [route] to curve, to bend

(Composés) **∼ de niveau** contour line; **∼ de température** temperature chart

courber /kuRbe/ [1]

A vtr to bend [rameau, barre, corps, partie du corps]; **courbant la tête sur son livre** bending over her book; **courbant le dos** or **les épaules pour** bending down in order to; ∼ **la tête** or **le front** or **le dos** fig to bow down

B vi ∼ **sous le poids** to be bowed down under the weight

C se courber vpr (se baisser) to bend down; (avec l'âge) to become bent with age

courbette /kuRbεt/ nf [1] (low) bow; **faire des ∼s** fig to bow and scrape (**devant** to); [2] (en équitation) curvet

courbure /kuRbyR/ nf curve

coureur, **-euse** /kuRœR, øz/ nm,f ▸ p. 372 Sport (en course à pied) runner

(Composés) **∼ automobile** racing driver; **∼ cycliste** racing cyclist; **∼ de haies** hurdler; **∼ de jupons** philanderer; **∼ motocycliste** motorcycle racer

courge /kuRʒ/ nf Bot (terme générique) gourd; (fruit) (vegetable) marrow

courgette /kuRʒεt/ nf courgette GB, zucchini US

courir /kuRiR/ [26]

A vtr [1] Sport to compete in [épreuve]; [2] (parcourir en tous sens) ∼ **la campagne/les océans/le monde** to roam the countryside/the oceans/the world; **j'ai couru tout Paris pour trouver ton cadeau** I searched the whole of Paris for your present; [3] (fréquenter) ∼ **les théâtres** to do the round of the theatres, ∼ **les boutiques** to do the round of the shops GB ou stores US; [4] (s'exposer à) ∼ **un (grand) danger** to be in (great) danger; **faire ∼ un (grand) danger à qn/qch** to put sb/sth in (serious) danger; ∼ **un (gros) risque** to run a (big) risk; **faire ∼ un risque à qn** to put sb at risk; **c'est un risque à ∼** it's a risk one has to take; [5] ○(chercher à séduire)

~ **les filles/garçons** to chase after girls/boys

B vi **1** gén [*personne, animal*] to run; **sortir en courant** to run out; **'va chercher ton frère'—'j'y cours'** 'go and get your brother'–'I'm going'; **tout le monde court voir leur spectacle** everybody is rushing to see their show; **les voleurs courent toujours** fig the thieves are still at large; **2** Sport (à pied) [*athlète, cheval*] to run; (en vélo, voiture, moto) to race; ~ **sur une balle** (au tennis) to run for a ball; **3** (se presser) [*personne*] to rush; **en courant** hastily, in a rush; ~ **(tout droit) à la catastrophe/faillite** to be heading (straight) for disaster/bankruptcy; **4** (chercher à rattraper) ~ **après qn/qch** gén to run after sb/sth; (poursuivre) to chase after [*voleur, gloire*]; **s'il ne veut pas me voir je ne vais pas lui** ~ **après** fig if he doesn't want to see me I'm not going to go chasing after him; **5** (se mouvoir rapidement) [*ruisseau*] to rush (**dans** through); [*nuages, flammes*] to race (**dans** across); **6** (parcourir) ~ **le long de** [*sentier*] to run along; [*veine*] to run down; **7** (se propager) [*rumeur*] to go around; **c'est un bruit qui court** it's a rumour^{GB}; **faire** ~ **un bruit** to spread a rumour^{GB}; **8** (être en vigueur) [*intérêts*] to accrue; [*bail, contrat*] to run (**jusqu'à** to); **9** (s'écouler) **le mois/ l'année qui court** the current *ou* present month/year; **10** [*navire*] to run, to sail

(Idiomes) **tu peux toujours** ~[○]! you can go whistle for it[○]!; **laisser** ~[○] to let things ride; **laisse** ~[○]! forget it!

courlis /kuʀli/ nm inv curlew

couronne /kuʀɔn/ nf **1** (de roi) crown; (de noble) coronet; **2** (de fleurs, feuilles) ~ **de fleurs** garland; (pour enterrement) wreath; ~ **de lauriers** laurel wreath; **3** (de dent) crown; **4** (cercle) ring; **5** (pouvoir) **la** ~ the Crown; **6** (monnaie) crown; **7** (pain) ring-shaped loaf; **8** (banlieue de Paris) **la petite** ~ the inner suburbs; **la grande** ~ the outer suburbs

couronnement /kuʀɔnmã/ nm (de souverain) coronation; (de saint, héros) crowning; **c'est le** ~ **de leur carrière** fig it's their crowning achievement

couronner /kuʀɔne/ [1] vtr **1** (coiffer d'une couronne, sacrer) to crown [*roi*] (**de** with); **enfant à la tête couronnée de roses** child wearing a garland of roses on his/her head; **pic couronné de neige** liter snow-capped peak; **2** (donner un prix à) to award a prize to [*personne, œuvre*]; (récompenser) **être couronné de succès** to be crowned with success; **cela couronne dix années de recherches** this is the crowning achievement of ten years' research; **et pour** ~ **le tout** hum and to crown it all; **3** (en dentisterie) to crown

courre /kuʀ/ vtr **chasse à** ~ hunting

courriel /kuʀjɛl/ nm Can email

courrier /kuʀje/ nm (lettres) mail, post GB; (une lettre) letter; **faire son** ~ to write some letters; **par retour du** ~ by return (of post) GB, by return mail

(Composés) ~ **du cœur** problem page; ~ **de la mode/ littéraire** fashion/book page; ~ **électronique** Ordinat electronic mail; ~ **des lecteurs** letters to the editor

courriériste /kuʀjeʀist/ nmf columnist

courroie /kuʀwa/ nf **1** (lien) strap; **2** (sur une machine) belt

courroucé, ~**e** /kuʀuse/ adj liter wrathful sout

courroux /kuʀu/ nm inv liter wrath sout, ire sout

cours /kuʀ/ nm inv **1** (session d'enseignement) Scol lesson, class; Univ class; (magistral) lecture; (hors cadre scolaire) class; (en privé) lesson; (ensemble de sessions) course; **avoir** ~ to have a class; **suivre un** ~ to do *ou* take a course; **faire** ~ to teach; **qui vous fait** ~ **en chimie?** who teaches chemistry; **faire un** ~ **sur qch** (une fois) to give a class in sth; (plusieurs fois) to teach a course in sth; **il nous a fait un véritable** ~ **sur la gastronomie** he gave us a real lecture on gastronomy; **donner des** ~ **de français** (dans l'enseignement) to teach French; (en privé) to give French lessons; **2** (manuel) Scol, Univ course book, textbook; (notes) notes; **3** (établissement) school; ~ **de théâtre** drama school; **4** Fin (taux de négociation) (de denrée, valeur) price; (de devise) exchange rate; **avoir** ~ Fin [*monnaie*] to be legal tender; fig [*théorie, pratique*] to be current; [*terme*] to be used; **ne plus avoir** ~ Fin [*monnaie*] to be no longer legal tender; fig [*théorie, pratique*] to be no longer accepted; [*terme*] to be no longer used; **5** (de rivière) (parcours) course; (débit) flow; **6** (enchaînement) (de récit, carrière, d'événements) course; (d'idées) flow; **les choses suivent leur** ~ things are taking their course; **la vie reprend son** ~ life returns to normal; **donner libre** ~ **à** to give free rein to [*imagination*]; to give way to [*peine*]; to give vent to [*colère*]; **au** *or* **dans le** ~ **de** in the course of, during;

en ~ [*mois, semaine, année*] current; [*processus, projet*] under way (*après n*); [*travail, négociations, changements*] in progress (*après n*); **en** ~ **de journée/saison** in the course of the day/ season; **en** ~ **de fabrication/rénovation** in the process of being manufactured/renovated; **le pont en** ~ **de construction** the bridge being built *ou* under construction; **en** ~ **de route** along the way; **en** ~ **de cuisson** during cooking

(Composés) ~ **d'eau** watercourse; ~ **élémentaire deuxième année**, CE2 *third year of primary school, age 8–9*; ~ **élémentaire première année**, CE1 *second year of primary school, age 7–8*; ~ **magistral** lecture; ~ **moyen deuxième année**, CM2 *fifth year of primary school, age 10–11*; ~ **moyen première année**, CM1 *fourth year of primary school, age 9–10*; ~ **d'initiation** introductory course; ~ **par correspondance** correspondence course; ~ **particulier(s)** private tuition **𝒞** GB, private tutoring **𝒞** US (**en**, **de** in); ~ **de perfectionnement** improvers' course; ~ **préparatoire**, CP *first year of primary school, age 6–7*; ~ **de rattrapage** remedial course; ~ **de remise à niveau** refresher course; ~ **du soir** evening class

course /kuʀs/

A nf **1** (mode de déplacement) running; **faire la** ~ **avec qn** lit, fig to race sb; **être rapide à la** ~ to be a fast runner; **2** (trajet) (de personne) run; (de taxi) journey; **c'est 10 euros la** ~ the fare is 10 euros; **3** [○](précipitation) rush; **ça va être la** ~ **pour rendre le rapport dans les délais** it'll be a rush getting the report in before the deadline; **4** (compétition) race; **la** ~ **au profit/aux voix** the race for profit/for votes; **être en** ~ Sport to be in the race; fig to be in the running; **être hors** ~ Sport, fig to be out of the race; **5** (activité) (en athlétisme) running; (avec un véhicule, animal) racing; (épreuve) race; (en alpinisme) climb; **6** (démarche) errand; **faire une** ~ to run an errand; **7** (achat, commission) **j'ai une** ~ **à faire** I've got to go and get something; **j'ai deux ou trois** ~**s à faire** I've got some shopping to do; **8** (trajectoire) (d'astre, de planète, comète) path; (de nuages) passage; (de fusée, projectile) flight path; **9** (passage) liter **la** ~ **du temps/des années** the passing of time/of the years

B courses nfpl **1** (achats) shopping **𝒞**; **je vais faire des** ~**s** I'm going shopping; **2** (de chevaux) races

(Composés) ~ **de haies** (en athlétisme) hurdles (*pl*); (à cheval) steeplechase; ~ **d'obstacles** obstacle race; fig obstacle course; ~ **à pied** running; ~ **de taureaux** (corrida) bull-fight; (dans la rue) bull run; ~ **de vitesse** (en athlétisme) sprint; (en moto) speedway race

(Idiomes) **ne plus être dans la** ~ to be out of touch; **être en fin de** ~ to be on the decline; **être à bout de** ~ to be worn out

coursier, -ière /kuʀsje, ɛʀ/

A ▸ p. 372 nm,f messenger

B nm Hist charger, warhorse

coursive /kuʀsiv/ nf passageway

court, ~**e** /kuʀ, kuʀt/

A adj **1** (de taille, en durée) short; **dans le délai le plus** ~ in the shortest possible time; **de** ~**e durée** [*victoire, joie, espoir*] short-lived; [*prêt, emploi, maladie*] short-term; **s'arrêter, souffle** ~ to get out of breath and stop; **avoir le souffle** ~ to get out of breath easily; **prendre au plus** ~ to take the shortest route; **2** (insuffisant) [*connaissances*] limited; **une heure/trois pages c'est (un peu)** ~ one hour/three pages, that's not really enough; **3** (faible) [*défaite, victoire, majorité*] narrow; **gagner d'une** ~**e tête** [*cheval*] to win by a short head; [*candidat*] to win by a narrow margin

B adv **s'habiller** ~ to wear short skirts; **jouer** ~ to play short balls; **couper qch** ~ to cut sth short; **couper** ~ (en parlant) to cut the conversation short; **couper** ~ **à qch** (abréger) to cut sth short; (faire cesser) to put paid to sth; **tourner** ~ to come to a sudden end; **s'arrêter** ~ to stop short

C nm **1** (style vestimentaire) **le** ~ short skirts (*pl*); **2** Sport ~ **de tennis** tennis court

(Composés) ~ **métrage** Cin short (film); ~**e échelle** leg up[○]; **faire la** ~**e échelle à qn** to give sb a leg up[○]

(Idiomes) **être à** ~ **de** to be short of [*argent*]; to be short on [*idées*]; **prendre qn de** ~ to catch sb on the hop[○] GB *ou* unprepared

courtaud, ~**e** /kuʀto, od/ adj [*personne*] shortish

court-circuit, pl ~**s** /kuʀsiʀkɥi/ nm shortcircuit

court-circuiter /kuʀsiʀkɥite/ [1] *vtr* ① lit to short-circuit; ② ○fig to bypass [*intermédiaire*]

courtier, -ière /kuʀtje, ɛʀ/ ▸ p. 372 *nm,f* broker

courtisan /kuʀtizã/ *nm* ① (flatteur) sycophant; **attitude de** ∼ fawning ℂ; ② Hist courtier

courtisane /kuʀtizan/ *nf* courtesan

courtiser /kuʀtize/ [1] *vtr* to woo

courtois, ∼**e** /kuʀtwa, az/ *adj* courteous; Littérat courtly

courtoisie /kuʀtwazi/ *nf* courtesy

court-vêtu, ∼**e**, *mpl* ∼**s** /kuʀvety/ *adj* **une femme** ∼**e** a woman in a short skirt

couru, ∼**e** /kuʀy/ *adj* ① [*endroit*] popular; ② (aux courses) **vingt partants, tous** ∼ twenty at the start, all ran

(Idiome) **c'est** ∼○ **d'avance** it's a foregone conclusion

cousin, ∼**e** /kuzɛ̃, in/
Ⓐ *nm,f* cousin; ∼ **germain** first cousin
Ⓑ *nm* Zool mosquito

(Idiomes) **être** ∼**s à la mode de Bretagne** hum to be distantly related; **le roi n'est pas son** ∼ he thinks he is the cat's whiskers

coussin /kusɛ̃/ *nm* (pour divan) cushion

(Composés) ∼ **d'air** air cushion; ∼ **de sécurité** air bag

coussinet /kusinɛ/ *nm* (de divan) small cushion

(Composé) ∼ **plantaire** Zool pad

cousu, ∼**e** /kuzy/ ▸ **coudre**

coût /ku/ *nm* cost (**de** of; **en** in)

coûtant /kutã/ *adj* **prix** ∼ cost price

couteau, *pl* ∼**x** /kuto/ *nm* ① gén knife; (de mixeur) blade; **c'est un coup de** ∼ (blessure) it's a knife wound; **jouer** *or* **manier du** ∼ to use a knife (*in a fight*); **donner un coup de** ∼ **à qn** to stab sb; **tuer qn à coups de** ∼ to stab sb to death; ② (coquillage) razor shell GB *ou* clam US

(Composé) ∼ **à cran d'arrêt** flick knife GB, switchblade US

(Idiomes) **être à** ∼**x tirés**○ **avec qn** to be at daggers drawn with sb; **avoir le** ∼ **sous la gorge** to have a pistol to one's head; **tendre la gorge au** ∼ to lay one's head on the block

coutelas /kutla/ *nm* (de cuisine) large (kitchen) knife; (sabre) cutlass

coutelier, -ière /kutəlje, ɛʀ/ ▸ p. 372 *nm,f* cutler

coutellerie /kutɛlʀi/ *nf* (magasin) cutlery shop; (fabrique) cutlery works (*pl*); (industrie) cutlery industry; (commerce) cutlery trade *ou* business; (objets) cutlery

coûter /kute/ [1]
Ⓐ *vtr* to cost; ∼ **la vie à qn** to cost sb his/her life
Ⓑ *vi* to cost; ∼ **dix euros** to cost ten euros; **combien coûte ce livre?** how much is this book?; **cela me coûte d'aller le voir** fig it's hard for me to go and see him; ∼ **cher** to be expensive; **ne pas** ∼ **cher** to be cheap, not to cost a lot; ∼ **cher à qn** lit to cost sb a lot; fig [*erreur, action*] to cost sb dear(ly)
Ⓒ *v impers* **il en coûte à qn de faire** it's hard for sb to do; **il t'en coûtera d'avoir fait cela** you will pay for doing this; **coûte que coûte, quoi qu'il en coûte** at all costs

(Idiomes) **il n'y a que le premier pas qui coûte** the first step is the hardest; ∼ **les yeux de la tête**○ to cost an arm and a leg○

coûteux, -euse /kutø, øz/ *adj* costly

coutil /kuti/ *nm* (pour vêtement) (cotton) drill; (pour matelas) ticking

coutume /kutym/ *nf* (habitude) custom; **selon la** ∼ according to custom; **avoir** ∼ **de faire qch** to be in the habit of doing sth; **la** ∼ **le veut** it is the custom; **de** ∼ as a rule; **comme de** ∼ as usual

(Idiome) **une fois n'est pas** ∼ it does no harm just this once

coutumier, -ière /kutymje, ɛʀ/ *adj* customary

couture /kutyʀ/ *nf* ① (activité, chose à coudre) sewing; (activité professionnelle) dressmaking; **faire de la** ∼ to sew; **haute** ∼ haute couture; ② (bords cousus) seam

(Idiomes) **le petit doigt sur la** ∼ **du pantalon** standing stiffly to attention; **regarder qch sous toutes les** ∼**s** to examine sth from every angle; **battre qn à plates** ∼**s** to beat sb hollow

couturier /kutyʀje/ *nm* ▸ p. 372 dress designer; **grand** ∼ couturier

couturière /kutyʀjɛʀ/ *nf* ▸ p. 372 dressmaker

couvée /kuve/ *nf* (d'oisillons, enfants) brood; (d'œufs) clutch

couvent /kuvã/ *nm* ① (pour femmes) convent; (pour hommes) monastery; **entrer au** ∼ to enter a convent; ② (école) convent school

couver /kuve/ [1]
Ⓐ *vtr* ① Zool to sit on [*œufs*]; **la poule couve** the hen is brooding; ② (protéger) to overprotect; ∼ **qn/qch du regard** (avec tendresse) to look fondly at sb/sth; (avec envie) to gaze longingly at sb/sth; ③ (être atteint de) to be coming down with [*maladie*]; ④ (préparer) to hatch [*complot*]; to plot [*vengeance*]
Ⓑ *vi* [*révolte*] to brew; [*feu, colère, jalousie*] to smoulder; [*racisme, fanatisme*] to lie dormant

couvercle /kuvɛʀkl/ *nm* lid; (qui se visse) screwtop

couvert, ∼**e** /kuvɛʀ, ɛʀt/
Ⓐ *pp* ▸ **couvrir**
Ⓑ *pp adj* ① (plein) covered (**de** in, with); **être** ∼ **de diplômes** to have a lot of qualifications; ② (en intérieur) [*piscine*] indoor; [*marché, stade, passage*] covered; ③ Météo [*ciel, temps*] overcast
Ⓒ *nm* ① (accessoires pour un repas) place setting; **une table de 6** ∼**s** a table set for 6; **mettre le** ∼ to lay the table; **avoir son** ∼ **chez qn** fig to be a frequent dinner guest at sb's house; **un** ∼ **en argent** a silver knife, fork and spoon; **ils mangent avec des** ∼**s en argent** they eat with silver cutlery; ② (à payer au restaurant) cover charge; ③ (abri) cover; **sous le** ∼ **d'un arbre/bois** under the cover of a tree/wood
Ⓓ **à couvert** *loc adv* under cover; **se mettre à** ∼ to take cover
Ⓔ **sous le couvert de** *loc prép* (apparence) under the pretence GB of; **sous** ∼ **de la plaisanterie** under the guise of a joke

couverture /kuvɛʀtyʀ/ *nf* ① (de lit) blanket; (plus petit) rug GB, lap robe US; ② (de livre) cover; ③ (dans la presse) coverage; **assurer la** ∼ **d'un événement** to cover an event; ④ (toiture) roofing ℂ, roof; ⑤ (ce qui protège d'un risque, d'un danger) cover; ∼ **aérienne** air cover; **taux de** ∼ (dans les échanges commerciaux) import-export ratio

(Composés) ∼ **chauffante** electric blanket; ∼ **maladie universelle, CMU** free health care for people on low incomes; ∼ **sociale** social security cover; ∼ **végétale** plant cover; ∼ **de voyage** travelling rug GB, lap robe US

(Idiome) **tirer la** ∼ **à soi** to turn a situation to one's own advantage

> ⓘ **Couverture maladie universelle** Since January 2000, the social security cover guaranteed by the *CMU* provides 6 million low-income earners in France with free medical care. In addition, those eligible for full medical cover are entitled to free consultations.

couveuse /kuvøz/ *nf* ① (appareil) incubator; ② (poule) brood hen

couvre-chef, *pl* ∼**s** /kuvʀəʃɛf/ *nm* hum headgear ℂ, hat

couvre-feu, *pl* ∼**x** /kuvʀəfø/ *nm* curfew

couvre-lit, *pl* ∼**s** /kuvʀəli/ *nm* bedspread

couvre-pieds /kuvʀəpje/ *nm inv* small quilt

couvreur /kuvʀœʀ/ ▸ p. 372 *nm* roofer

couvrir /kuvʀiʀ/ [32]
Ⓐ *vtr* ① (recouvrir) gén to cover (**de** with); to roof [*maison*]; (aux cartes) to cover; ∼ **un toit d'ardoises/de tuiles** to slate/to tile a roof; ∼ **des pages et des pages d'une écriture serrée** to fill page after page in closely written script; **une peinture qui couvre bien** a paint that gives good coverage; ② (être plus fort que) [*son, musique*] to drown out; ③ (desservir) [*émetteur, inspecteur*] to cover [*région*]; ④ (contre le froid) (avec des vêtements) to wrap [sb] up; (au lit) to cover [sb] up; **il est trop couvert** (vêtu) he's got too many clothes on; (au lit) he's got too many blankets on; ⑤ (donner en grande quantité) ∼ **qn de qch** (d'honneurs, de bijoux, compliments) to shower sb with sth, to shower sth on sb; (de baisers) to cover sb with sth; ⑥ (protéger) to cover up for [*faute, personne*]; (avec une arme) to cover [*soldat, retraite*]; ⑦ (parcourir) to cover [*distance*]; ⑧ (rendre compte de) [*livre, auteur, presse*] to cover [*sujet, période, événement*]; ⑨ (pourvoir à) ∼ **les besoins de qn** to meet sb's needs; ⑩ Fin [*somme*] to cover [*dépenses*]; ∼ **une enchère** to make a higher bid; ⑪ (garantir) to cover [*dégât,*

risque, personne]; [12] Zool [*mâle*] to cover [*femelle*]

B **se couvrir** *vpr* [1] (s'habiller) to wrap up; (d'un chapeau) to put on a hat; **elle se couvrit les épaules d'un châle** she covered her shoulders with a shawl; **rester couvert** to keep one's hat on; [2] Météo [*ciel*] to become cloudy *ou* overcast; [3] (se remplir) **se ~ de** (de plaques, boutons) to become covered with; **l'arbre se couvre de fleurs/feuilles** the tree comes into bloom/leaf; **son visage se couvrit de larmes** tears poured down her face; [4] (se protéger) (de critiques, d'accusations) to cover oneself; (de coups) to protect oneself; **se ~ contre** to cover oneself against

CP /sepe/ *nm: abbr* ▸ **cours**

CPI *nf* (*abbr* = **Cour Pénale Internationale**) International Criminal Court, ICC

CQFD /sekyefde/ (*abbr* = **ce qu'il fallait démontrer**) QED

crabe /kʀab/ *nm* Zool crab; **marcher en ~** to sidle along

crac /kʀak/ *nm* (*also onomat*) (cassure) crack; (déchirure) rip; (bruit) cracking sound; **et puis ~! elle a changé d'idée** and then, bang! she changed her mind

crachat /kʀaʃa/ *nm* spit **ℂ**

crachement /kʀaʃmɑ̃/ *nm* [1] (de salive, etc) spitting **ℂ**; [2] (de fumée) belching **ℂ**; (d'étincelles) shower; (de flammes) burst; [3] (bruit) crackling **ℂ**

cracher /kʀaʃe/ [1]
A *vtr* [1] (ce qui est dans la bouche) to spit out [*noyau, aliment*]; **~ du sang** to spit blood; **c'est le portrait de sa mère tout craché** fig she's the spitting image of her mother; **c'est lui tout craché** fig that's just like him; [2] (dire) **~ des injures à qn** to hurl abuse at sb; [3] (émettre) to belch (out) [*flammes, fumée*]; to spit out [*balles*]
B *vi* [1] [*personne*] to spit; **je ne cracherais pas dessus** hum I wouldn't turn up my nose at it; [2] [*robinet, stylo*] to splutter; [*radio*] to crackle

(Idiome) **c'est comme si on crachait en l'air** it's a complete waste of time

cracheur /kʀaʃœʀ/ *nm* **~ de feu** fire-eater

crachin /kʀaʃɛ̃/ *nm* drizzle

crachoir /kʀaʃwaʀ/ *nm* spittoon

(Idiome) **tenir le ~ à qn** to talk on and on at sb

crachoter /kʀaʃɔte/ [1] *vi* [1] [*personne*] to cough and splutter; [2] [*robinet*] to splutter; [3] [*micro*] to crackle

crack /kʀak/ *nm* [1] (cheval) champion horse; [2] (génie) ace; [3] (drogue) crack

craie /kʀɛ/ *nf* (roche, bâton) chalk

craindre /kʀɛ̃dʀ/ [54] *vtr* [1] (redouter) to fear, to be afraid of; **~ le pire** to fear the worst; **ne craignez rien** don't be afraid; **oui, je le crains** yes, I'm afraid so; **~ de faire** to be afraid of doing; **une explosion est à ~** there's some danger of an explosion; [2] (être sensible à) [*personne, peau*] to be sensitive to [*froid, savon*]; [*plante*] to dislike [*soleil*]

crainte /kʀɛ̃t/ *nf* [1] (peur) fear (**de** of; **de faire** of doing); **sans ~** without fear; **avec ~** fearfully; [2] (inquiétude) fear; **avoir des ~s au sujet de qn** to be worried about sb

(Idiome) **la ~ est le commencement de la sagesse** Prov only a fool knows no fear

craintif, -ive /kʀɛ̃tif, iv/ *adj* [*personne, voix*] timorous; [*animal*] timid

craintivement /kʀɛ̃tivmɑ̃/ *adv* timidly

cramoisi, ~e /kʀamwazi/ ▸ p. 140 *adj* crimson

crampe /kʀɑ̃p/ *nf* cramp

crampon /kʀɑ̃pɔ̃/ *nm* [1] (d'alpiniste) crampon; **chaussures à ~s** (de football) boots with studs GB *ou* cleats US; (de course) spiked shoes; [2] (pour assembler) cramp (iron), clamp

cramponner: se cramponner /kʀɑ̃pɔne/ [1] *vpr* to hold on tightly; **se ~ à qch/qn** lit, fig to cling to sth/sb

cran /kʀɑ̃/
A *nm* [1] (encoche) notch; (sur ceinture, courroie) hole; **se mettre un ~ à la ceinture** fig to tighten one's belt; **monter d'un ~** fig [*cote de popularité*] to go up a notch; [*personne*] (dans l'estime) to move up a notch; (dans une hiérarchie) to move up a rung; **pousse-toi d'un ~** move up one (place); [2] (entaille, repère) nick; [3] (courage) **avoir du ~** to have guts; [4] (en coiffure) wave
B à **cran** *loc adv* **être à ~, avoir les nerfs à ~** to be on edge

(Composés) **~ d'arrêt** flick knife GB, switchblade US; **~ de sûreté** safety catch

crâne /kʀɑn/ ▸ p. 136 *nm* [1] Anat skull; [2] (tête) head; **ne rien avoir dans le ~** to have no brains

(Idiome) **bourrer le ~ à qn** to brainwash sb

crânement /kʀɑnmɑ̃/ *adv* (bravement) gallantly; (fièrement) proudly

crâner /kʀɑne/ [1] *vi* to show off

crâneur, -euse /kʀɑnœʀ, øz/
A *adj* pretentious
B *nm,f* show-off; **faire le ~** to show off

crânien, -ienne /kʀanjɛ̃, ɛn/ *adj* cranial; **boîte crânienne** cranium

cranter /kʀɑ̃te/ [1] *vtr* [1] (entailler) to notch; [2] (en coiffure) to crimp

crapaud /kʀapo/ *nm* [1] Zool toad; [2] (de diamant) flaw

(Idiome) **la bave du ~ n'atteint pas la blanche colombe** hum ≈ sticks and stones (may break my bones but words will never hurt me)

crapule /kʀapyl/ *nf* pej (individu) crook

crapuleux, -euse /kʀapylø, øz/ *adj* villainous

craquant, ~e /kʀakɑ̃, ɑ̃t/ *adj* [*personne*] irresistible

craqueler /kʀakle/ [19]
A *vtr* to crackle [*céramique*]
B **se craqueler** *vpr* to crack

craquelure /kʀaklyʀ/ *nf* crack; **~s** (en céramique) (accidentelles) crazing **ℂ**; (délibérées) crackle **ℂ**; Art craquelure **ℂ**

craquement /kʀakmɑ̃/ *nm* (grincement) creaking sound, creak; (bruit de cassure) cracking sound, crack; (de feuilles mortes) crackle **ℂ**

craquer /kʀake/ [1]
A *vtr* [1] (déchirer) to split [*vêtement*]; to rip [*collant*]; to break [*sangle, poignée*]; [2] (frotter) to strike [*allumette*]
B *vi* [1] (se rompre) [*couture*] to split; [*vêtement*] to split (at the seams); [*collant*] to rip; [*branche, vitre*] to crack; [*sac*] to burst; **faire ~ une branche** to break a branch; [2] (faire un bruit) [*plancher, mât*] to creak; [*neige*] to crunch; [*feuilles*] to rustle; [*branchages*] to crack; **qui craque sous la dent** crunchy; **faire ~ ses articulations** to crack one's joints; [3] (pour allumer) **faire ~ une allumette** to strike a match; [4] (ne pas résister) [*entreprise*] to collapse; [*personne*] (de tension nerveuse) to crack up; (dans un effort) to give up

crasse /kʀas/
A *adj* [*ignorance, stupidité*] crass; [*impolitesse*] gross; **d'une ignorance ~** pig ignorant
B *nf* [1] (saleté) grime, filth; [2] (mauvais tour) dirty trick; [3] Tech (scorie) dross, slag; (résidus) scum **ℂ**

crasseux, -euse /kʀasø, øz/ *adj* filthy, grimy

crassier /kʀasje/ *nm* slag heap

cratère /kʀatɛʀ/ *nm* crater

cravache /kʀavaʃ/ *nf* whip; **donner un coup de ~ à** to whip

cravacher /kʀavaʃe/ [1] *vtr* to whip [*cheval*]

cravate /kʀavat/ *nf* [1] (pour chemise) tie; (insigne de décoration) ribbon; [2] (prise de catch) headlock

cravater /kʀavate/ [1] *vtr* [1] (saisir par le cou) to grab [sb] round the neck; (en sport) to put [sb] in a headlock; [2] (d'une cravate) **cravaté de soie** wearing a silk tie

crawl /kʀol/ *nm* crawl; **nager le ~** to do *ou* swim the crawl

crawler /kʀole/ [1] *vi* to do *ou* swim the crawl; **dos crawlé** backstroke

crayeux, -euse /kʀɛjø, øz/ *adj* gén chalky; [*teint*] chalk-white

crayon /kʀɛjɔ̃/ *nm* [1] (pour écrire, se farder) pencil; **au ~** in pencil; **avoir un bon coup de ~** to be good at drawing; **faire un portrait en trois coups de ~** to quickly sketch a portrait; [2] (dessin) pencil drawing

(Composés) **~ à bille** ballpoint pen; **~ de couleur** coloured^GB pencil; **~ feutre** felt-tip pen; **~ gras** soft pencil; **~ à lèvres** lip pencil; **~ noir** lead pencil; **~ optique** light pen; **~ à sourcils** eyebrow pencil; **~ pour les yeux** eyeliner

crayon-feutre, *pl* **crayons-feutres** /kʀɛjɔ̃føtʀ/ *nm* felt-tip pen

crayon-lecteur, *pl* **crayons-lecteurs** /kʀɛjɔ̃lɛktœʀ/ *nm* bar-code reader

crayonnage /kʀɛjɔnaʒ/ nm (croquis) pencil sketch; (gribouillage) **des ~s** scribbles

crayonner /kʀɛjɔne/ [1] vtr (dessiner) to make a pencil sketch of; (écrire) to scribble down

créance /kʀeɑ̃s/ nf ① (somme due) debt (owed by a debtor); (titre) letter of credit; ② (foi) liter credence sout; **perdre ~ auprès de qn** to lose credibility with sb

créancier, -ière /kʀeɑ̃sje, ɛʀ/ nm,f creditor

créateur, -trice /kʀeatœʀ, tʀis/
A adj creative
B nm,f (de parfum, genre littéraire, rôle) creator; (de produit) designer

Créateur /kʀeatœʀ/ nm Relig **le ~** the Creator

créatif, -ive /kʀeatif, iv/ adj creative

création /kʀeasjɔ̃/ nf ① (action de créer, produit original) creation; Comm (action) (produit) product; **la ~ d'une société/d'un comité** setting up a company/a committee; **la ~ d'emplois** job creation; **il y aura des ~s d'emplois** new jobs will be created; **encourager les ~s d'entreprises** to encourage business start-ups; ② Théât **c'est une ~** (rôle) the part has never been acted before; (pièce) the play is being staged for the first time

Création /kʀeasjɔ̃/ nf Bible **la ~ (du monde)** the Creation

créationnisme /kʀeasjɔnism/ nm creationism

créativité /kʀeativite/ nf creativity

créature /kʀeatyʀ/ nf gén creature

crécelle /kʀesɛl/ nf rattle; **voix de ~** shrill voice

crécerelle /kʀesʀɛl/ nf kestrel

crèche /kʀɛʃ/ nf ① (garderie) crèche GB, day-nursery; ② (de Noël) crib GB, crèche US

crédibilité /kʀedibilite/ nf credibility (**auprès de** with)

crédible /kʀedibl/ adj credible

crédit /kʀedi/ nm ① (somme allouée) funds (pl); **nous disposons d'un ~ de 2 000 euros** we have funds of 2,000 euros; **les ~s de la recherche/défense** research/defence GB funding ou budget; ② (avance de fonds) credit **C**; **accorder un ~ à qn** to grant credit terms ou facilities to sb; **faire ~ à qn** to give sb credit; **à ~** on credit; ③ Fin credit; **votre ~ est de 200 euros** you are 200 euros in credit; **porter une somme au ~ de qn** or **d'un compte** to credit sb's account with a sum of money; ④ (considération) credibility; **mettre** or **porter qch au ~ de qn** fig to give sb credit for sth

Composé **~ municipal** pawnshop

créditer /kʀedite/ [1] vtr to credit (**de** with)

créditeur, -trice /kʀeditœʀ, tʀis/ adj [compte, solde] credit (épith); [client, pays] in credit (après n); **être ~** to be in credit

crédit-relais, pl **crédits-relais** /kʀediʀəlɛ/ nm bridging loan

credo /kʀedo/ nm ① (principes) creed; ② Relig **le Credo** the Creed

crédule /kʀedyl/ adj gullible, credulous

crédulité /kʀedylite/ nf gullibility, credulity

créer /kʀee/ [11]
A vtr gén to design, to invent [produit]; to set up [compagnie, comité]; to create [problème]; ② Théât to create [rôle]; to put on [sth] (for the first time) [pièce, spectacle]
B se créer vpr **se ~ du travail** to create work for oneself; **se ~ des problèmes** to create problems for oneself

crémaillère /kʀemajɛʀ/ nf (de cheminée) trammel, chimney hook

Idiome **pendre la ~** to have a house-warming (party)

crémation /kʀemasjɔ̃/ nf cremation

crématoire /kʀematwaʀ/ nm crematorium; **four ~** crematorium furnace

crème¹ /kʀɛm/
A ▸ p. 140 adj inv cream
B nm ① ○(café) espresso with milk; ▸ **petit**; ② ▸ p. 140 (couleur) cream

crème² /kʀɛm/ nf ① (matière grasse) cream; **escalope à la ~** escalope with cream; ② (pour dessert; (pour fourrer un gâteau) cream; ③ (soupe) **~ d'asperges** cream of asparagus soup; ④ (liqueur) **~ de cassis/menthe** crème de cassis/menthe; ⑤ (pour la peau) cream; ⑥ ○(élite) **la ~** (socialement) the cream of society; **la ~ des linguistes** the very best linguists; **c'est la ~ des hommes** he's the perfect man

Composés **~ anglaise** ≈ custard; **~ Chantilly** whipped cream; **~ fleurette** ≈ whipping cream; **~ fouettée = ~ Chantilly**; **~ fraîche** crème fraîche, ≈ cream; **~ glacée** dairy ice cream; **~ de gruyère** ≈ cheese spread; **~ de marrons** chestnut purée; **~ pâtissière** confectioner's custard; **~ renversée** caramel custard

crémerie /kʀɛmʀi/ ▸ p. 372 nf cheese shop GB ou store US; **changer de ~**○ hum to take one's custom ou business elsewhere

crémeux, -euse /kʀemø, øz/ adj lit, fig creamy

crémier, -ière /kʀemje, ɛʀ/ ▸ p. 372 nm,f cheese seller

crémone /kʀemɔn/ nf espagnolette (bolt)

créneau, pl **~x** /kʀeno/ nm ① Aut parallel parking **C**; ② (moment) **tu as un ~ demain?** do you have any free time tomorrow?; ③ Comm market; (sur un marché) gap, niche (**sur** in); ④ Archit crenel; **les ~x** crenellations

Composés **~ horaire** time slot; **~ de lancement** Astronaut launch window; **~ publicitaire** Radio, TV advertising slot

Idiome **monter au ~** to intervene

créneler /kʀɛnle/ [19] vtr to crenellate [tour]; to mill [pièce de monnaie]

créole¹ /kʀeɔl/
A adj [accent, cuisine] creole
B ▸ p. 336 nm Ling Creole

créole² /kʀeɔl/ nf ① (boucle d'oreille) hoop earring; ② Culin **à la ~** creole

crêpage /kʀɛ(e)paʒ/ nm **~ de chignon**○ fight

crêpe¹ /kʀɛp/ nm ① (tissu) crepe; ② (de deuil) (voile) black veil; ③ (latex) crepe (rubber)

crêpe² /kʀɛp/ nf pancake, crêpe; **~ dentelle** very thin pancake; **faire sauter une ~** to toss a pancake

Idiome **s'aplatir comme une ~**○ pej to grovel (**devant qn** to sb)

crêper /kʀepe/ [1]
A vtr to backcomb GB, to tease
B se crêper vpr **se ~ les cheveux** to backcomb GB ou tease one's hair

Idiome **se ~ le chignon**○ (physiquement) to scratch each other's eyes out

crépi /kʀepi/ nm rendering

crépitement /kʀepitmɑ̃/ nm (de feu, flamme) crackling **C**; (d'huile) sizzling **C**; (de fusillade) crackle **C**; (d'appareils photo) clicking **C**

crépiter /kʀepite/ [1] vi [feu, bois] to crackle; [huile] to sizzle; [pluie, grêle] to patter

crépon /kʀepɔ̃/ nm (tissu) plissé; (papier) crepe paper

crépu, ~e /kʀepy/ adj [cheveux] frizzy

crépusculaire /kʀepyskylɛʀ/ adj lit, fig crepuscular

crépuscule /kʀepyskyl/ nm lit twilight, dusk; fig twilight

crescendo /kʀeʃɛndo/
A adv Mus [jouer] crescendo, to intensify; **aller ~** [bruit, protestations, douleur] to grow, to mount
B nm Mus crescendo

cresson /kʀesɔ̃, kʀəsɔ̃/ nm watercress

crête /kʀɛt/ nf ① Zool (de volaille) comb; (de lézard, d'oiseau) crest; ② (de montagne, vague) crest; (de mur, toit) ridge; ③ Électrotech peak value

Crète /kʀɛt/ ▸ p. 303 nprf Crete

crétin, ~e /kʀetɛ̃, in/ nm,f pej moron○ péj

crétinerie /kʀetinʀi/ nf ① ○(acte) idiotic prank; (parole) idiotic remark; ② (état) imbecility

crétinisme /kʀetinism/ nm Méd cretinism

crétois, ~e /kʀetwa, az/
A adj Cretan
B nm Cretan

creusement /kʀøzmɑ̃/ nm (de sol) digging

creuser /kʀøze/ [1]
A vtr ① (ôter de la matière dans) [personne] to dig a hole in [terre]; to hollow out [tronc, fruit]; to drill a hole in [dent]; to dig into [roche]; [mer, eau] to eat into, to erode [falaise]; ② (pratiquer) to dig [trou, canal, tombe, terrier]; to sink [puits]; to plough GB, to plow US [sillon] (**dans** in); to hollow out [lit]; ③ (marquer) [rides] to furrow [front, visage]; **elle avait le visage creusé par la faim/le chagrin** her face was

gaunt with hunger/grief; ④ (accentuer la cambrure de) ∼ **le dos** or **les reins** to arch one's back; ⑤ (accentuer) to deepen, to increase [*déficit, fossé*]; ∼ **l'écart entre** to widen the gap between; ⑥ (approfondir) [*personne*] to go into [sth] in depth [*sujet, théorie*]

B *vi* ∼ **dans la roche** to dig into the rock

C **se creuser** *vpr* [*joues, visage*] to become hollow; [*mer, vagues*] to be whipped up; [*rides*] to deepen; [*écart*] to widen

(Idiomes) **ça creuse**○ it really gives you an appetite; **se** ∼ **(la tête** or **la cervelle)**○ to rack one's brains

creuset /krøzɛ/ *nm* ① (récipient) crucible; ② fig (mélange de cultures, d'influences) melting pot

creux, -euse /krø, øz/
A *adj* ① (vide à l'intérieur) [*tronc, dent, tube*] hollow; [*son, voix*] hollow; [*estomac*] empty; ② (concave) [*joues, visage*] hollow; **un plat** ∼ a shallow dish; **assiette creuse** soup dish ou plate; ③ (vide de sens) [*discours*] empty; [*débat, analyse*] shallow; ④ (à l'activité réduite) [*jour, période*] slack, off-peak; **la saison creuse** the off-season

B *adv* **sonner** ∼ lit to make a hollow sound; fig to ring hollow

C *nm* ① (dépression) hollow; **le** ∼ **d'un arbre** the hollow of a tree; **le** ∼ **de l'épaule** the hollow of one's shoulder; **le** ∼ **des reins** or **du dos** the small of the back; **le** ∼ **de l'aisselle** the armpit; **au** ∼ **de l'estomac** in the pit of the stomach; **ça tient dans le** ∼ **de la main** it fits into the palm of the hand; **l'oiseau a mangé dans le** ∼ **de ma main** the bird ate from my hand; **le** ∼ **de la vague** lit the trough of the wave; **être au** ∼ **de la vague** fig to be at rock bottom; **au** ∼ **de la vallée** in the bottom of the valley; ② ○(petite faim) **avoir un (petit)** ∼ to feel peckish○ GB, to have the munchies○; ③ Art **en** ∼ [*fresque, motif*] incised; **gravure en** ∼ intaglio engraving; ④ (sur un graphique) trough; **la courbe fait un** ∼ there is a trough in the curve; ⑤ (ralentissement d'activité) slack period

crevaison /krəvɛzɔ̃/ *nf* puncture

crevant○, ∼**e** /krəvã, ãt/ *adj* killing○

crevasse /krəvas/ *nf* ① (de glacier) crevasse; ② (dans la terre, sur un mur) crack, fissure; ③ (gerçure) (sur les lèvres, mains) chapped skin; (sur les mamelons) crack

crevasser /krəvase/ [1]
A *vtr* to cause [sth] to crack [*terre, mur*]; to chap [*peau*]
B **se crevasser** *vpr* [*terre, mur*] to crack; [*peau*] to chap

crève○ /krɛv/ *nf* chill; **attraper la** ∼ to catch a chill ou one's death (of cold)

crevé, ∼e /krəve/ *adj* ① (percé) [*ballon, pneu*] punctured; [*tympan*] burst; ② ○(épuisé) done in○ GB, exhausted

crève-cœur /krɛvkœr/ *nm inv* heartbreak

crève-la-faim○ /krɛvlafɛ̃/ *nmf inv* down-and-out

crever /krəve/ [16]
A *vtr* ① (percer) to puncture, to burst [*pneu, ballon*]; to burst [*bulle, abcès, tympan*]; ∼ **les yeux de qn** (accidentellement) to blind sb; (volontairement) to put sb's eyes out; **ça te crève les yeux** fig it's staring you in the face; **ça crève les yeux** fig it's blindingly obvious; **ça crève le cœur** fig it's heartbreaking; ② ○(épuiser) [*travail, chaleur*] to wear [sb] out; [*patron*] to work [sb] into the ground; [*cheval*] (au galop) to ride a horse into the ground

B *vi* ① (se percer) [*pneu, nuage, abcès, tympan*] to burst; [*paquet*] to burst open; ② [*automobiliste, cycliste*] to have a puncture; ③ (mourir) [*plante, animal*] to die; **un chat crevé** a dead cat; ∼ **de faim/froid** to be starving/freezing; ④ (éclater) pej ∼ **d'envie/de jalousie** to be eaten up ou consumed with envy/with jealousy; ∼ **d'orgueil** to be terribly full of oneself

C **se crever** *vpr* **se** ∼ **un tympan** to burst an eardrum; **il s'est crevé un œil** he put his eye out

(Idiome) **marche ou crève** sink or swim

crevette /krəvɛt/ *nf* ∼ **grise** shrimp; ∼ **rose** prawn

cri /kri/ *nm* ① (de personne) cry; (plus fort) shout; (aigu) scream; **un** ∼ **de douleur/surprise** a cry of pain/surprise; **un** ∼ **de détresse** a cry for help; **un** ∼ **perçant** a piercing scream; **un** ∼ **aigu** a shriek; **à grands** ∼ loudly; **pousser un grand** ∼ to scream loudly; **pousser des** ∼**s de douleur/plaisir** to cry out in pain/pleasure; ② (d'animal) gén cry; (d'oiseau) call

(Idiome) **pousser** or **jeter les hauts** ∼**s** to protest loudly

criaillement /kri(j)ajmã/ *nm* ① (cri désagréable) squeal; ② Zool (d'oie) honk; (de paon) screech

criailler /kri(j)aje/ [1] *vi* ① (crier souvent) [*enfants*] to shriek; ② (rouspéter) to grouse (**après** at); ③ Zool (oie) to honk; [*paon*] to screech

criant, ∼e /krijã, ãt/ *adj* ① (manifeste) striking; ∼ **de vérité** [*description, peinture*] true to life (*jamais épith*); **il est** ∼ **de vérité dans le rôle** he's extremely convincing in the role; ② (scandaleux) [*inégalité, malhonnêteté*] blatant; [*injustice*] glaring; [*abus*] flagrant

criard, ∼e /kriar, ard/ *adj* [*voix*] shrill; [*couleur, affiche*] garish; **un enfant** ∼ a squawking child

crible /kribl/ *nm* Tech (pour minerai) screen; (pour sable) riddle; **passer au** ∼ fig to sift through

criblé, ∼e /krible/ *adj* ∼ **de** (de balles, trous, fautes) riddled with; (de flèches) bristling with; (de taches) covered in; (de dettes) crippled with

cribler /krible/ [1] *vtr* ① ∼ **qn/qch de balles** to riddle sb/sth with bullets; ∼ **qn de flèches/coups** to rain arrows/blows on sb; ② (accabler) ∼ **qn de reproches** to heap reproaches on sb

cric /krik/ *nm* (de voiture) jack

cricket /krikɛ(t)/ ▸ p. 327 *nm* Sport cricket

cricri /krikri/ *nm* (also onomat) ① (cri du grillon) chirping; ② (grillon) cricket

criée /krije/ *nf* (vente à la) ∼ auction; **vendre qch à la** ∼ to auction sth

crier /krije/ [2]
A *vtr* ① (pour dire) to shout (**à qn** to sb); ∼ **des slogans** to shout ou chant slogans; ② (pour proclamer) to proclaim [*indignation*]; to protest [*innocence*]
B **crier à** *vtr ind* **ils criaient à l'injustice** they protested that it was injustice; **on a crié au génie quand il a proposé sa théorie** so was proclaimed a genius when he put forward his theory; **on a crié au scandale quand...** there was an outcry when...
C *vi* ① [*personne*] to shout; (en pleurant) to cry; (de peur) to scream; ∼ **de joie** to shout for joy; ∼ **de peur/plaisir** to cry out in fear/delight; ∼ **après**○ **qn** to shout at sb; ② [*animal*] to give a cry; [*singe*] to chatter; [*mouette*] to cry; [*porc*] to squeal; [*craie, chaussure*] to squeak; [*planche, marche, gond*] to creak; [*pneu, frein*] to squeal

(Idiome) ∼ **comme un cochon qu'on égorge** or **un damné** to squeal like a stuck pig

crieur, -ieuse /krijœr, øz/ *nm,f* **les** ∼**s de slogans** slogan chanters

(Composés) ∼ **de journaux** news vendor; ∼ **public** Hist town crier

crime /krim/ *nm* ① (acte criminel répréhensible) gén, Jur crime; **ce serait un** ∼ **de faire** it would be a crime to do; ② (meurtre) murder; ∼ **crapuleux** murder for money; ∼ **passionnel** crime of passion, crime passionnel; ③ (actions criminelles) crime; **le** ∼ **ne paie pas** crime does not pay

(Composés) ∼ **contre l'humanité** crime against humanity; ∼ **d'État** crime against the State; ∼ **organisé** organized crime; ∼ **de sang** murder; ∼**s de guerre** war crimes

Crimée /krime/ ▸ p. 504 *nprf* Crimea; **guerre/presqu'île de** ∼ Crimean war/peninsula

criminaliste /kriminalist/ ▸ p. 372 *nmf* criminologist

criminalité /kriminalite/ *nf* crime

criminel, -elle /kriminɛl/
A *adj* criminal
B *nm,f* (coupable d'actes criminels) criminal; (meurtrier) murderer

(Composé) ∼ **de guerre** war criminal

criminologie /kriminɔlɔʒi/ *nf* criminology

criminologue /kriminɔlɔg/ ▸ p. 372 *nmf* criminologist

crin /krɛ̃/ *nm* (de cheval) horsehair; **à tout** ∼ fig dyed-in-the-wool

(Composé) ∼ **végétal** leaf fibre

crincrin /krɛ̃krɛ̃/ *nm* pej scratchy (old) violin

crinière /krinjɛr/ *nf* ① (de lion, cheval) mane; ② ○(chevelure) mane; ③ (de casque) plume

crinoline /krinɔlin/ *nf* crinoline

crique /krik/ *nf* Géog cove

criquet /krikɛ/ *nm* locust

crise /kʀiz/ nf **1** (phase difficile) crisis; **en (pleine)** ∼ [secteur, pays] in (the middle of a) crisis; **la** ∼ Écon the economic crisis; **la** ∼ **de 1929** the Great Depression; **2** (pénurie) shortage; ∼ **de main-d'œuvre** shortage of labour[GB]; ∼ **de l'emploi** job shortage; **3** Méd attack; ∼ **d'asthme** asthma attack; ∼ **d'appendicite** appendicitis; ∼ **d'épilepsie** epileptic fit; ∼ **de rhumatisme** bout of rheumatism; ∼ **de toux** coughing fit; **4** (accès) fit; ∼ **de larmes** crying fit; **elle a été prise d'une** ∼ **de rangement** she had a sudden urge to tidy up; **avoir une** ∼ **de fou rire** to get the giggles; **faire/piquer**○ **une** or **sa** ∼ [enfant] to have/to throw a tantrum; [adulte] to have/to throw a fit○

Composés ∼ **cardiaque** heart attack; ∼ **de foie** indigestion; ∼ **de nerfs** hysterics (pl)

crispant○, ∼**e** /kʀispɑ̃, ɑ̃t/ adj irritating

crispation /kʀispasjɔ̃/ nf **1** (de muscle, visage) tensing; (de mâchoires, main) clenching; **2** (tension nerveuse) state of tension; **3** fig (durcissement) tension

crispé, ∼**e** /kʀispe/ adj **1** (contracté) [doigts, mâchoires] clenched; [muscles, visage] tensed; **traits** ∼**s par la douleur/colère** features tense with pain/anger; **2** (tendu) [personne, sourire] tense, nervous

crisper /kʀispe/ [1]
A vtr **1** (contracter) **la colère crispait son visage** his/her face was tense with anger; **2** ○(irriter) ∼ **qn** to irritate sb, to get on sb's nerves○
B **se crisper** vpr **1** (se contracter) [mains, doigts] to clench; [visage, personne] to tense (up); [sourire] to freeze; **ne te crispe pas sur le volant!** don't clutch the wheel so hard!; **2** fig (devenir tendu) [personne] to get nervous, to tense up; **3** (se raidir) [régime, gouvernement] to take a hard line (**sur** on)

crissement /kʀismɑ̃/ nm (de chaussures, craie) squeak; (de neige) crunch; (de freins, pneus) screech; (de plume) scratching

crisser /kʀise/ [1] vi [chaussures, craie, ongles] to squeak; [neige] to crunch; [pneus, freins] to screech; [plume] to scratch

cristal, pl **-aux** /kʀistal, o/ nm **1** (matière) crystal; **eaux d'une limpidité de** ∼ crystal-clear waters; **voix de** ∼ crystal-clear voice; **2** (objet) piece of crystalware; **les cristaux** the crystal(ware) ¢; **les cristaux du lustre** the crystal pendants of the chandelier

Composé **cristaux (de soude)** (pour laver) washing soda ¢

cristallin, ∼**e** /kʀistalɛ̃, in/
A adj **1** (en géologie) [roche] crystalline; [massif] of crystalline rock; **2** Chimie, Phys [zone, structure] crystal; **3** (limpide) [eau] crystal clear; **elle avait un rire** ∼ her laugh was as clear as a bell
B nm Anat (crystalline) lens

cristalliser /kʀistalize/ [1] vtr, vi, **se cristalliser** vpr to crystallize

critère /kʀitɛʀ/ nm **1** (pour juger, pour sélectionner) criterion; (pour évaluer) standard; (pour identifier) indication, sign; **les** ∼**s du succès/de l'intelligence** the criteria for success/intelligence; ∼**s de gestion/de confort** standards of management/comfort; **le prix n'est pas un** ∼ **de qualité** price is no indication of quality; **le** ∼ **déterminant** the crucial factor; **2** (stipulation) specification; ∼**s d'âge et de diplôme** specifications of age and qualifications; **remplir les** ∼**s d'âge et de diplôme** to meet the requirements as far as age and qualifications are concerned

critérium /kʀitɛʀjɔm/ nm Sport (cycliste) rally

critiquable /kʀitikabl/ adj **1** (qu'on peut critiquer) open to criticism (après n); **2** (contestable) questionable

critique[1] /kʀitik/
A adj critical (**à l'égard de, envers** of)
B ▸ p. 372 nmf (commentateur) critic

critique[2] /kʀitik/ nf **1** (reproche) criticism; **accabler qn de** ∼**s** to heap criticism on sb; **faire une** ∼ or **des** ∼**s à qn** to criticize sb; **2** (désapprobation) criticism (**à l'égard de, à l'adresse de** of); **la** ∼ **est aisée** it's easy to criticize; **3** (art de juger) criticism; **la nouvelle** ∼ the new criticism; **4** (de livre, film) review (**de** of); **avoir une bonne/mauvaise** ∼ to get good/bad reviews; **faire la** ∼ **d'une pièce/d'un film** to review a play/a film; **5** (commentateurs) **la** ∼ the critics (pl)

critiquer /kʀitike/ [1] vtr **1** (condamner) to criticize; **il ne fait que** ∼ he finds fault with everything, he criticizes everything; **usage critiqué** Ling controversial usage;

2 (analyser) to make a critical study ou appraisal of [ouvrage]

croassement /kʀɔasmɑ̃/ nm cawing ¢

croasser /kʀɔase/ [1] vi to caw

croate /kʀɔat/ ▸ p. 392, p. 336
A adj Croatian
B nm Ling Croatian

Croatie /kʀɔasi/ ▸ p. 230 nprf Croatia

croc /kʀo/ nm **1** (d'animal) fang; **montrer les** ∼**s** fig to bare one's teeth; **2** (crochet) butcher's hook

croc-en-jambe, pl **crocs-en-jambe** /kʀɔkɑ̃ʒɑ̃b/ nm **faire un** ∼ **à qn** lit to trip sb up; fig to set sb up

croche /kʀɔʃ/ nf quaver GB, eighth note US; **double** ∼ semiquaver GB, sixteenth note US; **triple** ∼ demisemiquaver GB, thirty-second note US; **quadruple** ∼ hemidemisemiquaver GB, sixty-fourth note US

croche-pied○, pl ∼**s** /kʀɔʃpje/ nm **faire un** ∼ **à qn** to trip sb up

crochet /kʀɔʃɛ/ nm **1** Tech hook; (d'appareil dentaire) clasp; **2** (de serrurier) picklock; **3** (en couture) (instrument) crochet hook; (technique) crochet; **faire qch au** ∼ to crochet sth; **4** (parenthèse) **mettre entre** ∼**s** to put [sth] in square brackets; **5** (détour) lit, fig detour; **faire un** ∼ to make a detour (**par** via); **6** (écart) swerve; **faire un** ∼ to swerve; **7** Sport (en boxe) hook; **8** Radio (pour chanteur) talent contest; **9** (de serpent) fang

Idiome **vivre aux** ∼**s de qn** to sponge off○ sb

crocheter /kʀɔʃte/ [18] vtr **1** to crochet [gilet]; **2** to pick [serrure]; **3** Sport to side-step

crochu, ∼**e** /kʀɔʃy/ adj [bec] hooked; [doigt] clawed

Idiome **avoir les doigts** ∼**s** to be tight-fisted

crocodile /kʀɔkɔdil/ nm (animal, peau) crocodile

crocus /kʀɔkys/ nm inv crocus; **des** ∼ crocuses

croire /kʀwaʀ/ [71]
A vtr **1** (trouver crédible) to believe [histoire, personne]; **faire** ∼ **à qn** to make sb believe; **tu me croiras si tu veux** believe it or not; **2** (penser) to think; **j'ai cru mourir** I thought I was dying; **je crois rêver!** I must be dreaming!; **je crois n'avoir rien oublié** I don't think I've forgotten anything; **je crois bien que non** I don't think so; **je crois savoir que** I happen to know that; **il faut** ∼ **qu'il avait vraiment besoin de repos** it would seem that he really needed a rest; **il est malin, (il ne) faut pas**○ ∼**!** he's clever, believe me!; **c'est à** ∼ **qu'elle le fait exprès** anyone would think she was doing it on purpose; **je ne suis pas celui que vous croyez** I'm not what you think I am; **tu ne crois pas si bien dire** you don't know how right you are; **on croirait de la soie/un diamant** it looks like silk/a diamond; **3** (se fier à) **en** ∼ to believe; **si l'on en croit l'auteur, à en** ∼ **l'auteur** if we are to believe the author; **à en** ∼ **les sondages, elle va remporter les élections** if the polls are anything to go by, she will win the election; **crois-en mon expérience** take my word for it
B **croire à** vtr ind ∼ **à** to believe [histoire]; to believe in [fantômes, justice, progrès]; ∼ **à la médecine** to have faith in doctors; **nous avons cru à la victoire** we thought we'd win; **'veuillez** ∼ **à ma sympathie'** 'with deepest sympathy'; **faire** ∼ **à un accident** to make people believe ou think it was an accident
C **croire en** vtr ind ∼ **en Dieu** to believe in God
D vi Relig to believe
E **se croire** vpr **il se croit beau** he thinks he's handsome; **il se croit quelqu'un** he thinks he's really somebody; **on se croirait à New York** you'd think you were in New York

croisade /kʀwazad/ nf lit, fig crusade

croisé, ∼**e**[1] /kʀwaze/
A adj **1** (se chevauchant) [bâtons, fils, jambes] crossed; [bras, mains] folded; **conversations** ∼**es** Télécom crossed lines; **2** (métissé) [sang] mixed; [chien] crossbred; **race** ∼**e** crossbreed; **pollinisation** ∼**e** cross-pollination; **3** (style vestimentaire) [costume, veste] double-breasted; [dos, corsage] crossover (épith); **4** (réciproque) [accords, alliances] reciprocal; [taux] cross (épith); **5** Littérat [rimes, vers] alternate; **6** Sport **volée** ∼**e** cross-court volley; **passe** ∼**e** reverse pass
B nm **1** Hist crusader; **2** (tissu) twill

croisée[2] /kʀwaze/ nf **1** (intersection) junction (**de** of); **à la** ∼ **des chemins** lit, fig at the crossroads; **2** (fenêtre) liter window

croisement /kʀwazmɑ̃/ nm [1] (de routes) (carrefour) crossroads (+ v sg); (point d'intersection) crossing, junction; **au ~ de la route et de la voie ferrée** where the road crosses the railway line; [2] (de fils, lanières) crossing; [3] (de véhicules) **le ~ de deux trains** two trains passing one another; [4] (d'espèces) (méthode) crossing *Ȼ* (**avec** with), crossbreeding *Ȼ* (**avec** with); (spécimen obtenu) hybrid, cross(breed); **faire des ~s (d'espèces)** to crossbreed species; **faire un ~ entre A et B** to cross A with B

croiser /kʀwaze/ [1]
A vtr [1] (mettre l'un sur l'autre) to cross [objets, jambes]; **~ les bras/mains** to fold one's arms/hands; **~ les doigts** fig to keep one's fingers crossed; [2] (couper) [rue, voie] to cross [rue, voie]; [3] (passer à côté de) [véhicule, piéton] **~ qn/qch** to pass sb/sth (coming the other way); (rencontrer) to meet; **mon regard croisa le sien** our eyes met, my gaze met his/hers; [4] Biol to cross(breed) [espèces, animaux]
B vi [1] [bretelles] to cross; [veste] to cross over; [2] [navire] gén to cruise; (pour surveiller) to be on patrol
C **se croiser** vpr [piétons, véhicules] to pass each other; [lettres] to cross (in the post GB ou mail US); [routes] to cross; **nos regards se sont croisés** our eyes met

croiseur /kʀwazœʀ/ nm cruiser (warship)

croisière /kʀwazjɛʀ/ nf cruise; **faire une ou partir en ~** to go on a cruise; **régime de ~** lit cruising speed; **en régime de ~, nous produirons 10 tonnes par mois** fig once we're up and running° we'll produce 10 tons a month

croisillon /kʀwazijɔ̃/ nm (de croix) crosspiece; **~s** (de fenêtre) lattice work; (sur une tarte) lattice pattern

croissance /kʀwasɑ̃s/ nf growth; **~ de 7%** 7% growth; **en pleine ~** [enfant] growing; [secteur] fast-growing (épith), growing fast (jamais épith)

croissant, ~e /kʀwasɑ̃, ɑ̃t/
A adj [1] (en expansion) growing; **de manière ~e** increasingly; [2] Math [fonction, suite] monotonic
B nm [1] Culin croissant; [2] (forme) crescent; **en forme de ~** crescent-shaped
(Composé) **~ de lune** crescent moon

croître /kʀwatʀ/ [72] vi [1] (se développer) [animal, personne, plante] to grow; **faire ~** to grow; [2] (en nombre, en importance) [colère, abstentionnisme] to grow; [bruit] to get ou grow louder; **aller ~** to increase; [3] (augmenter) [production, vente] to grow (**de** by); [jour] to get longer; **~ de 3%** to grow by 3%; [4] Math to increase; **faire ~** to increase

croix /kʀwa/ nf inv cross; **disposé en ~** arranged crosswise; **bras en ~** arms out on either side of the body; **être mis en ~** [condamné] to be crucified; **chacun porte sa ~** fig we all have our cross to bear
(Composé) **~ gammée** swastika
(Idiomes) **ton argent, tu peux faire une ~ dessus°** you can kiss your money goodbye; **faire une ~ sur son passé** to leave the past behind; **un jour à marquer d'une ~ blanche** a red-letter day, a day to remember; **~ de bois, ~ de fer (si je mens, je vais en enfer)** cross my heart (and hope to die)

Croix-du-Sud /kʀwadysyd/ nprf **la ~** the Southern Cross

Croix-Rouge /kʀwaʀuʒ/ nf **la ~** the Red Cross

croquant, ~e /kʀɔkɑ̃, ɑ̃t/ adj crunchy

croque: à la croque au sel /alakʀɔkosɛl/ loc adv with just a sprinkling of salt

croque-madame /kʀɔkmadam/ nm inv: toasted ham and cheese sandwich topped with a fried egg

croquemitaine /kʀɔkmitɛn/ nm bogeyman; hum ogre

croque-monsieur /kʀɔkməsjø/ nm inv: toasted ham and cheese sandwich

croque-mort°, pl **~s** /kʀɔkmɔʀ/ nm undertaker

croquer /kʀɔke/ [1]
A vtr [1] (manger) to crunch [biscuit, pomme]; [2] °(dilapider) to squander [fortune, argent]; [3] (esquisser) to sketch [personne]; fig (décrire) to give a thumbnail sketch of [personne]; **elle est (jolie ou belle) à ~** she's as pretty as a picture
B vi [1] [pomme, biscuit] to be crunchy; [2] [personne] **~ dans une pomme** to bite into an apple

croquet /kʀɔke/ nm [1] ▸ p. 327 Jeux croquet; [2] (galon) rickrack braid GB, rickrack US; [3] (gâteau) almond biscuit GB ou cookie US

croquis /kʀɔki/ nm inv [1] (dessin) sketch; **faire le ~ d'une maison** to draw a sketch of a house; [2] (description) outline;

faire un ~ de la situation to give an outline of the situation

cross(-country) /kʀɔs(kuntʀi)/ nm inv (course) (à pied, à cheval) cross country race; (à moto) motocross event

crosse /kʀɔs/ nf [1] (de fusil) butt; (de revolver) grip; **à coups de ~** (de fusil) with the butt of a rifle; [2] (d'évêque) crozier; [3] Sport stick; **~ de hockey** hockey stick; [4] (extrémité recourbée) (de fougère) crozier; (de canne) crook; (de violon) head; (d'aorte) arch

crotale /kʀɔtal/ nm rattlesnake

crotte /kʀɔt/ nf [1] (de souris, lapin, chèvre) dropping; **ce sont des ~s or c'est de la ~ de souris** they're mouse droppings; **c'est de la ~ de chien/chat** it's dog/cat mess *Ȼ* ou muck *Ȼ*; [2] †(boue) mud
(Composé) **~ en chocolat** Culin chocolate drop

crotter /kʀɔte/ [1] vtr to muddy; **bottes crottées** muddy boots

crottin /kʀɔtɛ̃/ nm [1] (de cheval) dung; [2] (fromage) (small round) goat's cheese

croulant, ~e /kʀulɑ̃, ɑ̃t/ adj [bâtiment] crumbling

crouler /kʀule/ [1] vi [1] (s'effondrer) to collapse; (se désagréger) to crumble; [2] (être submergé) **~ sous** [personne] to be weighed down by; **~ sous les applaudissements** to resound with applause; **~ sous le poids de** to groan under the weight of

croupe /kʀup/ nf [1] (de cheval) croup; **monter en ~** to ride pillion; [2] °(postérieur) behind°; [3] (de colline, montagne) (rounded) top

croupetons: à croupetons /akʀuptɔ̃/ loc adv **être à ~** to be squatting; **se mettre à ~** to squat down

croupi, ~e /kʀupi/ adj [eau] stagnant

croupier /kʀupje/ ▸ p. 372 nm croupier

croupion /kʀupjɔ̃/ nm [1] (d'oiseau) rump; fig **parti/parlement ~** rump party/parliament; [2] Culin (de volaille) parson's nose

croupir /kʀupiʀ/ [3] vi [1] [eau] to stagnate; [détritus] to rot; [2] [personne] **~ en prison** to rot in jail; **~ dans la misère** to languish in poverty

croupissant, ~e /kʀupisɑ̃, ɑ̃t/ adj [eau] stagnant

CROUS /kʀus/ nm (abbr = **Centre régional d'œuvres universitaires et sociales**) French student welfare organization

croustillant, ~e /kʀustijɑ̃, ɑ̃t/ adj [1] [pain, peau grillée] crispy; [biscuit, toast] crunchy; [2] [histoire, détails] spicy

croustiller /kʀustije/ [1] vi [pain] to be crusty; [viande grillée, chips] to be crisp; [chocolat] to be crunchy

croûte /kʀut/ nf [1] (surface épaisse) (de pain) crust; (de fromage) rind; **~ de pain** a crust; [2] (couche) (de peinture) (sur un mur) old layers (pl); (dans un pot) skin; (de glace) crust; [3] Culin **pâté en ~** pâté en croute ou in pastry; [4] Méd scab; [5] °(tableau) daub
(Composé) **la ~ terrestre** the earth's crust
(Idiomes) **casser la ~°** to have a bite to eat; **gagner sa ~°** to earn a crust°

croûton /kʀutɔ̃/ nm [1] (d'un pain) crust; [2] Culin crouton

croyable /kʀwajabl/ adj **pas ~** unbelievable

croyance /kʀwajɑ̃s/ nf belief (**en** in)

croyant, ~e /kʀwajɑ̃, ɑ̃t/ adj **être ~** to be a believer

CRS /sɛɛʀɛs/ (abbr = **compagnie républicaine de sécurité**) nm **un ~** a member of the French riot police; **compagnie de ~** riot squad

cru, ~e¹ /kʀy/
A adj [1] Culin gén raw; [pâte à tarte] uncooked; [lait] unpasteurized; **se faire manger or dévorer tout ~°** fig to be eaten alive°; [2] (intense) [lumière, couleur] harsh; [3] (direct) [description, réalisme, réponse, termes] blunt; [détail] raw; [représentation] graphic; [vérité] harsh; [4] (osé) [langage] crude
B adv [1] (sans ménagement) [parler] bluntly; [2] (en équitation) **monter à ~** to ride bareback
C nm (vignoble) vineyard; (vin) vintage; (année) vintage year; **de grand or du meilleur ~** fig [disque, collection] vintage (épith); **du ~** local; **de son (propre) ~** [recette] of one's own invention; [expression] of one's coinage

cruauté /kʀyote/ nf [1] (caractère) cruelty (**envers** to); [2] (action cruelle) act of cruelty

cruche /kʀyʃ/ nf [1] (contenant) jug GB, pitcher US; (contenu) jugful, pitcherful US; [2] °(niais) dope°, twit° GB

(Idiome) **tant va la ~ à l'eau qu'à la fin elle se casse** Prov that's what comes of taking things for granted

cruchon /kʀyʃɔ̃/ nm small jug GB, small pitcher US

crucial, **~e**, mpl **-iaux** /kʀysjal, o/ adj crucial

crucifier /kʀysifje/ [2] vtr lit, fig to crucify

crucifix /kʀysifi/ nm crucifix

crucifixion /kʀysifiksjɔ̃/ nf crucifixion

cruciforme /kʀysifɔʀm/ adj gén cruciform; [vis, tournevis] cross-head

cruciverbiste /kʀysivɛʀbist/ nmf crossword fan

crudité /kʀydite/ nf [1] Culin **~s** raw vegetables, crudités; [2] (d'aliments) rawness; [3] (de couleur) garishness; (de lumière) harshness; [4] (de langage) crudeness

crue² /kʀy/
A adj f ▸ **cru A**
B nf (montée des eaux) rise in water level; (inondation) flood; **emporté par les ~s** swept away by the flood waters; **en ~** in spate

cruel, **-elle** /kʀyɛl/ adj cruel (**envers**, **avec** to)

cruellement /kʀyɛlmɑ̃/ adv [1] (avec cruauté) cruelly; [2] (beaucoup) desperately; **manquer ~ de qch** to be desperately short of sth; [3] (douloureusement) [ressentir] terribly; **la pénurie de carburant se fait ~ sentir** the fuel shortage is being sorely felt; **être ~ ramené à la réalité** to be brought back to earth painfully

crûment /kʀymɑ̃/ adv [1] (sans ménagement) bluntly; [2] (de façon choquante) crudely

crustacé /kʀystase/ nm shellfish (inv)

crypte /kʀipt(ə)/ nf crypt

crypté, **~e** /kʀipte/ adj coded; Ordinat encrypted; TV scrambled

crypter /kʀipte/ [1] vtr to encrypt

CSA /seɛsa/ nm: abbr ▸ **conseil**

Cuba /kyba/ ▸ p. 303, p. 230 nprf Cuba

cubage /kybaʒ/ nm (d'eau, d'air) volume

cubain, **~e** /kybɛ̃, ɛn/ ▸ p. 392 adj Cuban

cube /kyb/
A ▸ p. 628 adj cubic
B nm gén, Math cube; (jouet) building block; **le ~ de 3 est 27** 3 cubed is 27; **mettre au ~** to cube

cubique /kybik/ adj [1] Math [racine] cubic; [2] **de forme ~** cube-shaped

cubisme /kybism/ nm Cubism

cubitus /kybitys/ nm inv Anat ulna

cucul° /kyky/
A adj péj [histoire, film] corny°; [personne] silly
B nmf (personne) péj twit° GB, jerk° US

(Composé) **~ la praline** corny°

cueillette /kœjɛt/ nf [1] (ramassage) (de fruits, fleurs) picking; fig (d'idées, de chiffres) gathering together; **~ du coton** cotton-picking; **ils vivent de chasse et de ~** they are hunter-gatherers; [2] (produit) crop

cueillir /kœjiʀ/ [27] vtr [1] (ramasser) to pick [fruits, fleurs]; [2] fig to gather [informations]; [3] °(prendre) to pick up°, to arrest [malfaiteur]; to pick up° [ami]; [4] °(atteindre) [projectile] to catch

cui-cui /kɥikɥi/ nm inv (also onomat) twitter; **faire ~** to go tweet! tweet!

cuiller, **cuillère** /kɥijɛʀ/ nf [1] (pour manger) spoon; (contenu) spoonful; **petite ~** ≈ teaspoon; [2] Mus spoon; **jouer des ~s** to play the spoons; [3] (pour pêcher) spoon; **pêche à la ~** spoonbait fishing

(Composés) **~ à café** ≈ teaspoon; (très petite) coffee spoon; **~ à dessert** dessertspoon; **~ à soupe** soupspoon; (pour mesurer) ≈ tablespoon

(Idiomes) **il n'y va pas avec le dos de la ~**° (en parlant) he doesn't pull his punches; (en agissant) he doesn't do things by halves; **on l'a ramassé à la ~**° they had to scrape her up off the road; **faire qch en deux ou trois coups de ~ à pot** to do sth in two shakes of a lamb's tail°

cuillerée /kɥij(ə)ʀe/ nf spoonful

cuir /kɥiʀ/ nm [1] (peau traitée) leather; **c'est du ~** it's leather; **sac en or de ~** leather bag; **le travail du ~** leatherwork; [2] (peau non traitée) rawhide; (peau de gros mammifère) hide; **~ de vache** cowhide; [3] °(peau humaine) hum

hide; **avoir le ~ épais** to be thick-skinned

(Composés) **~ chevelu** scalp; **~ naturel** natural leather

cuirasse /kɥiʀas/ nf (armure) breast-plate; (blindage) armour^GB plating; fig (d'indifférence) front

cuirassé, **~e** /kɥiʀase/
A adj [véhicule, division] armoured^GB
B nm battleship

cuirassier /kɥiʀasje/ nm (soldat) cuirassier; (régiment) **le premier ~** the first armoured^GB division

cuire /kɥiʀ/ [69]
A vtr [1] Culin [personne] (sur le feu) to cook; (au four) gén to bake; to roast [viande]; to cook [daube]; **~ à la vapeur** to steam; **~ à la poêle** to fry; **~ au gril** to grill; **~ qch à feu doux** to cook sth gently; [2] to fire [porcelaine, émaux]; [3] (chauffer) [soleil] to bake [terre]; to burn [peau]; **le soleil me cuit le dos** the sun is burning my back
B vi [1] [aliment, repas] to cook; **mets les légumes à ~** put the vegetables on (to cook); **faire or laisser ~ qch 20 minutes** to cook sth for 20 minutes; **laissez ~ à petit feu** allow to simmer gently; **tu l'as trop peu/trop fait ~** it's undercooked/overcooked; **à ~** [chocolat, pomme] cooking; [fruit] stewing; [2] °(avoir chaud) [personne] **on cuit sur la plage** it's baking (hot) on the beach; **j'ai cuit au soleil toute la matinée** I spent the morning roasting in the sun; [3] (faire mal) **ça me cuit** it stings; **les joues me cuisaient** (de honte, après un coup de soleil) my cheeks were burning; (après des gifles) my cheeks were stinging ou smarting

cuisant, **~e** /kɥizɑ̃, ɑ̃t/ adj [1] (humiliant) [défaite] bitter; [remarque] stinging; [2] (douloureux) [douleur] (qui brûle) burning; (qui pique) stinging; [froid] biting

cuisine /kɥizin/
A nf [1] (pièce) kitchen; Naut galley; [2] (mobilier) kitchen furniture **C**; [3] (préparation des aliments) (art) cookery; (activité) cooking; **apprendre la ~** Scol to do cookery; **il sait faire la ~** he can cook; **faire la ~** to do the cooking; [4] (méthode) cooking; (aliments) food; **tu n'aimes pas ma ~?** don't you like my cooking?; **~ au beurre** (méthode) cooking in butter; (aliments) food cooked in butter; **la ~ française** (méthode, art) French cooking; (aliments) French food; [5] (personnel) **la ~** the kitchen staff; **~** °(magouillage) intrigues (pl); **~ électorale** dubious electioneering tactics; **faire sa petite ~** to be on the fiddle° GB ou on the take°
B cuisines nfpl (de restaurant, d'hôpital, d'école) kitchens

(Composés) **~ familiale** home cooking; **~ intégrée** fully fitted kitchen; ▸ **grand**

cuisiner /kɥizine/ [1]
A vtr [1] Culin to cook; [2] °(interroger) to grill°
B vi to cook; **bien ~** to be a good cook

cuisinette /kɥizinɛt/ nf kitchenette

cuisinier, **-ière¹** /kɥizinje, ɛʀ/ ▸ p. 372 nm,f (chez des particuliers) cook; (dans un restaurant) chef

cuisinière² /kɥizinjɛʀ/ nf (à gaz, électrique) cooker

cuissarde /kɥisaʀd/ nf (de caoutchouc) wader; (de cuir, daim) thighboot

cuisse /kɥis/ ▸ p. 136 nf [1] Anat thigh; [2] Culin (de poulet) thigh; (de chevreuil) haunch; **des ~s de grenouille** frogs' legs

cuisseau, pl **~x** /kɥiso/ nm **~ de veau** haunch of veal

cuissettes /kɥisɛt/ nfpl H (short) sports shorts

cuisson /kɥisɔ̃/ nf [1] Culin gén cooking; (au four) (de pain, gâteau, poisson) baking; (de rôti, poulet) roasting; **temps de ~** cooking time; **la ~ de la viande est très longue** meat takes a long time to cook; [2] (de poterie, d'émaux) firing; **mettre qch à la ~** to fire sth

cuissot /kɥiso/ nm (de chevreuil) haunch

cuistot° /kɥisto/ nm cook

cuit, **~e¹** /kɥi, kɥit/
A pp ▸ **cuire**
B pp adj [1] [aliment] cooked; [viande, poisson, gâteau] done (jamais épith); [abricot] stewed; **trop ~** [gigot, steak] overdone; **bien ~** well done; **pas assez ~** underdone; [2] [poterie, argile] fired; [3] °(par le soleil) [gazon, plante] scorched; [peau] burned

(Idiomes) **c'est ~**° we've had it°; **sinon, on était ~s**° otherwise, we were done for°; **c'est du tout ~**° (facile) it's a piece of cake°; (assuré) it's in the bag°; **ce n'est pas du tout ~**° it's not all cut and dried; **elle attend que ça (lui) tombe tout ~**° she expects things to fall straight into her lap

cuite² /kɥit/ *nf* ① ○(ivresse) **quelle ~!** what a booze-up○ GB *ou* bender○!; **tenir/prendre une ~** to be/to get plastered○; ② Tech (cuisson) firing

cuiter○: **se cuiter** /kɥite/ [1] *vpr* to get plastered○

cuivre /kɥivʀ/

A *nm* (métal) **~ (rouge)** copper; **~ (jaune)** brass

B cuivres *nmpl* ① (objets) (en cuivre rouge) copperware; (en cuivre jaune) brass; ② Mus **les ~s** the brass (*sg*); **ensemble de ~s** brass ensemble

cuivré, **~e** /kɥivʀe/ ▶ p. 140 *adj* [peau] copper-coloured^GB; (par le soleil) bronzed; **aux reflets ~s** with coppery glints

cul /ky/

A *adj inv* [personne] simple; [film] twee○

B *nm* ① ●(postérieur) bottom, arse● GB, ass●○; **~ nu** (à moitié nu) bare-bottomed; (entièrement nu) stark naked; ② ●(sexe) sex; **histoire de ~** (blague) dirty joke; (texte) dirty story; (liaison) affair; ③ Zool rump; ④ ○(arrière) (de voiture, camion) back end; ⑤ (base) (de lampe, bouteille) bottom; **~ de bouteille** bottom of a bottle; **~ sec**○! bottoms up!○; **faire ~ sec**○ to down it in one

(Idiomes) **avoir qn au ~**○ to have sb on one's tail; **se bouger le ~**○ (se dépêcher) to get moving○; **en rester** *or* **tomber sur le ~**● to be gobsmacked○

culasse /kylas/ *nf* (de moteur) cylinder head; (d'arme) breechblock

culbute /kylbyt/ *nf* ① (galipette) somersault; **faire une ~** to somersault; ② (chute) tumble; **faire une ~ dans l'escalier** to tumble down the stairs

culbuter /kylbyte/ [1]

A *vtr* (faire tomber) to knock [sb/sth] over

B *vi* (se renverser) [personne] to take a tumble; [véhicule] to overturn; **la voiture a culbuté dans le ravin** the car fell into the ravine

cul-cul○ = **cucul**

cul-de-jatte, *pl* **culs-de-jatte** /kydʒat/ *nmf* person who has had both legs amputated

cul-de-poule, *pl* **culs-de-poule** /kydpul/ *nm* (récipient) mixing bowl; **avoir la bouche en ~** to have a small pursed mouth

cul-de-sac, *pl* **culs-de-sac** /kydsak/ *nm* (rue) cul-de-sac; (situation) dead end; (emploi sans avenir) dead-end job

culinaire /kylinɛʀ/ *adj* culinary; **préparation ~** dish

culminant, **~e** /kylminã, ãt/ *adj* **point ~** (de montagne) highest point *ou* peak; (de carrière) peak; (de gloire) height; (de réunion, vacances, soirée) high point

culminer /kylmine/ [1] *vi* ① [sommet, massif] **~ au-dessus de qch** to tower above sth; ② fig [inflation, chômage] to reach its peak; [crise, carrière] to reach its height; [soirée] to reach its climax; **l'inflation a culminé à 5% en mai** inflation peaked at 5% in May

culot /kylo/ *nm* ① ○(aplomb) cheek○; **avoir un sacré ~** *or* **un ~ monstre** to have a hell○ of a nerve; **y aller au ~** to bluff○; ② Tech (de bougie) Aut shell; (de douille, cartouche, d'ampoule) base

culotte /kylɔt/ *nf* ① (sous-vêtement féminin) pants (*pl*) GB, drawers (*pl*), panties (*pl*) US; **une ~** (pour femme) a pair of pants GB *ou* panties US *ou* drawers; **où est la ~ de mon maillot de bain?** where are my bikini bottoms?; **faire dans sa ~**○ (déféquer) to dirty one's pants; (uriner) to wet one's pants; fig to wet oneself; ② (pantalon mi-long) breeches (*pl*); (pantalon) trousers (*pl*), pants (*pl*) US; **en ~(s) courte(s)** in short trousers GB *ou* pants US

(Composés) **~ bouffante** bloomers (*pl*); **~ de cheval** (pantalon) riding breeches (*pl*); (cellulite) flabby thighs (*pl*); **~ de golf** plus-fours (*pl*)

(Idiomes) **c'est elle qui porte la ~**○ she's the one who wears the trousers GB *ou* pants US; **baisser ~**○ fig to back down

culotté○, **~e** /kylɔte/ *adj* [personne] cheeky

culpabilisation /kylpabilizasjɔ̃/ *nf* (action) making guilty; (résultat) feeling of guilt

culpabiliser /kylpabilize/ [1]

A *vtr* to make [sb] feel guilty

B *vi* to feel guilty

culpabilité /kylpabilite/ *nf* guilt

culte /kylt/

A *nm* ① Relig gén cult; (adoration) worship; **rendre un ~ à** to worship; ② (ensemble de pratiques) religion; ③ (adoration profane) cult, worship; **avoir le ~ de qch** to worship sth

B (-)culte (*in compounds*) **film-~** cult film

cultivateur, **-trice** /kyltivatœʀ, tʀis/

A ▶ p. 372 *nm,f* farmer

B *nm* (machine) cultivator

cultivé, **~e** /kyltive/ *adj* Agric cultivated; (raffiné) cultured, cultivated

cultiver /kyltive/ [1]

A *vtr* ① Agric to grow [plante]; to cultivate [champ]; ② (entretenir) to cultivate

B **se cultiver** *vpr* ① (devoir être entretenu) [amitié, don] to need to be cultivated; ② (s'instruire) [personne] to improve one's mind; ③ [plante] to be grown; [terre] to be cultivated

culture /kyltyʀ/

A *nf* ① (action de cultiver) cultivation; **la ~ du blé** wheat growing; ② (espèce cultivée) crop; **~ d'hiver** winter crop; ③ Biol culture; **~ in vitro** in vitro culture; (d'une civilisation) culture; **~ de masse** mass culture; ④ (connaissances) knowledge; **~ classique** classical education; **homme de (grande) ~** man of (great) learning; **avoir de la ~** to be cultured; **ne pas avoir de ~** to be uncultured; ⑤ (arts) arts (*pl*); **subventionner la ~** to subsidize the arts

B cultures *nfpl* (terres cultivées) cultivated land **₡**

(Composés) **~ extensive** extensive farming; **~ intensive** intensive farming; **~ physique** Scol physical education; Sport physical exercise

culturel, **-elle** /kyltyʀɛl/ *adj* cultural

culturisme /kyltyʀism/ ▶ p. 327 *nm* body-building

culturiste /kyltyʀist/ *nmf* body-builder

cumin /kymɛ̃/ *nm* cumin

cumul /kymyl/ *nm* ① (accumulation) **~ d'avantages** accumulation of advantages; **~ de fonctions** holding of several posts concurrently; **~ de salaires** drawing several salaries concurrently; ② Jur **~ des peines** ≈ consecutive sentence

cumulable /kymylabl/ *adj* [fonctions, mandats] which can be held concurrently (*après n*); [traitement, allocations] which can be drawn concurrently (*après n*)

cumulatif, **-ive** /kymylatif, iv/ *adj* cumulative

cumuler /kymyle/ [1]

A *vtr* ① (avoir en même temps) to hold [sth] concurrently [fonctions]; to draw [sth] concurrently [salaires]; **~ deux pensions** to draw two separate pensions; **il cumule les fonctions de gestionnaire avec celles de concepteur** he combines the post of manager with that of designer; ② (accumuler) to accumulate [handicaps, diplômes]; ③ (réunir) to combine [résultats]; (ajouter) to add up [sommes]; **intérêts cumulés** accrued interest; **~ qch avec qch** (réunir) to combine sth with sth; (ajouter) to add sth to sth

B **se cumuler** *vpr* **ces réductions ne peuvent pas se ~** you may claim only one of these discounts

cumulus /kymylys/ *nm inv* cumulus

cunéiforme /kyneifɔʀm/ *adj*, *nm* cuneiform

cupide /kypid/ *adj* [personne, esprit] grasping

cupidité /kypidite/ *nf* cupidity

Cupidon /kypidɔ̃/ *npr* Cupid

curable /kyʀabl/ *adj* [maladie] curable

curage /kyʀaʒ/ *nm* (de puits) cleaning out; (de rivière, d'étang) dredging

curare /kyʀaʀ/ *nm* curare

cure /kyʀ/ *nf* ① (dans une station thermale) course of treatment in *ou* at a spa; **faire une ~** to go for a course of treatment in a spa; ② (traitement) course of treatment; **faire une ~ de** to take a course of; ③ (grande consommation) course; **faire une ~ de raisin** to eat a lot of grapes; **j'ai fait une ~ de soleil** I did nothing but soak up the sun

(Composés) **~ d'amaigrissement** slimming course GB, reducing treatment US; **~ de désintoxication** detoxification; **~ de repos** rest cure; **~ de sommeil** sleep therapy

curé /kyʀe/ *nm* (parish) priest; **se faire ~**○ to become a priest; **bouffer du ~**○ to be anticlerical

cure-dents /kyʀdɑ̃/ *nm inv* toothpick

curée /kyʀe/ *nf* ① (à la chasse) (portion of) quarry (*fed to hounds*); ② fig scramble for the spoils; **se précipiter à la ~** to scramble for the spoils

cure-pipes /kyʀpip/ *nm inv* pipe cleaner

curer /kyʀe/ [1]

A *vtr* to clean out [pipe, étang]

B se curer *vpr* se ~ les ongles to clean one's nails; se ~ les dents/le nez to pick one's teeth/nose

curetage /kyʀtaʒ/ *nm* Méd D and C, curettage; **on lui a fait un** ~ she's had a D and C spéc

curie /kyʀi/ *nf* Relig la ~ the Curia

curieusement /kyʀjøzmã/ *adv* (modifiant un verbe ou un adjectif) oddly, strangely; (adverbe de phrase) curiously enough, oddly enough

curieux, -ieuse /kyʀjø, øz/
A *adj* [1] (comme défaut) [*personne*] inquisitive, curious; [*yeux*] inquisitive; **regarder qn d'un œil** ~ to look curiously at sb; [2] (étrange) strange; **un** ~ **paradoxe** a curious paradox; **et, chose curieuse, elle était seule** and, curiously enough, she was alone; [3] (intellectuellement) **esprit** ~ person with an inquiring mind; **être** ~ **de** to be very interested in; **être** ~ **d'apprendre** to be keen to learn; **je suis** ~ **de voir…** (une réaction) I am curious to see…; (une collection, un objet) I am keen to see…; [4] (intéressant) interesting
B *nm,f* [1] (personne indiscrète) **c'est un** ~ he's nosy○; **aller quelque part en** ~ to go somewhere (just) out of curiosity; [2] (passant) onlooker
C *nm* (chose étrange) **le** ~ **de l'histoire c'est que** the funny *ou* curious thing about it is that

curiosité /kyʀjozite/ *nf* [1] (défaut) curiosity; **par** ~ out of curiosity; **il est d'une** ~! he is so curious!; **la** ~ **est un vilain défaut** curiosity killed the cat; [2] (désir de connaître) curiosity (pour about); **avec** ~ [*dévisager, regarder*] curiously; [3] (objet) strange object; [4] (étrangeté) **objet d'une grande** ~ very curious object

curiste /kyʀist/ *nmf* person having hydrotherapy

curriculum vitae /kyʀikylɔmvite/ *nm inv* curriculum vitae, résumé US

curry /kyʀi/ *nm* [1] (assaisonnement) curry powder; **riz au** ~ curried rice; [2] (plat) curry

curseur /kyʀsœʀ/ *nm* Ordinat cursor; (de règle à calcul) cursor; (de fermeture à glissière) slider

cursif, -ive /kyʀsif, iv/ *adj* [*écriture*] cursive; [*lecture*] cursory

cursus /kyʀsys/ *nm inv* course

cutané, ~e /kytane/ *adj* skin (épith)

cuti /kyti/ *nf* skin test; **virer sa** ~ (changer de comportement sexuel) to switch over

cutter /kytœʀ/ *nm* Stanley knife®

cuve /kyv/ *nf* (pour fermentation, teinture, blanchissage) vat; (à eau, mazout) tank; (de lave-linge, lave-vaisselle) interior; Phot developing tank

cuvée /kyve/ *nf* [1] (vin de toute une vigne) vintage; **la** ~ **1959** the 1959 vintage; ~ **du patron** house wine; [2] (contenu) vatful; [3] fig (de romans, films) crop; (d'élèves) year group

cuver○ /kyve/ [1] *vtr* ~ **son vin** to sleep it off○

cuvette /kyvet/ *nf* [1] (en plastique, métal) bowl; ~ **des wc** (lavatory) bowl *ou* pan; [2] Géog basin; ~ **océanique** deep sea floor

CV /seve/ *nm* [1] (*abbr* = **curriculum vitae**) CV GB, résumé US; [2] (written *abbr* = **cheval-vapeur**) HP

cyanure /sjanyʀ/ *nm* cyanide

cybernétique /sibɛʀnetik/
A *adj* cybernetic
B *nf* cybernetics (+ *v sg*)

cyclable /siklabl/ *adj* **piste** ~ cycle track

cyclamen /siklamɛn/ *nm* cyclamen

cycle /sikl/ *nm* [1] (de phénomènes, changements) cycle; ~ **infernal** fig vicious cycle; [2] (série) gén series (+ *v sg*); **deux** ~**s de dix sessions** two series of ten sessions; [3] Littérat cycle; ~ **de la Table ronde** Arthurian cycle; ~ **de chansons** song cycle; [4] Univ **premier** ~ first two years of a degree course; **deuxième** ~ final two years of a degree course; **troisième** ~ postgraduate GB *ou* graduate US studies; [5] (bicyclette) cycle; **magasin de** ~**s** cycle shop
⎯(Composé) ~ **de formation** training course

cyclique /siklik/ *adj* cyclic

cyclisme /siklism/ ▸ p. 327 *nm* gén cycling; (de compétition) cycle racing; **faire du** ~ to go cycling *or* cycle racing

cycliste /siklist/
A *adj* [*club, saison*] cycling (épith); [*course*] cycle (épith); **coureur** ~ racing cyclist
B *nmf* cyclist; **short de** ~ cycling shorts (pl)

cyclo-cross /siklokʀɔs/ ▸ p. 327 *nm inv* (sport) cyclo-cross; **faire du** ~ to do cyclo-cross racing

cyclomoteur /siklomɔtœʀ/ *nm* moped

cyclomotoriste /siklomɔtɔʀist/ *nmf* moped rider

cyclone /siklon/ *nm* (typhon) cyclone; (zone de basse pression) depression; fig whirlwind; **arriver comme un** ~ to sweep in like a whirlwind

Cyclope /siklɔp/ *npr* Cyclops

cyclotourisme /sikloturism/ ▸ p. 327 *nm* cycle touring; **faire du** ~ to go long-distance cycling

cyclotouriste /sikloturist/ *nmf* (touring) cyclist

cygne /siɲ/ *nm* gén swan; ~ **mâle** cob; ~ **femelle** pen; **jeune** ~ cygnet; **chant du** ~ swansong

cylindrage /silɛ̃dʀaʒ/ *nm* (de route) rolling; (au tour) turning

cylindre /silɛ̃dʀ/ *nm* (objet cylindrique) cylinder; Tech (pour compresser, laminer) roller; (pour imprimer) cylinder; Math, Aut cylinder

cylindrée /silɛ̃dʀe/ *nf* [1] (volume) capacity, size; ~ **de 1200 cm³** 1200 cc engine; **voiture de petite/grosse** ~ car with a small/powerful engine; [2] (moto, voiture) **petite** ~ (voiture) car with a small engine; (moto) light motorcycle; **grosse** ~ (voiture) powerful car; (moto) powerful motorcycle

cylindrique /silɛ̃dʀik/ *adj* cylindrical

cymbale /sɛ̃bal/ ▸ p. 389 *nm* cymbal; **coup de** ~**s** clash of cymbals

cymbalier, -ière /sɛ̃balje, ɛʀ/ ▸ p. 372 *nm,f* cymbal player

cynique /sinik/
A *adj* gén cynical; Philos Cynic
B *nmf* gén cynic; Philos Cynic

cynisme /sinism/ *nm* gén cynicism; Philos Cynicism

cyprès /sipʀɛ/ *nm* cypress

cypriote /sipʀijɔt/ ▸ p. 392 *adj* Cypriot

cyrillique /siʀilik/ *adj* Cyrillic

cystite /sistit/ ▸ p. 195 *nf* cystitis **₵**

Cythère /sitɛʀ/ *npr* Cythera

cytomégalovirus /sitomegaloviʀys/ *nm inv* cytomegalovirus

Dd

d

d, D /de/ *nm inv* d, D

d' ▸ **de**

DAB /deabe/ *nm: abbr* ▸ **distributeur**

d'abord ▸ **abord**

dactylo¹ /daktilo/ ▸ p. 372 *nmf* (*abbr* = **dactylographe**) typist

dactylo² /daktilo/ *nf* (*abbr* = **dactylographie**) typing

dactylographe /daktilɔgʀaf/ *nmf* typist

dactylographie /daktilɔgʀafi/ *nf* (technique) typing

dactylographier /daktilɔgʀafje/ [2] *vtr* to type (out)

dada /dada/
A *adj* Art, Littérat Dada
B *nm* ①ᵒ(cheval) baby talk horsie lang enfantin; ② ᵒ(passe-temps) hobby; (idée fixe) hobbyhorse; **enfourcher son** ∼ to get on one's hobbyhorse

dadaisᵒ /dadɛ/ *nm inv* clumsy youth; **espèce de grand** ∼**!** you great oaf!

dague /dag/ *nf* (épée courte) dagger; (de cerf) spike

Daguestan /dagɛstã/ ▸ p. 230 *nprm* Dagestan

daigner /deɲe/ [1] *vtr* to deign (**faire** to do)

daim /dɛ̃/ *nm* ① (animal) (fallow) deer; ② (viande) venison; ③ (cuir de daim) buckskin; ④ (cuir de veau) suede; **chaussures en** ∼ suede shoes

dalaï-lama /dalailama/ *nm* Dalai Lama

dallage /dalaʒ/ *nm* ① (revêtement) paving; ② (action) flagging, paving

dalle /dal/ *nf* ① (de pierre, marbre) slab; (dans église, maison) flagstone; ② Constr (à même le sol) concrete foundation slab; (d'étage) suspended slab; ∼ **de moquette** carpet tile; ③ (en alpinisme) wall; ④ **que** ∼⁰ nothing at all, zilchᵒ
(Composé) ∼ **funèbre** *or* **funéraire** tombstone
(Idiomes) **avoir** *or* **crever la** ∼ᵒ to be ravenous; **casser la** ∼ᵒ to eat

daller /dale/ [1] *vtr* to pave

dalmate /dalmat/ *adj, nm* Dalmatian

dalmatien /dalmasjɛ̃/ *nm* (chien) Dalmatian

daltonien, -ienne /daltɔnjɛ̃, ɛn/ *adj* colour^GB-blind

dam /dɑm/ *nm* **au grand** ∼ **de** to the great displeasure of

damas /dama(s)/ *nm inv* ① (tissu) damask; ② (prune) damson

Damas /damas/ ▸ p. 621 *npr* Damascus

dame /dam/
A *nf* ① (femme) lady; (de la noblesse) lady; **la première** ∼ **de France** France's First Lady; **la** ∼ **de son cœur** liter his lady-love; **de** ∼ lady's; **pour** ∼**s** ladies'; **jouer les grandes** ∼**s** to behave like a princess; **c'est une grande** ∼ **du cinéma** she's a grande dame of the screen; **ma bonne** *or* **petite** ∼ᵒ my dear; ② (épouse)ᵒ lady; ③ (dans fables, contes) ∼ **belette** Old Mother Weasel; **Dame Nature** Mother Nature; ④ Jeux (aux cartes, échecs) queen; (aux dames) King; ⑤ Jur Mrs
B ᵒ†excl ∼ **oui!/non!** my word yes!/no!
C **dames** *nfpl* ① ▸ p. 327 Jeux draughts (+ *v sg*) GB, checkers (+ *v sg*) US; ② (inscription) ladies'; ③ Sport **le simple** ∼**s** the women's singles
(Composés) ∼ **de compagnie** live-in companion; ∼ **d'honneur** lady-in-waiting; **une** ∼ **de petite vertu** a woman of easy virtue

damier /damje/ *nm* draughtboard GB, checkerboard US; **étoffe en** *or* **à** ∼ checked material

damnation /danasjɔ̃/ *nf* (tous contextes) damnation

damné, ∼e /dane/
A *pp* ▸ **damner**
B *pp adj* ① ᵒ(maudit) (*before n*) cursed; ② Relig damned
C *nm,f* ① Relig damned soul; **les** ∼**s** the damned; ② (réprouvé) outcast
(Idiome) **souffrir comme un** ∼ to suffer horribly

damner /dane/ [1]
A *vtr* to damn
B **se damner** *vpr* ① Relig to damn oneself; ② ᵒhum **se** ∼ **pour qn/qch** to sell one's soul for sb/sth

dancing /dãsiŋ/ *nm* dance hall

dandiner: **se dandiner** /dãdine/ [1] *vpr* [canard] to waddle; **se** ∼ **d'un pied sur l'autre** to shift from one foot to the other

Danemark /danmaʀk/ ▸ p. 230 *nprm* Denmark

danger /dãʒe/ *nm* ① (risque général) danger; **être en** ∼ to be in danger; **tout** ∼ **est écarté maintenant** the danger is past now; **hors de** ∼ out of danger; **mettre qn/qch en** ∼ to endanger sb/sth; **sans** ∼ safe; **(en)** ∼ **de faire** (in) danger of doing; **il y a** ∼ **à faire** there's a danger in doing; **(il n'y a) pas de** ∼ **qu'il fasse** no danger of him doing; '∼ **de chute'** 'Danger: steep drop'; '∼ **d'éboulement'** 'risk of landslide'; '∼ **de noyade'** 'Danger: unsafe for bathing'; **'attention** ∼**!'** 'Danger!'; ② (risque ponctuel) danger; (personne) menace; **au volant c'est un vrai** ∼ he is a real menace at the wheel; **un** ∼ **pour qn/qch** a danger to sb/sth; **courir un (grand)** ∼ to be in (great) danger; **faire courir un (grand)** ∼ **à qn** to put sb in (serious) danger; ∼ **de la route** (obstacle) road hazard; (personne) menace behind the wheel
(Composé) ∼ **public** lit danger to the public; fig iron menace

dangereusement /dãʒʀøzmã/ *adv* dangerously

dangereux, -euse /dãʒʀø, øz/ *adj* dangerous (**pour** to); **zone dangereuse** danger zone

danois, ∼e /danwa, az/
A ▸ p. 392 *adj* Danish
B *nm* ① ▸ p. 336 Ling Danish; ② (chien) Great Dane

Danois, ∼e /danwa, az/ ▸ p. 392 *nm,f* Dane

dans /dã/

⚠ *Généralités*
La préposition *dans* est présentée ici dans ses grandes lignes. Les expressions courantes comme *dans l'abondance, dans le genre, être dans le pétrin* etc sont traitées respectivement dans les articles **abondance, genre, pétrin**.
On trouvera ci-dessous des exemples illustrant les principales utilisations de la préposition mais il sera toujours prudent de consulter l'entrée du nom introduit par *dans*.
Par ailleurs, la consultation des notes d'usage dont la liste est donnée ▸ p. 1411 pourra apporter des réponses à certains problèmes bien précis.

prép ① (lieu, sans déplacement) in; ∼ **un avion/bus** on a plane/bus; ∼ **une voiture/un taxi** in a car/a taxi; **boire** ∼ **un verre** to drink out of a glass; **fouiller** ∼ **un tiroir** to rummage through a drawer; **prendre une casserole** ∼ **un placard** to take a pan out of a cupboard; **vider qch** ∼ **l'évier** to pour sth down the sink; **qu'est-ce que je fais** ∼ **tout ça**ᵒ**?** what am I doing in all this?; ∼ **l'ensemble** by and large; ∼ **le fond** in fact; ② (avec des verbes de mouvement) **aller** ∼ **la cuisine** to go to the kitchen; **entrer** ∼ **une pièce** to go into a room; **voler ~ les airs** to fly in the air; **descendre ~ un puits** to go down a well; **monter ~ un avion** to get on a plane; ③ (temps) **~ ma jeunesse** in my youth; **~ deux heures** in two hours; **je t'appellerai ~ la journée** I'll call you during the day; **~ la minute qui a suivi** the next moment; **l'heure qui suivit** within the hour; **finir qch ~ les temps**○ to finish sth in time; ④ (domaine) in; **être ~ les affaires** to be in business; ⑤ (état) **~ la misère/ le silence** in poverty/silence; ⑥ (but) **~ un esprit de vengeance** in a spirit of revenge; **~ l'intention de faire** with the intention of doing; ⑦ (approximation) about; **~ les 3 euros** about 3 euros

dansant, ~e /dɑ̃sɑ̃, ɑ̃t/ adj (entraînant) [reflet] dancing; (où l'on danse) **thé ~** tea dance

danse /dɑ̃s/ nf ① (style) dance; (activité) dancing; **faire de la ~** to take dancing classes; **accorder une ~ à qn** to give sb a dance; **de ~** [festival] dance; [club, piste, troupe] dance (épith); **cours de ~** (pour adultes) dance class; (pour enfants) dancing class; **école de ~** school of dance; **professeur de ~** gén dancing teacher; (de ballet) ballet teacher; **contempler la ~ des flammes dans l'âtre** to watch the flames dancing in the hearth; ② ○(correction) hiding○

(Composés) **~ classique** classical ballet; **~ classique** to do ballet dancing; **~ du feu/de la pluie** (ritual) fire-/rain-dance; **~ guerrière** war dance; **~ macabre** dance of death; **~ nuptiale** Zool courtship display; **~ du ventre** lit belly dancing

(Idiomes) **entrer dans la ~** lit to join the dance; fig to join in; **mener la ~** fig to run the show fig; **avoir la ~ de Saint-Guy** fig to have the fidgets; Méd to have St Vitus's dance

danser /dɑ̃se/ [1]
A vtr to dance
B vi gén to dance; [barque] to bob; **~ sur une musique** to dance to a tune; **~ de joie** to dance with joy; **faire ~ qn** to have a dance with sb
(Idiome) **ne pas savoir sur quel pied ~** not to know what to do

danseur, -euse /dɑ̃sœʀ, øz/ nm,f dancer; **en danseuse** Sport standing on the pedals
(Composé) **~ étoile** principal dancer

dard /daʀ/ nm (aiguillon) sting; (arme) spear

darder /daʀde/ [1] vtr liter **le soleil darde ses rayons** the sun is beaming down

dare-dare○ /daʀdaʀ/ adv double quick

darne /daʀn/ nf (fish) steak

dartre /daʀtʀ/ nf scurf patch

datation /datasjɔ̃/ nf (attribution d'une date) dating; (date attribuée) date

date /dat/ nf ① (moment précis) date; **~ de décès** date of death; **~ d'expiration** expiry date GB, expiration date US; **~ d'arrivée** date of arrival; **~ de départ** departure date; **~ de clôture** closing date; **prendre ~** to set a date; **à une ~ ultérieure** at some future date; **à ~ fixe** on a set date; **~ anniversaire** anniversary; **depuis 1962, ~ à laquelle...** since 1962, in which year...; **~ limite** deadline; **~ limite de consommation vente** eat-by sell-by date; **~ limite d'envoi des dossiers** final date for sending the documents; **~ limite d'inscription** closing date for registration; ② (époque) time; **à/depuis cette ~** at/from that time; **jusqu'à une ~ récente** until recently; **un ami de fraîche/ longue ~** a recent/longstanding friend; **le dernier scandale en ~** the latest scandal

dater /date/ [1]
A vtr ① (donner une date à) to date; **la circulaire est datée du...** the circular is dated the...; **à ~ du 31 juillet** as from 31 July; ② (attribuer une date à) to date [fossile, objet]
B vi ① (exister depuis) **~ de** to date from; **de quand date cette réforme?** what was the date of this reform?; **de quand date votre séparation?** when did you separate?; **cela ne date pas d'hier**○ it's not exactly new; ② (être démodé) to be dated

dateur /datœʀ, øz/ adj [tampon, timbre] date (épith)

datif /datif/ nm Ling dative; **au ~** in the dative

dation /dasjɔ̃/ nf **~ (en paiement)** payment in kind

datte /dat/ nf date

dattier /datje/ nm date palm

daube /dob/ nf casserole

dauphin /dofɛ̃/ nm ① Zool dolphin; ② (successeur) heir apparent; Hist dauphin

daurade /doʀad/ nf **~ (royale)** gilt-head bream

davantage /davɑ̃taʒ/
A adv ① (plus) more; **il est rusé mais elle l'est ~** he's crafty but she's (even) more so; **il ne travaille pas ~** (en effort) he isn't working any harder; (en quantité) he doesn't do any more work; **après trois mois de cours je n'en sais pas ~** after three months of classes I don't know any more than I did before; **je ne peux pas la supporter et ses enfants pas ~** I can't stand her or her children either; **sinon ~** if not more; **rien ne me plaît ~ que** controv I like nothing better than; ② (plus longtemps) longer; **le projet prendra cinq ans et peut-être ~** the project will take five years and perhaps (even) more; **si vous vous exposez ~ aux radiations** if you are further exposed to radiation
B dét indéf **~ de** more; **en voulez-vous ~?** would you like some more?; **le système a ~ de succès à la campagne** the system is more successful in the country

DCA /desea/ nf (abbr = **défense contre les aéronefs**) antiaircraft defence^{GB}

DDASS /das/ nf (abbr = **Direction départementale de l'action sanitaire et sociale**) regional social services department

de (**d'** before vowel or mute h) /də, d/ prép ① (indiquant l'origine) from; **le train ~ Bruxelles** the train from Brussels; **il arrive du Japon** he's just come from Japan; **à 20 mètres ~ là** 20 metres^{GB} from there; **un enfant ~ mon premier mari** a child by my first husband; **un vin ~ Grèce** (rapporté de là-bas) a wine from Greece; (fait là-bas) a Greek wine; **né ~ parents immigrés** born of immigrant parents; **il est ~ père italien** his father is Italian; **~ méfiant il est devenu paranoïaque** he went from being suspicious to being paranoid; ② (indiquant la progression) **~...à, ~...en** from...to; **~ 8 à 10 heures** from 8 to 10 (o'clock); **du matin au soir** from morning till night; **d'heure en heure** from hour to hour; ③ (indiquant la destination) to; ④ (indiquant la cause) **mourir ~ soif** to die of thirst; **pleurer ~ rage** to cry with rage; **trembler ~ froid** to shiver with cold; ⑤ (indiquant la manière) in; **parler d'un ton monocorde** to speak in a monotone; **tirer ~ toutes ses forces** to pull with all one's might; ⑥ (indiquant le moyen) with; **pousser qch du pied** to push sth aside with one's foot; **vivre ~ saucisses** to live on sausages; ⑦ (indiquant l'agent) by; **un poème ~ Victor Hugo** a poem by Victor Hugo; **avoir un enfant ~ qn** to have a child by sb; ⑧ (indiquant la durée) **travailler ~ nuit/~ jour** to work at night/ during the day; **ne rien faire ~ la journée** to do nothing all day; ⑨ (indiquant l'appartenance, la dépendance) **les chapeaux ~ Paul** Paul's hats; **un élève du professeur Talbin** one of professor Talbin's students; **l'immensité ~ la mer** the immensity of the sea; **le toit ~ la maison** the roof of the house; **la porte ~ la chambre** the bedroom door; **le cadran du téléphone** the dial on the telephone; **c'est bien ~ lui** it's just like him; ⑩ (détermination par le contenant) **le foin ~ la grange** the hay in the barn; **le vin du tonneau** (qui s'y trouve) the wine in the barrel; (qu'on a tiré) the wine from the barrel; ⑪ (détermination par le contenu) of; **une tasse ~ café** a cup of coffee; ⑫ (détermination par la quantité) of; **une minute ~ silence** one minute of silence, a minute's silence; ⑬ (détermination par le lieu) of; **les pyramides d'Égypte** the pyramids of Egypt; ⑭ (détermination par le temps) of; **le 20 du mois** the 20th of the month; **la réunion ~ samedi** Saturday's meeting; **la réunion du 20 juin** the meeting on 20 June; **le train ~ 15 heures** the 3 o'clock train; **les ventes ~ juin** the June sales; ⑮ (détermination par la dimension, la mesure) **un livre ~ 200 pages** a 200-page book; **être long ~ 20 mètres** to be 20 metres^{GB} long; **7 euros ~ l'heure** 7 euros an hour; **trop lourd ~ trois kilos** three kilos too heavy; ⑯ (détermination par la nature, fonction, matière) **un billet ~ train** a train ticket; **une robe ~ coton rouge** a red cotton dress; **une bulle d'air** an air bubble; ⑰ (apposition) of; **le mois ~ juillet** the month of July; **le nom ~ Flore** the name Flore; ⑱ (avec attribut du nom ou du pronom) **trois personnes ~ tuées** three people killed; **deux heures ~ libres** two hours free; **20 euros ~ plus** 20 euros more; **l'ourlet a deux centimètres ~ trop** the hem is two centimetres^{GB} too long; **quelque chose/rien ~ nouveau** something/nothing new; **c'est quelqu'un ~ célèbre** he's/she's famous; **c'est ça ~ fait**○ that's that out of the way; ⑲ (avec un infinitif) **ça me peinait ~ la voir ainsi** it upset me to see her like that; **et eux ~ rire** and they laughed; ⑳ (après un déverbal) **le filtrage ~ l'eau pose de gros problèmes** filtering water

La date

Noter

- *Les noms de mois et les noms de jours prennent toujours une majuscule en anglais; pour les abréviations des noms de mois et de jours fréquemment utilisées en anglais ▸ p. 380 et ▸ p. 545.*

- *En anglais parlé, on utilise presque toujours le nombre ordinal (par ex. fifth et non five) pour indiquer le jour du mois; pour les abréviations des nombres ordinaux ▸ p. 398.*

■ *En anglais, il y a quatre façons d'écrire la date, et trois façons de la dire: ces options sont toutes indiquées pour la première date du tableau suivant. Pour écrire la date, les deux premières façons (May 1st ou May 1) sont acceptées dans tous les pays anglophones. Dans le tableau on utilisera indifféremment l'une ou l'autre de ces deux formes.*

■ *Pour dire la date, la première des formes données (May the first) est acceptée partout, et c'est cette forme qu'on utilisera dans le tableau. Les deux autres ne sont pas aussi répandues.*

	écrire	dire
1er mai	May 1 *ou* May 1st (*US & GB*) 1st May *ou* 1 May (*GB*)	May the first (*GB & US*) *ou* the first of May (*GB*) *ou* May first (*US*)
2 avril	April 2 (*etc.*) *abrév.* Apr 2	April the second (*etc.*)
lundi 3 mai	Monday, May 3	Monday, May the third
4 mai 1927	May 4th 1927	May the fourth, nineteen twenty-seven
31.7.65	31.7.65* (*GB*) *ou* 7.31.65* (*US*)	July the thirty-first nineteen sixty-five
jeudi 5 mai 1994	Thursday, May 5 1994	Thursday, May the fifth, nineteen ninety-four
1968	1968	nineteen sixty-eight
1900	1900	nineteen hundred
l'an 2000	the year 2000	the year two thousand
2005	2005	two thousand and five
45 ap. J.-C.	45 AD†	forty-five AD [eɪdiː]
250 av. J.-C.	250 BC‡	two hundred and fifty BC [biːsiː]
le XVIe siècle	the 16th§ century	the sixteenth century

* *L'anglais britannique, comme le français, place le chiffre du jour avant celui du mois; l'anglais américain commence par le chiffre du mois.*
† *AD signifie* anno domini *(l'année de notre Seigneur).*
‡ *BC signifie* before Christ *(avant Jésus-Christ).*
§ *Noter que l'anglais utilise les chiffres arabes pour les siècles.*

Quel jour?

le combien sommes-nous aujourd'hui?
= what's the date today?

nous sommes le 10
= it's the tenth

nous sommes le lundi 10
= it's Monday 10th (*dire* Monday the tenth)

nous sommes le 10 mai
= it's May 10 (*dire* it's the tenth of May)

■ *Pour indiquer la date à laquelle il s'est passé ou se passera quelque chose, l'anglais utilise normalement la préposition* on *devant le quantième du mois.*

on se voit le 10
= see you on the 10th

c'est arrivé le 10
= it happened on the 10th

c'est arrivé le 10 décembre
= it happened on 10th December
  (*dire* the tenth of December)

le 10 de chaque mois
= on the 10th of every month

■ *L'anglais emploie* on *même en début de phrase.*

le lundi 5 mai, il atteignit Tombouctou
= on Monday May 5, he reached Timbuktu

■ *Mais on peut aussi utiliser d'autres prépositions:*

à partir du 10
= from the 10th onwards

jusqu'au 10
= till *ou* until the 10th

attendez le 10
= wait till the 10th

avant le 10 mai
= before May 10 (*dire* before May the tenth)

aux environs du 10 mai
= around 10 May (*dire* around the tenth of May)

du 10 au 16 mai
= from 10th to 16th May (*GB*)
  (*dire* from the tenth to the sixteenth of May)
  ou from 10th through 16th May (*US*)
  (*dire* from the tenth through the sixteenth of May)

■ *Devant les noms de mois et les chiffres des années et des siècles, l'anglais utilise normalement* in.

en mai = in May	*en 1945* = in 1945

je suis né en mai 1914 | *il est mort en 1616*
= I was born in May 1914 | = he died in 1616

Shakespeare (1564–1616)
= Shakespeare (**1564–1616**)
  (*dire* Shakespeare fifteen sixty-four to sixteen sixteen)
  ou Shakespeare, b. 1564–d. 1616 (*dire* Shakespeare born in fifteen sixty-four and died in sixteen sixteen)

la révolution de 1789
= the 1789 revolution

les émeutes de 68
= the riots of '68 (*dire* of sixty-eight)

en mai 45
= in May '45 (*dire* in May forty-five)

dans les années 50
= in the fifties *ou* in the 1950s (*dire* in the nineteen fifties)

au début des années 50
= in the early fifties

à la fin des années 50
= in the late fifties

au XVIIe siècle
= in the 17th century (*dire* in the seventeenth century)

au début du XXIe siècle
= in the early twenty-first century

à la fin du XIIe siècle
= in the late twelfth century

■ *Le mot* century *ne peut pas être omis en anglais:*

à partir du XIIe
= from the 12th century onwards
  (*dire* from the twelfth century onwards)

les romanciers du XIXe
= 19th-century novelists
  (*dire* nineteenth century novelists)

d

de

La préposition

Certains emplois de la préposition *de* sont traités ailleurs dans le dictionnaire, notamment:

lorsque *de* introduit le complément de verbes transitifs indirects comme *douter de*, *jouer de*, de verbes à double complément comme *recevoir qch de qn*, de certains noms comme *désir de*, *obligation de*, de certains adjectifs comme *fier de*, *plein de*;

lorsque *de* fait partie de locutions comme *d'abord*, *de travers* ou de composés comme *chemin de fer*, *pomme de terre*;

lorsque *de* est utilisé dans la structure de déterminants indéfinis comme *peu de*, *moins de* etc.;

lorsque *de* fait suite à *être* dans certaines tournures, voir **être**.

D'autres renvois essentiels apparaissent dans l'entrée ci-dessous, mais on se reportera également aux notes d'usage répertoriées **p. 1355** pour certaines constructions.

L'article indéfini

de article indéfini pluriel est traité sous **un**.

L'article partitif: *de, de l', de la, du*

Lorsqu'il exprime une généralité non quantifiée ou une alternative, *de*, article partitif, ne se traduit pas:

manger de la viande/du lapin/des œufs
= to eat meat/rabbit/eggs

il ne boit jamais de vin
= he never drinks wine

tu prends du café au petit déjeuner?
= do you have coffee for breakfast?

voulez-vous de la bière ou du vin?
= would you like beer or wine?

il ne veut pas de vin mais de la bière
= he doesn't want wine, he wants beer

Lorsque l'idée de quantité est présente, il se traduit par *some* ou *any*:

achète de la bière
= buy some beer

achète des bananes
= buy some bananas

voulez-vous de la bière?
= would you like some beer?

évidemment, tu leur as donné de l'argent?
= of course, you gave them some money?

y a-t-il du soleil?
= is there any sun?

il n'y a pas de soleil
= there isn't any sun, there's no sun

il y a rarement du soleil
= there's seldom any sun

il n'y a jamais de soleil
= there's never any sun

il n'y a plus de vin
= there isn't any more wine

Et lorsqu'il s'agit d'une partie déterminée d'un tout, il se traduit par *some of* ou *any of*:

a-t-elle bu du vin que j'ai apporté?
= did she drink any of the wine I brought?

je ne prendrai plus de ce mélange
= I won't take any more of this mixture

---

poses big problems; ⟨21⟩ (après un superlatif) gén of; (avec un lieu ou ensemble assimilé) in; **le plus grand restaurant ∼ la ville** the biggest restaurant in the town; ⟨22⟩ ○(en corrélation avec le pronom un, une) **pour une gaffe, c'en est une, ∼ gaffe!** as blunders go, that was a real one!; ⟨23⟩ (dans une comparaison chiffrée) then; **plus/moins ∼ 10** more/less than 10

dé /de/ *nm* ⟨1⟩ Jeux dice (*inv*); **jeter les ∼s** to throw the dice; **les ∼s sont jetés** the die is cast; **couper de la viande en ∼s** to dice meat; **coup de ∼** lit, fig throw of the dice; ⟨2⟩ (pour coudre) **∼ (à coudre)** lit thimble; (mesure) thimbleful

DEA /deəa/ *nm* (*abbr* = **diplôme d'études approfondies**) postgraduate certificate (*prior to doctoral thesis*)

dealer[1]○ /dilœʀ/ *nm* pusher○, (drug) dealer

dealer[2]○ /dile/ [1] *vi* to deal (in drugs)

déambulateur /deãbylatœʀ/ *nm* zimmer® (frame) GB, walker US

déambuler /deãbyle/ [1] *vi* to wander (about)

débâcle /debɑkl/ *nf* Géog breaking up; Mil rout; fig collapse

déballage○ /debalaʒ/ *nm* (désordre) jumble; (aveu public) outpouring

déballer /debale/ [1] *vtr* to unpack [*marchandise, caisse*]; to open [*paquet, cadeau*]; (étaler) to display [*marchandise*]

débandade /debɑ̃dad/ *nf* ⟨1⟩ (déroute) stampede; **soldats en pleine ∼** soldiers fleeing in disarray; ⟨2⟩ fig disarray

débaptiser /debatize/ [1] *vtr* to rename [*rue, ville*]

débarbouiller /debaʀbuje/ [1]
A *vtr* to wash
B **se débarbouiller** *vpr* to wash one's face

débarcadère /debaʀkadɛʀ/ *nm* landing stage, jetty

débardeur /debaʀdœʀ/ *nm* (pull sans manches) tank top; (d'été) sleeveless tee-shirt

débarquement /debaʀkəmɑ̃/ *nm* ⟨1⟩ (de marchandises) unloading; (de passagers) disembarkation; ⟨2⟩ Mil landing

débarquer /debaʀke/ [1]
A *vtr* to unload [*marchandise*] (**de** from; **sur** onto); to land [*personne*]
B *vi* ⟨1⟩ (descendre à terre) [*passagers*] to disembark; **∼ du train** to get off the train; ⟨2⟩ Mil to land (**sur** on; **en** in); ⟨3⟩ ○(arriver) (en masse) to descend (**à** upon); (à l'improviste) to turn up○ (**chez qn** at sb's place); ⟨4⟩ ○(ne pas être au courant) **il débarque toujours** he never has a clue○ (what's going on)

débarras /debaʀa/ *nm inv* (endroit) junk room; **bon ∼○!** good riddance!

débarrasser /debaʀase/ [1]
A *vtr* ⟨1⟩ (vider) to clear out [*pièce, placard*]; to clear [*bureau, table, jardin*]; **∼ une pièce de qch** to clear sth out of a room; **∼ (la table)** (après le repas) to clear the table; ⟨2⟩ (libérer) **∼ qn de** to free sb from [*complexe*]; to release sb from [obligation]; to rid sb of [*dictateur*]; ⟨3⟩ **∼ qn (de son manteau)** to take sb's coat
B **se débarrasser** *vpr* ⟨1⟩ (se séparer) **se ∼ de** to get rid of; **se ∼ des déchets** to dispose of waste; ⟨2⟩ **se ∼ (de son manteau)** to take off one's coat
(Idiome) **∼ le plancher**○ to clear off○

débat /deba/
A *nm* ⟨1⟩ (discussion) debate (**sur** on); **entrer dans le cœur du ∼** to get to the heart of the matter; ⟨2⟩ (conflit moral) crisis; **∼ intérieur** crisis of conscience
B **débats** *nmpl* ⟨1⟩ Pol debates; ⟨2⟩ Jur closing submissions and summing-up

débattre /debatʀ/ [61]
A *vtr* (négocier) to negotiate; **prix à ∼** price negotiable
B **débattre de** *or* **sur** *vtr ind* (discuter) to discuss; (au Parlement, à la télévision) to debate
C **se débattre** *vpr* ⟨1⟩ lit [*animal*] to struggle; [*personne*] to

put up a struggle; **se ~ contre** to struggle with; **2** fig to struggle (**dans** with)

débauche /deboʃ/ nf **1** (dépravation) debauchery; **un lieu de ~** a den of vice; **2** (profusion) profusion

débauché, **~e** /deboʃe/
A pp ▸ **débaucher**
B pp adj [personne] debauched
C nm,f debauchee; **mener une vie de ~** to lead a dissolute life

débaucher /deboʃe/ [1] vtr **1** (licencier) to lay off [employé]; **2** ○(distraire) to tempt [sb] away

débile /debil/
A ○adj (idiot) [personne] moronic; [film, raisonnement] daft○; **c'est ~** it's daft○
B nmf **~ mental** Méd retarded person

débilité /debilite/ nf **1** Méd debility; **2** ○(de film, discours) stupidity

débiner○ /debine/ [1]
A vtr to badmouth○
B se débiner vpr **1** (partir) to clear off○; (pour se dérober à qch) to make oneself scarce○; **2** (se disloquer) [choses] to fall apart

débit /debi/ nm **1** (en comptabilité) debit; **la somme est inscrite au ~** gén the sum has been debited; **2** (en parlant, récitant) delivery; **il a un de ces ~s!** (bavard) he never stops talking!; **3** (de cours d'eau) rate of flow; **4** (de liquide) flow; (de gaz) output; **5** (de ligne d'assemblage) output; **6** (de magasin) turnover (of stock); (de restaurant) customer turnover; **produit qui a un bon ~** product which sells well; **7** Télécom throughput; **bas**/**haut ~** low bandwidth/broadband

(Composés) **~ de boissons** (bar) bar; **~ de tabac** tobacconist GB

débiter /debite/ [1] vtr **1** Fin to debit [compte, client]; **~ un compte de 100 euros** to debit an account with 100 euros; **2** (dire) pej to reel off [texte]; **~ des bêtises** to talk a lot of nonsense; **3** (découper) to cut up; **4** (vendre) to sell; **5** (produire) to produce; **6** (fournir en liquide) **~ tant par heure** [fleuve] to have a flow of so much per hour; [pompe] to discharge so much per hour

débiteur, -trice /debitœr, tris/
A adj [compte, solde] debit (épith); [entreprise, pays] which is in debt
B nm,f debtor

déblais /deblɛ/ nmpl (décombres) rubble ¢; (sol) earth ¢

déblayer /debleje/ [21] vtr (dégager) to clear away [terre, neige]; to clear [lieu, porte] (**de qch** of sth); (ranger) to tidy up [pièce]; **~ le plancher**○ to clear off○; **~ le terrain** to do the groundwork

déblocage /debloka3/ nm (de fonds) releasing; (de salaires) unfreezing; (de prix) deregulating

débloquer /debloke/ [1]
A vtr **1** (libérer) to release [frein]; to unlock [volant, roue]; to unjam [machine, mécanisme]; **2** (libérer) to unfreeze [salaires, prix]; to release [fonds, crédits, dossiers, marchandises]; to end the deadlock in [situation, négociation]; **3** (dégager) to make [sth] available [crédits, subventions]; to create [poste]; **4** (ouvrir) to clear [rue, entrée]
B ○vi to be off one's rocker○
C se débloquer vpr **la situation s'est débloquée** the deadlock has been broken

déboires /debwar/ nmpl **1** (déceptions) disappointments; **2** (ennuis) trials; **3** (échecs) setbacks; **essuyer des ~** to meet with setbacks

déboiser /debwaze/ [1] vtr (dégager) to clear [sth] of trees [terrain]; to deforest [région]

déboîtement /debwatmā/ nm **1** Méd dislocation; **2** Aut **accident dû au ~ d'une voiture** accident caused by a car pulling out

déboîter /debwate/ [1]
A vtr (disloquer) to dislocate [os]; to dislodge [objet]; to disconnect [tubes]
B vi (sortir d'un alignement) [personne] to move out of line; [groupe] to break out of column; [voiture] to pull out
C se déboîter vpr **se ~ le genou** to dislocate one's knee

débonnaire /debonɛr/ adj [personne] good-humoured^{GB}; [air] kindly

débordant, **~e** /debordā, āt/ adj **1** (extrême) [imagination] overactive; [joie] overflowing; **être d'une activité ~e** to be extremely active; **2** (abondant) **~ de** brimming with [vitalité, énergie]; bursting with [santé]

débordé, **~e** /deborde/
A pp ▸ **déborder**
B pp adj **1** (dépassé) overwhelmed; **2** (surchargé) overloaded (**de** with)

débordement /debordəmā/
A nm (d'insultes, de protestations) flood; (d'enthousiasme) excess
B débordements nmpl liter excesses

déborder /deborde/ [1]
A vtr **1** (sortir de) [problème]; to go beyond [domaine]; **2** (submerger) to overwhelm; **se laisser ~** to let oneself be overwhelmed; **3** Mil, Pol, Sport to outflank; **4** (saillir de) to jut out from
B déborder de vtr ind (être plein de) to be overflowing with [personnes, détails]; to be brimming over with [joie, amour]; to be bursting with [santé]; **~ de vie**/**d'activité** to be full of life/of activity
C vi **1** (sortir des bords) [liquide, rivière] to overflow; (en bouillant) to boil over; **2** (laisser répandre) [récipient] to overflow; (en bouillant) to boil over; **la coupe déborde** fig it's the last straw; **3** (dépasser) to spill out (**de** of); **la pierre déborde de dix centimètres** the stone juts out ten centimetres^{GB}; **elle déborde en coloriant** she goes over the lines when she's colouring^{GB} in
D se déborder vpr (au lit) to become untucked

débouché /debuʃe/ nm **1** (ouverture commerciale) (pays, région) market (**dans** in; **pour** for); (créneau) outlet (**dans** in; **pour** for); **trouver de nouveaux ~s à l'exportation** to find new export outlets; **2** (perspective d'avenir) job opportunity (**en** in); **3** (de vallée) mouth

déboucher /debuʃe/ [1]
A vtr (dégager) to unblock; (ouvrir) to open
B vi **1** lit, fig (arriver) [personne, véhicule] to come out (**de** from; **sur** onto; **dans** into); (brusquement) to appear; **2** (ouvrir) **~ sur** or **dans** [rue] to open onto; **3** (mener) **~ sur** [études, débat] to lead to
C se déboucher vpr [évier, conduit] to come unblocked; **2** **se ~ le nez** to unblock one's nose

déboucheur /debuʃœr/ nm (produit) drain clearing product

déboucler /debukle/ [1] vtr to unbuckle [ceinture]

débouler /debule/ [1]
A vtr (dévaler) to charge down
B vi **1** (dégringoler) to tumble down; **2** ○(venir rapidement) **~ de** [personne] to come charging along from; **~ sur qn** to burst in on sb

déboulonner /debulone/ [1] vtr to unbolt [roue]; **~ une statue** [ouvrier] to remove a statue; [manifestants] to topple a statue

déboursement /debursəmā/ nm paying out (**de** of)

débourser /deburse/ [1] vtr to pay out

déboussoler○ /debusole/ [1] vtr to throw○, to confuse [personne]

debout /dəbu/
A adv, adj inv **1** (vertical, sur pied) [personne] standing; **les personnes ~** the people standing; **'assis: 40, ~: 10'** (dans un bus) 'seated: 40, standing: 10'; **rester ~** to stand; (veiller) to stay up; **j'ai dû voyager ~** I had to stand all the way; **ne restez pas ~, asseyez-vous** do take a seat; **être** or **se tenir ~** to stand; **se mettre ~** to stand up; **ça bougeait tellement que personne ne pouvait se tenir ~** it was moving so much that no-one could stay on their feet; **je ne tiens plus ~, je vais me coucher** I'm falling asleep on my feet, I'm going to go to bed; **aidez-la à se mettre ~** help her to get up; **2** (hors du lit) [personne] up; **tu es déjà ~!** you're already up!; **3** (qui se maintient) [bâtiment, mur] standing; **le bâtiment ne tient plus ~** the building is falling down; **ton histoire tient ~**○ your story seems likely; **4** (vertical, sur une extrémité) [animal] on its hind legs; [objet] upright; **poser un tonneau ~** to put a barrel upright; **nous avons remis la statue ~** we stood the statue back up; **5** (guéri) **grâce à votre médicament, il était ~ en deux jours** thanks to your medicine, he was up and about in two days
B excl get up!

déboutonner /debutone/ [1]
A vtr to unbutton [vêtement]; **tu es déboutonné** your buttons are undone

B se **déboutonner** vpr [personne] to unbutton one's clothes; [vêtement] to come undone

débraillé, ~e /debʀaje/
A adj [personne] dishevelled^GB; [tenue, style] sloppy
B nm sortir en ~ to go out sloppily dressed

débrancher /debʀɑ̃ʃe/ [1] vtr to unplug [appareil]; to disconnect [système d'alarme]; to pull out [prise]

débrayage /debʀɛjaʒ/ nm **1** Aut declutching; **pédale de** ~ clutch pedal; **2** (grève) stoppage

débrayer /debʀeje/ [21] vi Aut to declutch; (cesser le travail) to stop work

débridé, ~e /debʀide/ adj [imagination] unbridled

débris /debʀi/
A nm inv **1** (d'objet brisé) fragment; **des** ~ **de verre** broken glass **𝒞**; **2** (de véhicule accidenté) piece of wreckage; **parmi les** ~ **de l'avion** among the wreckage from the plane
B nmpl (ordures) rubbish GB (**𝒞**), garbage US (**𝒞**); (restes) scraps; (d'armée, de fortune) remnants

débrouillard, ~e /debʀujaʀ, aʀd/ adj resourceful

débrouillardise /debʀujaʀdiz/ nf resourcefulness

débrouiller /debʀuje/ [1]
A vtr (démêler) to disentangle; (éclaircir) to solve [énigme]; (enseigner les bases à)^○ to teach [sb] the basics (**en**, **à** of)
B se **débrouiller** vpr **1** (s'arranger) to manage; **se** ~ **avec qn** to sort it out with sb; **se** ~ **pour faire** to manage to do; **se** ~ **pour que** to arrange it so that; **débrouille-toi pour que** make sure that; **se** ~ **pour ne pas faire** to weasel out of doing sth^○; **2** (s'en sortir) to get by; **il faut savoir se** ~ you have to learn to stand on your own two feet; **il se débrouille en espagnol** he gets by in Spanish; **débrouille-toi tout seul** you'll have to manage on your own

débroussailler /debʀusaje/ [1] vtr Agric to clear the undergrowth from; (éclaircir) to do the groundwork on [texte, problème]

débusquer /debyske/ [1] vtr to flush out [animal, personne]

début /deby/
A nm (de film, mois, discours) beginning; (de crise, négociations, d'épidémie) start; **au tout** ~ at the very beginning; **au** ~ at first; **au/en** ~ **de** at the beginning of; ~ **mars** early in March; **dès le** ~ from the very beginning; **depuis le** ~ **(de)** since the beginning (of); **je le savais depuis le** ~ I knew all along; **du** ~ **(jusqu')à la fin** from start to finish; **il y a un** ~ **à tout** you have to start somewhere; **pour un** ~, **ce n'est pas mal** it's not bad for starters; **un** ~ **de solution** the beginnings of a solution
B débuts nmpl **1** (de comédien, musicien) debut (sg); **à mes** ~s when I started out; **2** (de parti politique, média) early stages; **depuis ses** ~s **en 1962, le mouvement a évolué** since its inception in 1962, the movement has evolved

débutant, ~e /debytɑ̃, ɑ̃t/
A adj [conducteur, skieur, artiste] novice (épith); [ingénieur, cadre] recently qualified; **elle est** ~e she's a beginner
B nm,f gén beginner (**en** in); Cin, Théât actor/actress making his/her debut; **c'est une** ~e she's a beginner

débuter /debyte/ [1]
A vtr contro to begin
B vi **1** (commencer) [journée, roman, séance] to begin, to start (**avec**, **par**, **sur** with); [personne] to start off (**avec**, **par**, **sur** with); **2** (faire ses premiers pas) gén to start out (**comme** as); [acteur, comédien] to make one's debut (**dans** in)

déca^○ /deka/ nm decaf^○, sanka® US

deçà /dəsa/
A adv ~, **delà** here and there
B en **deçà** loc adv on this side
C en **deçà de** loc prép **1** (de ce côté-ci de) on this side of [montagne, rivière]; **2** fig (en dessous de) below; **le résultat est (très) en** ~ **de notre objectif** the result falls (far) short of our target

décacheter /dekaʃte/ [20] vtr to unseal

décade /dekad/ nf (dix jours) 10-day period; (décennie) controv decade

décadence /dekadɑ̃s/ nf (état) decadence; (déclin) decline

décadent, ~e /dekadɑ̃, ɑ̃t/ adj (en état de dégénérescence) decadent; (en déclin) in decline (après n); Littérat Decadent

décaféiné, ~e /dekafeine/
A adj decaffeinated
B nm decaffeinated coffee

décalage /dekalaʒ/ nm **1** (différence) (écart) gap; (désaccord) discrepancy; **se sentir en** ~ **(par rapport aux autres)** to feel out of step (with the others); **2** (intervalle dans le temps) interval; **3** (glissement dans le temps) (avance) move forward; (retard) move back; **4** (dans l'espace) shift; ~ **des lignes de départ** Sport staggering of starting lines; **il y a un** ~ **de 10 centimètres entre les deux tableaux** there's a 10 centimetre^GB difference in the height at which the two pictures are hung; **5** Ordinat shift

(Composé) ~ **horaire** (entre deux lieux) time difference; **mal supporter le** ~ **horaire** to suffer from jet-lag

décalcifier /dekalsifje/ [1]
A vtr to decalcify
B se **décalcifier** vpr to be decalcified

décalcomanie /dekalkɔmani/ nf transfer GB, decal US

décaler /dekale/ [1]
A vtr **1** (dans le temps) (avancer) to bring [sth] forward [date, départ]; (reculer) to put GB ou move US [sth] back; **les avions sont tous décalés d'une heure** (en retard) the planes are all taking off an hour later; **2** (dans l'espace) (avancer) to move [sth] forward [objet]; (reculer) to move [sth] back; ~ **qn/qch d'un rang** (reculer) to move sb/sth back a row; **poteau décalé (par rapport aux autres)** post out of line (with the others); **lignes décalées** staggered lines
B se **décaler** vpr se ~ **sur la droite** to move ou shift to the right

décalitre /dekalitʀ/ ▸ p. 87 nm (unité) decalitre^GB

décalque /dekalk/ nm Art tracing; (imitation) carbon copy

décalquer /dekalke/ [1] vtr **1** Art (par transparence) to trace (**sur** from); (reporter) to transfer (**sur** onto); **2** fig (imiter) to copy (**sur** onto)

décamètre /dekamɛtʀ/ ▸ p. 347 nm (unité) decametre^GB

décamper^○ /dekɑ̃pe/ [1] vi (s'enfuir) to run off; (partir) to clear off^○; **faire** ~ **qn** to chase sb away

décantage /dekɑ̃taʒ/ nm, **décantation** /dekɑ̃tasjɔ̃/ nf (procédé) decantation; (action) (de liquide) (settling and) decanting

décanter /dekɑ̃te/ [1]
A vtr (laisser reposer) to allow [sth] to settle [liquide]; to clarify [eaux usées]
B se **décanter** vpr **1** [liquide] to settle; [eaux usées] to clarify; **2** [situation, idées] to become clearer; **laisser les choses se** ~ to allow the dust to settle

décapage /dekapaʒ/ nm **1** (de meuble, plancher) gén cleaning; (avec un abrasif) scouring; (avec un produit) stripping; (à la brosse) scrubbing; (à la ponceuse) sanding; **2** Tech (de métal) pickling

décapant, ~e /dekapɑ̃, ɑ̃t/
A adj **1** (abrasif) scouring; **produit** ~ (produit pour enlever la peinture, le vernis) paint stripper; (acide) pickle; **2** ^○fig (caustique) [humour] abrasive, caustic
B nm (abrasif) scouring agent; (pour peinture) paint stripper; (acide) pickle

décaper /dekape/ [1] vtr **1** (nettoyer) gén to clean; (enlever la peinture) to strip; ~ **à la brosse** to scrub; ~ **avec un abrasif** to scour; **2** ^○[shampooing, savon] to be harsh

décapitation /dekapitasjɔ̃/ nf (de personne) (accident) decapitation; (exécution) beheading

décapiter /dekapite/ [1] vtr (tuer) to behead; (accidentellement) to decapitate; fig to remove the leaders from [parti, organisation]

décapotable /dekapɔtabl/ adj convertible

décapsuler /dekapsyle/ [1] vtr to take the top off

décapsuleur /dekapsylœʀ/ nm bottle-opener

décarcasser^○: se **décarcasser** /dekaʀkase/ [1] vpr to put oneself to a lot of trouble

décathlon /dekatlɔ̃/ ▸ p. 327 nm decathlon

décatir: se décatir /dekatiʀ/ [3] vpr to become decrepit; **décati** decrepit

décéder /desede/ [14] vi to die; **X récemment décédé** X who died recently; ~ **d'un cancer** to die of cancer

décelable /deslabl/ adj detectable

déceler /desle/ [17] vtr **1** (distinguer) to detect; **2** (indiquer) to reveal [sentiment]; to indicate [présence]

décélération /deseleʀasjɔ̃/ nf (de vitesse) deceleration

décembre /desɑ̃bʀ/ ▸ p. 380 nm December

décemment /desamɑ̃/ adv ①> (selon les normes) [se conduire, être logé] decently; ②> (avec compétence) [travailler, jouer] reasonably well; ③> (raisonnablement) reasonably

décence /desɑ̃s/ nf (bienséance) decency

décennal, ~e, mpl **-aux** /desenal, o/ adj ten-year

décennie /deseni/ nf decade

décent, ~e /desɑ̃, ɑ̃t/ adj ①> (bienséant) decent; ②> (correct) proper, right; ③> (acceptable) decent, reasonable

décentraliser /desɑ̃tralize/ [1]
A vtr to decentralize
B se décentraliser vpr to become decentralized

décentrer /desɑ̃tre/ [1]
A vtr to move [sth] away from the centre^{GB}
B se décentrer vpr to move away (**par rapport à** from); **décentré** off-centre^{GB}

déception /desɛpsjɔ̃/ nf disappointment

décerner /deserne/ [1] vtr to award

décès /desɛ/ nm inv death; **fermé pour cause de** ~ closed owing to bereavement

décevant, ~e /desəvɑ̃, ɑ̃t/ adj disappointing

décevoir /desəvwar/ [5] vtr ①> (ne pas répondre aux espoirs de) to disappoint; **tu me déçois (beaucoup)** I'm (very) disappointed in you; **ne pas** ~ to live up to expectations; ②> (tromper) to fail to fulfil^{GB} [espoir]

déchaîné, ~e /deʃene/
A pp ▸ déchaîner
B pp adj ①> (violent) [mer, vent] raging; ②> (très énervé) [personne, foule] wild; [opinion] stirred up (jamais épith); ~ **contre** furious with

déchaînement /deʃɛnmɑ̃/ nm ①> (de tempête) raging; ②> (explosion) **le** ~ **de l'opinion publique** the public outcry (**contre** against)

déchaîner /deʃene/ [1]
A vtr to rouse [sentiments]; to excite [personnes]
B se déchaîner vpr ①> [phénomènes naturels] to rage; [sentiments] to burst out; ②> [foule] to go wild; ③> [personne] to fly into a rage

déchanter /deʃɑ̃te/ [1] vi to become disenchanted; **elle a dû** ~ she was brought down to earth; **faire** ~ to disappoint

décharge /deʃarʒ/ nf ①> (d'arme à feu) discharge; ②> (d'ordures) rubbish GB ou garbage US dump; ~ **municipale** municipal dump; ③> (d'électricité) **recevoir une** ~ to get an electric shock; ④> Jur (d'accusé) acquittal; ⑤> (de responsabilités) **signer une** ~ to sign a discharge

déchargement /deʃarʒəmɑ̃/ nm (de véhicule, d'arme à feu) unloading

décharger /deʃarʒe/ [13]
A vtr ①> (débarrasser de sa charge) to unload [navire, véhicule]; to relieve [personne] (**de** of); ②> (enlever un chargement) to unload [marchandises, passagers]; ③> (ôter la charge de) to unload [arme à feu]; (tirer avec) to fire [arme]; ④> (libérer) ~ **qn de** to relieve sb of [tâche, obligation]; ⑤> (en électricité) [personne] to discharge [batterie]; ⑥> (soulager) to unburden [conscience, cœur] (**auprès de qn** to sb)
B se décharger vpr ①> (se libérer) **se** ~ **de qch** to off-load sth (**sur qn** onto sb); ②> [batterie] to run down; **la batterie est déchargée** the battery is flat

décharné, ~e /deʃarne/ adj [corps, bras, visage] emaciated; [doigt] bony

décharner /deʃarne/ [1] vtr to emaciate

déchaussé, ~e /deʃose/
A pp ▸ déchausser
B pp adj [personne] barefoot; **dents** ~**es** receding gums

déchausser /deʃose/ [1]
A vtr gén ~ **qn** to take sb's shoes off; Sport ~ (**ses skis**) to take off one's skis
B se déchausser vpr ①> (enlever ses chaussures) to take off one's shoes; ②> [dent] to work loose due to receding gums

dèche /dɛʃ/ nf **être dans la** ~ to be broke[○]

déchéance /deʃeɑ̃s/ nf ①> (décadence morale) decline; **tomber dans la** ~ to go into total decline; ②> (décrépitude) degeneration; ③> (déclin) (d'une nation) decline

déchet /deʃɛ/
A nm ①> (morceau inutilisé) scrap; ②> (perte) waste; **il y a du** ~ (dans la marchandise) there's some waste; (parmi des candidats) there are failures ou duds[○]; ③> (épave) fig wreck; **les** ~**s de** **la société** the dregs of society
B déchets nmpl (résidus) waste material **C**; (ordures) waste **C**; ~**s d'activité de soins** biowaste **C**; ~**s ménagers** household refuse **C**; ~**s industriels** industrial waste

déchetterie /deʃɛtri/ nf waste reception centre^{GB}

déchiffrage /deʃifraʒ/ nm gén deciphering; Mus sight-reading

déchiffrement /deʃifrəmɑ̃/ nm (de message codé) decoding; (de texte, d'écriture) deciphering

déchiffrer /deʃifre/ [1] vtr (lire) to decipher; (interpréter) to fathom out; Mus to sight-read [partition]

déchiqueté, ~e /deʃikte/ adj [côte, relief] jagged, ragged

déchiqueter /deʃikte/ [20] vtr ①> (réduire en lambeaux) to tear [sth] to shreds; ②> (mutiler) to mutilate [membre]; ③> (tuer) [machine, animal] to tear [sb] to pieces; [explosion] to blow [sb] to pieces

déchirant, ~e /deʃirɑ̃, ɑ̃t/ adj ①> (émouvant) heartrending; ②> (difficile) agonizing; ③> [lutte] divisive

déchirement /deʃirmɑ̃/ nm ①> (souffrance) heartbreak; ②> (conflit) rift (**entre** between)

déchirer /deʃire/ [1]
A vtr ①> (mettre en morceaux) to tear [sth] up [papier, tissu]; to rip [sth] up [chair]; to break [sth] up [surface]; ~ **un contrat** fig to go back on a contract; ②> (détériorer) to tear [vêtement, sac]; ③> liter (troubler) [bruit] to shatter [silence]; [éclair] to rend; ④> (diviser) [conflit] to split [groupe, pays]; **couple déchiré** divided couple; **déchiré entre son devoir et son désir de rester** torn between his duty and his desire to stay; ⑤> (faire souffrir) to torture [personne]
B se déchirer vpr ①> (se rompre) [papier, tissu, vêtement] to tear; ②> Méd **se** ~ **un muscle** to tear a muscle; ③> (s'affronter) [personnes] to tear each other apart; ④> liter (souffrir) [cœur] to break

déchirure /deʃiryr/ nf ①> Méd tear; ~ **à la cuisse** muscle tear in the thigh; ②> (accroc) tear (**de** in); ③> (rupture) break (**de** in); ④> (conflit) rift (**de** within)

déchoir /deʃwar/ [51]
A vtr Jur (priver) to strip [sb] of [droit]
B vi (tomber dans un état inférieur) [personne] to demean oneself; ~ **de son rang** to come down in the world

déchu, ~e /deʃy/
A pp ▸ déchoir
B pp adj [monarque, dictateur] deposed; [ange] fallen

de-ci /dəsi/ adv ~ **de-là** here and there

décibel /desibɛl/ nm decibel

décidé, ~e /deside/
A pp ▸ décider
B pp adj ①> (arrêté) **c'est** ~, **je m'en vais** it's settled, I'm leaving; ②> (résolu) [personne] determined; [allure, air] resolute

décidément /desidemɑ̃/ adv really

décider /deside/ [1]
A vtr ①> (prendre la décision de) to decide; ~ **une politique** to decide on a policy; **c'est toi qui décides, c'est à toi de** ~ it's for you ou up to you to decide; ~ **si** to decide whether; ~ **qui contacter** to decide who to contact; **c'est ce qui a décidé sa perte** it's what led to his downfall; ②> (persuader) to persuade (**à faire** to do)
B décider de vtr ind to decide on [date, mesure, lieu]; to fix [prix]; **le hasard en décida autrement** fate decided otherwise; ~ **du sort de qn** to seal sb's fate
C se décider vpr ①> (prendre une décision) to make up one's mind; **tu te décides à parler?** are you going to speak?; **elle s'est enfin décidée à s'excuser** she apologized at last; **être décidé à faire** to be determined to do; ②> (choisir) **se** ~ **pour** to decide on; ③> (être fixé) [accord, réunion] to be decided on; [date] to be set; **tout s'est décidé très vite** it all happened very quickly

décideur /desidœr/ nm decision-maker

décigramme /desigram/ ▸ p. 453 nm decigram

décilitre /desilitr/ ▸ p. 87 nm decilitre^{GB}

décimal, ~e, mpl **-aux** /desimal, o/ adj Math decimal; Chimie decinormal

décimer /desime/ [1] vtr to decimate

décimètre /desimɛtr/ nm ①> ▸ p. 347 (unité) decimetre^{GB}; ②> (instrument) (decimetre^{GB}) ruler; **double** ~ (20 centimetre^{GB}) ruler

décisif, **-ive** /desizif, iv/ adj gén decisive; [preuve] conclusive; [ton, voix] authoritative

décision /desizjɔ̃/ *nf* [1] (résolution) decision; **prendre une** ~ **to make a decision; prendre la** ~ **de faire** to decide to do; [2] (fait de décider) **avoir le pouvoir de** ~ to be the one who makes the decisions; [3] (détermination) decisiveness

décisionnel, -elle /desizjɔnɛl/ *adj* [*système, processus*] decision-making (*épith*); **pouvoir** ~ power to make decisions

déclamer /deklame/ [1] *vtr* to declaim

déclaration /deklarasjɔ̃/ *nf* [1] (communication publique) gén statement; (officielle) declaration (**sur** about); ~ **de guerre** declaration of war; ~ **(d'amour)** declaration of love; **faire sa** ~ **à qn** to declare one's love to sb; [2] Admin notification; ~ **de naissance** (enregistrement) registration of birth; (information) notification of birth; [3] Jur statement; ~ **de vol/perte** report of theft/loss; ~ **sous serment** sworn statement

(Composé) ~ **d'impôts** *or* **de revenus** (income-)tax return

déclaré, ~**e** /deklare/ *adj* [*ennemi*] avowed; [*haine*] professed; [*maladie*] full-blown

déclarer /deklare/ [1]
A *vtr* [1] (dire, proclamer) to declare [*indépendance, intentions*]; ~ **son amour** to declare one's love; ~ **qn vainqueur** to declare sb the winner; **il a été déclaré coupable** he was found guilty; ~ **la séance ouverte** to declare the meeting open; ~ **que** to declare that; ~ **à qn que** to tell sb that; ~ **la guerre à** to declare war on; [2] Admin to declare [*marchandise, revenus, employé*]; to report [*vol*]; to register [*naissance, décès*]; **non déclaré** [*somme*] undeclared; [*travail*] illegal
B **se déclarer** *vpr* [1] (commencer) [*incendie, épidémie*] to break out; [*fièvre*] to start; [*maladie*] to manifest itself; [2] (se dire) **se** ~ **convaincu** to declare oneself convinced; **se** ~ **pour/contre qch** to come out for/against sth; [3] (avouer son amour) to declare one's love (**à qn** to sb)

déclasser /deklase/ [1] *vtr* [1] (rétrograder) to downgrade; [2] (mettre en désordre) to jumble up

déclenchement /deklɑ̃ʃmɑ̃/ *nm* (de mécanisme) release; (d'avalanche) start; (de maladie) onset; (de réaction) start; (de conflit, grève) outbreak

déclencher /deklɑ̃ʃe/ [1]
A *vtr* [1] (entraîner) to spark (off) [*protestation*]; to prompt [*décision*]; to cause [*réaction, explosion*]; to start [*avalanche*]; to lead to [*larmes*]; ~ **les larmes de qn** to make sb burst into tears; ~ **un éclat de rire général** to provoke general laughter; [2] (commencer) to launch [*offensive*]; to begin [*hostilités*]; to start [*grève, polémique*]; [3] (actionner) to set off [*mécanisme*]; [4] Ordinat to initiate [*opération*]
B **se déclencher** *vpr* [1] (se mettre en marche) [*alarme*] to go off; [*signal, mécanisme*] to be activated; [2] (commencer) [*douleur, réaction, contractions*] to start; [*grève, guerre*] to break out; [*opération*] to begin

déclencheur /deklɑ̃ʃœr/ *nm* Phot shutter release

déclic /deklik/ *nm* [1] (mécanisme) trigger; [2] (bruit) click

déclin /deklɛ̃/ *nm* gén decline; (de sentiment, passion) waning; ~ **de la demande** decline in demand; **popularité en** ~ declining popularity; **être en** *or* **sur le** ~ [*civilisation, industrie*] to be in decline; [*popularité, prestige*] to be waning; **être sur le** *or* **son** ~ [*homme d'État*] to be on the way out; **le soleil est à son** ~ the sun is going down; **au** ~ **du jour** at the close of day; **au** ~ **de la vie** in the twilight of life

déclinaison /deklinɛzɔ̃/ *nf* Ling declension

déclinant, ~**e** /deklinɑ̃, ɑ̃t/ *adj* [*forces*] waning; [*santé*] failing

décliner /dekline/ [1]
A *vtr* [1] (refuser) to decline [*invitation*]; to turn down [*offre*]; ~ **toute responsabilité** to disclaim all responsibility; [2] Ling to decline; [3] (dire) ~ **son identité** to give one's name
B *vi* [*lumière*] to fade; [*vue, santé*] to deteriorate; [*talent*] to fade; [*enthousiasme*] to wane; [*soleil*] to go down
C **se décliner** *vpr* Ling to decline

déclivité /deklivite/ *nf* gradient; **habiter sur une** ~ to live on a hill

décocher /dekɔʃe/ [1] *vtr* to shoot [*flèche*] (**à** at); ~ **un coup de poing à qn** to punch sb

décoction /dekɔksjɔ̃/ *nf* brew, decoction

décoder /dekɔde/ [1] *vtr* to decode

décodeur /dekɔdœr/ *nm* (appareil) decoder

décoiffer /dekwafe/ [1]
A *vtr* (dépeigner) ~ **qn** to ruffle sb's hair; **elle est toute décoiffée** her hair is in a mess; **tu me décoiffes** you are messing up my hair
B **se décoiffer** *vpr* (se découvrir) to doff one's hat

décoincer /dekwɛ̃se/ [12]
A *vtr* (débloquer) to unjam [*mécanisme, tiroir, porte*]; to free [*clé*]; to get [sth] back to normal [*dos, cou*]
B **se décoincer** *vpr* [*mécanisme*] to come free

décolérer /dekɔlere/ [14] *vi* **ne pas** ~ **de la soirée** to stay angry all evening; **sans** ~ without letting up

décollage /dekɔlaʒ/ *nm* [1] (d'avion) take-off; (de fusée) lift-off; [2] (d'enterprise) take-off; [3] (d'affiche, étiquette) peeling off

décoller /dekɔle/ [1]
A *vtr* (détacher) to peel off [*étiquette, affiche*]; to remove [*adhésif*]; ~ **une étiquette en la laissant tremper** to soak a label off; ~ **à la vapeur** to steam [sth] off [*étiquette, papier*]; to steam [sth] open [*enveloppe*]
B *vi* [1] (s'envoler) [*avion*] to take off (**de** from); [*fusée*] to lift off (**de** from); [2] (démarrer) [*industrie*] to take off; [*spectacle*] to get going
C **se décoller** *vpr* to come off

décolleté, ~**e** /dekɔlte/
A *adj* [*vêtement*] low-cut; **pas assez** ~ too high-cut; **une robe** ~ **en V** a V-neck dress
B *nm* [1] (partie de vêtement) low neckline; ~ **plongeant** plunging neckline; [2] (partie du corps) cleavage; **dans son** ~ down her cleavage

décolleter /dekɔlte/ [20] *vtr* Ind to cut (from the bar) [*vis, boulons*]

décolleuse /dekɔløz/ *nf* steam stripper

décolonisation /dekɔlɔnizasjɔ̃/ *nf* decolonization

décolorant, ~**e** /dekɔlɔrɑ̃, ɑ̃t/
A *adj* [*agent*] bleaching
B *nm* bleaching agent

décoloration /dekɔlɔrasjɔ̃/ *nf* gén discoloration; (de tissu) fading

décolorer /dekɔlɔre/ [1]
A *vtr* [*substance*] to bleach [*tissu, cheveux*]; [*lumière, lavage*] to cause [sth] to fade
B **se décolorer** *vpr* [*tapis, rideau*] to fade

décombres /dekɔ̃br/ *nmpl* rubble **¢**

décommander /dekɔmɑ̃de/ [1]
A *vtr* to call off [*rendez-vous*]
B **se décommander** *vpr* to cry off GB, to beg off

décomposer /dekɔ̃poze/ [1]
A *vtr* [1] (analyser) to break [sth] down [*raisonnement, phrase*] (**en** into); to break down [*eau*]; to disperse [*lumière*]; to resolve [*force*]; Math to factorize [*expression*]; [2] (déformer) to distort [*traits, visage*]; **visage décomposé** distraught face
B **se décomposer** *vpr* [1] (pourrir) [*matière organique*] to decompose; [*société, parti*] to fall apart; [2] (se déformer) [*visage, traits*] to become distorted

décomposition /dekɔ̃pozisjɔ̃/ *nf* [1] (de matière) decomposition; **en** ~ decomposing; [2] (de société) disintegration; **en** ~ decaying

décompresser○ /dekɔ̃prese/ [1] *vi* to unwind

décompte /dekɔ̃t/ *nm* [1] (déduction) discount; [2] (calcul détaillé) count; **faire le** ~ **de** to count [sth] up [*votes, points*]; [3] (relevé) statement

décompter /dekɔ̃te/ [1] *vtr* [1] (déduire) to deduct (**de** from); [2] (calculer) to work out [*frais*]; to count [*votes, points, personnes*]

déconcentrer /dekɔ̃sɑ̃tre/ [1]
A *vtr* (distraire) to distract
B **se déconcentrer** *vpr* [*personne*] to lose one's concentration

déconcertant, ~**e** /dekɔ̃sɛrtɑ̃, ɑ̃t/ *adj* disconcerting; **d'une facilité** ~**e** ridiculously easy

déconcerter /dekɔ̃sɛrte/ [1] *vtr* to disconcert

déconfit, ~**e** /dekɔ̃fi, it/ *adj* [*air, mine*] crestfallen

déconfiture /dekɔ̃fityr/ *nf* [1] (échec) (de personne) failure; (de parti, d'équipe) defeat; [2] (faillite) (d'entreprise) collapse

décongeler /dekɔ̃ʒle/ [17] *vtr, vi* to defrost

décongestionner /dekɔ̃ʒɛstjone/ [1]
A *vtr* [1] gén to ease the pressure on [*universités, services*]; [*auto-*

route] to relieve congestion in [rue, ville]; **2** Méd [médicament] to relieve congestion in [organe]; to clear [nez]
B se **décongestionner** vpr to clear

déconnecté, **~e** /dekɔnɛkte/ adj [personne] out of touch (**de** with)

déconnecter /dekɔnɛkte/ [1] vtr **1** to disconnect [appareil]; to break [circuit]; **2** fig to dissociate (**de** from)

déconner° /dekɔne/ [1] vi **1** [personne] (plaisanter) to kid around°; (dire des bêtises) to talk crap°; (faire l'idiot) to mess around°; **sans ~!** no kidding°!; **2** [appareil] to play up°

déconseillé, **~e** /dekɔseje/
A pp ▸ **déconseiller**
B pp adj [action] inadvisable; [médicament, boisson, nourriture] not recommended (**à** for); **départ ~ samedi** you are advised not to travel on Saturday

déconseiller /dekɔseje/ [1] vtr **~ qch à qn** to advise sb against sth; **~ à qn de faire** to advise sb against doing; **à ~ aux âmes sensibles** not for the squeamish

déconsidérer /dekɔ̃sideʀe/ [14]
A vtr to discredit
B se **déconsidérer** vpr [journal] to lower its tone; **tu t'es déconsidéré** it was unworthy of you

décontaminer /dekɔ̃tamine/ [1] vtr to decontaminate

décontenancer /dekɔ̃tnɑ̃se/ [12] vtr to disconcert

décontractant, **~e** /dekɔ̃tʀaktɑ̃, ɑ̃t/
A adj relaxing
B nm relaxant

décontracté, **~e** /dekɔ̃tʀakte/
A pp ▸ **décontracter**
B pp adj **1** (détendu) [personne, soirée] relaxed; [mode] casual; **2** (désinvolte) [attitude] laid-back°

décontracter /dekɔ̃tʀakte/ [1] vtr, se **décontracter** vpr to relax

décontraction /dekɔ̃tʀaksjɔ̃/ nf **1** (relaxation) relaxation; **2** (aisance) ease; **3** (désinvolture) casual attitude

déconvenue /dekɔ̃vəny/ nf disappointment

décor /dekɔʀ/ nm **1** (de pièce) decor; (d'objet) decoration; **2** (cadre) setting; **j'ai besoin de changer de ~** I need a change of scene; **3** Cin, Théât **le ~**, **les ~s** the set; **film tourné en ~ naturel** film shot on location

décorateur, **-trice** /dekɔʀatœʀ, tʀis/ ▸ p. 372 nm,f **1** (de maison) interior decorator; (de vitrine) window dresser; **2** Cin, Théât (concepteur) set designer; (peintre) scene painter

décoratif, **-ive** /dekɔʀatif, iv/ adj **1** (destiné à la décoration) ornamental; **2** (qui décore bien) decorative

décoration /dekɔʀasjɔ̃/ nf **1** (action) decorating; **2** (garniture) decoration; **~s de Noël** Christmas decorations; **3** (médaille) decoration; **4** (métier) (d'intérieur) interior design; Cin set design; Théât stage design

décorer /dekɔʀe/ [1] vtr **1** (orner) to decorate (**de** with); (en couture) to trim (**de** with); **2** (médailler) to decorate; **il a été décoré de la médaille militaire** he has been awarded the military medal

décortiquer /dekɔʀtike/ [1] vtr **1** to shell [noix, crabe]; to peel [crevette]; to hull, to husk [riz, graine]; **2** to dissect [texte]

décorum /dekɔʀɔm/ nm (bienséance) **observer le ~** to observe the proprieties

décote /dekɔt/ nf Fin (baisse) drop

découcher /dekuʃe/ [1] vi to spend the night away from home

découdre /dekudʀ/ [76]
A vtr to take [sth] to pieces [vêtement, rideau]; to take off [bouton]; to undo [ourlet]
B vi **en ~** to have a fight (**avec** with)
C se **découdre** vpr [couture, ourlet] to come undone; [bouton] to come off

découler /dekule/ [1] vi **1** (s'ensuivre) to follow (**de** from); **2** (provenir) to result (**de** from)

découpage /dekupaʒ/ nm **1** (image découpée) cut-out; **2** (de métal) cutting up; **3** Cin shooting script

(Composé) **~ électoral** Pol division into constituencies GB, districting US

découpé, **~e** /dekupe/ adj [feuille] lobed; [côte] indented
découper /dekupe/ [1]
A vtr **1** (diviser) to cut up [tarte]; to carve [rôti, volaille]; to

divide up [territoire, domaine]; **~ qch en tranches** to cut sth into slices; **2** (extraire) to cut out [article, photo]; **~ une photo dans un journal** to cut a photo out of a newspaper; **3** (délimiter) **la lampe découpe des ombres sur le mur** the lamp throws shadows on the wall
B se **découper** vpr (se profiler) liter se **~ sur** to stand out against

découragé, **~e** /dekuʀaʒe/ adj [personne] disheartened; [air] despondent; [ton] dejected

décourageant, **~e** /dekuʀaʒɑ̃, ɑ̃t/ adj disheartening

découragement /dekuʀaʒmɑ̃/ nm discouragement, despondency

décourager /dekuʀaʒe/ [13]
A vtr **1** (déprimer) to dishearten; **se laisser ~** to give up (**par** because of); **2** (déconseiller) **~ qn de faire** to discourage sb from doing; **3** (rebuter) to discourage [épargne, initiative]; to deter [malfaiteur]; **la pluie va en ~ plusieurs** the rain will put some people off
B se **décourager** vpr to get discouraged; **ne te décourage pas** don't give up

décousu, **~e** /dekuzy/
A pp ▸ **découdre**
B pp adj [vêtement, ourlet] which has come undone (épith, après n)
C adj (sans cohésion) [histoire, discours, exposé] rambling; (décontracté) [conversation] casual

découvert, **~e**[1] /dekuvɛʀ, ɛʀt/
A pp ▸ **découvrir**
B pp adj **1** (nu) [épaules] bare; **avoir la tête ~e** to be bareheaded; **2** (dégagé) [terrain, pays] open; **3** (non fermé) [camion, wagon] open; [voiture] open-topped
C nm Fin overdraft; **~ budgétaire** budget deficit
D à **découvert** loc adv **1** Fin **être à ~** [client, compte] to be overdrawn; **2** (sans protection) [combattre] out in the open

découverte[2] /dekuvɛʀt/ nf discovery; **partir** or **aller à la ~ de qch** to set off to explore sth

découvrir /dekuvʀiʀ/ [32]
A vtr **1** (trouver) gén to discover; to expose [complot]; **faire ~ qch à qn** to introduce sb to sth; **je vais leur faire ~ Paris** I'm going to show them Paris; **2** (montrer) to show [partie du corps]; to unveil [statue]; **~ son jeu** to show one's hand; **3** (priver de protection) to leave [sth] exposed [frontière, pièce d'échec]; (voir) to see [château, vallée]
B se **découvrir** vpr **1** (enlever son chapeau) to remove one's hat; **2** (trouver en soi) **elle s'est découvert un talent** she found she had a talent; **3** (s'exposer) (volontairement) **ne te découvre pas trop** keep covered up; (involontairement) [dormeur] to kick off one's bedclothes

décrassage /dekʀasaʒ/ nm (de moteur) cleaning; (de mur) scrubbing

décrasser /dekʀase/ [1]
A vtr (nettoyer) to get [sb/sth] clean
B se **décrasser** vpr (se laver) to clean oneself up; **se ~ les mains** to scrub one's hands clean; **se ~ les poumons**° to get some fresh air into one's lungs

décrêper /dekʀepe/ [1] vtr to straighten [cheveux]

décrépit, **~e** /dekʀepi, it/ adj [personne] decrepit; [bâtiment] dilapidated; [mur] crumbling

décrépitude /dekʀepityd/ nf (de mœurs) degeneration; (de régime) decay; (de personne) decrepitude; **tomber en ~** [idéologie, système] to degenerate; [lieu, monument] to crumble

décret /dekʀɛ/ nm decree

décréter /dekʀete/ [14] vtr **1** (par décret) to order; **~ le couvre-feu** to impose a curfew; **2** (autoritairement) to decree (**que** that); (dire avec force) to declare

décret-loi, pl **décrets-lois** /dekʀɛlwa/ nm government decree

décrier /dekʀije/ [2] vtr **le roman a été très décrié** the novel met with a harsh reception; **après avoir été tant décrié, le mariage redevient à la mode** after getting a bad press for so long, marriage is back

décrire /dekʀiʀ/ [67] vtr **1** (dépeindre) to describe; **2** (suivre) to describe [courbe]; to follow [trajectoire]

décrochement /dekʀɔʃmɑ̃/ nm (discontinuité) (en creux) indentation; (en saillie) projection

décrocher /dekʀɔʃe/ [1]
A vtr **1** (détacher) to take down [tableau, jambon, tenture]; to uncouple [wagon]; **~ son téléphone** (pour parler) to pick up the receiver; (pour ne pas être dérangé) to take the phone off

the hook; [2] ○(obtenir) to clinch○, to get [*marché*]; to land○, to get [*contrat, poste, rôle*]; to get [*diplôme*]; to win [*titre*]

B *vi* [1] ○(cesser une activité) to give up; [2] ○(en parlant de tabac, drogue) to kick○ the habit; [3] ○(cesser de s'intéresser) to switch off GB, to tune out US; [4] Mil to disengage; [5] Aviat to stall

C se décrocher *vpr* [*tableau*] to come off its hook; [*rideau*] to come down; [*jupe*] to come undone

(Idiome) **~ le gros lot** to hit the jackpot

décroiser /dekʀwaze/ [1] *vtr* **~ les bras** to unfold one's arms; Tech to uncross [*fils*]

décroissant, **~e** /dekʀwasɑ̃, ɑ̃t/ *adj* [*bruit*] fading; [*intensité*] lessening; [*fortune, pouvoir*] declining; [*vitesse, nombre*] decreasing; [*lune*] waning; **par** *or* **en ordre ~** in descending order

décroître /dekʀwɑtʀ/ [72] *vi* [1] (baisser) [*niveau*] to fall; [*eau, rivière*] to go down; [*lune*] to wane; [2] (diminuer) [*jour*] to get shorter; [*lumière, bruit*] to fade; [*inflation, chômage*] to go down; [*influence, force*] to decline

décrotter /dekʀɔte/ [1] *vtr* [1] to scrape the dirt off [*chaussures*]; [2] ○to civilize○ [*personne*]

décrue /dekʀy/ *nf* (d'eaux) fall *ou* drop in the (water) level; **le fleuve est en ~** the level of the river is falling

décrypter /dekʀipte/ [1] *vtr* [1] (décoder) to decipher [*signes, langue*]; [2] (interpréter) to interpret [*propos*]

déçu, **~e** /desy/

A *pp* ▸ **décevoir**

B *pp adj* [*personne*] disappointed (de *or* par by); [*espoir*] thwarted, foiled; **être ~ dans ses attentes** to feel let down

C *nm,f* disillusioned person

déculotter /dekylɔte/ [1] *vtr* **~ qn** to take off sb's trousers GB *ou* pants US

déculpabiliser /dekylpabilize/ [1]

A *vtr* to free [sb] of guilt [*personne*]

B se déculpabiliser *vpr* [*personne*] to stop feeling guilty

décuple /dekypl/

A *adj* **une somme ~ d'une autre** a sum ten times greater than another

B *nm* **ma mise m'a rapporté le ~** I got back ten times my original stake

décupler /dekyple/ [1]

A *vtr* [1] Math to multiply [sth] by ten; [2] fig to increase *ou* to multiply [sth] tenfold [*énergie, forces*]; **~ les forces de qn** to give sb the strength of ten

B *vi* [*population, ressources*] to increase tenfold

dédaigner /dedeɲe/ [1] *vtr* gén to despise [*personne, gloire, richesse*]; **ce n'est pas à ~** (somme, titre) it's not to be sneezed at *ou* despised; **dédaigné de ses contemporains** spurned by his/her contemporaries; **il ne dédaigne pas la bonne chère** he's not averse to good food

dédaigneusement /dedɛɲøzmɑ̃/ *adv* [*regarder, parler*] disdainfully; [*accueillir*] with disdain

dédaigneux, -euse /dedɛɲø, øz/ *adj* [*ton, sourire, air*] disdainful, scornful; **être ~ du danger** to be unmindful of danger; **être ~ des honneurs** to have no interest in glory

dédain /dedɛ̃/ *nm* contempt (de for), disdain (de for)

dédale /dedal/ *nm* [1] (de couloirs, bâtiments) maze; [2] (de lois, formalités) labyrinth

Dédale /dedal/ *npr* Daedalus

dedans /dədɑ̃/

A *adv* inside; **il vaut mieux dîner ~** it would be better to eat inside *ou* indoors; **j'ai perdu mon sac et mes clés étaient ~** I've lost my bag and my keys were in it; **essaie ce fauteuil, on est très bien ~** try this armchair, it's very comfortable; **il n'y a rien ~** there's nothing in it *ou* inside

B **en dedans** *loc adv* (à l'intérieur) inside

dédicace /dedikas/ *nf* (inscription) (imprimée) dedication (à qn to sb); (manuscrite) inscription (à qn to sb); **faire une ~ à qn** to sign sth for sb

dédicacer /dedikase/ [12] *vtr* [1] (dédier) to dedicate (à to); [2] (signer) to sign [*ouvrage, photographie*] (à for)

dédier /dedje/ [2] *vtr* [1] (offrir en hommage) to dedicate [*œuvre, pensées*] (à to); [2] (consacrer) to dedicate [*vie, efforts*] (à to); to devote [*soirée*] (à to); [3] Relig to dedicate [*chapelle*] (à to)

dédire: se dédire /dediʀ/ [65] *vpr* to back out

dédommagement /dedɔmaʒmɑ̃/ *nm* compensation **C** (de for); **à titre de ~** in compensation (**pour** for)

dédommager /dedɔmaʒe/ [13] *vtr* [1] (indemniser) to compensate (de for); **être dédommagé** to get compensation; [2] (offrir une compensation à) **~ qn de qch** to make it up to sb for sth

dédouanement /dedwanmɑ̃/ *nm* customs clearance

dédouaner /dedwane/ [1]

A *vtr* [1] Comm to clear [sth] through customs [*marchandises*]; [2] (disculper) to clear (**de** of; **auprès de** in the eyes of)

B se dédouaner *vpr* to rehabilitate oneself

dédoublement /dedubləmɑ̃/ *nm* **~ de la personnalité** split personality

dédoubler /deduble/ [1]

A *vtr* (diviser) to split [sth] in two [*groupe*]; to separate [sth] into strands [*câble*]

B se dédoubler *vpr* (se diviser) [*groupe*] to split in two; [*ongle*] to split; [*rayon, image*] to split in two; [*fil, laine, câble*] to come apart

dédramatiser /dedʀamatize/ [1]

A *vtr* to make [sth] less traumatic [*divorce, examen*]; to play [sth] down [*maladie, situation*]; to play down the significance of [*événement*]

B *vi* to play things down

déductible /dedyktibl/ *adj* deductible (**de** from); **~ des impôts** tax-deductible

déduction /dedyksjɔ̃/ *nf* [1] (raisonnement) deduction; **par ~** by deduction; [2] (conclusion) deduction; [3] (soustraction) deduction; **après ~ de, ~ faite de** after deducting; **venir en ~** to be deducted (**de** from)

déduire /dedɥiʀ/ [69]

A *vtr* [1] (tirer la conséquence) to deduce (**de** from; **que** that); [2] (supposer) to infer (**de** from; **que** that); [3] (soustraire) to deduct (**de** from); **frais déduits, une fois déduits les frais** after deduction of expenses

B se déduire *vpr* [1] (être induit) to be inferred (**de** from); [2] (découler) to be deduced (**de** from); [3] (être soustrait) to be deducted (**de** from)

déesse /deɛs/ *nf* goddess

défaillance /defajɑ̃s/ *nf* [1] (mauvais fonctionnement) failure; [2] (moment de faiblesse) **il a eu une ~ à 100 mètres de l'arrivée** he began to flag 100 metres GB from the line; **volonté sans ~** iron will

défaillant, **~e** /defajɑ̃, ɑ̃t/ *adj* [1] (qui fonctionne mal) [*moteur, système*] faulty; [2] (inefficace) [*organisation, service, pouvoir*] inefficient; [3] (qui faiblit) [*santé, mémoire*] failing; (près de s'évanouir) [*personne*] fainting

défaillir /defajiʀ/ [28] *vi* [1] (s'évanouir) to faint; **se sentir ~** to feel faint; **~ de faim** to feel faint with hunger; **~ de bonheur** to be overwhelmed with joy; [2] (faiblir) [*mémoire, santé*] to fail; **soutenir qn sans ~** to show unflinching support for sb

défaire /defɛʀ/ [10]

A *vtr* [1] (ce qui est fait) to undo [*paquet, chignon, ourlet, couture, assemblage*]; to unwind [*pelote*]; to unravel [*tricot, écheveau*]; to break [sth] up [*puzzle*]; to unpack [*valise*]; **le lit n'était pas défait** the bed hadn't been slept in; [2] (détacher) to undo [*cravate, bouton, ceinture, soutien-gorge*]; to untie [*lacet, nœud*]; **ta jupe est défaite** your skirt has come undone; [3] (casser) to break up [*union, alliance*]; [4] (infliger une défaite) to defeat [*armée, adversaire*]; [5] (délivrer) **~ qn de** to free sb from [*liens*]; to rid sb of [*habitudes, préjugés, illusions*]

B se défaire *vpr* [1] (ce qui était fait) [*nœud, ourlet*] to come undone; [2] (se casser) [*alliance, amitié*] to break up; [3] (se débarrasser) **se ~ de** (volontairement) to get rid of [*objet, animal, importun*]; to rid oneself of [*croyance, habitude*]; (à regret) to part with [*objet, animal*]; [4] (se troubler) [*visage, mine*] to fall; **le visage défait** looking haggard

défaite /defɛt/ *nf* defeat

défaitisme /defetism/ *nm* defeatism

défalquer /defalke/ [1] *vtr* to deduct (**de** from)

défaut /defo/

A *nm* [1] (moral) fault; **n'avoir aucun ~** to be perfect; **se mettre en ~** to put oneself in the wrong; **prendre qn en ~** to catch sb out; [2] (physique, matériel, esthétique) gén defect; (de tissu, verre, gemme) flaw (**de** in); (de théorie, raisonnement, d'œuvre d'art) flaw (**de** in); **avoir** *or* **présenter des ~s** [*machine, construction*] to be faulty; **sans ~** [*système, machine*] perfect; [*rubis, raisonnement*] flawless; **le ~ de la cuirasse de qn** fig the chink in sb's armour GB; [3] (insuffisance) shortage (**de** of); (absence) lack (**de** of); **faire ~** [*argent, ressources*] to be lacking; [*signature, document*] to be missing; **le talent leur**

fait ~ they lack talent; **le courage leur a fait** ~ their courage failed them; **le temps m'a fait** ~ I didn't have enough time; ④ Jur ~ **de paiement** non-payment; **par** ~ [*condamné, jugé*] in absentia; **faire** ~ [*accusé, témoin*] to fail to appear in court

⑤ à défaut de *loc prép* **à** ~ **de miel, utilisez du sucre** if you have no honey, use sugar; **à** ~ **de paiement immédiat** failing prompt payment; **à** ~ **de quoi** failing which; **à** ~ **de mieux** for want of anything better

(Composés) ~ **de construction** structural defect; ~ **de fabrication** manufacturing fault; ~ **de prononciation** speech impediment

défaveur /defavœʀ/ *nf* ① (perte d'estime) **être en** ~ **auprès de qn** to be out of favour^GB with sb; ② (désavantage) **il s'est trompé de 3 euros en ma** ~ he overcharged me 3 euros; **mon âge a joué en ma** ~ my age went against me

défavorable /defavɔʀabl/ *adj* [*situation, conditions*] unfavourable^GB (**à** to); [*personne, gouvernement*] opposed (**à** to)

défavorablement /defavɔʀabləmã/ *adv* unfavourably^GB; **juger** ~ to have an unfavourable^GB opinion of

défavorisé, ~e /defavɔʀize/
Ⓐ *pp* ▸ **défavoriser**
Ⓑ *pp adj* [*milieu, personne*] underprivileged; [*région, pays*] disadvantaged
Ⓒ *nm,f* underprivileged person

défavoriser /defavɔʀize/ [1] *vtr* ① (léser) [*impôt, mesure sociale*] to discriminate against; ② (handicaper) [*difformité physique, défaut*] to put [sb] at a disadvantage; ③ (être injuste envers) [*examinateur*] to put [sb] at a disadvantage

défection /defɛksjɔ̃/ *nf* ① (abandon) (d'alliés) desertion; (pour un autre parti, pays) defection; **faire** ~ to defect; ② (absence) nonappearance; **faire** ~ to back out

défectueux, -euse /defɛktɥø, øz/ *adj* [*matériel*] faulty, defective; [*raisonnement*] flawed; [*organisation*] poor

défendable /defãdabl/ *adj* Mil [*position, ville*] defensible; [*point de vue*] tenable; [*conduite*] justifiable; **pas** ~ [*ville*] indefensible; [*thèse*] untenable; [*conduite*] indefensible, inexcusable; **l'accusé n'est pas** ~ the defendant has no case

défendant: **à son corps défendant** /asɔ̃kɔʀdefãdã/ *loc adv* unwillingly

défendre /defãdʀ/ [6]
Ⓐ *vtr* ① (interdire) ~ **qch à qn** to forbid sb sth; ~ **à qn de faire** to forbid sb to do; **ne fume pas ici, c'est défendu** you can't smoke here; **l'alcool/le tabac m'est défendu** I'm not allowed to drink/to smoke; ② (protéger) (généralement) to defend [*personne, pays, honneur, intérêts*] (**contre** against); to fight for [*droit*]; (dans une circonstance) to stand up for [*ami, idées, principe*]; Jur to defend [*accusé*]; Sport to defend [*titre, but*]; ~ **qn/qch au péril de sa vie** to risk one's life in defence^GB of sb/sth; ~ **une cause** to champion a cause
Ⓑ **se défendre** *vpr* ① (lutter) (généralement) to defend oneself (**contre** against); (dans une circonstance) to stand up for oneself (**contre** against); ② (être défendable) [*argument, thèse*] to be tenable; **cette opinion se défend** it's a valid opinion; **il préfère attendre, et ça se défend** he'd rather wait, and he's got a point; ③ (se protéger) to protect oneself (**de** or **contre** from or against); **se** ~ **contre le désespoir** to ward off despair; ④ ○(se débrouiller) to get by; **se** ~ **en français** to be quite good at French; **se** ~ **bien en affaires** to do very well in business; ⑤ (nier) **se** ~ **d'être jaloux** to deny being jealous; ⑥ (s'empêcher) **se** ~ **de faire qch** to refrain from doing sth; **on ne peut se** ~ **de penser que...** one can't help thinking that...

défense /defãs/ *nf* ① (interdiction) '~ **de pêcher/fumer**' 'no fishing/smoking'; '~ **d'entrer**' 'no entry'; '~ **de toucher**' '(please) do not touch'; ~ **d'en parler devant lui** don't mention it in front of him; ② (contre un agresseur) gén, Mil, Sport defence^GB (**contre** against); (moyens, ouvrages) ~**s** defences^GB; **courir à la** ~ **de qn** to leap to sb's defence^GB; **pour sa** ~**, elle a dit que...** in her defence^GB, she said that...; **le budget de la** ~ **(nationale)** the defence^GB budget; **armes de** ~ defensive weapons; **assurer la** ~ **du territoire** to defend the country; **sans** ~ (faible) helpless; (sans protection) unprotected; **la** ~ **de l'environnement** the protection of the environment; **la** ~ **de la langue française** the preservation of the French language; **association pour la** ~ **des consommateurs** consumer rights organization; **faire grève pour la** ~ **de l'emploi** to strike against job cuts; **prendre la** ~ **de qn/qch** to stand up for sb/sth; ③ Méd, Psych defence^GB; **les** ~**s de l'organisme** the body's defences^GB; **les** ~**s immunitaires** the immune system; ④ Zool (d'éléphant, de sanglier, morse) tusk

défenseur /defãsœʀ/ *nm* defender; **se faire le** ~ **des faibles** to defend the weak

défensive /defãsiv/ *nf* **être** *or* **se tenir sur la** ~ to be on the defensive

déférence /deferãs/ *nf* deference (**pour, envers** to); **par** ~ **pour** out of *ou* in deference to

déférent, ~e /deferã, ãt/ *adj* **se montrer** ~ to show respect (**envers, à l'égard de** for)

déferlement /defɛʀləmã/ *nm* (d'articles, images) flood; (de violence, protestations) upsurge (**de** in); (de passion) surge; (de paroles) torrent; (de louanges) flood; **un** ~ **de critiques** a barrage of criticism

déferler /defɛʀle/ [1] *vi* [*vague*] to break (**sur** on); [*violence, protestations*] to erupt; [*injures*] to pour out; [*articles*] to flood in; [*personnes*] to pour (**sur** into; **dans** through); **une vague de racisme déferle sur la France** a wave of racism is sweeping through France

défi /defi/ *nm* ① (gageure) challenge; **lancer un** ~ **à qn** to challenge sb; **relever un** ~ to take up a challenge; **c'est un** ~ **aux lois de l'équilibre** it defies the laws of gravity; ② (provocation) act of defiance

défiance /defjãs/ *nf* distrust, mistrust; **avec** ~ warily; **sans** ~ unsuspectingly, trustingly

défiant, ~e /defjã, ãt/ *adj* distrustful, wary

déficeler /defisle/ [19] *vtr* to untie [*paquet*]

déficience /defisjãs/ *nf* ① Méd deficiency; ~ **en calcium** calcium deficiency; ~ **physique** physical handicap; ~ **immunitaire** immunodeficiency; ② (défaut) deficiency; **les** ~**s de l'intrigue** weaknesses in the plot

déficient, ~e /defisjã, ãt/ *adj* ① Méd [*cœur, muscle*] deficient; **mentalement** ~ mentally defective; ② (insuffisant) [*système, contrôle*] inadequate

déficit /defisit/ *nm* ① Comm, Écon, Fin deficit; ② Méd deficiency

déficitaire /defisitɛʀ/ *adj* [*budget, compte*] showing a deficit (*jamais épith*); [*entreprise*] showing a loss (*jamais épith*); [*activité, secteur*] loss-making (*épith*); [*ressources*] showing a shortfall (*jamais épith*)

défier /defje/ [2] *vtr* ① (provoquer) to challenge [*rival, adversaire*]; ~ **qn en combat singulier** to challenge sb to single combat; ~ **qn de prouver** to defy sb to prove; **je te défie de plonger** I dare you to dive; ~ **qn du regard** to stare defiantly at sb; ② (braver) to defy [*danger, mort, opinion*]; **cela défie la raison** *or* **l'entendement** it is beyond belief; **prix défiant toute concurrence** unbeatable price

défigurer /defigyʀe/ [1] *vtr* gén to disfigure; to mutilate [*texte*]; to distort [*pensée, propos*]

défilé /defile/ *nm* ① (de fête) parade; (de manifestants) march; ② (de visiteurs, candidats) stream; ③ Géog gorge

(Composés) ~ **aérien** flypast GB, flyover US; ~ **militaire** march-past; ~ **de mode** fashion show

défiler /defile/ [1]
Ⓐ *vi* ① (marcher en rangs) (pour célébrer) to parade; (pour manifester) to march; ② (se succéder) [*personnes*] to come and go; [*minutes, kilomètres*] to add up; ~ **devant** (devant un cercueil, un lieu) to file past; [*mannequin*] to parade in front of; **les souvenirs défilaient dans ma mémoire** memories thronged in; ③ (se dérouler) [*images, paysage*] to unfold; ~ **rapidement** to flash past; **voir** ~ **sa vie en quelques secondes** to see one's life flash before one's eyes; ④ Ordinat [*texte*] to scroll (**vers le bas** down; **vers le haut** up)
Ⓑ **se défiler**○ *vpr* **se** ~ **au moment de faire qch** to get out of doing sth

défini, ~e /defini/ *adj* ① gén clearly defined; **mal** ~ [*sentiment*] vague; [*contour, image, circonstances*] ill-defined; **bien** ~ well-defined (*épith*); ② Ling [*article*] definite

définir /definiʀ/ [3] *vtr* to define [*mot, politique*]; to define [*personne*] (**comme** as); ~ **qch comme une priorité** to make sth top priority; ~ **la gestion comme un art** to see management as an art

définitif, -ive /definitif, iv/
Ⓐ *adj* [*comptes, rapport, accord*] final; [*édition*] definitive; [*refus*] flat; **rien de** ~ nothing definite; **renvoi** ~ Scol expulsion

(de from); **'fermeture définitive'** Comm 'closing down'
B **en définitive** *loc adv* at the end of the day

définition /definisjɔ̃/ *nf* gén definition; (de mots croisés) clue; **par** ~ by definition

définitivement /definitivmɑ̃/ *adv* [*fermer, séparer, cesser*] for good

défiscalisé, ~**e** /defiskalize/ *adj* tax-exempt (*épith*)

déflagration /deflagʀasjɔ̃/ *nf* (explosion) detonation

défoncé, ~**e** /defɔ̃se/ *adj* [*fauteuil, divan*] sagging (*épith*); [*chaise*] with a broken seat (*épith, après n*); [*chemin*] pot-holed, full of potholes (*après n*); [*trottoir*] full of holes (*après n*)

défoncer /defɔ̃se/ [12] *vtr* to smash [*vitrine, barricade*]; to break [*sth*] down [*porte*]; to break the springs of [*divan, sommier*]; to smash [*sth*] in [*aile, arrière d'une voiture*]; to dent [*chapeau*]; **il lui a défoncé la mâchoire**○ he broke his jaw; **la pluie a défoncé le terrain** the rain has churned up the ground

déformant, ~**e** /defɔʀmɑ̃, ɑ̃t/ *adj* [*miroir*] distorting

déformation /defɔʀmasjɔ̃/ *nf* (d'objet, image, de fait, propos) distortion; ~ **de la colonne vertébrale** spinal deformity; **c'est de la** ~ **professionnelle** it's a habit that comes from the job

déformé, ~**e** /defɔʀme/ *adj* [*visage, traits, image, vérité*] distorted; [*objet*] warped; [*corps, membre*] misshapen; [*vêtement*] shapeless; [*esprit*] warped; **traits** ~**s par la douleur/colère** features contorted with pain/anger; **mains** ~**es par l'âge** hands gnarled with age; **chaussée** ~**e** uneven (road) surface

déformer /defɔʀme/ [1]
A *vtr* **1** (endommager) to bend [*sth*] (out of shape) [*pare-chocs, aile d'avion*]; **tu vas le** ~ you'll get it out of shape; **2** (transformer) to distort [*image, traits*]; **3** (fausser) to distort [*vérité, faits*]; **on a déformé mes propos** (par erreur) I've been misquoted; (à dessein) my words have been twisted
B **se déformer** *vpr* gén to lose its shape; [*pantalon*] to go GB *ou* become baggy

défoulement /defulmɑ̃/ *nm* letting off steam **¢**

défouler /defule/ [1]
A *vtr* **1** [*activité*] to release tension in [*personne*]; **2** [*personne*] ~ **sa colère contre qn** to vent one's anger on sb
B **se défouler** *vpr* (dépenser de l'énergie) to let off steam; (se détendre) to let one's hair down○; **se** ~ **sur qn** to take it out on sb

défraîchi, ~**e** /defʀeʃi/ *adj* [*vêtement, rideau*] worn; [*tissu, beauté, couleur*] faded

défrayer /defʀeje/ [21] *vtr* **1** (être le sujet de) ~ **la conversation** to be the main topic of conversation; ~ **la chronique** to be the talk of the town; **2** (rembourser) ~ **qn** to pay sb's expenses

défricher /defʀiʃe/ [1] *vtr* to clear [*bois, terre*]; ~ **le terrain** fig to do the groundwork

défriser /defʀize/ [1] *vtr* to straighten [*cheveux*]

défroisser /defʀwase/ [1] *vtr* to smooth out [*vêtement, papier*]

défroque /defʀɔk/ *nf* (vêtements ridicules) ridiculous outfit

défroqué, ~**e** /defʀɔke/ *adj* [*prêtre*] defrocked

défunt, ~**e** /defœ̃, œ̃t/
A *adj* [*personne*] late; [*empire, grandeur*] former; [*idéologie*] defunct
B *nm,f* **le** ~, **la** ~**e** the deceased

dégagé, ~**e** /degaʒe/ *adj* [*vue, passage, route, ciel*] clear; [*cou, front*] bare; [*air, allure*] casual

dégagement /degaʒmɑ̃/ *nm* **1** (d'un lieu) clearing (**de** of); **2** (de vestiges) digging out (**de** of); **3** Sport (au football) clearance (**de qn** by sb)

dégager /degaʒe/ [13]
A *vtr* **1** (libérer physiquement) to free; **2** (débarrasser) to clear [*bureau, route, passage*]; **'dégagez, s'il vous plaît'** (ordre de la police) 'move along please'; **dégage**○! GB, **get lost**○!; **demande au coiffeur de te** ~ **les oreilles** ask the hairdresser to cut your hair away from your ears; **3** (extraire) to find [*idée, morale, sens*]; ~ **les grands axes d'une politique** to highlight the main points of a policy; **4** (laisser échapper) [*volcan, voiture*] to emit [*odeur, gaz*]; [*casserole*] to let out [*vapeur*]; ~ **de la chaleur** to give off heat; **5** Fin ~ **des crédits pour la construction d'une école** to make funds available for a school to be built; ~ **des bénéfices** to make a profit; ~ **un excédent commercial** to

show a trade surplus; **6** (racheter ce qui était en gage) ~ **une montre du mont-de-piété** to redeem a watch from the pawnbroker; **7** (libérer moralement) ~ **qn d'une responsabilité** to relieve sb of a responsibility; ~ **qn d'une obligation** to release sb from an obligation; **8** (au football, rugby) ~ **la balle** to clear the ball; **9** (déboucher) to unblock [*nez, sinus*]; to clear [*bronches*]
B **se dégager** *vpr* **1** (se libérer) to free oneself/itself; **se** ~ **d'une situation piégée** to get out of a tricky situation; **2** Météo [*temps, ciel*] to clear; **3** (émaner) **se** ~ **de** [*chaleur, gaz, fumée*] to come out of; [*odeur, parfum*] to emanate from; **4** (apparaître) **un charme désuet se dégage du roman** the novel has an element of old world charm about it; **la conclusion qui se dégage de la discussion** the outcome of the debate

dégaine○ /degɛn/ *nf* (allure) odd appearance; (démarche) odd walk; **avoir une** ~ **de cow-boy** (allure) to look like a cowboy; (démarche) to walk like a cowboy

dégainer /degene/ [1] *vtr* **1** (sortir de son étui) to draw [*arme*]; **2** Électrotech to strip [*câble*]

dégarni, ~**e** /degaʀni/ *adj* **1** (sans cheveux) **avoir le crâne** ~ to be balding; **front** ~ receding hairline; **2** (vide) [*rayons, magasin*] bare; [*compte*] empty

dégarnir /degaʀniʀ/ [3]
A *vtr* to empty [*rayon*]
B **se dégarnir** *vpr* **1** (perdre ses cheveux) **il a le front qui se dégarnit** his hair is receding, he's got a receding hair line; **2** (se vider) [*rue, salle*] to empty

dégât /dega/ *nm* damage **¢**; **limiter les** ~**s** to limit the damage; **faire des** ~**s** [*personne*] to do damage; [*explosion*] to cause damage

dégel /deʒɛl/ *nm* **1** Météo thaw; **c'est le** ~ it's thawing; **2** (de tensions) thaw; (de crédits) unfreezing

dégeler /deʒle/ [17]
A *vtr* **1** (détendre) to improve [*relations*]; to warm up [*public*]; ~ **l'atmosphère** to break the ice; **2** (débloquer) to unfreeze [*crédits*]
B *vi* [*sol, lac*] to thaw (out)
C **se dégeler** *vpr* [*relations, situation*] to thaw; [*public*] to warm up; [*personne*] to thaw out

dégénéré, ~**e** /deʒenere/ *adj, nm,f* degenerate

dégénérer /deʒenere/ [14] *vi* **1** (mal tourner) [*bagarre, incident*] to get out of hand; ~ **en** to degenerate into; **2** (s'abâtardir) [*race, plante, espèce*] to degenerate

dégénérescence /deʒeneresɑ̃s/ *nf* (d'organe, espèce) degeneration; **en pleine** ~ [*pays*] in decline

dégingandé, ~**e** /deʒɛ̃gɑ̃de/ *adj* lanky

dégivrage /deʒivʀaʒ/ *nm* **1** Aut, Aviat de-icing; **2** (de réfrigérateur) defrosting

dégivrer /deʒivʀe/ [1] *vtr* to de-ice [*pare-brise, serrure*]; to defrost [*réfrigérateur*]

déglacer /deglase/ [12] *vtr* Culin to deglaze

déglingué○, ~**e** /deglɛ̃ge/ *adj* dilapidated

déglinguer○ /deglɛ̃ge/ [1]
A *vtr* to bust○, to break [*appareil, objet*]
B **se déglinguer** *vpr* [*mécanisme*] to go wrong; [*appareil*] to break down; **se** ~ **la santé** to wreck○ one's health

déglutir /deglytiʀ/ [3] *vtr, vi* to swallow

dégommer○ /degɔme/ [1] *vtr* **1** (licencier) to fire; **2** (décrier) **se faire** ~ **(en flèche)** to get a terrible telling-off; **3** (atteindre) to hit (**avec** with)

dégonflé, ~**e** /degɔ̃fle/
A *adj* [*ballon*] deflated; [*pneu*] flat
B○ *nm,f* chicken○, coward

dégonfler /degɔ̃fle/ [1]
A *vtr* **1** (vider de son air) to deflate [*pneu, ballon*]; **2**○ (réduire) to streamline [*effectifs*]; to reduce [*masse monétaire*]
B *vi* (désenfler) [*cheville, bosse*] to go down
C **se dégonfler** *vpr* **1** (se vider de son air) [*bouée*] to deflate; [*pneu, ballon*] to go down; **2**○ (manquer de courage) [*personne*] to chicken out○, to lose one's nerve

dégot(t)er○ /degɔte/ [1] *vtr* to find

dégouliner /deguline/ [1] *vi* **1** [*liquide*] to trickle; **2** [*personne, objet*] to drip (**de** with)

dégoupiller /degupije/ [1] *vtr* ~ **une grenade** to pull the pin out of a grenade

dégourdi, ~**e** /deguʀdi/ *adj* (débrouillard) smart

dégourdir /deguʀdiʀ/ [3]
A *vtr* **1** (réchauffer) to warm [*sth*] up [*doigts, pieds*];

② (assouplir) to loosen [sth] up [*doigts, membres*]; ③ (rendre plus hardi) ~ **des enfants** to bring children out of themselves

B **se dégourdir** *vpr* ① (se détendre) **se** ~ **(les jambes)** to stretch one's legs; ② (devenir plus hardi) to come out of oneself

dégoût /degu/ *nm* ① (répulsion) disgust (**devant** at; **pour** for); **avec un profond** ~ with absolute disgust; ② (lassitude) weariness; ~ **de la vie** world-weariness; ③ (satiété) nausea; **boire jusqu'au** ~ to drink until one feels sick

dégoûtant, ~**e** /degutã, ãt/ *adj* ① (sale) filthy; ② ○(scandaleux) disgusting; ③ (répugnant) [*habitude*] revolting; [*créature*] disgusting; **il fait un temps** ~ **aujourd'hui** the weather is foul today

dégoûté, ~**e** /degute/ *adj* [*commentaire, ton*] disgusted; **d'un air** ~ with disgust; **être** ~ **de qch** to have had enough of sth; **ne pas être** ~ to have a strong stomach; **faire le** ~ to turn one's nose up

dégoûter /degute/ [1]
A *vtr* ① (répugner) to disgust; (écœurer) to make [sb] feel sick; **ça me dégoûte** it's disgusting; ② (ôter l'envie) to put [sb] off; ~ **qn de qch/de faire** to put sb off sth/off doing; ③ (scandaliser) to sicken; **ça me dégoûte (de voir) que/de voir comment** it makes me sick (to see) that/the way
B **se dégoûter** *vpr* (se lasser) **se** ~ **de** to get tired of

dégradant, ~**e** /degradã, ãt/ *adj* [*activité, travail*] degrading

dégradation /degradasjõ/ *nf* ① (dégât provoqué) damage **Ȼ**; **la** ~ **du site** the damage caused to the area; ② (usure naturelle) deterioration; ③ (détérioration) (de situation) deterioration (**de** in); (de mœurs) decline (**de** in); **la** ~ **des conditions de vie** the deterioration in the standard of living; **la** ~ **du pouvoir d'achat** the erosion in purchasing power

⟨Composé⟩ ~ **civique** loss of civil rights; ~ **militaire** dishonourable[GB] discharge

dégradé, ~**e** /degrade/
A *adj* **tons** ~**s** shaded tones; **coupe** ~**e** layered cut
B *nm* ① (de couleurs) gradation; **peint en** ~ painted in shaded tones; ② (en coiffure) layered cut

dégrader /degrade/ [1]
A *vtr* ① (détériorer) to damage; ② Mil (destituer) to cashier [*officier*]; ③ Art to shade [sth] from dark to light [*tons, couleurs*]; ④ (avilir) [*vice*] to degrade [*personne*]
B **se dégrader** *vpr* (se détériorer) to deteriorate

dégrafer /degrafe/ [1]
A *vtr* to undo
B **se dégrafer** *vpr* to come undone

dégraissage /degresaʒ/ *nm* (d'effectifs) reduction (**de** in); (d'entreprise) streamlining **Ȼ** (**de** of); ~**s de personnel** staff cuts

dégraissant, ~**e** /degresã, ãt/ *adj* [*produit, liquide*] grease-removing (épith)

dégraisser /degrese/ [1] *vtr* ○(réduire le personnel) to streamline [*effectifs*]; ② (nettoyer) to dry-clean [*vêtement*]

degré /degre/ *nm* ① ▸ p. 581 (d'angle, de température) degree; **il fait 15** ~**s dehors** it's 15 degrees outside; ② (concentration) **ce vin fait 12°** this wine contains 12% alcohol; **cette boisson fait combien de** ~**s?** what is the alcohol content of this drink?; ③ (niveau) degree (**de** of); (stade d'une évolution) stage; **par** ~**s** gradually; **à un moindre** ~ to a lesser extent; **jusqu'à un certain** ~ up to a point; **susceptible au dernier** *or* **au plus haut** ~ extremely touchy; **un tel** ~ **de cruauté est-il possible?** is it possible that anyone could be so cruel?; ④ (dans un classement) degree; **brûlures du premier** ~ first-degree burns; **cousins au premier/second** ~ first/second cousins; **enseignement du premier/second** ~ primary/secondary education; ⑤ (dans une interprétation) **premier/deuxième** *or* **second** ~ literal/hidden meaning; **prendre ce que quelqu'un dit au premier** ~ to take what somebody says literally; **tout discours politique est à interpréter au deuxième** *or* **second** ~ you need to read between the lines of any political speech; ⑥ (marche) step; **les** ~**s de l'échelle sociale** the rungs of the social ladder

⟨Composés⟩ ~ **Celsius** degree Celsius; ~ **Fahrenheit** degree Fahrenheit; ~ **de parenté** degree of kinship

dégressif, -ive /degresif, iv/ *adj* [*impôt*] graduated; **tarifs** ~**s** tapering charges

dégrèvement /degrɛvmã/ *nm* ~ **(fiscal)** tax relief

dégriffé, ~**e** /degrife/ *adj* **robe/veste** ~**e** marked-down designer dress/jacket

dégringolade○ /degrĩgɔlad/ *nf* ① (de personne, d'objets) fall; ② (de cours, prix) collapse

dégringoler○ /degrĩgɔle/ [1]
A *vtr* to race down [*escalier, pente*]
B *vi* ① (tomber) [*personne*] to tumble; [*livres, tuiles*] to tumble down (**de** off); [*pluie*] to pour down; ② (baisser) [*prix, température*] to fall sharply; [*production*] to drop sharply; [*popularité*] to slump

dégripper /degripe/ [1] *vtr* to lubricate [*moteur*]; to unjam [*mécanisme*]

dégriser /degrize/ [1]
A *vtr* ① (dessoûler) to sober [sb] up; ② (ramener à la réalité) to bring [sb] to his/her senses
B **se dégriser** *vpr* ① (dessoûler) to sober up; ② (revenir à la réalité) to come to one's senses

dégrossi, ~**e** /degrosi/ *adj* [*planches*] rough-hewn; **mal** ~ [*personne*] coarse péj

dégrossir /degrosir/ [3] *vtr* to rough-hew [*pierre*]; to break the back of [*travail*]; to knock a few corners off [*personne*]

dégrouiller○: **se dégrouiller** /degruje/ [1] *vpr* to hurry up, to get a move on○

déguerpir /degɛrpir/ [3] *vi* to leave; **faire** ~ **qn** to drive sb off

déguisé, ~**e** /degize/ *adj* ① (vêtu d'un déguisement) (pour s'amuser) in fancy dress (*jamais épith*); (pour duper) in disguise (*jamais épith*); ~ **en pirate** dressed up as a pirate; ② (où l'on se déguise) [*soirée, défilé*] fancy dress (*épith*); ③ (camouflé) [*appui, subvention, tentative*] concealed; [*compliment*] disguised; [*critique*] veiled; **une façon** ~**e de faire** a roundabout way of doing; **non** ~ undisguised

déguisement /degizmã/ *nm* ① (costume) (pour s'amuser) costume; (pour duper) disguise; ② (de pensée, vérité) concealment; **sans** ~ openly

déguiser /degize/ [1]
A *vtr* ① (mettre un déguisement à) (pour s'amuser) to dress [sb] up (**en** as); (pour duper) to disguise (**en** as); ② (altérer) to disguise [*visage, voix, écriture*]; ③ (camoufler) to conceal [*intentions, ambition*]
B **se déguiser** *vpr* (pour s'amuser) to dress up (**en** as); (pour duper) to disguise oneself (**en** as)

dégurgiter /degyrʒite/ [1] *vtr* ① (vomir) to bring up [*aliment*]; ② (dire) to spew out [*insultes*]; to regurgitate [*leçon*]

dégustation /degystasjõ/ *nf* tasting

déguster /degyste/ [1] *vtr* (savourer) to savour[GB] [*boisson, aliment, victoire*]; to enjoy [*spectacle*]

déhanchement /deãʃmã/ *nm* ① (naturel) swaying hips (*pl*); ② (d'infirme) lopsidedness; ③ Méd dislocation of the hip

déhancher: **se déhancher** /deãʃe/ [1] *vpr* gén to sway one's hips; (exagérément) to wiggle one's hips

dehors /dəɔr/
A *adv* outside; **passer la nuit** ~ (occasionnellement) to spend the night outdoors; [*clochard*] to sleep rough; **j'ai été** ~ **toute la journée** I was out all day; **mettre qn** ~ gén to throw sb out; (d'un travail) to fire sb; (d'un établissement scolaire) to expel [*élève*]; **de** ~ [*voir, arriver*] from outside
B *excl* get out!
C *nm inv* **les bruits du** ~ noise from outside; **quelqu'un du** ~ **ne peut pas comprendre** an outsider can't understand; **ses** ~ **bourrus cachent un cœur d'or** his/her rough exterior hides a heart of gold
D **en dehors** *loc adv* ① (à l'extérieur) outside; ② fig (non impliqué) **rester en** ~ to stay out of it
E **en dehors de** *loc prép* ① (à l'extérieur de) outside; **en** ~ **du pays** outside the country; ② (mis à part) apart from; ③ (hors de) outside; **en** ~ **des heures de travail** outside working hours; **il est resté en** ~ **du coup** he stayed out of the whole business; **c'est en** ~ **du sujet** Scol it's off the subject; **c'est en** ~ **de mes attributions** that's outside my jurisdiction sout, that's not my job; **en** ~ **des limites de la loi** beyond the limits of the law

déifier /deifje/ [2] *vtr* ① (diviniser) to deify [*personne, animal*]; ② (vénérer) to worship [*argent, progrès*]; to idolize [*jeunesse, vedette*]

déjà /deʒa/ *adv* ⓵ (dès maintenant) already; **il est ~ tard** it is already late, it is late already; **sans cela, j'aurais ~ fini** if it hadn't been for that, I would have finished already *ou* I'd be finished by now; **elle serait ~ mariée, si elle l'avait voulu** she could have been married by now if she'd wanted; ⓶ (précédemment) before, already; **je te l'ai ~ dit** I told you before, I've already told you once; ⓷ ○(pour renforcer) **c'est ~ un joli salaire!** that's a pretty good salary!; **être second, c'est ~ très bien!** even to come second is pretty good!; **c'est ~ beaucoup d'avoir la santé** good health is the main thing; **il s'est excusé, c'est ~ quelque chose** at least he apologized, that's something; ⓸ ○(pour protester) **elle est ~ assez riche (comme ça)!** she's rich enough as it is; ⓹ ○(pour faire répéter) again; **c'est combien, ~?** how much was it again?

déjà-vu /deʒavy/ *nm inv* ⓵ ○**c'est du ~** we've seen it all before; ⓶ Psych déjà vu

déjeuner¹ /deʒœne/ [1] *vi* ⓵ (à midi) to have lunch; **inviter qn à ~** to invite sb to lunch; **restez ~** stay for lunch; **~ d'un sandwich** to have a sandwich for lunch; ⓶ (le matin) dial, B, C to have breakfast

déjeuner² /deʒœne/ *nm* ⓵ (repas de midi) lunch; **~ d'affaires** business lunch; **prendre son ~** to have lunch; **l'heure du ~** lunchtime; **le ~ est servi** lunch is ready; **après ~** after lunch; ⓶ (petit déjeuner) dial, B, C breakfast

(Composé) **~ sur l'herbe** picnic lunch

déjouer /deʒwe/ [1] *vtr* to frustrate [*astuce, précaution*]; to foil [*plan, conspiration*]; to evade [*surveillance, contrôle*]; **~ les pièges de l'ennemi** to avoid the traps set by the enemy; **~ les manœuvres de qn** to outmanoeuvre sb

déjuger: se déjuger /deʒyʒe/ [13] *vpr* to go back on one's decision

delà /dəla/ *adv* **deçà, ~** here and there

de-là /dəla/ *adv* **de-ci, ~** here and there

délabré, ~e /delabre/ *adj* [*maison, équipement*] dilapidated; [*plafond, mur*] crumbling; [*vêtements*] ragged; [*santé, esprit*] damaged

délabrement /delabrəmɑ̃/ *nm* (de maison, d'équipement) dilapidation; (de santé, pays) poor state

délabrer /delabre/ [1]
A *vtr* to ruin [*maison, équipement*]
B **se délabrer** *vpr* [*maison, équipement, économie, pays*] to become run-down; [*affaires*] to go to rack and ruin; [*santé*] to deteriorate

délacer /delase/ [12]
A *vtr* to undo [*chaussures*]; to unlace [*corsage*]
B **se délacer** *vpr* [*chaussure*] to come undone

délai /delɛ/ *nm* ⓵ (période accordée) **tu as un ~ de 20 jours pour payer** you have 20 days to pay; **dans un ~ de 24 heures** within 24 hours; **faire qch dans le ~ prescrit** to do sth within the allotted time; **rester dans les ~s** to meet the deadline; **les ~s sont trop courts** *or* **serrés** there isn't enough time; **fixer un ~** to set a deadline; **respecter un ~** to meet a deadline; **dernier ~ pour les inscriptions** final date for registration; ⓶ (période d'attente) **abaisser un ~** to cut the waiting time; **le ~ moyen tourne autour de six mois** the average wait is about six months; **comptez trois semaines de ~ pour la livraison** allow three weeks for delivery; **dans les meilleurs** *or* **plus brefs ~s** as soon as possible; **sans ~** [*agir*] immediately; ⓶ (période supplémentaire) extension; **obtenir un ~** to get an extension; **demander un ~** to ask for extra time; **proroger un ~** to extend a deadline

(Composés) **~ de grâce** grace period; **~ de livraison** delivery *ou* lead time (**pour** on); **~ de préavis** (period of) notice; **~ de réflexion** time to think

délaissé, ~e /delese/ *adj* ⓵ (abandonné) [*épouse*] deserted; [*maîtresse, enfant, terres*] abandoned; ⓶ (négligé) [*personne*] neglected

délaisser /delese/ [1] *vtr* ⓵ (abandonner) to leave [*épouse*]; to abandon [*lieu, activité*]; ⓶ (négliger) to neglect [*amis, études*]

délassant, ~e /delasɑ̃, ɑ̃t/ *adj* [*bain, activité physique*] relaxing; [*film*] entertaining

délassement /delasmɑ̃/ *nm* relaxation

délasser /delase/ [1]
A *vtr* [*bain*] to relax [*corps*]; **cela m'a délassé de faire** I feel more relaxed after doing; **ça délasse** it's relaxing
B **se délasser** *vpr* to relax (**en faisant** by doing)

délateur, -trice /delatœr, tris/ *nm,f* informer

délation /delasjɔ̃/ *nf* informing

délavé, ~e /delave/ *adj* ⓵ (décoloré) [*couleur, ciel*] washedout; [*jean, affiche*] faded; ⓶ (imprégné d'eau) [*terre*] waterlogged

délayer /deleje/ [21] *vtr* ⓵ (diluer) to thin [*peinture*] (**avec** with); to mix [*farine*] (**dans** with); ⓶ (trop étirer) **un rapport trop délayé** a waffling report○

delco® /dɛlko/ *nm* distributor

délectation /delɛktasjɔ̃/ *nf* (plaisir) delight

délecter: se délecter /delɛkte/ [1] *vpr* **se ~ à faire/en faisant** to delight in doing; **se ~ de qch** to enjoy sth thoroughly; **se ~ à l'avance de qch/de faire** to be thoroughly looking forward to sth/to doing

délégation /delegasjɔ̃/ *nf* ⓵ (groupe) delegation (**auprès de** to); **aller voir qn en ~** to form a delegation to go and see sb; ⓶ Jur authority; **signer par ~** to sign on sb's authority; **recevoir ~ (de qn) pour faire qch** to be authorized to do sth (by sb); ⓷ (transmission) delegation (**à qn** to sb)

délégué, ~e /delege/
A *adj* [*administrateur, directeur*] acting (*épith*)
B *nm,f* ⓵ (à une réunion) delegate; ⓶ (responsable) director

(Composés) **~ du personnel** workers' representative; **~ syndical** union representative

déléguer /delege/ [14] *vtr* ⓵ (charger d'une mission) to appoint [sb] as a delegate (**auprès de** to); ⓶ (transmettre) to delegate [*autorité, responsabilités*] (**à** to)

délestage /delɛstaʒ/ *nm* ⓵ (de navire, d'aérostat) unloading of the ballast; ⓶ (d'axe routier) diversion (*to relieve a road of heavy traffic*); ⓷ Électrotech power cut

délester /delɛste/ [1]
A *vtr* ⓵ (alléger) to get rid of the ballast from [*navire, aérostat*]; **~ un véhicule de six sacs** to take six bags out of a vehicle; **se faire ~ de son portefeuille** hum to have one's wallet pinched; ⓶ (décongestionner) to divert traffic away from [*route*]
B **se délester** *vpr* **se ~ de** [*personne*] to get rid of [*bagages*]; to off-load [*responsabilité*] (**sur** onto)

délibératif, -ive /deliberatif, iv/ *adj* **voix délibérative** voting powers (*pl*)

délibération /deliberasjɔ̃/ *nf* (discussion) deliberation; **être en ~** to be deliberating

délibéré, ~e /delibere/
A *adj* [*acte, violation*] deliberate; [*choix, volonté, politique*] conscious
B *nm* Jur deliberation

délibérément /deliberemɑ̃/ *adv* [*blesser, provoquer*] deliberately; [*accepter, choisir*] consciously

délibérer /delibere/ [14]
A **délibérer de** *or* **sur** *vtr ind* to discuss
B *vi* ⓵ (tenir conseil) [*assemblée*] to be in session; ⓶ (réfléchir) *fml* to think carefully

délicat, ~e /delika, at/
A *adj* ⓵ (raffiné) [*mets*] subtle; [*palais*] discriminating; [*personne*] refined; **manières ~es** refinement (*sg*); ⓶ (plein de tact) tactful; (attentionné) thoughtful; **quelle attention ~e!** what a kind thought!; **des procédés peu ~s** unscrupulous means; ⓷ (complexe, difficile) [*équilibre, négociations, tâche*] delicate; [*affaire, dossier, point, moment*] sensitive; [*mission, manœuvre*] tricky; ⓸ (fragile) [*peau, mécanisme, instrument*] delicate; [*estomac, oreille*] sensitive; **elle est de santé ~e** she's delicate
B *nm,f* **faire le ~** to be fussy

délicatement /delikatmɑ̃/ *adv* ⓵ (avec finesse, subtilité) [*dessiner, graver, sculpter*] finely, delicately; [*parfumer*] delicately; ⓶ (avec légèreté) [*appuyer, caresser, saisir*] delicately

délicatesse /delikatɛs/ *nf* ⓵ (de saveur, coloris, parfum, sentiments) delicacy; **la ~ de ses traits** his/her fine features; **une œuvre sans ~** a crude piece of work; **un style sans ~** a coarse style; ⓶ (fragilité) *gén* delicacy; (de peau) sensitivity; ⓷ (tact) delicacy; **manquer de ~** to be heavy-handed; **il a eu la ~ de ne pas poser la question** he was tactful enough not to ask; **montrer de la ~ à l'égard de qn** to show kindness and consideration to sb; ⓸ (complexité) (d'opération, de négociations) delicacy; (de problème, cas, situation) trickiness; ⓹ (précaution) **manipuler qch avec ~** to handle sth with care; ⓺ (attention) **avoir des ~s pour qn** to be very attentive to sb

d

(Idiome) **être en ~ avec qn** to be at odds with sb

délice /delis/ *nm* delight; **avec ~** with delight; **un vrai ~ ton poulet** your chicken is quite delicious; **faire ses ~s de qch** to delight in sth; **faire les ~s de qn** to delight sb

délicieusement /delisjøzmɑ̃/ *adv* gén delightfully; (au goût) deliciously; **~ parfumé** [*bain*] deliciously scented; [*fruit*] sweet-smelling (*épith*)

délicieux, -ieuse /delisjø, øz/ *adj* [*repas, goût, odeur, frisson*] delicious; [*sensation, endroit, humour, souvenir, musique*] delightful; [*joie*] exquisite; [*personne*] sweet

délié, ~e /delje/
A *adj* 1 [*taille*] slender; 2 [*mouvement*] loose; 3 [*esprit*] nimble
B *nm* (en calligraphie) upstroke

(Idiome) **avoir la langue ~e** to have the gift of the gab○

délier /delje/ [2] *vtr* to untie [*personne, gerbe, poignets*]; **~ qn de** to release sb from [*promesse*]

(Idiomes) **sans bourse ~** without paying a penny; **les langues se délient** people are starting to talk

délimiter /delimite/ [1] *vtr* 1 (déterminer les limites de) [*clôture*] to mark the boundary of [*domaine*]; [*montagnes*] to form the boundary of [*pays*]; 2 (définir) to define [*rôle, frontière*]; to define the scope of [*sujet, question*]

délinquance /delɛ̃kɑ̃s/ *nf* crime; **la petite ~** petty crime; **la ~ juvénile** juvenile delinquency

délinquant, ~e /delɛ̃kɑ̃, ɑ̃t/
A *adj* delinquent; **l'enfance ~e** child offenders (*pl*)
B *nm,f* offender; **un petit ~** a petty criminal

déliquescence /delikesɑ̃s/ *nf* decline; **être en pleine ~** to be degenerating

déliquescent, ~e /delikesɑ̃, ɑ̃t/ *adj* [*mœurs*] declining; [*style*] lifeless; [*esprit*] failing; [*industrie*] in decline (*après n*)

délirant, ~e /delirɑ̃, ɑ̃t/ *adj* 1 (exubérant) [*accueil, foule*] ecstatic; 2 ○(loufoque) [*personne, scénario, soirée*] crazy○; 3 (déraisonnable) [*prix*] outrageous; 4 Méd [*personne, état*] delirious

délire /delir/ *nm* 1 Méd, Psych delirium; **en proie au ~** suffering from delirium; 2 ○(folie) madness; **travailler autant, c'est du ~!** it's crazy○ to work that hard!; 3 (enthousiasme) frenzy; **salle en ~** ecstatic audience; 4 (frénésie) frenzy; **~ verbal** verbal excess

délirer /delire/ [1] *vi* 1 Méd to be delirious; 2 ○fig to be off one's rocker○

délit /deli/ *nm* offence^{GB}

(Composé) **~ de fuite** hit-and-run offence^{GB}

délivrance /delivrɑ̃s/ *nf* 1 (soulagement) relief; **la mort fut pour elle une ~** her death was a merciful release; 2 (remise) (de certificat, brevet, passeport, d'ordonnance) issue; (de diplôme, prix) award

délivrer /delivre/ [1]
A *vtr* 1 (libérer) to free [*captif*]; to liberate [*pays, peuple*]; **~ qn de** to free sb from [*chaînes*]; to release sb from [*obligation*]; to relieve sb of [*souci*]; to rid sb of [*obsession*]; **vous me délivrez d'un grand poids** you have taken a great weight off my shoulders; **délivre-nous du mal** Relig deliver us from evil; 2 (donner) to issue document; to award [*diplôme, prix*]; to provide [*soins*]
B **se délivrer** *vpr* (se libérer) [*captif*] to free oneself; **se ~ de** to free oneself from [*chaînes, obligation*]; to rid oneself of [*angoisse*]

délocalisation /delɔkalizasjɔ̃/ *nf* relocation

déloger /delɔʒe/ [13] *vtr* (chasser) to evict [*locataire*] (**de** from); to flush out [*rebelles, gibier*] (**de** from); to remove [*poussière*] (**de** from)

déloyal, ~e, *mpl* **-aux** /delwajal, o/ *adj* [*ami, collègue*] disloyal (**envers** to); [*concurrence*] unfair; [*acte, conduite, méthode, procédé*] underhand

delta /dɛlta/ *nm inv* (tous contextes) delta

deltaplane /dɛltaplan/, ▸ p. 327 *nm* 1 (engin) hang-glider; 2 (activité) hang-gliding

déluge /delyʒ/ *nm* 1 (pluie) downpour, deluge; 2 (profusion) (de coups, d'insultes) hail (**de** of); (de larmes, plaintes) flood (**de** of); (de mots) torrent (**de** of); (de compliments) shower (**de** of); (de fleurs) profusion (**de** of); (de malheurs) spate (**de** of)

Déluge /delyʒ/ *nm* **le ~** the Flood, the Deluge

(Idiomes) **ça remonte au ~** it goes back to the year dot *ou* one; **après moi le ~** I don't care what happens after I'm gone

déluré, ~e /delyre/ *adj* 1 (dégourdi) smart; 2 (effronté) forward; péj fast (*jamais épith*)

démagogie /demagɔʒi/ *nf* gén popularity seeking; (électoraliste) electioneering, demagogy sout; **faire de la ~** to try to gain popularity

démagogique /demagɔʒik/ *adj* gén popularity-seeking (*épith*); (en politique) electioneering (*épith*)

démagogue /demagɔg/ *nmf* popularity-seeker, demagogue sout

demain /dəmɛ̃/
A *adv* tomorrow; **~ toute la journée** all day tomorrow; **~ en huit/en quinze** a week/two weeks tomorrow
B *nm* tomorrow; **à ~!** see you tomorrow; **de quoi ~ sera-t-il fait?** who knows what tomorrow may bring?; **l'Europe de ~** the Europe of the future

(Idiomes) **~ il fera jour** tomorrow is another day; **ce n'est pas ~ la veille!** that's not going to happen in a hurry!

démancher /demɑ̃ʃe/ [1]
A *vtr* 1 (ôter le manche de) to take the handle off; 2 ○(disloquer) to dislocate [*membre, mâchoire*]
B **se démancher** *vpr* 1 (perdre son manche) to come off its handle; 2 ○(se disloquer) [*membre, mâchoire*] to be dislocated

demande /dəmɑ̃d/ *nf* 1 (sollicitation) request; **répondre à la ~ de qn** to grant sb's request; 2 (démarche) application; **faire une ~ de mutation** to apply for a transfer; **gratuit sur (simple) ~** free on request; **remboursement sur simple ~ écrite** refund on application; 3 Admin (formulaire) application form; **une ~ d'inscription** a registration form; 4 Écon demand; 5 Jur **~ (en justice)** claim; **~ de divorce** petition for divorce

(Composés) **~ d'asile** application for asylum; **~ d'emploi** (démarche) job application; **'~s d'emploi'** (rubrique) 'situations wanted'; **~ en mariage** marriage proposal

demandé, ~e /dəmɑ̃de/ *adj* **très ~** [*destination, sport, personne*] very popular; [*service, qualification, produit*] in great demand

demander /dəmɑ̃de/ [1]
A *vtr* 1 (solliciter) to ask for [*conseil, argent, aide*]; **~ l'asile politique** to apply for political asylum; **~ la main de qn** to ask for sb's hand; **~ qn en mariage** to propose to sb; **le numéro que vous demandez n'est plus en service'** 'the number you have dialled^{GB} is unobtainable'; **on demande un plombier** (dans une offre d'emploi) plumber wanted; **fais ce qu'on te demande!** do as you're told!; **il n'en demandait pas tant** he didn't expect all that; **je ne demande pas mieux que de partir** there's nothing I would like better than to go; **je ne demande que ça!** that's exactly what I want!; **il ne demande qu'à te croire** he'd really like to believe you; **je demande à voir**○ that'll be the day○; 2 (interroger sur) **~ qch à qn** to ask sb sth; **je ne t'ai rien demandé**○! I wasn't talking to you!; 3 (faire venir) to send for [*médecin, prêtre*]; **'un vendeur est demandé à l'accueil'** 'would a salesman please come to reception'; **le patron vous demande** (dans son bureau) the boss wants to see you; (au téléphone) the boss wants to speak to you; 4 (nécessiter) [*travail, tâche*] to require [*effort, qualification*]; [*plante, animal*] to need [*attention*] ; **~ à être revu** [*sujet, texte*] to need revision; 5 (requérir) to call for [*peine, réformes*]; Jur to sue for [*divorce, dommages-intérêts*]
B **se demander** *vpr* 1 (s'interroger) **se ~ si/pourquoi** to wonder whether/why; 2 (être demandé) **ce genre de choses ne se demande pas** it's not the kind of thing you ask

demandeur¹, -euse /dəmɑ̃dœr, øz/
A *adj* Comm, Écon **le pays est très ~ de matières premières** raw materials are very much in demand in the country
B *nm,f* gén, Admin applicant

(Composés) **~ d'asile** asylum-seeker; **~ d'emploi** job-seeker

demandeur², -eresse /dəmɑ̃dœr, d(ə)rɛs/ *nm,f* Jur plaintiff

démangeaison /demɑ̃ʒɛzɔ̃/ *nf* (irritation) itch ⊄; **provoquer des ~s** to cause itching

démanger /demãʒe/ [13] vtr ① lit (irriter) **ça me démange** I'm itchy; ② fig **l'envie de le gifler me démangeait** I was itching to slap him

démantèlement /demãtɛlmã/ nm (de laboratoire, service) dismantling (**de** of); (de forces nucléaires) destruction

démanteler /demãtle/ [17] vtr to dismantle [service, institution, armes, frontières]; to break up [gang]

démantibuler○ /demãtibyle/ [1] vtr to bust○, to break up [meuble]

démaquillage /demakijaʒ/ nm make-up removal

démaquillant, ~e /demakijã, ãt/
A adj [lait, gel] cleansing (épith)
B nm make-up remover

démaquiller: se démaquiller /demakije/ [1] vpr to remove one's make-up

démarcation /demarkasjõ/ nf demarcation

démarchage /demarʃaʒ/ nm door-to-door selling; **~ électoral** canvassing; **~ téléphonique** cold calling

démarche /demarʃ/ nf ① (allure) walk; **avoir une ~ assurée** to walk with a confident step; **avoir une ~ de canard** to waddle like a duck; ② (tentative) step; **faire** or **tenter une ~ auprès de qn** to approach sb; **faire des ~s pour obtenir qch** to take steps to obtain sth; **~ commune** or **collective** joint representation; **plusieurs ~s sont possibles** there are several possible courses of action open to you; **les ~s à effectuer sont les suivantes** the correct procedure is as follows; ③ (attitude) approach; ④ (raisonnement) reasoning; (évolution) **~ de la pensée** thought process

démarcher /demarʃe/ [1] vtr ① (vendre) to sell [sth] door-to-door [produit]; ② (solliciter) to canvass [client, entreprise]

démarcheur, -euse /demarʃœr, øz/ nm,f (door-to-door) salesman

démarque /demark/ nf (de marchandises) mark-down (**de** of)

démarquer /demarke/ [1]
A vtr ① (rendre anonyme) **~ un article** to cut out the label from an item (so as to lower the price); ② (solder) to mark down [marchandises]; ③ Sport to free [sb] from a marker
B se démarquer vpr ① (se distinguer) **se ~ de qn/qch** to distance oneself from sb/sth; ② Sport to get free of one's marker

démarrage /demaraʒ/ nm ① lit, fig starting up; **j'ai peur de caler au ~** I'm afraid of stalling as I pull away; ② (en course à pied) spurt, burst of speed

(Composé) **~ en côte** hill start

démarrer /demare/ [1]
A vtr ① lit to start (up) [moteur, véhicule]; ② fig to start [roman, émission]; to get [sth] off the ground [projet]
B vi ① (se mettre en marche) [véhicule] to pull away; [moteur] to start; ② (mettre en marche) [chauffeur] to drive off; ③ (débuter) [affaire, entreprise] to start up; [campagne électorale] to get under way; [personne] to start off; ④ (en course à pied) to put on a spurt

démarreur /demarœr/ nm Aut starter

démasquer /demaske/ [1]
A vtr ① fig to unmask [traître]; to expose [hypocrisie]; to uncover [complot]; ② lit **~ qn** to remove sb's mask
B se démasquer vpr ① fig (involontairement) to betray oneself; (volontairement) to reveal oneself; ② lit to remove one's mask

démâter /demate/ [1]
A vtr [équipage] to unstep the mast of [navire]; [tempête] to dismast [navire]
B vi [voilier] to lose its mast

dématérialiser: se dématérialiser /dematerjalize/ [1] vpr to vanish, to disappear

démazouter /demazute/ [1] vtr to clean the oil from [plage]

démêlant, ~e /demelã, ãt/ adj [shampooing, baume] detangling

démêlé /demele/ nm wrangle; **avoir des ~s avec la justice** to get into trouble with the law

démêler /demele/ [1]
A vtr ① lit to disentangle [fils, pelote]; to untangle [cheveux]; ② fig (éclaircir) to sort out [affaire, situation]; **~ les fils d'une intrigue** to unravel the threads of a plot
B se démêler vpr ① (être clarifié) [situation] to get sorted out;

② (se dépêtrer) [personne] **se ~ de qch** to extricate oneself from sth

démêloir /demelwar/ nm wide-toothed comb

démembrement /demãbrəmã/ nm ① (de pays, compagnie) break-up (**de** of); ② (de propriété) division (**de** of)

démembrer /demãbre/ [1] vtr (morceler) to divide up, to dismember [domaine, empire]

déménagement /demenaʒmã/ nm ① (action de déménager) move; ② (changement de domicile) moving house **ℂ**; ③ (changement de bureaux) relocation; ④ (transport) removal; ⑤ (action de vider) clearing **ℂ**

déménager /demenaʒe/ [13]
A vtr ① (déplacer) to move [meubles, livres]; to relocate [bureaux]; ② (vider) to clear [pièce]
B vi ① (changer de domicile) to move house; ② (changer de bureaux) to relocate; ③ ○(partir) to push off○, to leave; ④ ○(déraisonner) to be off one's rocker○

(Idiome) **~ à la cloche de bois** to do a moonlight flit GB

déménageur, -euse /demenaʒœr, øz/ ▸ p. 372 nm,f (ouvrier) removal GB ou moving US man/woman; (patron) furniture remover GB ou mover US; **épaules de ~** muscular shoulders

démence /demãs/ nf madness, insanity

démener: se démener /dem(ə)ne/ [16] vpr ① (s'agiter) to thrash about; [prisonnier] to struggle; ② (se donner du mal) to put oneself out; **se ~ pour faire** to put oneself to some trouble to do; **elle se démène du matin au soir** she slaves away from morning till night

(Idiome) **se ~ comme un beau diable** (pour se libérer) to thrash about; (pour avoir qch) to do one's utmost

dément, ~e /demã, ãt/
A adj ① (fou) mad, insane; ② ○[spectacle] terrific○; [événement] amazing; [prix] outrageous
B nm,f mentally ill person

démenti /demãti/ nm denial; **cette rumeur est restée sans ~** the rumour GB has not been denied

démentiel, -ielle /demãsjɛl/ adj ① ○[inflation, rythme] insane; [prix] outrageous; ② Psych insane

démentir /demãtir/ [30]
A vtr ① (nier) to deny [information, accusation]; ② (contredire) [personne] to refute [propos, déclaration]; [fait] to give the lie to [propos, déclaration]; to contradict [point de vue, prévision]; to belie [apparence]
B se démentir vpr [courage, intérêt] to flag

démerder○: **se démerder** /demɛrde/ [1] vpr ① (se débrouiller) to manage; **se ~ pour faire** to manage to do; **se ~ avec ses problèmes** to sort out one's own problems; ② (se dépêcher) **démerde-toi un peu!** get your arse GB ou ass US in gear○!

démériter /demerite/ [1] vi to prove oneself unworthy

démesure /demazyr/ nf ① (d'ambition, de prétentions) excesses (pl); ② (taille exagérée) excessive size

démesuré, ~e /demazyre/ adj ① [taille] excessive; ② [orgueil, appétit] immoderate; [ambition] excessive

démesurément /demazyremã/ adv excessively, inordinately

démettre /demɛtr/ [60]
A vtr ① (déboîter) **~ l'épaule de qn** to dislocate sb's shoulder; ② (révoquer) to dismiss [personne]; **~ qn de ses fonctions** to relieve sb of his/her duties
B se démettre vpr ① (se déboîter) **il s'est démis l'épaule** he dislocated his shoulder; ② (démissionner) to resign

demeurant: au demeurant /odəmœrã/ loc adv as it happens, besides, for all that

demeure /dəmœr/
A nf ① (habitation) residence; **~ ancestrale** ancestral home; ② **mettre qn en ~ de faire** gén to require sb to do; Jur to give sb formal notice to do; **mise en ~** gén demand; Jur formal notice (**de faire** to do)
B à demeure loc adv permanently

(Idiome) **il n'y a pas péril en la ~** there's no rush

demeuré, ~e /dəmœre/
A adj retarded
B nm,f simpleton

demeurer /dəmœre/ [1]
A vi ① (+ v avoir) (résider) to reside; ② (+ v être) (rester) to remain

B *v impers* **il n'en demeure pas moins que** nonetheless, the fact remains that

demi, ∼e¹ /d(ə)mi/ ▸ p. 296
A **et demi, et demie** *loc adj* and a half; **trois et** ∼ **pour cent** three and a half per cent; **il est trois heures et** ∼**e** it's half past three
B *nm,f* half
C *nm* ① (verre de bière) glass of beer, ≈ half-pint GB; ② Sport half; ∼ **de mêlée** scrum half; ∼ **d'ouverture** stand-off half
D **à demi** *loc adv* half; **je ne suis qu'à** ∼ **éveillé** I'm only half awake; **je ne suis qu'à** ∼ **satisfait** I'm not entirely satisfied
E **demi-** (in compounds) ① (à moitié) half; **une** ∼**-pomme** half an apple; **trois** ∼**-pommes** three half apples; ② (incomplet) partial

demi-botte, *pl* ∼**s** /d(ə)mibɔt/ *nf* calf-length boot
demi-centre /d(ə)misɑ̃tʀ/ *nm* halfback
demi-cercle, *pl* ∼**s** /d(ə)misɛʀkl/ *nm* semicircle; **en** ∼ [objet] semicircular
demi-deuil, *pl* ∼**s** /d(ə)midœj/ *nm* half-mourning (wearing grey)
demi-dieu, *pl* ∼**x** /d(ə)midjø/ *nm* demigod
demi-douzaine, *pl* ∼**s** /d(ə)miduzɛn/ *nf* half a dozen; **une** ∼ **d'œufs** half a dozen eggs
demi-droite, *pl* ∼**s** /d(ə)midʀwat/ *nf* half-line
demie² /d(ə)mi/
A *adj f* ▸ demi A
B *nf* (d'heure) half hour; **il est déjà la** ∼ it's already half past
demi-échec /d(ə)mieʃɛk/ *nm* **un** ∼ something of a failure
demi-écrémé, ∼**e**, *mpl* ∼**s** /d(ə)miekʀeme/ *adj* semi-skimmed
demi-finale, *pl* ∼**s** /d(ə)mifinal/ *nf* semifinal
demi-fond, *pl* ∼**s** /d(ə)mifɔ̃/ *nm* (spécialité) middle-distance running
demi-franc, *pl* ∼**s** /d(ə)mifʀɑ̃/ *nm* Hist half a franc, fifty centimes
demi-frère, *pl* ∼**s** /d(ə)mifʀɛʀ/ *nm* half-brother
demi-gros /d(ə)migʀo/ *nm inv* wholesale direct to the public
demi-heure, *pl* ∼**s** /d(ə)mijœʀ/ *nf* half an hour
demi-journée, *pl* ∼**s** /d(ə)miʒuʀne/ *nf* half a day; **à la** ∼ on a half-day basis
démilitariser /demilitaʀize/ [1] *vtr* to demilitarize
demi-litre, *pl* ∼**s** /d(ə)militʀ/ *nm* half a litre^GB
demi-longueur, *pl* ∼**s** /d(ə)milɔ̃gœʀ/ *nf* half-length
demi-lune, *pl* ∼**s** /d(ə)milyn/ *nf* ① lit half-moon; ② (objet) half-circle
demi-mal /d(ə)mimal/ *nm* **il n'y a que** ∼ it's not as bad as all that
demi-mesure, *pl* ∼**s** /d(ə)mim(ə)zyʀ/ *nf* lit, fig half-measure
demi-mot: **à demi-mot** /ad(ə)mimo/ *loc adv* **j'ai compris à** ∼ I didn't need to have it spelt out
déminage /deminaʒ/ *nm* (de terrain) (land)mine clearance; (de mer) minesweeping
déminer /demine/ [1] *vtr* ① to clear [sth] of mines [terrain]; to sweep [sth] of mines [estuaire]; ② fig to defuse [conflit, situation]
déminéraliser: **se déminéraliser** /demineʀalize/ [1] *vpr* [personne] to suffer from a mineral deficiency
démineur /deminœʀ/ *nm* mine clearance expert
demi-pause, *pl* ∼**s** /d(ə)mipoz/ *nf* minim rest GB, half rest US
demi-pension /d(ə)mipɑ̃sjɔ̃/ *nf* (régime, prix) half board; **être en** ∼ (à l'hôtel) to stay half board; (à l'école) to have school lunches
demi-pensionnaire, *pl* ∼**s** /d(ə)mipɑ̃sjɔnɛʀ/ *nmf* Scol pupil who has school lunches
demi-place, *pl* ∼**s** /d(ə)miplas/ *nf* **payer** ∼ (en voyage) to pay half-fare; (au spectacle) to pay half-price
demi-queue, *pl* ∼**s** /d(ə)mikø/ *nm* (piano) ∼ boudoir grand piano
démis, ∼**e** /demi, iz/
A *pp* ▸ démettre

B *pp adj* [articulation] dislocated
demi-saison, *pl* ∼**s** /d(ə)misɛzɔ̃/ *nf* **manteau de** ∼ lightweight coat
demi-sel /d(ə)misɛl/ *adj inv* [beurre] slightly salted
demi-siècle, *pl* ∼**s** /d(ə)misjɛkl/ *nm* half a century
demi-sœur, *pl* ∼**s** /d(ə)misœʀ/ *nf* half-sister
demi-solde, *pl* ∼**s** /d(ə)misɔld/ *nf* half-pay
demi-sommeil, *pl* ∼**s** /d(ə)misɔmɛj/ *nm* **être dans un** ∼ to be half-asleep
demi-soupir, *pl* ∼**s** /d(ə)misupiʀ/ *nm* quaver GB *ou* eighth US rest
démission /demisjɔ̃/ *nf* ① lit resignation (**de** from); ② fig failure to take responsibility
démissionnaire /demisjɔnɛʀ/ *adj* resigning (épith)
démissionner /demisjɔne/ [1]
A ○*vtr* hum to oust
B *vi* ① (quitter son poste) to resign (**de** from); ② (renoncer) to give up; (renier ses responsabilités) to abdicate one's responsibilities
demi-succès /d(ə)misyksɛ/ *nm inv* qualified success
demi-tarif, *pl* ∼**s** /d(ə)mitaʀif/
A *adj inv* half-price (épith)
B *adv* **payer** ∼ to pay half-price
C *nm* (billet) half-price ticket; **voyager à** ∼ to travel half-fare
demi-teinte, *pl* ∼**s** /d(ə)mitɛ̃t/ *nf* **en** ∼**s** lit in muted colours^GB; fig in a subdued style
demi-ton, *pl* ∼**s** /d(ə)mitɔ̃/ *nm* semitone
demi-tour, *pl* ∼**s** /d(ə)mituʀ/ *nm* (dans l'espace) Aut U-turn; Mil about-turn GB, about face US; **faire** ∼ gén to turn back
demi-volée, *pl* ∼**s** /d(ə)mivɔle/ *nf* half-volley
démobiliser /demɔbilize/ [1] *vtr* ① Mil to demobilize; ② fig to demotivate [électorat, partisan]
démocrate /demɔkʀat/
A *adj* ① gén democratic; ② (aux États-Unis) [parti, sénateur] Democratic
B *nmf* ① gén democrat; ② (aux États-Unis) Democrat
démocrate-chrétien, -ienne, *pl* **démocrates-chrétiens, -iennes** /demɔkʀatkʀetjɛ̃, ɛn/ *adj, nm,f* Christian Democrat
démocratie /demɔkʀasi/ *nf* democracy
démocratique /demɔkʀatik/ *adj* ① Pol [régime, débat] democratic; ② (accessible à tous) accessible
démocratiser /demɔkʀatize/ [1]
A *vtr* Pol, fig to democratize [régime, enseignement]
B **se démocratiser** *vpr* ① Pol [régime] to become more democratic; ② [enseignement] to become more accessible
démodé, ∼**e** /demɔde/ *adj* old-fashioned
démoder: **se démoder** /demɔde/ [1] *vpr* to go out of fashion
démographie /demɔgʀafi/ *nf* demography
démographique /demɔgʀafik/ *adj* demographic
demoiselle /d(ə)mwazɛl/ *nf* ① (jeune fille) fml or iron young lady; ② †(célibataire) single lady; **elle est restée** ∼ she remained single; ③ (libellule) damselfly
(Composés) ∼ **de compagnie** female companion; ∼ **d'honneur** (de mariée) bridesmaid; (à la cour) maid of honour^GB
démolir /demɔliʀ/ [3]
A *vtr* ① (détruire) to demolish [quartier, bâtiment]; (détériorer) to wreck [appareil, jouet]; ② fig to destroy [système, réputation]; to demolish [argumentation, politicien]; to wreck [carrière]; ③ ○(rosser) to beat [sb] up○ [personne]; (épuiser) [effort] to whack [sb] out○ [personne]
B **se démolir** *vpr* **se** ∼○ **la santé** to ruin one's health
démolisseur, -euse /demɔlisœʀ, øz/ *nm,f* ① ▸ p. 372 (personne) demolition worker; (entreprise) demolition contractor GB, wrecker US; ② (destructeur) wrecker
démolition /demɔlisjɔ̃/
A *nf* ① (de construction) demolition; ② fig destruction
B **démolitions** *nfpl* rubble **₵**
démon /demɔ̃/ *nm* ① Relig devil; ② (esprit) spirit; **poussé par son** ∼ **intérieur** (bon) prompted by his guiding spirit; (mauvais) driven by the demon inside him; ③ (personne) devil; ④ fig **le** ∼ **de la boisson** *or* **de l'alcool** the demon drink
(Composé) ∼ **de midi** ≈ middle-age lust

d

démoniaque /demɔnjak/ adj demonic

démonstrateur, -trice /demɔ̃stratœr, tris/ ▸ p. 372 nm,f Comm demonstrator

démonstratif, -ive /demɔ̃stratif, iv/
A adj gén, Ling demonstrative; [geste] expressive; [joie] uninhibited
B nm Ling demonstrative

démonstration /demɔ̃strasjɔ̃/ nf **1** (manifestation) display; **faire des ~s d'amitié à qn** to make a show of friendship toward(s) sb; **2** (leçon pratique) demonstration; **faire la ~ d'un appareil** to demonstrate an appliance; **3** (de théorie) demonstration; (de théorème) proof

démontable /demɔ̃tabl/ adj [meuble] that can be taken apart

démontage /demɔ̃taʒ/ nm **1** (d'échafaudage) taking down; (de meuble) taking apart; (de moteur) stripping down; (de pendule) dismantling; (de roue) removal; **2** fig (explication) **procéder au ~ de mécanismes psychologiques** to describe the functioning of psychological mechanisms

démonté, ~e /demɔ̃te/ adj [mer] stormy

démonte-pneu, pl **~s** /demɔ̃t(ə)pnø/ nm Aut tyre-lever GB, tire iron US

démonter /demɔ̃te/ **1**
A vtr **1** to dismantle [assemblage]; to take [sth] to pieces [machine]; **2** (enlever) to remove [roue]; to take off [porte]; to take down [rideau]; **3** °(déconcerter) to fluster
B se **démonter** vpr **1** (être démontable) **le buffet se démonte facilement** the sideboard can be taken apart GB ou knocked down US easily; **2** (se disloquer) to come apart; **3** °(perdre son sang-froid) to become flustered

démontrable /demɔ̃trabl/ adj demonstrable

démontrer /demɔ̃tre/ **1** vtr **1** (avec preuve) to demonstrate [intérêt, absurdité]; to prove [théorème]; **2** (indiquer) to prove, to demonstrate

démoraliser /demɔralize/ **1**
A vtr to demoralize
B se **démoraliser** vpr to get demoralized

démordre: **démordre de** /demɔrdr/ **6** vtr ind **je n'en démords pas** (d'une idée, opinion) I stick by it; (d'une déclaration, décision) I'm sticking to it

démoulage /demulaʒ/ nm **1** (de pâtisserie) turning out; **2** Art, Tech (d'objet) removal from the mould GB ou mold US; (de moule) turning out of the mould GB ou mold US

démouler /demule/ **1** vtr to turn [sth] out of the tin GB ou pan US [gâteau]; to turn [sth] out of the mould GB ou mold US [flan]; to remove [sth] from the mould GB ou mold US [statue]

démultiplication /demyltiplikasjɔ̃/ nf (effet) gearing down; (rapport) reduction ratio

démultiplier /demyltiplije/ **2** vtr **1** to reduce [vitesse]; **2** to increase [pouvoirs, capacité]

démuni, ~e /demyni/ adj **1** (pauvre) impoverished; (à court d'argent) penniless; **2** (vulnérable) helpless; **3** (à court de stock) out of stock (jamais épith); **4** (privé) **~ de** devoid of [talent]; lacking [diplômes]

démunir /demynir/ **3**
A vtr (dégarnir) to divest (de of)
B se **démunir** vpr (se dessaisir) se **~ de qch** to leave oneself without sth

démystifier /demistifje/ **2** vtr **1** **~ qn** to dispel sb's illusions; **2** to demystify [discipline]

démythifier /demitifje/ **2** vtr to demythologize

dénatalité /denatalite/ nf fall in the birthrate

dénationaliser /denasjɔnalize/ **1** vtr to denationalize

dénaturé, ~e /denatyre/ adj **1** [alcool] denatured; **2** (dépravé) warped; **3** (indigne) [parents, enfants] unnatural; **4** (déformé) distorted

dénaturer /denatyre/ **1** vtr **1** Tech, Ind to denature; **2** (déformer) to distort [faits]; **3** (altérer) to spoil [goût, sauce]

dénégation /denegasjɔ̃/ nf gén, Jur denial

déneiger /deneʒe/ **13** vtr to clear the snow off [route]

déni /deni/ nm denial (de of)

déniaiser /denjeze/ **1** vtr **1** (dégourdir) to make [sb] more worldly-wise; **2** °(initier sexuellement) to initiate [sb] sexually

dénicher /deniʃe/ **1** vtr **1** °(découvrir) to dig out° [objet]; to track down [personne]; to discover [bonne adresse];

dénicheur, -euse /deniʃœr, øz/ nm,f **1** (d'objets, de talents) **~ de** person who is good at spotting [talent]; **2** (d'œufs) bird's-nester

denier /dənje/
A nm **1** Fin, Hist (français) denier; (romain) denarius; **2** (de collants) denier
B **deniers** nmpl money; **~s publics** or **de l'État** public funds
⌐Composés⌐ **~ du culte** Relig funds collected annually for a parish; **~ de saint Pierre** Relig Peter's pence

dénier /denje/ **2** vtr to deny

dénigrement /denigrəmã/ nm denigration; **par ~** disparagingly; **esprit de ~** disparaging mentality

dénigrer /denigre/ **1** vtr to denigrate

dénivelé /denivle/ nm, **dénivelée** nf difference in altitude

dénivellation /denivɛlasjɔ̃/ nf **1** (écart d'altitude) difference in altitude; (écart de niveau) difference in level; **2** (inclinaison) gradient; **3** (inégalité de terrain) unevenness; **4** (changement du niveau) alteration of level

dénombrable /denɔ̃brabl/ adj Ling, Math countable, count (épith); **non ~** uncountable

dénombrer /denɔ̃bre/ **1** vtr to count

dénominateur /denɔminatœr/ nm denominator

dénomination /denɔminasjɔ̃/ nf **1** gén name; **2** Relig denomination
⌐Composés⌐ **~ commune** generic name; **~ sociale** Admin registered company name

dénommé, ~e /denɔme/ adj Admin **le ~ Pierre** the person by the name of Pierre

dénommer /denɔme/ **1** vtr **1** Jur to name; **2** (appeler) to call; **3** (désigner) to designate

dénoncer /denɔ̃se/ **12**
A vtr **1** (signaler) to denounce [personne, abus]; **2** Jur (rompre) to break [traité, contrat]
B se **dénoncer** vpr to give oneself up

dénonciateur, -trice /denɔ̃sjatœr, tris/
A adj [lettre, article] denunciatory
B nm,f (de coupable) informer; (d'injustice) campaigner (de against)

dénonciation /denɔ̃sjasjɔ̃/ nf **1** (de coupable, d'injustice) denunciation; **2** Jur (de traité) (rupture) termination; (signification légale) notice

dénoter /denɔte/ **1** vtr denote

dénouement /denumã/ nm **1** Théât denouement; **2** (d'une affaire, d'un conflit) outcome, conclusion; **un heureux ~** a happy ending

dénouer /denwe/ **1**
A vtr **1** (détacher) to undo [nœud, cravate]; to let down [cheveux]; to disentangle [fils]; **2** (débrouiller) to unravel [intrigue]; to resolve [crise]
B se **dénouer** vpr **1** [lacet, corde] to come undone; **2** [crise] to resolve itself; [intrigue] to unravel

dénoyauter /denwajote/ **1** vtr to stone GB, to pit US

denrée /dãre/ nf **1** (produit) **~ de base** staple; **~s alimentaires** foodstuffs; **2** fig commodity

dense /dãs/ adj gén, Phys dense; [réseau] concentrated; [programme, tir] heavy

densité /dãsite/ nf **1** gén, Ordinat density; **~ démographique** density of population; **à forte ~** densely populated; **2** Phys relative density; **3** (de végétation, brouillard) denseness

dent /dã/ nf **1** Anat, Zool tooth; **~s de devant** front teeth; **entre ses ~s** [murmurer] under one's breath; **parler entre ses ~s** to mumble; **mal** ou **rage de ~s** toothache; **à pleines ~s** or **à belles ~s** [croquer] with relish; **rire de toutes ses ~s** to laugh heartily; **manger du bout des ~s** to pick at one's food; **rire du bout des ~s** to laugh half-heartedly; **accepter du bout des ~s** to accept reluctantly; **faire ses (premières) ~s, percer ses ~s** to teethe; **elle vient de percer une ~** she has just cut a tooth; **jusqu'aux ~s** [être armé] to the teeth; **ne rien avoir à se mettre sous la ~** to have nothing to eat; **montrer les ~s** lit, fig to bare one's teeth; **serrer les ~s** to grit one's teeth; **2** (de peigne) tooth; (de fourchette) prong; (de timbre) serration; **en ~s de scie** [bord, lame] serrated; [carrière] full of ups and downs;

[*résultats*] which go up and down; **3)** (sommet) crag

(Composés) ~ **de lait** milk tooth; ~ **de sagesse** wisdom tooth

(Idiomes) **avoir** *or* **conserver une** ~ **contre qn** to bear sb a grudge; **avoir les** ~**s longues** to be ambitious; **avoir la** ~ **dure** to be scathing; **avoir la** ~○ to feel peckish○; **se casser les** ~**s (sur qch)** to come to grief (over sth); **être sur les** ~**s** to be on edge

dentaire /dɑ̃tɛʀ/ *adj* dental

denté, ~**e** /dɑ̃te/ *adj* Tech, Zool toothed; Bot dentate

dentelé, ~**e** /dɑ̃t(ə)le/ *adj* [*côte*] indented; [*crête*] jagged; [*tissu*] pinked; [*papier, lame*] serrated; [*timbre*] perforated; Bot dentate

dentelle /dɑ̃tɛl/ *nf* lace

(Idiome) **il ne fait pas dans la** ~ he's not one to bother with niceties

dentellière /dɑ̃təljɛʀ/ *nf* **1)** (personne) lacemaker; **2)** (machine) lacemaking machine

dentelure /dɑ̃tlyʀ/ *nf* (de timbre) perforation; (de tissu) pinked edge; (de papier, lame) serrated edge; (de côte) indentation; (de crête) jagged outline; Bot serration; Archit dentils (*pl*)

dentier /dɑ̃tje/ *nm* dentures (*pl*)

dentifrice /dɑ̃tifʀis/ *nm* toothpaste

dentiste /dɑ̃tist/ ▸ p. 372 *nmf* dentist

dentition /dɑ̃tisjɔ̃/ *nf* dentition

denture /dɑ̃tyʀ/ *nf* **1)** (disposition) dentition; (dents) set of teeth; **2)** Tech teeth (*pl*), cogs (*pl*)

dénucléariser /denyklearize/ [1] *vtr* to denuclearize

dénuder /denyde/ [1]
A *vtr* **1)** Électrotech to strip [*câble, fil*]; **2)** [*mouvement*] to reveal [*corps*]; **3)** Méd to bare [*nerf, veine*]; to strip [*os*] (**de** of)
B se dénuder *vpr* **1)** (se dévêtir) to strip (off); **2)** (perdre sa verdure) to become bare; **3)** (perdre ses cheveux) **son crâne se dénude** he's going bald

dénué, ~**e** /denɥe/ *adj* ~ **de** lacking in; **un acte** ~ **de sens** a senseless act; **accusation** ~**e de fondement** groundless accusation; ~ **de toute utilité** utterly useless; ~ **de tout** destitute

dénuement /denymɑ̃/ *nm* (de personne) destitution; (de pièce) bareness

dénutrition /denytrisjɔ̃/ *nf* malnutrition

déodorant, ~**e** /deɔdɔʀɑ̃, ɑ̃t/
A *adj* deodorant
B *nm* deodorant

déontologie /deɔ̃tɔlɔʒi/ *nf* (de profession) ethics (+ *v sg*); Philos deontology

déontologique /deɔ̃tɔlɔʒik/ *adj* Philos deontological; Méd ethical; **code** ~ **des médecins** code of practice governing doctors GB, medical code of ethics

dépannage /depanaʒ/ *nm* (réparation) repair; ~**s à domicile** home repairs; ~ **24 heures sur 24** 24 hour repair service; **faire un** ~ to do a repair job

dépanner /depane/ [1] *vtr* **1)** (réparer) to fix [*voiture, appareil*]; **2)** (remorquer) to tow away; **3)** ○(aider) to help [sb] out

dépanneur, -**euse**[1] /depanœr, øz/ ▸ p. 372 *nmf* (personne) engineer

dépanneuse[2] /depanøz/ *nf* (véhicule) breakdown truck GB, tow truck US

dépaqueter /depakte/ [20] *vtr* to unpack

dépareillé, ~**e** /depareje/ *adj* **1)** (isolé) odd (*épith*); **un volume** ~ an odd volume; **articles** ~**s** oddments; **2)** (disparate) [*service, ensemble*] odd; **un service de verres** ~ a set of odd glasses; **3)** (incomplet) incomplete

déparer /depare/ [1] *vtr* to spoil [*lieu*]; to mar [*beauté*]

départ /depaʀ/ *nm* **1)** (d'un lieu) departure; ~ **des grandes lignes/des lignes de banlieue** Rail (platforms for) main line/suburban departures; **téléphone avant ton** ~ phone before you leave; **se donner rendez-vous au** ~ **du car** (au lieu) to arrange to meet at the bus; **vols quotidiens au** ~ **de Nice** daily flights from Nice; **le train a pris du retard au** ~ **de Lyon** the train was late leaving Lyons; **être sur le** ~ to be about to leave; **il n'y a qu'un** ~ **du courrier par jour** the post GB *ou* mail US only goes once a day; **2)** (exode) exodus (**vers** to); **3)** (d'une fonction, organisation) departure; (démission) resignation; **le** ~ **en retraite** retirement; **4)** Sport

start; ~ **arrêté/décalé/lancé** standing/staggered/flying start; **prendre le** ~ (d'une course) to be among the starters; **prendre un nouveau** ~ fig to make a fresh start; **5)** (début) start; **au** ~ (d'abord) at first; (au début) at the outset; **langue de** ~ source language; **salaire de** ~ starting salary; **capital de** ~ start-up capital

départager /depaʀtaʒe/ [13] *vtr* to decide between [*concurrents*]; **le vote du président va** ~ **les voix** the chairman has the casting vote; ~ **un jury** to bring the members of a jury to agreement

département /depaʀtəmɑ̃/ *nm* **1)** Admin (administrative) department (*French territorial division*); **2)** (branche d'une administration) department

ⓘ **Département** An administrative unit (of which there are 96 in Metropolitan France) based on a division dating from the Revolutionary period. Most are named after rivers or mountains within their border. The main town is the seat of the *préfet*, and is often called the *préfecture*. Each *département* has a number and this appears as the first two digits in postcodes for addresses within the *département* and as the two-digit number at the end of registration numbers on motor vehicles.

départemental, ~**e**[1], *mpl* -**aux** /depaʀtəmɑ̃tal, o/ *adj* [*budget, élection*] local, regional

départementale[2] /depaʀtəmɑ̃tal/ *nf* (route) secondary road, ≈ B road GB

départir: **se départir** /depaʀtiʀ/ [30] *vpr* **se** ~ **de** to lose [*calme, sourire*]; to swerve from [*opinion*]; to abandon [*réserve*]; to break [*silence*]

dépassé, ~**e** /depase/ *adj* **1)** (qui n'a plus cours) outdated, outmoded; **2)** (vieux jeu) [*personne*] out-of-date (*épith*); **3)** ○(débordé) [*personne*] overwhelmed; **être** ~ **par les événements** to be overtaken by events

dépassement /depasmɑ̃/ *nm* **1)** (sur route) overtaking GB, passing US; **2)** (de budget) overrun; ~ **d'horaire** overrunning the schedule; **le** ~ **de la dose prescrite peut entraîner des effets secondaires** exceeding the stated dose can produce side-effects; **3)** (fait de se surpasser) ~ **de soi** surpassing oneself

(Composés) ~ **budgétaire** cost overrun; ~ **de capacité** Ordinat overflow

dépasser /depase/ [1]
A *vtr* **1)** (passer devant) to overtake GB, to pass US; **2)** (excéder) to exceed; ~ **qch en hauteur** to be taller than sth; **certaines classes dépassent 30 élèves** some classes have over 30 pupils; **il a dépassé la cinquantaine** he's over *ou* past fifty; **3)** (aller au-delà de) lit to go past [*cible, lieu*]; fig to exceed [*espérances, attributions*]; **quand vous aurez dépassé le village, tournez à droite** when you've gone through the village, turn right; **je ne peux pas acheter cette maison, elle dépasse mes moyens** I can't buy that house, it's more than I can afford; **nous avons dépassé les difficultés de base** we have got over the basic difficulties; ~ **la mesure** *or* **les bornes** *or* **les limites** to go too far; **4)** (montrer une supériorité sur) to be ahead of, to outstrip; ~ **qn en bêtise** to surpass sb in stupidity; **ça me dépasse!** (incompréhensible) it's beyond me!; (choquant) it's beyond belief!
B *vi* **1)** (être plus grand) to jut out; **2)** (sortir) to stick out; **fais attention de ne pas** ~ **en coloriant** be careful not to colour○ᴳᴮ over the lines; **3)** (se faire voir) to show
C se dépasser *vpr* **1)** (soi-même) to surpass oneself; **2)** (l'un l'autre) to overtake each other

dépassionner /depasjone/ [1] *vtr* to defuse [*débat, discussion*]; **réflexion dépassionnée** dispassionate reflection

dépatouiller○: **se dépatouiller** /depatuje/ [1] *vpr* to get by; **se** ~ **de** to pull oneself out of [*situation*]

dépaver /depave/ [1] *vtr* to take up the paving stones from [*rue*]

dépaysé, ~**e** /depeize/ *adj* **il est complètement** ~ he's like a fish out of water; **il n'est pas** ~ **ici** he feels at home here

dépaysement /depeizmɑ̃/ *nm* (changement volontaire) change of scenery; (changement désagréable) disorientation

dépayser /depeize/ [1] *vtr* (agréablement) to provide [sb] with a pleasant change of scenery; (désagréablement) to disorient

dépecer /dep(ə)se/ [16] *vtr* to tear [sth] apart [*proie*]; to cut up [*victime*]; to carve up [*propriété*]

dépêche /depɛʃ/ *nf* dispatch
⬭ Composé ⬭ ~ **d'Ems** Hist Ems telegram

dépêcher /depeʃe/ [16]
A *vtr* to dispatch (**à** to)
B **se dépêcher** *vpr* to hurry up

dépeigné, ~**e** /depeɲe/ *adj* dishevelled^{GB}

dépeigner /depeɲe/ [1] *vtr* ~ **qn** to make sb's hair untidy

dépeindre /depɛ̃dʀ/ [55] *vtr* to depict (**comme** as)

dépenaillé, ~**e** /depənaje/ *adj* ragged

dépénaliser /depenalize/ [1] *vtr* to decriminalize

dépendance /depɑ̃dɑ̃s/ *nf* ⬭**1**⬭ (sujétion) dependence; **maintenir qn dans la** ~ to keep sb dependent; ⬭**2**⬭ (lien) link; ⬭**3**⬭ (de malade, drogué) dependency; ⬭**4**⬭ (bâtiment) outbuilding; ⬭**5**⬭ Hist, Pol dependency

dépendant, ~**e** /depɑ̃dɑ̃, ɑ̃t/ *adj gén* dependent (**de** on); **être** ~ **de qn** (dans un emploi) to be responsible to sb; **organisme** ~ **du ministère** body which comes under the authority of the ministry; **les personnes** ~**es** dependants

dépendre /depɑ̃dʀ/ [6]
A *vtr* to take down [*tableau*]
B **dépendre de** *vtr ind* ⬭**1**⬭ (reposer sur) ~ **de** to depend on; **ça dépend de toi** it's up to you; ⬭**2**⬭ (avoir besoin de) ~ **de** to be dependent on; ⬭**3**⬭ (être sous l'autorité de) ~ **de** [*organisme, région*] to come under the control of; [*personne*] to be responsible to; ⬭**4**⬭ (être la responsabilité de) ~ **de** to be the responsibility of; ⬭**5**⬭ (être un territoire de) ~ **de** to be a dependency of; ⬭**6**⬭ (être une dépendance de) ~ **de** [*bâtiment, terre*] to belong to

dépens /depɑ̃/ *nmpl* ⬭**1**⬭ (détriment) **aux** ~ **de** at the expense of; **victoire aux** ~ **de l'équipe favorite** win over the favourite^{GB} team; **réussir aux** ~ **des autres** to walk over people to get to the top; **apprendre à ses** ~ to learn to one's cost; ⬭**2**⬭ (frais) **vivre aux** ~ **des autres** to live off other people; ⬭**3**⬭ Jur (frais de justice) legal costs

dépense /depɑ̃s/ *nf* ⬭**1**⬭ (emploi d'argent) spending, expenditure; **pousser qn à la** ~ to make sb spend money; **ça vaut la** ~ it's worth the outlay; **regarder à la** ~ to watch one's spending; **ne pas regarder à la** ~ to spare no expense; ⬭**2**⬭ (somme déboursée) outlay; **avoir beaucoup de** ~**s** to have a lot of expenses; **faire des** ~**s inconsidérées** to indulge in reckless spending; **être une source de** ~**s** to be a drain on one's resources; ⬭**3**⬭ (quantité utilisée) (d'essence, électricité) consumption; ~ **d'énergie physique** expenditure of physical energy; **cela représente une** ~ **de temps trop importante** it takes too much time
⬭ Composés ⬭ **la** ~ **publique** public expenditure; ~**s courantes** running costs

dépenser /depɑ̃se/ [1]
A *vtr* ⬭**1**⬭ (employer de l'argent) to spend [*salaire, fortune*]; ~ **sans compter** to spend (money) freely; ⬭**2**⬭ (consommer) to use up [*carburant*]; to use [*tissu, papier*]; to spend [*temps*]; **ils ont dépensé des trésors d'imagination pour faire** they've really used their imagination doing
B **se dépenser** *vpr* ⬭**1**⬭ (faire de l'exercice) to get (enough) exercise; ⬭**2**⬭ (se donner du mal) **se** ~ **pour faire** to put a lot of energy into doing

dépensier, -ière /depɑ̃sje, ɛʀ/
A *adj* extravagant
B *nmf* spendthrift

déperdition /depɛʀdisjɔ̃/ *nf* (perte) loss

dépérir /depeʀiʀ/ [3] *vi* [*personne, animal*] lit to waste away; fig to fade away; [*plante*] to wilt; [*économie*] to be on the decline

dépérissement /depeʀismɑ̃/ *nm* (de personne) deterioration; (de plante) wilting; (d'économie) decline

dépêtrer /depetʀe/ [1]
A *vtr* to extricate (**de** from)
B **se dépêtrer** *vtr* **se** ~ **de** to extricate oneself from [*situation*]; to get rid of [*personne*]

dépeuplement /depœpləmɑ̃/ *nm* depopulation

dépeupler /depœple/ [1] *vtr* ⬭**1**⬭ Géog, Sociol to depopulate; ⬭**2**⬭ (vider temporairement) to empty; ⬭**3**⬭ Écol to reduce the wildlife in [*forêt, rivière*]

déphasé, ~**e** /defaze/ *adj* ⬭**1**⬭ ○(décalé) out of step (**par rapport à** with); **je suis complètement** ~**e** I'm not with it at all; ⬭**2**⬭ Phys out of phase

déphaser /defaze/ [1] *vtr* ⬭**1**⬭ ○(décaler) to disorientate; ⬭**2**⬭ Électrotech to shift phase

dépiauter○ /depjote/ [1] *vtr* ⬭**1**⬭ (analyser) to dissect [*document*]; ⬭**2**⬭ (ôter la peau de) to skin [*animal*]

dépilation /depilasjɔ̃/ *nf* ⬭**1**⬭ (élimination) hair removal, depilation; ⬭**2**⬭ (chute) hair loss

dépilatoire /depilatwaʀ/ *adj, nm* depilatory

dépistable /depistabl/ *adj* detectable

dépistage /depistaʒ/ *nm* (de maladie) screening; ~ **systématique du sida** mass screening for Aids; **test de** ~ **du sida** Aids test; ~ **précoce** early detection; **test de** ~ **génétique** genetic testing

dépister /depiste/ [1] *vtr* ⬭**1**⬭ (découvrir) to track down [*criminel*]; to identify [*problème*]; to detect [*maladie*]; ⬭**2**⬭ liter (détourner) ~ **les recherches** to put people off the scent; to deflect [*soupçons*]; ⬭**3**⬭ to spoor [*gibier*]

dépit /depi/
A *nm* (déception) bitter disappointment, chagrin; (ressentiment) pique; **par** ~ in ou out of pique; **par** ~ **amoureux** on the rebound
B **en dépit de** *loc prép* in spite of; **faire qch en** ~ **du bon sens** to do sth in a very illogical way

dépité, ~**e** /depite/ *adj* piqued (**de** at); **avoir une mine** ~**e** to look really disappointed ou upset

dépiter /depite/ [1] *vtr* to upset [*personne*]

déplacé, ~**e** /deplase/ *adj* ⬭**1**⬭ Sociol [*population*] displaced; ⬭**2**⬭ (pas adapté) inappropriate; **c'est** ~ (malséant) it's out of place; (inopportun) it's uncalled for; ⬭**3**⬭ (impoli) improper

déplacement /deplasmɑ̃/ *nm* ⬭**1**⬭ (voyage) trip; **au cours de mes** ~**s** when I'm travelling^{GB}; **elle a fait le** ~ she made the effort to go/to come; ⬭**2**⬭ (pour le travail) business trip; ⬭**3**⬭ (frais) **payer pour le** ~ (de médecin, d'artisan) to pay a call-out fee; ⬭**4**⬭ (action de déplacer) moving; (d'attention, de problème) shifting; (de l'âge de la retraite) changing; **le** ~ **des voix sur un autre parti** the swing of votes to another party; ⬭**5**⬭ (de population) displacement (**vers** to); (de service) transfer (**vers** to); ⬭**6**⬭ Ling, Naut, Psych displacement

déplacer /deplase/ [12]
A *vtr* ⬭**1**⬭ (volontairement) to move [*objet, personne*]; (par accident) to dislodge [*tuile*]; to dislocate [*os*]; ⬭**2**⬭ (de lieu, réunion, cours) to change [*âge de la retraite*]; ⬭**3**⬭ (faire porter sur autre chose) to shift [*débat, problème, attention*]; ⬭**4**⬭ (muter) to move; (faire migrer) to displace; (attirer) to bring in [*foules*]
B **se déplacer** *vpr* ⬭**1**⬭ (changer de position) to move; ⬭**2**⬭ (être mis ailleurs) to be moved; [*tuile*] to be dislodged; **se** ~ **une vertèbre** to slip a disc; ⬭**3**⬭ (avancer) to get about; (voyager) to travel; (aller quelque part) to go; (venir) to come; **se** ~ **en fauteuil roulant** to be in a wheelchair; **se** ~ **avec difficulté** to have difficulty getting about; ⬭**4**⬭ [*médecin, artisan*] to go out on call
⬭ Idiome ⬭ ~ **de l'air** or **beaucoup d'air**○ to like to make one's presence felt

déplafonner /deplafɔne/ [1] *vtr* fig to lift the ceiling on

déplaire /deplɛʀ/ [59]
A *vi* ⬭**1**⬭ (ne pas avoir de succès) **le spectacle a déplu/n'a pas déplu** the show was not well received/was moderately successful; ⬭**2**⬭ (rebuter) **elle déplaît** she is not liked
B **déplaire à** *vtr ind* **cela m'a déplu** I didn't like it
C *v impers* **il me déplairait de vous voir partir** fml I should be sorry to see you go; **il ne me déplairait pas de les voir partir** I'd be quite happy to see them go; **je le ferai, ne vous en déplaise** iron I shall do it whether you like it or not

déplaisant, ~**e** /deplɛzɑ̃, ɑ̃t/ *adj* unpleasant, disagreeable

déplâtrer /deplɑtʀe/ [1] *vtr* ⬭**1**⬭ Constr to strip the plaster off; ⬭**2**⬭ Méd to remove the cast from [*membre*]

dépliant /deplijɑ̃/ *nm* (prospectus) leaflet; (dans un livre) gatefold; ~ **hors-texte** foldout

déplier /deplije/ [2]
A *vtr* to unfold [*journal*]; to open out [*carte*]; to display [*marchandise*]; ~ **les jambes** to stretch one's legs out
B **se déplier** *vpr* ⬭**1**⬭ [*parachute*] to unfold; [*drapeau*] to unfurl; ⬭**2**⬭ ○[*personne*] to rise to one's feet

déploiement /deplwamɑ̃/ nm **1** (démonstration) (de solidarité) display; (de mesures) deployment; **2** Mil deployment; **3** (d'aile) spreading; (de voile) unfurling; (de panneau) opening out

déplorable /deplɔRabl/ adj **1** (fâcheux) regrettable; **2** (très mauvais) appalling, deplorable

déplorer /deplɔRe/ **1** vtr to deplore [événement]; ~ **que** to bemoan the fact that

déployer /deplwaje/ [23]
A vtr **1** (montrer) to display [talent]; ~ **toute son énergie pour faire** to expend all one's energy to do; **2** Mil to deploy [troupes]; **3** (déplier) to spread [ailes]; to unfurl [voile]; to open out [panneau]
B se déployer vpr **1** (s'éparpiller) [policiers] to fan out; **2** Mil [troupes] to be deployed; **3** (se déplier) [ailes] to spread; [voile] to unfurl; [panneau] to open out

dépoli, ~**e** /depɔli/ adj **verre** ~ gén frosted glass; Phot ground glass

dépolir /depɔliR/ [3] vtr to frost [verre]; to take the gloss off [vernis]; to texture [marbre]

dépolitiser /depɔlitize/ [1] vtr to depoliticize [débat, groupe]

dépolluer /depɔlɥe/ [1] vtr to rid [sth] of pollution [rivière]

dépollution /depɔlysjɔ̃/ nf cleanup

déportation /depɔRtasjɔ̃/ nf **1** (dans un camp de concentration) internment in a concentration camp; **2** (bannissement) deportation, transportation

déporté, ~**e** /depɔRte/ nm,f **1** (dans un camp de concentration) prisoner interned in a concentration camp; **2** (personne bannie) transported convict

déporter /depɔRte/ [1]
A vtr **1** (interner) to send [sb] to a concentration camp; **2** (faire dévier d'une trajectoire) to make [sth] swerve; **3** Hist (bannir) to deport
B se déporter vpr to swerve

déposant, ~**e** /depozɑ̃, ɑ̃t/ nm,f **1** Fin depositor; **2** Jur (témoin) deponent

déposer /depoze/ [1]
A vtr **1** (poser) to put down [fardeau]; to dump [ordures]; to lay [gerbe]; **'défense de** ~ **des ordures'** 'no dumping'; **il déposa un baiser sur sa joue** he kissed his/her cheek; ~ **les armes** fig to lay down one's arms; **2** (laisser) to leave [objet, lettre]; (au passage) to drop off, to leave [paquet, passager]; **3** (verser) gén, Fin to deposit [argent, bijoux]; ~ **sa signature à la banque** to give the bank a specimen signature; **4** (faire enregistrer) to register [marque]; to submit [dossier, offre]; to propose [amendement]; to introduce [projet de loi]; to file [requête]; to lodge [plainte]; ~ **son bilan** Fin to file a petition in bankruptcy; ~ **sa candidature** [chercheur d'emploi] to apply; [homme politique] to run; ~ **une motion de censure** Pol to move a vote of no confidence; ~ **un préavis de grève** to give notice of strike action; **5** (laisser un dépôt) to deposit [alluvions]; **6** (destituer) to depose [souverain]; **7** (enlever) to remove [moteur]; to take up [tapis]; to take down [rideau]
B vi **1** Jur (devant un juge) to testify; (au commissariat) to make a statement; **2** [vin] to leave a sediment
C se déposer vpr [poussière] to settle; [calcaire] to collect

dépositaire /depoziteR/ nmf **1** Comm ~ **(exclusif)** (sole) agent; ~ **agréé** authorized dealer; **2** (d'objet) trustee; Jur (de biens) bailee; fig (de secret) guardian

déposition /depozisjɔ̃/ nf **1** Jur (au tribunal) evidence ℂ; (recueillie) statement; (par écrit) deposition; **2** (destitution) (de souverain) deposition; (de magistrat) removal from office; **3** Art ~ **de croix** Deposition (from the Cross)

déposséder /deposede/ [14] vtr ~ **qn de qch** to dispossess sb of sth

dépossession /deposesjɔ̃/ nf dispossession

dépôt /depo/ nm **1** (entrepôt) warehouse; (plus petit) store; Rail depot; (à la douane) bonded warehouse; Mil (de garnison) depot; **2** Comm (succursale) outlet; **l'épicerie fait** ~ **de pain** the grocer's sells bread; **3** Admin, Jur (d'acte) filing ℂ; (de marque) registration; (de projet de loi) introduction; (d'amendement) proposal; **4** (remise en un lieu) **nous recommandons le** ~ **des documents chez un notaire** we recommend that the documents be deposited with a notary; **5** Fin (de fonds) deposit; (de titres) lodging ℂ; **en** ~ [fonds] on deposit; [bijoux] in a safe at the bank; **6** (sédiment) deposit; **7** (prison) police cells

---

⟮Composés⟯ ~ **d'armes** arms store; (clandestin) arms cache; ~ **de bilan** voluntary liquidation; ~ **légal** formal deposit of a copy of a book, film, record, etc with an institution; ~ **de marchandises** Rail goods GB ou freight US depot; ~ **de munitions** Mil munitions store; (au rebut) munitions dump; ~ **d'ordures** (rubbish) tip ou dump GB, garbage dump US

dépoter /depote/ [1] vtr **1** (en jardinage) to remove a plant from its pot; **2** Tech (décharger) to strip

dépotoir /depotwaR/ nm **1** (d'ordures) rubbish dump, rubbish tip GB, garbage dump US; **2** ○(lieu en désordre) shambles○ (sg)

dépôt-vente, pl **dépôts-ventes** /depovɑ̃t/ nm secondhand shop GB ou store (where goods are sold on commission)

dépouille /depuj/
A nf **1** (peau) skin; (de gros mammifère) hide; (de serpent) slough; **2** (cadavre) body; ~ **(mortelle)** mortal remains (pl)
B dépouilles nfpl (butin) spoils

dépouillé, ~**e** /depuje/ adj **1** (sobre) [style] spare; **2** (écorché) [animal] skinned; **3** (dénudé) [arbre] bare

dépouillement /depujmɑ̃/ nm **1** (examen) **assister au** ~ **du scrutin** to be present when the votes are counted; **procéder au** ~ **du courrier** to go through the mail; **2** (ascèse) asceticism; **vivre dans le plus grand** ~ to live a very ascetic ou spartan life; **3** (sobriété) sobriety

dépouiller /depuje/ [1]
A vtr **1** (dépecer) to skin [animal]; **2** (dénuder) to lay [sth] bare [champ, région]; **3** (déposséder) to rob [voyageur]; hum to fleece○ [contribuable]; ~ **qn de ses biens** to strip sb of his/her possessions; **4** to open [courrier]; to count [scrutin]; to go through [documents]
B se dépouiller vpr **1** (se démunir) [personne] **se** ~ **de** to shed [vêtements]; to divest oneself of [biens]; fig to cast off [morgue]; **2** Zool (muer) [serpent] to slough; **3** (se dénuder) [arbre] to shed its leaves; [style] to become spare

dépourvu, ~**e** /depuRvy/
A adj ~ **de** devoid of, lacking in [intérêt, charme, talent]; devoid of [arrière-pensées]; without [chauffage, rideaux, accessoire]
B nm **prendre qn au** ~ to take sb by surprise

dépoussiérant /depusjerɑ̃/ nm furniture polish

dépoussiérer /depusjere/ [14] vtr lit to dust; fig to revamp [idéologie, loi]

dépravation /depRavasjɔ̃/ nf depravity

dépravé, ~**e** /depRave/ adj depraved

dépraver /depRave/ [1] vtr to deprave

dépréciation /depResjasjɔ̃/ nf depreciation

déprécier /depResje/ [2] vtr **1** Écon, Fin to depreciate; **2** (rabaisser) to disparage, to depreciate

déprédateur -trice /depRedatœR, tRis/
A adj destructive
B nm,f vandal

déprédation /depRedasjɔ̃/ nf ~**s** (pillage) pillaging ℂ; (dégâts) damage ℂ

dépressif, -ive /depResif, iv/ adj, nm,f depressive

dépression /depResjɔ̃/ nf ▸ p. 195 (tous contextes) depression

⟮Composé⟯ ~ **nerveuse** nervous breakdown

dépressionnaire /depResjɔneR/ adj **zone** ~ area of low pressure

dépressurisation /depResyRizasjɔ̃/ nf (volontaire) depressurization; (accidentelle) loss of pressure

dépressuriser /depResyRize/ [1] vtr to depressurize

déprimant, ~**e** /depRimɑ̃, ɑ̃t/ adj depressing

déprime○ /depRim/ nf depression; **il est en pleine** ~ he's really depressed

déprimer /depRime/ [1]
A vtr (démoraliser) to depress
B ○vi to be depressed

déprogrammer /depRɔgRame/ [1] vtr to cancel

depuis /dəpɥi/
A adv since
B prép **1** (marquant le point de départ) since; **elle fait de la danse** ~ **l'âge de 6 ans** she has been dancing since she was 6 years old; ~ **quand vis-tu là-bas?** how long have you been living there ?; ~ **ta naissance** since you were born; **c'est ce que je te répète** ~ **le début** that's what I've been telling

d

depuis

L'adverbe

depuis se traduit généralement par *since*:

elle a démontré, depuis, qu'elle pouvait le faire
= she has since demonstrated that she could do it

Lorsqu'on veut insister sur le temps qui s'est écoulé depuis l'action dont on parle, on peut renforcer *since* par *ever*:

nous nous sommes disputés hier, depuis il me fait la tête
= we had an argument yesterday, he's been sulking ever since

Attention, cette construction ne marche pas à la forme négative:

depuis il ne me parle plus
= he hasn't talked to me since

. . . .

La préposition

depuis, préposition de temps, se traduit par *since* lorsqu'il sert à indiquer un point de départ, une date, une heure précise:

depuis 1789
= since 1789

depuis 2 heures du matin
= since 2 am

depuis le début
= since the beginning

et par *for* lorsqu'il sert à indiquer une durée, un nombre de jours, d'heures:

depuis deux heures
= for two hours

depuis six ans
= for six years

depuis quelques mois
= for a few months

. . . .

depuis + date

j'apprends l'anglais depuis l'âge de 12 ans
= I've been learning English since I was 12

cette maison nous appartient depuis 1876
= we've owned this house since 1876

je le connais depuis l'été dernier
= I've known him since last summer

je n'ai rien mangé depuis hier soir
= I haven't eaten since yesterday evening

il a fait trois films depuis le début de sa carrière
= he's made three films since the beginning of his career

il neigeait depuis midi
= it had been snowing since midday

il n'avait pas plu depuis dimanche
= it hadn't rained since Sunday

On notera l'emploi de la forme progressive:

il habite ici depuis 1990
= he's lived here since 1990
ou he's been living here since 1990

il habite ici depuis le mois de janvier
= he's been living here since January

. . . .

depuis + durée

il travaille ici depuis quelques années
= he's worked here for a few years

il travaille ici depuis dix ans
= he's worked here for ten years

nous marchons depuis deux heures
= we've been walking for two hours

je n'ai pas eu de nouvelles depuis six mois
= I haven't had any news for six months

je dormais depuis une heure
= I had been sleeping for an hour

je ne les avais pas vus depuis cinq ans
= I hadn't seen them for five years

On trouvera des exemples supplémentaires et les autres emplois de la préposition *depuis* et de la locution conjonctive *depuis que* dans l'entrée.

---

you all along; ∼ **le début jusqu'à la fin** from start to finish; [2] (marquant la durée) for; **il pleut ∼ trois jours** it's been raining for three days; ∼ **quand** *or* **combien de temps est-ce qu'elle enseigne?** how long has she been teaching?; ∼ **longtemps** for a long time; ∼ **peu** recently; ∼ **toujours** always; **on pratique cette coutume ∼ toujours** this custom has been observed from time immemorial; [3] (marquant le lieu) from; ∼ **ma fenêtre** from my window; ∼ **Dijon il faut deux heures** from Dijon it takes two hours; [4] (dans une série) from; ∼ **le premier jusqu'au dernier** from first to last

G depuis que *loc conj* gén since; (pour renforcer) ever since; **il pleut ∼ que nous sommes arrivés** it's been raining ever since we arrived

députation /depytasjɔ̃/ *nf* [1] (délégation) deputation; [2] (mandat de député) Pol post of deputy

député /depyte/ *nm* [1] Pol deputy; ∼ **britannique** (British) MP; **être ∼ au Parlement européen** to be a Euro-MP GB *ou* member of the European Parliament; [2] (envoyé) representative, delegate

député-maire, *pl* **députés-maires** /depytemɛʀ/ *nm* deputy and mayor

députer /depyte/ [1] *vtr* ∼ **qn auprès d'un comité** to send sb as a representative to serve on a committee; ∼ **qn pour faire qch** to delegate sb to do sth

déqualifier /dekalifje/ [2] *vtr* to deskill

der○ /dɛʀ/ *nf* last; **la ∼ des ∼s** Hist the war to end all wars; **dix de ∼** Jeux bonus of 10 points awarded to player who takes the last trick in game of belote

déraciné, **∼e** /deʀasine/ *nm,f* uprooted person

déracinement /deʀasinmã/ *nm* [1] (d'arbre) uprooting; [2] (d'immigré) (processus) uprooting; (résultat) rootlessness

déraciner /deʀasine/ [1] *vtr* [1] lit to uproot [arbre, plante]; [2] fig to uproot [personne]; [3] (faire disparaître) to eradicate [préjugé, abus]

déraillement /deʀajmã/ *nm* derailment

dérailler /deʀaje/ [1] *vi* [1] Rail to be derailed; **faire ∼ un train** to derail a train; [2] ○(perdre l'esprit) [vieillard] to go senile, to lose one's marbles○; (tenir des propos incohérents) to rave, to ramble; (se tromper) to talk through one's hat○; [3] [voix] (chantée) to waver; (parlée) to crack; [instrument] to go out of pitch

dérailleur /deʀajœʀ/ *nm* [1] (de bicyclette) derailleur; [2] Rail derailing stop

déraison /deʀɛzɔ̃/ *nf* liter madness

déraisonnable /deʀɛzɔnabl/ *adj* (impensable) unrealistic; (peu sage) senseless; (excessif) unreasonable

déraisonner /deʀɛzɔne/ [1] *vi* liter (dire des bêtises) to talk nonsense

dérangé, **~e** /deʀɑ̃ʒe/ adj ☐ [estomac] upset; ☐ ○(fou) **être ~**, **avoir l'esprit ~** to be deranged

dérangeant, **~e** /deʀɑ̃ʒɑ̃, ɑ̃t/ adj [idée, livre, film] disturbing

dérangement /deʀɑ̃ʒmɑ̃/
A nm ☐ (inconvénient) trouble, inconvenience; **excusez le ~** sorry to bother you; ☐ (dérèglement) ~ **intestinal** stomach upset; **être en ~** [ascenseur, téléphone] to be out of order
B **dérangements** nmpl Télécom fault reporting service (sg)

déranger /deʀɑ̃ʒe/ [13]
A vtr ☐ (importuner) [visiteur, téléphone] to disturb [personne]; **'(prière de) ne pas ~'** 'do not disturb'; **excusez-moi de vous ~** (I'm) sorry to bother you; ☐ (gêner) [bruit, fumée] to bother [personne]; **et alors, ça te dérange que je sorte?** so, what's it to you if I go out?; ☐ (surprendre) to disturb [animal, voleur]; ☐ (faire déplacer) to disturb [spectateurs assis]; (faire venir) to call out [médecin, plombier]; ☐ (contrarier) to upset [personne, habitudes]; (troubler) to disturb [personne]; ☐ (mettre en désordre) to disturb [livres]; to ruffle, to mess up [coiffure] ; to turn [sth] upside down [pièce]; ☐ (dérégler) to upset [estomac]; to affect [esprit]
B **se déranger** vpr ☐ (se déplacer) (aller) to go out; (venir) to come out; ☐ (se lever) to get up; (changer de place) to move; ☐ (faire un effort) to put oneself out; **ne te vous dérange pas pour moi** don't go to any trouble on my account

dérapage /deʀapaʒ/ nm ☐ (de véhicule) skid; **traces de ~** skid marks; ☐ (erreur) blunder; ☐ (augmentation) escalation; **~ des prix** escalation of prices; ☐ (perte de contrôle) loss of control; **les risques de ~ demeurent** the risk of things getting out of control remains; **~ verbal** slip; ☐ (sur skis) sideslip

déraper /deʀape/ [1] vi ☐ [prix, débat] to get out of control; ☐ [couteau] to slip; ☐ [personne, voiture] to skid; ☐ (à skis) to sideslip

dératé○, **~e** /deʀate/ nm,f **courir comme un ~** to run like crazy

dératisation /deʀatizasjɔ̃/ nf pest control (for rats)

derechef /dəʀəʃɛf/ adv fml once again

déréglé, **~e** /deʀegle/ adj [esprit] unbalanced; [vie] irregular; **avoir le sommeil ~** to have a disrupted sleep pattern

dérèglement /deʀɛɡləmɑ̃/
A nm (de machine) fault; Météo disturbance; (psychologique) disturbance; (physiologique) disorder; (socio-économique) imbalance
B **dérèglements** mpl fml excesses

déréglementation /deʀegləmɑ̃tasjɔ̃/ nf deregulation

déréglementer /deʀegləmɑ̃te/ [1] vtr to deregulate

dérégler /deʀegle/ [14] vtr to affect [temps, organe]; to upset [déroulement]; **~ la télévision** to lose the channel on the TV; **~ le réveil** to set the alarm clock wrong

dérégulation /deʀegylasjɔ̃/ nf Écon deregulation

dérider /deʀide/ [1]
A vtr to cheer [sb] up
B **se dérider** vpr to start smiling

dérision /deʀizjɔ̃/ nf scorn, derision; **avec ~** scornfully, derisively; **tourner qn/qch en ~** to ridicule sb/sth

dérisoire /deʀizwaʀ/ adj [pouvoir] pathetic; [somme] trivial, derisory

dérivatif, -ive /deʀivatif, iv/
A adj Ling derivative
B nm ☐ gén diversion (à from); ☐ Méd derivative

dérivation /deʀivasjɔ̃/ nf ☐ (de cours d'eau) diversion; ☐ (routière) diversion GB, detour US; ☐ Électrotech shunt; **en ~ in parallel**; ☐ Ling derivation

dérive /deʀiv/ nf ☐ fig drift; **à la ~** drifting; **aller** or **partir à la ~** to drift away; **leur affaire va à la ~** their business is going downhill; ☐ Écon slide; ☐ Naut (aileron) centreboard**GB**; (déviation) deviation; **être à la ~** to be adrift; ☐ Aviat (déviation) drift; (gouvernail) (vertical) fin

dérivé, **~e** /deʀive/
A adj Chimie, Ling **corps/mot ~** derivative
B nm ☐ gén spin-off; ☐ (produit) by-product; ☐ Chimie, Ling derivative

dériver /deʀive/ [1]
A vtr ☐ (détourner) to divert [rivière]; ☐ Math to obtain the derivative of [fonction]
B **dériver de** vtr ind ☐ gén **~ de** to stem from; ☐ Ling **~ de** to be derived from

C vi ☐ lit, fig to drift; ☐ Math to differentiate

dériveur /deʀivœʀ/ nm ☐ (de plaisance) (sailing) dinghy; ☐ (de pêche) drifter; ☐ (voile) stormsail

dermatologie /dɛʀmatɔlɔʒi/ nf dermatology

derme /dɛʀm/ nm dermis

dernier, -ière[1] /dɛʀnje, ɛʀ/
A adj ☐ (qui termine une série) gén last; [étage, étagère] top; **arriver ~** (dans une course) to come last; **être bon ~** to come well and truly last; **un ~ mot avant que vous ne partiez** a final word before you go;**la dissertation est pour le 20 juin ~** the deadline for this essay is 20 June; **de la dernière chance** final; ☐ (précédent) last; **l'an ~** last year; ☐ (le plus récent) [roman, nouvelles] latest; **ces ~ temps** recently; ☐ (extrême) **le ~ degré de** the height of; **être du ~ ridicule** to be utterly ridiculous; **c'était la dernière chose à faire** it was the worst possible thing to do; **le ~ choix** the poorest quality
B nmf ☐ (qui est à la fin) last; **les ~s** the last; **arriver le ~** to arrive last; **tu es toujours le ~** you are always last; **c'est le ~ qui me reste** it's my last one; **le ~ qui** (personne) the last person who; **c'est le ~ de mes soucis** that is the least of my worries; **être le ~ de la classe** to be bottom of the class; **le petit ~** the youngest child; **est-ce votre ~?** is that your youngest?; **ce ~**, **ces ~s** (de plusieurs) the latter; **dans ce ~ cas** in the latter case; ☐ (le pire) **c'est le ~ des imbéciles** or **idiots** he's a complete idiot; **le ~ des ~s** the lowest of the low
C **en dernier** loc adv last

(Composés) **~ cri** latest fashion; **dernière demeure** final resting place; **dernières volontés** last requests

dernière[2] /dɛʀnjɛʀ/ nf ☐ (histoire, nouvelle) **la ~** the latest; ☐ (d'un spectacle) last performance

dernièrement /dɛʀnjɛʀmɑ̃/ adv recently, lately

dernier-né, **dernière-née**, mpl **derniers-nés** /dɛʀnjene, dɛʀnjɛʀne/ nm,f ☐ (enfant) youngest; ☐ (modèle) latest model

dérobade /deʀɔbad/ nf gén evasion; (d'un cheval) running out

dérobé, **~e** /deʀɔbe/
A adj [porte, escalier] concealed
B **à la dérobée** loc adv furtively

dérober /deʀɔbe/ [1]
A vtr ☐ liter (voler) to steal; ☐ liter (cacher) to hide
B **se dérober** vpr ☐ (se soustraire aux questions) to be evasive; ☐ (se soustraire à son devoir) to shirk responsibility; ☐ (se soustraire) **se ~ à** to shirk [responsabilités, devoir]; to evade [question, justice]; **se ~ à un engagement** to get out of a commitment; ☐ (céder) [sol] to give way (**sous** under)

dérogation /deʀɔgasjɔ̃/ nf ☐ (autorisation) (special) dispensation; ☐ (contravention) infringement (**à** of)

dérogatoire /deʀɔgatwaʀ/ adj [régime, cas] special; **clause ~** derogation clause

déroger /deʀɔʒe/ [13] vtr ind **~ à** to infringe [loi, droit]; to depart from [principes, politique]; to ignore [obligation]; to break with [tradition]

dérouillée○ /deʀuje/ nf ☐ (volée de coups) hiding○, beating; ☐ (défaite sportive) thrashing○, defeat

dérouiller○ /deʀuje/ [1]
A vtr (dégourdir) [sport] to loosen up [jambes]; to limber [sb] up [personne]
B vi (recevoir des coups) to get a hiding○ ou beating; (souffrir) to suffer
C **se dérouiller** vpr **se ~ les jambes** to loosen up one's legs

déroulement /deʀulmɑ̃/ nm **le ~ des événements** the sequence of events; **veiller au bon ~ de** to make sure [sth] goes smoothly [cérémonie, négociations]; **expliquer le ~ de la cérémonie** to explain the procedure for the ceremony; **~ de carrière** career development; **le ~ de l'intrigue** the unfolding of the plot

dérouler /deʀule/ [1]
A vtr (étendre) to unroll [tapis, tuyau, manuscrit]; to let down [chevelure]; to uncoil [corde]; (autour d'une bobine) to unwind [fil, pellicule]
B **se dérouler** vpr ☐ (avoir lieu) to take place; ☐ (progresser) [négociations] to proceed sout, to go; [histoire, événements] to unfold; (être déroulé) [tapis] to be unrolled; [pellicule] to be unwound; [carte] to unroll; **les images qui se déroulent dans ma tête** the images going through my head

d

dérouleur /deʀulœʀ/ *nm* **1** gén holder; **2** Tech (de câble, papier) unwinding machine; **3** Ordinat ~ **de bande** tape drive

déroutant, ~e /deʀutɑ̃, ɑ̃t/ *adj* puzzling

déroute /deʀut/ *nf* **1** (défaite) crushing defeat; **mettre qn en** ~ to defeat sb; **2** (débandade) rout; **en** ~ in full flight; **mettre en** ~ to put [sb] to flight, to rout sb; **3** (crise profonde) disarray; **en** ~ in disarray

dérouter /deʀute/ [1] *vtr* **1** (déconcerter) to puzzle; **2** Aviat, Naut to divert

derrière¹ /deʀjɛʀ/
A *prép* **1** (en arrière de) behind; **l'un** ~ **l'autre** one behind the other; **il ne fait rien par lui-même, il faut toujours être** ~ **lui** fig he never gets anything done unless you keep after him; **il a les syndicats** ~ **lui** fig the unions are behind him; **2** (sous) behind; ~ **les apparences** (de personne) behind the façade; (de situation) beneath the surface
B *adv* (à l'arrière) behind; (dans le fond) at the back; (à l'arrière d'une voiture) in the back; **qu'y a-t-il** ~? fig what's behind it?; **ne poussez pas** ~! stop pushing at the back!, stop pushing back there!

derrière² /deʀjɛʀ/ *nm* **1** (de maison, véhicule, d'objet) back; **de** ~ [*chambre, porte*] back; **2** ○(de personne, d'animal) behind○, backside○

derviche /dɛʀviʃ/ *nm* dervish; ~ **tourneur** whirling dervish

des /de/ *art indéf pl* ▶ **un A**

dès /dɛ/
A *prép* **1** (indique le point de départ dans le temps) from; ~ **(l'âge de) huit ans** from the age of eight; ~ **aujourd'hui** [*faisable*] from today; [*écrire, se renseigner*] this very day; ~ **maintenant** [*s'inscrire, commencer*] straight away; ~ **le départ** *or* **début** (right) from the start *ou* beginning; ~ **l'instant** *or* **le moment où** from the very moment when; **je vous téléphone** ~ **mon arrivée** I'll phone *ou* call you as soon as I arrive; **je lui en parlerai** ~ **lundi** I'll talk to him about it on Monday; **2** (indique le point de départ dans l'espace) from; ~ **Versailles il y a des embouteillages** there are traffic jams from Versailles onwards; **vous serez pris en charge par les organisateurs** ~ **l'aéroport** organizers will take care of you as soon as you get to the airport
B **dès que** *loc conj* as soon as; ~ **que possible** as soon as possible
C **dès lors** *loc adv* (à partir de ce moment) from then on, from that time on, henceforth; (de ce fait) therefore, consequently
D **dès lors que** *loc conj* (à partir du moment où) once, from the moment that; (puisque) since

désabusé, ~e /dezabyze/
A *pp* ▶ **désabuser**
B *pp adj* [*personne*] disillusioned; [*air, ton, parole*] cynical

désabuser /dezabyze/ [1] *vtr* **1** (désillusionner) to disenchant (**de** with); **2** (détromper) to disabuse (**de** about)

désaccord /dezakɔʀ/ *nm* **1** (divergence) disagreement (**avec** with; **sur** over); **exprimer son** ~ to express (one's) disagreement; **en** ~ in disagreement; **être en** ~ to disagree (**avec** with; **sur** over); **2** (contradiction) discrepancy

désaccordé, ~e /dezakɔʀde/ *adj* Mus out-of-tune (*épith*); **ton piano est** ~ your piano is out of tune

désaccoutumer /dezakutyme/ [1]
A *vtr* ~ **qn de qch** to cure sb's addiction to sth [*tabac, drogue*]; ~ **qn de faire** to cure sb of doing
B **se désaccoutumer** *vpr* **se** ~ **de qch** to break one's dependence on sth [*tabac, alcool*]

désaffecté, ~e /dezafɛkte/ *adj* disused

désaffection /dezafɛksjɔ̃/ *nf* disaffection (**pour** with)

désagréable /dezagʀeabl/ *adj* unpleasant, disagreeable

désagrégation /dezagʀegasjɔ̃/ *nf* **1** (décomposition) disintegration; (écroulement) collapse; (dislocation) break-up; **2** (de roche) disintegration; **3** Psych collapse

désagréger /dezagʀeʒe/ [15]
A *vtr* to disintegrate
B **se désagréger** *vpr* **1** (se décomposer) to disintegrate; (s'écrouler) to collapse; (se disloquer) to break up; **2** [*roche*] to disintegrate

désagrément /dezagʀemɑ̃/ *nm* **1** (gêne) inconvenience; **2** (embêtement) annoyance, inconvenience

désaltérant, ~e /dezalteʀɑ̃, ɑ̃t/ *adj* thirst-quenching

désaltérer /dezalteʀe/ [14]
A *vtr* ~ **qn** to quench sb's thirst
B **se désaltérer** *vpr* to quench one's thirst

désamorçage /dezamɔʀsaʒ/ *nm* **1** (d'explosif, de crise) defusing; **2** (de pompe) draining

désamorcer /dezamɔʀse/ [12] *vtr* to defuse [*explosif, crise*]; to drain [*pompe*]

désappointement /dezapwɛ̃tmɑ̃/ *nm* disappointment

désappointer /dezapwɛ̃te/ [1] *vtr* to disappoint

désapprobateur, -trice /dezapʀɔbatœʀ, tʀis/ *adj* disapproving; **d'un air** ~ disapprovingly

désapprobation /dezapʀɔbasjɔ̃/ *nf* disapproval

désapprouver /dezapʀuve/ [1] *vtr* to disapprove of

désarçonner /dezaʀsɔne/ [1] *vtr* **1** (déséquilibrer) [*cheval*] to throw [*cavalier*]; **2** (déconcerter) to take [sb] aback [*personne*]; **se faire** ~ to be thrown (**par** by)

désargenté○, ~e /dezaʀʒɑ̃te/ *adj* (pauvre) hard up○, penniless

désarmant, ~e /dezaʀmɑ̃, ɑ̃t/ *adj* disarming

désarmement /dezaʀməmɑ̃/ *nm* **1** Mil (de pays, région) disarmament; **2** Naut (de navire) laying up

désarmer /dezaʀme/ [1]
A *vtr* **1** (rendre inoffensif) gén, Mil to disarm; **2** (décontenancer) to disarm [*personne*]; (désamorcer) to defuse [*colère*]; **3** Naut to lay up [*navire*]; to ship [*avirons*]
B *vi* **1** Mil to disarm; **2** (abandonner une lutte) [*personne*] to give up the fight; (cesser) [*colère, haine*] to abate

désarroi /dezaʀwa/ *nm* (trouble moral) distress; (désordre) confusion; **au grand** ~ **de** much to the distress of; **jeter qn dans le** ~ to throw sb into confusion

désarticulé, ~e /dezaʀtikyle/
A *pp* ▶ **désarticuler**
B *pp adj* [*fauteuil*] wrecked; [*pantin*] with broken joints (*épith, après n*)

désarticuler /dezaʀtikyle/ [1] *vtr* **1** (déboîter) to dislocate [*membre*]; **2** Méd (amputer) to amputate

désastre /dezastʀ/ *nm* (tous contextes) disaster

désastreux, -euse /dezastʀø, øz/ *adj* disastrous

désavantage /dezavɑ̃taʒ/ *nm* **1** (handicap) disadvantage; **avoir un** ~ **par rapport à qn** to be at a disadvantage compared to sb; **être/tourner au** ~ **de** to be/to turn to sb's disadvantage; **2** (inconvénient) drawback, disadvantage

désavantager /dezavɑ̃taʒe/ [13] *vtr* to put [sb/sth] at a disadvantage, to disadvantage [*personne, entreprise*]

désavantageux, -euse /dezavɑ̃taʒø, øz/ *adj* [*affaire, prix*] unfavourableᴳᴮ, disadvantageous

désaveu /dezavø/ *nm* **1** (reniement) denial; **2** (condamnation) rejection

désavouer /dezavwe/ [1] *vtr* **1** (ne pas reconnaître comme sien) to deny [*acte, propos*]; **2** (rejeter) to disown [*personne, candidat*]; **3** Jur to disown [*enfant*]

désaxé, ~e /dezakse/
A *adj* [*personne*] deranged
B *nm,f* deranged person

desceller /desele/ [1]
A *vtr* **1** Constr to work [sth] free [*lavabo, pierre*]; **2** (ouvrir) to unseal [*acte, lettre*]
B **se desceller** *vpr* [*lavabo, pierre*] to work loose

descendance /desɑ̃dɑ̃s/ *nf* **1** (lignée) descendants (*pl*); **2** †(origine familiale) descent

descendant, ~e /desɑ̃dɑ̃, ɑ̃t/
A *adj* [*cabine, courbe*] downward; **train** ~ Rail down train
B *nm,f* descendant (**de** of)

descendre /dɛsɑ̃dʀ/ [6]
A *vtr* (+ *v avoir*) **1** (transporter) (en bas) gén to take [sb/sth] down (**à** to); (d'en haut) gén to bring [sb/sth] down (**de** from); **je peux vous** ~ **au village** I can take you down to the village; **descends-moi mes pantoufles** bring my slippers down for me; **2** (placer plus bas) to put [sth] down [*objet*]; (en abaissant) gén to lower [sth] (**de** by); (avec une manivelle) to wind [sth] down; **descends le store** put the blind down; ~ **un seau dans un puits** to lower a bucket into a well; **3** (réussir à mettre plus bas) to get [sth] down [*objet*]; **comment va-t-on** ~ **le piano?** (de l'étage) how are we going to get the piano downstairs?; **4** (parcourir) (en allant) to go down; (en venant) to come down [*pente, rue, marches, fleuve*]; ~ **la colline en rampant/à bicyclette** to crawl/to cycle down the hill; ~ **la rivière en pagayant/à la nage** to paddle/to swim down the river;

5⟩ ○(éliminer) to bump off○ [*personne*]; to shoot down [*avion*]; **on l'a descendu d'une balle dans la tête** he was shot in the head and killed; **6⟩** ○(malmener) to tear [sb/sth] to pieces; **7⟩** ○(boire) [*personne*] to down [*bouteille*]

B *vi* (+ *v être*) **1⟩** (se déplacer) [*personne*] (en allant) gén to go down (**à** to); (en venant) gén to come down (**de** from); [*ascenseur, avion*] (en allant) to go down; (en venant) to come down; [*oiseau*] to fly down; [*soleil*] to set (**sur** over); [*nuit*] to fall; [*brouillard*] to come down (**sur** over); **peux-tu ∼ chercher mon sac?** can you go downstairs and get my bag?; **il est descendu fumer** he went downstairs to smoke; **tu es descendu à pied?** did you walk down?; **nous sommes descendus par la route** (à pied) we walked down by the road; (à cheval) we rode down by the road; **descends, je te suis** go on down, I'll follow you; **∼ de** to step off [*trottoir, marche*]; to climb down from [*mur, tabouret, échelle*]; **∼ aux Enfers** Relig to descend into Hell; **descends de là!** get down from there!; **faites-les ∼** send them down [*clients, marchandises*]; **faire ∼ sa jupe** to pull one's skirt down; **2⟩** (d'un moyen de transport) **∼ d'une voiture** to get out of a car; **∼ d'un train/bus/avion** to get off a train/bus/plane; **∼ de bicyclette** to get off one's bicycle; **∼ de cheval** to get off one's horse, to dismount *sout*; **∼ à Marseille** (d'avion, de bateau, bus, train) to get off at Marseilles; **3⟩** (s'étendre de haut en bas) [*route, voie ferrée*] to go downhill, to go down; [*terrain*] to go down; **∼ jusqu'à la mer** [*route, rivière*] to go right down to the sea; **∼ en lacets** [*route*] to wind its way down; **∼ en pente douce** [*terrain, route*] to slope down gently; **∼ en pente raide** [*terrain, route*] to drop steeply; **4⟩** (atteindre) [*vêtement, cheveux*] to come down (**jusqu'à** to); **5⟩** (baisser) [*niveau, baromètre, température, pression, prix, taux*] to drop, to go down (**à** to; **de** by); [*marée*] to go out; **l'euro est** *or* **a descendu par rapport à la livre** the euro has dropped *ou* gone down against the pound; **ça fait ∼ la température** gén it lowers the temperature; Méd it brings one's temperature down; **ça ne fera pas ∼ le taux de chômage** it won't bring the unemployment rate down; **6⟩** (se rendre, séjourner) **∼ dans le Midi** to go down to the South (of France); **∼ dans un hôtel** to stay at a hotel; **∼ dans la rue** Pol to take to the streets; **7⟩** (être issu) **∼ de** gén to come from; (génétiquement) to be descended from

descente /desɑ̃t/ *nf* **1⟩** (parcours d'un véhicule, d'une personne) descent; **la ∼ a pris une heure** it took an hour to come down; **freiner dans les ∼s** to brake going downhill; **tomber dans la ∼** to fall on the way down; **faire la ∼ d'une rivière en canoë** to canoe down a river; **2⟩** (sortie) **à ma ∼ du train** when I got off the train; **accueillir qn à sa ∼ d'avion** to meet sb off the plane; **3⟩** Sport (en ski) (épreuve) downhill (event); (parcours) run; **∼ hommes/dames** men's/women's downhill; **4⟩** Sport (en alpinisme, cyclisme, spéléologie) descent; **5⟩** (raid) raid (**dans en**); **la police a fait une ∼ dans l'immeuble/le bar** the police raided the building/bar

Composés   **∼ de croix** Art, Relig descent from the cross; **∼ aux enfers** descent into hell; **∼ de lit** (tapis) (bedside) rug; **∼ d'organe** Méd prolapse

descriptible /deskʁiptibl/ *adj* describable

descriptif, -ive /deskʁiptif, iv/
A *adj* (tous contextes) descriptive
B *nm* (notice explicative) gén detailed description; Constr specification

description /deskʁipsjɔ̃/ *nf* gén description; **faire une ∼ de qch** to give a description of sth, to describe sth

désemparé, ∼e /dezɑ̃paʁe/
A *pp* ▸ **désemparer**
B *pp adj* **1⟩** (dérouté) [*personne*] distraught, at a loss (*jamais épith*); **2⟩** [*avion, navire*] in distress

désemparer /dezɑ̃paʁe/ [1]
A *vtr* (dérouter) to throw [sb] into confusion
B *vi* **sans ∼** without let-up

désemplir /dezɑ̃pliʁ/ [3] *vi* **ce restaurant ne désemplit pas** this restaurant is always full

désenchanté, ∼e /dezɑ̃ʃɑ̃te/ *adj* disillusioned, disenchanted (**de** with)

désenchantement /dezɑ̃ʃɑ̃tmɑ̃/ *nm* disillusionment, disenchantment

désenclaver /dezɑ̃klave/ [1] *vtr* to open up [*région*]

désendettement /dezɑ̃dɛtmɑ̃/ *nm* (partiel) reduction of the debt; (complet) rescuing from debt

désenfler /dezɑ̃fle/ [1] *vi* to become less swollen, to go down

désengagement /dezɑ̃gaʒmɑ̃/ *nm* **1⟩** Écon, Pol disengagement; **2⟩** Mil withdrawal (**de** from)

désengager: se désengager /dezɑ̃gaʒe/ [13] *vpr* Écon, Mil, Pol to withdraw (**de** from)

désensibiliser /desɑ̃sibilize/ [1] *vtr* Phot, Méd to desensitize

désenvoûter /dezɑ̃vute/ [1] *vtr* to break the spell on

désépaissir /dezepesiʁ/ [3] *vtr* **1⟩** Culin to thin [*sauce*]; **2⟩** (en coiffure) to thin [sth] out [*chevelure*]

déséquilibre /dezekilibʁ/ *nm* **1⟩** lit (de personne) loss of balance; (de meuble, objet) rocking; **en ∼** [*table*] unstable; [*personne*] off balance; **2⟩** fig (d'ordre économique, social, écologique) imbalance; **3⟩** Psych lack of balance

déséquilibré, ∼e /dezekilibʁe/
A *pp* ▸ **déséquilibrer**
B *pp adj* Psych (perturbé) unbalanced; (fou) crazy
C *nm,f* Psych lunatic

déséquilibrer /dezekilibʁe/ [1] *vtr* **1⟩** lit [*personne, choc, coup*] to make [sb] lose their balance [*personne*]; [*poids*] to make [sth] unstable [*barque, meuble*]; **être déséquilibré par qch** [*personne*] to be thrown off balance by sth; [*meuble, objet*] to be made unstable by sth; **2⟩** fig to destabilize [*pays*]; **3⟩** Psych to unbalance [*personne*]

désert, ∼e /dezɛʁ, ɛʁt/
A *adj* **1⟩** (inhabité) uninhabited; **île ∼e** desert island; **2⟩** (vide) deserted
B *nm* lit, fig desert

déserter /dezɛʁte/ [1] *vtr* to desert

déserteur /dezɛʁtœʁ/ *nm* deserter

désertion /dezɛʁsjɔ̃/ *nf* **1⟩** Mil desertion; **2⟩** Pol defection (**vers** to)

désertique /dezɛʁtik/ *adj* **1⟩** (du désert) [*paysage, climat, région*] desert (*épith*); **2⟩** (vide) [*étendue*] barren

désespérant, ∼e /dezespeʁɑ̃, ɑ̃t/ *adj* [*personne, situation*] hopeless; [*nouvelle*] heart-breaking

désespéré, ∼e /dezespeʁe/
A *pp* ▸ **désespérer**
B *pp adj* [*personne, population*] in despair (*épith, après n*); [*situation, cas*] hopeless; [*tentative, appel*] desperate; [*regard, geste*] despairing
C *nm,f* desperate person

désespérément /dezespeʁemɑ̃/ *adv* **1⟩** (avec désespoir) [*attendre*] despairingly; [*regretter*] desperately; **2⟩** (avec acharnement) desperately; **3⟩** (à en pleurer) hopelessly

désespérer /dezespeʁe/ [14]
A *vtr* to drive [sb] to despair (**avec, par** with); **ça me désespère de voir...** if fills me with despair to see...; **il ne désespère pas qu'elle revienne un jour** he has not given up hope that she will come back one day
B **désespérer de** *vtr ind* **∼ de qn/qch** to despair of sb/sth; **il ne désespère pas de le sauver** he hasn't given up hope of saving him
C *vi* to despair, to lose hope; **c'est à ∼** it's hopeless
D **se désespérer** *vpr* to despair

désespoir /dezespwaʁ/ *nm* despair; **mettre** *or* **réduire qn au ∼** to drive sb to despair; **être** *ou* **faire le ∼ de** [*enfant, bêtise*] to be the despair of; **en ∼ de cause** out of *ou* in desperation

déshabillé /dezabije/ *nm* (vêtement) negligee

déshabiller /dezabije/ [1]
A *vtr* to undress [*personne*]
B **se déshabiller** *vpr* **1⟩** (complètement) to undress; **2⟩** (ôter son manteau) to take one's coat off

déshabituer /dezabitɥe/ [1]
A *vtr* **∼ qn du tabac/de fumer** to get sb out of the habit of smoking
B **se déshabituer** *vpr* **se ∼ de l'alcool** to break oneself of the habit of drinking

désherbant /dezɛʁbɑ̃/ *nm* weedkiller

désherber /dezɛʁbe/ [1] *vtr* (à la main) to weed [*allée*]; (avec un désherbant) to apply weedkiller to [*allée*]

déshérité, ∼e /dezeʁite/
A *pp* ▸ **déshériter**
B *pp adj* (pauvre) [*personne*] underprivileged; [*pays*] disadvantaged; [*région, quartier*] deprived
C *nm,f* **les ∼s** the underprivileged

déshériter /dezeʁite/ [1] *vtr* to disinherit

déshonneur /dezɔnœʁ/ *nm* disgrace

déshonorant, **~e** /dezɔnɔrɑ̃, ɑ̃t/ *adj* dishonourable[GB], degrading

déshonorer /dezɔnɔre/ [1]
A *vtr* **1** (apporter le déshonneur à) to bring disgrace on [*personne, famille*]; to bring [sth] into disrepute [*doctrine, pays*]; **2** †(séduire) to dishonour[GB] [*femme, jeune fille*]
B **se déshonorer** *vpr* to disgrace oneself

déshumaniser /dezymanize/ [1]
A *vtr* to dehumanize
B **se déshumaniser** *vpr* to become dehumanized

déshydratation /dezidratasjɔ̃/ *nf* **1** Méd dehydration; **2** Tech drying; **~ à froid** freeze-drying

déshydrater /dezidrate/ [1]
A *vtr* **1** Méd to dehydrate; **2** Tech to dry [*aliment*]
B **se déshydrater** *vpr* [*malade*] to dehydrate; [*peau*] to dry out

desiderata /deziderata/ *nmpl* wishes

désigner /dezine/ [1] *vtr* **1** (faire référence à) [*mot, expression*] to designate; [*triangle, couleur*] to represent; **2** (indiquer) (d'un geste) to point out; (en nommant) to name; **~ qch du menton** *or* **d'un mouvement de tête** to indicate sth with a jerk of one's head; **~ du doigt** to point to; **~ nommément** to name; **~ qn comme responsable** to hold sb responsible; **3** (choisir) gén to choose, to designate (**comme, en qualité de** as); (à un emploi) to appoint (**comme** as); **être tout désigné pour** to be just right for

désillusion /dezil(l)yzjɔ̃/ *nf* disillusion

désincarcérer /dezɛ̃karsere/ [14] *vtr* to free

désincarné, **~e** /dezɛ̃karne/ *adj* **1** lit disembodied; **2** fig liter [*théorie*] not anchored in reality (*jamais épith*)

désinence /dezinɑ̃s/ *nf* Ling ending

désinfectant, **~e** /dezɛ̃fɛktɑ̃, ɑ̃t/
A *adj* disinfecting
B *nm* disinfectant

désinfecter /dezɛ̃fɛkte/ [1] *vtr* to disinfect

désinformation /dezɛ̃fɔrmasjɔ̃/ *nf* disinformation; **il y a une ~ du public sur ce point** the public is being deliberately misinformed on that matter

désinformer /dezɛ̃fɔrme/ [1] *vtr* to misinform deliberately

désinhiber /dezinibe/ [1] *vtr* to disinhibit

désinstaller /dezɛ̃stale/ [1] *vtr* Ordinat to uninstall

désintégration /dezɛ̃tegrasjɔ̃/ *nf* **1** (destruction) disintegration; **2** Phys disintegration; **3** (de roche) crumbling

désintégrer /dezɛ̃tegre/ [14] *vtr*, **se désintégrer** *vpr* to disintegrate

désintéressé, **~e** /dezɛ̃terese/
A *pp* ▸ **désintéresser**
B *pp adj* [*personne, acte*] selfless, unselfish; [*conseil, jugement*] disinterested; **il l'a aidée de façon ~e** he had no ulterior motive for helping her

désintéressement /dezɛ̃teresmɑ̃/ *nm* **1** (détachement) disinterestedness; **agir avec ~** to act disinterestedly; **2** Fin (remboursement) paying off

désintéresser /dezɛ̃terese/ [1]
A *vtr* Fin to pay off [*créancier*]
B **se désintéresser** *vpr* **se ~ de qch/qn** to lose interest in sth/sb

désintérêt /dezɛ̃tere/ *nm* (indifférence) lack of interest (**pour** in); (baisse d'intérêt) loss of interest (**pour** in)

désintoxication /dezɛ̃tɔksikasjɔ̃/ *nf* detoxification

désintoxiquer /dezɛ̃tɔksike/ [1] *vtr* Méd to detoxify [*alcoolique, toxicomane*]

désinvestissement /dezɛ̃vestismɑ̃/ *nm* Écon (dans un secteur économique) divestiture; (dans les biens d'équipement) disinvestment

désinvolte /dezɛ̃vɔlt/ *adj* [*personne, remarque, geste*] (cavalier) offhand; (à l'aise) casual

désinvolture /dezɛ̃vɔltyr/ *nf* **1** (sans-gêne) offhand manner; **avec ~** in an offhand manner; **2** (manière dégagée) casual manner; **avec ~** casually

désir /dezir/ *nm* **1** (souhait) desire (**de** for; **de faire** to do); **~s du défunt/public** wishes of the deceased/public; **prendre ses ~s pour des réalités** to delude oneself; **2** (attirance sexuelle) desire

désirer /dezire/ [1] *vtr* **1** (vouloir) to want (**faire** to do); **s'il le désire** if he wants; **effets non désirés** unwanted effects;

que désirez-vous? what would you like?; **tu te fais ~** you don't come to see me/us etc very often; **2** (vouloir sexuellement) to want, to desire

désireux, **-euse** /dezirø, øz/ *adj* **~ de faire/que** anxious to do/that

désistement /dezistəmɑ̃/ *nm* withdrawal

désister: **se désister** /deziste/ [1] *vpr* to stand down GB, to withdraw (**en faveur de** in favour[GB] of)

désobéir /dezɔbeir/ [3] *vtr ind* to be disobedient, to disobey; **~ à un ordre** to disobey sb/an order

désobéissant, **~e** /dezɔbeisɑ̃, ɑ̃t/ *adj* disobedient

désobligeant, **~e** /dezɔbliʒɑ̃, ɑ̃t/ *adj* disagreeable

désobliger /dezɔbliʒe/ [13] *vtr* to offend

désodorisant, **~e** /dezɔdɔrizɑ̃, ɑ̃t/
A *adj* deodorant
B *nm* (pour le corps) deodorant; (pour la maison) air freshener

désodoriser /dezɔdɔrize/ [1] *vtr* to freshen

désœuvré, **~e** /dezœvre/ *adj* at a loose end○ GB, at loose ends○ US (*jamais épith*)

désœuvrement /dezœvrəmɑ̃/ *nm* **faire qch par ~** to do sth for lack of anything better to do

désolant, **~e** /dezɔlɑ̃, ɑ̃t/ *adj* **1** (attristant) distressing, upsetting; **2** (consternant) depressing

désolation /dezɔlasjɔ̃/ *nf* **1** (affliction) grief; **2** (caractère dévasté) desolation

désolé, **~e** /dezɔle/ *adj* **1** (au regret) sorry; **être ~ que** to be sorry that; **2** (très affligé) [*personne*] desolate; **3** (vide) [*village, plaine*] desolate

désoler /dezɔle/ [1]
A *vtr* **1** (attrister) to upset, to distress; **2** (consterner) to depress
B **se désoler** *vpr* to be upset (**de qch** about)

désolidariser: **se désolidariser** /desɔlidarize/ [1] *vpr* to dissociate oneself (**de** from)

désopilant, **~e** /dezɔpilɑ̃, ɑ̃t/ *adj* hilarious

désordonné, **~e** /dezɔrdɔne/ *adj* **1** (désorganisé) [*personne*] untidy; [*article, paroles, pensée*] muddled; [*réunion, activité, combat*] disorderly; [*gestes*] uncoordinated; **2** (déréglé) [*conduite, existence*] wild

désordre /dezɔrdr/
A ○*adj inv* **faire ~** to look untidy *ou* messy; **être très ~** to be very untidy
B *nm* **1** (fouillis) mess; **pièce/maison en ~** untidy room/house; **laisser tout en ~** to leave everything in a mess; **quel ~!** what a mess!; **2** (manque de cohérence) chaos ¢; **semer le ~** to cause chaos; **se retirer dans le ~** Mil to retreat in disorder; **3** (trouble) disorder; **le ~ de sa maison** his/her untidy house; **4** (ordre aléatoire) **dans le ~** in any order; **gagner dans le ~** (aux courses) to win with a combination forecast; **5** (trouble) disorder; **~s sociaux** social disorder; **~s mentaux** mental disorders

désorganisation /dezɔrganizasjɔ̃/ *nf* (action) disruption; (résultat) disorganization

désorganisé, **~e** /dezɔrganize/ *adj* disorganized

désorienter /dezɔrjɑ̃te/ [1] *vtr* **1** (déconcerter) to confuse, to bewilder; **2** (faire perdre le sens de l'orientation) to disorientate[GB]

désormais /dezɔrmɛ/ *adv* (au présent) from now on, henceforth; (au passé) from then on, henceforth

désosser /dezɔse/ [1] *vtr* Culin to bone

despote /dɛspɔt/ *nm* despot

despotique /dɛspɔtik/ *adj* despotic

desquelles ▸ **lequel**

desquels ▸ **lequel**

DESS /deɛsɛs/ *nm* (*abbr* = **diplôme d'études supérieures spécialisées**) postgraduate degree taken after Master's

dessaisir /desezir/ [3]
A *vtr* **1** (priver) to relieve sb of sth [*responsabilité*]; **~ un juge d'un dossier** to take a judge off a case; **~ un tribunal d'une affaire** Jur to remove a case from a court; **2** (déposséder) **~ qn de** to divest sb of [*bien*]
B **se dessaisir** *vpr* **se ~ de** to relinquish

dessaler /desale/ [1]
A *vtr* **1** ○(initier) to teach [sb] the ways of the world; **2** (extraire le sel de) to desalinate [*eau de mer*]; to desalt [*mets*]
B *vi* **1** Culin to desalt; **2** ○Naut to capsize

C se dessaler° *vpr* to lose one's innocence

dessèchement /desɛʃmɑ̃/ *nm* (état) dryness; (processus) drying out

dessécher /deseʃe/ [14]

A *vtr* ① (déshydrater) to dry [sth] out; **le soleil dessèche la peau** the sun makes your skin dry; **arbre desséché** withered tree; ② (rendre insensible) to harden [*personne, cœur*]; to deaden [*imagination*]

B se dessécher *vpr* ① (se déshydrater) [*cheveux, lèvres*] to become dry; [*végétation*] to wither; [*sol*] to dry out; ② fig (maigrir) [*personne*] to wither

dessein /desɛ̃/ *nm* (projet) design; (intention) intention; **grand ~ grand** design; **noirs ~s** liter dark designs; **avoir/former le ~ de faire** to have/form the intention of doing; **à ~** deliberately, by design

desseller /desele/ [1] *vtr* to unsaddle

desserré, ~e /deseRe/ *adj* loose

desserrement /desɛRmɑ̃/ *nm* ① Tech loosening; ② Écon relaxation; **~ du crédit** relaxation of credit

desserrer /deseRe/ [1]

A *vtr* ① lit to loosen [*col, cravate, vis*]; to release [*frein*]; to undo [*nœud*]; ② fig to relax [*étau, étreinte, crédit*]; **~ les rangs** to break ranks

B se desserrer *vpr* ① [*ceinture, col, cravate*] to come loose; [*écrou, vis*] to work loose; [*nœud*] to come undone; ② [*étau, étreinte*] to slacken

(Idiome) **il n'a pas desserré les dents** he never once opened his mouth

dessert /desɛR/ *nm* ① (plat) dessert; **en** or **comme ~** for dessert; ② (moment) **au ~** at dessert

desserte /desɛRt/ *nf* ① (service de transport) service; **~ ferroviaire** rail or train service; ② (fait de desservir une localité) **la ~ aérienne des Antilles** flights to and from the Antilles; **chemin de ~** access road; ③ (meuble) sideboard

desservir /desɛRviR/ [30] *vtr* ① (relier) to serve [*ville, village*]; **quartier bien/mal desservi** well-/badly-served district; ② (conduire à) to lead to [*chambre, étage*]; ③ (être au service de) to serve

dessin /desɛ̃/ *nm* ① Art (activité) drawing; **~ au crayon/pinceau** pencil/brush drawing; **faire du ~** to draw; **école/professeur de ~** art school/teacher; ② (résultat) drawing; **faire un ~** to do a drawing; **tu veux que je te fasse un ~?** fig, iron do I have to spell it out for you?; ③ Art, Ind (conception) design; ④ (motif) pattern; ⑤ (organisation) layout; ⑥ (contour) outline; ⑦ (grandes lignes) outline

(Composés) **~ animé** Cin cartoon; **~ industriel** technical drawing

dessinateur, -trice /desinatœR, tRis/ ▸ p. 372 *nm,f* ① Art draughtsman GB, draftsman US; ② Ind **~ (industriel)** draughtsman GB; ③ Art, Ind (concepteur) designer

(Composés) **~ de bande dessinée** Art (strip) cartoonist; **~ humoristique** Presse cartoonist; **~ de presse** illustrator

dessiner /desine/ [1]

A *vtr* ① Art (représenter) to draw; **~ au crayon/à la plume** to draw in pencil/in pen and ink; ② (concevoir) to design [*tissu, décor, timbre*]; to draw up [*plans*]; **~ les grandes lignes de** to outline [*plan, programme*]; ③ (faire ressortir) **robe qui dessine la silhouette** figure-hugging dress

B *vi* Art to draw; **savoir ~** to be able to draw

C se dessiner *vpr* ① (se faire jour) to take shape; ② (apparaître) **se ~ à l'horizon** [*ruines, cavalier*] to appear on the horizon

dessoûler /desule/ [1]

A *vtr* to sober up [*personne*]

B *vi* to sober up; **il n'a pas dessoûlé pendant trois jours** he's been drunk for three days

dessous¹ /dəsu/

A *adv* underneath; **j'ai soulevé le livre, mes clés étaient ~** I lifted the book and my keys were underneath; **quand je vois une échelle, je ne passe jamais ~** when I see a ladder, I never walk under it

B en dessous *loc adj* (inférieur) **la taille/le modèle en ~** the next size down

C en dessous *loc adv* ① (sous quelque chose) underneath; **mets une chemise en ~** put a shirt on underneath; **il habite juste en ~** he lives on the floor below; **va voir à l'étage en ~** go and have a look downstairs;

② (sournoisement) **agir en ~** to act in an underhand way; **regarder qn en ~** to look at sb sidelong

D par en dessous *loc adv* underneath; **passer par en ~** to go underneath; **prendre qch par en ~** to lift sth up from underneath

E en dessous de *loc prép* (sous) below; **en ~ de la fenêtre** below the window; **15 degrés en ~ de zéro** 15 degrees below zero; **les enfants en ~ de 13 ans** children under 13

dessous² /dəsu/

A *nm inv* (de langue, vase) underside; (des bras) inside (part); **le ~ du pied** the sole of the foot; **de ~, du ~** [*drap*] bottom; **l'étagère de** or **du ~** (sous une autre) the shelf below; (la dernière) the bottom shelf; **l'étage du ~** the floor below

B *nmpl* ① (sous-vêtements) underwear **C**; ② (la face cachée) (de scandale, cas, succès) inside story (sg) (de on); **on ignore les ~ de l'affaire** we don't know what's behind this affair

(Idiome) **avoir le ~** to come off worst

dessous-de-bouteille /d(ə)sudbutɛj/ *nm inv* drip mat (for bottle)

dessous-de-plat /d(ə)sudpla/ *nm inv* (en vannerie, en bois) table mat; (à pieds) plate stand; (en métal) trivet

dessous-de-table /d(ə)sudtabl/ *nm inv* (entre particuliers) under-the-counter payment; (pot-de-vin) bribe, backhander° GB

dessous-de-verre /d(ə)sudvɛR/ *nm inv* coaster

dessus¹ /dəsy/

⚠ Lorsque *dessus* est utilisé avec un verbe d'action tel que *marcher, taper, tirer, compter etc* on se reportera au verbe correspondant; de même pour certaines expressions telles que *mettre la main dessus, avoir le nez dessus etc* on se reportera aux entrées **main, nez** etc. Les usages particuliers sont traités dans l'entrée ci-dessous.

adv **passe ~** go over it; **tu vois la pile, le livre doit être ~** you see that pile over there, the book should be on top of it; **un gâteau avec du chocolat ~** a cake with chocolate on top; **le prix est marqué ~** the price is on it; **'ton rapport est fini?'—'non , je travaille** or **suis ~'** 'is your report finished?'—'no, I'm working on it'

dessus² /dəsy/ *nm inv* (de chaussure) upper; (de table, tête, panier) top; **l'étage du ~** the floor above; **le drap de ~** the top sheet

(Idiome) **reprendre le ~** (dans un débat, une lutte) to regain the upper hand; (après une maladie, un chagrin) to get back on one's feet

dessus-de-lit /d(ə)sydli/ *nm inv* bedspread

déstabiliser /destabilize/ [1] *vtr* to unsettle [*personne*]; to destabilize [*situation, pays*]

destin /dɛstɛ̃/ *nm* ① (fatalité) fate; **c'est le ~!** that's life!; ② (existence) destiny

destinataire /dɛstinatɛR/ *nmf* ① Postes (de lettre) addressee; ② (bénéficiaire de crédit, d'aide) beneficiary; (de mandat) payee

destination /dɛstinasjɔ̃/

A *nf* ① gén (destination) **arriver à ~** [*personne*] to reach one's destination; [*lettre, train*] to reach its destination; ② (rôle, fonction) purpose

B à destination de *loc prép* [*avion, bateau, train*] bound for [*lieu*]; **'vol Air France 810 à ~ de Londres'** 'Air France flight 810 to London'

destiné, ~e¹ /dɛstine/

A *pp* ▸ destiner

B *pp adj* ① (prévu) **~ à faire** intended to do, meant to do; ② (promis) **~ à une belle carrière** destined for a successful career

destinée² /dɛstine/ *nf* destiny

destiner /dɛstine/ [1]

A *vtr* ① (concevoir pour) **~ qch à qn** to design sth for sb; **être destiné à faire** [*objet, système*] to be designed or intended to do; ② (réserver) **l'argent destiné à mes enfants** the money intended for my children; **produits destinés à l'exportation** goods (destined) for export; ③ (adresser) **la bombe était destinée à quelqu'un d'autre** the bomb was meant ou intended for somebody else; ④ (vouer) **être destiné à qch/à faire** [*personne*] to be destined for sth/to do; ⑤ (par le destin) **on ne peut pas savoir ce qui nous est destiné** we never know what fate has in store for us

B se destiner *vpr* **elle se destine à une carrière de juriste**

d

she's decided on a legal career

destituer /dɛstitɥe/ [1] vtr to discharge [officier]; to depose [souverain]; ~ qn de ses fonctions to relieve sb of their duties

destitution /dɛstitysjɔ̃/ nf (d'officier) discharge; (d'homme politique) deposition

dé-stresser /destʀese/ [1] vtr to de-stress

destructeur, -trice /dɛstʀyktœʀ, tʀis/
A adj destructive
B nm,f destroyer

destruction /dɛstʀyksjɔ̃/ nf destruction ₵

désuet, -ète /dezɥɛ, ɛt/ adj ① (vieillot) [décor, charme] old-world, quaint; [manière, style] old-fashioned; ② (dépassé) [mot] obsolete; [technique] outmoded

désuétude /desɥetyd/ nf obsolescence; **tomber en ~** to become obsolete

désunion /dezynjɔ̃/ nf ① (de parti) division, dissension; ② (dans la famille, le couple) discord

désunir /dezyniʀ/ [3] vtr (diviser) [dispute] to divide, to break up [famille, groupe]

détachant /detaʃɑ̃/ nm stain remover

détaché, ~e /detaʃe/
A pp ▸ détacher
B pp adj ① (indifférent) detached, unconcerned; ② Admin [professeur, diplomate, militaire] on secondment GB (après n), transferred [jamais épith] (auprès de to)

détachement /detaʃmɑ̃/ nm ① (indifférence) detachment; ② Admin (de fonctionnaire) secondment GB, transfer (auprès de to); ③ Mil (troupe) detachment

détacher /detaʃe/ [1]
A vtr ① (ôter les liens de) to untie [personne, animal, barque, cheveux, paquet] (de from); ② (défaire un lien) to unfasten [ceinture, collier]; to undo [chaussure, bouton]; to untie, to undo [nœud, corde]; **détachez-lui ses menottes** remove his/her handcuffs; ③ (défaire d'un support) [personne] to tear [sth] off [timbre, coupon, chèque]; [vent] to tear [sth] off [affiche]; **détachez selon** ou **suivant le pointillé** tear along the dotted line; ④ (éloigner) ~ qn de to turn ou drive sb away from [personne, famille]; ⑤ (détourner) ~ les yeux ou le regard de qch to take one's eyes off sth; ~ son attention de qch to turn one's attention away from sth; ⑥ (affecter) [administration] to second GB, to transfer [enseignant, diplomate, militaire]; **demander à être détaché en Asie** to ask to be seconded to Asia; ⑦ (faire ressortir) [orateur] to articulate [mot, syllabe]; [musicien] to detach [note]; [imprimeur, designer] to make [sth] stand out [lettre, titre, mot]; ⑧ (enlever les taches de) to remove the stain(s) from [vêtement]
B se détacher vpr ① (se défaire de ses liens) [prisonnier, animal] to break loose (de from); [bateau] to come untied (de from); ② (se défaire) [nœud, lien] to come undone; [se séparer d'un support] [coupon, feuillet] to come out (de of); [papier peint, affiche] to come away (de from), to peel (de off); **les fruits se détachent facilement des branches** the fruit comes off the branches easily; ④ (se désintéresser) se ~ de to turn one's back on [monde]; to grow away from [personne]; ⑤ (ressortir) [motif, titre, objet, silhouette] to stand out (dans in; sur against); ⑥ (s'éloigner) se ~ de [individu, invité] to detach oneself from [groupe]; [coureur, cheval] to pull away from [groupe]; [membre, pays] to break away from [organisation, pays]

détail /detaj/ nm ① (petit élément) detail; **étudier dans les moindres ~s** to study in minute detail; ② (analyse précise) breakdown; **expliquer en ~** to explain in detail; **entrer dans les ~s** to go into detail; **raconter qch en ~** to give a detailed account of sth; **analyse de ~** detailed analysis; ③ Comm retail; **acheter/vendre (qch) au ~** to buy/sell (sth) retail

détaillant, ~e /detajɑ̃, ɑ̃t/ nm,f retailer

détaillé, ~e /detaje/
A pp ▸ détailler
B pp adj [analyse, liste, plan] detailed; [facture] itemized; **très ~** very detailed

détailler /detaje/ [1] vtr ① (exposer) to detail [projet, problème]; ② (regarder) to scrutinize [personne, objet]

détaler○ /detale/ [1] vi ① (lapin) to bolt; ② [personne] to scarper○ GB, to decamp

détartrant, ~e /detaʀtʀɑ̃, ɑ̃t/
A adj descaling

B nm descaler

détartrer /detaʀtʀe/ [1] vtr ① to descale [bouilloire, chaudière]; ② to scale [dents]

détaxe /detaks/ nf (suppression de taxe) tax removal; (remboursement de taxe) tax refund; (ristourne d'exportation) export rebate

détecter /detɛkte/ [1] vtr to detect

détecteur /detɛktœʀ/ nm detector; ~ de mines mine detector

détection /detɛksjɔ̃/ nf detection

détective /detɛktiv/ ▸ p. 372 nm detective

déteindre /detɛ̃dʀ/ [55]
A vtr to fade [tissu]
B vi ① lit (au soleil) to fade; (dans l'eau) to run; ② fig (influer) to rub off (sur on)

dételer /detle/ [19]
A vtr to unharness [cheval]; to unyoke [bœuf]; to unhitch [charrue, wagon]
B ○vi (arrêter de travailler) to knock off○; sans ~ without a break

détendre /detɑ̃dʀ/ [6]
A vtr ① (faire jouer) to release [ressort]; ② (relâcher) to slacken [ressort, corde]; ③ (reposer) to relax [muscle]; to calm [atmosphère, esprit]; ④ (distraire) to entertain [public]
B vi ① (reposer) [pause, thé] to be relaxing; ② (distraire) [comédie] to be entertaining
C se détendre vpr ① (s'étirer) [corde, ressort] to slacken; ② (se relaxer) [personne, muscle] to relax

détendu, ~e /detɑ̃dy/
A pp ▸ détendre
B pp adj (étiré) [ressort, corde] slack
C adj (calme) [personne, ambiance, relation] relaxed

détenir /det(ə)niʀ/ [36] vtr ① (posséder) to keep [objets]; to hold [pouvoir, capital, record]; to possess [armes]; to have [moyen, secret, preuve]; ~ la vérité to possess the truth; ② Jur to detain [criminel, suspect]

détente /detɑ̃t/ nf ① (repos) relaxation; ② Pol détente; ③ Tech (d'arme) trigger; ④ Sport avoir une bonne ~ [joueur de tennis, gardien de but] to have quick reflexes; [athlète] to have a good take-off
⌐Idiome⌐ être dur à la ~○ to be slow on the uptake

détention /detɑ̃sjɔ̃/ nf ① (possession) (d'actions, de drogue, passeport, record) holding; (d'armes, de secret) possession; ② Jur (privation de liberté) detention
⌐Composé⌐ ~ préventive or provisoire Jur custody; placer qn en ~ préventive to remand sb in custody

détenu, ~e /detny/ nm,f prisoner

détergent /detɛʀʒɑ̃/ nm detergent

détérioration /deteʀjɔʀasjɔ̃/ nf ① (dégât) damage (de to); ② (usure) wear and tear (de on); ③ (déclin) deterioration (de in)

détériorer /deteʀjɔʀe/ [1]
A vtr to damage
B se détériorer vpr gén to deteriorate; [denrée] to go bad; [monnaie] to weaken

déterminant, ~e /detɛʀminɑ̃, ɑ̃t/ adj decisive

détermination /detɛʀminasjɔ̃/ nf determination

déterminé, ~e /detɛʀmine/
A pp ▸ déterminer
B pp adj ① (résolu) [personne] determined; ② (causé) determined (par by); ③ (établi) [corrélation] demonstrated (jamais épith); **il est mort dans des circonstances mal ~es** the circumstances in which he died are not yet clear ou established; ④ (donné) [durée, objectif] given

déterminer /detɛʀmine/ [1] vtr ① (établir) to determine [raison, responsabilité]; ② (fixer) to work out [mesures, modalités]; ③ (causer) to determine [attitude, choix]; ④ (décider) ~ qn à faire to make sb decide to do

déterré, ~e /detere/ nm,f avoir une tête or mine de ~ to look like death warmed up

déterrer /detere/ [1] vtr to dig up [plante, os]

détestable /detɛstabl/ adj [caractère, style, temps] appalling; [habitudes] revolting

détester /detɛste/ [1]
A vtr ① (exécrer) to detest, to loathe [personne]; se faire ~ de qn to arouse sb's hatred; ② (ne pas supporter) to hate
B se détester vpr ① (soi-même) to hate oneself; ② (l'un l'autre) to hate each other

détonant, ~**e** /detɔnɑ̃, ɑ̃t/ adj lit, fig explosive

détonateur /detɔnatœR/ nm ① (amorce d'explosif) detonator; ② fig catalyst

détonation /detɔnasjɔ̃/ nf detonation

détoner /detɔne/ [1] vi to go off, to detonate

détonner /detɔne/ [1] vi (jurer) [personne, comportement, meuble] to be out of place (**au milieu de** among)

détordre /detɔRdR/ [6] vtr to untwist [barre de fer]; to unwind [câble]

détour /detuR/ nm ① (trajet) detour; **faire un** ~ **par Oxford** to make a detour via Oxford; **ça vaut le** ~ it's worth the trip; ② (moyen indirect) roundabout means; (dans le langage) circumlocution; **être sans** ~**s** (explication) to be straight and to the point; (personne) to be plain-speaking; **il me l'a dit sans** ~**s** he told me straight; ③ (tournant) bend

détourné, ~**e** /detuRne/
A pp ▸ **détourner**
B pp adj [allusion] oblique; [moyen] indirect; **d'une façon** or **manière** ~**e** in a roundabout way

détournement /detuRnəmɑ̃/ nm ① (de recette, dividendes) misappropriation; ② (d'avion, de navire) hijacking; ③ (de circulation, rivière) diversion

Composés ~ **de fonds** embezzlement, misappropriation of funds; ~ **de mineur** (incitation à la débauche) corruption of a minor

détourner /detuRne/ [1]
A vtr ① (écarter) to divert [attention] (**de** from); ~ **les yeux** or **le regard** or **la tête** to look away (**de** from); ~ **les soupçons sur qn d'autre** to make suspicion fall on sb else; ② (éloigner) ~ **de** to distract [sb] from [objectif]; ③ (modifier le cours de) to divert [rivière, circulation]; ~ **la conversation** to change the subject; ④ (modifier la destination de) to divert [vol, navire, ressources] (**sur, vers** to); ⑤ (à des fins criminelles) to hijack [avion, navire]; to misappropriate, to embezzle [fonds]
B se détourner vpr ① (renoncer) se ~ de to turn away from [client, ami]; ② (tourner la tête) to look away

détracteur, **-trice** /detRaktœR, tRis/ nm,f detractor

détraqué, ~**e** /detRake/
A pp ▸ **détraquer**
B pp adj ① [mécanisme, moteur] broken down, on the blink○; [organisation, système] broken down; [temps] unsettled; ② ○**être** ~ or **avoir l'estomac** ~ to have an upset stomach
C ○ nm,f deranged person

détraquer /detRake/ [1]
A vtr ① [personne] to bust○ [mécanisme, montre]; [poussière, rouille, humidité] to make [sth] go wrong [mécanisme, montre]; ② ○ [médicament, alcool] to upset [estomac]; to damage [santé]
B se détraquer vpr [mécanisme, moteur] to break down, to go on the blink○; [montre, horloge] to go wrong; [temps] to break

détremper /detRɑ̃pe/ [1] vtr (imprégner) to saturate [sol]; to soak [vêtement]; **le terrain est détrempé** the ground is waterlogged

détresse /detRɛs/ nf distress; **dans la** ~ in distress; **lancer un appel de** ~ to send out a distress call; **en** ~ [navire, avion] in distress; [entreprise, train] in difficulties

détriment : **au détriment de** /odetRimɑ̃də/ loc prép to the detriment of

détritus /detRity(s)/ nmpl (ordures) refuse ₵, rubbish GB ₵, garbage US ₵

détroit /detRwa/ nm Géog straits (pl); **le** ~ **de Gibraltar** the Straits of Gibraltar

détromper /detRɔ̃pe/ [1]
A vtr to set [sb] straight
B se détromper vpr **si tu crois qu'il va nous attendre, détrompe-toi!** if you think he's going to wait for us, you'd better think again!

détrôner /detRone/ [1] vtr lit, fig to dethrone

détrousser /detRuse/ [1] vtr to rob

détruire /detRɥiR/ [69]
A vtr lit, fig to destroy
B se détruire vpr ① (soi-même) to destroy oneself; ② (l'un l'autre) to destroy each other

dette /dɛt/ nf debt; ~ **publique/extérieure** Écon national/foreign debt; **avoir 100 euros de** ~**s** to have debts of 100

euros; ~ **de jeu** gambling debt; **être en** ~ **envers qn** lit, fig to be indebted to sb

DEUG /dœg/ nm (abbr = **diplôme d'études universitaires générales**) university diploma taken after two years' study

deuil /dœj/ nm ① (décès) bereavement; **être frappé par un** ~ to be bereaved, to suffer a bereavement; ② (douleur) mourning ₵, grief; ③ (tenue) mourning (clothes); **être/se mettre en** ~ to be in/go into mourning; **prendre/porter le** ~ **de qn** to go into/wear mourning for sb; ④ (période) period of mourning; ⑤ (cortège) funeral procession

Idiome **faire son** ~ **de qch**○ to kiss sth goodbye○

deux /dø/ ▸ p. 398, p. 296, p. 155
A adj inv ① (précisément) two; **prendre qch à** ~ **mains** to take sth with both hands; ~ **fois** twice; **des** ~ **côtés de la rue** on either side ou both sides of the street; **tous les** ~ **jours** every other day, every two days; '~ **m'** (en épelant) 'double m' GB, 'two ms'; **à nous** ~ (je suis à vous) I'm all yours; (parlons sérieusement) let's talk; (à un ennemi) it's just you and me now; ② (quelques) a few, a couple of; **c'est à** ~ **minutes d'ici** it's a couple of ou two minutes from here; **l'arrêt de bus est à** ~ **pas** the bus stop is a stone's throw away; ③ (dans une date) second
B pron **je vais essayer les** ~ I'll try both of them
C nm (chiffre) two; **une fois sur** ~ 50% of the time; **il travaille un week-end sur** ~ he works every other weekend; **faire qch en moins de** ~○ to do sth very quickly ou in two ticks○ GB

Idiomes **faire** ~ **poids,** ~ **mesures** to have double standards; **un tiens vaut mieux que** ~ **tu l'auras** Prov a bird in the hand is worth two in the bush Prov; **en** ~ **temps, trois mouvements** very quickly, in two ticks○ GB; **lui et moi, ça fait** ~ we're two different people; **je n'ai fait ni une ni** ~ I didn't have a second's hesitation

deuxième /døzjɛm/ ▸ p. 398, p. 155 adj second; **dans un** ~ **temps nous étudierons...** subsequently, we will study...; **c'est à prendre au** ~ **degré** it is not to be taken literally

Composé ~ **classe** (soldat) private; (dans les transports) second class, standard class GB

deuxièmement /døzjɛmmɑ̃/ adv secondly, second

deux-points /døpwɛ̃/ nm inv Ling colon

deux-roues /døRu/ nm inv two-wheeled vehicle, two-wheeler

deux-temps /døtɑ̃/ adj, nm inv Tech two-stroke

dévaler /devale/ [1]
A vtr [animal, rocher] to hurtle down [pente]; [personne] to tear down [pente, rue]; ~ **les escaliers** to rush downstairs
B vi **la lave dévale vers le village** the lava is pouring down toward(s) the village

dévaliser /devalize/ [1] vtr ① [voleur] to rob [personne, banque, coffre]; to clean out○ [appartement]; ② [clients] to clean out○ [boutique]

dévalorisation /devalɔRizasjɔ̃/ nf ① (de monnaie, compétence) depreciation; ② (de politique, diplôme) devaluation

dévaloriser /devalɔRize/ [1]
A vtr ① Écon, Fin (diminuer la valeur de) to reduce the value of [monnaie, produit]; ② (diminuer le prestige de) to depreciate [objet]; to belittle [personne]
B se dévaloriser vpr ① (en valeur) to lose value; (en prestige) to lose prestige; ② (se déprécier soi-même) to put oneself down

dévaluation /devalɥasjɔ̃/ nf Écon devaluation

dévaluer /devalɥe/ [1]
A vtr Écon to devalue [monnaie]
B se dévaluer vpr to become devalued

devancer /dəvɑ̃se/ [12] vtr ① (avoir de l'avance sur) to be ahead of, to outstrip [adversaire, concurrent]; ② (précéder) **les pompiers ont devancé la police sur les lieux de l'accident** the fire brigade got to the scene of the accident ahead of ou before the police; ③ (anticiper sur) to anticipate [revendication, désir]; to forestall, to pre-empt [attaque, critiques]; ④ (faire avant la date prévue) ~ **l'appel** to enlist for military service before call-up

devancier, **-ière** /dəvɑ̃sje, ɛR/ nm,f precursor

devant[1] /dəvɑ̃/
A prép ① (en face de) ~ **qn/qch** in front of sb/sth; **le bus est passé** ~ **moi sans s'arrêter** the bus went straight past me without stopping; **regarder/marcher droit** ~ **soi** to look/walk straight ahead; ② (près de) outside; **cela s'est passé**

d

∼ **chez moi** it happened in front of *ou* outside my house; **il attendait** ∼ **la porte** (à l'extérieur) he was waiting outside the door; (à l'intérieur) he was waiting by the door; ③ (en présence de) **il l'a dit** ∼ **moi** he said it in front of me; **tous les hommes sont égaux** ∼ **la loi** all men are equal in the eyes of the law; **je jure** ∼ **Dieu** I swear before God; **cela s'est passé** ∼ **nous/nos yeux** it took place in front of us/before our very eyes; ④ (face à) **fuir** ∼ **le danger** to run away from danger, to flee in the face of danger; **hésiter** ∼ **le danger** to hesitate in the face of danger; **je recule** ∼ **ce genre de responsabilité** I shy away from that kind of responsibility; ∼ **l'inévitable** faced with the inevitable; **l'impuissance des mots** ∼ **le malheur** the inadequacy of language when confronted with misfortune; ⑤ (en avant de) **la voiture** ∼ **nous** the car ahead *ou* in front of us; **il était si fatigué qu'il ne pouvait plus mettre un pied** ∼ **l'autre** he was so tired he could hardly put one foot in front of the other; **elle est passée** ∼ **moi, elle m'est passée** ∼○ (dans une file) she jumped the queue GB *ou* cut in line US and went ahead of me; **laisser passer quelqu'un** ∼ (**soi**) to let somebody go first; ⑥ (de reste) **avoir du temps** ∼ **soi** to have plenty of time; **avoir de l'argent** ∼ **soi** to have some money to spare; **avoir toute la vie** ∼ **soi** to have one's whole life ahead of one

B *adv* ① (en face) **'où est la poste?'—'tu es juste** ∼' 'where's the post office?'—'you're right in front of it'; ② (en tête) **je passe** ∼, **si vous le permettez** (pour montrer le chemin) I'll go ahead of you, if you don't mind; ③ (à l'avant) (dans une salle, un théâtre) at the front; (dans une voiture) in the front

devant² /dəvɑ̃/ *nm* (de vêtement, maison, scène) front; **une chambre sur le** ∼ a room at the front; **de** ∼ [*dents, chambre, porte*] front

⌐Idiome⌐ **prendre les** ∼**s** to take the initiative

devanture /dəvɑ̃tyʀ/ *nf* ① (façade de magasin) front, frontage; ② (vitrine) shop *ou* store US window; ③ (étalage) window-dressing; **en** ∼ in the window

dévastateur, -trice /devastatœʀ, tʀis/ *adj* devastating

dévastation /devastasjɔ̃/ *nf* devastation ℂ, havoc ℂ

dévaster /devaste/ [1] *vtr* ① (détruire) [*armée*] to lay waste to [*pays*]; [*orage, feu*] to destroy [*récoltes*]; ② (saccager) [*cambrioleur*] to wreck [*habitation*]

déveine○ /devɛn/ *nf* rotten luck○, bad luck

développement /devlɔpmɑ̃/ *nm* ① (de faculté, science, pensée, d'organisme) development (**de** of); ② (d'entreprise, économie, de pays) development, expansion (**de** of); **pays en voie de** ∼ developing nation; **l'entreprise a connu un fort** ∼ **dans les années 80** the firm expanded greatly in the eighties; **en plein** ∼ [*pays*] rapidly developing (*épith*); [*industrie*] fast-growing (*épith*); [*ville, université*] rapidly expanding (*épith*); ③ (de produit, technique, stratégie) development; ④ Phot developing; **détail qui est apparu au** ∼ detail which appeared when the picture was developed

⌐Composé⌐ ∼ **durable** sustainable development

développer /devlɔpe/ [1]
A *vtr* ① (faire croître) to develop [*muscle, faculté, pays*]; to expand [*importations, réseau, connaissances*]; ② (amplifier) to develop, to expand [*sujet, chapitre, récit*]; ③ (innover) to develop [*stratégie, politique, modèle*]; ④ Phot to develop [*cliché*]; **donner qch à** ∼ to have *ou* get sth developed

B **se développer** *vpr* [*corps, faculté*] to develop; [*plante*] to grow; [*entreprise, ville, économie*] to grow, to expand; [*mœurs, usage*] to become widespread

développeur, -euse /devəlɔpœʀ, øz/ ▶ p. 372 *nm,f* Ordinat software developer

devenir¹ /dəvniʀ/ [36] *vi* to become; ∼ **réalité** to become a reality; **qu'est-ce que je vais** ∼○?, **que vais-je** ∼? what is to become of me?; **et Paul, qu'est-ce qu'il devient**○ *or* **que devient-il?** and what is Paul up to these days?; **il devient urgent de faire** it has become necessary to do; **la concurrence devient sévère** the competition is getting fierce

devenir² /dəvniʀ/ *nm* (avenir) future

dévergonder: se dévergonder /devɛʀgɔ̃de/ [1] *vpr* to be going to the bad

déversement /devɛʀsəmɑ̃/ *nm* ① (de trop-plein) draining-off, pouring-out; (d'effluents, de pétrole) dumping; ∼ **accidentel** spillage; ② Constr deflection

déverser /devɛʀse/ [1]
A *vtr* ① lit to pour [*liquide*] (**dans** into); to drop [*bombes*] (**sur**

on); to dump [*ordures, sable*] (**dans** into; **sur** on); to discharge [*effluents*] (**dans** into); to disgorge [*foule, touristes*] (**dans** onto); ∼ **du pétrole** (volontairement) to dump oil (**dans** into); (accidentellement) to spill oil (**dans** into); ② fig to pour out [*insultes*]

B **se déverser** *vpr* [*fleuve, rivière*] to flow (**dans** into); [*égout, foule*] to pour (**dans** into)

dévêtir /devɛtiʀ/ [33]
A *vtr* to undress
B **se dévêtir** *vpr* to get undressed

déviation /devjasjɔ̃/ *nf* ① (de circulation, réseau) diversion GB, detour US; ② (altération) departure (**par rapport à** from); ③ (de boussole) deviation; ④ (optique) deflection

dévider /devide/ [1] *vtr* ① (dérouler) to unwind [*fil, bobine*]; ② ○(raconter) to pour out [*histoire, souvenirs*]

dévier /devje/ [2]
A *vtr* to deflect [*ballon, trajectoire*]; to divert [*circulation*]
B *vi* ① [*balle de fusil, ballon*] to deflect; [*véhicule*] to veer off course; ∼ **d'une trajectoire** to veer off course; ② fig ∼ **de** to deviate from, to depart from [*projet, plan*]; ③ [*outil*] to slip; ④ [*conversation*] to drift

devin /dəvɛ̃/ *nm* soothsayer, seer; **je ne suis pas** ∼! I'm not psychic○!

deviner /dəvine/ [1] *vtr* ① (parvenir à connaître) to guess [*secret*]; to foresee, to tell [*avenir*]; ② (soupçonner) to sense [*danger*]; ③ (apercevoir) to make out

devinette /dəvinɛt/ *nf* riddle

devis /d(ə)vi/ *nm inv* estimate, quote; **établir/faire faire un** ∼ to draw up/to ask for an estimate *ou* quote

dévisager /devizaʒe/ [13] *vtr* ∼ **qn** to stare at sb

devise /dəviz/ *nf* ① (monnaie d'un pays) currency; **une** ∼ **forte** a strong *ou* hard currency; ② (monnaie étrangère) (foreign) currency ℂ; **acheter des** ∼**s** to buy foreign currency; ③ (maxime) motto

deviser /dəvize/ [1] *vi* to converse (**de** about)

dévisser /devise/ [1]
A *vtr* to unscrew [*boulon*]
B *vi* (en alpinisme) to fall
C **se dévisser** *vtr* (être amovible) to unscrew

dévitaliser /devitalize/ [1] *vtr* to do root canal work on [*dent*]

dévoiler /devwale/ [1] *vtr* ① lit to unveil [*statue*]; ② fig to reveal [*intentions*] (**à qn** to sb); to uncover [*scandale*]

devoir /dəvwaʀ/ [44]

┌───┐
⚠️ Lorsque *devoir* est utilisé comme auxiliaire pour exprimer une obligation posée comme directive, une recommandation, une hypothèse ou un objectif, il se traduit par *must* suivi de l'infinitif sans *to*: *je dois finir ma traduction aujourd'hui* = I must finish my translation today; *tu dois avoir faim!* = you must be hungry!

Lorsqu'il exprime une obligation imposée par les circonstances extérieures, il se traduit par *to have* suivi de l'infinitif: *je dois me lever tous les matins à sept heures* = I have to get up at seven o'clock every morning.

Les autres sens du verbe auxiliaire, et *devoir* verbe transitif et verbe pronominal, sont présentés ci-dessous.
└───┘

A *v aux* ① (obligation, recommandation, hypothèse) **tu dois te brosser les dents au moins deux fois par jour** you must brush your teeth at least twice a day; **je dois aller travailler** I've got to go to work; **il a dû accepter** (obligation) he had to accept; (hypothèse) he must have accepted; **tu ne dois pas montrer du doigt!** you shouldn't point!; **ces mesures doivent permettre une amélioration du niveau de vie** these measures should allow an improvement in the standard of living; **il doit absolument éviter l'alcool** it's imperative that he avoid alcohol, he really must avoid alcohol; **je dois dire/reconnaître que cela ne m'étonne pas** I have to *ou* I must say/admit I'm not surprised; **elle ne doit pas être fière!** she must be ashamed of herself; **je devais avoir 12 ans à ce moment-là** I must have been 12 at the time; **ils doivent arriver d'une minute à l'autre** they're due to arrive any minute; ② (être dans la nécessité de) **l'entreprise va** ∼ **fermer** the company will have to close; **dois-je prendre un parapluie?** do I need to take an umbrella?; **dussé-je en mourir** liter even if I die for it; **il a cru** ∼ **partir** he felt obliged to leave; ③ (exprime une prévision) **elles devaient en**

parler they were to talk about it; **le contrat doit être signé à 16 h** the contract is to be signed at 4 pm; **à quelle heure doit-il rentrer?** what time should he be home?; **je dois m'absenter prochainement** I'll have to leave shortly; **4** (exprime la fatalité) **ce qui devait arriver arriva** the inevitable happened; **cela devait arriver** it was bound *ou* it had to happen; **nous devons tous mourir un jour** we all have to die some day; **elle devait mourir dans un accident de voiture** she was to die in a car crash

B *vtr* **1** (avoir à payer) to owe [*argent, repas*]; **~ qch à qn** to owe sth to sb, to owe sb sth; **combien vous dois-je?** (pour un service) how much do I owe you?; (pour un achat) how much is it?; **2** (être redevable de) **~ qch à qn** to owe sth to sb, to owe sb sth; **je te dois d'avoir gagné** it's thanks to you that I won; **3** (avoir une obligation morale) **~ qch à qn** to owe sb sth; **il me doit des excuses** he owes me an apology

C **se devoir** *vpr* **1** (avoir une obligation morale) **se ~ à qn/son pays** to have a duty to sb/one's country; **2** (réciproquement) **les époux se doivent fidélité** spouses owe it to each other to be faithful; **3** (par convention) **un homme de son rang se doit d'avoir un chauffeur** a man of his standing has to have a chauffeur

D **comme il se doit** *loc adv* **1** (comme le veut l'usage) **faire qch/agir comme il se doit** to do sth/to act in the correct way; **2** (comme prévu) **comme il se doit, elle est en retard!** as you might expect, she's late!

devoir² /dəvwaʀ/ *nm* (obligation morale) duty; **faire son ~** to do one's duty; **le ~ m'appelle!** duty calls!; **il est de mon ~ de** it's my duty to; Scol (exercice fait en classe) test; (fait à la maison) homework **¢**

(Composé) **~ surveillé** *or* **sur table** Scol written test

dévolu, ~e /devɔly/
A *adj* **1** (échu par droit) devolved (**à** to); **2** (réservé) reserved (**à** for)
B *nm* **jeter son ~ sur** to set one's heart on [*objet*]; to set one's cap at [*personne*]

dévorant, ~e /devɔʀɑ̃, ɑ̃t/ *adj* [*faim*] voracious; [*soif*] raging; [*flamme, passion, amour*] all-consuming

dévorer /devɔʀe/ [1] *vtr* **1** (consommer) to devour [*nourriture, proie, livre*]; **être dévoré par les moustiques** to be eaten alive by mosquitoes; **~ qn de baisers** to smother sb with kisses; **2** (miner) [*obsession, sentiment*] to consume; **3** (consumer) to eat up [*kilomètres*]

dévot, ~e /devo, ɔt/
A *adj* (très pieux) devout
B *nm,f* *pej* sanctimonious person

dévotion /devosjɔ̃/ *nf* **1** (ferveur) devoutness; (culte) devotion (**à** to); **avec ~** devotedly; **2** (adoration) passion

dévoué, ~e /devwe/ *adj* devoted (**à** to)

dévouement /devumɑ̃/ *nm* devotion

dévouer: se dévouer /devwe/ [1] *vpr* **1** (se consacrer) to devote oneself (**à** to); **2** (faire abnégation) to put oneself out (**pour qn/qch** for sb/sth; **pour faire** to do)

dévoyé, ~e /devwaje/ *nm,f* depraved person

dévoyer /devwaje/ [23]
A *vtr* to deprave, to lead [sb] astray [*personne*]
B **se dévoyer** *vpr* to go astray

dextérité /dɛksteʀite/ *nf* (adresse manuelle) dexterity, skill; (adresse de l'esprit) **avec ~** with skill, skilfullyᴳᴮ

diabète /djabɛt/ ▸ p. 195 *nm* diabetes

diabétique /djabetik/ *adj, nmf* diabetic

diable /djɑbl/
A *nm* **1** Mythol, Relig devil; **le Diable** the Devil; **avoir un mal du ~** *or* **de tous les ~s à faire** to have a devil *ou* a hell○ of a job doing; **du ~** [*courage, peur*] terrific; **il fait un froid du ~ or de tous les ~s** it's hellishly cold; **un ~ d'homme** quite a man; **en ~** [*difficile*] diabolically; [*beau*] devastatingly; [*intelligent*] fiendishly; **2** (enfant) **un (petit) ~** a little devil; **3** (individu) **un pauvre ~** a poor devil; **4** (jouet) **~ (en boîte)** jack-in-the-box; **5** Tech (chariot) two-wheeled trolley GB, hand truck US
B *excl* **que ~!** damn it○!; **qui/où ~** who/where on earth; **au ~ l'avarice!** hang the expense!; **au ~ les scrupules!** to hell○ with scruples!

(Idiomes) **habiter au ~** *or* **à tous les ~s** to live miles from anywhere; **qu'il aille au ~!** he can go to the devil!; **que le ~ t'emporte!** to hell with you!; **(que) le ~ m'emporte si je me trompe** I'll eat my hat if I'm wrong; **ce n'est pas le ~!** it's not that difficult!; **ce serait tenter le ~** that would be

asking for it; **avoir le ~ au corps** to be like someone possessed; **tirer le ~ par la queue** to live from hand to mouth

diablement /djɑbləmɑ̃/ *adv* [*courageux, sévère*] terrifically; [*intelligent*] fiendishly; [*beau*] devastatingly

diabolique /djabɔlik/ *adj* **1** Relig diabolic; **2** (malveillant) [*personne, sourire*] demonic; [*machination, idée, ruse*] devilish; **3** (pénible, difficile) [*problème, situation*] diabolical; **4** (extrême) [*précision, habileté*] uncanny

diaboliquement /djabɔlikmɑ̃/ *adv* fiendishly

diabolo /djabɔlo/ *nm* **1** (jouet) diabolo; **2** **~ menthe** mint cordial and lemonade GB *ou* soda US

diacre /djakʀ/ *nm* deacon

diadème /djadɛm/ *nm* **1** (parure) tiara; **2** Hist diadem

diagnostic /djagnɔstik/ *nm* **1** Méd diagnosis; **bon/mauvais ~** correct/wrong diagnosis; **établir** *or* **poser un ~** to make a diagnosis; **avoir un bon ~** to be good at making diagnoses; **2** (évaluation) diagnosis; **~ d'un expert** expert opinion

(Composé) **~ préimplantatoire** pre-implantation genetic diagnosis

diagnostique /djagnɔstik/ *adj* diagnostic

diagnostiquer /djagnɔstike/ [1] *vtr* lit, fig to diagnose

diagonal, ~e¹, mpl -aux /djagɔnal, o/ *adj* diagonal

diagonale² /djagɔnal/ *nf* diagonal; **en ~** diagonally; **lire qch en ~** to skim through sth

diagramme /djagʀam/ *nm* graph

dialecte /djalɛkt/ *nm* dialect

dialectique /djalɛktik/
A *adj* dialectical
B *nf* dialectic

dialogue /djalɔg/ *nm* dialogueᴳᴮ

(Composé) **un ~ de sourds** a dialogueᴳᴮ of the deaf

dialoguer /djalɔge/ [1] *vi* to have talks

dialoguiste /djalɔgist/ ▸ p. 372 *nmf* Cin screenwriter, dialogist

dialyse /djaliz/ *nf* dialysis

diamant /djamɑ̃/ *nm* **1** (pierre précieuse) diamond; **2** (de tête de lecture) stylus

diamantaire /djamɑ̃tɛʀ/ ▸ p. 372 *nm* (tailleur) diamond cutter; (commerçant) diamond merchant

diamétralement /djametʀalmɑ̃/ *adv* diametrically

diamètre /djamɛtʀ/ *nm* diameter

diapason /djapazɔ̃/ *nm* Mus **1** (note) diapason; **2** (instrument) **~ (à branches)** tuning fork

(Idiomes) **se mettre au ~** to fall in step (**de** with); **être au ~** to be in tune

diaphane /djafan/ *adj* liter [*teint*] pallid; [*brume*] hazy; [*tissu*] diaphanous; [*papier*] translucent

diaphragme /djafʀagm/ *nm* diaphragm

diapo○ /djapo/ *nf* (*abbr* = **diapositive**) slide

diaporama /djapɔʀama/ *nm* slide show

diapositive /djapozitiv/ *nf* slide

diarrhée /djaʀe/ *nf* diarrhoea

diatonique /djatɔnik/ *adj* diatonic

diatribe /djatʀib/ *nf* diatribe (**contre** against)

dichotomie /dikɔtɔmi/ *nf* dichotomy

dico○ /diko/ *nm* (*abbr* = **dictionnaire**) dictionary

dictateur /diktatœʀ/ *nm* dictator

dictatorial, ~e, mpl -iaux /diktatɔʀjal, o/ *adj* dictatorial

dictature /diktatyʀ/ *nf* dictatorship

dictée /dikte/ *nf* **1** Scol (exercice) dictation; **2** (action de dicter) **écrire sous la ~ de qn** [*élève, secrétaire*] to take down sb's dictation; (sous la contrainte) to write down what sb dictates

dicter /dikte/ [1] *vtr* **1** (à haute voix) to dictate; **~ qch à qn** to dictate sth to sb; **2** (motiver) to motivate; **le souci d'aider autrui dicte notre action** our action is motivated by the desire to help others; **3** (imposer) to dictate (**à** to)

diction /diksjɔ̃/ *nf* **1** gén diction; **2** Cin, Théât elocution

dictionnaire /diksjɔnɛʀ/ *nm* gén dictionary

(Composé) **~ analogique** ≈ thesaurus

dicton /diktɔ̃/ *nm* saying; **comme le dit le ~** as the saying goes

didacticiel /didaktisjɛl/ nm educational software program

didactique /didaktik/ adj didactic

dièse /djɛz/ adj, nm sharp; **do** ∼ **C** sharp

diesel /djezɛl/ nm **1** (moteur) **(moteur)** ∼ diesel (engine); **2** (véhicule) diesel; **voiture** ∼ diesel car

diète /djɛt/ nf **1** Méd light diet; **2** Hist diet

diététicien, -ienne /djetetisjɛ̃, ɛn/ ▸ p. 372 nm,f dietician

diététique /djetetik/
A adj dietary (épith); **ce n'est pas très** ∼ **de manger du pain avec des pâtes** it's not very healthy to eat bread with pasta
B nf dietetics (+ v sg); **magasin de** ∼ health food shop GB ou store US

dieu, pl ∼**x** /djø/ nm **1** Mythol, Relig god; **le** ∼ **des mers** the god of the sea; **2** (personne talentueuse) **le** ∼ **du tennis** the greatest tennis player

⸤Idiomes⸥ **être beau comme un** ∼ to look like a Greek god; **nager comme un** ∼ to be a superb swimmer; **jurer ses grands** ∼**x que...** to swear to God that...; **être dans le secret des** ∼**x** to be privy to the secrets of those on high

Dieu /djø/ nm Relig God; ∼ **le père** God the Father; **le bon** ∼ the good Lord; **mon** ∼! my God!; **bon** ∼ᵒ**!** for God's sake!; ∼ **merci!** thank God!; ∼ **me pardonne!** God forgive me!; ∼ **vous entende!** may God hear your prayer!; ∼ **soit loué** or **béni!** thanks be to God!; ∼ **m'en garde!** God forbid!; ∼ **ait son âme!** God rest his/her soul; **c'est pas** ∼ **possible**ᵒ**!** good God, it's not possible!; ∼ **sait si je l'avais prévenu!** God knows I warned him!; ∼ **sait pourquoi/ quand!** goodness (only) knows why/when; ∼ **seul le sait** goodness only knows; **si** ∼ **le veut** God willing

⸤Idiomes⸥ **se prendre pour** ∼ **le père** to think one is God Almighty; **chaque jour que** ∼ **fait** day in, day out; **il vaut mieux s'adresser à** ∼ **qu'à ses saints** Prov always go straight to the top; **c'est la maison du bon** ∼ **ici!** it's open house here!

diffamation /difamasjɔ̃/ nf gén, Jur (par écrit) libel; (oralement) slander

diffamatoire /difamatwaʀ/ adj gén, Jur (par écrit) libellousᴳᴮ; (oralement) slanderous; **écrit** ∼ libel

diffamer /difame/ [1] vtr gén, Jur (par écrit) to libel; (oralement) to slander

différé, ∼e /difeʀe/
A pp ▸ différer
B pp adj **1** (remis) postponed; **2** Fin deferred; **3** Radio, TV pre-recorded
C nm recording; **match en** ∼ recording of the match; **en léger** ∼ recorded moments before

différemment /difeʀamɑ̃/ adv differently (de from); **il en va** ∼ **de** or **pour** it's a different matter for

différence /difeʀɑ̃s/ nf **1** (écart) difference; ∼ **d'âge** difference; ∼ **de taille/statut** difference in height/status; ∼ **d'opinion** difference of opinion; **à une** ∼ **près** with one difference; ∼ **de** (distinction) difference; **faire la** ∼ to tell the difference; **à la** ∼ **de** unlike; **à la** ∼ **que, à cette** ∼ **que** with the difference that; **2** (discrimination) differentiation Ȼ; **faire des** ∼**s entre ses enfants** to differentiate between one's children; **4** (spécificité) difference; **le droit à la** ∼ the right to be different; **5** Math difference

différenciation /difeʀɑ̃sjasjɔ̃/ nf differentiation

différencier /difeʀɑ̃sje/ [2]
A vtr **1** (distinguer) to differentiate (de from); **rien ne les différencie** there's no way of telling them apart; **2** (créer une différence) to make [sb/sth] different (de from); **3** (voir une différence) to differentiate between
B se **différencier** vpr **1** (se rendre différent) [personne, organisation] to differentiate oneself (de from); **2** (pouvoir être distingué) to differ (de from); **3** (devenir différent) to become different (de from)

différend /difeʀɑ̃/ nm disagreement (entre between; sur over)

différent, ∼e /difeʀɑ̃, ɑ̃t/ adj **1** (dissemblable) different (de from); **2** (varié) different, various; **pour** ∼**es raisons** for various reasons; **à** ∼**s moments** at various times; **en** ∼**s endroits** in different places

différentiel, -ielle /difeʀɑ̃sjɛl/
A adj (tous contextes) differential

B nm Écon, Tech differential

différer /difeʀe/ [14]
A vtr to postpone [départ, réunion, décision]; to defer [paiement, remboursement]
B vi (être différent) to differ (de from); ∼ **peu** to differ little; ∼ **en ce que** to differ in that

difficile /difisil/ adj **1** (malaisé, pénible) gén difficult; [victoire] hard-won (épith); **le plus** ∼ **reste à faire** the worst is yet to come; **2** (indocile) [personne, caractère] difficult; **être** ∼ **à vivre** to be difficult to live with; **3** (exigeant) fussy (sur about); **est-ce que ce cadeau va lui plaire? elle est si** ∼**!** will she like this present? she's so hard to please!; **faire le** ∼ to be fussy

difficilement /difisilmɑ̃/ adv with difficulty; **je pouvais** ∼ **dire non** I couldn't very well say no; ∼ **supportable** hard to bear

difficulté /difikylte/ nf **1** (peine) difficulty (**à faire** in doing); **aimer la** ∼ to enjoy difficulties; **reconnaître la** ∼ **d'une tâche** to admit that a task is difficult; **avec** ∼ with difficulty; **en** ∼ in difficulties ou trouble; **2** (obstacle) difficulty; **avoir des** ∼**s scolaires** to have problems at school; **sans** ∼**(s)** without any difficulty; **non sans** ∼**s** not without difficulty; ∼**s à** or **pour faire** difficulty (in) doing; **avoir des** ∼**s de logement** to have problems with housing; **3** (objection) **faire des** ∼**s** to raise objections

difforme /difɔʀm/ adj [corps, dos] deformed; [objet] strangely shaped (épith); [arbre] twisted

difformité /difɔʀmite/ nf deformity

diffus, ∼e /dify, yz/ adj [lumière, chaleur] diffuse; [sentiment, impression] vague; [style, exposé] pej diffuse, loose

diffuser /difyze/ [1]
A vtr **1** Radio, TV to broadcast; **diffusé en direct** broadcast live; **diffusé en différé** broadcast; **2** (propager) to spread; ∼ **le signalement de qn** to send out a description of sb; **3** (distribuer) to distribute [article]; **4** (émettre) to diffuse [lumière, chaleur]
B se **diffuser** vpr [nouvelle, information] to spread; [chaleur, lumière] to be diffused

diffuseur /difyzœʀ/ nm (d'ouvrages) distributor

diffusion /difyzjɔ̃/ nf **1** Radio, TV, Cin broadcasting; **la** ∼ **du film** the showing of the film; **2** (de connaissances) dissemination; **3** (distribution) distribution; **4** Presse circulation; **5** Méd, Phys diffusion

digérer /diʒeʀe/ [14] vtr **1** (après un repas) to digest; **bien/ mal** ∼ to have good/bad digestion; **2** (assimiler) to digest [lecture, connaissances]; **3** ᵒ(accepter) to swallow [affront]; to stomach [défaite]; **il a du mal à** ∼ **son échec** he finds it hard to come to terms with his failure

digeste /diʒɛst/ adj easily digestible, easy to digest

digestif, -ive /diʒɛstif, iv/
A adj digestive
B nm (liqueur) liqueur (taken after dinner); (eau-de-vie) brandy

digestion /diʒɛstjɔ̃/ nf digestion

digicode® /diʒikɔd/ nm digital (access) lock

digital, ∼e¹, mpl -aux /diʒital, o/ adj digital

digitale² /diʒital/ nf Bot digitalis; ∼ **pourprée** foxglove

digne /diɲ/ adj **1** (plein de dignité) dignified; **2** (approprié) worthy; (méritant) ∼ **de confiance** or **de foi** trustworthy; ∼ **d'être souligné** noteworthy; ∼ **d'envie** enviable; **4** (à la hauteur de) ∼ **de** worthy of

dignement /diɲmɑ̃/ adv **1** (avec dignité) with dignity; **2** (comme il convient) fittingly

dignitaire /diɲitɛʀ/ nm dignitary

dignité /diɲite/ nf **1** (qualité) dignity; **rendre sa** ∼ **à** to restore dignity to; **avoir sa** ∼ to have one's pride; **2** (fonction) dignity

digramme /digʀam/ nm digraph

digression /digʀesjɔ̃/ nf (s'écartant du sujet) digression (sur about); **faire une** ∼, **faire des** ∼**s** to digress

digue /dig/ nf (au bord de la mer) sea wall; (pour polder) dyke GB, dike US; (autour d'un port) harbourᴳᴮ wall; (barrière morale) barrier

dilapidateur, -trice /dilapidatœʀ, tʀis/ adj, nm,f spendthrift

dilapider /dilapide/ [1] vtr to squander [argent, fortune]

dilatation /dilatasjɔ̃/ nf **1** (de corps, gaz) expansion; **2** (de pupille, vaisseau, d'organe, orifice) dilation

185

dilater ▸ dire

dilater /dilate/ [1]
A vtr (agrandir) to dilate [orifice, pupille, vaisseau]; to distend [estomac]; Phys to expand [corps, gaz]
B se dilater vpr [1] (s'agrandir) [pupille, vaisseau, orifice] to dilate (de with); [estomac] to be distended; [2] Phys [corps, gaz] to expand

dilatoire /dilatwaʀ/ adj [1] (pour gagner du temps) [tactique] delaying; [mesure, réponse, conduite] intended to gain time; [2] Jur dilatory

dilemme /dilɛm/ nm dilemma

dilettante /diletɑ̃t/ nmf gén amateur, dilettante péj; **écrire des romans en ~** to be an amateur novelist

dilettantisme /diletɑ̃tism/ nm gén amateurism; péj dilettantism

diligence /diliʒɑ̃s/ nf [1] (véhicule) stagecoach; [2] (empressement) haste; **faire qch avec ~** to do sth posthaste

diligent, **~e** /diliʒɑ̃, ɑ̃t/ adj diligent

diluant /diɫɥɑ̃/ nm Tech thinner

diluer /diɫɥe/ [1] vtr [1] (diminuer la concentration de) to dilute (avec with; dans in); [2] (rendre plus liquide) to thin [sth] down

dilution /dilysjɔ̃/ nf [1] (pour diminuer la concentration) dilution; (pour liquéfier) thinning down; [2] (solution) solution

diluvien, **-ienne** /dilyvjɛ̃, ɛn/ adj [1] (torrentiel) **pluies diluviennes** torrential rain; [2] (du déluge) diluvian

dimanche /dimɑ̃ʃ/ ▸ p. 545 nm Sunday; **habits or toilette du ~** Sunday best; **peintre du ~** weekend ou amateur painter
⟨Idiome⟩ **ce n'est pas tous les jours ~** not every day is a holiday

dimension /dimɑ̃sjɔ̃/ nf [1] Math, Phys dimension; **object à trois ~s** three-dimensional object; **film en trois ~s** three-D film; [2] (mesure) dimension; [3] (taille, grandeur) size; **de toutes les ~s** of all sizes; **un objet de petite/grande ~** a small/large object; **de ~s standard** standard-size; [4] (aspect, caractère) dimension, aspect; [5] (importance, ampleur) dimensions (pl)

diminué, **~e** /diminɥe/
A pp ▸ diminuer
B pp adj (affaibli) [personne, adversaire] weak

diminuer /diminɥe/ [1]
A vtr [1] (réduire) to reduce [quantité, durée, niveau, frais, risques] (à to; de by); to lower [taux, taxe, salaire]; [2] (modérer) to dampen [enthousiasme, courage]; [3] (rabaisser) [personne] to belittle [exploit, personne]; [fait] **~ les mérites/le talent de qn** to detract from sb's merits/talent; [4] (affaiblir) to weaken [personne]; to sap [forces]; [5] (en tricot) to decrease [mailles]
B vi [1] (se réduire) [facture, chômage, taux, prix] to come ou go down (de by); [pouvoir d'achat] to be reduced; [salaire] to fall; [écart] to close; [réserves, consommation, quantité] to decrease; [croissance, volume, déficit, différence] to decrease; [production, ventes, demande] to fall off; [bougie, bouteille] to go down; **les jours diminuent** the days are getting shorter; [2] (faiblir) [activité, intérêt, attaques, violence] to fall off; [pression, tension] to decrease; [bruit, flamme, orage, rire, rumeurs, colère] to die down; [forces, capacités] to diminish; [courage] to fail; [ardeur] to cool; [température, fièvre] to go down

diminutif, **-ive** /diminytif, iv/
A adj [suffixe] diminutive
B nm (en diminutive; (familier) pet name

diminution /diminysjɔ̃/ nf [1] (réduction) gén (provoquée ou contrôlée) reduction (de in); (constatée) decrease (de in); (de production, d'activités commerciales) fall-off (de in); **être en ~** gén to be decreasing; [production, exportations] to be falling off; **être en ~ de 7%** to be down by 7%; [2] (affaiblissement) diminishing; [3] (en tricot) **commencer les ~s** start decreasing

dinde /dɛ̃d/ nf [1] Zool gén turkey; (femelle) turkey hen; [2] Culin turkey; **~ aux marrons** turkey with chestnuts; [3] ○(femme stupide) (silly) goose○

dindon /dɛ̃dɔ̃/ nm [1] Zool turkey (cock); [2] ○(homme stupide) dope○

dindonneau, pl **~x** /dɛ̃dono/ nm turkey; **un rôti de ~** turkey roast

dîner¹ /dine/ [1] vi [1] (prendre le repas du soir) to have dinner; **~ d'une soupe** to have soup for dinner; [2] (prendre le repas de midi) dial, B, C to have lunch

⟨Idiome⟩ **qui dort dîne** Prov when you're asleep you don't feel hungry

dîner² /dine/ nm [1] (repas du soir) dinner; **l'heure du ~** dinner time; **préparer le ~** to get dinner ready; **le ~ est servi** dinner is ready; **après ~** after dinner; [2] (repas de midi) dial, B, C lunch

dînette /dinɛt/ nf (service miniature) doll's tea set; **jouer à la ~** to play at tea parties

dingo○ /dɛ̃go/
A adj inv crazy○
B nm Zool dingo

dingue○ /dɛ̃g/
A adj [1] (idiot) [personne] crazy○; [2] (fou) [bruit, succès] wild; [prix, vitesse] ridiculous; **c'est ~!** (inadmissible) it's crazy!; (incroyable) it's amazing!; [3] (passionné) **être ~ de qch** to be crazy○ about sth
B nmf [1] (fou) nutcase○; **il est chez les ~s** he's in a loony bin○; [2] (passionné) **être un ~ de musique** to be a music freak○

dinguer⁰ /dɛ̃ge/ [1] vi **envoyer qn ~** (pousser) to send sb flying; [chasser] to send sb packing○

dinosaure /dinozɔʀ/ nm dinosaur

diocésain, **~e** /djɔsezɛ̃, ɛn/ adj, nm,f diocesan

diocèse /djɔsɛz/ nm diocese

diphtérie /difteʀi/ ▸ p. 195 nf Méd diphtheria

diphtongue /diftɔ̃g/ nf diphthong

diplomate /diplɔmat/
A adj diplomatic
B ▸ p. 372 nmf diplomat
C nm Culin dessert of glacé fruits and custard on a sponge base

diplomatie /diplɔmasi/ nf diplomacy

diplomatique /diplɔmatik/ adj diplomatic

diplôme /diplom/ nm [1] Scol certificate, diploma; **il n'a aucun ~** he hasn't got any qualifications; **quels ~s faut-il pour faire?** what qualifications are needed to do?; [2] (d'université, de grande école) degree; (d'autre institution) diploma; **~ d'ingénieur** engineering degree; **~ d'architecte** degree in architecture; [3] (dans l'armée, la police) staff exam; [4] (nécessaire à l'exercice d'une activité) certificate; [5] (épreuves) exam; **passer un ~** to take an exam; [6] (document) certificate

diplômé, **~e** /diplome/
A pp ▸ diplômer
B pp adj **il est ~ de l'université de Lille** he's a graduate of the university of Lille; **elle est ~e en droit** she has a degree in law; **une infirmière ~e** a qualified nurse
C nm,f graduate

diplômer /diplome/ [1] vtr gén to award a diploma to; Univ to award a degree to [étudiant]

dircom○ /diʀkɔm/ ▸ p. 372 nmf Entr director of public relations

dire¹ /diʀ/ [65]
A vtr [1] (faire entendre) to say [mots, prière]; to tell [histoire, blague]; **'entrez' dit-elle** 'come in,' she said; **sans mot ~** without saying a word; **ce n'est pas une chose à ~** you don't say that sort of thing; **~ des bêtises** to talk nonsense; **~ qch à voix basse** to whisper sth; **~ qch entre ses dents** to mutter sth; **ne plus savoir que ~** to be at a loss for words; **j'ai mon mot à ~ là-dessus** I've got something to say about that; **~ ce qu'on a à ~** to say one's piece; [2] (faire savoir) to tell; **~ des mensonges** to tell lies; **~ qch à qn** to tell sb sth; **je veux l'avais bien dit!** I told you so!; **c'est ce qu'on m'a dit** so I've been told; **faire ~ à qn que** to let sb know that; **je me suis laissé ~ que...** I heard that...; **tenez-vous le pour dit!** I don't want to have to tell you again!; **c'est moi qui vous le dis**○ I'm telling you; **permets-moi de te ~ que tu vas le regretter**○! you'll regret this, I can tell you!; **je ne te dis que ça**○ I'll say no more; **c'est pas pour ~, mais**○ I don't want to make a big deal of it, but○...; **à qui le dites-vous**○! don't I know it!; **je ne vous le fais pas ~**○! you don't need to tell me!; **ne pas se le faire ~ deux fois** not to need to be told twice; **dis, tu me crois**○? tell me, do you believe me?; **dis donc, où tu te crois**○? hey! where do you think you are?; **à vous de ~** Jeux your bid; [3] (affirmer) to say (que that); **elle dit pouvoir le faire** she says she can do it; **ne fais pas attention, il ne sait pas ce qu'il dit** don't mind him, he doesn't know what he's talking about; **on dit que...** it is said that...; **on le dit marié** he is said to be married; **j'irai jusqu'à ~ que** I'd go as far as to say that; **c'est le moins qu'on puisse ~**

that's the least one can say; **si l'on peut ~** if one might say so; **si je puis ~** if I may put it like that; **on peut ~ qu'elle a du toupet celle-là!** she's really got a nerve[○]!; **on ne peut pas ~ qu'il se soit fatigué!** he certainly didn't overtax himself; **autant ~ que** you might as well say that, in other words; **si j'ose ~** if I may say so; **ce n'est pas à moi de le ~** it's not for me to say; **cela va sans ~** it goes without saying; **il faut ~ que** one should say that; **c'est (tout) ~!** need I say more?; **cela dit** having said that; **c'est vous qui le dites!** that's what you say!; **disons, demain** let's say tomorrow; **c'est difficile à ~** it's hard to tell; **je sais ce que je dis** I know what I'm talking about; **à vrai ~** actually; **entre nous soit dit** between you and me; **soit dit en passant** incidentally; **c'est ~ si j'ai raison** it just goes to show I'm right; **c'est beaucoup ~** that's going a bit far; **c'est peu ~** that's an understatement; **c'est vite dit** that's easy for you to say; **ce n'est pas dit** I'm not that sure; **c'est plus facile à ~ qu'à faire** it's easier said than done; **il est dit que je ne partirai jamais** I'm destined never to leave; **tu l'as dit**[○]!, **comme tu dis**[○]! you said it[○]!; ④ (formuler) **voilà qui est bien dit!** well said!; **comment ~?** how shall I put it?; **tu ne crois pas si bien ~** you don't know how true that is; **pour ainsi ~** so to speak; **autrement dit** in other words; **lent, pour ne pas ~ ennuyeux** slow, not to say boring; **comme dirait l'autre**[○] as they say; **disons que je suis préoccupé** let's say I'm worried; **un lien disons social** a link which we could call social; ⑤ (indiquer) [loi] to state (**que** that); [appareil de mesure] to show (**que** that); **vouloir ~** to mean; **quelque chose me dit que** something tells me that; **qu'est-ce que ça veut ~ tout ce bruit**[○]**?** what's the meaning of all this noise?; ⑥ (demander) **~ à qn de faire** to tell sb to do; **fais ce qu'on te dit!** do as you're told!; ⑦ (objecter) **qu'avez-vous à ~ à cela?** what have you got to say to that?; **je n'ai rien à ~ no** comment; **il n'y a pas à ~**[○], **elle est belle** you have to admit, she's beautiful; **il n'y a rien à ~**, **tout est en ordre** I have no complaint, everything's fine; **tu n'as rien à ~!** (ne te plains pas) don't complain!; (tais-toi) don't say a word!; ⑧ (penser) to think; **qu'en dites-vous?** what do you think?; **que diriez-vous d'une promenade?** how about a walk?; **on dirait qu'il va pleuvoir** it looks as if it's going to rain; **on dirait un fou** you'd think he was mad; **on dirait du Bach** it sounds like Bach; **~ qu'hier encore il était parmi nous!** it's odd to think (that) he was still with us yesterday!; ⑨ (inspirer) **ça ne me dit rien de faire** I don't feel like doing; **notre nouveau jardinier ne me dit rien (qui vaille)** I don't think much of our new gardener

B se dire vpr ① (penser) to tell oneself (**que** that); **il faut (bien) se ~ que...** one must realize that...; **il faut te ~ que...** you must understand that...; ② (échanger) to exchange [insultes, mots doux]; **se ~ adieu** to say goodbye to each other; ③ (se prétendre) to claim to be; ④ (se déclarer) **il s'est dit favorable à** he says he's in favour^{GB} of; ⑤ (être exprimé) **ça ne se dit pas** you can't say that

C se dire v impers **il ne s'est rien dit d'intéressant** nothing of interest was said

dire² /diʀ/
A nm **au ~ de** according to; **au ~ de tous** by all accounts
B dires nmpl statements; **selon les ~s de** according to

direct /diʀɛkt/
A adj ① (sans intermédiaire) direct; (immédiat) [supérieur] immediate; ② [route, accès] direct; **train ~** through train; **ce train est ~ pour Lille** this train is nonstop to Lille; ③ (franc) direct; ④ (en grammaire) direct
B nm ① Radio, TV live broadcasting **☾**; **en ~ de** live from; ② (en boxe) jab; **~ du gauche** left jab; ③ (train) express (train)

directement /diʀɛktəmɑ̃/ adv ① (sans détour) straight; **je suis venu ~** I came straight here; ② (personnellement) [concerner, affecter] directly; **ça ne dépend pas ~ de lui** it's not entirely up to him; ③ (sans intermédiaire) directly; **~ du producteur au consommateur** straight from the producer to the consumer

directeur, -trice¹ /diʀɛktœʀ, tʀis/
A adj (central) **principe ~** guiding principle; **idée directrice d'un ouvrage** central theme of a book; **les lignes directrices d'une politique** the guidelines of a policy
B ▸ p. 372 nm,f ① (d'école) headmaster/headmistress GB, principal US; (d'établissement privé) principal; ② (d'hôtel, de cinéma) manager/manageress; ③ (administrateur) director; (chef) head (**de** of)

Composés **~ de banque** bank manager; **~ commercial** sales manager; **~ général** managing director US; Admin director general; **~ général adjoint** assistant general manager; **~ de journal** newspaper editor; **~ de prison** prison governor GB, warden US; **~ de la rédaction** Presse managing editor; **~ sportif** (team) manager; **~ d'usine** plant manager

direction /diʀɛksjɔ̃/ nf ① (chemin) direction; **se tromper de ~** to go in the wrong direction; **être** or **aller dans la bonne/mauvaise ~** lit, fig to be heading in the right/wrong direction; **quelle ~ ont-ils prise?** which way did they go?; **il a pris la ~ du nord** he headed north; **dans la ~ de, en ~ de** [aller, regarder] toward(s); **un village dans la ~ de Clermont** a village on the way to Clermont; **demander la ~** to ask the way to; **indiquer la ~ à qn** to tell sb the way; **prenez la ~ Nation** (d'autobus) take the bus going to 'Nation'; (de métro) take the train going to 'Nation'; **la ~ Lille** (route) the Lille road; **train en ~ de Toulouse** Toulouse train; **faire un pas** or **geste en ~ de qn** fig to make an overture to sb; ② (fonction de directeur) (gestion) management; (supervision) supervision; (de journal) editorship; (de parti, mouvement) leadership; **confier la ~ de qch à qn** to put sb in charge of sth; **nommé à la ~ de l'usine** appointed manager of the factory; **assurer la ~ de** (d'entreprise, de service) to manage, to run; (de projet, travaux) to be in charge of; **orchestre sous la ~ de** orchestra conducted by; ③ (personnes) management; ④ (lieu) manager's office; (siège social) head office; ⑤ (service) department; ⑥ (de véhicule) steering; **~ à crémaillère/assistée** rack-and-pinion/power steering

directive /diʀɛktiv/ nf (instruction) directive

directorial, ~e, mpl **-iaux** /diʀɛktɔʀjal, o/ adj managerial

directrice² /diʀɛktʀis/
A adj f ▸ **directeur A**
B nf ① Math directrix; ② (profession) ▸ **directeur B**

dirigeable /diʀiʒabl/ nm dirigible, airship

dirigeant, ~e /diʀiʒɑ̃, ɑ̃t/
A adj [classe] ruling; [rôle] leading
B nm (de pays, parti) leader; (gérant) manager

diriger /diʀiʒe/ [13]
A vtr ① (être responsable de) to be in charge of [personnes]; to run [service, école, journal, parti, pays]; to manage [usine, entreprise, théâtre]; to lead [discussion, débat, enquête]; to direct [opération]; to supervise [recherches, travaux]; **mal ~ une entreprise** to mismanage a business; **il veut tout ~** he wants to be in charge of everything; ② (conduire) to steer [véhicule, navire] (**vers** toward(s)); to pilot [avion] (**vers** toward(s)); **il vous dirigera dans la ville** he'll guide you around the town; ③ (orienter) lit to turn [lumière, lampe, jet, regard] (**vers** toward(s); **sur** on); to point [arme, télescope] (**sur** at); fig to direct [critiques, attaques] (**contre** against); **~ des étudiants dans leurs recherches** to guide students in their research; **~ qn vers un service** to send sb to a department; ④ (expédier) to dispatch [marchandises] (**vers, sur** to); to direct [convoi] (**vers, sur** to); ⑤ (motiver) **la volonté de plaire dirige tous leurs actes** all their actions are motivated by the desire to be liked; ⑥ Mus to conduct; ⑦ Cin, Théât to direct [acteurs]; to manage [troupe]
B **se diriger** vpr ① (aller) **se ~ vers** to make for; **se ~ droit sur** to head ou make straight for; **tu devrais te ~ dans cette voie** fig that's the way to go; ② (s'orienter) **se ~ d'après les étoiles** [navigateur] to sail by the stars; [promeneur] to be guided by the stars; **avoir du mal à se ~ dans le noir** to have difficulty finding one's way in the dark

dirigisme /diʀiʒism/ nm planned economy

discale /diskal/ adj f **hernie ~** slipped disc

discernable /disɛʀnabl/ adj discernible, detectable

discernement /disɛʀnəmɑ̃/ nm judgment; **choisir avec/ sans ~** to be discriminating/undiscriminating in one's choice

discerner /disɛʀne/ [1] vtr ① (par un effort d'attention) to detect [signe, odeur, expression]; to make out [silhouette, bruit]; ② (par un effort de réflexion) to make out [mobiles, intentions]; **~ le vrai du faux** to discriminate between truth and untruth; **~ le bien du mal** to be able to tell right from wrong

disciple /disipl/ nmf ① (partisan) follower; ② (élève) disciple; **les ~s de Jésus** the disciples of Jesus

disciplinaire /disiplinɛʀ/ adj disciplinary

discipline /disiplin/ nf **1** (règle) discipline; **2** (spécialité) discipline; **3** Scol (matière) subject; **4** Sport sport

discipliner /disipline/ [1]
A vtr **1** (faire obéir) to discipline [personne]; **2** (maîtriser) to control [troupes]; to discipline [pensées, passions]; **3** (faire tenir en place) to keep [sth] under control [cheveux]
B se discipliner vpr to discipline oneself

disco /disko/
A adj inv disco; **soirée** ~ disco night
B nm disco music

discontinu, ~e /diskɔ̃tiny/ adj **1** (intermittent) [effort, mouvement] intermittent; [ligne] broken; **2** Ling, Math discontinuous

discordance /diskɔrdɑ̃s/ nf (d'opinions) conflict; (de couleurs) clash; (de sons) dissonance

discordant, ~e /diskɔrdɑ̃, ɑ̃t/ adj (qui ne s'accordent pas) [couleurs] clashing; (désagréable) [son, instrument] discordant; [voix] strident [opinions, caractères] conflicting

discorde /diskɔrd/ nf discord, dissension

discothèque /diskɔtɛk/ nf (organisme de prêt) music library; (collection de disques) record collection; (boîte de nuit) discotheque

discourir /diskurir/ [26] vi ~ **de** or **sur qch** to hold forth on sth

discours /diskur/ nm inv **1** (exposé) speech (**sur** on); **2** (paroles) talk; **assez de** ~, **des actes!** let's have less talk and more action!; **fais ce que je te dis et pas de** ~! do what I say and no argument!; **tenir de longs** ~ **sur qch** to talk at great length about sth; **3** (propos) views (pl); Pol position; **il tient toujours le même** ~ his views haven't changed; **4** Ling (utilisation de la langue) speech; (énoncé) discourse

discourtois, ~e /diskurtwa, az/ adj discourteous

discrédit /diskredi/ nm disrepute; **jeter le** ~ **sur** to discredit

discréditer /diskredite/ [1]
A vtr to discredit
B se discréditer vpr to discredit oneself (**auprès de qn, aux yeux de qn** in sb's eyes)

discret, -ète /diskrɛ, ɛt/ adj **1** (qu'on remarque peu) [personne] unassuming; [vêtement, couleur] sober; [allusion, charme, maquillage] subtle; [éclairage] subdued; [sourire, signe, surveillance, parfum, bijou] discreet; [lieu] quiet; **2** (qui garde les secrets) discreet (**sur** about); **3** (qui n'est pas curieux) not inquisitive

discrètement /diskrɛtmɑ̃/ adv (sans publicité) [agir] discreetly; (sobrement) [se vêtir] soberly; (sans bruit) quietly

discrétion /diskresjɔ̃/
A nf (réserve) discretion; **dans la plus grande** ~ in the greatest secrecy; **entourer qch de (la plus grande)** ~ to shroud sth in (the greatest) secrecy; **garder la plus grande** ~ **sur qch** to keep sth a closely-guarded secret
B à discrétion loc [vin, pain] unlimited
C à la discrétion de loc at the discretion of

discriminant, ~e /diskriminɑ̃, ɑ̃t/ adj **1** (qui différencie) [caractère, facteur] differential; **2** (discriminatoire) discriminatory

discrimination /diskriminasjɔ̃/ nf (principe) discrimination (**contre, envers, à l'égard de** against)
(Composé) ~ **positive** positive discrimination

discriminatoire /diskriminatwar/ adj discriminatory (**à l'encontre de** against)

discriminer /diskrimine/ [1] vtr liter to discriminate between [choses, personnes]

disculper /diskylpe/ [1]
A vtr to exculpate
B se disculper vpr to vindicate oneself; **se** ~ **auprès de qn** to vindicate oneself in sb's eyes

discussion /diskysjɔ̃/ nf **1** (débat) discussion (**sur** about); **le texte est en** ~ the text is under discussion; **nous sommes en** ~ **avec eux** we're having discussions with them; **relancer la** ~ to revive the debate; **2** (échange de vues) discussion (**sur** about); **avoir une** ~ **avec qn** (conversation) to have a discussion with sb; (dispute) to have an argument with sb; **3** (contestation) argument; **pas de** ~! no argument!

discutable /diskytabl/ adj (prêtant à discussion) [question, proportion] debatable; (critiquable) [manière, choix] questionable

discuté, ~e /diskyte/
A pp ▸ discuter
B pp adj [problème, programme, proposition] controversial; **question très** ~e vexed question

discuter /diskyte/ [1]
A vtr **1** (examiner) to discuss [question, problème, accord]; to debate [texte, mesure]; **2** (contester) to question
B discuter de vtr ind to discuss [projet, prix]
C vi **1** (converser) to talk (**avec qn** to sb); **2** (protester) to argue; **on ne discute pas!** no arguing!; **il a dit trois heures et il n'y a pas à** ~ he said three o'clock and that's all there is to it
D se discuter vpr ça se discute that's debatable

disette /dizɛt/ nf (famine) famine, food shortage

diseur, -euse /dizœr, øz/ nm,f ~ **de bonne aventure** fortune-teller

disgrâce /disgrɑs/ nf (défaveur) disgrace; **tomber en** ~ to fall into disgrace

disgracier /disgrasje/ [2] vtr fml to dismiss [sb] from one's favour^GB

disgracieux, -ieuse /disgrasjø, øz/ adj [visage, enfant] ugly; [bouton, poil] unsightly; [démarche] awkward

disjoindre /diszwɛ̃dr/ [56]
A vtr **1** (écarter) to loosen; **2** (isoler) to separate
B se disjoindre vpr to come loose

disjoncter /diszɔ̃kte/ [1]
A vtr to trip
B vi [circuit] to trip out; fig [système, usine] to grind to a halt

disjoncteur /diszɔ̃ktœr/ nm circuit breaker

dislocation /dislɔkasjɔ̃/ nf (d'empire) dismemberment; (de pacte, groupe) breaking up; Méd ~ **(articulaire)** dislocation (of a joint)

disloquer /dislɔke/ [1]
A vtr **1** (démembrer) to dismember [empire, État]; **2** (déboîter) to dislocate [membre]; **3** (démonter) to break up
B se disloquer vpr **1** (se démembrer) [État, groupe] to break up; **2** (se déboîter) [personne] **se** ~ **l'épaule** to dislocate one's shoulder; **3** (se casser) [navire, mécanisme] to break up

disparaître /disparɛtr/ [73] vi **1** (devenir invisible) to disappear; **disparaissez!** out of my sight!; **le soleil disparaît à l'horizon** the sun is dipping below the horizon; **faire** ~ **tout un gâteau** to gobble up○ a whole cake; **2** (devenir introuvable) [objet, personne] to disappear; (soudainement) to vanish; **des centaines de personnes disparaissent chaque année** hundreds of people go missing every year; **faire** ~ **qch** to remove sth [objet]; **3** (être supprimé) [douleur, odeur] to go; [tache] to come out; [difficulté] to disappear; [craintes] to vanish; [fièvre] to subside; **faire** ~ to get rid of [douleur, pellicules, pauvreté, trouble]; to remove [tache]; to make [sth] extinct [espèce]; **4** euph (mourir) to die; (cesser d'exister) [civilisation] to die out; [espèce] to become extinct; **faire** ~ **qn** euph to get rid of sb; **voir** ~ to witness the end of [civilisation, culture]; **quand j'aurai disparu** when I'm gone

disparate /disparat/ adj [ensemble, mobilier] ill-assorted; [foule] mixed

disparité /disparite/ nf (caractère différent) disparity sout (**de** in); (différence) difference

disparition /disparisjɔ̃/ nf **1** gén disappearance; (d'espèce) extinction; **en voie de** ~ [civilisation, art] dying (épith); [espèce] endangered; **2** euph (mort) death

disparu, ~e /dispary/
A pp ▸ disparaître
B pp adj **1** [personne] (enlevé, présumé mort etc) missing; **porté** ~ Mil missing in action; **être porté** ~ to be reported missing; **2** (perdu) gén lost; [espèce] extinct; **3** euph (mort) dead; **marin** ~ **en mer** sailor lost at sea
C nm,f **1** (personne introuvable) missing person; **2** euph (mort) **les** ~s the dead

dispendieux, -ieuse /dispɑ̃djø, øz/ adj expensive, extravagant

dispense /dispɑ̃s/ nf (exemption) exemption (**de** from); (certificat d'exemption) certificate of exemption; Relig dispensation
(Composé) ~ **d'âge** exemption from statutory age limit

dispenser /dispɑ̃se/ [1]
A vtr **1** (donner) to hand out [largesses] (**à** to); to bestow sout [honneurs, compliments] (**à** on); **2** (exempter) ~ **qn de (faire) qch** to exempt sb from (doing) sth; **3** (épargner) ~ **qn de (faire) qch** to excuse sb from (doing) sth; **cela ne vous**

d

d

dispense pas d'étudier this does not make it any the less necessary for you to study; **se faire ~ d'un cours** to be excused from a lesson; **je vous dispense de (tout) commentaire** I don't need any comment from you

B **se dispenser** *vpr* (se passer de) **se ~ de (faire) qch** to spare oneself (the trouble of doing) sth; **j'ai décidé de me ~ de vos services** I've decided to dispense with your services

disperser /dispɛRse/ [1]
A *vtr* to scatter [*objets, famille*]; to disperse [*foule, fumée*]; to break up [*rassemblement, collection*]; **~ ses efforts** to spread oneself too thin
B **se disperser** *vpr* [*famille, fumée*] to disperse; [*foule, manifestants*] (volontairement) to disperse; (par nécessité) to scatter; [*rassemblement*] to break up

dispersion /dispɛRsjɔ̃/ *nf* (de manifestants, collection, fumée) dispersal; (de famille) scattering; (de tir, troupe) dispersion

disponibilité /disponibilite/
A *nf* **1** (temps libre) availability; **2** Comm (d'un produit) availability; **3** Admin temporary leave of absence; **en ~ on** leave of absence
B **disponibilités** *nfpl* (argent) available funds

disponible /disponibl/ *adj* **1** (libre) available (**pour** for); **2** Comm (à disposition) available (**auprès de** from)

dispos, ~e /dispo, oz/ *adj* (reposé) refreshed; (en bonne forme) in good form; **frais et ~** fresh as a daisy

disposé, ~e /dispoze/
A *pp* ▸ **disposer**
B *pp adj* **1** (agencé) [*meubles, fleurs*] arranged; [*appartement, pièce, jardin*] laid out; **2** (prêt) **~ à** willing to; **3** (favorable) **être bien/mal ~** to be in a good/bad mood; **être bien/mal ~ à l'égard de** *or* **envers qn** to be well-/ill-disposed toward(s) sb

disposer /dispoze/ [1]
A *vtr* (placer) to arrange [*objets*]; to position [*personnes*]
B **disposer de** *vtr ind* **1** (avoir) **~ de** to have; **les machines dont nous disposons** the machines we have at our disposal; **je ne dispose que de quelques minutes pour vous recevoir** I can only spare you a few minutes; **2** (se servir de) **~ de** to use; **3** (partir) **merci, vous pouvez ~** thank you, you may go
C **se disposer** *vpr* **1** (se préparer) **se ~ à faire** to be about to do; **2** (se placer) **se ~ en cercle autour de qn** to form a circle around sb

dispositif /dispozitif/ *nm* **1** (mécanisme) device; (système) system; **2** (ensemble de mesures) operation

disposition /dispozisjɔ̃/
A *nf* **1** (arrangement) arrangement; (d'appartement, de salle) layout; (place) position; **2** (possibilité d'utiliser) **c'est à ta ~** it's at your disposal; **à la ~ du public** for public use; **se tenir à la ~ de qn** to be at sb's disposal (**pour qch** for sth; **pour faire** to do); **je suis à votre entière ~** I am entirely at your disposal; **se mettre à la ~ de la justice** [*témoin*] to make oneself available to the court; **il a été mis à la ~ de la justice** he was remanded in custody; **3** (mesure) measure, step; **j'ai pris mes ~s pour arriver à l'heure** I made arrangements to arrive on time; **4** (tendance) *fml* tendency (**à** to); **5** (clause) clause
B **dispositions** *nfpl* **1** (aptitudes) aptitude; **2** (humeur) **elle n'était pas dans de bonnes ~s ce jour-là** she wasn't in a good mood that day

disproportion /dispRopoRsjɔ̃/ *nf* lack of proportion

disproportionné, ~e /dispRopoRsjone/ *adj* [*effort, demande, réaction*] disproportionate; [*nez, bouche*] disproportionately large; [*bras, jambes, tête*] out of proportion with one's body (*jamais épith*)

dispute /dispyt/ *nf* (querelle) argument (**sur** about); **un sujet de ~** a cause for argument

disputé, ~e /dispyte/ *adj* **1** (objet de lutte) keenly contested (*épith*); **2** (recherché) sought-after (**de** by); **3** (contesté) controversial

disputer /dispyte/ [1]
A *vtr* **1** (participer à) to compete in [*épreuve, tournoi*]; to compete for [*coupe*]; to play [*match*]; to run [*course*]; to take part in [*combat*]; **2** (lutter pour obtenir) **~ qch à qn** to compete with sb for sth [*honneur, prix, titre*]; to contend with sb for sth [*trône, pouvoir*]; **3** ○(réprimander) to tell [sb] off
B **se disputer** *vpr* **1** (se quereller) to argue (**à propos de, sur, au sujet de** about); **nous nous sommes disputés** we had an argument; **se ~ pour qch** to argue over sth; **2** (lutter pour obtenir) to fight over [*héritage, os*]; to contest [*siège*]; to

compete for [*honneur, place*]; to contend for [*trône, titre, pouvoir*]; **3** (avoir lieu) to take place

disquaire /diskɛR/ ▸ p. 372 *nmf* record dealer

disqualifier /diskalifje/ [2]
A *vtr* (exclure d'une compétition) to disqualify; **se faire ~ (par)** to be disqualified (by)
B **se disqualifier** *vpr* to discredit oneself (**en faisant** by doing)

disque /disk/ *nm* **1** Mus record; **passer un ~** to play a record; **change de ~**! *fig* give it a rest *ou* break○!; lit put another record on; **2** Tech disc; **3** ▸ p. 327 Sport discus; **le lancer du ~** the discus; **4** (objet rond) disc; **5** Ordinat disk
(Composés) **~ compact** compact disc; **~ dur** Ordinat hard disk; **~ d'embrayage** Aut clutch disc; **~ laser** laser disc; **~ numérique** digital disk; **~ d'or** gold disc; **~ souple** (de présentation, en cadeau) flexi disc; Ordinat floppy disk; **~ de stationnement** Aut parking disc

disquette /diskɛt/ *nf* diskette, floppy disk; **~ de sauvegarde** back-up disk; **lecteur de ~s** disk drive

dissection /disɛksjɔ̃/ *nf* dissection

dissemblable /disãblabl/ *adj* dissimilar, different

dissémination /diseminasjɔ̃/ *nf* (de germe, virus) spread; (de pollen, troupes) dispersal; (de maisons) scattering; (d'idée) dissemination

disséminé, ~e /disemine/
A *pp* ▸ **disséminer**
B *pp adj* [*maisons, population, entreprises*] scattered

disséminer /disemine/ [1]
A *vtr* to spread [*germe, idée*]; to disperse [*pollen*]; to distribute [*personnes, troupes*]
B **se disséminer** *vpr* [*personnes*] to scatter; [*germe, idée*] to spread

dissension /disãsjɔ̃/ *nf* **1** (discorde) dissension *sout*; **2** (désaccord) disagreement (**au sein de** within)

disséquer /diseke/ [14] *vtr* to dissect

dissertation /disɛRtasjɔ̃/ *nf* Scol, Univ (devoir) essay; **faire une ~** to write an essay

disserter /disɛRte/ [1] *vi* (discourir) to speak (**sur** on)

dissidence /disidãs/ *nf* **1** (opposition) Philos, Relig dissent; Pol dissidence; (insubordination civile) rebellion; **entrer en ~ contre** (contre un régime) to enter into rebellion against; (contre un parti) to break away from; **2** (opposants) **la ~** the dissidents

dissident, ~e /disidã, ãt/
A *adj* **1** Pol [*personne*] dissident; [*groupe*] break-away; **2** Relig [*secte*] dissenting
B *nm,f* **1** Pol dissident; **2** Philos, Relig dissenter

dissimulateur, -trice /disimylatœR, tRis/
A *adj* secretive
B *nm,f* dissembler

dissimulation /disimylasjɔ̃/ *nf* (de sentiment) dissimulation; (d'information) concealment; (caractère) secretiveness

dissimulé, ~e /disimyle/
A *pp* ▸ **dissimuler**
B *pp adj* concealed; **mal ~** ill-concealed; **fierté non ~e** undisguised pride

dissimuler /disimyle/ [1]
A *vtr* to conceal (**qch à qn** sth from sb); **mal ~** to conceal badly
B **se dissimuler** *vpr* [*personne*] (se cacher) to hide; (ne pas vouloir voir) to close one's eyes to

dissipation /disipasjɔ̃/ *nf* **1** (de malentendu) clearing up; **2** (de brouillard, nuages) clearing; **après ~ des brumes matinales** after the early morning mist has cleared; **3** (d'attention) wandering; **4** (d'élève) restlessness

dissipé, ~e /disipe/ *adj* [*élève*] badly-behaved (*épith*); [*vie*] dissipated

dissiper /disipe/ [1]
A *vtr* to dispel [*doute, illusion, fatigue*]; to clear up [*malentendu*]; to disperse [*fumée*]; to distract [*personne*]
B **se dissiper** *vpr* **1** (disparaître) [*menace*] to recede; [*illusion, doute, malaise*] to vanish; [*malentendu*] to be cleared up; [*brume*] to clear; **2** (s'agiter) [*élève*] to behave badly

dissociable /disɔsjabl/ *adj* [*questions, événements*] dissociable; **les deux causes ne sont pas ~s** the two causes can't be separated

dissocier /disɔsje/ [2]
A *vtr* (séparer) to separate (**de** from)

B **se dissocier** *vpr* **se ∼ de** to dissociate oneself from

dissolu, **∼e** /disɔly/ *adj* [*vie*] dissolute; [*mœurs*] loose

dissolution /disɔlysjɔ̃/ *nf* (d'assemblée, organisation, de mariage) dissolution; (de substance) dissolution (**dans** in); (écroulement) (de système politique) disintegration; (de famille) break-up

dissolvant, **∼e** /disɔlvã, ãt/
A *adj* solvent
B *nm* (en cosmétique) nail varnish remover; Chimie solvent

dissonant, **∼e** /disɔnã, ãt/ *adj* (discordant) [*voix, sons*] dissonant; [*couleurs, tons*] clashing, jarring

dissoudre /disudʀ/ [75]
A *vtr* **1** to dissolve [*assemblée, mariage, compagnie*]; to disband [*mouvement*]; **2** Chimie to dissolve [*substance*] (**dans** in); **faire ∼** to dissolve; **3** (briser) to break up [*empire, institutions, alliance*]; to destroy [*cohésion, unité*]
B **se dissoudre** *vpr* **1** [*organisation, parti*] to disband; **2** [*substance*] to dissolve (**dans** in)

dissuader /disɥade/ [1] *vtr* **∼ qn de faire** [*personne*] to dissuade sb from doing; [*publicité, maladie, temps*] to put sb off doing; **∼ l'ennemi** to deter the enemy

dissuasif, -ive /disɥazif, iv/ *adj* **1** (qui dissuade) [*argument, idée*] dissuasive; [*armes, force*] deterrent; **avoir un effet ∼ sur qn** to act as a deterrent to sb; **2** (élevé) prohibitive

dissuasion /disɥazjɔ̃/ *nf* **1** Mil, Pol deterrence; **force de ∼** deterrent force; **2** (action de dissuader) dissuasion

dissymétrie /disimetʀi/ *nf* asymmetry

distance /distãs/ ▸ p. 347 *nf* **1** (intervalle spatial) distance; **Paris est à quelle ∼ de Londres?** how far is Paris from London?; **à quelle ∼ est-ce?** how far is it?; **transporter 100 passagers sur une ∼ de** to transport 100 passengers over a distance of; **j'ai couru sur une ∼ de deux kilomètres** I ran for two kilometres^{GB}; **à une ∼ de 10 kilomètres** 10 kilometres^{GB} away; **les deux frères vivent à 1 000 kilomètres de ∼** the two brothers live 1,000 kilometres^{GB} apart; **être à faible ∼ de** not to be far (away) from; **gardez vos ∼s** Aut keep your distance; **prendre ses ∼s avec** fig to distance oneself from; **tenir qn/qch à ∼** to keep sb/sth at a distance; **tenir** *or* **garder ses ∼s** fig [*supérieur*] to stand aloof; [*inférieur*] to know one's place; **tenir la ∼** [*sportif*] to stay the course; **appel longue ∼** Télécom long-distance call; **à ∼** [*agir, communiquer, observer*] from a distance; [*commande, accès*] remote (*épith*); **se tenir à bonne ∼ de qch** to keep a good distance from sth; **2** (intervalle temporel) gap; **à une semaine de ∼** one week apart; **3** (recul) distance

(Composés) **∼ focale** focal length; **∼ de freinage** braking distance

distancer /distãse/ [12] *vtr* Sport gén to outdistance; (en course à pied, à cheval) to outrun; **il a largement distancé son rival** fig he left his rival standing; **se faire** *or* **se laisser ∼** to get left behind

distancier: se distancier /distãsje/ [2] *vpr* to distance oneself (**de** from)

distant, **∼e** /distã, ãt/ *adj* **1** (éloigné dans l'espace) distant; **un village ∼ de trois kilomètres** a village three kilometres^{GB} away; **∼s de trois kilomètres** three kilometres^{GB} apart; **2** (réservé) [*personne, regard*] distant; [*attitude*] reserved; [*rapports*] cool; **∼ avec/envers** distant with/toward(s); **3** (éloigné dans le temps) **à une époque ∼e de la nôtre** in the distant past; **des événements ∼s de plusieurs années** (entre eux) events that are several years apart; (par rapport à aujourd'hui) events that took place several years ago

distendre /distãdʀ/ [6]
A *vtr* **1** (étirer) to distend [*estomac*]; to stretch [*peau*]; to overstretch [*ressort*]; **2** (relâcher) to weaken [*liens*]
B **se distendre** *vpr* **1** (se relâcher) [*peau, ressort*] to slacken; **2** (s'affaiblir) [*liens*] to cool

distendu, **∼e** /distãdy/
A *pp* ▸ **distendre**
B *pp adj* **1** (étiré) [*estomac*] distended; **2** (relâché) [*peau, ressort, câble*] slack; **3** (affaibli) [*liens, relations*] cool

distillation /distilasjɔ̃/ *nf* distillation

distiller /distile/ [1]
A *vtr* **1** Chimie to distil^{GB} [*fruit, alcool*]; **2** (secréter) to secrete [*suc, poison, résine*]; **3** (répandre) to disclose [sth] little by little [*idée*]
B *vi* Chimie to evaporate (**à** at)

distillerie /distilʀi/ *nf* (usine) distillery; (production) distilling

distinct, **∼e** /distɛ̃, ɛ̃kt/ *adj* **1** (différent) distinct (**de** from); **2** (qui se perçoit nettement) [*forme, son*] distinct; [*voix*] clear; **3** (sans liens) [*société, entreprise*] separate

distinctement /distɛ̃ktəmã/ *adv* clearly

distinctif, -ive /distɛ̃ktif, iv/ *adj* [*signe, caractère*] distinguishing; [*trait*] distinctive

distinction /distɛ̃ksjɔ̃/ *nf* **1** (différence) distinction; **sans ∼** [*agir, récompenser*] without discrimination; [*massacrer, nuire*] indiscriminately; **sans ∼ d'origine ou de religion** irrespective of colour^{GB} or creed; **2** (récompense) honour^{GB}; **remettre/recevoir une ∼** to confer/to be awarded an honour^{GB}; **∼ honorifique** award; **3** (élégance) distinction; **il n'a aucune ∼** he lacks refinement; **avoir de la ∼** to be distinguished; **d'une grande ∼** of great distinction (*épith, après n*)

distingué, **∼e** /distɛ̃ge/
A *pp* ▸ **distinguer**
B *pp adj* **1** (élégant) distinguished; **2** (éminent) distinguished; **3** (en correspondance) **veuillez agréer mes salutations ∼es** (à une personne non nommée) yours faithfully; (à une personne nommée) yours sincerely

distinguer /distɛ̃ge/ [1]
A *vtr* **1** (séparer) to distinguish between [*choses, personnes*]; **∼ A de B** to distinguish A from B; **il est difficile de ∼ les deux jumeaux** it's difficult to tell the twins apart; **2** (par la vue, l'ouïe) (percevoir les différences) to distinguish; (percevoir avec difficulté) to make out; **3** (percevoir intellectuellement) to discern; **je distinguerais trois points** (dans un exposé) I would like to bring out three main points; **4** (différencier) [*détail, trait*] to set [sb] apart [*personnes, animaux*]; to make [sth] different [*objets*] (**de** from); **aucune caractéristique physique ne les distingue** physically, they have no distinguishing features; **5** (r écompenser) [*jury*] to single out [sb] for an honour^{GB} [*personne*]; [*prix*] to be awarded to [*personne, œuvre*]
B *vi* **il faut savoir ∼** you have to be able to tell the difference; **∼ s'il s'agit d'un besoin réel ou d'un caprice** to judge whether it's a question of real need or of a whim
C **se distinguer** *vpr* **1** (différer) **se ∼ de** (par ses qualités) to differ from; (par ses actes) to set oneself apart from; **il vaut mieux éviter de se ∼** it's best not to be conspicuous; **2** (s'illustrer) [*chercheur, sportif, candidat*] to distinguish oneself; **l'auteur se distingue par son originalité** the author is noted for his originality; **3** (être perçu) to be distinguishable; **4** (se faire remarquer) pej to draw attention to oneself

distordre /distɔʀdʀ/ [6]
A *vtr* [*colère, douleur*] to contort; **distordu par** contorted with
B **se distordre** *vpr* [*visage*] to become contorted

distorsion /distɔʀsjɔ̃/ *nf* distortion

distraction /distraksjɔ̃/ *nf* **1** (activité) leisure **℄**, entertainment **℄**; **c'est ma seule ∼** it's my only form of leisure; **cette ville manque de ∼s** there's not much in the way of entertainment in this town; **2** (détente) recreation; **la lecture est un moyen de ∼** reading is a means of relaxation; **j'ai besoin de ∼** I need some form of relaxation; **3** (étourderie) absent-mindedness **℄**; **par ∼** through absent-mindedness; **avec ∼** absent-mindedly

distraire /distreR/ [58]
A *vtr* **1** (divertir) (en amusant) to amuse; (en occupant) to entertain; **cela m'a distrait un moment** (amusé) it kept me amused for a while; **2** (soulager) **∼ qn de** to take sb's mind off [*problème*]; **3** (déconcentrer) to distract [*personne*] (**de** from; **par** by)
B **se distraire** *vpr* **1** (s'amuser) to amuse oneself; (prendre du bon temps) to enjoy oneself; **que fais-tu pour te ∼?** what do you do for entertainment?; **2** (se changer les idées) **j'ai besoin de me ∼** I need to take my mind off things

distrait, **∼e** /distrɛ, ɛt/
A *pp* ▸ **distraire**
B *pp adj* [*personne*] (trait de caractère) absent-minded; (occasionnellement) inattentive; [*élève*] inattentive; [*air, manière*] distracted; [*regard, sourire*] vague; **regarder qn d'un œil ∼** to look vaguely at sb

distraitement /distretmã/ *adv* absent-mindedly; [*écouter*] with half an ear; [*lire*] with half an eye

distrayant, **∼e** /distrejã, ãt/ *adj* entertaining

distribuer /distʀibɥe/ [1] *vtr* ① (donner) to distribute [*prospectus*] (**à** to); to pay out [*dividende*] (**à** to); to hand out [*compliments, poignées de main*] (**à** to); to allocate [*crédits, tâches*] (**à** to); ~ **les cartes** to deal; ~ **le courrier** to deliver the mail; ~ **les récompenses** to give out the awards; ② (vendre) [*personne*] to distribute; [*machine*] to dispense; ③ to supply [*eau, chaleur*]

distributeur, -trice /distʀibytœʀ, tʀis/ ▸ p. 372
A *adj* Comm distributing
B *nm,f* distributor; ~ **exclusif** sole distributor
C *nm* ① (machine automatique) dispenser; (payant) vending machine; ~ **de tickets** ticket machine; ~ **de billets (de banque)** cash dispenser; ② (compagnie du secteur de la distribution) retailing group
(Composés) ~ **automatique de billets**, **DAB** automatic teller machine, ATM

distributif, -ive /distʀibytif, iv/ *adj* distributive

distribution /distʀibysjɔ̃/ *nf* ① (secteur) retailing; **la ~ alimentaire** food retailing; ② (commercialisation) distribution; **se réserver l'exclusivité de la ~** to keep exclusive distribution rights (**de** for); ③ (d'eau, électricité) supply; ④ (fourniture) (d'objets) distribution; (de tâches, rôles) allocation; ⑤ (disposition) distribution; ~ **d'une maison** layout of a house; ⑥ Cin, Théât (choix effectué) casting; (liste) cast
(Composés) ~ **d'actions gratuites** allocation of bonus shares; ~ **automatique** automatic dispensing; ~ **des cartes** deal; ~ **du courrier** postal delivery

dithyrambique /ditiʀɑ̃bik/ *adj* [*discours, article, propos*] ecstatic; [*louange*] extravagant

diurétique /djyʀetik/ *adj, nm* diuretic

diurne /djyʀn/ *adj* [*fleur, animal*] diurnal

divagation /divagasjɔ̃/ *nf* (de fou, malade) ravings (*pl*); (élucubration) rambling ¢

divaguer /divage/ [1] *vi* ① (délirer) [*malade*] to rave; **la fièvre le fait** ~ he's delirious; ② (déraisonner) to ramble; (dire des bêtises) to talk nonsense; ③ Jur [*animal*] to stray

divan /divɑ̃/ *nm* (siège) divan; (de psychanalyste) couch

divergence /divɛʀʒɑ̃s/ *nf* (d'opinions) divergence; (de politique, goûts) difference

diverger /divɛʀʒe/ [13] *vi* ① (être en désaccord) [*idées, intérêts*] to diverge (**de** from); [*lois, goûts*] to differ (**de** from; **sur** on); **les témoignages divergent sur l'heure à laquelle le suspect a été vu** testimonies differ as to the time at which the suspect was seen; ② (se séparer) to diverge

divers, ~e /divɛʀ, ɛʀs/
A *adj* ① (varié, plusieurs) various; **à ~es reprises** on various *ou* several occasions; **les gens les plus ~** all sorts of people; ② (indéfini) [*frais*] miscellaneous; **dépenses ~es** sundries
B *nmpl* (rubrique) miscellaneous
(Composés) ~ **droite** Pol minor right-wing parties; ~ **gauche** Pol minor left-wing parties

diversement /divɛʀsəmɑ̃/ *adv* variously, in different ways; **le film a été ~ accueilli** the film had a mixed reception

diversification /divɛʀsifikasjɔ̃/ *nf* diversification; **une entreprise en voie de ~** a company in the process of diversifying; **une ~ de la clientèle** targeting a wider clientele

diversifier /divɛʀsifje/ [2]
A *vtr* (varier) to vary [*occupations, lectures*]; to widen the range of [*produits, activités*]; to widen [*clientèle*]; to diversify [*investissements*]; **des méthodes diversifiées** varied methods
B **se diversifier** *vpr* [*entreprise*] to diversify; [*produits, activités*] to be diversified

diversion /divɛʀsjɔ̃/ *nf* ① Mil diversion; **une manœuvre de ~** a diversionary move; **une tentative de ~** an attempt at diversion; ② (dittir) (distraction) diversion, distraction

diversité /divɛʀsite/ *nf* (de personnes, paysages) diversity; (de couleurs, produits, cultures) diversity; (de goûts, d'opinions, intérêts) variety

divertir /divɛʀtiʀ/ [3]
A *vtr* (distraire) (en occupant) to entertain; (en amusant) to amuse
B *vi* littér to entertain
C **se divertir** *vpr* (en s'amusant) to amuse oneself; (en prenant du bon temps) to enjoy oneself; **faire qch pour se ~** (en jouant, plaisantant) to do sth for fun; (à cause d'ennuis) to do sth to take one's mind off things

divertissant, ~e /divɛʀtisɑ̃, ɑ̃t/ *adj* (qui fait rire) amusing; (qui occupe) entertaining; (plaisant) enjoyable

divertissement /divɛʀtismɑ̃/ *nm* (action) entertainment ¢; (distraction) recreation; Mus divertimento; Théât divertissement

dividende /dividɑ̃d/ *nm* dividend

divin, ~e /divɛ̃, in/ *adj* divine; **le ~ Enfant** the Holy Child

diviniser /divinize/ [1] *vtr* (tous contextes) to deify

divinité /divinite/ *nf* (être divin) deity; Relig (nature) divinity

diviser /divize/ [1]
A *vtr* ① (désunir) to divide; **être divisé sur** to be divided over; ~ **pour régner** divide and rule; ② Math to divide (**en** into)
B **se diviser** *vpr* ① (se désunir) to become divided (**sur** over); ② (être séparé) to be divided (**en** into); ③ Math to be divisible (**par** by); ④ (se ramifier) [*cellule, branche, fleuve*] to divide; [*route*] to fork

diviseur /divizœʀ/ *nm* divisor

division /divizjɔ̃/ *nf* (tous contextes) division

divisionnaire /divizjonɛʀ/ *adj* **commissaire ~** Admin ≈ Chief Superintendent

divorce /divɔʀs/ *nm* ① Jur divorce (**d'avec** from); **prononcer le ~ entre deux époux** to grant a divorce to a couple; **gagner le ~** to win a divorce suit; **être en instance de ~** to be getting divorced *ou* a divorce; ② fig (rupture) divorce

divorcé, ~e /divɔʀse/ *nm,f* divorcee

divorcer /divɔʀse/ [12] *vi* ① Jur to get divorced; **il a divorcé d'avec** *ou* **de sa femme** he has divorced his wife; **elle veut ~** she wants a divorce; ② fig (rompre) to split (**d'avec, de** from)

divulgation /divylgasjɔ̃/ *nf* disclosure

divulguer /divylge/ [1]
A *vtr* to disclose
B **se divulguer** *vpr* to become known

dix /dis, *but before consonant* di, *before vowel* diz/ ▸ p. 398, p. 296, p. 155 *adj inv, pron* ten
(Idiomes) **ne rien savoir faire de ses ~ doigts** to be useless; **un de perdu, ~ de retrouvés** Prov there's plenty more fish in the sea Prov

dix-huit /dizɥit/ ▸ p. 398, p. 296, p. 155 *adj inv, pron* eighteen

dix-huitième /dizɥitjɛm/ ▸ p. 155, p. 398 *adj* eighteenth

dixième /dizjɛm/ ▸ p. 155, p. 398 *adj* tenth

dix-neuf /diznœf/ ▸ p. 398, p. 296, p. 155 *adj inv, pron* nineteen

dix-neuvième /diznœvjɛm/ ▸ p. 155, p. 398 *adj* nineteenth

dix-sept /dis(s)ɛt/ ▸ p. 398, p. 296, p. 155 *adj inv, pron* seventeen

dix-septième /dis(s)ɛtjɛm/ ▸ p. 155, p. 398 *adj* seventeenth

dizaine /dizɛn/ *nf* ① (nombre) ten; **la colonne des ~s** the tens column; ② (environ dix) about ten; **ça a duré une bonne ~ d'années** it went on for over ten years; **plus d'une ~ de victimes** at least ten casualties; **des ~s de personnes** dozens of people

djihad /dʒiad/ *nm* jihad

dm *written abbr* = **décimètre 1**

DM ▸ p. 34 (*written abbr* = **Deutsche Mark**) DM

DMLA /deɛmɛla/ *nf* (*abbr* = **dégénérescence maculaire liée à l'âge**) age-related macular degeneration

do /do/ *nm inv* Mus (note) C; (en solfiant) doh

docile /dɔsil/ *adj* [*animal, personne, élève*] docile; [*cheveux*] manageable

docilement /dɔsilmɑ̃/ *adv* [*écouter*] obediently; [*sourire, obéir*] meekly

docilité /dɔsilite/ *nf* obedience

dock /dɔk/ *nm* ① (bassin de chargement) dock; ② (entrepôt) warehouse

docte /dɔkt/ *adj* [*réflexions, personne*] learned

docteur /dɔktœʀ/ ▸ p. 590 *nm* ① (en médecine) doctor; **le ~ Lagrange** Doctor Lagrange; ② Univ Doctor; ~ **en droit** Doctor of Law

doctoral, ~e, *mpl* **-aux** /dɔktɔʀal, o/ *adj* (pédant) péj pompous

doctorat /dɔktɔʀa/ *nm* PhD, doctorate (**ès, en** in)

doctrinaire /dɔktRinɛR/ adj [attitude] doctrinaire pej; [ton] sententious; [discussion] doctrinal

doctrinal, ∼e, mpl **-aux** /dɔktRinal, o/ adj [revirement, référence] Relig doctrinal; Pol ideological

doctrine /dɔktRin/ nf doctrine

document /dɔkymɑ̃/ nm **1** (pour information, témoignage) document (**sur** on); **∼ sonore/vidéo** audio/video material **¢**; **avec ∼s à l'appui** with documentary evidence; **l'exposition est un ∼ sur notre époque** the exhibition is a record of our times; **2** (papier officiel) document, paper; **3** Scol **vous n'avez droit à aucun ∼ pour cette épreuve** no books or notes are allowed for this exam

documentaire /dɔkymɑ̃tɛR/
A adj [caractère, intérêt] documentary (épith); [centre] information (épith)
B nm documentary (**sur** on, about)

documentaliste /dɔkymɑ̃talist/ ▸ p. 372 nmf (en entreprise) information officer; Presse, TV researcher; Scol (school) librarian

documentation /dɔkymɑ̃tasjɔ̃/ nf **1** (documents) material (**sur** on); **nous avons toute une ∼ sur la ville** we can provide information about the town; **2** (information) research; **3** (brochures) brochures (pl) (**sur** on); **4** (activité) (en entreprise) information; (dans un journal, à la télévision) research; **centre de ∼** resource centre**GB**; **5** Scol **la ∼** the (school) library; **6** Univ (discipline) studies in librarianship

documenter /dɔkymɑ̃te/ **1**
A vtr **1** (fournir des renseignements à) to provide [sb] with information; **2** (fournir des renseignements pour) to research
B **se documenter** vpr **se ∼ sur qch** to research sth

dodeliner /dɔdline/ **1** vi **il dodelinait de la tête** his head was nodding

dodo /dodo/ nm baby talk **faire ∼** to sleep

dodu, -e /dɔdy/ adj plump

dogmatique /dɔgmatik/ adj dogmatic

dogme /dɔgm/ nm dogma

dogue /dɔg/ nm mastiff

doigt /dwa/ ▸ p. 136 nm (de main, gant) finger; **petit ∼** little finger GB, pinkie US; **lever le ∼** to put one's hand up; **bout des ∼s** fingertips (pl); **du bout des ∼s** lit with one's fingertips; fig reluctantly; **être français jusqu'au bout des ∼s** to be French through and through; **connaître une ville sur le bout des ∼s** to know a city like the back of one's hand; **savoir son vocabulaire sur le bout des ∼s** to know one's vocabulary off pat; **désigner** or **montrer du ∼** lit to point at; fig to point the finger at; **toucher du ∼** (vraiment sentir) to experience at first hand; (atteindre) to come close to touching

(Composé) **∼ de pied** Anat toe

(Idiomes) **se brûler les ∼s** to get one's fingers burned; **être à deux ∼s de qch/de faire** to be a whisker away from sth/ from doing; **filer entre les ∼s** [affaire, argent, voleur] to slip through one's fingers; [temps] to slip away from sb; **ne pas lever le petit ∼** not to lift a finger; **mon petit ∼ me dit que** a little bird tells me that; **se faire taper sur les ∼s** to get one's knuckles rapped

doigté /dwate/ nm **1** (diplomatie) tact; **avoir du ∼** to be tactful; **2** (adresse manuelle) light touch; **avoir du ∼** to have a light touch; **manquer de ∼** to be heavy-handed; **3** Mus fingering

doigtier /dwatje/ nm fingerstall

doléance /dɔleɑ̃s/ nf complaint

dolent, ∼e /dɔlɑ̃, ɑ̃t/ adj [air, personne] doleful; [ville] lifeless

dollar /dɔlaR/ ▸ p. 34 nm dollar

DOM /dɔm/ nm inv (abbr = **département d'outre-mer**) French overseas (department)

domaine /dɔmɛn/ nm **1** (terres) estate; **∼ vinicole** vineyards (pl); **2** (spécialité) field, domain; **dans le ∼ financier** in the field of finance; **3** ○(territoire) **le grenier c'est mon ∼ (réservé)** the attic is my territory; **4** Admin **le Domaine** state(-owned) property

(Composés) **∼ public** public domain; **tomber dans le ∼ public** Jur [œuvres d'art, invention] to be in the public domain; [œuvre littéraire] to be out of copyright; **∼ réservé** Pol, Jur reserved domain

domanial, ∼e, mpl **-iaux** /dɔmanjal, o/ adj [forêt, terrain, biens] state-owned (épith)

dôme /dom/ nm dome; **une tente ∼** a dome tent

domesticité /dɔmɛstisite/ nf **1** (ensemble des domestiques) (household) staff; **2** (condition de domestique) domestic service

domestique /dɔmɛstik/
A adj **1** [soucis, vie, personnel, tâche] domestic; **les travaux ∼s** housework; **les accidents ∼s** accidents in the home; **2** (domestiqué) [animal] domestic; **3** Écon, Ind [marché, consommation] domestic, home
B nmf servant

domestiquer /dɔmɛstike/ **1** vtr to domesticate [animal, espèce]; to harness [atome, marée]

domicile /dɔmisil/
A nm (d'une personne) place of residence, domicile; (d'une société) registered address; **ils ont regagné leur ∼** they went back home; **changer de ∼** to move (house)
B **à domicile** loc adj **travail à ∼** working at ou from home; **donner des soins à ∼** to give home care; **'livraisons à ∼'** 'home deliveries'

domiciliaire /dɔmisiljɛR/ adj Jur **visite ∼** domiciliary visit; **perquisition ∼** house search

domicilié, ∼e /dɔmisilje/ adj **être ∼ à Arras** to live in Arras; Admin to be resident in Arras; **j'habite à Paris, mais je suis ∼e à Rennes** I live in Paris, but my official address is in Rennes

dominance /dɔminɑ̃s/ nf dominance

dominant, ∼e[1] /dɔminɑ̃, ɑ̃t/ adj **1** (principal) [couleur, ton, rôle] dominant; [courant, opinion] prevailing; [trait, idée] main; **2** (au pouvoir) [classe] ruling; **3** Biol [caractère, gène] dominant

dominante[2] /dɔminɑ̃t/ nf **1** (trait) dominant feature; (couleur) main colour**GB**; **2** Mus dominant (note); **3** Univ main subject, major US

dominateur, -trice /dɔminatœR, tRis/
A adj [personne] domineering; [manières, attitude] overbearing; [geste, ton] imperious
B nm,f ruler

domination /dɔminasjɔ̃/ nf domination; **être sous la ∼ de** to be dominated by; **pays sous ∼ étrangère** (influence) country dominated by a foreign power; (autorité) country under foreign rule; **il est sous la ∼ de sa femme** he's completely under his wife's thumb

dominer /dɔmine/ **1**
A vtr **1** (surplomber) [maison, montagne] to dominate [ville, vallée]; (dépasser) [gratte-ciel, sommet] to tower above [quartier, montagnes]; **de là, on domine toute la vallée** from there you get a view of the whole valley; **il est tellement grand qu'il domine tout le monde** he's so tall that he towers over everyone; **2** (s'imposer dans, contre) to dominate [match, sport, débat]; to overshadow [adversaire]; **3** (prévaloir dans) [thème, problème] to dominate [œuvre, débat]; **4** (maîtriser) to master [langue, technique, sujet]; to overcome [peur, timidité]; to control [colère]; **∼ la situation** to be in control of the situation; **5** (avoir la haute main sur) to dominate [marché, secteur]; **6** Pol (gouverner) to rule [pays]
B vi **1** (exercer son pouvoir) [pays, peuple] to rule, to hold sway; **2** (être en tête) [équipe, concurrent] to be in the lead; **3** (prévaloir) [impression, idée] to prevail; [couleur, goût, parfum] to stand out; **c'est la persévérance qui domine chez lui** his chief characteristic is perseverance
C **se dominer** vpr [personne] to control oneself

dominicain, ∼e /dɔminikɛ̃, ɛn/ adj **1** ▸ p. 230, p. 392 Dominican; **2** Relig Dominican

dominical, ∼e, mpl **-aux** /dɔminikal, o/ adj Sunday (épith)

domino /dɔmino/ nm ▸ p. 327 Jeux domino

dommage /dɔmaʒ/ nm **1** (chose regrettable) **c'est très** ou **vraiment ∼** it's a great shame ou pity (**de faire** to do); **2** (dégât) damage **¢**; **3** Jur (préjudice) harm

(Composés) **∼s corporels** personal injury **¢**; **∼s et intérêts** Jur damages; **∼s de guerre** Jur war damage **¢**

dommageable /dɔmaʒabl/ adj harmful (**pour** to)

dommages-intérêts /dɔmaʒɛteRɛ/ nmpl damages; **1 500 euros de ∼** 1,500 euros in damages

domptage /dɔ̃taʒ/ nm taming (**de** of)

dompter /dɔ̃te/ **1** vtr to tame [fauve, nature, eaux]; to bring [sb] to heel [indiscipliné]; to crush, to put down [insurgés, insurrection]; to overcome, to master [orgueil, passion]

dompteur, -euse /dɔ̃tœR, øz/ ▸ p. 372 nm,f tamer

DOM-TOM /dɔmtɔm/ *nmpl* (*abbr* = **départements et ter-**
ritoires d'outre-mer) *French overseas administrative depart-*
ments and territories

don /dɔ̃/ *nm* ① (donation) donation; **faire ~ de** to give (**à** to);
~ de soi self-sacrifice; ② (talent) gift (**de qch** for sth); **avoir**
le ~ de faire to have a talent for doing

(Composé) **~ du sang** blood donation

donataire /dɔnatɛʀ/ *nmf* donee

donateur, -trice /dɔnatœʀ, tʀis/ *nm,f* donor

donation /dɔnasjɔ̃/ *nf* ① (cadeau) donation; ② Jur gift

donc /dɔ̃k/ *conj* ① (indiquant une conséquence) so, therefore;
(dans une déduction logique, un syllogisme) therefore; **il avait une**
réunion, il n'a ~ pas pu venir he had a meeting, so he was
unable to come; **je pense ~ je suis** I think, therefore I
am; ② (marquant la surprise) so; **c'est ~ pour ça qu'il n'est**
pas venu! so that's why he didn't come!; ③ (après interruption, digression) so; **nous disions ~?** so, where were we?; **je**
disais ~ que... as I was saying...; ④ (pour renforcer une affirmation, un ordre, une question) **tais-toi ~!** be quiet, will you?;
entrez ~! do come in!; **mais où est-il ~ passé?** where on
earth has he gone?; **allons ~!** come on!

donjon /dɔ̃ʒɔ̃/ *nm* keep, donjon

don Juan, *pl* **dons Juans** /dɔ̃ʒɥɑ̃/ *nm* **un ~** a Casanova

Don Juan /dɔ̃ʒɥɑ̃/ *npr* ① Littérat Don Juan; ② Mus Don
Giovanni

donne /dɔn/ *nf* ① (aux cartes) deal; **mauvaise** *ou* **fausse ~**
misdeal; ② (rapport de forces) order

donné, ~e¹ /dɔne/

A *pp* ▸ **donner**

B *pp adj* ① (possible) **il n'est pas ~ à tout le monde de faire**
not everyone can do *ou* is capable of doing; **il m'a été ~ de**
travailler avec lui I had the chance to work with him;
② (déterminé) [*quantité, durée, endroit, situation*] given; **à un**
moment ~ gén at one point; (soudain) all of a sudden;
③ (bon marché) cheap

C **étant donné** *loc adj* given

D **étant donné que** *loc conj* given that

donnée² /dɔne/ *nf* ① (élément d'information) fact, element;
nous n'avons aucune ~ sur cette question we have no
information on this issue; ② (élément défini) data (+ *v pl ou*
sg); **les ~s informatiques/statistiques** computer/
statistical data; **en ~s brutes** in raw data; **après correc-**
tion des ~s saisonnières Écon with seasonally adjusted
figures

donner /dɔne/ [1]

A *vtr* ① (gén) **~ qch à qn** to give sth to sb, to give sb sth [*livre,*
adresse, emploi, temps, autorisation, conseil, courage, rhume];
Jeux to deal [*cartes*] (**à** to); **~ pour les œuvres** to give to
charity; **~ l'heure à qn** to tell sb the time; **je lui donne 40**
ans I'd say he/she was 40; **on ne lui donne pas d'âge** you
can't tell how old he/she is; **~ froid/faim à qn** to make sb
feel cold/hungry; **~ à croire** *ou* **penser** *ou* **comprendre**
que... to suggest that...; **~ à qn à penser/croire que...** to
make sb think/believe that...; **donne-moi ton genou que**
j'examine cette blessure let me see your knee so that I
can look at that wound; ② (confier) to give [*objet, tâche*] (**à**
faire to do); **elle donne sa fille à garder à mes parents** she
has my parents look after her daughter; **j'ai donné ma**
voiture à réparer I've taken my car in to be repaired;
③ (présenter) [*salle, cinéma*] to show [*film*]; [*théâtre*] to put on
[*pièce*]; [*troupe*] to give [*spectacle, représentation*]; **qu'est-ce**
qu'on donne au Marignan? Cin what's showing *ou* on at
the Marignan?; Théât what's playing at the Marignan?;
④ (organiser) to give [*dîner, gala*] (**pour qn** for sb); ⑤ (assurer)
to give [*cours, exposé*] (**à, devant** to); ⑥ (considérer) to give
[*personne, œuvre*] (**comme, pour** as); **les sondages le don-**
nent en tête the polls put him in the lead; ⑦ (produire) to
give [*sentiment, impression*]; to show [*ombre, aspect, teinte*]; to
produce, to yield [*fruits, jus*]; to produce [*résultats*]; **leur**
intervention n'a rien donné their intervention didn't have
any effect; ⑧ (manifester) to show [*signes*] (**à** to);
⑨ ○(dénoncer) to inform on [*complice*] (**à** to); ⑩ (entreprendre)
~ l'assaut à qn to attack sb; **~ la charge contre qn** to
charge at sb

B *vi* ① (produire) **le poirier va bien ~ cette année** the pear
tree will produce GB *ou* yield a good crop this year;
② (retentir un son) [*radio*] to be playing; **~ du cor** (à la chasse)
to sound the horn; ③ (heurter) **~ sur** *ou* **contre** [*personne,*
animal, véhicule] to hit, to run into; **~ de la tête** *ou* **du front**

contre qch to hit one's head against sth; **ne plus savoir où**
~ de la tête fig not to know which way to turn; ④ (être
orienté) **~ sur** [*chambre, fenêtre*] to overlook [*mer, rue*]; [*porte*]
to give onto; **~ au nord/sud** [*façade, pièce*] to face *ou* look
north/south; **la cuisine donne dans le salon** the kitchen
leads into the living-room; ⑤ (avoir tendance à) **~ dans** to
tend toward(s); **en ce moment, il donne dans la musique**
baroque at the moment, he's into○ baroque music; ⑥ (se
lancer) **~ dans un piège** to fall into a trap; ⑦ (consacrer)
~ de soi-même *ou* **de sa personne** to give of oneself;
⑧ (attaquer) [*troupe, chars*] to attack, to go into action

C **se donner** *vpr* ① (se livrer) **se ~ à** to devote oneself to
[*travail, cause*]; **se ~ à fond dans qch** to give one's all to
sth; ② (s'octroyer) **se ~ le temps de faire** to give oneself
time to do; **se ~ les moyens de faire** to find the means to
do; **pays qui se donne un nouveau président** country
which is getting a new president; ③ (s'imposer) **se ~ pour**
or **comme but/mission de faire** to make it one's aim/
mission to do; **se ~ pour tâche de faire** to set oneself the
task of doing; ④ (affecter) **se ~ pour intelligent/pacifiste** to
make oneself out to be intelligent/a pacifist; **se ~ de**
grands airs to give oneself airs; ⑤ (échanger) **se ~ des**
coups to exchange blows; **se ~ des baisers** to kiss one
another; **se ~ rendez-vous** to arrange to meet; **se ~ le**
mot to pass the word on

(Idiomes) **donnant donnant: je garde ton chat à Noël, tu**
gardes le mien à Pâques fair's fair: I keep your cat at
Christmas, you keep mine at Easter; **avec lui, c'est don-**
nant donnant he never does anything for nothing; **je te le**
donne en mille○ you'll never guess

donneur, -euse /dɔnœʀ, øz/ *nm,f* ① Méd donor; ② Jeux
dealer; ③ (personne qui aime donner) **les ~s de bons conseils**
people who like to give advice

don Quichotte /dɔ̃kiʃɔt/ *npr* Don Quixote

dont /dɔ̃/ *pron rel*

> ⚠ Lorsque la traduction de *dont* fait intervenir une
> préposition en anglais, deux tournures sont pos-
> sibles: *c'est un enfant dont je suis fier* = he's a child
> I'm proud of; = he's a child of whom I am proud. La
> première traduction est utilisée dans la langue cou-
> rante, parlée ou écrite; la seconde traduction relève de
> la langue soutenue, surtout écrite, et n'est pas tou-
> jours acceptable: *le livre dont tu m'as parlé* = the book
> you told me about.

① (en fonction d'objet indirect) **la jeune fille ~ on nous disait**
qu'elle avait 20 ans the girl who they said was 20 *ou* who
was said to be 20; **Sylvaine est quelqu'un ~ on se**
souvient Sylvaine is somebody (that) you remember; **la**
maladie ~ il souffre the illness which he's suffering from;
② (en fonction de complément d'un adjectif) **des élèves ~ je suis**
satisfait pupils I'm satisfied with, pupils with whom I am
satisfied; **des renseignements ~ nous ne sommes pas**
certains information which we are not sure about; ③ (en
fonction de complément circonstanciel) **une voix ~ elle sait admira-**
blement se servir a voice which she really knows how to
use; **la manière ~ elle s'habille** the way (in which) she
dresses; **la façon ~ il a été traité** the way he has been
treated; **la famille ~ il descend** the family from which he
is descended; ④ (en fonction de complément de nom) **un canapé**
~ les housses sont amovibles a sofa whose covers are
removable; **un concours ~ le lauréat gagnera...** a competition the winner of which will receive...; **une personne**
~ il prétend être l'ami a person whose friend he claims to
be; ⑤ (parmi lesquels) **il y a eu plusieurs victimes ~ mon**
père there were several victims, one of whom was my
father; **l'organisation propose diverses activités ~ l'équi-**
tation, la natation et le tricot the organization offers various activities including horse riding, swimming and
knitting; **des boîtes ~ la plupart sont vides** boxes, most
of which are empty

dopage /dɔpaʒ/ *nm* (de chevaux) doping; (d'athlète) illegal
drug-taking *ou* drug use

dopant /dɔpɑ̃/ *nm* drug

doper /dɔpe/ [1] *vtr* lit to dope [*cheval, sportif*]; fig to boost
[*monnaie, marché*]

dorade /dɔʀad/ *nf* sea bream

doré, ~e /dɔʀe/

A *pp* ▸ **dorer**

B ▸ p. 140 *pp adj* ① (qui rappelle l'or) [*peinture, papier*] gold
(épith); [*bronze*] gold-colouredᴳᴮ; [*cadre, chaise*] gilt (épith);

② (avec de l'or) [*coupole*] gilded; ~ **sur tranche** [*feuille, livre*] gilt-edged (*épith*); ③ (blond cuivré) [*cheveux, lumière*] golden; [*peau*] tanned; [*pain, poulet*] golden brown; ④ (dans la richesse) [*exil*] luxurious; **jeunesse** ~**e** gilded youth
C *nm* gilt

dorénavant /dɔʀenavɑ̃/ *adv* henceforth

dorer /dɔʀe/ [1]
A *vtr* ① (couvrir d'or) to gild [*cadre*]; ~ **qch à l'or fin** to gild sth with gold leaf; ② Culin to glaze [*tourte, pâte*]; ③ (changer la couleur de) [*soleil*] to turn [sth] to gold [*feuillage, blés*]
B *vi* ① Culin [*poulet*] to brown; **faire** ~ **qch** to brown sth; ② liter [*moissons, raisins*] to turn golden
C **se dorer** *vpr* **se** ~ **au soleil** to sunbathe

doreur, -euse /dɔʀœʀ, øz/ ▸ p. 372 *nm,f* gilder

dorique /dɔʀik/ *adj* Doric

dorloter /dɔʀlɔte/ [1] *vtr* to pamper

dormant, -e /dɔʀmɑ̃, ɑ̃t/ *adj* **eaux** ~**es** still waters

dormeur, -euse /dɔʀmœʀ, øz/
A *nm,f* (personne) sleeper; **c'est un gros** ~ he sleeps a lot
B *nm* Zool (tourteau) (edible) crab

dormir /dɔʀmiʀ/ [30] *vi* ① to sleep; **il dort** he's sleeping, he's asleep; ~ **profondément** to sleep soundly; ~ **d'un sommeil léger/lourd** to be in a light/deep sleep; ~ **debout** [*animal*] to sleep standing up; [*personne*] to be asleep on one's feet; fig (être épuisé) to be dead on one's feet; **ça m'empêche de** ~ it keeps me awake; **il n'en dort plus** he's losing sleep over it; ② Fin [*argent*] to lie idle
(Idiomes) **ne** ~ **que d'un œil** to sleep with one eye open; ~ **sur ses deux oreilles**, ~ **tranquille** to rest easy; ~ **comme un loir** *or* **une marmotte** *or* **une souche** *or* **un bienheureux** to sleep like a log; ~ **à poings fermés** to be fast asleep; **la fortune vient en dormant** Prov good luck comes when you're not looking for it

dorsal, mpl -aux /dɔʀsal, o/ *adj* [*douleur, muscle*] back; [*vertèbre, nageoire*] dorsal

dortoir /dɔʀtwaʀ/
A *nm* dormitory
B (-)**dortoir** (in compounds) **ville-/banlieue-**~ dormitory town/suburb

dorure /dɔʀyʀ/ *nf* (revêtement) gilt **C**; (technique) gilding

doryphore /dɔʀifɔʀ/ *nm* Colorado beetle

dos /do/ ▸ p. 136 *nm inv* gén back; (de livre) spine; (de lame) blunt edge; **être sur le** ~ to be (lying) on one's back; **avoir le** ~ **rond** *or* **voûté** to stoop, to have round shoulders; **mal de** ~ backache; **voir qn de** ~ to see sb from behind; **au** ~ **de** (chèque, carte) on the back of; **robe décolletée dans le** ~ dress with a low back; **voyager à** ~ **d'âne** to travel riding on a donkey; **faire qch dans** *or* **derrière le** ~ **de qn** to do sth when sb's back is turned; **ils sont arrivés, sac au** ~ they arrived, with their rucksacks on their backs; **il n'a rien sur le** ~° he's wearing hardly anything; ~ **à** ~ lit back to back; **renvoyer deux parties** ~ **à** ~ fig to refuse to come out in favour^{GB} of either party; **tourner le** ~ **à** (position) to have one's back to; (mouvement) to turn one's back to; fig to turn one's back on; **faire le gros** ~ [*chat*] to arch its back; fig [*personne*] to keep one's head down
(Idiomes) **courber le** ~ to bow and scrape; **mettre qch sur le** ~ **de qch/qn**° to blame sth on sth/sb; **j'ai bon** ~ it's always me; **se mettre qn à** ~° to get on the wrong side of sb

dosage /dozaʒ/ *nm* ① (en chimie, pharmacie) (quantité) amount, proportion; (mesure) measurement; ② (combinaison) mix; (action de mélanger) mixing; ③ fig (contrôle) controlled use; ④ (proportions) proportions (*pl*)

dos-d'âne /dodɑn/ *nm inv* hump; **pont en** ~ humpback bridge

dose /doz/ *nf* ① (quantité) lit, fig dose; **à petites** ~**s** in small doses; **à** ~ **homéopathique** in tiny doses; **avoir une bonne** ~ **de bêtise/d'égoïsme** not to be short on stupidity/selfishness; **forcer la** ~° to go a bit far°; ② (mesure) measure

doser /doze/ [1] *vtr* ① (déterminer la quantité) to measure; (introduire une quantité) to measure out; **dosé à 100 mg** containing 100 mg (**par** per); ② (contrôler) to use [sth] in a controlled way; ~ **ses efforts** to pace oneself

doseur /dozœʀ/ *nm* measuring glass

dossard /dosaʀ/ *nm* number (worn by an athlete)

dossier /dosje/ *nm* ① gén file; ~ **personnel** personal file; **constituer** *or* **établir un** ~ **sur qn/qch** [*policier*] to draw up a

file on sb/sth; [*écolier, étudiant*] to do a project on sb/sth; **faire un** ~ **de demande de prêt** to make an application for a loan; ~ **médical/scolaire** medical/school records (*pl*); ~ **d'inscription** Scol, Univ registration form; **sélection sur** ~ selection by written application; ② Jur (documents) file; (affaire) case; ③ (sujet) **le** ~ **brûlant de la pollution** the controversial problem of pollution; **notre** ~ **sur l'alcoolisme** Presse our (special) feature on alcoholism; ④ (classeur) file, folder; ⑤ (de chaise, fauteuil) back
(Composé) ~ **de presse** press pack

dot /dɔt/ *nf* (de jeune fille, religieuse) dowry

dotation /dɔtasjɔ̃/ *nf* ① (somme allouée) allocation; (matériel) endowment; ② (revenu de chef d'État) salary

doté, -e /dɔte/
A *pp* ▸ **doter**
B *pp adj* **richement** ~ [*fondation*] richly endowed; [*fille*] with a large dowry (*après n*); **pays mal** ~ poor country

doter /dɔte/
A *vtr* ① (accorder une somme à) ~ **qn de qch** to allocate sth to sb; ② (fournir en équipement) ~ **qn/qch de** to equip sb/sth with; ③ fig (accorder) ~ **qn/qch de** to endow sb/sth with; **elle est dotée d'un grand talent** she's endowed with great talent; **la CEE est dotée d'un président** the EEC has a president
B **se doter** *vpr* **se** ~ **de** to acquire [*revenu*]; to create, set up [*service*]

douairière /dwɛʀjɛʀ/ *nf* dowager

douane /dwan/ *nf* ① (service) customs (+ *v sg ou pl*); **passer (à) la** ~ to go through customs; **passer des marchandises en** ~ to clear goods through customs; **marchandises (entreposées) en** ~ bonded goods; ② (taxe) duty; **exempt de** ~ duty-free; **soumis aux droits de** ~ dutiable

douanier, -ière /dwanje, ɛʀ/
A *adj* customs (*épith*)
B ▸ p. 372 *nm* customs officer

doublage /dublaʒ/ *nm* ① Cin dubbing; ② (de revêtement, fil) doubling; ③ (de vêtement, cloison) lining

double /dubl/
A *adj* [*quantité, somme, dose, épaisseur, consonne*] double; **à** ~ **effet** dual *ou* double action (*épith*); **outil à** ~ **usage** dual-purpose tool; **cassette** ~ **durée** double-play cassette; **l'avantage est** ~ the advantage is twofold; **rue à** ~ **sens** two-way street; **valise à** ~ **fond** suitcase with a false bottom; **mouchoirs** ~ **épaisseur** two-ply tissues GB *ou* Kleenex®; ~ **nationalité** dual citizenship, dual nationality; **avoir le don de** ~ **vue** to have second sight; **en** ~ **exemplaire** in duplicate
B *adv* [*compter, voir*] double
C *nm* ① (deux fois plus) double; **c'est le** ~ **de ce que j'ai payé!** that's double *ou* twice what I paid!; **30 est le** ~ **de 15** 30 is twice 15; **leur piscine fait le** ~ **de la nôtre** their swimming-pool is twice as big as ours *ou* is twice the size of ours; ② (exemplaire supplémentaire) (de document) copy; (de personne) double; **avoir un** ~ **des clés** to have a spare set of keys; **prends ce livre, je l'ai en** ~ take this book, I've got two copies of it; ③ Sport (au tennis) doubles (*pl*)

doublé, -e /duble/
A *pp* ▸ **doubler**
B *pp adj* ① [*vêtement*] lined (**de** with); ② Cin [*film*] dubbed; ③ (en plus de) **un imbécile** ~ **d'un lâche** a coward as well as a fool
C *nm* Sport (deux victoires successives) double

double-cliquer /dublklike/ [1] *vi* Ordinat to double-click (**sur** on)

double-crème, pl doubles-crèmes /dubləkʀɛm/ *nm* cream cheese

doublement /dubləmɑ̃/
A *adv* (à double titre) in two ways; **il est** ~ **coupable** he's doubly guilty, he's guilty on two counts
B *nm* (de quantité, chiffres) doubling

double peine /dublpɛn/ *nf*: *deporting of a foreign national from a country, after he/she has served a prison sentence for a crime committed there.*

doubler /duble/ [1]
A *vtr* ① (multiplier par deux) to double [*effectifs, prix, capacité*]; ~ **le pas** to quicken one's pace; ~ **la mise** Jeux to double the stakes; fig to up the stakes; ② (garnir d'une doublure, d'un revêtement) to line [*vêtement, cloison*] (**de** with); ③ (plier en deux) to fold [sth] in two [*papier, couverture*]; to double [*ficelle*]; ④ Cin to dub [*film, acteur*]; ⑤ Cin, Théât (pour

d

remplacement) (dans une scène périlleuse, un plan secondaire) to stand in for [*acteur*]; (pour indisponibilité) to understudy [*acteur*]; **6** (dépasser) to overtake GB, to pass US [*véhicule*]; **'défense de ∼'** 'no overtaking' GB, 'no passing' US; **7** Naut to double [*cap*]; **8** Mus to double; **∼ une partie** to double a part

B vi gén [*quantité, chiffre*] to double, to increase twofold; **∼ de valeur** to double in value

C se doubler vpr **se ∼ de qch** to be coupled with sth

doublure /dublyʀ/ nf **1** (pour un vêtement) lining; **2** Théât understudy; Cin (dans une scène périlleuse) double; (dans un plan secondaire) stand-in

douce ▸ doux

douce-amère ▸ doux-amer

douceâtre /dusɑtʀ/ adj sickly sweet

doucement /dusmɑ̃/ adv **1** (sans brusquer) gén gently; **il marchait ∼ pour ne pas faire craquer le plancher** he walked softly so that the floorboards wouldn't creak; **holà! ∼ avec le vin!** hey! go easy on the wine!; **∼! je n'ai pas dit ça!** hang on a minute! I never said that!; **∼, les enfants!** (calmez-vous) calm down, children!; (faites attention) careful, children!; **ça va ∼, sans plus** things are so-so○; **2** (sans bruit) quietly; **3** (lentement) slowly, quietly

doucereux, -euse /dusʀø, øz/ adj pej [*manières, personne*] smooth; [*paroles*] sugary; [*sourire*] sickly

douceur /dusœʀ/ nf **1** (de matière, tissu, cheveux, peau) softness, smoothness; (de saveur, d'odeur) mildness; (de fruit, vin) mellowness; (de liqueur, d'alcool) smoothness; (de lumière, couleur, musique, son) softness; **2** (de climat, temps, soleil) mildness; **∼ de vivre** relaxed rhythm of life; **3** (de visage, traits, ton, voix, gestes, paroles) gentleness; **employer la ∼ avec** to use the gentle approach with, to be gentle with; **avec ∼** [*parler, agir*] gently; **en ∼** [*conduire, atterrir*] smoothly; [*atterrissage, transition*] smooth; **4** (de relief, paysage) softness; **5** (friandise) sweet GB, candy US

(Idiome) **plus fait ∼ que violence** Prov gentleness works better than violence

douche /duʃ/ nf **1** (pour se laver) shower; **prendre une ∼** to have GB ou take US a shower; **être sous la ∼** to be in the shower; **2** ○(déception) letdown○

(Composé) **∼ écossaise** lit alternating hot and cold shower; fig bucket of cold water

doucher /duʃe/ [1]

A vtr **1** (laver) to give [sb] a shower [*personne*]; **2** ○(calmer) to dampen [*enthousiasme*]; to cool off [*personne*]; **3** ○(mouiller) [*pluie*] to soak [*personne*]; **se faire ∼** to get a soaking

B se doucher vpr to take a shower

douchette /duʃɛt/ nf **1** (dans salle de bains) shower head; **2** ○(pour scanner) hand-held scanner

doudou○ /dudu/ nm baby talk cuddly blanket○, security blanket

doué, ∼e /dwe/ adj **1** (talentueux) gifted, talented (en in, at); **être ∼ pour** to have a gift for [*théâtre, études*]; **être ∼ pour les chiffres** to have a good head for figures; **2** (pourvu) **∼ de** endowed ou gifted with [*qualité*]

douille /duj/ nf **1** (de cartouche) cartridge (case); **2** Électrotech socket

douillet, -ette /dujɛ, ɛt/ adj **1** (sensible) pej [*personne*] oversensitive to pain (*jamais épith*); **2** (confortable) [*existence, appartement*] cosy GB, cozy US

douleur /dulœʀ/ nf **1** ▸ p. 195 (physique) pain; **une ∼ aiguë/sourde** a sharp/dull pain; **médicament contre la ∼** a painkiller; **2** (morale) pain; (causée par un deuil) grief; **accablé de ∼** grief-stricken; **nous avons la ∼ de vous faire part du décès de** it is with great sorrow that we have to inform you of the death of

douloureuse[1] /duluʀøz/

A adj f ▸ douloureux

B ○nf bill

douloureusement /duluʀøzmɑ̃/ adv **1** (avec douleur morale) grievously; **2** (avec douleur physique) painfully

douloureux, -euse[2] /duluʀø, øz/ adj **1** [*sensation, piqûre*] painful; **2** [*dent, tête*] aching; **3** (moralement) [*spectacle, événement*] distressing; [*attente, décision, question*] painful; [*expression, sourire*] sorrowful

doute /dut/

A nm **1** (incertitude) doubt; **laisser qn dans le ∼** to leave sb in a state of uncertainty; **cela est hors de ∼** it's beyond doubt; **jeter le ∼ sur** to cast doubt on; **mettre qch en ∼** to

call sth into question; **être dans le ∼** to be doubtful, to have misgivings (**au sujet de** about); **2** (soupçon) doubt; **avoir des ∼s** to have doubts ou misgivings (**sur, au sujet de** about); **j'ai des ∼s!** I have my doubts!; **il fait peu de ∼ que, il ne fait guère de ∼ que** there's little doubt that; **sa culpabilité ne fait aucun ∼** there's no doubt as to his/her guilt; **3** Philos, Relig doubt

B sans doute loc adv probably; **sans aucun ∼, sans nul ∼** without any doubt

douter /dute/ [1]

A vtr **∼ que** to doubt that ou whether

B douter de vtr ind to have doubts about; **j'en doute!** I have my doubts!; **je n'ai jamais douté de toi** I never doubted you; **à n'en pas ∼** undoubtedly, without a doubt; **elle ne doute de rien**○! iron she's so sure of herself!

C vi Philos, Relig to doubt

D se douter vpr **se ∼ de qch** to suspect sth; **se ∼ que** to suspect that; **je m'en doutais!** I thought so!, I suspected as much!; **je m'en doute!** iron (c'est évident) obviously! iron; **je me doute (bien) qu'il devait être furieux** I can (well) imagine that he was furious; **nous étions loin de nous ∼ que** we didn't have the least idea that; **il aurait dû se ∼ que…** he should have known that…

douteux, -euse /dutø, øz/ adj **1** (peu certain) [*résultat, succès*] uncertain; **il est ∼ qu'il ait pu s'échapper** it is unlikely that he was able to escape; **2** (ambigu) [*sens, réponse*] ambiguous; **3** (sujet à caution) [*honnêteté, renseignements*] dubious; **4** (suspect) [*affaire, individu*] shady; [*hygiène, viande*] dubious; **plaisanterie d'un goût ∼** joke in dubious taste

douve /duv/ nf **1** (fossé) (de château) moat; Agric drainage ditch; **2** (de tonneau) stave

Douvres /duvʀ/ ▸ p. 621 npr Dover

doux, douce /du, dus/ adj **1** (aux sens) [*matière, peau, lumière, voix*] soft; [*vin, cidre*] sweet; [*fromage, piment, tabac*] mild; [*shampooing*] mild; **2** (pas froid) [*climat, temps, saison, température*] mild; **il fait ∼** it's mild; **3** (pas abrupt) [*relief, pente*] gentle; **4** (léger) [*punition*] mild; **5** (gentil) [*personne, animal, regard, geste, visage*] gentle; **6** liter (agréable) [*pensée, souvenir, rêve*] pleasant; [*baisers, caresses*] sweet, gentle; **7** Écol [*technologie, énergie*] environmentally friendly

(Idiomes) **filer ∼**○ to keep a low profile; **se la couler douce**○ to take it easy; **faire qch en douce**○ to do sth on the sly

doux-amer, douce-amère, mpl **∼s**, fpl **douces-amères** /duzamɛʀ, dusamɛʀ/ adj fig [*propos*] bittersweet, barbed

douzaine /duzɛn/ nf **1** (douze) dozen (inv); **deux ∼s d'œufs** two dozen eggs; **à la ∼** by the dozen; **2** (environ douze) about twelve, a dozen or so

douze /duz/ ▸ p. 398, p. 296, p. 155 adj inv, pron gén twelve

douzième /duzjɛm/ ▸ p. 398, p. 155 adj twelfth

doyen, -enne /dwajɛ̃, ɛn/ nmf **1** (en âge) **∼ (d'âge)** oldest person; **2** (en ancienneté) the (most) senior member; **3** Relig, Univ dean

Dr (written abbr = **docteur**) Dr

drachme /dʀakm/ ▸ p. 34 nf drachma

draconien, -ienne /dʀakɔnjɛ̃, ɛn/ adj [*loi, attitude, punition*] draconian; [*régime, traitement*] very strict

dragage /dʀagaʒ/ nm (nettoyage) dredging; (fouille) dragging; **∼ de mines** minesweeping

dragée /dʀaʒe/ nf **1** (bonbon) sugared almond; **2** (pilule) sugar-coated pill; **3** Agric mixed provender

(Idiomes) **la ∼ est amère** it's a bitter pill to swallow; **tenir la ∼ haute à qn** to hold out on sb

dragon /dʀagɔ̃/ nm **1** (animal) dragon; **un ∼ de vertu** fig a dragon of virtue; **2** Mil, Hist dragoon

drague /dʀag/ nf **1** Tech (machine) dredge; (chaland) dredger; **2** (filet de pêche) dragnet

(Composé) **∼ télématique** Minitel dating service

draguer /dʀage/ [1] vtr **1** ○to chat [sb] up○ GB, to come on to○; **2** Tech (pour nettoyer) to dredge; (pour fouiller) to drag; **3** (à la pêche) to catch [sth] with a dragnet; **∼ au chalut** to trawl; **4** Mil to sweep [*mines*]; Naut **l'ancre drague le fond** the ship is dragging its anchor

dragueur, -euse /dʀagœʀ, øz/

A ○nmf **c'est un drôle de ∼**○ he's a terrible flirt

B nm (pêcheur) dredge fisherman; (ouvrier) dredge-man; (chaland) dredger

Les douleurs et les maladies

Où est-ce que ça vous fait mal?

où avez-vous mal?
= where does it hurt?

■ *Pour traduire* avoir mal à, *l'anglais utilise un possessif devant le nom de la partie du corps (alors que le français a un article défini), et un verbe qui peut être* hurt *ou* ache (faire mal). hurt *est toujours possible:*

il a mal à la jambe
= his leg hurts

il a mal aux yeux
= his eyes hurt

sa jambe lui fait mal
= his leg hurts

il a mal aux oreilles
= his ears hurt

il a mal au dos
= his back hurts

■ ache *est utilisé avec les membres, les articulations, la tête, les dents et les oreilles:*

il a mal au bras
= his arm aches

■ *On peut aussi traduire par* have a pain in*:*

il a mal à la jambe
= he has a pain in his leg

■ *Pour quelques parties du corps, l'anglais utilise un composé avec* -ache*:*

avoir mal aux dents
= to have toothache

avoir mal aux oreilles
= to have earache

avoir mal au dos
= to have backache

avoir mal au ventre
= to have stomachache

avoir mal à la tête
= to have a headache (*noter l'article indéfini*)

■ *Attention à:*

il a mal au cœur
= he feels sick

il a mal aux reins
= he has backache

qui n'affectent pas la partie du corps désignée en français.

Les accidents

■ *Là où le français a des formes pronominales (*se faire mal à *etc.) avec l'article défini, l'anglais utilise des verbes transitifs, avec des adjectifs possessifs:*

il s'est cassé la jambe
= he broke his leg

il s'est fait mal au pied
= he hurt his foot

■ *Noter:*

il a eu la jambe cassée
= his leg was broken

Les faiblesses chroniques

■ *Le français* avoir le X fragile *peut se traduire par* to have something wrong with one's X *ou* to have X trouble:

avoir le cœur fragile
= to have something wrong with one's heart
  ou to have heart trouble

avoir les reins fragiles
= to have something wrong with one's kidneys
  ou to have kidney trouble

■ *Pour certaines parties du corps (*le cœur, les chevilles*), on peut aussi utiliser l'adjectif* weak:

avoir le cœur fragile
= to have a weak heart

■ *Noter que l'anglais utilise l'article indéfini dans cette tournure.*

Les maladies

■ *L'anglais utilise tous les noms de maladie sans article:*

avoir la grippe
= to have flu

avoir les oreillons
= to have mumps

avoir un cancer
= to have cancer

être au lit avec la grippe
= to be in bed with flu

avoir une hépatite
= to have hepatitis

guérir de la grippe
= to recover from flu

avoir de l'asthme
= to have asthma

mourir du choléra
= to die of cholera

■ *Même les noms de maladies suivies d'un complément ne prennent pas toujours d'article:*

avoir un cancer du foie
= to have cancer of the liver

Mais:

avoir un ulcère à l'estomac
= to have a stomach ulcer

■ *Et attention à* a cold (un rhume), *qui n'est pas vraiment une maladie:*

avoir un rhume
= to have a cold

■ *L'anglais utilise moins volontiers les adjectifs dérivés des noms de maladies, si bien qu'on peut avoir:*

être asthmatique
= to have asthma *ou* to be asthmatic

être épileptique
= to have epilepsy *ou* to be epileptic

être rachitique
= to have rickets

■ *Noter:*

quelqu'un qui a la malaria
= someone with malaria

quelqu'un qui a un cancer
= someone with cancer

les gens qui ont le Sida
= people with Aids

■ *Les gens qui se font soigner pour une maladie sont désignés par* a X patient:

quelqu'un qui se fait soigner pour un cancer
= a cancer patient

Les attaques de la maladie

■ *Le français* attraper *se traduit par* to get *ou* to catch.

attraper la grippe
= to get flu *ou* to catch flu

attraper une bronchite
= to get bronchitis *ou* to catch bronchitis

■ *Mais* get *est utilisable aussi pour ce qui n'est pas infectieux:*

développer un ulcère à l'estomac
= to get a stomach ulcer

■ Avoir *peut se traduire par* develop *lorsqu'il s'agit de l'apparition progressive d'une maladie:*

avoir un cancer
= to develop cancer

☛ Voir page suivante

d

d

Les douleurs et les maladies *suite*

avoir un début d'ulcère
= to develop an ulcer

■ *Pour une crise passagère, et qui peut se reproduire, on traduira* avoir un/une ... *par* to have an attack of ... *ou* a bout of ...:

avoir une crise d'asthme
= to have an asthma attack

avoir une bronchite
= to have an attack of bronchitis

avoir une crise de malaria
= to have a bout of malaria

■ *Noter aussi:*

avoir une crise d'épilepsie
= to have an epileptic fit

prescrire un médicament contre la toux
= to prescribe something for a cough

des cachets contre la malaria
= malaria tablets

se faire vacciner contre la grippe
= to have a flu injection

vacciner qn contre le tétanos
= to give sb a tetanus injection

se faire vacciner contre le choléra
= to have a cholera vaccination

un vaccin contre la grippe
= a flu vaccine ou an anti-flu vaccine

Mais noter:

prendre des médicaments contre la grippe
= to take something for flu

■ *Noter l'utilisation de la préposition anglaise* on *avec le verbe* operate:

se faire opérer d'un cancer
= to be operated on for cancer

le chirurgien l'a opéré d'un cancer
= the surgeon operated on him for cancer

Les traitements

■ *Le français* contre *ne se traduit pas toujours par* against.

prendre quelque chose contre le rhume des foins
= to take something for hay fever

prendre un médicament contre la toux
= to be taking something for a cough

---

drain /drɛ̃/ *nm* drain

drainage /drɛnaʒ/ *nm* ①: Tech, Agric drainage; ②: Méd draining (off); ③: fig drain; ~ **des cerveaux** brain drain

drainer /drɛne/ [1] *vtr* ①: Agric, Méd to drain; ②: fig to siphon off [*capitaux*] (**vers** to); [*spectacle, annonce*] to attract [*public*] (**vers** to)

drakkar /drakar/ *nm* drakkar, Viking longship

dramatique /dramatik/
Ⓐ *adj* ①: (tragique) [*problème, situation*] tragic; ②: Théât, Littérat [*création, effet*] dramatic; **art** ~ drama; **auteur** ~ playwright
Ⓑ *nf* TV, Radio play, drama

dramatiquement /dramatikmɑ̃/ *adv* tragically

dramatiser /dramatize/ [1] *vtr* to dramatize

dramaturge /dramatyrʒ/ ▸ p. 372 *nmf* playwright

dramaturgie /dramatyrʒi/ *nf* (art) dramatic art

drame /dram/ *nm* ①: (événement tragique) tragedy; **tourner au** ~ to take a tragic turn; **tu ne vas pas en faire un** ~! don't make a drama out of it!; ②: Cin, Littérat, Théât (genre) drama; (pièce) play
(Composé) ~ **lyrique** Mus opera

drap /dra/ *nm* ①: (de lit) sheet; ②: (tissu) woollenᴳᴮ fabric
(Composés) ~ **de bain** bath sheet; ~ **funéraire** pall
(Idiome) **se mettre dans de beaux** ~**s** to land oneself in a fine mess

drapé /drape/ *nm* drape

drapeau, *pl* ~**x** /drapo/ *nm* flag; **être sous les** ~**x** to be doing military service
(Composé) ~ **tricolore** (drapeau français) tricolourᴳᴮ

draper /drape/ [1]
Ⓐ *vtr* to drape [*tissu*]; (envelopper) to drape [*personne*]
Ⓑ **se draper** *vpr* ①: lit **se** ~ **dans** to wrap oneself in [*châle*]; ②: fig **se** ~ **dans sa dignité** to stand on one's dignity

drap-housse, *pl* **draps-housses** /draus/ *nm* fitted sheet

drapier, -ière /drapje, ɛr/ ▸ p. 372 *nm,f* (fabricant) cloth manufacturer

drastique /drastik/ *adj* fml [*mesure*] drastic

dressage /drɛsaʒ/ *nm* ①: (d'animal) training; ②: (de jeune cheval) breaking in; (discipline) dressage

dresser /drese/ [1]
Ⓐ *vtr* ①: (faire obéir) to train [*animal*]; to break in [*cheval*]; ②: (ériger) to put up [*tente, échafaudage, statue*]; ③: (lever) to raise [*tête, queue*]; ~ **l'oreille** [*animal*] to prick up its ears; fig to prick up one's ears; ④: (établir) to draw up [*carte géographique, inventaire, contrat*]; to write out [*procès-verbal*]; ⑤: (installer) to lay, to set [*table, piège*]; to lay out [*buffet*]; ⑥: (préparer) Culin to garnish [*plat*]; ⑦: (influencer) ~ **qn contre** to set sb against
Ⓑ **se dresser** *vpr* ①: (se mettre droit) to stand up; ②: (s'insurger) **se** ~ **contre** to rebel against [*injustice*]; ③: (s'élever) [*statue, obstacle*] to stand; (dominer) to tower up

dresseur, -euse /drɛsœr, øz/ ▸ p. 372 *nm,f* (d'animal) trainer

dribbler /drible/ [1] *vi* Sport to dribble

drille○ /drij/ *nm* **joyeux** ~ jolly fellow

driver /drive/ [1]
Ⓐ *vtr* to drive [*balle, cheval*]
Ⓑ *vi* (en tennis) to drive; (en golf) to drive off

drogue /drɔg/ *nf* ①: (stupéfiant) drug; **la** ~ drugs; **c'est devenu une** ~ fig it has become an addiction; ②: †(remède) drug; (de charlatan) quack remedy

drogué, ~e /drɔge/ *nm,f* drug-addict, junkie○

droguer /drɔge/ [1]
Ⓐ *vtr* ①: péj [*médecin*] (avec sédatif) to dope; (en prescrivant) to dish out○ drugs to; ②: (illégalement) to dope [*animal, sportif*]; to drug [*victime*]; to doctor [*boisson*]
Ⓑ **se droguer** *vpr* ①: péj (avec des médicaments) to dope oneself (à, de with); ②: (avec des stupéfiants) to take drugs; **se** ~ **à l'héroïne** to be on heroin

droguerie /drɔgri/ ▸ p. 372 *nf* (magasin) hardware shop GB *ou* store US; (commerce) hardware trade

droguiste /drɔgist/ ▸ p. 372 *nmf* (propriétaire) owner of a hardware shop GB *ou* store US

droit, ~e¹ /drwa, at/ ▸ p. 324
Ⓐ *adj* ①: (pas courbe, pas tordu) [*ligne, route, barre, cheveux, mur, nez*] straight; (pas penché) [*écriture*] up-and-down; **se tenir** ~ (debout) to stand up straight; (assis) to sit up straight; **s'écarter du** ~ **chemin** fig to stray from the straight and narrow; **descendre en** ~**e ligne de** to be a direct descendant of; ②: (contraire de gauche) right; ③: (honnête) [*personne*] straight, upright; [*vie*] blameless; ④: (sensé) [*jugement*] sound; ⑤: (en couture) [*jupe*] straight; [*veste*] single-breasted; ⑥: Math [*cône, angle, prisme*] right
Ⓑ *adv* [*aller, rouler*] straight; **continuez tout** ~ carry straight on; **aller** ~ **au but** *ou* **fait** fig to go straight to the point; **aller** ~ **à la catastrophe** to be heading straight for disaster; **ça m'est allé** ~ **au cœur** fig it really touched me; **marcher** *or* **filer**○ ~ fig to toe the line; **venir tout** ~ **de** [*expression,*

citation] to come straight out of [*auteur, œuvre*]

C nm **1** (prérogative) right; **avoir des ~s sur qn/qch** to have rights over sb/sth; **de quel ~ est-ce que tu me juges?** what gives you the right to judge me?; **être dans son (bon) ~** to be within one's rights; **de (plein) ~** by right(s); **de ~ divin** by divine right; **cela leur revient de ~** it's theirs by right; **avoir ~ à** to have the right to [*liberté, nationalité*]; to be entitled to [*bourse, indemnité*]; **il a eu ~ à une amende** iron he got a fine; **avoir le ~ de faire** (la permission) to be allowed to do; (selon la morale, la justice) to have the right to do; **avoir le ~ de vie ou de mort sur qn** to have (the) power of life and death over sb; **il s'imagine qu'il a tous les ~s** he thinks he can do whatever he likes; **être en ~ de** to be entitled to; **à bon ~** [*se plaindre*] with good reason; **'à qui de ~'** 'to whom it may concern'; **j'en parlerai à qui de ~**○ I'll speak to the appropriate person; **faire ~ à** to grant [*requête*]; **2** Jur (ensemble de lois) law; **faire son ~** to study law; **3** (redevance) fee; **~ d'inscription** registration fee; **4** (en boxe) right; **direct du ~** straight right; **crochet/uppercut du ~** right hook/uppercut

(Composés) **~ d'aînesse** Jur birthright, primogeniture; **~ d'antenne** broadcasting right; **~ de cité** Jur (right of) citizenship; fig acceptance; **acquérir ~ de cité** fig to gain acceptance; **avoir ~ de cité** to be accepted; **~ commun** (prisonnier) nonpolitical; **~ d'entrée** Comm import duty; (pour une personne) entrance fee; **~ de passage** Jur right of way GB, easement US; **~ de port** Fin port dues; **~ de propriété** right of possession; **~ de regard** Fin right of inspection; gén **avoir ~ de regard sur** to have a say in; **~ de timbre** Fin stamp duty; **~ de vote** Pol right to vote; **~s d'auteur** royalties; **~s civiques** Pol civil rights; **~s de douane** Comm, Fin customs duties; **les ~s de l'homme** human rights; **~s de succession** Fin inheritance tax

(Idiome) **se tenir ~ comme un i** *or* **un piquet** to hold oneself very erect

droite² /dʀwat/ nf **1** (opposé à gauche) **la ~** the right; **rouler à ~** to drive on the right; **tenir sa ~** Aut to keep (to the) right; **à ta ~, sur ta ~** on your right; **à ~ de** to the right of; **demander à ~ et à gauche** (partout) to ask everywhere *ou* all over the place; (à tous) to ask everybody; **2** Pol right; **voter à ~** to vote for the right; **de ~** [*parti, personne, gouvernement*] right-wing; **3** Math straight line

droitier, -ière /dʀwatje, ɛʀ/ nm,f **1** (qui se sert de la main droite) right-hander; **2** ○Pol right-winger

droiture /dʀwatyʀ/ nf honesty, uprightness

drôle /dʀol/ adj **1** (bizarre) funny, odd; **c'est un ~ de type** he's odd; **c'est ~ de faire/que** it's odd to do/that; **ce qui est** *or* **ce qu'il y a de ~ c'est que** the funny thing is that; **faire (tout) ~ à qn** to give sb a funny feeling; **faire une ~ de tête** to make a bit of a face; **de remerciement/consolation!** some thanks/consolation!; **2** (amusant) funny, amusing; **vous êtes ~, vous!** iron don't make me laugh!; **3** ○(grand) **un ~ de courage/travail** a lot of courage/work

(Composé) **~ de guerre** Hist phoney war

(Idiomes) **j'en ai entendu de ~s** I heard some funny things; **en faire voir de ~s à qn** to lead sb a merry dance

drôlement /dʀolmã/ adv **1** ○(très, beaucoup) really; **2** (bizarrement) oddly

drôlerie /dʀolʀi/ nf avec **~** amusingly

dromadaire /dʀomadɛʀ/ nm dromedary

dru, ~e /dʀy/
A adj [*cheveux, blés*] thick; [*averse*] heavy
B adv [*pousser*] thickly; [*pleuvoir*] heavily

DS /deɛs/ nf: Citroen car of the 1950s

DST /deɛste/ nf (abbr = **Direction de la surveillance du territoire**) French counterintelligence agency

du /dy/ ▸ **de**

dû, due, mpl dus /dy/
A pp ▸ **devoir¹**
B pp adj **1** (à payer) owed (*après n*), owing (*après n*), due (*après n*) (**à** to); (exigible) due (*après n*); **les intérêts dus** the interest due; **respect ~ à qn/qch** respect due to sb/sth; **en bonne et due forme** in due form; **2** (attribuable) **~ à** due to
C nm réclamer son **~** to claim one's due; **payer son ~** to pay one's dues

(Idiomes) **chose promise chose due** a promise is a promise; **à chacun son ~** credit where credit is due

dualisme /dɥalism/ nm **1** Philos dualism; **2** Pol **le ~ des partis** the two-party system

dualité /dɥalite/ nf duality

dubitatif, -ive /dybitatif, iv/ adj sceptical GB, skeptical US

duc /dyk/ ▸ p. 590 nm (titre) duke

duché /dyʃe/ nm (seigneurie) dukedom; (domaine) duchy

duchesse /dyʃɛs/ nf ▸ p. 590 duchess

duègne /dɥɛɲ/ nf duenna

duel /dɥɛl/ nm **1** (avec des armes) duel (**à** with); **se battre en ~** to fight a duel; **2** (en paroles) battle; **3** Ling dual

duettiste /dɥetist/ nmf duettist

dulcinée /dylsine/ nf hum lady-love

dûment /dymã/ adv duly; **je vous ai ~ averti** I gave you due warning

dune /dyn/ nf dune

dunette /dynɛt/ nf poop

duo /dyo, dɥo/ nm **1** Mus (œuvre) duet; (formation) **un ~ pour violon** a violin duet; **en ~** as a duo; **2** Théât double act GB, duo US; **3** ○(couple) pair

dupe /dyp/
A adj **être ~** to be fooled (**de** by)
B nf dupe; **un marché de ~s** a fool's bargain

duper /dype/ [1] vtr to fool; **facile à ~** gullible

duperie /dypʀi/ nf trickery **C**

duplex /dyplɛks/ nm inv **1** (appartement) maisonette GB, duplex apartment US; **2** Radio, Télécom, TV duplex

duplicata /dyplikata/ nm inv duplicate

duplication /dyplikasjɔ̃/ nf Tech duplication; Biol replication

duplicité /dyplisite/ nf duplicity

duquel ▸ **lequel**

dur, ~e /dyʀ/
A adj **1** (difficile à entamer) [*matériau, pain, siège, matelas*] hard; [*viande*] tough; (rigide) [*pinceau, poil, cuir, carton*] stiff; [*brosse à dents*] hard; [*plastique*] rigid; [*ressort*] hard; **2** (malaisé à manipuler) [*fermeture, poignée, pédale*] stiff; [*direction, volant*] heavy; **3** (résistant) [*personne*] **~ au mal** tough; **elle est ~e à la tâche** *ou* **au travail** she's a hard worker; **4** (anguleux) [*profil, traits*] hard; **5** (blessant) [*son, voix, ton, parole, lumière, couleur*] harsh; **6** (hostile) [*visage, expression*] severe; **7** (intransigeant) [*parents, patron*] (en général) hard; [*régime*] hard; [*faction, politique*] hardline (*épith*); **il est très ~ avec ses élèves** (comme défaut) he's very hard on his pupils; **il est ~ mais juste** (comme qualité) he's tough but fair; **la droite/gauche ~e** the hard Right/Left; **8** (contraignant) [*loi naturelle, conditions de vie*] harsh; [*conditions de crédit, termes de sécurité*] tough; **9** (éprouvant) [*métier*] gén hard; (physiquement) tough; [*climat, nécessité*] harsh; [*concurrence, sport, ascension*] hard, tough; **cela a été une ~e épreuve** it was quite an ordeal; **c'est la ~e réalité** it's the grim reality; **les temps sont ~s** times are hard; **10** (difficile) [*examen, problème*] hard; **il est ~ à supporter** he's heavy going; **11** (sans fard) [*film, reportage*] hard-hitting (*épith*); **12** (calcaire) [*eau*] hard
B nm,f **1** (personne solide) tough nut○; **jouer les ~s** to act tough; **2** Pol (partisan) hardliner
C adv [*travailler, frapper*] hard
D nm permanent structure
E **à la dure** loc adv the hard way

(Idiomes) **être ~ d'oreille**⊙ to be hard of hearing; **avoir la tête ~e** (obstiné) to be stubborn; (obtus) to be dense; **avoir la vie ~e** [*insectes*] to be difficult to get rid of; [*habitude, préjugé*] to die hard; **elle a la vie ~e** she has a hard life; **mener la vie ~e à qn** to give sb a hard time; **en faire voir de ~ à ses parents** to give one's parents a hard time

durable /dyʀabl/ adj **1** (stable) [*amélioration, amitié, impression, hausse, victoire*] lasting; [*attrait, intérêt*] enduring; [*situation*] long-standing; [*matériau*] durable; **développement ~** sustainable development; **2** Écon [*marchandise*] durable

durablement /dyʀabləmã/ adv [*s'installer*] on a permanent basis

durant /dyʀã/ prép **1** (exprimant une durée) for; **des heures ~** for hours and hours, for hours on end; **l'été ~** the whole summer; **plus d'une heure ~** for over an hour; **sa vie ~** throughout his/her life; **2** (au cours de) during; **~ le match** during the match

durcir /dyʀsiʀ/ [3]

A vtr **1** (rendre dur) [sécheresse, froid] to harden [sol, pâte]; **2** (rendre sévère) [maquillage] to harden [traits]; **3** (radicaliser) to harden [position]; to intensify [mouvement de grève]

B vi [argile] to harden; [ciment, colle] to set; [pain] to go hard; [artères] to harden

C se durcir vpr [argile, artères] to harden; [ton, régime] to become harsher; [conflit] to intensify

durcissement /dyʀsismɑ̃/ nm **1** (d'argile, artère) hardening; (de ciment, colle) setting; (d'attitude, de position) hardening; (de mouvement, grève) intensification

durcisseur /dyʀsisœʀ/ nm hardener

durée /dyʀe/ nf **1** (période) (de spectacle, séjour, règne, d'études) length; (de contrat) term; (de disque, cassette) playing time; **pour** or **pendant (toute) la ∼ de** for the duration of; **séjour d'une ∼ de trois mois** three-month stay; **ils n'ont pas précisé la ∼ du projet** they didn't specify how long the project would last; **pendant une ∼ limitée/fixée** over a limited/set period; **contrat à ∼ déterminée** fixed-term contract; **de courte ∼** [amitié, paix, reprise économique] short-lived; [orage, absence] brief; [bail, prêt] short-term; **de longue ∼** [bail, prêt, chômage, contrat] long-term; [absence] long; **2** (longévité) ∼ **(de vie)** life; ∼ **d'utilisation** useful life; **pile longue ∼** long-life battery; **3** Mus (de note) value; **4** Philos duration

durement /dyʀmɑ̃/ adv **1** (de façon éprouvante) **être ∼ touché** (affectivement) to be deeply affected; (économiquement) to be badly hit; **gagner ∼ sa vie** to earn one's living the hard way; **2** (sans aménité) [punir, parler] harshly; [regarder] severely; **3** [frapper] hard

durer /dyʀe/ [1] vi **1** (avoir une durée de) to last; **ne ∼ qu'un instant** only to last a moment; **2** (se prolonger) to go on; ∼ **indéfiniment** to go on forever; **3** (se passer) [conférence, festival] to run; **4** (être durable) to last; **faire ∼ ses vêtements** to make one's clothes last; **pourvu que ça dure** long may it last; **5** (se prolonger longtemps) to go on for long; **faire ∼** to prolong [réunion]; **faire ∼ le plaisir** iron to prolong the agony

dures /dyʀ/ nfpl **en faire voir de ∼ à ses parents** to give one's parents a hard time

dureté /dyʀte/ nf (fermeté) (de matériau, siège) hardness; (de viande) toughness; (de carton, poils, pinceau) stiffness; (de traits, visage) hardness; (d'expression, de ton, punition, paroles, métier, climat) harshness; (de regard) severity; (de tâche) difficulty; **avec ∼** [regarder] severely

durillon /dyʀijɔ̃/ nm callus

durite /dyʀit/ nf radiator hose

DUT /deyte/ nm (abbr = **diplôme universitaire de technologie**) two-year diploma from a university institute of technology

duvet /dyvɛ/ nm **1** (plumes, poils) down; **le ∼ d'oie** goosedown; **2** (sac de couchage) sleeping bag

duveté, ∼e /dyvte/ adj downy

duveteux, -euse /dyvtø, øz/ adj [joue] downy; [pelage] fluffy; [fruit] downy GB, fuzzy US

DVD /devede/ nm (abbr = **digital versatile disc**) DVD

DVD-Rom /devederɔm/ nm (abbr = **digital versatile disc read only memory**) DVD-ROM

dynamique /dinamik/

A adj gén Phys dynamic; [match] lively

B nf **1** Phys, Psych dynamics (+ v sg); **2** (processus) process

dynamiser /dinamize/ [1] vtr to make [sb/sth] more dynamic; (de nouveau) to revitalize

dynamisme /dinamism/ nm dynamism; **être plein de ∼** to be very dynamic

dynamite /dinamit/ nf lit, fig dynamite

dynamiter /dinamite/ [1] vtr lit to dynamite [pont]; fig to destroy

dynastie /dinasti/ nf dynasty

dysfonctionnement /disfɔ̃ksjɔnmɑ̃/ nm **1** Méd dysfunction; **2** (de système) malfunctioning

dyslexie /dislɛksi/ nf dyslexia

e, E /ə/ nm inv e, E; **e dans l'a** a and e joined together

EAO /əao/ nm: abbr ▸ **enseignement**

eau, pl **~x** /o/

A nf **1** gén water; **l'~ de source/du robinet** spring/tap water; **~ de pluie** rainwater **Ȼ**; **pastis sans ~** neat pastis; **2** (masse) water; **l'~ du lac** the water in the lake; **prendre l'~** [chaussure] to let in water; **être en ~** lit [réservoir] to be full of water; fig [personne] to be dripping with sweat; **mettre à l'~** to launch [bateau]; **se jeter à l'~** fig to take the plunge; **tomber à l'~** fig [projet] to fall through; **nettoyer le sol à grande ~** to sluice the floor down; **3** (approvisionnement) water; **~ courante** running water; **4** (pluie) rain; **5** (de pierre précieuse) water; **émeraude de la plus belle ~** emerald of the finest quality

B **eaux** nfpl **1** Géog (niveau) water (sg); (masse) waters; **2** (liquide amniotique) waters; **elle a perdu ses ~x** her waters have broken

⌐(Composés)⌐ **~ bénite** holy water; **~ de chaux** limewater; **~ douce** fresh water; **~ de Javel** ≈ (chloride) bleach; **~ lourde** heavy water; **~ de mer** seawater; **~ oxygénée** hydrogen peroxide; **~ plate** (du robinet) plain water; (minérale) still mineral water; **~ de rose** rose water; **à l'~ de rose** [roman] sentimental; **~ de vaisselle** lit, fig dishwater; **~ vive** white water; **~x et forêts** Admin forestry commission (sg); **~x usées** waste water **Ȼ**

⌐(Idiomes)⌐ **mettre l'~ à la bouche de qn** to make sb's mouth water; **c'est l'~ et le feu** they are like chalk and cheese; **être de la même ~** to be of the same ilk; **ou dans ces ~x-là**○ or thereabouts; **vivre d'amour et d'~ fraîche** to live on love alone

EAU written abbr ▸ **Émirats**

eau-de-vie, pl **eaux-de-vie** /odvi/ nf brandy, eau de vie

eau-forte, pl **eaux-fortes** /ofɔʀt/ nf etching

ébahir /ebaiʀ/ [3]
A vtr to dumbfound
B **s'ébahir** vpr to be dumbfounded (**de, devant** by)

ébats /eba/ nmpl (d'enfants) frolics; (de sportifs) movements

ébattre: s'ébattre /ebatʀ/ [61] vpr [enfants] to frolic (about); [animaux] to frisk about

ébauche /eboʃ/ nf **1** (objet, sculpture) rough shape; (dessin) preliminary sketch; (roman, réforme) preliminary draft; **2** (action) (de sculpture) rough-hewing; (de dessin) sketching out; (de roman, réforme) drafting; **être encore à l'état d'~** to be still at an early stage; **3** fig (début) **l'~ d'une amitié** the beginnings (pl) of a friendship; **l'~ d'un sourire** a hint of a smile; **l'~ d'un geste** an arrested gesture

ébaucher /eboʃe/ [1]
A vtr to sketch out [tableau, solution]; to draft [roman, projet]; to rough-hew [statue]; to begin [conversation]
B **s'ébaucher** vpr [solution, roman] to begin to take shape; [amitié] to begin to develop; [négociations] to start; [image] to begin to form

ébène /ebɛn/ nf ebony; **des cheveux d'~** fig jet-black hair

ébéniste /ebenist/ ▸ p. 372 nmf cabinetmaker

éberluer /ebɛʀlɥe/ [1] vtr [nouvelle] to dumbfound

éblouir /ebluiʀ/ [3] vtr lit, fig to dazzle (**de** with)

éblouissant, ~e /ebluisɑ̃, ɑ̃t/ adj lit, fig dazzling

éblouissement /ebluismɑ̃/ nm **1** (par une lumière vive) dazzle **Ȼ**; **2** fig dazzling experience; **3** (vertige) dizzy spell

éborgner /ebɔʀɲe/ [1] vtr (blesser) **~ qn** to blind sb in one eye

éboueur /ebuœʀ/ ▸ p. 372 nm dustman GB, garbageman US

ébouillanter /ebujɑ̃te/ [1] vtr to scald [personne, volaille]; to warm [théière]; to blanch [légumes]

éboulement /ebulmɑ̃/ nm (de mur, falaise) collapse; (de matériaux) fall; **~ (de rochers)** (chute) rockfall; (résultat) fallen rocks (pl)

ébouler: s'ébouler /ebule/ [1] vpr [mur, falaise] to collapse; [rochers] to fall

éboulis /ebuli/ nm inv (rochers) mass of fallen rocks; (terre) heap of fallen earth

ébouriffer /eburife/ [1] vtr [vent] to tousle [cheveux]; to ruffle [plumes, poils]; [personne] to ruffle [cheveux]

ébranler /ebʀɑ̃le/ [1]
A vtr **1** (faire vibrer) to rattle [vitre]; to shake [maison]; (rendre chancelant) to weaken [construction]; **2** (émouvoir) to shake [personne, pays]; (affaiblir) to undermine [santé, régime]; to shake [personne, nerfs, conviction, confiance]; to disturb [esprit]
B **s'ébranler** vpr [convoi, train] to move off

ébrécher /ebʀeʃe/ [14] vtr **1** to chip [vaisselle, dent]; to make a nick in [lame]; to damage [scie]; fig to tarnish [réputation]; **2** (entamer) to make a hole in [économies]

ébriété /ebʀijete/ nf intoxication; **en état d'~** in a state of intoxication, under the influence (of alcohol)

ébrouer: s'ébrouer /ebʀue/ [1] vpr **1** [cheval] to snort; **2** [personne, chien] to shake oneself/itself; [gros oiseau] to flap its wings; [petit oiseau] to flutter its wings

ébruitement /ebʀɥitmɑ̃/ nm disclosure

ébruiter /ebʀɥite/ [1]
A vtr to divulge
B **s'ébruiter** vpr [nouvelle] to get out

EBS /əbeɛs/ nf (abbr = **encéphalite bovine spongiforme**) BSE, bovine spongiform encephalopathy

ébullition /ebylisjɔ̃/ nf (de liquide) boiling; **porter à ~** to bring to the GB ou a US boil

⌐(Idiome)⌐ **être en ~** [maisonnée, foule] to be in a fever of excitement; [pays, cerveau] to be in a ferment

écaille /ekaj/ nf **1** (de poisson) scale; (d'huître) shell; **2** (pour peignes) tortoiseshell; **lunettes en ~** horn-rimmed glasses; **3** (parcelle) flake; **4** Bot (de bourgeon, d'oignon) scale

écailler[1] /ekaje/ [1]
A vtr **1** Culin to scale [poisson]; to open [huître]; **2** (endommager) **~ qch** [personne] to chip [sth] off
B **s'écailler** vpr [vernis, plâtre] to flake away

écailler[2], **-ère** /ekaje, ɛʀ/ ▸ p. 372 nm,f oyster seller

écale /ekal/ nf (de noix) nutshell

écaler /ekale/ [1] vtr to shell [noix]

écarlate /ekaʀlat/ ▸ p. 140 nf scarlet

écarquiller /ekaʀkije/ [1] vtr **~ les yeux** to open one's eyes wide (**devant** at)

écart /ekaʀ/
A nm **1** (distance) (entre des objets) distance, gap (**entre** between); (entre des dates) interval; (entre des concepts) gap; (entre des versions) difference; **2** (variation) difference; **~ des salaires** pay differential; **~ par rapport à la normale** deviation from the norm; **3** (mouvement brusque) **faire un ~** [cheval] to shy; [voiture] to swerve; [piéton] to leap aside; **4** (faute) lapse; **il fait des ~s de régime** he doesn't stick to

his diet; **~s de langage** bad language **₵**; **5** (aux cartes) discard

B **à l'écart** loc adv **être à l'~** to be isolated; **ils bavardaient dans le jardin, à l'~** they were talking in the garden GB ou yard US, off by themselves; **se tenir à l'~** (éloigné) to stand apart; (refuser de se mêler) to keep oneself to oneself; (ne pas participer) not to join in; **mettre qn à l'~** (éloigner) to push sb aside; (mettre au ban) to ostracize sb

C **à l'écart de** loc prép away from; **tenir qn à l'~ de** to keep sb away from [lieu]; to keep sb out of [activité, négociations]

écarté, ~e /ekaʀte/

A pp ▸ **écarter**

B pp adj **1** (espacé) [doigts] spread (épith, après n); [bras] wide apart (épith, après n); [jambes] apart (épith, après n); [yeux] widely set; **2** (isolé) [lieu] isolated

C ▸ p. 327 Jeux ⬧ écarté

écarteler /ekaʀtəle/ [17] vtr **1** fig (déchirer) **écartelé entre** torn between; **2** (supplicier) to quarter

écartement /ekaʀtəmɑ̃/ nm (distance) distance, space

écarter /ekaʀte/ [1]

A vtr **1** (séparer) to move [sth] further apart [objets]; to open [rideaux]; to spread [bras, jambes, doigts]; to part [lèvres, feuillage]; **2** (éloigner) to move [sth] aside [chaise]; to brush [sth] aside [mèche]; to remove [obstacle]; to push [sb] aside [personne]; to move [sb] on [badauds]; **ce chemin nous écarte trop** this path takes us too far out of our way; **3** (détourner) **~ qn de son devoir** to distract sb from his duty; **4** (éliminer) to dispel [soupçon]; to remove [tentation]; to eliminate [risque, concurrent]; **tout danger est écarté** the danger is over; **5** (rejeter) to reject [idée, candidature]; to rule out [possibilité]; **~ qn de** (empêcher) to exclude sb from; (exclure) to remove sb from

B **s'écarter** vpr **1** (se séparer) [foule, nuages] to part; [volets] to open; **2** (s'éloigner) to move away (**de** from); **écartez-vous** move out of the way; **écartez-vous les uns des autres** spread out a bit; **3** (dévier) lit, fig **s'~ de** to move away from [direction, norme]; to stray from [chemin, sujet]; to diverge from [vérité]; **s'~ de son devoir** to fail in one's duty

ecchymose /ekimoz/ nf bruise

ecclésiastique /eklezjastik/

A adj (du clergé) ecclesiastical; [ordres, état] holy

B nm cleric

écervelé, ~e /esɛʀvəle/

A adj featherbrained

B nm,f featherbrain

échafaud /eʃafo/ nm **1** (lieu) scaffold; **2** (peine capitale) guillotine

échafaudage /eʃafodaʒ/ nm **1** Constr scaffolding **₵**; **2** (tas) stack; **3** fig (montage) edifice

échafauder /eʃafode/ [1]

A vtr **1** (élaborer) to put [sth] together [plan, théorie]; to build up [fortune]; **2** (empiler) to stack [sth] up

B vi Constr to put up scaffolding

échalas /eʃala/ nm inv **1** (pieu) cane; **2** ○(personne) beanpole○

(Idiome) **maigre comme un ~** as thin as a rake

échalote /eʃalɔt/ nf shallot

échancré, ~e /eʃɑ̃kʀe/

A pp ▸ **échancrer**

B pp adj **1** [robe] low-cut; [culotte] cut high on the thigh (jamais épith); **2** (ouvert) [chemise] open-necked; **3** [côte] indented

échancrer /eʃɑ̃kʀe/ [1] vtr to cut away [encolure, emmanchure]; **~ une robe sur le devant/sous les bras** to cut a dress low at the front/under the arms

échange /eʃɑ̃ʒ/ nm **1** gén exchange (**entre** between; **contre** for); **il y a eu un ~ de coups** blows were exchanged; **faire un ~ de prisonniers** to exchange prisoners; **en ~** in exchange, in return; **en ~ de quoi** in exchange for which; **2** Écon, Comm trade **₵**; **~s commerciaux** trade **₵**; **3** (relations, séjour linguistique) exchange; **4** Biol, Phys exchange; **5** (au tennis, tennis de table) rally; **6** (aux échecs) exchange

(Composés) **~ de bons procédés** quid pro quo; **~ de logements** Tourisme home exchange, home swap; **~ standard** replacement by a reconditioned part

échanger /eʃɑ̃ʒe/ [13] vtr **1** gén to exchange (**contre** for); **~ des insultes** to trade insults; **~ des remerciements** to

thank each other; **elle et sa sœur échangent souvent leurs vêtements** she often swaps clothes with her sister; **'ni repris ni échangés'** 'no exchanges or returns'; **2** (au tennis, tennis de table) **~ des balles** to rally

échangeur /eʃɑ̃ʒœʀ/ nm **1** (intersection) interchange GB, grade separation US; **2** Tech exchanger

échantillon /eʃɑ̃tijɔ̃/ nm sample

échantillonnage /eʃɑ̃tijɔnaʒ/ nm **1** (prélèvement) sampling; (ensemble) selection; **2** Mus sampling

échantillonner /eʃɑ̃tijɔne/ [1] vtr gén to take a sample of; Ordinat, Télécom to sample

échappatoire /eʃapatwaʀ/ nf way out (**à** of); **répondre par une ~** to answer evasively

échappée /eʃape/ nf Sport break

échappement /eʃapmɑ̃/ nm **1** (de gaz) (dispositif) **(tuyau d')~** exhaust (pipe); (expulsion) release; **en ~ libre** without a silencer GB ou muffler US; **2** (d'horlogerie) escapement

échapper /eʃape/ [1]

A **échapper à** vtr ind **1** (se dérober à) **~ à** (par la fuite) to get away from [poursuivant]; (par la ruse) to elude [enquêteur, chasseur]; **2** (éviter) **~ à** to escape [mort, faillite]; (to manage) to avoid [accident, châtiment]; **~ à tout contrôle** not to be subject to any control; **~ à une taxation** (légalement) to be exempt from tax; (illégalement) to evade a tax; **~ aux réunions de famille/à l'obligation de faire** to get out of family gatherings/of having to do; **3** (se libérer de) **~ à** to escape from [milieu social]; to shake off [angoisse, désespoir]; **je sens qu'il m'échappe** (mari, amant) I feel he is drifting away from me; (enfant) I feel he's growing away from me; **4** (tomber) **~ à qn** or **des mains de qn** [objet] to slip out of sb's hands; **5** (être produit involontairement) **un soupir m'a échappé** I let out a sigh; **6** (intellectuellement) **~ à** to escape; **le titre m'échappe** the title escapes me; **7** (ne pas suivre) **~ à** to defy [classification, logique]; **~ à la règle** to be an exception to the rule

B **s'échapper** vpr **1** (s'enfuir) [personne, animal] to run away (**de** from); [oiseau] to fly away (**de** from); (d'un lieu clos) to escape (**de** from); (ne pas être pris) to get away; **laisser ~** [personne] to let [sb] get away [personne, animal]; to let [sth] slip between one's fingers [victoire]; to let [sth] slip [occasion]; **2** (se répandre) [gaz, fumée] to escape (**de, par** from); [eau] to leak (**de, par** from); **3** (partir) to get away; **4** (être produit) **laisser ~** to shed [larmes]; to let out [parole, soupir]; **5** Sport to break away

(Idiome) **l'~ belle** to have a narrow escape

écharde /eʃaʀd/ nf splinter

écharpe /eʃaʀp/ nf (cache-col) scarf; (d'officiel) sash; (bandage) sling

écharper /eʃaʀpe/ [1] vtr to tear to pieces

échasse /eʃas/ nf **1** (pour marcher) stilt; **2** (oiseau) stilt

échassier /eʃasje/ nm wading bird

échauder /eʃode/ [1] vtr **1** (décourager) to put [sb] off; **2** (ébouillanter) to scald

(Idiome) **chat échaudé craint l'eau froide** Prov once bitten, twice shy Prov

échauffement /eʃofmɑ̃/ nm **1** Sport warm-up; **2** fig (excitation) heat (**de** of); **3** Tech (de moteur) overheating; (de sol) warming; **4** Bot (de foin, bois) fermentation

échauffer /eʃofe/ [1] vtr **1** Sport to warm up; **2** fig (animer) to stir [imagination]; to stir up [personne, débat]; **3** (rendre chaud) to overheat [corps, liquide, pièce]; to warm [sol]; **4** (produire une fermentation) to start [sth] fermenting

(Idiome) **~ les oreilles** or **la bile de qn** to vex sb

échauffourée /eʃofuʀe/ nf brawl

échéance /eʃeɑ̃s/ nf **1** (date d'exigibilité) (de dette, facture) due date; (d'action, assurance) maturity date; (d'emprunt) redemption date; **arriver à** [emprunt] to fall due; [assurance, placement] to mature; **2** (date d'expiration) expiry date; **arriver à** to expire; **3** (délai) currency; **à longue/brève ~** [bon, prévision] long-/short-term (avant n); [renforcer, changer] in the long/short term; **4** (somme due) (de facture) payment; (d'emprunt) repayment; **faire face à de lourdes ~** to have heavy financial commitments; **5** (d'événement) date; (date limite) deadline; **~ électorale** polling GB ou election day

échéancier /eʃeɑ̃sje/ nm (ensemble d'échéances) schedule of due dates; (calendrier d'échéances) schedule of repayments

échéant: le cas échéant /ləkazeʃeɑ̃/ loc adv if need be, should the case arise

échec /eʃɛk/
A *nm* 1⃝ Scol, Univ failure (**à** in GB, on US); 2⃝ (fait de ne pas atteindre son but) failure; (remédiable) setback; **subir un ~** to fail; (temporairement) to suffer a setback; **voué à l'~** doomed to failure; **faire ~ à qn/aux projets de qn** to thwart sb/sb's plans; **tenir l'ennemi en ~** to hold the enemy in check; 3⃝ (défaite) Pol, Sport defeat; Mil reverse; **essuyer** *or* **subir un ~** to suffer a defeat *ou* setback; 4⃝ Jeux **~ au roi** check; **~ et mat** checkmate
B ▸ p. 327 **échecs** *nmpl* **les ~s** (jeu) chess; (échiquier et pièces) chess set; (pièces) chessmen

échelle /eʃɛl/ *nf* 1⃝ (pour grimper) ladder; **monter à une ~** to climb a ladder; **faire la courte ~ à qn** to give sb a leg up; 2⃝ (de plan, maquette) scale; **plan à l'~** scale plan; **carte à l'~ de 1/10 000°** map on a scale of 1:10,000; 3⃝ (système de gradation) scale; **~ de Richter** Richter scale; 4⃝ fig (dans un milieu social) scale, ladder; (dans une entreprise) hierarchy, ladder; **s'élever dans l'~ sociale** to rise up the social scale; **~ des prix** scale of prices; **~ mobile des salaires** sliding pay-scale; 5⃝ Mus scale; 6⃝ ○(accroc à un collant) ladder

échelon /eʃlɔ̃/ *nm* 1⃝ (d'échelle) rung; 2⃝ Admin (rang) grade; **sauter les ~s** to get accelerated promotion; 3⃝ (niveau) level; **à l'~ ministériel** at ministerial level; 4⃝ Mil (unité) echelon

échelonner /eʃlɔne/ [1]
A *vtr* 1⃝ (espacer) to space [sth] out [balises]; 2⃝ (répartir) to spread [paiements, travail] (**sur** over); to stagger [congés, départs] (**sur** over); 3⃝ (graduer) to grade [exercices]; to build up [arguments]; 4⃝ Mil to deploy [sth] in echelon [troupes]
B **s'échelonner** *vpr* 1⃝ [objets, personnes] to be positioned at intervals (**sur** over); 2⃝ [paiements, travaux] to be spread (**sur** over); [congés, départs] to be staggered (**sur** over)

écheveau, *pl* **~x** /eʃvo/ *nm* 1⃝ (de laine) hank; (de fil) skein; 2⃝ fig (enchevêtrement) tangle

échevelé, **~e** /eʃəvle/ *adj* 1⃝ (décoiffé) tousled; 2⃝ fig [rythme] frenzied; [romantisme] unbridled

échevin /eʃ(ə)vɛ̃/ *nm* 1⃝ Hist municipal magistrate; 2⃝ (en Belgique) deputy burgomaster

échine /eʃin/ *nf* 1⃝ (colonne vertébrale) spine; 2⃝ Culin (de porc) ≈ spare rib
Idiome **courber l'~ devant** to submit to

échiner: **s'échiner** /eʃine/ [1] *vpr* **s'~ à faire** to make a great effort to do

échiquier /eʃikje/ *nm* 1⃝ (aux échecs) chessboard; 2⃝ fig (terrain) arena; 3⃝ (motif) chequered GB *ou* checkered US pattern

Échiquier /eʃikje/ *nprm* **l'~** the Exchequer

écho /eko/ *nm* 1⃝ (de son) echo; **faire ~ à qch, se faire l'~ de qch** to echo sth; 2⃝ (réaction) response (**à** to); **ne trouver aucun ~** to fail to elicit any response; 3⃝ (information) **nous n'avons eu aucun ~ des pourparlers** we have heard nothing about the talks; 4⃝ (anecdote) piece of gossip

échographie /ekoɡʀafi/ *nf* scan

échoir /eʃwaʀ/ [51]
A *vi* [loyer] to fall due; [traite] to be payable
B **échoir à** *vtr ind* **~ à qn** to fall to sb's share

échoppe /eʃɔp/ *nf* stall

échouer /eʃwe/ [1]
A *vtr* Naut to beach [bateau]
B **échouer à** *vtr ind* to fail [examen, épreuve]
C *vi* 1⃝ (ne pas réussir) [personne, tentative] to fail; **faire ~** to cause [sth] to fail [négociations, projet]; 2⃝ (se retrouver) [personne, dossier] to end up; 3⃝ [bateau] to run aground; **un pétrolier échoué sur les récifs** an oil tanker stranded on the reef
D **s'échouer** *vpr* [bateau] to run aground (**sur** on); [baleine] to be beached

échu, **~e** /eʃy/
A *pp* ▸ **échoir**
B *adj* expired; **payer à terme ~** to pay in arrears

éclabousser /eklabuse/ [1] *vtr* 1⃝ (mouiller) to splash (**avec** with); (salir) to spatter (**de** with); 2⃝ (compromettre) **il a été éclaboussé par ces rumeurs** the rumours GB have damaged his reputation

éclair /eklɛʀ/
A *adj inv* **rencontre ~** brief meeting; **visite ~** flying visit;

attaque ~ lightning strike; **guerre ~** blitzkrieg; **repas ~** quick meal
B *nm* 1⃝ Météo flash of lightning; **passer comme un ~** to flash past; 2⃝ (éclat) (d'explosion, de bijou) flash; (de regard) glint; **leurs yeux lançaient des ~s de colère** their eyes were flashing with anger; 3⃝ (de lucidité, triomphe) moment; 4⃝ Culin éclair
Composé **~ de chaleur** sheet lightning **₵**

éclairage /eklɛʀaʒ/ *nm* (manière d'éclairer) lighting; (lumière) light; **~ au gaz** gaslight; **faible ~** dim light

éclairagiste /eklɛʀaʒist/ ▸ p. 372 *nm* electrician

éclairant, **~e** /eklɛʀɑ̃, ɑ̃t/ *adj* [fusée, bombe] flare (épith)

éclaircie /eklɛʀsi/ *nf* 1⃝ Météo (espace clair) sunny spell; (embellie) break in the weather; 2⃝ (de situation, conflit) liter respite sout

éclaircir /eklɛʀsiʀ/ [3]
A *vtr* 1⃝ (rendre moins sombre) to lighten [couleur]; to lighten the colour GB of [cheveux]; to improve [teint]; 2⃝ (élucider) to shed light on [mystère]; 3⃝ (rendre moins épais) to thin [sauce, futaie]
B **s'éclaircir** *vpr* 1⃝ Météo [temps] to clear; **l'horizon s'éclaircit** lit the horizon is clearing; fig the outlook is getting brighter; 2⃝ (pâlir) [couleur] to fade; [teint] to improve; [cheveux] to get lighter; 3⃝ (s'élucider) [situation, mystère] to become clearer; 4⃝ (se clairsemer) [foule, forêt] to thin out; 5⃝ (rendre clair) **s'~ les cheveux** to lighten one's hair; **s'~ la voix** *or* **la gorge** to clear one's throat

éclaircissement /eklɛʀsismɑ̃/ *nm* (explication) explanation; (clarification) clarification **₵**

éclairé, **~e** /eklɛʀe/ *adj* [homme] enlightened; [amateur] well-informed

éclairer /eklɛʀe/ [1]
A *vtr* 1⃝ (donner de la lumière à) [lampe] to light [lieu]; [soleil, phare] to light up [lieu, objet]; 2⃝ (avec une lampe) to give [sb] some light; (pour montrer le chemin) to light the way for; 3⃝ (expliquer) [remarque] to throw light on [texte, situation]; 4⃝ (instruire) to enlighten [personne] (**sur** as to); 5⃝ Mil to reconnoitre GB [route]; to reconnoitre GB for [convoi]
B *vi* [lampe, bougie] to give light
C **s'éclairer** *vpr* 1⃝ (s'illuminer) [écran] to light up; fig [visage] to light up (**de** with); 2⃝ (se donner de la lumière) **s'~ à l'électricité** to have electric lighting; 3⃝ (s'éclaircir) [situation] to become clearer; [question] to be cleared up

éclaireur, **-euse** /eklɛʀœʀ, øz/ *nm,f* 1⃝ (en scoutisme) (garçon) scout GB, Boy Scout US; (fille) guide GB, Girl Guide US; 2⃝ Mil scout

éclat /ekla/ *nm* 1⃝ (fragment) splinter; **un ~ d'obus** a piece of shrapnel; **voler en ~s** lit, fig to shatter; 2⃝ (de lumière, d'astre) brightness; (de phare, projecteur) glare; (de neige, diamant) sparkle; 3⃝ (de couleur, tissu) brilliance; (de fleur) brightness; (de cheveux, plumes) shine, sheen; (de métal) lustre GB; (du teint) radiance; (de chaussure, meuble) shine; **redonner de l'~ à** to make [sth] look like new [tissu]; to put the shine back into [meuble, cheveux]; 4⃝ (de visage, sourire) radiance; (de regard) sparkle; **sans ~** [regard] dull; [beauté] lifeless; 5⃝ (grandeur) splendour GB; **avec ~** [annoncer] dramatically; [fêter] with great pomp; **manquer d'~** [cérémonie, discours] to lack sparkle; **sans ~** [personnage, soirée] dull; **action** *or* **coup d'~** (admirable) remarkable feat; (qui attire l'attention) grand gesture; 6⃝ (esclandre) scene
Composés **~ de colère** fit of anger; **~ de rire** roar of laughter; **des ~s de voix** raised voices
Idiome **rire aux ~s** to roar with laughter

éclatant, **~e** /eklatɑ̃, ɑ̃t/ *adj* 1⃝ (très brillant) [lumière] dazzling; [soleil] blazing; 2⃝ (vif) [couleur, teinte, plumage] bright; **dents d'une blancheur ~e** sparkling white teeth; **avoir une mine ~e** to be glowing with health; 3⃝ (admirable) [beauté, sourire, santé] radiant; [victoire, réussite] brilliant; 4⃝ (manifeste) [preuve, démonstration] striking; 5⃝ (très bruyant) [bruit, son] deafening; [rire, voix] ringing

éclaté, **~e** /eklate/ *adj* 1⃝ (fragmenté) gén fragmented; [famille] divided; 2⃝ Art [dessin, vue] exploded

éclatement /eklatmɑ̃/ *nm* 1⃝ (rupture) (de tuyau) bursting; (de rate, foie) rupture; 2⃝ (explosion) (de grenade) explosion; (de pneu) blow-out; 3⃝ (de groupe) break-up (**en** into)

éclater /eklate/ [1] *vi* 1⃝ (exploser) [pneu, bulle, chaudière] to burst; [obus, pétard] to explode; [bouteille] to shatter; [personne] to burst [bulle, ballon]; to detonate [bombe, grenade]; to let off [pétard]; 2⃝ (se rompre) [canalisation, abcès] to

e

burst; [*organe*] to rupture; ③ (retentir) [*applaudissements, rire, fusillade*] to break out; [*coup de feu*] to ring out; ④ (être révélé) [*scandale, nouvelle*] to break; [*vérité*] to come out; **faire ∼ qch au grand jour** to bring sth to light; ⑤ (survenir) [*guerre, grève, polémique*] to break out; [*orage*] to break; [*crise*] to erupt; ⑥ (être exprimé) [*colère*] to erupt; **laisser ∼ sa colère** to give vent to one's anger; ⑦ (se fragmenter) [*coalition, royaume*] to break up (**en** into); [*parti*] to split (**en** into); ⑧ (se mettre en colère) [*personne*] to lose one's temper; **∼ de rire** to burst out laughing; **∼ en sanglots** to burst into tears

éclectisme /eklɛktism/ *nm* eclecticism

éclipse /eklips/ *nf* lit, fig eclipse

éclipser /eklipse/ [1]
A *vtr* ① (en astronomie) to eclipse; ② (cacher) to obscure; ③ (surpasser) to outshine
B **s'éclipser**○ *vpr* to slip away

éclopé, ∼e /eklɔpe/
A *adj* injured, lame
B *nm,f* person with slight injuries

éclore /eklɔr/ [79] *vi* ① [*poussin, œuf*] to hatch; [*fleur*] to bloom; ② [*idée*] to dawn; [*talent*] to bloom

écluse /eklyz/ *nf* lock

éclusier, -ière /eklyzje, ɛʀ/ ▸ p. 372 *nm,f* lockkeeper

écœurant, ∼e /ekœrɑ̃, ɑ̃t/ *adj* ① (physiquement) [*gâteau, odeur, liqueur*] sickly; [*plat*] over-rich; ② (révoltant) nauseating; ③ (décourageant) sickening

écœurement /ekœrmɑ̃/ *nm* lit nausea; fig disgust

écœurer /ekœre/ [1] *vtr* ① (physiquement) [*nourriture, odeur*] to make [sb] feel sick; ② (moralement) to sicken

écolabel /ekɔlabɛl/ *nm* eco-label

école /ekɔl/ *nf* ① Scol (établissement, ensemble des élèves) school; **être à l'∼** to be at GB *ou* in US school; **la grande/petite ∼** primary/nursery school; ② (enseignement) school; **dès l'∼** from the very first days at school; ③ (système) education system; ④ Univ **(grande) ∼** higher education institution with competitive entrance examination; **une ∼ d'ingénieurs** a Grande École of Engineering; ⑤ (source de formation) training (**de** in); **l'∼ de la vie** the university of life; ⑥ (mouvement) school; **∼ flamande** Flemish school; **∼ de pensée** school of thought; **faire ∼** to gain a following

Composés　**∼ élémentaire** primary school; **∼ de gestion** Univ business school, school of business and management GB; **∼ hôtelière** hotel management school; **∼ d'infirmières** nursing college; **∼ libre** (système) independent education; (établissement) independent school; **∼ maternelle** nursery school; **∼ militaire** military academy; **∼ normale, EN** primary teacher training college; **∼ de police** police college GB, police academy US; **∼ primaire** primary school; **∼ publique** (établissement) state school GB, public school US; (système) state education GB, public education US; **∼ de secrétariat** secretarial college; **École nationale d'administration, ENA** *Grande École for top civil servants*; **École normale supérieure, ENS** *Grande École from which the educational élite is recruited*

ⓘ **École** *The French school system has three tiers: l'école maternelle (from the age of two); l'école primaire comprising cours préparatoire (CP), cours élémentaire 1 et 2 (CE1, CE2), cours moyen 1 et 2 (CM1, CM2); and l'école secondaire (collège and lycée). School attendance is compulsory between the ages of 6 and 16.*

écolier, -ière /ekɔlje, ɛʀ/ *nm,f* schoolchild, schoolboy/schoolgirl

écologie /ekɔlɔʒi/ *nf* (science) ecology

écologique /ekɔlɔʒik/ *adj* ① [*équilibre, catastrophe*] ecological; [*discours*] on the environment (*épith, après n*); ② [*impact, intérêt, conscience*] environmental; ③ [*produit*] environment-friendly

écologiste /ekɔlɔʒist/
A *adj* ① [*candidat*] Green; ② [*mesure*] ecological
B *nm,f* ① (partisan) environmentalist; (candidat) Green; ② (chercheur) ecologist

écomusée /ekomyze/ *nm* ≈ open air museum

éconduire /ekɔ̃dɥiʀ/ [69] *vtr* to turn [sb] away

économat /ekɔnɔma/ *nm* ① (local) bursar's office; ② (charge) office of bursar

économe /ekɔnɔm/
A *adj* thrifty
B ▸ p. 372 *nmf* bursar

économie /ekɔnɔmi/
A *nf* ① (de pays, région) economy; ② (discipline) economics (+ *v sg*); ③ (somme économisée) saving; **réaliser une ∼ de 5 euros** to save 5 euros; **faire l'∼ de** to save the cost of [*voyage, repas*]; ④ (action d'économiser) economy; **par ∼** to save money; ⑤ (sobriété) economy
B **économies** *nfpl* savings; **faire des ∼s** (épargner) to save up; (dépenser moins) to cut back on spending

Composés　**∼ d'entreprise** managerial economics; **∼ de marché** free market (economy); **∼ solidaire** solidarity economy

Idiome　**il n'y a pas de petites ∼s** every little helps

économique /ekɔnɔmik/ *adj* ① Écon [*politique, crise*] economic; ② (peu coûteux) economical

économiser /ekɔnɔmize/ [1] *vtr* ① (épargner) to save (up) [*argent*]; **∼ ses forces** to pace oneself; ② (réduire la consommation de) to save [*essence, eau, énergie*]; ③ (réduire ses dépenses) to economize (**sur** on)

économiseur /ekɔnɔmizœr/ *nm*
Composé　**∼ d'écran** Ordinat screensaver

économiste /ekɔnɔmist/ ▸ p. 372 *nmf* economist

écoper /ekɔpe/ [1]
A *vtr* Naut to bail out
B **écoper○ de** *vtr ind* to get [*punition, amende*]
C ○*vi* to take the rap○

écoproduit /ekopʀɔdɥi/ *nm* environment-friendly product

écorce /ekɔʀs/ *nf* (d'arbre) bark; (de fruit) peel; (de châtaigne) skin

Composé　**∼ terrestre** earth's crust

écorché, ∼e /ekɔʀʃe/
A *nm,f* **c'est un ∼** (vif) fig he's hypersensitive
B *nm* ① Anat écorché; ② Tech cutaway (diagram)

écorcher /ekɔʀʃe/ [1] *vtr* ① (dépecer) to skin [*animal*]; to flay [*victime*]; ② (blesser) to graze [*visage, jambe*]; ③ (estropier) to mispronounce [*mot*]; to murder [*chanson, langue*]; ④ ○(voler) to fleece○ [*client*]

écorchure /ekɔʀʃyʀ/ *nf* graze

écorner /ekɔʀne/ [1] *vtr* ① (entamer) to dent [*image de marque*]; to make a hole in [*capital*]; ② (abîmer) to make [sth] dog-eared GB, to dogear [*livre*]

écossais, ∼e /ekɔsɛ, ɛz/ ▸ p. 336, p. 504
A *adj* [*caractère, personne, paysage*] Scottish; [*whisky*] Scotch; [*langue*] Scots; [*jupe*] tartan
B *nm* ① Ling (dialecte anglais) Scots; (dialecte gaélique) (Scottish) Gaelic; ② (tissu) tartan (cloth)

Écossais, ∼e /ekɔsɛ, ɛz/ *nm,f* Scotsman/Scotswoman, Scot

Écosse /ekɔs/ ▸ p. 504 *nprf* Scotland

écosser /ekɔse/ [1] *vtr* to shell

écot /eko/ *nm* share

écotaxe /ekotaks/ *nf* eco-tax, environmental tax

écotourisme /ekotuʀism/ *nm* ecotourism

écoulement /ekulmɑ̃/ *nm* ① (d'eau, de circulation) flow; (de temps) passing; ② Méd discharge; **∼ de sang** bleeding; ③ Comm distribution and sale

écouler /ekule/ [1]
A *vtr* ① Comm to sell [*produit, stock*]; **les stocks sont écoulés** stocks are exhausted; ② (trafiquer) to pass [*billet, drogue*]; to fence [*butin*]
B **s'écouler** *vpr* ① (passer) [*temps, vie*] to pass; **la semaine écoulée** the past week; **le délai écoulé** the time which has elapsed; ② (circuler) [*eau, rivière*] to flow; ③ (sortir accidentellement) [*pétrole, eau*] to escape (**de** from; **dans** into); ④ (être évacué) [*eau*] to drain away; ⑤ Comm [*produit*] to move

écourter /ekuʀte/ [1] *vtr* (abréger) to cut short [*séjour*] (**de dix jours** by ten days); to shorten [*discours*]

écoute /ekut/ *nf* ① (fait d'écouter) **l'∼ de** listening to [*cassette, personne*]; **être à l'∼ de** lit to be listening (**à** to) [*émission*]; (être attentif à) to be (always) ready to listen to [*problèmes*]; **restez à l'∼ (de nos programmes)** stay tuned; **la qualité**

d'~ (de réception d'un émetteur) reception; (du son) sound quality; **2)** (audience) audience; **heure de grande ~** Radio peak listening time; TV peak viewing time; **3)** Tech **un appareil d'~** a listening device; **centre d'~(s)** monitoring centre^GB; **~s téléphoniques** phone-tapping ¢

écouter /ekute/ [1]
A vtr **1)** (s'appliquer à entendre) to listen to [*conversation, musique*]; **~ qn chanter** to listen to sb singing; **écoute, ne sois pas ridicule!** come on, don't be ridiculous!; **~ aux portes** to eavesdrop; **2)** (accepter d'entendre) to listen to [*explications, témoin*]; **3)** (tenir compte de) to listen to [*conseil, personne*]; **4)** (se laisser guider par) **~ son cœur** to follow one's own inclination; **~ sa conscience** to be guided by one's conscience
B s'écouter vpr **1)** s'~ **parler** to like the sound of one's own voice; **2)** (se dorloter) to cosset oneself; **3)** (faire à sa guise) **si je m'écoutais** if I had my way

écouteur /ekutœʀ/ nm **1)** (de téléphone) earpiece; **2)** (de stéréo) earphones (*pl*); (plus grand) headphones (*pl*)

écoutille /ekutij/ nf hatch

écrabouiller° /ekʀabuje/ [1] vtr to squash [*fruit, animal*]

écran /ekʀɑ̃/ nm **1)** Cin (surface) screen; (salle) cinema GB, movie theater US; (art) cinema; **porter une œuvre à l'~** to adapt a work for the cinema; **crever l'~** to have a great screen presence; **2)** Ordinat, TV screen; Électrotech display; **une vedette du petit ~** a TV star; **3)** (pour masquer) lit, fig screen; **crème ~ total** sun block; **4)** (pour protéger) screen; (nucléaire) shielding
(Composés) **~ antibruit** soundproofing; **~ à cristaux liquides** liquid crystal display, LCD; **~ de fumée** lit screen of smoke; fig, Mil smokescreen; **~ solaire** sunscreen; **~ tactile** touch screen; **~ de visualisation** VDU screen

écrasant, ~e /ekʀɑzɑ̃, ɑ̃t/ adj **1)** lit [*poids*] enormous; **2)** fig [*chaleur*] sweltering; [*défaite, dette*] crushing; [*victoire*] resounding; [*supériorité*] overwhelming; [*responsabilité*] heavy

écrasé, ~e /ekʀɑze/ adj (accablé) **~ de fatigue/remords** [*personne*] overcome with exhaustion/remorse; **~ par le travail** overwhelmed by work

écraser /ekʀɑze/ [1]
A vtr **1)** (blesser, tuer) [*machine, porte*] to crush [*doigt, personne*]; [*personne*] to squash [*insecte*]; (avec un véhicule) to run over [*piéton, animal*]; **se faire ~** to get run over; **2)** (endommager) [*personne*] to squash [*boîte, fruit*]; (plus endommagé) to crush; [*éléphant, tank*] to flatten [*végétation*]; **3)** Culin [*personne*] to mash [*légumes, fraises*]; to crush [*gousse d'ail*]; **4)** (aplatir délibérément) gén to squash; **~ sa cigarette** to stub out one's cigarette; **~ une larme** to wipe away a tear; **5)** (presser) [*personne*] to press [*nez, visage*] (**contre** against); **6)** (anéantir) to crush [*révolte*]; to thrash° [*équipe*]; **7)** (en étant meilleur) [*personne*] to outshine; **8)** (humilier) to put [sb] down [*personne*]; **9)** (accabler) [*chagrin, remords*] to overwhelm [*personne*]; [*fatigue, chaleur*] to overcome [*personne*]
B s'écraser vpr **1)** (avoir un accident) [*voiture, train*] to crash (**contre** into); [*automobiliste, motocycliste*] to have a crash; [*insectes*] to splatter (**contre** on); s'~ **(au sol)** [*avion*] to crash (to the ground); **2)** °(se taire) to shut up°; **3)** °(se soumettre) to keep one's head down

écrémer /ekʀeme/ [14] vtr **1)** to skim [*lait*]; **2)** to cream off the best of [*candidats*]

écrevisse /ekʀəvis/ nf crayfish GB, crawfish US
(Idiome) **rouge comme une ~** as red as a beetroot GB, as red as a beet US

écrier: s'écrier /ekʀije/ [2] vpr to exclaim

écrin /ekʀɛ̃/ nm **1)** (boîte) case; **2)** liter (environnement) setting

écrire /ekʀiʀ/ [67]
A vtr **1)** (rédiger) to write (**à** to); **2)** (orthographier) to spell
B vi gén to write
C s'écrire vpr **1)** (être rédigé) to be written; **2)** (être orthographié) to be spelled

écrit, ~e /ekʀi, it/
A adj written; **règle non ~e** unwritten rule; **c'était ~** fig it was bound to happen
B nm **1)** (œuvre) work, piece of writing; **2)** (document) document; **par ~** in writing; **3)** Scol, Univ (examen) written examination; (travail) written work

(Idiome) **les paroles s'envolent, les ~s restent** (il ne faut pas s'engager par écrit) never put anything in writing; (faites promettre par écrit) get it in writing

écriteau, pl **~x** /ekʀito/ nm sign

écritoire /ekʀitwaʀ/ nf writing case

écriture /ekʀityʀ/
A nf **1)** (manière) handwriting; **2)** (en imprimerie) hand; **3)** (texte) writing; **4)** Ling script; **~ phonétique** phonetic script; **5)** Littérat (activité) writing; **6)** (style) style; **7)** Comm (inscription) entry
B écritures nfpl Comm accounts

Écriture /ekʀityʀ/ nf Relig Scripture

écrivain /ekʀivɛ̃/ ▸ **p. 372** nm writer
(Composé) **~ public** letter-writer

écrou /ekʀu/ nm Tech nut

écrouer /ekʀue/ [1] vtr Jur to commit [sb] to prison

écroulé, ~e /ekʀule/ adj **1)** [*personne*] overwhelmed; **2)** [*maison, mur, pont*] in a state of collapse

écrouler: s'écrouler /ekʀule/ [1] vpr [*mur, personne, régime*] to collapse; [*espoir, espérance*] to fade; [*rêve, illusion*] to crumble

écru, ~e /ekʀy/ adj **1)** (brut) [*toile*] unbleached; [*laine*] undyed; [*soie*] raw; **2)** ▸ **p. 140** (couleur) ecru

ECU /eky/ ▸ **p. 34** nm (abbr = **European currency unit**) ECU

écu /eky/ nm **1)** ▸ **p. 34** (unité monétaire de la CEE) ecu; **2)** (en numismatique) ≈ crown; **3)** (bouclier) shield; **4)** (blason) escutcheon

écueil /ekœj/ nm **1)** Naut reef; **2)** fig (danger) pitfall

écuelle /ekɥɛl/ nf **1)** (récipient) bowl; **2)** (contenu) bowlful

éculé, ~e /ekyle/ adj **1)** **chaussure ~e** shoe with a worn-down heel; **2)** [*plaisanterie, théorie*] hackneyed

écume /ekym/ nf **1)** (sur l'eau) foam; (de bouillon, confiture) scum; (de bière, d'eau savonneuse) froth; (de métal) dross; **2)** (bave) foam
(Composé) **~ de mer** (magnésite) meerschaum

écumer /ekyme/ [1]
A vtr **1)** (enlever l'écume) to skim [*bouillon*]; to skim [*métal*]; **2)** (parcourir) to scour
B vi **1)** (se couvrir d'écume) [*mer, lac*] to foam; [*vin*] to froth; **2)** (baver) to foam

écumoire /ekymwaʀ/ nf skimming ladle, skimmer

écureuil /ekyʀœj/ nm squirrel

écurie /ekyʀi/ nf **1)** (de chevaux) stable; **2)** (de voitures) stable; **3)** (lieu sale) pigsty
(Idiome) **sentir l'~** to know one is nearly there

écusson /ekysɔ̃/ nm **1)** gén badge; (de soldat) flash GB; (de voiture) insignia; **2)** (en héraldique) escutcheon

écuyer, -ère /ekɥije, ɛʀ/
A ▸ **p. 372** nm,f **1)** (cavalier) horseman/horsewoman; (instructeur) riding instructor; **2)** (dans un cirque) bareback rider
B nm Hist (gentilhomme) squire; (responsable des écuries) equerry

eczéma /egzema/ ▸ **p. 195** nm eczema ¢

éden /edɛn/ nm fig paradise; **l'Éden** Relig Eden

édenté, ~e /edɑ̃te/ adj (sans dents) toothless; (avec des dents en moins) gap-toothed; [*peigne*] broken

EDF /œdeɛf/ nf (abbr = **Électricité de France**) French electricity board

édicter /edikte/ [1] vtr to enact [*loi, statut*]; to lay down [*peine, règle*]

édifiant, ~e /edifjɑ̃, ɑ̃t/ adj **1)** (exemplaire) edifying; **2)** (instructif) enlightening

édification /edifikasjɔ̃/ nf **1)** (de bâtiment, pays) building; **2)** (d'œuvre) creation; **3)** (instruction) enlightenment

édifice /edifis/ nm **1)** (bâtiment) building; **2)** (vaste ensemble organisé) structure

édifier /edifje/ [2] vtr **1)** to build [*bâtiment, ville*]; **2)** to build [*empire*]; to create [*œuvre*]; **3)** (porter à la vertu) to edify; **4)** (renseigner) to enlighten

édile /edil/ nm **1)** (conseiller municipal) town councillor^GB; **2)** aedile

Édimbourg /edɛ̃buʀ/ ▸ **p. 621** npr Edinburgh

édit /edi/ nm edict

e

éditer /edite/ [1] *vtr* **1** (publier) to publish [*livre, auteur*]; to release [*disque*]; **2** (présenter et annoter) to edit; **3** Ordinat to edit

éditeur, -trice /editœʀ, tʀis/ ▸ p. 372
A *nm,f* (qui présente et annote des textes) editor
B *nm* **1** (de livre, photo, musique) publisher; **2** Ordinat editor

édition /edisjɔ̃/
A *nf* **1** (action de publier et de diffuser) (de livre) publication; (de disque) release; **2** (texte, livre, gravure) edition; (disque) release; **3** (secteur) publishing; **société d'~** publishing firm; **4** (correction, annotation) editing; **5** (de journal) edition; **l'~ de 20 heures du journal télévisé** the eight o'clock (edition of the) news
B **éditions** *nfpl* **les ~s Hachette** Hachette (sg)

éditorial, ~e, *mpl* **-iaux** /editɔʀjal, o/
A *adj* [*politique, service*] editorial
B *nm* Presse editorial, leader

édredon /edʀədɔ̃/ *nm* eiderdown

éducateur, -trice /edykatœʀ, tʀis/
A *adj* educational
B ▸ p. 372 *nm,f* **~** (spécialisé) youth worker

éducatif, -ive /edykatif, iv/ *adj* educational

éducation /edykasjɔ̃/ *nf* **1** (enseignement) education; **2** (formation de personne) education; **faire l'~ de** to educate; **3** (entraînement) training; **4** (bonnes manières) manners (*pl*); **être sans ~** to be ill-mannered

(Composés) **Éducation nationale, EN** (ministère) Ministry of Education; (système) state education; **~ physique** physical education, PE GB, phys ed US

édulcorant, ~e /edylkɔʀɑ̃, ɑ̃t/ *nm* sweetener

édulcorer /edylkɔʀe/ [1] *vtr* **1** lit to sweeten [*boisson, mets*]; **2** fig (atténuer) to tone down [*propos*]

éduquer /edyke/ [1] *vtr* to educate [*personne, peuple*]; to train [*chien*]; **bien/mal éduqué** well/badly brought up

effaçable /efasabl/ *adj* [*cassette*] erasable; [*tache*] removable

effacé, ~e /efase/ *adj* [*personne*] retiring

effacement /efasmɑ̃/ *nm* **1** (de mots) deletion; **touche d'~** delete key; **2** (de cassette) erasure; **3** (d'une personne) (en général) self-effacement; (devant un rival) withdrawal

effacer /efase/ [12]
A *vtr* **1** (faire disparaître) (avec une gomme, un chiffon) to rub out [*mot, dessin*]; (avec un effaceur) to remove [*mot, phrase*]; (sur un traitement de texte) to delete [*mot, paragraphe*]; to erase [*enregistrement, film*]; **2** (rendre propre) to wipe [*bande magnétique, cassette*]; to clear [*écran, fichier*]; to clean [*tableau noir*]; **3** (rendre moins visible) [*soleil*] to fade [*couleur*]; [*pluie*] to erase [*traces, pas*]; [*neige*] to cover (up) [*traces, pas*]; [*crème*] to remove [*rides*]; **l'usure** *or* **le temps a effacé l'inscription** the inscription has worn away with time; **4** (faire oublier) to blot out [*souvenir, image*]; to dispel [*doute, regret*]; to remove [*différence, distinctions*]; **on efface tout et on recommence** fig (oublier, pardonner) let's wipe the slate clean and start all over again; (repartir à zéro) let's start afresh; **5** to write off [*dette, pertes*]
B **s'effacer** *vpr* **1** (avec une gomme) **ça s'efface** you can rub it out; **2** (avec le temps) [*inscription, couleur, dessin*] to fade; **3** (cesser) [*souvenir, sourire, haine*] to fade; [*impression*] to wear off; [*doute, crainte*] to disappear; **4** (personne) (pour laisser passer) to step aside; (rester discret) to stay in the background; **s'~ devant un rival** to give way to a rival

effaceur /efasœʀ/ *nm* **~ (d'encre)** correction pen

effarant, ~e /efaʀɑ̃, ɑ̃t/ *adj* astounding

effarement /efaʀmɑ̃/ *nm* alarm

effarer /efaʀe/ [1] *vtr* to alarm

effaroucher /efaʀuʃe/ [1]
A *vtr* **1** (faire fuir) to frighten [sth] away [*personne, animal*]; **2** (inquiéter) to alarm
B **s'effaroucher** *vpr* to take fright (**de, à** at)

effectif, -ive /efɛktif, iv/
A *adj* (réel) [*contrôle, aide*] real; **durée effective du travail** actual time worked; **devenir ~** [*mesure*] to come into effect
B *nm* (d'école) number of pupils; (d'entreprise) workforce; (d'une armée) strength; **un ~ de 200 élèves** 200 pupils on the roll GB, an enrollment of 200 pupils US

effectivement /efɛktivmɑ̃/ *adv* **1** (en effet) indeed; **2** (réellement) actually, really

effectuer /efɛktɥe/ [1] *vtr* to do [*calcul, réparations, travail*]; to make [*paiement, changement, choix, atterrissage*]; to carry

out [*transaction*]; to conduct [*sondage*]; to serve [*peine*]; to complete [*visite, voyage*]; **~ son apprentissage** to serve an apprenticeship

efféminé, ~e /efemine/ *adj* effeminate

effervescence /efɛʀvesɑ̃s/ *nf* **1** (bouillonnement) effervescence; **2** (émoi) turmoil; **il avait l'esprit en ~** his mind was in a ferment

effervescent, ~e /efɛʀvesɑ̃, ɑ̃t/ *adj* **1** lit [*comprimé*] effervescent; **2** fig [*foule*] seething; [*caractère*] effervescent

effet /efɛ/
A *nm* **1** (conséquence) effect; **faire de l'~** [*médicament*] to work; [*commentaire*] to have some effect; **prendre ~** [*mesure*] to take effect; **sous l'~ de l'alcool** under the influence of alcohol; **sous l'~ de la passion** in a fit of passion; **sous l'~ de la colère** in a rage; **2** (impression) impression; **faire bon/mauvais ~** to make a good/bad impression; **être du meilleur ~** [*vêtement*] to look extremely nice; **être du plus mauvais ~** to be in the worst possible taste; **quel ~ cela te fait-il d'être père?** how does it feel to be a father?; **faire un drôle d'~** [*vitesse, alcool, rencontre*] to make one feel strange; **il me fait l'~ d'un homme honnête** he looks like an honest man to me; **leur réponse m'a fait l'~ d'une douche froide** their answer came as a real shock to me; **un ~ de surprise** an element of surprise; **3** (procédé) effect; **couper tous ses ~s à qn** to steal sb's thunder; **4** (but) **à cet ~** for that purpose; **5** (phénomène) **l'~ Maastricht** the Maastricht effect; **6** Sport spin
B **en effet** *loc adv* indeed
C **effets** *nmpl* (vêtements) things

(Composés) **~ de serre** greenhouse effect; **~ spécial** special effect; **~s secondaires** side effects

effeuiller /efœje/ [1] *vtr* [*personne*] to thin out the foliage of [*arbre*]; to strip the leaves off [*légume*]; [*vent*] to blow the leaves off [*arbre*]

(Idiome) **~ la marguerite** to play 'he loves me, he loves me not'

efficace /efikas/ *adj* [*action, méthode*] effective; [*remède*] effective; [*personne, dispositif*] efficient

efficacement /efikasmɑ̃/ *adv* [*travailler, fonctionner*] efficiently; [*intervenir, soigner*] effectively

efficacité /efikasite/ *nf* (d'action, de méthode, remède) effectiveness; (de personne, dispositif) efficiency

efficience /efisjɑ̃s/ *nf* efficiency

effigie /efiʒi/ *nf* **1** (représentation) effigy; **à l'~ de** [*médaille, timbre*] with the head of; **2** (symbole) logo

effilé, ~e /efile/ *adj* **1** [*amandes*] flaked; **2** [*doigt*] slender

effiler /efile/ [1]
A *vtr* **1** to sharpen [*lame, pointe*]; **2** to thin out [*cheveux*]; **3** to string [*haricots verts*]
B **s'effiler** *vpr* (s'effranger) to fray

effilocher: s'effilocher /efilɔʃe/ [1] *vpr* [*tissu*] to fray

efflanqué, ~e /eflɑ̃ke/ *adj* emaciated

effleurer /eflœʀe/ [1] *vtr* (frôler) to touch lightly, to brush (against); (égratigner) to graze; **l'idée ne m'a même pas effleuré** fig the idea didn't even cross my mind; **le livre ne fait qu'~ la question** fig the book only skims over the subject

efflorescence /eflɔʀesɑ̃s/ *nf* **1** Chimie, Méd efflorescence; **2** Bot bloom

effluent /eflyɑ̃/ *nm* (eaux usées) effluent; **~s radioactifs** radioactive discharge **¢**

effluve /eflyv/ *nm* (nauséabond) unpleasant smell; (agréable) fragrance

effondrement /efɔ̃dʀəmɑ̃/ *nm* **1** lit (de toit, pont) collapse; **2** (de terrain) subsidence; **3** (de régime, d'économie) collapse

effondrer: s'effondrer /efɔ̃dʀe/ [1] *vpr* **1** (s'écrouler) [*toit, personne, régime, prix*] to collapse; [*rêve*] to crumble; [*espoir*] to fall; [*popularité*] to fall drastically; **2** (nerveusement) to collapse; **s'~ en larmes** to dissolve into tears; **s'~ de chagrin** to be distracted with grief; **être effondré par la nouvelle** to be distraught at the news

efforcer: s'efforcer /efɔʀse/ [12] *vpr* to try hard (**de faire** to do)

effort /efɔʀ/ *nm* **1** (physique, intellectuel) effort; **après bien des ~s** after a great deal of effort; **un ~ de mémoire** an effort to remember; **fais un petit ~ d'imagination!** use a bit of imagination!; **avec mon dos, je ne peux pas faire d'~** with this back of mine, I can't do anything strenuous; **allons, encore un petit ~!** (près du bout) come on, you're almost there!; **sans ~** effortlessly; ② (subvention, aide) financial aid; (mise de fonds) investment, (financial) outlay; ③ Phys (force exercée) stress; (force subie) strain

effraction /efʀaksjɔ̃/ *nf* Jur breaking and entering; **ils sont entrés dans la maison par ~** they broke into the house

(Composé) **~ informatique** computer hacking

effranger /efʀɑ̃ʒe/ [13] *vtr*, **s'effranger** *vpr* to fray

effrayant, ~e /efʀɛjɑ̃, ɑ̃t/ *adj* ① (qui fait peur) [vision, laideur] frightening; [maigreur, pâleur] dreadful; ② ᴼ(excessif) [chaleur, prix] terrible

effrayer /efʀeje/ [21] *vtr* ① (faire peur à) to frighten; (alarmer) to alarm; ② (rebuter) to put [sb] off

effréné, ~e /efʀene/ *adj* [course, rythme, concurrence] frenzied; [ambition, luxe, gaspillage] wild

effriter /efʀite/ [1]
A *vtr* to crumble [gâteau]; to break up [motte de terre]
B **s'effriter** *vpr* lit, fig to crumble (away)

effroi /efʀwa/ *nm* dread, terror

effronté, ~e /efʀɔ̃te/
A *adj* [enfant, regard, remarque] cheeky; [adulte] (éhonté) shameless; (hardi) cheeky
B *nm,f* cheeky boy/girl

effronterie /efʀɔ̃tʀi/ *nf* cheek, effrontery sout

effroyable /efʀwajabl/ *adj* dreadful

effusion /efyzjɔ̃/ *nf* effusion; **avec ~** [remercier, parler] effusively; **sans ~** [parler] unemotionally

(Composé) **~ de sang** bloodshed

égailler: s'égailler /egaje/ [1] *vpr* to disperse

égal, ~e, *mpl* **-aux** /egal, o/
A *adj* ① (identique) equal (à to); **à travail ~, salaire ~** equal work for equal pay; **~ à lui-même, il...** true to form, he...; ② (régulier) [terrain] level; [lumière] even; [teinte] uniform; [temps] settled; [pouls, respiration] steady; **d'un pas ~** at an even pace; **avoir un tempérament ~** to be even-tempered; ③ (indifférent) **ça m'est ~** (je n'ai pas de préférence) I don't mind either way; (je m'en moque) I don't care; **c'est ~**ᴼ all the same; (équitable) **la partie n'est pas ~e (entre eux)** they are not evenly matched
B *nm,f* equal; **traiter d'~ à ~ avec qn** to deal with sb as an equal; **il est d'une beauté sans ~e** to be supremely beautiful; **il fera un piètre ministre, à l'~ de son prédécesseur** he'll make a poor minister, just like his predecessor

(Idiomes) **rester ~ à soi-même** to be one's usual self; **combattre à armes ~es** to be on an equal footing

égalable /egalabl/ *adj* **difficilement ~** [beauté, bêtise] unparalleled; [technique] incomparably superior

également /egalmɑ̃/ *adv* ① (aussi) also, too; ② (au même degré) equally

égaler /egale/ [1] *vtr* ① (atteindre) to equal [record]; to be as good as [personne]; to be as high as [prix]; **~ les meilleurs** to rank with the best; **technique jamais encore égalée** hitherto unequalled^GB technique; ② (valoir) **rien n'égale un coucher de soleil** nothing can compare with a sunset; **leur intelligence égale leur charme** they're as clever as they're charming; ③ Math **trois plus trois égalent six** three plus three equals six *ou* is six

égalisation /egalizasjɔ̃/ *nf* ① (des revenus, de surface, sol) levelling^GB out; ② Sport **rater l'~** to fail to score the equalizer

égaliser /egalize/ [1]
A *vtr* ① (en nivelant) to level [terrain]; to level out [prix, revenus]; ② (en taillant) to even up the ends of [cheveux]; to make [sth] the same size [planches]
B *vi* Sport to equalize GB, to tie US

égalitaire /egalitɛʀ/ *adj*, *nmf* egalitarian

égalité /egalite/ *nf* ① (parité) gén, Pol equality; ② Sport **être à ~** to be level GB, to be tied US; **~!** (au tennis) deuce!; ③ (uniformité) (de terrain) flatness; (de climat) temperate nature; (d'humeur) evenness; ④ Math equality

égard /egaʀ/
A *nm* ① (considération) consideration ¢; **sans ~ pour** without regard for; **par ~ pour** out of consideration for; ② (rapport) **à l'~ de qn** toward(s) sb; **à l'~ de qch** regarding; **à cet ~** in this respect; **eu ~ à qch** in view of sth

B **égards** *nmpl* (marques d'estime) **avec des ~s** with respect; **manquer d'~s envers qn** to be disrespectful toward(s) sb

égaré, ~e /egaʀe/ *adj* ① [animal] stray (épith); ② [air, yeux] wild, distracted

égarement /egaʀmɑ̃/ *nm* ① (trouble) distraction; ② (dérèglement) (état) confusion; (comportement) erratic behaviour^GB

égarer /egaʀe/ [1]
A *vtr* ① lit, fig (faire perdre) to lead [sb] astray [personne]; ② (perdre) to mislay [objet]
B **s'égarer** *vpr* ① (se perdre) [personne, animal] to get lost; ② (être perdu) [lettre, colis] to get lost; ③ (errer) [esprit] to wander; [personne] to ramble

égayer /egeje/ [21] *vtr* to enliven [conversation, soirée]; to cheer [sb] up [malade]; to amuse [convives, assemblée]; to brighten [sth] up [maison, robe]; to lighten [ouvrage, style]; to brighten [journée, vie]

Égée /eʒe/ ▸ p. 406 *npr* Aegeus; **mer ~** Aegean Sea

égérie /eʒeʀi/ *nf* muse

égide /eʒid/ *nf* aegis

églantine /eglɑ̃tin/ *nf* wild rose, dog-rose

églefin /eglafɛ̃/ *nm* haddock

église /egliz/ *nf* church; **aller à l'~** to go to church

Église /egliz/ *nf* Church; **homme d'~** cleric

égocentrique /egosɑ̃tʀik/ *adj*, *nmf* egocentric

égocentrisme /egosɑ̃tʀism/ *nm* self-centredness^GB

égoïsme /egoism/ *nm* selfishness

égoïste /egoist/
A *adj* selfish
B *nmf* selfish man/woman

égorger /egɔʀʒe/ [13] *vtr* **~ qn** to cut sb's throat

égosiller: s'égosiller /egozije/ [1] *vpr* ① (se fatiguer la voix) to shout oneself hoarse; ② (chanter fort) to sing at the top of one's voice; (crier) to yell

égotiste /egotist/
A *adj* egotistical
B *nmf* egotist

égout /egu/ *nm* sewer

égoutier, -ière /egutje, ɛʀ/ ▸ p. 372 *nm,f* sewage worker

égoutter /egute/ [1]
A *vtr* to drain [vaisselle, riz, légumes, frites]; to strain [fromage]; to hang up [sth] to drip dry [linge]
B *vi* [vaisselle, riz, fromage] to drain; [linge] to drip
C **s'égoutter** *vpr* [vaisselle, riz, légumes, fromage] to drain; [linge] to drip dry

égouttoir /egutwaʀ/ *nm* draining rack GB, (dish) drainer US

égratigner /egʀatiɲe/ [1]
A *vtr* ① (griffer) to scratch [jambe, meuble]; (écorcher) to graze [jambe]; ② fig to hurt [personne]
B **s'égratigner** *vpr* (sur des ronces, un objet pointu) to scratch oneself; (par frottement) to graze oneself

égratignure /egʀatiɲyʀ/ *nf* (en griffant) scratch; (par frottement) graze; **se sortir de qch sans une ~** lit to come out of sth without a scratch; fig to come out of sth with one's reputation unscathed

égrener /egʀəne/ [16] *vtr* ① Culin to shell [pois]; to remove the seeds from [tomate, melon]; ② to chime out [notes, heures]; to drone out [chiffres, chanson]; **~ son chapelet** to tell one's beads

égrillard, ~e /egʀijaʀ, aʀd/ *adj* [personne] dirty-minded; [air, histoire] bawdy

Égypte /eʒipt/ ▸ p. 230 *nprf* Egypt

égyptien, -ienne /eʒipsjɛ̃, ɛn/ ▸ p. 336, p. 392
A *adj* Egyptian
B *nm* Ling Egyptian

eh /e/ *excl* (pour attirer l'attention) hey; **~ bien** well; **~ oui** (ton résigné) so there we are; (pour insister) I'm afraid so

éhonté, ~e /eɔ̃te/ *adj* [menteur, mensonge] brazen; [demande] shameless

Éire /ɛʀ/ *npr* Éire, Republic of Ireland

éjaculer /eʒakyle/ [1] *vi* to ejaculate

éjectable /eʒɛktabl/ *adj* **siège ~** ejector seat GB, ejection seat US

éjecter /eʒɛkte/ [1] *vtr* ① (dans un accident) to throw [sb/sth] out; ② ᴼ(expulser) to chuck^ᴼ [sb] out [personne] (**de** of); ③ Tech to eject

éjection /eʒɛksjɔ̃/ nf [1] (de pilote, fluide, cartouche) ejection; [2] ○(expulsion) expulsion

élaboration /elabɔrasjɔ̃/ nf [1] (de projet) development; (de solution) working out; (de document) drafting; (de journal) putting together; [2] Bot elaboration

élaboré, ~**e** /elabɔre/ adj [cuisine] sophisticated

élaborer /elabɔre/ [1] vtr (préparer) to work [sth] out [stratégie, solution]; to draw up [document]; to put [sth] together [brochure]

élaguer /elage/ [1] vtr lit, fig to prune

élan /elɑ̃/ nm [1] Sport (pour sauter) run up; **saut avec/sans ~** running/standing jump; [2] (force) lit, fig momentum; [3] (impulsion) impetus; [4] (enthousiasme) enthusiasm; [5] (mouvement affectif) impulse; ~ **de colère** surge of anger; [6] Zool elk

élancé, ~**e** /elɑ̃se/ adj [personne, édifice] slender

élancement /elɑ̃smɑ̃/ nm [1] (douleur) throbbing pain; [2] (aspiration) yearning

élancer /elɑ̃se/ [12]
A vi **mon doigt m'élance** I've got a throbbing pain in my finger
B s'**élancer** vpr [1] (bondir) [personne] to dash forward; **s'~ à l'assaut** to launch an assault (**de** on); [2] (partir) [personne, voiture] to shoot off○; [3] (se dresser) **s'~ vers le ciel** [arbre, cathédrale] to soar up toward(s) the sky

élargi, ~**e** /elarʒi/ adj [format] enlarged; [gouvernement] expanded

élargir /elarʒir/ [3]
A vtr [1] (rendre plus large) to widen [chaussée]; to let [sth] out [vêtement]; [2] (déformer) [personne] to stretch [chaussures, pull]; [3] (étendre) to widen [débat]; to extend [contacts, audience, droit]; to broaden [connaissances, idées, activités]; to increase [majorité]; to expand [moyens, secteur]; [4] Jur (libérer) to release [détenu]
B s'**élargir** vpr [groupe] to expand; [écart] to increase; [débat, route, fleuve] to widen; [personne] to fill out; [épaules] to become broader; [vêtement] to stretch

élastique /elastik/
A adj [1] (extensible) [bretelle, taille] elasticated GB, elasticized US; [2] Phys [gaz, métal, fibre] elastic; **une démarche ~** a springy walk; [3] [règlement, horaire] flexible; [budget] elastic
B nm [1] (lien circulaire) rubber band; (en mercerie) elastic; [2] (jeu d'enfant) **jouer à l'~** to play elastics; [3] ▸ p. 327 Sport (pour sauter) bungee cord; **sauter à l'~** to do a bungee jump

électeur, **-trice** /elɛktœr, tris/ nm,f voter

élection /elɛksjɔ̃/ nf [1] Pol election (**à** to); ~ **partielle** by-election GB, off-year election US; **après son ~** after being elected; [2] (choix) choice; **mon pays d'~** my chosen country

> ℹ️ **Élection** Public elections are held on Sundays, with a week's delay (two weeks in the *élections présidentielles*) between first and second rounds if absolute majority is not achieved immediately. Voters, who must present their *carte d'électeur* and proof of identity, collect slips and in the privacy of the polling booth choose the slip containing the name of their preferred candidate or list and place it in an envelope and then in the polling box or *urne*.

électoral, ~**e**, mpl **-aux** /elɛktɔral, o/ adj [programme, réforme, calendrier, promesse] electoral; [affiche, dépense, période] election (épith); [victoire, campagne] election (épith), electoral

électoralisme /elɛktɔralism/ nm electioneering

électoraliste /elɛktɔralist/ adj electioneering

électorat /elɛktɔra/ nm electorate, voters (pl)

électricien, **-ienne** /elɛktrisjɛ̃, ɛn/ ▸ p. 372 nm,f electrician

électricité /elɛktrisite/ nf lit, fig electricity; **marcher à l'~** to run on electricity; **l'atmosphère était chargée d'~** fig the atmosphere was electric

électrifier /elɛktrifje/ [2] vtr to bring electricity to [village]; to electrify [voie ferrée]

électrique /elɛktrik/ adj [1] [appareil] electric; [installation] electrical; [réseau] electricity (épith); [2] fig [atmosphère] electric

électrisant, ~**e** /elɛktrizɑ̃, ɑ̃t/ adj fig electrifying

électriser /elɛktrize/ [1] vtr [1] Phys to charge [sth] with electricity; [2] (exalter) to electrify

électro(-) /elɛktro/ préf electro; ~**-aimant** electromagnet; ~**cardiogramme** electrocardiogram

électrochoc /elɛktroʃɔk/ nm [1] Méd ~**s** electroshock therapy (sg), EST; [2] fig shock treatment **₵**

électrocuter /elɛktrokyte/ [1]
A vtr to electrocute
B s'**électrocuter** vpr (accidentellement) to be electrocuted

électrode /elɛktrɔd/ nf electrode

électrogène /elɛktrɔʒɛn/ adj **groupe ~** (electricity) generator

électrolyse /elɛktrɔliz/ nf electrolysis

électromécanicien, **-ienne** /elɛktromekanisjɛ̃, ɛn/ ▸ p. 372 nm,f electrical engineer

électroménager /elɛktromenaʒe/
A adj m **appareil ~** electrical domestic ou household appliance
B nm [1] (appareils) electrical domestic ou household appliances (pl); [2] (industrie) electrical goods industry

électromoteur, **-trice** /elɛktromotœr, tris/ adj electromotive

électron /elɛktrɔ̃/ nm electron

électronicien, **-ienne** /elɛktrɔnisjɛ̃, ɛn/ ▸ p. 372 nm,f electronics engineer

électronique /elɛktrɔnik/
A adj [1] [circuit, composant] electronic; [2] [microscope, télescope] electron (épith)
B nf electronics (+ v sg)

électrophone /elɛktrɔfɔn/ nm record player

électrostatique /elɛktrostatik/
A adj electrostatic
B nf electrostatics (+ v sg)

électrotechnique /elɛktroteknik/ nf electrical engineering; (discipline) electrotechnology

élégamment /elegamɑ̃/ adv [s'habiller] elegantly; [se conduire] courteously

élégance /elegɑ̃s/ nf (qualité) elegance; **d'une grande ~** extremely elegant; **avec ~** [s'habiller] elegantly; [perdre] gracefully; [se conduire] honourably^GB; [résoudre un problème] neatly

élégant, ~**e** /elegɑ̃, ɑ̃t/
A adj [personne, vêtement, écriture] elegant; [solution] neat, elegant; **ce n'est pas très ~ de ta part** it's not very decent of you
B nm,f dandy/elegant lady

élégie /eleʒi/ nf elegy

élément /elemɑ̃/
A nm [1] (constituant) (d'ensemble, de structure) element; (d'appareil) component; (de mélange) ingredient; (de problème) element; (facteur) factor, element; ~ **décisif** deciding factor; **l'~ humain** the human element ou factor; ~ **moteur** (personne) driving force; [2] (de mobilier) unit; ~**s de cuisine** kitchen units; [3] (fait) fact; [4] (individu) **bon ~** (élève) good pupil; (joueur) good player; [5] Tech (de pile) cell; [6] Chimie element
B **éléments** nmpl [1] (rudiments) (premiers) ~**s** basics; [2] Météo elements

élémentaire /elemɑ̃tɛr/ adj (de base) [principe, besoin] basic; Scol [niveau] elementary; (simple) elementary

éléphant /elefɑ̃/ nm elephant

(Idiome) **avoir une mémoire d'~** never to forget a thing

éléphante /elefɑ̃t/ nf cow elephant

éléphanteau, pl ~**x** /elefɑ̃to/ nm (elephant) calf

éléphantesque /elefɑ̃tɛsk/ adj elephantine, enormous

élevage /elvaʒ/ nm [1] (de bétail) livestock farming; ~ **de saumons** salmon farming; **faire de l'~** to breed GB ou raise US livestock; **faire de l'~ de chevaux** to breed horses; **produits de l'~** meat and dairy products; **d'~** [huîtres, poisson] farmed; [caille, faisan] captive-bred; [2] (installation) farm; **un ~ de visons** a mink farm; [3] (ensemble des animaux) stock (**de** of)

élévateur /elevatœr/ nm (engin, muscle) elevator

élévation /elevasjɔ̃/ nf [1] (de niveau) rise (**de** in); [2] (promotion) elevation; [3] (sur un plan) elevation; [4] Géog ~ **de terrain** rise in the ground; [5] Relig Elevation (of the Host)

e

élève /elɛv/ *nmf* gén student; Scol pupil

(Composé) ~ **officier** trainee officer

élevé, ~**e** /elve/ *adj* ① [*niveau, prix, grade, rang*] high; **plus** ~ higher; **moins** ~ lower; **peu** ~ low; ② [*plateau*] high; **habiter un étage** ~ to live on an upper floor; ③ (noble) [*sentiment*] fine; [*principes*] high; [*idéal*] lofty; [*langage*] elevated

élever /elve/ [16]

A *vtr* ① (construire) to put up [*barrière, mur*]; to erect [*statue*]; ~ **des obstacles** fig to make things difficult; ② (porter à un degré supérieur) to raise [*température, taux, niveau*]; ~ **la voix** or **le ton** lit to raise one's voice; ③ (lever) to raise [*bras*]; (soulever) to raise, to lift [*chargement*]; ④ (ennoblir) **la poésie élève l'âme** or **l'esprit** poetry is elevating; ⑤ (formuler) to raise [*objection*]; to voice [*doutes*]; ⑥ (éduquer) to bring up [*enfant*]; **enfant bien/mal élevé** well/badly brought up child; **c'est mal élevé** it's bad manners (**de faire** to do); ⑦ Agric to rear [*bétail*]; to keep [*volaille, abeilles*]

B **s'élever** *vpr* ① (augmenter) [*température, taux*] to rise; ② (atteindre) **s'**~ **à** [*bénéfices, dépenses*] to come to; [*chiffre d'affaires, nombre de victimes*] to stand at; ③ (se hausser) to rise; **s'**~ **dans les airs** or **le ciel** [*fumée*] to rise up into the air; [*oiseau*] to soar into the air; **s'**~ **dans la hiérarchie** to rise in the hierarchy; ④ [*protestations, voix*] to be heard; ⑤ (prendre parti) **s'**~ **contre qch** to protest against sth; ⑥ (se dresser) [*clocher, statue*] to stand; **s'**~ **au-dessus de qch** [*clocher, falaise*] to rise above sth

éleveur, -euse /elvœʀ, øz/ ▸ p. 372 *nm,f* breeder

elfe /ɛlf/ *nm* elf

élider /elide/ [1] *vtr*, **s'élider** *vpr* to elide

éligibilité /eliʒibilite/ *nf* eligibility (**à** for election to)

éligible /eliʒibl/ *adj* eligible for office

élimé /elime/ *adj* [*vêtement*] threadbare

élimer /elime/ [1] *vtr* to wear [sth] thin [*tissu*]

éliminatoire /eliminatwaʀ/

A *adj* [*question, match*] qualifying (*épith*); [*note*] eliminatory

B *nf* qualifier

éliminer /elimine/ [1] *vtr* to eliminate [*candidat, équipe, toxines, erreurs*]; to rule out [*possibilité*]

élire /eliʀ/ [66] *vtr* to elect [*maire, représentant*]; ~ **qn président** to elect sb president; **se faire** ~ to be elected; **être élue Miss Monde** to be voted Miss World; ~ **domicile** gén to take up residence; Jur to elect domicile

élisabéthain, ~**e** /elizabetɛ̃, ɛn/ *adj* Elizabethan

élision /elizjɔ̃/ *nf* elision

élite /elit/ *nf* **l'**~ the elite; **d'**~ [*troupes, unité*] elite (*épith*), crack; [*athlète, étudiant*] high-flying (*épith*); **sujet d'**~ highflier

élitisme /elitism/ *nm* elitism

elle /ɛl/ *pron pers f* ① (sujet) (personne, animal familier) she; (objet, concept, pays, animal) it; ~**s** they; **ta mère est-**~ **arrivée?** has your mother arrived?; **j'aime le jazz,** ~ **aussi** I like jazz, so does she; ~ **qui aime tant le ballet, quel dommage qu'**~ **ne soit pas là** she loves ballet so much, it's a pity she isn't here; **est-ce** ~ **qui a bu le vin?** was she the one who drank the wine?; **ses collègues et** ~ **étaient enchantés** she and her colleagues were delighted; ~**, ne dit rien** she never says a word; **'je n'aime pas ça!'—'**~ **non plus'** 'I don't like that!'—'she doesn't either'; **la pie vole tout ce qu'**~ **trouve** the magpie steals everything it finds; **l'heure a-t-**~ **sonné?** has the clock struck the hour?; **le Portugal a signé, l'Espagne,** ~**, n'a pas encore donné son accord** Portugal has signed while Spain has not yet agreed; ② (dans une comparaison) her; **je suis plus jeune qu'**~ I'm younger than she is *ou* than her; **je les vois plus souvent qu'**~ (qu'elle ne les voit) I see them more often than she does; (que je ne la vois) I see them more often than her; ③ (après une préposition) (personne, animal familier) her; (objet, animal) it; **à cause d'**~ because of her; **pour** ~, **c'est un fou** she thinks he's mad; **je ne pense plus à** ~ I don't think about her any more; **à** ~ (dans une séquence) it's her turn; **c'est à** ~ **de choisir** (son tour) it's her turn to choose; (sa responsabilité) it's up to her to choose; (marquant la possession) **des amis à** ~ friends of hers; **elle n'a pas de coin à** ~ **dans la maison** she doesn't have a room of her own in the house; **le bol bleu est à** ~ the blue bowl is hers

ellébore /elebɔʀ/ *nm* helebore

elle-même, *pl* **elles-mêmes** /ɛlmɛm/ *pron pers f* ① (personne) herself; **elles-mêmes** themselves; **en** ~ **elle se** disait que she told herself that; **'Madame Dubois?'—'**~**'** (au téléphone) 'Mrs Dubois?'—'speaking'; ② (objet, idée, concept) itself; **elles-mêmes** themselves; **en** ~ in itself; **les taches sont parties d'elles-mêmes** the stains came out by themselves

elles *pron pers fpl* ▸ **elle**

ellipse /elips/ *nf* ① Math ellipse; ② Ling ellipsis

elliptique /eliptik/ *adj* Math elliptic; Ling elliptical

élocution /elɔkysjɔ̃/ *nf* diction; **avoir une** ~ **lente** to speak slowly; **défaut d'**~ speech impediment

éloge /elɔʒ/ *nm* ① (louange) praise; **faire l'**~ **de qn/qch** to sing the praises of sb/sth; **faire l'**~ **du crime/de la drogue** to extol^GB crime/drugs; **être digne d'**~**s** [*personne*] to deserve praise; [*action*] to be praiseworthy; **il a été couvert d'**~**s par** he was showered with praise by; **décerner des** ~**s à qn** to commend sb; **être tout à l'**~ **de qn** to do sb great credit; ② Littérat (discours) eulogy

(Composé) ~ **funèbre** funeral oration

élogieux, -ieuse /elɔʒjø, øz/ *adj* [*personne*] full of praise; [*article*] laudatory; **en termes** ~ in glowing terms

éloigné, ~**e** /elwaɲe/ *adj* ① (dans l'espace) distant; ~ **de tout** remote; **un hameau** ~ **de cinq kilomètres** a hamlet five kilometres^GB away; **deux usines** ~**es de cinq kilomètres** two factories five kilometres^GB apart; **c'est trop** ~ it's too far away; ② (dans le temps) [*souvenirs*] distant; [*événement*] remote (*jamais épith*); ~ **dans le temps** distant (in time); **dans un futur peu** ~ in the not too distant future; **dans un passé peu** ~ not (so) long ago; ③ (dans la famille) [*cousin*] distant; ④ (différent) [*positions, opinions*] poles apart; **très** ~ **de la réalité** far removed from reality

éloignement /elwaɲmɑ̃/ *nm* ① (dans l'espace) distance; ② (dans le temps) remoteness; **avec l'**~, **l'événement prend tout son sens** in retrospect, the full significance of the event becomes apparent; ③ (écart) **son** ~ **des milieux littéraires** his/her lack of contact with literary circles

éloigner /elwaɲe/ [1]

A *vtr* ① lit to move [sb/sth] away (**de** from); ~ **les badauds** to move onlookers on; ② fig **ils font tout pour l'**~ **de moi** they are doing everything to drive us apart; ~ **une menace/un danger** to remove a threat/a danger

B **s'éloigner** *vpr* ① lit to move away (**de** from); **l'orage s'éloigne** the storm is moving away; **il s'éloigne à pas lents** he walks away slowly; ② fig **s'**~ **de** [*personne*] to move away from; [*idéologie, ligne politique*]; to wander from, to stray from [*sujet*]; **le texte s'éloigne du schéma de base sur deux points** the text differs from the basic pattern on two points

élongation /elɔ̃gasjɔ̃/ *nf* ① Méd (accidentelle) pulled muscle; (thérapeutique) traction; ② (en astronomie) elongation; ③ Phys displacement

éloquence /elɔkɑ̃s/ *nf* eloquence **⊄**

éloquent, ~**e** /elɔkɑ̃, ɑ̃t/ *adj* [*personne, paroles*] eloquent; **le score est** ~ the score speaks for itself

élu, ~**e** /ely/ *nm,f* ① Pol elected representative; ② (personne aimée) beloved; **l'**~ **de mon cœur** the one I love; ③ (choisi par Dieu) **les** ~**s** the elect (+ *v pl*)

élucidation /elysidasjɔ̃/ *nf* clarification

élucider /elyside/ [1] *vtr* to solve [*crime, problème*]; to clarify [*circonstances, conditions*]; **crime non élucidé** unsolved crime

élucubrations /elykybʀasjɔ̃/ *nfpl* rantings

élucubrer /elykybʀe/ [1] *vtr* pej to dream up [*plan*]

éluder /elyde/ [1] *vtr* to evade

Élysée /elize/ *nprm* ① Pol **(palais de l')**~ Élysée Palace (*the official residence of the French President*); ② Mythol Elysium

élytre /elitʀ/ *nm* elytron

émacier: s'émacier /emasje/ [2] *vpr* to become emaciated

e-mail /imɛl/ *nm* email, e-mail

émail, *pl* **-aux** /emaj, o/ *nm* (matière, objet) enamel

émaillé, ~**e** /emaje/ *adj* [*ustensile*] enamel (*épith*); [*métal*] enamelled

émailler /emaje/ [1] *vtr* ① to enamel [*objet*]; ② fig **discours émaillé d'allusions** speech sprinkled with allusions

émanation /emanasjɔ̃/ *nf* (effluve) emanation; ~**s de gaz** gas fumes

émancipateur, -trice /emɑ̃sipatœʀ, tʀis/ adj liberating

émancipation /emɑ̃sipasjɔ̃/ nf emancipation

émanciper /emɑ̃sipe/ [1]
A vtr to emancipate [peuple, mineur]; to liberate [pays] (de from)
B s'émanciper vpr to become emancipated; hum to become very independent; **femme émancipée** liberated woman

émaner /emane/ [1]
A vi ~ de [chaleur, odeur] to emanate from; [ordre] to come from
B v impers **il émane d'elle un charme fou** she exudes charm

émarger /emaʀʒe/ [13]
A vtr **1** (rogner) to trim [page]; **2** (signer) to sign
B vi ~ à l'**université** to be on the payroll of the university; ~ **à 2 000 euros** to draw 2,000 euros

émasculer /emaskyle/ [1] vtr lit, fig to emasculate

émaux ▸ émail

emballage /ɑ̃balaʒ/ nm **1** (dans du carton) packaging; (dans du papier) wrapping; (dans une caisse) packing; **2** (papier) wrapping; (carton) packaging
⌐Composé⌐ ~ **sous vide** vacuum packing

emballant○, ~**e** /ɑ̃balɑ̃, ɑ̃t/ adj exciting

emballement /ɑ̃balmɑ̃/ nm **1** (enthousiasme) fit of enthusiasm (**pour** for); (colère) outburst of anger; **2** (de prix, d'inflation) rapid rise; **3** (de cheval) bolting; **4** (de moteur) racing

emballer /ɑ̃bale/ [1]
A vtr **1** (dans une boîte) to pack; (envelopper) to wrap; **2** ○(enthousiasmer) **cette idée m'emballe** I am really taken with this idea; **être emballé par** to be taken with; **3** to race [moteur]
B s'emballer vpr **1** [cheval] to bolt; **2** ○(se passionner) to get carried away (**pour** by); **ça ne m'emballe pas d'aller à Londres** I'm not too keen on going to London; **3** (s'énerver) to get all worked up○; **4** ○[moteur] to race; **5** [prix, inflation] to shoot up; [monnaie] to shoot up in value

embarcadère /ɑ̃baʀkadɛʀ/ nm (de passagers) pier; (de marchandises) wharf

embarcation /ɑ̃baʀkasjɔ̃/ nf boat

embardée /ɑ̃baʀde/ nf (d'auto) swerve; (de bateau) yaw; **faire une** ~ [auto] to swerve; [bateau] to yaw

embargo /ɑ̃baʀgo/ nm embargo (**contre, sur** on)

embarqué, ~e /ɑ̃baʀke/
A pp ▸ embarquer
B pp adj [équipement, système] on-board

embarquement /ɑ̃baʀkəmɑ̃/ nm (de passagers) boarding; **formalités d'**~ boarding procedures; **port d'**~ port of embarkation

embarquer /ɑ̃baʀke/ [1]
A vtr **1** Aviat, Naut (charger) to load [marchandises]; to take on board [passager]; **2** ○(emmener) to take [objet]; [police] to pick up [malfaiteur]; **3** ○(engager) ~ **qn dans un projet** to get sb involved in a project
B vi (monter à bord) to board; Naut (partir en voyage) to sail (**pour** for); ~ **à bord de** to board
C s'embarquer vpr **1** Naut = **embarquer B**; **2** ○(se lancer) **s'**~ **dans** to launch into [explication]

embarras /ɑ̃baʀa/ nm inv **1** (trouble) embarrassment; **2** (gêne financière) ~ **d'argent** or **financiers** financial difficulties; **ton chèque m'a tiré d'**~ your cheque GB ou check US helped me out; **3** (situation délicate) awkward position; **tirer qn d'**~ to get sb out of a difficult situation; **4** (incertitude) **être dans l'**~ to be in a quandary; **je conçois votre** ~ I understand your dilemma; **n'avoir que l'**~ **du choix** to be spoiled for choice GB, to have too much to choose from; **5** †(obstacle) **il craint d'être un** ~ **pour vous** he's afraid of being a nuisance (to you); **les** ~ **de la circulation** road congestion **C**
⌐Composé⌐ ~ **gastrique** Méd stomach upset

embarrassant, ~e /ɑ̃baʀasɑ̃, ɑ̃t/ adj **1** [problème, silence, choix] awkward; [situation] embarrassing; **2** [bagages] cumbersome

embarrassé, ~e /ɑ̃baʀase/
A pp ▸ embarrasser
B pp adj **1** [personne, silence] embarrassed; **être bien** ~ **pour répondre/expliquer** to be at a loss for an answer/explanation; **2** [explication] confused; **3** [pièce, bureau]

cluttered (**de** with); **4** Méd [estomac] upset

embarrasser /ɑ̃baʀase/ [1]
A vtr **1** (mettre mal à l'aise) to embarrass [personne]; **ça m'embarrasse de te le rappeler, mais...** I'm sorry to have to remind you, but...; **2** (encombrer) to clutter (up) [pièce, table] (**de** with); **cette armoire m'embarrasse plutôt qu'autre chose** this wardrobe is more of a nuisance than anything else
B s'embarrasser vpr (s'encombrer) **s'**~ **de** to burden oneself with [paquet, personne]; to weigh oneself down with [scrupules]; to worry about [détails]

embauche /ɑ̃boʃ/ nf appointment GB, hiring **C** US; **salaire d'**~ starting salary; **aides à l'**~ employment incentives

embaucher /ɑ̃boʃe/ [1] vtr **1** (pour un emploi) to hire [ouvrier]; **2** ○(pour une corvée) to recruit

embaumer /ɑ̃bome/ [1]
A vtr **1** [odeur] to fill [lieu]; [lieu] to smell of [lavande, cire]; **2** to embalm [cadavre]
B vi [air, fleurs] to be fragrant

embaumeur, -euse /ɑ̃bomœʀ, øz/ ▸ p. 372 nm,f embalmer

embellie /ɑ̃bɛli/ nf **1** (dans le temps) bright spell; Naut lull; **2** fig improvement

embellir /ɑ̃bɛliʀ/ [3]
A vtr **1** to improve [ville]; to make [sb] more attractive [personne]; **2** to embellish [récit, vérité]
B vi to become more attractive

embellissement /ɑ̃bɛlismɑ̃/ nm **1** (de pièce, maison) improving; **travaux d'**~ improvements; **2** (élément amélioré) improvement, embellishment; **3** (inexactitude) embellishment

emberlificoté○, ~**e** /ɑ̃bɛʀlifikɔte/ adj [texte] muddled; [situation] confused

emberlificoter○ /ɑ̃bɛʀlifikɔte/ [1]
A vtr **1** (embrouiller) to entangle [fil]; **2** (duper) to take [sb] in○ [personne]
B s'emberlificoter vpr **1** lit to get entangled (**dans** in); **2** fig to get mixed up (**dans** in)

embêtant, ~e /ɑ̃bɛtɑ̃, ɑ̃t/ adj **1** (fâcheux) gén annoying; [situation] awkward; **c'est** ~ **ça!** that's a real nuisance!; **2** (agaçant) annoying; **3** (lassant) boring

embêtement /ɑ̃bɛtmɑ̃/ nm problem

embêter /ɑ̃bɛte/ [1]
A vtr **1** (contrarier) to bother; **2** (importuner) to pester; (agacer) to annoy; **3** (lasser) to bore
B s'embêter vpr **1** (s'ennuyer) to be bored; **un hôtel quatre étoiles! tu ne t'embêtes pas**○! a four-star hotel! you're doing all right for yourself!; **2** (se compliquer la vie) **s'**~ **à faire** to go to all the bother of doing; **ne t'embête pas avec ça** don't bother with that!

emblée: d'emblée /dɑ̃ble/ loc adv (aussitôt) straightaway; [détester] at first sight

emblématique /ɑ̃blematik/ adj [dessin, décoration] emblematic; [personnage, figure] symbolic

emblème /ɑ̃blɛm/ nm emblem

embobiner○ /ɑ̃bɔbine/ [1] vtr **1** ○(tromper) to hoodwink; **2** (enrouler) to wind

emboîter /ɑ̃bwate/ [1]
A vtr to fit together [pièces]
B s'emboîter vpr to fit (**dans** into)
⌐Idiome⌐ ~ **le pas à qn** lit, fig to fall in behind sb

embolie /ɑ̃bɔli/ ▸ p. 195 nf embolism

embonpoint /ɑ̃bɔ̃pwɛ̃/ nm **avoir de l'**~ to be stout

embouché, ~e /ɑ̃buʃe/ adj **mal** ~ (grossier) coarse; (de mauvaise humeur) in a foul mood

embouchure /ɑ̃buʃyʀ/ nf (de rivière) mouth; (d'instrument) mouthpiece; (de tuyau) opening

embourber: s'embourber /ɑ̃buʀbe/ [1] vpr **1** (dans la boue) to get stuck in the mud; **2** (dans des difficultés) to get bogged down (**dans** in)

embourgeoiser: s'embourgeoiser /ɑ̃buʀʒwaze/ [1] vpr [personne] to become middle-class; [quartier] to become gentrified

embout /ɑ̃bu/ nm (de canne, cigare) tip; (de tuyau) nozzle; (de pipe) mouthpiece

embouteillage /ɑ̃butejaʒ/ nm **1** (en ville) traffic jam; (sur l'autoroute) tailback; **2** (de système) bottleneck

emboutir /ɑ̃butiʀ/ [3] *vtr* **1** Tech to stamp [*métal*]; **2** Aut to crash into [*véhicule, obstacle*]

embranchement /ɑ̃bʀɑ̃ʃmɑ̃/ *nm* **1** (point de jonction) junction; **2** (voie) (routière) side road; (ferrée) branch line; **3** Bot, Zool branch

embrasé, **~e** /ɑ̃bʀɑze/ *adj* **1** (en feu) burning; **2** (illuminé) glowing

embrasement /ɑ̃bʀazmɑ̃/ *nm* **1** (incendie) blaze; **2** (illumination) dazzling illumination; **3** (agitation sociale) unrest **✿**

embraser /ɑ̃bʀaze/ [1]

A *vtr* **1** (mettre le feu) to set [sth] ablaze [*bâtiment*]; **2** (agiter) to set [sth] alight [*ville, pays*]; **3** (illuminer) to set [sth] ablaze [*ciel, ville*]; **4** (emplir de passion) to set [sb] on fire [*personne*]

B s'embraser *vpr* **1** (prendre feu) to catch fire; **2** (pays, ville) to erupt into violence; **3** (devenir illuminé) to be set ablaze; **4** (s'emplir de passion) to burn with desire

embrassade /ɑ̃bʀasad/ *nf* hugging and kissing **✿**

embrasse /ɑ̃bʀas/ *nf* tieback

embrasser /ɑ̃bʀase/ [1]

A *vtr* **1** (donner un baiser à) to kiss; **je t'embrasse** (en fin de lettre) lots of love; **2** (étreindre) to embrace [*personnalité*]; to hug [*ami*]; **3** (choisir) to take up [*carrière*]; to embrace [*cause, religion*]; **4** (inclure) [*étude*] to take in [*période, question*]; [*regard*] to take in [*paysage*]; [*auteur*] to cover [*sujet*]

B s'embrasser *vpr* to kiss (each other)

embrasure /ɑ̃bʀazyʀ/ *nf* (dans un mur) opening

(Composés) **~ de fenêtre** window; **~ de porte** doorway

embrayage /ɑ̃bʀɛjaʒ/ *nm* **1** (dispositif) clutch; **2** (communication entre deux pièces) engaging; (par l'automobiliste) letting out the clutch; **3** (pédale) clutch pedal

embrayer /ɑ̃bʀeje/ [21] *vi* Aut to engage the clutch; Tech to engage

embrigader /ɑ̃bʀigade/ [1] *vtr* **1** (enrôler) to recruit (**dans** into; **comme** as); **2** Mil to brigade

embrocher /ɑ̃bʀɔʃe/ [1]

A *vtr* **1** Culin to put [sth] on a spit [*animal*]; to skewer [*morceau, gigot*]; **2** ○(transpercer) to run [sb] through [*adversaire*]

B s'embrocher○ *vpr* to impale oneself (**sur** on)

embrouillamini○ /ɑ̃bʀujamini/ *nm* muddle

embrouille○ /ɑ̃bʀuj/ *nf* shady goings-on○ (*pl*)

embrouillement /ɑ̃bʀujmɑ̃/ *nm* (de fils) (action) tangling; (résultat) tangle

embrouiller /ɑ̃bʀuje/ [1]

A *vtr* to tangle [*fils*]; to confuse [*affaire, personne*]

B s'embrouiller *vpr* [*fils, cheveux*] to become tangled; [*idées, affaire, personne*] to become confused; **s'~ dans** to get into a muddle with [*comptes*]; to get tangled up in [*explications*]

embroussaillé, **~e** /ɑ̃bʀusaje/ *adj* [*chemin*] overgrown; [*cheveux, sourcils*] bushy; [*barbe*] shaggy

embrumé, **~e** /ɑ̃bʀyme/ *adj* **1** [*temps*] misty; [*ciel, paysage*] hazy; **2** [*esprit*] befuddled; [*regard*] glazed; [*voix*] hoarse

embruns /ɑ̃bʀœ̃/ *nmpl* spray **✿**

embryogenèse /ɑ̃bʀijɔʒənɛz/ *nf* embryogenesis

embryon /ɑ̃bʀijɔ̃/ *nm* embryo

embryonnaire /ɑ̃bʀijɔnɛʀ/ *adj* lit, fig embryonic

embûche /ɑ̃byʃ/ *nf* **1** (machination) trap; **dresser des ~s** to set traps; **2** (danger) hazard; (difficulté) pitfall; **plein d'~s** lit hazardous; fig fraught with pitfalls

embuer /ɑ̃bɥe/ [1]

A *vtr* to mist up, to fog up US [*vitre*]

B s'embuer *vpr* [*vitre*] to mist up, to fog up US; [*yeux*] to mist over

embuscade /ɑ̃byskad/ *nf* ambush

embusquer: **s'embusquer** /ɑ̃byske/ [1] *vpr* to lie in ambush

éméché○, **~e** /emeʃe/ *adj* tipsy

émeraude¹ /emʀod/ ▸ p. 140 *adj inv*, *nm* (couleur) emerald green

émeraude² /emʀod/ *nf* (pierre) emerald

émergence /emɛʀʒɑ̃s/ *nf* emergence

émergent, **~e** /emɛʀʒɑ̃, ɑ̃t/ *adj* emergent; **les marchés ~s** emerging markets

émerger /emɛʀʒe/ [13] *vi* **1** (apparaître) to emerge; **2** ○(se réveiller) to surface

émeri /emʀi/ *nm* emery; **bouché à l'~** fig as thick as two short planks GB, dumb

émérite /emeʀit/ *adj* **1** [*joueur, acteur*] outstanding; **2 professeur ~** (titre) emeritus professor

émerveillement /emɛʀvɛjmɑ̃/ *nm* wonder (**devant** at); **il fait l'~ de ses professeurs** his teachers are greatly impressed by him; **la nature est un ~ perpétuel** nature is an eternal source of wonder

émerveiller /emɛʀveje/ [1]

A *vtr* **~ qn** to fill sb with wonder; **être émerveillé par** to marvel at, to be filled with wonder by

B s'émerveiller *vpr* **s'~ de** *or* **devant qch** to marvel at sth; **il s'émerveillait qu'elle ait pu faire cela aussi vite** he was amazed *ou* impressed that she had been able to do it so quickly

émétique /emetik/ *adj*, *nm* emetic

émetteur, **-trice** /emetœʀ, tʀis/

A *adj* **1** Radio, TV broadcasting; **2** [*banque, bureau*] issuing

B *nm* **1** Radio, TV transmitter; **2** (d'emprunt, de carte) issuer; **3** Ling sender

émettre /emɛtʀ/ [60] *vtr* **1** (exprimer) to express [*avis*]; to put forward [*hypothèse*]; to raise [*objection*]; **2** (produire) to utter [*cri*]; to produce [*son, chaleur*]; to give off [*odeur*]; **3** (mettre en circulation) to issue [*timbre, monnaie*]; **4** [*banque*] to float [*emprunt*]; **5** Radio, TV to broadcast [*programme*]; **6** [*avion, bateau*] to send out [*signal*]; **7** Phys to emit [*radiation*]

émeu /emø/ *nm* Zool emu

émeute /emøt/ *nf* riot

émeutier, **-ière** /emøtje, ɛʀ/ *nm,f* rioter

émietter /emjete/ [1]

A *vtr* **1** to crumble [*pain, motte de terre*]; **2** to split [sth] up [*domaine, fortune*]; **3** to dissipate [*forces, activités*]; to fritter away [*temps*]

B s'émietter *vpr* **1** [*pain, roche*] to crumble; **2** [*pouvoir*] to crumble; **3** [*héritage*] to be split up

émigrant, **~e** /emigʀɑ̃, ɑ̃t/ *nm,f* emigrant

émigration /emigʀasjɔ̃/ *nf* emigration

émigré, **~e** /emigʀe/ *nm,f* gén emigrant; Hist émigré

émigrer /emigʀe/ [1] *vi* **1** [*personne*] to emigrate; **2** [*oiseau*] to migrate

émincer /emɛ̃se/ [12] *vtr* to slice [sth] thinly

éminemment /eminamɑ̃/ *adv* eminently

éminence /eminɑ̃s/ *nf* **1** (monticule) hillock littér; **2** Anat protuberance

Éminence /eminɑ̃s/ *nf* Relig Eminence

(Composé) **~ grise** éminence grise, grey GB *ou* gray US eminence

éminent, **~e** /eminɑ̃, ɑ̃t/ *adj* distinguished, eminent

émirat /emiʀa/ *nm* emirate

émirati, **~e** /emiʀati/ ▸ p. 392 *adj* from the United Arab Emirates

Émirati, **~e** /emiʀati/ ▸ p. 392 *nm,f* native of the United Arab Emirates

Émirats /emiʀa/ ▸ p. 230 *nprmpl* **~ arabes unis**, **EAU** United Arab Emirates

émissaire /emisɛʀ/ *nm* emissary

émission /emisjɔ̃/ *nf* **1** Radio, TV programme^GB (**sur** about, on); **2** (de document, monnaie, timbre) issue; **3** (d'ondes, de signaux) emission

emmagasiner /ɑ̃magazine/ [1] *vtr* **1** (mettre en magasin) to store; **2** (accumuler) to stockpile [*marchandises*]; to store [*énergie*]; to store up [*connaissances*]

emmancher /ɑ̃mɑ̃ʃe/ [1]

A *vtr* **1** to fit a handle to [*outil*]; **2** ○to set [sth] up [*affaire, négociation*]

B s'emmancher○ *vpr* **s'~ bien/mal** [*affaire*] to get off to a good/bad start

emmanchure /ɑ̃mɑ̃ʃyʀ/ *nf* armhole

emmêler /ɑ̃mɛle/ [1]

A *vtr* **1** to tangle [*cheveux, fils*]; **2** to confuse [*affaire*]

B s'emmêler *vpr* [*fils*] to get tangled up; **s'~ les pieds dans** [*personne*] to get one's feet caught in

emménager /ɑ̃menaʒe/ [13] *vi* to move in

emmener /ɑ̃mne/ [16] *vtr* **1** (mener) to take [*personne*] (**à, jusqu'à** to); **~ qn faire des courses/promener** to take sb shopping/for a walk; **emmène-moi chez toi!** take me home with you!; **veux-tu que je t'emmène en voiture?** do you want a lift GB *ou* a ride US?; **2** ⃝(emporter) controv to take [*parapluie, livre*]; **3** (arrêter) [*police*] to take [sb] away [*personne*]; **4** (entraîner) [*chef, capitaine*] to lead [*équipe, troupe*]

emmerder⃝ /ɑ̃mɛʀde/ [1]

A *vtr* **1** (importuner) to annoy, to hassle⃝; **tu m'emmerdes** you're a pain⃝; **je les emmerde** to hell⃝ with them; **2** (ennuyer) to bore [sb] stiff⃝

B **s'emmerder** *vpr* **1** (s'ennuyer) to be bored (stiff)⃝; **2** (se compliquer la vie) **s'~ à faire** to go to the trouble *ou* bother of doing; **je n'ai pas envie de m'~ avec un chien** I don't want all the trouble *ou* hassle⃝ of a dog; **t'emmerde pas avec ça!** (avec la finition) don't bother with that!; (avec ce que les gens vont penser) don't waste your time worrying about that!; **un hôtel cinq étoiles, tu t'emmerdes pas!** a 5-star hotel! you're doing all right for yourself!; **tu as fouillé dans mes tiroirs, tu t'emmerdes pas!** you went through my drawers, you've got a nerve *ou* a bloody cheek⃝! GB

emmitoufler /ɑ̃mitufle/ [1]

A *vtr* to wrap [sb/sth] up warmly

B **s'emmitoufler** *vpr* to wrap (oneself) up warmly

emmurer /ɑ̃myʀe/ [1] *vtr* to wall [sb/sth] in

émoi /emwa/ *nm* agitation, turmoil; **la nouvelle a mis toute la ville en ~** the news threw the whole city into turmoil; **l'arrivée du jeune homme l'avait mise en ~** the young man's arrival had thrown her into a state of confusion

émollient, ~e /emɔljɑ̃, ɑ̃t/ *adj* emollient

émoluments /emɔlymɑ̃/ *nmpl* remuneration

émonder /emɔ̃de/ [1] *vtr* to prune

émotif, -ive /emɔtif, iv/

A *adj* emotional

B *nm,f* emotional person

émotion /emosjɔ̃/ *nf* (réaction affective) emotion; (peur) fright; (sensibilité) emotion; **rougir d'~** to blush with emotion; **donner des ~s à qn** to give sb a fright; **tu es remis de tes ~s**⃝? have you recovered from the shock?; **dans la salle d'audience, l'~ était à son comble** the atmosphere in the courtroom was extremely emotional

émotivité /emɔtivite/ *nf* **enfant d'une grande ~** highly emotional child

émoulu, ~e /emuly/ *adj* **frais ~ de** fresh from

émousser /emuse/ [1]

A *vtr* **1** to blunt [*lame*]; **2** to dull [*curiosité, sensibilité*]

B **s'émousser** *vpr* **1** [*lame*] to become *ou* get blunt; **2** [*curiosité, sensibilité*] to become dulled

émoustiller /emustije/ [1] *vtr* **1** (égayer) to exhilarate; **2** (exciter) to titillate

émouvant, ~e /emuvɑ̃, ɑ̃t/ *adj* moving

émouvoir /emuvwaʀ/ [43]

A *vtr* (attendrir) to move; (toucher) to touch; **~ qn (jusqu')aux larmes** to move sb to tears; **se laisser ~ par les larmes de qn** to be swayed by sb's tears; **~ l'opinion** to cause a stir

B **s'émouvoir** *vpr* **1** (être touché) to be touched; **s'~ à la vue/au souvenir de** to be touched by the sight/memory of; **2** (s'inquiéter) **le gouvernement s'émeut des troubles paysans** the government is becoming concerned about the farmers' unrest; **répondre sans s'~** to reply calmly

empailler /ɑ̃paje/ [1] *vtr* **1** to seat [sth] (with straw) [*chaise*]; **2** to stuff [*animal*]

empailleur, -euse /ɑ̃pajœʀ, øz/ ▸ p. 372 *nm* **1** (d'animaux) taxidermist; **2** (de chaise) chair seater

empaler /ɑ̃pale/ [1]

A *vtr* to impale [*personne*]

B **s'empaler** *vpr* to become impaled (**sur** on)

empaqueter /ɑ̃pakte/ [20] *vtr* (dans une boîte) to package; (dans du papier) to wrap [sth] up

emparer: s'emparer /ɑ̃paʀe/ [1] *vpr* **1** (prendre) **s'~ de** [*personne*] to take over [*ville, pays, record*]; to seize [*pouvoir, personne, prétexte*]; to gain possession of [*ballon*]; to get hold of [*rumeur, micro, volant*]; **2** (envahir) **s'~ de** [*torpeur*] to take hold of [*personne, pays*]

empâter: s'empâter /ɑ̃pate/ *vpr* [1] [*visage*] to become puffy; [*personne*] to put on weight; [*corps*] to thicken out

empêché, ~e /ɑ̃peʃe/

A *pp* ▸ **empêcher**

B *pp adj* **1** (retenu) **le Président, ~, a dû se décommander** the President has been detained and has had to cancel; **2** (incapable) fml **l'électeur ~ d'aller voter** the voter unable to go and vote

empêchement /ɑ̃peʃmɑ̃/ *nm* **1** (contretemps) unforeseen difficulty; **j'ai un ~, peux-tu reporter notre rendez-vous?** something's cropped up, can you make it another time?; **2** Jur impediment

empêcher /ɑ̃peʃe/ [1]

A *vtr* **1** to prevent, to stop; **~ un crime** to prevent a crime; **~ qn de faire** to prevent *ou* stop sb (from) doing; **rien ne t'en empêche** no-one's stopping you; **la pauvreté n'empêche pas la générosité** poverty does not preclude generosity; **une disposition qui empêche les fonctionnaires de faire grève** a clause that prevents civil servants from striking; **pour ~ toute tentative d'OPA** to stave off *ou* ward off any takeover attempt

B **s'empêcher** *vpr* **je n'ai pu m'~ de rire** I couldn't help laughing

C *v impers* **(il) n'empêche** all the same; **il n'empêche que** nonetheless, the fact remains that

empêcheur, -euse /ɑ̃peʃœʀ, øz/ *nm,f* **~ de tourner** *or* **danser en rond** spoilsport, killjoy

empeigne /ɑ̃pɛɲ/ *nf* upper

empennage /ɑ̃pɛnaʒ/ *nm* **1** (d'avion) tail; **2** (de flèche) flighting

empereur /ɑ̃pʀœʀ/ ▸ p. 590 *nm* emperor

empesé, ~e /ɑ̃pəze/ *adj* [*col*] starched; [*air, style, personne*] starchy

empester /ɑ̃pɛste/ [16]

A *vtr* to stink [sth] out GB, to stink up US [*endroit*]

B *vi* to stink; **ça empeste ici!** it stinks in here!

empêtrer: s'empêtrer /ɑ̃petʀe/ [1] *vpr* **1** **s'~ dans** to get entangled in [*ronces, cordages*]; to get tangled up in [*mensonges, discours*]; to get mixed up in [*affaire*]; to get bogged down in [*comptes, problème*]; **2** ⃝**s'~ de qn** to get stuck⃝ with sb

emphase /ɑ̃faz/ *nf* **1** (exagération) grandiloquence; **plein d'~** grandiloquent; **parler sans ~** to speak without affectation; **2** Ling emphasis

emphatique /ɑ̃fatik/ *adj* **1** (pompeux) grandiloquent; **2** Ling emphatic

empiècement /ɑ̃pjɛsmɑ̃/ *nm* (de vêtement) yoke

empierrer /ɑ̃pjeʀe/ [1] *vtr* to metal [*route*]; to ballast [*voie ferrée*]

empiéter /ɑ̃pjete/ [14] *vtr ind* **~ sur** lit, fig to encroach upon

empiffrer⃝: **s'empiffrer** /ɑ̃pifʀe/ [1] *vpr* to stuff oneself (**de** with)

empiler /ɑ̃pile/ [1]

A *vtr* to pile [sth] (up)

B **s'empiler** *vpr* [*livres*] to pile up; **s'~ dans** [*personnes*] to pile into

empire /ɑ̃piʀ/ *nm* **1** Pol empire; **pas pour un ~!** not for the world!; **2** (entreprise) empire; **3** (ascendant) fml influence (**sur** over); **agir sous l'~ de la colère** to act in a fit of anger

Empire /ɑ̃piʀ/ *nm* (règne de Napoléon Ier) **l'~** the Empire; **mobilier/style ~** Empire furniture/style

⌐Composés⌐ **l'~ céleste** the Celestial Empire; **l'~ du Milieu** the Middle Kingdom; **l'~ d'Orient** the Byzantine Empire; **l'~ (romain) d'Occident** the Western (Roman) Empire; **l'~ du Soleil Levant** the land of the Rising Sun

empirer /ɑ̃piʀe/ [1] *vi* to get worse

empirique /ɑ̃piʀik/ *adj* gén empirical

empirisme /ɑ̃piʀism/ *nm* empiricism

emplacement /ɑ̃plasmɑ̃/ *nm* **1** (site) site; **2** (de stationnement) parking space

⌐Composé⌐ **~ publicitaire** advertising space

emplâtre /ɑ̃plɑtʀ/ *nm* **1** Méd medicated plaster; **2** ⃝(personne) good-for-nothing⃝

emplette /ɑ̃plɛt/ *nf* purchase; **faire quelques ~s** to make a few purchases

emplir /ɑ̃pliʀ/ [3] *vtr*, **s'emplir** *vpr* to fill (**de** with)

emploi /ɑ̃plwa/ *nm* **1** (poste de travail) job; **changer d'~** to change jobs; **un ~ de chauffeur** a job as a driver; **sans ~**

unemployed; **②** (embauche) employment; **stimuler l'~** to stimulate employment; **③** (utilisation) use; **l'~ d'armes/de fonds** the use of weapons/of funds; **téléviseur couleur à vendre, cause double ~** colour^{GB} TV for sale, surplus to requirements; **④** Ling usage

(Composé) **~ du temps** timetable

(Idiome) **avoir la tête de l'~** to look the part

emploi-jeunes, pl **emplois-jeunes** /ɑ̃plwaʒœn/ nm: *job created for a young unemployed person*

employé, **~e** /ɑ̃plwaje/ ▸ p. 372 nm,f employee

(Composés) **~ de banque** bank clerk; **~ de bureau** office clerk; **~ aux écritures** ledger clerk; **~ de maison** domestic employee; **~ municipal** local authority employee

employer /ɑ̃plwaje/ [23]
A vtr to employ [personne] (**comme** as); to use [mot, méthode, produit]
B **s'employer** vpr **①** [produit, mot] to be used; **②** **s'~ à faire** [personne] to apply oneself to doing

employeur, **-euse** /ɑ̃plwajœr, øz/ nm,f employer

empocher /ɑ̃pɔʃe/ [1] vtr to pocket

empoignade○ /ɑ̃pwaɲad/ nf (bagarre) scrap○; (dispute) row

empoigne /ɑ̃pwaɲ/ nf **c'était la foire d'~** it was a free-for-all

empoigner /ɑ̃pwaɲe/ [1]
A vtr to grab (hold of) (**par, au** by)
B **s'empoigner** vpr **①** (se battre) **s'~ avec qn** to grapple with sb; **②** (se quereller) to clash

empoisonnant○, **~e** /ɑ̃pwazɔnɑ̃, ɑ̃t/ adj (fâcheux) annoying; (agaçant) irritating

empoisonné, **~e** /ɑ̃pwazɔne/
A pp ▸ empoisonner
B pp adj [aliment, flèche] poisoned (**à** with); [atmosphère, relations] sour; [querelle] venomous; [mot] barbed

empoisonnement /ɑ̃pwazɔnmɑ̃/ nm **①** lit poisoning **¢**; **~ au gaz** gas poisoning; **②** ○(ennui) trouble **¢**

empoisonner /ɑ̃pwazɔne/ [1]
A vtr **①** (pour tuer) to poison [personne, animal]; **②** (intoxiquer) to poison [sang]; **être empoisonné par des champignons** to get food poisoning from mushrooms; **③** (polluer) to poison [rivière]; **④** fig to poison [relations, atmosphère]; **arrête de m'~**○! stop bugging○ me!; **~ la vie de qn** to make sb's life a misery
B **s'empoisonner** vpr **①** (volontairement) to poison oneself (**à** with); (accidentellement) **il s'est empoisonné avec une huître pas fraîche** he got food poisoning from eating a bad oyster; **②** ○(se rendre malheureux) **s'~ la vie** or **l'existence** to make one's life a misery

empoisonneur, **-euse** /ɑ̃pwazɔnœr, øz/ nm,f **①** (criminel) poisoner; **②** ○(importun) nuisance

emporté, **~e** /ɑ̃pɔrte/ adj **être ~, avoir un caractère ~** to be quick-tempered

emportement /ɑ̃pɔrtəmɑ̃/ nm fit of anger; **dans mon ~ je l'ai frappé** I hit him in a fit of anger

emporte-pièce /ɑ̃pɔrtəpjɛs/ nm inv **①** Tech punch; **découper qch à l'~** to punch sth; **jugement à l'~** fig rash judgment; **②** Culin pastry cutter

emporter /ɑ̃pɔrte/ [1]
A vtr **①** (prendre avec soi) [personne] to take [objet]; **pizzas à ~** takeaway pizzas GB, pizzas to go US; **②** (transporter) [ambulance, sauveteurs] to take [sb] away; [bateau, train, avion] to carry away [passager, fret]; **se laisser ~ par son élan** to get carried away; **se laisser ~ par la colère** to let one's anger get the better of one; **③** (entraîner, arracher) [vent, rivière] to sweep away [personne, feuilles, pont]; [obus, balle] to take [sth] off [oreille, bras]; **④** (causer la mort) **une leucémie l'a emporté** he died of leukaemia; **⑤** (conquérir) to win [position]; **~ l'adhésion de qn** to win sb over; **⑥** (triompher) **l'~** [équipe, candidat] to win; [idée, bon sens] to prevail; **l'~ sur qn** to beat sb; **l'~ sur qch** to overcome sth
B **s'emporter** vpr to lose one's temper

(Idiome) **~ la bouche**○ to take the roof off one's mouth○

empoté○, **~e** /ɑ̃pɔte/
A adj clumsy, awkward
B nm,f clumsy oaf

empourprer: **s'empourprer** /ɑ̃purpre/ [1] vpr [ciel] to turn crimson; [visage] to flush (**de** with)

empreindre /ɑ̃prɛ̃dr/ [55]
A vtr **①** (marquer) to imprint; **②** (remplir de) to imbue sout (**de** with)
B **s'empreindre** vpr to become marked (**de** by), to become imbued (**de** with); **empreint de tristesse** [personnalité] imbued with sadness; [visage] marked by sadness

empreinte /ɑ̃prɛ̃t/ nf **①** (de pas) footprint; (d'animal) track; **②** (de milieu, culture) stamp, mark

(Composés) **~s digitales** fingerprints; **~s génétiques** genetic fingerprints

empressé, **~e** /ɑ̃prese/ adj **①** (marquant la hâte) [soins] prompt; **②** (prévenant) [admirateur] attentive

empressement /ɑ̃prɛsmɑ̃/ nm **①** (hâte) eagerness (**à faire** to do); **avec ~** eagerly; **②** (prévenance) attentiveness; **manifester de l'~** to be attentive

empresser: **s'empresser** /ɑ̃prese/ [1] vpr **s'~ de faire** to hasten to do; **s'~ autour** or **auprès de qn** to fuss over sb

emprise /ɑ̃priz/ nf hold, influence

emprisonnement /ɑ̃prizɔnmɑ̃/ nm imprisonment; **peine d'~** prison sentence

(Composé) **~ cellulaire** solitary confinement

emprisonner /ɑ̃prizɔne/ [1] vtr **①** (mettre en prison) to imprison (**à, dans** in); fig **être emprisonné dans** to be the prisoner of; **②** (retenir) to keep [sb] prisoner (**à, dans** in); **③** (enfermer) to clasp [personne, main]

emprunt /ɑ̃prœ̃/ nm **①** (somme) loan; **faire un ~** to take out a loan; **un ~ à 10% sur 15 ans** a loan at 10% (repayable) over 15 years; **un ~ d'État** a public loan; **②** (action) borrowing; **financé par l'~** financed by borrowing; **d'~** [voiture, nom] borrowed; **③** (objet) loan; **un ~ fait à un musée** a loan from a museum; **④** (d'idée, de style, mot) borrowing

emprunté, **~e** /ɑ̃prœ̃te/ adj (embarrassé) awkward

emprunter /ɑ̃prœ̃te/ [1] vtr **①** to borrow [argent, objet, idée] (**à qn** from sb); **②** (imiter) to imitate [voix, manière]; **③** (prendre) to take [route, métro]

emprunteur, **-euse** /ɑ̃prœ̃tœr, øz/
A adj [organisme] borrowing the money (après n)
B nm,f borrower

empuantir /ɑ̃pɥɑ̃tir/ [3] vtr to stink out GB, to stink up US

ému, **~e** /emy/
A pp ▸ émouvoir
B pp adj (attendri) moved; (reconnaissant) touched; (intimidé) nervous
C adj [paroles, regard] full of emotion (après n); [souvenir] fond; **d'une voix ~e** with a catch in his/her voice

émule /emyl/ nm,f imitator; **être l'~ de qn** to model oneself on sb

émuler /emyle/ [1] vtr Ordinat to emulate

émulsifiant, **~e** /emylsifjɑ̃, ɑ̃t/
A adj emulsifying
B nm emulsifier

émulsion /emylsjɔ̃/ nf emulsion

en /ɑ̃/
A prép **①** (lieu) (où l'on est) in; (où l'on va) to; (mouvement vers l'intérieur) into; **vivre ~ France/ville** to live in France/town; **aller ~ Allemagne** to go to Germany; **monter ~ voiture** to get into a car; **aller ~ ville** to go into town; **se promener ~ ville** to stroll around town; **②** (temps) (époque) in; (moment déterminé) in; (en l'espace de) in; **~ hiver/1991** in winter/1991; **~ semaine** during the week; **③** (moyens de transport) by; **voyager ~ train/voiture** to travel by train ou rail/car; **aller à Nice ~ avion/voiture** to fly/to drive to Nice; **descendre la rivière ~ aviron** to row down the river; **④** (manière, état) **elle était tout ~ vert** she was all in green; **il est toujours ~ manteau** he always wears a coat; **un ouvrage ~ vers/français/trois volumes** a work in verse/French/three volumes; **⑤** (comme) (en qualité de) as; (de la même manière que) **je vous parle ~ ami** I'm speaking (to you) as a friend; **agir ~ traître** to act like a traitor; **⑥** (transformation) into; **ils se séparèrent ~ plusieurs groupes** they broke up into several groups; **traduire ~ anglais** to translate into English; **changer des euros ~ dollars** to change euros into dollars; **⑦** (matière) made of; **c'est ~ quoi?** what is it made of?; **c'est ~ or** it's (made of) gold; **⑧** (pour indiquer une variante) **le même ~ plus grand** the same only bigger; **la même ~ bleu** the same in blue; **⑨** (indique le domaine, la discipline) in; **~ politique/affaires** in politics/business; **~ théorie** in

en

Généralités

en, préposition et pronom, est présenté ici dans ses grandes lignes. Les expressions courantes du genre *en vitrine, être en colère, ne pas s'en faire, s'en aller* sont traitées respectivement dans les articles **vitrine, colère, faire, aller**; de même on trouvera les expressions avec *il y en a* avec **avoir** et les expressions avec *en être à* avec **être**.

Pour les traductions de *en*, préposition, associée à des noms de couleurs, pays, régions, et de *en*, pronom, quand il sert à exprimer des quantités, on consultera aussi les notes d'usage pertinentes. Voir la liste ▸ **p. 1355**

La préposition

en + gérondif

La traduction sera différente selon les nuances exprimées.

La simultanéité

L'action est brève:

en ouvrant la porte, je me suis souvenue que
= as I opened the door, I remembered that

je l'ai croisé en sortant
= I met him as I was leaving

L'action dure:

prends un café en attendant
= have a cup of coffee while you're waiting

elle travaille en chantant
= she sings while she works

il sifflait en lavant sa voiture
= he was whistling while he was cleaning his car

L'antériorité

en arrivant chez moi, je leur ai téléphoné
= when I got back home (*ou* on getting back home), I telephoned them

en la voyant, il rougit
= when he saw (*ou* on seeing) her, he blushed

Le déroulement d'une action 'cadre'

en faisant les courses, peux-tu acheter le journal?
= while you're doing the shopping, can you buy the paper?

en rangeant, j'ai retrouvé la lettre
= while (*ou* as) I was tidying up, I found the letter

La manière

Il n'y a pas de traduction systématique:

l'enfant se réveilla en hurlant
= the child woke up screaming

il marchait en bombant le torse
= he was walking with his chest stuck out

Avec les verbes de mouvement, on optera pour un verbe à particule:

partir/entrer/monter/descendre en courant
= to run off/in/up/down

Le moyen

je m'en suis sorti en racontant un mensonge
= I got out of it by telling a lie

ouvrez cette caisse en soulevant le couvercle
= open this box by lifting the lid

endormir un enfant en lui chantant une berceuse
= to sing a child to sleep with a lullaby

Une explication

Dans ce cas, la traduction dépendra de la construction générée par ce qui précède:

elle a fait une erreur en acceptant ce poste
= she made a mistake in accepting the job

il a gâché sa vie en l'épousant
= he ruined his life by marrying her

il mentait en disant que c'était moi
= he was lying when he said it was me

La cause

La cause donnera lieu également à des traductions variées:

il s'est tordu le pied en tombant
= he twisted his foot when (*ou* as) he fell

il s'est étranglé en avalant
= he choked on his food

elle s'est enrouée en chantant
= she made herself hoarse with singing

La condition

tu aurais moins chaud en enlevant ta veste
= you'd be cooler (*ou* less hot) if you took your jacket off

en prenant des vitamines, tu serais plus en forme
= if you took vitamins you'd feel fitter

Le pronom

en = de lui/d'elle/d'eux/d'elles

en représente un être humain ou un animal familier:

j'en suis content
= I am pleased with him/her/them

ils aiment leurs enfants et ils en sont aimés
= they love their children and they are loved by them

j'en suis fier (*de mes enfants*)
= I'm proud of them

en représente un animal, un concept, un objet:

j'en suis content
= I am pleased with it/them

je m'en souviens
= I remember it

deux ans après, on en parlait encore
= two years later, we were still talking about it

nous en sommes très peinés
= we're very upset about it

j'en suis fier
= I'm proud of it

regarde cette robe, j'en aime beaucoup la forme
= look at that dress, I like its shape (*ou* the shape of it) a lot

Mais attention, le nom ne se traduit pas toujours littéralement en anglais:

j'ai reçu la facture de téléphone; ça t'intéresserait d'en connaître le montant?
= I got the phone bill; would you like to know how much it was for?

☛ Voir page suivante

en *suite*

Les locutions telles que *en voilà, de … en, en sorte que, en tant que* sont sous **voilà, de, sorte, tant** etc.

en représente le lieu d'où l'on vient:

'tu as été voir ta mère?' 'oui, j'en viens'
= 'have you been to see your mother?' 'yes, I've just come from there'

il entra dans le café comme j'en sortais
= he entered the café as I was coming out

Expression de quantité

en, pronom, peut remplacer des noms dénombrables ou non-dénombrables:

'veux-tu des oranges?'
= 'would you like some oranges?'

'oui, j'en veux'
= 'yes, I'd like some'

'non, je n'en veux pas'
= 'no, I don't want any'

'veux-tu du vin?'
= 'would you like some wine?'

'oui, j'en veux'
= 'yes, I'd like some'

'non, je n'en veux pas'
= 'no, I don't want any'

il en reste encore (*des oranges*)
= there are some left

(*du vin*)
= there is some left

il n'en reste pas beaucoup (*des oranges*)
= there aren't many (of them) left
(*du vin*)
= there isn't much (of it) left

il n'en reste plus (*des oranges*)
= there aren't any left
(*du vin*)
= there isn't any left

prends-en plusieurs
= take several *ou* take a few

prends-en un peu
= take some

tu as emporté des livres?
= have you brought any books?

oui, j'en ai un passionnant
= yes, I've got one which is really good

oui, j'en ai deux
= yes, I've got two

oui, j'en ai même trop
= yes, too many in fact

il n'en a pas lu la moitié (*du roman*)
= he didn't even read half of it
(*des articles*)
= he didn't even read half of them

---

theory; **licencié ~ droit** bachelor of law; **docteur ~ médecine** doctor of medicine; **être bon ~ histoire** to be good at history; ⑩ (mesures, dimensions) in; **compter ~ secondes** to count in seconds; **les draps se font ~ 90 et ~ 140** the sheets are available in single and double; **~ profondeur/ hauteur, il y a assez d'espace** the space is deep/high enough; **~ largeur/longueur, il y a la place** widthwise/ lengthwise, there's (enough) room
B *pron* ① (le moyen) **si les abricots sont abîmés, fais-~ de la confiture** if the apricots are bruised make jam with them; **prends cette couverture et couvre-t'~** take this blanket and cover yourself with it; ② (la cause) **ça l'a tellement bouleversé qu'il ~ est tombé malade** it distressed him so much that he fell ill GB *ou* became sick US; **il a eu un cancer et il ~ est mort** he got cancer and died; ③ ᴼ(emphatique) **tu ~ as un beau chapeau!** what a nice hat you've got!; **on s'~ souviendra de ce dimanche!** we won't forget this Sunday in a hurry!; **et moi, je n'~ ai pas des soucis, peut-être?** do you think I haven't got worries too?; **j'~ connais qui seraient contents** I know some who would be pleased
EN /œɛn/ *nf* ① *abbr* ▸ **école**; ② *abbr* ▸ **éducation**
ENA /ena/ *nf*: *abbr* ▸ **école**

> ⓘ **ENA** The *grande école*, based in Strasbourg, which trains the élite force of public administrators. There are about 1,500 applicants for 150 places, drawn from the graduates of a university or another *grande école*. Entry is by competitive examination or *concours*, and requires applicants to commit themselves to ten years' work for the state.

enamourer: s'enamourer /ãnamuʀe/ [1] *vpr* **s'~ de** to become enamoured^GB of *littér*
énarque /enaʀk/ *nmf* graduate of the ENA
en-avant /ãnavã/ *nm inv* (au rugby) knock-on
encablure /ãkablyʀ/ *nf* **à quelques ~s de là** a few hundred yards away
encadré /ãkadʀe/ *nm* (dans un journal) box; **~ publicitaire** display ad
encadrement /ãkadʀəmã/ *nm* ① (supervision) supervision; ② (personnel de supervision) supervisory staff; (cadres) managerial staff; Mil (officiers) officers (*pl*); ③ Mil (de tir) straddling; ④ Écon control; ⑤ Art (mise en cadre) framing;

(cadre) frame; (tableau) framed picture; ⑥ Archit frame
encadrer /ãkadʀe/ [1] *vtr* ① (superviser) to supervise [*personnel*]; to train [*soldat*]; ② (entourer) to flank [*personne*]; to frame [*visage, fenêtre*]; to surround [*vallée*]; **~ de rouge** to outline [sth] in red; ③ (contrôler) to restrict [*crédit*]; to control [*prix*]; ④ Art to frame [*tableau*]; **être à ~**ᴼ *hum* to be priceless^○
encadreur /ãkadʀœʀ/ ▸ p. 372 *nm* picture framer
encaissé, ~e /ãkese/ *adj* [*vallée, rivière*] steep-sided; [*chemin*] cut deep into the hillside (*après n*)
encaissement /ãkesmã/ *nm* ① (de cotisation) collection; (de chèque) cashing; (de dividende) receipt; **frais d'~** transaction costs; ② Géog steeply sided setting
encaisser /ãkese/ [1]
A *vtr* ① to cash [*somme, chèque*]; ② ᴼto take [*coup, défaite*]; **je ne peux pas ~ ton frère** I can't stand your brother
B ᴼ*vi* (résister) to take it; **il sait ~** he can take it
(Idiome) **~ le coup**^○ to take it all in one's stride
encaisseur, -euse /ãkesœʀ/ ▸ p. 372 *nm,f* collector
encanailler: s'encanailler /ãkanaje/ [1] *vpr* [*personne*] to slum it; [*style, ton*] to become vulgar
encart /ãkaʀ/ *nm* insert
(Composé) **~ publicitaire** promotional insert
en-cas /ãka/ *nm inv* snack
encastrable /ãkastʀabl/ *adj* [*four*] that can be built in (*épith, après n*); [*lavabo*] that can be fitted GB *ou* fit US (*épith, après n*)
encastrer /ãkastʀe/ [1]
A *vtr* to build in [*four, réfrigérateur*]; to fit [*table de cuisson, lavabo*]; (en retrait) to recess; (dans le sol) to sink; **four encastré** built-in oven; **baignoire encastrée (dans le sol)** sunken bath
B **s'encastrer** *vpr* [*élément*] to fit (**dans** into); **la voiture est venue s'~ sous le camion** the car crashed into the truck *ou* lorry GB and got jammed underneath it
encaustique /ãkostik/ *nf* ① (cire) wax polish; **passer à l'~** to wax; ② Art (procédé) encaustic painting
enceinte /ãsɛ̃t/
A *adj f* [*femme*] pregnant; **être ~ de trois mois** to be three months pregnant; **être ~ de jumeaux** to be pregnant with twins; **vêtements pour femmes ~s** maternity clothes

B *nf* **①** (mur) surrounding wall; ∼ **de fossés/haies** surrounding ditches/hedges; **②** (espace) (de prison, palais, d'aéroport) compound; (de tribunal, d'église) interior; (dans une cérémonie, fête) enclosure

encens /ɑ̃sɑ̃/ *nm inv* incense *C*

encenser /ɑ̃sɑse/ [1] *vtr* **①** Relig to cense; **②** (flatter) to sing the praises of [*personne*]; to acclaim [*œuvre*]

encensoir /ɑ̃sɑswaʀ/ *nm* censer

⸢Idiome⸣ **savoir manier l'∼** to be good at flattery

encéphale /ɑ̃sefal/ *nm* encephalon

encéphalite /ɑ̃sefalit/ ▸ p. 195 *nf* Méd encephalitis

encéphalopathie /ɑ̃sefalɔpati/ *nf* encephalopathy; ∼ **spongiforme bovine, ESB** Bovine Spongiform Encephalopathy

encerclement /ɑ̃sɛʀkləmɑ̃/ *nm* surrounding, encirclement

encercler /ɑ̃sɛʀkle/ [1] *vtr* **①** Mil to surround, to encircle; **②** (avec un trait) to circle

enchaînement /ɑ̃ʃɛnmɑ̃/ *nm* **①** (d'événements liés entre eux) chain; **②** (suite) sequence; ∼ **de réponses** sequence of answers; **③** (coordination) coordination (**entre** between); **④** Mus, Sport transition

enchaîner /ɑ̃ʃɛne/ [1]
A *vtr* **①** to chain up [*personne, animal*]; ∼ **à** to chain to; **②** to put [sth] together [*idées, mots*]; **③** to enslave [*humanité, peuple*]; to shackle [*presse*]
B *vi* (poursuivre) to go on; ∼ **sur l'économie** to move on to the economy
C **s'enchaîner** *vpr* **①** [*personne*] to chain oneself (**à** to); **②** [*plans, séquences*] to follow on

enchantement /ɑ̃ʃɑ̃tmɑ̃/ *nm* **①** (expérience agréable) delight; **②** (sortilège) enchantment, spell; **comme par ∼** as if by magic

enchanter /ɑ̃ʃɑ̃te/ [1] *vtr* **①** (faire plaisir à) **l'idée de te voir m'enchante** I'm delighted at the thought of seeing you; **ça ne m'enchante guère** it doesn't exactly thrill me; **enchanté (de faire votre connaissance)!** how do you do!; **②** (ensorceler) to enchant

enchanteur, -eresse /ɑ̃ʃɑ̃tœʀ, tʀɛs/
A *adj* enchanting
B *nm,f* **①** (magicien) enchanter/enchantress; **②** fig charmer

enchâsser /ɑ̃ʃase/ [1] *vtr* **①** to enshrine [*reliques*]; to set [*pierre précieuse*]; **②** Ling to embed

enchère /ɑ̃ʃɛʀ/
A *nf* (offre) bid; (activité) bidding; **faire une ∼** to bid, to make a bid
B **enchères** *nfpl* **vente aux ∼s** auction

enchérir /ɑ̃ʃeʀiʀ/ [3] *vi* Comm, Jeux to bid; ∼ **sur qn** to bid more than sb; ∼ **sur une offre** to make a higher bid

enchevêtrement /ɑ̃ʃ(ə)vɛtʀəmɑ̃/ *nm* (de fils, branches) tangle; (de couloirs, ruelles) labyrinth; (d'idées) muddle

enchevêtrer /ɑ̃ʃ(ə)vetʀe/ [1]
A *vtr* **①** lit to tangle [sth] up [*fils*]; **②** fig **être enchevêtré** [*phrase, intrigue*] to be muddled; [*problème, affaire*] to be complicated
B **s'enchevêtrer** *vpr* **①** [*branches, fils*] to get tangled; **②** [*phrases, idées*] to become muddled; **③** [*personne*] **s'∼ dans** to get tangled up in

enclave /ɑ̃klav/ *nf* lit, fig enclave

enclavement /ɑ̃klavmɑ̃/ *nm* (situation) enclosure; (processus) enclosing *C*

enclaver /ɑ̃klave/ [1] *vtr* to hem in [*terrain*]; **un pays enclavé** a landlocked country

enclenchement /ɑ̃klɑ̃ʃmɑ̃/ *nm* (de mécanisme) engagement

enclencher /ɑ̃klɑ̃ʃe/ [1]
A *vtr* **①** fig to launch, to set [sth] in motion [*processus*]; **②** lit to set [*minuterie*]; to engage [*mécanisme*]
B **s'enclencher** *vpr* **①** fig [*processus, cycle*] to get under way; **②** lit [*mécanisme*] to engage

enclin, ∼e /ɑ̃klɛ̃, in/ *adj* inclined (**à** to; **à faire** to do)

enclos /ɑ̃klo/ *nm inv* gén enclosure; (pour animaux) pen

enclume /ɑ̃klym/ *nf* Anat, Tech anvil

⸢Idiome⸣ **être entre l'∼ et le marteau** to be between the devil and the deep blue sea

encoche /ɑ̃kɔʃ/ *nf* (entaille) notch

encoder /ɑ̃kɔde/ [1] *vtr* to encode

---

encore

Lorsqu'il signifie *toujours*, *encore* se traduit généralement par *still* dans une phrase affirmative ou interrogative:

il était encore étudiant quand il s'est marié
= he was still a student when he got married

habite-t-elle encore ici?
= does she still live here?

pas encore se traduit par *not yet*:

elle n'était pas encore mariée quand elle a eu son premier bébé
= she wasn't yet married when she had her first baby
ou she was still unmarried when she had her first baby

il n'est pas encore rentré
= he hasn't come home yet
ou he still hasn't come home

Dans ce dernier cas, *still* marque l'étonnement ou l'exaspération, alors que *yet* indique un énoncé neutre des faits.

Des exceptions aux traductions fournies ci-dessus et les autres sens de *encore* sont traités ci-dessous.

---

encodeur /ɑ̃kɔdœʀ/ *nm* Ordinat encoder

encoignure /ɑ̃kwaɲyʀ/ *nf* **①** (angle) corner; **②** (placard) corner cupboard; (étagères) set of corner shelves

encoller /ɑ̃kɔle/ [1] *vtr* to paste [*papier peint*]

encolure /ɑ̃kɔlyʀ/ *nf* **①** ▸ p. 575 (de vêtement) (partie échancrée) neckline; (dimension) collar size; **②** (d'animal) neck

encombrant, ∼e /ɑ̃kɔ̃bʀɑ̃, ɑ̃t/ *adj* **①** [*meuble*] bulky; [*paquet, valise*] cumbersome; **②** [*personne, affaire*] troublesome

encombre: **sans encombre** /sɑ̃zɑ̃kɔ̃bʀ/ *loc adv* without a hitch

encombré, ∼e /ɑ̃kɔ̃bʀe/ *adj* [*route, ciel*] congested (**de** with); [*pièce, meuble*] cluttered (**de** with); [*conduit*] obstructed; [*lignes téléphoniques*] blocked; [*standard*] jammed; [*marché*] saturated (**de** with); [*profession*] overcrowded

encombrement /ɑ̃kɔ̃bʀəmɑ̃/ *nm* **①** (de la circulation) (ralentissement) traffic congestion *C*; (embouteillage) traffic jam; **②** (de standard, fréquences) jamming; **③** (de passage) obstruction; **④** (de pièce) cluttering; (des tribunaux) congestion; **⑤** (de profession) overcrowding; (de marché) saturation; **⑥** (volume) bulk; **d'un ∼ réduit** compact

encombrer /ɑ̃kɔ̃bʀe/ [1]
A *vtr* to clutter up [*pièce, mémoire, esprit*]; (obstruer) to obstruct [*route, passage*]; Télécom to block [*lignes*]; to overcrowd [*profession*]; to saturate [*marché*]
B **s'encombrer** *vpr* **s'∼ de** lit, fig to burden oneself with; **s'∼ l'esprit** to clutter up one's mind

encontre: **à l'encontre de** /alɑ̃kɔ̃tʀədə/ *loc prép* **①** (contrairement à) contrary to; **②** (en opposition à) counter to; **③** (activement contre) against; **aller à l'∼ de la politique gouvernementale** to go against government policy; **④** (envers) toward(s)

encorbellement /ɑ̃kɔʀbɛlmɑ̃/ *nm* (de fenêtre) corbel

encorder: **s'encorder** /ɑ̃kɔʀde/ [1] *vpr* to rope up

encore /ɑ̃kɔʀ/
A *adv* **①** (toujours) still; **je m'en souviens ∼** I still remember; **il n'est ∼ que midi** it's only midday; **tu en es ∼ là?** fig haven't you got GB *ou* gotten US beyond that by now?; **qu'il soit impoli passe ∼, mais...** the fact that he's rude is one thing, but...; ∼ **heureux** *or* **une chance que je m'en sois aperçu** it's lucky that I realized; **②** (toujours pas) **pas ∼** not yet; **tu n'as ∼ rien vu** you haven't seen anything yet; **cela ne s'est ∼ jamais vu/fait** it has never been seen/done before; **les abricots ne sont pas ∼ assez mûrs** the apricots aren't ripe enough yet; **③** (de nouveau) again; **les prix ont ∼ augmenté** prices have gone up again; ∼ **toi!** you again!; ∼**!** (à un spectacle) more!; ∼ **une fois** once more; **qu'est-ce que j'ai ∼ fait?** what have I done now?; **elle s'est ∼ acheté une nouvelle robe** she has bought herself yet

another new dress; **4** (davantage) more; **j'en veux ~** I want some more; **tu devrais ~ raccourcir ta robe** you should take your dress up a little more; **cela va ~ aggraver les choses** it's going to make things even worse; **c'est ~ mieux/moins** it's even better/less; **5** (en plus) **~ un gâteau?** another cake?; **pendant ~ trois jours** for another three days; **il me reste ~ 50 euros** I've still got 50 euros left; **que dois-je prendre ~?** what else shall I take?; **qu'est-ce qu'il te faut ~?** fig what more do you need *ou* want?; **et puis quoi ~?** what next?; **que dire ~?** what else can be said?; **ou ~** or else; **6** (toutefois) **il ne suffit pas d'avoir de bonnes idées, ~ faut-il savoir les exprimer** it's not enough to have good ideas, one must be able to articulate them; **~ faut-il qu'elle accepte** but she still has to accept; **si ~ il était généreux!** if he were at least generous!; **7** (seulement) only, just; **il y a ~ trois mois** only *ou* just three months ago

B et encore *loc adv* if that

C encore que *loc conj* (bien que) even though

encoubler /ãkuble/ [1] H
A *vtr* (gêner) **tu m'encoubles** you're getting under my feet
B s'encoubler *vpr* (se prendre les pieds) **s'~ dans qch** to catch one's feet in sth

encourageant, ~e /ãkuraʒã, ãt/ *adj* encouraging

encouragement /ãkuraʒmã/ *nm* encouragement **C**

encourager /ãkuraʒe/ [13] *vtr* **1** (pousser) to encourage (**à faire** to do); **2** (de la voix) to cheer [sb] on [*équipe, sportif*]

encourir /ãkurir/ [26] *vtr* to incur

encrasser /ãkrase/ [1]
A *vtr* **1** (obstruer) to clog [sth] (up) [*filtre, moteur, artère*]; to make [sth] sooty [*cheminée*]; **2** (salir) to dirty; Aut to foul up [*bougies*]
B s'encrasser *vpr* **1** (s'obstruer) to clog up; [*cheminée*] to get sooty; **2** (se salir) to get dirty; [*bougie*] to foul up

encre /ãkr/ *nf* ink; **~ d'imprimerie** printer's ink
(Composés) **~ de Chine** Indian GB *ou* India US ink; **~ sympathique** invisible ink
(Idiomes) **cela a fait couler beaucoup d'~** a lot of ink has been spilled over this; **se faire un sang d'~** to be worried stiff

encrer /ãkre/ [1] *vtr* to ink

encrier /ãkrije/ *nm* (encastré) inkwell; (pot) ink pot

encroûter○: **s'encroûter** /ãkrute/ [1] *vpr* [*personne*] to get in a rut; **il est complètement encroûté dans ses habitudes** he's very set in his ways

encyclopédie /ãsiklɔpedi/ *nf* encyclopedia

endémique /ãdemik/ *adj* endemic

endetté, ~e /ãdete/ *adj* in debt (*jamais épith*); **très ~** heavily in debt

endettement /ãdɛtmã/ *nm* debt; **~ public/extérieur** national/foreign debt

endetter /ãdete/ [1]
A *vtr* to put [sb] into debt
B s'endetter *vpr* to get into debt (**auprès de** with)

endeuiller /ãdœje/ [1] *vtr* to plunge [sb] into mourning [*famille*]; to cast a shadow over [*cérémonie, réunion sportive*]; **pays endeuillé** griefstricken country

endiablé, ~e /ãdjable/ *adj* [*rythme*] (très vif) furious; [*enfant*] boisterous

endiguer /ãdige/ [1] *vtr* to confine [*cours d'eau*]; to contain [*manifestants, groupe*]; to curb [*spéculation, mécontentement*]

endimanché, ~e /ãdimãʃe/ *adj* in one's Sunday best (*après n*)

endive /ãdiv/ *nf* chicory **C** GB, endive US

endocrine /ãdɔkrin/ *adj* endocrine

endoctrinement /ãdɔktrinmã/ *nm* indoctrination

endoctriner /ãdɔktrine/ [1] *vtr* to indoctrinate

endolori, ~e /ãdɔlɔri/ *adj* aching

endommagement /ãdɔmaʒmã/ *nm* (action) damaging; (résultat) damage

endommager /ãdɔmaʒe/ [13] *vtr* to damage

endormant, ~e /ãdɔrmã, ãt/ *adj* [*travail, film*] mind-numbing

endormi, ~e /ãdɔrmi/ *adj* **1** [*personne, animal*] sleeping (*épith*), asleep (*jamais épith*); **2** fig [*village, yeux, cerveau, élève*] sleepy; [*économie, marché*] sluggish; [*public*] lethargic

endormir /ãdɔrmir/ [30]
A *vtr* **1** (naturellement) [*personne*] to send [sb] to sleep [*enfant*]; (chimiquement) [*personne, substance*] to put [sb] to sleep [*patient*]; **2** (donner envie de dormir) [*personne, discours*] to send [sb] to sleep [*personne*] (**avec** with); **3** (tromper) to dupe [*personne, opinion, ennemi*] (**avec** with); **4** (atténuer) to lessen [*vigilance*]; to allay [*soupçon*]; to numb [*faculté*]
B s'endormir *vpr* **1** (s'assoupir) to fall asleep; (trouver le sommeil) to get to sleep; **2** (se laisser aller) to sit back; **3** (décéder) fml to pass away

endoscopie /ãdɔskɔpi/ *nf* endoscopy

endossable /ãdosabl/ *adj* [*chèque*] endorsable

endossement /ãdosmã/ *nm* Fin endorsement

endosser /ãdose/ [1] *vtr* **1** (mettre) to put on; **2** (assumer) to take on [*responsabilité, rôle*]; to shoulder [*conséquence*]; **3** Fin to endorse [*chèque*]; **4** (en reliure) to back [*livre*]

endroit /ãdrwa/
A *nm* **1** (lieu) place; **par ~s** in places; **à quel ~?** where?; **2** (de tissu, pull) right side
B à l'endroit de *loc prép* toward(s)

enduire /ãdɥir/ [69]
A *vtr* to coat (**de** with)
B s'enduire *vpr* **s'~ de** to put [sth] on

enduit /ãdɥi/ *nm* (pour couvrir) coating; (pour boucher) filler

endurance /ãdyrãs/ *nf* **1** (de personne) stamina; **2** (de véhicule) endurance

endurant, ~e /ãdyrã, ãt/ *adj* [*personne*] tough, with stamina (*épith, après n*); [*moteur*] hard-wearing

endurci, ~e /ãdyrsi/ *adj* **1** (dur) tough; **2** (invétéré) [*célibataire*] confirmed; [*criminel*] hardened

endurcir /ãdyrsir/ [3]
A *vtr* **1** (rendre plus robuste) [*travail, sport*] to strengthen [*corps, caractère*]; **~ qn contre** to build up sb's resistance to; **2** (rendre insensible) [*épreuve, égoïsme*] to harden
B s'endurcir *vpr* **1** (devenir plus robuste) to become stronger; **2** (devenir insensible) to become hardened

endurer /ãdyre/ [1] *vtr* **1** (supporter physiquement) to endure; **faire ~ qch à qn** to put sb through sth; **2** (tolérer) to put up with

énergétique /enɛrʒetik/ *adj* **1** Écon energy (*épith*); **besoins ~s** energy requirements; **2** [*aliment, produit*] high-calorie (*épith*); **aliment peu ~** low-calorie food; **3** Phys energy; **bilan ~** energetics (+ *v sg*)

énergie /enɛrʒi/ *nf* **1** Écon energy; **faire des économies d'~** to save energy; **2** Phys energy; Tech energy, power; **~ nucléaire** nuclear power *ou* energy; **~ éolienne** windpower; **3** (force) energy; **dépenser son ~ à faire** to use up one's energy doing; **avec l'~ du désespoir** driven on by despair; **avec ~** [*travailler*] energetically; [*agir*] forcefully; [*protester*] strongly

énergique /enɛrʒik/ *adj* **1** (physiquement) [*personne*] energetic; [*poignée de main*] vigorous; [*visage*] resolute; **2** fig [*action*] tough; [*objection*] strong; [*refus*] firm; [*intervention, tentative*] forceful

énergisant, ~e /enɛrʒizã, ãt/
A *adj* [*médicament, effet, activité*] energizing; **boisson ~e** energy drink
B *nm* (stimulant) stimulant

énergumène /enɛrgymɛn/ *nmf* (personne exaltée) oddball

énervant, ~e /enɛrvã, ãt/ *adj* irritating

énervé, ~e /enɛrve/ *adj* **1** (irrité) irritated; **2** (agité) nervous; [*enfant*] overexcited

énervement /enɛrvəmã/ *nm* **1** (irritation) irritation; **2** (agitation) agitation; **elle pleura d'~** she was so on edge that she cried

énerver /enɛrve/ [1]
A *vtr* **1** (agiter) to put [sb] on edge; **2** (irriter) **~ qn** to get on sb's nerves, to irritate sb
B s'énerver *vpr* to get worked up (**pour** over)

enfance /ãfãs/ *nf* **1** (période) childhood; (de garçon) boyhood; (de fille) girlhood; **la petite ~** early childhood; **2** (enfants) children (*pl*); **3** (début) dawn
(Idiomes) **retomber en ~** to lapse into second childhood; **c'est l'~ de l'art** it's child's play

enfant /ãfã/ *nmf* **1** (jeune être humain) child; (très jeune) infant; **c'est une ~ terrible** lit she's an unruly child; **l'~ terrible du cinéma français** the enfant terrible of French cinema; **faire l'~** to act like a child; **mes rêves d'~**

my childhood dreams; **elle est restée très ~** she is still very childlike; ▸ **vérité**; **2** (fils, fille) child; **être ~ unique** to be an only child; **couple sans ~** childless couple; **faire un ~**○ (avoir) to have a child; **faire un ~ à qn**○ to make sb pregnant; **ce roman, c'est son ~** that novel is his/her baby; **3** (terme d'affection) **mon ~** my child; **4** (marquant l'origine) child; **un ~ du peuple** a child of the people

(Composés) **~ de l'amour** love child; **~ de chœur** altar boy; **ce n'est pas un ~ de chœur** fig he's no angel

enfantement /ɑ̃fɑ̃tmɑ̃/ nm lit childbirth; fig giving birth (**de** to)

enfanter /ɑ̃fɑ̃te/ [1] vtr lit, fig to give birth to

enfantillage /ɑ̃fɑ̃tijaʒ/ nm **1** (caprice) **cesse tes ~s!** stop being childish!; **2** (défaut) childishness

enfantin, **~e** /ɑ̃fɑ̃tɛ̃, in/ adj **1** (simple) simple, easy; **2** (d'un enfant) [geste] childish; **les émotions ~es** children's emotions; **3** (pour enfant) [classe] infant GB, for young children; **mode ~e** children's fashion; **4** (digne d'un enfant) childish péj, childlike

enfarger: **s'enfarger** /ɑ̃faʀʒe/ [13] vpr C (trébucher) **s'~ dans qch** to catch one's foot in sth; **s'~ dans sa phrase** to get one's words mixed up

enfariné, **~e** /ɑ̃faʀine/ adj **1** (saupoudré de farine) covered with flour; **2** (poudré) [visage] powdered

enfer /ɑ̃fɛʀ/ nm **1** Relig Hell; Mythol **les ~s** Hell (sg), the Underworld (sg); **2** fig hell (**de** of); **un ~ de souffrance** a living hell; **l'~ de la guerre** the hell of war; **vision d'~** vision of hell, hellish sight; **aller à un train d'~**○ to go to hell for leather○; **soirée d'~**○ hell of a○ party

(Idiome) **croix de bois croix de fer, si je mens je vais en ~** ≈ cross my heart and hope to die

enfermer /ɑ̃fɛʀme/ [1]

A vtr **1** (dans un lieu) to shut [sth] in [animal]; (à clé) to lock [sth] up [bijou] (**dans** in); to lock [sb] up, to put [sb] away○ [criminel, aliéné] (**dans** in); **elle est bonne à ~**○ she's stark raving mad○; **2** (bloquer) **~ qn dans une situation** to trap sb in a situation; **3** (contenir) **~ une théorie en une seule formule** to encapsulate a theory in a single formula; **4** Mil, Sport to box [sb] in [adversaire]

B s'enfermer vpr **1** gén to lock oneself in; (pour s'isoler) to shut oneself away; (accidentellement) to get locked in; **ne reste pas enfermé toute la journée!** don't stay cooped up indoors all day!; **ça fait deux heures qu'ils sont enfermés dans le bureau à discuter** they've been closeted in the study for two hours; **2** (se confiner) **s'~ dans** to retreat into; **s'~ dans le mutisme** to remain obstinately silent

enferrer: **s'enferrer** /ɑ̃fɛʀe/ [1] vpr **1** to tie oneself up in knots; **s'~ dans des mensonges/une déposition** to get tangled up in lies/a statement; **2** lit to impale oneself (**sur, à** on)

enfiévré, **~e** /ɑ̃fjevʀe/ adj [imagination] fevered (épith); [atmosphère] feverish; [discours] fiery

enfilade /ɑ̃filad/ nf **1** (de pièces) succession; (de maisons, tables) row; **maison en ~** interconnecting house GB, shotgun house US; **2** Archit enfilade

enfiler /ɑ̃file/ [1]

A vtr **1** (mettre) to slip on; **2** to thread [aiguille]; **3** (entrer dans) to slide [rue]; **4** (dire) to spout [phrases]

B s'enfiler vpr **1** ○(avaler) to guzzle down; fig to devour; **2** ○(faire) to get landed○ with [corvée]

enfin /ɑ̃fɛ̃/ adv **1** (en dernier lieu) (dans un développement, un discours) finally; (dans une énumération) lastly; **~ et surtout** last but not least; **2** (marquant le soulagement) at last; **~ seuls!** alone at last!; **3** (marquant la résignation) oh well; **~, puisque tu y tiens** oh well, as you insist; **4** (marquant l'impatience) for heaven's sake; **mais ~, cessez de vous disputer!** for heaven's sake, stop arguing!; **5** (en d'autres termes) in short, in other words; **6** (introduit un correctif) well, at least; **il pleut tous les jours, ~ presque** it rains every day, well almost; **7** (tout bien considéré) **car ~** after all; **8** (marquant la perplexité) (**mais**) **~, que signifie toute cette histoire?** what on earth does it all mean?

enflammé, **~e** /ɑ̃flame/ adj **1** lit burning; **2** fig [personne, déclaration] passionate; [discours] impassioned, fiery; **3** Méd [gorge, blessure] inflamed; **4** (rouge) [joues, visage] burning (**de** with); [ciel] ablaze (jamais épith), blazing

enflammer /ɑ̃flame/ [1]

A vtr **1** (mettre le feu à) to set fire to; **2** (exciter) to inflame [opinion, esprit, cœur]; to fire [imagination]; to fuel [colère]

B s'enflammer vpr **1** (prendre feu) [maison, papier] to go up

in flames; [essence, bois] to catch fire; **2** (s'exciter) [regard] to blaze; [imagination] to be fired (**de** with; **à la vue de** by); [pays, peuple] to explode; **s'~ pour qn** to become passionate about sb

enflé, **~e** /ɑ̃fle/ adj **1** lit [poignet] swollen; **2** [style] bombastic

enfler /ɑ̃fle/ [1]

A vtr **1** fig to exaggerate [récit, événements]; **~ la voix** to raise one's voice; **2** lit to swell

B vi **1** [partie du corps] to swell; **2** [rivière, mer] to swell

enflure /ɑ̃flyʀ/ nf Méd swelling

enfoncé, **~e** /ɑ̃fɔ̃se/ adj **1** (défoncé) [siège] sagging; **2** (rentré) [yeux] deep-set

enfoncement /ɑ̃fɔ̃smɑ̃/ nm **1** (creux) (dans un mur) recess; (sur un terrain) dip; **2** Méd crushing **Ȼ**; **3** Mil (déroute) collapse; **4** (enlisement) **l'~ du pays dans la récession** the country's slide into recession

enfoncer /ɑ̃fɔ̃se/ [12]

A vtr **1** (faire entrer sans outil) to push in [piquet, bouchon]; (avec un outil) **~ un clou dans qch** to knock a nail into sth; **~ les mains dans ses poches** to dig one's hands into one's pockets; **~ son chapeau jusqu'aux yeux** to pull one's hat down over one's eyes; **~ son doigt** to stick one's finger (**dans** into); **2** (faire céder) to break down [porte]; to break through [adversaire]; (accidentellement) to crash through [obstacle]; to break [cage thoracique]; to smash in [aile de voiture]; **~ des portes ouvertes** fig to state the obvious; **3** (vaincre) to defeat [armée]; to beat [concurrent]; **4** (abaisser) **ne m'enfonce pas davantage** don't rub it in

B vi (s'enliser) to sink

C s'enfoncer vpr **1** (s'enliser) **s'~ dans la neige/le sable** to sink in the snow/the sand; **être enfoncé dans un fauteuil** (confortablement) to be settled cosily GB ou cozily US in an armchair; **s'~ dans l'erreur** to make error after error; **2** (couler) **s'~ dans l'eau** to sink; **3** (pénétrer) **les piquets s'enfoncent facilement** the posts go in easily; **4** (se mettre) **s'~ une épine dans le doigt** to get a thorn in one's finger; **5** (aller) **s'~ dans la forêt** to go into the forest; **s'~ dans le brouillard** to disappear into the fog; **s'~ dans les** or **à l'intérieur des terres** to go inland; **6** (se creuser) [chaussée, terre] to give way; **7** ○(aggraver son cas) to make things worse for oneself

(Idiome) **~ qch dans le crâne**○ or **la tête de qn** to get sth into sb's head

enfouir /ɑ̃fwiʀ/ [3]

A vtr **1** (enterrer) to bury; **2** (dissimuler) **~ son visage dans les coussins** to bury one's face in the cushions; **~ qch dans un sac** (sans soin) to shove sth into a bag; (avec soin) to tuck sth away in a bag

B s'enfouir vpr (se blottir) **s'~ sous les couvertures** to burrow under the blankets; (s'enterrer) to bury oneself (**dans** in)

enfourcher /ɑ̃fuʀʃe/ [1] vtr to mount [cheval]; to get on [moto]

enfourner /ɑ̃fuʀne/ [1] vtr **1** (pour cuire) to put [sth] in the oven; **2** ○(manger) to stuff down; **3** ○(introduire) **~ qch dans** to stuff sth into

enfreindre /ɑ̃fʀɛ̃dʀ/ [55] vtr to infringe, to break

enfuir: **s'enfuir** /ɑ̃fɥiʀ/ [9] vpr **1** lit to run away (**de** from); [oiseau] to fly away; (d'un lieu clos) to escape (**de** from); **s'~ à Paris** to run off to Paris; **s'~ vers la frontière** to make off toward/s the border; **s'~ par les toits** to escape over the rooftops; **2** fig [temps] to fly

enfumer /ɑ̃fyme/ [1] vtr to fill [sth] with smoke

engagé, **~e** /ɑ̃gaʒe/

A adj (politically) committed

B nm,f enlisted man/woman

engageant, **~e** /ɑ̃gaʒɑ̃, ɑ̃t/ adj [personne, manières] welcoming; [offre] attractive; [plat, lieu] inviting

engagement /ɑ̃gaʒmɑ̃/ nm **1** (promesse) commitment; **prendre l'~ de faire** to undertake to do; **remplir ses ~s** to honour^GB one's commitments; **sans ~ de votre part** with no obligation on your part; **2** (participation) involvement; **3** Mil (fait de s'engager, durée) enlistment; (combat) engagement; **4** (contrat) engagement

(Composés) **~ contractuel** contractual obligation; **~ volontaire** volunteering

engager /ɑ̃gaʒe/ [13]

A vtr **1** (recruter) to hire [personnel]; to enlist [soldat]; to

engage [artiste]; **2** (commencer) to begin [processus]; **nous avons engagé la conversation** we struck up a conversation; ~ **le combat** to go into combat; ~ **la partie** (au football) to kick off; ~ **une action judiciaire** to take legal action; **3** (obliger) to commit [personne]; **votre signature vous engage** your signature is binding; **4** (mettre en jeu) to stake [réputation]; ~ **sa parole** to give one's word; **5** (introduire) ~ **qch dans** to put sth in; **6** (amener) ~ **une voiture dans une petite route** to take a car into a country road; **7** Écon to lay out [capitaux]; ~ **des dépenses** to undertake expenditure; **8** ~ **qn à faire** (exhorter) to urge sb to do; (conseiller) to advise sb to do; **9** Sport ~ **qn dans une compétition** to enter sb for a competition; **10** (donner en gage) to pawn [objet précieux]

B s'engager vpr **1** (promettre) to promise (**à faire** to do); **elle s'est engagée à fond** she is fully committed; **s'~ vis-à-vis de qn** to take on a commitment to sb; **2** (entreprendre) **s'~ dans un projet** to embark on a project; **s'~ dans la bataille** to go into action; **s'~ dans des dépenses** to incur expenses; **3** (s'impliquer) to get involved; **4** (p énétrer) **s'~ sur une route** to go into a road; **s'~ sur un pont** to go onto a bridge; **avant de s'~ dans un carrefour** before going across an intersection; **5** (être amorcé) [action judiciaire, processus, négociations] to begin; **6** (se faire recruter) to enlist; **s'~ dans l'armée/la police** to join the army/the police; **s'~ dans une compétition** to enter a competition

engelure /ɑ̃ʒlyʀ/ nf chilblain (**à** on)

engendrer /ɑ̃ʒɑ̃dʀe/ [1] vtr **1** (provoquer) to engender; **2** Ling, Math to generate; **3** (mettre au monde) fml [femme] to give birth to; [homme] to father

engin /ɑ̃ʒɛ̃/ nm **1** (machine, objet, instrument) device; **qu'est-ce que c'est que cet** ~○? what's that contraption?; **2** (véhicule) vehicle; (machine) piece of equipment; ~**s de levage** lifting equipment; **3** Mil (missile) missile; (bombe) device; (véhicule) vehicle

englober /ɑ̃glɔbe/ [1] vtr to include

engloutir /ɑ̃glutiʀ/ [3] vtr **1** (faire disparaître) [mer, tempête, brouillard] to engulf, to swallow up; **2** ○(dévorer) to gulp [sth] down; **3** (dépenser) to squander [argent, somme]; (coûter) to swallow up [argent, somme]

engloutissement /ɑ̃glutismɑ̃/ nm swallowing up

engluer /ɑ̃glye/ [1]
A vtr (pour attraper) to lime [branche, oiseau]
B s'engluer vpr **s'~ dans qch** to become bogged down in sth

engoncé, ~e /ɑ̃gɔ̃se/ adj **il était ~ dans une veste trop étroite** he was squeezed into a tight jacket

engorgement /ɑ̃gɔʀʒəmɑ̃/ nm (de canalisation) blocking; (de route, d'organe) congestion

engorger /ɑ̃gɔʀʒe/ [13]
A vtr to block (up) [canalisation]; to clog up [routes]; Comm to glut [marché]; Méd to congest [organe]
B s'engorger vpr [tuyau] to be blocked (up)

engouement /ɑ̃gumɑ̃/ nm (pour une chose) passion (**pour** for); (pour une personne) infatuation (**pour** for)

engouer: s'engouer /ɑ̃gwe/ [1] vpr **s'~ de** to become infatuated with [personne]; to develop a passion for [artiste, peinture, musique]

engouffrer /ɑ̃gufʀe/ [1]
A vtr **1** ○(manger) to gobble up; **2** (dépenser) to sink; (coûter) [projet, affaire] to swallow up; **3** (mettre) to stuff (**dans** into)
B s'engouffrer vpr **1** lit (dans une pièce, un passage) [personne, vent, eau] to rush (**dans** in); (dans un taxi, le métro) to dive (**dans** into); **2** fig **s'~ dans** (pour en profiter) to rush to take advantage of; (pour combler un vide) to rush into

engourdi, ~e /ɑ̃guʀdi/ adj (ankylosé, transi) numb (**par, de** with); (somnolent) [personne] drowsy; fig [ville] sleepy, drowsy; (hébété) [cerveau] dull(ed)

engourdir /ɑ̃guʀdiʀ/ [3]
A vtr **1** (rendre gourd) to make [sb/sth] numb; **2** (endormir) to make [sb/sth] drowsy [personne, esprit]; to deaden [douleur]; **3** (hébéter) to dull
B s'engourdir vpr [membre] to go numb, to go to sleep; [corps] to go numb; [cerveau] to grow dull

engourdissement /ɑ̃guʀdismɑ̃/ nm **1** (état) (physique) numbness; (mental) (torpeur) drowsiness; (affaiblissement) dullness; **2** (action) (du corps) numbing; (de l'esprit) dulling

engrais /ɑ̃gʀɛ/ nm inv (animal) manure; (chimique) fertilizer

engraissage /ɑ̃gʀɛsaʒ/ nm, **engraissement** /ɑ̃gʀɛsmɑ̃/ nm (de bétail) fattening

engraisser /ɑ̃gʀɛse/ [1]
A vtr **1** to fatten [bétail]; **2** to fertilize [sol]; **3** ○to make [sb] rich
B vi (grossir) to get fat
C s'engraisser○ vpr (s'enrichir) to grow fat○

engranger /ɑ̃gʀɑ̃ʒe/ [13] vtr lit to gather in; fig to store [données]; to store up [souvenirs, argent]

engrenage /ɑ̃gʀənaʒ/ nm **1** (mécanique) gears (pl); **2** fig (de violence, difficultés) spiral; **être pris dans l'~ (de qch)** to get caught up in a spiral (of sth)

engueuler❜ /ɑ̃gœle/ [1]
A vtr to tell [sb] off [enfant]; to give [sb] an earful○ [adulte]
B s'engueuler vpr to have a row (**avec qn** with sb)

enguirlander /ɑ̃giʀlɑ̃de/ [1]
A vtr to tell [sb] off [enfant]; to give sb an earful○ [adulte]; **se faire ~** to get told off (**par** by), to get an earful○ (**par** from)
B s'enguirlander vpr to have a row

enhardir /ɑ̃aʀdiʀ/ [3]
A vtr to embolden
B s'enhardir vpr to become bolder

énième /ɛnjɛm/ adj umpteenth

énigmatique /enigmatik/ adj enigmatic

énigme /enigm/ nf **1** (mystère) enigma, mystery; **2** (devinette) riddle; **parler par ~s** to speak in riddles

enivrant, ~e /ɑ̃nivʀɑ̃, ɑ̃t/ adj intoxicating

enivrement /ɑ̃nivʀəmɑ̃/ nm intoxication

enivrer /ɑ̃nivʀe/ [1]
A vtr **1** [alcool] to intoxicate sout, make [sb] drunk; [air, altitude, mer] to intoxicate sout; **2** ~ **qn** [succès] to go to sb's head
B s'enivrer vpr **1** lit (se soûler) to get intoxicated sout; **2** fig to become intoxicated (**de** with)

enjambée /ɑ̃ʒɑ̃be/ nf stride; **s'éloigner à grandes ~s** to stride off

enjamber /ɑ̃ʒɑ̃be/ [1] vtr **1** [personne] to step over [obstacle]; **2** [pont] to span [rivière]

enjeu, pl ~x /ɑ̃ʒø/ nm **1** Jeux stake; **2** (ce qui est en jeu) what is at stake; **3** (problème) issue; **un ~ économique** an economic issue

enjoindre /ɑ̃ʒwɛ̃dʀ/ [56] vtr ~ **à qn de faire** to enjoin sout sb to do

enjôler /ɑ̃ʒole/ [1] vtr to beguile; **se laisser ~ par** to be taken in ou beguiled (**par** by)

enjoliver /ɑ̃ʒɔlive/ [1] vtr to embellish

enjoliveur /ɑ̃ʒɔlivœʀ/ nm hubcap

enjoué, ~e /ɑ̃ʒwe/ adj [caractère] cheerful; [ton] light-hearted

enlacé, ~e /ɑ̃lɑse/ adj **1** [corps, amants] entwined (jamais épith); **2** [fils, initiales] interlacing

enlacer /ɑ̃lɑse/ [12]
A vtr [personne] to embrace [personne]; [serpent] to wrap itself around [proie]
B s'enlacer vpr [personnes] to embrace; [corps] to intertwine

enlaidir /ɑ̃lediʀ/ [3]
A vtr to spoil [paysage]; to make [sb] look ugly [personne]
B vi to become ugly
C s'enlaidir vpr [personne] to make oneself (look) ugly

enlevé, ~e /ɑ̃lve/ adj [morceau, rythme] lively

enlèvement /ɑ̃lɛvmɑ̃/ nm **1** (délit) kidnapping^GB, abduction; **2** (de colis) removal; (d'ordures) collection

enlever /ɑ̃lve/ [16]
A vtr **1** (ôter) gén to remove; to take [sth] down [rideaux]; to take [sth] off [vêtement]; to move [véhicule] (**de** from); **enlève tes affaires de là/tes pieds du fauteuil** get○ your things out of here/your feet off the armchair; **2** (supprimer) to remove (**de** from); **3** (priver de) to take [sb/sth] away [personnes, objet] (**à** from); ~ **à qn l'envie de faire** to put sb off doing; ~ **toute signification à qch** to make sth totally meaningless; **cela n'enlève rien à l'estime que j'ai pour elle** it doesn't make me think any the less of her; **4** (ravir) to kidnap; [amant] to carry [sb] off [bien-aimée]; **5** (gagner) to carry [sth] off [coupe, prix]; to capture [marché]; **6** (avec brio) to give a brilliant rendering of [morceau de musique]
B s'enlever vpr **1** (disparaître) [vernis, papier peint] to come

off; [*tache*] to come out; **2**▸ (être séparable) [*pièce*] to be detachable; **ça s'enlève comment?** [*vêtement*] how do you take it off?; **3**▸ ○(partir) **enlève-toi de là** get off○

enlisement /ãlizmã/ *nm* lit sinking; fig (de négociations) stalemate; (de mouvement) collapse

enliser /ãlize/ [1]
A *vtr* to get [sth] stuck (**dans** in)
B **s'enliser** *vpr* **1**▸ [*bateau, véhicule*] to get stuck (**dans** in); **2**▸ fig [*enquête, négociations*] to drag on; **s'~ dans** to sink into; **être enlisé dans** (dans un conflit, des difficultés) to be embroiled in

enluminure /ãlyminyʀ/ *nf* Art illumination

enneigé, ~e /ãneʒe/ *adj* [*sommet, paysage*] snowy (*épith*); [*route*] covered in snow (*après n*)

enneigement /ãnɛʒmã/ *nm* bulletin d'~ snow report; **l'~ des pistes est insuffisant** there isn't enough snow on the slopes

ennemi, ~e /ɛnmi/
A *adj* **1**▸ Mil enemy (*épith*); **2**▸ (hostile) hostile; **être ~ de qch** to be opposed to sth
B *nm,f* **1**▸ (de personne, groupe) enemy; **se faire des ~s** to make enemies; **2**▸ (d'idée) opponent; **3**▸ (élément nocif) **la censure est l'~e de la liberté** censorship is the enemy of a free society
C *nm* Mil enemy; **~ héréditaire** traditional enemy; **passer à l'~** to go over to the enemy
(Idiome) **le mieux est l'~ du bien** perfectionism can be counter-productive

ennoblir /ãnɔbliʀ/ [3] *vtr* to ennoble

ennui /ãnɥi/ *nm* **1**▸ (sentiment) boredom; **tromper l'~** to escape from boredom; **c'est à mourir d'~** it's enough to bore you stiff *ou* to death; **2**▸ (problème) problem; **j'ai des ~s avec la police** I'm in trouble with the police; **créer des ~s à qn** to make trouble for sb; **s'attirer des ~s** to run into trouble

ennuyé, ~e /ãnɥije/ *adj* **1**▸ (embarrassé) embarrassed; **j'étais très ~ de laisser les enfants seuls** I felt awful *ou* terrible about leaving the children on their own; **2**▸ (dans une situation difficile) **j'aurais été très ~ si je n'avais pas eu la clé** I would have been in real trouble if I hadn't had the key

ennuyer /ãnɥije/ [22]
A *vtr* **1**▸ (lasser) to bore; **voyager m'ennuie** I find travelling^GB boring; **2**▸ (déranger) to bother; **ce qui m'ennuie avec lui c'est que** what bothers me about him is that; **si ça ne vous ennuie pas trop** if you don't mind; **3**▸ (irriter) to annoy; **4**▸ (harceler) to hassle○
B **s'ennuyer** *vpr* **1**▸ (être las) to be bored; **s'~ mortellement** to be bored stiff; **avoir l'air de s'~** to look bored; **2**▸ (se lasser) to get bored; **je me suis franchement ennuyée** I got really bored; ▸ **rat, sou**; **3**▸ (languir) **s'~ de** to miss

ennuyeux, -euse /ãnɥijø, øz/ *adj* **1**▸ (lassant) boring; **2**▸ (pénible) tedious; **3**▸ (agaçant) annoying; **l'~ c'est que** the annoying thing is that
(Idiome) **être ~ comme la pluie** to be as dull as ditchwater

énoncé /enɔse/ *nm* **1**▸ (de problème, sujet) wording (**de** of); **l'~ d'une théorie** the exposition of a theory; **2**▸ (de fait) statement (**de** of); **3**▸ Jur pronouncement (**de** of); **à l'~ du verdict** when the verdict was pronounced; **4**▸ Ling utterance

énoncer /enɔse/ [12] *vtr* to pronounce [*jugement*]; to set out, to state [*faits, principes*]; to expound [*théorie*]

enorgueillir /ãnɔʀgœjiʀ/ [3]
A *vtr* to make [sb] proud [*personne*]
B **s'enorgueillir** *vpr* to pride oneself (**de** on)

énorme /enɔʀm/ *adj* **1**▸ (par la taille, la quantité) [*objet, personne*] huge, enormous; [*dépense*] huge, vast; **2**▸ (par l'intensité) [*succès, effort*] tremendous; [*erreur, gaffe*] terrible; [*mensonge*] outrageous; [*rire*] hearty; **la différence est ~** there's a world of difference; **ça vous ferait un bien ~** it would do you a power of good; **c'est déjà ~ qu'il les voie** for him to even see them is quite something

énormément /enɔʀmemã/ *adv* [*manger, boire*] a tremendous amount; [*parler, changer*] a great deal; **il a ~ grossi** he's put on a tremendous amount of weight; **~ de temps** a tremendous amount of time; **ça m'a ~ plu** I liked it immensely; **ça l'a ~ fatigué** it made him tremendously tired; **ça a ~ progressé** it's come on a lot; **il travaille ~** he works very hard; **il gagne ~** he earns a fortune

énormité /enɔʀmite/ *nf* **1**▸ (de chiffre, taille) hugeness; (de faute, mensonge) enormity; **2**▸ (propos aberrant) outrageous remark

enquérir: s'enquérir /ãkeʀiʀ/ [35] *vpr* **s'~ de** to inquire about sth

enquête /ãkɛt/ *nf* **1**▸ Admin, Jur inquiry, investigation (**sur** into); (après une mort) inquest (**sur** into); **ouvrir une ~** to open *ou* set up an investigation; **mener une ~** to lead an investigation; **2**▸ Presse, Sociol (reportage) investigation (**sur** into); (sondage) survey (**sur** about)
(Composés) **~ administrative** public inquiry; **~ d'opinion** gén survey; (pour des élections) opinion poll

enquêter /ãkete/ [1] *vi* [*policier*] to carry out an investigation (**sur** into), to investigate; [*expert, commission*] to hold an inquiry (**sur** into)

enquêteur, -trice /ãketœʀ, tʀis/ ▸ p. 372 *nm,f* **1**▸ (de police) investigating officer; **2**▸ (pour sondage politique) pollster; (pour sondage commercial) (market research) interviewer

enquiquinant○, ~e /ãkikinã, ãt/ *adj* **1**▸ (agaçant) annoying; **2**▸ (ennuyeux) boring

enquiquiner○ /ãkikine/ [1]
A *vtr* **~ qn** (agacer) to get on sb's nerves, to irritate sb; (importuner) to pester sb
B **s'enquiquiner** *vpr* **s'~ à faire** to go to the trouble of doing

enquiquineur○, -euse /ãkikinœʀ, øz/ *nm,f* pain○, nuisance

enracinement /ãʀasinmã/ *nm* **1**▸ Agric, Bot taking root, rooting; **2**▸ (de peuple) settling; **3**▸ (d'habitude, idée, de parti) (processus) taking root; (situation) deep-rootedness

enraciner /ãʀasine/ [1]
A *vtr* **1**▸ Agric, Bot to root; **2**▸ (installer) to establish [*peuple*]; **3**▸ (fixer dans l'esprit) to implant [*idées*]
B **s'enraciner** *vpr* **1**▸ Agric, Bot to take root; **2**▸ (dans un lieu, pays) [*personne*] to put down roots; [*coutume, idée*] to take root

enragé, ~e /ãʀaʒe/
A *adj* **1**▸ (passionné) fanatical; **2**▸ (furieux) enraged; **3**▸ Méd rabid
B *nm,f* (passionné, révolté) fanatic
(Idiome) **manger de la vache ~e○** to go through hard times

enrageant, ~e /ãʀaʒã, ãt/ *adj* infuriating

enrager /ãʀaʒe/ [13] *vi* to be furious; **j'enrage de voir** I'm furious to see; **faire ~ qn** (taquiner) to tease sb; (ennuyer) to annoy sb

enrayer /ãʀeje/ [21]
A *vtr* **1**▸ (maîtriser) to check [*épidémie, développement*]; to curb [*inflation, chômage*]; to stop [sth] escalating [*crise, violence*]; **2**▸ (bloquer) to jam
B **s'enrayer** *vpr* lit, fig to get jammed

enregistrement /ãʀeʒistʀəmã/ *nm* **1**▸ Audio, Vidéo recording; **2**▸ (de plainte, données) recording; (de personnes, livres) registration; (de commande) taking down; **3**▸ Jur registration; **4**▸ (de bagages) check-in; **5**▸ Ordinat record

enregistrer /ãʀeʒistʀe/ [1] *vtr* **1**▸ Audio, Vidéo to record [*disque, cassette*]; **~ qch sur bande magnétique/vidéo** to tape/to videotape sth; **2**▸ (constater) to note [*progrès, échec, phénomène*]; to record [*hausse, baisse*]; **3**▸ (consigner) to make a record of [*dépenses*]; to take [*commande*]; to record [*données*]; to set [*record*]; **4**▸ to register [*déclaration, naissance*]; **5**▸ to check in [*bagages*]; **6**▸ (mémoriser) to take in; **c'est enregistré** I've made a mental note of it

enrhumer /ãʀyme/ [1]
A *vtr* to give [sb] a cold [*personne*]
B **s'enrhumer** *vpr* to catch a cold; **s'~ facilement** to catch colds easily; **être enrhumé** to have a cold

enrichi, ~e /ãʀiʃi/ *adj* [*substance*] enriched (**en** with); **formule ~e** improved formula

enrichir /ãʀiʃiʀ/ [3]
A *vtr* **1**▸ (financièrement) to make [sb] rich [*personne*]; to bring wealth to [*pays*]; **2**▸ (augmenter) to enrich, to enhance [*collection, ouvrage*] (**de** with); **3**▸ Tech to enrich
B **s'enrichir** *vpr* **1**▸ (devenir riche) [*personne*] to become rich; **2**▸ (être agrémenté) to be enriched (**de** with)

enrichissant, ~e /ãʀiʃisã, ãt/ *adj* [*expérience, lecture*] rewarding; [*relation*] fulfilling

enrichissement /ɑ̃ʁiʃismɑ̃/ nm [1] (en argent) (de pays) enrichment; (de personne) accumulation of wealth; [2] Tech enrichment

enrober /ɑ̃ʁɔbe/ [1] vtr [1] lit to coat [gâteau] (de with); [2] fig to wrap up [paroles] (de in)

enrôlement /ɑ̃ʁolmɑ̃/ nm (dans l'armée) enlistment (dans in); (dans un parti) enrolment^GB (dans in); ~ forcé impressment

enrôler /ɑ̃ʁole/ [1]
A vtr gén to recruit; Mil to enlist, to recruit
B s'enrôler vpr to enrol^GB, to enlist (dans in)

enroué, ~e /ɑ̃ʁwe/ adj hoarse, husky

enrouer: s'enrouer /ɑ̃ʁwe/ [1] vpr [voix] to go hoarse; [personne] to make oneself hoarse

enroulement /ɑ̃ʁulmɑ̃/ nm [1] (action de s'enrouler) winding, rolling up; [2] (disposition) curling (up); [3] Art, Archit scroll; [4] Électrotech coil

enrouler /ɑ̃ʁule/ [1]
A vtr [1] (autour d'un axe) to wind (autour de round GB, around); [2] (envelopper) to wrap
B s'enrouler vpr [1] [bande, fil] to wind (sur onto; autour de round GB, around); [2] [personne, animal] to curl up

enrubanner /ɑ̃ʁybane/ [1] vtr [1] (pour décorer) to decorate [sth] with ribbon; [2] (pour attacher) to tie [sth] up with ribbons

ensabler /ɑ̃sable/ [1]
A vtr [1] to get [sth] stuck in the sand [véhicule]; to strand [sth] on a sandbank [bateau]; [2] to silt up [port, canal]
B s'ensabler vpr [véhicule] to get stuck in the sand; [bateau] to get stranded (on a sandbank); [2] [canal, port] to silt up

ensanglanté, ~e /ɑ̃sɑ̃ɡlɑ̃te/ adj [corps, couteau] bloodstained, bloody; [blessure] bloody

ensanglanter /ɑ̃sɑ̃ɡlɑ̃te/ [1] vtr [1] (couvrir de sang) to cover [sth] with blood; [2] (ravager) to bring bloodshed to [pays, époque]

enseignant, ~e /ɑ̃seɲɑ̃, ɑ̃t/ ▸ p. 372
A adj corps ~ teaching profession
B nm,f Scol teacher; Univ lecturer

enseigne /ɑ̃sɛɲ/
A nf [1] (de magasin) (shop) sign; ~ lumineuse neon sign; [2] Mil, Naut (drapeau) ensign
B à telle enseigne que loc conj so much so that

(Idiome) nous sommes logés à la même ~ we are in the same boat

enseignement /ɑ̃sɛɲmɑ̃/ nm [1] (institution) education; l'~ supérieur higher education; réforme de l'~ educational reform; [2] (activité) teaching; méthodes d'~ teaching methods; entrer dans l'~ to enter the teaching profession; [3] (formation) instruction; l'~ pratique practical instruction; [4] (cours) tuition; dispenser un ~ to give tuition; [5] (leçon) lesson

(Composés) ~ assisté par ordinateur, EAO computer-aided learning, CAL; ~ par correspondance or à distance distance learning; ~ général mainstream education; ~ ménager domestic science; ~ mixte coeducation; ~ professionnel vocational training ou education; ~ religieux religious instruction; ~ technique technical education

enseigner /ɑ̃seɲe/ [1] vtr to teach; ~ qch à qn to teach sth to sb, to teach sb sth

ensemble /ɑ̃sɑ̃bl/
A adv [1] (l'un avec l'autre) together; ils iraient bien ~ ces deux-là○! they'd make a fine pair, those two○!; [2] (simultanément) at the same time; (à la fois) liter tout ~ at once
B nm [1] (éléments regroupés) group; un ~ de personnes a group of people; l'~ des élèves de la classe all the pupils (pl) in the class; l'~ de l'œuvre d'un écrivain the whole of a writer's work; une vue d'~ an overall view; plan d'~ d'une ville general plan of a town; dans l'~ by and large; dans l'~ de throughout; dans son or leur ~ as a whole; [2] (éléments assortis) set; [3] (cohésion) unity, cohesion; former un bel ~ to form a harmonious whole; [4] (synchronisation) (de gestes) coordination; (de sons) unison; [5] Math set; théorie des ~s set theory; [6] (formation musicale) ensemble; [7] Constr (de bureaux) complex; ~ industriel industrial estate GB ou park US; ▸ grand; [8] (vêtements) outfit; (tailleur) suit

ensemblier /ɑ̃sɑ̃blije/ ▸ p. 372 nm (décorateur) interior designer; (au cinéma) assistant set designer

ensemencer /ɑ̃smɑ̃se/ [12] vtr to sow; ~ une rivière to stock a river with young fish

enserrer /ɑ̃seʁe/ [1] vtr [1] (mouler) to fit tightly round; [2] (serrer fortement) il lui enserra la taille he clasped him/her around the waist; la pieuvre enserra sa proie the octopus gripped its prey tightly

ensevelir /ɑ̃savəliʁ/ [3] vtr [1] (enterrer) to bury, to inter sout; [2] (recouvrir) to bury; [3] (cacher) liter [personne] to hide; [temps] to enshroud sout

ensevelissement /ɑ̃savəlismɑ̃/ nm [1] (enterrement) fml burial; [2] (recouvrement) liter burying

ensoleillé, ~e /ɑ̃sɔleje/ adj sunny

ensoleillement /ɑ̃sɔlɛjmɑ̃/ nm [1] (exposition au soleil) la pièce jouit d'un bon ~ the room gets a lot of sun; [2] Météo l'~ moyen de la région est de 2 000 heures par an on average the region gets 2,000 hours of sunshine a year

ensommeillé, ~e /ɑ̃sɔmeje/ adj [personne, voix] sleepy, drowsy

ensorceler /ɑ̃sɔʁsəle/ [19] vtr [1] (jeter un sort) to cast ou to put a spell on; [2] (captiver) to bewitch, to enchant

ensorceleur, -euse /ɑ̃sɔʁsəlœʁ, øz/
A adj [1] (séduisant) bewitching, enchanting; [2] (magique) magic
B nm,f (personne séduisante) charmer

ensorcellement /ɑ̃sɔʁsɛlmɑ̃/ nm [1] (en jetant un sort) bewitchment; [2] (en séduisant) charm, enchantment

ensuite /ɑ̃sɥit/ adv [1] (après) then; (ultérieurement) later, subsequently; très bien, mais ~? fine, but then what?; [2] (en second lieu) secondly

ensuivre: s'ensuivre /ɑ̃sɥivʁ/ [19] vpr to follow, to ensue; jusqu'à ce que mort s'ensuive until one is dead

entaché, ~e /ɑ̃taʃe/ adj Jur acte ~ d'un vice de forme act vitiated by a formal flaw; ~ de nullité Jur null and void

entacher /ɑ̃taʃe/ [1] vtr fml to sully littér, to besmirch littér [réputation, honneur]; to mar [relations, rapports]

entaille /ɑ̃taj/ nf [1] (blessure) cut; (profonde) gash; (petite) nick; [2] (encoche) notch

entailler /ɑ̃taje/ [1]
A vtr to cut into; (profondément) to make a gash in
B s'entailler vpr s'~ le doigt to cut one's finger; (profondément) to gash one's finger

entame /ɑ̃tam/ nf (tranche) first slice; (carte) lead

entamé, ~e /ɑ̃tame/ adj [1] (avancé) under way; [2] (commencé) le sandwich était à peine ~ the sandwich had hardly been touched

entamer /ɑ̃tame/ [1] vtr [1] (démarrer) to start [activité, journée]; to initiate [procédure]; to enter into [bataille, entretien]; to open [réunion, négociation]; [2] (affaiblir) to undermine [crédibilité, moral]; to shake [détermination]; [3] (rogner) to eat into [économies]; [4] (commencer à consommer) to cut into [pain, rôti]; to open [bouteille, pot]; to start eating [dessert, sandwich]; [5] (entailler) to cut into; [6] (ronger) to eat into [métal]

entartrer /ɑ̃taʁtʁe/ [1]
A vtr to fur up GB, to scale up
B s'entartrer vpr to scale; [dents] to be covered in tartar

entassement /ɑ̃tɑsmɑ̃/ nm [1] (action) (de choses) piling up; (de personnes) cramming together; [2] (résultat) (d'objets) pile; (plus gros) heap

entasser /ɑ̃tɑse/ [1]
A vtr [1] (empiler) to pile [livres, vêtements] (dans into; sur onto); [2] (amasser) to hoard [argent, vieilleries]; [3] (serrer) to pack, to cram [personnes, objets] (dans into)
B s'entasser vpr [objets] to pile up; [personnes] to crowd, to squeeze (dans into; sur onto)

entendement /ɑ̃tɑ̃dmɑ̃/ nm understanding; cela dépasse l'~ it's beyond belief

entendeur /ɑ̃tɑ̃dœʁ/ nm à bon ~, salut! you've been warned!

entendre /ɑ̃tɑ̃dʁ/ [6]
A vtr [1] (percevoir par l'ouïe) to hear [bruit, mot]; ~ qn pleurer to hear sb crying; réussir à se faire ~ to manage to make oneself heard; elle entend mal she's hard of hearing; faire ~ un cri to give a cry; j'ai entendu dire que I've heard (say) that; je n'en ai jamais entendu parler I've never heard of it; vous entendrez parler de moi!

e

(menace) you haven't heard the last of it!; **2** (prêter attention à) [*juge, police*] to hear [*témoin, témoignage*]; [*dieu*] to hear [*prières, croyant*]; **à t'~, tout va bien** according to you, everything is fine; **raconter qch à qui veut l'~** to tell sth to anyone who'll listen; **(que) le ciel vous entende!** let's hope that's how it turns out!; **elle ne veut rien ~** she won't listen; **3** *fml* (comprendre) to understand; **il agit comme il l'entend** he does as he likes; **fais comme tu l'entends** do as you think best; **elle m'a laissé** *or* **donné à** *or* **fait ~ que** she gave me to understand that; **elle a laissé ~ que** she intimated that; **ils ne l'entendent pas de la sorte** *or* **de cette oreille** they don't see it that way; **4** (signifier) to mean; **qu'entends-tu par là?** what do you mean by that?; **5** *fml* (avoir l'intention de) **~ faire** to intend doing; **j'entends qu'on fasse ce que je dis** I expect people to do what I say

B s'entendre *vpr* **1** (sympathiser) to get on *ou* along (**avec** with); **2** (se mettre d'accord) to agree (**sur** on); **on leur dit la vérité ou pas? il faudrait s'~** shall we tell them the truth or not? let's get it straight; **3** (être perçu par l'oreille) [*bruit*] to be heard; (soi-même) to hear oneself; (les uns les autres) to hear each other; **4** (être compris) **phrase qui peut s'~ de plusieurs façons** sentence which can be taken in several different ways; **5** (être compétent) **s'y ~ en meubles anciens** to know about antiques; **pour te faire culpabiliser, elle s'y entend**○! when it comes to making you feel guilty, she's an expert!

entendu, ~e /ɑ̃tɑ̃dy/

A *pp* ▸ **entendre**

B *pp adj* (décidé) **c'est une affaire ~e** it's settled; **'tu viens demain?'—'~!'** 'will you come tomorrow?'—'OK○!'; **je fais ceci étant ~ que** I'm doing this on the understanding that

C *adj* (de connivence) knowing; **d'un air ~** with a knowing look

D bien entendu *loc adv* of course; **elle a oublié, (comme de)**○ **bien ~** she's forgotten, of course; **il est bien ~ qu'elle ne sait rien** of course, she knows nothing

entente /ɑ̃tɑ̃t/ *nf* **1** (bon rapport) harmony; **la bonne ~ de nos deux pays** the friendly relationship between our two countries; **vivre en bonne ~ avec qn** to be on good terms with sb; **2** (alliance) understanding; **3** (accord) arrangement

(Composé) **l'Entente cordiale** *Hist* the entente cordiale

entériner /ɑ̃teʀine/ [1] *vtr* (ratifier) to ratify; (admettre) to confirm

entérite /ɑ̃teʀit/ ▸ p. 195 *nf* Méd enteritis

enterré, ~e /ɑ̃teʀe/ *adj* **1** (sous terre) buried; **2** (oublié) **~ (depuis longtemps)** long-forgotten (*épith*)

enterrement /ɑ̃teʀmɑ̃/ *nm* **1** (inhumation) burial (**de** of); **2** (obsèques) funeral; **faire une tête d'~**○ to look gloomy; **3** (mise à l'écart) shelving

enterrer /ɑ̃teʀe/ [1]

A *vtr* **1** (inhumer) to bury; **2** (mettre sous terre) to bury; ▸ **hache**; **3** (renoncer à) to say goodbye to; **4** (mettre à l'écart) to shelve

B s'enterrer○ *vpr* to go and hole up○

(Idiome) **~ sa vie de garçon** to have a stag party

entêtant, ~e /ɑ̃tɛtɑ̃, ɑ̃t/ *adj* [*parfum*] heady; [*musique*] insistent

en-tête, *pl* **~s** /ɑ̃tɛt/ *nm* **1** (de papier) heading; **papier à lettres à ~** headed writing paper; **2** Ordinat header-block

entêté, ~e /ɑ̃tete/ *adj* stubborn, obstinate

entêtement /ɑ̃tɛtmɑ̃/ *nm* stubbornness, obstinacy

entêter: s'entêter /ɑ̃tete/ [1] *vpr* to be stubborn; **s'~ dans qch/à faire** to persist in sth/in doing

enthousiasmant, ~e /ɑ̃tuzjasmɑ̃, ɑ̃t/ *adj* exciting

enthousiasme /ɑ̃tuzjasm/ *nm* enthusiasm **C** (**pour** for); **susciter l'~** to arouse enthusiasm; **refroidir les ~s** to dampen enthusiasm

enthousiasmer /ɑ̃tuzjasme/ [1]

A *vtr* to fill [sb] with enthusiasm; **j'ai été enthousiasmé par le concert** I found the concert exciting

B s'enthousiasmer *vpr* to get enthusiastic (**pour** about)

enthousiaste /ɑ̃tuzjast/

A *adj* enthusiastic

B *nmf* enthusiast

enticher: s'enticher /ɑ̃tiʃe/ [1] *vpr* **s'~ de** to become infatuated with [*personne*]; to become passionate about [*objet, idée*]

entier, -ière /ɑ̃tje, ɛʀ/

A *adj* **1** (dans sa totalité) whole; **l'Europe (tout) entière** the whole of Europe; **il l'a fait cuire tout ~** he cooked it whole; **(pendant) des heures entières** for hours on end; **dans le monde ~** (partout dans le monde) all over the world; (au monde) in the whole world; **ils arrivent par trains ~s** they arrive by the trainload; **par caisses entières** by the crate; **lait ~** full-fat milk; **2** (complet) [*réussite, satisfaction*] complete; **avoir l'entière responsabilité de qch** to have full responsibility for sth; **avoir une entière confiance en qn** to have every confidence in sb; **3** (inaltéré) [*objet, réputation*] intact; **le problème de l'information reste ~** we have not even begun to address the information problem; **le mystère reste ~** the mystery remains unsolved; **4** (sans réserve) **se donner** *or* **dévouer tout ~ à une cause** to devote oneself wholeheartedly to a cause; **avoir un caractère ~, être ~** to be uncompromising

B *nm* **1** Math (nombre) integer; **2** (totalité) **en ~, dans son ~** in its entirety; **le pays dans son ~** the whole *ou* entire country

entièrement /ɑ̃tjɛʀmɑ̃/ *adv* entirely, completely; **~ équipé** fully equipped; **jouer ~ un morceau** to play a piece of music all the way through; **je partage ~ vos doutes** I share your doubts wholeheartedly

entité /ɑ̃tite/ *nf* entity

entoiler /ɑ̃twale/ [1] *vtr* **1** (en couture) to put interfacing in [*vêtement*]; **2** (fixer sur une toile) to mount [sth] on canvas; **3** (relier en toile) to bind [sth] in canvas [*livre*]

entomologie /ɑ̃tɔmɔlɔʒi/ *nf* entomology

entonner /ɑ̃tɔne/ [1] *vtr* to start singing [*chanson, air*]; to launch into [*thème, discours*]

entonnoir /ɑ̃tɔnwaʀ/ *nm* (ustensile) funnel; (cavité) crater

entorse /ɑ̃tɔʀs/ *nf* **1** Méd sprain; **se faire une ~ à la cheville/au genou** to sprain one's ankle/knee; **2** *fig* (manquement) infringement (**à** of); **faire une ~ au règlement** to bend *ou* stretch the rules

entortillement /ɑ̃tɔʀtijmɑ̃/ *nm* **1** (de fils) (processus) tangling; (résultat) tangle; **2** (de phrases, style) muddle

entortiller /ɑ̃tɔʀtije/ [1]

A *vtr* **1** (pour entourer) to wind (**autour de qch** round^{GB} sth); **2** (emmêler) to tangle up; **3** ○*fig* (embrouiller) to muddle up [*explications*]; **4** ○*fig* (emboîner) to get round^{GB} [sb], to win [sb] over GB; **se faire ~** to let oneself be won over

B s'entortiller *vpr* **1** (s'emmêler) [*fils, laine*] to get entangled (**dans** in); **2** (s'enrouler) [*plante*] to twist

entourage /ɑ̃tuʀaʒ/ *nm* (famille) family circle; (amis) circle (of friends); (conseillers, courtisans) entourage

entouré, ~e /ɑ̃tuʀe/ *adj* **1** (populaire) [*président, femme*] popular; **2** (soutenu) **nos patients sont très ~s** our patients are well looked after

entourer /ɑ̃tuʀe/ [1]

A *vtr* **1** (être autour) [*bâtiments, clôture, personnes*] to surround; **entouré de** [*lieu*] surrounded by *ou* with; **les gens/objets qui nous entourent** the people/things around us; **2** (placer autour) **~ qch de qch** to put sth around sth; **~ qch de mystère** to shroud sth in mystery; **~ qn d'affection** to surround sb with love; **~ un mot** to circle a word; **3** (soutenir) to rally round GB *ou* around US [*malade, veuve*]

B s'entourer *vpr* **1** (réunir autour de soi) **s'~ d'amis** to surround oneself with friends; **s'~ de précautions** to take every possible precaution; **2** (se mettre) **s'~ d'un châle** to wrap oneself (up) in a shawl

entourloupe○ /ɑ̃tuʀlup/ *nf* dirty trick

entournure /ɑ̃tuʀnyʀ/ *nf* **être gêné aux ~s** *fig* (mal à l'aise) to be in an awkward position; (financièrement) to feel the pinch○

entracte /ɑ̃tʀakt/ *nm* **1** (au théâtre, concert) interval GB, intermission; (au cinéma) intermission; **2** (divertissement) interlude

entraide /ɑ̃tʀɛd/ *nf* mutual aid (**entre** between)

entraider: s'entraider /ɑ̃tʀede/ [1] *vpr* to help each other *ou* one another

entrailles /ɑ̃tʀɑj/ *nfpl* **1** (d'animal) innards, entrails; **2** (de mère) *liter* womb; **3** (profondeurs) *liter* bowels

entrain /ɑ̃tʀɛ̃/ *nm* **1** (de personne) spirit, go○ GB; **elle est pleine d'~** she's full of go *ou* life; **manquer d'~** to have no go; **retrouver son ~** to cheer up; **2** (de soirée, musique, discussion) liveliness; **être plein/manquer d'~** to be/not to be very lively; **sans** ~ half-hearted

entraînant, ~e /ɑ̃tʀɛnɑ̃, ɑ̃t/ *adj* lively

entraînement /ɑ̃tʀɛnmɑ̃/ *nm* [1] (formation) training; (séance) training session; **d'**~ [*match, jours*] training (*épith*); [2] (habitude) practice^GB; **manquer d'**~ (être inexpérimenté) to lack practice^GB; (avoir perdu l'habitude) to be out of practice^GB

entraîner /ɑ̃tʀene/ [1]
A *vtr* [1] (provoquer) to lead to; **une panne a entraîné l'arrêt de la production** a breakdown brought production to a standstill; [2] (emporter) [*courant, rivière*] to carry [sth/sb] away; **il a entraîné qn/qch dans sa chute** *lit, fig* he dragged sb/sth down with him; [3] (conduire) to take [*personne*]; ~ **qn à faire qch** [*personne*] to make sb do sth; [*circonstances*] to lead sb to do sth; **ce sont ses camarades qui l'ont entraîné** his friends dragged him into it; [4] *fig* (stimuler) to carry [sb] away [*personne, groupe*]; [5] (former) to train, to coach [*sportif*] (**à** for); to train [*cheval, soldat*] (**à** for); [6] (actionner) [*moteur*] to drive [*machine*]
B s'entraîner *vpr* [1] (se former) [*sportif, soldats*] to train (**à** for); **s'**~ **au maniement des armes/au tir** to practise^GB handling weapons/shooting; [2] (s'exercer) to prepare oneself (**à qch** for sth); to train oneself (**à faire** to do); [3] (s'encourager) to encourage each other (**à faire** to do)

entraîneur, -euse[1] /ɑ̃tʀɛnœʀ, øz/ ▸ p. 372 *nm,f* (de sportif, d'équipe) coach, trainer; (de cheval) trainer

entraîneuse[2] /ɑ̃tʀɛnøz/ *nf* (dans un bar) hostess

entrapercevoir /ɑ̃tʀapɛʀsəvwaʀ/ [5] *vtr* to catch a glimpse of [*personne, phénomène*]; to glimpse [*solution, possibilité*]

entrave /ɑ̃tʀav/
A *nf* (gêne) hindrance (**à** to); (à la liberté) restriction (**à** of); **s'exprimer sans** ~ to speak freely; **pour** ~ **à la liberté du culte** *Jur* for failing to respect freedom of worship
B entraves *nfpl* (d'animal) hobble (*sg*); (de forçat) shackles, fetters *littér*

entraver /ɑ̃tʀave/ [1] *vtr* [1] (gêner) to hinder, to impede; [2] (attacher) to hobble [*animal*]; to shackle [*forçat*]

entre /ɑ̃tʀ/ *prép*

> ⚠ *Entre* se traduit par *between* sauf lorsqu'il signifie *parmi* (▸ 4) auquel cas il se traduit généralement par *among*.
> Exemples et exceptions sont présentés dans l'article ci-dessous.
> Les expressions telles que *entre parenthèses*, *entre deux guerres*, *lire entre les lignes* sont traitées respectivement sous **parenthèse, porte, lire**[1]; de même *entre ciel et terre* se trouve sous **ciel**, *entre la vie et la mort* sous **vie** etc.

[1] (dans l'espace, le temps) between; ~ **midi et deux** at lunchtime; [2] (pour désigner un état intermédiaire) between; **'doux ou très épicé?'—'**~ **les deux'** 'mild or very spicy?'—'in between'; ▸ **quatre**; [3] (à travers) between; **passer la main** ~ **les barreaux** to slip one's hand between *ou* through the bars; [4] (parmi) among; **choisir** ~ **plusieurs solutions** to choose between *ou* from among several solutions; ~ **tous ces romans, lequel préfères-tu?** out of all these novels, which one do you like best?; **chacune d'**~ **elles** each of them; [5] (pour désigner un groupe de personnes) **organiser une soirée** ~ **amis** to organize a party among friends; ~ **hommes** as one man to another; ~ **nous** between you and me, between ourselves; **nous sommes** ~ **nous** (deux personnes) there's just the two of us; (plus de deux) we're among friends; [6] (pour marquer la distribution) between; ~ **son travail et l'informatique, il n'a pas le temps de sortir** what with work and his computer he doesn't have time to go out; [7] (pour exprimer une relation) between; **les enfants sont souvent cruels** ~ **eux** children are often cruel to each other; **ces motifs peuvent se combiner** ~ **eux** these patterns can be combined (with each other); **deux d'**~ **eux sont cassés** two of them are broken

entrebâillement /ɑ̃tʀəbɑjmɑ̃/ *nm* (de porte) gap (**de** in)

entrebâiller /ɑ̃tʀəbɑje/ [1] *vtr* to half-open

entrechoquer /ɑ̃tʀəʃɔke/ [1]
A *vtr* to clatter [*vaisselle*]; to clink, to chink [*verres*]; to crash [*cymbales*]; to knock *ou* bang [sth] together [*cailloux, cuillères*]
B s'entrechoquer *vpr* [1] [*verres*] to clink, to chink; [*dents*] to chatter; [*casseroles*] to clatter; [2] [*idées, passions*] to clash

entrecôte /ɑ̃tʀəkot/ *nf* (portion servie) entrecôte (steak); (pièce de boucherie) rib steak

entrecouper /ɑ̃tʀəkupe/ [1]
A *vtr* to punctuate (**de** by); **film entrecoupé de publicité** film interrupted by advertisements; **voix entrecoupée de sanglots** voice broken with sobs
B s'entrecouper *vpr* [*lignes, routes*] to intersect

entrecroiser /ɑ̃tʀəkʀwaze/ [1] *vtr*, **s'entrecroiser** *vpr* to intertwine

entre-déchirer: s'entre-déchirer /ɑ̃tʀədeʃiʀe/ [1] *vpr* *lit* to tear each other to pieces; *fig* to tear each other apart

entre-deux-guerres /ɑ̃tʀədøgɛʀ/ *nm ou f inv* interwar period

entrée /ɑ̃tʀe/ *nf* [1] (point d'accès) entrance (**de** to); **à l'**~ at the entrance; **à l'**~ **de la ville** on the outskirts of the town; **il y a une pharmacie à l'**~ **de la rue** there's a chemist's where you turn into the street; **se retrouver à l'**~ **du bureau** to meet outside the office; [2] (d'autoroute) (entry) slip road GB, on-ramp US; [3] (vestibule) gén hall; (d'hôtel, de lieu public) lobby; (porte, grille) entry; [4] (moment initial) **trois mois après mon** ~ **à l'université** three months after I went to university; [5] (admission) **l'**~ **d'un pays dans une organisation** (accueil) the admission of a country to an organization; (adhésion) the entry of a country into an organization; **'**~ **libre'** (gratuité) 'admission free'; (publique) (dans un magasin) 'browsers welcome'; (dans un monument) 'visitors welcome'; **l'**~ **est payante** there's an admission charge; **refuser l'**~ **à qn** to refuse sb entry; **'**~ **interdite'** 'no admittance', 'no entry'; [6] (place) ticket; **nous avons fait 300** ~**s** (d'exposition) we had 300 visitors; (de théâtre) we sold 300 tickets; [7] (arrivée) (de personne) gén, Théât entrance; (de véhicule, marchandises) entry; **réussir son** ~ [*acteur*] to enter on cue; **faire son** ~ **dans le monde** to enter society; [8] (commencement) **à l'**~ **de l'hiver** at the beginning of winter; **d'**~ **(de jeu)** from the very start; [9] Culin (plat) starter; [10] Tech input ¢; [11] Ling (de dictionnaire) entry; [12] (de capitaux) inflow; [13] (en comptabilité) ~**s** receipts
• (Composés) ~ **des artistes** Théât stage door; ~ **en matière** introduction; ~ **de service** tradesmen's entrance GB, service entrance
• (Idiome) **avoir ses** ~**s chez le ministre** to be an intimate of the minister

entrée-sortie, *pl* **entrées-sorties** /ɑ̃tʀesɔʀti/ *nf* Ordinat input-output

entrefaites: sur ces entrefaites /syʀsezɑ̃tʀəfɛt/ *loc adv* at that moment, just then

entrefilet /ɑ̃tʀəfilɛ/ *nm* Presse brief article

entrejambes /ɑ̃tʀəʒɑ̃b/ *nm inv* [1] (de vêtement) (fond) crotch; (longueur de pantalon) inside leg GB, inseam US; [2] euph (partie du corps) crotch

entrelacer /ɑ̃tʀəlase/ [12] *vtr*, **s'entrelacer** *vpr* to intertwine, to interlace

entrelacs /ɑ̃tʀəlɑ/ *nm inv* tracery

entrelarder /ɑ̃tʀəlaʀde/ [1] *vtr lit, fig* ~ **qch de qch** to lard sth with sth

entremêler /ɑ̃tʀəmele/ [1]
A *vtr* to mix [*objets*]; to interweave [*fils*]
B s'entremêler *vpr* gén to be mixed; [*branches, cheveux*] to get tangled

entremets /ɑ̃tʀəmɛ/ *nm inv* dessert

entremetteur, -euse /ɑ̃tʀəmɛtœʀ, øz/ *nm,f* [1] (marieur) matchmaker; (proxénète) procurer/procuress; [2] (intermédiaire) go-between

entremettre: s'entremettre /ɑ̃tʀəmɛtʀ/ [60] *vpr* (intervenir) to act as mediator, to mediate (**dans** in; **entre** between)

entremise /ɑ̃tʀəmiz/ *nf* intervention (**auprès de** with); **il l'a su par mon** ~ he heard of it through me

entreposer /ɑ̃tʀəpoze/ [1] *vtr* [1] (dans un entrepôt) to store; (en douane) to bond; [2] (chez quelqu'un) to store (**chez** at)

entrepôt /ɑ̃tʀəpo/ *nm* (bâtiment) warehouse; (arrière-boutique) stockroom; ~ **de douane** bonded warehouse; ~ **frigorifique** cold storage plant

entreprenant, ~e /ɑ̃tʀəpʀənɑ̃, ɑ̃t/ *adj* (hardi) enterprising; (avec les femmes) **être** ~ to be forward with the ladies

entreprendre /ɑ̃tʀəpʀɑ̃dʀ/ [52] *vtr* [1] (commencer) to start, to undertake [*recherches, rénovation*]; ~ **de faire** (se mettre à) to set about doing; (se donner pour tâche de) to undertake to do; **2** (adresser la parole à) ~ **qn** (pour séduire) to set about seducing sb; (pour bavarder) to engage sb in conversation (**sur qch** about sth)

entrepreneur, -euse /ɑ̃tʀəpʀənœʀ, øz/ ▸ p. 372 nm,f **1** Constr builder; (de travaux) contractor; ~ **en bâtiment** building contractor; ~ **de pompes funèbres** undertaker, mortician US; **3** (chef d'entreprise) owner-manager (*of a small firm*)

entreprise /ɑ̃tʀəpʀiz/ nf **1** (société) firm, business; **petites et moyennes** ~**s** small and medium enterprises; ~ **de pompes funèbres** undertaker's business, funeral home US; ~ **de transports routiers** haulage contractor GB, trucking company US; **création d'**~**s** business start-ups; **la culture d'**~ corporate culture; **2** (secteur) business, industry; **3** (projet) undertaking, enterprise; (risqué) venture; **la libre** ~ free enterprise

(Composés) ~ **unipersonnelle à responsabilité limitée, EURL** company owned by a sole proprietor

entrer /ɑ̃tʀe/ [1]
A vtr (+ v avoir) **1** (transporter) (vu de l'intérieur) to bring [sth] in; (vu de l'extérieur) to take [sth] in; **2** (enfoncer) to stick (**dans** into); **3** Ordinat to enter; **4** Sport to score [but]
B vi (+ v être) **1** (pénétrer) gén to get in, to enter; (en allant) to go in; (en venant) to come in; (en roulant) to drive in; **l'eau est entrée par une fissure** the water came in ou got in through a crack; **je suis entré dans Paris par le sud** (en voiture) I drove into Paris from the south; **entrez!** come in!; **'défense d'**~**'** (sur une porte) 'no entry'; (sur une barrière) 'no trespassing'; **je ne fais qu'**~ **et sortir** I can only stay a minute; **laisser** ~ **qn** to let sb in; **faire** ~ **la table par la fenêtre** (vu de l'intérieur) to bring the table in through the window; (vu de l'extérieur) to take the table in through the window; **fais-la** ~ show her in; **2** (tenir, s'adapter) to fit; **faire** ~ **qch dans qch** to fit ou get sth into sth; **je n'arrive pas à faire** ~ **la pièce dans la fente** I can't get the coin into the slot; **3** (s'intégrer, commencer) ~ **dans** to enter [débat, période]; to join [opposition, gouvernement, armée]; ~ **à** to enter [école, hit-parade]; to get into [université]; ~ **en** to enter into [pourparlers, négociations]; **il entre en deuxième année** he's going into his second year; **il entre dans sa quarantième année** he's turned thirty-nine; ~ **dans la vie de qn** to come into sb's life; **n'entrons pas dans les détails** let's not go into the details; **il m'a fait** ~ **au ministère** he got me into the ministry; **il entre dans la catégorie des...** he comes into the category of...; **expression entrée dans l'usage** expression which has come into the language; ~ **dans l'histoire** to go down in history; ~ **dans la légende** [personne] to become a legend; [fait] to become legendary; **j'ai fait** ~ **tes dépenses dans les frais généraux** I've included your expenses in the overheads; ~ **en fusion** to begin to melt; ~ **dans une colère noire** to fly into a blind rage; **4** (être un élément de) **le carbone entre pour moitié dans ce composé** carbon makes up half (of) this compound
C v impers **il n'entre pas dans mes intentions de faire** I have no intention of doing

entresol /ɑ̃tʀəsɔl/ nm mezzanine

entre-temps /ɑ̃tʀətɑ̃/ adv meanwhile, in the meantime

entretenir /ɑ̃tʀətniʀ/ [36]
A **1** (garder en bon état) to look after [tapis, intérieur, vêtement]; to maintain [route, machine, édifice]; **les mots croisés entretiennent la mémoire** crosswords keep the mind active; ~ **sa forme** to keep in shape; **2** (faire vivre) to support [famille, indigent]; to keep [maîtresse]; **se faire** ~ **par qn** (par un amant) to be kept by sb; (par des amis, parents) to live off sb; **3** (maintenir) to keep up [correspondance]; **4** (alimenter) to keep [sth] going [feu, conversation, rivalités]; to keep [sth] alive [amitié]; to fuel [tensions]; **5** (informer) ~ **qn de qch** to speak to sb about sth
B s'entretenir vpr (converser) **s'**~ **de qch** to discuss sth

entretenu, ~e /ɑ̃tʀətny/ adj [personne] kept (épith); **bien/mal** ~ [intérieur, plante] well-/badly-kept; [voiture, bâtiment] well-/badly-maintained

entretien /ɑ̃tʀətjɛ̃/ nm **1** (soins) (de maison, jardin) upkeep; (de voiture, route, d'immeuble) maintenance; (de vêtement, plante, peau) care; **frais d'**~ maintenance costs; **demander peu d'**~ [plante, jardin, tapis] to need little looking after; **d'un** ~ **facile** [intérieur, jardin] easy to look after; [bâtiment, voiture] easy to maintain; [tissu] easy-care (épith); **2** (nettoyage) cleaning; **3** (conversation) gén discussion; (pour un emploi)

interview; Presse interview; Pol talks (pl); **accorder un** ~ **à qn** to give sb an interview; **4** (soutien financier) **assurer l'**~ **d'un enfant** to support a child

(Composés) ~ **d'appréciation** or **de carrière** job appraisal; ~ **d'embauche** job interview; **faire passer un** ~ **d'embauche** to interview

entre-tuer: **s'entre-tuer** /ɑ̃tʀətɥe/ [1] vpr to kill each other

entrevoir /ɑ̃tʀəvwaʀ/ [46] vtr **1** (voir) (brièvement) to catch a glimpse of; (indistinctement) to make out; **2** (discerner, deviner) to glimpse; (présager) to foresee; ~ **un espoir de paix** to see a glimmer of hope for peace; **commencer à** ~**...** to begin to see...; **laisser** ~ **que** [signe, résultat] to indicate that

entrevue /ɑ̃tʀəvy/ nf (entretien) meeting; (discussion) Pol talks (pl)

entrouvert, ~e /ɑ̃tʀuvɛʀ/ adj [porte] ajar (jamais épith), half open; [lèvres] parted

entrouvrir /ɑ̃tʀuvʀiʀ/ [32]
A vtr to open [sth] a little
B s'entrouvrir vpr gén [porte, pays] to half-open; [lèvres] to part

énumération /enymeʀasjɔ̃/ nf (action) listing; (liste) catalogue[GB]

énumérer /enymeʀe/ [14] vtr to enumerate, to list

envahir /ɑ̃vaiʀ/ [3] vtr (pénétrer dans) [troupes, foule] to invade; [animal, plante] to overrun; [publicité] to pervade; [marchandise] to flood [marché]

envahissant, ~e /ɑ̃vaisɑ̃, ɑ̃t/ adj **1** (gênant) [personne] intrusive; **2** [doctrine, sentiment] pervasive; [musique, odeur, plante] invasive

envahisseur /ɑ̃vaisœʀ/ nm invader

envaser /ɑ̃vaze/ [1]
A vtr to silt up [estuaire, port]
B s'envaser vpr [estuaire, port] to silt up; [barque] to get stuck in the mud

enveloppant, ~e /ɑ̃vlɔpɑ̃, ɑ̃t/ adj [membrane] enveloping; [chaussure] high-cut; [manteau] big and loose

enveloppe /ɑ̃vlɔp/ nf **1** (de lettre) envelope; **sous** ~ in an envelope; **2** (emballage) wrapping; (gaine) sheath; (tégument) husk; (cosse) pod; (d'organe) membrane; (peau) skin; (coquille, carapace) shell; ~ **charnelle** or **mortelle** mortal coil; **3** (budget) budget; **4** (gratification) bonus; (indemnité de départ) golden handshake; (pot-de-vin) bribe

enveloppé, ~e /ɑ̃vlɔpe/ adj (gros) [personne] plump

envelopper /ɑ̃vlɔpe/ [1]
A vtr **1** (recouvrir) [personne] to wrap [sb/sth] (up); [housse] to cover; **le papier qui enveloppait le vase** the paper around the vase; **2** (entourer) [brouillard, silence, nuit] to envelop; [brume] to veil; [mystère, secret] to surround
B s'envelopper vpr to wrap oneself (up); **s'**~ **la tête d'un turban** (le mettre) to wrap one's head in a turban; (le porter) to wear a turban

enveloppe-réponse, pl **enveloppes-réponse** /ɑ̃vlɔpʀepɔ̃s/ nf freepost envelope GB, postpaid envelope US

envenimé, ~e /ɑ̃vnime/ adj [plume, paroles] poisoned; [dispute] bitter

envenimer /ɑ̃vnime/ [1]
A vtr (aviver) to inflame [débat]; to fan the flames of [colère]; to aggravate [situation]; ~ **les choses** to make matters worse
B s'envenimer vpr [dispute] to worsen; [situation] to turn ugly

envergure /ɑ̃vɛʀgyʀ/ nf **1** (d'ailes) wingspan; **de 20 mètres d'**~ with a wingspan of 20 metres[GB]; **2** fig (de personne) stature; (de projet, d'entreprise) scale; **un projet de grande** ~ a large-scale project; **d'**~ **internationale** [projet, œuvre] of international scope; **prendre une** ~ **telle que...** to swell to such proportions that...; **sans** ~ [projet, débat] limited; [personne] of no account

envers[1] /ɑ̃vɛʀ/ prép **cruauté** ~ **qn** cruelty towards GB ou to sb; **méfiant/méprisant** ~ **qn** mistrustful/scornful of sb; **exigeant** ~ **qn** demanding with sb; **reconnaissance** ~ **qn** gratitude to sb; **cruel** ~ **qn** cruel to sb; **engagements** ~ **qn** obligations towards GB ou to sb

(Idiome) ~ **et contre tous/tout** in spite of everyone/everything

envers[2] /ɑ̃vɛʀ/
A nm inv (de papier) back; (de tissu) wrong side; (de vêtement)

inside; (de monnaie) reverse; **l'~ du décor** fig the other side (of the picture)

B **à l'envers** loc adv ①| (inadéquatement) the wrong way; ②| (le haut en bas) upside down; ③| (l'intérieur à l'extérieur) inside out; ④| (le devant derrière) back to front; **tenir des jumelles à l'~** to hold binoculars back to front; ⑤| (la droite à gauche) the wrong way round GB ou around US; ⑥| (à rebours) **passer un film à l'~** to run a film backward(s)

envi: **à l'envi** /ãlãvi/ loc adv [répéter, souligner, rappeler] at every possible opportunity

enviable /ãvjabl/ adj [situation, sort] enviable; **une situation peu ~** an unenviable position

envie /ãvi/ nf ①| gén urge (**de faire** to do); (de choses à manger) craving (**de** for); **~ folle** insane urge; **l'~ m'a prise de te téléphoner** I got the urge to phone you; **des ~s de femme enceinte** the cravings of a pregnant woman; **avoir des ~s de meurtre** to feel like killing somebody; **ce n'est pas l'~ qui me manque** don't think I haven't thought of it!; **avoir ~ de qch** to feel like sth; **avoir ~ de faire** (fortement) to want to do; (passagèrement) to feel like doing; **il n'a qu'une ~, (c'est de) partir** all he wants is to leave; **avoir ~ de rire** to feel like laughing; **avoir ~ de vomir** to feel sick; **il a ~ que je parte** he wants me to leave; **mourir d'~ de faire** to be dying○ to do; **donner (l')~ à qn de faire** to make sb want to do; ②| (convoitise) envy; **leur piscine fait ~ à** their swimming pool is the envy of; **il te fait ~ ce jouet?** would you like that toy?; ③| (angiome) birthmark; ▸ **pisser**

(Idiome) **avoir une ~ pressante** to need to go to the toilet

envier /ãvje/ [2] vtr to envy; **des musées que le monde entier nous envie** our museums that are the envy of the world

envieux, -ieuse /ãvjø, øz/

A adj envious

B nm,f envious person; **faire des ~** to make people jealous

environ /ãvirõ/ adv about; **tous les deux ans ~** about every two years; **à ~ dix mètres** about ten metres^{GB} away

environnant, ~e /ãvirɔnã, ãt/ adj surrounding

environnement /ãvirɔnmã/ nm environment

environner /ãvirɔne/ [1] vtr to surround

environs /ãvirõ/ nmpl **être des ~** to be from the area; **aux ~ de** (dans l'espace) in the vicinity of; (dans le temps) around; (en grandeur) in the region of

envisageable /ãvizaʒabl/ adj possible

envisager /ãvizaʒe/ [13] vtr ①| (projeter) to plan (**de faire** to do); ②| (imaginer) to envisage [hypothèse, situation]; **~ le pire** to imagine the worst; [problème, possibilité]; ③| (considérer) to consider

envoi /ãvwa/ nm ①| (expédition) **tous les ~s de colis sont suspendus** parcel post is suspended; **date d'~** dispatch date GB, mailing date US; **faire un ~ de** to send [fleurs, livres]; **date limite d'~ de qch** deadline for posting GB ou mailing US sth; **frais d'~** postage; ②| (ce qui est expédié) **nous attendons un ~ important** we're expecting a large consignment; **les ~s de plus de deux kilos** parcels over two kilos; ③| (déplacement) **demander l'~ (immédiat) de troupes** to ask for troops to be dispatched (immediately); ④| Sport **coup d'~** kick-off; **donner le coup d'~ de** to kick off [match, campagne]; to open [festival, fête]

(Composés) **~ en nombre** bulk dispatch GB ou mailing US; **~ recommandé** registered post ₵ GB ou mail ₵ US; **~ contre remboursement** cash on delivery, COD

envol /ãvɔl/ nm (d'oiseau, imagination) flight; (d'avion) takeoff; **prendre son ~** [oiseau] to take flight; [avion] to take off; [adolescent] to leave the nest

envolée /ãvɔle/ nf (discours) flight of fancy; (des prix) surge (**de** in); (de parti) rise

envoler: **s'envoler** /ãvɔle/ [1] vpr ①| (partir) [oiseau] to fly off (**pour** to); [avion, passager] to take off (**pour** for); [papier, chapeau] to be blown away; **mon portefeuille ne s'est tout de même pas envolé**○ my wallet didn't just disappear; ②| (augmenter) [prix] to soar; ③| (disparaître) to vanish; ④| ○(s'enfuir) to fly off○, to escape

envoûtant, ~e /ãvutã, ãt/ adj [film, livre] spellbinding; [atmosphère, musique] enchanting; [sourire, beauté] bewitching

envoûtement /ãvutmã/ nm (action) bewitchment; (sortilège) spell

envoûter /ãvute/ [1] vtr to bewitch; **~ son auditoire** fig to hold the audience spellbound

envoûteur, -euse /ãvutœr, øz/ nm,f sorcerer/sorceress

envoyé, ~e /ãvwaje/

A adj **ça c'est (bien) ~**○! well said!

B nm,f envoy; **~ spécial** (journaliste) special correspondent

envoyer /ãvwaje/ [24]

A vtr ①| (expédier, faire déplacer) to send (**à** to); **il vous envoie ses amitiés** he sends (you) his regards; **qui vous envoie?** who sent you?; **~ qn chercher le journal** to send sb out to get the paper; ②| (lancer) to throw [caillou]; to fire [missile] (**sur** at); **~ le ballon dans les buts** to put the ball in the net; ③| (asséner) **~ un coup de pied à qn** to kick sb; **il m'a envoyé son poing dans la figure** he punched me in the face; ④| (transmettre) to send

B **s'envoyer** vpr ①| (échanger) to exchange; **s'~ des baisers** (par gestes) to blow each other kisses; ②| ○(avaler) to guzzle [boisson]; to wolf down [repas]

(Idiomes) **~ qn promener**○ to send sb packing○; **tout ~ promener**○ to drop the lot○

envoyeur /ãvwajœr/ nm **retour à l'~** return to sender

éolien, -ienne[1] /eɔljɛ̃, ɛn/ adj [érosion, générateur] wind (épith)

éolienne[2] /eɔljɛn/ nf (aeolian) windmill

épagneul /epaɲœl/ nm spaniel

épais, épaisse /epɛ, ɛs/

A ▸ p. 347 adj ①| (pas mince) thick; **il n'est pas bien ~ ce petit**○! he's a skinny little fellow!; ②| (pas subtil) [esprit] dull; ③| (pâteux) thick; ④| (dense) thick; ⑤| (profond) [nuit, silence] deep

B adv a lot, much; **tu en as mis trop ~** you've put too much on

épaisseur /epɛsœr/ nf ①| ▸ p. 347 (dimension, densité) thickness; **un mur de deux mètres d'~** a wall two metres^{GB} thick; **de faible ~** thin; ②| (de liquide) thickness; ③| (profondeur) depths (pl); **dans l'~ de la nuit** in the depths of night; ④| fig (de personnage, projet) substance; ⑤| (couche) layer

épaissir /epesir/ [3]

A vtr ①| (rendre consistant) to thicken; ②| (déformer) [âge, graisse] to thicken [traits, taille]; [vêtement] to broaden [silhouette]; ③| (obscurcir) to deepen [mystère]

B vi ①| (devenir plus consistant) [sauce] to thicken; [gelée] to set; **faire ~** cook mixture until it thickens; ②| (grossir) to put on weight

C **s'épaissir** vpr [sauce, brume, taille] to thicken; [mystère] to deepen

épanchement /epãʃmã/

A nm Méd (de sang) effusion; **avoir un ~ de synovie** to have water on the knee

B **épanchements** nmpl (confidences) outpourings

épancher: **s'épancher** /epãʃe/ [1] vpr [personne] to open one's heart (**auprès de** to)

épandage /epãdaʒ/ nm (action) spreading; Tech sewage farming

épandre /epãdr/ [6] vtr to spread

épanoui, ~e /epanwi/ adj [fleur] in full bloom (après n); [sourire, visage] beaming; [personne, personnalité] well-adjusted; [corps] ample

épanouir: **s'épanouir** /epanwir/ [3] vpr [fleur] to bloom; [visage] to light up; [personne] to blossom; **permettre aux gens de s'~** to enable people to fulfil^{GB} their potential

épanouissant, ~e /epanwisã, ãt/ adj fulfilling

épanouissement /epanwismã/ nm (de fleur) blooming; (développement) gén development; (de talent) flowering; **favoriser/empêcher l'~ de qn/qch** to foster/to hamper the development of sb/sth

épargnant, ~e /eparɲã, ãt/ nm,f saver

épargne /eparɲ/ nf savings (pl); **un compte (d') ~** a savings account

(Composé) **~ salariale** company saving scheme

épargner /eparɲe/ [1]

A vtr ①| (économiser) to save [argent]; ②| (ne pas affecter) to spare [lieu, personne, institution]; ③| (éviter) **~ qch à qn** to spare sb sth

B vi to save

C **s'épargner** vpr to save oneself [attente, effort]

éparpillement /eparpijmã/ nm scattering

éparpiller /eparpije/ [1]

A vtr lit to scatter; fig to fail to concentrate [forces, attention]

B **s'éparpiller** vpr [cendres, foule] to scatter

épars, ∼e /epaʀ, aʀs/ adj scattered

épatant○, ∼e /epatã, ãt/ adj marvellous^{GB}

épate○ /epat/ nf showing off

épaté, ∼e /epate/ adj ① nez ∼ pug nose, flat nose; ② ○(surpris) amazed (**de** by)

épater○ /epate/ [1]
A vtr ① (impressionner) to impress; **ça t'épate, hein?** surprised, aren't you?; ② (étonner) to amaze
B s'épater vpr (s'étonner) to marvel (**de** at)

épaule /epol/ nf ▸ p. 136 Anat shoulder; **large d'∼s** broad-shouldered; **rentrer la tête dans les ∼s** to hunch one's shoulders; ∼ **d'agneau** shoulder of lamb
Idiomes **changer son fusil d'∼** to change one's tactics; **avoir la tête sur les ∼s** to have one's head screwed on○

épauler /epole/ [1]
A vtr ① (aider) to help; ② to take aim with [fusil]
B vi to take aim

épaulette /epolɛt/ nf (rembourrage) shoulder-pad; (bretelle) (shoulder-)strap; Mil epaulette

épave /epav/ nf ① lit, fig wreck; ② (débris) bit of wreckage

épée /epe/ nf sword; **c'est un coup d'∼ dans l'eau** fig it was a complete waste of effort

épeler /eple/ [19] vtr to spell [mot]

éperdu, ∼e /epɛʀdy/ adj [besoin, désir] overwhelming; [cri] frantic; [regard] desperate; [fuite] headlong (épith); [amour, reconnaissance] boundless

éperdument /epɛʀdymã/ adv [crier] frantically; [amoureux] madly; **je me moque ∼ de ce qu'il pense** I couldn't care less about what he thinks

éperon /epʀɔ̃/ nm spur

éperonner /epʀɔne/ [1] vtr lit, fig to spur on

épervier /epɛʀvje/ nm (oiseau) sparrowhawk

éphèbe /efɛb/ nm ① hum Adonis; ② Hist ephebe

éphémère /efemɛʀ/ adj [bonheur] fleeting; [succès, produit, insecte] short-lived; **de manière ∼** fleetingly

éphéméride /efemeʀid/ nf (calendrier) block calendar

épi /epi/ nm ① Bot (de blé, d'avoine) ear; (de fleur) spike; ② (mèche) (unmanageable) tuft of hair GB, cow-lick US
Composé ∼ **de maïs** corn cob

épice /epis/ nf spice

épicé, ∼e /epise/ adj (parfumé, grivois) spicy; (fort) hot

épicéa /episea/ nm spruce

épicentre /episãtʀ/ nm epicentre

épicer /epise/ [12] vtr (en cuisine) to spice; fig to add spice to

épicerie /episʀi/ ▸ p. 372 nf ① (boutique) grocer's (shop) GB, grocery (store) US; **à l'∼** at the grocer's; ② (commerce) grocery trade; ③ (produits) groceries (pl)
Composé ∼ **fine** delicatessen

épicier, -ière /episje, ɛʀ/ ▸ p. 372 nm,f grocer

épicurien, -ienne /epikyʀjɛ̃, ɛn/ adj Philos Epicurean

épidémie /epidemi/ nf Méd, fig epidemic

épidémique /epidemik/ adj epidemic

épiderme /epidɛʀm/ nm (peau) skin

épidermique /epidɛʀmik/ adj lit skin (épith); [blessure] skin-deep; fig [sensibilité] extreme; **réaction ∼** gut reaction

épier /epje/ [2] vtr ① (observer) to spy on [personne, comportement]; ② (attendre) to be on the lookout for

épigramme /epigʀam/ nf epigram

épilation /epilasjɔ̃/ nf removal of unwanted hair; (à la cire) waxing

épilepsie /epilɛpsi/ ▸ p. 195 nf epilepsy; **crise d'∼** epileptic fit

épileptique /epilɛptik/ adj, nmf epileptic

épiler /epile/ [1]
A vtr to remove unwanted hair from [jambe]; (à la cire) to wax; to pluck [sourcils]
B s'épiler vpr **s'∼ les sourcils** to pluck one's eyebrows; **s'∼ le menton** to remove the hairs from one's chin

épilogue /epilɔg/ nm Littérat epilogue^{GB}; fig outcome

épiloguer /epilɔge/ [1] vi to go on and on (**sur** about)

épinard /epinaʀ/ nm spinach **¢**
Idiome **ça met du beurre dans les ∼s**○ it makes life that little bit easier

épine /epin/ nf thorn; **sans ∼s** thornless
Composé ∼ **dorsale** Anat spine; fig backbone
Idiome **ôter à qn une ∼ du pied** to take a weight off sb's shoulders

épinette /epinɛt/ nf ① Mus spinet; ② Bot spruce

épineux, -euse /epinø, øz/ adj [tige] prickly; [problème, situation] tricky; [question] vexed; [caractère] prickly

épingle /epɛ̃gl/ nf pin
Composés ∼ **à chapeau** hatpin; ∼ **à cheveux** hairpin; **virage en ∼ à cheveux** hairpin bend; ∼ **de** or **à nourrice**, ∼ **de sûreté** safety pin
Idiomes **monter qch en** ∼ to blow sth up out of proportion; **être tiré à quatre ∼s**○ to be immaculately dressed; **tirer son ∼ du jeu** to get out while the going is good

épingler /epɛ̃gle/ [1] vtr ① (fixer) to pin [affiche] (**à** to); to pin [sth] together [billets]; ② ○(arrêter) to collar○

épinière /epinjɛʀ/ adj f **moelle** ∼ spinal cord

épiphyse /epifiz/ nf epiphysis

épique /epik/ adj epic; **poème** ∼ epic; **c'était** ∼○ hum it was quite something○

épiscopat /episkɔpa/ nm episcopate, episcopacy

épiscope /episkɔp/ nm ① (appareil optique) episcope GB, opaque projector US; ② Mil periscope

épisode /epizɔd/ nm episode; **roman à ∼s** serialized novel

épisodique /epizɔdik/ adj (secondaire) minor; (intermittent) [crises] sporadic; [rôle] occasional

épisodiquement /epizɔdikmã/ adv sporadically

épistémologie /epistemɔlɔʒi/ nf epistemology

épistolaire /epistɔlɛʀ/ adj [genre] epistolary; **ils ont des relations ∼s** they correspond

épitaphe /epitaf/ nf epitaph; **en** ∼ as an epitaph

épithète /epitɛt/ nf Ling attributive adjective; (qualificatif) epithet

épître /epitʀ/ nf epistle

éploré, ∼e /eplɔʀe/ adj (affligé) grief-stricken; (en pleurs) tearful

épluche-légume, pl ∼s /eplyʃlegym/ nm potato peeler

éplucher /eplyʃe/ [1] vtr lit to peel [fruit]; fig to go through [sth] with a fine-tooth comb

épluchure /eplyʃyʀ/ nf ∼ **de pomme** piece of apple peel; ∼**s** peelings

EPO /əpeo/ nm (abbr = **érythropoïétine**) erythropoietin

éponge /epɔ̃ʒ/ nf ① (animal) sponge; ② (pour la maison) sponge; ③ (tissu) terry-towelling^{GB}
Composé ∼ **métallique** (pan) scourer
Idiomes **passer l'∼** to forget the past; **passer l'∼ sur qch** to forget all about sth

éponger /epɔ̃ʒe/ [13]
A vtr to mop up [liquide]; to mop [sueur, surface]; to absorb [déficit]; to pay off [dettes]
B s'éponger vpr **s'∼ le front** to mop one's brow

éponyme /epɔnim/
A adj eponymous
B nm eponym

épopée /epɔpe/ nf (en poésie) epic; (suite d'événements) saga

époque /epɔk/ nf ① (période quelconque) time; **à l'∼** at that time; **à l'∼ où** at the time when; **à cette ∼ de l'année** (présent) at this time of the year; (passé, futur) at that time of the year; **d'une autre ∼** from another time; **il est d'une autre ∼** he belongs to another time; **vivre avec son ∼** to move with the times; **l'∼ est au pragmatisme** pragmatism is the order of the day; **quelle ∼!** what's the world coming to!; **à mon ∼** in my day; **à notre ∼** (aujourd'hui) these days; ② (période historique) era; ③ (période stylistique) period; **d'∼ Renaissance** from the Renaissance period; **des meubles d'∼** antique furniture; ④ (en géologie) epoch

époumoner○: **s'époumoner** /epumɔne/ [1] vpr lit, fig to shout oneself hoarse, to shout one's head off○; (en chantant) to sing oneself hoarse

épouse /epuz/ nf wife, spouse

épouser /epuze/ [1] vtr ① to marry [personne]; ② to adopt [cause, idée]

épousseter /epuste/ [20] vtr to dust

époustoufler○ /epustufle/ [1] *vtr* to amaze

épouvantable /epuvɑ̃tabl/ *adj* gén dreadful; (atroce) appalling

épouvantail /epuvɑ̃taj/ *nm* (à oiseaux) scarecrow; (personne laide)○ fright; (menace) spectre^{GB}

épouvante /epuvɑ̃t/ *nf* (terreur) terror; (horreur) horror; **glacé d'~** paralyzed with terror; **film d'~** horror film; **vision d'~** terrifying vision

épouvanter /epuvɑ̃te/ [1] *vtr* (terrifier) to terrify; (horrifier) to horrify

époux /epu/
A *nm inv* husband
B *nmpl* **les ~** the (married) couple; **les jeunes ~** the newly weds; **les ~ Martin** Mr and Mrs Martin

éprendre: s'éprendre /epʀɑ̃dʀ/ [52] *vpr* **s'~ de** to fall in love with [*personne*]

épreuve /epʀœv/ *nf* [1] (moment pénible) ordeal; **subir de dures ~s** to go through terrible ordeals; [2] (testant la valeur, résistance) test; **mettre à l'~** to put [sth/sb] to the test; **mettre à rude ~** to put [sb] to a severe test; to be very hard on [*voiture, chaussures*]; to tax [*patience, nerfs*]; to put a strain on [*amitié, relation*]; **soumettre qch à l'~ de** to subject sth to the test of; **à toute ~** unfailing (*épith*); **résister à l'~ du temps** to stand the test of time; **à l'~ du feu/des balles** fire/bullet-proof; [3] (partie d'examen) (part of an) examination; **~ écrite/orale** written/oral examination; **~ d'histoire** history examination; [4] Sport **~ d'athlétisme** athletics event; **~s éliminatoires** heats; **~s de sélection** trials; [5] (photo, estampe) proof

〔Composé〕 **~ de vérité** acid test

épris, **~e** /epʀi, iz/ *adj* (amoureux) in love (**de** with); (passionné) **être ~ de voyages** to have a great love of travelling

éprouvant, **~e** /epʀuvɑ̃, ɑ̃t/ *adj* [*attente, période, travail*] gruelling^{GB}; [*bruit, climat, situation*] trying

éprouver /epʀuve/ [1] *vtr* [1] (ressentir) to feel [*regret, amour*]; to have [*sensation, doute, difficulté*]; **~ le désir de faire** to feel a desire to do; **~ de la colère contre** to feel angry with; **~ du plaisir à faire** to get pleasure out of doing; [2] (tester) to test; **une technique éprouvée** a tried and tested technique; [3] (toucher) [*décès, événement*] to distress; [*épidémie, tempête, crise*] to hit

éprouvette /epʀuvɛt/ *nf* (tube) test tube; (échantillon) sample; **bébé ~** test-tube baby

épuisant, **~e** /epɥizɑ̃, ɑ̃t/ *adj* exhausting

épuisé, **~e** /epɥize/ *adj* (non disponible) [*livre*] out of print; [*article*] out of stock; **notre stock est ~** we're sold out; (consommé) [*stock, vivres*] exhausted

épuisement /epɥizmɑ̃/ *nm* exhaustion; **jusqu'à ~ des stocks** while stocks last

épuiser /epɥize/ [1]
A *vtr* [1] (fatiguer) [*activité*] to exhaust; [*souci, personne*] to wear [sb] out; **épuisé nerveusement** emotionally drained; [2] (finir) to exhaust [*sujet, mine*]; [3] (appauvrir) to impoverish [*sol*]
B **s'épuiser** *vpr* [1] (se fatiguer) [*personne*] to exhaust oneself; **s'~ à faire qch** to wear oneself out doing sth; [2] (s'amenuiser) [*réserves*] to become exhausted

épuisette /epɥizɛt/ *nf* landing net; (à crevettes) shrimp net

épurateur /epyʀatœʀ/ *nm* purifier

épuration /epyʀasjɔ̃/ *nf* (de gaz, liquide) purification; (de pétrole) refining; (d'eaux usées) treatment; (de groupe, parti) purge

〔Composé〕 **~ ethnique** Pol ethnic cleansing

épurer /epyʀe/ [1] *vtr* [1] Chimie to purify [*eau, gaz*]; [2] to purge [*parti*]; to clean up [*mœurs*]; to refine [*style, goût*]; to expurgate [*texte*]

équarrir /ekaʀiʀ/ [3] *vtr* (tailler) to square (off) [*pierre, bois*]; **mal équarri** lit, fig rough-hewn

équateur /ekwatœʀ/ *nm* Equator

équation /ekwɑsjɔ̃/ *nf* equation

équatorial, **~e**, *mpl* **-iaux** /ekwatɔʀjal, o/ *adj* equatorial

équatorien, **-ienne** /ekwatɔʀjɛ̃, ɛn/ ▸ p. 392 *adj* Ecuadorian, Ecuadoran

équerre /ekeʀ/ *nf* [1] (à dessin) set square; [2] (support) (en T) flat T-bracket; (en L) flat angle bracket

équestre /ekɛstʀ/ *adj* equestrian

équeuter /ekøte/ [1] *vtr* to remove the stalk from GB, to stem US [*cerise*]; to hull GB, to stem US [*fraise*]

équilibre /ekilibʀ/ *nm* [1] (fait de ne pas tomber) balance; **garder l'~** to keep one's balance; **être en ~ sur** [*objet*] to be balanced on; [*personne*] to balance on; **numéro d'~** balancing act; [2] (entre deux éléments, poids) balance; (stabilité) stability; **l'~ des forces** (en politique) the balance of power; **être en ~** [*objets*] to be balanced; [3] (bien-être, santé mentale) equilibrium; **manquer d'~** to be unstable; [4] (bonne combinaison) (de formes, phrase, d'alimentation) balance; [5] Chimie, Phys equilibrium

équilibrer /ekilibʀe/ [1]
A *vtr* to balance; **~ son alimentation** to have a balanced diet; **~ une façade** (en elle-même) to give balance to a façade; (avec un nouvel élément) to balance a façade; **un enfant équilibré** a well-balanced child; **le chargement est mal équilibré** the load is unevenly distributed
B **s'équilibrer** *vpr* [*facteurs, coûts*] to balance each other

équilibriste /ekilibʀist/ *nmf* lit, fig acrobat

équinoxe /ekinɔks/ *nm* equinox

équipage /ekipaʒ/ *nm* gén crew; (attelage) horse and carriage

équipe /ekip/ *nf* (groupe) team; (en usine) shift; (de rameurs) crew; **travailler en ~** to work as a team; **~ de secours** rescue team; **~ de dépannage** breakdown crew; **~ de télévision** television crew; **~ de tournage** Cin film unit; **faire ~ avec qn** to team up with sb (**pour faire** to do); **l'~ dirigeante** the management team; **l'~ de nuit** the night shift; **travailler en ~s** to work in shifts

équipé, **~e**¹ /ekipe/ *adj* equipped (**de, en** with; **pour** for; **pour faire** to do); **cuisine ~e** fitted kitchen

équipée² /ekipe/ *nf* (aventure) escapade

équipement /ekipmɑ̃/ *nm* [1] (matériel) (d'usine, de cuisine) equipment; (de sportif) kit; [2] (infrastructure) **~s** facilities; **~ hôtelier** accommodation facilities (*pl*); **~s collectifs** public facilities; [3] (processus) (d'armée) equipping; (de soldat, sportif) kitting out; **l'~ de la région a coûté...** improving the region's facilities cost...

équipementier /ekipmɑ̃tje/ *nm* equipment manufacturer

équiper /ekipe/ [1]
A *vtr* to equip [*hôpital, véhicule, armée*] (**de** with); to provide [*ville*] (**de** with); to fit out [*personne*] (**de** with)
B **s'équiper** *vpr* to equip oneself (**de, en** with; **pour** for; **pour faire** to do)

équipier, **-ière** /ekipje, ɛʀ/ *nm,f* gén team member; (rameur, marin) crew member

équitable /ekitabl/ *adj* [*personne*] fair-minded; [*décision*] fair

équitablement /ekitabləmɑ̃/ *adv* equitably, fairly

équitation /ekitasjɔ̃/ ▸ p. 327 *nf* (horse-)riding

équité /ekite/ *nf* equity; **en toute ~** in all fairness

équivalence /ekivalɑ̃s/ *nf* [1] (valeur identique) equivalence; [2] Univ **demander une ~** to ask for recognition of one's qualifications GB, to ask for advanced standing US

équivalent, **~e** /ekivalɑ̃, ɑ̃t/
A *adj* (égal) equivalent (**à** to); (identique) identical (**à** to)
B *nm* equivalent

équivaloir /ekivalwaʀ/ [45] *vtr ind* **~ à** to be equivalent to [*quantité*]; to amount to [*effet*]; to be tantamount to [*effet négatif*]

équivoque /ekivɔk/
A *adj* (ambigu) ambiguous; (suspect) [*réputation*] dubious; [*conduite*] questionable
B *nf* (ambiguïté) ambiguity; **sans ~** [*réponse*] unequivocal; [*répondre*] unequivocally

érable /eʀabl/ *nm* maple; **sirop d'~** maple syrup

éradication /eʀadikasjɔ̃/ *nf* eradication

érafler /eʀafle/ [1] *vtr* to scratch

éraflure /eʀaflyʀ/ *nf* scratch

éraillé, **~e** /eʀaje/ *adj* [*voix*] rasping (*épith*)

érailler: s'érailler /eʀaje/ [1] *vpr* [*voix*] to become hoarse

ère /ɛʀ/ *nf* [1] (historique, géologique) era; **cent ans avant notre ~** 100 years BC; **en l'an 10 de notre ~** in the year 10 AD; [2] (époque) age; **à l'~ atomique** in the nuclear age

érection /eʀɛksjɔ̃/ *nf* erection

éreintant, ~**e** /erɛ̃tɑ̃, ɑ̃t/ adj exhausting, killing○

éreinter /erɛ̃te/ [1]
A vtr (fatiguer) to exhaust
B s'**éreinter** vpr to wear oneself out

ergot /ɛRgo/ nm (de coq) spur; (de chien) dewclaw; (de seigle) ergot

ergoter /ɛRgɔte/ [1] vi péj to split hairs

ériger /eRiʒe/ [13]
A vtr to erect [statue, bâtiment]; to establish, to set up [tribunal, société]
B s'**ériger** vpr s'~ **en** to set oneself up as

ermitage /ɛRmitaʒ/ nm lit hermitage; fig retreat

ermite /ɛRmit/ nm ① lit hermit; ② fig recluse; **vivre en** ~ fig to live the life of a recluse

éroder /eRɔde/ [1]
A vtr lit, fig to erode; to erode the value of [monnaie]; to undermine [argument]
B s'**éroder** vpr fig to become eroded

érogène /eRɔʒɛn/ adj erogenous

érosion /eRozjɔ̃/ nf erosion; ~ **monétaire** depreciation of the currency

érotique /eRɔtik/ adj erotic

érotisme /eRɔtism/ nm eroticism

errant, ~**e** /eRɑ̃, ɑ̃t/ adj (par nécessité) wandering; (par choix) rootless; **chien** ~ stray dog

errements /ɛRmɑ̃/ nmpl fml transgressions

errer /eRe/ [1] vi [personne] to wander (**par** about); [imagination] to wander (**sur** over); [animal] to roam

erreur /eRœR/ nf ① (inexactitude, idée fausse) mistake; ~ **de date** mistake about the date; ~ **de jugement/de méthode** error of judgment/of method; ~ **de calcul/de stratégie** calculation/strategic error; ~ **de traduction** mistranslation; **je le croyais riche mais c'était une** ~ I thought he was rich but I was mistaken; **sauf** ~ **ou omission** errors and omissions excepted; ② (acte regrettable) mistake; **une** ~ **de jeunesse** a youthful mistake; ③ (confusion, fait de se tromper) **par** ~ by mistake; **induire qn en** ~ to mislead sb; **sauf** ~ **de ma part** if I'm not mistaken; **vous faites** ~ you are mistaken; **il n'y a pas d'**~ **possible** there's no mistake; **il y a** ~ **sur la personne** fml it's a case of mistaken identity sout; **le droit à l'**~ the right to make mistakes; (des scientifiques) the right to error; ④ Jur error

erroné, ~**e** /eRɔne/ adj incorrect; **'code** ~' 'code not valid'

ersatz /ɛRzats/ nm lit, fig ersatz

éructer /eRykte/ [1]
A vtr to spit out [injures]
B vi to eructate

érudit, ~**e** /eRydi, it/
A adj erudite, scholarly
B nm,f scholar, erudite person

érudition /eRydisjɔ̃/ nf erudition, scholarship

éruption /eRypsjɔ̃/ nf eruption; **entrer en** ~ to erupt

érythréen, **-éenne** /eRitRee, ɛn/ adj Eritrean

ès /ɛs/ prép **licence** ~ **lettres** ≈ arts degree, B.A. (degree)

esbroufe○ /ɛzbRuf/ nf **c'est de l'**~ it's all a lot of swank○; **faire de l'**~ to swank○, to show off

escabeau pl ~**x** /ɛskabo/ nm (échelle) stepladder; (tabouret avec marches) kitchen steps

escadre /ɛskadR/ nf squadron

escadrille /ɛskadRij/ nf squadron

escadron /ɛskadRɔ̃/ nm Mil company; ~ **de la mort** death squad

escalade /ɛskalad/ ▸ p. 327 nf ① (activité) climbing; (de montagne) ascent; **faire de l'**~ to go climbing; ② (intensification) Mil, gén escalation

escalader /ɛskalade/ [1] vtr to scale [mur, clôture]; to climb [montagne]

escale /ɛskal/ nf ① (arrêt, durée) gén stopover; **faire** ~ **à Rio** Naut [navire] to call at Rio; [passager] to stop off in Rio; Aviat [avion, passager] to stop over in Rio; **faire Londres-Rio sans** ~ [navire] to sail London-Rio direct; [avion] to fly London-Rio nonstop; ② (lieu) Naut port of call; Aviat stopover

Composé ~ **technique** Aviat refuelling^GB stop; Naut overhaul

escalier /ɛskalje/ nm ① (ensemble architectural) staircase; ② (ensemble de marches) stairs (pl); **monter l'**~ or **les** ~**s en courant** to run up the stairs

Composés ~ **en colimaçon** spiral staircase; ~ **d'honneur** grand staircase; ~ **mécanique** or **roulant** escalator; ~ **de secours** emergency staircase; ~ **de service** backstairs (pl), service stairs (pl)

escamotable /ɛskamɔtabl/ adj (train d'atterrissage) retractable; [meuble, échelle] foldaway (épith)

escamotage /ɛskamɔtaʒ/ nm (de roues) retraction; (de fait, preuve) cover-up; (de personne) spiriting away

escamoter /ɛskamɔte/ [1] vtr ① [illusionniste] to make [sth] disappear; ② (replier) to retract [roues]; ~ **un lit** to fold a bed away; ③ [fait, preuve] to cover up; ④ (éluder) to evade [problème]

escampette○ /ɛskɑ̃pet/ nf **prendre la poudre d'**~ to scarper○ GB, to skedaddle○

escapade /ɛskapad/ nf escapade; **faire une** ~ (fugue) to run away

escargot /ɛskaRgo/ nm snail

escarpé, ~**e** /ɛskaRpe/ adj [chemin, pente] steep; [rocher] craggy

escarpement /ɛskaRpəmɑ̃/ nm (versant) steep slope; (raideur) steepness

escarpin /ɛskaRpɛ̃/ nm court shoe GB, pump US

escarre /ɛskaR/ nf bedsore

escient /ɛsjɑ̃/ nm **à bon** ~ [agir] wittingly, advisedly; **à mauvais** ~ [agir] ill-advisedly

esclaffer: s'esclaffer /ɛsklafe/ [1] vpr to guffaw

esclandre /ɛsklɑ̃dR/ nm scene

esclavage /ɛsklavaʒ/ nm ① slavery; **réduire qn en** ~ to reduce sb to slavery; ② (contrainte) tyranny (**de** of)

esclavagisme /ɛsklavaʒism/ nm (doctrine) pro-slavery doctrine; (système) slavery

esclavagiste /ɛsklavaʒist/
A adj [politique] pro-slavery (épith); [État] slave (épith)
B nmf pro-slaver, person in favour^GB of slavery

esclave /ɛsklav/
A adj (asservi) enslaved; (servile) servile; **être** ~ **de la mode** to be a slave to fashion
B nmf slave

escompte /ɛskɔ̃t/ nm discount

escompter /ɛskɔ̃te/ [1] vtr ① to discount [effet, traite]; ② (espérer) to anticipate; ~ **faire** to count on doing

escorte /ɛskɔRt/ nf Mil, Naut escort; (suite) retinue; fig accompaniment; **sous bonne** ~ under escort

escorter /ɛskɔRte/ [1] vtr to escort

escorteur /ɛskɔRtœR/ nm escort vessel

escrime /ɛskRim/ ▸ p. 327 nf fencing

escrimer○: **s'escrimer** /ɛskRime/ [1] vpr **s'**~ **à faire** to knock○ ou wear oneself out trying to do

escrimeur, **-euse** /ɛskRimœR, øz/ nm,f fencer

escroc /ɛskRo/ nm swindler, crook

escroquer /ɛskRɔke/ [1] vtr to swindle; ~ **qch à qn**, ~ **qn de qch** to swindle sb out of sth

escroquerie /ɛskRɔkRi/ nf ① (action) fraud, swindling; tentative ~ attempted fraud; **c'est de l'**~**!** it's daylight robbery; ② (résultat) swindle

escudo /ɛskudo/ ▸ p. 34 nm escudo

ESEU /œesəy/ nm: abbr ▸ **examen**

ésotérique /ezɔteRik/ adj [propos] esoteric; [cercle] closed

espace /ɛspas/ nm ① (place, cosmos) space; ② (lieu réservé à une activité) ~ **de loisirs** leisure complex; ③ (sphère) arena; ④ (zone) area; ~ **économique** economic area; ⑤ (intervalle) gap; ⑥ (laps de temps) **en l'**~ **de** in the space of; **l'**~ **d'un instant** for a moment

Composés ~ **aérien** airspace; ~ **commercial** commercial space ¢; ~ **publicitaire** advertising space ¢

espacement /ɛspasmɑ̃/ nm ① gén (processus) spacing out; (situation) growing infrequency; ② (dans un texte) spacing; **barre d'**~ space bar

espacer /ɛspase/ [12]
A vtr to space [sth] out
B s'**espacer** vpr to become less frequent

espadon /ɛspadɔ̃/ nm swordfish

Espagne /ɛspaɲ/ ▸ p. 230 *nprf* Spain

Idiome **bâtir des châteaux en** ~ to build castles in the air

espagnol, ~**e** /ɛspaɲɔl/ ▸ p. 392
A *adj* Spanish
B ▸ p. 336 *nm* Ling Spanish

espalier /ɛspalje/ *nm* (treillis) espalier; (mur) fruit-wall; (méthode) espalier cultivation

espèce /ɛspɛs/
A *nf* **1** (en biologie) species; **une** ~ **rare** a rare species; **l'**~ **humaine** mankind; **2** (type) kind; **de toute** ~ of every kind; **de la pire** *or* **de la plus belle** ~ of the worst sort; **3** (dans une description approximative) sort; **il y avait des** ~**s de colonnes** there were some kind *ou* sort of columns; **cela n'a aucune** ~ **d'importance** that is of absolutely no importance; ~ **d'idiot!** you idiot!
B **espèces** *nfpl* **en** ~**s** [*payer, règlement*] in cash

espérance /ɛspeʀɑ̃s/
A *nf* hope
B **espérances** *nfpl* (aspirations) expectations

Composé ~ **de vie** life expectancy

espérer /ɛspeʀe/ [14]
A *vtr* **1** (appeler de ses vœux) ~ **qch** to hope for sth; ~ **faire** to hope to do; **j'espère avoir bien fait** I hope (that) I did the right thing; **j'espère que oui/que non** I hope so/not; **que peut-on** ~ **de plus?** what more can you hope for?; **2** (escompter) to expect (de from); **je n'en espérais pas tant** it's more than I expected; **je ne t'espérais plus** I had given up on you
B *vi* to hope

espiègle /ɛspjɛgl/
A *adj* mischievous
B *nmf* imp, little monkey○

espièglerie /ɛspjɛgləʀi/ *nf* (caractère) mischievousness

espion, **-ionne** /ɛspjɔ̃, ɔn/ ▸ p. 372 *nm,f* spy

espionnage /ɛspjɔnaʒ/ *nm* espionage, spying; **film/roman d'**~ spy film/story

Composé ~ **industriel** industrial espionage

espionner /ɛspjɔne/ [1] *vtr* to spy on

espionnite /ɛspjɔnit/ *nf* spy mania

esplanade /ɛsplanad/ *nf* esplanade

espoir /ɛspwaʀ/ *nm* (fait, raison d'espérer) hope (**de** of); **rendre** ~ to rekindle hope; **reprendre** ~ to feel hopeful again; **dans l'**~ **de faire qch** in the hope of doing sth; **dans l'**~ **de te lire bientôt** hoping to hear from you soon; **avoir l'**~ **de faire qch** to hope to do sth; **avec** ~ hopefully, in a hopeful way; **c'est sans** ~ it's hopeless; **je garde** ~ I am still hopeful

Idiome **tant qu'il y a de la vie il y a de l'**~ where there's life there's hope

esprit /ɛspʀi/ *nm* **1** (caractère) mind; **avoir l'**~ **vif** to have a quick mind; **avoir l'**~ **mal placé** to have a dirty mind○; **avoir l'**~ **d'aventure** to be adventurous; **avoir un** ~ **de synthèse** to be good at synthesizing; **avoir l'**~ **de contradiction** to be contrary; **2** (cerveau) mind; **l'idée m'a traversé l'**~ the idea crossed my mind; **mettre un doute dans l'**~ **de qn** to sow the seeds of doubt in sb's mind; **cela m'était totalement sorti de l'**~ it completely slipped my mind; **garder qch à l'**~ to keep sth in mind; **cela ne t'est jamais venu à l'**~? didn't it ever occur to you?; **avoir l'**~ **dérangé** to be disturbed; **avoir l'**~ **ailleurs** to be miles away; **3** (humour) wit; **avoir de l'**~ to be witty; **une réponse pleine d'**~ a witty reply; **faire de l'**~ to try to be witty; **4** (humeur) mood; (disposition) spirit; (ambiance) atmosphere; **je n'ai pas l'**~ **à rire** I'm in no mood for laughing; **dans un** ~ **de vengeance** in a spirit of revenge; **5** (personne) individual; **l'un des plus grands** ~**s de son temps** one of the greatest minds of his/her time; **calmer les** ~**s** to calm people down; **6** (caractéristique) spirit; **conforme à l'**~ **de l'entreprise** in accordance with the company ethic; **7** Philos, Relig, Mythol spirit; **les choses de l'**~ spiritual matters; **croire aux** ~**s** to believe in ghosts; **'**~ **es-tu là?** 'is there anybody there?'

Composés ~ **d'à-propos** ready wit; ~ **de corps** solidarity; ~ **d'équipe** team spirit; ~ **de famille** family solidarity; **ils ont l'**~ **de famille** they're a very close family; **je n'ai pas l'**~ **de famille** I'm not very family-oriented

Idiomes **perdre ses** ~**s** (s'évanouir) to faint; (être très troublé) to take leave of one's senses; **retrouver** *or* **reprendre ses** ~**s** (après un malaise) to regain consciousness; (après une émotion) to collect one's wits; **les grands** ~**s se rencontrent** great minds think alike

esquimau, **-aude**, *mpl* ~**x** /ɛskimo, od/
A *adj* Eskimo; **chien** ~ husky
B *nm* **1** Ling Eskimo; **2** ®(glace) chocolate-covered ice lolly GB, ice-cream bar US

esquinter○ /ɛskɛ̃te/ [1]
A *vtr* **1** (amocher) to damage [*voiture*]; to hurt [*personne*]; **2** (critiquer) to slate [*auteur*]; **3** (fatiguer) to wear [sb] out
B **s'esquinter** *vpr* **1** (se blesser) to hurt oneself; **s'**~ **la santé** to ruin one's health; **2** (se fatiguer) to wear oneself out (**à faire** doing)

esquisse /ɛskis/ *nf* (de dessin) sketch; (de programme) outline

esquisser /ɛskise/ [1]
A *vtr* to sketch [*portrait*]; to outline [*programme*]
B **s'esquisser** *vpr* [*solution*] to emerge

esquiver /ɛskive/ [1]
A *vtr* to duck [*coup*]; to sidestep [*question, attaque*]; to dodge [*responsabilité, difficulté*]
B **s'esquiver** *vpr* (partir) to slip away; (se dérober) to shy away

essai /ɛse/
A *nm* **1** Tech (expérimentation) trial; **faire des** ~**s** to run trials; **être à l'**~ to undergo trials; **vol d'**~ test flight; ~ **sur route** road test; **2** Tech (analyse, expérience) test; ~ **de laboratoire** laboratory test; **3** (tentative) try; **un coup d'**~ a try; **faire un** ~ to have a try; **je serai à l'**~ **pendant un mois** I'll work a month on a trial basis; **4** (en littérature) essay (**sur** on); **5** (en athlétisme) attempt; (au rugby) try; **transformer un** ~ to convert (a try)
B **essais** *nmpl* (en courses) qualifying round (*sg*)

essaim /esɛ̃/ *nm* lit, fig swarm

essayage /esɛjaʒ/ *nm* fitting

essayer /eseje/ [21]
A *vtr* **1** (tenter) to try; ~ **une voiture** (pour le plaisir) to try a car; (avant d'acheter) to test-drive a car; ~ **sa force** to test one's strength; **2** Tech (soumettre à des tests) [*technicien*] to test [*arme, avion, mécanisme, matériau*]; [*technicien*] to run trials on [*voiture, machine*]; [*client*] to try out [*voiture, arme*]; **3** to try on [*vêtement, chaussures*]; to try [*taille, couleur*]; **acheter sans** ~ to buy without trying on
B **s'essayer** *vpr* **s'**~ **à** to have a go at [*sport*] ; to try one's hand at [*art, littérature*]

essayiste /esejist/ ▸ p. 372 *nmf* essayist

esse /ɛs/ *nf* (crochet) (S-shaped) hook; (de violon) f-hole

essence /esɑ̃s/ *nf* **1** (carburant) petrol GB, gasoline US; **2** (extrait) essential oil; **3** (espèce d'arbre) tree species

Composés ~ **à briquet** lighter fuel GB, lighter fluid US; ~ **ordinaire** ≈ 2-star petrol GB, regular gasoline US; ~ **sans plomb** unleaded petrol GB *ou* gasoline US; ~ **super** ≈ 4-star petrol GB, premium gasoline US

essentiel, **-ielle** /esɑ̃sjɛl/
A *adj* **1** (très important) essential; **2** (central) key (*épith*), essential; **rôle** ~ key role
B *nm* **1** (chose principale) **c'est l'**~ that's the main thing; **aller à l'**~ to get to the heart of the matter; **2** (partie la plus importante) bulk; **pour l'**~ mainly; **3** (objets indispensables) basics (*pl*); **en voyage je n'emporte que l'**~ when travelling^GB I only ever take the bare minimum

essentiellement /esɑ̃sjɛlmɑ̃/ *adv* **1** (pour la plus grande partie) mainly; **2** (dans ses aspects les plus importants) essentially

esseulé, ~**e** /esœle/ *adj* forlorn

essieu, *pl* ~**x** /esjø/ *nm* axle

essor /esɔʀ/ *nm* (d'oiseau, imagination) flight; (de commerce, région) development; (de mode, sport) increasing popularity; **prendre son** ~ [*oiseau*] to fly off; [*entreprise*] to take off; **être en plein** ~ to be booming

essorage /esɔʀaʒ/ *nm* (à la main) wringing; (en machine) spin-drying

essorer /esɔʀe/ [1] *vtr* (en tordant) to wring; (par centrifugation) to spin-dry [*linge*]; to spin [*salade*]

essoreuse /esɔʀøz/ *nf* (à tambour) spin-drier GB, spin-dryer US; ~ **à salade** salad spinner

essoufflement /esufləmɑ̃/ *nm* lit breathlessness; fig loss of impetus

e

essouffler /esufle/ [1]
A *vtr* lit to leave [sb] breathless; **être essoufflé** to be out of breath
B **s'essouffler** *vpr* lit to get breathless; fig [économie, projet] to run out of steam

ESST /ɛsɛste/ *nf* (*abbr* = **encéphalopathie spongiforme subaiguë transmissible**) TSE, transmissible spongiform encephalopathy

essuie-glace, *pl* ~**s** /esɥiɡlas/ *nm* windscreen wiper GB, windshield wiper US

essuie-mains /esɥimɛ̃/ *nm inv* hand towel

essuie-tout /esɥitu/ *nm inv* (en rouleau) kitchen roll; (en feuilles) kitchen paper

essuyer /esɥije/ [22]
A *vtr* **1** (rendre sec) to dry [verre, mains, enfant, chien]; to wipe [table]; ~ **la vaisselle** to dry up; **2** (pour nettoyer) to wipe; **3** (éponger) to wipe up; ~ **ses larmes** to wipe away one's tears; **4** (subir) to run into [orage]; to suffer [défaite, pertes, affront]
B **s'essuyer** *vpr* (tout le corps) to dry oneself, to towel off US; (une partie du corps) (sécher) to dry; (nettoyer) to wipe; **s'~ les mains** to dry one's hands

est /ɛst/ ▸ p. 454
A *adj inv* [façade, versant, côte] east; [frontière, zone] eastern
B *nm* **1** (point cardinal, région) east; **2** (en géographie) **l'Est** the East; **de l'Est** [ville, accent] eastern

estafette /ɛstafɛt/ *nf* **1** ®Aut van; **2** Mil dispatch rider

estampe /ɛstɑ̃p/ *nf* Art (sur planche gravée) engraving; (par lithographie) print

estamper○ /ɛstɑ̃pe/ [1] *vtr* (escroquer) to rip [sb] off○

estampille /ɛstɑ̃pij/ *nf* lit (cachet, signature) stamp; (label) trademark; fig mark

est-ce ▸ **être¹**

esthète /ɛstɛt/ *nmf* aesthete

esthéticienne /ɛstetisjɛn/ ▸ p. 372 *nf* beautician

esthétique /ɛstetik/
A *adj* [sens] aesthetic; [décor] aesthetically pleasing; [pose, geste] graceful
B *nf* (théorie) aesthetics (+ *v sg*); (de décor) aesthetic quality; (de geste) grace

esthétisme /ɛstetism/ *nm* aestheticism

estimable /ɛstimabl/ *adj* **1** (honorable) [personne] worthy; **2** (admirable) [travail, résultat, effort] laudable; **3** **difficilement ~** [fortune] hard to estimate

estimation /ɛstimasjɔ̃/ *nf* **1** (de coût) estimate; (valeur) valuation; (de dégâts) assessment; **2** (de distance, temps, d'efficacité) estimate; **3** (en statistique) estimate

estime /ɛstim/ *nf* respect; **baisser dans l'~ de qn** to go down in sb's estimation

estimer /ɛstime/ [1]
A *vtr* **1** (penser) to consider (**que** that); ~ **nécessaire/de son devoir de faire** to consider it necessary/one's duty to do; **2** (respecter) to think highly of [ami, artiste]; **3** (chiffrer) to value [tableau, propriété]; to assess [dégâts]; ~ **qch au-dessus/au-dessous de sa valeur** to overvalue/ undervalue sth; ~ **qch à** to value sth at; ~ **qn à sa juste valeur** to recognize sb's real worth; **4** (calculer approximativement) to estimate (**à** at); **une vitesse estimée à 150 km/h** an estimated speed of 150 kph; **5** (deviner) to reckon
B **s'estimer** *vpr* **estimez-vous heureux** think yourself lucky; **je m'estime satisfait de lui** I am satisfied with him

estival, ~**e**, *mpl* **-aux** /ɛstival, o/ *adj* (d'été) summer (épith); (évoquant l'été) summery

estivant, ~**e** /ɛstivɑ̃, ɑ̃t/ *nm,f* summer visitor

estocade /ɛstokad/ *nf* lit fatal sword thrust; fig final blow

estomac /ɛstoma/ *nm* **1** Anat stomach; **avoir mal à l'~** to have stomach ache GB *ou* a stomachache US; ~ **bien rempli** full stomach; **j'ai un poids sur l'~** my stomach feels heavy; **avoir l'~ bien accroché** to have a strong stomach; **leur refus m'est resté sur l'~**○ their refusal left a nasty taste in my mouth; **2** ○fig (courage) guts○ (*pl*)
(Idiome) **avoir l'~ dans les talons**○ to be famished

estomaquer○ /ɛstomake/ [1] *vtr* to flabbergast

estomper /ɛstɔ̃pe/ [1]
A *vtr* to blur [paysage, formes]; fig to gloss over [détails]

B **s'estomper** *vpr* [paysage] to become blurred; [couleur, haine, souvenirs] to fade

estonien, **-ienne** /ɛstɔnjɛ̃, ɛn/ ▸ p. 392, p. 336
A *adj* Estonian
B *nm* Ling Estonian

estrade /ɛstʀad/ *nf* platform

estragon /ɛstʀaɡɔ̃/ *nm* tarragon

estropié, ~**e** /ɛstʀɔpje/
A *adj* crippled
B *nm,f* cripple

estropier /ɛstʀɔpje/ [2] *vtr* **1** lit to maim; **2** fig (en prononçant) to mispronounce; (en écrivant) to misspell; (en jouant) to mangle [sonate]

estuaire /ɛstɥɛʀ/ *nm* estuary

esturgeon /ɛstyʀʒɔ̃/ *nm* sturgeon

et /e/ *conj* and; **mon père ~ ma mère** my father and mother; **lui ~ son frère sont alcooliques** both he and his brother are alcoholics; **un homme grand ~ fort** a tall strong man; ~ **voilà qu'il sort un couteau de sa poche!** and next thing he whips a knife out of his pocket!; **il y a expert ~ expert** (ils ne se valent pas tous) there are experts and experts; **et tu en es fier?** (exprimant la désapprobation) and you're proud of it?; ~ **moi de répondre...** so I replied...; ~ **le pourboire (alors)?** what about the tip?; **moi j'y vais,** ~ **toi?** I'm going, are you? *ou* what about you?; ~ **alors?,** ~ **après?** so what?

étable /etabl/ *nf* cowshed

établi, ~**e** /etabli/
A *pp* ▸ **établir**
B *pp adj* **1** (solide, ancré) [réputation, usage] established; **il est/a été ~ que** it has been/was established that; **2** (en place) [pouvoir] ruling; [ordre, autorité] established
C *nm* (table de travail) workbench

établir /etabliʀ/ [3]
A *vtr* **1** (fixer) to set up [résidence]; ~ **son domicile à Londres** to set up home in London; ~ **le prix (de vente) de** to price; **2** (instituer) to establish [règlement, hiérarchie, régime, lien]; to introduce [impôt, discipline]; to set up [gouvernement]; to set [record, norme]; **3** (mettre en forme) to draw up [liste, plan, bilan, budget, dossier]; to make out [compte, chèque, facture]; to prepare [devis]; to set up [fiches]; to make [diagnostic]; to draw [parallèle]; **4** (assurer) to establish [réputation, fortune, influence]; **5** (prouver) to establish [fait, identité, innocence]
B **s'établir** *vpr* **1** (se fixer) [personne] to settle (**à, en** in); [organisme] to set up; **s'~ (comme) antiquaire** to set up as an antique dealer; **s'~ à son compte** to set up one's own business; **2** [indice, taux, hausse] to be set (**à** at); **3** (s'instituer) [liens] to develop (**sur** out of); [domination, pouvoir] to become established (**sur** on)

établissement /etablismɑ̃/ *nm* **1** (entreprise, organisme) gén organization; (institué) institution; (bâtiments) premises (*pl*); **2** (ville, village) settlement; **3** (mise en place) (de relations, hiérarchie, régime) establishment; (de norme) setting; (de gouvernement) formation; (de personne) settlement; (de taxe, sanction) introduction; **4** (mise en forme) (de liste, plan, dossier) drawing up; **5** (démonstration) **l'~ de leur culpabilité** proving they are guilty

(Composés) ~ **commercial** commercial establishment; ~ **de crédit** finance company; ~ **d'enseignement supérieur** higher education institution; ~ **hospitalier** hospital; ~ **pénitentiaire** penal institution; ~ **privé** (école) private school; ~ **scolaire** school; ~ **spécialisé** institution; ~ **thermal** hydrotherapy centre^GB; ~ **d'utilité publique** public service corporation

étage /etaʒ/ *nm* **1** (d'immeuble) floor; **le premier ~** the first floor GB, the second floor US; **le dernier ~** the top floor; **à tous les ~s** on every floor; **à l'~ au-dessus/au-dessous** on the floor above/below; **dans les ~s** on (one of) the floors above; **à l'~** upstairs; **une maison sans ~** a single-storey(ed) house GB, a single-story house US; **2** (division) (de tour) level; (d'aqueduc, de gâteau, coiffure) tier; (de fusée) stage; **3** (de terrain) terrace; **terrain en ~s** terraced land

étager /etaʒe/ [13]
A *vtr* to plant [sth] in tiers [fleurs]; to stagger [augmentations]
B **s'étager** *vpr* [cultures, jardins] to rise in terraces

étagère /etaʒɛʀ/ *nf* shelf; **des ~s** shelves

étain /etɛ̃/ *nm* **1** (métal) tin; **2** (matière) pewter; **3** (objet) piece of pewter ware; **les ~s** pewter ware ¢

étal /etal/ *nm* [1] (de marché) stall; [2] (de boucher) butcher's block

étalage /etalaʒ/ *nm* [1] Comm (de magasin) window display; (de marché) stall; [2] (de luxe, richesses) display; **faire ~ de** to flaunt

étalagiste /etalaʒist/ ▸ p. 372 *nmf* (décorateur) window dresser

étalement /etalmɑ̃/ *nm* [1] (dans le temps) staggering; [2] (dans l'espace) sprawl

étaler /etale/ [1]

A *vtr* [1] (déployer) to spread out [*document, drap*]; to spread [*tapis*]; to roll [sth] out [*pâte*]; [2] (éparpiller) to scatter; [3] (répandre) to spread [*beurre, pâté, colle*]; to apply [*peinture, pommade*]; [4] (échelonner) to spread [*travaux, réformes, remboursements*] (**sur** over); to stagger [*départs, horaires*] (**sur** over); [5] (montrer) to display [*articles*]; péj to flaunt [*richesse, savoir*]; ~ **au grand jour** to bring [sth] out into the open [*vie privée*]

B **s'étaler** *vpr* [1] (s'échelonner) [*programme, paiement*] to be spread (**sur** over); [*départs*] to be staggered (**sur** over); [2] (s'exhiber) **s'~ en première page** to be splashed all over the front page; **s'~ (au grand jour)** to be plain for all to see; [3] (s'étendre) [*paysage*] to sprawl; [4] (se vautrer) [*personne*] to sprawl; (prendre de la place) [*personne*] to spread out; [5] ○(tomber) to go sprawling○; **s'~ de tout son long** to fall flat on one's face; [6] ○(échouer) **s'~** *or* **se faire ~ à un examen** to fail *ou* flunk ○ an exam

étalon /etalɔ̃/

A *nm* [1] (cheval) stallion; [2] (modèle) standard; fig yardstick

B **(-)étalon** (*in compounds*) **métal(-)~** standard metal; **mètre(-)~** standard metre^{GB}

étalonnage /etalɔnaʒ/ *nm*, **étalonnement** /etalɔnmɑ̃/ *nm* calibration

étalonner /etalɔne/ [1] *vtr* (vérifier) to test; (graduer) to calibrate

étalon-or /etalɔ̃ɔʀ/ *nm inv* gold standard

étamer /etame/ [1] *vtr* to tin [*casserole*]; to tin-plate [*métal*]

étamine /etamin/ *nf* (de fleur) stamen

étanche /etɑ̃ʃ/ *adj* [1] lit ~ (**à l'eau**) [*montre, combinaison*] waterproof; [*tonneau, embarcation*] watertight; ~ (**à l'air**) airtight; [2] fig impenetrable

étanchéité /etɑ̃ʃeite/ *nf* ~ (**à l'eau**) (de montre) waterproof quality; (de citerne) watertightness; ~ (**à l'air**) airtightness

étancher /etɑ̃ʃe/ [1] *vtr* to quench [*soif*]

étang /etɑ̃/ *nm* pond

étant /etɑ̃/ ▸ **donné C, D, entendu, être**¹

étape /etap/ *nf* [1] (lieu d'arrêt) stop; [2] (section de trajet) stage; (dans une course) leg; [3] fig (phase) stage; (palier) step

(Idiome) **brûler les ~s** to go too far too fast

état /eta/

A *nm* [1] (condition physique) condition; **être/ne pas être en ~ de faire** to be in a/no fit state to do; **mettre qn hors d'~ de faire qch** to render sb incapable of doing sth; **mettre qn hors d'~ de nuire** (légalement) to put sb out of harm's way; (physiquement) to incapacitate sb; **leur ~ de santé** their (state of) health; **en piteux○ ~** in a pitiful state; [2] (condition psychique) state; **être dans un drôle○ d'~** to be in a hell of a state○; **ne pas être dans son ~ normal** not to be oneself; **ne te mets pas dans des ~s pareils!** don't get into such a state○!; **être dans un ~ second** to be in a trance; [3] (de voiture, livre, tapis) condition; **l'~ des routes** (conditions climatiques) road conditions (*pl*); (qualité) the state of the roads; **en bon/mauvais ~** [*maison, cœur*] in good/poor condition; **avoir les dents en mauvais ~** to have bad teeth; **hors d'~ de marche** [*voiture*] off the road; [*appareil*] out of order; **remettre qch en ~** to mend *ou* repair sth; **remettre une maison en ~** to do up a house; **j'ai laissé les choses en l'~** I left everything as it was; **à l'~ brut** [*pétrole*] in its raw state; **à l'~ de ruines** in a state of ruin; **à l'~ neuf** as good as new; **une voiture en ~ de rouler** a roadworthy car; [4] (d'affaires, économie, de finances, pays) state; **dans l'~ actuel des choses** in the present state of affairs; [5] (en sciences) (de corps) state; [6] (situation sociale) state; **être boulanger de son ~** to be a baker by trade; ▸ **tiers**; [7] Sociol state; **naissance d'un nouvel ~ social** birth of a new social order; [8] (en comptabilité) statement; [9] Jur (statut) state; [10] Hist (catégorie sociale) estate

B **faire état de** *loc verbale* [1] (arguer) to cite [*document, loi*]; [2] (mentionner) to mention ~ [*conversation, découverte*];

[3] (exposer) to state [*préférences, privilèges*]; to air [*soupçon, idée*]; [4] (se prévaloir de) to make a point of mentioning [*succès, courage*]

(Composés) ~ **d'alerte** Mil state of alert; ~ **d'âme** (scrupule) qualm; (sentiment) feeling; ~ **de choc** Méd, Psych state of shock; ~ **civil** Admin registry office GB; (de personne) civil status; ~ **de crise** Pol, Sociol state of crisis; ~ **d'esprit** state *ou* frame of mind; ~ **de fait** fact; ~ **de grâce** Relig state of grace; **en ~ de grâce** fig inspired; ~ **des lieux** Jur inventory and statement of state of repair; fig appraisal; ~ **de siège** state of siege; ~ **d'urgence** state of emergency; ~ **voyou** rogue state; **les ~s généraux** Hist the Estates General; ~**s de service** service record

(Idiome) **être/se mettre dans tous ses ~s**○ to be in/to get into a state○

État /eta/ *nm* [1] (nation) state, State; **coup d'~** coup d'état; [2] (gouvernement) state, government; **demander une aide de l'~** to apply for state aid; **un emprunt d'~** a public loan; [3] (territoire autonome) state

(Composé) ~ **de droit** Pol legally constituted state

étatique /etatik/ *adj* [*financement, gestion*] state GB (*épith*), public US (*épith*); [*contrôle*] state (*épith*)

étatiser /etatize/ [1] *vtr* to bring [sth] under state control

état-major, *pl* **états-majors** /etamaʒɔʀ/ *nm* [1] Mil (officiers) staff (+ *v pl*); (lieu) headquarters; [2] Pol administrative staff

États-Unis /etazyni/ ▸ p. 230 *nprmpl* ~ (**d'Amérique**) United States (of America)

étau, *pl* ~**x** /eto/ *nm* Tech vice GB; fig stranglehold (**autour de** on); **être pris en ~** to be caught in a vice-like GB *ou* vise-like US grip; **l'~ se resserre** the net is tightening (**autour de** around)

étayer /eteje/ [21] *vtr* [1] Constr to shore up, to prop up [*mur, plafond*]; [2] fig to support [*théorie, démonstration*] (**de, par** with)

été /ete/ ▸ p. 536 *nm* summer; ~ **comme hiver** all year round

éteignoir /etɛɲwaʀ/ *nm* (de bougie) snuffer

éteindre /etɛ̃dʀ/ [55]

A *vtr* [1] to put out [*feu, cigare, poêle*]; (en soufflant) to blow out [*bougie*]; [2] to switch off [*lampe, téléviseur, chauffage, phare*]; to turn off [*gaz*]; **c'est éteint chez elle** her lights are off; **tous feux éteints** [*rouler*] without lights; [3] (calmer) to subdue [*colère, désir*]; to quell [*ardeur*]

B **s'éteindre** *vpr* [1] [*cigare, feu*] to go out; (par accident) [*lumière*] to go out; [*radio*] to go off; [2] [*pièce, fenêtre*] to go dark; [3] (mourir) euph to pass away *ou* on; [4] [*famille, nom*] to die out; [5] [*son*] to die away; [*voix*] to become lifeless; [*désir, passion*] to fade; [*colère*] to subside

éteint, ~**e** /etɛ̃, ɛ̃t/

A *pp* ▸ **éteindre**

B *pp adj* [1] [*regard*] dull; [2] [*volcan*] extinct; [*astre*] extinct, dead

étendard /etɑ̃daʀ/ *nm* standard, flag; **se ranger sous l'~ de** to rally to the cause of

étendre /etɑ̃dʀ/ [6]

A *vtr* [1] (allonger) to stretch [*bras, jambe*]; **il a étendu les bras** he stretched his arms; [2] (déployer) to spread (out) [*bâche, nappe*]; ~ **du linge** (dehors) to hang out washing; (dedans) to hang up washing; [3] (coucher) to lay [sb] down; ~ **qn (sur le carreau)**○ (blesser) to lay sb out cold○, to floor^{GB} sb; [4] (étaler) to spread [*enduit, peinture*]; Culin to roll out [*pâte*]; [5] (accroître) to extend [*emprise, pouvoir*] (**sur** over); to extend [*allocation, embargo*] (**à** to)

B **s'étendre** *vpr* [1] (occuper un espace) to stretch (**sur** over); [2] (augmenter) [*grève, épidémie*] to spread (**à** to); [*ville*] to expand, to grow; [3] (s'appliquer) [*loi, mesure*] **s'~ à** to apply to; [4] (durer) to stretch (**sur** over), to last; [5] (s'allonger) to lie down; [6] (s'appesantir) **s'~ sur** to dwell on [*sujet, point*]

étendu, ~**e**¹ /etɑ̃dy/ *adj* [*ville*] sprawling; [*région, plaine*] vast; [*connaissances, dégâts*] extensive

étendue² /etɑ̃dy/ *nf* [1] (de terrain) expanse, area; (de sable, d'eau) expanse; [2] (de pays, collection) size; **sur toute l'~ du pays** throughout the country; [3] (de dégâts) scale, extent; (de connaissances) range; (d'ignorance) depth

(Composé) ~ **territoriale** (de contrat) territorial limits (*pl*)

Les États, les pays et les continents

■ Les adjectifs comme anglais *peuvent aussi qualifier des personnes (par ex. un touriste anglais ▸ p. 392) et des langues (par ex. un mot anglais ▸ p. 336.)*

Les noms de pays

■ *L'anglais n'utilise pas d'article défini devant les noms de pays et de continents, sauf pour les noms qui ont une forme de pluriel (the United States, the Netherlands, the Philippines etc.) et quelques rares exceptions (the Congo, the Gambia). En cas de doute, consulter l'article dans le dictionnaire.*

la France	**l'Afrique**
= France	= Africa
le Brésil	**aimer la France**
= Brazil	= to like France
Cuba	**aimer l'Afrique**
= Cuba	= to like Africa

■ *Attention: les noms qui ont une forme de pluriel se comportent en général comme des noms singuliers.*

les États-Unis sont un pays riche
= the United States is a rich country

■ *Noter que les noms de continents et de pays qui utilisent les points cardinaux ne prennent pas d'article défini non plus:*

l'Amérique du Nord	**la Corée du Sud**
= North America	= South Korea

À, au, aux, en

■ *À, au, aux et en se traduisent par* to *avec les verbes de mouvement (par ex. aller, se rendre etc) et par* in *avec les autres verbes (par ex. être, habiter etc.).*

aller au Brésil	**vivre au Brésil**
= to go to Brazil	= to live in Brazil
aller en Afrique	**vivre en Afrique**
= to go to Africa	= to live in Africa

De avec les noms de pays et de continents

■ *Les expressions françaises avec de se traduisent en général en anglais par l'emploi de l'adjectif. Mais voir ci-dessous quelques exceptions.*

■ *Attention: l'anglais emploie toujours la majuscule pour les adjectifs ethniques.*

l'ambassade de France
= the French embassy

les campagnes de la France
= the French countryside

le climat de la France
= the French climate

l'équipe de France
= the French team

les fleuves et rivières de France
= French rivers

l'histoire de France
= French history

Mais noter:

l'ambassadeur de France
= the French ambassador *ou* the ambassador of France

la capitale de la France
= the capital of France

les peuples de l'Afrique
= the peoples of Africa

une carte de France
= a map of France

Traduction des adjectifs

l'argent français	**la littérature française**
= French money	= French literature
l'armée française	**la marine française**
= the French army	= the French navy
l'aviation française	**le peuple français**
= the French air force	= the French nation
la cuisine française	**la politique française**
= French cooking	= French politics
la douane française	**les traditions françaises**
= the French Customs	= French traditions
le gouvernement français	**la vie politique française**
= the French government	= French politics
la langue française	**une ville française**
= the French language	= a French town

■ *En anglais, dans quelques rares cas, on trouve aussi le nom du pays ou du continent utilisé en position d'adjectif: the England team, the Africa question etc. Il est préférable de ne pas imiter ces tournures.*

éternel, -elle /etɛʀnɛl/
A *adj* [*problème*] endless; [*vérité*] eternal; [*optimiste*] eternal; [*sourire*] inevitable
B *nm* eternal; **l'~ féminin** the eternal feminine
Éternel /etɛʀnɛl/ *nm* Eternal; **l'~** the Lord

éternellement /etɛʀnɛlmɑ̃/ *adv* (jusqu'à la fin des temps) forever; (continûment) permanently; (de manière répétée) perpetually, continually; Relig eternally

éterniser: s'éterniser /etɛʀnize/ [1] *vpr* (se prolonger) to drag on; (s'attarder) to stay for ages○

éternité /etɛʀnite/ *nf* eternity; **de toute ~** from time immemorial

éternuement /etɛʀnymɑ̃/ *nm* sneeze

éternuer /etɛʀnɥe/ [1] *vi* to sneeze

étêter /etete/ [1] *vtr* **1** to top, to pollard [*arbre*]; **2** to remove the head of [*clou, sardine*]

éther /etɛʀ/ *nm* **1** Chimie ether; **2** (ciel) liter **l'~** the ether

éthéré, ~e /eteʀe/ *adj* ethereal

éthiopien, -ienne /etjɔpjɛ̃, ɛn/ ▸ p. 392 *adj* Ethiopian

éthique /etik/
A *adj* ethical
B *nf* Philos ethics (+ *v sg*); (conception morale) code of ethics; **l'~ capitaliste** the capitalist ethic

ethnie /ɛtni/ *nf* ethnic group

ethnique /ɛtnik/ *adj* ethnic

ethnographie /ɛtnɔgʀafi/ *nf* ethnography

ethnologie /ɛtnɔlɔʒi/ *nf* ethnology

ethnologue /ɛtnɔlɔg/ ▸ p. 372 *nmf* ethnologist

éthylique /etilik/
A *adj* **1** (alcoolique) alcoholic; **2** Chimie **alcool ~** ethyl alcohol
B *nmf* alcoholic

éthylisme /etilism/ ▸ p. 195 *nm* alcoholism

étincelant, ~e /etɛ̃selɑ̃, ɑ̃t/ *adj* **1** (lumineux) [*soleil*] blazing; [*étoile*] twinkling; [*pierreries, verre*] sparkling; [*plumage, couleur*] brilliant; **2** (remarquable) brilliant

étinceler /etɛ̃sle/ [19] *vi* [*étoile*] to twinkle; [*soleil, pierre précieuse, métal*] to sparkle; [*yeux*] (de colère) to flash (**de**

with); (de joie) to sparkle (**de** with)

étincelle /etɛ̃sɛl/ *nf* **1** (incandescence) spark; **2** (lueur) (sur une lame) flash; (sur un diamant) sparkle; (dans le regard) (d'humour) twinkle; (de colère) glint; **jeter des ~s** to glitter; **3** (manifestation fugitive) flash (**de** of)

(Idiomes) **ça va faire des ~s**○ fig that will make sparks fly; **faire des ~s** (dans l'action) to do brilliantly; **c'est l'~ qui a mis le feu aux poudres** fig it's what sparked off the crisis

étioler: s'étioler /etjɔle/ [1] *vpr* [*plante*] to wilt

étiquetage /etiktaʒ/ *nm* lit, fig labelling^{GB}

(Composé) **~ génétique** gene tagging

étiqueter /etikte/ [20] *vtr* lit, fig to label

étiquette /etikɛt/ *nf* **1** (à coller) label; (à attacher) tag; **porter une ~** to be labelled^{GB}; **2** (protocole) etiquette; **3** Ordinat tag

étirement /etiʀmɑ̃/ *nm* Sport stretching exercise

étirer /etiʀe/ [1]
A *vtr* (pour détendre) to stretch
B **s'étirer** *vpr* **1** [*personne*] to stretch; **2** [*procession, chemin*] to stretch out; [*journée*] to seem endless

étoffe /etɔf/ *nf* **1** (tissu) fabric; **2** fig substance; **avoir l'~ d'un grand homme** to have the makings of a great man

étoffer /etɔfe/ [1]
A *vtr* to expand [*récit, développement*]; **un récit bien étoffé** a well-developed story
B **s'étoffer** *vpr* [*personne*] to put on weight

étoile /etwal/ *nf* **1** (astre) star; **ciel sans ~s** starless sky; **à la lueur des ~s** by starlight; **2** (forme) star; **~ à cinq branches** five-pointed star; **3** (artiste) star

(Composés) **l'~ du berger** the evening star; **~ filante** shooting star; **~ polaire** Pole Star

(Idiomes) **être né sous une bonne/mauvaise ~** to be born under a lucky/an unlucky star; **coucher** *or* **dormir à la belle ~** to sleep out in the open

étoilé, ~e /etwale/ *adj* **1** [*ciel*] starry; **2** [*verre*] crazed

étole /etɔl/ *nf* stole

étonnamment /etɔnamɑ̃/ *adv* surprisingly

étonnant, ~e /etɔnɑ̃, ɑ̃t/ *adj* **1** (inattendu) surprising; **pas ~ qu'il soit malade**○ no wonder he's ill; **2** (extraordinaire) amazing

étonnement /etɔnmɑ̃/ *nm* surprise; **à mon grand ~** to my amazement

étonner /etɔne/ [1]
A *vtr* to surprise; **ça m'étonnerait (fort)** I'd be (very) surprised; **tu m'étonneras toujours!** you never cease to amaze me!
B **s'étonner** *vpr* to be surprised (**que** that; **de qch** at sth); **il ne faut pas s'~ que** it should come as no surprise that

étouffant, ~e /etufɑ̃, ɑ̃t/ *adj* **1** (suffocant) stifling; **2** (pesant) oppressive

étouffé, ~e[1] /etufe/ *adj* **1** (assourdi) [*son, voix*] muffled (**par** by); **2** (retenu) [*sanglot*] choked; [*rire, cri*] suppressed; [*soupir*] discreet

étouffée[2] /etufe/ *nf* **à l'~** [*légume, viande*] braised

étouffer /etufe/ [1]
A *vtr* **1** (entraver) to stifle [*carrière, création*]; to suppress [*protestation*]; **2** (dissimuler) to hush up [*scandale*]; **3** (asphyxier) to suffocate [*victime*]; [*bâillon*] to stifle; to choke [*plante*]; **la générosité ne les étouffe pas** they won't be accused of generosity; **4** (arrêter) to smother [*feu*]; **5** (retenir) to stifle [*bâillement*]; to hold back [*soupir*]; **6** (atténuer) to deaden [*bruits*]
B *vi* (ne pas à l'aise) to feel stifled; **on étouffe ici!**○ it's stifling in here!; **mourir étouffé** (par gaz etc) to die of suffocation; (par obstruction de la trachée) to choke to death
C **s'étouffer** *vpr* (suffoquer) to choke

étoupe /etup/ *nf* (de chanvre) tow; Naut oakum

étourderie /etuʀdeʀi/ *nf* absent-mindedness

étourdi, ~e /etuʀdi/
A *adj* **1** [*personne*] absent-minded; **2** [*réponse, paroles*] unthinking
B *nm,f* scatterbrain

étourdir /etuʀdiʀ/ [3]
A *vtr* **1** (assommer) to stun, to daze; **2** (fatiguer) **~ qn** [*vacarme, circulation*] to make sb's head spin
B **s'étourdir** *vpr* **s'~ de paroles** to become intoxicated with words

étourdissant, ~e /etuʀdisɑ̃, ɑ̃t/ *adj* [*bruit*] deafening; [*réussite*] stunning; [*vitesse*] dizzying

étourdissement /etuʀdismɑ̃/ *nm* dizzy spell

étourneau, *pl* **~x** /etuʀno/ *nm* **1** (oiseau) starling; **2** ○(étourdi) scatterbrain○

étrange /etʀɑ̃ʒ/
A *adj* strange; **trouver ~ que** to find it strange that; **chose ~ elle n'a pas répondu** strangely enough she didn't answer
B *nm* (caractère surprenant) strangeness; (bizarrerie) bizarre

étrangement /etʀɑ̃ʒmɑ̃/ *adv* **1** (fort curieusement) curiously; **vous me rappelez ~ un ami** it's strange *ou* uncanny but you remind me of a friend; **2** (remarquablement) surprisingly

étranger, -ère /etʀɑ̃ʒe, ɛʀ/
A *adj* **1** (d'un autre pays) foreign; **2** (extérieur) **~ à** [*personne*] not involved in (après n) [*affaire*]; outside (après n) [*groupe*]; [*fait*] with no bearing on (après n); [*comportement*] unrelated to (après n); **se sentir ~** to feel like an outsider; **3** (inconnu) [*personne, voix, théorie*] unfamiliar (**à** to); **votre visage ne m'est pas ~** I know your face; **le domaine ne m'est pas ~** I am quite familiar with the field; **la peur leur est étrangère** they know no fear
B *nm,f* **1** (d'un autre pays) foreigner; **2** (d'un autre groupe) outsider; **3** (inconnu) stranger
C *nm* **1** (autres pays) **l'~** foreign countries (*pl*); **à l'~** [*aller*] abroad; **2** (gens d'ailleurs) foreigners (*pl*)

étrangeté /etʀɑ̃ʒte/ *nf* strangeness

étranglé, ~e /etʀɑ̃gle/ *adj* **1** [*voix*] choked; [*son*] muffled; **2** [*rue, vallée*] narrow

étranglement /etʀɑ̃gləmɑ̃/ *nm* **1** (de victime) strangulation; **2** (de vallée) (fait) narrowing; (endroit) narrow section

étrangler /etʀɑ̃gle/ [1]
A *vtr* **1** lit to strangle [*victime*]; **j'ai envie de les ~!** fig I feel like throttling them!; **2** (gêner) [*col, cravate*] to choke, to throttle; **3** (comprimer) to pinch in [*taille*]; **4** [*colère, émotion*] to choke [*personne*]; **5** (écraser) to cripple [*entreprise, économie*]; **6** (museler) to stifle [*groupe politique, presse*]
B **s'étrangler** *vpr* **1** (avec une corde, un foulard) to strangle oneself; **2** (ne pas pouvoir respirer) to choke; **s'~ de rage/de rire** to choke with rage/laughter; **3** [*cri*] to die in one's throat

étrangleur, -euse /etʀɑ̃glœʀ, øz/ *nm,f* strangler

être[1] /etʀ/ [7] *vi* (+ v avoir) **1** **il n'est pas jusqu'à l'Antarctique qui ne soit pollué** even the Antarctic is polluted; **il en est de Pierre comme de Paul** it is the same with Pierre as with Paul; **voilà ce qu'il en est** (présentation) this is how it is; (conclusion) that's how it is; **il n'en est rien** this isn't at all the case; **il en sera toujours ainsi** it will always be so; **il en a été de même** it was the same; **qu'en est-il de…?** what's the news on…?; **2** **je suis à vous tout de suite/dans un instant** I'll be with you right away/in a minute; **je suis à vous** I'm all yours; **être à ce qu'on fait** to have one's mind on what one is doing; **elle est toujours à se plaindre** she's always complaining; **3** **il n'est plus** euph he's no longer with us; **ce temps n'est plus** these days are gone; **fût-il duc/en cristal** even if he were a duke/it were made of crystal; **n'était leur grand âge** were it not for their advanced age; **ne serait-ce qu'en faisant** if only by doing; **ne fût-ce qu'un instant** if only for a moment; **fût-ce pour des raisons humanitaires** if only on humanitarian grounds

(Idiome) **on ne peut pas ~ et avoir été** Prov you can't stay young forever

être[2] /etʀ/ *nm* **1** (organisme vivant) being; **~ humain** human being; **les ~s animés et inanimés** animate and inanimate things; **les ~s et les choses** living things and objects; **un ~ sans défense** a defenceless^{GB} creature; **2** (personne) person; **un ~ d'exception** an exceptional person; **un ~ cher** *or* **aimé** a loved one; **un ~ sensible** a sensitive soul; **3** (nature intime) being; **de tout son ~** with one's whole being; **blessé au plus profond de son ~** hurt to the core; **4** Philos **l'~** being

étreindre /etʀɛ̃dʀ/ [55]
A *vtr* **1** to embrace, to hug [*ami*]; to clasp [*adversaire*]; **la peur l'étreignait** he/she was constrained by fear
B **s'étreindre** *vpr* [*amis, amants*] to embrace (each other)

(Idiome) **qui trop embrasse mal étreint** ≈ grasp all, lose all

être¹

Généralités

Dans la plupart des situations exprimant l'existence, l'identité, la localisation, la qualité, *être* sera traduit par *to be*:

je pense donc je suis
= I think therefore I am

j'étais chez moi
= I was at home

le soleil est une étoile
= the sun is a star

l'eau est froide
= the water is cold

Les locutions figées contenant *être* sont traitées sous l'entrée appropriée. Ainsi *être en train de/sur le point de/hors de soi* etc. sont respectivement sous **train, point, hors** etc.; *comme si de rien n'était* et *quoi qu'il en soit* sous **comme** et **quoi**. Selon le même principe, l'emploi facultatif de *étant* après *considérer comme* et *présenter comme* est traité sous ces verbes; *étant donné (que)* et *étant entendu que* sont sous **donné** et **entendu**. La plupart des autres emplois de *étant* se traduisent par *being*:

cela (ou ceci) étant
= this being so

En revanche, *c'est-à-dire, n'est-ce pas, peut-être* et *soit* sont des entrées à part entière, traitées à leur place dans le dictionnaire.

Par ailleurs, on consultera utilement les notes d'usage répertoriées ▸ **p. 1355**.

être = verbe auxiliaire

De la voix passive

être auxiliaire de la voix passive se traduit par *to be*. On notera l'emploi des divers temps en anglais.

Au présent

où sont les épreuves? elles sont révisées par le traducteur
= where are the proofs? they are being revised by the translator

votre voiture est réparée
= your car has been repaired

les portes sont repeintes chaque année
= the doors are repainted every year

Au passé

les épreuves ont été révisées en juin
= the proofs were revised in June

les épreuves ont été révisées plusieurs fois
= the proofs have been revised several times

les épreuves ont été révisées bien avant ma démission
= the proofs had been revised long before I resigned

Du passé dans les temps composés

être se traduit par *to have* si le temps est également composé en anglais – ce qui est beaucoup moins fréquent qu'en français (voir ci-dessus) – sauf avec *naître*. Dans certains contextes, on peut avoir:

elles sont tombées
= they have fallen

ils se sont enfuis
= they have escaped

elle s'était vengée
= she had taken her revenge

Les verbes traduits par une construction passive ou attributive en anglais suivent les mêmes règles au passé:

se vendre
= to be sold

tous les livres se sont vendus
= all the books have been sold

s'indigner
= to be indignant

elle se serait indignée
= she would have been indignant

Noter que la forme pronominale à valeur passive est souvent mieux rendue en anglais par une forme intransitive:

les livres se sont bien vendus
= the books have sold well

être = aller

Lorsqu'il signifie *aller*, *être* se traduit par *to be* en anglais, mais seulement s'il est directement suivi d'un complément de lieu:

je n'ai jamais été en Chine
= I've never been to China

Suivi d'un infinitif, il se rend par *to go to*:

il a été voir son ami
= he's gone to see his friend

j'ai été manger au restaurant
= I went to eat in a restaurant

Dans le sens de *s'en aller*, on notera les tournures recherchées:

ils s'en furent au théâtre
= they went to the theatre

ils s'en furent (déçus)
= they left (disappointed)

c'est

Interrogation

est-ce, ou sa variante plus familière *c'est*, se traduit généralement par *is it*:

est-ce leur voiture?
= is it their car?

c'est grave?
= is it serious?

c'est toi ou ton frère?
= is it you or your brother?

Quand ce garde sa valeur démonstrative, l'anglais précise la référence:

est-ce clair?
= is that clear?

qui est-ce?
= who is he/she?
(en montrant une personne)
= who is that?

(mais, en parlant de quelqu'un qui vous appelle au téléphone, ou à quelqu'un qui frappe à la porte):

qui est-ce?
= who is it?

est-ce n'est généralement pas traduit dans les tournures emphatiques ou permettant d'éviter l'inversion du sujet en français:

est-ce que tu parles russe?
= do you speak Russian?

☞ Voir page suivante

être[1] *suite*

est-ce leur fils, ce garçon?
= is this boy their son?

qui est-ce qui l'a fait?
= who did it?

qui est-ce que tu as rencontré?
= who did you meet?

quand est-ce que tu manges?
= when do you eat?

qu'est-ce que c'est?
= what is it?
(*ou comme vu plus haut*)
= what is this/that? (*selon que l'on montre un objet
proche ou éloigné*)

Néanmoins, la tournure emphatique est également
possible en anglais dans certaines expressions:

qu'est-ce que j'entends?
= what's this I hear?

est-ce bien ce qu'il a voulu dire?
= is that what he really meant?

Affirmation

c'est se traduit, selon les contextes, *it is* (*it's*), *this is*,
that is (*that's*):

c'est facile (*de critiquer*)
= it's easy
(*ce que tu me demandes, ce travail*)
= that's easy

c'est moi (*réponse à 'qui est-ce?'*)
= it's me
(*réponse à 'qui le fait?'*)
= I do
(*réponse à 'qui l'a fait?'*)
= I did
(*pour me désigner sur une photo, ou comme étant le
personnage dont il est question*)
= that's me (*traduit également ça, c'est moi*)

c'est eux, ce sont eux
(*qui sont là-bas, que je montre*)
= it's them
(*qui le font*)
= they do
(*qui l'ont fait*)
= they did
(*qui arrivent*)
= here they are

ce sont mes enfants (*que je vous présente*)
= these are my children
(*qui sont là-bas*)
= they are my children

c'est cela
= that's right

c'est ça! tu crois que je vais faire le travail tout seul?
= what's this! do you think I'm going to do the work all by
myself?

Lorsqu'il reprend un nom, un infinitif ou une proposition
qui le précède *c'est* se traduit seulement par *is*:

réussir, c'est une question de volonté
= succeeding is a question of will-power

sortir par ce temps, c'est de la folie
= going out in this weather is sheer madness

eux, ce sont mes amis
= they are my friends

De même, lorsque *c'est que* reprend un groupe nominal
ou une proposition, il se traduit simplement par *is that*:

le comique, c'est que ...
= the funny thing is that ...

On se reportera à l'entrée appropriée, comme **comique**,
fort etc.

Lorsque *c'est que* sert à donner une explication il se rend
généralement, et selon le temps, par *it is that*, *it was that*,
mais aussi, pour insister sur l'explication, par *it is/was
because*:

si j'ai fait ça, c'est que je ne pouvais pas faire autrement
= if I did that, it was because I couldn't do otherwise
  ce n'est pas que se traduit la plupart du temps par *it
  is/was not that* (la contraction est *it's not* plutôt que *it
  isn't*):

ce n'est pas qu'il soit bête, mais ...
= it's not that he is stupid, but ...

En corrélation avec un pronom relatif, *c'est* peut soit
garder sa valeur de présentatif (voir plus haut) et se
rendre par *that's*:

c'est le journaliste qui m'a interviewé
= that's the journalist who interviewed me

c'est le journaliste dont je te parlais
= that's the journalist I was telling you about

c'est le château où je suis né
= that's the castle where I was born

c'est ce qui me fait croire que ...
= that's what makes me think that ...

c'est justement ce que je disais
= that's exactly what I was saying

soit constituer une tournure emphatique qui se rend en
anglais selon la nuance:

c'est de la même femme que nous parlons
= we're talking about the same woman

c'était d'en parler devant elle qui me gênait
= talking about it in front of her was what made me feel
  uneasy *ou* what made me feel uneasy was talking
  about it in front of her

c'est lui/Paul qui l'a cassé
(*je le dénonce*)
= he/Paul broke it
(*je l'accuse*)
= he/Paul is the one who broke it

c'est mon frère qui l'a écrit
= it was my brother who wrote it
  ou my brother's the one who wrote it

c'est de ta sœur que je parlais, pas de toi
= it was your sister I was talking about, not you

c'est cette voiture qui m'intéresse
= this is the car (that) I am interested in

c'est lui le coupable
= he is the culprit

ce sont eux les meurtriers
= they are the murderers

c'est à suivi d'un infinitif se traduit parfois par
it is suivi de l'adjectif correspondant si cette même
transformation est possible en français:

c'est à désespérer ou c'est désespérant
= it's hopeless

mais c'est rare, et il est conseillé de se reporter à l'infinitif
en question ou à l'un des autres termes obtenus à partir
de transformations semblables.

c'est à ... de faire (ou parfois *à faire*) se traduira de deux
manières:

c'est à Pierre/lui de choisir
(*c'est son tour*)
= it's Pierre's/his turn to choose
(*c'est sa responsabilité*)
= it's up to Pierre/to him to choose

☛ Voir page suivante

être¹ *suite*

La notion de rivalité contenue dans *c'est à qui* suivi du futur doit être rendue explicite en anglais:

c'est à qui proposera le plus de réformes
= each is trying to suggest more reforms than the other

c'était à qui des deux aurait le dernier mot
= they were each trying to get in the last word

c'était à qui trouverait le plus d'erreurs dans le texte
= they were vying with each other to find the most mistakes in the text

c'est, équivalent de *ça fait* dans le compte d'une somme, se rend par *it is*:

c'est 30 euros
= it's 30 euros

c'est combien?
= how much is it?

ce sera avec valeur modale de *ce doit être* se traduit *it must be*:

ce sera mon professeur de piano
= it must be my piano teacher

....

être = verbe impersonnel

il est facile de critiquer
= it is easy to criticize

il serait nécessaire de faire
= it would be necessary to do

il est des gens bizarres
= there are some strange people

il n'est pas de jour/d'heure sans qu'il se plaigne
= not a day/an hour goes by without him complaining

On se référera par ailleurs aux notes d'usage concernant l'heure et la date; voir aussi les entrées **temps** et **fois**.

il est à suivi d'un infinitif se rend différemment, selon les nuances qu'impose le contexte, par *it must be*, *it has to be*, *it should be*, *it can be* suivis du participe passé. Pour plus de sûreté, on se reportera à l'infinitif en question, où cette construction est généralement traitée.

il est de suivi d'un substantif ou d'un groupe nominal se rend souvent par *it is* suivi directement d'un adjectif ou d'un substantif précédé d'un déterminant (article, pronom):

il est de coutume de faire ou **qu'on fasse**
= it is customary (*ou* the custom) to do

il est de notre responsabilité de faire
= it is our responsibility to do

Mais ce n'est pas une règle absolue, et il est préférable de consulter des entrées telles que **goût**, **règle**, **notoriété** etc. pour avoir des traductions adéquates. Voir également sous l'entrée **pour** des exemples supplémentaires.

....

Emplois avec *en*

en être

Certains cas sont traités sous la rubrique 'être = verbe impersonnel'; d'autres, expressions figées, le sont sous l'entrée appropriée; voir par exemple **poche** et **frais** pour *en être de sa poche/pour ses frais*. Enfin, quand l'antécédent de *en* est exprimé dans la phrase, l'expression est traitée plus bas sous *être de*:

où en étais-je?
= where was I?

je ne sais plus où j'en suis
= I'm lost

'où en es-tu de tes recherches?' 'j'en suis à mi-chemin/au début'
= 'how far have you got in your research?' 'I'm halfway through/at the beginning'

elle a eu plusieurs amants/accidents: elle en est à son quatrième
= she has had several lovers/accidents: this is her fourth

j'en suis à me demander si ...
= I'm beginning to wonder whether ...

j'en étais à ne pouvoir distinguer le vrai du faux
= I'd got to the point where I couldn't distinguish between truth and falsehood

être en

Suivie d'un substantif représentant un vêtement, l'expression peut être traduite *to be in*, mais on consultera l'entrée appropriée pour s'en assurer. Si l'on dit *to be in uniform* ou éventuellement *to be wearing a uniform* pour *être en uniforme*, l'anglais préfère généralement *to be wearing a suit* à *to be in a suit* pour *être en costume* (de même pour *robe*, *tailleur* etc.). Dans le cas d'un déguisement, on a *to be dressed up as*:

être en pirate
= to be dressed up as a pirate.

....

emplois avec *y*

j'y suis
(*je vous comprends*)
= I'm with you
(*plus général mais un peu familier*)
= I get it

je n'y suis pas (*je ne comprends pas*)
= I don't get it

vous y êtes?
(*vous comprenez?*)
= are you with me?
(*vous êtes prêt(e)?*)
= are you ready?

3 000 euros? vous n'y êtes pas!
= 3,000 euros? you're a long way out!

tu n'y es pas, c'est plus compliqué que ça
= you don't realize, it's a lot more complicated than that

Voir aussi les entrées **y**, adverbe de lieu, et **pour**.

....

être + prépositions

La plupart des cas (*être dans, sur, devant, pour, après, avec* etc.) sont traités sous la préposition correspondante. Ne sont retenus ici que les cas particuliers de *être à* et *être de*.

être à

Les cas où l'on peut faire l'ellipse de *être* ou le remplacer par un autre verbe sont traités sous la préposition **à**; ceux de *en être à* sous la rubrique 'en être', et ceux de *c'est à* sous la rubrique 'c'est'.

Les emplois de *être à* suivi d'un groupe nominal et signifiant 'tendre vers' sont généralement traités sous le substantif approprié, comme **temps**, **hausse**, **agonie** etc. dans les expressions *le temps est à la pluie*, *être à la hausse*, *être à l'agonie*. De même, quand *être à* signifie un état, c'est sous le substantif ou l'adjectif approprié, comme **bout**, **disposition**, **quai**, **vif** etc., qu'on trouvera la ou les traductions de l'expression correspondante.

☛ Voir page suivante

être¹ *suite*

Suivi d'un infinitif et signifiant *devoir être, être à* peut généralement se traduire, en observant les mêmes nuances qu'avec *devoir*, par *must be, have to be* ou *should be* suivi du participe passé du verbe anglais. Il reste conseillé de consulter l'infinitif en question, comme **plaindre, prendre** etc. On en trouve également un traitement succinct sous les rubriques 'être = verbe impersonnel' et 'c'est'.

Au sens de *appartenir à*, l'anglais utilise *to be* suivi du cas possessif quand le possesseur est un être animé ou d'un pronom possessif si celui-ci est représenté par un pronom objet. Si le cas possessif n'est pas d'usage, on utilise de préférence *to belong to*:

ce livre est à moi
= this book is mine

ce livre est à mon frère
= this book is my brother's

ces dictionnaires sont au service de traduction
= these dictionaries belong to the translation department

à qui est ce chien?
= who does this dog belong to? *ou* whose dog is this?

être de

Quand elle exprime un état ou une situation, la tournure *être de* suivie d'un substantif sans déterminant est traduite sous le substantif en question, notamment **avis**, **garde**, **service** etc. De même, certaines expressions où la présence de déterminant est variable, comme dans *être de mauvaise foi/d'une incroyable mauvaise foi* sont traitées sous l'entrée appropriée, en l'occurrence, **foi**; voir aussi **humeur, poil** etc.

La construction *être d'un/d'une* suivie d'un adjectif substantivé ou d'un substantif exprimant une qualité ou un défaut peut généralement être rendue par *to be so* suivi de l'adjectif correspondant en anglais, si le substantif est seul:

elle est d'un ridicule!
= she's so ridiculous!

elle est d'une prétention!
= she's so pretentious!

Si le substantif est qualifié, l'adjectif devient généralement un adverbe en anglais:

il est d'une exquise courtoisie
= he's exquisitely courteous

il est d'une incompétence rare
= he's exceptionally incompetent

Mais il n'est pas inutile de vérifier les traductions des adjectifs et substantifs à leur entrée avant d'adopter cette construction.

Au sens de *participer à, faire partie de*, la tournure *être de* se traduit de façon très variable (voir aussi **partie**):

il est des nôtres *(il vient avec nous)*
= he's with us
(il est de notre clan, agit et pense comme nous)
= he's one of us

serez-vous des nôtres?
= will you be (coming) with us?

êtes-vous des nôtres?
= are you coming with us? (ici, *coming* est nécessaire, pour éviter l'ambiguïté de *are you with us?*)

les journalistes ne sont pas du voyage
= the journalists aren't coming on the trip

les journalistes ne seront pas du voyage
= the journalists won't be coming on the trip

ils ont organisé une expédition mais je n'en étais pas
= they organized an expedition but I wasn't part of it

il y avait un congrès mais il n'en était pas
= there was a congress but he didn't take part

Suivi d'un infinitif et précédé de noms abstraits avec l'article défini (*l'idéal*, etc.) ou de superlatifs (*le plus simple*), *être de* se traduit généralement par *to be* suivi de l'infinitif avec *to*:

le plus simple serait de tout recommencer
= the simplest thing to do would be to start all over again

étreinte /etʀɛt/ *nf* **1)** (affectueuse) embrace; (violente) grip; **2)** fig grip

(Composé) ~ **fatale** Ordinat deadly embrace

étrenner /etʀene/ **1)** *vtr* to wear [sth] for the first time [*vêtement*]; to use [sth] for the first time [*objet, voiture*]

étrennes /etʀɛn/ *nfpl* (cadeau) gift; (argent) money

étrier /etʀije/ *nm* (de cavalier) stirrup; (de ski) front binding

(Idiomes) **boire le coup de l'~**° to have one for the road°; **mettre à qn le pied à l'~** to get sb started

étriller /etʀije/ **1)** *vtr* **1)** (nettoyer) to curry; **2)** (critiquer) to tear to pieces

étriper /etʀipe/ **1)**
A *vtr* to gut [*animal*]
B **s'étriper**° *vpr* to murder each other

étriqué, ~e /etʀike/ *adj* [*veste*] skimpy; [*vie*] restricted

étroit, ~e /etʀwa, at/
A *adj* **1)** (pas large) narrow; **2)** (restreint) [*cercle d'amis, conception*] narrow; **avoir l'esprit ~** to be narrow-minded; **3)** (intime) [*rapport, liaison*] close (*épith*); **4)** (rigoureux) **sous ~e surveillance** (de la police) under close surveillance
B **à l'étroit** *loc adv* **nous sommes un peu à l'~** we're a bit cramped

étroitement /etʀwatmã/ *adv* [*surveiller*] closely

étroitesse /etʀwates/ *nf* lit, fig narrowness; **~ d'esprit** narrow-mindedness

étron /etʀɔ̃/ *nm* excreta (*pl*), turd°

étrusque /etʀysk/ *adj, nm* Etruscan

étude /etyd/
A *nf* **1)** (recherche) study (**sur** on); (enquête) survey (**sur** of); ~ **réalisée par** study carried out by; **2)** (observation) study (**de** of); **3)** (prise en considération) (**mise à l'**)~ consideration; **à l'~** under consideration; **4)** (apprentissage) study; **5)** (d'avoué, de notaire) (bureau) office; (charge) practice; **6)** Mus étude; **7)** Art study; **8)** Scol (salle) study room GB, study hall US; (période) study period
B **études** *nfpl* Scol, Univ studies; **faire des ~s** to be a student; **faire** *or* **poursuivre des ~s de médecine** to study medicine; **je n'ai pas fait d'~s (supérieures)** I didn't go to university *ou* college; **~s primaires** primary education **¢**

(Composés) ~ **de cas** case study; ~ **de marché** market research **¢**

étudiant, ~e /etydjã, ãt/ *adj, nm,f* student

étudié, ~e /etydje/ *adj* **1)** [*discours*] carefully prepared; **2)** [*démarche*] studied

étudier /etydje/ **2)**
A *vtr* **1)** (se pencher sur) to examine [*dossier, situation*]; to study [*carte, plan*]; **2)** (prendre en considération) to consider [*création*]; **3)** (faire une recherche sur) to study; [*science*] to deal with [*problème*]; **4)** (apprendre) to study [*langue*]; to learn [*leçon*]; **5)** (observer) to study [*personne, réaction*]; **6)** (concevoir) to design [*nouveau moteur*]
B *vi* **1)** (faire des études) to be a student; **2)** (apprendre) to be studying

étui /etɥi/ *nm* case; ~ **à revolver** holster

étuve /etyv/ *nf* **1)** (bain de vapeur) steam room; **2)** (en microbiologie) incubator

étuvée /etyve/ **à l'~** braised

étymologie /etimɔlɔʒi/ *nf* etymology

étymologique /etimɔlɔʒik/ *adj* etymological

eucharistie /økaʀisti/ *nf* (sacrifice) Eucharist; (pain, vin) Sacrament

eugénique /øʒenik/
A *adj* eugenic
B *nf* eugenics (+ *v sg*)

eunuque /ønyk/ *nm* eunuch

euphémisme /øfemism/ *nm* euphemism

euphorie /øfɔʀi/ *nf* euphoria

euphorique /øfɔʀik/ *adj* [*personne*] euphoric; [*marché*] bullish

euphorisant, **~e** /øfɔʀizɑ̃, ɑ̃t/
A *adj* [*boisson*] stimulating; [*qualité, atmosphère*] uplifting; [*substance, drogue*] euphoriant
B *nm* Méd stimulant

eurafricain, **~e** /øʀafʀikɛ̃, ɛn/ *adj* [*personne*] Eurafrican; [*entreprise*] Euro-African

eurasien, **-ienne** /øʀazjɛ̃, ɛn/ *adj* Eurasian

Euratom /øʀatɔm/ *nf* (*abbr* ▸ **European atomic energy commission**) Euratom

EURL /œyɛʀɛl/ *nf: abbr* ▸ **entreprise**

euro /øʀo/ ▸ p. 34 *nm* euro

eurochèque /øʀoʃɛk/ *nm* Eurocheque

euroconnecteur /øʀokɔnɛktœʀ/ *nm* (femelle) scart socket; (mâle) scart plug

eurodéputé, **~e** /øʀodepyte/ *nm,f* Euro-MP

euromarché /øʀomaʀʃe/ *nm* Euromarket

Europe /øʀɔp/ ▸ p. 230 *nprf* Europe; **l'~ communautaire** the European community; **l'~ de l'espace** the joint European space venture; **faire l'~** to build Europe

européaniser /øʀopeanize/ [1]
A *vtr* to europeanize [*pays*]; **~ un débat** to broaden a debate to a European level
B **s'européaniser** *vpr* [*pays*] to become europeanized; [*économie*] to become adapted to a European framework

européen, **-éenne** /øʀopeɛ̃, ɛn/ *adj* European

Européen, **-éenne** /øʀopeɛ̃, ɛn/ *nm,f* [1] Géog (habitant) European; [2] Pol (partisan) pro-European

Eurotunnel /øʀotynɛl/ *nm* Eurotunnel

euthanasie /øtanazi/ *nf* euthanasia

eux /ø/ *pron pers* [1] (sujet) they; **~ seuls ont le droit de parler** they alone have the right to speak; **ce sont ~, je les reconnais** it's them, I recognize them; **je sais que ce n'est pas ~ qui ont fait ça** I know they weren't the ones who did it; [2] (dans une comparaison) them; [3] (objet) **les inviter, ~, quelle idée!** invite THEM, what an idea!; **~, il faut les enfermer** they should be locked up; [4] (après une préposition) them; **à cause d'~** because of them; **à ~, je peux dire la vérité** I can tell THEM the truth; **ce sont des amis à ~** they're friends of theirs; **ils n'ont pas encore de voiture à ~** they don't have their own car yet; **c'est à ~** (appartenance) it's theirs, it belongs to them; **c'est à ~ de faire** (leur tour) it's their turn to do; (leur responsabilité) it's up to them to do

eux-mêmes /ømɛm/ *pron pers* themselves; **les experts ~ reconnaissent que...** even the experts admit that...; **ils me l'ont dit d'~** they volunteered the information, they told me themselves

évacuateur, **-trice** /evakɥatœʀ, tʀis/
A *adj* [*canal*] discharge
B *nm* sluice

évacuation /evakɥasjɔ̃/ *nf* [1] (de liquide) discharge; **il y a un problème d'~ de l'eau** the water doesn't drain away; [2] (de lieu, personnes) evacuation

(Composé) **~ sanitaire** medical evacuation

évacué, **~e** /evakɥe/ *nm,f* evacuee

évacuer /evakɥe/ [1] *vtr* [1] to evacuate [*personne*]; to evacuate [*lieu*]; to drain off [*eaux usées*]; Méd to evacuate [*excréments*]; [2] fig to shrug off [*problème*]

évadé, **~e** /evade/ *nm,f* escapee

évader: s'évader /evade/ [1] *vpr* [1] (s'enfuir) to escape (de from); [2] fig to get away (de from)

évaluable /evalɥabl/ *adj* assessable

évaluation /evalɥasjɔ̃/ *nf* [1] (de collection, maison) valuation; [2] (de coûts, dégâts) (action) assessment; (résultat) estimate, appraisal US; [3] (d'employé) appraisal

évaluer /evalɥe/ [1] *vtr* [1] (approximativement) to estimate [*grandeur, durée*] (à at); to assess [*risques, dégâts, coût*];

[2] (déterminer la valeur de) to value, to appraise US [*meuble, patrimoine*]; [3] (juger) to assess [*employé, élève*]

évangéliser /evɑ̃ʒelize/ [1] *vtr* evangelize

Évangile /evɑ̃ʒil/ *nm* (message, livre) Gospel (**selon** according to); **parole d'~** fig gospel truth

évanouir: s'évanouir /evanwiʀ/ [3] *vpr* [1] lit to faint (**de** with); [2] fig [*sentiment*] to fade

évanouissement /evanwismɑ̃/ *nm* [1] Méd blackout; [2] fig fading

évaporation /evapɔʀasjɔ̃/ *nf* evaporation

évaporé, **~e** /evapɔʀe/
A *adj* pej [*personne*] giddy
B *nm,f* pej birdbrain○ péj

évaporer: s'évaporer /evapɔʀe/ [1] *vpr* to evaporate; ○fig to vanish

évaser /evaze/ [1]
A *vtr* to widen [sth] at the mouth [*conduit, trou*]; to flare [*vêtement*]
B **s'évaser** *vpr* [*conduit*] to open out; [*jupe*] to be flared

évasif, **-ive** /evazif, iv/ *adj* evasive

évasion /evazjɔ̃/ *nf* lit, fig escape

(Composés) **~ des capitaux** flight of capital; **~ fiscale** tax avoidance

Ève /ɛv/ *nprf* Eve; **en tenue d'~** in one's birthday suit hum

(Idiome) **elle ne le connaît ni d'~ ni d'Adam** she doesn't know him from Adam

évêché /eveʃe/ *nm* [1] (territoire) diocese; [2] (résidence) bishop's palace

éveil /evɛj/ *nm* (de nature, dormeur, d'intelligence) awakening; (d'amour) dawning

éveiller /eveje/ [1]
A *vtr* [1] to arouse [*intérêt, curiosité, méfiance*]; to stimulate [*intelligence, imagination*]; to awaken [*conscience, goût*]; **sans ~ l'attention** without attracting attention; **un enfant éveillé** a bright child; [2] (du sommeil) to wake [*dormeur*]
B **s'éveiller** *vpr* [1] lit to awake; [2] fig [*imagination, intelligence*] to start to develop

événement /evenmɑ̃/ *nm* event; **être dépassé par les ~s** to be overwhelmed; **riche en ~s** eventful

événementiel, **-ielle** /evenmɑ̃sjɛl/ *adj* factual

éventail /evɑ̃taj/ *nm* [1] (objet) fan; [2] (série) range

(Idiome) **avoir les doigts de pied en ~**○ to laze about

éventaire /evɑ̃tɛʀ/ *nm* (devanture) stall; (de marchand ambulant) tray

éventer /evɑ̃te/ [1]
A *vtr* [1] (révéler) to give away [*secret*]; [2] (avec un éventail) to fan
B **s'éventer** *vpr* [1] (pour se rafraîchir) to fan oneself; [2] [*parfum, café*] to go stale; [*vin*] to pass its best; [*bière, limonade*] to go flat

éventré, **~e** /evɑ̃tʀe/ *adj* [1] [*animal*] gutted; [2] fig [*fauteuil*] burst

éventrer /evɑ̃tʀe/ [1]
A *vtr* [1] (blesser) [*personne*] to disembowel; [*taureau*] to gore; [2] (ouvrir) to rip [sth] open [*matelas, sac*]; to burst [sth] open [*malle*]; to force [sth] open [*coffre*]; to shatter [*mur*]
B **s'éventrer** *vpr* [1] (se blesser) [*personne*] (dans un accident) to cut one's stomach open; [2] (s'ouvrir) [*sac*] to burst open

éventreur /evɑ̃tʀœʀ/ *nm* **Jack l'~** Jack the Ripper

éventualité /evɑ̃tɥalite/ *nf* [1] (événement possible) eventuality; [2] (hypothèse) possibility; **dans l'~ de** in the event of

éventuel, **-elle** /evɑ̃tɥɛl/ *adj* [1] (possible) possible; [2] Jur conditional

éventuellement /evɑ̃tɥɛlmɑ̃/ *adv* [1] (peut-être) possibly; [2] (si nécessaire) if necessary

évêque /evɛk/ ▸ p. 590 *nm* bishop (**de** of)

évertuer: s'évertuer /evɛʀtɥe/ [1] *vpr* to try one's best (**à faire** to do), to strive (**à faire** to do)

éviction /eviksjɔ̃/ *nf* [1] (expulsion) ousting (**de** from); [2] Jur (dépossession) eviction

évidemment /evidamɑ̃/ *adv* of course

évidence /evidɑ̃s/
A *nf* (fait d'être évident) obviousness; (vérité évidente) obvious fact; **se rendre à l'~** to face the facts; **de toute ~, à l'~** obviously

B en **évidence** *loc* **laisser/mettre** qch en ~ lit (pour être vu) to leave/put sth in an obvious or a prominent place; **mettre en ~** fig to highlight [*faiblesse, utilité*]

évident, **~e** /evidɑ̃, ɑ̃t/ *adj* **1** gén obvious; [*progrès*] marked (*épith*); [*preuves*] clear (*épith*); **2** ○**ce n'est pas** ~○ (ce n'est pas si sûr) not necessarily; (ce n'est pas si facile) it's not so easy

évider /evide/ [1] *vtr* (creuser) to hollow out; Culin to scoop out

évier /evje/ *nm* sink

évincer /evɛ̃se/ [12] *vtr* (écarter) to oust [*rival*]

éviter /evite/ [1] *vtr* **1** (esquiver) to avoid [*obstacle, piéton*]; to dodge [*balle, coup*]; **2** (se soustraire à) to avoid [*crise, erreur*]; **3** (s'abstenir de) ~ qch/de faire to avoid sth/doing; **4** (épargner) ~ qch à qn to save sb sth; **je voulais t'~ une dépense** I wanted to spare you the expense; ~ **à qn de faire** to save sb (from) doing

évocateur, **-trice** /evɔkatœʀ, tʀis/ *adj* **1** (suggestif) evocative; **2** (significatif) significant

évocation /evɔkasjɔ̃/ *nf* **1** (remémoration) (action) evocation; (résultat) reminiscence; **2** (mention) mention (**de** of)

évolué, **~e** /evɔlɥe/ *adj* **1** ○(éclairé) **il n'est pas très ~!** he's not very bright!; **2** (avancé) [*pays, peuple*] civilized; **3** Biol [*espèces*] evolved

évoluer /evɔlɥe/ [1] *vi* **1** (progresser) [*groupe, individu, goûts*] to evolve, to change; [*idée*] to evolve; [*technique, science*] to advance, to evolve; [*situation*] to develop; **faire ~ la situation** to bring about some change in the situation; **2** (se déplacer gracieusement) [*danseurs*] to glide; [*avion*] to wheel

évolutif, **-ive** /evɔlytif, iv/ *adj* gén, Méd progressive; **une situation évolutive** a changing situation

évolution /evɔlysjɔ̃/ *nf* **1** Biol evolution; **2** (progrès) evolution (**de** of); (de langue, situation) development (**de** of); (de la science) advancement (**de** of); (d'enquête, étude) progress (**de** of); (de maladie) progression (**de** of); ~ **démographique** demographical change; ~ **de carrière** career advancement; **être en pleine ~** to be undergoing rapid change; **3** (changement) change

évolutionniste /evɔlysjɔnist/
A *adj* evolutionary
B *nmf* evolutionist

évoquer /evɔke/ [1] *vtr* **1** (se remémorer) [*personne*] to recall [*passé, amis, souvenirs*]; **2** (mentionner) to mention, to bring up [*problème, question*]; **3** (faire penser à) [*objet, son, image*] to bring back [*souvenir*]; to conjure up [*image*]; to be reminiscent of [*printemps, enfance*]; **4** (raconter) [*auteur, musicien*] to evoke [*lieu, moment*]; **5** (par magie) to invoke

ex ○/eks/
A ○*nmf inv* (ancien conjoint, concubin, compagnon) ex; (ancien membre) ex-member
B *nm* **1** (written *abbr* = **exemple**) eg; **2** (written *abbr* = **exemplaire**) copy; **25 ~** 25 copies

ex- /eks/ *préf* ~**actrice/champion** former actress/champion

exacerbation /ɛgzasɛʀbasjɔ̃/ *nf* exacerbation

exacerber /ɛgzasɛʀbe/ [1] *vtr* to exacerbate

exact, **~e** /ɛgza(kt), akt/ *adj* **1** (juste) correct; **2** (précis) exact; **pour être plus ~** to be more precise; **3** (ponctuel) punctual

exactement /ɛgzaktəmɑ̃/ *adv* gén exactly

exaction /ɛgzaksjɔ̃/
A *nf* exaction
B **exactions** *nfpl* gén barbaric acts, acts of violence; (en temps de guerre) atrocities

exactitude /ɛgzaktityd/ *nf* **1** (justesse) correctness; (de prévision) accuracy; **2** (précision) (de définition, description, dimension) accuracy; (de reproduction) exactness; (de montre) accuracy; **avec ~** [*mesurer, raconter*] accurately; **3** (ponctualité) punctuality; ▸ **politesse**

ex æquo /ɛgzeko/
A *adj inv* (tous contextes) equally placed
B *adv* **ils sont premiers/deuxièmes ~** Sport they've tied for first/second place

exagération /ɛgzaʒeʀasjɔ̃/ *nf* exaggeration

exagéré, **~e** /ɛgzaʒeʀe/ *adj* **1** (outré) exaggerated; **2** (excessif) excessive; **d'une sensibilité ~e** oversensitive; **c'est un peu ~!** that's a bit much○!

exagérément /ɛgzaʒeʀemɑ̃/ *adv* excessively

exagérer /ɛgzaʒeʀe/ [14]
A *vtr* to exaggerate; **sans ~** without exaggeration
B *vi* to go too far, to push one's luck
C **s'exagérer** *vpr* [*personne*] to overestimate

exaltant, **~e** /ɛgzaltɑ̃, ɑ̃t/ *adj* [*aventure, lecture*] thrilling; [*projet, travail, musique*] inspiring

exaltation /ɛgzaltasjɔ̃/ *nf* **1** (vive excitation) elation; **parler avec ~** to speak elatedly; **2** (intensification) (d'imagination) stimulation; (de différence) heightening; **3** (glorification) glorification

exalté, **~e** /ɛgzalte/
A *pp* ▸ **exalter**
B *pp adj* (surexcité) [*discours, esprit*] impassioned
C *nm,f* fanatic

exalter /ɛgzalte/ [1]
A *vtr* **1** (transporter) to elate, to thrill [*personne, foule*]; **2** (intensifier) to heighten [*qualité*]; **3** (glorifier) liter to glorify
B **s'exalter** *vpr* (s'enthousiasmer) to enthuse

examen /ɛgzamɛ̃/ *nm* **1** Scol, Univ examination, exam○; **passer un ~** to take or to sit (for) GB an exam○; ~ **de rattrapage** retake, resit GB; **2** Méd examination; **passer des ~s** to have some tests done; **3** (de cas, dossier) examination; (de question) consideration; (de situation) gén examination; (avant un changement) review; **à l'~ on** examination; **être en cours d'~** [*dossier*] to be under review; [*question*] to be under consideration; [*cas*] to be under investigation; **4** (inspection) (de bleu) inspection; (d'objet) examination

(Composés) ~ **blanc** mock (exam○); ~ **de conscience** gén self-examination; ~ **spécial d'entrée à l'université**, **ESEU** university entrance exam for students not having the baccalaureate

examinateur, **-trice** /ɛgzaminatœʀ, tʀis/ *nm,f* examiner

examiner /ɛgzamine/ [1] *vtr* **1** (étudier) gén to examine; (pour faire des changements) to review [*situation*]; ~ qch de près to have a close look at sth; ~ qn de la tête aux pieds to look sb up and down; **2** (observer) to examine [*marchandise, visage*]; ~ **le ciel** to scan the sky; **3** Méd to examine [*malade, blessure*]

exaspération /ɛgzaspeʀasjɔ̃/ *nf* **1** (d'humeur) exasperation; **2** (de besoin, douleur) intensification

exaspérer /ɛgzaspeʀe/ [14] *vtr* **1** (irriter) to exasperate, to infuriate; **2** (exacerber) to exacerbate

exaucer /ɛgzose/ [12] *vtr* to grant [*prière, requête*]

excavation /ɛkskavasjɔ̃/ *nf* excavation

excavatrice /ɛkskavatʀis/ *nf* Tech excavator

excédant, **~e** /ɛksedɑ̃, ɑ̃t/ *adj* exasperating, infuriating

excédent /ɛksedɑ̃/ *nm* surplus (**sur** over); **l'~ des dépenses sur les recettes** excess of expenditure over receipts; ~ **de bagages** excess baggage

excédentaire /ɛksedɑ̃tɛʀ/ *adj* surplus (*épith*)

excéder /ɛksede/ [14] *vtr* **1** (dépasser) to exceed [*quantité, durée*] (**de** by); **2** (agacer) to infuriate

excellence /ɛksɛlɑ̃s/ *nf* excellence

Excellence /ɛksɛlɑ̃s/ *nf* **Son ~, l'ambassadeur de France** His/Her Excellency, the French Ambassador

excellent, **~e** /ɛksɛlɑ̃, ɑ̃t/ *adj* excellent; **~!** great○!

exceller /ɛksele/ [1] *vi* to excel (**dans** in)

excentré, **~e** /ɛksɑ̃tʀe/ *adj* **1** (loin du centre-ville) [*quartier*] outlying (*épith*); **l'école est (très) ~e** the school is (quite) some distance from the town centre^{GB}; **2** Tech **être ~** [*axe*] to be off-centre^{GB}

excentricité /ɛksɑ̃tʀisite/ *nf* (de personne, comportement) eccentricity

excentrique /ɛksɑ̃tʀik/
A *adj* **1** [*personne, idée*] eccentric; **2** [*quartier*] outlying; **3** [*courbe*] eccentric
B *nmf* eccentric

excepté, **~e** /ɛksɛpte/
A *pp* ▸ **excepter**
B *pp adj* (sauf) except
C *prép* (sauf) except; ~ **quand** except when

excepter /ɛksɛpte/ [1] *vtr* **si l'on excepte** except for, apart from

exception /ɛksɛpsjɔ̃/ *nf* exception; **faire une ~** to make an exception; **faire ~** to be an exception; ~ **à la règle**

exception to the rule; **à l'~ de**, **~ faite de** except for, with the exception of; **à quelques ~s près** with a few exceptions; **d'~** [*personne, destin*] exceptional; [*loi, tribunal*] emergency; **c'est l'~ qui confirme la règle** it's the exception that proves the rule

(Composé) **~ d'euthanasie** Jur legal provision for performing euthanasia in terminal cases

exceptionnel, -elle /ɛksɛpsjɔnɛl/ adj [1] [*congé, subvention*] exceptional; [*autorisation*] special (*épith*); [*prix*] bargain (*épith*); [*réunion*] extraordinary (*épith*); **à titre ~** exceptionally; [2] [*circonstances, personne*] exceptional

exceptionnellement /ɛksɛpsjɔnɛlmɑ̃/ adv exceptionally; **~, le magasin restera ouvert** today only the shop GB ou store US will stay open

excès /ɛksɛ/ nm inv [1] (surplus) excess; **ôtez l'~ de colle** remove the excess glue; **en ~** excess (*épith*); [2] (abus) excess; **commettre des ~** to go too far; **faire des ~ de boisson** to drink excessively; **à l'~** excessively; [3] (extrême) **tomber dans l'~/dans l'~ inverse** to go too far/to the opposite extreme; **~ de confiance** overconfidence; **~ de prudence** excessive caution

(Composé) **~ de vitesse** Jur speeding; **faire un ~ de vitesse** to break the speed limit

excessif, -ive /ɛksesif, iv/ adj [1] (qui dépasse la mesure) excessive; **être d'un optimisme ~** to be overoptimistic; **sans enthousiasme ~** without too much enthusiasm; [2] (qui manque de modération) extreme

excessivement /ɛksesivmɑ̃/ adv (trop) excessively

excipient /ɛksipjɑ̃/ nm excipient

exciser /ɛksize/ [1] vtr [1] Méd to excise; [2] (retirer le clitoris) to circumcise

excision /ɛksizjɔ̃/ nf [1] Méd excision; [2] (du clitoris) female circumcision

excitable /ɛksitabl/ adj [1] (irritable) edgy; [2] [*muscle, organe*] excitable

excitant, ~e /ɛksitɑ̃, ɑ̃t/
A adj [1] (stimulant) [*substance*] stimulating (*épith*); [2] (palpitant) [*perspective, époque*] exciting; [*roman, aventure*] thrilling
B nm (substance) stimulant

excitation /ɛksitasjɔ̃/ nf [1] (enthousiasme) excitement; [2] (sexuelle) arousal; (stimulation) stimulation

excité, ~e /ɛksite/
A adj [1] (déchaîné) [*foule, presse*] frenzied (*épith*), in a frenzy (*jamais épith*); [*atmosphère*] frenzied; [2] (enthousiaste) [*personne*] thrilled; [3] (émoustillé) (sexuellement) [*personne, sens*] aroused; (par l'alcool) elated
B nm,f pej [1] (fauteur de troubles) rowdy; [2] (fanatique) fanatic; [3] (nerveux) neurotic

(Idiome) **être ~ comme une puce**○ to be like a cat on a hot tin roof

exciter /ɛksite/ [1]
A vtr [1] (attiser) to stir up [*colère*]; to kindle [*désir*]; [2] (enthousiasmer) to thrill; [3] (émoustiller) to arouse [*personne*]; [4] (énerver) [*personne*] to tease [*animal*]; to get [sb] excited [*enfant*]; [*café*] to make [sb] nervy [*personne*]; [*alcool*] to excite [*personne*]; [5] (stimuler) to stimulate [*palais*]; to excite [*nerf, tissu*]
B s'exciter vpr (s'enthousiasmer) to get excited

exclamatif, -ive /ɛksklamatif, iv/ adj exclamatory

exclamation /ɛksklamasjɔ̃/ nf cry, exclamation

exclamer: s'exclamer /ɛksklame/ [1] vpr (s'écrier) to exclaim, to cry (**de** with); (avec admiration) **s'~ sur** to exclaim over

exclu, ~e /ɛkskly/
A pp ▸ exclure
B pp adj (non admis) [*personne*] excluded (**de** from); [*hypothèse, idée*] ruled out; **c'est tout à fait ~!** it's absolutely out of the question!; **il n'est pas ~ que** it's not impossible that; **se sentir ~** to feel left out

exclure /ɛksklyʀ/ [78] vtr [1] (ne pas inclure) to exclude [*personne*] (**de** from); to rule out [*hypothèse, possibilité*]; **~ que qn fasse** to prohibit sb from doing; [2] (rejeter) to expel [*membre de groupe*] (**de** from); to oust [*dirigeant, chef*]; to send [sb] down [*étudiant*]

exclusif, -ive /ɛksklyzif, iv/ adj [1] Presse [*document*] exclusive; [2] Comm [*concessionnaire*] sole; [*produit*] exclusive; [3] (d'un seul) exclusive

exclusion /ɛksklyzjɔ̃/
A nf [1] (non-admission) exclusion (**de** from); [2] (expulsion) (défini-

tive) expulsion; (temporaire) suspension; [3] (clause contractuelle) exclusion

B à l'exclusion de loc prép with the exception of

exclusivement /ɛksklyzivmɑ̃/ adv exclusively

exclusivité /ɛksklyzivite/ nf [1] (droits) Comm, Cin, Presse exclusive rights (*pl*); **l'~ d'une marque** the exclusive rights to a brand; **en ~** [*publier*] exclusively; [*produit*] exclusive; [2] (objet, produit) **c'est une ~ de notre entreprise** it's exclusive to our company

excommunier /ɛkskɔmynje/ [2] vtr to excommunicate

excrément /ɛkskʀemɑ̃/ nm excrement ¢

excrétion /ɛkskʀesjɔ̃/ nf (évacuation) excretion

excroissance /ɛkskʀwasɑ̃s/ nf [1] Méd growth; [2] Bot outgrowth

excursion /ɛkskyʀsjɔ̃/ nf gén excursion, trip

excusable /ɛkskyzabl/ adj excusable, forgivable

excuse /ɛkskyz/ nf [1] (justification) excuse (**à qch** for sth); **ce n'est pas une ~ pour faire** it's no excuse for doing; **en guise d'~** by way of an excuse; [2] (regret) apology; **faire or présenter des ~s à qn** to offer one's apologies to sb; **exiger des ~s (de la part de qn)** to demand an apology from sb; **mille ~s** I'm terribly sorry

excuser /ɛkskyze/ [1]
A vtr [1] (pardonner) to forgive [*erreur, absence*]; to pardon [*faute*]; **excusez-moi** I'm sorry; **excusez mon retard** excuse me for being late; **vous êtes tout excusé** it's all right; [2] (justifier) to excuse; **rien n'excuse la cruauté** there is no excuse for cruelty; [3] (dispenser) to excuse [*personne*]
B s'excuser vpr to apologize (**auprès de** to; **de** for; **d'avoir fait** for doing); **je m'excuse de vous déranger** I'm sorry to disturb you

exécrable /ɛgzekʀabl/ adj (épouvantable) dreadful

exécrer /ɛgzekʀe/ [14] vtr fml to loathe

exécutable /ɛgzekytabl/ adj [*projet*] practicable; [*tâche*] manageable

exécutant, ~e /ɛgzekytɑ̃, ɑ̃t/ nm,f [1] Mus performer; **orchestre de 60 ~s** 60-piece orchestra; [2] (agent) **il dit n'avoir été qu'un ~** he claims he was only obeying orders

exécuter /ɛgzekyte/ [1]
A vtr [1] (faire) to carry out [*tâche, travaux*]; to do [*exercice*]; **faire ~ des travaux** to have work done; [2] (appliquer) to carry out [*ordre, dessein, menace*]; to fulfil^GB [*promesse*]; Comm to fill [*commande*]; Jur to fulfil^GB [*contrat*]; to enforce [*loi, jugement*]; [3] (tuer) to execute [*condamné, otage*]; [4] Mus to perform, to play [*morceau*]; [5] Ordinat to run [*programme*]; to execute [*instruction*]
B s'exécuter vpr (obéir) to comply

exécutif, -ive /ɛgzekytif, ive/
A adj Pol executive
B nm executive

exécution /ɛgzekysjɔ̃/ nf [1] (application) (d'ordre) execution; (de menace) carrying out ¢; (de décision, plan) implementation; Jur (de loi, jugement) enforcement; (d'obligation, de contrat) fulfilment^GB; **mettre à ~** to carry out [*menace*]; to implement [*programme*]; [2] (réalisation) (de travaux) execution; (de projet) implementation; Art (de tableau) painting ¢, execution; Mus (de morceau) performance, execution; **veiller à la bonne ~ d'une tâche** to see that a job is done well; **d'~ facile** [*mouvement*] easy to do; [*morceau*] easy to play; [3] (mise à mort) execution; [4] Ordinat execution

exemplaire /ɛgzɑ̃plɛʀ/
A adj [1] (modèle) [*conduite*] exemplary; [*élève*] model (*épith*); [*atterrissage*] textbook (*épith*); **de façon ~** in exemplary fashion; **la gestion de l'entreprise est ~** the firm is a model of good management; [2] (pour l'exemple) [*peine*] exemplary sout
B nm [1] (livre, document) copy; **en deux/trois ~s** in duplicate/triplicate; [2] (spécimen) specimen, example

exemplarité /ɛgzɑ̃plaʀite/ nf (de peine) deterrent nature (**de** of)

exemple /ɛgzɑ̃pl/
A nm [1] (cas) example; **prenez l'~ du Japon** take the case of Japan, take Japan for example; **sans ~** [*situation*] unprecedented; [2] (leçon) warning (**pour** to); **on a voulu faire de lui un ~** the intention was to make an example of him; [3] (image) example (**de** of); **donner l'~ du courage à qn** to set sb an example of courage; **prendre ~ sur qn, prendre qn en ~** to take sb as a model; [4] (idéal) model (**de** of); **être**

l'∼ **de la gentillesse** to be a model of kindness; **donner** or **citer qn en** ∼ to hold sb up as an example

B par exemple loc adv 1⟩ (pour illustrer) for example; 2⟩ (marquant l'étonnement) **(ça) par** ∼**!** how amazing!; 3⟩ (marquant l'indignation) **ça par** ∼**!** well, honestly!

exemplifier /ɛgzɑ̃plifje/ [2] vtr to exemplify

exempt, ∼e /ɛgzɑ̃, ɑ̃t/ adj 1⟩ (dispensé) exempt (**de** from); ∼ **d'impôt** tax-free; ∼ **de droits de douane** duty-free; 2⟩ (dépourvu) free (**de** from); 3⟩ (à l'abri) immune (**de** to)

exempter /ɛgzɑ̃te/ [1] vtr 1⟩ (dispenser) to exempt (**de** from; **de faire** from doing); 2⟩ (mettre à l'abri) to preserve (**de** from)

exemption /ɛgzɑ̃psjɔ̃/ nf exemption

exercé, ∼e /ɛgzɛʀse/ adj [main] deft, skilled; [oreille] trained; [œil] expert, practised[GB]; [personne] experienced

exercer /ɛgzɛʀse/ [12]

A vtr 1⟩ (appliquer) to exercise [droit, responsabilité] (**sur** over); to exert [pression, autorité] (**sur** on); to have [effet] (**sur** on); 2⟩ (pratiquer) to exercise [profession]; to practise[GB] [art]; ∼ **un métier** to have a job; 3⟩ (entraîner) to train, to exercise [corps, esprit]; (donner de l'exercice à) to exercise [corps, muscle]

B vi (travailler) [travailleur, employé] to work; [médecin, juriste, architecte] to practise[GB]

C s'exercer vpr 1⟩ (s'entraîner) [athlète] to train; [musicien] to practise[GB]; **s'∼ à la plongée** to practise[GB] diving; **s'∼ au calme** to make an effort to stay calm; 2⟩ (agir) [influence, force] to be exerted (**sur** on)

exercice /ɛgzɛʀsis/ nm 1⟩ (d'entraînement) exercise; **faire un** ∼ to do an exercise; ∼ **de prononciation** pronunciation drill; 2⟩ (activité physique) exercise; **faire de l'**∼ to get some exercise; 3⟩ (activité professionnelle) **avoir dix ans d'**∼ to have been working for ten years; **dans l'**∼ **de ses fonctions** [soldat, policier] while on duty; [travailleur] while at work; **être en** ∼ [fonctionnaire] to be in office; [médecin] to be in practice; **en** ∼ [ministre, président] incumbent; **entrer en** ∼ to take up one's duties; 4⟩ (usage) exercise (**de** of); 5⟩ Mil (instruction) drill

(Composés) ∼ **d'application** practical exercise; ∼ **d'évacuation** gén emergency evacuation exercise; (en cas d'incendie) fire drill; ∼ **de tir** shooting practice ⊄ GB, target practice ⊄; ∼**s structuraux** Ling structure drills

exergue /ɛgzɛʀg/ nm 1⟩ (sur un ouvrage) epigraph; 2⟩ (sur une médaille, une pièce) inscription

exhaler /ɛgzale/ [1] fml

A vtr (dégager) to exhale [parfum]; to give off [relent]

B s'exhaler vpr [parfum] to waft (**de** from)

exhausser /ɛgzose/ [1] vtr to raise

exhaustif, -ive /ɛgzostif, iv/ adj exhaustive

exhiber /ɛgzibe/ [1]

A vtr to flaunt [toilettes, richesse, objet]; to show [animal]; to expose [partie du corps]

B s'exhiber vpr 1⟩ pej (se montrer) to flaunt oneself; 2⟩ (indécemment) to expose oneself

exhibition /ɛgzibisjɔ̃/ nf 1⟩ (d'animaux) display; 2⟩ Sport demonstration; 3⟩ (étalage) (de richesse, toilettes) parade; (de sentiment) display

exhibitionniste /ɛgzibisjɔnist/ adj, nmf exhibitionist

exhortation /ɛgzɔʀtasjɔ̃/ nf exhortation (**à faire** to do); ∼ **au calme** call for calm

exhorter /ɛgzɔʀte/ [1] vtr ∼ **qn à faire** [personne] to urge ou exhort sb to do; ∼ **qn au calme** to ask sb to remain calm

exhumation /ɛgzymasjɔ̃/ nf 1⟩ (de cadavre) exhumation; (de ruines) excavation; 2⟩ (de document) unearthing; (du passé) resurrection

exhumer /ɛgzyme/ [1] vtr 1⟩ (déterrer) to exhume [cadavre]; to excavate [ruines]; 2⟩ (tirer de l'oubli) to unearth [document] (**de** from); to resurrect [souvenir]

exigeant, ∼e /ɛgziʒɑ̃, ɑ̃t/ adj demanding; **être ∼ avec** ou **envers qn** to demand a lot of sb

exigence /ɛgziʒɑ̃s/ nf 1⟩ (demande) demand (**de qch** for sth); 2⟩ (obligation) demand; Admin requirement; ∼**s de sécurité** security requirements; 3⟩ (trait de caractère) **le chef est d'une telle** ∼ the boss is so demanding

exiger /ɛgziʒe/ [13] vtr 1⟩ (demander impérativement) to demand [réponse, réformes, excuses]; ∼ **de qn qu'il fasse** to demand that sb do; **vous exigez trop d'eux** you're too demanding of them; 2⟩ (nécessiter) to require; 3⟩ (rendre obligatoire) to require; **comme l'exige la loi** as required by

---

law; **'expérience exigée'** 'experience required'; **'anglais/ permis de conduire exigé'** 'English/driver's licence[GB] essential'; **'tenue de soirée exigée'** 'black tie'

exigibilité /ɛgziʒibilite/ nf (d'impôt, de traite) payability; (de dette) repayability

exigible /ɛgziʒibl/ adj [impôt, traite] due (**après** n)

exigu, -uë /ɛgzigy/ adj [pièce, dimensions] cramped; [entrée] narrow; [espace] confined

exiguïté /ɛgziɡɥite/ nf smallness, pokiness péj

exil /ɛgzil/ nm exile; **en** ∼ in exile

exilé, ∼e /ɛgzile/ nm,f exile

exiler /ɛgzile/ [1]

A vtr to exile

B s'exiler vpr 1⟩ (s'expatrier) to go into exile; 2⟩ (se retirer) to bury oneself; **s'∼ loin du monde** to cut oneself off from the world

existant, ∼e /ɛgzistɑ̃, ɑ̃t/ adj gén existing; [besoins, produits] current; **non** ∼ nonexistent

existence /ɛgzistɑ̃s/ nf 1⟩ (réalité) existence; 2⟩ ○(vie) life; **ne te complique pas l'**∼ don't make life difficult for yourself; 3⟩ (mode de vie) lifestyle

existentialisme /ɛgzistɑ̃sjalism/ nm existentialism

exister /ɛgziste/ [1]

A vi to exist; **ce risque existe** this is a very real risk; **le savon/la courtoisie, ça existe!** hum there's such a thing as soap/manners, you know!; **si le paradis/la justice existe** if there is such a place as heaven/such a thing as justice; **la maison existe encore/n'existe plus** the house is still standing/is no longer standing; **la loi existe depuis dix ans** the law has been in existence for ten years; ∼ **en trois tailles** [article, produit] to be available in three sizes; **ces plantes n'existent que dans les Alpes** these plants are found only in the Alps; **les enfants me donnent une raison d'**∼ the children give me a reason for living

B v impers to be; **il existe un lieu/des lieux où...** there is a place/there are places where...

exocet /ɛgzɔsɛ/ nm Zool flying fish

exocrine /ɛgzɔkʀin/ adj exocrine

exode /ɛgzɔd/ nm lit, fig exodus

(Composé) ∼ **rural** rural depopulation

ⓘ **Exode rural** This refers to the population drift from rural to urban areas which took place on a massive scale in the post-war decades.

exonération /ɛgzɔneʀasjɔ̃/ nf exemption (**de** from)

exonérer /ɛgzɔneʀe/ [14] vtr to exempt (**de** from)

exorbitant, ∼e /ɛgzɔʀbitɑ̃, ɑ̃t/ adj [prix, agios] exorbitant; [exigence, privilège] outrageous; [pouvoir] inordinate (épith)

exorbité, ∼e /ɛgzɔʀbite/ adj bulging (**de** with)

exorciser /ɛgzɔʀsize/ [1] vtr to exorcize

exotique /ɛgzɔtik/ adj exotic

expansible /ɛkspɑ̃sibl/ adj expansive

expansif, -ive /ɛkspɑ̃sif, iv/ adj 1⟩ [personne] communicative, outgoing; 2⟩ Tech expansive

expansion /ɛkspɑ̃sjɔ̃/ nf 1⟩ (d'économie, de région) growth; **en (pleine)** ∼ [organisme, filiale, marché] (rapidly) growing; [activité, monnaie] (rapidly) increasing; **secteurs en** ∼ growth sectors; 2⟩ (de corps, pays) expansion; ∼ **coloniale** colonial expansion; 3⟩ (d'idées, épidémie) spread

expansivité /ɛkspɑ̃sivite/ nf expansiveness

expatriation /ɛkspatʀijasjɔ̃/ nf expatriation

expatrié, ∼e /ɛkspatʀije/ adj, nm,f expatriate

expatrier /ɛkspatʀije/ [2]

A vtr to deport

B s'expatrier vpr to emigrate (**en, à** to)

expectative /ɛkspɛktativ/ nf (attente prudente) prudent approach; **rester dans l'**∼ to wait and see

expectorer /ɛkspɛktɔʀe/ [1] vtr to expectorate

expédient /ɛkspedjɑ̃/ nm expedient; **user d'**∼**s** to resort to expedients; **vivre d'**∼**s** to live by one's wits

expédier /ɛkspedje/ [2] vtr 1⟩ gén to send; (par la poste) to post GB, to mail US [lettres, colis]; (faire partir) to dispatch [marchandises, commande]; ∼ **qch à qn** to send sb sth, to send sth to sb; ∼ **par bateau** to send [sth] by surface mail [lettre, colis]; to ship [marchandises]; 2⟩ (envoyer) to send, to dispatch [personne] (**à** to); 3⟩ ○(se débarrasser de) to get rid of [*importun*]; (bâcler) to polish off [*travail, repas*]; ∼ **un entretien en une heure** pej to get an interview over within one hour; **④** (régler) to deal with; ∼ **les affaires courantes** to deal with ou dispatch daily business

expéditeur, -trice /ɛkspeditœʀ, tʀis/
A adj [*bureau, gare*] of dispatch (*après n*)
B nm,f sender; **retour à l'**∼ return to sender

expéditif, -ive /ɛkspeditif, iv/ adj [*personne*] brisk, efficient; [*méthode, procédé*] cursory, expeditious sout; **un jugement** ∼ a hasty verdict; **une justice expéditive** summary justice

expédition /ɛkspedisjɔ̃/ nf **①** (de lettre, marchandises) dispatching, sending; (par bateau) shipping; **②** (chose expédiée) gén consignment, shipment US; (par bateau) shipment; **③** (mission) expedition; **④** Jur (de jugement, d'acte notarié) authenticated copy

expéditionnaire /ɛkspedisjɔnɛʀ/
A adj [*corps, armée, forces*] expeditionary
B ▶ p. 372 nm,f **①** Comm forwarding agent; **②** Admin copyist

expérience /ɛkspeʀjɑ̃s/ nf **①** (pratique) experience; **je sais par** ∼ I know from experience; ∼ **professionnelle** work experience; **avoir de l'**∼ to be experienced; **ne pas avoir d'**∼ to be inexperienced; **faire l'**∼ **de qch** to experience sth; **j'en ai fait l'**∼ **à mes dépens** I learned that lesson at my own expense; **②** (essai) experiment (**de** in)

expérimental, ∼e, mpl **-aux** /ɛkspeʀimɑ̃tal, o/ adj experimental

expérimentateur, -trice /ɛkspeʀimɑ̃tatœʀ, tʀis/ nm,f experimenter

expérimentation /ɛkspeʀimɑ̃tasjɔ̃/ nf experimentation

expérimenté, ∼e /ɛkspeʀimɑ̃te/ adj experienced

expérimenter /ɛkspeʀimɑ̃te/ [1] vtr to test [*médicament*] (**sur** on); to try out [*méthode, procédé*]

expert, ∼e /ɛkspɛʀ, ɛʀt/
A adj expert
B ▶ p. 372 nm **①** (spécialiste) expert (**en** on); **l'avis d'un** ∼ expert advice; **②** (dans les assurances) adjuster

expert-comptable, pl **experts-comptables** /ɛkspɛʀkɔ̃tabl/ ▶ p. 372 nm ≈ chartered accountant GB, certified public accountant US

expertise /ɛkspɛʀtiz/ nf **①** (de bijou) valuation GB, appraisal US; (de dégâts) assessment; **rapport d'**∼ expert's report; **②** (compétence) expertise

expertiser /ɛkspɛʀtize/ [1] vtr **①** (évaluer) to value GB, to appraise US [*bijou*]; to assess [*dégâts*]; **②** (authentifier) to authenticate [*tableau*]

expiation /ɛkspjasjɔ̃/ nf atonement (**de** for), expiation (**de** of)

expier /ɛkspje/ [2] vtr **①** (réparer) to atone for, to expiate [*crime, faute*] (**par** with); **②** (être puni de) to pay for [*erreur*] (**par** with)

expiration /ɛkspiʀasjɔ̃/ nf **①** (d'air) exhalation; **②** (échéance) expiry GB, expiration US; **venir** or **arriver à** ∼ to expire

expirer /ɛkspiʀe/ [1]
A vtr to exhale [*air*]
B vi **①** (arriver à son terme) to expire; **②** (souffler) to breathe out; **③** (mourir) liter to expire

explicatif, -ive /ɛksplikatif, iv/ adj [*note, lettre*] explanatory

explication /ɛksplikasjɔ̃/ nf **①** (éclaircissement) explanation **¢**; **je n'ai pas d'**∼**s à vous donner** I don't have to explain; **nous avons eu une bonne** ∼ we've just had things through; **②** (cause) explanation (**de** for); **③** (altercation) argument

(Composé) ∼ **de texte** Scol textual analysis

explicite /ɛksplisit/ adj [*texte, titre, film*] explicit; [*réponse*] definite; **peu** or **pas très** ∼ unclear

explicitement /ɛksplisitmɑ̃/ adv [*mentionner*] explicitly; [*condamner*] unequivocally; [*demander*] specifically

expliciter /ɛksplisite/ [1] vtr to clarify, to explain

expliquer /ɛksplike/ [1]
A vtr **①** (enseigner) to explain (**à** to); **②** (être la raison) to account for; **③** Scol to analyze [*passage*]
B s'**expliquer** vpr **①** (comprendre) **s'**∼ **qch** to understand sth; **②** (être compréhensible) to be understandable; **tout finira par s'**∼ everything will become clear; **la chose s'explique**

d'elle-même it is self-explanatory; **③** (exposer sa pensée) **je m'explique** let me explain; **sans doute me suis-je mal expliqué** perhaps I didn't make myself clear; **④** (se justifier) to explain (oneself) (**auprès de, devant** to); **⑤** (résoudre un conflit) **ils se sont expliqués** they talked things through; **s'**∼ **à coups de poings** to fight it out

exploit /ɛksplwa/ nm exploit, feat

exploitant, ∼e /ɛksplwatɑ̃, ɑ̃t/ nm,f **①** (de ferme) farmer; **②** Cin cinema owner GB, exhibitor US; **③** Comm manager

(Composé) ∼ **agricole** farmer

exploitation /ɛksplwatasjɔ̃/ nf **①** (traitement injuste) exploitation; **②** (ferme) ∼ **(agricole)** farm; **③** (entreprise) concern; **④** (de mine) working; (de gisement de charbon, de fer) mining; (de gisement, de fer) exploitation; (de ferme, d'entreprise) running; (de réseau, liaison aérienne, maritime) operation; (de brevet) using

exploiter /ɛksplwate/ [1] vtr **①** (abuser de) to exploit [*personne*]; **②** (faire valoir) to work [*mine*]; to mine [*gisement de charbon, fer*]; to exploit [*gisement, forêt, source thermale*]; to run [*entreprise*]; to operate [*réseau, liaison aérienne*]; to use [*brevet*]; **il exploite 17 hectares** he farms 17 hectares; **③** (utiliser) to make the most of [*don, connaissances*]; péj to exploit [*crédulité, rivalités*]; ∼ **une situation** to capitalize on a situation

exploiteur, -euse /ɛksplwatœʀ, øz/ nm,f exploiter

explorateur, -trice /ɛksplɔʀatœʀ, tʀis/
A ▶ p. 372 nm,f (personne) explorer
B nm Méd endoscope

exploration /ɛksplɔʀasjɔ̃/ nf exploration

explorer /ɛksplɔʀe/ [1] vtr to explore

exploser /ɛksploze/ [1] vi **①** lit [*bombe, mine, appareil*] to explode; [*véhicule, immeuble*] to blow up; **faire** ∼ [*personne, dispositif*] to blow up [*avion, voiture*]; to explode [*bombe, mine*]; [*gaz, court-circuit*] to cause [sth] to blow up [*immeuble*]; **②** fig [*joie*] to burst forth; **laisser** ∼ **sa colère** to give vent to one's anger; **③** (augmenter) [*prix*] to soar, to rocket○; [*ventes*] to boom, to rocket○

explosif, -ive /ɛksplozif, iv/
A adj explosive
B nm explosive

explosion /ɛksplozjɔ̃/ nf **①** lit explosion; **faire** ∼ to explode; **②** (de haine, colère, violence) explosion; **③** (de population, fraudes) explosion (**de** of); **④** (de marché) boom (**de** in)

exponentiel, -ielle /ɛksponɑ̃sjɛl/ adj exponential

export /ɛkspɔʀ/ nm export

exportateur, -trice /ɛkspɔʀtatœʀ, tʀis/
A adj [*pays*] exporting; [*marché, industrie, société*] export (épith)
B ▶ p. 372 nm,f exporter

exportation /ɛkspɔʀtasjɔ̃/ nf export; **faire l'**∼ **de qch** to export sth

exporter /ɛkspɔʀte/ [1] vtr to export

exposant, ∼e /ɛkspozɑ̃, ɑ̃t/
A nm,f exhibitor
B nm Math exponent

exposé, ∼e /ɛkspoze/
A pp ▶ **exposer**
B pp adj **①** (situé) [*maison, endroit*] exposed; **maison** ∼**e au sud** south-facing house; **maison bien** ∼**e** house with a good aspect; **②** (montré) [*tableau*] on show (après n); [*denrée*] on display (après n); **liste des œuvres** ∼**es** list of exhibits
C nm **①** (compte rendu) ∼ **de** account of [*situation*]; **faire l'**∼ **des faits** to give a statement of the facts; **②** (conférence) talk (**sur** on); **faire un** ∼ to give a talk

exposer /ɛkspoze/ [1]
A vtr **①** (montrer) to exhibit [*œuvre d'art*]; to put [sth] on display [*marchandise*]; **②** (décrire) to state [*faits*]; to outline [*idée, plan*]; to list [*griefs*]; to explain [*situation*]; to expound [*argument*]; Littérat to set out [*sujet*]; **③** Phot to expose; **④** (mettre en danger) to risk [*vie, réputation*]; Jur to abandon a child; **⑤** (soumettre à) to expose (**à** to); **ne reste pas exposé au soleil** stay out of the sun
B s'**exposer** vpr **①** (se rendre vulnérable) to put oneself at risk; **s'**∼ **à** to risk [*rechute, mort*], to lay oneself open to [*poursuites, critiques*]; **②** (se placer) **s'**∼ **au soleil** to go out in the sun

exposition /ɛkspozisjɔ̃/ nf **①** (de tableaux, photos, d'objets d'art) exhibition; (d'animaux, de plantes, marchandises) show; (d'objets à vendre) fair; **②** (dans un magasin) display; **③** (de thèse, situation, faits) exposition; **4** (orientation) aspect; **la terrasse jouit d'une bonne ~** the terrace has a pleasant aspect; **5** (soumission à un effet) Phot exposure; **l'~ aux radiations/au soleil** exposure to radiation/to sunlight

exprès¹ /ɛksprɛ/ *adv* **1** (délibérément) deliberately; **je ne l'ai pas fait ~** I didn't do it on purpose; **'la porte se referme toute seule'—'c'est fait ~'** 'the door shuts itself'—'that's what it's designed to do!'; **comme par un fait ~** as ill-luck would have it; **2** (spécialement) specially

exprès², -esse /ɛksprɛs/
A *adj* [ordre, condition, clause] express; **défense expresse d'en parler** all mention of it is expressly forbidden
B **exprès** *adj inv* Postes special delivery

express /ɛksprɛs/
A *adj inv* **1** [train] express; **2** [nettoyage] express; [déjeuner] quick
B *nm inv* **1** Rail express; **2** (café) espresso

expressément /ɛksprɛsemɑ̃/ *adv* expressly

expressif, -ive /ɛksprɛsif, iv/ *adj* expressive

expression /ɛksprɛsjɔ̃/ *nf* **1** gén expression; [yeux, visage] expressive; **sans ~** expressionless; **avec ~** [réciter, chanter] with feeling; **réduire qch à sa plus simple ~** fig to reduce sth to a minimum; **2** (groupe de mots) expression; **~ figée, ~ toute faite** set phrase; **passez-moi l'~!** if you'll pardon the expression!; **d'~ française/ anglaise** French-speaking/English-speaking
(Composé) **~ corporelle** self-expression through movement

expressionnisme /ɛksprɛsjɔnism/ *nm* expressionism

expressivité /ɛksprɛsivite/ *nf* expressiveness

exprimable /ɛksprimabl/ *adj* possible to express; **difficilement ~** [sentiment, impression] hard to express

exprimer /ɛksprime/ [1]
A *vtr* **1** (dire, montrer) to express; **~ qch en pourcentage** to give sth as a percentage; **2** (extraire) to squeeze [liquide] (**de** out of)
B **s'exprimer** *vpr* **1** [personne] to express oneself; **si j'ose m'~ ainsi** if I can put it this way; **s'~ en français** to speak in French; **2** [sentiment, état d'esprit] to be expressed

expropriation /ɛksprɔprijasjɔ̃/ *nf* (de propriété) compulsory purchase; (de personne) expropriation

exproprier /ɛksprɔprije/ [2] *vtr* **~ qn** to put a compulsory purchase order on sb's property

expulser /ɛkspylse/ [1] *vtr* **1** (renvoyer) to evict [locataire] (**de** from); to deport [immigré] (**de** from; **en, vers** to); to expel [élève, diplomate, dissident, membre] (**de** from); **2** Sport to send [sb] off [joueur]; **3** Méd to expel [calcul]; to excrete [déchets]

expulsion /ɛkspylsjɔ̃/ *nf* **1** (de locataire) eviction (**de** from); (d'immigré) deportation (**de** from); (d'élève, de diplomate, dissident) expulsion (**de** from); (de locataire) eviction order; **2** Sport sending-off (**de** from)

expurger /ɛkspyrʒe/ [13] *vtr* **1** to expurgate, to bowdlerize [texte]; **2** Pol to purge [parti]

exquis, ~e /ɛkski, iz/ *adj* gén exquisite; [personne] delightful

exsangue /ɛgzɑ̃g/ *adj* lit bloodless

exsuder /ɛksyde/ [1]
A *vtr* lit, fig to exude
B *vi* lit, fig to ooze (**de** from)

extase /ɛkstaz/ *nf* lit, fig ecstasy

extasier: s'extasier /ɛkstazje/ [2] *vpr* to go into ecstasy *ou* raptures (**devant, sur** over)

extatique /ɛkstatik/ *adj* ecstatic

extensible /ɛkstɑ̃sibl/ *adj* **1** lit [métal, tissu, matière] extensible; **2** fig [liste] extendable

extensif, -ive /ɛkstɑ̃sif, iv/ *adj* **1** [culture] extensive; **2** [sens] wider; [signification, usage] extended

extension /ɛkstɑ̃sjɔ̃/ *nf* **1** (de bras, jambe, muscle) stretching, extension; **faire des mouvements d'~ et de flexion** to stretch and bend; **quand votre jambe est en ~** when your leg is extended; **2** Méd extension; **3** (d'industrie) expansion; (de grève, zone, pouvoirs, loi) extension (**à** to); **prendre de l'~** [industrie] to expand; [grève] to spread, to extend; **4** (de ressort, métal) stretching; **5** Ordinat (de fichier) file extension; (module) plug-in

exténuer /ɛkstenɥe/ [1]
A *vtr* to exhaust

B **s'exténuer** *vpr* to wear oneself out (**à faire** doing)

extérieur, ~e /ɛksterjœr/
A *adj* **1** gén outside; **2** (périphérique) [couche, mur] outer; **3** (étranger) [commerce, relations, aide] foreign; **4** (apparent) [joie, calme] outward; **aspect ~** (de personne) outward appearance; (de bâtiment) outside
B *nm* **1** gén outside; **à l'~** outside, outdoors; **à l'~ de qch** outside sth; **d'~** outdoor (épith); **2** (monde autour de soi) outside world; **3** (étranger) foreign countries (+ v pl); **4** (apparence) exterior, appearance; **5** Cin **les ~s** outdoor location shots; **en ~** on location

extérieurement /ɛksterjœrmɑ̃/ *adv* **1** (vu du dehors) on the outside, externally; **2** (en apparence) outwardly

extérioriser /ɛksterjɔrize/ [1]
A *vtr* to show
B **s'extérioriser** *vpr* [personne] to express oneself

extermination /ɛkstɛrminasjɔ̃/ *nf* extermination

exterminer /ɛkstɛrmine/ [1] *vtr* to exterminate [peuple, animaux]; to wipe out [armée, rebelles]

externat /ɛkstɛrna/ *nm* **1** Scol (école) day school; **2** Méd, Univ **préparer l'~** to prepare for medical school entrance exams; **faire son ~** to be a nonresident student doctor (in a hospital) GB, to be an extern US

externe /ɛkstɛrn/
A *adj* **1** (extérieur) [cause, problème, croissance] external; [face] outside; [partie] exterior; **2** Méd external
B *nmf* **1** Scol day pupil; **2** Méd, Univ **~ (des hôpitaux)** non-residential medical student GB, extern US

extincteur /ɛkstɛ̃ktœr/ *nm* fire extinguisher

extinction /ɛkstɛ̃ksjɔ̃/ *nf* **1** Méd **avoir une ~ de voix** to have lost one's voice; **2** (d'espèce, de race) extinction; **espèce en voie d'~** endangered species; **3** (action d'éteindre) **après l'~ de l'incendie** after the fire was put out; **après l'~ des feux** after lights out

extirper /ɛkstirpe/ [1] *vtr* **1** ○(faire sortir) to drag [personne] (**de** out of, from); **2** (faire disparaître) to eradicate

extorquer /ɛkstɔrke/ [1] *vtr* to extort (**à qn** from sb)

extorsion /ɛkstɔrsjɔ̃/ *nf* extortion

extra /ɛkstra/
A *adj inv* **1** ○(remarquable) great○; **2** Comm **huile d'olive ~ vierge** extra virgin olive oil
B *nm inv* **1** (dépense imprévue) extra; **se payer un petit ~** to have a little treat; **2** (travail) **faire des ~** (petits travaux) to do bits and pieces; (travail supplémentaire) to do a few extra jobs; **3** (personne) extra worker

extra-atmosphérique, *pl* **~s** /ɛkstraatmɔsferik/ *adj* **espace ~** outer space

extracommunautaire, *pl* **~s** /ɛkstrakɔmynotɛr/ *adj* non-EEC (épith)

extraction /ɛkstraksjɔ̃/ *nf* **1** (de minerai, pétrole, gaz) extraction; (de charbon, diamants) mining; (d'ardoise, de marbre) quarrying; **2** Méd (de balle, dent) extraction (**de** from); **3** (origine) extraction sout; **être d'~ bourgeoise** to be from a middle-class background

extrader /ɛkstrade/ [1] *vtr* to extradite

extra-fin, ~e, *mpl* **~s** /ɛkstrafɛ̃, in/ *adj* [collants] ultra-fine; **petits pois ~s** petits pois

extraire /ɛkstrɛr/ [58]
A *vtr* **1** (exploiter) to extract [minerai]; to mine [or, houille]; to quarry [ardoise, marbre]; **2** (enlever) to extract, to pull out [dent]; to remove [balle, épine] (**de** from); to extract [substance, élément] (**de** from)
B **s'extraire** *vpr* **s'~ de** to climb out of [fauteuil, cabine de pilotage]; hum to struggle out of [vêtement]

extrait /ɛkstrɛ/ *nm* **1** (de livre, film) extract, excerpt; (de discours) extract; **2** (substance) essence, extract
(Composés) **~ (d'acte) de naissance** birth certificate; **~ de casier judiciaire (de qn)** copy of (sb's) criminal record; **~ de compte** abstract of accounts

extra-long, -longue, *mpl* **~s** /ɛkstralɔ̃, ɔ̃g/ *adj* [cigarette] king-size; [vêtement] extra-long

extralucide /ɛkstralysid/ *adj* clairvoyant

extraordinaire /ɛkstraɔrdinɛr/ *adj* **1** (qui surprend) [question, phénomène] extraordinary; (qui plaît et surprend) [sensation, paysage, personne] amazing; (admirable) [personne, film] remarkable; (qui plaît beaucoup) [personne, film] fantastic○; **si par ~...** and if by some extraordinary twist of fate...; **c'est quand même ~!** it's incredible!; **2** (non prévu) [dépenses, mesure, assemblée] extraordinary

extraordinairement /ɛkstʀaɔʀdinɛʀmɑ̃/ *adv* amazingly, extraordinarily

extrapoler /ɛkstʀapɔle/ [1] *vtr, vi* to extrapolate

extrascolaire /ɛkstʀaskɔlɛʀ/ *adj* [*activités*] extra-curricular

extraterrestre /ɛkstʀatɛʀɛstʀ/
A *adj* [*invasion*] extraterrestrial; **espace** ~ outer space
B *nmf* extraterrestrial, alien

extra-utérin, ~**e**, *mpl* ~**s** /ɛkstʀayteʀɛ̃, in/ *adj* **grossesse** ~**e** ectopic pregnancy

extravagance /ɛkstʀavagɑ̃s/ *nf* [1] (de personne) eccentricity; [2] (de projet, comportement, mode, d'idées) extravagance; [3] (acte) extravagance

extravagant, ~**e** /ɛkstʀavagɑ̃, ɑ̃t/ *adj* [1] [*comportement*] eccentric; [2] [*idée, mode*] extravagant; [3] [*prix*] exorbitant

extraverti, ~**e** /ɛkstʀavɛʀti/ *adj, nm,f* extrovert

extrême /ɛkstʀɛm/
A *adj* [1] (le plus distant) furthest; **dans l'**~ **sud du pays** in the extreme South of the country; [2] (très grand) [*simplicité, prudence*] extreme; [*pureté*] very great; **l'**~ **jeunesse du candidat** the candidate's extreme youth; **leur** ~ **vieillesse** their very great age; **avec un plaisir** ~ with the greatest pleasure; **d'une complexité** ~ extremely complex; [3] (immodéré) [*opinion, situation, comportement*] extreme; [*décision, remède*] drastic; **il est** ~ **en tout, c'est quelqu'un d'**~ he always goes to extremes; [4] Pol [*parti*] extremist; [*droite, gauche*] far, extreme

B *nm* [1] (ce qui est excessif) extreme; **c'est pousser la logique à l'**~ that's taking logic to extremes; **courageux à l'**~ extremely brave; **événement médiatisé à l'**~ event which was given a lot of media hype°; [2] (opposé) extreme; **à l'**~ **opposé** *or* **inverse** at the other extreme; [3] Météo extreme

extrêmement /ɛkstʀɛmmɑ̃/ *adv* extremely

extrême-onction, *pl* **extrêmes-onctions** /ɛkstʀɛmɔ̃ksjɔ̃/ *nf* extreme unction

Extrême-Orient /ɛkstʀɛmɔʀjɑ̃/ ▸ p. 504 *nprm* l'~ the Far East

extrémiste /ɛkstʀemist/ *adj, nmf* extremist

extrémité /ɛkstʀemite/ *nf* [1] gén end; (de doigt) tip; (de mât, clocher) top; (de surface, champ, ville) edge; **aux deux** ~**s** at both ends; [2] (mort) **(en) être à la dernière** ~ to be on the point of death, to be close to death; [3] fig (acte désespéré) extreme; **pousser qn jusqu'à la dernière** ~ to push sb to the brink; [4] (de membre) extremity; **avoir de petites** ~**s** to have small hands and feet

extrusion /ɛkstʀyzjɔ̃/ *nf* Ind, Tech (procédé) extrusion

exubérance /ɛgzybeʀɑ̃s/ *nf* exuberance

exubérant, ~**e** /ɛgzybeʀɑ̃, ɑ̃t/ *adj* exuberant

exultation /ɛgzyltasjɔ̃/ *nf* exultation

exulter /ɛgzylte/ [1] *vi* to be exultant (**de** with), to exult (**de faire** at doing)

exutoire /ɛgzytwaʀ/ *nm* [1] fig outlet; **servir d'**~ **à** to be an outlet for; [2] Tech outlet

ex-voto /ɛksvoto/ *nm inv* thanksgiving plaque

Ff

f, F /ɛf/ nm inv [1] (lettre) f, F; [2] (appartement) **F3** 2-bedroom flat GB ou apartment; [3] (written abbr = **franc**) **50 F** 50 F
fa /fa/ nm inv (note) F, fa; (en solfiant) fa; ~ **dièse** F sharp
fable /fɑbl/ nf [1] (récit) tale; [2] Littérat fable; [3] (mensonge) tall story
(Idiome) **être la ~ de la ville** (le sujet de conversation) to be the talk of the town; (la risée) to be a laughing stock
fabricant /fabʀikɑ̃/ nm manufacturer
fabrication /fabʀikasjɔ̃/ nf gén making; (pour le commerce) manufacture; **procédé de ~** manufacturing process; **il y a un défaut de ~** (tissu) it's imperfect; (machine) it's faulty; **de ~ française** French-made; **~ en série** mass production
(Composés) **~ assistée par ordinateur, FAO** computer-aided manufacturing, CAM
fabrique /fabʀik/ nf (usine) factory
fabriquer /fabʀike/ [1]
A vtr [1] (produire) gén to make; (industriellement) to manufacture; **'fabriqué en France'** 'made in France'; **fabriqué en série** mass-produced; [2] (pour tromper) to forge [faux papiers]; to invent [alibi]; **c'est fabriqué de toutes pièces** it's a complete fabrication; [3] ○(faire) **qu'est-ce que tu fabriques ici?** what are you doing here?
B se fabriquer vpr [1] (pour soi) to make [sth] for oneself; [2] Comm, Ind to be manufactured
fabulateur, -trice /fabylatœʀ, tʀis/ nm,f compulsive liar
fabulation /fabylasjɔ̃/ nf [1] (fable) lie, tale; [2] (mythomanie) compulsive lying
fabuler /fabyle/ [1] vi [1] (inventer) to make things up; [2] Psych to confabulate
fabuleusement /fabyløzmɑ̃/ adv fabulously
fabuleux, -euse /fabylø, øz/ adj [beauté, temps, richesse] fabulous; [somme] fantastic; [être] mythical
fabuliste /fabylist/ nmf fabulist
fac○ /fak/ nf [1] (faculté) faculty; [2] (université) university
façade /fasad/ nf [1] (de bâtiment) front; **chambres en ~** front bedrooms; **la ~ arrière** the back; **~ nord** north side; [2] (apparence) façade
face /fas/
A nf [1] (visage) face; **~ à ~** face to face; (étendu) **~ contre terre** lying face downward(s); **à la ~ de qn** [proclamer, jeter] in sb's face; **les muscles/os de la ~** the facial muscles/bones; **le côté ~ d'une pièce** the heads side of a coin; [2] (côté) side; [3] (aspect) side; **une question à plusieurs ~s** a multifaceted question; **la ~ cachée de la politique** the underside of politics; [4] (front) **faire ~** (résister) to face up to things; **se faire ~** (être vis-à-vis) [personnes] to face each other; [objets, maisons] to be opposite one another; (s'affronter) to confront each other; **faire ~ à** [maison, chambre] to face [lieu]; [personne] to face [adversaire, défi, accusation]; to cope with [exigences, dépenses]; to meet [besoin, dette]; to measure up to [concurrence]; **faire ~ à l'inflation** to tackle inflation
B de face loc [photo] fullface (épith); [éclairage] frontal; **elle est plus jolie de ~** she's prettier from the front; **aborder un problème de ~** to tackle a problem head-on; **prendre une loge de ~** Théât to take a box facing the stage
C en face loc **il habite en ~** he lives opposite; **les gens d'en ~** the people opposite; **avoir le soleil en ~** to have the sun in one's eyes; **voir les choses en ~** to see things as they are; **je leur ai dit la vérité en ~** I told them the truth straight out; **l'équipe d'en ~** the opposing team

D en face de loc prép [1] (devant) **en ~ de l'église** opposite the church GB, across from the church; **le couple en ~ de moi** the couple opposite me; **ils étaient assis l'un en ~ de l'autre** or **en ~ l'un de l'autre** they were sitting opposite ou facing each other; ▸ **trou**; [2] (en présence de) **ne dis pas ça en ~ des enfants** don't say that in front of the children; **en ~ de difficultés imprévues** faced with unexpected difficulties; [3] (comparé à) compared with
E face à loc prép [1] (devant) **parler ~ aux caméras** to speak facing the cameras; **mon lit est ~ à la fenêtre** my bed faces the window; [2] (confronté à) **~ à cette situation** in view of this situation
(Idiome) **se voiler la ~** not to face facts
face-à-face /fasafas/ nm inv (débat) one-to-one debate GB, one-on-one debate US; (confrontation) encounter
facétie /fasesi/ nf (plaisanterie) facetious remark; (farce) practical joke
facétieux, -ieuse /fasesjø, øz/ adj mischievous
facette /fasɛt/ nf facet; **à plusieurs ~s** multifaceted
fâché, ~e /fɑʃe/ adj [1] (en colère) angry (contre with); [2] (brouillé) **être ~ avec qn** to have fallen out with sb; [3] †(désolé) sorry (de about)
fâcher /fɑʃe/ [1]
A †vtr (irriter) to make [sb] angry
B se fâcher vpr [1] (se mettre en colère) to get angry (contre qn with sb; pour qch about sth); [2] (se brouiller) to fall out (avec qn with sb; pour qch over sth)
(Idiome) **se ~ tout rouge**○ to be hopping mad○
fâcheusement /fɑʃøzmɑ̃/ adv unfortunately
fâcheux, -euse /fɑʃø, øz/
A adj [influence, exemple] detrimental; [retard, initiative] unfortunate; [effet] unpleasing; [nouvelle, événement] distressing
B †nm,f irritating person
facial, ~e, mpl **-iaux** /fasjal, o/ adj Anat facial
faciès /fasjɛs/ nm inv (expression) face
facile /fasil/
A adj [1] (sans difficulté) easy; **rien de plus ~ (que)** nothing could be easier (than); ~ **comme tout** as easy as pie; **c'est plus ~ à dire qu'à faire** that's easier said than done; [2] (spontané) **avoir la larme ~** to be quick to cry; [3] (docile) easy-going; [4] (médiocre) facile
B ○adv (facilement) easily; **il a soixante ans ~** he's easily sixty
facilement /fasilmɑ̃/ adv [1] (sans difficultés) easily; **~ explicable** easy to explain; **elle rit très ~** she's very quick to laugh; [2] ○ (largement) **j'ai mis ~ deux heures** it took me a good two hours
facilité /fasilite/
A nf [1] (de travail, jeu) easiness; (d'acte, utilisation, entretien) ease; **avec ~** with ease; **d'une ~ déconcertante** surprisingly easy; [2] (d'expression, de style) fluency; **avec ~** fluently; [3] (médiocrité) **tomber dans/éviter la ~** to tend to take/to tend not to take the easy way out
B facilités nfpl [1] (possibilités) **~s d'importation** import opportunities; **toutes ~s pour faire** every opportunity to do; [2] Fin **~s (de paiement)** easy terms; **~s de caisse/prêt** overdraft/loan facility (sg)
faciliter /fasilite/ [1] vtr to make [sth] easier [tâche, choses] (à for)
façon /fasɔ̃/
A nf [1] (manière) way; **la ~ dont tu manges** the way you eat; **d'une ~ ou d'une autre** one way or another; **c'est une**

~ comme une autre de faire it's one way of doing; **d'une certaine ~** in a way; **de toute ~, de toutes les ~s** anyway; **de toutes les ~s possibles** in every possible way; **agir de la même ~** to do the same; **de telle ~ que personne n'a compris** so that nobody understood; **de ~ inattendue** unexpectedly; **à ma ~** my (own) way; **à la ~ de** like; **de ~ à faire** (en vue de) in order to do; (de telle manière que) in such a way as to do; **de ~ (à ce) qu'elle fasse** so (that) she does; **elle nous a joué un tour à sa ~** she played a trick of her own on us; **je vais leur dire ma ~ de penser** I'll tell them exactly what I think; **cette ~ de faire ne te/leur ressemble pas** that's not like you/them; **~ de parler** so to speak; **de quelle ~ est-il tombé?** how did he fall?; [2] (imitation) **un peigne ~ ivoire** an imitation ivory comb; **sac ~ sellier** saddle-stitched bag; **doublure ~ soie** silk-look lining; [3] (style) style; **spectacle ~ années 70** 70's-style show; [4] (main-d'œuvre) **on m'a donné le tissu et j'ai payé la ~** the cloth was a present and I paid for the making-up; **travailler à ~** to work to order (with supplied materials)

B **façons** nfpl [1] (attitude) **tes ~s me déplaisent** I don't like the way you behave; **en voilà des ~s!** what a way to behave!; [2] (excès de politesse) **faire des ~s** to stand on ceremony; **sans ~s** [repas] informal; [personne] unpretentious; **non merci, sans ~s** no thank you, really

faconde /fakɔd/ nf fml loquacity

façonnage /fasɔnaʒ/ nm (du bois) hewing; (de la pierre) cutting; (du cuir) sleeking; (du papier) converting; (du pétrole) processing

façonner /fasɔne/ [1] vtr [1] (fabriquer) to manufacture [outil, pièce]; to make [chapeau, objet artisanal]; [2] Ind to hew [bois]; to cut [pierre]; to fashion [argile]; to sleek [cuir]; [3] (former) (par l'éducation) to shape; (par les épreuves) to mould GB, to mold US

fac-similé, pl **~s** /faksimile/ nm facsimile

facteur, -trice /faktœʀ, tʀis/ ▸ p. 372

A nm,f postman/postwoman, mailman/mailwoman US

B nm [1] (élément) factor; **~ de risque** risk factor; **le ~ chance** the element of chance; [2] Math factor; **mettre en ~s** to factorize, to factor US; [3] Mus **~ d'orgues** organ builder; **~ de pianos** piano maker

factice /faktis/ adj [gaieté, sourire] forced; [style] contrived; [bijoux] imitation (épith); [fleur, beauté] artificial; [étalage] dummy (épith)

factieux, -ieuse /faksjø, øz/

A adj seditious

B nm,f dissident

faction /faksjɔ̃/ nf [1] Pol faction; [2] Mil guard duty; **être de** or **en ~** gén to keep watch; Mil to be on guard duty; [3] (poste de travail) shift

factoriel, -ielle[1] /faktɔʀjɛl/ adj factorial; **analyse factorielle** factor analysis

factorielle[2] /faktɔʀjɛl/ nf factorial

factotum /faktɔtɔm/ nm general handyman, factotum hum

factrice ▸ **facteur A**

factuel, -elle /faktɥɛl/ adj factual

facturation /faktyʀasjɔ̃/ nf [1] (opération) invoicing; [2] (service) invoicing department

facture /faktyʀ/ nf [1] gén bill; (détaillée) invoice; **faire** or **établir une ~** to make out a bill ou an invoice; ▸ **faux**[1]; [2] (dépense) bill; **~ pétrolière** oil bill; [3] (technique) (d'artisan) craftsmanship; (d'artiste) technique; [4] Mus (d'orgues) building; (d'instruments) making

(Composé) **~ détaillée** itemized invoice

facturer /faktyʀe/ [1] vtr [1] (dresser une facture pour) to invoice [marchandises]; [2] (faire payer) to charge for

facturette /faktyʀɛt/ nf credit card slip

facturier, -ière[1] /faktyʀje, ɛʀ/ ▸ p. 372

A nm,f (employé) invoice clerk

B nm (registre) invoice book

facturière[2] /faktyʀjɛʀ/ nf (machine) invoicing machine

facultatif, -ive /fakyltatif, iv/ adj optional

faculté /fakylte/ nf [1] (aptitude) (sensorielle, intellectuelle) faculty; (physique) ability; [2] (liberté) option (de faire of doing); [3] Univ faculty; [4] Jur (droit) right (de faire to do)

fada /fada/

A adj crazy° (de about), nuts° (de about)

B nmf nutcase°

fadaises /fadɛz/ nfpl twaddle° ¢, silly chatter ¢

fadasse° /fadas/ adj tasteless, drab, dull

fade /fad/ adj [aliment] tasteless; [couleur] drab; [blondeur] dull; [odeur] sickly; [œuvre, personne] dull

fadeur /fadœʀ/ nf (de goût) blandness; (de style) dreariness

fagot /fago/ nm bundle of firewood

(Idiome) **de derrière les ~s**° very special

fagoter° /fagɔte/ [1]

A vtr (habiller) to do [sb] up°

B **se fagoter** vpr to do oneself up°; **(être) mal fagoté** (to be) badly dressed

faiblard°, **~e** /fɛblaʀ, aʀd/ adj pej [personne, organisme] weak; [rendement, spectacle] (pretty) poor

faible /fɛbl/

A adj [1] (sans force) [malade, structure, résistance, monnaie, marché] weak; [vue] poor; **un enfant ~ de** or **de ~ constitution** a child with a frail constitution; [2] (sans fermeté) [parents, gouvernement] weak; **être ~ avec qn** to be soft with sb, to be too soft on sb; [3] (bas, léger, médiocre) [proportion, progression] small; [coût, revenu] low; [moyens, portée] limited; [avantage] slight; [chance] slim; [bruit, lueur, vibrations] faint; [éclairage] dim; [vent, pluie] light; [résultat] poor; [score] low; [argument] feeble; [production] weak; [élève, classe] slow; **à ~ vitesse** at a low speed; **à ~ profondeur** at a shallow depth; **de ~ profondeur** shallow; **il n'a qu'une ~ idée de** he has only a vague idea of; **de ~ importance** of little importance; **c'est une ~ consolation** it's small ou little consolation; **elle est ~ en anglais** she's weak in English; **~ d'esprit** feeble-minded; [mot, expression] inadequate; **c'est un imbécile et le mot est ~!** he's a fool and that's putting it mildly!

B nmf weak-willed person

C nm (penchant) weakness; **avoir un ~ pour** (pour un aliment, objet) to have a weakness for; (pour une personne) to have a soft spot for

D **faibles** nmpl **les ~s** the weak (+ v pl)

faiblement /fɛbləmã/ adv [se défendre, sourire] weakly; [frapper] gently; [éclairer] dimly; [influencer, augmenter] slightly; [développé, qualifié] poorly; [fréquenté] barely

faiblesse /fɛblɛs/ nf [1] (manque de force) gén weakness; (d'infirme, de vieillard) frailty; **mes jambes tremblaient de ~** my legs were so weak they trembled; [2] (manque de fermeté) weakness (envers toward(s)); **sans ~** [réprimer] ruthlessly; [répression] ruthless; **avoir la ~ de faire** to be weak enough to do; [3] (insuffisance) inadequacy; **la ~ de nos revenus** our low level of income; [4] (de voix) faintness; (d'éclairage) dimness; (de précipitations) lightness; [5] (défaut, médiocrité) weakness; [6] (défaillance) **avoir une ~** or **des ~s** to feel faint; **être pris de ~(s)** to feel faint; [7] (acte réprouvé) moment of weakness

faiblir /fɛbliʀ/ [3] vi [1] (perdre de sa force) to get weaker; **ma vue faiblit** my eyesight is failing; (perdre de sa fermeté) to weaken; [3] (baisser de niveau) [sportif] to flag; [roman, jeu] to decline; [mémoire] to fail; [attention, envie] to wane; [espoir] to fade; [rendement] to dwindle; [vitesse] to slacken; **quel humour, ma parole, tu faiblis**°! that wasn't very funny, I think you're losing your touch!; [4] (diminuer d'intensité) [pluie] to abate; [bruit] to grow faint; [éclairage] to grow dim

faïence /fajãs/ nf [1] (matière) earthenware; **de** or **en ~** earthenware (épith); [2] (objet) piece of earthenware

(Idiome) **se regarder en chiens de ~** to look daggers at each other

faïencerie /fajãsʀi/ ▸ p. 372 nf [1] (usine) pottery; [2] (objets) glazed earthenware ou pottery; [3] (magasin) china shop

faille /faj/ nf [1] (cassure) fault; [2] (lacune) flaw; **sans ~** unfailing; [3] (rupture) rift

faillir /fajiʀ/ [28] vi [1] **elle a failli mourir** she almost ou (very) nearly died; [2] (manquer) liter **sans ~** unfailingly; **~ à ses engagements** to fail in one's commitments; **~ à sa réputation** to fall short of one's reputation; **ne pas ~ à la tradition** to live up to the tradition

faillite /fajit/ nf [1] Comm, Jur bankruptcy; **se mettre en ~** to file for bankruptcy; **être en ~** to be bankrupt; **faire ~** to go bankrupt; [2] (échec) failure

(Composé) **~ frauduleuse** fraudulent bankruptcy

faim /fɛ̃/ nf hunger (de for); **avoir ~** to be hungry; **avoir ~ de** fig to hunger for; **avoir une ~ de loup** to be ravenous;

donner ∼ à qn to give sb an appetite; **manger à sa** ∼ to have enough to eat; **tromper sa** ∼ to stave off (one's) hunger; **mourir de** ∼ lit to die of starvation; fig to be starving; **je suis resté sur ma** ∼ fig I was disappointed

fainéant, ∼e /feneɑ̃, ɑ̃t/
A adj lazy
B nm,f layabout⁺ GB, lazybones (+ v sg)
fainéanter /feneɑ̃te/ [1] vi to laze about
fainéantise /feneɑ̃tiz/ nf laziness
faire /fɛʀ/ [10]

A vtr **1)** (produire) to make; **trois et deux font cinq** three and two make five; **combien font 13 fois 13?** what's 13 times 13?; **œil fait yeux au pluriel** œil is yeux in the plural; **2)** (façonner) to shape [histoire, période]; **3)** (étudier) to do [licence, sujet]; ∼ **du violon** to study ou play the violin; **tu as fait ton piano?** have you practised your piano?; ∼ **une école de commerce** to go to business school; **4)** (préparer) to make [soupe, thé], to prepare [salade]; ∼ **du poulet** to cook a chicken; **5)** (nettoyer) to do, to clean [vitres]; to clean, to polish [chaussures]; **6)** Comm (proposer) to do [service, marque]; (vendre) to do, to sell [article]; **ils ne font pas le petit déjeuner** they don't do breakfast; **l'hôtel fait-il restaurant?** does the hotel have a restaurant?; **7)** (cultiver) ∼ **des céréales** [personne] to grow ou do cereals; [région] to produce cereals; **8)** (se fournir en) ∼ **de l'eau** Naut, Rail to take on water; ∼ **(de) l'essence**⁺ Aut to get petrol GB ou gas US; **9)** (parcourir) to do [distance, trajet]; to go round [magasins, agences]; (visiter) to do⁺ [région, musées]; ∼ **toute la ville** to go all over town; ∼ **l'Écosse** to visit Scotland; **j'ai fait tous les tiroirs** I went through all the drawers; **10)** (souffrir de) to have [diabète, tension, complexe]; ∼ **une crise cardiaque** to have a heart attack; **11)** (demander un prix) ∼ **qch à 30 francs** to sell sth for 30 francs, to charge 30 francs for sth; **12)** (servir de) to serve as; **13)** (user, disposer de) to do; **qu'as-tu fait du billet?** what have you done with the ticket?; **pour quoi** ∼? for what?; **je n'ai que** ∼ **de** I have no need for; **je n'en ai rien à** ∼⁺ I couldn't care less; **14)** (avoir un effet) **que veux-tu que j'y fasse?** what do you want me to do about it?, what am I supposed to do about it?; **ça y fait**⁺ it has an effect; **leur départ ne m'a rien fait** their departure didn't affect me at all; **ça me fait quelque chose de la voir dans cet état** it upsets me to see her in that state; **pour ce que ça fait**⁺ for all the good it does!; **ça ne fait rien à la chose** it makes no difference; **qu'est-ce que ça peut bien te** ∼⁺? what is it to you?; **15)** (entraîner, causer) ∼ **des jaloux** to make some people jealous; **l'explosion a fait 12 morts** the explosion killed 12 people, the explosion left 12 people dead; **ça ne fait rien!** (pas grave) it doesn't matter!; **ça m'est égal que fait que j'ai oublié**⁺ as a result I forgot; **16)** (transformer) to make; **elle en a fait sa confidente** she's made ou her her confidante; ∼ **d'un garage un atelier** to make ou turn a garage into a workshop; **17)** (proclamer) ∼ **qn général** to make sb a general; **18)** (imiter) ∼ **le courageux** to pretend to be brave; ∼ **le dictateur** to act the dictator; **19)** (tenir le rôle de) to be; **quel plaisantin vous faites!** what a joker you are!; **20)** (dans un souhait) **mon Dieu, faites qu'il réussisse!** God, please let him succeed!; **21)** (tromper) **je m'en l'a fait au baratin** he talked me into it; **on ne me la fait pas!** I'm not a fool!; **22)** (dire) to say; **'bien sûr,' fit-elle** 'of course,' she said; **le canard fait 'coin-coin'** the duck says ou goes 'quack'

B vi **1)** (agir) to do, to act; **fais comme tu veux** do as you like; ∼ **vite** to act quickly; **vas-y, mais fais vite!** go, but be quick about it!; **fais comme chez toi** lit, iron make yourself at home; **2)** (paraître) to look; ∼ **jeune** to look young; **3)** ⁺(être) to be; **il veut** ∼ **pompier** he wants to be a fireman; **4)** (durer) to last; **sa robe lui a fait deux ans** her dress lasted her two years; **5)** (valoir) **ça fait cher** it's expensive; **6)** (pour les besoins naturels) to go; **tu as fait?** have you been?; **7)** ∼ **avec** (se contenter de) to make do with; (supporter) to put up with

C se faire vpr **1)** se ∼ **un café** to make oneself a coffee; **se** ∼ **des amis** to make friends; **se** ∼ **la cuisine soi-même** to do one's own cooking; **combien se fait-il**⁺ **par mois?** how much does he make a month?; **2)** (devenir) to get, to become; **il se fait tard** it's getting late; **3)** (se rendre) **se** ∼ **tout petit** to make oneself very small; **4)** (s'inquiéter) **s'en** ∼ to worry; **il ne s'en fait pas!** (sans inquiétude) he's not the sort of person to worry about things!; (pas gêné) he's got a nerve!; **5)** (s'habituer) **se** ∼ **à** to get used to [lieu, situation, idée]; **6)** (être d'usage) **ça se fait encore ici** it's still done here; **ça ne se fait pas** it's not the done thing (**de faire** to

do); **7)** (être à la mode) to be in (fashion); **ça ne se fait plus** it's no longer fashionable, it's out of fashion; **8)** (être produit) **c'est ce qui se fait de mieux** it's the best there is; **le pont se fera bien un jour** the bridge will be built one day; **9)** (emploi impersonnel) **il se fit que** it (so) happened that; **il se fit un grand silence** there was complete silence; **comment se fait-il que...?** how is it that...?; **10)** [fromage] to ripen; [vin] to mature; **11)** ⁺**il faut se le** ∼, **son copain!** his/her mate is a real pain!; **12)** (avec infinitif) **se** ∼ **couler un bain** to run oneself a bath; **se** ∼ **comprendre** to make oneself understood

faire-part /fɛʀpaʀ/ nm inv announcement
faire-valoir /fɛʀvalwaʀ/ nm inv **1)** Cin, Théât foil; **être le** ∼ **de** to be a foil for; **2)** Agric farming
fair-play /fɛʀplɛ/ controv
A adj inv sporting
B nm **le** ∼ sportsmanship, (sense of) fair play
faisabilité /fəzabilite/ nf feasibility; **étude de** ∼ feasability study
faisable /fəzabl/ adj **c'est/ce n'est pas** ∼ it can/it can't be done
faisan /fəzɑ̃/ nm Zool (cock) pheasant
faisandé, ∼e /fəzɑ̃de/ adj Culin gamey, high
faisane /fəzan/ nf (poule) ∼ hen pheasant
faisceau, pl ∼**x** /fɛso/ nm **1)** (de rayon) beam; ∼ **lumineux** beam of light; **2)** (gerbe) bundle; **3)** (de preuves) body; (d'indices) array; **4)** Anat fasciculus; **5)** Mil stack; **6)** Hist fasces
(Composé) ∼ **hertzien** radio link
faiseur, -euse /fəzœʀ, øz/ nm,f ∼ **de miracles** miracle-worker; ∼ **de rimes** rhymester péj; **c'est un** ∼ **d'histoires** he's a fusspot; ∼ **de bons mots** pej punster, wag; ∼ **d'intrigues** pej schemer; ∼ **de tours** conjuror
fait, ∼e /fɛ, fɛt/
A pp ▸ faire
B pp adj **1)** (réalisé, accompli) [tâche] done; **bien/mal** ∼ well/badly done; **c'en est** ∼ **de** that's the end of; **c'est bien** ∼⁺ **(pour toi)!** it serves you right!; **2)** (constitué) ∼ **de** or **en** (d'un élément) made of; (composite) made up of; **idée toute** ∼**e** ready-made idea; **formules toutes** ∼**es** clichés; **elle est bien** ∼**e** she's got a great figure; **elle a la taille bien** ∼**e** she has a shapely waist; **je suis ainsi** ∼ that's how I am; **la vie est ainsi** ∼**e!** life's like that!; **la vie est mal** ∼**e** life is unfair; **3)** (adapté) ∼ **pour qch/pour faire** meant for sth/to do; **ta remarque n'était pas** ∼**e pour arranger les choses** your comment certainly didn't help matters; **4)** (conçu) [programme, dispositif] designed; **bien/mal** ∼ well-/badly-designed; **5)** ⁺(pris) done for; **6)** (mûr) **un fromage bien** ∼ a ripe cheese
C nm **1)** (élément de réalité, acte) fact; **le** ∼ **d'avoir** the fact of having; **le** ∼ **d'être heureux** being happy; **le** ∼ **est là** that's the fact of the matter; **il a réussi, c'est un** ∼, **mais...** he has succeeded, certainly, but...; **les** ∼**s et gestes de qn** sb's movements; **les menus** ∼**s de la vie quotidienne** the tiny details of everyday life; **2)** (cause) **de ce** ∼ because of this ou that; **du** ∼ **de qch** due to sth; **du** ∼ **même que** due to the very fact that; **être le** ∼ **de** to be due to; **3)** (événement) event; **au moment des** ∼**s** at the time of (the) events; **4)** (sujet) point; **au** ∼, **je te prie!** get to the point, please!; **aller droit au** ∼ to go straight to the point; **elle lui a dit son** ∼ she told him/her straight; **5)** (trait) **mentir n'est pas son** ∼ it isn't like him/her to lie; **6)** (exploit) feat, exploit; **les hauts** ∼**s** heroic deeds
D au fait /ofɛt/ loc adv by the way
E de fait loc (situation, pouvoir) de facto (épith); [exister, entraîner] effectively; (en effet) indeed
F en fait loc adv in fact, actually
G en fait de loc prép as regards; **en** ∼ **de réforme, il s'agit plutôt d'une...** it isn't so much a reform as a...; **en** ∼ **de rénovation du système, ils (en) ont seulement changé quelques éléments** they haven't so much renovated the system as tinkered about at the edges
(Composés) ∼ **accompli** fait accompli; ∼ **d'actualité** news item; ∼ **d'armes** feat of arms; ∼ **divers** (short) news item; **la rubrique (des) '**∼**s divers'** the 'news in brief' column; ∼ **de guerre** exploit of war; ∼ **du prince** fiat; ∼ **de société** fact of life
(Idiomes) **être au** ∼ to be informed; **mettre qn au** ∼ to inform sb; **être sûr de son** ∼ to be sure of one's facts; **prendre qn sur le** ∼ to catch sb in the act

faire

Un très grand nombre de tournures et locutions contenant ce verbe sont traitées ailleurs, généralement sous le terme qui suit *faire*, en particulier:

– les expressions décrivant les tâches domestiques, agricoles (*faire la cuisine/ moisson*), les occupations manuelles (*faire du tricot/bricolage*), les activités professionnelles ou de loisir (*faire du théâtre, de la photo*), le type d'études (*faire médecine*). Pour ce qui est des jeux, sports et loisirs, voir également la note d'usage correspondante

– les locutions décrivant un mouvement, l'expression, un comportement (*faire un geste/une grimace/le pitre*)

– les expressions dans lesquelles *faire* signifie 'formuler' (*faire une promesse/offre* etc.)

– les expressions décrivant la qualité de la lumière (*il fait jour/sombre*) ou l'état du temps

– les expressions contenant une mesure (*faire 20 mètres de long/15 kilos/20°/15 kilomètres à l'heure* etc.) pour lesquelles on consultera les notes d'usage

– les expressions décrivant une démarche de l'esprit (*se faire une opinion/du souci* etc.)

– les expressions indiquant l'effet produit (*faire peur/mal/plaisir/du tort* etc., *faire cuire/sécher/tomber* etc.)

– *faire + venir/entrer/sortir* etc.

– les locutions telles que *faire semblant/ exprès, se faire avoir* etc.

– les expressions familières (*faire un enfant* etc.)

par ailleurs, pour les expressions décrivant:

– une activité sportive (*faire du tennis/de la marche/du parapente*)

– une durée (*ça fait 15 ans*)

La consultation des notes d'usage vous fournira des traductions utiles. Voir la liste ▸ **p. 1355**. En outre, certaines entrées telles que **combien, ce, que, comment, laisser, rien, mieux, bien** etc. fourniront également des traductions utiles.

....

To make ou to do?

Les principales traductions de *faire* sont *to make* et *to do* mais elles ne sont pas interchangeables.

to make traduit *faire* + objet dénotant ce qui est créé, confectionné, composé, réalisé, obtenu; l'objet est le résultat de l'action:

faire son lit
= to make one's bed

faire des confitures
= to make jam

faire un discours
= to make a speech

faire une faute
= to make a mistake

faire un bénéfice
= to make a profit

je me suis fait un café
= I made myself a coffee

to do a le sens plus vague de se livrer à une activité, s'occuper à quelque chose; l'objet peut préciser la nature de l'activité:

faire de la recherche
= to do research

faire un exercice
= to do an exercise

faire son devoir
= to do one's duty

ou bien la nature de l'activité reste indéterminée:

que fait-il (dans la vie)?
= what does he do (for a living)?

qu'est-ce que tu fais ce soir?
= what are you doing tonight?

la science peut tout faire
= science can do anything

j'ai à faire
= I have things to do

ou encore le contexte suggère la nature de l'activité:

faire une pièce
= to do a room

peut vouloir dire la nettoyer, la ranger, la peindre.

Si *faire* remplace un verbe plus précis, on traduira fréquemment par celui-ci:

faire une maison
= to build a house

faire un nid
= to build a nest

faire une lettre
= to write a letter

faire une visite
= to pay a visit

faire un numéro de téléphone
= to dial a number

Les périphrases verbales sont parfois rendues par un seul verbe:

faire voir (= *montrer*)
= to show

faire du tissage (= *tisser*)
= to weave

Mais:

faire un peu de tissage
= to do a bit of weaving

....

Faire + infinitif + qn

faire + infinitif + qn, c'est-à-dire obtenir de quelqu'un qu'il agisse d'une certaine manière, se traduit selon le sens de *faire*, par:

to make sb do sth (forcer, être cause que):

fais-la lever
= make her get up

ça m'a fait rire
= it made me laugh

ça fait dormir
= it makes you sleep

to get sb to do sth (inciter):

fais-leur prendre un rendez-vous
= get them to make an appointment

to help sb to do sth (aider):

faire traverser la rue à un vieillard
= to help an old man across the street

Mais:

faire manger un bébé
= to feed a child

☛ Voir page suivante

faire *suite*

Dans l'exemple *ça fait dormir* on notera qu'en anglais le sujet du verbe est toujours exprimé, ce qui n'est pas le cas en français.

(se) faire faire qch (par qn) se traduit par *to have sth done* ou *made (by sb)*, ou, dans une langue plus familière, *to get sth done* ou *made (by sb)*:

(se) faire construire une maison
= to have a house built

(se) faire réparer sa voiture
= to have ou get one's car repaired

c'est la table qu'il a fait faire
= it's the table he had made

elle fait exécuter les travaux par un ami
= she's having the work done by a friend

Ne faire que

exprime soit la continuité:

il ne fait que pleuvoir
= it never stops raining *ou* it rains all the time

soit la restriction:

je ne fais qu'obéir aux ordres
= I'm only obeying orders

Faire reprend un autre verbe

Dans ce cas il sera généralement traduit par *to do*:

'je peux regarder?' 'faites ou faites je vous en prie'
= 'may I look?' 'please do'

il souffla, comme il avait vu faire son père
= he blew, as he had seen his father do

on veut que je parte, mais je n'en ferai rien
= they want me to leave, but I'll do nothing of the sort

Vous trouverez d'autres exemples dans l'entrée *faire*.

f

---

faîte /fɛt/ nm [1] (sommet) (de montagne) summit; (de maison) rooftop; (d'arbre) top; [2] Constr (faîtage) ridgepole; [3] fig (apogée) pinnacle

faitout /fɛtu/ nm stockpot

falaise /falɛz/ nf cliff

fallacieux, -ieuse /falasjø, øz/ adj [argument] fallacious; [promesse, prétexte] false; [ressemblance] deceptive; [espoir] illusory; **il est ~ de penser que...** it's a fallacy to think that...

falloir /falwaʀ/ [50]
A v impers [1] **il faut qch/qn** gén we need sth/sb (**pour faire** to do); (sans bénéficiaire) sth/sb is needed (**pour faire** to do); **ce qu'il faut** what is needed; **il va ~ plusieurs personnes** it will take several people (**pour faire** to do); **il en faut pour qu'il se fâche** it takes a lot to make him angry; **c'est plus qu'il n'en faut** it's more than enough; [2] **il leur faut qch** they need sth; **il leur faut faire** they have to do, they must do; **il m'a fallu trois heures pour finir** it took me three hours to finish; **il me faut (absolument) ce livre!** I've got to have that book!; **pas assez grand? qu'est-ce qu'il te faut?** not big enough? what more do you want?; [3] **il faut faire** (nécessité) we've/you've etc got to do, we/you etc have to do; (autorité) we/you etc must do; (conseil, suggestion) we/you etc should do; (convenance, reproche) we/you etc ought to do; **il ne faut pas faire** (autorité) we/you etc mustn't do; (conseil) we/you etc shouldn't do; **'tu vas payer?'—'il faut bien!'** 'are you going to pay?'—'I have to!'; **il ne faut pas la déranger** she mustn't be disturbed; **faudrait pas me prendre pour un imbécile○!** do you think I'm a fool?; **qu'est-ce qu'il ne faut pas entendre!** what a lot of nonsense!; **s'il fallait croire tout ce qu'on raconte!** you can't believe everything people say!; **il faut dire que** I/you/we etc have to ou must say that; **il faut vous dire que** you should know that; **fallait le dire plus tôt○!** why didn't you say so before?; **nous ne savions pas encore, faut-il le rappeler, qu'il serait élu** it must be remembered that we didn't know then that he would be elected; **il fallait le faire** it had to be done; **(il) faut/fallait le faire○!** (c'est remarquable) it takes/took a bit of doing!; (c'est stupide) would you believe it?; **puisqu'il le faut** since it has to be done; **s'il le faut** (nécessité) if necessary; (obligation) if I/we/they etc have to; **il ne fallait pas!** (politesse) you shouldn't have!; **comme il faut** [se tenir] properly; **elle est très comme il faut** she's very proper; **encore faudra-t-il trouver de l'argent** we/you/they etc will still have to find the money; **encore faut-il préciser que** it should be added that; [4] **il faut que tu fasses** (obligation) you must do, you've got to do, you have to do; (conseil) you should do; (convenance, reproche) you ought to do; **il fallait que ce soit fait** it had to be done; **s'il faut qu'elle l'aime pour le croire!** she must love him to believe him!; **encore faut-il qu'elle accepte** she's still got to agree

B **s'en falloir** vpr loin or tant s'en faut far from it; **peu s'en faut** very nearly; **il s'en faut de beaucoup** very far from it; **elle a perdu, mais il s'en est fallu de peu** she lost, but only just; **il s'en est fallu d'un rien** or **de presque rien** there was almost nothing in it

(Idiomes) **il faut ce qu'il faut!** there's no point in skimping!; **en moins de temps qu'il ne faut pour le dire** before you could say Jack Robinson

falot, ~e /falo, ɔt/
A adj [personne] insignificant
B nm lantern

falsification /falsifikasjɔ̃/ nf [1] (altération) falsification; [2] (imitation) forging

falsifier /falsifje/ [2] vtr [1] (altérer) to falsify, to tamper with [document, chèque]; to distort, to falsify [faits]; [2] (contrefaire) to forge [signature, monnaie]

famé, ~e /fame/ adj **un quartier mal ~** a disreputable ou seedy area

famélique /famelik/ adj [personne] emaciated; [animal] scrawny

fameusement /famøzmɑ̃/ adv remarkably

fameux, -euse /famø, øz/ adj [1] (dont on a parlé) much talked-about; [2] (connu de tous) famous; [3] (véritable) real, right; [4] (excellent) excellent; **pas ~** not great

familial, ~e[1], mpl **-iaux** /familjal, o/ adj [1] (de famille) family (épith); **la cellule ~e** the family unit; [2] Aut **berline ~e** estate car GB, station wagon US

familiale[2] /familjal/ nf Aut estate car GB, station wagon US

familiariser /familjaʀize/ [1]
A vtr to familiarize
B **se familiariser** vpr to familiarize oneself

familiarité /familjaʀite/ nf familiarity ¢; **il s'est permis des ~s** he was too familiar

familier, -ière /familje, ɛʀ/
A adj [1] (connu) [visage, paysage, nom] familiar (**à** to); [2] Ling [mot, style] informal, colloquial; [3] (sans façon) [entretien, attitude] informal; [personne, geste] familiar; [4] (domestique) **animal ~** pet; [5] (informé) familiar (**de** with)
B nm [1] (ami) close friend (**de** of); [2] (habitué) regular

familièrement /familjɛʀmɑ̃/ adv (communément) commonly; (sans façon) informally; (de manière inconvenante) with undue familiarity

famille /famij/ nf [1] Sociol family; **~ monoparentale/nucléaire** one-parent/nuclear family; **une ~ de musiciens** a musical family; **air de ~** family resemblance; **c'est de ~** it runs in the family; **faire partie de la ~** to be one of the family; **nous partons en ~** we're going as a family; **de ~** [photo, histoire] family (épith); **ne pas avoir de ~** to have no relatives; **ma seule ∼ est un vieil oncle** my only relative is an old uncle; **rentrer dans sa ∼ tous les samedis** to go back home every Saturday; **un petit vin des ∼s**○ a nice little wine; **2** Art, Pol, Relig (communauté) body; **une ∼ politique** a political persuasion; **3** Biol, Bot, Ling, Zool family

(Composés) **∼ d'accueil** host family; **∼ nombreuse** family with more than two children; **∼ de placement** foster family

famine /famin/ *nf* famine; **salaire de ∼** starvation wages (*pl*); **crier ∼** to be starving

fana○ /fana/
A *adj* mad keen○ GB (**de** about), crazy○ (**de** about)
B *nmf* fanatic; **un ∼ de cinéma** a film buff

fanal, *pl* **-aux** /fanal, o/ *nm* gén lamp; Naut lantern; Rail headlamp

fanatique /fanatik/
A *adj* [*militant, mouvement*] fanatical; [*admiration, amour*] ardent, unbridled
B *nmf* **1** (extrémiste) fanatic; **2** (enthousiaste)○ enthusiast, freak○

fanatiser /fanatize/ [1] *vtr* to fanaticize, to inflame
fanatisme /fanatism/ *nm* fanaticism
faner /fane/ [1]
A *vtr* **1** to wither [*plante*]; **2** to fade [*couleur*]; **3** to toss [*herbe*]
B *vi* **1** [*plantes*] to wither; **2** Agric to make hay
C **se faner** *vpr* **1** [*fleurs, plantes*] to wither, to wilt; **2** [*beauté, couleur*] to fade
faneur, -euse[1] /fanœr, øz/ ▸ p. 372 *nm,f* haymaker
faneuse[2] /fanøz/ *nf* (machine) tedder
fanfare /fɑ̃far/ *nf* **1** (orchestre) brass band; **annoncer qch en ∼** to trumpet sth, to give sth great publicity; **faire une entrée en ∼** to make a spectacular entry; **réveiller qn en ∼** to wake sb up with a great commotion; **2** (air) fanfare

fanfaron, -onne /fɑ̃farɔ̃, ɔn/
A *adj* boastful
B *nm,f* boaster, swaggerer; **faire le ∼** to boast, to talk big○
fanfaronnade /fɑ̃faronad/ *nf* boasting **₵**
fanfaronner /fɑ̃farɔne/ [1] *vi* to boast
fanfreluches /fɑ̃frəlyʃ/ *nfpl* frills and flounces
fange /fɑ̃ʒ/ *nf* mud, mire
fanion /fanjɔ̃/ *nm* pennant
fanon /fanɔ̃/ *nm* (de baleine) baleen plate; **les ∼s** whalebone **₵**; (de reptile, dindon) wattle; (de bovin, chien) dewlap; (de cheval) fetlock

fantaisie /fɑ̃tezi/ *nf* **1** (qualité) imaginativeness; **être plein de ∼** [*personne*] to be full of marvellous○ GB ideas; [*roman*] to be highly imaginative; [*logement*] to be unconventional; **manquer de ∼** [*personne*] to be staid; [*logement*] to be conventional; [*vie*] to be dull; **2** (caprice) whim, fancy; **vivre selon sa ∼** to do as one pleases; **ne pouvoir se permettre aucune ∼** (dans son habillement) to have to dress in a very conventional way; (dans ses dépenses) to be unable to afford any extra expenses; **3** (de peu de valeur) **s'offrir une petite ∼** (objet) to buy oneself a little something; (sortie) to spoil oneself; **un bijou ∼** a piece of costume jewellery GB *ou* jewelry US; **accessoires ∼** fun accessories; **verres ∼** novelty glasses; **4** Mus fantasia, fantasy; **5** Littérat fantasy

fantaisiste /fɑ̃tezist/
A *adj* **1** (peu fiable) [*personne, renseignement, horaires*] unreliable; [*chiffres, analyse*] doubtful; **2** (excentrique) [*idée*] farfetched; [*procédé*] odd; [*personne*] eccentric
B *nmf* mildly eccentric person
fantasmagorie /fɑ̃tasmagɔri/ *nf* phantasmagoria
fantasme /fɑ̃tasm/ *nm* fantasy
fantasmer /fɑ̃tasme/ [1] *vi* to fantasize (**sur** about)
fantasque /fɑ̃task/ *adj* [*personnage, comportement*] unpredictable; [*image, récit*] fanciful
fantassin /fɑ̃tasɛ̃/ *nm* infantryman, footsoldier; **les ∼s** the infantry (+ *v pl*)
fantastique /fɑ̃tastik/
A *adj* fantastic; **le cinéma ∼** fantasy films (*pl*)
B *nm* Art, Cin, Littérat (genre) **le ∼** fantasy
fantoche /fɑ̃tɔʃ/
A *adj* puppet (*épith*)
B *nm* puppet

fantomatique /fɑ̃tɔmatik/ *adj* ghostly
fantôme /fɑ̃tom/
A *nm* ghost
B (-)**fantôme** (*in compounds*) **cabinet-∼** shadow cabinet GB, ≈ minority leadership US; **image(-)∼** TV ghost; **membre(-)∼** Méd phantom limb; **société(-)∼** Jur dummy company; **train(-)∼** ghost train; **ville(-)∼** ghost town
FAO /ɛfao/ *nf* **1** Écon, Pol (*abbr* = **Food and Agriculture Organization**) FAO; **2** Ordinat *abbr* ▸ **fabrication**
faon /fɑ̃/ *nm* fawn
FAQ *nf* (*written abbr* = **foire aux questions**) FAQ, frequently asked questions
faramineux○, **-euse** /faraminø, øz/ *adj* [*prix, somme*] colossal, staggering; [*bêtise*] incredible
farandole /farɑ̃dɔl/ *nf* (folklorique) farandole; (de soirée) ≈ conga
farce /fars/ *nf* **1** (tour) practical joke; **faire une ∼ à qn** to play a practical joke on sb; **magasin de ∼s et attrapes** joke shop GB, novelty store US; **2** (plaisanterie) joke; **3** (bouffonnerie) farce; **4** Théât farce; **5** Culin stuffing, forcemeat
farceur, -euse /farsœr, øz/ *nm,f* **1** (plaisantin) practical joker; **2** (personne peu sérieuse) joker○
farcir /farsir/ [3]
A *vtr* **1** Culin to stuff (**de** with); **2** ○(surcharger) to cram (**de** with)
B **se farcir** *vpr* **1** ○(accomplir) to get stuck with○; **2** ●(supporter) to put up with; **il faut se ∼** he's a real pain in the neck○!; **3** (surcharger) to cram (**de** with); **elle se farcit la tête de détails inutiles** she crams her head with useless facts; **4** ○(ingurgiter) to polish off○
fard /far/ *nm* make-up; **sans ∼** [*beauté*] natural; [*vérité*] simple; [*avouer*] openly
(Composés) **∼ à joues** blusher; **∼ à paupières** eyeshadow
(Idiome) **piquer un ∼**○ to go as red as a beetroot GB, to turn as red as a beet US
farde /fard/ *nf* B (dossier) folder
fardeau, *pl* **∼x** /fardo/ *nm* lit, fig burden
farder /farde/ [1]
A *vtr* **1** fig to disguise [*vérité*]; **2** lit to put make-up on [*visage*]; **visage outrageusement fardé** face caked in make-up
B **se farder** *vpr* [*acteur*] to make up; [*femme*] (tous les jours) to use make-up; (un jour) to put on make-up; **elle s'est fardé les joues** she's put blusher on her cheeks
farfadet /farfadɛ/ *nm* elf; **des ∼s** elves
farfelu, **∼e** /farfəly/
A *adj* [*projet, idée*] harebrained○; [*histoire*] far-fetched; [*personne*] scatterbrained○; [*spectacle*] bizarre
B *nm,f* scatterbrain○
farfouiller○ /farfuje/ [1] *vi* to rummage around *ou* about (**dans** in)
faribole† /faribɔl/ *nf* piece of nonsense; **des ∼s** nonsense **₵**
farine /farin/ *nf* flour; (pour nourrisson) baby cereal
(Composés) **∼ d'avoine** oatmeal; **∼ de blé dur** durum wheat flour; **∼ complète** wholemeal flour GB, wholewheat flour US; **∼ de froment** wheat flour; **∼ lactée** ≈ baby cereal; **∼ de maïs** cornflour GB, cornstarch US; **∼ d'orge** barley meal; **∼ d'os** bone meal; **∼ de poisson** fish meal; **∼ de seigle** rye flour
(Idiomes) **de la même ∼** as bad as each other; **rouler qn dans la ∼**○ to pull a fast one on sb○; **se faire rouler dans la ∼**○ to be had○
farineux, -euse /farinø, øz/ *adj* [*aliment*] starchy; [*aspect, goût, pommes de terre, pain*] floury; [*fruit*] mealy
farniente /farnjɛnte/ *nm* **le ∼** lazing about, lazing around
farouche /faruʃ/ *adj* **1** [*enfant, animal*] timid, shy; [*adulte*] unsociable; **2** [*regard*] fierce; [*guerrier*] savage; **3** [*ennemi, haine*] bitter; [*adversaire, résolution*] fierce; [*partisan*] staunch; [*ambition*] driving; [*volonté*] iron; **4** liter [*paysage, côte*] wild
farouchement /faruʃmɑ̃/ *adv* gén fiercely; [*refuser*] doggedly
fart /fart/ *nm* (ski-)wax
farter /farte/ [1] *vtr* to wax [*skis*]

fascicule /fasikyl/ *nm* (brochure) booklet; **paraître en ~s** to come out in parts

fascinant, ~e /fasinã, ãt/ *adj* [*personne, film*] fascinating; [*charme*] spellbinding; [*beauté*] bewitching

fascination /fasinasjõ/ *nf* fascination (**pour qch** with sth); **exercer une ~ sur qn** [*personne, musique*] to hold sb in one's *ou* its spell; [*télévision, mer*] to hold a fascination for sb

fasciner /fasine/ [1] *vtr* ① (captiver) to fascinate; **il regardait, fasciné** he watched in fascination; ② (envoûter) [*orateur, musique*] to hold [sb] spellbound; [*mer, personne*] to fascinate; ③ (hypnotiser) [*regard, spectacle*] to mesmerize; [*serpent*] to hypnotize

fascisant, ~e /faʃizã, ãt/ *adj* fascistic

fascisme /faʃism/ *nm* fascism

faste /fast/
A *adj* auspicious
B *nm* splendour[GB], pomp; **avec ~** with pomp

fastidieux, -ieuse /fastidjø, øz/ *adj* tedious, tiresome

fastueux, -euse /fastɥø, øz/ *adj* sumptuous

fat, ~e /fa, at/
A *adj* [*homme, air, manières*] conceited
B *nm* conceited man

fatal, ~e /fatal/ *adj* ① (inévitable) inevitable; **il était ~ que cela se produise** it was bound to happen; ② (désastreux) fatal (**à qn/qch** to sb/sth), disastrous (**à qn/qch** for sb/sth); ③ (mortel) fatal; ④ (fatidique) [*moment, jour*] fateful

fatalement /fatalmã/ *adv* inevitably

fatalisme /fatalism/ *nm* fatalism

fataliste /fatalist/
A *adj* fatalistic
B *nmf* fatalist

fatalité /fatalite/ *nf* ① (sort) **la ~** fate; ② (caractère inévitable) inevitability

fatidique /fatidik/ *adj* fateful

fatigant, ~e /fatigã, ãt/ *adj* [*sport, voyage*] tiring; [*climat*] wearing; [*travail*] arduous; **mon travail est ~ pour les yeux** my job is a strain on the eyes; [*personne*] tiresome; [*film, conversation*] tedious

fatigue /fatig/ *nf* ① gén tiredness; **excès de ~** overtiredness; **être mort de ~, tomber de ~** to be dead tired; ② Méd fatigue **C**; **~ visuelle** eyestrain; ③ Tech (de matériau) fatigue; (mécanique) wear and tear

fatigué, ~e /fatige/
A *pp* ▸ **fatiguer**
B *pp adj* ① gén tired (**de faire** of doing); ② Méd [*personne*] suffering from fatigue (*après n*); [*cœur*] weak
C *adj* ① [*voix*] strained; [*visage, yeux, sourire*] weary; ② [*vêtement, chaussure*] worn; [*moteur, voiture*] suffering from wear and tear (*après n*); [*couleur*] faded

fatiguer /fatige/ [1]
A *vtr* ① (physiquement) to make [sb] tired [*personne*]; to strain [*yeux*]; to weaken [*cœur*]; to tire [*cheval*]; ② (intellectuellement) to tire [sb] out; ③ (ennuyer) to wear [sb] out; ④ (mécaniquement) to wear out [*moteur*]; to put a strain on [*matériau, structure*]; ⑤ Culin to toss [*salade*]; ⑥ Agric to exhaust [*terre*]
B *vi* ① ○(physiquement, intellectuellement) to get tired; ② [*moteur, voiture*] to be labouring[GB]; [*matériau, structure*] to show signs of strain
C **se fatiguer** *vpr* ① (devenir fatigué) to get tired (**de** of); ② (se rendre fatigué) to tire oneself out; **se ~ en recherches/en démarches** to wear oneself out doing research/dealing with red tape; ③ (rendre fatigué) **se ~ les yeux** to strain one's eyes; **se ~ les jambes** to tire one's legs; ④ (s'évertuer) **se ~ à faire** to bother doing

fatras /fatra/ *nm inv* jumble

fatuité /fatɥite/ *nf* self-conceit; **avec ~** conceitedly

faubourg /fobur/ *nm* ① (banlieue ouvrière) working class area (on the outskirts); ② Hist part of a town outside its walls or former walls; ③ (artère) faubourg

fauche /foʃ/ *nf* ① ○(vol) petty thieving; ② = **fauchage**

fauché○, **~e** /foʃe/
A *adj* (sans argent) broke○ (*jamais épith*), penniless
B *nm,f* **c'est un ~** he's always broke○

(Idiome) **être ~ comme les blés** to be flat broke○

faucher /foʃe/ [1] *vtr* ① (couper) (avec une faucheuse) to mow, to cut; (à la faux) to scythe; ② (abattre) [*cyclone, explosion*] to

---

flatten [*arbres, bâtiment*]; [*véhicule, tir*] to mow down [*personne*]; ③ ○(voler) to pinch○ GB, to steal [*argent, place*]

faucheur, -euse[1] /foʃœr, øz/
A *nm,f* ① (moissonneur) reaper; ② ○(voleur) petty thief
B *nm* (araignée) harvestman

faucheuse[2] /foʃøz/ *nf* (machine) mowing machine

faucheux /foʃø/ *nm inv* (araignée) harvestman

faucille /fosij/ *nf* sickle

faucon /fokõ/ *nm* ① Zool falcon, hawk US; ② Pol hawk

faudra /fodra/ ▸ **falloir**

faufil /fofil/ *nm* basting thread

faufiler /fofile/ [1]
A *vtr* (en couture) to baste
B **se faufiler** *vpr* ① (se frayer un chemin) **se ~ à l'intérieur** to squeeze in; **se ~ à l'extérieur** to slip out; **se ~ à travers** to thread one's way through; **se ~ par une ouverture** to squeeze through an opening; ② (s'insinuer) **se ~ dans** [*élément*] to creep into [*discours*]; ③ (serpenter) [*route*] to snake in and out (**entre** between)

faune[1] /fon/ *nm* faun

faune[2] /fon/ *nf* ① Zool wildlife, fauna; **la ~ du désert** desert wildlife *ou* fauna; **la ~ marine** marine life; ② (personnes) pej set, crowd

faussaire /foser/ *nmf* forger

fausse ▸ **faux**[1] A

faussement /fosmã/ *adv* ① (à tort) falsely, wrongfully; ② (hypocritement) deceptively; **attitude ~ soumise** attitude of feigned submission

fausser /fose/ [1] *vtr* to distort [*résultat*]; to damage [*serrure*]; to bend [*clé, axe*]; to buckle [*lame*]

(Idiome) **~ compagnie à qn** to give sb the slip

fausset /fose/ *nm* Mus falsetto; **d'une voix de ~** in a falsetto

fausseté /foste/ *nf* (d'argument, de nouvelle) falseness; (de personne) duplicity; (de sentiment) insincerity

faut /fo/ ▸ **falloir**

faute /fot/ *nf* ① (erreur) mistake, error; **~ d'orthographe** spelling mistake; **~ d'étourderie** *or* **d'inattention** careless mistake; **~ de français** mistake in French; **~ de frappe** keying error; **~ d'impression** misprint; **~ de calcul** miscalculation; **~ de jugement** error of judgment; **il a fait un (parcours) sans ~** (en équitation) he had a clear round; fig he's never put a foot wrong; ② (action coupable) gén misdemeanour[GB]; Jur civil wrong; Relig sin; **être en ~** to be at fault; **prendre qn en ~** to catch sb out; ③ (responsabilité) fault; **c'est (de) ma ~** it's my fault, I'm to blame; **par la ~ de qn** because of sb; **rejeter la ~ sur qn** to lay the blame on sb; ④ (manque) **~ de temps** through lack of time; **~ de preuves** for lack of evidence; **~ de garanties** in the absence of any guarantees; **~ de mieux** for want of anything better; **ce n'est pourtant pas ~ d'essayer** it's not for want of trying; **~ de quoi** otherwise, failing which; **sans ~** without fail; ⑤ Sport gén foul; (au tennis) fault

(Composés) **~ contractuelle** breach of contract; **~ délictuelle** tort; **~ grave** gross misconduct; **~ professionnelle** professional misconduct **C**

fauteuil /fotœj/ *nm* ① (siège) chair; (bas, rembourré) armchair; ② Cin, Théât (place) seat; ③ fig (siège) seat; (présidence d'une assemblée) **le ~** the chair; **~ de député** seat in parliament

(Composés) **~ à bascule** rocking chair; **~ crapaud** chunky armchair; **~ dentaire** dentist's chair; **~ relax** recliner; **~ roulant** wheelchair; **~ tournant** swivel chair

fauteur, -trice /fotœr, tris/ *nm* **~ de troubles** troublemaker; **~ de guerre** warmonger

fautif, -ive /fotif, iv/
A *adj* ① (coupable) [*personne*] guilty, at fault (*après n*); [*véhicule*] at fault (*après n*), in the wrong (*après n*); ② (erroné) [*mémoire, édition*] faulty; [*référence*] inaccurate; [*tournure*] incorrect
B *nm,f* culprit

fauve /fov/
A *adj* ① ▸ p. 140 [*couleur*] tawny; ② [*odeur*] musky; ③ Art [*période*] Fauve
B *nm* ① (animal féroce) wild animal; (félin) big cat; **les ~s** big

cats; **sentir le** ∼○ to stink○; **2** (couleur) fawn; **3** Art Fauvist, Fauve

fauvette /fovɛt/ *nf* warbler

faux¹, fausse /fo, fos/

A *adj* **1** [*résultat, numéro, idée*] wrong; [*impression*] false; [*balance*] inaccurate; **il est ∼ de dire** it's not true to say; **2** [*nez, barbe, dent, cils*] false; **3** [*bois, marbre, diamant*] imitation (*épith*); (*pour tromper*) fake (*épith*); [*porte, tiroir, cloison*] false; **c'est du ∼ Louis XV** it's reproduction Louis Quinze; **4** (contrefait) [*billet, document*] forged; **5** [*science, savoir*] pseudo (*épith*); [*liberté, besoin*] false; [*policier, évêque*] bogus (*épith*); [*candeur, humilité*] feigned; **c'est un ∼ problème** it's not really a problem at all; **6** [*espoir*] false; [*certitude*] mistaken; [*crainte*] groundless; [*réputation*] quite unfounded; **7** [*prétexte, promesse, accusation*] false; **8** [*personne, regard*] deceitful

B *adv* [*jouer, chanter*] out of tune; **sonner ∼** [*rire, parole*] to have a hollow ring; [*discours*] to sound false

C à faux *loc adv* **porter à ∼** to be off balance

D *nm inv* **1) le vrai et le ∼** truth and falsehood; **2** (objet, tableau) fake; (document) forgery; **∼ et usage de ∼** Jur forgery and use of false documents

(Composés) **fausse alerte** false alarm; **fausse blonde** dyed blonde; **fausse couche** Méd miscarriage; **fausse dent** false tooth; **fausse facture** bogus invoice; **fausse fenêtre** blind window; **fausse joie** ill-founded joy; **faire une fausse joie à qn** to raise sb's hopes in vain; **fausse manœuvre** false move; **fausse monnaie** forged *ou* counterfeit currency; **fausse note** Mus wrong note; fig jarring note; **fausse nouvelle** false report; **fausse piste** wrong track; **∼ ami** Ling faux ami (*foreign word which looks deceptively like a word in one's own language*); **∼ bruit** false rumour○ᴳᴮ; **∼ col** (de chemise) detachable collar; (de bière) head; **∼ contact** Électrotech faulty connection; **∼ débutant** false beginner; **∼ départ** false start; **∼ en écriture(s)** falsification **C** of accounts; **∼ frais** extras; **∼ frère** hum false friend; **∼ jeton**○ two-faced person; **∼ jour** lit deceptive light; fig **sous un ∼ jour** in a false light; **∼ mouvement** false move; **∼ nom** assumed name; **∼ pas** lit slip; fig (erreur) mistake; (gaffe) faux pas; **∼ plafond** false ceiling; **∼ pli** crease; **∼ seins** falsies○; **∼ témoignage** Jur (déposition) false *ou* perjured evidence; (délit) perjury **C**; **faire un ∼ témoignage** to bear false witness, to commit perjury

faux² /fo/ *nf inv* scythe

faux-bourdon, *pl* **∼s** /foburdɔ̃/ *nm* **1** Zool drone; **2** Mus faux bourdon

faux-filet, *pl* **∼s** /fofilɛ/ *nm* sirloin

faux-fuyant, *pl* **∼s** /fofɥijɑ̃/ *nm* **chercher un ∼** to try to evade the issue; **user de ∼s** to evade the issue, to prevaricate

faux-monnayeur, *pl* **∼s** /fomɔnɛjœr/ *nm* forger, counterfeiter

faux-semblant, *pl* **∼s** /fosɑ̃blɑ̃/ *nm* **les ∼s** pretenceᴳᴮ (*sg*); **user de ∼s** to put up a pretenceᴳᴮ, to put on an act

faux-sens /fosɑ̃s/ *nm inv* mistranslation

faveur /favœr/

A *nf* **1** (bienfait) favourᴳᴮ; **il nous a fait la ∼ d'une visite** he honouredᴳᴮ us with a visit; **avoir les ∼s de qn** to be in favourᴳᴮ with sb; **par ∼** as a favour; **régime** *or* **traitement de ∼** preferential treatment; **2** (ruban) favourᴳᴮ, ribbon

B en faveur de *loc prép* **1** (à l'avantage de) **le jugement a été rendu en sa ∼** the court decided in his/her favourᴳᴮ; **les votes en ∼ du candidat de l'opposition** the votes for the opposition candidate; **2** (pour aider) **en ∼ des handicapés** to help the disabled; **en ∼ de l'emploi** to promote employment; **intervenir en ∼ de qn** to intervene on sb's behalf

C à la faveur de *loc prép* thanks to; **à la ∼ de la nuit** under cover of darkness

favorable /favɔrabl/ *adj* favourableᴳᴮ; **être ∼ à** (partisan de) to be in favourᴳᴮ of; (propice à) to be favourableᴳᴮ to

favorablement /favɔrabləmɑ̃/ *adv* favourablyᴳᴮ

favori, -ite /favɔri, it/

A *adj* favouriteᴳᴮ

B *nm,f* favouriteᴳᴮ; **c'est le ∼ du professeur** he's the teacher's pet

C *nm* (sportif, cheval) favouriteᴳᴮ; **partir ∼** to be the favouriteᴳᴮ

D favoris *nmpl* (barbe) sideburns

favoriser /favɔrize/ [1] *vtr* **1** (avantager) to favourᴳᴮ (**par rapport à** over); **les circonstances l'ont favorisé** circumstances were in his favourᴳᴮ; **les milieux favorisés** the privileged classes; **2** (encourager) to encourage; (activement) to promote

favorite ► favori A, B

favoritisme /favɔritism/ *nm* favouritismᴳᴮ

fax /faks/ *nm inv* (document) fax; (machine) fax machine; **envoyer qch par ∼** to send sth by fax, to fax sth

fayot¹○ /fajo/ *nm* Culin bean

fayot²○, **-otte** /fajo, ɔt/ *nm,f* creep○, crawler○

FB (written abbr = **franc belge**) BFr

FCP /fsepe/ *nm* (abbr = **fonds commun de placement**) unit trust GB, mutual fund US

fébrile /febril/ *adj* **1** [*sentiment, geste, moment, œuvre*] feverish; [*personne, équipe*] nervous; **2** Méd feverish

fébrilement /febrilmɑ̃/ *adv* feverishly

fébrilité /febrilite/ *nf* **1** (agitation) agitation; **avec ∼** agitatedly; **2** (nervosité) nervousness

fécal, ∼e, *mpl* **-aux** /fekal, o/ *adj* faecal

fécond, ∼e /fekɔ̃, ɔ̃d/ *adj* [*femme, sol, esprit, imagination*] fertile; [*période, effort, travail, idée*] fruitful; **année ∼e en incidents** eventful year

fécondable /fekɔ̃dabl/ *adj* [*femelle*] fertile; [*ovule*] fertilizable

fécondation /fekɔ̃dasjɔ̃/ *nf* (de femme, femelle) impregnation; (de plante) pollination; (d'œuf) fertilization

(Composés) **∼ artificielle** artificial insemination; **∼ croisée** cross-fertilization; **∼ in vitro, FIV** in vitro fertilization, IVF

féconder /fekɔ̃de/ [1] *vtr* **1** to impregnate [*femme, femelle*]; (par insémination) to inseminate [*animal*]; to pollinate [*plante*]; to fertilize [*œuf*]; [*fleuve*] to make [*sth*] fertile [*terre*]; **2** fig to enrich [*esprit*]

fécondité /fekɔ̃dite/ *nf* **1** (de femme, femelle, sol) fertility; **2** fig (d'idée) potential; (d'auteur) productivity

fécule /fekyl/ *nf* starch **C**

féculent, ∼e /fekylɑ̃, ɑ̃t/

A *adj* starchy

B *nm* starch, starchy food **C**; **les ∼s** starches

fédéral, ∼e, *mpl* **-aux** /federal, o/ *adj* [*république, police, budget*] federal; [*association*] federated

fédéralisme /federalism/ *nm* federalism

fédérateur, -trice /federatœr, tris/

A *adj* federal

B *nm,f* unifier

fédératif, -ive /federatif, iv/ *adj* federal

fédération /federasjɔ̃/ *nf* federation

fédérer /federe/ [14]

A *vtr* to federate [*États*]

B se fédérer *vpr* [*États*] to federate; [*comités, entreprises*] to form an association

fée /fe/ *nf* fairy; **méchante ∼** wicked fairy

(Composé) **∼ du logis** perfect housewife

(Idiome) **avoir des doigts** *or* **mains de ∼** to have nimble fingers

féerie /fe(e)ri/ *nf* **1** (spectacle merveilleux) **c'est une vraie ∼** it's magical; **2** Théât extravaganza

féerique /fe(e)rik/ *adj* [*beauté, vision*] enchanting; [*monde, paysage, moment*] enchanted

feignant, ∼e /feɲɑ̃, ɑ̃t/ = **fainéant**

feindre /fɛ̃dr/ [55]

A *vtr* to feign [*émotion, maladie*]; **∼ de faire/d'être** to pretend to do/to be

B *vi* to pretend; **inutile de ∼** it's no use pretending

feint, ∼e¹ /fɛ̃, ɛ̃t/ *adj* [*émotion, état*] feigned; [*sourire*] false; **non ∼** genuine

feinte² /fɛ̃t/ *nf* **1** (manœuvre) gén, Mil, Sport feint; **2** ○(attrape) trick, ruse; **faire une ∼ à qn** to trick sb

feinter /fɛ̃te/ [1]

A *vtr* **1** Sport **∼ l'adversaire** (en boxe, escrime) to feint at one's opponent; (au football, rugby) to sell one's opponent a dummy GB, to fake out one's opponent US; **2** ○(tromper) to trick [*personne*]

B *vi* (en escrime) to make a feint; (en boxe) to feint; (au football, rugby) to dummy GB, to fake US

fêlé○, ~e /fɛle/
A *adj* (fou) cracked○ (*jamais épith*)
B *nm,f* loony○; **un ~ du ski/jazz** a ski/jazz freak○

fêler /fele/ [1]
A *vtr* to crack [*tasse, os*]
B se fêler *vpr* [*tasse, os*] to crack; **d'une voix fêlée** in a cracked voice

félicitations /felisitasjɔ̃/ *nfpl* congratulations (**pour** on; **à** to); **être reçu avec les ~ du jury** Scol, Univ to pass with distinction

félicité /felisite/ *nf* bliss

féliciter /felisite/ [1]
A *vtr* to congratulate (**pour** on); **je te félicite!** congratulations!; **je ne te félicite pas!** it's nothing to be proud of!
B se féliciter *vpr* **se ~ de qch** to be very pleased about sth

félin, ~e /felɛ̃, in/
A *adj* [1] Zool [*race*] feline; [*exposition*] cat (*épith*); [2] *fig* [*grâce*] feline; [*yeux*] catlike
B *nm* feline; **les ~s** felines, the cat family *sg*

félon, -onne /felɔ̃, ɔn/ *fml*
A *adj* perfidious
B *nm,f* traitor/traitress

fêlure /fɛlyʀ/ *nf* crack

femelle /fəmɛl/
A *adj* [1] Biol, Bot female; [2] Zool *gén* female; [*baleine, éléphant*] cow; [*moineau, perroquet*] hen; **cygne ~** pen; [3] Électrotech [*prise*] female
B *nf* female; (partenaire sexuel) mate

féminin, ~e /feminɛ̃, in/
A *adj* [*corps, sexe, rôle, population*] female; [*activité, magazine, lingerie, record*] women's; [*allure*] feminine; [*nom, rime*] feminine
B *nm* Ling feminine; **au ~** in the feminine

féminiser /feminize/ [1]
A *vtr* [1] to open [sth] up to women [*profession*]; [2] to make [sb/sth] more feminine [*personne, vêtement*]; [3] Biol to feminize
B se féminiser *vpr* [*profession*] (s'ouvrir aux femmes) to become more open to women; (avoir moins d'hommes) to become predominantly female

féministe /feminist/ *adj, nmf* feminist

féminité /feminite/ *nf* femininity

femme /fam/
A *nf* [1] woman; **vêtements pour ~s** women's *ou* ladies' clothes; **c'est la ~ de sa vie** she's the love of his life; **elle fait très ~** (jeune fille) she looks quite grown-up; **elle est très ~** (adulte) she's very feminine; **elle n'est pas ~ à mentir** she's not a woman to lie; [2] (épouse) wife
B femme(-) (*in compounds*) **~(-)écrivain** woman writer; **~(-)prêtre** woman priest; **~(-)soldat** woman soldier; **~-objet** sex object; **femme-femme** very feminine woman

(Composés) **~ active** working woman; **~ d'affaires** businesswoman; **~ à barbe** (au cirque) bearded lady; **~ battue** battered wife; **~ de chambre** (employée d'hôtel, de maison) chambermaid; (attachée au service d'une dame) lady's maid, personal maid; **~ de charge** housekeeper; **~ de cœur** caring person; **~ enfant** little-girlish woman; **~ fatale** femme fatale; **~ au foyer** housewife; **~ galante** courtesan; **~ d'intérieur** homemaker; **~ de lettres** woman of letters; **~ de mauvaise vie** loose woman; **~ de ménage** cleaner, cleaning woman *ou* lady; **~ du monde** well-bred lady; **~ de petite vertu** woman of easy virtue; **~ de service** cleaner, cleaning lady; **~ de tête** assertive woman; ▸ **bon, jeune**

(Idiomes) **ce que ~ veut, Dieu le veut** Prov what a woman wants, a woman gets; **souvent ~ varie (bien fol est celui qui s'y fie)** Prov woman is fickle

femmelette /famlɛt/ *nf* wimp○, weakling

fémur /femyʀ/ *nm* thighbone; **se casser le col du ~** to break one's hip

FEN /fɛn/ *nf* (*abbr = Fédération de l'éducation nationale*) FEN (*French teachers' union*)

fenaison /fənɛzɔ̃/ *nf* (saison) haymaking time; (action) haymaking

fendiller /fɑ̃dije/ [1]
A *vtr* to chap [*peau, lèvres*]; to craze [*terre*]; to crack [*bois, meuble*]

B se fendiller *vpr* [*peau, lèvres*] to chap; [*terre*] to craze over; [*bois, meuble*] to crack

fendre /fɑ̃dʀ/ [6]
A *vtr* [1] (couper) to chop [*bois*]; to split [*pierre*]; to slit [*tissu*]; [2] (ouvrir) (légèrement) to chap [*lèvre*]; to crack [*mur, pierre*]; (profondément) to split [*lèvre*]; to split [sth] open [*crâne*]; [3] *fig* **~ le cœur à qn** to break sb's heart; **récit à ~ l'âme** heartbreaking story; **~ l'air** to slice through the air; **~ la foule** to push one's way through the crowd
B se fendre *vpr* [1] (se craqueler) to crack; [2] *fig* [*cœur*] to break; [3] ○**tu ne t'es pas fendu!** that didn't break the bank!; **se ~ de** to manage [*sourire, discours*]; to come up with [*cadeau, brochure*]; to cough up○ [*somme d'argent*]; [4] Sport (escrime) to lunge

(Idiomes) **~ la bise** to run like lightning; **se ~ la pêche○** *or* **poire○** to split one's sides○; **avoir la bouche fendue jusqu'aux oreilles** to be grinning from ear to ear

fenêtre /fənɛtʀ/ *nf* [1] Archit window; ▸ **faux¹**; [2] (d'enveloppe) window; [3] (dans un document) space; [4] Ordinat window

(Composés) **~ basculante** tilt-and-turn window; **~ à croisillons** lattice window; **~ à guillotine** sash window; **~ de lancement** Astronaut launch window; **~ en saillie** bay window; (arrondie) bow window; **~ de toit** roof light

(Idiome) **jeter l'argent par les ~s** to throw money away

fenouil /fənuj/ *nm* fennel

fente /fɑ̃t/ *nf* [1] (ouverture) *gén* slit; (pour insérer une pièce, carte, lettre) slot; (de veste) vent; [2] (fissure) *gén* crack; (de bois) split; (de rocher) crevice

féodal, ~e, *mpl* **-aux** /feɔdal, o/
A *adj* feudal
B *nm* feudal landowner

féodalisme /feɔdalism/ *nm* feudalism

féodalité /feɔdalite/ *nf* [1] Hist (caractère) feudalism; (système) feudal system; [2] Pol (fief) fiefdom

fer /fɛʀ/
A *nm* [1] (métal) iron; [2] *fig* **de ~** [*discipline, volonté*] iron (*épith*); [3] (de chaussure) steel tip; (pour marquer) branding iron; (de relieur) blocking tool; [4] (épée) sword; (lame) blade; **croiser le ~ avec** to cross swords with; [5] (train) rail transport; **par ~** by rail
B fers *nmpl* [1] Méd forceps; [2] (de prisonnier) irons; **être dans les ~s** *lit* to be in irons; *fig* to be in chains

(Composés) **~ à cheval** horseshoe; **en ~ à cheval** horseshoe-shaped; **~ forgé** wrought iron; **~ à friser** curling iron; **~ de lance** *lit, fig* spearhead; **~ à repasser** (pour les vêtements) iron; (pour carte de paiement) manual imprinter (*for credit card transactions*); **~ (à repasser) à vapeur** steam iron; **~ à souder** soldering iron

(Idiomes) **croire dur comme ~** to believe wholeheartedly; **il faut battre le ~ pendant** *or* **tant qu'il est chaud** Prov strike while the iron is hot; **tomber les quatre ~s en l'air** to fall flat on one's back

fer-blanc, *pl* **fers-blancs** /fɛʀblɑ̃/ *nm* tinplate

ferblanterie /fɛʀblɑ̃tʀi/ ▸ p. 372 *nf* [1] (ustensiles) tinware; [2] (secteur) tin trade; [3] (boutique) ironmonger's GB, hardware store US

férié, ~e /feʀje/ *adj* **jour ~** public holiday GB, holiday US

férir /feʀiʀ/ *vtr* **sans coup ~** meeting no resistance

fermage /fɛʀmaʒ/ *nm* (mode) tenant farming; (bail) farm tenancy; (redevance) farm rent

ferme¹ /fɛʀm/
A *adj* [1] (résistant) [*chair, sol*] firm; [*blanc d'œuf, crème*] stiff; [2] (assuré) [*pas, voix, attitude, écriture*] firm; [*geste, exécution*] confident; **être ~ sur ses jambes** to be steady on one's legs; **d'une main ~** [*diriger, saisir*] with a firm hand; [*écrire*] in a firm hand; **rester ~ dans ses résolutions** to be steadfast in one's resolutions; [3] (inflexible) firm; [4] [*marché, commande, prix*] firm; [5] *Jur* **peine de prison** custodial sentence; **cinq ans de prison ~, cinq ans ~○** a five-year sentence with no remission
B *adv* [1] (discuter, batailler) vigorously; (croire) firmly; **tenir ~** to stand one's ground; **s'ennuyer ~** to be bored stiff; [2] (de façon définitive) **commander ~** to put in a firm order for [*avion, voiture*]

(Idiomes) **attendre de pied ~** to be ready and waiting; **je les attends de pied ~** I'm ready for them

ferme² /fɛʀm/ *nf* [1] (exploitation) farm; (maison) farmhouse; **à la** ~ on the farm; [2] (contrat) (**bail à**) ~ farming lease; (domaine affermé) leasehold; **donner qch à** ~ to lease sth; [3] Constr truss

(Composés) ~ **école** *farm attached to an agricultural college*; ~ **éolienne** windfarm

fermé, ~**e** /fɛʀme/
A *pp* ▸ **fermer**
B *pp adj* [1] (hermétique) **être** ~ **à l'art moderne** to be totally uninterested in modern art; **visage** ~ inscrutable face; [2] (élitiste) exclusive; [3] Math closed

ferme-auberge, *pl* **fermes-auberges** /fɛʀmobɛʀʒ/ *nf* farmhouse inn (*serving home-grown produce*)

fermement /fɛʀməmɑ̃/ *adv* firmly

ferment /fɛʀmɑ̃/ *nm* lit, fig ferment

fermentation /fɛʀmɑ̃tasjɔ̃/ *nf* [1] Biol fermentation; [2] (agitation) ferment

fermenter /fɛʀmɑ̃te/ [1] *vi* [1] Biol to ferment; [2] (être en effervescence) to be in ferment

fermentescible /fɛʀmɑ̃tɛsibl/ *adj* fermentable

fermer /fɛʀme/ [1]
A *vtr* [1] gén to close, to shut [porte, fenêtre, livre, parapluie]; to close, to shut [yeux, bouche]; to clench [poing]; to draw [rideau]; to seal [lettre]; to turn off [robinet, gaz, radio]; to switch off [électricité]; to do up [vêtement]; to close off [passage]; ~ **à clé** to lock up [maison]; to lock [voiture, valise]; ~ **à double tour** lit to double-lock [maison]; fig to lock securely [voiture, valise]; ~ **le jeu** Sport to play a defensive game; [2] Admin, Comm (temporairement) to close [magasin, aéroport, frontière]; (définitivement) to close down [entreprise]; to close [mine, compte bancaire]; [3] (terminer) to bring [sth] to a close [débat]
B *vi* (temporairement) to close; (définitivement) to close down
C **se fermer** *vpr* [1] lit [porte] to shut; [fleur] to close up; [manteau, bracelet] to fasten; [2] fig [personne] to clam up; [visage] to harden

(Idiome) ~ **les yeux sur** to turn a blind eye to

fermeté /fɛʀməte/ *nf* firmness

fermette /fɛʀmɛt/ *nf* farmhouse-style cottage

fermeture /fɛʀmətyʀ/ *nf* [1] gén (de magasin, d'usine) (brève) closing; (longue) closure; (définitive) closing down; (de compte en banque) closing; '**attention à la ~ des portes**' 'mind the doors'; [2] Tech (dispositif) (de porte) latch; (de fenêtre, meuble) catch; (de sac à main) clasp; (de vêtement) fastening; ~ **automatique** automatic locking system; [3] (en phonétique) closure

(Composés) ~ **à baïonnette** bayonet clutch; ~ **éclair**® or **à glissière** zip GB, zipper US

fermier, -**ière¹** /fɛʀmje, ɛʀ/
A *adj* [beurre, fromage] farm (épith); [poulet, œufs] free-range (épith); **exploitation fermière** (activité) farming; (ferme) farm
B ▸ p. 372 *nm,f* (agriculteur) farmer
C *nm* Comm, Jur leaseholder

fermière² /fɛʀmjɛʀ/ *nf* (épouse de fermier) farmer's wife

fermoir /fɛʀmwaʀ/ *nm* (de bijou, sac, reliure) clasp

féroce /feʀɔs/ *adj* [1] (cruel) [animal] ferocious; [rire, répression] savage; [personne, air] fierce; [2] (acharné) [bataille] fierce; [3] (violent) [appétit] voracious; [envie, désir] violent

férocement /feʀɔsmɑ̃/ *adv* [1] (avec cruauté) savagely; [2] (violemment) fiercely

férocité /feʀɔsite/ *nf* [1] (d'animal) ferociousness; [2] (de réplique, rire) savagery; [3] (de personne, regard) fierceness

ferraille /feʀɑj/ *nf* [1] (morceaux de fer) scrap iron; (morceaux de métal) scrap metal; [2] (dépôt) scrapheap; [3] ○(monnaie) small change

ferrailleur /feʀɑjœʀ/ *nm* [1] ▸ p. 372 (récupérateur) scrap (metal) dealer; [2] (batailleur) swashbuckler

ferré, ~**e** /feʀe/
A *pp* ▸ **ferrer**
B *pp adj* [1] (muni de ferrures) [animal] shoed; [chaussure, bâton] steel-tipped; [roue] rimmed with steel; [lacet] tagged; [coffre] ironbound; [2] ○(instruit) **être** ~ **en** or **sur** to be well up on○

ferrer /feʀe/ [1] *vtr* [1] to shoe [cheval]; (munir de ferrures) to fit steel tips on [chaussure]; to rim [sth] with steel [roue]; to tip [sth] with steel [bâton]; to tag [lacet]; to reinforce [sth] with steel [porte]; [2] to hook [poisson]

ferreux, -**euse** /feʀø, øz/ *adj* ferrous; **métaux non** ~ non-ferrous metals

ferronnerie /feʀɔnʀi/ *nf* [1] (lieu) ironworks; **atelier de** ~ wrought iron workshop; [2] (travail) (du fer forgé) wrought ironwork; (du fer) ironwork

ferronnier /feʀɔnje/ ▸ p. 372 *nm* [1] (fabricant) iron craftsman; [2] (commerçant) iron work merchant

ferroviaire /feʀɔvjɛʀ/ *adj* [transport, collision, trafic] rail (épith); [gare, tunnel, compagnie] railway GB (épith), railroad US (épith)

ferrugineux, -**euse** /feʀyʒinø, øz/ *adj* ferruginous

ferrure /feʀyʀ/ *nf* [1] (de porte, fenêtre) metal fittings (pl); (de meuble, coffre) metal band; [2] (de cheval) shoes (pl)

ferry-boat, *pl* ~**s** /feʀibot/ *nm* gén ferry; (pour véhicules) (car) ferry

fertile /fɛʀtil/ *adj* [sol, plaine] fertile; [imagination] fertile; [année] productive; **année** ~ **en événements** eventful year; **journée** ~ **en émotions** day filled with emotion

fertilisant /fɛʀtilizɑ̃/ *nm* (engrais) fertilizer

fertiliser /fɛʀtilize/ [1] *vtr* to fertilize

fertilité /fɛʀtilite/ *nf* fertility

féru, ~**e** /feʀy/ *adj* **être** ~ **de qch** to be very keen on sth

férule /feʀyl/ *nf* **être sous la** ~ **de qn** to be under sb's iron rule

fervent, ~**e** /fɛʀvɑ̃, ɑ̃t/
A *adj* [croyant, prière] fervent; [admirateur, amour] ardent
B *nm,f* ~ **de tennis** tennis enthusiast GB, tennis buff US; ~ **de musique/théâtre** music/theatre^{GB} lover

ferveur /fɛʀvœʀ/ *nf* (de prière) fervour^{GB}; (d'amour) ardour^{GB}

fesse /fɛs/ *nf* Anat buttock

(Idiomes) **attention à tes** ~**s**○ watch your step; **avoir la police aux** ~**s**○ to have the police hot on one's trail; **avoir chaud aux** ~**s**○ to have a narrow escape○; **coûter la peau des** ~**s**○ to cost an arm and a leg○; **pousse tes** ~**s**⦾! shove over○! GB, scoot over○! US; **serrer les** ~**s**⦾ to be scared stiff

fessée /fese/ *nf* smack on the bottom, spanking

fessier /fesje/ *nm* [1] ○(fesses) backside○, behind○; [2] Anat (muscle) gluteus

festin /fɛstɛ̃/ *nm* feast; **faire un** ~ to have a feast

festival /fɛstival/ *nm* festival; **pièce hors** ~ play on the fringe

festivalier, -**ière** /fɛstivalje, ɛʀ/ *nm,f* festival-goer

festivités /fɛstivite/ *nfpl* festivities

feston /fɛstɔ̃/ *nm* [1] (guirlande) festoon; [2] Archit festoon; [3] (point de broderie) scallop; **à** ~**s** scalloped

festoyer /fɛstwaje/ [23] *vi* to feast

fêtard○, ~**e** /fɛtaʀ, aʀd/ *nm,f* reveller

fête /fɛt/ *nf* [1] (jour chômé) (jour) public holiday GB, holiday US; [2] (jour du saint patron) **c'est ma** ~ it's my (saint's) name-day; **ça va être ma** ~○! iron I'm going to cop it○!; **la** ~ **des pompiers** the festival of the patron saint of firemen; [3] (solennité religieuse) festival; [4] (célébration) (day of) celebration; [5] (réjouissances privées) party; **faire la** ~ to live it up○; **je serai de la** ~! fig I'll be there!; **air de** ~ festive look; **avoir le cœur en** ~ to feel incredibly happy; **être à la** ~ fig to have a field day; **ne pas être à la** ~ fig to be having a bad time; [6] (foire) fair; (kermesse) fête, fair; (manifestation culturelle) festival; (réjouissances officielles) celebrations (pl)

(Composés) ~ **de bienfaisance** charity bazaar; ~ **fixe** fixed feast; ~ **foraine** funfair; ~ **légale** public holiday GB, legal holiday US; ~ **des Mères** Mothers' Day; ~ **mobile** movable feast; **la** ~ **des morts** All Souls' Day ~ **Nationale** national holiday; (en France) Bastille Day; ~ **des Pères** Fathers' Day; ~ **des Rois (Mages)** Twelfth Night, Epiphany; ~ **du travail** Labour Day, 1 May

(Idiomes) **faire sa** ~○ **à qn** to give sb a working over○; **ce n'est pas tous les jours la** ~ Prov life is not a bed of roses

ℹ **Fête nationale** France's *fête nationale* is celebrated annually on the 14th July with nationwide firework displays, street parties, dancing and other local festivities. The date was chosen because of its symbolic significance, commemorating the fall of the Bastille in 1789 which signalled the end of the *Ancien Régime*.

f

Fête-Dieu /fɛtdjø/ nf Corpus Christi

fêter /fete/ [1] vtr to celebrate [anniversaire]; to fete [champion]

fétiche /fetiʃ/
A adj lucky; **jour** ~ lucky day
B nm [1] (mascotte) mascot; [2] Psych, Relig fetish

fétichiste /fetiʃist/
A adj fetishistic
B nmf fetishist

fétide /fetid/ adj [1] (malodorant) [odeur] foul; [lieu] foul-smelling; [2] (répugnant) [personne] repulsive

fétu /fety/ nm ~ **(de paille)** wisp of straw

feu[1], ~e /fø/ adj late; ~ **la reine, la** ~**e reine** the late queen

feu[2], pl ~**x** /fø/
A ▸ p. 140 adj inv (de couleur) ~ flame-colouredGB; **rouge** ~ fiery red
B nm [1] (combustion, incendie) fire; ~ **de braises** glowing embers (pl); **au** ~! fire!; **mise à** ~ (de fusée) blast-off; **au coin du** ~ [s'asseoir, bavarder] by the fire; [causerie, rêverie] fireside (épith); ▸ **huile, marron**; [2] (lumière) light; **les** ~**x de la rampe** the footlights; **sous le** ~ **des projecteurs** lit under the glare of the spotlights; fig in the spotlight; [3] (éclat) **briller de mille** ~**x** [chandelier, diamant] to sparkle brilliantly; **les** ~**x du couchant** the fiery glow of the setting sun; [4] Aut, Aviat, Naut (signal) light; **tous** ~**x éteints** without lights; [5] (à un carrefour) traffic light; ~ **orange** amber GB ou yellow US light; **j'ai le** ~ **vert de mon patron** my boss has given me the go-ahead; [6] Culin (de cuisinière) ring GB, burner US; (chaleur) heat; **j'ai oublié la soupe sur le** ~ I've left the soup on the stove; **j'ai quelque chose sur le** ~ I've got something cooking; [7] (allumettes, briquet) **avez-vous du** ~? have you got a light?; [8] (sensation de brûlure) **épice qui met la bouche en** ~ spice that burns your mouth; **elle avait les joues en** ~ her cheeks were burning ou on fire; **pour apaiser le** ~ **du rasoir** to soothe shaving burn; [9] (enthousiasme) passion; **avoir un tempérament de** ~ to have a fiery temperament; **dans le** ~ **de la discussion** in the heat of the discussion; [10] (tir) ~! fire!; **faire** ~ to fire (**sur** at); **coup de** ~ shot; **le coup de** ~ **de midi** (dans un restaurant) the lunchtime rush; **être pris entre deux** ~**x** lit, fig to be caught in the crossfire; [11] (combat) action; **aller au** ~ to go into action; [12] ○(pistolet) gun
(Composés) ~ **d'artifice** (spectacle) fireworks display; (fusée) firework; ~ **de Bengale** Bengal light; ~ **de camp** campfire; ~ **de cheminée** (incendie) chimney fire; (pour chauffer) open fire; ~ **d'encombrement** marker lamp ou light; ~ **follet** lit, fig will-o'-the-wisp; ~ **de gabarit** ~ **d'encombrement**; ~ **de joie** bonfire; ~ **de paille** fig flash in the pan; ~ **de signalisation** traffic light; ~ **tricolore** traffic light; ~**x de croisement** dipped GB headlights; dimmed headlights US; ~**x de détresse** warning lights; ~**x de position** Aut sidelights GB, parking lights US; ~**x de recul** reversing GB ou back-up US lights; ~**x de route** headlights; ~**x de stationnement** sidelights GB, parking lights US
(Idiomes) **il n'y a pas le** ~○! there's no rush!; **jouer avec le** ~ to play with fire; **faire long** ~ [projectile, projet] to misfire; **ne pas faire long** ~○ not to last long; **il n'y a vu que du** ~○ he fell for it; **mourir à petit** ~ to die a slow death; **avoir le** ~ **au derrière**○ or **aux fesses**○ (être pressé) to be in a rush

feuillage /fœjaʒ/ nm [1] Bot foliage ⊄, leaves (pl); [2] (décor) leafage ⊄; (branches coupées) cut branches (pl)

feuille /fœj/ nf [1] (d'arbre) leaf; ~**s d'érable** maple leaves; **arbre à** ~**s persistantes** evergreen; **arbre à** ~**s caduques** deciduous tree; [2] (de papier, carton) sheet; [3] (de métal, plastique) (plaque mince) sheet; (pellicule) foil ⊄; ~ **d'étain** tinfoil ⊄; ~ **d'argent** silver leaf ⊄; [4] (de placage) veneer ⊄; [5] (de dorure) ~ **d'or, en** ~**s** gold leaf ⊄; **dorer à la** ~ to gild; [6] (formulaire) form; [7] ○(journal) paper
(Composés) ~ **blanche** blank sheet; ~ **de chêne** Culin oak-leaf lettuce; ~ **de chou**○ (journal) rag○, newspaper; ~ **de chou farcie** Culin stuffed cabbage roll; **avoir les oreilles en** ~ **de chou** to have cauliflower ears; ~ **d'impôts** (déclaration) tax return; (avis de débit) tax demand GB, tax statement US; ~ **de maladie** a form for reclaiming medical expenses from the social security office; ~ **de notes** school report; ~ **de paie** payslip GB, pay stub US; ~ **de présence** attendance sheet; ~ **de route** Mil movement

order; (pour la paix, le développement) road map; ~ **de vigne** Bot vine leaf; Art fig leaf; ~ **volante** loose sheet

feuillet /fœjɛ/ nm (feuille) leaf; (page) page
(Composés) ~ **détachable** tear sheet; **bloc à** ~**s détachables** tear-off pad; ~ **intercalaire** interleaf

feuilleté, ~e /fœjte/
A adj [1] (en géologie) [roche] foliated; [2] Ind [verre] laminated; [3] Culin **pâte** ~**e** puff pastry
B nm Culin savouryGB pasty (made with puff pastry); ~**s au jambon/fromage** ham/cheese pasties

feuilleter /fœjte/ [20] vtr to leaf through [livre]

feuilleton /fœjtɔ̃/ nm [1] Radio, TV, Littér serial; (à rebondissements) soap (opera); **publié en** ~ serialized; **c'est un vrai** ~ it's a real saga; [2] (chronique) column

feuillu, ~e /fœjy/
A adj [1] (touffu) leafy; [2] Bot [arbre] broad-leaved (épith)
B nm Bot broad-leaved tree

feulement /følmã/ nm growl (of a tiger)

feutre /føtʀ/ nm [1] (matière) felt ⊄; [2] (chapeau) felt hat; [3] (stylo) felt-tip (pen)

feutré, ~e /føtʀe/ adj [1] (étouffé) [ambiance, lieu] hushed; [son] muffled; **marcher à pas** ~**s** to pad along; [2] (garni de feutre) [bureau] felt-topped

feutrer /føtʀe/ [1]
A vtr [1] (traiter) to felt [poils, laine]; **un tissu feutré** felt material; [2] (détériorer) to felt [étoffe]; **un pull feutré** a felted sweater; [3] (garnir) to felt [selle]
B vi [lainage] to become felted

feutrine /føtʀin/ nf (pour vêtements) fine felt fabric; (pour ameublement, table de billard) baize

fève /fɛv/ nf [1] Bot, Culin broad bean; [2] C (haricot) bean; ~**s au lard** baked beans; [3] (figurine) lucky charm (hidden in Twelfth Night cake)

février /fevʀije/ ▸ p. 380 nm February

FF (written abbr = **franc français**) FFr

fg written abbr = **faubourg** 3

fi /fi/ excl pooh!
(Idiome) **faire** ~ **de qch** to treat sth with disdain

fiabilité /fjabilite/ nf reliability

fiable /fjabl/ adj [machine, compagnie] reliable; [personne] (sérieuse) reliable; (de confiance) trustworthy

fiançailles /fjɑ̃saj/ nfpl engagement (sg)

fiancé, ~e /fjɑ̃se/ nm,f fiancé/fiancée

fiancer: se fiancer /fjɑ̃se/ [12] vpr to get engaged (**à, avec** to)

fiasque /fjask/ nf straw-sheathed flask

fibre /fibʀ/ nf [1] lit fibreGB; [2] fig (sensibilité) streak; **avoir la** ~ **maternelle** to have a strong maternal streak
(Composés) ~ **optique** fibreGB optics (+ v sg); ~ **de verre** fibreglassGB

fibreux, -euse /fibʀø, øz/ adj (texture) fibrous; (consistance) sinewy

ficeler /fisle/ [19] vtr to tie up [paquet]; to tie [mains, pieds]; **bien/mal ficelé** [intrigue, roman] well/badly put together; [projet, enquête] badly organized
(Idiome) ~ **qn comme un saucisson** to truss sb up like a chicken GB, to hogtie sb US

ficelle /fisɛl/ nf [1] (corde) string; [2] (astuce) trick; **la** ~ **est un peu grosse** it's a bit obvious; [3] Culin (baguette mince) thin baguette
(Idiomes) **avec des bouts de** ~ on a shoestring; **tirer sur la** ~ to push one's luck

fiche[1]○ /fiʃ/ vtr, **se fiche** vpr = **ficher** A 3, 4, 5; B 2, 3, 4

fiche[2] /fiʃ/ nf [1] (à classer) (en carton) index card; (en papier) (petite) slip; (grande) sheet; ~ **médicale** medical card; ~ **pratique** card with practical hints; [2] (formulaire) form; ~ **d'inscription** enrolmentGB form; [3] Électrotech (prise) plug; (broche) pin; **prise à trois** ~**s** three-pin plug
(Composés) ~ **(individuelle) d'état civil** Admin record of personal details for administrative purposes; ~ **de lecture** notes pl (from a book); ~ **de paie** payslip GB, pay stub US; ~ **technique** technical data sheet

ficher /fiʃe/ [1]
A vtr [1] (répertorier) to put [sth] on a file [œuvre]; to open a file on [personne]; **être fiché par la police** to be on police files;

f

[2] (enfoncer) to drive [*piquet, clou*] (**dans** into); **[3]** ᴼ(faire) to do; **ne rien ~** to do nothing; **n'en avoir rien à ~** not to give a damnᴼ; **[4]** ᴼ(donner) **~ un coup à qn** lit to wallop sb; fig to be a real blow to sb; **~ la trouille⊘ à qn** to scare the hell out of sb; **[5]** ᴼ(mettre) **où est-ce qu'il a bien pu ~ mon journal?** where the hell⊘ has he put my newspaper?; **son arrivée a fichu la soirée par terre** or **en l'air** his/her arrival ruined the party; **~ qn dehors** or **à la porte** (congédier) to give sb the bootᴼ; (faire sortir) to kick sb outᴼ; **~ qn dedans** (induire en erreur) to make sb screw upᴼ; **~ la paix à qn** to leave sb alone

B se ficher *vpr* **[1]** (se planter) [*flèche, couteau*] to stick (**dans** in); **[2]** ᴼ(se mettre) **se ~ en colère** to fly off the handleᴼ; **se ~ dedans** to screw upᴼ; **[3]** ᴼ(ridiculiser) **se ~ de qn** (se moquer) to make fun of sb; (manquer de respect) to mess sb aboutᴼ; **le repas était excellent, ils ne se sont pas fichus de nous** the meal was excellent, they did us proud; **se ~ du monde** [*personne*] to have a hell of a nerveᴼ; **[4]** ᴼ(être indifférent) **se ~ de ce que qn fait** not to give a damnᴼ (about) what sb does

fichier /fiʃje/ *nm* **[1]** (liste) file; (plusieurs listes) files (*pl*); (dans une bibliothèque) index; **[2]** (meuble) filing cabinet; (boîte) card index file; **[3]** Ordinat file

fichu /fiʃy/
A ᴼ*pp* ▸ **ficher A 3, 4, 5, B 2, 3, 4**
B ᴼ*adj* **[1]** (détestable) (*before n*) [*temps*] rottenᴼ; [*pluie*] dreadful; [*voiture, télévision*] damnedᴼ, blastedᴼ; [*caractère*] nasty; [*métier*] rottenᴼ; **[2]** (condamné) [*personne*] done forᴼ; (usé, cassé) [*vêtements, véhicule, machine*] done forᴼ; **s'il pleut c'est ~** if it rains that's the end of that; **c'est la troisième ampoule de ~e** that's the third bulb that's gone; **[3]** (fait) **comment c'est ~ ce truc?** how's this thing made?; **être bien ~** [*femme*] to be shapely; [*homme*] to be well built; **être bien/mal ~** (conçu) [*dispositif*] to be well/badly designed; [*appartement*] to be well/badly laid out; [*vêtement*] to be well made/badly cut; **être mal ~** (malade) to feel lousyᴼ; **[4]** (considérable) **une ~e différence** to be a heck of a difference; **[5]** (capable) **être ~ de faire** to be quite capable of doing; **il n'est pas ~ d'écrire une lettre** he can't even write a letter
C *nm* (châle) shawl

fictif, -ive /fiktif, iv/ *adj* **[1]** (inventé) [*personnage, récit*] fictitious, imaginary; [*promesse, identité*] false; **[2]** Fin [*actif, dividende*] fictitious; [*valeur*] conventional

fiction /fiksjɔ̃/ *nf* **[1]** gén fiction; **la réalité dépasse la ~** truth is stranger than fiction; **[2]** TV (émission) (TV) drama

ficus /fikys/ *nm inv* ficus

fidèle /fidɛl/
A *adj* **[1]** (constant) [*personne, chien*] faithful (**à** to); **être ~ au poste** to be always there; **[2]** (loyal) loyal (**à** to); **[3]** (identique) true (**à** to); **[4]** (conforme) [*traduction*] faithful (**à** to); **[5]** (fiable) [*instrument*] reliable
B *nmf* **[1]** (compagnon) loyal supporter; **[2]** (personne constante) faithful friend; **[3]** Relig **les ~s** the faithful (+ *v pl*); **quelques ~s** some of the faithful

fidèlement /fidɛlmɑ̃/ *adv* **[1]** (avec exactitude) faithfully; **[2]** (avec loyauté) loyally

fidéliser /fidelize/ **[1]** *vtr* to secure the loyalty of [*clients, adhérents*]

fidélité /fidelite/ *nf* **[1]** (dans un couple) fidelity; **[2]** (d'ami, de client) loyalty (**à** to); **[3]** (de celui qui promet) faithfulness; **[4]** (de traduction) accuracy; **[5]** (de mesure) reliability

fidjien, -ienne /fidʒjɛ̃, ɛn/ ▸ p. 392 *adj* Fijian

fiduciaire /fidysjɛʀ/ *adj* [*émission, circulation*] fiduciary; **société ~** trust company

fief /fjɛf/ *nm* **[1]** Hist fief; **[2]** (espace) territory; (de parti) stronghold

fieffé, ~e /fjefe/ *adj* **~ menteur** incorrigible liar

fiel /fjɛl/ *nm* **[1]** (hargne) venom; **[2]** Méd bile

fielleux, -euse /fjɛlø, øz/ *adj* venomous

fiente /fjɑ̃t/ *nf* droppings (*pl*)

fier¹, fière /fjɛʀ/ *adj* **[1]** (satisfait) proud; **tu peux être ~ de toi** lit you have every right to be proud; iron you must be very proud of yourself; **[2]** (hautain) proud, haughty; (prétentieux) stuck-up; **il n'était pas si ~ à l'examen!** he wasn't so cocky⊘ in the exam!; **[3]** (noble) [*caractère*] proud; **avoir fière allure** to cut a fine figure

(Idiomes) **~ comme Artaban** or **un coq** or **un paon** proud as a peacock; **faire le ~** to be haughty

fier²: se fier /fje/ **[2]** *vpr* **[1]** (placer sa confiance en) **se ~ à** to trust [*personne, promesse*]; **ne te fie pas à ce qu'il dit/aux apparences** don't go by what he says/by appearances; **[2]** (compter sur) **se ~ à** to rely on [*personne, mémoire, calculs*]; **to trust to** [*chance, destin*]

fier-à-bras, *pl* **fiers-à-bras** /fjɛʀabʀa/ *nm* braggart

fièrement /fjɛʀmɑ̃/ *adv* proudly

fierté /fjɛʀte/ *nf* pride; **tirer ~ de** to take pride in

fiestaᴼ /fjɛsta/ *nf* party; **faire la ~** to rave it upᴼ

fièvre /fjɛvʀ/ *nf* **[1]** Méd (high) temperature; **avoir de la ~** to have a (high) temperature; **[2]** (agitation) frenzy; **pris de ~** caught up in a frenzy; **[3]** (ardeur) fervourᴳᴮ; **[4]** (passion) fever; **~ électorale** election fever; **la ~ monte** the temperature is rising

(Composés) **~ de cheval**ᴼ raging fever; **~ jaune** yellow fever

fiévreusement /fjevʀøzmɑ̃/ *adv* [*chercher, préparer*] frantically; [*parler*] feverishly

fiévreux, -euse /fjevʀø, øz/ *adj* **[1]** Méd feverish; **[2]** (agité) frantic; **[3]** (passionné) feverish

fifilleᴼ /fifij/ *nf* little girl

fifre /fifʀ/ *nm* **[1]** ▸ p. 389 (instrument) fife; **[2]** (personne) fife player

figé, ~e /fiʒe/
A *pp* ▸ **figer**
B *pp adj* **[1]** (immobile) [*attitude, personne*] frozen; [*situation, sourire*] fixed; **[2]** (rigide) [*société*] fossilized; [*situation*] deadlocked; **être ~ dans ses habitudes** to be set in one's ways; **[3]** Ling [*expression*] set

figer /fiʒe/ **[13]**
A *vtr* **[1]** (immobiliser) **la peur figeait leurs visages/traits** their faces/features were frozen with fear; **[2]** (solidifier) to congeal [*graisse*]; to thicken [*sauce*]; to clot [*sang*]
B **se figer** *vpr* **[1]** [*attitude, sourire, personne*] to freeze (**de** with); **[2]** (se scléroser) [*idéologie, société, personne*] to become fossilized; **[3]** (se solidifier) [*graisse, sauce*] to congeal; [*sang*] lit to clot; fig to freeze

fignoler /fiɲole/ **[1]**
A *vtr* **[1]** (terminer) to put the finishing touches to; **[2]** (soigner) to take great pains over
B *vi* to fiddle about

figue /fig/ *nf* fig

(Composé) **~ de Barbarie** prickly pear

figuier /figje/ *nm* fig tree

figurant, ~e /figyʀɑ̃, ɑ̃t/ *nm,f* (acteur) Cin extra; Théât bit player; **n'être qu'un ~** fig to have a token role

figuratif, -ive /figyʀatif, iv/ *adj* Art figurative, representational; **artiste non ~** abstract artist; **poésie figurative** emblematic *ou* figured verse

figuration /figyʀasjɔ̃/ *nf* **faire de la ~** Théât to do bit parts; Cin to be an extra; fig to have a token role

figure /figyʀ/ *nf* **[1]** (visage, mine) face; **ma ~ s'allongea** my face fell; **elle changea de ~** her face fell; **[2]** (apparence) **faire ~ d'amateur** to look like an amateur; **ne plus avoir ~ humaine** to be unrecognizable; **reprendre ~ humaine** hum to look half-human again; **[3]** (personnalité) figure; **[4]** (schéma, photo, dessin) figure; **[5]** Jeux (carte) court card

(Composés) **~ imposée** compulsory figure; **~ de proue** lit figurehead; fig key figure; **~ de rhétorique** gén figure of speech; Littérat rhetorical figure; **~ de style** stylistic device; **~ libres** freestyle ℂ

(Idiomes) **prendre ~** to take shape; **faire bonne ~** (garder le sourire) to keep an air of composure; (faire bonne impression) to make the right impression; (réussir) to do well; **faire piètre** or **triste ~** (avoir l'air misérable) to look *ou* cut a sorry figure; (faire mauvaise impression) to make a bad impression

figuré, ~e /figyʀe/
A *adj* **sens ~** figurative sense
B *nm* Ling figurative sense

figurer /figyʀe/ **[1]**
A *vtr* to represent
B *vi* [*nom, chose*] to appear; **faire ~ qch dans un rapport** to include sth in a report; **un pompier figure parmi les victimes** a fireman is among the casualties
C **se figurer** *vpr* to imagine; **j'avais compris, figurez-vous!** I had actually got the point!; **figure-toi que je l'ai revu dix ans après!** I saw him again ten years later, can you imagine!

figurine /figyʀin/ nf figurine

fil /fil/
A nm [1] (brin) thread, cotton **C** GB; [2] (fibre naturelle) yarn; (fibre synthétique) filament; [3] (câble, corde) (en fibre) string; (métallique) wire; (de pêche) line; Sport (d'arrivée) tape; [4] Électrotech, Télécom (ligne) wire; (de micro, combiné, d'appareil électrique) flex GB, cord US; (de téléphone) lead; **sans ~** [micro, téléphone] cordless; **coup de ~**○ (phone) call; **au bout du ~**○ on the phone; ▸ **inventer**; [5] (lin) linen **C**; [6] (enchaînement de texte, conversation) thread; **perdre le ~ des événements** to lose track of events; **~ de la pensée** train of thought; [7] Culin (de haricot, céleri) string; **haricots sans ~s** stringless beans; [8] (d'araignée) thread; [9] (de bois) grain; [10] (tranchant) edge
B au fil de loc prép **au ~ des ans** over the years; **au ~ de l'enquête** in the course of the investigation; **au ~ des kilomètres, le paysage change** the scenery changes as you travel along; **aller au ~ de l'eau** lit, fig to go with the flow
(Composés) **~ d'Ariane** Mythol Ariadne's thread; fig vital clue; **~ conducteur** Électrotech conductor; (de roman) thread; (d'enquête) lead; **~ à couper le beurre** Culin cheese wire; **il n'a pas inventé le ~ à couper le beurre** fig he's not very bright; **~ dentaire** dental floss; **~ directeur** guiding principle; **~ de fer** wire; **~ à plomb** plumb line; **~ de la Vierge** gossamer thread
(Idiomes) **ne tenir qu'à un ~** to hang by a thread; **être mince comme un ~** to be as thin as a rake; **être sur le ~ du rasoir** to be on a knife edge

filage /filaʒ/ nm [1] (de laine etc) spinning; [2] Théât run through

filament /filamã/ nm [1] gén filament; **viande pleine de ~s** stringy meat; [2] Électrotech filament

filandreux, -euse /filãdʀø, øz/ adj [1] (plein de fils) [légume, viande] stringy; [2] (confus) rambling

filasse /filas/
A adj inv **cheveux (blond) ~** dirty yellow hair **C**
B nf (de lin, chanvre) tow

filature /filatyʀ/ nf [1] (usine) textile mill; [2] (surveillance) tailing **C**; **prendre qn en ~** to tail sb○

file /fil/ nf [1] (queue) **~ (d'attente)** queue GB, line US; [2] (alignement) line; **sortir/entrer en ~** to file out/in; **à la ~** (successivement) in a row; [3] (sur une chaussée) lane; **se garer en double ~** to double-park
(Composé) **~ indienne** single file

filer /file/ [1]
A vtr [1] (transformer en fil) to spin [laine, coton]; to draw [métal]; [2] Zool [araignée, chenille] to spin [toile, cocon]; [3] (démailler) to get a run in [collant]; [4] Naut (dérouler) to play out [ligne]; **~ 20 nœuds** [navire] to do 20 knots; [5] Mus to hold [note]; Théât to run straight through [scène]; Littérat to extend [métaphore]; [6] (suivre) to tail○ [suspect]; **~ le train**○ **à qn** to be on sb's tail○; [7] ○(donner) to give
B vi [1] Culin (couler) [sirop] to thread; [fromage fondu] to go stringy; [2] (se démailler) [collant] to ladder GB, to run US; [3] Naut (se dérouler) [cordage] to unwind; **laisser ~ un câble** to play out a cable; [4] ○(s'éloigner) [véhicule, animal] to go off; [personne] to leave; **~ à toute allure** [véhicule] to speed off; [animal] to run off; [personne] to dash off; **file, et que je ne te revoie plus!** clear off○, and don't come back!; [5] ○(aller) to rush; [6] ○(disparaître) [temps, journée] to fly past; [prisonnier] to get away; **~ entre les mains** [personne, argent, occasion] to slip through one's fingers
(Idiomes) **~ comme le vent** or **une flèche** to go like the wind; **~ des jours heureux** to lead a happy life

filet /filɛ/ nm [1] (objet en maille) net; **attirer** or **prendre qn dans ses ~s** fig to get sb in one's clutches; **coup de ~** (par la police) raid; **travailler sans ~** fig to take risks; [2] Tech (matériau) (textile) netting **C**; (métallique) mesh **C**; [3] Culin (de viande, poisson) fillet; [4] (d'eau) trickle; (de gaz) breath; (de fumée) wisp; **~ de citron** dash of lemon juice; **un ~ de voix** a faint voice; [5] (trait fin) rule; (sur une reliure) fillet; Art thin line; [6] (article de presse) snippet
(Composés) **~ à bagages** luggage rack; **~ à papillons** butterfly net; **~ de pêche** fishing net; **~ de protection** safety net; **~ à provisions** string bag

fileur, -euse /filœʀ, øz/ ▸ p. 372 nm,f (de laine, lin) spinner

filial, ~e[1], mpl **-iaux** /filjal, o/ adj filial

filiale[2] /filjal/ nf subsidiary

filiation /filjasjɔ̃/ nf filiation; **descendre de qn par ~ directe** to be a direct descendant of sb

filière /filjɛʀ/ nf [1] Univ (domaine d'études) course of study; **suivre une ~ scientifique/littéraire** to study science/arts; [2] Écon (domaine d'activité) field; [3] (étapes de carrière) **la ~ habituelle** the usual career ladder; [4] (suite de formalités) official channels (pl); [5] (de la drogue) **~ (clandestine)** ring; [6] Ordinat card throat

filiforme /filifɔʀm/ adj (mince) [personne, jambes, sculpture] spindly; [insecte, pattes] threadlike

filigrane /filigʀan/ nm [1] (de papier) watermark; **lire en ~** fig to read between the lines; **être en ~ dans** fig to be implicit in; [2] (en orfèvrerie, verrerie) filigree

filin /filɛ̃/ nm Naut rope

fille /fij/ nf [1] (descendante) daughter; **elle a eu une petite ~** she's had a little girl; **ma ~** gén my girl; Relig my child; ▸ **superstition**; [2] (jeune femme) girl; **elle fait encore très petite ~** she's still very much a little girl
(Composés) **~ de (bonne) famille** girl from a good family; **~ de ferme** farm girl; **~ mère**† unmarried mother; **~ spirituelle** spiritual heir
(Idiomes) **jouer les ~s de l'air**○ to vanish into thin air; **la plus belle ~ du monde ne peut donner que ce qu'elle a** with the best will in the world one can only go so far

fillette /fijɛt/ nf [1] (petite fille) little girl; **rayon ~** Comm girlswear department; [2] ○(bouteille) half bottle
(Idiome) **chausser du 45 ~**○ to have feet like boats○

filleul /fijœl/ nm godson, godchild

filleule /fijœl/ nf goddaughter, godchild

film /film/ nm [1] (œuvre) film, movie US; **un ~ à succès** a box-office success; **~ parlant** talking film; **~ muet** silent film; [2] (déroulement d'événements) course, sequence; [3] (pellicule) film; [4] (mince couche) film
(Composés) **~ d'animation** cartoon; **~ catastrophe** disaster film; **~ d'épouvante** or **d'horreur** horror film; **~ noir** film noir; **~ policier** detective film; **~ publicitaire** publicity film

filmé, ~e /filme/
A pp ▸ **filmer**
B pp adj on film; **la version ~e de Hamlet** the film version of Hamlet

filmer /filme/ [1] vtr to film

filmique /filmik/ adj film (épith)

filon /filɔ̃/ nm [1] (de roches) vein, seam, lode; **~ d'or** vein of gold; **exploiter un ~** lit, fig to mine a seam; [2] ○(pactole) bonanza; (travail lucratif) cushy number○; **avoir trouvé le bon ~** to be on to a good thing

filou /filu/ nm (escroc) crook; (tricheur) cheat; (enfant malin) rascal

fils /fis/ nm inv son; **Alexandre Dumas ~** Alexandre Dumas the younger; **Dupont ~** (entreprise) Dupont Junior; **Dupont et ~** (entreprise) Dupont and Son(s); **mon ~** gén my boy; Relig my son
(Composés) **~ de (bonne) famille** boy from a good family; **Fils de Dieu** Relig Son of God; **Fils prodigue** Bible Prodigal Son; **~ spirituel** spiritual heir

filtrant, ~e /filtʀã, ãt/ adj [papier, corps, couche] filter (épith)

filtre /filtʀ/ nm filter; **cigarette avec/sans ~** filter-tip/ untipped cigarette
(Composés) **~ à air** air filter; **~ à café** coffee filter; **~ à huile** oil filter; **~ solaire** sun screen

filtrer /filtʀe/ [1]
A vtr [1] (purifier) to filter; [2] (tamiser) to filter [bruit, lumière]; [3] (sélectionner) to screen [visiteurs, appels téléphoniques]
B vi [1] (émerger) [informations] (lentement) to filter through; (malgré les précautions) to leak out; [idée] to filter through; [2] (s'écouler) [liquide] to filter through; [3] (passer) [son, lumière] to filter

fin[1], **fine**[1] /fɛ̃, fin/
A adj [1] [sable, pluie] fine; [fil, écriture, pinceau, pointe] fine; [tranche, couche, verre] thin; [petit pois, haricots verts] quality (épith); **très ~s** top-quality (épith); [2] (délicat) [cheville, taille] slender; [traits] fine; [bijou, dentelle] delicate, fine; [vins, aliments] fine; [plat] delicate; [4] (subtil) [personne] perceptive; [esprit] shrewd; [allusion, interprétation, humour] subtle; [goût] delicate, subtle; **vraiment c'est ~!** iron that's

really clever! iron; **jouer au plus ~ avec qn** to try to outsmart sb; **avoir l'air ~**○ to look a fool; **tu as l'air ~**○ **avec ce chapeau!** you look a sight○ in that hat!; **5)** (sensible) **avoir l'ouïe ~e** to have a keen sense of hearing; **avoir le nez ~** to have a keen sense of smell; **6)** (remarquable) excellent; **la ~ fleur des économistes** the top *ou* best economists; **7)** (ultime) **au ~ fond de** in the remotest part of [*pays, région*]; at the very bottom of [*tiroir, armoire*]; **le ~ mot de l'histoire** the truth of the matter

B *adv* **1)** (complètement) **être ~ prêt** to be all set; **~ soûl**○ completely drunk; **2)** (finement) [*écrire, moudre*] finely; [*couper*] thinly

C *nm* **le ~ du ~** the ultimate (**de** in)

(Composés) **~ limier** super-sleuth; **~ renard** sly customer○; **~e gueule**○ gourmet; **~e mouche = ~ renard**; **~es herbes** mixed herbs, fines herbes

fin² /fɛ̃/ *nf* **1)** (terme) end; (de réunion, période) close, end; (façon dont se termine quelque chose) ending; **à la ~ des années 70** in the late '70s; **en ~ de matinée** late in the morning; **jusqu'à la ~** to the (very) end; **toucher** *or* **tirer à sa ~** to be coming *ou* drawing to an end; **prendre ~** to come to an end; **avoir des ~s de mois difficiles** to find it hard to make ends meet at the end of the month; **c'est la ~ de tout** it's the last straw; **mener qch à bonne ~** to bring sth to a successful conclusion; **sans ~** [*discussions*] endless; [*discuter*] endlessly; **tu vas te taire à la ~**○! for God's sake, be quiet!; **tu m'ennuies à la ~**○! you're really getting on my nerves!; **chômeur en ~ de droits** *unemployed person no longer eligible for benefit*; **~ de siècle** *pej* decadent, fin-de-siècle; **2)** (mort) end, death; **3)** (but) end, aim, purpose; **à toutes ~s utiles** for whatever purpose it may serve; **arriver à ses ~s** to achieve one's aims

(Composés) **~ de semaine** weekend; **~ de série** Comm oddment

final, ~e¹, *mpl* **-aux** /final, o/ *adj* final

finale² /final/ *nm* Mus finale

finale³ /final/ *nf* **1)** Sport final; **quart de ~** quarterfinal; **2)** Ling final; **en ~** in final position

finalement /finalmɑ̃/ *adv* **1)** (à la fin) in the end, finally; **2)** (en définitive) in fact, actually; **~ on a tout à y gagner** after all, we have everything to gain by it

finaliser /finalize/ [1] *vtr* to finalize [*accords*]; to complete [*transaction*]

finaliste /finalist/ *adj, nmf* finalist

finalité /finalite/ *nf* **1)** gén purpose, aim; **2)** Philos finality

finance /finɑ̃s/

A *nf* **1)** (activité) **la ~** finance; **un homme de ~** financier; **2)** (milieu) financiers (*pl*)

B finances *nfpl* **les ~s** finances; **moyennant ~s** for a consideration; **les ~s sont à sec**○ funds are exhausted; **mes ~s sont à sec**○ I'm broke○; **les Finances**○ (ministère) the Ministry (*sg*) of Finance

financement /finɑ̃smɑ̃/ *nm* financing **¢**

financer /finɑ̃se/ [12]

A *vtr* to finance

B ○*vi* (payer) to fork out○

financier, -ière /finɑ̃sje, ɛʀ/

A *adj* [*directeur, crise*] financial; **compagnie financière** finance company

B *nm* **1)** (personne) financier; **2)** Culin small cake (made with ground almonds and egg whites)

finasser /finase/ [1] *vi* to scheme, to use trickery

finaud, ~e /fino, od/

A *adj* cunning, wily

B *nm,f* (homme) wily bird○; (femme) crafty minx

fine² /fin/ *nf* (boisson) brandy

finement /finmɑ̃/ *adv* **1)** [*ouvragé, tissé*] finely, delicately; [*hacher, couper*] finely; **2)** (avec subtilité) cleverly; **c'est ~ joué!** that's a smart *ou* shrewd move!; **3)** (avec précision) [*mesurer*] accurately, precisely

finesse /finɛs/ *nf* **1)** (minceur) (d'aiguille, écriture, de fil, cheveux) fineness; (de couche, papier) thinness; (de lame) keenness, sharpness; **2)** (délicatesse) (de broderie, bijou, parfum, d'aliment) delicacy; (de visage) fineness, delicacy; (de chevilles, taille) slenderness; **3)** (perspicacité) (de personne, remarque) perceptiveness; (d'acteur, interprétation) sensitivity, finesse; **4)** (acuité des sens) keenness, sharpness; **5)** (subtilité) **les ~s d'une langue** the subtleties of a language

finette /finɛt/ *nf* brushed cotton

fini, ~e /fini/

A *pp* ▸ **finir**

B *pp adj* **1)** (terminé) **être ~** to be over, to be finished; **~ de rire!**, **~e la rigolade**○! the party's over!; **c'en est ~ de leurs espoirs** it's the end of their hopes; **2)** (ouvragé) finished; **produits ~s** finished products; **3)** ○(invétéré) [*menteur, alcoolique*] out-and-out, complete; **4)** ○(usé) [*artiste, politicien*] finished; **5)** Math [*ensemble, univers*] finite

C *nm* finish

finir /finiʀ/ [3]

A *vtr* **1)** (achever) to finish (off), to complete [*travail, tâche*]; (conclure) to end [*journée, nuit, discours*]; **~ de faire** to finish doing; **finissez vos querelles!** put a stop to your quarrelling GB!; **pour ~, je dirai que** in conclusion I'll say that; **vous n'avez pas fini de vous disputer?** for goodness sake stop arguing!; **tu n'as pas fini de te plaindre?** have you quite finished complaining?; **elle n'a pas fini de s'inquiéter** her worries are only just beginning; **tu n'as pas fini d'en entendre parler!** you haven't heard the last of it!; **2)** (consommer jusqu'au bout) to use up [*provisions, produit*]; to finish [*plat*]

B *vi* to finish, to end; **le film finit bien/mal** the film has a happy/an unhappy ending; **ça va mal ~!** it'll end in tears!; **il finira mal ce garçon** that boy will come to a bad end; **sa barbe finit en pointe** his beard tapers to a point; **~ en prison** to end up in prison; **tu vas ~ par te blesser** you'll end up hurting yourself; **ils finiront bien par céder** they're bound to give in in the end; **il a fini par** he eventually made up his mind; **finissons-en!** let's get it over with!; **il faut en ~ avec cette situation** we must put an end to this situation; **l'hiver n'en finit pas** the winter seems endless; **il n'en finit pas de se préparer** she takes ages○ to get ready; **des discussions à n'en plus ~** endless discussions; ▸ **queue**

finish /finiʃ/ *nm* Sport finish; **il l'a emporté au ~** he won at the finishing-line

finissant, ~e /finisɑ̃, ɑ̃t/ *adj* **une époque ~e** an era which is drawing to an end; **à l'été ~** in the last days of the summer

finition /finisjɔ̃/ *nf* (processus) finishing; (résultat) finish; **faire les ~s** to add the finishing touches (**de** to); **travaux de ~** finishing

finlandais, ~e /fɛ̃lɑ̃dɛ, ɛz/ ▸ p. 392 *adj* Finnish

Finlandais, ~e /fɛ̃lɑ̃dɛ, ɛz/ ▸ p. 392 *nm,f* Finn

Finlande /fɛ̃lɑ̃d/ ▸ p. 230 *nprf* Finland

finnois, ~e /finwa, az/ ▸ p. 336

A *adj* Finnish

B *nm* Ling Finnish

fiole /fjɔl/ *nf* (flacon) phial

fion○ /fjɔ̃/ *nm* H (mot blessant) cutting remark

fioriture /fjɔʀityʀ/ *nf* **1)** (ornement) embellishment; **sans ~s** [*meuble, pièce*] unadorned; [*écriture*] plain; [*parler, écrire*] plainly; **2)** Mus ornamentation

fioul /fjul/ *nm* fuel oil

(Composé) **~ domestique** heating oil

firmament /fiʀmamɑ̃/ *nm* **1)** (ciel) firmament; **2)** fig **au ~ du succès** at the pinnacle of success

firme /fiʀm/ *nf* firm

fisc /fisk/ *nm* tax office

fiscal, ~e, *mpl* **-aux** /fiskal, o/ *adj* fiscal, tax (épith)

fiscaliser /fiskalize/ [1] *vtr* **1)** (imposer) to tax; **2)** (financer par l'impôt) to fund [sth] by taxation

fiscalité /fiskalite/ *nf* **1)** (fait d'imposer) taxation; **2)** (système) tax system

fissible /fisibl/ *adj* fissionable, fissile

fission /fisjɔ̃/ *nf* fission; **~ nucléaire** nuclear fission

fissionner /fisjone/ [1] *vtr, vi* to split

fissure /fisyʀ/ *nf* **1)** (fente) crack; **2)** Anat fissure; **3)** fig rift

fissurer /fisyʀe/ [1] *vtr* **1)** (fendiller) to crack, to fissure spéc; **2)** (diviser) to cause a rift in [*amitié, union*]

fiston○ /fistɔ̃/ *nm* sonny○, son

fitness /fitnɛs/ *nm* fitness training; **un club de ~** a gym, a health club

FIV /fiv/ *nf: abbr* ▸ **fécondation**

fixateur /fiksatœr/ *nm* [1] Art, Phot (produit) fixative; (appareil) (à main) fixative sprayer; (à bouche) fixative mouth blower; [2] (après une permanente) neutralizing solution; (laque) fixative; (de parfum) fixative; [3] Biol (pour analyse) fixative

fixation /fiksasjɔ̃/ *nf* [1] (mise en place) fixing; (attache) fastening; [2] (détermination) setting; ~ **de la peine** Jur determination of penalty; ~ **des cours** (en Bourse) fixing; [3] Sport (de ski) binding; [4] (d'azote, oxygène) fixation; [5] Bot, Zool (processus) attachment; (attache) (de plante) stem; (de mollusque) foot; [6] Art, Phot (de pastel, photo) fixing; [7] Ling fossilization; [8] (de population) settling; [9] Psych fixation

fixe /fiks/
A *adj* [1] (immobile) [*caméra, point*] fixed; **avoir le regard** *or* **l'œil** ~ to have a fixed stare; [2] (invariable) [*prix, taux*] fixed; [*poste, résidence*] permanent; **à heures** ~**s** at set times
B *nm* (salaire) basic salary GB, base pay US
C *excl* Mil attention!

fixé, ~e /fikse/
A *pp* ▸ **fixer**
B *pp adj* [1] (renseigné) **tu es** ~ **maintenant!** you've got the picture now○!; **nous ne sommes pas encore** ~**s sur leur sort** we are still uncertain about their fate; [2] (certain) **nous ne sommes pas encore très** ~**s** we haven't really decided yet; [3] (orienté) **le monde entier a les yeux** ~**s sur vous** the whole world is watching you; [4] (installé) [*famille*] settled
C *nm* Art glass-picture

fixement /fiksəmɑ̃/ *adv* [*regarder*] fixedly

fixer /fikse/ [1]
A *vtr* [1] (attacher) to fix [*objet*] (**à** to; **sur** on); ~ **avec des boulons/des vis/de la colle** to bolt/to screw/to stick (**sur** to); [2] (décider) to set [*date, prix, conditions*]; ~ **son choix sur qch/qn** to decide on sth/sb; **au jour fixé** on the appointed day; [3] (établir) ~ **son domicile en France** to make one's home in France; ~ **le siège de l'organisation à Paris** to base the organization's headquarters in Paris; [4] (stabiliser) to fix [*couleur, émulsion*]; to establish [*frontières, forme littéraire*]; to regulate [*orthographe, langue*]; ~ **ses idées par écrit** to set one's ideas down in writing; [5] (concentrer) to focus [*attention, regard*]; [6] (observer) to stare at [*personne, objet*]
B **se fixer** *vpr* [1] Tech (s'attacher) [*pièce*] to be attached (**à** to); [2] (décider) to set oneself [*but, limite*]; [3] (s'installer) [*personne*] to settle; (se ranger) [*personne*] to settle down; [4] (se figer) **se** ~ **dans l'esprit/la mémoire de qn** to stick in sb's mind/ memory; **leur système d'écriture s'est fixé dès l'antiquité** their writing system was established in ancient times; [5] Zool [*coquillage, moule*] to attach itself (**à, sur** to)

fjord /fjɔrd/ *nm* fjord

flacon /flakɔ̃/ *nm* (bouteille) (small) bottle; (carafe) decanter; Chimie flask

flagada○ /flagada/ *adj inv* whacked○, exhausted

flagellation /flaʒɛlasjɔ̃/ *nf* gén flogging, scourging; Relig flagellation

flageller /flaʒele/ [1] *vtr* to flog; Relig to flagellate

flageoler /flaʒɔle/ [1] *vi* [1] **on les jambes qui flageolent** to feel wobbly; [2] [*amitié*] to crumble

flageolet /flaʒɔlɛ/ *nm* [1] (haricot) flageolet; [2] ▸ p. 389 (flûte) flageolet

flagorner /flagɔrne/ [1] *vtr* to fawn on, to toady to [*personne*]; to curry favour[GB] with [*groupe, public*]

flagornerie /flagɔrnəri/ *nf* toadying ¢, sycophantic behaviour[GB] ¢

flagrant, ~e /flagrɑ̃, ɑ̃t/ *adj* [*preuve*] obvious; [*injustice*] flagrant; [*mensonge*] blatant; [*erreur, exemple*] glaring

(Composé) ~ **délit** Jur *case requiring no further collection of evidence*; **en** ~ **délit** in flagrante delicto; **prendre qn en** ~ **délit** to catch sb red-handed

flair /flɛr/ *nm* [1] (odorat) nose; **avoir du** ~ to have a good nose; [2] (intuition) intuition

flairer /flɛre/ [1] *vtr* [1] (renifler) to sniff [*objet, vêtement*]; **le chien a flairé une piste** the dog has picked up a scent; [2] (sentir) [*animal*] to scent [*gibier, personne*]; [*personne*] to smell [*odeur*]; [3] (discerner) to sense [*danger*]

(Idiome) ~ **le vent** to see which way the wind is blowing

flamand, ~e /flamɑ̃, ɑ̃d/
A *adj* Flemish
B ▸ p. 336 *nm* Ling Flemish

flamant /flamɑ̃/ *nm* flamingo

(Composé) ~ **rose** pink flamingo

flambant /flɑ̃bɑ̃/ *adv* ~ **neuf** brand new

flambeau, *pl* ~**x** /flɑ̃bo/ *nm* [1] (torche) torch; **retraite aux** ~**x** torchlight procession; [2] fig torch (**de** of); [3] (chandelier) candlestick

flambée /flɑ̃be/ *nf* [1] (feu) fire; **faire une** ~ to light a fire; [2] (de violence) flare-up; (des prix) explosion (**de** in)

flamber /flɑ̃be/ [1]
A *vtr* [1] Culin (à la flamme) to singe [*volaille*]; (avec de l'alcool) to flambé [*crêpe, omelette*] (**à** in); [2] Méd to sterilize [sth] in a flame; [3] ○(dépenser) to blow [*argent, économies*]
B *vi* [1] lit [*combustible*] to burn; [*maison*] to burn down; [2] (augmenter) [*prix, cours*] to soar

flambeur○**, -euse** /flɑ̃bœr, øz/ *nm,f* [1] (dépensier) big spender; [2] (joueur) big-time gambler

flamboiement /flɑ̃bwamɑ̃/ *nm* (de feu) blaze; **le** ~ **des arbres en automne** fig the flaming colours[GB] (*pl*) of the trees in autumn GB *ou* the fall US

flamboyant, ~e /flɑ̃bwajɑ̃, ɑ̃t/
A *adj* [1] gén [*feu, lumière*] blazing; [*couleur*] flaming; [*ciel, coucher de soleil*] fiery; **chevelure** ~**e** flaming red hair; [2] Archit **gothique** ~ Flamboyant Gothic
B *nm* [1] Bot flame tree; [2] Archit Flamboyant (Gothic) style

flamboyer /flɑ̃bwaje/ [23] *vi* [*incendie, soleil, couleur*] to blaze; [*yeux*] gén to flash; (de colère) to blaze (**de** with); [*épée*] to gleam

flamingant, ~e /flamɛ̃gɑ̃, ɑ̃t/
A *adj* Ling [*population, région*] Flemish-speaking
B *nm,f* [1] Ling Flemish speaker; [2] Pol Flemish nationalist

flamme /flam/
A *nf* [1] (feu) flame; **passer une volaille à la** ~ to singe a fowl; [2] (passion amoureuse) love; [3] (ardeur) **parler avec** ~ to speak passionately; **ranimer la** ~ **d'une tradition** to rekindle a tradition; [4] (marque postale) postmark caption
B **flammes** *nfpl* (feu) fire ¢; **en** ~**s** on fire

(Idiomes) **descendre qn/qch en** ~**s** to shoot sb/sth down; **jeter feu et** ~ [*personne*] to be raging; **être tout feu tout** ~ [*personne*] to be wildly enthusiastic

flammèche /flamɛʃ/ *nf* spark

flan /flɑ̃/ *nm* Culin (crème) ≈ custard; (tarte) custard tart GB *ou* flan US

(Idiomes) **faire qch au**○ to do sth brazenly; **y aller au**○ to bluff; **en rester comme deux ronds de** ~○ to be dumbfounded

flanc /flɑ̃/ *nm* [1] Anat (de personne) side; (d'animal) flank, side; **le cheval battait des** ~**s** the horse was panting; **être sur le** ~○ to be exhausted; [2] (entrailles) gén entrails (*pl*); (de femme) womb; [3] (de montagne) side; [4] (de navire) side, beam end; [5] Mil flank

(Idiomes) **se battre les** ~**s**○ to strive in vain; **tirer au** ~○ to shirk, to skive○ GB; **prêter le** ~ **à la critique** to lay oneself open to criticism

flancher○ /flɑ̃ʃe/ [1] *vi* [1] (manquer de courage) to lose one's nerve; (ne plus faire face) to crack up; (devant une décision) to crack; [2] (faiblir) [*cœur, moteur*] to give out; [*mémoire*] to let [sb] down; [*jambes*] to go wobbly

flanchet /flɑ̃ʃe/ *nm* Culin flank

flanelle /flanɛl/ *nf* flannel; **jupe de** ~ flannel skirt

(Composé) ~ **de coton** flannelette

flâner /flɑne/ [1] *vi* [1] (se promener) to stroll; (s'attarder) to dawdle; [2] (paresser) to loaf around

flânerie /flɑnri/ *nf* [1] (promenade) stroll; [2] (inaction) lazing around

flâneur, -euse /flɑnœr, øz/ *nm,f* [1] (promeneur) stroller; [2] (paresseux) loafer○, idler US

flanquer /flɑ̃ke/ [1]
A *vtr* [1] (garnir) to flank [*construction, meuble*] (**de** by); **il est toujours flanqué de son adjoint** his assistant never leaves his side; [2] ○(mettre) to give [*coup, gifle, amende*]; ~ **qch par terre** (jeter) to throw sth to the ground; (faire tomber) to knock sth to the ground; ~ **la frousse**○ *or* **la trouille**○ **à qn** to give sb a fright; ~ **qn dehors** *or* **à la porte** (d'un travail) to fire sb; (d'un lieu) to chuck○ sb out
B **se flanquer**○ *vpr* **se** ~ **dans** to run into; **se** ~ **sous un train** to throw oneself under a train; **se** ~ **par terre** to fall flat on one's face

flapi○, **~e** /flapi/ adj fagged out○ GB, shot○ US, worn out

flaque /flak/ nf ~ **(d'eau)** puddle; ~ **d'huile** pool of oil

flash, pl **~es** /flaʃ/ nm [1] Phot flash; [2] Radio, TV ~ **(d'information)** (programmé) news headlines (pl); (exceptionnel) news flash

(Composé) ~ **publicitaire** advert GB, commercial US

flasher○ /flaʃe/ [1] vi ~ **sur** to fall in love with

flasque¹ /flask/ adj [peau] flabby; [traits] slack

flasque² /flask/ nf (flacon) flask

flatter /flate/ [1]

A vtr [1] (complimenter) to flatter [personne]; ~ **bassement qn** to toady to sb; [2] (honorer) **leur visite a flatté tout le village** the whole village felt honoured^GB by their visit; [3] (encourager) to encourage [sentiment, vice]; ~ **qn dans son amour-propre** to boost sb's ego; [4] (caresser) to pat [animal]; [5] (être agréable) to delight [narines, regard]; [6] (avantager) [vêtement, éclairage] to flatter [personne]

B se flatter vpr [1] (prétendre) **je me flatte de m'exprimer au moins de façon claire** I flatter myself that I'm at least articulate; [2] (tirer vanité) to pride oneself (**de** on; **de faire** on doing)

flatterie /flatri/ nf flattery ¢; **de basses ~s** toadying ¢

flatteur, -euse /flatœʀ, øz/

A adj [1] (avantageux) [portrait, éclairage] flattering; [distinction, récompense] gratifying; **sous un jour ~** in a favourable^GB light; [2] (obséquieux) [personne, paroles] sycophantic

B nm,f toady, sycophant

flatulence /flatylɑ̃s/ nf wind ¢, flatulence ¢ spéc

fléau, pl **~x** /fleo/ nm [1] (calamité) scourge; **le ~ de Dieu** the scourge of God; [2] (nuisance) (chose) curse; (personne) pest; [3] (outil agricole) flail; [4] (de balance) beam

(Composé) ~ **d'armes** Hist flail

flèche /flɛʃ/ nf [1] (arme) arrow; **pointe de ~** arrowhead; **les ~s de l'Amour** Love's darts; **partir/passer en** or **comme une ~** to shoot off/to shoot past; **monter en ~** [fusée] to shoot upward(s); [prix] to soar; ▸ **Parthe**; [2] (signe) arrow; [3] (raillerie) barbed remark; [4] (d'église) spire

(Idiome) **il fait ~ de tout bois** it's all grist to his mill

flécher /fleʃe/ [14] vtr to signpost

fléchette /fleʃɛt/ ▸ p. 327 nf (objet) dart; (activité) darts (+ v sg)

fléchi, **~e** /fleʃi/ adj Ling inflected

fléchir /fleʃiʀ/ [3]

A vtr [1] (plier) to bend; [2] (ébranler) to sway [personne, opinion]; to weaken [volonté]

B vi [1] (ployer) [poutre] to sag; [genoux] to bend; [jambes] to give way; [2] (faiblir) [attention] to flag; [courage] to waver; [volonté] to weaken; [production, demande] to fall off; [prix] to fall (**de** by); [3] (céder) [personne, armée] to yield; (s'adoucir) [personne] to relent; **sans ~** (stoïquement) unflinchingly; (obstinément) stubbornly

flegmatique /flɛgmatik/ adj phlegmatic

flegme /flɛgm/ nm (placidité) phlegm, composure

flémingite○ /flemɛ̃ʒit/ nf hum bone idleness; **il a une ~ aiguë** he's suffering from acute bone idleness

flemmard○, **~e** /flemaʀ, aʀd/

A adj bone idle (jamais épith)

B nm,f lazybones○ (+ v sg), lazy devil○

flemmarder○ /flemaʀde/ [1] vi to loaf○ around; ~ **au lit** to lie in

flemme○ /flɛm/ nf laziness; **j'ai la ~ de faire** I'm too lazy to do; **tirer sa ~** to laze around

flétan /fletɑ̃/ nm halibut

flétrir /fletʀiʀ/ [3]

A vtr [1] (faner) **le temps a flétri sa beauté** her beauty has faded with time; [2] (stigmatiser) to blacken [nom]; [3] (souiller) to corrupt [enfant]

B se flétrir vpr [1] [plante] to wither; [fleur] to fade; [fruit] to shrivel; [2] [beauté, peau] to fade

flétrissement /fletʀismɑ̃/ nm [1] (de peau) withering; [2] Bot wilt

fleur /flœʀ/ nf [1] Bot flower; **être en ~s** [jardin] to be full of flowers; [camélia] to be in bloom ou flowering; [poirier, lilas] to be in blossom; **à ~s** flowery; [2] (le meilleur) **la (fine) ~ des arts** the flower of the art world; **dans la ~ de l'âge** in the prime of life; [3] (niveau) **à ~ d'eau** [rocher] just above the water; [4] (de cuir) grain; **côté ~** grain layer

(Composés) ~ **des champs** wild flower; ~ **de farine** superfine white flour; ~ **de lys** fleur-de-lis, heraldic lily; ~ **d'oranger** (fleurs) orange blossom; (arôme) orange flower water

(Idiomes) **être ~ bleue** to be starry-eyed ou romantic; **avoir une sensibilité à ~ de peau** to be hypersensitive; **avoir les nerfs à ~ de peau** to be a bundle of nerves; **couvrir qn de ~s** to shower sb with compliments; **envoyer des ~s à qn**○ to pat sb on the back; **faire une ~ à qn**○ to do sb a favour^GB; **arriver** or **s'amener**○ **comme une ~** to turn up just like that

fleurdelisé, **~e** /flœʀdəlize/ adj gén [drapeau, manteau] decorated with fleurs-de-lis (après n)

fleurer /flœʀe/ [1] vtr to be fragrant with

fleuret /flœʀɛ/ ▸ p. 327 nm Sport (épée) foil; (discipline) foil

(Composé) ~ **moucheté** buttoned foil

fleurette /flœʀɛt/ nf Culin **crème ~** whipping cream

(Idiome) **conter ~† à qn** to woo† sb

fleurettiste /flœʀɛtist/ nmf Sport foil fencer

fleuri, **~e** /flœʀi/

A pp ▸ **fleurir**

B pp adj [1] [champs, jardin] full of flowers; [arbre] (de petites fleurs) in blossom; (de grosses fleurs) in bloom; [2] (décoré) [table] decorated with flowers; [papier] flowery; [3] [teint] florid, ruddy; [nez] spotty GB, pimply; **barbe ~e** hoary beard; [4] [style] flowery péj

fleurir /flœʀiʀ/ [3]

A vtr to decorate [sth] with flowers [maison, table]; to put flowers on [tombe]; to put a flower in [boutonnière]

B vi [1] [rosier] to flower, to bloom; [cerisier] to blossom; [2] (apparaître) [supermarchés] to spring up; [affiches] to appear; [3] (prospérer) to thrive; [4] (se couvrir de boutons) [visage] to come out in spots GB ou pimples

fleuriste /flœʀist/ ▸ p. 372

A nmf (commerçant) florist

B nm (magasin) flower shop, florist's

fleuron /flœʀɔ̃/ nm [1] fig (joyau) jewel (in the crown); [2] gén, Archit fleuron; (de pignon) finial; [3] Bot floret

fleuve /flœv/

A nm [1] Géog river; [2] (flot de boue, lave) river (**de** of); ~ **de larmes** flood of tears

B (-)**fleuve** (in compounds) **discours/procès(-)~** interminable speech/trial

(Composés) ~ **Bleu** Yangtze, Chang Jiang; ~ **Jaune** Yellow River, Huang He; ~ **Rouge** Red River, Song Koi

flexible /flɛksibl/

A adj [1] (souple) [branche] pliable; [lame, tuyau] flexible; [corps] supple; [2] (adaptable) flexible; [3] (docile) [personne, caractère] malleable

B nm (tuyau souple) ~ **de cimentation** cementing hose; ~ **de douche** shower hose; ~ **de gaz** rubber gas pipe; ~ **de robinet** nozzle

flexion /flɛksjɔ̃/ nf [1] (d'objet) bending; (de bras, jambe) flexing; [2] Ling inflection

flexionnel, **-elle** /flɛksjɔnɛl/ adj [langue] inflected; [forme, marque] inflectional

flibustier /flibystje/ nm [1] Hist (pirate) freebooter; [2] (escroc) swindler

flic○ /flik/ nm pej cop○, policeman

flip /flip/ nm [1] ○(dépression) **être le ~** [film] to be a real downer○; [lieu] to be creepy○; **être en plein ~** [drogué] to freak out○; [2] **porto ~** egg flip (with port)

flipper¹ /flipœʀ/ ▸ p. 327 nm Jeux (billard électrique) pinball machine; (pièce mobile) flipper; (jeu) pinball

flipper²○ /flipe/ [1] vi (être perturbé) to freak out○; (être déprimé) to be depressed ou down○; **complètement flippé** off his head○; **ta maison me fait ~** your house gives me the creeps○

flirt /flœʀt/ nm [1] (activité) flirting (**avec** with); [2] (relation) lit flirtation, brief romance; fig flirtation; [3] (personne) boyfriend/girlfriend

flirter /flœʀte/ [1] vi to flirt (**avec** with)

flocon /flɔkɔ̃/ nm (de neige, savon) flake; (de poussière) speck; (de laine) bit; (de fumée) wisp

(Composés) **~s d'avoine** oat flakes GB, oatmeal ¢ US; **~s de pomme de terre** instant mashed potato mix (sg)

Les fleuves et les rivières

■ *L'anglais ne distingue pas entre fleuve et rivière; dans les deux cas, c'est le mot river qui est utilisé, avec ou sans majuscule.*

Les noms de fleuves et de rivières

■ *L'anglais utilise toujours l'article défini devant les noms de fleuves et de rivières.*

le Nil
= the Nile

l'Amazone
= the Amazon

la Saône
= the Saône

■ *Le mot river est parfois utilisé, mais n'est jamais obligatoire. En anglais britannique, il est avant le nom propre, en anglais américain il est après.*

la Tamise
= the River Thames (*GB*) *ou* the river Thames

le Potomac
= the Potomac River (*US*) *ou* the Potomac river

De avec les noms de fleuves et de rivières

■ *Les expressions françaises avec de se traduisent en général par l'emploi des noms de fleuves et de rivières en position d'adjectifs.*

un affluent de la Tamise
= a Thames tributary

l'eau de la Seine
= Seine water

l'estuaire de la Tamise
= the Thames estuary

les industries de la Tamise
= Thames industries

les péniches de la Tamise
= Thames barges

Mais:

l'embouchure de la Tamise
= the mouth of the Thames

la source de la Tamise
= the source of the Thames

---

floconneux, -euse /flɔkɔnø, øz/ *adj* **1** gén [*laine, nuage*] fleecy; [*neige*] powdery; **2** Chimie [*précipité*] flocculent

flonflons /flɔ̃flɔ̃/ *nmpl* **1** Mus brass band music ¢; **2** fig **il a été accueilli sous les ~** they put out the red carpet for him

flop○ /flɔp/ *nm* (échec) flop; **faire un ~** to flop

flopée○ /flɔpe/ *nf* **(toute) une ~ de gamins/livres** a whole load○ GB *ou* slew○ US of kids/books, masses (*pl*) of kids/books

floraison /flɔRɛzɔ̃/ *nf* **1** (de fleurs) flowering, blooming; **2** (de talents) flowering; (d'entreprises) rash

floral, ~e, *mpl* **-aux** /flɔRal, o/ *adj* [*exposition, composition*] flower (*épith*); [*art, organe*] floral

floralies /flɔRali/ *nfpl* flower show

flore /flɔR/ *nf* **1** (végétation) flora; **2** (ouvrage) flora, botanical handbook
⟨Composé⟩ **~ intestinale** intestinal flora

florentin, ~e /flɔRɑ̃tɛ̃, in/
A ▶ p. 621 *adj* Florentine
B *nm* Culin Florentine

florilège /flɔRilɛʒ/ *nm* anthology

florin /flɔRɛ̃/ ▶ p. 34 *nm* **1** (monnaie des Pays-Bas) guilder; **2** Hist (ancienne monnaie) florin

florissant, ~e /flɔRisɑ̃, ɑ̃t/ *adj* **1** [*activité, économie, pays*] thriving; [*théorie*] fashionable; **2** [*teint*] ruddy; **il est d'une santé ~e** he's blooming

flot /flo/
A *nm* **1** (grande quantité) (de courrier, réfugiés) flood; (de questions, visiteurs) stream; (de critique) torrent; **2** (marée) liter tide; **3** (en équitation) rosette
B **à flot** *loc adv* **couler à ~(s)** lit, fig to flow; **être à ~** lit, fig to be buoyant; **remettre un navire à ~** to refloat a boat; **remettre qn/qch à ~** fig to put sb/sth back on their/its feet
C **flots** *nmpl* liter **les ~s** the billows littér, the deep (*sg*) littér

flottaison /flɔtɛzɔ̃/ *nf* Naut **ligne de ~** waterline

flottant, ~e /flɔtɑ̃, ɑ̃t/ *adj* **1** [*bois, ligne, mine*] floating; [*nuage*] drifting; **2** [*vêtements, cheveux*] flowing

flotte /flɔt/ *nf* **1** Aviat, Naut fleet; **2** ○(pluie) rain; **3** ○(eau) water; **4** (flotteur) float
⟨Composés⟩ **~ aérienne** air fleet; **~ de guerre** Mil naval fleet

flottement /flɔtmɑ̃/ *nm* (indécision) wavering ¢

flotter /flɔte/
A *vi* **1** (sur un liquide) to float (**sur** on; **dans** in); **~ à la dérive** to drift; **2** (dans l'air) [*brume*] to drift; [*drapeau*] to fly; **un**

sourire flottait sur ses lèvres a smile hovered on his/her lips; **~ au vent** [*drapeau*] to flutter in the wind; [*cheveux*] to stream in the wind; **elle flotte dans ses vêtements** her clothes are hanging off her; **3** Fin [*monnaie*] to float
B ○*v impers* (pleuvoir) to rain

flotteur /flɔtœR/ *nm* (de ligne, filet, d'hydravion) float; (de chasse d'eau) ballcock

flottille /flɔtij/ *nf* flotilla
⟨Composé⟩ **~ de pêche** fishing fleet

flou, ~e /flu/
A *adj* **1** lit [*photo*] blurred; [*coiffure*] soft; [*vêtement*] loose; **2** fig [*concept, style*] vague, woolly péj; [*souvenir, personnage*] vague; [*passé*] hazy
B *nm* **1** lit (de contour) fuzziness; **2** fig vagueness
⟨Composé⟩ **~ artistique** Cin, Phot soft focus; fig artistry

flouer○ /flue/ [1] *vtr* to cheat [*personne*]; **se faire ~** to be had○

fluctuant, ~e /flyktɥɑ̃, ɑ̃t/ *adj* [*cours, opinion*] fluctuating; [*personne, temps*] fickle; [*opinion*] fluctuating

fluet, -ette /flyɛ, ɛt/ *adj* [*corps, personne*] slight; [*bras, jambe*] frail; [*voix*] thin

fluide /flɥid/
A *adj* [*huile, peinture*] fluid; [*style*] fluent; [*circulation*] moving freely [*jamais épith*]; [*situation*] fluid
B *nm* **1** Phys fluid; **2** (de médium) (psychic) powers (*pl*)

fluidifier /flɥidifje/ [2] *vtr* to thin [*sang*]; to loosen [*mucosité*]

fluidité /flɥidite/ *nf* **1** Phys fluidity; **2** (de style, diction) fluency; (de vêtement) flowing lines (*pl*)

fluo○ /flyo/
A ▶ p. 140 *adj inv* fluorescent
B *nm* **la mode du ~** the fashion for Day-glo®

fluor /flyɔR/ *nm* fluorine; **dentifrice au ~** fluoride toothpaste

fluoré, ~e /flyɔRe/ *adj* fluoride (*épith*)

fluorescent, ~e /flyɔResɑ̃, ɑ̃t/ *adj* fluorescent

flûte /flyt/
A *nf* **1** ▶ p. 389 Mus flute; **petite ~** piccolo; **2** (verre) (champagne) flute; **3** (pain) French loaf; **4** ○(jambe) leg
B *excl* damn○!, darn it○!
⟨Composés⟩ **~ à bec** recorder; **~ de Pan** panpipes (*pl*); **~ traversière** (transverse) flute

flûté, ~e /flyte/ *adj* [*voix, son*] piping (*épith*)

flûtiau, *pl* **~x** /flytjo/ ▶ p. 389 *nm* **1** (flûte champêtre) pipe; **2** (flûte d'enfant) penny whistle

flûtiste /flytist/ ▶ p. 372 *nmf* flautist, flutist US

fluvial, **~e**, *mpl* **-iaux** /flyvjal, o/ *adj* [*érosion, plaine*] fluvial; [*port, bassin, transport*] river (*épith*)

flux /fly/ *nm inv* ①⃝ (écoulement) flow; ②⃝ Phys flux; ③⃝ Écon flow; ④⃝ (marée) flood tide; **le ~ et le reflux** lit flood tide and ebb tide; fig the ebb and flow; ⑤⃝ (mouvement) influx; **~ migratoire** influx of immigrants

FMI /ɛfɛmi/ *nm*: *abbr* ▸ **fonds**

FO /ɛfo/ *nf*: *abbr* ▸ **force**

foc /fɔk/ *nm* jib

focal, **~e¹**, *mpl* **-aux** /fɔkal, o/ *adj* focal

focale² /fɔkal/ *nf* (distance) focal length; (objectif)° lens

focaliser /fɔkalize/ [1] *vtr* ①⃝ Phys to focus [*rayons*]; to focalize [*faisceau d'électrons*]; ②⃝ (concentrer) to focus [*espoirs, attention*]; to concentrate [*efforts*]

fœtus /fetys/ *nm inv* foetus

fofolle ▸ **foufou**

foi /fwa/ *nf* ①⃝ Relig faith; **avoir la ~** to be a believer; ▸ **montagne**; ②⃝ (confiance) faith; **ajouter ~ à qch** to put faith in sth; ③⃝ (sincérité) **ma ~ oui** well yes; **faire qch de bonne ~** or **en toute bonne ~** to be made GB ou crazy with the best intentions; **en toute bonne ~ je crois que** in all sincerity, I believe that; **il est de bonne ~** he is genuine; **bonne/mauvaise ~** Philos good/bad faith; **de bonne ~** Jur bona fide (*épith*); **elle est d'une incroyable mauvaise ~** she's so insincere; ④⃝ (assurance) **sur la ~ de témoins** on the evidence of witnesses; **sur la ~ de documents** on the strength of documents; **en ~ de quoi** in witness whereof; **qui fait** or **faisant ~** [*texte, signature*] authentic; **sous la ~ du serment** under oath

(Idiomes) **voir avec les yeux de la ~** to see only what one wants to see; **sans ~ ni loi** fearing neither God nor man

foie /fwa/ *nm* ①⃝ Anat liver; **avoir mal au ~** ≈ to have an upset stomach; **crise de ~** indigestion; ②⃝ Culin liver; **~ gras** foie gras

(Idiome) **se ronger les ~s**° to worry

foin /fwɛ̃/

Ⓐ *nm* ①⃝ (herbe) hay Ⓒ; **tas de ~** haystack; **faire les ~s** to make hay; **saison des ~s** haymaking season; ▸ **bête**; ②⃝ °(tabac sans goût) old socks° (*pl*)

Ⓑ ‡*excl* **~ de vos conseils/richesses!** I pour scorn on your advice/wealth!

(Composé) **~ d'artichaut** choke

(Idiome) **faire du ~**° (faire du bruit) to make a hell of a racket ou noise°; (faire du scandale) to cause a scandal

foire /fwaR/ *nf* ①⃝ Comm fair; ②⃝ (fête foraine) fun fair; ③⃝ °(bruit, confusion) bedlam; **faire la ~**° to live it up°; ▸ **larron**

fois /fwa/

Ⓐ *nf inv* time; **une ~** once; **deux ~** twice; **trois ~** three times; **deux ou trois ~** two or three times; **deux ~ et demie** two and a half times; **quatre ~ trois font douze** four times three is twelve; **la plupart des ~** most of the time, more often than not; **une (bonne) ~ pour toutes** once and for all; **il faudrait qu'il neige une bonne ~** what we need is one good fall of snow; **une ~ sur deux** half the time; **une ~ sur trois** every third time; **deux ~ sur cinq** two times out of five; **toutes les ~ que** every time (that); **ça va pour cette ~, mais ne recommencez pas!** it's all right this once but don't do it again!; **comme (à) chaque ~** as usual; **deux ~ plus petit** half as big; **deux ~ plus cher** twice as expensive; **deux ~ moins lourd** half the weight; **deux ~ moins cher** half as expensive; **par deux ~** twice; **il vaut mieux le dire deux ~ plutôt qu'une** it needs saying twice; **c'est dix ~ trop lourd!** it's far too heavy!; **régler en trois ~** to pay in three instalments^GB; **pour la énième ~** for the hundredth time; **la première ~ que je vous ai parlé** when I first talked to you

Ⓑ **à la fois** *loc* **deux à la ~** two at a time; **porter trois valises à la ~** to carry three suitcases at the same time; **elle est à la ~ intelligente et travailleuse** she's both clever and hardworking; **pour des raisons à la ~ culturelles, sociales et religieuses** for cultural, social and religious reasons; **ne répondez pas tous à la ~!** lit, iron don't all answer at once! lit, iron

Ⓒ **des fois** *loc* (parfois) sometimes; **y a des ~ où there are times**° **when**; **tu n'as pas vu mon chien, des ~?** you wouldn't have seen my dog, by any chance?; **des ~ que** in case; **non mais des ~!** (indignation) well really!

(Idiomes) **il était** or **il y avait une ~** once upon a time there was; **je t'ai déjà dit cent** or **trente-six ~ de ne pas faire ça!** I've already told you a hundred ou a thousand times not to do that!

foisonner /fwazɔne/ [1] *vi* [*idées, erreurs*] to abound; **~ de** or **en** to have an abundance of

fol ▸ **fou** A

folâtre /fɔlɑtR/ *adj* [*personne, humeur*] playful

folâtrer /fɔlɑtRe/ [1] *vi* [*personne*] to romp about; [*animal*] to frisk

folichon°, **-onne** /fɔliʃɔ̃, ɔn/ *adj* **pas ~** far from brilliant

folie /fɔli/ *nf* ①⃝ (déraison) madness; **crise** or **coup de ~** brainstorm; **être pris de ~** to go mad GB ou crazy; **aimer qn/qch à la ~** to be mad GB ou crazy about sb/sth; **spectateurs en ~** ecstatic crowd *sg*; ②⃝ (acte déraisonnable) **cette ~ leur a coûté la vie** it was an act of folly which cost them their lives; **elle a fait une ~ en acceptant** she was mad to accept; ③⃝ (passion) **avoir la ~ des antiquités** to be mad GB ou crazy about antiques; ④⃝ (dépense inconsidérée) extravagance; **faire une ~, faire des ~s** to be extravagant

(Composés) **~ douce** sheer madness; **~ furieuse** stark raving madness; **être pris de ~ furieuse** to go berserk; **~ des grandeurs** delusions (*pl*) of grandeur

folk /fɔlk/

Ⓐ *adj inv* [*festival, musique*] folk

Ⓑ *nm* **le ~** folk music; **chanteur de ~** folk singer

folklo° /fɔlklo/ *adj* [*personne*] eccentric; [*soirée*] crazy°; **ça va être ~!** it'll be some laugh°!

folklore /fɔlklɔR/ *nm* ①⃝ (traditions) folklore; ②⃝ °(rituel) razzmatazz°

folklorique /fɔlklɔRik/ *adj* ①⃝ (traditionnel) [*musique, coutume*] folk (*épith*); [*costume*] traditional; ②⃝ °(loufoque) [*personnage*] eccentric; [*voiture, soirée*] crazy°

folle ▸ **fou** A, B

follement /fɔlmɑ̃/ *adv* **s'amuser ~** to have a terrific time; **un spectacle ~ drôle** a terribly funny show

follet /fɔlɛ/ *adj m* **feu ~** will-o'-the-wisp; **esprit ~** flighty creature

follicule /fɔlikyl/ *nm* Anat, Bot follicle

fomenter /fɔmɑ̃te/ [1] *vtr* to instigate

foncé, **~e** /fɔ̃se/ ▸ p. 140 *adj* [*couleur*] gén dark; [*rose, mauve*] deep; **avoir la peau ~e/les cheveux ~s** to be dark-skinned/dark-haired

foncer /fɔ̃se/ [12]

Ⓐ *vtr* (assombrir) to make [sth] darker [*couleur*]; to make [sth] deeper [*rose, mauve*]

Ⓑ *vi* ①⃝ °(aller très vite) [*chauffeur, voiture, coureur*] to tear along° (vers toward(s)); **fonce!** get a move on°!; **il va falloir ~ pour terminer à temps** we'll have to rush to finish in time; ②⃝ °(se précipiter) **~ vers/dans** to rush toward(s)/into; **~ sur qch/vers la sortie** to make a dash for sth/for the exit; **~ sur qn** (en attaquant) to charge at sb; **~ tête baissée dans la bagarre** to rush headlong into the fray; **~ à New York** to dash over to New York; **il n'est pas du genre à ~** (prudent) he's not the type to rush into things; **fonce!** (n'hésite pas) go for it°!; ③⃝ (s'assombrir) [*couleur*] to darken; [*rose, mauve*] to deepen; [*tissu*] to go darker; **~ au soleil** [*lunettes*] to go darker in the sun

fonceur°, **-euse** /fɔ̃sœR, øz/

Ⓐ *adj* dynamic

Ⓑ *nm,f* go-getter°

foncier, **-ière** /fɔ̃sje, ɛR/ *adj* ①⃝ [*impôt*] land; [*revenu*] from land (*après n*); **propriétaire ~** landowner; ②⃝ (inhérent) intrinsic

foncièrement /fɔ̃sjɛRmɑ̃/ *adv* fundamentally

fonction /fɔ̃ksjɔ̃/ *nf* ①⃝ (dans l'administration, une entreprise) (poste) post; (activité) duties (*pl*); **prendre ses ~s, entrer en ~s** to take up one's post; **dans le cadre de mes ~s** as part of my duties; **occuper la ~ de** to hold the position of; **quitter ses ~s** to leave one's job; **logement de ~** accommodation provided with the job; **voiture de ~** company car; **occuper d'importantes ~s** to hold important office; ②⃝ (dépendance) **en ~ de** according to; **être ~ de** to vary according to; ③⃝ (rôle) function; **~ d'une machine** function of a machine; **avoir pour ~ de faire** to be designed to do; **faire ~ de** to serve as; ④⃝ Math, Ordinat, Chimie, Biol function; **~ acide** acid function; **la ~ crée l'organe** the organ is shaped by its function; **5**▸ (secteur) profession; ~ **enseignante** teaching profession; **6**▸ Tech function; **la ~ avance rapide est en panne** the fast forward function does not work; **7**▸ Ling function

(Composés) ~ **primitive** Math primitive; ~ **publique** Admin civil service

fonctionnaire /fɔ̃ksjɔnɛR/ ▸ p. 372 *nmf* (petit, moyen) civil servant; (haut) government official; **haut ~** senior civil servant; ~ **international** international official

fonctionnalité /fɔ̃ksjɔnalite/ *nf* Ordinat functionality **₵**

fonctionnariser /fɔ̃ksjɔnaRize/ [1] *vtr* to make [sb/sth] work for the state

fonctionnel, -elle /fɔ̃ksjɔnɛl/ *adj* functional

fonctionnement /fɔ̃ksjɔnmɑ̃/ *nm* **1**▸ (d'institution, organe, du marché) functioning; ~ **quotidien** everyday functioning; **bon ~** smooth functioning; **2**▸ (d'équipement) working; **mauvais ~** malfunction; **en ~** in service; **entrer en ~** to come into service; **en état de ~** in working order

fonctionner /fɔ̃ksjɔne/ [1] *vi* to work; ~ **à merveille** to work perfectly; ~ **à l'essence** to run on petrol GB ou gas US; ~ **comme un alibi** to be used as an excuse; ~ **comme une société anonyme** to operate as a public company; ~ **comme un système d'alarme** to serve as an alarm signal; ~ **à la vodka** hum [*personne*] to live on vodka

fond /fɔ̃/
A *nm* **1**▸ (partie inférieure) bottom; **au ~ du verre** in the bottom of the glass; **au ~ du tiroir** at the bottom of the drawer; **vider les ~s de bouteilles** to empty out all the old bottles; **toucher le ~** (dans l'eau) to touch the bottom; fig to hit rock bottom; **descendre au ~ d'un puits** to go down a well; **2**▸ (paroi) (horizontale) bottom; (verticale) back; **le ~ du placard** the back of the cupboard; **valise à double ~** suitcase with a false bottom; ~ **de la mer** seabed; ~ **de l'océan** ocean floor; **3**▸ (partie reculée) (de cour, magasin) back; (de couloir, pièce) far end; **au ~ de l'armoire** in the back of the wardrobe; **la chambre du ~** the back bedroom; **au ~ des bois** deep in the woods; **avancer dans le ~** (dans un bus) to move up the bus; **de ~ en comble** from top to bottom; **4**▸ (essence) **quel est le ~ du problème?** what is the problem exactly?; **les problèmes de ~** the basic problems; **aller au ~ des choses** to get to the bottom of things; **un débat de ~** an in-depth debate; **au ~ or dans le ~, le problème est simple** the problem is simple, in fact; **dans le ~, tu as raison** you're right, really; **5**▸ (de texte) content; **le ~ et la forme** form and content; **6**▸ (intérieur) **regarder qn au ~ des yeux** (avec amour) to look deep into sb's eyes; (avec suspicion) to give sb a searching look; **du ~ du cœur** from the bottom of my heart; **elle a un bon ~** she's very good at heart; **il a un mauvais ~** he's got a nasty streak; **7**▸ (arrière-plan) background; **sur ~ noir** on a black background; ~ **musical** background music; **8**▸ (petite quantité) **un ~ de porto** a drop of port; **laisser un ~ de bouteille** to leave a drop in the bottle; **il n'y a pas assez de ~** the water is not deep enough; **il y a 20 mètres de ~** the water is 20 metresᴳᴮ deep; **l'épave gisait par 30 mètres de ~** the wreck lay 30 metresᴳᴮ down; **9**▸ Sport **épreuve de ~** long-distance event; **11**▸ (de pantalon) seat
B à fond *loc adv* **1**▸ (complètement) **connaître son domaine à ~** to be an expert in one's field; ~ **à fond** to commit oneself totally; **soutenir qn/qch à ~, être à ~° pour qn/qch** to support sb/sth wholeheartedly; **nettoyer qch à ~** to give sth a thorough cleaning; **respirer à ~** to breathe deeply; **mettre la radio à ~** to turn the radio right up; **2**▸ °(vite) **rouler à ~** to drive at top speed; **il est arrivé à ~** he came rushing in

(Composés) ~ **d'artichaut** artichoke bottom; ~ **de tarte** pastry case; ~ **de teint** foundation GB, make-up base US; ~**s marins** depths of the sea

(Idiome) **user ses ~s de culotte sur le même banc** fig to be at school together

fondamental, ~e, *mpl* **-aux** /fɔ̃damɑ̃tal, o/ *adj* **1**▸ (essentiel) [*droit, question, différence, élément*] basic; [*objectif, besoin, idée, raison, vocabulaire*] basic; [*cause, changement, conflit, importance, rôle*] fundamental; [*atout*] crucial; **libertés ~es** basic liberties, fundamental freedoms; **ce qui est ~ c'est que** the essential is that; **2**▸ Mus [*note*] fundamental

fondamentalement /fɔ̃damɑ̃talmɑ̃/ *adv* **1**▸ (au fond) fundamentally; **2**▸ (totalement) radically

fondant, ~e /fɔ̃dɑ̃, ɑ̃t/ *adj* [*neige, glace*] melting; [*poire, biscuit*] which melts in the mouth (épith, après n); **bonbon ~** fondant

fondateur, -trice /fɔ̃datœR, tRis/ *nm,f* gén founder; **groupe ~** founding group; **membre ~** founder member; **les pères ~s** the founding fathers

fondation /fɔ̃dasjɔ̃/
A *nf* (action, organisme) foundation
B fondations *nfpl* lit, fig foundations; **creuser les ~s de qch** to lay the foundations of sth

fondé, ~e /fɔ̃de/ *adj* (légitime) [*réclamation*] justifiable; [*crainte*] well-founded; [*demande*] legitimate; **vos reproches ne sont pas ~s** your criticisms are unfounded; **ce que tu dis n'est pas ~** what you say has no justification; **non ~, mal ~** [*accusation*] groundless

(Composé) ~ **de pouvoir** Jur (de personne) proxy; (de société) authorized representative; (de banque) manager

fondement /fɔ̃dmɑ̃/ *nm* (bases) foundation; **être dénué de** or **sans ~** to be unfounded

fonder /fɔ̃de/ [1]
A *vtr* **1**▸ (créer) to found [*ville, parti, journal*]; to establish [*prix, entreprise*]; ~ **un foyer** to get married; **2**▸ (baser) to base (sur qch); ~ **ses espoirs sur qch/qn** to place one's hopes in sth/sb
B se fonder *vpr* **se ~ sur** [*théorie, méthode*] to be based on; [*personne*] to go on; **sur quoi te fondes-tu?** what have you got to go on?

fonderie /fɔ̃dRi/ *nf* (atelier) foundry

fondeur, -euse /fɔ̃dœR, øz/
A *nm,f* Sport cross-country skier
B ▸ p. 372 *nm* (ouvrier) foundry worker

fondre /fɔ̃dR/ [6]
A *vtr* **1**▸ (liquéfier) to melt down [*métal*]; to smelt [*minerai*]; **2**▸ (fabriquer) to cast [*statue, caractère, lingot*]
B *vi* **1**▸ (se liquéfier) [*neige, métal, beurre*] to melt; **faire ~** to melt; **2**▸ (se dissoudre) [*sucre*] to dissolve; **faire ~** to dissolve; **3**▸ (baisser) [*réserve, économies*] to melt away; **4**▸ (maigrir) [*personne*] to waste away; **avoir fondu de dix kilos** to have lost ten kilos; **5**▸ (s'attendrir) to soften; **il fond devant sa petite-fille** his heart melts when he sees his granddaughter; ~ **en larmes** or **pleurs** to dissolve into tears; **6**▸ (s'abattre) fml ~ **sur** [*troupe, oiseau*] to swoop down on; [*malheur*] to overwhelm; [*calamité*] to ravage
C se fondre *vpr* **se ~ dans** [*personne, silhouette*] to blend in with

fonds /fɔ̃/
A *nm inv* **1**▸ (collection) collection; **2**▸ (capital) fund
B *nmpl* (capitaux) funds; **recueillir des ~** to raise money; **mise de ~** capital outlay; **rentrer dans ses ~** to recover outlay; **à ~ perdus** at a loss

(Composés) ~ **d'amortissement** sinking fund; ~ **bloqués** frozen assets; ~ **de commerce** business; ~ **commun de placement** unit trust GB, mutual fund US; ~ **d'investissement** investment fund; ~ **de pension** pension fund; ~ **de placement** investment fund; ~ **de prévoyance** provident fund; ~ **propres** equity capital; ~ **de roulement** working capital; ~ **de solidarité** mutual aid fund; ~ **spéculatif** hedge fund; **Fonds monétaire international, FMI** International Monetary Fund, IMF

fondu, ~e¹ /fɔ̃dy/
A *pp* ▸ **fondre**
B *pp adj* [*beurre*] melted; [*métal*] molten; [*sucre*] dissolved
C fondue *nf* Culin gén fondue; (au fromage) (cheese) fondue

fondue² /fɔ̃dy/ *nf* Culin fondue

(Composés) ~ **bourguignonne** fondue bourguignonne (*meat dipped in hot oil*), meat fondue US; ~ **savoyarde** cheese fondue

fontaine /fɔ̃tɛn/ *nf* gén fountain; (pour boire) drinking fountain; (source) spring

fonte /fɔ̃t/ *nf* **1**▸ (métal) cast iron; **de** or **en ~** cast-iron (épith); **2**▸ (de métal) melting down; (de minerai) smelting; **3**▸ Météo (de cours d'eau, glace, neige) thawing; **4**▸ (fabrication de cloche, statue) casting

(Composé) ~ **des neiges** thaw; **à la ~ des neiges** when the snow thaws

fonts /fɔ̃/ *nmpl* ~ **baptismaux** font (sg)

foot° /fut/ *nm* = **football**

football /futbol/ ▸ p. 327 *nm* football GB, soccer

Composé ~ **américain** american football GB, football US

footballeur, -euse /futbolœʀ, øz/ ▸ p. 372 *nm,f* football GB *ou* soccer player

footing /futiŋ/ ▸ p. 327 *nm* jogging; **faire un ~** to go for a jog

for /fɔʀ/ *nm* **dans** *or* **en son ~ intérieur** deep down

forage /fɔʀaʒ/ *nm* drilling; **le ~ d'un puits** the sinking of a well; **faire des ~s** to drill

forain, -aine /fɔʀɛ̃, ɛn/
A *adj* fairground
B *nm* (marchand) stallkeeper; **les ~s** fairground people

forçat /fɔʀsa/ *nm* (bagnard) convict; (galérien) galley slave

force /fɔʀs/
A *nf* **1** (de personne) **~s** strength ¢; **avoir de la ~** to be strong; **ne plus avoir de ~** to have no strength left; **la ~ de marcher** the strength to walk; **mes ~s m'abandonnent** I'm getting weak; **être à bout de ~s** to feel drained; **c'est au-dessus de mes ~s** it's too much for me; **de toutes ses ~s** [*lancer*] with all one's might; [*désirer*] with all one's heart; **dans la ~ de l'âge** in the prime of life; **avec ~** [*nier*] strongly; [*affirmer*] firmly; **2** (contrainte) force; **~ armée** armed force; **de ~** by force; **faire faire qch à qn de ~** to force sb to do sth; **entrer de ~ dans un lieu** to force one's way into a place; **par la ~ des choses** through force of circumstance; **coup de ~** Mil strike; **3** (puissance) (de pays, groupe, secteur, personne) strength; (d'expression) force; **c'est ce qui fait leur ~** that's where their strength lies; **ils sont de même ~** *or* **de ~ égale aux échecs** they are evenly matched at chess; **être de ~ à faire** to be up to doing; **tu n'es pas de ~ à t'attaquer à lui** you're no match for him; **revenir en ~** to make a strong comeback; **faire un retour en ~** to make a strong comeback; **4** (poids) (d'argument, accusation, de conviction) force; **5** Phys, fig force; **les ~s du mal** the forces of evil; **6** (intensité) (de choc, séisme, vent) force; (de désir, sentiment) strength; **7** (ensemble humain) force; **~s d'opposition** opposition forces; **arriver en ~** to arrive in force; **8** Mil (corps) force; (effectifs) **~s** forces; **~s navales** navy (*sg*); **~s terrestres** army (*sg*); **d'importantes ~s de police** large numbers of police
B à force° *loc adv* **à ~, elle l'a cassé** she ended up breaking it
C à force de *loc prép* **réussir à ~ de travail** to succeed by dint of hard work; **à ~ d'économiser, elle a pu l'acheter** by saving very hard, she was able to buy it; **il est aphone à ~ de crier** he shouted so much (that) he lost his voice; **à ~ de frotter, tu vas le déchirer** if you keep on rubbing it, you'll tear it
Composés **~ de dissuasion** Mil deterrent force; fig deterrent; **~ de frappe** (arme nucléaire) nuclear weapons (*pl*); (groupe) strike force; **~ d'interposition** Mil peacekeeping force; **~ d'intervention** Mil task force; **~ de la nature** (real) Goliath; **~ publique** police force; **~s de l'ordre** forces of law and order; **~s vives** life blood ¢; **Force ouvrière, FO** *French trade union*

forcé, ~e /fɔʀse/
A *pp* ▸ **forcer**
B *pp adj* **1** (contraint) forced; (accidentel) unintentional; **2** (artificiel) [*gaieté, sourire, comparaison*] forced; **3** °(inéluctable) **c'est ~!** there's no way around it°; **c'est ~ qu'il/elle fasse** he's/she's bound to do

forcément /fɔʀsemɑ̃/ *adv* inevitably; **elle viendra ~ tôt ou tard** she is bound to come sooner or later; **pas ~** not necessarily; **'j'ai faim'—'~, tu n'as pas déjeuné!'** 'I'm hungry'—'well, it's hardly surprising, you had no lunch!'

forcené, ~e /fɔʀsəne/
A *adj* [*rythme*] furious; [*activité*] frenzied
B *nm,f* (enragé) maniac; (armé) crazed gunman

forceps /fɔʀsɛps/ *nm inv* forceps (*pl*)

forcer /fɔʀse/ [12]
A *vtr* **1** (contraindre) to force; **être forcé à l'exil** to be forced into exile; **2** (faire céder) to force [*porte, serrure*]; **~ la porte de qn** fig to force one's way into sb's house; **3** (passer au travers) to break through [*barrière*]; **~ le passage** to force one's way through; **~ l'entrée** to force one's way in; **4** (imposer) to force [*négociation, décision*]; **5** (pousser) to force [*allure*]; **~ le ton** to raise one's voice
B forcer sur *vtr ind* **1** (abuser) **~ sur** to overdo [*vin, sel,*

couleur]; **2** Tech **~ sur** to overtighten [*vis*]; to force [*mécanisme*]
C *vi* **1** (faire trop d'efforts) **j'ai trop forcé** I overdid it; **gagner sans ~** to win easily; **2** (exercer une pression) **ne force pas, tu vas le casser** don't force it or you'll break it; **serrez sans ~** do not tighten too much
D se forcer *vpr* (se contraindre) to force oneself (**à faire** to do); (faire des efforts) **il se force pour manger** it's a real effort for him to eat
Idiome **~ la main à qn** to force sb's hand

forcing° /fɔʀsiŋ/ *nm* **faire du ~** to go all out

forcir /fɔʀsiʀ/ [3] *vi* [*vent*] to become stronger

forer /fɔʀe/ [1] *vtr* to drill; **~ un puits** to sink a well

forestier, -ière /fɔʀɛstje, ɛʀ/ *adj* **1** [*région, massif*] forested; [*chemin, paysage, ressources*] forest (*épith*); **exploitation forestière** (travail) forestry; (site) forestry plantation; **industrie forestière** timber industry; **2** Culin [*escalope*] with mushrooms (*après n*)

foret /fɔʀɛ/ *nm* drill

forêt /fɔʀɛ/ *nf* lit, fig forest; **~ tropicale** rain forest
Idiome **c'est l'arbre qui cache la ~** you can't see the wood for the trees

Forêt-Noire /fɔʀɛnwaʀ/ *nprf* **1** ▸ p. 504 (région) **la ~** the Black Forest; **2** (gâteau) Black Forest gâteau GB *ou* cake

foreuse /fɔʀøz/ *nf* drill

forfait /fɔʀfɛ/ *nm* **1** (prix global) fixed rate; **être payé au ~** to be paid a fixed rate; **~ hebdomadaire** weekly rate; **un ~ de 25 euros pour trois concerts** a 25 euro flat-rate ticket covering three concerts; **2** Tourisme (séjour) package; **~ avion-auto** fly-drive package; **le ~ comprend le voyage et cinq nuits d'hôtel** the all-in package covers travel and five nights' hotel accommodation; **3** (carte d'accès) pass; **~ skieur** ski pass; **4** Télécom package; **5** (d'un joueur, une équipe) withdrawal; **gagner par ~** to win by default; **déclarer ~** gén to give up; Sport to withdraw; **6** (pour les impôts) **être au ~** to be taxed at a rate calculated according to estimated turnover
Composé **~ journalier** individual contribution to cost of state hospital care

forfaitaire /fɔʀfɛtɛʀ/ *adj* **prix ~** contract *ou* all-inclusive price; **tarif ~** flat fare *ou* fee; **taxe ~** flat-rate tax; **somme ~** lump sum; **indemnité ~** basic allowance

forge /fɔʀʒ/ *nf* (atelier) forge; (feu) forge; (aciérie) ironworks

forgé, ~e /fɔʀʒe/
A *pp* ▸ **forger**
B *pp adj* [*objet, métal*] wrought; **fer ~** wrought iron; **grille en fer ~** wrought-iron gate

forger /fɔʀʒe/ [13]
A *vtr* **1** (dans une forge) to forge; **2** to form [*caractère*]; to invent [*théorie*]; to create [*métaphore*]; **une histoire forgée de toutes pièces** a complete fabrication
B se forger *vpr* **se ~ un alibi** to invent an alibi (for oneself)

forgeron /fɔʀʒəʀɔ̃/ ▸ p. 372 *nm* blacksmith
Idiome **c'est en forgeant qu'on devient ~** Prov practice makes perfect Prov

formaliser: se formaliser /fɔʀmalize/ [1] *vpr* to take offence^GB (**de** to); **se ~ d'un rien** to be easily offended

formalisme /fɔʀmalism/ *nm* **1** péj formality; **2** (en art, philosophie) formalism

formaliste /fɔʀmalist/
A *adj* **1** péj [*personne*] formal; **il est très ~** he's a stickler for form; **2** (en art, philosophie) formalist
B *nmf* formalist

formalité /fɔʀmalite/ *nf* Admin formality; **les ~s à accomplir pour obtenir un visa** the necessary procedure to obtain a visa; **simplifier les ~s** to simplify procedure; **ce n'est qu'une ~** it's a mere formality; **par pure ~** as a matter of form

format /fɔʀma/ *nm* **1** (de journal, disquette) format; (de livre, photo, d'objet) size; **de grand/très grand ~** large/extra large; **2** Ordinat (mode d'enregistrement) format

formatage /fɔʀmataʒ/ *nm* Ordinat formatting; **faire un ~** to format

formater /fɔʀmate/ [1] *vtr* Ordinat to format

formateur, -trice /fɔʀmatœʀ, tʀis/ *adj* formative

formation /fɔʀmasjɔ̃/ *nf* **1** (instruction) (scolaire) education; (professionnelle) training (**en** in); **ingénieur de** ~ engineer by training; **il a reçu une** ~ **d'ingénieur** he was trained as an engineer; **avoir une** ~ **littéraire** to have an arts background; **la** ~ **des jeunes** youth education; **en** ~ undergoing training (*après n*); '~ **assurée**' 'training provided'; **2** (cours) training course; **3** (de gouvernement, parti, d'équipe) forming; **il a été chargé de la** ~ **du gouvernement** he was asked to form the government; **4** (apparition) formation; **au moment de la** ~ **des glaciers** when the glaciers were (being) formed; **5** (ensemble) formation; **une** ~ **nuageuse** a cloud formation; **6** (groupe) group; **7** Mil (détachement) detachment; (disposition) formation; ~ **aérienne** aerial formation

⬭ Composés ~ **en alternance** sandwich course; ~ **continue**, ~ **permanente** adult continuing education; ~ **professionnelle** professional training; ~ **sur le tas** on-the-job training

forme /fɔʀm/
A *nf* **1** (concrète) shape; (abstraite) form; **une** ~ **de vie** a form of life; **prendre** ~ to take shape; **de** ~ **ronde** round; **sous** ~ **de** in the form of; **sous une autre** ~ in another form; **juger sur la** ~ to judge on form; **sans** ~ shapeless; **2** (modalité) (de gouvernement, contrat, violence) form; (de paiement, recrutement) method; **3** (procédé, condition) form; **en bonne et due** ~ in due form; **pour la** ~ as a matter of form; **pour la bonne** ~ to formalize things; **de pure** ~ purely formal; **4** (en grammaire) form; **à la** ~ **négative** in the negative (form); **5** (état général) form; **en** ~ on form; **en grande** ~ in peak form; **perdre/ne plus avoir la** ~ to go off/to be off form; **en pleine** ~ in great shape; **une séance de remise en** ~ a fitness session
B **formes** *nfpl* **1** (corps humain) figure (*sg*); **elle a des** ~**s rondes** she has a rounded figure; **pull qui moule les** ~**s** figure-hugging sweater; **2** (d'objet, de bâtiment) lines; **3** (règles) **faire qch dans les** ~**s** to do sth in the correct manner; **y mettre les** ~**s** to be tactful; **respecter les** ~**s** respect convention

formé, ~**e** /fɔʀme/
A *pp* ▸ **former**
B *pp adj* **1** (composé) made up (**de** of); (dessiné) formed (**de** from); **2** (instruit) educated; (professionnellement) trained; **3** (façonné) formed; **bien** ~ well-formed; **mal** ~ badly-formed; **4** (mûr) (*caractère, goût*) formed

formel, -elle /fɔʀmɛl/ *adj* **1** (*refus, démenti*) categorical, flat; (*promesse*) definite; (*ordre*) strict; **être** ~ **sur** (*personne*) to be definite about; (*loi*) to be clear on; **il a dit 20 heures, je suis** ~ he said 8 pm, I'm quite positive about it; **2** (en art, philosophie) formal; **3** (superficiel) (*politesse*) formal

formellement /fɔʀmɛlmɑ̃/ *adv* **1** (expressément) (*démentir*) categorically; (*interdire*) strictly; **2** (de façon officielle) officially; ~ **identifié** clearly identified

former /fɔʀme/
A *vtr* **1** (prendre l'aspect de) to form (*rectangle*); **2** (constituer) to form; **ils forment un couple très uni** they are a very close couple; **il forme avec son partenaire une brillante équipe** he and his partner make a brilliant team; **formez des groupes de cinq** get into groups of five; **3** (donner une formation à) to train (*personnel*); (à faire to do); (éduquer) to educate (*personne, goût*); to develop (*intelligence*); **to form** (*opinion*); ~ **qn au traitement de texte** to train sb in word processing; **4** (produire) to form (*abcès, pellicule*); **5** (mettre en forme) to form (*lettres, phrases*)
B **se former** *vpr* **1** (se créer) to form; **un caillot s'est formé** a clot has formed; **2** (être créé) to be formed; **3** (acquérir une formation) to train, to be trained (**à** in); **se** ~ **à la vente** to train in sales; **4** (s'éduquer) (*caractère, personnalité, style*) to develop; (*personne*) to educate oneself; **5** (concevoir) to form

formidable /fɔʀmidabl/ *adj* **1** (considérable) (*force, croissance*) tremendous; (*explosion*) enormous; **2** ○(épatant) (*spectacle, livre*) great○; (*personne*) marvellous^GB; **être** ~ **de patience avec qn** to be wonderfully patient with sb; **être** ~ **avec qn** (généreux) to be wonderful to sb; (patient) to be wonderful with sb; **3** ○(incroyable) **c'est quand même** ~ **qu'elle n'ait pas téléphoné!** it's incredible she hasn't phoned!

formidablement /fɔʀmidabləmɑ̃/ *adj* awfully; **il joue** ~ **bien**○ he plays tremendously well

formol /fɔʀmɔl/ *nm* formalin

formulaire /fɔʀmylɛʀ/ *nm* (imprimé) form

formulation /fɔʀmylasjɔ̃/ *nf* (action) formulation; (chose formulée) wording; **la** ~ **de cette idée est difficile** it's not easy to express that idea

formule /fɔʀmyl/ *nf* **1** (expression) expression; ~ **toute faite** set phrase; **2** (option) option; **3** (méthode) method; **la bonne** ~ **pour s'enrichir** a good way of making money; **4** (conception) concept; **5** (en science) formula; **6** (automobile) ~ **un/deux/trois** Formula One/Two/Three; **7** (d'émission, de magazine) format

⬭ Composés ~ **magique** (en magie) magic words (*pl*); fig magic formula; ~ **de politesse** gén polite phrase; (à la fin d'une lettre) letter ending

formuler /fɔʀmyle/ **1** *vtr* gén to express (*réserves*); to put (*sth*) into words (*idée*); to set out (*grief*); to draw up (*contrat*); ~ **une réponse** to give an answer

forniquer /fɔʀnike/ **1** *vi* to fornicate

fort, ~**e** /fɔʀ, fɔʀt/
A *adj* **1** (puissant) strong; **armée** ~**e de 10 000 hommes** 10,000-strong army; ~ **d'un chiffre d'affaires en hausse** boasting an increased turnover; ~**s de leur expérience...** boosted by their experience...; **le roi est plus** ~ **que la dame** a king is worth more than a queen; **trouver plus** ~ **que soi** to meet one's match; **s'attaquer à plus** ~ **que soi** to take on someone bigger than oneself; **2** (résistant) strong; **3** (intense) (*bruit*) loud; (*lumière*) bright; (*chaleur, activité, pression*) intense; (*crampe*) bad; (*fièvre*) high; (*soupçon*) strong; (*crainte, colère*) deep; **une** ~**e grippe** a bad attack of flu; **avoir une** ~**e envie de faire** to feel a strong desire to do; **4** (violent) (*coup*) hard; (*pluie*) heavy; (*vent*) strong; **5** (concentré) (*café, cigarette, alcool*) strong; (*épice*) hot; **6** (net) (*accent, personnalité, odeur, tendance, impression*) strong; (*pente*) steep; (*somme, majorité, réduction*) large; (*taux, inflation, consommation*) high; (*expansion, pénurie*) great; (*baisse, augmentation*) sharp; (*différence*) big; (*contingent, dose, croissance*) strong; ~**e émigration** high level of emigration; **7** (doué) good (**en**, **à** at; **pour faire** at doing); **il est** ~ **pour ne rien faire** hum he's good at doing nothing; **8** (ferme) (*personne*) strong; **9** (gros) (*personne*) stout; (*hanches*) broad; (*poitrine*) large; (*cuisses*) big; **être** ~**e de poitrine** to have a large bust; **10** ○(exagéré) **c'est un peu** ~! that's a bit much○!; **le plus** ~, **c'est que...** (surprenant) the most amazing thing is that...; (absurde) the most ridiculous thing is that...
B *adv* **1** (très) (*bon, déçu, émouvant*) extremely; (*bien, vite*) very; **c'est** ~ **dommage** it's a great pity; **2** (beaucoup) (*douter*) very much; **j'ai eu** ~ **à faire**○ **pour le convaincre** I had a hard job convincing him; **3** (avec force) (*frapper, tirer, frotter*) hard; (*serrer*) tight; (*respirer*) deeply; (*parler, crier*) loudly; (*sentir*) strongly; **souffle** ~! blow hard!; **le vent souffle** ~ there's a strong wind; **parler de plus en plus** ~ to speak louder and louder; **mon cœur bat trop** ~ my heart is beating too fast; **le chauffage marche trop** ~ the heating is turned up too high; **y aller un peu** ~○ to go a bit too far; **y aller un peu** ~ **sur la moutarde** to overdo the mustard; **4** (bien) well; **il ne va pas très** ~ he's not very well; **faire** *or* **frapper (très)** ~○ to do (really) well; **attaquer très** ~○ to start off really well
C *nm* **1** (ouvrage fortifié) fort; **2** (personne puissante) strong person; **3** (domaine d'excellence) strong point, forte
D **au plus fort de** *loc prép* **au plus** ~ **de l'été** at the height of summer; **au plus** ~ **de l'hiver** in the depths of winter; **au plus** ~ **de la bataille** in the thick of the fighting

⬭ Composés ~ **en thème**○ Scol swot○ GB, grind○ US; ~**e tête** rebel

⬭ Idiomes ~ **comme un bœuf** *or* **Turc** strong as an ox; **c'est plus** ~ **que moi/qu'elle** (incontrôlable) I/she just can't help it; **c'est plus** ~ **que l'as de pique**○ *or* **que de jouer au bouchon**○ that beats it all, that takes the biscuit○

fortement /fɔʀtəmɑ̃/ *adv* (avec force) (*encourager, critiquer*) strongly; (de façon très marquée) (*augmenter, accélérer*) sharply; (à un haut niveau) (*centralisé, industrialisé*) highly; (profondément) (*ébranlé*) deeply; (*endommagé, pollué*) badly; (*déplaire*) greatly; (lourdement) (*armé*) heavily; **il est** ~ **question de démolir l'usine** demolition of the factory is being seriously considered

forteresse /fɔʀtəʀɛs/ *nf* stronghold

fortiche○ /fɔʀtiʃ/
A *adj* smart, clever (**en** at)
B *nmf* brain○

fortifiant, ~e /fɔʀtifjɑ̃, ɑ̃t/
A *adj* [*boisson, médicament*] fortifying; [*air*] bracing
B *nm* Méd tonic

fortification /fɔʀtifikasjɔ̃/ *nf* fortification

fortifier /fɔʀtifje/ [2]
A *vtr* ① (donner de la robustesse) to strengthen [*cheveux*]; ② (donner des forces) [*repas*] to fortify; [*vacances, vitamines*] to do [*sb*] good; ③ (consolider) to strengthen [*foi, régime*]; ④ Mil to fortify [*ville*]
B **se fortifier** *vpr* (se consolider) [*régime*] to get stronger; [*foi*] to grow stronger

fortuit, ~e /fɔʀtɥi, it/ *adj* [*rencontre*] accidental; [*incident, circonstance*] fortuitous; [*remarque, découverte*] fortuitous, chance (*épith*); [*occasion*] unexpected; '**toute ressemblance serait purement ~e**' 'any similarity is purely coincidental'

fortune /fɔʀtyn/ *nf* ① (richesse) fortune; **grandes ~s** large fortunes; **faire ~** to make a fortune; **une des plus grosses ~s du Venezuela** one of Venezuela's wealthiest people; ② (chance) **(bonne)** ~ good fortune; **mauvaise ~** bad luck; ③ (destinée) fortunes (*pl*); ④ **de ~** (improvisé) makeshift (*épith*)
(Idiome) **faire contre mauvaise ~ bon cœur** to put on a brave face

fortuné, ~e /fɔʀtyne/ *adj* (riche) wealthy

fosse /fos/ *nf* ① (cavité) pit; ② (tombe) grave; ③ (pour le saut) sandpit; ④ (de garage) inspection pit
(Composés) **~ d'aisances** earth closet; **~ commune** communal grave; **~ aux lions** lions' den; **~ océanique** oceanic trench; **~ d'orchestre** orchestra pit; **~ septique** septic tank; **~s nasales** nasal passages

fossé /fose/ *nm* ① gén ditch; (de château) moat; **tomber dans le** or **au ~** to go into the ditch; ② fig (écart) gap; (désaccord) rift; **ça a creusé un ~ entre eux** it caused a rift between them
(Composé) **~ des générations** generation gap

fossette /fosɛt/ *nf* dimple

fossile /fɔsil/ *adj, nm* fossil

fossiliser /fɔsilize/ [1] *vtr,* **se fossiliser** *vpr* to fossilize

fossoyeur /foswajœʀ/ *nm* lit gravedigger; fig destroyer (**de** of)

fou (**fol** *before vowel or mute h*), **folle** /fu, fɔl/
A *adj* ① (dément) mad; **devenir ~** to go mad; **un tueur ~** a crazed killer; ② (insensé) [*personne, idée*] crazy; [*regard*] wild; [*soirée, histoire*] crazy; **tu n'es pas un peu ~?** are you mad *ou* crazy?; **réaliser ses rêves les plus ~s** to see one's wildest dreams come true; **être ~ furieux** to be raving mad; **être ~ à lier** to be stark raving mad; **entre eux c'est l'amour ~** they're madly in love; **~ de colère** mad with rage; **~ de joie** wild with joy; **~ de qn** crazy about sb; **~ de musique** mad about music; ③ (considérable) [*gaieté, enthousiasme*] mad; [*succès*] huge; **un monde ~** a huge crowd; **à une vitesse folle** at a crazy speed; **avoir un mal ~ à faire** to find it incredibly difficult to do; **mettre un temps ~ pour faire** to take an incredibly long time to do; **coûter un prix ~** to cost a fortune; **gagner un argent ~** to earn a fortune; **c'est ~ ce que le temps passe vite!** it's amazing how time flies!; ④ (incontrôlable) [*véhicule, cheval*] runaway; [*terreur*] wild; [*mèche*] stray; [*cheveux*] straggly; [*course*] headlong; **avoir le ~ rire** to have a fit of the giggles
B *nm,f* madman/madwoman; **envoyer qn chez les ~s** to send sb to the nuthouse; **courir comme un ~** to run like mad; **rire comme un ~** to laugh one's head off; **c'est un ~ d'art contemporain** he's mad about contemporary art; **un ~ du volant** a car freak; **une bande de ~s** a bunch of lunatics
C *nm* Hist (à la cour) fool, court jester; Jeux (aux échecs) bishop
(Idiomes) **faire les ~s** to fool about; **plus on est de ~s plus on rit** the more the merrier

foudre /fudʀ/
A *nf* lightning; **frappé par la ~** struck by lightning; **coup de ~** love at first sight; **avoir le coup de ~ pour qn/qch** to be really taken with sb/sth
B **foudres** fml *nfpl* wrath ¢; **s'attirer les ~s de qn** to incur sb's wrath

foudroyant, ~e /fudʀwajɑ̃, ɑ̃t/ *adj* [*attaque, progrès*] lightning (*épith*), sudden; [*succès*] meteoric; [*regard*] furious; [*mort*] sudden; **victime d'une leucémie ~e** struck down by leukemia

foudroyer /fudʀwaje/ [23] *vtr* ① (frapper) [*orage*] to strike [*arbre*]; **mort foudroyé** struck dead by lightning; **~ du regard** to look daggers at; ② (abattre) [*maladie*] to strike down; [*nouvelle*] to devastate

fouet /fwɛ/ *nm* ① (à lanières) whip; **dix coups de ~** ten lashes of the whip; **donner le ~ à qn** to flog sb; **coup de ~** lit whip lash; fig boost; **le grand air m'a donné un coup de ~** the fresh air invigorated me; **se heurter de plein ~** to collide head-on; ② Culin whisk; **~ mécanique** hand whisk

fouettard /fwɛtaʀ/ *adj m* **le père ~** ≈ the bogeyman

fouetter /fwɛte/ [1]
A *vtr* ① (frapper avec un fouet) to flog [*personne*]; to whip [*animal*]; **~ jusqu'au sang** to flog [*sb*] until the blood runs; ② (frapper) **la pluie leur fouettait le visage** the rain lashed their faces; ③ Culin to whisk GB, to beat US
B *vi* (battre) **la pluie fouettait contre les vitres** the rain lashed the windows
(Idiomes) **il n'y a pas de quoi ~ un chat** it's no big deal; **avoir d'autres chats à ~** to have other fish to fry

foufou, fofolle /fufu, fɔfɔl/
A *adj* scatterbrained
B *nm,f* scatterbrain

fougère /fuʒɛʀ/ *nf* (plante) fern; (végétation) bracken ¢

fougue /fug/ *nf* enthusiasm

fougueusement /fugøzmɑ̃/ *adv* enthusiastically

fougueux, -euse /fugø, øz/ *adj* [*cheval*] spirited; [*personne, élan, déclaration*] enthusiastic

fouille /fuj/ *nf* ① (de lieu, personne, bagages) search; **~ corporelle** body search; ② (en archéologie) excavation; **champ de ~s** archaeological site

fouillé, ~e /fuje/
A *pp* ▸ **fouiller**
B *pp adj* [*travail, étude, portrait*] detailed; [*style*] elaborate

fouiller /fuje/ [1]
A *vtr* ① (explorer) to search; ② (en archéologie) to dig [*site*]
B *vi* (chercher) **~ dans** to rummage through [*poches, armoire*]; to search [*mémoire*]; to sift through [*souvenirs*]; to delve into [*passé*]

fouillis /fuji/ *nm inv* (désordre) mess; (ensemble désordonné) jumble; **~ d'idées** jumble of ideas

fouine /fwin/ *nf* ① Zool stone marten; **tête de ~** weasel face; ② (curieux) snooper

fouiner /fwine/ [1] *vi* ① (sans but) to forage about; ② **~ dans** to rummage through [*objets, papiers*]; to poke one's nose into [*vie, passé*]

fouineur, -euse /fwinœʀ, øz/
A *adj* inquisitive
B *nm,f* ① (chineur) bargain hunter; ② (indiscret) snooper

foulard /fulaʀ/ *nm* scarf, headscarf

foule /ful/ *nf* ① (multitude de personnes) gén crowd; (menaçante) mob; **la ~ des acheteurs** the crowds of shoppers; **il n'y a pas ~ aujourd'hui** there isn't exactly a crowd today; **il y avait ~ à la réunion** there were masses of people at the meeting; **attirer les ~s** [*spectacle, chanteur*] to be a crowd-puller; **ils sont venus en ~ à la conférence** they flocked to the lecture; ② (grand nombre) mass; **une ~ de détails** a mass of details; **une ~ de gens** a crowd of people

foulée /fule/ *nf* (enjambée) stride; **rester** or **courir dans la ~ de qn** Sport to tail sb; **dans la ~ de leurs prédécesseurs** fig in the wake of their predecessors; **dans la ~ il a...** while he was at it, he...

fouler /fule/ [1]
A *vtr* ① to tread [*raisin*]; ② (marcher sur) **~ le sol de Mars** to set foot on Mars; **~ qch aux pieds** lit to trample sth underfoot; **~ aux pieds les usages** to ride roughshod over customs
B **se fouler** *vpr* ① Méd **se ~ le poignet** to sprain one's wrist; **avoir la cheville foulée** to have a sprained ankle; ② (se fatiguer) to strain oneself; **tu ne t'es pas foulé** you didn't kill yourself

foulure /fulyʀ/ *nf* sprain; **une ~ du poignet** a sprained wrist

four /fuʀ/ *nm* ① (de boulanger, cuisine) oven; **à ~ moyen** in a medium oven; **cuire au ~** to roast [*viande*]; to bake [*gâteau,* *poisson*]; **poulet au** ~ roast chicken; ② Ind furnace; (à céramique) kiln

(Composés) ~ **à catalyse** oven with self-clean linings; ~ **à chaleur tournante** fan(-assisted) oven; ~ **créma-toire** crematory (furnace); ~ **à micro-ondes** microwave oven; ~ **à pyrolyse** self-cleaning oven

(Idiome) **il fait noir comme dans un** ~ it's pitch dark in here

fourbi○ /furbi/ *nm* (objets) gear○; (désordre) shambles○ (+ *v sg*)

fourbu, ~**e** /furby/ *adj* (épuisé) exhausted

fourche /furʃ/ *nf* fork; **faire une** ~ to fork

fourcher /furʃe/ [1] *vi* **ma langue a fourché** it was a slip of the tongue

fourchette /furʃɛt/ *nf* ① (de table) fork; ② (gamme) (de prix, température) range; (de revenus, d'âge) bracket; ~ **horaire** period

(Idiome) **avoir un bon coup de** ~○ to have a hearty appe-tite

fourchu, ~**e** /furʃy/ *adj* [*langue, branche*] forked; [*sabot*] cloven; [*menton*] cleft; **cheveux** ~**s** split ends

fourgon /furɡɔ̃/ *nm* ① (camion) van; ② Rail goods wagon GB, freight car US; ~ **de tête** leading wagon GB, first car US; ~ **de queue** last wagon GB, caboose US

(Composés) ~ **à bagages** luggage van GB, baggage car US; ~ **à bestiaux** cattle truck; ~ **cellulaire** police van GB, patrol wagon US; ~ **mortuaire** hearse; ~ **postal** mail van GB, mail truck US

fourgonnette /furɡɔnɛt/ *nf* (small) van

fourguer❶ /furɡe/ [1] *vtr* to flog○ (**à** to) GB, to sell [sth] off (**à** to)

fourmi /furmi/ *nf* Zool ant; ~ **volante** flying ant; **travail de** ~ laborious task

(Idiome) **avoir des** ~**s dans les jambes** (avoir des picotements) to have pins and needles in one's legs

fourmilier /furmilje/ *nm* anteater

fourmilière /furmiljɛr/ *nf* Zool ant hill; fig hive of activity

fourmillement /furmijmɑ̃/ *nm* ① (abondance) **un** ~ **de gens** a mass of people; **un** ~ **d'idées** a host of ideas; ② (picotement) tingling sensation

fourmiller /furmije/ [1]

Ⓐ **fourmiller de** *vtr ind* ~ **de** to be chock-full of [*erreurs*]; to be swarming with [*visiteurs*]; to be teeming with [*animaux*]

Ⓑ *vi* ① (abonder) to abound (**dans** in); **les rats fourmillent dans le quartier** the neighbourhood^{GB} is swarming with rats; **livre où fourmillent les exemples** book bursting with examples; ② (picoter) **j'ai les jambes qui fourmillent** I've got pins and needles in my legs

fournaise /furnɛz/ *nf* ① (endroit chaud) blaze; **le bureau est une vraie** ~! the office is like an oven!; **la ville est une** ~ **en été** the town is baking hot in summer; ② C (chau-dière) boiler GB, furnace US

fourneau, *pl* ~**x** /furno/ *nm* Tech furnace; (cuisinière) stove; **être à ses** ~**x** to be doing the cooking

fournée /furne/ *nf* batch

fourni, ~**e** /furni/

Ⓐ *pp* ▸ **fournir**

Ⓑ *pp adj* **bien** ~ [*magasin*] well-stocked (**en** with)

Ⓒ *adj* (dense) [*barbe*] bushy; [*chevelure*] thick; [*herbe*] lush; [*emploi du temps*] busy

fourniment○ /furnimɑ̃/ *nm* clutter

fournir /furnir/ [3]

Ⓐ *vtr* ① (donner) to supply [*dossier, équipement, secours, informa-tion, argent*]; to give [*exemple, travail*]; to provide [*excuse, éner-gie, service*]; to contribute [*effort*]; to produce [*preuve, alibi*]; ~ **à qn** to supply sb with [*biens, données*]; to give [sth] to sb [*exemple*]; to provide sb with [*occasion, moyen*]; ~ **qn en** to supply sb with [*biens*]

Ⓑ **se fournir** *vpr* **se** ~ **chez** or **auprès de** to get [sth] from

fournisseur, **-euse** /furnisœr, øz/

Ⓐ *adj* **pays** ~ exporting country

Ⓑ *nm* supplier; **premier/deuxième** ~ **de** largest/second-largest supplier of; **chez votre** ~ from your supplier; ~ **attitré** official supplier; ~ **de drogue** drug dealer; ~ **de la famille impériale** purveyor to the imperial family

(Composé) ~ **d'accès Internet** Ordinat Internet Service Pro-vider, ISP

fourniture /furnityr/ *nf* ① Comm (vente) supply ℂ; ~ **d'armes** supply of arms; ~**s chinoises de coton** Chi-nese sales of cotton; ② (équipement) ~**s** equipment ℂ

(Composés) ~**s de bureau** office stationery ℂ; ~**s de laboratoire** (en sciences, dans l'industrie) laboratory equip-ment; ~**s scolaires** school stationery

fourrage /furaʒ/ *nm* forage; ~ **sec** fodder

fourre /fur/ *nf* H (couverture protectrice) cover

fourré, ~**e** /fure/

Ⓐ *pp* ▸ **fourrer**

Ⓑ *pp adj* ① Culin filled (**à** with); ~ **au chocolat** with choc-olate filling (*après n*); ② (de fourrure) fur-lined; (d'étoffe, de peau) lined (**de, en** with); ③ ○(installé) **toujours** ~ **au café** always hanging about at the café; **où étais-tu** ~? where have you been hiding?

Ⓒ *nm* (buisson) thicket

fourrer /fure/ [1]

Ⓐ *vtr* ① ○(mettre) to stick○; ~ **qch dans la tête de qn** to put sth into sb's head; ② (en cuisine) to fill (**avec, de** with); ③ to line [*vêtement*]

Ⓑ **se fourrer** *vpr* (se mettre) **se** ~ **dans un coin** to get into a corner; **aller se** ~ **dans** [*objet*] to get stuck in; **se** ~ **dans les jambes de qn** to get under sb's feet; **se** ~ **une idée dans la tête** to get an idea into one's head; **ne plus savoir où se** ~ not to know where to put oneself; **se** ~ **dans une sale histoire** to get mixed up in a bad business

fourre-tout /furtu/

Ⓐ *adj inv* ① [*solution*] cover-all; **groupe** ~ ragbag; ② [*pièce, placard*] storage; **sac** ~ holdall GB, carryall US

Ⓑ *nm inv* (trousse) pencil case

fourreur /furœr, ▸ p. 372 *nm* furrier

fourrière /furjɛr/ *nf* (pour animaux, véhicules) pound; **mettre une voiture à la** ~ to impound a car

fourrure /furyr/ *nf* ① (pour vêtement) fur; **fausse** ~ imi-tation fur; ~ **polaire** fleece; ② Zool coat

fourvoyer: **se fourvoyer** /furvwaje/ [23] *vpr* (se tromper) to make a mistake

foutoir○ /futwar/ *nm* (désordre) shambles○ (*sg*); (agitation) complete chaos

foutre❶ /futr/ [6]

Ⓐ *vtr* ① (faire) to do; **qu'est-ce qu'il fout?** what the hell's he doing❶?; **qu'est-ce que ça peut** ~? what the hell does it matter❶?; **n'en avoir rien à** ~ not to give a damn○ *ou* shit❶; ② (donner) ~ **un coup à qn** lit to wallop sb○; **sa mort nous a foutu un coup** his/her death was a terrible blow to us; ③ (mettre) ~ **qch quelque part** to stick○ sth some-where; **son nez partout** to stick one's nose into every-thing; ~ **qn dehors** *or* **à la porte** to kick sb out○; ~ **le camp** [*personne*] to bugger off❶ GB, to split○ US; [*choses*] to fall apart; **fous(-moi) le camp d'ici!** get lost○!; **tout fout le camp** everything's falling apart; **ça la fout mal** it makes a lousy○ impression

Ⓑ **se foutre** *vpr* ① (se mettre) **se** ~ **en colère** to fly off the handle○; **s'en** ~ **plein les poches** to rake it in○; **se** ~ **en l'air** (en voiture) to have an accident; (se suicider) to top one-self○; ② (se donner) **je me foutrais des claques!** sometimes I could kick myself!; ③ (ridiculiser) **se** ~ **de (la gueule de) qn** to take the piss out of sb❶; **il ne s'est pas foutu de toi!** he's been very generous!; **se** ~ **du monde** to have a bloody GB *ou* hell of a❶ US nerve; ④ (être indifférent) not to give a damn○ (**de** about); **je m'en fous** I don't give a damn○

foutu❶, ~**e** /futy/

Ⓐ *pp* ▸ **foutre**

Ⓑ *pp adj* ① (mauvais) (*before n*) [*temps*] bloody awful❶ GB, damned US; [*caractère*] bloody awful❶ GB; ~**e voiture** bloody❶ car GB, damned US car; ② (condamné) **être** ~ [*per-sonne, vêtement*] to have had it○; [*machine*] to be knack-ered❶ GB, to be shot○ US; **s'il me trouve, je suis** ~ if he finds me I've had it○; **être mal** ~ (*laid*) [*personne*] to be unattractive; (*malade*) [*personne*] to feel lousy○; ③ (capable) **être** ~ **de faire** to be totally capable of doing; **il n'est même pas** ~ **de répondre** he can't even bloody❶ well answer GB, he can't be bothered○ to answer

(Idiome) **café bouillu café** ~○ boiled coffee is ruined coffee

fox-terrier, *pl* ~**s** /fɔksterje/ *nm* fox terrier

foyer /fwaje/ *nm* ① (domicile) home; **rester au** ~ to stay at home; **fonder un** ~ to get married; ② (famille) household;

3 (résidence) hostel; **4** (club) club; **5** Cin, Théât (point de rencontre) foyer; **6** (de cheminée) hearth; **7** (centre actif) (de résistance) pocket; (d'intrigue) hotbed; **8** (centre de propagation) (d'incendie) seat; (d'épidémie) source; (de rébellion) seat; **9** Phys focus; **lunettes à double ~** bifocals

Composés ~ **fiscal** household for tax purposes; ~ **de placement** foster home

frac /fʀak/ nm morning coat

fracas /fʀaka/ nm inv (de chute) crash; (de vagues) roar; (de ville, bataille) din; **tomber avec ~** to fall with a crash; **lancer un produit à grand ~** fig to launch a product in a blaze of publicity; **renvoyé avec perte(s) et ~** summarily dismissed

fracassant, ~**e** /fʀakasɑ̃, ɑ̃t/ adj (violent) [bruit] deafening; (sensationnel) [entrée, déclaration] sensational; [succès, débuts] stunning

fracasser /fʀakase/ [1]
A vtr to smash [vitrine, crâne]
B se fracasser vpr to crash (**contre, sur** against)

fraction /fʀaksjɔ̃/ nf **1** Math fraction; **2** (partie) (de terrain, somme) part; (de société, jeunesse) section; (de produits, d'électeurs) proportion; **en une ~ de seconde** in a split second, in a fraction of a second

fractionnement /fʀaksjɔnmɑ̃/ nm (division) division; (morcellement) fragmentation

fractionner /fʀaksjɔne/ [1] vtr **1** (diviser) to divide up [travail, groupe]; to split [parti, opposition]; **2** (échelonner) to stagger [envois]; to spread [paiements]

fracture /fʀaktyʀ/ nf fracture; ~ **du poignet** fractured wrist; ~ **ouverte** compound fracture

Composé ~ **sociale** social divide

fracturer /fʀaktyʀe/ [1]
A vtr **1** to fracture [os]; **2** (pour pénétrer) to break down [porte]; to break [fenêtre]; to force [serrure, coffre]
B se fracturer vpr se ~ **la cheville** to break one's ankle

fragile /fʀaʒil/ adj **1** (cassable) fragile; **2** (faible) [personne, constitution] frail; [peau, œil] sensitive; [estomac, foie] delicate; [cœur] weak; **il est ~ du foie** he has a delicate liver; **avoir une santé ~** to have poor health; **3** (instable) [esprit, personne] fragile

Idiome ~ **comme du verre** very fragile

fragiliser /fʀaʒilize/ [1] vtr lit, fig to weaken

fragilité /fʀaʒilite/ nf **1** (aptitude à se briser) fragility; **2** (de personne, constitution, santé) frailty

fragment /fʀagmɑ̃/ nm **1** (morceau isolé) (de tasse, d'os) fragment; (de tissu) bit; **des ~s de conversation** snatches of conversation; **2** (d'œuvre) passage

fragmentaire /fʀagmɑ̃tɛʀ/ adj [connaissance] patchy; [vue, exposé] sketchy; [action, effort] sporadic

fragmentation /fʀagmɑ̃tasjɔ̃/ nf **1** fig (division) division; (morcellement) splitting up; **2** lit (de pierre) fragmentation

fragmenter /fʀagmɑ̃te/ [1]
A vtr (casser) to break up [substance]; (morceler) to split up [domaine, parti]; to divide up [travail]; to break up [vacances, texte]
B se fragmenter vpr [pierre] to break (**en** into)

fraîche ▸ frais A, E

fraîchement /fʀɛʃmɑ̃/ adv **1** (récemment) [creusé, repeint] freshly; [nommé] newly; ~ **cueillies** freshly cut; **2** (sans empressement) [recevoir] coldly; **elle a été ~ accueillie** she was given a cool welcome; **3** ○'**comment allez-vous?'—'~**' 'how are you?'—'cold'

fraîcheur /fʀɛʃœʀ/ nf **1** (température) (agréable) coolness; (plus froide) coldness; **donner une sensation de ~ à** to make [sb] feel cool; **la ~ du soir** the cold evening air; **2** (d'aliment) freshness; ~ **garantie** guaranteed fresh; **3** (teint) freshness; **pour redonner de la ~ à votre teint** to rejuvenate your complexion

frais, fraîche /fʀɛ, fʀɛʃ/
A adj **1** (légèrement froid) cool; (trop froid) cold; '**servir ~**' 'serve chilled'; **il fait ~ ce matin** (c'est agréable) it's cool this morning; (il fait froid) it's chilly this morning; **le fond de l'air est ~** there's a chill in the air; **2** (récent) [nouvelles, traces, neige] fresh; [peinture] wet; **de fraîche date** [membre] recent; **3** [produit] fresh; **4** (jeune) [teint, peau] fresh; [voix] young; **une fraîche jeune fille** a fresh-faced girl; **5** (nouveau) [troupes, équipe] fresh; **apporter un peu d'air ~ à qch** to bring a breath of fresh air to sth; **de l'argent ~** more money;

6 (léger) [parfum, décor, couleur] fresh; **7** (sans chaleur) [accueil, ambiance] cool
B adv (depuis peu) ~ **rasé** freshly shaved; **un livre tout ~ paru** a newly-published book
C nm (fraîcheur) **se tenir au ~** to stay in the cool; **prendre le ~** to get some fresh air; **mettre qch au ~** (pour le conserver) to put sth in a cool place; (pour le refroidir) to put sth to cool; **mettre qn au ~**○ (en prison) to put sb inside○
D nmpl **1** gén (dépenses) expenses; **aux ~ de l'entreprise** paid for by the company; **le voyage est à vos ~** you'll have to pay for the trip yourself; **vivre aux ~ de la société** to live off society; **aux ~ de qn** fig at sb's expense; **partager les ~** to share the cost; **faire des ~** [personne] to spend a lot of money; **rentrer dans ses ~** to cover one's expenses; **en être pour ses ~**○ lit to have to pay; fig to get nothing for one's pains; **faire les ~ de qch** to bear the brunt of sth; **arrêter les ~** fig to stop wasting one's time; **2** (coûts d'un service professionnel) fees; ~ **d'agence** agency fees; **3** (coûts d'un service commercial, commission) charges; **4** (en comptabilité) (coûts) costs; ~ **fixes/variables** fixed/variable costs
E à la fraîche loc adv (le matin) in the cool of the morning; (le soir) in the cool of the evening

Composés ~ **d'annulation** cancellation fees; ~ **de déplacement** (d'employé) travel expenses; (de réparateur) call-out charge (sg); ~ **divers** miscellaneous costs; ~ **d'expédition** (de colis) postage and packing; (de marchandise) freight; ~ **de fonctionnement** running costs; ~ **de garde** childminding fees; ~ **généraux** overheads; ~ **d'inscription** gén registration fees; Univ tuition fees, academic fees GB; ~ **de port** postage ¢; ~ **professionnels** professional expenses; ~ **de scolarité** tuition fees, school fees GB

Idiomes **être ~ comme une rose** to be as fresh as a daisy; **nous voilà ~**○! now we're in a fix○!

fraise /fʀɛz/
A ▸ p. 140 adj inv strawberry-pink
B nf **1** (fruit) strawberry; ~ **des bois** wild strawberry; **2** (en boucherie) ~ **de veau** calf's caul; **3** (angiome) strawberry mark; **4** (collerette) ruff; **5** (outil) (pour aléser) reamer; (machine) (pour couper) milling-cutter; (pour forer) drill

Idiome **ramener sa ~**○ to stick one's nose in○

fraiser /fʀɛze/ [1] vtr to ream [cylindre]; to mill [pièce]

fraiseur, -euse¹ /fʀɛzœʀ, øz/ ▸ p. 372 nm,f (ouvrier) cutter

fraiseuse² /fʀɛzøz/ nf (machine) milling machine

fraisier /fʀɛzje/ nm (plante) strawberry plant; Culin (gâteau) strawberry gateau

framboise /fʀɑ̃bwaz/
A ▸ p. 140 adj inv (couleur) raspberry-colouredGB
B nf (fruit) raspberry; (liqueur) raspberry liqueur

framboisier /fʀɑ̃bwazje/ nm (cultivé) raspberry cane; (sauvage) raspberry bush

franc¹, franche /fʀɑ̃, fʀɑ̃ʃ/
A adj **1** (honnête) [personne] frank, straight; [réponse] straight; [rire, regard] open, honest; **je vais être ~ avec vous** I'm going to be straight with you; **il n'est pas ~** he doesn't play straight; **jouer ~ jeu** to play fair; **2** (sans ambiguïté) (before n) [victoire, aversion] out-and-out; [gaieté] open, uninhibited; **3** (exempt) ~ **de port** postage paid
B adv parler ~ to be perfectly frank
C ▸ p. 34 nm (monnaie) franc; **un ~ symbolique de dommages et intérêts** Jur ≈ nominal damages (pl)

Composés ~ **belge** Hist Belgian franc; ~ **français** Hist French franc; ~ **lourd** Hist new franc; ~ **suisse** Swiss franc

franc², franque /fʀɑ̃, fʀɑ̃k/ adj Frankish

Franc, Franque /fʀɑ̃, fʀɑ̃k/ nm,f Frank

français, ~**e** /fʀɑ̃sɛ, ɛz/ ▸ p. 392, p. 336
A adj French; **à la ~e** French-style (épith)
B nm Ling French

Français, ~**e** /fʀɑ̃sɛ, ɛz/ ▸ p. 392 nm,f Frenchman/Frenchwoman; **le ~ moyen** gén the average Frenchman; péj the typical Frenchman

France /fʀɑ̃s/ ▸ p. 230 nprf France; **la ~ libre** Hist Free France

franche ▸ franc¹ A

franchement /fʀɑ̃ʃmɑ̃/ adv **1** (honnêtement) [parler, dire] frankly; [répondre] candidly; **je lui ai demandé ~ ce qu'il comptait faire** I asked him straight out what he intended to do; ~ **non, je n'ai pas beaucoup aimé** to be frank *ou* honest I didn't like it very much; ② (sans hésiter) [*appuyer*] firmly; [*entrer*] boldly; **servez-vous** ~ take a good helping; **versez** ~! don't be afraid of pouring in too much!; ③ (complètement) really; **il m'a** ~ **agacé** he really annoyed me; **elle est** ~ **bête** she is downright *ou* plain stupid; ④ (exclamatif) really, honestly

franchir /fʀɑ̃ʃiʀ/ [3] *vtr* to cross [*fossé, seuil, montagne*]; to get over [*mur, barrière*]; to cover [*distance*]; ~ **un obstacle** lit to clear an obstacle; fig to overcome an obstacle; ~ **le cap des quarts de finale** to get past the quarterfinals; ~ **le cap de la cinquantaine** to turn fifty

(Idiome) ~ **le pas** to take the plunge

franchise /fʀɑ̃ʃiz/ *nf* ① (qualité) (de personne, regard, d'aveu) frankness; (de ton) sincerity; ② (exemption) exemption; ③ (en assurance) excess GB, deductible US; ④ Comm franchise; ⑤ Hist (de ville) charter

(Composés) ~ **de bagages** Aviat baggage allowance; ~ **fiscale** tax exemption; ~ **postale** (sur une enveloppe) 'postage paid'; **en** ~ **postale** post free

franchiser /fʀɑ̃ʃize/ [1] *vtr* to franchise

franchissement /fʀɑ̃ʃismɑ̃/ *nm* (de col, rivière, ravin, seuil) crossing ℂ; (d'obstacle, de haie) clearing ℂ; ~ **de la ligne continue** Aut crossing the white line

francisation /fʀɑ̃sizasjɔ̃/ *nf* (de mot) gallicization

franciser /fʀɑ̃size/ [1] *vtr* to gallicize [*mot*]

franc-jeu /fʀɑ̃ʒø/ *nm* fair play

franc-maçon, -onne, *pl* **francs-maçons, franc-maçonnes** /fʀɑ̃masɔ̃, ɔn/ *nm,f* Freemason

franc-maçonnerie, *pl* ~**s** /fʀɑ̃masɔnʀi/ *nf* **la** ~ Freemasonry

franco /fʀɑ̃ko/ *adv* ① Comm ~ **de port** [*lettre, colis*] postage paid; [*livraisons*] carriage paid; ② ○(sans hésiter) **y aller** ~ (explication) to go right to the point; (action) to go right ahead

francophone /fʀɑ̃kɔfɔn/
A *adj* [*pays, personne*] French-speaking; **littérature** ~ literature in the French language
B *nmf* French speaker

francophonie /fʀɑ̃kɔfɔni/ *nf* (ensemble des francophones) French-speaking world

franc-parler, *pl* **francs-parlers** /fʀɑ̃paʀle/ *nm* frankness; **avoir son** ~ to speak one's mind

franc-tireur, *pl* **francs-tireurs** /fʀɑ̃tiʀœʀ/ *nm* ① (tireur isolé) sniper; ② (personne indépendante) maverick

frange /fʀɑ̃ʒ/ *nf* ① (en tissu, laine) fringe; ② (de cheveux) fringe GB, bangs (*pl*) US

frangin○ /fʀɑ̃ʒɛ̃/ *nm* brother

frangine○ /fʀɑ̃ʒin/ *nf* sister

franque ▸ **franc²**

franquette○: **à la bonne franquette** /alabɔnfʀɑ̃kɛt/ *loc adv* **c'est à la bonne** ~ it's just an informal meal

frappant, ~e /fʀapɑ̃, ɑ̃t/ *adj* striking

frappe /fʀap/ *nf* ① (de monnaie, médaille) (action) striking; (empreinte) impression; ② (de texte) typing; **le texte est à la** ~ the text is being typed out; ③ Sport (de footballeur) kick; (de boxeur) punch

(Composé) ~ **chirurgicale** Mil surgical strike

frappé, ~e /fʀape/
A *pp* ▸ **frapper**
B *pp adj* ① (rafraîchi) [*champagne, vin blanc*] chilled; [*cocktail*] frappé, mixed with crushed ice; [*café*] iced; ② ○(fou) crazy○, nuts○

frapper /fʀape/ [1]
A *vtr* ① (taper sur) gén to hit, to strike; ~ **le sol du pied** to stamp one's foot; ~ **qn à coups de matraque** to club sb; ~ **qn/qch à coups de pied** to kick sb/sth; ~ **qn/qch à coups de poing** to punch sb/sth; ~ **un coup** (à la porte) to knock (once); ~ **fort** *or* **un grand coup** lit to hit hard; (à la porte) to knock hard; fig to pull out all the stops; ② Tech to strike [*monnaie, médaille*]; ③ (affecter) [*chômage, épidémie, impôt*] to hit; **le malheur qui les frappe** the misfortune which has befallen them; **être frappé par le malheur** to be stricken by misfortune; **être frappé d'apoplexie** to have a stroke; **être frappé de mutisme** to be dumbstruck; **les taxes qui frappent les produits de luxe** duties imposed on luxury goods; ④ (marquer) to strike; **ce qui me frappe le plus c'est...** what strikes me most is...; **j'ai été frappé de**

voir que... I was amazed to see that...; ~ **l'imagination de qn** to catch sb's imagination; ⑤ (rafraîchir) to chill [*champagne, vin*]
B *vi* ① gén to hit, to strike; ~ **du poing sur la table** to bang one's fist on the table; ~ **du pied** to stamp one's foot; ~ **dans ses mains** to clap one's hands; ~ **à** to knock on *ou* at [*porte, fenêtre*]; **on a frappé** there was a knock at the door; ② (sévir) to strike

frasque /fʀask/ *nf* escapade; **faire des** ~**s** to get up to mischief; ~**s de jeunesse** youthful indiscretions

fraternel, -elle /fʀatɛʀnɛl/ *adj* fraternal, brotherly

fraternellement /fʀatɛʀnɛlmɑ̃/ *adv* in a brotherly fashion

fraternisation /fʀatɛʀnizasjɔ̃/ *nf* fraternizing

fraterniser /fʀatɛʀnize/ [1] *vi* to fraternize

fraternité /fʀatɛʀnite/ *nf* fraternity, brotherhood

fratricide /fʀatʀisid/
A *adj* fratricidal
B *nm* (crime) fratricide

fraude /fʀod/ *nf* ① Jur fraud ℂ; ~ **fiscale** tax fraud; ~ **électorale** vote *ou* election rigging; **passer qch/qn en** ~ to smuggle sth/sb in; **sortir qch en** ~ to smuggle sth out; **entrer** *or* **passer en** ~ (dans un pays) to enter illegally; ② Scol, Univ cheating ℂ

frauder /fʀode/ [1] *vi* (dans le métro) to travel without a ticket; (au cinéma) to slip in without paying

fraudeur, -euse /fʀodœʀ, øz/ *nm,f* gén swindler; (du fisc) tax evader; (à un examen) cheat

frauduleux, -euse /fʀodylø, øz/ *adj* fraudulent

frayer /fʀeje/ [21]
A *vtr* ~ **un passage à qn** to clear a path for sb; ~ **le chemin** *or* **la voie à qch** fig to pave the way for sth
B *vi* ① (entretenir des relations) **il ne fraye pas avec ces gens-là** he doesn't mix with that sort of person; ② Zool [*femelle*] to spawn; [*mâle*] to fertilize the eggs
C **se frayer** *vpr* lit (s'ouvrir) **se** ~ **un chemin dans** *or* **à travers** to make one's way through

frayeur /fʀejœʀ/ *nf* **il poussait des cris de** ~ he was screaming in fear; **j'ai eu une de ces** ~**s!** I got such a fright!

fredaine /fʀədɛn/ *nf* **faire des** ~**s** to have amorous adventures

fredonner /fʀədɔne/ [1] *vtr* to hum

free-lance /fʀilɑ̃s/ *nmf* freelance, freelancer; **travailler en** ~ to work freelance *ou* as a freelancer

freezer /fʀizœʀ/ *nm* freezer compartment GB, icebox

frégate /fʀegat/ *nf* ① Naut frigate; ② Zool frigate bird

frein /fʀɛ̃/ *nm* ① (de véhicule) brake; **la voiture n'a plus de** ~**s** the brakes are not working; **donner un coup de** ~ to brake hard; **utilisez le** ~ **moteur** keep in low gear; ② (entrave) **mettre un** ~ **à** to curb [*expansion, optimisme*]; ③ †(mors) bit

(Composés) ~ **à disques** disc brake; ~ **à main** hand brake; ~ **à tambour** drum brake

(Idiome) **ronger son** ~ to champ at the bit

freinage /fʀɛnaʒ/ *nm* braking

freiner /fʀɛne/ [1]
A *vtr* ① (faire ralentir) to slow down [*véhicule, parachute*]; ② (gêner) to impede [*personne, avance*]; ③ (modérer) to curb [*consommation*]
B *vi* ① (en voiture, à moto, vélo) to brake; ~ **à bloc** *or* **à fond** to slam on the brakes; ② (à ski) to slow down

frelaté, ~e /fʀəlate/ *adj* ① [*alcool*] adulterated; [*goût*] unnatural; ② [*milieu, plaisirs*] dubious

frêle /fʀɛl/ *adj* frail

frelon /fʀəlɔ̃/ *nm* hornet

freluquet† /fʀəlykɛ/ *nm* little squirt○, whippersnapper†

frémir /fʀemiʀ/ [3] *vi* ① (trembler) [*voile, feuille*] to quiver; [*eau du lac*] to ripple; ② (sous l'effet d'une émotion) [*lèvre, narine*] to tremble; [*personne*] (d'impatience, de colère, plaisir) to quiver (**de** with); (de dégoût, d'effroi) to shudder (**de** with); ③ Culin [*liquide*] to start to come to the boil

frémissant, ~e /fʀemisɑ̃, ɑ̃t/ *adj* **faire cuire dans l'eau** ~**e** simmer gently in water

frémissement /fʀemismɑ̃/ *nm* ① (vibration) quiver, tremor; **le** ~ **du vent dans les arbres** the rustle of the wind in the trees; **2** (d'émotion) (de narine, lèvre, main) trembling **C**; (de personne, corps) (dû à la joie, la colère, au plaisir) quiver; (dû à l'effroi, au dégoût) shudder

frêne /fʀɛn/ *nm* **1** (arbre) ash (tree); **2** (bois) ash (wood)

frénésie /fʀenezi/ *nf* frenzy; **avec ~** [*lutter*] frantically; [*danser*] frenziedly; [*applaudir*] wildly

frénétique /fʀenetik/ *adj* [*applaudissements, lutte, activité*] frenzied; [*joueur*] frenetic

frénétiquement /fʀenetikmɑ̃/ *adv* [*lutter, secouer*] frantically; [*danser*] frenziedly; [*applaudir*] wildly

fréquemment /fʀekamɑ̃/ *adv* frequently

fréquence /fʀekɑ̃s/ *nf* gén, Phys frequency; **à ~ vocale** Télécom tone dialling

fréquent, **~e** /fʀekɑ̃, ɑ̃t/ *adj* **1** (dans le temps) frequent; **il est ~ que cela arrive** it happens frequently; **2** (répandu) [*maladie, attitude*] common

fréquentable /fʀekɑ̃tabl/ *adj* (de bonne réputation) respectable; **ce ne sont pas des gens ~s** they are not the sort of people one should associate with

fréquentation /fʀekɑ̃tasjɔ̃/ *nf* **1** (amis) company **C**; **avoir de mauvaises ~s** to keep bad company; **c'est une mauvaise ~ pour toi** that's not the sort of person you should associate with; **2** (présence) **~ de l'église/des théâtres** churchgoing/theatregoing^{GB}; **record de ~ des théâtres** record theatre^{GB} audiences (*pl*); **la ~ des théâtres est en baisse/hausse** fewer/more people are going to the theatre^{GB}

fréquenté, **~e** /fʀekɑ̃te/
A *pp* ▸ **fréquenter**
B *pp adj* [*café, plage, théâtre*] popular; [*rue*] busy; **lieu bien/mal ~ place** that attracts the right/wrong sort of people; **la plage/cantine est peu ~e** not many people go to the beach/canteen

fréquenter /fʀekɑ̃te/ [1]
A *vtr* **1** (côtoyer) to associate with [*genre de personne*]; to see [sb] frequently [*amis, famille*]; to move in [*milieu*]; **~ les grands auteurs** fml to read the works of great writers; **2** (sortir avec) to go out with; **3** (aller à) to attend [*école*]; to visit [*musée*]; to go to [*plage*]; to frequent [*clubs*]; **il fréquente les bars** he hangs about[○] in bars
B **se fréquenter** *vpr* **1** (se voir) [*amis*] to see one another; **2** (sortir ensemble) to go out together

frère /fʀɛʀ/ *nm* gén, Relig brother; **~s ennemis** rivals within the same camp; **mes biens chers ~s** Relig my dear brethren; **vieux ~** old pal; **peuple** *or* **pays ~** fellow nation; **~ Jacques** Relig Brother Jacques; **être élevé chez les ~s** Relig to be educated by the brothers (*in a Catholic school*)

⌐Composés⌐ **~ d'armes** brother-in-arms; **~ de lait** foster brother

fresque /fʀɛsk/ *nf* **1** Art fresco; **2** fig panorama

fret /fʀɛt/ *nm* freight

fréter /fʀete/ [14] *vtr* **1** (donner en location) to charter out; **2** (prendre en location) to charter

frétillement /fʀetijmɑ̃/ *nm* (de poisson) wriggling **C**; (de queue de chien) wagging **C**

frétiller /fʀetije/ [1] *vi* **1** [*poisson*] to wriggle; **~ de la queue** [*chien*] to wag its tail; **2** fig **~ d'aise** to be quivering with pleasure

fretin /fʀətɛ̃/ *nm* lit, fig **(menu) ~** small fry

freudien, **-ienne** /fʀødjɛ̃, ɛn/ *adj, nm,f* Freudian

freux /fʀø/ *nm inv* Zool rook

friable /fʀijabl/ *adj* [*roche, pâte*] crumbly; [*terre*] friable

friand, **~e** /fʀijɑ̃, ɑ̃d/
A *adj* **être ~ de qch** to be very fond of sth
B *nm* Culin puff; **~ au fromage** cheese puff

friandise /fʀijɑ̃diz/ *nf* bonbon) sweet GB, candy US

fric[○] /fʀik/ *nm* dough[○], money; **être bourré de ~** to be loaded[○]

friche /fʀiʃ/ *nf* Agric waste land; **en ~** [*terre*] uncultivated, waste (*épith*)
⌐Composé⌐ **~ industrielle** industrial wasteland

friction /fʀiksjɔ̃/ *nf* **1** Méd rub; **2** (désaccord) friction **C**; **3** (en physique, mécanique) friction

frictionner /fʀiksjone/ [1]
A *vtr* to give [sb] a rub [*personne*]; to rub [*pieds, tête*]
B **se frictionner** *vpr* to rub oneself down

frigidaire® /fʀiʒidɛʀ/ *nm* refrigerator

frigide /fʀiʒid/ *adj* frigid

frigidité /fʀiʒidite/ *nf* frigidity

frigo[○] /fʀigo/ *nm* fridge[○]

frigorifié, **~e** /fʀigɔʀifje/ *adj* frozen

frigorifier /fʀigɔʀifje/ [2] *vtr* to freeze

frigorifique /fʀigɔʀifik/ *adj* [*vitrine, camion*] refrigerated; **machine ~** refrigeration system

frileux, **-euse** /fʀilø, øz/ *adj* **1** (sensible au froid) sensitive to the cold; **être (très) ~** [*personne*] to feel the cold; **2** (timoré) [*attitude, politique*] cautious

frimas /fʀima/ *nmpl* cold weather **C**

frime[○] /fʀim/ *nf* **1** (ostentation) **pour la ~** for show; **arrête ta ~!** stop showing off; **2** (simulation) pretence^{GB}; **c'est de la ~** it's all an act

frimer[○] /fʀime/ [1] *vi* to show off[○]

frimousse[○] /fʀimus/ *nf* little face

fringale[○] /fʀɛ̃gal/ *nf* **j'ai la ~** I'm absolutely starving

fringant, **~e** /fʀɛ̃gɑ̃, ɑ̃t/ *adj* [*cheval*] spirited; [*personne*] dashing; [*allure*] brisk

fringuer[○]: **se fringuer** /fʀɛ̃ge/ [1] *vpr* to dress

fringues[○] /fʀɛ̃g/ *nfpl* gear **C**, clothes

fripé, **~e** /fʀipe/ *adj* [*tissu*] crumpled; [*visage, bébé*] wrinkled

friper /fʀipe/ [1] *vtr*, **se friper** *vpr* to crease, to crumple

fripon[○], **-onne** /fʀipɔ̃, ɔn/
A *adj* mischievous
B *nm,f* rascal

fripouille[○] /fʀipuj/ *nf* **1** (escroc) crook[○]; **2** (affectueusement) **(petite) ~!** (little) monkey!

friqué[○], **~e** /fʀike/ *adj* loaded[○], very rich

frire /fʀiʀ/ [64] *vtr, vi* to fry

frisé, **~e¹** /fʀize/ *adj* [*cheveux*] curly; **elle est frisée** she has curly hair

frisée² /fʀize/ *nf* (salade) curly endive, frisée

friser /fʀize/ [1]
A *vtr* **1** (boucler) to curl [*cheveux, moustache*]; **se faire ~** to have one's hair curled; **2** (frôler) [*remarque, attitude*] to border on [*insolence, grossièreté*]; **il frise les quarante ans** he's getting on for forty; **cela frise les 10%** it's approaching 10%
B *vi* [*cheveux*] to curl; [*personne*] to have curly hair
C **se friser** *vpr* **se ~ les cheveux** to curl one's hair

frisette[○] /fʀizɛt/ *nf* little curl

frisquet[○], **-ette** /fʀiskɛ, ɛt/ *adj* chilly

frisson /fʀisɔ̃/ *nm* **1** (de froid, fièvre, plaisir) shiver (**de** of); (de peur) shudder; **avoir un ~ de** (de froid, fièvre) to shiver with; (de plaisir) to tremble with; (de peur) to shudder with; **j'ai des ~s** I keep shivering; **grand ~** great thrill; **2** (de feuillage) rustling; (de l'eau) rippling

frissonnement /fʀisɔnmɑ̃/ *nm* **1** (de feuillage) rustling; **2** (de froid, fièvre, plaisir) shivering (**de** of); (de peur) shuddering (**de** of)

frissonner /fʀisɔne/ [1] *vi* **1** (de fièvre, froid) to shiver (**de** with); (de peur) to shudder (**de** with); (de plaisir, d'orgueil) to tremble (**de** with); **2** [*feuillage*] to tremble; [*lac*] to ripple; **3** (commencer à bouillir) to simmer

frite /fʀit/ *nf* **1** Culin chip GB, French fry US; **2** [○](forme) **avoir la ~** to be feeling great, to be feeling chipper US

friterie /fʀitʀi/ *nf* chip shop GB, French-fries stall US

friteuse /fʀitøz/ *nf* chip pan GB, deep fat fryer US

friture /fʀityʀ/ *nf* **1** Culin (méthode) frying; (huile) oil; (aliment) fried food; poissons) ≈ whitebait (*pl*); **2** (parasites) crackling

frivole /fʀivɔl/ *adj* frivolous

frivolité /fʀivɔlite/ *nf* **1** (caractère) frivolousness; **2** (chose sans importance) trivial matter; **3** (dentelle) tatting

froc /fʀɔk/ *nm* **1** [○](pantalon) trousers (*pl*) GB, pants (*pl*) US; **2** Relig habit

froid, **~e** /fʀwa, fʀwad/
A *adj* **1** (à basse température) cold; **2** fig [*personne, lumière, beauté*] cold; [*accueil, manières, ton*] cool; [*humour*] deadpan; [*colère*] controlled; **laisser ~** to leave [sb] cold
B *nm* **1** (basse température) cold; **il fait ~** it's cold; **avoir ~** to be cold; **avoir ~ aux pieds** to have cold feet; **attraper** *or* **prendre ~** to catch a cold; **coup de ~** Méd chill; **2** (distance) coldness; **il y a un certain ~ dans nos relations**

there's a certain coolness in our relationship; **ils sont en ~ avec moi** relations between them and me are strained; **jeter un ~** to cast a chill (**dans, sur** over)

C à froid *loc adv* **démarrage à ~** cold start; **plaisanterie à ~** spontaneous joke; **analyse à ~** impartial analysis

(Idiomes) **il fait un ~ de canard**○ it is bitterly cold; **avoir/ faire** *or* **donner ~ dans le dos** to feel/to send a shiver down the spine; **ne pas avoir ~ aux yeux** to be fearless; **garder la tête ~e** to keep a cool head

froidement /fʀwadmɑ̃/ *adv* **1** (sans émotion) coolly; **abattre ~** to shoot [sb] down in cold blood [*personne*]; **2** (calmement) with a cool head; **regarder les choses ~** to look at things coolly

froideur /fʀwadœʀ/ *nf* coolness

froissement /fʀwasmɑ̃/ *nm* **1** (de tissu, papier, feuille) (action) crumpling; (bruit) rustling; **2** Méd strain

froisser /fʀwase/ [1]
A *vtr* **1** lit (chiffonner) to crease, to crumple [*tissu, vêtement*]; to crumple [*papier*]; **il n'y a eu que de la tôle froissée**○ the car was damaged but no-one was hurt; **2** (blesser) to hurt [*personne, sensibilité*]; **3** Méd to strain [*muscle, nerf*]
B se froisser *vpr* **1** (se chiffonner) [*tissu, vêtement, papier*] to crease; **2** (s'offusquer) to be hurt (**de** by); **3** Méd to strain

frôlement /fʀolmɑ̃/ *nm* **1** (contact) brushing **C**; **2** (de feuille, papier, tissu) rustling; (d'ailes) fluttering

frôler /fʀole/ [1]
A *vtr* **1** (toucher) [*personne, main, genou*] to brush; [*projectile*] to graze; **2** (passer près) [*balle, pierre, voiture*] to miss narrowly; [*personne*] to brush past [*personne*]; to brush against [*objet, mur*]; **il a frôlé la mort** he very nearly died; **~ le mauvais goût** to border on bad taste; **~ les 200 km/h** to nearly touch 200km per hour
B se frôler *vpr* **1** (se toucher) [*personnes, mains, genoux*] to brush against each other; **2** (sans se toucher) [*objets, voitures, conducteurs*] to just miss each other; [*personnes*] to brush past each other

fromage /fʀomaʒ/ *nm* **1** cheese; **2** ○(situation rentable) **il a trouvé un bon ~** he's found a nice little earner GB, he's hit pay dirt US; **se partager le ~** to split the profits

(Composés) **~ blanc** *or* **frais** fromage frais; **~ maigre** low-fat cheese; **~ à tartiner** cheese spread; **~ de tête** brawn GB, head cheese US

(Idiome) **faire un ~ de qch**○ to make a big deal○ out of sth

fromager, -ère /fʀomaʒe, ɛʀ/
A *adj* cheese (*épith*)
B ▸ p. 372 *nm* (fabricant) cheesemaker; (commerçant) cheese seller

fromagerie /fʀomaʒʀi/ ▸ p. 372 *nf* (fabrique) dairy; (magasin) cheese shop; (rayon) ~ cheese counter

froment /fʀomɑ̃/ *nm* wheat

fronce /fʀɔ̃s/ *nf* gather; **jupe à ~s** gathered skirt

froncement /fʀɔ̃smɑ̃/ *nm* **avoir un léger ~ de sourcils** to frown slightly

froncer /fʀɔ̃se/ [12]
A *vtr* **1** (en couture) to gather; **2** **~ les sourcils** to frown; **~ le nez** to wrinkle one's nose
B se froncer *vpr* **ses sourcils se froncèrent** he/she frowned

frondaison /fʀɔ̃dɛzɔ̃/ *nf* **1** (feuillage) liter foliage **C**; **2** Bot foliation

fronde /fʀɔ̃d/ *nf* **1** (arme) sling; (jouet) catapult GB, slingshot US; **2** (révolte) revolt

frondeur, -euse /fʀɔ̃dœʀ, øz/
A *adj* [*personne, esprit*] rebellious; [*propos*] anti-authoritarian
B *nm* troublemaker

front /fʀɔ̃/
A *nm* **1** Anat forehead, brow littér; **2** Mil front; **sur le ~ de l'emploi** fig on the job front; **faire ~ commun contre l'ennemi** to make a united stand against the enemy; **3** (façade) façade; **4** Météo front; **5** (en politique) front
B de front *loc adv* **aborder un problème de ~** to tackle a problem head-on; **les voitures se sont heurtées de ~** the cars collided head-on; **ils marchaient à quatre de ~** they were walking four abreast; **mener plusieurs tâches de ~** to have several jobs on the go

(Composés) **~ de mer** seafront; **Front populaire** Hist Popular Front

(Idiome) **avoir le ~ de faire qch** to have the face *ou* effrontery to do sth

frontal, -e, *mpl* **-aux** /fʀɔ̃tal, o/ *adj* [*attaque*] frontal; [*choc, collision*] head-on (*épith*)

frontalier, -ière /fʀɔ̃talje, ɛʀ/
A *adj* border (*épith*); **travailleur ~** person who works across the border
B *nm,f* person living near the border

frontière /fʀɔ̃tjɛʀ/ *nf* **1** Géog, Pol frontier, border; **à l'intérieur de nos ~s** at home; **hors de nos ~s** abroad; **2** (limite) ~s entre les disciplines boundaries between disciplines; **faire reculer les ~s de la connaissance** to push back the frontiers of knowledge; **au-delà des ~s du possible** beyond the realms of possibility

fronton /fʀɔ̃tɔ̃/ *nm* Archit pediment

frottement /fʀɔtmɑ̃/ *nm* **1** (mouvement) rubbing **C**; **2** (bruit) **j'entends des ~s** I can hear something rubbing; **3** (en mécanique, physique) friction **C**; **résistance de ~** frictional resistance

frotter /fʀɔte/ [1]
A *vtr* **1** (masser) to rub; **~ une allumette** to strike a match; **2** (nettoyer) to scrub [*peau, parquet, linge, tapis*]; to polish [*argenterie*]
B *vi* to rub; **le bas de la porte frotte** the bottom of the door is scraping against the floor
C se frotter *vpr* **1** (se frictionner) **se ~ les yeux** to rub one's eyes; **se ~ les mains** lit, fig to rub one's hands; **2** (se nettoyer) **se ~ les mains** to scrub one's hands; **3** (se mesurer) **se ~ à** to take on

(Idiomes) **se faire ~ les oreilles**○ to have one's ears boxed; **qui s'y frotte s'y pique** if you go looking for trouble, you'll find it

frottis /fʀɔti/ *nm inv* **1** (en biologie) smear; **2** Art scumble

froussard○, **-e** /fʀusaʀ, aʀd/ *nm,f* chicken○, coward

frousse /fʀus/ *nf* fright; **avoir la ~** to be scared

fructifier /fʀyktifje/ [2] *vi* [*capital*] to yield a profit; [*affaire*] to flourish; **faire ~ son argent** to make one's money grow

fructueux, -euse /fʀyktɥø, øz/ *adj* (fécond) [*relation, réunion*] fruitful; [*essai, carrière*] successful; [*travail*] productive; (lucratif) profitable

frugal, -e, *mpl* **-aux** /fʀygal, o/ *adj* frugal

frugalité /fʀygalite/ *nf* frugality; **avec ~** frugally

fruit /fʀɥi/ *nm* **1** gén, Culin fruit **C**; **voulez-vous un ~?** would you like some fruit?; **aimer les ~s** to like fruit; **2** (résultat) fruit; **les ~s de ses efforts** the fruits of one's efforts; **le ~ de mes entrailles** the fruit of my womb; **porter ses ~s** to bear fruit

(Composés) **~ confit** candied *ou* glacé fruit; **~ défendu** Bible forbidden fruit; **~ de la passion** passion fruit; **~ sec** Culin dried fruit; fig (personne) disappointment; **~s de mer** seafood **C**; **~s rouges** soft fruit **C** GB, berries US

fruité, ~e /fʀɥite/ *adj* [*alcool, parfum*] fruity

fruitier, -ière /fʀɥitje, ɛʀ/
A *adj* fruit (*épith*)
B ▸ p. 372 *nm,f* fruiterer GB, fruit seller US

frusques○ /fʀysk/ *nfpl* gear○ **C**, clothes; **de vieilles ~** old clothes

fruste /fʀyst/ *adj* unsophisticated

frustrant, ~e /fʀystʀɑ̃, ɑ̃t/ *adj* frustrating

frustration /fʀystʀasjɔ̃/ *nf* frustration

frustré, ~e /fʀystʀe/
A *adj* frustrated
B *nm,f* malcontent

frustrer /fʀystʀe/ [1] *vtr* **1** (décevoir) **~ les efforts de qn** to thwart sb's efforts; **~ qn dans son attente** to disappoint sb's hopes; **2** (priver) **~ qn de qch** to deprive sb of sth; (malhonnêtement) to cheat sb (out) of sth; **3** Psych to frustrate

fuel /fjul/ *nm* = fioul

fugace /fygas/ *adj* [*sensation, souvenir, reflet, instant, odeur*] fleeting; [*symptôme*] elusive

fugitif, -ive /fyʒitif, iv/
A *adj* **1** (échappé) [*prisonnier*] escaped; [*esclave*] runaway (*épith*); **2** (bref) [*sensation, pensée, ombre, espoir*] fleeting; [*plaisir, joie*] elusive
B *nm,f* fugitive

f

fugue /fyg/ *nf* [1] (escapade) **faire une** ∼ to run away; **c'est sa première** ∼ it's the first time he/she has run away; [2] Mus fugue

fuguer /fyge/ [1] *vi* to run away

fugueur, -euse /fygœʀ, øz/ *nm,f* runaway (child)

fuir /fɥiʀ/ [29]

A *vtr* [1] (quitter) to flee [*pays, ville, oppression*]; to flee from [*combats, amour*]; [2] (éviter) to escape [*hiver*]; to avoid [*responsabilité, personne*]; to steer clear of [*problème, foule*]; to stay out of [*soleil*]

B *vi* [1] (partir) [*personne, soldat, capitaux*] to flee; [*animal*] to run away; ∼ **à toutes jambes** to run for it; **faire** ∼ to scare [sb] off [*personne*]; [2] (suinter) [*robinet, gaz, toit, stylo*] to leak; [3] (se dérober) ∼ **devant ses responsabilités** not to face up to one's responsibilities; [4] (défiler et disparaître) [*nuages*] to sail by; [*temps*] to fly by

fuite /fɥit/ *nf* [1] (mouvement) gén flight; (de fugitif) escape; **prendre la** ∼ [*personne*] to flee; [*fugitif*] to escape; ∼ **des cerveaux** brain drain; ∼ **de capitaux** outflow of capital; [2] (d'information) leak; ∼**s avant l'examen** leaks before the examination; [3] Tech (suintement) leak; ∼ **d'eau** water leak

fulgurant, ∼e /fylgyʀɑ̃, ɑ̃t/ *adj* [*réflexes, attaque*] lightning (épith); [*ascension, progression*] dazzling; [*imagination*] brilliant; [*douleur*] searing (épith); **ses progrès ont été** ∼**s** he/she has made terrific progress; **regards** ∼**s** blazing eyes

fulminer /fylmine/ [1] *vi* (enrager) to fulminate (**contre** against); **il fulminait intérieurement** he was seething

fumant, ∼e /fymɑ̃, ɑ̃t/ *adj* [1] (dégageant de la fumée) smoking; (dégageant de la vapeur) steaming; [2] °(sensationnel) terrific°; **faire un coup** ∼ to pull off a real coup (**à qn** on sb); **préparer un coup** ∼ **contre** *or* **à qn** to have a nasty surprise in store for sb

fumasse° /fymas/ *adj* **être** ∼ to be fuming

fumé, ∼e¹ /fyme/

A *pp* ▸ **fumer**

B *pp adj* [1] Culin [*viande, poisson*] smoked; [2] (teinté) [*vitre, lunettes*] tinted; [*verre*] smoked; **des lunettes à verres** ∼**s** tinted glasses

fume-cigarette /fymsigaʀɛt/ *nm inv* cigarette holder

fumée² /fyme/

A *pp adj f* ▸ **fumé**

B *nf* [1] (de feu) smoke; (d'usine, d'échappement) ∼**s** fumes; **partir en** ∼ fig to go up in smoke; [2] (vapeur) steam

(Idiome) **il n'y a pas de** ∼ **sans feu** Prov there's no smoke without fire

fumer /fyme/ [1]

A *vtr* [1] [*fumeur*] to smoke; [2] Culin to smoke [*viande, poisson*]; [3] Agric to manure [*sol*]

B *vi* [1] [*fumeur*] to smoke; [2] [*volcan, cheminée*] to smoke; [*potage*] to steam; [*acide*] to give off fumes

(Idiome) ∼ **comme un pompier** *or* **sapeur** to smoke like a chimney

fumet /fymɛ/ *nm* [1] Culin (de viande) aroma; (de vin) bouquet; (sauce) fumet; [2] (forte odeur) smell, odour^{GB}

fumeur, -euse¹ /fymœʀ, øz/ *nm,f* smoker; **un grand** ∼ a heavy smoker; **zone** ∼**s/non** ∼**s** smoking/non-smoking area

fumeux, -euse² /fymø, øz/ *adj* [*théorie, propos*] woolly GB, wooly US; [*personne*] woolly-minded

fumier /fymje/ *nm* [1] Agric manure; **tas de** ∼ dunghill; [2] °(salaud) offensive bastard injur

fumigène /fymiʒɛn/

A *adj* Mil [*grenade*] smoke

B *nm* Mil smoke device; Agric fumigator

fumiste /fymist/ *nm,f* [1] ° (charlatan) phoney°; (paresseux) shirker; [2] ▸ **p. 372** (technicien) (pour cheminées) chimney specialist; (de chauffage) stove fitter

fumisterie /fymistəʀi/ *nf* [1] °(action peu sérieuse) joke; **c'est une** *or* **de la** ∼ it's a joke; [2] (profession) (pour cheminées) chimney engineering; (pour les appareils de chauffage) stove fitting

fumoir /fymwaʀ/ *nm* smoking-room

funambule /fynɑ̃byl/ ▸ **p. 372** *nmf* tightrope walker; **un numéro de** ∼**(s)** a tightrope act

funèbre /fynɛbʀ/ *adj* [1] (funéraire) funeral; [2] (lugubre) gloomy

funérailles /fyneʀɑj/ *nfpl* funeral (sg)

funéraire /fyneʀɛʀ/ *adj* [*cérémonie, frais*] funeral; [*objet, monument*] funerary; **dalle** *or* **stèle** ∼ tombstone, gravestone GB

funeste /fynɛst/ *adj* [*erreur, conseil*] fatal; [*décision, jour*] fateful; [*conséquence*] dire; **être** ∼ **à qn/qch** to be fatal to sb/sth; **cela nous a été** ∼ it was fatal

funiculaire /fynikylɛʀ/ *nm* funicular

fur: **au fur et à mesure** /ofyʀeaməzyʀ/ *loc adv* **passe-moi les livres, je les rangerai au** ∼ **et à mesure** pass me the books, I'll put them away as I go along; **au** ∼ **et à mesure de leurs besoins** as and when they need it; **la championne joue de mieux en mieux au** ∼ **et à mesure des rencontres** the champion is playing better and better with each match; **au** ∼ **et à mesure que la soirée avançait, il devenait de plus en plus animé** as the evening went on, he became more and more animated

furax° /fyʀaks/ *adj inv* (hopping) mad° (*jamais épith*); **être** ∼ **de devoir faire qch** to be mad° at having to do sth; **je suis** ∼ **d'avoir dit ça** I could kick myself for saying that°

furet /fyʀɛ/ *nm* ferret

fureter /fyʀte/ [18] *vi* to rummage, to ferret around

fureur /fyʀœʀ/ *nf* [1] (colère) rage, fury; ∼ **aveugle/noire** blind/unholy rage; **être en** ∼ **contre qn/contre qch** to be in a rage with sb/about sth; **se mettre en** ∼ **contre qn/qch** to fly into a rage with sb/sth; [2] (passion) frenzy; **s'adonner au jeu avec** ∼ to gamble frenziedly; ∼ **de vivre** lust for life; **avoir la** ∼ **du jeu** to be addicted to gambling; **faire** ∼ to be all the rage

furibond, ∼e /fyʀibɔ̃, ɔ̃d/ *adj* furious

furie /fyʀi/ *nf* [1] (rage) rage, fury; **mettre qn en** ∼ to make sb furious; **entrer en** ∼ to get furious, to fly into a rage; [2] (harpie) fury

furieusement /fyʀjøzmɑ̃/ *adv* [1] (violemment) [*attaquer, cogner*] furiously; [*injurier*] violently; [*répondre*] angrily; [2] °(extrêmement) **j'ai** ∼ **envie de dormir** I'm dying to go to sleep; **elle ressemble** ∼ **à son père** she's incredibly like her father

furieux, -ieuse /fyʀjø, øz/ *adj* [1] (irrité) [*personne, geste, air, ton*] furious; [*foule, animal, cris*] angry; **être** ∼ **contre qn** to be furious with sb; **être** ∼ **de qch** to be infuriated by sth; [2] °(intense) [*envie*] terrible; [3] (violent) [*combat*] intense; [*tempête, torrent*] raging

furoncle /fyʀɔ̃kl/ *nm* boil, furuncle spéc

furtif, -ive /fyʀtif, iv/ *adj* [1] (discret, rapide) furtive; **marcher d'un pas** ∼ to creep along; [2] (passager) [*soupçon, joie, émotion*] fleeting; [3] Mil (indétectable) **avion** ∼ Stealth bomber

furtivement /fyʀtivmɑ̃/ *adv* furtively

fusain /fyzɛ̃/ *nm* [1] (arbuste) spindle tree; [2] Art (matière) charcoal, fusain spéc; (crayon) charcoal crayon; (dessin) charcoal drawing; **au** ∼ [*dessiner*] in charcoal; [*dessin*] charcoal (épith)

fuseau, pl ∼**x** /fyzo/ *nm* [1] (pour filer) spindle; **en** ∼ [*jambe de pantalon, muscle*] tapering; [2] (à dentelle) lace bobbin; [3] (pantalon) ∼**(x) (de ski)** ski pants (pl)

(Composé) ∼ **horaire** time zone

fusée /fyze/ *nf* [1] (en astronautique, pyrotechnie) rocket; [2] Mil (missile) rocket, missile; [3] Aut stub axle

(Composés) ∼ **antichar** antitank rocket *ou* missile; ∼ **éclairante** flare; ∼ **porteuse** carrier rocket; ∼ **sol-air** surface-to-air missile

(Idiome) **partir comme une** ∼ to set off like a rocket

fuselage /fyzlaʒ/ *nm* fuselage

fuselé, ∼e /fyzle/ *adj* [*muscle, doigt*] tapering; [*arbre, colonne, structure*] spindle-shaped

fuser /fyze/ [1] *vi* [1] (retentir) to ring out; **les rires fusaient** laughter came from all sides; [2] (jaillir) [*objet*] to rocket; [*lumière*] to stream out

fusible /fyzibl/

A *adj* fusible

B *nm* (fil, cartouche) fuse

fusil /fyzi/ *nm* [1] (arme) gun, shotgun; Mil rifle; **coup de** ∼ lit gunshot; **dans ce restaurant c'est le coup de** ∼° fig they really sting you in that restaurant; [2] (tireur) **être un bon** ∼ to be a good shot; [3] (pour aiguiser) sharpening steel

(Idiome) **partir la fleur au** ∼ to set off without a care in the world

fusilier /fyzi(l)je/ *nm* rifleman, fusilier; Hist fusilier
(Composé) ~ **marin** marine

fusillade /fyzijad/ *nf* (bruit) gunfire **₵**; (bataille) shoot-out

fusiller /fyzije/ [1] *vtr* **1** (exécuter) to shoot; **2** ○(abîmer) to wreck
(Idiome) ~ **qn du regard** to look daggers at sb

fusil-mitrailleur, *pl* **fusils-mitrailleurs** /fyzimitraʒœʀ/ *nm* light machine gun

fusion /fyzjɔ̃/ *nf* **1** (liquéfaction) (de métal) melting, fusion spéc; (de glace) melting; **roche/métal en** ~ molten rock/metal; **2** Biol, Phys fusion; ~ **(thermo)nucléaire** nuclear fusion; **3** Ling fusion; **4** (union) (d'entreprises, de partis, listes, professions) merger (**entre** between); (de systèmes, cultures, théories) fusion (**entre** of); (de peuples, races) mixing (**entre** of)

fusion-acquisition, *pl* **fusions-acquisitions** /fyzjɔ̃akizisjɔ̃/ *nf* merger; **des fusions-acquisitions** mergers and acquisitions, M & A

fusionner /fyzjɔne/ [1] *vtr*, *vi* to merge

fustiger /fystiʒe/ [13] *vtr* **1** (condamner) to castigate, to lambast; **2** (battre) to thrash

fût /fy/ *nm* **1** (tonneau) cask, barrel; (pour produits chimiques) drum; **2** (d'arbre) trunk; **3** (de colonne) shaft

futaie /fytɛ/ *nf* (forêt) forest of tall trees

futé, ~**e** /fyte/
A *adj* [*personne, animal*] wily, crafty péj; [*sourire, réponse*] crafty; **ce n'est pas très** ~ that isn't/wasn't very clever
B *nm,f* **(petit)** ~ cunning little devil

futile /fytil/ *adj* [*projet, prétexte, distraction*] trivial; [*personne, existence, propos*] superficial

futilité /fytilite/
A *nf* (insignifiance) superficiality
B **futilités** *nfpl* (paroles) banalities; (objets) trifles; (actions) meaningless activities; (détails) trivial details

futur, ~**e** /fytyʀ/
A *adj* future; **son** ~ **mari** her future husband; **les** ~**s époux** the engaged couple (*sg*); **les** ~**es mères** expectant mothers; **cet enfant, c'est un** ~ **artiste/champion** that child has the makings of an artist/a champion
B *nm* **1** (avenir) future; **le train du** ~ the train of the future; **2** Ling future; **au** ~ in the future (tense)
(Composés) ~ **antérieur** Ling future perfect; ~ **simple** Ling future tense

futuriste /fytyʀist/ *adj* **1** (ultramoderne) [*décor, voiture, vision*] futuristic; **2** Art, Littérat futurist

futurologue /fytyʀɔlɔg/ ▸ p. 372 *nmf* futurologist

fuyant, ~**e** /fɥijɑ̃, ɑ̃t/ *adj* [*regard*] shifty; [*caractère*] slippery○; [*point, horizon*] receding; [*bonheur*] elusive; **front/profil** ~ receding forehead/profile

fuyard, ~**e** /fɥijaʀ, aʀd/ *nm,f* **1** (fugitif) runaway; **2** (déserteur) deserter

Gg

g, G /ʒe/ *nm inv* **1** (lettre) g, G; **2** (*written abbr* = **gramme**) 250 g 250 g; **3** G7 *abbr* ► **groupe**

gabardine /gabaʀdin/ *nf* gabardine

gabarit /gabaʀi/ *nm* **1** (de véhicule) size; **véhicule hors ~** oversize vehicle; **2** ○(de personne) (corpulence) build; (aptitudes) calibre^{GB}

gabegie /gabʒi/ *nf* (gaspillage) waste (due to mismanagement); (désordre) muddle

gabonais, ~e /gabɔnɛ, ɛz/ ► p. 392 *adj* Gabonese

gâcher /gaʃe/ **1** *vtr* to waste [*nourriture*]; to throw away [*vie*]; to spoil [*spectacle*]; to ruin [*affaire*]
⟨Idiome⟩ **~ le métier** to ruin the trade (*by undercutting prices*)

gâchette /gaʃɛt/ *nf* (d'arme) tumbler; (détente) controv trigger; **appuyer sur la ~** to pull the trigger; **avoir la ~ facile** to be trigger-happy

gâchis /gaʃi/ *nm inv* (gaspillage) waste ¢; (pagaille) mess

gadget /gadʒɛt/ *nm* gadget

gadin ○ /gadɛ̃/ *nm* **ramasser** *or* **prendre un ~** to fall flat on one's face

gadoue ○ /gadu/ *nf* (boue) mud

gaélique /gaelik/ ► p. 336 *adj, nm* Gaelic

gaffe /gaf/ *nf* **1** ○(acte) boob○ GB, blooper○ US, blunder; (parole) clanger○ GB, blooper○ US; **faire ~** to watch out (**à** for); **faire ~ que** to be careful that; **2** Naut boathook; **3** (pour accrocher le poisson) gaff

gaffeur ○, **-euse** /gafœʀ, øz/ *nm,f* blunderer

gag /gag/ *nm* **1** gag; **2** (incident drôle) joke

gaga ○ /gaga/
A *adj inv* (gâteux) gaga○; (débile) daft○ GB, silly; **devenir ~** to go gaga
B *nmf* dodderer○

gage /gaʒ/
A *nm* **1** (garantie) security ¢, surety ¢; **prêter sur ~s** to lend against surety; **mettre qch en ~** to pawn sth; **ta ténacité est le ~ de ta réussite future** your tenacity is a guarantee of your future success; **2** Jeux (pénitence) forfeit; **3** (d'amour, de fidélité, bonne foi) pledge; **donner des ~s d'amitié à qn** to pledge friendship to sb
B **gages†** *nmpl* (salaire) wages; **tueur à ~s** hired killer

gager /gaʒe/ [13] *vtr* **1** (supposer) fml **~ que** to suppose that, to wager† that; **2** (mettre en gage) to pawn

gageure /gaʒyʀ/ *nf* challenge

gagnant, ~e /gaɲɑ̃, ɑ̃t/
A *adj* [*numéro, équipe*] winning (*épith*); **donner un cheval/qn ~** to tip a horse/sb to win; **partir ~** to be on to a winner; **être** *or* **sortir ~** to come out on top (**de** in)
B *nm,f* (personne, cheval) winner

gagne-pain /gaɲpɛ̃/ *nm inv* livelihood

gagne-petit /gaɲpəti/
A *adj inv* pej **être ~** to be after every last penny
B *nmf inv* low-wage earner

gagner /gaɲe/ [1]
A *vtr* **1** (remporter) to win [*compétition, guerre, procès*]; **~ aux points** to win on points; **pour lui, rien n'est encore gagné** fig he's not there yet, he's still got a long way to go; **c'est gagné!** lit we've done it!; iron well done!; **à tous les coups on gagne!** every one a winner!; **2** (percevoir, mériter) to earn; **~ 10 000 francs par mois** to earn 10,000 francs a month; **il gagne bien sa vie** he makes a good living; **il a gagné une fortune sur la vente du tableau** he made a fortune from

the sale of the picture; **les sommes gagnées au jeu** gambling gains; **c'est toujours ça de gagné!** well, that's something anyway!; **3** (acquérir) to gain [*réputation, avantage*]; **~ du temps** (atermoyer) to gain time; **~ du terrain** [*personne, armée, idées*] to gain ground (**sur** on); [*incendie*] to spread; **~ de la vitesse** to gather speed; **il a gagné de l'assurance** he has gained in self-confidence; **elle a gagné 5 cm en un an** she's grown 5 cm in a year; **il a gagné 9 kilos** he's put on 9 kilos; **l'équipe a gagné trois places** the team has moved up three places; **4** (économiser) to save [*temps*]; **~ de la place en faisant** to make more room by doing; **5** (attirer) to win [sb] over (**à** to); **6** (atteindre) [*voyageur, véhicule*] to reach, to get to [*lieu*]; **7** (atteindre) [*incendie, maladie, troubles, chômage*] to spread to [*lieu*]; **8** (s'emparer de) [*peur, émotion, découragement*] to overcome [*personne*]; **la fatigue me gagnait peu à peu** I was gradually overcome with fatigue; **je sentais le froid me ~** I started to feel cold; **9** (battre) **~ qn de vitesse** to outstrip sb
B *vi* **1** (réussir) to win; **~ aux élections** to win the election; **2** (tirer avantage) **le film gagne à être vu en version originale** the film is best seen in the original version; **vous gagneriez à diversifier vos produits** it would be to your advantage to diversify; **elle gagne à être connue** she improves on acquaintance; **3** (acquérir plus) to gain (**en** in); **les entreprises ont gagné en productivité** firms have improved their productivity; **4** (être bénéficiaire) **y ~** to come off better; **y ~ en** to gain in; **5** (recouvrir) [*mer*] to encroach (**sur** on)

gagneur, -euse /gaɲœʀ, øz/ *nm,f* winner

gai, ~e /gɛ/
A *adj* **1** (joyeux) [*personne, visage*] happy; [*caractère, regard*] cheerful; [*réunion, œuvre*] light-hearted; [*couleur*] bright, cheerful; **2** (plaisant) iron **c'est ~** great! iron; **ça promet d'être ~** that'll be fun! iron; **3** (éméché) merry; **4** ○(homosexuel) controv gay
B ○ *nm* (homosexuel) controv gay

gaiement /gɛmɑ̃/ *adv* [*partir, chanter*] cheerfully, merrily; [*décoré*] gaily; **allons-y ~** hum let's get on with it

gaieté /gete/ *nf* (de personne, lieu, d'histoire) gaiety, cheerfulness; **il ne l'a pas fait de ~ de cœur** he wasn't very happy about doing it

gaillard, ~e /gajaʀ, aʀd/
A *adj* **1** (vigoureux) [*personne*] strapping; **2** (grivois) [*chanson*] ribald
B *nm,f* strapping lad/girl; **viens ici, mon ~!** come here, lad○ GB, over here buddy○ US!
C ○ *nm* (lascar) sly customer○
⟨Composés⟩ **~ d'arrière** Naut poop; **~ d'avant** Naut (en marine ancienne) forecastle; (en marine moderne) forward superstructure

gain /gɛ̃/ *nm* **1** (argent) earnings (*pl*); **tirer un ~ médiocre de ses efforts** to get a meagre^{GB} return for one's efforts; **cette maison représente les ~s de toute une vie de labeur** this house represents the fruits of a lifetime's hard work; **mes ~s au jeu** my gambling gains; **2** (profit en Bourse) gain; **3** (économie) saving; **c'est un ~ de temps considérable** it saves a considerable amount of time

gaine /gɛn/ *nf* **1** (de poignard) sheath; **2** (sous-vêtement) girdle; **3** Tech (de fil électrique) sheathing; (de tuyau) casing; **4** Bot sheath

gainer /gene/ [1] *vtr* **1** (mouler) [*robe*] to sheathe [*corps*]; **2** Tech to sheathe [*fil électrique*]

gala /gala/ *nm* gala; **tenue de ~** evening dress ¢

galamment /galamɑ̃/ adv gallantly

galant, **~e** /galɑ̃, ɑ̃t/
A adj **1** (délicat envers les femmes) gallant, gentlemanly; **2** (obligeant) **soyez ~** be a gentleman; **3** (amoureux) [rendez-vous] romantic; **elle était en ~e compagnie** she was in the company of a gentleman; **4** Art, Mus [style] galant
B †nm (fiancé) beau†

galanterie /galɑ̃tʀi/ nf **1** (courtoisie) gallantry; **2** †(propos flatteur) flattering remark

galaxie /galaksi/ nf galaxy

galbe /galb/ nm curve

galbé, **~e** /galbe/ adj [colonne] with entasis (épith, après n); [pied de meuble] curved; **épaule bien ~e** shapely shoulder

galber /galbe/ **1** vtr to shape

gale /gal/ ▸ p. 195 nf **1** (de personne) scabies ℂ; **je n'ai pas la ~**◦ hum I'm not contagious; **2** (du chien, chat) mange; (du mouton) scab; **3** Bot scab

(Idiome) **il est mauvais** or **méchant comme la ~**◦ he's a nasty customer◦

galéjade /galeʒad/ nf tall story

galère /galɛʀ/ nf **1** Hist (vaisseau) galley; **condamné aux ~s** (à ramer) sentenced to the galleys; (aux travaux forcés) sentenced to hard labour^GB; **2** ◦(situation pénible) hell◦; **c'est (la) ~!** it's a real pain◦!; **être dans la même ~** to be in the same boat

galérer◦ /galeʀe/ **14** vi **1** (peiner) to have a hard time; **2** (travailler) to slave away, to slog away◦

galerie /galʀi/ nf **1** Archit (de maison, musée) gallery; **2** Art (magasin, musée) gallery; (de mine, grotte) gallery; (de taupe) tunnel; **4** Aut (pour bagages) roof rack; **5** (de théâtre) gallery; **amuser la ~**◦ to play to the gallery; **pour épater la ~**◦ (in order) to impress the crowd

(Composés) **~ marchande** shopping arcade; **Galerie des Glaces** hall of mirrors

galérien /galeʀjɛ̃/ nm Hist (sur une galère) galley slave; (au bagne) convict

galet /galɛ/ nm **1** (caillou) pebble; **2** Tech roller

galette /galɛt/ nf (gâteau) plain round flat cake; (crêpe) pancake

(Composé) **~ des Rois** Twelfth Night cake (containing bean or lucky charm)

galeux, **-euse** /galø, øz/
A adj **1** (atteint de gale) [personne] with scabies (épith, après n); [chien] mangy; [mouton] scabby; [arbre] covered with scab (après n); **2** (décrépit) [mur] peeling; [bâtiment, quartier] slummy
B nm,f **1** lit person with scabies; **2** ◦fig scum◦ ℂ

galimatias /galimatja/ nm inv (parlé) gibberish; (écrit) rubbish

galipette◦ /galipɛt/ nf (cabriole) somersault

Galles /gal/ ▸ p. 504 nprfpl **le pays de ~** Wales (sg)

gallicisme /galisism/ nm (dans une langue étrangère) gallicism; (en français) French idiom

gallois, **~e** /galwa, az/ ▸ p. 336
A adj Welsh
B nm Ling Welsh

Gallois, **~e** /galwa, az/ nm,f Welshman/Welshwoman; **les ~** the Welsh

gallon /galɔ̃/ ▸ p. 87 nm gallon

galoche /galɔʃ/ nf (sabot, godillot) clog; **menton en ~** protruding chin

galon /galɔ̃/ nm **1** (ruban) braid ℂ; **2** Mil stripe; **gagner ses ~s** to win promotion; **prendre du ~** to be promoted

galonné, **~e** /galɔne/
A adj **1** (bordé de galon) trimmed with braid; **2** Mil [militaire] of officer class (épith, après n); [manche] displaying the insignia of rank (épith, après n)
B ◦nm soldiers' slang brass hat◦

galop /galo/ nm **1** (d'équidé) gallop; **petit ~** canter; **grand ~** full gallop; **cheval au ~** galloping horse; **partir au ~** to set off at a gallop; **faire du ~** to gallop; **au ~!** gallop!; **s'enfuir au (triple) ~**◦ [personne] to run off double-quick; **au ~!** hurry up!; **2** Mus galop

(Composé) **~ d'essai** trial run

(Idiome) **chassez le naturel il revient au ~** Prov what's bred in the bone will come out in the flesh Prov

galopade /galopad/ nf **1** (de chevaux) gallop; **2** ◦fig (course précipitée) stampede

galopant, **~e** /galopɑ̃, ɑ̃t/ adj [inflation] galloping; [prolifération, démographie] soaring

galoper /galope/ **1** vi **1** [cheval, cavalier] to gallop; **ne laisse pas ~ ton imagination** fig don't let your imagination run away with you; **2** ◦(en faisant du bruit) [enfant] to charge (around); **3** ◦(se dépêcher) to dash (around)

galopin /galopɛ̃/ nm (enfant) rascal

galvaniser /galvanize/ **1** vtr lit, fig to galvanize

galvauder /galvode/ **1** vtr to sully [réputation]; to dull [gloire]; to waste [talent]; to overwork [idée]; to squander [fortune]; **expression galvaudée** hackneyed expression

gamba /gɑ̃ba/ pl as/ nf large (Mediterranean) prawn

gambader /gɑ̃bade/ **1** vi [animal, enfant] to gambol

gamberger◦ /gɑ̃bɛʀʒe/ **13** vi to think hard

gamelle /gamɛl/ nf (de soldat) dixie GB, mess kit; (de campeur) billycan GB, tin dish; (d'ouvrier) lunchbox; (d'animal) dish

(Idiome) **prendre** or **ramasser une ~**◦ (tomber) to fall flat on one's face◦; (échouer) to come a cropper

gamin, **~e** /gamɛ̃, in/
A adj [air, allure] youthful; [caractère, attitude] childish
B nm,f kid◦; **~ des rues** street urchin

gaminerie /gaminʀi/ nf (action, propos) childish behaviour^GB ℂ

gamme /gam/ nf **1** Mus scale; **2** (série) range; **produit (de) bas de ~** (en qualité) low quality product; (en prix) cheap product; **modèle (de) haut de ~** upmarket model; **viser le haut/bas de ~** to aim at the top/lower end of the market

gammée /game/ adj f **croix ~** swastika

ganache /ganaʃ/ nf **1** Culin chocolate cream filling; **2** (de cheval) lower jaw; **3** †(idiot) **vieille ~** old fool

Gand /gɑ̃/ ▸ p. 621 npr Ghent

ganglion /gɑ̃glijɔ̃/ nm ganglion; **avoir des ~s**◦ to have swollen glands

gangrène /gɑ̃gʀɛn/ ▸ p. 195 nf **1** (maladie) gangrene; **2** fig (corruption) canker

gangrener /gɑ̃gʀəne/ **16**
A vtr fig to corrupt [pays, société]
B se gangrener vpr **1** [plaie] to become gangrenous; **2** fig [société] to become corrupt

gangster /gɑ̃gstɛʀ/ nm **1** (bandit) gangster; **2** (escroc) swindler

gangstérisme /gɑ̃gsteʀism/ nm organized crime

gangue /gɑ̃g/ nf **1** lit (substance) gangue; **~ de boue** coating of mud; **2** fig **extraire les idées de leur ~** to pick out the good ideas and discard the dross

gant /gɑ̃/ nm glove; **~s de cuir** leather gloves

(Composés) **~ de boxe** boxing glove; **~ de crin** massage glove; **~ de ménage** rubber glove; **~ de toilette** ≈ (face) flannel GB, wash cloth US

(Idiomes) **son tailleur lui va comme un ~** her suit fits her like a glove; **tes nouvelles fonctions te vont comme un ~** your new duties suit you down to the ground; **mettre** or **prendre des ~s avec qn** to handle sb with kid gloves; **elle n'a pas pris de ~s pour m'annoncer mon renvoi** she didn't pull any punches when telling me I was fired; **jeter/relever le ~** to throw down/to take up the gauntlet; ▸ **velours**

ganté, **~e** /gɑ̃te/ adj [main] gloved; [personne] wearing gloves (après n)

gantelet /gɑ̃tlɛ/ nm **1** Hist Mil gauntlet; **2** (en fauconnerie) hawking glove

garage /gaʀaʒ/ nm **1** (pour se garer) garage; **2** ▸ p. 372 (station-service) garage

(Composés) **~ d'autobus** bus depot; **~ à vélos** bicycle shed; (dans un bâtiment) bicycle storage area

garagiste /gaʀaʒist/ ▸ p. 372 nmf (propriétaire) garage owner; (ouvrier) car mechanic

garant, **~e** /gaʀɑ̃, ɑ̃t/
A adj **être** or **se porter ~ de qch/qn** to vouch for sth/sb
B nm,f Jur, Pol guarantor; **être le ~ d'un prêt** to stand guarantor for a loan

g

garanti, ~e¹ /gaʀɑ̃ti/ adj ⊡ (protégé) with a guarantee (épith, après n); **c'est ~ six mois** it has a six-month guarantee; ⊡ (certifié) guaranteed; **fromage ~ pur chèvre** guaranteed pure goat's milk cheese; **prix ~** guaranteed price

garantie² /gaʀɑ̃ti/ nf ⊡ Comm guarantee, warranty; **bon de ~** guarantee; ⊡ (en finance) (négociable) security **₵**; (fiduciaire) guarantee; **en ~** as security; ⊡ (en assurance) cover **₵**; **~ responsabilité civile** third-party cover; **montant des ~s** sum insured; ⊡ (certitude) guarantee (de of); ⊡ Jur guarantee

garantir /gaʀɑ̃tiʀ/ [3] vtr ⊡ (promettre) to guarantee; **~ à qn qch/que** to guarantee sb sth/that; ⊡ (protéger) to safeguard [sécurité, indépendance, droit]; ⊡ (assurer) **~ qch à qn** to guarantee sb sth; **~** to guarantee [emprunt, paiement]; ⊡ Comm to guarantee [produit]

garçon /gaʀsɔ̃/ nm ⊡ (enfant, fils) boy; ⊡ (jeune homme) young man; **un brave or gentil ~** a nice chap GB ou guy US; **être beau or joli ~** to be good-looking; ▸ **bon, mauvais**; ⊡ (célibataire) bachelor; ⊡ ▸ p. 372 (serveur) **~ (de café)** waiter; (employé de magasin) (shop) assistant GB, salesclerk US

(Composés) **~ d'ascenseur** lift GB ou elevator US attendant; **~ de cabine** Naut cabin steward; **~ de courses** messenger; **~ d'écurie** stableboy; **~ d'étage** floor supervisor; **~ de ferme** farmhand; **~ d'honneur** best man; **~ manqué** tomboy

garçonne /gaʀsɔn/ nf **être coiffée à la ~** to have an urchin cut

garçonnet /gaʀsɔnɛ/ nm little boy; **taille/rayon ~** boys' size/department

garçonnière /gaʀsɔnjɛʀ/ nf bachelor flat GB ou apartment US

garde¹ /gaʀd/ ▸ p. 372 nm ⊡ (soldat, policier) guard; ⊡ (de malade) carer; (de prison) warder

(Composés) **~ champêtre** ≈ local policeman (appointed by the municipality); **~ du corps** bodyguard; **~ forestier** forest warden, forest ranger; **Garde des Sceaux** French Minister of Justice

garde² /gaʀd/ nf ⊡ (infirmière) nurse; ⊡ (groupe) guard; ⊡ (surveillance, protection) **monter la ~** [soldat] to mount guard; **monter la ~ auprès de** to keep watch over [prisonnier, malade]; to stand guard over [enfant, homme politique]; **mettre sous bonne ~** to put [sb] under guard [suspect, prisonnier]; **être sous la ~ de qn** [prisonnier] to be guarded by sb; [enfant, objet de valeur] to be looked after by sb; Jur to be in sb's custody; ⊡ (service) **être de ~** [médecin] to be on call; [soldat, sentinelle] to be on guard duty; **pharmacie de ~** duty chemist's GB, emergency drugstore US; ⊡ (position de défense) guard, on-guard position; **en ~!** on guard!; **se mettre en ~** to square up; **mettre qn en ~** to warn sb; **mise en ~** warning; **prendre ~** (se méfier) to watch out (à for); (se soucier) to be careful (de faire to do); **sans y prendre ~** inadvertently; **n'avoir ~ de faire** fml to be careful not to do; ⊡ (d'épée) hilt; **jusqu'à la ~** up to the hilt; ⊡ (de livre, cahier) **(page de) ~** endpaper

(Composés) **~ d'enfant** childminder GB, day-care lady US; **~ à vue** ≈ police custody; **placer qn en ~ à vue** to hold sb for questioning

garde-à-vous /gaʀdavu/ nm inv **se mettre au ~** to stand to attention

garde-barrière, pl **~s** /gaʀdbaʀjɛʀ/ ▸ p. 372 nmf level-crossing keeper GB, gateman (at grade crossing) US

garde-boue /gaʀdbu/ nm inv mudguard

garde-chasse, pl **~s** /gaʀdəʃas/ ▸ p. 372 nm (de domaine public) game warden; (de domaine privé) gamekeeper

garde-chiourme /gaʀdəʃjuʀm/ nm inv ⊡ Hist overseer; ⊡ (surveillant) prison warder

garde-côte, pl **~s** /gaʀdəkot/ nm (bateau) coastguard ship

garde-feu /gaʀdəfø/ nm inv fire screen

garde-fou, pl **~s** /gaʀdəfu/ nm ⊡ (parapet) parapet; ⊡ fig safeguard

garde-frontière, pl **gardes-frontières** /gaʀdfʀɔ̃tjɛʀ/ ▸ p. 372 nm (personne) border guard

garde-malade, pl **gardes-malades** /gaʀdmalad/ ▸ p. 372 nmf home nurse

garde-manger /gaʀdmɑ̃ʒe/ nm inv ⊡ (armoire grillagée) meat safe; ⊡ (placard) pantry, larder

garde-meubles /gaʀdəmœbl/ nm inv furniture storage warehouse; **mettre qch au ~** to put sth in store ou storage

garder /gaʀde/ [1]

A vtr ⊡ (conserver) to keep [argent, objet]; to keep [sth] on [chapeau, vêtement]; to keep [sb] on [employé]; **~ pour soi** to keep [sth] to oneself [secret, critiques]; **gardez à votre teint toute sa fraîcheur** keep your complexion fresh; **un secret bien gardé** a well-kept secret; **ils gardent la suprématie en matière d'électronique** they retain the lead in electronics; **ils nous ont gentiment gardés à dîner** they kindly asked us to stay on for dinner; **~ le lit/la chambre** to stay in bed/in one's room; ⊡ (surveiller, protéger) [gardien] to guard; [personne] to look after [maison, enfant]; **parking gardé** supervised ou attended car park; **l'entrepôt est gardé** there's a security guard at the warehouse

B se garder vpr ⊡ (éviter) **se ~ de faire** to be careful not to do; **je me garde de toute interprétation hâtive** I'm wary of making any hasty interpretation; ⊡ (se conserver) [aliment] to keep

garderie /gaʀdəʀi/ nf ⊡ (local) day nursery; ⊡ (service) after-school child-minding facility

garde-robe, pl **~s** /gaʀdəʀɔb/ nf (vêtements, armoire) wardrobe

gardien, -ienne¹ /gaʀdjɛ̃, ɛn/ nm,f ⊡ (de locaux) security guard; (d'immeuble) caretaker GB, janitor US; (de parc) keeper; (de prison) warder; (de musée, parking) attendant; ⊡ Sport keeper; ⊡ (personne qui préserve) fml guardian; **se faire le ~ des traditions** to set oneself up as a guardian of tradition

(Composés) **~ de but** goalkeeper; **~ de nuit** night watchman; **~ de la paix** police officer

gardiennage /gaʀdjɛnaʒ/ nm (de locaux) security; (d'immeuble) caretaking; **société de ~** security firm

gardienne² /gaʀdjɛn/ nf **~ (d'enfant)** childminder GB, day-care lady US

gardon /gaʀdɔ̃/ nm roach

(Idiome) **être frais comme un ~** to be as fresh as a daisy

gare /gaʀ/

A nf (railway) station; **être en ~** [train] to be in the station; **entrer en ~** [train] to arrive

B excl ⊡ (pour prévenir) **~ (à toi)!** watch out!; **~ à ton portefeuille!** watch your wallet!; **~ aux voleurs!** watch out for thieves!; **~ à ta réputation!** mind your reputation!; ⊡ (pour menacer) **~ à toi!** careful!, watch it⊙!; **~ aux tricheurs!** anyone who cheats will be in trouble!

(Composés) **~ de marchandises** goods station GB, freight station US; **~ maritime** harbour^GB station; **~ routière** (cars) coach station GB, bus station US; (camions) truck depot; **~ de triage** marshalling^GB yard; **~ de voyageurs** passenger station

(Idiome) **sans crier ~** without any warning

garenne /gaʀɛn/ nf (de lapins) (rabbit) warren

garer /gaʀe/ [1]

A vtr to park [véhicule]

B se garer vpr ⊡ (stationner) to park; ⊡ (s'écarter) [véhicule] to pull over; [piéton] to move out of the way

gargantuesque /gaʀgɑ̃tɥɛsk/ adj gargantuan

gargariser: se gargariser /gaʀgaʀize/ [1] vpr ⊡ Méd to gargle; ⊡ ⊙fig **se ~ de** to revel in

gargarisme /gaʀgaʀism/ nm (action) gargling; (solution) gargle, mouthwash

gargote /gaʀgɔt/ nf cheap eating place, greasy spoon⊙

gargouille /gaʀguj/ nf (décoratif) gargoyle; (pour la pluie) waterspout

gargouiller /gaʀguje/ [1] vi [eau, fontaine] to gurgle; [ventre] to rumble, to growl US

garnement /gaʀnəmɑ̃/ nm tearaway GB, brat⊙

garni, ~e /gaʀni/ adj (rempli) **bien ~** [portefeuille] full; [réfrigérateur] well-stocked (épith); [buffet] copious; **une assiette bien ~e** a plateful; **plat ~** dish served with trimmings

garnir /gaʀniʀ/ [3]

A vtr ⊡ (remplir) [objets] to fill [pièce]; [personne] to stock [rayons, congélateur]; ⊡ (rembourrer) to stuff [coussin, fauteuil]; ⊡ (couvrir) to cover [siège]; (orner) to trim [robe]; (doubler) to line [vêtement, tiroir]; ⊡ Culin (décorer) to decorate [gâteau, table]; to garnish [*viande, poisson*]; (accompagner) to serve [*plat*]

B **se garnir** *vpr* [*salle, stade*] to fill up (**de** with)

garnison /garnizɔ̃/ *nf* Mil garrison; **ville de** ~ garrison town

garniture /garnityr, øz/ *nf* **1** Culin (accompagnement) side dish; (décoration) (de dessert) decoration; (de viande, poisson) garnish; **servir avec une** ~ **de légumes** serve with vegetables as a side dish; **2** (sur un chapeau, une robe) trimming; (dans un coffret, tiroir) lining

(*Composés*) ~ **de bureau** desk accessories (*pl*); ~ **de cheminée** mantelpiece ornaments (*pl*); ~ **de foyer** fire irons (*pl*)

garrigue /garig/ *nf* garrigue, scrubland (*in southern France*)

garrot /garo/ *nm* **1** Méd tourniquet; **2** Zool (de quadrupède) withers (*pl*); **le cheval mesure 1, 50 m au** ~ ≈ the horse is 15 hands; **3** (instrument de supplice) garrotte

garrotter /garɔte/ [1] *vtr* **1** (lier) to tie up [*prisonnier*]; to bind [*bras, jambes*]; **2** fig (bâillonner) to muzzle [*peuple*]; to stifle [*opposition*]; **3** (supplicier) to garrotte

gars○ /ga/ *nm inv* (garçon, jeune homme) lad GB, boy; (adulte) chap○ GB, guy○ US

Gascogne /gaskɔɲ/ ▸ p. 504 *nprf* **la** ~ Gascony; **le golfe de** ~ the Bay of Biscay

Gascon, -onne /gaskɔ̃, ɔn/ *nm,f* Gascon

(*Idiome*) **c'est une offre de** ~ it's not a serious offer

gas-oil /gazwal/ *nm* diesel (oil) GB, fuel oil US

gaspacho /gaspatʃo/ *nm* gazpacho

gaspillage /gaspijaʒ/ *nm* **1** (par négligence) (action) wasting; (conséquence) waste; **quel** ~! what a waste!; **c'est du** ~ it's wasteful; **2** (par prodigalité) squandering

gaspiller /gaspije/ [1] *vtr* **1** (gâcher) to waste [*temps, argent, nourriture*]; **ne gaspille pas tant** don't be so wasteful; **2** (dissiper) to squander [*forces, ressources*]

gastrite /gastrit/ ▸ p. 195 *nf* gastritis **C**

gastronome /gastrɔnɔm/ *nmf* gourmet, gastronome

gastronomie /gastrɔnɔmi/ *nf* gastronomy

gâteau, pl ~**x** /gato/

A *adj inv* [*papa*] doting

B *nm* cake; ~ **d'anniversaire** birthday cake; **se tailler une part du** ~○ fig to take one's share of the loot

(*Composés*) ~ **apéritif** cocktail biscuit; ~ **de cire** honeycomb; ~ **marbré** marble cake; ~ **de miel** = ~ **de cire**; ~ **de riz** ≈ rice pudding; ~ **salé** = ~ **apéritif**; ~ **sec** biscuit GB, cookie US; ~ **de semoule** semolina pudding

(*Idiomes*) **c'est du** ~○! it's a piece of cake○!; **c'est pas du** ~○! it's no picnic!

gâter /gate/ [1]

A *vtr* **1** (choyer) to spoil [*personne*]; **enfant gâté** spoiled child; **on a été gâtés côté temps** we've been very lucky with the weather; **il n'a pas été gâté par la nature** hum he hasn't been blessed by Nature; **2** (abîmer) to spoil [*fruit*]; to ruin [*dent*]; to spoil [*paysage*]; **3** (gâcher) to spoil [*plaisir*]

B **se gâter** *vpr* **1** (s'abîmer) [*viande*] to go bad; [*fruit, dent*] to rot; **avoir les dents gâtées** to have bad teeth; **2** (se détériorer) [*situation*] to take a turn for the worse; [*temps*] to change for the worse; **ça se gâte!** (situation) there's going to be trouble!

gâterie /gatri/ *nf* little treat

gâteux, -euse /gatø, øz/

A *adj* (avec l'âge) senile; **il est** ~○ **avec sa fille** fig he's dotty about his daughter○

B *nm,f* senile person; **vieux** ~○ old dodderer○

gauche¹ /goʃ/ ▸ p. 324

A *adj* **1** gén [*œil, main etc*] left; **le côté** ~ **de qch** the left-hand side of sth; **2** (maladroit) [*personne, manières*] awkward; [*style*] clumsy

B *nm* (en boxe) left-hander

(*Idiome*) **se lever du pied** ~○ to get out of bed on the wrong side GB, to get up on the wrong side of the bed US

gauche² /goʃ/ ▸ p. 324 *nf* **1** (côté) **la** ~ the left; **à** ~ [*rouler*] on the left; [*aller, regarder*] to the left; [*tourner*] left; **tenir sa** ~ to keep to the left; **en bas à** ~ in the bottom left-hand corner; **de** ~ [*page, mur, file*] left-hand; **2** Pol Left; **de** ~ left-wing; **la** ~ **du parti libéral** the left wing of the liberal party

---

(*Idiomes*) **passer l'arme à** ~○ to kick the bucket○; **jusqu'à la** ~○ completely, thoroughly; **avoir de l'argent à** ~○ to have money stashed away; **mettre de l'argent à** ~○ to put money aside

gauchement /goʃmã/ *adv* awkwardly

gaucher, -ère /goʃe, ɛr/

A *adj* left-handed

B *nm,f* left-handed person; ~ **contrarié** naturally left-handed person (*forced to write with their right hand*)

gaucherie /goʃri/ *nf* awkwardness

gauchisant, -e /goʃizã, ãt/ *adj* [*journal, groupe*] leftish (épith); **être** ~ to have leftish tendencies

gauchiste /goʃist/ *adj, nmf* leftist

gaufre /gofr/ *nf* **1** Culin waffle; **2** Zool honeycomb

gaufrer /gofre/ [1] *vtr* (imprimer en relief) to emboss; (donner un aspect froissé) to crinkle

gaufrette /gofrɛt/ *nf* wafer

gaufrier /gofrije/ *nm* waffle iron US

gaule /gol/ *nf* **1** (pour récolter les noix) long thin pole; (de bouvier, vacher) switch; **2** (de pêcheur) fishing rod

Gaule /gol/ *nprf* Gaul

gauler /gole/ [1] *vtr* **1** ~ **les noix** to knock the nuts out of a walnut tree; **2** ○(prendre) to catch; **se faire** ~ to get caught

gaulois, -e /golwa, az/

A *adj* Gallic

B ▸ p. 336 *nm* Ling Gaulish

Gaulois, -e /golwa, az/ *nm,f* Gaul

gausser: se gausser /gose/ [1] *vpr* (railler) liter **se** ~ **de** to laugh at, to mock

gavage /gavaʒ/ *nm* (des oies) force-feeding

gaver /gave/ [1]

A *vtr* to force-feed [*oies*]; to stuff [sb] with food [*personne*]; **être gavé** to be full up; ~ **qn d'âneries** to cram sb's head with silly ideas; ~ **qn de publicité** to bombard sb with advertising

B **se gaver** *vpr* **1** (se nourrir) to stuff oneself (**de** with); **2** fig **se** ~ **de** to devour [*romans, émissions*]

gavroche /gavrɔʃ/ *nm* street urchin

gay /gɛ/ *adj inv, nm* gay, homosexual

gaz /gaz/

A *nm inv* **1** (domestique) gas; **baisser le** ~ to turn down the gas; **se chauffer au** ~ to have gas heating; **2** Chimie gas; **à l'état de** ~ in its gaseous state

B *nmpl* **1** Aut air-fuel mixture (sg); **mettre les** ~○ to step on the gas○; **rouler à pleins** ~○ to go at full throttle; **2** (flatulence) wind (sg)

(*Composés*) ~ **butane** butane gas; ~ **carbonique** carbon dioxide; ~ **de combat** poison gas **C**; ~ **d'échappement** exhaust fumes (*pl*); ~ **hilarant** laughing gas; ~ **lacrymogène** teargas; ~ **de ville** mains gas

(*Idiome*) **il y a de l'eau dans le** ~○ there's trouble brewing

gaze /gaz/ *nf* gauze; **une bande de** ~ a gauze bandage

gazé, -e /gaze/ *nm,f* gas victim

gazéifier /gazeifje/ [2] *vtr* **1** (rendre pétillant) to carbonate [*boisson*]; **2** (transformer en gaz) to gasify

gazelle /gazɛl/ *nf* gazelle; **des yeux de** ~ doe eyes

gazer /gaze/ [1]

A *vtr* (asphyxier) to gas

B ○*v impers* **ça gaze?** how's things○?; **oui, ça gaze** things are fine

gazette /gazɛt/ *nf* **1** (journal) newspaper; hum rag; **2** (personne) gossip; **la** ~ **du quartier** the local gossip

gazeux, -euse /gazø, øz/ *adj* **1** [*boisson*] fizzy; **eau gazeuse** (naturelle) sparkling mineral water; (gazéifiée) carbonated water; **2** Chimie, Phys gaseous

gazinière /gazinjɛr/ *nf* gas cooker GB, gas stove

gazoduc /gazɔdyk/ *nm* gas pipeline

gazogène /gazɔʒɛn/ *nm* (générateur) gas generator

gazole /gazɔl/ *nm* diesel (oil) GB, fuel oil US

gazon /gazɔ̃/ *nm* **1** (herbe) grass, turf; (en plaque) turf; **2** (pelouse) lawn; **tennis sur** ~ lawn tennis; **jouer sur** ~ to play on grass courts

gazouillement /gazujmã/ *nm* (d'oiseau) twittering **C**; (de bébé, source) babbling **C**

g

gazouiller /gazuje/ [1] *vi* [*oiseau*] to twitter; [*bébé, source*] to babble

gazouillis /gazuji/ *nm inv* = **gazouillement**

GDF /ʒedeɛf/ (*abbr* = **Gaz de France**) French gas board

geai /ʒɛ/ *nm* jay

géant, ~e /ʒeɑ̃, ɑ̃t/
A *adj* **1** (démesuré) huge, enormous; **2** (de grande taille) giant; **raie ~e** giant ray; **3** Comm [*paquet*] jumbo; **4** ○(extraordinaire) **c'est ~!** it's brilliant GB *ou* great!
B *nm,f* giant/giantess; **~ de l'industrie** industrial giant

geignard, ~e /ʒɛɲaʀ, aʀd/ *adj* [*personne*] moaning; [*enfant*] whining; [*ton, musique*] wailing

geignement /ʒɛɲəmɑ̃/ *nm* (plainte) moan, groan

geindre /ʒɛ̃dʀ/ [55] *vi* [*malade*] to moan, to groan; (faiblement) to whimper; [*pleurnichard*] to whine; [*mécontent*] to moan; [*violon*] to wail; [*meuble*] to creak

gel /ʒɛl/ *nm* **1** Météo frost; **résistant au ~** frost-resistant; **2** Écon **~ des subventions** freeze on subsidies; **~ des prix/salaires** price/wage freeze; **~ des terres** set-aside **~ des avoirs** freezing of assets; **3** (suspension) **après le ~ du projet** after the project had been put on ice; **4** (produit) gel

gélatine /ʒelatin/ *nf* gelatine GB, gelatin US

gélatineux, -euse /ʒelatinø, øz/ *adj* gelatinous

gelé, ~e¹ /ʒəle/
A *pp* ▸ **geler**
B *pp adj* **1** (durci par le froid) [*eau, sol*] frozen; Méd [*orteil*] frostbitten; **2** (très froid) **j'ai les oreilles ~es** my ears are frozen; **3** (bloqué) [*prix, négociation*] frozen

gelée² /ʒəle/ *nf* **1** Culin (de fruit) jelly; (de viande, poisson) (suc naturel) gelatinous stock; (préparation) aspic; **œuf/poulet en ~** egg/chicken in aspic; **2** (cosmétique) gel; **3** Météo frost

(Composés) **~ blanche** hoarfrost; **~ royale** royal jelly

geler /ʒəle/ [17]
A *vtr* **1** (durcir) to freeze [*eau, sol*]; **2** (endommager) to freeze [*doigt*]; to nip [*plante*]; **3** (bloquer) to freeze [*salaire, prix, avoirs*]; to suspend [*projet, production*]
B *vi* **1** (se solidifier) [*eau, sol*] to freeze; **2** (être endommagé) [*doigt, pied*] to freeze; [*plante*] to be frosted; **3** ○(avoir froid) to be freezing; **on gèle** it's freezing
C *se geler*○ *vpr* (avoir froid) to freeze
D *v impers* **il** *or* **ça gèle** it's freezing; **il gèle à pierre fendre** it's absolutely freezing

gélifiant /ʒelifjɑ̃/ *nm* gelling agent

gélule /ʒelyl/ *nf* capsule

Gémeaux /ʒemo/ ▸ p. 635 *nprmpl* Gemini

gémir /ʒemiʀ/ [3] *vi* [*malade*] to moan, to groan (**de** with); (faiblement) to whimper; [*pleurnichard*] to moan; [*plancher, meuble*] to creak; (sous un poids) to groan; [*vent*] to moan

gémissement /ʒemismɑ̃/ *nm* (de personne) moan; (prolongé) moaning ¢; (de plancher) creak; (prolongé) creaking ¢; (du vent) moaning

gemme /ʒɛm/ *nf* **1** (pierre) gem, gemstone; **2** (résine) resin

gémonies /ʒemɔni/ *nfpl* **vouer qn aux ~** to expose sb to public contempt

gênant, ~e /ʒɛnɑ̃, ɑ̃t/ *adj* **1** (incommode) [*meuble, carton*] cumbersome; [*problème, bruit*] annoying; [*odeur*] unpleasant; **2** (qui met mal à l'aise) [*question, témoin*] embarrassing; **c'est gênant** it's awkward

gencive /ʒɑ̃siv/ *nf* gum

(Idiome) **prendre un coup dans les ~s**○ to be kicked in the teeth○

gendarme /ʒɑ̃daʀm/ ▸ p. 372 *nm* **1** Mil gendarme, French policeman; **jouer aux ~s et aux voleurs** to play cops and robbers; **la peur du ~** fig the fear of authority; **jouer les ~s du monde** fig to act the role of world policeman; **2** (personne autoritaire) **quel ~!** what a bossy person! **je n'ai pas envie de faire le ~** I don't want to have to lay down the law; **3** (organe de surveillance) watchdog; **4** Zool (punaise) stinkbug; **5** Culin (saucisson) dried sausage

(Composés) **~ couché** road hump, sleeping policeman GB; **~ mobile** member of mobile police unit

gendarmerie /ʒɑ̃daʀm(ə)ʀi/ *nf* **1** (bureaux) police station; **2** (logement) police quarters (*pl*); **3** (corps) **~ (nationale)** gendarmerie, French police force

(Composé) **~ mobile** mobile police unit

gendre /ʒɑ̃dʀ/ *nm* son-in-law

gène /ʒɛn/ *nm* gene

gêne /ʒɛn/ *nf* **1** (embarras) embarrassment; **il n'y a pas de ~ à avoir** there's nothing to be embarrassed about; **2** (physique) discomfort; **éprouver une ~ en avalant** to have difficulty swallowing; **~ respiratoire** breathing difficulties (*pl*); **3** (nuisance) inconvenience; **~ visuelle** visual disturbance; **4** (pauvreté) poverty

(Idiome) **là où il y a de la ~ il n'y a pas de plaisir**○ you can't have fun if you're minding your p's and q's

gêné, ~e /ʒɛne/ *adj* **1** (mal à l'aise) embarrassed; **2** (engoncé) **il est ~ dans sa veste** his jacket is too tight for him; **3** (désargenté) short of money

généalogie /ʒenealɔʒi/ *nf* genealogy

généalogique /ʒenealɔʒik/ *adj* genealogical; **livre ~** Biol herd book, stud book; **arbre ~** family tree

gêner /ʒɛne/ [1]
A *vtr* **1** [*personne*] (déranger sérieusement) to disturb; (déranger par sa présence) to bother; **ça te gêne si j'allume?** do you mind if I switch the light on?; **2** (incommoder) [*fumée, bruit*] to bother; **3** (mettre mal à l'aise) [*question, personne*] to embarrass; **cela me gêne d'avoir à te le rappeler mais...** I hate to have to remind you, but...; **4** (entraver) to disrupt [*événement*]; to block [*circulation*]; to restrict [*respiration*]; to get in the way of [*discussion, progrès*]; to hamper [*progression*]; **pousse-toi, tu me gênes** get out of my way; **les chiffres gênent la compréhension du texte** the figures make the text difficult to understand; **5** (faire mal) [*caillou, ceinture*] to hurt [*personne*]; **quelque chose dans ma chaussure me gêne** I've something in my shoe
B *se gêner* *vpr* **1** (se bousculer) [*personnes*] to get in each other's way; **on tient à quatre sans se ~** it can hold four people comfortably; **2** (faire des façons) **pourquoi se ~?** why hesitate?; **je ne me suis pas gênée pour le leur rappeler**○ I made a point of reminding them; **je vais me ~, tiens**○ iron see if I don't; **ne vous gênez pas pour moi, continuez** iron don't mind me, carry on GB *ou* continue

général, ~e¹, *mpl* **-aux** /ʒeneʀal, o/
A *adj* **1** (collectif) [*avis*] **de l'avis ~** in most people's opinion; **dans l'intérêt ~** in the public interest; **à la surprise ~e** to everyone's surprise; **2** (d'ensemble) general; **en ~, de façon** *or* **d'une manière ~e** generally, in general; **en règle ~e** as a rule
B *nm* **1** ▸ p. 283 Mil general; **mon ~!** general!; **2** Relig (supérieur) general; **3** Philos **le ~ et le particulier** the general and the particular

générale² /ʒeneʀal/ *nf* **1** Théât dress rehearsal; **2** (épouse de général) general's wife

généralement /ʒeneʀalmɑ̃/ *adv* generally

généralisable /ʒeneʀalizabl/ *adj* **l'expérience est ~ à d'autres domaines** the experiment can be applied to other fields

généralisation /ʒeneʀalizasjɔ̃/ *nf* **1** (systématisation) (de politique) general implementation; (de vaccination) widespread use; (de langue) general use; **2** (déduction) generalization; **3** (de maladie, grève) spread

généralisé, ~e /ʒeneʀalize/ *adj* [*conflit, pessimisme, corruption*] widespread; [*surproduction*] general; [*cancer*] generalized

généraliser /ʒeneʀalize/ [1]
A *vtr* to bring [sth] into general use [*impôt, vaccination, examen*]; to put [sth] into general use [*méthode*]
B *vi* to generalize
C *se généraliser* *vpr* [*technique*] to become standard; [*impôt*] to become widely applicable; [*grève, maladie*] to spread (à to)

généraliste /ʒeneʀalist/
A *adj* [*chaîne, revue, ingénieur*] non-specialized; [*conception*] broad; **médecin ~** general practitioner
B ▸ p. 372 *nmf* general practitioner, GP GB

généralité /ʒeneʀalite/ *nf* **1** (notion générale) generality; **2** (règle générale) **devenir ~** to become general

générateur, -trice /ʒeneʀatœʀ, tʀis/
A *adj* **1** (créateur) **être ~ de** to generate; **2** (servant à engendrer) generative
B *nm* Ordinat, Tech generator

génération /ʒeneʀasjɔ̃/ *nf* **1** (dans une famille) generation; **le fossé des ~s** the generation gap; **2** (personnes du même âge) generation; **la nouvelle ~** the new generation;

③ (d'avions, ordinateurs) generation; **④** (d'énergie, électricité) generation; **⑤** Biol generation

générer /ʒeneRe/ |14| vtr to generate

généreusement /ʒeneRøzmɑ̃/ adv (noblement) generously; (libéralement) liberally

généreux, -euse /ʒeneRø, øz/ adj **①** (plein de largesse) generous (envers to); **②** (plein de grandeur d'âme) [personne, caractère] generous; [idée, geste] noble; **③** (copieux) [portion] generous; **poitrine généreuse** large bust; **femme aux formes généreuses** well-rounded woman; **④** (fertile) liter [terre] bountiful littér

générique /ʒeneRik/
A adj generic
B nf Cin, Radio, TV **①** (liste) credits (pl); **le ~ de début/fin** opening/closing credits; **②** (présentation) titles (pl)

générosité /ʒeneRozite/ nf **①** (largesse) generosity (envers to, toward(s)); **②** (grandeur d'âme) generosity of spirit; **agir avec ~** to show generosity of spirit

Gênes /ʒɛn/ ▸ p. 621 npr Genoa

genèse /ʒənɛz/ nf **①** (d'œuvre d'art, de projet) genesis; (d'État) birth; **②** Bible **la Genèse** Genesis

genêt /ʒənɛ/ nm Bot broom

généticien, -ienne /ʒenetisjɛ̃, ɛn/ ▸ p. 372 nm,f geneticist

génétique /ʒenetik/
A adj genetic
B nf genetics (+ v sg)

gêneur, -euse /ʒɛnœR, øz/ nm,f troublemaker

Genève /ʒənɛv/ ▸ p. 621 npr Geneva

genévrier /ʒənevRije/ nm juniper

génial, ~e, mpl **-iaux** /ʒenjal, o/ adj **①** (ayant du génie) brilliant; **②** (inspiré par le génie) [idée, invention, découverte] brilliant; **③** (fantastique) [spectacle, livre] brilliant○ GB, great○; [personne] great○

génie /ʒeni/ nm **①** (aptitude) genius; **avoir du ~** to be a genius; **avoir un coup de ~** to have a flash of inspiration; **idée de ~** brainwave; **②** (personne) genius; **③** (talent) **avoir le ~ du commerce** to have a great gift for business; **④** Mythol (esprit) spirit; (dans les contes) genie; **être le bon/mauvais ~ de qn** to be sb's guiding/evil spirit; **⑤** (ingénierie) engineering; **⑥** Mil (activité) military engineering; (personnel) **le ~** the Engineers (pl)

(Composés) **~ civil** (activité) civil engineering; (personnel) civil engineers (pl); **~ génétique** genetic engineering

genièvre /ʒənjɛvR/ nm (arbuste) juniper; (baie) juniper berry; (eau-de-vie) Dutch gin

génisse /ʒenis/ nf heifer; **foie de ~** beef liver

génital, ~e, mpl **-aux** /ʒenital, o/ adj genital

géniteur, -trice /ʒenitœR, tRis/
A nm,f (parent) hum parent, pater/mater hum
B nm Zool (reproducteur) sire

génitif /ʒenitif/ nm Ling genitive

génocide /ʒenɔsid/ nm genocide

génoise /ʒenwaz/ nf Culin ≈ sponge cake

genou, pl **~x** /ʒ(ə)nu/ ▸ p. 136
A nm **①** (d'homme, animal) knee; **donner un coup de ~ à qn** to knee sb; **mettre (un) ~ à terre devant qn** lit to kneel down in front of sb; fig to pay homage to sb; **②** (de pantalon, collant) knee; **③** Naut, Tech knee
B **à genoux** loc adv **se mettre à ~x** gén to kneel down; (pour implorer) to go down on one's knees; **être à ~x devant qn** fig to worship sb

(Idiomes) **faire du ~ à qn○** to play footsie○ with sb; **être sur les ~x○** [personne] to be on one's last legs; **mettre qn sur les ~x○** to wear sb out

genouillère /ʒənujɛR/ nf Sport knee pad; Méd knee support ou bandage; (pour un animal) knee boot

genre /ʒɑ̃R/ nm **①** (sorte) sort, kind, type (de of); **c'est ce qu'on fait de mieux dans le ~** it's the best of its kind; **c'est le ~ rabat-joie** he/she's a killjoy; **tu vois le ~!** you know the type!; **elle n'est pas mal dans son ~** she's quite pretty in her way; **un peu dans le ~ de ta robe** a bit like your dress; **②** (comportement) **ce n'est pas mon ~ de tricher** cheating is not my style; **c'est bien son ~** it's just like him/her; **③** (allure) **pour se donner un ~** to make oneself look different; **④** Ling gender; **⑤** Art, Littérat genre; **peinture de ~** genre painting; **⑥** Bot, Zool genus

(Composé) **le ~ humain** mankind

gens /ʒɑ̃/ nmpl **①** (personnes) people; **les ~ du coin** the local people, the locals péj; **les ~ sans histoires** ordinary people; **②** (domestiques) servants, household (sg); (escorte) retinue (sg)

(Composés) **~ d'église** clergymen; **~ de lettres** writers; **~ de loi** lawyers; **~ de maison** servants; **~ du monde** polite society (sg); **~ de théâtre** actors; **~ du voyage** travelling^GB people.

⚠ When used with gens, the adjectives bon, mauvais, petit, vieux, vilain are placed before gens and in the feminine: (toutes) les vieilles gens. But the gender of gens itself does not change: les bonnes gens sont heureux. All other adjectives behave normally: (tous) les braves gens.

gent† /ʒɑ̃/ nf **la ~ masculine/féminine** mankind/womankind, men (pl)/women (pl)

gentiane /ʒɑ̃sjan/ nf **①** (fleur) gentian; **②** (liqueur) gentian liqueur

gentil, -ille /ʒɑ̃ti, ij/
A adj **①** (agréable) kind, nice (avec to); **aide-moi, tu seras ~** give me a hand, will you?; **c'est ~, je vous remercie** that's very kind of you, thank you; **sois ~, réponds au téléphone** do me a favour^GB, answer the phone; **②** (obéissant) good; **③** péj **le spectacle/film était ~** the show/film was harmless enough; **c'est bien ~ tout ça, mais...** that's all very well, but...; **il est (bien) ~** he's nice enough; **④** (non négligeable) [somme, récompense] fair
B nm Hist Relig gentile

gentilhomme, pl **gentilshommes** /ʒɑ̃tijɔm, ʒɑ̃tizɔm/ nm Hist gentleman; **~ campagnard** country gentleman

gentilhommière /ʒɑ̃tijɔmjɛR/ nf country house

gentille ▸ gentil A

gentillesse /ʒɑ̃tijɛs/ nf kindness (envers to); **faites-moi la ~ de...** would you do me the favour^GB of...?; **échanger des ~s** iron to exchange insults; **dire des ~s sur qn** iron to say unpleasant things about sb

gentillet, -ette /ʒɑ̃tijɛ, ɛt/ adj **①** (agréable) **être ~** [enfant] to be a sweetie; **②** péj [personne, livre, film] nice enough

gentiment /ʒɑ̃timɑ̃/ adv **①** (aimablement) kindly; **se moquer ~ de qn** to tease sb playfully; **je leur ai fait ~ comprendre** in the nicest possible way I made them understand; **②** (sagement) quietly

génuflexion /ʒenyflɛksjɔ̃/ nf genuflection

géode /ʒeɔd/ nf geode

géodésie /ʒeɔdezi/ nf geodesy

géographe /ʒeɔgRaf/ ▸ p. 372 nmf geographer

géographie /ʒeɔgRafi/ nf geography

geôle /ʒol/ nf liter jail

geôlier, -ière /ʒolje, ɛR/ nm,f liter jailer

géologie /ʒeɔlɔʒi/ nf geology

géologue /ʒeɔlɔg/ ▸ p. 372 nmf geologist

géomètre /ʒeɔmɛtR/ ▸ p. 372 nmf **①** Tech land surveyor; **②** †Math geometrician

géométrie /ʒeɔmetRi/ nf geometry; **~ dans l'espace** solid geometry; **à ~ variable** fig [doctrine] flexible

géométrique /ʒeɔmetRik/ adj [forme] geometric; [démonstration] geometrical

géophysique /ʒeɔfizik/
A adj geophysical
B nf geophysics (+ v sg)

géopolitique /ʒeɔpɔlitik/
A adj geopolitical
B nf geopolitics (+ v sg)

Géorgie /ʒeɔRʒi/ nprf **①** ▸ p. 504 (État américain) Georgia; **②** ▸ p. 230 (État indépendant) Georgia

(Composé) **~ du Sud** (île) South Georgia

géostationnaire /ʒeɔstasjɔnɛR/ adj geostationary

géothermie /ʒeɔtɛRmi/ nf (énergie) geothermal power

gérable /ʒeRabl/ adj manageable; **situation difficilement ~** a situation which is hard to handle

gérance /ʒeRɑ̃s/ nf management; **mettre en ~** to appoint a manager for [magasin, société]; to appoint a managing agent for [immeuble]; **assurer la ~ de qch** to manage sth

géranium /ʒeRanjɔm/ nm geranium

g

gérant, ∼**e** /ʒeRɑ̃, ɑ̃t/ *nm,f* ① (de magasin, d'usine) manager; (d'immeubles) (managing) agent; **'nouveau** ∼**'** 'under new management'; ② Presse editor

gerbe /ʒɛRb/ *nf* ① (bouquet enveloppé) bouquet; ∼ **de fleurs** bunch of flowers; (mortuaire) wreath; ② (d'eau) spray; ③ (de blé) sheaf

gerboise /ʒɛRbwaz/ *nf* jerboa

gercer /ʒɛRse/ [12]
A *vtr* to chap [main, lèvres]
B *vi* [lèvres, mains] to become chapped

gerçure /ʒɛRsyR/ *nf* crack; **avoir les mains pleines de** ∼**s** to have badly chapped hands

gérer /ʒeRe/ [14] *vtr* ① (administrer) to manage [production, temps]; to manage, to run [entreprise]; to run [pays]; ② (traiter) to handle [situation, information]; ③ Ordinat to manage [fichiers, bases de données]

gerfaut /ʒɛRfo/ *nm* gyrfalcon

gériatrie /ʒeRjatRi/ *nf* geriatrics (+ v sg); **(service de)** ∼ geriatric ward

germain, ∼**e** /ʒɛRmɛ̃, ɛn/ *adj* ① (dans la famille) **(cousin)** ∼ first cousin; ② Hist Germanic

germanique /ʒɛRmanik/ *adj, nm* Germanic

germaniste /ʒɛRmanist/ *nmf* Germanist

germanophone /ʒɛRmanɔfɔn/
A *adj* German-speaking (épith); **être** ∼ to speak German
B *nmf* German speaker

germe /ʒɛRm/ *nm* ① (d'embryon, de graine) germ; (d'œuf) germinal disc; (de pomme de terre) sprout; ∼ **de blé** wheat germ; ∼**s de soja** bean sprouts; ② (début) (de crise) seed; (d'idée) embryonic form, germ

(Composé) ∼ **dentaire** tooth bud

germer /ʒɛRme/ [1] *vi* ① fig (naître) [idée, soupçon] to form; ② Bot [blé] to germinate

germination /ʒɛRminasjɔ̃/ *nf* germination

gérondif /ʒeRɔ̃dif/ *nm* (nom verbal latin, anglais) gerund; (adjectif verbal latin) gerundive; (forme verbale en français) gerund

gérontologie /ʒeRɔ̃tɔlɔʒi/ *nf* gerontology

gésier /ʒezje/ *nm* gizzard

gésir /ʒeziR/ [37] *vi fml* ① (être couché) [personne] to be lying; **elle gît/gisait sur son lit** she is/was lying on her bed; ② (être abandonné) [vêtements] to be lying about ou around; ③ fig (se trouver) [solution] to lie

gestation /ʒɛstasjɔ̃/ *nf* gestation

geste¹ /ʒɛst/ *nm* ① (mouvement) movement; (mouvement expressif) gesture; **un** ∼ **brusque** a sudden movement; **il nous a fait signe d'avancer d'un** ∼ **de la main** he waved to us to come forward; **pas un** ∼**!** don't move!; **il n'a pas fait un** ∼ **pour m'aider** fig he didn't make any move to help me; **il pourrait faire un** ∼ **quand même!** fig he could at least show that he cares; **joindre le** ∼ **à la parole** to suit the action to the word; ② (acte) gesture, act; **un** ∼ **désespéré** a desperate act; **un** ∼ **symbolique** a token gesture; **un beau** ∼ a noble gesture

geste² /ʒɛst/ *nf* Littér *set of French epic poems of the Middle Ages*

gesticuler /ʒɛstikyle/ [1] *vtr* ① (en parlant) to gesticulate; ② (s'agiter) to fidget

gestion /ʒɛstjɔ̃/ *nf* ① (administration) management; **la** ∼ **de la production** production control; ② (de situation, crise, d'information) handling; ③ (discipline) management; **faire de la** ∼ to study management; ④ Ordinat management

(Composés) ∼ **administrative** administration; ∼ **prévisionnelle** (forward) planning; ∼ **de la production assistée par ordinateur** computer-aided production management; ∼ **des stocks** stock control GB, inventory control US

gestionnaire /ʒɛstjɔnɛR/
A *adj* Écon [technique, organisme] administrative
B *nmf* administrator

(Composés) ∼ **de fichiers** Ordinat file-management system; ∼ **de périphérique** Ordinat driver; ∼ **de portefeuille** Fin portfolio manager

gestuel, **-elle¹** /ʒɛstɥɛl/ *adj* gestural; **peinture gestuelle** action painting

gestuelle² /ʒɛstɥɛl/ *nf* body language

geyser /ʒezɛR/ *nm* geyser

ghanéen, **-éenne** /ɡaneɛ̃, ɛn/ ▸ p. 392 *adj* Ghanaian

ghetto /ɡeto/ *nm* lit, fig ghetto

gibecière /ʒibsjɛR/ *nf* gamebag; Scol satchel

gibet /ʒibɛ/ *nm* gallows (+ v sg)

gibier /ʒibje/ *nm* game; **gros** ∼ lit big game; fig big time criminals (pl); **être un** ∼ **facile pour les escrocs** fig to be an easy target for conmen; **c'est du** ∼ **de potence** he'll/she'll/they'll come to a bad end

(Composés) ∼ **d'eau** water fowl (+ v pl); ∼ **à plumes** game birds (pl); ∼ **à poil** game animals (pl)

giboulée /ʒibule/ *nf* shower; **les** ∼**s de mars** ≈ April showers GB

giboyeux, **-euse** /ʒibwajø, øz/ *adj* [région, plaine, réserve] full of game (après n)

gibus /ʒibys/ *nm inv* opera hat

GIC /ʒeise/ *nm: abbr* ▸ **grand**

giclée /ʒikle/ *nf* (d'eau, de sang) spurt; (d'encre) squirt

gicler /ʒikle/ [1] *vi* (jaillir) [sang, eau] to spurt (**de** from); [jus] to squirt (**sur** onto); **la voiture a fait** ∼ **de la boue** the car sprayed up mud

gicleur /ʒiklœR/ *nm* ① (de carburateur) jet; ② (de lave-vaisselle) spray

gifle /ʒifl/ *nf* ① (claque) slap in the face; **donner une bonne** ∼ **à qn** to whack sb in the face; **flanquer**○ **une paire de** ∼**s à qn** to clip sb around the ears○; ② (affront) slap in the face

gifler /ʒifle/ [1] *vtr* ① (frapper) to slap [personne]; ② (cingler) [pluie, vent] to lash

GIG /ʒeiʒe/ *nm: abbr* ▸ **grand**

gigantesque /ʒiɡɑ̃tɛsk/ *adj* huge, gigantic

gigantisme /ʒiɡɑ̃tism/ *nm* ① (de bâtiment, ville, statue) colossal size; (de projet, spectacle) giant scale; ② Bot, Méd gigantism

giga-octet, *pl* ∼**s** /ʒiɡaɔktɛ/ *nm* gigabyte

GIGN /ʒeiʒeɛn/ *nm* (abbr = **Groupe d'intervention de la gendarmerie nationale**) *branch of the police specialized in cases of armed robbery, terrorism etc*

gigogne /ʒiɡɔɲ/ *adj* lit ∼ hideaway bed; **tables** ∼**s** nest sg of tables

gigot /ʒiɡo/ *nm* (d'agneau) leg of lamb; **tranche de** ∼ slice of lamb; ∼ **de mouton** leg of mutton; ∼ **de chevreuil** haunch of venison

gigoter /ʒiɡɔte/ [1] *vi* gén to wriggle; (nerveusement) to fidget

gigue /ʒiɡ/ *nf* ① Culin haunch; ② ○(fille) **une grande** ∼ a great beanpole○ of a girl; ③ (air) gigue; (danse) jig

gilet /ʒilɛ/ *nm* ① (en tricot) cardigan; ∼ **sans manches** knitted waistcoat; ② (en tissu, cuir) waistcoat GB, vest US

(Composés) ∼ **pare-balles** bulletproof vest; ∼ **de sauvetage** lifejacket

gin /dʒin/ *nm* gin; ∼ **tonic** gin and tonic

gingembre /ʒɛ̃ʒɑ̃bR/ *nm* ginger

ginkgo /ʒinko/ *nm* ginkgo, maidenhair tree

girafe /ʒiRaf/ *nf* ① Zool giraffe; **avoir un cou de** ∼ to have a long neck; ② ○(personne) hum beanpole○

girafon /ʒiRafɔ̃/ *nm* baby giraffe

giratoire /ʒiRatwaR/ *adj* [mouvement] gyratory; **carrefour** ∼ roundabout GB, traffic circle US

girofle /ʒiRɔfl/ *nm* clove; **clou de** ∼ clove

giroflée /ʒiRɔfle/ *nf* wallflower

girolle /ʒiRɔl/ *nf* chanterelle

giron /ʒiRɔ̃/ *nm* ① (genoux) lap; ② fig (environnement) bosom

girondin, ∼**e** /ʒiRɔ̃dɛ̃, in/ *adj* ① Géog of the Gironde (après n); ② Hist [parti, politique] Girondist

girouette /ʒiRwɛt/ *nf* ① windvane; ② fig **c'est une vraie girouette** he/she is very capricious

gisant /ʒizɑ̃/ *nm* recumbent effigy

gisement /ʒizmɑ̃/ *nm* (de pétrole, minerai) deposit

gît ▸ **gésir**

gitan, ∼**e** /ʒitɑ̃, an/
A *adj* gypsy
B *nm,f* Gypsyᴳᴮ

gîte /ʒit/ *nm* ① (refuge) shelter; (demeure) home; (de lièvre) form; **le** ∼ **et le couvert** board and lodging GB, room and lodging US; ② (en boucherie) ∼ **(à la noix)** ≈ top rump

(Composé) ∼ **rural** self-catering cottage

givrant /ʒivʀɑ̃/ adj m brouillard ~ freezing fog

givre /ʒivʀ/ nm (sur le sol, une plante) frost; (sur un pare-brise, une hélice) ice

givré, ~e /ʒivʀe/ adj [1] (couvert de givre) [vitre] frosty; [branche, arbre] covered in frost (jamais épith); [neige] frozen; [2] ○(fou) crazy; [3] (avec du sucre) [verre] frosted

givrer /ʒivʀe/ [1] vi, **se givrer** vpr to frost over

glabre /glabʀ/ adj (imberbe) beardless; (rasé) clean-shaven

glaçage /glasaʒ/ nm [1] (de papier) glazing; [2] Culin (de viande) glazing; (de dessert) (au sucre) icing; (au blanc d'œuf) glazing

glace /glas/
A nf [1] (eau congelée) ice; **de ~** fig [accueil] icy; [visage] stony; [2] (dessert) ice cream; **à l'eau** water ice; [3] (miroir) mirror; **tu ferais mieux de te regarder dans une ~** fig you'd better take a long hard look at yourself; **~ sans tain** two-way mirror; [4] (panneau de verre) (plaque) sheet of glass; (de vitrine) glass; (de voiture) window
B glaces nfpl (de montagne) ice field (sg); (des pôles) ice sheet (sg); **pris dans les ~s** icebound
(Idiome) **rester de ~** to remain unmoved

glacé, ~e /glase/ adj [1] (très froid) [pluie, vent, air] ice-cold, icy; [douche, boisson] ice-cold; [mains] frozen; [personne] freezing; **thé/café ~** iced tea/coffee; [2] Culin [gâteau] iced; [fruit] glacé (épith); [3] (intimidant) [accueil, atmosphère] frosty, icy; [sourire] chilly; [voix] cold; [4] (brillant) [papier] glossy; [5] (gelé) frozen

glacer /glase/ [12]
A vtr [1] (transir) to freeze [corps]; to chill [sb] to the bone [personne]; [2] (rafraîchir) to chill [boisson, fruit]; [3] (intimider) [personne, regard] to intimidate; **~ qn d'effroi**, **~ le sang de qn** to make sb's blood run cold; **~ qn de peur** to fill sb with fear
B se glacer vpr [sourire, expression] to freeze; **mon sang se glaça dans mes veines** my blood froze

glaciaire /glasjɛʀ/ adj glacial; **calotte ~** icecap

glacial, ~e, mpl ~s or **-iaux** /glasjal, o/ adj [1] (froid) [froid, temps] icy; [pluie, journée, vent] icy, freezing cold; [2] fig (hostile) [personne, accueil] frosty; [silence] stony; [regard] icy

glaciation /glasjasjɔ̃/ nf glaciation

glacier /glasje/ nm [1] Géog glacier; [2] ▸ p. 372 (fabricant) ice-cream maker; (établissement) ice-cream parlour^GB

glacière /glasjɛʀ/ nf coolbox GB, cooler, ice chest US

glacis /glasi/ nm inv Art glaze

glaçon /glasɔ̃/ nm [1] ice cube; **avec des/sans ~s** with/without ice; [2] (dans une rivière) block of ice; (sur un toit, arbre) icicle; [3] ○(personne) pej iceberg

gladiateur /gladjatœʀ/ nm gladiator

glaïeul /glajœl/ nm gladiolus

glaire /glɛʀ/ nf [1] (sécrétion) mucus; **avoir des ~s** to have catarrh; [2] (blanc d'œuf) albumen

glaise /glɛz/ nf clay

glaive /glɛv/ nm double-edged sword; **le ~ et la balance** fig the sword and the scales of justice

gland /glɑ̃/ nm [1] Bot (de chêne) acorn; [2] Anat glans; [3] (décoration) tassel

glande /glɑ̃d/ nf gland

glaner /glane/ [1] vtr to glean [renseignements, grains, champ]

glapir /glapiʀ/ [3]
A vtr to screech [injures]
B vi [1] Zool [chiot] to yap; [renard] to bark; [grue] to whoop; [2] (hurler) [personne] to shriek; [haut-parleur, radio] to blare

glas /glɑ/ nm inv toll, knell; **sonner le ~** lit [personne] to toll the bell; [cloche] to toll; fig to sound the death knell (de for)

glauque /glok/ adj [eaux, lumière] murky; [rue] squalid; [film, ambiance] grim

glissade /glisad/ nf [1] lit (jeu) slide; (dérapage) skid; **faire une ~** [enfant] to slide; [joueur] to slip; [véhicule] to skid; [2] fig (de prix, monnaie) slide

glissant, ~e /glisɑ̃, ɑ̃t/ adj slippery

glisse /glis/ nf [1] (ski, skieur) glide; [2] ○(ski) skiing

glissement /glismɑ̃/ nm [1] (déplacement) sliding; **les deux pièces se superposent par ~** the two parts slide over each other; [2] (évolution) (de sens) shift; (d'électorat, opinion) swing; (de prix) fall

(Composé) **~ de terrain** landslide

glisser /glise/ [1]
A vtr [1] (mettre) to slip [objet] (**dans** into); **~ un oreiller sous la tête d'un malade** to slide a pillow under a patient's head; **elle a glissé la main dans mes cheveux** she ran her fingers through my hair; [2] (introduire) to slip in [remarque]; **~ qch à l'oreille de qn** to whisper sth in sb's ear
B vi [1] (être glissant) [route, savon] to be slippery; [2] (être déstabilisé) [personne] to slip; [chapeau, écharpe] to slip (down); [outil] to slip; [véhicule] to skid; **~ des mains de qn** [savon, bouteille] to slip out of sb's hands; **une tuile a glissé du toit** a tile fell off the roof; [3] (se déplacer) gén to slide; (avec grâce) to glide; **se laisser ~ le long d'une corde** to slide down a rope; [4] (ne pas accrocher) [tiroir, cloison] to slide; **leur regard glissait sur l'assistance** they surveyed the people present; **~ sur** fig (ne pas affecter) [critique] to have no effect on [personne]; (ne pas approfondir) [personne] to skate over [sujet]; [5] (passer) **~ dans l'ennui** to become bored; **l'électorat glisse à droite** there's a swing to the right among the electorate; **le roman glisse de la comédie au drame** the novel moves imperceptibly from comedy to drama
C se glisser vpr [1] (s'introduire) to slip; **se ~ dans** gén to slip into; (furtivement) to sneak into; **se ~ dans la foule** to slip through the crowd; **se ~ parmi les invités** to slip in among the guests; **se ~ parmi les badauds** to edge through the onlookers; **le chat s'est glissé sous la voiture** the cat crept under the car; [2] (s'insinuer) [sentiment, erreur] to creep into [personne, texte]

glissière /glisjɛʀ/ nf Tech slide; (d'autoroute) **~ (de sécurité)** crash barrier; **à ~** [porte, fenêtre] sliding (épith); **fermeture à ~** zip GB, zipper US

global, ~e, mpl -aux /glɔbal, o/ adj [somme, effectif] total; [résultat, coût] overall; [accord, vision, solution] global; [étude] comprehensive

globalement /glɔbalmɑ̃/ adv on the whole

globalité /glɔbalite/ nf **considérer qch dans sa ~** to consider sth in its entirety

globe /glɔb/ nm [1] (Terre) earth, globe; **stratégie à l'échelle du ~** worldwide strategy; **parcourir le ~** to globe-trot; [2] (sphère en verre) (de lampe) round glass lampshade; (de protection) glass case; [3] Archit dome

(Composé) **~ terrestre** (mappemonde) globe; (Terre) earth

globulaire /glɔbylɛʀ/ adj **numération ~** blood count

globule /glɔbyl/ nm (du sang) blood cell

(Composés) **~ blanc** white cell; **~ rouge** red cell

globuleux, -euse /glɔbylø, øz/ adj [œil] protruding

gloire /glwaʀ/ nf [1] (renom) glory, fame; **c'est ce qui a fait leur ~** that's what made them famous; **faire qch pour la ~** to do sth (just) for the sake of it; [2] (hommage) **à Dieu!** glory be to God; **rendre ~ à qn/au courage de qn** to pay tribute to sb/to sb's courage; [sujet de fierté] **tirer ~ de** to pride oneself on; [4] (personne) celebrity; (dans le monde du spectacle) star; [5] (splendeur) glory; **le Christ en ~** Art Christ in majesty

glorieusement /glɔʀjøzmɑ̃/ adv [combattre] with glory; **tomber ~ au champ d'honneur** to fall gloriously on the field of battle; **triompher ~** to have a great triumph

glorieux, -ieuse /glɔʀjø, øz/ adj glorious

glorifier /glɔʀifje/ [2]
A vtr to glorify
B se glorifier vpr to glory (de in), to boast (de about)

gloriole /glɔʀjɔl/ nf pej misplaced pride, vainglory littér

glose /gloz/ nf (annotation, développement) gloss; (note explicative) note

gloser /gloze/ [1]
A vtr to annotate [texte]
B vi (discourir) to ramble on (sur about)

glossaire /glɔsɛʀ/ nm glossary

glotte /glɔt/ nf glottis; **coup de ~** Ling glottal stop

glouglou /gluglu/ nm [1] ○(de liquide) gurgling sound; [2] (cri du dindon) gobbling sound

glouglouter /gluglute/ [1] vi [1] ○[liquide] to gurgle; [2] [dindon] to gobble

gloussement /glusmɑ̃/ nm (de poule) clucking ₵; (de personne) chuckle; **avec des ~s de satisfaction** with a satisfied chuckle

glousser /gluse/ [1] vi [*poule*] to cluck; [*personne*] to chuckle

glouton, -onne /glutɔ̃, ɔn/
A adj [*personne*] gluttonous; [*appétit*] voracious
B nm,f glutton
C nm Zool wolverine

gloutonnerie /glutɔnʀi/ nf gluttony; **manger avec ~** to wolf down one's food

glu /gly/ nf **1** bird lime; **prendre des oiseaux à la ~** to lime birds; **2** (colle) glue

gluant, ~e /glyɑ̃, ɑ̃t/ adj **1** (collant) [*main, pâtes*] sticky; [*poisson, mur, boue*] slimy; **2** ○(obséquieux) [*personne*] slimy

glucide /glysid/ nm carbohydrate

glycémie /glisemi/ nf **taux de ~** blood sugar level

glycérine /gliseʀin/ nf glycerin

glycine /glisin/ nf wisteria

gnangnan○ /nɑ̃nɑ̃/ adj inv silly

gnognotte○ /nɔnɔt/ nf **c'est de la ~!** (c'est facile) it's dead easy○; **c'est pas de la ~!** (de bonne qualité) it's not your common or garden variety○; (difficile) it's quite a business○

gnome /gnom/ nm gnome

gnon○ /nɔ̃/ nm (bosse sur une voiture) dent; (ecchymose) bruise; **il m'a flanqué un ~** he socked me; **prendre un ~** to get hit

gnostique /gnɔstik/ adj, nmf gnostic

gnou /gnu/ nm gnu

gnouf○ /nuf/ nm prison, nick○ GB

go /go/
A ▸ p. 327 nm Jeux go
B **tout de go** loc adv **tout de ~** [*dire*] straight out

goal /gol/ nm goalkeeper, goalie○

gobelet /gɔblɛ/ nm **1** (en plastique, carton) cup; (en verre) tumbler; (en métal) beaker; **~ en carton** paper cup; **2** Jeux shaker

gobe-mouche, pl **~s** /gɔbmuʃ/ nm Zool flycatcher

gober /gɔbe/ [1] vtr **1** (avaler) to suck [*œuf*]; to swallow [sth] whole [*huître*]; **2** ○(croire) to swallow, to fall for○ [*mensonge*]; **~ le morceau** to fall for it○

godasse○ /gɔdas/ nf shoe

goder /gɔde/ [1] vi (vêtement) to ruck up; (papier peint) to wrinkle

godet /gɔdɛ/ nm **1** (pour boire) goblet; (petit récipient) pot; (à dés) shaker; **2** (faux pli) crease; (pan de jupe) gore

godiche○ /gɔdiʃ/ adj **avoir un air ~** to look silly

godille /gɔdij/ nf **1** (aviron) steering oar; **2** (à ski) wedeln

godiller /gɔdije/ [1] vi (à skis) to wedeln

godillot /gɔdijo/ nm **1** ○(soulier) clodhopper○; **2** †Mil (brodequin) combat boot

goéland /gɔelɑ̃/ nm gull

goélette /gɔelɛt/ nf schooner

goémon /gɔemɔ̃/ nm (algues) wrack; (engrais) seaweed fertilizer

gogo○ /gogo/
A nm (dupe) sucker○
B **à gogo** loc adv **vin à ~** wine galore; **de l'argent, il en a à ~** he's got loads of money

goguenard, ~e /gɔgnaʀ, aʀd/ adj quietly ironic

goguette○: **en goguette** /ɑ̃gɔgɛt/
A loc adj (ivre) tipsy
B loc adv **partir en ~** to go on a spree

goinfre /gwɛ̃fʀ/ nmf greedy pig○

goinfrer○: **se goinfrer** /gwɛ̃fʀe/ [1] vpr to stuff oneself○ (de with)

goitre /gwatʀ/ nm goitre^GB

golden /gɔldɛn/ nf inv Golden Delicious (apple)

golf /gɔlf/ ▸ p. 327 nm **1** (sport) golf; **2** (terrain) golf course

golfe /gɔlf/ nm (grand) gulf; (petit) bay

golfeur, -euse /gɔlfœʀ, øz/ ▸ p. 372 nm,f golfer

gomina® /gɔmina/ nf hair cream

gominer: **se gominer** /gɔmine/ [1] vpr to slick one's hair back; **cheveux gominés** slicked-back hair

gommage /gɔmaʒ/ nm **1** (action d'effacer) rubbing-out, erasing; **2** (action d'enduire) gumming; **3** (produit de beauté, action) scrub

gomme /gɔm/
A nf **1** (pour effacer) eraser, rubber GB; **2** (substance) gum; **3** (bonbon) gum drop; **4** C (chewing-gum) **~ (à mâcher)** chewing gum; **5** Méd gumma
B **à la gomme**○ loc adj pej [*idée, personne, renseignement, machine*] useless; [*projet*] hopeless

(Composés) **~ adhésive** blu-tack®; **~ arabique** gum arabic; **~ à encre** ink eraser

(Idiome) **mettre (toute) la ~**○ (en voiture, à moto) to step on it○; (en avion, bateau) to give it full throttle○; (avec une radio) to turn it up full blast

gommer /gɔme/ [1] vtr **1** (effacer) to rub [sth] out [*mot*]; **2** (faire disparaître) to smooth out [*ride*]; to erase [*passé, frontière*]; to iron out [*différence*]; to soothe away [*fatigue*]; **3** (enduire) to gum; **papier gommé** gummed paper; **4** to scrub [*peau*]

gommier /gɔmje/ nm gum tree

gond /gɔ̃/ nm hinge; **sortir de ses ~s** [*porte*] to come off its hinges; fig [*personne*] to fly off the handle○

gondole /gɔ̃dɔl/ nf **1** (embarcation) gondola; **en ~** in a gondola; **2** (de supermarché) sales shelf, gondola spéc

gondoler: **se gondoler** /gɔ̃dɔle/ [1] vpr **1** [*papier*] to crinkle; [*bois*] to warp; [*métal*] to buckle; **2** ○(rire) to laugh

gondolier /gɔ̃dɔlje/ ▸ p. 372 nm gondolier

gonflable /gɔ̃flabl/ adj inflatable

gonflage /gɔ̃flaʒ/ nm (de pneu, ballon) inflation; **station de ~** Aut air point (for pumping up tyres)

gonflé, ~e /gɔ̃fle/ adj **1** (plein d'air) [*pneu, ballon*] inflated; [*joue*] puffed out; **2** (enflé) [*bourgeon, veine, bras*] swollen (de with); [*ventre*] (après un repas) bloated; (de malade) swollen; [*yeux, visage*] puffy, swollen; [*muscle*] bulging, flexed; [*sac*] bulging (de with); **yeux ~s de sommeil/de larmes** eyes heavy with sleep/swollen with tears; **éponge ~e d'eau** sponge saturated with water; **3** ○Aut [*moteur*] souped-up (épith); **voiture au moteur ~** hot rod GB, muscle car US; **4** ○(courageux) gutsy○; **être ~** to have guts○; **5** ○(impudent) cheeky○; **être ~** to have a nerve○

gonfler /gɔ̃fle/ [1]
A vtr **1** (remplir d'air) (avec la bouche) to blow up [*ballon*]; to fill [*poumon*] (de with); to puff out [*joue*]; (avec une pompe) to inflate [*pneu*]; **être gonflé à bloc** [*pneu*] to be fully inflated; fig [*personne*] to be raring○ to go; **le vent gonfle la voile** the wind swells ou fills the sail; **le vent gonfle ma chemise** the wind makes my shirt billow; **2** (faire grossir) [*personne*] to flex [*muscle*]; [*objet*] to make [sth] bulge [*poche*]; [*eau*] to saturate [*éponge*]; [*pluie*] to make [sth] swollen [*rivière*]; [*sève*] to swell [*bourgeon*]; **la limonade gonfle l'estomac** lemonade makes you feel bloated; **3** fig **la joie gonflait mon cœur** my heart was bursting with joy; **il est gonflé d'orgueil** he's full of his own importance; **4** (augmenter) to increase [*effectifs*]; to push up [*prix*]; to inflate [*statistiques*]; to exaggerate [*importance*]; **5** ○Aut to soup up [*moteur, voiture*]
B vi **1** (enfler) [*pied, paupière*] to swell (up); [*riz, bois, éponge*] to swell; [*gâteau, pâte*] to rise; **2** (augmenter) [*effectifs*] to increase; **faire ~ les prix** to push prices up

gonflette○ /gɔ̃flɛt/ nf pej **faire de la ~** to pump iron○, to go body-building

gong /gɔ̃g/ nm **1** ▸ p. 389 Mus gong; **2** (en boxe) bell

gordien /gɔʀdjɛ̃/ adj m **trancher le nœud ~** to cut the Gordian knot

goret /gɔʀɛ/ nm **1** Zool piglet; **2** ○(enfant) little pig○

gorge /gɔʀʒ/ nf **1** ▸ p. 136 Anat throat; **avoir mal à la ~** to have a sore throat; **voix de ~** throaty voice; **je suis pris à la ~, je n'ai plus un sou** I'm in a fix○, I haven't got a penny; **tenir qn à la ~** fig to have a stranglehold over sb; **avoir la ~ serrée** ou **nouée** (d'émotion) to have a lump in one's throat; (de peur) to have one's heart in one's mouth; **à ~ déployée, à pleine ~** [*chanter*] at the top of one's voice; [*rire*] uproariously; **je te ferai rentrer tes mots dans la ~!** I'll make you eat your words!; **ta remarque m'est restée en travers de la ~** I found your comment hard to swallow ou very hard to take; **ma question m'est restée dans la ~** I couldn't get the question out; **2** (poitrine) bosom, breast; **3** Géog gorge

(Idiome) **faire des ~s chaudes de qch** to laugh sth to scorn

gorgé, ~e /gɔʀʒe/
A pp ▸ **gorger**

B *pp adj* ~ **de nourriture** glutted with food; ~ **d'eau** [*terre*] waterlogged; [*éponge*] saturated with water (*jamais épith*); **fruit** ~ **de soleil** fruit bursting with sunshine

gorgée /gɔRʒe/ *nf* (petite) sip; (grande) gulp

gorger /gɔRʒe/ [13]

A *vtr* ~ **qn de nourriture** to stuff⁰ sb with food

B **se gorger** *vpr* **se** ~ **de nourriture** to gorge oneself; **la terre se gorge d'eau** the soil soaks up water

gorille /gɔRij/ *nm* **1** Zool gorilla; **2** ⁰(garde du corps) bodyguard

gosier /gozje/ *nm* throat, gullet; **ce vin (m')écorche le** ~⁰ hum this wine is like paint stripper; **ça m'est resté en travers du** ~⁰ it stuck in my throat

⟮Idiomes⟯ **s'humecter le** ~⁰ to wet one's whistle; **chanter à plein** ~ to sing at the top of one's voice

gospel /gɔspɛl/ *nm* **1** (style) gospel music; **2** (chant) gospel song

gosse⁰ /gɔs/ *nmf* (enfant) kid⁰, child; **sale** ~ brat⁰; **c'est un grand** ~ he's still a kid at heart; **il est beau** ~ he's a good-looking fellow

gotha /gɔta/ *nm* (noblesse) aristocracy; (haute société) high society

gothique /gɔtik/ *adj, nm* Gothic

gouache /gwaʃ/ *nf* (peinture, tableau) gouache

gouaille /gwaj/ *nf* (esprit moqueur) cheek

gouailleur, -euse /gwajœR, øz/ *adj* cheeky

goudron /gudRɔ̃/ *nm* **1** Chimie tar; '~**s 12 mg'** '12 mg tar'; **2** ⁰(pour revêtement) tar, tarmac® GB

goudronner /gudRɔne/ [1] *vtr* to tarmac

gouffre /gufR/ *nm* **1** (fosse) chasm, abyss; **le** ~ **de Padirac** the caves (*pl*) of Padirac; **2** fig **le** ~ **de l'oubli** the pit of oblivion; **le pays est au bord du** ~ the country is on the brink of the abyss; **leur maison est un** ~ their house is a real drain on their finances

gouille /guj/ *nf* H (flaque) puddle

goujat /guʒa/ *nm* boor; **comme un** ~ boorishly

goujaterie /guʒatRi/ *nf* boorishness

goujon /guʒɔ̃/ *nm* Zool gudgeon; **taquiner le** ~⁰ to do the odd bit of fishing

goulée⁰ /gule/ *nf* (de liquide) gulp

goulet /gulɛ/ *nm* (de port) narrows (*pl*); (en montagne) gully

⟮Composé⟯ ~ **d'étranglement** bottleneck

goulot /gulo/ *nm* (de bouteille) neck; **boire au** ~ to drink from the bottle

⟮Composé⟯ ~ **d'étranglement** bottleneck

goulu, ~e /guly/
A *adj* greedy
B *nm,f* glutton

goulûment /gulymɑ̃/ *adv* greedily

goupille /gupij/ *nf* pin

goupiller⁰: **se goupiller** /gupije/ [1] *vpr* **ça s'est bien/mal goupillé** it turned out well/badly

goupillon /gupijɔ̃/ *nm* **1** (brosse) bottle brush; **2** Relig holy water sprinkler, aspergillum

gourd, ~e¹ /guR, guRd/ *adj* (engourdi) numb

gourde² /guRd/
A ⁰*adj* (niais) dumb⁰, gormless⁰ GB
B *nf* **1** (pour liquide) gén flask; (en cuir, écorce) gourd; **2** ⁰(sot) dope⁰

gourdin /guRdɛ̃/ *nm* bludgeon, cudgel; **frapper qn à coups de** ~ to bludgeon sb

gourer⁰: **se gourer** /guRe/ [1] *vpr* (dans un calcul) to make a mistake; (dans une supposition) to be mistaken; **se** ~ **de jour** to get the day wrong

gourmand, ~e /guRmɑ̃, ɑ̃d/ *adj* **1** (amateur) fond of good food (*jamais épith*); (glouton) greedy; **je ne suis pas** ~**e** I'm not that interested in food; **il est** ~ **(de sucreries)** he has a sweet tooth; **2** (d'argent) grasping

gourmander /guRmɑ̃de/ [1] *vtr* to scold

gourmandise /guRmɑ̃diz/
A *nf* (pour les sucreries) weakness for sweet things; (pour la nourriture) weakness for good food; (défaut) greed; (péché) gluttony; **avec** ~ greedily
B **gourmandises** *nfpl* (friandises) sweets GB, candies US

gourme /guRm/ *nf* **jeter sa** ~ to sow one's wild oats

gourmet /guRmɛ/ *nm* gourmet

gourmette /guRmɛt/ *nf* (de poignet) chain bracelet

gourou /guRu/ *nm* guru

gousse /gus/ *nf* Bot pod; ~ **d'ail** clove of garlic

gousset /gusɛ/ *nm* **1** (poche) fob; **2** (de collant) gusset; **3** Tech gusset

goût /gu/ *nm* **1** (sens) taste; (appréciation) palate; **agréable au** ~ pleasant-tasting; **2** (saveur) taste; **avoir un** ~ **sucré** to taste sweet, to have a sweet taste; **avoir un** ~ **de brûlé/de pêche** to taste burned/of peaches; **avoir mauvais** ~ to taste unpleasant; **avoir un petit** ~ to taste a bit strange; **donner du** ~ **à qch** to give sth flavour⁰ᴮ; **n'avoir aucun** ~ to be tasteless; **3** (discernement) taste; **avoir du** ~ to have taste; **avoir un** ~ **très sûr** to have unfailingly good taste; **de bon/mauvais** ~ in good/bad taste (*après n*); **d'un** ~ **douteux** [*décor, plaisanterie, scène*] in dubious taste (*après n*); **avec/sans** ~ [*décorer*] tastefully/tastelessly; **s'habiller avec/sans** ~ to have good/no dress sense; **avoir le mauvais** ~ **de faire** to be tactless enough to do; **4** (gré) liking; **avoir du** ~ **pour qch** to have a liking for sth; **ne pas être du** ~ **de tout le monde** [*situation*] not to be to everyone's liking; [*décor, aliment*] not to be to everyone's cup of tea; **je n'ai rien trouvé à mon** ~ I didn't find anything I liked; **je n'ai plus** ~ **à rien** I've lost interest in everything; **elle reprend** ~ **à la vie** she's starting to enjoy life again; **être au** ~ **du jour** to be trendy; **se mettre au** ~ **du jour** to update one's image; **remettre qch au** ~ **du jour** to bring sth back into fashion; **il a pris** ~ **à la pêche** he's taken to fishing; **faire qch par** ~ to do sth for pleasure; **5** (préférence) taste; **avoir des** ~**s de luxe** to have expensive tastes; **chacun ses** ~**s** each to his own

⟮Idiomes⟯ **avoir un** ~ **de trop peu** *or* **pas assez** to be on the stingy side; **tous les** ~**s sont dans la nature** Prov it takes all sorts to make a world Prov; **des** ~**s et des couleurs on ne discute pas** Prov there's no accounting for taste

goûter¹ /gute/ [1]
A *vtr* **1** (essayer) to taste, to try; **2** (apprécier) to enjoy [*paix, solitude, spectacle*]; **je goûte fort peu ce genre de plaisanterie** I don't appreciate that kind of joke at all
B **goûter à** *vtr ind* **1** (essayer) ~ **à** to try [*aliment, boisson*]; **mais tu y as à peine goûté!** but you've hardly touched it!; **2** (faire l'expérience de) ~ **à** to have a taste of [*liberté, pouvoir*]; ~ **aux joies de qch** to sample the joys of sth
C **goûter de** *vtr ind* ~ **de** to have a taste of; **avoir goûté de la prison** to have had a taste of life in prison
D *vi* to have one's mid-afternoon snack

goûter² /gute/ *nm* **1** (nourriture) snack; **2** (réunion d'enfants) children's party; ~ **d'anniversaire** children's birthday party

goûteur, -euse /gutœR, øz/ ▸ p. 372 *nm,f* taster; ~ **d'eau** water taster

goutte /gut/
A *nf* **1** (de liquide) drop (**de** of); ~ **de pluie** raindrop; ~ **de rosée** dewdrop; ~ **à** ~ drop by drop; **couler** *or* **tomber** ~ **à** ~ to drip; **à grosses** ~**s** [*pleuvoir*] heavily; [*transpirer*] profusely; **hier il est tombé quelques** ~**s** there were a few spots of rain yesterday; ~ **de sueur** bead of sweat; ▸ **vase**¹; **2** ⁰(eau-de-vie) eau-de-vie; **3** ▸ p. 195 Méd gout
B **gouttes** *nfpl* (médicament) drops

⟮Idiomes⟯ **se ressembler comme deux** ~**s d'eau** to be as alike as two peas in a pod; **c'est une** ~ **d'eau dans la mer** *or* **l'océan** it's a drop in the ocean; **avoir la** ~ **au nez** to have a runny nose; **on n'y voit** ~ you can't see a thing

goutte-à-goutte /gutagut/ *nm inv* Méd drip

gouttelette /gutlɛt/ *nf* droplet

goutter /gute/ [1] *vi* to drip (**de** from)

gouttière /gutjɛR/ *nf* (de toit) gutter; (de descente) drainpipe

gouvernail /guvɛRnaj/ *nm* **1** Naut rudder; **2** fig helm; **tenir le** ~ to be at the helm

gouvernant, ~e¹ /guvɛRnɑ̃, ɑ̃t/
A *adj* [*classe, parti*] ruling
B **gouvernants** *nmpl* **les** ~**s** the government (*sg*)

gouvernante² /guvɛRnɑ̃t/ *nf* **1** (institutrice) governess; **2** (domestique) housekeeper

gouverne /guvɛRn/ *nf* **pour votre** ~ for your information

gouvernement /guvɛRnəmɑ̃/ *nm* government; **être au** ~ to be a member of the government

gouvernemental, ~e, *mpl* **-aux** /guvɛʀnəmãtal, o/ *adj* (du gouvernement) [*arrêté, politique*] government (*épith*); [*responsabilité*] governmental; **l'équipe** ~e the government; **non** ~ non-governmental

gouverner /guvɛʀne/ [1]
A *vtr* **1** Pol to govern, to rule [*pays, peuple*]; **le parti qui gouverne** the ruling party; **2** (dominer) [*intérêt*] to rule [*hommes*]; **3** Naut to steer [*ship*]
B se gouverner *vpr* **le droit des peuples à se** ~ the right of peoples to self-government

gouverneur /guvɛʀnœʀ/ ▸ p. 590 *nm* governor

goyave /gɔjav/ *nf* guava

GPS /ʒepeɛs/ *nm* (*abbr* = **global positioning system**) GPS

Graal /gʀal/ *nm* Grail

grabat /gʀaba/ *nm* pallet

grabataire /gʀabatɛʀ/
A *adj* bedridden
B *nmf* bedridden invalid; **les** ~**s** the bedridden

grabuge○ /gʀabyʒ/ *nm* **il y a avoir du** ~ there's going to be trouble; **faire du** ~ to raise hell○

grâce /gʀas/
A *nf* **1** (de geste, personne) grace; (de paysage) charm; (de style) elegance; **sans** ~ [*geste*] ungraceful; [*style*] inelegant; **se mouvoir avec/sans** ~ to move gracefully/awkwardly; **2** (volonté) **bonne/mauvaise** ~ good/bad grace; **de bonne/mauvaise** ~ willingly/grudgingly; **3** (faveur) favourᴳᴮ; **chercher/gagner les bonnes** ~**s de qn** to seek/to win sb's favourᴳᴮ; **faire à qn la** ~ **d'accepter** *fml* to do sb the honourᴳᴮ of accepting; **à la** ~ **de Dieu!** it's in God's hands!; **de** ~ *fml* please; (avec impatience) for pity's sake; **donner le coup de** ~ **à qn** *lit, fig* to deal sb the death blow; **ce fut le coup de** ~ that was the final stroke; **4** (pardon) mercy; Jur (free) pardon; **demander/crier** ~ to beg/to cry for mercy; ~ **présidentielle** Jur presidential pardon; ~**!** (have) mercy!; **je vous fais** ~ **des détails** I'll spare you the details; **5** (bonté divine) grace; **être touché par la** ~ to be touched by God's grace; ~ **à Dieu!** thank God!; **dire les** ~**s** to say grace (after a meal)
B grâce à *loc prép* thanks to

Grâce /gʀas/ *nf* Grace; **votre** ~ your Grace

gracier /gʀasje/ [2] *vtr* to pardon, to reprieve

gracieusement /gʀasjøzmã/ *adv* **1** (gratuitement) free of charge; **un billet vous sera** ~ **offert** you will be given a free ticket; **2** (élégamment) [*danser*] gracefully

gracieux, -ieuse /gʀasjø, øz/ *adj* **1** (beau) [*geste, personne*] graceful; **Sa gracieuse Majesté** *fml* his/her gracious Majesty; **2** (avenant) [*personne, sourire*] gracious

gracile /gʀasil/ *adj* slender

gradation /gʀadasjɔ̃/ *nf* gén, Art, Phot gradation; ~ **descendante** anticlimax

grade /gʀad/ *nm* rank; **monter en** ~ to be promoted; **en prendre pour son** ~○ to be hauled over the coals

gradé, ~e /gʀade/ *nm,f* Mil noncommissioned officer

gradin /gʀadɛ̃/ *nm* (de salle) tier; (d'arène) terrace; (de stade) **les** ~**s** the terraces GB, the bleachers US; **en** ~**s** [*terrain*] terraced

graduation /gʀaduasjɔ̃/ *nf* (d'instrument) graduation

gradué, ~e /gʀadɥe/ *adj* **règle** ~e ruler; **verre** ~ measuring cup; (avec bec verseur) measuring jug

graduel, -elle /gʀadɥɛl/ *adj* gradual

graduer /gʀadɥe/ [1] *vtr* **1** gén to increase [*difficulté*]; to grade GB, to graduate US [*exercices*]; **2** Tech to graduate [*instrument*]

graffeur, -euse /gʀafœʀ, øz/ ▸ p. 372 *nm,f* street artist (*working with graffiti and tags*)

graffiti /gʀafiti/ *nmpl* graffiti

graillon○ /gʀajɔ̃/ *nm* **ça sent le** ~ it smells of stale fat

grain /gʀɛ̃/ *nm* **1** (céréales) grain; **nourri au** ~ corn-fed, grain-fed; **2** (de céréale, sel, sable) grain; ~ **de poivre** peppercorn; ~ **de café** coffee bean; ~ **de moutarde** mustard seed; ~ **de cassis** blackcurrant; ~ **de raisin** grape; **3** (de chapelet) bead; **4** (de poussière) speck (**de** of); **5** *fig* **un** ~ **de folie** a touch of madness; **6** (texture) **le** ~ the grain; **7** (averse) heavy shower; **8** Naut squall

Composé ~ **de beauté** beauty spot, mole

Idiomes **avoir un** ~○ to be loony○; **mettre son** ~ **de sel**○ to put *ou* stick one's oar in○; **avoir du** ~ **à moudre** to have enough to be getting on with

graine /gʀɛn/ *nf* **1** (grosses ou individuelles) seeds; (pour semence) seed **C**; (pour oiseaux) birdseed **C**; **monter en** ~ [*légume*] to run to seed; *hum* [*enfant*] to shoot up; **ton fils, c'est de la mauvaise** ~ your son is a bad lot○

Idiomes **casser la** ~○ to have a bite to eat; **prends-en de la** ~○ let that be an example to you

grainetier /gʀɛntje/ ▸ p. 372 *nm* seedsman GB, feedstore manager US

graissage /gʀesaʒ/ *nm* lubrication

graisse /gʀes/ *nf* **1** (tissu adipeux) fat; (de baleine, phoque) blubber; **2** Culin fat; **mangez moins de** ~**s** eat less fat; **3** (lubrifiant) grease

graisser /gʀese/ [1] *vtr* to grease [*poêle*]; to lubricate [*rouage*]; ~ **la patte**○ **à qn** *fig* to grease sb's palm *fig*

graisseux, -euse /gʀesø, øz/ *adj* gén greasy; Méd [*tissu*] fatty

graminée /gʀamine/ *nf* **une** ~ a grass; **les** ~**s** grasses

grammaire /gʀamɛʀ/ *nf* **1** (science) grammar; **2** (manuel) grammar

grammairien, -ienne /gʀamɛʀjɛ̃, ɛn/ ▸ p. 372 *nm,f* grammarian

grammatical, ~e, *mpl* **-aux** /gʀamatikal, o/ *adj* grammatical

gramme /gʀam/ ▸ p. 453 *nm* gram; **il n'a pas un** ~ **de bon sens** he hasn't an ounce of common sense

grand, ~e /gʀã, gʀãd/
A *adj* **1** (de dimensions importantes) (en hauteur) tall; (en longueur, durée) long; (en largeur) wide; (en étendue, volume) big; **plus** ~ **que nature** larger than life; **ouvrir de** ~**s yeux** to open one's eyes wide; **2** (nombreux, abondant) large, big; **pas** ~ **monde** not many people; **il fait** ~ **jour** it's broad daylight; **laver à** ~e **eau** to wash [*sth*] in plenty of running water [*légumes*]; to wash [*sth*] down [*sol*]; **3** (à un degré élevé) [*rêveur, collectionneur, ami*] great; [*tricheur, joueur*] big; [*buveur, fumeur*] heavy; **c'est un** ~ **timide** he's very shy; **les** ~**s malades** very sick people; **les** ~**s blessés** the seriously injured; **4** (important) [*découverte, expédition, nouvelle*] great; [*date*] important; [*rôle*] major; [*problème, décision*] big; **c'est un** ~ **jour pour elle** it's a big day for her; **la** ~e **majorité** the great *ou* vast majority; **5** (principal) main; **les** ~**es lignes d'une politique** the broad lines of a policy; **6** (de premier plan) [*société, marque*] leading; **les** ~**es industries** the big industries; **7** (brillant, remarquable) [*peintre, vin, cause*] great; [*cœur, âme*] noble; **c'est un** ~ **homme** he's a great man; **Louis le Grand** Louis the Great; ▸ **esprit**; **8** (âgé) [*frère, sœur*] elder; [*élève*] senior GB, older; (adulte) **les** ~**es personnes** grown-ups; **les** ~**es classes** Scol the senior forms GB, the upper classes US; **une** ~e **fille comme toi!** a big girl like you!; **assez** ~ **pour faire** old enough to do; **9** (qualifiant une mesure) [*hauteur, longueur, distance, valeur*] great; [*pointure, quantité, étendue*] large; [*vitesse*] high; **il est** ~ **temps que tu partes** it's high time you went; **10** (extrême, fort) [*bonté, amitié, danger, intérêt*] great; [*bruit*] loud; [*froid*] severe; [*chaleur*] intense; [*vent*] strong, high; [*tempête*] big, violent; **d'une** ~e **timidité** very shy; **à ma** ~e **surprise** much to my surprise; **sans** ~ **espoir** without much hope; **ça te ferait le plus** ~ **bien** it would do you a world of good; **à** ~**s cris** loudly; ▸ **cas**, **remède**; **11** (de rang social élevé) [*famille, nom*] great; **la** ~e **bourgeoisie** the upper middle class; **12** (grandiose) [*réception, projet*] grand; **avoir** ~e **allure** to look very impressive; **13** (emphatique) [*mot*] big; [*phrase*] high-sounding; **un** ~ **merci** a big thank you; **faire de** ~**s gestes** to wave one's arms about; **et voilà, tout de suite les** ~**s mots** there you go, straight off the deep end
B *nm,f* (enfant) big boy/girl; Scol senior GB *ou* older pupil; **pour les** ~**s et les petits** for old and young alike
C *adv* wide; **ouvrir** ~ **les bras** to throw one's arms open; **ouvrir la porte toute** ~e to open the door wide; **ouvrir** ~ **ses oreilles** *fig* to prick up one's ears; **leurs vêtements taillent** ~ their clothes are cut on the large side; **voir** ~ to think big
D *nm* **les** ~**s de ce monde** the great and the good; **les cinq** ~**s** Pol the Big Five; **les** ~**s de l'automobile** the top car manufacturers
E en grand *loc adv* **faire de l'élevage en** ~ to breed animals

Les grades

■ *La liste suivante regroupe les grades des trois armes, armée de terre, marine et aviation du Royaume-Uni et des États-Unis. Pour les traductions, consulter les articles dans le dictionnaire.*

■ *En anglais comme en français, l'armée de terre et l'armée de l'air distinguent deux catégories: les officiers,* commissioned officers (*GB*) *ou* warrant officers (*US*), *à partir du grade de* Second Lieutenant/Pilot Officer, *et tous les autres, à l'exception de* Private/Aircraftman/Airman, *non-commissioned officers (the NCOs, dire* [ðɪ ensiːˈəʊz]*:*

Royaume-Uni

L'armée de terre

Royaume-Uni	États-Unis
the British Army	the United States Army
Field Marshal (FM)*	General of the Army (GEN)
General (Gen)	General (GEN)
Lieutenant†-General (Lt-Gen)	Lieutenant† General (LTG)
Major-General (Maj-Gen)	Major General (MG)
Brigadier (Brig)	Brigadier General (BG)
Colonel (Col)	Colonel (COL)
Lieutenant†-Colonel (Lt-Col)	Lieutenant† Colonel (LTC)
Major (Maj)	Major (MAJ)
Captain (Capt)	Captain (CAPT)
Lieutenant† (Lieut)	First Lieutenant† (1LT)
Second Lieutenant† (2nd Lt)	Second Lieutenant† (2Lt)
—	Chief Warrant Officer (CWO)
	Warrant Officer (WO)
Regimental Sergeant Major (RSM)	Command Sergeant Major (CSM)
Company Sergeant Major (CSM)	Staff Sergeant Major (SSM)
	1st Sergeant (1 SG)
	Master Sergeant (MSG)
	Sergeant 1st Class (SFC)
Staff Sergeant‡ (S/Sgt) *ou* Colour Sergeant‡ (C/Sgt)‡	Staff Sergeant (SSG)
Sergeant (Sgt)	Sergeant (SGT)
Corporal (Cpl)	Corporal (CPL)
Lance Corporal (L/Cpl)	Private First Class (P1C)
Private (Pte) *ou* Rifleman (Rfm) *ou* Guardsman (Gdm)‡	Private (PVT)

La marine

Royaume-Uni	États-Unis
the Royal Navy (RN)§	the United States Navy (USN)§
Admiral of the Fleet	Fleet Admiral
Admiral (Adm)*	Admiral (ADM)
Vice-Admiral (V-Adm)	Vice Admiral (VADM)
Rear-Admiral (Rear-Adm)	Rear Admiral (RADM)
Commodore (Cdre)	Commodore (CDRE)
Captain (Capt)	Captain (CAPT)
Commander (Cdr)	Commander (CDR)
Lieutenant†-Commander (Lt-Cdr)	Lieutenant† Commander (LCDR)
Lieutenant† (Lt)	Lieutenant† (LT)
Sub-Lieutenant† (Sub-Lt)	Lieutenant† Junior Grade (LTJG)
Acting Sub-Lieutenant† (Act Sub-Lt)	Ensign (ENS)
Midshipman	Chief Warrant Officer (CWO)
Fleet Chief Petty Officer (FCPO)	Midshipman
—	—
	Master Chief Petty Officer (MCPO)
—	Senior Chief Petty Officer (SCPO)
Chief Petty Officer (CPO)	Chief Petty Officer (CPO)
—	Petty Officer 1st Class (PO1)

Royaume-Uni	États-Unis
—	Petty Officer 2nd Class (PO2)
Petty Officer (PO)	Petty Officer 3rd Class (PO3)
Leading Seaman (LS)	Seaman (SN)
Able Seaman (AB)	—
Ordinary Seaman (OD)	
Junior Seaman (JS)	Seaman Apprentice (SA)
	Seaman Recruit (SR)

Royaume-Uni

L'armée de l'air

États-Unis

Royaume-Uni	États-Unis
the Royal Air Force (RAF)¶	the United States Air Force (USAF)‖
Marshal of the Royal Air Force	General of the Air Force
Air Chief Marshal (ACM)*	General (GEN)
Air Marshal (AM)	Lieutenant† General (LTG)
Air Vice-Marshal (AVM)	Major General (MG)
Air Commodore (Air Cdre)	Brigadier General (BG)
Group Captain (Gp Capt)	Colonel (COL)
Wing Commander (Wing Cdr)	Lieutenant† Colonel (LTC)
Squadron Leader (Sqn Ldr)	Major (MAJ)
Flight Lieutenant† (Flt Lt)	Captain (CAPT)
Flying Officer (FO)	First Lieutenant† (1LT)
Pilot Officer (PO)	Second Lieutenant† (2LT)
Warrant Officer (WO)	—
Flight Sergeant (FS)	Chief Master Sergeant (CMSGT)
	Senior Master Sergeant (SMSGT)
—	Master Sergeant (MSGT)
Chief Technician (Chf Tech)	Technical Sergeant (TSGT)
Sergeant (Sgt)	Staff Sergeant (SSGT)
Corporal (Cpl)	Sergeant (SGT)
Junior Technician (Jnr Tech)	
Senior Aircraftman (SAC) *ou* Senior Aircraftwoman	—
Leading Aircraftman (LAC) *ou* Leading Aircraftwoman	Airman First Class (A1C) *ou* Airwoman First Class
Aircraftman *ou* Aircraftwoman	Airman Basic (AB)

Comment parler des militaires

■ *L'anglais emploie l'article indéfini pour les noms de grades utilisés avec les verbes* to be (*être*), to become (*devenir*)*, à* to make (*faire*) *etc.*

■ *Dans les expressions suivantes,* colonel *est pris comme exemple; les autres noms de grades s'utilisent de la même façon.*

il est colonel
= he is a colonel

il est colonel dans l'armée de terre
= he is a colonel in the army

devenir colonel
= to become a colonel

on l'a nommé colonel
= he was made a colonel

■ *Mais avec le verbe* to promote *ou dans l'expression* the rank of…*, l'anglais n'emploie pas l'article indéfini:*

être promu colonel
= to be promoted colonel *ou* to be promoted to colonel

il a le grade de colonel
= he has the rank of colonel

■ *L'anglais n'emploie pas non plus l'article défini lorsque le grade est suivi du nom propre:*

☛ Voir page suivante

g

Les grades *suite*

le colonel Jones est arrivé
= Colonel Jones has arrived

Comparer:

le colonel est arrivé
= the colonel has arrived

■ *Noter que le mot* Colonel *prend une majuscule en anglais devant le nom propre, mais rarement dans les autres cas.*

Comment s'adresser aux militaires

■ *D'un militaire à son supérieur:*

oui, mon colonel
= yes, sir

oui, colonel
= yes, ma'am

■ *D'un militaire à son inférieur en grade:*

oui, sergent
= yes, sergeant

* *Les abréviations sont utilisées uniquement par écrit et avec les noms propres, par ex.:* Capt. Jones.

† *Noter la prononciation (GB):* [lef 'tenənt], *(US):* [lu:'tenənt].

‡ *Le mot varie selon le régiment.*

§ *Les abréviations* RN *et* USN *ne sont utilisés que par écrit.*

¶ *Pour* the RAF, *dire* [ðɪɑːreɪef].

‖ *L'abréviation* USAF *n'est utilisée que par écrit. Dire* the US Air Force.

---

on a large scale; **faire les choses en** ~ to do things on the grand scale

(Composés) ~ **banditisme** organized crime; ~ **bassin** (de piscine) main pool; ~ **couturier** couturier; ~ **duc** Zool eagle owl; ~ **écart** Sport splits (sg); **le** ~ **écran** the big screen; ~ **ensemble** high-density housing complex; ~ **invalide civil, GIC** civilian who is registered severely disabled; ~ **invalide de guerre, GIG** ex-serviceman who is registered severely disabled; **le** ~ **large** Naut the high seas (pl); ~ **magasin** department store; ~ **maître** (aux échecs) grand master; **le** ~ **mât** mainmast; **le** ~ **monde** high society; **le Grand Nord** the Far North; ~ **panda** giant panda; **Grand Pardon** Day of Atonement; ~ **patron** Méd senior consultant GB, head doctor US; ~ **prêtre** Relig, fig high priest; **le** ~ **public** the general public; Comm **produit** ~ **public** consumer product; ~ **quotidien** big national daily; ~ **teint** colourfast^GB; ~ **tourisme** Aut GT, gran turismo; **la** ~**e banlieue** the outer suburbs (pl); **la** ~**e cuisine** haute cuisine; ~**e distribution** volume retailing; ~**e école** higher education institution; **la Grande Guerre** the First World War; ~**e gueule**○ loud mouth○; **la** ~**e muraille de Chine** the Great Wall of China; ~**e personne** grown-up, adult; **la** ~**e presse** the popular dailies (pl); ~**e puissance** Pol superpower; ~**e roue** (de foire) big wheel GB, Ferris wheel US; ~**e série** Comm mass production; **fabriqué en** ~**e série** mass-produced; ~**e surface** Comm supermarket; ~**es eaux** fountains; **dès qu'on la gronde, ce sont les** ~**es eaux** fig the minute you tell her off, she turns on the waterworks; ~**es lignes** Rail main train routes; ~**es marées** spring tides; ~**es ondes** long wave (sg); ~**s espaces** open spaces; ~**s fauves** big cats; ~**s fonds** ocean depths; **Grands Lacs** Great Lakes; ~**s singes** great apes; ▸ **voyage**

ⓘ **Grande école** A prestigious third-level institution where admission is usually by competitive entrance examination or *concours*. Places are much sought after as they are widely considered to guarantee more promising career prospects than the standard university institutions. Many *grandes écoles* specialize in particular disciplines or fields of study, e.g. ENA, *Sciences Po*, etc.

grand-angle, pl **grands-angles** /grãtãgl, grãzãgl/, **grand-angulaire**, pl **grands-angulaires** /grãtãgylɛr, grãzãgylɛr/ adj wide-angle; **un (objectif)** ~ a wide-angle lens

grand-chose /grãʃoz/ pron indéf **pas** ~ not much, not a lot; **ça ne sert pas à** ~ it's not much use; **je n'ai pas vu** ~ **d'intéressant** I didn't see anything much of interest; **il n'y a plus** ~ **à faire** there isn't much left to do; **'tu t'es fait mal?'—'ce n'est pas** ~**'** 'have you hurt yourself?'—'it's nothing much'

grand-duc, pl **grands-ducs** /grãdyk/ ▸ p. 590 nm grand duke; **faire la tournée des grands-ducs** fig to have a night on the town

grand-duché, pl **grands-duchés** /grãdyʃe/ nm grand duchy

Grande-Bretagne /grãdbrətaɲ/ ▸ p. 303 nprf Great Britain

grand-duchesse, pl **grandes-duchesses** /grãdyʃɛs/ ▸ p. 590 nf grand duchess

grandement /grãdmã/ adv [intéresser] greatly; [aider] a great deal; [reconnaissant] extremely

grandeur /grãdœr/ nf [1] (taille) size; **être de la** ~ **de** to be the size of; ~ **nature** [reproduction] full-scale; [portrait] life-size; **de première** ~ lit, fig of the first magnitude; [2] (énormité) scale; [3] (élévation, gloire) greatness; **la** ~ **de leur sacrifice** their great sacrifice; **politique de** ~ politics of national greatness; **par** ~ **d'âme** out of generosity of spirit

(Idiome) **regarder qn du haut de sa** ~ to look down one's nose at sb

Grand-Guignol /grãgiɲɔl/ nm **le** ~ Grand Guignol; **c'est du** ~ fig it's farcical

grandiloquence /grãdilɔkãs/ nf pomposity, grandiloquence sout

grandiloquent, ~**e** /grãdilɔkã, ãt/ adj pompous, grandiloquent

grandiose /grãdjoz/ adj [site, édifice] grandiose; [réussite, fête] spectacular; [personnage] grand

grandir /grãdir/ [3]
Ⓐ vtr [loupe] to magnify; [talons] to make [sb] look taller; **sortir grandi d'une épreuve** to come out of an ordeal with increased stature
Ⓑ vi [1] (en taille) [plante, enfant] to grow; (en âge) [enfant] to grow up; ~ **de 20 cm** to grow 20 cms; ~ **dans l'estime de qn** fig to go up in sb's esteem; [2] (en importance) [entreprise] to expand; [rumeur, foule] to grow; **aller grandissant** liter [inquiétude] to become greater and greater; [bruit] to become louder and louder
Ⓒ se grandir vpr lit to make oneself (look) taller

grandissant, ~**e** /grãdisã, ãt/ adj growing

grand-maman, pl **grands-mamans** /grãmamã/ nf grandma

grand-mère, pl **grands-mères** /grãmɛr/ nf grandmother

grand-messe, pl ~**s** /grãmɛs/ nf [1] Relig High Mass; [2] fig ritual gathering

grand-oncle, pl **grands-oncles** /grãtɔ̃kl, grãzɔ̃kl/ nm great-uncle

grand-papa, pl **grands-papas** /grãpapa/ nm grandpa○, granddad○

grand-peine /grãpɛn/
Ⓐ nf avoir ~ à faire to have great difficulty doing
Ⓑ à grand-peine loc adv à ~ with great difficulty

grand-père, pl **grands-pères** /grãpɛr/ nm grandfather

grand-route, pl ~**s** /grãrut/ nf main road

grand-rue, pl ∿**s** /gʀɑ̃ʀy/ nf High Street GB, Main Street US

grands-parents /gʀɑ̃paʀɑ̃/ nmpl grandparents

grand-tante, pl **grand(s)-tantes** /gʀɑ̃tɑ̃t/ nf great-aunt

grand-voile, pl **grand(s)-voiles** /gʀɑ̃vwal/ nf mainsail

grange /gʀɑ̃ʒ/ nf barn

granit(e) /gʀanit/ nm granite

granité, ∿**e** /gʀanite/ adj grained

granitique /gʀanitik/ adj granite (épith), granitic

granule /gʀanyl/ nm granule

granulé /gʀanyle/ nm granule

granuleux, -euse /gʀanylø, øz/ adj [roche] granular; [papier] grained; [peau, cuir] grainy

graphie /gʀafi/ nf [1] (écriture) written form; [2] (orthographe) spelling

graphique /gʀafik/
A adj [1] Art, Math [forme, œuvre] graphic; [2] Ordinat [écran, tablette] graphic; [mode, mémoire, logiciel] graphics (épith)
B nm graph; ∿ **à bandes** or **en colonnes** bar chart ou graph

graphisme /gʀafism/ nm [1] (d'un artiste) style of drawing; [2] (écriture) handwriting; [3] (design) graphic design

graphiste /gʀafist/ ▸ p. 372 nmf graphic designer

graphite /gʀafit/ nm graphite

graphologie /gʀafɔlɔʒi/ nf graphology

graphologue /gʀafɔlɔɡ/ ▸ p. 372 nmf graphologist

grappe /gʀap/ nf (de fruits) bunch; (de fleurs) cluster

grappiller /gʀapije/ [1] vtr to pick up [fruits]; to glean [renseignements]; ∿ **quelques sous** to scrape together some money

grappin /gʀapɛ̃/ nm (crochet) grappling irons (pl)

(Idiome) **mettre le** ∿○ **sur qn** to get sb in one's clutches

gras, grasse /gʀɑ, gʀɑs/
A adj [1] gén [substance] fatty; [poisson] oily; [fromage] full fat; [papier, cheveux] greasy; ▸ **veau**; [2] (vulgaire) coarse; [3] (abondant) liter [salaire] fat; [récolte] bumper (épith); [4] (en typographie) [caractère] bold
B adv **cuisiner** ∿ to use a lot of fat in cooking; **manger** ∿ to eat fatty foods
C nm [1] (de viande) fat; [2] (corps huileux) grease; [3] (de bras, mollet) **le** ∿ the fleshy part (**de** of)

grassement /gʀɑsmɑ̃/ adv (généreusement) [payer] handsomely; [noter] generously; [nourrir] lavishly

grasseyement /gʀasɛjmɑ̃/ nm guttural pronunciation

grassouillet○, -ette /gʀasujɛ, ɛt/ adj chubby, plump

gratifiant, ∿**e** /gʀatifjɑ̃, ɑ̃t/ adj gratifying; **travail** ∿ rewarding job

gratification /gʀatifikasjɔ̃/ nf [1] (satisfaction) gratification; [2] (prime) bonus

gratifier /gʀatifje/ [2] vtr ∿ **qn de qch** to give sb sth; **se sentir gratifié** to feel gratified

gratin /gʀatɛ̃/ nm [1] Culin gratin (breadcrumbs and cheese); **macaroni au** ∿ macaroni cheese GB, macaroni and cheese US; ∿ **de pommes de terre** potatoes au gratin; [2] ○(élite) **le** ∿ the upper crust

gratiné, ∿**e** /gʀatine/ adj [1] Culin au gratin (après n); [2] ○fig [personne, style] weird; [problème] mind-bending○

gratiner /gʀatine/ [1] vtr (faire) ∿ **un plat** to brown a dish

gratis /gʀatis/
A adj inv free
B adv free GB, for free

gratitude /gʀatityd/ nf gratitude; **éprouver de la** ∿ **envers qn** to be grateful to sb

gratouiller○ /gʀatuje/ [1] vtr **j'ai la gorge qui me gratouille** I've got a tickle in my throat

grattage /gʀataʒ/ nm [1] (pour nettoyer) (de papier) scratching; (de métal, bois) scraping; [2] (pour enlever) (sur papier) scratching out; (sur métal, bois) scraping off; (de case sur un coupon) scratching

gratte-ciel /gʀatsjɛl/ nm inv skyscraper

gratte-cul○, pl ∿**s** /gʀatky/ nm rosehip

gratte-papier○ /gʀatpapje/ nm inv pen pusher○ GB, pencil pusher○ US

gratter /gʀate/ [1]
A vtr [1] (frotter) to scratch; (pour nettoyer) to scrape; (pour enlever) to scrape off [peinture, boue]; [2] (démanger) **ça me gratte partout** I'm itching all over; [3] ○(gagner) ∿ **quelques euros** to fiddle a few euros (**sur** from); ∿ **un quart d'heure sur son temps de travail** to work a quarter of an hour less than one is supposed to
B gratter de○ vtr ind ∿ **de la guitare** to strum the guitar
C vi ∿ **à la porte** to scratch at the door
D se gratter vpr to scratch

(Idiome) **il peut (toujours) se** ∿○ he can go and jump in a lake

grattoir /gʀatwaʀ/ nm [1] gén scraper; [2] (de boîte d'allumettes) striking strip

gratuit, ∿**e** /gʀatɥi, it/ adj [1] (non payant) free; **numéro d'appel** ∿ Freefone® number GB, toll-free number US; [2] (injustifié) [violence, remarque] gratuitous; [accusation] spurious; [exercice] pointless; [3] (désintéressé) [compliment] disinterested

gratuité /gʀatɥite/ nf [1] (caractère non payant) **la** ∿ **de l'enseignement** free education; [2] (caractère injustifié) unwarranted nature, gratuitous nature

gratuitement /gʀatɥitmɑ̃/ adv [1] (gratis) free GB, for free US; [2] (sans rétribution) [travailler, réparer] for nothing; [3] (sans motif) gratuitously

gravats /gʀava/ nmpl rubble ₵

grave /gʀav/
A adj [1] (préoccupant) [problème, blessure] serious; **deux blessés** ∿**s** two people seriously injured; [2] (digne) [air, visage] grave, solemn; [3] (de basse fréquence) [voix] deep; [note, registre] low; [son] low-pitched
B adv○ seriously
C graves nmpl (d'amplificateur) **les** ∿**s** the bass (sg)

graveleux, -euse /gʀavlø, øz/ adj (obscène) [histoire] smutty; [propos] indecent

gravement /gʀavmɑ̃/ adv [1] (avec solennité) gravely, solemnly; [2] (de façon importante) seriously

graver /gʀave/ [1] vtr [1] to engrave [inscription, motif] (**sur** on); **il a gravé son nom sur l'arbre** he carved his name on the tree; **l'épisode est gravé à jamais dans leur mémoire** the episode is engraved on their memory forever; [2] Ordinat to burn [CD]

graveur, -euse /gʀavœʀ, øz/ ▸ p. 372 nm,f engraver; ∿ **sur bois** wood engraver

(Composés) ∿ **de CD** CD burner; ∿ **de CD-R** CD-R burner

gravier /gʀavje/ nm du ∿ gravel ₵

gravillon /gʀavijɔ̃/ nm (petits cailloux) grit ₵; **un** ∿ a bit of grit

gravir /gʀaviʀ/ [3] vtr to climb up; ∿ **les échelons de la hiérarchie** to move up through the hierarchy

gravissime /gʀavisim/ adj extremely serious

gravitation /gʀavitasjɔ̃/ nf gravitation

(Composé) ∿ **universelle** Phys Newton's law of gravitation

gravité /gʀavite/ nf [1] (caractère préoccupant) seriousness; **une blessure sans** ∿ a minor injury; [2] (caractère solennel) solemnity; [3] Phys gravity

graviter /gʀavite/ [1] vi [astre] to orbit

gravure /gʀavyʀ/ nf [1] (procédé) **la** ∿ engraving; [2] (estampe) engraving; [3] (reproduction) print

(Composé) ∿ **à l'eau-forte** etching

gré /gʀe/ nm [1] (convenance) **être au** ∿ **de qn** [qualité, objet] to be to sb's liking; **contre le** ∿ **de qn** against sb's will; **de plein** ∿ willingly; **de mon/ton plein** ∿ of my/your own free will; **de bon** ∿ gladly; **de mauvais** ∿ reluctantly; **bon** ∿ **mal** ∿ willy-nilly; **de** ∿ **ou de force** one way or another; [2] (gratitude) fml **savoir** ∿ **à qn de qch** to be grateful to sb for sth; [3] (hasard) **j'ai flâné au** ∿ **de mon humeur** I strolled where the mood took me; **au** ∿ **des circonstances** as circumstances dictate

grec, grecque¹ /gʀɛk/
A ▸ p. 392 adj [1] [file, art] Greek; [2] [nez, profil] Grecian
B ▸ p. 336 nm Ling Greek; **le** ∿ **ancien/moderne** Ancient/Modern Greek

Grèce /gʀɛs/ ▸ p. 230 nprf Greece; ∿ **antique** Ancient Greece

g

gréco-romain, ~e, *mpl* ~s /gʀekoʀɔmɛ̃, ɛn/ *adj* Graeco-Roman GB, Greco-Roman US; **lutte** ~e Graeco-Roman

grecque² /gʀɛk/
A *adj* ▸ **grec**
B *nf* **1** Art Greek key; **2** Culin **à la** ~ à la grecque

gredin, ~e /gʀədɛ̃, in/ *nm,f* **1** hum rascal; **2** †(crapule) scoundrel†

gréer /gʀee/ [11] *vtr* to rig

greffe /gʀɛf/ *nf* **1** Méd (d'organe) transplant; (de peau) graft; **2** Agric (opération) grafting **ℂ**; (résultat) graft

greffer /gʀefe/ [1]
A *vtr* **1** Méd to transplant [*organe*]; to graft [*tissu*]; **on lui a greffé un rein** he's/she's had a kidney transplant; **2** Agric to graft
B **se greffer** *vpr* **se** ~ **sur qch** *fig* to come along on top of sth

greffier, -ière /gʀefje, ɛʀ/ ▸ p. 372 *nm,f* clerk of the court GB, court clerk US

greffon /gʀefɔ̃/ *nm* Agric graft, scion

grégaire /gʀegɛʀ/ *adj* **instinct** ~ herd instinct

grège /gʀɛʒ/ ▸ p. 140 *adj, nm* oatmeal

grégorien, -ienne /gʀegɔʀjɛ̃, ɛn/ *adj* Gregorian

grêle /gʀɛl/
A *adj* **1** (mince) [*silhouette*] skinny; [*jambes*] spindly; **2** (aigu) [*voix*] reedy; [*son*] thin
B *nf* **1** Météo hail **ℂ**; **orage de** ~ hailstorm; **il tombe de la** ~ it's hailing; **2** (volée) **recevoir une** ~ **de coups** to be showered with blows

grêlé, ~e /gʀɛle/ *adj* [*visage, peau*] pockmarked

grêler /gʀɛle/ [1] *v impers* to hail; **il grêle** it's hailing; **il a grêlé sur les vignes** the vines were hit by hail

grêlon /gʀɛlɔ̃/ *nm* hailstone

grelot /gʀəlo/ *nm* small bell

grelotter /gʀəlɔte/ [1] *vi* to shiver (**de** with); **on grelotte ici**○! we're freezing in here!

grenade /gʀənad/ *nf* **1** Mil (engin) grenade; **2** Bot, Culin pomegranate

Grenade /gʀənad/
A ▸ p. 621 *npr* (en Espagne) Granada
B ▸ p. 230 *nprf* (État) **la** ~ Grenada

grenadier /gʀənadje/ *nm* **1** Bot pomegranate tree; **2** Mil grenadier

grenadine /gʀənadin/ *nf* **(sirop de)** ~ grenadine

grenaille /gʀənaj/ *nf* (de plomb) lead shot

grenat /gʀəna/ ▸ p. 140
A *adj inv* dark red
B *nm* **1** (pierre) garnet; **2** (couleur) dark red

grenier /gʀənje/ *nm* **1** (de maison) attic, loft; (grange) loft; ~ **à foin** hay loft; ~ **à grain** granary; ~ **(à blé)** *fig* breadbasket

grenouille /gʀənuj/ *nf* frog
Composé ~ **de bénitier**○ holy Joe○

grenouillère /gʀənujɛʀ/ *nf* stretch suit GB, creepers (*pl*) US

grenu, ~e /gʀəny/ *adj* [*papier, peau*] grained

grès /gʀɛ/ *nm inv* **1** (roche) sandstone; **2** (céramique) stoneware; **3** (objet) piece of stoneware

grésil /gʀezil/ *nm* hail

grésillement /gʀezijmɑ̃/ *nm* **1** (à la radio) crackling; **2** (de beurre) sizzling

grésiller /gʀezije/ [1]
A *vi* **1** [*radio, téléphone*] to crackle; **2** [*beurre, huile*] to sizzle
B *v impers* to hail

grève /gʀɛv/ *nf* **1** (cessation du travail) strike; **être en** ~ to be on strike; **se mettre en** ~ to go on strike; **déclencher un mouvement de** ~ to take industrial action; **2** (rivage) shore
Composés ~ **de la faim** hunger strike; ~ **sur le tas** sit-down strike; ~ **tournante** staggered strike; ~ **du zèle** work-to-rule

grever /gʀəve/ [16] *vtr* to be a burden on [*pays, contribuable*]; to put a strain on [*budget*]; **l'entreprise est grevée de charges** the company has crippling overheads

gréviste /gʀevist/ *nmf* striker; **les mineurs** ~s the striking miners

Composé ~ **de la faim** hunger striker

gribiche /gʀibiʃ/ *adj* **sauce** ~ *mayonnaise made of a chopped hard-boiled egg, capers and herbs*

gribouillage○ /gʀibujaʒ/ *nm* scribble; **faire des** ~s to doodle

gribouiller○ /gʀibuje/ [1]
A *vtr* to scribble (**sur** on)
B *vi* to doodle (**sur** on)

gribouillis○ /gʀibuji/ *nm inv* = **gribouillage**

grief /gʀijɛf/ *nm* grievance; **je ne t'en fais pas** ~ I don't hold it against you

grièvement /gʀijɛvmɑ̃/ *adv* [*blessé*] seriously; [*brûlé*] badly; [*atteint*] severely; **être** ~ **blessé à la tête** to sustain serious head injuries

griffe /gʀif/ *nf* **1** Zool claw; **coup de** ~ scratch; **toutes** ~s **dehors** lit, fig ready to pounce; **tomber entre les** ~s **de qn** fig to fall into sb's clutches; **2** Comm (marque) label; **3** (empreinte) signature stamp; **4** (en bijouterie) claw

griffé, ~e /gʀife/ *adj* [*vêtements*] designer (*épith*)

griffer /gʀife/ [1]
A *vtr* (égratigner) to scratch
B **se griffer** *vpr* [*personne*] to scratch oneself

griffonnage /gʀifɔnaʒ/ *nm* scribble

griffonner /gʀifɔne/ [1] *vtr* **1** (écrire) to scrawl; **2** (dessiner) to sketch; ~ **un plan** to draw a rough map

griffure /gʀifyʀ/ *nf* scratch

grignotage /gʀiɲɔtaʒ/ *nm* **1** (fait de manger) nibbling **ℂ**; **2** (de libertés, capital) erosion (**de** of); (de terres) encroachment (**de** on)

grignoter /gʀiɲɔte/ [1]
A *vtr* **1** (manger un peu) to nibble; **tu n'as pas quelque chose à** ~? have you got anything to nibble? GB, do you have anything to snack on? US; **2** (empiéter) to encroach on [*terres*]; to conquer [*part de marché*]; **3** (entamer) to fritter away [*héritage*]; **4** (gagner) [*coureur*] to gain [*secondes*]
B *vi* to nibble

gri-gri, *pl* **gris-gris** /gʀigʀi/ *nm* lucky charm, talisman

gril /gʀil/ *nm* (de cuisinière) grill GB, broiler US; (plaque) grill pan GB, broiler US; **être sur le** ~ *fig* to be on tenterhooks

grillade /gʀijad/ *nf* grilled meat (**ℂ**)

grillage /gʀijaʒ/ *nm* (pour clôture) wire netting; (à gros trous hexagonaux) chicken wire; (à trous fins) wire mesh

grillagé, ~e /gʀijaʒe/ *adj* [*enclos*] fenced with wire (*après n*); [*porte*] covered with wire mesh (*après n*)

grillager /gʀijaʒe/ [13] *vtr* to fit a screen to [*fenêtre*]; to put chicken wire around [*poulailler*]

grille /gʀij/ *nf* **1** (clôture) railings (*pl*); (porte) (iron) gate; (d'évier, égout) drain; (de bouche d'aération, confessionnal) grille; (de four) shelf; (de poêle) grate; **2** (de mots croisés, d'horaires) grid; **3** Radio, TV programme^GB; **4** (système d'interprétation) model; **5** Admin scale

grillé, ~e /gʀije/
A *pp* ▸ **griller**
B *pp adj* **1** (cuit) [*viande, maïs*] grilled; [*pain*] toasted; [*amandes*] roasted; **2** (hors d'usage) burned out; **l'ampoule est** ~e the bulb has blown; **3** ○(révélé) [*espion*] exposed; **je suis** ~ my cover is blown

grille-pain /gʀijpɛ̃/ *nm inv* toaster

griller /gʀije/ [1]
A *vtr* **1** Culin to grill [*viande, maïs*]; to toast [*pain*]; to roast [*amandes*]; **2** (fumer) to smoke [*cigarette*]; **3** (mettre hors d'usage) to burn out [*appareil électrique*]; to blow [*ampoule*]; **4** ○(ne pas respecter) to jump○ [*feu rouge*]; to ignore [*priorité*]; **5** ○(révéler) **il s'est fait** ~ they blew his cover; **6** ○(dépasser) ~ **un adversaire** to manage to get ahead of one's opponent
B *vi* **1** Culin **faire** ~ to grill [*viande, maïs*]; to toast [*pain*]; to roast [*amandes*]; **2** [*ampoule*] to blow

grillon /gʀijɔ̃/ *nm* cricket

grimaçant, ~e /gʀimasɑ̃, ɑ̃t/ *adj* grimacing

grimace /gʀimas/ *nf* (expression) grimace; (comique) funny face; **faire des** ~s lit to make faces; fig to be fussy; **faire une** ~ **à qn** to make *ou* pull a face at sb; **faire la** ~ (devant un prix élevé) to wince; (de réticence) to make *ou* pull a face; ▸ **singe**

grimacer /gʀimase/ [12]
A *vtr* ~ **un sourire** to force a smile

B *vi* to grimace; **le soleil le faisait** ～ he screwed up his eyes in the sun

grimer: **se grimer** /gʀime/ [1] *vpr* to make oneself up (**en** as)

grimoire /gʀimwaʀ/ *nm* (écrit obscur) arcane text

grimpant, ～**e** /gʀɛ̃pɑ̃, ɑ̃t/ *adj* [plante] climbing

grimpée /gʀɛ̃pe/ *nf* climb

grimper¹ /gʀɛ̃pe/ [1]
A *vtr* (gravir) to climb
B *vi* **1** (escalader) ～ **aux arbres** to climb (up) trees; **dans un arbre** to climb up a tree; ～ **à la corde** to climb the rope; ～ **sur la scène/les genoux de qn** to climb up onto the stage/sb's knees; **grimpe sur mon dos** get on my back; **grimpe dans ton lit** get into bed; **2** ○(suivre une pente raide) [route] to be steep; **3** ○(augmenter) [température, prix] to climb (**de** by); **4** ○(progresser) ～ **de sept places** to go up seven places

grimper² /gʀɛ̃pe/ *nm* ～ **(à la corde)** rope-climbing **₵**

grimpeur, **-euse** /gʀɛ̃pœʀ, øz/ *nm,f* (alpiniste) rock climber

grinçant, ～**e** /gʀɛ̃sɑ̃, ɑ̃t/ *adj* **1** (bruyant) [serrure] creaking; [musique] grating; **2** (acerbe) [ton] scathing; [plaisanterie] caustic; [rire] nasty

grincement /gʀɛ̃smɑ̃/ *nm* **1** (type de bruit) (de porte) creaking **₵**; (de craie) squeaking **₵**; (de violon) screeching **₵**; **2** (bruit) (de porte) creak; (de craie) squeak; (de violon) screech

grincer /gʀɛ̃se/ [12] *vi* [porte] to creak; [violon] to screech; [craie] to squeak; ～ **des dents** lit to grind one's teeth; fig to gnash one's teeth; **faire** ～ **les dents à qn** [bruit] to set sb's teeth on edge

grincheux, **-euse** /gʀɛ̃ʃø, øz/
A *adj* grumpy GB, grouchy○
B *nm,f* (old) misery○ GB, grouch○

gringalet /gʀɛ̃galɛ/
A *adj m* puny
B *nm* runt

griotte /gʀijɔt/ *nf* Bot, Culin morello cherry

grippal, ～**e**, *mpl* **-aux** /gʀipal, o/ *adj* **affection** ～**e**, **état** ～ flu

grippe /gʀip/ ▸ p. 195 *nf* flu **₵**; **avoir la** ～ to have flu GB, to have the flu
(Composé) ～ **intestinale** gastric flu GB, intestinal flu US
(Idiome) **prendre qn/qch en** ～○ to take a sudden dislike to sb/sth

grippé, ～**e** /gʀipe/ *adj* Méd **être** ～ to have flu GB, to have the flu

gripper /gʀipe/ [1] *vtr* to make [sth] seize up [piston]; **le moteur est grippé** the engine has seized up

grippe-sou○, *pl* ～**s** /gʀipsu/ *nm* skinflint○ GB, tight-wad○ US

gris, ～**e** /gʀi, iz/ ▸ p. 140
A *adj* **1** (couleur) grey GB, gray US; ～ **bleu** blue-grey GB, blue-gray US; **2** (morne) [banlieue, rue] dreary; [existence] dull; **il fait** ～ it's a grey GB ou gray US day; **3** (ivre) tipsy
B *nm inv* **1** (couleur) grey GB, gray US; **2** (tabac) cheap tobacco
(Composés) ～ **anthracite** charcoal grey GB ou gray US; ～ **ardoise** slate grey GB ou gray US; ～ **perle** pearl grey GB ou gray US; ～ **souris** mid-grey GB, mid-gray US; ～ **tourterelle** dove grey GB ou gray US
(Idiomes) **faire** ～**e mine** to be none too pleased; **la nuit tous les chats sont** ～ Prov all cats are grey GB ou gray US in the dark

grisaille /gʀizaj/ *nf* **1** (ennui) **la** ～ **quotidienne** the daily grind; **2** (temps gris) greyness GB, grayness US

grisant, ～**e** /gʀizɑ̃, ɑ̃t/ *adj* **1** (exaltant) [vitesse, plaisir] exhilarating; [succès, danger] intoxicating; **2** (enivrant) [parfum] heady

grisâtre /gʀizɑtʀ/ ▸ p. 140 *adj* [couleur, ciel] greyish GB, grayish US; [linge] dirty white; [matin] dull

griser /gʀize/ [1]
A *vtr* [vitesse, plaisir] to exhilarate; [succès, danger, parfum] to intoxicate; **se laisser** ～ **par le pouvoir** to let power go to one's head
B se griser *vpr* **se** ～ **de** to get drunk on [vin, succès, pouvoir]

griserie /gʀizʀi/ *nf* (exaltation) exhilaration (**de** of)

grisonnant, ～**e** /gʀizɔnɑ̃, ɑ̃t/ *adj* greying GB, graying US

grisonner /gʀizɔne/ [1] *vi* to go grey GB, to gray US

Grisons /gʀizɔ̃/ ▸ p. 504 *nprmpl* Géog **le canton des** ～, **les** ～ the canton of Graubünden; **viande des** ～ dried beef (served in thin slices)

grisou /gʀizu/ *nm* firedamp; **coup de** ～ firedamp explosion

grive /gʀiv/ *nf* thrush
(Idiome) **faute de** ～**s on mange des merles** Prov half a loaf is better than no bread Prov

grivois, ～**e** /gʀivwa, az/ *adj* [chanson] bawdy; [plaisanterie] coarse; **être d'humeur** ～**e** to be in a saucy mood

grivoiserie /gʀivwazʀi/ *nf* (propos) suggestive remark

grizzli, **grizzly** /gʀizli/ *nm* grizzly bear

Groenland /gʀɔɛnlɑ̃d/ *nprm* Greenland

groenlandais, ～**e** /gʀɔɛnlɑ̃dɛ, ɛz/ *adj* Greenland (épith)

grogne○ /gʀɔɲ/ *nf* discontent

grognement /gʀɔɲəmɑ̃/ *nm* (de personne) grunt; (de chien, lion, d'ours) growl; (cri du cochon) grunt; **pousser des** ～**s de plaisir** to grunt with pleasure

grogner /gʀɔɲe/ [1]
A *vtr* to mutter [insultes]
B *vi* **1** [personne] lit to groan; fig to grumble; ～ **de douleur** to groan with pain; **2** Zool [cochon] to grunt; [ours, chien, lion] to growl

grognon /gʀɔɲɔ̃/ *nm* moaner GB, grouch○

groin /gʀwɛ̃/ *nm* snout

grommeler /gʀɔmle/ [19]
A *vtr* to mutter [insultes]; to murmur [compliment]
B *vi* **1** [personne] to grumble (**contre** about); **2** [sanglier] to snort

grommellement /gʀɔmɛlmɑ̃/ *nm* (de personne) groan; (de sanglier) snort

grondement /gʀɔ̃dmɑ̃/ *nm* (d'avalanche, canon) rumble; (de torrent, machine) roar; (de chien, d'ours) growl; (de foule) angry murmur

gronder /gʀɔ̃de/ [1]
A *vtr* (réprimander) to tell [sb] off
B *vi* **1** (tonner) [tonnerre] to rumble; [machine, vent] to roar; **2** (être menaçant) [révolte] to be brewing

groom /gʀum/ ▸ p. 372 *nm* (valet) bellboy GB, bellhop US

gros, **grosse** /gʀo, gʀos/
A *adj* **1** gén big, large; **2** (épais) thick; **3** (gras) fat; **4** (important) big, large; **5** (grave) [problème, erreur] serious, big; [déception, défaut] big, major; **6** (fort) [rhume] bad; [sanglots] loud; [soupir, voix] deep; [pluie, chute de neige] heavy; [orage] big; [temps, mer] rough; [buveur, fumeur] heavy; **avoir une grosse fièvre** to have a very high temperature; **avoir une grosse faim** to be very hungry; **pendant les grosses chaleurs** when the weather is at its hottest; ～ **malin**○! you silly fool○!; **7** (rude) [rire] coarse; [drap, laine] coarse
B *nm,f* fat man/woman
C *adv* **1** (en grands caractères) [écrire] big; **écrire moins** ～ to write smaller; **2** (beaucoup) [miser, perdre] lit a lot of money; fig a lot; **jouer** ～ lit, fig to play for high stakes; **il y a** ～ **à parier que...** it's a good bet that...
D *nm inv* **1** (plupart) **le** ～ **de** the majority ou bulk of [spectateurs, passagers]; the main body of [manifestants, expédition]; the bulk of [travail]; most of [hiver, saison]; most of [déficit]; **2** Comm wholesale trade; **de** ～ [magasin, prix] wholesale; **3** **la pêche au** ～ game fishing
E en gros *loc adv* **1** (dans les grandes lignes) roughly; **en** ～ **je suis d'accord** basically, I agree; **2** Comm [acheter] wholesale; **3** (en grands caractères) in big letters
(Composés) ～ **bétail** large livestock; ～ **bonnet**○ big shot○; ～ **lot** Jeux first prize, jackpot; **gagner** or **décrocher le** ～ **lot** lit, fig to hit the jackpot; ～ **mot** swearword; **dire des** ～ **mots** to swear; ～ **œuvre** shell (of a building); ～ **plan** Cin close-up; ～ **sel** cooking salt; ～ **titre** headline; **être en** ～ **titres dans les journaux** to hit the headlines; **grosse caisse** bass drum; **grosse légume**○ = ～ **bonnet**; **grosse tête**○ brain box○ GB, brain○

g

Idiomes avoir le cœur ~ to have a heavy heart; en avoir ~ sur le cœur *or* la patate○ to be very upset; ~ comme le poing as big as my fist; ~ comme une tête d'épingle no bigger than a pinhead; c'est un peu ~ comme histoire! that's a bit of a tall story!; il dit des bêtises grosses comme lui he says the most ridiculous things

groseille /gʀozɛj/
A ▸ p. 140 *adj inv* red
B *nf* redcurrant

Composés ~ blanche white currant; ~ à maquereau gooseberry

groseillier /gʀozeje/ *nm* redcurrant bush

Gros-Jean /gʀoʒɑ̃/ *nm* être ~ comme devant to be left feeling a real mug○

gros-porteur, *pl* ~**s** /gʀopɔʀtœʀ/ *nm* Aviat jumbo jet

grosse ▸ gros

grossesse /gʀosɛs/ *nf* pregnancy; ~ à risques risk pregnancy; robe de ~ maternity dress

Composé ~ nerveuse phantom pregnancy GB, false pregnancy

grosseur /gʀosœʀ/ *nf* **1** (volume) size; de la ~ d'une orange the size of an orange; **2** (épaisseur) thickness; **3** (bosse, kyste) lump

grossier, -ière /gʀosje, ɛʀ/ *adj* **1** (impoli) [*personne, geste*] rude; [*langage*] bad; **2** (sans finesse) [*esprit, rire, traits*] coarse; [*formes*] crude; [*médiocre*] [*copie, imitation*] crude; [*étoffe*] coarse; [*mobilier*] basic; **4** (rudimentaire) [*nettoyage*] cursory; [*ébauche, idée, estimation*] rough; [*travail*] crude; **5** (flagrant) [*ignorance*] crass; [*erreur*] glaring; [*procédé*] crude

grossièrement /gʀosjɛʀmɑ̃/ *adv* **1** (de façon sommaire) roughly; **2** (sans soin particulier) crudely; **3** (avec impolitesse) rudely; **4** (lourdement) se tromper ~ to be utterly mistaken

grossièreté /gʀosjɛʀte/ *nf* **1** (inconvenance) rudeness; ils sont d'une ~! they're so rude!; **2** (mot grossier) rude word GB, dirty word; dire des ~s to use bad language GB, to talk dirty

grossir /gʀosiʀ/ [3]
A *vtr* **1** (agrandir) to enlarge [*image*]; **2** (faire augmenter) to increase [*effectifs*]; to boost [*nombre, profits*]; ~ les rangs *or* la foule to swell the ranks; **3** (exagérer) to exaggerate [*incident*]; **4** (faire paraître plus gros) to make [sb] look fat [*personne*]
B *vi* **1** (prendre du poids) to put on weight; ~ de cinq kilos to put on five kilos; ça fait ~ it's fattening; **2** (devenir plus grand) gén to grow; [*fleuve*] to swell; **3** (s'intensifier) [*tempête*] to get worse; [*rumeur*] to grow

grossissant, ~e /gʀosisɑ̃, ɑ̃t/ *adj* [*verre*] magnifying; **2** [*flot*] swelling

grossissement /gʀosismɑ̃/ *nm* **1** (fait de grossir) enlargement; un ~ anormal du foie an abnormally enlarged liver; **2** (exagération) exaggeration; le ~ des faits par la presse distortion of the facts in the press; **3** (en optique) magnification

grossiste /gʀosist/ ▸ p. 372 *nmf* wholesaler

grosso modo /gʀosomodo/ *adv* roughly; ~, je suis satisfaite broadly speaking I am satisfied

grotesque /gʀɔtɛsk/
A *adj* **1** (risible) [*personne, coiffure*] ridiculous; [*idée, histoire, remarque*] ridiculous, preposterous; **2** Art, Littérat grotesque
B *nm* **1** (caractère risible) ridiculous aspect; être d'un ~ absolu [*histoire, situation*] to be utterly ridiculous; [*personne*] to be absolutely ludicrous; **2** Art, Littérat le ~ the grotesque

grotte /gʀɔt/ *nf* **1** Géog cave; **2** Archit grotto

grouillement /gʀujmɑ̃/ *nm* swarming ¢

grouiller /gʀuje/ [1]
A *vi* [*vers, insectes*] to swarm about; [*gens*] to mill about; ~ de to be swarming with; ~ d'asticots to be crawling with maggots
B se grouiller○ *vpr* to get a move on○

groupage /gʀupaʒ/ *nm* (pour transporter) bulking; envoi en ~ collective shipment

groupe /gʀup/ *nm* **1** (ensemble de personnes) group (de of); en ~ in a group; par ~s de deux in pairs, in twos; former un ~ autour de qn [*badauds*] to form a group around sb;

2 (ensemble d'objets) group; (plus petit) cluster (de of); un ~ d'arbres a cluster *ou* clump of trees; **3** Fin, Ind, Presse group

Composés ~ d'autodéfense vigilante group, vigilance committee; ~ de combat combat unit; ~ électrogène (electricity) generator; ~ de presse newspaper group; ~ de pression pressure group; ~ sanguin blood group; ~ scolaire school; ~ des Huit, G8 group of Eight, G8 countries (*pl*); ~ de travail working party

groupement /gʀupmɑ̃/ *nm* **1** (association) association, group; un ~ politique a political grouping; **2** (classification) grouping (de of)

grouper /gʀupe/ [1]
A *vtr* to put [sth] together [*factures, chèques*]; ~ ses achats (dans un même magasin) to make all one's purchases in the same store; (à plusieurs acheteurs) to make a group purchase; sauter en groupant les genoux to jump with one's knees held against one's chest
B se grouper *vpr* **1** (physiquement) [*personnes*] to gather (autour de around); groupez-vous par classes get into your class groups; se ~ par trois to form groups of three; **2** (s'organiser) to form a group (autour de around); restez groupés keep together; ne restez pas groupés scatter; avancer groupés to march in a group

groupuscule /gʀupyskyl/ *nm* (very) small group

gruau *pl* ~**x** /gʀyo/ *nm* **1** Culin (bouillie) gruel; **2** (fleur de froment) fine wheat flour

grue /gʀy/ *nf* **1** Tech crane; **2** Zool crane

Idiome faire le pied de ~○ to hang around

gruger○ /gʀyʒe/ [13] *vtr* to dupe; se faire ~ to be duped

grumeau *pl* ~**x** /gʀymo/ *nm* lump; faire des ~**x** [*sauce*] to go lumpy

grumeleux, -euse /gʀymlø, øz/ *adj* [*sauce, pâte*] lumpy

grutier, -ière /gʀytje, ɛʀ/ ▸ p. 372 *nm,f* crane operator

Guadeloupe /gwadlup/ ▸ p. 303, p. 504 *nprf* la ~ Guadeloupe

guadeloupéen, -éenne /gwadlupeɛ̃, ɛn/ *adj* Guadeloupian

guatémaltèque /gwatemaltɛk/ ▸ p. 392 *adj* Guatemalan

gué /ge/ *nm* ford; passer un ruisseau à ~ to ford a stream

Idiome on ne change pas de chevaux au milieu du ~ Prov you can't swap horses in midstream

guenille /gənij/ *nf* rag; en ~s in rags

guenon /gənɔ̃/ *nf* female monkey

guépard /gepaʀ/ *nm* cheetah

guêpe /gɛp/ *nf* wasp

Idiome pas folle la ~○! I'm/she's etc not just a pretty face○!

guêpier /gepje/ *nm* **1** (nid de guêpes) wasps' nest; **2** (situation difficile) tight corner; dans quel ~ es-tu allé te fourrer○? what kind of mess have you got GB *ou* gotten US yourself into?

guêpière /gepjɛʀ/ *nf* basque, bodyshaper with suspenders GB *ou* garters US

guère /gɛʀ/ *adv* **1** (modifiant un adjectif) hardly; les résultats n'étaient ~ meilleurs the results were hardly any better; les étudiants ne sont ~ préparés the students aren't really prepared; **2** (modifiant un adverbe) ça n'a ~ été mieux it was hardly any better; l'appareil ne coûte ~ plus de 30 euros the appliance doesn't cost much more than 30 euros; **3** (avec un verbe) hardly; il n'a ~ mangé he hardly ate anything; je n'ai ~ eu de mal à les convaincre I didn't have much trouble convincing them; il n'apprécie ~ ta décontraction he doesn't much care for your casual attitude; il n'avait ~ le choix he didn't really have a choice, he had little choice; ils ne se font ~ d'illusions sur leur avenir they don't hold out much hope for their future; il ne fait ~ de doute que there is little doubt that

guéridon /geʀidɔ̃/ *nm* pedestal table

guérilla /geʀija/ *nf* (forme de combat) guerilla warfare

guérillero /geʀijeʀo/ *nm* guerilla

guérir /geʀiʀ/ [3]
A *vtr* **1** Méd to cure [*personne, maladie*]; to heal [*blessure*]; cela

soulage mais ne guérit pas it brings relief but it isn't a cure; **2**▸ fig ~ **qn de** to cure sb of

B vi Méd [*personne, animal*] to recover, to get well; [*blessure*] to heal; [*entorse, rhume*] to get better; ~ **de qch** to recover from sth

C **se guérir** vpr fig **se** ~ **de** to overcome [*timidité*]

guérison /geʀizɔ̃/ nf (de malade, maladie) recovery; (de blessure) healing

guérissable /geʀisabl/ adj [*malade, maladie*] curable

guérisseur, -euse /geʀisœʀ, øz/ ▸ p. 372 nm,f healer

guérite /geʀit/ nf (de sentinelle) sentry box; (de péage) booth

guerre /gɛʀ/ nf (conflit) war; (technique) warfare; **entrer en** ~ to go to war (**contre** against); **être en** ~ to be at war (**avec** with); **faire la** ~ to wage war (**à** against, on); **mon grand-père a fait la** ~ my grandfather was ou fought in the war; **les pays en** ~ the warring nations; **c'est la** ~ **ouverte** it's open warfare; **les candidats se livrent une** ~ **sans merci** it's out-and-out war between the candidates; **elle lui fait la** ~ she's fighting a running battle with him; **les enfants jouent à la** ~ the children are playing at GB ou playing soldiers; ▸ **grand**

Composés ~ **chimique** (conflit) chemical war; (technique) chemical warfare; ~ **éclair** blitzkrieg, lightning war; ~ **d'Espagne** Spanish Civil War; ~ **des étoiles** Star Wars; ~ **froide** Cold War; ~ **mondiale** world war; **Première/Deuxième** or **Seconde Guerre mondiale** World War I/II, First/Second World War; ~ **des nerfs** war of nerves; ~ **psychologique** psychological warfare; ~ **de 14** 1914–18 war; ~ **de Sécession** American Civil War; ~ **de Troie** Trojan War; ~ **d'usure** war of attrition

Idiomes **à la** ~ **comme à la** ~ in time of hardship you have to make the best of things; **c'est de bonne** ~ it's only fair, it's fair enough; **être sur le pied de** ~ to be on a war footing; **de** ~ **lasse, elle renonça à la convaincre** realizing that she was fighting a losing battle, she gave up trying to convince him

guerrier, -ière /geʀje, ɛʀ/
A adj [*peuple*] warlike; [*exploit*] war (épith)
B nm,f warrior

guerroyer /geʀwaje/ [23] vi to wage war (**contre** against, on)

guet /gɛ/ nm **1**▸ gén lookout; **faire le** ~ to be on the lookout; **2**▸ Mil watch

guet-apens, pl **guets-apens** /gɛtapɑ̃/ nm lit ambush; fig trap; **tomber dans un** ~ lit to be caught in an ambush; fig to fall into a trap

guêtre /gɛtʀ/ nf (de laine) leggings (pl); (de cuir, tissu) gaiter

guetter /gete/ [1] vtr **1**▸ (surveiller) to watch [*proie, malfaiteur, réaction*]; to watch out for [*signe*]; to look out for [*facteur, ami*]; **je guettais le moindre bruit** I was alert for the slightest noise; ~ **l'arrivée de l'ennemi** to lie in wait for the enemy; **2**▸ (menacer) [*déclin, danger*] to threaten; **la folie le guette** he is on the brink of madness; **la fatigue guette les conducteurs** tiredness is a threat for drivers

guetteur, -euse /gɛtœʀ, øz/
A nm,f lookout
B nm Hist watchman

gueule /gœl/ nf **1**▸ ○(visage) face; **casser la** ~ **à qn** to beat sb up; **c'est bien fait pour leur** ~ (it) serves them right; **il en fait une** ~! (mélancolique) he looks really down; (furieux) he looks absolutely livid!; **il a la** ~ **de l'emploi** he really looks the part; **ta** ~! (bouche humaine) mouth; (ferme) **ta** ~! shut your face○ GB ou mouth○!; **être** or **avoir une grande** ~ to be a bigmouth○; ▸ **fin¹**; **3**▸ ○(aspect) look; **le gâteau a une drôle de** ~ the cake looks weird; **4**▸ Zool (bouche d'animal) mouth; ▸ **loup**; **5**▸ (de tunnel, four, canon) mouth

Composé ~ **de bois** hangover

Idiomes **faire** or **tirer la** ~○ to be sulking; **se bourrer** or **soûler la** ~○ to get blind drunk

gueule-de-loup, pl **gueules-de-loup** /gœldəlu/ nf snapdragon

gueuler○ /gœle/ [1]
A vtr (crier) to yell [*insultes*]; to bawl out [*réponse*]; (chanter) to bellow out
B vi [*personne*] (crier) to yell, to bawl; (chanter) to bawl, to howl; (protester) to kick up a real fuss; ~ **de douleur** to scream

with pain; **après qn** to have a go at sb○; ~ **contre qch** to moan about sth

Idiome ~ **comme un âne** or **putois** or **perdu** to scream blue GB ou bloody US murder○

gueux†, gueuse /gø, gøz/ nm,f (pauvre) beggar; (personne vile) rogue

Idiome **courir la gueuse**○ to go looking for a bit of skirt○

gui /gi/ nm **1**▸ Bot mistletoe; **2**▸ Naut boom

guichet /giʃɛ/ nm **1**▸ (comptoir vitré) window; (comptoir ouvert) (de banque) counter; (de stade, musée, gare) ticket office; (de théâtre, cinéma) box office, ticket office; **la pièce se jouera à** ~**s fermés** the play is sold out; **2**▸ (dans mur, porte) grille

Composé ~ **automatique** automatic teller machine, ATM

guichetier, -ière /giʃtje, ɛʀ/ ▸ p. 372 nm,f ticket clerk

guidage /gidaʒ/ nm **1**▸ Aviat guidance; **2**▸ Tech guide

guide /gid/ nm **1**▸ (accompagnateur) guide; ~ **de haute montagne** mountain guide; **2**▸ (ouvrage) guide; ~ **pratique** practical guide

guide-interprète, pl **guides-interprètes** /gidɛtɛʀpʀɛt, gidzɛtɛʀpʀɛt/ ▸ p. 372 nm,f tour guide and interpreter

guider /gide/ [1]
A vtr **1**▸ (montrer le chemin) to show [sb] the way (**vers** to); ~ **jusque** to take [sb] to, to lead [sb] to; ~ **à travers** to take [sb] around; **il m'a guidé dans les couloirs** he showed me the way through the corridors; **2**▸ (orienter) [étoile] to guide; [*flair, trace*] to lead; [*panneau indicateur*] to guide, to direct; **le chien guide l'aveugle** the dog guides the blind man; **3**▸ (diriger) to guide [*cheval, avion*]; **4**▸ (conseiller) to guide
B **se guider** vpr **se** ~ **sur qch** to set one's course by sth

guidon /gidɔ̃/ nm (de bicyclette, moto) handlebars (pl)

guigne○ /giɲ/ nf bad luck; **avoir la** ~ to be dogged by bad luck

Idiome **se soucier** or **se moquer de qch/qn comme d'une** ~ not to give a fig○ about sth/sb

guignol /giɲɔl/ nm **1**▸ (spectacle de marionnettes) puppet show, ≈ Punch and Judy show; **c'est du** ~ fig it's farcical, it's a complete farce; **2**▸ (personne peu sérieuse) pej clown, joker; **faire le** ~ to clown around

guilde /gild/ nf guild

Guillaume /gijom/ npr ~ **le Conquérant** William the Conqueror; ~ **d'Orange** William of Orange; ~ **Tell** William Tell

guillemets /gijmɛ/ nmpl inverted commas GB, quotation marks; **entre** ~ in inverted commas

guilleret, -ette /gijʀɛ, ɛt/ adj [*personne, air*] perky, jaunty

guillotine /gijɔtin/ nf guillotine

guimauve /gimov/ nf Bot (marsh) mallow; Culin marshmallow

guimbarde /gɛ̃baʀd/ nf **1**▸ ○(vieille voiture) old banger GB ou crate○; **2**▸ Mus Jew's harp

guindé, ~e /gɛ̃de/ adj formal

guingois: de guingois /degɛ̃gwa/ loc adv **être de** ~ [*meuble, maison*] to be lopsided; **aller de** ~ to go askew

guinguette /gɛ̃gɛt/ nf: small restaurant with music and dancing

guirlande /giʀlɑ̃d/ nf (de fleurs) garland; (de Noël) tinsel; (de papier) paper chain; (en plein air) bunting **C**

Composé ~ **électrique** set ou string of fairy lights

guise /giz/ nf **1**▸ **'à votre** ~' 'just as you like ou please'; **n'en faire qu'à sa** ~ to do exactly as one pleases ou likes; **2**▸ **en** ~ **de** by way of

guitare /gitaʀ/ ▸ p. 389 nf guitar

guitariste /gitaʀist/ ▸ p. 372 nm,f guitarist

gustatif, -ive /gystatif, iv/ adj [*organe*] taste

guttural, ~e, mpl **-aux** /gytyʀal, o/ adj guttural

Guyana /gɥijana/ ▸ p. 230 nprf Guyana; **République de** ~ Republic of Guyana

Guyane /gɥijan/ ▸ p. 504 nprf Guyana; ~ **française** French Guyana; ~ **hollandaise** Hist Dutch Guiana

gym○ /ʒim/ ▸ p. 327 *nf* Scol physical education, PE, phys ed○ US; Sport gymnastics (+ *v sg*)

gymkhana /ʒimkana/ *nm* ①⟩ (en voiture, à moto) rally; ②⟩ (à pied) lit obstacle race; fig obstacle course

gymnase /ʒimnɑz/ *nm* gymnasium

gymnaste /ʒimnast/ *nmf* gymnast

gymnastique /ʒimnastik/ ▸ p. 327 *nf* (discipline) gymnastics (+ *v sg*); (exercices) exercises (*pl*); **je fais 20 minutes de ~ tous les matins** I exercise for 20 minutes every morning; **~ de l'esprit** fig mental exercise

⟨Composés⟩ **~ aquatique** aquagym; **~ corrective** ≈ physiotherapy exercises (*pl*); **~ d'entretien** keep fit; **~ rythmique et sportive** eurythmics (+ *v sg*); **~ suédoise** callisthenics (+ *v sg*)

gymnique /ʒimnik/ *adj* [exercice] gymnastic

gynécologie /ʒinekɔlɔʒi/ *nf* gynaecology

gynécologue /ʒinekɔlɔg/ ▸ p. 372 *nmf* gynaecologist

gyrophare /ʒiʀɔfaʀ/ *nm* flashing light, emergency rotating light

gyroscope /ʒiʀɔskɔp/ *nm* gyroscope

g

h, H /aʃ/ *nm inv* [1] (lettre) h, H; **h aspiré** aspirate, aspirated h; **h muet** mute h, silent h; [2] (*written abbr* = **heure**) **9 h 10** 9.10

ha /'a/ (*written abbr* = **hectare**) ha

habile /abil/ *adj* [1] (adroit) [*bricoleur, policier, écrivain*] clever; [*avocat, diplomate*] skilful^{GB}; [*politicien*] smart; ~ **à** good at; **être** ~ **de ses mains** *or* **doigts** to be clever with one's hands; [2] (fait avec adresse) clever

habilement /abilmã/ *adv* (adroitement) skilfully^{GB}; (intelligemment) cleverly

habileté /abilte/ *nf* (de personne) skill; (de discours, manœuvre) skilfulness^{GB}

habiliter /abilite/ [1] *vtr* to authorize (**à faire** to do)

habillé, ~**e** /abije/ *adj* [*robe*] smart; [*soirée*] formal

habillement /abijmã/ *nm* [1] (activité) clothing; [2] (vêtements) clothing

habiller /abije/ [1]
A *vtr* [1] (mettre des vêtements à) to dress [*personne*] (**de** in); [2] (déguiser) to dress [sb] up (**en** as); [3] (fournir en vêtements) to clothe [*enfant*]; to provide [sb] with clothing [*acteur, personnel*]; [4] (faire des vêtements pour) to clothe [*enfant, famille*]; to dress [*acteur, personnel*]; [5] (convenir) [*vêtements*] to suit [*personne*]; [6] (revêtir) to cover [*mur, siège*] (**de** with); to encase [*appareil, tuyauterie*]
B **s'habiller** *vpr* [1] (mettre ses vêtements) to get dressed; [2] (choisir son style) to dress; **s'**~ **long/court** to wear long/short clothes; [3] (se vêtir élégamment) to dress up; [4] (se fournir en vêtements) to get one's clothes; **s'**~ **sur mesure** to have one's clothes made to measure; [5] (se travestir) to dress up (**en** as)

habilleur, -euse /abijœʀ, øz/ ▸ p. 372 *nm,f* dresser

habit /abi/
A *nm* [1] (de marié) (queue-de-pie) tails (*pl*), morning coat; (tenue) morning dress; [2] (déguisement) (de professionnel) outfit; (de personnage) costume; [3] Relig (de moine, nonne) habit; **prendre l'**~ to take the cloth; **quitter l'**~ to leave the priesthood
B **habits** *nmpl* clothes
(Composés) ~ **ecclésiastique** Relig clerical dress; ~**s du dimanche** Sunday best

habitable /abitabl/ *adj* [1] (pouvant être habité) habitable; **logement** ~ **immédiatement** accommodation ready to move into; [2] (servant à l'habitation) **surface** *or* **espace** ~ living space

habitacle /abitakl/ *nm* [1] Aviat cockpit; Astronaut cabin; [2] Aut interior; [3] Naut binnacle

habitant, ~**e** /abitã, ãt/ *nm,f* [1] (personne) (de ville, pays, région) inhabitant; (de quartier, d'immeuble) resident; **loger chez l'**~ Tourisme to stay as a paying guest; [2] liter (personne) dweller; (animal) beast

habitat /abita/ *nm* [1] (milieu) habitat; [2] (mode de peuplement) settlement; [3] (mode de logement) housing

habitation /abitasjõ/ *nf* [1] (construction) house, dwelling; [2] (résidence) home; [3] (fait d'habiter) living; **immeuble d'**~ block of flats GB, apartment building US
(Composés) ~ **à loyer modéré, HLM** (appartement) ≈ council flat GB, low-rent apartment US; (immeuble) ≈ block of council flats GB, low-rent apartment building US; (maison) ≈ council house GB, low rent house US

ⓘ **Habitation à loyer modéré** A type of public housing, usually an apartment in an estate, available for a relatively low rent with an option to buy as long as the property is retained for a minimum of five ▸▸▸

years. *HLM* are built and managed either by public bodies, by the private sector supported by state loans, or by cooperatives. About 13 million people live in *HLM*.

habité, ~**e** /abite/ *adj* [1] [*territoire*] inhabited; [2] Astronaut manned

habiter /abite/ [1]
A *vtr* [1] (résider à) to live in; **il habite une maison/Paris/la campagne** he lives in a house/in Paris/in the country; [2] fml [*sentiment*] to dwell in [*personne, cœur*]
B *vi* [1] (résider) ~ **à** *or* **en** to live in; ~ **à l'étranger** to live abroad; ~ **au 6 rue de la Paix** to live at 6 rue de la Paix; ~ **chez ses parents** to live with one's parents; [2] fig **être habité par** to be filled with

habitude /abityd/
A *nf* [1] (manière d'agir) habit; **faire qch par** ~ to do sth out of habit; **ce n'est pas dans mes** ~**s d'être en retard** it's not like me to be late; **avoir ses (petites)** ~**s** (routine) to have got GB *ou* gotten US into a routine; (manière de faire) to have one's own way of doing things; **ne perdons pas les bonnes** ~**s** let's stick to what we usually do; **comme à leur** ~, **suivant leur** ~ as they usually do; [2] (fait d'être accoutumé) habit; **avoir l'**~ **de** to be used to; [3] (coutume) (de pays, région) custom; (de personnes) habit
B **d'habitude** *loc adv* usually

habitué, ~**e** /abitye/ *nm,f* (de café) regular (customer); (de stade, musée) regular; (ami) regular (visitor)

habituel, -elle /abityɛl/ *adj* usual

habituellement /abityɛlmã/ *adv* usually, generally

habituer /abitye/ [1]
A *vtr* [1] (accoutumer) to get [sb/sth] used (**à** to; **à faire** to doing); [2] (former) to teach (**à faire** to do)
B **s'habituer** *vpr* to get used *ou* accustomed (**à** to)

hâbleur, -euse /'ablœʀ, øz/
A *adj* boastful
B *nm,f* boaster; **c'est un** ~ he's always boasting

hache /'aʃ/ *nf* axe GB, ax US; **visage taillé à la** ~ angular face
(Composés) ~ **d'abordage** poleaxe; ~ **de guerre** gén battle-axe GB *ou* ax US; (d'indien) tomahawk
(Idiomes) **enterrer la** ~ **de guerre** to bury the hatchet; **déterrer la** ~ **de guerre** to go on the warpath

haché, ~**e** /'aʃe/ *adj* [1] Culin **bifteck** ~ hamburger; **viande** ~**e** mince; [2] (saccadé) [*style, phrase, discours*] disjointed

hacher /'aʃe/ [1] *vtr* [1] (couper) to mince [*viande*]; to chop [*oignon, persil*]; ~ **au couteau** to chop [sth] up with a knife; [2] (broyer) to crush [*récolte, feuille*]; to cut [sb/sth] to pieces [*personne, chair*]

hachette /'aʃɛt/ *nf* hatchet

hachis /'aʃi/ *nm inv* Culin ~ **de viande** minced meat; ~ **d'échalotes** chopped shallots
(Composé) ~ **Parmentier** ≈ shepherd's pie

hachisch /'aʃiʃ/ *nm* hashish

hachoir /'aʃwaʀ/ *nm* [1] (appareil) mincer; ~ **électrique** electric mincer; [2] (couteau) (food) chopper, mincing knife; [3] (planche) chopping board

hachurer /'aʃyʀe/ [1] *vtr* Art to hatch

haddock /'adɔk/ *nm* smoked haddock

hagard, ~**e** /'agaʀ, aʀd/ *adj* [*air, personne*] dazed; [*yeux*] wild

haie /'ɛ/ nf **1** Bot hedge; **une ~ de cyprès** a cypress hedge; **2** Sport (en athlétisme) hurdle; (en hippisme) fence; **course de ~s** (en athlétisme) hurdle race, hurdles; (en hippisme) steeple chase; **3** (rangée) (de personnes) line; (d'objets) row

(Idiome) **former** or **faire une ~ d'honneur** to form a guard of honour^{GB}

haïku /'ajku/ nm haiku

haillon /'ajɔ̃/ nm rag; **vêtu de ~s** dressed in rags

haine /'ɛn/ nf hatred; **s'attirer la ~ de qn** to earn oneself sb's hatred

haineux, -euse /'ɛnø, øz/ adj full of hatred (après n)

haïr /'aiʀ/ [25]
A vtr to hate [personne, chose] (**de faire** for doing); **~ que** to hate it when
B **se haïr** vpr **1** [ennemis] to hate each other; **2** [soi-même] to hate onself

haïssable /'aisabl/ adj detestable, hateful

haïtien, -ienne /aisjɛ̃, ɛn/ ▸ p. 392, p. 336
A adj Haitian
B nm Ling Haitian

halage /'alaʒ/ nm towing; **chemin de ~** towpath

hâle /'al/ nm (sun)tan

hâlé, ~e /'ale/ adj (par le soleil) suntanned; (par l'air, une lampe) tanned

haleine /alɛn/ nf **1** (air expiré) breath; **2** (respiration) breathing; **être hors d'~** to be out of breath; **à perdre ~** until one is out of breath; **reprendre ~** lit to get one's breath back; fig to have a rest; **tenir qn en ~** (fasciné) to hold sb spellbound; (dans l'incertitude) to keep sb in suspense; **un travail de longue ~** a long-drawn-out job

haler /'ale/ [1] vtr to tow [bateau]; to haul in [chaîne]

haletant, ~e /'altɑ̃, ɑ̃t/ adj [personne] panting, breathless; [animal] panting; [voix] breathless

haleter /'alte/ [18] vi **1** to pant (**de** with); **2** [machine] to puff; [poitrine] to heave

hall /'ol/ nm entrance hall GB, lobby US; **~ (de gare)** lit concourse; **on dirait un ~ de gare** pej it looks like the inside of a railway station

(Composés) **~ d'accueil** reception; **~ d'exposition** exhibition hall

hallali /'alali/ nm (en chasse à courre) mort

halle /'al/
A nf market hall
B **halles** nfpl covered market

(Composés) **~ aux grains** corn exchange; **~ à marchandises** goods depot

hallebarde /'aləbaʀd/ nf halberd

(Idiome) **il pleut des ~s** it's raining cats and dogs

hallucinant^O, ~e /alysinɑ̃, ɑ̃t/ adj astounding

hallucination /alysinasjɔ̃/ nf hallucination; **avoir des ~s** lit to hallucinate; fig to be seeing things

halluciné, ~e /alysine/
A adj **1** (hagard) [regard] wild; **2** [malade] suffering from hallucinations (après n)
B nm,f **1** ^O(illuminé) crank; **2** person suffering from hallucinations

halluciner^O /al(l)ysine/ vi **une patinoire dans le désert, ça m'a vraiment fait ~** an ice-rink in the desert? that really blew my mind

hallucinogène /alysinoʒɛn/ adj hallucinogenic

halo /'alo/ nm **1** (de phares, lampe) **~ (de lumière)** circle of light; **entouré d'un ~ de mystère** shrouded in mystery; **2** (d'astre) halo

halogène /alɔʒɛn/ adj **1** Chimie halogenous; **2** [lampe, éclairage] halogen (épith)

halte /'alt/
A nf **1** (temps d'arrêt) stop; **faire une ~** to stop somewhere; **2** (lieu d'arrêt) stop
B excl gén stop!; Mil halt!; **~ à la vivisection!** stop vivisection!

halte-garderie, pl **haltes-garderies** /'altəgaʀdəʀi/ nf ≈ playgroup

haltère /alterʀ/ nm (pour une main) dumbbell; (à deux mains) barbell; **faire des ~s** to do weightlifting

haltérophilie /alterofili/ ▸ p. 327 nf weightlifting

hamac /'amak/ nm hammock

hameau, pl **~x** /'amo/ nm hamlet

hameçon /amsɔ̃/ nm hook

(Idiome) **mordre à l'~** to take the bait

hampe /'ɑ̃p/ nf **1** (de drapeau, parasol) pole; (d'arme) shaft; **2** Bot scape; **3** (de lettre) vertical stroke; **4** (de bœuf) flank

hanche /'ɑ̃ʃ/ ▸ p. 136, p. 575 nf **1** Anat hip; **prothèse de la ~** hip replacement; **2** (de cheval) haunch

handball /'ɑ̃dbal, 'ɑ̃dbol/ ▸ p. 327 nm handball

handicap /'ɑ̃dikap/ nm lit, fig handicap; (course) handicap (race)

handicapant, ~e /'ɑ̃dikapɑ̃, ɑ̃t/ adj disabling

handicapé, ~e /'ɑ̃dikape/
A adj **1** (infirme) disabled, handicapped; **à vie** permanently disabled; **2** (désavantagé) **être ~** to be at a disadvantage
B nm,f disabled person; **~ moteur** person with motor disability

handicaper /'ɑ̃dikape/ [1] vtr to handicap

handisport /'ɑ̃dispoʀ/ adj wheelchair (épith)

hangar /'ɑ̃gaʀ/ nm gén (large) shed; (entrepôt) warehouse

(Composés) **~ d'aviation** hangar; **~ à bateaux** boathouse

hanneton /'antɔ̃/ nm cockchafer GB, June bug US; ▸ piquer

hanter /'ɑ̃te/ [1] vtr (tous contextes) to haunt; **lieu hanté** haunted place

hantise /'ɑ̃tiz/ nf dread; **avoir la ~ de qch** to dread sth

happer /'ape/ [1] vtr to catch [nourriture, insecte]; to seize [animal, bras]; **être happé par** (pris) to be caught up in [machine]; (fauché) to be hit by [voiture, train]; fig to be swallowed up by [bouche de métro, foule]

haranguer /'aʀɑ̃ge/ [1] vtr to harangue

haras /'aʀa/ nm inv stud farm

harassement /'aʀasmɑ̃/ nm fml exhaustion

harasser /'aʀase/ [1] vtr to exhaust

harcèlement /'aʀsɛlmɑ̃/ nm harassment

(Composés) **~ moral** psychological abuse; **~ psychologique** psychological abuse; **~ sexuel** sexual harassment

harceler /'aʀsəle/ [17] vtr **1** (importuner) [démarcheur, mendiant, journaliste] to pester [personne] (**de** with; **pour faire** to do); **les remords le harcèlent** he's plagued by remorse; **2** (poursuivre) to harass [ennemi]

harde /'aʀd/
A nf **1** (d'animaux sauvages) herd; **2** (de chiens) pack
B **hardes** nfpl liter rags

hardi, ~e /'aʀdi/ adj **1** (intrépide, osé) bold; **2** [plaisanterie] risqué

hardiesse /'aʀdjɛs/ nf **1** (intrépidité, originalité) boldness; **2** liter (impudence) brazenness

hareng /'aʀɑ̃/ nm herring

(Composé) **~ saur** smoked herring

(Idiome) **sec comme un ~ saur** as thin as a rake

hargne /'aʀɲ/ nf aggression; **avec ~** aggressively

hargneux, -euse /'aʀɲø, øz/ adj aggressive

haricot /'aʀiko/ nm (plante, graine) bean

(Composés) **~ beurre** wax bean; **~ blanc** haricot bean; **~ à écosser** bean for shelling; **~ rouge** red kidney bean; **~ vert** French bean

(Idiome) **c'est la fin des ~s** we've had it^O

harki /'aʀki/ nm: Algerian soldier who fought on the French side in the war of independence

harmonica /aʀmɔnika/ ▸ p. 389 nm mouth organ

harmonie /aʀmɔni/ nf **1** (entente) harmony; **en ~ avec** gén in harmony with; **2** Mus (connaissance des accords) harmony; (fanfare) brass band

(Composés) **~ imitative** Littérat onomatopoeia; **~ vocalique** Ling vowel harmony

harmonieux, -ieuse /aʀmɔnjø, øz/ adj **1** (agréable) harmonious; **2** (en accord) [couleurs, courbes] harmonious; [gestes] graceful; [vie, mélange] harmonious; **ils forment un couple ~** they are very well suited

harmonique /aʀmɔnik/ adj, nm harmonic

harmonisation /aʀmɔnizasjɔ̃/ *nf* gén harmonization; Ling vowel harmony

harmoniser /aʀmɔnize/ [1]
A *vtr* ① (rendre harmonieux) to coordinate [*couleurs*]; ② (rendre cohérents) to make [sth] consistent [*règles*]; ③ Mus to harmonize
B s'harmoniser *vpr* bien s'~ to go together well

harnachement /'aʀnaʃmɑ̃/ *nm* ① (de cheval) (pièces) harness; (action) harnessing; ② ○(de personne) get-up○

harnacher /'aʀnaʃe/ [1] *vtr* ① to harness [*cheval*]; ② ○(équiper) to rig out○ [*personne*]

harnais /'aʀnɛ/ *nm inv* harness

harpagon /aʀpagɔ̃/ *nm* liter miser, Scrooge

harpe /'aʀp/ ▸ p. 389 *nf* harp

harpie /'aʀpi/ *nf* ① Mythol harpy; les Harpies the Harpies; ② (femme acariâtre) harpy; ③ (aigle) harpy eagle

harpon /'aʀpɔ̃/ *nm* harpoon

harponner /'aʀpɔne/ [1] *vtr* ① to harpoon [*baleine*]; ② (arrêter)○ to waylay [*badaud*]; to nab○ [*malfaiteur*]

hasard /'azaʀ/ *nm* (cause imprévisible) chance; le ~ nous a fait découvrir que… we discovered by chance that…; ce n'est pas un ~ si… it's no accident that…; s'en remettre au ~, compter sur le ~ to trust to luck (pour as regards; pour faire to do); au ~ [*choisir, tirer*] at random; [*marcher*] aimlessly; répondre au ~ to answer off the top of one's head; au ~ de mes promenades on my walks; par ~ by chance; par un curieux ~ by a curious coincidence; par un heureux ~ by a stroke of luck; comme par ~, il a oublié son argent iron surprise, surprise, he's forgotten his money; à tout ~ (par précaution) just in case; (pour une tentative) on the off chance; les ~s de la vie the fortunes of life
(Idiome) le ~ fait bien les choses fate is a great provider

hasarder /'azaʀde/ [1]
A *vtr* ① (avancer) to venture [*conseil, explication*]; ② liter (risquer) to risk [*vie*]
B se hasarder *vpr* to venture (à faire to do)

hasardeux, -euse /'azaʀdø, øz/ *adj* (peu sûr) risky; (dangereux) hazardous

hase /'az/ *nf* doe-hare

hâte /'ɑt/ *nf* ① (précipitation) haste; en toute ~ in great haste; à la ~ hastily; ② (impatience) j'ai ~ de partir/qu'elle vienne I can't wait to leave/for her to come

hâter /'ate/ [1]
A *vtr* to hasten; ~ le pas to quicken one's step
B se hâter *vpr* to hurry, to rush

hâtif, -ive /'atif, iv/ *adj* ① (rapide) [*jugement, recrutement*] hasty, hurried; ② [*variété, plante*] early

hâtivement /'ativmɑ̃/ *adv* hurriedly, hastily

hauban /'obɑ̃/ *nm* ① Naut shroud; ② Tech (souple) stay; (rigide) brace

hausse /'os/ *nf* ① (augmentation) (de prix, salaires) increase (de in); (de dépenses, chômage, température) rise (de in); être en ~ [*prix, température*] to be rising; [*marchandise*] to be going up in price; subir une forte ~ to rocket; en ~ de 10% up 10%; réviser à la ~ to revise upward(s); ② (en Bourse) rise (de in); être à la ~ [*devise*] to be rising; [*tendance*] to be upward(s); [*marché*] to be on the uptrend

haussement /'osmɑ̃/ *nm* (d'épaules) shrug; il marqua son intérêt par un ~ de sourcils he raised his eyebrows in an interested way

hausser /'ose/ [1]
A *vtr* ① (élever) to shrug [*épaules*]; to raise [*sourcils*]; ~ le ton or la voix lit to raise one's voice; fig to adopt an aggressive tone; ② (augmenter) to raise [*prix*]; to increase [*exigences, prétentions*]; ③ (surélever) to raise [*mur, maison*]
B se hausser *vpr* se ~ au niveau de to rise up to the level of; se ~ sur la pointe des pieds to stand on tiptoe

haut, ~e¹ /'o, 'ot/
A *adj* ① ▸ p. 347 [*montagne, mur, talon*] high; [*arbre, monument*] tall; [*herbe*] long, tall; attention, la première marche est ~e be careful, the first step is steep; ② (situé en altitude) high; la partie ~e d'un mur the top part of a wall; l'étagère la plus ~e the top shelf; une robe à taille ~e a high-waisted dress; ③ (dans une échelle de valeurs) [*température, salaires, précision*] high; [*note, ton*] high, high-pitched; parler à ~e voix to speak loudly; lire à ~e voix to read out loud; au plus ~ point immensely; ④ (dans une hiérarchie) (before n) [*personnage, poste*] high-ranking; [*clergé,

magistrat*] senior; [*société*] high; [*responsabilités*] big; [*dirigeant, responsable*] senior, high-ranking; ~ Comité/Conseil National Committee/Council; ~e surveillance close supervision; ⑤ Géog upper; la ~e Égypte Upper Egypt; ⑥ Hist de la plus ~e antiquité from earliest antiquity; le ~ Moyen Âge the early Middle Ages
B *adv* ① (à un niveau élevé) [*monter, voler*] high; un personnage ~ placé a person in a high position; de ~ from above; ② (dans le temps) far back; ③ (dans un texte) plus ~ above; colle-le plus ~ sur la page stick it higher up on the page; ④ (fort) loudly; dire qch bien ~ to say sth loud(ly); mettre la radio plus ~ to turn the radio up; tout ~ out loud; parler ~ et clair fig to speak unambiguously; n'avoir jamais un mot plus ~ que l'autre never to raise one's voice
C *nm* ① (partie élevée) top; le ~ du visage the top part of the face; le ~ du corps the top half of the body; l'étagère du ~ the top shelf; les pièces du ~ the upstairs rooms; prendre qch par le ~ to get hold of the top of sth; parler du ~ d'un balcon to speak from a balcony; ② (hauteur) faire 50 mètres de ~ to be 50 metres^GB high
D en haut *loc* (à l'étage supérieur) upstairs; (à un étage supérieur) on an upper floor; (de rideau, mur, page) at the top; (le ciel, le paradis) above; ~ passer par en ~ (par la route) to take the top road; les voleurs sont entrés par en ~ (par l'étage) the thieves got in upstairs
E hauts *nmpl* heights

(Composés) ~ en couleur [*personnage, tableau, texte*] colourful^GB; ~ fait heroic deed; ~ fonctionnaire senior civil servant; ~ lieu de centre^GB of ou for; en ~ lieu in high places; une décision prise en ~ lieu a decision taken at a high level; ~e mer Naut open sea; ~es eaux high water (sg); ~es sphères high social circles; ~es terres Géog highlands

(Idiomes) marcher la tête ~e to walk with one's head held high; voir les choses de ~ (avec sérénité) to have a detached view of things; tomber de ~ to be dumbfounded; regarder qn de ~ en bas to look sb up and down; avoir or connaître des ~s et des bas to have one's ups and downs; ~ les mains! hands up!; l'emporter or gagner or vaincre ~ la main to win hands down; prendre qn de ~ to look down one's nose at sb; ▸ cri, pavé

hautain, ~e /'otɛ̃, ɛn/ *adj* haughty

hautbois /'obwa/ ▸ p. 389 *nm inv* ① (instrument) oboe; ② (instrumentiste) oboist

hautboïste /'oboist/ ▸ p. 389, p. 372 *nmf* oboist

haut-de-chausse(s), *pl* **hauts-de-chausses** /'odʃos/ *nm* (knee) breeches

haut-de-forme, *pl* **hauts-de-formes** /'odfɔʀm/ *nm* top hat

haute² /'ot/
A *adj f* ▸ haut A
B ○*nf* (les gens de) la ~ the upper crust

haute-contre, *pl* **hautes-contre** /'otkɔ̃tʀ/ ▸ p. 98 *nf* Mus counter tenor

haute(-)fidélité /'otfidelite/ *nf* Électrotech ① (qualité) chaîne ~ hi-fi system; ② (technique) ¢ la ~ hi-fi, high fidelity

hautement /'otmɑ̃/ *adv* (à un haut degré) highly

hauteur /'otœʀ/
A *nf* ① ▸ p. 347 (dimension verticale) height; prendre de la ~ lit [*avion, oiseau*] to climb; dans le sens de la ~ upright; à ~ d'homme at about the height of a person; à ~ des yeux at eye level; ② (profondeur) depth; ~ d'eau Naut depth of water; ③ Sport le saut en ~ high jump; ④ (de robe, jupe) length; ⑤ (éminence) hill; gagner les ~s to reach high ground; il y a encore de la neige sur les ~s there is still some snow on the upper slopes; les ~s de la ville the upper part of the town; ⑥ Math height; ⑦ (qualité morale) nobility; ⑧ péj (arrogance) haughtiness; ⑨ (en acoustique) pitch; ⑩ (d'astre) altitude
B à la hauteur de *loc* ① (au niveau) arriver à la ~ de to come up to; raccourcir une jupe à la ~ des genoux to shorten a dress to knee-level; ② (à côté) arriver à la ~ de to draw level with; un déraillement s'est produit à la ~ de Rouen there was a derailment near Rouen; ③ fig être à la ~ to measure up; être à la ~ de qn to match up to sb; être à la ~ de sa tâche to be equal to one's job; être à la ~ des espérances de qn to live up to sb's hopes; être à la ~ du talent de qn [*scénario*] to do justice to sb's talent; ④ (en

h

valeur, quantité) **à (la)** ~ **de 10%** up to 10%

Idiomes **tomber de toute sa** ~ to fall headlong; **se dresser de toute sa** ~ [*personne*] to draw oneself up to one's full height; [*animal*] to stand on its hind legs

Haute-Volta /'otvɔlta/ *nprf* Hist Upper Volta

haut-fond, *pl* **hauts-fonds** /'ofɔ̃/ *nm* Naut shallows (*pl*)

haut(-)fourneau, *pl* **hauts(-)fourneaux** /'ofuRno/ *nm* Ind blast furnace

haut-le-cœur /'olkœR/ *nm inv* retching ₵, heaving ₵; **en voyant les images nous avons eu un** ~ fig the pictures turned our stomachs

haut-le-corps /'olkɔR/ *nm inv* start, jump

haut-parleur, *pl* ~**s** /'oparlœR/ *nm* loudspeaker

Composés ~ **d'aigus** tweeter; ~ **de graves** boomer

haut-relief, *pl* **hauts-reliefs** /'oRəljɛf/ *nm* Archit, Art high relief

hauturier, -ière /'otyRje, ɛR/ *adj* [*pêche*] deep-sea; [*navire*] ocean-going

havane /'avan/
Ⓐ ▸ p. 140 *adj inv* tobacco-brown
Ⓑ *nm* ① (tabac) Havana tobacco; ② (cigare) Havana cigar

hâve /'av/ *adj fml* [*visage*] haggard, gaunt

havre /'avR/ *nm* liter, fig haven

Haye /'ɛ/ ▸ p. 621 *npr* **la** ~ the Hague

heaume /'om/ *nm* helmet

hebdomadaire /ɛbdomadɛR/
Ⓐ *adj* [*départ*] weekly
Ⓑ *nm* weekly (magazine)

hébergement /ebɛRʒəmã/ *nm* ① (commercial) accommodation; ② (social) housing

héberger /ebɛRʒe/ [13] *vtr* ① (loger) [*personne*] to put [sb] up [*amis*]; to accommodate [*touristes*]; [*pays*] to take [sb] in [*réfugiés*]; ③ (abriter) [*bâtiment*] to accommodate [*touristes*]; [*refuge*] to provide shelter for [*montagnards, sans-abri*]; ④ Ordinat to host [*site*]

hébergeur /ebɛRʒœR/ *nm* Ordinat host

hébété, ~e /ebete/ *adj* [*regard*] stupid; **d'un air** ~ stupidly; ~ **par** stupefied by [*alcool, travail*]; ~ **de douleur** numb with grief

hébraïque /ebRaik/ *adj* [*études*] Hebrew

hébreu, *pl* ~**x** /ebRø/ ▸ p. 336
Ⓐ *adj m* Hebrew; **l'État** ~ the State of Israel
Ⓑ *nm* Ling Hebrew

Idiome **pour moi, c'est de l'**~ it's all Greek to me

Hébreu, *pl* ~**x** /ebRø/ *nm* Hebrew

HEC /aʃəse/ *nf* (abbr = **Hautes études commerciales**) *major business school*

hécatombe /ekatɔ̃b/ *nf* ① (massacre) massacre, slaughter; **l'examen a été une** ~ fig lots of people failed the exam; ② (dans l'antiquité) hecatomb

hectare /ɛktaR/ ▸ p. 568 *nm* hectare

hecto /ɛkto/
Ⓐ *nm* (abbr = **hectogramme**) hectogram
Ⓑ **hecto(-)** (in *compounds*) hecto

hectolitre /ɛktɔlitR/ ▸ p. 87 *nm* hectolitre^GB

hectopascal /ɛktɔpaskal/ *nm* milibar

hégémonie /eʒemɔni/ *nf* hegemony

hein○ /'ɛ̃/ *excl* (pour faire répéter) what○?, sorry?; **ça t'étonne,** ~? that's surprised you, hasn't it?

hélas /'elas/ *excl* alas; ~ **non!** unfortunately not!

héler /ele/ [14] *vtr* to hail [*taxi*]; to call [*personne*]

hélice /elis/ *nf* ① Naut, Aviat (screw) propeller; ② Archit, Biol, Math helix; ③ Tech (de ventilateur) blades (*pl*)

hélicoïdal, ~e, *mpl* **-aux** /elikɔidal, o/ *adj* ① Math, Tech [*mouvement, axe*] helical; [*escalier*] spiral; ② Bot helicoid

hélicoptère /elikɔptɛR/ *nm* helicopter

héliogravure /eljɔgRavyR/ *nf* ① (procédé) gravure printing; ② (image) gravure

héliport /elipɔR/ *nm* heliport

héliporté, ~e /elipɔRte/ *adj* helicopter-borne

hélitreuiller /elitRœje/ [1] *vtr* to winch [sb] to safety (*by helicopter*)

hellène /ellɛn/ *adj* [*peuple, voilier*] Hellenic

helvète /ɛlvɛt/ *adj* Helvetian

helvétique /ɛlvetik/ *adj* Helvetic, Swiss; **la Confédération** ~ Switzerland

helvétisme /ɛlvetism/ *nm* Swiss French expression

hématie /emati, emasi/ *nf* red blood cell

hématome /ematom/ *nm* ① bruise; ② haematoma

hémicycle /emisikl/ *nm* (de théâtre) semicircular auditorium; (salle quelconque) semicircular room

hémiplégie /emipleʒi/ *nf* paralysis of one side of the body, hemiplegia spéc

hémisphère /emisfɛR/ *nm* Anat, Géog hemisphere; **l'**~ **Nord** Géog the northern hemisphere

hémisphérique /emisfeRik/ *adj* hemispherical

hémistiche /emistiʃ/ *nm* (moitié de vers) hemistich; **coupe à l'**~ caesura

hémoglobine /emoglobin/ *nf* ① (pigment des globules rouges) haemoglobin; ② ○(sang) blood

hémophile /emɔfil/
Ⓐ *adj* haemophilic
Ⓑ *nmf* haemophiliac

hémorragie /emoRaʒi/ *nf* ① Méd bleeding ₵; ② (fuite) (de capitaux) massive outflow; (de populations, clients) exodus; ③ (pertes humaines) massive loss of (human) life

hémorroïdes /emoRoid/ ▸ p. 195 *nfpl* piles, haemorrhoids

henné /'ene/ *nm* henna

hennir /'eniR/ [3] *vi* [*cheval*] to neigh, to whinny

hennissement /'enismã/ *nm* neigh, whinnying ₵

hépatique /epatik/
Ⓐ *adj* hepatic
Ⓑ *nmf* person with a liver complaint

hépatite /epatit/ ▸ p. 195 *nf* hepatitis

héraldique /eRaldik/
Ⓐ *adj* heraldic
Ⓑ *nf* heraldry

héraut /'eRo/ *nm* ① (annonciateur) liter harbinger; ② Hist (officier) ~ **d'armes** herald

herbage /ɛRbaʒ/ *nm* pasture

herbe /ɛRb/
Ⓐ *nf* ① (revêtement végétal) grass; ② Bot (plante) **C hautes** ~**s** tall grass ₵; **mauvaise** ~ weed; ③ Bot, Culin aromatic herb
Ⓑ **en herbe** *loc adj* ① (encore vert) [*blé, avoine*] in the blade (*après n*); ② (jeune) [*musicien*] budding

Composé ~**s folles** wild grass

Idiome **couper l'**~ **sous le pied de qn** to pull the rug from under sb's feet

herbeux, -euse /ɛRbø, øz/ *adj* grassy

herbicide /ɛRbisid/
Ⓐ *adj* [*produit*] herbicidal
Ⓑ *nm* weed killer, herbicide

herbier /ɛRbje/ *nm* (de plantes séchées) herbarium

herbivore /ɛRbivɔR/
Ⓐ *adj* herbivorous
Ⓑ *nm* herbivore

herboriste /ɛRbɔRist/ ▸ p. 372 *nmf* herbalist

herboristerie /ɛRbɔRistəRi/ ▸ p. 372 *nf* ① (vente) herb trade; ② (boutique) herbalist's shop GB *ou* store US

Hercule /ɛRkyl/ *npr* Hercules; **les travaux d'**~ Mythol the Labours of Hercules; **c'est un travail d'**~ fig it's a Herculean task

hère /'ɛR/ *nm* liter **un pauvre** ~ a poor wretch

héréditaire /eReditɛR/ *adj* Biol, Jur, Méd hereditary; **l'ennemi** ~ fig the traditional enemy

hérédité /eRedite/ *nf* ① Biol heredity; ② (origines) background; ③ Jur (de possession) hereditary nature

hérésie /eRezi/ *nf* ① Relig heresy; **tomber en** ~ to become a heretic; ② (opinion, théorie) heresy; hum (action) sacrilege

hérétique /eRetik/
Ⓐ *adj* heretical
Ⓑ *nmf* heretic

hérissé, ~e /'eRise/ *adj* **il a les cheveux** ~**s** (volontairement) he's got spiky hair; (involontairement) his hair sticks up

hérisser /'eRise/ [1]
Ⓐ *vtr* ① (dresser) [*oiseau*] to ruffle (up) [*plumes*]; [*hérisson*] to

raise [*piquants*]; **2** (garnir) ~ **qch de** to spike sth with; **question hérissée de difficultés** fig question fraught with difficulties; **3** ○(irriter) ~ **qn** to make sb's hackles rise

B se hérisser vpr **1** (se dresser) [*poils, cheveux*] to stand on end; [*animal*] to bristle; **2** ○(s'irriter) to bristle

hérisson /eʀisɔ̃/ nm **1** Zool hedgehog; **2** (de ramoneur) (chimney sweep's) brush; **3** (égouttoir à bouteilles) bottle-drainer; **4** Mil hedgehog

héritage /eʀitaʒ/ nm **1** (biens légués) inheritance; **faire un** ~ to come into an inheritance; **une tante à** ~ a wealthy aunt; **recevoir qch en** ~ to inherit sth; **2** (survivance du passé) (concret) inheritance; (abstrait) heritage, legacy

hériter /eʀite/ [1]
A vtr to inherit
B hériter de vtr ind **1** Jur to inherit [*argent, bien*]; **la maison dont il a hérité** the house he inherited; **2** ○(se retrouver encombré de) to be landed with
C vi (être légataire) to inherit; (faire un héritage) to come into an inheritance; ~ **de qn** to receive an inheritance from sb

héritier, -ière /eʀitje, ɛʀ/ nmf Jur heir/heiress (**de** to)

(Composé) ~ **testamentaire** Jur legatee

hermaphrodite /ɛʀmafʀɔdit/ nm hermaphrodite

hermétique /ɛʀmetik/ adj **1** lit (étanche) [*joint, récipient*] hermetic; [*fermeture*] (aux gaz) airtight; (aux liquides) watertight; **2** (impénétrable) [*frontière*] closed, sealed-off [*jamais épith*]; [*milieu, société*] impenetrable; [*blocus, embargo*] solid; **3** (indéchiffrable) [*poésie, auteur*] abstruse; [*visage, expression*] inscrutable; **il est** ~ **au cricket** cricket is a closed book to him

hermétiquement /ɛʀmetikmɑ̃/ adv **1** [*fermé*] hermetically; **2** [*s'exprimer*] abstrusely

hermétisme /ɛʀmetism/ nm **1** (caractère indéchiffrable) abstruseness; **2** (doctrine) hermeticism

hermine /ɛʀmin/ nf **1** (animal) stoat; **2** (fourrure) ermine

hernie /ɛʀni/ nf **1** Méd hernia; **2** (de pneu) bulge

héroïne /eʀɔin/ nf **1** (personnage) heroine; **2** (drogue) heroin

héroïnomane /eʀɔinɔman/ nmf heroin addict

héroïque /eʀɔik/ adj [*personne*] heroic; [*poème*] epic

héroïsme /eʀɔism/ nm heroism

héron /eʀɔ̃/ nm heron

héros /eʀo/ nm inv hero; **mourir en** ~ to die a hero's death

herse /ɛʀs/ nf **1** Agric harrow; **2** (grille d'entrée) portcullis; **3** Théât (éclairage) batten GB, bank of floodlights US; **4** Mil (barrage routier) caltrop barrier

hertzien, -ienne /ɛʀtzjɛ̃, ɛn/ adj [*onde*] Hertzian; [*station, système, liaison*] radio-relay

hésitant, -e /ezitɑ̃, ɑ̃t/ adj [*geste, dessin*] hesitant; [*pas, voix*] hesitant, faltering; [*démarrage*] shaky

hésitation /ezitasjɔ̃/ nf **1** (indécision) indecision, hesitancy; **il a eu une seconde d'**~ he hesitated for a second; **2** (signe d'incertitude) hesitation ¢; **lever les dernières** ~**s de qn** to overcome sb's final doubts

hésiter /ezite/ [1] vi to hesitate (**sur** over; **devant** before); **elle hésite encore** she's still undecided; **il n'y a pas à** ~ it's got to be done; **'alors, tu viens?'—'j'hésite'** 'are you coming?'—'I can't make up my mind'; **j'hésite entre plusieurs possibilités** I can't decide between several possibilities; **j'hésite à interrompre leur conversation** I don't like to interrupt their conversation; **les docteurs hésitent à l'opérer** the doctors are reluctant to operate on him/her

hétéro○ /eteʀo/ adj, nmf (abbr = **hétérosexuel**) straight○

hétéroclite /eteʀɔklit/ adj [*population, œuvre*] heterogeneous; [*objets, matériaux*] miscellaneous

hétérogène /eteʀɔʒɛn/ adj [*groupe, ensemble*] mixed, heterogeneous sout; [*nombre*] mixed

hétérosexuel, -elle /eteʀɔsɛksɥɛl/ adj, nmf heterosexual

hêtre /ɛtʀ/ nm **1** (arbre) beech (tree); **2** (bois) beechwood

heure /œʀ/ ▸ p. 296, p. 582, p. 624 nf **1** (soixante minutes) hour; **24** ~**s sur 24** lit, fig 24 hours a day; **dans l'**~ **qui a suivi** within the hour; **d'**~ **en** [*augmenter, empirer*] by

the hour; **deux** ~**s d'attente** a two-hour wait; **toutes les deux** ~**s** every two hours; **toutes les** ~**s** every hour; **après trois** ~**s d'avion** after three hours on the plane; **être à trois** ~**s d'avion de Paris** to be three hours away from Paris by plane; **faire trois** ~**s de bateau** to be on the boat for three hours; **faire du 60 à l'**~○, **faire 60 km à l'**~ to do 60 km per hour; **payé à l'**~ paid by the hour; **25 euros de l'**~ 25 euros an hour; **la semaine de 35** ~**s** the 35-hour week; **une petite** ~ an hour at the most; **une bonne** ~ a good hour; **2** (indication) time; **à 11** ~**s**, ~ **de Paris** at 11, Paris time; **il ne sait pas lire l'**~ he can't tell the time; **se tromper d'**~ to get the time wrong; **il est 10** ~**s** it's 10 (o'clock); **il est 10** ~**s 20** it's 20 past 10; **il est 10** ~**s moins 20** it's 20 to 10; **à 4** ~**s pile** or **tapantes**○ at 4 o'clock sharp; **mettre sa montre à l'**~ to set one's watch; **l'**~ **tourne** time is passing; **3** (point dans le temps) time; **l'**~ **d'arrivée** the arrival time; ~**s d'ouverture** opening times; **être à l'**~ to be on time; **'sandwiches à toute** ~**'** 'sandwiches available at any time'; **à une** ~ **avancée (de la nuit)** late at night; **de bonne** ~ [*se lever, partir*] early; **il doit être loin à l'**~ **qu'il est** he must be a long way off by now; **c'est son** ~ it's his/her usual time; **à l'**~ **où je te parle** while I'm speaking to you; **de la première** ~ [*résistant, militant*] from the very beginning; **à la première** ~ at first light; **de dernière** ~ [*manœuvre, décision*] last-minute; **un résistant de la dernière** ~ a late convert to the resistance; **ta dernière** ~ **est arrivée** your time has come; **4** (période, époque) time; **à l'**~ **actuelle, pour l'**~ at the present time; **à l'**~ **de la pause** during the break; **l'**~ **du déjeuner/thé/d** ˈner lunchtime/teatime/dinnertime; **aux** ~**s des repas** at mealtimes; **l'**~ **n'est pas à la polémique** this is no time for controversy; **l'**~ **est grave** the situation is serious; **il est peintre à ses** ~**s** he paints in his spare time; **à la bonne** ~**!** well done!; **5** (ère) era; **vivre à l'**~ **des satellites** to live in the satellite era

(Composés) ~ **d'affluence** peak hour; ~ **d'été** Admin summer time GB, daylight saving(s) time; ~ **H** Mil, fig zero hour; ~ **d'hiver** Admin winter time GB, standard time; ~ **légale** Admin standard time; ~ **de pointe** rush hour; ~**s supplémentaires** overtime

(Idiomes) **avant l'**~, **c'est pas l'**~, **après l'**~, **c'est plus l'**~○ there's no time but the right time; **vivre à cent à l'**~○ fig to be always on the go○

heureusement /œʀøzmɑ̃/ adv **1** (par chance) fortunately (**pour** for); ~ **que tu es là!** it's a good job you're here!; **2** (avec bonheur) fml [*réparti*] successfully; [*terminé, conclu*] nicely

heureux, -euse /œʀø, øz/ adj **1** (satisfait) [*personne, visage, enfance*] happy; **être** ~ **de vivre** to be happy with life; ~ **en ménage** happily married; **très** ~ **de faire votre connaissance** (very) pleased to meet you; **2** (satisfaisant) [*fin*] happy; [*surprise*] pleasant; **3** (optimiste) [*nature, caractère*] happy; **4** (chanceux) lucky; **'il a réussi!'—'encore** ~**!'** 'he succeeded!'—'just as well!'; **l'**~ **propriétaire de...** the proud owner of...; **5** (réussi) [*idée*] happy; [*proportions*] pleasing; [*formulation*] happy, felicitous sout; **ce n'est pas très** ~ **comme choix de mots** it's an unfortunate ou unhappy choice of words

(Composé) **l'**~ **élu** (en amour) the lucky man; (à un jeu) the lucky winner

(Idiome) **être** ~ **comme un roi** or **un pape** to be happy as a lark ou as Larry

heurt /œʀ/ nm **1** (friction) (différend) conflict; (accrochage) clash; **faire qch sans** ~ to do sth smoothly; **leur relation ne va pas sans** ~**s** their relationship has its ups and downs; **2** (contraste) clash

heurté, -e /œʀte/ adj [*style, rythme*] jerky, uneven; [*sons, couleurs, tons*] clashing

heurter /œʀte/ [1]
A vtr **1** (cogner contre) [*objet*] to hit; [*personne*] to collide with [*passant, véhicule*]; to bump into [*objet, personne à l'arrêt*]; ~ **qn avec qch** to knock sb with sth; **il a heurté la table avec sa valise** he knocked against the table with his suitcase; **2** (cogner) ~ **qch avec** or **contre qch** to knock sth against sth; **3** (offenser) to offend [*personne, morale*]; to go against [*convenances*]; to hurt [*sentiment*]; ~ **l'opinion publique** [*action*] to run counter to public opinion; [*personne*] to conflict with public opinion; ~ **qn de front** to clash with sb head-on
B vi ~ **contre** to strike

L'heure

Quelle heure est-il?

■ *En anglais, on donne l'heure en utilisant les prépositions* past *et* to (*ou* after *et de* of *aux États-Unis*). *Par ex., pour* 4 h 05, five past four, five after four (*US*), *pour* 4 h 50, ten to five, ten of five (*US*) *etc. Dans un style plus officiel, on juxtapose les chiffres des heures et des minutes: par ex., pour* 4 h 10, four ten. *Dans les horaires de train etc, on utilise aussi l'horloge de vingt-quatre heures: par ex, pour* 16 h 23, sixteen twenty-three. *Dans le tableau suivant,* past *peut être remplacé par* after (*US*) *et* to *peut être remplacé par* of (*US*).

il est ...	it is ...	dire
4 h	4 o'clock	four o'clock *ou* four
4 h du matin	4 am	four o'clock* *ou* four am [eɪ em] *ou* four o'clock in the morning
4 h de l'après-midi	4 pm	four o'clock *ou* four pm [pi: em] *ou* four o'clock in the afternoon
4 h 02	4.02	two minutes past four[†] *ou* four oh two
4 h 05	4.05	five past four[†] *ou* four oh five
4 h 10	4.10	ten past four *ou* four ten
quatre heures et quart	4.15	a quarter past four
4 h 15	4.15	four fifteen
4 h 20	4.20	twenty past four *ou* four twenty
4 h 23	4.23	twenty-three minutes past four *ou* four twenty-three
4 h 25	4.25	twenty-five past four *ou* four twenty-five
quatre heures et demie	4.30	half past four
4 h 30	4.30	four thirty
4 h 37	4.37	four thirty-seven
cinq heures moins vingt	4.40	twenty to five
4 h 40	4.40	four forty
cinq heures moins le quart	4.45	a quarter to five
4 h 45	4.45	four forty-five
cinq heures moins dix	4.50	ten to five
4 h 50	4.50	four fifty
cinq heures moins cinq	4.55	five to five
4 h 55	4.55	four fifty-five
17 h 00	5 pm	five o'clock in the afternoon*
17 h 15	5.15 pm	a quarter past five *ou* five fifteen
17 h 23	5.23 pm	twenty-three minutes past five *ou* five twenty-three
18 h 00	6 pm	six o'clock *ou* six [pi: em]
12 h	12.00	twelve o'clock
midi	12.00	noon *ou* twelve noon
minuit	12.00	midnight *ou* twelve midnight
zéro heure *ou* 00 h 00	00.00	midnight

quelle heure est-il?
= what time is it?

il est quatre heures à ma montre
= my watch says four o'clock

pouvez-vous me donner l'heure?
= could you tell me the time?

il est quatre heures juste
= it's exactly four o'clock

il est environ quatre heures
= it's about four o'clock *ou* it's about four[‡]

il va être quatre heures
= it's nearly four o'clock

il est presque quatre heures
= it's almost four o'clock

il est à peine plus de quatre heures
= it's just after four o'clock

il est quatre heures passées
= it's gone four[‡]

....

Quand?

à quelle heure cela est-il arrivé?
= what time did it happen? *ou* what time did it happen at?

à quelle heure va-t-il venir?
= what time will he come? *ou* what time will he come at?

c'est arrivé à quatre heures
= it happened at four o'clock

il viendra à quatre heures
= he's coming at four o'clock

à quatre heures dix
= at ten past four

à quatre heures et demie
= at half past four (*GB*), at half after four (*US*)

à quatre heures précises
= at four o'clock exactly

soyez là à quatre heures pile
= be there at four o'clock on the dot

aux environs de quatre heures
= at about four o'clock

à quatre heures au plus tard
= at four o'clock at the latest

un peu après quatre heures
= shortly after four o'clock

il faut que ce soit prêt avant quatre heures
= it must be ready by four

je serai là jusqu'à quatre heures
= I'll be there until four

je ne serai pas là avant quatre heures
= I won't be there until four

de 7 h à 9 h
= from seven till nine

ouvert de 9 h à 5 h
= open from nine to five

fermé entre treize et quatorze heures
= closed from 1 to 2 pm

toutes les heures à l'heure juste
= every hour on the hour

toutes les heures à dix
= at ten past every hour

* *Lorsqu'il s'agit d'horaires de trains, d'avions etc, on peut écrire* 0400, *qui est prononcé* oh four hundred hours, *de même* sixteen hundred hours, twenty-four hundred hours *etc.*

† *Le mot* minutes *ne peut être omis qu'avec les multiples de 5.*

‡ *Dans la conversation,* o'clock *est souvent omis.*

C **se heurter** *vpr* **1** (se cogner) [*véhicules, personnes*] to collide; [*tasses*] to knock against each other; **les idées se heurtaient dans sa tête** ideas were whirling about in his head; **se ~ contre** *or* **à qn/qch** to bump into sb/sth; **2** (rencontrer) **se ~ à** to come up against [*préjugé, refus*]; **3** (s'affronter) to clash (**à** with)

heurtoir /ˈœʀtwaʀ/ nm 1▸ (marteau de porte) (door) knocker; 2▸ Rail buffers (pl)

hévéa /evea/ nm rubber tree, hevea spéc

hexagonal, ~e, mpl **-aux** /ɛgzagɔnal, o/ adj 1▸ Math hexagonal; 2▸ ○(français) French

hexagone /ɛgzagon/ nm 1▸ Math hexagon; 2▸ ○(France métropolitaine) l'**Hexagone** France

hiatus /ˈjatys/ nm inv 1▸ Anat, Ling hiatus; 2▸ fig (interruption) hiatus, break; (décalage) discrepancy

hibernation /ibɛʀnasjɔ̃/ nf Biol, Zool hibernation

hiberner /ibɛʀne/ [1] vi to hibernate

hibou, pl ~**x** /ˈibu/ nm owl

hic○ /ˈik/ nm snag; **c'est bien là le ~** there's the snag

hideux, **-euse** /ˈidø, øz/ adj hideous

hier /jɛʀ/ adv yesterday; **toute la journée d'~** all day yesterday; **ce problème ne date pas d'~** this problem is nothing new

hiérarchie /ˈjeʀaʀʃi/ nf hierarchy

hiérarchique /ˈjeʀaʀʃik/ adj [organisation] hierarchical; **mon supérieur ~** my immediate superior; **mes supérieurs ~s** my superiors; **par la voie ~** through the correct channels

hiérarchiser /ˈjeʀaʀʃize/ [1] vtr to organize [sth] into a hierarchy [structure]; to prioritize [tâches]; **~ les salaires** to establish a wages hierarchy

hiératique /jeʀatik/ adj hieratic

hiéroglyphe /ˈjeʀɔglif/ nm 1▸ (caractère) hieroglyph; 2▸ (système) **les ~s** hieroglyphics (+ v sg)

hi-fi /ˈifi/
A adj inv hi-fi; **une chaîne ~** a hi-fi system
B nf inv **la ~** hi-fi equipment

hilarant, ~e /ilaʀɑ̃, ɑ̃t/ adj hilarious; **gaz ~** laughing gas

hilare /ilaʀ/ adj **être ~** to be laughing

hilarité /ilaʀite/ nf mirth, hilarity

hindi /ˈindi/ ▸ p. 336 adj, nm Hindi

hindou, ~e /ɛ̃du/ adj, nm,f Hindu

hindouisme /ɛ̃duism/ nm Hinduism

hippique /ipik/ adj [sport] equestrian; **concours ~** show-jumping event GB, horse show US; **club ~** riding school; **journaliste ~** racing journalist

hippisme /ipism/ nm equestrianism

hippocampe /ipokɑ̃p/ nm Zool sea horse

hippodrome /ipodʀom/ nm racecourse GB, racetrack US

hippopotame /ipopotam/ nm hippopotamus

hirondelle /iʀɔ̃dɛl/ nf Zool swallow

hirsute /ˈiʀsyt/ adj (peu soigné) [personne, apparence] dishevelled^GB, tousled; [cheveux, barbe] unkempt

hispanique /ispanik/ ▸ p. 336 adj, nmf Hispanic

hispaniste /ispanist/ nmf Hispanicist

hispano-américain, ~e, mpl ~**s** /ispanoameʀikɛ̃, ɛn/ ▸ p. 336 adj Hispanic-American, Spanish-American

hispanophone /ispanofon/
A adj Spanish-speaking
B nmf Spanish speaker

hisse /ˈis/ excl **oh ~!** heave-ho!

hisser /ˈise/ [1]
A vtr 1▸ (faire monter) to hoist [charge, drapeau]; to hoist [sb] (up) [personne]; 2▸ fig **~ qn au rang de** to push sb to the rank of
B se hisser vpr 1▸ (monter avec effort) to heave oneself up; 2▸ fig (parvenir) to pull oneself up (**jusqu'à** to (the level of))

histoire /istwaʀ/ nf 1▸ (discipline) history; l'**~ de France**/**Chine** French/Chinese history; l'**~ de l'art**/**de la littérature** the history of art/of literature; **entrer dans** or **marquer l'~** to go down in history; **un lieu chargé d'~** a place steeped in history; l'**~ jugera** posterity will be the judge; **c'est de l'~ ancienne** (c'est sans intérêt) that's ancient history; (mieux vaut l'oublier) that was a long time ago; **la petite ~ veut que...** it is said that...; 2▸ (récit) story; **tout ça, c'est des ~s**○! that's all fiction!; **une ~ à dormir debout** a tall story; **raconter des ~s** to tell fibs; **c'est une ~ de fous** (c'est incroyable) it's absolutely crazy!; (sur les fous) it's a joke about mad people; 3▸ (aventure, affaire) **~ d'amour** love affair; **~ de famille**

family matter; **c'est sûrement une ~ d'argent** there must be money involved; **il m'est arrivé une drôle d'~** a funny thing happened to me; 4▸ (embarras) fuss **₵**; (ennuis) trouble **₵**; **en voilà des ~s!** what a to-do!, what a fuss!; **elle fait toujours des ~s** she's always making a fuss; **ça va faire des ~s** it will cause trouble; **il n'y a pas de quoi en faire une ~** there's no need to get worked up about it; **c'est une femme à ~s** she's a troublemaker; **une vie sans ~s** an uneventful life; **ça va faire des ~s avec elle si...** she'll be upset if...; **ça a été toute une ~ pour faire** it was a terrible job doing; **chercher des ~s à qn** to go on○ at sb; **au travail, et pas d'~s**○! get on with it, no messing about○!; 5▸ ○**prends quelques jours de repos, ~ de te changer les idées** take a few days' rest, just to have a break from everything; **~ de rire** or **s'amuser** just for fun

historien, **-ienne** /istɔʀjɛ̃, ɛn/ ▸ p. 372 nm,f historian

historique /istɔʀik/
A adj 1▸ (relatif au passé) historical; 2▸ (important) historic; 3▸ Ling **passé ~** past historic; **présent ~** historic present
B nm **faire l'~ du cinéma** to trace the history of the cinema; **faire l'~ d'une institution** to tell the story of an institution

hitlérien, **-ienne** /itleʀjɛ̃, ɛn/
A adj Hitlerian
B nm,f Hitlerite

hit-parade, pl ~**s** /ˈitpaʀad/ nm charts (pl)

HIV /aʃive/ nm (abbr = **Human Immunodeficiency Virus**) HIV

hiver /ivɛʀ/ ▸ p. 536 nm winter; **au cœur de l'~**, **au plus fort de l'~** in the depths of winter; **été comme ~** in summer and winter alike

hivernage /ivɛʀnaʒ/ nm 1▸ (de bétail) wintering; 2▸ (de navires) over wintering

hivernal, ~e, mpl **-aux** /ivɛʀnal, o/ adj 1▸ (d'hiver) winter (épith); 2▸ (comme en hiver) [jour, temps] wintry

hiverner /ivɛʀne/ [1]
A vtr to winter [bétail]
B vi (passer l'hiver) [animaux, bateaux] to winter; [personnes] to spend the winter

HLM /aʃɛlɛm/ nm ou f: abbr ▸ **habitation**

hobereau, pl ~**x** /ɔbʀo/ nm 1▸ (gentilhomme) country squire; 2▸ (faucon) hobby

hochement /ˈɔʃmɑ̃/ nm ~ (**de tête**) (de haut en bas) nod; (de droite à gauche) shake of the head

hocher /ˈɔʃe/ [1] vtr ~ **la tête** (de haut en bas) to nod; (de droite à gauche) to shake one's head

hochet /ˈɔʃɛ/ nm rattle

hockey /ˈɔkɛ/ ▸ p. 327 nm ~ (**sur glace**) ice hockey; ~ **sur gazon** hockey GB, field hockey US

hockeyeur, **-euse** /ˈɔkɛjœʀ, øz/ nm,f hockey player

holà /ˈɔla/ excl 1▸ (pour appeler) hey (there)!; 2▸ (pour arrêter un animal) whoa!
(Idiome) **mettre le ~ à qch** to put an end ou to sth

holding /ˈɔldiŋ/ nm ou f holding company

hold-up, pl ~ ou ~**s** /ˈɔldœp/ nm hold-up (**de qch** at sth); **commettre un ~** to stage a hold-up

hollandais, ~e /ˈɔlɑ̃dɛ, ɛz/ ▸ p. 336
A adj Dutch
B nm Ling Dutch

Hollandais, ~e /ˈɔlɑ̃dɛ, ɛz/ ▸ p. 392, p. 336 nm,f Dutchman/Dutchwoman; **les ~** the Dutch

Hollande /ˈɔlɑ̃d/ ▸ p. 504 nprf Holland

holocauste /ɔlɔkost/ nm 1▸ Hist (génocide) holocaust; 2▸ Relig holocaust, burned offering; 3▸ fig (total) sacrifice

homard /ˈɔmaʀ/ nm lobster
(Idiome) **rouge comme un ~** as red as a beetroot

homélie /ɔmeli/ nf homily

homéopathie /ɔmeopati/ nf homeopathy

homéopathique /ɔmeopatik/ adj [traitement, préparation] homeopathic; **à doses ~s** fig in small doses

homérique /ɔmeʀik/ adj Homeric

homicide /ɔmisid/
A adj homicidal
B nmf (personne) homicide

C nm (crime) homicide

⟨Composés⟩ ~ **involontaire** Jur unintentional manslaughter; ~ **avec préméditation** Jur premeditated murder; ~ **volontaire** Jur intentional manslaughter

hommage /ɔmaʒ/

A nm **1** (témoignage de respect) homage, tribute; **rendre ~ à qn/qch** to pay tribute to sb/sth; **c'est lui faire trop d'~** it's making too much of him/her; **2** (don) **faire ~ de qch à qn** to present sb with sth; **'~ de l'auteur'** 'with the author's compliments'; **3** Hist homage

B **hommages** nmpl **1** (salutations) respects; **2** (compliments) compliments

hommasse /ɔmas/ adj mannish

homme /ɔm/ nm **1** (espèce) **l'~** man; **l'~ de Néanderthal** Neanderthal man; **2** (genre humain) **l'~** mankind; **3** (être humain) human being; **un ~ à la mer!** Naut man overboard!; **comme un seul ~** as one; **4** (adulte de sexe masculin) man; **l'~ de la réunification** the man who achieved reunification; **l'~ de la situation** the right man for the job; **être l'~ de confiance de qn** to be sb's right-hand man; **il n'est pas ~ à se venger** he's not the type to want revenge; **l'~ du jour** the man of the moment

⟨Composés⟩ ~ **d'affaires** businessman; ~ **de bien** philanthropist; ~ **des bois** wild man; ~ **des cavernes** caveman; ~ **d'Église** man of the cloth; ~ **d'équipage** Naut crewman; ~ **d'esprit** wit; ~ **d'État** Pol statesman; ~ **à femmes** womanizer; ~ **au foyer** house-husband; ~ **de loi** lawyer; ~ **de main** hired hand; ~ **du monde** gentleman; ~ **de l'ombre** behind-the-scenes operator; ~ **de paille** front, straw man US; ~ **de peine** labourer^{GB}; ~ **de plume** writer; ~ **politique** Pol politician; ~ **de robe** lawyer; ~ **de terrain** man with practical experience; Pol grass-roots politician; ~ **à tout faire** handyman; ~ **de troupe** Mil private; ~ **en blanc** surgeons

⟨Idiome⟩ **un ~ averti en vaut deux** Prov forewarned is forearmed

homme-grenouille, pl **hommes-grenouilles** /ɔmɡRənuj/ nm frogman

homme-orchestre, pl **hommes-orchestres** /ɔmɔRkɛstR/ nm lit, fig one-man band

homo○ /omo/ adj, nmf (abbr = **homosexuel**) gay○

homogène /ɔmɔʒɛn/ adj **1** (uniforme) homogeneous; **2** (cohérent) [équipe] united, harmonious; [base] consistent

homogénéiser /ɔmɔʒeneize/ [1] vtr to homogenize

homogénéité /ɔmɔʒeneite/ nf homogeneity

homographe /ɔmɔɡRaf/

A adj [mots] homographic

B nm homograph

homologue /ɔmɔlɔɡ/

A adj homologous

B nmf **1** (personne) counterpart, opposite number; **2** Chimie (composé) homologue^{GB}

homologuer /ɔmɔlɔɡe/ [1] vtr **1** Admin (déclarer conforme à) to approve [produit, appareil]; **2** Sport (enregistrer) to recognize officially [record, performance]

homonyme /ɔmɔnim/

A adj Ling homonymous

B nm **1** Ling homonym; **2** (personne) namesake

homophobe /ɔmɔfɔb/

A adj homophobic

B nmf homophobe

homophone /ɔmɔfɔn/

A adj **1** Ling homophonous; **2** Mus homophonic

B nm Ling homophone

homosexualité /ɔmɔsɛksɥalite/ nf homosexuality

homosexuel, ~**elle** /ɔmɔsɛksɥɛl/ adj, nm,f homosexual

hongrois, ~**e** /'ɔ̃ɡRwa, az/

A ▸ p. 392 adj Hungarian

B ▸ p. 336 nm Ling Hungarian

honnête /ɔnɛt/ adj **1** (intègre) [personne, réponse] honest; [élections] fair; **2** (honorable) [personne] decent, respectable; [moyens] honest; [intention] honourable^{GB}; **c'est une proposition ~** it's a genuine offer; **3** (juste) [arbitre, prix, marché] fair; **4** (moyen) [travail, salaire, repas] reasonable; [résultat] fair

⟨Composés⟩ ~ **femme†** respectable woman; ~ **homme†** gentleman

honnêtement /ɔnɛtmɑ̃/ adv **1** (avec probité) [gérer, dire] honestly; [répondre] frankly; [agir] properly; [juger] fairly; [reconnaître] freely; **2** (convenablement) [rétribuer] fairly; **gagner ~ sa vie** to earn a decent living; **travail ~ payé** reasonably well-paid job

honnêteté /ɔnɛtte/ nf (probité) honesty

honneur /ɔnœR/

A nm **1** (fierté) honour^{GB} **C**; **s'être engagé sur l'~ à faire** to be honour^{GB} bound to do; **l'~ national** national pride; **sauver l'~** to save face; **faire ~ à sa parole** to honour^{GB} one's promise; **avec ~** [servir] honourably^{GB}; **dans l'~** [capituler, se réconcilier] honourably^{GB}; **jouer pour l'~** to play for the love of it; **combattre pour l'~** to fight as a matter of honour^{GB}; **être l'~ de sa famille** [personne] to be a credit to one's family; **2** (mérite) credit; **ce fut tout à leur ~** it was all credit to them; **3** (privilège) honour^{GB}; **se disputer l'~ de faire** to fight over the honour^{GB} of; **à qui ai-je l'~?** fml to whom do I have the honour^{GB} of speaking? sout; **~ au perdant!** loser goes first!; **à toi l'~!** you do the honours^{GB}; **vous me faites trop d'~** you flatter me; **j'ai l'~ de vous informer que** I beg to inform you that; **d'~** [escalier, cour] main; ▸ **seigneur**; **4** (célébration) **être (mis) à l'~** [personne] to be honoured^{GB}; **mettre qn à l'~** to honour^{GB} sb; **être à l'** or **en ~** [chose] to be in favour^{GB}; **être remis à l'~** [tradition, usage, discipline] to regain favour^{GB}; **faire** or **rendre ~ à** [personne] to do justice to a meal; **~ à ceux qui** all praise to those who; **en quel ~?** iron any particular reason why?; **5** Jeux (carte haute) honour^{GB}

B **honneurs** nmpl (distinction) honours^{GB}; **être accueilli avec les ~s réservés aux chefs d'État** to be received with the ceremony reserved for heads of State; **rendre les ~s à** Mil (funèbres) to pay the last honours^{GB} to; (militaires) to honour^{GB}; **la richesse et les ~s** wealth and glory; **faire les ~s de la maison à qn** to show sb around the house; **avoir les ~s de la presse** to be mentioned in the press

⟨Idiomes⟩ **en tout bien tout ~** (sans arrière-pensées) with no hidden motive; **il est venu prendre un verre, mais c'était en tout bien tout ~** he came round for a drink but that's all there was to it

honnir /'ɔniR/ [3] vtr liter to execrate

⟨Idiome⟩ **honni soit qui mal y pense** evil unto him who evil thinks

honorabilité /ɔnɔRabilite/ nf integrity

honorable /ɔnɔRabl/ adj **1** (respectable) [personne, métier, reddition] honourable^{GB}; [compagnie, marque] venerable; **2** (suffisant) [classement, score] creditable; [moyens financiers, nombre, proportion] sizable; [salaire] decent

honorablement /ɔnɔRabləmɑ̃/ adv **1** (de façon respectable) honourably^{GB}; ~ **connu** [famille] highly respected; [compagnie] venerable; **2** (suffisamment) decently; **gagner ~ sa vie** to earn a decent living

honoraire /ɔnɔRɛR/

A adj [membre] honorary

B **honoraires** nmpl (rétributions) fee (sg)

honorer /ɔnɔRe/ [1]

A vtr **1** (rendre hommage) to honour^{GB} [Dieu, personne, équipe, mémoire]; ~ **qn de sa confiance** to honour^{GB} sb with one's trust; **2** (acquitter) to honour^{GB} [promesse, dette]; **3** (procurer de la fierté) [personne] to be a credit to [pays, profession, parents]; **4** (donner du mérite) **votre courage vous honore** your bravery does you credit

B **s'honorer** vpr **1** (être fier) to be proud; **2** (s'attirer de la considération) to bring credit on oneself

honorifique /ɔnɔRifik/ adj honorary; **nommé président à titre ~** appointed honorary president

honoris causa /ɔnɔRiskoza/ loc adj [docteur] honorary; **être nommé docteur ~** to be awarded an honorary doctorate

honte /'ɔ̃t/ nf **1** (gêne) shame; **rougir de ~** to blush with shame; **avoir ~** to be ashamed of; **faire ~ à qn** to make sb ashamed; **sans ~** fml shamelessly; **à ma (grande) ~** to my (great) embarrassment; **avouer qch sans ~** to acknowledge sth openly; **2** (discrédit) disgrace; **faire la ~ de** to be a disgrace; **jeter la ~ sur** to bring disgrace upon

honteusement /'ɔ̃tøzmɑ̃/ adv (ignoblement) [traiter, trahir] shamefully; (sans honte) [tricher] shamelessly

honteux, -euse /'ɔ̃tø, øz/ adj **1** (déshonorant) [conduite, secret] disgraceful; **2** (gêné) [personne] ashamed (**de qn/qch** of sb/sth)

hôpital, *pl* **-aux** /ɔpital, o/ *nm* hospital; ~ **de campagne** field hospital

Composé ~ **de jour** outpatient clinic

Idiome **c'est l'~ qui se moque de la charité** it's the pot calling the kettle black

hoquet /'ɔkɛ/ *nm* hiccup; **avoir le ~** to have hiccups; **avoir un ~ de frayeur** to gulp with fright

hoqueter /'ɔkte/ [20] *vi* [*personne*] to hiccup; [*moteur*] to sputter

horaire /ɔRƐR/

A *adj* [*salaire, débit, tarif*] per hour; **tranche** *or* **plage ~** time-slot

B *nm* **1** (de train, bus) timetable GB, schedule US; (d'avion, de vols) schedule; **les ~s de train** the train times; **2** (emploi du temps) timetable, schedule; **les ~s de travail** working hours; **les ~s libres** *or* **à la carte** flexitime

horde /'ɔRd/ *nf* (de barbares) horde; (de chiens, loups) pack

horizon /ɔRiʒɔ̃/ *nm* **1** (limite de la vue) horizon; **l'~ est bouché** lit there are clouds on the horizon; fig the road ahead is not clear; **2** fig (avenir) outlook; **des réformes se profilent à l'~** reforms are appearing on the horizon; **cet emploi m'ouvre de nouveaux ~s** this job opens up new horizons for me; **3** fig (univers) horizons (*pl*); **changer d'~** to have a change of scene; **ils viennent d'~s très divers** they come from very varied backgrounds

horizontal, **~e**[1], *mpl* **-aux** /ɔRizɔ̃tal, o/ *adj* horizontal

horizontale[2] /ɔRizɔ̃tal/ *nf* Math (ligne) horizontal; **à l'~** in a horizontal position

horloge /ɔRlɔʒ/ *nf* clock

horloger, -ère /ɔRlɔʒe, ƐR/

A *adj* watchmaking; **B** ▸ p. 372 *nm,f* watchmaker

horlogerie /ɔRlɔʒRi/ ▸ p. 372 *nf* (industrie) watchmaking; (boutique) watchmaker's (shop); (produits) clocks and watches (*pl*); **pièce d'~** watch component

hormis /'ɔRmi/ *prép* fml save sout, except (for)

hormonal, **~e**, *mpl* **-aux** /ɔRmɔnal, o/ *adj* [*problème*] hormonal; [*traitement*] hormone (*épith*)

hormone /ɔRmon/ *nf* hormone

hormonothérapie /ɔRmɔnoteRapi/ *nf* hormone therapy

horodateur /ɔRodatœR/ *nm* parking ticket machine

horoscope /ɔRɔskɔp/ *nm* horoscope

horreur /ɔRœR/ *nf* **1** (atrocité) horror; **2** (parole méchante) awful thing; **3** (épouvante) horror; **être glacé d'~** to be frozen with horror; **être saisi d'~** to be horror-struck; **être une ~** [*personne, chose, œuvre*] to be horrible; **quelle ~!** how horrible!; **4** (aversion) loathing; **avoir ~ de qn/qch**, **avoir qn/qch en ~** to loathe sb/sth; **avoir ~ de faire** to hate doing; **ton attitude me fait ~** your attitude horrifies me

Idiome **c'est (vraiment) l'~**○ it's (really) the pits○

horrible /ɔRibl/ *adj* **1** (abominable) [*cri, maladie*] horrible; [*temps*] filthy; [*moment, séjour*] dreadful; [*meurtre, scène*] horrific; [*douleur, bruit*] terrible; [*pensée*] horrible; [*paroles, personne*] nasty; **2** (répugnant) [*goût, odeur*] revolting; [*créature*] horrid; [*nourriture*] dreadful; **3** (laid) [*visage, objet, cicatrice*] hideous

horriblement /ɔRibləmɑ̃/ *adv* **1** (effroyablement) [*brûlé*] horribly; **2** (terriblement) [*dangereux, froid*] terribly

horrifier /ɔRifje/ [2] *vtr* to horrify

horripiler /ɔRipile/ [1] *vtr* to exasperate

hors /'ɔR/

⚠ Lorsque *hors* et *hors de* sont suivis d'un nom sans article reportez-vous à ce nom. Ainsi *hors catégorie* est traité sous **catégorie** et *hors d'atteinte* sous **atteinte**. Une expression telle que *mettre qn hors la loi* figure sous **loi**. *hors-la-loi* est une entrée à part.
  Les autres emplois de *hors* sont présentés dans l'article ci-dessous.

A *prép* liter apart from, save sout

B **hors de** *loc prép* (dans l'espace) (position fixe) outside; (avec mouvement) out of; fig outside; **~ d'ici!** get out of here!; **~ de chez soi** away from home

Composé ~ **tout** overall; **longueur ~ tout** overall length

Idiomes **être ~ de soi** to be beside oneself; **cela m'a mis ~ de moi** it infuriated me

hors-bord /'ɔRbɔR/

A *adj* [*moteur*] outboard

B *nm inv* powerboat, speedboat; **faire du ~** to go speedboating

hors-d'œuvre /'ɔRdœvR/ *nm inv* **1** Culin starter, hors d'oeuvre; **2** ○fig foretaste

hors-jeu /'ɔRʒø/ *nm inv* (pour) ~ for offside

hors-la-loi /'ɔRlalwa/ *nm inv* outlaw

hors-piste /'ɔRpist/ *nm inv* off-piste skiing

hors-série /'ɔRseRi/ **1** *adj inv* **un numéro ~** a special issue; **2** *nm* special issue; **~ sur le cinéma indien** Indian cinema special

hors-sol /'ɔRsɔl/ *nm inv* **1** (culture) soilless culture; **2** (élevage) industrial husbandry

hortensia /ɔRtɑ̃sja/ *nm* hydrangea

horticole /ɔRtikɔl/ *adj* horticultural

horticulteur, -trice /ɔRtikyltœR, tRis/ ▸ p. 372 *nm,f* horticulturist

hospice /ɔspis/ *nm* **1** (asile) home; **finir à l'~** to end up in the poorhouse; **2** †Relig hospice†

Composé ~ **de vieillards** old people's home

hospitalier, -ière /ɔspitalje, ƐR/ *adj* **1** Méd hospital (*épith*); **centre ~** hospital; **2** (accueillant) hospitable; **3** Relig [*ordre*] charitable

hospitalisation /ɔspitalizasjɔ̃/ *nf* hospitalization

Composé ~ **à domicile** home (medical) care

hospitaliser /ɔspitalize/ [1] *vtr* to hospitalize

hospitalité /ɔspitalite/ *nf* hospitality; **demander l'~ à qn** to ask sb for shelter

hospitalo-universitaire, *pl* **~s** /ɔspitaloyniveRsiteR/ *adj* **centre ~** teaching hospital

hostellerie /ɔstɛlRi/ *nf* (country) inn

hostie /ɔsti/ *nf* Relig Host

hostile /ɔstil/ *adj* hostile (à to)

hostilité /ɔstilite/ *nf* hostility; **les ~s** Mil hostilities

hosto○ /ɔsto/ *nm* (abbr = **hôpital**) hospital

hôte /ot/

A *nm* **1** (personne qui invite) host; **2** (résident) (personne) occupant; (animal) inhabitant; **3** Biol host

B *nmf* **1** (personne invitée) guest; **2** (d'appartement) occupant; (d'hôtel) guest

hôtel /otɛl/ *nm* hotel

Composés ~ **des impôts** tax office; ~ **de la Monnaie** Admin (French) Mint; ~ **particulier** Archit town house; ~ **de tourisme** Tourisme tourist hotel; ~ **des ventes** Comm saleroom; ~ **de ville** Admin ≈ town hall

hôtel-club, *pl* **hôtels-clubs** /otɛlklœb/ *nm* (hotel-based) holiday club

hôtel-Dieu, *pl* **hôtels-Dieu** /otɛldjø/ *nm* main hospital

hôtelier, -ière /otəlje, ƐR/ ▸ p. 372

A *adj* [*industrie, chaîne*] hotel (*épith*); [*école*] hotel management

B *nm,f* hotelkeeper

hôtellerie /otɛlRi/ *nf* (profession) hotel business

hôtesse /otɛs/ ▸ p. 372 *nf* **1** (professionnelle) (de société, magasin) receptionist; (d'exposition) hostess; (de train, bateau) stewardess; **2** (personne qui invite) hostess

Composés ~ **d'accueil** receptionist; ~ **de l'air** Aviat stewardess; ~ **au sol** Aviat ground attendant

hotte /'ɔt/ *nf* **1** (de vendangeur) basket (carried on the back); **2** (de cheminée) hood; **3** (de cuisinière) hood GB, range hood US

Composés ~ **aspirante** extractor hood GB, ventilator US; **la ~ du Père Noël** Father Christmas's sack GB, Santa Claus's sack US

houblon /'ublɔ̃/ *nm* hop C

houe /'u/ *nf* hoe

houille /'uj/ *nf* (charbon) coal

Composé ~ **blanche** hydroelectric power

houiller, -ère[1] /'uje, ƐR/ *adj* [*gisement, industrie*] coal (*épith*); [*terrain*] coal-bearing; [*région*] coalmining

houillère[2] /'ujƐR/ *nf* **1** (dépôt) coalmine; **2** (exploitation) colliery

houle /'ul/ *nf* swell

houlette /'ulɛt/ *nf* **1** (de berger) crook; **sous la ~ de** fig under the leadership of; **2** (de jardinier) trowel

houleux, -euse /'ulø, øz/ *adj* **1** [*mer*] rough; **2** [*réunion, débat*] stormy

houppe /'up/ *nf* **1** (de cheveux) tuft; (de fils) tassel; **2** (à poudrer) powder puff

houppelande /'uplãd/ *nf* greatcoat

houppette /'upɛt/ *nf* **1** (à poudrer) powder puff; **2** (de cheveux) little tuft (of hair)

hourra /'uRA/
A *nm* (acclamation) cheer; **pousser des ~s** to cheer; **pousser un ~ de joie** to give a shout of joy
B *excl* hurrah!; **hip hip hip ~!** hip hip hurrah!

houspiller /'uspije/ [1] *vtr* to scold; **se faire ~** to be scolded

housse /'us/ *nf* gén cover; (de chaise, sofa) slipcover; (de siège de voiture) seat cover; (de vêtements) garment bag; (de machine à écrire) dust cover
Composé ~ **de couette** duvet cover, quilt cover

houx /'u/ *nm inv* holly

HS○ /'aʃɛs/ *adj* (*abbr* = **hors service**) [*machine*] on the blink○; [*personne*] knackered◑ GB, shot○ US

HT (*written abbr* = **hors taxes**) exclusive of tax; **2** (*written abbr* = **haute tension**) HV

hublot /'yblo/ *nm* (de bateau) porthole; (d'avion) window; (de machine à laver) door

huche /'yʃ/ *nf* (coffre) chest
Composé ~ **à pain** bread bin

huées /'ɥe/ *nfpl* booing 𝒞

huer /'ɥe/ [1]
A *vtr* to boo [*auteur, discours*]
B *vi* [*hibou*] to hoot

huile /ɥil/ *nf* **1** (substance) oil; **sardines à l'~** sardines in vegetable oil; **pommes à l'~** potato salad; **2** Art (tableau) oil painting; **3** ○(personnage important) big shot○, bigwig○
Composés ~ **d'arachide** peanut oil; ~ **de coude** hum elbow grease; ~ **de graissage** lubricating oil; ~ **de paraffine** liquid paraffin; ~ **de ricin** castor oil; ~ **solaire** suntan oil
Idiomes **tout/ça baigne dans l'~**○ everything/it is going smoothly; **jeter** *or* **verser de l'~ sur le feu** to add fuel to the fire

huiler /ɥile/ [1] *vtr* to oil [*peau, mécanisme, poêle*]; **bien huilé** [*mécanisme, machine*] lit, fig well-oiled; [*reportage, scénario*] fig slick

huilerie /ɥilRi/ *nf* **1** (usine) oil mill; **2** (commerce) oil trade

huileux, -euse /ɥilø, øz/ *adj* oily

huilier /ɥilje/ *nm* (oil and vinegar) cruet

huis /'ɥi/ *nm inv* Jur ~ **clos** closed hearing; **à ~ clos** Jur in camera; fig behind closed doors

huisserie /ɥisRi/ *nf* (de porte) doorframe; (de fenêtre) window frame

huissier /ɥisje/ ▸ p. 372 *nm* **1** Jur ~ **(de justice)** bailiff; **2** (portier) porter; (de tribunal) usher

huit /'ɥit, but before consonant 'ɥi/ ▸ p. 398, p. 296, p. 155
A *adj inv* eight; ~ **jours** (semaine) a week; (précisément) eight days; **mardi en ~** a week on Tuesday; **donner ses ~ jours à qn** to give sb a week's notice
B *pron* eight
C *nm inv* **1** (numéro) eight; **2** (trajectoire) a figure of eight

huitaine /'ɥitɛn/ *nf* **1** (semaine) about a week; **sous ~** within a week; **2** (environ huit) about eight

huitième /'ɥitjɛm/ ▸ p. 398, p. 155
A *adj* eighth
B *nf* Scol fourth year of primary school, age 9-10
Composés **le ~ art** television; ~ **de finale** Sport round before the quarter finals

huître /ɥitR/ *nf* oyster

huîtrier, -ière¹ /ɥitRije, ɛR/
A *adj* oyster (*épith*)
B *nm* (oiseau) oystercatcher

huîtrière² /ɥitRijɛR/ *nf* (banc) oyster bed; (parc) oyster farm

hululement /'ylylmã/ *nm* hooting 𝒞

hululer /'ylyle/ [1] *vi* to hoot

humain, ~e /ymɛ̃, ɛn/
A *adj* **1** gén human; **pertes ~es** loss of life 𝒞; **marée ~e** tide of humanity; **2** (clément) [*solution, régime*] humane; [*personne*] human
B *nm* **1** (personne) human being; **2** (être terrestre) human; **3** Philos **l'~ et le divin** the human and the divine
Idiome **l'erreur est ~e** to err is human

humainement /ymɛnmã/ *adv* **1** [*possible, impossible*] humanly; **2** [*traiter, se comporter*] humanely

humanisation /ymanizasjõ/ *nf* (de prison, conditions de vie) humanization; (de politique) softening

humaniser /ymanize/ [1]
A *vtr* to humanize [*conditions de vie*]; to make [sb/sth] more human [*ville*]
B **s'humaniser** *vpr* to become more human

humaniste /ymanist/ *adj, nmf* humanist

humanitaire /ymanitɛR/ *adj* humanitarian

humanité /ymanite/ *nf* **1** (genre humain) humanity; **2** (altruisme) humanity; **avec ~** [*traiter*] humanely

humble /œbl/
A *adj* [*personne*] (par soi-même) unassuming; (vis-à-vis d'autres) humble; [*ton, manières*] unassuming; [*travail, origine*] humble; [*maison*] modest; **se faire ~ devant qn** to humble oneself before sb
B **humbles** *nmpl* **les ~s** the common people

humblement /œbləmã/ *adv* humbly

humecter /ymɛkte/ [1] *vtr* to moisten [*visage, gâteau*] (**de, avec** with); to dampen [*linge*]

humer /'yme/ [1] *vtr* **1** to sniff [*air*]; **2** liter to smell [*fleur, potage*]

humérus /ymeRys/ *nm inv* humerus

humeur /ymœR/ *nf* **1** (disposition passagère) mood; **être de bonne/mauvaise ~** to be in a good/bad mood; **être/ne pas être d'~ à faire** to be in the mood/in no mood to do; **2** (disposition dominante) temper; **d'~ égale** even-tempered; **d'~ inégale** moody; **un spectacle plein de bonne ~** a fun-filled show; **3** (mauvaise disposition) bad temper; **geste d'~** bad-tempered gesture

humide /ymid/ *adj* **1** [*linge, cheveux, maison*] damp; **il avait le regard ~** his eyes were moist with tears; **2** [*région, air*] humid; [*saison*] rainy; **il fait froid et ~** it's cold and damp; **il fait une chaleur ~** it's muggy

humidificateur /ymidifikatœR/ *nm* humidifier

humidifier /ymidifje/ [2] *vtr* to dampen [*linge, papier*]; to spray [sth] (with water) [*peau*]; to humidify [*air*]

humidité /ymidite/ *nf* **1** (de lieu) dampness, damp; **'craint l'~'** 'should be stored in a dry place'; **le livre est resté à l'~** the book has been left in a damp place; **2** (résultat) damp; **prendre l'~** to be affected by damp; **3** (de climat, région) humidity

humiliation /ymiljasjõ/ *nf* humiliation

humilier /ymilje/ [2] *vtr* to humiliate; **se sentir humilié** to feel humiliated (**par** by; **de faire** doing)

humilité /ymilite/ *nf* **1** (de personne) humility; **en toute/ avec ~** in all/with humility; **2** (de condition, tâche) humble nature

humoriste /ymɔRist/ ▸ p. 372 *nmf* **1** (auteur) humorist; **2** (farceur) joker

humoristique /ymɔRistik/ *adj* humorous; **dessin ~** cartoon

humour /ymuR/ *nm* (de personne, situation) humour^GB; ~ **noir** black humour^GB; **ne pas avoir le sens de l'~** to have no sense of humour^GB; **avec ~** humorously; **savoir faire preuve d'~** to take things in good part; **il n'a pas su apprécier l'~ de la situation** he couldn't see the funny side of it; **faire de l'~** to make jokes

huppé, ~e /'ype/ *adj* **1** ○(mondain) upper-crust (*épith*); **2** [*oiseau*] crested

hure /'yR/ *nf* (tête, trophée) head

hurlement /'yRləmã/ *nm* (d'animal) howl, howling 𝒞; (de personne) yell, howl; (de sirène) wail, wailing 𝒞; **pousser un ~ de douleur** to howl with pain

hurler /'yRle/ [1]
A *vtr* **1** [*personne*] to yell (**à qn** at sb); **2** [*télévision, radio, magnétophone*] to blare out

B *vi* **1** (pousser des cris) to howl; ∼ **de douleur** to howl with pain; ∼ **de rire** to roar with laughter; ∼ **au scandale** to be outraged; **2** (parler fort) to yell; **3** (faire du bruit) [*sirène*] to wail; [*vent*] to roar; [*radio*] to blare

(Idiomes) ∼ **avec les loups** to follow the crowd; ∼ **à la mort** to bay at the moon

hurluberlu, ∼**e** /yʀlybɛʀly/ *nm,f* oddball○

hutte /ˈyt/ *nf* hut

hybride /ibʀid/ *adj*, *nm* lit, fig hybrid

hydratant, ∼**e** /idʀatɑ̃, ɑ̃t/
A *adj* moisturizing
B *nm* moisturizer

hydratation /idʀatasjɔ̃/ *nf* **1** (de la peau) moisturizing; **2** (du corps) hydration; **3** Chimie hydration

hydrate /idʀat/ *nm* hydrate
(Composé) ∼ **de carbone** carbohydrate

hydrater /idʀate/ [1]
A *vtr* **1** to moisturize [*peau*]; **2** to hydrate [*tissu, organisme*]; **3** Chimie to hydrate
B **s'hydrater** *vpr* **1** [*personne*] **bien s'**∼ to take plenty of fluids; **2** Chimie to undergo hydration

hydraulique /idʀolik/
A *adj* hydraulic
B *nf* hydraulics (+ *v sg*)

hydravion /idʀavjɔ̃/ *nm* seaplane, hydroplane

hydre /idʀ/ *nf* Mythol Hydra

hydro /idʀo/ *préf* hydro; ∼**céphale** hydrocephalic; ∼**électrique** hydroelectric

hydrocarbure /idʀokaʀbyʀ/ *nm* hydrocarbon

hydrocution /idʀokysjɔ̃/ *nf* immersion hypothermia

hydrofuge /idʀofyʒ/ *adj* [*mastic*] water-repellent

hydrogène /idʀoʒɛn/ *nm* hydrogen
(Composé) ∼ **lourd** Chimie deuterium

hydroglisseur /idʀoglisœʀ/ *nm* hydroplane

hydromel /idʀomɛl/ *nm* mead

hydrophile /idʀofil/ *adj* [*tissu, matière*] absorbent

hydroptère /idʀoptɛʀ/ *nm* hydrofoil

hydrorésistant, ∼**e** /idʀoʀezistɑ̃, ɑ̃t/ *adj* water resistant

hydroxyde /idʀoksid/ *nm* hydroxide

hyène /ˈjɛn/ *nf* hyena

hygiaphone® /iʒjafon/ *nm* grill (*perforated communication panel*)

hygiène /iʒjɛn/ *nf* hygiene; **contraire à l'**∼ unhygienic; **par mesure d'**∼ for (the sake of) hygiene; ∼ **scolaire** health guidelines for schools; **une bonne** ∼ **alimentaire** a healthy diet
(Composés) ∼ **corporelle** personal hygiene; ∼ **mentale** mental health

hygiénique /iʒjenik/ *adj* **1** (propre) hygienic; **2** (sain) healthy; **promenade** ∼ constitutional

hymen /imɛn/ *nm* **1** Anat hymen; **2** (mariage) liter nuptial bond

hymne /imn/ *nm* Littérat, Mus, fig hymn; ∼ **à la vie** fig hymn to life
(Composé) ∼ **national** national anthem

hyperactif, -ive /ipɛʀaktif, iv/ *adj* hyperactive

hyperbole /ipɛʀbɔl/ *nf* **1** Math hyperbola; **2** Littérat hyperbole

hypercalorique /ipɛʀkalɔʀik/ *adj* high in calories (*jamais épith*), high-calorie (*épith*)

hyperclassique /ipɛʀklasik/ *adj* [*situation, réaction*] absolutely classic; **roman** or **pièce** or **film** ∼ great classic

hyperconnu, ∼**e** /ipɛʀkɔny/ *adj* extremely famous

hyperdoué, ∼**e** /ipɛʀdwe/ *adj* exceptionally gifted

hyperinformé, ∼**e** /ipɛʀɛ̃fɔʀme/ *adj* very well informed

hypermarché /ipɛʀmaʀʃe/ *nm* large supermarket

hypermétrope /ipɛʀmetʀɔp/ *adj* longsighted

hypernerveux, -euse /ipɛʀnɛʀvø, øz/ *adj* highly strung

hyperpuissance /ipɛʀpɥisɑ̃s/ *nf* superpower

hyperpuissant, ∼**e** /ipɛʀpɥisɑ̃, ɑ̃t/ *adj* [*voiture, moteur*] extremely powerful

hypersensible /ipɛʀsɑ̃sibl/ *adj* hypersensitive

hypersophistiqué, ∼**e** /ipɛʀsofistike/ *adj* [*personne, vêtement*] very sophisticated; [*théorie*] highly sophisticated

hyperspécialisé, ∼**e** /ipɛʀspesjalize/ *adj* highly specialized

hypertendu, ∼**e** /ipɛʀtɑ̃dy/ *adj* **1** ○extremely tense; **2** Méd suffering from high blood pressure

hypertension /ipɛʀtɑ̃sjɔ̃/ *nf* ∼ **(artérielle)** high blood pressure, hypertension spéc

hypertrophie /ipɛʀtʀofi/ *nf* **1** Méd enlargement, hypertrophy spéc; **2** (de ville) overdevelopment

hypertrophier: s'hypertrophier /ipɛʀtʀofje/ [2] *vpr* **1** Méd to hypertrophy; **2** [*administration, ville, sentiment*] to become overdeveloped

hypnose /ipnoz/ *nf* hypnosis

hypnotiser /ipnotize/ [1] *vtr* lit to hypnotize; fig to mesmerize

hypnotiseur, -euse /ipnotizœʀ, øz/ ▸ p. 372 *nm,f* hypnotist

hypocagne = **hypokhâgne**

hypocalorique /ipokalɔʀik/ *adj* low-calorie (*épith*), low in calories (*jamais épith*)

hypocondriaque /ipokɔ̃dʀijak/ *adj*, *nmf* hypochondriac

hypocrisie /ipokʀizi/ *nf* hypocrisy

hypocrite /ipokʀit/
A *adj* hypocritical
B *nmf* hypocrite

hypodermique /ipodɛʀmik/ *adj* hypodermic

hypoglucidique /ipoglysidik/ *adj* [*aliment*] low-carbohydrate (*épith*)

hypokhâgne /ipokaɲ/ *nf* students' slang first year preparatory class in humanities for entrance to École normale supérieure

hypophyse /ipofiz/ *nf* pituitary gland

hyposodé, ∼**e** /iposode/ *adj* low-salt (*épith*)

hypotaupe /ipotop/ *nf* students' slang first year preparatory class in mathematics and science for entrance to Grandes Écoles

hypotendu, ∼**e** /ipotɑ̃dy/ *adj* suffering from low blood pressure ou hypotension spéc

hypotension /ipotɑ̃sjɔ̃/ *nf* ∼ **(artérielle)** low blood pressure, hypotension spéc

hypoténuse /ipotenyz/ *nf* hypotenuse

hypothécaire /ipotekɛʀ/ *adj* mortgage (*épith*); **créancier/débiteur** ∼ mortgagee/mortgager

hypothèque /ipotɛk/ *nf* **1** mortgage; **2** fig (obstacle) obstacle

hypothéquer /ipoteke/ [14] *vtr* to mortgage; fig to endanger [*chances*]; ∼ **l'avenir** fig to mortgage one's future

hypothèse /ipotɛz/ *nf* hypothesis; ∼ **de travail** working hypothesis; **se refuser à la moindre** ∼ to refuse to speculate; **écarter l'**∼ **de l'accident** to rule out the possibility of an accident

hypothétique /ipotetik/ *adj* hypothetical

hystérie /isteʀi/ *nf* hysteria; ∼ **collective** mass hysteria

hystérique /isteʀik/
A *adj* hysterical
B *nmf* **1** (nerveux) pej bundle of nerves; **2** Méd, Psych hysteric

h

Ii

i, I /i/ nm inv i, I

(Idiome) **mettre les points sur les i** to dot the i's and cross the t's

ibérique /ibeʀik/ adj Iberian; **la péninsule ~** the Iberian peninsula

iceberg /ajsbɛʀɡ, isbɛʀɡ/ nm iceberg; **la partie visible de l'~** fig the tip of the iceberg

ici /isi/ adv **1** (dans l'espace) here; **c'est ~ que…** this is where…; **c'est ~ même que…** it was in this very place that…; **par ~ la sortie** this way out; **par ~!** j'ai trouvé **quelque chose!** over here! I've found something!; **les gens sont plutôt méfiants par ~** the people around here are a bit wary; **il y a une belle église par ~** there is a beautiful church near here; **les gens d'~** the locals; **~ Grovagnard** (au téléphone, à la radio) this is Grovagnard; **je vois ça d'~!** I can just picture it!; **vous êtes ~ chez vous!** make yourself at home!; **2** (dans le temps) **jusqu'~** (au présent) until now; (dans le passé) until then; **d'~ peu** shortly; **d'~ demain** by tomorrow; **d'~ deux jours** two days from now; **je te téléphone ce soir, d'~ là, tâche de te reposer** I'll phone you tonight, in the meantime try and rest; **d'~ là, on sera tous morts** by then, we'll all be dead; **d'~ à ce qu'il change d'avis, il n'y a pas loin** it won't be long before he changes his mind; **il l'aime bien, mais d'~ à ce qu'il l'épouse…** he likes her, but as for marrying her…

ici-bas /isiba/ adv here below

icône /ikon/ nf icon

iconographie /ikɔnɔɡʀafi/ nf (sur un thème) iconography; (illustrations) illustrations (pl)

idéal, ~e, mpl **-aux** /ideal, o/
A adj ideal
B nm ideal; **ce n'est pas l'~** it's not ideal; **dans l'~** ideally

idéalement /idealmɑ̃/ adv ideally

idée /ide/ nf **1** (inspiration, projet) idea (**de faire** of doing); **une ~ de cadeau** an idea for a present; **il y a de l'~ dans ce projet** there are some good ideas in the project; **avoir de l'~** to be inventive; **avoir une ~ derrière la tête** to have something in mind; **il n'a qu'une ~ en tête, apprendre à piloter** all he can think about is learning to fly; **2** (opinion) idea (**sur** about); (réflexion) thought; **j'ai ma petite ~ sur le sujet** I have my own theory about that; **avoir ~ que** to think that; **se faire une haute ~ de** to think a lot of; **se faire des ~s** to imagine things; **mettre de l'ordre dans ses ~s** (dans l'immédiat) to gather one's thoughts; (à long terme) to order one's thoughts; **avoir les ~s larges** to be broad-minded; **ça te changera les ~s** it'll take your mind off things; **changer d'~** to change one's mind; **avoir de la suite dans les ~s** (savoir ce que l'on veut) to be single-minded; (être entêté) not to be easily deterred; **faire à son ~** to do as one thinks best; **3** (esprit) **avoir dans l'~ que** to have an idea that; **avoir dans l'~ de faire** to plan to do; **il n'est venu à l'~ de personne de faire** nobody has thought of doing; **il ne leur viendrait jamais à l'~ de faire** it would never occur to them to do; **je reste dans l'~ que… I still think that…; il s'est mis dans l'~ de faire** he's taken it into his head to do

(Composés) **~ fixe** idée fixe, obsession; **c'est une ~ fixe chez lui** he's got a fixation about it; **~ force** key idea; **~ de génie** brainwave○; **~ noire** dark thought; **~ toute faite** second-hand idea

idem /idem/ adv ditto; **tu seras puni et lui ~**○ you'll be punished and so will he

identification /idɑ̃tifikasjɔ̃/ nf identification

identifier /idɑ̃tifje/ [2]
A vtr **1** (reconnaître) to identify; **non identifié** unidentified; **2** (assimiler) to identify (**à, avec, et** with)
B s'**identifier** vpr (être comparable) to become identified (**à** with); (vouloir ressembler) to identify (**à** with)

identique /idɑ̃tik/ adj **1** (pareil) identical (**à** to); **2** (constant) unchanged

identiquement /idɑ̃tikmɑ̃/ adv identically

identitaire /idɑ̃titɛʀ/ adj [crise, révolution, marqueur] identity; **~ d'emprunt** assumed identity; [affirmation, question] of identity

identité /idɑ̃tite/ nf **1** Math, Philos, Psych identity; **2** (état civil) identity; **~ d'emprunt** assumed identity; **(les services de) l'~ judiciaire** the French criminal records office; **3** (similarité) similarity; **~ de vues** similar views (pl)

idéogramme /ideɔɡʀam/ nm ideogram

idéologie /ideɔlɔʒi/ nf ideology

idéologue /ideɔlɔɡ/ nmf ideologist

idiomatique /idjɔmatik/ adj idiomatic

idiome /idjom/ nm idiom

idiosyncrasie /idjosɛ̃kʀazi/ nf idiosyncrasy

idiot, ~e /idjo, ɔt/
A adj stupid
B nm **1** gén idiot; **l'~ du village** the village idiot; **faire l'~** (sans simuler) to behave like an idiot; (en simulant) to play the fool, to act innocent GB, to act dumb; **2** †Méd idiot†

idiotie /idjɔsi/ nf **1** (parole) stupid thing; **2** (ânerie) rubbish ℂ GB, garbage ℂ US; **3** (caractère) stupidity; **4** †Méd idiocy†

idiotisme /idjɔtism/ nm Ling idiom

idoine /idwan/ adj suitable

idolâtre /idolɑtʀ/
A adj idolatrous
B nmf idolator

idolâtrer /idolɑtʀe/ [1] vtr to idolize

idolâtrie /idolɑtʀi/ nf idolatry

idole /idɔl/ nf idol

idylle /idil/ nf **1** (liaison) love affair; **2** (poème) idyll

idyllique /idilik/ adj idyllic

if /if/ nm **1** (arbre) yew; **2** (bois) yew

IFOP /ifɔp/ nm (abbr = **Institut français d'opinion publique**) French institute for opinion polls

ignare /iɲaʀ/
A adj ignorant
B nmf ignoramus

ignifuge /iɲifyʒ/ adj [produit] fireproofing (épith)

ignifuger /iɲifyʒe/ [13] vtr to fireproof; **un mur ignifugé** a fireproof wall

ignoble /iɲɔbl/ adj **1** [personne, procédé] vile; **2** [lieu] squalid; [nourriture, œuvre] revolting

ignominie /iɲɔmini/ nf **1** (état) ignominy; **traiter qn avec ~** to treat sb abominably; **2** (acte, parole) dreadful thing; **c'est une ~!** it's an outrage!

ignorance /iɲɔʀɑ̃s/ nf ignorance; **être dans l'~** to be in the dark (**de** about)

ignorant, ~e /iɲɔʀɑ̃, ɑ̃t/
A adj ignorant; **être ~ de tout** to know nothing about anything
B nm,f ignoramus; **faire l'~** to feign ignorance

ignoré, ~e /iɲɔʀe/ adj (inconnu) unknown (**de** to); (méprisé) ignored (**de** by); **vivre ~** to live in obscurity

Les îles

Article ou pas article?

■ *En anglais, les noms d'îles se comportent comme les noms de pays: seuls les noms pluriels prennent un article (pour les îles qui sont aussi des pays ▸ p. 230).*

Chypre
= Cyprus

aimer Chypre
= to like Cyprus

la Corse
= Corsica

aimer la Corse
= to like Corsica

les Baléares
= the Balearics

aimer les Baléares
= to like the Balearics

■ *Noter que certains noms d'îles sont pluriels en français mais singuliers en anglais, et ne prennent donc pas d'article.*

les îles Fidji
= Fiji

j'aime les îles Fidji
= I like Fiji

les Samoas occidentales
= Western Samoa

En, à, aux

■ *En, à et aux se traduisent par* to *avec les verbes de mouvement (par ex.* aller, se rendre *etc.):*

aller à Chypre
= to go to Cyprus

aller à Sainte-Hélène
= to go to St Helena

aller en Corse
= to go to Corsica

aller aux Baléares
= to go to the Balearics

■ *Avec les autres verbes (par ex.* être, habiter, *etc.), en, à et aux se traduisent normalement par* in. *Cependant, pour les toutes petites îles, on traduira par* on.

vivre en Corse
= to live in Corsica

vivre à Chypre
= to live in Cyprus

vivre aux Baléares
= to live in the Balearics

vivre à Naxos
= to live on Naxos

■ *Pour la traduction des expressions avec de ▸ p. 156.*

Avec ou sans *island*

■ *L'anglais utilise toujours les mots* island *ou* islands *dans les cas où le français utilise* île *ou* îles.

l'île de Guernesey
= the island of Guernsey

les îles Baléares
= the Balearic Islands

les Baléares
= the Balearics

■ *Noter que* isle *n'est plus utilisé que dans quelques noms d'îles, comme la* Isle of Man, *la* Isle of Wight, *etc.*

---

ignorer /iɲɔʀe/ [1]
A *vtr* ⓵ (ne pas savoir) not to know; ∼ **tout de qch** to know nothing of *ou* about sth; **ne rien** ∼ **de qch** to know everything about sth; ⓶ (ne pas connaître) **il ignore le savon** hum he's never heard of soap; ∼ **l'existence de** to be unaware of the existence of; ⓷ (ne pas tenir compte de) to ignore [*personne, règle, recherches*]; **tu n'as qu'à l'**∼ just ignore him/her; ⓸ (ne pas éprouver) not to feel [*émotion, sentiment*]; **il ignorait la peur** he didn't know what fear was
B **s'ignorer** *vpr* **vous êtes un poète qui s'ignore** you are a poet without knowing it

iguane /igwan/ *nm* iguana

il /il/

⚠ *Il pronom personnel masculin représentant une personne du sexe masculin ou un animal familier mâle se traduit par* he (1); *lorsqu'il représente un objet, un concept, un animal non familier,* il *se traduit par* it; *il peut également se traduire par* she *lorsqu'il représente un navire.*

il pronom personnel neutre sujet d'un verbe impersonnel se traduit généralement par it. *On se reportera au verbe.*

A *pron pers m* ⓵ (personne, animal familier) he; ∼**s** they; **Pierre a-t-**∼ **téléphoné?** has Pierre phoned?; ⓶ (objet, concept, animal) it; ∼**s** they; **le Japon a annoncé qu'**∼ **participerait à la réunion** Japan announced that it would be taking part in the meeting
B *pron pers neutre* it; ∼ **pleut** it's raining

île /il/ *nf* island
⟮Composés⟯ **l'**∼ **de Beauté** Corsica; ∼ **flottante** Culin floating island

illégal, ∼**e,** *mpl* **-aux** /ilegal, o/ *adj* illegal

illégalité /ilegalite/ *nf* ⓵ (caractère) illegality **Ȼ**; **être dans l'**∼ to be in breach of the law; **entrer dans l'**∼ to start breaking the law; ⓶ (acte illégal) breach of the law

illégitime /ileʒitim/ *adj* ⓵ (hors mariage) [*union, amour*] illicit; [*enfant*] illegitimate; ⓶ (injustifié) [*prétention, revendication*] unjustified

illégitimité /ileʒitimite/ *nf* gén illegitimacy; (d'amour) illicitness

illettré, ∼**e** /iletʀe/ *adj, nm,f* illiterate

illettrisme /iletʀism/ *nm* illiteracy

illicite /ilisit/ *adj* [*vente, gain, amour, plaisir*] illicit; [*pratique, contrat, trafic*] unlawful

illico○ /iliko/ *adv* straightaway, sharpish○; ∼ **presto** pronto○

illimité, ∼**e** /ilimite/ *adj* unlimited

illisible /ilizibl/ *adj* ⓵ [*écriture, mot, document*] illegible; ⓶ [*œuvre, auteur*] unreadable

illogique /iloʒik/ *adj* illogical

illumination /ilyminasjɔ̃/
A *nf* ⓵ (action d'éclairer) floodlighting; ⓶ (inspiration) gén flash of inspiration; Relig spiritual enlightenment **Ȼ**
B **illuminations** *nfpl* (de ville, rue, bâtiment) illuminations; (de sapin, fête) lights

illuminé, ∼**e** /ilymine/
A *adj* ⓵ [*monument, site*] floodlit; ⓶ [*regard, visage*] radiant; ⓷ [*poète, prédicateur*] inspired
B *nm,f* gén visionary; péj crank

illuminer /ilymine/ [1]
A *vtr* ⓵ gén to illuminate; (avec des projecteurs) to floodlight; ⓶ fig [*sourire*] to light up [*visage*]; [*foi, passion*] to illuminate
B **s'illuminer** *vpr* ⓵ (s'éclairer) [*ville, rue*] to light up; ⓶ (prendre de l'éclat) [*visage*] to light up (**de** with)

illusion /ilyzjɔ̃/ *nf* ⓵ (croyance) illusions (*pl*) (**sur** about); **ne pas se faire d'**∼**s** to have no illusions; **je ne me fais guère** *or* **pas trop d'**∼**s** I don't hold out much hope; **se faire des** ∼**s** to delude oneself (**sur** about); **il se donne l'**∼ **de dominer la situation** he likes to think that he's in control of the situation; **entretenir qn dans l'**∼ **que...** to let sb labour under the illusion that...; ⓶ (apparence trompeuse) illusion; **il ne fait pas** ∼ he doesn't fool anyone
⟮Composé⟯ ∼ **d'optique** optical illusion

illusionner: s'illusionner /ilyzjɔne/ [1] *vpr* to delude oneself (**sur qch/qn** about sth/sb)

illusionnisme /ilyzjɔnism/ *nm* ⓵ (art du prestidigitateur) conjuring; ⓶ Art, Pol (effet) illusionism

illusionniste /ilyzjɔnist/ *nmf* ▸ p. 372 (prestidigitateur) conjuror, illusionist

illusoire /ilyzwaʀ/ *adj* illusory; **il serait** ∼ **de croire que...** it would be an illusion to believe that...

illustrateur, -trice /ilystʀatœʀ, tʀis/ ▸ p. 372 *nm,f* illustrator

illustration /ilystʀasjɔ̃/ *nf* illustration

illustre /ilystʀ/ *adj* illustrious; **un** ∼ **inconnu** a perfect nobody

illustré /ilystʀe/ *nm* (journal) comic

illustrer /ilystʀe/ [1]
A vtr to illustrate (**de with**)
B s'**illustrer** vpr [personne] to distinguish oneself

îlot /ilo/ nm ①▸ (petite île) islet; ②▸ (espace réduit) ~s **de**
végétation isolated patches of vegetation; ~ **de paix**
haven of peace; ③▸ (habitations) block
⸨Composé⸩ ~ **directionnel** traffic island

ilote /ilɔt/ nmf Helot

îlotier /ilɔtje/ nm Admin community policeman

ils ► il

image /imaʒ/ nf ①▸ (reproduction) picture; ②▸ (sur une pellicule)
frame; (qualité de réglage) picture; (qualité artistique) photography; ③▸ (reflet) reflection, image; Phys image;
④▸ (représentation) picture; **à l'~ de ses prédécesseurs...**
just like his/her predecessors...; ⑤▸ Littérat image
⸨Composés⸩ ~ **d'Épinal** lit simplistic print of traditional French
life; fig clichéd image; ~ **de marque** (de produit) brand
image; (de société) corporate image; (de politicien, personnalité)
(public) image

imagé, ~**e** /imaʒe/ adj [langage, style] colourful^GB

imagerie /imaʒʀi/ nf ①▸ (thématique) imagery;
②▸ (scientifique) imaging; ~ **médicale** medical imaging

imaginable /imaʒinabl/ adj conceivable, imaginable

imaginaire /imaʒinɛʀ/
A adj gén, Math imaginary
B nm imagination; **l'~ d'un auteur** the imaginative world of
an author

imaginatif, -ive /imaʒinatif, iv/ adj imaginative

imagination /imaʒinasjɔ̃/ nf imagination; **un enfant**
plein d'~ a very imaginative child; **des chiffres qui**
dépassent or **défient l'~** mind-boggling° figures

imaginer /imaʒine/ [1]
A vtr ①▸ (se représenter) to imagine, to picture [personne, chose,
scène]; **je l'imaginais plus grand** I imagined him to be
taller; **imagine sa tête quand...** just picture his/her face
when...; ②▸ (supposer) to suppose; ③▸ (inventer) to devise, to
think up [méthode, moyen]; **que vas-tu ~?** how can you
think such a thing?
B s'**imaginer** vpr ①▸ (se représenter) to imagine, to picture
[chose, personne]; ②▸ (se voir) to picture oneself; ③▸ (croire) to
think (**que** that)

imbattable /ɛ̃batabl/ adj unbeatable

imbécile /ɛ̃besil/
A adj idiotic
B nmf fool; **passer pour un ~** to look a fool; **faire l'~** to play
the fool; **jouer les ~s** to play dumb; **un ~ heureux** a
happy idiot

imbécillité /ɛ̃besilite/ nf stupidity; **avoir l'~ de faire** to
be stupid enough to do; **quelle ~!** (acte) what a stupid
thing to do!; (œuvre) what rubbish! GB, what garbage! US;
(propos) what nonsense!

imberbe /ɛ̃bɛʀb/ adj beardless

imbiber /ɛ̃bibe/ [1]
A vtr to soak (**de** in)
B s'**imbiber** vpr to become soaked (**de** with)

imbrication /ɛ̃bʀikasjɔ̃/ nf ①▸ (d'objets) interlocking ¢; (de
tuiles) overlapping ¢; ②▸ Ordinat interleaving

imbriquer /ɛ̃bʀike/ [1]
A vtr ①▸ (faire se chevaucher) to overlap; **tuiles imbriquées** overlapping tiles; ②▸ (faire s'enchevêtrer) to interlock; ③▸ Ordinat to
interleave
B s'**imbriquer** vpr [tuiles, écailles] to overlap; [chapitres] to be
interwoven; [questions] to be interlinked; [pièces] to interlock

imbroglio /ɛ̃bʀɔ(g)lijo/ nm imbroglio

imbu, ~**e** /ɛ̃by/ adj ~ **de sa personne** full of oneself

imbuvable /ɛ̃byvabl/ adj ①▸ [liquide] undrinkable;
②▸ °[personne, discours, spectacle] unbearable

imitable /imitabl/ adj **facilement ~** easy to imitate
(jamais épith)

imitateur, -trice /imitatœʀ, tʀis/ nmf ①▸ ► p. 372
(comédien) impressionist; ②▸ Art imitator

imitation /imitasjɔ̃/ nf ①▸ gén imitation; (de personne)
impression; **faire un numéro d'~** to do impressions;
②▸ Comm imitation; **sac ~ crocodile** imitation crocodile
handbag

imiter /imite/ [1] vtr ①▸ (copier) to imitate [geste, cri, maître];
to forge [signature]; **un revêtement de sol qui imite le bois**

an imitation parquet flooring; ②▸ Théât to do an impression of [personne]; ③▸ (faire pareil) **il part, je vais l'~** he's
leaving and I'm going to do the same

immaculé, ~**e** /imakyle/ adj immaculate

immanent, ~**e** /imanɑ̃, ɑ̃t/ adj immanent

immangeable /ɛ̃mɑ̃ʒabl/ adj inedible

immanquable /ɛ̃mɑ̃kabl/ adj [panneau, cible] impossible
to miss (jamais épith); [succès] guaranteed

immanquablement /ɛ̃mɑ̃kabləmɑ̃/ adv inevitably

immatériel, -ielle /imateʀjɛl/ adj immaterial; **biens ~s**
Jur intangible assets

immatriculation /imatʀikylasjɔ̃/ nf gén, Admin registration; **d'~** (numéro) registration (épith) GB, license (épith) US

immatriculer /imatʀikyle/ [1] vtr gén, Admin to register
[personne, société]; to register GB ou license US [véhicule]; **se**
faire ~ au consulat to register with the consulate; **faire**
~ **un véhicule** to have a vehicle registered GB ou
licensed US

immédiat, ~**e** /imedja, at/
A adj immediate
B nm **l'~** the present; **dans l'~** for the time being

immédiatement /imedjatmɑ̃/ adv immediately

immense /imɑ̃s/ adj gén huge; [douleur, regret] immense;
[joie, courage] great; **l'~ majorité des gens** the vast majority of people

immensément /imɑ̃semɑ̃/ adv immensely

immensité /imɑ̃site/ nf (de lieu) immensity; (de
connaissances) breadth

immergé, ~**e** /imɛʀʒe/ adj [corps, objet] submerged;
[terres, récifs] sunken

immerger /imɛʀʒe/ [13]
A vtr to immerse [objet]; to bury [sth] at sea [cadavre]; to
dump [sth] in the sea [déchets]
B s'**immerger** vpr ①▸ lit [sous-marin] to dive; ②▸ fig [personne]
to immerse oneself (**dans** in)

immérité, ~**e** /imeʀite/ adj undeserved

immersion /imɛʀsjɔ̃/ nf ①▸ (de corps, d'objet) immersion; (de
cadavre) burial at sea; (de déchets) dumping; ②▸ Géog (de terres)
flooding; ③▸ Scol immersion (**dans** in)

immettable° /ɛ̃metabl/ adj [vêtement] unwearable

immeuble /imœbl/ nm ①▸ (bâtiment) building; ②▸ Jur real
asset
⸨Composés⸩ ~ **de bureaux** office block GB, office building;
~ **d'habitation** residential block GB, apartment building
US; ~ **de rapport** rented property GB, rental building US

immigrant, ~**e** /imigʀɑ̃, ɑ̃t/ adj, nmf immigrant

immigration /imigʀasjɔ̃/ nf immigration

immigré, ~**e** /imigʀe/ adj, nmf immigrant

immigrer /imigʀe/ [1] vi to immigrate

imminent, ~**e** /iminɑ̃, ɑ̃t/ adj imminent

immiscer: s'immiscer /imise/ [12] vpr to interfere
(**dans** in)

immobile /imɔbil/ adj gén motionless; [véhicule] stationary; [regard] fixed

immobilier, -ière /imɔbilje, ɛʀ/
A adj property (épith) GB, real-estate (épith) US
B nm **l'~** property GB, real estate US

immobilisation /imɔbilizasjɔ̃/ nf ①▸ lit (action) immobil-
ization; (résultat) immobility; ②▸ Fin (de capital) tying up

immobiliser /imɔbilize/ [1]
A vtr ①▸ (arrêter) to bring [sth] to a standstill [véhicule]; to stop
[machine, cheval]; to immobilize [armée]; ②▸ (maintenir immobile) to immobilize [personne, membre]; ③▸ (paralyser) to bring
[sth] to a halt [économie, pays]; ④▸ Fin to tie up [capitaux]
B s'**immobiliser** vpr (volontairement) to stop; (involontairement) to
come to a halt

immobilisme /imɔbilism/ nm opposition to change

immobilité /imɔbilite/ nf (de personne, d'animal) immobility;
(d'eau, air, de paysage, feuillage) stillness

immodéré, ~**e** /imɔdeʀe/ adj [besoin, goût, amour,
dépenses] excessive; [propos, attitude] immoderate; **faire un**
usage ~ de l'alcool to abuse alcohol

immolation /imɔlasjɔ̃/ nf immolation

immoler /imɔle/ [1] vtr to sacrifice (**à** to)

immonde /imɔ̃d/ adj ①▸ (sale) filthy; ②▸ (révoltant)
revolting

immondices /imɔ̃dis/ *nfpl* refuse **¢** GB, trash **¢** US

immoral, ~e, *mpl* **-aux** /imɔʀal, o/ *adj* immoral

immortaliser /imɔʀtalize/ [1]
A *vtr* to immortalize
B **s'immortaliser** *vpr* to achieve immortality

immortalité /imɔʀtalite/ *nf* immortality

immortel, -elle[1] /imɔʀtɛl/ *adj* immortal

immortelle[2] /imɔʀtɛl/ *nf* Bot everlasting (flower)

immotivé, ~e /imɔtive/ *adj* [colère, action] unmotivated; [réclamation, crainte] groundless

immuable /imɥabl/ *adj* [loi, cycle, geste] immutable; [tradition, paysage] unchanging; [bonheur] perpetual

immuniser /imynize/ [1] *vtr* **[1]** Méd to immunize (**contre** against); **[2]** fig **~ qn contre** to make sb immune to

immunitaire /imynitɛʀ/ *adj* Méd immune

immunité /imynite/ *nf* immunity

immunodéficience /imynodefisjɑ̃s/ *nf* immunodeficiency

immunodéprimé, ~e /imynodeprime/ *adj* immunodepressed

immunologie /imynɔlɔʒi/ *nf* immunology

impact /ɛ̃pakt/ *nm* (choc, effet) impact; (trace) mark; **des ~s de balles** bullet holes

impair, ~e /ɛ̃pɛʀ/
A *adj* **[1]** Math [nombre, numéro] odd; [jour, année] odd-numbered; **[2]** Anat unpaired
B *nm* (gaffe) indiscretion, faux pas

imparable /ɛ̃paʀabl/ *adj* [coup] unstoppable; [riposte] unanswerable; [argument] irrefutable

impardonnable /ɛ̃paʀdɔnabl/ *adj* unforgivable

imparfait, ~e /ɛ̃paʀfɛ, ɛt/
A *adj* **[1]** (défectueux) imperfect; **[2]** (incomplet) [connaissance, guérison] partial; [travail] unfinished; **[3]** Ling imperfect
B *nm* Ling imperfect

impartial, ~e, *mpl* **-iaux** /ɛ̃paʀsjal, o/ *adj* impartial

impartir /ɛ̃paʀtiʀ/ [3] *vtr* **~ un délai à qn** to give sb a set time; **dans les temps impartis** within the given time

impasse /ɛ̃pas/ *nf* **[1]** (cul-de-sac) dead end, cul-de-sac GB; **[2]** (situation sans issue) deadlock; **[3]** Scol, Univ **faire une ~** to skip parts of one's revision GB *ou* review US; **[4]** Jeux finesse

impassibilité /ɛ̃pasibilite/ *nf* impassivity

impassible /ɛ̃pasibl/ *adj* impassive

impatience /ɛ̃pasjɑ̃s/ *nf* impatience; **avec ~** impatiently; **mourir** *or* **brûler d'~ de faire** to be dying to do

impatient, ~e[1] /ɛ̃pasjɑ̃, ɑ̃t/ *adj* impatient

impatiente[2] /ɛ̃pasjɑ̃t/ *nf* Bot busy lizzie

impatienter /ɛ̃pasjɑ̃te/ [1]
A *vtr* to irritate
B **s'impatienter** *vpr* to get impatient

impavide /ɛ̃pavid/ *adj* unperturbed

impayable° /ɛ̃pɛjabl/ *adj* (drôle) priceless

impayé, ~e /ɛ̃pɛje/
A *adj* unpaid
B *nm* **les ~s** unpaid debts, outstanding debts

impeccable /ɛ̃pekabl/ *adj* [travail, style] perfect, faultless; [vêtement] impeccable; [maison] spotless; [rue] spotlessly clean; [tapis] in perfect condition; **il est toujours ~** he's always impeccably dressed

impeccablement /ɛ̃pekabləmɑ̃/ *adv* [repassé, vêtu] impeccably; [enveloppé] beautifully; **~ nettoyé** spotlessly clean; **travail ~ fait** perfect *ou* faultless job; **il parle ~ le français** he speaks perfect French

impénétrable /ɛ̃penetʀabl/ *adj* **[1]** [végétation, mystère] impenetrable; **[2]** [personne, visage] inscrutable

Idiome) **les voies du Seigneur sont ~s** God moves in mysterious ways

impénitent, ~e /ɛ̃penitɑ̃, ɑ̃t/ *adj* **[1]** [buveur, fumeur] inveterate; [célibataire] confirmed; **[2]** Relig impenitent sout, unrepentant

impensable /ɛ̃pɑ̃sabl/ *adj* unthinkable, unimaginable

imper° /ɛ̃pɛʀ/ *nm* raincoat, mac° GB

impératif, -ive /ɛ̃peʀatif, iv/
A *adj* imperative
B *nm* **[1]** (de situation) imperative; (de qualité) necessity; (d'emploi

du temps) constraint; **[2]** Ling imperative

impérativement /ɛ̃peʀativmɑ̃/ *adv* **il faut ~ faire** it is imperative *ou* absolutely necessary to do

impératrice /ɛ̃peʀatʀis/ *nf* empress

imperceptible /ɛ̃pɛʀsɛptibl/ *adj* imperceptible

imperceptiblement /ɛ̃pɛʀsɛptibləmɑ̃/ *adv* imperceptibly

imperfection /ɛ̃pɛʀfɛksjɔ̃/ *nf* (état) imperfection; (petit défaut) flaw

impérial, ~e[1], *mpl* **-iaux** /ɛ̃peʀjal, o/ *adj* imperial

impériale[2] /ɛ̃peʀjal/ *nf* **[1]** (de bus) upper deck; **autobus à ~** double-decker bus; **[2]** (barbe) imperial

impérialisme /ɛ̃peʀjalism/ *nm* imperialism

impérieux, -ieuse /ɛ̃peʀjø, øz/ *adj* **[1]** (autoritaire) imperious; **[2]** (urgent) pressing

impérissable /ɛ̃peʀisabl/ *adj* imperishable

imperméabiliser /ɛ̃pɛʀmeabilize/ [1] *vtr* to waterproof

imperméable /ɛ̃pɛʀmeabl/
A *adj* **[1]** [tissu, peinture] waterproof; [sol] impermeable; **[2]** (insensible) impervious (**à** to)
B *nm* raincoat

impersonnel, -elle /ɛ̃pɛʀsɔnɛl/ *adj* impersonal

impertinence /ɛ̃pɛʀtinɑ̃s/ *nf* **[1]** (caractère) impertinence; **avec ~** impertinently; **[2]** (parole) impertinent remark

impertinent, ~e /ɛ̃pɛʀtinɑ̃, ɑ̃t/
A *adj* impertinent (**envers** to)
B *nm,f* impertinent person

imperturbable /ɛ̃pɛʀtyʀbabl/ *adj* imperturbable, unruffled

imperturbablement /ɛ̃pɛʀtyʀbabləmɑ̃/ *adv* [continuer, écouter] unperturbed; [sérieux] invariably

impétrant, ~e /ɛ̃petʀɑ̃, ɑ̃t/ *nm,f* **[1]** (de diplôme) person receiving a qualification; **[2]** (candidat) controv applicant

impétueusement /ɛ̃petɥøzmɑ̃/ *adv* impetuously

impétueux, -euse /ɛ̃petɥø, øz/ *adj* [orateur] impassioned; [caractère, jeunesse] impetuous; [vent, torrent] raging

impétuosité /ɛ̃petɥozite/ *nf* (de personnes) impetuousness; (de vent, torrent) fury

impie /ɛ̃pi/
A *adj* [paroles, actes] impious
B *nmf* impious person

impiété /ɛ̃pjete/ *nf* impiousness

impitoyable /ɛ̃pitwajabl/ *adj* [personne, tribunal] merciless, pitiless; [lutte, loi] relentless; [sélection, châtiment] ruthless

implacable /ɛ̃plakabl/ *adj* [logique, critique] implacable; [négociateur] tough; [répression, verdict] harsh

implacablement /ɛ̃plakabləmɑ̃/ *adv* [progresser, continuer] relentlessly; [réprimer] ruthlessly

implantation /ɛ̃plɑ̃tasjɔ̃/ *nf* **[1]** (mise en place) (de secte, d'industrie) establishment; (d'entreprise) setting up; (d'équipement) installation; (de cheveux) implantation; (de personnes) settlement; **[2]** (entreprise) site; **[3]** (disposition) (de bâtiments, machines) layout; **[4]** Méd implantation

implanté, ~e /ɛ̃plɑ̃te/ *adj* [usine, parti, personne] established; [population] settled; **préjugé solidement ~ chez** a deeply rooted prejudice; **dents bien/mal ~es** straight/crooked teeth

implanter /ɛ̃plɑ̃te/ [1]
A *vtr* **[1]** (établir) to establish [usine]; to build [hypermarché, cinéma]; to open [agence, cafétéria]; to install [équipements]; to introduce [produit, système, mode]; **[2]** Méd to implant
B **s'implanter** *vpr* [entreprise, système] to establish itself; [usine] to be built; [personne] to settle; [parti, doctrine] to gain a following; **s'~ sur un marché** to gain a foothold in a market

implication /ɛ̃plikasjɔ̃/ *nf* **[1]** (participation) involvement; **[2]** (conséquence) implication; **[3]** (engagement personnel) commitment

implicite /ɛ̃plisit/ *adj* implicit

implicitement /ɛ̃plisitmɑ̃/ *adv* gén implicitly; Ordinat by default

impliquer /ɛ̃plike/ [1]
A *vtr* **[1]** (mêler) to implicate [personne]; **[2]** (faire participer) to involve [personnel]; **[3]** (imposer) to involve (**de faire** doing); **[4]** (signifier) to mean
B **s'impliquer** *vpr* to get involved

implorer /ɛ̃plɔʀe/ [1] vtr **1** (supplier) to beseech, to implore [personne, dieux]; **2** (demander) to beg for [délai, faveur]

imploser /ɛ̃ploze/ [1] vi to implode

implosion /ɛ̃plozjɔ̃/ nf **1** Tech implosion; **2** fig collapse

impoli, ~e /ɛ̃pɔli/ adj rude, impolite

impolitesse /ɛ̃pɔlites/ nf rudeness; **avec** ~ rudely; **commettre de graves** ~s to behave very rudely

impopulaire /ɛ̃pɔpylɛʀ/ adj unpopular

impopularité /ɛ̃pɔpylaʀite/ nf unpopularity

importance /ɛ̃pɔʀtɑ̃s/ nf **1** (gravité) importance; **prendre de l'**~ [événement] to gain in importance; **sans** ~ [détail] unimportant; **cela est sans** ~ it's not important; **d'**~ [problème] important; **quelle** ~? what does it matter? **2** (taille) (de réduction, société) size; (de travail, d'effort) amount; (de massacres, dégâts) extent; **prendre de l'**~ [société, ville] to increase in size; **ville d'**~ **moyenne** medium-sized town; **d'une certaine** ~ sizeable; **3** (influence) importance; **prendre de l'**~ [personne] to become more important; **pour se donner de l'**~ to make oneself look important

important, ~e /ɛ̃pɔʀtɑ̃, ɑ̃t/
A adj **1** (essentiel) important; **2** (considérable) [hausse, baisse] significant; [nombre, effort, écart] considerable; [communauté, héritage] sizeable; [ville, société] large; [retard] lengthy; [actionnaire] major; **3** (influent) important; **prendre un air** ~ to adopt a self-important manner
B nm,f faire l'~, jouer les ~s to act important○

importateur, **-trice** /ɛ̃pɔʀtatœʀ, tʀis/
A adj [pays] importing (épith); [société] import (épith); **pays** ~s **de pétrole** oil-importing countries
B nm,f importer

importation /ɛ̃pɔʀtasjɔ̃/ nf **1** (introduction) importation; **d'**~ [coûts, compagnie, quotas] import (épith); [produit, article] imported; ~s **de luxe** luxury imports

importer /ɛ̃pɔʀte/ [1]
A vtr to import [marchandise, main-d'œuvre, mode]; to introduce [espèce végétale]
B v impers cela importe peu it doesn't really matter; **ce qui importe c'est que...** what matters is that...; **peu importe** or **qu'importe que...** it doesn't matter ou what does it matter if...; **'il pleut!'—'peu importe!'** 'it's raining!'—'never mind!'; **'lequel?'—'n'importe'** 'which one?'—'it doesn't matter'; **n'importe quel enfant** any child; **à n'importe quel moment** at any time; **n'importe qui** anybody, anyone; **n'importe lequel** any; **n'importe où** anywhere; **viens n'importe quand** come anytime; **prends n'importe quoi** take anything; **n'importe quoi de tranchant** any sharp object; **elle dit n'importe quoi** she talks nonsense; **c'est (du) n'importe quoi**○ it's rubbish; **c'est fait n'importe comment** it's done any old how○

import-export /ɛ̃pɔʀɛkspɔʀ/ nm inv import-export trade

importun, ~e /ɛ̃pɔʀtœ̃, yn/
A adj **1** [personne] (gênant) troublesome; (irritant) tiresome; (indésirable) unwelcome; **je ne voudrais pas être** ~ I don't wish to intrude; **2** [visite, intervention] ill-timed; [remarque] ill-chosen; [question] awkward
B nm,f (visiteur) unwelcome visitor; (gêneur) tiresome individual

importuner /ɛ̃pɔʀtyne/ [1] vtr **1** (ennuyer) to bother; **2** (déranger) to disturb

imposable /ɛ̃pozabl/ adj [personne] liable to tax (après n); [revenu, bénéfice] taxable

imposant, ~e /ɛ̃pozɑ̃, ɑ̃t/ adj [stature, monument] imposing; [cérémonie, œuvre] impressive

imposé, ~e /ɛ̃poze/ adj **1** (fixé) [tarif, délai] fixed; **2** (obligatoire) [thème, travail, figure] set

imposer /ɛ̃poze/ [1]
A vtr **1** (rendre obligatoire) [personne] to impose [sanctions, délai, personne] (à on); to lay down [règlement]; [situation] to require [mesures, changement]; ~ **le port de lunettes protectrices** to make it obligatory to wear protective goggles; **il nous a imposé sa présence** he forced his presence on us; **elle nous a imposé le silence** she made us be quiet; **2** (faire admettre) to impose [idée, volonté]; to set; **3** (inspirer) to command [respect, admiration]; **4** (soumettre à l'impôt) to tax
B en imposer vtr ind elle en impose par son calme her calm is impressive; **elle en impose à ses élèves** she inspires respect in her pupils; **ne t'en laisse pas** ~ don't let yourself be overawed

C s'imposer vpr **1** (être évident) [choix, solution] to be obvious (à to); (être requis) [prudence, mesure, changement] to be called for; **une visite au Louvre s'impose** a visit to the Louvre is a must; **s'**~ **comme évident** to be obvious; **2** (s'astreindre à) to impose [sth] on oneself [horaires, discipline]; **s'**~ **un sacrifice** to force oneself to make a sacrifice; **s'**~ **de travailler le soir** to make it a rule to work in the evening; **3** (déranger) to impose (à qn on sb); **4** (se faire admettre) **s'**~ **comme leader** to establish oneself as the leader; **s'**~ **comme langue officielle** to become established as the official language; **s'**~ **dans un domaine** [personne] to make a name for oneself in a field; **s'**~ **sur un marché** [produit, firme] to establish itself in a market; **s'**~ **par son intelligence** to stand out because of one's intelligence; **s'**~ **comme le plus grand architecte contemporain** to be universally acknowledged as the greatest contemporary architect; **5** (pour dominer) [personne] to make one's presence felt; [volonté] to impose itself

imposition /ɛ̃pozisjɔ̃/ nf taxation

impossibilité /ɛ̃pɔsibilite/ nf impossibility; **être dans l'**~ **de faire** to be unable to do; **mettre qn dans l'**~ **de faire** to make it impossible for sb to do

impossible /ɛ̃pɔsibl/
A adj **1** gén impossible (à faire to do); **il est** ~ **qu'il soit déjà arrivé** he cannot possibly have arrived yet; **cela m'est** ~ I really can't; ~! out of the question!; **2** ○[personne, goût, heure, habitude, nom] impossible; **rendre la vie** ~ **à qn** to make life impossible for sb
B nm l'~ the impossible; **faire** or **tenter l'**~ to do everything one can
(Idiomes) **à l'**~ **nul n'est tenu** Prov nobody can be expected to do the impossible; ~ **n'est pas français** there's no such word as 'can't'

imposteur /ɛ̃pɔstœʀ/ nm impostor

imposture /ɛ̃pɔstyʀ/ nf **1** (action de tromper) deception, imposture sout; **2** (acte de tromperie) fraud

impôt /ɛ̃po/ nm tax; **payer ses** ~s to pay one's taxes; **avant/après** ~ before/after tax; **payer des** ~s to pay tax
(Composés) ~ **additionnel** surtax; ~ **foncier** property tax; ~ **sur les plus-values** capital gains tax; ~ **sur le revenu** income tax; ~ **sur les sociétés** corporate tax, company tax; ~s **locaux** local taxes

impotence /ɛ̃pɔtɑ̃s/ nf lack of mobility

impotent, ~e /ɛ̃pɔtɑ̃, ɑ̃t/
A adj infirm
B nm,f person with impaired mobility

impraticable /ɛ̃pʀatikabl/ adj **1** [chemin, route] impassable; **2** [projet] unworkable, impracticable

imprécis, ~e /ɛ̃pʀesi, iz/ adj [forme, souvenir, renseignement] vague; [idée] hazy; [résultats, statistiques] imprecise; [personne] vague

imprécision /ɛ̃pʀesizjɔ̃/ nf (de connaissances) imprecision; (de données, document) vagueness; (de tir, coup) inaccuracy

imprégnation /ɛ̃pʀeɲasjɔ̃/ nf **1** (de bois, tissu) impregnation; **2** fig **apprendre une langue par** ~ to learn a language by immersing oneself in it

imprégner /ɛ̃pʀeɲe/ [14]
A vtr **1** to impregnate [tissu, bois] (de with); to dye [cuir]; **une forte odeur de tabac imprégnait leurs vêtements** their clothes smelled strongly of tobacco; **2** fig **une doctrine imprégnée de christianisme** a doctrine heavily influenced by Christian thinking
B s'imprégner vpr [étudiant] to immerse oneself

imprenable /ɛ̃pʀənabl/ adj [citadelle] impregnable; **avec vue** ~ with unobstructed view guaranteed

imprésario /ɛ̃pʀesaʀjo/ ▸ p. 372 nm agent, impresario

impression /ɛ̃pʀesjɔ̃/ nf **1** (sentiment, sensation) impression; **avoir l'**~ **de faire** to feel one is doing; **j'ai l'**~ **d'être surveillé** I feel I am being watched; **j'ai (comme**○**) l'**~ **que/d'avoir...** I've got a (funny) feeling that/I have...; **le film laisse une** ~ **de malaise** this film leaves one feeling uneasy; **ça m'a fait une drôle d'**~ **de les revoir** it was a strange feeling seeing them again; **2** (de textes, tissus) printing; **faire de l'**~ **sur tissu** to print on fabric; **l'ouvrage est à l'**~ the book is with the printers; **3** (motif imprimé) pattern; **4** Phot exposure

impressionnable /ɛ̃pʀesjɔnabl/ adj **1** (sensible) sensitive; (influençable) impressionable; **il est peu** ~ he's not easily shocked; **2** Phot [papier, plaque] sensitized

impressionnant, **~e** /ɛ̃pʀesjɔnɑ̃, ɑ̃t/ *adj*
[1] (remarquable) [*résultat, spectacle, joueur*] impressive; [*arsenal, défi*] formidable; **~ de bêtise** amazingly stupid;
[2] (troublant) disturbing

impressionner /ɛ̃pʀesjɔne/ [1] *vtr* [1] (faire de l'effet) [*personne, qualité, spectacle*] to impress; **se laisser facilement ~** to be easily impressed; **ne te laisse pas ~ par les examinateurs** don't be overawed by the examiners; [2] (troubler) to disturb; [3] (sensibiliser) to act on [*rétine, pellicule*]

impressionnisme /ɛ̃pʀesjɔnism/ *nm* Impressionism

impressionniste /ɛ̃pʀesjɔnist/
A *adj* [1] Art Impressionist; [2] Littér, Mus impressionistic
B *nmf* Impressionist

imprévisible /ɛ̃pʀevizibl/ *adj* unpredictable

imprévoyance /ɛ̃pʀevwajɑ̃s/ *nf* lack of foresight

imprévoyant, **~e** /ɛ̃pʀevwajɑ̃, ɑ̃t/
A *adj* improvident
B *nm,f* improvident person

imprévu, **~e** /ɛ̃pʀevy/
A *adj* [1] (non prévu) unforeseen; [2] (non prévisible) unexpected
B *nm* [1] (incident) hitch; **~ de dernière minute** last-minute hitch; **sauf ~** barring accidents; [2] (choses inattendues) **l'~** the unexpected; **plein d'~** [*personne, film*] quirky; [*vacances, voyage*] with a few surprises (*épith, après n*); [*métier*] never dull (*jamais épith*), which is never dull (*épith, après n*); [3] (dépense exceptionnelle) unforeseen expense

imprimante /ɛ̃pʀimɑ̃t/ *nf* printer
(Composés) **~ à jet d'encre** ink-jet printer; **~ (à) laser** laser printer; **~ à marguerite** daisywheel printer; **~ matricielle** dot matrix printer

imprimé, **~e** /ɛ̃pʀime/
A *pp* ▸ **imprimer**
B *pp adj* [*image, papier, tissu*] printed (**de** with)
C *nm* [1] (formulaire) form; [2] (papier imprimé) printed matter ¢; [3] (tissu) print; **un ~ à fleurs** a floral print; **l'~ et l'uni** printed and plain fabrics

imprimer /ɛ̃pʀime/ [1] *vtr* [1] (marquer d'un motif) to print [*texte, étiquettes*]; to print a design on [*tissu*]; [2] (publier) to publish [*texte, auteur*]; [3] (reproduire) to put [*cachet*] (**sur** on); to print [*initiales*] (**sur** on); [4] (transmettre) [*personne*] to give [*style, direction, cadence*] (**à** to); to transmit [*impulsion*] (**à** to); [5] (laisser une empreinte) [*personne*] to leave an imprint of [*forme*]; [6] (graver) **être imprimé dans la mémoire de qn** to be engraved in sb's memory; **être imprimé sur le visage de qn** to be written all over sb's face

imprimerie /ɛ̃pʀimʀi/ *nf* [1] (technique) printing; **atelier d'~** printing shop; [2] (entreprise) printing works (+ *v sg*); **~ d'étiquettes** label-printing company; **une ~ clandestine** an underground printing press
(Composé) **Imprimerie nationale** government publications office

imprimeur /ɛ̃pʀimœʀ/ ▸ p. 372 *nm* [1] (directeur) printer; **~ éditeur** printer and publisher; [2] (ouvrier) **(ouvrier) ~** print worker, printer

improbable /ɛ̃pʀɔbabl/ *adj* unlikely, improbable

improductif, **-ive** /ɛ̃pʀɔdyktif, iv/ *adj* unproductive; **capitaux ~s** idle capital (*sg*)

impromptu, **~e** /ɛ̃pʀɔ̃pty/ *adj, adv, nm* impromptu

imprononçable /ɛ̃pʀɔnɔ̃sabl/ *adj* unpronounceable

impropre /ɛ̃pʀɔpʀ/ *adj* [*terme, tournure, usage*] incorrect; **~ à** unfit for [*consommation*]

improprement /ɛ̃pʀɔpʀəmɑ̃/ *adv* incorrectly

impropriété /ɛ̃pʀɔpʀijete/ *nf* [1] (caractère impropre) incorrectness; [2] (mot impropre) incorrect usage

improvisation /ɛ̃pʀɔvizasjɔ̃/ *nf* improvisation; **tout laisser à l'~** to improvise all the way through

improvisé, **~e** /ɛ̃pʀɔvize/ *adj* (non préparé) [*discours, civière*] improvised; [*repas, rencontre*] impromptu (*épith*); [*moyens, réforme*] makeshift (*épith*); [*solution*] ad hoc; [*chauffeur, cuisinier*] stand-in (*épith*)

improviser /ɛ̃pʀɔvize/ [1]
A *vtr* to improvise [*civière, repas, discours*]; to concoct [*excuse, alibi*]; **~ un hôpital** to set up a makeshift hospital; **~ une rencontre** to set up an impromptu meeting
B *vi* to improvise; **~ à l'orgue** to improvise on the organ
C **s'improviser** *vpr* [1] (se faire) [*personne*] **s'~ cuisinier/avocat** to act as a cook/lawyer; [2] (se créer) **un camp pour**

réfugiés **ne s'improvise pas** you can't create a refugee camp just like that

improviste: **à l'improviste** /alɛ̃pʀɔvist/ *loc adv* unexpectedly

imprudemment /ɛ̃pʀydamɑ̃/ *adv* [*parler, traverser*] carelessly; [*agir, annoncer*] unwisely; [*conduire*] recklessly

imprudence /ɛ̃pʀydɑ̃s/ *nf* [1] (témérité) carelessness; **avoir l'~ de faire** to be foolish enough to do; **être d'une grande ~** to be very careless; [2] (acte) **commettre une ~** to do something foolish; **pas d'~s surtout** make sure you don't do anything foolish

imprudent, **~e** /ɛ̃pʀydɑ̃, ɑ̃t/
A *adj* [*personne, parole*] careless; [*action, comportement*] rash
B *nm,f* foolhardy person; **les ~s** the foolhardy

impubère /ɛ̃pybɛʀ/ *adj* pre-pubescent

impudence /ɛ̃pydɑ̃s/ *nf* (effronterie) impudence

impudent, **~e** /ɛ̃pydɑ̃, ɑ̃t/ *adj* impudent

impudeur /ɛ̃pydœʀ/ *nf* (physique) immodesty; (de sentiments) shamelessness

impudique /ɛ̃pydik/ *adj* [*geste, parole*] obscene; [*vêtement*] indecent; [*personne*] shameless

impudiquement /ɛ̃pydikmɑ̃/ *adv* shamelessly, brazenly

impuissance /ɛ̃pɥisɑ̃s/ *nf* [1] gén impotence; **~ à faire** inability to do; **réduire qn à l'~** to render sb powerless; [2] Méd impotence

impuissant, **~e** /ɛ̃pɥisɑ̃, ɑ̃t/
A *adj* [1] gén powerless, helpless; [*effort*] vain; **~ à faire** powerless to do; **assister ~ à qch** to watch sth helplessly; [2] Méd impotent
B *nm* Méd impotent man

impulsif, **-ive** /ɛ̃pylsif, iv/ *adj* impulsive

impulsion /ɛ̃pylsjɔ̃/ *nf* [1] (force) impetus; **donner une (nouvelle) ~ à** to give fresh impetus to; [2] (désir) impulse; **~ brusque** sudden impulse; [3] Psych drive; [4] (en dynamique) impulse; [5] Électrotech, Phys, Télécom pulse

impulsivité /ɛ̃pylsivite/ *nf* impulsiveness; **avec ~** impulsively

impunément /ɛ̃pynemɑ̃/ *adv* with impunity; **on ne joue pas ~ avec sa santé** you don't play fast and loose with your health and get away with it

impuni, **~e** /ɛ̃pyni/ *adj* unpunished; **rester ~** to go unpunished

impunité /ɛ̃pynite/ *nf* impunity; **en toute ~** with complete impunity; **bénéficier d'une totale ~** to be granted immunity from prosecution

impur, **~e** /ɛ̃pyʀ/ *adj* [1] [*cœur, pensées*] impure; [2] [*eau, air*] dirty; [*sang*] tainted; [3] [*minerai*] impure; [4] Relig unclean

impureté /ɛ̃pyʀte/ *nf* impurity

imputable /ɛ̃pytabl/ *adj* [1] [*erreur, accident, échec*] attributable (**à** to); [2] [*somme*] chargeable (**sur** to)

imputation /ɛ̃pytasjɔ̃/ *nf* [1] (accusation) accusation, imputation *sout*

imputer /ɛ̃pyte/ [1] *vtr* [1] (attribuer) to attribute, to impute *sout*; [2] (en comptabilité) to charge (**sur** to)

imputrescible /ɛ̃pytʀesibl/ *adj* rotproof

inabordable /inabɔʀdabl/ *adj* [1] [*sommet*] inaccessible; [*personne*] unapproachable; [2] [*prix*] prohibitive; [*produit, service*] prohibitively priced

inacceptable /inaksɛptabl/ *adj* unacceptable

inaccessible /inaksesibl/ *adj* [*lieu*] inaccessible; [*personne*] unapproachable; [*vérité*] unattainable; [*rêve*] impossible; **ce livre est ~ pour lui** this book is beyond him; **~ à la pitié** incapable of pity

inaccompli, **~e** /inakɔ̃pli/ *adj* [1] gén [*travail*] unfinished; [*désir*] unfulfilled; [2] Ling imperfective

inaccoutumé, **~e** /inakutyme/ *adj* unusual

inachevé, **~e** /inaʃve/ *adj* unfinished

inachèvement /inaʃɛvmɑ̃/ *nm* incompleteness

inactif, **-ive** /inaktif, iv/
A *adj* [1] gén [*personne, cerveau, journée*] idle; [2] Sociol [*personne*] inactive; [*population*] non-working; [3] Fin [*capital*] idle; [*marché*] slow; [*compte*] dormant; [4] [*volcan*] inactive
B *nm,f* Sociol non-worker; **les ~s** the non-working population ¢

inaction /inaksjɔ̃/ *nf* inactivity

inactivité /inaktivite/ nf **1** (manque d'activité) inactivity; ~ **forcée** enforced inactivity; **2** Admin, Mil inactivity; **être en ~** to be out of active service

inadaptation /inadaptasjɔ̃/ nf **1** gén (de loi, d'équipement) inappropriateness (**à** for); **2** Psych, Sociol maladjustment (**à** to)

inadapté, **~e** /inadapte/
A adj **1** Psych, Sociol [enfant] maladjusted; **2** (qui ne convient pas) [moyen] inappropriate (**à** for); [outil] unsuitable (**à** for); [système, loi] ill-adapted (**à** to); **3** (mal préparé) [personne] ill-equipped (**à** for)
B nm,f maladjusted person

inadéquat, **~e** /inadekwa, at/ adj [système, moyen, réponse] inadequate; [structure, bâtiment] unsuitable

inadéquation /inadekwasjɔ̃/ nf (inadaptation) unsuitability; (décalage) disparity, discrepancy

inadmissible /inadmisibl/ adj **1** (intolérable) [comportement, erreur, situation] intolerable; **2** (inacceptable) [proposition] unacceptable; **3** Jur [preuve] inadmissible

inadvertance: **par inadvertance** /paʁinadvɛʁtɑ̃s/ loc adv inadvertently

inaliénable /inaljenabl/ adj Jur inalienable

inaltérabilité /inalteʁabilite/ nf **1** (résistance) (de matière, substance) unalterability; (de couleur) fastness; **2** (permanence) permanence, immutability

inaltérable /inalteʁabl/ adj **1** (résistant) [matériau] unalterable, non-corroding; [couleur] fade-resistant; **~ à** resistant to the effects of; **2** (immuable) [ciel] unchanging; [caractère] constant; [principe] immutable; [espoir, règle] steadfast; [sentiment, humour] unfailing

inamical, **~e**, mpl **-aux** /inamikal, o/ adj unfriendly

inamovible /inamɔvibl/ adj **1** [fonctionnaire, magistrat] irremovable; [poste, charge] for life (après n); **être ~** hum [personne] to be a permanent fixture; **2** [panneau, élément] fixed; **3** [règle] immutable

inanimé, **~e** /inanime/ adj [matière] inanimate; [personne] (inconscient) unconscious; (sans vie) lifeless

inanité /inanite/ nf **1** (vanité) inanity; **2** (inutilité) futility, pointlessness

inanition /inanisjɔ̃/ nf starvation

inaperçu, **~e** /inapɛʁsy/ adj **passer ~** to go unnoticed

inapplicable /inaplikabl/ adj [théorie, réforme] unworkable; [clause, traité] unenforceable

inapplication /inaplikasjɔ̃/ nf (de loi, réglementation) **~ de** failure to enforce GB, nonenforcement of US

inappliqué, **~e** /inaplike/ adj **1** [élève] lacking application (après n); **2** [loi, réglementation] unenforced

inappréciable /inapresjabl/ adj (exceptionnel) [service, soutien] invaluable; [avantage] inestimable

inapte /inapt/ adj **1** gén unfit (**à** for; **à faire** to do); **2** Mil **~ (au service militaire)** unfit (for military service)

inaptitude /inaptityd/ nf unfitness

inarticulé, **~e** /inaʁtikyle/ adj inarticulate

inassouvi, **~e** /inasuvi/ adj [appétit] insatiable; [soif] unquenchable (épith); [personne, corps] unsatisfied; [ambition, âme] unfulfilled; [haine] enduring

inattaquable /inatakabl/ adj **1** Mil unassailable; **2** [personne, conduite, réputation] irreproachable; **3** [argumentation, jugement] irrefutable; [droit] unchallengeable; [honnêteté] indisputable; **4** [matériau, substance] (par la rouille) rust-proof; (par les vers) woodworm-proof; (par le temps) weatherproof

inattendu, **~e** /inatɑ̃dy/
A adj unexpected
B nm **l'~** (ce qui est imprévu) the unexpected; (caractère imprévisible) the unexpectedness

inattentif, **-ive** /inatɑ̃tif, iv/ adj **1** (distrait) [enfant] inattentive; [air] distracted; **2** (indifférent) [personne] heedless (**à** of)

inattention /inatɑ̃sjɔ̃/ nf inattention; **moment d'~ (de qn)** lapse of concentration (on the part of sb); **faute d'~** careless mistake

inaudible /inodibl/ adj inaudible

inaugural, **~e**, mpl **-aux** /inogyʁal, o/ adj **1** (d'ouverture) [cérémonie] inauguration (épith); [discours, séance] inaugural; **2** (tout premier) [vol, voyage] maiden

inauguration /inogyʁasjɔ̃/ nf (statue) unveiling; de route, bâtiment) inauguration; (de congrès) opening; (de politique)

launching; **discours d'~** inaugural speech

inaugurer /inogyʁe/ [1] vtr **1** (par une cérémonie) to unveil [statue, plaque]; to open [autoroute, musée, école]; **2** (ouvrir) to open [congrès, débat, exposition]; to inaugurate [série d'articles]; to launch [politique]; **3** (marquer le début) [événement, politique] to mark the start of [période]; **4** ○to christen○ [vêtement, voiture]

inavouable /inavwabl/ adj shameful

inavoué, **~e** /inavwe/ adj [vice] unconfessed; [but] undisclosed; [peur] hidden; [amour] undeclared

INC /iɛns/ nm (abbr = **Institut national de la consommation**) French consumer organization

incalculable /ɛ̃kalkylabl/ adj **1** (impossible à compter) innumerable; **2** (considérable) incalculable

incandescence /ɛ̃kɑ̃desɑ̃s/ nf incandescence; **porter qch à ~** to heat sth until it's red hot

incandescent, **~e** /ɛ̃kɑ̃desɑ̃, ɑ̃t/ adj [filament] incandescent; [métal] white-hot; [braises, lave] glowing

incapable /ɛ̃kapabl/
A adj **1** (par nature) incapable (**de faire** of doing); (temporairement) unable (**de faire** to do); **2** (incompétent) incompetent
B nmf incompetent; **c'est un ~!** he's useless!

incapacité /ɛ̃kapasite/ nf **1** (impossibilité) inability (**à faire** to do); **être dans l'~ de faire** to be unable to do; **2** (incompétence) incompetence (**en matière de** as regards); **3** (invalidité) disability; **4** Jur incapacity; **~ de travail** unfitness for work; **~s électorales** cases leading to disenfranchisement

incarcération /ɛ̃kaʁseʁasjɔ̃/ nf imprisonment

incarcérer /ɛ̃kaʁseʁe/ [14] vtr to imprison, to jail

incarnat, **~e** /ɛ̃kaʁna, at/ ▸ p. 140
A adj incarnadine
B nm incarnadine

incarnation /ɛ̃kaʁnasjɔ̃/ nf incarnation; **être l'~ du mal** to be evil personified

incarné, **~e** /ɛ̃kaʁne/ adj **1** (personnifié) incarnate (après n); **c'est la bêtise ~e** he/she is stupidity itself; **2** Relig incarnate (après n); **3** [ongle] ingrowing

incarner /ɛ̃kaʁne/ [1]
A vtr **1** to embody [tendance, espoir]; **2** to play, to portray [personnage]
B s'incarner vpr **1** (être représenté) to be embodied (**dans** in); **2** Relig to become incarnate (**dans** in)

incartade /ɛ̃kaʁtad/ nf **1** (écart de conduite) misdemeanour^GB; **2** (de cheval) shy; **faire une ~** to shy

incassable /ɛ̃kasabl/ adj unbreakable

incendiaire /ɛ̃sɑ̃djɛʁ/
A adj **1** [matière, bombe] incendiary; **2** [déclaration] inflammatory
B nmf arsonist

incendie /ɛ̃sɑ̃di/ nm fire; **lutte contre l'~** firefighting
(Composé) **~ criminel** arson

incendié, **~e** /ɛ̃sɑ̃dje/
A adj [bâtiment] burned-out; [forêt] burned
B nm,f person affected by the fire

incendier /ɛ̃sɑ̃dje/ [2] vtr **1** (brûler) to burn down, to torch [bâtiment]; to burn, to torch [véhicule, ville, forêt, récolte]; **2** ○(réprimander) to give [sb] a talking-to; **se faire ~** to be hauled over the coals; **~ qn du regard** to glower at sb

incertain, **~e** /ɛ̃sɛʁtɛ̃, ɛn/ adj **1** (indéterminé) [date, durée, origine] uncertain; [effet] unknown; [contours] blurred; [couleur] indeterminate; [sourire, sentiment] vague; **2** (aléatoire) [résultat, entreprise, profit] uncertain; [temps] unsettled; **3** (hésitant) [personne] uncertain; [électeur] undecided; [pas, voix] hesitant

incertitude /ɛ̃sɛʁtityd/ nf uncertainty; **vivre dans l'~** to live in a state of uncertainty; **vivre dans l'~ du lendemain** to live from day to day; **être dans l'~ sur ce que l'on doit faire** not to be sure what to do

incessamment /ɛ̃sesamɑ̃/ adv very shortly; **~ sous peu**○ hum in next to no time

incessant, **~e** /ɛ̃sesɑ̃, ɑ̃t/ adj [bruit, pluie, appels, querelles] incessant; [effort, activité] unceasing; [critiques] unremitting; [changements] constant

inceste /ɛ̃sɛst/ nm incest; **commettre un ~** to commit incest

incestueux, -euse /ɛ̃sɛstɥø, øz/ adj ①‣ (coupable ou entaché d'inceste) incestuous; ②‣ (né d'un inceste) born of an incestuous liaison

inchangé, **~e** /ɛ̃ʃɑ̃ʒe/ adj unchanged

incidemment /ɛ̃sidamɑ̃/ adv ①‣ (au passage) in passing; ②‣ (par hasard) by chance

incidence /ɛ̃sidɑ̃s/ nf ①‣ (effet) impact; ②‣ Méd, Phys incidence

incident, **~e**[1] /ɛ̃sidɑ̃, ɑ̃t/
Ⓐ adj ①‣ (peu important) incidental; ②‣ Ling [proposition] parenthetical; ③‣ Phys [lumière] incident
Ⓑ nm ①‣ (événement fortuit) incident; **en cas d'~** if anything should happen; ②‣ (perturbation) **~ (de parcours)** hitch; **~ de séance** procedural hitch; **l'~ est clos** the matter is closed

incidente[2] /ɛ̃sidɑ̃t/ nf Ling ①‣ (parenthèse) parenthetical clause; ②‣ (dans un discours rapporté) comment clause

incinérateur /ɛ̃sineratœr/ nm ①‣ (pour déchets) incinerator; ②‣ (crématoire) crematorium GB, crematory US

incinération /ɛ̃sinerasjɔ̃/ nf (de déchets) incineration; (de corps) cremation

incinérer /ɛ̃sinere/ [14] vtr to burn [bois]; to incinerate [déchets]; to cremate [corps]; **choisir de se faire ~** to choose to be cremated

incise /ɛ̃siz/ nf ①‣ Mus phrase; ②‣ Ling (parenthèse) parenthetical clause; (dans un discours) comment clause

inciser /ɛ̃size/ [1] vtr to make an incision in [bois, peau]; to lance [abcès]

incisif, -ive[1] /ɛ̃sizif, iv/ adj [critique] incisive; [portrait] telling; [regard] piercing; [instrument] sharp

incision /ɛ̃sizjɔ̃/ nf (de peau, d'écorce) incision; (d'abcès) lancing ₵

incisive[2] /ɛ̃siziv/ nf (dent) incisor

incitatif, -ive /ɛ̃sitatif, iv/ adj incentive (épith)

incitation /ɛ̃sitasjɔ̃/ nf ①‣ (encouragement) incentive (à to); ②‣ Jur incitement (à to)

inciter /ɛ̃site/ [1] vtr [personne, situation, attitude] to encourage; [événement, décision] to prompt; **~ qn à la prudence** to make sb cautious; **~ vivement** to urge; **~ à la haine raciale** to stir up racial hatred

inclassable /ɛ̃klasabl/ adj unclassifiable

inclinable /ɛ̃klinabl/ adj [dossier] adjustable; **fauteuil (à dossier) ~** reclining chair GB, recliner US

inclinaison /ɛ̃klinɛzɔ̃/ nf ①‣ (de route, pente) incline; (de mur, siège) angle; (de toit) slope; (de bateau) list; ②‣ Math angle

inclination /ɛ̃klinasjɔ̃/ nf ①‣ (disposition naturelle) inclination (à faire to do); ②‣ (de la tête) nod; (du buste) bow; ③‣ (amour) liter inclination

incliné, **~e** /ɛ̃kline/ adj ①‣ (non horizontal) [plateau, fonds marins] sloping; [toit] steep; **le plancher est ~** the floor slopes; ②‣ (non vertical) [mur, tour] leaning; **tenir qch ~** to hold sth at an angle

incliner /ɛ̃kline/ [1]
Ⓐ vtr ①‣ (pencher) to tilt [parasol]; to tip up [flacon]; **~ le buste** to lean forward; ②‣ (inciter) fml **cela m'incline à penser que** this leads me to think that
Ⓑ vi fml to be inclined (**à faire** to do)
Ⓒ nmf **s'incliner** ①‣ (se pencher en avant) to lean forward; (par politesse) to bow; ②‣ (ne pas contester) **s'~ devant qch** to bow to sth, to accept sth; **s'~ devant les faits** to accept the facts; ③‣ (s'avouer vaincu) to give in○ (**devant** to); **Pau s'incline devant Dax** Sport Pau lost to Dax; ④‣ (témoigner du respect) **s'~ devant le courage de qn** to admire sb's courage; ⑤‣ (se pencher sur le côté) [moto] to lean over

inclure /ɛ̃klyr/ [78] vtr ①‣ (intégrer) to include [nom, personne]; ②‣ (contenir) [liste, prix] to include; ③‣ (joindre) to enclose [document, argent]; ④‣ (ajouter) to insert [correction, clause]; ⑤‣ Math to include

inclus, **~e** /ɛ̃kly, yz/
Ⓐ pp ► **inclure**
Ⓑ pp adj ①‣ (compris) **il y avait 20 personnes, enfants ~** there were 20 people, including children; **jusqu'au second chapitre ~** up to and including chapter two; **jusqu'à jeudi ~** up to and including Thursday GB, through Thursday US; **les taxes sont ~es dans le prix** taxes are included in the price; ②‣ (joint) enclosed; ③‣ Math **B est ~ dans A** B is a subset of A

inclusion /ɛ̃klyzjɔ̃/ nf inclusion

inclusivement /ɛ̃klyzivmɑ̃/ adv **jusqu'au 4 mai ~** till 4 May inclusive

incognito /ɛ̃kɔɲito/
Ⓐ adv incognito
Ⓑ nm **garder l'~** to remain incognito

incohérence /ɛ̃kɔerɑ̃s/ nf ①‣ (manque de logique) incoherence ₵; **avec ~** incoherently; ②‣ (contradiction) discrepancy

incohérent, **~e** /ɛ̃kɔerɑ̃, ɑ̃t/ adj [propos, comportement, personne] incoherent; [attitude, raisonnement] illogical; **il se montre plutôt ~ dans ses décisions** he tends to be inconsistent in his decisions

incollable /ɛ̃kɔlabl/ adj ①‣ ○(qui a réponse à tout) [personne] impossible to catch out (jamais épith); **elle est ~ en latin** you can't catch her out in Latin; ②‣ Culin **riz ~** easy-cook rice

incolore /ɛ̃kɔlɔr/ adj ①‣ (sans couleur) [liquide, gaz, gel] colourlessGB; [vernis, verre] clear; ②‣ (sans originalité) colourlessGB

incomber /ɛ̃kɔ̃be/ [1]
Ⓐ vtr ind **~ à** [devoir, tâche, mission, dépense] to fall to; [responsabilité, faute] to lie with; **la faute en incombe à...** the fault lies with...
Ⓑ v impers **il incombe à qn de faire** it is incumbent upon sb to do sout; Jur it rests with sb to do

incommensurable /ɛ̃kɔmɑ̃syrabl/ adj ①‣ (immense) boundless; ②‣ Math incommensurable

incommode /ɛ̃kɔmɔd/ adj ①‣ (peu pratique) [équipement] inconvenient; [installation] awkward; [horaire] unsatisfactory; ②‣ (inconfortable) uncomfortable

incommodé, **~e** /ɛ̃kɔmɔde/ adj unwell, indisposed sout

incommoder /ɛ̃kɔmɔde/ [1] vtr to bother

incomparable /ɛ̃kɔ̃parabl/ adj [site, mérite, artiste] incomparable; **d'un charme ~** extremely charming

incompatibilité /ɛ̃kɔ̃patibilite/ nf incompatibility (**de qch et qch** of sth with sth); **il y a ~ entre leur politique et la nôtre** our policies are incompatible

incompatible /ɛ̃kɔ̃patibl/ adj incompatible

incompétence /ɛ̃kɔ̃petɑ̃s/ nf gén incompetence; Jur incompetency

incompétent, **~e** /ɛ̃kɔ̃petɑ̃, ɑ̃t/ adj incompetent

incomplet, -ète /ɛ̃kɔ̃plɛ, ɛt/ adj incomplete

incompréhensible /ɛ̃kɔ̃preɑ̃sibl/ adj incomprehensible (**à, pour** to)

incompréhension /ɛ̃kɔ̃preɑ̃sjɔ̃/ nf (intellectuelle) incomprehension; (affective) lack of understanding

incompressible /ɛ̃kɔ̃presibl/ adj ①‣ Phys [matière] incompressible; ②‣ Écon [dépenses, charges] fixed; ③‣ Jur **peine ~** sentence without possibility of remittance

incompris, **~e** /ɛ̃kɔ̃pri, iz/
Ⓐ adj **un artiste ~** an artist whose work is not understood
Ⓑ nmf misunderstood person

inconcevable /ɛ̃kɔ̃svabl/ adj inconceivable

inconditionnel, -elle /ɛ̃kɔ̃disjɔnɛl/
Ⓐ adj [reddition] unconditional; [appui] unqualified; [obéissance] absolute; [adhésion] wholehearted; [amateur] dedicated
Ⓑ nmf (fanatique) fan; **je suis un ~ de Mozart** I'm absolutely mad○ about Mozart

inconduite /ɛ̃kɔ̃dɥit/ nf gén misbehaviourGB; Jur misconduct

inconfort /ɛ̃kɔ̃fɔr/ nm lack of comfort

inconfortable /ɛ̃kɔ̃fɔrtabl/ adj ①‣ (sans confort) uncomfortable; ②‣ (désagréable) awkward

incongru, **~e** /ɛ̃kɔ̃gry/ adj [comportement] unseemly; [remarque] incongruous, unseemly

incongruité /ɛ̃kɔ̃grɥite/ nf ①‣ (étrangeté) incongruity; ②‣ (acte) faux-pas; (parole) incongruous remark

inconnu, **~e**[1] /ɛ̃kɔny/
Ⓐ adj gén unknown (**de** to); [territoires] unexplored; **~ à cette adresse** not known at this address; **votre visage ne m'est pas ~** your face is familiar
Ⓑ nmf ①‣ (personne non célèbre) unknown (person); ②‣ (étranger) stranger; **il s'est épris d'une ~e** he fell in love with a complete stranger
Ⓒ nm **l'~** the unknown

inconnue[2] /ɛ̃kɔny/ nf gén, Math unknown

inconsciemment /ɛ̃kɔ̃sjamã/ *adv* (sans le savoir) subconsciously; (sans le vouloir) unintentionally, unconsciously

inconscience /ɛ̃kɔ̃sjɑ̃s/ *nf* **1** (absence de jugement) recklessness; **c'est de l'∼!** it's sheer madness!; **2** Méd unconsciousness

inconscient, ∼e /ɛ̃kɔ̃sjɑ̃, ɑ̃t/
A *adj* **1** (sans jugement) unthinking; (devant un danger) foolhardy; **être ∼ de** to be unaware of; **il faut être ∼ pour rouler à cette vitesse** you have to be mad○ to drive at that speed; **2** Méd (sans connaissance) unconscious; **3** Psych [*acte, geste*] unconscious, automatic; [*sentiment*] subconscious; [*réaction*] unconscious
B *nm,f* **c'est un ∼** he's totally irresponsible
C *nm* Psych **l'∼** the unconscious

inconséquence /ɛ̃kɔ̃sekɑ̃s/ *nf* (de raisonnement) inconsistency; (de conduite) fecklessness

inconséquent, ∼e /ɛ̃kɔ̃sekɑ̃, ɑ̃t/ *adj* inconsistent

inconsidéré, ∼e /ɛ̃kɔ̃sidere/ *adj* **1** (irréfléchi) [*propos, geste, action*] ill-considered; [*prêt*] ill-advised; **2** (excessif) [*usage, consommation*] excessive

inconsidérément /ɛ̃kɔ̃sideremã/ *adv* **1** (imprudemment) [*dire, promettre*] rashly; [*prêter*] ill-advisedly; **2** (excessivement) [*boire*] to excess; [*dépenser*] wildly

inconsistance /ɛ̃kɔ̃sistɑ̃s/ *nf* (d'œuvre) lack of substance; (de personne) lack of character

inconsistant, ∼e /ɛ̃kɔ̃sistɑ̃, ɑ̃t/ *adj* [*raisonnement, argumentation, scénario*] flimsy; [*programme*] lacking in substance (épith); [*personne*] characterless

inconsolable /ɛ̃kɔ̃sɔlabl/ *adj* inconsolable

inconstance /ɛ̃kɔ̃stɑ̃s/ *nf* fickleness

inconstant, ∼e /ɛ̃kɔ̃stɑ̃, ɑ̃t/ *adj* fickle

incontestable /ɛ̃kɔ̃tɛstabl/ *adj* unquestionable, indisputable

incontestablement /ɛ̃kɔ̃tɛstabləmã/ *adv* unquestionably

incontesté, ∼e /ɛ̃kɔ̃tɛste/ *adj* [*victoire, champion*] undisputed; [*droit, fait*] uncontested

incontinence /ɛ̃kɔ̃tinɑ̃s/ *nf* Méd incontinence

incontournable /ɛ̃kɔ̃tuʀnabl/ *adj* [*question, problème*] that must be addressed (épith, après n); [*chiffres, faits*] that cannot be ignored (épith, après n); [*personne*] to be reckoned with (épith, après n); [*livre*] considered to be essential reading (épith, après n)

incontrôlable /ɛ̃kɔ̃tʀolabl/ *adj* **1** (invérifiable) unverifiable; **2** (que l'on ne peut maîtriser) uncontrollable

incontrôlé, ∼e /ɛ̃kɔ̃tʀole/ *adj* **1** (non vérifié) [*information, affirmation*] unverified, unchecked; **2** (non maîtrisé) [*individus, actes, violence*] uncontrolled

inconvenance /ɛ̃kɔ̃vnɑ̃s/ *nf* **1** (de discours, proposition) impropriety, unseemliness; **2** (acte) impropriety

inconvenant, ∼e /ɛ̃kɔ̃vnɑ̃, ɑ̃t/ *adj* [*terme*] unsuitable; [*attitude, propos, discours*] improper, unseemly

inconvénient /ɛ̃kɔ̃venjɑ̃/ *nm* drawback, disadvantage; **si vous n'y voyez pas d'∼** if you have no objection; **je ne vois pas d'∼ à ce qu'il reste dîner** I see no reason why he should not stay for dinner; **il n'y a aucun ∼ à reporter la réunion** the meeting can easily be postponed

incorporation /ɛ̃kɔʀpɔʀasjɔ̃/ *nf* Mil enlistment GB, induction US

incorporé, ∼e /ɛ̃kɔʀpɔʀe/ *adj* [*micro, antenne, cellule*] built-in

incorporer /ɛ̃kɔʀpɔʀe/ [1] *vtr* **1** Culin to blend (**à** into; **dans** with); **2** (faire entrer dans un ensemble) to incorporate [*chapitre*]; **3** Mil to enlist GB, to induct US [*recrue*]

incorrect, ∼e /ɛ̃kɔʀɛkt/ *adj* **1** (comportant des fautes) [*terme, langue, interprétation*] incorrect; [*montage*] faulty, incorrect; [*prévisions*] inaccurate; **2** (inconvenant) [*conduite*] improper; [*terme*] unsuitable; [*personne*] impolite; **être ∼ avec qn** to be rude *ou* impolite to sb; **3** (déloyal) [*personne, procédé*] unfair

incorrection /ɛ̃kɔʀɛksjɔ̃/ *nf* **1** (de style, langue) incorrectness; (de conduite, comportement) impropriety; **2** (faute) inaccuracy

incorrigible /ɛ̃kɔʀiʒibl/ *adj* incorrigible

incorruptible /ɛ̃kɔʀyptibl/
A *adj* incorruptible
B *nmf* incorruptible person

incrédule /ɛ̃kʀedyl/
A *adj* **1** (sceptique) [*personne*] incredulous; [*expression, air*] of disbelief (après n), incredulous; **2** (en matière religieuse) unbelieving (épith)
B *nmf* unbeliever, nonbeliever

incrédulité /ɛ̃kʀedylite/ *nf* **1** gén incredulity; **faire preuve d'∼** to be incredulous; **un sourire d'∼** an incredulous smile; **2** Relig lack of belief

incrémenter /ɛ̃kʀemɑ̃te/ [1] *vtr* to increment

increvable /ɛ̃kʀəvabl/ *adj* **1** ○(inépuisable) [*personne*] tireless; **2** (qui ne peut être crevé) [*pneu*] puncture-proof

incriminer /ɛ̃kʀimine/ [1] *vtr* [*personne*] to accuse [*personne*]; [*preuve, indice*] to incriminate [*personne*]; **l'article incriminé** the offending article

incroyable /ɛ̃kʀwajabl/ *adj* **1** (impossible ou difficile à croire) [*récit, nouvelle*] incredible, unbelievable; **∼ mais vrai** strange but true; **2** (hors du commun) [*chance, courage*] incredible, amazing; [*cruauté, paresse, bêtise*] incredible; **il est d'une intelligence/ignorance ∼** he's incredibly intelligent/ignorant

incroyablement /ɛ̃kʀwajabləmã/ *adv* incredibly, unbelievably

incroyance /ɛ̃kʀwajɑ̃s/ *nf* unbelief

incrustation /ɛ̃kʀystasjɔ̃/ *nf* **1** Art (procédé) inlaying; (résultat) inlay; **2** (dépôt) encrustation

incruster /ɛ̃kʀyste/ [1]
A *vtr* **1** Art to inlay [*objet*] (**de** with); **2** (en couture) **robe incrustée de diamants** dress encrusted with diamonds
B **s'incruster** *vpr* (s'agglomérer) [*caillou, coquillage*] to become embedded *ou* encrusted (**dans** in)

incubateur /ɛ̃kybatœʀ/ *nm* incubator

incubation /ɛ̃kybasjɔ̃/ *nf* **1** (de maladie, d'œuf) incubation; **2** (de révolution, d'insurrection) hatching

incuber /ɛ̃kybe/ [1] *vtr* to incubate, to hatch

inculpation /ɛ̃kylpasjɔ̃/ *nf* Jur charge (**de, pour** of); **être sous le coup d'une ∼** to be facing charges

inculpé, ∼e /ɛ̃kylpe/ *nm,f* ≈ accused; **les ∼s** the accused

inculper /ɛ̃kylpe/ [1] *vtr* to charge (**de, pour** with)

inculquer /ɛ̃kylke/ [1] *vtr* to inculcate (**à** in), to instil GB (**à** in)

inculte /ɛ̃kylt/ *adj* **1** [*personne*] uncultivated; **2** [*terres*] uncultivated

incultivable /ɛ̃kyltivabl/ *adj* unworkable, unfarmable

inculture /ɛ̃kyltyʀ/ *nf* lack of culture

incurable /ɛ̃kyʀabl/ *adj, nmf* incurable

incurie /ɛ̃kyʀi/ *nf* negligence, carelessness

incursion /ɛ̃kyʀsjɔ̃/ *nf* incursion, foray

incurver /ɛ̃kyʀve/ [1] *vtr*, **s'incurver** *vpr* to curve, to bend

Inde /ɛ̃d/ ▸ p. 230 *nprf* India

indécemment /ɛ̃desamã/ *adv* indecently

indécence /ɛ̃desɑ̃s/ *nf* **1** (manque de décence) (de tenue, attitude) indecency; (de propos) impropriety; **ce luxe, quelle ∼!** such luxury is quite obscene; **2** (acte) act of indecency; (parole) obscenity

indécent, ∼e /ɛ̃desɑ̃, ɑ̃t/ *adj* **1** [*joie*] improper, indecent; **2** [*tenue, geste, propos, spectacle*] indecent; **3** [*chance, succès, luxe*] obscene, indecent; **avoir une chance ∼e** to be disgustingly lucky

indéchiffrable /ɛ̃deʃifʀabl/ *adj* **1** (indécryptable) indecipherable; **2** (énigmatique) incomprehensible

indécis, ∼e /ɛ̃desi, iz/
A *adj* **1** (ponctuellement) **il est encore ∼** he hasn't decided yet; **2** (de nature) [*personne, caractère*] indecisive; **3** (incertain) [*résultats, victoire*] uncertain
B *nm,f* indecisive person; (électeur) floating voter

indécision /ɛ̃desizjɔ̃/ *nf* **1** (hésitation) indecision, uncertainty; **2** (trait de caractère) indecisiveness○

indécrottable /ɛ̃dekʀɔtabl/ *adj* (incorrigible) hopeless○

indéfectible /ɛ̃defɛktibl/ *adj* [*attachement, amitié, lien*] indissoluble, indefectible; [*soutien*] unfailing

indéfendable /ɛ̃defɑ̃dabl/ *adj* indefensible

indéfini, ∼e /ɛ̃defini/ *adj* **1** (sans limites) [*nombre*] indeterminate; **2** (vague) [*tristesse, mélancolie*] undefined; [*malaise*] vague; [*durée*] indeterminate, indefinite; **3** Ling indefinite

indéfiniment /ɛ̃definimɑ̃/ *adv* indefinitely

indéfinissable /ɛ̃definisabl/ *adj* undefinable

indélébile /ɛ̃delebil/ *adj* indelible

indélicat, **~e** /ɛ̃delika, at/ *adj* ①ǀ (impoli) tactless; ②ǀ (malhonnête) dishonest

indélicatesse /ɛ̃delikatɛs/ *nf* ①ǀ (impolitesse) indelicacy, tactlessness; ②ǀ (malhonnêteté) dishonesty; ③ǀ (acte malhonnête) act of dishonesty

indemne /ɛ̃dɛmn/ *adj* unscathed, unharmed

indemnisation /ɛ̃dɛmnizasjɔ̃/ *nf* ①ǀ (paiement) indemnification; ②ǀ (somme versée) indemnity, compensation **₵**

indemniser /ɛ̃dɛmnize/ [1] *vtr* to indemnify (**de** for), to compensate (**de** for); **se faire ~** to receive compensation

indemnité /ɛ̃dɛmnite/ *nf* ①ǀ Jur (dédommagement) indemnity, compensation **₵**; **verser des ~s** to pay compensation; ②ǀ (allocation) allowance

(Composés) **~ de chômage** unemployment benefit; **~ de déménagement** relocation expenses (+ *v pl*); **~ journalière** sick pay; **~ de licenciement** severance pay **₵**, redundancy payment GB; **~ parlementaire** French deputy's allowances (*pl*)

indémontrable /ɛ̃demɔ̃trabl/ *adj* undemonstrable

indéniable /ɛ̃denjabl/ *adj* undeniable, unquestionable

indentation /ɛ̃dɑ̃tasjɔ̃/ *nf* indentation

indépendamment /ɛ̃depɑ̃damɑ̃/
🅰 *adv* independently
🅱 **indépendamment de** *loc prép* ①ǀ (en faisant abstraction de) regardless of; ②ǀ (outre) in addition to

indépendance /ɛ̃depɑ̃dɑ̃s/ *nf* independence; **elle tient à son ~** she likes her independence

indépendant, **~e** /ɛ̃depɑ̃dɑ̃, ɑ̃t/
🅰 *adj* ①ǀ [*personne*] independent (**de** of); ②ǀ [*chambre, entrée*] separate; **maison ~** detached house
🅱 *nm,f* ①ǀ (travailleur) self-employed person; **travailler en ~** to be self-employed; ②ǀ (candidat) independent

indépendantiste /ɛ̃depɑ̃dɑ̃tist/
🅰 *adj* [*mouvement, organisation*] (pro-)independence (*épith*)
🅱 *nmf* ①ǀ (combattant) freedom fighter; ②ǀ (militant) member of an independence movement

indéracinable /ɛ̃derasinabl/ *adj* ineradicable

Indes† /ɛ̃d/ *nprfpl* Hist **les ~** the Indies

(Composés) **~ occidentales** Hist West Indies; **~ orientales** Hist East Indies

indescriptible /ɛ̃dɛskriptibl/ *adj* indescribable

indésirable /ɛ̃dezirabl/
🅰 *adj* [*personne*] undesirable; **effets ~s** Méd adverse reactions
🅱 *nmf* undesirable

indestructible /ɛ̃dɛstryktibl/ *adj* indestructible

indétermination /ɛ̃detɛrminasjɔ̃/ *nf* ①ǀ (indécision) indecision; ②ǀ (imprécision) vagueness

indéterminé, **~e** /ɛ̃detɛrmine/ *adj* ①ǀ (non précisé) [*forme, quantité*] indeterminate; [*raison, nombre*] unspecified; **l'origine de l'incendie reste ~e** the cause of the fire has not yet been identified; ②ǀ (hésitant) (de caractère) indecisive; (ponctuellement) undecided; ③ǀ Math indeterminate

index /ɛ̃dɛks/ *nm inv* ①ǀ (table alphabétique) index; **mettre qch/qn à l'~** to blacklist sth/sb; ②ǀ Ordinat index; ③ǀ ▸ p. 136 Anat forefinger; ④ǀ Tech pointer

indexation /ɛ̃dɛksasjɔ̃/ *nf* ①ǀ Écon indexation; ②ǀ (pour classer) indexing

indexer /ɛ̃dɛkse/ [1] *vtr* ①ǀ Écon to index-link [*salaire, taux*]; **~ qch sur qch** to index sth to sth; ②ǀ (classer) to index; ③ǀ Ordinat to index

indicateur, **-trice** /ɛ̃dikatœr, tris/
🅰 *adj* **panneau** or **poteau ~** signpost
🅱 *nm* ①ǀ (délateur) informer; ②ǀ (indice) indicator; **~ de tendance** market indicator; ③ǀ (brochure) (de rues) directory; (d'horaires) timetable; ④ǀ Tech gauge, indicator; **~ de niveau d'huile** oil gauge; **~ lumineux** (warning) light; **~ de vitesse** speed indicator; **~ (de changement) de direction** Aut (direction) indicator

indicatif, **-ive** /ɛ̃dikatif, iv/
🅰 *adj* indicative
🅱 *nm* ①ǀ Ling indicative; **à l'~** in the indicative; **le futur de l'~** the future indicative; ②ǀ Télécom (téléphonique) dialling^GB code; **~ de pays** country code; ③ǀ Radio, TV (d'émission) theme tune

indication /ɛ̃dikasjɔ̃/ *nf* ①ǀ (action d'indiquer) indication; **il n'y a pas d'~ d'origine** the place of origin is not indicated; **il n'y a pas d'~ de date/lieu** no date/place is specified; ②ǀ (renseignement) information **₵**; **sauf ~ contraire** unless otherwise indicated; ③ǀ (instruction) instruction; **se conformer aux** or **suivre les ~s** to follow the instructions; ④ǀ (indice) indication

(Composé) **~ scénique** stage direction

indice /ɛ̃dis/ *nm* ①ǀ (signe apparent) sign, indication; ②ǀ (dans une enquête) clue; ③ǀ Écon, Fin index; ④ǀ (évaluation) **~ de popularité** popularity rating; **l'~ d'écoute** audience ratings (*pl*)

(Composés) **~ des prix à la consommation** retail price index GB, consumer price index US; **~ de protection (solaire)** sun protection factor, SPF

indicible /ɛ̃disibl/ *adj* inexpressible

indien, **-ienne¹** /ɛ̃djɛ̃, ɛn/ ▸ p. 392 *adj* (d'Inde, d'Amérique) Indian

Indien /ɛ̃djɛ̃/ ▸ p. 406 *adj* **l'océan ~** the Indian Ocean

indienne² /ɛ̃djɛn/ *nf* ①ǀ (tissu) (printed) calico; ②ǀ (nage) sidestroke

indifféremment /ɛ̃diferamɑ̃/ *adv* ①ǀ (sans distinction) equally; ②ǀ (selon les cas) **servir ~ de salon ou de bureau** to be used either as a living room or a study

indifférence /ɛ̃diferɑ̃s/ *nf* indifference

indifférencié, **~e** /ɛ̃diferɑ̃sje/ *adj* ①ǀ (indistinct) indistinct; ②ǀ Biol undifferentiated

indifférent, **~e** /ɛ̃diferɑ̃, ɑ̃t/ *adj* ①ǀ (impassible) indifferent (**à** to); **laisser qn ~** [*œuvre, événement*] to leave sb cold; **ça m'est tout à fait ~** it makes absolutely no difference to me; ②ǀ (sans importance) [*âge, sexe*] irrelevant

indifférer /ɛ̃difere/ [14] *vtr* to leave [sb] indifferent

indigence /ɛ̃diʒɑ̃s/ *nf* destitution, extreme poverty

indigène /ɛ̃diʒɛn/
🅰 *adj* ①ǀ Bot, Zool [*faune, flore*] indigenous; ②ǀ [*population, coutume, langue*] (du pays) local; (d'une colonie) native
🅱 *nmf* (natif du pays) local, native hum; (d'une colonie) native

indigent, **~e** /ɛ̃diʒɑ̃, ɑ̃t/
🅰 *adj* destitute
🅱 *nm,f* pauper; **les ~s** the destitute, the poor

indigeste /ɛ̃diʒɛst/ *adj* [*aliment, roman*] indigestible

indigestion /ɛ̃diʒɛstjɔ̃/ *nf* ①ǀ Méd indigestion **₵**; ②ǀ fig **avoir une ~ de qch** to be fed up○ with sth

indignation /ɛ̃diɲasjɔ̃/ *nf* indignation (**devant** at)

indigne /ɛ̃diɲ/ *adj* ①ǀ (méprisable) [*conduite, procédé*] disgraceful; [*mère, fils*] bad; ②ǀ (pas digne) **~ de qn** [*propos, acte*] unworthy of sb; **elle est ~ de ton amitié** she is unworthy of your friendship, she doesn't deserve your friendship; **il est ~ de représenter son pays** he's unfit to represent his country

indigné, **~e** /ɛ̃diɲe/ *adj* indignant (**de** at)

indigner /ɛ̃diɲe/ [1]
🅰 *vtr* to make [sb] indignant, to outrage [*personne*]
🅱 **s'indigner** *vpr* to be indignant (**de** about)

indignité /ɛ̃diɲite/ *nf* ①ǀ (caractère) despicableness; ②ǀ (action) despicable act, disgraceful act

indigo /ɛ̃digo/ ▸ p. 140 *adj inv*, *nm* indigo

indiqué, **~e** /ɛ̃dike/
🅰 *pp* ▸ **indiquer**
🅱 *pp adj* ①ǀ (recommandé) [*traitement*] recommended; **ça n'est pas très ~** [*aliment, trajet*] it's better avoided; **le moyen tout ~ d'échouer** the sure way to fail; ②ǀ (convenu) **à l'heure ~e** at the specified time; (signalisé) **le village est très mal/bien indiqué** the village is very badly/well signposted

indiquer /ɛ̃dike/ [1] *vtr* ①ǀ (montrer où se trouve) [*personne*] to point out, to point to [*objet, lieu*]; [*pancarte*] to show the way to [*ville, magasin*]; **il indiqua l'endroit du doigt** he pointed out the place; **la carte n'indique que les grandes routes** the map only shows the main roads; **pouvez-vous m'~ la banque la plus proche?** can you tell me where the nearest bank is?; ②ǀ (être un indice de) to indicate (**que** that); **rien n'indique que les deux affaires soient liées** there is nothing to indicate or suggest that the two matters are connected; **les chiffres indiquent une légère reprise** the figures show a slight recovery; ③ǀ (conseiller) **je peux t'~ un bon médecin** I can give you the name of a good doctor; ④ǀ (signaler, dire) **indique-moi ton heure d'arrivée** tell me what time you are arriving; **l'heure indiquée sur le programme est fausse** the time given on the programme^{GB} is wrong; **comme il l'indique dans son introduction...** as he says in his introduction...; **on m'a indiqué la marche à suivre** I've been told the procedure

indirect, ∼e /ɛ̃diʀɛkt/ *adj* indirect

indirectement /ɛ̃diʀɛktəmɑ̃/ *adv* indirectly

indiscipline /ɛ̃disiplin/ *nf* lack of discipline

indiscipliné, ∼e /ɛ̃disipline/ *adj* undisciplined, unruly

indiscret, -ète /ɛ̃diskʀɛ, ɛt/ *adj* [1] (trop curieux) [*question*] indiscreet; [*personne*] inquisitive; **combien gagnez-vous, si ce n'est pas ∼?** how much do you earn, if you don't mind my asking?; **à l'abri des regards ∼s** away from prying eyes; [2] (qui ne sait pas garder un secret) [*propos, personne*] indiscreet

indiscrètement /ɛ̃diskʀɛtmɑ̃/ *adv* [*révéler*] indiscreetly; [*demander*] inquisitively

indiscrétion /ɛ̃diskʀesjɔ̃/ *nf* [1] (curiosité) inquisitiveness; **sans ∼, combien gagnez-vous?** if you don't mind my asking, how much do you earn?; [2] (tendance à trop parler) lack of discretion; **elle est d'une grande ∼** she's very indiscreet; [3] (parole indiscrète) indiscreet remark

indiscutable /ɛ̃diskytabl/ *adj* indisputable, unquestionable

indiscutablement /ɛ̃diskytabləmɑ̃/ *adv* unquestionably

indispensable /ɛ̃dispɑ̃sabl/
A *adj* gén essential (à to; pour for); [*argent*] necessary (épith), essential (jamais épith); **être ∼ à qn** to be indispensable to sb; **c'est ∼** it's essential
B *nm* **l'∼** essentials (pl); **n'emporte que l'∼** only take the essentials with you; **faire l'∼** to do what is necessary

indisponible /ɛ̃dispɔnibl/ *adj* unavailable

indisposé, ∼e /ɛ̃dispoze/ *adj* unwell, indisposed sout

indisposer /ɛ̃dispoze/ [1] *vtr* [1] (agacer) to annoy; [2] (rendre légèrement malade) to upset, to make [sb] feel ill

indisposition /ɛ̃dispozisjɔ̃/ *nf* indisposition; **souffrir d'une légère ∼** to be slightly indisposed

indissociable /ɛ̃disɔsjabl/ *adj* inseparable (de from)

indistinct, ∼e /ɛ̃distɛ̃, ɛ̃kt/ *adj* indistinct

individu /ɛ̃dividy/ *nm* [1] (personne privée) individual; **la société écrase l'∼** society crushes the individual; [2] (personne physique) human being, person; [3] (homme suspect) individual; **un sinistre/dangereux ∼** a sinister/dangerous individual ou character; **un ∼ armé** an armed man; [4] (unité) subject

individualisé, ∼e /ɛ̃dividɥalize/ *adj* [*enseignement, formation*] tailored to individual needs (après n), individualized US; [*salaire*] negotiated on an individual basis (après n)

individualiser /ɛ̃dividɥalize/ [1]
A *vtr* (adapter) to tailor [sth] to individual needs, to individualize US [*enseignement, horaire*]
B **s'individualiser** *vpr* to become more individual

individualiste /ɛ̃dividɥalist/
A *adj* individualistic
B *nmf* individualist

individuel, -elle /ɛ̃dividɥɛl/
A *adj* [1] (pour une personne) [*portion, cours*] individual; [*voiture*] private; [*chambre*] single (épith); **maison individuelle** (detached) house; [2] (d'une seule personne) [*initiative, réussite*] individual; [3] (qui concerne l'individu) [*propriété*] private; [*responsabilité*] personal
B *nm* [1] Sport **il a obtenu de bons résultats en ∼** he did well in the individual events; [2] Tourisme **voyage en groupe ou en ∼** group or individual travel

individuellement /ɛ̃dividɥɛlmɑ̃/ *adv* individually

indivisible /ɛ̃divizibl/ *adj* indivisible; **une et ∼** one and indivisible

indochinois, ∼e /ɛ̃dɔʃinwa, az/ *adj* Indochinese

indo-européen, -éenne /ɛ̃dooʀɔpeɛ̃, ɛn/ *mpl* ∼s
A *adj* Indo-European
B *nm* Ling Indo-European

indolence /ɛ̃dɔlɑ̃s/ *nf* (de personne) laziness, indolence sout; (d'administration) apathy, indifference

indolent, ∼e /ɛ̃dɔlɑ̃, ɑ̃t/ *adj* lazy, indolent

indolore /ɛ̃dɔlɔʀ/ *adj* painless

indomptable /ɛ̃dɔ̃tabl/ *adj* [*tempérament, peuple, courage*] indomitable; [*colère, passion*] uncontrollable, ungovernable; [*personnes*] uncontrollable; [*animaux*] untamable; **avec une énergie ∼** with tireless energy

indompté, ∼e /ɛ̃dɔ̃te/ *adj* unsubdued, untamed

indonésien, -ienne /ɛ̃dɔnezjɛ̃, ɛn/ ▸ p. 336, p. 392
A *adj* Indonesian
B *nm* Ling Indonesian

indu, ∼e /ɛ̃dy/ *adj* [1] (inconvenant) [*heure*] ungodly[○], unearthly; [*propos, réaction*] inappropriate, unseemly; [2] (sans fondement) [*somme*] unwarranted, unjustified

indubitable /ɛ̃dybitabl/ *adj* indubitable; **il nous cache quelque chose, c'est ∼** he's hiding something from us, there's no doubt about it

indubitablement /ɛ̃dybitabləmɑ̃/ *adv* undoubtedly

induction /ɛ̃dyksjɔ̃/ *nf* induction

induire /ɛ̃dɥiʀ/ [69] *vtr* [1] (entraîner) [*événement, mesures, phénomène*] to lead to, to bring about; [2] (conclure) to infer, to conclude (de qch from sth); [3] (inciter) to induce (à faire to do); **∼ qn en erreur** to mislead sb; [4] (en électricité) to induce [*courant*]

indulgence /ɛ̃dylʒɑ̃s/ *nf* [1] (de parent, public) indulgence; [2] (de jury, d'examinateur) leniency

indulgent, ∼e /ɛ̃dylʒɑ̃, ɑ̃t/ *adj* [*parent, public*] indulgent; [*jury, examinateur*] lenient

industrialisation /ɛ̃dystʀializasjɔ̃/ *nf* industrialization

industrialisé, ∼e /ɛ̃dystʀijalize/ *adj* **pays ∼s** industrialized countries

industrialiser /ɛ̃dystʀialize/ [1]
A *vtr* to industrialize
B **s'industrialiser** *vpr* to become industrialized

industrie /ɛ̃dystʀi/ *nf* [1] (secteur) industry; **∼ automobile/d'armement** car/arms industry; **l'∼ hôtelière** the hotel trade; [2] (entreprise) industrial concern ou firm

industriel, -ielle /ɛ̃dystʀijɛl/
A *adj* industrial; [*pain*] factory-made, factory-baked; **en quantité industrielle** in vast ou huge amounts
B *nm,f* industrialist, manufacturer

industriellement /ɛ̃dystʀijɛlmɑ̃/ *adv* industrially

industrieux, -ieuse /ɛ̃dystʀijø, øz/ *adj* liter industrious

inébranlable /inebʀɑ̃labl/ *adj* [1] [*personne, conviction, résolution*] unshakeable, unwavering; **rester ∼ dans ses convictions** to stick firmly to one's convictions; [2] [*roc, construction*] immovable

inédit, ∼e /inedi, it/
A *adj* [1] (jamais publié) [*livre, pièce, traduction*] (previously) unpublished; [*disque, film*] (previously) unreleased; [2] (original) [*procédé, information, spectacle, situation*] (totally) new
B *nm* [1] (ouvrage) (previously) unpublished work ou article; **un ∼ de Diderot** a previously unpublished work by Diderot; [2] (nouveau) **voilà de l'∼** that's something completely new

ineffable /inefabl/ *adj* ineffable, unutterable

inefficace /inefikas/ *adj* [*traitement, médicament, mesure*] ineffective; [*méthode, système, service, appareil, travailleur*] inefficient

inefficacité /inefikasite/ *nf* [1] (absence de résultats) ineffectiveness, inefficacy sout; [2] (rendement insuffisant) inefficiency

inégal, ∼e /inegal/ *mpl* -aux /inegal, o/ *adj* [1] (dissemblable) unequal; **de force ∼e** of unequal strength; [2] (déséquilibré) [*lutte, partage*] unequal; [*partie*] uneven; [3] (irrégulier) [*rythme*] irregular, uneven; [*surface*] uneven; [4] (variable) [*humeur*] changeable, erratic; [*auteur, œuvre*] uneven; **il a un jeu ∼** he is an inconsistent player; **avec un bonheur ∼** with mixed success

inégalable /inegalabl/ *adj* incomparable, matchless

inégalé, ∼e /inegale/ *adj* unequalled^{GB}, unrivalled^{GB}

inégalement /inegalmɑ̃/ *adv* [1] (de manière dissemblable) unequally; (de manière irrégulière) unevenly; **une œuvre ∼ appréciée** a work which received a mixed reception

inégalitaire /inegalitɛʀ/ *adj* non-egalitarian

inégalité /inegalite/ *nf* [1] (disproportion) disparity (entre between; de in); [2] (iniquité) inequality; **les ∼s sociales** social inequalities; [3] (irrégularité) (d'humeur) changeability; (de terrain, surface) unevenness

inélégant, **~e** /inelegã, ãt/ adj [1] (mal habillé) inelegant; [2] (mesquin) [procédé, comportement] shabby

inéligible /ineliʒibl/ adj ineligible

inéluctable /inelyktabl/ adj, nm inevitable, ineluctable sout

inénarrable /inenaʀabl/ adj hilarious

inepte /inɛpt/ adj [personne, gouvernement] inept; [jugement] inane; [film, remarque] idiotic

ineptie /inɛpsi/ nf [1] (caractère inepte) inanity; **des propos d'une ~ totale** totally idiotic remarks; [2] (parole stupide) idiotic remark

inépuisable /inepɥizabl/ adj inexhaustible

inerte /inɛʀt/ adj [1] (sans réaction) [corps, membre, personne] inert; [2] Chimie, Phys inert; [3] (apathique) [personne, groupe] apathetic

inertie /inɛʀsi/ nf [1] Chimie, Phys inertia; [2] (passivité) apathy, inertia

inespéré, **~e** /inɛspeʀe/ adj [victoire] unhoped for; **c'est une occasion ~e de faire** this is a heaven-sent opportunity to do

inesthétique /inɛstetik/ adj (laid) unsightly; (au niveau artistique) unaesthetic

inestimable /inɛstimabl/ adj [fortune, valeur] inestimable; [dommages] incalculable; [tableau, cadeau] priceless; [aide, service] invaluable

inévitable /inevitabl/
A adj [1] (certain) inevitable; [2] (incontournable) hum **l'~ Paul était là** Paul was there, as always; **il y avait l'~ clown** there was the inevitable clown
B nm **l'~** the inevitable

inévitablement /inevitabləmã/ adv inevitably

inexact, **~e** /inegza, akt/ adj inaccurate; **c'est ~!** that's not accurate!

inexactitude /inegzaktityd/ nf [1] (erreur) inaccuracy; [2] (manque de ponctualité) unpunctuality

inexcusable /inɛkskyzabl/ adj inexcusable; **tu es ~** there's no excuse for it!

inexistant, **~e** /inegzistã, ãt/ adj [moyens, aide] non-existent; **les risques ne sont pas ~s** there are certain risks

inexorable /inɛgzɔʀabl/ adj inexorable

inexpérimenté, **~e** /inɛkspeʀimãte/ adj inexperienced

inexplicable /inɛksplikabl/ adj inexplicable

inexpliqué, **~e** /inɛksplike/ adj unexplained

inexploitable /inɛksplwatabl/ adj [gisement] unworkable; [renseignements, documents] unusable

inexploité, **~e** /inɛksplwate/ adj [richesses, sol] unexploited; [ressources, marché, créneau] untapped, unexploited; [documents] unused

inexploré, **~e** /inɛksplɔʀe/ adj unexplored

inexprimable /inɛkspʀimabl/ adj inexpressible

inextinguible /inɛkstɛ̃gibl/ adj [feu, incendie] inextinguishable; [2] [passion, ardeur] inextinguishable; [soif] unquenchable

in extremis /inɛkstʀemis/
A loc adj inv (de dernière minute) [sauvetage, accord] last-minute
B loc adv (au dernier moment) at the last minute

inextricable /inɛkstʀikabl/ adj inextricable

inextricablement /inɛkstʀikabləmã/ adv inextricably

infaillible /ɛ̃fajibl/ adj infallible

infaisable /ɛ̃fəzabl/ adj unfeasible, impossible

infalsifiable /ɛ̃falsifjabl/ adj impossible to forge

infamant, **~e** /ɛ̃famã, ãt/ adj [1] [propos] defamatory sout; [acte] infamous

infâme /ɛ̃fam/ adj [1] (répugnant) [nourriture, odeur, boisson] revolting, disgusting; [2] (ignoble) [individu] despicable; [trahison, bassesse] base; [crime] odious

infamie /ɛ̃fami/ nf [1] (caractère) infamy; [2] (acte vil) act of infamy; (calomnie) slanderous remark

infanterie /ɛ̃fãtʀi/ nf infantry

infantile /ɛ̃fãtil/ adj [1] (relatif aux enfants) [maladie] childhood; [mortalité] infant; [psychologie, protection] child; [2] (puéril) infantile, childish

infantilisme /ɛ̃fãtilism/ nm [1] péj childishness; [2] Méd infantilism

infarctus /ɛ̃faʀktys/ ▸ p. 195 nm inv Méd (du myocarde) heart attack, myocardial infarction spéc; **faire**○ or **avoir un ~** to have a coronary, to have a heart attack

infatigable /ɛ̃fatigabl/ adj [personne, esprit] tireless

infatigablement /ɛ̃fatigabləmã/ adv tirelessly

infatué, **~e** /ɛ̃fatɥe/ adj **être ~ de sa personne** or **soi-même** to be full of oneself

infatuer: s'infatuer /ɛ̃fatɥe/ [1] vpr fml to become infatuated (**de qn** with sb)

infect, **~e** /ɛ̃fɛkt/ adj [temps, odeur, humeur] foul; [plat] revolting; [personne, attitude, lieu] horrible

infecter /ɛ̃fɛkte/ [1]
A vtr [1] Méd to infect; [2] fig to poison
B s'infecter vpr to become infected, to go septic

infectieux, **-ieuse** /ɛ̃fɛksjø, øz/ adj infectious

infection /ɛ̃fɛksjɔ̃/ nf [1] Méd infection; [2] fig **c'est une ~!** (puanteur) it stinks to high heaven○!; (chose répugnante) it's disgusting!

⬭ Composé⬭ **~ nosocomiale** (hospital) superbug

inférer /ɛ̃feʀe/ [14] vtr to infer (**de** from)

inférieur, **~e** /ɛ̃feʀjœʀ/
A adj [1] (dans l'espace, dans une hiérarchie) lower; **dans le coin ~ gauche** in the bottom left-hand corner; **on l'a rétrogradé au rang ~** he was demoted to the next rank down; [2] (en valeur) [température, vitesse, coût, salaire, nombre] lower (**à** than); [taille] smaller (**à** than); [durée] shorter (**à** than); **~ à la moyenne** below average; **des coûts de production ~s à la moyenne** lower than average production costs; **être en nombre ~** to be fewer in number; [3] (de qualité moindre) [travail, ouvrage, qualité] inferior (**à** to); [4] Math **si a est ~ à b** if a is less than b
B nm,f inferior

infériorité /ɛ̃feʀjɔʀite/ nf inferiority; **être en position d'~** to be in an inferior position

infernal, **~e**, mpl **-aux** /ɛ̃fɛʀnal, o/ adj [1] (insupportable) [bruit, cadence, chaleur] infernal; **cycle ~** unstoppable chain of events; [2] [situation, circulation] diabolical; **ce gosse est ~**○ that child is a monster; [3] Mythol infernal

infertile /ɛ̃fɛʀtil/ adj barren, infertile

infester /ɛ̃fɛste/ [1] vtr to infest, to overrun; **infesté de rats/requins** rat-/shark-infested; **infesté de puces** flea-ridden (épith); **jardin infesté d'orties** garden overrun with nettles

infidèle /ɛ̃fidɛl/
A adj [1] (inconstant) [mari, maîtresse] unfaithful (**à qn** to sb); [ami] disloyal; [2] (non conforme) [traduction, récit] inaccurate; [3] Relig infidel
B nm,f Relig infidel

infidélité /ɛ̃fidelite/ nf [1] (dans un couple) infidelity (**à** to); **faire des ~s à** to be unfaithful to; [2] (d'ami, allié) disloyalty (**à** to); [3] (de traduction) inaccuracy

infiltration /ɛ̃filtʀasjɔ̃/ nf [1] (de liquide) **~s d'eau** water seepage ₵; **il y a des ~s dans le mur** water is seeping into the wall; [2] (d'espions) infiltration (**dans** into); [3] (piqûre) **~s de cortisone** cortisone injections

infiltrer /ɛ̃filtʀe/ [1]
A vtr to infiltrate [organisation]
B s'infiltrer vpr [1] [liquide] to leak (**dans** into); [lumière, froid] to filter in; **le doute s'infiltra dans mon esprit** I began to have doubts; [2] [personne] **s'~ dans** to infiltrate [groupe, lieu]

infime /ɛ̃fim/ adj (petit) tiny, minute; **chance ~** very remote chance

infini, **~e** /ɛ̃fini/
A adj infinite; **avec d'~es précautions** with infinite care
B nm Math, Phot **l'~** infinity

infiniment /ɛ̃finimã/ adv (énormément) immensely; **~ reconnaissant** immensely grateful; **~ plus** infinitely more

infinité /ɛ̃finite/ nf **l'~** infinity; **une ~ de** an endless number of

infinitésimal, **~e**, mpl **-aux** /ɛ̃finitezimal, o/ adj infinitesimal

infinitif, **-ive** /ɛ̃finitif, iv/
A adj infinitive
B nm infinitive; **à l'~** in the infinitive

infirmation /ɛ̃fiʀmasjɔ̃/ nf quashing, invalidation

infirme /ɛ̃fiʀm/
A *adj* gén disabled; (par l'âge) infirm
B *nmf* disabled person; **les ∼s** the disabled
infirmer /ɛ̃fiʀme/ [1] *vtr* gén, Jur to invalidate
infirmerie /ɛ̃fiʀməʀi/ *nf* gén infirmary; (d'école) sick room; (de bateau) sick bay
infirmier /ɛ̃fiʀmje/ ▶ p. 372 *nm* male nurse
infirmière /ɛ̃fiʀmjɛʀ/ ▶ p. 372 *nf* nurse
infirmité /ɛ̃fiʀmite/ *nf* [1] gén disability; (de vieillesse) infirmity; [2] (imperfection) weakness
inflammable /ɛ̃flamabl/ *adj* flammable
inflammation /ɛ̃flamasjɔ̃/ *nf* Méd inflammation
inflammatoire /ɛ̃flamatwaʀ/ *adj* Méd inflammatory
inflation /ɛ̃flasjɔ̃/ *nf* inflation
inflationniste /ɛ̃flasjɔnist/ *adj* inflationary; **tensions ∼s** inflationary pressures
infléchir /ɛ̃fleʃiʀ/ [3]
A *vtr* [1] (assouplir) to soften [position, politique]; [2] (faire dévier) to deflect [trajectoire]; **∼ la courbe des dépenses** to curb spending
B **s'infléchir** *vpr* [1] (s'assouplir) [position, politique] to soften; [2] (se courber) [tige, route] to bend; [poutre] to sag; [3] (dévier) [trajectoire] to deflect; [4] (commencer à baisser) [courbe] to level off; [5] Math [courbe] to inflect
inflexibilité /ɛ̃flɛksibilite/ *nf* inflexibility
inflexible /ɛ̃flɛksibl/ *adj* inflexible
inflexion /ɛ̃flɛksjɔ̃/ *nf* [1] (changement) change (**de, dans** in); [2] (baisse) slight drop (**de** in); [3] (mouvement) **∼ du corps** bow; **∼ de la tête** bow; [4] (vocale) inflection
infliger /ɛ̃fliʒe/ [13] *vtr* [1] (faire subir) to inflict [défaite, mauvais traitements] (**à** on); [2] Jur to impose [amende, punition] (**à** on); to give [avertissement] (**à** to)
influençable /ɛ̃flyɑ̃sabl/ *adj* impressionable
influence /ɛ̃flyɑ̃s/ *nf* [1] (effet) influence (**sur** on); **il a une mauvaise ∼ sur son frère** he is a bad influence on his brother; **avoir une ∼ néfaste** [facteur, phénomène] to have a detrimental effect (**sur** on); [2] (pouvoir) influence ¢; [3] Art, Littérat influence (**sur** on); [4] Pol (rôle) influence ¢
influencer /ɛ̃flyɑ̃se/ [12] *vtr* to influence [enfant, électeur, artiste]; to affect [économie, situation]
influent, ∼e /ɛ̃flyɑ̃, ɑ̃t/ *adj* influential
influer /ɛ̃flye/ [1] *vtr ind* **∼ sur** to have an influence on
influx /ɛ̃fly/ *nm inv* **∼ nerveux** nerve impulse
infographie® /ɛ̃fografi/ *nf* computer graphics (+ *v sg*)
infographiste /ɛ̃fografist/ ▶ p. 372 *nmf* computer graphics specialist
informateur, -trice /ɛ̃fɔʀmatœʀ, tʀis/ *nmf* [1] gén informant; [2] (indicateur de police) informer
informaticien, -ienne /ɛ̃fɔʀmatisjɛ̃, ɛn/ ▶ p. 372 *nmf* computer scientist
information /ɛ̃fɔʀmasjɔ̃/ *nf* [1] (renseignement) information ¢; **une ∼** a piece of information; **ces ∼s sont confidentielles** this is confidential information; [2] Presse, Radio, TV (nouvelle) piece of news, news item; **écouter les ∼s** to listen to the news; [3] Presse, Radio, TV (activité) reporting; (résultat) information; (médias) media; **de meilleurs journalistes pour une meilleure ∼** better journalists for a better standard of reporting; **défendre le droit à l'∼** to defend freedom of information; **contrôler l'∼** to control the media; [4] Ordinat information; **le traitement de l'∼** data *ou* information processing; [5] Jur inquiry; **∼ judiciaire** judicial inquiry
informatique /ɛ̃fɔʀmatik/
A *adj* [système, équipement] computer
B *nf* (science) computer science, computing; (techniques) information technology
informatisation /ɛ̃fɔʀmatizasjɔ̃/ *nf* computerization
informatiser /ɛ̃fɔʀmatize/ [1]
A *vtr* to computerize
B **s'informatiser** *vpr* to become computerized
informe /ɛ̃fɔʀm/ *adj* shapeless
informer /ɛ̃fɔʀme/ [1]
A *vtr* (mettre au courant) to inform [personne, groupe] (**de** about; **que** that); **les journaux bien informés** the serious press; **les milieux bien informés** well-informed circles; **de source bien informée** from a reliable source
B *vi* Jur to hold an inquiry *ou* investigation

C **s'informer** *vpr* [1] (suivre l'actualité) to keep oneself informed; [2] (se mettre au courant) **s'∼ de qch** to inquire about sth; [3] (prendre des renseignements) **s'∼ sur qn** to make inquiries about sb
infortune /ɛ̃fɔʀtyn/ *nf* misfortune; **compagnon d'∼** companion in adversity
infortuné, ∼e /ɛ̃fɔʀtyne/
A *adj* ill-fated
B *nm,f* unfortunate
infos° /ɛ̃fo/ *nfpl* news (*sg*)
infra /ɛ̃fʀa/ *adv* below; **voir ∼** see below
infraction /ɛ̃fʀaksjɔ̃/ *nf* Jur offenceᴳᴮ; **être en ∼ avec la loi** [personne] to be in breach of the law
infranchissable /ɛ̃fʀɑ̃ʃisabl/ *adj* [obstacle] insurmountable; [frontière] impassable
infrarouge /ɛ̃fʀaʀuʒ/ *adj, nm* infrared; **missile guidé par ∼** heat-seeking missile
infrastructure /ɛ̃fʀastʀyktyʀ/ *nf* [1] (équipements) facilities (*pl*); **∼ hôtelière/médicale** hotel/medical facilities; [2] Écon infrastructure; [3] Constr substructure
infructueux, -euse /ɛ̃fʀyktɥø, øz/ *adj* fruitless
infuser /ɛ̃fyze/ [1]
A *vtr* Culin to brew, to infuse [thé]; to infuse [tisane]
B *vi* [thé] to brew, to infuse; [tisane] to infuse
infusion /ɛ̃fyzjɔ̃/ *nf* [1] (tisane) herbal tea; **∼ de camomille** camomile tea; **boîte de 20 ∼s** box of 20 herbal tea bags; [2] (processus) infusion
ingénier: s'ingénier /ɛ̃ʒenje/ [2] *vpr* to do one's utmost (**à faire** to do)
ingénierie /ɛ̃ʒeniʀi/ *nf* engineering
ingénieur /ɛ̃ʒenjœʀ/ ▶ p. 372 *nm* engineer; **∼ agronome/ chimiste/électricien/du son** agricultural/chemical/ electrical/sound engineer; **∼ des travaux publics** civil engineer
ingénieur-conseil, *pl* **ingénieurs-conseils** /ɛ̃ʒenjœʀkɔ̃sɛj/ *nm* consulting engineer
ingénieux, -ieuse /ɛ̃ʒenjø, øz/ *adj* ingenious
ingéniosité /ɛ̃ʒenjozite/ *nf* ingenuity
ingénu, ∼e /ɛ̃ʒeny/
A *adj* ingenuous
B *nm,f* **un ∼** an ingenuous man; **une ∼e** an ingénue
ingénuité /ɛ̃ʒenɥite/ *nf* ingenuousness; **avec ∼** ingenuously; **en toute ∼** in all innocence
ingérence /ɛ̃ʒeʀɑ̃s/ *nf* interference ¢ (**dans** in)
ingérer /ɛ̃ʒeʀe/ [14]
A *vtr* to ingest
B **s'ingérer** *vpr* to interfere (**dans** in)
ingestion /ɛ̃ʒɛstjɔ̃/ *nf* ingestion
Ingouchie /ɛ̃guʃi/ ▶ p. 230 *nprf* Ingush Republic
ingrat, ∼e /ɛ̃gʀa, at/
A *adj* [1] (sans reconnaissance) ungrateful; [2] (sans agrément) [œuvre] arid; [lieu, paysage] unwelcoming; [visage, physique] unattractive; [3] (sans récompense) [métier, tâche, rôle] thankless; [terre] unproductive
B *nm,f* ungrateful person
ingratitude /ɛ̃gʀatityd/ *nf* (manque de reconnaissance) ingratitude (**envers** to); **faire preuve d'∼** to show ingratitude, to be ungrateful
ingrédient /ɛ̃gʀedjɑ̃/ *nm* ingredient
ingurgiter /ɛ̃gyʀʒite/ [1] *vtr* [1] (avaler) to gulp down [boisson, aliment]; to swallow [médicament]; [2] (assimiler) to take in [donnée]; to learn [programme]
inhabitable /inabitabl/ *adj* uninhabitable
inhabité, ∼e /inabite/ *adj* [1] (sans habitants) [maison, région] uninhabited; [2] Astronaut [engin, vol] unmanned
inhabituel, -elle /inabitɥɛl/ *adj* unusual (**de la part de** for)
inhalateur /inalatœʀ/ *nm* inhaler
inhalation /inalasjɔ̃/ *nf* inhalation; **faire des ∼s** to have inhalations
inhaler /inale/ [1] *vtr* to inhale
inhérent, ∼e /ineʀɑ̃, ɑ̃t/ *adj* inherent (**à** in)
inhiber /inibe/ [1] *vtr* to inhibit
inhibition /inibisjɔ̃/ *nf* inhibition
inhospitalier, -ière /inɔspitalje, ɛʀ/ *adj* inhospitable
inhumain, ∼e /inymɛ̃, ɛn/ *adj* inhuman

inhumation /inymasjɔ̃/ *nf* ①▸ (mise en terre) burial; ②▸ (cérémonie) funeral

inhumer /inyme/ [1] *vtr* to bury

inimaginable /inimaʒinabl/ *adj* ①▸ (impossible à imaginer) unimaginable; ②▸ (impossible à concevoir) unthinkable

inimitable /inimitabl/ *adj* inimitable

ininflammable /inɛ̃flamabl/ *adj* nonflammable

inintelligible /inɛ̃teliʒibl/ *adj* unintelligible

inintéressant, **~e** /inɛ̃teresɑ̃, ɑ̃t/ *adj* uninteresting; **pas ~** not without interest

ininterrompu, **~e** /inɛ̃tɛRɔ̃py/ *adj* ①▸ (continu dans le temps) [*processus*] uninterrupted; [*chute, hausse*] continuous; [*bruit, circulation*] endless; ②▸ (continu dans l'espace) [*procession*] unbroken

iniquité /inikite/ *nf* iniquity

initial, **~e**[1], *mpl* **-iaux** /inisjal, o/ *adj* initial

initiale[2] /inisjal/ *nf* initial; **à l'~** in initial position (*après n*)

initiateur, **-trice** /inisjatœʀ, tʀis/ *nm,f* ①▸ (de projet, mode) originator; (de publication, mobilisation) instigator; ②▸ (de personne) instructor

initiation /inisjasjɔ̃/ *nf* ①▸ (formation) introduction (**à** to); **~ à l'anglais/la gestion** introduction to English/management; ②▸ (admission à la connaissance) initiation; **rites d'~** initiation rites

initiatique /inisjatik/ *adj* initiatory

initiative /inisjativ/ *nf* initiative; **à l'~ de qn** on sb's initiative; **avoir de l'~**, **avoir l'esprit d'~** to have initiative

initié, **~e** /inisje/ *nm,f* ①▸ (formé et admis) initiate; ②▸ Fin insider trader

initier /inisje/ [2]
Ⓐ *vtr* ①▸ (former) to introduce (**à** to); ②▸ (admettre à la connaissance) to initiate (**à** into); ③▸ (être à l'origine de) to initiate [*projet, réforme*]
Ⓑ **s'initier** *vpr* **s'~ à qch** to learn sth

injectable /ɛ̃ʒɛktabl/ *adj* injectable

injecter /ɛ̃ʒɛkte/ [2]
Ⓐ *vtr* to inject (**dans** into); **~ qch à qn** to inject sb with sth
Ⓑ **s'injecter** *vpr* [*personne*] to inject oneself with; [*médicament*] to be injected; **injecté de sang** bloodshot

injection /ɛ̃ʒɛksjɔ̃/ *nf* injection; **en ~(s)** by injection; **~ de capitaux** *or* **crédits** injection of funds; **se faire une ~ de** to inject oneself with

injoignable /ɛ̃ʒwaɲabl/ *adj* incommunicado

injonction /ɛ̃ʒɔ̃ksjɔ̃/ *nf* injunction

injure /ɛ̃ʒyʀ/ *nf* (insulte) abuse ₵; (offense) insult; **couvrir qn d'~s** to heap abuse on sb; **faire ~ à qn** to insult sb

injurier /ɛ̃ʒyʀje/ [1] *vtr* to insult, to swear at; **se faire ~** to be sworn at (**par** by)

injurieux, **-ieuse** /ɛ̃ʒyʀjø, øz/ *adj* [*parole, écrit*] abusive, offensive; [*attitude*] insulting

injuste /ɛ̃ʒyst/ *adj* unfair (**envers** to)

injustement /ɛ̃ʒystəmɑ̃/ *adv* [*accusé, condamné*] unjustly; [*méconnu, négligé*] unfairly

injustice /ɛ̃ʒystis/ *nf* ①▸ (caractère injuste) (d'impôt, de société) injustice; (de personne) unfairness; ②▸ (absence de justice) injustice; **combattre l'~** to fight injustice; ③▸ (acte injuste) injustice; **réparer une ~** to right a wrong; **quelle ~!** how unfair!

injustifiable /ɛ̃ʒystifjabl/ *adj* unjustifiable

injustifié, **~e** /ɛ̃ʒystifje/ *adj* unjustified

inlassable /ɛ̃lasabl/ *adj* [*personne*] tireless; [*curiosité*] insatiable; [*efforts*] unremitting

inlassablement /ɛ̃lasabləmɑ̃/ *adv* tirelessly

inné, **~e** /inne/ *adj* innate

innocemment /inɔsamɑ̃/ *adv* innocently; **pas ~** disingenuously

innocence /inɔsɑ̃s/ *nf* innocence

innocent, **~e** /inɔsɑ̃, ɑ̃t/
Ⓐ *adj* innocent (**de** of)
Ⓑ *nm,f* ①▸ (être pur) innocent; ②▸ (personne non coupable) innocent person; **une ~e** an innocent woman

innocenter /inɔsɑ̃te/ [1] *vtr* to prove [sb] innocent (**de** of), to clear (**de** of)

innocuité /inɔkɥite/ *nf* harmlessness; **en toute ~** without any risks

innombrable /innɔ̃bʀabl/ *adj* ①▸ (multiple) countless; ②▸ (immense) [*foule, armée*] vast

innommable /innɔmabl/ *adj* [*comportement, saleté, terreur*] unspeakable; [*plat, boisson*] revolting

innovateur, **-trice** /inɔvatœʀ, tʀis/
Ⓐ *adj* innovative
Ⓑ *nm,f* innovator

innovation /inɔvasjɔ̃/ *nf* innovation

innover /inɔve/ [1] *vi* [*personne, entreprise*] to innovate (**en matière de** in); [*équipement*] to break new ground

inoccupé, **~e** /inɔkype/ *adj* unoccupied

inoculer /inɔkyle/ [1] *vtr* ①▸ (vacciner) to inoculate (**contre** against); **~ qch à qn** to inoculate sb with sth; ②▸ (contaminer) **~ à qn** to infect sb with [*virus, maladie, idée*]

inodore /inɔdɔʀ/ *adj* [*substance*] odourless[GB]; [*fleur*] scentless

inoffensif, **-ive** /inɔfɑ̃sif, iv/ *adj* harmless

inondation /inɔ̃dasjɔ̃/ *nf* ①▸ (situation) flood; ②▸ (processus) flooding

inonder /inɔ̃de/ [1] *vtr* ①▸ (submerger) to flood [*lieu*]; ②▸ (baigner) [*soleil, lumière*] to flood [*lieu*]; **inondé de sueur/sang** bathed in sweat/blood; **les larmes lui inondaient le visage**, **il avait le visage inondé de larmes** tears were streaming down his face; ③▸ (envahir) [*commerçants, marque*] to flood [*marché*] (**de** with); to inundate [*clients*] (**de** with); [*produit*] to flood [*marché*]

inopérant, **~e** /inɔpeʀɑ̃, ɑ̃t/ *adj* ineffective

inopiné, **~e** /inɔpine/ *adj* unexpected

inopinément /inɔpinemɑ̃/ *adv* unexpectedly

inopportun, **~e** /inɔpɔʀtœ̃, yn/ *adj* ①▸ (non souhaitable) inappropriate; ②▸ (mal à propos) ill-timed

inoubliable /inublijabl/ *adj* unforgettable

inouï, **~e** /inwi/ *adj* [*événement*] unprecedented; [*succès, violence*] incredible, tremendous; **c'est ~** that's unheard of; **chose ~e** something unheard of

inox /inɔks/ *nm inv* stainless steel

inoxydable /inɔksidabl/
Ⓐ *adj* [*métal*] non-oxidizing; **acier ~** stainless steel
Ⓑ *nm* stainless steel

inqualifiable /ɛ̃kalifjabl/ *adj* unspeakable

inquiet, **-iète** /ɛ̃kjɛ, ɛt/
Ⓐ *adj* ①▸ (de nature) anxious; ②▸ (alarmé) worried (**pour** about); ③▸ (empli de crainte) [*air, regard*] anxious, worried
Ⓑ *nm,f* worrier; **c'est un (éternel) ~** he's a (perpetual) worrier

inquiétant, **~e** /ɛ̃kjetɑ̃, ɑ̃t/ *adj* ①▸ (alarmant) worrying; ②▸ (effrayant) frightening

inquiéter /ɛ̃kjete/ [14]
Ⓐ *vtr* ①▸ to worry; **ce que vous venez de me dire m'inquiète un peu** I find what you've just told me rather worrying; **le phénomène commence à ~ les spécialistes** specialists are beginning to be concerned about the phenomenon; ②▸ (demander des comptes à) **les douaniers ne l'ont pas inquiété** the customs officers didn't bother him; **quitter le pays sans être inquiété** to leave the country without any trouble; ③▸ (harceler) fml to harass [*pays, région*]; ④▸ ○(mettre en difficulté) to threaten [*adversaire*]
Ⓑ **s'inquiéter** *vpr* ①▸ (s'alarmer) to worry, to get worried; **il n'y a pas de quoi s'~** there's nothing to get worried about *ou* to worry about; ②▸ (se soucier) **ne t'inquiète pas pour elle** don't worry about her; ③▸ (s'enquérir) **s'~ de qch** to inquire about sth; **s'~ de savoir si/combien** to inquire about whether/how much

inquiétude /ɛ̃kjetyd/ *nf* ①▸ (état) anxiety, concern; **être un sujet d'~** to give cause for concern *ou* anxiety; **être fou d'~** to be beside oneself with worry; **soyez sans ~** don't worry; ②▸ (trouble) worry; **il n'y a pas d'~ à avoir** there's nothing to worry *ou* be concerned about

inquisiteur, **-trice** /ɛ̃kizitœʀ, tʀis/
Ⓐ *adj* inquisitive
Ⓑ *nm,f* inquisitor; **grand ~** Grand Inquisitor

inquisition /ɛ̃kizisjɔ̃/ *nf* inquisition

insaisissable /ɛ̃sezisabl/ *adj* [*voleur, animal, caractère*] elusive; [*nuance, image*] imperceptible

insalubre /ɛ̃salybʀ/ *adj* insanitary

insanité /ɛ̃sanite/ *nf* (propos insensé) rubbish **⊄**; **c'est une ~** it's rubbish; **proférer** *or* **débiter des ~s** to come out with a lot of rubbish (**sur** about)

insatiable /ɛ̃sasjabl/ *adj* insatiable

insatisfaction /ɛ̃satisfaksjɔ̃/ *nf* dissatisfaction **⊄** (**quant à** with)

insatisfait, ~e /ɛ̃satisfɛ, ɛt/
A *adj* [*personne*] dissatisfied (**de** with); [*désir, ambition, requête*] unsatisfied
B *nm,f* **c'est un ~** he's never satisfied

inscription /ɛ̃skripsjɔ̃/ *nf* **1** Scol enrolment^{GB}; Univ registration; **il y a mille nouvelles ~s par an** a thousand new students register every year; **2** (enregistrement) **~ à un tournoi** entering for a tournament; **l'~ coûte 20 euros** the membership fee costs 20 euros; **~ électorale** registration as a voter; **3** (chose écrite, gravée) (élaborée) inscription; (graffiti) graffiti

inscrire /ɛ̃skrir/ [67]
A *vtr* **1** (enregistrer) [*institution, enseignant*] to enrol^{GB} [*élève*]; to register [*étudiant*]; **~ qn sur une liste** to enter sb's name on a list; **~ une question à l'ordre du jour** to place an item on the agenda; **faites-vous ~ à la mairie pour le tournoi** put your name down at the Town Hall for the tournament; **2** (écrire) to write down [*nom, rendez-vous*]
B **s'inscrire** *vpr* **1** (faire enregistrer) Scol to enrol^{GB}; Univ to register; **s'~ à un parti/club** to join a party/club; **s'~ à un examen** to enter for an exam; **s'~ au chômage** to register as unemployed; **s'~ sur les listes électorales** to get oneself put on the electoral roll; **2** (faire partie de) **s'~ dans le cadre de** to be in line with; **s'~ dans la logique de** to fit into the scheme of; **s'~ dans une stratégie** to be part of a strategy; **3** **s'~ en faux contre qch** to dispute the validity of sth

inscrit, ~e /ɛ̃skri, it/
A *pp* ▸ **inscrire**
B *pp adj* lit Scol enrolled; Univ registered; **les personnes ~es sur la liste d'attente** those on the waiting list; **le débat ~ à l'ordre du jour** the debate on the agenda; **les personnes non ~es au club** non-members of the club; **60% des électeurs ~s** 60% of registered voters; **les députés non ~s** independent members of the French Parliament
C *nm,f* (élève) registered student; (électeur) registered voter

insecte /ɛ̃sɛkt/ *nm* insect

insecticide /ɛ̃sɛktisid/
A *adj* insecticidal
B *nm* insecticide

insécurité /ɛ̃sekyrite/ *nf* insecurity **⊄**

insémination /ɛ̃seminasjɔ̃/ *nf* insemination; **~ artificielle** artificial insemination

inséminer /ɛ̃semine/ [1] *vtr* to inseminate

insensé, ~e /ɛ̃sãse/ *adj* **1** (extravagant) [*pari, histoire, projet*] insane; **c'est ~!** that's insane!; **tenir des discours ~s** to talk complete nonsense; **2** °(excessif) [*cohue, embouteillage, gains*] phenomenal

insensibilisation /ɛ̃sãsibilizasjɔ̃/ *nf* anaesthetization

insensibiliser /ɛ̃sãsibilize/ [1] *vtr* to anaesthetize

insensibilité /ɛ̃sãsibilite/ *nf* insensitivity (**à** to)

insensible /ɛ̃sãsibl/ *adj* **1** (sans réaction) impervious (**à** to); **2** (indifférent) insensitive (**à** to)

insensiblement /ɛ̃sãsibləmã/ *adv* imperceptibly

inséparable /ɛ̃separabl/ *adj* inseparable

insérer /ɛ̃sere/ [14]
A *vtr* to insert (**dans** in)
B **s'insérer** *vpr* [*encart, disquette*] to be inserted; **cette mesure s'insère dans un contexte de rigueur** this measure is to be seen in the context of austerity

insertion /ɛ̃sɛrsjɔ̃/ *nf* **1** (d'objet, annonce, de clause) insertion; **2** (intégration) integration; **faciliter l'~ des immigrés** to facilitate the integration of immigrants; **~ sociale** social integration

insidieusement /ɛ̃sidjøzmã/ *adv* insidiously

insidieux, -ieuse /ɛ̃sidjø, øz/ *adj* insidious

insigne /ɛ̃siɲ/
A *adj* fml [*honneur, faveur, privilège*] great, signal sout (*épith*); [*service*] distinguished; [*maladresse*] remarkable iron; **avoir l'~ honneur de faire** to have the great honour^{GB} of doing
B *nm* (signe distinctif) badge
C **insignes** *nmpl* (emblème) insignia (*pl*)

insignifiance /ɛ̃siɲifjãs/ *nf* insignificance

insignifiant, ~e /ɛ̃siɲifjã, ãt/ *adj* insignificant

insinuation /ɛ̃sinɥasjɔ̃/ *nf* insinuation

insinuer /ɛ̃sinɥe/ [1]
A *vtr* **1** (suggérer) to insinuate (**que** that); **2** (introduire) to slip (**dans** into)
B **s'insinuer** *vpr* [*personne*] (physiquement) to slip; (socialement) to ingratiate oneself (**auprès de qn** with sb); [*sentiment, idée*] to creep; [*liquide, odeur*] to seep; **le doute s'insinuait en eux** *or* **dans leur esprit** doubt crept into their minds

insipide /ɛ̃sipid/ *adj* lit, fig insipid

insistance /ɛ̃sistãs/ *nf* insistence; **avec ~** insistently

insistant, ~e /ɛ̃sistã, ãt/ *adj* insistent

insister /ɛ̃siste/ [1] *vi* **1** (persévérer) to insist; **entendu, je n'insiste pas!** all right *ou* OK, I won't insist!; **j'ai dû ~ pour qu'il vienne** I had to press him to come; **inutile d'~, ils doivent être sortis** it's pointless to keep on trying, they must be out; **inutile d'~, il est têtu** there's no point in insisting, he's stubborn; **il est parti sans ~** he left without further ado; **2** (mettre l'accent) **~ sur** to stress [*danger, besoin*]; to put the emphasis on [*orthographe, attitude*]; **n'insistons pas sur cette question** let's not dwell on this question; **3** (repasser plusieurs fois) **~ sur** to pay particular attention to [*tache, défaut, aspérité*]

insolation /ɛ̃sɔlasjɔ̃/ *nf* **1** ▸ p. 195 (coup de soleil) sunstroke **⊄**; **2** (exposition) exposure to the sun, insolation spéc; Phot (de plaque, film) exposure; **3** Météo (ensoleillement) sunny period

insolence /ɛ̃sɔlãs/ *nf* (irrespect) insolence

insolent, ~e /ɛ̃sɔlã, ãt/
A *adj* **1** (irrespectueux) [*enfant, ton, attitude*] insolent, cheeky; **2** (arrogant) [*rival, vainqueur*] arrogant; **3** (provocant) [*personne, jeunesse*] brazen; [*luxe, succès, fortune, joie*] unashamed
B *nm,f* insolent person

insolite /ɛ̃sɔlit/ *adj, nm* unusual; **goût de l'~** taste for the unusual

insoluble /ɛ̃sɔlybl/ *adj* **1** [*matière*] insoluble; **2** [*problème, question*] insoluble

insolvabilité /ɛ̃sɔlvabilite/ *nf* insolvency

insolvable /ɛ̃sɔlvabl/ *adj* insolvent

insomniaque /ɛ̃sɔmnjak/ *adj, nmf* insomniac

insomnie /ɛ̃sɔmni/ *nf* **1** ▸ p. 195 (trouble) insomnia **⊄**; **avoir des ~s** to have insomnia; **2** (nuit sans sommeil) sleepless night

insondable /ɛ̃sɔ̃dabl/ *adj* [*abîme, mystère*] unfathomable; [*tristesse, désespoir, bêtise*] immense

insonorisation /ɛ̃sɔnɔrizasjɔ̃/ *nf* soundproofing

insonoriser /ɛ̃sɔnɔrize/ [1] *vtr* to soundproof; **mal insonorisé** poorly soundproofed

insouciance /ɛ̃susjãs/ *nf* carefreeness, insouciance sout; **vivre dans l'~** to lead a carefree life

insouciant, ~e /ɛ̃susjã, ãt/ *adj* carefree; **~ du lendemain** without a thought for the future (*épith, après n*)

insoumis, ~e /ɛ̃sumi, iz/
A *adj* (rebelle) [*contrée, peuple*] unsubdued; **soldat ~** draft dodger
B *nm,f* Mil draft dodger

insoumission /ɛ̃sumisjɔ̃/ *nf* **1** (rébellion) insubordination; **2** Mil avoidance of the draft

insoupçonnable /ɛ̃supsɔnabl/ *adj* beyond suspicion (*après n*)

insoupçonné, ~e /ɛ̃supsɔne/ *adj* [*ressources, force, menace, difficultés*] unsuspected; [*richesses, perspectives, horizons*] undreamed of

insoutenable /ɛ̃sutnabl/ *adj* **1** (intolérable) [*violence, douleur*] unbearable; **un film d'une violence ~** an unbearably violent film; **2** (impossible à suivre) [*cadence*] impossible; **3** (indéfendable) [*opinion*] untenable

inspecter /ɛ̃spɛkte/ [1] *vtr* to inspect

inspecteur, -trice /ɛ̃spɛktœr, tris/ ▸ p. 372, p. 590 *nm,f* inspector

(Composés) **~ de police** ≈ detective constable GB; **~ du travail** Admin government inspector (*concerned with health and safety and respect of labour laws*); **~ des travaux finis**° hum skiver° GB, shirker°

inspection /ɛ̃spɛksjɔ̃/ *nf* 1 (contrôle) inspection; **faire l'~ de qch** to inspect sth; 2 (ensemble d'inspecteurs) inspectorate

(Composés) **~ académique** ≈ local schools inspectorate; **~ du travail** ≈ labour^{GB} inspectorate

inspirateur, -trice /ɛ̃spiratœr, tris/ *nm,f* 1 (d'idée, de théorie) initiator; (de complot) instigator; 2 (d'artiste, œuvre) inspiration

inspiration /ɛ̃spirasjɔ̃/ *nf* 1 (souffle créateur) inspiration **℃; auteur sans ~** uninspired author; 2 (influence) inspiration; **œuvre d'~ romantique** work of romantic inspiration; 3 (idée) inspiration; **soudain, il eut une ~** he had a sudden inspiration, he had a brainwave^{O}; 4 (inhalation) inspiration

inspiré, ~e /ɛ̃spire/ *adj* [*auteur, artiste, œuvre*] inspired; **être bien/mal ~ de faire** to be well-/ill-advised to do; **un roman ~ des vieux contes populaires** a novel based on old folk tales

inspirer /ɛ̃spire/ [1]
A *vtr* 1 (donner de l'inspiration à) to inspire [*personne*]; 2 (donner envie à) to appeal to; **ça ne m'inspire pas** that doesn't appeal to me; 3 (susciter) to inspire; **~ la méfiance à qn** to inspire distrust in sb; **il ne m'inspire pas confiance** I don't have much confidence in him; **vos remarques m'ont inspiré plusieurs réflexions** your remarks made me think of several things
B *vi* (inhaler) to breathe in, to inhale
C **s'inspirer** *vpr* 1 (prendre son inspiration) **s'~ de** to draw one's inspiration from; **la révolution s'est inspirée de ces idéaux** the revolution was inspired by these ideals; 2 (prendre exemple) **s'~ de qn** to follow sb's example, to take a leaf out of sb's book; **inspirez-vous d'elle!** follow her example!

instabilité /ɛ̃stabilite/ *nf* 1 (de situation, pays, prix) instability; (de temps) changeability; 2 (de personne) (emotional) instability; 3 Chimie, Phys instability

instable /ɛ̃stabl/ *adj* 1 [*monnaie, économie*] unstable; [*construction*] unstable, unsteady; [*temps*] unsettled; 2 [*personne, caractère*] unstable, unsteady

installateur, -trice /ɛ̃stalatœr, tris/ ▸ p. 372 *nm,f* fitter

installation /ɛ̃stalasjɔ̃/
A *nf* 1 (mise en place) (d'appareil ménager, de téléphone, gaz) installation, putting in; (de toilettes publiques, douches, canalisations) putting in; (de système de sécurité, d'équipement informatique, usine) installation; (de table pliante, chevalet) putting up; **~ gratuite** 'free installation'; 2 (appareils) system; 3 (manière d'être installé) **notre ~ est temporaire** we're not permanently settled; 4 (usine) plant; 5 (arrivée) **depuis mon ~ à Paris** since I moved to Paris; **dès leur ~ au pouvoir, les insurgés...** as soon as they came to power, the rebels...; **quelques jours après l'~ du nouveau gouvernement** a few days after the new government took office
B **installations** *nfpl* (équipements) facilities

(Composés) **~ électrique** electric wiring; **~ téléphonique** telephone system; **~s militaires** military installations

installé, ~e /ɛ̃stale/
A *pp* ▸ **installer**
B *pp adj* (établi) [*personne*] living (**à** in); [*organisme, société*] based (**à** in); **être bien ~ dans un fauteuil** to be ensconced *ou* comfortably installed in an armchair; **ils sont bien ~s dans leur nouvelle maison** they're very snug in their new home; **c'est un homme ~** fig he's very nicely set up

installer /ɛ̃stale/ [1]
A *vtr* 1 (mettre en place) to install, to put in [*lave-vaisselle, évier, chauffage central*]; to put up [*table pliante, étagère*]; to set up [*infrastructure militaire*]; (raccorder) to connect [*gaz, téléphone, électricité*]; **faire ~ une antenne parabolique** to have a satellite dish put up *ou* installed; **~ le bureau près de la fenêtre** to put the desk near the window; 2 (aménager) to do up [*cuisine*]; **~ une chambre dans le grenier** to make a bedroom in the attic; 3 (implanter) to set up [*usine*]; 4 (loger) to put [*invité*] (**dans** in); **~ qn dans un fauteuil** to sit sb in an armchair; 5 Admin **il a été installé dans ses fonctions** he took up his duties; **~ qn à un poste** to appoint sb to a post
B **s'installer** *vpr* 1 (devenir durable) [*régime*] to become established; [*morosité, récession*] to set in; **le doute s'installe dans leur esprit** they're beginning to have doubts;

2 (professionnellement) to set oneself up in business; **s'~ à son compte** to set up one's own business; 3 (pour vivre) to settle; **partir s'~ à l'étranger** to go and live abroad; **s'~ temporairement chez des amis** to move in temporarily with friends; **je viendrai te voir quand tu seras installé** I'll come and see you when you're settled in; 4 (se mettre à l'aise) **s'~ dans un fauteuil** to settle into an armchair; **s'~ au soleil** to sit in the sun; **s'~ pour travailler/à son bureau** to settle down to work/at one's desk; **tu es bien installé?** are you sitting comfortably?; **installe-toi, j'arrive!** make yourself at home, I'm coming!; **on est mal installé sur ces chaises** these chairs are uncomfortable; 5 (être mis en place) **l'appareil s'installe facilement** the appliance is easy to install; **des usines étrangères vont s'~ dans la région** foreign companies are going to open factories in the area

instamment /ɛ̃stamɑ̃/ *adv* insistently

instance /ɛ̃stɑ̃s/ *nf* 1 (autorité) authority; **l'~ supérieure** the higher authority; **en dernière ~** in the final analysis; **les ~s d'un parti politique** the leaders of a political party; 2 (demande) entreaty; **il m'a demandé avec ~ de venir** he pleaded with me to come; 3 Jur (action) legal proceedings (*pl*); (juridiction) level of jurisdiction; **être en ~ de divorce** to be engaged in divorce proceedings; **en seconde ~** on appeal; 4 (attente) **l'affaire est en ~** the matter is pending; **courrier en ~** mail pending attention

instant, ~e /ɛ̃stɑ̃, ɑ̃t/
A *adj* [*demande*] insistent
B *nm* moment, instant; **un ~!** just a minute!; **à tout** *or* **chaque ~** all the time; **ne pas perdre un ~** not to waste any time; **d'~ en ~** every minute; **par ~s** at times; **pour l'~** for the moment; **il devrait arriver d'un ~ à l'autre** he should arrive any minute now; **à l'~** (même) this instant *ou* minute; **à l'~ même où** just when; **au même ~** at that very moment

instantané, ~e /ɛ̃stɑ̃tane/
A *adj* [*réponse, effet*] instantaneous, instant (*épith*); [*mort*] instantaneous; [*boisson, potage*] instant; [*vision, lueur*] momentary
B *nm* Phot snapshot

instar: à l'instar de /alɛ̃stardə/ *loc prép* following the example of

instaurer /ɛ̃store/ [1]
A *vtr* to institute [*taxe, contrôle*]; to establish [*régime, dialogue*]; to impose [*couvre-feu*]
B **s'instaurer** *vpr* to be established

instigateur, -trice /ɛ̃stigatœr, tris/ *nm,f* (de troubles) instigator; (de mouvement) originator

instigation /ɛ̃stigasjɔ̃/ *nf* **à l'~ de qn** at sb's instigation

instiller /ɛ̃stile/ [1] *vtr* to instil^{GB} (**à, dans** into)

instinct /ɛ̃stɛ̃/ *nm* instinct; **d'~** instinctively; **l'~ de conservation** the instinct of self-preservation

instinctif, -ive /ɛ̃stɛ̃ktif, iv/ *adj* instinctive; **c'est quelqu'un d'~** he/she's someone who relies on instinct

instituer /ɛ̃stitɥe/ [1] *vtr* (créer) to institute

institut /ɛ̃stity/ *nm* institute

(Composé) **~ de beauté** beauty salon *ou* parlour^{GB}

instituteur, -trice /ɛ̃stitytœr, tris/ ▸ p. 372 *nm,f* (d'école primaire) (primary school) teacher; (d'école maternelle) (nursery school) teacher

institution /ɛ̃stitysjɔ̃/
A *nf* 1 (administration) institution; 2 (établissement d'enseignement) private school; 3 (action) institution (**de** of); 4 (établissement pour enfants, vieillards, malades) institution
B **institutions** *nfpl* Pol institutions

institutionnel, -elle /ɛ̃stitysjɔnɛl/ *adj* institutional

institutrice ▸ **instituteur**

instructeur /ɛ̃stryktœr/
A *adj* Jur examining; Mil drill
B *nm* gén, Mil instructor

instructif, -ive /ɛ̃stryktif, iv/ *adj* [*rencontre, histoire*] instructive; [*voyage, livre*] informative; [*expérience*] enlightening

instruction /ɛ̃stryksjɔ̃/
A *nf* 1 (formation) education **℃**; Mil training; 2 (connaissances) education **℃; niveau d'~ insuffisant** poor level of education; **homme sans ~** uneducated man; **manquer d'~** to be uneducated; **avoir de l'~** to be well-educated;

i

3 (circulaire) directive; **4** Jur preparation of a case for eventual judgment
B instructions nfpl (directives) instructions
(Composés) ~ **civique** civics (+ v sg); ~ **religieuse** religious instruction
instruire /ɛ̃stʀɥiʀ/ [69]
A vtr **1** (former) [personne] to teach [enfant]; to train [soldats]; **ce film ne vise pas à** ~ this film is not intended to be educational; **2** Jur ~ **une affaire** to prepare a case for judgment; **3** (informer) fml ~ **qn de qch** to inform sb of sth
B s'instruire vpr (apprendre) to learn; **on s'instruit à tout âge** it's never too late to learn
instruit, ~**e** /ɛ̃stʀɥi, it/
A pp ▸ **instruire**
B pp adj [personne] educated
instrument /ɛ̃stʀymɑ̃/ nm **1** (objet) instrument; ~**s de chirurgie** surgical instruments; ~ **à cordes** string instrument; **3** (agent) tool; (moyen) instrument; **être l'**~ **de qn** to be sb's tool; **être l'**~ **de la vengeance de qn** to be the instrument of sb's revenge
(Composés) ~ **ancien** Mus period instrument; ~ **de musique** musical instrument; ~**s de bord** controls
insu: **à l'insu de** /alɛ̃syda/ loc prép **1** (sans le dire) **je suis parti à leur** ~ I left without their knowing; **2** (sans le savoir) without knowing it; **ils ont été filmés à leur** ~ they were filmed without (their) knowing it
insubmersible /ɛ̃sybmɛʀsibl/ adj unsinkable
insubordonné, ~**e** /ɛ̃sybɔʀdɔne/ adj gén rebellious, insubordinate sout; Mil insubordinate
insuffisamment /ɛ̃syfizamɑ̃/ adv (pas assez) insufficiently; (mal) inadequately
insuffisance /ɛ̃syfizɑ̃s/ nf **1** (pénurie) insufficiency, shortage; **2** (médiocrité) poor standard; **3** (déficit) shortfall; **l'**~ **de la production** the shortfall in production; **4** (lacune) shortcoming; **5** Méd insufficiency
insuffisant, ~**e** /ɛ̃syfizɑ̃, ɑ̃t/ adj **1** (quantitativement) insufficient; **ils sont en nombre** ~ there aren't enough of them; **2** (qualitativement) inadequate; **tes résultats sont** ~**s** your results are not good enough
insuffler /ɛ̃syfle/ [1] vtr **1** to instil^GB (**à** into); ~ **la vie à qn** to breathe life into sb; **2** Méd to insufflate [oxygène] (**à**, **dans** into)
insulaire /ɛ̃sylɛʀ/
A adj [population, traditions] island (épith); [mentalité] insular péj
B nmf islander
insuline /ɛ̃sylin/ nf insulin
insultant, ~**e** /ɛ̃syltɑ̃, ɑ̃t/ adj insulting
insulte /ɛ̃sylt/ nf insult; **c'est une** ~ **à leur mémoire** it is an insult to their memory; **une lettre d'**~**s** an insulting letter; **dire des** ~**s à qn** to insult sb; **faire à qn l'**~ **de refuser** to insult sb by refusing
insulter /ɛ̃sylte/ [1]
A vtr (injurier) to insult, to shout abuse at [personne]; (offenser) [personne] to insult; [attitude] to be an insult to; **se faire** ~ to get a stream of abuse (**par** from)
B s'insulter vpr to exchange insults
insupportable /ɛ̃sypɔʀtabl/ adj unbearable
insurgé, ~**e** /ɛ̃syʀʒe/ adj, nmf insurgent, rebel
insurger: **s'insurger** /ɛ̃syʀʒe/ [13] vpr (se soulever) to rise up; (protester) to protest
insurmontable /ɛ̃syʀmɔ̃tabl/ adj [problème, dette] insurmountable; [désaccord] insuperable; [timidité] unconquerable
insurrection /ɛ̃syʀɛksjɔ̃/ nf **1** (de population) insurrection, uprising; **mouvements d'**~ rebel movements; **2** fig revolt (**contre** against)
insurrectionnel, -**elle** /ɛ̃syʀɛksjɔnɛl/ adj insurrectionary
intact, ~**e** /ɛ̃takt/ adj intact (jamais épith)
intangible /ɛ̃tɑ̃ʒibl/ adj (inviolable) [lois, principes] inviolable
intarissable /ɛ̃taʀisabl/ adj [imagination, bavard] inexhaustible; [bavardage, larmes] endless; [source] fig never-ending; **elle est** ~ she can go on forever (**sur** about)
intégral, ~**e**¹, mpl -**aux** /ɛ̃tegʀal, o/ adj **1** [paiement] full, in full (après n); [bronzage] all-over (épith); **2** [édition,

texte] complete, unabridged; **voir un film en version** ~**e** to see the uncut version of a film
intégrale² /ɛ̃tegʀal/ nf **1** Mus **l'**~ **des concertos pour piano** the complete piano concertos (pl); **2** Math integral
intégralement /ɛ̃tegʀalmɑ̃/ adv [payer, citer, publier] in full; [refuser, rejeter] completely
intégralité /ɛ̃tegʀalite/ nf **l'**~ **de leur salaire** their entire salary; **payer une dette dans son** ~ to pay a debt in full; **diffuser un opéra dans son** ~ to broadcast an opera in its entirety
intégrante /ɛ̃tegʀɑ̃t/ adj f **faire partie** ~ **de qch** to be an integral part of sth
intégration /ɛ̃tegʀasjɔ̃/ nf gén integration (**à**, **dans** into); ~ **sociale** integration into society
intègre /ɛ̃tɛgʀ/ adj [personne, caractère, vie] honest; **un homme** ~ a man of integrity
intégrer /ɛ̃tegʀe/ [14]
A vtr **1** (insérer) to insert (**à**, **dans** into); **une architecture bien intégrée dans l'environnement** architecture which blends with the surroundings; **2** (assimiler) to integrate [communauté, population] (**à**, **dans** into); **3** ^○ (entrer dans) **il a intégré la garde présidentielle** he joined the presidential guard; **il vient d'**~ **Harvard** he has just got into Harvard
B s'intégrer vpr **1** [population] to integrate (**à**, **dans** with); **2** [immeuble] to fit in (**à**, **dans** with)
intégrisme /ɛ̃tegʀism/ nm fundamentalism
intégrité /ɛ̃tegʀite/ nf integrity
intellect /ɛ̃telɛkt/ nm intellect
intellectuel, -**elle** /ɛ̃telɛktɥɛl/
A adj [travail, facultés, milieu] intellectual; [fatigue, effort] mental; [goût, musique] highbrow
B nm,f intellectual
intelligence /ɛ̃teliʒɑ̃s/ nf **1** (aptitude) intelligence **avec** ~ intelligently; **2** (compréhension) understanding; **3** agreement; **agir d'**~ **avec qn** to act in agreement with sb; **faire des signes d'**~ **à qn** to make signs of complicity to sb
(Composé) ~ **artificielle** Ordinat artificial intelligence
intelligent, ~**e** /ɛ̃teliʒɑ̃, ɑ̃t/ adj [personne] intelligent, clever; [réponse, regard] intelligent; **ce n'est pas** ~ **de ta part d'avoir fait** it wasn't very clever of you to do; **c'est** ~! iron that's clever!
intelligible /ɛ̃teliʒibl/ adj intelligible (**à** to); **parler à haute et** ~ **voix** to speak loudly and clearly
intempéries /ɛ̃tɑ̃peʀi/ nfpl bad weather **C**
intempestif, -**ive** /ɛ̃tɑ̃pɛstif, iv/ adj [démarche, arrivée] untimely; [curiosité, joie, zèle] misplaced
intemporel, -**elle** /ɛ̃tɑ̃pɔʀɛl/ adj (immuable) timeless
intenable /ɛ̃t(ə)nabl/ adj [odeur, chaleur, situation] unbearable; (indiscipliné) difficult; (indéfendable) untenable
intendance /ɛ̃tɑ̃dɑ̃s/ nf Scol (service) administration; (bureau, personnel) administrative offices (pl); **l'**~ **ne suit pas** the backup is not forthcoming
intendant, ~**e** /ɛ̃tɑ̃dɑ̃, ɑ̃t/
A nm,f Scol bursar
B nm Mil (général) quartermaster; (financier) paymaster
intense /ɛ̃tɑ̃s/ adj intense
intensif, -**ive** /ɛ̃tɑ̃sif, iv/ adj intensive
intensification /ɛ̃tɑ̃sifikasjɔ̃/ nf intensification
intensifier /ɛ̃tɑ̃sifje/ [2] vtr, **s'intensifier** vpr to intensify
intensité /ɛ̃tɑ̃site/ nf **1** (force) intensity; **la tempête diminue d'**~ the storm is dying down; **2** Phys (électrique) current
intensivement /ɛ̃tɑ̃sivmɑ̃/ adv intensively
intenter /ɛ̃tɑ̃te/ [1] vtr ~ **un procès à qn** to sue sb; ~ **une action contre** to bring an action against
intention /ɛ̃tɑ̃sjɔ̃/ nf intention; **les meilleures** ~**s du monde** the best of intentions; **avoir l'**~ **de faire** to intend to do; **c'est l'**~ **qui compte** it's the thought that counts; **dans l'**~ **de faire** with the intention of doing; **à l'**~ **de qn** [déclaration, geste] aimed at sb; [œuvre] intended for sb; [fête] in sb's honour^GB
intentionné, ~**e** /ɛ̃tɑ̃sjɔne/ adj **bien/mal** ~ well-/ill-intentioned
intentionnel, -**elle** /ɛ̃tɑ̃sjɔnɛl/ adj intentional
interactif, -**ive** /ɛ̃teʀaktif, iv/ adj interactive

interaction /ɛ̃tɛraksjɔ̃/ nf interaction

interactivité /ɛ̃tɛraktivite/ nf interactivity

interallié, ∼e /ɛ̃tɛralje/ adj [état-major, force] joint allied

interarmées /ɛ̃tɛrarme/ adj inv [état-major, force] joint

interbancaire /ɛ̃tɛrbɑ̃kɛr/ adj interbank (épith)

interbibliothèques /ɛ̃tɛrbiblijɔtɛk/ adj inv **prêt** ∼ interlibrary loan

intercalaire /ɛ̃tɛrkalɛr/
A adj **feuille** or **feuillet** ∼ insert
B nm (de séparation) divider

intercaler /ɛ̃tɛrkale/ [1]
A vtr ⓵ (insérer) to insert (**dans** into); ⓶ (ajouter) to intercalate [jour, mois]
B s'intercaler vpr [rendez-vous] to fit; [feuillet, exemple] to be inserted; [personne, véhicule] to come

intercéder /ɛ̃tɛrsede/ [14] vi to intercede (**auprès de qn** with sb; **en faveur de qn** on sb's behalf)

intercepter /ɛ̃tɛrsɛpte/ [1] vtr to intercept

interception /ɛ̃tɛrsɛpsjɔ̃/ nf interception

intercession /ɛ̃tɛrsesjɔ̃/ nf intercession

interchangeable /ɛ̃tɛrʃɑ̃ʒabl/ adj interchangeable

interclasse /ɛ̃tɛrklas/ nm break (between classes)

intercommunal, ∼e, mpl **-aux** /ɛ̃tɛrkɔmynal, o/ adj [coopération] between local councils (épith, après n); [équipement] district (épith)

intercommunautaire /ɛ̃tɛrkɔmynotɛr/ adj within the EU (après n)

intercontinental, ∼e, mpl **-aux** /ɛ̃tɛrkɔ̃tinɑ̃tal, o/ adj intercontinental

intercostal, ∼e, mpl **-aux** /ɛ̃tɛrkɔstal, o/ adj [nerf] intercostal; [douleur] in the ribs (après n)

interdiction /ɛ̃tɛrdiksjɔ̃/ nf ⓵ (action d'interdire) banning; **demander l'**∼ **de qch** to ask for sth to be banned; '∼ **de fumer**' 'no smoking'; **condamné avec** ∼ **d'exercer sa profession** found guilty and banned from practising^GB; ⓶ (chose interdite) ban; **lever une** ∼ to lift a ban

(Composé) ∼ **de séjour** prohibition on residence

interdire /ɛ̃tɛrdir/ [65]
A vtr ⓵ (ne pas autoriser) to ban; ∼ **à qn l'entrée de sa maison** to refuse sb entry to one's house; **le médecin m'a interdit l'alcool** the doctor has told me not to drink alcohol; **interdit d'antenne** banned from broadcasting; ∼ **à qn de faire**, ∼ **que qn fasse** to forbid sb to do; **il est interdit de parler au chauffeur** it is forbidden to talk to the driver; **il est interdit de fumer** (sur une pancarte) no smoking; ⓶ (rendre impossible) **mon état de santé m'interdit l'alcool** I can't drink alcohol on account of my health; ∼ **à qn de faire** to prevent sb from doing
B s'interdire vpr **s'**∼ **le chocolat** to keep off chocolate; **s'**∼ **les sorties** to refrain from going out

interdisciplinaire /ɛ̃tɛrdisiplinɛr/ adj Scol [cours, activité] cross-curricular; Univ interdisciplinary

interdit, ∼e /ɛ̃tɛrdi, it/
A pp ▸ interdire
B pp adj ⓵ (défendu) prohibited, forbidden; **baignade/chasse** ∼e swimming/hunting prohibited; **entrée** ∼e no entry ou admittance; **film** ∼ **aux moins de 13 ans** film unsuitable for children under 13; **film** ∼ **aux moins de 18 ans** film for adults over 18 only; **être** ∼ **de séjour** Jur to be subject to a prohibition on residence; fig to be banned (**dans** from)
C adj (stupéfait) dumbfounded
D nm ⓵ (chose interdite) (par les lois) proscription; (par les conventions) taboo; ⓶ (condamnation) bar; **jeter l'**∼ **sur qn** to debar ou bar sb

intéressant, ∼e /ɛ̃tɛresɑ̃, ɑ̃t/
A adj ⓵ (qui retient l'attention) interesting (**de faire** to do); ⓶ (qui offre des ressources) interesting; ⓷ (avantageux) [prix, conditions] attractive; **c'est une affaire** ∼e it's an attractive proposition; **il est plus** ∼ **de payer au comptant** it's better to pay in cash
B nm,f **faire l'**∼ or **son** ∼ to show off

intéressé, ∼e /ɛ̃tɛrese/
A pp ▸ intéresser
B pp adj ⓵ (attiré) interested (**par** in); **il est peu** ∼ **par l'affaire** he has little interest in the matter; **se dire** ∼ **par qch** to express an interest in sth; ⓶ (captivé) attentive; ⓷ (concerné) **les parties** ∼es those concerned; **toute personne** ∼e

all those interested (+ v pl); **les personnes** ∼**es aux bénéfices** people with a share in the profits; ⓸ (qui vise un profit) [personne, avis, démarche] self-interested (épith); **il est** ∼ he acts out of self-interest; **ses conseils étaient** ∼**s** he/she had a selfish motive for giving that advice
C nm,f person concerned; **les** ∼**s** people concerned; **le principal** ∼ the person most directly concerned; **les principaux** ∼**s** those most directly concerned

intéressement /ɛ̃tɛresmɑ̃/ nm (système) profit-sharing; (revenu) share in the profits

intéresser /ɛ̃tɛrese/ [1]
A vtr ⓵ (retenir l'attention) to interest; **ça ne m'intéresse pas** I'm not interested (**de faire** in doing); ⓶ (concerner) [problème, décision, mesures] to concern; **la protection du site intéresse tout le monde** the protection of the site is of concern to all; ⓷ ∼ **les salariés aux bénéfices** to offer a profit-sharing scheme to employees
B s'intéresser vpr **s'**∼ **à** gén to be interested in; (en s'engageant) to take an interest in; **ils s'intéressent à l'environnement** they are taking an interest in the environment

intérêt /ɛ̃tɛrɛ/ nm ⓵ (attention) interest (**pour** in); ⓶ (attrait) interest; **recherche digne d'**∼ worthwhile research; **livre plein d'**∼ book of exceptional interest; **sans** ∼ uninteresting; **n'avoir pas grand** ∼ not to have much to recommend it; ⓷ (avantage, utilité) interest; **d'**∼ **général** of general interest; **l'**∼ **supérieur de la nation** the higher good of the country; **elle a tout** ∼ **à faire** it is in her best interest to do; **être du plus grand** ∼ to be of particular interest (**pour** to); **tu as** ∼ **à faire** you'd be well advised to do; **quel** ∼ **auraient-ils à faire?** what would be the point in their doing?; **y a** ∼^⚪**!** you bet!; **je ne vois pas l'**∼ **de cette réforme/de faire** I can't see the point of this reform/of doing; **par** ∼ [agir] out of self-interest; [se marier] for money; ⓸ Fin interest **¢**; **prêt sans** ∼**s** interest-free loan; ⓹ (part) interest; **des** ∼**s dans le sucre** interests in sugar

interethnique /ɛ̃tɛrɛtnik/ adj [relations] between ethnic communities (après n); [violence, affrontements] (entre tribus) intertribal; (entre communautés) racial

interférence /ɛ̃tɛrferɑ̃s/ nf interference

interférer /ɛ̃tɛrfere/ [14] vi to interfere (**avec** with)

intérieur, ∼e /ɛ̃tɛrjœr/
A adj ⓵ (au-dedans) [mur, escalier, température] internal, interior; [cour] inner; [mer] inland; [poche] inside; [frontière] internal; **le côté** ∼ the inside; **pour l'aménagement** ∼ **de votre maison** for the interior decoration of your house; **lire notre article en pages** ∼**es** read our article inside; ⓶ (d'un pays) domestic; **sur le plan** ∼ on the domestic front; ⓷ (d'une organisation) internal; ⓸ (intime) inner
B nm ⓵ (de boîte, journal, d'enveloppe, armoire) inside; (de voiture) interior; **fermé de l'**∼ locked from the inside; **à l'**∼ inside, indoors; **à l'**∼ **de** inside; **à l'**∼ **des terres** inland; ⓶ (habitation) interior; **fière de son** ∼ proud of her home; **d'**∼ [jeu] indoor; **plante d'**∼ houseplant, indoor plant; ⓷ (de pays) interior; **à l'**∼ **du pays** inland; **les villes de l'**∼ the inland towns

intérieurement /ɛ̃tɛrjœrmɑ̃/ adv (en soi-même) inwardly; (au-dedans) **verrouillé/doublé** ∼ bolted from the/lined on the inside

intérim /ɛ̃tɛrim/ nm ⓵ (période) interim (period); **par** ∼ on an interim basis; **président par** ∼ acting president; ⓶ (fonction) interim duties (pl); **assurer l'**∼ **de** to stand in for; ⓷ (travail temporaire) temporary work; **société** or **agence d'**∼ gén temporary employment agency; (de secrétariat) temping agency; **travailler en** ∼ to do temporary work, to temp^⚪

intérimaire /ɛ̃tɛrimɛr/
A adj [fonction, comité] interim; [ministre] acting, interim; [emploi, personnel] temporary
B nmf gén worker from a temporary employment agency; (secrétaire) temporary secretary, temp^⚪

intérioriser /ɛ̃tɛrjɔrize/ [1] vtr to internalize

interjection /ɛ̃tɛrʒɛksjɔ̃/ nf Ling interjection

interligne /ɛ̃tɛrliɲ/ nm (espace) line space; **ajouter un mot dans l'**∼ to add a word between the lines; **double** ∼ double spacing

interlocuteur, **-trice** /ɛ̃tɛrlɔkytœr, tris/ nm,f ⓵ (dans une conversation) interlocutor sout; **mon** ∼ the person I am talking to; **2** (dans une négociation) representative; **reconnaî-tre qn comme un ~ valable** to acknowledge sb as a recognized spokesperson; **3** (contact) **Louis est notre seul ~** Louis is our only contact; **l'~ privilégié du gouvernement** the person the government prefers to deal with

interloquer /ɛ̃tɛʀlɔke/ [1] *vtr* to take [sb] aback; **rester interloqué** to be taken aback

interlude /ɛ̃tɛʀlyd/ *nm* TV, Mus interlude

intermède /ɛ̃tɛʀmɛd/ *nm* interlude

intermédiaire /ɛ̃tɛʀmedjɛʀ/
A *adj* [taux, étape] intermediate; **il n'existe pas de structure ~ entre la prison et l'hôpital psychiatrique** there's no halfway house between prison and a psychiatric hospital; **avez-vous la taille ~?** do you have a size in between?
B *nmf* (dans des négociations) go-between; (dans l'industrie) middleman
C *nm* **sans ~** [faire, agir] without any intermediary; [traiter, vendre] direct; **par l'~ de** through

interminable /ɛ̃tɛʀminabl/ *adj* (qui dure) interminable, never-ending; (long) [lettre, file, plage] endless

intermittence /ɛ̃tɛʀmitɑ̃s/ *nf* **1** **par ~** [pleuvoir] on and off; [travailler] intermittently; **2** Méd (rémission) remission

intermittent, ~e /ɛ̃tɛʀmitɑ̃, ɑ̃t/ *adj* [pluie, fièvre] intermittent; [bruit, effort] sporadic

internat /ɛ̃tɛʀna/ *nm* **1** (école) boarding school; (dortoirs) dormitories (*pl*); (élèves) boarders (*pl*); **2** Univ (concours) examination for the post of houseman GB *ou* intern US; (stage) period as houseman GB, internship US

international, ~e, *mpl* **-aux** /ɛ̃tɛʀnasjɔnal, o/
A *adj* international
B *nm,f* (athlète) international
C **internationaux** *nmpl* Sport internationals

internationalisme /ɛ̃tɛʀnasjɔnalism/ *nm* internationalism

interne /ɛ̃tɛʀn/
A *adj* **1** (intérieur) [crise, règlement, concours] internal; [formation] in-house (épith); **~ à** within; **2** Anat, Méd [paroi, organe, hémorragie] internal; [oreille] inner; **à usage ~** for internal use
B *nmf* **1** Scol boarder; **je suis ~** I'm a boarder; **2** Univ **~ (en médecine)** houseman GB, intern US

internement /ɛ̃tɛʀnəmɑ̃/ *nm* (de prisonnier, dissident) internment; (de malade mental) committal (to a psychiatric institution); **demander l'~ de qn** to request that sb be committed

interner /ɛ̃tɛʀne/ [1] *vtr* to intern [prisonnier politique]; to commit [malade]; **faire ~ qn** to have sb committed; **il est bon à ~** hum he ought to be in a loony bin○

interparlementaire /ɛ̃tɛʀpaʀləmɑ̃tɛʀ/ *adj* interparliamentary GB, joint (épith)

interpellation /ɛ̃tɛʀpelasjɔ̃/ *nf* **1** (action policière) questioning ¢; **il y a eu quinze ~s** fifteen people have been questioned by the police; **procéder à des ~s** to take people in for questioning; **2** (adresse) calling out (**de** to); **3** Pol interpellation

interpeller /ɛ̃tɛʀpele/ [1]
A *vtr* **1** (appeler) to call out to; (apostropher) to shout at; **2** (interroger sur place) to question; (emmener au poste) to take [sb] in for questioning; **3** Pol to interpellate
B **s'interpeller** *vpr* [personnes] (amicalement) to shout to one another; (agressivement) to shout at one another

interphone® /ɛ̃tɛʀfɔn/ *nm* **1** (dans un bureau) intercom; **parler par l'~** to speak over the intercom; **2** (dans un immeuble) entry phone

interplanétaire /ɛ̃tɛʀplanetɛʀ/ *adj* interplanetary

interposer /ɛ̃tɛʀpoze/ [1]
A *vtr* to interpose sout (**entre** between); **par personne interposée** through an intermediary
B **s'interposer** *vpr* to intervene

interprétariat /ɛ̃tɛʀpʀetaʀja/ *nm* interpreting

interprétation /ɛ̃tɛʀpʀetasjɔ̃/ *nf* **1** (explication) interpretation (**de** of); **mauvaise ~** misinterpretation; **on peut donner plusieurs ~s à ce phénomène** this phenomenon can be interpreted in several ways; **2** Mus, Théât interpretation; **3** (métier) interpreting

interprète /ɛ̃tɛʀpʀɛt/ *nmf* **1** ▸ p. 372 (traducteur) interpreter; **servir d'~ à qn** to act as an interpreter for sb; **2** Mus (exécutant) performer; (soliste) soloist; **3** Cin, Théât performer; **les ~s d'une pièce** the cast (*sg*) of a play; **4** (porte-parole)

spokesperson; **se faire l'~ de qn** to act as sb's spokesperson; **5** (de texte) exponent; (de présage, rêve) interpreter

interpréter /ɛ̃tɛʀpʀete/ [14]
A *vtr* **1** to play [rôle]; to sing [chanson]; to perform [sonate, morceau]; **2** (tirer une signification de) to interpret; **ne pas savoir comment ~ qch** not to know what to make of sth; **mal ~ qch** to misinterpret sth
B **s'interpréter** *vpr* to be interpreted

interpréteur /ɛ̃tɛʀpʀetœʀ/ *nm* Ordinat interpreter

interrogateur, -trice /ɛ̃tɛʀɔgatœʀ, tʀis/ *adj* inquiring; **d'un air ~** inquiringly

interrogatif, -ive /ɛ̃tɛʀɔgatif, iv/ *adj* interrogative

interrogation /ɛ̃tɛʀɔgasjɔ̃/ *nf* **1** (de témoin) questioning (**sur** about); **2** Ling question; **3** Scol test; **~ orale** oral test; **4** Ordinat query

interrogatoire /ɛ̃tɛʀɔgatwaʀ/ *nm* gén interrogation; (par la police) questioning

interrogeable /ɛ̃tɛʀɔʒabl/ *adj* which can be interrogated; **répondeur ~ à distance** remote-access answering machine

interroger /ɛ̃tɛʀɔʒe/ [13]
A *vtr* **1** (questionner) gén to question (**sur** about); (pour un renseignement) to ask; [police] to question, to interrogate [suspect]; [journaliste] to put questions to (**sur** on); fig to search [mémoire]; to examine [conscience]; **50% des personnes interrogées** 50% of those questioned; **quand on l'a interrogé sur ses intentions** when he was asked about his intentions; **être interrogé comme témoin** to be called as a witness; **2** (consulter) to query [ordinateur]; **~ son répondeur** to check one's calls; **3** Scol to test (**sur** on)
B **s'interroger** *vpr* **s'~ sur** to wonder about

interrompre /ɛ̃tɛʀɔ̃pʀ/ [53]
A *vtr* **1** (momentanément) to interrupt [émission, repas, conversation]; to break off [relations, dialogue]; to disrupt [circulation]; to cut off [distribution d'eau]; to cease [activité]; **~ son repas pour faire** to stop eating to do; **2** (définitivement) to put an end to [carrière, études, vacances]; to stop [traitement]; **3** (couper la parole à) to interrupt; **ne m'interromps pas tout le temps!** stop interrupting all the time!
B **s'interrompre** *vpr* **1** (soi-même) **s'~ dans son travail** to stop working (**pour faire** to do); **2** (l'un l'autre) to interrupt each other; **3** (s'arrêter) [pluie, fête] to stop

interrupteur /ɛ̃tɛʀyptœʀ/ *nm* switch

interruption /ɛ̃tɛʀypsjɔ̃/ *nf* **1** (arrêt) break (**de** in); **une ~ de trois mois** a three-month break; **sans ~** continuously; **j'ai travaillé sans ~ jusqu'à minuit** I worked nonstop until midnight; **2** (fin) ending (**de** of); **l'~ du dialogue entre** the breaking off of the dialogue GB between
○ **Composés** **~ volontaire de grossesse, IVG** termination of pregnancy

intersaison /ɛ̃tɛʀsɛzɔ̃/ *nf* Tourisme low season; Sport off-season

intersection /ɛ̃tɛʀsɛksjɔ̃/ *nf* intersection

intersidéral, ~e, *mpl* **-aux** /ɛ̃tɛʀsideʀal, o/ *adj* interstellar

interstellaire /ɛ̃tɛʀstelɛʀ/ *adj* interstellar

interstice /ɛ̃tɛʀstis/ *nm* (de plancher) crack; (de volets, stores) chink

intersyndical, ~e, *mpl* **-aux** /ɛ̃tɛʀsɛ̃dikal, o/ *adj* inter-union

intertitre /ɛ̃tɛʀtitʀ/ *nm* Cin insert title

interurbain, ~e /ɛ̃tɛʀyʀbɛ̃, ɛn/
A *adj* [liaisons, transports] interurban; (au téléphone) [communications] trunk; [appel] trunk, long distance
B *nm* **l'~** long distance telephone service

intervalle /ɛ̃tɛʀval/ *nm* **1** (dans l'espace) space; **à ~s réguliers** at regular intervals; **2** (dans le temps) interval; **dans l'~** meanwhile; **3** Mus interval

intervenir /ɛ̃tɛʀvəniʀ/ [36] *vi* (+ *v* être) **1** (se produire) [changements] to take place; [accord] to be reached; [augmentation] to occur; **2** (prendre part) [orateur] to speak (**dans** in); **~ sur le marché** to intervene in the market; **3** (agir en urgence) [armée, police, pompiers] to intervene; **le chirurgien a décidé d'~** the surgeon decided to operate; **4** (intercéder) to intercede; **~ auprès de qn** to intercede with sb; **~ comme médiateur** to play the role of mediator

intervention /ɛ̃tɛʀvɑ̃sjɔ̃/ nf [1] (engagement) intervention (**en faveur de** on behalf of; **auprès de** with); ~ **de l'armée** military intervention; [2] (d'orateur) speech; (de conférencier) lecture; [3] (opération) operation; ~ **chirurgicale** operation (**sur qn** on sb); **une petite** ~ a minor operation

interventionnisme /ɛ̃tɛʀvɑ̃sjɔnism/ nm interventionism

interversion /ɛ̃tɛʀvɛʀsjɔ̃/ nf inversion

intervertir /ɛ̃tɛʀvɛʀtiʀ/ [3] vtr to invert [objets, mots]

interviewer /ɛ̃tɛʀvjuve/ [1] vtr to interview

intestin /ɛ̃tɛstɛ̃/ nm bowel, intestine

intestinal, ~**e**, mpl -**aux** /ɛ̃tɛstinal, o/ adj intestinal; **problèmes intestinaux** bowel problems

intime /ɛ̃tim/
A adj [1] (personnel) [vie, journal] private; [ami, rapports] intimate; [hygiène] personal; **avoir des relations** ~**s avec qn** to be on intimate terms with sb; [2] (entre proches) [fête, dîner] intimate; [conversation] private; [cérémonie] quiet; [3] (douillet) [pièce] cosy; [4] (profond) [connaissance] intimate; [conviction] deep; **j'ai la conviction** ~ **que...** I firmly believe that...
B nmf close friend, intimate; **c'est Jojo pour les** ~**s** my friends call me/him Jojo

intimement /ɛ̃timmɑ̃/ adv intimately; **je suis** ~ **convaincu que...** I'm absolutely convinced that...

intimer /ɛ̃time/ [1] vtr ~ **à qn l'ordre de faire** to order sb to do

intimidable /ɛ̃timidabl/ adj **être** ~ to be easily intimidated

intimidation /ɛ̃timidasjɔ̃/ nf intimidation; **d'**~ [mesure, parole] intimidatory; **céder à des mesures d'**~ to allow oneself to be intimidated

intimider /ɛ̃timide/ [1] vtr to intimidate; **se laisser** ~ **par** to be intimidated by

intimité /ɛ̃timite/ nf [1] (lien) intimacy; [2] (privé) privacy; **ils ont fêté Noël dans l'**~ they had a quiet Christmas; **dans l'**~ **il est beaucoup plus chaleureux** in private he is much warmer; [3] (vie privée) private life; [4] (de maison, pièce, cadre) cosiness

intitulé /ɛ̃tityle/ nm title, heading

intituler /ɛ̃tityle/ [1]
A vtr to call
B s'**intituler** vpr to be called, to be entitled

intolérable /ɛ̃tɔleʀabl/ adj [souffrance, vacarme, attitude] intolerable; [images] deeply shocking; **de façon** ~ intolerably

intolérance /ɛ̃tɔleʀɑ̃s/ nf intolerance; Méd allergy

intolérant, ~**e** /ɛ̃tɔleʀɑ̃, ɑ̃t/ adj intolerant

intonation /ɛ̃tɔnasjɔ̃/ nf intonation

intouchable /ɛ̃tuʃabl/ adj, nmf untouchable

intox(e)○ /ɛ̃tɔks/ nf inv disinformation; **faire de l'**~ to spread disinformation

intoxication /ɛ̃tɔksikasjɔ̃/ nf [1] Méd poisoning; ~ **alimentaire** Méd food poisoning; ~ **par les champignons** poisoning caused by eating fungi; **17** ~**s mortelles** 17 deaths due to poisoning; [2] (propagande) disinformation

intoxiquer /ɛ̃tɔksike/ [1]
A vtr (empoisonner) to poison; fig (abrutir) to brainwash
B s'**intoxiquer** vpr to poison oneself

intraduisible /ɛ̃tʀadɥizibl/ adj [1] (qu'on ne peut traduire) untranslatable; [2] (inexprimable) inexpressible

intraitable /ɛ̃tʀɛtabl/ adj inflexible; **je serai** ~ **là-dessus** I will not budge on this

intra-muros /ɛ̃tʀamyʀos/
A loc adj inv **Paris** ~ Paris itself
B loc adv [habiter] in ou within the town itself

intranet /ɛ̃tʀanɛt/ nm intranet

intransigeance /ɛ̃tʀɑ̃ziʒɑ̃s/ nf intransigence

intransigeant, ~**e** /ɛ̃tʀɑ̃ziʒɑ̃, ɑ̃t/ adj [attitude, principe] uncompromising; [personne] intransigent (**sur** on); [partisan] staunch

intransitif, -**ive** /ɛ̃tʀɑ̃zitif, iv/
A adj intransitive
B nm intransitive verb

intransmissible /ɛ̃tʀɑ̃smisibl/ adj [maladie] non-infectious; [savoir] incommunicable

intransportable /ɛ̃tʀɑ̃spɔʀtabl/ adj [marchandises] untransportable; [blessé] who should not be moved (épith, après n)

intra-utérin, ~**e**, mpl ~**s** /ɛ̃tʀayteʀɛ̃, in/ adj intra-uterine

intraveineuse[1] /ɛ̃tʀavɛnøz/ nf intravenous injection

intraveineux, -**euse**[2] /ɛ̃tʀavɛnø, øz/ adj intravenous

intrépide /ɛ̃tʀepid/ adj intrepid, bold

intrépidité /ɛ̃tʀepidite/ nf boldness, intrepidity; **avec** ~ boldly

intrigant, ~**e** /ɛ̃tʀigɑ̃, ɑ̃t/ nm,f schemer

intrigue /ɛ̃tʀig/ nf [1] (machination) intrigue; [2] Littérat plot; **une** ~ **policière** a detective story

intriguer /ɛ̃tʀige/ [1] vtr to intrigue; **elle m'intrigue** I find her intriguing

intrinsèque /ɛ̃tʀɛ̃sɛk/ adj [valeur, contenu] intrinsic

introducteur, -**trice** /ɛ̃tʀɔdyktœʀ, tʀis/ nm,f (personne qui introduit) **l'**~ **du tabac en France** the man who introduced tobacco to France

introduction /ɛ̃tʀɔdyksjɔ̃/ nf [1] Littérat, Mus (préliminaire) introduction (**à, de** to); [2] (d'objet, sonde, clé) insertion (**dans** into); [3] (de visiteur) ushering (**dans** into); [4] (présentation) **une lettre d'**~ **auprès de qn** a letter of introduction to sb; [5] (de mode, produit, mesure) introduction; [6] (importation illicite) ~ **de substances illicites** smuggling in illegal substances; [7] (initiation) introduction (**à** to)

introduire /ɛ̃tʀɔdɥiʀ/ [69]
A vtr [1] (insérer) to insert [objet]; [2] (faire entrer) (en grande pompe) to usher [sb] in [personne]; (clandestinement) to smuggle; [3] (présenter) to introduce [personne] (**auprès de** to); [4] (faire adopter) to introduce [produit, idée] (**dans** into); [5] (importer illicitement) to smuggle
B s'**introduire** vpr [1] (pénétrer) s'~ **dans** to get into; s'~ **dans une maison par effraction** to break into a house; [2] (se faire admettre) [personne] to gain admittance (**dans** to)

introduit, ~**e** /ɛ̃tʀɔdɥi, it/
A pp ▸ introduire
B pp adj **être** ~ **dans les milieux bancaires** to know a lot of people in banking circles; **être bien** ~ **auprès de qn** to have access to sb

introniser /ɛ̃tʀɔnize/ [1] vtr to enthrone [évêque]

introspection /ɛ̃tʀɔspɛksjɔ̃/ nf introspection

introuvable /ɛ̃tʀuvabl/ adj [1] (qu'on ne peut trouver) [personne] untraceable; [objet] that cannot be found (épith, après n); [endroit] that is impossible to find (épith, après n); **le voleur reste** ~ the thief has still not been found; **mon portefeuille est** ~ I can't find my wallet anywhere; [2] (rare) [spécialiste] that is hard to come by (épith, après n); [livre, antiquité] that is impossible to get hold of (épith, après n)

introversion /ɛ̃tʀɔvɛʀsjɔ̃/ nf introversion

introverti, ~**e** /ɛ̃tʀɔvɛʀti/
A adj introverted
B nm,f introvert

intrus, ~**e** /ɛ̃tʀy, yz/ nm,f intruder; **'cherchez l'**~**'** Jeux 'spot the odd one out' GB, 'pick the one that doesn't fit' US

intrusion /ɛ̃tʀyzjɔ̃/ nf (irruption) intrusion (**dans** into); (ingérence) (de personne, pays) interference (**dans** in); (d'objet, idée) intrusion

intuitif, -**ive** /ɛ̃tɥitif, iv/ adj intuitive; **connaissance intuitive de qch** intuitive understanding of sth

intuition /ɛ̃tɥisjɔ̃/ nf intuition; **avoir l'**~ **de** to have an intuition about

inusable /inyzabl/ adj hardwearing

inusité, ~**e** /inyzite/ adj Ling (non utilisé) not used (jamais épith); (rare) uncommon, not in common use (jamais épith)

inutile /inytil/ adj [1] [objet, développement] useless; [travail, discussion] pointless; [crainte] needless; (**il est**) ~ **de faire** there's no point in doing; ~ **de dire que** needless to say; ~ **de me demander si** it's no use asking me whether; ~ **de rincer** no need to rinse; **sans risques** ~**s** without unnecessary risks; **mes efforts sont restés** ~**s** my efforts were in vain; [2] [personne] useless

inutilement /inytilmɑ̃/ adv [se fatiguer] unnecessarily; [s'inquiéter, souffrir] needlessly; [attendre, chercher] in vain

inutilisable /inytilizabl/ *adj* unusable

inutilisé, ~e /inytilize/ *adj* unused

inutilité /inytilite/ *nf* (d'objet, effort, de personne) uselessness; (de démarche, dépense) pointlessness

invalide /ẽvalid/
A *adj* disabled
B *nmf* disabled person; **les ~s** the disabled

(Composé) **~ de guerre** registered disabled ex-serviceman

invalider /ẽvalide/ [1] *vtr* to invalidate

invalidité /ẽvalidite/ *nf* Méd disability; Jur invalidity

invariable /ẽvaʀjabl/ *adj* invariable

invasif, -ive /ẽvazif, iv/ *adj* invasive

invasion /ẽvazjõ/ *nf* Mil, fig invasion

invective /ẽvɛktiv/ *nf* invective ¢, abuse ¢; **se répandre en ~s** to pour out abuse (**contre** against)

invendable /ẽvãdabl/ *adj* unsaleable

invendu, ~e /ẽvãdy/
A *adj* unsold
B *nm* gén unsold item; (journal) unsold copy; (livre) remaindered copy

inventaire /ẽvãtɛʀ/ *nm* ① Comm (opération) stocktaking GB, inventory US; (liste) stocklist GB, inventory US; **faire l'~** to do the stocktaking GB, to take inventory US; ② (de valise, garde-robe) list of contents; (de collection) inventory; **faire l'~ de sa valise** (vérifier le contenu) to go through one's suitcase

inventer /ẽvãte/ [1]
A *vtr* to invent [*machine, technique, remède*]; to devise [*moyen*]; to invent [*excuse, raison*]; **histoire inventée** made-up story; **tu inventes** you're making it up; **je n'invente rien** I'm not making it up; **je ne sais plus quoi ~ pour te faire plaisir**○ I can't think what else to do to make you happy
B *s'inventer vpr* **il s'est inventé une enfance malheureuse** he's invented an unhappy childhood for himself; **elle s'invente toujours des excuses** she can always find an excuse; **ça ne s'invente pas** that has to be true

(Idiome) **il n'a pas inventé la poudre**○ *or* **l'eau tiède**○ *or* **le fil à couper le beurre**○ he is not very bright

inventeur, -trice /ẽvãtœʀ, tʀis/ *nmf* ① ▸ p. 372 inventor; ② Jur (découvreur d'un bien) finder

inventif, -ive /ẽvãtif, iv/ *adj* (novateur) inventive; (débrouillard) resourceful

invention /ẽvãsjõ/ *nf* ① (création) invention; **elle nous a servi un plat de son ~** she served us a dish she'd invented herself; ② (mensonge) fabrication; **c'est de l'~ pure** it's a complete fabrication; **ce ne sont que des ~s** it's not true at all

inventorier /ẽvãtɔʀje/ [2] *vtr* to make out a stocklist GB *ou* an inventory US of [*marchandises*]; to draw up an inventory of [*biens, succession*]

inverse /ẽvɛʀs/
A *adj* gén [*direction, effet, démarche*] opposite; **on s'est retrouvé dans la situation ~** (de la vôtre) the exact opposite happened to us; (de la précédente) the situation was reversed; **en sens ~** [*aller, repartir*] in the opposite direction; [*venir, arriver*] from the opposite direction; **attention aux voitures qui arrivent en sens ~** beware of oncoming traffic; **une voiture a heurté un camion roulant en sens ~** a car was in collision with a truck coming the opposite way; **dans l'ordre ~** (sur une liste) in reverse order
B *nm* ① gén **l'~** the opposite; **à l'~** conversely; **aller à l'~ de** to be the opposite of; **à l'~ de ce qui s'est passé l'an dernier** unlike last year; **à l'~ de ce qu'il croyait** contrary to what he thought; **c'est comme ça qu'il faut faire et non l'~** that's how it should be done, not the other way around; ② Math inverse

inversement /ẽvɛʀsəmã/ *adv* gén conversely; Math inversely; **et ~** and vice-versa; **~ proportionnel** in inverse proportion (**à** to)

inverser /ẽvɛʀse/ [1]
A *vtr* ① (intervertir) to invert [*position, termes*]; to reverse [*tendance, rôles, ordre*]; **image inversée** mirror image; ② to reverse [*courant*]
B *s'inverser vpr* to be reversed

inversion /ẽvɛʀsjõ/ *nf* ① (d'éléments, de rôles, valeurs) inversion; (de tendance, processus) reversal; ② Anat, Chimie, Ling, Psych inversion; ③ Électrotech reversal

invertébré, ~e /ẽvɛʀtebʀe/
A *adj* invertebrate
B *nm* invertebrate; **les ~s** invertebrates

invertir /ẽvɛʀtiʀ/ [3] *vtr* ① (inverser) to switch [sth] round [*termes*]; to reverse [*ordre*]; ② to reverse [*courant*]

investigateur, -trice /ẽvɛstigatœʀ, tʀis/
A *adj* inquiring
B *nm,f* investigator

investigation /ẽvɛstigasjõ/ *nf* investigation; **d'~** investigative

investir /ẽvɛstiʀ/ [3]
A *vtr* ① (placer) to invest [*capitaux*] (**dans** in); **~ en Bourse** to invest on the Stock Exchange; ② (charger) to invest [*personne, ambassadeur*] (**de** with); ③ (se répandre dans) [*policiers*] to go into; [*touristes, manifestants*] to take over; ④ (encercler) [*armée*] to besiege
B *s'investir vpr* **s'~ dans** (énergiquement) to put a lot of oneself into; (sentimentalement) to invest emotionally in

investissement /ẽvɛstismã/ *nm* ① gén investment (**dans** in); **un énorme ~ de temps** an enormous investment in terms of time; ② Mil (encerclement) investing (**de** of)

investisseur /ẽvɛstisœʀ/ *nm* investor

investiture /ẽvɛstityʀ/ *nf* investiture

invétéré, ~e /ẽvetere/ *adj* [*buveur, voleur, tricheur*] inveterate; [*menteur*] compulsive; [*haine, habitude, mal*] deep-rooted

invincibilité /ẽvẽsibilite/ *nf* invincibility

invincible /ẽvẽsibl/ *adj* (qui ne peut être vaincu) invincible; (irréfutable) irrefutable

inviolabilité /ẽvjɔlabilite/ *nf* ① (de règle, frontière, territoire) inviolability; ② (de forteresse, coffre) impregnability

inviolable /ẽvjɔlabl/ *adj* [*loi, secret, frontière, refuge*] inviolable; [*coffre, porte*] impregnable

invisible /ẽvizibl/
A *adj* ① (non perceptible) invisible; ② (hors de vue) **la route était ~ depuis la maison** the road could not be seen from the house; ③ (non disponible) [*personne*] unavailable; ④ (caché, secret) [*vestiges*] hidden; [*danger, menace*] unseen
B *nm* **l'~** the invisible

invitation /ẽvitasjõ/ *nf* (prière, exhortation) invitation (**à** to); (document) invitation; **à** *or* **sur l'~ de qn** at sb's invitation; **carte** *or* **carton d'~** invitation card; **c'est une ~ à la révolte** it's an open invitation to revolt

invité, ~e /ẽvite/ *nm,f* guest; **~ d'honneur** guest of honour^GB; **~ de marque** distinguished guest

inviter /ẽvite/ [1]
A *vtr* ① (prier de venir) to invite; ② (payer) **~ qn à déjeuner/à prendre un verre** to take sb out for lunch/for a drink; ③ (engager) to invite (**à faire** to do); (demander) to ask (**à faire** to do); **le temps n'invite guère à la promenade** it's not particularly nice weather for a walk; **cela invite à la réflexion** it is thought-provoking
B *s'inviter vpr* [*personne*] to invite oneself

in vitro /invitʀo/ *loc adj, loc adv* in vitro

invivable /ẽvivabl/ *adj* unbearable

invocation /ẽvɔkasjõ/ *nf* invocation (**de** of)

involontaire /ẽvɔlõtɛʀ/ *adj* (incontrôlé) [*réaction, cri, geste*] involuntary; [*mensonge, faute*] unintentional; (fortuit) [*intermédiaire, héros, témoin*] unwitting

involontairement /ẽvɔlõtɛʀmã/ *adv* (sans le vouloir) [*soupirer, crier, sourire*] involuntarily; (sans préméditation) [*blesser, casser*] unintentionally; **si je vous ai blessé, c'est bien ~** I didn't mean to hurt you

invoquer /ẽvɔke/ [1] *vtr* to invoke

invraisemblable /ẽvʀesãblabl/ *adj* ① (non crédible) [*événement, histoire*] unlikely; [*hypothèse, aventure*] improbable; [*explication*] implausible; ② ○(inouï) fantastic, incredible

invraisemblance /ẽvʀesãblãs/ *nf* (caractère) unlikelihood; (détail) improbability

invulnérabilité /ẽvylneʀabilite/ *nf* invulnerability

invulnérable /ẽvylneʀabl/ *adj* invulnerable

iode /jɔd/ *nm* iodine

ioder /jɔde/ [1] *vtr* to iodize; **eau iodée** iodized water

ion /jõ/ *nm* ion

iota /jɔta/ nm inv iota

(Idiomes) ne pas changer d'un ~ not to change one iota; ne pas bouger d'un ~ not to move an inch

irakien, -ienne /iʀakjɛ̃, ɛn/ ▸ p. 392 adj Iraqi

iranien, -ienne /iʀanjɛ̃, ɛn/ ▸ p. 336, p. 392
A adj Iranian
B nm Ling Iranian

irascible /iʀasibl/ adj [personne] irascible sout, quick-tempered; avoir un caractère ~ to be quick-tempered

iris /iʀis/ nm inv (fleur) iris; (de l'œil) iris; (diaphragme) iris diaphragm

irisé, ~e /iʀize/ adj iridescent

irlandais, ~e /iʀlɑ̃dɛ, ɛz/ ▸ p. 336, p. 392
A adj Irish
B nm Ling Irish

Irlandais, ~e /iʀlɑ̃dɛ, ɛz/ ▸ p. 392 nm,f Irishman/Irishwoman; les ~ du Nord the northern Irish

Irlande /iʀlɑ̃d/ ▸ p. 230 nprf Ireland; la République d'~ the Republic of Ireland; l'~ du Nord Northern Ireland

IRM /iɛʀɛm/ nf (abbr = imagerie par résonance magnétique) MRI, magnetic resonance imaging

ironie /iʀɔni/ nf irony; l'~ du sort the irony of fate; faire de l'~ to be ironic

ironique /iʀɔnik/ adj ironic

ironiser /iʀɔnize/ [1] vi to be ironic (sur about); 'tu es déjà prête!' ironisa-t-il 'ready so soon!' he said ironically

iroquois, ~e /iʀɔkwa, az/ ▸ p. 336
A adj Iroquois
B nm Ling Iroquois

irradiation /iʀadjasjɔ̃/ nf **1** (nucléaire) radiation; dix morts par ~ ten deaths through ou from radiation; **2** Ind, Phys irradiation

irradier /iʀadje/ [2]
A vtr (exposer aux radiations) to irradiate; déchets irradiés radioactive waste ⊄
B vi (se propager) to radiate (dans through)

irrationnel, -elle /iʀasjɔnɛl/
A adj irrational
B nm l'~ the irrational

irréalisable /iʀealizabl/ adj [entreprise, idée, rêve] impossible; [projet] unworkable

irrecevable /iʀəsəvabl/ adj Jur inadmissible

irréconciliable /iʀekɔ̃siljabl/ adj irreconcilable

irrécupérable /iʀekypeʀabl/ adj **1** (que l'on ne peut recouvrer) irrecoverable; (que l'on ne peut réparer) damaged beyond repair (après n); voiture ~ write-off; **2** [délinquant] beyond help (après n)

irrécusable /iʀekyzabl/ adj [preuve] indisputable; [témoin] unimpeachable

irréductible /iʀedyktibl/
A adj [opposition, volonté] implacable; [personne] indomitable; [conflit] relentless
B nmf diehard

irréel, -elle /iʀeɛl/
A adj unreal
B nm l'~ the unreal

irréfléchi, ~e /iʀefleʃi/ adj (précipité) [action, propos] ill-considered; (étourdi) [personne] careless

irréfutable /iʀefytabl/ adj irrefutable

irrégularité /iʀegylaʀite/ nf **1** (acte critiquable) irregularity; **2** (en quantité) l'~ de la production the irregular production; **3** (en qualité) irregularity, unevenness; **4** (défaut) irregularity; (de surface) unevenness; les ~s du sol the uneven ground (sg); **5** Ling irregularity

irrégulier, -ière /iʀegylje, ɛʀ/ adj **1** (sans régularité) [forme, traits, croissance, pouls, respiration] irregular; [écriture, résultats, qualité, sol] uneven; **2** (illégal) [procédure, transaction] irregular; [travailleur, vente] illegal; immigré en situation irrégulière illegal immigrant; être en situation irrégulière to be in breach of the regulations; **3** (inégal) [élève, athlète] whose performance is uneven (épith, après n); **4** Mil irregular; **5** Ling [verbe, pluriel] irregular

irrégulièrement /iʀegyljɛʀmɑ̃/ adv **1** (illégalement) illegally; **2** (sans régularité) [décomposer, se conjuguer] irregularly; [répartir] unevenly; [travailler] erratically

irrémédiable /iʀ(ʀ)emedjabl/ adj [perte, faute] irreparable; [déclin, situation] irremediable sout

irremplaçable /iʀɑ̃plasabl/ adj irreplaceable

irréparable /iʀepaʀabl/
A adj [voiture, appareil] beyond repair (après n); [dégât] irreparable; [tort, crime] irreparable
B nm commettre l'~ to go beyond the point of no return

irrépressible /iʀepʀesibl/ adj [sourire, désir, rire] irrepressible; [larmes] uncontrollable

irréprochable /iʀepʀɔʃabl/ adj [conduite, vie, employé] irreproachable, beyond reproach (après n); [travail] perfect, impeccable; [goût, manières] impeccable

irrésistible /iʀezistibl/ adj [séducteur, charme, essor] irresistible; [besoin] compelling; [envie, passion] overpowering; [personne, blague] hilarious

irrésolu, ~e /iʀezɔly/ adj (indécis) [personne] indecisive; (sans solution) unsolved

irrespectueux, -euse /iʀɛspɛktɥø, øz/ adj disrespectful (envers to, toward(s))

irrespirable /iʀɛspiʀabl/ adj [air, gaz] unbreathable; [climat, ambiance, atmosphère] stifling

irresponsable /iʀɛspɔ̃sabl/ adj **1** (qui agit avec légèreté) [personne, attitude] irresponsible; de façon ~ irresponsibly; **2** Jur non-accountable

irrévérencieux, -ieuse /iʀʀeveʀɑ̃sjø, øz/ adj irreverent (envers to, toward(s))

irréversible /iʀeveʀsibl/ adj gén, Chimie, Phys irreversible; [engrenage, mécanisme] non-reversible

irrévocable /iʀevɔkabl/ adj irrevocable

irrigateur /iʀigatœʀ/
A adj m irrigating
B nm irrigator

irrigation /iʀigasjɔ̃/ nf **1** Agric irrigation; **2** Méd (de plaie, cavité) irrigation; (en sang) supply of blood; une mauvaise ~ du cerveau an insufficient blood supply to the brain

irriguer /iʀige/ [1] vtr Agric, Méd to irrigate; le sang irrigue les organes organs are supplied with blood

irritable /iʀitabl/ adj irritable

irritant, -e /iʀitɑ̃, ɑ̃t/ adj (agaçant) irritating; Méd irritant

irritation /iʀitasjɔ̃/ nf (agacement) irritation; Méd irritation

irriter /iʀite/ [1]
A vtr **1** (agacer) to irritate, to annoy; très irrité very annoyed; **2** Méd to irritate
B s'irriter vpr **1** (s'énerver) to get annoyed (de about, over), to get angry (de about, over); **2** Méd to become irritated, to become inflamed

irruption /iʀypsjɔ̃/ nf (apparition) irruption sout; faire ~ dans to burst into; ils ont fait ~ dans le monde du rock il y a dix ans they burst onto the rock scene ten years ago

islam /islam/ nm l'~ Islam

islamique /islamik/ adj Islamic

islamisme /islamism/ nm Islamism

islamiste /islamist/
A adj Islamist, Islamic
B nmf Islamist

islandais, ~e /islɑ̃dɛ, ɛz/ ▸ p. 336, p. 392
A adj Icelandic
B nm Ling Icelandic

Islande /islɑ̃d/ ▸ p. 230 nprf Iceland

isocèle /izosɛl/ adj triangle ~ isosceles triangle

isolant, ~e /izolɑ̃, ɑ̃t/
A adj [matériau] insulating; la laine de verre est très ~e fibreglass^GB is a very good insulator
B nm insulating material; ~ thermique thermal insulator

isolation /izolasjɔ̃/ nf **1** insulation; ~ acoustique soundproofing; **2** Psych isolation

isolé, ~e /izole/
A pp ▸ isoler
B pp adj **1** (très éloigné) remote; **2** (un peu à l'écart) isolated (de from); **3** [cas, événement] isolated; tireur ~ lone gunman, sniper; des tirs ~s sniper fire ⊄; **4** (seul, sans alliés) isolated

isolement /izolmɑ̃/ nm **1** (de village, région) remoteness; (de maison) isolated location; **2** (absence de contacts) (de malade, chômeur) isolation; (de pays, politicien) isolation; **3** (mise à l'écart) (de malade) isolation; (de prisonnier) solitary confinement; **4** (de gène, substance, virus) isolation; **5** (en électricité) insulation

isolément /izɔlemɑ̃/ adv in isolation

isoler /izɔle/ [1]
A vtr ⒈ to isolate [malade, politicien, dissident] (**de** from); to put [sb] in solitary confinement [prisonnier]; ⒉ (séparer d'un ensemble) to isolate [gène, substance, élément]; ~ **une citation de son contexte** to take a quote out of context; ⒊ (contre le bruit) to soundproof; (contre la chaleur, le froid) to insulate (**contre** against); ⒋ (en électricité) to insulate
B **s'isoler** vpr ⒈ to isolate oneself (**de** from); **s'~ dans un coin pour lire une lettre** to withdraw into a corner to read a letter

isoloir /izɔlwaʀ/ nm voting ou polling GB booth

isomère /izɔmɛʀ/
A adj isomeric
B nm isomer

isomorphe /izɔmɔʀf/ adj isomorphic

isorel® /izɔʀɛl/ nm hardboard

isotherme /izɔtɛʀm/ adj [camion, wagon] refrigerated; **boîte** ~ ice box; **bouteille** ~ insulated bottle; **sac** ~ cool bag

isotope /izɔtɔp/ nm isotope

Israël /isʀaɛl/ ▸ p. 230 nprm Israel; **en** ~ in Israel

israélien, -ienne /isʀaeljɛ̃, ɛn/ ▸ p. 392 adj Israeli

israélite /isʀaelit/
A adj Jewish
B nmf Hist Israelite; (juif) Jew

issu, ~e¹ /isy/ adj ⒈ (originaire) **être** ~ **de** to come from; **les jeunes ~s de familles pauvres** young people from poor families; ⒉ (résultant) **être** ~ **de** to result from

issue² /isy/ nf ⒈ (sortie) exit; **'sans ~'** 'no exit'; ⒉ (solution) solution (**à** to); **situation sans** ~ situation with no solution; ⒊ (dénouement) outcome; **à l'~ de** at the end of; **à l'~ de trois jours de pourparlers** at the close of three days of talks
(Composé) ~ **de secours** emergency exit

isthme /ism/ nm isthmus

Italie /itali/ ▸ p. 230 nprf Italy

italien, -ienne /italjɛ̃, ɛn/ ▸ p. 336, p. 392
A adj Italian
B nm Ling Italian

italique /italik/ nm italics (pl)

item /itɛm/ adv ditto

itinéraire /itineʀɛʀ/ nm ⒈ (de voyage) route; (détaillé) itinerary; ⒉ fig career
(Composés) ~ **bis** alternative route, holiday GB ou vacation US route; ~ **de délestage** relief route

itinérant, ~e /itineʀɑ̃, ɑ̃t/ adj [musicien, artiste] itinerant; [spectacle, exposition] touring; [vie, personnel] peripatetic; [cirque] travellingGB

IUFM /iyɛfɛm/ nm (abbr = **institut universitaire de formation des maîtres**) university teacher-training faculty

ⓘ **IUFM** A teacher-training establishment, introduced in 1990, incorporating the role of the former école normale and providing training for concours for teaching qualifications like the CAPES. Each IUFM is attached to a university.

IUT /iyte/ nm (abbr = **Institut universitaire de technologie**) university institute of technology

IVG /iveʒe/ nf: abbr ▸ **interruption**

ivoire /ivwaʀ/ ▸ p. 140
A adj inv ivory
B nm ⒈ (d'éléphant) ivory; **en** ~, **d'**~ ivory (épith); ⒉ (de dent) dentine GB, dentin US

ivoirien, -ienne /ivwaʀjɛ̃, ɛn/ ▸ p. 392 adj of the Ivory Coast

ivraie /ivʀɛ/ nf rye-grass; **séparer le bon grain de l'~** fig to separate the wheat from the chaff

ivre /ivʀ/ adj ⒈ (par l'alcool) intoxicated, drunk; ~ **mort** dead drunk; ⒉ (transporté) drunk (**de** with); ~ **de liberté** exhilarated ou intoxicated by freedom; ~ **de bonheur** drunk with happiness; ~ **de rage** wild with rage

ivresse /ivʀɛs/ nf ⒈ (ébriété) intoxication; **conduite en état d'**~ driving while intoxicated, drunken driving; ⒉ (exaltation) exhilaration
(Composé) ~ **des profondeurs** decompression sickness

ivrogne /ivʀɔɲ/ nmf drunkard

ivrognerie /ivʀɔɲəʀi/ nf drinking

j, J /ʒi/ *nm inv* j, J; **le jour J** D-day; **jour J moins dix** ten days to D-day

j' ▶ je

jabot /ʒabo/ *nm* (d'oiseau, abeille) crop; (de chemise) jabot

jacasser /ʒakase/ [1] *vi* to chatter

jachère /ʒaʃɛʀ/ *nf* (pratique, état) fallow; (terrain) fallow land ₵; **en ~** lying fallow

jacinthe /ʒasɛ̃t/ *nf* (fleur) hyacinth

jackpot /(d)ʒakpɔt/ *nm* [1] (combinaison gagnante) jackpot; **gagner le ~** to hit the jackpot; [2] (machine) slot machine

jacobin, ~e /ʒakɔbɛ̃, in/ *adj, nm,f* Hist Jacobin; Pol radical

jacquerie /ʒakʀi/ *nf* Hist peasant revolt, jacquerie

Jacques /ʒak/
A *nm* **faire le ~** to play the fool
B *npr* James

jacquet /ʒakɛ/ ▶ p. 327 *nm* (jeu) backgammon; (tablette) backgammon board

jacter⁹ /ʒakte/ [1] *vi* (parler) to jaw○, to talk

jacuzzi® /ʒakyzi/ *nm* jacuzzi®

jade /ʒad/ *nm* [1] (pierre) jade; [2] (objet) piece of jade

jadis /ʒadis/ *adv* formerly, in the past; **~, la vie était différente** in the past, life was different; **les mœurs de ~** the customs of long ago

jaguar /ʒagwaʀ/ *nm* jaguar

jaillir /ʒajiʀ/ [3] *vi* [1] (sortir impétueusement) [*liquide, gaz*] to gush out (**de** of); [*larmes*] to flow (**de** from); [*flamme, étincelle*] to shoot up (**de** from); [2] (apparaître subitement) [*personne, animal*] to spring up (**de** from); (en sortant) to spring out (**de** from); [*voiture*] to shoot out (**de** from); [3] [*rires, cris, plaisanteries*] to burst out (**de** from); [4] (s'élever) [*clocher, arbre*] to thrust up, to tower up (**au-dessus de** above); [5] (se révéler) [*idée, vérité*] to emerge (**de** from)

jais /ʒɛ/ *nm inv* [1] (pierre) jet; [2] ▶ p. 140 (couleur) (noir) **de ~** jet-black (*épith*), jet black (*jamais épith*)

jalon /ʒalɔ̃/ *nm* (piquet) marker; fig **poser les ~s de** to prepare the ground for; **~ important** milestone

jalonner /ʒalɔne/ [1] *vtr* [1] (marquer) to punctuate [*vie, histoire*]; **une journée jalonnée de péripéties** a day full of incidents; [2] (border) to line [*route*]; [3] (délimiter avec une marque) [*personne*] to mark out [*route*]

jalousement /ʒaluzmɑ̃/ *adv* [1] (avec jalousie) jealously; (avec envie) enviously; [2] (avec un soin inquiet) jealously

jalouser /ʒaluze/ [1] *vtr* to be jealous of

jalousie /ʒaluzi/ *nf* [1] (sentiment) jealousy ₵ (**à l'égard de, envers** toward(s)); **susciter des ~s chez les concurrents** to arouse jealousy among competitors; [2] (persienne) (à lattes verticales) vertical blind; (à lattes horizontales) Venetian blind; [3] (œillet) sweet william

jaloux, -ouse /ʒalu, uz/
A *adj* jealous (**de** of); **avec un soin ~** with meticulous care
B *nm,f* jealous man/woman; **faire des ~** to make people jealous

jamaïcain, ~e, jamaïquain, jamaïquaine /ʒamaikɛ̃, ɛn/ ▶ p. 392 *adj* Jamaican

Jamaïcain, ~e, Jamaïquain, Jamaïquaine /ʒamaikɛ̃, ɛn/ ▶ p. 392 *nm,f* Jamaican

jamais /ʒamɛ/ *adv* [1] (à aucun moment) never; **il n'écrit ~** he never writes; **n'écrit-il ~?** doesn't he ever write?; **je n'écrirai ~ plus** *or* **plus ~** I'll never write again; **ce n'est ~ assez** it's never enough; **~ plus!** never again!; **rien** n'est ~ **certain** nothing is ever certain; **sans ~ comprendre** without ever understanding; **sait-on ~?** you never know; **~ de la vie!** never!; **c'est le moment ou ~** it's now or never; [2] (à tout autre moment) ever; **plus belle que ~** prettier than ever; **si ~ tu passes à Oxford, viens me voir** if you are ever in Oxford, come and see me; **on a ce qu'il faut si ~ il pleut** we have everything we need in case it rains; [3] (toujours) **à ~, à tout ~** forever; [4] (seulement) **ce n'est ~ que** it is only

jambage /ʒɑ̃baʒ/ *nm* (de lettre) downstroke; (support) jamb

jambe /ʒɑ̃b/ *nf* [1] ▶ p. 136 leg; **avoir des ~s bien faites** to have nice *ou* good legs; **avoir de bonnes ~s** to have strong legs; **plier les ~s** (debout) to bend one's knees; (assis) to draw one's legs up; **croiser les ~s** to cross one's legs; **il avait les ~s écartées** his legs were wide apart; **aller** *or* **courir à toutes ~s** to run as fast as one's legs can carry one; **j'ai mal aux ~s** my legs are hurting; **j'ai les ~s lourdes** my legs feel heavy; **tomber les ~s en l'air** to fall flat on one's back; **j'ai les ~s comme du coton**○ I feel weak at the knees; **traîner la ~**○ to trudge along

〔Composé〕 **~ de bois** wooden leg

〔Idiomes〕 **cela me fait une belle ~**○ a fat lot of good○ that does me; **il ne tient plus sur ses ~s** he can hardly stand up; **prendre ses ~s à son cou** to take to one's heels; **parlez-lui de mariage et il prendra ses ~s à son cou** mention marriage and you won't see him for dust○; **avoir qn dans les ~s** to have sb under one's feet; **tenir la ~ à qn** to keep talking to sb; **faire qch par-dessus** *or* **par-dessous la ~** to do sth in a slipshod manner

jambière /ʒɑ̃bjɛʀ/ *nf* (de randonneur) legging; (de joueur de hockey) pad; (de danseur) leg-warmer; (de soldat) greave

jambon /ʒɑ̃bɔ̃/ *nm* ham

〔Composés〕 **~ beurre** (buttered) ham sandwich; **~ blanc** *or* **cuit** cooked ham; **~ fumé** smoked ham; **~ de Paris** = **~ blanc**

jambonneau, *pl* **~x** /ʒɑ̃bono/ *nm* knuckle of ham

jansénisme /ʒɑ̃senism/ *nm* Jansenism

jante /ʒɑ̃t/ *nf* (bord de roue) rim; (roue sans pneu) wheel

janvier /ʒɑ̃vje/ ▶ p. 380 *nm* January; **du premier ~ à la Saint-Sylvestre** from New Year's Day to New Year's Eve

Japon /ʒapɔ̃/ ▶ p. 230 *nprm* Japan

japonais, ~e /ʒapɔnɛ, ɛz/ ▶ p. 392, p. 336
A *adj* Japanese
B *nm* Ling Japanese

jappement /ʒapmɑ̃/ *nm* yapping ₵

japper /ʒape/ [1] *vi* to yap

jaquette /ʒakɛt/ *nf* (d'homme) morning coat; (de livre) dust jacket; (de dent) crown

jardin /ʒaʀdɛ̃/ *nm* [1] (privé) garden GB, yard US; **faire son ~** to work in one's garden GB *ou* in the yard US; [2] (parc) gardens (*pl*), park; **le ~ des Oliviers** the Garden of Gethsemane

〔Composés〕 **~ d'acclimatation** = **~ zoologique; ~ d'agrément** ornamental *ou* pleasure garden; **~ anglais** landscape garden; **~ d'enfants** kindergarten; **~ à la française** formal garden; **~ japonais** Japanese garden; **~ potager** vegetable garden; **~ public** park; **~ secret** private domain; **~ zoologique** zoo

jardinage /ʒaʀdinaʒ/ *nm* gardening

jardiner /ʒaʀdine/ [1] *vi* to do some gardening; **il aime ~** he enjoys gardening

jardinier, -ière¹ /ʒaʀdinje, ɛʀ/
A adj garden
B ▸ p. 372 nm,f (personne) gardener; **outils de** ~ garden tools; ~ **paysagiste** landscape gardener

jardinière² /ʒaʀdinjɛʀ/ nf (plat) ~ **(de légumes)** jardinière; (bac à fleurs) jardinière; ~ **d'enfants** Scol kindergarten teacher

jargon /ʒaʀgɔ̃/ nm [1] (langue de métier) jargon; ~ **administratif** officialese; [2] (langage incorrect) ungrammatical language; (langue étrangère) foreign language

Jarnac /ʒaʀnak/ npr **coup de** ~ decisive and unexpected blow

jarre /ʒaʀ/ nf (earthenware) jar

jarret /ʒaʀɛ/ nm [1] (d'humain) ham, hollow of the knee; [2] (d'animal) hock; [3] (en cuisine) ~ **de veau/porc** knuckle of veal/pork

jarretelle /ʒaʀtɛl/ nf suspender GB, garter US

jars /ʒaʀ/ nm inv gander

jaser /ʒaze/ [1] vi [1] (médire) to gossip (**sur** about); **ça fait** ~ it sets people talking; [2] C (bavarder) to chat

jasmin /ʒasmɛ̃/ nm (arbuste, parfum) jasmine

jaspe /ʒasp/ nm (pierre) jasper

jatte /ʒat/ nf bowl, basin

jauge /ʒoʒ/ nf gauge; ~ **d'huile** dipstick

jauger /ʒoʒe/ [13] vtr [1] (évaluer) to get the measure of [candidat, élève]; [2] to measure [capacité, volume]; ~ **un réservoir** to measure the capacity of a tank

jaunâtre /ʒonɑtʀ/ ▸ p. 140 adj yellowish; [teint, peau] sallow

jaune /ʒon/ ▸ p. 140
A adj [1] (couleur) yellow; ~ **orange** orangy⁶ᴮ yellow; ~ **canari/citron/moutarde** canary/lemon/mustard yellow; ~ **d'or** golden yellow; ~ **paille** straw-coloured⁶ᴮ; ~ **poussin/safran** bright/saffron yellow; **il a le teint** ~ he's got a sallow complexion; [2] (asiatique) East Asian
B nm [1] (couleur) yellow; [2] Culin ~ **(d'œuf)** (egg) yolk; [3] (briseur de grève) pej blackleg péj GB, scab péj
(Idiome) **rire** ~° to give a forced laugh

jaunir /ʒoniʀ/ [3]
A vtr [soleil] to turn [sth] yellow [papier, herbe]; [thé] to make [sth] go yellow [dents]; [nicotine] to stain [doigts]; **le temps a jauni les photos** the photos have gone yellow with age; **doigts jaunis par la nicotine** nicotine-stained fingers
B vi to go yellow

jaunisse /ʒonis/ ▸ p. 195 nf Méd jaundice; **il va en faire une** ~° that'll put his nose out of joint!

java /ʒava/ nf [1] (danse) popular dance; [2] °(fête) rave-up°; **faire la** ~ to rave it up°

javanais, -e /ʒavanɛ, ɛz/ ▸ p. 336
A adj Javanese
B nm Ling Javanese

Javel /ʒavɛl/ nf **(eau de)** ~ ≈ bleach

javelliser /ʒavelize/ [1] vtr to chlorinate

javelot /ʒavlo/ ▸ p. 327 nm (objet) javelin; (discipline) **(lancer du)** ~ javelin

jazz /dʒaz/ nm jazz; **musique de** ~ jazz (music)

J-C (written abbr = Jésus-Christ) **avant** ~ BC; **après** ~ AD

je (**j'** before vowel or mute h) /ʒ(ə)/ pron pers I

jean /dʒin/ nm [1] (pantalon) jeans (pl); **un** ~ a pair of jeans; [2] (tissu) denim

Jean /ʒɑ̃/ npr John; **saint** ~-**Baptiste** St John the Baptist; **saint** ~ **de la Croix** St John of the Cross

jeannette /ʒanɛt/ nf (pour repasser) sleeve board; (en scoutisme) ≈ Brownie

je-ne-sais-quoi /ʒənsɛkwa/ nm inv **avoir un** ~ to have a certain something

jérémiades /ʒeʀemjad/ nfpl moaning ⊄; **cesse tes** ~ stop moaning

jerrican /ʒeʀikan/ nm five-gallon container, jerrycan

jersey /ʒɛʀzɛ/ nm [1] (point) stocking stitch; [2] (tissu) jersey; **jupe en** ~ jersey skirt

jésuite /ʒezɥit/ adj, nm Relig Jesuit

Jésus /ʒezy/ npr Jesus; **le petit** ~ baby Jesus

jet¹ /ʒɛ/ nm [1] (lancer) (action) throwing ⊄; (distance) throw; **un** ~ **de 30 mètres au disque** Sport a 30-metre⁶ᴮ discus-throw;

à un ~ **de pierre** a stone's throw away (**de** from); [2] (jaillissement) (de liquide, vapeur) jet; (de salive) spurt; (de flammes) burst; **premier** ~ fig first sketch; **passer au** ~ to hose down [voiture, sol]; [3] Tech (coulage) cast(ing); **d'un seul** ~ [couler] in one piece; [écrire] in one go
(Composé) ~ **d'eau** (fontaine, jaillissement) fountain; (de tuyau) hosepipe

jet² /dʒɛt/ nm Aviat jet

jetable /ʒətabl/ adj [briquet, rasoir, couche] disposable

jeté, ~**e¹** /ʒəte/
A °adj (fou) crazy
B nm (en tricot) **une maille envers, un** ~ purl one, wool round needle (once)
(Composés) ~ **de lit** bedspread; ~ **de table** runner

jetée² /ʒəte/ nf (sur l'eau) pier; (plus petite) jetty

jeter /ʒəte/ [20]
A vtr [1] (lancer) to throw [caillou, dé]; (avec force) to hurl, to fling [objet]; ~ **qch à qn** (pour qu'il l'attrape) to throw sth to sb; (pour faire mal, peur) to throw sth at sb; ~ **qch par terre/en l'air** to throw sth to the ground/(up) in the air; ~ **le buste en avant/la tête en arrière** to throw one's chest out/one's head back; [2] (placer rapidement) to throw (**dans** into; **sur** over); (étaler) ~ **une couverture sur un blessé** to throw a blanket over an injured person; ~ **quelques idées sur le papier** fig to jot down a few ideas; [3] (mettre au rebut) to throw away ou out; ~ **qch à la poubelle** to throw sth out; **être bon à** ~ to be fit for the bin GB ou the garbage US; ▸ **fenêtre**; [4] (expédier) ~ **qn dehors/par la fenêtre** to throw sb out/out of the window; ~ **qn en prison** to throw sb in jail; **se faire** ~° to get thrown out; ~ **qn°** to throw sb out; [5] (émettre) to give [cri]; ~ **un vif éclat** to shine brightly; **en** ~° [personne, voiture] to be quite something°; [6] (construire) to lay [fondations]; [7] (causer) to create [confusion]; to cause [consternation]; to sow [terreur]; ~ **l'émoi dans la ville** to throw the town into turmoil; [8] (plonger) ~ **qn dans** to throw sb into [désespoir]; [9] (lancer en paroles) to hurl [insultes] (**à** qn to sb); **'tu es fou,' jeta-t-elle** 'you must be mad,' she said; ~ **quelques commentaires** (dans une discussion) to put in a few comments; ~ **à la tête** or **au visage de qn** to throw [sth] in sb's face [vérité, défi]
B **se jeter** vpr [1] (se précipiter) [personne] to throw oneself; **se** ~ **dans les bras de qn** to throw oneself into sb's arms; **se** ~ **sur** to fall upon [adversaire]; to pounce on [proie, nourriture, journal]; **se** ~ **au cou de qn** to fling oneself around sb's neck; **se** ~ **à l'eau** lit to jump into the water; fig to take the plunge; **se** ~ **tête baissée dans qch** to rush headlong into sth; [2] (être jetable) to be disposable; [3] (être mis au rebut) to be disposed of; [4] [cours d'eau] to flow (**dans** into)
(Idiome) **n'en jetez plus (la cour est pleine)**° hold your horses°

jeteur, -euse /ʒətœʀ, øz/ nm,f thrower
(Composés) ~ **de sort** sorcerer; **jeteuse de sort** sorceress

jeton /ʒ(ə)tɔ̃/ nm (pour un appareil) token; (pour un jeu de société) counter; (au casino) chip; ▸ **faux¹**

jeu, pl ~**x** /ʒø/ ▸ p. 327 nm [1] Jeux, Sport (activité) **le** ~ gén play ⊄; (avec de l'argent) gambling ⊄; (type) **un** ~ a game; **on va faire un** ~ let's play a game; **jouer (un) double** ~ fig to be guilty of double dealing; **à quel** ~ **joue-t-il?** fig what's his game?; **il fait ça par** ~ he does it for fun; **ton avenir est en** ~ your future is at stake; **entrer en** ~ fig to come into the picture; **d'entrée de** ~ fig right from the start; **se prendre** or **se piquer au** ~ to get hooked; **mettre en** ~ to bring [sth] into play [éléments]; to stake [somme, titre, honneur]; **remise en** ~ (au football, après une touche) throw; (au hockey, après un but) face-off; **être hors** ~ (au football) to be offside; **ils ont beau** ~ **de me critiquer** it's easy for them to criticize me; [2] Jeux, Sport (manche) game; **il a gagné (par) trois** ~**x à deux** he won by three games to two; [3] Jeux (main aux cartes) hand; **cacher bien son** ~ fig to keep it quiet; [4] Comm, Jeux (matériel) (d'échecs, de dames) set; (de cartes) deck; (de société) game; [5] (manière de jouer) (d'acteur) acting ⊄; (de musicien) playing ⊄; (de footballeur, joueur de tennis) game; [6] (série) set; ~ **de clés** set of keys; [7] (effet) (de reflets, vagues, d'ombres) play; (de forces, d'alliances) interplay; [8] Tech (possibilité de mouvement) play; **donner du** ~ **à** to loosen
(Composés) ~ **d'adresse** game of skill; ~ **d'argent** game played for money; **jouer à des** ~**x d'argent** to gamble; ~ **de caractères** Ordinat character set; ~ **de construction** (pièces) construction set; ~ **d'éveil** early-

Les jeux et les sports

Les noms de jeux et de sports

■ *En anglais, tous les noms de jeux et de sports sont singuliers. Ils ne prennent pas d'article défini.*

le football
= football

j'aime le football
= I like football

les échecs
= chess

j'aime les échecs
= I like chess

les règles des échecs
= the rules of chess

jouer aux échecs
= to play chess

savez-vous jouer aux échecs?
= can you play chess?

faire une partie d'échecs
= to play a game of chess

faire un bridge
= to have a game of bridge

■ *Certains noms de jeux et de sports ont une forme de pluriel, mais ils se comportent tout de même comme des singuliers:* billiards, bowls, checkers, darts, dominoes, draughts *etc.*

les dominos sont un jeu facile
= dominoes is easy

le jeu de boules est pratiqué par les dames et les messieurs
= bowls is played both by men and women

Les noms des joueurs

■ *Certains noms de sportifs en anglais se forment en ajoutant* -er *au nom du sport.*

un footballeur
= a footballer

un golfeur
= a golfer

un coureur de 100 mètres
= a 100-metre runner

un coureur de haies
= a hurdler

■ *Mais ceci n'est pas toujours possible. Par contre, pour les sports d'équipe, on peut toujours utiliser le mot* player *précédé du nom du sport.*

un joueur de football
= a football player

un joueur de rugby
= a rugby player

■ *En cas de doute, consulter l'article dans le dictionnaire.*

■ *Pour les noms de personnes qui jouent à des jeux, on utilise la même construction avec* player.

un joueur d'échecs
= a chess player

■ *Noter que dans les exemples suivants* chess *peut être remplacé par presque tous les noms de sports et de jeux. En cas de doute, consulter l'article dans le dictionnaire.*

il joue très bien aux échecs
= he's very good at chess
ou he's a very good chess player

un champion d'échecs
= a chess champion

le champion du monde d'échecs
= the world chess champion

je ne joue pas aux échecs
= I am not a chess player *ou* I don't play chess

Les événements

une partie d'échecs
= a game of chess

jouer aux échecs avec qn
= to play chess with sb

jouer aux échecs contre qn
= to play chess against sb

gagner une partie d'échecs
= to win a game of chess

battre qn aux échecs
= to beat sb at chess

perdre une partie d'échecs
= to lose a game of chess

jouer dans l'équipe d'Angleterre
= to play for England

gagner le championnat de Grande-Bretagne
= to win the British championship

j'espère que l'Angleterre va gagner
= I hope England wins

Douai a perdu 2 à zéro
= Douai lost 2 nil

Nantes 2–Lyon 0
= Nantes two, Lyons nil

il est arrivé quatrième
= he came fourth

■ *De avec les noms de jeux et de sports:*

un championnat d'échecs
= a chess championship

un club d'échecs
= a chess club

l'équipe d'Angleterre d'échecs
= the English chess team

un fan d'échecs
= a chess enthusiast

■ *L'anglais utilise la même construction dans des cas où le français a un mot différent, par ex.:*

un échiquier
= a chess board

Mais:

les règles des échecs
= the rules of chess

une partie d'échecs
= a game of chess (a chess game *est possible, mais moins fréquent*)

■ *En cas de doute, consulter l'article dans le dictionnaire.*

Activités sportives

■ *Les jeux:*

faire du tennis/rugby
= to play tennis/rugby

■ *Les arts martiaux et disciplines:*

faire du judo/de la boxe/de la gymnastique
= to do judo/boxing/gymnastics

■ *Les activités de plein air:*

faire de l'équitation/de l'aviron/du jogging
= to go riding/rowing/jogging

Les jeux de cartes

■ *Noter que dans les exemples suivants* clubs *pourrait être remplacé par* hearts, spades *ou* diamonds.

le huit de trèfle
= the eight of clubs

l'as de trèfle
= the ace of clubs

jouer le huit de trèfle
= to play the eight of clubs

l'atout est trèfle
= clubs are trumps

demander du trèfle
= to call clubs

as-tu du trèfle?
= do you have clubs?

learning game; **~ de hasard** Jeux game of chance; **~ de jambes** Sport footwork; **~ de massacre** Jeux ≈ coconut shy GB; **~ de mots** pun; **~ de l'oie** ≈ snakes and ladders GB; **~ radiophonique** radio game show; **~ de rôles** role playing ◖; **~ de société** (échecs, monopoly® etc) board game; (charades etc) party game; **~ télévisé** (TV) game show; **~ à XIII** Sport rugby league; **~ vidéo** video game; **~x Olympiques, JO** Olympic Games, Olympics

(Idiomes) **jouer le ~** to play the game; **jouer le grand ~** to pull all the stops out○; **c'est pas de** or **du ~**○! that's not fair!

jeudi /ʒødi/ ▸ p. 545 *nm* Thursday

(Composés) **~ de l'Ascension** Ascension day; **~ saint** Maundy Thursday

(Idiome) **ça aura lieu la semaine des quatre ~s**○! never in a month of Sundays!

jeun: à jeun /aʒœ̃/ *loc adv* **[1]** (l'estomac vide) [*partir, boire, fumer*] on an empty stomach; **soyez à ~** don't eat or drink anything; **[2]** ○(sans avoir bu d'alcool) sober

jeune /ʒœn/
A *adj* **[1]** (non vieux) gén young; [*industrie*] new; [*allure, coiffure, visage*] youthful; **il est tout ~** he's very young; **elle n'est plus très ~** she's not so young any more; **nos ~s années** our youth; **le ~ âge** youth; **couple ~** young couple; **le ~ marié** the groom; **la ~ mariée** the bride; **[2]** (cadet) [*frère, sœur, fils, fille, génération*] younger; **être moins ~ que qn** to be older than sb; **Pline le Jeune** Pliny the Younger; **[3]** (nouveau dans son état) **les ~s mariés** the newlyweds
B *nmf* young person; **un ~** a young man; **les ~s** young people
C *adv* **s'habiller ~** to wear young styles; **faire ~** [*personne*] to look young

(Composés) **~ femme** young woman; **~ fille** girl; **~ homme** young man; **~ loup** up-and-coming executive; **~ premier** Cin, Théât romantic lead

jeûne /ʒøn/ *nm* **[1]** (privation) fasting; **observer le ~** to fast; **jour de ~** fast day; **[2]** (période) period of fasting

jeûner /ʒøne/ **[1]** *vi* to fast

jeunesse /ʒœnɛs/ *nf* **[1]** (période) youth; **la première** or **prime ~** early youth; **une seconde ~** a new lease of life; **il n'a pas eu de ~** he didn't have a proper youth; **mon amour de ~** my first love; **une erreur de ~** a youthful indiscretion; **il n'est plus de la première ~** hum he's no longer in the first flush of youth hum; **[2]** (état) youth; **quand on a la ~** when you are young; **[3]** (les jeunes) young people (*pl*); **la ~ étudiante** students (*pl*)

(Idiomes) **il faut que ~ se passe** youth will have its course; **les voyages forment la ~** travel broadens the mind

jeunet○, **-ette** /ʒœnɛ, ɛt/
A *adj* young
B *nm,f* (garçon) young lad; (fille) young girl

jf *written abbr* = **jeune femme** or **fille**

jh *written abbr* = **jeune homme**

JO /ʒio/
A *nm: abbr* ▸ **journal**
B *nmpl: abbr* ▸ **jeu**

joaillerie /ʒɔajri/ *nf* **[1]** ▸ p. 372 (magasin) jeweller's shop GB, jewelry store US; **[2]** (articles) jewellery GB, jewelry US

joaillier, -ière /ʒɔalje, ɛʀ/ ▸ p. 372 *nm,f* jeweller

Joconde /ʒɔkɔ̃d/ *npr* **la ~** the Mona Lisa

joggeur, -euse /dʒɔgœʀ, øz/ *nm,f* jogger

joie /ʒwa/ *nf* **[1]** (bonheur) joy; **être au comble de la ~** to be overjoyed; **~ sans mélange** or **sans partage** pure joy; **faire la ~ de qn** to make sb happy; **cette enfant fait la ~ de ses parents** the child is her parents' pride and joy; **il y a eu des explosions de ~ dans toute la ville** the whole town erupted with joy; **quelle ~!** iron wonderful! iron; **être ivre de ~** to be drunk with happiness *ou* delight; **pleurer de ~** to cry for joy; **[2]** (plaisir) pleasure; **avoir la ~ de faire** to have the pleasure of doing; **se faire une ~ de faire** (envisager avec plaisir) to look forward to doing; (faire avec plaisir) to be delighted to do; **leurs seules ~s** their only pleasures; ▸ **faux¹**

(Idiome) **s'en donner à cœur ~** lit to enjoy oneself to the full; fig to have a field day

joignable /ʒwaɲabl/ *adj* **il n'est pas ~ en ce moment** he's not available at the moment

joindre /ʒwɛ̃dʀ/ **[56]**
A *vtr* **[1]** (communiquer avec) to get hold of [*personne*]; **~ qn au téléphone** to get sb on the phone; **[2]** (ajouter) (dans une lettre, un paquet) to enclose [*timbre, chèque*] (**à** with); (en agrafant, fixant) to attach (**à** to); (par courrier électronique) to attach [*fichier*] (**à** to); **~ sa voix au concert de protestations** to add one's voice to the chorus of protest; **[3]** (relier) [*rue, pont, passage*] **~ qch à qch** to link sth with sth; **[4]** (mettre ensemble) to put [sth] together [*planches, tôles*]; **~ les pieds** to put one's feet together
B *se joindre vpr* **[1]** (se mêler) **se ~ à** to join [*personne, groupe*]; to join with [*parti*]; to mix with [*sentiment, émotion*]; **toute la famille se joint à moi pour vous souhaiter une bonne année** all the family join me in wishing you a happy New Year; **se ~ à la conversation** to join in the conversation; **[2]** (s'unir) [*lèvres*] to meet; [*mains*] to join

(Idiome) **~ les deux bouts**○ to make ends meet

joint /ʒwɛ̃/ *nm* Tech (de planches, fenêtres) joint; (de robinet) washer; (de tuyauterie) seal; (de carrelage, briques) joint

(Composés) **~ de cardan** cardan joint; **~ de culasse** cylinder head gasket; **~ de dilatation** expansion joint; **~ d'étanchéité** seal

jointoyer /ʒwɛ̃twaje/ **[23]** *vtr* Constr to point

jointure /ʒwɛ̃tyʀ/ *nf* Anat, Tech joint

jojo○ /ʒoʒo/
A *adj inv* **il n'est pas ~ ton chapeau** your hat isn't very nice; **ce n'est pas ~ ce qu'ils lui ont fait** (moralement) what they did to him/her wasn't very nice; (physiquement) they made a mess of him/her○
B *nm* **un affreux ~** (enfant) a horrible brat○; (drôle d'individu) a weirdo○

joli, -e /ʒɔli/
A *adj* [*personne, visage, fleur*] pretty; [*animal, objet, lieu, vêtement, visage, yeux*] nice, lovely; [*somme, bénéfice*] nice; [*situation*] good; [*coup de publicité, résultat, but*] great○; **faire ~** to look nice, to look good; **ce n'est pas ~ (de faire)** it's not nice (to do); **ce n'était pas ~ à voir** it wasn't a pretty sight; **c'est ~ de dire du mal de ses parents** iron that's a fine thing, saying nasty things about one's parents iron
B *nm* **le plus ~ c'est que** the funniest thing is (that); **c'est du ~!** iron very nice! iron

(Composé) **~ cœur** smooth talker; **faire le ~ cœur** to play Romeo

(Idiome) **être ~ à croquer** or **comme un cœur** to be as pretty as a picture

joliment /ʒɔlimɑ̃/ *adv* **[1]** (agréablement) [*meublé, illustré, décoré*] prettily, nicely; [*dire*] nicely; **comme l'a ~ dit Sue** as Sue put it so neatly; **[2]** ○(remarquablement) [*content, bien*] really; [*manœuvrer*] nicely; **il s'est fait ~ recevoir** iron he got a fine reception iron

jonc /ʒɔ̃/ *nm* Bot rush

joncher /ʒɔ̃ʃe/ **[1]** *vtr* to be strewn over [*sol*]; **être jonché de** to be strewn with

jonction /ʒɔ̃ksjɔ̃/ *nf* **[1]** (point de rencontre) junction; **[2]** (rencontre) link-up; **établir** or **réaliser la ~ entre A et B** to link up A and B; **opérer une ~** [*armée, manifestants*] to link up; **point de ~** meeting point

jongler /ʒɔ̃gle/ **[1]** *vi* to juggle (**avec** with); **~ avec les chiffres/horaires** fig to juggle figures/timetables

jongleur, -euse /ʒɔ̃glœʀ, øz/ ▸ p. 372 *nm,f* juggler

jonque /ʒɔ̃k/ *nf* junk

jonquille /ʒɔ̃kij/
A ▸ p. 140 *adj inv* (couleur) daffodil yellow
B *nf* Bot daffodil

jouable /ʒwabl/ *adj* **[1]** (faisable) feasible; **le pari est ~** the gamble might pay off; **[2]** (qu'on peut jouer) [*musique*] playable; **une pièce qui n'est pas ~** a play that's impossible to stage

joue /ʒu/ *nf* **[1]** Anat cheek; **~ contre ~** cheek to cheek; **avoir de bonnes ~s** to have plump cheeks; **[2]** Mil **en ~!** aim!; **mettre qn en ~** to take aim at sb; **tenir qn en ~** to train one's gun on sb

jouer /ʒwe/
A *vtr* **[1]** Jeux, Sport to play [*match, jeu, carte*]; to back [*cheval, favori*]; to stake [*argent*]; to risk [*réputation, vie*]; **c'est joué d'avance** it's a foregone conclusion; **tout n'est pas encore joué** the game isn't over yet; **~ le tout pour le tout** to go for broke○; **[2]** Mus to play [*morceau, compositeur, disque*]; **[3]** Cin, Théât [*personne*] to perform [*pièce*]; [*personne*] to act

[*Shakespeare*]; [*personne*] to play [*rôle*]; [*cinéma*] to show [*film*]; [*théâtre*] to put on [*pièce*]; **∼ Figaro** to play Figaro; **∼ une pièce** to stage a play; **quel film joue-t-on au Rex?** what film is showing at the Rex?; **④** (incarner) **∼ les imbéciles** to play dumb; **∼ la surprise** to pretend to be surprised; **∼ les héros** to take unnecessary risks

B jouer à *vtr ind* **∼ à** to play [*tennis, échecs, roulette*]; to play with [*poupée*]; to play [*cowboy, Tarzan*]; **à quoi jouez-vous?** lit what are you playing?; fig what are you playing at?; **∼ à qui perd gagne** to play 'loser takes all'; **∼ à la marchande/au docteur** to play shops/doctors and nurses

C jouer de *vtr ind* **①** Mus **∼ de** to play [*instrument*]; **∼ du violon** to play the violin; **②** (se servir de) **∼ de** to use [*influence*] (**pour faire** to do)

D *vi* **①** (s'amuser) [*enfant, animal*] to play (**avec** with); **allez ∼ dehors!** go and play outside!; **arrête de ∼ avec ta bague!** stop fiddling with your ring!; **c'était pour ∼, ne le prenez pas mal!** I/he etc was only joking, don't be offended!; **②** (pratiquer un jeu) to play; (avec de l'argent) to gamble; **∼ pour de l'argent** to play for money; **à toi de ∼!** (au jeu) your turn!; fig the ball's in your court!; **bien joué!** (au jeu) well played!; fig well done!; **j'en ai assez, je ne joue plus!** I've had enough, count me out!; **③** (traiter à la légère) **∼ avec** to gamble with [*vie, santé*]; to put [sth] on the line [*réputation*]; to play with [*sentiments*]; **④** (spéculer) to gamble; **∼ en Bourse** to gamble on the stock exchange; **∼ aux courses** to bet on the horses; **∼ sur** to play on [*crédulité, lassitude*]; to speculate in [*valeur boursière*]; **⑤** Cin, Mus, Théât [*acteur*] to act; [*musicien, radio*] to play; **⑥** (produire des effets) [*lumière, flammes, vent*] to play (**sur** on; **dans** in); **⑦** (intervenir) [*argument, clause*] to apply; [*âge, qualification*] to matter; **les questions d'argent ne jouent pas entre eux** money is not a problem in their relationship; **∼ en faveur de qn** to work in sb's favour^GB; **∼ comme un déclic** to serve as the trigger; **faire ∼ la clé dans la serrure** to jiggle the key in the lock; **faire ∼ ses relations** to make use of one's connections; **⑧** (être mal ajusté) to be loose; **le contrevent a joué** the shutter has worked loose

E se jouer *vpr* **①** Cin, Mus, Théât [*musique*] to be played; [*film*] to be shown; [*pièce*] to be performed; **②** Jeux, Sport [*jeu, sport*] to be played; [*partie, rencontre*] (amicalement) to be played; (avec enjeu) to be played out; **③** (être en jeu) [*avenir, sort, paix*] to be at stake; **c'est l'avenir du pays qui se joue** the future of the country is at stake; **le sort des réfugiés va se ∼ à la conférence sur la paix** the fate of the refugees hangs on the peace conference; **④** (triompher de) **se ∼ de** to make light of [*difficulté*]; to defy [*pesanteur, gravité*]; to make light work of [*obstacle*]

jouet /ʒwɛ/ *nm* **①** (objet pour enfant) toy; **②** (victime) plaything; **être le ∼ d'une hallucination** to be in the grip of an hallucination; **être le ∼ des vagues** to be at the mercy of the waves

joueur, -euse /ʒwœR, øz/
A *adj* **①** (qui aime s'amuser) playful; **②** (qui risque de l'argent) **être ∼/joueuse** to be a gambling man/woman
B ▸ p. 372 *nm,f* **①** Mus, Jeux, Sport player; **une joueuse de tennis** a woman tennis player; **un ∼ de mandoline** a mandolin player; **un ∼ de cornemuse** a piper; **être beau/mauvais ∼** to be a good/bad loser; **②** (personne qui joue de l'argent) gambler

joufflu, ∼e /ʒufly/ *adj* [*personne*] chubby-cheeked; [*visage*] chubby

joug /ʒu/ *nm* **①** Agric yoke; **②** (sujétion) yoke; **③** (de balance) beam

jouir /ʒwiR/ [3]
A jouir de *vtr ind* (bénéficier) **∼ de** [*personne*] to enjoy [*soutien, avantage*]; to enjoy the use of [*bien*]; [*lieu*] to have [*climat, vue*]; **∼ de toutes ses facultés** to have the use of all one's faculties
B *vi* (sexuellement) to have an orgasm

jouissance /ʒwisɑ̃s/ *nf* **①** Jur (usage) use; **avoir la ∼ de qch** to have the use of sth; **②** (plaisir) pleasure; **③** (orgasme) orgasm

jouisseur, -euse /ʒwisœR, øz/ *nm,f* hedonist

joujou, *pl* **∼x** /ʒuʒu/ *nm* baby talk toy; **faire ∼** to play (**avec** with)

jour /ʒuR/ **▸** p. 582 *nm* **①** (période de vingt-quatre heures) day; **en un ∼** in one day; **dans les trois ∼s** within three days; **ces derniers ∼s** these last few days; **d'un ∼** [*bonheur, espoir*] fleeting; [*mode*] passing; [*reine*] for a day; **des ∼s et des ∼s** for ever and ever; **dès le premier ∼** right from the start;

∼ après ∼ (quotidiennement) day after day; (progressivement) little by little; **vivre au ∼ le ∼** to live one day at a time; **▸ ressembler, Rome**; **②** (date) day; **ce ∼-là** that day; **quel ∼ sommes-nous?** what day is it today?; **un ∼ ou l'autre** some day; **tous les ∼s** every day; **∼ pour ∼** to the day; **de ∼ en ∼** from day to day; **à ce ∼** to date; **à ∼** up to date; **mettre à ∼** (actualiser) to bring up to date [*courrier, travail*]; to revise [*édition*]; (révéler) to expose, to reveal [*mystère, secret, trafic, problème*]; **mise à ∼** (actualisation) (d'édition, de données, statistiques) updating (**de** of); (découverte) (de secret, trafic) revelation (**de** of); **édition mise à ∼** revised edition; **tenir à ∼** to keep up to date; **jusqu'à ce ∼** (maintenant) until now; (alors) until then; **de nos ∼s** nowadays; **d'un ∼ à l'autre** [*être attendu*] any day now; [*changer*] from one day to the next; **du ∼ au lendemain** overnight; **nouvelle/mode du ∼** latest news/fashion; **③** (du lever au coucher du soleil) day; **les ∼s raccourcissent** the days are getting shorter; **pendant le ∼** during the day; **nuit et ∼** night and day; **le ∼ se lève** it's getting light; **lumière du ∼** daylight; **au lever** or **point du ∼** at daybreak; **le petit ∼** the early morning; **se lever avec le ∼** to get up at the crack of dawn; **travailler de ∼** to work days; **④** (clarté) daylight; **il fait ∼** it's daylight; **en plein ∼** in broad daylight; **faire qch au grand ∼** to do sth for all to see; **se faire ∼** [*vérité*] to come to light; **mettre au ∼** to unearth [*vestige*]; to bring [sth] to light [*vérité*]; **jeter un ∼ nouveau sur qch, éclairer qch d'un ∼ nouveau** to shed new light on sth; **▸ faux^1**; **⑤** (aspect) **sous ton meilleur/pire ∼** at your best/worst; **je ne te connaissais pas sous ce ∼** I knew nothing of that side of you; **je t'ai vu sous ton vrai ∼** I saw you in your true colours^GB; **sous un ∼ avantageux** in a favourable^GB light; **⑥** fig **donner le ∼ à qn** to bring sb into the world; **voir le ∼** [*personne*] to come into the world; [*œuvre, projet*] to see the light of day; [*organisme*] to come into being; **mes ∼s sont comptés** my days are numbered; **finir ses ∼s à la campagne** to end one's days in the country; **des ∼s difficiles** hard times; **attenter à ses ∼s** to make a suicide attempt; **avoir encore de beaux ∼s devant soi** still to have a future; **les beaux ∼s reviennent** spring will soon be here; **⑦** Constr (ouverture) gap; **∼ entre les tuiles** gap between tiles; **⑧** (de broderie) **∼s** openwork (embroidery) **Ⓒ**

Composés **∼ de l'An** New Year's Day; **∼ de deuil national** national day of mourning; **∼ férié** bank holiday GB, legal holiday US; **∼ de fermeture** closing day; **∼ des morts** Relig All Souls' Day; **∼ ouvrable** working day

Idiomes **Rome ne s'est pas faite en un ∼** Rome wasn't built in a day; **beau comme le ∼** very good-looking; **être dans un bon ∼** to be in a good mood; **être dans un mauvais ∼** to be having an off day; **il y a des ∼s avec et des ∼s sans^○** there are good days and bad days

journal, *pl* **-aux** /ʒuRnal, o/ *nm* **①** (quotidien) newspaper, paper; (revue) magazine; (bureaux) newspaper office; **②** Radio, TV news bulletin, news **Ⓒ**; **③** Littérat journal

Composés **∼ de bord** logbook; **∼ intime** diary; **Journal officiel, JO** government publication listing new acts, laws etc

journalier, -ière /ʒuRnalje, ɛR/
A *adj* [*taux, variation*] daily
B *nm* day labourer^GB

journalisme /ʒuRnalism/ *nm* journalism

journaliste /ʒuRnalist/ **▸** p. 372 *nmf* journalist

journalistique /ʒuRnalistik/ *adj* journalistic; **style ∼** journalese

journée /ʒuRne/ **▸** p. 582 *nf* day; **∼ de repos** day off; **dans la ∼** during the day; **à longueur de ∼** all day long; **la ∼ d'hier** yesterday; **la ∼ de mardi** Tuesday; **faire des ∼s de huit heures** to work an eight-hour day; **j'ai gagné ma ∼!** iron I may as well pack up and go home!

Composés **∼ continue** Entr continuous working day; **faire la ∼ continue** to work with a short lunch break; **∼ d'études** conference; **∼ d'information** awareness day; **∼ du patrimoine** national heritage open day; **∼ portes ouvertes** open day GB, open house US

journellement /ʒuRnɛlmɑ̃/ *adv* (fréquemment) all the time

joute /ʒut/ *nf* **①** (duel) fig jousting **Ⓒ**, battle; **∼ oratoire** or **verbale** sparring match; **②** Sport, Hist joust

jouter /ʒute/ [1] *vi* (à cheval) to joust (**contre** against, with); (sur des barques) to joust (*in water tournament*)

jouvence /ʒuvɑ̃s/ *nf* **fontaine de ∼** Fountain of Youth

jouxter /ʒukste/ [1] *vtr* to adjoin [*bâtiment, terrain*]

jovial, ∼**e**, *mpl* ∼**s** *ou* **-iaux** /ʒɔvjal, o/ *adj* jovial

jovialité /ʒɔvjalite/ *nf* joviality

joyau, *pl* ∼**x** /ʒwajo/ *nm* lit, fig jewel, gem

joyeusement /ʒwajøzmɑ̃/ *adv* [1] [*gambader*] merrily; [*saluer*] cheerfully; [2] iron happily

joyeux, -euse /ʒwajø, øz/ *adj* [*musique*] cheerful; **c'est ∼!** iron that's great! iron

jubilation /ʒybilasjɔ̃/ *nf* joy, jubilation

jubilé /ʒybile/ *nm* jubilee

jubiler /ʒybile/ [1] *vi* to be jubilant, to rejoice (**de faire** to do); (avec arrogance) to gloat

jucher /ʒyʃe/ [1]
A *vtr* to perch (**sur** on)
B **se jucher** *vpr* **se ∼ sur** to perch on

judaïsme /ʒydaism/ *nm* Judaism

judas /ʒyda/ *nm inv* (dans une porte) peephole

Judée /ʒyde/ ▸ p. 504 *nprf* Judaea; **arbre de ∼** Judas tree

judiciaire /ʒydisjɛʀ/ *adj* [*acte, institution, erreur*] judicial

judicieux, -ieuse /ʒydisjø, øz/ *adj* [*conseil, idée, choix*] sound; [*utilisation, critique*] judicious; **il semblerait ∼ de faire** it would seem wise to do

judo /ʒydo/ ▸ p. 327 *nm* judo

juge /ʒyʒ/ *nm* [1] ▸ p. 372, p. 590 Jur judge; **elle est ∼** she is a judge; **le ∼ Morin** gén Judge Morin; (des juridictions supérieures) Mr *ou* Mrs Justice Morin; **oui, Monsieur le ∼** yes, Your Honour^{GB}; **comparaître devant le ∼** to appear before the court; [2] (de jeu, concours) judge; [3] (personne compétente) judge; **tu es seul ∼** only you can tell

<u>Composés</u> ∼ **d'instruction** examining magistrate; ∼ **de touche** Sport linesman

jugé: au jugé /oʒyʒe/ *loc adv* [*évaluer*] by guesswork; **avancer au ∼** to follow one's nose

jugement /ʒyʒmɑ̃/ *nm* [1] (opinion) judgment; ∼ **de valeur** value judgment; [2] (aptitude) judgment; **n'avoir aucun ∼** to lack judgment; [3] Jur (décision) (pour un crime) verdict; (pour un délit) judgment, decision; **passer en ∼** [*affaire*] to come to court

jugeote[○] /ʒyʒɔt/ *nf* common sense

juger /ʒyʒe/ [13]
A *vtr* [1] (former une opinion sur) to judge; **ce n'est pas à moi de ∼** how should I know?; [2] (considérer) to consider; **ne le juge pas mal** don't think badly of him; **je t'avais mal jugé** I misjudged you; [3] Jur (examiner) to try [*affaire, personne*]; (décider) to judge [*affaire*]; to arbitrate in [*différend, litige*]; **l'affaire sera jugée demain** the case will be heard *ou* tried tomorrow; **l'affaire est jugée** the case is closed; **le tribunal jugera** the court will decide; [4] (pour un concours) to judge [*candidats, films*]
B **juger de** *vtr ind* [1] (évaluer) ∼ **de** to assess [*niveau, valeur, capacité*]; **j'en jugerai par moi-même** I'll judge for myself; **à en ∼ par tes réponses** judging by *ou* from your answers; [2] (imaginer) **jugez de ma colère** imagine my anger
C **se juger** *vpr* [1] (se considérer) to consider oneself; [2] Jur [*affaire*] to be heard

juguler /ʒygyle/ [1] *vtr* to stamp out [*épidémie, chômage, fléau*]; to check [*hémorragie*]; to curb [*inflation*]

juif, juive /ʒɥif, ʒɥiv/
A *adj* [*religion, communauté*] Jewish
B *nm,f* (personne) Jew

juillet /ʒɥijɛ/ ▸ p. 380 *nm* July; **le 14 ∼** the Fourteenth of July, Bastille Day

juin /ʒɥɛ̃/ ▸ p. 380 *nm* June

juive ▸ **juif**

jumeau, -elle¹, *mpl* ∼**x** /ʒymo, ɛl/
A *adj* [1] [*frère, sœur*] twin; [*fruits*] double; [2] [*lits*] twin; [3] [*ville*] twin
B *nm,f* (personne) twin

jumelage /ʒymlaʒ/ *nm* (de communes, clubs) twinning

jumelé, ∼**e** /ʒymle/ *adj* [*billet*] double; [*fenêtres, colonnes*] twin

jumeler /ʒymle/ [19] *vtr* to twin [*communes, clubs*] (**à** with); to combine [*événements*]

jumelle² /ʒymɛl/ *nf* binoculars (*pl*); **une paire de ∼s, des ∼s** (a pair of) binoculars; **à la ∼** through binoculars

<u>Composé</u> ∼**s de théâtre** opera glasses

jument /ʒymɑ̃/ *nf* mare

jumping /dʒœmpiŋ/ *nm* showjumping

jungle /ʒœ̃gl/ *nf* jungle

junior /ʒynjɔʀ/ *adj inv, nmf* Sport junior

junte /ʒœ̃t/ *nf* junta

jupe /ʒyp/ *nf* [1] (vêtement) skirt; ∼ **plissée** pleated skirt; [2] Tech skirt

<u>Idiome</u> **il est toujours dans les ∼s de sa mère** he's tied to his mother's apron strings

jupe-culotte, *pl* **jupes-culottes** /ʒypkylɔt/ *nf* culottes (*pl*)

jupette /ʒypɛt/ *nf* short skirt; ∼ **de tennis** tennis skirt

jupon /ʒypɔ̃/ *nm* petticoat

<u>Idiome</u> **courir le ∼** to womanize

jurassien, -ienne /ʒyʀasjɛ̃, ɛn/ *adj* of the Jura (Mountains)

jurassique /ʒyʀasik/ *adj, nm* Jurassic

juré, ∼e /ʒyʀe/
A *pp* ▸ **jurer**
B *pp adj* [1] (assermenté) [*expert*] on oath (après *n*); [*traducteur*] sworn-in (épith); [2] (éternel) [*fidélité, ennemi*] sworn
C *nm* [1] Jur juror; [2] Art, Sport judge

jurer /ʒyʀe/ [1]
A *vtr* to swear (**de faire** to do); **jure-moi de ne rien dire** swear you won't say anything; **on leur a fait ∼ le secret** they were sworn to secrecy; **jure-le!** swear!; **on jurerait (que c'est) de la soie** you'd swear it was silk; ∼ **de tuer qn** (à soi-même) to vow to kill sb; **ah mais je te jure**[○]**!** (indignation) honestly[○]!
B **jurer de** *vtr ind* to swear to; **j'en jurerais** I would swear to it
C *vi* [1] (dire des jurons) to swear (**après, contre** at); [2] (détonner) [*couleurs*] to clash (**avec** with); [*détail, construction*] to look out of place (**avec** in); [3] (être partisan de) **ne ∼ que par** to swear by
D **se jurer** *vpr* [1] (l'un l'autre) to swear [sth] to one another [*fidélité*]; [2] (à soi-même) to vow

<u>Idiome</u> **il ne faut ∼ de rien** Prov never say never

juridiction /ʒyʀidiksjɔ̃/ *nf* [1] (pouvoir) jurisdiction; **sous ma ∼** within my jurisdiction; [2] (tribunaux) courts (*pl*); ∼ **civile** civil courts (*pl*); ∼ **administrative** administrative tribunals (*pl*)

juridique /ʒyʀidik/ *adj* [*statut, langue, formation*] legal; **agir sur le plan ∼** to take legal action; **vide ∼** gap in the law

juridiquement /ʒyʀidikmɑ̃/ *adv* legally

jurisprudence /ʒyʀispʀydɑ̃s/ *nf* case law; **faire ∼** to set a legal precedent

juriste /ʒyʀist/ *nmf* [1] (qui étudie le droit) jurist; [2] (qui pratique le droit) lawyer

juron /ʒyʀɔ̃/ *nm* swearword

jury /ʒyʀi/ *nm* [1] Jur jury; **président du ∼** foreman of the jury; [2] Art, Sport panel of judges; [3] Univ board of examiners

jus /ʒy/ *nm inv* [1] (de fruit) juice; ∼ **de pomme** apple juice; [2] (de viande) (qui exsude) juices (*pl*); (sauce servie) gravy; **cuire qch au ∼** to cook sth in the juices from the meat; **laisser qn mijoter dans son ∼**[○] fig to let sb stew in his own juice; [3] [○](café) coffee; [4] [○](courant électrique) juice[○], electricity; **il n'y a plus de ∼** the power's off; **prendre le ∼** to get a shock

jusqu'au-boutiste, *pl* ∼**s** /ʒyskobutist/ *nmf* gén hardliner; péj extremist

jusque (jusqu' *before vowel*) /ʒysk/
A *prép* [1] (dans l'espace) **aller jusqu'à Paris/jusqu'en Amérique** (insistant sur la destination atteinte) to go as far as Paris/America; (insistant sur la distance parcourue) to go all the way to Paris/America; **courir jusqu'au bout du jardin** to run right down to the bottom of the garden GB *ou* the end of the yard US; **suivre qn ∼ dans sa chambre** to follow sb right into his/her room; **la nouvelle n'était pas officiellement arrivée jusqu'à nous** the news hadn't reached us officially; **ils l'ont suivi ∼ chez lui** they followed him all the way home *ou* right up to his front door; **descendre jusqu'à 100 mètres de profondeur** to go down to a depth of 100 metres^{GB}; **jusqu'où comptez-vous aller?** lit, fig how far do you intend to go?; [2] (dans le temps) until, till; **je t'ai attendu jusqu'à huit heures** I waited for you until *ou* till eight o'clock; **jusqu'alors** until then; **jusqu'à présent** *or* **maintenant, jusqu'ici** (up) until now; **jusqu'à quand**

restes-tu à Oxford? how long are you staying in Oxford?; ③ (limite supérieure) up to; (limite inférieure) down to; **il peut soulever jusqu'à dix kilos** he can lift up to ten kilos; **avoir de l'eau jusqu'aux chevilles** to be up to one's ankles in water; **je le suivrai jusqu'au bout** fig I'll follow him all the way; ④ (avec une notion d'exagération) to the point of; **aller jusqu'à faire** to go so far as to do; ⑤ (y compris) even; **des détritus ~ sous la table** rubbish everywhere, even under the table; **ils sont venus, jusqu'au dernier** every last one of them came

B jusqu'à ce que loc conj until; **jusqu'à ce qu'il s'endorme** until he is asleep

jusque-là /ʒyskəla/ adv ① (dans le temps) until then, up to then; **~ je ne peux rien dire** until then ou in the meantime I have nothing to say; ② (dans l'espace) up to here; (plus loin) up to there; **on avait de l'eau ~** (aux genoux etc) the water was up to here; **l'eau est montée ~** (en pointant vers un objet) the water came up to there

(Idiomes) **en avoir ~ de qch/qn**○ to have had it up to here with sth/sb○; **en avoir ~ de faire**○ to be sick and tired of doing○; **s'en mettre ~**○ to stuff one's face○

jusques liter = jusque

jusquiame /ʒyskjam/ nf henbane

justaucorps /ʒystokɔr/ nm inv ① (pour la danse) leotard; ② (sous-vêtement) body stocking; ③ Hist doublet

juste /ʒyst/
A adj ① (impartial) [personne] fair; ② (équitable) [règlement, partage] fair; [récompense, sanction, cause] just; **ce n'est pas ~!** it's not fair!; **~ retour des choses, il a été renvoyé** it was poetic justice that he got expelled; **trouver un ~ milieu** to find a happy medium; **~ ciel!** good heavens!; ③ (légitime) [colère, certitude] righteous (épith); [revendication] legitimate; [crainte] justifiable; [raisonnement, remarque, comparaison] valid; **à ~ raison** or **titre** with good reason; **dire des choses ~s** to make some valid points; ④ (adéquat) right; **trouver le mot ~** to find the right word; **comme de ~**○ il **était en retard** of course , he was late; ⑤ (exact) [calcul, proportion, heure, analyse] correct; **avoir l'heure ~** to have the correct time; **le ~ prix des choses** fig the true value of things; **apprécier qn à sa ~ valeur** to get a fair picture of sb; ⑥ (précis) [instrument de mesure] accurate; ⑦ Mus [piano, voix] in tune (jamais épith); [note] true; **ton piano n'est pas ~** your piano is out of tune; ⑧ (trop ajusté) [vêtement, chaussure] tight; **un peu ~** a bit tight; ⑨ (à la limite) **un poulet pour six c'est un peu ~** one chicken for six people is stretching it a bit; **une heure pour y aller c'est un peu ~** one hour to get there is cutting it a bit fine; **nous sommes un peu ~s**○ **en ce moment** money is a bit tight○ at the moment

B adv ① (sans erreur) [chanter] in tune; [sonner] true; [deviner] right; **elle a vu ~** she was right; **viser ~** lit to aim straight; fig to hit the nail on the head; ② (précisément) just; **~ à temps** just in time; ③ (seulement) just; **~ un** just one; ④ (depuis peu) (tout) **~** only just; **j'arrive ~** I've only just arrived; ⑤ (à peine) hardly; **c'est tout ~ s'il sait lire** he can hardly read; **j'ai réussi à éviter le bus mais ça a été ~**○ I managed to avoid the bus but it was a close shave○

C au juste loc adv exactly; **que s'est-il passé au ~?** what happened exactly?

D nm righteous man; **les ~s** the righteous

justement /ʒystəmɑ̃/ adv ① (précisément) precisely; **c'est ~ ce qu'il ne fallait pas dire** that's precisely what one shouldn't have said; ② (à l'instant) just; **je parlais ~ de toi** I was just talking about you; ③ (avec justesse) [dire, répondre]

correctly; **comme l'a fort ~ souligné Nina** as Nina so correctly pointed out; ④ (légitimement) [se flatter, s'inquiéter] justifiably

justesse /ʒystɛs/
A nf ① (pertinence) **être convaincu de la ~ d'une décision** to be sure that a decision is correct; **avec ~** [souligner, remarquer] correctly; ② (précision) accuracy; **avec ~** [analyser, prévoir, mesurer] accurately

B de justesse loc adv only just; **on a évité la catastrophe de ~** we only just avoided disaster; **s'en sortir de ~** to have a narrow escape

justice /ʒystis/ nf ① (principe) justice; (équité) fairness; **en toute ~** in all fairness; **ce n'est que ~** it is only fair; ② (application) justice; **rendre la ~** to dispense justice; **il faut leur rendre** or **faire cette ~ qu'ils sont...** one has to acknowledge that they are...; **se faire ~ (à soi-même)** (se venger) to take the law into one's own hands; (se suicider) to take one's own life; ③ (pouvoir) **la ~** (lois) the law; (institution) the legal system; (tribunaux) the courts (pl); **être livré à la ~** to be handed over to the law; **aller en ~** to go to court; **poursuivre qn en ~** to take sb to court; **être traduit en ~** to be brought before the courts; **action en ~** legal action

(Composé) **~ militaire** military law

justicier, -ière /ʒystisje, ɛR/ nm,f righter of wrongs

justificatif, -ive /ʒystifikatif, iv/
A adj [facture, document] supporting; **pièce justificative** documentary evidence ¢
B nm documentary evidence ¢; **~ de domicile** proof of domicile; **~ de frais** receipt

justification /ʒystifikasjɔ̃/ nf ① (action) justification; ② (preuve) (orale) explanation; (écrite) documentary evidence; ③ (en imprimerie) justification

justifié, -e /ʒystifje/
A pp ▸ justifier
B pp adj ① (légitime) [inquiétude, choix] justified; **non ~** unjustified; ② (expliqué) justified

justifier /ʒystifje/ [2]
A vtr ① (rendre acceptable) to justify [méthode, politique, thèse, décision] (par by); ② (confirmer après coup) to vindicate; **les faits ont justifié nos craintes** events proved our fears to have been justified; ③ (excuser) to vindicate [coupable]; to justify [comportement, retard, absence]; to explain [ignorance]; **tu essaies toujours de la ~** you are always making excuses for her
B justifier de vtr ind to give proof of [domicile, identité]; to have [expérience, connaissance]
C se justifier vpr ① (se disculper) (devant un tribunal) to clear oneself; (devant une personne) to make excuses; ② (être explicable) to be justified (par by); **ta décision peut se ~** there are good reasons for your decision

jute /ʒyt/ nm ① (fibre) jute; **toile de ~** hessian; ② (tissu) hessian

juteux, -euse /ʒytø, øz/ adj ① [fruit] juicy; ② ○[affaire, projet] profitable, juicy○

juvénile /ʒyvenil/ adj [sourire, caractère] youthful; [délinquance, mortalité] juvenile; [public] young; [assemblée] of young people (épith, après n)

juxtaposer /ʒykstapoze/ [1] vtr to juxtapose [termes, idées]

juxtaposition /ʒykstapozisjɔ̃/ nf (de termes, d'idées) juxtaposition

Kk

k, K /ka/ *nm inv* k, K

kabbale /kabal/ *nf* cabala

kafkaïen, -ïenne /kafkajɛ̃, ɛn/ *adj* ① [*ambiance*] Kafkaesque; ② [*études*] Kafka (*épith*)

kakatoès /kakatɔɛs/ *nm inv* cockatoo

kaki /kaki/
Ⓐ ▸ p. 140 *adj inv* khaki
Ⓑ *nm* ① (fruit) persimmon; ② (couleur) khaki

kaléidoscope /kaleidɔskɔp/ *nm* kaleidoscope

kanak = canaque

kangourou /kɑ̃guru/
Ⓐ *adj inv* **poche** ~ front pocket; **slip** ~ pouch-front briefs (*pl*)
Ⓑ *nm* ① Zool kangaroo; ② ®(sac pour bébé) baby carrier

kaput○ /kaput/ *adj inv* [*personne*] dog-tired○; [*objet, machine*] kaput○

karaoké /karaɔke/ *nm* karaoke

karaté /karate/ ▸ p. 327 *nm* karate

karcher® /karʃɛr/ *nm* pressurized water gun

karité /karite/ *nm* shea; **beurre de** ~ shea butter

kart /kart/ *nm* go-kart

karting /kartiŋ/ ▸ p. 327 *nm* go-karting; **faire du** ~ to go karting

kasher /kaʃɛr/ *adj inv* kosher

kayak /kajak/ ▸ p. 327 *nm* kayak; **faire du** ~ to go canoeing

kazakh, ~e /kazak/
Ⓐ ▸ p. 392 *adj* Kazak
Ⓑ ▸ p. 336 *nm* Kazak

kényan, ~e /kenjɑ̃, an/ ▸ p. 392 *adj* Kenyan

képi /kepi/ *nm* kepi

kératine /keratin/ *nf* keratin

kermesse /kɛrmɛs/ *nf* fête GB

kérosène /kerɔzɛn/ *nm* kerosene

ketchup /kɛtʃœp/ *nm* ketchup, catsup US

keuf○ /kœf/ *nm* cop○ ▸ verlan

keum○ /kœm/ *nm* guy○, bloke○ ▸ verlan

kF *written abbr* = **kilofranc**

kg (*written abbr* = **kilogramme**) kg

khi /ki/ *nm inv* chi

Khmer, -ère /kmɛr/ *nm,f* Khmer; **les** ~**s rouges** Khmer Rouge (+ *v pl*)

kibboutz, *pl* **-tzim** /kibuts, kibutsim/ *nm* kibbutz

kick /kik/ *nm* kick-start

kidnapper /kidnape/ [1] *vtr* to kidnap; **se faire** ~ to be kidnapped GB

kidnappeur, -euse /kidnapœr, øz/ *nm,f* kidnapper GB

kiffer○ /kife/
Ⓐ *vt* to like; **cette fille, il la kiffe grave** that girl really does it for him
Ⓑ *vi* **on a trop kiffé au concert!** the concert was awesome!; **ça le fait** ~ he gets a kick out of it.

kif-kif○ /kifkif/ *adj inv* **c'est** ~ **(bourricot)** it's all the same

kilo¹ /kilo/ *préf* kilo

kilo² /kilo/ ▸ p. 453 *nm* (*abbr* = **kilogramme**) kilo; **prendre des** ~**s** to put on weight

kilofranc /kilɔfrɑ̃/ *nm* Hist 1,000 French francs

kilogramme /kilɔgram/ ▸ p. 453 *nm* kilogram

kilométrage /kilɔmetraʒ/ *nm* ≈ mileage

kilomètre /kilɔmɛtr/ ▸ p. 347, p. 568, p. 624 *nm* kilometreGB; **marcher des** ~**s** to walk for miles

kilomètre-heure *pl* **kilomètres-heure** /kilɔmɛtrœr/ ▸ p. 624 kilometreGB per hour

kilométrique /kilɔmetrik/ *adj* [*distance*] in kilometresGB; [*prix, coût*] per kilometreGB

kilo-octet /kilɔɔktɛ/ *nm* kilobyte

kilotonne /kilɔtɔn/ *nf* kiloton

kilowattheure /kilɔwatœr/ *nm* kilowatt-hour

kimono /kimɔno/ *nm* gén kimono; Sport ≈ judo suit

kinésithérapeute /kineziterapøt/ ▸ p. 372 *nmf* physiotherapist GB, physical therapist US

kinésithérapie /kineziterapi/ *nf* physiotherapy GB, physical therapy US

kinesthésie /kinɛstezi/ *nf* kinesthesia

kiosque /kjɔsk/ *nm* (à journaux) kiosk
(Composé) ~ **à musique** bandstand

kirghiz, ~e /kirgiz/
Ⓐ ▸ p. 392 *adj* Kirghiz
Ⓑ ▸ p. 336 *nm* Kirghiz

kiwi /kiwi/ *nm* ① (fruit) kiwi; ② Zool kiwi

klaxon® /klaksɔn/ *nm* (car) horn

klaxonner /klaksɔne/ [1]
Ⓐ *vtr* to hoot GB, to honk
Ⓑ *vi* to sound one's horn GB, to honk the horn US

kleptomane /klɛptɔman/ *adj, nmf* kleptomaniac

kleptomanie /klɛptɔmani/ *nf* kleptomania

km (*written abbr* = **kilomètre**) km

knock-out /nɔkaut/
Ⓐ *adj inv* [*boxeur*] knocked out (jamais *épith*)
Ⓑ *nm* knockout; **gagner par** ~ to win by a knockout

Ko (*written abbr* = **kilo-octet**) KB

KO /kao/
Ⓐ *adj inv* (*abbr* = **knocked out**) ① Sport KO'd○; **mettre qn** ~ **to KO**○ sb; ② ○(épuisé) exhausted
Ⓑ *nm* (*abbr* = **knockout**) KO○

koala /kɔala/ *nm* koala (bear)

kôhl /kol/ *nm* kohl

kolkhoze /kɔlkoz/ *nm* kolkhoz

kopeck /kɔpɛk/ ▸ p. 34 *nm* kopeck; **ça ne vaut pas un** ~ it's not worth a penny

kosovar /kɔsɔvar/ ▸ p. 392 *adj* Kosovan

Kosovar /kɔsɔvar/ ▸ p. 392 *nmf* Kosovar

Kosovo /kɔsɔvo/ ▸ p. 230 *nprm* Kosovo

kouglof /kuglɔf/ *nm* kugelhopf

koweïtien, -ienne /kɔwetjɛ̃, ɛn/ ▸ p. 392 *adj* Kuwaiti

krach /krak/ *nm* (boursier) crash

kraft /kraft/ *nm* (**papier**) ~ brown paper

kremlinologue /krɛmlinɔlɔg/ *nmf* Kremlinologist

kurde /kyrd/ ▸ p. 336 *adj, nm* Kurdish

Kurde /kyrd/ *nmf* Kurd

kW (*written abbr* = **kilowatt**) kW

K-way® /kawe/ *nm* windcheater GB, windbreaker US

kyrielle /kirjɛl/ *nf* **une** ~ **de** a string of

kyste /kist/ *nm* cyst

l, L /ɛl/ *nm inv* **1** (lettre) l, L; **2** (*written abbr* = **litre**) 20 l
20 l

l' ▸ **le**

la /la/
A *art déf, pron* ▸ **le**
B *nm* Mus (note) A; (en solfiant) lah; **donner le** ~ *lit* to give an A;
fig to set the tone

là /la/

> ⚠ Lorsque *là* est employé par opposition à *ici* il se
> traduit par *(over) there*: ne le mets pas ici, mets-
> le là = don't put it here, put it there; lorsque *là* signifie
> *ici* il se traduit par *(over) here*: viens là = come (over)
> here.
> Lorsque *là* est utilisé avec un sens temporel il se
> traduit par *then*: et là, le téléphone a sonné = and
> then the phone rang.
> Pour les autres emplois voir l'article ci-dessous.
> *celle-là*, *celui-là* etc sont traités séparément à leur
> place dans l'ordre alphabétique.

adv **1** (désignant un lieu) (par opposition à ici) there; (ici) here; **tu
étais** ~ **quand c'est arrivé?** were you there when it happened?; **il n'est pas** ~ **pour l'instant** he's not here at the
moment; ~ **où j'habite** where I live; **par** ~ (par ici) here;
(dans cette direction) this way; (dans cette zone) around there; **de**
~ (de cet endroit) from there; (pour cette raison) hence; **rester**
~ **à ne rien faire** to hang around doing nothing; **2** (à ce
moment) then; **d'ici** ~ between now and then; **il n'en est
pas encore** ~ he hasn't yet reached that stage; **s'il en est
(arrivé)** ~, **c'est que…** if he's reduced to that, it's
because…; **3** (pour renforcer l'énoncé) ~ **d'accord, j'ai eu tort**
OK then, I was wrong; **alors** ~ **tu exagères!** now you're
going too far!; ~, **c'est fini, ne pleure plus** there now, it's
over, don't cry; ~ **c'est différent** that's a different matter;
c'est bien ~ **ce qui me chagrine** that's precisely what's
bothering me; **4** (dans cela, en cela) **je ne vois** ~ **rien
d'anormal** I don't see anything unusual in that; **que me
dites-vous** ~? what are you telling me?; **il veut réussir**
~ **où personne n'a osé se lancer** he wants to succeed
where no-one has dared venture before; **il a fallu en
passer par** ~ there was no alternative; **qu'entendez-vous
par** ~? what do you mean by that?; **5** (à ce point) **je vais
m'en tenir** ~ I'll leave it at that; **nous n'en sommes pas** ~
(près du but) we haven't got that far; (ce n'est pas si
catastrophique) we haven't reached that point yet; **6** (pour
renforcer un adjectif démonstratif) **en ce temps-**~ in those days;
ce jour-~ that day

là-bas /labɑ/ *adv* **1** *gén* over there; **2** (pour renforcer) over;
~ **au Pérou** over in Peru

labeur /labœʀ/ *nm* liter hard work

labo○ /labo/ *nm* lab○

laborantin, **-e** /labɔʀɑ̃tɛ̃, in/ ▸ p. 372 *nm,f* laboratory
assistant

laboratoire /labɔʀatwaʀ/ *nm* laboratory; **de** ~ [*animal,
appareil*] laboratory (*épith*)
(Composés) ~ **d'analyses médicales** medical laboratory; ~ **de langues** language laboratory; ~ **orbital**
skylab; ~ **pharmaceutique** pharmaceutical company

laborieusement /labɔʀjøzmɑ̃/ *adv* laboriously

laborieux, -ieuse /labɔʀjø, øz/ *adj* **1** *gén* [*travail,
processus*] arduous; [*accouchement*] difficult; [*style*] laboured;
[*victoire*] hard-won (*épith*); **c'est** ~ **de leur faire faire leurs
devoirs!** it's hard work getting them to do their homework!; **2** Sociol [*classes*] working

---

Les lacs

Les noms de lacs

■ *L'anglais n'utilise pas l'article défini devant les noms
de lacs. Le mot* Lake *prend une majuscule lorsqu'il est
utilisé devant le nom propre.*

le lac Supérieur	**le lac Victoria**
= Lake Superior	= Lake Victoria

■ *Les mots* Loch *et* Lough *s'utilisent de la même façon.*

le loch Ness	**le lough Erne**
= Loch Ness	= Lough Erne

■ *Le* de *utilisé en français pour les lacs qui portent des
noms de villes n'est pas traduit en anglais.*

le lac de Constance	**le lac d'Annecy**
= Lake Constance	= Lake Annecy

■ *Dans ce cas, l'anglais utilise toujours le mot* Lake.
Dans d'autres cas, Lake *peut être omis:*

le lac Balaton	**le lac Titicaca**
= Balaton *ou* Lake Balaton	= Titicaca *ou* Lake Titicaca

■ *En cas de doute, il est toujours préférable d'employer*
Lake.

---

labour /labuʀ/ *nm* (travail) ploughing **C** GB, plowing **C** US;
cheval de ~ plough GB *ou* plow US horse

labourage /labuʀaʒ/ *nm* ploughing GB, plowing US

labourer /labuʀe/ [1] *vtr* to plough GB, to plow US

laboureur /labuʀœʀ/ ▸ p. 372 *nm* **1** ploughman GB,
plowman US; **2** †(cultivateur) farmer

labyrinthe /labiʀɛ̃t/ *nm* **1** Archit maze; **2** Mythol labyrinth; **3** *fig* labyrinth, maze

lac /lak/ *nm* (naturel) lake; (artificiel) reservoir

lacer /lase/ [12] *vtr* to lace up [*chaussures, corset*]

lacérer /laseʀe/ [14] *vtr* to lacerate [*peau, chair*]; to slash
[*vêtement, tableau, affiche*]

lacet /lase/ *nm* **1** (de soulier, corset) lace; **chaussures à** ~**s**
lace-up shoes; **2** (de route) hairpin bend; **route en** ~**s**
twisting road

lâche /lɑʃ/
A *adj* **1** (sans courage) [*personne, attitude, crime*] cowardly;
2 (distendu) [*ceinture, nœud*] loose; **3** (sans rigueur) [*règlement*]
lax; [*style, scénario*] woolly
B *nmf* coward

lâchement /lɑʃmɑ̃/ *adv* **ils se sont** ~ **enfuis** they fled
like cowards; **il a été** ~ **assassiné** he was foully murdered

lâcher¹ /lɑʃe/ [1]
A *vtr* **1** (cesser de tenir) to drop [*objet*]; to let go of [*corde, main*];
lâche-moi *lit* let go of me; *fig*○ give me a break○, leave me
alone; ~ **prise** to lose one's grip; **2** (produire) to come out
with [*mot*]; to reveal [*information*]; to let out [*cri*]; **il n'a pas
lâché un mot de toute la soirée** he didn't utter a word all
evening; **3** (laisser partir) to let [sb/sth] go [*personne,
animal*]; **elle a lâché ses chiens sur lui** she set her dogs on
him; **il ne la lâche pas des yeux** he never takes his eyes off

her; **4** (abandonner) to drop [ami, activité]; **5** Sport (distancer) to break away from [concurrent]

B vi (céder) [lien, nœud] to give way; [freins] to fail

C se lâcher vpr ○(se décontracter) to let it all hang out○, to let one's hair down

lâcher² /lɑʃe/ nm (de ballons, d'oiseaux) release

lâcheté /lɑʃte/ nf **1** (défaut) cowardice **C**; **par ~** out of cowardice; **2** (acte) cowardly act

lâcheur○, **-euse** /lɑʃœʀ, øz/ nm,f unreliable person

laconique /lakɔnik/ adj [style] laconic; [réponse] terse

lacrymal, **~e**, mpl **-aux** /lakʀimal, o/ adj lachrymal

lacrymogène /lakʀimɔʒɛn/ adj [grenade, bombe] teargas; **gaz ~** teargas

lacté, **~e** /lakte/ adj **1** (qui contient du lait) [produit, alimentation] milk (épith); **2** (laiteux) [liquide, blanc] milky; **la voie ~e** the Milky Way

lacune /lakyn/ nf (dans un manuscrit) lacuna; (dans les connaissances, la loi) gap; (dans une argumentation) hole

lacustre /lakystʀ/ adj **cité ~** lake dwelling

là-dedans /lad(ə)dɑ̃/ adv

> ⚠ De même que là se traduit soit par here soit par there, là-dedans, au sens littéral, se traduit par in here ou in there suivant que l'objet dont on parle se trouve près ou non du locuteur.

(près) in here; (plus loin) in there; **mets ça ~** (près) put this in here; (plus loin) put that in there; **debout ~**○! get up!; **et moi ~ qu'est-ce que je fais**○? and where do I come in?

là-dessous /lad(ə)su/ adv

> ⚠ De même que là se traduit soit par here soit par there, là-dessous, au sens littéral, se traduit par under here ou under there suivant que l'objet se trouve près ou non du locuteur.

(près) under here; (plus loin) under there; **il y a qch de louche ~**○ there's something fishy○ about all this

là-dessus /lad(ə)sy/ adv

> ⚠ De même que là se traduit soit par here soit par there, là-dessus, au sens littéral, se traduit par on here ou on there suivant que l'objet dont on parle se trouve près ou non du locuteur.

1 (sur une surface) (près) on here; (plus loin) on there; **2** (sur ce sujet) **nous sommes d'accord ~** we agree; **qu'as-tu à dire ~?** what have you got to say about it?; **il y a un bon livre ~** there's a good book on it; **3** (alors) **~ il a raccroché** with that he hung up; **nous nous sommes quittés ~** we parted at that point

ladite ▶ ledit

ladre /ladʀ/

A adj liter [personne] miserly

B nm (avare) liter miser

lagon /lagɔ̃/ nm lagoon

lagune /lagyn/ nf lagoon

là-haut /lao/ adv

> ⚠ De même que là se traduit soit par here soit par there, là-haut, au sens littéral, se traduit par up here ou up there suivant que l'objet dont on parle se trouve près ou non du locuteur.

1 (en hauteur) (près) up here; (plus loin) up there; **~ dans le ciel** up in the sky; **il veut grimper ~** he wants to climb up there; **de ~** from up there; **2** (à l'étage) upstairs; **3** (au paradis) in heaven

laïc /laik/ nm layman

laïcité /laisite/ nf (concept) secularism; (nature) secularity

laid, **~e** /lɛ, lɛd/ adj **1** (pas beau) ugly; **2** (choquant) disgusting

laideur /lɛdœʀ/ nf ugliness

lainage /lɛnaʒ/ nm **1** (étoffe) woollen^GB material; **2** (vêtement) woollen^GB garment

laine /lɛn/ nf **1** wool; **de** or **en ~** woollen^GB, wool (épith); **2** ○(vêtement) **une (petite) ~** a woolly

Composés **~ peignée** worsted; **~ à repriser** darning wool; **~ à tapisserie** tapestry wool; **~ à tricoter** knitting wool; **~ de verre** glass wool; **~ vierge** new wool GB, virgin wool

laineux, **-euse** /lɛnø, øz/ adj woolly

lainier, **-ière** /lɛnje, ɛʀ/ adj [industrie] wool (épith); [région] wool-producing

laïque /laik/

A adj [école, enseignement] nondenominational GB, public US; [État, esprit] secular

B nmf layman/laywoman; **les ~s** lay people

laisse /lɛs/ nf (pour chien) lead GB, leash US

laissé-pour-compte, **laissée-pour-compte**, mpl **laissés-pour-compte** /lesepuʀkɔ̃t/ nm,f outcast

laisser /lese/ [1]

A vtr **1** to leave [parapluie, pourboire, marge, trace]; **~ qch à qn** to leave sb sth; **~ la liberté à qn** to let sb go free; **je te laisse** I must go; **laisse tes livres et viens te balader** put your books away and come for a stroll; **~ le choix à qn** to give sb the choice; **laisse ce jouet à ton frère** let your brother have the toy; **tu y laisseras ta santé** you'll ruin your health; **je ne veux pas y ~ ma peau**○ I don't want it to kill me; **laisse-le, ça lui passera** ignore him, he'll get over it; **je te laisse à tes occupations** I'll let you get on; **cela me laisse sceptique** I'm sceptical; **2** (cesser) liter **cela ne laisse pas d'étonner** it is a continual source of amazement

B v aux **~ qn/qch faire** to let sb/sth do; **laisse-moi faire** (ne m'aide pas) let me do it; (je m'en occupe) leave it to me; **laisse-la faire!** (ne t'en mêle pas) let her get on with it!; **laisse-la faire, elle reviendra toute seule** just leave her, she'll come back of her own accord

C se laisser vpr **se ~ bercer par les vagues** to be lulled by the waves; **il se laisse insulter** he puts up with insults; **elle n'est pas du genre à se ~ faire** (laisser abuser) she won't be pushed around; **il ne veut pas se ~ faire** (coiffer, laver etc) he won't let you touch him; **se ~ aller** to let oneself go; **ça se laisse manger**○! euph it's quite palatable

laisser-aller /leseale/ nm inv **1** (dans la tenue) scruffiness; **2** (dans le travail) sloppiness

laissez-passer /lesepase/ nm inv pass

lait /lɛ/ nm milk; **frère/sœur de ~** foster brother/sister (who has had the same wet nurse); **~ de soja** soya milk

Composés **~ de chaux** whitewash; **~ concentré non sucré** evaporated milk; **~ concentré sucré** sweetened condensed milk; **~ condensé = ~ concentré**; **~ instantané** instant dried milk; **~ maternel** breastmilk; **~ de poule** Culin eggnog

Idiome **on lui pressait le nez il en sortirait du ~**○ he's/she's still wet behind the ears

laitage /lɛtaʒ/ nm dairy product

laitance /lɛtɑ̃s/ nf Culin, Zool soft roe

laiterie /lɛtʀi/ nf **1** (usine) dairy; **2** (industrie) dairy industry; **3** †(crémerie) dairy

laiteux, **-euse** /lɛtø, øz/ adj [liquide, blanc, lueur] milky; [teint, peau] creamy; [mur, peinture] milk-white

laitier, **-ière** /lɛtje, ɛʀ/

A adj [industrie, produit] dairy (épith); [production, vache] milk

B ▶ p. 372 nm,f **1** (livreur) milkman/milkwoman; **2** †(crémier) dairyman/dairymaid

laiton /lɛtɔ̃/ nm brass

laitue /lɛty/ nf lettuce

laïus○ /lajys/ nm inv speech

lama /lama/ nm **1** (animal) llama; **2** (religieux) lama

lamantin /lamɑ̃tɛ̃/ nm manatee

lambda /lɑ̃bda/

A ○adj inv [individu, lecteur] average

B nm inv lambda

lambeau, pl **~x** /lɑ̃bo/ nm **1** (d'étoffe) rag; (de papier, peau, cuir) strip; (de chair) bit; **mettre qch en ~x** to tear sth to pieces; **2** fig (de patrimoine) scraps (pl); **fortune qui part en ~x** fortune which is being frittered away

lambin○, **~e** /lɑ̃bɛ̃, in/

A adj slow

B nm,f slowcoach○ GB, slowpoke○ US

lambris /lɑ̃bʀi/ nm inv (en bois) panelling^GB **C**; (en marbre) marble walls (pl); (au plafond) mouldings^GB (pl)

lambrisser /lɑ̃bʀise/ [1] vtr (avec du bois) to panel

lame /lam/ nf **1** (de couteau, scie, tournevis) blade; **visage en ~ de couteau** hatchet face; **2** (couteau) knife; (épée) sword; (personne) **une fine ~** an expert swordsman; **3** (plaque mince) (de métal, bois, etc) strip; (de store) slat; (de ressort) leaf; **4** (vague) breaker

laisser

Verbe transitif

laisser, verbe transitif, se traduit généralement par *to leave*. On trouvera la traduction des expressions comme *laisser la parole à qn, laisser qch en suspens, laisser à qn le soin de, laisser qn pour mort* etc. sous le nom ou l'adjectif. Attention, *to leave* verbe transitif ne s'utilise jamais sans complément:

laisse, si tu n'as plus faim!
= leave it if you've had enough!

laisse, c'est trop lourd pour toi!
= leave it, it's too heavy for you!

non merci, je laisse, c'est trop cher
= no thank you, I think I'll leave it, it's too expensive

Voir **A.**

laisser + sujet + infinitif

On trouvera la traduction des expressions comme *laisser voir, laisser courir, laisser à penser* etc. sous le deuxième verbe.

Lorsque *laisser* signifie *permettre de* ou *ne pas empêcher de*, on pourra le traduire par *to let*:

vous avez laissé pousser des mauvaises herbes
= you've let weeds grow

il ne laisse pas ses enfants regarder la télévision
= he doesn't let his children watch television

laisse-le pleurer/critiquer/dormir
= let him cry/criticize/sleep

ne laisse pas le chat monter sur le canapé
= don't let the cat climb on the settee

ne laisse pas brûler la sauce
= don't let the sauce burn

quand on laisse le repassage s'accumuler
= if you let the ironing mount up

Voir **B.**

se laisser + infinitif

De façon très générale, le verbe pronominal suivi d'un verbe à l'infinitif peut se traduire par *to let oneself*:

laisse-toi couler jusqu'au fond
= let yourself sink to the bottom

Quand la structure signifie plus précisément *accepter l'action d'autrui* on traduira par *to let sb do sth*:

il s'est laissé coiffer
= he let me/her etc. do his hair

il ne se laisse pas caresser
= he won't let you stroke him

Quand *se laisser* peut être remplacé par *être* on traduira par *to be*:

se laisser envahir par un sentiment de bien-être
= to be overcome by a feeling of well-being

Voir **C.**

(Composés) ~ **de fond** lit ground swell; fig upheaval; ~ **de parquet** (longue) parquet strip; (courte) parquet block; ~ **de rasoir** razor blade

lamé /lame/ *nm* lamé; **en** ~ lamé (*épith*)

lamelle /lamɛl/ *nf* ⓵ (de bois, métal) small strip; ⓶ Culin (de truffe, fromage) sliver; **découper en fines** ~**s** to slice thinly; ⓷ Bot (de champignon) gill

lamentable /lamãtabl/ *adj* ⓵ (minable) [*résultat, jeu*] pathetic; ⓶ (pitoyable) [*spectacle, cri*] pitiful; [*mort, accident*] terrible; [*voix, ton*] plaintive

lamentablement /lamãtabləmã/ *adv* [*échouer*] miserably; [*pleurer*] piteously

lamentation /lamãtasjõ/ *nf* wailing ¢

lamenter: se lamenter /lamãte/ [1] *vpr* to moan

laminer /lamine/ [1] *vtr* to roll

laminoir /laminwaʀ/ *nm* rolling mill

lampadaire /lãpadɛʀ/ *nm* (de salon) standard lamp GB, floor lamp US; (de rue) streetlight

lampe /lãp/ *nf* gén lamp, light; (ampoule) bulb; (tube électronique)† valve GB, electron tube US

(Composés) ~ **à bronzer** sun lamp; ~ **de bureau** desk light *ou* lamp; ~ **de chevet** bedside light *ou* lamp; ~ **électrique** torch GB, flashlight US; ~ **à pétrole** paraffin lamp GB, kerosene lamp US; ~ **de poche** pocket torch GB, flashlight US; ~ **à souder** blow lamp GB, blow torch; ~ **témoin** indicator light; ~ **tempête** hurricane lamp

lampion /lãpjõ/ *nm* paper lantern

lance /lãs/ *nf* (de chasse, guerre) spear; (de tournoi) lance

(Composé) ~ **d'incendie** fire hose nozzle

lancée /lãse/ *nf* **sur ma** ~ while I was at it; **continuer sur sa** ~ (dans une activité) to continue to forge ahead; (dans un discours) to continue in the same vein

lance-flammes /lãsflam/ *nm inv* flame-thrower

lancement /lãsmã/ *nm* ⓵ (mise en route) (de navire, compagnie, campagne, d'offensive) launching; (de programme, processus) setting up; ⓶ (mise sur le marché) (de produit, livre, film) launch; (d'emprunt) floating; (d'acteur, écrivain) promotion; ⓷ (de missile,

satellite) (processus) launching; (action) launch

lance-pierres /lãspjɛʀ/ *nm inv* catapult

(Idiomes) **manger au** ~° to gobble one's food; **payer qn avec un** ~° to pay sb peanuts°

lancer¹ /lãse/ [12]

A *vtr* ⓵ (jeter) to throw [*ballon, caillou, javelot*]; ~ **un coup de pied/poing à qn** to kick/to punch sb; ⓶ (envoyer, mettre en route) to launch [*satellite, fusée, navire*]; to fire [*flèche, missile*] (**sur** at); to drop [*bombe*]; to launch [*offensive, projet, enquête, produit, chanteur*]; to start up [*engine*]; to take [*sth*] to full speed [*véhicule*]; ~ **une voiture à 150 km/h** to take a car up to 150 kph; ⓷ (émettre) to throw out [*fumée, flammes*]; to give [*regard, cri*]; to put about [*rumeur*]; to issue [*avis, ultimatum*]; to send out [*invitation*]; to float [*emprunt*]; ⓸ (proférer) to hurl [*insulte*] (**à** at); to make [*menace, accusation*]; to let out [*juron*]; to crack [*plaisanterie*]; ~ **une accusation à qn** to level an accusation at sb; **lança-t-il** he said

B °*vi* (élancer) to throb

C **se lancer** *vpr* ⓵ (s'engager) **se** ~ **dans une explication** to launch into an explanation; **se** ~ **dans l'informatique** to take up computing; **se** ~ **dans les affaires** to go into business; ⓶ (sauter) **se** ~ **dans le vide** to jump; ⓷ (s'envoyer) (pour attraper) to throw [sth] to each other [*ballon*]; (pour faire mal) to throw [sth] at each other [*pierre*]; to exchange [*insultes*]; ⓸ (se faire connaître) [*acteur*] to make a name for oneself

lancer² /lãse/ *nm* ⓵ Sport ~ **du disque** discus event; ~ **du poids** shot put (event); ⓶ (à la pêche) **le** ~, **la pêche au** ~ rod and reel fishing

lance-roquettes /lãsʀɔkɛt/ *nm inv* rocket launcher

lancinant, ~**e** /lãsinã, ãt/ *adj* [*douleur*] shooting (*épith*); [*musique*] insistent; [*problème*] nagging (*épith*)

lanciner /lãsine/ [1] *vtr* (tourmenter) [*idée, remords*] to torment

landau /lãdo/ *nm* (d'enfant) pram GB, baby carriage US

lande /lãd/ *nf* moor

langage /lãgaʒ/ *nm* language; **elle m'a tenu un tout autre** ~ she said something completely different to me

Les langues

■ *Les adjectifs comme* anglais *peuvent aussi qualifier des personnes:* un touriste anglais (► p. 392) *et des choses:* la cuisine anglaise (► p. 230). *Dans les expressions suivantes,* English *est pris comme exemple; les autres noms de langues s'utilisent de la même façon.*

Les noms de langues

■ *L'anglais n'utilise pas l'article défini devant les noms de langues. Noter aussi l'emploi de la majuscule, obligatoire en anglais.*

apprendre l'anglais
= to learn English

étudier l'anglais
= to study English

l'anglais est facile
= English is easy

j'aime l'anglais
= I like English

parler anglais
= to speak English

parler couramment l'anglais
= to speak good English *ou* to speak English fluently

je ne parle pas très bien l'anglais
= I don't speak very good English
ou my English isn't very good

En avec les noms de langues

■ *Avec un verbe,* en anglais *se traduit par* in English:

dis-le en anglais
= say it in English

■ *Après un nom,* en anglais *se traduit par* in English *ou par l'adjectif* English. *Noter l'emploi de la majuscule, obligatoire pour l'adjectif et le nom.*

un livre en anglais
= a book in English *ou* an English book*

une émission en anglais
= an English-language broadcast

* *Noter que* an English book *est ambigu, tout comme* un livre français, *qui peut signifier* un livre en français *ou* un livre qui vient de France.

Mais attention:

traduire en anglais
= to translate into English

De avec les noms de langues

■ *Les expressions françaises avec de se traduisent en général en utilisant l'adjectif.*

un cours d'anglais   **un manuel d'anglais**
= an English class   = an English textbook

un dictionnaire d'anglais   **un professeur d'anglais**
= an English dictionary   = an English teacher

une leçon d'anglais
= an English lesson

■ *Noter que ceci peut signifier aussi* un professeur anglais. *Pour éviter l'ambiguïté, on peut dire* a teacher of English.

La traduction de l'adjectif français

l'accent anglais   **un mot anglais**
= an English accent   = an English word

une expression anglaise   **un proverbe anglais**
= an English expression   = an English proverb

la langue anglaise
= the English language

■ *L'anglais a peu d'équivalents simples des adjectifs et des noms en* -phone.

un arabophone   **l'Afrique anglophone**
= an Arabic speaker   = English-speaking Africa

il est arabophone
= he is an Arabic speaker

(Composés) ~ **administratif** official jargon; ~ **journalistique** journalese; ~ **de programmation** programming^{GB} language; ~ **des sourds-muets** sign language

lange /lɑ̃ʒ/ *nm* ① (pour emmailloter) swaddling clothes (*pl*); ② (couche de change) nappy GB, diaper US

langer /lɑ̃ʒe/ [13] *vtr* ① (emmailloter) to wrap [sb] in swaddling clothes [*bébé*]; ② (mettre une couche) to put a nappy GB *ou* diaper US on [*bébé*]

langoureux, -euse /lɑ̃guʀø, øz/ *adj* languorous

langouste /lɑ̃gust/ *nf* spiny lobster

langoustine /lɑ̃gustin/ *nf* langoustine

langue /lɑ̃g/ *nf* ① ► p. 136 Anat tongue; **tirer la** ~ (comme insulte) to stick out one's tongue (**à qn** at sb); (au médecin) to put out one's tongue; (avoir soif) to be dying of thirst; (avoir des problèmes d'argent) to struggle financially; ② Ling (système) language; (discours) speech; **aimer les** ~s to love languages; **en** ~ **familière** in informal speech; ③ (personne) **les** ~s **vont aller bon train** people will talk; **mauvaise** ~ malicious gossip; ④ (forme allongée) ~ **de terre** spit of land
(Composés) ~ **de bois** political cant; ~ **maternelle** mother tongue; ~ **d'origine** native language; ~ **verte** slang
(Idiomes) **avoir la** ~ **bien pendue**° to be very talkative; **avoir qch sur le bout de la** ~ to have sth on the tip of one's tongue

languette /lɑ̃gɛt/ *nf* (de soulier) tongue; (de cartable) strap; (de fermoir) flap; (de pain) long narrow strip

langueur /lɑ̃gœʀ/ *nf* languor

languir /lɑ̃giʀ/ [3]
A *vi* ① (manquer d'énergie) [*conversation*] to languish; [*économie*] to be sluggish; ② (souffrir d'attendre) ~ **après** *or* **pour qn** to pine for sb; **je languis de vous revoir** I'm longing to see you; **faire** ~ **qn** to keep sb in suspense
B se languir *vpr* to pine (**de qn** for sb)

languissant, ~**e** /lɑ̃gisɑ̃, ɑ̃t/ *adj* [*personne*] listless; [*économie*] sluggish; [*conversation*] desultory

lanière /lanjɛʀ/ *nf* (attache) strap; (de fouet) lash

lanterne /lɑ̃tɛʀn/ *nf* ① (lampe) lantern; ② Aut (feu de position) sidelight GB, parking light US
(Idiomes) **être la** ~ **rouge** to bring up the rear; **éclairer la** ~ **de qn** to enlighten sb (**sur qch** about sth)

lapalissade /lapalisad/ *nf* truism

laper /lape/ [1] *vtr* to lap (up) [*soupe, lait*]

lapidaire /lapidɛʀ/ *adj* [*formule, style*] pithy

lapidation /lapidasjɔ̃/ *nf* stoning

lapider /lapide/ [1] *vtr* ① (tuer) to stone [sb] to death [*personne*]; ② (attaquer) to throw stones at [*personne*]

lapin /lapɛ̃/ *nm* ① (animal, viande) rabbit; **coup du** ~ (coup asséné) rabbit punch; (choc en voiture) whiplash injury; **cage** *or* **cabane à** ~s lit rabbit hutch; fig° (immeuble) tower block; ② (fourrure) rabbit(skin)
(Composé) ~ **de garenne** wild rabbit

Idiomes **poser un ~ à qn**° to stand sb up; **se faire tirer comme des ~s**° to be picked off like flies; **c'est un chaud ~°** he's a randy devil

lapine /lapin/ *nf* doe rabbit
lapon, ~e /lapɔ̃, ɔn/ ▸ p. 336
A *adj* Géog Lapp
B *nm* Ling Lapp
Laponie /laponi/ ▸ p. 504 *nprf* **la** ~ Lapland
laps /laps/ *nm inv* ~ **de temps** period of time
lapsus /lapsys/ *nm inv* slip; ~ **révélateur** Freudian slip
laquais /lakɛ/ *nm inv* lackey
laque /lak/ *nf* [1] (pour cheveux) hairspray; [2] (résine, vernis) lacquer; (peinture) gloss paint GB, enamel US
laqué, ~e /lake/ *adj* [1] [*peinture*] gloss; [2] Culin **canard** ~ Peking duck; **porc** ~ roast glazed pork
laquelle /lakɛl/ ▸ **lequel**
laquer /lake/ [1]
A *vtr* to lacquer [*meuble*]; to paint [sth] in gloss GB *ou* enamel US [*porte*]
B **se laquer** *vpr* **se** ~ **les cheveux** to put hairspray on one's hair; **cheveux laqués** lacquered hair
larbin° /laʁbɛ̃/ *nm* (domestique) pej servant; fig flunkey
larcin /laʁsɛ̃/ *nm* [1] (vol) petty theft; [2] (produit du vol) loot
lard /laʁ/ *nm* ≈ fat streaky bacon
Idiome **je ne sais pas si c'est du ~ ou du cochon**° I don't know what to think
larder /laʁde/ [1] *vtr* Culin to lard (**de** with); ~ **qn de coups de couteau** fig to stab sb repeatedly
lardon /laʁdɔ̃/ *nm* Culin bacon cube
large /laʁʒ/
A *adj* [1] ▸ p. 347 (de grande dimension) [*épaules, hanches, paumes*] broad; [*couloir, avenue, rivière, lit*] wide; [*sillon*] broad; [*manteau*] loose-fitting; [*pantalon*] loose; [*jupe, cape*] full; [*chandail*] big; [*geste, mouvement*] sweeping; [*sourire*] broad; [*courbe, détour*] long; **un ~ cercle** a big circle; ~ **de trois mètres** three metresGB wide; [2] (important) [*avance, bénéfice*] substantial; [*choix, public*] wide; [*concertation, coalition*] broad; [*extrait, majorité*] large; **au sens** ~ in a broad sense; **bénéficier d'un ~ soutien** to have widespread support; [3] (généreux) [*personne*] generous (**avec** to); [4] (ais é) [*vie*] comfortable; [5] (ouvert) **avoir les idées ~s, être ~ d'esprit** to be broad-minded
B *adv* [1] (généreusement) [*prévoir*] on a generous scale; [*calculer, mesurer*] on the generous side; [2] **s'habiller** ~ to wear loose-fitting clothes
C *nm* [1] (largeur) **faire quatre mètres de** ~ to be four metresGB wide; [2] Naut open sea; **au** ~ offshore; **au** ~ **de Marseille** off Marseilles; **l'air du** ~ the sea air; **prendre le** ~ Naut to sail; ▸ **grand**
Idiome **ne pas en mener** ~° to be worried stiff°
largement /laʁʒəmɑ̃/ *adv* [1] (massivement) [*admis, approuvé, représenté*] widely; [*disperser, irriguer, répandre*] widely; **se prononcer** ~ **en faveur de/contre qch** to come out largely in favourGB of/against sth; [2] (en grande partie) largely, to a large extent; **l'opposition a** ~ **remporté les élections** the opposition won the elections by a wide margin; **être** ~ **majoritaire** to have a comfortable majority; **arriver** ~ **en tête** to be a clear winner; ~ **en dessous/au-dessus de la limite** well under/over the limit; **il dépasse** ~ **les autres** (en taille) he's much taller than the others; [4] (amplement) **tu as** ~ **le temps** you've got plenty of time; **c'est** ~ **suffisant, cela suffit** ~ that's more than enough, that's plenty; [5] (au moins) easily; **une chaîne en or vaudrait** ~ **le double** a gold chain would easily be worth double; [6] (généreusement) [*indemniser, contribuer*] generously; [7] (dans l'aisance) [*vivre*] comfortably
largesse /laʁʒɛs/
A *nf* generosity; **être d'une grande** ~ **avec qn** to be very generous with sb
B **largesses** *nfpl* generous gifts
largeur /laʁʒœʁ/ *nf* [1] ▸ p. 347 (dimension) gén width, breadth; (en géométrie) breadth; **occuper toute la** ~ **de qch** to take up the full width of sth; **en petite/grande** ~ in a narrow/broad width; **être déchiré sur toute la** ~ to be torn right across; **dans le sens de la** ~ widthwise; [2] (ouverture) ~ **d'esprit** *or* **de vues** broad-mindedness
largué°, ~**e** /laʁge/ *adj* [1] (dépassé) (par un raisonnement) lost; (par les événements) out of touch; [2] (marginal) spaced out°

larguer /laʁge/ [1] *vtr* [1] Mil, Aviat to drop [*bombe, missile*]; to drop [*parachutiste*]; to release [*satellite, navette*]; [2] Naut to unfurl [*voile*]; ~ **les amarres** lit to cast off; fig to set off; [3] °(abandonner) to give up [*études, appartement*]; to leave [*travail*]; to chuck°, to leave [*petit ami*]
larme /laʁm/ *nf* [1] lit tear; **elle a ri aux ~s** she laughed till she cried; **pleurer à chaudes ~s** to cry as though one's heart would break; **avoir la ~ à l'œil** to be a bit weepy; **pleurer toutes les ~s de son corps** to cry one's eyes out; [2] °fig (petite quantité) drop (**de** of)
larmoyant, ~e /laʁmwajɑ̃, ɑ̃t/ *adj* [1] (qui pleure) [*personne*] tearful; [*yeux*] full of tears (après n); [2] (qui veut attendrir) [*ton, voix*] whining; [*discours*] maudlin; [*personne*] snivellingGB
larmoyer /laʁmwaje/ [23] *vi* [1] [*yeux*] to water; [2] (pleurnicher) to whine (**sur qch** about sth)
larron /laʁɔ̃/ *nm* [1] hum scoundrel; [2] thief
Idiomes **s'entendre comme ~s en foire** to be as thick as thieves; **l'occasion fait le** ~ Prov opportunity makes the thief
larvaire /laʁvɛʁ/ *adj* fig [*état*] embryonic
larve /laʁv/ *nf* [1] Zool larva; [2] (être humain) pej (sans volonté) wimp°; (sans dignité) worm péj
larvé, ~e /laʁve/ *adj* [1] gén latent; [2] Méd atypical
laryngite /laʁɛ̃ʒit/ ▸ p. 195 *nf* laryngitis
larynx /laʁɛ̃ks/ *nm inv* larynx
las, lasse /lɑ, lɑs/ *adj* weary (**de** of)
lasagnes /lazaɲ/ *nfpl* lasagna **¢**
lascar° /laskaʁ/ *nm* (gaillard) fellow; (enfant) devil
lascif, -ive /lasif, iv/ *adj* liter [*personne, pose, regard*] lascivious; [*tempérament*] lustful
lascivité /lasivite/ *nf* liter lasciviousness
laser /lazɛʁ/ *nm* laser
lassant, ~e /lasɑ̃, ɑ̃t/ *adj* [1] (ennuyeux) [*discours*] tedious; [*reproches*] tiresome; [2] (fatigant) tiring
lasser /lɑse/ [1]
A *vtr* (ennuyer) to bore [*personne, audience*]; (excéder) to weary [*personne, audience*]
B **se lasser** *vpr* [*personne*] to grow tired (**de qn/qch** of sb/sth; **de faire** of doing); **sans se** ~ (infatigablement) without tiring; (patiemment) patiently
lassitude /lasityd/ *nf* weariness; **avec** ~ wearily
latence /latɑ̃s/ *nf* latency; Psych latency (period)
latent, ~e /latɑ̃, ɑ̃t/ *adj* [*danger, maladie, possibilité*] latent; [*angoisse, jalousie*] underlying
latéral, ~e, *mpl* **-aux** /lateʁal, o/ *adj* (sur le côté) [*porte, sortie*] side (épith); (parallèle) [*nef, tunnel*] lateral
latéralement /lateʁalmɑ̃/ *adv* lit (de côté) [*arriver*] from the side; (sur le côté) [*placer*] sideways
latin, ~e /latɛ̃, in/
A *adj* [1] [*auteurs, textes*] Latin; [2] (méditerranéen) [*tempérament*] Latin; [*culture*] Mediterranean; [3] Ling **langues ~es** Romance languages
B ▸ p. 336 *nm* Ling Latin
Idiome **c'est à y perdre son** ~ one can't make head or tail of it
latinisme /latinism/ *nm* Latinism
latiniste /latinist/ *nmf* Latinist
latino-américain, ~e, *mpl* **~s** /latinoameʁikɛ̃, ɛn/ *adj* Latin-American
latitude /latityd/
A *nf* [1] Géog latitude; **par 38° de** ~ **nord** at latitude 38° north; [2] (liberté) latitude; **avoir toute** ~ **de faire** to be entirely free to do
B **latitudes** *nfpl* (régions, climats) latitudes
latte /lat/ *nf* [1] Constr (de plafond, mur) lath; (de plancher) board; [2] (de sommier, siège) slat
latter /late/ [1] *vtr* to lath
laudateur, -trice /lodatœʁ, tʁis/ *fml*
A *adj* laudatory sout
B *nm,f* adulator
laudatif, -ive /lodatif, iv/ *adj* laudatory
lauréat, ~e /loʁea, at/ *nm,f* [1] (de compétition) winner; [2] Scol, Univ successful candidate
laurier /loʁje/
A *nm* [1] Bot laurel; ~ **commun** bay (tree); [2] Culin **feuille de** ~ bay leaf

le

Article

le, la, les article défini se traduit par *the* (invariable) quand le nom qu'il précède est déterminé par un contexte supposé connu de l'interlocuteur:

passe-moi le sel
= pass me the salt

le déjeuner d'anniversaire
= the birthday lunch

le courage de faire
= the courage to do

Il ne se traduit pas quand ce nom exprime une généralité ou que son contexte est indéterminé:

le sel de mer
= sea salt

pendant le déjeuner
= during lunch

le courage seul ne suffit pas
= courage alone isn't enough

the se prononce /ðə/ devant consonne et h aspiré, /ðɪ/ devant voyelle et h muet (hour, honest, honour, heir), et /ðiː/ quand il est employé de manière emphatique pour indiquer l'excellence (comme **le** en français dans *c'est le poète de la liberté*).

Ne sont traités ci-dessous que les cas où l'article se traduit différemment de *the*, ou ne se traduit pas, ou se rend par une structure particulière, à l'exclusion de ceux qui sont développés dans les notes d'usage répertoriées ▸ p. 1355, notamment celles concernant **les jours de la semaine, les douleurs et les maladies, les jeux et les sports, les nationalités, les langues, les pays, les nombres, les titres de politesse** etc.

Dans la composition du superlatif, l'anglais ne répète pas l'article:

l'homme le plus riche du monde
= the richest man in the world

l'homme le plus intelligent du monde
= the most intelligent man in the world

Les noms de plats sur un menu ne prennent pas d'article:

le steak au poivre vert
= steak with green peppercorns

Il n'y a pas d'article après *whose*:

les enfants dont la mère ...
= the children whose mother ...

L'article se traduit avec les noms d'inventions:

la charrue
= the plough

l'ordinateur
= the computer

Noter:

la Terre est ronde
= the Earth is round

sur la planète Terre
= on planet Earth

au contraire de la Terre, Mars ...
= unlike Earth, Mars ...

Pronom personnel

Le pronom personnel se traduit selon le genre et le nombre de l'antécédent en anglais: *him* pour représenter une personne de sexe masculin, un animal familier mâle; *her* pour une personne de sexe féminin, un animal familier femelle, un bateau, un véhicule qu'on aime bien ou dont on parle avec ironie; *it* pour une chose, un concept, un pays, une institution, un animal; *them* pour un antécédent régissant un verbe au pluriel.

B lauriers *nmpl* laurels; **se couvrir de ~s** [*soldat*] to distinguish oneself; [*écrivain*] to win many awards; [*candidat*] to perform outstandingly; **s'endormir** *or* **se reposer sur ses ~s** to rest on one's laurels

laurier-rose, *pl* **lauriers-roses** /lɔʀjəʀoz/ *nm* oleander

lavable /lavabl/ *adj* washable; **~ en machine** machine washable

lavabo /lavabo/ *nm* (cuvette) washbasin, washbowl

lavage /lavaʒ/ *nm* ① (de linge, sol, mains) washing; (de plaie) cleaning; **le ~ des vitres** window cleaning; ② (cycle de machine à laver) wash; **un ~** a wash

(Composé) **~ de cerveau** brainwashing; **faire un ~ d'estomac à qn** to pump sb's stomach (out)

lavande /lavɑ̃d/ ▸ p. 140 *adj inv, nf* lavender

lavandière /lavɑ̃djɛʀ/ *nf* ① (oiseau) wagtail; ② ▸ p. 372 (blanchisseuse) washerwoman

lavasse○ /lavas/ *nf* **c'est de la ~** (soupe, café) it tastes like dishwater

lave /lav/ *nf* lava **¢**; **coulée de ~** lava flow

lave-auto, *pl* **~s** /lavoto/ *nm* C car wash

lave-glace, *pl* **~s** /lavglas/ *nm* windscreen GB *ou* windshield US washer

lave-linge /lavlɛ̃ʒ/ *nm inv* washing machine

lave-mains /lavmɛ̃/ *nm inv* washbasin

lavement /lavmɑ̃/ *nm* Méd enema

laver /lave/ [1]
A *vtr* ① (nettoyer) to wash [*vêtement, enfant, voiture*]; **~ son linge** to do one's washing; **~ la vaisselle** to do the dishes, to do the washing-up GB; **~ qch à grande eau** to wash sth down; **~ qch au jet** to hose sth down; **~ qch à la brosse** to scrub sth; ② (désinfecter) to clean [*plaie*]; ③ liter [*pluie,* *orage*] to wash [*rue, ciel*]; ④ (innocenter) to clear; ⑤ (venger) liter to wash away [*humiliation, péché*]; ⑥ Art to wash

B se laver *vpr* ① (soi-même) to wash; **se ~ les dents** to brush one's teeth; ② [*tissu, vêtement*] to be washable; **se ~ en machine** to be machine washable; ③ fig, liter **se ~ d'un affront** to take revenge for an insult

(Idiome) **je m'en lave les mains** I'm washing my hands of it

laverie /lavʀi/ ▸ p. 372 *nf* **~ (automatique)** launderette, laundromat® US

lavette /lavɛt/ *nf* ① (pour la vaisselle) dishcloth; ② ○(personne) péj wimp○ péj; ③ H (de toilette) flannel GB, wash cloth US

laveur, -euse /lavœʀ, øz/ ▸ p. 372 *nm,f* cleaner

lave-vaisselle /lavvɛsɛl/ *nm inv* dishwasher

lavis /lavi/ *nm inv* (technique) wash; (dessin) wash drawing

lavoir /lavwaʀ/ *nm* (pour la lessive) wash house

laxatif, -ive /laksatif, iv/
A *adj* laxative
B *nm* laxative

laxisme /laksism/ *nm* laxity

laxiste /laksist/ *adj* lax (**à l'égard de, avec** with)

layette /lɛjɛt/ *nf* baby clothes (*pl*), layette

lazaret /lazaʀɛ/ *nm* (dans un port) lazaretto; (dans un hôpital) isolation ward

le, la¹ (**l'** before vowel or mute h), *pl* **les** /lə, la, l, lɛ/
A *art déf* ① (avec complément de nom) **la jupe/fille de ma sœur** my sister's skirt/daughter; **les chapitres du livre** the chapters of the book; **la table de la cuisine** the kitchen table; ② (en parlant d'une personne) **il est arrivé les mains dans les poches** he arrived with his hands in his pockets; **elle s'est cogné ~ bras** she banged her arm; **elle m'a pris par ~ bras** she took me by the arm; ③ (avec un nom d'espèce)

l'homme préhistorique/de Cro-Magnon prehistoric/Cro-Magnon man; **les droits de l'enfant** children's rights; **elle aime les chevaux** she likes horses; **4** (avec un nom propre) **les Dupont** the Duponts; **la Noël** Christmas; **la Saint-Michel** St. Michael's day; **~ roi Olaf** King Olaf; **5** (avec un adjectif) **je prendrai la bleue** I'll take the blue one; **~ ridicule de cette affaire** what is ridiculous about this matter; **les pauvres** the poor; **6** (avec préposition et nombre) **dans les 5 euros** about 5 euros; **7** (pour donner un prix, une fréquence etc) a, an; **3 euros ~ kilo** 3 euros a kilo; **8** (dans les exclamations) **l'imbécile!** the fool!; **la pauvre!** the poor thing!; **(oh) la jolie robe!** what a pretty dress!

B pron pers **je ne ~/la/les comprends pas** I don't understand him/her/them

C pron neutre **1** (complément) **je ~ savais** (j'étais au courant) **I** knew; (j'aurais dû m'en douter) I knew it; **je ne veux pas ~ savoir** I don't want to know (about it); **si je ne ~ fais pas, qui ~ fera?** if I don't do it, who will?; **je ~ croyais aussi, mais...** I thought so too, but...; **si c'est lui qui ~ dit...** if HE says so...; **'ils auront fini demain'—'espérons-~!'** 'they'll have finished tomorrow'—'let's hope so!'; **2** (attribut) **'est-elle satisfaite?'—'je ne crois pas qu'elle ~ soit'** 'is she satisfied?'—'I don't think so'

lé /le/ nm **1** (de papier peint) width; **2** (de jupe) panel

LEA /ɛloa/ nfpl (abbr = **langues étrangères appliquées**) university language course with emphasis on business and management

leadership /lidœRʃip/ nm **1** (rôle de leader) leading role; **2** (suprématie) supremacy

lèche-bottes○ /lɛʃbɔt/ nm (servilité) **le ~** crawling○ GB, bootlicking○; **faire du ~** to be a crawler GB ou bootlicker○

lèchefrite /lɛʃfRit/ nf dripping pan

lécher /leʃe/ [1]
A vtr **1** (avec la langue) to lick [cuillère, assiette]; **2** (effleurer) [flamme] to lick; [mer] to lap against; **3** ○(peaufiner) to polish [œuvre]; **4** **~ les vitrines** to go window-shopping
B se lécher vpr **se ~ les doigts** to lick one's fingers
(Idiome) **~ les bottes**○ **de qn** to lick sb's boots○, to brown-nose sb◑ US

lécheur○, **-euse** /leʃœR, øz/ nm,f pej crawler○ GB, brown-noser◑ US

lèche-vitrines /lɛʃvitRin/ nm inv window-shopping

leçon /ləsɔ̃/ nf **1** Scol lesson; **~ particulière** private lesson; **2** (punition, avis) lesson; **elle m'a fait la ~** she lectured me; **elle pourrait nous donner des ~s en matière de courage** she could teach us a thing or two about courage; **3** (conclusion) lesson; **la ~ de la fable** the moral of the story

lecteur, **-trice** /lɛktœR, tRis/
A ▸ p. 372 nm,f **1** gén reader; **2** Univ (language) teaching assistant
B nm **1** Ordinat reader; **~ optique** optical scanner ou reader; **~ de disquettes** disk drive; **2** Audio player; **~ laser** CD player

lectorat /lɛktɔRa/ nm **1** (public) readership; **2** Univ post of lecteur/-trice

lecture /lɛktyR/ nf **1** (de livre, journal) reading; **livre d'une ~ ardue** book which is difficult to read; **faire la ~ à qn** to read to sb; **donner ~ de qch** fml to read out sth; **2** (interprétation) reading, interpretation; **3** (ce qu'on lit) reading material; **ce sont mes ~s préférées** it's my favourite○ (kind of) reading; **4** (de musique, radiographie, graphique) reading; **5** Pol reading; **6** Audio play; **7** Ordinat reading

ledit, **ladite**, pl **lesdits**, **lesdites** /lədi, ladit, ledi, ledit/ adj the aforementioned

légal, **~e**, mpl **-aux** /legal, o/ adj [âge, définition, voies] legal; [activité, possession] lawful; **monnaie ~e** legal tender; **domicile ~** official residence

légalement /legalmɑ̃/ adv (selon la loi) legally; (sans enfreindre la loi) lawfully

légaliser /legalize/ [1] vtr (rendre légal) to legalize; (certifier) to authenticate

légalité /legalite/ nf (conformité à la loi) legality; (légitimité) lawfulness; **rester dans la ~** to remain within the law

légat /lega/ nm legate

légataire /legatɛR/ nmf legatee; **~ universel** sole legatee

légendaire /leʒɑ̃dɛR/ adj legendary

légende /leʒɑ̃d/ nf **1** (fable) legend; **entrer dans la ~** to become legendary; **2** (inscription) (d'illustration) caption; (de carte) key; **3** (mensonge) tall story

léger, **-ère** /leʒe, ɛR/
A adj **1** (peu pesant) light; **se sentir plus ~** fig to have a great weight off one's mind; **2** Culin light; **3** (souple) [danseur] nimble; [démarche] light; [pas] springy; [mouvement] nimble; **4** (faible) [rire] gentle; [coup] soft, gentle; [blessure, progrès, baisse, faute, retard] slight; [crainte, condamnation] mild; [goût, odeur, tremblement, espoir] faint; [vent, pluie, brume] light; [accent, bruit] faint, slight; [couche, nuage] thin; [blessure] minor; **5** (peu concentré) [café, thé, alcool] weak; [parfum, vin] light; [tabac] mild GB, light US; **6** (superficiel) [action, initiative] ill-considered; [jugement, propos] thoughtless, careless; [argument, preuve] weak, flimsy; **7** ○(insuffisant) **c'est un peu ~** it's a bit skimpy; **8** (frivole) [femme] loose; [mœurs] loose, lax; [mari, caractère, humeur] fickle; **9** Mil [arme, division] light
B adv [voyager] light
C **à la légère** loc adv [agir] without thinking; **prendre qch à la ~** not to take sth seriously

légèrement /leʒɛRmɑ̃/ adv **1** (faiblement) [appuyer, bouger] gently; [masser, gratter] gently, lightly; [parfumer] lightly, slightly; [trembler, blessé, teinté] slightly; **être habillé ~** to be dressed for warm weather; **2** Culin [manger] lightly; **3** (avec souplesse) [marcher, courir] lightly, nimbly; **4** (avec désinvolture) [agir, parler, se conduire] without thinking

légèreté /leʒɛRte/ nf **1** lit lightness; **2** Culin lightness; **3** (souplesse) (de personne) lightness, nimbleness; (de démarche, mouvement, style) lightness; **avec ~** lightly; **4** (superficialité) (de jugement, propos) lack of thought (**de qch** behind sth); **faire preuve de ~ dans qch** (dans la conduite) to show irresponsibility in sth; (dans les propos) to show a lack of depth in sth; **5** (frivolité) **la ~ de ses mœurs** his/her loose morals (pl); (caractère volage) fickleness

légion /leʒjɔ̃/ nf **1** Hist, Mil legion; **2** (multitude) army (**de** of); **ils sont ~** they are legion
(Composés) **la Légion (étrangère)** the Foreign Legion; **la Légion d'honneur** the Legion of Honour^GB

> **ⓘ** **Légion d'honneur** The system of honours awarded by the state for meritorious achievement. The *Président de la République* is the *Grand maître*. The basic rank is *Chevalier*. Holders of the *Légion d'honneur* are entitled to wear a small red lapel ribbon or *une rosette*.

légionellose /leʒjɔneloz/ nf Méd legionnaire's disease

légionnaire /leʒjɔnɛR/
A nmf (qui a la Légion d'honneur) member of the Legion of Honour^GB
B nm (romain) legionary; (de la Légion étrangère) legionnaire

législateur, **-trice** /leʒislatœR, tRis/ nm,f legislator, lawmaker

législatif, **-ive** /leʒislatif, iv/
A adj legislative; **élections législatives** ≈ general election (sg)
B nm legislature

législation /leʒislasjɔ̃/ nf legislation

législature /leʒislatyR/ nf **1** (durée) term of office; **2** (assemblée) legislature

légiste /leʒist/ ▸ p. 372 nm jurist

légitime /leʒitim/ adj **1** (selon la loi) [enfant, droit, pouvoir] legitimate; [union, époux, héritier] lawful; **2** (justifié) [grief, revendication, action] legitimate; [colère] justifiable; **3** (juste) [salaire] fair; [récompense] just
(Composé) **~ défense** self-defence^GB

légitimité /leʒitimite/ nf **1** Jur legitimacy; **2** (d'une action) lawfulness

legs /lɛg/ nm inv **1** Jur (de biens mobiliers) legacy; (de terres, biens immobiliers) devise; (d'effets personnels) bequest; (à une fondation) bequest; **2** fig legacy

léguer /lege/ [14] vtr **1** (par testament) to leave sth (**à qn** to sb); **2** (transmettre) to hand down [traditions]; to pass on [qualité, défaut]

légume /legym/ nm **1** lit vegetable; **~s verts** green vegetables; **~s secs** pulses; **2** ○fig pej vegetable

Léman /lemɑ̃/ ▸ p. 333 npr **le lac ~** Lake Geneva

lendemain /lɑ̃dəmɛ̃/
A nm ① (jour suivant) **le ~, la journée du ~** the following day; **dès le ~** the (very) next day; **le ~ de l'accident** the day after the accident; **le ~ matin/soir** the following morning/evening; **du jour au ~** overnight; ② (période qui suit) **au ~ de** (in the period) after; ③ (avenir) **le ~** tomorrow, the future; **sans ~** [bonheur, succès] short-lived
B **lendemains** nmpl ① (issue) outcome (sg); (conséquences) consequences; ② (perspectives) future (sg); **des ~s difficiles** difficult days ahead

(Idiome) **il ne faut jamais remettre au ~ ce qu'on peut faire le jour même** Prov never put off till tomorrow what you can do today

lénifiant, ~e /lenifjɑ̃, ɑ̃t/ adj [médicament, remarque] soothing

lent, ~e¹ /lɑ̃, ɑ̃t/ adj gén slow; [film, véhicule] slow-moving; [poison] slow-acting; **être ~ au travail** to be a slow worker; **avoir l'esprit ~** to be slow-witted

lente² /lɑ̃t/ nf Zool nit

lentement /lɑ̃t(ə)mɑ̃/ adv slowly

(Idiome) **qui va ~ va sûrement** Prov slowly but surely

lenteur /lɑ̃tœʀ/ nf slowness (**à faire** to do, in doing); **avec ~** slowly

lentille /lɑ̃tij/ nf ① Bot, Culin lentil; ② (optique) lens; **~s de contact** contact lenses

lentivirus /lɑ̃tiviʀys/ nm inv lentivirus, slow virus

léopard /leɔpaʀ/ nm ① (animal) leopard; ② (fourrure) leopardskin

lèpre /lɛpʀ/ ▸ p. 195 nf Méd leprosy

lépreux, -euse /lepʀø, øz/
A adj Méd leprous
B nm,f leper

léproserie /lepʀɔzʀi/ nf leper hospital

lequel /ləkɛl/, **laquelle** /lakɛl/, **lesquels** mpl, **lesquelles** fpl /lekɛl/, (avec à) **auquel, auxquels** mpl, **auxquelles** fpl /okɛl/, (avec de) **duquel** /dykɛl/, **desquels** mpl, **desquelles** fpl /dekɛl/

> ⚠ Lorsque la traduction du verbe de la proposition relative introduite par lequel, laquelle etc fait intervenir une préposition en anglais, trois traductions sont possibles: le carton dans lequel tu as mis les bouteilles = the box you put the bottles in; = the box that ou which you put the bottles in; = the box in which you put the bottles. Les deux premières traductions relèvent de la langue courante, parlée ou écrite; la troisième traduction sera préférée dans une langue plus soutenue, surtout écrite.
> La forme interrogative fonctionne de la même façon, avec seulement deux possibilités, la seconde étant préférée dans la langue écrite soutenue: dans lequel de ces cartons as-tu mis les bouteilles? = which of these boxes did you put the bottles in?; = in which of these boxes did you put the bottles?

A lequel, laquelle, lesquels, lesquelles adj (avec personne) who; (autres cas) which; **elle a envoyé son dossier au service des inscriptions, ~ dossier a été perdu** she sent her file to the registration office, and it got lost; **auquel cas** in which case
B pron rel ① (en fonction de sujet) (représentant une personne) who; (dans les autres cas) which; **il a donné le colis au réceptionniste, ~ me l'a remis** he gave the package to the receptionist, who gave it to me; ② (en fonction d'objet) (représentant une personne) whom; (dans les autres cas) which; **l'ami auquel tu as écrit** the friend to whom you wrote, the friend (who) you wrote to; **les gens contre lesquels ils luttaient** the people against whom they were fighting; **la table sur laquelle tu as posé la tasse** the table (which) you put the cup on; **les gens chez lesquels nous sommes allés** the people whose house we went to
C pron inter which; **de tous ces employés, lesquels sont les plus compétents?** of all these employees, which are the most competent?; **auquel de tes amis as-tu écrit?** which of your friends did you write to?; **'j'ai vu un film de Chaplin hier'—'~?'** 'I saw a Charlie Chaplin film yesterday'—'which one?'

les ▸ le

lesbienne /lɛsbjɛn/ nf lesbian

lesdites ▸ ledit

lesdits ▸ ledit

léser /leze/ [14] vtr ① (causer du tort à) to wrong [personne]; to prejudice [intérêts]; ② fig to hurt [sentiment]

lésiner /lezine/ [1] vi **ne pas ~ sur** to be liberal with [ingrédient, argent, compliments]; **ne pas ~ sur la dépense** to spare no expense

lésion /lezjɔ̃/ nf Méd lesion

lesquels, lesquelles /lekɛl/ ▸ lequel

lessivable /lesivabl/ adj washable

lessive /lesiv/ nf ① (produit) (en poudre) washing powder; (liquide) washing liquid; ② (tâche ménagère, linge) washing; **faire deux ~s par semaine** to do two washes a week

lessiver /lesive/ [1] vtr ① (laver) to wash; ② ○(épuiser) **être lessivé**○ hum to be washed out○

lessiveuse /lesivøz/ nf boiler, copper GB

lest /lɛst/ nm ① Naut, Aviat ballast; **lâcher du ~** fig to make concessions; ② (sur un filet) weight

leste /lɛst/ adj ① (souple) [personne, animal] agile; [démarche, pas] nimble; ② (osé) [propos, plaisanterie] risqué

lestement /lɛstəmɑ̃/ adv (avec souplesse) nimbly

lester /lɛste/ [1] vtr ① Naut, Aviat to ballast; ② ○(charger) to stuff sth (**de** with)

léthargie /letaʀʒi/ nf ① (engourdissement) lethargy; ② Méd lethargy

léthargique /letaʀʒik/ adj ① [personne] lethargic; [industrie, économie] sluggish; ② Méd lethargic

letton, -onne /letɔ̃, ɔn/
A ▸ p. 392 adj Latvian
B ▸ p. 336 nm Ling **le ~** Latvian

Lettonie /letɔni/ ▸ p. 230 nprf Latvia

lettre /letʀ/
A nf ① (signe graphique) letter; **~ minuscule** small letter; **~ majuscule** or **capitale** capital letter; **~ d'imprimerie** block letter; **un mot de trois ~s** a three-letter word; **en toutes ~s** lit in full; **c'est écrit en toutes ~s dans le rapport** fig it's down in black and white in the report; **les Romains furent des urbanistes avant la ~** the Romans were city planners before the concept was invented; ② (écrit adressé) letter; **~ de réclamation** letter of complaint; **~ de rupture** letter ending a relationship; **une petite ~** a note; ③ (contenu d'un texte) letter; **à la ~, au pied de la ~** [appliquer, suivre] to the letter; **il prend à la ~ tout ce qu'on lui dit** he takes everything you say literally
B **lettres** nfpl ① Univ, Scol (français) French; (plus général) arts GB, humanities US; **étudiant en ~s** (français) student reading French GB, student majoring in French US; (plus général) arts GB ou humanities US student; **docteur ès ~s** ≈ Doctor of Philosophy; ② (culture littéraire) letters; **femme de ~s** woman of letters; **les gens de ~s** writers; **avoir des ~s** to be well read

(Composés) **~ de cadrage** Pol scoping document (outlining issues for inclusion in the next budget); **~ ouverte** open letter (**à** to); **~ recommandée** registered letter; **~s classiques** French and Latin; **~s modernes** French language and literature

(Idiomes) **passer comme une ~ à la poste**○ [réforme] to go through smoothly; [excuse] to be accepted without any questions; **devenir ~ morte** to become a dead letter; **rester ~ morte** to go unheeded

lettré, ~e /letʀe/
A adj [personne] well-read; [milieu] literary
B nm,f man/woman of letters

leucémie /løsemi/ ▸ p. 195 nf leukaemia

leucocyte /løkɔsit/ nm leucocyte GB, leukocyte US

leur, (pl **leurs**) /lœʀ/

> ⚠ En anglais, on ne répète pas le possessif coordonné: leur nom et leur adresse = their names and addresses.

A pron pers inv them; **promesse ~ a été faite que** they were given a promise that; **il ~ a expliqué le fonctionnement de l'appareil** he told them how the machine worked; **il ~ a fallu faire** they had to do
B adj poss mf, pl **~s** their; **elles ressemblent à ~ père** they look like their father; **un de ~s amis** a friend of theirs; **ils sont partis chacun de ~ côté** they went their separate ways; **à ~ arrivée/départ** when they arrived/left
C **le leur, la leur, les leurs** pron poss theirs; **celui-là, c'est**

le ~ that's theirs; **qu'ils aient chacun le ~** let them have one each; **il est des ~s** (de leur groupe) he's one of them; **ils vivent loin des ~s** (de leur famille) they live far away from their families

leurre /lœʀ/ nm **1** (tromperie) illusion; **2** (à la pêche, chasse) lure; **3** Mil decoy

leurrer /lœʀe/ [1]
A vtr (tromper) to delude (**par** with)
B se leurrer vpr to delude oneself (**de** with; **au sujet de** about)

levage /ləvaʒ/ nm Tech (de charge) lifting

levain /ləvɛ̃/ nm **1** Culin leaven GB, sourdough US; **pain au/sans ~** leavened/unleavened bread; **2** Biol, Ind (agent de fermentation) starter; **3** (force) catalyst

levant /ləvɑ̃/
A adj m **soleil ~** rising sun; **au soleil ~** at sunrise
B nm east; **au ~** in the east

levé, **~e**[1] /ləve/
A pp ▸ **lever**[1]
B pp adj **1** (dressé) **voter à main ~e** to vote by a show of hands; **2** (hors du lit) up; **elle est toujours la première ~e** she's always the first up
C nm Géog (relevé) survey
(Idiome) **faire qch au pied ~** to do sth off the cuff

levée[2] /ləve/ nf **1** (suppression) (d'embargo, de loi martiale, préavis de grève, peine) lifting (**de** of); (de siège) raising; (de mesures, quotas) suspension (**de** of); (d'immunité parlementaire) removal (**de** of); (d'anonymat, de secret, tabou) ending (**de** of); (de séance) close (**de** of); **2** (de courrier) collection; **3** Jeux (aux cartes) trick; **4** Géog (remblai) levee; **5** Mil (recrutement) levying
(Composé) **~ de boucliers** outcry

lever[1] /ləve/ [16]
A vtr **1** (dresser) gén to raise; **~ la main** or **le doigt** (pour parler) to put up one's hand; **~ la main sur qn** (frapper) to raise a hand to sb; **~ les bras au ciel** to throw up one's hands (**de** in); **lève les pieds quand tu marches!** don't drag your feet!; **~ les yeux** or **la tête** (regarder) to look up (**sur, vers** at); **sans ~ les yeux** [dire, répondre] without looking up; [travailler, étudier] without a break; **2** (soulever) to lift [objet]; to raise [barrière]; **~ son verre** to raise one's glass (**à** to); **~ le rideau** Théât to raise the curtain; **~ les filets** (à la pêche) to haul in the nets; **3** (sortir du lit) to get [sb] up [enfants, malade]; **4** (mettre fin à) to lift [embargo, contrôle]; to raise [siège]; to dispel [doute, mystère]; to end [tabou, secret, audience]; to remove [obstacle, difficultés]; to close [séance]; **5** (collecter) to raise [capitaux, fonds]; to levy [impôt]; **6** (recruter) to levy [troupes]; **7** (débusquer) to flush out [gibier]; **~ un lièvre** lit to start a hare
B vi **1** Culin [pâte] to rise; **2** Agric [semis, blé] to come up
C se lever vpr **1** (sortir du lit) to get up; **il faut se ~ de bonne heure○ pour comprendre ce qu'il dit** fig you need to be pretty○ clever to understand what he says; **2** (se mettre debout) to stand up; **se ~ de sa chaise** to rise from one's chair; **se ~ de table** to leave the table; **'accusé, levez-vous!'** Jur 'the accused will stand'; **3** (s'insurger) [personne, peuple] to rise up (**contre** against); **4** (apparaître) [soleil, lune] to rise (**sur** over); **le jour se lève** it's getting light; **5** (s'agiter) [vent] to rise; [brise] to get up; (s'éclaircir) [nuages, brume] to clear; [temps] to clear

lever[2] /ləve/ nm **1** (sortie du lit) **être là au ~ des enfants** to be there when the children get up; **2** Géog **= levé C**
(Composés) **~ du jour** daybreak; **au ~ du jour** at daybreak; **~ de rideau** (début de la représentation) curtain up; (prélude) curtain raiser; **~ du soleil** sunrise

lève-tard /lɛvtaʀ/ nmf inv late riser

lève-tôt /lɛvto/ nmf inv early riser, early bird○

levier /ləvje/ nm lit, fig lever
(Composés) **~ de changement de vitesse** Aut gear lever GB, gear stick US; (de bicyclette) gear switch; **~ de commande** Aviat control stick; **être aux ~s de commande** fig to be in the driving seat

levraut /ləvʀo/ nm leveret

lèvre /lɛvʀ/ nf **1** (sur le visage) lip; **avoir le sourire aux ~s** to be smiling; **du bout des ~s** [rire, manger] half-heartedly; [parler, répondre] grudgingly; **2** (de la vulve) labium; **petites/grandes ~s** labia minora/majora; **3** (de faille, plaie) lip, edge
(Idiome) **être suspendu aux ~s de qn** to hang on sb's every word

levrette /ləvʀɛt/ nf **1** (femelle du lévrier) greyhound bitch; **2** (lévrier d'Italie) Italian greyhound

lévrier /levʀije/ nm greyhound
(Composé) **~ afghan** Afghan hound

levure /ləvyʀ/ nf yeast; **~ chimique** baking powder

lexème /lɛksɛm/ nm lexeme

lexical, **~e**, mpl **-aux** /lɛksikal, o/ adj lexical

lexicaliser /lɛksikalize/ [1]
A vtr **1** Ling to lexicalize; **2** Ordinat to sort
B se lexicaliser vpr Ling to become lexicalized

lexicographie /lɛksikɔgʀafi/ nf lexicography

lexique /lɛksik/ nm **1** (unilingue) glossary; (bilingue) vocabulary (book); **2** Ling lexicon, lexis

lézard /lezaʀ/ nm **1** (animal) lizard; **2** (peau) lizard(skin)

lézarde /lezaʀd/ nf lit, fig crack

lézarder /lezaʀde/ [1]
A vtr to crack
B ○vi **~ au soleil** to bask in the sun
C se lézarder vpr lit, fig to crack

liaison /ljezɔ̃/ nf **1** (ligne) link; **la ~ Calais–Douvres** the Calais–Dover line ou route; **2** Radio, Télécom **~ radio** radio contact; **~ satellite/téléphonique** satellite/telephone link; **être en ~ avec qn** to be in contact with sb; **3** (contact) **assurer la ~ entre différents services** to liaise between different services; **travailler/agir en ~ avec** to work/act in collaboration with; **4** (rapport logique) connection; **5** (relation amoureuse) affair; **6** Ling liaison

liane /ljan/ nf creeper, liana

liant, **~e** /ljɑ̃, ɑ̃t/ adj (sociable) sociable

liasse /ljas/ nf (de billets) wad; (de lettres, papiers, documents) bundle

Liban /libɑ̃/ ▸ p. 230 nprm Lebanon

libanais, **~e** /libanɛ, ɛz/ ▸ p. 392 adj Lebanese

libation /libasjɔ̃/ nf libation (**à** to)

libellé /libɛlle/ nm (de jugement, lettre) wording

libeller /libɛlle/ [1] vtr **1** Admin to draw up [acte, contrat]; **2** fml to word [lettre, demande, article]; **3** to make out [chèque, mandat]

libellule /libɛllyl/ nf dragonfly

libérable /libeʀabl/ adj **1** Jur **détenu ~** (à l'issue de sa peine) prisoner due for release; (par remise de peine) prisoner eligible for release; **prévenu ~** defendant to be discharged; **2** Mil [conscrit, contingent] to be discharged soon (**après** n)

libéral, **~e**, mpl **-aux** /libeʀal, o/
A adj **1** (tolérant) [personne, morale] liberal; **2** (favorable aux libertés) liberal; **3** Pol Liberal; **4** Écon free-market (épith)
B nm,f **1** Pol Liberal; **2** Écon free marketeer

libéralisation /libeʀalizasjɔ̃/ nf Écon, Pol liberalization; **~ des mœurs** relaxation of moral standards

libéraliser /libeʀalize/ [1]
A vtr to liberalize [commerce, économie, transports, loi, pays]
B se libéraliser vpr [pays, mœurs] to become more liberal

libéralisme /libeʀalism/ nm liberalism

libéralité /libeʀalite/ nf (générosité) liberality

libérateur, **-trice** /libeʀatœʀ, tʀis/
A adj liberating
B nm,f (de pays, ville, personne) liberator

libération /libeʀasjɔ̃/ nf **1** (de prisonnier, d'otage) release; **2** (de pays, ville, peuple) liberation; **3** (affranchissement) liberation; **4** (soulagement) relief; **5** Écon (de prix) deregulation; (d'échanges) freeing; **6** Fin (d'actions, de capital) paying up; **7** Mil discharge; **8** Phys (d'énergie) release

Libération /libeʀasjɔ̃/ nf Hist (de 1944) **la ~** the Liberation; **à la ~** at the time of the Liberation

libéré, **~e** /libeʀe/
A pp ▸ **libérer**
B pp adj **1** (émancipé) [homme, femme] liberated; **2** (délivré) [pays, zone, ville] free; **3** (disponible) [poste, lieux] vacant; **4** (affranchi) [personne, entreprise] free

libérer /libeʀe/ [14]
A vtr **1** (délivrer) to liberate [pays, ville] (**de** from); to free [compagnon, otage] (**de** from); **2** (relâcher) to release [otage, détenu] (**de** from); to free [esclave, animal] (**de** from); **3** (laisser partir) to allow [sb] to go [employé, élève]; **4** (affranchir) (de contraintes) to liberate [personne, imagination] (**de** from); (de fonctions) to relieve [ministre, employé] (**de** of); (de service militaire)

to discharge [*soldat*] (**de** from); ~ **un associé de ses obligations** to release a partner from his obligations; ~ **qn de l'emprise de qn** to get sb away from sb's influence; [5] (ne pas retenir) to release [*émotion, énergie*]; to give free rein to [*instinct, imagination*]; [6] (soulager) to relieve [*esprit, personne*] (**de** of); ~ **sa conscience** to unburden oneself; [7] (débarrasser) to vacate [*appartement, bureau*]; to clear [*passage, trottoir*] (**de** of); ~ **la chambre avant midi** (dans un hôtel) to check out before noon; [8] (dégager) to free [*bras, main*] (**de** from); to release [*ressort, cran*]; [9] Écon (libéraliser) to liberalize [*économie, échanges*]; (débloquer) to deregulate [*prix*]; ~ **les loyers/tarifs** to lift rent/tariff controls; [10] Chimie, Phys (produire) to release [*gaz, énergie, électrons*]

B se libérer *vpr* [1] (se délivrer) [*personne*] to free oneself (**de** from); [*pays, entreprise*] to free itself (**de** from); [2] (se rendre disponible) **j'essaierai de me ~ mercredi** I'll try and be free on Wednesday

libertaire /libɛʀtɛʀ/ *adj, nmf* libertarian

liberté /libɛʀte/ *nf* [1] (condition, état) freedom ¢; **Statue de la ~** Statue of Liberty; **~, égalité, fraternité** Liberty, Equality, Fraternity; **espèce vivant en ~** species in the wild; **être en ~** to be free; **l'assassin est toujours en ~** the killer is still at large; [2] (latitude) freedom ¢; **en toute ~** with complete freedom; **avoir toute ~ pour faire** to be quite free to do; **n'avoir aucune ~ de manœuvre** to have no room for manoeuvre GB *ou* maneuver US; [3] (hardiesse) freedom; ~ **de ton** outspokenness; **prendre la ~ de faire** to take the liberty of doing; [4] (droit) freedom; ~ **de pensée/d'expression** freedom of thought/of expression; **~s individuelles** individual liberties

(Composés) ~ **conditionnelle** Jur parole; ~ **de la presse** Pol freedom of the press; ~ **provisoire** Jur provisional release (*pending trial*); **mettre en ~ provisoire** to release provisionally; ~ **surveillée** Jur probation; **mise en ~ surveillée** release on probation

libertin, ~e /libɛʀtɛ̃, in/ *adj, nm,f* libertine

libidineux, -euse /libidinø, øz/ *adj* libidinous, lustful

libraire /libʀɛʀ/ ▸ p. 372 *nmf* bookseller

librairie /libʀɛʀi/ ▸ p. 372 *nf* [1] (magasin) bookshop GB, bookstore; [2] (activité) bookselling business

librairie-papeterie, *pl* **librairies-papeteries** /libʀɛʀipapɛtʀi/ ▸ p. 372 *nf* stationer's and bookshop GB *ou* bookstore

libre /libʀ/ *adj* [1] gén [*personne, condition, pays*] free (**de faire** to do); **être ~ de ses décisions/choix** to be free to decide/choose; ~ **à elle de partir** it's up to her whether she goes or not; **être ~ de ses actes** to do as one wishes; [2] (dénué) free (**de** from); ~ **de préjugés** free from prejudice; **être ~ de soucis** to enjoy peace of mind; [3] (direct) [*personne*] free and easy; [*manière*] free; [*allure*] easy; [*opinion*] candid; [*morale*] easygoing; [4] (dégagé) [*main, pouce*] free; [*route, voie*] lit, fig clear; **avoir les mains ~s** lit to have one's hands free; fig to be a free agent; [5] (disponible) [*personne, chambre*] available; [*siège, place*] free; **'~ de suite'** (dans une annonce) 'available immediately'; [6] (non occupé) [*WC*] vacant; **la ligne n'est pas ~** (au téléphone) the number is engaged GB *ou* busy US

(Composés) ~ **arbitre** Philos free will; ~ **concurrence** Écon free competition; ~ **entreprise** Écon free enterprise

(Idiome) **être ~ comme l'air** to be as free as a bird

libre-échange /libʀeʃɑ̃ʒ/ *nm* free trade

librement /libʀəmɑ̃/ *adv* freely

libre-penseur, *pl* **libres-penseurs** /libʀəpɑ̃sœʀ/ *nm* freethinker

libre-service, *pl* **libres-services** /libʀəsɛʀvis/
A *adj inv* self-service (*épith*)
B *nm* [1] (système) **le ~** self-service; [2] (magasin) self-service shop GB *ou* store US; (restaurant) self-service restaurant

(Composé) ~ **bancaire** automatic teller

lice /lis/ *nf* lists (*pl*); **entrer en ~** to enter the lists

licence /lisɑ̃s/ *nf* [1] Univ (bachelor's) degree; ~ **en droit** law degree; **préparer une ~ d'anglais** to do a degree in English; **être en ~ d'anglais** to be in the final year of an English degree; [2] Comm, Jur licence^GB; ~ **de fabrication** manufacturing licence^GB; ~ **d'importation** import licence^GB; **produit sous ~** licensed product; [3] Sport **avoir sa ~ de tennis** to be a member of the national tennis federation; [4] (liberté) licence^GB; **avoir toute ~ de faire** to have a free hand to do

licencié, ~e /lisɑ̃sje/
A *pp* ▸ **licencier**
B *pp adj* [*étudiant*] graduate (*épith*)
C *nm,f* [1] Univ graduate GB, college graduate US; [2] Sport member (*of a sports federation*); [3] Écon ~ **(économique)** person made redundant GB, laid-off worker

licenciement /lisɑ̃simɑ̃/ *nm* (pour faute) dismissal; ~ **(économique)** redundancy GB, lay-off; ~ **collectif** mass redundancy, mass lay-offs (*pl*)

(Composé) ~ **sec** compulsory redundancy (*without compensation*)

licencier /lisɑ̃sje/ [2] *vtr* (pour raisons économiques) to make [sb] redundant GB, to lay [sb] off; (pour faute) to dismiss GB, to let [sb] go

licencieux, -ieuse /lisɑ̃sjø, øz/ *adj* licentious

lichen /likɛn/ *nm* lichen

licite /lisit/ *adj* lawful

licorne /likɔʀn/ *nf* Mythol unicorn

lie /li/ *nf* lit, fig dregs (*pl*); ~ **de vin** wine dregs

lie-de-vin /lidvɛ̃/ ▸ p. 140 *adj inv* wine, wine-coloured^GB

liège /ljɛʒ/ *nm* cork; **bouchon en ~** cork

liégeois, ~e /ljeʒwa, az/ ▸ p. 621 *adj* of Liège; **café ~** iced coffee topped with whipped cream

lien /ljɛ̃/ *nm* [1] (attache) strap; (plus fin) string; fig bond; **se libérer de ses ~s** lit to free oneself of one's bonds; fig to shake off one's ties; [2] (rapport) connection, link; [3] (relation) gén link, tie; (d'ordre affectif) tie, bond; **ses ~s avec la pègre** his/her connections *ou* links with the underworld; ~ **d'amitié** ties of friendship; **~s de parenté** family ties; **il n'a aucun ~ de parenté avec elle** he's not related to her at all; **être uni par les ~s du mariage** to be joined *ou* united in marriage

lier /lje/ [1]
A *vtr* [1] (attacher) to tie [sb/sth] up [*personne, fleurs, paille*]; **il avait les mains liées** lit, fig his hands were tied; **être pieds et poings liés** lit to be bound hand and foot; fig to have one's hands tied; [2] (unir) to bind; **ils sont très liés** they are very close; [3] (établir un rapport) to link [*idées, événements*] (**à** to); [4] (commencer) ~ **amitié avec qn** to strike up a friendship with sb; [5] Culin to thicken [*sauce*]; [6] Mus to slur [*notes*]

B se lier *vpr* to make friends (**avec qn** with sb)

lierre /ljɛʀ/ *nm* ivy

liesse /ljɛs/ *nf* jubilation; **en ~** jubilant

lieu /ljø/
A *nm* [1] (*pl* **~s**) (poisson) ~ **(noir)** coley, black pollock; [2] (*pl* **~x**) (endroit) place; **complément de ~** adverbial of place; **en ~ sûr** in a safe place; ~ **de rendez-vous** *or* **de rencontre** meeting place; ~ **d'habitation/de naissance** place of residence/of birth; ~ **de vente** retail outlet, point of sale; **sur le ~ de travail** in the workplace; ~ **de passage** thoroughfare; **sur le ~ du drame** at the scene of the tragedy; **en tous ~x** everywhere; **en ~ et place de qn** [*signer, agir*] on behalf of sb; **en premier ~** in the first place, firstly; **en second ~** secondly; **en dernier ~** lastly; **avoir ~** to take place; **tenir ~ de** to serve as [*réfectoire, chambre*]; **il y a ~ de s'inquiéter** there is cause for anxiety; **cela n'a pas ~ d'être** it shouldn't be so; **donner ~ à** to cause *ou* give rise to [*scandale*]; ▸ **haut**

B au lieu de *loc prép* instead of

C lieux *nmpl* [1] (endroit) parts; **repérer les ~x** to have a scout around; **sur les ~x** [*être*] at the scene; [*arriver*] on the scene; [2] (habitation) premises

(Composés) ~ **commun** platitude; ~ **jaune** yellow pollock; ~ **public** public place; ~ **saint** holy place

lieue /ljø/ ▸ p. 347 *nf* Hist league; ~ **marine** league

(Idiome) **j'étais à cent** *or* **mille ~s d'imaginer** I never for a moment imagined

lieutenant /ljøtnɑ̃/ ▸ p. 283 *nm* [1] Mil (dans l'armée de terre) ≈ lieutenant GB, ≈ first lieutenant US; (dans l'armée de l'air) ≈ flying officer GB, ≈ first lieutenant US; [2] Naut first officer

lieutenant-colonel, *pl* **lieutenants-colonels** /ljøtnɑ̃kɔlɔnɛl/ ▸ p. 283 *nm* (dans l'armée de terre) ≈ lieutenant-colonel; (dans l'armée de l'air) ≈ wing commander GB, ≈ lieutenant colonel US

lièvre /ljɛvʀ/ nm [1] Zool hare; [2] Sport pacemaker

(Idiome) **courir plusieurs ~s à la fois** to have several irons in the fire

lifter /lifte/ [1] vtr to put topspin on [balle]

lifting /liftiŋ/ nm Méd, fig face-lift

ligament /ligamã/ nm ligament

ligature /ligatyʀ/ nf Méd (opération) tying; (résultat) ligature

ligaturer /ligatyʀe/ [1] vtr Méd to tie; **se faire ~ les trompes** to have one's tubes tied

lignage /liɲaʒ/ nm [1] (de famille) lineage; [2] (en imprimerie) linage

ligne /liɲ/ nf [1] (trait) line; **~ blanche/continue/ discontinue** Aut white/solid/broken line; **~ de départ/ d'arrivée** Sport starting/finishing line; **lire les ~s de la main de qn** to read sb's palm; **~ droite** gén straight line; (de route) straight piece of road; **la dernière ~ droite avant l'arrivée** the home straight; [2] (d'écriture) line; **je vous écris ces quelques ~s pour vous dire...** this is just a quick note to tell you...; **à la ~!** (dans une dictée) new paragraph!; [3] (de bus, bateau, d'avion) (service) service; (parcours) route; (de métro, train) line; **la ~ Paris-Rome** Aviat the Paris to Rome route; Rail the Paris to Rome line; **~ de chemin de fer** railway line; **~s intérieures** Aviat domestic flights; [4] Électrotech (câble) cable; [5] Télécom line; **la ~ est mauvaise** it's a bad line; **il y a quelqu'un d'autre sur la ~** we've got a crossed line; **avoir** or **obtenir la ~** to get through; [6] (silhouette) figure; **avoir/garder la ~** to be/to stay slim; **retrouver la ~** to get back one's figure; [7] (contour) (de corps) contours (pl); (de visage) shape; (de collines) outline; **la ~ aérodynamique d'une voiture** the aerodynamic lines (pl) of a car; [8] (allure générale) (de mobilier, style, vêtement) look; [9] Comm (gamme) line; [10] (idée, point) outline; **raconter un événement dans ses grandes ~s** to give an outline of events; [11] (orientation) (de parti politique) line; [12] (à la pêche) fishing line; **pêche à la ~** angling; [13] (alignement) line; (rangée) row; **les ~s ennemies** Mil the enemy lines; **ils sont en ~ pour le départ** they are lined up for the start; [14] Ordinat **en ~** on line; [15] (en généalogie) line; [16] TV (définition) line

(Composés) **~ de but** Sport goal line; **~ de conduite** (politique) policy; (position) line; (attitude) attitude; (stratégie) strategy; **~ de démarcation** boundary; Mil demarcation line; **~ de mire** line of sight; **~ de tir** line of fire; **~ de touche** Sport gén touchline; (au basket) boundary line

(Idiomes) **être en première ~** lit, Mil to be in the front line; fig to be in the firing line; **entrer en ~ de compte** to be taken into account ou consideration

lignée /liɲe/ nf [1] (descendants) descendants (pl); (famille) line of descent; **de haute ~** of noble descent; [2] (filiation spirituelle) tradition

lignite /liɲit/ nm brown coal, lignite spéc

ligoter /ligɔte/ [1] vtr to truss [sb] up [personne]

ligue /lig/ nf league

liguer /lige/ [1]

A vtr **~ des gens/nations contre** to unite people/countries against

B se liguer vpr [personnes] to join forces; **être ligué avec/ contre** to be in league with/against

lilas /lila/ ▸ p. 140 adj inv, nm inv lilac

lilliputien, -ienne /lilipysjɛ̃, ɛn/ adj, nm,f Lilliputian

limace /limas/ nf Zool slug

(Idiome) **se traîner comme une ~** to crawl along at a snail's pace

limaçon /limasɔ̃/ nm [1] Zool snail; [2] Anat cochlea

limaille /limaj/ nf filings (pl)

limande /limɑ̃d/ nf dab; **filet de ~** fillet of dab

limande-sole, pl **limandes-soles** /limɑ̃dsɔl/ nf lemon sole

lime /lim/ nf [1] Tech file; **à la ~** with a file; **~ à ongles** nail file; [2] Bot lime; [3] Zool lima

limer /lime/ [1]

A vtr [1] (façonner) to file [ongle, métal]; to file down [clé, aspérité]; [2] (couper) to file through [barreau]

B se limer vpr **se ~ les ongles** to file one's nails

limier /limje/ nm [1] (chien) bloodhound; [2] ○(détective, policier) sleuth; **un fin ~** a super-sleuth

limitatif, -ive /limitatif, iv/ adj limiting, restrictive

limitation /limitasjɔ̃/ nf (de pouvoir, liberté) limitation, restriction; (de prix, taux d'intérêt) control ⊄

(Composé) **~ de vitesse** Aut speed limit

limite /limit/ [1]

A nf [1] (ligne de séparation) border; [2] (partie extrême) (de domaine, terrain) boundary; (de forêt, village) edge; [3] (borne) limit; **aller jusqu'à la ~ de ses forces** to push oneself to the limit; **ma patience a des ~s** there are limits to my patience; **connaître ses ~s** to know one's (own) limitations; **franchir les ~s de la décence** to go beyond the bounds of decency; **vraiment, il dépasse les ~s!** he's really going too far!; **à la ~, je préférerais qu'il refuse** I'd almost prefer it if he refused; [4] (bord) **à la ~ de** on the verge of; **plaisanterie à la ~ du mauvais goût** joke bordering on bad taste; **un spectacle à la ~ du supportable** an almost unbearable sight; [5] (cadre) **dans une certaine ~** up to a point, to a certain extent; **dans la ~ de, dans les ~s de** within the limits of; **nous vous aiderons dans la ~ de nos moyens** we will help you as much as we can; **accepter des spectateurs dans la ~ des places disponibles** to admit spectators subject to the availability of seats; **dans la ~ du possible** as far as possible

B (-)**limite** (in compounds) **âge(-)~** maximum age; **date(-)~** deadline; **date(-)~ de vente** sell-by date

(Composé) **~ d'âge** age limit

limité, ~e /limite/

A pp ▸ limiter

B pp adj (restreint) [possibilité, conversation, ressources, intérêt, choix] limited; **devoir en temps ~** question to be answered within a set time limit

limiter /limite/ [1]

A vtr [1] (restreindre) to limit, to restrict [pouvoir, dépenses, durée, nombre]; (à to); **la vitesse est limitée à 90 km/h** the speed limit is 90 kph; **~ les dégâts** to minimize the damage; [2] (border) **la clôture qui limite notre propriété** the enclosure which marks the boundaries of our property

B se limiter vpr [1] (se restreindre) **se ~ à deux verres de bière par jour** to limit oneself to two glasses of beer a day; [2] (se résumer) **se ~ à** to be limited to; **la vie ne se limite pas au travail** there's more to life than work

limitrophe /limitʀɔf/ adj [pays, État, département, province] adjacent; [ville] border (épith)

limoger /limɔʒe/ [13] vtr (destituer) to dismiss; (déplacer) to transfer

limon /limɔ̃/ nm [1] (dépôt) silt; [2] (de voiture à cheval) shaft

limonade /limɔnad/ nf lemonade GB, lemon soda US

limoneux, -euse /limɔnø, øz/ adj [terre] silty; [eau] silt-laden

limousine /limuzin/ nf Aut limousine

limpide /lɛ̃pid/ adj [1] lit clear, limpid; [2] fig [explication, style] clear, lucid

limpidité /lɛ̃pidite/ nf [1] lit clarity; [2] fig clarity, lucidity

lin /lɛ̃/ nm [1] (fibre, plante) flax; [2] (tissu) linen

linceul /lɛ̃sœl/ nm lit, fig shroud

linéaire /lineɛʀ/ adj linear

linge /lɛ̃ʒ/ nm [1] (domestique) linen; **~ sale** dirty linen; **~ de couleur** coloureds^{GB} (pl); [2] (lessive) washing; **corde** or **fil à ~** clothes line; [3] (sous-vêtements) underwear; [4] (torchon) cloth

(Composés) **~ de corps** underwear; **~ de maison** household linen; **~ de toilette** bathroom linen

(Idiomes) **être blanc comme un ~** to be as white as a sheet; **déballer son ~ sale**○ to reveal one's guilty secret

lingère /lɛ̃ʒɛʀ/ nf (personne) laundry woman

lingerie /lɛ̃ʒʀi/ nf [1] (local) linen room; [2] (linge de corps) ~ fine fine lingerie; [3] (industrie) lingerie industry

lingette /lɛ̃ʒɛt/ nf wipe

lingot /lɛ̃go/ nm ingot; **~ de métal** metal ingot

(Composé) **~ d'or** gold ingot (weighing 1 kg)

linguiste /lɛ̃gɥist/ ▸ p. 372 nmf linguist

linguistique /lɛ̃gɥistik/

A adj linguistic; **communauté ~** speech community

B nf linguistics (+ v sg)

linotte /linɔt/ nf linnet

linteau, pl **~x** /lɛ̃to/ nm lintel

lion /ljɔ̃/ nm lion; **la part du ~** the lion's share

(Idiomes) **se battre** or **se défendre comme un ~** to fight like a tiger; **avoir mangé du ~**○ to be full of beans○ GB, to be full of pep○ US

Lion /ljɔ̃/ ▸ p. 635 *nprm* Leo

lionceau, *pl* ~**x** /ljɔ̃so/ *nm* lion cub

lionne /ljɔn/ *nf* lioness

lipide /lipid/ *nm* lipid

lippu, ~**e** /lipy/ *adj* [*bouche, personne*] full-lipped; [*lèvre*] full

liquéfier /likefje/ [2]
A *vtr* to liquefy
B se liquéfier *vpr* **1** lit to liquefy; **2** ○(avoir peur) to turn to jelly

liquette○ /likɛt/ *nf* shirt

liquidation /likidasjɔ̃/ *nf* **1** Comm, Jur (d'entreprise, de bien) liquidation; (de dettes, comptes, succession) settlement, selling off; ~ **judiciaire** *or* **forcée** compulsory liquidation; **société en** ~ company in liquidation; **2** Comm (vente) clearance

liquide /likid/
A *adj* liquid; **trop** ~ [*colle, sauce*] too runny; **argent** ~ cash; **miel** ~ clear honey
B *nm* **1** (substance) liquid; **2** (argent) cash
Composés ~ **correcteur** correction fluid, white-out (fluid) US; ~ **de frein** brake fluid; ~ **de refroidissement** coolant

liquider /likide/ [1] *vtr* **1** Jur to settle [*comptes*]; to liquidate [*société, commerce*]; to realize [*biens*]; to liquidate, to settle [*dettes*]; **2** Comm (vendre) to clear [*marchandises, stock*]; **3** ○(régler) to settle [*problèmes, querelles*]; **4** ○(se débarrasser de) to liquidate○ [*adversaire, témoin*]; **5** ○(consommer complètement) to demolish [*plat*]; to empty [*verre*]; to clear [*assiette*]

liquidité /likidite/ *nf* **1** (caractère liquide) liquidity; **2** Fin liquidity; **des** ~**s** liquid assets

lire¹ /liʀ/ [66] *vtr* **1** (déchiffrer) to read; ~ **qch à qn** to read sth to sb; **apprendre à** ~ to learn to read; **elle sait** ~ she can read; ~ **à voix haute** to read aloud; ~ **Platon dans le texte** to read Plato in the original; '**lu et approuvé**' 'read and approved'; ~ **qch en diagonale** to skim through sth, to scan sth; ~ **sur les lèvres de qn** to lip-read what sb is saying; **dans l'espoir de vous** ~ **bientôt** hoping to hear from you soon; **2** Méd, Mus to read [*radiographie, musique*]; **3** Audio, Ordinat to read; **4** (discerner) to read [*avenir*]; ~ **les lignes de la main** to read palms; ~ **dans les pensées de qn** to read sb's mind
Idiome ~ **entre les lignes** to read between the lines

lire² /liʀ/ ▸ p. 34 *nf* lira

lirette /liʀɛt/ *nf* **tapis en** ~ rag rug

lis /lis/ *nm inv* lily

liseré /lizʀe/ *nm*, **liséré** /lizeʀe/ *nm* (raie) edging; (ruban) piping

liseron /lizʀɔ̃/ *nm* bindweed, convolvulus

liseuse /lizøz/ *nf* **1** (veste) bed jacket; **2** (couvrant un livre) book cover; **3** (lampe) small reading lamp

lisible /lizibl/ *adj* **1** [*écriture, manuscrit*] legible; **2** [*auteur, roman*] readable

lisière /lizjɛʀ/ *nf* **1** (de bois, champ) edge; (de village) outskirts; fig (bord) verge; **2** (de tissu) selvage

lisse /lis/ *adj* [*surface, cheveux*] smooth; [*pneu*] worn

lisser /lise/ [1] *vtr* to smooth [*cheveux*]; to stroke [*barbe, moustache*]; to smooth (out) [*vêtement, nappe*]; to smooth [*cuir*]; **l'oiseau lisse ses plumes** the bird is preening its feathers *ou* itself

liste /list/ *nf* gén list (de of); Pol list (of candidates) GB, ticket US; **dresser** *or* **établir une** ~ to draw up a list; **faire la** ~ **de** to list, to make a list of
Composés ~ **d'attente** waiting list; ~ **de contrôle** checklist; ~ **électorale** electoral roll
Idiome **être sur (la)** ~ **rouge** to be ex-directory GB, to have an unlisted number US

listel /listɛl/ *nm* **1** Archit listel, fillet; **2** (de pièce, médaille) rim; **3** (de livre) fillet

lister /liste/ [1] *vtr* to list

lit /li/ *nm* **1** (meuble) bed; ~ **à une place** *or* **d'une personne** single bed; ~ **à deux places** *or* **de deux personnes** double bed; **aller** *or* **se mettre au** ~ to go to bed; **garder le** ~ to stay in bed; **mettre qn au** ~ to put sb to bed; **tirer qn du** ~ to drag sb out of bed; **au** ~! (à un enfant) bedtime!; **2** (structure) bed; ~ **métallique** iron bedstead; **3** (literie) bed; **le** ~ **n'était pas défait** the bed had not been slept in;

4 (unité d'accueil) bed; **un hôpital de 300** ~**s** a 300-bed hospital; **5** Jur (mariage) marriage; **6** Culin (couche) bed; **7** Géog (de cours d'eau) bed; **la rivière est sortie de son** ~ the river has overflowed its banks
Composés ~ **à baldaquin** four-poster bed; ~ **de camp** camp bed GB, cot US; ~ **d'enfant** cot GB, crib US; ~ **de mort** death-bed; ~ **en portefeuille** apple-pie bed; ~**s superposés** bunk bed (sg)
Idiome **comme on fait son** ~ **on se couche** Prov as you make your bed so you must lie in it Prov

litanie /litani/ *nf* lit, fig litany

liteau, *pl* ~**x** /lito/ *nm* **1** (en bois) (de toiture) batten; (d'étagère) bracket; **2** (de nappe) coloured^{GB} stripe

literie /litʀi/ *nf* bedding

lithographe /litɔgʀaf/ ▸ p. 372 *nmf* lithographer

lithographie /litɔgʀafi/ *nf* **1** (technique) lithography; **2** (estampe) lithograph

litière /litjɛʀ/ *nf* (de vaches) litter; (de chevaux) bedding; (pour chats) cat litter, kitty litter US

litige /litiʒ/ *nm* dispute; **point de** ~ gén bone of contention; Jur point at issue; **être en** ~ Jur to be involved in litigation; **les parties en** ~ the litigants

litigieux, -ieuse /litiʒjø, øz/ *adj* [*affaire, point, hypothèse, argument*] contentious; [*personne*] litigious

litote /litɔt/ *nf* gén, hum understatement; (en rhétorique) litotes (+ v sg)

litre /litʀ/ ▸ p. 87 *nm* (mesure) litre^{GB}; (bouteille) litre^{GB} bottle; **être vendu au** ~ to be sold by the litre^{GB}

littéraire /liteʀɛʀ/
A *adj* [*œuvre, critique, prix*] literary; [*études*] arts (épith), liberal arts (épith) US
B *nm,f* (par penchant) literary person; (étudiant) arts *ou* liberal arts US student

littéral, ~**e**, *mpl* -**aux** /liteʀal, o/ *adj* gén literal

littéralement /liteʀalmɑ̃/ *adv* **1** (signifier, traduire) literally; (citer) verbatim

littérature /liteʀatyʀ/ *nf* **1** gén literature; **2** (métier d'écrivain) **se lancer dans la** ~ to become a writer; **3** (documentation) literature

littoral, ~**e**, *mpl* -**aux** /litɔʀal/
A *adj* [*navigation, eaux*] coastal (épith); [*faune, flore*] inshore (épith)
B *nm* coast

liturgie /lityʀʒi/ *nf* liturgy

livide /livid/ *adj* [*personne, visage*] deathly pale; [*pâleur*] ghastly; liter [*aube, teint, lueur*] livid

living /liviŋ/ *nm* (pièce) living-room

Livourne /livuʀn/ *npr* Leghorn, Livorno

livraison /livʀɛzɔ̃/ *nf* **1** (de marchandise) delivery; '~**s à domicile**' 'we deliver'; **il est venu prendre** ~ **de la commande** he came to pick up the order; **2** (marchandises) delivery

livre¹ /livʀ/ *nm* **1** (volume publié) book; ~ **pour enfants** children's book; ~ **de chevet** fig bedside reading; fig bible; **2** (registre) book; (de comptabilité) (account) book, ledger; **3** (tome) book; **4** (industrie) **le** ~, **l'industrie du** ~ the book trade
Composés ~ **blanc** blue book; ~ **de bord** logbook; ~ **de caisse** cash book; ~ **électronique** e-book; ~ **de l'élève** pupil's book; ~ **de lecture** reading book, reader; ~ **du maître** teacher's book; ~ **de messe** missal, mass book; ~ **d'or** visitors' book; ~ **de poche**® paperback; ~ **scolaire** schoolbook, textbook

livre² /livʀ/ *nf* **1** **1** (monnaie) pound; ~ **sterling** pound sterling; ~ **irlandaise** Irish pound, punt; **2** ▸ p. 453 (unité de masse) (demi-kilo) half a kilo; (anglo-saxonne) pound

livrée /livʀe/ *nf* (de domestique) livery; **en** ~ in livery

livrer /livʀe/
A *vtr* **1** Comm to deliver [*marchandises*] (**to** à); **se faire** ~ **qch** to have sth delivered; ~ **qn** to deliver sb's order; **2** (remettre) to hand [sb] over [*criminel, prisonnier*] (**à** to); (en trahissant) to betray [*complice, secret*] (**to** à); to pass [sth] on [*document, renseignement*] (**à** to); **3** (abandonner) **ils ont livré le meurtrier à la colère de la foule** they turned the murderer over to the mob; **être livré à soi-même** to be left to one's own devices; **4** (confier) **il nous livre un peu de lui-même** he reveals something of himself

B se livrer vpr ⓵ (s'adonner) **se ~ à un trafic de drogue** to engage in drug trafficking; ⓶ (se rendre) **se ~ à** [*terroristes, bandits*] to give oneself up to, to surrender to; ⓷ (se confier) **se ~ à un ami** to confide in a friend; **il ne se livre pas facilement** he doesn't open up easily

Ⓘ(Idiome) **~ bataille (à qn)** to fight (sb)

livret /livʁɛ/ nm ⓵ (livre) booklet; ⓶ (d'opéra) libretto

Ⓒ(Composés) **~ de caisse d'épargne** ≈ savings book GB, bankbook (*for a savings account*) US; **~ de famille** family record book (*of births, marriages and deaths*); **~ scolaire** school report book

livreur, -euse ▸ p. 372 /livʁœʁ, øz/ nm,f delivery man/woman

lobe /lɔb/ nm Anat, Bot, Géog, Zool lobe

lobé, ~e /lɔbe/ adj ⓵ Bot lobed, sinuate; ⓶ Archit foiled, foliated

lober /lɔbe/ [1] vtr, vi to lob

local, ~e, pl **-aux** /lɔkal, o/
Ⓐ adj gén local; [*journal, industrie, autorités*] local; [*douleur, averses*] localized; **contraceptif ~** barrier method of contraception including spermicidal creams etc; **22 heures heure ~e** 22.00 local time
Ⓑ nm ⓵ (pièce quelconque) place; ⓶ (pièce à usage déterminé) **~ (à usage) commercial** commercial premises (*pl*); **locaux habitables** residential units; **dans les locaux du lycée** on school premises; **dans les locaux de la gendarmerie** at the police station; **les locaux du journal** the newspaper offices

localement /lɔkalmɑ̃/ adv gén on a local level; **appliquer la crème** ~ apply the cream locally

localisation /lɔkalizasjɔ̃/ nf ⓵ (emplacement) location; ⓶ (limitation) **la ~ d'un incendie** localizing a fire

localiser /lɔkalize/ [1] vtr ⓵ (repérer) to locate [*personne, bruit, fuite, panne*]; ⓶ (circonscrire) to localize [*incendie, conflit*]

localité /lɔkalite/ nf Biol, Géog locality

locataire /lɔkatɛʁ/ nmf tenant; **être ~** to be renting

locatif, -ive /lɔkatif, iv/
Ⓐ adj [*revenu, secteur, valeur*] rental
Ⓑ nm Ling locative; **au ~** in the locative

location /lɔkasjɔ̃/ nf ⓵ (d'immobilier) (par le propriétaire) renting out; (par le locataire) renting; **agence de ~** rental agency; **donner** ou **mettre en ~** to rent out, to let GB; **maison en ~** rented house; ⓶ (logement) rented accommodation ⓒ; ⓷ (loyer) rent; ⓸ (de matériel) **~ de voitures** car hire, car rental; **véhicule de ~** hire vehicle; **contrat de ~** rental agreement; **~ de téléviseurs/cassettes vidéos** TV/video rental; **coût de ~** cost of hiring; ⓹ (de spectacle) reservation, booking GB; **faire les ~s** to reserve, to book GB the seats; **guichet de ~** box office

location-vente, pl **locations-ventes** /lɔkasjɔ̃vɑ̃t/ nf (d'immobilier) 100% mortgage scheme

locomoteur, -trice /lɔkɔmɔtœʁ, tʁis/ adj locomotive

locomotion /lɔkɔmɔsjɔ̃/ nf locomotion

locomotive /lɔkɔmɔtiv/ nf ⓵ Rail engine, locomotive; **~ à vapeur** steam engine; ⓶ fig (meneur) driving force; (personne, région dynamique) powerhouse

Ⓘ(Idiome) **souffler comme une ~**○ to puff and pant

locuteur, -trice /lɔkytœʁ, tʁis/ nm,f speaker

locution /lɔkysjɔ̃/ nf (grammaticale) phrase; (expression) idiom; **~ toute faite** set phrase

loden /lɔdɛn/ nm ⓵ (tissu) loden; ⓶ (manteau) loden coat

logarithme /lɔgaʁitm/ nm logarithm, log

loge /lɔʒ/ nf ⓵ (de gardien) lodge; ⓶ Théât (d'artiste) dressing room; (de spectateur) box; ⓷ (de franc-maçons) Lodge; ⓸ Archit loggia

Ⓘ(Idiome) **être aux premières ~s**○ to be in an ideal position

logé, ~e /lɔʒe/
Ⓐ pp ▸ loger
Ⓑ pp adj housed; **être ~, nourri, blanchi** to have bed, board and one's laundry done

logement /lɔʒmɑ̃/ nm ⓵ (local d'habitation) accommodation ⓒ; **l'achat d'un ~** (appartement) buying a flat GB ou an apartment US; (maison) buying a house; ⓶ (fait de loger) housing; **la crise du ~** the housing crisis

Ⓒ(Composé) **~ social** local authority housing GB, public housing US

loger /lɔʒe/ [13]
Ⓐ vtr ⓵ (fournir un logement permanent à) [*mairie, service social*] to house [*famille, étudiant, réfugié*]; ⓶ (héberger temporairement) [*personne*] to put [sb] up [*ami*]; [*mairie, école*] to provide accommodation for [*sinistrés, stagiaires*]; ⓷ (contenir) [*hôtel, pensionnat*] to have accommodation for; ⓸ (placer) **~ qch dans un placard** to put sth in a cupboard [*objet, livres*]; **je n'ai pas pu ~ tous mes meubles dans le salon** I couldn't fit all my furniture in the living room; ⓹ (faire pénétrer) **~ une balle dans la tête de qn** to shoot sb in the head
Ⓑ vi ⓵ (habiter) to live; **~ chez un particulier** to have a room in a private house; ⓶ (résider temporairement) to stay; **~ à l'hôtel** to stay at a hotel; **~ chez qn** to stay with sb
Ⓒ **se loger** vpr ⓵ (avoir un lieu d'habitation) **avec cette somme, je dois me nourrir et me ~** with that I have to pay for food and accommodation ou housing; ⓶ (se placer) **se ~ dans qch** (en se fixant) to get stuck in sth; [*poussière, saletés*] to collect in sth; **la balle est venue se ~ dans le genou** the bullet lodged in his/her knee

logeur, -euse /lɔʒœʁ, øz/ nm,f lodger

logiciel, -ielle /lɔʒisjɛl/
Ⓐ adj software (*épith*)
Ⓑ nm ⓵ (ensemble de programmes) software ⓒ; **~ de base** system(s) software; **~ contributif** shareware; **~ public** freeware; ⓶ (programme) program

logicien, -ienne /lɔʒisjɛ̃, ɛn/ nm,f logician

logique /lɔʒik/
Ⓐ adj ⓵ gén logical; **il n'est pas ~ avec lui-même** he is not consistent; ⓶ ○(compréhensible) reasonable
Ⓑ nf ⓵ gén logic (**de** of); **manquer de ~** to be illogical; **avec ~** in a logical way; **c'est dans la ~ des choses** it's in the nature of things; **~ déductive** deductive reasoning; **en toute ~** logically; ⓶ Math, Ordinat, Philos logic

logiquement /lɔʒikmɑ̃/ adv logically

logis /lɔʒi/ nm inv liter home, dwelling

logistique /lɔʒistik/
Ⓐ adj logistical
Ⓑ nf logistics (+ *v sg*) (**de** of)

logo /lɔgo/ nm, **logotype** /lɔgɔtip/ nm logo

loi /lwa/ nf ⓵ (règle) law (**sur** on; **contre** against); **voter/abroger une ~** to pass/to repeal a law; **être au-dessus des ~s** to be above the law; ⓶ (corps de textes) **la ~** the law; **enfreindre la ~** to break the law; **avoir la ~ pour soi** to have the law on one's side; **subir la ~ de qn** to be ruled by sb; **d'après la ~ française** under French law; **mettre qn/qch hors la ~** to outlaw sb/sth; **tomber sous le coup de la ~** to be ou constitute an offence^{GB}; **faire la ~** fig to lay down the law; ⓷ (principe) law; **c'est la ~ des séries** things always happen in a row; ⓸ (convention) rule; **les ~s de l'hospitalité** the rules of hospitality; **~ du silence** (règle de conduite) code of silence; (pour protéger) conspiracy of silence

Ⓒ(Composés) **~ d'amnistie** act granting amnesty to some offenders; **~ communautaire** community law; **~ divine** divine law; **~ de la jungle** law of the jungle; **~ d'orientation** framework law; **~s d'exception** emergency legislation

loin /lwɛ̃/
Ⓐ adv ⓵ (dans l'espace) a long way, far (away); **c'est ~** it's a long way; **c'est trop ~** it's too far; **elle ne peut pas être bien ~** she can't be too far away ou off; **est-ce ~?** is it far (away)?; **il habite plus ~** he lives further ou farther away; **aussi** or **du plus ~ que l'on regarde** however far you look; **aussi ~ que l'on pouvait voir** as far as the eye could see; **voir plus ~** (dans un texte) see below; **plus ~ dans le roman** at a later point in the novel; ▸ **monture**; ⓶ (dans le temps) **tout cela est bien ~** that was all a long time ago; **aussi ~ que je me souvienne** as far back ou as long as I can remember; **les vacances sont déjà ~** it's a long time since the holidays GB ou the vacation US now; **c'est encore ~ (dans l'avenir)** it's still a long way off (in the future); **le temps n'est pas si ~ où...** it's not so long since...; ⓷ fig **il y a ~ d'une idée à sa réalisation** there's a wide gap between an idea and its fulfilment^{GB}; **de là à dire qu'il est incompétent, il n'y a pas ~** that comes close to saying he's incompetent; **tu sembles si ~** (distant) you seem so distant; (absorbé) you seem miles away; **il n'est pas bête, ~ s'en faut!** he's not stupid, far from it!; **ce film ne va très pas ~**

this film GB *ou* movie US is a bit shallow; **la décentralisation n'est pas allée très ~** decentralization didn't get very far; **votre fille est brillante, elle ira ~** your daughter is brilliant, she'll go far

B **loin de** *loc prép* **1** (dans l'espace) far from; **est-ce encore ~ d'ici?** is it much further *ou* farther from here?; **2** (dans le temps) far from; **cette époque n'est pas si ~ de nous** we're not so far from that time; **ils veulent aller plus ~ dans leur coopération** they want to extend their cooperation; **il ne peut pas aller plus ~ dans son soutien** he can't increase his support; **on est encore ~ d'avoir fini** we're still far from finished, we're still a long way off finishing; **il n'est pas ~ de 11 heures** it's not far off 11 o'clock; **cela ne fait pas ~ de quatre ans que je suis ici** I've been here for almost four years now; **je me sens ~ de tout cela** I feel detached from all that; **~ de moi cette idée!** nothing could be further from my mind!; **avec l'imprimante, il faut compter pas ~ de 900 euros** if you include the printer, you're talking about 900 euros or thereabouts

C **de loin** *loc adv* **1** (d'un endroit éloigné) from a distance, from afar *littér*; **je ne vois pas très bien de ~** I can't see very well at a distance; **2** *fig* from a distance; **il voit les choses de ~** he sees things from a distance; **c'est de ~ ton meilleur roman** it's by far your best novel

D **au loin** *loc adv* **(tout) au ~** (far away) in the distance

E **de loin en loin** *loc adv* **1** (séparé dans l'espace) **on pouvait voir des maisons de ~** you could see houses scattered here and there; **2** (de temps en temps) every now and then

(Idiome) **~ des yeux, ~ du cœur** *Prov* out of sight, out of mind *Prov*

lointain, ~e /lwɛ̃tɛ̃, ɛn/

A *adj* **1** (dans l'espace) distant; **2** (dans le temps) distant; **les jours ~s où...** the far-off days when...; **3** (indirect) [*ressemblance, rapport*] remote; [*cause*] indirect; **4** (détaché) [*personne, air*] distant

B *nm* background; **dans le ~** [*apercevoir, entendre*] in the distance

loir /lwar/ *nm* (edible) dormouse

(Idiome) **être paresseux comme un ~** to be bone idle

loisir /lwazir/ *nm* **1** (temps libre) spare time **C**; **pendant mes ~s** in my spare time; **(tout) à ~** at (great) leisure; **2** (possibilité) **avoir tout ~ de faire** to have plenty of time to do; **3** (activité) leisure activity; **civilisation des ~s** leisure society

lombaire /lɔ̃bɛr/ *nf* lumbar vertebra

londonien, -ienne /lɔ̃dɔnjɛ̃, ɛn/ ► p. 621 *adj* of London

Londonien, -ienne /lɔ̃dɔnjɛ̃, ɛn/ *nm,f* Londoner

Londres /lɔ̃dr/ ► p. 621 *npr* London

long, longue /lɔ̃, lɔ̃g/ ► p. 347

A *adj* **1** (dans l'espace) [*tige, cils, patte, lettre, robe, table, distance*] long; **une chemise à manches longues** a shirt with long sleeves, a long-sleeved shirt; **un tuyau ~ de trois mètres** a pipe three metres^{GB} long, a three-metre^{GB} long pipe; **au ~ cours** *Naut* [*voyage, navigation*] ocean; [*capitaine*] fully-licensed; **2** (dans le temps) [*moment, vie, voyage, exil, film, silence*] long; [*amitié*] long-standing; **ta longue habitude des enfants** your great experience of children; **une traversée longue de 40 minutes** a 40 minute crossing; **être ~ (à faire)** [*personne*] to be slow (to do); **je ne serai pas ~ (pour aller quelque part)** I won't be long; (pour un discours) I will be brief; **aliment ~ à cuire** food that takes a long time to cook; **être en longue maladie** to be on extended sick leave; **être ~ à la détente** to be slow on the uptake[○]; **il trouve le temps ~** time hangs heavy on his hands; **pendant de longues heures/années** for hours/years; **3** *Ling* (voyelle) long

B *adv* **1** (beaucoup) **en dire ~/trop ~/plus ~** to say a lot/too much/more (**sur qch/qn** about sth/sb); **2** **s'habiller ~** to wear longer skirts

C *nm* **1** (longueur) **un câble de six mètres ~** a cable six metres ^{GB} long, a six-metre^{GB} long cable; **en ~** [*découper, fendre*] lengthwise; **en ~ et en large** [*raconter*] in great detail; **marcher de ~ en large** to pace up and down; **en ~, en large et en travers**[○] [*raconter*] at great length; **le ~ du mur** (en longueur) along the wall; (en hauteur) up *ou* down the wall; **tout le ~ de qch** (dans l'espace) all along sth; (dans le temps) all the way through sth; **courir tout le ~ du chemin** to run all the way; **tomber de tout son ~** to fall flat (on one's face)

D **à la longue** *loc adv* in the end, eventually

(Composé) **~ métrage** *Cin* feature-length film

long-courrier, *pl* **~s** /lɔ̃kurje/ *nm* (navire) ocean-going ship; (avion) long-haul aircraft

longe /lɔ̃ʒ/ *nf* (de cheval) (pour attacher) tether; (pour mener) rein; **mener un cheval à la ~** to lead a horse

longer /lɔ̃ʒe/ [13] *vtr* **1** (aller le long de) [*personne, train*] to go along [*forêt, côte*]; to follow [*rivière*]; [*bateau*] to sail along [*côte*]; **2** (s'étendre le long de) [*jardin, route*] to run alongside [*lac, champ*]

longévité /lɔ̃ʒevite/ *nf* lit, fig longevity

longiligne /lɔ̃ʒiliɲ/ *adj* lanky, rangy

longitude /lɔ̃ʒityd/ *nf* longitude; **à** *or* **par 30° de ~ est/ouest** at longitude 30° east/west

longitudinal, ~e, *mpl* **-aux** /lɔ̃ʒitydinal, o/ *adj gén* longitudinal; [*axe, coupe, fibres, cassure*] longitudinal, lengthwise

longtemps /lɔ̃tɑ̃/ *adv* **1** [*attendre, dormir etc*] (for) a long time; (avec négation, dans question) (for) long; **j'y ai vécu ~** I lived there for a long time; **il n'a pas mis ~** it didn't take him long; **tu en as pour ~?** will you be long/much longer?; **il n'en a plus pour ~** (à vivre) he won't last much longer; **prévoir qch ~ à l'avance** to plan sth a long time ahead; **~ avant/après** long before/after; **avant ~** (d'ici peu) before long; **pas avant ~** not for a long time; **j'ai attendu trop ~** I waited too long; **je peux le garder plus ~?** can I keep it a bit longer?; **durer assez ~** (suffisamment) to last long enough; (une longue période) to last quite a long time; **une lettre ~ attendue** a long-awaited letter; **2** (avec il y a, depuis, cela fait) (marquant la continuité) (for) a long time, (for) long; (quand l'action est terminée) a long time ago, long ago; **il y a** *or* **cela fait ~ que je le connais, je le connais depuis ~** I've known him for a long time; **il ne travaille pas ici depuis ~, il n'y a pas ~ qu'il travaille ici** he hasn't worked *ou* been working here (for) long; **ça fait ~ qu'il n'a pas téléphoné** he hasn't phoned for ages[○]; **il n'y a plus ~ à attendre** it won't be much longer now; **il est mort depuis ~** he died a long time ago; **il ne conduisait plus depuis ~** he had stopped driving long before then; **il n'y a pas si ~ c'était encore possible** it was still possible until quite recently

longue ► long A, D

longuement /lɔ̃gmɑ̃/ *adv* (pendant longtemps) [*hésiter, cuire*] for a long time; (en détail) [*expliquer*] at length; **j'y ai ~ réfléchi** I've given it a lot of thought

longueur /lɔ̃gœr/

A *nf* **1** (dimension) length; **dans (le sens de) la ~** lengthways GB, lengthwise US; **être déchiré/fendu sur toute la ~** to be ripped/cracked along the whole length; **la maison est tout en ~** the house is long and narrow; **un câble de trois mètres de ~** a cable three metres^{GB} long, a three-metre^{GB} long cable; **2** (distance entre deux concurrents) length; **avoir une ~ d'avance sur qn** *Sport* to be one length ahead of sb; fig to be ahead of sb; **3** ► p. 327 *Sport* (en natation) length; (en athlétisme) **le saut en ~** the long *ou* broad US jump; **4** (durée) length; **traîner en ~** [*film*] to go on forever

B **longueurs** *nfpl* (dans un film, livre, discours) overlong passages

C **à longueur de** *loc prép* **~ de journée** all day long; **à ~ d'année** all year round; **à ~ de temps** all the time

(Composé) **~ d'onde** *Phys*, fig wavelength

longue-vue, *pl* **longues-vues** /lɔ̃gvy/ *nf* telescope

look[○] /luk/ *nm* (allure, style) look; (image) image

looping /lupiŋ/ *nm* loop; **faire un ~** to loop the loop

lopin /lɔpɛ̃/ *nm* **~ (de terre)** patch of land, plot

loquace /lɔkas/ *adj* talkative, loquacious

loque /lɔk/

A *nf* **~ (humaine)** (human) wreck

B **loques** *nfpl* (guenilles) rags

loquet /lɔkɛ/ *nm* latch

loqueteux, -euse /lɔktø, øz/ *adj* fml [*vêtement, livre*] tattered; [*personne*] ragged (épith)

lorgner[○] /lɔrɲe/ [1] *vtr* to give [sb] the eye[○] [*personne*]; to cast longing glances at [*bijou, gâteau*]; to have one's eye on [*héritage, poste*]

lorgnette /lɔrɲɛt/ *nf* (d'opéra) opera-glasses (*pl*); (de marine) spy-glass

Les mesures de longueur

Les unités

■ *Le système métrique est de plus en plus utilisé en Grande-Bretagne et aux États-Unis pour les mesures de longueur. Mais les anciennes mesures ont encore cours, et sont quelquefois préférées, notamment pour les distances, exprimées en miles, et non en kilomètres. Les commerçants utilisent en général les deux systèmes.*

Équivalences

1 inch	=	2,54 cm		
1 foot	=	12 inches	=	30,48 cm
1 yard	=	3 feet	=	91,44 cm
1 furlong	=	220 yards	=	201,17 m
1 mile	=	1760 yards	=	1,61 km

Pour la prononciation des nombres, voir **les nombres** ▸ **p. 398.**

dire			**dire**
one millimetre	1 mm	0.04 in*	*inches*
one centimetre	1 cm	0.39 in	
one metre	1 m	39.37 ins	
		3.28 ft	*feet†*
		1.09 yds	*yards*
one kilometre‡	1 km	1094 yds	
		0.62 ml	*miles*

* *Le symbole de inch est ": 4 inches = 4 ".*

† *Le symbole de foot et feet est ': 5 feet 4 inches = 5' 4 ".*

‡ *Deux prononciations possibles:* [kɪˈlɒmɪtə(r)] *ou* [ˈkɪləmiːtə(r)]

Pour l'écriture, noter:

– *on écrit* -metre *en anglais britannique, mais* -meter *en anglais américain;*

– *pour le système métrique, les abréviations sont les mêmes en anglais qu'en français;*

– *l'anglais utilise un point là où le français a une virgule.*

il y a 100 centimètres dans un mètre
= there are 100 centimetres in one metre

il y a douze pouces dans un pied
= there are twelve inches in one foot

il y a trois pieds dans un yard
= there are three feet in one yard

La distance

quelle distance y a-t-il entre A et B?
= what's the distance from A to B?
 ou how far is it from A to B?

à quelle distance de l'église se trouve l'école?
= how far is the school from the church?

il y a 2 km
= it is 2 kilometres

il y a environ 2 km
= it is about 2 kilometres

la distance est de 2 km
= the distance is 2 kilometres

il y a 2 km entre A et B
= it is 2 kilometres from A to B

A est à 2 km de B
= A is 2 kilometres from B

■ *(Noter l'absence d'équivalent anglais de la préposition française à avant le chiffre dans le dernier exemple.)*

à peu près 2 km
= about 2 kilometres

presque 3 km
= almost 3 kilometres

plus de 2 km
= more than 2 kilometres *ou* over 2 kilometres

moins de 3 km
= less than 3 kilometres *ou* under 3 kilometres

A est plus loin de B que C de D
= it is further from A to B than from C to D
 ou A is further away from B than C is from D

C est plus près de B que A
= C is nearer to B than A is

A est plus près de B que de C
= A is nearer to B than to C

A est aussi loin que B
= A is as far away as B

A et B sont à la même distance
= A and B are the same distance away

■ *Noter l'ordre des mots dans l'adjectif composé anglais, et l'utilisation du trait d'union. Noter aussi que* kilometre, *employé comme adjectif, ne prend pas la marque du pluriel.*

une promenade de 10 kilomètres
= a 10-kilometre walk

La longueur

combien mesure la corde?
= how long is the rope?

elle mesure 10 m de long
= it is 10 metres long

elle fait 10 m de long
= it is 10 metres in length

une corde d'environ 10 m de long
= a rope about 10 metres long *ou* 10 metres in length

à peu près 10 m
= about 10 metres

presque 11 m
= almost 11 metres

plus de 10 m
= more than 10 metres

moins de 11 m
= less than 11 metres

A est plus long que B
= A is longer than B

B est plus court que A
= B is shorter than A

A est aussi long que B
= A is as long as B

A et B ont la même longueur
= A and B are the same length

A a la même longueur que B
= A is the same length as B

10 mètres de corde
= 10 metres of rope

6 mètres de soie
= 6 metres of silk

vendu au mètre
= sold by the metre

■ *Noter l'ordre des mots dans les adjectifs composés anglais, et l'utilisation du trait d'union. Noter aussi que* metre *et* foot, *employés comme adjectifs, ne prennent pas la marque du pluriel.*

☛ Voir page suivante

l

Les mesures de longueur *suite*

une corde de 10 mètres
= a 10-metre rope *ou* a rope 10 metres long

un python de six pieds de long
= a six-foot-long python *ou* a python six feet long

....

La hauteur

La taille des personnes

combien mesure-t-il?
= how tall is he?
 ou (si l'on veut obtenir un chiffre précis) what is his
 height?

■ *En anglais, la taille des personnes est donnée en pieds*
(feet) *et en pouces* (inches), *jamais en yards. En gros,*
1,50 m = cinq pieds, et 1,80 m = six pieds.

il mesure 1,80 m
= he is 6 feet tall *ou* he is 6 feet *ou* he is 1.80 m

il mesure 1,75 m
= he is 5 feet 10 inches *ou* he is 5 feet 10 *ou* he is 1.75 m

■ *Dans la conversation courante, on utilise souvent* foot
au lieu de feet. *On peut donc dire:* he is 5 foot 10 inches
ou 5 foot 10.

à peu près 1,80 m
= about 6 ft

presque 1,80 m
= almost 6 ft

plus de 1,75 m
= more than 5 ft 10 ins

moins de 1,85 m
= less than 6 ft 3 ins

Pierre est plus grand que Paul
= Pierre is taller than Paul

Paul est plus petit que Pierre
= Paul is smaller than Pierre *ou* Paul is shorter than Pierre

Pierre est aussi grand que Paul
= Pierre is as tall as Paul

Pierre a la même taille que Paul
= Pierre is the same height as Paul

Pierre et Paul ont la même taille
= Pierre and Paul are the same height

■ *Noter l'ordre des mots dans l'adjectif composé anglais,*
et l'utilisation du trait d'union. Noter également que foot,
employé comme adjectif, ne prend pas la marque du
pluriel.

un athlète d'un mètre quatre-vingts
= a six-foot athlete

■ *On peut aussi dire* an athlete six feet tall. *De même,* a
footballer over six feet in height, *etc.*

La hauteur des choses

quelle est la hauteur de la tour?
= what is the height of the tower?

combien mesure la tour?
= what is the height of the tower?

elle fait 23 mètres de haut
= it is 23 metres high

elle mesure 23 mètres de hauteur
= it is 23 metres high *ou* it is 23 metres in height

elle a une hauteur de 23 m
= its height is 23 metres

une tour d'environ 25 m de haut
= a tower about 25 metres high
 ou about 25 metres in height

à une hauteur de 20 mètres
= at a height of 20 metres

A est plus haut que B
= A is higher than B

B est moins haut que A
= B is lower than A

A est aussi haut que B
= A is as high as B

A et B sont de la même hauteur
= A and B are the same height

A est de la même hauteur que B
= A is the same height as B

■ *Noter l'ordre des mots dans l'adjectif composé anglais,*
et l'utilisation du trait d'union. Noter aussi que metre,
employé comme adjectif, ne prend pas la marque du
pluriel.

une tour haute de 23 mètres
= a 23-metre-high tower

■ *On peut aussi dire:* a tower 23 metres high. *De même,*
a mountain over 4,000 metres in height, *etc.*

à quelle altitude est l'avion?
= how high is the plane?

à quelle altitude vole l'avion?
= what height is the plane flying at?

l'avion vole à 5000 m d'altitude
= the plane is flying at 5,000 metres

son altitude est de 5000 m
= its altitude is 5,000 metres

à une altitude de 5000 m
= at an altitude of 5,000 metres

....

La largeur

■ *L'anglais dispose de deux mots pour la largeur:* wide
mesure la distance entre deux limites (a wide valley; *le*
nom est width), *alors que* broad *décrit ce qui remplit un*
espace d'une certaine largeur (a broad avenue; *le nom*
est breadth).

■ *Les expressions suivantes utilisent* wide *et* width, *mais*
broad *et* breadth *s'emploient de la même façon.*

quelle est la largeur de la rivière?
= how wide is the river? *ou* what width is the river?

elle fait 7 m
= it is 7 metres

elle fait 7 m de large
= it is 7 metres wide *ou* it is 7 metres in width
 ou it is 7 metres across

elle fait environ 7 m de large
= it is about 7 metres wide

A est plus large que B
= A is wider than B

B est plus étroit que A
= B is narrower than A

A est aussi large que B
= A is as wide as B

A et B sont de la même largeur
= A and B are the same width

A est de la même largeur que B
= A is the same width as B

■ *Noter l'ordre des mots dans l'adjectif composé anglais,*
et l'utilisation du trait d'union. Noter aussi que metre,
employé comme adjectif, ne prend pas la marque du
pluriel.

☛ Voir page suivante

Les mesures de longueur *suite*

une rivière de 7 m de large
= a seven-metre-wide river

■ *On peut aussi dire:* a river seven metres wide. *De même,* a ditch two metres wide, a piece of cloth two metres in width, *etc.*

....

La profondeur

quelle est la profondeur du lac?
= how deep is the lake? *ou* what depth is the lake? *ou* what is the depth of the lake?

il fait 4 m
= it is 4 metres deep

il fait 4 m de profondeur
= it is 4 metres in depth

il fait environ 4 m de profondeur
= it is about 4 metres deep

un lac de 4 mètres de profondeur
= a lake four metres deep *ou* a lake four metres in depth

■ *Noter l'absence d'équivalent anglais de la préposition française de avant le chiffre dans les expressions de ce genre. Mais:*

à une profondeur de dix mètres
= at a depth of ten metres

A est plus profond que B
= A is deeper than B

B est moins profond que A
= B is shallower* than A

A est aussi profond que B
= A is as deep as B

A et B ont la même profondeur
= A and B are the same depth

A a la même profondeur que B
= A is the same depth as B

un puits de 7 m de profondeur
= a well seven metres deep

* *Noter que l'adjectif* shallow (*peu profond*) *n'a pas d'équivalent simple en français.*

Idiome **regarder la situation par le petit bout de la** ~ to take a very simplistic view of the situation

lorgnon /lɔʀɲɔ̃/ *nm* (face-à-main) lorgnette; (pince-nez) pince-nez

loriot /lɔʀjo/ *nm* oriole

lors /lɔʀ/
A **lors de** *loc prép* [1] (pendant) during; [2] (au moment de) at the time of
B **lors même que** *loc conj* even if

lorsque (**lorsqu'** *before vowel or mute h*) /lɔʀsk(ə)/ *conj* when.

⚠ *Lorsque se traduit par* when: lorsque je suis allé au Portugal = when I went to Portugal; *lorsqu'elle travaille, elle n'aime pas être dérangée* = she doesn't like to be disturbed when she's working.
Attention, on n'utilise jamais le futur après when: *lorsqu'il aura terminé* = when he's finished.

losange /lɔzɑ̃ʒ/ *nm* rhomb, lozenge; **en** ~ diamond-shaped

lot /lo/ *nm* [1] (portion) (de succession, partage) share, portion Jur; (d'émotions) share; (de terrain) plot; [2] (à la loterie) prize; **gagner le gros** ~ lit, fig© to hit the jackpot; [3] (d'objets en vente) gén batch; (aux enchères) lot; [4] (de personnes) **être au-dessus du** ~ to be above the average; [5] Ordinat batch; [6] (destin) fate, lot

loterie /lɔtʀi/ *nf* (avec lots) raffle; (de fête foraine) tombola GB, raffle US; (à grande échelle) lottery; **jouer à la** ~ to have a go© on the lottery

loti, ~**e** /lɔti/ *adj* **bien/mal** ~ well/badly off; **me voilà bien** ~**e avec un patron pareil!** iron just my luck to land up with a boss like him! iron

lotion /losjɔ̃/ *nf* lotion; ~ **après rasage** after-shave

lotir /lɔtiʀ/ [3] *vtr* [1] (répartir) to share out [*biens, immeubles*]; **terrain(s) à** ~ plots *ou* lots US for sale; [2] (attribuer) to allot (**qn de qch** sth to sb)

lotissement /lɔtismɑ̃/ *nm* housing estate GB, subdivision US

loto /lɔto/ ▸ p. 327 *nm* lotto; **le** ~ **sportif** ≈ the national sport lottery

lotte /lɔt/ *nf* (de mer) monkfish, angler fish; (de rivière) burbot

louable /luabl/ *adj* [*intention, effort*] commendable, praiseworthy

louage /luaʒ/ *nm* ~ **de services** contract of employment; **voiture de** ~ rented car GB, rental car US

louange /luɑ̃ʒ/ *nf* praise; **chanter les** ~**s de qn/de qch** to sing sb's/sth's praises; **à la** ~ **de** in praise of; **digne de** ~ praiseworthy

loubard© /lubaʀ/ *nm* hooligan, delinquent youth

louche /luʃ/
A *adj* (équivoque) [*individu, passé*] shady; [*lieu*] seedy; **il y a quelque chose de** ~ **dans cette histoire** there is something fishy© about this business
B *nf* (ustensile) ladle; (contenu) ladleful

loucher /luʃe/ [1]
A *vi* to have a squint
B **loucher sur**© *vtr ind* (convoiter) to eye [*filles*]; to have one's eye on [*héritage*]

louer /lue/ [1]
A *vtr* [1] (donner en location) to let GB, to rent out [*maison, terrain*] (**à** to); to hire [*salle*]; to hire out GB, to rent out [*équipement, film*] (**à** to); '**à** ~' 'for rent', 'to let' GB; [2] (prendre en location) to rent [*maison, terrain*] (**à** from); to hire [*salle*]; to hire GB, to rent [*équipement, film*] (**à** from); [3] (embaucher) to hire [*personnel*]; [4] (rendre grâce à) to praise (**de, pour** for); **Dieu soit loué** thank God
B **se louer** *vpr* **la chambre se loue à la semaine** the room is rented on a weekly basis; **l'appartement se loue 300 euros par mois** the rent for this apartment is 300 euros per month; (se féliciter) liter **se** ~ **d'avoir fait** to congratulate oneself on doing

loufoque© /lufɔk/ *adj* crazy©

loukoum /lukum/ *nm* Turkish delight ₵

loulou /lulu/ *nm* [1] (chien) spitz; [2] ©(voyou) hooligan, delinquent youth; [3] ©(terme d'affection) pet© GB, honey US

loup /lu/ *nm* [1] (mammifère) wolf; **à pas de** ~ stealthily; **crier au** ~ lit, fig to cry wolf; ~ **solitaire** lone wolf; ▸ **jeune** [2] (poisson) ~ (**de mer**) (sea) bass; [3] (masque) domino, mask

Composé (vieux) ~ **de mer** old salt, old tar

Idiomes **avoir une faim de** ~ to be ravenous; **être connu comme le** ~ **blanc** to be known to everybody; **se jeter dans la gueule du** ~ to stick one's head in the lion's mouth; **faire entrer le** ~ **dans la bergerie** to let the wolf into the fold; **elle a vu le** ~ hum she's lost her virginity; **les** ~**s ne se mangent pas entre eux** Prov (there is) honour^{GB} among thieves; **la faim fait sortir le** ~ **du bois** Prov needs must (when the devil drives); **quand on parle du** ~ (**on en voit la queue** *or* **il sort du bois**) Prov speak of the devil; **l'homme est un** ~ **pour l'homme** Prov dog eat dog

loupe /lup/ *nf* (lentille) magnifying glass

louper© /lupe/ [1]
A *vtr* [1] (manquer) to miss [*train, occasion, personne*]; **la prochaine fois, ils ne le louperont pas** next time they'll get you; **il n'en loupe pas une** he's always opening his big mouth; [2] (ne pas réussir) to flunk© [*examen*]; to screw up© [*sauce, ouvrage*]; to bungle [*entrée en scène*]; **il a loupé son coup** he botched it; **la soirée est complètement loupée** the evening is a wash-out

B *vi* **j'avais dit que ça se casserait, ça n'a pas loupé** I said it would break, and sure enough it did; **tu vas tout faire ~** you'll mess everything up

loup-garou, *pl* **loups-garous** /lugaʀu/ *nm* werewolf

loupiote○ /lupjɔt/ *nf* small lamp

lourd, ~e¹ /luʀ, luʀd/

A *adj* **1** (d'un poids élevé) [*personne, objet, métal*] heavy; **~ à transporter** heavy to carry; **2** (donnant une sensation de pesanteur) [*estomac, jambe, tête, pas*] heavy; [*geste*] clumsy, ungainly; **j'ai les jambes ~es** my legs feel heavy, my legs ache; **il a les yeux ~s de sommeil** his eyes are heavy with sleep; **3** (indigeste) [*repas, aliment*] heavy; [*vin*] heady; **~ à digérer** heavy on the stomach; **4** (dense) [*protection*] heavy; [*chevelure*] thick; **5** Ind, Mil [*armement, équipement*] heavy; **6** (onéreux) [*amende, fiscalité*] heavy; **7** (grave) [*perte, défaite, responsabilité*] heavy; [*présomption, erreur*] serious; **8** (encombrant) [*administration, structure*] unwieldy; [*effectifs*] great; **9** (massif) [*personne, animal*] ungainly; [*corps, objet, architecture, poitrine*] heavy; [*bâtiment*] squat; **10** (sans finesse) [*personne*] oafish; [*voix*] thick; [*plaisanterie*] flat; [*style*] clumsy; **11** (pénible) [*ciel, atmosphère, silence*] heavy; [*chaleur*] sultry; **12** (chargé) (de danger, conséquences) fraught (**de** with); (de menaces) charged (**de** with); **13** (difficilement praticable) [*piste, sol, terrain*] heavy; **14** Fin (médiocre) [*marché, tendance*] sluggish

B *adv* **1** peser **~** (être d'un poids élevé) to weigh heavy; (compter beaucoup) **peser/ne pas peser ~** to carry a lot of/not to carry very much weight (**sur** with); **2** Météo **il fait ~** it's close; **3** ○(beaucoup) **pas ~** not a lot, not much; **elle n'en fait/sait pas ~** she doesn't do/know a lot *ou* much; **rachète du beurre, il n'en reste pas ~** buy some more butter, there's hardly any left

⸢Idiomes⸣ **avoir le cœur ~** to have a heavy heart; **être ~ comme du plomb** to be (as) heavy as lead; **avoir la main ~e** (avec taxes, punitions) to be heavy-handed; **avoir la main ~e avec le sel/le parfum** to overdo the salt/the perfume

lourdaud, ~e /luʀdo, od/

A *adj* [*personne*] oafish; [*esprit*] dull; [*discours*] clumsy

B *nm,f* oaf

lourde² /luʀd/

A *adj f ▸* lourd A

B ○*nf* (porte) door

lourdement /luʀdəmɑ̃/ *adv* **1** (fortement) heavily; **se tromper ~** to be gravely mistaken; **2** (sans finesse) **marcher/se déplacer ~** to walk/move clumsily; **insister ~** to labour^GB the point; **insister ~ sur** to keep going on about

lourder⊕ /luʀde/ [1] *vtr* (congédier) to kick [sb] out○

lourdeur /luʀdœʀ/ *nf* **1** (d'organisation, de secteur, réseau) complexity; **2** (sensation de pesanteur) heaviness; **avoir des ~s d'estomac** to feel bloated; **3** (maladresse) (de style) clumsiness; (dans un texte) clumsy expression; **4** (importance) (de condamnation) heaviness, stiffness; **la ~ des subventions/impôts/pertes** the heavy subsidies (*pl*)/taxes (*pl*)/losses (*pl*); **5** (poids élevé) weight; **6** (manque de raffinement) (de personne) oafishness; (de plaisanterie) poorness; (d'architecture) ungainliness; **7** (de temps) closeness, mugginess; (d'ambiance) heaviness; **8** (de marché) sluggishness

loustic○ /lustik/ *nm* pej chap, guy

loutre /lutʀ/ *nf* **1** (animal) otter; **2** (fourrure) otterskin

louve /luv/ *nf* she-wolf

louveteau, *pl* **~x** /luvto/ *nm* Zool wolf cub

louvoyer /luvwaje/ [23] *vi* **1** Naut to beat to windward, to tack; **2** (biaiser) to manoeuvre GB, to maneuver US; (tergiverser) to hedge

lover: se lover /love/ [1] *vpr* [*serpent*] to coil itself up; [*personne*] to curl up

loyal, ~e, mpl -aux /lwajal, o/ *adj* **1** (fidèle) [*ami*] true; [*serviteur*] loyal, faithful; **bons et loyaux services** good and faithful service; **2** (honnête) [*procédé, conduite*] honest; [*concurrence, jeu*] fair

loyalement /lwajalmɑ̃/ *adv* [*servir*] faithfully; [*se battre*] fairly; [*informer*] honestly

loyalisme /lwajalism/ *nm* loyalty

loyaliste /lwajalist/ *adj, nmf* loyalist

loyauté /lwajote/ *nf* **1** (fidélité) loyalty (**envers** to); **2** (honnêteté) (de personne, conduite) honesty; (de procédé) honesty, fairness

loyer /lwaje/ *nm* rent

lubie /lybi/ *nf* whim; **avoir des ~s** to have whims

lubricité /lybʀisite/ *nf* (de personne) lustfulness, lechery; (de propos, conduite) lewdness

lubrifiant, ~e /lybʀifjɑ̃, ɑ̃t/ *nm* lubricant

lubrifier /lybʀifje/ [2] *vtr* to lubricate

lubrique /lybʀik/ *adj* [*personne*] lecherous; [*œil, danse*] lewd

lucarne /lykaʀn/ *nf* (fenêtre) (small) window; (dans un toit) skylight

lucide /lysid/ *adj* [*personne, politique*] clear-sighted; Méd lucid; [*esprit, analyse*] lucid

lucidité /lysidite/ *nf* **1** Méd lucidity; **moments de ~** lucid moments; **il a toute sa ~** he has all his wits about him; **2** (perspicacité) (de personne) clear-headedness; (d'esprit) clarity; **raisonner avec ~** to think clearly; **il a agi en toute ~** he knew perfectly well what he was doing

luciole /lysjɔl/ *nf* firefly

lucratif, -ive /lykʀatif, iv/ *adj* lucrative; **assez ~** [*emploi*] fairly well-paid; [*opération*] fairly profitable

ludique /lydik/ *adj* **1** [*activité*] play (épith); **2** Psych ludic

ludothèque /lydɔtɛk/ *nf* toy library

luette /lɥɛt/ *nf* uvula

lueur /lɥœʀ/ *nf* **1** (faible clarté) (faint) light (**de** of); **les premières ~s de l'aube** the first light (sg) of dawn; **pas la moindre ~ d'espoir** fig not the faintest glimmer of hope; **à la ~ des étoiles/d'une bougie** by starlight/candlelight; **à la ~ des événements d'hier** fig in the light of yesterday's events; **jeter une faible ~** to cast a poor light; **2** (rougeoiement) glow; **les dernières ~s du soleil couchant** the dying glow of the sunset; **3** (éclat fugitif) lit, fig gleam, flash

luge /lyʒ/ *▸* p. 327 *nf* **1** (objet) sledge GB, sled US; **2** (sport) luge

lugubre /lygybʀ/ *adj* [*paysage, pensée*] gloomy; [*son, chant*] mournful

lui /lɥi/ *pron pers*

⚠ Lorsqu'il représente une personne de sexe masculin ou un animal familier mâle, *lui* peut avoir plusieurs fonctions et se traduira différemment selon les cas: *lui, c'est un menteur* = HE's a liar; *donne-lui à boire* = give him something to drink. Voir A.

Lorsqu'il représente un objet, un concept, une plante, un animal mâle ou femelle, quel que soit le genre du mot, *lui* se traduira par *it* ou ne se traduira pas. Voir B.

Lorsqu'il représente une personne de sexe féminin ou un animal familier femelle, *lui* se traduira par *her: je ne lui dirai rien* = I won't say anything to her. Voir C.

A *pron pers m* (personne, animal familier) **1** (en fonction sujet) **elle lit, ~ regarde la télévision** she's reading, he's watching TV; **~ et moi avons longuement discuté** he and I had a long chat; **~ seul a le droit de parler** he alone has the right to talk; **c'est ~** (à la porte) it's him; **~ c'est ~ et moi c'est moi**○ he and I are different; **je sais que ce n'est pas ~ qui a fait ça** I know it wasn't he *ou* him who did it; **2** (dans une comparaison) him; **je travaille plus que ~** I work more than him *ou* than he does; **je les vois plus souvent que ~** (qu' il ne les voit) I see them more often than he does; (que je ne le vois) I see them more often than I see him; **3** (en fonction d'objet) **le frapper, ~, quelle idée!** hit HIM? what a thought!; **~, il faut l'enfermer** HE should be locked away; **4** (après une préposition) **à cause de/autour de/après ~** because of/around/after him; **à ~** (en jouant) his turn; **ce sont des amis à ~** they're friends of his; **il n'a pas encore de voiture à ~** he doesn't have his own car yet; (appartenance) it's his, it belongs to him; (tour de rôle) it's his turn; **c'est à ~ de choisir** (sa responsabilité) it's up to him to choose

B *pron pers mf* (objet, concept, animal, plante) it; **le parti/l'association lance un appel, apportez-~ votre soutien** the party/the association is launching an appeal—give it your support; **l'Espagne a signé, le Portugal, ~, n'a pas encore donné son accord** Spain has signed while Portugal hasn't yet agreed; **le toit, ~, n'a pas besoin d'être réparé** the ROOF doesn't need to be repaired; **l'appartement, ~, a été vendu** the apartment was sold

C *pron pers f* (personne, animal familier) her; **je l'ai rencontrée hier**

et ~ ai annoncé la nouvelle I met her yesterday and told her the news

lui-même /lɥimɛm/ *pron pers* **1** (personne) himself; **il me l'a dit** ~ he told me himself; **en** ~ **il se disait que** he told himself that; **'M. Greiner?'**—**'~'** (au téléphone) 'Mr Greiner?'–'speaking'; **2** (objet, idée, concept) itself; **l'objet n'a pas de valeur en** ~ the object has no value in itself

luire /lɥiʀ/ [69] *vi* (soleil, surface polie) to shine; (braises) to glow; **les yeux du loup luisaient dans l'obscurité** the wolf's eyes gleamed in the dark; ~ **de sueur** to glisten with sweat; **leur regard luisait de colère** their eyes shone with anger

luisant, ~**e** /lɥizɑ̃, ɑ̃t/ *adj* gén (surface polie) shining (**de** with); (surface mouillée) glistening (**de** with); (yeux) gleaming

lumbago /lœbago/ ▸ p. 195 *nm* back pain

lumière /lymjɛʀ/

A *nf* **1** gén, Phys light; ~ **naturelle** natural light; **la** ~ **des étoiles** starlight; **la** ~ **du soleil** sunlight; **la** ~ **du jour** daylight; **il y a de la** ~ **dans la cuisine** there's a light on in the kitchen; **les** ~ **de la ville** the city lights; **il a éteint toutes les** ~s he put all the lights out; **à la** ~ **d'une chandelle** by candlelight; **2** fig light; **à la** ~ **des récents événements** in the light of recent events; **mettre qch en** ~ (mettre en évidence) to highlight sth; (révéler) to bring sth to light; **agir en pleine** ~ to act openly; **faire (toute) la** ~ **sur une affaire** to bring the truth about a matter to light; **3** (personne) **ce n'est pas une** ~ he'll never set the world on fire

B **lumières** *nfpl* **1** (feux d'un véhicule) lights; **2** ○(connaissances) **j'ai besoin de vos** ~s I need to pick your brains; **aider qn de ses** ~s to give sb the benefit of one's wisdom; **avoir des** ~s **sur qch** to have some knowledge of a subject

Lumières /lymjɛʀ/ *nfpl* **les** ~ the Enlightenment (sg); **le siècle des** ~ the Age of Enlightenment

lumignon /lymiɲɔ̃/ *nm* (lampe) (dim) lamp

luminaire /lyminɛʀ/ *nm* (lampe) light (fitting)

lumineux, **-euse** /lyminø, øz/ *adj* **1** (qui émet de la lumière) (corps, point) luminous; **panneau** ~ electronic display (board); **enseigne lumineuse** neon sign; **faisceau** ~ beam of light, light beam; **rayon** ~ ray of light; **2** (clair) (exposé, explication) clear, lucid; **idée lumineuse** brilliant idea, brainwave○; **3** (radieux) (teint, regard) radiant

luminosité /lyminozite/ *nf* gén brightness, luminosity littér

lump /lœmp/ *nm* **œufs de** ~ lumpfish roe ₵

lunaire /lynɛʀ/ *adj* (de lune) lunar

lunatique /lynatik/ *nmf* moody person

lunch /lœʃ/ *nm* (dans la journée) buffet (lunch); (en soirée) buffet (supper)

lundi /lœdi/ ▸ p. 545 *nm* Monday; **le** ~ **de Pâques/de Pentecôte** Easter/Whit Monday

lune /lyn/ *nf* moon; **pleine** ~ full moon; **nuit sans** ~ moonless night; **nouvelle** ~ new moon

(Composés) ~ **de miel** honeymoon; ~ **rousse** ≈ April moon

(Idiomes) **être dans la** ~○ to have one's head in the clouds; **avoir l'air de tomber de la** ~ to look blank; **demander la** ~○ to cry for the moon; **promettre la** ~○ to promise the earth *ou* the moon; **décrocher la** ~ to do the impossible

luné○, ~**e** /lyne/ *adj* **bien** ~ cheerful; **mal** ~ grumpy

lunette /lynɛt/

A *nf* **1** Archit lunette; **2** (siège de toilettes) lavatory seat

B **lunettes** *nfpl* **1** (optiques) glasses; **mettre ses** ~s to put on one's glasses; **porter des** ~s to wear glasses; **2** (de protection) goggles

(Composés) ~ **d'approche** telescope; ~ **arrière** Aut rear window; ~s **noires** dark glasses; ~s **de soleil** sunglasses

lunule /lynyl/ *nf* (de l'ongle) half-moon

lupanar /lypanaʀ/ *nm* house of ill repute

lupin /lypɛ̃/ *nm* lupin GB, lupine US

lurette○ /lyʀɛt/ *nf* **il y a** *or* **cela fait belle** ~ **qu'elle a tout dépensé** she spent it all ages○ ago; **il y a** *or* **cela fait belle**

~ **que je ne l'ai pas vue** it's been ages○ since I last saw her; **il n'a rien publié depuis belle** ~ he has not published anything for ages○

luron /lyʀɔ̃/ *nm* fellow; **gai** *or* **joyeux** ~ jolly fellow

lustrage /lystʀaʒ/ *nm* **1** (processus) (de bois, métal, cuir) buffing; (de textile) lustring; (de voiture) polishing; **2** (résultat) sheen

lustre /lystʀ/

A *nm* **1** (au plafond) gén (decorative) ceiling light; (en cristal) chandelier; **2** (éclat) (de surface) sheen; (de cheveux) shine; **3** (de lieu, d'institution) prestigious image; **perdre de son** ~ to become rather lacklustre

B **lustres**○ *nmpl* **depuis des** ~s for a long time, for ages○

lustré, ~**e** /lystʀe/ *adj* **1** (naturellement) glossy; (par l'usure) shiny; **2** (tissu) glazed

lustrer /lystʀe/ [1] *vtr* (faire briller) to polish (chaussure, miroir); to make (sth) shine (cheveux, vêtement)

luth /lyt/ *nm* **1** ▸ p. 389 Mus lute; **2** Zool leatherback

luthérien, **-ienne** /lyteʀjɛ̃, ɛn/ *adj*, *nm,f* Lutheran

luthier /lytje/ ▸ p. 372 *nm* stringed instrument maker

luthiste /lytist/ ▸ p. 389 *nmf* lutenist

lutin /lytɛ̃/ *nm* **1** (démon) goblin; **2** (enfant) imp

lutte /lyt/ *nf* **1** (opposition entre personnes) conflict; (plus pénible) struggle; ~ **d'influence** power struggle; **être en** ~ **contre qn** to be in conflict with sb; **une** ~ **sans merci** a ruthless battle; **2** (action énergique) fight; (plus pénible) struggle; **la** ~ **contre le cancer** the fight against cancer; **être en** ~ to be fighting *ou* struggling; **de haute** ~ fml (gagner, obtenir) after a hard-fought struggle; **3** ▸ p. 327 Sport wrestling; **faire de la** ~ to wrestle

(Composés) ~ **armée** armed conflict; ~ **de classes** class war; ~ **d'intérêts** clash of interests; ~ **pour la vie** struggle for existence

lutter /lyte/ [1] *vi* **1** (s'opposer) (partie, peuple, pays) to struggle; ~ **contre qn** to fight against sb; **2** (agir énergiquement) (personne, groupe) to fight (**pour faire** to do); ~ **contre** to fight (crime, pollution, chômage); to fight against (violence); to contend with (intempéries, bruit); **aider le malade à** ~ **contre la maladie** to help the sick person fight back; ~ **contre l'abus d'alcool** to combat alcohol abuse; **Louis luttait contre le sommeil** Louis was fighting off sleep

lutteur, **-euse** /lytœʀ, øz/ *nm,f* **1** gén fighter; **2** Sport wrestler

luxation /lyksasjɔ̃/ *nf* Méd dislocation

luxe /lyks/ *nm* luxury; **vivre dans le** ~ to live in luxury; **voitures de** ~ luxury cars; **s'offrir le** ~ **de faire** (financièrement) to afford the luxury of doing; fig to give oneself the satisfaction of doing; **il peut se payer ce** ~ he can afford it; **ce n'est pas du** ~○ it has to be done; **je l'ai nettoyé et ce n'était pas du** ~○ I gave it a much needed clean; **avoir des goûts de** ~ to have expensive tastes

Luxembourg /lyksɑ̃buʀ/ ▸ p. 621, p. 230, p. 504 *nprm* Luxembourg; **grand-duché de** ~ Grand Duchy of Luxembourg

luxembourgeois, ~**e** /lyksɑ̃buʀʒwa, az/

A *adj* **1** ▸ p. 392 (du Luxembourg) of Luxembourg; **2** ▸ p. 621 (de Luxembourg) Luxembourg

B ▸ p. 336 *nm* Ling German dialect spoken in Luxembourg

luxer /lykse/ [1]

A *vtr* to dislocate

B **se luxer** *vpr* **se** ~ **l'épaule** to dislocate one's shoulder

luxueux, **-euse** /lyksɥø, øz/ *adj* (appartement) luxurious; (magazine) glossy

luxure /lyksyʀ/ *nf* lust

luxuriant, ~**e** /lyksyʀjɑ̃, ɑ̃t/ *adj* luxuriant

luxurieux, **-ieuse** /lyksyʀjø, øz/ *adj* liter lustful

luzerne /lyzɛʀn/ *nf* alfalfa, lucerne GB

lycée /lise/ *nm* secondary school (school preparing students aged 15–18 for the baccalaureat)

(Composés) ~ **agricole** agricultural college; ~ (**d'enseignement**) **professionnel, L(E)P** vocational school

lycéen, **-éenne** /liseɛ̃, ɛn/ *nm,f* secondary school student

lymphatique /lɛ̃fatik/ *adj* **1** (nonchalant) lethargic; **2** Anat lymphatic

lymphe /lɛ̃f/ *nf* lymph
lyncher /lɛ̃ʃe/ [1] *vtr* to lynch
lynx /lɛ̃ks/ *nm inv* lynx
(Idiome) **avoir des yeux de** ~ to be lynx-eyed
lyophiliser /ljɔfilize/ [1] *vtr* to freeze-dry
lyre /liʀ/ ▸ p. 389 *nf* lyre

lyrique /liʀik/ *adj* [1] Mus [*chant, compositeur*] operatic; [*chanteur, saison*] opera; **opéra** ~ lyric opera; [2] Littérat [*poésie, poète*] lyric; [*contenu, élan*] lyrical
lyrisme /liʀism/ *nm* lyricism; **avec** ~ lyrically
lys /lis/ *nm inv* lily
(Idiome) **blanc comme un** ~ lily-white

m, M /ɛm/ *nm inv* [1] (lettre) m, M; [2] ▸ p. 347 (*written abbr =* **mètre**) **30 m** 30 m

m' ▸ **me**

M. ▸ p. 590 (*written abbr =* **Monsieur**) Mr

ma ▸ **mon**

MA /ɛma/ *nmf* (*abbr =* **maître auxiliaire**) *secondary teacher without tenure*

macabre /makabʀ/ *adj* macabre

macadam /makadam/ *nm* tarmac®

macaque /makak/ *nm* [1] Zool macaque; [2] ○(homme laid) ugly man

macaron /makaʀɔ̃/ *nm* [1] (gâteau) macaroon; [2] (insigne) lapel badge; (étiquette autocollante) sticker; [3] (natte) coiled plait GB *ou* braid US

maccarthysme /makkaʀtism/ *nm* McCarthyism

macédoine /masedwan/ *nf* mixed diced vegetables (*pl*)

Macédoine /masedwan/ ▸ p. 504 *nprf* **la ~** Macedonia

macédonien, -ienne /masedɔnjɛ̃, ɛn/ *adj* Macedonian

macération /maseʀasjɔ̃/ *nf* (de fruits) soaking

macérer /maseʀe/ [14] *vi* [*plante, fruit*] to soak; [*viande*] to marinate; (dans du vinaigre) [*cornichon*] to pickle; **faire ~** to steep, to soak

Mach /mak/ *nm* Mach; **voler à ~ 2** to fly at Mach 2

mâche /maʃ/ *nf* lamb's lettuce

mâcher /maʃe/ [1] *vtr* to chew [*aliments, objet*]

(Idiomes) **~ la besogne** *or* **le travail à qn** to break the back of the work for sb; **il ne mâche pas ses mots** he doesn't mince his words

machette /maʃɛt/ *nf* machete

machiavélique /makjavelik/ *adj* Machiavellian

machin○ /maʃɛ̃/ *nm* [1] (objet dont on ne trouve pas le nom) thing, thingummy○, whatsit○; **qu'est-ce que c'est que ce ~-là?** what on earth's that?; [2] (chose) thing; **ce sont des ~s dangereux** they're dangerous things; [3] (personne) old fogey

Machin○, **~e** /maʃɛ̃, in/ *nmf* what's-his-name○/what's-her-name○; **la mère ~** Mrs whatsit

machinal, ~e, *mpl* **-aux** /maʃinal, o/ *adj* [*geste, réaction*] mechanical; **jeter un coup d'œil ~** to glance absent-mindedly

machinalement /maʃinalmã/ *adv* mechanically, without thinking

machination /maʃinasjɔ̃/ *nf* plot; **des ~s** plots, machinations

machine /maʃin/ *nf* [1] Tech (appareil) machine; **taper une lettre à la ~** to type a letter; **coudre un ourlet à la ~** to machine-sew a hem; **lavable en ~** machine-washable; **langage ~** Ordinat machine language; [2] (moteur) engine; **faire ~ arrière** Naut to go astern; fig to back-pedal; [3] (système) machine; **la ~ sociale/économique** the social/economic machine; [4] ○(lavage) **faire deux ~s (de linge)** to do two loads of washing

(Composés) **~ agricole** agricultural machine; **~ à calculer** calculating machine; **~ à coudre** sewing machine; **~ à écrire** typewriter; **~ infernale** (engin explosif) infernal machine; (bombe) time bomb; **~ à laver** washing machine; **~ à laver la vaisselle** dishwasher; **~ à sous** fruit machine GB, slot machine, one-armed bandit; **~ à vapeur** steam engine

machine-outil, *pl* **machines-outils** /maʃinuti/ *nf* machine tool

machinerie /maʃinʀi/ *nf* [1] (ensemble) machinery; [2] (local) gén machine room; Naut engine room; [3] Théât stage machinery

machinisme /maʃinism/ *nm* mechanization

machiniste /maʃinist/ ▸ p. 372 *nmf* [1] Théât stagehand; Cin, TV scene shifter; [2] (conducteur) driver

machisme /ma(t)ʃism/ *nm* male chauvinism

macho○ /matʃo/
A *adj* macho
B *nm* macho man

mâchoire /maʃwaʀ/ *nf* jaw

(Composé) **~ de frein** Aut brake shoe

(Idiome) **bâiller à s'en décrocher la ~** to yawn one's head off

mâchonner /maʃɔne/ [1] *vtr* to chew

mâchouiller○ /maʃuje/ [1] *vtr* to chew (on)

maçon /masɔ̃/ ▸ p. 372 *nm* gén, Constr bricklayer; (entrepreneur) builder; (qui construit en pierre) mason

maçonnerie /masɔnʀi/ *nf* (travaux) building; **travaux de ~** building work ⊄; (ouvrage) masonry-work ⊄

maçonnique /masɔnik/ *adj* masonic

macramé /makʀame/ *nm* macramé

macrobiotique /makʀɔbjɔtik/
A *adj* macrobiotic
B *nf* macrobiotics (+ *v sg*)

macrocosme /makʀɔkɔsm/ *nm* macrocosm

maculer /makyle/ [1] *vtr* to smudge [*devoir, feuille*] (**de** with); **~ qch de sang/boue** to spatter sth with blood/mud

madame, *pl* **mesdames** /madam, medam/ ▸ p. 590
[1] (titre donné à une inconnue) **Madame** (dans une lettre) Dear Madam; **Madame, Monsieur** Dear Sir or Madam; **bonsoir ~** good evening!; **mesdames et messieurs bonsoir** good evening ladies and gentlemen; [2] (titre donné à une femme dont on connaît le nom, par exemple Bon) **bonjour, ~** good morning, Ms *ou* Mrs Bon; **Chère Madame** (dans une lettre) Dear Ms *ou* Mrs Bon; **Madame Blanc** (sur une enveloppe) Ms *ou* Mrs Blanc; **Madame le Ministre** (en lui parlant) Minister; (dans une lettre) Dear Minister; [3] (formule de respect) **oui, Madame** yes, madam; **veuillez m'annoncer à Madame** tell your mistress that I am here; **Madame est servie!** dinner is served; [4] Hist Madame.

⚠ L'anglais possède un équivalent féminin de monsieur, Ms /mɪz/, qui permet de faire référence à une femme dont on connaît le nom sans préciser sa situation de famille: Ms X

madeleine /madlɛn/ *nf* madeleine

(Idiome) **pleurer comme une Madeleine** to cry one's eyes out

mademoiselle, *pl* **mesdemoiselles** /madmwazɛl, medmwazɛl/ ▸ p. 590 *nf* [1] (titre donné à une inconnue) **Mademoiselle** (dans une lettre) Dear Madam; **~** good morning; **entrez, mesdemoiselles** do come in; **occupez-vous de ~** (dans un magasin) could you attend to this lady, please?; **et pour ~, comme d'habitude?** (au café, bar etc) will it be the usual, madam?; **mesdames, mesdemoiselles, messieurs** ladies and gentlemen; [2] (titre donné à une jeune fille dont on connaît le nom, par exemple Bon) Ms Bon, Miss Bon; **Chère Mademoiselle** (dans une lettre) Dear Ms *ou* Miss Bon; **bonjour, ~** good morning Ms *ou* Miss Bon; **Mademoiselle Brun** (sur une enveloppe) Ms Brun, Miss Brun; [3] (formule de respect) ∼ **votre fille**† your daughter; ∼ **boude?** hum madam's sulking, is she? hum.

⚠️ L'anglais possède un équivalent féminin de monsieur, Ms /miz/, qui permet de faire référence à une femme dont on connaît le nom sans préciser sa situation de famille: Ms X

madère /madɛʀ/ nm madeira

madone /madɔn/ nf Art madonna; **un visage de** ∼ a serenely beautiful face

madras /madʀas/ nm inv (tissu) madras cotton

madrier /madʀije/ nm beam

madrigal, pl **-aux** /madʀigal, o/ nm Mus madrigal

madrilène /madʀilɛn/ ▸ p. 621 adj of Madrid

maelström /malstʀɔm/ nm Météo, fig maelstrom

maestria /maɛstʀija/ nf brilliance, panache; **avec** ∼ with great panache

maf(f)ia /mafja/ nf mafia; **la Mafia** the Mafia

maf(f)ieux, **-ieuse** /mafjø, øz/ adj mafia (épith)

magasin /magazɛ̃/ nm ⓵ (boutique) shop GB, store US; (plus grand) store; **grand** ∼ department store; ∼**s spécialisés** specialist shops GB ou stores US; **faire les** ∼**s** to go shopping; ∼ **d'alimentation** food shop GB ou store US; ⓶ Ind store, storehouse; **avoir en** ∼ to have in stock

(Composé) ∼ **d'armes** Mil armoury^{GB}; Comm gunsmith's

magasiner /magazine/ [1] vi C **aller** ∼ to go shopping

magasinier, **-ière** /magazinje, ɛʀ/ ▸ p. 372 nm,f ⓵ (dans une entreprise) stock controller; ⓶ (gardien de dépôt) warehouse keeper

magazine /magazin/ nm (journal, émission) magazine

mage /maʒ/ nm magus; **les rois** ∼**s** the (Three) Wise Men

magenta /maʒɛ̃ta/ ▸ p. 140 adj, nm magenta

Maghreb /magʀɛb/ ▸ p. 504 nprm **le** ∼ the Maghreb

ℹ️ **Maghreb** Collectively refers to Morocco, Algeria and Tunisia in North Africa which have been a major source of immigration to metropolitan France since the 1960s and which were previously French colonial territories.

maghrébin, ∼**e** /magʀebɛ̃, in/ adj North African, Maghrebi

magicien, **-ienne** /maʒisjɛ̃, ɛn/ ▸ p. 372 nm,f magician; **un** ∼ **de l'économie** fig an economic wizard

magie /maʒi/ nf ⓵ (science, effet) magic; **comme par** ∼ as if by magic; ⓶ (dans un spectacle) conjuring

magique /maʒik/ adj ⓵ lit magic (épith), magical; **formule** ∼ magic words (pl); ⓶ fig [décor] magical

magistère /maʒistɛʀ/ nm: high-level University degree combining academic coursework with work experience in industry

magistral, ∼**e**, mpl **-aux** /maʒistʀal, o/ adj ⓵ (remarquable) brilliant; **un coup** ∼ a masterstroke; ⓶ (doctoral) [ton] magisterial; ⓷ hum [gifle] tremendous

magistrat /maʒistʀa/ nm magistrate

magistrature /maʒistʀatyʀ/ nf ⓵ Jur magistracy; ⓶ Admin (fonction) public office; **arriver à la** ∼ **suprême** to reach the highest office in the land

magma /magma/ nm ⓵ (en géologie) magma; ⓶ fig jumble

magnanime /maɲanim/ adj magnanimous

magnanimité /maɲanimite/ nf magnanimity

magnat /maɲa/ nm magnate, tycoon

magner○: **se magner** /maɲe/ [1] vpr to get a move on○

magnésie /maɲezi/ nf magnesia

magnésium /maɲezjɔm/ nm magnesium

magnétique /maɲetik/ adj magnetic

magnétiser /maɲetize/ [1] vtr ⓵ Phys, Méd to magnetize; ⓶ (charmer) to hypnotize, to mesmerize

magnétiseur, **-euse** /maɲetizœʀ, øz/ ▸ p. 372 nm,f (magnetic) healer

magnétisme /maɲetism/ nm gén magnetism; **le** ∼ **d'un discours** the magnetic power of a speech

magnétophone /maɲetɔfɔn/ nm (à cassette) cassette (tape) recorder; (à bande) tape recorder

magnétoscope /maɲetɔskɔp/ nm video recorder, VCR

magnificence /maɲifisɑ̃s/ nf ⓵ (splendeur) magnificence, splendour^{GB}; ⓶ (générosité) **recevoir qn avec** ∼ to entertain sb lavishly

magnifier /maɲifje/ [1] vtr ⓵ (élever) to idealize [souvenir, sentiment]; ⓶ (célébrer) to glorify [héroisme, exploit]

magnifique /maɲifik/ adj magnificent, splendid

magnitude /maɲityd/ nf (de séisme) strength; **séisme de** ∼ **5,6** earthquake measuring 5.6 (on the Richter scale)

magnolia /maɲɔlja/ nm magnolia (tree)

magnum /magnɔm/ nm magnum (bottle)

magot○ /mago/ nm pile○ (of money)

magouillage○ /maguʒaʒ/ nm wangling○, fiddling○

magouille○ /maguj/ nf ⓵ (procédé) wangling○, fiddling○; ⓶ (résultat) trick; **de sombres** ∼**s** dirty tricks; ∼**s politiques** political skulduggery ¢; ∼**s électorales** election rigging ¢

magouiller○ /maguje/ [1] vi to wangle○, to fiddle○

magret /magʀɛ/ nm ∼ **de canard** duck breast

Mahomet /maɔme/ npr Mohammed

mai /mɛ/ ▸ p. 380 nm May; **le premier** ∼ May Day

maigre /mɛgʀ/
A adj ⓵ [personne] thin, skinny; ⓶ Culin [viande] lean; [fromage] low-fat; ⓷ Relig [jour] without meat; **faire** or **manger** ∼ to abstain from meat; ⓸ (médiocre) [résultat] poor; [talents, repas, économies] meagre^{GB}; [espoir] slim; [applaudissements] scant; ⓹ (peu volumineux) [filet d'eau] thin; [gazon, chevelure] sparse, thin
B nmf thin man/woman; **c'est une fausse** ∼ she looks thinner than she is

(Idiome) ∼ **comme un clou**○ as thin as a rake

maigrement /mɛgʀəmɑ̃/ adv [payé] poorly

maigreur /mɛgʀœʀ/ nf ⓵ (de personne) thinness; **d'une grande** ∼ very thin; ⓶ (faible quantité) meagreness^{GB}

maigrichon, **-onne** /mɛgʀiʃɔ̃, ɔn/ adj skinny

maigrir /mɛgʀiʀ/ [3] vi to lose weight; ∼ **de trois kilos** to lose three kilos; **il a maigri du visage** his face has got GB ou gotten US thinner; **pour** ∼ [cachet] slimming GB, reducing US

mail¹ /maj/ nm ⓵ (allée) mall, avenue; ⓶ ▸ p. 327 (jeu) pall-mall

mail² /mɛl/ nm email, e-mail

mailing /mɛliŋ/ nm controv ⓵ (principe) direct mail advertising; ⓶ (envoi) mail shot; ⓷ (document) mailing pack

maillage /majaʒ/ nm ⓵ (de filet) mesh size; ⓶ (création de réseau) creation of a network; (réseau créé) network

maille /maj/ nf ⓵ (de tricot) stitch; ∼ **(à l') endroit/envers** plain/purl stitch; **à fines/grosses** ∼**s** fine-/loose-knit (épith); **une** ∼ **qui file** (sur un collant) a ladder; **monter 20** ∼**s** to cast on 20 stitches; ⓶ (de filet) mesh; **passer à travers les** ∼**s** lit to pass through the net; fig to slip through the net; ⓷ (de chaînette) link

(Idiome) **avoir** ∼ **à partir avec qn** to have a brush with sb

maillet /majɛ/ nm mallet

mailloche /majɔʃ/ nf ⓵ (maillet) mallet, beetle; ⓶ Mus beater

maillon /majɔ̃/ nm link; ∼ **de la chaîne** link in the chain

maillot /majo/ nm ⓵ ∼ **(de corps)** vest GB, undershirt US; ⓶ (de rugby) shirt; (de cyclisme) jersey; ⓷ ∼ **(de bain)** swimsuit

(Composé) **le** ∼ **jaune** (cycliste) the leader in the Tour de France

main /mɛ̃/ ▸ p. 136 nf ⓵ Anat hand; **saluer qn de la** ∼ to wave at sb; **la** ∼ **dans la** ∼ lit hand in hand; **avoir les** ∼**s liées** lit, fig to have one's hands tied; **haut les** ∼**s!** hands up!; **se tenir la** ∼ to hold hands; **demander la** ∼ **de qn** to ask for sb's hand in marriage; **ramasser qch à pleines** ∼**s** to pick up handfuls of sth; **saisir qch à pleines** ∼**s** to take a firm hold of sth; **avoir qch bien en** ∼**(s)** lit to hold sth firmly; fig to have sth well in hand; **être adroit de ses** ∼**s** to be good with one's hands; **si tu lèves la** ∼ **sur elle** if you lay a finger on her; **faire qch à la** ∼ to do sth by hand; **fait** ∼ [produit] handmade; **tricoté** ∼ hand-knitted; **à la** ∼ [régler] manually; **jouer du piano à quatre** ∼**s** to play a duet on the piano; **à** ∼ **levée** [dessiner] freehand; [voter] by a show of hands; **vol à** ∼ **armée** armed robbery; **donner un coup de** ∼ **à qn** to give sb a hand; **dix secondes montre**

en ~ ten seconds exactly; ▸ vilain; **2** (personne) **une ~ secourable** a helping hand; **une ~ criminelle** someone with criminal intentions; **3** (dénotant le contrôle, la possession) **changer de ~s** to change hands; **avoir qch sous la ~** to have sth to hand; **c'est ce que j'avais sous la ~** it's what I had; **cela m'est tombé sous la ~** I just happened to come across it; **mettre la ~ sur qch** (s'approprier) to get one's hands on sth; **je n'arrive pas à mettre la ~ dessus** I can't lay my hands on it; **je l'ai eu entre les ~s mais** I did have it but; **être entre les ~s de qn** [pouvoir, responsabilité] to be in the hands of sb; **prendre en ~s** to take [sth] in hand; **se prendre par la ~** (soi-même) to take oneself in hand; **prendre qn par la ~** lit, fig to take sb by the hand; **avoir la ~ haute sur** to have control over; **avoir les choses en ~** to have things in hand; **à ne pas mettre entre toutes les ~s** [livre] not for general reading; **tomber entre les ~s de qn** to fall into sb's hands; **repartir avec un contrat en ~(s)** to leave with a signed contract; **elle est arrivée preuve en ~** she had concrete proof; **les ~s vides** empty-handed; **je le lui ai remis en ~s propres** I gave it to him/her in person; **de la ~ à la ~** [vendre, acheter] privately; **être payé de la ~ à la ~** to be paid cash (in hand); **de seconde ~** second-hand; **de première ~** (dans une annonce) 'one owner'; **avoir des renseignements de première ~** to have first-hand information; ▸ **velours**; **4** (origine) **écrit de la ~ du président** written by the president himself/herself; **reconnaître la ~ d'un artiste** to recognize an artist's style; **de ma plus belle ~** (écriture) in my best handwriting; **5** (dénotant l'habileté) **avoir le coup de ~** to have the knack; **il faut d'abord se faire la ~** you have to learn how to do it first; **avoir la ~ légère** to have a light touch; **6** Zool (de primate) hand; **7** (longueur) **une ~** a hand's width; **8** Sport (au football) handball; **9** Jeux (cartes de chacun) hand; (tour de jeu) deal; **perdre la ~** fig to lose one's touch; **garder la ~** fig to keep one's hand in; **10** (direction) **à ~ droite/gauche** on the right/left

(Composé) **~ courante** Constr handrail; (en comptabilité) day-book

(Idiomes) **j'en mettrais ma ~ au feu** or **à couper** I'd swear to it; **d'une ~ de fer** [gouverner] with an iron rod; **il n'y est pas allé de ~ morte**○! he didn't pull his punches!; **avoir la ~ leste** to be always ready with a slap; **laisser les ~s libres à qn** to give sb a free hand ou rein; **passer la ~** to step down (à in favour^GB of); **faire ~ basse sur** to help oneself to [biens]; to take over [marché]; **en venir aux ~s** to come to blows; **avoir la ~ heureuse/malheureuse** to be lucky/unlucky; **mettre la dernière ~ à** to put the finishing touches to; **ils peuvent se donner la ~** pej (deux personnes) they're both the same

mainate /mɛnat/ nm mynah bird

main-d'œuvre, pl **mains-d'œuvre** /mɛ̃dœvʀ/ nf (travailleurs, travail) labour^GB ȼ; **coût de la ~** labour^GB costs (pl)

main-forte /mɛ̃fɔʀt/ nf inv **prêter ~ à qn** to come to sb's aid

mainmise /mɛ̃miz/ nf **1** (domination) control (**sur** over); **avoir la ~ sur qch** to have control over sth; **2** Jur seizure

maint, **~e** /mɛ̃, mɛ̃t/ adj indéf many (+ pl), many a (+ sg); **pour ~ lecteur** for many a reader; **dans ~e famille** in many families; **~es et ~es fois** time and (time) again; **à ~es reprises** many times

maintenance /mɛ̃tnɑ̃s/ nf maintenance

maintenant /mɛ̃t(ə)nɑ̃/ adv now; **jusqu'à ~** up until now; **à partir de ~** from now on; **~ que** now that; **commence dès ~** start straightaway; **c'est ~ qu'il faut planter vos rosiers** now is the time to plant your rose bushes; **imaginons ~ que** now let's imagine that; **il doit avoir fini ~** he must have finished by now; **la jeunesse de ~** the youth of today; **les mœurs de ~** today's social mores; **~ les choses se font différemment** nowadays people do things differently; **je t'ai averti, ~ tu fais ce que tu veux** I've warned you, now do what you want

maintenir /mɛ̃t(ə)niʀ/ [36]
A vtr **1** (faire durer) to maintain [situation, équilibre, privilège]; to keep [paix, cessez-le-feu]; to keep up [coutumes]; **ils ont maintenu le secret** they kept it secret; **~ les prix** to keep prices stable; **2** (soutenir) to support [mur, cheville]; **3** (conserver en l'état) to keep; **~ la tête hors de l'eau** to keep one's head above the water; **~ qch debout** to hold sth upright; **~ la température** to maintain the temperature; **4** (ne pas retirer) to stand by [décision, accusation]; **~ que** to maintain

that; **~ sa candidature** (pour un emploi) to go through with one's application; Pol not to withdraw one's candidacy

B **se maintenir** vpr [amélioration, tendance] to persist; [prix] to remain stable; [système politique] to remain in force; [monnaie] to hold steady (à at); [temps] to hold; [personne] to remain in good health; **se ~ au pouvoir** to remain in power

maintien /mɛ̃tjɛ̃/ nm **1** (d'état de fait, de système) maintaining; **notre but c'est le ~ des prix** our aim is to keep prices stable; **assurer le ~ de l'ordre** to maintain order; **2** (de poitrine, tête) support; **3** Pol **le ~ de sa candidature est peu probable** it is unlikely that he will continue to stand GB ou run US; **4** (allure) deportment

maire /mɛʀ/ nm mayor
(Composé) **~ adjoint** deputy mayor

mairie /mɛʀi/ nf **1** (administration) gén town council GB ou hall US; (dans une grande ville) city council; **être élu à la ~ de** to be elected mayor of; **2** (bureaux) town hall

mais /mɛ/ conj but; **incroyable ~ vrai** strange but true; **~ ne t'inquiète donc pas!** don't you worry about it!; **il est bête, ~ bête**○! he's so incredibly stupid!; **je n'ai rien compris, ~ vraiment rien!** I understood absolutely nothing!; **'est-ce que je peux venir aussi?'—'~ oui!** 'can I come too?'—'of course!'; **~ où est-il passé?** where on earth○ has he got to?; **~ vas-tu te taire!** can't you just shut up○?; **~, vous pleurez!** good heavens, you're crying!; **~ alors, vous m'avez menti!** so you lied to me!; **~ j'y pense** now that I come to think of it; **~ dis-moi, tu le connais aussi?** so you know him too?; **il n' y a pas de ~** there are no buts about it

maïs /mais/ nm inv **1** Agric maize GB, corn US; **2** Culin sweetcorn; **épi de ~** corn on the cob

maison /mɛzɔ̃/
A adj inv **1** (fait chez soi, comme chez soi) home-made; **2** (d'une entreprise) **notre formation ~** our very own training scheme

B nf **1** (bâtisse) house; **2** (domicile familial) home; **rester à la ~** to stay at home; **elle tient la ~** she runs the house; **3** (maisonnée) household; (famille) family; **la ~ du roi** the royal household; **le fils de la ~** the son of the family; **faire la jeune fille de la ~** hum to do the honours^GB; **gens de ~** domestic staff ȼ; **c'est une ~ de fous!** it's a madhouse!; **4** (lignée) family; **~ d'Orange** House of Orange; **5** (société) firm; **avoir 15 ans de ~** to have been with the firm for 15 years; **~ d'édition** publishing house; **~ de production** production company; **~ de confiance** reliable company; **'la ~ ne fait pas crédit'** 'no credit given'; **6** (en astrologie) house

(Composés) **~ d'arrêt** prison; **~ bourgeoise** imposing town house; **~ de campagne** house in the country; **~ close** brothel; **~ de correction** institution for young offenders; **~ de la culture** ≈ community arts centre^GB; **~ des jeunes et de la culture**, **MJC** ≈ youth club; **~ de jeu** gaming house; **~ maternelle** home for single mothers; **~ mère** (siège) headquarters (pl); (établissement principal) main branch; **~ de passe** brothel; **~ de poupée** doll's^GB ou doll US house; **~ de retraite** old people's ou retirement home; **~ de santé** nursing home; **la Maison Blanche** the White House

(Idiomes) **c'est gros comme une ~**○ it sticks out a mile; **avoir un pied dans la ~** to have a foot in the door; **c'est la ~ du bon Dieu** it's open house

maisonnée /mɛzɔne/ nf gén household; (famille) family

maître, -esse[1] /mɛtʀ, ɛs/ ▸ p. 283
A adj **1** (en contrôle) **être ~ de soi** (calme) to have self-control; **être ~ de faire** to be free to do; **être ~ de ses émotions** to keep one's emotions under control; **être ~ chez soi** to be master in one's own house; **être ~ de son (propre) destin** to be master of one's destiny; **rester ~ de la décision** to retain control over the decision; **être ~ de son véhicule** to be in control of one's vehicle; **se rendre ~ d'une ville** to take over a city; **2** (principal) **idée maîtresse** key idea; **~ mot** catchword; **ouvrage** or **œuvre maîtresse** magnum opus; **qualité maîtresse** main quality

B nmf **1** Scol teacher; **2** (de maison) master/mistress; **3** (d'animal) owner; **un chien et son ~** a dog and its master

C nm **1** (dirigeant) **être (le) seul ~ à bord** lit, fig to be in sole command; **être le ~ du pays** to rule the country; **être son propre ~** to be one's own master/mistress; **régner en**

~ **absolu** to reign supreme (**sur** over); **être le** ~ **du jeu** to have the upper hand; **2** (expert) **tu es un** ~ you're an expert; **Hitchcock, le** ~ **du suspense** Hitchcock, the master of suspense; **être passé** ~ **dans l'art de faire** to be a past master at doing; **en** ~ masterfully; **de main de** ~ in a masterly fashion; **coup de** ~ masterstroke; ▸ **grand**; **3** (guide, enseignant) master; **4** Art, Littérat master; **5** (titre) Maître; **6** Jeux **être** ~ **à carreau** to hold the master card in diamonds

Composés ~ **d'armes** Sport fencing instructor; ~ **d'hôtel** maître d'hôtel GB, maître d' US; ~ **d'œuvre** Constr project manager; ~ **d'ouvrage** (privé) employer; (public) contracting authority; ~ **à penser** mentor; **maîtresse femme** strong-minded woman

Idiomes **trouver son** ~ to meet one's match; **nul ne peut servir deux** ~s a man cannot serve two masters

maître-assistant, ~**e,** mpl **maîtres-assistants** /mɛtRasistɑ̃, ɑ̃t/ nm,f Univ ≈ senior lecturer GB, senior instructor US

maître-autel, pl **maîtres-autels** /mɛtRotɛl/ nm high altar

maître-chanteur, pl **maîtres-chanteurs** /mɛtRəʃɑ̃tœR/ nm blackmailer

maître-chien, pl **maîtres-chiens** /mɛtRəʃjɛ̃/ nm dog-handler

maître-nageur, pl **maîtres-nageurs** /mɛtRənaʒœR/ ▸ p. 372 nm (enseignant) swimming instructor; (surveillant) pool attendant

Composé ~ **sauveteur** lifeguard

maîtresse² /mɛtRɛs/
A adj f ▸ **maître A**
B nf (amante) mistress

maîtrise /mɛtRiz/ nf **1** (virtuosité) mastery ¢; **avec** ~ masterfully; **2** (connaissance approfondie) perfect command; **3** (calme) ~ **(de soi)** self-control ¢; **4** (contrôle) control; **5** (exploitation) harnessing; ~ **de l'atome** harnessing of nuclear energy; **6** Mil (domination) supremacy; **7** Univ master's degree

maîtriser /mɛtRize/ [1]
A vtr **1** (contenir) to control [sentiment, rire, personne]; to get [sth] under control [épidémie]; to bring [sth] under control [incendie]; to overcome [adversaire]; to handle [problème]; **2** (connaître parfaitement) to master [langue, technique]
B se maîtriser vpr to have self-control; **ne plus se** ~ to have lost one's self-control

maïzena® /maizena/ nf cornflour

majesté /maʒɛste/ nf majesty; **un air de** ~ an air of dignity; **sa Majesté** His/Her Majesty

majestueux, -euse /maʒɛstɥø, øz/ adj [bâtiment, avenue] majestic; [personne, démarche] stately

majeur, ~**e** /maʒœR/
A adj **1** **être** ~ to be over 18 ou of age Jur; **elle sera** ~**e en mai** she will be 18 in May ou come of age in May; **2** (le plus important) [cause, défi] main, major; **un problème** ~ a major problem; **le problème** ~ the main problem; **en** ~**e partie** for the most part; **3** Mus major
B nm (doigt) middle finger

Majeur /maʒœR/ ▸ p. 333 npr **le lac** ~ Lake Maggiore

major /maʒɔR/ nm **1** Univ **sortir** ~ **de sa promotion** to come first in one's year; **2** ▸ p. 283 Mil (dans l'armée de terre, de l'air) French rank above that of warrant officer GB ou chief warrant officer US; (dans la marine) French rank above that of fleet chief petty officer GB ou chief warrant officer US

majoration /maʒɔRasjɔ̃/ nf increase

majordome /maʒɔRdɔm/ nm butler, majordomo

majorer /maʒɔRe/ [1] vtr to increase

majorette /maʒɔRɛt/ nf majorette

majoritaire /maʒɔRitɛR/ adj majority (épith)

majoritairement /maʒɔRitɛRmɑ̃/ adv **1** (à la majorité) [décider] by a majority (vote); **2** (en majorité) **province** ~ **catholique** predominantly Catholic province

majorité /maʒɔRite/ nf **1** (dans un vote) majority; **avoir la** ~ to have a majority; **la** ~ **silencieuse** the silent majority; **2** (des gens, choses) majority; **la** ~ **de la population** most of the population; **ils sont en** ~ they are in the majority; **ce sont, en** ~, **des enfants** they are, for the most part, children; **3** (parti majoritaire) **la** ~ the government, the party in power

majuscule /maʒyskyl/
A adj capital
B nf capital (letter)

mal, mpl **maux** /mal, mo/
A adj inv **1** (répréhensible) wrong; **qu'a-t-elle fait de** ~? what has she done wrong?; **2** (mauvais) bad; **ce ne serait pas** ~ **de déménager** it wouldn't be a bad idea to move out; ~ **an;** **3** ○**un film pas** ~ a rather good film; **elle est pas** ~ (physiquement) she's rather good looking
B nm **1** (peine) trouble, difficulty; **sans** ~ easily; **avoir du** ~ **à faire** to have trouble doing; **se donner beaucoup de** ~ **pour qn** to go to a great deal of trouble on sb's account; **ne te donne pas ce** ~! don't bother!; **donne-toi un peu de** ~! make some effort!; **2** ▸ p. 195 (douleur) pain; **faire** ~ lit, fig to hurt; **se faire** ~ to hurt oneself; **j'ai** ~ it hurts; **avoir** ~ **partout** to ache all over; **elle avait très** ~ she was in pain; **ces bottes me font** ~ **aux pieds** these boots hurt my feet; **avoir** ~ **à la gorge** to have a sore throat; **j'ai** ~ **aux yeux** my eyes are sore; **ça me fait** ~ **au ventre** lit it gives me a stomach-ache; **3** (maladie) illness, disease; ~ **sans gravité** minor illness; ~ **incurable** incurable disease; **tu vas attraper du** ~○ you'll catch something; ▸ **remède, patience;** **4** (manque) **être en** ~ **d'inspiration** to be short of inspiration; **être en** ~ **d'affection** to be lacking in affection; **5** (dommage) harm; **le** ~ **est fait** the harm is done; **faire du** ~ **à** (durablement) to harm; (momentanément) to hurt [personne, économie]; **il n'y a pas de** ~ (formule de politesse) there's no harm done; **une douche ne te ferait pas de** ~ hum a shower wouldn't do you any harm; **mettre à** ~ **qch** to damage sth; **6** (calamité) **qu'elle parte, est-ce vraiment un** ~? is it really a bad thing that she is leaving?; **un** ~ **à combattre** an evil that must be fought; **7** (méchanceté) **penser à** ~ to have evil intentions; **sans penser à** ~ without meaning any harm; **dire du** ~ **de qn** to speak ill of sb; **8** Philos, Relig evil
C adv **1** (avec incompétence) [fait, écrit] badly; **elle travaille** ~ her work isn't good; **elle joue** ~ (maintenant) she's playing badly; (en général) she's not a good player; **s'y prendre** ~ **avec qn** to deal with sb the wrong way; ▸ **étreindre;** **2** (de manière défectueuse) ~ **fonctionner** not to work properly; **elle est** ~ **en point** she's not too good; (très grave) she's in a bad way; **dire quelque chose** ~ **à propos** to make an inappropriate remark; **3** (difficilement) **on voit** ~ **comment** it's difficult to see how; **marcher** ~ [personne] to walk with difficulty; **4** (insuffisamment) [éclairé, payé] poorly; **j'ai t'entends** ~ I can't hear you very well; ~ **entretenu** neglected; ▸ **cordonnier;** **5** (sans goût) [s'habiller] badly; **6** (de manière erronée) [diagnostiqué, adressé] wrongly; **j'avais** ~ **compris** I had misunderstood; ~ **informé** ill-informed; **7** (défavorablement) **aller** ~ [personne] not to be well; [affaires] to go badly; [vêtement] not to fit well; **se trouver** ~ to faint; **être** ~ (assis ou couché) not to be comfortable; **être au plus** ~ to be critically ill; **ne le prenez pas** ~ don't take it badly ou the wrong way; **être** ~ **avec qn** to be on bad terms with sb; **se mettre** ~ **avec qn** to fall out with sb; **8** (de manière criticable) [se conduire] badly; ~ **faire** to do wrong; **se tenir** ~ (grossièrement) to have bad manners; (voûté) to have a bad posture; **il serait** ~ **venu de faire** it would be unseemly to do; ▸ **acquis**
D **pas mal**○ loc adv (beaucoup) **il a pas** ~ **bu** he's had quite a lot to drink; **elle a pas** ~ **d'amis** she has quite a few friends; **il est pas** ~ **violent** he's rather violent

Composés ~ **de l'air** airsickness; ~ **des grands ensembles** social problems attendant on high-density housing; ~ **de mer** seasickness; **avoir le** ~ **de mer** (ponctuellement) to feel seasick; (généralement) to suffer from seasickness; ~ **du pays** homesickness; **avoir le** ~ **du pays** to feel homesick; ~ **du siècle** world-weariness; ~ **des transports** travel sickness; **avoir le** ~ **des transports** to be prone to travel sickness

Idiomes **ça me ferait** ~○ (d'étonnement) I'd be amazed; (d'écœurement) it would really piss me off○; **entre or de deux maux il faut choisir le moindre** Prov it's a matter of choosing the lesser of two evils

Malacca /malaka/ npr **presqu'île de** ~ Malay peninsula

malade /malad/
A adj **1** [personne] ill, sick; [animal] sick; [plante] diseased; **tomber** ~ to fall ill ou sick, to get sick US; **être** ~ **en voiture/en avion** to get carsick/airsick; **j'en suis** ~○ fig it makes me sick; ~ **de peur** sick with fear; **être** ~ **d'inquiétude** to be worried sick; **se faire porter** ~ to

report sick; **2)** [*poumons, œil*] diseased; [*dent*] bad; **3)** ○(fou) **être ~ (de la tête)** to be crazy

B *nm,f* gén sick man/woman; (dans un cadre médical) patient; **les ~s** the sick (+ *v pl*), the patients

(Composés) **~ imaginaire** hypochondriac; **~ mental** mentally ill person; **les ~s mentaux** the mentally ill (+ *v pl*); **c'est un ~ mental** he's mentally ill

(Idiome) **être ~ comme un chien**○ to be as sick as a dog

maladie /maladi/ ▸ p. 195 *nf* **1)** (d'un malade) illness, disease; **pendant sa longue ~** during his/her long illness; **~s contagieuses** contagious diseases; **~ des poumons** lung disease; **une ~ mentale** a mental illness; **il va en faire une ~**○ fig he'll have a fit○; **2)** (de végétal, d'animal) disease; **3)** ○(manie) **avoir la ~ du rangement** to have a mania for tidiness

(Composés) **~ honteuse** Méd† venereal disease; fig shameful disease; **~ orpheline** orphan disease; **~ professionnelle** occupational disease; **~ sexuellement transmissible, MST** sexually transmitted disease, STD

maladif, -ive /maladif, iv/ *adj* [*enfant, air*] sickly; [*jalousie*] pathological; **être d'une pâleur maladive** to be unhealthily pale

maladresse /maladʀɛs/ *nf* **1)** (manque d'adresse) clumsiness; **2)** (manque de tact) tactlessness; **il a agi avec ~ envers elle** he was tactless with her; **3)** (manque d'aisance) awkwardness; **avec ~** awkwardly; **4)** (erreur) (de personne) mistake; (dans un texte) **des ~s de style** infelicities of style; **5)** (bévue) blunder

maladroit, ~e /maladʀwa, wat/

A *adj* **1)** (malhabile) [*personne, geste, traduction*] clumsy; [*écriture*] faltering; **2)** (sans tact) tactless

B *nm,f* (personne gauche) clumsy person; (gaffeur) tactless person

maladroitement /maladʀwatmɑ̃/ *adv* (sans adresse) clumsily; (sans tact) tactlessly; (sans aisance) awkwardly; (sans finesse) ineptly

mal-aimé, ~e, *mpl* **~s** /malɛme/ *adj* **être ~** to be starved of affection

malais, ~e[1] /malɛ, ɛz/ ▸ p. 392, p. 336

A *adj* Malay

B *nm* Malay

malaise[2] /malɛz/ *nm* **1)** Méd dizzy turn; **avoir un ~** to feel faint; **2)** (gêne) uneasiness; **il y a (comme) un ~**○ there's a bit of a problem; **3)** (état de crise) unrest (**chez** among)

(Composé) **~ cardiaque** mild heart attack

malaisé, ~e /malɛze/ *adj* difficult (**à faire, de faire** to do)

malappris†, ~e /malapʀi, iz/ *nm,f* lout

malaria /malaʀja/ ▸ p. 195 *nf* malaria

malawien, -ienne /malawjɛ̃, ɛn/ ▸ p. 392 *adj* Malawian

malaxer /malakse/ [1] *vtr* **1)** (pétrir) to cream [*beurre*]; to knead [*pâte*]; **2)** (mélanger) to mix

malbouffe○ /malbuf/ *nf* unhealthy eating

malchance /malʃɑ̃s/ *nf* bad luck, misfortune; **jouer de ~** to be dogged by bad luck; **par ~** as ill luck would have it

malchanceux, -euse /malʃɑ̃sø, øz/ *adj* unlucky

maldonne /maldɔn/ *nf* (aux cartes) misdeal; (malentendu) misunderstanding

mâle /mɑl/

A *adj* **1)** Biol, Bot male; **2)** Zool gén male; [*éléphant, baleine*] bull; [*antilope, lièvre, lapin*] buck; [*moineau, perroquet*] cock; **cygne ~** cob; **canard ~** drake; **3)** Électrotech [*fiche, prise*] male; **4)** (viril) manly

B *nm* **1)** Zool male; **2)** (homme viril) hum he-man○

malédiction /malediksjɔ̃/ *nf* curse; **la ~ pèse sur eux** there's a curse on them

maléfice /malefis/ *nm* evil spell

maléfique /malefik/ *adj* evil

malencontreusement /malɑ̃kɔ̃tʀøzmɑ̃/ *adv* [*survenir*] inopportunely; [*annoncer*] inappropriately; [*oublier*] unfortunately

malencontreux, -euse /malɑ̃kɔ̃tʀø, øz/ *adj* unfortunate

malentendant, ~e /malɑ̃tɑ̃dɑ̃, ɑ̃t/

A *adj* **être ~** to be hard of hearing

B *nm,f* **les ~s** the hearing-impaired

malentendu /malɑ̃tɑ̃dy/ *nm* misunderstanding

malfaçon /malfasɔ̃/ *nf* defect (*caused by bad workmanship*)

malfaisant, ~e /malfəzɑ̃, ɑ̃t/ *adj* [*personne*] evil; [*influence, idéologie*] harmful

malfaiteur /malfɛtœʀ/ *nm* criminal

malformation /malfɔʀmasjɔ̃/ *nf* malformation

malgache /malgaʃ/ ▸ p. 392, p. 336 *adj, nm* Malagasy

malgré /malgʀe/ *prép* in spite of, despite; **~ les apparences** in spite of appearances; **elle l'a épousé ~ son âge** she married him in spite of his age; **~ le fait que** in spite of *ou* despite the fact that; **~ d'incontestables progrès** although there has been clear progress; **~ l'absence de liens diplomatiques entre les deux pays** although the two countries have no diplomatic ties; **~ cela, ~ tout** nevertheless; **~ qn** against sb's wishes; **(presque) ~ soi** reluctantly; **j'ai entendu leur conversation ~ moi** I overheard their conversation without wishing to *ou* by accident

malhabile /malabil/ *adj* clumsy

malheur /malœʀ/ *nm* **1)** (adversité) adversity, misfortune; **tomber dans le ~** to be struck by misfortune; **faire le ~ de qn** to bring sb nothing but unhappiness; ▸ **bonheur; 2)** (coup du sort) misfortune; (grave) tragedy; (accident) accident; **une série de ~s** a series of misfortunes; **le grand ~ de ma jeunesse** the great tragedy of my youth; **un ~ est si vite arrivé!** accidents can so easily happen!; **il leur arrivera ~!** something terrible will happen to them!; **raconter ses ~s à qn** to tell sb one's troubles; **le grand ~!** iron so what!; **3)** (malchance) misfortune; **ceux qui ont le ~ de faire** those who are unfortunate enough to do; **j'ai eu le ~ de le leur dire** I made the mistake of telling them; **pour mon ~** unfortunately for me; **par ~, le ~ a voulu que** as bad *ou* ill luck would have it; **si par ~ la guerre éclatait** if, God forbid, war should break out; **porter ~** to be *ou* bring bad luck; **le ~, c'est que...** the trouble is,...

(Idiomes) **il va faire un ~**○ (avoir du succès) he'll be a sensation; (faire un éclat) he'll cause a scene; **un ~ n'arrive jamais seul** Prov it never rains but it pours; **à quelque chose ~ est bon** Prov every cloud has a silver lining Prov

malheureusement /malœʀøzmɑ̃/ *adv* unfortunately

malheureux, -euse /malœʀø, øz/

A *adj* **1)** (pas heureux) unhappy; (plus fort) miserable; **ne prends pas cet air ~!** don't look so miserable; **si c'est pas ~**○ de **voir...;** isn't it awful to see...; **2)** (à plaindre) [*victime*] unfortunate; **3)** (malchanceux) [*personne*] unlucky (en in); [*coïncidence*] unfortunate; [*passion*] ill-fated; **4)** (regrettable) [*mot, geste, choix*] unfortunate; **c'est ~ que** it's a pity *ou* shame that; **5)** ○(négligeable) paltry, pathetic; **pour trois ~ euros** for a paltry three euros; **seulement dix ~ visiteurs** only a pathetic ten visitors

B *nm,f* **1)** (personne peu chanceuse) **le ~!** poor man!; **ne fais pas cela, malheureuse!** don't do that, for heaven's sake!; **2)** (indigent) poor person; **les ~** the poor

(Idiome) **être ~ comme les pierres** to be as miserable as sin

malhonnête /malɔnɛt/

A *adj* **1)** (indélicat) dishonest; **2)** (inconvenant) [*proposition*] improper

B *nmf* **1)** (personne indélicate) dishonest person; **2)** (personne) rude person

malhonnêteté /malɔnɛtte/ *nf* dishonesty

malice /malis/ *nf* **1)** (taquinerie) mischief; **avec ~** mischievously; **2)** †(malveillance) malice; **être sans ~** to be harmless

malicieux, -ieuse /malisjø, øz/ *adj* mischievous

malin, maligne /malɛ̃, maliɲ/

A *adj* **1)** (intelligent) clever; **elle n'est pas très maligne** she isn't very bright; **j'ai eu l'air ~!** iron I looked like a total fool!; **2)** ○(difficile) **ce n'est pas bien ~** it's not exactly difficult; **3)** (méchant) **prendre un ~ plaisir à faire** to take malicious pleasure in doing; **4)** Méd [*tumeur*] malignant

B *nm,f* **1)** (personne rusée) **c'est un ~** he's a crafty one; **faire le** *ou* **son ~**○ to show off; **jouer au plus ~**○ to play the wise guy○; **2)** Littérat **le Malin** Satan, the Devil

(Idiome) **à ~, ~ et demi** Prov there's always someone who will outwit you

malingre /malɛ̃gʀ/ *adj* puny

malintentionné, ~e /malɛ̃tɑ̃sjɔne/ *adj* malicious

m

malle /mal/ *nf* **1** (coffre, valise) trunk; **se faire la** ~⁹ to clear off°; **2** Aut ~ **(arrière)** boot GB, trunk US

malléabilité /maleabilite/ *nf* malleability

mallette /malɛt/ *nf* (pour le bureau) briefcase

malmener /malməne/ [16] *vtr* **1** (maltraiter) to manhandle [*personne*]; **2** (mettre en difficulté) to give [sb] a rough ride; **3** [*auteur*] to misuse [*langue*]

malnutrition /malnytRisjɔ̃/ *nf* malnutrition

malodorant, ~e /malɔdɔRɑ̃, ɑ̃t/ *adj* foul-smelling (*épith*)

malotru, ~e /malɔtRy/ *nm,f* boor

malouin, ~e /malwɛ̃, in/ ▸ p. 621 *adj* of Saint-Malo

Malouines /malwin/ ▸ p. 303 *nprfpl* **les (îles)** ~ the Falklands, the Falkland Islands

malpoli, ~e /malpɔli/ *adj* rude

malpropre /malpRɔpR/
A *adj* (sale) dirty
B *nmf* **se faire renvoyer comme un** ~ to be chucked out°

malsain, ~e /malsɛ̃, ɛn/ *adj* lit, fig unhealthy

malséant, ~e /malseɑ̃, ɑ̃t/ *adj* unseemly

malt /malt/ *nm* malt; **de** ~ malt (*épith*)

malthusianisme /maltyzjanism/ *nm* Malthusianism

maltraitance /maltRɛtɑ̃s/ *nf* abuse; ~ **d'enfants** child abuse

maltraiter /maltRɛte/ [1] *vtr* to mistreat [*personne, animal*]; to misuse [*langue, grammaire*]

malus /malys/ *nm inv* (surprime) loaded premium

malveillance /malvɛjɑ̃s/ *nf* **1** (antipathie) malice; **2** (intention de nuire) malicious intent; **incendie dû à la** ~ malicious arson

malveillant, ~e /malvɛjɑ̃, ɑ̃t/ *adj* malicious

malvenu, ~e /malvəny/ *adj* [*propos, intervention*] out of place (*jamais épith*); **tu es** ~ **de te plaindre** you're in no position to complain

malversation /malvɛRsasjɔ̃/ *nf gén* malpractice **₵**; Fin embezzlement **₵**

malvoyant, ~e /malvwajɑ̃, ɑ̃t/ *nmf* partially sighted person

maman /mamɑ̃/ *nf* mum° GB, mom° US, mummy° GB, mommy° US, mother

mamelle /mamɛl/ *nf* Zool *gén* teat; (pis) udder

mamelon /mamlɔ̃/ *nm* **1** Anat nipple; **2** Géog hillock

mamie /mami/ *nf* (grand-mère) granny°, grandma°

mammaire /mamɛR/ *adj* mammary

mammectomie /mamɛktɔmi/ *nf* mastectomy

mammifère /mamifɛR/ *nm* mammal

mammographie /mamɔgRafi/ *nf* mammography

mammouth /mamut/ *nm* mammoth

mam'selle°, mam'zelle° /mamzɛl/ *nf* miss

mamy = mamie

manager¹ /manaʒœR/ = manageur

manager² /manaʒe/ [13] *vtr* to manage

manageur /manaʒœR/ ▸ p. 372 *nm* manager

manant† /manɑ̃/ *nm* Hist (paysan) peasant

manche¹ /mɑ̃ʃ/ *nm* **1** (d'outil) handle; (de violon) neck; ▸ **cognée**; **2** °(maladroit) clumsy idiot; **jouer comme un** ~ to be a hopeless player; **il s'y est pris comme un** ~ he set about it in a clumsy fashion

(*Composé*) ~ **à balai** lit broomhandle; (de sorcière) broomstick; Aviat joystick

manche² /mɑ̃ʃ/ *nf* **1** (de vêtement) sleeve; **à** ~**s longues** long-sleeved; **sans** ~**s** sleeveless; **2** Sport round; (aux cartes) hand; (au bridge) game; **3** °(quête) **faire la** ~ [*mendiant*] to beg

(*Idiomes*) **avoir qn dans la** ~ to have sb in one's pocket; **se faire tirer par la** ~ to need coaxing; **c'est une autre paire de** ~**s**° it's a different ball game°

Manche /mɑ̃ʃ/ *nprf* **1** ▸ p. 406 (mer) **la** ~ the (English) Channel; **le tunnel sous la** ~ the Channel tunnel; **2** ▸ p. 504 (département) **la** ~ the Manche

manchette /mɑ̃ʃɛt/ *nf* **1** (de chemise) double cuff; (de protection) oversleeve; (garniture) cuff; **2** (titre) headline

manchon /mɑ̃ʃɔ̃/ *nm* muff

manchot, -otte /mɑ̃ʃo, ɔt/
A *adj* (d'un bras) one-armed; (d'une main) one-handed; **il est** ~

(d'un bras) he's only got one arm; **ne pas être** ~° to be pretty good with one's hands°
B *nm,f* (personne) (d'un bras) one-armed person; (d'une main) one-handed person
C *nm* Zool penguin

mandarin /mɑ̃daRɛ̃/ *nm* **1** Hist, fig mandarin; **2** ▸ p. 336 Ling Mandarin (Chinese)

mandarine /mɑ̃daRin/ *nf* mandarin orange

mandarinier /mɑ̃daRinje/ *nm* mandarin tree

mandat /mɑ̃da/ *nm* **1** ~ **(postal)** money order; **2** (fonction, charge) term of office; **exercer son** ~ to be in office; **3** (pouvoir) mandate, authorization; **donner** ~ **à qn de faire** to authorize sb to do

(*Composés*) ~ **d'amener** summons (+ *v sg*); ~ **d'arrêt** (arrest) warrant; ~ **d'expulsion** (hors d'un pays) expulsion order; (hors d'une maison) eviction order; ~ **international** Jur mandate; (postal) international money order; ~ **de perquisition** search warrant; ~ **télégraphique** telegraphic money order

mandataire /mɑ̃datɛR/ *nmf* **1** Jur proxy; **2** (représentant) representative; Comm agent

mandat-carte, *pl* **mandats-cartes** /mɑ̃dakaRt/ *nm* postal order (*in the form of a postcard*)

mandater /mɑ̃date/ [1] *vtr* to appoint [sb] as one's representative [*personne*]; (pour une mission) to give a mandate to

mandat-lettre, *pl* **mandats-lettres** /mɑ̃dalɛtR/ *nm* postal order

mandchou, ~e /mɑ̃dʃu/
A *adj* Manchu
B ▸ p. 336 *nm* Ling Manchu

mandibule /mɑ̃dibyl/ *nf* **1** Anat, Zool mandible; **2** °(mâchoire) jaw

mandoline /mɑ̃dɔlin/ ▸ p. 389 *nf* mandolin

mandrin /mɑ̃dRɛ̃/ *nm* (de perceuse) chuck

manège /manɛʒ/ *nm* **1** (de fête foraine) merry-go-round; **faire un tour de** ~ to have a ride on the merry-go-round; **2** (centre équestre) riding school; (piste) ~ **(couvert)** indoor school *ou* arena; **3** (manœuvre habile) (little) trick, (little) game; **j'ai bien observé ton** ~ I know what you are up to

mânes /mɑn/ *nmpl* manes

manette /manɛt/ *nf* **1** *gén* lever; (de jeu) joystick; ~ **des gaz** throttle; **2** fig (commande) ~**s** controls; **être aux** ~**s** to be in control

manganèse /mɑ̃ganɛz/ *nm* manganese

mangeable /mɑ̃ʒabl/ *adj* edible

mangeoire /mɑ̃ʒwaR/ *nf* (pour chevaux, bovins) manger; (pour porcs) trough; (pour poules) feeding trough; (pour oiseaux) feeding tray

manger /mɑ̃ʒe/ [13]
A *vtr* **1** (consommer) to eat; **il n'y a rien à** ~ **dans la maison** there's no food in the house; **qu'est-ce qu'on mange à midi?** what's for lunch?; **je ne vais pas te** ~°! fig I won't eat you°!; ▸ **enragé, grive, soupe**; **2** (dépenser) to use up [*économies*]; to go through [*héritage*]; [*activité*] to take up [*temps*]; **3** (attaquer) [*rouille, acide*] to eat away [*métal*]; [*mites*] to eat [*laine*]; **être mangé aux** *or* **par les rats** to be gnawed by rats; **se faire** ~ **par les moustiques** to be eaten alive by mosquitoes; **se faire** ~ **par son concurrent** to be devoured by one's competitor; **4** (mal articuler) ~ **ses mots** to mumble
B *vi* (se nourrir) to eat; **ils viendront te** ~ **dans la main** lit, fig you'll have them eating out of your hand; ~ **à sa faim** to eat one's fill; **donner à** ~ **à** to feed [*bébé*]; to give [sb] something to eat [*pauvre*]; **faire à** ~ to cook; ~ **froid** (un plat refroidi) to eat [sth] cold; (un repas froid) to have a cold meal; **inviter qn à** ~ to invite sb for a meal; **je vous invite à** ~ **dimanche midi** (au restaurant) let me take you to lunch on Sunday; (chez soi) come to lunch on Sunday; ~ **chinois** to have a Chinese meal; ~ **au restaurant** to eat out; **on mange mal ici** the food is not good here
C **se manger** *vpr* **le gaspacho se mange froid** gazpacho is served cold; **le poulet peut se** ~ **avec les doigts** you can eat chicken with your fingers; ▸ **loup**

(*Idiome*) ~ **la consigne** to forget one's orders

mangeur, -euse /mɑ̃ʒœR, øz/ *nm,f* **bon/gros** ~ good/big eater

(*Composé*) **mangeuse d'hommes** man-eater

mangouste /mãgust/ *nf* ① Zool mongoose; ② Bot mangosteen

mangue /mãg/ *nf* mango

manguier /mãgje/ *nm* mango (tree)

maniabilité /manjabilite/ *nf* (de véhicule) manoeuvrability GB, maneuvrability US; **notre voiture allie la ~ à la puissance** our car is both easy to handle and powerful

maniable /manjabl/ *adj* [objet, voiture] easy to handle (*jamais épith*)

maniaco-dépressif, -ive, *mpl* **~s** /manjakodepResif, iv/ *adj, nm,f* manic-depressive

maniaque /manjak/
Ⓐ *adj* ① (tatillon) particular, fussy; (qui a des marottes) cranky; ② Méd manic
Ⓑ *nm,f* ① (personne excentrique) crank; (personne tatillonne) fusspot GB, fussbudget US; ② (fanatique) fanatic; **c'est un ~ de l'ordre** he's obsessive about tidiness; ③ (détraqué) maniac
(Composé) **~ sexuel** sex maniac

maniaquerie /manjakRi/ *nf* (caractère) fussiness

manichéen, -éenne /manikeẽ, ɛn/ *adj* Philos, Relig Manichean; (en) dualistic

manichéisme /manikeism/ *nm* Manicheism

manie /mani/ *nf* ① (habitude) habit (**de faire** of doing); **avoir la ~ de tout garder** to be a compulsive hoarder; **c'est une vraie ~** it's an absolute obsession; ② (marotte) quirk, idiosyncrasy; ③ Méd mania; **~ de la persécution** persecution mania

maniement /manimã/ *nm* ① (manipulation) gén handling; (de machine) operation; (de langue) command; **d'un ~ aisé** [outil] easy to handle; [machine] easy to operate; ② (gestion) management
(Composé) **~ d'armes** Mil arms drill

manier /manje/ [2]
Ⓐ *vtr* gén to handle; **bien ~ le pinceau** fig to be a good painter
Ⓑ **se manier** *vpr* **se ~ aisément** [outil] to be easy to handle; [voiture] to handle well
(Idiomes) **~ la fourchette avec entrain**○ hum to have a hearty appetite; **il sait ~ la brosse à reluire**○ he's good at buttering people up○

manière /manjeR/
Ⓐ *nf* ① (façon) way; **d'une ~ ou d'une autre** in one way or another; **d'une certaine ~** in a way; **la bonne ~ de s'y prendre** the right way to go about it; **leur ~ de vivre/penser** their way of life/thinking; **leur ~ d'être** the way they are; **de toutes les ~s possibles** in every possible way; **de telle ~ que** in such a way that; **de ~ à faire** so as to do; **en aucune ~** in no way; **de la même ~** [travailler] in the same way; [agir] the same way; **à ma ~** my (own) way; **de ~ décisive** in a decisive way; **de quelle ~ peut-on résoudre le problème?** how can one solve the problem?; **de toute ~, de toutes ~s** anyway, in any case; ② (méthode) **employer la ~ forte** to use strong-arm tactics; **il ne reste plus que la ~ forte** there's no alternative but to use force; **utiliser la ~ douce** to use kid gloves; ③ (style) **à la ~ de qn/qch** in the style of sb/sth
Ⓑ **manières** *nfpl* ① (savoir-vivre) manners; **bonnes/mauvaises ~s** good/bad manners; **il n'a pas de ~s** he has no manners; **qu'est-ce que c'est que ces ~s!** what manners!; **je vais t'apprendre les bonnes ~s** I'll teach you some manners; ② (excès de politesse) **faire des ~s** to stand on ceremony

maniéré, ~e /manjeRe/ *adj* pej affected

maniérisme /manjeRism/ *nm* Art mannerism

manifestant, ~e /manifɛstã, ãt/ *nm,f* demonstrator

manifestation /manifɛstasjõ/ *nf* ① (pour protester) demonstration (**contre** against; **pour** for); ② (réunion) event; **~s sportives** sporting events; ③ (de phénomène) appearance; ④ (de sentiment) expression, manifestation
(Composés) **~ silencieuse** vigil; **~ de soutien** rally (**en faveur de** for)

manifeste /manifɛst/
Ⓐ *adj* obvious, manifest
Ⓑ *nm* Art, Pol manifesto

manifester /manifɛste/ [1]
Ⓐ *vtr* (faire connaître) to show, to demonstrate [soutien]; to show [curiosité, sentiment, qualité]; (exprimer) to express [désir, crainte]; **~ de l'humeur** to show irritation; **~ sa présence**

to make one's presence known
Ⓑ *vi* to demonstrate
Ⓒ **se manifester** *vpr* ① (devenir apparent) [symptôme] to manifest itself; [phénomène] to appear; [maladie, inquiétude] to show itself; **une tendance au changement se manifeste** a tendency for change can be seen; ② (faire signe) **il ne s'est pas encore manifesté** (en personne) there is still no sign of him; (par lettre, téléphone) we still haven't heard from him; ③ (répondre à un appel) [témoin] to come forward

manigance /manigãs/ *nf* little scheme

manigancer /manigãse/ [12] *vtr* **~ quelque chose** to be up to something; **qu'est-ce qu'elle manigance encore?** what's she up to now?; **~ un mauvais coup** to hatch up a scheme

manille /manij/ *nf* ▸ p. 327 Jeux manille

manipulateur, -trice /manipylatœR, tRis/ *nm,f* ① ▸ p. 372 (technicien) technician; ② (provocateur) pej manipulator

manipulation /manipylasjõ/ *nf* ① (d'objet, de produit) handling; ② (d'opinion, de personne) manipulation *C*; **~s électorales** electoral rigging *C*; ③ Méd manipulation *C*; ④ (sur une substance) operation; Scol, Univ (expérience) experiment

manipuler /manipyle/ [1] *vtr* ① (avec les mains) to handle [objet, véhicule]; to manipulate [bouton]; ② (utiliser) to handle [chiffres]; to use [mots]; ③ (falsifier) to massage [données, chiffres]; ④ (influencer) to manipulate [opinion, personne]; ⑤ Théât to operate [marionnettes]

manitou /manitu/ *nm* ① ○fig big noise○; **un grand ~ de la finance** a big noise in the financial world; ② Relig manitou

manivelle /manivɛl/ *nf* handle
(Idiome) **donner le premier tour de ~** Cin to start filming

manne /man/ *nf* (aubaine) godsend; **~ céleste** manna from Heaven

mannequin /manke/ *nm* ① ▸ p. 372 (de mode) model; ② (de vitrine, musée) dummy

manœuvre¹ /manœvR/ ▸ p. 372 *nm* unskilled worker

manœuvre² /manœvR/ *nf* ① (avec véhicule) (opération) manoeuvre GB, maneuver US; (maniement) manoeuvring GB, maneuvering US; **effectuer ou faire une ~** to carry out a manoeuvre GB ou maneuver US; **fausse ~** mistake; ▸ **faux¹**; ② (d'appareil, de dispositif) operation; ③ (pour obtenir quelque chose) tactic; **~s électorales** electoral tactics; ④ Mil manoeuvre GB, maneuver US; **partir en ~s** to go on manoeuvres GB ou maneuvers US; **champ de ~s** military training area; ⑤ Rail (manœuvre) shunting GB, switching US

manœuvrer /manœvRe/ [1]
Ⓐ *vtr* ① (déplacer) to manoeuvre GB, to maneuver US [véhicule]; ② (actionner) to operate [dispositif, machine]; ③ (manipuler) to manipulate [personne]
Ⓑ *vi* **j'ai dû ~ pour sortir la voiture** I had to carry out a tricky manoeuvre GB ou maneuver US to get the car out

manoir /manwaR/ *nm* manor (house)

manomètre /manɔmɛtR/ *nm* pressure gauge

manouche○ /manuʃ/ *nm,f* gypsy

manquant, ~e /mãkã, ãt/ *adj* missing

manque /mãk/
Ⓐ *nm* ① (insuffisance) gén lack (**de** of); (de personnel) shortage (**de** of); **par ~ de ressources** for ou through lack of resources; **quel ~ de chance!** what bad luck!; **~ de chance, il est tombé malade** just his luck, he fell ill; ② (lacune) gap; ③ (privation) **ressentir un ~** to feel an emptiness; **être en ~ d'affection** to be in need of affection; **être en (état de) ~** [drogué] to be suffering from withdrawal symptoms
Ⓑ **à la manque**○ *loc adj* **un héros à la ~** a would-be hero; **une idée à la ~** a useless idea
(Composé) **~ à gagner** loss of earnings

manqué, ~e /mãke/
Ⓐ *pp* ▸ **manquer**
Ⓑ *pp adj* [tentative] failed; [occasion] missed
Ⓒ *adj* **c'est un poète ~** he should have been a poet

manquement /mãkmã/ *nm* **~ à la discipline** breach of discipline; **~ à une promesse** failure to keep a promise

manquer /mãke/ [1]
Ⓐ *vtr* ① (ne pas atteindre, ne pas voir) to miss [cible, spectacle, train, personne]; **~ l'école** to miss school; **un film à ne pas ~** a film not to be missed; **vous l'avez manquée de cinq**

minutes you missed her/it by five minutes; **2** (ne pas réussir) **elle a manqué son solo** she made a mess of her solo; **ça nous a fait ~ plusieurs contrats** it has lost us several contracts; **~ son coup**○ to fail; **3** ○(ne pas sanctionner) **la prochaine fois je ne le manquerai pas** next time I won't let him get away with it

B manquer à *vtr ind* **1** **la Bretagne/ma tante me manque** I miss Brittany/my aunt; **2** **~ à ses promesses** to fail to keep one's promises; **~ à sa parole** to break one's word

C manquer de *vtr ind* **1** (avoir en quantité insuffisante) **~ de** to lack [*patience, argent, expérience, pratique*]; **on ne manque de rien** we don't want ou lack for anything; **ma cousine ne manque pas d'humour** my cousin's got a good sense of humour^GB; **elle ne manque pas de charme** she's not without charm; **on manque d'air ici** it's stuffy in here; **il manque de magnésium** he has a magnesium deficiency; **2** (toujours à la forme négative) **je ne manquerai pas de vous le faire savoir** I'll be sure to let you know; **'remercie-le de ma part'—'je n'y manquerai pas'** 'thank him for me'—'I won't forget'; **et évidemment, ça n'a pas manqué**○! and sure enough that's what happened!; **3** (faillir) **il a manqué (de) casser un carreau** he almost broke a windowpane

D *vi* **1** (faire défaut) **trois soldats manquaient à l'appel** three soldiers were missing at roll call; **les vivres vinrent à ~** supplies ran out ou short; **ce ne sont pas les occasions qui manquent** there's no lack of opportunity; **le courage leur manqua** their courage failed them; **les mots me manquent** words fail me; **les mots me manquent pour exprimer ma joie** I can't find the words to express my joy; **ce n'est pas l'envie qui me manque de faire** it's not that I don't want to do; **2** (être absent) [*élève, personne*] to be absent

E *v impers* **il manquait deux fourchettes** two forks were missing; **il lui manque un doigt** he's got a finger missing; **il nous manque deux joueurs pour former une équipe** we're two players short of a team; **ça manque d'animation ici!** it's not very lively here!; **il ne manquerait plus que ça**○! that would be the last straw!; **il ne manquerait plus qu'il se mette à pleuvoir** all (that) we need now is for it to start raining

F se manquer *vpr* **1** (soi-même) to bungle one's suicide attempt; **2** (ne pas se voir) to miss each other

mansarde /mɑ̃saʀd/ *nf* (pièce) attic room

mansardé, ~e /mɑ̃saʀde/ *adj* [*pièce*] attic (épith)

mansuétude /mɑ̃sɥetyd/ *nf* indulgence

mante /mɑ̃t/ *nf* **~ religieuse** Zool praying mantis; fig man-eater

manteau, *pl* **~x** /mɑ̃to/ *nm* **1** (vêtement) coat; **2** (de brume, de neige) blanket

(Composé) **~ de cheminée** mantelpiece

(Idiome) **sous le ~** illicitly

mantille /mɑ̃tij/ *nf* mantilla

manucure /manykyʀ/
A ▸ p. 372 *nmf* (personne) manicurist
B *nf* (soins, technique) manicure; **se faire faire une ~** to have a manicure

manuel, -elle /manɥɛl/
A *adj* manual
B *nm,f* **1** (par métier) manual worker; **2** (par goût) **c'est une manuelle** she likes working with her hands; (par don) she is good with her hands
C *nm* Scol textbook

(Composés) **~ de conversation** phrase book; **~ d'utilisation** instruction manual; **~ scolaire** school textbook

manuellement /manɥɛlmɑ̃/ *adv* **1** Tech manually; **2** (avec les mains) [*travailler*] with one's hands

manufacture /manyfaktyʀ/ *nf* **1** (établissement) factory; **2** (fabrication) manufacture

manufacturer /manyfaktyʀe/ [1] *vtr* to manufacture

manu militari /manymilitaʀi/ *adv* forcibly

manuscrit, ~e /manyskʀi, it/
A *adj* handwritten
B *nm* manuscript

manutention /manytɑ̃sjɔ̃/ *nf* (activité) handling

manutentionnaire /manytɑ̃sjɔnɛʀ/ ▸ p. 372 *nm* warehouseman

maoïsme /maoism/ *nm* Maoism

maori /maoʀi/ ▸ p. 336 *nm* Ling Maori

mappemonde /mapmɔ̃d/ *nf* **1** (carte) map of the world (in two hemispheres); **2** (globe) globe

maquereau, *pl* **~x** /makʀo/ *nm* Zool mackerel

maquette /makɛt/ *nf* **1** (modèle réduit) (scale) model; **2** (grandeur nature) mock-up

maquignon /makiɲɔ̃/ *nm* **1** lit horse dealer; **2** péj shady operator

maquignonnage /makiɲɔnaʒ/ *nm* **1** lit horse dealing; **2** péj sharp practice

maquillage /makijaʒ/ *nm* **1** (action) making-up; **2** (résultat) make-up; **2** (fard) make-up

(Composé) **~ de théâtre** greasepaint

maquiller /makije/ [1]
A *vtr* **1** (farder) to make [sb/sth] up [*acteur, visage*]; **2** (déguiser) to doctor [*document, vérité*]; **~ un crime en accident** to disguise a crime as an accident
B se maquiller *vpr* (mettre du fard) to put make-up on; (porter du fard) to wear make-up

maquilleur, -euse /makijœʀ, øz/ ▸ p. 372 *nm,f* Théât make-up artist

maquis /maki/ *nm* *inv* Géog, Hist maquis; **prendre le ~** [*résistant*] to join the maquis; [*fuyard*] to go underground

maquisard, ~e /makizaʀ, aʀd/ *nm,f* Hist member of the Resistance

marabout /maʀabu/ *nm* **1** Zool marabou; **2** Relig marabout

maraîchage /maʀɛʃaʒ/ *nm* market gardening GB, truck farming US

maraîcher, -ère /maʀeʃe, ɛʀ/
A *adj* **produits ~s** market garden produce ¢ GB, truck ¢ US; **la culture maraîchère** market gardening GB, truck farming US
B ▸ p. 372 *nm,f* market gardener GB, truck farmer US

marais /maʀɛ/ *nm* *inv* marsh, swamp

(Composé) **~ salant** saltern

marasme /maʀasm/ *nm* Écon, Pol stagnation; **être dans le** or **en plein ~** to be in the doldrums

marathon /maʀatɔ̃/ *nm* marathon

marathonien, -ienne /maʀatɔnjɛ̃, ɛn/ *nm,f* marathon runner

marâtre /maʀɑtʀ/ *nf* péj cruel mother

maraude /maʀod/ *nf* (pillage) pilfering; **en ~** [*taxi*] cruising for fares (après n); [*voyou*] on the prowl (jamais épith).

marauder /maʀode/ [1] *vi* **1** (voler) to pilfer; **2** (être à l'affût) [*taxi*] to cruise for fares; [*voyou*] to prowl around

maraudeur, -euse /maʀodœʀ, øz/ *nm,f* petty thief

marbre /maʀbʀ/ *nm* **1** (roche) marble; **2** (plaque de meuble) marble top; (statue) marble statue; **3** (en imprimerie) **livre sur le ~** book at press

(Idiomes) **rester de ~** (impassible) to remain stony-faced; **la nouvelle les laissa de ~** they were completely unmoved by the news

marbrer /maʀbʀe/ [1] *vtr* **1** Tech to marble [*papier, cuir*]; **2** (marquer) **le froid lui marbrait le visage** his/her face was blotchy with the cold; **peau marbrée** mottled skin; **il avait le dos marbré de coups** or **de bleus** his back was mottled with bruises; **pelage roux marbré de noir** red coat mottled with black

marbrerie /maʀbʀəʀi/ *nf* **1** (industrie) marble industry; (travail du marbre) marble masonry; **~ funéraire** monumental masonry; **2** (atelier) marble mason's workshop

marbrier, -ière¹ /maʀbʀije, ɛʀ/ ▸ p. 372 *nm* (ouvrier, entrepreneur) marble mason; **~ funéraire** monumental mason; **~ d'art** artist in marble

marbrière² /maʀbʀijɛʀ/ *nf* marble quarry

marbrure /maʀbʀyʀ/ *nf* (sur papier, cuir) marbling ¢; (sur la peau) blotchiness ¢; (hématomes) mottling ¢

marc /maʀ/ *nm* marc; **~ de raisin** grape marc

(Composé) **~ de café** coffee grounds (pl)

marcassin /maʀkasɛ̃/ *nm* young wild boar

marchand, ~e /maʀʃɑ̃, ɑ̃d/
A *adj* Comm [*denrée, qualité*] marketable; [*secteur, économie*] trade; [*valeur*] market
B ▸ p. 372 *nm,f* **1** (commerçant) trader; (négociant) dealer, merchant; (dans une boutique) shopkeeper; (sur un marché) stallholder; **~ d'armes/de bestiaux** arms/cattle dealer; **~ de**

soie/vins silk/wine merchant; **jouer à la ~e** to play shops; ② Hist merchant

☐ Composés ~ **ambulant** hawker; ~ **de couleurs** ironmonger GB, hardware merchant; ~ **de glaces** ice cream vendor; ~ **en gros** wholesaler; ~ **de journaux** (dans un magasin) newsagent; (dans la rue) newsvendor; ~ **des quatre saisons** costermonger GB, fruit and vegetable merchant; ~ **de sable** fig sandman; **le ~ de sable est passé** the sandman has been; ~ **à la sauvette** street vendor; ~ **de tableaux** art dealer; ~ **de tapis** carpet salesman; **c'est un vrai ~ de tapis**○ pej he's just a petty wrangler

marchandage /maʁʃɑ̃daʒ/ nm (sur le prix) haggling (de over); **après un long ~** after lengthy haggling; **faire du ~** to haggle

marchander /maʁʃɑ̃de/ [1] vtr ① to haggle over [marchandise, prix]; to haggle for [rabais]; **sans ~** without haggling; ② fig ~ **son accord** to give one's approval grudgingly; ~ **sa peine** not to put oneself out; **il n'a pas marchandé ses éloges** he was not sparing in his praises

marchandise /maʁʃɑ̃diz/ nf ① (articles) **des ~s** goods, merchandise **℃**; **~s en gros/au détail** wholesale/retail goods; ② (produit) (pl) **livrer la ~** to deliver the goods; **tromper** or **voler qn sur la ~** to swindle sb

☐ Idiomes **il a essayé de nous vendre sa ~**○ he tried to win us over; **vanter** or **étaler sa ~**○ to parade one's wares

marche /maʁʃ/ nf ① ▸ p. 327 (activité, sport) walking; (trajet) walk; **faire de la ~** to go walking; **la ~ à pied** walking; **faire une petite ~** to take a short walk; **à 10 minutes de ~** 10 minutes' walk away; **ralentir la ~** to walk slower; ② Mil, Pol march; ~ **de protestation** protest march; **soldats en ~** soldiers on the march; **fermer la ~** to bring up the rear; **ouvrir la ~** to be at the head of the march; ③ (fonctionnement de véhicule) progress; **la ~ du train a été gênée** the progress of the train was hampered; **prendre un bus en ~** to climb aboard a moving bus; **dans le sens contraire de la ~** facing backward(s); ④ (fonctionnement de mécanisme) operation; **bonne ~** smooth operation; **en état de ~** in working order; **mettre en ~** to start [machine, moteur]; to start up [chaudière, réacteur]; to switch on [téléviseur, ordinateur]; **se mettre en ~** [appareil, véhicule] to start up; **être en ~** [machine, moteur] to be running; [téléviseur, radio] to be on; ⑤ (fonctionnement d'organisme) running; **bonne ~ de l'entreprise** smooth running of the company; ⑥ (déroulement) course; **la ~ du temps/du progrès** the march of time/of progress; **la ~ à suivre** procedure (**pour faire** for doing); ⑦ Constr (d'escalier, de train, bus) step; **les ~s** the stairs; ⑧ Mus march

☐ Composés ~ **arrière** Aut reverse; **passer la ~ arrière** to go into reverse; **sortir en ~ arrière** to reverse out; **faire ~ arrière** fig to backpedal; ~ **avant** forward; ~ **forcée** Mil forced march

☐ Idiome **prendre le train en ~** (par hasard) to join halfway through; (par intérêt) to climb onto the bandwagon

marché /maʁʃe/ nm ① Comm market; ~ **aux fleurs** flower market; **vendre ses pommes au ~** to sell one's apples at the market; **les jours de ~** market days; **faire son ~** to do one's shopping at the market; **il fait les ~s de la région** he does the rounds of the markets in the area; **mettre qch sur le ~** to put sth on the market; ② Écon, Fin market; ~ **boursier** stock market; **le ~ de l'immobilier** the property market; **pénétrer un ~** to break into a market; ③ (arrangement) deal; **conclure un ~ avec qn** to strike a deal with sb; ~ **conclu!** it's a deal!; **bon/meilleur ~** [produit] cheap/cheaper; **par-dessus le ~**○ to top it all

☐ Composés ~ **des changes** Fin foreign exchange market; ~ **de l'emploi** job market; ~ **extérieur** foreign market; ~ **intérieur** (national) domestic ou home market; (de l'UE) internal market; ~ **libre** free market; ~ **noir** black market; ~ **public** Admin public works contract; ~ **aux puces** flea market; ~ **à terme** forward market; ~ **du travail** labour^GB market; ~ **des valeurs** stock market; **Marché commun** Hist Common Market

☐ Idiome **faire bon ~ de qch** to set little value on sth

marchepied /maʁʃəpje/ nm ① (de véhicule) step; ② (escabeau) steps (pl); ③ fig **servir de ~ à qn** to be a stepping stone for sb

marcher /maʁʃe/ [1] vi ① (utiliser ses pieds) [personne, animal, robot] to walk; **allons ~ un peu** let's go for a little walk; ② (poser le pied) to tread (**dans** in; **sur** on); ~ **sur les**

pieds de qn to tread on sb's toes; **tu m'as marché sur le pied** you stood on my foot; **se laisser ~ sur les pieds** fig to let oneself be walked over; ③ (avancer) to go; ~ **sur les mains** [gymnaste] to walk on one's hands; ~ **en tête de cortège** to march at the head of the procession; ~ **sur le palais présidentiel** to march on the presidential palace; ④ (fonctionner) [mécanisme, réforme, procédé] to work; **ma radio marche bien/marche mal** my radio works well/doesn't work properly; **faire ~ qch** to get sth to work; **ma montre ne marche plus** my watch has stopped working; **la poste marche de mieux en mieux** the postal service is getting better and better; ~ **au gaz** to run on gas; **les bus ne marchent pas le dimanche** the buses don't run on Sundays; ⑤ ○(aller) ~ **(bien)/~ mal** [travail, relations, examen] to go well/not to go well; [affaires, film, élève] to do well/not to do well; **comment marchent les affaires?** how is business?; ⑥ ○(être d'accord) to go for it; **je marche** I'll go for it; **c'est trop risqué, je ne marche pas** it's too risky, count me out; **ça marche!** (marché conclu) it's a deal!; (la commande est prise) coming up!; ⑦ ○(croire naïvement) to fall for it; **tu verras, elle marchera à tous les coups** you'll see, she falls for it every time; **faire ~ qn** to pull sb's leg; **elle fait ~ sa mère comme elle veut** she's got her mother wrapped round her little finger; ⑧ ○(obéir) **faire ~ son monde** to be good at giving orders

☐ Idiomes **il ne marche pas, il court**○! he's as gullible as they come; ~ **sur la tête de qn**○ to walk all over sb

marcheur, -euse /maʁʃœʁ, øz/ nm,f walker

mardi /maʁdi/ ▸ p. 545 nm Tuesday; ~ **gras** Shrove Tuesday

mare /maʁ/ nf ① (étang) pond; ~ **aux canards** duck pond; ② (grande quantité) pool (de of)

marécage /maʁekaʒ/ nm ① lit marsh; (sous les tropiques) swamp; ② fig quagmire

marécageux, -euse /maʁekaʒø, øz/ adj ① lit [sol] marshy, swampy; [faune, flore] marsh (épith); ② fig [terrain, situation] sticky○

maréchal, pl **-aux** /maʁeʃal, o/ ▸ p. 283 nm ≈ field marshal GB, general of the army US

☐ Composé ~ **de France** marshal of France

maréchal-ferrant, pl **maréchaux-ferrants** /maʁeʃalferɑ̃, maʁeʃoferɑ̃/ ▸ p. 372 nm farrier

maréchaussée /maʁeʃose/ nf Hist mounted police (+ v pl)

marée /maʁe/ nf ① Géog tide; **la ~ monte/descend** the tide is coming in/is going out; **les grandes ~s** the spring tides; **à ~ haute/basse** at high/low tide; **la ~ montante/descendante** the rising/ebbing tide; ② fig **une ~ humaine** a human tide; ③ (produits pêchés) fresh fish

☐ Composés ~ **noire** oil slick; ~ **verte** aquatic weed pollution

☐ Idiome **contre vents et ~s** (à l'avenir) come hell or high water; (dans le passé) against all odds

marelle /maʁɛl/ ▸ p. 327 nf hopscotch

marémoteur, -trice /maʁemɔtœʁ, tʁis/ adj tidal; **usine marémotrice** tidal power station

mareyeur, -euse /maʁɛjœʁ, øz/ ▸ p. 372 nm,f fish wholesaler

margarine /maʁgaʁin/ nf margarine

marge /maʁʒ/

Ⓐ nf ① (espace) margin; ~ **de gauche/du bas** left/bottom margin; ② (écart) leeway; **on a 10 minutes de ~** we've got 10 minutes leeway; **le train n'est qu'à midi, on a de la ~** the train isn't until midday, we've got plenty of leeway; **se sentir en ~** to feel like an outsider; ③ (latitude) scope; **tu devrais me laisser plus de ~ de décision** you should give me more scope for making decisions; ④ (profit, écart) profit margin; (pourcentage) mark-up

Ⓑ en marge de loc prép ① (à l'écart) **vivre en ~ de la société** to live on the fringes of society; **vivre en ~ de la loi** to live outside the law; ② (parallèlement) **en ~ de la conférence** outside the conference proper; **en ~ de l'accord de septembre** alongside September's agreement

☐ Composés ~ **bénéficiaire** profit margin; ~ **commerciale** gross profit; ~ **d'erreur** margin of error; ~ **de manœuvre** room for manoeuvre GB ou maneuver US; ~ **de sécurité** safety margin; ~ **de tolérance** tolerance margin

margelle /maʁʒɛl/ nf edge, rim (**de** of)

margeur /maʀʒœʀ/ nm (de machine à écrire) margin stop; (machine) machine feeder

marginal, **~e**, mpl **-aux** /maʀʒinal, o/
A adj **1** (secondaire) [occupations] marginal; **2** (non conformiste) [artiste] fringe (épith); **3** (en marge de la société) on the margins of society (après n)
B nm,f dropout; **les marginaux** the fringe elements of society

marginaliser /maʀʒinalize/ [1]
A vtr to marginalize
B se marginaliser vpr [communauté] to put itself on the fringes of society; [artiste] to put oneself on the fringe

marginalité /maʀʒinalite/ nf marginality; **vivre dans la ~** to live on the fringes of society; **le parti est sorti de la ~** the party has come in from the cold

marguerite /maʀgəʀit/ nf daisy

⟨Idiome⟩ **effeuiller la ~** to play he/she loves me, he/she loves me not

mari /maʀi/ nm husband

mariage /maʀjaʒ/ nm **1** (union) marriage; **au début de leur ~** in the early days of their marriage; **né d'un premier ~** from a previous marriage; **faire un ~ de raison** to enter into a marriage of convenience; **faire un ~ d'amour/ d'argent** to marry for love/money; **faire un riche ~** to marry into money; **né hors ~** born out of wedlock; **2** (cérémonie) wedding; **un ~ en blanc** a white wedding; **le ~ a été célébré à la mairie** the wedding took place at the Town Hall; **leur ~ a été célébré à l'église** their marriage was followed by a church service; **3** fig (association) (de couleurs) marriage; (d'entreprises) merger; (de partis) alliance; (de techniques) fusion

⟨Composés⟩ **~ blanc** (contrat) marriage in name only; **faire un ~ blanc** (contractuel) to marry in name only; (ne pas le consommer) to have an unconsummated marriage; **~ civil** civil wedding; **~ religieux** church wedding

Marianne /maʀjan/ npr Marianne (female figure personifying the French Republic)

ⓘ **Marianne** The symbolic female figure often used to represent the French Republic. There are statues of her in public places all over France and she also appears on the standard French stamp. She is always depicted wearing the Phrygian bonnet, a pointed cap which became one of the symbols of liberty as represented by the 1789 Revolution.

marié, **~e** /maʀje/
A pp ▸ **marier**
B pp adj [personne, couple] married (à, avec to); **être bien/mal ~** to have made a good/bad marriage
C nm,f **le (jeune) ~** the (bride)groom; **la (jeune) ~e** the bride; **les (jeunes) ~s** the newlyweds

marier /maʀje/ [2]
A vtr **1** (unir) to marry (à, avec to); **on l'a mariée de force** she was forced into marriage; **nous avons encore un fils à ~** we still have one unmarried son; **2** (associer) to marry [couleurs, styles]
B se marier vpr **1** [personne] to get married (avec qn to sb); **2** [tissus, couleurs] to go well together

marigot /maʀigo/ nm marshland

marijuana /maʀiʀwana/ nf marijuana

marin, **~e**[1] /maʀɛ̃, in/
A adj **1** (de mer) [courant, faune] marine (épith); [air, sel, monstre] sea (épith); [prospection] offshore (épith); [bateau] seaworthy; **2** (de marin) **pull ~** seaman's jersey; **costume ~** sailor suit
B nm sailor; **peuple de ~s** seafaring nation

⟨Composés⟩ **~ d'eau douce** fair-weather sailor; **~ pêcheur** fisherman

⟨Idiome⟩ **avoir le pied ~** to be a good sailor

marine[2] /maʀin/
A ▸ p. 140 adj inv (couleur) navy (blue)
B nm (soldat) marine

marine[3] /maʀin/ nf **1** Mil, Naut navy; **~ marchande** merchant navy; **de ~** [instrument] nautical; **2** Art seascape

mariner /maʀine/ [1]
A vtr gén to marinate; **harengs marinés** pickled herrings

B vi **1** Culin to marinate; **2** ○(attendre) **laisser** or **faire ~ qn** to let sb stew

marinier /maʀinje/ ▸ p. 372 nm bargee GB, bargeman US

marinière /maʀinjɛʀ/ nf (blouse) smock

marionnette /maʀjɔnɛt/
A nf lit, fig puppet
B marionnettes nfpl puppet show (sg)

marionnettiste /maʀjɔnetist/ ▸ p. 372 nmf puppeteer

maritalement /maʀitalmɑ̃/ adv **vivre ~** to live as man and wife

maritime /maʀitim/ adj gén maritime; [région] coastal; [compagnie, droit] shipping

marivaudage /maʀivodaʒ/ nm **1** (badinage) gallant sophisticated banter; **2** Littérat refined affectation (in the style of Marivaux)

marjolaine /maʀʒɔlɛn/ nf marjoram

mark /maʀk/ ▸ p. 34 nm mark

marmaille○ /maʀmaj/ nf rabble of kids○ péj

marmelade /maʀməlad/ nf Culin stewed fruit; **~ d'abricots** stewed apricots; **en ~** [aliments cuits] cooked to a mush; **réduire qn en ~**○ to beat sb to a pulp○; **j'ai le dos en ~**○ my back is killing○ me

marmite /maʀmit/ nf **1** (ustensile) pot; **2** (contenu) potful

⟨Idiome⟩ **faire bouillir la ~**○ to bring home the bacon

marmiton /maʀmitɔ̃/ nm chef's assistant

marmonner /maʀmɔne/ [1] vtr to mumble [excuse]; to mutter [injure]

marmoréen, **-éenne** /maʀmɔʀeɛ̃, ɛn/ adj **1** [roche] marble; **2** [beauté] marble-like; [froideur] marmoreal

marmot○ /maʀmo/ nm kid○, brat○ péj

marmotte /maʀmɔt/ nf **1** Zool marmot; **2** fig sleepy-head○

⟨Idiome⟩ **dormir comme une ~** to sleep like a log

marmotter /maʀmɔte/ [1] vtr to mumble [excuse]; to mutter [injure]

Maroc /maʀɔk/ ▸ p. 230 nprm Morocco

marocain, **~e** /maʀɔkɛ̃, ɛn/ ▸ p. 392 adj Moroccan

maroquin /maʀɔkɛ̃/ nm (cuir) morocco (leather)

maroquinerie /maʀɔkinʀi/ ▸ p. 372 nf **1** (magasin) leather shop; **2** (commerce) leather trade; (articles) leather goods (pl)

maroquinier /maʀɔkinje/ ▸ p. 372 nm **1** (commerçant) trader in fine leather goods; **2** (artisan) fine leather craftsman

marotte /maʀɔt/ nf **1** (thème favori) pet subject, hobby horse; (occupation) pet ou favourite[GB] hobby; **il a la ~ des mots croisés** doing crosswords is his pet hobby

marquant, **~e** /maʀkɑ̃, ɑ̃t/ adj [fait] memorable; [souvenir] lasting; [personnalité, œuvre] outstanding

marque /maʀk/ nf **1** Comm, Ind (de produit) brand; (de machine, matériel, voiture) make; **des voitures de ~ japonaise** Japanese cars; **produits de ~** branded goods; **2** (trace) mark; (indice) sign; **faire une ~ au couteau** to make a notch with a knife; **les ~s du bétail** the brands on cattle; **on voit encore les ~s** (de coups) you can still see the bruises; **~s d'usure** signs of wear; **~ de naissance** birthmark; **~ de doigts** fingermarks (pl); **~ de pas** footprint; **~ de brûlure** (sur un tissu) scorch mark; (sur la peau) burn; **3** (preuve) sign; **il l'a fait en ~ d'estime** he did it as a mark of his esteem; **4** (particularité) mark; **laisser sa ~** to make one's mark; **5** (haut niveau) **invité de ~** distinguished guest, VIP; **personnage de ~** eminent person; **6** Jeux, Sport (décompte) score; **à vos ~s, prêts, partez!** on your marks, get set, go!; **7** Ling marker; **~ du pluriel** plural marker

⟨Composés⟩ **~ déposée** registered trademark; **~ de fabricant** or **fabrication** manufacturer's brand name; **~ de fabrique** trademark; **~ d'infamie** stigma

marqué, **~e** /maʀke/
A pp ▸ **marquer**
B pp adj **1** (affecté) **il a le corps ~ de traces de coups** he's bruised all over; **elle est restée ~e par la guerre** the war left its mark on her; **c'est un homme ~** he's been through the mill; **visage ~** worn face; **2** (affirmé) [différence, préférence] marked; **3** (jalonné) marked; **une époque ~e par les conflits sociaux** a period marked by social unrest; **4** Ling marked; **non ~** unmarked

marque-page, ∼s /maʀkpaʒ/ nm bookmark

marquer /maʀke/ [1]

A vtr ① (étiqueter) to mark [article]; to brand [bétail]; to mark out [emplacement, limite]; ∼ **des vêtements au nom d'un enfant** to put nametapes on a child's clothes; ∼ **d'une croix** to mark with a cross; ② (signaler) to mark, to signal [début, rupture]; ③ (laisser une trace sur) [personne, coup] to mark [corps, objet]; ④ (influencer) [événement, œuvre] to leave its mark on [personne, esprit]; **c'est quelqu'un qui m'a beaucoup marqué** he/she was a strong influence on me; ⑤ (écrire) to mark [prix]; to write [sth] (down) [renseignement]; **marquez cela sur mon compte** put it on my account; **qu'est-ce qu'il y a de marqué?** what does it say?; ⑥ (indiquer) [montre] to say [heure]; [jauge, chiffres] to show [pression, température]; **l'horloge marque dix heures** the clock says ten o'clock; **il marquait ses propos d'un hochement de tête** he nodded emphatically as he spoke; ∼ **la mesure** Mus to beat time; ⑦ (exprimer) to show [volonté, désapprobation, sentiment]; **il faut** ∼ **le coup** (célébrer) let's celebrate; (exprimer le mécontentement) we can't let it go just like that; ⑧ ∼ **un temps (d'arrêt)** to pause; ∼ **un silence** to fall silent; ⑨ Sport to score [but, point]; to mark [adversaire]

B vi ① (laisser une trace) to leave a mark (**sur** on); ② Sport to score

marqueterie /maʀkɛtʀi/ nf (art) marquetry; (produit) inlay; **en** ∼ inlaid

marqueur /maʀkœʀ/ nm ① (stylo) marker (pen); ② Biol, Ling marker

marquis, ∼e[1] /maʀki, iz/ nm,f (titre) marquis/ marchioness

marquise[2] /maʀkiz/ nf ① (auvent) glass canopy GB, marquee US; ② (siège) ≈ Gainsborough chair

marraine /maʀɛn/ nf ① Relig (d'enfant) godmother; **être (la)** ∼ **de qn** to be godmother to sb; ② (d'enfant défavorisé) sponsor.

⚠ En anglais *godmother* n'est jamais une forme d'adresse.

(Composé) ∼ **de guerre** *soldier's wartime female penfriend*

marrant○, ∼e /maʀɑ̃, ɑ̃t/ adj ① (amusant) funny; **il/ce n'est pas** ∼ (ennuyeux) he's/it's not much fun; (pénible) he's/ it's a real pain○; ② (bizarre) funny, odd

marre○ /maʀ/ adv **en avoir** ∼ to be fed up○ (**de qch** with sth; **de faire** with doing)

marrer○: **se marrer** /maʀe/ [1] vpr (s'amuser) to have a great time; (rire) to have a good laugh; **il n'y a pas de quoi se** ∼ there's nothing to laugh about

marri†, ∼e /maʀi/ adj saddened, grieved†

marron, **-onne** /maʀɔ̃, ɔn/

A adj (malhonnête) bent○, crooked

B ▸ p. 140 adj inv (couleur) brown

C nm ① Bot ∼ (**d'Inde**) horse chestnut; (châtaigne) chestnut; ② (couleur) brown; ③ ○(coup) thump○

(Composés) ∼ **glacé** marron glacé; ∼s **chauds** roast chestnuts

(Idiomes) **tirer les** ∼s **du feu** (faire son profit) to reap the benefits; **je suis** ∼○ (dupé) I've been had○; (coincé) I'm stuck○

marronnier /maʀɔnje/ nm chestnut (tree)

(Composé) ∼ **d'Inde** horse chestnut (tree)

mars /maʀs/ ▸ p. 380 nm inv March

(Idiome) **arriver comme** ∼ **en carême** to come as sure as night follows day

marseillais, ∼e /maʀsɛjɛ, ɛz/ ▸ p. 621 adj of Marseilles; **une histoire** ∼e ≈ a tall story

Marseillaise /maʀsɛjɛz/ nf Marseillaise (French national anthem)

ℹ **La Marseillaise** The popular name of the French national anthem, composed by Claude-Joseph Rouget de Lisle in 1792. It was adopted as a marching song by a group of republican volunteers from Marseilles and marked their entry into Paris.

marsouin /maʀswɛ̃/ nm Zool porpoise

marsupial, pl **-iaux** /maʀsypjal, o/ nm marsupial

marteau, pl ∼**x** /maʀto/

A ○adj cracked○

B nm gén, Sport hammer; (de juge) gavel; (de porte) knocker; **un coup de** ∼ a blow from a hammer; **donner un coup de** ∼ **à qch** to hit sth with a hammer; **enfoncer qch à coups de** ∼ to hammer sth in; **casser qch à coups de** ∼ to take a hammer to sth

martel† /maʀtɛl/ nm **se mettre** ∼ **en tête** to get worried

marteler /maʀtəle/ [17] vtr ① to beat [métal]; [poings, artillerie] to pound; ② (scander) to rap out [syllabes]

martial, ∼**e**, mpl **-iaux** /maʀsjal, o/ adj [air, pas] military

martien, **-ienne** /maʀsjɛ̃, ɛn/ adj, nm,f Martian

martinet /maʀtinɛ/ nm ① Zool swift; ② (fouet) ≈ whip

martingale /maʀtɛ̃gal/ nf ① (de vêtement) half belt; ② (de cheval) martingale

Martinique /maʀtinik/ ▸ p. 504, p. 303 nprf **la** ∼ Martinique

martin-pêcheur, pl **martins-pêcheurs** /maʀtɛ̃pɛʃœʀ/ nm kingfisher

martre /maʀtʀ/ nf ① (animal) marten; ② (fourrure) sable

martyr, ∼**e**[1] /maʀtiʀ/

A adj [héros, nation] martyred littér; **enfant** ∼ battered child

B nm,f martyr (**d'une cause** to a cause); **se donner des airs de** ∼ to put on a martyred look

martyre[2] /maʀtiʀ/ nm (supplice) Relig, fig martyrdom; (souffrance) agony, suffering; **souffrir le** ∼ to suffer agony; **je souffre le** ∼ **dans ces chaussures** these shoes are sheer torture

martyriser /maʀtiʀize/ [1] vtr ① (torturer) to torment [victime, animal]; to batter [enfant]; ② Relig to martyr

marxisme /maʀksism/ nm Marxism

mas /mɑ/ nm inv farmhouse (in Provence)

mascara /maskaʀa/ nm mascara

mascarade /maskaʀad/ nf ① (pour duper) farce; ∼ **de justice** travesty of justice; ② (bal) masquerade; (accoutrement) pej fancy dress

mascotte /maskɔt/ nf mascot

masculin, ∼**e** /maskylɛ̃, in/

A adj ① Biol [sexualité, hormone] male; **le sexe** ∼ the male sex; **un enfant de sexe** ∼ a male child; ② (pour hommes) [revue] men's; [activité] man's, for men; [contraception] male; **le seul rôle** ∼ the only male part; ③ (composé d'hommes) [population] male; Sport [équipe, record] men's; ④ (viril) [visage, allure] masculine; ⑤ Ling [nom, rime] masculine

B nm Ling masculine

masculinité /maskylinite/ nf ① (qualité) masculinity; ② (en démographie) **rapport de** ∼ male to female ratio

masochisme /mazɔʃism/ nm masochism

masochiste /mazɔʃist/

A adj masochistic

B nmf masochist

masque /mask/ nm ① (sur le visage) mask; **il portait un** ∼ **de chien** he was wearing a dog mask; ∼ **de gaze** surgical mask; ② (de beauté) face-pack; ③ (expression) **prendre un** ∼ **tragique** to put on a tragic expression; **se couvrir d'un** ∼ **de la vertu** to hide behind the appearance of virtue; ④ Ordinat mask

(Composés) ∼ **d'apiculteur** beekeeper's veil; ∼ **funé**... funeral mask; ∼ **à gaz** gas mask; ∼ **de gros** mask of pregnancy; ∼ **mortuaire** death mask; ∼ **plongée** diving mask; ∼ **de soudeur** face s... **Masque de fer** the Iron Mask

(Idiomes) **jeter le** ∼ to show one's true colour ∼**s!** no more pretending now

masqué, ∼**e** /maske/

A pp ▸ **masquer**

B adj ① (avec un masque) masked; **il est ap**... he appeared wearing a mask; ② fig [v... [voix] disguised

masquer /maske/ [1]

A vtr ① (cacher) to conceal [défaut] (**à** fr... (**à** from); to mask [sentiment, problèm... block [orifice, lumière]; ③ Mil to mas...

B **se masquer** vpr to hide [sth] fro...

massacrante /masakʀɑ̃t/ adj... a foul mood

massacre /masakʀ/ nm ①... **¢**; (d'animaux) slaughter **¢** ③ ○(gâchis) botch(-up)○

ⓘ**Idiomes** **faire un ~**○ [*chanteur*] to be a roaring○ success; [*homme d'affaires*] to make a killing; **arrêtez le ~**○**!** stop making such a mess of things!

massacrer /masakʀe/ [1] *vtr* **1** (tuer) to slaughter; **2** ○(écraser) to slaughter○ [*adversaire*]; **3** ○(abîmer) to wreck; **4** ○(maltraiter) to make a complete mess of [*musique*]; to botch [*travail*]; **5** ○(critiquer) to savage GB, to trash US [*auteur, œuvre*]

massage /masaʒ/ *nm* massage; **faire un ~ à qn** to give sb a massage

ⓒ**Composé** **~ cardiaque** heart massage

masse /mas/ *nf* **1** (ensemble) mass; **~ rocheuse** rocky mass; **~ d'air chaud** mass of warm air; **~ d'eau** body of water; **une ~ humaine** a mass of humanity; **la ~ croissante des chômeurs** the swelling ranks (*pl*) of the unemployed; **2** (grande quantité) **une ~ de** a lot of; **départs/exécutions en ~** mass exodus (*sg*)/executions; **ils sont venus en ~** they came in droves; **produire qch en ~** to mass-produce sth; **production de ~** mass production; **la population a voté en ~** there was a high turnout at the election; **les manifestants ont envahi le stade en ~** the demonstrators invaded the stadium en masse; **il a des ~s**○ **d'argent/de copains** he's got masses *ou* loads○ of money/of friends; **'tu as aimé ce livre?'—'pas des ~s'**○ 'did you like this book?'—'not much'; **la ~ des électeurs demeure indécise** the bulk of the electorate remains undecided; **3** (peuple) **la ~** the masses (*pl*); **~s laborieuses** working classes; **les ~s paysannes** the peasantry; **culture de ~** mass culture; **enseignement/loisirs de ~** education/leisure activities for the masses; **4** Phys mass; **~ atomique** atomic mass; **5** (en électricité) earth GB, ground US; **6** (maillet) sledgehammer

ⓒ**Composés** **~ d'armes** mace; **~ monétaire** money supply; **~ salariale** (total) wage bill

ⓘ**Idiomes** **se noyer** *or* **fondre dans la ~** to get lost in the crowd; **(se laisser) tomber comme une ~** to collapse; **dormir comme une ~** to sleep like a log○

massepain /maspɛ̃/ *nm* marzipan cake

masser /mase/ [1]
A *vtr* **1** (assembler) to assemble [*personnes*]; to mass [*troupes*]; **2** (frictionner) to massage; **se faire ~** to have a massage
B se masser *vpr* **1** (s'assembler) to mass; **2** (frictionner) **se ~ les jambes** to massage one's legs

masseur, -euse /masœʀ, øz/ ▸ p. 372 *nm,f* masseur/masseuse

massicot /masiko/ *nm* (à papier) guillotine

massif, -ive /masif, iv/
A *adj* **1** (d'aspect lourd) [*meuble, traits*] heavy; [*personne*] heavily built; [*silhouette*] massive; **2** (par la quantité, le nombre) [*attaque, dose, foule, publicité*] massive; [*licenciements*] mass (*épith*); **3** (pur) **or/argent/noyer ~** solid gold/silver/walnut
B *nm* **1** Géog massif; **2** (de fleurs) (groupe) clump; (parterre) bed

massivement /masivmã/ *adv* [*embaucher, manifester*] in great numbers; [*injecter*] in massive doses; [*absorber*] in large quantities; [*approuver*] overwhelmingly

mass media /masmedja/ *nmpl* mass media

massue /masy/ *nf* gén, Sport club; **coup de ~** lit blow with a club; (événement) crushing blow; (somme) staggering sum

mastic /mastik/
A ▸ p. 140 *adj inv* (couleur) putty-coloured^GB
B *nm* **1** (pour vitres) putty; (pour trous) filler; (pour arbres) grafting wax; **2** (résine) mastic; **3** (erreur) transposition

mastiquer /mastike/ [1] *vtr* **1** (mâcher) to chew, to masticate; **2** (boucher) to putty [*vitre*]; to fill in [*fente*]; to plug [*fuite*]

mastoc○ /mastɔk/ *adj inv* bulky

mastodonte /mastɔdɔ̃t/ *nm* **1** fig (personne) colossus; (animal) monster; (objet) huge thing; **2** Zool mastodon

[m]asturber /mastyʀbe/ [1] *vtr*, **se masturber** *vpr* to masturbate

[p]'as-tu-vu○ /matyvy/
[a]dj inv showy
[n]mf inv show-off

[...]sure /mazyʀ/ *nf* hovel

[...], ~e /mat/
[**1**] [*peinture, papier*] matt; **2** [*teint*] olive (*épith*); [*son*] dull
[aux échecs] **~!, échec et ~!** checkmate!; **faire qn/être ~**

to put sb/to be in checkmate

mât /ma/ *nm* **1** Naut mast; ▸ **grand; 2** (perche, pylône) gén pole; Sport climbing pole; **~ de drapeau** flagpole

ⓒ**Composé** **~ de cocagne** greasy pole

matador /matadɔʀ/ ▸ p. 372 *nm* matador

matamore /matamɔʀ/ *nm* braggart; **faire le ~** to swagger

match /matʃ/ *nm* Sport (jeux d'équipe) match GB, game US; (de boxe, lutte, tennis) match; **~ nul** draw GB, tie US; **faire ~ nul** to draw GB, to tie US

ⓒ**Composés** **~ amical** friendly match; **~ avancé** match GB *ou* game that has been brought forward; **~ de classement** league match

matelas /matla/ *nm inv* **1** (de lit) mattress; **~ à ressorts** spring mattress; **2** (de feuilles) bed

ⓒ**Composés** **~ d'eau** water bed; **~ à langer** changing mat; **~ de plage** inflatable mattress, Lilo®; **~ pneumatique** air bed

matelassé, ~e /matlase/
A *pp* ▸ **matelasser**
B *pp adj* [*tissu*] quilted; **porte ~e** (de cuir) padded door; (de tissu) baize door

matelasser /matlase/ [1] *vtr* to pad [*porte*]; to upholster [*siège*]; to quilt [*tissu, vêtement*]

matelot /matlo/ ▸ p. 283 *nm* seaman, sailor; Mil Naut ≈ ordinary seaman GB, ≈ seaman apprentice US

matelote /matlɔt/ *nf* **1** Culin matelote, fish stew; **2** (danse) hornpipe

mater /mate/ [1] *vtr* to put down [*révolte*]; to bring [sb] into line [*rebelles*]; to take [sb] in hand [*enfant, cheval*]

mâter /mate/ [1] *vtr* to mast

matérialisation /mateʀjalizasjɔ̃/ *nf* **1** (de projet, d'idée, espoir) realization; **2** (signalisation) marking; **3** (en spiritisme) materialization

matérialiser /mateʀjalize/ [1]
A *vtr* **1** (concrétiser) to realize [*rêve*]; to fulfil^GB [*espoir*]; to make [sth] happen [*projet*]; **des décisions qui seront matérialisées par un traité** decisions that will be embodied in a treaty; **le fleuve matérialise la frontière** the river forms the border; **2** (signaliser) to mark; **'chaussée non matérialisée sur 3 km'** 'no road markings for 3 km'
B se matérialiser *vpr* [*projet*] to materialize

matérialisme /mateʀjalism/ *nm* materialism

matérialiste /mateʀjalist/
A *adj* **1** Philos materialist; **2** (terre à terre) materialistic
B *nmf* materialist

matériau, *pl* **~x** /mateʀjo/ *nm* **1** (documentation) material **¢**; **2** Constr material; **~x de construction** building materials

matériel, -ielle /mateʀjɛl/
A *adj* **1** gén [*conditions, biens, dégâts*] material; [*plaisirs*] worldly; [*problème, moyens*] practical; [*obstacle*] tangible, concrete; **sur le plan ~** in practical terms; **2** (matérialiste) materialistic; **3** Philos material
B *nm* **1** (équipement) equipment; **~ agricole** farm machinery; **2** (documentation) material

ⓒ**Composé** **~ informatique** hardware

matériellement /mateʀjɛlmã/ *adv* **1** (physiquement) **c'est ~ possible** it can be done; **c'est impossible ~** it's a physical impossibility; **2** (financièrement) financially; **aider ~ qn** to give material assistance to sb; **~, c'est un peu difficile** things are a bit tight○ financially

maternel, -elle¹ /mateʀnɛl/ *adj* **1** (d'une mère) [*instinct*] maternal; [*amour*] motherly; **2** (de la mère) **biens/conseils ~s** mother's property **¢**/advice **¢**; **3** (dans la famille) [*ligne, tante, grand-père*] maternal; **du côté ~** on the mother's *ou* maternal side

maternelle² /mateʀnɛl/ *nf* Scol nursery school

materner /mateʀne/ [1] *vtr* to mother; (à l'excès) to mollycoddle, to baby

maternité /mateʀnite/ *nf* **1** (état de mère) motherhood; **2** (grossesse) pregnancy; **de ~** [*allocation, congé*] maternity; **3** (établissement) maternity hospital; (service) maternity ward

mathématicien, -ienne /matematisjɛ̃, ɛn/ ▸ p. 372 *nm,f* mathematician

mathématique /matematik/ *adj* **1** Math mathematical; **2** fig **c'est ~** (logique) it follows; (certain) it's dead certain

mathématiquement /matematikmã/ *adv* [1] Math [*démontrer*] mathematically; [2] fig (logiquement) logically

mathématiques /matematik/ *nfpl* mathematics (+ *v sg*)

matheux○, **-euse** /matø, øz/ *nm,f* mathematician

maths○ /mat/ *nfpl* maths○ (+ *v sg*) GB, math○ (*sg*) US

matière /matjɛʀ/ *nf* [1] (substance) material; **mes voyages me fournissent la ~ de mes romans** my travels provide me with material for my novels; [2] Biol, Chimie, Philos, Phys matter; **la ~ vivante** organic matter; [3] (sujet) matter ¢; **en ~ littéraire** as far as literature is concerned; **donner ~ à plaisanterie** to make people smile; **~ à réflexion** food for thought; **il n'y a pas là ~ à plaisanter** it's no laughing matter; **il n'y a pas là ~ à se féliciter** there's no call for complacency; [4] Scol, Univ (discipline) subject

(Composés) **~s fécales** faeces; **~s grasses** fat ¢; **~ grise** grey GB *ou* gray US matter; **~ plastique** plastic; **~ première** raw material

Matignon /matiɲɔ̃/ *npr: offices of the French Prime Minister*

matin /matɛ̃/ *nm* morning; **travailler le ~** to work in the morning, to work mornings; **5 heures du ~** gén 5 (o'clock) in the morning; (pour un horaire) 5 am; **le ~ du 3, le 3 au ~** on the morning of the 3rd; **au ~ il avait oublié** by morning he had forgotten; **brume du ~** morning mist; **de bon ~** early in the morning; **de grand ~** at daybreak; **au petit ~** in the early hours; **à prendre ~, midi et soir** Méd to be taken three times a day

(Idiomes) **être du ~** to be a morning person; **un de ces quatre ~s**○ one of these days

matinal, **~e**, *mpl* **-aux** /matinal, o/ *adj* [*toilette, promenade*] morning (*épith*); [*brume, gelée*] (early) morning (*épith*); **heure ~e** early hour; **il est ~** (d'habitude) he is an early riser; (aujourd'hui) he's up early

mâtiné, **~e** /matine/ *adj* (mélangé) **un anglais ~ de français** a mixture of English and French

matinée /matine/ *nf* [1] (période) morning; **dans la ~** in the morning; **(toute) une ~ de travail** a (whole) morning's work; [2] Cin, Théât matinée

(Idiome) **faire la grasse ~** to sleep in

matines /matin/ *nfpl* matins

matois, **~e** /matwa, az/ *adj* wily, sly

matou /matu/ *nm* tomcat

matraquage /matʀakaʒ/ *nm* [1] lit bludgeoning; [2] fig **~ publicitaire** hype○; **faire du ~ pour un produit** to plug○ a product

matraque /matʀak/ *nf* gén club; (de policier) truncheon GB, billy US; (de malfaiteur) cosh GB, blackjack US; **recevoir un coup de ~** [*manifestant*] to be hit with a truncheon; **il m'a donné deux coups de ~** he clubbed me twice; **c'est le coup de ~**○ fig it costs a fortune

matraquer /matʀake/ [1] *vtr* [1] (assommer) [*policier*] to club; [*malfaiteur*] to cosh GB, to blackjack US; [2] (étourdir) [*médias*] to bombard (**de** with); [3] ○(escroquer) to rip off○

matriarcal, **~e**, *mpl* **-aux** /matʀijaʀkal, o/ *adj* matriarchal

matrice /matʀis/ *nf* Math, Ordinat matrix; Tech (moule) die; (pour disque) matrix

matriciel, **-ielle** /matʀisjel/ *adj* Math matrix (*épith*)

matricule /matʀikyl/ *nm* (numéro) Mil service number; Admin reference number

matrimonial, **~e**, *mpl*, **-iaux** /matʀimɔnjal, o/ *adj* marriage (*épith*), matrimonial

matrone /matʀon/ *nf* matronly woman

maturation /matyʀasjɔ̃/ *nf* (de fruit, fromage) ripening; (du vin) maturing; (de cellule, d'abcès) maturation; (d'idée) development

maturité /matyʀite/ *nf* gén maturity; **~ d'esprit** (psychological) maturity; **manquer de ~** to be immature; **en pleine ~** [*homme*] of mature years (*épith, après n*); [*auteur*] at the height of one's powers (*après n*)

maudire /modiʀ/ [80] *vtr* to curse

maudit, **~e** /modi, it/
A *pp* ▸ **maudire**
B *adj* [1] ○(satané) (before n) blasted○; [2] (rejeté) (after n) [*écrivain*] cursed (**de** by); **~s soient-ils** a curse on them
C *nm,f* damned soul; **les ~s** the damned

Maudit /modi/ *nprm* **le ~** the evil one

maugréer /mogʀee/ [11] *vi* to grumble (**contre** about)

maure /mɔʀ/ *adj* Moorish

mauresque /mɔʀɛsk/ *adj* Moorish

mauricien, **-ienne** /mɔʀisjɛ̃, ɛn/ ▸ p. 392 *adj* Mauritian

mauritanien, **-ienne** /mɔʀitanjɛ̃, ɛn/ ▸ p. 392 *adj* Mauritanian

mausolée /mozole/ *nm* mausoleum

maussade /mosad/ *adj* [*voix, humeur*] sullen; [*temps*] dull; [*paysage, perspective*] bleak

maussaderie /mosadʀi/ *nf* sullenness

mauvais, **~e** /mɔvɛ, ɛz/
A *adj* [1] (d'un goût désagréable) **être ~** to be horrible; **ne pas être ~** to be quite good; [2] (de qualité inférieure) [*repas, restaurant*] poor; [*tabac, alcool, café*] cheap; [*spectacle*] terrible; [*nourriture, hébergement, livre*] bad; [*dictionnaire, lycée, enregistrement*] poor; **ne pas être ~** to be all right; [3] (mal fait) [*cuisine, travail, gestion, éducation*] poor; [*prononciation, départ*] bad; [4] (inadéquat) [*conseil, définition, exemple, conditions de travail*] bad; [*projet*] flawed; [*renseignement*] wrong; [*éclairage, vue, mémoire, santé*] poor; **il ne serait pas ~ de faire** it wouldn't be a bad idea to do; **~ pour la santé** bad for one's health; [5] (inapproprié) wrong; [6] (incompétent) [*auteur, cuisinier, menteur, équipe*] bad (**en** at); [*élève, nageur, chasseur*] poor; [*avocat, médecin*] incompetent; **être ~ en français** [*élève*] to be bad at French; [7] (déplaisant) [*nuit, rêve, nouvelle, journée, situation*] bad; [*surprise*] nasty; [*vacances*] terrible; [8] (méchant) [*animal*] vicious; [*personne, sourire, remarque*] nasty; **~ coup** (méchanceté) dirty trick; (blessure) nasty knock; (revers) terrible blow; **préparer un ~ coup** to be up to mischief; [9] (grave) [*fièvre, rhume*] nasty; [10] (peu lucratif) [*rendement, terre*] poor; [*salaire*] low; [*récolte, saison*] bad; [11] (peu flatteur) [*résultat, opinion*] poor; [*chiffres, critique*] bad; [12] (répréhensible) [*père, comportement*] bad; [*chrétien*] poor; [*instinct*] base; [*génie, intention, pensée*] evil; [13] (pénible) [*vent, pluie*] nasty; [*traversée, mer*] rough; [*météo*] bad; **▸ numéro, pas²**
B *adv* **sentir ~** lit to smell; fig○ to look bad; **sentir très ~** lit to stink; fig to stink○; **ouvre la fenêtre, ça sent ~** open the window, there's a nasty smell; **il fait ~** the weather is bad
C *nm* (mauvais côté) **le bon et le ~** the good and the bad; **il n'y a pas que du ~ dans le projet** the project isn't all bad

(Composés) **~ esprit** (personne) scoffing person; (attitude) scoffing attitude; **faire du ~ esprit** to scoff; **~ garçon** tough guy; **~ plaisant** person with a warped sense of humour^GB; **~ traitements** ill-treatment ¢; **~ herbe** weed; **~es rencontres** bad company ¢; **faire de ~es rencontres** to get into bad company

(Idiome) **la trouver** *or* **l'avoir ~e**○ to be furious

mauve¹ /mov/ ▸ p. 140 *adj, nm* mauve

mauve² /mov/ *nf* mallow

mauviette /movjɛt/ *nf* pej wimp○

maux ▸ mal

maxi- /maksi/ *préf* **~-bouteille** one-and-a-half litre^GB bottle; **il y a un ~-choix**○ there's a huge choice; **~-jupe** maxiskirt

maxillaire /maksilɛʀ/
A *adj* maxillary
B *nm* jawbone; **~ inférieur/supérieur** lower/upper jawbone

maxima ▸ maximum

maximal, **~e**, *mpl* **-aux** /maksimal, o/ *adj* maximum

maximaliser /maksimalize/ [1] *vtr* to maximize

maximaliste /maksimalist/ *adj* [*discours*] uncompromising; [*attitude, personne*] hard-line (*épith*)

maxime /maksim/ *nf* maxim

maximiser /maksimize/ [1] *vtr* to maximize

maximum, *pl* **~s** *or* **maxima** /maksimɔm, maksima/
A *adj* maximum
B *nm* [1] (limite supérieure) maximum; **un prêt jusqu'à un ~ de...** a loan for a maximum amount of...; **un ~ de 11 jours, 11 jours (au) ~** eleven days at (the) most; **au grand ~** at the very most; **au ~** [*travailler, développer*] to the maximum; [*réduire*] as much as possible; **détenir 20% du capital au ~** to hold 20% of the capital at the outside *ou* at most; **rouler au ~** to drive flat out○; **obtenir le ~ d'avantages** to get as many advantages as possible; **faire le ~** to do one's utmost; **atteindre son ~** [*bruit, inflation*] to reach its peak; [*douleur*] to be at its worst;

2 Météo **~ (de température)** maximum temperature; **3** ᴼ(grande quantité) **un ~ a** lot; **faire un ~ de bruit** to be as noisy as possible; **coûter le** *or* **un ~** to cost a bundleᴼ; **obtenir le** *or* **un ~** (dans une transaction) to get the best possible deal; **4** Jur maximum sentence

maya /maja/
A *adj* Mayan
B ▸ p. 336 *nm* Ling Maya

Maya /maja/ *nmf* Maya

Mayence /majɑ̃s/ ▸ p. 621 *npr* Mainz

mayonnaise /majɔnɛz/ *nf* mayonnaise

mazagran /mazagrɑ̃/ *nm*: thick china goblet for coffee

mazout /mazut/ *nm* (fuel) oil; **cuve à ~** oil tank; **chauffage au ~** oil-fired heating

MCJ /ɛmseʒi/ *nf* (*abbr* = **maladie de Creutzfeld-Jakob**) CJD, Creutzfeld-Jakob disease

me (**m'** before vowel or mute h) /m(ə)/ *pron pers* **1** (objet) me; **2** (à moi) me; **tu m'as fait mal** you hurt me; **3** (pronom réfléchi) myself; **je ~ lave (les mains)** I wash (my hands); **je m'en veux** I'm angry with myself

Me written abbr = **maître** C 5

méandre /meɑ̃dʀ/ *nm* **1** Géog meander. **2** fig **les ~s de l'administration** the maze (*sg*) of officialdom; **les ~s de ta pensée** the rambling development (*sg*) of your ideas

mecᴼ /mɛk/ *nm* guyᴼ; **beau ~** gorgeous guy; **mon ~** my manᴼ

mécanicien, -ienne /mekanisjɛ̃, ɛn/
A *adj* mechanical
B ▸ p. 372 *nm,f* (ouvrier) mechanic
C *nm* Rail engine driver GB, (locomotive) engineer US; Aviat flight engineer; Naut engineer; **~ navigant** Aviat flight engineer

mécanique /mekanik/
A *adj* **1** (manuel) [hachoir, tondeuse] hand (épith); [jouet] clockwork (épith); **2** (doté d'une machine) mechanical; **3** (fait à la machine) machine (épith); **4** (de machine) [panne] mechanical; **se déplacer de façon ~** to move mechanically; **industrie ~** engineering industry; **5** Phys mechanical; **6** (irréfléchi) [geste] mechanical; [rire] empty
B *nf* **1** (discipline) mechanics (+ v sg); **un terme de ~** a mechanical term; **une merveille de ~** a marvel of engineering; **2** (fonctionnement) mechanics (pl); **la ~ d'une campagne électorale** the mechanics of running a campaign; **3** ᴼ(machine, véhicule) machine

mécaniquement /mekanikmɑ̃/ *adv* lit, fig mechanically; **fabriqué ~** machine-made

mécaniser /mekanize/ [1] *vtr*, **se mécaniser** *vpr* to mechanize

mécanisme /mekanism/ *nm* mechanism

mécanoᴼ /mekano/ *nm* mechanic

mécanographe /mekanɔgʀaf/ ▸ p. 372 *nmf* punch-card operator

meccano® /mekano/ *nm* Meccano® GB, erector set US

mécénat /mesenɑ/ *nm* **1** (artistique) patronage; **~ d'entreprise** corporate patronage; **2** (parrainage) sponsorship

mécène /mesɛn/ *nm* (des arts) patron of the arts; (parrain) sponsor

méchamment /meʃamɑ̃/ *adv* **1** (avec méchanceté) [faire, parler, sourire] spitefully, maliciously; [frapper] viciously; **traiter qn ~** to treat sb badly; **2** ᴼ(extrêmement) [travailler] terribly hard; [abîmer] badly; **ils nous en veulent ~** they're terribly angry with us

méchanceté /meʃɑ̃ste/ *nf* **1** (de personne) nastiness; **par pure ~** out of pure spite *ou* malice; **avec ~** spitefully, nastily; **sans ~** without malice; **2** (de propos, regard, d'acte) maliciousness; (plus fort) viciousness; **3** (acte) malicious act; (propos) malicious remark; **dire des ~s** to say malicious *ou* nasty things

méchant, ~e /meʃɑ̃, ɑ̃t/
A *adj* **1** (malveillant) nasty, malicious; **ce n'est pas une ~e femme** she's not such a bad woman; **avoir l'air ~** to look mean; **être ~ avec qn** to be horrible *ou* mean to sb; **2** (dangereux) [animal, personne] vicious; **quand il a bu, il devient ~** he gets nasty when he's been drinking; **attention chien ~!** beware of the dog!; **3** (grave) [blessure, grippe, affaire] nasty, bad; **ce n'est pas bien ~** it's not very bad; **4** ᴼ(extraordinaire) fantasticᴼ

B *nm,f* (au cinéma) villain; (enfant) naughty boy/girl

mèche /mɛʃ/ *nf* **1** (de cheveux) lock; (teinte) streak; **se faire faire des ~s** to have streaks put in one's hair; **2** (de bougie, lampe, briquet) wick; **3** Méd packing **C**; **4** (d'explosif, arme, de fusée) fuse; **5** (outil) (drill) bit

(Composés) **~ folle** stray lock; **~ rebelle** wayward lock
(Idiomes) **être de ~ avec qn**ᴼ to be in cahootsᴼ with sb; **vendre la ~** to let the cat out of the bag

méchoui /meʃwi/ *nm* (repas) North African style barbecue; (viande grillée) spit-roast lamb; **faire un ~** to spit-roast a lamb

méconnaissable /mekɔnɛsabl/ *adj* unrecognizable; (presque) barely recognizable

méconnaissance /mekɔnesɑ̃s/ *nf* liter **1** (ignorance) (total) ignorance; **2** (sous-estimation) misreading

méconnaître /mekɔnɛtʀ/ [73] *vtr* (se méprendre sur) to misread [situation]; to be mistaken about [cause]

méconnu, ~e /mekɔny/
A *adj* [artiste, œuvre] neglected; [talent] undervalued; [valeur] unrecognized
B *nm,f* **un grand ~** a neglected genius

mécontent, ~e /mekɔ̃tɑ̃, ɑ̃t/
A *adj* gén dissatisfied; [électeur] discontented; **pas ~ de lui/d'avoir fini** rather pleased with him/to have finished
B *nm,f* malcontent

mécontentement /mekɔ̃tɑ̃tmɑ̃/ *nm* (insatisfaction) dissatisfaction; (déception) discontent; (irritation) annoyance; (déplaisir) displeasure

mécontenter /mekɔ̃tɑ̃te/ [1] *vtr* (irriter) to annoy; (courroucer) [décision] to anger [peuple]

Mecque /mɛk/ ▸ p. 621 *npr* **la ~** Mecca

médaille /medaj/ *nf* **1** (récompense) medal; **~ d'or** gold medal; **2** (pièce) coin; **3** (bijou) medallion

médaillé, ~e /medaje/
A *pp* ▸ **médailler**
B *pp adj* [sportif] medal-winning (épith); [animal, vin] prize-winning (épith); [soldat] decorated (épith); **un champion plusieurs fois ~** a champion with several medals to his credit
C *nm,f* (sportif) medallistᴳᴮ; gén person who has received a medal

médailler /medaje/ [1] *vtr* **1** Sport to award a medal to; **2** Mil to decorate; **3** to award a prize to [animal, vin]

médaillon /medajɔ̃/ *nm* **1** (bijou) locket; **2** Art, Culin medallion; **3** (sur une image) **en ~** inset

médecin /medsɛ̃/ ▸ p. 372 *nm* doctor; **aller chez le ~** to go to the doctor's; **~ traitant** general practitioner, GP GB

(Composés) **~ acupuncteur** acupuncturist; **~ de famille** family doctor; **~ de garde** duty doctor; **~ homéopathe** homeopath; **~ légiste** forensic surgeon; **~ militaire** army doctor

médecine /medsin/ *nf* **1** (discipline) medicine; **faire (des études de) ~** to study medicine; **étudiant en ~** medical student; **2** (profession) medicine

(Composés) **~ légale** forensic medicine; **~ par les plantes** herbal medicine; **~ scolaire** ≈ school health service; **~ sportive** sports medicine; **~ du travail** ≈ occupational medicine; **~s douces** *or* **parallèles** alternative medicine **C**

MEDEF /medɛf/ *nm* (*abbr* = **Mouvement des entreprises de France**) French business confederation

média /medja/
A *nm* medium
B *médias nmpl* **les ~s** the media

médian, ~e[1] /medjɑ̃, an/ *adj* median (épith)

médiane[2] /medjan/ *nf* Math median

médiateur, -trice[1] /medjatœʀ, tʀis/
A *adj* mediatory
B *nm* gén mediator; (entre le public et l'administration) ombudsman

médiathèque /medjatɛk/ *nf* multimedia library

médiation /medjasjɔ̃/ *nf* mediation

médiatique /medjatik/ *adj* **1** (par les médias) [exploitation] by the media; **2** (dans les médias) [succès] media (épith); **3** (attirant l'attention des médias) media (épith); **geste ~** publicity stunt; **4** (utilisant les médias) [personne] media-conscious; [campagne électorale] conducted through the media; **5** (des médias) **milieu ~** media (pl); **chef-d'œuvre ~** media success

médiatisation /medjatizasjɔ̃/ *nf* media coverage

médiatiser /medjatize/ [1] *vtr* to give |sth| publicity in the media

médiatrice² /medjatʀis/
A *adj f* ▸ **médiateur**
B *nf* Math perpendicular bisector

médical, ~e, *mpl* **-aux** /medikal, o/ *adj* medical

médicament /medikamɑ̃/ *nm* medicine, drug (**pour** for; **contre** to prevent); **mes** ~**s** my medicine (sg)

médicamenteux, **-euse** /medikamɑ̃tø, øz/ *adj* |*produit*| medicinal; |*traitement*| drug (*épith*); |*eczéma, allergie*| drug-related

médication /medikasjɔ̃/ *nf* medication **⊄**

médicinal, ~e, *mpl* **-aux** /medisinal, o/ *adj* medicinal

médico-légal, ~e, *mpl* **-aux** /medikolegal, o/ *adj* forensic; **certificat** ~ autopsy report; **institut** ~ forensic science laboratory

médico-pédagogique, *pl* ~**s** /medikopedagɔʒik/ *adj* **institut** ~ special school

médico-social, ~e, *mpl* **-iaux** /medikosɔsjal, o/ *adj* **centre** ~ ≈ community health centre^{GB}

médiéval, ~e, *mpl* **-aux** /medjeval, o/ *adj* medieval

médiocre /medjɔkʀ/
A *adj* **1** (aux capacités insuffisantes) |*personne, ouvrier*| mediocre, second-rate; |*élève, intelligence*| below-average; **2** (de qualité insuffisante) |*travail, qualité, résultat*| mediocre; |*terrain, nourriture, temps*| poor; (sans valeur) |*œuvre, carrière*| mediocre; |*vie*| humdrum; (sans intensité) |*plaisir, intérêt, succès, ambition*| limited; **3** (en quantité insuffisante) |*revenu, rentabilité*| meagre^{GB}; |*lumière, résultat*| poor
B *nmf* |*personne*| loser, no-hoper[○] GB

médiocrement /medjɔkʀəmɑ̃/ *adv* rather badly

médiocrité /medjɔkʀite/ *nf* **1** (de personne, travail, sentiment) mediocrity; **2** (de revenus, résultats, lumière) meagreness^{GB}

médire /mediʀ/ [65] *vtr ind* ~ **de** to speak ill of

médisance /medizɑ̃s/ *nf* malicious gossip **⊄**

médisant, ~e /medizɑ̃, ɑ̃t/ *adj* malicious

méditatif, **-ive** /meditatif, iv/ *adj* meditative

méditation /meditasjɔ̃/ *nf* meditation (**sur** on)

méditer /medite/ [1]
A *vtr* (projeter) to contemplate (**de faire** doing); (évaluer) to mull over |*paroles*|; **un projet longuement médité** a carefully considered project
B *vi* to meditate; ~ **sur** (sur l'existence, Dieu) to meditate on; (sur un problème) to ponder on *ou* over

Méditerranée /mediteʀane/ ▸ p. 406 *nprf* **la (mer)** ~ the Mediterranean (Sea)

méditerranéen, **-éenne** /mediteʀaneɛ̃, ɛn/ *adj* Mediterranean

médium /medjɔm/ *nm* **1** (voyant) medium; **2** Mus middle register

médius /medjys/ *nm inv* middle finger

méduse /medyz/ *nf* Zool jellyfish

méduser /medyze/ [1] *vtr* to dumbfound; **en rester médusé** to be dumbfounded

meeting /mitiŋ/ *nm* meeting; ~ **aérien** air show

méfait /mefɛ/ *nm* **1** (de personne) misdemeanour^{GB}; (plus grave) crime; **2** (du tabac, d'une politique) ~**s** harmful effects

méfiance /mefjɑ̃s/ *nf* mistrust, suspicion; **éveiller/ apaiser la** ~ **de qn** to arouse/to allay sb's suspicions; **avoir de la** ~ **pour** to be wary of; **avec** ~ warily; **faire qch sans** ~ to do sth unsuspectingly; **être sans** ~ (de nature) to be naïve; ~ **de qn envers** sb's wariness of

méfiant, ~e /mefjɑ̃, ɑ̃t/ *adj* suspicious; **elle est d'un naturel** *or* **caractère** ~ she's always very wary; **d'un œil** ~ suspiciously

méfier: se **méfier** /mefje/ [2] *vpr* **1** (ne pas faire confiance) **se** ~ **de qn/qch** not to trust sb/sth; **sans se** ~ quite trustingly; **2** (faire attention) to be careful; **se** ~ **de qch** to be wary of sth; **ne pas se** ~ **de** not to watch out for; **méfie-toi!** be careful! the road is slippery; **méfietoi, tu vas recevoir une gifle** watch it! you'll get a slap; **tu aurais dû te** ~ you should have been more careful

méga¹ /mega/ *préf* **1** (un million) mega; ~**watt** megawatt; **2** ○ mega; ~**entreprise** mega-firm

méga²[○] /mega/ *adj inv* mega[○]

mégalo[○] /megalo/ *adj, nmf* megalomaniac

mégalomane /megalɔman/ *adj, nmf* megalomaniac

mégaphone /megafɔn/ *nm* (avec amplificateur) loudhailer; (porte-voix) megaphone

mégarde: **par mégarde** /parmegard/ *loc adv* inadvertently

mégère /meʒɛʀ/ *nf* shrew

mégot /mego/ *nm* (de cigarette) cigarette butt *ou* end; (de cigare) stub

meilleur, ~**e¹** /mɛjœʀ/
A *adj* **1** (comparatif) better (**que** than); **tu devrais en acheter une** ~**e** you should buy a better one; **en attendant des jours** ~**s** hoping for better days; **jamais il n'avait mangé (de)** ~ **choucroute** he'd never eaten better sauerkraut; **2** (superlatif) best; **le** ~ **des deux** the better of the two; **c'est le** ~ **de l'équipe** he's the best in the team; **les** ~**s amis du monde** the best of friends; **ta plaisanterie n'était pas du** ~ **goût** your joke wasn't in the best of taste; **c'est le** ~ **des pères** he's the best of fathers; **c'est sur terre battue qu'il est le** ~ he's at his best on clay; **tu ne manges pas la croûte? c'est pourtant ce qu'il y a de** ~**!** aren't you going to eat the crust? but it's the best bit!; **au** ~ **prix** |*acheter*| at the lowest price; |*vendre*| at the highest price
B *nm,f* **le** ~, **la** ~**e** the best one; **ce sont toujours les** ~**s qui s'en vont** it's always the best who go first; **que le** ~ **gagne** may the best man win
C *adv* better; **il fait** ~ **qu'hier** the weather is better than it was yesterday
D *nm* **mange donc la croûte, c'est le** ~**!** eat the crust, it's the best bit!; **donner le** ~ **de soi-même** to give of one's best; **pour le** ~ **et pour le pire** for better or for worse; **garder le** ~ **pour la fin** to keep the best bit till last; **et le** ~ **c'est que...!** and the best bit of it is that...!

meilleure² /mɛjœʀ/ *nf* **tu connais la** ~**?** have you heard the best one yet?; **ça c'est la** ~**!** that's the best one yet!; **j'en passe et des** ~**s!** that's the least of it, I could go on!

mélancolie /melɑ̃kɔli/ *nf* melancholy; Méd melancholia

mélancolique /melɑ̃kɔlik/
A *adj* melancholy
B *nmf* Méd melancholic

mélancoliquement /melɑ̃kɔlikmɑ̃/ *adv* melancholically, in a melancholy fashion

mélange /melɑ̃ʒ/ *nm* **1** (action) gén mixing; (de thés, tabacs) blending; **bonheur/joie sans** ~ unadulterated happiness/ joy; **2** (résultat) (de thés, tabacs) blend; (de légumes, produits, d'idées) combination; (de couleurs, céréales, sentiments) mixture; **un** ~ **explosif** an explosive mixture; **c'est un** ~ (**coton et synthétique**) it's a mix (of cotton and synthetic fibres^{GB})

mélanger /melɑ̃ʒe/ [13]
A *vtr* **1** (pour former un tout) to blend |*tabacs, alcools, thés, huiles*|; to mix |*couleurs, peintures, liquides*|; ~ **les œufs et le sucre** to mix the eggs and the sugar together; **2** (associer) to put together |*styles, personnes*|; **3** (mettre en désordre) to mix up; ~ **les cartes** to shuffle (the cards); **4** (confondre) to mix up; **mais non! tu mélanges tout!** no! you're getting it all mixed up
B **se mélanger** *vpr* **1** (pour former un tout) |*tabacs, thés, huiles*| to blend; |*couleurs, peintures*| to mix; **2** (en créant une confusion) **les souvenirs se mélangent dans ma tête** the memories are getting muddled (up) in my head

mélangeur /melɑ̃ʒœʀ/ *nm* Tech **1** (appareil) mixer; **2** (robinet) (**robinet**) ~ mixer tap GB, mixer faucet US

mélasse /melas/ *nf* **1** Culin black treacle GB, molasses (*pl*); **2** ○ (boue) muck; (brouillard) murk; **3** ○ (confusion) shambles[○] (sg), mess

mêlé, ~**e¹** /mele/
A *pp* ▸ **mêler**
B *pp adj* |*éléments, public, société*| mixed; |*sons, eaux*| mingled; ~ **de** mingled with

mêlée² /mele/ *nf* **1** (bataille, cohue) mêlée; ~ **générale** free-for-all; **la** ~ **devint générale** it turned into a free-for-all; **2** Sport (au rugby) scrum; **3** fig (contestation) fray; **rester en dehors** *ou* **au-dessus de la** ~ to keep out of the fray

mêler /mele/ [1]
A *vtr* **1** (mélanger) to mix |*produits, couleurs*|; to blend |*ingrédients, cultures*|; to combine |*thèmes, influences*|; ~ **le vrai et le faux** to mix truth and falsehood; ~ **ironie et tendresse** to combine irony and tenderness; **2** (allier en soi) ~ **l'utile à l'agréable** to be both useful and pleasurable; ~ **l'ironie à la colère** to be ironic and angry at the same time;

m

③ (impliquer) ~ **qn à** (à un scandale) to get sb involved in; (à des négociations) to involve sb in; (à une conversation) to bring sb into; **être mêlé à** (à un scandale, des négociations) to be involved in; (à une conversation) to be included in

B se mêler *vpr* ① (s'unir) [*cultures, religions*] to mix; [*odeurs, voix, eaux*] to mingle; ② **se ~ à** (se joindre à) to mingle with; (être sociable) to mix with; (participer à) to join in; ③ (s'occuper) **se ~ de** to meddle in; **il se mêle de tout** he interferes in everything; **mêle-toi de tes affaires**⊘ or **oignons**⦿ mind your own business; **de quoi je me mêle**⊘! what's it got to do with you?; **se ~ de faire** to take it upon oneself to do; **quand l'amour s'en mêle!** when love comes into it!

méli-mélo, *pl* **mélis-mélos** /melimelo/ *nm* (mélange) hotchpotch GB, hodgepodge US; (fouillis) jumble, mess; (imbroglio) muddle

mélo⊘ /melo/

A *adj* slushy⊘, schmaltzy⊘; **feuilleton ~** soap (opera)

B *nm* melodrama; **c'est du pur ~** (film, pièce) it's pure schmaltz⊘

mélodie /melɔdi/ *nf* ① Mus melody; (air) tune; (pièce vocale) song; ② (de vers) melodiousness

mélodieux, -ieuse /melɔdjø, øz/ *adj* melodious

mélodique /melɔdik/ *adj* melodic

mélodrame /melɔdʀam/ *nm* melodrama

mélomane /melɔman/

A *adj* **être ~** to be a music lover

B *nmf* music lover

melon /mɔlɔ̃/ *nm* ① (fruit) melon; **~ d'hiver** honeydew melon; ② (chapeau) bowler (hat) GB, derby (hat) US

membrane /mɑ̃bʀan/ *nf* gén membrane

membre /mɑ̃bʀ/ *nm* ① (personne) member; **devenir ~ d'un club** to join a club; **le parti a perdu beaucoup de ~s** the party's membership has fallen considerably; **les pays non ~s** the nonmember countries; ② Anat, Zool limb; **~ antérieur** forelimb; ③ (d'équation, expression) member

Composés **~ fantôme** Méd phantom limb; **~ de phrase** part of a sentence; **~ viril** male member

même /mɛm/

A *adj* ① (identique) same; **en ~ temps** at the same time; **être de la ~ taille** to be the same size; **c'est toujours la ~ chose** it's always the same; ② (suprême) [*bonté, dévouement*] itself; **il est la perfection ~** he's perfection itself; ③ (exact) **à l'heure ~ où** at the very moment when; **les lieux ~s du meurtre** the (actual) scene of the murder; **ce sont les termes ~s qu'il a employés** those were his very words

B *adv* ① (pour renchérir) even; **je ne m'en souviens ~ plus** I can't even remember now; ② (précisément) very; **aujourd'-hui ~** this very day; **c'est cela ~** that's it exactly; ③ **à ~ la peau** next to the skin; **boire à ~ la bouteille** to drink straight from the bottle; **coucher à ~ le sol** to sleep on the bare ground

C **de même** *loc adv* **agir de ~** to do the same; **il a refusé et sa sœur de ~** he refused and so did his sister; **il n'en est plus de ~ depuis 1970** this is no longer the case since 1970; **cette remarque ne s'adresse pas qu'à lui, il en est de ~ pour vous** this comment isn't just aimed at him, it goes for you too; **(de la même manière) de ~ en France l'armée...** similarly in France, the army...

D **de même que** *loc conj* **de ~ que la première entreprise a fait faillite, la seconde n'a pas duré très longtemps** just as the first business went bankrupt, the second one didn't last very long either; **le prix du café, de ~ que celui du tabac, a augmenté de 10%** the price of coffee, as well as that of tobacco, has risen by 10%

E **à même de** *loc prép* **être à ~ de faire** to be able *ou* in a position to do

F **même si** *loc conj* even if

G **même que**⦿ *loc conj* **il roulait à toute allure, ~ qu'il a failli avoir un accident** he was driving so fast that he nearly had an accident

H *pron indéf* **le ~, la ~, les ~s** the same; **j'ai le ~** I've got the same one; **le ~ que celui de Pierre** the same as Pierre's; **le groupe est le ~ qu'en 1980** the group is the same as it was in 1980; **ce sont les ~s qui disaient** these are the same people who said; **Smirnov, le ~ que l'on soupçonne aujourd'hui** Smirnov, the same person suspected today

mémé⊘ /meme/ *nf* (grand-mère) gran⊘, granny⊘; (vieille femme) pej old granny⊘

mémento /memɛ̃to/ *nm* guide

mémère⊘ /memɛʀ/ *nf* (vieille femme) pej old granny⊘; (grand-mère) granny⊘

mémo⊘ /memo/ *nm* note

Mémo-Appel /memoapɛl/ *nm* Télécom reminder call service (*in France*)

mémoire¹ /memwaʀ/ *nm* ① (rapport) memo; Univ (exposé) dissertation (**sur** on); ② (souvenirs) memoirs

mémoire² /memwaʀ/ *nf* ① (faculté) memory; **avoir de la ~** to have a good memory; **si j'ai bonne ~** if I remember rightly; **ne pas avoir de ~** to have a bad memory; **avoir la ~ des dates** to have a good memory for dates; **gravé dans ma ~** engraved on my memory; **des faits qui sont dans toutes les ~s** facts that everyone remembers; **ça m'est soudain revenu en ~** it suddenly came back to me; **chacun a gardé en ~ cette image** everyone remembers that image; **citer de ~** to quote from memory; **de ~ d'homme** in living memory; **de ~ de journaliste, on n'avait jamais vu cela** no journalist could remember such a thing happening before; ② (souvenir) memory (**de** of); (réputation) reputation (**de** of); **en ~ de** to the memory of, in memory of; **d'illustre ~** [*personnage, fait*] illustrious; **pour ~** (à titre de rappel) for the record; (pour conserver) for reference; ③ Ordinat (espace adressable) memory; (unité fonctionnelle) storage; **mettre en ~** to input; **calculatrice à ~** calculator with a memory

Composés **~ centrale** main storage *ou* memory; **~ de maîtrise** Univ dissertation (*which constitutes part of the French master's degree*); **~ morte** read-only memory, ROM; **~ vidéo** video RAM, VRAM, video memory; **~ vive** random access memory, RAM

Idiome **avoir la ~ courte** to have a short memory

Mémophone /memɔfɔn/ *nm* Télécom public voice mail service

mémorable /memɔʀabl/ *adj* memorable

mémorandum /memɔʀɑ̃dɔm/ *nm* memorandum

mémorial, ~e, *mpl* **-iaux** /memɔʀjal, o/ *nm* Archit memorial; Littérat memorials (*pl*)

mémoriser /memɔʀize/ [1] *vtr* ① to memorize; ② Ordinat to store

menaçant, ~e /mənasɑ̃, ɑ̃t/ *adj* menacing; **être ~, dire des paroles ~es** to make threats; **se faire ~** [*personne*] to start to make threats; [*temps*] to look threatening

menace /mənas/ *nf* threat; **~s de mort** death threats; **faire peser une ~ sur** to pose a threat to; **~s en l'air** idle threats; **obtenir de l'argent par la ~** to obtain money with menaces; **sous la ~** under duress; **sous la ~ d'une arme** at gunpoint

menacer /mənase/ [12] *vtr* ① (terroriser) to threaten (**de** with); ② (agiter une menace) to threaten (**de faire** to do); **~ qn d'une amende** to threaten sb with a fine; **~ qn de mort** to threaten to kill sb; **la pluie menace** rain is threatening; ③ (mettre en danger) to pose a threat to; **être menacé** [*équilibre, économie*] to be in jeopardy; [*vie*] to be in danger; [*tranquillité*] to be threatened; [*carrière*] to be on the line; **toute la population est menacée** the entire population is at risk; ④ (risquer) **la chaudière menace d'exploser** the boiler could explode at any moment; **le retard menace d'être long** the delay threatens to be long

ménage /menaʒ/ *nm* ① (foyer) household; ② (couple) couple; (rapports) relationship; **rien ne va plus dans leur ~** their relationship doesn't work any more; **se mettre en ~ avec qn** to set up home with sb; **ils sont** *ou* **vivent en ~** they're living together; **scènes de ~** domestic rows; ③ (administration domestique) **tenir son ~** to look after the house; **monter son ~** to buy the household goods; **pain de ~** home-baked bread; ④ (entretien d'intérieur) housework; **faire le ~** lit to do the cleaning; fig (dans une organisation) to do the cleaning up; **faire des ~s** to do domestic cleaning work

Composé **~ à trois** ménage à trois

Idiome **faire bon ~** [*personnes*] to get on well (**avec** with); [*choses*] to be compatible (**avec** with)

ménagement /menaʒmɑ̃/ *nm* **avec ~s** gently; **sans ~s** [*dire, annoncer, parler*] bluntly; [*jeter, pousser*] roughly, unceremoniously; **traite-le avec ~** (malade) be gentle with him; (personnage puissant) handle him very carefully; **la police l'a embarqué sans aucun ~** the police bundled him unceremoniously into the van

ménager¹ /menaʒe/ [13]
A vtr **1** (traiter avec précaution) to handle [sb] carefully
[collaborateur]; to deal carefully with [adversaire]; to be
gentle with, to treat [sb] gently [personne âgée, malade]; to
be careful with [machine]; **ils savent ~ leurs alliés** they're
careful not to upset their allies; **~ la susceptibilité de qn**
to humour^{GB} sb; **les critiques n'ont pas ménagé le
cinéaste** the critics didn't spare the film director; **~ sa
santé** to look after one's health; **2** (employer avec économie)
to be careful with [vêtements, économies]; to save [forces]; **elle
ne nous a pas ménagé les critiques** she wasn't sparing in
her criticism of us; **il ne ménage pas ses efforts** or **sa
peine** he spares no effort; **3** (installer) **~ un passage** to
make an opening; **~ un espace pour** to make some space
for; **4** (régler avec soin) to organize [entrevue]; **~ un temps de
pause entre les séquences** to allow for breaks between
sequences; **je lui ménage une petite surprise** iron I'm arranging a little surprise for him; **l'auteur ménage ses effets**
the author saves his/her best effects until the end
B **se ménager** vpr (s'économiser) [personne] to take it easy

ménager², **-ère¹** /menaʒe, ɛR/ adj [tâches] domestic;
[équipement] household; **appareils ~s** domestic appliances; **travaux ~s** housework **₵**

ménagère² /menaʒɛR/ nf (personne) housewife; (couverts)
canteen of cutlery

ménagerie /menaʒRi/ nf menagerie

mendiant, **~e** /mãdjã, ãt/ nm,f beggar

mendicité /mãdisite/ nf begging

mendier /mãdje/ [2]
A vtr to beg for; **~ qch auprès de qn** to beg sb for sth
B vi to beg

mener /məne/ [16]
A vtr **1** (accompagner) gén **~ qn quelque part** to take sb somewhere; (en voiture) to drive sb somewhere; **2** (guider) to lead;
3 (commander) to lead [hommes, pays]; to run [entreprise]; **il
ne se laisse pas ~ par sa grande sœur** he won't be bossed
about⁰ by his sister; **se laisser ~ par son seul intérêt** to
be motivated by pure self-interest; **4** (avoir l'avantage) to
lead; **la France mène le championnat devant l'Allemagne
par trois points** France is leading the championship three
points ahead of Germany; **5** (aller, faire aller) [route] **~ au
village** to go ou lead to the village; **~ qn quelque part** to
take sb somewhere; **6** (faire aboutir) **~ à** to lead to; **je ne
vois pas où cela nous mène** I can't see where this is getting ou leading us; **cela mène à tout** it leads to all kinds of
things; **cela ne mène à rien** it doesn't lead anywhere;
parler ne mène à rien talking won't get you anywhere;
cette histoire peut te ~ loin (avoir des conséquences graves) it
could be a very nasty business; **10 euros, cela ne nous
mènera pas loin** 10 euros, that won't get us very far; **~ à
bien** or **à (son) terme** to complete [sth] successfully [projet];
to bring [sth] to a successful conclusion [négociation,
enquête]; to handle [sth] successfully [opération délicate];
7 (poursuivre) to carry out [étude, réforme]; to pursue
[politique]; to run [campagne]; **~ une enquête** gén to hold an
investigation; **~ une vie misérable** to lead a wretched
existence; **~ sa vie comme on l'entend** to live as one
pleases; **~ une guerre sans pitié** to wage a bitter war
B vi Sport to be in the lead; **~ par trois buts à un** to lead by
three goals to one

(Idiomes) **~ la danse** or **le jeu** to call the tune; **~ la grande
vie** to live it up

ménestrel /menɛstRɛl/ nm minstrel

meneur, **-euse** /mənœR, øz/ nm,f leader; **qualités de ~**
leadership qualities; **~ d'hommes** leader of men

menhir /meniR/ nm menhir

méninge /menɛ̃ʒ/
A nf Anat meninx
B **méninges**⁰ nfpl brains⁰; **se creuser les ~s** to rack one's
brains

méningite /menɛ̃ʒit/ ▸ p. 195 nf meningitis

ménisque /menisk/ nm meniscus

ménopause /menɔpoz/ nf menopause

menotte /mənɔt/
A nf (petite main) tiny hand
B **menottes** nfpl handcuffs; **avoir les ~s aux poignets** to be
handcuffed; **passer les ~s à qn** to handcuff sb

mensonge /mãsɔ̃ʒ/ nm **1** (assertion fausse) lie; **dire des ~s
à qn** to tell sb lies; **2** (principe) **le ~** lying

mensonger, **-ère** /mãsɔ̃ʒe, ɛR/ adj [propos, accusations]
false; [publicité] misleading; [campagne] dishonest

mensualisé, **~e** /mãsɥalize/ adj [paiement] monthly
(épith); [salaire, employé] paid monthly (jamais épith)

mensualiser /mãsɥalize/ [1] vtr (étaler) **~ des versements**
to pay in monthly instalments^{GB}

mensualité /mãsɥalite/ nf (versement) monthly
instalment^{GB}; **par ~s** in monthly instalments^{GB}

mensuel, **-elle** /mãsɥɛl/
A adj monthly
B nm (revue) monthly magazine

mensuellement /mãsɥɛlmã/ adv once a month,
monthly

mensurations /mãsyRasjɔ̃/ nfpl measurements

mental, **~e**, mpl **-aux** /mãtal, o/ adj mental; **handicapé
~** mentally handicapped person

mentalement /mãtalmã/ adv (par la pensée) in one's head;
(sur le plan mental) mentally

mentalité /mãtalite/ nf mentality; **belle ~!** iron the mentality of some people!

menteur, **-euse** /mãtœR, øz/
A adj [personne] untruthful; **être ~** to be a liar
B nm,f liar; **menteuse!** you liar!

menthe /mãt/ nf **1** (plante) mint; **à la ~** mint (épith);
~ poivrée peppermint; **~ verte** spearmint; **2** (infusion)
mint tea; **3** (sirop) **~ (à l'eau)** mint cordial

menthol /mɛ̃tɔl/ nm menthol

mentholé, **~e** /mɛ̃tole/ adj mentholated; [bonbon, cigarette, dentifrice] menthol (épith)

mention /mãsjɔ̃/ nf **1** (action de citer) mention; **sans ~ de**
with no mention of; **faire ~ de qch** to mention sth; **ne
pas faire ~ de qch** to make no mention of sth; **2** Scol,
Univ **~ passable** pass with 50 to 60%; **~ assez bien** pass with
60 to 70%; **~ bien** pass with 70 to 80%; **~ très bien** pass with
80% upwards; **réussir avec ~** to pass with distinction;
3 (indication) note; **dossier portant la ~ 'secret'** file
marked 'secret'; **rayer la ~ inutile** delete as appropriate

mentionner /mãsjɔne/ [1] vtr to mention

mentir /mãtiR/ [30]
A vi **1** (ne pas dire la vérité) [personne] to lie (**sur** about), to tell
lies (**sur** about; **à qn** to sb); **sans ~, le poisson était grand
comme ça!** no lie, the fish was this big!; ▸ **arracheur**
2 (être trompeur) to be misleading; **faire ~ le proverbe** to
give the lie to the proverb
B **se mentir** vpr **1** (à soi-même) to fool oneself (**sur** about);
2 (l'un l'autre) to lie to one another (**sur** about)

menton /mãtɔ̃/ ▸ p. 136 nm chin

mentonnière /mãtɔnjɛR/ nf (de couvre-chef) chinstrap; (de
violon) chin rest

menu, **~e** /məny/
A adj **1** (petit) [personne] slight; [pied, morceau] tiny; [brindille,
écriture] small; **2** (sans importance) [corvées, travaux] small;
[frais, soucis] minor; [détails] minute
B adv [écrire] small; [hacher] finely
C nm **1** (liste) menu; **le ~ à 15 euros** the 15-euro menu;
~ dégustation special house menu; **le ~ du jour** today's
menu; **~ gastronomique/touristique** gourmet/middle-
price menu; **au ~** on the menu; **2** (repas) meal;
3 (régime) diet; **4** (programme) programme^{GB}; **5** Ordinat
menu
D **par le menu** loc adv in (great) detail

(Composés) **~ fretin** lit, fig small fry; **~e monnaie** small
change

menuet /mənɥɛ/ nm minuet

menuiserie /mənɥizRi/ nf **1** (travail du bois, profession) joinery; (discipline, passe-temps) woodwork; **un atelier de ~** a joiner's workshop; **2** (boiseries) woodwork **₵**

menuisier /mənɥizje/ ▸ p. 372 nm joiner GB, finish carpenter

méprendre: **se méprendre** /mepRãdR/ [52] vpr fml to be
mistaken (**sur** about); **elles se ressemblent tellement, c'est
à s'y ~** they're so much alike, it's hard to tell them
apart

mépris /mepRi/ nm inv **1** (dédain) contempt (**de** for); **avoir
du ~ pour** to despise; **sourire de ~** contemptuous smile;
2 (indifférence) **~ de** (d'argent, de succès) contempt for; (de
danger, des convenances) disregard for; **au ~ de la loi** regardless of the law

méprisable /mepʀizabl/ *adj* contemptible; (plus fort) despicable

méprisant, ~e /mepʀizɑ̃, ɑ̃t/ *adj* [geste, sourire] contemptuous; [personne] disdainful

méprise /mepʀiz/ *nf* mistake; **par ~** by mistake

mépriser /mepʀize/ [1] *vtr* to despise [personne, argent]; to scorn [danger, conseils, offre]

mer /mɛʀ/ ▸ p. 406 *nf* **1** (étendue d'eau) sea; **niveau de la ~** sea level; **~ d'huile** glassy sea; **en pleine ~** out at sea; **être en ~** to be at sea; **prendre la ~** to go to sea; **un homme à la ~!** man overboard!; **en bord de ~** by the sea; **mettre un bateau à la ~** to launch a boat; **eau de ~** seawater; **~ Morte** Dead Sea; **~ Noire** Black Sea; **~ du Nord** North Sea; **~ Rouge** Red Sea; **2** (zone côtière) seaside; **aller à la ~** to go to the seaside; **3** (marée) tide; **la ~ monte** the tide is coming in

(Idiome) **ce n'est pas la ~ à boire** it's not all that difficult

mercantile /mɛʀkɑ̃til/ *adj* pej mercenary péj

mercantilisme /mɛʀkɑ̃tilism/ *nm* (en économie) mercantilism; (mentalité) pej mercenary mentality

mercenaire /mɛʀsənɛʀ/ *adj, nmf* mercenary

mercerie /mɛʀsəʀi/ ▸ p. 372 *nf* (boutique) haberdasher's shop GB, notions store US

merci¹ /mɛʀsi/
A *nm* thank you; **tu leur diras un grand ~ de ma part** give them a big thank you from me; **mille ~s** thank you so much
B *excl* thank you, thanks○ (à to; de, pour for; de faire, d'avoir fait for doing); **~ beaucoup** thank you very much; **~ à vous!** (repartie) thank YOU!; **Dieu ~** thank God

merci² /mɛʀsi/ *nf* mercy; **sans ~** [lutte] merciless (épith); **à leur ~** at their mercy; **on est toujours à la ~ d'un changement de dernière minute** there's always the risk of a last minute change

mercredi /mɛʀkʀədi/ ▸ p. 545 *nm* Wednesday; **~ des Cendres** Ash Wednesday

mercure /mɛʀkyʀ/ *nm* mercury

mercurochrome® /mɛʀkyʀokʀom/ *nm* Mercurochrome®, antiseptic

merde /mɛʀd/
A ●*nf* **1** (matière) shit○; **2** (étron) turd○; **3** (objet de mauvaise qualité) crap○; **chaussures de ~** crap○ shoes; **4** (pagaille) mess○
B ○*excl* shit○!; **dire ~ à qn** to tell sb to piss off○

merdique○ /mɛʀdik/ *adj* [film, livre] crappy○; [voiture, appareil, pays] crap○

mère /mɛʀ/
A *nf* **1** (génitrice) mother; **elles sont sages-femmes de ~ en fille** they have been midwives for generations; **mariée et ~ de deux enfants** married with two children; **2** ○(femme) **la ~ Michel** old mother Michel; **3** (dans un couvent) **~ supérieure** Mother Superior
B (-)**mère** (in compounds) **cellule/maison ~** parent cell/ company
(Composés) **~ adoptive** foster mother; **~ célibataire** single mother; **~ de famille** gén mother; (ménagère) housewife; **~ patrie** motherland; **~ porteuse** surrogate mother; **~ poule** hum mother hen
(Idiome) **il tuerait père et ~ pour avoir qch** he'd kill to get sth

merguez /mɛʀgɛz/ *nf inv* spicy sausage

méridien, -ienne /meʀidjɛ̃, ɛn/
A *adj* meridian
B *nm* meridian

méridional, ~e, *mpl* **-aux** /meʀidjɔnal, o/
A *adj* (du Midi) Southern; [versant, côte] southern
B *nm,f* Southerner

meringue /məʀɛ̃g/ *nf* meringue

mérinos /meʀinos/ *nm inv* merino

merise /məʀiz/ *nf* wild cherry

merisier /məʀizje/ *nm* (arbre) wild cherry tree; (bois) cherry wood

méritant, ~e /meʀitɑ̃, ɑ̃t/ *adj* deserving

mérite /meʀit/ *nm* (vertu permanente) merit; (pour un événement ponctuel) credit; (qualité) merit, quality; **il a au moins le ~ d'être sincère** but at least he's sincere; **au ~** according to merit; **avoir du ~ à faire qch** to deserve credit for doing

sth; **il n'y a aucun ~ à faire** there's no merit in doing; **vous n'en avez que plus de ~** you deserve all the more credit for it; **cette voiture n'est pas très belle mais elle a le ~ de rouler** this car isn't much to look at but at least it goes GB ou runs US; **vanter les ~s de** to sing the praises of; **avoir le double ~ d'être confortable et puissant** to be both comfortable and powerful

mériter /meʀite/ [1]
A *vtr* to deserve; **il mériterait qu'on lui fasse subir le même sort** he deserves the same treatment; **tu n'as que ce que tu mérites** you've got GB ou gotten US what you deserve; **~ réflexion/d'être lu** to be worth considering/reading; **le détour** to be worth the detour; **il a reçu une gifle et il l'a bien méritée** he got a slap in the face and it was nothing less than he deserved; **succès (bien) mérité** well-deserved success; **sa lettre mérite une réponse** his/her letter merits a reply
B **se mériter** *vpr* **c'est quelque chose qui se mérite** it's something that has to be earned

méritoire /meʀitwaʀ/ *adj* praiseworthy

merlan /mɛʀlɑ̃/ *nm* whiting

merle /mɛʀl/ *nm* blackbird

merlu /mɛʀly/ *nm* hake

merluche /mɛʀlyʃ/ *nf* (merlu) hake; (morue séchée) stockfish

mérou /meʀu/ *nm* grouper

merveille /mɛʀvɛj/
A *nf* (chose admirable) marvel, wonder; **c'est une pure ~** it's marvellous GB; **les sept ~s du monde** the seven wonders of the world; **la ~ des ~s** the most wonderful thing in the world; **une ~ de finesse** a marvel ou miracle of delicacy; **faire ~** or **des ~s** to work wonders
B **à merveille** *loc adv* wonderfully; **la voiture marche à ~** the car goes like a dream; **se porter à ~** to be in excellent health

merveilleusement /mɛʀvɛjøzmɑ̃/ *adv* marvellously GB, wonderfully

merveilleux, -euse /mɛʀvɛjø, øz/
A *adj* (admirable) marvellous GB, wonderful; [conte] fabulous
B *nm* **le ~** the fabulous

mes ▸ mon

mésange /mezɑ̃ʒ/ *nf* tit; **~ bleue** blue tit

mésaventure /mezavɑ̃tyʀ/ *nf* misadventure, unfortunate experience; **par ~** by some misfortune

mesdames ▸ madame

mesdemoiselles ▸ mademoiselle

mésentente /mezɑ̃tɑ̃t/ *nf* dissension; (moins grave) disagreement

mésestimer /mezɛstime/ [1] *vtr* liter to underrate [artiste, œuvre]; to underestimate [collaborateur, qualité, difficulté]

mesquin, ~e /mɛskɛ̃, in/ *adj* **1** (vil) [personne] meanminded, petty-minded; [esprit, attitude] petty; **2** (chiche) [personne] mean GB, cheap○ US; [récompense] stingy

mesquinerie /mɛskinʀi/ *nf* **1** (caractère) (bassesse) meanness; (avarice) stinginess; **2** (action) mean trick; (remarque) mean remark

mess /mɛs/ *nm inv* Mil mess

message /mesaʒ/ *nm* message; **~ de détresse** SOS message
(Composés) **~ électronique** email; **~ publicitaire** commercial

messager, -ère /mesaʒe, ɛʀ/ *nm,f* (qui transmet) messenger; (en diplomatie) envoy; (qui présage) liter herald

messagerie /mesaʒʀi/ *nf* (transport de marchandises) freight forwarding; Télécom messaging; **~ vocale** voice messaging, voice mail; **~s aériennes** air freight service (sg)

messe /mɛs/ *nf* Relig, Mus Mass (en in); **aller à la ~** to go to mass; **~ basse** low mass; fig **~s basses** whispering ¢; **arrêtez de faire des ~s basses**○! stop whispering together!; **~ de minuit** midnight mass

Messeigneurs ▸ Monseigneur

messie /mesi/ *nm* messiah; **le Messie** the Messiah

messieurs ▸ monsieur

mesurable /məzyʀabl/ *adj* measurable; **non ~** unmeasurable; **ce n'est pas ~** it can't be measured

mesure /məzyʀ/ *nf* **1** (initiative) measure; **par ~ d'économie** as an economy measure, to save money; **prendre des ~s** gén to take measures; (autoritairement) to take

m

steps; **par ~ de sécurité** as a safety precaution; **2** (dimension) measurement; **prendre les ~s de qn** [*couturière*] to take sb's measurements; **faire prendre ses ~s** to be measured up; **(fait) sur ~** [*vêtement*] made-to-measure (*épith*); [*chaussures*] handmade; **le sur ~** made-to-measure clothes (*pl*); **tu as un emploi sur ~** the job is tailor-made for you; **emploi à la ~ de ses ambitions** job which is commensurate with one's ambition; **c'est une adversaire à ta ~** she is a match for you; **pour faire bonne ~** for good measure; **3** (évaluation) measurement; **unité de ~** unit of measurement; **instrument de ~** measuring device; **4** (unité) measure; ▸ **deux**; **5** (récipient, contenu) measure; **deux ~s de lait pour une ~ d'eau** two parts milk to one of water; **6** (modération) moderation; **parler avec ~** to weigh one's words; **agir avec ~** to behave in a moderate way; **sans ~** [*dépenser*] wildly; [*boire*] to excess; **dépasser la ~** to go too far; **7** Mus bar; **c'est une ~ à trois temps** it's in three time; **battre la ~** to beat time; **en ~** [*jouer*] in time; [*danser*] in time to the music; **8** (situation) **être en ~ de rembourser** to be in a position to reimburse; **le malade n'est pas en ~ de vous parler** the patient cannot talk to you; **9** (limite) **je t'aiderai, dans la ~ où je le pourrai** or **de mes moyens** I'll help you as much as I can; **dans la ~ du possible** as far as possible; **dans une certaine ~** to some extent; **dans une large ~** to a large extent; **dans la ~ où** insofar as

mesuré, ~e /məzyʀe/
A *pp* ▸ **mesurer**
B *pp adj* [*propos*] measured; [*attitude*] moderate; **être ~ dans ses propos** to weigh one's words

mesurer /məzyʀe/ **1** ▸ p. 347, p. 568, p. 575
A *vtr* **1** (avec un instrument) gén to measure [*longueur, quantité, objet, lieu*] (**en** in); (pour prélever une partie) to measure off [*longueur*]; to measure out [*poids, volume*]; (avant travaux) to measure up [*recoin*]; **~ le tour de cou de qn** to take sb's neck measurement; **2** (évaluer) to measure [*productivité, écart*]; to assess [*risques, effets*]; to consider [*conséquences*] ; **~ sa force contre** or **avec qn** to pit one's strength against sb; **mal ~ la portée de qch** to miscalculate the implications of sth; **~ ses paroles** to weigh one's words; **ne pas ~ ses propos** to speak without restraint; **3** (donner sans générosité) **le temps nous est mesuré** our time is limited; **ne pas ~ ses efforts** to try one's utmost
B *vi* **~ 20 mètres carrés** to be 20 metres^GB square; **~ 2 mètres de haut** to be 2 metres^GB high; **elle mesure 1,60 m** she's 1.60 m tall
C *se mesurer* **1** (se calculer) **se ~ en mètres** to be measured in metres^GB; **2** (s'affronter) **se ~ à** or **avec qn** to pit one's strength against sb

métabolique /metabɔlik/ *adj* metabolic

métacarpe /metakaʀp/ *nm* metacarpus

métal, *pl* **-aux** /metal, o/ *nm* metal; **pièce de** or **en ~** metal coin; **~ jaune** gold

métallique /metalik/ *adj* **1** lit (en métal) metal (*épith*); (ressemblant au métal) metallic; **2** fig metallic; **le bruit ~ des clés** the clink of keys

métallisé /metalize/ *adj* [*vert, bleu*] metallic; **peinture ~e** paint with a metallic finish

métalloïde /metalɔid/ *nm* metalloid

métallurgie /metalyʀʒi/ *nf* (technique) metallurgy; (industrie) metalworking industry

métallurgique /metalyʀʒik/ *adj* metallurgical

métallurgiste /metalyʀʒist/ ▸ p. 372 *nm* (ouvrier) metalworker; (industriel) metallurgist

métamorphose /metamɔʀfoz/ *nf* metamorphosis

métamorphoser /metamɔʀfoze/ **1**
A *vtr* to transform completely; **~ qn en qch** to turn sb into sth
B *se métamorphoser* *vpr* to be completely transformed; **se ~ en** to metamorphose into

métaphore /metafɔʀ/ *nf* metaphor

métaphorique /metafɔʀik/ *adj* metaphorical

métaphysique /metafizik/
A *adj* metaphysical
B *nf* Philos metaphysics (+ *v sg*)

métastase /metastaz/ *nf* metastasis

métatarse /metataʀs/ *nm* metatarsus

métayage /metejaʒ/ *nm* tenant farming GB, sharecropping US

métayer, -ère /meteje, ɛʀ/ *nmf* tenant farmer GB, sharecropper US

météo /meteo/
A *adj inv* weather (*épith*)
B *nf* **1** (organisme) Met Office GB, Weather Service US; **que dit la ~?** what's the forecast?; **2** (prévisions) weather forecast; **~ marine** shipping forecast

météore /meteɔʀ/ *nm* meteor; **passer comme un ~** (avoir un bref succès) to be a flash in the pan; (faire une visite éclair) to be gone in a flash

météorique /meteɔʀik/ *adj* meteoric

météorite /meteɔʀit/ *nm ou f* meteorite

météorologie /meteɔʀɔlɔʒi/ *nf* meteorology; **la ~ nationale** the Meteorological Office GB, the Weather Service US

météorologique /meteɔʀɔlɔʒik/ *adj* [*phénomène*] meteorological; **conditions ~s** weather conditions

météorologiste /meteɔʀɔlɔʒist/, **météorologue** /meteɔʀɔlɔg/ ▸ p. 372 *nmf* meteorologist

métèque /metɛk/ *nm* offensive foreigner, dago○

méthane /metan/ *nm* methane

méthode /metɔd/ *nf* **1** gén, Philos method; **~ de gestion** management method; **2** (ordre) **procéder avec ~** to proceed methodically; **il manque de ~** he's not methodical; **avoir de la ~** to be methodical; **3** (manuel) (de musique) method; (de langues) course book GB, textbook US; **4** (système) way; **j'ai ma ~ pour le convaincre** I've got a way of convincing him; **il n'y a pas de ~ miracle pour réussir** there is no magic formula for success

méthodique /metɔdik/ *adj* methodical

méthodiquement /metɔdikmɑ̃/ *adv* methodically; **procédons ~** let's take things step by step

méthodisme /metɔdism/ *nm* Methodism

méthyle /metil/ *nm* methyl

méthylique /metilik/ *adj* **alcool ~** methyl alcohol

méticuleux, -euse /metikylø, øz/ *adj* [*personne, soin*] meticulous; [*travail, choix*] painstaking

métier /metje/ *nm* **1** (activité rémunérée) job; (intellectuel) profession; (manuel) trade; (artisanal) craft; **c'est mon ~ (de faire ça)!** it's my job!; **il a fait tous les ~s** he's tried his hand at everything; **apprendre un ~** (manuel) to learn a trade; **il est cuisinier de son ~** he's a cook by trade; **un maçon de ~** a professional mason; **terme de ~** specialized term; **les gens du ~** (manuels) people in the trade; (intellectuels) the professionals; **ne t'inquiète pas, elle est du ~** don't worry, she knows what she's doing; **2** (rôle) job; **faire son ~ de reine/mère** to do one's job as queen/a mother; **3** (expérience) **avoir du ~** to be experienced; **avoir 20 ans de ~** to have 20 years' experience; **4** (objet) loom; **~ à tisser** weaving loom

(Idiome) **faire le plus vieux ~ du monde** euph to practise^GB the oldest profession

métis, -isse /metis/
A *adj* **1** [*famille, enfant*] mixed-race (*épith*); [*animal, plante*] hybrid; **2** [*toile*] union (*épith*)
B *nmf* (personne) person of mixed-race
C *nm inv* cotton and linen cloth

métissage /metisaʒ/ *nm* (de personnes) miscegenation; (de plantes, d'animaux) crossing; **~ culturel** cultural cross-fertilization

métrage /metʀaʒ/ *nm* **1** (de tissu) length; **2** (de mur, parquet) length in metres^GB; **3** (de film) length; **long/court ~** feature(-length)/short film

mètre /mɛtʀ/ *nm* **1** ▸ p. 347, p. 568, p. 575, p. 624, p. 628 (unité de mesure) metre^GB; **ça se vend au ~** it's sold by the metre^GB; (en sport) **le 60 ~s** the 60 metres^GB; **piquer un cent ~s○** fig to break into a run; **2** (instrument de mesure) (metre^GB) rule GB, yardstick US; **3** Littérat metre^GB

(Composés) **~ carré** square metre^GB; **~ de couturière** tape measure; **~ cube** cubic metre^GB; **~ enrouleur** retractable tape measure; **~ étalon** standard metre^GB; **~ pliant** folding (metre^GB) rule; **~ ruban** tape measure

métrique /metʀik/ *adj* metric

métro /metʀo/ *nm* **1** (réseau) underground GB, subway US; **prendre le ~** to take the underground; **2** (rame) underground train GB, subway train US; **j'ai raté le dernier ~** I've missed the last train; **~ aérien** elevated railway

(Idiome) **~, boulot, dodo○** the daily grind

Les métiers et les professions

Les personnes

que fait-il dans la vie?
= what does he do? *ou* what's his job?

■ *Au singulier l'anglais emploie l'article indéfini devant les noms de métiers et de professions utilisés avec les verbes to be* (être), *to become* (devenir), *etc., ou avec as.*

il est mécanicien
= he is a mechanic

elle est dentiste
= she is a dentist

elle est professeur d'histoire
= she is a history teacher

c'est un bon boucher
= he is a good butcher

il travaille comme boucher
= he works as a butcher

il est employé comme mécanicien
= he works as a mechanic

elle veut devenir architecte
= she wants to be an architect

ils sont bouchers
= they are butchers

ce sont de bons bouchers
= they are good butchers

Les lieux

■ *S'il y a un nom en anglais pour désigner la personne* (the butcher, the baker, the chemist *etc.*), *on peut utiliser ce nom pour désigner le lieu où elle travaille.*

aller chez le boucher
= to go to the butcher's* *ou* to go to the butcher's shop†

travailler dans une boucherie
= to work at a butcher's *ou* to work at a butcher's shop

acheter quelque chose chez le boucher
= to buy something at the butcher's
ou to buy something at the butcher's shop

■ *Dans les cas où le lieu ne s'appelle pas* shop *ou* store, *la première de ces deux formes est toujours possible.*

aller chez le coiffeur
= to go to the hairdresser's

■ *On peut aussi employer* surgery *pour les professions médicales ou* office *pour les architectes, les avocats, les comptables, etc.*

aller chez le médecin
= to go to the doctor's surgery (*GB*) *ou* office (*US*)

aller chez l'avocat
= to go to the lawyer's office

■ *On peut, dans certains cas, utiliser le nom particulier du lieu, s'il existe* (bakery, grocery *etc.*).

aller à la boulangerie
= to go to the bakery

■ *Dans les cas où le français dit* chez le marchand de X, *on peut, en général, dire en anglais* at/to the X shop.

aller chez le marchand de poissons
= to go to the fish shop

acheter quelque chose chez le marchand de fruits
= to buy something at the fruit shop

■ *De même* shoe shop (chaussures), *toy shop* (jouets), wine shop (vin) *etc.*

* *Au lieu de* to the butcher's, *on peut aussi dire* to the butcher. *Mais la forme avec* 's *est préférable.*

† *Attention: ce qui s'appelle* shop *en anglais britannique s'appelle en général* store *en anglais américain.*

---

métronome /metʀɔnɔm/ *nm* metronome

métropole /metʀɔpɔl/ *nf* **1** (capitale) metropolis; (grande ville) major city; **2** (France métropolitaine) Metropolitan France

métropolitain, **~e** /metʀɔpɔlitɛ̃, ɛn/ *adj* **1** [réseau] underground GB, subway US; **2** [culture, investisseur] from Metropolitan France

métropolite /metʀɔpɔlit/ *nm* metropolitan

mets /mɛ/ *nm inv* dish, delicacy

mettable /mɛtabl/ *adj* [vêtement] wearable

metteur /mɛtœʀ/ *nm* **~ en pages** make-up man; **~ en scène** director

mettre /mɛtʀ/ [60]

A *vtr* **1** (placer dans un endroit, une position) to put; **on m'a mis devant** they put me at the front; **je mets les enfants à la crèche** I send the children to a creche; **2** (projeter involontairement) to drop [confiture, beurre] (**sur** on); to spill [liquide, poudre] (**sur** on); **3** (placer sur le corps) to put on [écharpe, fard]; **4** (placer dans le corps) to put in; **on m'a mis un plombage** I had a filling; **5** (porter habituellement sur le corps) to wear; **je ne mets jamais de chapeau** I never wear a hat; **6** (placer dans une situation, un état) **~ qn en colère** to make sb angry; **~ qn de bonne humeur** to put sb in a good mood; **~ qn au travail** to put sb to work; **~ le riz à cuire** to put the rice on; **~ le linge à sécher** to put the washing out to dry; **7** (classer) **~ qch avant tout le reste** *ou* **au-dessus de tout** to put sth; **8** (disposer) **~ les assiettes** to put the plates on the table; **~ les verres** to put out the glasses; **~ une autre chaise** to bring another chair; **~ une nappe** to put on a tablecloth; **je t'ai mis des draps propres** I've put clean sheets on for you; **9** (faire fonctionner) **~ la radio/les nouvelles** to put the radio/the news on; **mets plus/moins fort!** turn it up/down!; **~ les phares** to switch on the headlights; **~ le réveil** to set the alarm; **~ le verrou** to bolt the door; **10** (installer) to put in [chauffage, douche, téléphone, placard]; to put up [rideau, lustre, étagère]; **faire ~ le téléphone** to have a telephone put in; **~ du carrelage/de la moquette** to lay tiles/a carpet; **faire ~ de la moquette** (dans plusieurs pièces) to have carpets laid; **11** (écrire) to put up [inscription]; **il met que tout va bien** (dans une lettre) he says *ou* writes that everything's fine; **qu'est-ce que je dois ~?** what shall I put?; **~ au passif/en anglais** to put into the passive/into English; **est-ce qu'on met un trait d'union à 'multinational'?** is there a hyphen in 'multinational'?; **il faut ~ un trait d'union** you must put a hyphen in; **mettez votre signature ici** sign here; **mettez le pronom qui convient** (remplacez) replace with the appropriate pronoun; (bouchez les trous) insert the appropriate pronoun; **~ en musique** to set to music; **12** (ajouter) to add [ingrédient] (**dans** to); to put [accessoire]; **~ du sel dans la soupe** to put some salt in the soup; **13** (consacrer) **~ tout son cœur dans son travail** to put one's heart into one's work; **y ~ du sien** to put oneself into it; **~ toute son énergie à faire** to put all one's energy into doing; **14** (investir, dépenser) to put [argent] (**dans, sur** into); **combien pouvez-vous ~?** (pour acheter) how much can you afford?; (pour contribuer) how much can you put in?; **15** (prendre) (du temps) **elle a (bien) mis une heure** it took her (easily) an hour; **~ un temps fou**⚪ to take ages⚪; **16** ⚪(vendre) **je vous mets des tomates?** would you like some tomatoes?; **17** (attribuer) to give [note]; **18** ⚪(dire) **mettons dix dollars/à dix heures** let's say ten dollars/at ten; **19** ⚪(supposer) **mettons qu'il vienne** supposing he comes; **20** ⚫(ficher) **tu peux te le ~ où je pense** *or* **quelque part** you know where you can put it⚪

B *vi* **~ bas** gén [vache] to calve; [brebis] to lamb; [jument] to foal

C **se mettre** *vpr* **1** (se placer dans un endroit, une position) **se ~ devant la fenêtre** (debout) to stand in front of the window; (assis) to sit down in front of the window; **se**

~ **sur les mains** to stand on one's hands; **se ~ sur le dos** to lie on one's back; **se ~ au lit** to go to bed; **se ~ debout** to stand up; **ne plus savoir où se ~** not to know where to put oneself; **se ~ les mains sur la tête** to put one's hands on one's head; **se ~ les doigts dans le nez** to pick one's nose; **où est-ce que ça se met?** where does this go?; ② (projeter involontairement sur soi) to spill [sth] on oneself [*liquide, poudre*]; **se ~ de la confiture** to get jam on oneself; **s'en ~ partout** to get it all over oneself; ③ (placer sur son corps) to put on [*veste, fard*]; **je ne sais pas quoi me ~** I don't know what to put on; ④ (placer dans son corps) to put in; ⑤ (commencer) **se ~ à l'anglais** to take up English; **elle s'est mise à leur recherche** she started looking for them **il va se ~ à pleuvoir** it's going to start raining; **il se met à faire du vent** it's starting to get windy; ⑥ (tourner) **le temps s'est mis au froid/à la pluie** the weather has turned cold/ to rain; ⑦ (se placer dans une situation, un état) **se ~ en tort** to put oneself in the wrong; **se ~ dans une situation impossible** to get (oneself) into an impossible situation; **se ~ dans une sale affaire** to get involved in some shady business; **je me mets de ton côté** I'm on your side; **je préfère me ~ bien avec lui** I prefer to get on the right side of him; **se ~ à l'aise** to make oneself comfortable; **on va se ~ ensemble**○ (sous le même toit) we're going to live together; ⑧ (s'habiller) **se ~ en tenue d'été** to put on summer clothes; **se ~ en jaune** to wear yellow; ⑨ (se grouper) **ce n'est pas la peine de vous (y) ~ à dix** there's no need for ten of you; **ils s'y sont mis à au moins trente** there were at least thirty of them

meuble /mœbl/
A *adj* [*sol*] loose
B *nm* un ~ a piece of furniture; **des ~s** furniture **℄**; **un ~ de jardin** a piece of garden furniture; **~ hi-fi** hi-fi unit; **~ de cuisine/salle de bains/rangement** kitchen/ bathroom/storage unit
(Idiomes) **sauver les ~s** to salvage something; **faire partie des ~s** to be part of the furniture; **être dans ses ~s** to have a home of one's own

meublé, ~e /mœble/
A *pp* ▸ **meubler**
B *pp adj* furnished; **non ~** unfurnished
C *nm* furnished flat GB *ou* apartment

meubler /mœble/ [1]
A *vtr* ① [*personne*] to furnish (**de, avec** with); ② (décorer) **un simple lit meuble la chambre** the room is furnished only with a bed; **la plante meuble la pièce** the plant makes the room look more cosy GB *ou* cozy US
B **se meubler** *vpr* to furnish one's home

meuf○ /mœf/ *nf* gén woman; (petite amie) girlfriend

meugler /møgle/ [1] *vi* to moo

meuh /mø/ *nm* (also onomat) moo

meule /møl/ *nf* ① (de moulin) millstone; (pour aiguiser) grindstone; ② (fromage) round; ③ Agric **~ de foin** haystack; **~ de paille** rick of straw

meunier, -ière[1] /mønje, ɛR/
A *adj* flour-milling
B ▸ p. 372 *nm,f* miller

meunière[2] /mønjɛR/ *nf* ① (épouse de meunier) miller's wife; ② Culin **sole (à la) ~** sole meunière

meurtre /mœRtR/ *nm* murder

meurtrier, -ière /mœRtRije, ɛR/
A *adj* [*combats, répression*] bloody; [*explosion, accident*] fatal; [*épidémie*] deadly; [*arme*] lethal; [*rage*] murderous; [*route, carrefour*] very dangerous; **le lundi de Pâques a été très ~ sur la route** there were many deaths on the roads on Easter Monday; **les derniers séismes ont été très ~s** recent earthquakes have claimed many lives
B *nm,f* murderer

meurtrir /mœRtRiR/ [3] *vtr* ① (faire mal) to hurt; (contusionner) to bruise; ② (endommager) to bruise [*fruit*]; ③ (blesser moralement) to wound

meurtrissure /mœRtRisyR/ *nf* lit, fig bruise

meute /møt/ *nf* ① (chiens) pack of hounds; ② fig pack; **la ~ des créanciers** the pack of creditors

mexicain, ~e /mɛksikɛ̃, ɛn/ ▸ p. 392 *adj* Mexican

Mexico /mɛksiko/ ▸ p. 621 *npr* Mexico City

Mexique /mɛksik/ ▸ p. 230 *nprm* Mexico

mezzanine /medzanin/ *nf* Constr mezzanine; Cin balcony; Théât circle GB, mezzanine US

MF /ɛmɛf/ *nf: abbr* ▸ **modulation**

Mgr ▸ p. 590 (written *abbr* = **Monseigneur**) Mgr

mi /mi/ *nm inv* (note) E; (en solfiant) mi, me

mi- /mi/ *préf* **~-chinois, ~-français** [*personne*] half Chinese, half French; [*style, objet*] part Chinese, part French; **à ~-combat/carrière** in mid-fight/-career; **à ~-journée** halfway through the day; **à la ~-mai/saison** in mid-May/-season; **à ~-parcours** in the middle; **à ~-pente** halfway up the hill

miam-miam○ /mjammjam/ *excl* yum-yum○!, yummy○!

miaou /mjau/ *nm* (also onomat) miaow GB, meow; **faire ~** to go miaow GB *ou* meow

miauler /mjole/ [1] *vi* to miaow GB, to meow

mi-bas /miba/ *nm inv* knee sock, long sock

mica /mika/ *nm* mica

mi-carême /mikaRɛm/ *nf*: Thursday of the third week in Lent

miche /miʃ/ *nf* round loaf; H (petit pain) roll

mi-chemin: **à mi-chemin** /amiʃmɛ̃/ *loc adv* lit halfway; fig halfway through; **à ~ de chez moi** halfway home

mi-clos, ~e /miklo, oz/ *adj* half-closed

micmac /mikmak/ *nm* ① (intrigue) shady○ goings-on (*pl*); **faire des ~s** to wheel and deal○; ② (désordre) mess○

mi-côte: **à mi-côte** /amikot/ *loc adv* (en montant) halfway up; (en descendant) halfway down

mi-course: **à mi-course** /amikuRs/ *loc adv* Sport halfway through the race; fig halfway through

micro[1] /mikRo/ *préf* **~biologie** microbiology; **~chirurgie** microsurgery

micro[2] /mikRo/ *nm* ① (microphone) microphone, mike○; **parler dans le ~** to speak into the microphone; **dire qch au ~** to say sth into the microphone; **une annonce au ~** an announcement over the microphone; **annoncer au ~ de la BBC que** to announce on the BBC that; **mettre des ~s dans une pièce** to bug a room; ② ○(micro-ordinateur) micro○, microcomputer
(Composé) **~ caché** bug

micro[3] /mikRo/ *nf* (micro-informatique) microcomputing

microbe /mikRɔb/ *nm* ① (organisme) germ, bug○, microbe spéc; ② ○(petite personne) offensive squirt○

microbien, -ienne /mikRɔbjɛ̃, ɛn/ *adj* microbic

microclimat /mikRoklima/ *nm* microclimate

microcosme /mikRɔkɔsm/ *nm* microcosm

micro-cravate, *pl* **micros-cravates** /mikRokRavat/ *nm* lapel-microphone

microcrédit /mikRokRedi/ *nm* microcredit

micro-édition /mikRoedisjɔ̃/ *nf* desktop publishing

microfiche /mikRofiʃ/ *nf* microfiche

microfilm /mikRofilm/ *nm* microfilm

micro-informatique /mikRoɛ̃fɔRmatik/ *nf* microcomputing

micron /mikRɔ̃/ ▸ p. 347 *nm* micron

micro-onde, *pl* **~s** /mikRoɔ̃d/ *nf* microwave; **à ~s** microwave (*épith*)

micro-ondes /mikRoɔ̃d/ *nm inv* (four) microwave○

micro-ordinateur, *pl* **~s** /mikRoɔRdinatœR/ *nm* microcomputer

microphone /mikRofon/ *nm* microphone

micropilule /mikRopilyl/ *nf* mini-pill

microprocesseur /mikRopRɔsesœR/ *nm* microprocessor

microscope /mikRɔskɔp/ *nm* microscope; **examiner qch au ~** lit to examine sth under a microscope; fig to scrutinize sth
(Composé) **~ électronique** electron microscope

microscopique /mikRɔskɔpik/ *adj* lit microscopic; fig tiny

microsillon /mikRɔsijɔ̃/ *nm* (disque) **~** microgroove record

microtraumatisme /mikRotRomatism/ *nm* strain injury

mi-cuisse: **à mi-cuisse** /amikɥis/ *loc adv* above one's knees

midi /midi/

A *adj inv* midi; **chaîne ~** midi system

B *nm* ▸ p. 296 **1** (heure) twelve o'clock, midday, noon; **je fais mes courses entre ~ et deux**° I go shopping in my lunch hour; **2** (heure du déjeuner) lunchtime; **on mange ensemble à ~?** shall we have lunch together?; **qu'est-ce qu'on mange à ~?** what are we having for lunch?; **3** (point cardinal) south

(Idiome) **chacun voit ~ à sa porte** everybody has their own way of looking at things

Midi /midi/ ▸ p. 504 *nm* **le ~ (de la France)** the South (of France)

midinette /midinɛt/ *nf* feather-brained young girl, bimbo°; **elle a une âme** *or* **un cœur de ~** she's a romantic schoolgirl at heart

mi-distance: **à mi-distance** /amidistãs/ *loc adv* halfway

mie /mi/ *nf* bread without the crusts; **de la ~ (de pain)** fresh breadcrumbs (*pl*)

miel /mjɛl/ *nm* honey; **au ~** made with honey; **tes paroles sont de ~** fig your words are soothing

(Idiomes) **être tout sucre tout ~** to be as sweet *ou* nice as pie°; **faire son ~ de qch** to turn sth to one's advantage

mielleusement /mjɛløzmɑ̃/ *adv* unctuously

mielleux, -euse /mjɛlø, øz/ *adj* fig [*ton, paroles*] unctuous, honeyed; [*personne*] fawning

mien, mienne /mjɛ̃, mjɛn/

A *adj poss* **ces idées, je les ai faites miennes** I adopted these ideas; **tu seras mienne** (mon épouse) you will be mine

B **le mien, la mienne, les miens, les miennes** *pron poss* mine; **votre prix sera le ~** name your price; **les ~s** (ma famille) my family (*sg*)

miette /mjɛt/ *nf* crumb; **juste une ~** fig just a little bit; **ne pas laisser une ~ de** not to leave a scrap of; **réduire en ~s** to smash [sth] to bits [*vase*]; to shatter [*bonheur*]; to reduce [sth] to shreds [*théorie*]; **elle n'en perd pas une ~**° she's taking it all in; **nous n'avons eu que les ~s** we only had the leftovers

mieux /mjø/

A *adj inv* better; **le ~, la ~, les ~** (de plusieurs) gén the best; (de caractère) the nicest; (d'aspect) the most attractive; **le ~ des deux** the better one; **ce qu'il y a de ~** the best

B *adv* **1** (comparatif) better; **je ne peux pas te dire ~** that's all I can tell you; **qui dit ~?** gén any other offers?; (dans une vente aux enchères) any advance on that bid?; **tu serais ~ au lit** you'd be better off in bed; **elle est ~ portante** she's in better health; **j'aime ~ rester ici** I'd rather stay here; **il vaudrait ~ rester** it would be best to stay; **qui ~ est** moreover; **de ~ en ~** gén better and better; **parler anglais de ~ en ~** to get better and better at (speaking) English; **aller de ~ en ~** [*malade*] to be getting stronger all the time; **tu n'as pas d'argent? de ~ en ~** iron you've no money now? that's absolutely great°! iron; **ils criaient à qui ~ ~** they were all shouting, each one louder than the other; **on la critiquait à qui ~ ~** each person criticized her more harshly than the last; **c'est ~ que bien, c'est merveilleux** it's not just good, it's marvellous^{GB}!; **c'est on ne peut ~** it couldn't be better; **2** (superlatif) **le ~, la ~, les ~** (de plusieurs) the best; (de deux) the better; **c'est ici qu'on mange le ~** this is the best place to eat; **je me porte le ~ du monde** I'm feeling absolutely fine; **être des ~ payés** to be extremely well paid

C *nm inv* **le ~ est de refuser** the best thing is to refuse; **il y a du ~** there is some improvement; **il y a ~** it's nothing special; **il n'y a pas ~** it's the best there is; **tu ne trouveras pas ~** it's as good as you'll get; **je ne demande pas ~ que de rester ici** I'm perfectly happy staying here; **fais pour le ~, fais au ~** do whatever is best; **tout va pour le ~** everything's fine; **elle est au ~ avec sa voisine** she is on very good terms with her neighbour^{GB}; **elle est au ~ de sa forme** she's on GB *ou* in US top form; **c'est le même, en ~** it's the same, only better; **changer en ~** to change for the better

mieux-vivre /mjøvivʀ/ *nm inv* improved living standards (*pl*)

mièvre /mjɛvʀ/ *adj* [*personne, remarque*] vapid; [*sourire*] sickly; [*roman, musique*] soppy

mièvrerie /mjɛvʀəʀi/ *nf* **1** (de personne, parole, sourire) vapidity; (de roman, musique) soppiness; (de compliment, d'excuse)

---

feebleness; **2** (parole, action) **tes ~s m'agacent** your simpering ways get on my nerves

mi-figue /mifig/ *adj inv* **~ mi-raisin** [*sourire*] half-hearted; [*compliment*] ambiguous; [*remarque*] half-humourous^{GB}; [*accueil*] mixed; **d'un ton ~ mi-raisin** half in jest half in earnest

mi-fin, *pl* **~s** /mifɛ̃/ *adj m* [*haricot, petit pois*] medium-sized

mignon, -onne /miɲɔ̃, ɔn/ *adj* **1** (joli) cute; **2** (gentil) sweet, kind; **sois ~, va fermer la porte** be a dear and close the door

migraine /migʀɛn/ *nf* splitting headache; (plus fort) migraine; **donner la ~ à qn** fig to give sb a headache

migrant, ~e /migʀɑ̃, ɑ̃t/ *adj, nm,f* migrant

migrateur, -trice /migʀatœʀ, tʀis/ *adj* migratory

migration /migʀasjɔ̃/ *nf* migration; **~ saisonnière** (d'ouvriers) seasonal migration; (de vacanciers) seasonal departures (*pl*); **~ journalière** *or* **quotidienne** commuting

migratoire /migʀatwaʀ/ *adj* migratory

migrer /migʀe/ [1] *vi* to migrate (**à, en, vers** to)

mi-hauteur: **à mi-hauteur** /amiotœʀ/ *loc adv* (en montant) halfway up; (en descendant) halfway down

mi-jambe: **à mi-jambe** /amiʒɑ̃b/ *loc adv* (up) to one's knees

mijaurée /miʒoʀe/ *nf* **ne fais pas ta ~** don't put on such airs; **petite ~!** little madam!

mijoter /miʒɔte/ [1]

A *vtr* **1** Culin to prepare [*plat*]; **2** °(manigancer) to cook up

B *vi* Culin to simmer

(Idiome) **laisser qn ~ dans son jus**° to let sb stew in his/her own juice

mijoteuse® /miʒɔtøz/ *nf* slow cooker

mikado /mikado/ ▸ p. 327 *nm* spillikins (+ *v sg*)

mil /mil/

A *adj* **= mille A**

B *nm* millet

milan /milɑ̃/ *nm* Zool kite

mildiou /mildju/ *nm* mildew

milice /milis/ *nf* militia; **~ de quartier** local vigilante group

Milice /milis/ *nf* **la ~** the Milice (*French wartime paramilitary organization which collaborated with the Germans against the Resistance*)

milicien, -ienne /milisjɛ̃, ɛn/ *nm,f* **1** Mil militiaman/militiawoman; **2** Hist member of the Milice

milieu, *pl* **~x** /miljø/

A *nm* **1** (dans l'espace) middle; **au beau** *or* **en plein ~** right in the middle; **2** (dans le temps) middle; **au ~ de** in the middle of, halfway through; **3** (moyen terme) middle ground; **c'est vrai ou faux, il n'y a pas de ~** it's either right or wrong, there's no in-between; **4** (environnement) environment; **le ~ familial** the home environment; **en ~ rural** in the country; **en ~ urbain/scolaire** in towns/schools; **le ~ carcéral** prison life; **5** (origine sociale) background, milieu; (groupe) circle; **des gens de tous les ~x** people from every walk of life; **les ~x universitaires** academic circles; **un ~ professionnel très conservateur** a very conservative sector; **le ~ de l'édition** the world of publishing; **le ~** (pègre) the underworld; **6** Math (de segment) midpoint

B **au milieu de** *loc prép* **1** (parmi) among; **être au ~ de ses amis** to be with one's friends; **2** (entouré de) surrounded by; **travailler au ~ du bruit** to work surrounded by noise; **au ~ du désastre** in the midst of disaster

(Composés) **~ de culture** breeding ground; **~ de terrain** (joueur) midfield player; (endroit) midfield

militaire /militɛʀ/

A *adj* gén military; [*médecin, vie, camion*] army (épith); **école ~** military academy

B ▸ p. 372 *nm* serviceman; **un ~ de carrière** a career soldier; **être ~** to be in the army

militairement /militɛʀmɑ̃/ *adv* **1** lit by military means; **zone occupée ~ militairement** military occupied zone; **2** fig (efficacement) with military efficiency; péj along military lines

militant, ~e /militɑ̃, ɑ̃t/

A *adj* militant

B *nm,f* (de syndicat, parti) active member, activist; (de cause) campaigner; **les ~s de base** the rank-and-file members

militantisme /militãtism/ *nm* political activism

militarisation /militaʀizasjõ/ *nf* militarization

militariste /militaʀist/
A *adj* militaristic
B *nmf* militarist

militer /milite/ [1] *vi* **1** (agir) gén to campaign; (dans un parti) to be a political activist; **2** (constituer un argument) **~ pour** or **en faveur de** to argue in favour^{GB} of; **~ contre** to militate against

mille /mil/
A ▸ p. 398, p. 155 *adj inv* a thousand, one thousand; **deux/trois ~** two/three thousand
B *nm inv* **1** Comm, Math a thousand, one thousand; **2** Sport (cible) bull's eye; **mettre** or **taper dans le ~** lit to hit the bull's-eye; fig to hit the nail on the head
C ▸ p. 347, p. 624 *nm* Naut **~ (marin** or **nautique)** (nautical) mile; Aviat (air) mile
D **pour mille** *loc adj* per thousand
⟨Idiomes⟩ **je ne gagne pas des ~ et des cents** I don't earn very much; **je vous le donne en ~** you'll never guess (in a million years)

millefeuille /milfœj/ *nm* millefeuille (*small layered cake made of puff pastry filled with custard and cream*)

millénaire /milenɛʀ/
A *adj* **1** (de mille ans) **un arbre ~** a one thousand year old tree, a tree that is one thousand years old; **2** (vieux) [*tradition*] age-old
B *nm* **1** (période) millennium; **pendant des ~s** for thousands of years; **2** (anniversaire) millennium, millenary

mille-pattes /milpat/ *nm inv* centipede, millipede

millésime /milezim/ *nm* **1** (de vin) vintage, year; (de monnaie, médaille) date; **2** Aut year of manufacture; **3** (dans une date) millennial figure

millésimé, ~e /milezime/ *adj* [*vin*] vintage (*épith*); [*monnaie*] bearing a date (*épith, après n*)

millet /mijɛ/ *nm* millet
⟨Composé⟩ **~ des oiseaux** birdseed, millet

milli /mili/ *préf* milli; **~bar** millibar; **~gramme** milligram; **~litre** millilitre^{GB}; **~mètre** millimetre^{GB}

milliard /miljaʀ/ ▸ p. 398 *nm* billion

milliardaire /miljaʀdɛʀ/ *nmf* multimillionaire, billionaire

milliardième /miljaʀdjɛm/ ▸ p. 398 *adj* billionth

millième /miljɛm/ ▸ p. 398 *adj* thousandth

millier /milje/ *nm* **1** (mille) thousand; **2** (environ mille) **un ~** about a thousand

millimétré, ~e /milimetʀe/ *adj* graduated in millimetres^{GB}; **papier ~** graph paper

million /miljõ/ ▸ p. 398 *nm* million; **être riche à ~s** to be worth millions

millionième /miljɔnjɛm/ ▸ p. 398 *adj* millionth; **au ~** to the sixth decimal place

millionnaire /miljɔnɛʀ/
A *adj* **être ~** [*entreprise, société*] to be worth millions; [*personne*] to be a millionaire
B *nmf* millionaire

mi-lourd, *pl* **~s** /miluʀ/ *nm* light heavyweight

mime /mim/ ▸ p. 372 *nm* **1** Théât mime; **2** (imitateur) mimic

mimer /mime/ [1] *vtr* **1** Théât to mime; **2** (imiter) to mimic

mimétisme /mimetism/ *nm* **1** Zool mimicry; **2** (imitation) **par ~** through unconscious imitation

mimique /mimik/ *nf* **1** (expression comique) funny face; **2** (gestes et expressions) expressions and gestures (*pl*); (des sourds-muets) sign language

mimodrame /mimɔdram/ *nm* mime

mimosa /mimoza/ *nm* mimosa

minable[○] /minabl/
A *adj* **1** (médiocre) pathetic; [*délit*] petty; **2** (misérable) [*personne*] wretched; [*logement*] crummy[○]; [*existence*] miserable
B *nmf* pej (médiocre) pathetic[○] character; (raté) loser[○]

minage /minaʒ/ *nm* Mil mining

minaret /minaʀɛ/ *nm* minaret

minauder /minode/ [1] *vi* (dans l'allure) to mince about; (de la voix, du sourire) to simper

minauderies /minodʀi/ *nfpl* affected mannerisms

mince /mɛ̃s/
A *adj* **1** (fin) [*personne, jambe*] slim, slender; [*cou, bras*] slender; [*visage*] thin; [*tranche, lame*] thin; [*livre*] slim; **2** (faible) [*consolation*] small; [*espoir, chance*] slim; [*indice*] tenuous; [*revenus*] meagre; **ce n'est pas une ~ affaire** (difficile) that's no small task; (important) that's no trivial matter
B *excl* **~ (alors)!** (étonnement) wow[○]!; (dépit) damn[○]!

minceur /mɛ̃sœʀ/
A *adj inv* **cuisine ~** low-calorie dishes (*pl*)
B *nf* **1** (de personne, jambes) slimness, slenderness; (de cou, bras) slenderness; (de visage, tranche) thinness; **2** (d'indice) tenuousness; (de revenus) meagreness^{GB}

mincir /mɛ̃siʀ/ [3] *vi* to lose weight; **il a minci de visage** his face has got GB *ou* gotten US thinner

mine /min/
A *nf* **1** (expression) expression; (aspect) look; **faire triste ~** to have a gloomy expression, to look gloomy; **juger sur la ~** to judge by appearances; **faire ~ d'accepter** to pretend to accept; **faire ~ de partir** to make as if to go; **elle nous a dit, ~ de rien**[○]**, que** she told us, casually, that; **il est doué, ~ de rien**[○] it may not be obvious, but he's very clever; **2** (apparence) **avoir mauvaise ~, avoir une sale**[○] or **petite ~** to look a bit off-colour^{GB}; **avoir une ~ resplendissante** to be glowing with health; **avoir une ~ de papier mâché** to look washed out; **avoir bonne ~** [*personne*] to look well; [*tarte, rôti*] to look appetizing; **j'aurais bonne ~!** iron I would look really stupid!; **3** (pour dessiner) lead; **crayon à ~ dure/grasse** hard/soft pencil; **4** (gisement) mine; **~ d'or** lit, fig gold mine; **5** (source) source; **~ d'informations** fig mine of information; **6** Mil mine
B **mines** *nfpl* (minauderies) simpering **¢**; **faire des ~s** to simper
⟨Composés⟩ **~ de crayon** lead; **~ de plomb** graphite **¢**
⟨Idiome⟩ **ne pas payer de ~**[○] not to look anything special[○]

miner /mine/ [1] *vtr* **1** (affaiblir) to sap [*moral, énergie*]; to undermine [*santé, gouvernement*]; **cela me mine** it's wearing me down; (plus fort) it's eating me alive; **2** Mil to mine; **le terrain est miné** lit the ground is mined; fig it's a minefield

minerai /minʀɛ/ *nm* ore; **~ de fer** iron ore

minéral, ~e, *mpl* **-aux** /mineʀal, o/
A *adj* **1** [*huile, eau, règne*] mineral; [*chimie*] inorganic; **2** fig [*paysage*] barren
B *nm* mineral

minéralogie /mineʀalɔʒi/ *nf* mineralogy

minéralogique /mineʀalɔʒik/ *adj* **1** (en géologie) mineralogical; **2** Admin, Aut **numéro ~** registration number GB, license number US; **plaque ~** number plate GB, license plate US

minerve /minɛʀv/ *nf* Méd surgical collar GB, neck brace US

minet /minɛ/ *nm* **1** (chat) pussycat lang enfantin; **2** [○](jeune dandy) pretty boy[○]

minette /minɛt/ *nf* **1** (chatte) pussycat lang enfantin; **2** [○](jeune fille) cool chick[○]

mineur, ~e /minœʀ/
A *adj* **1** Jur under 18 (*après n*); **2** (peu important) minor; **3** Mus minor
B *nm,f* Jur person under 18, minor *spéc*
C *nm* **1** ▸ p. 372 (ouvrier) miner; **~ de fond** pit worker; **2** (soldat) soldier who lays mines

mini /mini/
A [○]*adj inv* (minuscule) tiny
B *nm* **1** (jupes courtes) **s'habiller en ~** to wear mini-skirts; **2** [○]Ordinat minicomputer, mini[○]

mini- /mini/ *préf* mini; **~-révolution** mini-revolution

miniature /minjatyʀ/
A *adj* miniature (*épith*)
B *nf* gén, Art miniature

miniaturisation /minjatyʀizasjõ/ *nf* miniaturization

minibus /minibys/ *nm inv* minibus

minicassette® /minikasɛt/ *nf* mini-cassette®

minier, -ière /minje, ɛʀ/ *adj* mining

mini-golf, *pl* **~s** /minigɔlf/ ▸ p. 327 *nm* mini-golf

mini-informatique /miniɛ̃fɔʀmatik/ *nf* mini-computing

m

mini-jupe, pl ～s /miniʒyp/ nf mini-skirt

minima ▸ minimum

minimal, ～e, mpl **-aux** /minimal, o/ adj minimal, minimum

minimalisme /minimalism/ nm minimalism

minime /minim/
A adj [dégâts, différence, dépenses] negligible; [chance] slim, slender; [rôle] minor
B nmf Sport junior (7 to 13 years old)

mini message /minimesaʒ/ nm Télécom text message, text

minimiser /minimize/ [1] vtr to minimize, to play down

minimum, pl ～s or **minima** /minimɔm, minima/
A adj minimum; un an, c'est le délai ～ it will take one year at least
B nm [1] (limite inférieure) minimum; en faire un ～ to do as little as possible; il faut travailler un ～ si tu veux réussir you have to do a bit of work if you want to succeed; un ～ de bon sens a certain amount of common sense; un ～ d'hygiène a basic level of hygiene; avec un ～ d'efforts with a minimum of effort; prendre le ～ de risques to take as few risks as possible; il faut au ～ deux heures pour faire le trajet the journey takes at least two hours; [2] Jur minimum sentence
Composés **minima sociaux** raft of benefit payments for those on the lowest incomes; ～ **vital** subsistence level

mini-ordinateur, pl ～s /miniɔrdinatœr/ nm minicomputer

minipilule /minipilyl/ nf low-dose combined pill

ministère /minister/ nm [1] Pol gén ministry; (au Royaume-Uni, aux États-Unis) department; (charge) ministership; [2] Pol (équipe gouvernementale) cabinet, government; [3] Jur le ～ **public** (service) the public prosecutor's office; (magistrat) the prosecuting magistrate, the prosecution; [4] Relig ministry

ministériel, -ielle /ministerjɛl/ adj ministerial

ministre /ministr/ nm [1] Pol gén minister; (au Royaume-Uni) Secretary of State; (aux États-Unis) Secretary; ～ **délégué** minister of state GB, under-secretary US (auprès de to); les ～s the cabinet; Madame le ～ Minister GB, Madam Secretary US; Monsieur le ～ Minister GB, Mr Secretary US; ▸ premier; [2] (en diplomatie) envoy; [3] Relig minister

Minitel® /minitel/ nm Minitel (terminal linking phone users to a database); sur or au ～ on Minitel; par le ～ by Minitel

minivague /minivag/ nf soft perm

minois /minwa/ nm inv fresh young face; joli petit ～ pretty little face

minon○ /minɔ̃/ nm H (poussière) fluff ₵

minoration /minɔrasjɔ̃/ nf [1] (sous-estimation) undervaluation; (de prix) underestimation; [2] (réduction) reduction; ～ **des prix** cut in prices

minorer /minɔre/ [1] vtr [1] (réduire) to reduce [prix, taux] (de by); [2] (sous-estimer) to undervalue [biens]; to underestimate [montant]

minoritaire /minɔriter/
A adj minority (épith)
B nmf member of a minority group; les ～s those in the minority

minorité /minɔrite/ nf [1] (groupe) minority; être en ～ to be in the minority; être mis en ～ to be defeated; [2] (petit nombre) minority (de of); [3] (d'âge) minority; ～ **pénale** Jur ≈ legal infancy
Composé ～ **de blocage** Fin blocking minority

minoterie /minɔtri/ nf [1] (usine) flour mill; [2] (industrie) flour-milling (industry)

minotier /minɔtje/ ▸ p. 372 nm miller

minou /minu/ nm [1] (chat) pussycat lang enfantin; (pour appeler un chat) ～～! puss puss○!; [2] (terme d'affection) mon gros ～ my sweetie○

minuit /minɥi/ ▸ p. 296 nm midnight; de ～ [messe, soleil] midnight (épith)

minus○ /minys/ nmf inv pej moron○

minuscule /minyskyl/
A adj [1] (tout petit) tiny; [2] (en écriture) small; (en imprimerie) lower-case
B nf (en écriture) small letter; (en imprimerie) lower-case letter

minutage /minytaʒ/ nm (precise) timing

minute /minyt/ ▸ p. 296, p. 582
A nf [1] (unité de temps) minute; [2] (court moment) minute, moment; hé! ～○!, ～ papillon○! hang on a minute○!; il peut arriver d'une ～ à l'autre he may arrive any minute now; j'en ai pour une ～ I won't be a minute; l'angoisse monte de ～ en ～ fear is mounting by the minute; on vient de me l'apporter à la ～ it has just been brought to me this very second; c'est pas à la ～○ it's not desperate ou urgent; à la ～ où je vous parle just as I'm speaking to you; [3] Jur ～ d'un jugement record of a decision; ～s d'un procès minutes of a trial; [4] (unité d'angle) minute
B (-)minute (in compounds) 'clés-～' 'keys cut while you wait'; 'nettoyage-～' 'same day dry cleaning'
Composés ～ **de silence** minute's silence; la ～ **de vérité** the moment of truth

minuter /minyte/ [1] vtr (chronométrer) to time; (prévoir) to work out the timing of; l'opération doit être minutée à la seconde the operation requires split-second timing

minuterie /minytri/ nf (d'éclairage) (interrupteur) time-switch; (mécanisme) automatic lighting

minuteur /minytœr/ nm timer

minutie /minysi/ nf meticulousness

minutieusement /minysjøzmɑ̃/ adv (avec soin) with meticulous care; (dans le détail) in great detail

minutieux, -ieuse /minysjø, øz/ adj [ouvrier, soin, travail] meticulous; [étude, description] detailed

mioche○ /mjɔʃ/ nmf kid○; **sale** ～ horrible brat○

mirabelle /mirabɛl/ nf [1] (fruit) mirabelle (small yellow plum); [2] (eau-de-vie) plum brandy

miracle /mirakl/
A adj inv un médicament ～ a wonder drug; une méthode ～ a magic formula
B nm [1] gén miracle; accomplir or faire un ～ Relig to work a miracle; fig to work miracles; tenir du ～ to be a miracle; un ～ de l'architecture an architectural wonder; par ～ miraculously; comme par ～ as if by magic; [2] (drame sacré) miracle play

miraculé, -e /mirakyle/ Relig
A adj [malade] who is/was etc miraculously cured (épith, après n)
B nmf c'est un ～ he has been saved by a miracle; les ～s de la route people who have miraculously survived a road accident

miraculeusement /mirakyløzmɑ̃/ adv miraculously

miraculeux, -euse /mirakylø, øz/ adj gén miraculous; [remède] which works wonders (épith, après n)

mirador /miradɔr/ nm Mil watchtower

mirage /miraʒ/ nm (vision) mirage

mi-raisin /mirɛzɛ̃/ adj inv ▸ mi-figue

miraud○, **-e** /miro, od/ adj shortsighted

mire /mir/ nf [1] TV test card GB, test pattern US; [2] (en topographie) levelling^GB staff

mirer: se mirer /mire/ [1] vpr liter [personne] to gaze at one's reflection; [objet] to be reflected

mirifique /mirifik/ adj hum fabulous○

mirobolant○, **-e** /mirɔbolɑ̃, ɑ̃t/ adj fabulous○

miroir /mirwar/ nm lit, fig mirror
Composé ～ **aux alouettes** lit, fig lure

miroitement /mirwatmɑ̃/ nm liter (de vitre) sparkling ₵; (de l'eau) shimmering ₵

miroiter /mirwate/ [1] vi [objet] to sparkle; [eau] to shimmer; faire ～ qch à qn to hold out the prospect of sth to sb

mironton /mirɔ̃tɔ̃/, **miroton** /mirɔtɔ̃/ nm (bœuf) ～ beef stew (with onion sauce)

mis, ～e^1 /mi, miz/
A pp ▸ mettre
B pp adj être bien ～ to be well-dressed

misaine /mizɛn/ nf (voile de) ～ foresail

misanthrope /mizɑ̃trɔp/
A adj misanthropic
B nmf misanthropist, misanthrope

mise^2 /miz/
A pp adj f ▸ mis
B nf [1] (dans un pari, jeu) une ～ de cinq euros a five-euro bet; récupérer sa ～ to recover one's stake; [2] (tenue)

~ négligée sloppy appearance

(Composés) **~ de fonds** investment; **~ en plis** set

(Idiomes) **être de ~** [remarque] to be appropriate; **ne pas être de ~** to be out of place; **je t'ai sauvé la ~**⊖ I saved your bacon⊖.

> ⚠ Les expressions du type *mise en boîte, mise à feu, mise à mort* sont traitées sous le deuxième élément; on se reportera à *boîte, feu, mort* etc.

mise-bas, *pl* **mises-bas** /mizbɑ/ *nf* (d'animal) birth

miser /mize/ [1]
A *vtr* to bet [argent] (**sur** on)
B *vi* **1** (parier) **~ sur le 2** (au casino) to place a bet on the 2; **~ sur un cheval** to put money on a horse; **~ sur le mauvais cheval** fig to make the wrong choice; **2** (compter) **~ sur la qualité d'un produit** to bank on the quality of a product; **~ sur un événement/sa chance/ses efforts** to count on an event/one's luck/one's efforts; **~ sur qn** to place all one's hopes in sb

misérabilisme /mizeRabilism/ *nm* **1** (d'écrivain) sordid realism; **2** (d'individu) tendency to dwell on the dark side

misérable /mizeRabl/
A *adj* **1** (très pauvre) [personne] destitute; [habit] shabby; [vie, pays] poor, wretched; [maison] squalid; **2** (dérisoire) [salaire] meagreᴳᴮ; [affaire] pathetic; **3** (pitoyable) pitiful, miserable
B *nmf* **1** (indigent) pauper; **2** †(personne méprisable) scoundrel

misérablement /mizeRabləmɑ̃/ *adv* **1** (pauvrement) wretchedly, miserably; **2** (pitoyablement) miserably, pitifully

misère /mizɛR/ *nf* **1** (pauvreté) destitution; **être dans la ~** to be destitute; **réduire qn à la ~** to reduce sb to poverty; **2** (détresse) misery, wretchedness; **quelle ~!** isn't it awful!; **3** (ennui) trouble, woe; **petites ~s** little troubles; **4** (somme dérisoire) pittance; **5** Bot wandering Jew, tradescantia

(Composés) **~ intellectuelle** intellectual poverty; **~ noire** dire poverty

miséreux, -euse /mizeRø, øz/
A *adj* destitute
B *nm,f* destitute person; **les ~** the destitute

miséricorde /mizeRikɔRd/ *nf* Relig mercy

miséricordieux, -ieuse /mizeRikɔRdjø, øz/ *adj* merciful

misogyne /mizɔʒin/
A *adj* misogynous
B *nmf* misogynist

misogynie /mizɔʒini/ *nf* misogyny

missel /misɛl/ *nm* missal

missile /misil/ *nm* missile

mission /misjɔ̃/ *nf* **1** (tâche) mission, task; **il s'est donné pour ~ de faire** he has taken it upon himself to do; **2** (fonction temporaire) mission, assignment; **~ d'information, ~ d'enquête** special fact-finding mission; **être envoyé en ~** to be sent to sb on special assignment; **être envoyé en ~ d'étude** to be sent to make a study; **3** (groupe) mission, team; **~ d'experts** team of experts; **4** Mil (but) mission; **5** Relig gén mission; (groupe) missionary group

missionnaire /misjɔnɛR/ *adj, nmf* missionary

missive /misiv/ *nf* fml missive sout

mistigri /mistigRi/ *nm* **1** (aux cartes) mistigris; **2** ⊖(chat) pussycat⊖ lang enfantin

mistral /mistRal/ *nm* mistral

mitaine /mitɛn/ *nf* fingerless mitt

mite /mit/ *nf* (clothes) moth

mi-temps¹ /mitɑ̃/ *nm inv* **1** (emploi) part-time job; **2** (système) part-time work ⊄; **il est serveur à ~** he's a part-time waiter

mi-temps² /mitɑ̃/ *nf inv* Sport (arrêt) half-time; (moitié de match) half; **à la ~** at half-time

miteux, -euse /mitø, øz/ *adj* [quartier, hôtel] seedy; [vêtements] shabby; [personne] down-at-heel

mitigé, ~e /mitiʒe/ *adj* [accueil] lukewarm; [succès] qualified; [conclusions] ambivalent

mitonner /mitone/ [1]
A *vtr* to cook [sth] lovingly [plat]; to prepare the ground carefully for [projet]

B *vi* [plat] to cook slowly
C **se mitonner** *vpr* **se ~ un petit plat** to cook a nice little meal for oneself; **se ~ un bel avenir** to carve out a nice future for oneself

mitoyen, -enne /mitwajɛ̃, ɛn/ *adj* **1** Jur (en commun) [haie] dividing; **mur ~** party wall; **2** (contigu) controv [bâtiment] adjoining

mitraillage /mitRajaʒ/ *nm* **1** Mil machine-gunning (**de** of); **2** fig **~ (de questions)** quick-fire questioning

(Composé) **~ au sol** strafing

mitraille /mitRaj/ *nf* **1** Mil (d'artillerie) hail of bullets; **2** ⊖(monnaie) small change

mitrailler /mitRaje/ [1] *vtr* **1** Mil to machine-gun; **~ au sol** to strafe; **2** ⊖(bombarder) **~ qn de cailloux**⊖ to pelt sb with stones; **~ qn de questions** to fire questions at sb; **3** ⊖(photographier) to take photo after photo of [tableau, personne]; **se faire ~ par les photographes** to be besieged by photographers

mitraillette /mitRajɛt/ *nf* submachine gun

mitrailleuse /mitRajøz/ *nf* machine gun

mitre /mitR/ *nf* Relig mitreᴳᴮ

mitron /mitRɔ̃/ *nm* baker's boy

mi-voix: à mi-voix /amivwa/ *loc adv* in a low voice

mixage /miksaʒ/ *nm* sound mixing

mixer¹ /mikse/ [1] *vtr* Audio to mix

mixer² /miksɛR/ = **mixeur**

mixeur /miksœR/ *nm* (batteur) mixer; (broyeur) blender

mixité /miksite/ *nf* (à l'école) coeducation

mixte /mikst/ *adj* **1** (école) coeducational; [classe] mixed; [concours] open to both sexes (après n); [salon de coiffure] unisex; **enseignement ~** coeducation; **2** (hétérogène) gén mixed; [commission] joint (épith); [chaudière] dual-system (épith); [scrutin] dual; **entreprise** *or* **société ~** joint venture

mixture /mikstyR/ *nf* **1** (plat cuisiné) concoction; **2** (en pharmacie) mixture; **3** (mélange) mishmash⊖ péj

MJC /ɛmʒise/ *nf: abbr ►* **maison**

MLF /ɛmɛlɛf/ *nm* (abbr = **mouvement de libération des femmes**) ≈ Women's Lib

Mlle ► p. 590 (written abbr = **Mademoiselle**) Ms, Miss; **~ Lévy** Ms Lévy, Miss Lévy

Mlles ► p. 590 (written abbr = **Mesdemoiselles**) Misses

mm (written abbr = **millimètre**) mm

MM. ► p. 590 (written abbr = **Messieurs**) Messrs

Mme ► p. 590 (written abbr = **Madame**) Ms, Mrs

Mmes ► p. 590 (written abbr = **Mesdames**) **~ Huet et Cordelle** Ms Huet and Ms Cordelle, Mrs Huet and Mrs Cordelle

mnémotechnique /mnemɔtɛknik/ *adj* mnemonic

Mo (written abbr = **mégaoctet**) Mb, MB

mob⊖ /mɔb/ *nf* (vélomoteur) moped

mobile /mɔbil/
A *adj* gén mobile; [feuillet] loose; [fête] movable
B *nm* **1** (motif) motive; **2** Phys moving body; **3** Art mobile

mobilier, -ière /mɔbilje, ɛR/
A *adj* **biens ~s** movable property ⊄; **valeurs mobilières** securities
B *nm* furniture; **~ urbain** street furniture

mobilisateur, -trice /mɔbilizatœR, tRis/ *adj* [discours] rousing; [projet] stimulating; [personne] inspiring

mobilisation /mɔbilizasjɔ̃/ *nf* gén mobilization; **~ générale** Mil mobilization; fig all-out effort

mobiliser /mɔbilize/ [1]
A *vtr* **1** Mil to mobilize [militaire]; to call up [civil]; **2** (rassembler) to mobilize [militants]; **le projet a mobilisé l'attention des étudiants** the project caught the attention of the students; fig to rally [personne]; to summon up [courage]; to call on [raison]; **~ les énergies** to mobilize people to act
B **se mobiliser** *vpr* [militants, étudiants] to rally

mobilité /mɔbilite/ *nf* gén mobility

mobylette® /mɔbilɛt/ *nf* moped

mocassin /mɔkasɛ̃/ *nm* (chaussure) moccasin

moche⊖ /mɔʃ/ *adj* **1** (laid) [personne] ugly; [vêtement] ghastly; [couleur] awful; **2** (triste) dreadful; **3** (mesquin) nasty

m

Idiome ~ **comme un pou** as ugly as sin

mocheté° /mɔʃte/ nf (caractère) ugliness; (personne) horror

modal, ~**e**, mpl **-aux** /mɔdal, o/
A adj modal
B nm modal verb

modalité /mɔdalite/
A nf Ling, Mus, Philos modality
B **modalités** nfpl gén (conditions) terms; (façon de fonctionner) practical details; ~**s de financement** methods of funding; ~**s d'inscription** Scol, Univ enrolment^{GB} procedure **C**

mode¹ /mɔd/ nm **1)** (façon) way, mode; ~ **de vie** way of life; ~ **de transport** mode of transport; ~ **de paiement** method of payment; **le** ~ **de fonctionnement de qch** the way sth operates; **traiter le sujet sur le** ~ **comique** to treat the subject in a comic vein; **2)** Ling mood; **3)** Mus, Ordinat, Philos mode

Composé ~ **d'emploi** directions (pl) for use; (de plat cuisiné) cooking instructions (pl)

mode² /mɔd/ nf **1)** (en matière d'habillement, d'idées) fashion; **lancer une** ~ to start a trend; **une** ~ **passagère** a fad; **s'habiller à la dernière** ~ to wear the latest fashions; **c'était une** ~ it was fashionable; **coupe** ~ fashionable cut; **à la** ~ [vêtement, restaurant, style] fashionable; [romancier] who is in vogue (épith, après n); [chanteur] popular; **être à la** ~ [vêtement, style] to be in fashion; **2)** (secteur d'activité) fashion industry; **présentation de** ~ fashion show

modelage /mɔdlaʒ/ nm **1)** (activité) modelling; **2)** (objet) model

modèle /mɔdɛl/
A adj gén model (épith)
B nm **1)** (référence) gén model; (exemple) example; **prendre** ~ **sur qn** to do as sb does/did; **être un** ~ **de clarté** to be a model of clarity; ~ **à suivre** (personne) somebody to look up to, role model; **2)** Comm, Ind (type) model; (taille) size; **grand/petit** ~ large-/small-size (épith); ~ **familial** family-size (épith); **construit sur le même** ~ built to the same design; **3)** (de v êtement) (création) model; (type d'article) style; **essaie ce** ~ try this style; **4)** (échantillon) ~ **de signature** specimen signature; **compléter selon le** ~ Scol do the exercise following the example; **5)** ▸ p. 372 Art, Phot (personne) model; **6)** (reproductible) pattern; ~ **de conjugaison/tricot** conjugation/knitting pattern; **7)** (prototype) model

Composés ~ **déposé** Jur registered pattern; ~ **réduit** scale model; ~ **réduit d'avion** model plane

modelé, ~**e** /mɔdle/
A adj **bien** ~ [corps, jambe] shapely; [visage] finely-sculpted
B nm **1)** Art, Géog relief; **2)** (de visage, corps) contours (pl)

modeler /mɔdle/ [17] vtr (façonner) to model [argile, statue]; to shape [personne, caractère]

modélisme /mɔdelism/ nm modelling, model-making

modéliste /mɔdelist/ ▸ p. 372 nmf **1)** (de vêtements) (dress) designer; **2)** (de maquettes) model-maker

modérateur, -trice /mɔderatœr, tris/
A adj moderating (épith)
B nm,f (personne) moderating influence; (fonction) moderator
C nm (de pile atomique) moderator

modération /mɔderasjɔ̃/ nf **1)** (sens de la mesure) moderation; **2)** (de prix) reduction; **3)** (de peine) mitigation

modéré, ~**e** /mɔdere/
A adj gén moderate; [prix] reasonable; [tempérament] even; [enthousiasme] mild
B nm,f moderate

modérément /mɔderemɑ̃/ adv **1)** (moyennement) relatively; **2)** (avec retenue) in moderation; **3)** (légèrement) slightly

modérer /mɔdere/ [14]
A vtr to curb [dépenses, sentiments]; to soften [attitude]; to moderate [propos]; to reduce [vitesse]
B **se modérer** vpr to exercise self-restraint

moderne /mɔdɛrn/ adj modern

modernisateur, -trice /mɔdɛrnizatœr, tris/ adj, nm,f progressive

modernisation /mɔdɛrnizasjɔ̃/ nf modernization

moderniser /mɔdɛrnize/ [1] vtr to modernize [institution, secteur, matériel]; to update [loi, manuel]

modernisme /mɔdɛrnism/ nm **1)** (goût) modernity; **2)** (mouvement) modernism

modernité /mɔdɛrnite/ nf modernity

modern style /mɔdɛrnstil/ nm inv Art Deco style

modeste /mɔdɛst/ adj gén modest; [facture, coût] moderate; [famille, milieu] humble

modestement /mɔdɛstəmɑ̃/ adv **1)** (sans superflu) modestly; **être** ~ **vêtu** to be wearing cheap clothes; **2)** (sans orgueil) modestly

modestie /mɔdɛsti/ nf modesty

modicité /mɔdisite/ nf lowness; **la** ~ **des prix** the low prices (pl)

modificatif, -ive /mɔdifikatif, iv/
A adj **1)** Ling modifying; **2)** Admin **texte** ~ amendment
B nm Admin amendment

modification /mɔdifikasjɔ̃/ nf modification; (d'un projet de loi) amendments

modifier /mɔdifje/ [2] vtr gén to change; Tech to alter, to modify [moteur, système]; Pol to amend [projet de loi]; Ling to modify

modique /mɔdik/ adj [somme, ressources] modest

modiste /mɔdist/ ▸ p. 372 nf milliner

modulable /mɔdylabl/ adj [format, prélèvement] adjustable; [salle] multi-purpose; [horaire] flexible

modulation /mɔdylasjɔ̃/ nf **1)** Phys, Radio modulation; **2)** (flexibilité) flexibility; **3)** (adaptation) adjustment

Composés ~ **de fréquence, MF** frequency modulation, FM

module /mɔdyl/ nm **1)** gén, Univ module; (pour cuisine) unit; **2)** Math, Phys modulus

moduler /mɔdyle/ [1] vtr **1)** gén, Radio, Télécom to modulate; **2)** (adapter) to adjust [prix]; to adapt [politique]

moelle /mwal/ nf Anat, Culin, fig marrow

Composés ~ **épinière** spinal cord; ~ **osseuse** bone marrow

moelleux, -euse /mwalø, øz/ adj [tissu, couleur, ton] soft; [voix] mellifluous; [vin] mellow; [dessert] smooth; [viande] tender

moellon /mwalɔ̃/ nm Constr breeze block GB, cinder block US

mœurs /mœr(s)/ nfpl **1)** (usages) gén customs; (de milieu social) lifestyle (sg); **entrer dans les** ~ [usage] to become part of everyday life; **comédie de** ~ Littérat comedy of manners; **l'évolution des** ~ the change in attitudes; **2)** (habitudes de conduite) habits; **les** ~ **des renards** the habits of foxes; **3)** (moralité) morals; **la police des** ~ the vice squad; **une sordide affaire de** ~ a sordid sex case

Idiome **autres temps, autres** ~ other days, other ways

mohair /mɔɛr/ nm mohair

moi /mwa/ pron pers **1)** (sujet) I, me; **c'est** ~ (au téléphone) it's me; **c'est** ~ **qui ai cassé la vitre** I was the one who broke the windowpane; **il les voit plus souvent que** ~ (que je ne les vois) he sees them more often than I do; (qu'il ne me voit) he sees them more often than me ou than he sees me; **2)** (objet) me; **pour** ~ **il est fou** personally, I think he's mad; **à** ~ (à l'aide) help!; (à mon tour) it's my turn!; **des amis à** ~ friends of mine; **une pièce à** ~ a room of my own; **c'est à** ~ (appartenance) it's mine, it belongs to me; (tour) it's my turn; **c'est à** ~ **de choisir** (ma responsabilité) it's up to me to choose

moignon /mwaɲɔ̃/ nm stump

moi-même /mwamɛm/ pron pers myself; **en** ~ **je me disais que ça n'avait pas d'importance** I told myself that it didn't matter

moindre /mwɛ̃dr/ adj **1)** (comparatif) lesser; **dans une** ~ **mesure** to a lesser extent; **considérer qch comme un** ~ **mal** to consider sth as the lesser of two evils; **à** ~ **prix** more cheaply; **2)** (superlatif) **le** ~ the least; **c'est la** ~ **des choses** it's the least I/you etc could do; **ce serait la** ~ **des politesses de répondre à leur lettre** you/we etc could at least have the courtesy to reply to their letter; **je n'en ai pas la** ~ **idée** I haven't got the slightest idea; **de nombreux scientifiques, et non des** ~**s** many scientists, and highly respected ones at that; **dernier point à souligner et non des** ~**s** last but not least

moine /mwan/ nm Relig monk

Idiome **l'habit ne fait pas le** ~ Prov you can't judge a book by its cover

moins¹

Généralités

La traduction en anglais de *moins* est *less*.
Cependant, elle n'est utilisée que dans un nombre de cas assez restreint:

en moins de trois jours
= in less than three days

Très souvent, même quand une traduction avec *less* est possible, l'anglais a recours à d'autres moyens. Certains sont réguliers:

ma chambre est moins grande que la tienne
= my bedroom isn't as big as yours

j'ai moins d'expérience que toi
= I don't have as much experience as you (do)
ou I have less experience than you (do)

c'est moins compliqué que vous ne le croyez
= it's not as complicated as you think
ou it's less complicated than you think

D'autres ne le sont pas:

j'essaie de moins fumer
= I'm trying to cut down on my smoking
ou I'm trying to smoke less

··

moins de

Lorsque *moins de*, déterminant indéfini, est suivi d'un nom dénombrable, la règle voudrait que l'on traduise par *fewer* mais dans la langue parlée on utilise également *less*.

Les expressions *le moins possible*, *le moins du monde* sont traitées respectivement sous **possible** et **monde**.

On trouvera ci-contre exemples et exceptions illustrant les différentes fonctions de *moins*.

On pourra également se reporter aux notes d'usage portant notamment sur **les quantités**, l'expression de **l'âge** etc. Consulter l'index ▸ p. 1355.

··

moineau, *pl* ∼**x** /mwano/ *nm* (oiseau) sparrow
Idiome **il a une cervelle de** ∼ he is a featherbrain
moins¹ /mwɛ̃/
A *prép* **1** (dans une soustraction) minus); **2** (pour dire l'heure) to); **il est huit heures** ∼ **dix** it's ten (minutes) to eight; **il est** ∼ **vingt**○ it's twenty to○; **il était** ∼ **une**○ *or* ∼ **cinq**○ it was a close shave○; **3** (dans une température) minus
B *adv* **1** (modifiant un verbe) (comparatif) less; (superlatif) **le** ∼ **the least**; **ils sortent** ∼ they go out less often; **c'est** ∼ **une question d'argent qu'une question de principe** it's not so much a question of money as a question of principle; **de** ∼ **en** ∼ less and less; ∼ **je sors,** ∼ **j'ai envie de sortir** the less I go out, the less I feel like going out; **qui travaille le** ∼ **de tous?** who works the least of all?; **le film qui m'a le** ∼ **plu** the film I liked the least; **ce que j'aime le** ∼ **chez lui** what I like least about him; **2** (modifiant un adjectif) (comparatif) less; (superlatif) **le** ∼, **la** ∼, **les** ∼ (de deux) the less; (de plus de deux) the least; **il est** ∼ **grand que son père** he's not as tall as his father; **il est** ∼ **menteur que sa sœur** he's less of a liar than his sister; **les jeunes et les** ∼ **jeunes** the young and the not so young; **dans le livre il y a du bon et du** ∼ **bon** in the book, there are bits that are good and bits that are not so good; **il n'en est pas** ∼ **vrai que** it's nonetheless true that; **le même en** ∼ **gros** the same, only thinner; **un individu des** ∼ **recommandables** a most unsavoury individual; **3** (modifiant un adverbe) (comparatif) less; (superlatif) **le** ∼ least; **tu devrais rester** ∼ **longtemps dans le sauna** you shouldn't stay so long in the sauna; **elle chante** ∼ **bien qu'avant** she doesn't sing as well as she used to be; **le** ∼ **souvent** (the) least often
C **moins de** *dét indéf* **1** (avec un nom) ∼ **de livres** fewer

books; ∼ **de graisses** less fat; ∼ **de sucre/bruit** less sugar/noise; **il a parlé avec** ∼ **de hargne** he spoke less aggressively; **il y a** ∼ **de monde aujourd'hui qu'hier** there are fewer people today than there were yesterday; **c'est lui qui a le** ∼ **d'expérience des trois** of the three he's the one with the least experience; **2** (avec un numéral) **en** ∼ **de trois heures** in less than three hours; **il est** ∼ **de 3 heures** it's not quite 3 o'clock; **les** ∼ **de 20 ans** people under 20, the under-twenties
D **à moins** *loc adv* **on serait furieux à** ∼ it's more than enough to make one angry
E **à moins de** *loc prép* **à** ∼ **de partir maintenant** unless we/you etc leave now; **à** ∼ **d'un miracle** unless there's a miracle
F **à moins que** *loc conj* **à** ∼ **qu'il ne veuille venir** unless he wants to come
G **à tout le moins** *loc adv* to say the least
H **au moins** *loc adv* at least; **tout au** ∼ at least; **tu l'as remercié, au** ∼? you did thank him, didn't you?
I **de moins** *loc adv* **ça m'a pris deux heures de** ∼ it took me two hours less; **le kilo de pêches valait dix centimes de** ∼ **que la veille** a kilo of peaches cost 10 cents less than it had the day before; **j'ai un an de** ∼ **que lui** I'm a year younger than he is; **il a obtenu 25% de voix de** ∼ **que son adversaire** he got 25% fewer votes than his opponent
J **du moins** *loc adv* at least; **c'est du** ∼ **ce qu'il m'a raconté** at least that's what he told me; **si du** ∼ **tu es d'accord** that is if you agree
K **en moins** *loc adv* **il y avait deux fourchettes en** ∼ **dans la boîte** there were two forks missing from the box; **il est revenu du front avec une jambe en** ∼/**avec un doigt en** ∼ he came back from the front with only one leg/with a finger missing; **c'est tout le portrait de son père, la moustache en** ∼ he's the spitting image of his father without the moustache GB *ou* mustache US
L **pour le moins** *loc adv* to say the least
moins² /mwɛ̃/ *nm inv* **1** Math minus; **le signe** ∼ the minus sign; **2** ○(inconvénient) minus
Composé ∼ **que rien** good-for-nothing, nobody
moins-value, *pl* ∼**s** /mwɛ̃valy/ *nf* **1** (diminution de valeur) depreciation; **2** (déficit des recettes fiscales) shortfall
moire /mwaʀ/ *nf* (étoffe) moire
moiré, ∼**e** /mwaʀe/ *adj* [tissu] moiré; [soie, papier] watered
mois /mwa/ ▸ p. 13, p. 582 *nm inv* **1** (division de l'année) month; **au** ∼ **de juin** in June; **un bébé de trois** ∼ a three-month-old baby; **elle est enceinte de trois** ∼ she's three months pregnant; **à moins de deux** ∼ **du premier tour** with the first round less than two months away; **2** (salaire) monthly salary
Moïse /mɔiz/ *npr* Moses
moisi /mwazi/ *nm* mould GB, mold US; **odeur/goût de** ∼ musty smell/taste
moisir /mwaziʀ/ [3] *vi* **1** [aliment] to go mouldy GB *ou* moldy US; [objet, plante] to become mildewed; **2** ○ [personne] to stagnate; [argent, objet] to gather dust; **on va pas** ∼ **ici!** we're not going to hang around here all day!
moisissure /mwazisyʀ/ *nf* mould **₵** GB, mold **₵** US, mildew **₵**
moisson /mwasɔ̃/ *nf* **1** lit, gén harvest; (époque) harvest time; **faire la** ∼ to harvest; **2** fig harvest
moissonner /mwasɔne/ [1] *vtr* **1** lit to harvest; **2** fig to gather [renseignements]; to win [médailles]
moissonneur, -euse¹ /mwasɔnœʀ, øz/ *nm,f* (personne) harvester
moissonneuse² /mwasɔnøz/ *nf* (machine) reaper
moissonneuse-batteuse, *pl* **moissonneuses-batteuses** /mwasɔnøzbatøz/ *nf* combine harvester
moite /mwat/ *adj* [chaleur] muggy; [mur] damp; [peau] sweaty
moiteur /mwatœʀ/ *nf* (de l'air) mugginess; (de la peau) sweatiness
moitié /mwatje/ *nf* **1** gén half; **la peinture, c'est la** ∼ **de ma vie** half of my life is devoted to painting; **à** ∼ **vide** half empty; **dormir à** ∼○ to be half asleep; ∼ **prix** half-price; **s'arrêter à la** ∼ to stop halfway through; **à** ∼ **cassé** damaged; **je n'y crois qu'à** ∼ I don't entirely believe it; **il fait toujours les choses à** ∼ he never does anything properly; **être pour** ∼ **dans qch** to be instrumental in sth;

m

Les mois de l'année

Les noms des mois

■ *L'anglais emploie la majuscule pour les noms de mois. Les abréviations sont courantes en anglais familier écrit, par ex. dans une lettre à un ami:* I'll see you on Mon 17 Sept.

		abréviation anglaise
janvier	January	Jan
février	February	Feb
mars	March	Mar
avril	April	Apr
mai	May	May
juin	June	Jun
juillet	July	Jul
août	August	Aug
septembre	September	Sept
octobre	October	Oct
novembre	November	Nov
décembre	December	Dec

■ *Dans les expressions suivantes,* May *est pris comme exemple. Tous les autres noms de mois s'utilisent de la même façon.*

mai a été pluvieux
= May was wet

■ *L'anglais peut utiliser les noms de mois même là où le français a recours à l'expression* le mois de …

j'aime le mois de mai
= I like May

le mois de mai le plus chaud
= the warmest May

nous avons eu un beau mois de mai
= we had a lovely May

Quand?

■ *Pour l'expression de la date* ▸ p. 155.

nous sommes en mai
= it is May

■ *Avec les autres verbes que* be *(être),* en *se traduit normalement par* in.

en mai
= in May *or* (littéraire) in the month of May

je suis né en mai
= I was born in May

je te verrai en mai
= I'll see you in May

l'an prochain en mai
= in May next year

■ *Noter aussi:*

cette année-là en mai
= that May

en mai prochain
= next May

l'année dernière en mai
= last May

dans deux ans en mai
= the May after next

il y a deux ans en mai
= the May before last

tous les ans en mai
= every May

tous les deux ans en mai
= every other May

presque tous les ans en mai
= most Mays

■ *Comparer:*

un matin en mai
= one morning in May

un matin de mai
= one May morning *ou* on a May morning

début mai
= in early May

au début de mai
= at the beginning of May

fin mai
= in late May

à la fin de mai
= at the end of May

à la mi-mai
= in mid-May

depuis mai
= since May

pendant tout le mois de mai
= for the whole of May *ou* for the whole month of May

tout au long du mois de mai
= all through May *ou* throughout May

De avec les noms de mois

■ *Les expressions françaises avec de se traduisent par l'emploi du nom de mois en position d'adjectif.*

les fleurs de mai
= May flowers

la pluie du mois de mai
= the May rain

le soleil de mai
= the May sunshine

le temps du mois de mai
= May weather

les soldes du mois de mai
= the May sales

---

m

[2] ○(époux) **ma** ∼ my better half○

moitié-moitié /mwatjemwatje/ *adv* (en proportions égales) half-and-half; **partager** ∼ **avec qn** (dépense) to go halves with sb; (gains) to split the profits with sb

moka /mɔka/ *nm* [1] (café) mocha; [2] (gâteau) mocha cake

mol ▸ **mou** A

molaire /mɔlɛʀ/ *nf* (dent) molar

môle /mol/ *nm* [1] (brise-lames) breakwater; [2] (pour s'amarrer) pier, jetty

moléculaire /mɔlekylɛʀ/ *adj* molecular

molécule /mɔlekyl/ *nf* molecule

moleskine /mɔlɛskin/ *nf* [1] (imitant le cuir) imitation leather; [2] (pour doublures) moleskin; [3] (de café) wall seat

molester /mɔlɛste/ [1] *vtr* to manhandle

molette /mɔlɛt/ *nf* [1] Tech (de clé) adjusting knob; (pour découper) rotary cutter; [2] (de briquet) striker wheel

molière /mɔljɛʀ/ *nm: theatrical award*

mollasse○ /mɔlas/ *adj* (mou) pej lit sluggish; fig soft

molle ▸ **mou** A

mollement /mɔlmɑ̃/ *adv* [allongé] idly; [travailler] without much enthusiasm; [protester] half-heartedly; [tomber] softly; [couler] gently

mollesse /mɔlɛs/ *nf* [1] (caractère moelleux) softness; [2] (de chair) flabbiness; (de trait du visage) weakness; [3] (de personne) listlessness; (de poignée de main) limpness; [4] (manque d'autorité) **la** ∼ **du gouvernement face aux manifestants** the government's failure to stand up to the demonstrators; [5] fig (de personne, réponse) lack of conviction; (d'idée, de style) woolliness; (d'opposition) weakness; (de croissance) sluggishness

mollet /mɔlɛ/
A *adj m* **œuf** ∼ soft-boiled egg
B ▸ p. 136 *nm* calf; **des** ∼s **de coq** legs like sticks; **avoir des** ∼s **de cycliste** to have muscular calves

molletière /mɔltjɛʀ/
A *adj f* **bande** ∼ puttee
B *nf* legging

molleton /mɔltɔ̃/ nm **①** (en laine) flannel; (en coton) flannelette; **②** (pour une table) (table) felt; (pour une planche à repasser) (ironing board) cover

molletonner /mɔltɔne/ [1] vtr to line with fleece

mollir /mɔliʀ/ [3] vi **①** (céder) [courage] to fail; [autorité] to diminish; [enthousiasme] to cool; [ténacité] to flag; [résistance] to grow weaker; [personne] to soften; **②** Météo [vent] to die down, to abate

mollusque /mɔlysk/ nm **①** Zool mollusc GB, mollusk US; **②** ○(personne) drip○, wimp○

molosse /mɔlɔs/ nm huge dog

Molotov /mɔlɔtɔf/ npr cocktail ~ Molotov cocktail

môme○ /mom/ nmf (enfant) kid○; péj brat○

moment /mɔmɑ̃/ nm **①** (instant précis) moment; le ~ venu (dans l'avenir) when the time comes; (dans le passé) when the time came; il devrait arriver d'un ~ à l'autre he should arrive any minute now; à aucun ~ il n'a abordé le sujet at no time did he touch on the subject; à un ~ donné (quelconque) at some point; (fixé) at a given moment; sur le ~ j'ai cru qu'il plaisantait at first I thought he was joking; à ce ~-là (à l'époque) at that time; (au même instant) just then; (dans ce cas) in that case; au ~ de l'accident at the time of the accident; au ~ où gén at the time (when); au ~ où il quittait son domicile as he was leaving his home; jusqu'au ~ où until; du ~ que (pourvu que) as long as, provided; (puisque) since; du ~ que tu le dis! if you say so!; ce n'est pas le ~ gén it's not the right moment; (inopportun) now is not the time; il arrive toujours au bon iron or mauvais ~! he certainly picks his moment to call! iron; choisir son ~ pour faire iron to pick one's moment to do iron; **②** (temps bref) moment; j'ai eu un ~ d'incertitude I hesitated for a moment; **③** (temps long) pour le ~ for the time being; tu en as pour un ~ à avoir mal you'll feel uncomfortable for quite some time; ça va prendre un ~ it will take a while; au bout d'un ~, après un ~ after a while; du ~ [ennemi, préoccupations] of the moment; en ce ~ at the moment; par ~s at times; c'est le ~ de la journée où it's the time of day when; les ~s forts du film the film's highlights; cela a été un ~ fort (émouvant) it was a moment of intense emotion; dans ses meilleurs ~s, il fait penser à Orson Welles at his best, he reminds one of Orson Welles; à mes ~s perdus in my spare time

momentané, ~e /mɔmɑ̃tane/ adj momentary; interruption ~e du son temporary loss of sound

momentanément /mɔmɑ̃tanemɑ̃/ adv for a moment, momentarily

momie /mɔmi/ nf mummy

momifier /mɔmifje/ [2] vtr, se momifier vpr to mummify

mon, **ma**, pl **mes** /mɔ̃, ma, mɛ/ adj poss

⚠ Au vocatif, on n'emploie généralement pas le possessif en anglais: ma chérie! = darling!; oui mon général! yes, sir!; mes chers amis! = dear friends! On ne répète pas le possessif coordonné: mon café et mon cognac = my coffee and cognac.

my; ma mère à moi○ my mother; un de mes amis a friend of mine; j'ai ~ idée I have my own ideas about that; à ~ arrivée when I arrived; pendant ~ absence while I was away; j'ai ~ lundi (cette semaine) I'm off on Monday; (toutes les semaines) I have Mondays off

monacal, ~e, mpl -aux /mɔnakal, o/ adj lit, fig monastic

monarchie /mɔnaʀʃi/ nf monarchy

monarchiste /mɔnaʀʃist/ adj, nmf monarchist

monarque /mɔnaʀk/ nm monarch

monastère /mɔnastɛʀ/ nm monastery

monastique /mɔnastik/ adj monastic

monceau, pl ~x /mɔ̃so/ nm pile

mondain, ~e /mɔ̃dɛ̃, ɛn/
A adj [réception, vie] society (épith); conversation ~e polite conversation; il est très ~ he's a socialite
B nm,f socialite

mondanités /mɔ̃danite/ nfpl **①** (réceptions mondaines) society events; **②** (politesses) se faire des ~ to stand on ceremony

monde /mɔ̃d/ nm **①** gén world; ce sont les meilleurs amis du ~ they are the best of friends; le plus calmement du ~ quite calmly; pas le moins du ~ not in the least; si vous êtes le moins du ~ soucieux if you are (in) the least bit worried; s'il souffrait le moins du ~ if he felt any pain at all; se porter le mieux du ~ to be absolutely fine; aller or voyager de par le ~, parcourir le ~ to travel the world; il irait jusqu'au bout du ~ pour la retrouver he would go to the ends of the earth to find her again; c'est le bout du ~!, c'est au bout du ~! it's in the back of beyond!; mon père habite à l'autre bout du ~ my father lives halfway around the world; ce n'est pas le bout du ~! fig it' s not such a big deal!; comme le ~ est petit! it's a small world!; la faim dans le ~ world famine; à la face du ~ for all the world to see; les biens de ce ~ worldly goods; en ce bas ~ here below; elle n'est plus de ce ~ euph she's no longer with us euph; quand je ne serai plus de ce ~ euph when I have departed this world; la perfection n'est pas de ce ~ there is no such thing as perfection; le ~ des vivants the land of the living; je n'étais pas encore au ~ I wasn't yet born; ▸ grand; **②** (milieu) world; le ~ médical the medical world; le ~ animal the animal kingdom; ils ne sont pas du même ~ they are from different social backgrounds; cet événement marqua la fin d'un ~ this event marked the end of an era; un ~ nous sépare we are worlds apart; ▸ nouveau; **③** (gens) people; il n'y a pas grand ~ there aren't many people; tout le ~ everybody; voir beaucoup de ~ to have a busy social life; j'ai du ~ ce soir○ I'm having people round GB ou over US tonight; elle se moque du ~! what does she take us for?; tout mon petit ~ my family and friends (pl); **④** (bonne société) society; le beau or grand ~ high society

(Idiomes) se faire (tout) un ~ de qch to get all worked up about sth; ainsi va le ~ that's the way it goes; depuis que le ~ est ~ since the beginning of time; c'est le ~ à l'envers! whatever next!; c'est un ~○! that's a bit much!

mondial, ~e, mpl -iaux /mɔ̃djal, o/ adj [record, congrès, économie] world (épith); [problème, succès] worldwide; la capitale ~e du cinéma the cinema capital of the world; seconde guerre ~e Second World War

mondialement /mɔ̃djalmɑ̃/ adv être ~ connu to be known all over the world

mondialisation /mɔ̃djalizasjɔ̃/ nf (de marché, sport, phénomène) globalization; la ~ d'un conflit the worldwide spread of a conflict

mondialiser /mɔ̃djalize/ [1] vtr to globalize [marché, échanges]; to cause [sth] to spread worldwide [conflit]

mondialisme /mɔ̃djalism/ nm internationalism

mondovision /mɔ̃dɔvizjɔ̃/ nf satellite broadcasting; retransmettre en ~ to broadcast worldwide via satellite

monégasque /mɔnegask/ ▸ p. 392 adj Monegasque

monème /mɔnɛm/ nm moneme

monétaire /mɔnetɛʀ/ adj [système] monetary; [marché] money

monétariste /mɔnetaʀist/ adj, nmf monetarist

monétique /mɔnetik/ nf electronic banking

monétiser /mɔnetize/ [1] vtr to monetize

mongol, ~e /mɔ̃gɔl/
A ▸ p. 392 adj Géog Mongolian; l'empire ~ Hist the Mongol Empire
B ▸ p. 336 nm Ling Mongolian

Mongolie /mɔ̃gɔli/ ▸ p. 230 nprf Mongolia

Mongolie-Intérieure /mɔ̃gɔliɛ̃teʀjœʀ/ ▸ p. 504 nprf Inner Mongolia

mongolien, -ienne /mɔ̃gɔljɛ̃, ɛn/ controv
A adj Méd Down's syndrome (épith); être ~ to have Down's syndrome
B nm,f Méd (enfant) Down's syndrome child

mongolisme /mɔ̃gɔlism/ nm controv Méd le ~ Down's syndrome

moniteur, -trice /mɔnitœʀ, tʀis/
A ▸ p. 372 nm,f **①** (de sport, conduite) instructor; **②** (de colonie de vacances, centre aéré) group leader GB, counselor US
B nm TV monitor; Ordinat monitor system

(Composé) ~ cardiaque heart monitor

monitorat /mɔnitɔʀa/ nm Univ (activité) tutoring; (système) tutorial system

monnaie /mɔnɛ/ nf **①** (unité monétaire) currency; **②** (pièces et billets de faible valeur) change; faire de la ~ to get some change; **③** (appoint) change; **④** (pièce) coin; battre ~ to mint ou strike coins; frapper une ~ to strike coins ou a

coinage; ⑤ (bâtiment) **(l'hôtel de) la Monnaie** the Mint;
⑥ Écon (argent) money

(Idiomes) **rendre à qn la ~ de sa pièce** to pay sb back in his/
her own coin; **c'est ~ courante** it's commonplace

monnaie-du-pape, pl **monnaies-du-pape** /mɔnɛ-
dypap/ nf Bot honesty

monnayable /mɔnejabl/ adj ① [bon, billet] convertible;
② [diplôme, talent] marketable

monnayer /mɔneje/ [21] vtr ① lit to convert [sth] into
cash; ② fig to capitalize on [talent, expérience]; **~ qch
contre qch** to exchange sth for sth; **~ son silence** to exact
a price for one's silence

mono[1] /mono/ préf mono; **~chrome** monochrome; **~cul-
ture** monoculture; **~graphie** monograph; **~lingue** monolingual; **~lithique** monolithic; **~syllabe** monosyllable

mono[2] /mono/ nf Audio mono; **en ~** in mono

monobloc /monoblɔk/ adj inv cast in one piece (après n)

monocellulaire /monosɛlylɛʀ/ adj **famille ~** nuclear
family

monocle /mɔnɔkl/ nm monocle

monocoque /monokɔk/
Ⓐ adj [bateau] monohull; [voiture] monocoque
Ⓑ nm (bateau) monohull

monocorde /monokɔʀd/ adj [voix, discours] monotonous;
sur un or **d'un ton ~** in a monotone

monocylindrique /monosilɛ̃dʀik/ adj single-cylinder
(épith)

monogame /mɔnɔgam/
Ⓐ adj monogamous
Ⓑ nmf monogamist

monogamie /mɔnɔgami/ nf monogamy

monolithisme /mɔnɔlitism/ nm ① (de parti) monolithic
nature; ② Archit monolithic system

monologue /mɔnɔlɔg/ nm monologue

monologuer /mɔnɔlɔge/ [1] vi (parler seul) to deliver a
monologue; péj to hold forth

monôme /mɔnom/ nm Math monomial

monomoteur /monomɔtœʀ/ nm Aviat single-engined aircraft

mononucléose /mononykleoz/ ▸ p. 195 nf mononucle-
osis

(Composé) **~ infectieuse** glandular fever

monoparental, **~e**, mpl **-aux** /monopaʀɑ̃tal, o/ adj
famille ~e single-parent family

monoplace[1] /monoplas/ nm Aviat single-seater (aircraft)

monoplace[2] /monoplas/ nf Aut one-seater (car)

monoplan /monoplɑ̃/ nm monoplane

monopole /monopɔl/ nm lit, fig monopoly

monopoliser /monopolize/ [1] vtr to monopolize

monoprocesseur /monopʀɔsesœʀ/ nm single-chip
computer

monoski /monoski/ ▸ p. 327 nm (ski) monoski; (sport)
monoskiing

monospace /monospas/ nm Aut space cruiser

monothéiste /monoteist/
Ⓐ adj monotheistic
Ⓑ nmf monotheist

monotone /mɔnɔtɔn/ adj monotonous

monotonie /mɔnɔtɔni/ nf monotony

monozygote /monozigɔt/ adj monozygotic

Monseigneur, pl **Messeigneurs** /mɔsɛɲœʀ, mese-
ɲœʀ/ ▸ p. 590 nm ① (forme d'adresse) (à un prince) Your Highness; (à un membre de la famille royale) Your Royal Highness; (à un
cardinal) Your Eminence; (à un duc, archevêque) Your Grace; (à
un évêque) Your Lordship, My Lord (Bishop); ② (titre) **~ le
duc de Parme** His Grace, the duke of Parma

monsieur, pl **messieurs** /məsjø, mesjø/ ▸ p. 590 nm
① (titre donné à un inconnu) **Monsieur** (dans une lettre) Dear Sir;
bonjour, ~ good morning; ② (titre donné à un homme dont on
connaît le nom, par exemple Bon) **bonjour, ~** good morning, Mr
Bon; **cher Monsieur** (dans une lettre) Dear Mr Bon; **Monsieur
le curé** Father Bon; **Monsieur le ministre** (en lui parlant) Minister; **merci Monsieur le président** (de club, d'association)
thank you Mr Chairman; (de la République) thank you Mr
President; **moi Monsieur!** (à un enseignant) please sir!;

③ (homme) man; **c'était un (grand) ~!** he was a (true)
gentleman!; ④ (formule de respect utilisée avec un homme dont on
connaît le nom) **'Monsieur a sonné?'** 'you rang sir?'; **tu comprends, Monsieur a ses habitudes!** iron His Lordship is
rather set in his ways you see!; ⑤ Hist **Monsieur, frère du
roi** Monsieur, the king's brother

(Composé) **~ Tout le Monde** the man in the street

monstre /mɔ̃stʀ/
Ⓐ °adj [travail, succès] huge; [culot, publicité] colossal; **'soldes
~s'** 'mammoth sales'
Ⓑ nm ① lit, fig monster; **un ~ d'orgueil** a monstrously arrogant person; ② (être difforme) freak (of nature)

(Composés) **~ marin** sea monster; **~ sacré** superstar

monstrueusement /mɔ̃stʀyøzmɑ̃/ adv lit, fig [riche, bête,
intelligent] horrendously; **il est ~ gros** he's a monstrous
size

monstrueux, **-euse** /mɔ̃stʀyø, øz/ adj ① (choquant)
monstrous; ② (hideux) hideous; **d'une laideur monstrueuse** hideously ugly; ③ (énorme) colossal; **d'une bêtise
monstrueuse** incredibly stupid

monstruosité /mɔ̃stʀyozite/ nf ① (de crime) monstrous-
ness; ② (acte) atrocity; (objet) monstrosity; **dire des ~s** to
say preposterous things; ③ (difformité) deformity

mont /mɔ̃/ nm Géog gén mountain; (lieu) Mount;
▸ **promettre**, **val**

(Composés) **le ~ Blanc** Mont Blanc; **le ~ Everest** Mount
Everest; **le ~ des Oliviers** the Mount of Olives; **~ de
Vénus** Anat mons veneris

montage /mɔ̃taʒ/ nm ① (organisation) set-up; ② (de machine)
assembly; (de tente) putting up; (en couture) (de col) putting
on; (de manche) setting in; **atelier de ~** assembly shop;
③ Cin (de film) editing; **table de ~** cutting table; ④ (de
pierre précieuse) setting, mounting

(Composés) **~ photo** photomontage; **~ sonore** sound
montage

montagnard, **-e** /mɔ̃taɲaʀ, aʀd/
Ⓐ adj [peuple] mountain (épith); [coutume] highland (épith); **la
vie ~e** life in the mountains
Ⓑ nm,f mountain dweller

montagne /mɔ̃taɲ/ nf ① (élévation) mountain; **pays de ~s**
mountainous country; ② (région montagneuse) **la ~** the
mountains (pl); **de ~** [route, animal] mountain (épith); **il
neige en haute ~** it's snowing on the upper slopes; **village
de basse ~** village in the foothills of the mountains;
③ fig (grande quantité) mountain

(Composés) **les ~s Rocheuses** the Rocky Mountains, the
Rockies; **~s russes** big dipper (sg) GB, roller coaster (sg);
~ à vaches° fig easy walks (pl); (pour ski) easy slopes
(pl)

(Idiomes) **se faire une ~ de qch** to get really worked up
about sth; **faire battre des ~s** to stir up trouble; **la foi
déplace** or **soulève les ~s** faith can move mountains; **il
n'y a que les ~s qui ne se rencontrent pas** Prov there are
none so distant that fate cannot bring them together Prov;
c'est la ~ qui accouche d'une souris hum a great deal of
effort leading to nothing much

montagneux, **-euse** /mɔ̃taɲø, øz/ adj mountainous

montant, **~e** /mɔ̃tɑ̃, ɑ̃t/
Ⓐ adj ① [cabine, groupe] going up (après n); ② [rue] uphill;
[courbe] rising; ③ [col] high; [chaussettes] long; **chaussures
~es** ankle boots
Ⓑ nm ① (somme) sum; **un ~ global** a sum total; **le ~ des
pertes** the total losses (pl); **d'un** or **pour un ~ de** [déficit,
épargne] amounting to; [chèque] to the amount of;
[marchandises] for a total of; ② (d'échafaudage) pole; (d'échelle,
de porte) upright

(Composés) **~ de lit** bedpost; **~s compensatoires
(monétaires)** (monetary) compensatory amounts

mont-de-piété, pl **monts-de-piété** /mɔ̃dpjete/ nm
pawnshop, pawnbroker's; **mettre qch au ~** to pawn sth

monté°, **~e**[1] /mɔ̃te/ adj (équipé) equipped; **te voilà bien
~e avec un mari comme ça!** iron you're in a bad way with
a husband like that!

monte-charge /mɔ̃tʃaʀʒ/ nm inv goods lift GB ou elevator US

montée[2] /mɔ̃te/
Ⓐ adj f ▸ **monté**

B *nf* [1] (action de grimper) (d'escalier, de pente) climb; (de montagne) ascent; **'ne pas gêner la ~ des voyageurs'** 'do not obstruct passengers boarding'; [2] (d'avion, de ballon) climb, ascent; [3] (élévation de niveau) (action) rising (**de** of); (résultat) rise (**de** in); **la ~ des eaux** the rise in the water level; [4] Fin rise (**de** in); (de coûts, frais) increase (**de** in); [5] (augmentation) gén rise; (de dangers, risques) increase; **une ~ de l'inqui étude à travers le pays** a mounting concern throughout the country; [6] (pente) hill; [7] Sport **~ de Papin** Papin moves up the field

monte-plats /mɔ̃tpla/ *nm inv* dumbwaiter, small lift GB *ou* elevator US

monter /mɔ̃te/ [1]

A *vtr* (+ *v avoir*) [1] (transporter) (en haut) gén to take [sb/sth] up (**à** to); (à l'étage) to take [sb/sth] upstairs; [2] (placer plus haut) to put [sth] up [objet]; to raise [étagère] (**de** by); [3] (réussir à transporter) to get [sth] up [objet]; **impossible de ~ le piano par l'escalier** it's impossible to get the piano up the stairs; [4] (parcourir) to go up [escalier, pente, rue]; **~ la colline à bicyclette** to cycle up the hill; [5] (en valeur, intensité) to turn up [volume, thermostat]; Mus to raise the pitch of [instrument]; [6] Culin to beat, to whisk [blanc d'œuf, mayonnaise]; [7] (rendre hostile) **~ qn contre qn** to turn ou set sb against sb; [8] (chevaucher) to ride [cheval]; [9] (couvrir, saillir) to mount, to cover; [10] (assembler) to assemble [meuble, appareil]; to put up [tente, échafaudage]; to set, to mount [pierre précieuse]; to mount [gravure]; Mus to string [instrument]; **~ un film** to edit a film; [11] (en couture) to put [sth] in [col]; to set [sth] in [manche]; [12] (organiser) to hatch [complot]; to mount [attaque]; to set up [société]; Théât to stage [pièce]; **~ une histoire de toutes pièces** to concoct ou fabricate a story from beginning to end; [13] (fournir) **~ son ménage** to set up home; **~ sa garde-robe** to build up one's wardrobe

B *vi* (+ *v être*) [1] (se déplacer) (en allant) gén to go up; (à l'étage) to go upstairs; [avion, hélicoptère] to climb; [oiseau] to fly up; [soleil, brume] to rise; **tu es monté à pied?** gén did you walk up?; **il est monté au col à bicyclette/en voiture** he cycled/drove up to the pass; **~ sur** to get onto [trottoir]; to climb onto [mur]; **~ sur le toit** [enfant, chat] to go up onto the roof; **~ à l'échelle/l'arbre** to climb (up) the ladder/the tree; **~ au ciel** to ascend into Heaven; **l'air chaud fait ~ les ballons** warm air makes balloons rise; **faites-les ~** (clients, marchandises) send them up; [2] (sur un moyen de transport) **~ dans une voiture** to get in a car; **~ dans un train/bus/avion** to get on a train/bus/plane; **il a peur de ~ en avion** he's afraid of flying; **~ à bord** to get on board; **~ sur** to get on [cheval, bicyclette, tracteur]; [3] (s'étendre de bas en haut) [route, voie ferrée] to go uphill, to climb; [terrain] to rise; [canalisation, ligne téléphonique] (en allant) to go up; **~ en lacets** [route] to wind its way up; **~ en pente douce** [terrain, route] to slope up gently; **~ en pente raide** [terrain, route] to climb steeply; [4] (atteindre) [vêtement, liquide, neige] to come up; **il avait des chaussettes qui lui montaient aux genoux** he was wearing knee socks; [5] (augmenter) gén to rise, to go up (**à** to; **de** by); [marée] to come in; Mus [mélodie] to rise; **faire ~ les cours de 2%** to push prices up by 2%; [6] (se rendre, séjourner) **~ à** or **sur Paris** (de province) to go up to Paris; [7] (chevaucher) **~ (à cheval)** to ride; **~ à bicyclette/moto** to ride a bicycle/motorbike; [8] Mil **~ à l'assaut** or **l'attaque** to mount an attack (**de** on); **~ au front** to move up to the front; **~ en ligne** to move up the line; **~ au combat** to go into battle; [9] Jeux (aux cartes) to play a higher card; [10] (progresser) [employé, artiste] to rise; **à force de ~, il deviendra directeur** he'll work his way right up to director; **~ en puissance** [parti, politicien] to rise; [11] (gagner en intensité) [colère, émotion] to mount; [sanglots] to rise; [larmes] to well up; **le ton monta** (animation) the conversation became noisier; (énervement) the discussion became heated; [12] (saisir) **~ à la gorge de qn** [sanglots, cri] to rise (up) in sb's throat; **~ à la tête de qn** [vin, succès] to go to sb's head; **le rouge lui est monté au front** he/she went red in the face; [13] Aut, Tech **~ à 250 km/h** to go up to 250 kph

C *se monter vpr* [1] (s'élever) **se ~ à** [frais, facture] to amount to; [2] (s'équiper) to get oneself set up (**en** with)

Idiome **se ~ la tête**○ to get worked up○

monteur, -euse /mɔ̃tœʀ, øz/ ▸ p. 372 *nm,f* [1] Ind fitter; [2] Cin editor; [3] (en typographie) paste-up artist

montgolfière /mɔ̃ɡɔlfjɛʀ/ *nf* [1] (ballon) hot-air balloon; [2] ▸ p. 327 (sport) (hot-air) ballooning

---

monticule /mɔ̃tikyl/ *nm* [1] (butte) hillock; [2] (amas) mound (**de** of)

montrable /mɔ̃tʀabl/ *adj* [personne] presentable; [film] suitable for viewing (après n)

montre /mɔ̃tʀ/ *nf* [1] (objet) watch; **il est 5 heures à ma ~** it's 5 o'clock by my watch; **trois heures ~ en main** fig three hours exactly; **course contre la ~** race against the clock; [2] (action de montrer) fml **faire ~ de** to show [prudence, courage]; to display [esprit, habileté]; [3] (ostentation) liter **pour la ~** for show, for the sake of appearances; [4] Comm (présentation) display, show; **articles en ~** articles on display

Montréal /mɔ̃ʀeal/ ▸ p. 621 *npr* Montreal

montrer /mɔ̃tʀe/ [1]

A *vtr* [1] (faire voir) to show [objet, passeport]; **~ qch à qn** to show sth to sb; [2] (faire visiter) **laissez-moi vous ~ la maison** let me show you around the house; [3] (faire connaître) to show [problème, sentiments, connaissances]; to reveal [intentions]; **~ que** to show that; **~ à qn comment faire** to show sb how to do; [4] (indiquer) [personne] to point out [trace, lieu, objet]; [panneau] to point to [direction]; [tableau, sondage] to show [évolution, résultats]; **~ qch à qn** to point sth out to sb; **~ qch du doigt** or **d'un geste** to point to sth, to point sth out; **~ qn du doigt** lit to point at sb; fig to point the finger at sb; **~ le chemin à qn** lit, fig to show sb the way

B *se montrer vpr* [1] (se révéler) [personne] to show oneself to be; [choses] to prove (to be); **il s'est montré serviable** he was very helpful; **il faut se ~ optimiste** we must try to be optimistic; [2] (se faire voir) [personne] to show oneself; [soleil] to come out; **il n'ose pas se ~** he doesn't dare show his face; **elle n'osait pas se ~ avec lui** she didn't dare be seen with him; **on n'est pas obligés de rester mais il faut au moins se ~** we don't have to stay but we should at least put in an appearance

Idiomes **~ le poing à qn** to shake one's fist at sb; **~ les dents** to bare one's teeth; **~ le bout de son** or **du nez** [personne] to show one's face; [soleil] to peep through; [plantes] to poke through

montreur, -euse /mɔ̃tʀœʀ, øz/ ▸ p. 372 *nm,f* **~ d'animaux** animal trainer; **~ de marionnettes** puppeteer; **~ d'ours** bear tamer

monture /mɔ̃tyʀ/ *nf* [1] (animal) mount; [2] Tech mount; (de lunettes) frames (pl); (de bague) setting

Idiome **qui veut voyager loin ménage sa ~** Prov you have to learn to pace yourself

monument /mɔnymɑ̃/ *nm* [1] (commémoratif) monument; [2] (édifice) (historic) building; **visiter les ~s de Paris** to see the sights of Paris; [3] fig **être un ~ de bêtise** [personne] to be monumentally stupid; **un des ~s de la littérature européenne** a masterpiece of European literature

Composés **~ historique** ancient monument; **~ aux morts** war memorial

monumental, ~e, mpl ~aux /mɔnymɑ̃tal, o/ *adj* monumental; **il est d'une ignorance ~e** he's monumentally ignorant

moquer: se moquer /mɔke/ [1] *vpr* [1] (ridiculiser) to make fun (**de** of), to laugh (**de** at); **arrête de te ~!** stop poking fun!; [2] (être indifférent) **se ~ de** not to care about; **je me moque qu'ils viennent ou pas** I don't care whether they come or not; ▸ **chemise, guigne**; [3] (tromper) **se ~ de qn** to fool sb; **se ~ des gens** to take people for fools

moquerie /mɔkʀi/ *nf* [1] (remarque) mocking remark; **être en butte aux ~s** to be the target of mockery; [2] (action) mockery

moquette /mɔkɛt/ *nf* [1] (tapis) fitted carpet GB, wall-to-wall carpet; **faire poser une** or **de la ~** to have a carpet laid ou fitted; [2] (tissu) moquette

moquetter /mɔkete/ [1] *vtr* to carpet [pièce]

moqueur, -euse /mɔkœʀ, øz/ *adj* mocking

moral, ~e[1], mpl ~aux /mɔʀal, o/

A *adj* [1] (éthique) moral; **n'avoir aucun sens ~** to have no sense of right and wrong; **sur le plan ~** morally; [2] (mental) [torture] mental; [courage, soutien] moral; **douleur ~e** mental anguish; **force ~e** moral fibre GB; [3] (conforme aux bonnes mœurs) [œuvre, personne] moral; [conduite] ethical; **le conseil qu'il t'a donné n'était pas très ~** the advice he gave you was morally dubious; **ce n'est pas très ~ d'avoir fait cela** that was not a very ethical thing to do

B *nm* ① (disposition d'esprit) morale; **le ~ des troupes est bon/mauvais** the troops' morale is high/low; **avoir bon ~, avoir le ~** to be in good spirits; **ne pas avoir le ~** to feel down; **avoir le ~ à zéro**○ to feel very down; **remonter le ~ de qn** to raise sb's spirits *ou* morale, to cheer sb up; **garder le ~** to keep up one's morale; **saper le ~ de qn** to undermine sb's morale; ② (psychique) mind; **au ~ comme au physique** mentally and physically

morale² /mɔʀal/ *nf* ① (règles de conduite) morality; **contraire à la ~** immoral; **leur ~** their moral code; ② (enseignement) moral; **la ~ de tout ceci** the moral of all this; **faire la ~ à qn** *fig* to give sb a lecture; ③ Philos **la ~** moral philosophy, ethics

moralement /mɔʀalmɑ̃/ *adv* ① (conformément à la morale) morally; ② (psychiquement) psychologically

moralisant, ~e /mɔʀalizɑ̃, ɑ̃t/ *adj* moralizing

moralisateur, -trice /mɔʀalizatœʀ, tʀis/ *adj* [*personne, ton, discours*] moralizing, moralistic; [*histoire*] with a moral (*épith, après n*)

moraliser /mɔʀalize/ [1]
A *vtr* to clean up [*campagne électorale*]; to reform [*vie publique*]
B *vi* to moralize (**sur** about)

moraliste /mɔʀalist/ *nmf gén* moralist; *péj* moralizer; Philos moral philosopher

moralité /mɔʀalite/ *nf* ① (de personne, société) morals (*pl*), moral standards (*pl*); **un individu d'une ~ douteuse** an individual with dubious morals; ② (d'œuvre, action) morality; **la ~ publique** public morality; ③ (leçon) moral; **~, ne faites confiance à personne** the moral is, don't trust anybody

morbide /mɔʀbid/ *adj* morbid

morbidité /mɔʀbidite/ *nf* morbidity

morceau, pl ~x /mɔʀso/ *nm* ① (fragment) piece, bit; **être en ~x** Culin [*sucre*] to be in lumps; [*viande*] to be in cubes; (cassé) to be in pieces *ou* bits; **casser en mille ~x** to break into a thousand pieces; **manger un ~**○ to have a snack; ② Culin (en boucherie) cut; **bas ~** cheap cut; ③ Mus (œuvre) piece; **~ de piano** piano piece; ④ Littérat extract; ⑤ ○(partie) **le chapitre 8 est un sacré ~**○ chapter 8 is quite substantial

⟮Idiome⟯ **recoller les ~x** to patch things up

morceler /mɔʀsəle/ [19] *vtr* to divide up [*héritage, terrain*] (**en** into); to split up [*pays*]

morcellement /mɔʀsɛlmɑ̃/ *nm* ① (action) (d'héritage, de terrain) dividing up; (de pays) splitting up; ② (résultat) division; **le ~ des terres** the division of land into smaller units

mordant, ~e /mɔʀdɑ̃, ɑ̃t/
A *adj* ① [*ironie, ton*] caustic; [*personne*] scathing; ② [*froid*] biting
B *nm* ① (causticité) sarcasm; **avec ~** sarcastically; ② ○(énergie de personne, d'équipe) zip○

mordicus○ /mɔʀdikys/ *adv* pigheadedly○, stubbornly

mordiller /mɔʀdije/ [1] *vtr* to nibble at

mordoré, ~e /mɔʀdɔʀe/ *adj* golden brown

mordre /mɔʀdʀ/ [6]
A *vtr* ① [*animal, personne*] to bite; **~ qn au bras** to bite sb on the arm; **~ qn jusqu'au sang** to bite sb and draw blood; **se faire ~** to be bitten (**par** by); ② (entamer) [*lime*] to bite; [*acide, rouille*] to eat into
B **mordre à** *vtr ind* **~ à l'appât** *or* **l'hameçon** *lit, fig* to take the bait; **'ça mord?'** 'are the fish biting?'
C *vi* ① **~ dans une pomme** to bite into an apple; ② (empiéter) **~ sur** to go over [*ligne blanche*]; to encroach on [*territoire*]; ③ ○(croire naïvement) to fall for it○
D **se mordre** *vpr* **se ~ la langue** *lit, fig* to bite one's tongue

⟮Idiome⟯ **je m'en suis mordu les doigts** I could have kicked myself

mordu, ~e /mɔʀdy/
A ○*adj* ① (passionné) **être ~ de qch** to be mad○ about sth; ② (amoureux) smitten
B ○*nm,f* fan; **les ~s du ski** skiing fans *ou* buffs○

more, moresque = maure

morfondre: se morfondre /mɔʀfɔ̃dʀ/ [6] *vpr* ① **se ~ à attendre** *or* **en attendant** to wait dejectedly; ② (languir) to pine; **le pays se morfond dans la crise** *fig* the country is stagnating in recession

morganatique /mɔʀganatik/ *adj* morganatic

morgue /mɔʀg/ *nf* ① (lieu) morgue; (dans un hôpital) mortuary; ② arrogance

moribond, ~e /mɔʀibɔ̃, ɔ̃d/
A *adj lit* dying; *fig* moribund
B *nm,f* dying man/woman; **les ~s** the dying

moricaud○, **~e** /mɔʀiko, od/ *adj* swarthy

morigéner /mɔʀiʒene/ [14] *vtr* to reprimand

morille /mɔʀij/ *nf* morel (mushroom)

mormon, ~e /mɔʀmɔ̃, ɔn/ *adj, nm,f* Mormon

morne /mɔʀn/ *adj* ① [*personne, attitude, silence*] gloomy; [*visage*] glum; [*regard*] doleful; ② [*paysage, lieu, existence, débat, vacances*] dreary; [*temps, journée*] dismal; **une rue ~** a drab street

morose /mɔʀoz/ *adj* [*personne, vieillesse, humeur*] morose; [*journée, lieu, ton, atmosphère, vie*] gloomy

morosité /mɔʀozite/ *nf* gloom

Morphée /mɔʀfe/ *npr* Morpheus

⟮Idiome⟯ **être dans les bras de ~** to be in the arms of Morpheus

morphème /mɔʀfɛm/ *nm* morpheme

morphine /mɔʀfin/ *nf* morphine

morphinomane /mɔʀfinɔman/ *nmf* morphine addict

morphologie /mɔʀfɔlɔʒi/ *nf* morphology

morpion /mɔʀpjɔ̃/ *nm* ▸ p. 327 (jeu) noughts and crosses GB, tick-tack-toe US

mors /mɔʀ/ *nm inv* bit; **prendre le ~ aux dents** [*cheval*] to take the bit between its teeth; [*personne*] (colère subite) to fly off the handle○; (énergie subite) to take the bit between one's teeth

morse /mɔʀs/ *nm* ① Zool walrus; ② Télécom (code) **~** Morse code

morsure /mɔʀsyʀ/ *nf* ① (plaie) bite; **~ de chien** dogbite; ② (action) **la ~ du froid** the biting cold; **la ~ de l'acide** the bite of acid

mort¹ /mɔʀ/ *nf* death; **mourir de ~ naturelle** to die of natural causes; **mourir de sa belle ~** to die peacefully in old age; **vouloir la ~ de qn** to wish sb dead; **il n'y a pas eu ~ d'homme** there were no fatalities; **être à deux doigts de la ~** to be at death's door; **j'ai vu la ~ de près** I saw death close up; **lutter jusqu'à la ~** to fight to the death; **jusqu'à ce que ~ s'ensuive** [*battre*] to death; **trouver la ~** *liter* to die; **être en danger de ~** to be in mortal danger; **mettre qn à ~** to put sb to death; **mise à ~** (de condamné) killing; (de taureau) dispatch; **un engin de ~** a deadly contraption; **à ~** [*lutte*] to the death; [*guerre*] ruthless; [*freiner, serrer*] like mad○; [*frapper, lutter*] to death; [*blessé*] fatally; **je leur en veux à ~**○ I'll never forgive them; **on est fâchés à ~**○ we'll never have anything to do with each other again

⟮Composés⟯ **~ cérébrale** brain death; **~ subite** sudden death; **~ subite du nourrisson** cot death GB, crib death US; **un ~ vivant** one of the living dead; **tu as l'air d'un ~ vivant** you look like death warmed up GB *ou* over US

⟮Idiome⟯ **la ~ dans l'âme** with a heavy heart

mort², ~e /mɔʀ, mɔʀt/
A *pp* ▸ **mourir**
B *pp adj* ① (sans vie) dead; **laisser qn pour ~** to leave sb for dead; **être ~ de faim** *fig* to be starving; **je suis ~e de froid** I'm freezing to death; **il est ~ de sommeil** he's ready to drop; ② (très fatigué) half-dead; ③ (partie du corps) [*dent*] dead; **mes orteils sont comme ~s** my toes have gone numb; ④ (sans activité) [*quartier*] dead; [*saison*] slack; **eaux ~es** stagnant water ₵
C *nm,f* (défunt) dead person, dead man/woman; **les ~s** the dead; **jour des ~s** Relig All Souls' Day
D *nm* ① (victime) fatality; **il y a eu 12 ~s** there were 12 dead; **il n'y a pas eu de ~s** there were no fatalities, nobody was killed; **l'attentat n'a fait qu'un ~** the attack claimed only one life; ② (cadavre) body; **faire le ~** (être immobile) to play dead; (éviter les contacts) to lie low

⟮Idiomes⟯ **ne pas y aller de main ~e**○ not to pull any punches; **être à la place du ~**○ (en voiture) to sit in the front passenger seat

mortaise /mɔʀtɛz/ *nf* mortise

mortalité /mɔʀtalite/ *nf* mortality

mort-aux-rats /mɔʀoʀa/ *nf inv* rat poison

morte-eau, pl mortes-eaux /mɔʀto, mɔʀtzo/ *nf* neap(-tide)

mortel, -elle /mɔʀtɛl/
A *adj* **①** [*coup, maladie, chute*] fatal; [*poison, dose, gaz*] lethal; [*venin*] deadly; [*champignon*] deadly poisonous; **②** [*froid, pâleur, silence*] deathly; [*angoisse, frayeur*] mortal; **③** [*ennemi*] mortal; **④** [*spectacle, personne, attente*] deadly boring; **⑤** (susceptible de mourir) [*être*] mortal
B *nm,f* liter mortal

mortellement /mɔʀtɛlmɑ̃/ *adv* **①** [*blessé, atteint*] fatally; **②** [*ennuyeux*] deadly; [*pâle*] deathly

morte-saison, *pl* **mortes-saisons** /mɔʀt(ə)sɛzɔ̃/ *nf* off season

mortier /mɔʀtje/ *nm* (récipient, ciment, canon) mortar

mortification /mɔʀtifikasjɔ̃/ *nf* mortification

mortifier /mɔʀtifje/ [2] *vtr* to mortify

mort-né, ~**e**, *mpl* ~**s** /mɔʀne/ *adj* lit stillborn; fig abortive

mortuaire /mɔʀtɥɛʀ/ *adj* [*cérémonie*] funeral; **veillée** ~ wake

morue /mɔʀy/ *nf* cod

morutier /mɔʀytje/ *nm* **①** (navire) cod-fishing boat; **②** ▸ p. 372 (pêcheur) cod fisherman

morve /mɔʀv/ *nf* (sécrétion) nasal mucus

morveux, -euse /mɔʀvø, øz/ *adj* [*enfant*] snotty-nosed○ (épith); **se sentir** ~ to feel embarrassed

mosaïque /mɔzaik/ *nf* (assemblage, art) mosaic

Moscou /mɔsku/ ▸ p. 621 *npr* Moscow

mosquée /mɔske/ *nf* mosque

mot /mo/ *nm* **①** gén word; **faire du** ~ **à** ~ to translate word for word; **à** ~ **couverts** in veiled terms; **au bas** ~ at least; **en un** ~ in a word; **explique-moi en deux** ~**s** tell me briefly; **pour eux, l'amitié n'est pas un vain** ~ they take friendship seriously; **'manger', il n'a que ce** ~ **à la bouche** all he can talk about is eating; ▸ **gros**; **②** (parole) word; **dire un** ~ **à qn** to have a word with sb; **ne pas souffler** *or* **piper**○ ~ not to say a word; **ne pas pouvoir placer un** ~ to be unable to get a word in edgeways; **prendre qn au** ~ to take sb at their word; **toucher**○ **un** ~ **de qch à qn** to have a word with sb about sth; **glisser un** ~ **à qn** to have a quick word with sb; **des** ~**s que tout cela!** it's just hot air!; **si tu as besoin de moi tu n'as qu'un** ~ **à dire** if you need me you've only to say the word; **sur ces** ~**s il sortit** with that, he left; **il ne dit jamais un** ~ **plus haut que l'autre** he never raises his voice; **avoir son** ~ **à dire** to be entitled to one's say; **viens par ici, j'ai deux** ~**s à te dire!** euph come here, I've got a bone to pick with you!; **50 euros pour les deux c'est mon dernier** ~ 50 euros the pair but that's my last offer; **avoir toujours le** ~ **pour rire** to be a born joker; **c'est un** ~ **d'enfant** it's something only a child could say; **③** (petite lettre) note; **④** Ordinat word

(Composés) ~ **d'auteur** literary quotation; ~ **d'esprit** witticism, witty remark; ~ **de la fin** closing words (pl); **avoir le** ~ **de la fin** to have the last word; ~ **d'ordre** watchword; ~ **d'ordre de grève** strike call; ~ **de passe** password; ~**s croisés** crossword; ~**s doux** sweet nothings

(Idiomes) **avoir** *or* **échanger des** ~**s avec qn** euph to have words with sb; **ne pas avoir peur des** ~**s** to call a spade a spade; **se donner** *or* **passer le** ~ to pass the word around

motard, ~e /mɔtaʀ, aʀd/
A ○*nm,f* motorcyclist, biker○
B ▸ p. 372 *nm* (de police) police motorcyclist

mot-clé, *pl* **mots-clés** /mokle/ *nm* key word

moteur, -trice¹ /mɔtœʀ, tʀis/
A *adj* **①** [*force, principe*] driving (épith); **être l'élément** ~ **de qch** to be the driving force behind sth; **jouer un rôle** ~ **dans** to play a dynamic role in; **la voiture a quatre roues motrices** the car has four-wheel drive; **les roues motrices sont à l'avant** it's a front-wheel drive (car); **②** [*trouble, fibre*] motor (épith)
B *nm* **①** (électrique) motor; (autre) engine; **un véhicule à** ~ a motor vehicle; **②** fig driving force; **être le** ~ **de qch** to be the driving force behind sth

(Composé) ~ **de recherche** search engine.

motif /mɔtif/ *nm* **①** (raison) grounds (de for); **il y a des** ~**s d'espérer/de se réjouir** there are grounds for hope/for rejoicing; **②** (cause) reason (de for); **les** ~**s de notre retard** the reasons why we are/were late; **③** (motivation) motive;

sans ~ **apparent** for no apparent motive; **④** (dessin) pattern; **à** ~ **floral** with a floral pattern; **⑤** (thème) motif

motion /mɔsjɔ̃/ *nf* motion; ~ **de censure** motion of censure

motivant, ~e /mɔtivɑ̃, ɑ̃t/ *adj* [*salaire*] attractive; [*travail*] rewarding; [*raison*] worthwhile

motivation /mɔtivasjɔ̃/ *nf* **①** motivation; **②** motive

motivé, ~e /mɔtive/ *adj* **①** (enthousiaste) motivated (**pour** as regards; **pour faire** to do); **il est peu** ~ he lacks motivation; **②** (légitime) [*plainte*] justifiable

motiver /mɔtive/ [1] *vtr* **①** to motivate [*personne*] (**à faire** to do); **②** to lead to [*décision, action*]; **motivé par** caused by

moto /moto/ *nf* **①** (véhicule) (motor)bike; **à** ~ by motorbike; **②** (activité) motorcycling

motocross /motokʀɔs/ ▸ p. 327 *nm* inv motocross, scramble GB

motoculteur /motokyltœʀ/ *nm* rotary cultivator

motocyclette /motosiklɛt/ *nf* motorcycle

motocyclisme /motosiklism/ ▸ p. 327 *nm* motorcycle racing

motocycliste /motosiklist/
A *adj* [*rallye, brigade*] motorcycle (épith); **le sport** ~ the sport of motorcycling
B *nmf* motorcyclist

motonautisme /motonotism/ ▸ p. 327 *nm* speedboat racing

motoneige /motonɛʒ/ *nf* snowmobile

motopompe /motopɔ̃p/ *nf* power-driven pump

motorisation /motɔʀizasjɔ̃/ *nf* motorization; **taux de** ~ rate of car ownership

motoriser /motɔʀize/ [1] *vtr* to motorize [*véhicule, troupes*]; **être motorisé**○ to have transport GB *ou* transportation US

motoriste /motɔʀist/ ▸ p. 372 *nmf* **①** (constructeur) engine builder; **②** (mécanicien) mechanic

motrice² /motʀis/
A *adj f* ▸ **moteur**
B *nf* Rail (locomotive) engine

motte /mɔt/ *nf* ~ **(de terre)** clod (of earth); ~ **de gazon** sod, piece of turf; ~ **(de beurre)** slab of butter; **acheter du beurre en** ~ to buy butter by weight

motus○ /mɔtys/ *excl* ~ **(et bouche cousue)!** keep it under your hat!

mot-valise, *pl* **mots-valises** /movaliz/ *nm* portmanteau word

mou (mol before vowel or mute h**), molle** /mu, mɔl/
A *adj* **①** (pas ferme) [*coussin, matière*] soft; [*tige, étoffe*] limp; [*choc*] dull; **②** (sans tenue) [*trait du visage*] weak; [*chair, ventre*] flabby; [*cheveux*] limp; **③** (apathique) [*personne*] listless; [*poignée de main*] limp; [*croissance, reprise économique*] sluggish; **④** (sans énergie) [*parent, professeur*] soft; **⑤** (sans conviction) pej [*version, libéralisme*] watered-down; [*discours, résistance*] feeble
B *nm* **①** (personne) pej wimp○; **②** (en boucherie) lights (pl) GB, lungs (pl) US; **③** (de corde) **avoir du** ~ to be slack; **donner du** ~ to let (the rope) out a bit; **donner du** ~ **à qn** fig to give sb a bit of leeway

mouchard, ~e /muʃaʀ, aʀd/
A ○*nm,f* (de police) grass○; Scol sneak○
B *nm* **①** (appareil) tachograph; **②** (orifice) spyhole

moucharder /muʃaʀde/ [1] *vtr* ~ **qn** (pour la police) to inform on sb, to squeal○ on sb; Scol to sneak○ on sb

mouche /muʃ/ *nf* **①** (insecte) fly; **②** (sur le visage) patch; **③** (de cible) bull's eye; **faire** ~ lit to hit the bull's eye; fig to be right on target

(Composés) ~ **bleue** bluebottle; ~ **commune** *or* **domestique** housefly; ~ **à miel** bee; ~ **verte** greenbottle; ~ **du vinaigre** fruit fly

(Idiomes) **on entendrait une** ~ **voler** you could hear a pin drop; **quelle** ~ **les a piqués**○? what's got GB *ou* gotten US into them?; **regarder voler les** ~**s** to stare into space; **prendre la** ~ to fly off the handle

moucher /muʃe/ [1]
A *vtr* **①** ~ **qn** lit to blow sb's nose; fig○ to put sb in their place; **②** to snuff (out) [*chandelle*]
B **se moucher** *vpr* to blow one's nose

m

(Idiome) **il ne se mouche pas du pied**° *or* **du coude**° (mener grand train) he lives the high life; (être prétentieux) he's full of airs and graces

moucheron /muʃʀɔ̃/ *nm* (insecte) midge

moucheté, **~e** /muʃte/ *adj* **1** [*étoffe*] flecked; [*œuf*] speckled; [*pelage*] spotted; [*cheval*] dappled; **2** [*fleuret*] buttoned

mouchoir /muʃwaʀ/ *nm* handkerchief; (en papier) tissue GB, Kleenex®

(Idiome) **arriver dans un ~** [*candidats, concurrents*] to have a close finish

moudjahidin /mudʒaidin/ *nmpl* mujaheddin

moudre /mudʀ/ [77] *vtr* to grind

moue /mu/ *nf* pout; **faire la ~** (bouder) to pout; (pour exprimer un doute) to pull a face

mouette /mwɛt/ *nf* (sea) gull

mouf(f)ette /mufɛt/ *nf* skunk

moufle /mufl/ *nf* (gant) mitten

mouillage /mujaʒ/ *nm* Naut (manœuvre) anchoring; (emplacement) anchorage; **être au ~** to lie *ou* ride at anchor; **~ de mines** Mil minelaying

mouiller /muje/ [1]
A *vtr* **1** to wet [*cheveux, linge, sol*]; to get [sth] wet [*vêtements, chaussures*]; **2** to drop [*ancre*]; to lay [*mine*]; to cast [*ligne*]; **3** Culin to moisten; **4** to palatalize [*consonne*]
B *vi* Naut to anchor, to drop anchor
C **se mouiller** *vpr* **1** lit to get wet; **2** ° fig to stick one's neck out°

mouillette° /mujɛt/ *nf* soldier° GB, finger of bread (*eaten with a boiled egg*)

mouilleur /mujœʀ/ *nm* **1** (stamp) sponge; **2** Naut (dispositif) tumbler

(Composé) **~ de mines** minelayer

moujik /muʒik/ *nm* muzhik

moulage /mulaʒ/ *nm* (reproduction) casting; **faire un ~ de qch** to take a cast of sth

moulant, **~e** /mulɑ̃, ɑ̃t/ *adj* [*vêtement*] skin-tight

moule¹ /mul/ *nm* **1** Art, Ind, fig mould GB, mold US; **fait au ~** fig perfectly shaped; **2** Culin (pour gâteau, pain) tin, pan US; (pour gelées) mould GB, mold US

(Composé) **~ à gaufre** waffle iron

moule² /mul/ *nf* Zool mussel

mouler /mule/ [1] *vtr* **1** (fabriquer avec un moule) to mould GB, to mold US [*substance*]; to cast [*liquide*]; to mint [*médaille*]; **écriture moulée** fig copperplate handwriting; **2** (prendre une empreinte) to take a cast of; **3** (coller à) [*vêtement*] to hug [*corps*]; **moulée dans une robe de cuir** in a skin-tight leather dress

moulin /mulɛ̃/ *nm* (édifice, appareil) mill

(Composés) **~ à paroles** chatterbox; **~ à prières** prayer wheel; **~ à vent** windmill

(Idiomes) **apporter de l'eau au ~ de qn** to fuel sb's arguments; **on ne peut être à la fois au four et au ~** one can't be in two places at once; **on y entre comme dans un ~** one can just slip in; **se battre contre des ~s à vent** to tilt at windmills; **jeter son bonnet par-dessus les ~s** to let one's hair down

mouliner /muline/ [1] *vtr* **1** Culin to purée [*pommes de terre*]; to grind [*café*]; **2** [*pêcheur*] to reel in [*ligne*]

moulinet /mulinɛ/ *nm* **1** (de canne à pêche) reel; **2** (mouvement) **faire des ~s avec les bras** gén to wave one's arms about; **faire des ~s avec un bâton** to twirl a stick

moulinette® /mulinɛt/ *nf* (small) vegetable mill; **passer à la ~** lit, fig to put [sth/sb] through the mill

moulu, **~e** /muly/
A *pp* ▸ **moudre**
B *pp adj* [*café, poivre*] ground
C °*adj* fig **~ (de fatigue)** worn out; **~ (de coups)** beaten black and blue

moulure /mulyʀ/ *nf* moulding GB, molding US

moumoute° /mumut/ *nf* **1** (perruque) toupee; **2** (vêtement) sheepskin jacket

mourant, **~e** /muʀɑ̃, ɑ̃t/
A *adj* [*personne, animal*] dying (de of); [*entreprise*] moribund; [*voix*] faint
B *nm,f* dying person; **les ~s** the dying (+ v pl)

mourir /muʀiʀ/ [34]
A *vi* **1** (cesser d'exister) to die (**de** of); **~ de vieillesse** to die of old age; **~ de froid** (dehors) to die of exposure; (sous un toit) to die of cold; **je meurs de soif** fig I'm dying of thirst; **je meurs de faim** fig I'm starving; **je meurs de froid** fig I'm freezing to death; **je meurs de sommeil** fig I'm ready to drop; **c'était à ~ (de rire)!** it was hilarious!; **~ assassiné** to be murdered; **je meurs d'envie de faire** I'm dying to do; **se laisser ~ de faim** to starve oneself to death; **faire ~ qn** to kill sb; **2** (faiblir) liter [*jour*] to fade away littér; [*flamme*] to die down; [*conversation*] to die away; [*vagues*] to break and fall back
B **se mourir** *vpr* liter [*personne, civilisation*] to be dying; [*flamme, feu*] to die down

(Idiomes) **partir c'est ~ un peu** to say goodbye is to die a little; **je ne veux pas ~ idiot**° hum I want to know; **on n'en meurt pas**°!, **tu n'en mourras pas**°! hum it won't kill you!; **je veux bien ~** *or* **que je meure si...** I'll eat my hat if...

mouroir /muʀwaʀ/ *nm* pej old people's home, twilight home péj

mouron /muʀɔ̃/ *nm* Bot pimpernel

mousquetaire /muskətɛʀ/ *nm* musketeer

mousqueton /muskətɔ̃/ *nm* **1** Tech snap clasp; **2** (d'alpinisme) carabiner; **3** Mil carbine

moussaillon /musajɔ̃/ *nm* ship's apprentice

moussant, **~e** /musɑ̃, ɑ̃t/ *adj* [*gel*] foaming (épith); **non ~** [*savon, lessive*] low-lather

mousse¹ /mus/ *nm* Naut ship's apprentice

mousse² /mus/ *nf* **1** Bot moss; **2** (bulles) gén foam; (de savon, lessive) lather; (sur le lait, le café) froth; (sur la bière) head; **3** Culin mousse; **~ au chocolat** chocolate mousse; **4** (matière) (pour coussin) foam rubber; **chaussettes en ~** stretch socks

(Composés) **~ carbonique** (fire) foam; **~ de nylon**® stretch nylon; **~ à raser** shaving foam

(Idiome) **pierre qui roule n'amasse pas ~** Prov a rolling stone gathers no moss Prov

mousseline /muslin/ *nf* **1** (de coton) muslin; (de soie) chiffon; **2** Culin **sauce ~** mousseline sauce

mousser /muse/ [1] *vi* [*champagne*] to bubble; [*bière*] to foam; [*détergent, savon*] to lather; **faire ~** to work [sth] up into a lather [*savon, détergent*]

(Idiome) **se faire ~**° to sing one's own praises

mousseux, **-euse** /musø, øz/
A *adj* **1** lit [*vin*] sparkling; [*bière*] fizzy; **2** fig [*dentelle*] frothy
B *nm inv* (vin) sparkling wine

mousson /musɔ̃/ *nf* monsoon

moussu, **~e** /musy/ *adj* mossy

moustache /mustaʃ/ *nf* (d'homme) moustache GB, mustache US; (d'animal) **~s** whiskers

(Composés) **~ en brosse** toothbrush moustache GB *ou* mustache US; **~ à la gauloise** walrus moustache GB *ou* mustache US; **~ en guidon de vélo**° handlebar moustache GB *ou* mustache US

moustachu, **~e** /mustaʃy/ *adj* with a moustache GB *ou* mustache US (épith, après n)

moustiquaire /mustikɛʀ/ *nf* mosquito net

moustique /mustik/ *nm* Zool mosquito

moût /mu/ *nm* (de raisin, pomme) must; (de houblon, d'orge) wort

moutarde /mutaʀd/ *adj inv*, *nf* mustard

(Idiome) **la ~ me monte au nez**°! I'm beginning to see red!

moutardier /mutaʀdje/ *nm* (récipient) mustard pot

mouton /mutɔ̃/
A *nm* **1** Zool sheep; **2** Culin mutton; **3** (peau) sheepskin; **4** (personne) pej sheep péj
B **moutons** *nmpl* **1** (nuages) small fleecy clouds; **2** (petites vagues) white horses GB, whitecaps; **3** (poussière) fluff **C**

(Composés) **~ à cinq pattes** rare bird; **~ de Panurge** pej sheep péj; **ce sont des ~s de Panurge** they follow one another like sheep

(Idiome) **revenons à nos ~s**° let's get back to the subject *ou* point

moutonnement /mutɔnmɑ̃/ *nm* **le ~ du ciel** the sky breaking up into fleecy clouds; **le ~ des collines** the rolling hills (*pl*)

moutonneux, -euse /mutɔnø, øz/ *adj* [*toison*] curly; [*mer*] covered with white horses (*après n*)

moutonnier, -ière /mutɔnje, ɛʀ/ *adj* ① [*élevage*] sheep (*épith*); ② *pej* [*comportement*] sheeplike péj

mouvant, ~e /muvɑ̃, ɑ̃t/ *adj* ① (qui s'enfonce) [*sol*] unstable; ② (qui bouge) [*groupe*] shifting; **reflets ~s** shimmering reflections; ③ (qui évolue) [*situation, opinion*] changing; **électorat ~** floating voters

mouvement /muvmɑ̃/ *nm* ① (geste) movement; **faire un ~** to move, to make a move; **tu es libre de tes ~s** you can come and go as you please; ▶ **faux**¹; ② (déplacement) movement, motion; **le ~ des vagues** the movement of the waves; **~ perpétuel** perpetual motion; **le ~ de personnel dans une entreprise** staff changes in a company; **~ de retraite** withdrawal; **accélérer le ~** to speed up; **ralentir le ~** to slow down; **se mettre en ~** [*troupe*] to start moving; [*machine*] to start up; **mettre qch en ~**, **imprimer un ~ à qch** to set sth in motion; ③ (animation) bustle; **il y a du ~ dans la rue** there's a lot of bustle in the street; **une rue pleine de ~** a busy street; **suivre le ~** *fig* to follow the crowd; ④ (élan) impulse, reaction; **mon premier ~ a été de me mettre en colère** my initial reaction *ou* my first impulse was to get angry; **dans un ~ de générosité** on a generous impulse; **un ~ de colère/pitié** a surge of anger/pity; **un ~ de panique** a panic reaction; **un bon ~** a kind *ou* nice gesture; **agir de son propre ~** to act of one's own accord; ⑤ (action collective) movement; **le ~ étudiant** the student protest movement; **~ surréaliste** surrealist movement; **~ de grève** strike; ⑥ (évolution) **le ~ des idées** the evolution of ideas; **être dans le ~** to move with the times; **un milieu en ~** a changing environment; ⑦ Écon, Fin (fluctuation) fluctuation; (échange) transaction; (tendance) trend; **le ~ du marché** market fluctuations; **~ de hausse** upward trend; **un ~ de reprise** a movement toward(s) recovery; **~s financiers** financial transactions; **~ de fonds** movement of funds; ⑧ (de poème, d'œuvre musicale) movement; ⑨ (d'horloge) movement; **~ d'horlogerie** clockwork mechanism

mouvementé, ~e /muvmɑ̃te/ *adj* ① [*vie, semaine*] eventful, hectic; [*réunion*] lively; [*récit, voyage*] eventful; **l'histoire ~e d'un pays** a country's turbulent history; ② [*relief, terrain*] rough

mouvoir /muvwaʀ/ [43] *fml*
Ⓐ *vtr* ① [*personne*] to move; [*énergie, mécanisme*] to drive [*machine*]; ② [*sentiment, désir*] to drive
Ⓑ **se mouvoir** *vpr* to move

moyen, -enne¹ /mwajɛ̃, ɛn/
Ⓐ *adj* ① (intermédiaire en dimension, poids) [*taille, épaisseur*] medium; [*ville, entreprise, légume*] medium-sized; [*fil*] of medium thickness; [*prix*] moderate; **de grandeur moyenne** medium-sized; **de moyenne portée** medium-range; **le cours ~ d'un fleuve** the middle reaches of a river; ② (passable) [*élève, résultat*] average (**en** in); ③ (dans une hiérarchie) [*cadre, revenu*] middle; [*échelon*] intermediate; **les salaires ~s** (personnes) people on middle incomes; ④ (ordinaire) average; **le Français/lecteur ~** the average Frenchman/reader; ⑤ (après calcul) [*taux, température*] average, mean; ⑥ (de compromis) [*solution, position*] middle-of-the-road

Ⓑ *nm* ① (façon de procéder) (usg) **(de faire** of doing), way **(de faire** of doing); **c'est un ~ comme un autre** it's as good a way as any; **par tous les ~s** by every possible means; **par n'importe quel ~** by hook or by crook°; **tous les ~s sont bons** any means will do; **tous les ~s leur sont bons** they'll stop at nothing; **employer les grands ~s** to resort to drastic measures; ② (d'action, expression, de production) means; (d'investigation, de paiement) method; **~ de communication** means of communication; ③ (possibilité) way; **il y a un ~ de faire** there's a way of doing; **il y a ~ de s'en sortir** there's a way out; **n'y avait-il pas ~ de faire autrement?** was there no other way to go about it?; **(il n'y a) pas ~ de lui faire comprendre qu'il a tort** it's impossible to make him realize he's wrong

Ⓒ **au moyen de** *loc prép* by means of, by using

Ⓓ **par le moyen de** *loc prép* by means of, through

Ⓔ **moyens** *nmpl* ① (financiers) means; **manquer de ~s** to lack the resources (**pour faire** to do); **faute de ~s** through lack of money; **vivre au-dessus de ses ~s** to live beyond one's

means; **je n'ai pas les ~s de faire, mes ~s ne me permettent pas de faire** I can't afford to do; **avoir de petits/grands ~s** not to be/to be very well off; ② (matériels) resources; **la ville a mis d'énormes ~s à notre disposition** the town put vast resources at our disposal; **je n'ai ni le temps ni les ~s de taper ce texte** I have neither the time nor the equipment to type this text; **donner à qn les ~s de faire** to give sb the means to do; **j'ai dû y aller par mes propres ~s** I had to make my own way there; **se débrouiller par ses propres ~s** to manage on one's own; ③ (intellectuels) ability; **il a de petits ~s** he has limited ability; **être en possession de tous ses ~s** to be at the height of one's powers; **perdre ses ~s** to go to pieces

⬚ **Composés** **~ de locomotion** *or* **transport** means of transport GB *ou* transportation US; **~ métrage** Cin medium-length film; **Moyen Âge** Middle Ages (*pl*); **le bas/haut Moyen Âge** the late/early Middle Ages; **Moyen Empire** Middle Kingdom

moyenâgeux, -euse /mwajɛnaʒø, øz/ *adj* ① [*château*] medieval; ② *pej* [*idée*] antiquated

moyen-courrier, *pl* **~s** /mwajɛ̃kuʀje/ *nm* medium-haul airliner

moyennant /mwajɛnɑ̃/ *prép* for [*somme, rançon*]; in return for [*faveur*]; with [*effort, modification*]; **~ finances** for a fee *ou* a consideration; **~ quoi** (en conséquence de quoi) in view of which; (en échange de quoi) in return for which

moyenne² /mwajɛn/
Ⓐ *adj f* ▶ **moyen**
Ⓑ *nf* ① (norme) average; **au-dessous/au-dessus de la ~** below/above average; **être dans la ~** to be average; ② Scol (moitié de la note maximale) half marks GB, 50%; **j'ai eu tout juste la ~** (à un examen) I barely passed; (à un devoir) I just got half marks GB, I just got 50%; ③ (après calcul) average; **la ~ d'âge** the average age; **en ~** on average; ④ (vitesse) average speed

moyennement /mwajɛnmɑ̃/ *adv* [*intelligent, riche, cultivé*] moderately; [*réussir, comprendre*] moderately well; [*aimer, apprécier*] to a certain extent

Moyen-Orient /mwajɛnɔʀjɑ̃/ ▶ p. 504 *nprm* Middle East

moyeu, *pl* **~x** /mwajø/ *nm* hub

MST /ɛmɛste/ *nf: abbr* ▶ **maladie**

mû ▶ **mouvoir**

mucosité /mykozite/ *nf* mucus ₵

mucoviscidose /mykovisidoz/ ▶ p. 195 *nf* cystic fibrosis

mucus /mykys/ *nm inv* mucus

mue¹ ▶ **mouvoir**

mue² /my/ *nf* ① Zool (renouvellement) (d'insecte) metamorphosis; (de serpent, lézard) sloughing of the skin; (d'oiseau, de mammifère) moulting^{GB}; (de cerf) casting; ② Zool (dépouille) (d'insecte, de serpent) slough, sloughed skin; ③ (de voix) breaking GB *ou* changing US of voice; ④ (transformation) liter transformation

muer /mɥe/ [1]
Ⓐ *vtr* liter to transform (**en** into)
Ⓑ *vi* ① Zool [*insecte*] to metamorphose; [*serpent, lézard*] to slough its skin; [*oiseau, mammifère*] to moult^{GB}; [*cerf*] to cast its antlers; ② **sa voix mue, il mue** his voice is breaking GB *ou* changing US
Ⓒ **se muer** *vpr* (être transformé) to be transformed (**en** into); (activement) to transform oneself (**en** into)

muet, -ette /mɥɛ, ɛt/
Ⓐ *adj* ① [*personne*] gén dumb; (momentanément) speechless; **sous le choc, elle resta muette** the shock left her speechless; **~ de** (d'admiration, de terreur) speechless with; **rester ~ de** to be struck dumb with; ② (qui refuse de parler) [*témoin, presse, rapport*] silent (**sur, à propos de** on); **rester ~** to remain silent; ③ (inexprimé) [*reproche, douleur, cloche*] silent; [*voyelle, consonne*] mute, silent; ④ Cin [*cinéma, film*] silent; [*rôle*] non-speaking (*épith*); ⑤ (sans inscription) [*carte de géographie, page*] blank; [*menu*] unpriced
Ⓑ *nm,f* Méd mute; **les ~s** the dumb (+ *v pl*)
Ⓒ *nm* Cin **le ~** the silent screen

muette² /mɥɛt/ *nf* Hist **la grande ~** the army

mufle /myfl/
Ⓐ *adj* boorish, loutish
Ⓑ *nm* ① Zool (museau) (de ruminant) muffle; (de carnassier) muzzle; ② (malotru) boor, lout

muflerie /myfləʀi/ *nf* boorishness

mugir /myʒiʀ/ [3] vi **1** [vache] to low; [taureau, bœuf] to bellow; **2** [vent] to howl; [sirène] to wail; [mer, torrent] to roar

mugissement /myʒismɑ̃/ nm **1** (de vache) lowing **C**; (de taureau) bellowing **C**; **pousser des ~s** [vache] to moo; **2** (de vent) howling **C**; (de sirène) wailing **C**; (de vagues) roar **C**

muguet /mygɛ/ nm (fleur) lily of the valley

mulâtre /mylatʀ/ adj, nm mulatto

mulâtresse /mylatʀɛs/ nf mulatto

mule /myl/ nf **1** Zool female mule; **2** (pantoufle) mule; **3** (passeur de drogue) mule; **~ aveugle** unwitting drugs carrier

mulet /mylɛ/ nm **1** (équidé) (male) mule; **2** (poisson) grey mullet GB, mullet US; **3** Sport back-up car

muletier, -ière /myltje, ɛʀ/
A adj sentier or chemin **~** mule track
B ▸ p. 372 nm muleteer, mule skinner⊕ US

mulot /mylo/ nm fieldmouse

multi /mylti/ préf multi; **~colore** multicolouredᴳᴮ; **~couche** multi-layered; **~latéral** multilateral; **~media** multimedia; **~programmation** multiple programming

multicarte /myltikaʀt/ adj inv **représentant ~** (sales) representative for several firms

multifonction /myltifɔ̃ksjɔ̃/ adj inv gén multipurpose; Ordinat multifunction

multiforme /myltifɔʀm/ adj [aspect] multiform; [vie, danger] many-sided; [réalité] multifaceted

multipartite /myltipaʀtit/ adj **1** [réunion, traité] multipartite; **2** [élections] multi-party (épith)

multiple /myltipl/
A adj **1** (nombreux) [raisons, occasions] numerous, many; [naissances] multiple; **après de ~s spéculations/tergiversations** after much speculation/hesitation; **à usages ~s** multipurpose; **à choix ~** multiple-choice (épith); **2** (divers) [buts, causes, facettes] many, various; **3** Bot, Math, Phys multiple
B nm multiple

multiplexe /myltiplɛks/ nm multiplex

multipliable /myltiplijabl/ adj multiplicable

multiplicateur, -trice /myltiplikatœʀ, tʀis/
A adj multiplying
B nm multiplier

multiplication /myltiplikasjɔ̃/ nf **1** (augmentation) **~ de** increase in the number of; **2** Math (processus) multiplication **C**; (opération) multiplication **C**; **apprendre à faire des ~s** to learn to do multiplication; **il fait des ~s à longueur de journée** he does multiplications all day long; **faire une erreur de ~** to make a mistake in the multiplication; **3** Biol, Bot multiplication

multiplicité /myltiplisite/ nf multiplicity

multiplier /myltiplije/ [2]
A vtr **1** Math to multiply [chiffre] (**par** by); **2** (augmenter) to increase [risques, fortune]; to increase the number of [trains, accidents]; **~ les bénéfices par cinq/par cent** to increase profits fivefold/a hundredfold; **~ les risques d'accident par trois/dix** to make the risk of accident three/ten times more likely; **3** (faire en grand nombre) **~ les excuses** to give endless excuses; **~ les visites** to make endless visits
B se multiplier vpr **1** (augmenter) [succursales, villas] to grow in number; [incidents, arrestations] to be on the increase; [difficultés, obstacles] to increase; [contacts, disputes] to become more frequent; **2** (se reproduire) [animaux, microbes] to multiply

multiprise /myltipʀiz/ adj **pince ~** adjustable pliers (pl)

multipropriété /myltipʀɔpʀijete/ nf time-sharing; **acheter une villa en ~** to buy a time-share in a villa

multirisque /myltiʀisk/ adj **assurance ~** comprehensive insurance

multisalle /myltisal/ adj inv **cinéma ~** cinema complex GB, multiplex US

multitude /myltityd/ nf **1** (grand nombre) **une ~ de** (d'objets, de touristes) a mass of; (d'idées, de raisons) a lot of, many; **2** (foule de gens) multitude, throng

municipal, ~e, mpl **-aux** /mynisipal, o/ adj Admin [conseil, conseiller] (de petite ville) local, town (épith); (de grande ville) city (épith); [impôt, élections, arrêté] local; [parc, piscine, bibliothèque] municipal

municipales /mynisipal/ nfpl local elections

municipalité /mynisipalite/ nf **1** (ville) municipality; **2** (conseil) (de petite ville) town council; (de grande ville) city council

munificent, ~e /mynifisɑ̃, ɑ̃t/ adj munificent

munir /myniʀ/ [3]
A vtr **1** to provide [personne] (**de** with); **2** (équiper) **~ un bâtiment d'un escalier de secours** to put a fire escape on a building; **muni de** fitted with
B se munir vpr se **~ de** (apporter) to bring [argent, arme]; (emporter) to take; **manifestants munis de barres de fer** demonstrators carrying iron bars; **se ~ de patience** to summon up one's patience

munitions /mynisjɔ̃/ nfpl ammunition **C**, munitions

muqueuse /mykøz/ nf mucous membrane

mur /myʀ/
A nm wall; **rester** or **être entre quatre ~s** to be cooped up; **c'est à se taper⊕** or **cogner⊕ la tête contre les ~s** you feel like banging your head against the wall⊕; **un ~ de silence** a wall of silence; **parler à un ~** to be talking to a brick wall; **faire du ~** (au tennis) to practiseᴳᴮ hitting a ball against the wall; **faire les pieds au ~** lit to do a handstand against the wall; fig to tie oneself up in knots
B murs nmpl (local) premises; (d'entreprise) premises; (d'ambassade, de palais) confines; **être dans ses ~s** to own one's own house

(Composés) **~ d'appui** (de soutènement) retaining wall; (parapet) parapet; **~ portant** or **porteur** load-bearing wall; **~ du son** sound barrier; **franchir le ~ du son** to break the sound barrier; **~ de soutènement** retaining wall; **Mur des lamentations** Wailing Wall

(Idiomes) **faire le ~** (s'échapper) to go over the wall; (au football) to make a wall; **mettre qn au pied du ~** to call sb's bluff; **être au pied du ~** to be up against the wall; **aller dans le ~** to be heading for disaster

mûr, ~e¹ /myʀ/ adj **1** [fruit, blé] ripe; **2** (intellectuellement) mature; **être ~ pour son âge** to be mature for one's age; **l'âge ~** middle age; **après ~e réflexion** after careful consideration; **3** (psychologiquement) ready (**pour qch** for sth; **pour faire** to do); **il est ~ pour des aveux** he's ready to confess; **4** [affaire, situation] at a decisive stage (jamais épith); **5** [abcès, bouton] **être ~** to have come to a head

(Idiomes) **en voir des vertes et des pas ~es⊕** to go through a lot ou through some hard times; **en dire des vertes et des pas ~es⊕** (histoires osées) to tell some dirty jokes; (méchancetés) to say a lot of nasty things (**sur, au sujet de** about)

muraille /myʀaj/ nf lit, fig great wall; **la Grande Muraille de Chine** the Great Wall of China

mural, ~e, mpl **-aux** /myʀal, o/ adj [panneau, revêtement, carte] wall (épith); [plante] climbing; [four] wall-mounted; **peinture ~e** Art mural

mûre² /myʀ/
A adj f ▸ **mûr**
B nf blackberry

mûrement /myʀmɑ̃/ adv **~ réfléchi** carefully thought through

murène /myʀɛn/ nf moray eel

murer /myʀe/ [1]
A vtr to build a wall around [champ]; to brick up [porte]; to block off [pièce]; to wall [sb] up [personne]
B se murer vpr se **~ chez soi** to shut oneself away; **se ~ dans son obstination** to dig one's heels in; **se ~ dans la solitude** to retreat into isolation

muret /myʀɛ/ nm, **murette** /myʀɛt/ nf low wall

mûrier /myʀje/ nm mulberry tree

mûrir /myʀiʀ/ [3]
A vtr to ripen [fruit]; to mature [personne]; to develop [projet]
B vi [fruit] to ripen; **faire ~ des bananes** to ripen bananas; [personne, talent] to mature; [projet, idée] to evolve, to mature; [passion] to develop; [abcès, bouton] to come to a head

murmure /myʀmyʀ/ nm **1** (chuchotement) murmur; **~ d'indignation** murmur of protest; **2** (plainte sourde) **~s** mutterings; **3** (de vent) whisper; (de source) murmur, babbling; **4** (rumeur) rumourᴳᴮ

murmurer /myʀmyʀe/ [1]
A vtr **1** (chuchoter) to murmur; **~ qch à qn/à l'oreille de qn** to murmur sth to sb/into sb's ear; **2** (dire) to say; **on**

Les instruments de musique

Les instruments

■ *L'anglais emploie l'article défini devant les noms d'instruments de musique, même avec le verbe* to play *(jouer).*

apprendre le piano
= to learn the piano

étudier le piano
= to study the piano

jouer du piano
= to play the piano

Les morceaux de musique

un arrangement pour piano
= an arrangement for piano *ou* a piano arrangement

une sonate pour violon
= a violin sonata

un concerto pour piano et orchestre
= a concerto for piano and orchestra

la partie pour piano
= the piano part

Les musiciens

■ *Le suffixe anglais* -ist *correspond au suffixe français* -iste.

un violoniste	*un pianiste*
= a violinist	= a pianist

■ *Dans les autres cas; on peut toujours dire* a X player.

un corniste
= a horn player

■ *De même,* an oboe player, a piccolo player, *etc.*

■ *En anglais comme en français, le nom de l'instrument est parfois utilisé pour parler des musiciens.*

les trombones
= the trombones

De avec les noms d'instruments de musique

un cours de violon	*un professeur de violon*
= a violin class	= a violin teacher
une leçon de violon	*un solo de violon*
= a violin lesson	= a violin solo

---

murmure qu'il est riche he is rumoured^{GB} to be rich **B** *vi* **1** (chuchoter) [*personne*] [*vent*] to whisper; [*ruisseau*] to babble; **2** (se plaindre) to mutter; **obéir sans ~** to obey without a murmur; **3** (faire courir des bruits) to spread rumours^{GB}; **on murmure à leur sujet** there are rumours^{GB} about them

musaraigne /myzaʀɛɲ/ *nf* shrew

musarder /myzaʀde/ [1] *vi* to wander around

musc /mysk/ *nm* musk

muscade /myskad/ *nf* Bot, Culin nutmeg; **noix ~** nutmeg

muscardin /myskaʀdɛ̃/ *nm* (common) dormouse

muscle /myskl/ *nm* muscle

musclé, ~e /myskle/ *adj* **1** lit muscular; **2** fig (vigoureux) [*style*] sinewy; [*musique, discours*] powerful; [*réaction*] strong; (dur) [*discours, intervention, match*] tough; **3** Écon [*entreprise, économie*] competitive

muscler /myskle/ [1]
A *vtr* **1** lit **~ les bras/jambes** to develop the arm/leg muscles; **2** fig to strengthen; **~ l'industrie** to make industry more competitive
B se muscler *vpr* **1** [*personne*] to develop one's muscles; **2** [*entreprise*] to become more competitive

musculaire /myskylɛʀ/ *adj* [*tissu, fibre*] muscle (*épith*); [*force, faiblesse*] muscular

musculation /myskylasjɔ̃/ *nf* **(exercices de) ~** Sport bodybuilding; (après une maladie) exercises to strengthen the muscles; **salle de ~** weights room

musculature /myskylatyʀ/ *nf* musculature; **avoir une ~ bien développée** to have well developed muscles

musculeux, -euse /myskylø, øz/ *adj* **1** [*bras, personne*] muscular; **2** Anat [*tissu*] muscle (*épith*)

muse /myz/ *nf* **1** (divinité) Muse; **les neuf ~s** the Muses; **taquiner la ~** hum to dabble in verse; **2** (inspiration) muse

museau, *pl* **~x** /myzo/ *nm* **1** (de chien, bovin, d'ovin) muzzle; (de porc) snout; (de renard) nose; **2** [○](visage) face

musée /myze/ *nm* gén museum; (d'art) art gallery GB, art museum US; **leur maison, c'est le ~ des horreurs**[○] hum everything in their house is indescribably ugly; **une ville ~** a city of great historical and artistic importance

⸺ **Composé** ⸺ **~ de cire** waxworks, wax museum

museler /myzəle/ [19] *vtr* lit, fig to muzzle

muselière /myzəljɛʀ/ *nf* muzzle

muser† /myze/ [1] *vi* to wander around

musette¹ /myzɛt/ *nm* **1** Mus (style) accordion music; **2** (bal) dance (*where accordion music is played*)

musette² /myzɛt/ *nf* **1** (sac) (de soldat) haversack; (d'ouvrier) lunchbag; **2** Zool common shrew

muséum /myzeɔm/ *nm* **~ (d'histoire naturelle)** natural history museum

musical, ~e, *mpl* **-aux** /myzikal, o/ *adj* [*événement*] musical; [*revue, critique*] music (*épith*); [*choix*] of music (*épith, après n*)

musicalité /myzikalite/ *nf* musicality

music-hall, *pl* **~s** *nm* /myzikol/ music hall; **artiste/spectacle de ~** variety artist/show

musicien, -ienne /myzisjɛ̃, ɛn/
A *adj* musical
B ▸ p. 389 *nm,f* musician

musicographie /myzikɔgʀafi/ *nf* musicography

musicologie /myzikɔlɔʒi/ *nf* musicology

musique /myzik/ *nf* **1** (art, notes) music; **travailler en ~** to work with music in the background; **mettre en ~** to set [sth] to music; **faire de la ~** (savoir jouer) to play an instrument; **2** (œuvre) piece of music; **une ~ pour piano** a piece of piano music; **une ~ de film** a film score; **sur une ~ de** with music by; **3** (orchestre) band

⸺ **Idiomes** ⸺ **c'est toujours la même ~**[○] it's always the same old refrain; **connaître la ~**[○] to know the score[○]; **je ne peux pas aller plus vite que la ~**[○] I can't go any faster than I'm already going; **être réglé comme du papier à ~**[○] [*personne*] to be as regular as clockwork; [*congrès, projet*] to go very smoothly

musqué, ~e /myske/ *adj* **1** [*parfum*] musky; [*cheveux*] musk-scented; **2** Zool **bœuf ~** musk ox; **rat ~** muskrat

musulman, ~e /myzylmɑ̃, an/ *adj, nm,f* Muslim

mutabilité /mytabilite/ *nf* mutability

mutant, ~e /mytɑ̃, ɑ̃t/ *adj, nm,f* Biol, fig mutant

mutation /mytasjɔ̃/ *nf* **1** (transfert) transfer; **2** (transformation) transformation; **en pleine ~** undergoing radical transformation; **3** Biol, Ling, Mus mutation

⸺ **Composé** ⸺ **~ génétique** Biol genetic mutation

muter /myte/ [1]
A *vtr* to transfer [*fonctionnaire*]
B *vi* Biol to mutate

mutilation /mytilasjɔ̃/ *nf* (d'arbre, de membre, texte) mutilation

⸺ **Composé** ⸺ **~ volontaire** self-inflicted injury

m

mutilé, **~e** /mytile/ *nm,f* disabled person

(Composés) **~ de guerre** disabled war veteran; **~ du travail** *person disabled through an accident at work*

mutiler /mytile/ [1]

A *vtr* to mutilate

B **se mutiler** *vpr* to inflict an injury on oneself

mutin, **~e** /mytɛ̃, in/

A *adj* mischievous

B *nm* (soldat, marin) mutineer; (prisonnier) rioter

mutiné, **~e** /mytine/ *nm,f* (soldat, marin) mutineer; (prisonnier) rioter

mutiner: **se mutiner** /mytine/ [1] *vpr* [*marins, soldats*] to mutiny; [*prisonniers*] to riot; **équipage mutiné** mutinous crew

mutinerie /mytinʀi/ *nf* (de marins, soldats) mutiny; (de prisonniers) riot

mutisme /mytism/ *nm* (silence) silence

mutité /mytite/ *nf* muteness, dumbness

mutualiste /mytɥalist/

A *adj* mutualist

B *nmf* member of a mutual insurance company

mutuel, **-elle**[1] /mytɥɛl/ *adj* mutual

mutuelle[2] /mytɥɛl/ *nf* mutual insurance company

mutuellement /mytɥɛlmɑ̃/ *adv* mutually; **s'aider ~** to help each other

mycologie /mikɔlɔʒi/ *nf* mycology

myocarde /mjɔkaʀd/ *nm* myocardium

myopathe /mjɔpat/ *nmf* myopathy patient

myopathie /mjɔpati/ ▸ p. 195 *nf* myopathy

myope /mjɔp/ *adj* short-sighted, myopic *spéc*

(Idiome) **~ comme une taupe**○ as blind as a bat

myopie /mjɔpi/ *nf* lit, fig short-sightedness

myosotis /mjɔzɔtis/ *nm inv* forget-me-not

myriade /miʀjad/ *nf* liter myriad (**de** of)

myrmidon /miʀmidɔ̃/ *nm* pipsqueak○

myrrhe /miʀ/ *nf* myrrh

myrte /miʀt/ *nm* myrtle

myrtille /miʀtij/ *nf* bilberry, blueberry

mystère /mistɛʀ/ *nm* **1** (énigme) mystery; **auteur ~** mysterious author; **2** (fait de cacher) secrecy; **entourer qch de ~** to surround sth in secrecy; **je n'en fais pas (un) ~** I make no secret of it; **il n'est un ~ pour personne que** it's an open secret that; **3** Relig mystery; Littérat Mystery play; **4** (rite antique) rite

mystérieusement /misteʀjøzmɑ̃/ *adv* mysteriously

mystérieux, **-ieuse** /misteʀjø, øz/ *adj* mysterious; **faire le ~** to assume an air of mystery

mysticisme /mistisism/ *nm* mysticism

mystificateur, **-trice** /mistifikatœʀ, tʀis/

A *adj* [*personne*] who likes playing tricks; [*lettre, coup de fil*] hoax (*épith*); [*attitude*] intended to dupe (*après n*); **dans un esprit ~** for a hoax

B *nm,f* hoaxer

mystification /mistifikasjɔ̃/ *nf* **1** (canular) hoax; **2** (illusion) myth

mystifier /mistifje/ [2] *vtr* to hoodwink, to fool

mystique /mistik/

A *adj* mystical

B *nmf* mystic

C *nf* **1** (doctrine) mysticism; **2** (mystère) mystique; **3** (passion) blind belief (**de** in); **avoir la ~ révolutionnaire** to have a blind belief in revolution

mythe /mit/ *nm* gén myth; **le ~ d'Orphée** the myth of Orpheus; **le ~ de l'alcool qui fortifie** the myth that alcohol fortifies

mythique /mitik/ *adj* mythical

mythologie /mitɔlɔʒi/ *nf* mythology

mythologique /mitɔlɔʒik/ *adj* mythological

mythomane /mitɔman/ *adj, nmf* mythomaniac

mythomanie /mitɔmani/ *nf* mythomania

m

n, N /ɛn/
A *nm inv* **1** n, N; **2** **n°** (*written abbr* = **numéro**) no
B N *nf* (*abbr* = **nationale**) **sur la N7** on the N7

n' ▸ **ne**

nabab /nabab/ *nm* **1** (homme riche) mogul; **2** (en Inde) nabob

nabot, ~e /nabo, ɔt/ *nm,f* offensive dwarf injur

nacelle /nasɛl/ *nf* **1** (de ballon) gondola; **2** (de landau) carrycot GB, carrier US; **3** (d'ouvrier) cradle

nacre /nakʀ/ *nf* mother-of-pearl; **de ~** [teint, peau] pearly

nacré, ~e /nakʀe/ *adj* pearly

nage /naʒ/ *nf* **1** (natation) swimming; **200 mètres quatre ~s** 200 metres^GB medley; **regagner la rive à la ~** to swim back to shore; **2** (sueur) **être en ~** to be in a sweat; **3** Naut rowing; **4** Culin **à la ~** à la nage (*après n*) (*cooked in an aromatic court-bouillon*)

(Composés) **~ sur le dos** backstroke; **~ libre** freestyle

nageoire /naʒwaʀ/ *nf* **1** (de poisson) fin; **2** (de phoque, pingouin) flipper

nager /naʒe/ [13]
A *vtr* to swim; **~ le cent mètres** to swim the hundred metres^GB; **~ le crawl** to do the crawl
B *vi* **1** lit to swim; **les tomates nagent dans l'huile** the tomatoes are swimming in oil; **2** fig **~ dans le bonheur** to bask in contentment; **elle nage dans sa robe** her dress is far too big for her; **3** ○(mal comprendre) to be absolutely lost; **4** Naut to row

(Idiome) **~ entre deux eaux** to run with the hare and hunt with the hounds

nageur, -euse /naʒœʀ, øz/ *nm,f* **1** Sport swimmer; **2** (rameur) oarsman/oarswoman

naguère /nagɛʀ/ *adv* **1** (récemment) quite recently; **2** (autrefois) formerly

naïade /najad/ *nf* naiad

naïf, naïve /naif, iv/
A *adj* **1** [personne] (sans artifice) artless; (crédule) naïve; [réponse] naïve; **2** Art naïve
B *nm,f* innocent, gullible fool péj

nain, ~e /nɛ̃, nɛn/
A *adj* [arbre, étoile] dwarf (épith); [lapin, chien] miniature
B *nm,f* (personne) dwarf

(Composé) **le ~ jaune** Jeux pope Joan

naissance /nɛsɑ̃s/ *nf* **1** (d'enfant) birth; **de ~** [italien] by birth; [sourd] from birth; **c'est de ~ chez lui**○ he was born like that; **donner ~ à** to give birth to; **à la ~** at birth; **à ma/ta** when I was/you were born; **16% des ~s** 16% of births; **2** (d'œuvre, de courant, sentiment) birth; (de produit) first appearance; (de rumeur) start; **la ~ du jour** liter daybreak; **le mouvement a pris ~ dans le milieu ouvrier** the movement sprang up in the working classes; **l'idée a donné ~ à de multiples œuvres** the idea gave rise to many works; **3** (base) **à la ~ du cou** at the base of the neck

naissant, ~e /nɛsɑ̃, ɑ̃t/ *adj* [barbe, art, pays] new

naître /nɛtʀ/ [74] *vi* **1** [personne, animal] to be born; **elle est née le 5 juin 92** she was born on 5 June 92; **le bébé doit ~ à la fin du mois** the baby is due at the end of the month; **elle vient de ~** she's only just been born; **les bébés qui viennent de ~** newborn babies; **l'enfant à ~** the unborn baby *ou* child; **~ sourd** to be born deaf; **2** (commencer d'exister) [mouvement, projet] to be born; [entreprise] to come into existence; [amour, amitié] to spring up; [jour] to break; [soupçon] to arise; **~ de** to arise out of [désir]; **faire ~**

to give rise to [espoir, conflit]; **voir ~** to see the birth of [journal]; **3** liter **~ à** to awaken to [art, religion]

naïve ▸ **naïf**

naïvement /naivmɑ̃/ *adv* gén naively; (sans artifice) artlessly

naïveté /naivte/ *nf* gén naivety; (naturel) artlessness; **avoir la ~ de croire que...** to be naïve enough to believe that...

naja /naʒa/ *nm* cobra

nanisme /nanism/ *nm* dwarfism, nanism spéc

nanti, ~e /nɑ̃ti/
A *adj* (riche) well-off
B **nantis** *nmpl* **les ~s** péj the well-off (+ v pl)

nantir /nɑ̃tiʀ/ [3]
A *vtr* (pourvoir) liter **~ qn de** to provide sb with [objet]; to award [sth] to sb [titre]
B **se nantir** *vpr* (se munir de) liter **se ~ de** to provide oneself with [certificat, autorisation]; to equip oneself with [parapluie]

naphtaline /naftalin/ *nf* mothballs (pl); **boule de ~** mothball

napoléonien, -ienne /napɔleɔnjɛ̃, ɛn/ *adj* Napoleonic

nappe /nap/ *nf* **1** (de table) tablecloth; **2** (couche) (de pétrole, gaz, d'huile) layer; (d'eau) sheet; Culin layer; **~ de mazout** oil slick; **~ de feu** sheet of flames; **~ de brouillard** (en mer) fog bank; (sur terre) layer of fog

napper /nape/ [1] *vtr* Culin (avec de la sauce, du chocolat) to coat (de with); (avec de la confiture) to glaze

napperon /napʀɔ̃/ *nm* (pour couvert) place mat; (pour vase, lampe) mat

narcisse /naʀsis/ *nm* **1** (fleur) narcissus; **2** (vaniteux) péj narcissist

narcissisme /naʀsisism/ *nm* narcissism

narco(-) /naʀko/ *préf* drug; **~-dollars** drug money

narcotique /naʀkɔtik/ *adj*, *nm* narcotic

narcotouriste /naʀkoturist/ *nmf* narcotourist

narghilé /naʀgile/ *nm* hookah

narguer /naʀge/ [1] *vtr* to taunt [personne]; to flout [autorité]

narguilé /naʀgile/ *nm* hookah

narine /naʀin/ *nf* ▸ p. 136 nostril

narquois, ~e /naʀkwa, az/ *adj* mocking

narquoisement /naʀkwazmɑ̃/ *adv* mockingly

narrateur, -trice /naʀatœʀ, tʀis/ *nm,f* narrator

narratif, -ive /naʀatif, iv/ *adj* narrative

narration /naʀasjɔ̃/ *nf* narration

narrer /naʀe/ [1] *vtr* liter to relate

nasal, ~e, mpl -aux /nazal, o/ *adj* [cloison] nasal; [hémorragie, goutte] nose; [son, voix] nasal

naseau, pl ~x /nazo/ *nm* nostril

nasillard, ~e /nazijaʀ, aʀd/ *adj* [voix] nasal; [instrument] tinny

nasillement /nazijmɑ̃/ *nm* **1** (de personne) nasal twang; **2** (d'instrument) tinny sound; **3** (de canard) quack

nasiller /nazije/ [1] *vi* **1** [personne] to speak with a nasal voice; **2** [canard] to quack

nasse /nas/ *nf* **1** (pour la pêche) keepnet; **2** fig net

natal, ~e, mpl ~s /natal/ *adj* [pays, langue] native

nataliste /natalist/ *adj* [politique] pro-birth (épith)

natalité /natalite/ *nf* **(taux de) ~** birthrate

Les nationalités

■ *Les adjectifs ethniques comme* anglais *peuvent aussi qualifier des langues (par ex.* un mot anglais ▸ **p. 336)** *et des choses (par ex.* la cuisine anglaise ▸ **p. 230**).

■ *En anglais, les noms et les adjectifs ethniques se forment de plusieurs manières. On peut distinguer cinq groupes. Noter que l'anglais emploie la majuscule dans tous les cas, pour l'adjectif et pour le nom.*

1er groupe: le nom et l'adjectif ont la même forme. Le nom pluriel prend un s.

un Allemand
= a German *ou* (s'il est nécessaire de distinguer) a German man

une Allemande
= a German *ou* a German woman

les Allemands (*en général*)
= the Germans *ou* Germans *ou* German people

c'est un Allemand
= he's German *ou* he's a German

il est allemand
= he's German

■ *Dans ce groupe:* American, Angolan, Belgian, Brazilian, Chilean, Cypriot, Czech, Egyptian, Greek, Indian, Iranian, Italian, Jamaican, Mexican, Moroccan, Norwegian, Pakistani, Russian, Thai *etc.*

2e groupe: le nom s'obtient en ajoutant le mot man *ou* woman *à l'adjectif.*

un Japonais
= a Japanese man

une Japonaise
= a Japanese woman

les Japonais (*en général*)
= the Japanese* *ou* Japanese people

c'est un Japonais
= he's Japanese

il est japonais
= he's Japanese

* Japanese *est un adjectif utilisé comme nom: il prend toujours l'article défini et ne prend jamais de* s.

■ *Dans ce groupe:* Burmese, Chinese, Congolese, Lebanese, Portuguese, Sudanese, Vietnamese *etc.*

3e groupe: le nom s'obtient en ajoutant le suffixe -man *ou* -woman *à l'adjectif.*

un Anglais
= an Englishman

une Anglaise
= an Englishwoman

les Anglais (*en général*)
= the English† *ou* English people

c'est un Anglais
= he's English *ou* he's an Englishman

il est anglais
= he's English

† English *est un adjectif utilisé comme nom: il prend toujours l'article défini et ne prend jamais de* s.

■ *Dans ce groupe:* French, Dutch, Irish, Welsh *etc.*

4e groupe: le nom et l'adjectif sont des mots différents. Le nom pluriel prend un s.

un Danois
= a Dane *ou* a Danish man

une Danoise
= a Dane *ou* a Danish woman

les Danois (*en général*)
= Danes *ou* the Danes *ou* Danish people

c'est un Danois
= he's Danish *ou* he's a Dane

il est danois
= he's Danish

■ *Dans ce groupe:* Finn (*nom*): Finnish (*adjectif*); Icelander: Icelandic; Pole: Polish; Scot: Scottish; Spaniard: Spanish; Swede: Swedish; Turk: Turkish *etc.*

5e groupe: quelques cas particuliers, qui n'ont pas d'adjectif, par ex. la Nouvelle-Zélande:

un Néo-Zélandais
= a New Zealander

une Néo-Zélandaise
= a New Zealander

les Néo-Zélandais (*en général*)
= New Zealanders

c'est un Néo-Zélandais
= he's a New Zealander

il est néo-zélandais
= he's a New Zealander

■ *Quelques autres expressions permettant de parler de la nationalité de quelqu'un en anglais:*

il est né en Angleterre
= he was born in England

il vient d'Angleterre
= he comes from England

il est d'origine anglaise
= he's of English extraction

il est citoyen britannique
= he's a British citizen

il est citoyen néo-zélandais
= he's a New Zealand citizen

c'est un ressortissant britannique
= he's a British national

---

natation /natasjɔ̃/ ▸ p. 327 *nf* swimming
natif, -ive /natif, iv/ *adj* (originaire) ~ **de** native of
nation /nasjɔ̃/ *nf* nation
(Composé) **les Nations unies** the United Nations
national, ~e¹, *mpl* **-aux** /nasjɔnal, o/
A *adj* national
B nationaux *nmpl* nationals; **nationaux autrichiens/danois** Austrian/Danish nationals
nationale² /nasjɔnal/ *nf* (route) trunk road GB, ≈ A road GB, highway US
nationalement /nasjɔnalmɑ̃/ *adv* nationally
nationalisation /nasjɔnalizasjɔ̃/ *nf* nationalization
nationaliser /nasjɔnalize/ [1] *vtr* to nationalize
nationalisme /nasjɔnalism/ *nm* nationalism

nationalité /nasjɔnalite/ *nf* nationality
national-socialisme /nasjɔnalsɔsjalism/ *nm* National Socialism
nativité /nativite/ *nf* **1** Relig nativity; **2** Art Nativity scene
natte /nat/ *nf* **1** (tresse) plait; **2** (sur le sol) mat
natter /nate/ [1] *vtr* to plait
naturalisation /natyralizasjɔ̃/ *nf* **1** Jur naturalization; **2** (acclimatation) naturalization; **3** (taxidermie) stuffing
naturalisé, ~e /natyralize/ *adj* Jur naturalized
naturaliser /natyralize/ [1] *vtr* **1** Jur to naturalize [étranger]; **elle est naturalisée française** she's acquired French nationality; **2** (adopter) to assimilate [mot, coutume]; **3** (acclimater) to naturalize [espèce]; **4** (empailler) to stuff [animal]

naturaliste /natyʀalist/
A *adj* naturalist
B *nmf* [1] Art, Littérat, Philos naturalist; [2] ▸ p. 372 (taxidermiste) taxidermist

nature /natyʀ/
A *adj inv* [1] (sans additif) [*yaourt, fromage blanc*] natural; [*omelette*] plain; [*thé*] black; **à consommer avec du sucre ou ~** to be eaten with sugar or on its own; [2] ○(spontané) [*personne*] natural
B *nf* [1] (forces nous gouvernant) nature; **laisser faire la ~** to let nature take its course; **la ~ fait bien les choses** the ways of nature are wonderful; [2] (environnement) nature; **une merveille de la ~** a wonder of nature; **protection de la ~** protection of the environment; **une ~ hostile** a hostile environment; **en pleine ~** in the heart of the countryside; **lâcher qn dans la ~** (en pleine campagne) to leave sb in the middle of nowhere; fig to let sb loose; [3] (caractère) nature; **une ~ généreuse** a generous nature; **de ~ à faire** likely to do; **il est anxieux de ~, il est d'une ~ anxieuse** he's nervous by nature; **avoir une ~ fragile/robuste** to have a delicate/strong constitution; **de même ~** of the same nature; **des offres de toute ~** offers of all kinds; [4] (réalité) **peindre d'après ~** to paint from life; **plus petit/plus vrai que ~** smaller/more real than life; [5] (objets réels) **en ~** [*payer*] in kind; **avantages en ~** fringe benefits
(Composé) **~ morte** still life; ▸ **petit**
(Idiome) **partir** *or* **disparaître dans la ~**○ to vanish into thin air

naturel, -elle /natyʀɛl/
A *adj* natural
B *nm* [1] (caractère) nature; **être d'un ~ gai** to be naturally cheerful; [2] (spontanéité) **il manque de ~** he's not very natural; **avec le plus grand ~** in the most natural way; [3] Culin **au ~** [*riz*] plain; [*thon*] in brine

naturellement /natyʀɛlmã/ *adv* naturally

naturisme /natyʀism/ *nm* [1] (nudisme) naturism GB, nudism; **faire du ~** to be a naturist GB *ou* nudist; [2] Philos, Relig naturism

naturiste /natyʀist/ *nmf* (nudiste) naturist GB, nudist

naufrage /nofʀaʒ/ *nm* shipwreck, sinking ₵; **le ~ de l'économie** fig the collapse of the economy; **faire ~** [*navire*] to be wrecked; [*marin*] to be shipwrecked; [*entreprise*] to collapse

naufragé, ~e /nofʀaʒe/
A *adj* [*marin, équipage*] shipwrecked; **retrouver le navire ~** to find the wreck of the ship
B *nm,f* (rescapé) survivor (of a shipwreck); (sur une île, une côte déserte) castaway

nauséabond, ~e /nozeabõ, õd/ *adj* [*odeur*] sickening, nauseating

nausée /noze/ *nf* (dégoût) nausea ₵; **avoir la ~** to feel sick GB *ou* nauseous

nautique /notik/ *adj* [*science*] nautical; [*sports*] water (épith)

nautisme /notism/ *nm* (sports) water sports (*pl*)

naval, ~e, *mpl* **~s** /naval/ *adj* [1] Ind [*industrie, secteur*] shipbuilding; [2] Mil naval

navet /navɛ/ *nm* [1] (légume) turnip; [2] (film) pej rubbishy film GB, turkey○ US

navette /navɛt/ *nf* [1] (véhicule) shuttle; (liaison) shuttle (service); **faire la ~ entre Paris et Dijon** [*personne*] (pour le travail) to commute between Paris and Dijon; (pour raison personnelle) to travel back and forth between Paris and Dijon; **il y a un car qui fait la ~** there is a shuttle service; [2] (en tissage) shuttle
(Composé) **~ spatiale** space shuttle

navigabilité /navigabilite/ *nf* [1] (de rivière) navigability; [2] (de bateau) seaworthiness; (d'avion) airworthiness

navigable /navigabl/ *adj* navigable

navigant, ~e /navigã, ãt/ *adj* [*personnel*] Naut seagoing; Aviat flying; **mécanicien ~** flight engineer

navigateur, -trice /navigatœʀ, tʀis/
A *nm,f* [1] (qui guide) navigator; [2] (marin) sailor; (au long cours) navigator
B *nm* Ordinat browser
(Composé) **~ solitaire** solo yachtsman

navigation /navigasjõ/ *nf* [1] Aviat, Naut (techniques) navigation; **instrument de ~** navigational instrument; [2] (trafic sur l'eau) shipping, navigation; **~ intérieure** *or* **fluviale** inland navigation; **salon de la ~** boat show; [3] (voyage) **plusieurs semaines de ~** several weeks on the water; [4] Ordinat browsing
(Composé) **~ de plaisance** gén boating; (en voilier) sailing

naviguer /navige/ [1] *vi* [1] Naut [*bateau, marin, passager*] to sail; **en état de ~** [*navire*] seaworthy; [2] (guider un bateau, un avion) to navigate; [3] (voler) to fly; [4] Ordinat to browse

navire /naviʀ/
A *nm* ship
B **navire-** (in compounds) **~-école/-hôpital/-usine** training/hospital/factory ship; **~s-citernes** tankers
(Composés) **~ amiral** Mil flagship; **~ de commerce** merchant ship; **~ de guerre** warship; **~ marchand** merchant ship

navrant, ~e /navʀã, ãt/ *adj* [1] (consternant) depressing; [2] (attristant) distressing, upsetting

navré, ~e /navʀe/ *adj* [1] (dans une formule de politesse) **je suis vraiment ~** I am terribly sorry; [2] (triste, déçu) **avoir l'air ~** to look sad *ou* upset

navrer /navʀe/ [1] *vtr* liter (contrarier) to upset

nazi, ~e /nazi/ *adj, nm,f* Nazi

nazisme /nazism/ *nm* Nazism

NDLR *written abbr* ▸ **note**

ne /nə/ (**n'** before vowel or mute h) *adv*

⚠️ *Ne*, adverbe de négation, n'a pas d'équivalent exact en anglais.
   Généralement, la forme négative se construit avec un auxiliaire ou un verbe modal accompagné d'une négation: *je ne sais pas* = I don't know; *je ne peux pas* = I can't, I cannot; *il n'a pas répondu* = he didn't answer.
   Pour *ne* utilisé avec *pas, jamais, guère, rien, plus, aucun, personne* etc, on se reportera à l'article correspondant.
   ne + verbe + que est traité dans l'article ci-dessous.

je n'ai que 10 euros I've only got 10 euros; **ce n'est qu'une égratignure** it's only a scratch; **il n'y avait que lui dans la salle** there was nobody but him in the room; **tu n'avais qu'à le dire!** you only had to say so!; **il ne pense qu'à s'amuser** he only thinks of enjoying himself, he thinks of nothing but enjoying himself; **il n'y a qu'elle qui comprenne** only she understands; **il n'y a que lui pour être aussi désagréable** only he can be so unpleasant; **tu n'es qu'un raté** you're nothing but a loser○; **si l'avion est trop cher, il n'a qu'à prendre le train** if flying is too expensive he can take the train; **je n'ai que faire de tes conseils** you can keep your advice

né, ~e /ne/
A *pp* ▸ **naître**
B *pp adj* **bien/mal ~** highborn/lowborn (épith); **Madame Masson ~e Roux** Mrs Masson née Roux
C (-)né (in compounds) **un écrivain(-)~** a born writer

néanmoins /neãmwɛ̃/ *adv* nevertheless

néant /neã/ *nm* [1] Philos **le ~** nothingness; [2] (absence de valeur) emptiness; **réduire à ~** to negate [*efforts, progrès*]; to destroy [*argument, espoir, rêve*]; to wipe out [*majorité*]; **'revenus: ~'** 'income: nil'

nébuleuse[1] /nebyløz/ *nf* [1] (objet céleste) nebula; [2] fig amorphous grouping

nébuleux, -euse[2] /nebylø, øz/ *adj* [1] (obscurci) [*ciel*] cloudy, overcast; [*masse*] nebulous; [2] fig nebulous

nébulosité /nebylozite/ *nf* (de ciel, concept) nebulosity

nécessaire /nesesɛʀ/
A *adj* gén necessary (à for); **conditions ~s à la vie** conditions necessary for life; **juger ~ de faire** to consider it necessary to do; **~ ou pas** whether necessary or not; **il est ~ de faire** it is necessary to do; **il est ~ que tu y ailles** you have to go; **les voix ~s pour renverser le gouvernement** the votes needed in order to overthrow the government
B *nm* [1] (ce qui s'impose) **faire le ~** to do what is necessary *ou* what needs to be done; **as-tu fait le ~ pour les billets?** did you see about the tickets?; **j'ai fait le ~** I've seen to it; **le ~ et le superflu** what is necessary and what is superfluous; [2] (biens et services) essentials (*pl*); **manquer du ~** to lack the essentials

n

Composés ~ **de couture** sewing kit; ~ **à ongles** manicure set; ~ **de toilette** toiletries (*pl*)

nécessairement /nesesɛʀmɑ̃/ *adv* necessarily; **le progrès n'est pas** ~ **un bienfait** progress is not necessarily a blessing; **'y aura-t-il des licenciements?'—'pas** ~/**oui,** ~' 'will there be redundancies?'—'not necessarily/yes, it is unavoidable'; **cela finit** ~ **mal** it inevitably goes wrong; **passe-t-on** ~ **par Oslo?** do you have to go via Oslo?

nécessité /nesesite/ *nf* **1** (ce qui s'impose) necessity; **le téléphone est devenu une** ~ the telephone has become a necessity; ~ **absolue** *or* **impérative** absolute necessity; ~ **urgente/impérieuse** urgent/pressing need; ~ **de qch/de faire/d'être** need for sth/to do/to be; ~ **pour qn de qch/de faire** sb's need for sth to do; **je n'en vois pas la** ~ I don't see the need for it; **de première** ~ vital; **par** ~ out of necessity; **sans** ~ unnecessarily; **être dans la** ~ **de faire** to have no choice but to do; **2** (pauvreté) need; **être dans la** ~ to be in need; **3** (caractère inéluctable) necessity

Idiome ~ **fait loi** Prov necessity knows no law

nécessiter /nesesite/ **1** *vtr* to require; **la situation nécessite qu'elle intervienne** the situation calls for her intervention

nécessiteux, -euse /nesesitø, øz/
A *adj* needy
B *nm,f* needy person; **les** ~ the needy (+ *v pl*)

nec plus ultra /nɛkplyzyltʀa/ *nm inv* **le** ~ the last word (**de** in)

nécrologie /nekʀɔlɔʒi/ *nf* **1** (liste) deaths column, obituary column; **2** (article) obituary

nécrologique /nekʀɔlɔʒik/ *adj* obituary

nécrophage /nekʀɔfaʒ/ *adj* necrophagous

nécropole /nekʀɔpɔl/ *nf* necropolis

nécrose /nekʀoz/ *nf* necrosis

nécroser /nekʀoze/ **1** *vtr*, **se nécroser** *vpr* to necrose

nectar /nɛktaʀ/ *nm* nectar

néerlandais, ~**e** /neɛʀlɑ̃dɛ, ɛz/ ▸ p. 336, p. 392
A *adj* Dutch
B *nm* Ling Dutch

Néerlandais, ~**e** /neɛʀlɑ̃dɛ, ɛz/ ▸ p. 392 *nm,f* Dutchman/Dutchwoman; **les** ~ the Dutch (+ *v pl*)

nef /nɛf/ *nf* **1** Archit nave; **les** ~**s latérales** the side aisles; **2** †(embarcation) vessel, ship

néfaste /nefast/ *adj* (nuisible) harmful (**à** to)

négatif, -ive¹ /negatif, iv/
A *adj* **1** (non positif) negative; **2** (néfaste) negative, adverse
B *adv* Aviat, Mil negative

négation /negasjɔ̃/ *nf* **1** (action de nier) negation; **2** Ling negative

négative² /negativ/
A *adj* f ▸ **négatif**
B *nf* **répondre par la** ~ to reply in the negative; **dans la** ~, **nous aviserons** if not, we will think again

négligé, ~**e** /negliʒe/
A *adj* [*personne, vêtement*] sloppy, scruffy○; [*cheveux, barbe*] unkempt; [*maison*] neglected; [*travail*] careless, sloppy; [*blessure*] untreated
B *nm* (vêtement) negligée

négligeable /negliʒabl/ *adj* [*quantité, somme*] negligible, insignificant; [*personne*] insignificant; **non** ~ [*somme, atout*] considerable; [*détail, rôle*] significant

négligemment /negliʒamɑ̃/ *adv* (avec nonchalance) nonchalantly; (avec indifférence) carelessly

négligence /negliʒɑ̃s/ *nf* **1** (faute) negligence *Ȼ*; **il y aurait eu des** ~**s** negligence is alleged; **2** (laisser-aller) negligence, carelessness

négligent, ~**e** /negliʒɑ̃, ɑ̃t/ *adj* [*employé*] negligent, careless; [*élève, démarche*] careless; [*geste*] casual

négliger /negliʒe/ **13**
A *vtr* **1** to neglect [*santé, travail, personne*]; to leave untreated [*affection, rhume*]; **2** to ignore, to disregard [*résultat, règle*]; **il n'a rien négligé pour réussir** he tried everything possible to succeed; **une offre qui n'est pas à** ~ an offer which is worth considering; ~ **de faire** to fail to do
B **se négliger** *vpr* (dans sa tenue) not to take care over one's appearance; (pour sa santé) not to look after oneself

négoce /negɔs/ *nm* trade (**avec** with)

négociable /negɔsjabl/ *adj* negotiable

négociant, ~**e** /negɔsjɑ̃, ɑ̃t/ ▸ p. 372 *nm,f* gén merchant; (grossiste) wholesaler

négociateur, -trice /negɔsjatœʀ, tʀis/ *nm,f* negotiator

négociation /negɔsjasjɔ̃/ *nf* negotiation; **la table de** ~ the negotiating table

négocier /negɔsje/ **2**
A *vtr* **1** Comm, Pol to negotiate (**avec** with); **2** Sport ~ **un virage** to negotiate a bend
B *vi* to negotiate (**avec** with)

nègre /nɛgʀ/
A *adj* [*art, musique*] Negro
B *nm* **1** (Noir) offensive Negro injur; **2** (auteur occulte) ghostwriter

négresse /negʀɛs/ *nf* offensive Negress injur

négrier /negʀije/ *nm* Hist (personne) slave trader; (navire) slave ship

négritude /negʀityd/ *nf* black identity, negritude

neige /nɛʒ/ *nf* Météo snow; ~ **fondue** (au sol) slush; (pluie) sleet; **aller à la** ~ to go skiing; **paysage de** ~ snow-covered landscape; **blancs battus en** ~ stiffly beaten eggwhites

Idiomes **être blanc comme** ~ to be completely innocent; **fondre comme** ~ **au soleil** to melt away

neiger /neʒe/ **13** *v impers* to snow; **il neige** it's snowing

neigeux, -euse /neʒø, øz/ *adj* [*cime*] snow-covered; [*temps, hiver*] snowy

nénuphar /nenyfaʀ/ *nm* waterlily

néo /neo/ *préf* neo; ~**classicisme** neoclassicism

néo-calédonien, -ienne, *mpl* ~**s** /neokaledɔnjɛ̃, ɛn/ *adj* New Caledonian

néo-écossais, ~**e** /neoekɔsɛ, ɛz/ *adj* Nova Scotian

néologisme /neɔlɔʒism/ *nm* neologism

néon /neɔ̃/ *nm* **1** (gaz) neon; **2** (tube) neon light

néophyte /neofit/ *nmf* neophyte

néo-zélandais, ~**e** /neozelɑ̃dɛ, ɛz/ ▸ p. 392 *adj* New Zealand (*épith*)

Néo-Zélandais, ~**e** /neozelɑ̃dɛ, ɛz/ ▸ p. 392 *nm,f* New Zealander

népalais, ~**e** /nepalɛ, ɛz/ ▸ p. 336, p. 392
A *adj* Nepali
B *nm* Ling Nepali

néphrétique /nefʀetik/ *adj* nephritic; **coliques** ~**s** renal colic *Ȼ*

népotisme /nepotism/ *nm* nepotism

nerf /nɛʀ/
A *nm* **1** Anat nerve; ~ **optique** optic nerve; **2** (vigueur) spirit, go○; **redonner du** ~ **à qn** to put new heart into sb; **allez, du** ~○! come on, buck up○!
B **nerfs** *nmpl* (système nerveux) nerves; **être malade des** ~**s** to suffer from nerves

Composé ~ **de bœuf** pizzle

Idiomes **jouer avec les** ~**s de qn** to be deliberately annoying; **ses** ~**s ont lâché** he/she went to pieces; **avoir les** ~**s à fleur de peau** to have frayed nerves; **avoir les** ~**s en pelote**○ *or* **en boule**○ *or* **à vif** to be really wound up; **être sur les** ~**s, avoir ses** ~**s**○ to be on edge; **vivre sur les** ~**s** to live on one's nerves; **taper**○ **sur les** ~**s de qn** to get on sb's nerves; **être à bout de** ~**s** to be at the end of one's tether; **passer ses** ~**s sur**○ qn to take it out on sb; **l'argent est le** ~ **de la guerre** money is the sinews of war

nerveusement /nɛʀvøzmɑ̃/ *adv* **1** (avec impatience) nervously; **2** (psychologiquement) **être épuisé** ~ to be suffering from nervous exhaustion; **il n'est pas solide** ~ he's rather highly strung GB *ou* high-strung US; **il faut qu'il récupère** ~ he needs to have a good rest and calm down

nerveux, -euse /nɛʀvø, øz/
A *adj* **1** [*personne, animal, rire*] nervous; [*allure*] tense; **2** [*corps, main*] sinewy; [*moteur*] responsive; **3** (énergique) [*personne*] dynamic; [*style, écriture*] vigorous; **4** Anat [*cellule, centre*] nerve (*épith*); [*système, tension*] nervous
B *nm,f* Méd nervous person

nervosité /nɛʀvozite/ *nf* **1** (appréhension) nervousness; **on sentait la** ~ **ambiante** you could feel the tension in the air; **2** (surexcitation) excitability; **un cheval/enfant d'une grande** ~ a very excitable horse/child; **3** Aut (de moteur) liveliness, bite○

nervure /nɛʀvyʀ/ *nf* **1** Bot, Zool nervure; **2** Archit rib

nervuré, **~e** /nɛʀvyʀe/ adj [feuille, aile] veined

n'est-ce pas /nɛspɑ/ adv **1** (appelant l'approbation) **c'est joli, ~?** it's pretty, isn't it?; **tu es d'accord, ~?** you agree, don't you?; **~ qu'il est gentil?** isn't he nice?; **2** (pour renforcer) of course

net, **nette** /nɛt/
A adj **1** Écon, Fin (après déductions) net; **prix/salaire ~** net price/salary; **2** [changement, augmentation] marked; [baisse] sharp; [tendance, odeur] distinct; **3** [personne, victoire, souvenir] clear; [situation] clear-cut; [écriture] neat; [cassure] clean; **en avoir le cœur ~** to be clear in one's mind about it; **avoir la nette impression que** to have the distinct impression that; **4** (propre) lit [maison, vêtement] neat; [mains] clean; fig [personne] clean; [conscience] clear; **faire place nette** to clear everything away; **5** ᐤ(lucide) **pas (très) ~** not quite with itᐤ
B adv [s'arrêter] dead; [tuer] outright; [refuser] flatly; [dire] straight out; **refuser tout ~** to refuse point blank; **la corde a cassé ~** the rope snapped; **la clé s'est cassée ~** the key snapped in two
C nm **1** Écon, Fin (revenu) net income; (bénéfices) net earnings (pl); **2** (propre) **copie au ~** clean copy

netéconomie /nɛtekɔnɔmi/ nf e-economy

nétiquette /netikɛt/ nf netiquette

nettement /nɛtmɑ̃/ adv **1** [augmenter, se détériorer] markedly; [devancer] clearly; [préférer] definitely; **~ meilleur** decidedly better; **2** [voir, dire] clearly; [refuser] flatly; [se souvenir] distinctly

netteté /nɛtte/ nf **1** (de voix, ciel) clarity; (d'image) sharpness; (de résultat) definite nature; (de cassure) cleanness; **2** (de lieu) cleanness; (de travail) neatness

nettoiement /nɛtwamɑ̃/ nm **1** (nettoyage) cleaning 𝒞; **2** (enlèvement des ordures) refuse collection GB, garbage collection US; **service de ~** cleansing department GB, sanitation department US

nettoyage /nɛtwajaʒ/ nm **1** (opération) cleanup; **~ de printemps** spring-cleaning 𝒞; **2** (action) cleaning 𝒞; **~ à sec** dry-cleaning; **produit de ~** cleaning product; **3** (de la peau) cleansing 𝒞; **4** Mil mopping-up 𝒞
(Idiome) **faire le ~ par le vide** to have a good clearoutᐤ

nettoyant /nɛtwajɑ̃/ nm (produit) cleaning agent

nettoyer /nɛtwaje/ [23]
A vtr **1** lit to clean [lieu, objet, mains]; to clean up [jardin]; to clean out [rivière]; to clean off [tache]; **donner une robe à ~** to take a dress to the cleaner's; **faire ~ qch à sec** to have sth dry-cleaned; **2** fig to clean up [ville]; (dévaliser, ruiner) to clean outᐤ [appartement, personne]
B se nettoyer vpr **1** (se laver soi-même) **se ~ les mains** to clean one's hands; **2** (pouvoir être lavé) **la tache se nettoie à l'eau** the stain can be cleaned with water

neuf¹ /nœf/ ▸ p. 155, p. 296, p. 398
A adj inv, pron nine
B nm inv nine; **faire la preuve par ~** Math to cast out the nines

neuf², **neuve** /nœf, nœv/
A adj new; **comme ~** as new; **tout ~** brand new; **porter un regard ~ sur qch** to look at sth in a new light; **'état ~'** 'as new'
B nm inv new; **être habillé de ~** to be dressed in new clothes; **refaire qch à ~** to re-do sth completely; **faire du ~ avec du vieux** to revamp things
(Idiome) **faire peau neuve** [bâtiment] to undergo a transformation; [personne] to transform one's image

neurasthénie /nøʀasteni/ nf depression

neurasthénique /nøʀastenik/
A adj depressed; (chroniquement) depressive
B nmf depressive

neuro /nøʀo/ préf neuro; **~biologie** neurobiology; **~logie** neurology

neuronal, **~e**, mpl **-aux** /nøʀɔnal, o/ adj **1** Méd neuronal; **2** Ordinat neural

neurone /nøʀɔn/ nm neurone

neutralisation /nøtʀalizasjɔ̃/ nf neutralization

neutraliser /nøtʀalize/ [1] vtr **1** gén, Chimie to neutralize; **2** (empêcher d'agir) to overpower [forcené]

neutralité /nøtʀalite/ nf (d'État) neutrality; (d'individu) impartiality

neutre /nøtʀ/
A adj **1** gén, Chimie, Phys, Pol neutral; **2** Ling, Zool neuter

B nm Ling **le ~** the neuter

neutron /nøtʀɔ̃/ nm neutron

neuvième /nœvjɛm/
A ▸ p. 155, p. 398 adj ninth
B nf Scol third year of primary school, age 8–9

neveu, pl **~x** /n(ə)vø/ nm nephew

névralgie /nevʀalʒi/ nf neuralgia 𝒞

névralgique /nevʀalʒik/ adj **1** Méd [douleur] neuralgic; **2** fig **point ~** key point

névropathe /nevʀɔpat/ adj, nmf neurotic

névrose /nevʀoz/ ▸ p. 195 nf neurosis

névrosé, **~e** /nevʀoze/ adj, nm,f neurotic

New York /njujɔʀk/ npr **1** ▸ p. 621 (ville) New York City; **2** ▸ p. 504 **l'État de ~** New York (State)

nez /ne/ ▸ p. 136 nm nose; **~ en trompette** turned-up nose; **ça sent le parfum à plein ~**ᐤ there's a strong smell of perfume; **je n'ai pas mis le ~ dehors**ᐤ I didn't set foot outside; **mettre le ~ à la fenêtre**ᐤ to show one's face at the window; **lever à peine le ~** barely to look up; **ne pas lever le ~ de qch** never to lift one's head from sth; **tu as le ~ dessus**ᐤ it's staring you in the face; **avoir du ~, avoir le ~ fin** (odorat) to have a good sense of smell; (intuition) to be shrewd; **rire au ~ de qn** to laugh in sb's face

(Idiomes) **mener qn par le bout du ~**ᐤ (dans un couple) to have sb under one's thumb; (plus général) to have sb wrapped round one's little finger; **avoir qn dans le ~**ᐤ to have it in for sb; **avoir un coup** or **verre dans le ~**ᐤ to have had one too manyᐤ; **faire qch au ~ (et à la barbe) de qn** to do sth right under sb's nose; **filer** or **passer sous le ~ de qn** to slip through sb's fingers; **avoir le ~ creux**ᐤ to be canny; **se casser le ~**ᐤ (trouver porte close) to find nobody at home; (échouer) to fail, to come a cropperᐤ

NF /ɛnɛf/ adj, nf (abbr = **norme française**) French manufacturing standard

ni /ni/ conj

> ⚠ On observe que le français et l'anglais fonctionnent de la même façon: il ne jure ni ne se met en colère = he doesn't swear or lose his temper; ni il jure ni il se met en colère = he neither swears nor loses his temper; elle ne veut pas le voir ni lui parler = she doesn't wish to see him or talk to him; elle ne veut ni le voir ni lui parler = she neither wishes to see him nor talk to him.

elle ne veut ~ ne peut changer she doesn't want to change, nor can she; **il n'est ~ beau ~ laid** he's neither handsome nor ugly; **il ne parle ~ anglais, ~ allemand, ~ espagnol** he speaks neither English, nor German, nor Spanish; **~ l'un ~ l'autre** neither of them; **il ne m'a dit ~ oui ~ non** he didn't say yes or no; **~ plus ~ moins** no more and no less

(Idiomes) **faire qch ~ vu ~ connu**ᐤ to do sth on the sly; **c'est ~ fait ~ à faire**ᐤ it's a botchedᐤ job; **il n'a fait ~ une ~ deux**ᐤ he didn't have a second's hesitation

niais, **~e** /njɛ, njɛz/
A adj stupid
B nm,f idiot, simpleton

niaiserie /njɛzʀi/ nf **1** (caractère) stupidity, silliness; **2** (propos) stupid ou inane remark

niaiseux, **-euse** /njɛzø, øz/ C
A adj (stupide) moronic
B nm,f (imbécile) moronᐤ

nicaraguayen, **-enne** /nikaʀagwajɛ̃, ɛn/ ▸ p. 392 adj Nicaraguan

niche /niʃ/ nf **1** (de chien) kennel; **2** Archit (de statue) niche; (alcôve) recess; **3** ᐤ(farce) trick; **4** Comm niche market

nichée /niʃe/ nf (d'oisillons, enfants) brood; (de souris) litter

nicher /niʃe/ [1]
A vi **1** Zool to nest; **2** ᐤ(loger) to live
B se nicher vpr **1** Zool to nest; **2** (se blottir) [personne, chaumière] to nestle (**dans** in)

nickel /nikɛl/
A ᐤadj [objet] spotless; [logement] spick and span (jamais épith)
B nm nickel

nicotine /nikɔtin/ nf nicotine

nid /ni/ nm nest

Composés ~ **d'aigle** eyrie; ~ **de brigands** den of thieves; ~ **d'hirondelle** bird's nest; ~ **à poussière** dust trap; ~ **de résistance** pocket of resistance

nid-d'abeilles, pl **nids-d'abeilles** /nidabɛj/ nm honeycomb weave

nid-de-poule, pl **nids-de-poule** /nidpul/ nm pothole

nidification /nidifikasjɔ̃/ nf nesting

nièce /njɛs/ nf niece

nième /ɛnjɛm/ = **énième**

nier /nje/ [2] vtr to deny [fait, existence, signature]; to repudiate [dette]; ~ **une faute** to deny having made a mistake; ~ **l'évidence** to refuse to face up to the facts

nigaud, ~**e** /nigo, od/
A adj silly
B nm,f (silly) twit° GB, goof° US

nihiliste /niilist/ adj, nmf nihilist

nimbe /nɛ̃b/ nm nimbus, halo

nimber /nɛ̃be/ [1] vtr [soleil] to halo (**de** with); [brume] to swathe

nîmois, ~**e** /nimwa, az/ ▸ p. 621 adj of Nîmes

nipper°: **se nipper** /nipe/ [1] vpr to get rigged out° in one's Sunday best

nippes° /nip/ nfpl rags°, old clothes

nippon, -**onne** /nipɔ̃, ɔn/ adj Japanese

nitouche /nituʃ/ nf **sainte** ~ goody-goody°

nitrate /nitrat/ nm nitrate

nitrique /nitrik/ adj nitric; **acide** ~ nitric acid

niveau, pl ~**x** /nivo/ nm **1** (hauteur) level; ~ **de l'eau/d'huile** water/oil level; **au** ~ **du sol** at ground level; **être de** ~ to be level; **arrivé au** ~ **du bus** when he drew level with the bus; **au** ~ **du cou** [blessures] in the neck region; **accroc au** ~ **du genou** tear at the knee; **2** (étage) storey GB, story US; **bâtiment sur deux** ~**x** two-storey GB ou two-story US building; **3** (degré) (d'intelligence) level; (de connaissances) standard; ~ **intellectuel** intellectual level; **'~ bac + 3'** baccalaureate or equivalent plus 3 years' higher education; **remettre qn à** ~ to bring sb up to the required level; **de haut** ~ [athlète] top (épith); [candidat] high-calibre^{GB} (épith); ~ **des salaires** wage levels (pl); **4** (échelon) level; **au plus haut** ~ [discussion] top-level (épith); **les négociations se dérouleront au plus haut** ~ there will be negotiations at the highest level; **5** Ling register; **6** (instrument) level

Composés ~ **de langue** register; ~ **social** social status; ~ **sonore** sound level; ~ **de vie** standard of living, living standards (pl)

nivelage /nivlaʒ/ nm **1** (de sol) levelling^{GB}; **2** (égalisation) (économique) standardization; (social) levelling^{GB} out

niveler /nivle/ [19] vtr **1** (aplatir) to level [sol]; to flatten [relief]; **2** (égaliser) to bring [sth] to the same level [revenus]; ~ **par le bas/haut** to level down/up

nivellement /nivɛlmɑ̃/ nm **1** (du sol) levelling^{GB}; **2** (mesure) land survey; **3** (économique) standardization; (social) levelling^{GB}-out

nobiliaire /nɔbiljɛr/ adj [titre, particule] nobiliary

noble /nɔbl/
A adj **1** [personne] of noble birth; [famille] aristocratic; **2** [sentiments, maintien] noble; [cause] worthy, noble; **3** [matériau] (naturel) natural, non-synthetic; (raffiné) fine; [filière, section] prestigious; [sport] noble; **métaux** ~**s** precious metals
B nmf (personne) nobleman/noblewoman; **les** ~**s** the nobility (sg)

noblement /nɔbləmɑ̃/ adv **1** (avec noblesse) nobly; **2** (avec générosité) handsomely

noblesse /nɔblɛs/ nf **1** (qualité morale) nobility; **2** (aristocratie) **la** ~ the nobility; **la petite** ~ the gentry

nobliau, pl ~**x** /nɔblijo/ nm minor nobleman

noce /nɔs/
A nf **1** (fête) party; **faire la** ~° fig to live it up°, to party°; **aujourd'hui je n'étais pas à la** ~ fig today was no picnic; **2** (invités) wedding party
B noces nfpl wedding (sg); **nuit de** ~**s** wedding night; **en premières** ~**s, il a épousé...** his first wife was...

noceur°, -**euse** /nɔsœr, øz/ nm,f party animal°

nocif, -**ive** /nɔsif, iv/ adj [gaz] noxious; [théorie] harmful

nocivité /nɔsivite/ nf (de gaz) noxiousness

noctambule /nɔktɑ̃byl/
A adj [promeneur] late-night (épith)
B nmf night owl

nocturne¹ /nɔktyrn/
A adj [spectacle, attaque] night (épith); [animal] nocturnal; [sortie, promenade] late-night (épith); **la vie** ~ **à Londres** nightlife in London
B nm **1** Zool (oiseau) nocturnal bird; **2** Mus, Relig nocturne

nocturne² /nɔktyrn/ nf **1** Sport (course, match) evening fixture; **2** Comm (de magasin) late-night opening

Noé /noe/ npr Noah

noël /nɔɛl/ nm s2 (chant) Christmas carol

Noël /nɔɛl/ nm Christmas; **'Joyeux** ou **Happy Christmas'**; **de** ~ [arbre, cadeau] Christmas (épith)

nœud /nø/
A nm **1** (pour lier) knot; **faire un** ~ **de cravate** to tie a tie; **2** (pour orner) bow; **3** ▸ p. 624 Naut knot; ~**s marins** sailors' knots; **4** Bot knot; **5** (point essentiel) crux; **6** Littérat (de pièce, d'intrigue) core
B nœuds nmpl (d'amitié, affection) liter bonds, ties

Composés ~ **coulant** slipknot; ~ **papillon** bow tie; ~ **de vipères** nest of vipers; ~ **vital** Anat vital centre^{GB}

noir, ~**e¹** /nwar/
A adj **1** (couleur) [peinture, fumée, cheveux] black; [yeux] dark; **être** ~ **de coups** to be black and blue; **être** ~ **de monde** [rue, plage] to be swarming with people; **2** (sale) [mains, col] black, filthy; **être** ~ **de crasse** to be black with grime; **3** (obscur) [ruelle, cachot] dark; **il fait** ~ it's dark; **4** [personne, race, peau, quartier] black; **5** (bronzé) **être** ~, **avoir la peau** ~ to have a dark tan; **6** (catastrophique) [époque, année] bad, bleak; [misère] dire, abject; [désespoir] deep; [idée] gloomy, dark; **7** (méchant) [regard] black; [âme, dessein] dark; **entrer** or **se mettre dans une colère** ~**e** to fly into a towering rage
B nm **1** (couleur) black; **2** (crasse) dirt; (saleté, tache noire) **du** ~ a black mark; **3** (obscurité) dark; **4** (clandestinité) **au** ~ [acheter, vendre] on the black market; **travailler au** ~ gén to work without declaring one's earnings; (avoir un deuxième emploi, non déclaré) to moonlight°; **5** °(café) **un (petit)** ~ an espresso
Idiome **voir tout en** ~ to look on the black side (of things)

Noir, ~**e** /nwar/ nm,f black man/woman

noirâtre /nwarɑtr/ ▸ p. 140 adj blackish

noiraud, ~**e** /nwaro, od/ adj [personne, teint, visage] swarthy

noirceur /nwarsœr/ nf **1** (d'encre) blackness; (de cheveux, nuit, d'yeux) darkness; **2** (de personne, regard, projets, d'intentions) blackness; **3** C (obscurité) dark

noircir /nwarsir/ [3]
A vtr **1** (salir) [charbon] to make [sth] dirty; [fumée, pollution] to blacken; [encre] to stain [sth] black; ~ **du papier** fig to scribble away; **2** (assombrir) ~ **la situation** to paint a black picture of the situation; ~ **qn** to blacken sb's name
B vi (devenir noir) [banane] to go black; [mur] to get dirty; [métal] to tarnish
C se noircir vpr [ciel] to darken; [temps] to become threatening; **se** ~ **le visage** to blacken one's face

noircissure /nwarsisyr/ nf dark smudge

noire² /nwar/
A adj f ▸ noir
B nf Mus crotchet GB, quarter note US

noise /nwaz/ nf **chercher** ~ or **des** ~**s à qn** to pick a quarrel with sb

noisetier /nwaztje/ nm hazel (tree)

noisette /nwazɛt/
A ▸ p. 140 adj inv [couleur, yeux] hazel; [tissu] light brown
B nf **1** Bot, Culin hazelnut; **2** (morceau) small knob

noix /nwa/ nf inv Bot walnut GB, English walnut US; **pain aux** ~ walnut bread; **à la** ~° [histoire, artiste] crummy°; **une** ~ **de beurre** a knob of butter

Composés ~ **de cajou** cashew nut; ~ **de coco** coconut; ~ **(de) muscade** nutmeg

nom /nɔ̃/
A nm **1** (désignation) name; **connu sous le** ~ **de** known as; **donner un** ~ **à** to name; **sans** ~ pej unspeakable; **cela**

porte un ∼: **la fainéantise** there's a word for that: laziness; ∼ **de** ∼○, ∼ **d'un chien**○ or **d'une pipe**○ hell○; **2** (nom propre) name; (opposé à prénom) surname, second name; **porter le** ∼ **de son mari** to use one's husband's surname; **George Sand, de son vrai** ∼ **Aurore Dupin** George Sand, whose real name was Aurore Dupin; ∼ **et prénom** full name; ∼ **à coucher dehors**○ impossible name; ∼ **à rallonges**○ impossibly long name; **parler en son propre** ∼ to speak for oneself; **3** (réputation) name; **il s'est fait un** ∼ **dans la publicité** he made his name in advertising; **4** Ling (partie du discours) noun

B au nom de loc prép **1** (en vertu de) in the name of; **2** (de la part de) on behalf of

(Composés) ∼ **de baptême** Christian name; ∼ **de code** code name; ∼ **commercial** corporate name; ∼ **d'emprunt** pseudonym; ∼ **de famille** surname; ∼ **de jeune fille** maiden name; ∼ **de lieu** place-name; ∼ **de théâtre** stage name

(Idiomes) **traiter qn de tous les** ∼**s (d'oiseaux)**○ to call sb all the names under the sun; **appeler les choses par leur** ∼ to call a spade a spade

nomade /nɔmad/
A adj [personne, vie, tribu] nomadic
B nmf (du désert) nomad; **mener une vie de** ∼ to lead a nomadic existence

nombrable /nɔ̃bʀabl/ adj countable, numerable

nombre /nɔ̃bʀ/ nm **1** Ling, Math number; **un** ∼ **à deux chiffres** a two-digit number; **2** (quantité) number; **un certain** ∼ **de** some; **être en** ∼ **inférieur** [troupes, joueurs] to be fewer in number; [groupe] to be smaller; **être en** ∼ **supérieur** [troupes, joueurs] to be greater in number; [groupe] to be bigger; **dans le** ∼○ il y aura bien quelqu'un qui me prêtera de l'argent surely one of them will lend me some money; **ils étaient au** ∼ **de 30** there were 30 of them; **3** (grande quantité) numbers (pl); **être écrasé** or **succomber sous le** ∼ (de personnes) to be overcome by sheer weight of numbers; (de dossiers, lettres) to be defeated by the sheer volume; **sans** ∼ [ennemis] countless; [ennuis] endless; **bon** ∼ **de** a good many; ∼ **de fois** many times

(Composés) ∼ **impair** odd number; ∼ **ordinal** ordinal number; ∼ **pair** even number; ∼ **premier** prime number

nombrer /nɔ̃bʀe/ [1] vtr liter to number, to count

nombreux, -euse /nɔ̃bʀø, øz/ adj **1** (important) [population, collection] large; **la foule était nombreuse** there was a large ou vast crowd; **2** (en grand nombre) many (épith); **l'usine ne sera pas mise en service avant de nombreuses années** it will be many years before the factory is put into operation; **ils étaient peu** ∼ there were only a few of them; **ils ont répondu** ∼ **à l'appel** numerous people responded to the appeal; **ils arrivent toujours plus** ∼ they are arriving in ever greater numbers; **les touristes deviennent trop** ∼ the number of tourists is becoming excessive

nombril /nɔ̃bʀil/ nm navel; **elle se prend pour le** ∼ **du monde**○ she thinks she's God's gift to mankind

nombrilisme○ /nɔ̃bʀilism/ nm (de personne) pej navel-gazing○

nombriliste○ /nɔ̃bʀilist/ adj pej [personne] egocentric; [politique] inward-looking

nomenclature /nɔmɑ̃klatyʀ/ nf **1** (ensemble de termes) nomenclature; (de dictionnaire) word list; **2** Ordinat nomenclature

nominal, ∼e, mpl **-aux** /nɔminal, o/ adj **1** Écon, Fin [hausse, taux] nominal; **salaire** ∼ (en valeur absolue) nominal wage; (avant déductions) gross salary ou pay; **valeur** ∼**e** (d'action) par value; (de monnaie) face value; **2** (par nom) **liste** ∼**e** list of names; **appel** ∼ roll call; **3** Ling [forme, emploi] nominal

nominatif, -ive /nɔminatif, iv/
A adj [fichier, liste] of names; [invitation] personal; Fin [titre] registered
B nm Ling nominative; **au** ∼ in the nominative

nomination /nɔminasjɔ̃/ nf **1** (affectation) appointment; **2** (lettre d'affectation) letter of appointment; **3** (sélection) controv nomination

nominativement /nɔminativmɑ̃/ adv by name

nominer /nɔmine/ [1] vtr controv to nominate

nommément /nɔmemɑ̃/ adv specifically, by name

nommer /nɔme/ [1]
A vtr **1** (désigner pour une fonction) to appoint; **être nommé à Paris** to be posted to Paris; **2** (dénommer) to name [personne]; to call [chose]; **comment l'ont-ils nommé?** what did they call him?; **3** (citer) to name [complice, arbre, peintre]
B se nommer vpr **1** (s'appeler) to be called; **2** (donner son nom) to give one's name

non /nɔ̃/

⚠ En anglais la réponse no est généralement renforcée en reprenant le verbe utilisé pour poser la question: 'tu es déçu?'—'non' = 'are you disappointed?'—'no, I'm not'; 'est-ce que vous aimez les concombres?'—'non' = 'do you like cucumber?'—'no, I don't'

A adv **1** (marque le désaccord) no; **répondez par oui ou par** ∼ answer yes or no; **ah, ça** ∼**!** definitely not!, no way○!; **alors, c'est** ∼**?** so the answer is no?; **dire** ou **faire** ∼ **de la tête** to shake one's head; **2** (remplace une proposition) **je pense que** ∼ I don't think so; **je te dis que** ∼ no, I tell you; **il paraît que** ∼ apparently not; **tu trouves ça drôle? moi** ∼ do you think that's funny? I don't; **3** (dans une double négation) ∼ **sans raison** not without reason; **une situation** ∼ **moins triste** an equally sad situation; **4** (introduisant une rectification, nuance) ∼ **(pas) que je sois d'accord** not that I agree; **5** (dans une alternative) **qu'il soit d'accord ou** ∼ whether he agrees or not; **6** (interrogatif, exclamatif!) **c'est difficile,** ∼**?** (n'est-ce pas) it's difficult, isn't it?; ∼**?** (de scepticisme) oh no?; ∼**!** (de surprise) no!; **sois un peu plus poli,** ∼ **mais** ○! be a bit more polite, for heaven's sake!; **7** (avec adjectif) non; ∼ **alcoolisé** nonalcoholic; ∼ **négligeable** [somme] considerable; [rôle] important; **objet** ∼ **identifié** unidentified object

B nm inv **1** (désaccord) no; **un** ∼ **catégorique** an emphatic no; **2** (vote négatif) 'no' vote

C non plus loc adv **je ne suis pas d'accord** ∼ **plus** I don't agree either; **il n'a pas aimé le film, moi** ∼ **plus** he didn't like the film and neither did I

D non(-) (in compounds) ∼**-agression** nonaggression; ∼**-combattant** noncombatant; ∼**-dissémination** nonproliferation; ∼**-fumeur** nonsmoker; ∼**-responsabilité** nonliability; ∼**-syndiqué** non union member

non-aligné, ∼e, mpl ∼**s** /nɔnaliɲe/ nmf nonaligned country

nonante /nɔnɑ̃t/ ▸ p. 398, p. 155 adj inv, pron B, C, H ninety

nonantième /nɔnɑ̃tjɛm/ adj, nmf B, C, H ninetieth

non-assistance /nɔnasistɑ̃s/ nf ∼ **à personne en danger** failure to render assistance

nonchalance /nɔ̃ʃalɑ̃s/ nf nonchalance; **avec** ∼ nonchalantly

nonchalant, ∼e /nɔ̃ʃalɑ̃, ɑ̃t/ adj (personne) nonchalant; (enfant, élève) apathetic; **c'est un** ∼ he shows no enthusiasm for anything

non-dit /nɔ̃di/ nm inv **le** ∼ what is left unsaid

non-droit /nɔ̃dʀwa/ nm absence of legislation

non-emploi /nɔ̃ɑ̃plwa/ nm unemployment

non-figuratif, -ive, mpl ∼**s** /nɔ̃fiɡyʀatif, iv/ nmf abstract artist

non-fonctionnement /nɔ̃fɔ̃ksjɔnmɑ̃/ nm failure to operate

non-initié, ∼e, mpl ∼**s** /nɔninisje/ nmf gén layman, lay person; (dans une secte) uninitiated person

non-inscrit, ∼e, mpl ∼**s** /nɔnɛ̃skʀi, it/ nmf independent

non-lieu, pl ∼**x** /nɔ̃ljø/ nm Jur dismissal (of a charge); **il y a eu** ∼ the judge dismissed the case

nonne† /nɔn/ nf nun

nonnette /nɔnɛt/ nf Culin small iced gingerbread

nonobstant† /nɔnɔpstɑ̃/ adv, prép notwithstanding

non-recevoir /nɔ̃ʀəsəvwaʀ/ nm **fin de** ∼ flat refusal

non-reconduction, pl ∼**s** /nɔ̃ʀəkɔ̃dyksjɔ̃/ nf (de contrat, mesure) nonrenewal; (de personne) failure to reappoint

non-respect /nɔ̃ʀɛspɛ/ nm ∼ **de** failure to comply with [clause, accord]; failure to respect [personne]

non-sens /nɔ̃sɑ̃s/ nm inv **1** (absurdité) nonsense ⊄; **cette politique est un** ∼ this policy is nonsensical; **2** (dans une traduction) meaningless phrase

non-spécialiste, pl ∼**s** /nɔ̃spesjalist/ nmf layman

n

Les nombres

Les nombres cardinaux

```
 0  nought (GB)
    zero (US)*
 1  one
 2  two
 3  three
 4  four
 5  five
 6  six
 7  seven
 8  eight
 9  nine
10  ten
11  eleven
12  twelve
13  thirteen
14  fourteen
15  fifteen
16  sixteen
17  seventeen
18  eighteen
19  nineteen
20  twenty
21  twenty-one
22  twenty-two
30  thirty
31  thirty-one
32  thirty-two
40  forty†
50  fifty
60  sixty
70  seventy
73  seventy-three
80  eighty
84  eighty-four
90  ninety
95  ninety-five
100 a hundred ou one hundred‡
101 a hundred and one (GB)§
    a hundred one (US)
111 a hundred and eleven (GB)
    a hundred eleven (US)
123 a hundred and twenty-three (GB)
    a hundred twenty-three (US)
200 two hundred
```

Noter que l'anglais utilise une virgule là où le français a un espace.

```
      1,000  a thousand
      1,002  a thousand and two (GB)
             a thousand two (US)
      1,020  a thousand and twenty (GB)
             a thousand twenty (US)
      1,200  a thousand two hundred
     10,000  ten thousand
     10,200  ten thousand two hundred
    100,000  a hundred thousand
    102,000  a hundred and two thousand (GB)
             ou a hundred two thousand (US)
  1,000,000  one million
  1,200,000  one million two hundred thousand
  1,264,932  one million two hundred and sixty-
             four thousand nine hundred and
             thirty-two (GB) ou one million two
             hundred sixty-four thousand nine
             hundred thirty-two (US)
  2,000,000  two million¶
3,000,000,000  three thousand million (GB) ou three
             billion‖ (US)
4,000,000,000,000  four billion (GB) ou four thousand
             billion (US)
```

les nombres jusqu'à dix
= numbers up to ten

compter jusqu'à dix
= to count up to ten

* *En anglais, lorsqu'on énonce les chiffres un à un, on prononce en général le zéro oh: mon numéro de poste est le 403 = my extension number is 403 (dire four oh three). Pour la température, on utilise zero: il fait zéro = it's zero.*

  Pour les scores dans les jeux et les sports, on utilise en général nil (GB) zero (US), sauf au tennis, où zéro se dit love.

† *Noter que forty s'écrit sans u, alors que fourteen et fourth s'écrivent comme four.*

‡ *Les formes avec one s'utilisent lorsqu'on veut insister sur la précision du chiffre. Dans les autres cas, on utilise plutôt a.*

§ *Noter que and s'utilise en anglais britannique entre hundred ou thousand et le chiffre des dizaines ou des unités (mais pas entre thousand et le chiffre des centaines). Il ne s'utilise pas en anglais américain.*

¶ *Noter que million est invariable en anglais dans ce cas.*

‖ *Attention: un billion américain vaut un milliard (1 000 millions), alors qu'un billion britannique vaut 1 000 milliards. Le billion américain est de plus en plus utilisé en Grande-Bretagne.*

Les adresses, les numéros de téléphone, les dates, etc.

Les adresses

	dire
29 Park Road	twenty-nine Park Road
110 Park Road	a hundred and ten Park Road (GB)
	ou one ten Park Road (US)
1021 Park Road	one oh two one Park Road (GB)
	ou ten twenty-one Park Road (US)

Les numéros de téléphone

	dire
020 7392 1011	oh two oh, seven three nine two; one oh one one
	ou ... one oh double one
1-415-243 7620	one, four one five, two four three, seven six two oh
04 78 02 75 27	oh four, seven eight, oh two, seven five, two seven

Les dates ► p. 155

Combien?

combien d'enfants y a-t-il?
= how many children are there?

il y a vingt-trois enfants
= there are twenty-three children

■ *Noter que l'anglais n'a pas d'équivalent du pronom français en dans:*

combien est-ce qu'il y en a?
= how many are there?

il y en a vingt-trois
= there are twenty-three

nous viendrons à 8
= there'll be 8 of us coming

ils sont 8
= there are 8 of them

☞ Voir page suivante

Les nombres *suite*

ils étaient 10 au commencement
= there were 10 of them at the beginning

■ *L'anglais* million *s'utilise ici comme adjectif. Noter l'absence d'équivalent anglais de la préposition de après* million.

1 000 000 d'habitants
= 1,000,000 inhabitants (*dire* a million inhabitants *ou* one million inhabitants)

2 000 000 d'habitants
= two million inhabitants

■ *L'anglais utilise aussi les mots* hundreds, thousands, millions *etc. au pluriel, comme en français:*

j'en ai des centaines
= I've got hundreds

des milliers de livres
= thousands of books

les milliers de livres que j'ai lus
= the thousands of books I have read

des centaines et des centaines
= hundreds and hundreds

des milliers et des milliers
= thousands and thousands

■ *Pour les numéraux français en* -aine *(dizaine, douzaine, quinzaine, vingtaine, trentaine, quarantaine, cinquantaine, soixantaine et centaine) lorsqu'ils désignent une somme approximative, l'anglais utilise le chiffre avec la préposition* about *ou* around.

une dizaine de questions
= about ten questions

une quinzaine de personnes
= about fifteen people

une vingtaine
= about twenty

une centaine
= about a hundred

presque dix
= almost ten *ou* nearly ten

environ dix
= about ten

environ 400 pages
= about four hundred pages

moins de dix
= less than ten

plus de dix
= more than ten

tous les dix
= all ten of them *ou* all ten

ils s'y sont mis à cinq
= it took five of them
ou (*s'ils n'étaient que cinq en tout*) it took all five of them

■ *Noter l'ordre des mots dans:*

les deux autres
= the other two

les cinq prochaines semaines
= the next five weeks

mes dix derniers dollars
= my last ten dollars

Quel numéro? Lequel?

le volume numéro 8 de la série
= volume 8 of the series *ou* the 8th volume of the series

le cheval numéro 11
= horse number 11

miser sur le 11
= to bet on number 11

le nombre 7 porte bonheur
= 7 is a lucky number

la ligne 8 du métro
= line number 8 of the underground (*GB*) *ou* subway (*US*)

la (chambre numéro) 8 est libre
= room 8 is free

le 8 de pique
= the 8 of spades

Louis XIV
= Louis the Fourteenth

Les opérations

dire

$10 + 3 = 13$	ten and three are thirteen
	ou ten plus three make thirteen
$10 - 3 = 7$	ten minus three is seven
	and three from ten leaves seven
$10 \times 3 = 30$	ten times three is thirty
	ou ten threes are thirty
$30 \div 3 = 10*$	thirty divided by three is ten
	ou three into thirty is ten
3^2	three squared
3^3	three cubed *ou* three to the power of three
3^4	three to the fourth
	ou three to the power of four
3^{100}	three to the hundredth
	ou three to the power of a hundred
3^n	three to the nth (*dire* [enθ])
	ou three to the power of n
$\sqrt{12}$	the square root of 12
$\sqrt{25} = 5$	the square root of twenty-five is 5
$B > A$	B is greater than A
$A < B$	A is less than B

* *Noter que le signe* divisé par *est différent dans les deux langues: au* ":" *français correspond le* "÷" *anglais.*

Les nombres décimaux

■ *Noter que l'anglais utilise un point* (the decimal point) *là où le français a une virgule. Noter également qu'en anglais britannique* zéro *se dit* nought, *et en américain* zero.

dire

0.25	nought point two five *ou* point two five
0.05	nought point nought five *ou* point oh five
0.75	nought point seven five *ou* point seven five
3.33	three point three three
8.195	eight point one nine five
9.1567	nine point one five six seven

Les pourcentages

dire

25%	twenty-five per cent
50%	fifty per cent
100%	a hundred per cent *ou* one hundred per cent
200%	two hundred per cent
365%	three hundred and sixty-five per cent (*GB*)
	ou three hundred sixty-five per cent (*US*)
4.25%	four point two five per cent
4.025%	four point oh two five per cent

☛ Voir page suivante

Les nombres *suite*

Les fractions

	dire		dire
1/2	a half† *ou* one half	1/10	a tenth
1/3	a third *ou* one third	1/11	one eleventh
1/4	a quarter	1/12	one twelfth (*etc.*)
	ou one quarter etc.	2/3	two thirds
1/5	a fifth	2/5	two fifths
1/6	a sixth	2/10	two tenths (*etc.*)
1/7	a seventh	3/4	three quarters
1/8	an eighth	5/8	five eighths
1/9	a ninth	3/10	three tenths (*etc.*)

■ *Noter l'utilisation en anglais de l'article indéfini dans les expressions suivantes:*

$1\frac{1}{2}$	one and a half
$1\frac{1}{3}$	one and a third
$1\frac{1}{4}$	one and a quarter
$1\frac{1}{6}$	one and a sixth
$1\frac{1}{7}$	one and a seventh (etc.)
$5\frac{2}{3}$	five and two thirds
$5\frac{3}{4}$	five and three quarters
$5\frac{4}{5}$	five and four fifths (etc.)
$45/100$	forty-five hundredths

■ *Noter que l'anglais n'utilise pas l'article défini dans:*

les deux tiers d'entre eux
= two thirds of them

■ *Mais noter l'utilisation de l'article indéfini anglais dans:*

quarante-cinq centièmes de seconde
= forty-five hundredths of a second

dix sur cent
= ten out of a hundred

Les nombres ordinaux

français	abréviation	en toutes lettres anglaises
1er	1st	first
2e	2nd	second
3e	3rd	third
4e	4th	fourth
5e	5th	fifth
6e	6th	sixth
7e	7th	seventh
8e	8th	eighth
9e	9th	ninth
10e	10th	tenth
11e	11th	eleventh
12e	12th	twelfth
13e	13th	thirteenth
20e	20th	twentieth
21e	21st	twenty-first
22e	22nd	twenty-second
23e	23rd	twenty-third
24e	24th	twenty-fourth
30e	30th	thirtieth
40e	40th	fortieth
50e	50th	fiftieth
60e	60th	sixtieth
70e	70th	seventieth
80e	80th	eightieth
90e	90th	ninetieth
99e	99th	ninety-ninth
100e	100th	hundredth
101e	101st	hundred and first
102e	102nd	hundred and second (*GB*)
		hundred second (*US*)
103e	103rd	hundred and third (*GB*)
		hundred third (*US*)
196e	196th	hundred and ninety-sixth (*GB*)
		hundred ninety-sixth (*US*)
1 000e‡	1,000th	thousandth
1 000 000e‡	1,000,000th	millionth

le premier
= the first *ou* the first one

le quarante-deuxième
= the forty-second *ou* the forty-second one

il y en a un deuxième
= there is a second one

le second des deux
= the second of the two

■ *Noter l'ordre des mots dans:*

les trois premiers
= the first three

le troisième pays le plus riche du monde
= the third richest nation in the world

les quatre derniers
= the last four

† *Pour les fractions jusqu'à 1/10, on utilise normalement a (a third); on utilise one (one third) en mathématiques et pour les calculs précis.*
‡ *Noter que l'anglais utilise une virgule là où le français a un espace.*

---

n

---

non-violent, ~e, *mpl* ~s /nɔ̃vjɔlɑ̃, ɑ̃t/ *nm,f* advocate of nonviolence

non-voyant, ~e, *mpl* ~s /nɔ̃vwajɑ̃, ɑ̃t/ *nm,f* visually handicapped person; **les** ~s the visually handicapped

nord /nɔʀ/ ▸ p. 454
A *adj inv* [*façade, versant, côte*] north; [*frontière, zone*] northern
B *nm* ① (point cardinal) north; ② (région) north; **le** ~ **de l'Europe** northern Europe; ③ Géog, Pol **le Nord** the North; **du Nord** [*ville, accent*] northern
(Idiome) **il ne perd pas le** ~○! he' s got his head screwed on○!

nord-africain, ~e, *mpl* ~s /nɔʀafʀikɛ̃, ɛn/ *adj* North African

nord-américain, ~e, *mpl* ~s /nɔʀamerikɛ̃, ɛn/ *adj* North American

nord-coréen, **-éenne**, *mpl* ~s /nɔʀkɔreɛ̃, ɛn/ ▸ p. 392 *adj* North Korean

nord-est /nɔʀ(d)ɛst/ ▸ p. 454
A *adj inv* [*façade, versant*] northeast; [*frontière, zone*] northeastern
B *nm* northeast; **vent de** ~ northeasterly wind

nordique /nɔʀdik/ *adj* [*pays, langue*] Nordic

nord-ouest /nɔʀ(d)west/ ▸ p. 454
A *adj inv* [*façade, versant*] northwest; [*frontière, zone*] northwestern
B *nm* northwest; **vent de** ~ northwesterly wind

Nord-Sud /nɔʀsyd/ *adj inv* Pol North-South

nord-vietnamien, **-ienne**, *mpl* ~s /nɔʀvjɛtnamjɛ̃, ɛn/ *adj* North Vietnamese

normal, ~e¹, *mpl* **-aux** /nɔʀmal, o/ *adj* normal; **ne pas être dans son état** ~ not to be oneself; **il est** ~ **que** (+ *subj*) it is natural that; **il n'est pas** ~ **que** (+ *subj*) it is not right that

normale² /nɔʀmal/ *nf* ① (moyenne) average; ② (norme) norm; **retour à la** ~ return to normal

normalement /nɔʀmalmɑ̃/ *adv* [*marcher*] normally; ~ **elle devrait être là** she should be here by now

normalien, **-ienne** /nɔʀmaljɛ̃, ɛn/ *nm,f* student at an École normale supérieure

normalisation /nɔʀmalizasjɔ̃/ *nf* ① Pol (régularisation) normalization; ② Tech (standardisation) standardization

normaliser /nɔʀmalize/ [1] *vtr* ① Pol (régulariser) to normalize; ② Tech (standardiser) to standardize

normalité /nɔʀmalite/ *nf* normality

normand, ~e /nɔʀmɑ̃, ɑ̃d/
A ▸ p. 504 *adj* Hist [*conquête*] Norman
B *nm* Ling Norman (French)

Normand, ~e /nɔʀmɑ̃, ɑ̃d/ *nm,f* (de Normandie) Norman
⏵Idiome⏴ **une réponse de ~** a noncommittal reply

normatif, -ive /nɔʀmatif, iv/ *adj* normative

norme /nɔʀm/ *nf* ⚊1⚊ (*règle*) norm; ⚊2⚊ Comm, Tech standard; **~s de sécurité** safety standards; **hors ~** lit nonstandard; fig extraordinary; ⚊3⚊ Math norm

Norvège /nɔʀvɛʒ/ ▸ p. 230 *nprf* Norway

norvégien, -ienne /nɔʀveʒjɛ̃, ɛn/ ▸ p. 336, p. 392
A *adj* Norwegian
B *nm* Ling Norwegian

nos ▸ notre

nosocomial, ~e *adj* /nɔzɔkɔmjal, o/ Méd hospital-acquired

nostalgie /nɔstalʒi/ *nf* nostalgia (**de** for)

nostalgique /nɔstalʒik/
A *adj* (*mélancolique*) nostalgic (**de** for); (*loin de son pays*) homesick
B *nmf* **les ~s des années 20** those who are nostalgic for the 1920's

notabilité /nɔtabilite/ *nf* notability

notable /nɔtabl/
A *adj* [*fait*] notable; [*progrès*] significant
B *nm* notable

notablement /nɔtabləmɑ̃/ *adv* significantly

notaire /nɔtɛʀ/ ▸ p. 372 *nm* notary public

notamment /nɔtamɑ̃/ *adv* ⚊1⚊ (*entre autres*) notably; ⚊2⚊ (*plus particulièrement*) in particular, more particularly

notation /nɔtasjɔ̃/ *nf* ⚊1⚊ (*système*) notation; ⚊2⚊ (*d'élève*) marking GB, grading US; (*de fonctionnaire*) grading

note /nɔt/ *nf* ⚊1⚊ (*facture*) bill, check US; **faire la ~ de qn** to write out sb's bill GB *ou* check US; ⚊2⚊ Mus note; ⚊3⚊ (*évaluation*) mark GB, grade US; **~ éliminatoire** fail mark GB *ou* grade US; **c'est une bonne ~ pour lui** fig that's a point in his favour^GB; ⚊4⚊ (*communication écrite*) note; ⚊5⚊ (*transcription*) **~s de cours** (lecture) notes; **prendre qch en ~** to make a note of sth; **prendre (bonne) ~ de qch** fig to take (due) note of sth; ⚊6⚊ (*détail*) note; **une ~ d'originalité** a touch of originality; **forcer la ~** to overdo it; ⚊7⚊ (*commentaire*) note; **~ en bas de page** footnote
⏵Composés⏴ **~ de frais** expense account; **~ d'honoraires** bill; **~ interne** memorandum, memo^○; **~ de la rédaction, NDLR** editor's note; **~ de service = ~ interne**

noter /nɔte/ *vtr* ⚊1⚊ (*inscrire*) to note down [*renseignement*]; to write down [*idée, citation*]; **c'est (bien) noté?** have you got that?; ⚊2⚊ (*remarquer*) to notice [*changement, progrès, erreur*]; **ceci est à ~** this should be noted; **il me déplaît, notez bien que je n'ai rien à lui reprocher** I don't like him, though mind you I haven't got anything particular against him; **il faut quand même ~** it has to be said; ⚊3⚊ (*évaluer*) to mark GB, to grade US [*devoir*]; to give a mark GB *ou* grade US to [*élève*]; to grade [*employé*]; **élève bien/mal noté** pupil who got good/bad marks GB *ou* grades US; **fonctionnaire bien/mal noté** civil servant who obtains a high/low rating in progress reports; ⚊4⚊ (*marquer*) to mark [*texte*]; ⚊5⚊ Mus to write down [*air, notes*]

notice /nɔtis/ *nf* ⚊1⚊ (*exposé*) note; ⚊2⚊ (*instructions*) instructions (*pl*)

notification /nɔtifikasjɔ̃/ *nf* gén notification; Jur notice

notifier /nɔtifje/ [2] *vtr* **~ qch à qn** gén to notify sb of sth; Jur to give sb notice of sth

notion /nɔsjɔ̃/ *nf* ⚊1⚊ (*conscience*) notion; **perdre la ~ de qch** to lose all sense of sth; ⚊2⚊ (*concept*) notion; ⚊3⚊ (*de langue, science*) **~s** basic knowledge ⚿

notoire /nɔtwaʀ/ *adj* [*fait, position*] well-known; [*escroc, bêtise*] notorious; Jur [*inconduite*] manifest

notoirement /nɔtwaʀmɑ̃/ *adv* gén manifestly; péj notoriously

notoriété /nɔtɔʀjete/ *nf* ⚊1⚊ (*de personne, lieu, d'œuvre*) fame; (*de produit*) reputation; **il est de ~ (publique) que** it's common knowledge that; ⚊2⚊ (*personne célèbre*) celebrity

notre, *pl* **nos** /nɔtʀ, no/ *adj poss*

⚠ En anglais, on ne répète pas le possessif coordonné: *notre adresse et notre numéro de téléphone* = our address and phone number.

our; **nos enfants à nous**^○ our children; **à nos âges** at our age; **ils sont venus pendant ~ absence** they came while we were away; **~ retour s'est bien passé** we got back safely; **c'était ~ avis à tous** we all felt the same; **c'est ~ maître à tous** he's the master of us all

nôtre /notʀ/
A *adj poss* **nous avons fait ~s ces idées** we've adopted these ideas
B **le nôtre, la nôtre, les nôtres** *pron poss* ours; **quelle erreur était la ~!** how wrong we were!; **à la ~** cheers!; **soyez des ~s!** won't you join us?; **les ~s** (*notre peuple*) our own people; (*notre équipe*) our side (*sg*)

nouer /nwe/ [1]
A *vtr* ⚊1⚊ (*attacher*) to tie [*lacets, cravate*]; to tie up [*chaussure, colis*]; **~ ses cheveux** to tie one's hair back; **~ ses bras autour du cou** to put one's arms around sb's neck; ⚊2⚊ (*contracter*) **avoir la gorge nouée** to have a lump in one's throat; **avoir l'estomac noué** to have a knot in one's stomach; ⚊3⚊ (*établir*) to establish [*relations*]; to engage in [*dialogue*]; ⚊4⚊ Cin, Littérat, Théât to weave [*intrigue*]
B **se nouer** *vpr* ⚊1⚊ Cin, Littérat, Théât [*intrigue*] to take shape; ⚊2⚊ [*relations diplomatiques*] to be established; [*dialogue, amitié*] to begin

noueux, -euse /nuø, øz/ *adj* gnarled

nougat /nuga/ *nm* nougat

nouille /nuj/ *nf* ⚊1⚊ (*pâtes alimentaires*) **des ~s** noodles, pasta ⚿; ⚊2⚊ ^○(*niais*) noodle^○

nounou^○ /nunu/ *nf* nanny GB, nurse

nounours^○ /nunuʀs/ *nm inv* baby talk teddy bear

nourri, ~e /nuʀi/ *adj* ⚊1⚊ [*tir*] heavy; [*applaudissements*] sustained; ⚊2⚊ [*conversation*] lively

nourrice /nuʀis/ *nf* (*gardienne*) (*chez elle*) childminder GB, babysitter US; (*chez l'enfant*) nanny, babysitter US

nourricier, -ière /nuʀisje, ɛʀ/ *adj* ⚊1⚊ liter [*terre, sève*] nourishing; ⚊2⚊ †[*père*] foster

nourrir /nuʀiʀ/ [3]
A *vtr* ⚊1⚊ (*fournir des aliments à*) to feed [*personne, plante*]; to nourish [*cuir, peau*]; **bien nourri** well-fed; **mal nourri** undernourished; **~ au sein/au biberon** to breast-/to bottle-feed; ⚊2⚊ (*subvenir aux besoins de*) to keep [*famille*]; to provide a living for [*région*]; **mon travail ne me nourrit pas** I don't make enough to live on; ⚊3⚊ (*entretenir*) to harbour^GB [*espoir*]; to nurture [*projet*]; to feed [*incendie*]; to fuel [*passion*]; to feed [*idéologie*]; ⚊4⚊ (*enrichir*) to fuel [*discussion*]; to feed [*esprit*]; **elle fut nourrie d'histoire classique** she was brought up on classical history
B **se nourrir** *vpr* [*animal*] to feed (**de** on); [*personne*] to eat; **se ~ de** to live on [*légumes*]; to feed on [*illusions*]

nourrissant, ~e /nuʀisɑ̃, ɑ̃t/ *adj* nourishing

nourrisson /nuʀisɔ̃/ *nm* (*nouveau-né*) new-born baby; (*enfant jusqu'à deux ans*) infant

nourriture /nuʀityʀ/
A *nf* ⚊1⚊ (*aliments*) food; ⚊2⚊ (*régime*) diet
B **nourritures** *nfpl* liter nourishment ⚿

nous /nu/ *pron pers* ⚊1⚊ (*sujet*) we; **c'est ~ les premiers**^○ we're first; ⚊2⚊ (*dans une comparaison*) **il travaille plus que ~** he works more than we do *ou* than us; **ils les voient plus souvent que ~** (*que nous ne les voyons*) they see them more often than we do; (*qu'ils ne nous voient*) they see them more often than us; ⚊3⚊ (*objet*) us; **à cause de/autour de/après ~** because of/after us; **entre ~, il n'est pas très intelligent** between ourselves *ou* you and me, he isn't very intelligent; **à ~** (*en jouant*) our turn; **nous n'avons pas encore de maison à ~** we haven't got a house of our own yet; **c'est à ~** (*appartenance*) it's ours, it belongs to us; (*séquence*) it's our turn; **(c'est) à ~ de choisir** (*notre tour*) it's our turn to choose; (*notre responsabilité*) it's up to us to choose; ⚊4⚊ (*pronom réfléchi*) ourselves; **nous ne ~ soignons que par les plantes** we only use herbal medicines; ⚊5⚊ (*nous-mêmes*) ourselves

nous-même, *pl* **nous-mêmes** /numɛm/ *pron pers* ⚊1⚊ (*pluriel*) ourselves; ⚊2⚊ (*de majesté, modestie*) we

nouveau (**nouvel** before vowel or mute h), **nouvelle**[1], *mpl* **~x** /nuvo, nuvɛl/
A *adj* ⚊1⚊ (*qui remplace, succède*) [*modèle, locataire*] new; (*qui s'ajoute*) [*attentat, tentative*] fresh; **se faire faire un ~ costume** (*pour remplacer*) to have a new suit made; (*supplémentaire*) to have

another suit made; **il a subi une nouvelle opération** he's had another operation; **faire une nouvelle tentative** to make another *ou* a fresh attempt; **procéder à de nouvelles arrestations** to make further arrests; **une nouvelle fois** once again; ⟨2⟩ (d'apparition récente) [*mot, virus, science, ville*] new; (de la saison) [*pommes de terre, vin*] new; **tout ∼** brand-new; **les ∼x élus** the newly-elected members; **les ∼x mariés** the newlyweds; **la nouvelle venue** the newcomer; ⟨3⟩ (original) [*ligne, méthode*] new, original; **c'est une façon très nouvelle d'aborder le problème** it's a very novel approach to the problem; ⟨4⟩ (novice) **être ∼ dans le métier** to be new to the job

B *nm,f* (à l'école) new student; (dans une entreprise) new employee; (à l'armée) new recruit; **je ne sais pas, je suis ∼** I don't know, I'm new here

C *nm* (rebondissement) **téléphone-moi s'il y a du ∼** give me a call if there is anything new to report; **j'ai du ∼ pour toi** I've got some news for you; ⟨2⟩ (nouveauté) **il nous faut du ∼** we want something new

D **à nouveau, de nouveau** *loc adv* (once) again

⟨Composés⟩ **∼ franc** Hist new franc; **∼ riche** nouveau riche; **∼ roman** nouveau roman; **Nouveau Monde** New World; **Nouvel An** New Year; **nouvelle année** = **Nouvel An**

⟨Idiome⟩ **tout ∼ tout beau** the novelty will soon wear off

nouveau-né ∼**e,** *mpl* ∼**s** /nuvone/
A *adj* [*enfant, agneau*] newborn (*épith*)
B *nm,f* newborn baby

nouveauté /nuvote/ *nf* ⟨1⟩ (caractère récent) newness, novelty; (originalité) novelty; ⟨2⟩ (chose nouvelle) novelty; **être à la recherche de/aimer la ∼** to look for/to like novelty; **ce n'est pas une ∼!** that's nothing new!; ⟨3⟩ (objet nouveau) *gén* new thing; (livre) new publication; (disque) new release; (appareil, voiture) new model

nouvel ▸ nouveau A

nouvelle² /nuvel/
A *adj f* ▸ **nouveau**
B *nf* ⟨1⟩ (annonce d'un événement) news **C**; **une ∼** *gén* a piece of news; (aux informations) an item of news; **une bonne/mauvaise ∼** some good/bad news; **tu connais la ∼?** have you heard the news?; **première ∼°!** that's news to me!; ⟨2⟩ Littérat short story
C **nouvelles** *nfpl* ⟨1⟩ (renseignements) news (*sg*); **recevoir des ∼s de qn** (par la personne elle-même) to hear from sb; (par un intermédiaire) to hear news of sb; **il m'a demandé de tes ∼s** he asked after you; **je viens aux ∼s°** I've come to see what's happening; **il aura de mes ∼s°!** he'll be hearing from me!; **goûte ce vin, tu m'en diras des ∼s°** have a taste of this wine, it's really good!; ⟨2⟩ (informations) **les ∼s** the news (*sg*)

nouvellement /nuvelmɑ̃/ *adv* [*publié*] recently; [*bâti*] newly

nouvelliste /nuvelist/ ▸ p. 372 *nmf* short-story writer

novateur, -trice /nɔvatœʀ, tʀis/
A *adj* innovative
B *nm,f* innovator, pioneer

novembre /nɔvɑ̃bʀ/ ▸ p. 380 *nm* November

novice /nɔvis/
A *adj* inexperienced, green
B *nmf* ⟨1⟩ (débutant) novice; ⟨2⟩ Relig novice

noyade /nwajad/ *nf* (meurtre, accident) drowning **C**; **il y a eu 20 ∼s** there were 20 people drowned

noyau, *pl* ∼**x** /nwajo/ *nm* ⟨1⟩ (de fruit) stone GB, pit US; **fruits à ∼** stone fruit GB, fruit with pits US; ⟨2⟩ (groupe humain) small group; ∼**x de résistance** pockets of resistance; ⟨3⟩ (partie centrale) Biol, Phys nucleus; (de la Terre) core; Constr newel; Ling (de phrase) kernel; (d'intonation) nucleus; Ordinat kernel

noyauter /nwajote/ [1] *vtr* to infiltrate

noyé, ∼**e** /nwaje/
A *adj* ⟨1⟩ °fig (perdu) **mes enfants sont ∼s en algèbre** my children are out of their depth in algebra; ⟨2⟩ (couvert) liter **vallée** ∼**e dans la brume** valley shrouded in mist; **visage** ∼ **de larmes** face bathed in tears; **yeux** ∼**s de larmes** eyes swimming with tears
B *nm,f* drowned person

noyer¹ /nwaje/ [23]
A *vtr* ⟨1⟩ (tuer) to drown [*personne, animal*]; ⟨2⟩ (inonder) to flood [*village, champ*]; ⟨3⟩ (mettre trop de liquide) to flood [*moteur*]; to

drown [*pastis, whisky*]; to douse [*feu, incendie*]; **∼ son chagrin** *or* **sa peine dans l'alcool** to drown one's sorrows (in drink); ⟨4⟩ (accabler, étourdir) **∼ qn sous un flot de paroles** to talk sb's head off; ⟨5⟩ (faire disparaître) **∼ une idée dans qch** to lose *ou* bury an idea in sth; ⟨6⟩ Art to blend [*couleurs*]; to merge [*contours*]

B **se noyer** *vpr* ⟨1⟩ (accidentellement) to drown; (volontairement) to drown oneself; **mourir noyé** to die by drowning; ⟨2⟩ fig **mes cris se sont noyés dans le brouhaha général** my shouts were drowned (out) in the general hubbub; **quelques acteurs connus noyés dans la foule** some well-known actors lost in the crowd; **se ∼ dans des détails** to get bogged down in details

⟨Idiome⟩ **se ∼ dans un verre d'eau** to make a mountain out of a molehill

noyer² /nwaje/ *nm* ⟨1⟩ (arbre) walnut (tree); ⟨2⟩ (bois) walnut; **table en ∼** walnut table

NTIC /ɛnteise/ *nf pl* (*abbr* = **nouvelles technologies de l'information et de la communication**) ICT

nu, ∼**e** /ny/
A *adj* ⟨1⟩ (dévêtu) [*corps*] naked; [*partie du corps*] bare; **être ∼** to be naked; **être tout ∼** to be completely *ou* stark naked; **avoir la tête** ∼**e** to be bare-headed; **avoir les pieds** ∼**s** to be barefoot; **être torse ∼** to be stripped to the waist; ⟨2⟩ [*mur, pièce, arbre, fil électrique*] bare; [*style*] unadorned; **voilà la vérité toute** ∼**e** that is the plain truth
B *nm inv* (lettre) nu
C *nm* Art **le ∼** the nudes (*pl*); **un ∼** a nude
D **à nu** *loc adv* **être à ∼** [*fil électrique*] to be bare *ou* exposed; [*personne, vice*] to be exposed; **mettre à ∼** to strip [*fil électrique*]; to expose [*personne, vice*]; **mettre son cœur à ∼** to open one's heart

nuage /nɥaʒ/ *nm* lit, fig cloud; **sans** ∼**s** [*ciel*] cloudless; [*bonheur*] unclouded; **∼ de lait** dash of milk

⟨Idiomes⟩ **être dans les** ∼**s°** to have one's head in the clouds; **descendre de son ∼** to come back to earth

nuageux, -euse /nɥaʒø, øz/ *adj* [*ciel*] cloudy; [*masse*] cloud (*épith*)

nuance /nɥɑ̃s/ *nf* ⟨1⟩ (de couleur) shade; (de sens) nuance; **sans ∼** [*commentaire, bilan*] clearcut; [*personnalité*] straightforward; [*différence*] slight *ou* subtle difference; **à cette ∼ près que** with the small reservation that; ⟨4⟩ Mus nuance

nuancer /nɥɑ̃se/ [12] *vtr* ⟨1⟩ (avec un élément nouveau) to qualify [*avis*]; to modify [*vision des choses*]; **peu nuancé** unsubtle; ⟨2⟩ (modérer) to moderate [*propos*]

nucléaire /nykleɛʀ/
A *adj* nuclear (*épith*)
B *nm* **le ∼** (énergie) nuclear energy; (technologie) nuclear technology

nudité /nydite/ *nf* ⟨1⟩ (de personne) nakedness, nudity; ⟨2⟩ (de lieu, mur) bareness

nuée /nɥe/ *nf* ⟨1⟩ (multitude) (d'insectes) swarm; (de personnes) horde; ⟨2⟩ Météo dense cloud **C**

nues /ny/ *nfpl* **les ∼** (cieux) liter the heavens littér; (nuages) the clouds

⟨Idiomes⟩ **tomber des** ∼**°** to be flabbergasted°; **porter qn aux ∼** to praise sb to the skies

nuire /nɥiʀ/ [69]
A *vtr ind* **∼ à** to harm [*voisin, famille*]; to be harmful to [*santé, intérêts, réputation*]; to damage [*récoltes*]; to take away from [*plaisir, qualité, beauté*]; to be detrimental to [*déroulement*]
B **se nuire** *vpr* (mutuellement) to do each other a lot of harm; (à soi-même) to do oneself a lot of harm

⟨Idiome⟩ **trop parler nuit** you should know when to keep your mouth shut

nuisance /nɥizɑ̃s/ *nf* nuisance **C**

nuisible /nɥizibl/ *adj* [*déchets*] dangerous; [*influence*] harmful; **insecte ∼** (insect) pest; **∼ à** detrimental to

nuit /nɥi/ *nf* ⟨1⟩ (période) night; **cette ∼** tonight; **en pleine ∼** in the middle of the night; **au cœur de la ∼** at dead of night; **étudier la ∼** to study at night; **une ∼ d'hôtel** a night in a hotel; **voyager de ∼** to travel by night; **vol/équipe de ∼** night flight/shift; **faire sa ∼** to sleep right through the night; ⟨2⟩ (date) night; **par une ∼ d'orage** on a stormy night; ⟨3⟩ (obscurité) **la ∼ tombe** night is falling; **avant la ∼** before dark *ou* nightfall; **à la ∼ tombante, à la tombée de la ∼** at nightfall; **il fait ∼** it's dark; **il faisait ∼ noire, il faisait une ∼ d'encre** it was pitch dark; **ça se**

perd dans la ~ des temps it is lost in the mists of time; depuis la ~ des temps since the dawn of time; ▸ **gris**

(Composés) ~ **américaine** Cin day for night; ~ **blanche** sleepless night; ~ **bleue** *night of terrorist bomb attacks*

(Idiomes) **c'est le jour et la** ~ they're as different as chalk and cheese; **attends demain pour donner ta réponse: la** ~ **porte conseil** wait till tomorrow to give your answer: sleep on it first

nul, nulle /nyl/

A *adj* **1** ○[*personne*] hopeless, useless; [*travail, étude*] worthless; [*film, roman*] trashy○; **il est trop** ~ **pour ce travail** he's too useless for the job; **2** Jur [*contrat, mariage*] void; [*testament*] invalid; [*élections*] null and void; [*vote*] spoiled; **3** Sport, Jeux **match** ~ (égalité) tie, draw GB; (zéro partout) nil-all draw; **4** (qui n'existe pas) [*différence, effet*] nil (*jamais épith*); [*récolte*] nonexistent; **vent** ~ no wind

B *adj indéf* (aucun) [*homme, idée, pays*] no; ~ **autre que vous** no-one else but you; **sans** ~ **doute** without any doubt

C ○*nm,f* idiot○; **c'est un** ~ he's a dead loss○, he's completely useless

D *pron indéf* no-one; ~ **n'est censé ignorer la loi** ignorance of the law is no excuse; ~ **n'ignore que** everyone knows that; ▸ **impossible**

E **nulle part** *loc adv* nowhere

nullement /nylmɑ̃/ *adv* not at all; **n'avoir** ~ **l'intention de faire** to have absolutely no intention of doing

nullité /nylite/ *nf* **1** Jur nullity; **frapper de** ~ to render void; **sous peine de** ~ under pain of being declared null and void; **2** (d'argument, de théorie) invalidity; (d'œuvre, de personne)○ worthlessness; **c'est d'une totale** ~ it's absolutely awful; **3** ○(personne incapable) idiot○

numéraire /nymeʀɛʀ/ *nm* cash

numéral, ~e, *mpl* **-aux** /nymeʀal, o/ ▸ p. 398

A *adj* numeral

B *nm* numeral

numération /nymeʀasjɔ̃/ *nf* Math numeration

(Composé) ~ **globulaire** blood count

numérique /nymeʀik/ *adj* **1** Tech [*affichage*] digital; **clavier** ~ Télécom keypad; **commande** ~ numerical control; **2** Math [*valeur*] numerical

numériser /nymeʀize/ [1] *vtr* to digitize

numéro /nymeʀo/ *nm* **1** (nombre) number; ~ **de téléphone** telephone number; **2** (indiquant l'importance) **le** ~ **deux du parti** number two in the party; **objectif** ~ **un** primary objective; **le** ~ **un de l'opposition** the leader of the opposition; **3** (journal, magazine) issue; **un vieux** ~ a back number *ou* issue; **suite au prochain** ~ lit to be continued; fig watch this space; **4** (dans un spectacle) act; (de chant) number; **5** ○(personne drôle) **quel** ~**!** what a character!

(Composés) ~ **d'abonné** customer's number; ~ **d'appel** telephone number; ~ **d'appel gratuit** freefone number GB, toll-free number US; ~ **de série** serial number; ~ **d'urgence** hotline; ~ **vert** = ~ **d'appel gratuit**; ~ **zéro** (de périodique) trial issue

(Idiome) **tirer le bon/mauvais** ~ to be lucky/unlucky

numérologie /nymeʀɔlɔʒi/ *nf* numerology

numérotation /nymeʀɔtasjɔ̃/ *nf* numbering; ~ **téléphonique** telephone numbering system

numéroter /nymeʀɔte/ [1] *vtr* to number

numerus clausus /nymeʀysklozys/ *nm inv* quota

numismatique /nymismatik/

A *adj* numismatic

B *nf* numismatics (+ *v sg*), numismatology

nunuche○ /nynyʃ/ *adj pej* bird-brained○, silly

nu-pied, *pl* ~**s** /nypje/ *nm* (sandale) (open) sandal

nuptial, ~e, *mpl* **-iaux** /nypsjal, o/ *adj* [*messe*] nuptial; [*chambre*] bridal; **cérémonie** ~**e** wedding

nuque /nyk/ ▸ p. 136 *nf* nape (of the neck)

nurse /nœʀs/ *nf* nanny GB, nurse

nutritif, -ive /nytʀitif, iv/ *adj* [*aliment, repas*] nutritious; [*crème*] nourishing; [*valeur*] nutritive

nutrition /nytʀisjɔ̃/ *nf* nutrition

nyctalopie /niktalɔpi/ *nf* night vision

nylon® /nilɔ̃/ *nm* nylon

nymphe /nɛ̃f/ *nf* Mythol, Zool nymph; Anat nympha

nymphéa /nɛ̃fea/ *nm* waterlily

nymphomane /nɛ̃fɔman/ *adj, nf* nymphomaniac

n

Oo

o, O /o/ nm inv o, O

ô /o/ excl liter o!

oasis /ɔazis/ nf inv oasis

obédience /ɔbedjɑ̃s/ nf persuasion; **pays d'∼ catholique** Catholic country

obéir /ɔbeiʀ/ [3] vtr ind **1** (se soumettre) ∼ **à** to obey [ordre, devoir]; to follow [norme]; to observe [coutume]; to comply with [décision]; ∼ **à qn** [soldat] to obey sb; [enfant, employé] to do what one is told by sb; **elle se fait ∼ de ses enfants** her children always do as she says; **2** (être soumis) [freins] to respond (**à** to)

(Idiome) ∼ **à qn au doigt et à l'œil** to obey sb slavishly

obéissance /ɔbeisɑ̃s/ nf obedience (**à** to); ∼ **passive** blind obedience

obéissant, ∼e /ɔbeisɑ̃, ɑ̃t/ adj obedient

obélisque /ɔbelisk/ nm obelisk

obèse /ɔbɛz/ adj obese

objecter /ɔbʒɛkte/ [1] vtr to object

objecteur /ɔbʒɛktœʀ/ nm objector

(Composé) ∼ **de conscience** conscientious objector

objectif, -ive /ɔbʒɛktif, iv/
A adj objective
B nm **1** (dessein) objective; **se donner qch pour ∼** to set oneself sth as an objective; **2** Phot lens; (de microscope, jumelles, télescope) objective; ∼ **à focale variable** zoom lens; **braquer son ∼ sur qn** to point one's camera at sb; **3** (cible) target; (position à saisir) objective

objection /ɔbʒɛksjɔ̃/ nf objection

objectivement /ɔbʒɛktivmɑ̃/ adv **1** (de façon objective) objectively; **2** (évidemment) clearly

objectivité /ɔbʒɛktivite/ nf objectivity

objet /ɔbʒɛ/
A nm **1** (chose) object; ∼ **en bois** wooden object; ∼ **fragile** fragile item; ∼**s personnels** gén personal possessions; Admin personal effects; **2** (sujet) (de débat, recherches, science) subject; (de haine, d'amour) object; (de désaccord) source; **faire l'∼ de** to be the subject of [enquête, recherche]; to be subjected to [moquerie, surveillance]; to be the object of [convoitise, haine, lutte]; **être un ∼ de respect pour qn** to be respected by sb; **3** (but) purpose, object; **cette lettre a pour ∼ de faire** the purpose of this letter is to do; **'∼: réponse à votre lettre du...'** (en haut d'une lettre) 're: your letter of...'; **sans ∼** [réclamation, inquiétude] to be groundless; **4** Ling, Philos object; **5** Jur ∼ **d'un litige** matter at issue; ∼ **d'un procès** subject of an action
B **-objet** (in compounds) as an object (après n); **femme-∼** woman as an object

(Composés) ∼ **du culte** liturgical object; ∼ **du délit** hum offending object; ∼ **sexuel** sex object; ∼**s trouvés** lost property **¢**; ∼ **volant non identifié, ovni** unidentified flying object, UFO

objurgations /ɔbʒyʀgasjɔ̃/ nfpl **1** (reproches) objurgations sout; **2** (prières) entreaties

obligataire /ɔbligatɛʀ/ Fin
A adj [marché, émission, rendement] bond; **emprunt ∼** bond issue
B nmf bondholder

obligation /ɔbligasjɔ̃/ nf **1** (devoir) (professionnel, moral, familial) obligation, responsibility; (légal) obligation; (militaire) obligation, duty; **on n'est pas une ∼ de les inviter** you don't have to invite them; **se faire une ∼ de** to feel it one's duty to; **avoir une ∼ or des ∼s envers qn** to feel an obligation toward(s) sb; **2** (nécessité) necessity; **se voir** or **trouver dans l'∼ de faire** to be forced to do; **3** Fin bond; **4** Jur obligation; **5** (devoir de reconnaissance) liter obligation (**envers** toward(s))

(Composés) ∼ **scolaire** compulsory school attendance; ∼**s militaires** military service **¢**; **être dégagé des ∼s militaires** to have done one's military service

obligatoire /ɔbligatwaʀ/ adj **1** lit compulsory, obligatory; **l'étude du latin n'est pas ∼** Latin is not a compulsory subject; **tenue de soirée ∼** evening dress is obligatory; **2** ○(inévitable) inevitable

obligatoirement /ɔbligatwaʀmɑ̃/ adv **1** (par règlement) **une lettre doit ∼ accompagner la demande** the application must be accompanied by a letter; **2** (inévitablement) inevitably, necessarily

obligé, ∼e /ɔbliʒe/
A pp ▸ **obliger**
B pp adj **1** (contraint) **je suis ∼ de partir** I must go now, I have to go now; **se voir ∼ de faire** to be forced to do; **je suis bien ∼ de vous croire** I have no choice ou option but to believe you; **vous n'êtes pas ∼ d'accepter** you don't have to accept; **2** (reconnaissant) **être ∼ à qn de** to be obliged ou grateful to sb for; **3** ○(fatal) inevitable; **4** (indispensable) essential; **un passage ∼ (pour)** fig a prerequisite (for)
C nm,f **1** fml (personne) **être l'∼ de qn** to be obliged ou indebted to sb; **2** Jur (débiteur) obligor

obligeamment /ɔbliʒamɑ̃/ adv obligingly

obligeance /ɔbliʒɑ̃s/ nf **avec l'∼ de qn** through sb's good offices; **avoir l'∼ de** to be kind enough to

obligeant, ∼e /ɔbliʒɑ̃, ɑ̃t/ adj [personne] obliging; [manières] pleasing; [offre, mot] kind

obliger /ɔbliʒe/ [13]
A vtr **1** (contraindre) ∼ **qn à** [personne, police] to force sb to; [autorité, règlement] to make it compulsory for sb to; [devoir, prudence] to compel sb to; **comme la loi vous y oblige** as required by law; **rien ne t'oblige à accepter** you don't have to accept; **2** Jur [bail, contrat, accord] to bind [sb] legally [personne]; **le bail m'oblige à réparer les dégâts** the lease makes me legally responsible for repairs; **3** (rendre service à) to oblige
B s'obliger vpr **s'∼ à faire** to force oneself to do

oblique /ɔblik/ adj [trait, rayon] slanting; [regard] sidelong (épith); **en ∼** [avancer] diagonally; [poser] crosswise

obliquement /ɔblikmɑ̃/ adv [enfoncer, poser] at an angle; [déplacer] diagonally

obliquer /ɔblike/ [1] vi ∼ **vers la droite/gauche** (légèrement) to bear right/left; (nettement) to veer right/left

oblitération /ɔbliteʀasjɔ̃/ nf **1** (de timbre) (action) cancelling[GB] **¢**; (cachet d')∼ postmark; **2** Méd occlusion

oblitérer /ɔbliteʀe/ [14] vtr **1** to cancel, to obliterate [timbre]; Méd to obstruct [vaisseau]

obnubiler /ɔbnybile/ [1] vtr **1** (obséder) to obsess [personne]; **2** (obscurcir) to cloud [jugement, émotion]

obole /ɔbɔl/ nf small donation

obscène /ɔpsɛn/ adj obscene

obscur, ∼e /ɔpskyʀ/ adj **1** (sans lumière) dark; **2** (mystérieux) obscure; **3** (humble) lowly; **4** (vague) vague

obscurcir /ɔpskyʀsiʀ/ [3]
A vtr **1** lit to make [sth] dark [lieu]; to deepen [couleur]; **2** (ternir) to overshadow [relations]; to blur [situation]; to make [sth] obscure [texte, œuvre]; [fumée] to obscure [vue]
B s'obscurcir vpr **1** lit [ciel, lieu] to darken; **2** [regard] to

become sombre^{GB}; [*situation*] to become confused

obscurément /ɔpskyʀemɑ̃/ *adv* **1** [*sentir*] vaguely; **2** [*vivre*] in obscurity

obscurité /ɔpskyʀite/ *nf* **1** (de lieu) darkness; **2** (d'œuvre, de personne) obscurity; (de situation) vagueness

obsédant, **~e** /ɔpsedɑ̃, ɑ̃t/ *adj* [*souvenir, rêve, musique*] haunting; [*rythme*] insistent; [*problème*] nagging (*épith*)

obsédé, **~e** /ɔpsede/ *nm,f* **~ (sexuel)** sex maniac; **un ~ du vélo/du ski** a cycling/ski freak[○]

obséder /ɔpsede/ [14] *vtr* [*souvenir, rêve, remords*] to haunt; [*idée, problème*] to obsess; **il est obsédé** (sexuellement) he has sex on the brain[○]

obsèques /ɔpsɛk/ *nfpl* funeral (*sg*)

obséquieux, **-ieuse** /ɔpsekjø, øz/ *adj* obsequious

observateur, **-trice** /ɔpsɛʀvatœʀ, tʀis/
A *adj* observant
B *nm,f* observer

observation /ɔpsɛʀvasjɔ̃/ *nf* **1** gén, Méd (étude, surveillance) observation; **mission d'~** Pol observer mission; **l'~ des oiseaux** bird-watching; **2** (obéissance) observance; **3** (remarque) gén observation, remark; (sur un devoir) comment; **4** (reproche) reproach

observatoire /ɔpsɛʀvatwaʀ/ *nm* **1** (astronomique) observatory; **2** Mil observation post, look-out post; **3** (organisme) watchdog

observer /ɔpsɛʀve/ [1]
A *vtr* **1** (regarder) gén to observe; to watch [*personne, mouvement*]; **je me sens observé** I feel I'm being watched; **~ qch au microscope** lit to examine sth under a microscope; fig to scrutinize sth; **2** (remarquer) to notice, to observe [*chose, phénomène, réaction*]; **faire ~ qch à qn** to point sth out to sb; **3** (suivre) to observe [*règle, usage, repos, traité*]; to keep, to observe [*jeûne*]; to keep to [*régime*]; to maintain [*stratégie, politique, grève*]; **~ le silence** to keep *ou* remain quiet; **4** (contrôler) to watch [*propos, manières, gestes*]
B **s'observer** *vpr* **1** (se regarder) to watch each other; **2** (se surveiller) to keep a check on oneself

obsession /ɔpsɛsjɔ̃/ *nf* obsession

obsessionnel, **-elle** /ɔpsɛsjɔnɛl/ *adj* obsessional

obsolète /ɔpsɔlɛt/ *adj* obsolete

obstacle /ɔpstakl/ *nm* **1** (difficulté) obstacle (**à** to); **faire ~ aux négociations** to obstruct the negotiations; **elle a fait ~ à ma promotion** she stood in the way of my promotion; **2** (en équitation) fence

obstétricien, **-ienne** /ɔpstetʀisjɛ̃, ɛn/ ▸ p. 372 *nm,f* obstetrician

obstétrique /ɔpstetʀik/ *nf* obstetrics (*+ v sg*)

obstination /ɔpstinasjɔ̃/ *nf* obstinacy; **avec ~** stubbornly

obstiné, **~e** /ɔpstine/
A *adj* **1** (entêté) [*personne, caractère, refus*] stubborn; **2** (acharné) [*efforts*] dogged; [*chercheur*] dedicated; **3** (durable) [*pluie*] persistent
B *nm,f* pigheaded person *péj*

obstinément /ɔpstinemɑ̃/ *adv* obstinately

obstiner: s'obstiner /ɔpstine/ [1] *vpr* to persist (**dans** in; **à faire** in doing); **s'~ à ne pas faire qch** to refuse obstinately to do sth; **s'~ dans une opinion** to cling stubbornly to an opinion

obstruction /ɔpstʀyksjɔ̃/ *nf* gén, Méd, Pol, Sport obstruction; Tech (de conduit, canalisation) blockage; **faire ~ à qch** to obstruct sth

obstruer /ɔpstʀye/ [1]
A *vtr* to obstruct, to block [*conduit, passage*]; **les valises obstruent le passage** the suitcases are in the way
B **s'obstruer** *vpr* to get *ou* become blocked

obtempérer /ɔptɑ̃peʀe/ [14] *vtr ind* **~ à** to comply with; **refus/refuser d'~** refusal/to refuse to comply

obtenir /ɔptəniʀ/ [36]
A *vtr* to get, to obtain [*informations, prix, diplôme*]; to secure [*silence*]; to get, to arrive at [*total, somme*]; **~ qch de/pour qn** to get *ou* obtain sth from/for sb; **~ de faire** to gain *ou* get permission to do; **~ de qn qu'il fasse** to get sb to do
B **s'obtenir** *vpr* [*total, résultat*] to be arrived at, to be obtained

obtention /ɔptɑ̃sjɔ̃/ *nf* **l'~ d'un diplôme** getting a diploma; **l'~ d'un visa** obtaining a visa

obturateur, **-trice** /ɔptyʀatœʀ, tʀis/
A *adj* Tech obturating (*épith*)
B *nm* Phot shutter

obturation /ɔptyʀasjɔ̃/ *nf* **1** (accidentelle) blocking (up); (volontaire) stopping up; **2** (résultat) blockage

obturer /ɔptyʀe/ [1] *vtr* gén to block up [*trou*]

obtus, **~e** /ɔpty, yz/ *adj* obtuse

obus /ɔby/ *nm inv* Mil shell; **un éclat d'~** a piece of shrapnel; **des éclats d'~** shrapnel **℄**; **tirs d'~** shellfire **℄**

occasion /ɔkazjɔ̃/ *nf* **1** (circonstance) occasion; (moment favorable) opportunity, chance; **rater l'~** to miss one's opportunity *ou* chance; **à l'~** (si le cas se présente) some time; (parfois) occasionally; **à l'~ de** on the occasion of; **à *ou* en plusieurs ~s** on several occasions; **par la même ~** at the same time; **pour l'~** for the occasion; **les grandes ~s** special occasions; **avoir l'~ de faire** to have the opportunity *ou* chance to do *ou* of doing; **être l'~ de qch** to give rise to sth; **être l'~ de faire** to be a chance *ou* an opportunity to do; **profiter de l'~ pour faire** to take the opportunity to do; **d'~** [*héroïsme*] incidental; [*rencontre, aventure*] chance; **j'ai encore raté une bonne ~ de me taire** I should have kept my mouth shut; **2** (marché) **une voiture d'~** a second-hand car; **je l'ai acheté d'~** I bought it second-hand; **3** (objet) second-hand buy; (bonne affaire) bargain

occasionnel, **-elle** /ɔkazjɔnɛl/ *adj* occasional

occasionner /ɔkazjɔne/ [1] *vtr* to cause, to occasion sout

occident /ɔksidɑ̃/ *nm* **1** (direction) west; **2** (nations) **l'Occident** the West

occidental, **~e**, *mpl* **-aux** /ɔksidɑ̃tal, o/ *adj* **1** Géog western; **2** Pol Western

Occidental, **~e**, *mpl* **-aux** /ɔksidɑ̃tal, o/ *nm,f* Westerner

occitan, **~e** /ɔksitɑ̃, an/ *nm* Ling langue d'oc

occlusion /ɔklyzjɔ̃/ *nf* Méd occlusion; **~ intestinale** intestinal obstruction, obstruction of the bowels

occulte /ɔkylt/ *adj* **1** (relatif à l'occultisme) occult; **2** (secret) secret

occulter /ɔkylte/ [1] *vtr* (involontairement) to eclipse, to overshadow; (volontairement) to obscure [*sujet, problème*]; to conceal [*vérité, fait*]; to conceal, to mask [*malaise*]

occultisme /ɔkyltism/ *nm* occultism

occupant, **~e** /ɔkypɑ̃, ɑ̃t/
A *adj* [*troupes*] occupying
B *nm,f* (de maison) occupier, occupant; (de siège, véhicule) occupant
C *nm* Mil **l'~, les ~s** the occupying forces (*pl*)

occupation /ɔkypasjɔ̃/ *nf* **1** (passe-temps, tâche) occupation; (emploi) occupation, job; **mes ~s professionnelles** my professional activities; **2** (fait d'habiter un lieu) occupancy, occupation; **3** (pour protester) occupation; **décider l'~ des locaux** to decide to stage a sit-in; **4** Mil occupation; **l'armée d'~** the army of occupation; **l'Occupation** Hist the Occupation

occupé, **~e** /ɔkype/
A *pp* ▸ occuper
B *pp adj* **1** [*personne, vie*] busy; **être très ~** to be very busy; **2** [*siège*] taken; [*ligne téléphonique*] engaged GB, busy; [*toilettes*] engaged; **3** Mil [*pays*] occupied

occuper /ɔkype/ [1]
A *vtr* **1** (se trouver dans) to live in, to occupy [*appartement, maison*]; to be in [*douche, cellule*]; to sit in, to occupy [*siège*]; **il occupe les lieux depuis six mois** he's been in the premises for six months; **2** (remplir) [*local, meuble*] to take up, to occupy [*espace*]; [*activité*] to take up, to fill [*temps*]; **le jardin potager occupe tout mon temps** the kitchen garden takes up all my time; **le sport occupe une grande place dans ma vie** sport plays a large *ou* great part in my life; **~ son temps à faire** to spend one's time doing; **3** (donner une activité à) to occupy [*personne, esprit*]; **ça m'occupe!** it keeps me occupied *ou* busy!; **le sujet qui nous occupe** the matter which we are dealing with; **4** (exercer) to have [*emploi*]; to hold [*poste, fonctions*]; **5** (se rendre maître de) [*grévistes, armée*] to occupy [*lieu*]; **~ les locaux** to stage a sit-in
B **s'occuper** *vpr* **1** (ne pas être oisif) to keep oneself busy *ou* occupied; **j'ai de quoi m'~** I've got plenty to do; **trouver à s'~** to find sth to do; **2** (prendre en charge) **s'~ de** to see to, to take care of [*dîner, billets*]; **3** (consacrer ses efforts à) **s'~ de**

Les océans et les mers

Les noms d'océans et de mers

■ *En anglais, les mots* Ocean *et* Sea *prennent toujours une majuscule lorsqu'ils accompagnent un nom propre.*

l'océan Atlantique
= the Atlantic Ocean

la mer Baltique
= the Baltic Sea

■ Ocean *et* Sea *peuvent être omis dans la plupart des cas où* océan *et* mer *peuvent être omis en français.*

l'Atlantique
= the Atlantic

la Baltique
= the Baltic

■ *En cas de doute, consulter l'article dans le dictionnaire.*

De avec les noms d'océans et de mers

■ *Les expressions françaises avec de se traduisent en général par l'emploi des noms de mers et d'océans en position d'adjectifs.*

le climat de l'Atlantique
= the Atlantic climate

le climat de la mer du Nord
= the North Sea climate

une traversée de l'Atlantique
= an Atlantic crossing

une traversée de la mer du Nord
= a North Sea crossing

Noter aussi:

une croisière sur l'Atlantique
= an Atlantic cruise

une croisière en mer du Nord
= a North Sea cruise

to be dealing with [*dossier*]; **4** (prodiguer des soins à) **s'~ de** to take care of [*enfant, animal, plante*]; to attend to [*client*]; **on s'occupe de vous?** Comm are you being served?; **je m'occupe de vous tout de suite** I'll be with you in a minute; **5** (avoir pour emploi) **s'~ de** to be in charge of [*financement, bibliothèque*]; to work with [*handicapés, enfants*]; **6** (se mêler) **occupe-toi de tes affaires**° or **de ce qui te regarde**°! mind your own business°!; **ne t'occupe pas de ça!, t'occupe**°! keep your nose out°! GB, keep your butt out°! US; **ne t'occupe pas d'elle** don't take any notice of her

occurrence /ɔkyʀɑ̃s/ *nf* **1** (cas) case, instance; **en l'~** in this case *ou* instance; **2** Ling occurrence

OCDE /osedeø/ *nf* (abbr = **Organisation de coopération et de développement économiques**) OECD

océan /ɔseɑ̃/ ▸ p. 406 *nm* **1** lit ocean; **2** (en France) **l'Océan** the Atlantic; **3** fig **un ~ de** a sea of

océanien, -ienne /ɔseanjɛ̃, ɛn/ *adj, nm,f* Oceanian

océanique /ɔseanik/ *adj* oceanic

océanographe /ɔseanɔgʀaf/ ▸ p. 372 *nmf* oceanographer

ocelle /ɔsɛl/ *nm* ocellus

ocre[1] /ɔkʀ/ ▸ p. 140 *adj inv, nm* ochre GB, ocher US

ocre[2] /ɔkʀ/ *nf* (pigment) ochre GB, ocher US

octane /ɔktan/ *nm* octane

octante /ɔktɑ̃t/ ▸ p. 398 *adj inv, pron* B, C, H eighty

octave /ɔktav/ *nf* octave

octet /ɔktɛt/ *nm* **1** Ordinat byte; **2** Phys octet

octobre /ɔktɔbʀ/ ▸ p. 380 *nm* October; **à la mi-~** in mid-October

octogénaire /ɔktɔʒenɛʀ/
A *adj* **être ~** to be in one's eighties, to be an octogenarian
B *nmf* octogenarian

octogonal, ~e, *mpl* **-aux** /ɔktɔgɔnal, o/ *adj* octagonal

octosyllabe /ɔktɔsilab/
A *adj* octosyllabic
B *nm* octosyllable

octroi /ɔktʀwa/ *nm* **1** (attribution) granting; **2** Hist octroi

octroyer /ɔktʀwaje/ [23]
A *vtr* **~ à qn** to grant sb [*pardon*]; to award sb [*bourse*]; to allocate sb [*budget*]
B **s'octroyer** *vpr* to allow oneself [*répit, sursis*]; to win [*victoire, place*]; to achieve [*succès*]

oculaire /ɔkylɛʀ/ *adj* **1** Méd **avoir des troubles ~s** to have eye trouble; **2** **témoin ~** eyewitness

oculiste /ɔkylist/ ▸ p. 372 *nmf* oculist, ophthalmologist

ode /ɔd/ *nf* ode (**à qn** to sb; **à qch** to sth, on sth)

odeur /ɔdœʀ/ *nf* smell (**de** of); (bonne) **~** nice smell; (mauvaise) **~** smell; **dégager** *or* **avoir une bonne ~** to smell nice; **dégager** *or* **avoir une mauvaise ~** to smell nice; **chasser les mauvaises ~s** to get rid of unpleasant odours[GB]; **sans ~** [*crème, lotion*] fragrance-free; [*produit de nettoyage*] odourless[GB]

odieux, -ieuse /ɔdjø, øz/ *adj* **1** (abject) horrible, odious; **2** (insupportable) obnoxious (**avec qn** to sb)

odorant, ~e /ɔdɔʀɑ̃, ɑ̃t/ *adj* **1** (exhalant une odeur) odorous littér, which has a smell (*épith*); **2** (exhalant une bonne odeur) sweet-smelling

odorat /ɔdɔʀa/ *nm* sense of smell; **l'organe de l'~** the olfactory organ

OECE /oøsea/ *nf* (abbr = **Organisation européenne de coopération économique**) OEEC

œdème /edɛm/ ▸ p. 195 *nm* Méd oedema

œdipe /edip/ *nm* (complexe) Oedipus complex

œil, *pl* **yeux** /œj, jø/ *nm* ▸ p. 136 **1** Anat eye; **avoir de bons yeux** to have good eyesight *ou* eyes; **ouvrir un ~** lit to open one eye; **ouvrir l'~** fig to keep one's eyes open; **ouvrir les yeux à qn** fig to open sb's eyes; **fermer les yeux** lit to shut one's eyes; **fermer les yeux sur qch** fig to turn a blind eye to sth; **faire qch les yeux fermés** (très facilement) to be able to do sth with one's eyes closed; **acheter qch les yeux fermés** (avec confiance) to buy sth with complete confidence; **je n'ai pas fermé l'~ (de la nuit)** I didn't sleep a wink (all night); **il faut l'avoir à l'~** you have to keep an eye on him/her; **avoir l'~ à tout** to be vigilant; **cligner des yeux** to blink; **visible à l'~ nu** visible to the naked eye; **cela s'est passé sous mes yeux** it happened before my very eyes; **je n'en crois pas mes yeux** I can't believe my eyes; **il l'a suivie des yeux** his eyes followed her; **jeter un ~ à** *or* **sur qch** to have a quick look at sth; **n'avoir d'yeux que pour qn** to have eyes only for sb; **sans lever les yeux** [*parler, répondre*] without looking up; [*travailler*] without a break; **lever les yeux sur qch** to look up at sth; **je l'ai sous les yeux** I have it in front of me; **faire qch aux yeux de tous** to do sth openly; **les yeux dans les yeux** gazing into each other's eyes; **être agréable à l'~** to be easy on the eye° *ou* nice to look at; **coup d'~** (regard rapide) glance; (vue) view; **jette un coup d'~ pour voir s'il dort** have a quick look to see if he is asleep; **cela vaut le coup d'~** it's worth seeing; **avoir le coup d'~** to have a good eye; **yeux de biche** doe eyes; **yeux de chat** eyes like a cat; **yeux de cochon** piggy eyes; ▸ **obéir, taper**; **2** (exprimant des sentiments) eye; **des yeux rieurs/tristes** laughing/sad eyes; **elle le regardait d'un ~ amusé** she was looking at him with amusement in her eye; **d'un ~ méfiant** with a suspicious look, suspiciously; **d'un ~ inquiet** anxiously; **regarder qch d'un ~ neuf** to see sth in a new light; **voir qch d'un mauvais ~** to take a dim view of sth; **à mes yeux, il a tort** in my opinion he's wrong; **à leurs yeux, c'était un échec** in their eyes it was a failure; **voir qch d'un autre ~** to take a different view of sth; **3** (boucle, trou) gén eye; (dans une porte) peephole

Composés ▸ **poché**° black eye; **~ de verre** glass eye

Idiomes **mon ~**°! (marquant l'incrédulité) my eye°, my foot°; **à l'~**° [*manger, voyager*] for nothing, for free°; **faire les gros yeux à qn** to glare at sb; **dévorer qch/qn des yeux** to gaze longingly at sth/sb; **faire les yeux doux à qn** to make (sheep's) eyes at sb; **tourner de l'~**° to faint; **cela me sort**

par les yeux○ I 've had it up to here ○; **avoir bon pied bon ~** to be as fit as a fiddle; **sauter aux yeux** to be obvious

œil-de-bœuf, pl **œils-de-bœuf** /œjdəbœf/ nm (lucarne) bull's eye

œillade /œjad/ nf (clin d'œil) wink; (regard furtif) glance

œillère /œjɛʀ/ nf (du cheval) blinker, blinder US; **avoir** or **porter des ~s** fig to have a blinkered attitude

œillet /œjɛ/ nm ① Bot carnation; ② (de chaussure, bâche) eyelet; (de ceinture, bracelet) hole; (pour renforcer) reinforcement, reinforcing ring; (de métal) grommet

(Composés) **~ d'Inde** French marigold; **~ de poète** sweet william

œilleton /œjtɔ̃/ nm (de porte) peephole

œnologie /enɔlɔʒi/ nf oenology

œsophage /ezɔfaʒ/ nm oesophagus

œstrogène /ɛstʀɔʒɛn/
A adj oestrogenic
B nm oestrogen

œuf /œf, pl ø/ nm ① Culin, Zool egg; **en forme d'~** egg-shaped; **~s de cabillaud** cod's roe **¢**; ② ○(imbécile) idiot○; **faire l'~** to play the fool

(Composés) **~ à la coque** boiled egg; **~ dur** hard-boiled egg; **~ en gelée** egg in aspic; **~ mimosa** egg mimosa (chopped egg garnish); **~ mollet** soft-boiled egg; **~ au plat** or **sur le plat** fried egg; **~ poché** poached egg; **~ à repriser** darning egg; **~s brouillés** scrambled eggs; **~s à la neige** floating islands

(Idiomes) **plein comme un ~** full to bursting; **va te faire cuire un ~**○! go and take a running jump○!; **marcher sur des ~s** to be walking on eggs

œuvre /œvʀ/ nf ① Art, Littérat, Mus (production unique) work; (production générale) works (pl); **les ~s complètes** the complete works; **il a laissé une ~ imposante** he left an imposing body of work; ② (besogne) work; **se mettre à l'~** to get down to work; **voir qn à l'~** to see sb in action; **mettre en ~** to implement [programme, réforme]; to display [grande ingéniosité]; **mise en ~** (de programme) implementation; **tout mettre en ~ pour faire** to make every effort to do; ③ (résultat d'un travail) work; **être l'~ de** to be the work of

(Composés) **~ d'art** work of art; **~ de bienfaisance** or **de charité** charity

(Idiome) **être à pied d'~** to be ready to get down to work

off○ /ɔf/ adj inv Cin (hors écran) off-screen; **voix ~** voice-over; ② (hors programme officiel) alternative; **le festival ~** the fringe festival

offensant, ~e /ɔfɑ̃sɑ̃, ɑ̃t/ adj offensive (**pour** to)

offense /ɔfɑ̃s/ nf ① (affront) insult; **faire ~ à qn** to offend sb; ② Relig trespass

offenser /ɔfɑ̃se/ [1]
A vtr ① (blesser) to offend [personne, sensibilité, délicatesse]; to tarnish [souvenir, réputation]; ② Relig to offend against [Dieu, ciel]
B s'offenser vpr to take offence^{GB} (**de** at)

offensif, -ive[1] /ɔfɑ̃sif, iv/ adj Mil offensive

offensive[2] /ɔfɑ̃siv/ nf Mil, fig offensive (**contre** against); **l'~ du froid** the onslaught of the cold

office /ɔfis/
A nm ① (rôle) **remplir son ~** [objet] to fulfil^{GB} its purpose, to do the job○; [employé] to carry out one's duty; **faire ~ de table** to serve as a table; **faire ~ d'interprète** to act as an interpreter; ② Admin, Jur (charge) office; ③ Relig (cérémonie) service; (prières) office; ④ (salle) butlery
B d'office loc adv **d'~** (autoritairement) without consultation; **on m'a muté d'~ aux archives** I was transferred to records without being consulted; **nos propositions ont été rejetées d'~** our proposals were dismissed out of hand; **commis** or **nommé d'~** [avocat, expert] appointed by the court (après n)

(Composé) **~ du tourisme** tourist information office

officialiser /ɔfisjalize/ [1] vtr to make [sth] official

officiel, -ielle /ɔfisjɛl/
A adj gén official; **être en visite officielle** [envoyé] to be on an official visit; [chef d'État] to be on a state visit
B nm (fonctionnaire, organisateur) official

officier[1] /ɔfisje/ [2] vi Relig, hum to officiate

officier[2] /ɔfisje/ nm officer

officieusement /ɔfisjøzmɑ̃/ adv unofficially

officieux, -ieuse /ɔfisjø, øz/ adj unofficial; **à titre ~** unofficially

officinal, ~e, mpl **-aux** /ɔfisinal, o/ adj officinal

officine /ɔfisin/ nf ① (laboratoire) dispensary; (magasin) pharmacy; ② (organisation) organization

offrande /ɔfʀɑ̃d/ nf offering; **en ~** as an offering

offrant /ɔfʀɑ̃/ nm **vendre qch au plus ~** to sell sth to the highest bidder

offre /ɔfʀ/ nf ① (proposition) offer; **faire une ~** to make an offer; **'~ d'emploi'** 'situation vacant'; **répondre à une ~ d'emploi** to reply to a job advertisement; **faire paraître une ~ d'emploi** to advertise a job; **'cadres: ~s d'emploi'** 'managerial appointments'; **'locations: ~s'** 'accommodation to let' GB, 'rentals' US; ② Écon supply; **l'équilibre entre l'~ et la demande** the balance between supply and demand

(Composés) **~ d'achat** bid; **lancer une ~ d'achat** to launch a bid (**sur** for); **~ publique d'achat, OPA** takeover bid

offrir /ɔfʀiʀ/ [4]
A vtr ① (en cadeau) **~ qch à qn** to give sth to sb, to give sb sth; **c'est pour ~?** (cadeau) do you want it gift-wrapped?; (fleurs) would you like them specially wrapped?; ② (acheter) to buy (**à qn** for sb); **tu aimes ce chapeau? je te l'offre!** do you like this hat? I'll buy it for you!; **je t'offre un verre?** can I buy you a drink?; **j'offre la tournée** it's my round; ③ (mettre à la disposition) to offer [rôle, crédit]; **~ qch à qn** to offer sb sth; **~ à manger à qn** to offer sb something to eat; **il a offert de nous aider** he offered to help us; ④ (à titre d'échange) to offer [récompense]; **je t'en offre 30 euros** I'll give you 30 euros for it; ⑤ (présenter) to offer, to give [choix]; to offer [démission]; to present [difficultés]; **n'~ aucune résistance** to put up ou offer no resistance; **cela offre un avantage** there is one advantage; ⑥ (exposer) **~ son visage au vent** to turn one's face into the wind
B s'offrir vpr ① (se payer) **s'~** to buy oneself [chapeau, fleurs]; **ils ne peuvent pas s'~ le théâtre** they can't afford to go to the theatre^{GB}; **je me suis offert le restaurant** I treated myself to a meal out; ② (s'accorder) **s'~ un jour de vacances** to give oneself a day off; ③ (se présenter) [solution] to present itself (**à** to); **c'est une grande chance qui s'offre à toi** it's a wonderful opportunity for you; **le paysage qui s'offrait à nous était féerique** the landscape before us was magical; **s'~ en spectacle** to make an exhibition of oneself

offusquer /ɔfyske/ [1]
A vtr to offend
B s'offusquer vpr to be offended (**de** by)

ogival, ~e, mpl **-aux** /ɔʒival, o/ adj [arc, voûte] ribbed, ogival apex; [architecture, art] Gothic

ogive /ɔʒiv/ nf ① Archit rib; ② Mil nose cone

(Composé) **~ nucléaire** nuclear warhead

OGM /oʒeɛm/ nm (abbr = **organisme génétiquement modifié**) GMO, genetically modified organism

ogre /ɔgʀ/ nm ① (géant) ogre; ② (gros mangeur) big eater

(Idiome) **manger comme un ~** to eat like a horse

ogresse /ɔgʀɛs/ nf ① (géante) ogress; ② (grosse mangeuse) big eater

oh /o/
A nm inv **pousser un ~ de surprise** to give a cry of surprise; **pousser des ~** to cry out (**de** in)
B excl oh!; **~ hisse!** heave-ho!

oie /wa/ nf ① Zool goose; ② ○(personne) goose

(Composé) **~ blanche** naïve young girl

oignon /ɔɲɔ̃/ nm ① Bot, Culin onion; ② Bot (de fleur) bulb; ③ (montre) fob watch; ④ Méd bunion

(Idiomes) **faire qch aux petits ~s**○ to do sth with great attention to detail; **ce n'est pas tes ~s**○ it's none of your business○; **occupe-toi de tes ~s**○ mind your own business○

oindre /wɛ̃dʀ/ [56] vtr ① Relig to anoint; ② to rub [sb] with ointment [athlète]

oiseau, pl **~x** /wazo/ nm ① Zool bird; ② ○(personne) **un (drôle d')~** an oddball○

(Composés) **~ de malheur** or **de mauvais augure** bird of ill omen; **~ de nuit** night owl; **~ de passage** lit, fig bird of passage; **~ de proie** bird of prey

(Idiomes) trouver l'~ rare° to find the one person in a million; petit à petit l'~ fait son nid Prov with time and effort
you achieve your goals

oiseau-mouche, pl **oiseaux-mouches** /wazomuʃ/
nm hummingbird

oiseleur /wazlœʀ/ nm bird-catcher

oisellerie /wazɛlʀi/ nf (boutique) bird shop; (profession) selling of caged birds

oiseux, -euse /wazø, øz/ adj [propos] idle (épith); [dispute,
explication] pointless, unnecessary

oisif, -ive /wazif, iv/
A adj idle
B nm,f idler péj; **les** ~**s** the idle rich

oisillon /wazijɔ̃/ nm fledgling

oisiveté /wazivte/ nf idleness

(Idiome) l'~ **est (la) mère de tous les vices** Prov the devil
makes work for idle hands (to do) Prov

okapi /ɔkapi/ nm okapi

ola /ɔla/ nf Mexican wave

olé°: **olé olé** /ɔleɔle/ loc adj inv [plaisanterie] naughty
(épith); [personne] racy°

oléagineux, -euse /ɔleaʒinø, øz/
A adj oleaginous
B nm inv oleaginous plant

oléiculture /ɔleikyltyʀ/ nf olive-growing

oléoduc /ɔleɔdyk/ nm (oil) pipeline

olfactif, -ive /ɔlfaktif, iv/ adj olfactory

oligarchie /ɔligaʀʃi/ nf oligarchy

oligo-élément, pl ~**s** /ɔligoelemɑ̃/ nm trace element

olivâtre /ɔlivatʀ/ ▸ p. 140 adj gén olive-greenish; [teint]
sallow

olive /ɔliv/
A ▸ p. 140 adj inv olive; **vert** ~ olive green
B nf [1] (fruit) olive; [2] (interrupteur) switch

oliveraie /ɔlivʀɛ/ nf olive grove

olivette /ɔlivɛt/ nf (tomate) plum tomato

olivier /ɔlivje/ nm (arbre) olive tree; (bois) olive wood

Olympe /ɔlɛ̃p/ nprm l'~ Mount Olympus

olympiade /ɔlɛ̃pjad/
A nf (de l'antiquité) Olympiad
B olympiades nfpl Sport Olympics

olympique /ɔlɛ̃pik/ adj Olympic

ombilic /ɔ̃bilik/ nm Anat umbilicus, navel

ombilical, ~**e**, mpl **-aux** /ɔ̃bilikal, o/ adj umbilical

ombrage /ɔ̃bʀaʒ/ nm shade ¢

(Idiomes) **porter** ~ **à qn** to offend sb; **prendre** ~ **de qch** to
take umbrage at sth

ombrager /ɔ̃bʀaʒe/ [13] vtr [feuillage] to shade; **route
ombragée** shady road

ombrageux, -euse /ɔ̃bʀaʒø, øz/ adj [personne] tetchy

ombre /ɔ̃bʀ/ nf [1] (ombrage) shade; **30° à l'**~ 30° in the
shade; **à l'**~ **d'un figuier** in the shade of a fig tree; **tu leur
fais de l'**~ lit you're (standing) in their light; fig you're
putting them in the shade; **rester dans l'**~ **de qn** to be in
sb's shadow; [2] (forme portée) shadow; **suivre qn comme
une** ~ to be sb's shadow; **n'être plus que** or **être l'**~ **de soi-
même** to be a shadow of one's former self; [3] (pénombre)
liter darkness; [4] (anonymat, clandestinité) **laisser certains
détails dans l'**~ to be deliberately vague about certain
details; **agir dans l'**~ to operate behind the scenes; **rester
dans l'**~ [manipulateur] to stay behind the scenes; [poète]
to remain in obscurity; [5] (trace) liter hint; **une** ~ **de
moustache** a hint of a moustache; **l'**~ **d'un reproche/d'un
accord** a hint of reproach/of an agreement; **une** ~ **de
regret passa dans son regard** a shadow of regret crossed
his/her face; **sans l'**~ **d'un doute** without a shadow of a
doubt; **sans l'**~ **d'une preuve** without the slightest shred
of evidence; [6] Art **l'**~ (procédé) shading ¢; **faire des** ~**s** to
shade; [7] (silhouette indécise) shadowy figure

(Composés) ~ **chinoise** shadow puppet; ~ **à paupières**
eye shadow

(Idiomes) **passer comme une** ~ to be ephemeral; **courir
après une** ~ to chase rainbows; **il y a une** ~ **au tableau**
there is only one thing wrong; **la seule** ~ **au tableau** the
only snag

ombrelle /ɔ̃bʀɛl/ nf (objet) parasol, sunshade

OMC /ɔɛmse/ nf ▸ **organisation**

omelette /ɔmlɛt/ nf Culin omelette

(Composé) ~ **norvégienne** baked Alaska

(Idiome) **on ne fait pas d'**~ **sans casser des œufs** Prov your
can't make an omelette without breaking eggs Prov

omerta /ɔmɛʀta/ nf omertà

omettre /ɔmɛtʀ/ [60] vtr to leave out, to omit

omission /ɔmisjɔ̃/ nf omission

omnibus /ɔmnibys/ nm inv Rail slow ou local train

omnipotent, ~**e** /ɔmnipɔtɑ̃, ɑ̃t/ adj omnipotent

omnisports /ɔmnispɔʀ/ adj inv **salle** ~ sports hall

omnivore /ɔmnivɔʀ/
A adj omnivorous
B nmf omnivore

omoplate /ɔmɔplat/ nf shoulder blade

OMS /ɔɛmɛs/ nf (abbr = **Organisation mondiale de la
santé**) WHO

on /ɔ̃/ pron pers [1] (complètement indéfini) ~ **a refait la route** the
road was resurfaced; ~ **a prétendu que** it was claimed
that; **une démission dont** ~ **a beaucoup parlé** a much
talked-about resignation; ~ **le dit très malade** he's said to
be very ill; ~ **dit qu'il a une maîtresse** it's said he has a
mistress; **il pleut des cordes, comme** ~ **dit** it's raining cats
and dogs, as they say; [2] (nous) we; **mon copain et moi,**
~ **va en Afrique** my boyfriend and I are going to Africa;
au lycée ~ **n'a pas le droit de fumer** smoking is not
allowed at school; **toi et moi,** ~ **est faits pour s'entendre**
we're two of a kind; ~ **en parlait avec Janet hier** I was
discussing it with Janet yesterday; **qu'est-ce qu'**~ **mange
ce soir?** what's for dinner tonight?; ~ **recherche une
secrétaire de direction bilingue** bilingual personal assistant required; **il y a tellement de bruit qu'**~ **ne s'entend
plus** there's so much noise that you can't hear yourself
think; [3] (tu, vous) you; **alors,** ~ **se promène?** so you're
taking a stroll then?; ~ **se calme°!** calm down!; ~ **se
dépêche°!** hurry up!; **quand** ~ **veut,** ~ **peut** where
there's a will, there's a way; [4] (je) **on fait ce qu'**~ **peut!**
one does what one can!; **toi,** ~ **ne t'a rien demandé**
nobody asked you for your opinion; [5] (ils, elles) they;
~ **ne m'a pas demandé mon avis** they didn't ask me for
my opinion; **est-ce qu'**~ **nous a livré le piano?** has the
piano been delivered?; [6] (quelqu'un) ~ **t'appelle** someone's
calling you; ~ **a refusé de me laisser entrer** I was refused
admittance; ~ **frappe** there's someone at the door; **si**
~ **me demande, dites que je ne suis pas là** if anyone asks
for me, tell them I'm out; [7] (n'importe qui) ~ **ne peut pas
vivre avec 300 euros par mois** you can't live on 300 euros
a month; ~ **peut le dire** you can say that

onanisme /ɔnanism/ nm onanism

once /ɔ̃s/ nf [ounce](#) ▸ p. 453 nf ounce; **sans une** ~ **de méchanceté**
without an ounce of malice

oncle /ɔ̃kl/ nm uncle; **oui, mon** ~ yes uncle; **l'**~ **Robert**
Uncle Robert; ~ **d'Amérique** fig rich uncle

onction /ɔ̃ksjɔ̃/ nf Relig unction, anointing

onctueux, -euse /ɔ̃ktɥø, øz/ adj [1] [pâte, mélange]
smooth, creamy; [couleur] rich; [2] (mielleux) pej [gestes,
propos, personne] unctuous

onctuosité /ɔ̃ktɥozite/ nf smoothness

onde /ɔ̃d/ nf [1] (vibration) wave; **grandes** ~**s** long wave (sg);
sur les ~**s** on the air; **sur les** ~**s de la BBC** on the BBC;
[2] (vague marine) wave; [3] (eau) liter waters (pl) liter

(Composé) ~ **de choc** Phys, fig shock wave

ondée /ɔ̃de/ nf shower

ondine /ɔ̃din/ nf [1] Mythol undine; [2] (nageuse) female
swimmer

on-dit /ɔ̃di/ nm inv **les** ~ hearsay ¢

ondoiement /ɔ̃dwamɑ̃/ nm (de collines) undulation; (de blé,
d'herbes) swaying

ondoyant, ~**e** /ɔ̃dwajɑ̃, ɑ̃t/ adj [blé, chevelure] rippling;
[corps, personne] lithe; [démarche] swaying

ondoyer /ɔ̃dwaje/ [23] vi [paysage, chevelure] to undulate;
[démarche, blé] to sway; [flamme] to flutter

ondulant, ~**e** /ɔ̃dylɑ̃, ɑ̃t/ adj [démarche] swaying; [paysage]
undulating

ondulation /ɔ̃dylasjɔ̃/ nf [1] (mouvement) (de chevelure, musique) undulation; (de corps) swaying ¢; ~**s du corps** swaying movements of the body; [2] (courbe) (de contour) curves
(pl); (de chevelure) wave

ondulatoire /ɔ̃dylatwaʀ/ *adj* undulatory

ondulé, **~e** /ɔ̃dyle/ *adj* [*cheveux, forme*] wavy; [*collines, terrain*] undulating; [*carton, tôle*] corrugated

onduler /ɔ̃dyle/ [1] *vi* (ondoyer) [*route*] to roll; [*herbe*] to ripple; [*chevelure*] to fall in waves; [*corps*] to sway

onéreux, **-euse** /ɔneʀø, øz/ *adj* (coûteux) [*dépense*] onerous, heavy; [*achat*] expensive; [*entretien*] costly

ONG /ɔɛnʒe/ *nf* (*abbr* = **organisation non gouvernementale**) NGO

ongle /ɔ̃gl/ *nm* (de personne) nail; (de quadrupède) claw; (de rapace) talon; **~s des mains** fingernails; **~s des pieds** toenails; **se faire les ~s** to do one's nails

▸ (Idiomes) **défendre qch bec et ~s** to defend sth fiercely; **jusqu'au bout des ~s** through and through

onglée /ɔ̃gle/ *nf* **avoir l'~** to have fingers numb with cold

onglet /ɔ̃glɛ/ *nm* **1** (sur un livre) (échancré) thumb cut-out; (qui déborde) tab; **avec ~s** (échancrés) with thumb-index; (qui débordent) with step index; **2** Culin prime cut of beef; **3** (de lame, couvercle) groove

onguent /ɔ̃gɑ̃/ *nm* ointment, salve

onirique /ɔniʀik/ *adj* (analogue au rêve) [*scène, atmosphère*] dream-like, oneiric sout; (relatif au rêve) [*symbole*] dream (*épith*)

onomatopée /ɔnɔmatɔpe/ *nf* onomatopoeia

ONU /ɔny, ɔɛny/ *nf* (*abbr* = **Organisation des Nations unies**) UN, UNO

onyx /ɔniks/ *nm inv* onyx; **en ~** onyx (*épith*)

onze /ɔ̃z/ ▸ p. 398, p. 296, p. 155 *adj inv, pron* eleven; **~ novembre** Armistice Day GB, Remembrance Sunday GB, Veterans Day US

onzième /ɔ̃zjɛm/ ▸ p. 398, p. 155
A *adj* eleventh
B *nmf* Scol *first year of primary school, age 6–7*

OPA /opea/ *nf*: *abbr* ▶ **offre**

opacité /ɔpasite/ *nf* **1** lit opacity; **2** fig (de texte) opacity; (de nuit) darkness; (de forêt) impenetrability

opale /ɔpal/ *nf* opal

opalescent, **~e** /ɔpalɛsɑ̃, ɑ̃t/ *adj* opalescent

opaline /ɔpalin/ *nf* **1** (substance) opaline; **2** (objet) object made of opaline

opaque /ɔpak/ *adj* **1** lit opaque; **2** fig [*texte*] opaque; [*nuit*] dark; [*forêt, brouillard*] impenetrable

opéable /ɔpeabl/ *adj* ripe for a takeover bid (*après n*); **une société ~** a potential takeover target

OPEP /ɔpɛp/ *nf* (*abbr* = **Organisation des pays producteurs de pétrole**) OPEC; **un pays membre de l'~** an OPEC state

opéra /ɔpeʀa/ *nm* **1** Mus opera; **2** (bâtiment) opera house

opérable /ɔpeʀabl/ *adj* [*malade, tumeur*] operable

opérateur, **-trice** /ɔpeʀatœʀ, tʀis/
A ▸ p. 372 *nm,f* operator
B *nm* **1** Ling, Math operator; **2** Télécom (exploitant) private telecommunications company

(Composé) **~ de saisie** keyboarder

opération /ɔpeʀasjɔ̃/ *nf* **1** Méd **~ (chirurgicale)** operation, surgery **⊄**; **2** Math (type de calcul) operation; (calcul) calculation; **faire des ~s** (pour calculer) to do calculations; Scol to do sums; **3** (étape d'un processus) operation; **4** (fonctionnement) process; **l'~ de la digestion** the digestive process; **5** Fin (transaction) transaction; **~ boursière** stock transaction; **6** (suite d'actions concrètes) gén, Mil operation; **~ 'non à la misère'** anti-poverty campaign

(Composé) **~ à cœur ouvert** open-heart surgery **⊄**

opérationnel, **-elle** /ɔpeʀasjɔnɛl/ *adj* operational

opératoire /ɔpeʀatwaʀ/ *adj* **1** Méd [*technique*] surgical; [*risque*] in operating (*après n*); **les suites ~s** the after-effects of surgery; **2** (qui fonctionne) operative

opercule /ɔpɛʀkyl/ *nm* **1** Bot, Zool operculum; **2** (de hublot) deadlight; **3** (de pot) lid

opéré, **~e** /ɔpeʀe/ *nm,f* person who has had an operation

opérer /ɔpeʀe/ [14]
A *vtr* **1** Méd to operate on [*malade, organe*]; **~ qn du genou** to operate on sb's knee; **~ qn d'un kyste** to operate on sb to remove a cyst; **~ qn des amygdales** to remove sb's tonsils;

se faire **~** to have an operation; **on l'a opéré du cœur** he's had a heart operation; **2** (effectuer) to make [*choix, changement, distinction*]; to carry out [*restructuration*]; **3** (produire) to bring about [*changement*]
B *vi* **1** Méd to operate; **il faut ~** an operation is necessary; **2** (avoir un effet) [*remède, charme*] to work (**sur** on); **3** (procéder) to proceed; **leur façon d'~** the way they go about things; **4** (mener des activités) [*voleur*] to operate
C **s'opérer** *vpr* (se produire) to take place

opérette /ɔpeʀɛt/ *nf* operetta, light opera **⊄**

ophtalmologiste /ɔftalmɔlɔʒist/, **ophtalmologue** /ɔftalmɔlɔg/ ▶ p. 372 *nmf* ophthalmologist

opiacé, **~e** /ɔpjase/
A *adj* [*médicament*] opiate (*épith*); [*odeur*] of opium (*épith, après n*)
B *nm* opiate

opiner /ɔpine/ [1] *vi* **~ du bonnet** *or* **de la tête** to nod in agreement

opiniâtre /ɔpinjatʀ/ *adj* [*résistance*] dogged; [*travail*] relentless; [*personne*] tenacious; [*toux*] persistent

opinion /ɔpinjɔ̃/ *nf* **1** (jugement, idée) opinion; **il se moque de l'~ des autres** he doesn't care what other people think; **être de l'~ que** to be of the opinion that; **mon ~ est faite** my mind is made up; **se faire une ~** to form an opinion (**de, sur** on); **'sans ~'** (dans un sondage) 'don't know'; **2** (sentiment général) **l'~ (publique)** public opinion

opiomane /ɔpjɔman/ *nmf* opium addict

opium /ɔpjɔm/ *nm* opium

opportun, **~e** /ɔpɔʀtœ̃, yn/ *adj* [*moment*] opportune, appropriate; [*remarque, visite*] opportune

opportunisme /ɔpɔʀtynism/ *nm* opportunism

opportuniste /ɔpɔʀtynist/
A *adj* opportunistic
B *nmf* opportunist

opportunité /ɔpɔʀtynite/ *nf* **1** (bien-fondé) appropriateness; **2** (occasion) controv opportunity

opposant, **~e** /ɔpozɑ̃, ɑ̃t/
A *adj* Jur opposing
B *nm,f* Pol opponent (**à** of)

opposé, **~e** /ɔpoze/
A *adj* **1** (inverse) [*direction*] opposite; **2** (en contradiction) [*avis, opinion*] opposite; [*partis, forces, côtés*] opposing; [*intérêts, buts, stratégies*] conflicting; **les deux partis restent ~s** the two parties remain opposed to each other; **3** (défavorable) opposed (**à** to)
B *nm* opposite; **elle est l'~ de sa sœur** she's the opposite of her sister
C **à l'opposé** *loc* **1** (contrairement à) **à l'~ de mes frères** in contrast to my brothers; **à l'~ de ce qu'on pourrait croire** contrary to what one might think; **2** (dans l'autre sens) **il est parti exactement à l'~** he went off in exactly the opposite direction

opposer /ɔpoze/ [1]
A *vtr* **1** (poser en obstacle) to put up [*résistance, argument*]; **~ un refus à qn** to refuse sb; **~ un démenti à qch** to deny sth; **2** (mettre en compétition) **~ à** to match *ou* pit [sb] against [*personne, équipe*]; **la finale opposait deux Américains** the final was between two Americans; **3** (séparer) [*chose*] to divide [*personnes*]; **le conflit qui a opposé les deux pays** the conflict which set the two countries against each other; **4** (comparer) to compare (**à** to, with)
B **s'opposer** *vpr* **1** (ne pas accepter) **s'~ à qch** (montrer son désaccord) to be opposed to sth; (désapprouver activement) to oppose sth; **ils s'opposent fermement à ce que l'usine se construise** they are strongly opposing the building of the factory; **2** (empêcher) **s'~ à** to stand in the way of [*développement, changement*]; **3** (contraster) to contrast (**with** à); **4** (diverger) [*idées, opinions*] to conflict; [*personnes*] to disagree; [*partisans*] to be divided; **5** (s'affronter) [*équipes*] to confront each other

opposition /ɔpozisjɔ̃/ *nf* **1** (en politique) opposition; **les partis de l'~** the opposition parties; **être dans l'~** to be in the opposition; **d'~** [*député, parti*] opposition (*épith*); **journal d'~** newspaper of the opposition; **2** (désaccord) opposition; **être en ~ avec** to be in opposition to; **3** (contraste) contrast (**entre** between); **~ de couleurs** contrast in colours(GB); **par ~ à** in contrast with *ou* to; **4** Jur objection; **faire ~ à un chèque** to stop a cheque GB *ou* check US

oppressant, **~e** /ɔpʀesɑ̃, ɑ̃t/ *adj* oppressive

oppressé, **~e** /ɔpʀese/
A *pp* ▸ **oppresser**
B *pp adj* **être ~** (physiquement) to be breathless; (psychiquement) to be oppressed

oppresser /ɔpʀese/ [1] *vtr* to oppress; **la chaleur l'oppresse** he/she finds the heat oppressive

oppresseur /ɔpʀesœʀ/ *nm* oppressor

oppression /ɔpʀesjɔ̃/ *nf* oppression

opprimé, **~e** /ɔpʀime/
A *adj* [*peuple*, *classe*] oppressed
B *nm,f* **les ~s** the oppressed (+ *v pl*)

opprimer /ɔpʀime/ [1] *vtr* **1** to oppress [*peuple*]; **2** to stifle [*conscience*]

opprobre /ɔpʀɔbʀ/ *nm fml* (déshonneur) opprobrium sout; (déchéance) disgrace

opter /ɔpte/ [1] *vi* to opt (**pour** for)

opticien, **-ienne** /ɔptisjɛ̃, ɛn/ ▸ p. 372 *nm,f* optician

optimal, **~e**, *mpl* **-aux** /ɔptimal, o/ *adj* optimum

optimiser /ɔptimize/ [1] *vtr* to optimize

optimisme /ɔptimism/ *nm* optimism; **faire preuve d'un ~ prudent** to be cautiously optimistic

optimiste /ɔptimist/
A *adj* optimistic (**sur** about)
B *nmf* optimist

option /ɔpsjɔ̃/ *nf* **1** gén option (**sur** on); **le toit ouvrant est en ~** the sunroof is an optional extra *ou* an option US; **en ~** optional; **2** Fin option

optionnel, **-elle** /ɔpsjɔnɛl/ *adj* optional

optique /ɔptik/
A *adj* **1** Anat optic; **2** Phys, Tech optical
B *nf* **1** (étude, industrie) optics (+ *v sg*); **2** (point de vue) perspective; **dans cette ~** from this perspective; **3** (partie d'instrument) optical components (*pl*)

optométriste /ɔptɔmetʀist/ ▸ p. 372 *nmf* ophthalmic optician GB, optometrist

opulence /ɔpylɑ̃s/ *nf* (richesse) opulence

opulent, **~e** /ɔpylɑ̃, ɑ̃t/ *adj* **1** [*pays*] opulent, wealthy; [*train de vie*] affluent; **2** [*poitrine*] ample

or¹ /ɔʀ/ *conj* **1** (indiquant une opposition) and yet; **tu m'as dit que tu serais à la bibliothèque, ~ tu n'y étais pas** you told me you'd be at the library and you weren't there; **2** (introduisant un nouvel élément) **les musées sont fermés le mardi, ~ c'était justement un mardi** museums are closed on Tuesdays, and it just so happened that it was a Tuesday; **3** (pour récapituler) **~ donc, c'était la nuit et nous étions perdus** now, it was night and we were lost

or² /ɔʀ/
A ▸ p. 140 *adj inv* [*couleur*] gold; [*cheveux*] golden
B *nm* **1** (métal) gold **ℂ**; **gravé à l'~ fin** engraved in fine gold; **en ~** [*dent*, *bague*] gold (*épith*); [*patron*, *mari*] marvellous^GB; [*occasion*] golden; **avoir un cœur d'~** *or* **en ~** to have a heart of gold; **2** Archit, Art (d'encadrement, église, de dôme) gilding **ℂ**; **3** (couleur) golden; **cheveux d'~** golden hair (*sg*); **les ~s de l'automne** the golden tints of autumn

(Composés) **~ blanc** white gold; **~ jaune** yellow gold; **~ noir** black gold, oil

(Idiomes) **la parole est d'argent, le silence est d'~** Prov speech is silver, silence is golden Prov; **je ne le ferais pas pour tout l'~ du monde** I wouldn't do it for all the money in the world; **rouler sur l'~** to be rolling in it° *ou* in money

oracle /ɔʀakl/ *nm* oracle

orage /ɔʀaʒ/ *nm* storm; **le temps est à l'~, il y a de l'~ dans l'air** lit, fig there's a storm brewing; **pluie d'~** thundery shower GB, thundershower US; **ciel/vent d'~** stormy sky/wind; **l'~ de la passion** the tumult of passion

orageux, **-euse** /ɔʀaʒø, øz/ *adj* **1** [*été*] stormy; [*temps*] thundery; **zone orageuse** storm belt; **2** (agité) [*discussion*, *réunion*] stormy; [*ambiance*] threatening; [*humeur*] angry

oraison /ɔʀezɔ̃/ *nf* prayer

(Composé) **~ funèbre** funeral oration

oral, **~e**, *mpl* **-aux** /ɔʀal, o/
A *adj* **1** (non écrit) oral; **2** Méd **par voie ~e** orally
B *nm* Scol, Univ oral (examination)

oralement /ɔʀalmɑ̃/ *adv* **1** Méd orally; **2** (pas par écrit) verbally

orange¹ /ɔʀɑ̃ʒ/ ▸ p. 140
A *adj inv* orange; [*feu*] amber GB, yellow US
B *nm* (couleur) orange; **passer à l'~** to go through when the light is amber GB *ou* yellow US

orange² /ɔʀɑ̃ʒ/ *nf* (fruit) orange

orangeade /ɔʀɑ̃ʒad/ *nf* orangeade

oranger /ɔʀɑ̃ʒe/ *nm* orange tree; **fleur d'~** orange blossom

orangeraie /ɔʀɑ̃ʒʀɛ/ *nf* orange grove

orangerie /ɔʀɑ̃ʒʀi/ *nf* orangery

orateur, **-trice** /ɔʀatœʀ, tʀis/ *nm,f* (intervenant) speaker; (tribun) orator

oratoire /ɔʀatwaʀ/
A *adj* oratorical
B *nm* Relig oratory

orbite /ɔʀbit/ *nf* **1** (en astronomie) orbit; **en ~** in orbit; **mettre sur ~** to put [sth] into orbit [*satellite*]; fig to launch; **2** Anat eye-socket; **3** (zone d'influence) **être dans/tomber dans l'~ de** to be in/to fall within the sphere of influence of; **4** Phys orbit

orchestral, **~e**, *mpl* **-aux** /ɔʀkɛstʀal, o/ *adj* orchestral

orchestre /ɔʀkɛstʀ/ *nm* **1** (classique) orchestra; (de bal, d'harmonie) band; **~ de jazz** jazz band; **2** (fosse pour les musiciens) orchestra pit; **3** Cin, Théât (partie de la salle) orchestra stalls (*pl*) GB, orchestra US

orchestrer /ɔʀkɛstʀe/ [1] *vtr* to orchestrate

orchidée /ɔʀkide/ *nf* orchid

ordinaire /ɔʀdinɛʀ/
A *adj* **1** (ni spécial, ni anormal) gén ordinary; [*qualité*] standard; [*lecteur*, *touriste*] average, ordinary; [*journée*] normal, ordinary; **l'(essence) ~** 2-star (petrol) GB, regular (gasoline) US; **en temps ~** in normal times; **journée peu ~** unusual day; **2** (médiocre) pej [*vie*] humdrum (*épith*); **très ~** [*repas*, *vin*] very average; [*personne*] very ordinary; **3** (coutumier) [*qualité*, *défaut*] usual
B *nm* **1** (menu habituel) **l'~** everyday fare; **2** (moyenne) **l'~** the commonplace; **sortir de l'~** [*livre*, *film*] to be out of the ordinary
C **à l'ordinaire**, **d'ordinaire** *loc adv* usually; **plus tard que d'~** *ou* **qu'à l'~** later than usual; **comme à l'~** as usual

ordinal, **~e**, *mpl* **-aux** /ɔʀdinal, o/
A *adj* ordinal
B *nm* ordinal

ordinateur /ɔʀdinatœʀ/ *nm* computer; **travailler sur ~** to work with a computer; **~ central** mainframe; **création d'images par ~** computer-generated graphics; **assisté par ~** computer-aided

ordination /ɔʀdinasjɔ̃/ *nf* ordination

ordonnance /ɔʀdɔnɑ̃s/ *nf* **1** (document) prescription; **délivré uniquement sur ~** only available on prescription; **on peut l'acheter sans ~** you can buy it over the counter; **médicament vendu sans ~** over-the-counter medicine; **2** (agencement) (de salle, meubles) layout; (de cérémonie) order; **3** Jur ruling

ordonné, **~e¹** /ɔʀdɔne/ *adj* **1** (rangé) [*chambre*, *armoire*, *personne*] tidy; **2** (méthodique) [*personne*] methodical; **3** (pas désorganisé) [*manifestation*] orderly; **bien ~** [*texte*, *vie*] well-ordered; **4** Math ordered

ordonnée² /ɔʀdɔne/ *nf* Math ordinate

ordonner /ɔʀdɔne/ [1] *vtr* **1** (commander) gén to order; [*médecin*] to prescribe [*repos*]; **~ à qn de faire qch** to order sb to do sth; **2** (mettre en ordre) to put [sth] in order [*objets*]; to order [*paragraphes*]; **3** Relig to ordain

ordre /ɔʀdʀ/ *nm* **1** (commandement) order; **donner à qn l'~ de faire** to give sb the order to do; **je n'ai d'~ à recevoir de personne** I don't take orders from anybody; **j'ai des ~s** I'm acting under orders; **agir sur ~ de qn** to act on sb's orders; **travailler sous les ~s de qn** to work under sb; **elle a 30 personnes sous ses ~s** she has 30 people (working) under her; **prendre qn à ses ~s** to take sb on; **à vos ~s!** Mil yes, sir!; (à un ami, parent) hum at your service! hum; **jusqu'à nouvel ~** until further notice; **2** (disposition régulière) order; **par ~ alphabétique** in alphabetical order; **par ~ de préférence** in order of preference; **procédons par ~** let's do things in order; **en bon ~** [*être aligné*, *avancer*] in an orderly fashion; **avancer en ~ dispersé/serré** to advance in scattered/close formation; **3** Ordinat command; **4** (fait d'être rangé) tidiness, orderliness; (fait d'être bien organisé) order; **être en ~** [*maison*, *armoire*] to be tidy;

[comptes] to be in order; **tenir une pièce en ~** to keep a room tidy; **mettre de l'~ dans** to tidy up [pièce, placard]; **mettre de l'~ dans ses comptes** to get one's accounts in order; **mettre de l'~ dans ses idées** to get one's ideas straight; **mettre de l'~ dans sa vie** to set ou put one's life in order; **remettre une pièce en ~** to put everything back where it was in a room; **remise en ~** fig rationalization; **5}** (état stable et normal) order; **maintenir l'~ dans sa classe** to keep order in the classroom; **rappeler qn à l'~** to reprimand sb; **tout est rentré dans l'~** gén everything is back to normal; (après des émeutes) order has been restored; **l'~ public** public order; **maintenir l'~ (public)** to maintain law and order; **6}** (nature) nature; **c'est dans l'~ des choses** it's in the nature of things; **un problème de cet ~** a problem of that nature; **c'est un problème d'~ économique** it's a problem of an economic nature; **de l'~ de 30%** in the order of 30% GB, on the order of 30% US; **de premier ~** first-rate; **de second ~** second-rate; **dans le même ~ d'idées, je voudrais vous demander** talking of which, I would like to ask you; **c'est du même ~** it's the same kind of thing; **7}** Archit, Biol, Zool order; **8}** (confrérie) order; **9}** Relig order; **~ monastique** monastic order; **entrer dans les ~s** to take (holy) orders; **10}** Fin order; **~ d'achat** order to buy; **libellez le chèque à l'~ de X** make the cheque GB ou check US payable to X

(Composé) **~ du jour** (de réunion) agenda; **être à l'~ du jour** lit to be on the agenda; fig to be talked about

ordure /ɔRdyR/
A nf (abjection) liter filth; **se complaire dans l'~** to wallow in filth
B ordures nfpl **1}** (déchets) refuse ¢ GB, garbage ¢ US; **les ~s ménagères** household refuse GB ou garbage US; **jeter qch aux ~s** to put/to throw sth in the bin GB ou in the garbage US; **défense de déposer des ~s** no dumping; **tas d'~s** rubbish heap GB, pile of garbage US; **2}** (grossièretés) filth ¢

ordurier, -ière /ɔRdyRje, ɛR/ adj filthy

orée /ɔRe/ nf **1}** lit edge; **2}** fig start

oreille /ɔRɛj/ nf **1}** ► p. 136 Anat ear; **avoir les ~s décollées** to have sticking out ears; **dire qch à l'~ de qn** to whisper sth in sb's ear; **dresser l'~** lit, fig to prick up one's ears; **emmitouflé jusqu'aux ~s** all wrapped up; **tendre l'~** to strain one's ears; **c'est arrivé à leurs ~s** they got to hear of it; **n'écouter que d'une ~, écouter d'une ~ distraite** to half-listen, to listen with half an ear; **ouvre-bien les ~s!** listen carefully; **en avoir plein les ~s**○ **de qch** to have had an earful of sth; **arrête de crier, tu me casses les ~s**○ stop yelling, you're bursting my eardrums; **2}** (ouïe) hearing; **avoir l'~ fine** to have keen hearing ou sharp ears; **avoir de l'~** Mus to have a good ear (for music); **n'avoir pas d'~** Mus to be tone-deaf; **3}** (personne) **à l'abri** or **loin des ~s indiscrètes** where no-one can hear; **4}** (de marmite, plat) handle; (de vis, fauteuil) wing

(Idiomes) **avoir l'~ basse** to look sheepish; **tirer** or **frotter les ~s à qn** to tell sb off; **rougir jusqu'aux ~s** to blush to the roots of one's hair; **les ~s ont dû te siffler**○ or **tinter**○ or **sonner**○ your ears must have been burning

oreiller /ɔRɛje/ nm pillow

oreillette /ɔRɛjɛt/ nf **1}** Anat auricle; **2}** (de casquette) earflap

oreillons /ɔRɛjɔ̃/ ► p. 195 nmpl mumps

ores: d'ores et déjà /dɔRzedeʒa/ loc adv already

orfèvre /ɔRfɛvR/ ► p. 372 nmf goldsmith; **être ~ en la matière** fig to be an expert in the field

orfèvrerie /ɔRfɛvRəRi/ nf (métier) goldsmith's art; (commerce) goldsmith's and silversmith's; **pièce d'~** (en argent) piece of silverware; (en or) piece of gold work

organe /ɔRgan/ nm **1}** (de la vue, l'ouïe) organ; **2}** (publication) organ; **~ officiel d'un parti** official organ of a party; **3}** (institution) organ; **~ de presse** press organ; **4}** (en mécanique) system; **~s de freinage/direction** braking/steering system (sg); **5}** (voix) voice

organigramme /ɔRganigRam/ nm **1}** (d'entreprise) organization chart; **2}** Ordinat flowchart

organique /ɔRganik/ adj organic

organisateur, -trice /ɔRganizatœR, tRis/
A adj organizing (épith)
B nm,f organizer

organisation /ɔRganizasjɔ̃/ nf organization; **tu devrais faire un effort d'~** you should try to be more organized;

comité d'~ organizing committee

organiser /ɔRganize/ [1]
A vtr to organize
B s'organiser vpr **1}** (se regrouper) [dissidents, chômeurs, opposition] to get organized; **s'~ en** to organize oneself into; **2}** (être méthodique) to organize oneself; **3}** (être mis sur pied) [lutte, secours] to be organized; **4}** (être conçu) to be organized; **l'histoire s'organise autour de deux thèmes principaux** the plot revolves ou is organized around two main themes

organiseur /ɔRganizœR/ nm organizer; **~ électronique** electronic organizer

organisme /ɔRganism/ nm **1}** (corps humain) body; **2}** (être vivant) organism; **3}** (organisation) organization

organiste /ɔRganist/ ► p. 372 nmf organist

orgasme /ɔRgasm/ nm orgasm

orge /ɔRʒ/ nf barley

orgelet /ɔRʒəlɛ/ nm stye

orgie /ɔRʒi/ nf lit, fig orgy

orgue /ɔRg/ ► p. 389
A nm Mus organ; **tenir l'~** to be at the organ
B orgues nfpl Mus organ (sg)

orgueil /ɔRgœj/ nm pride; **être l'~ de qn** to be sb's pride and joy; **pécher par ~** to be too proud

orgueilleux, -euse /ɔRgœjø, øz/
A adj overproud
B nm,f **c'est un ~** he's overproud

orient /ɔRjɑ̃/ nm **1}** (direction) east; **2}** (pays) **l'Orient** the East

oriental, ~e, mpl **-aux** /ɔRjɑ̃tal, o/ adj [côte] eastern; [civilisation, langues, art, type] oriental

Oriental, ~e, mpl **-aux** /ɔRjɑ̃tal, o/ nm,f Asian; **les Orientaux** Asians

orientation /ɔRjɑ̃tasjɔ̃/ nf **1}** (position) (de maison) aspect; (d'antenne) angle; (de projecteur) direction; **la maison a une ~ plein sud** the house faces directly south; **2}** (d'enquête, de recherche, politique) direction; **les ~s de l'art moderne** trends in modern art; **3}** Scol, Univ **l'~** (conseils) advice to students on which courses to follow; **changer d'~** to change courses; **4}** (tendance politique) leanings (pl); **5}** (action de s'orienter) finding one's bearings

(Composé) **~ scolaire** curriculum counselling GB, counseling US

orienté, ~e /ɔRjɑ̃te/
A pp ► orienter
B pp adj **maison ~e d'est en ouest** house which has an east-west aspect; **bien/mal ~** [maison] in a good/bad position ou situation; **région ~e vers le tourisme** region geared to tourism

orienter /ɔRjɑ̃te/ [1]
A vtr **1}** (positionner) to decide on the aspect of [maison]; to adjust [antenne, lampe] (vers to); **~ la maison au sud** or **(face) au sud** to make the house south-facing; **~ le spot vers le fond** to direct the spotlight toward(s) the back; **~ l'antenne vers l'ouest** to make the aerial face west; **2}** (faire porter) to focus [enquête] (sur on); **~ la conversation sur** to bring the conversation around to; **3}** (politiser) to slant [cours]; **4}** (guider) to direct [personne] (vers to); **~ qn vers un spécialiste** to send sb to a specialist; **5}** Scol, Univ (conseiller) to give [sb] some career advice
B s'orienter vpr **1}** (se repérer) to get ou find one's bearings; **2}** (se diriger) **s'~ vers** lit to turn toward(s); fig [pays, mouvement] to move toward(s); [conversation] to turn to; **s'~ vers les carrières scientifiques** to go in for a career in science

orifice /ɔRifis/ nm **1}** Anat orifice; **2}** gén (de tuyau) mouth; (de puits) opening; (de tube) neck

originaire /ɔRiʒinɛR/ adj **1}** (provenant) [plante, animal] native (**de** to); **produit ~ d'Afrique** product from Africa; **famille ~ d'Asie** Asian family; **le pays dont il est ~** his native country; **2}** (d'origine) [tare, état] original; [déformation] inherent

original, ~e, mpl **-aux** /ɔRiʒinal, o/
A adj **1}** (authentique, créatif) original; **2}** (bizarre) eccentric
B nm,f (personne excentrique) eccentric, oddball○
C nm (œuvre primitive) original

originalité /ɔʀiʒinalite/ nf [1] (créativité) originality; [2] (aspect original) originality; [3] (excentricité) eccentricity

origine /ɔʀiʒin/ nf [1] (provenance) origin; **être d'~ modeste/noble** to come from a modest/noble background; **être d'~ paysanne** [personne] to come from a farming family; [2] (commencement) origin; **l'~ de l'univers** the origin of the universe; **l'~ des temps** the beginning of time; **dès l'~** (de projet, technique) right from the start; (du monde) from the very beginning; **à l'~** originally; **d'~** [pays] of origin; [moteur, vitraux] original; [3] (source) origin; **produit d'~ végétale** product of vegetable origin; **à l'~ du conflit il y a un problème frontalier** the conflict has its origins in a border dispute; [4] Math origin

originel, -elle /ɔʀiʒinɛl/ adj original

orignal, pl **-aux** /ɔʀiɲal, o/ nm moose (inv)

oripeaux /ɔʀipo/ nmpl faded finery ₵

orme /ɔʀm/ nm [1] (arbre) elm (tree); [2] (bois) elm (wood)

ormeau, pl **~x** /ɔʀmo/ nm [1] Bot young elm tree; [2] Zool abalone

orné, **~e** /ɔʀne/ adj [style] ornate

ornement /ɔʀnəmɑ̃/ nm [1] gén ornament; **jardin d'~** ornamental garden; [2] (de texte) embellishment; [3] Archit, Art decorative detail; [4] Mus ornament

ornemental, **~e**, mpl **-aux** /ɔʀnəmɑ̃tal, o/ adj ornamental

ornementer /ɔʀnəmɑ̃te/ [1] vtr to decorate (de with)

orner /ɔʀne/ [1] vtr [1] (décorer) [personne] to decorate [maison] (de with); to trim [vêtement] (de with); [2] (embellir) [ornement] to adorn [maison, vêtement]; [personne] to embellish [style, texte] (de with)

ornière /ɔʀnjɛʀ/ nf rut; **sortir de l'~** fig (de la routine) to get out of a rut; (d'une situation difficile) to get out of a difficult ou tricky○ situation

ornithologie /ɔʀnitɔlɔʒi/ nf ornithology

ornithologue /ɔʀnitɔlɔg/ ▸ p. 372 nmf ornithologist

ornithorynque /ɔʀnitɔʀɛ̃k/ nm (duck-billed) platypus, duckbill US

oronge /ɔʀɔ̃ʒ/ nf agaric; **fausse ~** fly agaric

orphelin, **~e** /ɔʀfəlɛ̃, in/
A adj [1] lit (de père et mère) orphan; **être ~** to be an orphan; **être ~ de père** to be fatherless; [2] fig **se sentir ~** to feel abandoned
B nm,f orphan

(Idiome) **défendre la veuve et l'~** to defend the weak

orphelinat /ɔʀfəlina/ nm orphanage

orque /ɔʀk/ nm ou f killer whale

orteil /ɔʀtɛj/ ▸ p. 136 nm toe; **gros ~** big toe

orthodoxe /ɔʀtɔdɔks/
A adj [1] (accepté) orthodox; **méthodes peu ~s** rather unorthodox methods; [2] Relig Orthodox
B nmf Relig Orthodox

orthographe /ɔʀtɔgʀaf/ ▸ p. 413 nf [1] (forme écrite) spelling; **quelle est l'~ de...?** how do you spell...?; **avoir une bonne/mauvaise ~** to be good/bad at spelling; [2] Scol (matière) spelling ₵

orthographier /ɔʀtɔgʀafje/ [2]
A vtr to spell; **mot mal orthographié** misspelled word
B s'orthographier vpr to be spelled

orthographique /ɔʀtɔgʀafik/ adj [règle] spelling (épith), orthographic; **correcteur ~** Ordinat spellchecker

orthopédiste /ɔʀtɔpedist/ ▸ p. 372 nmf [1] Méd orthopedic specialist, orthopedist; [2] (fabricant d'appareils) manufacturer of orthopedic appliances

orthophoniste /ɔʀtɔfɔnist/ ▸ p. 372 nmf speech therapist

orthoptie /ɔʀtɔpsi/ nf orthoptics (+ v sg)

orthoptiste /ɔʀtɔptist/ ▸ p. 372 nmf orthoptist

ortie /ɔʀti/ nf (stinging) nettle; **se piquer aux ~s** to get stung in the nettles

orvet /ɔʀvɛ/ nm slowworm, blindworm

os /ɔs, pl o/ nm inv [1] (élément) bone; **en chair et en ~** in the flesh; **n'avoir que la peau sur les ~** to be all skin and bone; **se rompre les ~**○ to break one's neck○; **de la viande vendue avec/sans ~** meat sold on/off the bone; [2] (matière) bone; **un peigne en ~** a bone comb

(Composés) **~ à moelle** Culin marrowbone; **~ de seiche** Zool cuttlebone

(Idiomes) **il y a un ~**○ there's a hitch; **jusqu'à l'~**○ completely; **tomber sur un ~**○ to come across a snag; **être trempé jusqu' aux ~**○ to be soaked to the skin○; **il ne va pas faire de vieux ~** he'll never make old bones

oscillation /ɔsilasjɔ̃/ nf [1] Phys, Télécom oscillation; [2] (balancement) (de pendule) swinging; (de navire) rocking; (du corps) swaying; [3] (variation) fluctuation

oscillatoire /ɔsilatwaʀ/ adj oscillatory

osciller /ɔsile/ [1] vi [1] (se balancer) [pendule] to swing; [navire] to rock; [foule] to sway; [2] (fluctuer) [monnaie] to fluctuate; [3] (hésiter) to vacillate (**entre** between)

osé, **~e** /oze/ adj [1] (licencieux) [livre, film] risqué; [2] (audacieux) [comportement] daring; [paroles] outspoken

oseille /ozɛj/ nf [1] Bot, Culin sorrel; [2] ○(argent) dough○, money; **avoir de l'~** to be rolling in it○

oser /oze/ [1] vtr to dare; **je n'ose pas demander** I daren't ask, I don't dare ask; **il a osé rester** he dared to stay; **ils n'ont pas osé répondre** they dared not answer, they didn't dare answer; **répète si tu l'oses!** don't you dare repeat that!; **je n'ose croire que** I hardly dare believe that; **j'ose espérer que** I would hope that; **si j'ose dire** if I may say so

osier /ozje/ nm [1] (arbre) osier; [2] (bois) osier, wicker

osmose /ɔsmoz/ nf lit, fig osmosis

ossature /ɔsatyʀ/ nf skeleton; **avoir une forte ~** to be big-boned; **~ du visage** bone structure

osselet /ɔslɛ/ nm [1] Anat small bone; **~ de l'oreille** ossicle; [2] ▸ p. 327 Jeux (pièce) jack, knucklebone; (jeu) les **~s** jacks

ossements /ɔsmɑ̃/ nmpl remains

osseux, -euse /ɔsø, øz/ adj [1] [personne, visage, charpente] bony; [2] [croissance, maladie] bone (épith)

ossifier /ɔsifje/ [2] vtr, **s'ossifier** vpr to ossify

ossu, **~e** /ɔsy/ adj big-boned

ossuaire /ɔsɥɛʀ/ nm ossuary

ostensible /ɔstɑ̃sibl/ adj obvious

ostentatoire /ɔstɑ̃tatwaʀ/ adj ostentatious

ostéopathe /ɔsteopat/ ▸ p. 372 nmf osteopath

ostracisme /ɔstʀasism/ nm ostracism; **être frappé d'~** Pol to be ostracized

ostréiculteur, -trice /ɔstʀeikyltœʀ, tʀis/ ▸ p. 372 nm,f oyster farmer

ostréiculture /ɔstʀeikyltyʀ/ nf oyster farming

otage /ɔtaʒ/ nm hostage; **être pris en ~** to be taken hostage; **prise d'~s** hostage-taking; **plusieurs prises d'~s** several instances of hostage-taking; **les grévistes tiennent les voyageurs en ~** fig the strikers are holding the passengers to ransom

OTAN /ɔtɑ̃/ nf (abbr = **Organisation du traité de l'Atlantique Nord**) NATO

otarie /ɔtaʀi/ nf eared seal, otary

ôter /ote/ [1]
A vtr [1] (se débarrasser de) to take off [vêtement, lunettes]; to remove [arête, tache] (de from); **ôte tes pieds du fauteuil** take your feet off the chair; [2] (retirer) fml **~ qch à qn** to take sth away from sb; **~ tout espoir à qn** to dash sb's hopes; **~ la vie à qn** to take sb's life; **on ne m'ôtera pas de l'idée qu'ils le savaient** I'm still convinced that they knew; [3] Math (retrancher) to take [sth] (à away from); **4 ôté de 9, il reste 5** 9 minus ou less ou take away 4 leaves 5
B s'ôter vpr [1] (s'enlever) **s'~ qch de l'esprit** or **la tête** to get sth out of one's mind ou head; [2] (se déplacer) **ôte-toi de là!** move!

otite /ɔtit/ ▸ p. 195 nf inflammation of the ear; **avoir une ~** to have earache

oto-rhino-laryngologiste, pl **~s** /ɔtoʀinolaʀɛ̃gɔlɔʒist/ ▸ p. 372 nmf ENT specialist

ou¹ /u/ conj [1] (choix) or; **tu pourrais lui offrir un collier, ~ (bien) une montre** you could give her a necklace, or (else) a watch; **est-ce que tu viens ~ pas?** are you coming or not?; **tu te moques de moi ~ quoi**○? are you making fun of me or what?; **tu peux venir me prendre chez moi, ~ alors on s'attend devant le cinéma** you can pick me up

L'orthographe et la ponctuation

L'alphabet anglais

■ *La liste suivante indique la prononciation de chaque lettre, et donne pour chacune un moyen, parmi d'autres, d'épeler clairement en cas de difficultés. Certains utilisent pour cela l'alphabet des pilotes, d'autres celui des téléphonistes présenté ci-dessous.*

A [eɪ]	A for Alfred		O [əʊ]	O for Oliver	
B [bi:]	B for beautiful		P [pi:]	P for Peter	
C [si:]	C for cat		Q [kju:]	Q for quite	
D [di:]	D for dog		R [ɑ:(r)]	R for Robert	
E [i:]	E for elephant		S [es]	S for sugar	
F [ef]	F for father		T [ti:]	T for Tommy	
G [dʒi:]*	G for George		U [ju:]	U for uncle	
H [eɪtʃ]	H for Harry		V [vi:]	V for victory	
I [aɪ]	I for Ireland		W ['dʌblju:]	W for Walter	
J [dʒeɪ]*	J for John		X [eks]	X for X-ray	
K [keɪ]	K for kangaroo		Y [waɪ]	Y for yellow	
L [el]	L for London		Z [zed] (GB)	Z for zoo	
M [em]	M for mother		ou [zi:] (US)		
N [en]	N for nothing				

Pour épeler

A majuscule
= capital A

a minuscule
= small a

ça s'écrit avec un A majuscule
= it has got a capital A

en majuscules
= in capital letters *ou* in capitals

à (a accent grave)	= a grave	[eɪ grɑ:v]
é (e accent aigu)	= e acute	[i: ə'kju:t]
è (e accent grave)	= e grave	[i: grɑ:v]
ê (e accent circonflexe)	= e circumflex	[i: 'sɜ:kəmfleks]
ë (e tréma)	= e diaeresis (on dira parfois, plus simplement: e with two dots)	[i: daɪ'erəsɪs]
ù (u accent grave)	= u grave	[ju: grɑ:v]
ç (c cédille)	= c cedilla	[si: sɪ'dɪlə]
l' (l apostrophe)	= l apostrophe	[el ə'pɒstrəfi]
d' (d apostrophe)	= d apostrophe	[di: ə'pɒstrəfi]
- (trait d'union)	= hyphen	['haɪfn]

en minuscules
= in small letters

deux l
= double l

deux n
= double n

deux t
= double t

"rase-mottes" s'écrit avec un trait d'union
= "rase-mottes" has a hyphen

Pour dicter la ponctuation

un point	.	= full stop (GB) *ou* period (US)
à la ligne		= new paragraph
virgule	,	= comma
deux points	:	= colon[†]
point-virgule	;	= semi-colon[†]
point d'exclamation	!	= exclamation mark (GB) *ou* exclamation point (US)[†]
point d'interrogation	?	= question mark[†]
ouvrez la parenthèse	(	= open brackets
fermez la parenthèse	)	= close brackets
entre parenthèses	()	= in brackets
entre crochets	[ ]	= in square brackets
tiret	-	= dash
points de suspension	...	= three dots (GB) *ou* suspension points (US)
ouvrez les guillemets	"*ou* '[‡]	= open inverted commas (GB) *ou* open quotation marks (US)
fermez les guillemets	"*ou* '	= close inverted commas (GB) *ou* close quotation marks (US)
entre guillemets	" " *ou* ' '	= in inverted commas (GB) *ou* in quotation marks (US) *ou* in quotes

La ponctuation des dialogues

■ *La ponctuation des dialogues n'est pas la même dans les deux langues.*

■ *En français, le dialogue commence par le signe « (maintenant souvent remplacé par un tiret, ou par "), chaque prise de parole est signalée par un tiret, le dialogue est clos par » (ou par ") et les interventions du narrateur (dit-il, remarqua-t-elle etc.) ne sont pas séparées du dialogue par un quelconque signe de ponctuation. En anglais, chaque prise de parole commence par " ou ', et se termine par " ou '. Ces mêmes signes sont utilisés avant et après chaque intervention du narrateur à l'intérieur d'une réplique. Exemple:*

"Well, I don't know," she said, "what to make of all this!"

* *Noter que les francophones confondent souvent les prononciations anglaises de G et de J.*
† *Noter qu'en anglais les deux points, le point-virgule, le point d'exclamation et le point d'interrogation ne sont pas précédés par un espace.*

Il a dit oui ; je ne sais pas pourquoi.
= He said he would; I don't know why.

Voici pourquoi : je n'ai pas pu !
= This is why: I could not!

‡ *Noter que les guillemets anglais (" " ou ' ') sont placés au dessus de la ligne*

---

at home or else we'll meet outside the cinema; **fatigué ~ pas, il faut bien rentrer à la maison** tired or not, we have to go home; **que ça vous plaise ~ non** whether you like it or not; **2** (choix unique) or; **~ (bien)... ~ (bien)...** either... or...; **~ bien il est très timide, ~ il est très impoli** he's either very shy or very rude; **3** (évaluation) or; **il y avait trois ~ quatre cents personnes** there were three or four hundred people

où² /u/
A *adv* **1** lit where; **je me demande ~...** I wonder where...; **~ est-ce que tu vas?** where are you going?; **~ ça?** where's that?; **je l'ai perdu je ne sais ~** I've lost it somewhere or other; **elle l'a rencontré je ne sais ~** God knows where she met him; **par ~ êtes-vous passés pour venir?** which way did you come?; **je ne sais pas d'~ elle vient** I don't know where she comes from; **2** fig where; **~ en étais-je?** where was I?; **~ en êtes-vous?** (à quel stade) where have you got to?; (comment ça va) how is it going?; **~ allons-nous?** (quelle époque!) what are things coming to!; **d'~ tenez-vous que?** where did you get the idea that?

B *pron rel* **1** (locatif) where; **le quartier ~ nous habitons** the area we live in, the area in which we live; **trouver un endroit ~ dormir** to find a place *ou* somewhere to sleep; **d'~ s'élevait de la fumée** out of which smoke was rising; **les villes par ~ nous sommes passés** the towns we passed through; **~ tu iras, j'irai** where *ou* wherever you go, I'll go; **~ qu'ils aillent/qu'elle soit** wherever they go/she is; **2** (abstrait) **la misère ~ elle se trouvait** the poverty in which she was living, the poverty she was living in; **l'école d'~ elle sort est très réputée** the school she went to is very well-known; **au train** or **au rythme** or **à l'allure ~ vont les choses** (at) the rate things are going; **le travail s'est accumulé, d'~ ce retard** there is a backlog of work, hence the delay; **d'~ l'on peut conclure que** from which we can conclude that; **3** (temporel) when; **il fut un temps ~ there** was a time when; **elle est à l'âge ~** she's at the age when *ou* where; **le matin ~ je l'ai rencontré** the morning I met him; **~ il se trompe, c'est lorsqu'il s'imagine que** where he goes wrong is in thinking that

ouah○ /wa/ *excl* wow○!

où

où adverbe de lieu se traduit généralement par *where* dans les interrogations directes ou indirectes:

où es-tu?
= where are you?

sais-tu où il est?
= do you know where he is?

Lorsque la traduction du verbe de la proposition relative introduite par *où* pronom relatif est un verbe à particule, trois traductions sont possibles:

la ville où nous sommes passés
= the town we passed through
ou the town that we passed through
ou the town which we passed through
ou the town through which we passed

Les trois premières traductions sont utilisées dans la langue courante, parlée ou écrite; la quatrième traduction sera préférée dans une langue plus soutenue, surtout écrite.

Pour simplifier la lecture des exemples, une seule traduction sera fournie mais il est toujours possible de générer les variantes sur les modèles donnés ci-dessus.

Lorsque *où* pronom relatif a une valeur temporelle, souvent il ne se traduit pas:

au moment où j'allais partir
= at the moment I was about to leave

ou bien il se traduit par *when*:

c'était l'époque où j'habitais à Oxford
= that was (the time) when I lived in Oxford

Attention, lorsque la proposition relative est au futur en français, elle est au présent en anglais:

le jour où elle arrivera
= the day she arrives

un jour où tu auras le temps
= one day when you have time

Pour les emplois abstraits et temporels de *où*, reportez-vous à l'entrée.

---

ouailles /waj/ *nfpl* flock *(sg)*; **une de mes** ~ one of my flock

ouate /wat/ *nf* [1] (de pharmacie) cotton wool GB, cotton US; [2] (garniture) wadding; **doublé d'**~ wadded

ouaté, ~**e** /wate/ *adj* [1] *[vêtement, tissu]* wadded; [2] fig *[ambiance]* cocoon-like; *[bruit, pas]* muffled

ouatine /watin/ *nf* wadding, padding

oubli /ubli/ *nm* [1] gén **de qch** gén forgetting sth; (de devoir) neglect of sth; **l'**~ **des autres** forgetting other people; **elle cherche l'**~ **dans la boisson** she drinks to forget; **le temps apporte l'**~ time passes and men forget; [2] (omission) omission; [3] (anonymat après la mort) oblivion; **tomber dans l'**~ to be completely forgotten, to sink into oblivion

oublier /ublije/ [2]

A *vtr* [1] (ne pas se souvenir de) to forget *[nom, date, fait]*; (ne pas penser à) to forget about *[soucis, famille, incident]*; (ne pas prendre) to leave; **j'ai oublié mes clés chez elle** I've left my keys at her house; **rien ne pourra me faire** ~ **ce moment** I shall never forget that moment; ~ **de faire/pourquoi/ comment** to forget to do/why/how; ~ **que** to forget that; **se faire** ~ to keep a low profile, to lie low○; [2] (omettre) to leave *[sth]* out, to forget *[personne, détail]*; **tu oublies de dire que** you forget ou mention that; [3] (négliger) to forget, to neglect *[devoir, ami]*.

B **s'oublier** *vpr* [1] *[souvenir]* to be forgotten; **ce sont des choses qui ne s'oublient pas** it's not the sort of thing you forget; [2] (négliger de se servir) to leave oneself out

oubliettes /ublijɛt/ *nfpl* oubliette *(sg)*

⟨Idiomes⟩ **tomber dans les** ~ to be forgotten; **mettre** *or* **jeter qch aux** ~ to consign sth to oblivion

---

oued /wɛd/ *nm* wadi

ouest /wɛst/ ▸ p. 454

A *adj inv* *[façade, versant, côte]* west; *[frontière, zone]* western
B *nm* [1] (point cardinal) west; [2] (région) west; [3] Géog, Pol **l'Ouest** the West; **de l'Ouest** *[ville, accent]* western

ouest-allemand, ~**e**, *mpl* ~**s** /wɛstalmɑ̃, ɑ̃d/ *adj* West German

ouf /uf/

A *nm* faire ~, **pousser un** ~ **(de soulagement)** to breathe a sigh of relief; **je n'ai pas eu le temps de dire** ~, **il était déjà parti** before I could say Jack Robinson, he'd gone
B *excl* phew!

oui /wi/

> ⚠ En anglais la réponse *yes* est généralement renforcée en reprenant le verbe utilisé pour poser la question: *are you happy? yes, I am*; *do you like Brahms? yes, I do.*

A *adv* [1] (marque l'accord) yes; **mais** ~! yes!; **bien sûr que** ~! yes, of course!; **alors c'est** ~? so the answer is yes?; **acceptera-t-il** ~ **ou non de me rencontrer?** will he agree to meet me or not?; **découvrir si** ~ **ou non** to discover whether or not; **êtes-vous d'accord? si** ~, **dites pourquoi** do you agree? if so, say why; **dire** ~ **à qch** (par conviction) to welcome sth; (par nécessité) to agree to sth; **faire** ~ **de la tête** to nod; [2] (renforce une constatation) yes; **lui, prudent? un lâche,** ~! him, cautious? a coward, more like○!; **elle est radin**○, ~, **radin**! she's stingy, really stingy!; **eh** ~, **c'est comme ça!** well, that's just the way it is!; **eh bien** ~, **j'ai triché, et alors?** OK, I cheated, so what?; [3] (interrogatif) **tu viens,** ~? are you coming?; **tu viens,** ~ **ou non?** are you coming? yes or no?; **c'est bientôt fini,** ~? are you going to stop that or not?; [4] (marque une transition) yes; ~, **tu disais?** yes, you were saying?; ~, ~, **tu dis ça et puis tu ne le feras pas** yeah, yeah○, that's what you say, but you won't do it; [5] (remplace une proposition) **je crois que** ~ I think so; **'ils sont partis?'—'je crains que** ~' 'have they left?'—'I'm afraid so'; **tu ne le crois pas, moi** ~ you don't believe it, but I do

B *nm inv* [1] (accord) yes; **le '**~ **mais' de M. Axel à notre proposition** Mr Axel's qualified 'yes' to our proposal; [2] (vote positif) 'yes' vote; **50** ~ **sur 57 votants** 50 votes in favour^GB out of 57 votes cast; **le** ~ **l'a emporté** the ayes have it

⟨Idiome⟩ **pour un** ~ **pour un non** *[s'énerver]* for the slightest thing; *[changer d'avis]* at the drop of a hat

ouï-dire /widiʀ/ *nm inv* hearsay; **par** ~ by hearsay

ouïe /wi/ *nf* [1] (sens) hearing **Ȼ**; **avoir l'**~ **fine** to have good hearing; **être tout** ~ to be all ears; [2] Zool (de poisson) gill; [3] Mus (de violon) sound hole

ouïr† /wiʀ/ [38] *vtr* **j'ai ouï dire que** word has reached me that; **oyez bonnes gens!** oyez! oyez! oyez!

ouistiti /wistiti/ *nm* [1] Zool marmoset; [2] ○(personne) **un (drôle de)** ~ a funny character

ouragan /uʀagɑ̃/ *nm* [1] Météo hurricane; [2] (tumulte) storm; **déclencher un** ~ to create a storm

⟨Idiome⟩ **arriver/passer comme un** ~ to arrive/to pass through like a hurricane

Oural /uʀal/ *nprm* [1] ▸ p. 504 (région) **l'**~ the Urals *(pl)*; [2] ▸ p. 259 (fleuve) **l'**~ the Ural

ourler /uʀle/ [1] *vtr* to hem

ourlet /uʀlɛ/ *nm* (en couture) hem; **faire un** ~ **à** to put a hem on

ours /uʀs/ *nm inv* [1] Zool bear; ▸ **cage**; [2] (personne) **il est un peu** ~ he's a bit surly

⟨Composés⟩ ~ **blanc** polar bear; ~ **brun** brown bear; ~ **mal léché** boor; ~ **de mer** Northern fur seal; ~ **en peluche** teddy bear; ~ **polaire** = ~ **blanc**

⟨Idiome⟩ **vendre la peau de l'**~ **avant de l'avoir tué** Prov to count one's chickens before they're hatched

ourse /uʀs/ *nf* Zool she-bear

Ourse /uʀs/ *nprf* **la Grande** ~ the Plough GB, the Big Dipper US; **la Petite** ~ the Little Bear GB, the Little Dipper US

oursin /uʀsɛ̃/ *nm* (sea) urchin

ourson /uʀsɔ̃/ *nm* bear cub

outil /uti/ *nm* tool; ~ **de travail** work tool

outillage /utijaʒ/ *nm* tools *(pl)*

o

outiller /utije/ [1] *vtr* to equip [*personne, usine*]

outrage /utraʒ/ *nm* insult; **faire ~ à** to be an insult to [*personne, réputation, mémoire*]; to be an affront to [*raison, morale*]

〔Composés〕 **~ à agent** *verbal assault of a policeman*; **~ aux bonnes mœurs** affront to public decency; **~ à magistrat** contempt ₵ of court

outragé, ~e /utraʒe/
A *pp* ▸ **outrager**
B *pp adj* [*personne, loyauté*] outraged; **prendre un air ~** to assume an air of outrage

outrageant, ~e /utraʒɑ̃, ɑ̃t/ *adj* offensive

outrager /utraʒe/ [13] *vtr* to offend [*personne*]

outrance /utrɑ̃s/ *nf* ① (*excès*) excess; ② (*caractère excessif*) excessiveness; **manger à ~** to eat excessively; **le sport à ~** excessive sport

outrancier, -ière /utrɑ̃sje, ɛʀ/ *adj* extreme

outre¹ /utʀ/
A *prép* (en plus de) in addition to; **~ (le fait) qu'il écrit, il illustre ses livres** as well as writing books, he also illustrates them
B *adv* **passer ~** to pay no heed; **passer ~ à** to disregard, to override [*loi, décision, objection*]
C **outre mesure** *loc adv* unduly; **cela ne m'inquiète pas ~ mesure** it doesn't worry me unduly
D **en outre** *loc adv* in addition

outre² /utʀ/ *nf* goatskin

〔Idiome〕 **être plein comme une ~°** to be full to bursting

outré, ~e /utre/
A *pp* ▸ **outrer**
B *pp adj* ① (*indigné*) outraged; **prendre un air ~** to look deeply offended; ② (*exagéré*) extravagant

outre-Atlantique /utʀatlɑ̃tik/ *adv* across the Atlantic; **d'~** American

outre-Manche /utʀəmɑ̃ʃ/ *adv* across the Channel, in Britain; **d'~** [*presse, chanteur*] British

outremer /utʀəmɛʀ/ ▸ p. 140 *adj inv, nm* ultramarine

outre-mer /utʀəmɛʀ/ *adv* overseas

outrepasser /utʀəpase/ [1] *vtr* to exceed [*droits, fonctions, devoir, pouvoir*]; to overstep [*limites, ordres*]

outrer /utre/ [1] *vtr* ① (*indigner*) to outrage; ② (*exagérer*) [*personne*] to exaggerate [*comportement, description*]

outre-tombe /utʀətɔ̃b/ *adv* **d'~** [*pâleur*] deathly; **une voix d'~** a voice from beyond the grave

ouvert, ~e /uvɛʀ, ɛʀt/
A *pp* ▸ **ouvrir**
B *pp adj* ① (non fermé) open; **rester ~** to stay open; **grand ~** wide open; **~ au public** open to the public; **~ à la circulation** open to traffic; **chemise à col ~** open-necked shirt; **(la) bouche ~e** [*rester, écouter*] gén with one's mouth open; (d'étonnement) open-mouthed; **avoir/garder les yeux ~s** (ne pas s'endormir) to be/to stay awake; (être attentif) to have/to keep one's eyes open; ② (en marche) [*lumière, gaz*] on (*jamais épith*); [*robinet*] running; **laisser le robinet ~** to leave the tap GB or faucet US running; ③ (inauguré) [*séance, tunnel*] open; ④ (destiné) **à** [*centre, service*] open to; ⑤ (déclaré) [*guerre*] open; ⑥ (franc) [*personne, jeu, dialogue*] open; ⑦ (réceptif) [*personne, esprit*] open (à to); ⑧ (épanoui) [*fleur*] open; ⑨ (non résolu) [*question*] open; ⑩ (non limitatif) [*série, programme*] open-ended; ⑪ Ling [*classe, voyelle, syllabe*] open

ouvertement /uvɛʀtəmɑ̃/ *adv* gén openly; (de manière éhontée) blatantly

ouverture /uvɛʀtyʀ/ *nf* ① (action d'ouvrir) opening; ② (fait de s'ouvrir) opening; **l'~ des vannes est automatique** the sluices open automatically; ③ (début) opening; **à l'~** at the opening; **~ de la chasse** opening of the shooting GB ou hunting US season; ④ (inauguration) opening; **cérémonie/jour d'~** opening ceremony/day; ⑤ Admin, Comm (fonctionnement) opening; **heures d'~** opening hours; **à l'~** at opening time; ⑥ (occasion) opportunity; ⑦ (mise en œuvre) opening; **~ de négociations** opening of negotiations; ⑧ Constr opening; **ménager une ~** to leave an opening; ⑨ (tolérance) openness (à to); **~ sur le monde** openness to the world; **~ d'esprit** open-mindedness; ⑩ Pol (transparence) openness; ⑪ Pol (libéralisation) opening-up; **~ à l'Ouest/à gauche** opening-up to the West/to the left; ⑫ Écon (de marché) opening (à to); ⑬ Mus overture;

⑭ Jeux (aux cartes) opening bid; (aux échecs) opening

ouvrable /uvʀabl/ *adj* [*jour*] working; [*heure*] business

ouvrage /uvʀaʒ/ *nm* ① (travail) work; **se mettre à l'~** to get down to work; ② (livre) book, work; (œuvre) work; **~ de référence** reference book; **~ collectif** joint publication; ③ (produit par un artisan, un ouvrier, un couturière) piece of work

〔Idiomes〕 **mettre** or **avoir du cœur à l'~** to work with a will; **ne pas avoir le cœur à l'~** not to have one's heart in one's work

ouvragé, ~e /uvʀaʒe/ *adj* finely wrought

ouvrant, ~e /uvʀɑ̃, ɑ̃t/ *adj* **toit ~** Aut sunroof

ouvré, ~e /uvʀe/ *adj* ① (ouvragé) finely worked; ② Admin, Jur **jour ~** working day

ouvre-boîtes /uvʀəbwat/ *nm inv* tin-opener GB, can-opener

ouvre-bouteilles /uvʀəbutɛj/ *nm inv* bottle-opener

ouvreur, -euse /uvʀœʀ, øz/ *nm,f* ① ▸ p. 372 Cin, Théât usher/usherette; ② Jeux (joueur qui commence) opener

ouvrier, -ière¹ /uvʀije, ɛʀ/
A *adj* ① Pol, Sociol [*contestation*] of the workers (*après n*); **classe ouvrière** working class; **syndicat ~** trade union; ② Zool [*abeille, fourmi*] worker (*épith*)
B ▸ p. 372 *nm,f* gén worker; (dans le bâtiment) workman; **les ~s du bâtiment** the construction workers

〔Composé〕 **~ agricole** agricultural labourer

ouvrière² /uvʀijeʀ/ *nf* Zool worker

ouvrir /uvʀiʀ/ [32]
A *vtr* ① gén to open [*boîte, porte, bouteille, tiroir, huître, lettre*]; to draw back [*verrou*]; to undo [*col, chemise*]; **ne pas ~ la bouche** or **le bec°** (ne rien dire) not to say a word; **~ ses oreilles** to keep one's ears open; **~ les bras** to open one's arms; **~ les bras à qn** (accueillir) to welcome sb with open arms; **~ sa maison à qn** to throw one's house open to sb; ② (commencer) to open [*débat, spectacle, cérémonie, chantier*]; to initiate [*période, dialogue, processus*]; ③ (mettre en marche) to turn on [*radio, chauffage*]; ④ (créer) to open [*compte, magasin, école*]; to open up [*possibilité, marché, passage*]; to initiate [*cours*]; **~ une route** to build a road; **~ la route** or **voie à qch** to pave the way for sth; ⑤ (élargir) to open [*capital, rangs*] (**à** to); to open up [*compétition, marché*] (**à** to); **~ l'esprit à qn** to open sb's mind; ⑥ (entailler) to open [*abcès*]; to cut open [*joue*]; **~ le ventre°** **à qn** (opérer) to cut sb open°
B *vi* ① (ouvrir la porte) to open the door (**à** to); **va ~** go and open the door; **ouvrez!** (injonction) open up!; **ouvre-moi** let me in!; **se faire ~** to be let in; ② (fonctionner) [*magasin, service*] to open; **~ le dimanche** to open on Sundays; ③ (être créé) [*magasin, service*] to be opened; ④ (déboucher) [*chambre, tunnel*] to open (**sur** onto); ⑤ Fin **la Bourse a ouvert en baisse** the exchange opened down; ⑥ (aux cartes, échecs) to open
C **s'ouvrir** *vpr* ① gén to open; (sous un souffle) [*fenêtre*] to blow open; (sous un choc) [*porte, boîte, sac*] to fly open; (inopinément) [*vêtement*] to come undone; ② (commencer) [*négociation, spectacle, chantier*] to open (**sur, avec** with); [*période, dialogue, processus*] to be initiated (**sur, avec** with); ③ (s'élargir) [*pays, économie, capital, institution*] to open up (**à, vers** to); ④ (se confier) to open one's heart (**à** to); ⑤ (être ouvrant) [*fenêtre, toit*] to open; **ma jupe s'ouvre sur le côté** my skirt opens at the side; ⑥ (être créé) [*magasin, métro, possibilité*] to open; **un garage va s'~ ici** there's going to be a garage here; ⑦ (créer pour soi) [*personne*] to open up [*passage*]; ⑧ (se dérouler) [*chemin, voie, espace*] to open up; ⑨ (s'épanouir) [*fleur*] to open; ⑩ (se fendre) [*sol, cicatrice*] to open; ⑪ (se blesser) [*personne*] to cut open [*crâne, pied*]; **s'~ les veines** or **poignets** (pour se suicider) to slash one's wrists

ovaire /ɔvɛʀ/ *nm* ovary; **un kyste de** or **à l'~** an ovarian cyst

ovale /ɔval/
A *adj* ① oval; ② (ayant trait au rugby) rugby
B *nm* oval

ovation /ɔvasjɔ̃/ *nf* ① (applaudissements) ovation; **faire une ~ à qn** to give sb an ovation; **il a fini son discours sous les ~s de la foule** he finished his speech to wild applause from the crowd; ② (reconnaissance) accolade

ovationner /ɔvasjɔne/ [1] *vtr* to greet [sb/sth] with wild applause; **ils se levèrent pour ~ le candidat** they gave the candidate a standing ovation

ovin, ∼e /ɔvɛ̃, in/
A *adj* ovine; **la viande** ∼e mutton; **les producteurs** ∼s sheep farmers
B *nm* sheep; **les** ∼s sheep

ovipare /ɔvipaʀ/ *nm* egg-laying animal

ovni /ɔvni/ *nm*: *abbr* ▸ **objet**

ovocyte /ɔvɔsit/ *nm* oocyte, egg

ovulation /ɔvylasjɔ̃/ *nf* ovulation

ovule /ɔvyl/ *nm* ①▸ Biol ovum; ②▸ Bot ovule; ③▸ (en pharmacie) pessary

oxydable /ɔksidabl/ *adj* [*métal*] liable to rust (*après n*)

oxydant, ∼e /ɔksidɑ̃, ɑ̃t/
A *adj* oxidizing
B *nm* oxidizer, oxidizing agent

oxydation /ɔksidasjɔ̃/ *nf* oxidation

oxyde /ɔksid/ *nm* oxide
(Composé) ∼ **de carbone** carbon monoxide

oxyder /ɔkside/ [1] *vtr*, **s'oxyder** *vpr* to oxidize

oxygène /ɔksiʒɛn/ *nm* ①▸ Chimie oxygen; **à** ∼ [*masque, tente*] oxygen (*épith*); ②▸ (air) air; **je manque d'**∼ **ici** I'm suffocating here

oxygéné, ∼e /ɔksiʒene/
A *pp* ▸ **oxygéner**
B *pp adj* **cheveux** ∼s peroxide (blond) hair; **eau** ∼e hydrogen peroxide

oxygéner /ɔksiʒene/ [14]
A *vtr* to oxygenate
B **s'oxygéner** *vpr* [*personne*] to get some fresh air

oyez /ɔje/ ▸ **ouïr**

ozone /ozon/ *nf* ozone; **la couche d'**∼ the ozone layer

o

p, P /pe/ *nm inv* p, P

pacage /pakaʒ/ *nm* **1** (lieu) pasture, grazing land; **2** (action) grazing

pacha /paʃa/ *nm* pasha

(Idiome) **mener une vie de ~**○ to live the life of Riley

pachyderme /paʃidɛʀm/ *nm* **1** Zool pachyderm; **2** (personne massive) elephant; **de ~** [*physique, pas*] heavy

pacificateur, -trice /pasifikatœʀ, tʀis/
A *adj* [*action, discours*] placatory; [*rôle*] peacemaking
B *nm,f* peacemaker

pacifier /pasifje/ [1] *vtr* to establish peace in, to pacify [*pays, région*]; **un monde pacifié** a world at peace

pacifique /pasifik/
A *adj* **1** [*coexistence, solution, manifestation*] peaceful; [*peuple, personne*] peaceful, peace-loving; **2** Géog Pacific
B *nmf* (personne) peace-loving person

Pacifique /pasifik/ ▸ p. 406 *nprm* **l'océan ~, le ~** the Pacific (Ocean); **le ~ Sud** the South Pacific

pacifiste /pasifist/ *adj, nmf* pacifist

pack /pak/ *nm* **1** (lot) pack (**de** of); **2** (au rugby) pack; **3** (de téléphone) mobile phone package

pacotille /pakɔtij/ *nf pej* **de la ~** cheap rubbish, junk○; **montre de ~** cheap watch; **héroïsme de ~** bogus heroism

PACS /paks/ *nm* (*abbr* = **pacte civil de solidarité**) contract of civil union

> **ℹ** PACS In force since November 1999, this new civil contract is designed to safeguard the common interests of partners living together either in mixed or in same-sex couples. The *PACS* does not apply to under 18s, to couples who are blood relatives or those already in another marriage or relationship. The *PACS* entails certain obligations on the part of the couple such as a commitment to mutual support and maintenance and shared responsibility for joint expenses. By the same token, couples have rights in the areas of accommodation, property, taxation, social security, employment and inheritance.

pacsé○, **~e** /pakse/ *nm,f* partner in a PACS

pacser: se pacser /pakse/ [1] *vpr* to sign a PACS

pacte /pakt/ *nm* pact

(Composé) **P~ de stabilité et de croissance** Stability and Growth Pact

pactiser /paktize/ [1] *vi* to treat (**avec qn** with sb)

pactole /paktɔl/ *nm* gold mine; **ramasser** *or* **toucher le ~**○ to make a fortune *ou* mint○

PAF /paf/
A *nm: abbr* ▸ **paysage**
B *nf: abbr* ▸ **police**

pagaie /pagɛ/ *nf* paddle

pagaille○ /pagɑj/
A *nf* mess; **elle a mis la ~ dans mes papiers** she messed up my papers; **la grève a semé la ~ dans le pays** the strike has caused chaos throughout the country
B en pagaille *loc adv* **1** (en désordre) in a mess; **2** (à profusion) **du poisson en ~** loads○ of fish

paganisme /paganism/ *nm* paganism

pagayer /pageje/ [21] *vi* to paddle

page¹ /paʒ/ *nm* page (boy)

page² /paʒ/ *nf* page; **tournez la ~ SVP** please turn over, PTO; **tourner la ~** *fig* to turn over a new leaf; **faire la mise en ~, mettre en ~** to make up a page; **mise en ~** (résultat) layout; **une ~ sombre de leur existence** a dark chapter in their lives

(Composé) **~ de publicité** Radio commercial break

(Idiomes) **être à la ~** to be up to date; **se mettre à la ~** to bring oneself up to date

pagination /paʒinasjɔ̃/ *nf* **1** (numérotation) pagination; **2** Ordinat paging

pagne /paɲ/ *nm* **1** (en tissu) loincloth; **2** (en paille) grass skirt

pagode /pagɔd/ *nf* pagoda

paie /pɛ/ *nf* pay; **ma ~ me suffit pour vivre** I can live on my pay *ou* wages; **toucher une bonne ~** to be well paid, to get a good wage; **bulletin** *or* **fiche** *or* **feuille de ~** payslip

(Idiome) **ça fait une ~**○ **que je ne l'ai pas vu** it's ages○ since I've seen him

paiement /pɛmɑ̃/ *nm* payment; **le ~ de la dette extérieure** repayment of the foreign debt

païen, -ienne /pajɛ̃, ɛn/ *adj, nm,f* pagan

paillard, ~e /pajaʀ, aʀd/ *adj* bawdy

paillasse /pajas/ *nf* **1** (matelas) straw mattress; **2** (de laboratoire) lab bench; (d'évier) draining board

paillasson /pajasɔ̃/ *nm* **1** (tapis) doormat; **2** (personne servile) doormat

paille /pɑj/
A ▸ p. 140 *adj inv* (couleur) **cheveux (couleur) ~** straw-colouredᴳᴮ hair; **jaune ~** straw yellow
B *nf* straw; **tapis de ~** straw mat; **~ de riz** rice straw; **boire avec une ~** to drink through a straw

(Composé) **~ de fer** steel wool

(Idiomes) **être sur la ~**○ to be penniless; **se retrouver sur la ~**○ to find oneself destitute; **tirer à la courte ~** to draw lots

pailleté, ~e /pajte/ *adj* **1** (avec des disques brillants) sequined, spangled US; **2** (avec de la poudre brillante) [*tissu*] glittery

paillette /pajɛt/ *nf* **1** (disque brillant) sequin, spangle US; **robe à ~s** a sequined *ou* spangled US dress; **2** (poudre brillante) glitter **Ȼ**; **3** (de roche) splinter; **savon en ~s** soap flakes (*pl*)

paillote /pajɔt/ *nf* grass hut

pain /pɛ̃/ *nm* **1** (aliment) bread **Ȼ**; **miettes de ~** breadcrumbs; **2** (miche) loaf; **acheter deux ~s** to buy two loaves; **un petit ~** a (bread) roll; **3** Culin **~ de légumes/viande** vegetable/meat loaf; **4** (bloc) (de savon, cire) bar; (de glace) block; (de dynamite) stick

(Composés) **~ blanc** white bread; **manger son ~ blanc (le premier)** to have it easy at the start; **~ brioché** brioche bread; **~ de campagne** farmhouse bread; (miche) farmhouse loaf; **~ complet** wholemeal bread; (miche) wholemeal loaf; **~ d'épices** gingerbread; **~ grillé** toast; **~ au lait** milk roll; **~ de mie** sandwich loaf; **~ perdu** French toast; **~ aux raisins** currant bun; **~ de seigle** rye bread; (miche) rye loaf; **~ de son** bran loaf; **~ de sucre** sugar loaf; **en ~ de sucre** (crâne) egg-shaped; (montagne) sugar loaf (*épith*)

(Idiomes) **se vendre comme des petits ~s** to sell like hot cakes; **ça ne mange pas de ~**○ it doesn't cost anything; **je ne mange pas de ce ~-là**○ I won't have anything to do with it, I want no part of it; **enlever le ~ de la bouche à qn** to take the bread out of sb's mouth

pair, **~e¹** /pɛʀ/
A adj [nombre, jours, fonction] even
B nm **1** (égal) peer; **c'est une cuisinière hors ~** she's an excellent cook; **elle a un mari hors ~!** she has a marvellous^{GB} husband!; **aller** or **marcher de ~ avec** to go hand in hand with; **2** Hist, Pol peer
C **au pair** loc travailler **au ~** to work as an au pair; **jeune fille au ~** au pair (girl)

paire² /pɛʀ/ nf pair; **donner une ~ de gifles à qn** to box sb's ears

(Idiome) **les deux font la ~!** they're two of a kind!

paisible /pɛzibl/ adj **1** (doux) gentle; **2** (tranquille) [vie, quartier] peaceful, quiet; [personne] calm, easygoing; [eau] calm, untroubled; [sommeil] peaceful; **il dormait d'un sommeil ~** he was sleeping peacefully

paisiblement /pɛzibləmã/ adv **1** (tranquillement) peacefully; **2** (sans s'inquiéter) quietly

paître /pɛtʀ/ [74] vi to graze

(Idiome) **envoyer ~**[○] to send [sb] packing[○]

paix /pɛ/ nf inv **1** Mil, Pol peace; **en temps de ~** in peacetime, in times of peace; **2** (calme intérieur) peace; **avoir l'esprit en ~** to have peace of mind; **3** (tranquillité) peace; **avoir la ~** to get some peace; **laisser qn en ~** to leave sb alone, to leave sb in peace; **ficher[○] la ~ à qn** to leave sb alone; **la ~[○]!** be quiet!

pakistanais, **~e** /pakistanɛ, ɛz/ ▸ p. 392 adj Pakistani

palabre /palabʀ/ nm ou f (discussion) endless discussion

palabrer /palabʀe/ [1] vi to discuss endlessly

palace /palas/ nm luxury hotel

palais /palɛ/ nm inv **1** Anat palate; **2** (goût) palate; **3** Archit (de souverain, particulier) palace; **4** Jur **~ de justice** law courts (pl)

(Composé) **~ des sports** sports centre^{GB}

palan /palã/ nm hoist

pale /pal/ nf **1** (d'hélice, de rame, roue) blade; **2** Tech (vanne) paddle

pâle /pal/ adj pale; **vert/bleu ~** pale green/blue; **tu es toute ~** you look really pale; **être ~ comme un linge** to be as white as a sheet; **une ~ imitation** a pale imitation; **faire ~ figure à côté de** to pale into insignificance beside

palefrenier, **-ière** /palfʀənje, ɛʀ/ nm,f groom

paléochrétien, **-ienne** /paleokʀetjɛ̃, ɛn/ adj [art] early Christian

paléolithique /paleɔlitik/ adj, nm Paleolithic

paléontologie /paleɔ̃tɔlɔʒi/ nf paleontology

paléontologiste /paleɔ̃tɔlɔʒist/, **paléontologue** /paleɔ̃tɔlɔg/ ▸ p. 372 nmf paleontologist

palestinien, **-ienne** /palɛstinjɛ̃, ɛn/ ▸ p. 504 adj Palestinian

palet /palɛ/ nm **1** Sport (au hockey sur glace) puck; **2** Jeux (pierre) quoit

paletot /palto/ nm jacket

(Idiome) **tomber sur le ~ de qn** to lay into sb[○]

palette /palɛt/ nf **1** Art (objet, couleurs) palette; **2** fig range; **une ~ d'activités** a range of activities; **la ~ d'un musicien/acteur** a musician's/an actor's range; **3** Culin (de porc, mouton) ≈ shoulder; **4** (plateau de chargement) pallet

(Composé) **~ de maquillage** make-up palette

palétuvier /paletyvje/ nm mangrove

pâleur /palœʀ/ nf **1** (de ciel) paleness; **2** (de malade) pallor

pâlichon[○], **-onne** /paliʃɔ̃, ɔn/ adj [personne, teint] peaky[○] GB, peaked US; [ciel, éclairage] watery

palier /palje/ nm **1** (d'escalier) landing; **mon voisin de ~** my neighbour^{GB} on the same floor; **2** (stade) level; (phase stable) plateau; **avancer par ~s** to proceed by stages; **3** Sport (en plongée) **~ (de décompression)** (decompression) stage

palière /paljɛʀ/ adj f **porte ~** entry door

pâlir /paliʀ/ [3] vi **1** [coloris, photo, jour] to fade; [ciel, soleil] to grow pale; [personne] to turn pale (de with); **faire ~ qn d'envie** or **de jalousie** to make sb green with envy; **2** [gloire, prestige] to fade

palissade /palisad/ nf (de jardin) fence; Mil palisade

pâlissant, **~e** /palisã, ãt/ adj [jour, lueur] fading

palliatif, **-ive** /paljatif, iv/
A adj palliative
B nm palliative

pallier /palje/ [2] vtr to compensate for

palmarès /palmaʀɛs/ nm inv **1** (classement) honours^{GB} list; (d'acteurs, auteurs) list of award winners; (de sportifs) list of winners; **2** (liste de succès) record of achievements; **il a trois tournois à son ~** he has three tournament wins to his credit; **3** (meilleures ventes) (de disques) hit parade; (de livres) bestsellers list

palme /palm/ nf **1** Bot (feuille) palm leaf; (palmier) palm; **2** Sport (pour nager) flipper; **3** Mil (décoration) ≈ bar; **4** fig prize; **remporter la ~** to take the prize

palmé, **~e** /palme/ adj **1** Zool webbed; **2** Bot palmate

palmeraie /palməʀɛ/ nf palm grove

palmier /palmje/ nm **1** Bot palm (tree); **~ dattier** date palm; **2** Culin (pâtisserie) large pastry biscuit

palmipède /palmipɛd/
A adj web-footed
B nm palmiped

palombe /palɔ̃b/ nf wood pigeon

pâlot[○], **-otte** /palo, ɔt/ adj rather pale

palourde /paluʀd/ nf clam

palpable /palpabl/ adj [objet, bonheur, brouillard] palpable; [vérité, preuve, avantage] tangible

palper /palpe/ [1] vtr [médecin] to palpate [partie du corps]; [client, aveugle] to feel [objet, fruit]

palpitant, **~e** /palpitã, ãt/ adj **1** (captivant) [histoire, vie] thrilling; **2** [cœur] fluttering; [chair, corps] twitching; **3** (qui respire par saccades) panting (de with)

palpitation /palpitasjɔ̃/ nf **1** Méd palpitation; **avoir des ~s** to have palpitations; **2** (de paupière, muscle) twitching; **3** (de lumière, flamme, d'étoile) liter flickering; (de feuille, voile) fluttering; (d'eau) quivering; **4** (exaltation) liter thrill (de of)

palpiter /palpite/ [1] vi **1** (battre) [cœur] to beat; [chair, corps] to twitch; [veine] to pulse; **2** (avoir des mouvements convulsifs) [cœur] to flutter; [paupière] to twitch; **3** (frémir) liter [personne, eau] to quiver (de with); [lumière, flamme] to flicker; [feuille, voile] to flutter

paludisme /palydism/ ▸ p. 195 nm malaria

pâmer: se pâmer /pame/ [1] vpr † or hum **se ~ de plaisir** to swoon with pleasure; **se ~ (d'admiration) devant qch** to swoon over sth

pâmoison /pamwazɔ̃/ nf † or hum swoon; **tomber en ~ (devant qch)** to swoon (over sth)

pamphlet /pãflɛ/ nm satirical tract

pamphlétaire /pãfletɛʀ/ nmf pamphleteer

pamplemousse /pãpləmus/ nm grapefruit

pan /pã/
A nm **1** (partie) (de falaise, maison) section; (de vie, problème) part; (d'obscurité, de ciel) patch; **~ de mur** section of wall; **~ de vitre** glass panel; **2** (côté) (de tour, prisme) side; **relever les ~s d'un rideau** to tie back the curtains; **~s d'un manteau** coat-tails
B excl (coup de feu) bang!; (coup de poing) thump!; (fessée) whack!

(Composé) **~ de chemise** shirt-tail

pan- /pã, pan/ préf Pol Pan; **~-européen** Pan-European; **~-russe** Pan-Russian

panacée /panase/ nf panacea

panache /panaʃ/ nm **1** (élégance) panache; **2** (plumes) plume

panaché, **~e** /panaʃe/
A adj [bouquet, salade] mixed; [tulipe, lierre] variegated
B nm (boisson) shandy

panacher /panaʃe/ [1] vtr to mix

panade /panad/ nf bread soup

(Idiome) **être dans la ~[○]** to be in the soup[○]

panama /panama/ nm (chapeau) panama (hat)

panaméen, **-éenne** /panameɛ̃, ɛn/ ▸ p. 392 adj Panamanian

panaris /panaʀi/ ▸ p. 195 nm inv whitlow

pancarte /pãkaʀt/ nf **1** (sur un mur) notice GB, sign US; (sur un piquet) sign; **2** (dans une manifestation) placard GB, sign US

pancréas /pãkʀeas/ nm inv pancreas

panda /pɑ̃da/ nm panda

panégyrique /paneʒirik/ nm panegyric

paner /pane/ [1] vtr to coat with ou in breadcrumbs

panier /panje/ nm **1** (en osier, rotin, etc) basket; (corbeille à papier) wastepaper basket; (dans un lave-vaisselle) rack; **mettre** or **jeter au ∼** lit to throw [sth] out; fig to get rid of; **2** Sport (au basket-ball) basket; **marquer un ∼** to score a basket; **3** (de jupe, robe) pannier; **robe à ∼s** dress with panniers

(Composé) **∼ à salade** (ustensile) salad shaker; (fourgon de police)○ Black Maria GB, paddy wagon US

(Idiomes) **être un ∼ percé** to spend money like water; **ils sont tous à mettre dans le même ∼**○ they are all much of a muchness GB, they are all about the same; **mettre tous ses œufs dans le même ∼**○ to put all one's eggs in one basket; **le haut** or **dessus du ∼**○ the pick of the bunch

panière /panjɛr/ nf large basket

panier-repas, pl **paniers-repas** /panjerəpa/ nm packed lunch GB, box lunch US

panique /panik/
A adj panic; **sensibilité ∼ au bruit** panic reaction to noise; **peur ∼ (de qch)** terror (of sth)
B nf panic; **mouvement de ∼** panic; **début de ∼** moment of panic; **pas de ∼!** don't panic!; **être pris de ∼** to panic

paniquer○ /panike/ [1]
A vtr to throw [sb] into a panic
B vi to panic; **il a paniqué** he panicked

panne /pan/ nf (de véhicule, machine) breakdown; (de moteur, d'électricité) failure; **∼ de courant** power failure; **la machine/ voiture est (tombée) en ∼** the machine/car has broken down; **tomber en ∼ sèche** or **d'essence** to run out of petrol GB ou gas US; **lorsque la ∼ survint...** (de voiture) when the car broke down...; (d'électricité) when the power failed...; **être en ∼ de**○ to be out of [objet, main-d'œuvre]; to have run out of [idées, imagination]

panneau, pl **∼x** /pano/ nm **1** (permanent) sign; (temporaire) board; (d'information) notice board; **2** (élément) panel; **∼ en bois** wooden panel; **3** Art panel

(Composés) **∼ d'affichage** notice board GB, bulletin board; **∼ indicateur** Aut signpost; **∼ publicitaire** hoarding GB, billboard; **∼ de signalisation routière** road sign; **∼ solaire** solar panel

(Idiome) **tomber** or **donner dans le ∼**○ to fall for it○

panonceau, pl **∼x** /panɔ̃so/ nm (permanent) sign; (temporaire) board

panoplie /panɔpli/ nf **1** Jeux (pour se déguiser) outfit; **2** (de professionnel) paraphernalia; **3** (ornementale) display of weapons; **4** (gamme) (d'objets usuels) array; (d'armements) arsenal; (de mesures, moyens) range

panorama /panɔrama/ nm **1** lit panorama; **2** fig (culturel) panorama; (politique) overview

panoramique /panɔramik/
A adj **1** gén [vue, visite, route] panoramic; **2** Aut [vitre, pare-brise] wrap-around; **3** Cin [écran] wide
B nm Cin pan (shot)

panosse /panɔs/ nf H **1** (serpillière) floor cloth; **2** (chiffon) cloth

panse /pɑ̃s/ nf **1** Zool paunch; **2** ○(estomac) hum belly○; **s'en mettre plein la ∼**○ to stuff one's face○; **3** (de cruche) belly

pansement /pɑ̃smɑ̃/ nm **1** (avec compresse) dressing; **∼ (adhésif)** plaster GB, Band-Aid®; **faire un ∼ à qn** to put a dressing on sb's wound; **2** (action) dressing

panser /pɑ̃se/ [1] vtr **1** Méd to dress [blessure]; to put a dressing on [partie du corps]; **2** fig [temps] to heal [blessure morale]; **∼ ses blessures** to lick one's wounds; **3** Agric (étriller) to groom [cheval]

pansu, **∼e** /pɑ̃sy/ adj [personne, objet] pot-bellied

pantagruélique /pɑ̃tagryelik/ adj Pantagruelian

pantalon /pɑ̃talɔ̃/ nm (culotte longue) trousers (pl) GB, pants (pl) US; **acheter un ∼** to buy a pair of trousers GB ou pants US; **∼ à pinces** pleat front trousers (pl) GB ou pants (pl) US; **∼ de pyjama** pyjama GB ou pajama US bottoms (pl)

pantalonnade /pɑ̃talɔnad/ nf **1** Théât slapstick comedy; **2** fig play-acting ₡

pantelant, **∼e** /pɑ̃tlɑ̃, ɑ̃t/ adj **1** (haletant) [personne] panting; (palpitant) [chair] quivering; **2** (ému) overcome (de with)

panthère /pɑ̃tɛr/ nf **1** (animal) panther; **2** (fourrure) panther skin

pantin /pɑ̃tɛ̃/ nm (jouet, fantoche) puppet

pantois, **∼e** /pɑ̃twa, az/ adj flabbergasted

pantomime /pɑ̃tɔmim/ nf (art) mime; (spectacle) mime show; **faire la ∼** fig to play it up

pantouflard○, **∼e** /pɑ̃tuflar, ard/ adj **qu'est-ce que tu es ∼!** what a stay-at-home you are!

pantoufle /pɑ̃tufl/ nf slipper

PAO /peao/ nf **1** abbr ▸ **production**; **2** abbr ▸ **publication**

paon /pɑ̃/ nm peacock; **faire le ∼** to strut around like a peacock

(Idiome) **être fier comme un ∼** to be as proud as a peacock

papa /papa/ nm dad○, daddy○, father; **fils** or **fille à ∼** spoiled little rich kid○

papauté /papote/ nf papacy

pape /pap/ nm **1** ▸ p. 590 Relig pope; **le ∼ Jean-Paul II** Pope John Paul II; **2** fig (personne influente) high priest (**de qch** of sth)

(Idiome) **être sérieux comme un ∼** to be solemn-faced

paperasse○ /papras/ nf pej **1** (papiers) bumph○ ₡ GB, documents (pl); **2** (activité) paperwork ₡

paperasserie○ /paprasri/ nf pej paperwork

papeterie /papetri/ nf **1** ▸ p. 372 (commerce) stationer's (shop), stationery shop GB ou store US; **2** (articles) stationery; **3** (industrie) papermaking industry; **4** (usine) paper mill

papetier, -ière /paptje, ɛr/
A adj papermaking
B ▸ p. 372 nm,f **1** (fabricant) papermaker; **2** (commerçant) stationer

papi○ /papi/ nm **1** (grand-père) granddad○, grandpa○; **2** (vieil homme) granddad○, old man

papier /papje/
A nm **1** (matière) paper; **sortie sur ∼** Ordinat hardcopy output; **pâte à ∼** pulp; **2** (document) paper; **∼s personnels** personal ou private papers; **3** ○(article de journal) article, piece○
B **papiers** nmpl Admin documents, papers; **∼s d'identité** (identity) papers ou documents

(Composés) **∼ absorbant** kitchen towel, paper towel US; **∼ alu○, ∼ (d')aluminium** (aluminium GB ou aluminum US) foil, kitchen foil; **∼ brouillon** rough paper GB, scrap paper; **∼ buvard** blotting paper; **∼ cadeau** gift wrap, wrapping paper; **∼ carbone** carbon paper; **∼ à cigarettes** cigarette paper; **∼ crépon** crepe paper; **∼ à dessin** drawing paper; **∼ d'emballage** wrapping paper; **∼ glacé** glossy ou shiny paper; **∼ hygiénique** toilet paper ou tissue; **∼ journal** newsprint; **∼ à lettres** writing paper, notepaper; **∼ mâché** papier-mâché; **∼ millimétré** graph paper; **∼ à musique** music paper; **être réglé comme du ∼ à musique** [vie] to be highly regimented; **∼ peint** wallpaper; **∼ pelure** onionskin (paper); **∼ de verre** sandpaper, glasspaper; **∼s gras** litter ₡

(Idiome) **être dans les petits ∼s de qn**○ to be in sb's good books

papier-calque, pl **papiers-calque** /papjekalk/ nm tracing paper

papille /papij/ nf papilla

(Composé) **∼s gustatives** taste buds

papillon /papijɔ̃/ nm **1** Zool butterfly; **∼ de nuit** moth; **2** ○(contravention) parking ticket; **3** Sport (brasse) **∼** butterfly (stroke); **4** (écrou) wing nut

papillonner /papijɔne/ [1] vi **1** (voleter) to flit about; **2** (être volage) to flirt incessantly

papillote /papijɔt/ nf **1** Culin (papier aluminium) foil parcel; (confiserie) chocolate sweet GB ou candy US (wrapped in silver paper); (sur une côtelette) frill; **faire du saumon en ∼** to cook salmon in a foil parcel; **2** (pour les cheveux) curlpaper; **3** (mèche) lock

papilloter /papijɔte/ [1] vi [lumière] to flicker; [personne, yeux] to blink; **∼ des paupières** to blink

papoter○ /papɔte/ [1] vi to chatter

paprika /paprika/ nm paprika

papy-boom○, pl **papy-booms** /papibum/ nm hum onset of retirement for the baby boom generation

pâque /pɑk/
A nf la ~ juive Passover
B **pâques** nfpl faire ses ~s to do one's Easter duty

paquebot /pakbo/ nm liner

pâquerette /pɑkʀɛt/ nf daisy
(Idiome) être au ras des ~s○ to be very basic

Pâques /pɑk/
A nm (date) Easter; **le lundi de** ~ Easter Monday
B nfpl (fête) Easter (sg)
C ▸ p. 303 nprf Géog **île de** ~ Easter Island

paquet /pakɛ/ nm **1** Comm (de sucre, lessive, riz) packet GB, package US; (de cigarettes, café) packet GB, pack US; (d'enveloppes) pack; (de bonbons) bag; **mettre en** ~ to package; **2** (colis) parcel; **3** (assemblage) (de vêtements, linge, billets) bundle; (de lettres) packet; **faire un** ~ **de journaux** to put together a bundle of newspapers; **4** ○(grande quantité) masses (pl); **5** ○(grosse somme) packet○ GB, bundle○ US; **6** Ordinat, Télécom packet
(Composés) ~ **de muscles**○ muscleman; ~ **de nerfs**○ bundle of nerves○
(Idiome) **mettre le** ~○ to pull out all the stops

paquetage /paktaʒ/ nm Mil pack

paquet-cadeau, pl **paquets-cadeaux** /pakɛkado/ nm gift-wrapped present; **est-ce que vous pouvez faire un** ~? could you gift-wrap it?

par /paʀ/
A prép **1** (indiquant un trajet) **entre** ~ **le garage/**~ **la porte du garage** come in through the garage/by the garage door; **il a pris** ~ **les champs** he cut across the fields; **il est passé** ~ **tous les échelons** fig he worked his way up through the ranks; **pour aller à Rome, je passe** ~ **Milan** to get to Rome, I go via ou through Milan; **elle est arrivée** ~ **la droite** she came from the right; **errer** ~ **les rues** to wander through the streets; **le peintre a terminé** or **fini** ~ **la cuisine** the painter did the kitchen last; **2** (indiquant un lieu) ~ **endroits** in places; **3** (indiquant une circonstance) ~ **le passé** in the past; ~ **une belle journée d'été** on a beautiful summer's day; ~ **ce froid** in this cold weather; **ils sortent même** ~ **moins 40°** they go outdoors even when it's minus 40°; ~ **deux/trois fois** on two/three occasions; **4** (indiquant une répartition) ~ **jour/semaine/an** a day/week/year; ~ **personne** ou **habitant** per person ou head; ~ **petits groupes** in small groups; **deux** ~ **deux** [travailler] in twos; [marcher] two by two; **les touristes sont arrivés** ~ **centaines** tourists arrived by the hundred; **5** (introduit un complément d'agent) by; **être pris** ~ **son travail** to be taken up with one's work; **6** (indiquant le moyen) by; **payer** ~ **carte de crédit** to pay by credit card; **7** (indiquant la manière) in; ~ **étapes** in stages; ~ **rafales** in gusts; **8** (indiquant la cause) **l'accident est arrivé** ~ **sa faute** it was his/her fault that the accident happened; ~ **ennui/jalousie** out of boredom/jealousy; **9** (indiquant un intermédiaire) through; **tu peux me faire passer le livre** ~ **ta sœur** you can get the book to me via your sister
B **de par** loc prép fml **1** (partout dans) throughout, all over; **voyager de** ~ **le monde** to travel all over ou throughout the world; **2** (à cause de) **de** ~ **leurs origines** by virtue of their origins

parabole /paʀabɔl/ nf **1** Bible parable; **2** Math parabola; **3** (antenne) satellite dish, satellite receiver

parachever /paʀaʃve/ [16] vtr (terminer) to complete; (fignoler) to put the finishing touches to

parachutage /paʀaʃytaʒ/ nm airdrop

parachute /paʀaʃyt/ nm **1** (voile) parachute; **sauter en** ~ to make a parachute jump; **2** ▸ p. 327 (sport) parachuting

parachuter /paʀaʃyte/ [1] vtr **1** Mil, Sport to parachute [soldat, vivres]; **2** ○(envoyer) **je n'ai pas envie d'être parachuté en Normandie** I don't want to be shunted off○ to Normandy

parachutisme /paʀaʃytism/ ▸ p. 327 nm parachuting

parachutiste /paʀaʃytist/ ▸ p. 372
A adj [troupes, escadron] parachute
B nmf **1** Sport parachutist; **2** Mil paratrooper

parade /paʀad/ nf **1** Mil, Théât (défilé) parade; **de** ~ [costume, uniforme] parade (épith); **faire une** ~ to parade; **2** Sport, fig (défense) parry; **3** (étalage) parade; **faire** ~ **de** to flaunt; **4** (d'animal) display

parader /paʀade/ [1] vi pej to strut about

paradis /paʀadi/ nm inv **1** Relig heaven; **2** (lieu idéal) paradise; **c'est le** ~ **sur terre** it's heavenly; **c'est un** ~ **perdu** it's a garden of Eden
(Composés) ~ **fiscal** tax haven; ~ **terrestre** Garden of Eden
(Idiome) **tu ne l'emporteras pas au** ~○ you'll live to regret it

paradisiaque /paʀadizjak/ adj heavenly

paradoxal, ~**e**, mpl **-aux** /paʀadɔksal, o/ adj paradoxical

paradoxe /paʀadɔks/ nm paradox

paraffine /paʀafin/ nf (liquide) paraffin GB, kerosene US; (solide) paraffin wax; **huile de** ~ paraffin oil GB, kerosene US

parages /paʀaʒ/ nmpl neighbourhood^GB (sg); **dans les** ~ around; **elle est dans les** ~ she is around somewhere

paragraphe /paʀagʀaf/ nm **1** (division) paragraph; **2** (signe typographique) section mark

paraître /paʀɛtʀ/ [73]
A vi **1** [publication] to come out, to be published; **faire** ~ **un article** to publish an article; **un article paru dans une revue** an article which appeared in a magazine; **'à** ~' 'forthcoming titles'; **prochains ouvrages à** ~ **dans cette collection** coming out soon in this collection; **2** (sembler) to appear, to seem; (avoir l'air) to look; **cela peut** ~ **ridicule** this may appear ou seem ridiculous; **il ne craint pas de** ~ **ridicule** he's not afraid of looking silly; **3** (devenir visible) [personne, objet, véhicule, soleil] to appear; **elle ne laisse rien** ~ **de ses sentiments** she doesn't let her feelings show at all; **sans qu'il n'y paraisse rien, elle a fini par gagner tout le monde à sa cause** without anyone realizing, she ended up winning everyone over to her cause; **4** (se montrer) to appear; ~ **à son avantage** to look one's best; **chercher à/aimer** ~ to try/to like to be noticed
B v impers **il paraît qu'il/elle** apparently he/she; **il paraîtrait que** it would seem that; **il me paraît inutile de faire** it seems useless to me to do; **paraît-il** so it seems; **oui, il paraît** so I hear; **il paraît que les Français adorent la musique** the French are supposed to love music; **à ce qu'il paraît** apparently

parallèle¹ /paʀalɛl/
A adj **1** [lignes, plans] parallel (à to); **la rue est** ~ **au fleuve** the street runs parallel to the river; **2** (distinct) parallel; (semblable) similar; **en** ~ **à** (distinctement) in parallel with; (semblablement) similarly to; **une manifestation** ~ a parallel demonstration; **nos concurrents ont suivi une démarche** ~ our competitors took similar steps; **3** (en marge) [marché, police] unofficial; [médecine, éducation] alternative; [monde, univers] parallel
B nm **1** (comparaison) parallel; **établir** or **dresser un** ~ to draw a parallel (**entre** between); **mettre deux événements en** ~ to draw a parallel between two events; **2** Géog parallel

parallèle² /paʀalɛl/ nf Math parallel line

parallèlement /paʀalɛlmɑ̃/ adv **1** Math ~ **à** parallel to; **2** (simultanément) at the same time (**à** as)

parallélépipède /paʀalelepiped/ nm parallelepiped

parallélisme /paʀalelism/ nm **1** Math parallelism; **2** Aut (wheel) alignment; **3** (correspondance) parallelism (**entre** between)

parallélogramme /paʀalelogʀam/ nm parallelogram

paralyser /paʀalize/ [1] vtr **1** Méd to paralyse; **2** (bloquer) to paralyse [pays, entreprise]; to bring [sth] to a halt [production]

paralysie /paʀalizi/ nf paralysis; **être frappé de** ~ to be paralysed

paralytique /paʀalitik/ adj, nmf paralytic

paramédical, ~**e**, mpl **-aux** /paʀamedikal, o/ adj paramedical

paramètre /paʀamɛtʀ/ nm parameter

paranoïaque /paʀanɔjak/ adj, nmf paranoiac

parapente /paʀapɑ̃t/ ▸ p. 327 nm **1** (engin) paraglider; **2** (sport) paragliding

parapet /paʀapɛ/ nm parapet

parapharmacie /paʀafaʀmasi/ nf toiletries and vitamins (pl)

paraphe /paʀaf/ *nm* (initiales) initials (*pl*); (trait de plume) flourish; (signature) signature

parapher /paʀafe/ [1] *vtr* **1** (avec ses initiales) to initial; **2** (d'un trait de plume) to put a flourish to; **3** (avec sa signature) *fml* to sign

paraphrase /paʀafʀɑz/ *nf* paraphrase

paraphraser /paʀafʀɑze/ [1] *vtr* to paraphrase

paraplégique /paʀapleʒik/ *adj, nmf* paraplegic

parapluie /paʀaplɥi/ *nm* lit, fig umbrella

parascolaire /paʀaskɔlɛʀ/ *adj* extracurricular

parasismique /paʀasismik/ *adj* **construction ~** earthquake-resistant construction

parasitaire /paʀazitɛʀ/ *adj* parasitic(al)

parasite /paʀazit/
A *adj* [*plante, organisme*] parasitic(al); [*idée*] intrusive; **bruits ~s** Radio, TV interference **ℂ**
B *nm* **1** lit, fig parasite; **2** Radio, Télécom, TV **~s** (brouillage) interference **ℂ**; (électricité statique) static **ℂ**; **provoquer** *or* **faire des ~s dans la radio** to cause interference on the radio

parasiter /paʀazite/ [1] *vtr* **1** Biol, Bot, Méd to live as a parasite on [*plante, animal*]; **2** (exploiter) to exploit

parasol /paʀasɔl/ *nm* **1** (de plage) beach umbrella; (de café, jardin) sun umbrella; **2** †(ombrelle) parasol, sunshade

paratonnerre /paʀatɔnɛʀ/ *nm* lightning conductor GB, lightning rod

paravent /paʀavɑ̃/ *nm* lit, fig screen

parc /paʀk/ *nm* **1** (jardin) park; **2** (enclos) (pour enfant) play-pen; (pour bestiaux) pen; **3** (ensemble) (d'installations) (total) number (**de** of); (de biens d'équipement) stock (**de** of); **~ automobile** (d'une entreprise) fleet of cars; (d'un pays) number of cars (on the road); **~ ferroviaire** rolling stock; **~ immobilier** housing stock

(Composés) **~ d'attractions** amusement *ou* theme park; **~ de loisirs** theme park; **~ naturel** nature park; **~ relais** park-and-ride

parce: **parce que** /paʀs(ə)k(ə)/ *loc conj* because; **'pourquoi est-ce que je ne peux pas aller à la plage avec eux?'—'~ quel'** 'why can't I go to the beach with them?'—'because I say so *ou* you can't!'; **'pourquoi ne lui as-tu pas téléphoné?'—'~ quel'** 'why haven't you phoned him/her?'—'because I haven't, that's why'; **c'est bien ~ que c'est toi!** only because it's you!; **ne serait-ce que ~ que** if only because

parcelle /paʀsɛl/ *nf* **1** (petit morceau) **~ de verre/plâtre** fragment of glass/plaster; **~ d'or** particle of gold; **2** (petite quantité) **une ~ de bonheur/d'autorité** a bit of happiness/of authority; **3** (terrain) plot (of land)

parchemin /paʀʃəmɛ̃/ *nm* (peau, document) parchment

parcheminé, ~e /paʀʃəmine/ *adj* **1** [*papier*] with a parchment finish (*épith*); **2** [*peau*] papery; **3** [*visage, main*] shrivelled^{GB}

par-ci /paʀsi/ *adv* **~ par-là** here and there; **un gâteau ~ un bonbon par-là** a cake here, a sweet GB *ou* candy US there

parcimonie /paʀsimɔni/ *nf* parsimony *sout*; **avec ~** sparingly, parsimoniously

parcimonieux, -ieuse /paʀsimɔnjø, øz/ *adj* [*personne*] sparing (*jamais épith*), parsimonious *sout*; [*répartition*] stingy (*jamais épith*)

parcmètre /paʀkmɛtʀ/ *nm* parking meter

parcourir /paʀkuʀiʀ/ [26] *vtr* **1** (sillonner) to travel all over [*pays, continent*]; **~ la ville** to go all over town; **~ un lieu à la recherche de** to scour a place in search of; **2** (franchir) to cover [*distance*]; **il reste un long chemin à ~** there's still a long way to go; **3** (traverser) **la chemin de fer parcourt toute la région** the railway runs right across the region; **un frisson me parcourut le dos** a shiver ran down my spine; **4** (examiner rapidement) to glance through, to skim [*lettre, offres d'emploi*]; to scan [*horizon*]; **~ un endroit des yeux** to have a quick glance around a place

parcours /paʀkuʀ/ *nm inv* **1** (trajet) (d'autobus, de personne) route; (de fleuve) course; **~ balisé** *or* **fléché** marked path; **2** Sport course; **~ de golf** round of golf; **elle a fait un excellent ~** (dans une course) she had an excellent race; **3** (cheminement professionnel) career; **incident de ~** hitch

par-delà /paʀdəla/ *prép liter* **1** (de l'autre côté de) beyond; **2** (à travers) **~ les siècles** down the centuries

par-derrière /paʀdɛʀjɛʀ/ *adv* **1** (par l'arrière) **passer ~** to go round GB *ou* to the back; **ils m'ont attaqué ~** they attacked me from behind; **2** (sournoisement) behind sb's back; **critiquer qn ~** to criticize sb behind their back

par-dessous /paʀdəsu/ *prép, adv* underneath

pardessus /paʀdəsy/ *nm inv* overcoat

par-dessus /paʀdəsy/
A *adv* **1** (dessus) **tu vas avoir froid en chemise, mets un pull ~** you'll be cold in a shirt, put a sweater on; **pose ton sac dans un coin et mets ton manteau ~** put your bag in a corner and put your coat on top of it; **2** (par le dessus) **le mur n'est pas haut, passe/saute ~** the wall isn't high, climb/jump over it
B *prép* over; **saute ~ le ruisseau** jump over the stream; **jeter qn/qch ~ bord** to throw sb/sth overboard; **ce que j'aime ~ tout, c'est voyager** what I like best of all is travelling^{GB}

par-devant /paʀdəvɑ̃/
A *adv* **1** (par l'avant) **passer ~** to come round by the front; **2** (en face) **il te fait des sourires ~ mais dit du mal de toi dans ton dos** he's all smiles to your face but says nasty things about you behind your back
B *prép* **~ notaire** in the presence of a notary

pardon /paʀdɔ̃/ *nm* **1** (fait de pardonner) forgiveness; Relig pardon; **je te demande ~** I'm sorry; **j'ai demandé ~?** did you apologize *ou* say you were sorry?; **2** (dans une formule de politesse) **~!** sorry!; **~? qu'est-ce que tu as dit?** sorry *ou* I beg your pardon GB, what did you say?; **~ madame, je cherche...** excuse me please, I'm looking for...; **~ de vous avoir interrompu** I'm sorry for interrupting you

pardonnable /paʀdɔnabl/ *adj* [*faute, délit*] forgivable; **ils ne sont pas ~s** it's unforgivable of them

pardonner /paʀdɔne/ [1]
A *vtr* **1** (accorder son pardon à) [*personne*] to forgive [*faute, erreur, écart*]; **~ à qn** to forgive sb; **~ qch à qn** to forgive sb sth; **~ à qn d'avoir fait** to forgive sb for doing; **2** (dans une formule de politesse) **pardonnez-moi, mais je voudrais intervenir** excuse me, but I'd like to say something
B *vi* **ne pas ~** [*maladie, erreur*] to be fatal
C **se pardonner** *vpr* **je ne me le pardonnerai jamais** I'll never forgive myself for that

(Idiome) **faute avouée est à moitié pardonnée** Prov a fault confessed is half redressed Prov

pare-balles /paʀbal/ *adj inv* bulletproof

pare-brise /paʀbʀiz/ *nm inv* windscreen GB, windshield US

pare-chocs /paʀʃɔk/ *nm inv* bumper

pare-feu /paʀfø/ *nm inv* (bande déboisée) firebreak

pareil, -eille /paʀɛj/
A *adj* **1** (semblable) similar (**à** to); **mon frère et ma sœur sont ~s** (l'un à l'autre) my brother and sister are alike; (que moi) my brother and sister are the same; **les deux chapeaux sont presque ~s** the two hats are almost identical; **je veux une robe pareille à la tienne** I want a dress the same as yours *ou* just like yours; **c'est toujours ~ avec toi** it's always the same with you; **pour moi, c'est ~** it's all the same to me; **ce n'est pas ~!** it's not the same thing!; **à nul autre ~** liter without equal; **2** (de telle nature) such; **je n'ai jamais dit une chose pareille** I never said any such thing; **je n'ai jamais rien vu de ~** I've never seen anything like it; **tu travailles encore à une heure pareille!** you're still working at this hour!; **par un temps ~** in weather like this
B *nm,f* (égal) equal; **c'est un homme sans ~** he's a man without equal; **il est d'un dynamisme sans ~** he's incredibly dynamic; **il n'a pas son ~ pour semer le doute** he's second to none for spreading doubt; **pour moi c'est du ~ au même**[○] it makes no odds GB *ou* difference to me
C *adv* **1** (identiquement) the same; **faire ~** to do the same; **nous étions habillées ~** we were dressed the same (way); **2** [○]C (néanmoins) all the same; **je l'ai fait ~** I did it all the same

pareillement /paʀɛjmɑ̃/ *adv* **1** (de la même manière) (in) the same way; **2** (également) too; **vous le pensez et moi ~** you think so and so do I *ou* and me too

parent, ~e /paʀɑ̃, ɑ̃t/
A *adj* [*conceptions, langues*] similar; **~ avec** [*personne*] related to
B *nm,f* relative, relation; **~s et amis** friends and relations; **plus proche ~(e)** next of kin
C *nm* **1** (le père ou la mère) parent; **mes ~s** my parents; **2** (ancêtres) liter **~s** forebears

P

(Composés) ~ **pauvre** poor relation; **faire figure de ~ pauvre** to look like a poor relation; **~s d'élèves** (pupils') parents; **réunion de ~s d'élèves** parents' evening

parental, ~e, mpl **-aux** /paʀɑtal, o/ adj parental

parenté /paʀɑ̃te/ nf **1)** (rapport) (entre personnes) blood relationship; (entre projets, histoires) connection; **l'importance des liens de ~** the importance of family ties; **il n'y a pas de lien de ~ entre eux** they are not related; **2)** (parents et alliés) relations (pl)

parenthèse /paʀɑ̃tɛz/ nf **1)** (digression) **ouvrir une ~** to digress; **refermons la ~** but to come back to what we were talking about; **(soit dit) par ~** or **entre ~s** incidentally; **2)** ▸ p. 413 (signe typographique) bracket; **mettre qch entre ~s** lit to put sth in brackets; fig to put sth aside; **3)** (épisode) interlude

parer /paʀe/ [1]

A vtr **1)** (esquiver) to ward off [coup, attaque]; **2)** (protéger) to protect; **3)** (orner) [objet] to adorn [chose, personne]; [personne] to adorn [chose, personne] (**de** with)

B parer à vtr ind **~ à** (prévenir) to guard against; (remédier à) to deal with; **~ à toute éventualité** to be prepared for all contingencies; **~ au plus pressé** to deal with the most urgent matters first

C se parer vpr **1)** (se protéger) to take precautions (**contre** against); **2)** (se vêtir) to adorn oneself; **3)** (être recouvert) to be bedecked (**de** with)

pare-soleil /paʀsɔlɛj/ nm inv Aut visor

paresse /paʀɛs/ nf laziness

paresser /paʀɛse/ [1] vi to laze; **arrête de ~!** stop lazing around!

paresseux, -euse /paʀɛsø, øz/
A adj gén lazy; [organe] sluggish
B nmf lazy person
C nm Zool sloth

parfaire /paʀfɛʀ/ [10] vtr to complete, to round off [éducation, œuvres]; to perfect [connaissance]

parfait, ~e /paʀfɛ, ɛt/
A adj **1)** (insurpassable) [personne, beauté, travail, accord] perfect; **elle est d'une beauté ~e** she is absolutely beautiful; **2)** (total) [ressemblance] exact; [imbécile] complete; [discrétion, égalité] absolute; [ignorance] total; **3)** (typique) [estivant, touriste] archetypal; [exemple] classic
B nm Ling perfect

(Idiome) **filer le ~ amour** to spin out love's sweet dream

parfaitement /paʀfɛtmɑ̃/ adv **1)** (à la perfection) perfectly; **2)** (absolument) [savoir] perfectly well; [tolérer, admettre] fully; [heureux, capable, simple] perfectly; [correct, égal] absolutely; [faux] totally; [absurde, choquant] utterly; **3)** (absolument) absolutely

parfois /paʀfwa/ adv sometimes

parfum /paʀfœ̃/ nm **1)** (pour se parfumer) perfume, scent; **2)** (senteur) (de fleur, forêt) scent; (de sels de bain) fragrance; (de vin) bouquet; (de fruit) scent, (sweet) smell; **3)** (goût) flavourᴳᴮ; **4)** fig **un ~ du terroir** a rural flavourᴳᴮ; **un ~ de scandale** a whiff of scandal

(Idiome) **mettre qn au ~**○ to put sb in the picture, to clue sb in○

parfumé, ~e /paʀfyme/ adj **1)** [fleur] sweet-scented; [thé] flavouredᴳᴮ; [fruit] fragrant; [air, chambre] fragrant; **2)** [mouchoir] scented; **3)** [glace] flavouredᴳᴮ

parfumer /paʀfyme/ [1]
A vtr **1)** (embaumer) **les fleurs parfument la pièce** the room is fragrant with flowers; **2)** (imprégner de parfum) to put scent on [mouchoir]; to put scent in [bain]; **3)** (aromatiser) to flavourᴳᴮ (**à** with)
B se parfumer vpr (en général) to wear perfume; (pour l'occasion) to put perfume on

parfumerie /paʀfymʀi/ ▸ p. 372 nf perfumery

parfumeur, -euse /paʀfymœʀ, øz/ ▸ p. 372 nm,f **1)** (vendeur) perfume salesman/saleswoman; **2)** (fabricant) perfumer

pari /paʀi/ nm **1)** Sport bet; (gageure) bet, wager; **un ~ de 50 euros** a 50-euro bet; **2)** (activité) betting **C**; **3)** (défi) gamble

parier /paʀje/ [2] vtr **1)** (faire un pari) to bet; **tu paries?** do you want to bet?; **~ qch avec qn** to bet sb sth; **2)** Sport to bet [argent]; **~ sur** to bet on, to back [cheval, boxeur]; **~ gros sur un cheval** to bet heavily on a horse, to place a large

bet on a horse; **il y a fort** or **gros à ~ que** it's a safe bet that, the odds are that; **3)** (compter) to bank (**sur** on); **4)** (être sûr) to bet; **je parie qu'il a encore oublié** I bet he has forgotten again; **je l'aurais parié!** I knew it!

parieur, -ieuse /paʀjœʀ, øz/ nm,f (joueur) gambler; (aux courses) better GB, bettor US, punter○ GB

Paris /paʀi/ ▸ p. 621 npr Paris

(Idiome) **avec des si, on mettrait ~ en bouteille** ≈ if wishes were horses, beggars would ride Prov

parisien, -ienne /paʀizjɛ̃, ɛn/ ▸ p. 621 adj [agglomération, accent, vie] Parisian; [bassin, banlieue, région] Paris (épith)

paritaire /paʀitɛʀ/ adj [commission] joint (épith)

parité /paʀite/ nf **1)** parity; **à ~** at parity; **2)** (en politique) male-female parity

---

ⓘ **Parité** The law of parité, passed in early 2000, stipulates that political parties should put forward an equal number of male and female candidates at all elections, from municipal to European levels. Parties failing to comply are subject to financial penalties which take the form of a reduction in their public funding. The law however only applies to communes with over 3500 inhabitants.

---

parjure /paʀʒyʀ/
A nmf (personne) perjurer
B nm (faux serment) perjury **C**; **commettre un ~** to commit perjury

parking /paʀkiŋ/ nm **1)** (parc de stationnement) car park GB, parking lot US; (place de stationnement) parking space; **2)** (stationnement) controv parking; **~ interdit** no parking

(Composé) **~ de dissuasion** park-and-ride

par-là /paʀla/ adv ▸ **par-ci**

parlant, ~e /paʀlɑ̃, ɑ̃t/ adj **1)** (éloquent) [attitude, geste] eloquent, meaningful; [comparaison] vivid; [preuve, chiffre, résultat, fait] which speaks for itself (jamais épith, après n); [portrait] lifelike; **les faits sont ~s** the facts speak for themselves; **ça me paraît suffisamment ~** it looks convincing enough to me; **2)** (accompagné de paroles) **le cinéma ~** the talkies○ (pl); **un film ~** a talking picture, a talkie○; **horloge ~e** speaking clock

parlé, ~e /paʀle/ adj [langue, style] spoken; (familier) colloquial

Parlement /paʀləmɑ̃/ nm Parliament

parlementaire /paʀləmɑ̃tɛʀ/
A adj parliamentary
B nmf (membre du Parlement) Member of Parliament

parlementer /paʀləmɑ̃te/ [1] vi to negotiate

parler¹ /paʀle/ [1]
A vtr **1)** (savoir manier) to speak [langue]; **~ (l')italien** to speak Italian; **2)** (discuter) **~ affaires/politique** to talk (about) business/politics; **~ littérature/cinéma** to talk (about) books/films

B parler à vtr ind **~ à** (s'adresser) to talk ou speak to; (ne pas être brouillé) to be on speaking terms with; **trouver à qui ~** fig to meet one's match; **moi qui vous parle, je n'aurais jamais cru ça**○! I'm telling you, I'd never have believed it!

C parler de vtr ind **1)** (discuter) **~ de** to talk about; (mentionner) **~ de** to mention; **~ de tout et de rien, ~ de choses et d'autres** to talk about this and that ou one thing and another; **toute la ville en parle** it's the talk of the town; **les journaux en ont parlé** it was in the papers; **faire ~ de soi** gén to get oneself talked about; (dans les médias) to make the news; **c'est d'épidémie qu'il faut ~** we're talking about an epidemic here; **on parle d'un gymnase** there's talk of a gymnasium; **on en parle** there's talk of it; **qui parle de vous expulser?** who said anything about throwing you out?; **tu parles d'une aubaine**○! talk about a bargain○!; **ta promesse/son travail, parlons-en!** some promise/work!; **n'en parlons plus!** (ça suffit) let's drop it; (c'est oublié, pardonné) that's the end of it; **finis-le, comme ça on n'en parle plus** finish it, then it's done; **2)** (traiter) [article, film, livre] **~ de** to be about; **3)** (s'entretenir) **~ de qch/qn avec qn** to talk to sb about sth/sb; **~ de qch/qn à qn** (l'entretenir de) to talk to sb about sth/sb, to tell sb about sth/sb; **il va ~ de toi à son chef** he'll put in a word for you with his boss; **il nous a parlé de vous** he's told us about you; **il ne m'a jamais parlé de sa famille** he's never mentioned his family to me; **on m'a beaucoup parlé de vous**

I've heard a lot about you; **la lecture? parle-lui plutôt de tennis!** books? he would rather hear about tennis! **D** vi **1** (articuler des mots) [*enfant, perroquet, poupée*] to talk; (d'une certaine façon) to speak, to talk; **elle a parlé à 14 mois** she started to talk at 14 months; **~ vite/fort/en russe** to speak *ou* talk fast/loudly/in Russian; **~ du nez/avec un accent** to speak with a nasal twang/with an accent; **2** (s'exprimer) to speak; **parle, on t'écoute** come on *ou* speak up, we're listening; **économiquement parlant** economically speaking; **laisser ~ son cœur** to speak from the heart; **~ par gestes** to communicate by means of gestures; **les muets parlent par signes** the speech-impaired use sign language; **~ en connaissance de cause** to know what one is talking about; **bien parlé!** well said!; **une prime? tu parles°!** a bonus? you must be joking!; **tu parles si je viens°!** (bien sûr) you bet I'm coming°!; **3** (bavarder) to talk; **~ avec qn** to talk *ou* speak to sb (**de** about); **~ pour ne rien dire** to talk for the sake of talking; **il s'écoute ~** he loves the sound of his own voice; **parlons peu et parlons bien** let's get down to business; **4** (faire des aveux) to talk
E **se parler** vpr **1** (communiquer) to talk *ou* speak (to each other); **2** (ne pas être brouillés) to be on speaking terms; **ils ne se parlent pas** they're not on speaking terms; **3** (être utilisé) [*langue*] to be spoken

parler² /paʀle/ nm **1** (manière de s'exprimer) way of talking; (langage) speech; **2** Ling dialect

parloir /paʀlwaʀ/ nm (d'école, hôpital) visitors' room; (de prison) visiting room; (pour avocat) interview room; (de maison, couvent) parlour^GB; (de théâtre) greenroom

parme /paʀm/ ▸ p. 140 adj inv, nm mauve

Parmentier /paʀmɑ̃tje/ npr **hachis ~** cottage pie, shepherd's pie

parmi /paʀmi/ prép among, amongst; **demain il sera ~ nous** he'll be with us tomorrow; **le plus important ~ les écrivains de ce siècle** the most important of this century's writers; **choisir ~ huit destinations** to choose from eight destinations

parodie /paʀɔdi/ nf **1** (pastiche) parody; **2** (simulacre) mockery; **une ~ de procès** a travesty of justice

parodier /paʀɔdje/ [2] vtr to parody

paroi /paʀwa/ nf **1** (face interne) (de tunnel) side; (de grotte) wall; (de tube, tuyau) inner surface; **2** Constr (cloison) wall; **3** (de montagne) **~ rocheuse** rock face; **la ~ nord** the north face; **4** Anat, Bot wall

paroisse /paʀwas/ nf parish

paroissial, ~e, mpl **-iaux** /paʀwasjal, o/ adj parish (épith)

paroissien, -ienne /paʀwasjɛ̃, ɛn/ nm,f parishioner

parole /paʀɔl/ nf **1** (faculté) speech; **perdre/retrouver la ~** to lose/to regain the power of speech, to lose/to regain one's speech; **avoir la ~ facile** to have the gift of the gab°; **avoir le don de la ~** to be a good talker; **2** (possibilité de s'exprimer) **avoir droit à la ~** to have the right to speak; **prendre la ~** to speak; **laisser la ~ à qn** to let sb speak; **temps de ~** speaking time; **et maintenant, je donne** *or* **laisse la ~ à mon collègue** and now I hand over to my colleague; **3** (mot) word; **il n'a pas dit une ~** he didn't say a word; **~s en l'air** empty words; **une ~ blessante** a hurtful remark; **joindre le geste à la ~** to suit the action to the word; **sur ces bonnes ~s, je m'en vais** hum on that (philosophical) note, I'm off; **4** (assurance verbale) word; **reprendre/manquer à/donner sa ~** to go back on/to break/to give one's word; **tenir ~** to keep one's word; **il n'a qu'une ~, c'est un homme de ~** he's a man of his word; **il n'a aucune ~** you can't trust him; **je t'ai cru sur ~** I took you at your word; **~ d'honneur!** cross my heart!, I promise!; **je te donne ma ~ d'honneur que ce n'est pas vrai** I swear it's not true; **ma ~!** (upon) my word!; **5** (sentence, aphorisme) words (pl); **prêcher la bonne ~** to spread the good word; **c'est ~ d'évangile** it's gospel truth, it's gospel°; **6** (texte) **~s** (de chanson) words, lyrics; (de dessin) words; **film sans ~s** silent film; **7** Ling speech

parolier, -ière /paʀɔlje, ɛʀ/ ▸ p. 372 nm,f (de chansons) lyric writer; (d'opéra) librettist

paroxysme /paʀɔksism/ nm **1** (plus haut degré) (de plaisir) paroxysm; (de bataille) climax; (de ridicule) height; **atteindre/être à son ~** [*douleur*] to reach/to be at its height; [*conflit, combat*] to reach/to be at its climax; **au ~ de la fureur** in a frenzy of rage; **2** Méd crisis

parpaing /paʀpɛ̃/ nm **1** (en béton) breeze-block GB, cinder block US; **2** (en pierre) perpend

Parque /paʀk/ npr **la ~** Fate; **les trois ~s** the three Fates

parquer /paʀke/ [1] vtr **1** (mettre dans un parc) to pen [*bestiaux*]; **2** (entasser) pej to coop up [*personnes*]; **3** (garer) to park [*voiture*]

parquet /paʀkɛ/ nm **1** (plancher) parquet (floor); **poser du** *or* **un ~** to lay parquet; **2** Jur **le ~ ≈** the prosecution; **3** (à la Bourse) **le ~** the floor

parrain /paʀɛ̃/ nm **1** Relig godfather; **être (le) ~ de qn** to be godfather to sb; **2** (de candidat, projet, d'enfant défavorisé, initiative) sponsor; (d'œuvre, de fondation) patron; **3** (de navire) *man who ceremonially launches a ship*; **4** (d'organisation criminelle) godfather.

⚠ En anglais *godfather* n'est jamais une forme d'adresse.

parrainage /paʀɛnaʒ/ nm **1** (caution morale) (de candidat, projet) sponsorship, backing ⊄; (de fondation) patronage; **2** (soutien financier) sponsorship; **sous le ~ de…** sponsored by…

parrainer /paʀene/ [1] vtr **1** (moralement) to be patron of; **2** (financièrement) to sponsor

parricide /paʀisid/
A nmf (personne) parricide
B nm (crime) parricide

parsemer /paʀsəme/ [16] vtr **parsemez-la de persil haché** sprinkle some chopped parsley over it; **une pelouse parsemée de fleurs** a lawn dotted with flowers; **les obstacles ont parsemé sa vie** his/her life was strewn with obstacles

part /paʀ/
A nf **1** (portion) (de tarte, gâteau) slice, portion; (de viande, riz) helping, portion; (d'héritage, de marché) share; **une ~ du gâteau** fig a slice *ou* share of the cake; **avoir sa ~ de misères** to have one's (fair) share of misfortunes; **2** (élément d'un tout) proportion; **une grande ~ de qch** a high proportion *ou* large part of sth; **une ~ de chance** an element of chance; **il y a une grande ~ de fiction dans son récit** his/her account is highly fictional; **le hasard n'a aucune ~ là-dedans** chance has nothing to do with it; **pour une bonne** *or* **grande ~** to a large *ou* great extent; **faire la ~ de qch** to take sth into account *ou* consideration; **faire la ~ belle à qn** to give sb the best deal; **à ~ entière** [*membre, citoyen*] full (épith); [*science, sujet*] in its own right; **participer aux discussions à ~ entière** to participate fully in the discussions; **3** (contribution) share; **payer sa ~** to pay one's share; **prendre ~ à** to take part in; **il m'a fait ~ de ses projets/son inquiétude** he told me about his plans/his concern; **je vous ferai ~ de mes intentions** I'll let you know my intentions; **faire ~ d'une naissance** to announce a birth; **4** (partie d'un lieu) **de toute(s) ~(s)** [*surgir, arriver*] from all sides; **de ~ et d'autre** on both sides, on either side; **de ~ en ~** [*traverser, transpercer*] right *ou* straight through; **5** (point de vue) **pour ma ~** for my part; **d'une ~…, d'autre ~…** (marquant une énumération) firstly…, secondly…; (marquant une opposition) on (the) one hand… on the other hand; **d'autre ~** (de plus) moreover; **prendre qch en bonne/mauvaise ~** to take sth in good part/take sth badly
B **à part** loc **1** (séparément) [*ranger, classer*] separately; **mettre qch à ~** to put sth to one side; **si on met à ~ cette partie de la population** leaving aside this section of the population; **prendre qn à ~** to take sb aside *ou* to one side; **2** (séparé) **une salle à ~** a separate room; **faire chambre à ~** to sleep in separate rooms; **3** (différent) **être un peu à ~** [*personne*] to be out of the ordinary; **un cas/lieu à ~** a special case/place; **4** (excepté) apart from; **à ~ ça, quoi de neuf°?** apart from that, what's new?; **à ~ que** apart from the fact that; **blague à ~** joking aside
C **de la part de** loc prép **1** (à la place de) **de la ~ de** [*agir, écrire, téléphoner*] on behalf of; **2** (venant de) **de la ~ de qn** from sb; **il y a un message de la ~ de ton père** there's a message from your father; **donne-leur le bonjour de ma ~** say hello to them for me; **ce n'est pas très gentil de ta ~** that's not very nice of you; **sans engagement de votre ~** with no obligation on your part; **de leur ~, rien ne m'étonne** nothing they do surprises me; **c'est de la ~ de qui?** (au téléphone) who's calling please?

partage ▸ partie

(Idiomes) faire la ∼ du feu to cut one's losses; faire la ∼ des choses to put things in perspective

partage /paʀtaʒ/ *nm* [1] (découpage) dividing, sharing; le ∼ des gains se fera entre 20 personnes the profits will be split between *ou* shared out among 20 people; des problèmes de ∼ familial problems in dividing up the inheritance; [2] (distribution) distribution; le ∼ des terres n'était pas équitable the land had not been shared out fairly; le ∼ du pain the breaking of the bread; [3] (répartition) sharing, division; régner/gouverner sans ∼ to reign/to govern absolutely; victoire sans ∼ total victory; le ∼ des voix Pol the division of votes; [4] (séparation) division, partition; un plan de ∼ d'un territoire en deux zones a plan to divide *ou* partition a territory into two zones; [5] (part) recevoir qch en ∼ to be left sth (in a will); il a reçu la malchance en ∼ fig his lot is an unhappy one

partagé, ∼e /paʀtaʒe/ *adj* [1] (divisé) [*avis, presse, syndicats*] divided (sur on); [2] (ambivalent) [*réactions, sentiments*] mixed; [3] (indécis) être ∼ [*personne*] to be torn (entre between); [4] (commun) [*chagrin*] shared; leurs torts sont ∼s they are both to blame; [5] (réciproque) [*tendresse*] mutual; amour ∼/non ∼ requited/unrequited love

partager /paʀtaʒe/ [13]
A *vtr* [1] (donner une partie de ce qui est à soi) to share [*jouets, nourriture*]; [2] (séparer) to divide [*pays, pièce*]; [3] (diviser) to divide [sth] (up), to split; je partage mon temps entre la lecture et la musique I divide my time between reading and music; [4] (avoir en commun) to share; (prendre part à) to share [*émotion, angoisse*]; ∼ les mêmes valeurs to have common values, to share values; je partage votre avis I agree with you, I'm of the same opinion; [5] (communiquer) to share [*chagrin, problème, joie*]; faire ∼ qch à qn to let sb share in sth; il sait nous faire ∼ ses émotions he knows how to get his feelings across; [6] (opposer) [*problème, question*] to divide, to split [*opinion publique*]
B se partager *vpr* [1] (se répartir) to share [*argent, travail, responsabilité*]; [2] (être divisé) to be divided (en into; entre between); to be split (en into); le mouvement se partage en deux grandes tendances the movement is divided *ou* split into two broad tendencies; [3] (se diviser) [*frais, responsabilités, nourriture*] to be shared; [*gâteau, tarte*] to be cut (up) (en into); [4] (se communiquer) to be shared; un tel chagrin ne peut se ∼ such grief cannot be shared

partance /paʀtɑ̃s/ *nf* en ∼ [*avion*] about to take off; [*navire*] about to sail; [*train, personne*] about to leave; être en ∼ pour *ou* vers [*avion, navire, train, voyageurs*] to be bound for

partant○, ∼e /paʀtɑ̃, ɑ̃t/ *adj* (enthousiaste) être ∼ to be game○ (pour faire to do)

partenaire /paʀtǝnɛʀ/
A *nmf* partner; qui était le ∼ d'Arletty? Cin, Théât who played opposite Arletty?
B *nm* Fin, Pol partner
(Composé) ∼s sociaux ≈ unions and management

partenariat /paʀtǝnaʀja/ *nm* partnership

parterre /paʀtɛʀ/ *nm* [1] (de jardin) bed; [2] Théât (places) stalls (*pl*) GB, orchestra US; (spectateurs) people in the stalls GB *ou* orchestra US; [3] (assemblée) panel; devant un ∼ de journalistes before a panel of journalists

Parthe /paʀt/ *nm* Parthian; les ∼s the Parthians
(Idiome) décocher la flèche du ∼ to fire a Parthian *ou* parting shot

parti, ∼e¹ /paʀti/
A○ *adj* (ivre) être ∼ to be tight○; être complètement ∼ to be plastered○
B *nm* [1] (groupe de personnes) group; Pol party; le ∼ des mécontents the malcontents (*pl*); [2] (solution) option; prendre ∼ to commit oneself; prendre ∼ contre qn to side against sb; prendre ∼ pour/contre qch to be for/against sth; prendre le ∼ de qn to side with sb; prendre ∼ de qch to opt for sth; il a pris le ∼ de ne rien dire he decided not to say anything; ne pas savoir quel ∼ prendre not to know what to do for the best; [3] †(personne à marier) suitable match
(Composé) ∼ pris bias; ∼ pris de réalisme/modernité bias toward(s) realism/modernity
(Idiomes) prendre son ∼ de qch to come to terms with sth; tirer ∼ de to take advantage of [*situation*]; to turn [sth] to good account [*leçon, invention*]

ⓘ **Partis politiques** In general, French political parties reflect a basic left/right divide. On the left, the main parties are the *parti socialiste* (*PS*) and the *parti communiste français* (*PCF*) while the principal parties on the right are the *Union pour un mouvement populaire* (*UMP*) and the *Union pour la démocratie française* (*UDF*). These two groups regularly run a joint list known as part of an electoral pact. There are in addition more extreme groupings at both ends of the political spectrum. Beyond the left/right divide generally, the ecological movement is represented by *Les Verts* and *Génération Écologie*.

---

partial, ∼e, *mpl* -iaux /paʀsjal, o/ *adj* biased^GB

partialité /paʀsjalite/ *nf* (de personne, jugement) bias; ∼ envers qn (au profit de) bias toward(s) sb; (au détriment de) bias against sb; avec ∼ in a biased^GB way; accuser qn de ∼ to accuse sb of being biased^GB

participant, ∼e /paʀtisipɑ̃, ɑ̃t/ *nm,f* (à un concours, une course) participant, entrant (à in); (à un débat, une cérémonie) participant, person taking part (à in)

participation /paʀtisipasjɔ̃/ *nf* [1] (à une réunion, un projet, festival, soulèvement) participation (à in); (à un complot, attentat) involvement (à in); la ∼ de plusieurs vedettes a attiré les photographes the presence of several stars drew the photographers; la ∼ aux élections a été faible there was a low turnout at the polls; [2] (contribution) contribution; ∼ aux frais (financial) contribution; [3] (part financière) stake, holding; ∼ de 17% 17% stake
(Composé) ∼ aux bénéfices profit-sharing

participe /paʀtisip/ *nm* participle; ∼ passé past participle

participer /paʀtisipe/ [1]
A participer à *vtr ind* [1] (personnellement) ∼ à to participate in, to take part in [*réunion, soulèvement*]; to be involved in [*crime, complot*]; il ne participe pas assez en classe he doesn't participate enough in class; ce projet est immoral, je n'y participerai pas this project is immoral, I will have no part in it; ∼ à la joie de qn to share sb's joy; [2] (financièrement) ∼ à to contribute to; ∼ aux frais to share in the cost
B participer de *vtr ind* fml ∼ de la névrose to be akin to *ou* to have some of the characteristics of neurosis; ∼ de l'idéologie dominante to draw on the dominant ideology

particularisme /paʀtikylaʀism/ *nm* distinctive identity

particularité /paʀtikylaʀite/ *nf* [1] (caractéristique) special feature; les ∼s historiques d'un pays a country's particular historical background (sg); [2] (de maladie, régime politique, situation) particular nature; (de coutume) uniqueness

particule /paʀtikyl/ *nf* [1] gén, Phys particle; [2] Ling particle; nom à ∼ aristocratic name

particulier, -ière /paʀtikylje, ɛʀ/
A *adj* [1] (propre) l'entreprise a une façon particulière de procéder the company has its own (particular) procedures; il a ceci de ∼ qu'il aime son indépendance the thing with him is that he likes his independence; [2] (spécifique) [*droits, statut, privilèges, rôle*] special; [*exemple, thème, objectif*] specific; [3] (personnel) [*voiture, secrétaire, collection*] private; [4] (inhabituel) [*cas, situation, phénomène, épisode*] unusual; [*talent, jour, effort*] special; [*mœurs*] odd; [*accent, style*] distinctive, unusual; il a examiné ce cas avec une attention particulière he gave this case his particular attention; c'est quelqu'un de très ∼ (admiratif) he's/she's somebody out of the ordinary; péj he's/she's weird; 'quoi de neuf?' —'rien de ∼' 'what's new?'—'nothing special'
B en particulier *loc adv* [1] (en privé) in private; [2] (séparément) individually; [3] (notamment) in particular, particularly
C *nm* (personne) (simple) ∼ private individual; loger chez des ∼s to stay with a family; vendre de ∼ à ∼ to sell privately

particulièrement /paʀtikyljɛʀmɑ̃/ *adv* [1] (hautement) [*fatigué, honteux, important*] particularly; [*intelligent*] exceptionally; [*aimer, souffrir*] really; [2] (spécialement) particularly, in particular; plus *ou* tout ∼ more particularly; je ne la connais pas ∼ I don't know her particularly well

partie² /paʀti/
A *adj f* ▸ parti
B *nf* [1] (élément d'un tout) gén part; (d'une somme, d'un salaire) proportion, part; une ∼ des électeurs a proportion of the

voters; **une bonne** *or* **grande ~ de** a good *ou* large number of [*personnes, objets*]; a high proportion of [*masse, ressources*]; **la majeure ~ des gens** most people (*pl*); **la majeure ~ de la population** the majority of the population; **en ~** partly, in part; **en grande ~** to a large *ou* great extent; **il fait ~ de la famille** he's one of the family; **faire ~ des premiers/derniers** to be among the first/last; [2] (division de l'espace) part; **dans cette ~ du monde** in this part of the world; [3] (division temporelle) part; **il a plu une ~ de la nuit** it rained for part of the night; **elle passe la majeure ~ de son temps au travail/à dormir** she spends most of her time at work/sleeping; [4] (profession) line (of work); **dans ma ~** in my line (of work); **il est de la ~** it's in his line (of work); [5] ▸ p. 327 Jeux, Sport game; **une ~ de tennis** a game of tennis; **une ~ de cache-cache** a game of hide-and-seek; **une ~ de golf** a round of golf; **faire une ~** to have a game; **gagner/perdre la ~** fig to win/to lose the day; **je fête mes trente ans, j'espère que tu seras de la ~** I'm having a thirtieth birthday party, I hope you can come; **ce n'est que ~ remise** maybe next time; [6] (dans une négociation, un contrat) party; **les ~s en présence** the parties involved; **être ~ prenante dans qch** to be actively involved in [*conflit, contrat, négociation*]; [7] Jur party; **la ~ adverse** the opposing party; [8] Mus part; [9] Math part
C parties○ *nfpl* privates○

Composés ~ **de chasse** hunting party; ~ **civile** Jur plaintiff; **se constituer** *or* **porter ~ civile** to take civil action; ~ **de pêche** fishing trip; ~ **de plaisir** fun **C**; **tu parles d'une ~ de plaisir!** that's not my idea of fun!

Idiomes **avoir affaire à forte ~** to have a tough opponent; **prendre qn à ~** to take sb to task

partiel, -ielle¹ /paʀsjɛl/
A adj [*paiement*] part (*épith*); [*montant, remboursement, destruction, accord, résultat*] partial; **des solutions partielles** incomplete solutions
B nm Univ exam based on a module

partielle² /paʀsjɛl/ nf by-election

partiellement /paʀsjɛlmɑ̃/ adv partly, partially

partir /paʀtiʀ/ [30]
A vi [1] (quitter un lieu) [*personne*] to leave, to go; **partez devant, je vous rejoins** go on ahead, I'll catch you up; **est-ce qu'ils sont partis en avion ou en train?** did they fly or did they take the train?; **j'espère que je ne vous fais pas ~?** I hope I'm not driving you away?; ~ **en courant/boitant/hurlant** to run off/to limp off/to go off screaming; ~ **fâché** to go off in a huff○; ~ **content** to go away happy; ~ **sans laisser d'adresse** (sans laisser de traces) to disappear without trace; [2] (pour une destination) to go; **il est parti en ville à bicyclette** he went to town on his bicycle; ~ **pour le Mexique/l'Australie** to leave for Mexico/Australia; **ils sont partis en Écosse en stop** (ils sont encore en voyage) they're hitchhiking to Scotland; (dans le passé) they hitchhiked to Scotland; ~ **à la guerre/au front** to go off to war/to the front; ~ **en tournée** to set off on tour GB *ou* on a tour; ~ **en retraite** to retire; [3] (se mettre en mouvement) [*personne, voiture, car, train*] to leave; [*avion*] to take off; [*moteur*] to start; **je pars** I'm off, I'm leaving; **les coureurs sont partis** the runners are off; **le train à destination de Dijon va ~** the train to Dijon is about to depart *ou* leave; **à vos marques, prêts, partez!** on your marks, get set, go!; [4] (être projeté) [*flèche, balle*] to be fired; [*bouchon*] to shoot out; [*capsule*] to shoot off; [*réplique*] to slip out; **le coup de feu est parti** the gun went off; **elle était tellement énervée que la gifle est partie toute seule** she was so angry that she slapped him/her before she realized what she was doing *ou* before she could stop herself; [5] (commencer) [*chemin, route*] to start; **les branches qui partent du tronc** the branches growing out from the trunk; **les avenues qui partent de la place de l'Étoile** the avenues which radiate outwards from the Place de l'Étoile; ~ **favori** [*concurrent, candidat*] to start favourite^{GB}; ~ **battu d'avance** to be doomed from the start; ~ **dernier** (dans une course) to start last; **le troisième en partant de la gauche** the third (starting) from the left; ~ **de rien** to start from nothing; **c'est parti!** (ordre) go!; **et voilà, c'est parti**○, **il pleut!** here we go, it's raining!; [*coureur, cheval, projet, travail, personne*] to have got GB *ou* gotten US off to a good start; **être bien parti pour gagner** to seem all set to win; **c'est mal parti**○ things don't look too good, it doesn't look too promising; **il a l'air parti**○ **pour réussir** he seems to be heading for success; **le mauvais temps est parti**○ **pour**

durer it looks as if the bad weather is here to stay; [6] (se fonder) ~ **de** to start from [*idée, observation*]; ~ **du principe que** to work on the assumption that; ~ **d'une bonne intention** to be well-meant; [7] (s'enlever) [*tache, saleté*] to come out; [*émail, peinture*] to come off; [*odeur*] to go; [*bouton, écusson, décoration*] to come off; **faire ~ une tache** to remove a stain; [8] (être expédié) [*colis, candidature*] to be sent (off); [9] (se lancer) **quand il est parti**○ **on ne l'arrête plus** once he starts *ou* gets going there's no stopping him; ~ **dans des explications** to launch into explanations; [10] (mourir) euph to go, to pass away euph
B à partir de loc prép from; **à ~ de maintenant** from now on; **à ~ du moment où** (sens temporel) as soon as; (sens conditionnel) as long as; **à ~ de là, tout a basculé** from then on everything changed radically; **les enfants ne sont admis qu'à ~ de huit ans** children under eight are not admitted; **faire une étude à ~ de statistiques** to base a study on statistics

partisan, ~e /paʀtizɑ̃, an/
A adj [1] pej [*esprit, querelle*] partisan; [2] (en faveur de) ~ **de qch/de faire** in favour^{GB} of sth/of doing; **être ~ du moindre effort**○ (être paresseux) to be lazy; (dans une décision) to go for the easy option
B nm,f gén supporter, partisan; Mil partisan

partitif, -ive /paʀtitif, iv/
A adj partitive
B nm partitive

partition /paʀtisjɔ̃/ nf [1] Mus score; [2] (partage) partition

partout /paʀtu/ adv [1] (en tous lieux) [*sévir, traîner, chercher*] everywhere; [*avoir mal, s'enduire*] all over; **un peu ~ dans le monde** more or less all over the world; **il y avait de la boue ~** there was mud all over the place; ~ **sur ton passage** wherever you go; ~ **où je vais** wherever I go; [2] (dans tous les domaines) **il est le premier ~** he's the best at everything; [3] Sport **trois (points** *or* **buts) ~** three all

Idiome **fourrer son nez ~**○ to stick one's nose into everything○

parure /paʀyʀ/ nf [1] (toilette) finery **C**; [2] (bijoux) set of jewels; ~ **de diamants** set of diamonds; [3] (ensemble assorti) set; ~ **de table** set of table linen

parution /paʀysjɔ̃/ nf (de livre, journal, revue) publication; **à sa ~, le livre a fait scandale** when it came out, the book caused a scandal; **la ~ a été reportée** the publication date has been put back

parvenir /paʀvəniʀ/ [36]
A parvenir à vtr ind [1] (atteindre) ~ **à** to reach; **un fruit parvenu à maturité** a fruit which has reached maturity; **faire ~ qch à qn** (par voie postale) to send sth to sb; (par messager) to get sth to sb; [2] (au prix d'efforts) ~ **à** to reach [*accord, solution*]; to gain [*pouvoir*]; to get [*poste*]; to achieve [*équilibre*]; ~ **à faire** to manage to do; ~ **à ses fins** to achieve one's ends
B vi (réussir socialement) to succeed

parvenu, ~e /paʀvəny/ nm,f pej upstart

parvis /paʀvi/ nm inv (d'église) square

pas¹ /pa/ adv

> ⚠ Dans la langue parlée ou familière, *not* utilisé avec un auxiliaire ou un modal prend parfois la forme *n't* qui est alors accolée à l'auxiliaire: *he hasn't finished, he couldn't come.* On notera que *will not* devient *won't*, que *shall not* devient *shan't* et *cannot* devient *can't*.

[1] gén **c'est un Autrichien, ~ un Allemand** he's an Austrian, not a German; **je ne prends ~ de sucre avec mon café** I don't take sugar in coffee; **ce n'est ~ un lâche** gén he isn't a coward; (pour insister) he's no coward; **ce n'est ~ une raison pour crier comme ça!** that's no reason to shout like that!; **il n'est ~ plus intelligent qu'un autre** he's no brighter than anybody else; **je ne pense ~ I** don't think so, I think not sout; **elle a aimé le film, mais lui ~** she liked the film but he didn't; **des tomates ~ mûres** unripe tomatoes; **des chaussures ~ cirées** unpolished shoes; **une radio ~ chère**○ a cheap radio; **non mais t'es ~ dingue**○**?** are you mad or what?; [2] (dans des expressions, exclamations) ~ **du tout** not at all; ~ **le moins du monde** not in the slightest *ou* in the least; **absolument ~** absolutely not; ~ **tellement** not much; ~ **tant que ça** not all that much; ~ **plus que ça** not all that much; ~ **d'histoires!** I don't want any arguments *ou* fuss!; ~ **de chance!** hard

luck!; ~ **possible**! I can't believe it!; ~ **vrai**○? gén isn't that so?; (n'est-ce pas) **on a bien travaillé**, ~ **vrai**○? we did good work, didn't we?

pas² /pɑ/ nm inv **1** (enjambée) step; **faire un grand ~** to take a small step; **avancer à grands ~** to stride along; **avancer à petits ~** to edge forward; **l'hiver arrive à grands ~** winter is fast approaching; **avancer à ~ de géant (dans qch)** to make giant strides (in sth); **marcher à ~ de loup** to move stealthily; **marcher à ~ feutrés** to walk softly; **faire ses premiers ~** [enfant] to take one's first steps; **faire ses premiers ~ dans la société mondaine** to make one's debut in society; **faire le premier ~** fig to make the first move; **suivre qn ~ à ~** to follow sb everywhere; **avancer ~ à ~** to proceed step by step; **de là à dire qu'il s'en fiche○, il n'y a qu'un ~** there's only a fine line between that and saying he doesn't care; **j'habite à deux ~ (d'ici)** I live just a step away (from here); **2** (allure) pace; **d'un bon ~** at a brisk pace; **d'un ~ lourd** with a heavy tread; **d'un ~ pressé** hurriedly; **marcher du même ~** to walk in step; **ralentir le ~** to slow down; **marcher au ~** (à pied) to march; (à cheval) to walk; **marquer le ~** Mil to mark time; **rouler au ~** to crawl (along); **'roulez au ~'** (panneau) 'dead slow' GB, '(very) slow' US; **mettre qn au ~** to bring sb to heel; **partir au ~ de course** to rush off, to race off; **faire qch au ~ de charge** to do sth in double-quick time; **j'y vais de ce ~** I'm on my way now; **3** (bruit) footstep; **reconnaître le ~ de qn** to recognize sb's footstep; **4** (trace de pied) footprint; **revenir** or **retourner sur ses ~** lit to retrace one's steps; fig to backtrack; **marcher sur les ~ de qn** fig to follow in sb's footsteps; **5** (de danse) step; **apprendre les ~ du tango** to learn how to tango

(Composé) **~ de porte** doorstep

(Idiomes) **tirer qn/se tirer d'un mauvais ~** to get sb/to get out of a tight corner; **faire** or **sauter le ~** to take the plunge; **céder le ~ à qn** to make way for sb; **prendre le ~ sur qch/qn** to overtake sth/sb

pascal, **~e**, mpl **~s** or **-aux** /paskal, o/
A adj Relig [fêtes] Easter (épith); [cierge, agneau] paschal
B nm (mesure) pascal

pas-de-porte /pɑdpɔʀt/ nm inv (somme) key money

passable /pɑsabl/ adj **1** [film, soirée] fairly good; [production] reasonable; **2** Scol (notation) fair

passablement /pɑsabləmɑ̃/ adv **1** (considérablement) [ivre, énervé, flou] rather; [boire, s'inquiéter] quite a lot; **2** (moyennement) [jouer au tennis] reasonably well

passade /pɑsad/ nf (engouement) fad

passage /pɑsaʒ/ nm **1** (circulation) **interdire le ~ des camions dans la ville** to ban trucks from (driving through) the town; **une rue où il y a beaucoup de ~** (véhicules) a street where there's a lot of traffic; **2** (séjour) **ton ~ dans la ville a été bref** your stay in the town was brief; **un petit ~ chez le teinturier ne lui ferait pas de mal** a visit to the dry-cleaners' wouldn't do it any harm; **après un bref ~ dans la fonction publique** after a short spell in the civil service; **3** (visite en chemin) **était-ce après le ~ du facteur?** was it after the postman had come ou been?; **manquer le ~ des cigognes** to miss the storks going over; **je peux te prendre au ~** I can pick you up on the way; **des hôtes de ~** short-stay guests; **4** (franchissement) '**~ interdit, voie privée**' 'no entry, private road'; **pour permettre le ~ de la lumière** in order to let the light in; **pour empêcher le ~ de l'air** in order to prevent draughts GB ou drafts US; **pour laisser** or **céder le ~ à l'ambulance** in order to let the ambulance go past; **on se retourne sur leur ~** people's heads turn as they go past; **notons au ~ que...** fig let's note in passing that...; **se servir au ~** lit (en passant) to help oneself; fig (légalement) to take a cut (of the profits); (illégalement) to pocket some of the profits; **~ en ferry** ferry crossing; **le ~ à gué du bras de mer est possible à marée basse** the sound can be forded at low tide; **5** (à la radio, télévision, au théâtre) **leur troisième ~ à l'Olympia** the third time they've been to the Olympia; **ton ~ sur scène a été remarqué** you made a great impact on stage; **chaque ~ de votre chanson à la radio** every time your song is played on the radio; **6** (chemin emprunté) (par une personne) way; (par une chose) path; **prévoir le ~ de câbles** to plan the route of cables; **7** (à une situation nouvelle) **~ (de qch) à qch** transition (from sth) to sth; **~ à la phase suivante** progression to the next phase; **son ~ dans la classe supérieure est compromis** he/she won't be allowed to move up into the next year GB ou grade US; **rites de ~** rites of passage;

8 (petite rue) alley; (dans un bâtiment) passageway; **9** (de roman, symphonie) passage; (de film) sequence

(Composés) **~ à l'acte** Psych acting out; **~ clouté**† = **~ pour piétons**; **~ à niveau** level crossing GB, grade crossing US; **~ obligé** prerequisite; **~ pour piétons** pedestrian crossing; **~ protégé** right of way; **~ souterrain** underground passage; (sous une rue) subway; **~ à tabac** beating; **~ à vide** gén bad patch; (pour un artiste) unproductive period

passager, **-ère** /pɑsaʒe, ɛʀ/
A adj (de courte durée) [situation, crise] temporary; [sentiment] passing; [averse] brief; [malaise] slight, short-lived (épith); [amours] casual; **sa mauvaise humeur n'est que passagère** his/her bad mood won't last long
B nm,f passenger

(Composé) **~ clandestin** stowaway

passant, **~e** /pɑsɑ̃, ɑ̃t/
A adj [rue] busy
B nm,f passer-by; **quelques ~s** a few passers-by
C nm (anneau de ceinture, de bracelet-montre) loop

passation /pɑsasjɔ̃/ nf **~ des pouvoirs** Jur, Pol transfer of power

passe¹○ /pɑs/ nm **1** (passe-partout) master key; **2** (laissez-passer) pass

passe² /pɑs/ nf **1** Sport pass; **faire une ~** to pass the ball (à to); **2** (de prestidigitateur, torero) pass; **3** (situation) **être dans une ~ difficile/une mauvaise ~** to be going through a difficult/a bad patch; **être en ~ de faire** to be (well) on the way to doing; **c'est une méthode révolue ou en ~ de l'être** it's an outdated method or soon will be

passé, **~e** /pɑse/
A adj **1** (révolu) [années, amours] past; **le temps ~** the past; **~ de mode** dated; **il était cinq heures ~es** it was past five o'clock; **2** (dernier en date) [an, semaine] last; **3** (usé par le temps) [couleur, tissu] faded
B nm **1** (division du temps) past; **dans** or **par le ~** in the past; **2** (de civilisation, d'individu) past; **mon ~ de syndicaliste/comédien** my past as a trade unionist/an actor; **3** Ling past (tense); **au ~** in the past tense
C prép after; **~ la poste c'est tout droit** after the post office you go straight on; **~ 8 heures il s'endort dans son fauteuil** come eight o'clock he goes to sleep in his armchair; **~ la rivière vous serez libre** once you've crossed the river, you'll be free

(Composés) **~ antérieur** past anterior; **~ composé** present perfect; **~ simple** past historic

passe-droit, pl **~s** /pɑsdʀwa/ nm **bénéficier d'un ~** to get preferential treatment

passéisme /pɑseism/ nm pej attachment to the past

passéiste /pɑseist/ adj pej [méthode] old-fashioned; [organisation, idée] backward-looking péj

passementerie /pɑsmɑ̃tʀi/ nf trimmings (pl)

passe-montagne, pl **~s** /pɑsmɔ̃taɲ/ nm balaclava

passe-partout /pɑspaʀtu/
A adj inv [formule, réponse] catch-all; [vêtement] for all occasions (après n)
B nm inv (clé) master key; (scie) two-man saw

passe-passe /pɑspas/ nm inv **tour de ~** conjuring trick; fig sleight of hand; **faire qch par des tours de ~ juridiques** to do sth by legal sleight of hand

passe-plat, pl **~s** /pɑspla/ nm serving hatch

passeport /pɑspɔʀ/ nm lit, fig passport

passer /pɑse/ [1]
A vtr **1** (franchir) to cross [fleuve, frontière]; to go through [porte, douane]; to get over [obstacle]; **ils ont fait ~ au troupeau** they took the herd across the river; **il m'a fait ~ la frontière** he got me across the border; **2** (faire franchir) **~ qch à la douane** to get sth through customs; **3** (dépasser) to go past, to pass; **quand vous aurez passé le feu, tournez à droite** turn right after the lights; **j'ai passé l'âge** I'm too old; **le malade ne passera pas la nuit** the patient won't last the night; **4** (mettre) **~ le doigt sur la table** to run one's finger over the table-top; **~ la tête à la fenêtre** to stick one's head out of the window; **elle m'a passé le bras autour des épaules** she put her arm around my shoulders; **5** (transmettre) to pass [objet] (à to); to pass [sth] on [consigne, maladie] (à to); (prêter)○ to lend (à qn to sb); (donner)○ to give (à qn to sb); **fais ~ la nouvelle à tes amis** pass the news on to your friends; **~ sa colère sur**

ses collègues to take one's anger out on one's colleagues; ⑥ (au téléphone) **tu peux me ~ Chris?** can you put Chris on?; **attends, je te la passe** hold on, here she is, I'll put her on; **je vous le passe** (sur un autre poste) I'm putting you through; **pourriez-vous me ~ le poste 4834?** could you put me through to extension 4834 please?; ⑦ (se présenter à) to take, to sit [*examen scolaire, test*]; to have [*visite médicale, entretien*]; **faire ~ un test à qn** to give sb a test; **c'est moi qui fais ~ l'oral de français aux nouveaux** I'm taking the new pupils for the French oral; ⑧ (réussir) to pass [*examen, test*]; ⑨ (dans le temps) to spend [*temps*] (à faire doing); **nous avons passé de bons moments ensemble** we've had some good times together; **dépêche-toi, on ne va pas y ~ la nuit**○! hurry up, or we'll be here all night!; ⑩ (pardonner) **elle leur passe tout** she lets them get away with murder; **il passe tous ses caprices à sa fille** he indulges his daughter's every whim; **passez-moi l'expression** if you'll pardon the expression; ⑪ (omettre) to skip [*mot, page, paragraphe*]; **je vous passe les détails** I'll spare you the details; **j'en passe et des meilleures**○ (après énumération) and so on and so forth, I could go on; ⑫ (utiliser) **~ un chiffon sur les meubles** to go over the furniture with a cloth; **~ un coup de fer sur une chemise** to give a shirt a quick iron; **~ l'aspirateur dans le salon** to hoover® GB *ou* vacuum the lounge; ⑬ (étendre) **~ un peu de baume sur une brûlure** to dab some ointment on a burn; **~ une couche de peinture sur qch** to give sth a coat of paint; ⑭ (soumettre) **~ qch à la flamme** to hold sth over a flame; **qu'est-ce qu'elle nous a passé**○! she really went for us○!; ⑮ (à travers une grille) to filter [*café*]; to strain [*jus, sauce*]; to purée [*légumes*]; ⑯ (enfiler) to slip [sth] on [*vêtement, anneau*]; to slip into [*robe*]; **ils ont essayé de me ~ la camisole** they tried to put me in a straitjacket; ⑰ (faire jouer) to play [*disque, cassette audio*]; (projeter) to show [*film, diapositives, cassette vidéo*]; (diffuser) to place [*annonce*]; ⑱ (signer) to sign [*contrat*]; to enter into [*accord*]; to place [*commande*]; to pass [*loi, décret*]; **~ un marché**○ to make a deal; ⑲ Aut (enclencher) **~ la troisième/la marche arrière** to go into third gear/into reverse; ⑳ Jeux **~ son tour** to pass

Ⓑ *vi* ① (parcourir son chemin) [*personne, animal, véhicule, ballon*] to go past *ou* by, to pass; **~ entre** to pass between; **nous sommes passés près du lac** we went past the lake; **~ sur un pont** to go over a bridge; **l'autobus vient juste de ~ le** bus has just gone; **le facteur n'est pas encore passé** the postman hasn't come *ou* been yet; **je suis passé à côté du monument** I passed the monument; **nous sommes passés près de chez toi** we were near your house; **~ à pied/à bicyclette** to walk/to cycle past; **un avion est passé** a plane flew overhead; **il est passé en courant** he ran past; **le ballon est passé tout près des buts** the ball narrowly missed the goal; ② (se trouver, s'étendre) **la route passe à côté du lac** the road runs alongside the lake; **ils ont fait ~ la route devant chez nous** they built the road in front of our house; **ligne qui passe par les centres de deux cercles** line that goes through the centres^{GB} of two circles; **en faisant ~ une ligne par ces deux villes** drawing a line through these two towns; ③ (faire un saut) **je ne fais que ~** I've just popped in GB *ou* dropped by for a minute; **quand je suis passé au marché** when I went down to the market; **il est passé déposer un dossier** he came to drop off a file; **~ dans la matinée** to call in the morning GB, to come over in the morning; **passe nous voir plus souvent!** come and see us more often!; **~ prendre qn/qch** to pick sb/sth up; ④ (se rendre) to go; **les contrebandiers sont passés en Espagne** the smugglers have crossed into Spain; **passez derrière moi** follow me; **il est passé devant moi** (dans une queue) he pushed in front of me; **~ devant une commission** to come before a committee; ⑤ (aller au-delà) to get through; **il est passé au rouge** he went through the red lights; **il n'a pas attendu le feu vert pour ~** he didn't wait for the lights to turn green; **il m'a fait signe de ~** he waved me on; **vas-y, ça passe!** go on, there's plenty of room!; **laisser ~ une ambulance** to let an ambulance through; **le volet laisse ~ un peu de lumière** the shutter lets in a chink of light; **la cloison laisse ~ le bruit** the partition doesn't keep the noise out; **~ par-dessus bord** to fall overboard; **il est passé par la fenêtre** (par accident) he fell out of the window; (pour entrer) he got in through the window; **il est passé sous un train** he was run over by a train; **~ derrière la maison** to go round GB *ou* around US the back of the house; ⑥ (transiter) **~ par** [*personne*] lit to pass through; fig to go through; **nous**

sommes passés par Édimbourg we went via Edinburgh; **~ par qn pour faire qch** to go through sb to do; **~ par de rudes épreuves** to go through the mill; **~ par une rue** to go along a street; **~ au bord de la faillite** to come very close to bankruptcy; **la formation par laquelle il est passé** the training (that) he had; **il dit tout ce qui lui passe par la tête** he always says the first thing that comes into his head; **je ne sais jamais ce qui te passe par la tête** I never know what's going on in your head; **une idée m'est passée par la tête** an idea occurred to me; **qu'est-ce qui lui est passé par la tête?** what was he/she thinking of?; **un sourire passa sur ses lèvres** he/she smiled briefly; **des reptiles à l'homme, en passant par le singe** from reptiles to man, including apes; ⑦ ○(avoir son tour) **il accuse le patron, ses collègues, bref, tout le monde y passe** he's accusing the boss, his colleagues—in other words, everyone in sight; **que ça te plaise ou non, il va falloir y ~** whether you like it or not, there's no alternative; **on ne peut pas faire autrement que d'en ~ par là** there is no other way around it; **je sais, j'en suis déjà passé par là** I know all about that, I've been there○; ⑧ (négliger) **je préfère ~ sur ce point** I'd rather not dwell on that point; **il est passé sur les détails** he didn't go into the details; **si l'on passe sur les frais de déplacement** if we ignore the travel expenses; **passons!** (injonction) let's hear no more about it!; **~ à côté d'une question** (involontairement) to miss the point; **laisser ~ qch** (délibérément) to overlook sth; **laisser ~ une occasion** to miss an opportunity; **laisser ~ plusieurs fautes** (par inadvertance) to let several mistakes slip through; ⑨ (ne pas approfondir) **notons en passant que** we should note in passing that; **soit dit en ~** incidentally; ⑩ (être admis, supporté) [*aliment, repas*] to go down; [*commentaires, discours, critiques*] to go down well (auprès de with); [*loi, candidat*] to get through; [*attitude, pensée*] to be accepted; **ce doit être le concombre qui passe mal** it must be the cucumber; **prends un peu de cognac, ça fait ~!** have a drop of brandy, it's good for the digestion; **vos critiques sont mal passées** your criticism went down badly; **ils n'ont jamais pu faire ~ leurs idées** they never managed to get their ideas accepted; **que je sois critiqué, passe encore, mais calomnié, non!** criticism is one thing, but I draw the line at slander; **avec lui, la flatterie, ça ne passe pas** flattery won't work with him; **~ au premier tour** Pol to be elected in the first round; **~ dans la classe supérieure** to move up to the next year *ou* grade US; **(ça) passe pour cette fois**○ I'll let it go this time; ⑪ (se déplacer) **~ de France en Espagne** to leave France and enter Spain; **~ de la salle à manger au salon** to move from the dining room to the lounge; **~ à l'ennemi** to go over to the enemy; **~ sous contrôle de l'ONU** to be taken over by the UN; **~ sous contrôle ennemi** to fall into enemy hands; **~ de main en main** to be passed around; **~ constamment d'un sujet à l'autre** to flit from one subject to another; **~ de la théorie à la pratique** to put theory into practice; **leur nombre pourrait ~ à 700** their number could reach 700; **~ à un taux supérieur** to go up to a higher rate; **faire ~ qch de 200 à 300** to increase sth from 200 to 300; ⑫ (être pris) **~ pour un imbécile** to look a fool; **il passe pour l'inventeur de l'ordinateur** he's supposed to have invented computers; **il pourrait ~ pour un Américain** he could be taken for an American; **il veut ~ pour un grand homme** he wants to be seen as a great man; **faire ~ qn/qch pour exceptionnel** to make sb/sth out to be exceptional; **se faire ~ pour malade** to pretend to be ill; **se faire ~ pour mort** to fake one's own death; **il se fait ~ pour mon frère** he passes himself off as my brother; ⑬ (disparaître) [*douleur, événement*] to pass; **quand l'orage sera** *or* **aura passé** lit when the storm is over; fig when the storm dies down; **ça passera** (sa mauvaise humeur) it'll pass; (ton chagrin) you'll get over it; **la première réaction passée** once we/they calmed down; **nous avons dû attendre que sa colère soit passée** we had to wait for his/her anger to subside; **~ de mode** to go out of fashion; **cette mode est vite passée** that fashion was short-lived; **faire ~ à qn l'envie de faire** to cure sb of the desire to do; **je vais leur faire ~ l'envie de tirer sur ma sonnette!** I'll teach them to ring my bell!; **ce médicament fait ~ les maux d'estomac** this medicine relieves stomach ache; **cette mauvaise habitude te passera** it's a bad habit you'll grow out of; ⑭ (apparaître, être projeté, diffusé) [*artiste, groupe*] (sur une scène) to be appearing; (à la télévision, radio) to be on; [*spectacle, film*] to be on; [*cassette, musique*] to be playing; ⑮ (être placé)

∼ **avant/après** (en importance) to come before/after; **la santé passe avant tout** health comes first; **il fait** ∼ **sa famille avant ses amis** he puts his family before his friends; ⑯ ○(disparaître) **où étais-tu (encore) passé?** where (on earth) did you get to?; **où est passé mon livre?** where has my book got to?; ⑰ (s'écouler) [*temps*] to pass, to go by; **deux ans ont passé** two years have passed; **je ne vois pas le temps** ∼ I don't know where the time goes; **le week-end a passé trop vite** the weekend went too quickly; ⑱ (se mettre à) to turn to; **passons aux choses sérieuses** let's turn to serious matters; ∼ **à l'étape suivante** to move on to the next stage; **passons à autre chose** let's change the subject; **nous allons** ∼ **au vote** let's vote now; ∼ **à l'offensive** to take the offensive; ⑲ (être transmis) ∼ **de père en fils** to be handed down from father to son; **l'expression est passée dans la langue** the expression has become part of the language; **ça finira par** ∼ **dans les mœurs** it'll eventually become common practice; **il a fait** ∼ **son émotion dans la salle** he transmitted his emotion to the audience; ⑳ (être promu) to be promoted to; **être passé maître dans l'art de faire** to be a past master at doing; **elle est passée maître dans l'art de mentir** she's an accomplished liar; ㉑ (être dépensé) [*argent, somme*] to go on *ou* in *ou* into; [*produit, matière*] to go into; ㉒ ○(mourir) **y** ∼ to die; **si tu continues à conduire comme ça, tu vas finir par y** ∼ if you keep driving like that, you'll kill yourself; **on y passera tous, mais le plus tard sera le mieux** we've all got to go sometime, the later the better; ㉓ (se décolorer) [*teinte, tissu*] to fade; ∼ **au soleil** to fade in the sun; ㉔ (filtrer) [*café*] to filter; **faire** ∼ **la soupe** to put the soup through a sieve; ㉕ (changer de vitesse) ∼ **en troisième/marche arrière** to go into third/reverse; **la troisième passe mal** *or* **a du mal à** ∼ third gear is a bit stiff; ㉖ Jeux (au bridge, poker) to pass

C se passer *vpr* ① (se produire) to happen; **tout se passe comme si l'euro avait été dévalué** it's as if the euro had been devalued; ② (être situé) to take place; **la scène se passe au Viêt Nam** the scene is set in Vietnam; ③ (se dérouler) [*opération, examen, négociations*] to go; **tout s'est passé très vite** it all happened very fast; **ça va mal se** ∼ **pour toi** you're going to be in trouble; **je ne passerai pas comme ça!** I won't leave it at that!; ④ (s'écouler) [*période*] to go by, to pass; **deux ans se sont passés depuis** that was two years ago; **attendons que ça se passe** let's wait till it's over; **nos soirées se passaient à regarder la télévision** we spent the evenings watching television; ⑤ (se dispenser) **se** ∼ **de** [*personne*] to do without [*objet, activité, personne*]; to go without [*repas, nourriture, sommeil*]; **se** ∼ **de commentaires** to speak for itself; **ne pas pouvoir se** ∼ **de faire** not to be able to help doing; ⑥ (se mettre) **se** ∼ **la langue sur les lèvres** to run one's tongue over one's lips; **se** ∼ **la main sur le front** to put a hand to one's forehead; ⑦ (l'un à l'autre) **ils se sont passé des documents** they exchanged some documents; **nous nous sommes passé le virus** we caught the virus from each other

passereau, *pl* ∼**x** /pasʀo/ *nm* ① gén passerine; ② †(moineau) sparrow

passerelle /pasʀɛl/ *nf* ① (petit pont) footbridge; ② fig (lien) link; **jeter une** ∼ **entre qch et qch** to provide a link between sth and sth; ③ (pour embarquer) Naut gangway; Aviat (escalier) steps (*pl*); (tunnel) gangway

passe-temps /pastɑ̃/ *nm inv* pastime, hobby

passeur, -euse /pasœʀ, øz/ *nm,f* ① ▸ p. 372 Naut ferryman/ferrywoman; ② (pour passer une frontière) smuggler; (de drogue) courier, mule○

passible /pasibl/ *adj* Jur ∼ **de** [*délit*] punishable by; [*personne*] liable to

passif, -ive /pasif, iv/
A *adj* ① gén [*personne*] passive (**devant, face à** in the face of); ② Ling passive
B *nm* ① Ling passive (voice); ② Fin debit; **mettre qch au** ∼ **de qn** fig to count sth amongst sb's failures

passiflore /pasiflɔʀ/ *nf* passionflower

passion /pasjɔ̃/ *nf* passion; **avoir la** ∼ **d'écrire** to have a passion for writing; **aimer à la** *or* **avec** ∼ to love passionately; **sans** ∼ (objectivement) dispassionately; (sans enthousiasme) without enthusiasm; **se prendre de** ∼ **pour qn** to become infatuated with sb; **se prendre de** ∼ **pour qch** to develop a passion for sth

passionnant, ∼e /pasjɔnɑ̃, ɑ̃t/ *adj* [*voyage, métier, match*] exciting; [*personne, roman, musée*] fascinating

passionné, ∼e /pasjɔne/
A *adj* [*amour*] passionate; [*débat*] impassioned; **être** ∼ **de** to have a passion for
B *nm,f* enthusiast; **un** ∼ **de tennis** a tennis enthusiast

passionnel, -elle /pasjɔnɛl/ *adj* [*débat*] passionate; [*sujet*] emotive; [*crime*] of passion (*après n*)

passionnément /pasjɔnemɑ̃/ *adv* passionately

passionner /pasjɔne/ [1]
A *vtr* ① (intéresser) to fascinate; **la botanique le passionne** he has a passion for botany; ② (rendre passionné) to inflame [*débat*]
B **se passionner** *vpr* to have a passion (**pour** for)

passivité /pasivite/ *nf* passivity

passoire /paswaʀ/ *nf* (pour légumes) colander; (pour infusion) strainer

pastel /pastɛl/
A *adj inv* [*teinte*] pastel
B *nm* ① (technique, crayon) pastel; ② (œuvre) pastel

pastèque /pastɛk/ *nf* watermelon

pasteur /pastœʀ/ ▸ p. 372 *nm* ① (protestant) minister; ② (prêtre) priest; ③ (berger) shepherd

pasteuriser /pastœʀize/ [1] *vtr* to pasteurize

pastiche /pastiʃ/ *nm* pastiche

pasticher /pastiʃe/ [1] *vtr* to imitate the style of [*auteur, œuvre*]; to imitate [*style*]

pastille /pastij/ *nf* ① (médicament) pastille, lozenge; ∼ **contre la toux** cough drop; ② (petit bonbon) ∼ **de chocolat** chocolate drop; ∼ **de menthe** peppermint; ③ (de tissu, caoutchouc) patch; (de plastique) disc

pastoral, ∼e¹, mpl -aux /pastɔʀal, o/ *adj* pastoral

pastorale² /pastɔʀal/ *nf* ① Littérat, Mus pastoral; ② Relig pastoralia (*pl*)

patachon○ /pataʃɔ̃/ *nm* **mener une vie de** ∼ to live in the fast lane

patata○ /patata/ *excl* ▸ **patati**

patate○ /patat/ *nf* ① ○(pomme de terre) spud○; ② ○(idiot) blockhead○, idiot

(Composé) ∼ **douce** sweet potato

(Idiomes) **se débrouiller comme une** ∼○ to make a complete hash of things; **ça m'est resté sur la** ∼○ it left me feeling bitter

patati○ /patati/ *excl* ∼, **patata** and so on and so forth

patatras○ /patatʀa/ *excl* crash○!

pataud /pato, od/ *adj* clumsy

pataugeoire /patoʒwaʀ/ *nf* paddling pool GB, baby pool US

patauger /patoʒe/ [13] *vi* ① (jouer) (dans une flaque) to splash about; (au bord de la mer) to paddle; ∼ **dans la boue/neige** to flounder in the mud/snow; ② (s'embrouiller) to flounder

patch /patʃ/ *nm* Méd patch; ∼ **antitabac** *or* **à la nicotine** nicotine patch

pâte /pɑt/
A *nf* ① Culin (à tarte) pastry; (levée) dough; (à friture, crêpes) batter; ② (substance) (**produit en**) ∼ **paste**
B **pâtes** *nfpl* Culin ∼**s (alimentaires)** pasta **C**

(Composés) ∼ **d'amandes** marzipan; ∼ **à beignets** batter; ∼ **de fruit(s)** fruit paste; ∼ **à modeler** modelling GB clay, Plasticine®; ∼ **à papier** pulp; ∼ **à tartiner** spread

(Idiome) **mettre la main à la** ∼ to pitch in

pâté /pɑte/ *nm* ① Culin pâté; ∼ **de campagne** farmhouse pâté GB, coarse pâté; ∼ **en croûte** ≈ pie; ② Constr ∼ **de maisons** block (of houses); ③ (tache d'encre) blot; ④ (à la plage) sandcastle

pâtée /pɑte/ *nf* ① (nourriture) (pour un chien) food; (pour les cochons) swill; (pour la volaille) mash; ② ○(râclée, défaite) hiding; **prendre la** ∼ to get a hiding

patelin, ∼e /patlɛ̃, in/
A †*adj* [*manières, voix*] oily
B ○*nm* small village

patent, ∼e¹ /patɑ̃, ɑ̃t/ *adj* fml manifest, obvious

patente² /patɑ̃t/ *nf* (permis) licence GB to exercise a trade or profession

patenté, ∼e /patɑ̃te/ *adj* ① (agréé) [*fournisseur, transporteur*] licensed, authorized; ② ○hum [*critique, défenseur*] established

patère /patɛʀ/ *nf* peg, hook

paternalisme /patɛʀnalism/ *nm* paternalism

paternaliste /patɛʀnalist/ *adj* paternalistic

paternel, -elle /patɛʀnɛl/ *adj* ① (du père) paternal; ② (affectueux) fatherly

paternellement /patɛʀnɛlmã/ *adv* in a fatherly way

paternité /patɛʀnite/ *nf* ① (état de père) fatherhood; Jur paternity; **recherche de ~ naturelle** paternity suit; ② (d'œuvre) authorship

pâteux, -euse /patø, øz/ *adj* ① [*substance*] doughy; [*bouillie*] mushy; ② [*voix*] thick; **j'ai la bouche pâteuse** my mouth feels all furry

pathétique /patetik/
Ⓐ *adj* (émouvant) moving
Ⓑ *nm* pathos

pathétiquement /patetikmã/ *adv* touchingly

pathologie /patɔlɔʒi/ *nf* pathology

pathologique /patɔlɔʒik/ *adj* pathological

pathos /patos/ *nm* pathos; **faire du ~** to pile[○] on the pathos

patibulaire /patibylɛʀ/ *adj* [*individu*] sinister-looking

patiemment /pasjamã/ *adv* patiently

patience /pasjãs/ *nf* ① (qualité) patience; **avoir de la ~** to be patient; **ma ~ a des limites** there are limits to my patience; **être d'une ~ infinie** to be endlessly patient; ② ▸ p. 327 Jeux patience ₵ GB, solitaire ₵ US

Ⓘ(Idiome) **prendre son mal en ~** to resign oneself to one's fate

patient, ~e /pasjã, ãt/ *adj*, *nm,f* patient

patienter /pasjãte/ [1] *vi* to wait; **puis-je vous demander de ~?** would you mind waiting?

patin /patɛ̃/ *nm* ① ▸ p. 327 (de patineur) skate; ② (pour parquet) felt pad used for walking on parquet floors; ③ Tech (de meuble) furniture glide; (d'hélicoptère) skid; (de luge) runner

(Composés) **~ à glace** (chaussure) ice skate; (activité) ice-skating; **~ de frein** Aut brake block; **~ à roulettes** (chaussure) roller skate; (activité) roller-skating

patinage /patinaʒ/ ▸ p. 327 *nm* (sport) skating; **~ sur glace** ice-skating

(Composés) **~ artistique** figure skating; **~ de vitesse** speed skating

patine /patin/ *nf* (naturelle) patina; (artificielle) finish, sheen; **la ~ du temps** *or* **de l'âge** the patina of age

patiner /patine/ [1]
Ⓐ *vtr* (artificiellement) to apply a finish to [*métal, meuble*]
Ⓑ *vi* ① Sport to skate; ② Aut [*roue*] to spin; [*embrayage*] to slip; **faire ~ l'embrayage** to slip the clutch
Ⓒ **se patiner** *vpr* [*bois, statue*] to acquire a patina; **chêne patiné** oak shiny with age

patinette /patinɛt/ *nf* (child's) scooter

patineur, -euse /patinœʀ, øz/ *nm,f* skater

patinoire /patinwaʀ/ *nf* ice rink

pâtir /patiʀ/ [3] *vi* **~ de** to suffer as a result of

pâtisserie /patisʀi/ *nf* ① ▸ p. 372 (magasin) cake shop, pâtisserie; ② (gâteau) pastry, cake; ③ (gâteaux) **la ~** pastries (*pl*), cakes (*pl*); **faire de la ~** to do some baking; ④ (secteur) confectionery

pâtissier, -ière /patisje, ɛʀ/ ▸ p. 372 *nm,f* confectioner, pastry cook

patois /patwa/ *nm inv* patois, dialect; **parler ~** to speak patois

patraque[○] /patʀak/ *adj* under the weather[○]

pâtre /patʀ/ *nm* shepherd

patriarcal, ~e, *mpl* **-aux** /patʀijaʀkal, o/ *adj* patriarchal

patriarcat /patʀijaʀka/ *nm* ① Relig patriarchate; ② Sociol patriarchy

patriarche /patʀijaʀʃ/ *nm* patriarch

patricien, -ienne /patʀisjɛ̃, ɛn/ *adj*, *nm,f* patrician

patrie /patʀi/ *nf* homeland, country

patrimoine /patʀimwan/ *nm* ① (de personne, famille) patrimony; (d'une entreprise) capital; **~ immobilier** property holdings (*pl*); ② (biens communs) heritage

(Composés) **~ génétique** gene pool; **~ héréditaire** genetic inheritance

patriote /patʀijɔt/ *nmf* patriot; **en ~** patriotically

patriotique /patʀijɔtik/ *adj* patriotic

patriotisme /patʀijɔtism/ *nm* patriotism

patron, -onne /patʀɔ̃, ɔn/
Ⓐ *nm,f* (directeur, gérant) manager, boss[○]; (propriétaire) owner, boss[○]; **être son propre ~** to be one's own boss[○]
Ⓑ *nm* ① (en couture) pattern; ② (taille) large; **grand ~** extra-large

(Composés) **~ d'industrie** captain of industry; **~ de pêche** skipper, master

patronage /patʀɔnaʒ/ *nm* ① (soutien) patronage; ② †(centre de loisirs) ≈ youth club

patronal, ~e, *mpl* **-aux** /patʀɔnal, o/ *adj* [*organisation, représentant*] employers'; [*cotisations*] employer

patronat /patʀɔna/ *nm* employers (*pl*)

patronne ▸ **patron**

patronner /patʀɔne/ [1] *vtr* to sponsor

patronnesse /patʀɔnɛs/ *adj* dame **~** Lady Bountiful

patronyme /patʀɔnim/ *nm* patronymic

patrouille /patʀuj/ *nf* patrol; **en ~** on patrol

patrouiller /patʀuje/ [1] *vi* to be on patrol; **~ dans la forêt** to patrol the forest

patte /pat/ *nf* ① Zool (jambe) leg; (pied) (de mammifère avec ongles ou griffes) paw; (d'oiseau) foot; **~ de devant** (jambe) foreleg; **~ de derrière** (jambe) hind leg; **donner la ~** to give its paw; **retomber sur ses ~s** [*chat*] to fall on its feet; fig [*personne*] to fall on one's feet; ② [○](jambe) leg; (pied) foot; (main) hand; **tu es toujours dans mes ~s** you are always getting under my feet; **marcher à quatre ~s** [*enfant, adulte*] to walk on all fours; [*bébé*] to crawl; **traîner la ~** to limp; **en avoir plein les ~s** to be dead on one's feet[○]; **bas les ~s!** (ne me touchez pas) keep your hands to yourself!; (n'y touchez pas) hands off!; ③ [○](style) hand; **on reconnaît ta ~** one can recognize your hand; ④ (languette) tab; (d'attache) lug; (de vêtement, bonnet) flap; (de col) tab; (de chaussure) tongue; ⑤ (favori) sideburn

(Composés) **~s d'éléphant** (de pantalon) flares; **~ folle**[○] gammy leg GB, game leg US; **~ de mouche** (écriture) spidery scrawl ₵; **faire des ~s de mouche** to write in a spidery scrawl

Ⓘ(Idiomes) **faire ~ de velours** [*chat*] to draw in its claws; [*personne*] to switch on the charm; **tomber dans les ~s de qn** to fall into sb's clutches; **montrer ~ blanche** to prove one is acceptable; **avoir un fil à la ~** to be tied down; **se tirer dans les ~s** to pull dirty tricks on each other

patte-d'oie, *pl* **pattes-d'oie** /patdwa/ *nf* ① (ride) crow's-foot; ② (carrefour) junction

pâturage /patyʀaʒ/ *nm* ① (terrain) pasture; ② (droit) pasturage

pâture /patyʀ/ *nf* (nourriture animale) feed; (terrain) pasture; **un scandale donné en ~ au public** fig a scandal used to satisfy the public's baser instincts; **être jeté en ~** fig to be thrown to the lions

paume /pom/ ▸ p. 136 *nf* palm (of the hand)

paumé[○], **~e** /pome/
Ⓐ *adj* ① [*personne*] (perdu) lost; (inadapté) mixed up GB, out of it[○] US; ② pej [*endroit*] godforsaken, jerkwater US
Ⓑ *nm,f* misfit

paumer[○] /pome/ [1]
Ⓐ *vtr*, *vi* to lose
Ⓑ **se paumer** *vpr* to get lost

paupière /popjɛʀ/ ▸ p. 136 *nf* eyelid; **battre des ~s** to flutter one's eyelashes

paupiette /popjɛt/ *nf* **~ de veau** stuffed escalope of veal

pause /poz/ *nf* ① (dans une activité) break; **~ publicitaire** commercial break; ② (période calme) pause; ③ Mus rest

pause-café, *pl* **pauses-café** /pozkafe/ *nf* coffee break

pauvre /povʀ/
Ⓐ *adj* ① (sans ressources) poor; ② (déficient) [*sol, alimentation, vocabulaire*] poor; [*végétation*] sparse; [*langue, style*] impoverished; **régime ~ en sucre** (insuffisant) diet lacking in sugar; (conseillé) low-sugar diet; **minerai ~ en métal** ore with a low metal content; ③ (malheureux) [*personne*] poor; [*sourire*] weak; **un ~ type**[○] (à plaindre) a poor chap[○] GB *ou* guy[○]; (incapable) a dead loss[○]; **~ de moi!** poor me!
Ⓑ [○]*nmf* **le/la ~!** (à plaindre) poor man/woman!; (attendri) poor

p

thing!; **ma ~, si tu m'avais vu!** well, my dear, you should have seen me!

C nm (indigent) **un ~** a poor man; **les ~s** the poor; **plat de ~** humble dish; **~ d'esprit** half-wit

pauvrement /povʀəmã/ adv poorly

pauvresse† /povʀɛs/ nf poor wretch, pauper

pauvreté /povʀəte/ nf **1** (de personne, pays) poverty; **2** (de mobilier, vêtements) shabbiness; **3** (de sol, vocabulaire, d'imagination) poverty; (de débat, programme) poor quality; (de raisonnement) thinness; **~ de moyens** lack of means; **la ~ de la récolte** the poor harvest

Idiome) **~ n'est pas vice** Prov poverty is no disgrace ou sin Prov

pavage /pavaʒ/ nm **1** (travail) paving; **2** (revêtement) paving

pavaner: se pavaner /pavane/ [1] vpr [personne] to strut about; [paon] to strut

pavé /pave/ nm cobblestone; **se retrouver sur le ~** to find oneself out on the street; **battre le ~** to wear out one's shoe leather

Idiomes) **lancer un ~ dans la mare** to set the cat among the pigeons; **sous les ~s, la plage** beneath the harsh reality lies a brighter tomorrow; **tenir le haut du ~** to head the field

paver /pave/ [1] vtr to lay [sth] with cobblestones

Idiome) **l'enfer est pavé de bonnes intentions** the road to hell is paved with good intentions

pavillon /pavijɔ̃/ nm **1** (maison) (detached) house; (d'exposition) pavilion; (d'hôpital) wing; (d'hôtel etc) chalet GB, bungalow US; **2** (d'oreille) auricle; (d'instrument) bell; (de haut-parleur, phonographe) horn; **3** Naut flag; **baisser ~** lit to lower the flag; fig to admit defeat (**devant qn** to sb); **battre ~ russe** Naut to fly the Russian flag

Composé) **~ de chasse** hunting lodge

pavillonnaire /pavijɔnɛʀ/ adj **zone ~** residential area; **banlieue ~** suburb consisting of houses (as opposed to high-rise buildings)

pavoiser /pavwaze/ [1]
A vtr to decorate [sth] with flags [édifice, rue]
B ○vi (chanter victoire) to crow péj

pavot /pavo/ nm poppy

payable /pɛjabl/ adj [somme] payable; **~ à la commande** cash with order

payant, ~e /pɛjã, ãt/ adj **1** (qui paie) [personne] paying; **2** (qu'il faut payer) [spectacle] not free (jamais épith); **l'entrée est-elle ~e?** is there a charge for admission?; **chaîne ~e** subscription channel; **3** (avantageux) [affaire] lucrative, profitable; [mesures] worthwhile; [effort] which pays off (épith, après n); **notre attente a été ~e** it was worth the wait

paye /pɛj/ = **paie**

payement /pɛjmã/ = **paiement**

payer /peje/ [21]
A vtr **1** (régler) to pay for [achat, travail]; to settle [facture]; to pay [somme]; **~ le téléphone** to pay the phone bill; **il m'a fait ~ 10 euros** he charged me 10 euros; **être payé avec un lance-pierres**○ to be paid peanuts○; **2** (s'acquitter envers) to pay [employé]; **être payé à ne rien faire** to be paid for doing nothing; **être trop peu payé** to be underpaid; **il est payé pour le savoir!** fig he knows that to his cost!; **3** ○(offrir) **~ qch à qn** to buy sb sth; **je te paie le restaurant** I'll treat you to a meal; **4** (subir des conséquences) to pay for [faute, imprudence]; **il a payé sa témérité de sa vie** his rashness cost him his life; **~ pour les autres** to take the rap○; **5** (compenser) to cover; **leur réussite la paie de tous ses sacrifices** their success makes all her sacrifices worthwhile
B vi **1** (rapporter) [efforts, peine, sacrifice] to pay off; [profession, activité] to pay; **c'est un métier qui paie bien** it's a job that pays well; **2** (prêter à rire) to look funny; **il payait dans son imitation du patron** he did a funny imitation of the boss
C se payer vpr **1** (être payable) [service, marchandise] to have to be paid for; [personne, salaire] to have to be paid; **2** ○(à soi-même) to treat oneself to [voyage, dîner]; hum to get [rhume, mauvaise note]; to get landed with [travail, importun]; **se ~ une cuite** to get plastered○; **se ~ un arbre** to crash into a tree; **3** (prendre son dû) **payez-vous sur ce billet** take what I owe you out of this note GB ou bill US

Idiomes) **~ qn de promesses** to fob sb off with promises; **se ~ de mots** to talk a lot of rubbish○; **se ~ d'illusions** to delude oneself; **se ~ du bon temps**○ to have a good time; **se ~ la tête**○ **de qn** (se moquer) to take the mickey○ out of sb GB, to razz○ sb US; (duper) to take sb for a ride; **il me déteste et il est payé de retour** he hates me and the feeling's mutual; **il a payé de sa personne** it cost him dear

payeur, -euse /pɛjœʀ, øz/
A adj **organisme ~** paying authority
B nm (trésorier) paymaster; **mauvais ~** bad debtor

pays /pei/ nm **1** (État) country; **dans mon ~** where I come from, in my country; **2** (région) **la Bourgogne est le ~ du bon vin** Burgundy is the home of good wine; **fromage du ~** locally-produced cheese; **gens/produit du ~** local people/product; **rentrer au ~** (vu du point de départ) to go back home; (vu du point d'arrivée) to come back home; **3** (village) village

Composés) **~ d'accueil** host country; **~ de cocagne** Cockaigne; **~ en (voie de) développement, PED** developing nation

Idiome) **voir du ~** to do some travelling GB

paysage /peizaʒ/ nm **1** (site) landscape; (vue) scenery **₵**, landscape; **~ urbain** lit, fig urban landscape GB, cityscape; **les cheminées gâchent le ~** the chimneys spoil the view; **le ~ politique** the political scene; **2** Art (genre, tableau) landscape (painting)

Composé) **~ audiovisuel français, PAF** French radio and TV scene

paysager, -ère /peizaʒe, ɛʀ/ adj **1** (relatif à l'environnement) environmental; **2** (aménagé) [parc] landscaped; [bureau] open-plan

paysagiste /peizaʒist/ nmf **1** (peintre) landscape artist, landscapist; **2** ▸ p. 372 (concepteur) (jardinier) **~** landscape gardener

paysan, -anne /peizã, an/
A adj **1** (agricole) [milieu] farming; [revendications] farmers'; **2** (de la campagne) [monde, vie] rural; [allure, façons] peasant; [soupe, pain] country
B nm,f ▸ p. 372 **1** (cultivateur) ≈ small farmer; (dans le tiers-monde) peasant farmer; Hist peasant/peasant woman; **2** (campagnard) péj peasant péj

paysannerie /peizanʀi/ nf small farmers (pl); Hist peasantry

Pays-Bas /peiba/ ▸ p. 230 nprmpl **les ~** The Netherlands

PC /pese/ nm **1** Ordinat (abbr = **personal computer**) PC; **2** (abbr = **poste de commandement**) (dans la police) division; Mil CP

pcc (written abbr = **pour copie conforme**) Admin certified true and accurate

PCF /peseɛf/ nm (abbr = **parti communiste français**) French Communist Party

PCV /peseve/ nm (abbr = **paiement contre vérification**) reverse charge call GB, collect call US; **appelle-moi en ~** phone me and reverse the charges GB, call me collect US

PDG /pedeʒe/ nm (abbr = **président-directeur général**) chairman and managing director GB, chief executive officer, CEO

péage /peaʒ/ nm **1** (taxe) toll; **à ~** toll (épith); **2** (lieu) tollbooth

peau, ~x /po/ nf **1** Anat skin; **avoir la ~ dure** fig to be thick-skinned; **n'avoir que la ~ sur les os** to be all skin and bone; **2** (d'animal) gén skin; (pour faire du cuir) hide; (fourrure) pelt; **sac en ~ de porc** pigskin bag; **gants/veste en** ou **de ~** leather gloves/jacket; **3** (de fruit, légume) skin, peel **₵**; (d'orange, de citron, pamplemousse) peel **₵**; **les oranges ont une ~ épaisse** oranges have thick peel ou a thick rind; **enlever la ~ d'un fruit** to peel a fruit; **4** (pellicule sur le lait, la peinture) skin; **5** ○(vie) **risquer sa ~** to risk one's life; **faire la ~ à qn** to kill sb; **tenir à sa ~** to value one's life; **vouloir la ~ de qn** to want sb dead; **changer de ~** to turn over a new leaf; ▸ **vieux**

Composés) **~ de banane** lit banana skin; fig trap; **~ de chagrin** shagreen **₵**; **rétrécir comme une ~ de chagrin** to shrink away to nothing; **~ de chamois** chamois leather **₵**, shammy (leather) **₵**; **~ d'orange** (cellulite) orange peel skin, cellulite; **~ de tambour** Mus drumhead; **~ de vache** lit cowhide; fig○ nasty piece of work GB, low-life○

(Idiomes) **je n'aimerais pas être dans sa** ∼ I wouldn't like to be in his/her shoes; **être bien dans sa** ∼○ (dans sa tête) to feel good about oneself; (dans son corps) to feel good; **être mal dans sa** ∼○ (physiquement) to feel lousy○; (gêné) to feel ill-at-ease; **avoir qn dans la** ∼○ to be crazy about sb; **prendre douze balles dans la** ∼○ to be shot by a firing squad

peaufiner /pofine/ [1] *vtr* to refine [*politique, système*]; to put the finishing touches to [*contrat, travail, texte*]

Peau-Rouge, *pl* **Peaux-Rouges** /poru3/ *nmf* Red Indian

peausserie /posRi/ *nf* leatherwork **℄**; **les** ∼**s** leather goods

peccadille /pekadij/ *nf* peccadillo

pêche /pɛʃ/
A ▸ p. 140 *adj inv* (couleur) peach
B *nf* **1** Bot peach; **2** (activité) fishing; **la** ∼ **est ouverte** the fishing season is open; **3** (poissons capturés) catch; **une belle** ∼ a good *ou* fine catch; **la** ∼ **a été bonne?** lit did you catch anything?; **4** ○(coup) clout○; **5** ○(forme) **avoir la** ∼ to be feeling great
(Composés) ∼ **à la baleine** whaling; ∼ **à la crevette** shrimping; ∼ **au lancer** casting; ∼ **à la ligne** angling; ∼ **miraculeuse** Relig miraculous draught of fishes; ∼ **à la mouche** fly-fishing; ∼ **aux moules** mussel gathering *ou* picking

péché /peʃe/ *nm* sin; **les sept** ∼**s capitaux** the seven deadly sins; **vivre dans le** ∼ to live a sinful life; ∼ **de jeunesse** youthful indiscretion; **ce serait un** ∼ **de rater ça** it would be a crime to miss that
(Composé) ∼ **mignon** (little) weakness

pécher /peʃe/ [14] *vi* **1** Relig to sin; **2** (ne pas être parfait) ∼ **par ignorance** to err through ignorance; ∼ **par excès de confiance** to be overconfident; **le roman pèche sur un point** the novel has one shortcoming

pêcher¹ /peʃe/ [1]
A *vtr* (chercher à prendre) to go fishing for [*poissons*]; to go catching [*crabes*]; (attraper) to catch; ∼ **la truite** to go fishing for trout; **où est il allé** ∼ **cette idée?**○ where did he get that idea from?
B *vi* to fish; ∼ **à la mouche** to fly-fish; ∼ **au vif** to fish with live bait; ∼ **en haute mer** to go deep-sea fishing; ∼ **à la ligne** to angle
(Idiome) ∼ **en eau trouble** to fish in troubled waters

pêcher² /peʃe/ *nm* Bot peach tree

pécheresse /peʃRɛs/ *nf* sinner

pêcherie /peʃRi/ *nf* **1** (usine) fish factory; **2** (zone de pêche) fishing ground

pécheur /peʃœR/ *nm* sinner

pêcheur /peʃœR/ ▸ p. 372 *nm* fisherman
(Composés) ∼ **de baleines** whaler; ∼ **de crevettes** shrimper; ∼ **à la ligne** angler; ∼ **de perles** pearl diver

pectoral, ∼**e**, *mpl* **-aux** /pɛktɔRal, o/
A *adj* pectoral
B *nm* pectoral muscle; **gonfler les pectoraux** to stick out one's chest

pécule /pekyl/ *nm* savings (*pl*), nest egg○; **amasser un petit** ∼ to put a little money by

pécuniaire /pekynjɛR/ *adj* financial

pédagogie /pedagɔ3i/ *nf* **1** (science) education, pedagogy; **2** (qualité de pédagogue) teaching skills (*pl*); **il a le sens de la** ∼ he's a born teacher; **3** (méthode) teaching method

pédagogique /pedagɔ3ik/ *adj* [*activité, but*] educational; [*système*] education (*épith*); [*matériel, méthode*] teaching (*épith*); **formation** ∼ teacher training

pédagogue /pedagɔg/
A *adj* good at explaining (*jamais épith*)
B *nmf* **1** (enseignant) teacher; **2** (spécialiste) educationalist

pédale /pedal/ *nf* (de bicyclette, piano, frein) pedal; (de machine à coudre, tour) treadle
(Idiome) **perdre les** ∼**s** (s'affoler) to lose one's grip

pédaler /pedale/ [1] *vi* **1** lit to pedal; **2** ○(se dépêcher) to get a move on○
(Idiome) ∼ **dans la choucroute**○ *or* **semoule**○ to flounder around

pédalier /pedalje/ *nm* (de bicyclette) chain transmission; (de piano) pedals (*pl*)

pédalo® /pedalo/ *nm* pedalo GB, pedal boat

pédant, ∼**e** /pedã, ãt/
A *adj* pedantic
B *nm,f* pedant

pédantisme /pedãtism/ *nm* pedantry

pédérastie /pederasti/ *nf* **1** (pédophilie) pederasty; **2** (homosexualité masculine) homosexuality

pédestre /pedɛstR/ *adj* **randonnée** ∼ ramble; **itinéraire** ∼ ramblers' route; **circuit** ∼ (signed) walk

pédiatre /pedjatR/ ▸ p. 372 *nmf* paediatrician

pédiatrie /pedjatRi/ *nf* paediatrics (+ *v sg*)

pédicure /pedikyR/ ▸ p. 372 *nmf* chiropodist GB, podiatrist US

pedigree /pedigRe/ *nm* pedigree

pédologue /pedɔlɔg/ ▸ p. 372 *nmf* pedologist

pédoncule /pedɔ̃kyl/ *nm* peduncle

pédophilie /pedɔfili/ *nf* paedophilia

pédopsychiatre /pedopsikjatR/ ▸ p. 372 *nmf* child psychiatrist

peeling /pilin/ *nm* exfoliation

pègre /pɛgR/ *nf* **la** ∼ the underworld

peigne /pɛɲ/ *nm* **1** (à cheveux) comb; **se donner un coup de** ∼ to comb one's hair; **2** (de métier à tisser) reed; (pour carder) carder
(Idiome) **passer qch au** ∼ **fin** to go over sth with a fine-tooth comb

peigner /peɲe/ [1]
A *vtr* **1** to comb [*cheveux*]; **bien peignés** neatly combed; **mal peignés** tousled; **2** to card [*laine*]
B *se peigner* *vpr* to comb one's hair
(Idiome) ∼ **la girafe**○ to fiddle about doing nothing GB, to do busy work US

peignoir /peɲwaR/ *nm* (déshabillé) dressing gown GB, robe US; (de boxeur) dressing gown; ∼ **de bain** bathrobe

peinard○, ∼**e** /penaR, aRd/ *adj* [*travail*] cushy○; [*endroit*] snug; **être** ∼ to take things easy; **père** ∼ easy-going guy; **en père** ∼ indolently

peindre /pɛ̃dR/ [55]
A *vtr* **1** (avec de la peinture) to paint; ∼ **qch en blanc** to paint sth white; **2** (avec des mots) to depict [*personnage, situation, époque*] (**comme** as)
B *vi* to paint
C *se peindre* *vpr* **1** [*peintre*] to paint a self-portrait; **2** [*auteur*] to depict oneself (**comme** as); **3** (apparaître) **se** ∼ **sur** [*gêne, joie*] to be written on

peine /pɛn/
A *nf* **1** (chagrin) sorrow, grief; **avoir de la** ∼ to feel sad *ou* upset; **faire de la** ∼ **à qn** [*personne*] to hurt sb; [*événement, remarque*] to upset sb; **il faisait** ∼ **à voir** he looked a sorry sight; **cela faisait** ∼ **à voir** it was sad to see; **2** (effort) effort, trouble; **c'est** ∼ **perdue** it's a waste of effort; **en être pour sa** ∼ to waste one's time and effort; **se donner de la** ∼ **pour faire** to go to a lot of trouble to do; **il ne s'est même pas donné la** ∼ **de nous prévenir** he didn't even bother to tell us; **donnez-vous** *or* **prenez la** ∼ **d'entrer** fml please do come in; **il n'est pas au bout de ses** ∼**s** (dans une situation pénible) his troubles are far from over; (pour accomplir une tâche) he's still got a long way to go; **se mettre en** ∼ **pour qn** to go out of one's way for sb; **ce n'est pas la** ∼ **de crier** (c'est inutile) there's no point shouting; (ton critique) there's no need to shout; **est-ce vraiment la** ∼ **que je vienne?** do I really need to come?; **ce n'est pas la** ∼ **d'aller voir ce film** that film's not worth seeing; **c'était bien la** ∼! what was the point!; **ça en valait vraiment la** ∼ it was really worth it; **concentrez vos efforts sur ce qui en vaut la** ∼ concentrate on worthwhile activities; **pour la** ∼ *or* **ta**/**votre** ∼ (en récompense) for your trouble; **3** (difficulté) difficulty; **sans** ∼ easily; **j'ai** ∼ **à le croire** I find it hard to believe; **l'allemand sans** ∼ German without tears; **il n'est pas en** ∼ **pour trouver du travail** he has no difficulty finding work; **il serait bien en** ∼ **de te prêter de l'argent** he would be hard put to lend you any money; **4** (punition) gén punishment; Jur penalty, sentence; **'défense de fumer sous** ∼ **d'amende'** 'no smoking, offenders will be fined'; **sous** ∼ **de perdre de l'argent** at the risk of losing money; **pour la** ∼ ∼ as punishment
B **à peine** *loc adv* hardly, barely; **une allusion à** ∼ **voilée** a thinly veiled allusion; **c'est à** ∼ **si je l'ai reconnu** I hardly recognized him; **il était à** ∼ **arrivé qu'il pensait déjà à**

repartir no sooner had he arrived than he was thinking of leaving again; **'je n'étais pas au courant'—'à** ~○**!'** (incrédulité) 'I didn't know about it'—'I don't believe it!' ou 'I don't buy that○!'

(Composés) ~ **capitale** capital punishment; **condamné à la** ~ **capitale** sentenced to death; ~ **de cœur** heartache **₵**; **il a des** ~**s de cœur** he's unhappy in love; ~ **de mort** death penalty

peiner /pene/ [1]
A vtr to sadden, to upset [*personne*]
B vi [*personne*] to struggle; [*machine, voiture*] to labour^{GB}

peintre /pɛ̃tʀ/ ▸ p. 372 nm **1** (artiste, artisan) painter; **2** fig (auteur) portrayer

(Composé) ~ **en bâtiment** house painter

peinture /pɛ̃tyʀ/ nf **1** (matériau) paint; **'**~ **fraîche'** 'wet paint'; **2** (revêtement) paintwork; **3** (art, technique) painting; ~ **au pistolet** spray painting; **investir dans la** ~ to invest in paintings; **faire de la** ~ to paint; **je ne peux pas le voir en** ~○ fig I can't stand the sight of him; **4** (tableau) painting; **5** fig (description) portrayal

(Composés) ~ **à l'eau** water-based paint; ~ **de genre** genre painting; ~ **gestuelle** action painting; ~ **à l'huile** (revêtement) oil paint; (technique) painting in oils; (tableau) oil painting; ~ **murale** mural

peinturlurer /pɛ̃tyʀlyʀe/ [1]
A vtr to daub; **un mur peinturluré** a wall that has been daubed with paint; **des clowns peinturlurés** clowns with their faces daubed in paint
B se peinturlurer vpr se ~ le visage [*acteur, clown*] to cake one's face in greasepaint; pej [*femme*] to cake one's face in make-up

péjoratif, -ive /peʒɔʀatif, iv/ adj pejorative

pékin○ = péquin

Pékin /pekɛ̃/ ▸ p. 621 npr Beijing, Peking

pékinois, ~e /pekinwa, az/
A ▸ p. 621 adj of Beijing, Pekinese
B nm **1** ▸ p. 336 Ling Pekinese; **2** Zool Pekinese

PEL /pøɛl/ nm: abbr ▸ **plan**

pelade /pəlad/ ▸ p. 195 nf alopecia

pelage /pəlaʒ/ nm coat, fur

pelé, ~e /pəle/ adj [*animal*] mangy; [*vêtement*] threadbare; [*colline*] bare

(Idiome) **il y avait quatre** or **trois** ~**s et un tondu**○ there was hardly anybody

pêle-mêle /pɛlmɛl/
A adv [*entasser*] higgledy-piggledy
B nm inv (désordre) jumble

peler /pəle/ [17]
A vtr to peel
B vi **1** [*peau, nez*] to peel; **2** ○(avoir froid) to freeze

pèlerin /pɛlʀɛ̃/ nm Relig pilgrim

pèlerinage /pɛlʀinaʒ/ nm **1** (voyage) pilgrimage; **2** (lieu) place of pilgrimage

pèlerine /pɛlʀin/ nf cape

pélican /pelikɑ̃/ nm pelican

pelisse /pəlis/ nf fur-trimmed coat, pelisse

pelle /pɛl/ nf gén shovel; (jouet) spade; (de boulanger) peel; **à la** ~○ fig by the dozen

(Composés) ~ **à gâteau** cake slice; ~ **à tarte** pie server

pelletée /pɛlte/ nf **1** lit shovelful; **2** ○fig heap

pelleterie /pɛltʀi/ nf (préparation) fur dressing; (commerce) fur trade; (fourrures) furs (pl)

pelleteuse /pɛltøz/ nf mechanical digger

pellicule /pelikyl/
A nf **1** Cin, Phot film; **2** (de poussière) film; (de givre) thin layer
B pellicules nfpl (dans les cheveux) dandruff **₵**

pelote /p(ə)lɔt/ nf **1** (de laine) ball; **2** ▸ p. 327 Sport (balle) pelota ball; (jeu) pelota

(Composés) ~ **basque** pelota; ~ **à épingles** pin cushion

peloton /p(ə)lɔtɔ̃/ nm **1** (de laine) ball; **2** Mil platoon; **3** (en cyclisme) pack; **dans le** ~ **de tête** Sport in the leading pack; fig [*entreprise*] up among the leaders

(Composé) ~ **d'exécution** firing squad

pelotonner: se pelotonner /pəlɔtɔne/ [1] vpr [*personne, chat*] (de bien-être) to snuggle up; (de peur) to huddle up

pelouse /p(ə)luz/ nf **1** (gazon) lawn; **'**~ **interdite'** 'keep off the grass'; **2** Sport (terrain) pitch GB, field US; (de champ de courses) public enclosure

peluche /p(ə)lyʃ/ nf **1** (matière) plush; **jouet en** ~ cuddly toy GB, stuffed animal US; **2** (sur un lainage) fluff

pelucher /p(ə)lyʃe/ [1] vi [*lainage*] to become fluffy

pelucheux, -euse /p(ə)lyʃø, øz/ adj fluffy

pelure /p(ə)lyʀ/ nf **1** (de légume, fruit) peel **₵**, piece of peel; (d'oignon) skin; **2** ○(manteau) coat

(Composé) ~ **d'oignon** adj inv (couleur) pale rosé; nm (vin) rosé (wine)

pelvis /pɛlvis/ nm inv pelvis

pénal, ~e, mpl **-aux** /penal, o/
A adj criminal
B nm (juridiction) criminal courts (pl)

pénalisation /penalizasjɔ̃/ nf **1** Sport (pénalité) penalty; (action) penalizing **₵**; **2** (sanction) ~ **(fiscale)** taxation

pénaliser /penalize/ [1] vtr to penalize

pénalité /penalite/ nf **1** Fin, Jur (sanction) penalty; **2** Sport penalty; **réussir une** ~ (en rugby) to score a penalty goal

penalty /penalti/ nm penalty; **siffler un** ~ to award a penalty

pénard, ~e = peinard

pénates○ /penat/ nmpl (domicile) hum home (sg)

penaud, ~e /pəno, od/ adj [*personne, air*] sheepish

penchant /pɑ̃ʃɑ̃/ nm **1** (inclination) fondness; (faible) weakness; **2** (disposition) tendency, inclination; **donner libre cours à ses mauvais** ~**s** to give way to one's baser instincts

penché, ~e /pɑ̃ʃe/ adj [*arbre, tour*] leaning; [*écriture*] slanting; **être** ~ [*personne*] to be bent over; [*mur, arbre*] to be leaning

pencher /pɑ̃ʃe/ [1]
A vtr to tilt [*meuble*]; to tip [*sth*] up [*bouteille*]; ~ **la tête en avant** to bend one's head forward(s); ~ **la tête en arrière/sur le côté** to tilt one's head back/to one side
B vi **1** (être incliné) [*tour, arbre, mur*] to lean; [*bateau*] to list; [*tableau*] to slant, to tilt; **2** (préférer) ~ **pour** to incline toward(s) [*opinion, théorie*]; to be in favour^{GB} of [*solution, fermeté*]
C se pencher vpr **1** (s'incliner) [*personne*] to lean; (se baisser) to bend down; **se** ~ **à la fenêtre** to lean out of the window; **se** ~ **sur qn/qch** to bend over sb/sth; **2** (analyser) **se** ~ **sur** to look into [*problème, passé*]

pendable /pɑ̃dabl/ adj **c'est un cas** ~ it's deplorable

(Idiome) **jouer un tour** ~ **à qn** to play a rotten trick on sb

pendaison /pɑ̃dɛzɔ̃/ nf hanging

(Composé) ~ **de crémaillère** house-warming (party)

pendant¹ /pɑ̃dɑ̃/
A prép for; **je t'ai attendu** ~ **des heures** I waited for you for hours; ~ **combien de temps avez-vous vécu à Versailles?** how long did you live in Versailles?; **avant la guerre et** ~ before and during the war; ~ **tout le trajet** throughout the journey; ~ **ce temps(-là)** meanwhile
B pendant que loc conj while; **voyage** ~ **qu'il est temps** travel while you have the chance; ~ **que tu y es** while you're at it

pendant², ~**e** /pɑ̃dɑ̃, ɑ̃t/
A adj **1** (qui pend) **être assis les jambes** ~**es** to be sitting with one's legs dangling; **l'oreille** ~**e** with one ear drooping; **le chien avait la langue** ~**e** the dog's tongue was hanging out; **2** (en instance) [*cas, procès*] pending; [*question*] outstanding
B nm **1** (bijou) ~ **(d'oreille)** drop earring; **2** (équivalent) **le** ~ **d'un vase** the matching vase

pendeloque /pɑ̃dlɔk/ nf (de bijou) pendant, drop (on earring)

pendentif /pɑ̃dɑ̃tif/ nm (bijou) pendant; Archit pendentive

penderie /pɑ̃dʀi/ nf (meuble) wardrobe; (local) walk-in cupboard GB ou closet US

Pendjab /pɛndʒab/ ▸ p. 504 nprm Punjab

pendouiller○ /pɑ̃duje/ [1] vi to dangle down

pendre /pɑ̃dʀ/ [6]
A vtr **1** (exécuter) to hang [*condamné*]; ~ **qn haut et court** to hang sb; **va te faire** ~○**!** go to hell○!; **je veux bien être pendu**○ **s'il rembourse ses dettes** if he pays off his debts I'll eat my hat; **2** (accrocher) to hang [*tableau, rideau*]; to hang up [*vêtement, clé*]

B vi **1** (être suspendu) [objet, vêtement] to hang (à from); [jambe, bras] to dangle; **2** (être tombant) [lambeaux, mèche] to hang down; [joue, sein] to sag; [pan de jupe] to droop

C se pendre vpr **1** (se tuer) to hang oneself; **2** (s'accrocher) se ~ à to hang from [branche]; se ~ au cou de qn to throw one's arms around sb's neck

⟨Idiome⟩ **ça te pend au (bout du) nez**○ you've got it coming to you

pendu, ~e /pãdy/
A pp ▸ pendre
B pp adj **1** (mort) [personne] hanged; **2** (accroché) [objet] hung (à on), hanging (à from); ~ **à son micro** fig clutching the microphone; ~ **au bras de sa femme** clinging to his wife's arm; **être ~ aux lèvres de qn** to hang on sb's every word; **être toujours ~ au téléphone** to spend all one's time on the telephone
C nm,f hanged man/woman
D ▸ p. 327 nm Jeux **jouer au ~** to play hangman

⟨Idiome⟩ **parler de corde dans la maison d'un ~** to make a tactless remark

pendulaire /pãdylεR/ adj [mouvement] pendular

pendule¹ /pãdyl/ nm pendulum

pendule² /pãdyl/ nf (horloge) clock

⟨Idiome⟩ **remettre les ~s à l'heure** to set the record straight

pendulette /pãdylεt/ nf small clock

pêne /pεn/ nm bolt

pénétrant, ~e /penetrã, ãt/ adj [vent] penetrating; [pluie] drenching; [froid] piercing; [humidité] pervasive; [remarque] shrewd; [esprit, regard] penetrating

pénétration /penetrasjõ/ nf lit, fig penetration; (des eaux) seepage

pénétré, ~e /penetre/ adj [air, ton] earnest, intense; **être ~ de** to be imbued with [sentiment]; **être ~ de son importance** to be full of one's own importance

pénétrer /penetre/ [14]
A vtr **1** (s'infiltrer dans) [pluie] to soak ou seep into [terre]; [soleil] to penetrate [feuillage]; **le froid m'a pénétré jusqu'aux os** the cold went right through me; **2** (percer à jour) to fathom [secret, pensée]; **3** (sexuellement) to penetrate; **4** (atteindre) [idée, mode] to reach [milieu]; **5** (remplir) ~ qn **d'admiration** to fill sb with admiration
B vi **1** (entrer) ~ **dans** or **à l'intérieur de** [personne, animal] to enter, to get into [lieu]; [balle] to penetrate [organe]; [armée] to penetrate [pays]; [personne] to penetrate [cercle, organisation]; ~ **dans une maison par effraction** to break into a house; **l'auteur nous fait ~ dans l'univers des sociétés secrètes** the author takes us into the world of secret societies; **2** (s'infiltrer) ~ **dans** to get into; **3** (s'imprégner) ~ **dans** to penetrate; **faire ~ la pommade** to rub the ointment in
C se pénétrer vpr se ~ **d'une idée** to get an idea firmly rooted in one's mind

pénible /penibl/ adj [effort, impression] painful; [travail] hard; [voyage] difficult; [personne] tiresome; **c'est un enfant ~** he's a difficult child; **c'est ~!** it's such a pain○!

péniblement /peniblǝmã/ adv **1** (tout juste) [atteindre] barely; **2** (avec peine) with difficulty

péniche /penif/
A nf barge
B ○**péniches** nfpl (chaussures) clodhoppers○, shoes

pénicilline /penisilin/ nf penicillin

péninsulaire /penẽsylεR/ adj peninsular

péninsule /penẽsyl/ nf peninsula

pénis /penis/ ▸ p. 136 nm inv penis

pénitence /penitãs/ nf **1** Relig (peine) penance; **2** (punition) punishment

pénitencier /penitãsje/ nm prison, penitentiary US

pénitent, ~e /penitã, ãt/ adj, nm,f penitent

pénitentiaire /penitãsjεR/ adj [établissement] penal; [régime] prison (épith)

penne /pεn/ nf **1** (d'oiseau) quill, penna spéc; **2** (de flèche) feather

pénombre /penõbR/ nf (obscurité) half-light

pensable /pãsabl/ adj; **ce n'est pas ~** it's unthinkable

pensant, ~e /pãsã, ãt/ adj thinking

pense-bête, pl **pense-bêtes** /pãsbεt/ nm reminder

pensée /pãse/ nf **1** gén, Philos thought; **être perdu dans ses ~s** to be lost in thought; **j'aimerais connaître le fond de ta ~** I'd like to know what you really think deep down; **dire sa ~** to speak one's mind; **j'ai eu une ~ émue pour mes grands-parents** I thought fondly of my grandparents; **2** (esprit) mind; **en ~, par la ~** [se représenter, voir] in one's mind; **nous serons avec vous par la ~** we'll be with you in spirit; **3** (manière de penser) thinking; ~ **claire** clear thinking; **4** (fleur) pansy

⟨Composé⟩ ~ **unique** dominant ideology

penser /pãse/ [1]
A vtr **1** (avoir une opinion) to think (de of, about); ~ **du bien/du mal de qn/qch** to think well/badly ou ill of sb/sth; **je n'en pense rien** I have no opinion about it; **qu'est-ce que tu penserais d'un week-end en Normandie?** what would you say to a weekend in Normandy?; **il ne disait rien mais n'en pensait pas moins** he said nothing but it didn't mean that he agreed; **2** (croire) to think; **c'est bien ce que je pensais!** I thought as much!; **je te le dis comme je le pense** I'm telling you (just) what I think; **elle ne pense pas un mot de ce qu'elle dit** she doesn't believe a word of what she's saying; **tu penses vraiment ce que tu dis?** do you really mean what you're saying?; **tout laisse** or **porte à ~ que** there's every indication that; **je pense bien!** you bet○!, for sure!; **vous pensez si j'étais content!** you can imagine how pleased I was!; **'il s'est excusé?'—'pensestu!'** 'did he apologize?'—'you must be joking!' ou 'some hope!'; **pensez donc!** just imagine!; **3** (se rappeler) **pense que ça ne sera pas facile** remember that it won't be easy; **ça me fait ~ qu'il faut que je lui écrive** that reminds me that I must write to him/her; **4** (avoir l'intention de) ~ **faire** to be thinking of doing, to intend to do; **5** (concevoir) to think [sth] up [dispositif, projet]; **c'est bien pensé!** it's well thought out!
B penser à vtr ind **1** (songer) ~ **à** to think of ou about [personne, endroit]; (réfléchir à) ~ **à** to think about [problème, proposition]; **dire qch sans y ~** to say sth without thinking; **c'est simple, il fallait y ~** or **il suffisait d'y ~** it's simple, it just required some thinking; **regardez le pendule et ne pensez plus à rien** look at the pendulum and empty your mind; **sans ~ à mal** without meaning any harm; **tu n'y penses pas! c'est trop dangereux!** you can't be serious! it's too dangerous!; **n'y pensons plus!** let's forget about it!; **il a reçu le ballon où je pense**○ the ball hit him you know where○; **il ne pense qu'à ça**○! he's got a one-track mind!; **2** (se souvenir) ~ **à** to remember; **pense à ton rendez-vous** remember your appointment; **mais j'y pense, c'est ton anniversaire aujourd'hui!** now I come to think of it, it's your birthday today!; **il me fait ~ à mon père** he reminds me of my father; **3** (envisager) ~ **à faire** to be thinking of doing
C vi to think; **façon de ~** way of thinking; **je lui ai dit ma façon de ~!** I gave him/her a piece of my mind!; **je pense comme vous** I agree with you

penseur /pãsœR/ nm thinker

pensif, -ive /pãsif, iv/ adj pensive, thoughtful

pension /pãsjõ/ nf **1** (rente) pension; **2** (hôtel) boarding house; (séjour) board; **frais de ~** accommodation charges; **prendre qn en ~** to take sb as a lodger; **3** Scol (école) boarding school; (frais) boarding fees (pl)

⟨Composés⟩ ~ **alimentaire** alimony; ~ **complète** full board; ~ **de famille** family hotel; ~ **de retraite** old-age pension

pensionnaire /pãsjonεR/ nmf **1** (résident) (d'hôtel) resident; (de prison) inmate; **2** Scol boarder; **3** Théât resident member

pensionnat /pãsjona/ nm boarding school

pensionné, ~e /pãsjone/
A adj pensioned-off
B nm,f pensioner

pensivement /pãsivmã/ adv pensively

pensum† /pεsɔm/ nm (punition) imposition GB, punishment; (tâche pénible) chore; (ouvrage ennuyeux) laborious book

pentagone /pεtagon/ nm pentagon

pentathlon /pεtatlõ/ nm pentathlon

pente /pãt/ nf **1** (déclivité) slope; **une ~ de 10%** a gradient of 1 in 10 GB, a 10% gradient US; **toit en ~** sloping roof; **jardin en ~** garden on a slope; **descendre** or **aller en ~ douce** to slope gently down; **2** Math gradient; **3** fig (direction) direction; (tendance) trend

P

⸤Idiomes⸥ **avoir la dalle** *or* **le gosier en** ~○ to drink like a fish○; **être sur la mauvaise** ~, **être sur une** ~ **savonneuse** [*délinquant*] to be on the slippery slope GB, to be going astray; [*entreprise*] to be going downhill; **remonter la** ~ to get back on one's feet

Pentecôte /pɑ̃tkot/ *nf* (événement) Pentecost; (période) Whitsun; **à la** ~ at Whitsun; **lundi de** ~ Whit Monday

pentu, ~e /pɑ̃ty/ *adj* [*toit*] pitched (*épith*), sloping; [*chemin*] steep

pénultième /penyltjɛm/ *nf* penultimate (syllable)

pénurie /penyʀi/ *nf* shortage

pépé○ /pepe/ *nm* ⃞1 (grand-père) grandpa○; ⃞2 (vieil homme) old man

pépère /pepɛʀ/
⃞A *adj* [*vie*] cushy○; [*endroit*] nice
⃞B *nm* ⃞1 (grand-père) granddad○, grandpa○; ⃞2 (vieillard) granddad○, old man; ⃞3 *fig* (homme) *pej* fatty○ *péj*; (bébé) chubby little chap

pépier /pepje/ [2] *vi* to chirp

pépin /pepɛ̃/ *nm* ⃞1 Bot pip; **sans** ~**s** seedless; ⃞2 ○(ennui) slight problem; ⃞3 ○(parapluie) brolly○ GB, umbrella

pépinière /pepinjɛʀ/ *nf* ⃞1 *lit* nursery; ⃞2 *fig* breeding-ground

pépiniériste /pepinjeʀist/ ▶ p. 372 *nmf* nurseryman/nurserywoman

pépite /pepit/ *nf* (d'or) nugget

⸤Composé⸥ ~**s de chocolat** chocolate chips

péplum /peplom/ *nm* ⃞1 (tunique) peplos; ⃞2 ○Cin historical epic

péquenaud○, ~**e** /pekno, od/ *nm,f pej* country bumpkin○

péquenot○ /pekno/ *nm pej* country bumpkin○

péquin○ /pekɛ̃/ *nm* ⃞1 soldiers' slang civvy○; ⃞2 (individu) fellow○

percale /pɛʀkal/ *nf* percale

perçant, ~e /pɛʀsɑ̃, ɑ̃t/ *adj* ⃞1 [*cri, voix*] shrill; [*regard*] piercing; ⃞2 [*vue*] sharp

percée /pɛʀse/ *nf* ⃞1 *lit* opening; ⃞2 *fig*, Mil breakthrough; ⃞3 Sport (au rugby) break

percement /pɛʀsəmɑ̃/ *nm* (de tunnel) boring; (de route) (ouverture) cutting; (construction) building

perce-neige /pɛʀsənɛʒ/ *nm ou f inv* snowdrop

perce-oreille, *pl* ~**s** /pɛʀsɔʀɛj/ *nm* earwig

percepteur /pɛʀsɛptœʀ/ ▶ p. 372 *nm* tax inspector

perceptible /pɛʀsɛptibl/ *adj* ⃞1 [*son*] perceptible; ⃞2 [*impôt*] payable

perception /pɛʀsɛpsjɔ̃/ *nf* ⃞1 (bureau) tax office; ⃞2 (d'impôt) collection; ⃞3 Psych perception

percer /pɛʀse/ [12]
⃞A *vtr* ⃞1 (transpercer) to pierce [*corps, surface*]; (crever) to burst [*abcès, tympan*]; **cela me perce le cœur** it breaks my heart; ⃞2 (faire un trou dans) ~ **un trou dans** *gén* to make a hole in; (avec une perceuse) to drill a hole through; (avec une pointe fine) to pierce a hole in; ~ **un coffre-fort** to break open a safe; **avoir des souliers percés** to have holes in one's shoes; ⃞3 (créer) to make [*fenêtre, porte*]; to build [*route, tunnel*]; ⃞4 (traverser) to pierce [*silence, air*]; to break through [*nuages*]; ~ **le front ennemi** to break through the enemy front lines; ⃞5 (découvrir) to penetrate [*secret*]; to uncover [*complot*]; ~ **qn à jour** to see through sb; ⃞6 ~ **ses dents** to be teething; ~ **une dent** to cut a tooth
⃞B *vi* ⃞1 (apparaître) [*soleil*] to break through; [*plante*] to come up; [*dent*] to come through; ⃞2 Mil, Sport to break through; ⃞3 (se révéler) [*inquiétude*] to show; ⃞4 (réussir) [*acteur, écrivain*] to become known

perceuse /pɛʀsøz/ *nf* drill

percevable /pɛʀsəvabl/ *adj* [*impôt*] payable

percevoir /pɛʀsəvwaʀ/ [5] *vtr* ⃞1 (encaisser) to collect [*impôt*]; to receive [*pension, loyer*]; ⃞2 (sentir) to perceive [*odeur, bruit*]; to experience [*sensation*]; to feel [*vibration*]; to appreciate [*signification*]; to perceive [*changement*]; **être perçu comme** to be seen as; **être bien/mal perçu** to be well/badly received

perche /pɛʀʃ/ *nf* ⃞1 (tige) *gén* pole; (de téléski) T-bar; (pour micro) (microphone) boom; ⃞2 (personne) (grande) ~ beanpole○; ⃞3 ▶ p. 327 Sport (activité) pole-vaulting; ⃞4 (poisson) perch

⸤Idiome⸥ **tendre la** ~ **à qn** to throw sb a line

perché, ~e /pɛʀʃe/ *adj* perched; **voix haut ~e** high-pitched voice; ~ **sur des échasses** standing on stilts; **ma valise est ~e en haut de l'armoire** my suitcase is on top of the wardrobe

percher /pɛʀʃe/ [1]
⃞A *vtr* ~ **qch sur une étagère** to stick sth up on a shelf
⃞B *vi* ⃞1 [*oiseau*] (se poser) to perch; (pour la nuit) to roost; ⃞2 ○[*personne*] (loger) to live; (passer la nuit) to crash○
⃞C **se percher** *vpr* to perch

perchiste /pɛʀʃist/ ▶ p. 372 *nmf* ⃞1 (sauteur) pole-vaulter; ⃞2 Cin, Radio, TV boom operator

perchoir /pɛʀʃwaʀ/ *nm* ⃞1 *lit, fig* perch; ⃞2 ○Pol Speaker's Chair

perclus, ~e /pɛʀkly, yz/ *adj* crippled; *fig* paralysed

percolateur /pɛʀkɔlatœʀ/ *nm* (espresso) coffee machine

percussion /pɛʀkysjɔ̃/ *nf* ~**s** (instruments) percussion instruments; (dans un orchestre) percussion section (*sg*); (tambours) drums

percussionniste /pɛʀkysjɔnist/ *nmf* ▶ p. 372 percussionist

percutant, ~e /pɛʀkytɑ̃, ɑ̃t/ *adj* ⃞1 *fig* [*critique*] hard-hitting; [*style*] trenchant; [*démonstration*] striking; [*personne*] forceful; [*slogan*] punchy○; ⃞2 Mus [*son*] percussive

percuter /pɛʀkyte/ [1]
⃞A *vtr* (voiture, chauffeur) to hit
⃞B *vi* ~ **contre** [*véhicule*] to crash into; [*obus*] to explode against
⃞C **se percuter** *vpr* [*véhicules*] to collide

perdant, ~e /pɛʀdɑ̃, ɑ̃t/
⃞A *adj* [*numéro*] losing (*épith*); **être** ~ (désavantagé) to have lost out; (ne pas gagner) to have lost; **partir** ~ (désavantagé) to be at a disadvantage from the word go; (défaitiste) to have a defeatist attitude from the word go
⃞B *nm,f* loser

perdition /pɛʀdisjɔ̃/ *nf* **lieu de** ~ den of iniquity; **en** ~ [*pays, entreprise*] in trouble (*après n*); [*navire*] in distress (*après n*)

perdre /pɛʀdʀ/ [6]
⃞A *vtr* ⃞1 *gén* to lose; ~ **qch/qn de vue** *lit, fig* to lose sight of sth/sb; **il a perdu de son arrogance** he's become more humble; ~ **de l'importance** to become less important; **leurs actions ont perdu 9%** their shares have dropped 9%; **sans** ~ **le sourire, elle a continué** still smiling, she went on; ⃞2 (to shed) [*feuilles, fleurs*]; **ton chien perd ses poils** your dog is moulting GB *ou* molting US; **la brosse perd ses poils** the brush is losing its bristles; ⃞3 (manquer) to miss [*chance*]; **tu n'as rien perdu (en ne venant pas)** you didn't miss anything (by not coming); **ne pas** ~ **un mot de ce que qn dit** to hang on sb's every word; ⃞4 (gaspiller) to waste [*journée, années*]; **perdre son temps** to waste one's time; **tu as de l'argent à** ~! you've got money to burn!; **elle a du temps à** ~ she's got nothing better to do; **sans** ~ **un instant** immediately; ⃞5 (mal retenir) **je perds mes chaussures** my shoes are too big; **je perds mon pantalon** my trousers are falling down; ⃞6 (ruiner) to bring [*sb*] down; **cet homme te perdra** that man will be your undoing
⃞B *vi* ⃞1 (être perdant) to lose; **j'y perds** I lose out; ⃞2 (diminuer) ~ **en gentillesse** to be less kind
⃞C **se perdre** *vpr* ⃞1 (s'égarer) to get lost; ⃞2 (s'embrouiller) to get mixed up; **ne vous perdez pas dans des détails** don't get bogged down in details; ⃞3 (être absorbé) **se** ~ **dans ses pensées** to be lost in thought; ⃞4 (disparaître) (cesser d'être vu) to disappear; (cesser d'être entendu) to be lost; ⃞5 [*aliment, récolte*] to go to waste; **il y a des claques qui se perdent**○! somebody's looking for a good smack!; ⃞6 [*tradition*] to die out

⸤Idiome⸥ ~ **la tête** *or* **la raison** *or* **l'esprit** (devenir fou) to go out of one's mind; (paniquer) to lose one's head

perdreau, *pl* ~**x** /pɛʀdʀo/ *nm* ⃞1 Zool young partridge; ⃞2 Culin partridge

perdrix /pɛʀdʀi/ *nf inv* partridge

perdu, ~e /pɛʀdy/
⃞A *pp* ▶ **perdre**
⃞B *pp adj* ⃞1 *gén* lost; **chien** ~ stray dog; **balle ~e** stray bullet; **tout est** ~ it's all over; **c'est** ~ **d'avance** it's hopeless; ⃞2 [*journée, occasion*] wasted; **c'est du temps** ~ it's a waste of time; **à tes moments ~s** in your spare time; ⃞3 [*récolte*]

ruined; [*aliment*] spoiled; **il est** ~ (condamné) there's no hope for him; **le regard** ~ **dans le vide** staring into space

C *adj* **1** (isolé) remote, isolated; **vivre dans un coin** ~ to live in a godforsaken spot; **salle** ~**e au bout d'un couloir** room tucked away at the end of a corridor; **2** (non réutilisable) disposable; (non consigné) non returnable

Idiomes **se lancer à corps** ~ **dans** to throw oneself head-long into; **ce n'est pas** ~ **pour tout le monde** somebody will do all right out of it; **crier/courir comme un** ~ to shout/to run like a madman

perdurer /pɛʀdyʀe/ [1] *vi liter* [*situation, conflit*] to continue; [*sentiment, phénomène*] to endure

père /pɛʀ/
A *nm* **1** lit, fig, Relig father; **ils sont banquiers de** ~ **en fils** they have been bankers for generations; **Dupont** ~ Dupont senior; **le** ~○ **Dupont** old○ Dupont; **2** (d'animal) gén male parent; (de chien, cheval) sire
B **pères** *nmpl* (ancêtres) forefathers

Composés ~ **abbé** abbot; ~ **de famille** father; **être** ~ **de famille** to have a family to look after; **en bon** ~ **de famille** as a responsible person; **le** ~ **Noël** Santa Claus; ~ **tranquille** mild-mannered fellow

pérégrinations /peʀegʀinasjɔ̃/ *nfpl* travels, peregrinations *sout*

péremption /peʀɑ̃psjɔ̃/ *nf* **date de** ~ use-by date

péremptoire /peʀɑ̃ptwaʀ/ *adj* peremptory

pérennité /peʀenite/ *nf liter* permanence

péréquation /peʀekwasjɔ̃/ *nf* adjustment

perfectif, -ive /pɛʀfɛktif, iv/ *adj* Ling perfective

perfection /pɛʀfɛksjɔ̃/ *nf* perfection

perfectionné, ~**e** /pɛʀfɛksjɔne/ *adj* advanced

perfectionnement /pɛʀfɛksjɔnmɑ̃/ *nm* improvement

perfectionner /pɛʀfɛksjɔne/ [1]
A *vtr* to perfect [*technique, machine*]; to refine [*art*]
B **se perfectionner** *vtr* [*technique, outils*] to improve; **se** ~ **en allemand** to improve one's German

perfectionniste /pɛʀfɛksjɔnist/ *adj, nmf* perfectionist

perfide /pɛʀfid/
A *adj liter* perfidious, treacherous
B *nmf liter* gén traitor; (amant) faithless lover

Composé **la** ~ **Albion** perfidious Albion

perfidie /pɛʀfidi/ *nf liter* perfidy *littér*, treachery

perforation /pɛʀfɔʀasjɔ̃/ *nf* **1** gén, Méd perforation; **2** Ordinat (opération) punching; (trou) punched hole

perforatrice /pɛʀfɔʀatʀis/ *nf* **1** (pour papier, carton) punch; **2** Tech (outil) drill; (machine) drilling machine

perforer /pɛʀfɔʀe/ [1] *vtr* **1** (percer) gén to pierce; (de trous réguliers) to perforate; **2** (poinçonner) to punch; **carte perforée** Ordinat punch card

performance /pɛʀfɔʀmɑ̃s/ *nf* (résultat) gén result, performance; (record, exploit) achievement; ~ **d'acteur** acting performance

performant, ~**e** /pɛʀfɔʀmɑ̃, ɑ̃t/ *adj* **1** Tech [*voiture, matériel*] high-performance (épith); [*personne, techniques*] efficient; **2** Fin [*action*] performing; [*investissement*] high-return (épith); **3** Écon [*entreprise*] competitive

perfusion /pɛʀfyzjɔ̃/ *nm* Méd drip GB, IV US

péricliter /peʀiklite/ [1] *vi* to be going downhill

péridurale /peʀidyʀal/ *nf* epidural

péril /peʀil/ *nm lit*re peril *littér*, danger; **au** ~ **de sa vie** at the risk of his/her life; **à ses risques et** ~**s** at his/her own risk; **il n'y a pas** ~ **en la demeure** what's the hurry?; **mettre en** ~ to jeopardize [*avenir, démocratie*]; to threaten [*survie, patrimoine*]; to endanger [*santé, qualité*]

périlleux, -euse /peʀijø, øz/ *adj liter* perilous *littér*, dangerous

périmé, ~**e** /peʀime/ *adj* **1** [*passeport, billet*] out-of-date (épith); **son passeport est** ~ his/her passport has expired; **2** Comm **ce produit est** ~ this product has passed its use-by date; **3** (désuet) [*idée, coutume, institution*] outdated

périmètre /peʀimɛtʀ/ *nm* **1** Math perimeter; **2** (espace enclos) area; **dans le** ~ **de l'usine** on the factory premises; **dans un** ~ **de 30 km** within a 30 km radius

périnée /peʀine/ *nm* perineum

période /peʀjɔd/ *nf* **1** gén period; **la** ~ **Brejnev** the Brezhnev era; **elle traverse une** ~ **Elvis** hum she's going through

an Elvis phase; **en** ~ **de crise** at times of crisis; **en** ~ **électorale** at election time; **nous sommes en pleine** ~ **de crise** we are right in the middle of a crisis; **par** ~**s** periodically; **2** Météo period; (plus court) spell; **3** Sport (mi-temps) half

périodique /peʀjɔdik/
A *adj* **1** Chimie, Phys periodic; **2** Méd [*fièvre*] recurring; **3** (hygiénique) [*protection*] sanitary
B *nm* (publication) periodical

périodiquement /peʀjɔdikmɑ̃/ *adv* periodically

péripétie /peʀipesi/ *nf* **1** (incident) incident; (événement) event; (aventure) adventure; **les** ~**s de** the eventful moments of; **2** Littérat, Théât **les** ~**s de l'intrigue** the twists and turns of the plot

périphérie /peʀifeʀi/ *nf* periphery

périphérique /peʀifeʀik/
A *adj* gén peripheral; [*quartier*] outlying (épith); **radio** ~ broadcasting station situated outside the territory to which it transmits
B *nm* **1** (boulevard) ring road GB, beltway US; **2** Ordinat peripheral; ~ **d'entrée/de sortie** input/output device

périphrase /peʀifʀɑz/ *nf* circumlocution, periphrasis *spéc*

périple /peʀipl/ *nm* gén journey; (en bateau) voyage

périr /peʀiʀ/ [3] *vi* **1** (mourir) liter to die, to perish *littér*; **2** Naut [*navire*] to go down; **3** (disparaître) liter [*œuvre*] to be destroyed; **4** (se détériorer) [*denrées*] to perish

périscolaire /peʀiskɔlɛʀ/ *adj* extracurricular

périscope /peʀiskɔp/ *nm* periscope

périssable /peʀisabl/ *adj* **1** Comm perishable; **2** fig [*œuvre*] ephemeral

Péritel® /peʀitɛl/ *nf* **prise** ~ (femelle) scart socket; (mâle) scart plug

péritonite /peʀitɔnit/ ▸ p. 195 *nf* peritonitis

perle /pɛʀl/ *nf* **1** lit (d'huître, de bijouterie) pearl; (de verre) bead; **2** fig gem; **épouser une** ~ to marry a wonderful man/woman; **ma femme de ménage est une vraie** ~ my cleaning lady is a real treasure; **3** ○(erreur grossière) howler○ (de in); **4** (goutte) liter ~ **de rosée** dewdrop; ~ **de sang** drop(let) of blood; ~ **de sueur** bead of sweat

Composés ~ **de culture** cultured pearl; ~ **fine** or **naturelle** real pearl; ~ **rare** fig real treasure

Idiomes **il n'est pas ici pour enfiler des** ~**s**○ he's not here to amuse himself; **jeter des** ~**s aux cochons** to cast one's pearls before swine

perlé, ~**e** /pɛʀle/ *adj* **1** [*orge*] pearl (épith); [*riz*] polished; **2** [*laine*] pearlized; [*broderie*] beaded; **coton** ~ pearl cotton; **3** fig **rire** ~ rippling laugh

perler /pɛʀle/ [1] *vi* [*goutte, larme*] to appear; **la sueur perlait sur son front** beads of sweat stood out on his/her brow

perlier, -ière /pɛʀlje, ɛʀ/ *adj* pearl (épith)

perlimpinpin /pɛʀlɛ̃pɛ̃pɛ̃/ *nm* **poudre de** ~ hum magical cure

perm○ /pɛʀm/ *nf* **1** soldiers' slang = **permission 2**; **2** schoolchildren's slang = **permanence A 4**

permanence /pɛʀmanɑ̃s/
A *nf* **1** (absence d'interruption) permanence; (répétition) persistence; **2** (service) '~ **de 8 à 9 heures**' 'open from 8 am till 9 am'; ~ **téléphonique** manned line; **assurer** or **tenir une** ~ [*personne*] to be on duty; [*député, avocat*] to hold a surgery GB, to have office hours US; **3** (local) permanently manned office; ~ **du parti** party offices (*pl*); **4** Scol (salle) (private) study room GB, study hall US; (période) (private) study period
B **en permanence** *loc adv* **1** (sans interruption) permanently; **2** (très fréquemment) constantly

permanent, ~**e**[1] /pɛʀmanɑ̃, ɑ̃t/
A *adj* **1** (durable) [*personnel, exposition*] permanent; [*comité, armée*] standing (épith); **2** (constant) [*danger*] constant; [*spectacle, formation*] continuous; [*invalidité*] permanent
B *nm,f* (employé) permanent employee; (membre) permanent member

permanente[2] /pɛʀmanɑ̃t/ *nf* (coiffure) perm; **se faire faire une** ~ to have one's hair permed

permanenter /pɛʀmanɑ̃te/ [1] *vtr* to perm [*cheveux*]

perméable /pɛʀmeabl/ *adj* **1** lit permeable (à to); **2** fig [*frontière*] easily crossed; [*marché*] easily penetrated; **être** ~ **à une influence** to be susceptible to an influence

P

permettre /pɛʀmɛtʀ/ [60]

A vtr **①** (donner l'autorisation) ~ **à qn de faire qch** to allow sb to do sth; **permets-moi de te dire que** let me tell you that; **permettez-moi d'ajouter que** I would like to add that; **vous permettez que j'ouvre la fenêtre?** do you mind if I open the window?; **(vous) permettez! j'étais là avant!** excuse me! I was here first!; **ça, permettez-moi d'en douter** I'm sorry, I have my doubts about that; **c'est pas permis○ d'être aussi hypocrite!** how can anyone be such a hypocrite?; **il est menteur comme c'est pas permis○** he's an incredible liar; **il est permis de se poser des questions** one is entitled to wonder; **tous les espoirs sont permis** there is every hope of success; **②** (donner les moyens) ~ **à qn de faire qch** to allow ou enable sb to do sth; **des mesures pour** ~ **une reprise rapide de l'économie** measures to ensure rapid economic recovery; **si le temps le permet** weather permitting; **je viendrai si mon emploi du temps (me) le permet** I'll come if my schedule allows ou permits; **ce procédé permet de consommer moins d'énergie** this system makes it possible to use less energy; **leurs moyens ne le leur permettent pas** they can't afford it; **ma santé ne me permet pas de faire du sport** my health prevents me from doing any sport; **autant qu'il est permis d'en juger** as far as one can tell

B se permettre vpr **je peux me** ~ **ce genre de plaisanterie avec lui** I can get away with telling him that kind of joke; **puis-je me** ~ **une remarque?** might I say something?; **se** ~ **de faire** to take the liberty of doing; **je ne peux pas me** ~ **d'acheter une nouvelle voiture** I can't afford to buy a new car; **puis-je me** ~ **de vous offrir un verre?** would you care for a drink?; **puis-je me** ~ **de vous raccompagner?** might I be allowed to escort you home?; **'je me permets de vous écrire au sujet de...'** 'I'm writing to you about...'

permis, ~e /pɛʀmi, iz/

A pp ▸ **permettre**

B pp adj [limites] permitted

C nm inv permit, licence GB, license US

(Composés) ~ **de conduire** (document) driver's licenceGB; (examen) driving test; ~ **de construire** planning permission GB, building permit US; ~ **de démolition** demolition consent; ~ **d'inhumer** burial certificate; ~ **moto** motorcycle licenceGB; ~ **de navigation** certificate of seaworthiness; ~ **poids lourd** heavy goods vehicle licence GB, articulated-vehicle license US; ~ **de port d'armes** gun licenceGB; ~ **de séjour** residence permit; ~ **de travail** work permit

permissif, -ive /pɛʀmisif, iv/ adj permissive

permission /pɛʀmisjɔ̃/ nf **①** gén permission; **②** Mil leave **₡**; **partir en** ~ to go on leave

(Composé) **la** ~ **de minuit** permission to stay out late

permissionnaire /pɛʀmisjɔnɛʀ/ nm soldier on leave

permutable /pɛʀmytabl/ adj [fonction] interchangeable

permutation /pɛʀmytasjɔ̃/ nf Admin, Mil exchange of posts

permuter /pɛʀmyte/ [1]

A vtr **①** gén to switch [sth] around [lettres, étiquettes]; **②** Math to permute

B vi [personnes] to exchange posts (**avec** with)

pernicieux, -ieuse /pɛʀnisjø, øz/ adj pernicious

péroné /peʀɔne/ nm fibula

pérorer /peʀɔʀe/ [1] vi pej to hold forth péj

Pérou /peʀu/ ▸ p. 230 nprm Peru

(Idiome) **ce n'est pas le** ~ it's not a fortune

perpendiculaire /pɛʀpɑ̃dikylɛʀ/ adj, nf perpendicular (**à** to)

perpendiculairement /pɛʀpɑ̃dikylɛʀmɑ̃/ adv **①** (à angle droit) at right angles (**à** to); **②** (verticalement) vertically

perpète○ /pɛʀpɛt/ nf **être condamné à** ~, **avoir la** ~ prisoners' slang to get life○; **habiter à** ~ to live miles away; **jusqu'à** ~ forever and a day○

perpétrer /pɛʀpetʀe/ [14] vtr to perpetrate

perpette = **perpète**

perpétuel, -elle /pɛʀpetɥɛl/ adj **①** gén perpetual; **②** (à vie) [poste, secrétaire] permanent; **réclusion perpétuelle** life imprisonment

perpétuellement /pɛʀpetɥɛlmɑ̃/ adv constantly, perpetually

perpétuer /pɛʀpetɥe/ [1] vtr to perpetuate

perpétuité /pɛʀpetɥite/ nf (durée) perpetuity; **à** ~ [réclusion] life; [concession] in perpetuity (après n)

perplexe /pɛʀplɛks/ adj perplexed, baffled; **rendre** ~ to perplex

perplexité /pɛʀplɛksite/ nf perplexity, confusion

perquisition /pɛʀkizisjɔ̃/ nf search

perquisitionner /pɛʀkizisjɔne/ [1]

A vtr to search

B vi to carry out a search

perron /peʀɔ̃/ nm flight of steps

perroquet /peʀɔkɛ/ nm **①** Zool parrot; **tout répéter comme un** ~ to repeat everything parrot-fashion; **②** Naut topgallant sail; **③** (apéritif) pastis with crème de menthe; **④** (porte-manteau) hat and coat stand

(Composé) ~ **de mer** (oiseau) puffin; (poisson) parrotfish

perruche /peʀyʃ/ nf **①** Zool budgerigar GB, budgie○ GB, parakeet US; **②** Naut mizzen topgallant sail

perruque /peʀyk/ nf (postiche) wig

persan, ~e /pɛʀsɑ̃, an/ adj [chat, tapis] Persian

perse /pɛʀs/ adj Persian

persécuté, -e /pɛʀsekyte/ nm,f **①** lit victim of persecution; **②** Psych person with a persecution complex

persécuter /pɛʀsekyte/ [1] vtr to persecute

persécuteur, -trice /pɛʀsekytœʀ, tʀis/ nm,f persecutor

persécution /pɛʀsekysjɔ̃/ nf persecution

persévérance /pɛʀseveʀɑ̃s/ nf perseverance

persévérant, ~e /pɛʀseveʀɑ̃, ɑ̃t/ adj [personne] persevering (épith); **tu n'es pas très** ~! you give up too easily!

persévérer /pɛʀseveʀe/ [14] vi **①** [personne, équipe] to persevere; **②** (persister) liter [fièvre] to persist

persienne /pɛʀsjɛn/ nf (louvredGB) shutter

persiflage /pɛʀsiflaʒ/ nm mockery, persiflage

persifleur, -euse /pɛʀsiflœʀ, øz/ adj liter [ton, propos] mocking

persil /pɛʀsi(l)/ nm parsley

persillade /pɛʀsijad/ nf parsley and garlic garnish

persillé, ~e /pɛʀsije/ adj garnished with chopped parsley (après n); **fromage** ~ blue cheese; **viande** ~e marbled meat

persique /pɛʀsik/ adj Persian; **le golfe Persique** the Persian Gulf

persistance /pɛʀsistɑ̃s/ nf persistence; **avec** ~ persistently

persistant, ~e /pɛʀsistɑ̃, ɑ̃t/ adj [chaleur, problème] continuing; [odeur, neige] lingering; [symptôme] persistent; **arbre à feuilles** ~es evergreen

persister /pɛʀsiste/ [1] vi **①** (durer) [symptôme, douleur] to persist; [mauvais temps, inflation] to continue; [doute, problème] to remain; [odeur] to linger; **②** (s'obstiner) ~ **dans son erreur** to persist in one's error; ~ **dans son refus** to continue to refuse; **je persiste à croire que...** I still think that...

(Idiome) **il persiste et signe○** he's sticking to his guns○

personnage /pɛʀsɔnaʒ/ nm **①** (personne fictive) character; **la distribution des** ~s Théât the cast, the dramatis personae (pl); **②** (personne représentée) figure; **③** (personne importante) figure; **un** ~ **haut placé** a high-placed person; **les** ~s **importants de la ville** the local dignitaries; **④** (personne curieuse) character; **⑤** (personnalité que l'on se crée) **se composer un** ~ to adopt a persona

personnaliser /pɛʀsɔnalize/ [1] vtr to add a personal touch to [maison]; to customize [voiture]; ~ **un contrat** to tailor a contract to an individual's needs; **lettre personnalisée** personal letter

personnalité /pɛʀsɔnalite/ nf **①** Psych personality; **②** (personne influente) important person

personne¹ /pɛʀsɔn/ pron indéf ~ **n'est parfait** nobody's ou no-one's perfect; **je n'ai parlé à** ~ I didn't talk to anybody ou anyone; ~ **de sensé ne ferait cela** no sensible person would do that; **ce n'est un mystère pour** ~ it's no mystery

personne² /pɛʀsɔn/ nf **①** (individu) person; **dix** ~s ten people; **50% des** ~s **interrogées** 50% of those interviewed; **un voyage pour deux** ~s a trip for two; lit/ **chambre d'une** ~ single bed/room; **la** ~ **aimée** the loved one; **les ~s âgées** the elderly; **une charmante jeune ~** a charming young lady; **une ~ de confiance** someone trustworthy; **il doit y avoir erreur sur la ~** it must be the wrong person *ou* a case of mistaken identity; **2** (individu en lui-même) **satisfait de sa (petite) ~** satisfied with oneself; **bien fait de sa ~** good-looking; **le respect de la ~ (humaine)** respect for the individual; **en ~** personally; **c'est la cupidité en ~** he/she is greed personified; **3** Ling person

(Composé) **~ à charge** dependant

personnel, -elle /pɛʀsɔnɛl/
A *adj* **1** (individuel) [*ami, effets*] personal; [*engagement, papiers*] private; **adresse personnelle** home *ou* private address; **c'est ~** it's confidential; **'personnelle'** (sur une lettre) 'private'; **'strictement personnelle'** (sur une lettre) 'private and confidential'; **2** (original) individual; **3** (égoiste) selfish; **4** Ling [*forme, pronom*] personal; [*mode*] finite
B *nm* (d'industrie, usine) workforce; (de compagnie, d'administration) employees (*pl*), personnel; (d'hôpital, hôtel) staff; **nous manquons de ~** we are understaffed; **~ navigant/au sol** flight/ground personnel

personnellement /pɛʀsɔnɛlmɑ̃/ *adv* personally; **il nous a reçus ~** he received us in person

personnification /pɛʀsɔnifikasjɔ̃/ *nf* personification

personnifier /pɛʀsɔnifje/ [2] *vtr* to personify

perspective /pɛʀspɛktiv/ *nf* **1** Archit, Art perspective; **en ~** [*dessin*] perspective (*épith*); [*dessiner*] in perspective; **2** (vue) view; **3** (optique) perspective, angle; **4** (éventualité) prospect

perspicace /pɛʀspikas/ *adj* perceptive, perspicacious

perspicacité /pɛʀspikasite/ *nf* insight, perspicacity

persuader /pɛʀsɥade/ [1] *vtr* to persuade; **j'en suis persuadé** I'm convinced of it

persuasif, -ive /pɛʀsɥazif, iv/ *adj* persuasive

persuasion /pɛʀsɥazjɔ̃/ *nf* persuasion

perte /pɛʀt/
A *nf* **1** gén loss; **être en ~ de vitesse** lit to be losing speed; fig to be slowing down; **avoir des ~s de sang** to bleed; **à ~ de vue** as far as the eye can see; **vendre à ~** to sell at a loss; **2** (gaspillage) waste; **~ d'énergie** (de personne) waste of energy; (de machine) energy loss; **ce serait en pure ~** (inutile) it would be futile; **agir en pure ~** to do something that is a complete waste of time; **3** (ruine) ruin; **courir** *ou* **aller à sa (propre) ~** to be heading for a fall; **vouloir la ~ de qn** to try to bring about sb's downfall
B *pertes nfpl* losses; **causer des ~s en vies humaines** to take a heavy toll in human life

(Composés) **~ sèche** Fin dead loss; **~s blanches** vaginal discharge ¢; **~s séminales** involuntary emission ¢ of semen

pertinemment /pɛʀtinamɑ̃/ *adv* **1** (avec justesse) pertinently; **2** (parfaitement) [*savoir*] perfectly well

pertinence /pɛʀtinɑ̃s/ *nf* pertinence

pertinent, ~e /pɛʀtinɑ̃, ɑ̃t/ *adj* **1** (à propos) [*question*] pertinent; **2** Ling **trait ~** relevant feature

perturbant, ~e /pɛʀtyʀbɑ̃, ɑ̃t/ *adj* disturbing

perturbateur, -trice /pɛʀtyʀbatœʀ, tʀis/ *nm,f* troublemaker

perturbation /pɛʀtyʀbasjɔ̃/ *nf* **1** (d'un service) disruption; **2** Météo disturbance; **3** (politique) upheaval; (sociale) disturbance

perturber /pɛʀtyʀbe/ [1] *vtr* **1** (dérégler) to disrupt [*trafic, marché*]; to interfere with [*sommeil, développement*]; **cela m'a un peu perturbé** it has unsettled me a bit; **être perturbé**° (mentalement) to be very disturbed; **2** (inquiéter) to perturb sout; **cela ne m'a pas perturbé** it didn't bother me; **3** (semer le trouble) to disrupt [*réunion, ordre*]

péruvien, -ienne /peʀyvjɛ̃, ɛn/ ▸ p. 392 *adj* Peruvian

pervenche /pɛʀvɑ̃ʃ/
A ▸ p. 140 *adj inv* (bleu) **~** periwinkle blue
B *nf* **1** (fleur) periwinkle; **2** °(contractuelle) (female) traffic warden GB, meter maid° US

pervers, ~e /pɛʀvɛʀ, ɛʀs/
A *adj* **1** (méchant) wicked; **2** (dépravé) perverted; **3** [*effet*] pernicious
B *nm,f* pervert

perversion /pɛʀvɛʀsjɔ̃/ *nf* perversion (**de** of)

perversité /pɛʀvɛʀsite/ *nf* perversity

pervertir /pɛʀvɛʀtiʀ/ [3] *vtr* to corrupt

pesamment /pəzamɑ̃/ *adv* [*tomber*] heavily; [*marcher*] with a heavy step

pesant, ~e /pəzɑ̃, ɑ̃t/ *adj* **1** (lourd) heavy; **2** (pénible) [*réglementation*] cumbersome; [*contrainte*] burdensome; [*atmosphère, silence*] oppressive; [*incertitude*] heavy; **3** (inélégant) [*architecture, personne*] ungainly; [*style*] heavy; **4** (ennuyeux) [*écrivain*] dull, ponderous

(Idiome) **valoir son ~ d'or** to be worth its weight in gold

pesanteur /pəzɑ̃tœʀ/ *nf* **1** (de style) heaviness; (d'esprit) dullness; (de bureaucratie) inertia ¢; **2** Phys gravity

pèse-bébé, *pl* **~s** /pɛzbebe/ *nm* baby scales (*pl*)

pesée /pəze/ ▸ p. 453 *nf* **1** (opération) weighing; **2** (poussée) shove; **3** (quantité) weight

pèse-lettre, *pl* **~s** /pɛzlɛtʀ/ *nm* letter scales (*pl*)

pèse-personne, *pl* **~s** /pɛzpɛʀsɔn/ *nm* bathroom scales (*pl*)

peser /pəze/ [16] ▸ p. 453
A *vtr* **1** lit to weigh [*personne, objet*]; **2** fig to weigh up; **~ le pour et le contre** to weigh up the pros and cons; **~ ses mots** to choose one's words carefully; **tout bien pesé** all things considered
B *vi* **1** (avoir un poids) to weigh; (être lourd) to be heavy; **~ lourd** to weigh a lot; **2** (avoir de l'importance) to carry weight; **~ dans/sur une décision** to have a decisive influence in/on a decision; **3** (faire sentir son poids) **~ sur** [*soupçons, risques*] to hang over [*personne, projet*]; [*impôts, charges*] to weigh [sb/sth] down [*personne, pays*]; [*personne, décision*] to influence (greatly) [*politique, situation*]; **faire ~ un danger sur** to be a danger to; **faire ~ un risque sur** to threaten; **la solitude me pèse** fig loneliness weighs heavily on me; **4** (exercer une poussée) **~ contre/sur** to push against/down on

C *se peser vpr* to weigh oneself

(Idiome) **envoyez, c'est pesé**°**!** off it goes!

peseta /pezeta/ ▸ p. 34 *nf* peseta

pessimisme /pesimism/ *nm* pessimism

pessimiste /pesimist/
A *adj* pessimistic
B *nmf* pessimist

peste /pɛst/ *nf* **1** ▸ p. 195 Méd plague; **2** °(personne insupportable) pest°

(Idiome) **je me méfie de lui comme de la ~**° I don't trust him an inch

pester /pɛste/ [1] *vi* **~ contre qn/qch** to curse sb/sth

pesticide /pɛstisid/
A *adj* pesticidal
B *nm* pesticide

pestiféré, ~e /pɛstifeʀe/ *adj* [*personne*] plague-stricken; [*lieu*] plague-infested

pestilence /pɛstilɑ̃s/ *nf* stench

pet° /pe/ *nm* fart°; **lâcher un ~** to fart°

(Idiomes) **ça ne vaut pas un ~ (de lapin)** it's not worth a damn°; **il a toujours un ~ de travers** he's always got something wrong with him

pétale /petal/ *nm* petal

pétanque /petɑ̃k/ ▸ p. 327 *nf* petanque (*game of bowls played in the South of France*)

pétant°, **~e** /petɑ̃, ɑ̃t/ *adj* on the dot (*après n*)

pétarade /petaʀad/ *nf* backfiring ¢

pétarader /petaʀade/ [1] *vi* to backfire, to sputter

pétard /petaʀ/ *nm* **1** (explosif) banger GB, firecracker US; **un ~ mouillé** fig a damp squib; **2** °(tapage) racket°; **faire du ~** (faire scandale) to make a hell of a row°; (protester) to kick up a fuss°; **être en ~** (en colère) to be hopping mad° GB, to be real mad° US

pet-de-nonne, *pl* **pets-de-nonne** /pɛdnɔn/ *nm* Culin fritter (*made from choux pastry*)

péter /pete/ [14]
A °*vtr* (casser) to bust° [*appareil*]; to snap [*fil*]
B *vi* **1** °(lâcher un pet) to fart°; **2** (éclater) lit [*ballon, tuyau*] to burst; [*explosif*] to go off; fig to blow up; °(casser) [*appareil, lampe*] to bust°; [*fil*] to snap; [*couture*] to burst

(Idiomes) **~ le feu**° [*personne*] to be full of beans°; **~ la santé**° to be bursting with health

pète-sec° /pɛtsɛk/
A *adj inv* [*ton, manières*] abrupt
B *nmf inv* pej abrupt person

péteux°, **-euse** /petø, øz/
A adj ①° (poltron) cowardly; ②° (prétentieux) stuck-up°
B nm,f ①° (poltron) coward; ②° (prétentieux) cocky (little) upstart°

pétillant, **-e** /petijɑ̃, ɑ̃t/ adj gén sparkling; [personne] bubbly

pétillement /petijmɑ̃/ nm (de champagne) fizziness; (de feu) crackling

pétiller /petije/ [1] vi [champagne] to fizz; [bois] to crackle; [yeux, regard] to sparkle (**de** with)

petiot°, **~e** /pətjo, ɔt/
A adj [enfant] tiny
B nm,f (enfant) little boy/little girl

petit, **~e** /p(ə)ti, it/
A adj ① (en taille) small, little; **~ et trapu** short and stocky; **une toute ~e pièce** a tiny room; **se faire tout ~** fig to try to make oneself inconspicuous; **c'est Versailles en plus ~** it's a miniature Versailles; ② (en longueur, durée) short; **par ~es étapes** in easy stages; ③ (en âge) young, little; **je t'ai connu ~** I knew you when you were little; **le ~ Jésus** baby Jesus; **une ~e Française** a French girl; **le ~ nouveau** the new boy; **c'est notre ~ dernier** he's our youngest; **~ chat** kitten; **~ chien** puppy; **~ ours/renard/lion** bear/fox/lion cub; ④ [appétit, quantité, groupe] small; [mangeur] light; [salaire] low; [averse] light; [cri, rire, souci] little; [chance, rhume] slight; [détail, défaut] minor; **ça a un ~ goût de cerise** it tastes slightly of cherries; **avoir une ~e santé** to have poor health; **un (tout) ~ peu de sel** (just) a little salt; ⑤ (dans une hiérarchie) [marque] lesser known; [emploi] modest; [fonctionnaire] low-ranking; [poète] minor; **les ~es routes** minor roads; **le ~ personnel** low-grade staff; **les ~es gens** ordinary people; **un ~ escroc** a small-time crook; ⑥ fig little; **mon ~ papa** darling daddy°; **un ~ imbécile** an idiot; **très préoccupée de sa ~e personne** very taken up with herself; **de bons ~s plats** tasty dishes; **un ~ coin tranquille** a quiet spot; **envoie-moi un ~ mot** drop me a line; **passe-moi un ~ coup de fil**° give me a call; **j'en ai pour une ~e minute** it won't take me a minute; **une ~e trentaine de personnes** under thirty people; ⑦ (mesquin) [personne, procédé] petty, mean; (étroit) [conception] narrow
B nm,f ① (enfant) little boy/girl, child; (benjamin) **le ~** (de deux) the younger one; (de plus de deux) the youngest one; **mes ~s** my children; **pauvre ~!** poor thing!; **la ~e Martin** the Martin girl; ② (adulte de petite taille) small man/woman
C adv **voir ~** (sous-estimer) to underestimate; (être sans ambition) to have no ambition; **tailler ~** to be small-fitting; **~ à ~** little by little
D nm ① (jeune animal) **~s** gén young (+ v pl); (chats) kittens; (chiens) puppies; **faire des ~s** [chienne] to have puppies; fig [argent] to grow; ② (personne modeste) **les ~s** ordinary people; **un ~ de la finance** a minor figure in the world of finance

(Composés) **~ ami** boyfriend; **~ bois** (d'allumage) kindling; **~ chef** petty tyrant; **jouer au ~ chef** to throw one's weight around°; **~ coin**° (toilettes) euph loo° GB, bathroom US; **~ crème** small espresso with milk; **~ déjeuner** breakfast; **~ linge** underwear; **~ noir**° coffee; **~ nom**° (prénom) first name; **~ pois** (garden) pea, petit pois; **~ pot** (pour bébés) jar of baby food; **~ rat de l'Opéra**) pupil at Paris Opéra's ballet school; **~ salé** streaky salted pork; **~e amie** girlfriend; **~e annonce** classified advertisement; **~e école**° ≈ nursery school; **~e main** seamstress (at a top fashion house); **~e nature** weakling; **~e souris** tooth fairy; **~e vérole** smallpox; **~e voiture** toy car; **~es annonces matrimoniales** personal ads; **~es et moyennes entreprises, PME** small and medium enterprises, SMEs; **~s chevaux** Jeux ≈ ludo (sg)

petit-beurre, pl **petits-beurre** /p(ə)tibœʀ/ nm petit beurre biscuit GB ou cookie US

petite-fille, pl **petites-filles** /p(ə)titfij/ nf granddaughter

petitement /p(ə)titmɑ̃/ adv ① (chichement) in a penny-pinching way; ② (avec mesquinerie) pettily

petitesse /p(ə)tites/ nf ① (mesquinerie) pettiness; ② (petite taille) small size

petit-fils, pl **petits-fils** /p(ə)tifis/ nm grandson

pétition /petisjɔ̃/ nf petition

petit-lait /p(ə)tilɛ/ nm whey
(Idiome) **ça se boit comme du ~!** it slips down nicely!

petit-nègre /p(ə)tinɛgʀ/ nm inv offensive pidgin French

petits-enfants /p(ə)tizɑ̃fɑ̃/ nmpl grandchildren

petit-suisse, pl **petits-suisses** /p(ə)tisɥis/ nm petit-suisse, individual fromage frais

pétoire° /petwaʀ/ nf (fusil) rusty old gun

peton /pətɔ̃/ nm tootsie lang enfantin, foot

pétoncle /petɔ̃kl/ nm small scallop

pétouiller° /petuje/ [1] vi H (avoir des problèmes) [personne] to be struggling; [voiture] to run rough

pétri /petʀi/ adj **~ de** pej steeped in [ignorance]; puffed up with [orgueil]; full of [contradictions]

pétrifiant, **-e** /petʀifjɑ̃, ɑ̃t/ adj petrifying

pétrifier /petʀifje/ [2]
A vtr ① lit to petrify; ② fig to transfix
B se pétrifier vpr ① lit to become petrified; ② fig [personne] to be transfixed; [cœur] to harden; [sourire] to freeze

pétrin /petʀɛ̃/ nm dough trough; **~ mécanique** kneading machine; **être dans le ~**° to be in a fix°

pétrir /petʀiʀ/ [3] vtr ① Culin to knead [pâte]; ② fig to mould GB ou mold US [personnalité]

pétrochimique /petʀoʃimik/ adj petrochemical

pétrole /petʀɔl/ nm oil, petroleum spéc; **~ brut** crude oil

pétrolette° /petʀɔlɛt/ nf (vélomoteur) moped

pétroleuse /petʀɔløz/ nf ① Hist (female) fire-raiser (during the Commune); ② (militante) (female) activist

pétrolier, **-ière** /petʀɔlje, ɛʀ/
A adj [prospection] oil; [produits] petroleum; [pays] oil-producing; [port] oil-exporting
B nm ① (navire) oil tanker; ② ▸ p. 372 (industriel) oil man; (ingénieur) petroleum engineer

pétrolifère /petʀɔlifɛʀ/ adj [roche] oil-bearing; [région] oil-producing; **gisement ~** oilfield

pétulant, **-e** /petylɑ̃, ɑ̃t/ adj exuberant

pétunia /petynja/ nm petunia

peu /pø/

> ⚠ Les emplois de peu avec avant, d'ici, depuis, sous sont traités respectivement sous chacun de ces mots.
> Il sera également utile de se reporter à la note d'usage sur les quantités ▸ p. 483.

A adv ① (modifiant un verbe) not much; **elle gagne assez ~** she doesn't earn very much; **elle gagne très ~** she earns very little; **le radiateur chauffe ~** the radiator doesn't give out much heat; **je sais me contenter de ~** I'm satisfied with very little; **deux semaines c'est trop ~** two weeks isn't long enough; **si ~ que ce soit** however little; **tu ne vas pas t'en faire pour si ~** you're not going to worry about such a little thing; **la catastrophe a été évitée de ~** disaster was only just avoided; **ça importe ~** it doesn't really matter; **c'est ~ dire** to say the least; **il est aussi borné que son père et ce n'est pas ~ dire**! he's as narrow-minded as his father and that's saying a lot!; **un homme comme on en voit ~** the kind of man you don't often come across; **très ~ pour moi**! fig no thanks°!; ② (modifiant un adjectif) not very; **assez ~ connu** little-known; **ils se sentent très ~ concernés par...** they feel quite unconcerned about...; **nous étions ~ nombreux** there weren't many of us; **un individu ~ recommandable** a disreputable character; **elle n'est pas ~ fière** she's more than a little proud
B pron indéf **~ leur font confiance** few ou not many people trust them
C **peu de** dét indéf ① (avec un nom dénombrable) **~ de mots** few words; ② (avec un nom non dénombrable) **~ de temps** little time; **en ~ de temps** in next to no time; **il y a ~ de bruit** there's not much noise; **c'est ~ de chose** it's not much; **avec ~ de chose elle a fait un repas délicieux** with very little she made a delicious meal; **on est bien ~ de chose!** we're so insignificant!
D **le ~** (petite quantité) **le ~ de** the little [confiance, liberté]; the few [livres, amis]; **il a voulu montrer le ~ d'importance qu'il attachait à l'affaire** he wanted to show how unimportant the matter was to him; ② (manque) **le ~ de** the lack of
E **un peu** loc adv ① (dans une mesure faible) a little, a bit; **reste encore un ~** stay a little longer; **'elle aime le fromage?'—'oui, pas qu'un ~**°!' 'does she like cheese?'—'does

she ever○!'; **2** (modifiant un adverbe) a little, a bit; **parle un ~ moins fort** keep your voice down; **elle se maquille un ~ trop** she wears a bit too much make-up; **un ~ plus de gens** a few more people; **un ~ moins de** slightly less [*pluie*]; slightly fewer [*gens*]; **amène tes amis, un ~ plus un ~ moins...** bring your friends, another two or three people won't make much difference; **'il avait l'air un ~ contrarié'—'un ~ beaucoup même**○' 'he looked a bit annoyed'—'more than a bit'; **3** (emploi stylistique) just; **répète un ~ pour voir**○! you just try saying that again!; **je vous demande un ~**○! I ask you!; **il sait un ~**○ **de quoi il parle** he does know what he's talking about; **4** (emploi par antiphrase) a little; **tu ne serais pas un ~ jaloux toi?** aren't you just a little jealous?; **5** ○(pour renforcer une affirmation) **il est un ~ bien ton copain!** your boyfriend is a bit of all right○ GB *ou* a good-looker○!; **'tu le ferais toi?'—'un ~ (que je le ferais)!'** 'would you do it?'—'I sure would○!'

F peu à peu *loc adv* gradually, little by little
G pour un peu *loc adv* **pour un ~ ils se seraient battus** they very nearly had a fight
H pour peu que *loc conj* if; **pour ~ qu'il ait bu, il va nous raconter sa vie** if he's had anything at all to drink, he'll tell us his life story

peuchère /pøʃɛʀ/ *excl* dial poor thing!

peuplade /pœplad/ *nf* small tribe

peuple /pœpl/ *nm* **1** Pol people; **le ~ de gauche** the left-wing element of the population; **2** Sociol **le ~** the people (+ *v pl*); **le ~ des campagnes** country people (+ *v pl*); **le ~ des villes** townspeople (+ *v pl*); **3** ○(foule) lots of people (*pl*)
Composé ~ **élu** Chosen People

peuplement /pœpləmɑ̃/ *nm* **1** (d'une région) (en habitants) populating; (en arbres) planting (with trees); (d'un lac) stocking; **2** (habitants) population

peupler /pœple/ [1]
A *vtr* **1** (faire occuper) to populate [*pays*] (**de** with); to stock [*bois, étang*] (**de** with); **2** (occuper) [*personnes*] to populate [*pays*]; [*animaux, plantes*] to colonize [*région*]; [*spectateurs, étudiants*] to fill [*salle, rue*]; **peuplé de** peopled with [*personnes*]; **3** (remplir) [*souvenirs, rêves*] to fill
B se peupler *vpr* [*ville, région*] to fill up (**de** with)

peuplier /pøplije/ *nm* poplar

peur /pœʀ/ *nf* gén fear; (soudaine) fright, scare; **être mort** *or* **vert**○ **de ~** to be scared to death; **une ~ panique s'empara de lui** he was panic-stricken; **avoir ~** to be afraid; **j'en ai bien ~** I'm afraid so; **il n'a ~ de rien** lit he's not afraid of anything, he's fearless; **il veut courir le marathon sans s'être préparé! il n'a pas ~**○! he wants to run the marathon without having trained? he's being very optimistic!; **n'ayez pas ~** (ne soyez pas effrayé) don't be afraid; (ne vous inquiétez pas) don't worry; **avoir plus de ~ que de mal** to be more frightened than hurt; **faire ~ à qn** to frighten sb; **tu ne me fais pas ~**! I'm not afraid of you!; **être laid à faire ~** to be hideously ugly; **maigre** *or* **d'une maigreur à faire ~** terribly thin; **le travail ne nous fait pas ~** we're not afraid of hard work; **il est poli ça fait ~**○! iron he's not exactly the most polite man in the world!

peureusement /pœʀøzmɑ̃/ *adv* fearfully

peureux, -euse /pœʀø, øz/
A *adj* fearful
B *nmf* fearful person

peut-être /pøtɛtʀ/ *adv* perhaps, maybe; **tu veux m'apprendre à conduire, ~?** iron I do know how to drive, you know!; **elle travaille ~ lentement mais avec soin** she might work slowly, but she's careful

pèze○ /pɛz/ *nm* dough○, money

phacochère /fakɔʃɛʀ/ *nm* warthog

phagocyter /fagɔsite/ [1] *vtr* **1** Biol to ingest by phagocytosis; **2** fig to swallow up

phalange /falɑ̃ʒ/ *nf* **1** Anat phalanx; **2** Hist phalanx; **3** Pol (en Espagne) Falange; (au Liban) **les ~s** the (Christian) Phalangists

phalangiste /falɑ̃ʒist/ *adj, nmf* (au Liban) Phalangist; (en Espagne) Falangist

phalène /falɛn/ *nf ou m* geometer moth

phallocrate /falɔkʀat/ *nm* male chauvinist, phallocrat

phalloïde /falɔid/ *adj* **amanite ~** death cap

phallus /falys/ *nm inv* phallus

phantasme = **fantasme**

---

pharamineux, -euse = **faramineux**

pharaon /faʀaɔ̃/ *nm* pharaoh

phare /faʀ/
A *nm* **1** Aut headlight, headlamp; **2** Naut lighthouse; **3** fig (guide) beacon
B (-)**phare** (*in compounds*) **société/industrie(-)~** flagship company/industry; **œuvre(-)~** seminal work; **pays(-)~** leading country; **année(-)~** key year
Composés ~ **antibrouillard** fog-light; ~ **à iode** quartz halogen light

pharmaceutique /faʀmasøtik/ *adj* pharmaceutical

pharmacie /faʀmasi/ *nf* **1** ▸ p. 372 Comm chemist's (shop) GB, drugstore US, pharmacy; **~ de nuit** duty chemist's GB, night pharmacy US; **~ de garde** duty chemist's GB, *pharmacy open on a Sunday or a holiday according to a rotating schedule*; **2** (dans un hôpital) dispensary, pharmacy; **3** (meuble) medicine cabinet; **4** (discipline) pharmacy; **elle est en troisième année de ~** she's in her third year studying pharmacy; **5** (produits) **la ~** medicines (*pl*); (dans un supermarché) health-care products (*pl*); Ind pharmaceuticals (*pl*)
Composé ~ **portative** *or* **de voyage** first-aid kit

pharmacien, -ienne /faʀmasjɛ̃, ɛn/ ▸ p. 372 *nm,f* (dans un magasin) (dispensing) chemist GB, pharmacist; (ailleurs) pharmacist

pharmacodépendance /faʀmakodepɑ̃dɑ̃s/ *nf* drug-dependence

pharmacologie /faʀmakɔlɔʒi/ *nf* pharmacology

pharmacopée /faʀmakɔpe/ *nf* pharmacopeia

pharyngite /faʀɛ̃ʒit/ ▸ p. 195 *nf* pharyngitis

pharynx /faʀɛ̃ks/ *nm inv* pharynx

phase /faz/ *nf* **1** (d'évolution) stage; **2** Chimie, Phys phase; **3** Électrotech (conducteur de) **~** live wire; **en ~** in phase; **être en ~ avec qn** fig to be on the same wavelength as sb

phénicien, -ienne /fenisjɛ̃, ɛn/
A *adj* Phoenician
B *nm* Ling Phoenician

phénix /feniks/ *nm inv* Mythol phoenix

phénoménal, ~e, *mpl* **-aux** /fenɔmenal, o/ *adj* phenomenal

phénomène /fenɔmɛn/ *nm* **1** (fait) phenomenon; **des ~s de racisme** manifestations of racism; **2** ○(original) character; **3** (de cirque) freak

philanthropie /filɑ̃tʀɔpi/ *nf* philanthropy

philatélie /filateli/ *nf* stamp collecting, philately spéc

philatéliste /filatelist/ *nmf* stamp collector, philatelist spéc

philharmonique /filaʀmɔnik/ *adj* philharmonic

Philippe /filip/ *npr* Philip
Composés ~ **Auguste** Philip Augustus; ~ **le Bel** Philip the Fair; ~ **le Bon** Philip the Good

philippin, ~e /filipɛ̃, in/ ▸ p. 392 *adj* Philippine (*épith*)

Philippin, ~e /filipɛ̃, in/ ▸ p. 392 *nm,f* Filipino

Philippines /filipin/ ▸ p. 406, p. 230 *nprfpl* **les ~** the Philippines; **mer des ~** Philippine Sea

philosophale /filɔzɔfal/ *adj f* **la pierre ~** the philosopher's stone

philosophe /filɔzɔf/
A *adj* philosophical
B *nmf* philosopher

philosopher /filɔzɔfe/ [1] *vi* to philosophize

philosophie /filɔzɔfi/ *nf* philosophy; **avec ~** philosophically

philosophique /filɔzɔfik/ *adj* philosophical

philtre /filtʀ/ *nm* philtre; **~ d'amour** love potion

phlébite /flebit/ ▸ p. 195 *nf* phlebitis

phlébologie /flebɔlɔʒi/ *nf* vascular medicine

phlegmon /flɛgmɔ̃/ ▸ p. 195 *nm* acute inflammation

phobie /fɔbi/ *nf* gén, Psych phobia (**de** about)

phocéen, -éenne /fɔseɛ̃, ɛn/ *nm,f* Phocean; **la cité phocéenne** Marseilles

phonématique /fɔnematik/ *nf* phonemics (+ *v sg*)

phonème /fɔnɛm/ *nm* phoneme

phonétique /fɔnetik/
A adj [transcription, alphabet] phonetic; **loi** ~ sound law; **altération** ~ sound change
B nf phonetics (+ v sg)

phonographe /fɔnɔgRaf/ nm gramophone GB, phonograph US

phonothèque /fɔnɔtɛk/ nf sound archive

phoque /fɔk/ nm **1** (animal) seal; **2** (peau) sealskin
(Idiome) **souffler comme un** ~○ to puff and pant

phosphate /fɔsfat/ nm phosphate

phosphore /fɔsfɔR/ nm phosphorus

phosphorescent, ~e /fɔsfɔResã, ãt/ adj phosphorescent

phosphoreux, -euse /fɔsfɔRø, øz/ adj [acide] phosphorous; [alliage] phosphor (épith)

photo /fɔto/ nf **1** (technique) photography; **faire de la** ~ (en amateur) to take photos; (en professionnel) to be a photographer; **2** (image) photo, picture; **être pris en** ~ to be photographed
(Composés) ~ **d'identité** passport photo; ~ **de mode** fashion photo
(Idiome) **(il) y a pas** ~○ it's clear-cut

photocomposeuse /fɔtokɔ̃pozøz/ nf filmsetter GB, photocomposer US

photocomposition /fɔtokɔ̃pozisjɔ̃/ nf film setting GB, photocomposition US

photocopie /fɔtokɔpi/ nf **1** (copie) photocopy; **2** (procédé) photocopying; **3** (service) photocopying service

photocopier /fɔtokɔpje/ [2] vtr to photocopy, to xerox® US

photocopieur /fɔtokɔpjœR/ nm photocopier

photocopieuse /fɔtokɔpjøz/ nf photocopier

photoélectrique /fɔtoelɛktRik/ adj photoelectric

photogénique /fɔtoʒenik/ adj photogenic

photographe /fɔtogRaf/ ▸ p. 372 nmf **1** (qui prend des photos) photographer; **2** (commerçant) **aller chez le** ~ to go to the camera shop GB ou store US
(Composé) ~ **de plateau** stills man

photographie /fɔtogRafi/ nf **1** (technique) photography; **2** (image) photograph, picture; **3** fig picture
(Composés) ~ **aérienne** (technique) aerial photography; (cliché) aerial photograph; ~ **d'art** art photography; ~ **de plateau** Cin still

photographier /fɔtogRafje/ [2] vtr **1** (prendre en photo) to photograph, to take a photo of [personne, lieu]; **se faire** ~ to have one's photo ou picture taken; **2** (mémoriser) to fix [sth/sb] in one's mind [endroit, personne]

photographique /fɔtogRafik/ adj photographic

photogravure /fɔtogRavyR/ nf photoengraving

photomaton® /fɔtomatɔ̃/ nm (appareil) photo booth

photophore /fɔtofɔR/ nm (de mineur, spéléologue) miner's lamp; (décoratif) (decorative) candle holder

photostyle /fɔtostil/ nm light pen

photothèque /fɔtotɛk/ nf **1** (lieu) picture library; **2** (collection) photographic collection

phrase /fRaz/ nf **1** Ling (assemblage de mots) sentence; **2** (propos) phrase; **avoir une** ~ **malheureuse** to say the wrong thing; **faire des** ~s **ou de grandes** ~s to use flowery language; **pas de** ~s no fine phrases; **tour de** ~ turn of phrase; **3** Mus phrase
(Composé) ~ **toute faite** stock phrase, set expression

phrasé /fRaze/ nm Mus phrasing

phrastique /fRastik/ adj phrasal

phréatique /fReatik/ adj **nappe** ~ ground water **C**

phtisie† /ftizi/ nf consumption, phthisis spéc

phylactère /filaktɛR/ nm **1** (de bande dessinée) speech ou thought bubble; **2** Art phylactery, scroll; **3** (étui) phylactery

physicien, -ienne /fizisjɛ̃, ɛn/ ▸ p. 372 nm,f physicist

physiologie /fizjɔlɔʒi/ nf **1** (science) physiology (de of); **2** (structure) liter anatomy (de of)

physiologique /fizjɔlɔʒik/ adj physiological

physiologiste /fizjɔlɔʒist/ ▸ p. 372 nmf physiologist

physionomie /fizjɔnɔmi/ nf (traits du visage) facial appearance, physiognomy sout; (visage) face; fig (de pays) face; (de quartier) appearance, look; ~ **politique d'un pays** political complexion of a country; ~ **du marché** Fin state of the market

physionomiste /fizjɔnɔmist/ nmf **1** gén **c'est un bon** ~ (doué de mémoire) he has a good memory for faces; (qui sait juger) he's a good judge of faces; **2** ▸ p. 372 (profession) casino employee responsible for recognizing people who are banned from gaming halls

physiothérapie /fizjoteRapi/ nf physiotherapy GB, physical therapy US

physique¹ /fizik/
A adj physical; **pour les cyclistes, c'est une étape très** ~ for cyclists, this stage is physically very taxing; **un acteur qui a un jeu très** ~ an actor with a very physical way of acting; **le squash provoque une énorme dépense** ~ squash is a very strenuous game
B nm (apparence) physical appearance; (corps) physique; **avoir un** ~ **séduisant** to look attractive; **jouer de son** ~ to play on one's good looks; **au** ~ physically
(Idiome) **avoir le** ~ **de l'emploi** to look the part

physique² /fizik/ nf (discipline) physics (+ v sg)

physiquement /fizikmã/ adv physically

phytothérapeute /fitoteRapøt/ ▸ p. 372 nmf herbalist

phytothérapie /fitoteRapi/ nf herbal medicine

piaf○ /pjaf/ nm (petit oiseau) little bird

piaffer /pjafe/ [1] vi **1** [cheval] to paw the ground; **2** [personne] to be impatient (**de faire** to do); ~ **d'impatience** to be champing at the bit

piailler /pjɑje/ [1] vi **1** [oiseau] to chirp; **2** [personne] to squeal

pianiste /pjanist/ nmf **1** ▸ p. 372 (professionnel) pianist; **un** ~ **de talent** a talented pianist; **2** (amateur) piano player

pianistique /pjanistik/ adj **1** (de pianiste) [technique, qualité] pianistic; **2** (de piano) [musique, études] piano

piano /pjano/
A nm **1** ▸ p. 389 (instrument) piano; **jouer qch au** ~ to play sth on the piano; **se mettre au** ~ (s'asseoir) to sit down at the piano; (apprendre) to take up the piano; **2** (passage joué doucement) piano passage
B adv **1** Mus piano; **2** ○fig gently; **vas-y** ~ take it easy
(Composés) ~ **bastringue** honky-tonk piano; ~ **de concert** concert grand (piano); ~ **crapaud** small baby grand; ~ **demi-queue** boudoir grand GB, parlor grand US; ~ **droit** upright piano; ~ **numérique** player piano; ~ **quart de queue** baby grand; ~ **à queue** grand piano

pianoforte /pjanofɔRte/ ▸ p. 389 nm pianoforte

pianoter /pjanɔte/ [1] vi **1** (sur un piano) to tinkle; **2** (sur un ordinateur, une machine à écrire) to tap (**sur** at); **je pianote sur mon clavier toute la journée** I tap away at the keyboard all day long; **3** (sur une table) to drum one's fingers

piastre /pjastR/ ▸ p. 34 nf **1** gén piastreᴳᴮ; **2** C (dollar) dollar

piauler /pjole/ [1] vi **1** (oiseau) to cheep; **2** ○(enfant) to bawl○

PIB /peibe/ nm: abbr ▸ **produit**

pic /pik/
A nm **1** (montagne, sommet) peak; **2** (outil) pick; (de mineur) pickaxeᴳᴮ; **3** (de courbe) peak; ~ **de pollution** air pollution peak; **4** (oiseau) woodpecker
B **à pic** loc adj [falaise] sheer; [ravin] very steep
C **à pic** loc adv **1** (en pente raide) **s'élever à** ~ to rise sheer; **tomber à** ~ to fall in a sheer drop; **couler à** ~ [personne, objet] to go straight down; **2** ○fig **tomber à** ~ to come just at the right time

pichenette /piʃnɛt/ nf flick; **enlever une poussière d'une** ~ to flick off a speck of dust

pichet /piʃɛ/ nm **1** (cruche) jug GB, pitcher; **2** (contenu) jugful GB, pitcherful

pick-up○ /pikœp/ nm inv record player

picorer /pikɔRe/ [1]
A vtr [oiseau] to peck at [graines]
B vi [oiseau] to peck about; [personne] to nibble

picotement /pikɔtmã/ nm (de peau, membres) tingling **C**; (de gorge) tickling **C**; (d'yeux) smarting **C**

picoter /pikɔte/ [1]
A vtr **1** (irriter) [fumée, gaz, vent] to sting, to make [sth] sting [yeux, nez]; to tickle [gorge]; **j'ai la gorge qui me picote** my

throat is tickling; **2** (piquer) [*oiseau*] to peck [*fruit, pain*]
B vi [*gorge*] to tickle; [*yeux*] to sting

picotin /pikɔtɛ̃/ nm **1** (ration) ~ **d'avoine** ration of oats; **2** (mesure) peck

picrate /pikʀat/ nm **1** ◑(vin) plonk◯ GB, cheap wine; **2** Chimie picrate

pictural, -e, *mpl* **-aux** /piktyʀal, o/ adj pictorial

pie /pi/
A ▸ p. 140 adj inv [*vache*] black and white; ~ **noir** [*cheval*] piebald; ~ **alezan** [*cheval*] skewbald; **la race** ~ **rouge** (bovin) breed of red and white cattle
B nf **1** (oiseau) magpie; **2** ◯(bavard) chatterbox◯

pièce /pjɛs/
A nf **1** (d'habitation) room; **maison de quatre** ~**s** four-room(ed) house (*excluding kitchen and bathroom*); **2** ▸ p. 34 (monnaie) ~ **(de monnaie)** coin; **donner** or **glisser la** ~ **à qn** to give sb a tip; **3** Théât play; Littérat, Mus piece; **4** (morceau) bit, piece; **en** ~**s** in bits; **mettre en** ~**s** (briser) to smash [sth] to pieces; (déchirer) to pull [sth] to pieces; fig to pull [sth/sb] to pieces; **5** (élément d'un assemblage) part; **créé de toutes** ~**s** fig created from nothing; **c'est forgé** or **inventé de toutes** ~**s** fig it's a complete fabrication; **6** (pour réparer) patch; **7** (document) document; **juger (avec)** ~**s à l'appui** to judge on the basis of supporting documents; ~**s jointes** enclosures; **juger sur** ~**s** to judge on the actual evidence; **8** (unité, objet) piece, item; (de jeu d'échecs, puzzle) piece; **vendu à la** ~ sold separately *ou* individually; **travailler à la** ~ or **aux** ~**s** to do piecework; **9** (d'étoffe) length; ~ **de bois** piece of timber; ~ **de viande** (large) piece of meat; ~ **de terre** field, piece of land; **une belle** ~ **de poisson** a fine fish
B **-pièces** (*in compounds*) **1** (habitation) **un trois-**~**s cuisine** a three-roomed flat GB *ou* apartment US with kitchen; **2** (vêtement) **un (maillot) deux-**~**s** a two-piece swimsuit
(Composés) ~ **d'artillerie** cannon; ~ **de collection** collector's item; ~ **à conviction** exhibit; ~ **d'eau** ornamental lake; (plus petit) ornamental pond; ~ **détachée** spare part; **en** ~**s détachées** (en kit) in kit form; (démonté) dismantled; ~ **d'identité** identity papers (*pl*); ~ **maîtresse** (de collection) showpiece; (de plaidoyer) key element; (de politique) cornerstone; ~ **montée** *pyramid-shaped arrangement of cream puffs*; ~ **de musée** museum piece; ~ **de théâtre** play; ~ **de vin** cask of wine
(Idiomes) **il est tout d'une** ~ he's a very straightforward man; **on n'est pas aux** ~**s** we're not in a sweat-shop

piécette /pjesɛt/ nf small coin

pied /pje/ nm **1** ▸ p. 136 gén foot; **marcher avec les** ~**s tournés en dedans/en dehors** to be pigeon-toed/splay-footed; **être** ~**s nus** to be barefoot(ed); **il était** ~**s nus dans ses chaussures** his feet were bare inside his shoes; **sauter à** ~**s joints** lit to jump with one's feet together; fig to jump in with both feet; **coup de** ~ kick; **donner un coup de** ~ **à qn** to kick sb; **casser qch à coups de** ~ to kick sth to pieces; **écarter qch d'un coup de** ~ to kick sth aside; **à** ~ gén on foot; **promenade à** ~ walk; **randonnée à** ~ ramble; **bottes aux** ~**s** wearing boots; **traîner les** ~**s** lit, fig to drag one's feet; **ne plus tenir sur ses** ~**s** to be about to keel over; **taper du** ~ (de colère) to stamp one's foot; (d'impatience) to tap one's feet; **mettre** ~ **à terre** to dismount; **de la tête aux** ~**s, des** ~**s à la tête, de** ~ **en cap** from head to foot, from top to toe; **portrait en** ~ full-length portrait; **statue en** ~ standing figure; **avoir un** ~ **dans l'édition** to have a foothold in publishing; **avoir conscience de là où on met les** ~**s**◯ fig to be aware of what one is letting oneself in for; **sur un** ~ **d'égalité** on an equal footing; **2** (d'animal) gén foot; (de cheval) hoof; Culin trotter; **animaux sur** ~ livestock **⊄** on the hoof; **3** (de colline, d'escalier) foot, bottom; (de colonne) foot, base; **4** (de meuble) (totalité) leg; (extrémité) foot; (de verre) stem; (de lampe) base; (d'appareil photo) gén stand; (trépied) tripod; (de champignon) stalk; **5** (plant) head; ~ **de vigne** vine; **récolte sur** ~ standing crop; **6** ▸ p. 347 (unité de longueur) foot
(Composés) ~ **à coulisse** calliper rule; ~ **de lit** footboard
(Idiomes) ~ **à** ~ inch by inch; **être sur** ~ [*personne*] to be up and about; [*affaires*] to be up and running; **mettre qch sur** ~ to set sth up; **j'ai** ~ I can touch the bottom; **je n'ai plus** ~ I'm out of my depth; **perdre** ~ lit to go out of one's depth; fig to lose ground; **être à** ~ **d'œuvre** to be ready to get down to work; **je me suis débrouillé comme un** ~◯

I've made a mess of it; **elle joue au tennis comme un** ~◯ she's hopeless at tennis; **faire un** ~ **de nez à qn** to thumb one's nose at sb; **faire un** ~ **de nez aux conventions** to cock a snook at conventions; **faire du** ~ **à qn** to play footsy with sb◯; **faire des** ~**s et des mains**◑ **pour obtenir qch** to work really hard at getting sth; **ça lui fera les** ~**s**◯ that will teach him/her a lesson; **c'est le** ~◯ (très bien) that's terrific◯; **c'est pas le** ~ **aujourd'hui**◑ things aren't so hot today◯; **prendre son** ~◑ to have a good time; **mettre à** ~ (mesure disciplinaire) to suspend; (mesure économique) to lay [sb] off; **lever le** ~◯ (aller moins vite) to slow down; (s'arrêter) to stop

pied-à-terre /pjetatɛʀ/ nm inv pied-à-terre

pied-bot, *pl* **pieds-bots** /pjebo/ nm club-footed person

pied-de-biche, *pl* **pieds-de-biche** /pjedbiʃ/ nm **1** (de machine à coudre) presser foot; **2** (levier) crowbar; **3** (arrache-clous) claw head

pied-de-poule, *pl* **pieds-de-poule** /pjedpul/ adj inv houndstooth

piédestal, *pl* **-aux** /pjedɛstal, o/ nm pedestal

pied-noir◯, *pl* **pieds-noirs** /pjenwaʀ/ nmf pied-noir (*French colonial born in Algeria*)

piège /pjɛʒ/ nm **1** lit, fig trap; **relever un** ~ to check a trap; **pris au** ~ trapped; **tendre un** ~ **à qn** to set a trap for sb; **être pris à son propre** ~ to fall into one's own trap; ~ **à loups** mantrap; **2** (difficulté) pitfall; **c'est un texte sans** ~ it's a straightforward text; ~**s orthographiques** tricky spellings

piégé, -e /pjeʒe/ adj [*objet, valise*] booby-trapped; **lettre** ~**e** letter bomb; **colis** ~ parcel GB *ou* package US bomb; **voiture** ~**e** car bomb

piéger /pjeʒe/ [15] vtr **1** lit to trap [*animal, criminel*]; **se faire** or **se laisser** ~ to get trapped; **2** (tromper) to trick, to trap [*personne*]; **3** to booby-trap [*lettre, voiture*]

pie-grièche, *pl* **pies-grièches** /piɡʀijɛʃ/ nf shrike

piercing /piʀsiŋ/ nm body piercing; **il a un** ~ **sur la langue** he has a tongue stud

pierraille /pjɛʀaj/ nf loose stones (*pl*)

pierre /pjɛʀ/ nf **1** (matière) stone; **2** (morceau) stone, rock; **un désert de** ~**s** a rocky *ou* stony wilderness; **'chute de** ~**s'** 'falling rocks'; **poser la première** ~ to lay the foundation stone; fig to lay the foundations (**de** of); **être amateur de vieilles** ~**s** fig to be fascinated by old buildings; **3** (immobilier) property GB, real-estate US
(Composés) ~ **à aiguiser** whetstone; ~ **angulaire** lit, fig cornerstone; ~ **à briquet** flint; ~ **fine** gemstone; ~ **à fusil** gun flint; ~ **de taille** dressed stone; ~ **tombale** tombstone, gravestone
(Idiomes) **jeter la** ~ **à qn** to accuse sb; **apporter sa** ~ **à qch** to make one's contribution to sth; **faire d'une** ~ **deux coups** to kill two birds with one stone

pierreries /pjɛʀʀi/ nfpl gems

pierreux, -euse /pjɛʀø, øz/ adj stony (épith)

piétaille /pjetaj/ nf pej **la** ~ the underlings (*pl*) péj

piété /pjete/ nf piety; **de** ~ [*articles*] devotional

piétinement /pjetinmɑ̃/ nm **1** (mouvement) **le** ~ **de la foule dans les rues en fête** the crowd shuffling through the festive streets; **2** (bruit) **les** ~**s dans le couloir** the sound (sg) of feet in the corridor; **3** (de négociations, d'enquête) lack of progress

piétiner /pjetine/ [1]
A vtr lit to trample [sth] underfoot [*bouquet, fraisiers*]; fig to trample on [*droits, croyances*]; ~ **le sol** to stamp one's feet
B vi **1** (sur place) ~ **d'impatience** to hop up and down with impatience; **2** (marcher lentement) (à cause de la foule) to shuffle along; (à cause de la neige) to trudge along; **3** fig [*négociations, enquête*] to make no headway; **je piétine** I'm not getting anywhere

piéton, -onne /pjetɔ̃, ɔn/
A adj [*rue, zone, voie*] pedestrianized
B nm,f pedestrian; **passage pour** ~**s** pedestrian crossing

piétonnier, -ière /pjetɔnje, ɛʀ/ adj **1** [*rue, zone, voie*] pedestrianized; **2** [*circulation*] pedestrian (épith)

piètre /pjɛtʀ/ adj [*acteur, écrivain*] very mediocre; [*santé, résultats*] very poor; [*avantage*] negligible; [*performance*] sorry; **c'est une** ~ **consolation** it's not much comfort; **avoir** ~ **allure** to cut a sorry figure

pieu, pl ~**x**¹ /pjø/ nm **1)** (poteau pointu) stake; **2)** Archit, Constr pile

pieuse ▸ pieux²

pieusement /pjøzmɑ̃/ adv **1)** Relig piously; **2)** (avec respect) devotedly; ~ **conservé** religiously kept

pieuvre /pjœvʀ/ nf **1)** Zool octopus; **2)** (entreprise tentaculaire) octopus

pieux², **pieuse** /pjø, øz/ adj **1)** Relig [personne] pious, religious; [livre] pious; [peinture] religious; **avoir une pensée pieuse pour qn** to remember sb in one's prayers; **2)** liter [devoirs] loving; [affection, silence] reverent

(Composé) ~ **mensonge** white lie

pif⁰ /pif/ nm **1)** (nez) nose, conk⁰ GB, schnozzle⁰ US; **2)** (flair) intuition; **j'ai eu du** ~ I had a hunch⁰; **au** ~ [mesurer] roughly; [trouver] by chance; [décider] just like that

(Idiome) **avoir qn dans le** ~ to have it in for sb⁰

pige /piʒ/ nf **1)** (dans la presse) **travailler à la** ~, **faire des** ~**s** to do freelance work; **2)** (tige) measuring rod; (longueur) length

pigeon /piʒɔ̃/ nm **1)** (oiseau) pigeon; **2)** ⁰(naïf) sucker⁰

(Composés) ~ **d'argile** clay pigeon; ~ **ramier** wood pigeon, ring dove; ~ **vole** Simon says; **jouer à** ~ **vole** to play Simon says; ~ **voyageur** carrier pigeon

pigeonnant, ~**e** /piʒɔnɑ̃, ɑ̃t/ adj [soutien-gorge] uplift (épith); [poitrine] with a lot of cleavage (épith, après n)

pigeonneau, pl ~**x** /piʒɔno/ nm young pigeon

pigeonnier /piʒɔnje/ nm **1)** (pour pigeons) gén pigeon house; (en haut d'un bâtiment) pigeon loft; (bâtiment circulaire) dovecote; **2)** (appartement) hum garret

piger⁰ /piʒe/ [13] vtr (comprendre) to understand; **tu as pigé?** did you get it?; **je ne pige rien à l'informatique** I haven't got a clue⁰ about computing

pigiste /piʒist/ nmf freelance

pigment /pigmɑ̃/ nm pigment

pigmenter /pigmɑ̃te/ [1] vtr [soleil, maladie] to alter the pigmentation of [peau]

pigne /piɲ/ nf pine cone

pignon /piɲɔ̃/ nm **1)** (de maison) gable; **2)** (roue dentée) gearwheel, cogwheel; (petite roue) pinion; **3)** (de pin) pine kernel

(Idiome) **avoir** ~ **sur rue** to be well-established

pilaf /pilaf/ nm pilau; **riz** ~ pilau rice

pile¹⁰ /pil/ adv **1)** (brusquement) **s'arrêter** ~ to stop dead; **2)** (exactement) exactly; **à 10 heures et demie** ~ at ten-thirty sharp ou on the dot⁰; **être** ~ **à l'heure** to be right on time; **tu tombes** ~ (au bon moment) you've come just at the right time; (la personne qu'il faut) you're just the person I wanted to see; **tu es tombé** ~ (en devinant) you hit the nail on the head⁰; **ça tombe** ~ (au bon moment) that's lucky; **elle est arrivée** ~ **au moment où je devais partir** she turned up precisely as I was about to leave; **c'est tombé** ~ **dans mon assiette** it fell right into my plate

pile² /pil/ nf **1)** (tas) (désordonné) pile; (régulier) stack; **2)** Électrotech ~ **(électrique)** battery; **à** ~**s** [jouet, réveil] battery-operated (épith); **3)** Archit (de pont) pier; **4)** (de monnaie) **le côté** ~ the reverse side; **jouer à** ~ **ou face** to play heads or tails; **ils ont décidé à** ~ **ou face** (choix de personne) they tossed for it; (choix d'option) they decided it on the flip ou toss of the coin

(Composés) ~ **bouton** button battery; ~ **solaire** solar cell

pile-poil⁰ /pilpwal/ adv exactly; **arriver** ~ to arrive bang on time⁰

piler /pile/ [1]
A vtr to grind [noix]; to crush [gousse d'ail, verre]
B ⁰vi (s'arrêter net) [voiture] to pull up short, to stop suddenly; [conducteur] to slam on the brakes

pileux, -**euse** /pilø, øz/ adj **système** ~ hair

pilier /pilje/ nm **1)** Constr pillar; **2)** fig (d'économie) mainstay; (personne) (de communauté) pillar; (de parti) stalwart; ~ **de bar** bar fly⁰; **3)** (au rugby) prop forward

pillage /pijaʒ/ nm **1)** (de ville, région) pillage, plundering; (de magasins) looting; **2)** (des caisses de l'État) pillaging; **3)** (plagiat) plagiarism

pillard, ~**e** /pijaʀ, aʀd/
A adj [hordes, bandes] pillaging, plundering; [oiseaux] thieving
B nm,f looter

piller /pije/ [1] vtr **1)** (dépouiller) to pillage [ville]; to loot [magasin]; to ransack [maison, réfrigérateur]; **2)** (voler) to pillage [objets d'art]; to plunder [temple, caisse]; **3)** (plagier) to plagiarize [œuvre, auteur]

pilleur, -**euse** /pijœʀ, øz/ nm,f (de magasin) looter; (d'église) plunderer

pilon /pilɔ̃/ nm **1)** (outil) pestle; **2)** (jambe de bois) wooden leg; **3)** (de volaille) drumstick; **4)** (dans l'édition) pulping; **mettre qch au** ~ to pulp sth

pilonnage /pilɔnaʒ/ nm Mil bombardment

pilonner /pilɔne/ [1] vtr **1)** Mil to bombard; **2)** (écraser) to grind, to pound [graines, céréales]; **3)** ⁰Sport to give [sb] a pounding⁰ [adversaire, équipe]; to pound away at [buts]; **4)** (dans l'édition) to pulp

pilori /piloʀi/ nm Hist stocks (pl); **mettre qn au** ~ fig to pillory sb

pilosité /pilozite/ nf hairiness **C**

pilotage /pilotaʒ/ nm **1)** Aviat, Naut piloting **C**; Aut driving **C**; **erreur de** ~ pilot error; **le** ~ **à trois** flying with two co-pilots; **2)** (gestion) (d'entreprise) running **C**; (de négociation) leading **C**

pilote /pilot/
A nm **1)** ▸ p. 372 Aviat, Naut pilot; Aut driver; **2)** (guide) guide; **servir de** ~ **à qn** to show sb around
B (-)**pilote** (in compounds) **projet(-)**~⁰ pilot project

(Composés) ~ **automatique** automatic pilot; ~ **automobile** racing driver; ~ **de chasse** fighter pilot; ~ **de course** = ~ **automobile**; ~ **d'essai** test pilot; ~ **de ligne** airline pilot

piloter /pilote/ [1]
A vtr **1)** lit to pilot [avion, navire]; to drive [voiture]; **2)** fig to show [sb] around [personne]; to run [entreprise]; to lead [négociation]
B vi **1)** Aviat to fly; ~ **à deux** to fly with dual controls; **2)** Aut to drive

pilotis /piloti/ nm inv stilts (pl), pilotis (pl) spéc

pilule /pilyl/ nf **1)** (médicament) pill; **2)** (contraceptif) ~ **(contraceptive)** (contraceptive) pill; ~ **abortive** abortion pill; **je prends la** ~ I'm on the pill

(Idiomes) **avaler la** ~⁰ to grin and bear it; **faire passer la** ~⁰ to sweeten the pill; **dorer la** ~ **à qn** to butter sb up; **se dorer la** ~⁰ to sunbathe

pilulier /pilylje/ nm pillbox

pimbêche /pɛ̃bɛʃ/ nf stuck-up madam⁰

piment /pimɑ̃/ nm **1)** (plante) capsicum; **2)** (condiment) hot pepper; **le risque met du** ~ **dans la vie** fig danger adds a bit of spice to life

(Composés) ~ **doux** sweet pepper; ~ **rouge** red hot pepper, chilli; ~ **vert** hot pepper

pimenter /pimɑ̃te/ [1] vtr **1)** Culin to put chilliesᴳᴮ in, to put chilliᴳᴮ powder in [plat]; **un plat très pimenté** a very hot dish; **2)** (animer) to give a bit of spice to [situation, réunion, spectacle]

pimpant, ~**e** /pɛ̃pɑ̃, ɑ̃t/ adj [personne] spruce, smart; [voiture] smart

pimprenelle /pɛ̃pʀənɛl/ nf burnet

pin /pɛ̃/ nm pine (tree); **du bois de** ~ pine

pinacle /pinakl/ nm Archit pinnacle

(Idiomes) **porter** or **mettre qn au** ~ to praise sb to the skies; **être au** ~ to be at the top

pinacothèque /pinakɔtɛk/ nf art gallery

pinailler⁰ /pinaje/ [1] vi to split hairs, to quibble (**sur** about)

pince /pɛ̃s/
A nf **1)** (outil) (de plombier, d'électricien) pliers (pl), pair of pliers; (de forgeron) tongs (pl), pair of tongs; **2)** (en couture) dart; **un pantalon à** ~**s** pleat front trousers (pl) GB ou pants (pl) US; **3)** (de crabe) pincer, claw; (dent de cheval) incisor; **4)** (levier) crowbar
B **pinces**⁰ nfpl **être à** ~**s** to be on foot

(Composés) ~ **à cheveux** hair grip; ~ **coupante** wire cutters (pl); ~ **crocodile** crocodile clip; ~ **à dessin** bulldog clip; ~ **à épiler** tweezers (pl); ~ **à escargot** snail tongs (*pl*); ~ **à glaçons** ice tongs (*pl*); ~ **à linge** clothes peg; ~ **multiprise** adjustable pliers (*pl*); ~ **à ongles** nail clippers (*pl*); ~ **à sucre** sugar tongs (*pl*); ~ **universelle** universal pliers (*pl*); ~ **à vélo** bicycle clip

pincé, ~**e¹** /pɛ̃se/ *adj* **1** (contraint) [*sourire*] tight-lipped; **prendre un air** ~ to become stiff *ou* starchy; **2** (serré) [*lèvres*] thin; [*narines*] pinched

pinceau, *pl* ~**x** /pɛ̃so/ *nm* **1** (instrument) (paint) brush; **donner un coup de** ~ **à qch** to give sth a lick of paint; **2** (manière de peindre) brushwork; **3** (faisceau) ~ **lumineux** pencil beam

pincée² /pɛ̃se/ *nf* (de poivre, sel) pinch (**de** of)

pincement /pɛ̃smɑ̃/ *nm* **1** (de peau) pinch; **avoir un** ~ **de cœur** fig to feel a twinge of sadness; **2** Mus (de corde) plucking

pince-monseigneur, *pl* **pinces-monseigneur** /pɛ̃smɔ̃sɛɲœʀ/ *nf* (levier) jemmy GB, slim jim US

pincer /pɛ̃se/ [12]
A *vtr* **1** (pour faire mal) [*personne*] to pinch; [*crabe*] to nip; **2** (attraper) to nab○, to catch [*voleur, criminel*]; **3** (serrer) ~ **les lèvres** *or* **la bouche** to purse (up) one's lips; **une veste qui pince la taille** a jacket which hugs the waist; **4** Mus to pluck [*corde*]
B ○*vi* [*vent, froid*] to be nippy○
C **se pincer** *vpr* **1** (accidentellement) to catch oneself; **elle s'est pincée en refermant le tiroir** she caught her fingers closing the drawer; **2** (volontairement) to pinch oneself; **j'ai dû me** ~ **pour y croire** I had to pinch myself to make sure I wasn't dreaming; **se** ~ **le nez** to hold one's nose

(Idiome) **en** ~○ **pour qn** to be stuck○ on sb, to be in love with sb

pince-sans-rire /pɛ̃sɑ̃ʀiʀ/ *nmf inv* **c'est un** ~ he has a deadpan sense of humour○ᴳᴮ

pincette /pɛ̃sɛt/ *nf* **1** (petite pince) tweezers (*pl*), pair of tweezers; **2** (de cheminée) fire tongs (*pl*)

(Idiome) **il n'est pas à prendre avec des** ~**s**○ he's like a bear with a sore head

pinçon /pɛ̃sɔ̃/ *nm* pinch-mark

pinède /pinɛd/ *nf* pine forest

pingouin /pɛ̃gwɛ̃/ *nm* auk; (manchot) controv penguin; **grand** ~ great auk; **petit** ~ razorbill

ping-pong®, *pl* ~**s** /piŋpɔ̃g/ ▸ p. 327 *nm* **1** (jeu) table tennis, ping-pong; **2** (table) table tennis table

pingre /pɛ̃gʀ/
A *adj* stingy, niggardly
B *nmf* skinflint

pingrerie /pɛ̃gʀəʀi/ *nf* stinginess

pin-pon /pɛ̃pɔ̃/ *nm* (also onomat) *sound of a two-tone siren*

pin's /pins/ *nm inv* controv lapel badge

pinson /pɛ̃sɔ̃/ *nm* chaffinch

(Idiome) **gai comme un** ~ as happy as a lark

pintade /pɛ̃tad/ *nf* guinea fowl

pintadeau, *pl* ~**x** /pɛ̃tado/ *nm* young guinea fowl

pinte /pɛ̃t/ *nf* ▸ p. 87 (mesure anglo-saxonne) pint; (ancienne mesure) ≈ US quart (= 0,94 litre)

(Idiome) **se payer une** ~ **de bon sang**○ (rire) to have a good laugh

pinter○: **se pinter** /pɛ̃te/ [1] *vpr* (s'enivrer) to get plastered○ *ou* drunk

pin-up /pinœp/ *nf inv* (personne) glamour girl

pioche /pjɔʃ/ *nf* **1** (de cultivateur) mattock; (de terrassier) pick-axe; **2** Jeux stock

piocher /pjɔʃe/ [1]
A *vtr* **1** (creuser) to dig [*sol*]; **2** ○(potasser) to work on [*sujet*]; **3** Jeux to take [sth] from the stock [*carte, domino*]
B *vi* **1** (creuser) to dig; **2** ○(potasser) to study; **3** (prendre) to take [sth] from the stock [*carte, domino*]; **pioche!** (aux cartes) take a card!; (à table) help yourself!, dive in○!; ~ **dans la caisse** to have one's hand in the till

piolet /pjɔlɛ/ *nm* ice axe GB *ou* ax US

pion, pionne /pjɔ̃, pjɔn/
A ○*nm,f* Scol *student paid to supervise pupils*
B *nm* **1** (aux échecs) pawn; (aux dames) draught GB, checker US; **2** fig pawn

pionnier, -ière /pjɔnje, ɛʀ/ *adj, nm,f* pioneer

pipe /pip/ *nf* (à fumer) pipe

(Idiomes) **casser sa** ~○ to die, to kick the bucket○; **se fendre la** ~○ to laugh one's head off○

pipeau, *pl* ~**x** /pipo/ *nm* **1** ▸ p. 389 (petite flûte) (reed-)pipe; **2** (appeau) birdcall

(Idiomes) **c'est du** ~○ it's no great shakes○; **c'est pas du** ~○ it's for real○

pipelette /piplɛt/ *nf* (bavard) gossip(monger)

pipeline /piplin, pajplajn/ *nm* controv pipeline

piper /pipe/ [1] *vtr* **1** ○(dire) **ne pas** ~ (**mot**) not to say a word; **2** Jeux to load [*dés*]; to mark [*cartes*]

piperade /pipeʀad/ *nf*: omelette made with tomatoes and peppers, ≈ Spanish omelette

pipette /pipɛt/ *nf* pipette

pipi○ /pipi/ *nm* wee○ GB, pee○; (langage enfantin) wee-wee○; **faire** ~ **dans sa culotte** to wet oneself; **c'est à faire** ~ **dans sa culotte** fig it's hilarious

(Idiome) **c'est du** ~ **de chat** (boisson) it's gnat's piss○; (spectacle, livre) it's as dull as dishwater

piquant, ~**e** /pikɑ̃, ɑ̃t/
A *adj* **1** [*tige, chardon*] prickly; [*clou*] sharp; [*barbe*] bristly; **2** [*moutarde, sauce*] hot; [*odeur*] pungent; [*vin, fromage*] sharp; **3** [*froid*] biting; [*air*] sharp; **4** [*remarque*] cutting, biting; **5** [*aventure*] spicy, piquant; [*charme*] heady
B *nm* **1** (de tige, chardon) prickle; (de hérisson, cactus) spine; (de barbelés) spike, barb; **2** fig (d'histoire) spiciness; (de situation) piquancy

pique¹ /pik/ *nm* Jeux (carte) spade; (couleur) spades (*pl*)

pique² /pik/ *nf* **1** (parole) cutting remark; **2** (arme) pike; (de picador) lance; **3** (à cocktail) swizzle stick

piqué, ~**e** /pike/
A *pp* ▸ **piquer**
B *pp adj* **1** [*couverture*] quilted; **2** (marqué) [*bois*] worm-eaten; [*linge, miroir, fruit*] spotted; [*papier, livre*] foxed; **un visage** ~ **de taches de rousseur** a face dotted with freckles; **3** (aigre) [*vin*] sour; **4** ○(fou) [*personne*] dotty, eccentric; **5** Mus [*note, phrase*] staccato
C ○*nm,f* (extravagant) nutcase○
D *nm* **1** (tissu) piqué; **2** Aviat (nose)dive; **3** (en danse) piqué; **4** (de photographie) sharpness

pique-assiette○ /pikasjɛt/ *nmf inv* sponger○, free-loader○

pique-feu /pikfø/ *nm inv* poker

pique-nique, *pl* ~**s** /piknik/ *nm* picnic

pique-niquer /piknike/ [1] *vi* to have a picnic

piquer /pike/ [1]
A *vtr* **1** (blesser) [*guêpe, ortie*] to sting; [*moustique, serpent*] to bite; [*chardon, rosier*] to prick; **2** (enfoncer une pointe) [*personne*] to prick [*animal, fruit*]; ~ **un couteau dans le gâteau** to prick the cake with a knife; ~ **des petits pois avec sa fourchette** to stab peas with one's fork; **3** Méd to give [sb] an injection; **je me suis fait** ~ **contre la grippe** I've had a flu injection; **faire** ~ **un animal** to have an animal put down; **4** Culin ~ **un gigot d'ail** to stud a leg of lamb with garlic; ~ **un oignon de clous de girofle** to stick an onion with cloves; **5** (fixer) to stick [*épingle*]; **6** (de trous) [*insecte, ver*] to make holes in [*bois, meuble*]; **7** (irriter) **mon pull me pique la peau** my sweater feels scratchy; **le froid me pique le visage** the cold is making my face tingle; **la fumée me pique la gorge** the smoke is stinging my throat; **ses yeux la piquaient** her eyes were stinging; **ça me pique partout** I'm itchy all over; **8** ○(voler) to pinch○ GB, to steal [*livre, idée*] (**à** from); (emprunter) to pinch○ GB, to borrow [*crayon, pull*]; **il pique (dans les magasins)** he's always pinching things (from shops GB *ou* stores US); **9** ○(arrêter) [*police*] to nab○, to nick○ GB [*bandit*]; (surprendre) to get [*personne*]; **ils se sont fait** ~ **à tricher pendant l'examen** they got caught cheating during the exam; **10** ○(attraper) to catch [*virus*]; **11** to stitch [*tissu, vêtement*]; **12** [*propos*] to needle [*personne*]; to sting [*orgueil, fierté*]; ~ **qn au vif** to cut sb to the quick; **13** (éveiller) to arouse [*curiosité, intérêt*]; ~ **une crise de nerfs** to throw a fit○; ~ **un cent mètres** to break into a run; ~ **un galop** to break into a gallop; **15** (plonger) ~ **une tête (dans l'eau)** to dive (into the water); **16** Mus ~ **une note** to play a note staccato
B *vi* **1** (irriter) [*barbe*] to be bristly; [*vêtement, laine*] to be scratchy; [*gorge, yeux*] to sting; [*vent, froid*] to be biting; **2** (exciter les sens) [*moutarde, sauce*] to be hot; [*vin, fromage*]

to be sharp; [*boisson, soda*]○ to be fizzy○ GB *ou* sparkling; **3** (descendre) [*oiseau*] to swoop down; [*avion*] to dive; **~ du nez** (s'endormir) to nod off, to doze off; (baisser la tête) to look down; (chuter) [*avion*] to go into a nosedive; [*marché, Bourse*] to take a nosedive; [*fleur*] to droop; **4** ○(prendre) **arrête de ~ dans le plat** stop picking (things out of the dish); **pique dans le tas si tu veux** help yourself from the pile; **5** (s'élancer) **le taureau piqua droit sur nous** the bull came straight for us; **il piqua à travers bois** he cut across the woods

C se piquer *vpr* **1** (se blesser) to prick oneself; **se ~ aux ronces** to scratch oneself on the brambles; **se ~ aux orties** to get stung by nettles; **2** (se faire une piqûre) to inject oneself; (se droguer)○ to shoot up○; **3** (se couvrir de taches) [*miroir, linge, métal*] to become spotted; [*papier, livre*] to become foxed; **4** (par prétention) *fml* **se ~ d'être philosophe** to like to pretend one is a philosopher; **se ~ de pouvoir réussir seul** to claim that one can manage on one's own; **5** (se vexer) to take offenceᴳᴮ (**de** at)

(Idiomes) **quelle mouche t'a piqué**○? what's eating○ you?; **son article n'était pas piqué des vers**○ *or* **hannetons**○ his/her article didn't pull any punches; **c'est une petite maison pas piquée des vers**○ *or* **hannetons**○ it's a really lovely little house

piquet /pikɛ/ *nm* **1** (pieu) stake; (très court) peg; (pour slalom) gate pole; (de parasol) pole; **2** (groupe de gens) picket; **3** (punition) **mettre un élève au ~** to make a pupil stand in the corner; **4** ▸ p. 327 (jeu de cartes) piquet

(Composé) **~ de grève** (strike) picket, picket line

(Idiomes) **rester planté comme un ~**○ to stand like a dummy; **raide comme un ~**○ stiff as a post

piqueter /pikte/ [20] *vtr* **1** (pour délimiter) to stake out; **2** (parsemer) to dot; **piqueté de (taches de) rouille** spotted with rust; **ciel piqueté d'étoiles** sky spangled with stars

piquette○ /pikɛt/ *nf* (vin) *pej* plonk○ GB, cheap wine

piqûre /pikyʀ/ *nf* **1** (injection) injection, shot; **faire une ~ à qn** to give sb an injection; **2** (d'épine, épingle) prick; (d'ortie, abeille) sting; (de moustique) bite; **~ d'amour-propre** wound to one's pride; **3** (dans le bois) hole; **4** (petite tache) spot; **~s de rouille** specks *ou* spots of rust; **5** (point) stitch; (couture) stitching **C**

(Composé) **~ de rappel** Méd booster (injection)

piratage /piʀataʒ/ *nm* piracy, pirating; **~ de cartes bancaires** credit card fraud; **~ informatique** (reproduction illégale) electronic piracy; (violation de réseau) computer hacking

pirate /piʀat/
A *adj* [*édition, radio*] pirate (*épith*)
B *nm* Naut pirate

(Composés) **~ de l'air** hijacker, skyjacker; **~ informatique** computer hacker

pirater /piʀate/ [1] *vtr* to pirate

piraterie /piʀatʀi/ *nf* (activité) piracy **C**; (acte) act of piracy

(Composés) **~ aérienne** hijacking, skyjacking; **~ informatique** computer hacking

pire /piʀ/
A *adj* **1** (comparatif) worse (**que** than); **2** (superlatif) worst; **les ~s mensonges** the most wicked lies; **le ~ des imbéciles** the biggest fool; **le ~ des deux** the worse of the two
B *nm* **le ~** the worst; **au ~** at the very worst

(Idiome) **il n'y a ~ eau que l'eau qui dort** Prov still waters run deep Prov

pirogue /piʀɔg/ *nf* dugout canoe, pirogue *spéc*

pirouette /piʀwɛt/ *nf* **1** (tour) pirouette; **les ~s d'un clown** the cavortings of a clown; **2** *fig* (réponse évasive) skilful evasion; (revirement) U-turn, flip-flopᵁˢ; **s'en tirer par une ~** to dodge the question skilfully

pirouetter /piʀwɛte/ [1] *vi* **1** [*danseur*] to pirouette; **~ sur ses talons** to spin on one's heels; **2** (faire volte-face) to do a U-turn

pis /pi/
A *adj inv* liter worse
B *adv* liter worse
C *nm inv* **1** (de vache) udder; **2** liter **le ~** the worst

(Idiome) **dire ~ que pendre de qn** to vilify sb

pis-aller /pizale/ *nm inv* lesser evil; **ces matériaux sont des ~** we'll have to make do with these materials

pisciculteur, -trice /pisikyltœʀ, tʀis/ ▸ p. 372 *nm,f* fish farmer, pisciculturist *spéc*

pisciculture /pisikyltyʀ/ *nf* fish farming, pisciculture *spéc*

piscine /pisin/ *nf* swimming pool; **~ couverte** indoor swimming pool

Pise /piz/ ▸ p. 621 *npr* Pisa

pisé /pize/ *nm* ≈ adobe

pisse• /pis/ *nf* piss•

(Idiome) **c'est de la ~ de chat** *or* **d'âne** (boisson) it's gnat's piss

pissenlit /pisɑ̃li/ *nm* dandelion

(Idiome) **manger les ~s par la racine**• to be pushing up the daisies○

pisser• /pise/ [1]
A *vtr* **~ du sang** to pass blood; **~ le sang** [*personne, nez, blessure*] to pour with blood; **mon moteur pissait l'huile** my engine was leaking oil all over the place
B *vi* **1** (uriner) [*personne, animal*] to pee○, to piss•; **rire à en ~ dans sa culotte** to wet *ou* piss• one's pants laughing; **~ au lit** to wet the bed; **2** (fuir) [*récipient*] to leak; **l'eau pisse de partout** water is pouring out from everywhere

(Idiomes) **il pleut comme vache qui pisse** it's pissing down•; **se regarder** *or* **s'écouter ~, ne plus se sentir ~** to be full of oneself; **ça lui a pris comme une envie de ~** he/she had a sudden urge to do it; **laisse ~!** forget it!

pisseux○, **-euse** /pisø, øz/ *adj* (sale, terne) *pej* dingy

pissotière○ /pisɔtjɛʀ/ *nf* street urinal, pissoir US

pistache /pistaʃ/ *nf* pistachio; **une ~** a pistachio nut

piste /pist/ *nf* **1** (trace) *lit, fig* trail; **être sur une fausse ~** to be on the wrong track; **2** (ensemble d'indices) lead; **3** (de stade, d'autodrome) track; (d'hippodrome) racecourse GB, racetrack US; (de danse) floor; (de patinage) rink; (de cirque) ring; (de ski) slope; (de ski de fond) trail; (pour course automobile) racetrack; **~ d'élan** (au ski) take-off ramp; **~ (de ski) pour débutants** nursery slope; **skier hors ~** to go off-piste skiing; **épreuve sur ~** track event; **faire un tour de ~** to do a lap; **entrer en ~** (au cirque) to come into the ring; *fig* to enter the fray; **en ~!** *fig* get cracking○!; **être en ~** *fig* to be in the running; **4** (chemin) (de brousse) track; (de désert) trail; **5** Aviat runway; **6** (de disque, cassette) track

(Composés) **~ artificielle** (avec neige artificielle) artificial slope; (en matière plastique) dry ski slope; **~ cavalière** bridle path, bridleway; **~ cyclable** (sur une route) cycle lane; (à côté d'une route) cycle way, cycle path; (à la campagne) cycle track

pister /piste/ [1] *vtr* to trail, to track

pistil /pistil/ *nm* pistil

pistolet /pistɔlɛ/ *nm* **1** (arme) pistol, gun; **tirer au ~** to fire a pistol; **2** Tech (outil) gun

(Composés) **~ d'alarme** alarm gun; **~ à peinture** spray gun

pistolet-mitrailleur, *pl* **pistolets-mitrailleurs** /pistɔlɛmitʀajœʀ/ *nm* submachine gun

piston /pistɔ̃/ *nm* **1** Tech piston; **moteur à ~s** piston engine; **2** ○(relations) contacts (*pl*); **avoir du ~** to have connections *ou* contacts in the right places; **il a obtenu son poste par ~** someone pulled strings to get him the job; **3** Mus (d'instrument) valve; **cornet à ~s** cornet

pistonner○ /pistɔne/ [1] *vtr pej* to pull strings for

pitance† /pitɑ̃s/ *nf* fare **C**

piteusement /pitøzmɑ̃/ *adv* pitifully, pathetically

piteux, -euse /pitø, øz/ *adj* **1** (piètre) [*résultats*] poor, pitiful; **en ~ état** in a sorry state; **2** (penaud) [*personne, air*] crestfallen

pitié /pitje/ *nf* (compassion) pity, mercy; **avoir ~ de qn** (plaindre) to feel sorry for sb; (se montrer charitable) to take pity on sb; **ayez ~ de nous!** (soyez bon) take *ou* have pity on us!; (épargnez-nous) have mercy on us!; **prendre qn en ~** to take pity on sb; **il me fait ~** I feel sorry for him; **il fait ~ (à voir)** he's a pitiful sight; **maigre à faire ~** pitifully thin; **ça me fait ~ de la voir dans cet état** it makes me sad to see her in that state; **sans ~** [*vainqueur*] merciless, pitiless; [*huer, critiquer*] mercilessly; [*concurrence*] ruthless; **un monde sans ~** a cruel world; **par ~, tais-toi!** for pity's sake, be quiet!; **~ pour nos forêts!** save our forests!; **~ pour mes pauvres oreilles!** think of my poor ears!; **regarder qn avec ~** to look pityingly at sb

piton /pitɔ̃/ *nm* ⚊ (à crochet) hook; (à anneau) eye; ⚋ (d'alpinisme) piton; ⚌ Géog peak

pitoyable /pitwajabl/ *adj* ⚊ (digne de pitié) pitiful; ⚋ (lamentable) pathetic

pitoyablement /pitwajabləmɑ̃/ *adv* ⚊ (de façon pitoyable) pitifully; ⚋ (lamentablement) [*échouer*] miserably; [*chanter*] pathetically

pitre /pitʀ/ *nm* clown, buffoon

pitrerie /pitʀəʀi/ *nf* clowning ¢

pittoresque /pitɔʀɛsk/
A *adj* [*lieu*] picturesque; [*personnage, scène*] colourfulᴳᴮ; [*expression, œuvre*] vivid
B *nm* le ~ the picturesque; le ~ de qch the picturesque quality of sth, the vividness of sth; le ~ dans tout cela the amusing thing about all that

pivert /pivɛʀ/ *nm* green woodpecker

pivoine /pivwan/ *nf* peony

⸤Idiome⸥ **être rouge comme une** ~ to be as red as a beetroot GB *ou* a beet US

pivot /pivo/ *nm* ⚊ Tech pivot; ⚋ fig (d'économie) linchpin; (de complot) kingpin; **société** ~ key firm; ⚌ Sport (joueur) pivot, post; ⚍ (de dent) post and core

pivotant, ~**e** /pivotɑ̃, ɑ̃t/ *adj* [*fauteuil*] swivel; [*panneau*] pivoting; [*porte*] revolving

pivoter /pivote/ [1] *vi* [*personne, animal*] to pivot, to turn; [*panneau, mur*] to pivot; [*porte, table*] to revolve; [*fauteuil, chaise*] to swivel

PJ /peʒi/ *nf: abbr* ▸ **police**

PL (*written abbr* = **poids lourd**) HGV GB, heavy truck US

placage /plakaʒ/ *nm* ⚊ (revêtement) (en bois) veneer; (en métal) plating; (en pierre) facing; ⚋ Sport tackling ¢

placard /plakaʀ/ *nm* ⚊ (meuble) cupboard; **ranger** *or* **mettre au** ~ fig (de côté) to put [sth] on ice [*projet*]; to shunt [sb] aside [*personne*]; (au rebut) to ditch [*projet*]; to pension [sb] off [*personne*]; **sortir du** ~ fig to come in from the cold; ⚋ (affiche) poster, bill; (dans un journal) ~ **publicitaire** display advertisement; ⚌ (épreuve) galley (proof); ⚍ ○(prison) clink○

placarder /plakaʀde/ [1] *vtr* ⚊ (afficher) to post, to stick [*avis, affiche, photo*]; ⚋ (décorer) to cover [sth] with posters [*mur*]

place /plas/ *nf* ⚊ (espace) room, space; **laisser de la** ~ to leave enough space; ⚋ (emplacement, espace défini) gén place; (pour s'asseoir) seat; **les dictionnaires ne sont pas à leur** ~ the dictionaries aren't where they should be; **deux** ~**s pour 'Le Lac des Cygnes'** two tickets for 'Swan Lake'; **la** ~ **d'un mot dans une phrase** the position of a word in a sentence; **il faut savoir rester à sa** ~ you must know your place; **tenir une grande** ~ **dans la vie de qn** to play a large part in sb's life; **faire une large** ~ **à qch** to put a lot of emphasis on sth; **notre travail laisse peu de** ~ **à l'imagination** our work leaves little room for the imagination; **faire** ~ **à** to give way to; ~ **aux jeunes** *or* **à la jeunesse!** lit, fig make way for the young!; **il reste une** ~ **en première** there's one seat left in first class; **une salle de 200** ~**s** a 200 seat auditorium; **payer sa** ~ (au cinéma, théâtre) to pay for one's ticket; (dans un train etc) to pay one's fare; **les** ~**s sont chères** fig (parking difficile) parking spaces are hard to find; (âpre concurrence dans l'emploi) jobs are hard to come by; **prenez** ~ (sur un siège) take a seat; (chacun à son siège) take your seats; (chacun à son poste) take your places; **sur** ~ [*aller*] to the scene; [*arriver*] on the scene; [*étudier*] on the spot; **on se retrouve sur** ~ we'll meet up there; **ouvrage à consulter sur** ~ reference book; **laisser qn sur** ~ to leave sb standing; **de** ~ **en** ~ here and there; **divan à trois** ~**s** three-seater sofa; **un parking de 500** ~**s** a car park for 500 cars; ⚌ (dans un classement) place; (dans un ordre) position; **il est dans les premières** ~**s** he's up toward(s) the top; ⚍ (substitution) **à la** ~ **de** instead of, in place of; **il a mis de la vodka à la** ~ **du cognac** he's used vodka instead of brandy; **qu'aurais-tu fait à ma** ~? what would you have done in my place?; **(si j'étais) à ta** ~ if I were in your position *ou* shoes; **je ne peux pas le faire à ta** ~! I can't do it for you!; **j'ai mis le vase à la** ~ **du cendrier** I put the vase where the ashtray was; ⚎ (situation définie) **en** ~ [*système, structures*] in place (*après n*); [*troupes*] in position (*après n*); [*dirigeant, parti*] ruling (*épith*); **les gens en** ~ the powers that be; **ne plus tenir en** ~ to be restless *ou* fidgety; **mettre en** ~ to put [sth] in place [*programme*]; to put [sth] in position [*équipe*]; to establish, to set up [*réseau,*

institution]; **to install** [*ligne téléphonique*]; ⚏ (dans une agglomération) square; **la** ~ **du village** the village square; **la** ~ **du marché** the marketplace; ⚐ Fin market; ~ **financière** financial market; ⚑ (emploi) job; **perdre sa** ~ to lose one's job; ⚒ (forteresse) **être dans la** ~ to be on the inside; **être maître de la** ~ lit to be in control; fig to rule the roost; **avoir un pied dans la** ~ fig to have a foot in the door

⸤Composés⸥ ~ **d'armes** parade ground; ~ **assise** seat; ~ **forte** fortified town; ~ **d'honneur** (à table) place *ou* seat of honourᴳᴮ; **sur la** ~ **publique** in public; **mettre qch sur la** ~ **publique** to bring sth out in the open

placé, ~**e** /plase/
A *pp* ▸ **placer**
B *pp adj* ⚊ (situé géographiquement) **être** ~ [*objet, robinet, fenêtre*] to be; [*chaise, table, statue*] to be placed; [*personne*] gén to be; (au théâtre, cinéma) to be sitting; **être bien/mal** [*objet*] to be in a good/bad position; [*bâtiment, boutique*] to be well/badly situated; [*personne*] (à table, à une cérémonie) to have a good/bad place; (au théâtre, cinéma) to have a good/bad seat; **être** ~ **face à** to be facing; ⚋ (dans une hiérarchie) **être bien/mal** ~ to be well/badly placed; **être bien** ~ **sur une liste** to have a good position on the list; **il est bien** ~ **pour le poste** he's a likely candidate for the job; **avoir des amis haut** ~**s** to have friends in high places; **être** ~ **sous la direction de** [*orchestre*] to be conducted by; [*troupe de théâtre*] to be directed by; ⚌ fig **mal** ~ [*orgueil, remarque*] misplaced; **être bien/mal** ~ **pour faire** (pour réussir) to be well/badly placed to do; (pour savoir, juger) to be in a (good)/in no position to do; ⚍ (aux courses) [*cheval*] placed; **jouer un cheval** ~ **et gagnant** to back a horse each way GB, to back a horse across the board US; **non** ~ unplaced

placebo /plasebo/ *nm* placebo

placement /plasmɑ̃/ *nm* ⚊ Fin investment; ⚋ (emploi) **assurer le** ~ **des diplômés** to ensure that graduates find employment; ⚌ (d'enfant) fostering

placenta /plasɛ̃ta/ *nm* placenta

placer /plase/ [12]
A *vtr* ⚊ (mettre à un endroit) to put, to place [*objet*]; to seat [*personne*]; **des gardes** to post guards; ~ **des hommes autour d'une maison** to position men around a house; ⚋ (mettre dans une situation) to put, to place; ~ **un service sous la responsabilité de qn** to make sb responsible for a department; ~ **qn/être placé devant un choix difficile** to present sb/to be faced with a difficult choice; ⚌ (procurer un emploi) to place, to find a job for; ⚍ Fin (investir) to invest; (mettre en dépôt) to deposit, to put; ⚎ (attribuer) ~ **sa confiance en qn** to put one's trust in sb; ⚏ (introduire) to slip in [*remarque, anecdote*]; **je n'arrive pas à en** ~ **une**○ **avec elle!** I can't get a word in edgeways GB *ou* edgewise US with her!; ⚐ (prendre en charge) to place [sb] in care [*enfant*]; ⚑ (vendre) to place, to sell [*marchandise*]
B *se placer vpr* ⚊ (à un endroit) **se** ~ **près de** (debout) to stand next to; (assis) to sit next to; **se** ~ **autour d'une maison** [*policiers*] to position oneself around a house; **où se placent les verres?** where do the glasses go?; ⚋ (dans une situation) **se** ~ **sous une perspective nouvelle** to look at things from a new perspective; **il s'est placé comme apprenti** he found himself an apprenticeshipᴳᴮ; **notre démarche se place dans le cadre de l'aide au tiers-monde** our action comes within the context of Third World aid; ⚌ (dans une hiérarchie) **il s'est placé dans les premiers** (en classe) he got one of the top places; (dans une course) he finished among the first

placeur, -**euse** /plasœʀ, øz/ ▸ **p. 372** *nm,f* usher/usherette

placide /plasid/ *adj* placid, calm

placier, -**ière** /plasje, ɛʀ/ ▸ **p. 372** *nm,f* ⚊ (représentant) sales representative; ⚋ (sur un marché) market superintendent

plafond /plafɔ̃/
A *nm* ⚊ (de pièce) ceiling; (de tente, véhicule, souterrain) roof; ~ **à caissons** coffered ceiling; **salle haute de** ~ high-ceilinged room; ~ **nuageux** cloud ceiling; ▸ **faux**¹; ⚋ (limite) ceiling, limit; **crever le** ~ (dépasser la limite) to go through the ceiling; (battre les records) to break all previous records
B (-)**plafond** (in *compounds*) **vitesse(-)**~ maximum speed

plafonnement /plafɔnmɑ̃/ *nm* ⚊ (action) setting a ceiling on [*salaires*]; setting a limit on [*dépenses*]; ⚋ (de salaires) ceiling (de on); (de dépenses) limitation (de of)

plafonner /plafɔne/ [1]

A *vtr* (limiter) to put a ceiling on [*prix, salaire, production*]; **l'augmentation des salaires est plafonnée à 3%** wage increases are limited to a maximum of 3%; **loyer plafonné** protected rent; **salaire plafonné** *upper limit of salary on which contributions are payable*

B *vi* [*production, dépenses*] to reach a ceiling; [*élève, employé*] to reach a maximum level of attainment; (se stabiliser) [*prix, chômage*] to level off; **la production plafonne autour de 15 tonnes par an** production remains constant at about 15 tons a year; **l'avion plafonne à 15 000 m** (est limité à) the plane has an absolute ceiling of 15,000 m; (culmine à) the plane has reached its ceiling of 15,000 m

plafonnier /plafɔnje/ *nm* (au plafond) flush-fitting ceiling light; (dans une voiture) interior light

plage /plaʒ/ *nf* **1** Géog beach; **sac de** ~ beach bag; **2** (zone) range; ~ **de prix** price range; **3** (tranche horaire) slot; **4** (de disque) track

(Composés) ~ **arrière** Aut rear window shelf; Naut quarterdeck; ~ **avant** Naut forecastle; ~ **horaire** Radio, TV time slot; ~ **musicale** Radio, TV musical interval; ~ **sous-marine** bank

plagiaire /plaʒjɛʀ/ *nmf* plagiarist

plagiat /plaʒja/ *nm* plagiarism

plagier /plaʒje/ [2] *vtr* to plagiarize [*œuvre, auteur*]

plagiste /plaʒist/ ▸ p. 372 *nmf* (employé) beach attendant; (exploitant) beach manager

plaid /plɛd/ *nm* (couverture) tartan rug GB, plaid blanket US

plaidant, ~e /plɛdɑ̃, ɑ̃t/ *adj* Jur [*parties*] litigant

plaider /plede/ [1]

A *vtr* to plead [*cause, affaire*]; ~ **la légitime défense** to plead self-defence^{GB}

B *vi* **1** lit to plead (**contre** against; **pour qn** on sb's behalf); **2** fig ~ **en faveur de qn** [*circonstances, qualités*] to speak in favour^{GB} of sb

plaideur, -euse /plɛdœʀ, øz/ *nm,f* Jur litigant

plaidoirie /plɛdwaʀi/ *nf* Jur plea

plaidoyer /plɛdwaje/ *nm* **1** Jur speech for the defence^{GB}; **2** fig plea

plaie /plɛ/ *nf* **1** (blessure physique) wound; (ulcération) sore; (coupure) cut; ~ **vive** open sore; **2** (blessure morale) wound; (calamité) scourge; **les sept** ~**s d'Égypte** the seven plagues of Egypt; **3** ○(chose ou personne pénible) pain○; **cet enfant, quelle** ~! that child is such a pain!

(Idiomes) ~ **d'argent n'est pas mortelle** Prov money isn't everything; **mettre le doigt sur la** ~ to put one's finger on the problem

plaignant, ~e /plɛɲɑ̃, ɑ̃t/

A *adj* Jur litigant

B *nm,f* Jur plaintiff, complainant

plaindre /plɛ̃dʀ/ [54]

A *vtr* to pity, to feel sorry for [*personne, animal*]; **elle aime se faire** ~ she likes to be pitied; **il est (bien) à** ~ he's (very much) to be pitied; **il n'est vraiment pas à** ~ (il mérite son sort) he got what he deserved; (il a de la chance) he's got nothing to complain about

B **se plaindre** *vpr* **1** (protester) to complain; (pleurnicher) to whinge○ péj, to complain; **se** ~ **à qn** to complain to sb; **je n'ai pas à me** ~ **de lui** I've no complaints about him; **2** (geindre) [*blessé, malade*] to moan

plaine /plɛn/ *nf* plain

plain-pied: de plain-pied /dəplɛ̃pje/

A *loc adj* **1** (à un étage) **un bâtiment/une maison de** ~ a single-storey GB ou single-story US building/house; **la cuisine est de** ~ **avec le jardin** the kitchen is at the same level as the garden GB ou yard US; **2** (à égalité) **être de** ~ **avec qn** to be on an equal footing with sb

B *loc adv* **entrer de** ~ **dans le monde politique** to have an easy passage into the world of politics

plainte /plɛ̃t/ *nf* **1** Jur complaint; ~ **contre X** complaint against person or persons unknown; **2** (de malade) moan, groan; **la** ~ **du vent** the moaning of the wind; **la** ~ **des violons** the wail of the violins

plaintif, -ive /plɛ̃tif, iv/ *adj* plaintive

plaintivement /plɛ̃tivmɑ̃/ *adv* plaintively, dolefully

plaire /plɛʀ/ [59]

A **plaire à** *vtr ind* **elle plaît aux hommes** men find her attractive; **elle m'a plu tout de suite** I liked her straight away; **il a tout pour** ~ lit he is attractive in every way; iron he is not exactly God's gift; **mon nouveau travail me plaît** I like my new job; **si ça ne te plaît pas, c'est pareil** or **c'est le même prix**○ if you don't like it, that's tough○ ou that's too bad; **offre-leur des fleurs, ça plaît toujours** give them flowers, they're always welcome; **un modèle qui plaît beaucoup** a very popular model

B **se plaire** *vpr* **1** (à soi-même) to like oneself; **2** (l'un l'autre) [*personnes, couple*] to like each other; **3** (être bien) **ils se plaisent ici** they like it here; **cette plante se plaît dans un environnement marécageux** this plant thrives in a marshy environment; **4** (aimer) **se** ~ **à faire** to enjoy doing; **il se plaît à dire qu'il est issu du peuple** he likes to say that he's a son of the people

C *v impers* **il me plaît de penser que** I like to think that; **s'il te plaît, s'il vous plaît** please; **plaît-il?** I beg your pardon?; **plût au ciel** or **à Dieu qu'il soit sain et sauf!** fml God grant he's safe and sound!

plaisamment /plɛzamɑ̃/ *adv* **1** (de manière agréable) agreeably; **2** (d'une manière comique) amusingly

plaisance /plɛzɑ̃s/ *nf* **la (navigation de)** ~ gén boating; (sur un voilier) sailing; **bateau de** ~ pleasure boat

plaisancier, -ière /plɛzɑ̃sje, ɛʀ/ *nm,f* amateur sailor

plaisant, ~e /plɛzɑ̃, ɑ̃t/ *adj* **1** (agréable) pleasant; **2** (amusant) amusing, funny; ▸ **mauvais**

plaisanter /plɛzɑ̃te/ [1]

A *vtr* (railler) to tease [*personne*] (**sur** about)

B *vi* **1** to joke (**sur, de** about); **dire qch pour** ~ to say sth as a joke; **on ne plaisante pas avec ces choses-là** these things are no laughing matter; **il ne faut pas** ~ **avec sa santé** one shouldn't take chances with one's health

plaisanterie /plɛzɑ̃tʀi/ *nf* **1** gén joke; **il ne comprend pas la** ~ he can't take a joke; **lancer des** ~**s** to crack jokes; **être l'objet des** ~**s de qn** to be a figure of fun to sb; **la** ~ **a assez duré!** this has gone on long enough!; **2** (chose facile à faire) **c'est une** ~ it's a piece of cake○

plaisantin /plɛzɑ̃tɛ̃/ *nm* **1** (blagueur) practical joker; **petit** ~**!** wise guy○!; **2** (fumiste) skiver○

plaisir /plɛziʀ/ *nm* **1** (sensation agréable) pleasure; **le** ~ **des sens/des yeux** sensual/aesthetic pleasure; **prendre** or **avoir (du)** ~ **à faire** to enjoy doing; **prendre un malin** ~ **à faire** to take a wicked delight in doing; **j'ai appris avec** ~ **que** I was delighted to hear that; **je ne te punis pas pour le** ~ **mais parce que tu le mérites** I'm not punishing you for the sake of it, but because you deserve it; **à** ~ [*se tourmenter, exagérer, mentir*] for the sake of it; **pour le plus grand** ~ **des auditeurs** for the enjoyment of the listeners; **faire** ~ **à qn** to please sb; **qu'est-ce qui te ferait** ~? what would you like?; **si ça peut te faire** ~ if it'll make you happy; **je viendrai, mais c'est bien pour te faire** ~ I'll come, but only because you want me to; **ça fait toujours** ~! iron isn't that nice!; **tu vas me faire le** ~ **de ranger ta chambre!** you'll tidy up your room if you know what's good for you!; **faites-moi le** ~ **de vous taire!** would you please shut up○!; **il se fera un** ~ **de vous aider** he will be delighted to help you; **faire durer le** ~ lit to make the pleasure last; iron to prolong the agony; **je vous souhaite bien du** ~ iron I wish you joy of it!; **2** (source d'agrément) pleasure; **une vie de** ~**s** a life devoted to pleasure; **aimer les** ~**s de la table** to enjoy good food

plan, ~e /plɑ̃, plan/

A *adj* **1** gén flat, even; **2** Math, Phys plane

B *nm* **1** (carte) (de ville, métro) map; (dans un bâtiment) plan, map; **2** Archit, Constr plan; **3** (de machine) (schéma directeur) blueprint; (après construction) plan; **4** Math, Phys plane; **5** (de dissertation) plan; **6** Cin, Phot (image) shot; **montage** ~ **par** ~ shot-to-shot editing; **premier** ~ foreground; **second** ~ middle-distance; ▸ **gros**; **7** (niveau) level; **au premier** ~ **de l'actualité** at the forefront of the news; **être relégué au second** ~ [*personne, problème*] to be relegated to the background; **de (tout) premier** ~ [*personnalité*] leading (épith); [*œuvre*] key, major; **de second** ~ second-rate; **sur le** ~ **politique** from a political point of view; **8** (projet) plan, programme^{GB}; ~ **de relance économique** plan to boost the economy; **j'ai un bon** ~○ **pour voyager pas cher** I know a good way of travelling^{GB} cheaply; **c'est (pas) le bon** ~○ it's (not) a good idea

(Composés) ~ **américain** Cin medium shot; ~ **directeur** Écon master plan; ~ **d'eau** (artificiel) artificial lake; (naturel) smooth expanse of water; ~ **d'ensemble** Cin long shot; ~ **d'épargne** savings plan; ~ **d'épargne-logement**, **PEL** *savings scheme entitling depositor to cheap mortgage*;

~ **d'épargne retraite** top-up pensions scheme; ~ **fixe** Cin static shot; ~ **moyen** Cin medium close-up; ~ **d'occupation des sols, POS** land use plan; ~ **rapproché** Cin medium close-up; ~ **social** Écon planned redundancy scheme GB, scheduled lay-off program US; ~ **de travail** (pour projet) working schedule; (surface) worktop; ~ **d'urbanisme** urban planning policy; ~ **de vol** flight plan

Ⓘ (Idiomes) **laisser qn en** ~° to leave sb in the lurch, to leave sb high and dry; **laisser qch en** ~° to leave sth unfinished; **il a tout laissé en** ~ he dropped everything

planant°, **~e** /planã, ãt/ adj mind-blowing°

planche /plãʃ/ nf 1 (pièce de bois) plank; (pour pétrir, laver etc) board; **faire la** ~ (en natation) to float on one's back; 2 (illustration) plate

(Composés) ~ **à billets** minting plate; **faire marcher la** ~ **à billets**° to print money; ~ **à découper** chopping-board; (plus épaisse) butcher's block; ~ **à dessin** drawing board; ~ **à repasser** ironing-board; ~ **à roulettes** Sport skateboard; ~ **de salut** lifeline; ~ **de surf** surfboard; ~ **à voile** (engin) windsurfing board; (activité) windsurfing

(Idiomes) **monter sur les** ~**s** Théât to go on the stage, to tread the boards; **brûler les** ~**s** Théât to bring the house down; **avoir du pain sur la** ~° to have one's work cut out

plancher¹° /plãʃe/ [1] vi students' slang to work

plancher² /plãʃe/
Ⓐ nm 1 (sol) floor; 2 Écon, Fin (seuil inférieur) floor, minimum; **atteindre un** ~ [prix, cours] to bottom out
Ⓑ (-)**plancher** (in compounds) **prix(-)**~ bottom price
(Composé) **le** ~ **des vaches**° land, terra firma
(Idiome) **mettre le pied au** ~° to put one's foot down on the accelerator

planchette /plãʃɛt/ nf 1 (petite planche) small board; 2 (rayon) (small) shelf

planchiste /plãʃist/ nmf windsurfer

plancton /plãktõ/ nm plankton

plané /plane/ adj m **vol** ~ lit glide; **faire un vol** ~ fig to go flying

planer /plane/ [1] vi 1 [avion, oiseau] to glide; [oiseau de proie] to hover; [vapeur] to float; 2 [tristesse, menace] to hang; **laisser** ~ **le doute** to allow uncertainty to persist; 3 ° [rêveur] to have one's head in the clouds; [drogué] to be spaced out°, to be high°

planétaire /planetɛʀ/ adj Phys, Tech planetary; fig global

planète /planɛt/ nf planet

planeur /planœʀ/ nm 1 (engin) glider; 2 ▸ p. 327 (sport) gliding

planification /planifikasjõ/ nf planning

planifier /planifje/ [2] vtr to plan [production, vacances]; to schedule [traitement]; ~ **à court terme** to draw up a short-term plan

planning° /planiŋ/ nm controv schedule
(Composé) ~ **familial** family planning service

planque° /plãk/ nf 1 (cachette) (de personne) hideout; (de chose) hidey-hole° GB, stash° US; 2 (emploi confortable) cushy number°

planqué° /plãke/ nm soldiers' slang skiver

planquer° /plãke/ [1]
Ⓐ vtr to hide [personne]; to hide [sth] away [objet]; ~ **de l'argent** to stash money away
Ⓑ **se planquer** vpr gén to hide; (longtemps) to go into hiding; (par lâcheté) to skive

plan-relief, pl **plans-reliefs** /plãʀəljɛf/ nm scale model

plan-séquence, pl **plans-séquences** /plãsekãs/ nm sequence shot

plant /plã/ nm 1 (plante) young plant; (plus jeune) seedling; **un** ~ **de vigne** a young vine; **des** ~**s de fleurs** bedding plants; 2 (plantation) plantation; ~ **de légumes** vegetable patch; ~ **de fleurs** flower bed

plantaire /plãtɛʀ/ adj Anat plantar

plantation /plãtasjõ/ nf (d'arbres, de café) plantation; (de fleurs) bed (de légumes) patch

plante /plãt/ nf 1 Bot plant; ~ **d'appartement** or **verte** houseplant; ~ **grasse** succulent; ~ **de serre** lit, fig hothouse plant; ~ **vivace** perennial; **soigner par les** ~**s** to

use herbal medicine; 2 Anat ~ (**des pieds**) sole (of the foot)

planté, **~e** /plãte/ adj 1 (enraciné) **dents bien/mal** ~**es** regular/uneven teeth; **avoir les cheveux** ~**s bas sur le front** to have a low forehead; 2 °(debout) standing; **ne reste pas** ~ **là!** don't just stand there!

planter /plãte/ [1]
Ⓐ vtr 1 to plant [tomates, jardin]; **route plantée d'arbres** road lined with trees; 2 (enfoncer) to drive in [pieu]; to knock in [clou]; ~ **un couteau dans** to stick a knife into; **clou mal planté** nail which has not gone in straight; ~ **un drapeau** to put a flag; 3 (dresser) to pitch [tente]; ~ **un décor** lit to put up a set; fig to set the scene; ~ **une échelle contre un mur** to stand a ladder against a wall; 4 °(mettre) to put, to stick°; ~ **la bouteille sur la table** to stick the bottle on the table; 5 °(abandonner) ~ **là** to drop [outil]; to abandon [voiture]; to pack in° [travail]; to walk out on [époux]; **il m'a planté là** he left me standing there
Ⓑ °vi Ordinat to crash
Ⓒ **se planter** vpr 1 [fleur, parterre] to be planted; 2 (s'enfoncer) [clou] to go in; 3 [personne] **se** ~ **une épine dans le pied** to get a thorn in one's foot; 4 °(se tenir) **aller se** ~ **devant qch** to go and stand in front of sth; 5 °(avoir un accident) to crash; **se** ~ **en vélo** to have a bicycle accident; 6 °(se tromper) to get it wrong; (se perdre) to get lost; **il s'est planté en histoire** he made a mess of the history exam

planteur /plãtœʀ/ ▸ p. 372 nm (exploitant) planter

plantoir /plãtwaʀ/ nm dibble

planton /plãtõ/ nm (sentinelle) sentry; (ordonnance) orderly; **faire le** ~ fig to wait around

plantureux, **-euse** /plãtyʀø, øz/ adj 1 [déjeuner] lavish; [poitrine] generous; [femme] buxom (épith), well-endowed hum; 2 [terre] fertile; [année, récolte] bumper (épith)

plaquage /plakaʒ/ nm Sport (technique) tackling ₵; **un** ~ a tackle

plaque /plak/ nf (de moisissure, d'humidité) patch; ~ **de verglas** patch of ice; (sur la peau) blotch; (de verre, métal) plate; (de marbre, chocolat) slab; (au jeu) chip; (de cabinet médical, d'étude de notaire) brass plate; (de policier) badge

(Composés) ~ **chauffante** hotplate; ~ **de cheminée** fireback; ~ **dentaire** plaque; ~ **d'égout** manhole cover; ~ **d'identité** (de soldat) ID tag; (de chien) name tag, dog tag; ~ **d'immatriculation** or **minéralogique** number plate GB, license plate US; ~ **tournante** lit turntable; fig crossroads (+ v sg)

(Idiomes) **être à côté de la** ~° (se tromper) to be completely mistaken; **elle répond toujours à côté de la** ~° her answers are always slightly off beam°

plaqué, **~e** /plake/
Ⓐ adj ~ **or** gold-plated; ~ **acajou** with a mahogany veneer (épith, après n); **poche** ~**e** patch pocket
Ⓑ nm **le** ~ (bijoux) plated jewellery GB ou jewelry US; (couverts) plated cutlery; **en** ~ plated

plaquer /plake/ [1]
Ⓐ vtr 1 (appuyer, aplatir) ~ **qn contre qch/au sol** to pin sb against sth/to the ground; ~ **sa main sur** to put one's hand on; **le vent plaquait sa jupe contre ses cuisses** the wind made her skirt cling to her legs; ~ **une mèche sur son front** to plaster a lock of hair onto one's forehead; 2 °(quitter) to leave [emploi, mari]; to chuck it all in° GB, to chuck everything° US; 3 (au rugby) to tackle; 4 (rajouter) pej to tack [citation, commentaire] (sur onto); 5 Tech to veneer [meuble, bois]; to plate [bijou, métal]; 6 Mus to strike [accord]
Ⓑ **se plaquer** vpr **se** ~ **contre un mur** to flatten oneself against a wall; **se** ~ **au sol** to lie flat on the ground; **se** ~ **contre qn** to press oneself up against sb

plaquette /plakɛt/ nf 1 (de chocolat) bar; (de beurre) packet; (de pilules) ≈ blister strip; (de métal) small plate; 2 (dans le sang) platelet; 3 (publicitaire) brochure; (en prose) pamphlet
(Composé) ~ **de frein** brake shoe

plastic /plastik/ nm plastic explosive; **attentat au** ~ bomb attack

plasticage /plastikaʒ/ nm bomb attack (**de** on)

plastifier /plastifje/ [2] vtr to coat [sth] with plastic

plastiquage = **plasticage**

plastique¹ /plastik/
Ⓐ adj plastic

B nm (matière) plastic; **c'est du ~** it's plastic

plastique² /plastik/ nf **1** (arts) **la ~** the plastic arts (pl); (sculpture) the art of sculpture; **2** (esthétique) (d'objet, de statue) formal beauty; (de personne) physique

plastiquer /plastike/ [1] vtr to carry out a bomb attack on

plastron /plastRɔ̃/ nm **1** (de chemise) shirt front; **2** (d'escrimeur) plastron; **3** (d'oiseau) breast-shield

plastronner /plastRɔne/ [1] vi to be full of oneself

plat, ~e /pla, plat/

A adj **1** (sans relief) [fond, surface, pays] flat; [mer] smooth; **être ~e, avoir la poitrine ~e** to be flat-chested; **2** (peu profond) [chapeau, caillou, paquet] flat; [bateau] flat-bottomed; [montre, briquet] slimline; [cheveux] limp; **3** (sans talon) [chaussure] flat; **4** fig [goût] bland; [vin] insipid; [style, description] lifeless; [traduction] flat; [texte] dull; **faire de ~es excuses à qn** to apologize abjectly to sb

B nm **1** (pour cuire, servir) dish; **2** (aliments servis) dish; **3** (partie d'un repas) course; **4** (partie plate) **le ~ de la main** the flat of one's hand; **5** (terrain plat) flat ground; **courir sur du ~** to run on the flat

C à plat loc adv **1** (horizontalement) **poser** or **mettre qch à ~** to lay sth down flat; **dormir à ~** to sleep without a pillow; **à ~ ventre** lit flat on one's stomach; **se mettre à ~ ventre devant qn** fig to grovel in front of sb; **tomber à ~** [plaisanterie] to fall flat; **2** (hors d'usage) **à ~** [pneu] flat; [batterie] flat GB, dead; **3** ○(sans énergie) **être à ~** [personne] to be run down; **sa maladie l'a mis à ~**○ his illness really took it out of him○; **4** (en ordre) **mettre à ~** to review [sth] from scratch [comptes, dossier]

〔Composés〕 **~ de côtes** top rib of beef; **~ cuisiné** ready-cooked meal; **~ du jour** today's special; **~ à poisson** serving dish for fish; **~ de résistance** Culin main course; fig main item

〔Idiomes〕 **faire un ~**○ (en natation) to do a belly flop○; **faire du ~ à qn**○ to chat sb up○ GB, to come on to sb○; **mettre les petits ~s dans les grands**○ to go to town on a meal○; **mettre les pieds dans le ~**○ to put one's foot in it; **faire tout un ~ de qch**○ to make a big deal about sth

platane /platan/ nm plane tree; **se payer un ~**○ to crash into a tree

plateau, pl ~x /plato/

A nm **1** (pour servir, porter) tray; **2** Théât stage; Cin, TV set; **et sur le ~ ici ce soir...** and in our panel tonight...; **3** (niveau constant) plateau; **arriver à un ~** [fièvre, inflation] to level off; [talent, capacités] to reach a plateau; **4** Géog plateau; **5** (de balance) pan; (de table) top; (de tourne-disques) turntable

B plateau(-) (in compounds) **~(-)télé**○ TV dinner

〔Composés〕 **~ continental** continental shelf; **~ à fromage** or **de fromages** cheeseboard; **~ de fruits de mer** seafood platter; **~ de tournage** film set

〔Idiome〕 **il faut qu'on t'apporte tout sur un ~?** do you expect everything to be handed to you on a plate?

plateau-repas, pl plateaux-repas /plato(ə)pɑ/ nm meal tray

plate-bande, pl plates-bandes /platbɑ̃d/ nf border, flower bed; **piétiner les plates-bandes de qn**○ fig to encroach on sb's territory

platée○ /plate/ nf plateful (de of)

plate-forme, pl plates-formes /platfɔRm/ nf gén platform; (pour marchandises) skid; **la ~ électorale** the party platform

〔Composés〕 **~ de forage** drilling rig; **~ littorale** coastal shelf; **~ pétrolière** oil rig

platement /platmɑ̃/ adv **s'excuser ~** to apologize abjectly

platine¹ /platin/ ▸ p. 140 adj inv, nm platinum

platine² /platin/ nf **1** (d'horloge, de serrure) plate; (de microscope) stage; **2** (tourne-disques) turntable

platiné, ~e /platine/ adj **1** (plaqué) platinum-plated; **2** ▸ p. 140 (blond) [cheveux] platinum blond

platitude /platityd/ nf **1** (de texte) banality; (de personne) dreariness; (de style) triteness; **2** (propos) platitude

platonique /platonik/ adj **1** [amour] platonic; **2** [revendication] token (épith)

plâtras /platRɑ/ nm inv Constr rubble ₡

plâtre /platR/ nm **1** Constr (matériau) plaster; **les ~s** plasterwork ₡; **2** Art, Méd (objet) plaster cast; **~ de marche** walking cast

〔Idiomes〕 **battre qn comme ~**○ to beat the living daylights out of sb○; **essuyer les ~s** to put up with the initial problems

plâtrer /platRe/ [1] vtr **1** Constr to plaster [mur]; **2** Méd **~ le bras de qn** to put sb's arm in a cast

plâtreux, -euse /platRø, øz/ adj **1** [mur] plastered; fig [teinte] chalky; **2** Culin [fromage] chalky

plâtrier, -ière¹ /platRije, ɛR/ ▸ p. 372 nm,f plasterer

plâtrière² /platRijeR/ nf (carrière) gypsum quarry; (four) gypsum kiln; (usine) plasterworks

plausible /plozibl/ adj plausible

playback /plɛbak/ nm inv miming, lip syncing; **chanter en ~** to mime to a tape, to lip-sync (a song)

plébiscite /plebisit/ nm plebiscite

plébisciter /plebisite/ [1] vtr **1** (élire) to elect [sb] with a huge majority; **2** (approuver) to vote overwhelmingly in favour^GB of [personne, mesure]; to acclaim [mode]

pléiade /plejad/ nf liter galaxy, pleiad

plein, ~e /plɛ̃, plɛn/

A adj **1** (rempli) full (de of); **une jupe ~e de taches** a skirt covered with stains; **2** **un ~ verre/panier** a glassful/basketful (de of); **saisir à ~es mains** to take hold of [sth] with both hands [objet massif]; to pick up a handful of [terre, sable, pièces]; **3** (non creux) [brique, mur] solid; [joues, visage] plump; [forme] rounded; **4** (total) [pouvoir, accord, effet] full; [succès, confiance] complete; **avoir la responsabilité ~e et entière de qch** to have full responsibility for sth; **5** (entier) [mois] whole, full; [lune] full; **6** (milieu) **en ~e poitrine/réunion/forêt** (right) in the middle of the chest/meeting/forest; **en ~ cœur** right in the heart; **en ~ jour** in broad daylight; **en ~ été** at the height of summer; **en ~ hiver** in the depths of winter; **en ~e mer** on the open sea; **être en ~e mutation** to be experiencing radical change; **7** Zool **~e** [femelle] pregnant; [vache] in calf (après n); [jument] in foal (après n); [truie] in pig (après n); **8** ○(ivre) sloshed, drunk; **9** (en parlant de cuir) **reliure ~e peau** full leather binding; **veste ~e peau** jacket made out of full skins

B adv **1** (exprimant une grande quantité) **avoir des billes ~ les poches** to have one's pockets full of marbles; **il a des idées ~ la tête** he's full of ideas; **2** (directement) **être orienté ~ sud** to face due south

C nm **1** (de réservoir) **faire le ~ de** lit to fill up with [eau, carburant]; fig to get a lot of [idées, voix, visiteurs]; **j'ai fait deux ~s** or **deux fois le ~ pour venir ici** I took two tankfuls to get here; **le ~ s'il vous plaît** fill it up please; **2** (en calligraphie) downstroke

D plein de○ dét indéf **~ de** lots of, loads○ of

E à plein loc adv [bénéficier, utiliser] fully; **tourner** or **marcher à ~** to work flat out, to work to capacity

F en plein loc adv **l'avion s'est écrasé en ~ sur l'immeuble** the plane crashed straight into the building; **il m'est rentré en ~ dedans** he crashed right into me

G tout plein○ loc adv really; **mignon tout ~** really sweet

〔Composés〕 **~e page** full page; **~e propriété** Jur freehold

〔Idiomes〕 **en avoir ~ les jambes**○ or **pattes**○ to be worn out, to be fit to drop○; **en avoir ~ le dos**○ or **les bottes❶** to be fed up (to the back teeth)○; **(s')en prendre ~ les gencives❶** to get it in the neck○

plein-air /plɛnɛR/ nm inv Scol (outdoor) games (pl)

pleinement /plɛnmɑ̃/ adv fully

plein-emploi /plɛnɑ̃plwa/ nm inv full employment

plein-temps, pl pleins-temps /plɛ̃tɑ̃/ nm gén full-time job; Méd full-time consultancy

plénier, -ière /plenje, ɛR/ adj plenary

plénipotentiaire /plenipotɑ̃sjɛR/ adj, nm plenipotentiary

plénitude /plenityd/ nf **1** (intégrité) **exercer la ~ de ses fonctions** to exercise one's functions to the full; **garder la ~ de ses droits** to retain all one's rights; **2** (bien-être) **un sentiment de ~** a blissful feeling; **3** (ampleur) liter fullness

pléonasme /pleonasm/ nm pleonasm

pléthore /pletoR/ nf superabundance, plethora

pléthorique /pletɔʀik/ adj [quantité, trafic] excessive; [classe] overcrowded; [personnel] surplus to requirement (jamais épith); **aux effectifs** ~**s** [société, service] overstaffed

pleurer /plœʀe/ [1]

A vtr [1] (regretter) to mourn [ami]; to lament [absence]; [2] ○(économiser) **ne pas** ~ **son argent** to spare no expense

B vi [1] (après une émotion) to cry, to weep; **j'en aurais pleuré!** I could have wept!; ~ **de rire, rire à en** ~ to laugh until one cries; **c'est une histoire triste/bête à** ~ this story is too sad/stupid for words; [2] (involontairement) [yeux] to water; **j'ai les yeux qui pleurent** my eyes are watering; [3] (s'affliger) ~ **sur qch/qn** to shed tears over sth/sb; **arrête de** ~ **sur ton sort!** stop feeling sorry for yourself!; [4] ○(se plaindre) [personne] to whine; **aller** ~ **auprès de qn** to go whining to sb; ~ **après** to beg for [augmentation, faveur]; [5] littér [violon] to sob; [vent] to sigh

(Idiome) **elle n'a que ses yeux pour** ~ all she can do is cry ou weep

pleurésie /plœʀezi/ ▸ p. 195 nf pleurisy

pleureur /plœʀœʀ/ adj m **saule** ~ weeping willow

pleureuse /plœʀøz/ nf (hired) mourner

pleurnichard○, ~**e** /plœʀniʃaʀ, aʀd/

A adj whining

B nm,f cry-baby○

pleurnicher○ /plœʀniʃe/ [1] vi to snivel

pleurnicheur○, **-euse** /plœʀniʃœʀ, øz/ nm,f sniveller^GB

pleurs /plœʀ/ nmpl tears; **en** ~ in tears; **il y aura des** ~ **et des grincements de dents** there will be wailing and gnashing of teeth

pleutre /pløtʀ/ nm liter coward

pleuvoir /pløvwaʀ/ [39]

A v impers to rain; **il pleut** it's raining; **il pleut à torrents** or **à seaux** it's pouring with rain; **il pleut des cordes**○ it's coming down in buckets; **des gâteaux comme s'il en pleuvait**○ loads○ of cakes

B vi [obus, coups] to rain down; [demandes d'emploi] to pour in; [questions, critiques] to come thick and fast

pli /pli/ nm [1] (de tissu, rideau, dépliant, soufflet) fold; (de pantalon) crease; (de jupe) pleat; **(faux)** ~ crease; **ta veste fait des** ~**s** your jacket is all creased; [2] (de bouche, d'yeux) line; (de ventre, double menton) fold; [3] (de terrain) fold; [4] Jeux (levée) trick; **faire un** ~ to take a trick; [5] (lettre) letter; **sous** ~ **cacheté** in a sealed envelope; **sous** ~ **séparé** under separate cover

(Idiomes) **ça ne fait pas un** ~○ there's no doubt about it; **c'est un** ~ **à prendre** it's something you've got to get used to; **il a pris un mauvais** ~ he's got into a bad habit

pliage /plijaʒ/ nm folding

pliant, ~**e** /plijã, ãt/

A adj folding

B nm folding stool, campstool

plie /pli/ nf plaice

plier /plije/ [2]

A vtr [1] (rabattre) to fold [papier, vêtement, parapluie]; to fold up [meuble, tente]; ~ **qch en deux** to fold sth in two; [2] (courber) to bend [tige, roseau]; **je n'arrive pas à** ~ **le bras** I can't bend my arm; [3] (ranger) to pack [affaires]; [4] (soumettre) to submit [à to]

B vi [1] (ployer) [arbre, branche, articulation] to bend; [planche, plancher] to sag; [2] (céder) to give in; **faire** ~ **qn** to make sb give in; ~ **sous les menaces de qn** to yield to sb's threats

C se plier vpr [1] (être pliant) to fold; [2] (se soumettre) **se** ~ **à** to submit to; **se** ~ **à des exigences** to bow to necessity

(Idiome) **être plié en deux**○ or **quatre**○ (de rire) to be doubled up with laughter; (de douleur) to be doubled up with pain

plinthe /plɛ̃t/ nf [1] (de mur) skirting board GB, baseboard US; [2] (de statue) plinth

plissage /plisaʒ/ nm pleating

plissé /plise/ nm pleats (pl)

plissement /plismã/ nm [1] ▸ **de terrain** fold; ~ **alpin** Alpine orogeny; [2] (des yeux) screwing up; (de peau) wrinkling

plisser /plise/ [1]

A vtr [1] (volontairement) to fold [papier]; to pleat [tissu]; [2] (involontairement) to crease [vêtement]; **ta robe est toute**

plissée your dress is all creased; [3] (froncer) ~ **le front** to knit one's brows; ~ **les yeux** to screw up one's eyes

B vi [bas] to wrinkle; [jupe, veste] to be creased ou puckered

C se plisser vpr [1] [vêtement, tissu] to crease, to get creased; [2] [nez] to wrinkle; [bouche] to pucker up

pliure /plijyʀ/ nf (de feuille, tissu) fold; **la** ~ **du genou** the back of the knee; **la** ~ **du coude** the crook of the elbow

plomb /plɔ̃/ nm [1] (métal) lead; **de** or **en** ~ lead (épith); **sans** ~ [essence] unleaded; **soleil de** ~ fig burning sun; **ciel de** ~ leaden sky; [2] (de chasse) **un** ~ a lead pellet; **du** ~ lead shot **₵**; **du gros** ~ buckshot **₵**; [3] (fusible) fuse; **faire sauter les** ~**s** to blow the fuses; [4] (en couture) piece of lead; (pour la pêche) sinker; [5] (sur un compteur) ~**s** seal (sg); [6] (de vitrail) lead; [7] (en typographie) type

(Idiomes) **avoir du** ~ **dans l'aile**○ to be in a bad way○; **cela va lui mettre du** ~ **dans la tête**○ or **cervelle**○ that will knock some sense into them; **péter les** ~**s**○ to lose it○

plombage /plɔ̃baʒ/ nm (dentaire) filling

plombé, ~**e** /plɔ̃be/

A pp ▸ **plomber**

B pp adj [dent] with a filling (épith, après n)

C adj [teint, visage] ashen; [couleur, ciel] leaden

plomber /plɔ̃be/ [1]

A vtr [1] to fill [dent]; [2] (sceller) to seal; [3] (pour alourdir) to weight [filet, rideau]

B se plomber vpr liter [ciel] to become leaden

plomberie /plɔ̃bʀi/ nf (tuyaux, métier) plumbing

plombier /plɔ̃bje/ ▸ p. 372 nm plumber

plombières /plɔ̃bjɛʀ/ nf inv tutti-frutti ice cream

plonge○ /plɔ̃ʒ/ nf washing up, dishwashing US

plongeant, ~**e** /plɔ̃ʒã, ãt/ adj [tir, décolleté] plunging; **une vue** ~**e** a bird's eye view (**sur** of)

plongée /plɔ̃ʒe/ nf [1] ▸ p. 327 (discipline) gén (skin) diving; (avec scaphandre) scuba diving; (avec tube) snorkelling^GB; ~ **sous-marine** deep-sea diving; **faire de la** ~ to go diving; [2] (séjour sous l'eau) dive; **un sous-marin en** ~ a submerged submarine; [3] Cin high-angle shot

plongeoir /plɔ̃ʒwaʀ/ nm gén diving-board; (planche) springboard

plongeon /plɔ̃ʒɔ̃/ nm [1] ▸ p. 327 (discipline) diving; [2] (de nageur, gardien de but) dive; [3] (chute) fall; [4] (oiseau) diver

plonger /plɔ̃ʒe/ [13]

A vtr to plunge; **elle plongea son regard dans le mien** she stared deep into my eyes; **il a plongé la tête dans le moteur** he stuck his head into the engine

B vi [1] gén to dive (**dans** into); [oiseau] to swoop down (**sur** on); [2] (péricliter) [affaire, commerce] to flounder; [action, monnaie] to take a dive; [élève] to go downhill

C se plonger vpr [1] lit to plunge (**dans** into); [2] fig to bury oneself (**dans** in); **être plongé dans ses pensées** to be deep in thought

plongeur, **-euse** /plɔ̃ʒœʀ, øz/

A ▸ p. 372 nm,f Sport diver; (laveur de vaisselle) dishwasher

B nm [1] Tech plunger piston; [2] (oiseau) diver

plot /plo/ nm [1] Électrotech contact; [2] (de bois) block

(Composé) ~ **de départ** Sport starting block

plouc○ /pluk/ pej nm country bumpkin○

plouf /pluf/

A nm inv splash; **faire un** ~ to go splash

B excl splash!

ployer /plwaje/ [23] liter

A vtr to bend [genou, branche]; to bow [tête]; **il ploya les épaules** his shoulders sagged

B vi [planche, toit] to sag; [branche, personne] to bend; [jambes, genoux] to buckle, to give way; ~ **sous un fardeau** to be weighed down by a burden; ~ **sous le joug** to bend under the yoke; **faire** ~ **l'ennemi** to force the enemy to yield

pluie /plɥi/ nf [1] Météo **la** ~ rain; **sous une** ~ **battante** in driving rain; **il tombait une** ~ **fine** it was drizzling; **jour de** ~ rainy day; **par temps de** ~ when it rains, in rainy weather; **des** ~**s violentes** heavy showers; **la saison des** ~**s** the rainy season, the rains (pl); [2] (de missiles, d'injures) hail; (d'étincelles, de cadeaux, compliments) shower; (de lettres, d'offres) lots (pl); **tomber en** ~ [projectiles, étincelles] to rain down

(Composé) ~**s acides** acid rain **₵**

(Idiomes) **il n'est pas né** or **tombé de la dernière** ~○ he wasn't born yesterday○; **parler de la** ~ **et du beau temps** to make small talk; **elle fait la** ~ **et le beau temps dans le**

parti she calls the shots○ in the party; **après la ~ le beau temps** Prov every cloud has a silver lining Prov

plume /plym/ nf ① (d'oiseau) feather; **chapeau à ~s** feathered hat; **oreiller de ~s** feather pillow; ② (pour écrire) (d'oiseau) quill (pen); (en métal) nib (pen); **prendre la ~ pour...** to put pen to paper to..., to take up one's pen to...; **d'un coup de ~** with a single stroke of the pen; **écrire au fil de la ~** to write as the thoughts come into one's head; **elle a la ~ facile** words flow easily from her pen; **vivre de sa ~** to earn a living by one's pen; **dessin à la ~** pen-and-ink drawing

Idiomes **elle y a laissé** or **perdu des ~s**○ she did not come off unscathed; **voler dans les ~s à** or **de qn** to fly at sb

plumeau /plymo/ nm ① (ustensile) feather duster; ② (touffe) tuft

plumer /plyme/ [1] vtr ① to pluck [oiseau]; ② ○to fleece○ [personne]; **se faire ~** to be ripped off○ ou fleeced○

plumier /plymje/ nm pencil box

plupart: **la plupart** /laplypar/ nf inv **la ~ des gens/oiseaux** most people/birds; **dans la ~ des cas** in most cases; **pour la ~** for the most part; **la ~ d'entre eux** most of them; **la ~ du temps** most of the time, mostly

pluridisciplinaire /plyridisipliner/ adj multidisciplinary

pluriel, -elle /plyrjɛl/
A adj plural
B nm plural

plurilinguisme /plyrilɛ̃gɥism/ nm multilingualism

plus¹ /ply, plys, plyz/
A prép ① **8 ~ 3 égale 11** 8 and ou plus 3 equals 11; **un dessert ~ du café** a dessert and coffee (as well); **~ 10°** plus 10°
B adv de comparaison ① (modifiant un verbe) (comparatif) more; (superlatif) the most; **je ne peux pas faire ~** I can do no more, I can't do any more; **elle est ~ que jolie** she's more than just pretty; **elle mange deux fois ~ que lui** she eats twice as much as he does; **~ j'y pense, moins je comprends** the more I think about it, the less I understand; **~ ça va** as time goes on; **qui ~ est** furthermore, what's more; **quel pays aimes-tu le ~?** which country do you like best?; **de ~ en ~** more and more; ② (modifiant un adjectif) (comparatif) more; (superlatif) most; **deux fois ~ cher** twice as expensive (que as); **c'est le même modèle en ~ petit** it's the same model, only smaller; **il est on ne peut ~ désagréable** he's as unpleasant as can be; **il est ~ ou moins artiste** he's an artist of sorts; **il a été ~ ou moins poli** he wasn't particularly polite; **ils étaient ~ ou moins ivres** they were a bit drunk; **un livre des ~ intéressants** a most interesting book; **de ~ en ~ difficile** more and more difficult; ③ (modifiant un adverbe) (comparatif) more; (superlatif) most; **trois heures ~ tôt/tard** three hours earlier/later; **deux fois ~ longtemps** twice as long (que as); **ils ne sont pas restés ~ longtemps que nous** they didn't stay any longer than we did ou than us; **il l'a fait ~ ou moins bien** he didn't do it very well; **de ~ en ~ loin** further and further; **~ tu te coucheras tôt, moins tu seras fatigué** the earlier you go to bed, the less tired you'll be
C adv de négation **elle ne fume ~** she doesn't smoke any more ou any longer, she no longer smokes; **~ jamais ça!** never again!; **~ besoin de se presser**○ there's no need to hurry any more; **il n'y a ~ d'œufs** there are no more eggs, there aren't any eggs left; **j'entre dans le garage, ~ de voiture!** I went into the garage, the car was gone!; **il n'y a ~ que lui qui puisse nous aider** only he can help us now; **~ que trois jours avant Noël!** only three days left ou to go until Christmas!
D **plus de** dét indéf ① (avec un nom dénombrable) **deux fois ~ de livres que** twice as many books as; **c'est lui qui a le ~ de livres** he's got the most books; **les gens qui posent le ~ de problèmes** the people who pose the most problems; **~ tu mangeras de bonbons, ~ tu auras de caries** the more sweets GB ou candy US you eat, the more cavities you'll have; **il y en a ~ d'un qui voudrait être à sa place** quite a few people would like to be in his/her position; ② (avec un nom non dénombrable) **je n'ai pas pris ~ de crème que toi** I didn't take any more cream than you did, I took no more cream than you did; **deux fois ~ de vin** twice as much wine (que as); ③ (avec un numéral) **elle n'a pas ~ de 50 disques** she has no more than 50 records; **les gens de ~ de 60 ans** people over 60; **il était déjà bien ~ de onze heures** it was already well past ou after eleven o'clock
E **au plus** loc adv at the most; **tout au ~** at the very most

F **de plus** loc adv ① (en outre) furthermore, moreover, what's more; ② (en supplément) **deux pommes de ~** two more apples; **une fois de ~** once more, once again; **9% de ~** 9% more

G **en plus** loc **en ~ (de cela)** on top of that; **le même modèle avec le toit ouvrant en ~** the same model, only with a sunroof; **il a reçu 300 euros en ~ de son salaire** he got 300 euros on top of his salary; **les taxes en ~** plus tax, tax not included.

⚠ A note on pronunciation:
plus/le plus used in comparison (meaning more/the most) is pronounced [ply] before a consonant and [plyz] before a vowel. It is pronounced [plys] when at the end of a clause. In the *plus de* and *plus que* structures both [ply] and [plys] are generally used.
plus used in *ne plus* (meaning no longer/not any more) is always pronounced [ply] except before a vowel, in which case it is pronounced [plyz]: *il n'habite plus ici* [plyzisi].

plus² /plys/ nm inv ① Math plus; **le signe ~** the plus sign; ② ○(avantage) plus○

plusieurs /plyzjœr/
A adj several; **une ou ~ personnes** one or more people
B pron indéf ① **ont déjà signé** several people have already signed; **vous êtes ~ à en vouloir** there are several of you who want some

plus-que-parfait /plyskəparfɛ/ nm inv pluperfect

plus-value, pl **~s** /plyvaly/ nf ① (de biens mobiliers) increase in value; (d'actif, de monnaie) appreciation; (profit à la vente) capital gain; ② Écon surplus value

Composé **~ financière** capital gain

plutôt /plyto/ adv ① (de préférence) rather; **pourquoi lui ~ qu'un autre?** why him rather than anybody else?; **~ le matin** in the morning preferably; ② (au lieu de) instead; **~ mourir (que d'accepter)!** I'd rather ou sooner die (than accept)!; **j'ai ~ tendance à ne pas m'en faire** I'm more the kind not to worry; ③ (plus précisément) rather; **elle est blonde ou ~ châtain clair** she's got blond, or rather light brown hair; **dis ~ que tu n'as pas envie de le faire** why don't you just say that you don't want to do it?; ④ (ayant une valeur intensive) rather; **la nouvelle a été ~ mal accueillie** the news went down rather badly; **'tu prends des vacances cet été?'—'~ oui!'** 'are you taking a vacation this summer?'—'too right○!' ou 'you bet○!'

pluvial, ~e, mpl **-iaux** /plyvjal, o/ adj pluvial

pluvieux, -ieuse /plyvjø, øz/ adj wet, rainy

PM /peɛm/ nm (abbr = **pistolet-mitrailleur**) submachine gun

PME /peɛmə/ nfpl: abbr ▸ **petit**

PMI /peɛmi/ nfpl (abbr = **petites et moyennes industries**) small and medium-sized industries

PMU /peɛmy/ nm (abbr = **Pari mutuel urbain**) French state-controlled betting system; **un ~** a betting office

PNB /peɛnbe/ nm: abbr ▸ **produit**

pneu /pnø/ nm ① Aut tyre GB, tire US; **~ clouté** or **à clous** studded tyre; **~ neige** snow tyre; **~ tendre** slick tyre; ② ○= **pneumatique B 1**

pneumatique /pnømatik/
A adj ① Tech pneumatic; ② (gonflable) inflatable
B nm ① (message) letter sent by pneumatic tube; ② †= **pneu 1**

pneumonie /pnømɔni/ ▸ p. 195 nf pneumonia

Composé **~ atypique** severe acute respiratory syndrome

pochard○, **~e** /pɔʃar, ard/ nm,f soak○, drunk

poche¹ /pɔʃ/ nm ① ○(livre) paperback; ② (format) pocket size; **paraître en ~** to come out in paperback

poche² /pɔʃ/ nf ① (de vêtement, sac, portefeuille) pocket; **il est revenu le contrat en ~** fig he came back with the contract in the bag○ ou all sewn up○; **son diplôme en ~, il est parti aux États-Unis** armed with his diploma, he set off for the States; **il avait 150 euros en ~** lit he had 150 euros on him; fig (à sa disposition) he had 150 euros available; **avoir de l'argent plein les ~s**○ to be loaded○, to have plenty of money; **s'en mettre plein** or **se remplir les ~s**○ to line one's pockets; **faire les ~s de qn** (vider) to empty out sb's pockets; (voler) to pick sb's pocket; **format de ~** pocket-size

plus¹

Formation du comparatif des adjectifs et des adverbes en anglais

Deux cas peuvent se présenter:

1 Adjectifs et adverbes courts

En règle générale on ajoute '*-er*' à la fin de l'adjectif/adverbe:

plus grand
= taller

plus longtemps
= longer

plus petit
= smaller

plus vite
= faster

plus simple
= simpler

Remarques:

Pour certains mots dont l'unique voyelle est une voyelle brève, on double la consonne finale:

big	→	bigger
sad	→	sadder
dim	→	dimmer
wet	→	wetter etc.

Attention aux adjectifs en '*-y*':

sunny	→	sunnier
pretty	→	prettier
happy	→	happier etc.

2 Adjectifs et adverbes longs

On ajoute *more* devant le mot:

plus beau
= more beautiful

plus facilement
= more easily

plus compétent
= more competent

plus sérieusement
= more seriously

plus intéressant
= more interesting

Remarques:

Certains mots de deux syllabes admettent les deux formes: *simple* peut produire *simpler* ou *more simple*

handsome	→	handsomer
		ou more handsome etc.

Certains mots de deux syllabes n'admettent que la forme avec *more*:

callous	→	more callous
cunning	→	more cunning

Les adverbes se terminant par '*-ly*' n'admettent que la forme avec *more*:

quickly	→	more quickly
slowly	→	more slowly etc.

On trouvera ci-contre exemples et exceptions illustrant les différentes fonctions de *plus*. On trouvera également des exemples de *plus* dans les notes d'usage répertoriées. **p. 1355.**

Formation du superlatif des adjectifs et des adverbes en anglais

Deux cas peuvent se présenter:

1 Adjectifs et adverbes courts

En règle générale on ajoute '*-(e)st*' à la fin du mot:

le plus grand
= the tallest

le plus longtemps
= the longest

le plus petit
= the smallest

le plus vite
= the fastest

le plus simple
= the simplest

Remarques:

Pour certains mots dont l'unique voyelle est une voyelle brève, on double la consonne finale:

big	→	the biggest
sad	→	the saddest
dim	→	the dimmest etc.

Attention aux adjectifs en '*-y*':

sunny	→	the sunniest
pretty	→	the prettiest
happy	→	the happiest etc.

2 Adjectifs et adverbes longs

On ajoute *the most* devant le mot:

le plus beau
= the most beautiful

le plus facilement
= the most easily

le plus compétent
= the most competent

le plus sérieusement
= the most seriously

le plus intéressant
= the most interesting

Remarques:

Certains mots de deux syllabes admettent les deux formes:

simple	→	the simplest ou the most simple
clever	→	the cleverest
		ou the most clever etc.

Certains mots de deux syllabes n'admettent que la forme avec *the most*:

callous	→	the most callous
cunning	→	the most cunning etc.

Les adverbes en '*-ly*' n'admettent que la forme avec *the most*:

quickly	→	the most quickly
slowly	→	the most slowly etc.

Attention: lorsque la comparaison ne porte que sur deux éléments on utilise la forme du comparatif:

le plus doué des deux
= the more gifted of the two

la voiture la plus rapide des deux
= the faster car

L'expression *le plus possible* est traitée avec **possible**.

(*épith*); **2** (sac) bag; **3** (accumulation) ～ **de gaz/d'air** gas/air pocket; **4** (déformation) **avoir des ～s sous les yeux** to have bags under one's eyes; **mon pantalon fait des ～s aux genoux** my trousers GB *ou* pants US are baggy at the knees; **5** Zool (de kangourou, pélican) pouch

(Composés) ～ **de glace** ice pack; ～ **revolver** hip pocket
(Idiomes) **mettre qn dans sa ～**○ to get sb on one's side; **c'est dans la ～**○ it's in the bag○, it's all sewn up○; **en être de sa ～**○ to be out of pocket; **ne pas avoir les yeux dans sa ～**○ not to miss a thing○; **connaître un endroit comme sa ～**○ to know a place like the back of one's hand

pocher /pɔʃe/ [1] *vtr* **1** Culin to poach; **2** (meurtrir) ～ **un œil à qn** to give sb a black eye; **se faire ～ un œil** to get a black eye

pochette /pɔʃɛt/ *nf* **1** (de crayons, compas) case; (de document) folder; (de disque) sleeve; (d'allumettes) book; **vendu sous ～ plastique** sold in a plastic cover; **2** (mouchoir) pocket handkerchief; **3** (sac à main) clutch bag; (pour papiers d'identité, argent) pouch

pochette-surprise, *pl* **pochettes-surprises** /pɔ-ʃɛtsyʀpʀiz/ *nf*: *child's novelty consisting of several small surprise items in a cone*

pochoir /pɔʃwaʀ/ *nm* stencil; **au ~** stencilled^{GB}

podium /pɔdjɔm/ *nm* gén podium; (de défilé de mannequins) catwalk GB, runway US; **monter sur le ~** to mount the podium

poêle¹ /pwal/ *nm* ① (pour chauffer) stove; ② (de cercueil) pall

poêle² /pwal/ *nf* frying pan; **passer à la ~** to fry

poêlon /pwalɔ̃/ *nm* heavy saucepan (*earthenware or cast iron*)

poème /pɔɛm/ *nm* poem; **c'est tout un ~** it's quite something

poésie /pɔezi/ *nf* ① (art) poetry; ② (poème) poem; ③ (qualité) **la ~ de son œuvre** the poetic quality of his/her work

poète /pɔɛt/ *nm* poet

poétesse† /pɔetɛs/ *nf* poetess†

poétique /pɔetik/
Ⓐ *adj* [*œuvre, lieu*] poetic; [*personne*] romantic
Ⓑ *nf* poetics (+ *v sg*)

poétiquement /pɔetikmɑ̃/ *adv* poetically

poids /pwa/ *nm inv* ① Phys weight; **peser son ~** to be very heavy; ② (importance) (de personne, pays, parti, d'électoral) influence; (de paroles) weight; **argument de ~** weighty argument; **adversaire de ~** opponent to be reckoned with; **il n'a aucun ~ politique** he hasn't got any political stature; **il ne fait pas le ~ devant un adversaire aussi redoutable** he's no match for such a formidable opponent; **je ne crois pas qu'il fera le ~ à ce poste** I don't think he's up to this job; ③ (fardeau) lit weight; fig burden; **être un ~ pour qn** to be a burden on sb; **avoir un ~ sur la conscience** to have a guilty conscience; ④ (pour peser, lester) weight; **des ~ en laiton** brass weights; ⑤ (en athlétisme) shot; **lancer le ~** to put the shot; **le lancer du ~** the shot put

⌐Composés⌐ **~ atomique** atomic weight; **~ brut** gross weight; **~ coq** Sport bantamweight; **~ et haltères** weightlifting Ⓒ; **~ léger** Sport lightweight; **~ lourd** Sport heavyweight; (camion) heavy goods vehicle GB, heavy truck; **~ mi-lourd** Sport light heavyweight; **~ mi-moyen** Sport welterweight; **~ mort** Tech, fig dead weight; **~ mouche** Sport flyweight; **~ moyen** Sport middleweight; **~ net** net weight; **~ net égoutté** net weight drained; **~ plume** Sport featherweight; **~ superléger** Sport light middleweight; **~ total en charge, PTC** gross weight; **~ total à vide, PTAV** tare; **~ welter** Sport welterweight

⌐Idiomes⌐ **faire bon ~** bonne mesure to be evenhanded; **avoir** *or* **faire deux ~ deux mesures** to have double standards

poignant, **~e** /pwaɲɑ̃, ɑ̃t/ *adj* (émouvant) poignant; (déchirant) heart-rending, harrowing

poignard /pwaɲaʀ/ *nm* dagger; **coup de ~** stab

poignarder /pwaɲaʀde/ [1] *vtr* (blesser) to stab, to knife; (tuer) to stab [sb] to death; **~ qn dans le dos** lit, fig to stab sb in the back

poigne /pwaɲ/ *nf* **avoir de la ~** lit to have a strong grip; fig to be firm-handed

poignée /pwaɲe/ *nf* ① (quantité) gén handful; (de billets) fistful; ② (de porte, tiroir, sac) handle; (de sabre) hilt

⌐Composé⌐ **~ de main** handshake; **échanger une ~ de main** to shake hands

poignet /pwaɲɛ/ *nm* ① ▸ p. 136 Anat wrist; **au ~** on the wrist; **à la force des ~s** [*se hisser*] using the strength of one's arms; **à la force du ~** [*réussir*] by sheer hard work; ② (de chemise) cuff

poil /pwal/ *nm* ① (chez l'être humain) hair; **avoir du ~ aux jambes** to have hairy legs; **avoir du ~ au menton** (être adulte) to be a grown man; **à ~** (nu) stark naked, starkers[○]; **se mettre à ~[○]** to strip, to strip off GB; **de tout ~** of all kinds; **'au (petit) ~[○]!'** 'fine!'; **être au ~[○]** [*objet*] to be just the ticket[○]; [*personne*] to be fantastic; **ça marche au ~[○]** it works like a dream; ② [○](cheveux) **avoir le ~ ras/rare** to have short/thin hair; ③ (d'animal) hair; **perdre ses ~s** to moult GB ou molt US, to shed (its) hairs; **animal à ~s** furry animal; **animal à ~ ras** short-haired animal; **animal au ~ soyeux** animal with a silky coat; **caresser dans le sens du ~** lit to stroke [sth] the way the fur lies; fig to butter [sb] up[○]; ④ Bot hair, down Ⓒ; ⑤ [○](petite quantité)

(d'humour, ironie) touch; (d'intelligence, de bon sens, courage) shred; **un ~ plus grand/trop petit** a shade larger/too small; **à un ~ près** by a whisker; **il s'en est fallu d'un ~ que je fasse** I was within a whisker of doing; ⑥ (de tapis) pile Ⓒ; (de tissu) nap Ⓒ; (de brosse, balai) bristle

⌐Composé⌐ **~ à gratter** itching powder

⌐Idiomes⌐ **être de bon/mauvais ~[○]** to be in a good/bad mood; **j'ai le ~ qui se hérisse[○]** my hackles rise; **hérisser le ~[○] de qn** to put sb's back up[○]; **avoir un ~ dans la main[○]** to be bone idle; **ne plus avoir un ~ sur le caillou[○]** to be as bald as a coot[○]; **ne plus avoir un ~ de sec[○]** to be soaked to the skin; **tomber sur le ~ de qn[○]** (se fâcher contre) to have a real go at sb[○]; (frapper) to give sb what's coming to him/her

poil-de-carotte /pwaldəkaʀɔt/ ▸ p. 140 *adj inv* (couleur) [*cheveux*] ginger

poilu, **~e** /pwaly/
Ⓐ *adj* hairy
Ⓑ [○]*nm*: *French soldier in World War I*

poinçon /pwɛ̃sɔ̃/ *nm* ① (de brodeuse) stiletto; (de cordonnier) awl; (de menuisier) bradawl; (de graveur) burin; (de sculpteur) punch; (de scribe) stylus; ② (pour marquer) die, stamp; (marque) hallmark; ③ (matrice) die

poinçonner /pwɛ̃sɔne/ [1] *vtr* ① (perforer) to punch, to clip [*billet*]; ② (marquer) to hallmark [*or, argent*]; to stamp [*marchandise*]

poinçonneur, **-euse**¹ /pwɛ̃sɔnœʀ, øz/ ▸ p. 372 *nm,f* (employé des transports) ticket-puncher; (ouvrier) punching-machine operator

poinçonneuse² /pwɛ̃sɔnøz/ *nf* (à billets) ticket-punch; (machine-outil) punching machine

poindre /pwɛ̃dʀ/ [56] *vi* [*jour*] to dawn, to break; [*aube*] to break; [*soleil*] to peep through; [*plante*] to peep through, to come up; [*idée, sentiment*] to dawn

poing /pwɛ̃/ *nm* fist; **coup de ~** punch; **donner un coup de ~ à qn** to punch sb; **les ~s sur les hanches** with (one's) arms akimbo; **être pieds et ~s liés** lit to be bound hand and foot; fig to have one's hands tied; **l'épée au ~** sword in hand

⌐Idiome⌐ **dormir à ~s fermés** to sleep like a log

point /pwɛ̃/
Ⓐ *nm* ① (endroit) point; **un ~ de rencontre** a meeting point; **~ de vente** (sales) outlet; ② (situation) point; Naut position; **être sur le ~ de faire** to be just about to do, to be on the point of doing; **j'en suis toujours au même ~ (qu'hier/qu'il y a un an)** I'm still exactly where I was (yesterday/last year); **au ~ où j'en suis, ça n'a pas d'importance!** I've reached the point where it doesn't matter any more!; **faire le ~** Naut to take bearings; fig to take stock of the situation; ③ (degré) **il m'agace au plus haut ~** he annoys me intensely; **je ne le pensais pas bête à ce ~** I didn't think he was that stupid; **'j'en aurais pleuré'—'ah bon, à ce ~?'** 'I could have cried'—'really? it was that bad?'; **si tu savais à quel ~ il m'agace!** if you only knew how much he annoys me!; **au ~ que** to the extent that; **à tel ~ que** to such an extent that; **douloureux au ~ que** so painful that; **il est têtu à un ~[○]!** he's so incredibly stubborn!; **jusqu'à un certain ~** up to a (certain) point, to a certain extent; ④ (question particulière) point; (dans un ordre du jour) item, point; **un programme en trois ~s** a three-point plan; **un ~ de détail** a minor point; **en tout ~, en tous ~s** in every respect ou way; ⑤ (marque visible) dot; **un ~ de colle** a spot of glue; **un ~ de rouille** a speck of rust; ⑥ Jeux, Sport point; **marquer/perdre des ~s** lit, fig to score/ to lose points; **compter les ~s** to keep (the) score; **un ~ partout!** one all!; **gagner aux ~s** to win on points; ⑦ (pour évaluer) mark GB, point US; **avoir sept ~s d'avance/de retard** to be seven marks ahead/behind; **obtenir** *or* **avoir 27 ~s sur 40** to get 27 out of 40; **être un bon ~ pour** to be a plus point for; **être un mauvais ~ pour qn/qch** to be a black mark against sb/sth; ⑧ (dans un système de calcul) point; **la livre a perdu trois ~s** the pound lost three points; **le permis à ~s** system whereby driving offender gets penalty points; ⑨ Math point; **~ d'intersection** point of intersection; ⑩ ▸ p. 413 Ling (en ponctuation) full stop GB, period US; **~ à la ligne** (dans une dictée) full stop, new paragraph; **~ final** (dans une dictée) full stop; **mettre un ~ à qch** fig to put a stop ou an end to sth; **je n'irai pas, ~ final[○]!** I'm not going, full stop GB ou period US!; **tu vas**

Le poids

dire				dire		
one gram	1 g*	= 0.35† oz	ounces			
one hundred grams	100 g	= 0.22 lbs	pounds‡			
		= 3.52 oz	ounces			
one kilogram	1 kg	= 2.20 lbs				
		= 35.26 oz				
one hundred kilograms	100 kg	= 220 lbs				
		= 15.76 st§	stones			
		= 1.96 cwt	hundredweight			
One ton ou one metric ton		= 0.98 ton¶	tons (GB)			
		= 1.10 tons‖	tons (US)			

* *Pour les mesures du système métrique, les abréviations sont les mêmes en anglais qu'en français. Mais attention à ton: voir ci-dessous.*

† *Noter que l'anglais a un point là où le français a une virgule. Pour la prononciation des nombres, voir* **les nombres ▸ p. 398**.

‡ *Noter que la pound anglaise, que nous appelons couramment* livre, *vaut en fait 454 grammes.*

§ *Les* stones *ne sont pas utilisées aux États-Unis.*

¶ *Il n'y a pas d'abréviation pour* ton.

‖ *La tonne anglaise et la tonne américaine ne correspondent pas au même poids. Attention, car les anglophones peuvent en outre utiliser le mot* ton *pour la tonne de 1000 kilos; pour éviter cette ambiguïté, on peut dire* metric ton.

■ *Les équivalences suivantes peuvent être utiles:*

1 oz	= 28,35 g			
1 lb	= 16 ozs	= 453,60 g		
1 st	= 14 lbs	= 6,35 kg		
1 cwt	= 8 st (GB)	= 112 lbs (GB)	= 50,73 kg	
		= 100 lbs (US)	= 45,36 kg	
1 ton	= 20 cwt (GB)	= 1014,6 kg		
	= 20 cwt (US)	= 907,2 kg		

Le poids des choses

combien pèse le colis?
= what does the parcel weigh?
ou how much does the parcel weigh?

quel est son poids?
= how much does it weigh? *ou* how heavy is it?
or what is its weight?

il pèse 5 kg
= it weighs 5 kilos *ou* it is 5 kilos in weight

le colis fait 5 kg
= the parcel weighs 5 kilos

il fait à peu près 5 kg
= it is about 5 kilos

presque 6 kg
= almost 6 kilos

plus de 5 kg
= more than 5 kilos

moins de 6 kg
= less than 6 kilos

A est plus lourd que B
= A is heavier than B

A pèse plus lourd que B
= A weighs more than B

B est plus léger que A
= B is lighter than A

B est moins lourd que A
= B is lighter than A

A est aussi lourd que B
= A is as heavy as B

A fait le même poids que B
= A is the same weight as B

A pèse autant que B
= A is the same weight as B

A et B font le même poids
= A and B are the same weight

A et B pèsent le même poids
= A and B are the same weight

Noter:

il pèse deux kilos de trop
= it is 2 kilos overweight

six kilos de sucre
= six kilos of sugar

vendu au kilo
= sold by the kilo

■ *Noter l'ordre des mots dans l'adjectif composé anglais, et l'utilisation du trait d'union. Noter aussi que* pound *et* kilo, *employés comme adjectifs, ne prennent pas la marque du pluriel.*

une pomme de terre de 3 livres
= a 3-lb potato (*dire* a three-pound potato)

un colis de 5 kg
= a 5-kilo parcel (*dire* a five-kilo parcel)

■ *On peut aussi dire* a parcel 5 kilos in weight.

Le poids des personnes

■ *En anglais britannique, le poids des personnes est donné en* stones, *chaque stone valant 6,35 kilos; en anglais américain, on le donne en* pounds (*livres*), *chaque livre valant 454 grammes.*

combien pèses-tu?
= how much do you weigh? *ou* what is your weight?

je pèse 63 kg 500
= I weigh 10 st (*ten stone*) (GB)
ou I weigh 140 lbs (*a hundred forty pounds*) (US)
ou I weigh 63 kg 500

il pèse 71 kg
= he weighs 10 st 3 (*ten stone three*) (GB)
ou he weighs 160 lbs (*a hundred sixty pounds*) (US)
ou he weighs 71 kg

il pèse 82 kg
= he weighs 13 st (*thirteen stone*) (GB)
ou he weighs 180 lbs (*a hundred eighty pounds*) (US)
ou he weighs 82 kg

il fait trois kilos de trop
= he is three kilos overweight

■ *Noter l'ordre des mots dans l'adjectif composé anglais, et l'utilisation du trait d'union. Noter aussi que* stone, *employé comme adjectif, ne prend pas la marque du pluriel.*

un athlète de 125 kg
= a 20-stone athlete *ou* a 125-kg athlete

p

te coucher un ~ c'est tout○! you're going to bed and that's final!; 11▸ Mus dot; 12▸ (en typographie) point; 13▸ Méd (douleur) pain; **avoir un ~ à l'aine** to have a pain in the groin; 14▸ (en couture, tricot) stitch; **faire un ~ à qch** to put a few stitches in sth; **dentelle au ~ de Venise** Venetian lace

Les points cardinaux

nord	north	N
sud	south	S
est	east	E
ouest	west	W

■ *Noter que la liste des quatre points cardinaux est traditionnellement donnée dans cet ordre dans les deux langues.*

nord-est	northeast	NE
nord-ouest	northwest	NW
nord-nord-est	north northeast	NNE
est-nord-est	east northeast	ENE
etc.		

■ *Dans les expressions suivantes,* nord *est pris comme exemple; les autres noms de points cardinaux s'utilisent de la même façon.*

Où?

vivre dans le Nord
= to live in the North

dans le nord de l'Écosse
= in the north of Scotland

au nord du village
= north of the village *ou* to the north of the village

à 7 km au nord
= 7 kilometres north *ou* 7 kilometres to the north

droit au nord
= due north

la côte nord
= the north coast

la face nord (*d'une montagne*)
= the north face

le mur nord
= the north wall

la porte nord
= the north door

passer au nord d'Oxford
= to go north of Oxford

Les mots en -*ern* et -*erner*

■ *Les mots anglais en* -ern *et* -erner *sont plus courants que les adjectifs français* septentrional, occidental, oriental *et* méridional.

une ville du Nord
= a northern town

l'accent du Nord
= a northern accent

le dialecte du Nord
= the northern dialect

l'avant-poste le plus au nord
= the most northerly outpost
  ou the northernmost outpost

quelqu'un qui habite dans le Nord
= a northerner

un homme du Nord
= a northerner

les gens du Nord
= northerners

■ *Les adjectifs en* -ern *sont normalement utilisés pour désigner des régions à l'intérieur d'un pays ou d'un continent* (▸ **p. 504**).

le nord de l'Europe
= northern Europe

l'est de la France
= eastern France

le sud de la Roumanie
= southern Romania

le nord d'Israël
= northern Israel

Mais noter:

l'Asie du Sud-Est
= South-East Asia

■ *Pour les noms de pays qui utilisent les points cardinaux* (Corée du Nord, Yémen du Sud), *se reporter au dictionnaire.*

Dans quelle direction?

Noter les adverbes en -*ward* ou -*wards* (*GB*) et les adjectifs en -*ward*, utilisés pour indiquer une direction vague.

aller vers le nord
= to go north *ou* to go northward
  ou to go in a northerly direction

naviguer vers le nord
= to sail north *ou* to sail northward

venir du nord
= to come from the north

un mouvement vers le nord
= a northward movement

■ *Pour décrire le déplacement d'un objet, on peut utiliser un composé avec* -bound.

un bateau qui se dirige vers le nord
= a northbound ship

les véhicules qui se dirigent vers le nord
= northbound traffic

Noter aussi:

les véhicules qui viennent du nord
= traffic coming from the north

des fenêtres qui donnent au nord
= north-facing windows *ou* windows facing north

une pente orientée au nord
= a north-facing slope

nord quart nord-est
= north by northeast

■ *Noter ces expressions servant à donner la direction des vents:*

le vent du nord
= the north wind

un vent de nord
= a northerly wind *ou* a northerly

des vents dominants de nord
= prevailing north winds

le vent est au nord
= the wind is northerly *ou* the wind is in the north

le vent vient du nord
= the wind is blowing from the north

B †*adv* not; **tu ne tueras** ∼ thou shalt not kill
C **à point** *loc adv* **1** (en temps voulu) just in time; **à** ∼ **nommé** just at the right moment; **2** Culin (**cuit**) **à** ∼ medium rare; **le camembert est à** ∼ the camembert is ready to eat
D **au point** *loc* **être au** ∼ [*système, machine*] to be well

designed; [*spectacle*] to be well put together; **leur système n'est pas encore très au** ～ their system still needs some working on; **le prototype n'est pas encore au** ～ the prototype isn't quite ready yet; **mettre au** ～ (*élaborer*) to perfect [*système*]; to work out, to devise [*accord, plan*]; to develop [*vaccin, appareil*]; (*régler*) to adjust; **finir de mettre qch au** ～ to put the finishing touches to sth; **mise au** ～ (*de système*) perfecting; (*de vaccin*) development; (*réglage*) adjusting; Phot focus; fig (*déclaration*) clarifying statement; **faire la mise au** ～ Phot to focus; **faire une mise au** ～ fig to set the record straight (**sur** about)

Composés ～ **d'ancrage** Aut anchor; fig base; ～ **d'appui** Mil base of operations; Phys fulcrum; gén support; ～ **d'attache** base; ～ **cardinal** compass *ou* cardinal point; ～ **chaud** trouble *ou* hot spot; ～ **de chute** fig port of call; ～ **commun** mutual interest; **nous avons beaucoup de** ～**s communs** we have a lot in common; ～ **de côté** (*douleur*) stitch; ～ **de départ** lit, fig starting point; **nous revoilà à notre** ～ **de départ** fig we're back to square one; ～ **d'eau** (*naturel*) watering place; (*robinet*) water tap GB *ou* faucet US; ～ **d'exclamation** exclamation mark; ～ **de fuite** vanishing point; ～ **de fusion** melting point; ～ **d'interrogation** question mark; ～ **du jour** daybreak; ～ **de mire** Mil target; fig focal point; **être au** ～ **mort** fig (*affaires, consommation*) to be at a standstill; [*négociations*] to be in a state of deadlock; ～ **noir** (*comédon*) blackhead; (*problème*) problem; (*sur la route*) blackspot; ～ **d'orgue** Mus pause sign; ～ **de penalty** penalty spot; ～ **de repère** (*spatial*) landmark; (*temporel, personnel*) point of reference; ～ **de suture** stitch; ～ **de vue** (*paysage*) viewpoint; (*opinion*) point of view; **du** ～ **de vue du sens** as far as meaning is concerned; ～**s de suspension** suspension points

Idiome **être mal en** ～ to be in a bad way

pointage /pwɛ̃taʒ/ nm [1] (*vérification*) gén checking; (en cochant) ticking off GB, checking off US; **la** ～ (dans un vote) the tally of the votes; [2] (de salarié) (en entrant) clocking in; (en sortant) clocking off; **feuille de** ～ time sheet

pointe /pwɛ̃t/
A nf [1] (extrémité) (de couteau, crayon) point; (de chaussure) toe; (des cheveux) end; (de grille) spike; (de lance, flèche) tip, point; **en** ～ pointed; **un casque à** ～ a spiked helmet; [2] fig **de** ～ [*technologie*] advanced, state-of-the-art; [*secteur, industrie*] high-tech; [*entreprise*] leading; **à la** ～ **du progrès** state-of-the-art (*épith*); [3] (maximum) high; **fortes** ～**s saisonnières** seasonal highs; **vitesse de** ～ maximum *ou* top speed; **heure de** ～ rush hour; **aux heures de** ～ at peak time; [4] (petite quantité) (d'ail, de cannelle) touch; (d'accent, ironie) hint; [5] (clou) nail; [6] (outil) (pour tailler) cutter; (pour graver) metal point; [7] (de chausson de danse) blocked shoe; (extrémité du chausson) point; [8] (allusion désagréable) pointed *ou* barbed remark; **lancer des** ～**s à qn** to level cutting remarks at sb
B pointes nfpl [1] Sport (chaussures à) ～**s** spikes; **courir avec des** ～**s** to run in spikes; [2] (en danse) **faire des** ～**s** to dance on points

Composés ～ **d'asperge** asparagus tip; ～ **de diamant** diamond cutter; ～ **du pied** tiptoe; **elle est entrée sur la** ～ **des pieds** she tiptoed in; **aborder une question sur la** ～ **des pieds** fig to broach a matter carefully; ～ **sèche** metal point; ～ **du sein** nipple

Idiome **tailler les oreilles en** ～ ○ **à qn** to give sb a thick ear

pointé, ～**e** /pwɛ̃te/ adj Mus [*note*] dotted

pointer¹ /pwɛ̃te/ [1]
A vtr [1] (en cochant) to tick off GB, to check off US [*noms, mots, chiffres*]; to check [*liste*]; [2] (diriger) to point [*arme*] (**sur** at); ～ **le doigt vers** to point at; ～ **son museau** [*animal*] to peep out; ～ **son nez** ○ to show one's face; [3] (dresser) ～ **ses oreilles** [*chien*] to prick up its ears
B vi [1] [*employé*] (en arrivant) to clock in; (en sortant) to clock out; ～ **à l'usine** ○ to work in a factory; ～ **à l'agence pour l'emploi** to sign on at the unemployment office; [2] (aux boules) *to aim at positioning a boule as close to the jack as possible*; [3] (se dresser) [*clocher, arbre, antenne*] to rise up; [*seins*] to stick out; ～ **à l'horizon** to rise up on the horizon; [4] (apparaître) [*soleil*] to come up, to rise; [*aube, jour*] to break; [*fleur, plante*] to come up; [*bourgeon*] to open
C se pointer ○ vpr [*personne*] to turn up (**à** at)

pointer² /pwɛ̃tɛʀ/ nm (chien) pointer

pointeur, **-euse¹** /pwɛ̃tœʀ, øz/
A nm,f gén checker; (en entreprise, sport) timekeeper; (aux boules) *player whose role is to position his own boule*
B nm Mil gun-layer

pointeuse² /pwɛ̃tøz/ nf time clock

pointillé, ～**e** /pwɛ̃tije/
A adj dotted (**de** with)
B nm [1] (ligne) dotted line; (perforation) perforation(s); **plier suivant le** ～ fold along the dotted line; **en** ～ lit dotted; **message en** ～ fig underlying message; [2] Art stippling; **dessin au** ～ stippled drawing

pointilleux, **-euse** /pwɛ̃tijø, øz/ adj pej [*personne*] fussy (**sur** about), pernickety

pointu, ～**e** /pwɛ̃ty/
A adj [1] [*bout*] pointed; [*ciseaux*] with a sharp point (*épith, après n*); [*toit, chapeau*] pointed; [*menton*] pointed, sharp péj; [2] [*contrôle*] close, thorough; [3] [*secteur, travail*] highly specialized; [*question*] precise; [4] [*voix*] piercing; [*ton*] shrill
B adv **parler** ～ *to sound like a Parisian to a native of the south of France*

pointure /pwɛ̃tyʀ/ ▸ p. 575 nf (de gant, chaussure) size

point-virgule, pl **points-virgules** /pwɛ̃viʀgyl/ ▸ p. 413 nm semicolon

poire /pwaʀ/ nf [1] (fruit) pear; **en forme de** ～ pear-shaped; [2] (en boucherie) *cut of topside of beef used for steaks*; [3] (interrupteur) (pear-shaped) light switch; [4] (en bijouterie) pear-shaped stone; [5] ⁰(visage) face; [6] ○(personne naïve) mug ○ GB, sucker ○

Composé ～ **à injections** *or* **à lavement** bulb syringe

Idiomes **couper la** ～ **en deux** to split the difference; **garder une** ～ **pour la soif** to save something for a rainy day

poireau, pl ～**x** /pwaʀo/ nm leek

poireauter ○ /pwaʀɔte/ [1] vi to hang about ○

poirier /pwaʀje/ nm [1] (arbre) pear (tree); [2] (bois) pear

Idiome **faire le** ～ to do a headstand

pois /pwa/ nm inv [1] Bot, Culin pea; **petit** ～ (garden) pea, petit pois; [2] (motif) dot; **à** ～ polka dot (*épith*), spotted

Composés ～ **cassé** split pea; ～ **chiche** chickpea; ～ **de senteur** sweet pea

poison /pwazɔ̃/
A ○nmf (personne agaçante) pest
B nm lit, fig poison

poisse ○ /pwas/ nf (malchance) rotten luck ○

poisseux, **-euse** /pwasø, øz/ adj [*mains, table*] sticky; [*atmosphère*] muggy; [*restaurant*] greasy

poisson /pwasɔ̃/ nm fish; **les** ～**s d'eau douce/de mer** freshwater/saltwater fish ⦰

Composés ～ **d'argent** (insecte) silverfish; ～ **d'avril** (exclamation) April fool!; (blague) April fool's joke; **faire un** ～ **d'avril à qn** to make an April fool of sb; ～ **pané** breaded fish; (en bâtonnets) fish fingers (*pl*); ～ **rouge** goldfish; ～ **volant** flying fish

Idiomes **être comme un** ～ **dans l'eau** to be in one's element; **essayer de noyer le** ～ ○ to fudge the issue; **petit** ～ **deviendra grand** mighty oaks from little acorns grow; **les gros** ～**s mangent les petits** it's the survival of the fittest

poissonnerie /pwasɔnʀi/ ▸ p. 372 nf [1] (magasin) fishmonger's (shop) GB, fish shop US; (dans un supermarché) fish counter, fish market US; [2] (industrie) fish trade

poissonneux, **-euse** /pwasɔnø, øz/ adj [*eaux, rivière*] well stocked with fish (*après n*)

poissonnier, **-ière** /pwasɔnje, ɛʀ/ ▸ p. 372 nm,f fishmonger GB, fish vendor US

Poissons /pwasɔ̃/ ▸ p. 635 nprmpl Pisces

poitrail /pwatʀɑj/ nm breast; (poitrine) hum chest

poitrine /pwatʀin/ ▸ p. 136, p. 575 nf [1] (thorax) chest; (seins) breasts (*pl*); **tour de** ～ (pour un homme) chest size; (pour une femme) bust size; **se frapper la** ～ fig to beat one's breast; **elle n'a pas beaucoup de** ～ she is rather flat-chested; [2] Culin breast; ～ **de bœuf** brisket; ～ **de porc** ≈ belly of pork

Composé ～ **fumée/salée** ≈ smoked/unsmoked streaky bacon

poivre /pwavʀ/ nm pepper; ~ **en grains** whole pepper-corns (pl); ~ **et sel** salt-and-pepper (épith)

poivré, **~e** /pwavʀe/ adj [sauce, odeur] peppery; [plaisanterie] racy

poivrer /pwavʀe/ [1] vtr to add pepper to [plat, sauce]

poivrier /pwavʀije/ nm **1** Culin (récipient) pepper-pot GB, pepper shaker US; (moulin) pepper mill; **2** Bot (arbuste) pepper tree

poivron /pwavʀɔ̃/ nm sweet pepper

poivrot○, **~e** /pwavʀo, ɔt/ nmf drunk, drunkard

poix /pwa/ nf inv pitch; ~ **bitumineuse** coal-tar pitch

poker /pɔkɛʀ/ ▸ p. 327 nm poker; **une partie de** ~ fig a game of bluff; **coup de** ~ fig gamble

polaire /pɔlɛʀ/
A adj **1** [faune, flore, région] polar; [froid, paysage] arctic; **2** Chimie, Math polar; **3** Tex **laine** or **fibre** ~ fleece
B nf Tex, Costume fleece

polar○ /pɔlaʀ/ nm detective novel

polariser /pɔlaʀize/ [1]
A vtr **1** Phys to polarize; **2** (concentrer) to focus [débat, opinion]; **3** (attirer à soi) to attract [regards]; to be a focus for [soupçons]
B se polariser vpr (se concentrer) [attention, débat] to focus; [personne] to focus one's attention

pôle /pol/ nm **1** Géog, Math, Phys pole; **2** fig (centre) centreGB; (tendance) pole

polémique /pɔlemik/
A adj polemical
B nf debate; **de violentes ~s** fierce debate ⊄

poli, **~e** /pɔli/
A pp ▸ polir
B pp adj lit, fig [métal, style] polished
C adj (courtois) polite (**avec qn** to sb)
D nm shine; **donner du** ~ **à qch** to polish sth up

police /pɔlis/ nf **1** (force) police (+ v pl); **toutes les ~s du pays** every police force in the country; **2** (organisme privé) security service; **3** (maintien de l'ordre) policing; **pouvoirs de** ~ powers to enforce law and order; **faire la** ~ to keep order; **4** (d'assurance) policy; **5** (en typographie) ~ **(de caractères)** fonts (pl); **6** (tribunal) **passer en simple** ~ to be tried in a police court

Composés ~ **de l'air et des frontières**, **PAF** border police; ~ **judiciaire**, **PJ** detective division of the French police force; ~ **des mœurs** or **mondaine** vice squad; ~ **montée** mounted police; ~ **municipale** city police; ~ **nationale** national police force; ~ **privée** private police force; ~ **de la route** traffic police; ~ **secours** ≈ emergency services (pl)

policer /pɔlise/ [12] vtr liter to civilize

polichinelle /pɔliʃinɛl/ nm (jouet) Punch

Polichinelle /pɔliʃinɛl/ npr Punchinello

policier, **-ière** /pɔlisje, ɛʀ/
A adj [surveillance, chien, régime, mesure, enquête] police; [film, roman] detective
B nm **1** ▸ p. 372 (personne) policeman; **femme** ~ police-woman; **2** ○(film) detective film; (roman) detective novel

policlinique /pɔliklinik/ nf ≈ outpatients' clinic

poliment /pɔlimã/ adv politely

polio /pɔljo/ ▸ p. 195 nf polio

poliomyélite /pɔljɔmjelit/ ▸ p. 195 nf poliomyelitis

poliomyélitique /pɔljɔmjelitik/
A adj handicapped by polio (jamais épith); [virus] polio (épith); **il est** ~ he has polio
B nmf polio sufferer

polir /pɔliʀ/ [3] vtr to polish [bois, pierre]; to polish (up) [style]; **se** ~ **les ongles** to buff one's nails

polisson, **-onne** /pɔlisɔ̃, ɔn/
A adj **1** [enfant] naughty; **2** (licencieux) naughty, saucy
B nmf (enfant) naughty child

polissonnerie /pɔlisɔnʀi/ nf **1** (d'enfant) naughty trick; **2** (propos licencieux) naughty remark

politesse /pɔlitɛs/ nf politeness; **par** ~ out of politeness; **le 'vous' de** ~ the polite 'vous' form; **tu pourrais avoir la** ~ **de t'excuser** you might have the decency to apologize; **rendre la** ~ **à qn** to return the compliment; **échanger des ~s** to exchange pleasantries; iron to exchange insults

Idiomes **l'exactitude est la** ~ **des rois** Prov punctuality is the hallmark of a gentleman; **brûler** or **griller la** ~ **à qn** to push in ahead of sb

politicard○ /pɔlitikaʀ/ nm pej political wheeler-dealer

politicien, **-ienne** /pɔlitisjɛ̃, ɛn/
A adj (purely) political; **politique politicienne** pej politicking pej
B nmf politician

politique¹ /pɔlitik/
A adj **1** gén political; **2** (habile) [concession] tactical; [comportement, acte] calculating
B nm **1** (aspect) political aspect; **2** (personne qui s'intéresse aux affaires de l'État) politician; **3** (personne habile) **un (fin)** ~ a shrewd operator

politique² /pɔlitik/ nf **1** (science, art) politics (+ v sg); **faire de la** ~ (en faire son métier) to go into politics, to be in polit-ics; (en tant que militant) to be involved in politics; **2** (manière de gouverner, stratégie) policy

Composé ~ **de la terre brûlée** scorched earth policy

Idiomes **pratiquer la** ~ **de l'autruche** to stick one's head in the sand; **pratiquer la** ~ **du pire** to envisage the worst-case scenario

politiquement /pɔlitikmã/ adv **1** lit politically; ~ **correct** politically correct; **2** (habilement) shrewdly

politiser /pɔlitize/ [1]
A vtr to politicize
B se politiser vpr to become politicized

politologue /pɔlitɔlɔg/ ▸ p. 372 nmf political scientist

pollen /pɔl(l)ɛn/ nm pollen

polluant, **~e** /pɔl(l)yã, ãt/
A adj polluting
B nm pollutant

polluer /pɔl(l)ye/ [1] vtr to pollute

pollueur, **-euse** /pɔl(l)yœʀ, øz/
A adj polluting
B nmf (usine) polluter, factory responsible for pollution

pollution /pɔl(l)ysjɔ̃/ nf lit, fig pollution ⊄

Composé ~ **nocturne** wet dream, nocturnal emission spéc

polo /pɔlo/ nm **1** (vêtement) polo shirt; **2** ▸ p. 327 (sport) polo

polochon○ /pɔlɔʃɔ̃/ nm bolster; **bataille (à coups) de ~s** pillow fight

Pologne /pɔlɔɲ/ ▸ p. 230 nprf Poland

polonais, **~e¹** /pɔlɔnɛ, ɛz/
A ▸ p. 392 adj Polish
B ▸ p. 336 nm Ling Polish

Polonais, **~e** /pɔlɔnɛ, ɛz/ ▸ p. 392 nmf Pole

polonaise² /pɔlɔnɛz/ nf **1** Mus polonaise; **2** Culin pastry with meringue topping, flavouredGB with Kirsch

poltron, **-onne** /pɔltʀɔ̃, ɔn/
A adj cowardly
B nmf coward

poltronnerie /pɔltʀɔnʀi/ nf cowardice

polyclinique /pɔliklinik/ nf private hospital

polycopie /pɔlikɔpi/ nf **1** (procédé) duplicating; **2** (feuille) duplicate copy

polycopié, **~e** /pɔlikɔpje/
A adj duplicated
B nm duplicated notes (pl)

polycopier /pɔlikɔpje/ [2] vtr to duplicate

polyculture /pɔlikyltyʀ/ nf mixed farming

polyèdre /pɔliɛdʀ/ nm polyhedron

polyéthylène /pɔlietilɛn/ nm polythene GB, polyethyl-ene US

polygame /pɔligam/
A adj polygamous
B nmf polygamist

polyglotte /pɔliglɔt/ adj, nmf polyglot

polygone /pɔligon/ nm **1** Math polygon; **2** Mil firing range

polyhandicapé, **~e** /pɔliãdikape/ nmf multiply handicapped person

Polynésie /pɔlinezi/ ▸ p. 504 nprf Polynesia

polynésien, **-ienne** /pɔlinezjɛ̃, ɛn/
A adj Polynesian

B *nm* Ling Polynesian

polysémique /pɔlisemik/ *adj* polysemous

polytechnicien, -ienne /pɔliteknisjɛ̃, ɛn/ *nm,f*: graduate of the École Polytechnique

Polytechnique /pɔliteknik/ *nf*: Grande École of Science and Technology

> **ⓘ** **Polytechnique** One of the most prestigious of all *grandes écoles*, founded in 1794, producing an élite force of engineers who work in the industry or public administration. Students, recruited by *concours*, have the rank of reserve military officers. *X*, as the *École Polytechnique* is nicknamed, is located at Palaiseau. ▸ **grande école**

polyvalence /pɔlivalɑ̃s/ *nf* **1** (d'appareil, de matériel) versatility; **2** (d'employé, de professeur) flexibility; **3** Chimie, Méd polyvalence

polyvalent, ∼e¹ /pɔlivalɑ̃, ɑ̃t/
A *adj* Chimie, Méd polyvalent; [matériel] multipurpose (épith); [employé] who does several jobs (après n); [professeur] teaching several subjects (après n)
B *nm* tax inspector (checking company tax returns)

polyvalente² /pɔlivalɑ̃t/ *nf* C comprehensive school

pommade /pɔmad/ *nf* Méd ointment

(Idiome) **passer de la ∼**○ **à qn** to butter sb up○

pomme /pɔm/ *nf* **1** (fruit) apple; **2** (d'arrosoir) rose; (de douche) shower-head; (de canne) pommel, knob; (de mât) truck; (d'escalier) knob; **3** ○(benêt) mug○ GB, sucker○; **4** ○(personne) **ça va encore être pour ma ∼** (ennui) I'm in for it again○; (tour de payer) it looks like it's my turn to pay again

(Composés) **∼ d'Adam** Adam's apple; **∼ d'amour** (confiserie) toffee apple GB, candy apple US; **∼ d'api** ≈ small apple; **∼ de discorde** bone of contention; **∼ de pin** pine cone; **∼ de terre** potato; **∼ de terre en robe des champs** (bouillie) potato boiled in its skin; (au four) jacket potato; **∼s allumettes** potato straws GB, shoestring potatoes US; **∼s chips** crisps GB, potato chips US; **∼s frites** chips GB, (French) fries; **∼s à l'huile** ≈ potato salad; **∼s vapeur** steamed potatoes

(Idiome) **tomber dans les ∼s** to faint, to pass out○

pommeau, *pl* **∼x** /pɔmo/ *nm* (de canne, rampe) knob; (d'épée, de selle) pommel

pommelé, ∼e /pɔmle/ *adj* **cheval ∼** dappled horse; **cheval gris ∼** dapple-grey GB *ou* dapple-gray US horse; **un ciel ∼** a mackerel sky

pommeraie /pɔmʀe/ *nf* apple orchard

pommette /pɔmɛt/ ▸ **p. 136** *nf* cheekbone

pommier /pɔmje/ *nm* (arbre) apple tree; (bois) apple, applewood

pompage /pɔ̃paʒ/ *nm* pumping

pompe /pɔ̃p/
A *nf* **1** (appareil) pump; **2** ○(chaussure) shoe; **3** (apparat) pomp; **4** ○Sport (exercice) press-up GB, push-up
B **pompes** *nfpl* Relig vanities; **les ∼s de Satan** Satan's pomps

(Composés) **∼ à essence** petrol pump GB, gas pump US; **∼ à incendie** fire engine; **∼s funèbres** (lieu) undertaker's (sg) GB, funeral home (sg) US; (entreprise) undertaker's GB, funeral director's

(Idiomes) **avoir un coup de ∼**○ to be knackered❶ GB *ou* pooped○; **à toute ∼**○ at top speed, as quickly as possible; **marcher** *or* **être à côté de ses ∼s**○ not to be with it, to be away with the fairies○

pomper /pɔ̃pe/ [1] *vtr* **1** (aspirer) to pump; (pour vider) to pump out; (pour faire monter) to pump up; **2** ○(copier) students' slang to copy (**sur** from), to crib (**sur** from)

(Idiome) **∼ l'air**○ **à qn** to get on sb's nerves

pompette○ /pɔ̃pɛt/ *adj* tipsy, drunk

pompeux, -euse /pɔ̃pø, øz/ *adj* pompous

pompier, -ière /pɔ̃pje, ɛʀ/
A *adj* pompous
B ▸ **p. 372** *nm* fireman, firefighter; **appeler les ∼s** to call the fire brigade GB *ou* fire department US

pompiste /pɔ̃pist/ ▸ **p. 372** *nmf* petrol GB *ou* gas US pump attendant

pompon /pɔ̃pɔ̃/ *nm* (de bonnet, frange) bobble; (de pantoufle) pompom

(Idiome) **remporter** *or* **décrocher le ∼**○ to come top, to win first prize

pomponner /pɔ̃pɔne/ [1]
A *vtr* **∼ un bébé** to get a baby dressed up
B **se pomponner** *vpr* to get dolled up

ponçage /pɔ̃saʒ/ *nm* **1** Tech (de bois, mur) sanding; (de cuir) smoothing; **2** (à la pierre ponce) pumicing

ponce /pɔ̃s/ *nf* **pierre ∼** pumice stone

poncer /pɔ̃se/ [12] *vtr* **1** Tech (pour décaper) to sand; **2** Art (pour reproduire) to pounce; **3** (à la pierre ponce) to pumice

ponceuse /pɔ̃søz/ *nf* sander; **∼ vibrante** orbital sander

poncif /pɔ̃sif/ *nm* (banalité) cliché, commonplace

ponction /pɔ̃ksjɔ̃/ *nf* **1** Méd puncture; **2** (en argent) levy

ponctionner /pɔ̃ksjɔne/ [1] *vtr* **1** Méd (perforer) to puncture; (extraire) to tap [liquide]; **2** (prélever) to levy [somme]

ponctualité /pɔ̃ktɥalite/ *nf* punctuality; **avec ∼** punctually

ponctuation /pɔ̃ktɥasjɔ̃/ ▸ **p. 413** *nf* Ling punctuation

ponctuel, -elle /pɔ̃ktɥɛl/ *adj* **1** (à l'heure) [personne] punctual; [paiement] prompt; **2** (ne portant pas sur l'ensemble) [action] (limité) limited; (localisé) localized; (ciblé) selective; [problème] isolated; **3** Ling punctual

ponctuellement /pɔ̃ktɥɛlmɑ̃/ *adj* **1** (à l'heure) [arriver, répondre] punctually; [payer] promptly; **2** (en ciblant) selectively

ponctuer /pɔ̃ktɥe/ [1] *vtr* to punctuate (**de** with)

pondérateur, -trice /pɔ̃deʀatœʀ, tʀis/ *adj* [élément] stabilizing

pondération /pɔ̃deʀasjɔ̃/ *nf* **1** (de personne) levelheadedness; **2** (équilibrage) balancing; (équilibre) balance (**entre** between); **3** (d'indice) weighting

pondéré, ∼e /pɔ̃deʀe/ *adj* **1** [personne, attitude] levelheaded; **2** [indice] weighted

pondérer /pɔ̃deʀe/ [14] *vtr* **1** (équilibrer) to balance; **2** to weight [indice]

pondre /pɔ̃dʀ/ [6] *vtr* **1** Zool to lay [œuf]; **où les oiseaux pondent-ils?** where do birds lay their eggs?; **2** ○(produire) to produce [poème, article]; to churn out○ péj [poèmes, articles]; to produce [enfant]

poney /pɔnɛ/ *nm* pony; **faire du ∼** to go pony-riding

pongiste /pɔ̃ʒist/ *nmf* table-tennis player

pont /pɔ̃/
A *nm* **1** Archit, Constr bridge; **2** (liens) link, tie; **couper les ∼s** to break off all contact; **il a coupé les ∼s avec sa famille** he has broken with his family; **3** (vacances) extended weekend (including day(s) between a public holiday and the weekend); **faire le ∼** to make a long weekend of it; **lundi je fais le ∼** I'm taking Monday off; **4** Naut deck; **bâtiment à deux ∼s** two-decker; **5** Aut axle; **6** Sport crab; **faire le ∼** to do the crab
B **ponts** *nmpl* **∼s (et chaussées)** highways department

(Composés) **∼ aérien** airlift; **∼ basculant** bascule bridge; **∼ flottant** pontoon bridge; **∼ levant** vertical-lift bridge; **∼ roulant** (overhead) travelling^GB crane; **∼ suspendu** suspension bridge; **∼ tournant** swing bridge

(Idiomes) **coucher sous les ∼s** to sleep rough; **il coulera beaucoup d'eau sous les ∼s avant que...** it will be a long time before...; **faire un ∼ d'or à qn** to offer sb a large sum to accept a job

pontage /pɔ̃taʒ/ *nm* Méd bypass (operation)

ponte¹ /pɔ̃t/ *nm* **1** ○(personnage) big shot○; **2** (au jeu) punter

ponte² /pɔ̃t/ *nf* (action) laying (of eggs); (œufs) clutch; **∼ ovulaire** ovulation

pontife /pɔ̃tif/ *nm* **1** Relig pontiff; **le souverain ∼** the pope; **2** ○(personnage important) pundit○

pontifical, ∼e, *mpl* **-aux** /pɔ̃tifikal, o/ *adj* [trône, autorité, garde] papal; [messe, célébration] pontifical

pontifier /pɔ̃tifje/ [2] *vi* to pontificate

pont-levis, *pl* **ponts-levis** /pɔ̃ləvi/ *nm* drawbridge

ponton /pɔ̃tɔ̃/ *nm* Naut (débarcadère) (floating) landing stage; (plate-forme) pontoon

pope /pɔp/ *nm* pope, orthodox priest

popeline /pɔplin/ *nf* poplin

popote○ /pɔpɔt/ *nf* (cuisine) cooking

popotin○ /pɔpɔtɛ̃/ *nm* bum○ GB, rear○, bottom

populace /pɔpylas/ nf la ~ the masses (pl)

populaire /pɔpylɛʀ/ adj ① (ouvrier) [quartier] working-class; [art, roman] popular; [édition] cheap; [restaurant] basic; **classe** ~ working class; ② (entériné par la tradition) [tradition] folk; **culture** ~ folklore; **le bon sens** ~ popular wisdom; ③ (estimé) popular (**chez, parmi** with); ④ (venant du peuple) [mouvement] popular; [volonté] of the people (après n); ⑤ Ling (utilisé par le peuple) popular; (grossier) vulgar; ⑥ Géog, Pol **République** ~ People's Republic

populariser /pɔpylaʀize/ [1]
Ⓐ vtr to popularize
Ⓑ **se populariser** vpr to become very popular

popularité /pɔpylaʀite/ nf popularity

population /pɔpylasjɔ̃/ nf population; ~ **active** working population

populeux, -euse /pɔpylø, øz/ adj densely populated, populous

porc /pɔʀ/ nm ① (animal) pig, hog US; ~ (viande) pork; (peau) pigskin; ② ○(personne) pej pig○

porcelaine /pɔʀsəlɛn/ nf ① (matière) porcelain, china; ~ **de Chine** china; ~ **de Sèvres** Sèvres china ou porcelain; ② (objet) piece of porcelain; ③ Zool cowrie

porcelet /pɔʀsəlɛ/ nm piglet

porc-épic, pl ~**s** /pɔʀkepik/ nm porcupine

porche /pɔʀʃ/ nm porch; **sous le** ~ in the porch

porcherie /pɔʀʃəʀi/ nf lit, fig pigsty

porcin, ~e /pɔʀsɛ̃, in/
Ⓐ adj ① Agric [race] porcine; **élevage** ~ pig breeding; **viande** ~**e** pork; ② fig [visage, yeux] piggy, porcine; [manières] swinish
Ⓑ nm pig; **les** ~**s** pigs

pore /pɔʀ/ nm pore; **suant la peur par tous les** ~**s** fig exuding fear

poreux, -euse /pɔʀø, øz/ adj porous

porno○ /pɔʀno/
Ⓐ adj porno○, porn○
Ⓑ nm Cin (genre) porn○; (film) blue movie○

pornographique /pɔʀnɔɡʀafik/ adj pornographic

port /pɔʀ/ nm ① (pour accoster) harbour^GB; (avec installations portuaires) port; ~ **fluvial** river port; **les restaurants du** ~ the restaurants along the harbour^GB; ② (ville portuaire) port; ③ (refuge) haven; ④ (fait de porter) **le** ~ **du casque est obligatoire** helmets must be worn at all times; ~ **d'armes** carrying arms; ⑤ (maintien) carriage; (démarche) bearing; **un joli** ~ **de tête** a graceful carriage of the head; ⑥ (transport) carriage; (par la poste) postage; ~ **dû/payé** gén carriage forward/paid; (par la poste) postage due/paid; ⑦ Ordinat port; ~ **USB** USB port

Ⓒᴏᴍᴘᴏ̄ꜱ́ꜱ ~ **d'aéroglisseurs** hoverport; ~ **d'attache** Naut port of registry; fig home base; ~ **d'escale** port of call; ~ **franc** free port; ~ **de pêche** (installations) fishing harbour^GB; (ville) fishing port; ~ **pétrolier** tanker terminal; ~ **de plaisance** marina; ~ **de salut** haven

Ⓘᴅɪᴏᴍᴇ **arriver à bon** ~ to arrive safe and sound

portable /pɔʀtabl/
Ⓐ adj ① (portatif) portable; ② (pas trop lourd) **c'est** ~ it can be carried; ③ (mettable) wearable
Ⓑ nm ① (téléphone) mobile (phone); ② (ordinateur) laptop.

portage /pɔʀtaʒ/ nm (transport à dos d'homme) porterage

Ⓒᴏᴍᴘᴏ̄ꜱ́ ~ **salarial** system which allows a self-employed person to obtain the social welfare advantages of employee status

portail /pɔʀtaj/ nm
Ⓐ (de parc, jardin) gate; (d'église, de temple) great door; ② Ordinat portal

portant, ~e /pɔʀtɑ̃, ɑ̃t/ adj ① [mur] load-bearing; [roue] carrying; ② [personne] **bien** ~ in good health; **être mieux** ~ to be in better health

Ⓘᴅɪᴏᴍᴇ **à bout** ~ at point-blank range

portatif, -ive /pɔʀtatif, iv/ adj portable; **ordinateur** ~ laptop computer

porte /pɔʀt/
Ⓐ adj [veine] portal
Ⓑ nf ① (entrée) (de bâtiment) door; (de parc, stade, ville) gate; **la** ~ **de derrière** the back door; **devant la** ~ **de l'hôpital** outside the hospital; **j'ai une gare à ma** ~ I have a station on my doorstep; **aux** ~**s du désert** at the edge of the desert; **passer la** ~ to enter the house; **ouvrir sa** ~ **à qn** to let sb

in; **c'est la** ~ **ouverte à la criminalité** it's an open invitation to crime; **ouvrir ses** ~**s (au public)** [salon, exposition, magasin] to open (to the public); **l'entreprise a fermé ses** ~**s** the company has gone out of business; **mettre à la** ~ (exclure d'un cours) to throw [sb] out; (renvoyer) to expel [élève]; to fire, to sack○ GB [employé]; **ce n'est pas la** ~ **à côté**○ it's quite far; **voir qn entre deux** ~**s** to see sb very briefly; **trouver** ~ **close** or **de bois** to find nobody in; **tu frappes à la bonne/mauvaise** ~ you've come to the right/wrong place; ② (moyen d'accès) gateway; **la victoire leur ouvre la** ~ **de la finale** the victory clears the way to the final for them; ③ (possibilité) door; **cela ouvre bien des** ~**s** it opens many doors; ④ (dans un aéroport) gate; ⑤ Sport (en ski) gate; ⑥ (portière) door; **une voiture à deux/cinq** ~**s** a two-/five-door car; ⑦ (en électronique) gate

Ⓒᴏᴍᴘᴏ̄ꜱ́ꜱ ~ **basculante** up-and-over door; ~ **battante** swing door; ~ **d'écluse** lock gate; ~ **d'entrée** (de maison) front door; (d'église, hôpital, immeuble) main entrance; ~ **de service** tradesmen's entrance GB, service entrance; ~ **de sortie** lit exit; fig escape route; ~ **à tambour** revolving door; ~**s ouvertes** open day GB, open house US

Ⓘᴅɪᴏᴍᴇꜱ **prendre la** ~ to leave; **entrer par la petite/grande** ~ to start at the bottom/top; **enfoncer une** ~ **ouverte** to state the obvious; **il faut qu'une** ~ **soit ouverte ou fermée** Prov you've got to decide one way or the other

porté, ~e¹ /pɔʀte/ adj **être** ~ **à se plaindre** to be inclined to complain; **être** ~ **sur qch** to be keen on sth; **être** ~ **sur la chose** euph to like it○, to be keen on sex

porte-à-faux /pɔʀtafo/ nm inv **être en porte à faux** lit [mur] to be out of plumb; [rocher] to be precariously balanced; Archit [construction] to be cantilevered; fig [personne] to be in an awkward position

porte-à-porte /pɔʀtapɔʀt/ nm inv Comm door-to-door selling; Pol door-to-door canvassing

porte-avions /pɔʀtavjɔ̃/ nm inv aircraft carrier

porte-bagages /pɔʀt(ə)baɡaʒ/ nm inv (sur un vélo) carrier; (dans un train) luggage rack; (sur un toit de voiture) roof rack

porte-bébé /pɔʀt(ə)bebe/ nm inv (panier) carrycot GB, carrier US; (kangourou®) (baby) sling, baby carrier; (sac à dos) baby carrier

porte-bonheur /pɔʀt(ə)bɔnœʀ/ nm inv lucky charm

porte-bouteilles /pɔʀt(ə)butɛj/ nm inv (panier) bottle-carrier, bottleholder; (égouttoir) bottle-drainer

porte-clés, **porte-clefs** /pɔʀt(ə)kle/ nm inv key ring

porte-couteau, pl ~**x** /pɔʀt(ə)kuto/ nm knife rest

porte-documents /pɔʀt(ə)dɔkymɑ̃/ nm inv briefcase, attaché case

porte-drapeau /pɔʀt(ə)dʀapo/ nm inv standard-bearer

portée² /pɔʀte/
Ⓐ adj f ▸ porté
Ⓑ nf ① (distance) range; **être hors de** ~ to be out of reach; **être à** ~ **de main** or **à la** ~ **de la main** (accessible) to be within reach; (dans endroit commode) to be to hand; **être à** ~ **de voix** to be within earshot; ② (niveau) **c'est à la** ~ **de n'importe qui** (faisable) anybody can do it; (compréhensible) anybody can understand it; (en prix) anybody can afford it; **se mettre à la** ~ **de qn** to come down to sb's level; ③ (effet) impact; ④ (d'animaux) litter; ⑤ Mus staff, stave GB

porte-fenêtre, pl **portes-fenêtres** /pɔʀt(ə)fənɛtʀ/ nf French window

portefeuille /pɔʀt(ə)fœj/
Ⓐ adj **jupe/robe** ~ wrap-over skirt/dress
Ⓑ nm ① (à billets) wallet, billfold US; ② Pol portfolio; ③ Fin portfolio

Ⓘᴅɪᴏᴍᴇꜱ **faire un lit en** ~ to make an apple pie bed; **avoir le** ~ **bien garni** to be well-off; **avoir toujours la main au** ~ to be very generous

porte-jarretelles /pɔʀt(ə)ʒaʀtɛl/ nm inv suspender belt GB, garter belt US

portemanteau, pl ~**x** /pɔʀt(ə)mɑ̃to/ nm ① (au mur) (patère) (coat) peg ou hook; (collectif) coat rack; (sur pied) coat stand, coat ou clothes tree US; ② (cintre) coat hanger

portemine /pɔʀt(ə)min/ nm propelling GB ou mechanical US pencil

porte-monnaie /pɔʀt(ə)mɔnɛ/ nm inv purse GB, coin purse US

porte-parapluies /pɔʀt(ə)paʀaplɥi/ *nm inv* umbrella stand

porte-parole /pɔʀt(ə)paʀɔl/ *nm inv* (personne) spokesperson, spokesman/spokeswoman; (journal) mouthpiece

porte-plume /pɔʀt(ə)plym/ *nm inv* penholder

porter /pɔʀte/ [1]

A *vtr* [1] (transporter) to carry [*chose, personne*]; ~ **qn sur son lit** to get sb into bed; [2] (apporter) ~ **qch quelque part** to take sth somewhere; ~ **des messages** to run messages; ~ **une affaire devant les tribunaux** to bring a case to court; [3] (soutenir) [*mur, chaise*] to carry, to bear [*poids*]; **l'eau te portera** the water will hold you up; ~ **qn à bout de bras** fig to take on sb's problems; ~ **l'espoir de millions d'hommes** to be the focus for the hopes of millions; [4] (avoir sur soi) to wear [*robe, bijou, verres de contact*]; to have [*cheveux longs, moustache*]; ~ **les armes** to bear arms; ~ **une arme** to be armed; [5] (avoir) to have [*initiales, date, titre*]; to bear [*sceau*]; **portant le numéro 300** with the number 300; **le document porte la mention 'secret'** the document is marked 'secret'; **ils ne portent pas le même nom** they have different names; **il porte bien son nom** the name suits him; **bien** ~ **son âge** to look good for one's age; ~ **des traces de sang** to be blood-stained; **portant une expression de découragement** looking discouraged; ~ **en soi une grande volonté de réussir** to be full of ambition; [6] (produire) to bear [*fleurs*]; ~ **des fruits** lit, ~ **ses fruits** fig to bear fruit; **l'enfant qu'elle porte** the child she is carrying; **le roman qu'il porte en lui** his great unwritten novel; [7] (amener) **cela porte le prix du billet à…** this brings the price of the ticket to…; ~ **un taux à** to put a rate up to; ~ **la température de l'eau à 80°C** to heat the water to 80°C; ~ **qn au pouvoir** to bring sb to power; [8] (diriger) ~ **son regard vers** to look at; ~ **qch à sa bouche** to raise sth to one's lips; **si tu portes la main sur elle** if you lay a finger on her; **l'estime qu'elle te porte** her respect for you; ~ **ses efforts sur qch** to devote one's energies to sth; ~ **un jugement sur qch** to pass judgment on sth; [9] (inscrire) ~ **qch sur un registre** to enter sth on a register; **être porté disparu** to be reported missing; **se faire** ~ **malade** *or* **pâle**⁰ *ou* report sick; [10] (inciter) ~ **qn à se méfier** to make sb cautious; **tout nous porte à croire que** everything leads us to believe that; [11] (donner, causer) ~ **bonheur** *or* **chance** to be lucky; ~ **malheur** to be unlucky; **ça m'a porté bonheur** it brought me luck; **ça m'a porté malheur** it was unlucky

B *porter sur vtr ind* [1] (concerner) ~ **sur** [*débat, article*] to be about; [*mesure, interdiction*] to apply to; [2] (reposer sur) ~ **sur** [*structure*] to be resting on; [3] (heurter) ~ **sur** to hit

C *vi* **une voix qui porte** a voice that carries; **le coup a porté** the blow hit home; **un canon qui porte à 500 mètres** a cannon with a range of 500 metres^{GB}

D *se porter vpr* [1] (se sentir) **se** ~ **bien/mal** [*personne*] to be well/ill; [*affaire*] to be going well/badly; **je ne m'en porte pas plus mal** I'm none the worse for it; **je me porte à merveille** I'm absolutely fine; [2] (être mis) **cela se porte avec des chaussures plates** you wear it with flat shoes; **cela ne se porte plus** it has gone out of fashion; [3] (se diriger) **se** ~ **sur** [*soupçon*] to fall on; **le choix se porta sur le vase** they/she etc chose the vase; **tous les regards se sont portés vers le ciel/vers lui** everyone looked toward(s) the sky/in his direction; [4] (se propager) **se** ~ **sur** to spread to

porte-revues /pɔʀt(ə)ʀəvy/ *nm inv* magazine rack

porte-savon /pɔʀt(ə)savɔ̃/ *nm inv* soapdish

porte-serviettes /pɔʀt(ə)sɛʀvjɛt/ *nm inv* towel rail

porteur, -euse /pɔʀtœʀ, øz/

A *adj* [1] gén **être** ~ **d'espoir** to bring hope; **être** ~ **d'un passeport grec** to hold a Greek passport; **être** ~ **d'un virus** to carry a virus; [2] Tech **mur/essieu** ~ load-bearing wall/axle; [3] Écon (en expansion) [*marché*] buoyant; [*métier*] booming; [4] Radio, Télécom [*courant, onde*] carrier (*épith*); [5] Ling **être** ~ **de sens** to have a meaning

B *nm,f* [1] (possesseur) holder, bearer; **les** ~**s de diplômes étrangers** people who hold foreign qualifications; [2] Méd carrier

C *nm* [1] ▸ p. 372 (de bagages) porter; (coursier) messenger; [2] Fin (de chèque) bearer; ~ **d'actions** shareholder

Composé ~ **sain** Méd symptom-free carrier

porte-voix /pɔʀt(ə)vwa/ *nm inv* megaphone; **les mains en** ~ his/her hands cupped around his/her mouth

portier /pɔʀtje/ *nm* [1] ▸ p. 372 (concierge) porter; [2] ⁰(gardien de but) goalkeeper

portière /pɔʀtjɛʀ/ *nf* Aut door

portillon /pɔʀtijɔ̃/ *nm* gate

Idiome **ça ne se bouscule pas au** ~⁰ people are not exactly queueing up GB *ou* lining up US

portion /pɔʀsjɔ̃/ *nf* [1] Culin (part) portion; (quantité servie) helping; [2] (dans un partage) share; [3] (partie) gén portion; (de route) stretch; (de territoire) part

Composé ~ **congrue** (nourriture) minute portion of food; (revenu) minimal income; **réduire qn à la** ~ **congrue** to give sb the strict minimum

portique /pɔʀtik/ *nm* [1] Archit portico; [2] Sport frame (in gym); [3] (pour enfants) swing frame

porto /pɔʀto/ *nm* port

portoricain, ~**e** /pɔʀtɔʀikɛ̃, ɛn/ ▸ p. 392 *adj* Puerto Rican

portrait /pɔʀtʀɛ/ *nm* [1] Art, Phot portrait; **c'est un** ~ **fidèle** it's a good likeness; [2] gén, Littérat (description) description, picture; **faire le** ~ **de** to paint a picture of; [3] (réplique) **tu es tout le** ~ **de ton père** you're the spitting image of your father; [4] ⁰(visage) face; **se faire tirer le** ~ to have one's photo taken

portrait-robot, *pl* **portraits-robots** /pɔʀtʀeʀɔbo/ *nm* photofit® (picture), identikit®

portuaire /pɔʀtɥeʀ/ *adj* port (*épith*)

portugais, ~**e** /pɔʀtygɛ, ɛz/

A ▸ p. 392 *adj* Portuguese

B ▸ p. 336 *nm* Ling Portuguese

Portugal /pɔʀtygal/ ▸ p. 230 *nprm* Portugal

POS /peɔɛs, pɔs/ *nm: abbr* ▸ **plan**

pose /poz/ *nf* [1] (mise en place) (de compteur, vitre) putting in, installation (**de** of); (de placard, dentier) fitting (**de** of); (de moquette) laying (**de** of); (de rideau) hanging, putting up (**de** of); Mil (de mine) laying (**de** of); [2] (manière de se tenir) pose; **prendre une** ~ **provocante** to strike a provocative pose; [3] Art pose; **une séance de** ~ a sitting; [4] (affectation) pretention; [5] Phot exposure

posé, ~**e** /poze/ *adj* [*air, personne*] composed; [*geste, voix*] controlled

posément /pozemɑ̃/ *adv* carefully, thoughtfully; **il parlait très** ~ he weighed his words (carefully)

poser /poze/ [1]

A *vtr* [1] (mettre) to put down; **pose ton manteau** put your coat somewhere; **ils ont posé un échafaudage contre le mur** they've put some scaffolding up against the wall; ~ **la main sur le bras de qn** to lay *ou* place one's hand on sb's arm; **j'ai posé une lettre sur votre bureau** I've put a letter on your desk; ~ **les yeux sur qn/qch** to look at sb/sth; [2] (mettre en place) to put in [*compteur, vitre*]; to install [*signalisation, radiateur*]; to fit [*serrure, prothèse*]; to lay [*carrelage, mine, pierre, câble*]; to plant [*bombe*]; to fit, to lay [*moquette*]; to put up [*papier peint, tableau, rideau, cloison, affiches*]; [3] (établir) to assert, to postulate sout [*hypothèse*]; to lay down [*règles, limites*]; ~ **sa candidature à un poste** to apply for a job; ~ **sa candidature à une élection** to stand GB *ou* run for election; **je pose 3 et je retiens 2** I put *ou* write down (the) 3 and carry (the) 2; ~ **comme hypothèse que** to put forward the theory that; [4] (soulever) to ask [*question*]; to set [*devinette*]; **la question reste posée** the question (still) remains; ~ **(un) problème à qn** to pose a problem for sb; **ça ne pose aucun problème** that's no problem at all; [5] Mus to place [*voix*]

B *vi* [1] Art, Phot to pose; ~ **nu** to pose (in the) nude; [2] (être affecté) to put on airs

C *se poser vpr* [1] [*oiseau, insecte*] to settle, to alight; [2] [*avion*] to land, to touch down; **se** ~ **en catastrophe** to make an emergency landing; [3] ⁰(s'asseoir) to plant oneself; **pose-toi quelque part et attends-moi** park⁰ yourself somewhere and wait for me; [4] (s'arrêter) [*yeux, regard*] to fall (upon); [5] (s'affirmer) **se** ~ **en** *ou* **comme** to claim to be; **se** ~ **en victime** to present oneself as a victim; [6] (se demander) **se** ~ **des questions** to ask oneself questions; **se** ~ **des questions au sujet de qn/qch** (s'interroger) to wonder about sb/sth; (douter) to have doubts about sb/sth; **ils vivent sans se** ~ **de questions** they accept things as they are; [7] (exister) [*question*] to arise; **la question ne se pose pas** (c'est impossible) there's no question of it; (c'est évident) it goes without saying

Ⓘdiome **comme imbécile il se pose là⊙!** he's a prime example of an idiot!

poseur, -euse /pozœʀ, øz/ *nm,f* (snob) poser⊙

Ⓒomposés **~ d'affiches** billsticker, billposter; **~ de bombes** bomber, bomb planter; **~ de carrelage** tiler; **~ de moquette** carpet fitter

positif, -ive /pozitif, iv/

Ⓐ *adj* ① (affirmatif) [*réponse*] affirmative; ② (constructif) [*entretien, climat*] constructive; [*évolution, effet*] positive; ③ (favorable) [*réaction, bilan*] favourable^{GB}; [*point, image*] positive; ④ (réaliste) [*personne, attitude*] positive; ⑤ Méd, Math, Électrotech, Phot positive

Ⓑ *nm* ① (résultat concret) **je veux du ~** I need something positive; ② (points favorables) positive points (*pl*); ③ Phot positive; ④ Ling positive (degree)

position /pozisjɔ̃/ *nf* ① (dans l'espace) position; **il faut revoir la ~ des joueurs** the positioning of the players has to be rethought; **en ~ horizontale/verticale** horizontally/vertically; **attention, l'échelle est en ~ instable** be careful, the ladder isn't steady; ② (posture) position; **la ~ des doigts sur une guitare** the positioning of the fingers on a guitar; **rien de pire que de rester en ~ assise toute la journée** there's nothing worse than sitting down all day; ④ (situation) position; **une ~ délicate** a tricky situation; **être en ~ dominante sur le marché** to be a market leader; ⑤ (professionnelle, sociale) position; ⑥ (au classement) place, position; ⑦ (point de vue) position, stance; **prendre ~ sur un problème** to take a stand on an issue; **prise de ~** stance, stand (**sur qch** on sth); **camper** *or* **rester sur ses ~s** to stand one's ground; ⑧ Fin (bank) balance; **être en ~ créditrice/débitrice** [*compte*] to be in credit/debit; ⑨ (en danse) position

positivement /pozitivmɑ̃/ *adv* [*répondre*] positively; [*réagir, juger*] favourably^{GB}

posologie /pozɔlɔʒi/ *nf* dosage

possédant, ~e /posedɑ̃, ɑ̃t/

Ⓐ *adj* wealthy

Ⓑ *nm,f* **les ~s** the rich (+ *v pl*), the wealthy (+ *v pl*)

posséder /posede/ [14]

Ⓐ *vtr* ① (détenir) *gén* to own, to possess; to hold [*charge*]; **sa famille ne possède plus rien** his/her family has nothing left; ② (être équipé de) to have; **un jardin qui possède un bassin** a garden with a fish pond; ③ (jouir de) to have [*connaissance, qualité*]; ④ (maîtriser) to speak [sth] fluently [*langue*]; to have a thorough knowledge of [*sujet, technique*]; ⑤ (sexuellement) to have, to possess *sout*; ⑥ (dominer) [*sentiment, douleur*] to overwhelm; ⑦ ⊙(duper) **il nous a bien possédés** he really had⊙ us there; **se faire ~ par qn** to be had⊙ by sb

Ⓑ **se poser** *vpr* (se dominer) *liter* to control oneself

possesseur /posesœʀ/ *nm* (de biens, d'objets) owner; (de diplôme, carte d'identité, d'actions) holder; (de secret) keeper; (de passeport) bearer

possessif, -ive /posesif, iv/

Ⓐ *adj* Ling, Psych possessive

Ⓑ *nm* Ling possessive

possession /posesjɔ̃/ *nf* ① (de maison, terres, fortune) possession, ownership; (de diplôme, drogue, d'arme) possession; **la ~ d'un passeport est obligatoire** you must have a passport; **prendre ~ d'un héritage** to come into one's inheritance; **être en pleine ~ de ses moyens** to be on top form; ② (maîtrise) (de langue) fluency (**de** in); (de métier, technique) mastery (**de** of); ③ (chose possédée) possession; ④ (ensorcellement) possession

possibilité /posibilite/

Ⓐ *nf* ① (éventualité) possibility; ② (occasion) opportunity; (solution) option; **les ~s de trouver un emploi** the chances of finding a job; **se réserver la ~ de faire** to reserve the right to do

Ⓑ **possibilités** *nfpl* ① (potentiel) (de personne) abilities; (d'appareil) potential *ou* possible uses; **avoir de nombreuses ~s** [*personne, appareil*] to be versatile; ② (moyens) resources

possible /posibl/

Ⓐ *adj* ① (réalisable) possible; **je viendrai chaque fois que cela sera ~** I'll come whenever I can; **ce n'est pas ~ autrement** there's no other way of doing it; **il ne me sera pas ~ de me déplacer aujourd'hui** I won't be able to get out today; **tout le courage ~** the utmost courage; **tous les cas ~s et imaginables** every conceivable case; **recule**

le plus ~ go back as far as you can; **limiter les déplacements autant que ~** to keep travelling^{GB} down to a minimum; ② (potentiel) possible; **il n'y a pas d'erreur ~, c'est lui** it's him, without a shadow of a doubt; **nous avons sélectionné de ~s candidats** we have selected some potential candidates; **(ce n'est) pas ~!** ⊙ (surprise) I don't believe it!; (ironie) you're joking!; **ce n'est pas ~ d'être aussi bête** how can anyone be so stupid?; **'tu vas acheter une voiture?'—'~'** 'are you going to buy a car?'—'maybe'; ③ ⊙(acceptable) **pas ~** impossible, awful; (croyable) **pas ~** unbelievable; **il a un accent pas ~** he has an atrocious accent; **être d'une lenteur pas ~** to be awfully slow; **il a une chance pas ~** he's incredibly lucky

Ⓑ *nm* **le ~** that which is possible; **rester dans le domaine du ~** to be within the realms of possibility; **faire (tout) son ~** to do one's best; **elle est bête au ~**⊙ she's as stupid as they come

post(-) /post/ *préf* post(-); **~-doctoral** postdoctoral; **~-romantique** post-Romantic

postal, ~e, *mpl* -aux /postal, o/ *adj* [*train, bateau, avion*] mail; [*fourgonnette, fourgon*] post office GB, mail US; [*services*] postal

poste¹ /post/ *nm* ① (fonction) (dans une entreprise) position, job; (dans la fonction publique) post; **suppression de ~** job cut; **trois ~s vacants** *or* **à pourvoir** three vacancies; **être en ~ à Moscou** [*diplomate*] to be posted to Moscow; ② Sport position; ③ (lieu) post; **~ (de travail)** work station; ④ (commissariat) **~ de police** police station; ⑤ Radio, TV (appareil) set; **~ de radio** radio (set); (station de radio) (radio) station; ⑥ Télécom (appareil) (tele)phone; (ligne) extension; ⑦ (période de travail) shift; ⑧ (en comptabilité) item; ⑨ Mil post; **~ de garde** *or* **police** guardhouse; **il est toujours fidèle au ~** you can always rely on him

Ⓒomposés **~ d'aiguillage** signal box; **~ budgétaire** budget item; **~ de contrôle** control centre^{GB}; **~ d'équipage** crew's quarters (*pl*); **~ de péage** toll booth; **~ de pilotage** Aviat flight deck; **~ de secours** first-aid post GB *ou* station; **~ de soudure** *or* **à souder** welding equipment

poste² /post/ *nf* ① (bureau) post office; **la Poste** the Post Office; **la ~** (service) the post GB, the mail US; **envoyer par la ~** to send [sth] by post GB, to mail US; **privatiser la ~** to privatize postal services; ② Hist mail

Ⓒomposés **~ aérienne** airmail; **~ restante** poste restante GB, general delivery US

poster¹ /poste/ [1]

Ⓐ *vtr* ① (expédier) to post GB, to mail US; ② (placer) to post, to station [*soldat, garde*]; to station [*complice*]; to put [sb] in place [*espion*]

Ⓑ **se poster** *vpr* **se ~ devant** (debout) to station oneself in front of; (assis) to sit in front of

poster² /postɛʀ/ *nm* (affiche) poster

postérieur, ~e /posterjœʀ/

Ⓐ *adj* ① (dans le temps) [*date*] later (*épith*); [*événement, œuvre*] subsequent (*épith*); **un écrivain ~ à Flaubert** a writer who came after Flaubert; **un événement ~ à la guerre** an event which took place after the war; ② (dans l'espace) [*partie, section*] posterior; [*pattes*] hind (*épith*); ③ [*phonème*] back

Ⓑ ⊙*nm* behind⊙, posterior *hum*

postérieurement /posterjœʀmɑ̃/ *adv* subsequently; **~ à** time, subsequent to *sout*

postérité /posterite/ *nf* ① (immortalité) posterity; **passer à** *or* **entrer dans la ~** [*nom, personne*] to go down in history; [*œuvre*] to become part of the cultural heritage; ② (lignée) descendants (*pl*)

posthume /postym/ *adj* posthumous

postiche /postiʃ/

Ⓐ *adj* (faux) [*barbe*] false

Ⓑ *nm* (de cheveux) hairpiece; (pour un chauve) toupee; (perruque) wig; (fausse moustache) false moustache GB *ou* mustache US; (fausse barbe) false beard

postier, -ière /postje, ɛʀ/ ▸ p. 372 *nm,f* postal worker

postillon /postijɔ̃/ *nm* ① ⊙(de salive) drop of saliva; ② ▸ p. 372 (cocher) postillion

postillonner⊙ /postijɔne/ [1] *vi* to spit (saliva)

postnatal, ~e, *mpl* ~s /postnatal/ *adj* postnatal; **allocation ~e** maternity allowance

postposer /postpoze/ [1] *vtr* to place [sth] after the verb [*sujet*]; to place [sth] after the noun [*adjectif*]

postscolaire /pɔstskɔlɛʀ/ *adj* **enseignement** ∼ continuing education

post-scriptum /pɔstskʀiptɔm/ *nm inv* postscript

postsynchroniser /pɔstsɛ̃kʀɔnize/ [1] *vtr* to dub, to add the soundtrack to

postulant, ∼**e** /pɔstylɑ̃, ɑ̃t/ *nm,f* **1)** gén candidate (**à** for); **2)** Relig postulant

postulat /pɔstyla/ *nm* gén premise; Math, Philos postulate

postuler /pɔstyle/ [1]
A *vtr* **1)** (solliciter) to apply for [*emploi*] (**auprès de** to); **2)** (affirmer) to postulate
B *vi* to apply (**à, pour** for)

posture /pɔstyʀ/ *nf* (pose) posture; (situation) position

pot /po/ *nm* **1)** (récipient, contenu) gén container; (en verre) jar; (en plastique) carton, tub; (en faïence, terre) pot; (pichet) jug; **mettre qch en** ∼ to put [sth] into jars [*confiture, fruits*]; to pot [*plante*]; **plante en** ∼ potted plant; **un** ∼ **de peinture** a tin of paint; **2)** (de chambre) pot; (de bébé) potty; **3)** ○(boisson) drink; **prendre un** ∼ to have a drink; **4)** ○(réunion) do○ GB, drinks party; **5)** ○(chance) luck; **avoir du** ∼ to be lucky

(Composés) ∼ **catalytique** catalytic converter; ∼ **de colle** tin pot of glue; fig○ leech; ∼ **à eau** water jug GB, pitcher US; ∼ **d'échappement** (silencieux) silencer GB, muffler US; (système) exhaust; ∼ **à tabac** lit tobacco jar; fig○ potbellied person

(Idiomes) **payer les** ∼**s cassés** to pick up the pieces; **c'est le** ∼ **de terre contre le** ∼ **de fer** it's an unequal contest; **découvrir le** ∼ **aux roses** to stumble on what's been going on; **être sourd comme un** ∼○ to be as deaf as a post; **tourner autour du** ∼○ to beat about the bush; **partir** *or* **démarrer plein** ∼○ to be off *ou* go off like a shot○

potable /pɔtabl/ *adj* **1)** (buvable) **eau** ∼ drinking water; **eau non** ∼ water unsuitable for drinking; **2)** ○(passable) decent

potage /pɔtaʒ/ *nm* soup

potager, -ère /pɔtaʒe, ɛʀ/
A *adj* [*plante, herbe, racine*] edible; **jardin** ∼ kitchen garden
B *nm* kitchen garden

potasser○ /pɔtase/ [1]
A *vtr* to mug up○ GB, to bone up on○ US [*dossier*]; to swot up○ GB, to bone up on○ US [*latin*]
B *vi* to swot○ GB, to bone up○ US

pot-au-feu /pɔtofø/ *nm inv* **1)** (plat) boiled beef (*with vegetables*); **2)** (viande) boiling beef

pot-de-vin, *pl* **pots-de-vin** /podvɛ̃/ *nm* bribe, backhander○ GB

pote○ /pɔt/ *nm* mate○ GB, pal○ US

poteau, *pl* ∼**x** /pɔto/ *nm* (grand piquet) post; (au football, rugby) goalpost; **coiffer qn au** ∼ lit, fig to overtake GB *ou* pass US sb at the finishing line; **avoir des jambes comme des** ∼**x**○ to have legs like tree trunks

(Composés) ∼ **électrique** electricity pole (*supplying domestic power lines*); ∼ **indicateur** signpost

potelé, ∼**e** /pɔtle/ *adj* chubby

potence /pɔtɑ̃s/ *nf* **1)** (gibet) gallows (+ *v sg*); (pendaison) gallows (+ *v sg*); **il mérite la** ∼ he deserves to hang; **2)** (équerre) bracket

potentialité /pɔtɑ̃sjalite/ *nf* **1)** (virtualité) potential; **2)** (possibilité) potentiality

potentiel, -ielle /pɔtɑ̃sjɛl/
A *adj* potential
B *nm* **1)** (possibilité) potential (**de** for); ∼ **de production** production capacity; **2)** Phys potential

poterie /pɔtʀi/ *nf* **1)** (production) pottery; **2)** (produit) piece of pottery; **des** ∼**s** pottery 𝐂; **3)** (atelier) pottery

potiche /pɔtiʃ/ *nf* **1)** (vase) vase; **2)** (en politique) pej **n'être qu'une** ∼ *or* **faire figure de** ∼ to be a mere puppet; **3)** (en société) pej **être une** ∼ to look merely decorative

potier, -ière /pɔtje, ɛʀ/ ▸ p. 372 *nm,f* potter

potin○ /pɔtɛ̃/ *nm* **1)** (commérage) gossip 𝐂; **2)** (tapage) **faire du** ∼ to make a din○

potion /posjɔ̃/ *nf* potion

potiron /pɔtiʀɔ̃/ *nm* pumpkin GB, winter squash US

pot-pourri, *pl* **pots-pourris** /popuʀi/ *nm* **1)** Mus medley; **2)** (pour parfumer) potpourri

pou, *pl* ∼**x** /pu/ *nm* louse; **des** ∼**x** lice

(Idiomes) **chercher des** ∼**x**○ to nitpick○; **chercher des** ∼**x dans la tête de qn**○ to find fault with sb; **être laid** *or* **moche**○ **comme un** ∼○ to be as ugly as sin; **être vexé comme un** ∼○ to be extremely offended

poubelle /pubɛl/ *nf* (de cuisine, salle de bains) bin GB, trash can US; (d'extérieur) dustbin GB, garbage can US; **mettre** *ou* **jeter qch à la** ∼ to throw sth away; **sortir la** ∼ to take the rubbish out; **faire les** ∼**s** to go through dustbins GB *ou* trash cans US

pouce /pus/
A *nm* **1)** ▸ p. 136 (de la main) thumb; (du pied) big toe; **2)** ▸ p. 347 (unité de mesure) inch; **ne pas bouger d'un** ∼ not to budge an inch
B *excl* schoolchildren's slang pax! GB, truce!

(Idiomes) **se tourner** *or* **rouler les** ∼**s**○ to twiddle one's thumbs; **manger sur le** ∼ to have a quick bite to eat; **donner un coup de** ∼ **à qn/à qch** (au départ) to help sb/sth get started; (pour relancer) to give sb/sth a boost

Poucet /pusɛ/ *npr* **le petit** ∼ Hop o' my Thumb

poudre /pudʀ/ *nf* **1)** gén powder; **réduire qch en** ∼ to grind sth to a powder; **2)** (cosmétique) powder; ∼ **compacte** pressed powder; **3)** (explosif) ∼ **(à canon)** gunpowder

(Composés) ∼ **à éternuer** sneezing powder; ∼ **à récurer** scouring powder; ∼ **de riz** (cosmétique) rice powder

(Idiomes) **mettre le feu aux** ∼**s** to bring things to a head; **jeter de la** ∼ **aux yeux** to try to impress; **se répandre comme une traînée de** ∼ to spread like wildfire

poudrer /pudʀe/ [1]
A *vtr* to powder
B **se poudrer** *vpr* to powder oneself; **se** ∼ **le visage/le nez** to powder one's face/one's nose

poudrerie /pudʀəʀi/ *nf* (d'explosifs) explosives factory

poudreuse¹ /pudʀøz/ *nf* (neige) powdery snow

poudreux, -euse² /pudʀø, øz/ *adj* [*neige*] powdery

poudrier /pudʀije/ *nm* powder compact

poudrière /pudʀijɛʀ/ *nf* **1)** (entrepôt) powder magazine; **2)** fig time bomb

pouët-pouët /pwɛtpwɛt/ *nm inv* (also onomat) honk-honk

pouf /puf/ *nm* **1)** (siège) pouffe; **2)** (bruit) **faire** ∼ to fall with a soft thud

pouffer /pufe/ [1] *vi* ∼ **(de rire)** to burst out laughing

Pouilles /puj/ *npr* ▸ p. 504 *nprfpl* Apulia (*sg*)

pouilleux, -euse /pujø, øz/ *adj* **1)** (sale) seedy; **2)** (couvert de poux) flea-ridden

poulailler /pulaje/ *nm* **1)** Agric (abri) henhouse; (enclos) hen run; (oiseaux) hens (*pl*); **2)** Théât (lieu) **le** ∼ the Gods (*pl*) GB, the gallery; (spectateurs) the audience in the Gods (*pl*) GB, the gallery

poulain /pulɛ̃/ *nm* **1)** Zool colt; (très jeune) foal; **2)** (débutant) protégé

poularde /pulaʀd/ *nf* fattened chicken

poule /pul/ *nf* **1)** Zool hen; **2)** Culin boiling fowl; **3)** ○(terme d'affection) ∼ **ma** ∼ my pet○, honey○ US; **4)** Sport (groupe d'adversaires) group; (tournoi) tournament; **5)** Jeux pool, kitty

(Composés) ∼ **d'eau** moorhen; ∼ **faisane** hen pheasant; ∼ **mouillée** pej wimp○ péj; ∼ **naine** bantam; ∼ **pondeuse** laying hen; ∼ **au pot** Culin boiled chicken

(Idiomes) **quand les** ∼**s auront des dents**○ when pigs fly; **se coucher avec les** ∼**s** to go to bed early; **tuer la** ∼ **pour avoir l'œuf, tuer la** ∼ **aux œufs d'or** to kill the goose that lays the golden egg

poulet /pulɛ/ *nm* **1)** Zool, Culin chicken; **2)** ○(terme d'affection) **mon** ∼ my pet○, honey○ US

(Composés) ∼ **d'élevage** ≈ battery chicken; ∼ **fermier** ≈ free-range chicken

poulette /pulɛt/ *nf* **1)** Zool young hen; Culin pullet; **2)** ○(terme d'affection) **ma** ∼ my pet○, honey○ US

pouliche /puliʃ/ *nf* filly

poulie /puli/ *nf* pulley; ∼ **de tension** idler

poulpe /pulp/ *nm* octopus

pouls /pu/ *nm inv* pulse

poumon /pumɔ̃/ *nm* Anat lung; **à pleins** ∼**s** [*crier*] at the top of one's voice; [*aspirer*] deeply

pour¹

| **pour + verbe** | **pour + nom ou pronom** |

pour + verbe

Lorsque *pour* sert à indiquer un but il se traduit généralement par *to* devant un verbe à l'infinitif:

sortir pour acheter un journal
= to go out to buy a newspaper

pour faire des meringues, il faut des œufs
= to make meringues, you need eggs

Il peut également se traduire par *in order to*, qui est plus soutenu:

pour mettre fin aux hostilités
= in order to put an end to hostilities

Quand *pour* est suivi d'une forme négative, il se traduira par *so as not to* ou *in order not to*:

pour ne pas oublier
= so as not to forget

pour ne pas rater le train
= so as not to miss the train
ou in order not to miss the train

Lorsque *pour* relie deux actions distinctes sans relation de cause à effet, il sera traduit par *and* et le verbe conjugué normalement:

elle s'endormit pour se réveiller deux heures plus tard
= she fell asleep and woke up two hours later

Quand la deuxième action n'est pas souhaitable ou qu'une notion de hasard malheureux est sous-entendue, on traduira par *only to*:

elle s'endormit pour se réveiller deux heures plus tard
= she fell asleep only to wake up two hours later

il partit à la guerre pour se faire tuer trois jours plus tard
= he went off to war only to be killed three days later

pour + nom ou pronom

Lorsque *pour* sert à indiquer la destination au sens large il se traduit généralement par *for*:

le train pour Pau   ***il travaille pour elle***
= the train for Pau   = he works for her

pour vendredi
= for Friday

Lorsque *pour* signifie *en ce qui concerne*, il se traduira le plus souvent par *about*:

tu te renseignes pour une assurance voiture?
= will you find out about car insurance?

tu te renseignes pour samedi?
= will you find out about Saturday?

Attention:

pour placé en début de phrase se traduira par *as regards*:

pour l'argent, rien n'est décidé
= as regards the money, nothing has been decided
ou nothing has been decided about the money

Lorsque *pour* signifie *comme*, il se traduit souvent par *as*:

je l'ai eu pour professeur
= I had him as a teacher

Attention à la présence de l'article en anglais.

Lorsque *pour* relie un terme redoublé, il se traduit parfois par *for*:

mot pour mot
= word for word

Mais ce n'est pas toujours le cas:

jour pour jour
= to the day

On se reportera au nom dans le dictionnaire.

On trouvera dans l'entrée exemples supplémentaires et exceptions.

---

poupe /pup/ *nf* stern; **avoir le vent en ~** lit, fig to have the wind in one's sails

poupée /pupe/ *nf* **1** ▸ p. 327 (jouet) doll; **jouer à la ~** to play dolls; **avoir un visage de ~** to have a doll-like face; **2** ○(forme d'adresse) poppet GB, toots○ US; **3** ○(pansement) finger bandage

(Composés) **~ mannequin** Barbie® doll; **~s gigognes** *or* **russes** set (sg) of Russian dolls

poupin, **~e** /pupɛ̃, in/ *adj* chubby

poupon /pupɔ̃/ *nm* (bébé) tiny baby; (jouet) baby doll

pouponner○ /pupɔne/ [1] *vi* (s'occuper d'un bébé) to play the doting father/mother

pouponnière /pupɔnjɛʀ/ *nf* children's home (*for under-threes*)

pour¹ /puʀ/ *prép* **1** (indiquant le but) to; **~ cela, il faudra faire** to do that, you'll have to do; **c'était ~ rire** *or* **plaisanter** it was a joke; **il est seul mais il a tout fait ~**○ he's on his own, but it's entirely his own doing; **~ que** so that; **~ ainsi dire** so to speak; **c'est fait** *or* **étudié ~**○**!** (c'est sa fonction) that's what it's for; **2** (indiquant une destination) for; **c'est le train ~ où?** where does this train go?; **il faut une heure ~ Oloron** it's an hour to Oloron; **3** (en ce qui concerne) **c'est bien payé mais ~ la sécurité de l'emploi...** the pay is good but as regards job security...; **oui, c'est ~ quoi?** yes, what is it?; **~ moi, il a tort** as far as I am concerned, he's wrong; **4** (en faveur de) for; **je suis ~**○ I'm in favour○ᴳᴮ; **être ~ qch/faire qch** génᴳᴮ to be in favour○ᴳᴮ of sth/doing sth; **5** (avec une indication de temps) for; **ce sera prêt ~ vendredi?** will it be ready by Friday?; **~ toujours** forever; **le bébé c'est ~ quand?** when is the baby due?; **6** (comme) **elle a ~ ambition d'être pilote** her ambition is to be a pilot; **ils ont ~ habitude de déjeuner tard** they usually have a late lunch; **7** (à la place de) for; **écrire qch ~ qch** to write sth instead of sth; **je l'ai pris ~ plus bête qu'il n'est** I thought he was more stupid than he really is; **8** (à son avantage) **elle avait ~ elle de savoir écouter** she had the merit of being a good listener; **9** (introduisant une concession) **~ intelligent qu'il soit** intelligent though he may be; **'il te parlera du Japon'—'~ ce que ça m'intéresse!'** 'he'll talk to you about Japan'—'I can't say I'm very interested'; **~ autant que je sache** as far as I know; **10** (marquant l'emphase) **~ être intelligente, ça elle l'est!** she really is intelligent!, intelligent she certainly is!; **11** (indiquant une quantité) **j'ai mis ~ 30 euros d'essence** I've put in 30 euros' worth of petrol GB *ou* gas US; **je n'y suis ~ rien** I had nothing to do with it; **elle y est ~ beaucoup s'il a réussi** if he has succeeded a lot of the credit should go to her; **je n'en ai pas ~ longtemps** it won't take long; **il n'en a plus ~ longtemps** (mourant) he doesn't have long to live; **j'en ai encore ~ deux heures** it'll take another two hours; **12** (indiquant une cause) for; **se battre ~ une femme** to fight over a woman; **13** (introduisant une proportion) **dix ~ cent** ten per cent; **une cuillère de vinaigre ~ quatre d'huile** one spoonful of vinegar to four of oil; **~ une large part** to a large extent

pour² /puʀ/ *nm* **le ~ et le contre** pros and cons (*pl*)

pourboire /puʀbwaʀ/ *nm* tip; **donner un ~ à qn** to tip sb

pourcentage /puʀsɑ̃taʒ/ *nm* **1** Math percentage; **2** (rémunération) commission; **payer qn au ~** to pay sb by commission; **3** (profit illicite) pej cut○

pourchasser /puʀʃase/ [1] *vtr* **1** (traquer) to hunt [*animal, criminel*]; **2** (harceler) to pursue

pourparlers /puʀpaʀle/ *nmpl* talks; **être en ~** [*personnes*] to be engaged in talks; [*affaire*] to be under discussion

pourpre¹ /puʀpʀ/ ▸ p. 140
A *adj* crimson
B *nm* ① (couleur) crimson; ② Zool murex

pourpre² /puʀpʀ/ *nf* (colorant) Tyrian purple; (étoffe, dignité) purple

pourpré, **~e** /puʀpʀe/ ▸ p. 140 *adj* crimson

pourquoi¹ /puʀkwa/
A *adv, conj* ① (dans une interrogation directe) why?; **~ ça?** why?; **~ donc?** but why?; **~ pas un week-end à Paris?** what *ou* how about a weekend in Paris?; ② (dans une interrogation indirecte) why; **dis-moi ~ tu pleures** tell me why you are crying; **va donc savoir ~!** God knows why!
B **c'est pourquoi** *loc adv* that's why; **il semble que vous n'avez pas reçu ma première lettre, c'est ~ je vous adresse ci-joint une photocopie** it appears that you didn't receive my first letter, so I enclose a photocopy

pourquoi² /puʀkwa/ *nm inv* **le ~ et le comment** the why and the wherefore; **quel est le ~ de toute cette agitation?** what is the reason for all this disturbance?

pourri, **~e** /puʀi/
A *adj* ① (avarié) [aliment] rotten; ② (décomposé) [végétal] decayed, rotting; [bois] rotten; [mur, roche] rotten, crumbling; ③ ᵒ(mauvais) [temps] rotten, dismal; ④ ᵒ(de mauvaise qualité) rotten, lousyᵒ; ⑤ (déplaisant) [lieu] awful; ⑥ ᵒ(corrompu) [personne, mentalité] crooked°, corrupt; [société] corrupt, rotten°; ⑦ ᵒ(gâté) [enfant] spoiled rotten° (jamais épith), spoiled
B *nm* rotten part; **ça sent le ~** it smells rotten

pourrir /puʀiʀ/ [3]
A *vtr* ① (faire se décomposer) [eau, humidité] to rot [bois]; ② (corrompre) to spoil [personne]; ③ ᵒ(gâter) to spoil [sb] rotten° [enfant]
B *vi* ① (s'abîmer) [œuf, viande] to go bad *ou* off GB; [fruit] to go bad, to rot; ② (se décomposer) to rot; ③ (végéter) to rot; ④ (se dégrader) [situation] to deteriorate

pourriture /puʀityʀ/ *nf* ① (décomposition) rot, decay; ② (corruption) corruption, rottenness; ③ Agric, Bot rot

poursuite /puʀsɥit/ *nf* ① (action de poursuivre) pursuit; **se lancer à la ~ de qn** to set off in pursuit of sb; ② (chasse) chase; **une folle ~** a wild chase; ③ (continuation) continuation; **la ~ d'un dialogue** the continuation of a dialogueᴳᴮ; ④ Sport (en cyclisme) pursuit; ⑤ Jur ~ (**judiciaire**) (judicial) proceedings (pl); **abandonner les ~s** to drop the charges

poursuivant, **~e** /puʀsɥivã, ãt/ *nm,f* (personne qui poursuit) pursuer

poursuivre /puʀsɥivʀ/ [62]
A *vtr* ① (traquer) to chase; ② (harceler) [personne] to hound [personne]; [cauchemar, rêve] to haunt [personne]; **~ qn de ses assiduités** liter to force one's attentions on sb; **cette histoire de vol m'a longtemps poursuivie** that stealing business dogged me for a long time; ③ (rechercher) to seek (after) [honneurs, vérité]; to pursue [but]; ④ (continuer) to continue [chemin]; to pursue [négociations, réflexion, tâche]; to continue [efforts, conflit]; **~ une enquête policière** to proceed with a police enquiry; **~ des** *or* **ses études** to continue studying *ou* one's studies; ⑤ Jur ~ **qn (en justice** *or* **devant les tribunaux)** (en droit civil) to sue sb; (en droit pénal) to take sb to court
B *vi* (continuer) [personne] to continue; **poursuivez, nous vous écoutons** please continue, we're listening
C **se poursuivre** *vpr* ① (continuer) to continue; **les combats se sont poursuivis dans la nuit** fighting continued into the night; ② (l'un l'autre) [enfants, adultes] to chase (after) each other

pourtant /puʀtã/ *adv* though; **et ~** and yet; **c'était ~ une bonne idée** and yet it was a good idea, it was a good idea though; **ce n'est ~ pas difficile!** (and yet) it's not so difficult!; **techniquement ~, le film est parfait** technically, however, the film is perfect

pourtour /puʀtuʀ/ *nm* ① (bords extérieurs) perimeter; (de cercle) circumference; ② (région avoisinante) surrounding area

pourvoi /puʀvwa/ *nm* appeal

pourvoir /puʀvwaʀ/ [40]
A *vtr* ① (attribuer) to fill [poste, siège]; **siège/poste à ~** available seat/position; ② (doter) **~ qn de** to endow sb with [qualité, trait, ressources]; **~ une maison en équipement** to fit out a house
B **pourvoir à** *vtr ind* (assurer) **~ à** to provide for [besoin,

dépense, sécurité]; **j'y pourvoirai** I'll see to it
C **se pourvoir** *vpr* ① (se munir) **se ~ de** to provide oneself with [monnaie]; to equip oneself with [véhicule, bottes]; ② Jur (faire appel) **se ~ en** *or* **devant** to appeal to

pourvoyeur, **-euse** /puʀvwajœʀ, øz/ *nm,f* ① (source) **~ de** source of; ② (fournisseur) **~ de** purveyor of

pourvu: **pourvu que** /puʀvyk(ə)/ *loc conj* ① (à condition que) provided (that), as long as; ② (espérons que) let's hope; **~ que ça dure!** let's hope it lasts!

pousse /pus/ *nf* ① (rejet) Bot shoot; fig offshoot; **~s de bambou** Culin bamboo shoots; ② (croissance) growth; ③ Bot (apparition) **la ~ des bourgeons/feuilles** the sprouting of buds/leaves

poussé, **~e¹** /puse/
A *pp* ▸ **pousser**
B *pp adj* ① (de haut niveau) [enquête] thorough; [formation, études] advanced; ② (exagéré) **être un peu ~** [plaisanterie] to go a bit too far; [comparaison] to be a bit forced; ③ Aut [moteur] modified, souped upᵒ

pousse-café /puskafe/ *nm inv* (after-dinner) liqueur

poussée² /puse/
A *pp adj f* ▸ **poussé**
B *nf* ① (pression, poids) (d'eau, de foule) pressure; (de vent) force; Phys (force) thrust; **~ verticale de l'eau** Phys buoyancy in water; **sous la ~ de** lit beneath the pressure of; fig under the pressure of; ② (bourrade) push, shove; Mil (avancée) thrust; **d'une ~** with a push *ou* shove; ③ Méd (accès) attack (de of); **~ de fièvre** sudden high temperature; **~ d'urticaire** rash; ④ (augmentation) (de prix) (sharp) rise *ou* increase (de in); (de racisme, violence, nationalisme) upsurge (de of); **~ démographique** rise in population; **~ inflationniste** inflationary trend

pousser /puse/ [1]
A *vtr* ① (déplacer) to push [vélo, meuble, personne]; (écarter ce qui gêne) to move, to shift, to push [sth] aside [objet]; **~ une porte** (pour la fermer) to push a door to; (pour l'ouvrir) to push *ou* slide a bolt home; **le vent poussait le bateau vers la côte** the wind was driving the boat toward(s) the shore; **~ les enfants vers la sortie** to hustle the children toward(s) the exit; **~ qn du coude** to give sb a dig *ou* to nudge sb with one's elbow; ② (entraîner) **poussé par la pitié** stirred by pity; **poussé par le désir de les aider** prompted by a desire to help them; **~ qn à faire qch** (encourager) to encourage sb to do sth; (vivement) to urge sb to do sth; (contraindre) [faim, désespoir, haine] to drive sb to do sth; **~ qn au suicide** to drive sb to suicide; **c'est ce qui m'a poussé vers l'enseignement** that's what made me take up teaching; **tout me pousse à croire que** everything leads me to believe that; **il n'a pas fallu le ~ beaucoup pour qu'il parle** he didn't need much prompting to talk; ③ (faire travailler plus) to push [élève]; to keep [sb] at it [employé]; to ride [sth] hard [monture]; to drive [sth] hard [voiture]; to flogᵒ [moteur]; ④ (promouvoir) to push [produit, protégé]; ⑤ (porter plus avant) to pursue [recherches, raisonnement]; **c'est ~ un peu loin la plaisanterie** that's carrying *ou* taking the joke a bit far; **~ le perfectionnisme à l'extrême** to be too much of a perfectionist; **~ la bêtise jusqu'à faire** to be stupid enough to do; ⑥ (émettre) to let out [cri]; to heave [soupir]; **~ un hurlement/miaulement** to howl/to miaow; **~ une gueulante** to yell and screamᵒ; **~ la chansonnette** to sing a song
B *vi* ① (croître) [enfant, plante, barbe, ongle] to grow; (apparaître) [plante] to sprout; [dent] to come through; [immeuble, ville] to spring up; **je fais ~ des légumes** I grow vegetables; **se laisser** *ou* **se faire ~ les cheveux** to grow one's hair; **se laisser** *ou* **se faire ~ la barbe** to grow a beard; ② (aller) **~ plus loin/jusqu'à la ville** to go on further/as far as the town; ③ (pour accoucher, aller à la selle) to push; ④ ᵒ(exagérer) to overdo it, to go too far; **tu ne crois pas que tu pousses un peu?** don't you think you're overdoing it?
C **se pousser** *vpr* (pour faire de la place) to move over

(Idiomes) **à la va comme je te pousse** any old how; **se ~ du col**ᵒ to push oneself forward, to be pushyᵒ

poussette /puset/ *nf* (de bébé) pushchair GB, stroller US

poussière /pusjɛʀ/ *nf* ① (poudre) dust; **~ d'or** gold dust; **tomber en ~** lit to crumble away; fig to fall to bits; **~ d'étoiles** stardust; ② (grain) speck of dust

(Idiomes) **10 euros/20 ans et des ~s**ᵒ just over 10 euros/20 years; **mordre la ~** to bite the dust

poussiéreux, -euse /pusjeʁø, øz/ adj lit dusty; fig pej [idée, bureaucratie] outdated, fossilized

poussif, -ive /pusif, iv/ adj **1** [personne, véhicule] wheezy; [cheval] broken-winded; **2** [allure] labouring^{GB}; **3** [film, discours] laboured^{GB}

poussin /pusɛ̃/ nm **1** Zool chick; **2** Culin poussin GB, spring chicken; **3** ○(terme d'affection) **mon ∼** my poppet○ GB, honey(bunch)○ US

poussoir /puswaʁ/ nm (bouton) (push) button

poutre /putʁ/ nf **1** Constr (en bois, béton) beam; (en métal) girder; **∼s apparentes** exposed beams; **2** Sport beam

poutrelle /putʁɛl/ nf girder

pouvoir¹ /puvwaʁ/ [49]

> ⚠ Can et may qui peuvent traduire le verbe pouvoir ne s'emploient ni à l'infinitif, ni au futur.

A v aux **1** (être capable de) to be able to; **peux-tu soulever cette boîte?** can you lift this box?; **dès que je pourrai** as soon as I can; **je suis content que vous ayez pu venir** I'm glad you could come; **il pourrait mieux faire** he could do better; **je n'en peux plus** (épuisement, exaspération) I've had it○; (satiété) I'm full○; **2** (être autorisé à) to be allowed to; **est-ce que je peux me servir de ta voiture?** can I use your car?; **puis-je m'asseoir?** may I sit down?; **est-ce qu'on peut fumer ici?** is smoking allowed here?; **3** (avoir le choix de) **on peut écrire clef ou clé** the word can be written clef or clé; **on peut ne pas faire l'accord** the agreement is optional; **il ne peut pas ne pas accepter** he has no option but to accept; **4** (avoir l'obligeance de) **pourriez-vous me tenir la porte s'il vous plaît?** can ou could you hold the door (open) for me please?; **5** (être susceptible de) **tout peut arriver** anything could happen; **il ne peut pas ne pas gagner** he's bound to win; **puisse cette nouvelle année exaucer vos vœux les plus chers** wishing you everything you could want for the new year; **qu'est-ce que cela peut (bien) te faire**○? what business is it of yours?; **on peut toujours espérer** there's no harm in wishing ou hoping; **s'il croit que je vais payer il peut toujours attendre** if he thinks I'm going to pay he's got another think coming; **ce qu'il peut être grand!** how tall he is!; **peux-tu être bête!** you can be so silly!

B vtr **que puis-je pour vous?** what can I do for you?; **je peux rien pour vous/contre eux** there's nothing I can do for you/about them; **je fais ce que je peux** I'm doing my best

C v impers **il peut faire très froid en janvier** it can get very cold in January; **il pouvait être 10 heures** it was probably about 10 o'clock; **il peut neiger comme il peut faire beau** it might snow or it might be fine; **c'est inimaginable ce qu'il a pu pleuvoir!** you can't imagine ou wouldn't believe how much it rained!

D il se peut vpr impers **il se peut que les prix augmentent en juin** prices may ou might rise in June; **se peut-il qu'il m'ait oublié?** can he really have forgotten me?; **'est-ce que tu viendras ce soir?'—'cela se peut'** 'are you coming this evening?'—'I may do'; **ça ne se peut pas**○ it's impossible

E on ne peut plus loc adv **il est on ne peut plus timide** he is as shy as can be; **il est on ne peut plus désagréable** he's thoroughly unpleasant

F on ne peut mieux loc adv **c'est on ne peut mieux** it couldn't be better; **ils s'entendent on ne peut mieux** they get on extremely well

(Idiome) **autant que faire se peut** as far as possible

pouvoir² /puvwaʁ/ nm **1** (puissance) power; **∼s surnaturels** supernatural powers; **2** (faculté) ability; **avoir le ∼ de faire** to be able to do; **3** (ascendant) power (sur over); **4** (autorité) power, authority; **je n'ai pas le ∼ de décider** it's not up to me to decide; **5** Pol power; **∼ absolu** absolute power; **après 15 ans au ∼** after 15 years in power; **donner tous ∼ à qn** to give sb full powers; **le ∼ en place** the government in power; **6** Admin, Jur power; **∼ par-devant notaire** power of attorney

(Composés) **∼ d'achat** purchasing power; **∼ exécutif** executive power; **le ∼ judiciaire** (corps) the judiciary; **∼ législatif** legislative power; **les ∼s constitués** the powers that be; **∼s publics** authorities

pragmatique /pʁagmatik/ adj pragmatic

praire /pʁɛʁ/ nf clam

prairie /pʁeʁi/ nf gén meadow; (aux États-Unis) **la ∼** the prairie(s)

pralin /pʁalɛ̃/ nm Culin praline

praline /pʁalin/ nf (amande) sugared GB ou sugar-coated US almond

praliné, ∼e /pʁaline/

A adj **1** (enrobé de sucre) sugared GB, sugar-coated US; **2** [crème] praline (épith)

B nm (mélange, arôme, bonbon) praline

praticable /pʁatikabl/ adj **1** (où l'on peut passer) [chemin, route] passable; **2** (réalisable) [sport] that can be played (épith, après n); [analyse] practicable sout

praticien, -ienne /pʁatisjɛ̃, ɛn/ nm,f **1** Méd general practitioner, GP; **demandez à votre ∼** ask your GP; **2** (personne de métier) practitioner

pratiquant, ∼e /pʁatikɑ̃, ɑ̃t/

A adj Relig [personne, catholique] practising^{GB}; **il n'est pas ∼** he doesn't practise^{GB} (his religion); **être très ∼** to be very devout

B nm,f (catholique) practising^{GB} Catholic; (musulman) practising^{GB} Muslim; (juif) practising^{GB} Jew

pratique /pʁatik/

A adj **1** (commode) [appareil, objet] handy, practical; [endroit, itinéraire] convenient; [technique, vêtement, meuble] practical; **2** (utile) practical; **3** (non théorique, concret) practical; **4** (pragmatique) practical; **avoir le sens** or **l'esprit ∼** to be practical

B nf **1** (exercice d'une activité) **la ∼ des arts martiaux est très répandue** many people practise^{GB} martial arts; **cela nécessite de longues heures de ∼** it takes hours of practice; **avoir une bonne ∼ de l'anglais** to have a good working knowledge of English; **2** (expérience) practical experience; **avoir la ∼ des affaires** to have practical business experience; **3** (application de principes) practice; **la théorie et la ∼** theory and practice; **4** (habitude) practice; **une ∼ courante** a common practice

pratiquement /pʁatikmɑ̃/ adv **1** (en pratique) in practice; **2** (quasiment) practically, virtually; **∼ jamais** hardly ever

pratiquer /pʁatike/ [1]

A vtr **1** (exercer régulièrement) to play [tennis, basket]; to do [athlétisme, canoë, yoga]; to take part in [activité, discipline]; to practise^{GB} [langue]; **∼ l'équitation/l'aviron/le ski** to ride/to row/to ski; **∼ la médecine** to practise^{GB} medicine; **il est croyant mais ne pratique pas** he believes in God but doesn't practise^{GB} his religion; **2** (recourir à) to use [méthode, chantage]; to pursue [politique]; to charge [taux d'intérêt]; **ils pratiquent des tarifs très compétitifs** they offer very competitive rates; **3** (effectuer) to carry out [examen, greffe]; to administer [soins]; to make [trou]; to clear [chemin]; to carry out [expulsion]

B se pratiquer vpr [tennis, billard] to be played; [technique, politique] to be used; [prix] to be charged; **un sport qui se pratique beaucoup** a very popular sport

pré¹ /pʁe/ préf pre(-); **∼accord** preliminary agreement; **∼classique** preclassical; **∼commande** advance order; **∼victorien** pre-Victorian

pré² /pʁe/ nm Agric meadow

préadolescent, ∼e /pʁeadɔlesɑ̃, ɑ̃t/ adj, nm,f pre-teen

pré-affranchi, ∼e /pʁeafʁɑ̃ʃi/ adj postage-paid

préalable /pʁealabl/

A adj (qui précède) [permission, avis] prior; (qui prépare) [entretien, étude] preliminary; **les entretiens ∼s aux négociations** the talks preceding the negotiations

B nm (condition) precondition (à for, of); (préliminaire) preliminary; **en ∼ à** (avant) prior to; (en préliminaire) as a preliminary to

C au préalable loc adv first, beforehand

préalablement /pʁealabləmɑ̃/ adv beforehand; **∼ à toute décision** prior to ou before any decision; **coupez en petits dés les légumes ∼ épluchés** dice the previously peeled vegetables

préambule /pʁeɑ̃byl/ nm **1** (introduction) preamble; **2** (avertissement) **sans ∼** with no forewarning

préau, pl **∼x** /pʁeo/ nm (d'école) covered playground; (de prison) exercise yard; (d'hôpital, de cloître) inner courtyard

préavis /pʁeavi/ nm inv notice; **déposer un ∼ de grève** to give notice of strike action

précaire /pʁekɛʁ/ adj **1** [existence, bonheur] precarious; [emploi] insecure; [construction] flimsy; **le travail ∼** casual work; **2** Jur [possession] precarious

précariser /pʀekaʀize/ [1]
A vtr ~ **l'emploi** to casualize labour^GB; ~ **la situation de qn** to make sb's position insecure
B se précariser vpr [emploi] to become insecure

précarité /pʀekaʀite/ nf gén, Jur precariousness; **la ~ de l'emploi** job insecurity

précaution /pʀekosjɔ̃/ nf **1** (mesure) precaution; ~**s d'hygiène** hygiene precautions; **les ~s d'emploi d'un médicament** the precautions to be taken in using a medicine; **prendre ses** ~**s** gén to take precautions; (en allant aux toilettes) euph to go to the toilet just in case; (avec un contraceptif) euph to take precautions euph; **2** (prévoyance) caution; **sans** ~ without caution; **avec** ~ (attention) with caution; (méfiance) cautiously; **par** ~ as a precaution

(Composé) ~**s oratoires** carefully chosen words

(Idiome) **deux** ~**s valent mieux qu'une** Prov better safe than sorry Prov

précautionneux, -euse /pʀekosjɔnø, øz/ adj fml careful

précédemment /pʀesedamɑ̃/ adv previously, before

précédent, ~e /pʀesedɑ̃, ɑ̃t/
A adj previous
B nm,f **le** ~, **la** ~**e** the previous one
C nm precedent; **sans** ~ without precedent

précéder /pʀesede/ [14] vtr **1** (dans un groupe en mouvement) [personne, groupe] to go in front of, to precede; [véhicule] to be in front of, to precede; **2** (dans un lieu) **il m'avait précédé de cinq minutes** he'd got there five minutes ahead of me; **on l'avait précédé** someone had got there first; **3** (être placé avant) [paragraphe, mot, chapitre] to precede; **dans le paragraphe qui précède** in the above ou preceding paragraph; **4** (se produire avant) to precede; **la semaine qui a précédé votre départ** the week before you left; **les générations qui nous ont précédés** the generations that came before us; **5** (dans un classement) **Pierre précède Paul au classement** Pierre comes before Paul in the ranking; **Tours précède Grenoble de trois points** Tours is three points ahead of Grenoble

précepte /pʀesɛpt/ nm precept

précepteur, -trice /pʀeseptœʀ, tʀis/ ▸ p. 372 nm,f (private) tutor

préchauffer /pʀeʃofe/ [1] vtr to preheat [aliment]; to warm up [moteur]; to heat [goudron, pièce à souder]

prêcher /pʀeʃe/ [1]
A vtr **1** Relig to preach [Évangile]; ~ **la bonne parole** to spread the Word; **2** (recommander) to advocate
B vi to preach

(Idiome) ~ **le faux pour savoir le vrai** to tell a lie in order to get at the truth

précieusement /pʀesjøzmɑ̃/ adv **1** [garder, conserver] carefully; [graver] minutely; **2** [parler] in an affected manner

précieux, -ieuse /pʀesjø, øz/ adj **1** (coûteux) [pierre, métal, livre] precious; [meuble] valuable; **2** (utile) [information] very useful; [collaborateur] valued; **votre aide m'a été précieuse** your help was most valuable; **3** (chéri) [amitié, droit, qualité] precious; [ami] very dear; **4** (affecté) [style, langage, geste] precious; **5** Littérat [littérature, salon] précieuse

précipice /pʀesipis/ nm precipice; **être au bord du** ~ fig to be on the brink of collapse

précipitamment /pʀesipitamɑ̃/ adv [partir, s'enfuir] hurriedly; **il nous a quittés** ~ he left us in a hurry

précipitation /pʀesipitasjɔ̃/
A nf **1** (hâte) haste; **avec** ~ hurriedly; **sans** ~ unhurriedly; **2** Chimie precipitation
B précipitations nfpl Météo rainfall ¢, precipitation ¢ spéc

précipité, ~e /pʀesipite/
A adj **1** (rapide) rapid; **2** (hâtif) hasty, precipitate; **un jugement** ~ a snap judgment
B nm Chimie precipitate

précipiter /pʀesipite/ [1]
A vtr **1** (jeter) ~ **qn d'un balcon** to push sb off a balcony; ~ **qn par la fenêtre** to push sb out of the window; ~ **qn dans le vide** (du haut d'un bâtiment, palier) to push sb off; (du haut d'une falaise) to push sb over; (par la fenêtre) to push sb out; ~ **qn contre** to throw sb against; **2** fig (plonger) ~ **qn dans le désarroi** to throw sb into confusion; **3** (hâter) to hasten [départ, décision]; to precipitate [révolte, événement]; ~ **les**

choses to rush things; **4** Chimie to precipitate [solution]
B vi Chimie to precipitate
C se précipiter vpr **1** (se jeter) **il s'est précipité dans le vide** he jumped off; **2** (se ruer) to rush; **se** ~ **dans les bras de qn** to throw oneself into sb's arms; **se** ~ **sur** [personne] to rush at, to throw oneself on [personne]; [animal] to rush at [personne]; to rush for [objet]; fig to pounce on [idée, théorie]; **3** (se dépêcher) to rush, to hurry; **4** (affluer) [clients] to pour in; [investisseurs] to come running; **5** (s'accélérer) [action, événement] to move faster

précis, ~e /pʀesi, iz/
A adj **1** (bien défini) [programme, critère, motif, réglementation] specific; [idée, engagement, date] definite; [moment] particular; **2** (exact) [personne, geste, langue, travail, horaire, réponse] precise; [chiffre, donnée] accurate; [souvenir] clear; [endroit, moment] exact; **à deux heures** ~**es** at exactly two o'clock; **3** (de précision) [instrument de mesure] accurate
B nm inv (manuel) handbook

précisément /pʀesizemɑ̃/ adv **1** (justement) precisely; **2** (avec précision) precisely; **3** (pour être précis) **à la page 6 plus** ~ on page 6 to be more precise; **l'Europe et plus** ~ **la France** Europe and more precisely France

préciser /pʀesize/ [1]
A vtr **1** (ajouter) [personne, rapport] to add (que that); **a-t-il précisé** he added; **faut-il le** ou **est-il besoin de** ~ needless to say; **2** (faire état de) [personne, communiqué] to state (que that); ~ **ses intentions** to state one's intentions; **3** (indiquer avec précision) to specify [lieu, date, nombre]; **pouvez-vous** ~? could you be more specific?; **4** (rendre plus précis) to clarify [idées, programme]
B se préciser vpr **1** (se concrétiser) [danger, avenir, menace] to become clearer; [projet, mariage, voyage] to take shape; **2** (devenir apparent) [forme, réalité] to become clear

précision /pʀesizjɔ̃/ nf **1** (minutie) precision; ~ **du détail** detailed precision; **2** (justesse) accuracy; **avec une** ~ **d'un millimètre** with an accuracy to within one millimetre^GB; **avec** ~ accurately; **localiser avec** ~ to pinpoint; **instrument de** ~ precision instrument; **3** (détail) detail; **apporter quelques** ~**s** to give a few details (**sur** about)

précité, ~e /pʀesite/ adj aforementioned (épith)

précoce /pʀekɔs/ adj **1** (mûr avant l'âge) [enfant, intelligence, sexualité] precocious; **2** (en avance) [légume, saison, diagnostic] early (épith); **3** (prématuré) [rides, sénilité] premature

précocité /pʀekɔsite/ nf **1** (d'enfant, intelligence) precociousness, precocity sout; **2** (d'action) **la** ~ **du dépistage** early detection; **3** (de fruit, saison) earliness

précompte /pʀekɔ̃t/ nm deduction; ~ **de l'impôt** deduction of tax at source

préconçu, ~e /pʀekɔ̃sy/ adj preconceived

préconiser /pʀekɔnize/ [1] vtr **1** (conseiller) to recommend [méthode, solution]; (prôner) to advocate [doctrine, jeûne]; **2** Relig to preconize [évêque]

précuit, ~e /pʀekɥi, it/ adj precooked

précurseur /pʀekyʀsœʀ/
A adj m precursory fml; **signes** ~**s de l'orage** signs that herald a storm
B nm (dans un domaine) pioneer; ~ **de** (discipline) forerunner of; (personne) precursor of

prédateur, -trice /pʀedatœʀ, tʀis/
A adj predatory
B nm **1** (animal) predator; **2** (homme préhistorique) hunter-gatherer

prédécesseur /pʀedesesœʀ/ nm predecessor

prédestiné, ~e /pʀedɛstine/ adj [nom, prénom] appropriate

prédestiner /pʀedɛstine/ [1] vtr to predestine

prédicat /pʀedika/ nm predicate

prédicateur, -trice /pʀedikatœʀ, tʀis/ nm,f preacher

prédication /pʀedikasjɔ̃/ nf **1** Ling, Philos predication; **2** Relig (fait de prêcher) preaching; (sermon) sermon

prédiction /pʀediksjɔ̃/ nf prediction

prédilection /pʀedilɛksjɔ̃/ nf predilection (**pour** for), liking (**pour** for); **de** ~ favourite^GB (épith)

prédire /pʀediʀ/ [65] vtr **1** (par divination) to predict [avenir]; ~ **qch à qn** to predict sth for sb; **2** (par réflexion) to predict

prédisposer /pʀedispoze/ [1] vtr to predispose (**à** to)

prédisposition /pʀedispozisjɔ̃/ *nf* predisposition (**à faire** to do); **montrer des ∼s pour la musique** to show a talent for music

prédominant, ∼e /pʀedɔminɑ̃, ɑ̃t/ *adj* predominant

prédominer /pʀedɔmine/ [1] *vi* to predominate

préélectoral, ∼e, *mpl* **-aux** /pʀeelɛktɔʀal, o/ *adj* pre-election (*épith*)

prééminent, ∼e /pʀeeminɑ̃, ɑ̃t/ *adj* preeminent

préencollé, ∼e /pʀeɑ̃kɔle/ *adj* [*papier peint*] prepasted

préétablir /pʀeetabliʀ/ [3] *vtr* to pre-establish

préexister /pʀeɛɡziste/ [1] *vi* to pre-exist; **∼ à qch** to pre-date sth

préfabriqué, ∼e /pʀefabʀike/
A *adj* prefabricated
B *nm* **1** (*matériau*) prefabricated material; **2** (*maison*) prefabricated house, prefab○; (*bâtiment*) prefabricated building, prefab○

préface /pʀefas/ *nf* preface

préfacer /pʀefase/ [12] *vtr* to write a *ou* the preface to

préfectoral, ∼e, *mpl* **-aux** /pʀefɛktɔʀal, o/ *adj* [*niveau, autorisation*] prefectoral; [*administration, locaux*] prefectural

préfecture /pʀefɛktyʀ/ *nf* **1** Admin prefecture; **2** (*chef-lieu*) main city *of a department*; **3** Naut ∼ **maritime** naval prefecture
Composé ∼ **de police** police headquarters *in some large French cities*

préférable /pʀefeʀabl/ *adj* preferable; **il est ∼ que** it is preferable *ou* better that; ∼ **à** preferable to

préféré, ∼e /pʀefeʀe/ *adj, nm,f* favourite^GB

préférence /pʀefeʀɑ̃s/ *nf* preference; **de ∼** preferably; **achète cette marque de ∼** if you can, buy this brand

préférentiel, -ielle /pʀefeʀɑ̃sjɛl/ *adj* preferential

préférer /pʀefeʀe/ [14] *vtr* to prefer; **(c'est) comme tu préfères** (it's) as you prefer *ou* wish; **j'aurais préféré ne jamais l'apprendre** I wish I'd never heard it

préfet /pʀefɛ/ *nm* prefect; ∼ **de police** prefect of police, police chief; ∼ **maritime** post admiral

préfigurer /pʀefiɡyʀe/ [1] *vtr* to prefigure

préfixe /pʀefiks/ *nm* prefix

préhistoire /pʀeistwaʀ/ *nf* prehistory

préhistorique /pʀeistɔʀik/ *adj* lit, fig prehistoric

préinscription /pʀeɛ̃skʀipsjɔ̃/ *nf* preregistration

préjudice /pʀeʒydis/ *nm* harm ¢, damage ¢; **un grave ∼** serious harm *ou* damage; ∼ **matériel** material loss; ∼ **moral** moral wrong; **porter ∼ à qn** to harm sb, to cause harm to sb; **porter ∼ à qch** gén to damage sth, to be detrimental to sth; Jur to be prejudicial to sth; **subir un ∼** to suffer harm; **au ∼ de qn** to the detriment of sb; **sans ∼ de** Jur without prejudice to

préjugé /pʀeʒyʒe/ *nm* prejudice; ∼**(s) en faveur de qn** bias (sg) in favour^GB of sb

préjuger /pʀeʒyʒe/ [13]
A *vtr* to prejudge
B **préjuger de** *vtr ind* ∼ **de** to prejudge; **nous ne pouvons ∼ de l'avenir** we can't tell what the future holds

prélasser: se prélasser /pʀelase/ [1] *vpr* to lounge; **se ∼ au soleil** to laze in the sun

prélat /pʀela/ *nm* prelate

prélavage /pʀelavaʒ/ *nm* prewash

prêle /pʀɛl/ *nf* Bot horsetail, equisetum

prélèvement /pʀelɛvmɑ̃/ *nm* **1** (*de roche, sang etc*) sampling; **faire** *or* **effectuer un ∼ de sang** to take a blood sample; **2** (*échantillon*) sample; **3** Fin (*opération*) debiting; (*somme*) debit; **faire** *or* **effectuer un ∼ bancaire** to make a debit
Composés ∼ **automatique** direct debit; ∼ **exceptionnel** exceptional levy; ∼ **fiscal** deduction of tax; ∼ **à la source** deduction at source

prélever /pʀelve/ [16] *vtr* **1** (*extraire*) (pour une analyse) to take a sample of [*sang, eau*]; (pour une greffe) to remove [*organe*]; **2** Fin (sur un compte bancaire) to debit; (sur un revenu) to deduct [*cotisation, impôt*]; **3** (*prendre*) to take [*argent, pourcentage*]; to remove [*pièce, matériel*]

préliminaire /pʀeliminɛʀ/
A *adj* preliminary (**à** to)

B **préliminaires** *nmpl* preliminaries

prélude /pʀelyd/ *nm* Mus, fig prelude

préluder /pʀelyde/ [1] **préluder à** *vtr ind* ∼ **à** to be a prelude to

prématuré, ∼e /pʀematyʀe/
A *adj* premature
B *nm,f* premature baby

préméditation /pʀemeditasjɔ̃/ *nf* premeditation; **avec/sans ∼** [*agir*] with/without premeditation; [*crime*] premeditated/unpremeditated

préméditer /pʀemedite/ [1] *vtr* to premeditate

prémices /pʀemis/ *nfpl* liter beginnings

premier, -ière¹ /pʀəmje, ɛʀ/ ▸ p. 155, p. 398
A *adj* **1** (dans le temps) first; **(dans) les ∼s temps** at first; **2** (dans l'espace) first; **3** (dans une série) first; **le ∼ janvier** the first of January; **'livre ∼'** 'book one'; **Napoléon I**^er Napoléon I, Napoleon the First; **4** (dans une hiérarchie) [*artiste, écrivain, puissance*] leading; [*élève, étudiant*] top; **être ∼** [*élève, étudiant*] to be top; [*coureur*] to be first; **une affaire de première urgence** a matter of the utmost urgency; **nos ∼s prix** *or* **tarifs** (pour voyages) our cheapest holidays GB *ou* package tours US; (pour billets) our cheapest tickets; **5** (*original*) [*impression*] first, initial; [*éclat*] initial; [*aspect*] original; **6** (*essentiel*) [*qualité*] prime; [*objectif, conséquence*] primary; **7** Philos [*terme, notion, donnée*] fundamental; [*vérité, principe*] first
B *nm,f* **1** (dans le temps) first; **2** (dans une énumération) first; **je préfère le ∼** I prefer the first one; **le ∼ de mes fils** (sur deux fils) my elder son; (sur plus de deux fils) my eldest son; **3** (dans un classement) **arriver le ∼** [*coureur*] to come first; **être le ∼ de la classe** [*élève*] to be top of the class
C *nm* **1** (dans un bâtiment) first floor GB, second floor US; **2** (jour du mois) first; **le ∼ de l'an** New Year's Day; **3** (arrondissement) first arrondissement
D **en premier** *loc adv* faire qch en ∼ to do sth first; **citons en ∼ le livre de notre collègue** first of all there's our colleague's book
E **de première**○ *loc adj* first-rate; **c'est de première** it's first-class *ou* first-rate
Composés ∼ **âge** [*produits, vêtements*] for babies up to six months (*après n*); ∼ **de cordée** leader; ∼ **danseur** leading dancer; ∼ **jet** first *ou* rough draft; ∼ **ministre** prime minister; **le ∼ venu** just anybody; **elle s'est jetée dans les bras du ∼ venu** she threw herself at the first man to come along; **première nouvelle**○! that's the first I've heard about it; ∼**s secours** first aid ¢

première² /pʀəmjɛʀ/ *nf* **1** (événement important, exploit) first; ∼ **mondiale** world first; **2** Théât, Cin première; **3** Scol sixth year of secondary school, age 16–17; **4** Aut first (gear); **5** ○(dans les transports) first class

premièrement /pʀəmjɛʀmɑ̃/ *adv* **1** (dans une énumération) firstly, first; **2** (introduisant une objection) for a start, for one thing

prémisse /pʀemis/ *nf* premise, premiss GB

prémolaire /pʀemɔlɛʀ/ *nf* premolar

prémonition /pʀemɔnisjɔ̃/ *nf* premonition

prémonitoire /pʀemɔnitwaʀ/ *adj* premonitory

prémunir /pʀemyniʀ/ [3]
A *vtr* (protéger) to protect
B **se prémunir** *vpr* to protect oneself

prenant, ∼e /pʀənɑ̃, ɑ̃t/ *adj* **1** (captivant) [*intrigue, spectacle*] fascinating; [*voix*] captivating; (absorbant) [*travail, métier*] absorbing; **2** Zool [*queue*] prehensile

prénatal, ∼e, *mpl* **∼s** /pʀenatal/ *adj* [*chirurgie*] prenatal; [*surveillance*] antenatal; **un examen ∼** an antenatal○

prendre /pʀɑ̃dʀ/ [52]
A *vtr* **1** (saisir) to take; ∼ **un vase sur l'étagère/dans le placard** to take a vase off the shelf/out of the cupboard; **2** (se donner, acquérir) ∼ **un accent** (involontairement) to pick up an accent; (volontairement) to put on an accent; ∼ **une habitude** to develop *ou* pick up a habit; ∼ **une voix grave** to adopt a solemn tone; ∼ **un rôle** to assume a role; **3** (dérober) to take; **on m'a pris tous mes bijoux** I had all my jewellery GB *ou* jewelry US stolen; **la guerre leur a pris deux fils** they lost two sons in the war; **4** (apporter) to bring; **je n'ai pas pris assez d'argent** I haven't brought enough money; **5** (emporter) to take; **j'ai pris ton parapluie** I took your umbrella; **6** (retirer) ∼ **de l'argent au**

distributeur to get some money out of the cash dispenser; ∼ **de l'eau au puits** to get water from the well; ∼ **quelques livres à la bibliothèque** to get a few books out of the library; ⟨7⟩ (consommer) to have [*boisson, aliment, repas*]; to take [*médicament, drogue*]; **je vais ∼ du poisson** I'll have fish; **aller ∼ un café/une bière** to go for a coffee/a beer; **je prends des calmants depuis la guerre** I've been on tranquillizers^{GB} since the war; **je ne prends jamais d'alcool** I never touch alcohol; ⟨8⟩ (s'accorder) to take; ∼ **un congé** to take some time off; **je vais ∼ mon mercredi**○ I'm going to take Wednesday off; **je vais ∼ mon mercredi**○ I'm going to take Wednesday off; ⟨9⟩ (choisir) to take [*objet*]; to choose [*sujet, question*]; **j'ai pris la question sur Zola** I chose the question on Zola; ∼ **qn pour époux/épouse** to take sb to be one's husband/wife; ⟨10⟩ (faire payer) to charge; **elle prend combien de l'heure?** how much does she charge an hour?; **il prend 15% au passage**○ he takes a cut of 15%; ⟨11⟩ (nécessiter) to take [*temps*]; (user) to take up [*espace, temps*]; **mes enfants me prennent tout mon temps** my children take up all my time; ⟨12⟩ (acheter, réserver, louer) to get [*aliments, essence, place*]; ∼ **une chambre en ville** to get a room in town; ⟨13⟩ (embaucher) (durablement) to take [sb] on [*employé, assistant, apprenti*]; (pour une mission) to engage [*personne*]; **ils ne m'ont pas pris** they didn't take me on; ∼ **qn comme nourrice** to take sb on as a nanny; ∼ **un avocat/ guide** to engage a lawyer/guide; ⟨14⟩ (accueillir) to take; **ils ont pris la petite chez eux** they took the little girl in; ∼ **un client** [*taxi*] to pick up a customer; ⟨15⟩ (ramasser au passage) to pick up [*personne, pain, clé, journal, ticket*]; ∼ **les enfants à l'école** to collect the children from school; ⟨16⟩ (emmener) to take [*personne*]; **je peux te ∼** (en voiture) I can give you a lift; ⟨17⟩ (attraper) to catch [*personne, animal*]; **elle s'est fait ∼ en train de voler** she got caught stealing; ∼ **un papillon avec ses doigts** to pick up a butterfly; **je vous y prends**○! caught you!; **on ne m'y prendra plus**○! (à faire) you won't catch me doing that again!; (à croire) I won't be taken in○ again!; **je ne me suis pas laissé ∼** (tromper) I wasn't going to be taken in○; ⟨18⟩ ○(assaillir) **qu'est-ce qui te prend?** what's the matter with you?; **ça te/leur prend souvent?** are you/they often like this?; ⟨19⟩ (captiver) to involve [*spectateur, lecteur*]; **être pris par un livre/film** to get involved in a book/film; ⟨20⟩ (subir) to get [*gifle, coup de soleil, décharge, contravention*]; to catch [*rhume*]; **j'ai pris le marteau sur le pied** the hammer hit me on the foot; ⟨21⟩ (utiliser) to take [*autobus, métro, train, ferry, autoroute*]; ⟨22⟩ (envisager) to take; **prenons par exemple Nina** take Nina, for example; **à tout ∼** all in all; ⟨23⟩ (considérer) to take; **ne le prends pas mal** don't take it the wrong way; **pour qui me prends-tu?** (grossière erreur) what do you take me for?; (manque de respect) who do you think you're talking to?; **excusez-moi, je vous ai pris pour quelqu'un d'autre** I'm sorry, I thought you were someone else; ⟨24⟩ (traiter) to handle; **il est très gentil quand on sait le ∼** he's very nice when you know how to handle him; ⟨25⟩ (mesurer) to take [*mensurations, température, tension, pouls*]; ⟨26⟩ (noter) to take down; **je vais ∼ votre adresse** let me just take down your address; ⟨27⟩ (apprendre) ∼ **que** to get the idea (that); **où a-t-il pris qu'ils allaient divorcer?** where did he get the idea they were going to get divorced?; ⟨28⟩ (accepter) to take; **il faut ∼ les gens comme ils sont** you must take people as you find them; ⟨29⟩ (endosser) to take over [*direction, pouvoir*]; to assume [*contrôle, poste*]; **je prends ça sur moi** I'll see to it; ∼ **sur soi de faire** to take it upon oneself to do, to undertake to do; ⟨30⟩ (accumuler) to put on [*poids*]; to gain [*avance*]; ∼ **des forces** to build up one's strength; ⟨31⟩ (contracter) to take on [*bail*]; to take [*emploi*]; ⟨32⟩ (défier) to take [sb] on [*concurrent*]; **je prends le gagnant** I'll take on the winner; ⟨33⟩ (conquérir) Mil to take, to seize [*ville, forteresse*]; to capture [*navire, tank*]; Jeux to take [*pièce, carte*]

B *vi* ⟨1⟩ (aller) ∼ **à gauche/vers le nord** to go left/north; **prenez tout droit** keep straight on; ∼ **par le littoral** to follow the coast; ⟨2⟩ (s'enflammer) [*feu, bois, mèche*] to catch; [*incendie*] to break out; ⟨3⟩ (se solidifier) [*gelée, flan, glace, ciment, plâtre, colle*] to set; [*blancs d'œufs*] to stiffen; [*mayonnaise*] to thicken; ⟨4⟩ (réussir) [*grève, innovation*] to be a success; [*idée, mode*] to catch on; [*teinture, bouture, vaccination, greffe*] to take; [*leçon*] to sink in; ⟨5⟩ (prélever) ∼ **sur son temps libre pour traduire un roman** to translate a novel in one's spare time; ⟨6⟩ (se contraindre) **j'ai pris sur moi pour les écouter** I made myself listen to them; **j'ai pris sur moi pour ne pas les insulter** I kept myself from insulting them; ⟨7⟩ ○(être cru) **ça ne prend pas!** it won't wash○ ou work!; ⟨8⟩ ○(subir) **c'est toujours moi qui prends!** I'm

always the one who gets it in the neck○!; **il en a pris pour 20 ans** he got 20 years

C **se prendre** *vpr* ⟨1⟩ (devoir être saisi, consommé, mesuré) **un marteau se prend par le manche** you hold a hammer by the handle; **en Chine le thé se prend sans sucre** in China they don't put sugar in their tea; **la vitamine C se prend de préférence le matin** vitamin C is best taken in the morning; ⟨2⟩ (pouvoir être acquis) **les mauvaises habitudes se prennent vite** bad habits are easily picked up; ⟨3⟩ (se tenir l'un l'autre) **se ∼ par la taille** to hold each other around the waist; ⟨4⟩ (se coincer) **se ∼ les doigts dans la porte** to catch one's fingers in the door; **mon écharpe s'est prise dans les rayons** my scarf got caught in the spokes; ⟨5⟩ ○(recevoir) **il s'est pris une gifle** he got a slap in the face; **je me suis pris une averse** I got caught in a shower; ⟨6⟩ (commencer) **se ∼ à faire** to find oneself doing; **se ∼ de sympathie pour qn** to take to sb; ⟨7⟩ (se considérer) **elle se prend pour un génie** she thinks she's a genius; ⟨8⟩ **s'en ∼ à** (par des reproches ou des critiques) to attack [*personne, presse, parti*]; (pour passer sa colère) to take it out on [*personne*]; (agresser verbalement ou physiquement) to go for [*personne*]; (blâmer) to blame [*personne, groupe, institution*]; **il ne pourra s'en ∼ qu'à lui-même** he will have only himself to blame; ⟨9⟩ (se comporter) **savoir s'y ∼ avec** to have a way with [*enfants, femmes, vieux*]; to know how to handle [*employés, élèves*]; ⟨10⟩ (agir) **il faut s'y ∼ à l'avance pour avoir des places** you have to book ahead to get seats; **tu t'y es pris trop tard** you left it too late; **il s'y est pris à plusieurs fois** he tried several times; **regarde comment elle s'y prend** look how she's doing it; **elle s'y prend bien/mal** she goes about it the right/wrong way

⟨Idiomes⟩ **c'est ∼ ou à laisser** take it or leave it; **tel est pris qui croyait ∼** the tables are turned

preneur, -euse /pʀənœʀ, øz/ *nm,f* Comm (acheteur) taker; **trouver ∼** [*article*] to attract a buyer; [*personne*] to find a buyer (**pour** for); **ne pas trouver ∼** [*article*] to remain unsold; **je suis ∼** I'll take it

prénom /pʀenɔ̃/ *nm* gén first name, christian name GB; Admin forename, given name; **deuxième ∼** middle name

prénommé, ∼e /pʀenɔme/
A *pp* ▸ **prénommer**
B *pp adj* **un ∼ Jules** somebody called Jules; **la ∼e Isabelle** the girl known as Isabelle
C *nm,f* Jur **le ∼, la ∼e** the aforementioned

prénommer /pʀenɔme/ [1]
A *vtr* to name, to call; **M. Martin, prénommé Henri** Mr Martin, first name Henri
B **se prénommer** *vpr* to be called

prénuptial, ∼e, *pl* **-iaux** /pʀenypsjal, o/ *adj* [*accord*] prenuptial; [*examen*] prior to marriage (*épith, après n*)

préoccupant, ∼e /pʀeɔkypɑ̃, ɑ̃t/ *adj* worrying; **son état de santé est ∼** his/her condition is giving cause for concern

préoccupation /pʀeɔkypasjɔ̃/ *nf* (souci) worry, concern; (pensée dominante) concern

préoccupé, ∼e /pʀeɔkype/
A *pp* ▸ **préoccuper**
B *pp adj* (soucieux) preoccupied; **être ∼ par qch** to be concerned about sth; **il semble peu ∼ par les problèmes de l'entreprise** he seems to have little concern for the company's problems

préoccuper /pʀeɔkype/ [1]
A *vtr* ⟨1⟩ (inquiéter) to worry; **ma santé le préoccupe** he's been worried about my health; ⟨2⟩ (occuper) to concern
B **se préoccuper** *vpr* **se ∼ de** to be concerned about [*problème, situation*]; to think about [*avenir, opinion*]; **il ne s'est pas préoccupé de savoir si cela m'arrangeait** he didn't think to ask if it would suit me; **se ∼ de sa petite personne** to think only of oneself, to be self-centred^{GB}

prépa○ /pʀepa/ *nf* students' slang preparatory classes for entrance to the Grandes Écoles

> **ⓘ** **Prépa** refers to an intensive two-year post-*baccalauréat* course of study, usually provided in a *lycée* and working towards the competitive entrance examinations or *concours* by which candidates are selected for admission to a *grande école* ▸ **grande école**

préparateur, -trice /pʀepaʀatœʀ, tʀis/ ▸ p. 372 *nm,f* ∼ **en pharmacie** pharmacist's assistant

préparatifs /pʀepaʀatif/ *nmpl* preparations (**de** for)

préparation /pʀepaʀasjɔ̃/ *nf* **1** (mise au point) preparation; **2** (résultat) preparation; **~ pharmaceutique** pharmaceutical preparation; **3** Scol homework

préparatoire /pʀepaʀatwaʀ/ *adj* [*réunion, entretien, phase*] preliminary; [*travail*] preparatory, preliminary

préparer /pʀepaʀe/ [1]
A *vtr* **1** (apprêter) to prepare [*affaires, chambre, cours, loi, plat, surprise*] (**pour** for); to get [sth] ready [*vêtements, outils, dossier*] (**pour** for); to prepare, to plan [*réunion, spectacle*]; to plan [*vacances, avenir*]; to prepare for [*rentrée*]; to draw up [*projet*]; to hatch [*complot*]; to prepare, to lay [*piège*]; **il est en train de ~ le dîner** he's getting dinner ready, he's fixing dinner US; **~ le terrain** fig to prepare the ground; **il est en train de ~ un mauvais coup** he's up to no good; **il prépare un disque pour l'année prochaine** he's working on a record to be released next year; **des plats préparés** ready-to-eat meals; **je me demande ce que l'avenir nous prépare** I wonder what the future has in store for us; **2** (mettre en condition) to prepare [*personne, pays, économie*] (**à** for); **~ qn à une épreuve sportive** to coach sb for a (sports) competition; **essaie de la ~ avant de lui annoncer la nouvelle** try and break the news to her gently; **3** Scol, Univ to prepare for, to study for [*examen, concours*]; **4** Tech to dress [*laine, cuir*]; **5** Culin to dress [*poisson, volaille*]
B se préparer *vpr* **1** (s'apprêter) to get ready; **2** (se mettre en condition) to prepare (**à** for); **je ne m'étais pas préparé à cette éventualité** I was not prepared for this to happen; **3** (être imminent) [*orage, malheurs*] to be brewing; [*changements*] to be in the offing; **un coup d'État se prépare** a coup d'état is imminent; **il se prépare quelque chose de louche** something fishy° is going on; **4** (faire pour soi) **se ~ une tasse de thé** to make *ou* fix US oneself a cup of tea

prépondérance /pʀepɔ̃deʀɑ̃s/ *nf* predominance

prépondérant, -e /pʀepɔ̃deʀɑ̃, ɑ̃t/ *adj* predominant

préposé, ~e /pʀepoze/ *nm,f* **1** gén official; **~ à qch** official responsible for sth; **~ des douanes** customs official; **~ au vestiaire** cloakroom attendant; **2** (facteur) postman/ postwoman

préposer /pʀepoze/ [1] *vtr* **~ à** to assign to

prépositif, -ive /pʀepozitif, iv/ *adj* prepositional

préposition /pʀepozisjɔ̃/ *nf* preposition

préprofessionnel, -elle /pʀepʀɔfɛsjɔnɛl/ *adj* vocational

prépuce /pʀepys/ *nm* foreskin

préretraite /pʀeʀətʀɛt/ *nf* **1** (situation) early retirement; **être en ~** to have taken early retirement; **2** (allocation) early retirement pension

prérogative /pʀeʀɔgativ/ *nf* prerogative; **~ de qn/qch sur** primacy of sb/sth over; **s'arroger des ~s** to claim prerogatives

près /pʀɛ/
A *adv* **1** (non loin dans l'espace) close; **la ville est tout ~** it's no distance to the town, the town is close by; **ce n'est pas tout ~** it's quite a way; **se raser de ~** to have a close shave; **2** fig **10 kg, à quelques grammes ~** 10 kg, give or take a few grammes; **ce roman est plutôt bon, à quelques détails ~** this novel is quite good, apart from the odd detail; **à ceci** *or* **cela ~ que** except that; **il m'a remboursé au centime ~** he paid me back to the very last penny; **à une voix ~, le projet aurait été adopté** the project would have been adopted but for one vote; **gagner à deux voix ~** to win by two votes; **prends ton temps, on n'est pas à cinq minutes ~** take your time, five minutes won't make any difference; **précis au millimètre ~** accurate to within a millimetre^{GB}; **à une exception ~** with only one exception; **à quelques exceptions ~** with a few rare exceptions
B près de *loc prép* **1** (dans l'espace) near; **elle habite ~ d'ici** she lives nearby *ou* near here; **être ~ du but** fig to be close to achieving one's goal; **j'aimerais être ~ de toi** I'd like to be with you; **elle est ~ de lui** (à ses côtés) she's at his side; **2** (dans le temps) near, nearly; **il est ~ de l'âge de la retraite** he's near retirement age; **il est ~ de minuit** it's nearly midnight; **être ~ de partir** to be about to do; **je suis ~ de penser que** I almost think that; **ils étaient ~ de la victoire** they were close to victory; **le problème n'est pas ~ d'être résolu** the problem is nowhere near solved; **3** (par les idées, les sentiments) close (**de** to); **ils sont très ~ l'un de l'autre** they are very close; **vivre ~ de la nature** to live

close to nature; **4** (presque) nearly, almost; **cela coûte ~ de 500 euros** it costs nearly *ou* almost 500 euros
C de près *loc adv* closely; **regarder de plus ~** to take a closer look; **suivre qn de ~** to follow sb closely; **surveiller qn/qch de ~** to keep a close eye on sb/sth; **vu de ~, cela ressemble à…** seen from close quarters, it looks like…; **les concurrents se suivent de ~** the competitors are close together; **s'intéresser de ~ à qch** to take a close interest in sth; **voir la mort de ~** to look death in the face, to come close to death; **à y regarder de plus ~** on closer examination
D à peu près *loc adv* (presque) **la rue est à peu ~ vide** the street is practically *ou* virtually empty; **cela coûte à peu ~ 20 euros** it costs about *ou* around 20 euros; **il y a à peu ~ une heure qu'il est parti** he left about an hour ago; **à peu ~ de la même façon** in much the same way; **à peu ~ semblables** pretty much the same; **cela désigne à peu ~ n'importe quoi** it refers to just about anything

présage /pʀezaʒ/ *nm* **1** (signe) omen; **2** (signe avant-coureur) harbinger; **3** (prédiction) prediction

présager /pʀezaʒe/ [13] *vtr* (annoncer) [*événement, nouvelle*] to presage; (prévoir) [*personne*] to predict; **laisser ~** to suggest (**à** to); **cela ne présage rien de bon** this does not bode well

presbyte /pʀɛsbit/
A *adj* longsighted GB, farsighted US
B *nmf* longsighted person GB, farsighted person US

presbytère /pʀɛsbiteʀ/ *nm* presbytery

presbytérien, -ienne /pʀɛsbiteʀjɛ̃, ɛn/ *adj, nm,f* Presbyterian

presbytie /pʀɛsbisi/ *nf* longsightedness GB, farsightedness US

prescience /pʀesjɑ̃s/ *nf* **1** (connaissance de l'avenir) foresight, prescience; **2** (intuition) premonition; **3** Relig prescience

préscolaire /pʀeskɔlɛʀ/ *adj* preschool

prescriptible /pʀɛskʀiptibl/ *adj* [*dette, droit*] subject to limitation of action by lapse of time; [*peine, crime*] time-barred

prescription /pʀɛskʀipsjɔ̃/ *nf* **1** Méd prescription; (sur un emballage) **'se conformer aux ~s du médecin'** 'to be taken in accordance with doctor's instructions'; **2** (ordre) prescript

prescrire /pʀɛskʀiʀ/ [67] *vtr* **1** Méd to prescribe [*médicament, repos*] (**à qn** for sb); **'ne pas dépasser la dose prescrite'** (sur un emballage) 'do not exceed stated dose'; **2** (imposer) to stipulate; **au jour prescrit** on the day stipulated; **3** (requérir) [*circonstance, événement*] to call for; **4** Jur to subject [sth] to limitation by lapse of time [*peine, crime, dette, droit*]

préséance /pʀeseɑ̃s/ *nf* precedence

présélecteur /pʀeselɛktœʀ/ *nm* **1** Aut preselector; **2** Tech preset device

présélection /pʀeselɛksjɔ̃/ *nf* **1** (de personnes, livres) shortlisting; **2** Tech presetting; **bouton de ~** preset button

présélectionner /pʀeselɛksjɔne/ [1] *vtr* **1** to shortlist [*personnes, livres*]; **2** Tech to preselect [*vitesse*]; TV, Radio to preset

présence /pʀezɑ̃s/ *nf* **1** (de personne) presence; (au bureau, à l'usine) attendance; **il ignore ta ~** he doesn't know you are here; **il fait de la ~, c'est tout** he's present and not much else; **en ~ d'une foule énorme** in front of a huge crowd; **les forces en ~** the forces involved in the conflict; **les parties en ~** Jur the litigants, the opposing parties; **mettre deux personnes en ~** to bring two people together *ou* face to face; **2** (de pays) presence; **3** (de substance, phénomène, d'industrie) presence (**dans** in); **4** (être animé) **sentir une ~** to feel a presence; **il a besoin d'une ~** he needs company; **5** (personnalité) presence

⎡Composé⎤ **~ d'esprit** presence of mind

présent, ~e¹ /pʀezɑ̃, ɑ̃t/
A *adj* **1** (sur les lieux) [*personne*] present; **les personnes ici ~es** the persons here present sout; **M. Glénat, ici ~** Mr Glénat, who is here with us; **il ne sera pas ~ à l'audience** Jur he will not appear in court; **'~!'** (à l'école) 'here!', 'present!'; **j'étais ~ en pensée** *or* **par le cœur** I was there in spirit; **2** (existant) present; **la faim est toujours ~e dans cette partie du monde** there's still hunger in that part of the world; **avoir ~ à l'esprit** to have [sth] in mind [*conseil*];

to have [sth] fresh in one's mind [*souvenir*]; **le souvenir toujours ~ de** the ever present memory of; **gardez** *or* **ayez bien ~ à l'esprit que** bear in mind that; **③** (actif) actively involved; **un chanteur très ~ sur scène** a singer with a strong stage presence; **④** (actuel) [*moment, situation, état*] present; **⑤** (en cause) present; **par la ~e lettre** by the present (letter), hereby Jur; **⑥** Ling [*temps, participe*] present

B *nm,f* (personne) **il n'y avait que 20 ~s** there were only 20 people present; **la liste des ~s** the list of those present

C *nm* **①** (période) **le ~** the present; **②** Ling (temps) present (tense); **③** (cadeau) gift, present; **faire ~ de qch à qn** to present sb with sth

D **à présent** *loc adv* (en ce moment) at present; (maintenant) now; **d'à ~ of** today; **à ~ que** now that

présentable /pʀezɑ̃tabl/ *adj* presentable

présentateur, -trice /pʀezɑ̃tatœʀ, tʀis/ ▸ p. 372 *nm,f* Radio, TV (de spectacle, d'émission) presenter, anchor; **le ~ (du journal)** the newsreader GB, the newscaster US

présentation /pʀezɑ̃tasjɔ̃/ *nf* **①** (d'ami, de conférencier) introduction; **faire les ~s** to make the introductions; **②** (apparence) appearance; **'excellente ~ exigée'** 'smart appearance required'; **③** (arrangement) presentation; **④** (manifestation, spectacle) show, showing; **~ de mode** fashion show; **⑤** (d'émission, de journal, jeu) presentation; **⑥** (de carte, ticket, bagage) production, showing; (de pièces justificatives) production, presentation; (de chèque) presentation; **sur ~ de** on production of; **⑦** (exposé) presentation; **⑧** Relig **la Présentation de l'Enfant Jésus** Presentation of the Child

présente² /pʀezɑ̃t/
A *adj f* ▸ **présent A**
B *nf* **①** (lettre) **par la ~** hereby; **joint à la ~** herewith; **②** ▸ **présent B**

présentement /pʀezɑ̃tmɑ̃/ *adv* at present GB, presently

présenter /pʀezɑ̃te/ [1]
A *vtr* **①** (faire connaître) to introduce (**à** to); (de manière officielle) to present (**à qn** to sb); **je vous présente mon fils** this is my son, may I introduce my son?; **il n'est pas nécessaire de vous ~ Pierre** Pierre needs no introduction from me; **②** (montrer) to show [*ticket, carte, menu*]; **~ une troupe à** to parade troops before; **'présentez armes!'** 'present arms!'; **③** (proposer au public) to present [*spectacle, vedette, rétrospective, collection*]; Radio, TV to present [*journal, émission*]; Comm to display [*marchandises*]; **④** (soumettre) to present [*facture, addition*]; to submit [*devis, rapport*]; to table [*motion*]; to introduce [*proposition, projet de loi*]; **~ qn à** to put sb forward for [*poste, élection*]; **~ une liste pour les élections** to put forward a list of (candidates) for the elections; **~ une proposition à un comité** to put a proposal to a committee; **⑤** (exposer) to present [*situation, budget*]; to expound, to present [*théorie*]; to set out [*point de vue*]; **~ qn comme (étant) un monstre** to portray sb as a monster; **être présenté comme miraculeux** to be described as miraculous; **être présenté comme un modèle** to be held up as a model; **comment allez-vous leur ~ l'affaire?** how are you going to put the matter to them?; **⑥** (exprimer) to offer [*condoléances*] (**à** to); **~ des excuses** to apologize (**à** to); **⑦** (comporter) to involve, to present [*risque, difficulté*]; to show [*différences, trace*]; to show, to present [*symptôme*]; to offer [*avantage*]; to have [*aspect, particularité, défaut*]; **~ un grand intérêt/peu d'intérêt** to be of great interest/of little interest; **⑧** (orienter) **~ son visage au soleil** to turn one's face to the sun; **~ le flanc à l'ennemi** Mil to offer its flank to the enemy

B *vi* **~ bien** to have a smart appearance; **~ mal** not to have a smart appearance

C **se présenter** *vpr* **①** (paraître) to appear; (aller) to go; (venir) to come; **se ~ à l'audience** Jur to appear in court; **en arrivant, il faut se ~ à la réception** when you arrive you must go *ou* report to reception; **comment oses-tu te ~ chez moi?** how dare you show your face at my house?; **②** (se faire connaître) to introduce oneself (**à** to); **se ~ comme le** *or* **en libérateur du pays** to make oneself out to be the country's saviour; **③** (se porter candidat) **se ~ à** to stand [*examen, concours*]; to stand for [*élections*]; **se ~ sur la même liste que** to stand GB *ou* run alongside sb; **④** (survenir) [*occasion, difficulté, problème*] to arise, to present itself; [*solution*] to emerge; **lire/manger tout ce qui se présente** to read/to eat anything that comes along; **les difficultés qui se présentent à nous** the difficulties with which we are faced *ou* confronted; **un spectacle étonnant se présenta à mes yeux** an amazing sight met my eyes; **⑤** (exister) [*médicament, produit*] **se ~ en, se ~ sous forme de** to come in the

---

form of; **⑥** (s'annoncer) **l'affaire se présente bien** things are looking good; **comment se présente la situation sur le front?** what is the situation at the front?; **⑦** Méd **comment se présente l'enfant?** how is the baby presenting?; **le bébé se présente par le siège** the baby is in the breech position

présentoir /pʀezɑ̃twaʀ/ *nm* (meuble) display stand *ou* unit; (rayon) display shelf

préservatif /pʀezɛʀvatif/ *nm* condom

préservation /pʀezɛʀvasjɔ̃/ *nf* preservation; **la ~ de la nature** nature conservation

préserver /pʀezɛʀve/ [1]
A *vtr* to preserve [*tradition, patrimoine, paix*] (**de** from, against); to protect [*intérêt, droit, emploi, environnement, corps*] (**de** from, against)
B **se préserver** *vpr* **se ~ de** to protect oneself against

présidence /pʀezidɑ̃s/ *nf* **①** (fonction) (d'État, association, de club, syndicat, tribunal) presidency; (d'entreprise, de parti, commission, jury, cour) chairmanship; (d'université) vice-chancellorship GB, presidency US; **être candidat à la ~** Pol to stand GB *ou* run for president; **②** (résidence) presidential palace; (bureaux) presidential offices (*pl*)

président /pʀezidɑ̃/ ▸ p. 590 *nm* (d'État, association, de club, syndicat) president; (d'entreprise, de conseil d'administration, parti, commission, jury) chairman, chairperson; (d'université) vice-chancellor GB, president US; **Monsieur le Président** Pol Mr President; (d'une entreprise) Mr Chairman; Jur Your Honour^GB

(Composé) **~ de la République** President of the Republic

ℹ️ Président de la République The president is the head of state and is elected for a term of 5 years. In the terms of the constitution of the *Cinquième République*, the president plays a strong executive role in the governing of the country.

président-directeur, *pl* **présidents-directeurs** /pʀezidɑ̃diʀɛktœʀ/ *nm* **~ général** chairman and managing director GB, chief executive officer

présidente /pʀezidɑ̃t/ ▸ p. 590 *nf* **①** (d'État, de club, syndicat) president; (de parti, commission) chairwoman, chairperson; (d'entreprise, de conseil d'administration) chairman; **②** (épouse du chef d'État) First Lady

présidentiel, -ielle¹ /pʀezidɑ̃sjɛl/ *adj* presidential; **l'entourage ~** the president's entourage

présidentielles² /pʀezidɑ̃sjɛl/ *nfpl* presidential election (*sg*), presidential elections

présider /pʀezide/ [1] *vtr* **①** (diriger) to chair [*commission, débat*]; **②** (être président de) to be the president of [*association*]; to be the chairman/chairwoman of [*parti, conseil d'administration*]; Jur to preside over [*cour*]; **~ un dîner** to be the guest of honour^GB at a dinner

présomption /pʀezɔ̃psjɔ̃/ *nf* **①** Jur presumption (**de** of); **condamner qn sur de simples ~s** to condemn sb on presumptive grounds alone; **②** (supposition) assumption; **③** (prétention) presumption

présomptueux, -euse /pʀezɔ̃ptɥø, øz/ *adj* [*personne, air*] arrogant; [*action, propos*] presumptuous

presque /pʀɛsk/ *adv* almost, nearly; **la même histoire ou ~** the same story or almost the same; **il n'y avait personne ou ~, il n'y avait ~ personne** there was hardly anyone there; **c'était le bonheur ou ~** it was as close to happiness as one can get; **il ne reste ~ rien** there's hardly anything left

presqu'île /pʀɛskil/ *nf* peninsula

pressant, ~e /pʀesɑ̃, ɑ̃t/ *adj* [*besoin, invitation, danger*] pressing; [*appel*] urgent; [*vendeur*] insistent

presse /pʀɛs/
A *nf* **①** (journaux) press; (journalistes) press; (magazines) magazines (*pl*); **que dit la ~?** what do the papers say?; **avoir bonne/mauvaise ~** fig to be well/not well thought of (**auprès de** among); **②** (machine à presser) press; **③** (machine à imprimer) press; **mettre sous ~** to send [sth] to press; **être mis sous ~** to go to press; **'sous ~'** 'in preparation'
B **presses** *nfpl* (maison d'édition) press (*sg*)

pressé, ~e /pʀese/ *adj* **①** (qui n'a pas le temps) [*personne*] in a hurry [*jamais épith*]; [*pas, air*] hurried; **les gens ~s dans la rue** people rushing about in the street; **②** (désireux) **~ de faire** keen to do; **③** (urgent) [*affaire*] urgent; **elle n'a**

rien eu de plus ~ **que de faire** she couldn't wait to do; **aller** or **parer au plus** ~ to do the most urgent thing(s) first

presse-citron /pʀɛsitʀɔ̃/ *nm inv* lemon squeezer

pressentiment /pʀesɑ̃timɑ̃/ *nm* premonition; **mes** ~**s se confirment** it's all turning out as I expected

pressentir /pʀesɑ̃tiʀ/ [30] *vtr* (deviner) to have a premonition about [*malheur, changement*]; ~ **que** to have a premonition that

presse-papiers /pʀɛspapje/ *nm inv* paperweight

presse-purée /pʀɛspyʀe/ *nm inv* potato masher

presser /pʀese/ [1]
A *vtr* ① (inciter) ~ **qn de faire** to urge sb to do; ② (harceler) [*personne*] to press [*personne, débiteur*]; [*armée*] to harry [*ennemi*]; **cessez de me** ~ stop pestering me; ~ **de questions** to ply [sb] with questions; ③ (éperonner) [*faim, nécessité*] to drive [sb] on [*personne*]; ④ (hâter) to increase [*cadence, rythme*]; ~ **le pas** or **mouvement** to hurry; ⑤ (appuyer sur) to press [*bouton*]; ⑥ (serrer) to squeeze [*main, bras, objet*]; ~ **qch contre** or **sur** to press sth against; ~ **qn contre sa poitrine** to clasp sb to one's chest; ⑦ (comprimer) to squeeze [*orange, éponge, peau*]; to press [*raisin*]; ⑧ Tech to press [*disque*]
B *vi* (être urgent) [*affaire*] to be pressing; [*travail, tâche*] to be urgent; **le temps presse** time is running out
C **se presser** *vpr* ① (se serrer) **se** ~ **sur** or **contre** to press oneself against; **se** ~ **autour de qn/qch** to press around sb/sth; ② (se hâter) to hurry up; **se** ~ **de faire** to hurry up and do; **pressons, pressons**○! get a move on○!; ③ (être en nombre) [*foule*] to throng; (aller en nombre) [*foule*] to flock (**à, dans, sur, vers** to)

pressing /pʀesiŋ/ ▸ p. 372 *nm* (teinturerie) dry-cleaner's

pression /pʀesjɔ̃/ *nf* ① (force physique) pressure **C**; ~ **artérielle** blood pressure; **sous** ~ (sans compression) under pressure; (avec compression) pressurized; ② (contrainte) pressure **C**; ~ **fiscale** tax burden; ③ (action d'appuyer) pressure; **exercer une (légère)** ~ **avec la main** to press (gently) with one's hand; ④ (bouton) press stud GB, popper GB, snap (fastener)

pressoir /pʀeswaʀ/ *nm* ① (bâtiment) pressing shed; ② (machine) press

pressurer /pʀesyʀe/ [1] *vtr* ① Agric (presser) to press; ② ○(exploiter) to milk○

pressuriser /pʀesyʀize/ [1] *vtr* to pressurize

prestance /pʀɛstɑ̃s/ *nf* **avoir de la** ~ to have great presence; **noble** ~ noble bearing

prestataire /pʀɛstatɛʀ/ *nm* ① Comm ~ **de service** (service) contractor, service provider; ② (bénéficiaire de prestations) recipient (*of a state benefit*)

prestation /pʀɛstasjɔ̃/ *nf* ① Admin (aide) benefit; ② Mil allowance (*paid to servicemen*); ③ (prêt, fourniture) provision; ~ **de service** (provision of a) service; ④ (service) service; ⑤ (de personne) controv performance; ~ **télévisée** televised appearance

prestement /pʀɛstəmɑ̃/ *adv* liter [*agir, répliquer*] promptly; [*se mouvoir*] nimbly

prestidigitateur, **-trice** /pʀestidiʒitatœʀ, tʀis/ ▸ p. 372 *nm,f* conjuror

prestidigitation /pʀestidiʒitasjɔ̃/ *nf* conjuring

prestige /pʀɛstiʒ/ *nm* prestige; **être sensible au** ~ **de l'uniforme** to be susceptible to the glamour of a uniform; **de** ~ [*réalisation, voiture*] prestige

prestigieux, **-ieuse** /pʀestiʒjø, øz/ *adj* prestigious

présumer /pʀezyme/ [1]
A *vtr* to presume, to assume; **le père présumé** the putative father; **le présumé coupable/terroriste** the alleged culprit/terrorist
B **présumer de** *vtr ind* (trop) ~ **de ses forces** to overestimate one's strength

présupposer /pʀesypoze/ [1] *vtr* to presuppose

présure /pʀezyʀ/ *nf* rennet

prêt, ~**e** /pʀɛ, pʀɛt/
A *adj* ① (préparé) ready; **être fin** ~ [*personne*] to be all set; ② (disposé) **être** ~ **à faire** to be ready ou prepared to do; **il est** ~ **à tout pour atteindre son but** he will stop at nothing ou he will do anything to get what he wants
B *nm* ① (action) lending; **le service de** ~ **de la bibliothèque** the library loans service; ② (somme) loan; Mil soldier's pay

prêt-à-porter /pʀɛtapɔʀte/ *nm* ready-to-wear, ready-to-wear clothes (*pl*); **acheter du** ~ to buy clothes off the peg GB ou rack US

prétendant, ~**e** /pʀetɑ̃dɑ̃, ɑ̃t/
A *nm,f* ① (à un titre, poste) candidate (**à** for); ② (royal) pretender
B *nm* (soupirant) suitor

prétendre /pʀetɑ̃dʀ/ [6]
A *vtr* to claim; **à ce qu'il prétend** according to him; **on le prétend très spirituel** he is said to be very witty; **il ne prétend pas rivaliser avec les favoris** he does not expect to keep up with the favourites^GB
B **prétendre à** *vtr ind* ~ **à des indemnités** to claim damages; ~ **à un poste** to aspire to a job
C **se prétendre** *vpr* **elle se prétend offensée** she claims she is offended; **il se prétend artiste** he makes out he is an artist

prétendu, ~**e** /pʀetɑ̃dy/ *adj* [*coupable, terroriste*] alleged; [*démocratie, égalité, crise*] alleged, so-called; [*médecin, policier, expert, artiste*] would-be

prétendument /pʀetɑ̃dymɑ̃/ *adv* supposedly, allegedly

prête-nom, *pl* ~**s** /pʀɛtnɔ̃/ *nm* (personne) frontman, man of straw; **société** ~ dummy ou fronting US company

prétentieux, **-ieuse** /pʀetɑ̃sjø, øz/
A *adj* pretentious
B *nm,f* pretentious person; **petit** ~ pretentious twit

prétention /pʀetɑ̃sjɔ̃/
A *nf* ① (vanité) pretentiousness, conceit; **être plein de** ~ to be very pretentious ou conceited; **être sans** ~ to be unpretentious ou unassuming; ② (revendication) claim; **avoir des** ~**s sur** or **à qch** to have a claim to sth; ③ (présomption) **avoir une** ~ **à l'élégance** to have pretentions to elegance; **avoir la** ~ **de faire** to claim to do
B **prétentions** *nfpl* (salaire demandé) **quelles sont vos** ~**s?** what salary are you asking for?

prêter /pʀɛte/ [1]
A *vtr* ① (fournir un bien matériel) to lend [*argent, objet*]; ~ **sur gages** to loan against security; ② (accorder) ~ **son assistance à qn** to give ou lend sb one's assistance; ~ **attention à** to pay attention to; ~ **la main à qn** to lend sb a hand; ~ **l'oreille** to listen, to lend an ear hum; ~ **serment** to take an oath; ~ **son nom à** to lend one's name to, to allow one's name to be used by; **si Dieu me prête vie** if God spares me; ③ (attribuer) ~ **à qch** to attribute ou ascribe [sth] to sb; **les intentions que l'on prête au président** the president's supposed intentions; **on me prête des propos que je n'ai jamais tenus** I'm credited with remarks I never made
B **prêter à** *vtr ind* ~ **à** to give rise to, to cause; **sujet qui prête à l'inquiétude** issue which is cause for concern; **son attitude prête à rire** his/her attitude is laughable ou ridiculous; **tout prête à croire** or **penser que** all the indications would suggest that
C **se prêter** *vpr* ① (consentir) **se** ~ **à** to take part in; ② (convenir) **se** ~ **à** to lend itself to; ③ (se donner) **se** ~ **assistance** [*personnes*] to assist one another

prétérit /pʀeteʀit/ *nm* preterite

prêteur, **-euse** /pʀɛtœʀ, øz/
A *adj* **il n'est pas** ~ he doesn't like lending his things
B ▸ p. 372 *nm,f* lender
(Composé) ~ **sur gages** pawnbroker

prétexte /pʀetɛkst/ *nm* excuse, pretext; **être le** ~ **de** to be used as an excuse for; **n'ouvrez la porte sous aucun** ~ don't open the door on any account

prétexter /pʀetɛkste/ [1]
A *vtr* to use [sth] as an excuse, to plead; **prétextant qu'il était trop vieux/qu'il faisait froid** using his age/the cold as an excuse; ~ **un rendez-vous urgent pour s'éclipser** to plead an urgent engagement in order to get away
B **prétexter de** *vtr ind* ~ **de qch pour faire** to use sth as an excuse for doing

prétimbré, ~**e** /pʀetɛ̃bʀe/ *adj* postage-paid

prétoire /pʀetwaʀ/ *nm* ① Jur courtroom; ② (tribunal) praetorium

prêtre /pʀɛtʀ/ *nm* priest

prêtresse /pʀɛtʀɛs/ *nf* priestess

prêtrise /pʀɛtʀiz/ *nf* priesthood

preuve /pʀœv/ *nf* ① (argument) proof **C**; **une** ~ a piece of evidence; **donner la** ~ **que** to prove that; **faire ses** ~**s**

[*personne*] to prove oneself; [*chose*] to prove itself; **jusqu'à ~ du contraire** until proved otherwise; **il doit être malade, la ~, c'est qu'il n'a pas mangé** he must be ill, the fact that he has not eaten proves it; ② (expression) demonstration; **~ d'amour** demonstration of love; **faire ~ de** to show; **~ de bonne volonté (de la part de)** goodwill gesture (from)

prévaloir /pʀevalwaʀ/ [45]

A *vi* to prevail; **faire ~ son point de vue** to gain acceptance for one's point of view

B **se prévaloir** *vpr* ① (se fonder) **se ~ d'un règlement/précédent** to cite a rule/precedent (**auprès de** to; **pour faire** as grounds for doing); **se ~ de son ancienneté** to claim seniority (**pour faire** as grounds for doing); ② (tirer vanité) **se ~ de** to boast [*succès, expérience, diplômes*]

prévenance /pʀevnɑ̃s/ *nf* consideration

prévenant, ~e /pʀevnɑ̃, ɑ̃t/ *adj* considerate

prévenir /pʀevniʀ/ [36] *vtr* ① (informer) to tell; **que** that); **partir sans ~** to leave without telling anybody; ② (téléphoner à) to call [*médecin, police*]; ③ (donner un avertissement) to warn; **je vous aurai prévenu!** I have warned you!; ④ (éviter) to prevent [*catastrophe, maladie*]; ⑤ (aller au devant de) to anticipate [*désir*]

Idiome mieux vaut ~ que guérir Prov prevention is better than cure Prov

préventif, -ive /pʀevɑ̃tif, iv/ *adj* preventive

prévention /pʀevɑ̃sjɔ̃/ *nf* ① (action préventive) prevention; **faire de la ~** to take preventive action; ② (préjugé) fml prejudice (**contre** against); ③ Jur (détention préventive) detention on suspicion; (temps de détention préventive) detention

préventivement /pʀevɑ̃tivmɑ̃/ *adv* as a precautionary measure; **agir ~** to take preventive action

prévenu, ~e /pʀevny/

A *adj* Jur **~ de** accused of

B *nm,f* Jur defendant

prévisible /pʀevizibl/ *adj* predictable; **un accident difficilement ~** an accident which could hardly have been foreseen

prévision /pʀevizjɔ̃/ *nf* ① (action de prévoir) forecasting; **faire des ~s** to make forecasts; **en ~ de** in anticipation of; ② (ce qu'on prévoit) gén prediction; Écon, Fin forecast; **les résultats vont au-delà de toutes nos ~s** the results go beyond all our expectations; **~s météorologiques** weather forecast (*sg*)

prévisionnel, -elle /pʀevizjɔnɛl/ *adj* projected

prévoir /pʀevwaʀ/ [42] *vtr* ① (annoncer comme probable) to predict [*changement, arrivée, inflation*]; to foresee [*échec, victoire*]; to anticipate [*conséquence*]; to forecast [*résultat, temps*]; **c'était à ~!** that was predictable!; ② Jur (envisager) [*loi*] to make provision for, to provide for; [*législateur*] to make provision for, to allow for; **les cas prévus par la loi** cases provided for by the law; ③ (fixer dans le temps) to plan [*réunion*]; to set the date for [*déménagement*]; **rendez-vous comme prévu le 17** meeting on the 17th as planned *ou* arranged; ④ (planifier) [*concepteur*] to plan; [*propriétaire, client*] to plan to have [*pièce*]; **nous devons ~ une salle de conférence** we must make provision for a conference room; **ce n'était pas prévu!** that wasn't meant to happen!; **rien n'est prévu pour l'année prochaine** there's no plan for next year; **je dois ~ un repas pour 30 personnes** I have to organize a meal for 30 people; **un plan de réorganisation prévoyant 500 suppressions d'emploi** a reorganization plan which entails the projected loss of 500 jobs; **remplissez le formulaire prévu à cet effet** fill in the appropriate form; **tout a été prévu pour qch/pour faire** all the arrangements have been made for sth/to do; **la salle a été prévue pour 100 personnes** the room has been designed for 100 people; ⑤ (se munir de) to make sure one takes [*vêtement, parapluie*]; **~ le repas de midi** to bring a packed lunch; ⑥ (s'attendre à) to expect [*personne*]; to expect, to anticipate [*postes d'emploi, pénurie, grève*]; ⑦ (allouer) to allow [*argent, temps*]

prévoyance /pʀevwajɑ̃s/ *nf* foresight

prévoyant, ~e /pʀevwajɑ̃, ɑ̃t/ *adj* far-sighted

prier /pʀije/ [2]

A *vtr* ① (demander à) **~ qn de faire** to ask sb to do; **je vous prie d'excuser mon retard** I'm so sorry I'm late; **je vous prie de vous taire** will you kindly be quiet; **vous êtes priés de vous abstenir de fumer** you are kindly requested to refrain from smoking; **vous êtes prié d'assister à**

l'inauguration you are invited to attend the opening; **pouvez-vous me passer le sel, je vous prie?** would you mind passing the salt, please?; **je vous en prie, laissez-nous** please, leave us alone; **'puis-je entrer?'—'je vous en prie'** 'may I come in?'—'please do!'; **je vous en prie, ce n'est rien** don't mention it, it's nothing; **elle ne s'est pas fait ~** she didn't have to be asked twice; **il aime se faire ~** he likes to be coaxed; **il a accepté sans se faire ~** he accepted without hesitation; ② Relig to pray to [*Dieu, saint*]; **~ que** to pray that

B *vi* Relig to pray; **~ pour qn/qch** to pray for sb/sth; **~ sur la tombe de qn** to pray at sb's grave

prière /pʀijɛʀ/ *nf* ① Relig prayer; **faire sa ~** to say one's prayers; ② (demande) request; (plus insistant) plea, entreaty; **~ de ne pas fumer** no smoking please

prieuré /pʀijœʀe/ *nm* (couvent) priory; (église) priory church; (maison du prieur) prior's house, priory

primaire /pʀimɛʀ/

A *adj* ① (par opposition à secondaire) primary; ② (simpliste) [*personne*] limited, of limited outlook (*après n*); [*réaction*] knee-jerk○ (*épith*); [*raisonnement, anticommunisme, opinion*] simplistic

B *nm* ① Scol **le ~** primary education; ② (en géologie) **le ~** the palaeozoic era

primat /pʀima/ *nm* ① (archevêque) primate; ② (primauté) primacy

primate /pʀimat/ *nm* primate; **les ~s** the primates

primauté /pʀimote/ *nf* ① (supériorité de fait) primacy, supremacy (**sur** over); ② (autorité) primacy

prime /pʀim/

A *adj* ① (premier) **de ~ abord** at first, initially; **dans sa ~ jeunesse** in the early days of his/her youth; **la ~ enfance** early childhood; ② Math prime; **A ~** A prime

B *nf* ① (récompense) bonus; **en ~ avec votre abonnement, recevez ce magnifique réveil** as a free gift to new subscribers, we're offering this fabulous alarm clock; **et en ~ il a reçu un coup de pied aux fesses** hum and, for good measure, he got a kick in the backside; ② (indemnité) allowance; ③ (subvention) subsidy; ④ (d'assurance) premium; ⑤ (en escrime) prime

Composés **~ de fin d'année** Christmas bonus; **~ de licenciement** redundancy payment GB, severance pay; **~ de risque** danger money; **~ de transport** transport allowance GB, transportation allowance US

primer /pʀime/ [1]

A *vtr* ① (l'emporter sur) to take precedence over, to prevail over; ② (récompenser) to award a prize to [*œuvre, animal*]; **film primé** award-winning film; **ce film a été primé** this film won an award

B **primer sur** *vtr ind* controv = **primer A 1**

C *vi* (dominer) **pour moi, c'est la qualité qui prime** what counts for me is quality; **dans ce sorbet, c'est le cassis qui prime** blackcurrant is the dominant flavour^{GB} in this sorbet

primesautier, -ière /pʀimsotje, ɛʀ/ *adj* impulsive

primeur /pʀimœʀ/

A *nf* ① (nouveauté) **avoir la ~ de qch** (apprendre) to be the first to hear sth; (bénéficier de) to be the first to benefit from sth; ② Comm **fruits/légumes de ~** new season's fruit/vegetables

B **primeurs** *nfpl* early fruit and vegetables, early produce **Ⓒ; marchand de ~s** greengrocer (*specializing in early produce*)

primevère /pʀimvɛʀ/ *nf* primrose

primitif, -ive /pʀimitif, iv/

A *adj* ① (d'origine) [*budget, différence*] initial; [*projet, état*] original; ② [*société, art*] primitive; ③ (peu évolué, rudimentaire) primitive; ④ (simpliste) [*personne*] primitive; [*raisonnement*] crude; ⑤ Math [*fonction*] primitive; ⑥ Ling [*temps*] basic

B *nm,f* ① †[*personne*] primitive; ② (personne fruste) uncouth person

C *nm* Art **~s italiens** Italian Primitives

primodélinquant, ~e /pʀimodelɛ̃kɑ̃, ɑ̃t/ *nm,f* first offender

primordial, ~e, *mpl* -iaux /pʀimɔʀdjal, o/ *adj* essential, vital

prince /pʀɛ̃s/ *nm* ▸ p. 590 prince; **le ~ de la mode** the king of fashion

Composés **le ~ charmant** Prince Charming; **~ héritier** crown prince

⸨Idiome⸩ **se montrer bon ~** to be magnanimous

prince-de-galles /prɛ̃sdəgal/ *adj inv* prince-of-wales check

princesse /prɛ̃sɛs/ ▸ p. 590 *nf* princess

⸨Idiome⸩ **aux frais de la ~**○ (de l'État) at the taxpayer's expense; (d'une société) at the company's expense; (d'une personne) at sb's expense

princier, -ière /prɛ̃sje, ɛR/ *adj* [*titre, goûts, somme*] princely; [*luxe*] dazzling

principal, ~e[1], *mpl* **-aux** /prɛ̃sipal, o/

A *adj* **1** (le plus important) [*facteur, danger, souci*] main; [*tâche, objection, autorité*] principal; **c'est l'œuvre ~e de l'auteur** it's the author's major work; **2** (de tête) [*pays, rôle, personnage*] leading; **3** Admin [*commissaire, inspecteur*] chief; **4** Ling [*proposition*] main.

B *nm* **1** (l'essentiel) **le ~** the main thing; **2** Scol principal; **3** Fin principal

principale[2] /prɛ̃sipal/ *nf* **1** Ling main clause; **2** Scol principal

principalement /prɛ̃sipalmɑ̃/ *adv* mainly

principauté /prɛ̃sipote/ *nf* principality

principe /prɛ̃sip/

A *nm* **1** (règle) principle; **pour le ~** as a matter of principle; **objection de ~** objection on the grounds of principle; **accord de ~** provisional agreement; **2** (hypothèse) assumption; **partir du ~ que** to work on the assumption that; **3** (concept) principle; **quel est le ~ de la machine à vapeur?** how does a steam engine work?; **les ~s d'une science/d'un art** (rudiments) the rudiments of a science/an art; **4** Chimie principle

B **en principe** *loc adv* **1** (habituellement) as a rule; **2** (en théorie) in theory

printanier, -ière /prɛ̃tanje, ɛR/ *adj* [*fleur, soleil*] spring (épith); [*temps, tenue, couleur*] springlike

printemps /prɛ̃tɑ̃/ ▸ p. 536 *nm inv* **1** (saison) spring; **au ~ de la vie** fig in the springtime of life; **2** ○(an) hum **mes 60 ~** my 60 summers

priori ▸ a priori

prioritaire /prijoritɛR/ *adj* **1** [*dossier, projet*] priority (épith); **être ~ to have priority;** [*voiture, chauffeur*] with right GB *ou* the right US of way (épith, après n); **être ~, être sur une route ~** to have right GB *ou* the right US of way

priorité /prijorite/ *nf* **1** (importance) priority; **en ~** (avant le reste) first; (par-dessus tout) first and foremost; **nous nous en occuperons en ~** we'll make it a priority; **2** (fait plus important) priority; **être la ~ numéro un** to be the top priority; **3** (en voiture) priority, right of way; **laisser/refuser la ~ à un véhicule** to give way to/to refuse to give way to a vehicle

pris, ~e[1] /pri, priz/

A *pp* ▸ prendre

B *pp adj* **1** (occupé) busy; **je suis ~** (pour l'instant) I'm busy; (pour la période qui vient) I've got something to do; **j'ai les mains ~es** I've got my hands full; **les places sont toutes ~es** all the seats are taken; **2** (gelé) frozen; **3** (encombré) [*nez*] stuffed up; [*bronches*] congested; **j'ai la gorge ~e** I'm hoarse; **4** (affecté) **~ de** overcome with; **~ de panique** panicstricken; **être ~ de nausées** to feel sick GB *ou* nauseous US

prise[2] /priz/ *nf* **1** (assaut) storming; **2** (à la chasse, pêche) catching *C*; **une belle ~** a fine catch; **3** Sport (au judo, catch) hold; **4** (point permettant de saisir) hold; **n'offrir aucune ~** (pour la main) to have no handholds; (pour le pied) to have no footholds; **avoir ~ sur qn** to have a hold over sb; **avoir ~ sur qch** to have leverage on sth; **donner** *or* **laisser ~ à** [*personne*] to lay oneself open to; **être en ~ avec qch** [*personne*] to be in touch with sth; **5** (absorption) **la ~ d'alcool est déconseillée pendant le traitement** do not take alcohol during the course of treatment; **6** Électrotech (femelle) socket GB, outlet US; (mâle) plug; **~ à deux fiches** two-pin plug; **~ multiple** (domino) (multiplug) adaptor; (sur une rallonge) trailing socket; **7** (en électronique) (femelle) jack; (mâle) plug

⸨Composés⸩ **~ de bec**○ row, argument; **~ en charge** (de frais) payment; **assurer la ~ en charge des frais de qn** to cover sb's expenses; **~ en compte** consideration (de of); **~ de conscience** realization; **~ de contact** initial contact; **~ de courant** (femelle) socket GB, outlet US; **~ de décision** decision-making *C*; **~ d'eau** water supply point; **~ d'otages** hostage-taking *C*; **~ de pouvoir**

takeover; **~ de position** stand; **~ de sang** blood test; **faire une ~ de sang à qn** to take a blood sample from sb; **~ de tête**○ nightmare; **quelle ~ de tête ce jeu/ce mec!** this game/that bloke does my head in!; **~ de vue** Cin, Vidéo shooting *C*; Phot shot

⸨Idiome⸩ **être aux ~s avec des difficultés** to be grappling with difficulties

priser /prize/ [1] *vtr* **1** (apprécier) liter to hold [sth] in esteem; **il prise fort/peu ce genre de divertissement** this kind of entertainment is very much/is not to his taste; **chanteur très prisé du public** singer very popular with the public; **2** (aspirer par le nez) to snort [*drogue*]; **~ (du tabac)** to take snuff

prisme /prism/ *nm* prism

prison /prizɔ̃/ *nf* lit, fig prison; **elle a fait de la ~** she has been in prison; **condamné à trois ans de ~** sentenced to three years' imprisonment

prisonnier, -ière /prizɔnje, ɛR/

A *adj* **il est ~** he is a prisoner; **être ~** to be held prisoner by [*personne, groupe*]; to be a prisoner of [*éducation, croyance*]; **ma main était prisonnière** my hand was trapped

B *nm,f* lit, fig prisoner

privatif, -ive /privatif, iv/ *adj* **1** (privé) private; **2** Jur (qui prive) privatory sout; **3** Ling privative

privation /privasjɔ̃/ *nf* **1** (suppression) (de droit, liberté) deprivation; (de salaire) suspension; **2** (manque) want, privation sout; **s'imposer des ~s** to make sacrifices; **économiser à force de ~s** to scrimp and save

privatisation /privatizasjɔ̃/ *nf* privatization

privatiser /privatize/ [1] *vtr* to privatize

privautés /privote/ *nfpl* fml liberties

privé, ~e /prive/

A *pp* ▸ priver

B *pp adj* **~ de** deprived of; **un style ~ d'humour** a humourless[GB] style; **je suis resté ~ de téléphone pendant deux jours** I had to do without a phone for two days; **tu seras ~ de dessert!** you'll go without dessert!

C *adj* **1** (non étatique) private; **2** (non destiné au public) private; **3** (non officiel) unofficial; **à titre ~** unofficially; **4** (personnel) private

D *nm* **1** (secteur) Écon private sector; **2** Scol **le ~** (secteur) private schools (pl); **3** (activité) **dans le ~, le maire est directeur d'une société** apart from his official position, the mayor is a company director; **en ~** (seul à seul) in private; (non officiellement) off the record; **4** ○(détective) private eye○, private detective

priver /prive/ [1]

A *vtr* **~ qn/qch de** to deprive sb/sth of; **~ qn de sorties** to forbid sb to go out; **son attaque l'a privée de l'usage d'un bras** she lost the use of an arm after her stroke; **l'orage nous a privés d'électricité** we had no electricity because of the thunderstorm

B **se priver** *vpr* **1** (s'abstenir) **se ~ pour ses enfants** to go without for the sake of one's children; **pourquoi se ~?** why deprive ourselves?; **se ~ de qch/de faire** to go *ou* do without sth/doing; **c'est gratuit, j'aurais tort de m'en ~!** it's free, I'd be a fool not to take it!; **elle ne se privera pas du plaisir de le raconter à tout le monde** she will enjoy telling everyone about it; **elle ne s'est pas privée de leur dire les choses en face** she didn't hesitate to tell them a few home truths; **2** (se défaire) **se ~ de** to do without [*personne*]; to dispense with [*services*]

privilège /privilɛʒ/ *nm* privilege; **j'ai le triste ~ de** it is my sad duty to

privilégié, ~e /privileʒje/

A *adj* **1** (avantagé) privileged; **être ~ par le sort** to be blessed by fortune; **2** (chanceux) fortunate; **3** (exceptionnel) [*moment, liens*] special; [*traitement*] preferential; [*position, conditions de travail*] privileged; **4** (préféré) [*cible*] preferred

B *nm,f* (favorisé) **un ~** a privileged person; **les ~s** the privileged

privilégier /privileʒje/ [2] *vtr* **1** (favoriser) to favour[GB]; **2** (donner priorité à) to give priority to

prix /pri/ *nm inv* **1** Écon, fig price; **~ de revient** cost price; **c'est à quel ~?** how much is it?; **ton ~ sera le mien** name your price; **c'est mon dernier ~** that's my final offer; **un ~ d'ami** a special price○; **qu'il soit d'accord ou pas, c'est le même ~**○! fig it doesn't matter whether he agrees or not!; **trouver qch dans ses ~** (fourchette de prix) to find sth within one's price range; (dans ses moyens) to find sth one can afford; **acheter une maison au ~ fort** to pay the top price for a house; **hors de ~** extremely expensive; **cela n'a pas de ~** it's priceless; **acheter qch à ~ d'or** to pay a small fortune for sth; **y mettre le ~** to pay for it; **mettre qch à ~ à 50 euros** [commissaire-priseur] to start the bidding for sth at 50 euros; **mettre à ~ la tête de qn** to put a price on sb's head; **à tout ~** at all costs; **au ~ de nombreux sacrifices** by making many sacrifices; **son amitié n'a pas de ~ pour moi** his/her friendship is very precious to me; **j'attache beaucoup de ~ à son amitié** I value his/her friendship highly ou greatly; **2** (honneur, récompense) prize; **obtenir le premier ~ d'interprétation** to get the award for best actor; **~ Nobel** (récompense) Nobel prize; (personne) Nobel prizewinner; **3** (course hippique) race

pro(-) /pʀo/ préf pro(-); **~-européen** pro-European

probabilité /pʀobabilite/ nf **1** (d'événement, accident) probability, likelihood; **2** Math probability **C**; **les ~s** probability theory (sg)

probable /pʀobabl/ adj **1** (vraisemblable) probable, likely; **c'est peu ~** it's unlikely; **il est ~ qu'il viendra** he'll probably come; **2** (prévisible) likely

probablement /pʀobabləmɑ̃/ adv probably

probant, ~e /pʀobɑ̃, ɑ̃t/ adj [argument, démonstration] convincing; [force, preuve] conclusive

probation /pʀobasjɔ̃/ nf Jur, Relig probation

probatoire /pʀobatwaʀ/ adj **examen ~** assessment test; **épreuve ~** aptitude test; **stage ~** probation period; **délai ~** Jur probation

probité /pʀobite/ nf integrity, probity

problématique /pʀoblematik/
A adj [situation] problematic; [issue, dénouement] uncertain
B nf problems (pl)

problème /pʀoblɛm/ nm (difficulté) problem; (sujet) issue; **ça pose un ~** it is a problem; **~ moral** moral issue; **peau à ~s** problem skin

procédé /pʀosede/ nm **1** (méthode) process; **2** (manière d'agir) practice^GB; **échange de bons ~s** exchange of courtesies; **3** Littérat device

procéder /pʀosede/ [14]
A procéder à vtr ind (se livrer) **~ à** to carry out [analyse, vérification, sondage]; to undertake [réforme, création d'emplois]; **~ à un tirage au sort/un vote** to hold a draw/a vote; **~ à l'arrestation de qn** to arrest sb
B procéder de vtr ind **~ de** to be a product of
C vi (agir) to go about things; **comment allez-vous ~?** how are you going to go about it?; **~ par élimination** to use a process of elimination

procédure /pʀosedyʀ/ nf **1** (action judiciaire) proceedings (pl); **2** (méthode) procedure

procédurier, -ière /pʀosedyʀje, ɛʀ/ pej
A adj [personne] litigious
B nm,f litigious person

procès /pʀosɛ/ nm inv **1** Jur (pénal) trial; (civil) lawsuit, case; **intenter un ~ à qn** to take sb to court, to sue sb; **2** (critique) indictment; **faire le ~ de qch/qn** to put sth/sb in the dock; **faire un mauvais ~ à qn** to accuse sb unjustly; **faire un ~ d'intention à qn** to judge sb on mere intent; **3** Ling process

(Idiome) **sans autre forme de ~** without further ado

processeur /pʀosesœʀ/ nm Ordinat processor

procession /pʀosesjɔ̃/ nf **1** (file) procession; **2** (défilé) fig stream; **3** Relig procession

processus /pʀosesys/ nm inv **1** gén process; **2** Méd (évolution) evolution

procès-verbal, pl **-aux** /pʀosɛvɛʀbal, o/ nm **1** (de réunion) minutes (pl); **2** Jur statement of offence^GB; **3** (amende) controv fine; **avoir un ~** to get a ticket

prochain, ~e /pʀoʃɛ̃, ɛn/
A adj **1** (suivant) next; **ce sera pour une ~e fois** some other time, then!; **à la ~e** ^○! see you^○!; **2** (imminent) [publication] forthcoming; [réunion] coming, forthcoming; [mort, départ, guerre] imminent, impending (épith); **un jour ~** one day soon
B nm gén fellow man; Relig neighbour^GB

prochainement /pʀoʃɛnmɑ̃/ adv soon, shortly

proche /pʀoʃ/
A adj **1** (dans l'espace) [bâtiment, maison, rue] nearby (épith); **~ de** close to, near; **le plus ~** the nearest; **assez ~** not far

away; **les bureaux sont très ~s les uns des autres** the desks are very close together; **2** (dans le futur) [événement] imminent; **la victoire est ~** victory is at hand; **la fin est ~** the end is (drawing) near; **3** (récent) [événement] recent; [souvenir] real, vivid; **4** (voisin) gén similar; [langues] closely related; **~ de** [chiffre, langue] close to; [idée, conclusion, parti] similar to; [attitude] verging on; **5** (sur le plan affectif) [personnes] close (**de** to); Admin (sur un formulaire) (**plus**) **~ parent** next of kin
B de proche en proche loc adv little by little, gradually
C nm (parent) close relative; (ami) close friend; (collègue, associé) close associate; **un ~ du président** a close aide to the president; **mes ~s** my nearest and dearest

Proche-Orient /pʀoʃoʀjɑ̃/ ▸ p. 504 nprm **le ~** the Near East

proclamation /pʀoklamasjɔ̃/ nf proclamation

proclamer /pʀoklame/ [1] vtr **1** (reconnaître officiellement) to proclaim; **2** (annoncer) to declare [confiance, intention, conviction]; to proclaim [innocence]

procréation /pʀokʀeasjɔ̃/ nf procreation

procréer /pʀokʀee/ [11] vi to procreate

procuration /pʀokyʀasjɔ̃/ nf **1** (pouvoir) power of attorney; (pour une élection) proxy; **par ~** [voter] by proxy; [vivre] vicariously; **2** (formulaire) power of attorney; (pour une élection) proxy form

procurer /pʀokyʀe/ [1]
A vtr **1** (apporter) to bring [plaisir, sensation]; to give [argent, avantages]; **2** (faire obtenir) [personne] **~ qch à qn** to get sb sth
B se procurer vpr (obtenir) to obtain; (acheter) to buy

procureur /pʀokyʀœʀ/ ▸ p. 372 nm prosecutor

prodigalité /pʀodigalite/ nf **1** (trait de caractère) extravagance; **2** (abondance) liter abundance (**de** of); **3** (dépenses) extravagance

prodige /pʀodiʒ/ nm **1** (génie) prodigy; **guitariste ~** guitar prodigy; **2** (exploit) feat; **faire des ~s** to work wonders; **~ technique** technical miracle

prodigieux, -ieuse /pʀodiʒjø, øz/ adj [intelligence, mémoire, quantité] prodigious; [personne] wonderful

prodigue /pʀodig/ adj **1** (gaspilleur) extravagant; **2** (libéral) **être ~ de compliments/de son argent** to be lavish with one's praise/one's money; **être ~ de son temps/ses efforts** to be generous with one's time/one's efforts; **3** Relig **le fils ~** the prodigal son

prodiguer /pʀodige/ [1] vtr **1** (distribuer sans compter) to lavish [affection, soins]; to make lots of [promesses]; to give lots of [conseils, encouragements]; **malgré les efforts prodigués par l'équipe** despite the team's heroic efforts; **2** (donner) to give [soins]

producteur, -trice /pʀodyktœʀ, tʀis/
A adj **région productrice de thé/café** tea-/coffee-growing area; **pays ~ de pétrole** oil-producing country
B nm,f **1** Écon (de matériel, pétrole, d'objet) producer; (de café, coton) grower, producer; **2** ▸ p. 372 Cin, TV (personne) producer; (société) production company

productif, -ive /pʀodyktif, iv/
A adj [travail, réunion, journée] productive; [investissement, capital] profitable
B nm **les ~s** people working in production

production /pʀodyksjɔ̃/ nf **1** (fait de produire) (de produit) production; (d'énergie) generation; **la ~ du nouveau modèle débutera le mois prochain** the new model will go into production next month; **arrêter la ~ d'un modèle** to stop producing a model; **2** (produits) gén products (pl), goods (pl); (produits agricoles) produce **C**; **3** (quantités produites) (de produits agricoles, matières premières) production; (de produits manufacturés, d'énergie) output, production; (dans une entreprise) (**service de**) **la ~** production; **5** Cin, TV (processus, film) production; **6** (d'auteur) (ouvrage) work; (ensemble de l'œuvre) works (pl); **7** (présentation) presentation

(Composés) **~ assistée par ordinateur, PAO** computer-aided manufacturing, CAM

productivité /pʀodyktivite/ nf productivity

produire /pʀodɥiʀ/ [69]
A vtr **1** (fabriquer) to produce; **cette usine produit peu** this factory has a low output; **2** (cultiver) to produce, to grow [céréales, café, coton]; (donner) [arbre, terre] to yield; [région, pays] to produce; **3** (causer, provoquer) to produce, to have [effet, résultat]; to produce, to bring about [changement]; to

create, to make [*impression*]; to cause, to create [*sensation, émotion*]; ④ (réaliser, créer) to produce; **un artiste/écrivain qui produit beaucoup** a prolific artist/writer; ⑤ Fin (rapporter) to bring in [*argent, richesse*]; to yield [*intérêt*]; ⑥ (montrer) to produce [*certificat*]

B se produire *vpr* ① (survenir) [*catastrophe, changement*] to occur, to happen; ② (donner un spectacle) [*groupe, chanteur*] to perform

produit /pʀɔdɥi/ *nm* ① (article) product; **des ~s** gén goods, products; Agric produce **℄**; **~s alimentaires** foodstuffs; **~s agricoles** agricultural *ou* farm produce **℄**; ② Fin (revenu) income; (d'investissement) yield, return; (bénéfice) profit; **vivre du ~ de sa terre** to live off the land; **le ~ de la vente** the proceeds (*pl*) of the sale; ③ (résultat) (de recherche) result; (d'activité, état, de hasard) product; **c'est le ~ de ton imagination** it's a figment of your imagination; **c'est un pur ~ des médias** he's/she's a media creation; ④ Biol, Chimie, Phys product; ⑤ Math product

(Composés) **~ de base** (aliment) staple food; **~ chimique** chemical; **~ d'entretien** cleaning product, household product; **~ intérieur brut**, **PIB** gross domestic product, GDP; **~ national brut**, **PNB** gross national product, GNP

proéminent, **~e** /pʀɔeminɑ̃, ɑ̃t/ *adj* prominent
profanateur, **-trice** /pʀɔfanatœʀ, tʀis/ *nm,f* profaner
profanation /pʀɔfanasjɔ̃/ *nf* (de temple, tombe) desecration; (de sentiment, mémoire, beauté) defilement; (de famille, d'institution) debasement
profane /pʀɔfan/
A *adj* ① (non religieux) secular; ② (non initié) **être ~ en la matière** to know nothing about the subject
B *nmf* ① (non-initié) layman/laywoman; ② Relig nonbeliever
C *nm* **le ~ et le sacré** the sacred and the profane
profaner /pʀɔfane/ [1] *vtr* to desecrate [*temple, tombe*]; to defile [*mémoire, nom, beauté*]; to debase [*institution*]
proférer /pʀɔfeʀe/ [14] *vtr* to hurl [*insultes, obscénités*]; to make [*menaces*] (**contre** against)
professer /pʀɔfese/ [1] *vtr* (déclarer) to declare [*admiration, amour*]; to profess [*idée*]
professeur /pʀɔfesœʀ/ ▸ p. 372 *nm* ① (enseignant) (de collège, lycée) teacher; (dans l'enseignement supérieur) lecturer GB, professor US; (titulaire d'une chaire) professor; **le ~ remplaçant** the supply GB *ou* substitute US teacher; ② ▸ p. 590 Univ (titre) professor
profession /pʀɔfesjɔ̃/ *nf* ① (métier) occupation; **exercer la ~ d'infirmière** to be a nurse by profession; **être sans ~** gén to have no occupation; [*femme au foyer*] to be a housewife; ② (corporation) profession; ③ (déclaration) declaration, profession; **faire ~ de libéralisme** to profess one's liberalism
(Composé) **~ libérale** profession
professionnalisme /pʀɔfesjɔnalism/ *nm* (qualité) professionalism
professionnel, **-elle** /pʀɔfesjɔnɛl/
A *adj* ① (relatif au métier) gén professional; [*vie, milieu*] working (épith, professional; [*maladie*] occupational; [*enseignement, formation*] vocational; [*exposition, salon*] trade; **revendications professionnelles** workers' demands; **l'avenir ~** career prospects (*pl*); **activité professionnelle** occupation; **en dehors de mes activités professionnelles** outside my work; **il s'occupe de leur réinsertion professionnelle** he's responsible for finding them jobs; **local à usage ~** business premises (*pl*); ② (non amateur) professional; **acteur, sportif non ~** amateur actor/sportsman
B *nm,f* ① (spécialiste d'un métier) professional; **le salon est réservé aux ~s** the fair is restricted to people in the trade; **un ~ du cinéma** a professional film-maker; **un ~ du bâtiment** a person working in the building trade; ② (non-amateur) professional
professionnellement /pʀɔfesjɔnɛlmɑ̃/ *adv* professionally
professoral, **~e**, *mpl* **-aux** /pʀɔfesɔʀal, o/ *adj* (dogmatique) professorial; (relatif aux professeurs) **le corps ~** the teaching profession
profil /pʀɔfil/ *nm* ① (contour, coupe) profile; **se mettre de ~** to turn sideways; ② (qualifications) **'~ exigé'** 'qualifications required'; **avoir un ~ de gestionnaire** to have the right profile for a manager; ③ Psych profile
profiler /pʀɔfile/ [1]
A *vtr* (présenter) **la tour profile sa silhouette dans le ciel** the

tower is silhouetted *ou* outlined against the sky
B se profiler *vpr* [*forme*] to stand out (**contre**, **sur** against); [*candidat, problème*] to emerge; [*événements*] to approach

profit /pʀɔfi/ *nm* ① (avantage) benefit, advantage; **faire qch avec ~** to benefit from doing sth; **vous consulterez ce guide avec ~** you'll find this guide very useful; **tirer ~ de** to make the most of, to take advantage of; **faire du ~** [*nourriture*] to go a long way; [*objet, appareil*] to be good value; **ce manteau m'a fait du ~** I've had a lot of wear out of this coat; **concert au ~ des handicapés** concert in aid of the handicapped; **espionnage au ~ d'une puissance étrangère** spying for a foreign country; **la réforme s'est faite au ~ des grands propriétaires** the reform benefited land owners; **abandonner le charbon au ~ du nucléaire** to drop coal in favour^{GB} of nuclear energy; **perdre des voix au ~ de** to lose votes to; **mettre à ~** to make the most of [*temps libre, stage*]; to turn [sth] to good account [*situation*]; **mettre à ~ qch** to make good use of [*idée, résultat*]; ② (gains) profit; **faire des ~s** to make a profit; **être une source de ~ pour** to be a source of wealth for

(Idiome) **il n'y a pas de petits ~s** Prov look after the pennies and the pounds will look after themselves Prov GB, a dollar is a dollar US

profitable /pʀɔfitabl/ *adj* (utile) beneficial (**à** to); **leur départ n'est ~ à personne** their leaving doesn't make things better for anybody
profiter /pʀɔfite/ [1]
A profiter à *vtr ind* (être utile) **~ à qn** to benefit sb; **ça profite toujours aux mêmes** it's always the same people who reap the benefit; **à qui profite le crime?** who benefits by *ou* from the crime?
B profiter de *vtr ind* **~ de** to use [*avantage*]; to make the most of [*situation*]; to take advantage of [*faiblesse, vente, personne*]; **profite bien de tes vacances!** have a good holiday!; **j'ai profité de ce qu'il était là pour lui demander de m'aider** since he was there I took the opportunity of asking him to help me; **il a profité de ce que je ne regardais pas** he took advantage of the fact that I was not looking; **~ de l'obscurité pour s'enfuir** to flee under cover of darkness; **les enfants ont profité de leurs vacances** the children got a lot out of their holidays GB *ou* vacation US
C *vi* [*personne, animal*] to grow; [*plante*] to thrive
profiteur, **-euse** /pʀɔfitœʀ, øz/ *nm,f* profiteer
profond, **~e** /pʀɔfɔ̃, ɔ̃d/
A *adj* ① ▸ p. 347 (haut) deep; **peu ~** shallow; **au plus ~ de** in the depths of; ② (intense) [*joie, désespoir*] overwhelming; [*ennui*] acute; [*soupir*] heavy; [*sentiment, sommeil*] deep; [*bleu*] deep; ③ (très grand) [*changement, désaccord*] profound; [*intérêt*] keen; [*mépris, ignorance*] profound; [*silence*] deep; ④ (pénétrant) [*esprit, remarque*] profound; [*regard*] penetrating; ⑤ (provincial) **la France ~e** provincial France; **l'Amérique ~e** small-town America
B *adv* deeply, deep down; **creuser ~** to dig deeply
profondément /pʀɔfɔ̃demɑ̃/ *adv* ① (loin) [*creuser, s'enfoncer*] deeply; ② (intensément) [*dormir, respirer, éprouver, aimer*] deeply; [*souffrir*] greatly; [*détester*] utterly; [*marqué, affecté*] profoundly; [*choqué, convaincu*] deeply; **s'ennuyer ~** to be profoundly bored
profondeur /pʀɔfɔ̃dœʀ/
A *nf* ① ▸ p. 347 (de mer, trou, d'armoire, étagères) depth; **avoir une ~ de 3 mètres** to be 3 metres deep; **creuser à 2 mètres de ~** to dig to 2 metres down; ② (de sentiment, d'amour) depth; (de remarque, d'œuvre) profundity; **en ~** [*analyse, réforme*] in-depth (épith); **travail en ~** thorough work
B profondeurs *nfpl* (de mer, forêt) liter depths
profusion /pʀɔfyzjɔ̃/ *nf* (de détails, couleurs) profusion; (de nourriture, boisson) abundance; **à ~** in abundance
progéniture /pʀɔʒenityʀ/ *nf* progeny
programmateur, **-trice** /pʀɔgʀamatœʀ, tʀis/
A ▸ p. 372 *nm,f* Radio, TV programme^{GB} planner
B *nm* (mécanique) timer
programmation /pʀɔgʀamasjɔ̃/ *nf* programming
programme /pʀɔgʀam/ *nm* ① Cin, Radio, Théât, TV programme^{GB}; **ce n'est pas au ~** lit it's not on the programme^{GB}; fig that wasn't planned; **changement de ~** lit change in the programme^{GB}; fig change of plan; ② (emploi du temps) programme^{GB}; **quel est le ~ des réjouissances aujourd'hui?** hum what delights are in store (for us) today?; ③ (projet) (d'action) plan; (de travail) programme^{GB}; **c'est tout un ~!** hum that'll take some doing!; ④ Scol, Univ

syllabus; **au ~ on the syllabus**; ⑤ Ordinat program

programmer /pʀɔgʀame/ [1] *vtr* ① (prévoir) to schedule [émission]; to plan [travail, vacances]; ② Ordinat to program

programmeur, -euse /pʀɔgʀamœʀ, øz/ ▸ p. 372 *nm,f* (computer) programmer

progrès /pʀɔgʀɛ/ *nm inv* ① (pas en avant) progress ⊄; **les ~ de la médecine** advances in medicine; **être en ~** [personne] to be making progress; [résultats] to be improving; **il y a du ~**⁰! things are improving!; ② (résultat chiffré) increase; **être en ~ de 10%** to be up by 10%; ③ (concept) **le ~ progress**; **on n'arrête pas le ~**! iron that's progress for you!; ④ (de maladie) progression; (d'homme politique) progress; (d'armée) advance

progresser /pʀɔgʀese/ [1] *vi* ① (atteindre un niveau supérieur) [taux, résultat, salaires, chômage] to rise; [pouvoir d'achat, budget] to increase; [économie] to improve; [entreprise] to make progress; [homme politique] to make gains; **nos ventes ont bien progressé ce mois-ci** there has been a marked increase in our sales this month; **~ de 3%** [production] to rise by 3%; [candidat, parti] to gain 3%; **l'euro a progressé de 3% par rapport à la livre** the euro has risen by 3% against the pound; ② (dans son développement) [relations] to improve; [pays, enquête, négociations] to make progress; [science] to progress; [connaissances] to increase; [gagner du terrain] [marcheur] to make progress; [armée] to move forward; **~ de 200 m** to advance 200 m; **~ dans sa carrière** to progress in one's career; ④ (se propager) [maladie] to spread; [idéologie] to gain ground; [criminalité, toxicomanie] to be on the increase; ⑤ (s'améliorer) to make progress

progressif, -ive /pʀɔgʀesif, iv/ *adj* progressive

progression /pʀɔgʀesjɔ̃/ *nf* ① (avancée) (de marcheur, d'alpiniste) progress; (d'ennemi, orage) advance; ② (propagation) (d'épidémie, idéologie) spread; (de criminalité) increase; ③ (résultats supérieurs) gén increase; (de candidat, parti) progress; **être en ~** [résultat] to be up; [tendance] to be increasing; **en ~ de 10%** up by 10%; ④ Math, Mus progression

progressiste /pʀɔgʀesist/ *adj, nmf* progressive

progressivement /pʀɔgʀesivmã/ *adv* progressively

prohibé, ~e /pʀɔibe/ *adj* [marchandise, substance, arme] prohibited; [commerce, action] illegal; **port d'arme ~** illegal possession of a firearm

prohiber /pʀɔibe/ [1] *vtr* to prohibit

prohibitif, -ive /pʀɔibitif, iv/ *adj* ① (excessif) [prix, taxe] prohibitive; ② (qui interdit) prohibition (épith)

prohibition /pʀɔibisjɔ̃/ *nf* prohibition

proie /pʀwa/ *nf* lit, fig prey; **il a été la ~ des journaux à scandale** he fell prey to the gutter press; **être la ~ des flammes** to be in flames; **être en ~ à l'angoisse** to be racked by anguish; **pays en ~ à la guerre civile** country in the grip of civil war; **entreprise en ~ à des difficultés insurmontables** company beset by overwhelming difficulties

projecteur /pʀɔʒɛktœʀ/ *nm* ① (pour éclairer) (de DCA, mirador) searchlight; (de stade) floodlight; **être sous les ~s** fig to be in the spotlight; ② Cin projector

projectile /pʀɔʒɛktil/ *nm* gén missile; (balle, obus) projectile

projection /pʀɔʒɛksjɔ̃/ *nf* ① (processus) **~ de cendres** discharge of ashes; **nettoyer qch par ~ de sable** to sandblast sth; ② (éclaboussures) **le cuisinier a reçu des ~s d'huile bouillante** the cook got spattered with scalding oil; ③ Cin (fait de projeter) projection; (séance) showing; **salle de ~** screening room; ④ Math, Psych projection (**sur** onto)

projectionniste /pʀɔʒɛksjɔnist/ ▸ p. 372 *nmf* projectionist

projet /pʀɔʒɛ/ *nm* ① (plan) plan; **en ~, à l'état de ~** at the planning stage, on the drawing board; **j'ai un film en ~** I'm planning a film; ② (entreprise en cours) project; ③ (esquisse de roman, contrat) (rough) draft

(Composés) **~ de loi** (government) bill; **~ de réforme** Pol reform bill

projeter /pʀɔʒte/ [20] *vtr* ① (lancer) [véhicule] to throw [gravillon] (**sur** up against); **~ du sable sur des bâtiments pour les nettoyer** to sandblast buildings; **le geyser projetait des gerbes d'eau** the geyser was spouting jets of water; **le choc l'a projeté par terre/par-dessus bord** the shock sent him hurtling to the ground/overboard; **~ des étincelles** to throw out sparks; ② (jeter) to cast [ombre, reflet] (**sur** on);

③ Cin, Phot to show [film, diapositives] (**sur** onto); ④ (prévoir) to plan; ⑤ Math, Psych to project (**sur** onto)

prolétaire /pʀɔletɛʀ/ *adj, nmf* proletarian

prolétariat /pʀɔletaʀja/ *nm* proletariat

prolétarien, -ienne /pʀɔletaʀjɛ̃, ɛn/ *adj* proletarian

proliférer /pʀɔlifeʀe/ [14] *vi* to proliferate

prolifique /pʀɔlifik/ *adj* prolific

prolixe /pʀɔliks/ *adj* verbose, prolix

prolo⁰ /pʀɔlo/
A *adj* [vêtement, style] modest, cheap and nasty péj; **ça fait ~** that's a bit common
B *nmf* pleb⁰, prole

prologue /pʀɔlɔg/ *nm* prologue

prolongation /pʀɔlɔ̃gasjɔ̃/ *nf* ① (de trêve, bataille) continuation; (de congé, spectacle) extension; ② Sport extra time; **jouer les ~s** to play ou go into extra time GB, to play overtime US

prolongé, ~e /pʀɔlɔ̃ʒe/ *adj* [effort] sustained; [arrêt] lengthy; [séjour] extended; [week-end] long; [exposition] prolonged; **'pas d'utilisation ~e sans avis médical'** 'if symptoms persist, consult your doctor'

prolongement /pʀɔlɔ̃ʒmã/ *nm* ① (agrandissement) extension; ② (direction) **la rue Berthollet se trouve dans le ~ de la rue de la Glacière** Rue de la Glacière becomes Rue Berthollet; ③ (suite) outcome; **une affaire aux ~s multiples** a case with wide-ranging repercussions

prolonger /pʀɔlɔ̃ʒe/ [13]
A *vtr* ① (faire durer) to extend [séjour, voyage]; to prolong [séance, vie]; to continue [traitement] (**de** for); ② (agrandir) to extend; ③ (être le prolongement de) to be an extension of
B **se prolonger** *vpr* ① (dans le temps) [maladie, effet] to persist; [situation, réunion] to go on; ② (dans l'espace) **se ~ jusqu'à** to go as far as

promenade /pʀɔmnad/ *nf* ① (sortie) (à pied) walk; (à cheval, moto, bicyclette) ride; (en voiture) drive; (en bateau) boat-ride; ② (lieu aménagé) gén walkway; (en bord de mer) promenade

promener /pʀɔmne/ [16]
A *vtr* ① (faire sortir) to take [sb] out [personne]; **il est sorti ~ le chien** he's taken the dog out for a walk; **nous l'avons promené partout** we took him all over the place; **va chez le boulanger, ça te promènera**⁰ go to the baker's, it'll get you out; ② (transporter) to carry; **il promène encore son ours en peluche** he still carries his teddy bear around with him; **~ son regard sur** to cast an eye over
B **se promener** *vpr* (à pied) to go for a walk; (en voiture) to go for a drive; (en bateau) to go out in a boat; (à bicyclette, à cheval) to go for a ride; **le dossier s'est promené**⁰ **dans toute l'usine** the file did the rounds of the factory

promeneur, -euse /pʀɔmnœʀ, øz/ *nm,f* walker; **quelques ~s attardés se trouvaient encore dans le parc** there were still a few people strolling in the park

promesse /pʀɔmɛs/ *nf* ① (engagement) promise; **faire de grandes ~s** to make fine promises; **avoir la ~ de qn** to have sb's word; ② Jur, Comm **honorer ses ~s** to honour^GB one's commitments; **~ de vente** agreement to sell; ③ (espérance) promise; **un magnifique coucher de soleil qui est la ~ de beau temps** a beautiful sunset which promises fine weather to come

(Composé) **~ en l'air** or **de Gascon** or **d'ivrogne** empty ou idle promise

prometteur, -euse /pʀɔmɛtœʀ, øz/ *adj* promising

promettre /pʀɔmɛtʀ/ [60]
A *vtr* ① (garantir) **~ qch à qn** to promise sb sth; **je ne (te) promets rien** I can't promise anything; **je te promets qu'il le regrettera** he'll regret it, I guarantee you; ② (annoncer) **une soirée qui promet bien des surprises** an evening that holds a few surprises in store; **voilà qui nous promet de nombreux débats télévisés** it looks as though we'll be getting a lot of televised debates; **cette grève nous promet une belle pagaille** this strike is guaranteed to cause chaos
B *vi* ① (avoir de l'avenir) to show promise; **un jeune musicien qui promet** a promising young musician; **un film qui promet** a film which sounds interesting; ② (présager des ennuis) iron **cet enfant promet!** that child is going to be a handful!; **ça promet!** that's going to be fun!; **ça promet pour l'hiver!** winter's got GB ou gotten US off to a good start!
C **se promettre** *vpr* ① (à soi-même) to promise oneself; **se**

∼ **du bon temps** to decide to have a bit of fun; [2] (être résolu) **se** ∼ **de faire** to resolve to do; [3] (l'un l'autre) [*personnes, couple*] **se** ∼ **de faire** to promise each other to do; **ils se sont promis de ne plus se quitter** they (have) vowed never to be parted

(Idiome) ∼ **monts et merveilles** *or* **la lune**○ **(à qn)** to promise (sb) the moon *ou* the earth

promiscuité /pʀɔmiskɥite/ *nf* lack of privacy

promo○ /pʀɔmo/ *nf* Comm (special) offer

promontoire /pʀɔmɔ̃twaʀ/ *nm* promontory

promoteur, **-trice** /pʀɔmɔtœʀ, tʀis/ *nm,f* [1] ▸ p. 372 Constr ∼ **(immobilier)** property developer; [2] (de théorie) instigator; (de mouvement, d'exposition) promoter

promotion /pʀɔmɔsjɔ̃/ *nf* [1] (avancement) promotion; (personnes promues) promotion list; [2] Comm (special) offer; **en** ∼ **on** (special) offer; [3] (développement) promotion; **assurer la** ∼ **de** to promote

promotionnel, **-elle** /pʀɔmɔsjɔnɛl/ *adj* promotional; **grande vente promotionnelle** big promotion GB, big sale US; **prix** ∼ special offer

promouvoir /pʀɔmuvwaʀ/ [43] *vtr* (faire la promotion de) to promote; (dans la hiérarchie) to promote; (honorifiquement) to elevate

prompt, **∼e** /pʀɔ̃, pʀɔ̃t/ *adj* [*réaction, coup d'œil*] swift; [*retournement, départ*] sudden; ∼ **rétablissement** speedy recovery; **être** ∼ **à agir** to act swiftly

promptement /pʀɔ̃təmɑ̃/ *adv* (sans délai) [*expédier, remplacer, licencier*] promptly; [*réagir, intervenir*] swiftly; (vite) [*juger, comprendre*] quickly

promptitude /pʀɔ̃tityd/ *nf* (de réponse, réaction, geste) swiftness; (de décision) rapidity; (de départ, changement) suddenness; **leur** ∼ **à réagir** their quick reaction

promulguer /pʀɔmylge/ [1] *vtr* to promulgate

prôner /pʀone/ [1] *vtr* to advocate, to extol the virtues of

pronom /pʀɔnɔ̃/ *nm* pronoun

prononçable /pʀɔnɔ̃sabl/ *adj* pronounceable; **c'est difficilement** ∼ it's difficult to pronounce

prononcé, **∼e** /pʀɔnɔ̃se/ *adj* [*accent, saveur, odeur*] strong; [*rides*] deep; **avoir un goût** ∼ **pour** to be particularly fond of

prononcer /pʀɔnɔ̃se/ [12]
A *vtr* [1] (émettre) to pronounce [*mot*]; **mal** ∼ to mispronounce, to pronounce wrongly; [2] (proférer) to mention [*nom*]; to say [*mot, phrase*]; [3] (dire publiquement) to deliver [*discours*]; [4] Jur (déclarer) to pronounce [*peine de mort*]; to pass [*mesure*]; ∼ **le divorce** to grant a divorce
B **se prononcer** *vpr* [1] (être émis) to be pronounced; [2] (faire connaître un avis) **se** ∼ **contre/en faveur de** *or* **pour qch** to declare oneself against/in favourGB of sth; **se** ∼ **sur qch** to give one's opinion on sth

prononciation /pʀɔnɔ̃sjasjɔ̃/ *nf* pronunciation; **la mauvaise** ∼ **du mot 'province'** the mispronunciation of the word 'province'

pronostic /pʀɔnɔstik/ *nm* [1] (sportif, financier) forecast; [2] (dans un conflit) prediction; [3] (médical) prognosis

pronostiquer /pʀɔnɔstike/ [1] *vtr* Sport to forecast [*résultat*]; (prévoir) to herald

pronostiqueur, **-euse** /pʀɔnɔstikœʀ, øz/ *nm,f* tipster

propagande /pʀɔpagɑ̃d/ *nf* propaganda; **faire de la** ∼ **pour** to campaign for [*cause*]; to plug, to push [*produit*]

propagateur, **-trice** /pʀɔpagatœʀ, tʀis/ *nm,f* proponent

propagation /pʀɔpagasjɔ̃/ *nf* gén spread; (de son, d'onde) propagation; (d'espèce) propagation

propager /pʀɔpaʒe/ [13]
A *vtr* to spread [*rumeur, haine, maladie*]; to propagate [*espèce*]; Phys to propagate [*onde, son*]
B **se propager** *vpr* gén to spread; Phys to propagate

propane /pʀɔpan/ *nm* propane

propension /pʀɔpɑ̃sjɔ̃/ *nf* propensity

prophète /pʀɔfɛt/ *nm* prophet; ∼ **de malheur** prophet of doom GB, doomsayer US

(Idiome) **nul n'est** ∼ **en son pays** Prov a prophet is not without honour, save in his own country

prophétesse /pʀɔfetɛs/ *nf* prophetess

prophétie /pʀɔfesi/ *nf* prophecy

prophétique /pʀɔfetik/ *adj* prophetic

prophétiser /pʀɔfetize/ [1] *vtr* to prophesy

propice /pʀɔpis/ *adj* favourableGB **(à** for); **peu** ∼ rather unfavourableGB; **trouver le moment** ∼ to find the right moment

proportion /pʀɔpɔʀsjɔ̃/ *nf* [1] gén proportion; **une** ∼ **de 10 chômeurs pour 35 salariés** 10 unemployed workers for every 35 in work; **dans une** ∼ **de cinq contre un** in a ratio of five to one; **c'est calculé en** ∼ it is calculated proportionately; **ramener le débat à de plus justes** ∼**s** to put things back in perspective; **cela a pris de telles** ∼**s que** it has become so serious that; **dans des** ∼**s considérables** considerably; **toutes** ∼**s gardées** relatively speaking; [2] Art, Archit proportion

proportionné, **∼e** /pʀɔpɔʀsjɔne/ *adj* **bien/mal** ∼ well-/badly-proportioned

proportionnel, **-elle¹** /pʀɔpɔʀsjɔnɛl/ *adj* proportional

proportionnelle² /pʀɔpɔʀsjɔnɛl/ *nf* Pol proportional representation

proportionnellement /pʀɔpɔʀsjɔnɛlmɑ̃/ *adv* proportionately

propos /pʀɔpo/
A *nm inv* [1] (sujet) **à** ∼ by the way; **à** ∼ **de** about; **à quel** ∼? what about?; **à** ∼ **de qui?** about who?; **à** ∼ **de rien** about nothing in particular; **à ce** ∼ in this connection; [2] (moment) **à** ∼ at the right moment; **mal à** ∼ at (just) the wrong moment; **à tout** ∼ constantly
B *nmpl* (paroles) comments; '∼ **recueillis par J. Brun**' 'interview by J. Brun'

proposer /pʀɔpoze/ [1]
A *vtr* [1] (suggérer) to suggest; [2] (offrir) to offer; '**que veux-tu manger?**'—'**qu'est-ce que tu me proposes?**' 'what would you like to eat?'—'what is there?'; **je te propose de travailler avec nous** why don't you come and work with us?; [3] (soumettre) to put forward [*solution, mesure*]; to propose [*stratégie, projet*]; ∼ **la candidature de qn** to put sb's name forward as a candidate; [4] (à un examen) to set [*sujet*]
B **se proposer** *vpr* [1] (être volontaire) **se** ∼ **pour faire** to offer to do; [2] (avoir l'intention) **se** ∼ **de faire** to intend to do

proposition /pʀɔpozisjɔ̃/ *nf* [1] (suggestion) suggestion; [2] (offre) proposal; **faire des** ∼**s à qn** euph to proposition sb; **sur (la)** ∼ **du maire** at the mayor's instigation; [3] Ling clause; ∼ **principale** main clause

(Composé) ∼ **de loi** ≈ bill

propre /pʀɔpʀ/
A *adj* [1] (sans souillure) clean; **la menuiserie est plus** ∼ **que la plomberie** carpentry is not such a dirty job as plumbing; **nous voilà** ∼**s!** fig, iron we're in a fine mess now!; [2] (soigné, soigneux) tidy, neat; [3] (moral) [*personne, vie*] decent; [*affaire*] honest; **des affaires pas très** ∼**s** unsavouryGB business (sg); [4] (personnel) own; **ce sont tes** ∼**s paroles** (rapport) you said so yourself; (insistance) those were your very words; [5] (spécifique) of one's own; **chaque pays a des lois qui lui sont** ∼**s** each country has its own particular laws; [6] (approprié) [*expression*] right; [7] (continent) [*bébé*] toilet-trained; [*animal*] housetrained GB, housebroken US
B **propre à** *loc adj* [1] (spécifique) ∼ **à** peculiar to; [2] (capable de) ∼ **à faire** (résultat attendu) likely to do; (résultat étonnant) liable to do; **mesures** ∼**s à limiter le chômage** measures to curb unemployment; [3] (adapté) ∼ **à** appropriate for; ∼ **à la consommation** fit for consumption
C *nm* [1] (nettoyé) **ça sent le** ∼ it smells nice and clean; [2] (recopié) **mettre qch au** ∼ to make a fair copy of sth; [3] (moral) **c'est du** ∼! iron that's very nice!; [4] (spécifique) **être le** ∼ **de** to be peculiar to; **la maison leur appartient en** ∼ they are the sole owners of the house; **disposer en** ∼ **d'un ordinateur** to have one's own individual computer; ∼ **à rien** good-for-nothing

(Idiome) **bon à tout**, ∼ **à rien** Prov Jack of all trades and master of none Prov

proprement /pʀɔpʀəmɑ̃/ *adv* [1] (au sens strict) purely; **à** ∼ **parler** strictly speaking; ∼ **dit** (sans considérations annexes) as such (*après n*); (au sens restreint) in the strict sense of the word (*après n*); **quant au procès** ∼ **dit** as for the trial itself; [2] (absolument) absolutely; [3] (véritablement) really; [4] (littéralement) literally; ∼ **irrespirable** literally unbreathable; [5] (spécifiquement) specifically; [6] (comme il faut) **le professeur l'a** ∼ **remis à sa place** he was well and truly put in his place by the teacher; [7] (avec soin) neatly; **travailler** ∼ to do a neat job; **mange** ∼! don't make a mess when you eat!; ⑧ (honnêtement) [*gagner sa vie*] honestly; [*agir*] decently

propreté /prɔprəte/ *nf* ① (absence de souillure) cleanliness; **d'une ~ douteuse** not very clean; **d'une ~ éblouissante** sparkling clean; **veiller à la ~ d'un bâtiment** to make sure that a building is kept clean; ② (honnêteté) honesty

propriétaire /prɔprijetɛr/ *nmf* ① owner; **un petit ~** a small-scale property owner; **il y a plus de ~s que de locataires** there are more homeowners than tenants; **ils sont ~s de leur maison** they own their own house; **ils font le tour du ~** to look round GB *ou* around US the house; **faire faire le tour du ~ à qn** to show sb round GB *ou* around US the house; ② (de propriété louée) landlord/landlady

propriété /prɔprijete/ *nf* ① (droit) ownership; ② (biens possédés) property; ③ (bien immobilier) *gén* property; (domaine) estate, property; (maison) house, property; ④ (caractéristique) property; ⑤ (exactitude) aptness

(Composés) **~ artistique et littéraire** intellectual property right, copyright; **~ foncière** landed estate; **~ immobilière** real estate ₵

propulser /prɔpylse/ [1] *vtr* ① (faire mouvoir) [*moteur*] to propel; ② ᴼ(promouvoir) to propel; ③ ᴼ(déplacer violemment) to hurl [*personne, objet*]

propulseur /prɔpylsœr/ *nm* (moteur) engine

(Composés) **~ à hélice** propeller; **~ à réaction** jet engine

propulsion /prɔpylsjɔ̃/ *nf* propulsion; **à ~ nucléaire** nuclear-powered

prorata /prɔrata/ *nm inv* **au ~ de** in proportion to

proroger /prɔrɔʒe/ [13] *vtr* (reculer) to defer [*date, échéance*]; (prolonger) to renew [*contrat, passeport*]; to extend [*validité, délai*]

prosaïque /prɔzaik/ *adj* prosaic

prosaïsme /prɔzaism/ *nm* mundaneness

prosateur /prɔzatœr/ *nm* prose writer

proscription /prɔskripsjɔ̃/ *nf* ① (interdiction) proscription; ② Pol (exil) banishment; **frapper qn de ~** to banish sb

proscrire /prɔskrir/ [67] *vtr* (interdire) to ban; (bannir) to banish

proscrit, ~e /prɔskri, it/ *nm,f* outcast

prose /proz/ *nf* ① (forme littéraire) prose; ② (style personnel) *hum* distinctive prose

prosélyte /prɔzelit/ *nmf* proselyte

prosélytisme /prɔzelitism/ *nm* proselytizing; **faire du ~ politique** to try to convert people to one's politics

prosodie /prɔzɔdi/ *nf* prosody

prospecter /prɔspɛkte/ [1] *vtr* ① (pour vendre) to canvass; ② (pour trouver) to prospect

prospecteur, -trice /prɔspɛktœr, tris/ *nm,f* ① Comm canvasser; ② (de terrain) prospector; ③ (d'idées) explorer

prospectif, -ive /prɔspɛktif, iv/ *adj* long-term

prospection /prɔspɛksjɔ̃/ *nf* Comm canvassing; Ind prospecting

prospectus /prɔspɛktys/ *nm inv* leaflet

prospère /prɔspɛr/ *adj* [*société, personne*] thriving; [*année, saison*] prosperous

prospérer /prɔspere/ [14] *vi* to thrive

prospérité /prɔsperite/ *nf* prosperity; **en pleine ~** (fortune) prosperous; (santé) in flourishing health

prostate /prɔstat/ *nf* prostate (gland)

prosternation /prɔstɛrnasjɔ̃/ *nf* ① lit prostration (**devant** before); ② fig self-abasement

prosterner: se prosterner /prɔstɛrne/ [1] *vpr* ① lit to prostrate oneself; **prosterné devant l'autel** prostrate before the altar; ② fig to grovel (**devant** to)

prostitué /prɔstitɥe/ ▸ p. 372 *nm* male prostitute GB, prostitute US

prostituée /prɔstitɥe/ ▸ p. 372 *nf* prostitute

prostituer /prɔstitɥe/ [1]
Ⓐ *vtr* ① lit to send [sb] out to work as a prostitute; ② fig to prostitute [*talent*]
Ⓑ **se prostituer** *vpr* lit, fig to prostitute oneself

prostitution /prɔstitysjɔ̃/ *nf* lit, fig prostitution

prostration /prɔstrasjɔ̃/ *nf* Méd, Relig prostration; **un état de ~** a state of shock

protagoniste /prɔtagɔnist/ *nmf* protagonist

protecteur, -trice /prɔtɛktœr, tris/
Ⓐ *adj* ① (qui protège) protective; **sous l'œil ~ de** under the protective gaze of; **trop ~** overprotective; ② (supérieur) patronizing
Ⓑ *nm,f* protector; **~ des arts** patron of the arts

protection /prɔtɛksjɔ̃/ *nf* ① (action de protéger) protection; **assurer la ~ de qn** to protect sb; **être sous haute ~** to be under tight security; **de ~** [*lunettes, mesures*] protective; [*zone, système*] protection; ② (dispositif qui protège) protective device; ③ (appui) **bénéficier de ~s** to have friends in high places

(Composés) **~ civile** civil defence^GB; **~ rapprochée** bodyguard; **~ sociale** social welfare system

protectionnisme /prɔtɛksjɔnism/ *nm* protectionism

protectionniste /prɔtɛksjɔnist/ *adj, nmf* protectionist

protège-cahier, *pl* **~s** /prɔtɛʒkaje/ *nm* exercise-book sleeve

protège-matelas /prɔtɛʒmatla/ *nm inv* mattress cover

protéger /prɔteʒe/ [15]
Ⓐ *vtr* ① (préserver) to protect; **le vaccin protège pour dix ans** the vaccine provides protection for ten years; ② (favoriser) to encourage [*art*]
Ⓑ **se protéger** *vpr* to protect oneself

protège-slip, *pl* **~s** /prɔtɛʒslip/ *nm* panty-liner

protège-tibia, *pl* **~s** /prɔtɛʒtibja/ *nm* shinpad

protéine /prɔtein/ *nf* protein

protestant, ~e /prɔtɛstɑ̃, ɑ̃t/ *adj, nm,f* Protestant

protestantisme /prɔtɛstɑ̃tism/ *nm* Protestantism

protestataire /prɔtɛstatɛr/
Ⓐ *adj* [*personne*] protesting (épith); [*défilé, mouvement*] protest (épith)
Ⓑ *nmf* protester

protestation /prɔtɛstasjɔ̃/ *nf* ① (réclamation) protest; ② (assurance) liter protestation

protester /prɔtɛste/ [1]
Ⓐ **protester de** *vtr ind* **~ de son innocence** to protest one's innocence
Ⓑ *vi* to protest

prothèse /prɔtɛz/ *nf* gén prosthesis; (membre artificiel) artificial limb; (dentier) dentures (*pl*); **~ auditive** hearing aid; **~ de la hanche** hip replacement

prothésiste /prɔtezist/ ▸ p. 372 *nmf* gén prosthetist; **~ dentaire** prosthodontist

protide† /prɔtid/ *nm* protein

protocolaire /prɔtɔkɔlɛr/ *adj* (cérémonieux) formal; (officiel) official; **question ~** question of protocol; **de façon peu ~** unceremoniously

protocole /prɔtɔkɔl/ *nm* ① (cérémonial) formalities (*pl*); (d'État) protocol; **sans ~** gén informally; hum unceremoniously; ② Pol (accord) protocol; **~ d'accord** draft agreement

prototype /prɔtɔtip/ *nm* prototype

protubérance /prɔtyberɑ̃s/ *nf* gén bump; Anat protuberance

protubérant, ~e /prɔtyberɑ̃, ɑ̃t/ *adj* protruding

prou /pru/ *adv* **peu ou ~** more or less

proue /pru/ *nf* prow, bow(s)

prouesse /pruɛs/ *nf* lit feat; iron exploit

prouver /pruve/ [1]
Ⓐ *vtr* ① (établir la réalité de) to prove; **il faudrait qu'il accepte, et ça n'est pas prouvé**ᴼ he has to accept and there's no guarantee that he will; ② (indiquer) to show; ③ (exprimer) to demonstrate [*sentiment*]
Ⓑ **se prouver** *vpr* ① (à soi-même) to prove to oneself; ② (être démontré) **un axiome ne se prouve pas** an axiom cannot be proved; ③ (l'un l'autre) **ils se sont prouvé qu'ils s'aimaient** they proved their love

(Idiome) **n'avoir plus rien à ~** to have proved oneself

provenance /prɔvnɑ̃s/ *nf* origin; **en ~ de** from

provençal, ~e, mpl -aux /prɔvɑ̃sal, o/
Ⓐ ▸ p. 504 *adj* Provençal; **à la ~e** Culin (à la) provençale (*après n*)
Ⓑ ▸ p. 336 *nm* Ling Provençal

provenir /prɔvnir/ [36] *vi* ① (venir) to come (**de** from); **provenant de** from; ② [*situation, déséquilibre*] to stem (**de** from)

proverbe /pʀɔvɛʀb/ *nm* proverb; **comme dit le ~** as the saying goes

proverbial, **~e**, *mpl* **-iaux** /pʀɔvɛʀbjal, o/ *adj* proverbial

providence /pʀɔvidɑ̃s/
A *nf* salvation; (bonté divine) providence
B **(-)providence** (*in compounds*) **État(-)~** welfare state

providentiel, **-ielle** /pʀɔvidɑ̃sjɛl/ *adj* providential

province /pʀɔvɛ̃s/ *nf* 1 (région) province; 2 (pays hormis la capitale) **la ~** the provinces (*pl*); **ville de ~** provincial town; **elle sort de sa ~** pej she's up from the country

provincial, **~e**, *mpl* **-iaux** /pʀɔvɛ̃sjal, o/
A *adj* provincial
B *nm,f* provincial; **les provinciaux** people from *ou* in the provinces

proviseur /pʀɔvizœʀ/ *nm* headteacher GB *ou* principal US (*of a lycée*)

provision /pʀɔvizjɔ̃/
A *nf* 1 (réserve) stock, supply; (d'eau) supply; **faire (une) ~ de qch** to stock up with sth; **faire (une) ~ d'énergie** [*personne*] to build up one's energy; 2 (acompte) deposit; (sur un compte en banque) credit (balance)
B **provisions** *nfpl* food shopping ₵; **faire ses ~s** to go food shopping

provisoire /pʀɔvizwaʀ/
A *adj* [*accord, bilan, gouvernement*] provisional; [*construction, solution, situation*] temporary; **à titre ~** on a temporary basis
B *nm* **s'installer dans le ~** to get stuck with what was originally temporary; **c'est du ~ qui dure** it was supposed to be only temporary

provisoirement /pʀɔvizwaʀmɑ̃/ *adv* provisionally

provocant, **~e** /pʀɔvɔkɑ̃, ɑ̃t/ *adj* provocative

provocateur, **-trice** /pʀɔvɔkatœʀ, tʀis/
A *adj* provocative
B *nm,f* agitator

provocation /pʀɔvɔkasjɔ̃/ *nf* provocation; **faire de la ~** to be provocative

provoquer /pʀɔvɔke/ [1] *vtr* 1 (causer) to cause [*accident, mort*]; to arouse [*curiosité*]; to provoke [*réaction, gaieté, colère*]; to trigger off [*discussion*]; to prompt [*explications*]; **~ l'accouchement** to induce labour; **~ une rencontre entre** to set up a meeting between; 2 (défier) to provoke; **~ qn en duel** to challenge sb to a duel; 3 (exciter sexuellement) to arouse

proxénète /pʀɔksenɛt/ *nm* procurer, pimp

proxénétisme /pʀɔksenetism/ *nm* procuring sout; **inculpé de ~** Jur charged with living off immoral earnings

proximité /pʀɔksimite/ *nf* 1 (voisinage) nearness, proximity; **à ~** nearby; **le commerce de ~** corner shops (*pl*) GB, convenience stores (*pl*) US; **à ~ de** near; 2 (imminence) imminence; **à cause de la ~ de Noël** because it is/was so close to Christmas

prude /pʀyd/ *adj* prudish

prudemment /pʀydamɑ̃/ *adv* [*conduire, observer*] carefully; [*réagir, progresser, attendre*] cautiously

prudence /pʀydɑ̃s/ *nf* caution; **donner des conseils de ~** to advise caution; **avec ~** [*avancer, parler, réagir*] cautiously; [*utiliser*] with caution; **par ~** as a precaution; **redoubler de ~** to be doubly careful; **automobilistes, ~!** drive safely!

prudent, **~e** /pʀydɑ̃, ɑ̃t/ *adj* 1 (soucieux de sa sécurité) careful; **ce n'est pas ~ de faire** it isn't safe to do; 2 (réservé) cautious; 3 (sage) wise; **juger ~ de ne pas accepter** to think it wiser to decline

prud'homme /pʀydɔm/ *nm* **Conseil des ~s** ≈ industrial tribunal GB, labor relations board US

prune /pʀyn/
A ▸ p. 140 *adj inv* (couleur) plum-coloured[GB]
B *nf* (fruit) plum; (eau-de-vie) plum brandy
(Idiomes) **des ~s**◑**!** no way○!; **pour des ~s**○ for nothing

pruneau, *pl* **~x** /pʀyno/ *nm* 1 (fruit) prune; 2 ◑(balle) slug○, bullet

prunelle /pʀynɛl/ *nf* 1 (fruit) sloe; (liqueur) ≈ sloe gin; 2 Anat pupil
(Idiome) **j'y tiens comme à la ~ de mes yeux** it's my pride and joy

prunellier /pʀynelje/ *nm* blackthorn

prunier /pʀynje/ *nm* plum (tree); **secouer qn comme un ~**○ to shake sb until their teeth rattle

prurit /pʀyʀit/ *nm* pruritus

Prusse /pʀys/ *nprf* Prussia
(Idiome) **travailler pour le roi de ~** to work for nothing

PS /peɛs/ *nm* (*abbr* = **post-scriptum**) PS

psalmodier /psalmɔdje/ [2]
A *vtr* to chant [*texte*]
B *vi* Relig (réciter) to say psalms; (chanter) to chant psalms

psaume /psom/ *nm* psalm

pseudo- /psødo/ *préf* pseudo; **~-équilibre** so-called balance; **~-savant** self-styled scientist

pseudonyme /psødɔnim/ *nm* pseudonym

psy○ /psi/ *nmf* shrink○, therapist

psychanalyse /psikanaliz/ *nf* psychoanalysis; **faire une ~** [*sujet*] to undergo analysis

psychanalyser /psikanalize/ [1] *vtr* to psychoanalyse[GB] [*personne*]

psychanalyste /psikanalist/ ▸ **p. 372** *nmf* psychoanalyst

psyché /psiʃe/ *nf* 1 (miroir) cheval glass; 2 Philos psyche

psychiatre /psikjatʀ/ ▸ **p. 372** *nmf* psychiatrist

psychiatrie /psikjatʀi/ *nf* psychiatry

psychiatrique /psikjatʀik/ *adj* psychiatric

psychique /psiʃik/ *adj* [*activité, troubles*] mental

psychisme /psiʃism/ *nm* psyche

psychologie /psikɔlɔʒi/ *nf* (discipline) psychology; (intuition) (psychological) insight; (mentalité) psychology

psychologique /psikɔlɔʒik/ *adj* psychological; **c'est ~!** it's all in the mind!

psychologue /psikɔlɔg/
A *adj* **il n'est pas très ~** he's not much of a psychologist; **être ~** to understand people very well
B ▸ p. 372 *nmf* psychologist

psychomoteur, **-trice** /psikomɔtœʀ, tʀis/ *adj* psychomotor

psychopathe /psikɔpat/ *nmf* psychopath

psychopédagogie /psikopedagɔʒi/ *nf* educational psychology

psychose /psikoz/ *nf* 1 Méd, Psych psychosis; 2 (obsession) **~ de la guerre** obsessive fear of war; **~ collective** mass panic

psychosomatique /psikosɔmatik/ *adj* psychosomatic

psychothérapeute /psikoteʀapøt/ ▸ **p. 372** *nmf* psychotherapist

psychothérapie /psikoteʀapi/ *nf* psychotherapy; **faire une ~** [*patient*] to be in *ou* have (psycho)therapy

psychotique /psikɔtik/ *adj, nmf* psychotic

PTAV *written abbr* ▸ **poids**

PTC *written abbr* ▸ **poids**

PTT /petete/ *nfpl* (*abbr* = **Administration des postes et télécommunications et de la télédiffusion**) *former French postal and telecommunications service*

puant, **~e** /pɥɑ̃, ɑ̃t/ *adj* 1 lit stinking, foul-smelling; [*fromage*] smelly; 2 ○fig (déplaisant) pej **un type ~** an incredibly arrogant guy○

puanteur /pɥɑ̃tœʀ/ *nf* stench

pub○ /pyb/ *nf*: *abbr* ▸ **publicité**

pubère /pybɛʀ/ *adj* pubescent

puberté /pybɛʀte/ *nf* puberty; **à la ~** at puberty

pubien, **-ienne** /pybjɛ̃, ɛn/ *adj* pubic

pubis /pybis/ *nm inv* (région) pubes; (os) pubis

public, **-ique** /pyblik/
A *adj* [*lieu, argent*] public; [*enseignement*] state (*épith*) GB, public US; [*entreprise, chaîne*] state-owned (*épith*); **la dette publique** the national debt; **les cours sont ~s** the lectures are open to the public; **homme** *or* **personnage ~** public figure
B *nm* 1 (tout le monde) public; **en ~** in public; **'interdit au ~'** 'no admittance'; 2 (de spectacle, conférence, d'émission) audience; (de manifestation sportive) spectators (*pl*); **être bon ~** to be a good audience; **être mauvais ~** to be hard to please; **tous ~s** for all ages; 3 (lecteurs) readership; 4 (adeptes) **avoir un ~** to have a following; **elle ne veut pas décevoir**

son ~ she doesn't want to disappoint her fans *ou* public; [5] (secteur) **le** ~ the public sector

publication /pyblikasjɔ̃/ *nf* [1] (parution) publication; **la** ~ **du livre est prévue pour mai** the book is due out in May; [2] (ouvrage) publication

(Composés) ~ **assistée par ordinateur, PAO** desktop publishing, DTP

publicitaire /pyblisitɛʀ/
A *adj* [campagne, budget] advertising; [objet, vente] promotional
B ▸ p. 372 *nmf* (personne) advertising executive; **il est** ~ he's in advertising
C *nm* (société) advertising agency

publicité /pyblisite/ *nf* [1] (activité, profession) advertising; **faire de la** ~ **pour** to advertise; **coup de** ~ publicity stunt; **c'était un beau coup de** ~ it was good publicity; [2] (annonce) advertisement, advert GB, ad○; [3] (diffusion) publicity; **faire une mauvaise** ~ **à qn/qch** to give sb/sth a bad press

(Composés) ~ **comparative** knocking copy○; ~ **mensongère** misleading advertising

publier /pyblije/ [2] *vtr* to publish [livre, auteur]; to issue [communiqué]; **se faire** ~ to get published

publiquement /pyblikmɑ̃/ *adv* publicly

puce /pys/ *nf* [1] Zool flea; [2] ○(terme d'affection) **ma** ~ my pet○; [3] ▸ p. 327 Jeux **jeu de** ~ tiddlywinks (+ *v sg*); [4] Ordinat (silicon) chip

(Idiome) **ça m'a mis la** ~ **à l'oreille** that set me thinking; **secoue-toi les** ~s○! get a move on○!; **secouer les** ~○ **à qn** (gronder) to bawl sb out○

puceau○, *pl* ~**x** /pyso/ *nm* virgin

pucelle○ /pysɛl/ *nf* virgin

puceron /pysʀɔ̃/ *nm* aphid

pudding /pudiŋ/ *nm* heavy fruit sponge

pudeur /pydœʀ/ *nf* [1] (relative au corps) sense of modesty; **sans** ~ shamelessly; [2] (relative aux sentiments) (considération) decency; (retenue) sense of propriety; **par** ~ **elle ne pleura pas** she did not like to cry in public

pudibond, ~**e** /pydibɔ̃, ɔ̃d/ *adj* pej prudish

pudique /pydik/ *adj* modest; (discret) discreet

pudiquement /pydikmɑ̃/ *adv* [1] (chastement) modestly; [2] (par timidité, discrétion) discreetly; [3] (en termes pudiques) discreetly

puer /pɥe/ [1]
A *vtr* to stink of [essence, gaz]; **il pue le parvenu** he is a real parvenu
B *vi* to stink; **il puait des pieds** his feet stank

puéricultrice /pɥerikyltʀis/ ▸ p. 372 *nf* pediatric nurse

puériculture /pɥerikyltyʀ/ *nf* childcare

puéril, ~**e** /pɥeril/ *adj* [conduite, réaction] childish; [attitude, activité] puerile

puérilement /pɥerilmɑ̃/ *adv* childishly

puis /pɥi/ *adv* [1] (ensuite) then; **et** ~**?** then what?; **des pommes, des poires et** ~ **des pêches** apples, pears and peaches; **et** ~ **quoi encore**○! what(ever) next?; [2] (d'ailleurs) **et** ~ **je m'en fiche**○! anyway, I don't care!; **il va être en colère? et** ~ **(après**○**)?** so what if he's angry!; **tu vas ranger ta chambre et** ~ **c'est tout!** you'll go and tidy your room and that's the end of the matter

puisard /pɥizaʀ/ *nm* soakaway GB, sink hole US

puiser /pɥize/ [1] *vtr* lit, fig ~ **qch dans qch** to draw sth from sth; ~ **à pleines mains dans qch** to draw heavily on sth; ~ **ses informations aux meilleures sources** to get one's information from the most reliable sources

puisque (**puisqu'** *before vowel or mute h*) /pɥisk(ə)/ *conj* since; ~ **c'est comme ça, je m'en vais** if that's how it is, I'm off; **mais** ~ **je te dis que c'est impossible** but I'm telling you it's impossible

puissance /pɥisɑ̃s/
A *nf* [1] Phys, Électrotech power; **un amplificateur d'une** ~ **de 60 watts** a 60-watt amplifier; **de forte** ~ very powerful; [2] (intensité) (de lumière) intensity; (de son) volume; [3] Math power; **dix** ~ **trois** ten to the power (of) three; [4] (pouvoir) power; **assassin en** ~ potential killer; [5] (capacité) power; **la** ~ **militaire** the military strength *ou* might; ~ **de concentration** powers (*pl*) of concentration; **il a une** ~ **de travail remarquable** his capacity for work is remarkable;

[6] (vigueur) power, strength; [7] (pays) power; **une grande** ~ a superpower
B *puissances nfpl* Relig **les** ~**s des ténèbres** the powers of darkness

puissant, ~**e** /pɥisɑ̃, ɑ̃t/
A *adj* gén powerful; [sentiment] strong
B *puissants nmpl* **les** ~**s** the powerful (+ *v pl*), the mighty (+ *v pl*)

puits /pɥi/ *nm inv* [1] (d'eau) well; ~ **de pétrole** oil well; [2] (conduit) shaft

(Composés) ~ **de mine** mine shaft; ~ **perdu** soakaway GB, sink hole US; ~ **de science** fount of knowledge

pull○ /pyl/ *nm* (tricot) sweater

pull-over, *pl* ~**s** /pylɔvɛʀ/ *nm* sweater

pullulement /pylylmɑ̃/ *nm* [1] (multiplication) proliferation; [2] (grand nombre) (d'insectes, de gens) swarm; (de fautes, problèmes) multitude

pulluler /pylyle/ [1] *vi* [1] (se multiplier) to proliferate; **depuis dix ans les romans de mauvaise qualité pullulent** over the last ten years there has been a glut of bad novels; [2] (grouiller) **les touristes pullulent dans la région** the area is swarming with tourists; **les poissons pullulent dans la rivière** the river is teeming with fish; **les erreurs pullulent dans le texte** the text is absolutely full of mistakes

pulmonaire /pylmɔnɛʀ/ *adj* [maladie, infection] lung (épith); [artère, veine] pulmonary

pulpe /pylp/ *nf* (de fruit) pulp; (de pomme de terre) flesh

pulpeux, -**euse** /pylpø, øz/ *adj* [corps, lèvres] luscious; [fruit] fleshy

pulsation /pylsasjɔ̃/ *nf* (battement) beat; ~**s cardiaques** (rythme) heartbeat (sg); (battements) heartbeats

pulsion /pylsjɔ̃/ *nf* impulse, urge; ~ **de mort** death wish

pulvérisateur /pylveʀizatœʀ/ *nm* gén spray; Agric sprayer

pulvérisation /pylveʀizasjɔ̃/ *nf* [1] (de liquide) spraying; **'utiliser en** ~**s nasales'** 'for use as nasal spray'; [2] (de matériau) pulverization GB

pulvériser /pylveʀize/ [1] *vtr* [1] (projeter) to spray [liquide]; [2] (broyer) to pulverize [solide]; [3] (anéantir) to pulverize [bâtiment, ennemi]; to demolish○ [argument]; [4] (battre) to shatter○ [record]

punaise /pynɛz/
A *nf* [1] (pointe) drawing pin GB, thumbtack US; [2] Zool bug
B *excl* (de surprise) blimey○! GB, gee○! US; (de dépit) heck○!

(Composés) ~ **des bois** stink bug; ~ **des lits** bedbug

punaiser○ /pyneze/ [1] *vtr* to pin *ou* tack US [sth] up

punch[1] /pɔ̃ʃ/ *nm* (boisson) punch

punch[2] /pœnʃ/ *nm* [1] (de boxeur) punch; **avoir du** ~ to pack quite a punch; [2] (énergie) energy; (dynamisme) drive; **manquer de** ~ [slogan, film] to lack punch; [personne] to lack drive; **avoir du** ~ [slogan, discours] to be punchy○; [personne] to have drive

punching-ball, *pl* ~**s** /pœnʃiŋbol/ *nm* punchball GB, punching bag US

punir /pyniʀ/ [3] *vtr* to punish

punitif, -**ive** /pynitif, iv/ *adj* punitive; **expédition punitive** punitive strike

punition /pynisjɔ̃/ *nf* [1] (châtiment) punishment; **infliger une** ~ **à qn** to punish sb; **avoir une** ~ to be punished; [2] (tâche) **il n'a pas fait sa** ~ he hasn't done the task he was given as punishment

pupille[1] /pypij/ *nmf* (mineur sous tutelle) ward; ~ **de l'État** child in care; ~ **de la Nation** war orphan

pupille[2] /pypij/ *nf* Anat pupil

pupitre /pypitʀ/ *nm* [1] (tableau de commande) control panel; Ordinat console; [2] (de musicien) music stand; (de piano) music rest; **qui est au** ~**?** who's conducting?; [3] (bureau) desk; [4] (d'orateur) lectern

pupitreur, -**euse** /pypitʀœʀ, øz/ ▸ p. 372 *nm,f* computer operator

pur, ~**e** /pyʀ/
A *adj* [1] (sans mélange) pure; (non dilué) straight; **boire son vin** ~ to drink one's wine undiluted; [2] (non altéré) [eau, air] pure; [diamant] flawless; [ciel, voix] clear; [3] (sans fioritures) [ligne, style] pure; [4] (total) [méchanceté, vérité] pure; [coïncidence, plaisir, folie] sheer; **en** ~**e perte** to no avail; **question de** ~**e forme** token question; ~ **et simple** outright; ~ **et**

dur hardline; **5** (théorique) pure; **6** (d'origine) [tradition] true; **un ~ produit de** lit, fig a typical product of; **à l'état ~** [génie, bêtise] sheer; **7** (sans défaut moral) pure
B nm,f **1** (personne irréprochable) virtuous person; **2** (fidèle à un parti) ~ **(et dur)** hardliner

purée /pyʀe/
A nf Culin (de fruits, légumes) purée; (aliment trop cuit) pej mush; ~ **(de pommes de terre)** mashed potatoes (pl); ~ **de marrons** chestnut purée
B ᵒexcl heckᵒ!
(Composés) ~ **en flocons** instant mashed potatoes (pl); ~ **de pois** (brouillard) pea souper GB, fog
(Idiome) **être dans la ~**ᵒ to be in a mess

purement /pyʀmɑ̃/ adv purely

pureté /pyʀte/ nf purity

purgatif, -ive /pyʀgatif, iv/
A adj purgative
B nm purgative

purgatoire /pyʀgatwaʀ/ nm Relig **le ~** purgatory; **faire son ~** fig to do one's penance

purge /pyʀʒ/ nf Méd purgative; Pol purge

purger /pyʀʒe/ [13]
A vtr **1** Méd to purge; **2** Tech to bleed [radiateur, freins]; to drain [tuyau]; to purify [métal]; **3** Jur to serve [peine]
B **se purger** vpr [personne] to take a laxative

purificateur /pyʀifikatœʀ/ nm ~ **d'atmosphère** or **d'air** air purifier

purification /pyʀifikasjɔ̃/ nf purification

purifier /pyʀifje/ [2]
A vtr **1** gén to purify [eau, air, sang]; to cleanse [peau]; to purify [langage]; **2** (moralement) liter to purify
B **se purifier** vpr [personne] to cleanse oneself

purin /pyʀɛ̃/ nm slurry

puriste /pyʀist/ nmf purist

puritain, ~e /pyʀitɛ̃, ɛn/
A adj (austère) puritanical; Relig Puritan
B nm,f (rigoriste) puritan; Relig Puritan

puritanisme /pyʀitanism/ nm puritanism

pur-sang /pyʀsɑ̃/ nm inv thoroughbred, purebred

purulent, ~e /pyʀylɑ̃, ɑ̃t/ adj purulent

pus /py/ nm inv pus

putois /pytwa/ nm inv (animal) polecat; (fourrure) skunk (fur)
(Idiome) **crier comme un ~**ᵒ to scream one's head off

putréfaction /pytʀefaksjɔ̃/ nf putrefaction; **odeur de ~** smell of rotting; **cadavre en état de ~** decomposing body

putréfier: se putréfier /pytʀefje/ [2] vpr [cadavre] to putrefy; [viande] to rot

putsch /putʃ/ nm putsch

putschiste /putʃist/
A adj involved in the putsch (après n)
B nmf **les ~s** those involved in the putsch

puzzle /pœzl, pyzl/ nm Jeux jigsaw puzzle; fig jigsaw

PVᵒ /peve/ nm (abbr = **procès-verbal**) gén fine; (pour stationnement illégal) parking ticket; (pour excès de vitesse) speeding ticket

pygmée /pigme/ nmf pygmy

pyjama /piʒama/ nm pyjamas (pl) GB, pajamas (pl) US, pair of pyjamas GB ou pajamas US

pylône /pilon/ nm pylon; Radio, TV mast; (de pont) tower

pyramidal, ~e, mpl **-aux** /piʀamidal, o/ adj lit pyramid-shaped; fig [hiérarchie] structured like a pyramid (après n)

pyramide /piʀamid/ nf lit, fig pyramid; ~ **des âges** age pyramid

pyrograveur, -euse /piʀogʀavœʀ, øz/ ▸ p. 372 nm,f pokerwork artist

pyrogravure /piʀogʀavyʀ/ nf pokerwork

pyrolyse /piʀoliz/ nf pyrolysis; **four à ~** self-cleaning oven

pyromane /piʀoman/ nmf gén pyromaniac; Jur arsonist

pyrotechnicien, -ienne /piʀotɛknisjɛ̃, ɛn/ ▸ p. 372 nm,f fireworks manufacturer

pyrotechnie /piʀotɛkni/ nf pyrotechnics (+ v sg)

Pyrrhus /piʀys/ npr Pyrrhus; **victoire à la ~** Pyrrhic victory

Pythagore /pitagoʀ/ npr Pythagoras; **théorème de ~** Pythagoras' theorem; **table de ~** multiplication table

python /pitɔ̃/ nm python

p

q, Q /ky/ *nm inv* q, Q

qatari, ~**e** /katari/ ▸ p. 392 *adj* Qatari

qcm /kysɛem/ *nm* (*abbr* = **questionnaire à choix multiple**) multiple-choice questionnaire, mcq

QI /kyi/ *nm*: *abbr* ▸ **quotient**

qu' ▸ que

quadragénaire /kwadraʒenɛr/
A *adj* **être** ~ to be in one's forties
B *nmf* person in his/her forties

quadrature /kwadratyr/ *nf* quadrature; **c'est la** ~ **du cercle** it's like squaring the circle

quadriennal, ~**e**, *mpl* **-aux** /kwadrijenal, o/ *adj* **1** (de quatre ans) [*plan*] four-year (*épith*); **2** (tous les quatre ans) quadrennial, four-yearly (*épith*)

quadrilatère /k(w)adrilatɛr/ *nm* quadrilateral

quadrillage /kadrijaʒ/ *nm* **1** (de papier) cross-ruling; **2** (occupation) **le** ~ **de la ville par l'armée** the systematic military takeover of the town; **le** ~ **du terrain** Mil the chequering of the terrain

quadrillé, ~**e** /kadrije/
A *pp* ▸ **quadriller**
B *pp adj* [*papier*] squared

quadriller /kadrije/ [1] *vtr* **1** (occuper) [*armée*] to take control of; [*police*] to spread one's net over; **2** (faire des carrés sur) to cross-rule [*papier*]

quadrimoteur /k(w)adrimɔtœr/
A *adj* four-engined
B *nm* four-engined plane

quadrithérapie /k(w)adriterapi/ *nf* Méd quadruple therapy

quadrupède /k(w)adryped/ *adj, nm* quadruped

quadruple /k(w)adrypl/
A *adj* [*nombre, rangée, somme*] quadruple
B *nm* **le nombre des sans-abri est le** ~ **de ce qu'il était il y a 20 ans** the number of homeless people is four times what it was twenty years ago

quadruplé, ~**e** /k(w)adryple/ *nm,f* quadruplet

quadrupler /k(w)adryple/ [1]
A *vtr* to quadruple
B *vi* to quadruple, to increase fourfold

quai /kɛ/ *nm* **1** Naut quay; **le navire est à** ~ the ship has docked; **2** (berge aménagée) bank; **3** (de gare, métro) platform

(Composés) ~ **de débarquement** Naut unloading dock; ~ **d'embarquement** Naut loading dock; **Quai des Orfèvres** criminal investigation department of the French police force; **Quai d'Orsay** French Foreign Office

quaker, **quakeresse** /kwɛkœr, kwɛkərɛs/ *nm,f* Quaker/Quakeress

qualifiable /kalifjabl/ *adj* Sport able to qualify (*jamais épith*)

qualificatif, **-ive** /kalifikatif, iv/
A *adj* qualifying
B *nm* Ling qualifier; (mot) term

qualification /kalifikasjɔ̃/ *nf* **1** Sport qualification (**pour** for); **un match de** ~ a qualifying match *ou* game; **2** (compétence pratique) skills (*pl*); (diplôme) qualification; **sans** ~ unskilled

qualifié, ~**e** /kalifje/
A *pp* ▸ **qualifier**

B *pp adj* **1** (compétent) skilled; (diplômé) qualified; **les jeunes non** ~**s** (sans diplôme) young people without qualifications; (sans compétences) young people without skills; **je ne suis pas** ~ **pour vous répondre** I'm not qualified to give you an answer; **2** (demandant des compétences) skilled; **3** Jur [*vol*] aggravated

qualifier /kalifje/ [2]
A *vtr* **1** (caractériser) to describe (**de** as); **2** (donner la compétence à) to qualify; **3** Sport [*victoire*] to qualify; **4** Ling [*adjectif*] to qualify [*nom*]
B **se qualifier** *vpr* [*joueur, pays*] to qualify; **l'équipe s'est qualifiée pour la finale** the team has qualified for the final

qualitatif, **-ive** /kalitatif, iv/ *adj* [*étude, enquête*] qualitative; **sur le plan** ~ in terms of quality

qualité /kalite/ *nf* **1** (valeur) quality; **de bonne** ~ good quality (*épith*); **de** ~ quality (*épith*); **de première** ~ of the highest quality; ~ **de la vie** quality of life; **2** (aptitude) quality; **avoir beaucoup de** ~**s** to have many (good) qualities; **ses** ~**s de gestionnaire** his/her skills as an administrator; **la franchise n'est pas sa** ~ **première** openness is not his/her strong point; **3** Ind quality; **4** (statut) status; (fonction) position; **sa** ~ **de directeur l'autorise à faire** his/her position as manager allows him/her to do; **en (sa)** ~ **de représentant** in his/her capacity as a representative; **nom, prénom et** ~ surname, first name and occupation; **5** (sorte) quality

quand /kɑ̃, kɑ̃t/

⚠ *When* traduisant *quand* conjonction ne peut pas être suivi du futur: *quand il aura terminé* = when he has finished; *quand je serai guérie, j'irai te voir* = when I'm better, I'll come and see you.

A *conj* **1** (lorsque) when; ~ **il arrivera, vous lui annoncerez la nouvelle** when he gets here, you can tell him the news; ~ **il prend son poste en 1980, la situation est déjà catastrophique** when he took up his post in 1980, the situation was already catastrophic; **tu auras ton dessert** ~ **tu auras fini ta viande** you'll have your dessert when you have finished your meat; **emporte une pomme pour** ~ **tu auras faim**○ take an apple with you in case you get hungry; **2** (valeur exclamative) ~ **je pense que ma fille va avoir dix ans!** to think that my daughter's almost ten (years old)!; ~ **je vous le disais!** I told you so!; **3** (toutes les fois que) whenever; ~ **il pleut plus de trois jours la cave est inondée** whenever it rains for more than three days, the cellar floods; **son attitude change** ~ **il s'agit de son fils** his/her attitude changes when it comes to his/her son; **4** (alors que) when; **tu oses te plaindre** ~ **des gens meurent de faim!** you dare to complain when there are people starving!; **5** (même si) even if; ~ **(bien même) la terre s'écroulerait, il continuerait à dormir** he'd sleep through an earthquake

B *adv* when; ~ **arrive-t-il/viendras-tu?** when does he arrive/will you come?; **depuis** ~ **habitez-vous ici?** how long have you been living here?; **ça date de** ~ **cette histoire?** when did all this happen?; **de** ~ **date votre dernière réunion?** when was your last meeting?; **de** ~ **est la lettre?** what is the date on the letter?; **c'est prévu pour** ~? when is it scheduled for?; **c'est pour** ~ **le bébé?** when is the baby due?; **à** ~○ **la semaine de 30 heures?** when will we get a 30-hour working week?

C **quand même** *loc adv* still; **ils étaient occupés mais ils nous ont** ~ **même rendu visite** they were busy but they still came to visit us; **ils ne veulent pas de moi, mais j'irai**

~ **même!** they don't want me, but I'm still going!; **elle est ~ même bête○ d'avoir fait ça!** it's really stupid of her to have done that!; ~ **même○, tu exagères!** (tu n'es pas objectif) come on, you're exaggerating!; (tu vas trop loin) come on, that's going too far!; **tu ne vas pas faire ça ~ même○?** you're not going to do that, are you?

quant: **quant à** /kɑ̃ta/ loc prép **1** (pour ce qui est de) as for; **la France, ~ à elle, n'a pas pris position** as for France, it did not take a stand; ~ **à partir, jamais!** as for leaving, never!; **2** (au sujet de) about; **elle ne a rien dit ~ à l'heure de la réunion** she didn't say anything about what time the meeting would be

quantifiable /kɑ̃tifjabl/ adj quantifiable

quantifier /kɑ̃tifje/ [2] vtr Écon, Math to quantify; Phys to quantize

quantique /kɑ̃tik/ adj Phys quantum

quantitatif, -ive /kɑ̃titatif, iv/ adj quantitative

quantité /kɑ̃tite/ ▸ p. 483 nf **1** (mesure) quantity (**de** of), amount (**de** of); **en grande ~** in large quantities; **faire qch en ~s industrielles** Ind to mass-produce sth; hum to make vast quantities of sth; ~ **négligeable** lit small ou negligible quantity; **être une ~ négligeable** [personne] to be dispensable; **2** (grand nombre) **des ~s de** (de personnes) scores of; (de choses) a lot of; **il y avait une ~ de gens incroyable** there was an incredible number of people; **du pain/vin en ~** plenty of bread/wine; **3** (en sciences, linguistique, musique) quantity

quarantaine /kaʁɑ̃tɛn/ nf **1** (environ quarante) about forty; **2** (âge) **il a la ~** he's in his forties; **elle approche la ~** she's getting on for forty; **3** Méd (isolement) quarantine; **être en ~** lit to be in quarantine; fig to be ostracized

quarante /kaʁɑ̃t/ ▸ p. 398, p. 155 adj inv, pron forty

quarante-cinq /kaʁɑ̃tsɛ̃k/ ▸ p. 398, p. 155 adj inv, pron forty-five

(Composé) ~ **tours** Audio single

quarantième /kaʁɑ̃tjɛm/ ▸ p. 398 adj fortieth

quart /kaʁ/ ▸ p. 296 nm **1** (quatrième partie) quarter (**de** of); **un ~ d'heure** lit a quarter of an hour; **faire passer un mauvais ~ d'heure○ à qn** to give sb a hard time; **un kilo un ~** a kilo and a quarter; **un ~ de siècle** a quarter of a century; **les trois ~s du temps○** most of the time; **les trois ~s des gens○** most people; **2** (bouteille) a quarter-litre^GB bottle (**de** of); (pichet) a quarter-litre^GB pitcher (**de** of); **3** (gobelet) beaker of (a quarter-litre^GB capacity); **4** Naut watch; **être de ~** to be on watch

(Composés) ~ **de cercle** quadrant; ~ **de tour** lit 90° ou ninety-degree turn; **faire qch au ~ de tour○** fig to do sth immediately

quarte /kaʁt/ nf Mus fourth

quarté /kaʁte/ nm: betting based on forecasting the first four horses in a race

quartier /kaʁtje/ nm **1** (partie d'une ville) area, district; (zone administrative) district; (zone ethnique) quarter; **le ~ des affaires** the business area ou district; **dans mon ~** in my area; **le plan du ~** a map of the area; **les beaux ~s** fashionable districts; **de ~** local; **la vie de ~** local community life; **les gens du ~** the locals; **êtes-vous du ~?** are you from around here?; **2** (portion) quarter; **un ~ de pommes** a slice of apple; **un ~ de bœuf** a quarter of beef; **un ~ d'orange** an orange segment; **3** (en astronomie) quarter; **le premier ~ de la lune** the moon's first quarter; **4** (de noblesse) quarter; **5** Mil ~s quarters; **avoir ~ libre** Mil to be off duty; fig to have time off ou free time

(Composés) ~ **général, QG** Mil, fig headquarters, HQ; ~ **résidentiel fermé** gated community

(Idiome) **ne pas faire de ~** to show no mercy

quartier-maître, pl **quartiers-maîtres** /kaʁtjemɛtʁ/ nm leading seaman GB, petty officer third class US

quart-monde /kaʁmɔ̃d/ nm inv underclass

quartz /kwaʁts/ nm quartz; **à ~** quartz (épith)

quasi /kazi/
A adv almost
B nm Culin ~ **(de veau)** fillet of veal
C quasi- (in compounds) ~-**monopole/indifférence** virtual monopoly/indifference; ~-**certitude** near certainty; **la ~-totalité de** almost all of

quasiment○ /kazimɑ̃/ adv practically

quaternaire /kwatɛʁnɛʁ/ adj, nm (en géologie) Quaternary

quatorze /katɔʁz/ ▸ p. 398, p. 296, p. 155 adj inv, pron fourteen

(Idiomes) **chercher midi à ~ heures○** to complicate matters; **c'est reparti comme en 14○!** here we go again!

quatorzième /katɔʁzjɛm/ ▸ p. 398, p. 155 adj fourteenth

quatrain /katʁɛ̃/ nm quatrain

quatre /katʁ/ ▸ p. 398, p. 296, p. 155 adj inv, pron, nm inv four

(Idiomes) **dire ses ~ vérités○ à qn** to tell sb a few home truths; **faire les ~ volontés de qn** to give in to sb's every whim; **être tiré à ~ épingles** to be dressed up to the nines○; **manger comme ~** to eat like a horse; **ne pas y aller par ~ chemins** not to beat about the bush; **je vais leur parler entre ~ yeux** or **quat'zyeux○** I'm going to talk to them face to face; **monter/descendre (un escalier) ~ à ~** to go up/to go down the stairs four at a time; **être entre ~ planches○** to be six feet under

quatre-cent-vingt-et-un /katsɑ̃vɛ̃teœ̃/ nm inv: game of dice

quatre-heures /katʁœʁ/ nm inv afternoon snack (for children)

quatre-mâts /katʁəmɑ/ nm inv four-master

quatre-quarts /kat(ʁə)kaʁ/ nm inv pound cake

quatre-vingt(s) /katʁəvɛ̃/ ▸ p. 398, p. 155 adj, pron eighty

quatre-vingt-dix /katʁəvɛ̃dis/ ▸ p. 398, p. 155 adj inv, pron ninety

quatre-vingt-dixième /katʁəvɛ̃dizjɛm/ ▸ p. 398 adj ninetieth

quatre-vingtième /katʁəvɛ̃tjɛm/ ▸ p. 398 adj eightieth

quatrième /katʁijɛm/ ▸ p. 398, p. 155
A adj fourth
B nf **1** Scol third year of secondary school, age 13–14; **2** Aut fourth gear; **passer en ~** to change ou go into fourth gear

(Composé) **le ~ âge** very old people (+ v pl)

(Idiome) **faire qch en ~ vitesse○** to do sth in double quick time○

quatuor /kwatɥɔʁ/ nm (œuvre, formation) quartet

quat'zyeux○ /katzjø/ ▸ **quatre**

que (**qu'** before vowel or mute h) /kə/
A conj **1** (reprenant une autre conjonction) **comme tu ne veux pas venir et ~ tu ne veux pas dire pourquoi** since you refuse to come and (since you) refuse to say why; **si vous venez et ~ vous ayez le temps** if you come and (if you) have the time; **2** **je crains ~ tu (ne) fasses une bêtise** I'm worried (that) you might do something silly; **qu'il soit le meilleur, nous nous en sommes déjà rendu compte** we were already well aware that he's the best; **approche, ~ je te regarde** come closer so I can look at you; ~ **vous le vouliez ou non, ~ cela vous plaise ou non** whether you like it or not; **il n'était pas sitôt parti qu'elle appela la police** no sooner had he left than she called the police; **j'avais déjà lu dix pages qu'il n'avait toujours pas commencé** I had already read ten pages while he hadn't even started; ~ **tout le monde sorte!** everyone must leave!; **qu'on veuille bien m'excuser mais...** you must excuse me but...; ~ **ceux qui n'ont pas compris le disent** let anyone who hasn't understood say so; **qu'on le pende!** hang him!; **qu'il crève○!** let him rot○!; ~ **je leur prête ma voiture!** you expect me to lend them my car!; ~ **je sache** as far as I know

B pron inter what; ~ **dire?** what can you ou one say?; ~ **faire?** (maintenant) what shall I/we do?; (au passé) what could I/we do?; **je ne sais pas ce qu'il a dit** I don't know what he said; **qu'est-ce que c'est que ça?** what's that?

C pron rel **1** (ayant un nom de personne pour antécédent) **Pierre, ~ je n'avais pas vu depuis 20 ans, est venu me voir hier** Pierre, whom I had not seen for 20 years, came to see me yesterday; **c'est la plus belle femme ~ j'aie jamais vue** she's the most beautiful woman (that) I've ever seen; **2** (ayant un nom de chose ou d'animal pour antécédent) **je n'aime pas la voiture ~ tu as achetée** I don't like the car (that) you've bought; **3** (employé comme attribut) that; **la vieille dame qu'elle est**

Les quantités

Dénombrables ou indénombrables?

■ *L'anglais, comme le français, distingue deux catégories de noms: ceux qui désignent des éléments pouvant se compter par unités, se dénombrer (les dénombrables), comme les pommes, les chaises etc., et ceux qui désignent des éléments toujours à l'état de masse, indénombrable en éléments séparés (les indénombrables), comme le lait ou le sable.*

■ *Comment distinguer un dénombrable d'un indénombrable? Précédés de «assez de», un dénombrable se met au pluriel (assez de pommes) et un indénombrable se met au singulier (assez de lait)* (**recette pour francophones uniquement**). *«beaucoup», «peu» et «moins» exigent, en anglais, des traductions différentes, selon qu'ils spécifient un nom dénombrable, ou un nom indénombrable.*

	pour les dénombrables	**pour les in- dénombrables**
beaucoup de =	a lot of *ou* lots of *ou* many*	a lot of *ou* lots of *ou* much*
peu =	few *ou* not many	little *ou* not much
plus =	more	more
moins =	fewer *ou* (*familier*) less	less
assez =	enough	enough

* *Attention:* not many *et* not much *s'emploient couramment, mais* many *et* much *sont peu utilisés à la forme affirmative.*

Les noms dénombrables

combien y a-t-il de pommes?
= how many apples are there?

il y a beaucoup de pommes
= there are lots of apples

■ *Noter l'absence d'équivalent anglais du français en dans les expressions suivantes:*

combien y en a-t-il ?
= how many are there?

il y en a beaucoup
= there are a lot

il y en a deux kilos
= there are two kilos (*on peut aussi dire, dans la conversation*, there's two kilos)

il y en a vingt
= there are twenty

j'en ai vingt
= I've got twenty

■ *Noter l'ordre des mots dans:*

quelques pommes de plus
= a few more apples

quelques personnes de plus
= a few more people

A a moins de pommes que B
= A doesn't have as many apples as B

beaucoup moins de pommes
= far fewer apples *ou* not nearly as many apples

Les noms indénombrables

combien y a-t-il de lait?
= how much milk is there?

il y a beaucoup de lait
= there is a lot of milk

■ *Noter l'absence d'équivalent anglais du français en dans les expressions suivantes.*

combien y en a-t-il?
= how much is there?

il n'y en a pas beaucoup
= there isn't much *ou* there's only a little

j'en ai deux kilos
= I've got two kilos

A a plus de lait que B
= A has got more milk than B

beaucoup plus de lait
= much more milk

un peu plus de lait
= a little more milk

A a moins de lait que B
= A has got less milk than B

beaucoup moins de lait
= much less milk *ou* far less milk

Quantités relatives

combien y en a-t-il par kilo?
= how many are there to the kilo?

il y en a dix par kilo
= there are ten to the kilo

il y en a cinq pour deux euros
= you get five for two euros

■ *Pour toutes les expressions utilisées pour donner un prix par unité de mesure (longueur, poids etc.), l'anglais utilise l'article indéfini là où le français utilise l'article défini.*

combien coûte le litre?
= how much does it cost a litre?
ou how much does a litre cost?

trois euros le litre
= three euros a litre

combien coûte le kilo de pommes?
= how much do apples cost a kilo?
ou how much does a kilo of apples cost?

elles sont à deux euros le kilo
= they are two euros a kilo

combien coûte le mètre?
= how much does it cost a metre?

dix livres le mètre
= £10 a metre

Mais noter:

la voiture fait huit litres aux cent
= the car does 35 miles to the gallon†

combien y a-t-il de verres par bouteille?
= how many glasses are there to the bottle?

il y a six verres par bouteille
= there are six glasses to the bottle

† *En anglais, on compte la consommation d'une voiture en mesurant non pas le nombre de litres nécessaires pour parcourir 100 kilomètres, mais la distance parcourue (en miles) avec 4,54 litres (un gallon) de carburant (mpg). Pour convertir la consommation exprimée en litres aux 100km en mpg (miles per gallon) et vice versa il suffit de diviser 280 par le chiffre connu.*

q

que

que conjonction de subordination se traduit généralement par *that*:

elle a dit qu'elle le ferait
= she said that she would do it

il est important qu'ils se rendent compte que ce n'est pas simple
= it's important that they should realize that it's not simple

On notera que *that* est souvent omis:

je pense qu'il devrait changer de métier
= I think he should change jobs

Quand *que* suit un verbe exprimant un souhait, une volonté, l'anglais utilise un infinitif:

je voudrais que tu ranges ta chambre
= I'd like you to tidy your room

elle veut qu'il fasse un stage de formation
= she wants him to do a training course

On trouvera ci-dessous quelques exemples supplémentaires mais on pourra toujours se reporter aux verbes, adjectifs et substantifs qui peuvent être suivis de *que*, comme **montrer, comprendre, apparaître, certain, évident, idée** etc. De même les locutions *ainsi que, alors*

que, bien que sont traitées respectivement à **ainsi, alors, bien**. Pour les emplois de *que* avec *ne, plus, moins* etc. on se reportera à **ne, plus, moins** etc.

que pronom relatif se traduit différemment selon qu'il a pour antécédent un nom de personne:

l'homme que je vois
= the man that I can see *ou* the man I can see
ou the man who I can see *ou* the man whom I can see

les amis que j'ai invités
= the friends that I've invited *ou* the friends I've invited
ou the friends who I have invited
ou the friends whom I have invited

(dans les deux cas ci-dessus la traduction avec *whom* appartient au registre de la langue écrite);

ou un nom de chose, concept, animal:

le chien que je vois
= the dog that I can see *ou* the dog I can see
ou the dog which I can see

l'invitation que j'ai reçue
= the invitation that I received *ou* the invitation I received
ou the invitation which I received

Voir **C p. 482**.

quel

quel déterminant interrogatif se traduit généralement par *who* lorsque la question porte sur des personnes:

quel est ce jeune homme?
= who is that young man?

et par *what* dans les autres cas:

quelle est la capitale du Togo?
= what is the capital of Togo?

Toutefois lorsque la question porte sur un nombre de possibilités que l'on sait restreint, on utilisera *which*:

quel est le musicien français qui a composé 'le Boléro'?
= what French musician composed the 'Bolero'?

mais:

quel est le musicien français qui a composé 'le Boléro'? Debussy, Ravel ou Poulenc?
= which French musician composed 'the Bolero'? Debussy, Ravel or Poulenc?

On remarquera par ailleurs que l'inversion du sujet dans les propositions interrogatives indirectes en français n'est pas reproduite en anglais:

je me demande quel est son avis sur la question
= I wonder what his opinion on the matter is

quel adjectif interrogatif se traduit soit par *what* lorsque le contexte est vague et les possibilités infinies:

quel musicien vas-tu écouter?
= what musician are you going to listen to?

soit par *which* lorsque le contexte est spécifique et le nombre de possibilités limité:

dans quel tiroir as-tu mis la lettre?
= which drawer did you put the letter in?

On remarquera qu'en anglais, lorsque la question comporte une préposition, plusieurs cas sont possibles:

dans quel pays habite-t-elle?
= what country does she live in?
ou in what country does she live?

La première traduction est utilisée dans la langue courante, parlée ou écrite. La deuxième sera préférée dans une langue plus soutenue, surtout écrite. Voir **B** ci-dessous.

Les autres fonctions de *quel* sont traitées ci-contre en **C** et **D**.

Par ailleurs certains emplois de *quel* sont traités dans les notes d'usage, notamment celles concernant **l'âge, l'heure** etc. ▸ **p. 1355**.

q

devenue the old lady she is today
D *adv* ~ **vous êtes jolie!** how pretty you are!; ~ **c'est difficile!** how difficult it is!; ~ **c'est joli!** it's so pretty!; **ce** ~ **vous êtes jolie!** you're so pretty!; ~ **de monde!** what a lot of people!; **'vous ne leur en avez pas parlé?'—'oh ~ si!'** 'haven't you spoken to them about it?'—'yes I have!'; **'tu en as besoin?'—'~ oui!'** 'do you need it'—'I certainly do!'

Québec /kebɛk/
A ▸ p. 504 *nprm* (province) **le** ~ Quebec
B ▸ p. 621 *npr* (ville) Quebec

québécois, ~e /kebekwa, az/ *adj* of Quebec

Québécois, ~e /kebekwa, az/ *nm,f* Quebecois, Quebecker

quel, quelle /kɛl/
A *dét inter* ~**s sont les pays membres de l'UE?** what are the

member countries of the EU?; **je me demande quelle est la meilleure solution** I wonder what the best solution is; **de ces deux médicaments, ~ est le plus efficace?** which of these two medicines is more effective?
B *adj inter* **dans ~s pays as-tu vécu?** what countries have you lived in?; **de ~ étage a-t-il sauté?** which floor did he jump from?; **quelle heure est-il?** what time is it?; **si tu savais à ~ point il m'agace!** if you only knew how much he irritates me!
C *adj excl* **~ what**; ~ **imbécile!** what an idiot!; **quelle coïncidence!** what a coincidence!; **quelle horreur!** how dreadful!
D *adj rel* **quelles qu'aient pu être tes raisons, tu n'aurais jamais dû faire cela** whatever your reasons may have been, you should never have done that; **quelle que soit la route que l'on prenne** whatever *ou* whichever road we take; **~ que soit le vainqueur** whoever the winner may be;

quelque

Remarques à propos de *quelque chose*

Dans les phrases affirmatives, *quelque chose* se traduit par *something*:

quelque chose m'a frappé
= something struck me

j'ai vu quelque chose qui va te plaire
= I saw something that you will like

Dans les phrases interrogatives et conditionnelles, l'anglais fait une distinction entre une vraie question dont la réponse peut être *oui* ou *non* ou une vraie supposition:

avez-vous quelque chose à ajouter?
= have you got anything to add?

si tu vois quelque chose de louche
= if you see anything suspicious

si quelque chose leur arrivait
= if anything happened to them

et une supposition formulée sous forme de question:

tu fais une drôle de tête, tu as quelque chose à dire?
= you don't look too pleased, have you got something to say?

ou de suggestion:

si tu as vu quelque chose que tu aimerais pour ton anniversaire
= if you have seen something that you'd like for your birthday

si quelque chose te déplaît, dis-le
= if there's something you don't like, say so.

Voir exemples supplémentaires et exceptions ci-dessous.

quelqu'un

Dans les phrases affirmatives, *quelqu'un* se traduit par *someone* ou *somebody*:

quelqu'un m'a dit qu'elle était malade
= someone told me she was ill

j'ai rencontré quelqu'un qui te connaissait
= I met someone who knew you

Dans les phrases interrogatives et conditionnelles, l'anglais fait une distinction entre une vraie question dont la réponse peut être *oui* ou *non* ou une vraie supposition:

est-ce que quelqu'un parle grec?
= does anybody speak Greek?

est-ce que quelqu'un a vu mes clés?
= has anybody seen my keys?

est-ce que quelqu'un connaît la réponse?
= does anyone know the answer?

si quelqu'un téléphone, dites que je serai absent jusqu'à demain
= if anyone calls, say that I'll be away until tomorrow

si quelqu'un touche à mon ordinateur, il sera puni
= if anyone touches my computer, they'll be punished

et une supposition, un soupçon formulé sous forme de question:

est-ce que quelqu'un a touché à mon ordinateur?
= has somebody been playing with my computer?

est-ce que quelqu'un t'a donné la réponse?
= did someone give you the answer?

ou bien une requête ou une offre polie:

est-ce que quelqu'un pourrait fermer la fenêtre?
= could somebody close the window?

est-ce que quelqu'un veut encore du gâteau?
= would somebody like another piece of cake?

si quelqu'un voulait bien ouvrir la porte au chien
= if someone would please let the dog in

Dans les deux derniers cas, la réponse attendue est *oui*.

Voir exemples supplémentaires et exceptions dans l'entrée **quelqu'un**.

q

~ que soit l'endroit où il se sont arrêtés wherever they stopped

quelconque /kɛlkɔ̃k/
A *adj* (ordinaire) [*personne*] ordinary; [*livre, acteur*] poor; [*restaurant, produit*] second-rate; [*endroit, décor*] characterless; (qui manque de charme) [*personne*] ordinary-looking; **j'ai trouvé le film très ~** I thought the film was very poor
B *adj indéf* (n'importe lequel) any; **je doute qu'il y ait un ~ rapport entre les deux événements** I doubt that there's any link between the two events; **si pour une raison ~** if for some reason or other

quelle ▸ **quel**

quelque /kɛlk/
A *adj indéf* **1** (au singulier) (dans les phrases affirmatives) some; (dans les phrases interrogatives) any; **il y aurait ~ contradiction à dire que** it would be somewhat contradictory to say that; **si pour ~ raison que ce soit** if for whatever reason; **de ~ côté que nous allions** whichever way we go; **2** (au pluriel) (dans les phrases affirmatives) some, a few; (dans les phrases interrogatives) any; **je voudrais ajouter ~s mots** I'd like to add a few words; **~s instants** a few moments; **est-ce qu'il vous reste ~s cartons?** do you have any boxes left?; **ça dure trois heures et ~s** it lasts over three hours
B *adv* **1** (environ) **les ~ deux mille spectateurs** the two thousand odd spectators, the two thousand or so spectators; **ça lui a coûté ~ 30 euros** it cost him about 30 euros; **2** (si) however; **~ admirable que soit son attitude** however admirable his/her attitude may be
C **quelque chose** *pron indéf inv* (dans les phrases affirmatives) something; **il y a ~ chose qui ne va pas** something's wrong; **ils y sont pour ~ chose** they've got something to do with it; **elle est restée ~ chose comme trois heures** she stayed for something like three hours; **il me reste ~ chose comme 20 euros** I've got about 20 euros left; **~ chose de mieux** something better; **il y aurait ~ chose d'absurde à refuser sa proposition** it would be ridiculous

to turn down his offer; **c'est ~ chose d'inimaginable!** it's unbelievable!; **il a ~ chose de son grand-père** he's got a look of his grandfather about him; **faire ~ chose à qn** [*événement, substance*] to have an effect on sb; **c'est ~ chose○! tu es toujours en retard!** for crying out loud! you're always late; **en ce temps-là, être instituteur, c'était ~ chose** in those days it was quite something to be a primary school teacher; **ça me dit ~ chose** it reminds me of something, it rings a bell
D **quelque part** *loc adv* somewhere; **il lui a mis son pied ~ part**○ *euph* he gave him/her a kick in the behind
E **quelque peu** *loc adv* somewhat; **il a accepté après avoir ~ peu hésité** he accepted after some hesitation

quelquefois /kɛlkəfwa/ *adv* sometimes

quelques-uns, **quelques-unes** /kɛlkəzœ̃, yn/ *pron indéf pl* some, a few

quelqu'un /kɛlkœ̃/ *pron indéf* **1** (dans les phrases affirmatives) someone, somebody; **~ d'autre** somebody else, someone else; **c'est ~ de compétent/de très doué** he/she is competent/very gifted; **un jour, il deviendra ~**○ one day, he'll be somebody; **cette fille-là, c'est ~**○! that girl isn't just anybody; **2** (dans les phrases interrogatives et conditionnelles) **il y a ~?** is there anybody here?; **le téléphone sonne, est-ce que ~ pourrait répondre?** the telephone is ringing, could somebody answer?

quémander /kemɑ̃de/ [1] *vtr* to beg; **~ qch auprès de qn** to beg sth from sb, to beg sb for sth

qu'en-dira-t-on /kɑ̃diratɔ̃/ *nm inv* gossip; **sans souci du ~** heedless of what people might say

qui

qui, pronom interrogatif sujet, se traduit par *who*:

qui est-ce?　　**qui a cassé la vitre?**
= who is it?　　= who broke the window?

qui vous a reçu?
= who met you?

qui, pronom interrogatif dans des fonctions autres que sujet, se traduit par *who* ou *whom*:

qui avez-vous rencontré?
= who did you meet? *ou* whom did you meet?

qui vas-tu inviter?
= who are you going to invite?
ou whom are you going to invite?

La traduction avec *whom* appartient au registre de la langue écrite.

Lorsque le pronom interrogatif est utilisé avec une préposition, deux cas sont possibles:

avec qui voulez-vous un rendez-vous?
= who do you want an appointment with?
ou with whom do you want an appointment?

pour qui as-tu acheté cette montre?
= who did you buy that watch for?
ou for whom did you buy that watch?

Voir la remarque ci-dessus concernant *whom*. Voir exemples supplémentaires et exceptions en **A** dans l'entrée **qui.**

qui, pronom relatif sujet, se traduit par *who* lorsqu'il remplace un nom de personne:

je remercie ceux qui m'ont aidé
= my thanks to those who helped me

j'ai rencontré Pierre qui m'a parlé de toi
= I met Pierre who talked to me about you

et par *that* ou *which* (ce dernier étant plus spécifique à l'anglais britannique) dans la plupart des autres cas:

le vase qui était sur la table
= the vase that (*ou* which) was on the table

une idée qui n'était pas mauvaise
= an idea that (*ou* which) wasn't bad

un chien qui avait l'air affamé
= a dog that (*ou* which) looked hungry

Voir exemples supplémentaires et exceptions en **B1.**

qui, pronom relatif ayant une fonction autre que sujet et remplaçant un nom de personne, se traduit par *that*, *who* ou *whom*, cette dernière traduction étant du domaine de la langue écrite:

un ami en qui je peux avoir confiance
= a friend that I can trust *ou* a friend who I can trust
ou a friend whom I can trust
ou (*le pronom relatif peut parfois s'omettre en anglais*)
a friend I can trust

---

quenelle /kənɛl/ *nf*: dumpling made of flour and egg, flavoured^GB with meat or fish

quenotte^○ /kənɔt/ *nf* toothy-peg^○ GB lang enfantin, tooth

quenouille /kənuj/ *nf* distaff

(Idiome) **tomber en ~** to die out

querelle /kərɛl/ *nf* [1] (dispute) quarrel (**entre** between); (chamaillerie) squabble; **chercher ~ à qn** to pick a quarrel with sb; **~s intestines** internal squabbling ¢; [2] (débat) dispute

(Composé) **~ d'amoureux** lovers' tiff

quereller /kərɛle/ [1]
A†*vtr* (gronder) to tell [sb] off
B se quereller *vpr* to quarrel

querelleur, -euse /kərɛlœr, øz/ *adj* quarrelsome

question /kɛstjɔ̃/ *nf* [1] (interrogation) question (**sur** about); **je ne me suis jamais posé la ~** I've never really thought about it; **je me posais justement la ~** I was just wondering about that; **je ne sais pas, pose-leur la ~** I don't know, ask them; **sans se poser de ~s** unthinkingly; [2] (sujet) matter, question; (ensemble de problèmes) issue, question; **~ d'habitude!** it's a matter of habit; **c'est une ~ de vie ou de mort** it's a matter of life and death; **il en fait une ~ de principe** he's making an issue of it; **la ~ n'est pas de savoir qui/comment/si** the question is not who/how/whether; **en ~** (dont il s'agit) in question; (qui pose problème) at issue; **(re)mettre en ~** (réexaminer) to reappraise; (repenser) to reassess; **se remettre en ~** to take a new look at oneself; **la ~ n'est pas là** that's not the point; **les ~s à l'ordre du jour** the items on the agenda; **il est ~ d'elle dans l'article** she's mentioned in the article; **il est ~ qu'il prenne sa retraite** there's some talk of him retiring; **il n'est pas ~ que tu partes** (à un invité) you can't possibly leave; **pas ~!** no way^○!; [3] ^○(pour ce qui est de) **~ argent/ santé, ça va** where money/health is concerned, things are OK; **la maison est jolie, mais ~ quartier...** the house is pretty, but as for the area...; [4] Hist (torture) question

(Composé) **~ de confiance** Pol vote of confidence; **poser la ~ de confiance** to call for a vote of confidence

(Idiome) **faire les ~s et les réponses** to do all the talking

questionnaire /kɛstjɔnɛr/ *nm* questionnaire

questionner /kɛstjɔne/ [1] *vtr* to question

quête /kɛt/ *nf* [1] (d'aumônes) collection; **faire la ~** (à l'église) to take the collection; [saltimbanque] to pass the hat

round; (pour une œuvre) to collect for charity; [2] (recherche) search (**de** for); **en ~ de nouvelles** in search of news; **être en ~ de qch** to be looking for sth; **la ~ du Graal** the quest for the Holy Grail

quêter /kete/ [1]
A *vtr* to look for, to seek [approbation, pitié, soutien]; to try to get [sourire]
B *vi* (à l'église) to take the collection; (pour une cause) **~ pour une œuvre** to collect for a charity

quetsche /kwɛtʃ/ *nf* (sweet purple) plum

queue /kø/ *nf* [1] Zool tail; [2] Bot (de feuille, fleur) stem; (de cerise, pomme) stalk GB, stem US; (de fraise) hull; [3] (manche) (de casserole, poêle) handle; [4] (de billard) cue; [5] (partie terminale) (d'animal, avion, de cerf-volant) tail; (de cortège, procession) tail(-end); (de train) rear, back; [6] (dans un classement) **ils arrivent en ~ (de peloton)** des grandes entreprises they come at the bottom of the league table of companies; [7] (file d'attente) queue GB, line US; **faire la ~** to stand in a queue GB, to stand in line US; **à la ~!** go to the back of the queue GB *ou* line US

(Idiomes) **une histoire sans ~ ni tête**^○ a cock and bull story; **ce film n'a ni ~ ni tête**^○ you can't make head or tail of this film; **la ~ basse** with one's tail between one's legs; **il n'y en avait pas la ~ d'un(e)**^○ there were none to be seen; **faire une ~ de poisson à qn** to cut in front of sb; **finir en ~ de poisson** to fizzle out, to peter out

queue-de-cheval, *pl* **queues-de-cheval** /kødʃəval/ *nf* ponytail; **elle se fait une ~** she puts her hair in a ponytail

queue-de-pie^○, *pl* **queues-de-pie** /kødpi/ *nf* tails (*pl*), tailcoat

queux† /kø/ *nm inv* **maître ~** chef

qui /ki/
A *pron inter* (fonction sujet) who; (fonction complément) whom; **~ veut-elle voir?** who does she want to speak to?; **à ~ sont ces livres?** whose books are these?; **de ~ est ce roman?** who is this novel by?; **dis-moi à ~ tu penses** tell me who you are thinking about
B *pron rel* [1] (fonction sujet) (l'antécédent est un nom de personne) who; (autres cas) that, which; **le gouvernement ~ a été formé par** the government (which was) formed by; **le chien, ~ m'avait reconnu...** the dog, which recognized me...; **lui ~ s'intéresse aux armes à feu devrait aimer cette exposition** interested in firearms as he is, he should enjoy

the exhibition; **toi ∼ pensais faire des économies!** and you were the one who thought you were going to save money!; **celui ∼ a pris le livre aurait pu le dire** whoever took the book could have said so; **[2]** (fonction autre que sujet) **invitez ∼ vous voulez** invite whoever *ou* anyone you like; **c'est à ∼ des deux criera le plus fort** each (one) is trying to shout the other down; **quelqu'un en ∼ j'ai confiance** someone I trust; **∼ que vous soyez** whoever you are; **∼ que ce soit** whoever it is, anybody; **je n'ai jamais frappé ∼ que ce soit** I've never hit anybody; **∼ que ce soit ∼ a fait cela** whoever (it was who) did that; **∼ que ce soit, je ne suis pas là** I'm not here for anybody; **[3]** *fml* **les enfants étaient déguisés ∼ en indien, ∼ en pirate** the children were dressed up, one as an Indian, one as a pirate

quiche /kiʃ/ *nf* quiche, flan

(Composé) **∼ lorraine** egg and bacon quiche

quiconque /kikɔ̃k/
A *pron rel* whoever, anyone who
B *pron indéf* anyone, anybody

quiétude /kjetyd/ *nf* tranquillity (**de** of); **travailler en toute ∼** to work undisturbed; **partez en toute ∼, je m'occupe des chats** don't worry about a thing, I'll look after the cats while you're away

quignon /kiɲɔ̃/ *nm* crusty end (of a loaf)

quille /kij/ *nf* **[1]** ▸ p. 327 (objet) skittle; **jouer aux ∼s** to play skittles; **[2]** *Naut* keel

(Idiome) **être reçu comme un chien dans un jeu de ∼s**○ to be given a very unfriendly welcome

quincaillerie /kɛ̃kajʀi/ *nf* **[1]** ▸ p. 000 (magasin) hardware shop GB *ou* store US, ironmonger's GB; **[2]** (articles) hardware; (industrie) hardware business

quincaillier, -ère /kɛ̃kaje, ɛʀ/ ▸ p. 372 *nm,f* owner of a hardware shop GB *ou* store US, ironmonger GB

quinconce /kɛ̃kɔ̃s/ *nm* **en ∼** in staggered rows

quinquagénaire /kɛ̃kaʒenɛʀ/
A *adj* **être ∼** to be in one's fifties
B *nmf* person in his/her fifties

quinquennal, ∼e, mpl -aux /kɛ̃kenal, o/ *adj* **[1]** (de cinq ans) [plan] five-year (épith); **[2]** (tous les cinq ans) five-yearly (épith)

quintal, pl -aux /kɛ̃tal, o/ ▸ p. 453 *nm* quintal

quinte /kɛ̃t/ *nf* **[1]** *Mus* fifth; **[2]** *Jeux* (aux cartes) quint; **∼ royale** royal flush; **[3]** *Sport* (en escrime) quinte; **[4]** *Méd* **une ∼ (de toux)** a coughing fit

quintessence /kɛ̃tesɑ̃s/ *nf* quintessence (**de** of)

quintette /kɛ̃tɛt/ *nm* *Mus* quintet

quintuple /kɛ̃typl/
A *adj* [nombre, rangée] quintuple; **une somme ∼ d'une autre** an amount five times more than another; **en ∼ exemplaire** in five copies
B *nm* **le ∼ de cette quantité** five times the amount

quintuplé, ∼e /kɛ̃typle/ *nm,f* quintuplet

quintupler /kɛ̃typle/ [1] *vtr, vi* to quintuple

quinzaine /kɛ̃zɛn/ *nf* **[1]** (environ quinze) about fifteen; ▸ **cinquantaine**; **[2]** (deux semaines) fortnight GB, two weeks; **∼ commerciale** two-week sale

quinze /kɛ̃z/ ▸ p. 398, p. 296, p. 155
A *adj inv* fifteen; **∼ jours** two weeks, a fortnight GB
B *pron* fifteen

quinzième /kɛ̃zjɛm/ ▸ p. 398, p. 155 *adj* fifteenth

quiproquo /kipʀɔko/ *nm* (sur des personnes) case of mistaken identity; (sur des choses) misunderstanding

quittance /kitɑ̃s/ *nf* (reçu) receipt; (facture) bill

quitte /kit/
A *adj* **[1]** (sans dette) **nous sommes ∼s, je suis ∼ avec lui** lit, fig we're quits; **[2]** **en être ∼ pour la peur/un rhume** to get off with a fright/a cold
B **quitte à** *loc prép* **[1]** (au risque de) **nous voulons un barrage, ∼ à inonder quelques fermes** we want a dam even if it means flooding a few farms; **[2]** (tant qu'à) **∼ à aller à Londres, autant que ce soit pour quelques jours** if you're

going to London anyway, you might as well go for a few days

(Composé) **∼ ou double** double or quits

quitter /kite/ [1]
A *vtr* **[1]** (sortir de) [personne] to leave [endroit, pays, ville, bureau]; **il faut ∼ la nationale 7 à Valence** you have to come off the nationale 7 at Valence; **[2]** (se séparer de) [personne] to leave [personne, famille]; **il faut que je vous quitte, j'ai une réunion** I must go now, I have a meeting; **[3]** (abandonner) to leave [travail, poste, service, parti, entreprise]; **∼ l'enseignement** to give up teaching; **∼ la politique** to retire from politics; **∼ la scène** fig [acteur] to give up acting; **tout en cuisinant, elle ne quittait pas ses enfants des yeux** while cooking, she didn't let the children out of her sight; **il ne l'a pas quittée des yeux de tout le repas** he didn't take his eyes off her throughout the meal; **ne quittez pas** (au téléphone) hold the line, please; **[4]** (déménager) [personne] to leave [lieu]; [entreprise] to move from [rue]; to move out of [bâtiment]; **[5]** (laisser en mourant) euph **un grand homme nous a quittés** a great man has passed away euph; **quand je vous aurai quittés...** when I've gone...; **[6]** (enlever) [personne] to take off [vêtement]; **∼ le deuil** to come out of mourning; **[7]** *Ordinat* to quit [application, programme]
B **se quitter** *vpr* (se séparer) to part; **nous nous sommes quittés bons amis** we parted the best of friends; **ils ne se quittent plus** they're inseparable now

qui-vive /kiviv/ *nm inv* **être sur le ∼** to be on the alert

quoi /kwa/
A *pron inter* what; **∼? je n'ai pas entendu** what? I didn't hear; **à ∼ penses-tu?** what are you thinking about?; **à ∼ bon recommencer?** what's the point of starting again?; **par ∼ voulez-vous commencer?** (à table) what would you like to start with?; (tâche, travail) where would you like to start?; **pour ∼ faire?** what for?; **∼ encore**○**?** what now?
B *pron rel* **il n'y a rien sur ∼ vous puissiez fonder vos accusations** there's nothing on which you can base your accusations; **voilà sur ∼ je fonde mes accusations** that's what I base my accusations on; **il prétend tout savoir, ce en ∼ il se trompe** he claims he knows everything, and that's where he's wrong; **il se moque de tout ce en ∼ elle croit** he laughs at everything she believes in; **ce en ∼ il avait raison** and he was quite right; **à ∼ il a répondu** to which he replied; **ce contre ∼ ils se battent** what they are fighting against; **(il n'y a) pas de ∼** think nothing of it, my pleasure; **il n'y a pas de ∼ crier** there's no reason to shout; **il n'a (même) pas de ∼ s'acheter un livre** he hasn't (even) got enough money to buy a book; **il a de ∼ être satisfait** he's got good reason to feel satisfied; **dis-nous avec ∼ tu as payé ta nouvelle voiture** tell us how you paid for your new car
C *pron indéf* **∼ qu'elle puisse en dire** whatever she may say; **si je peux faire ∼ que ce soit pour vous aider** if I can do anything to help you; **je ne m'étonne plus de ∼ que ce soit** nothing surprises me any more; **∼ qu'il en soit** be that as it may
D *excl* really, basically; **alors, ∼**○**!** really!; **il est prétentieux, stupide, pas du tout intéressant ∼**○**!** he's pretentious, stupid, a dead loss○ in fact!

quoique (**quoiqu'** before vowel or mute h) /kwak(ə)/ *conj* although, though; **nous sommes mieux ici qu'à Paris, ∼** we're better off here than in Paris, but then (again); **j'irai avec toi..., ∼, c'est assez loin** I'll come with you...it's quite a long way though

quota /kɔta/ *nm* quota (**sur** on)

quote-part, pl quotes-parts /kɔtpaʀ/ *nf* share

quotidien, -ienne /kɔtidjɛ̃, ɛn/
A *adj* (de chaque jour) daily; (ordinaire) everyday (épith); **les tâches quotidiennes** daily tasks
B *nm* **[1]** (journal) daily (paper); **[2]** (vie quotidienne) everyday life; **vivre la pauvreté au ∼** to experience real poverty on a daily basis

quotidiennement /kɔtidjɛnmɑ̃/ *adv* every day, daily

quotient /kɔsjɑ̃/ *nm* quotient

(Composés) **∼ intellectuel, QI** intelligence quotient, IQ

q

Rr

r, R /ɛʀ/ *nm inv* r, R; **rouler les** ~ to roll one's r's

rab° /ʀab/ *nm* **1** (ce qui est en trop) extra; **en** ~ extra (*épith*); **faire du** ~ (au travail) to do extra hours; **2** (portion supplémentaire) seconds

rabâcher /ʀabɑʃe/ [1]
A *vtr* to keep repeating [*histoires, faits*]
B *vi* to keep harping on

rabais /ʀabɛ/ *nm inv* discount; **obtenir un** ~ **de 20% sur qch** to get a 20% discount on sth; **au** ~ [*achat, vente*] at a discount; [*matériel*] cheap; [*travail*] badly paid; [*chef, acteur*] third-rate

rabaisser /ʀabese/ [1]
A *vtr* to belittle [*mérite, personne*]; ~ **les prétentions de qn** to humble sb's pride
B **se rabaisser** *vpr* (en paroles) to run oneself down; (par son comportement) to demean oneself

rabat /ʀaba/ *nm* (de sac, meuble, poche) flap

rabat-joie /ʀabaʒwa/ *adj inv* **être** ~ to be a killjoy

rabattable /ʀabatabl/ *adj* [*siège*] folding (*épith*)

rabatteur, -euse /ʀabatœʀ, øz/ *nm,f* (à la chasse) beater

rabattre /ʀabatʀ/ [61]
A *vtr* **1** (refermer) [*personne*] to shut [*capot, couvercle*]; to fold [*tablette*]; to put up [*strapontin*]; [*vent*] to blow [sth] back [*volet*]; **2** (plier) to turn [sth] down [*col*]; to take in [*coutures*]; to take up [*ourlet*]; to turn [sth] back [*couverture*]; to turn [sth] down [*drap*] (**sur** over); **3** (faire descendre) [*personne*] to pull [sth] down [*chapeau, jupe*] (**sur** over); [*vent*] to blow [sth] down [*fumée*]; [*joueur*] to smash [*balle*]; ~ **l'orgueil de qn** to humble sb's pride; **4** (retrancher) to knock [sth] off [*pourcentage, somme*]; **5** (à la chasse) to beat [*gibier*]; **6** (racoler) to tout for° [*clientèle*]
B **se rabattre** *vpr* **1** (se refermer) [*capot, couvercle*] to shut; [*tablette*] [*volet*] to bang to; **2** (rentrer dans sa file) [*automobiliste, véhicule*] to pull back in; **3** (s'accommoder) **se** ~ **sur** (faute de mieux) to make do with; (après réflexion) to settle for

rabbin /ʀabɛ̃/ ▸ p. 590 *nm* rabbi; **grand** ~ chief rabbi

rabibocher° /ʀabibɔʃe/ [1]
A *vtr* ~ **Pierre avec Paul** to bring Pierre and Paul together
B **se rabibocher** *vpr* to make up

râble /ʀɑbl/ *nm* (de lapin, lièvre) saddle

(Idiome) **ils nous sont tombés sur le** ~° they laid into us°

râblé, ~e /ʀɑble/ *adj* **1** [*animal*] sturdy; **2** [*personne*] stocky

rabot /ʀabo/ *nm* plane

raboter /ʀabɔte/ [1] *vtr* Tech to plane

rabougri /ʀabugʀi/ *adj* [*arbre, tronc*] stunted; [*fruit, adulte*] shrivelledᴳᴮ up; [*vieillard*] wizened

rabougrir: se rabougrir /ʀabugʀiʀ/ [3] *vpr* [*plante*] to become stunted; [*vieillard*] to become wizened

rabrouer /ʀabʀue/ [1] *vtr* to snub

racaille /ʀakaj/ *nf* scum

raccommoder /ʀakɔmɔde/ [1]
A *vtr* **1** to mend [*filet*]; to darn [*bas*]; **2** °to reconcile [*personnes*]
B °**se raccommoder** *vpr* (se réconcilier) to make it up° (**avec** with)

raccompagner /ʀakɔ̃paɲe/ [1] *vtr* (à pied) to walk [sb] (back) home; (en voiture) to drive [sb] (back) home

raccord /ʀakɔʀ/ *nm* **1** (de planche, papier peint) join; **faire un** ~ (en posant du papier peint) to line up the pattern; **2** (retouche en peinture) touch-up; **3** (transition) (dans un film) link shot; **4** Tech joint

raccordement /ʀakɔʀdəmɑ̃/ *nm* (jonction) (de route) link road; (de voie ferrée) loop line; Télécom connection, hookup US; (de tubes) joint

raccorder /ʀakɔʀde/ [1] *vtr* **1** gén to connect (**à** to); to link together [*chapitres, parties*]; to line up [*motifs de papier peint*]; **2** Télécom (par câble) to connect, to hook up US; (par satellite) to link up; **3** Cin to link [sth] together [*scènes, plans*]

raccourci /ʀakuʀsi/ *nm* **1** (chemin) shortcut; **prendre un** ~ to take a shortcut; **2** (image réductrice) **c'est un peu un** ~ it's a bit simplistic; **en** ~ in short

(Composé) ~ **clavier** Ordinat hot key, keyboard shortcut

raccourcir /ʀakuʀsiʀ/ [3]
A *vtr* gén to shorten (**de** by); to cut [*texte, discours*]; to cut short [*visite*]
B *vi* **1** [*vêtement*] (au lavage) to shrink (**de** by); (avec la mode) to get shorter; [*jours*] to get shorter (**de** by), to draw in

(Idiomes) **tomber sur qn à bras** ~s° fig to lay into sb

raccrocher /ʀakʀɔʃe/ [1]
A *vtr* **1** (remettre) to hang [sth] back up [*rideaux, manteau, tableau*] (**à, sur** on); **2** Télécom ~ **le combiné** to put the telephone down
B *vi* **1** Télécom to hang up; ~ **au nez de qn°** to hang up on sb; **2** °Sport to give up competition
C **se raccrocher** *vpr* **se** ~ **à** lit to grab hold of [*bras, rebord*]; fig to cling to [*personne, prétexte*]

race /ʀas/ *nf* **1** (d'êtres humains) race; **2** Zool breed; **cheval de** ~ thoroughbred (horse); **chien de** ~ pedigree (dog); **3** °(catégorie de personnes) **une** ~ **guerrière** a race of warriors

racé, ~e /ʀase/ *adj* **1** [*cheval*] thoroughbred; [*chien*] pedigree (*épith*); **2** [*objet*] classically elegant

rachat /ʀaʃa/ *nm* **1** (d'objet vendu) buying back, buyback; **2** (de société) buyout; **3** (d'actions) repurchase; **4** (de dette) redemption; **5** (pardon) redemption

racheter /ʀaʃte/ [18]
A *vtr* **1** (récupérer un objet vendu) to buy [sth] back; **2** (acheter encore) **je vais** ~ **du vin** I'll buy some more wine; **3** (pour renouveler) **mes draps sont usés, il faut que j'en rachète** my sheets are worn out, I'll have to buy new ones; **4** (acheter) to buy out [*société, usine*]; to buy up [*ensemble d'actions*]; **5** [*pécheur*] to atone for [*faute*] (**par** by); [*qualité*] to make up for [*défaut*]; **6** [*examinateur*] to mark up [*candidat, copie*]
B **se racheter** *vpr* to redeem oneself (**par** through)

rachitique /ʀaʃitik/ *adj* **1** Méd [*personne*] **il est** ~ he suffers from rickets; **2** (maigre) [*animal, plante, personne*] scrawny

rachitisme /ʀaʃitism/ *nm* rickets (+ *v sg*)

racial, ~e, mpl -iaux /ʀasjal, o/ *adj* racial; **émeutes/relations** ~es race riots/relations

racine /ʀasin/ *nf* (tous contextes) root; **prendre** ~ lit, fig to take root; **prendre** *or* **attaquer le mal à la** ~ to strike at the root of the problem; ~ **carrée/cubique** Math square/cube root

racisme /ʀasism/ *nm* **1** (doctrine) racism; **2** (discrimination) ~ **anti-étudiants** prejudice against students

raciste /ʀasist/ *adj, nmf* racist

racket /ʀakɛt/ *nm* (organisation) extortion racket; (activité) racketeering; **c'est du** ~! it's extortion!

raclée○ /ʀɑkle/ nf hiding○

racler /ʀɑkle/ [1]
A vtr ① (nettoyer) to scrape [sth] clean [plat]; ▸ tiroir; ② (enlever) to scrape off [rouille]; ③ (frotter) [pneu] to scrape against [trottoir]
B se racler vpr **se ~ la gorge** to clear one's throat

raclette /ʀɑklɛt/ nf ① Culin raclette; ② (racloir) scraper

racloir /ʀɑklwaʀ/ nm scraper

racolage /ʀakɔlaʒ/ nm ① (d'électeurs, de partisans) touting (**de** for); **le ~ publicitaire** canvassing; ② (par une prostituée) soliciting (**de** for)

racoler /ʀakɔle/ [1] vtr ① [politicien] to tout for [électeurs]; (pour un spectacle) to tout for, to bark for○ [passants]; ② [prostituée] to solicit for [clients]

racoleur, -euse /ʀakɔlœʀ, øz/ adj [affiche] eye-catching; [slogan] catchy; [regard, sourire] enticing

racontar○ /ʀakɔ̃taʀ/ nm piece of idle gossip

raconter /ʀakɔ̃te/ [1] vtr ① (relater) [personne] to tell [histoire]; [film, livre] to tell [histoire]; to describe [fait, épisode, rencontre, amitié, vie, accident]; **~ en détail** to describe in detail; **alors! raconte!** tell me all about it then! **il raconte bien** he's a good storyteller; **je suis tombée en panne, je te raconte pas**○! my car broke down, I'll spare you the details!; **tu racontes n'importe quoi!** you're talking nonsense!; ② (prétendre) to say; **on raconte que** they say that; ③ (dépeindre) liter [personne] to describe [époque, mœurs, pays]

racornir /ʀakɔʀniʀ/ [3]
A vtr (durcir) to harden [peau]; to stiffen [cuir]; fig to harden [personne, cœur]
B se racornir vpr (devenir dur) [peau] to harden; fig [cœur] to harden; [cuir] to stiffen

radar /ʀadaʀ/ nm radar; **au ~** by radar; **effectuer des contrôles ~** to carry out radar speed checks; **marcher au ~**○ fig to be on autopilot

rade /ʀad/ nf Naut roads (pl); **en ~ de Toulon** in the Toulon roads; **mouiller en ~** to lie at anchor
(Idiome) **rester en ~**○ [personne] to be left stranded; [projet] to be shelved

radeau, pl **~x** /ʀado/ nm (embarcation) raft

radiateur /ʀadjatœʀ/ nm radiator

radiation /ʀadjasjɔ̃/ nf ① Phys radiation; ② (de personne) gén expulsion; (de médecin) striking off from the register GB, loss of the license to practice medicine US; (d'avocat) disbarment

radical, ~e, mpl **-aux** /ʀadikal, o/ adj, nm,f gén, Pol radical

radicalement /ʀadikalmɑ̃/ adv [opposé, différent] radically; [nouveau] completely; [efficace] extremely; [changer] radically

radicaliser /ʀadikalize/ [1]
A vtr [syndicat, parti] to toughen [attitude]; to harden [politique]; to step up [revendications]
B se radicaliser vpr [personne] to become more radical

radicelle /ʀadisɛl/ nf rootlet

radié, ~e /ʀadje/ adj Bot rayed

radier /ʀadje/ [2] vtr **~ qn d'une liste** to remove sb from a list; **~ un médecin** to strike off a doctor GB, to take away a doctor's license US; **~ un avocat** to disbar a lawyer

radieux, -ieuse /ʀadjø, øz/ adj ① (éclatant) [soleil] dazzling; ② (ensoleillé) [temps, matinée] glorious; ③ (heureux) [visage, air, sourire] radiant; [personne] radiant with joy (jamais épith); [souvenir] glorious; ④ (prometteur) [avenir] brilliant

radin○, **~e** /ʀadɛ̃, in/
A adj stingy○
B nm,f skinflint○

radinerie○ /ʀadinʀi/ nf stinginess○

radio¹ /ʀadjo/
A adj inv [contact, signal] radio
B ▸ p. 372 nm (opérateur) radio operator

radio² /ʀadjo/ nf ① (appareil) radio; ② (radiodiffusion) radio; **poste de ~** radio; **à la ~** on the radio; ③ (station) radio station; ④ (radiographie) X-ray; **passer une ~ des poumons** to have a chest X-ray
(Composé) **~ libre** independent local radio station

radioactivité /ʀadjoaktivite/ nf radioactivity

radiocassette /ʀadjokasɛt/ nm ou f (lecteur) radio cassette player; (enregistreur) radio cassette recorder

radiocommande /ʀadjokɔmɑ̃d/ nf radio control

radiodiffuser /ʀadjodifyze/ [1] vtr to broadcast

radioélectricien, -ienne /ʀadjoelɛktʀisjɛ̃, ɛn/ ▸ p. 372 nm,f radio engineer

radiographie /ʀadjɔgʀafi/ nf ① (procédé) radiography, X-ray photography; ② (cliché) X-ray (photograph)

radiographier /ʀadjɔgʀafje/ [2] vtr to X-ray

radiographique /ʀadjɔgʀafik/ adj X-ray

radioguidage /ʀadjɔgidaʒ/ nm ① Aviat, Naut radio control; **~ des automobilistes** traffic information service

radioguider /ʀadjogide/ [1] vtr to control by radio

radiologie /ʀadjɔlɔʒi/ nf radiology

radiologiste /ʀadjɔlɔʒist/, **radiologue** /ʀadjɔlɔg/ ▸ p. 372 nmf radiologist

radiophonique /ʀadjofɔnik/ adj [programme, production] radio (épith); **techniques ~s** (radio) broadcasting techniques

radio-réveil, pl **radios-réveils** /ʀadjoʀevɛj/ nm clock radio

radioscopie /ʀadjɔskɔpi/ nf fluoroscopy

radiothérapie /ʀadjoteʀapi/ nf radiotherapy

radis /ʀadi/ nm inv radish; **~ noir** black radish
(Idiome) **je n'ai plus un ~**○ I haven't got a penny

radius /ʀadjys/ nm inv radius

radotage /ʀadotaʒ/ nm drivel ¢

radoter /ʀadote/ [1]
A vtr to tell [sth] again and again
B vi (se répéter) to repeat oneself; (dire des bêtises) to talk drivel○

radoteur, -euse /ʀadotœʀ, øz/ nm,f driveller^GB

radoucir /ʀadusiʀ/ [3]
A vtr to soften up [personne]
B se radoucir vpr [voix] to become softer; [personne] to soften up; [humeur] to improve; [temps] to turn milder

radoucissement /ʀadusismɑ̃/ nm **la météo annonce un ~** the forecast is for milder weather

rafale /ʀafal/ nf ① (de vent, pluie) gust; (de neige) flurry; **vent qui souffle en ~s** gusty wind; ② (de mitraillette) burst; **tir en ~s** bursts (pl) of gunfire

raffermir /ʀafɛʀmiʀ/ [3]
A vtr ① lit to tone [épiderme]; to tone up [musculature]; ② fig [personne] to strengthen [autorité, position]; to steady [marché]
B se raffermir vpr [tissus, peau] to become firmer; [voix] to become more assured; [cours boursier] to become steady; [sol] to harden

raffermissement /ʀafɛʀmismɑ̃/ nm ① (de peau) firming up; ② (de monnaie, taux) steadying; **le ~ de l'euro vis-à-vis du dollar** the strengthening of the euro against the dollar

raffinage /ʀafinaʒ/ nm refining

raffiné, ~e /ʀafine/ adj [personne, civilisation] refined; [cuisine] sophisticated; **un type**○ **pas très ~** a rather uncouth character; **un mets ~** a delicacy

raffinement /ʀafinmɑ̃/ nm ① (de personne, civilisation) refinement; ② (de décor, d'habillement) elegance (**de** of)

raffiner /ʀafine/ [1] vtr to refine

raffinerie /ʀafinʀi/ nf refinery

raffoler /ʀafɔle/ [1] vtr ind **~ de** to be crazy○ about

raffut○ /ʀafy/ nm ① (bruit) racket○; ② (scandale) stink○; **faire du ~** to raise a stink

rafiot○ /ʀafjo/ nm boat, (old) tub○

rafistolage○ /ʀafistɔlaʒ/ nm ① (action) patching up; ② (réparation) makeshift repair; fig stop-gap solution

rafistoler○ /ʀafistɔle/ [1] vtr to patch up

rafle /ʀɑfl/ nf (opération) raid; (arrestation massive) roundup; **faire une ~** to carry out a raid (**dans, chez** on)

rafler○ /ʀɑfle/ [1] vtr ① (emporter) to make off with, to swipe○ [bijoux, provisions]; ② (obtenir) to walk off with [médaille, récompense]; to snap up [contrat, marché]

rafraîchir /ʀafʀɛʃiʀ/
A vtr (refroidir) [pluie] to cool [atmosphère]; [glaçons] to chill [eau]; **le thé glacé te rafraîchira** the iced tea will cool you down

B **se rafraîchir** vpr [temps, atmosphère] to become ou get cooler; [personne] to refresh oneself

(Idiome) ~ la mémoire° de qn to refresh sb's memory

rafraîchissant, ~**e** /ʀafʀɛʃisɑ̃, ɑ̃t/ adj refreshing

rafraîchissement /ʀafʀɛʃismɑ̃/ nm **1** Météo drop in temperature; **2** (boisson) refreshment

ragaillardir /ʀagajaʀdiʀ/ [3] vtr to cheer [sb] up; **je me sens (tout) ragaillardi** I feel much brighter

rage /ʀaʒ/ nf **1** ▸ p. 195 Méd rabies ¢; **2** (fureur) rage; **être en ~ contre qn/contre qch** to be furious with sb/about sth; **être fou de ~** to be in a mad rage; **se mettre** or **entrer dans une ~ folle** to fly into a rage; **avoir la ~ au cœur** or **au ventre°** to (inwardly) seethe with rage; **mettre qn en ~** to make sb's blood boil; **faire ~** [maladie, concurrence] to be rife; [épidémie, incendie, bataille] to rage

(Composé) ~ **de dents** raging toothache

(Idiome) **qui veut noyer son chien l'accuse de la ~** give a dog a bad name and hang him

rageant°, ~**e** /ʀaʒɑ̃, ɑ̃t/ adj infuriating

rageur, -euse /ʀaʒœʀ, øz/ adj furious

rageusement /ʀaʒøzmɑ̃/ adv **1** (avec colère) [s'écrier] furiously; [écrire] angrily; **2** °(sans relâche) furiously

ragondin /ʀagɔ̃dɛ̃/ nm (animal, fourrure) coypu

ragot° /ʀago/ nm malicious gossip ¢

ragoût /ʀagu/ nm stew, ragout

ragoûtant, ~**e** /ʀagutɑ̃, ɑ̃t/ adj **peu** or **pas très ~** [cuisine, mets] rather unappetizing; [affaire] rather unsavoury[GB]

rai /ʀɛ/ nm ~ **de lumière** ray of light

raï /ʀaj/ nm: music from the Maghreb with Western influences

raid /ʀɛd/ nm **1** Mil raid; ~ **aérien** air raid; **2** Sport (à pied, ski, VTT) trek; **3** Fin raid (**sur** on)

raide /ʀɛd/

A adj **1** (sans souplesse) gén stiff; [cheveux] straight; (tendu) [corde] taut; **2** (à pic) [pente, escalier] steep; **3** °(exagéré) **je trouve ça un peu ~** that's a bit steep; **4** ⓝ(désargenté) **broke°**

B adv [monter, descendre] steeply

(Idiomes) **être/se tenir ~ comme un piquet** to be/to stand stiff as a ramrod; **tomber ~** (d'étonnement) to be flabbergasted; **tomber ~ mort** to drop dead

raideur /ʀɛdœʀ/ nf **1** (de jambe, dos) stiffness; **avec ~** [marcher, répondre] stiffly; **2** (de pente) steepness

raidir /ʀɛdiʀ/ [3]

A vtr **1** lit to tighten [cordage]; to tense [bras, corps]; **2** fig to harden [attitude]

B **se raidir** vpr **1** lit [cordage] to get tighter; [bras, corps] to tense up; [tissu] to stiffen; **2** fig **se ~ contre la douleur** to brace oneself against pain

raie /ʀɛ/ nf **1** (dans une coiffure) parting GB, part US; **2** (griffure) scratch; **3** (poisson) skate

rail /ʀaj/ nm **1** (de chemin de fer) rail, track; **sortir des ~s** lit to leave the track GB, to jump the track US; **2** (moyen de transport) **le ~** rail; **transport par ~** rail transport; **3** (de tringle, porte) rail

(Composé) ~ **de sécurité** crash barrier

railler /ʀaje/ [1]

A vtr to make fun of

B **se railler** vpr **se ~ de** to make fun of

raillerie /ʀajʀi/ nf **1** (attitude) mockery ¢; **dire qch sur le ton de la ~** to say sth in a mocking tone; **2** (propos) mocking remark; **être l'objet de ~s** to be a laughing stock; **être l'objet de ~s de qn** to be the butt of sb's jokes

railleur, -euse /ʀajœʀ, øz/

A adj mocking

B nm,f mocker

rainette /ʀɛnɛt/ nf tree frog

rainure /ʀenyʀ/ nf groove

raisin /ʀezɛ̃/ nm **1** (fruit) grapes (pl); **une grappe de ~** a bunch of grapes; **un grain de ~** a grape; **2** (variété) grape; **un ~ sucré** a sweet grape

(Composés) ~**s de Corinthe** currants; ~**s secs** raisins

raison /ʀezɔ̃/ nf **1** (motif) reason; **n'avoir aucune ~ de** to have no reason to; **pour ~(s) de santé** for health reasons; **pour des ~s d'hygiène** for reasons of hygiene; **on ne sait pour quelle ~** for unknown reasons; **il y a une ~ à cela** there's a reason for that; ~ **d'agir** reason for action; ~ **de**

plus pour faire all the more reason to do; **en ~ d'une panne** owing to a breakdown; **à plus forte ~** even more so; **à juste ~** quite rightly; **avec ~** justifiably; **comme de ~** as one might expect; ~ **d'inquiétude** cause for alarm; ~ **d'espoir** grounds (pl) for hope; **2** (opposé à tort) **avoir ~** to be right; **avoir un peu ~** to be partly right; **à** or **avec ~** rightly; **donner ~ à qn** to agree with sb; **obtenir ~** to obtain satisfaction; **3** (rationalité) reason ¢; **la folie l'a emporté sur la ~** folly won the day; **se rendre à la ~** to see reason; **faire entendre ~ à qn** to make sb see reason; **ramener qn à la ~** to bring sb to his/her senses; **perdre la ~** to lose one's mind; **se faire une ~ de qch** to resign oneself to sth; **plus que de ~** more than is sensible; **avoir ~ de qn/qch** to get the better of sb/sth; **à ~ de** at the rate of; ▸ **rime**

(Composés) ~ **d'État** reasons (pl) of State; ~ **d'être** (de vivre) reason for living; **n'avoir aucune ~ d'être** to have no justification; ~ **sociale** company ou corporate name

(Idiome) **la ~ du plus fort est toujours la meilleure** Prov might is right Prov

raisonnable /ʀezɔnabl/ adj **1** (pas trop élevé) [prix, distance, délais] reasonable; [consommation, natalité] moderate; **2** (mesuré) [personne, objectif] reasonable; [politique, enthousiasme] moderate; **3** (sensé) [personne, idée] sensible; **4** (doué de raison) rational

raisonnablement /ʀezɔnabləmɑ̃/ adv [expliquer] reasonably; [propre, confiant] reasonably; [boire, fumer] in moderation; [gérer, parler] sensibly

raisonné, ~**e** /ʀezɔne/

A pp ▸ **raisonner**

B pp adj **1** (prudent) [attitude] cautious; [décision] carefully thought out; **2** (contrôlé) [passion] controlled[GB]; [enthousiasme] measured

raisonnement /ʀezɔnmɑ̃/ nm **1** (suite d'arguments) reasoning ¢ (**sur** about); **selon le même ~** by the same token; **je ne tiens pas le même ~** I look at it differently; **avec ce genre de ~** with that sort of thinking; **2** (type de pensée) thinking; ~ **économique** economic thinking

(Composé) ~ **par l'absurde** reductio ad absurdum

raisonner /ʀezɔne/ [1]

A vtr to reason with [personne, enfant]; to rationalize [sentiment, peur]; **se laisser ~** to let oneself be talked round GB ou persuaded

B vi to think; ~ **à court terme** to think in the short term; ~ **avant d'agir** to think carefully before acting

C **se raisonner** vpr [personne] to be more sensible, to pull oneself together

rajeunir /ʀaʒœniʀ/ [3]

A vtr **1** (physiquement) to make [sb] look younger; (moralement) to make [sb] feel younger; **sa coiffure la rajeunit de cinq ans** that hairstyle makes her look five years younger ou takes five years off her; **2** (attribuer un âge moindre à) ~ **qn** to make sb out to be younger; **votre fils a 25 ans! cela ne nous rajeunit pas** your son is 25! we're not getting any younger; **3** (rendre plus moderne) to give a new look to, to brighten up [bâtiment, fauteuil]; to modernize [secteur économique, organisation, équipement]; to update, to bring [sth] up to date [livre, guide, règlement]; **4** (abaisser la moyenne d'âge) to bring ou inject new blood into [parti, profession]

B vi **1** (physiquement) [personne] to look younger; **2** (moralement) [personne] to feel younger

C **se rajeunir** vpr **1** (essayer de paraître plus jeune) to make oneself look younger; **2** (se dire plus jeune) to make oneself out to be younger (than one is)

rajeunissant, ~**e** /ʀaʒœnisɑ̃, ɑ̃t/ adj rejuvenating

rajeunissement /ʀaʒœnismɑ̃/ nm **1** (de groupe, population) **nous avons enregistré un ~ de la population** we see that the population is getting younger; **2** (d'entreprise, de bâtiment) modernization; (de livre, manuel, règlement) updating; **3** (de personnes) rejuvenation

rajouter /ʀaʒute/ [1] vtr to add (**à** to); **en ~°** (mentir) to exaggerate; (en faire trop) to overdo it

rajuster /ʀaʒyste/ [1] vtr to straighten [chapeau, vêtement]; to push [sth] back up [lunettes]

râle /ʀɑl/ nm **1** (bruit pulmonaire) rale; **2** (de mourant) death rattle

ralenti, ~**e** /ʀalɑ̃ti/

A pp ▸ **ralentir**

B pp adj [geste, rythme, croissance] slower

C nm Cin slow motion

D▶ au ralenti *loc adv* **fonctionner au ~** [*machine, entreprise*] to be just ticking over; [*personne*] to be running at half-speed; **tourner au ~** [*moteur*] to be ticking over GB, to idle

ralentir /ʀalɑ̃tiʀ/ [3] *vtr, vi,* **se ralentir** *vpr* to slow down

ralentissement /ʀalɑ̃tismɑ̃/ *nm* ①▶ (processus) slowing down; ②▶ (sur les routes) tailback

ralentisseur /ʀalɑ̃tisœʀ/ *nm* ①▶ (système de freins) engine brake; ②▶ (sur la chaussée) sleeping policeman GB, speed ramp

râler /ʀale/ [1] *vi* ①▶ ᴼ(protester) to moanᴼ (**contre** about); **ça me fait ~** it annoys *ou* bugsᴼ me; ②▶ [*mourant*] to give the death rattle

râleurᴼ, **-euse** /ʀalœʀ, øz/ *nm,f* moanerᴼ

ralliement /ʀalimɑ̃/ *nm* rallying (**de qn à qch** of sb to sth); **de ~** [*cri, point, signe*] rallying

rallier /ʀalje/ [2]

A▶ *vtr* ①▶ (rassembler) to rally [*troupes, navires*]; ②▶ (convaincre) to rally [*partisans*]; to win over [*opposants*] (**à** to); **solution qui rallie tous les suffrages** solution that has unanimous support; **~ qn à sa cause** to win sb over; ③▶ (adhérer à) to rejoin [*groupe, parti*]; ④▶ (rejoindre) [*militaire*] to rejoin [*poste*]; [*diplomate, fonctionnaire*] to take up [*poste*]; **~ la terre** [*navire*] to make landfall

B▶ se rallier *vpr* **se ~ à** to rally to [*républicains*]; to come round to [*opinion*]; **elle s'est ralliée à notre cause** she was won over

rallonge /ʀalɔ̃ʒ/ *nf* ①▶ (de fil électrique) extension cord, extension lead GB; (de table) leaf; **table à ~s** extending table; **nom à ~(s)**ᴼ double-barrelled name GB, hyphenated name; ②▶ ᴼ(d'argent) additional sum; (de temps) extension

rallonger /ʀalɔ̃ʒe/ [13]

A▶ *vtr* to extend [*fil, table, période*] (**de** by); to make [sth] longer [*paragraphe*]; **~ une jupe** (par l'ourlet) to let a skirt down; **~ la paie**ᴼ to increase wages (**de** by)

B▶ *vi* **les jours rallongent** the days are drawing out

C▶ se rallonger *vpr* to lie down again

rallumer /ʀalyme/ [1]

A▶ *vtr* to relight [*feu, pipe*]; **~ la lumière** to put the light on again

B▶ se rallumer *vpr* ①▶ [*incendie*] to flare up again; **les lumières se sont rallumées** the lights came back on; ②▶ fig [*querelles, passions, guerre*] to flare up again

rallye /ʀali/ *nm* ①▶ Sport (car) rally; ②▶ (réunion mondaine) party

ramadan /ʀamadɑ̃/ *nm* Ramadan; **faire le ~** to keep Ramadan

ramage /ʀamaʒ/
A▶ *nm* (d'oiseau) liter song
B▶ ramages *nmpl* (motif) foliage pattern

ramassage /ʀamasaʒ/ *nm* ①▶ (de coquillages, d'œufs) collecting; (de fruits, feuilles mortes, débris) picking up; ②▶ (fait de collecter) (de cahiers, copies) taking in, collection; (d'ordures ménagères) collection; (d'enfants) collection GB, picking up; **car de ~** (pour employés) works *ou* company bus; (scolaire) school bus

ramassé, ~e /ʀamase/
A▶ *pp* ▶ **ramasser**
B▶ *pp adj* ①▶ (trapu) stocky, squat; ②▶ (recroquevillé) **~ sur lui-même** hunched up; ③▶ (concis) [*style, expression*] concise

ramasser /ʀamase/ [1]

A▶ *vtr* ①▶ (prendre par terre) to collect [*bois, œufs*]; to pick up [*crayon*]; to dig up [*pommes de terre*]; **~ à la pelle** lit to shovel [sth] up [*terre*]; fig (en grande quantité) to get bucketfuls of [*argent*]; ②▶ (collecter) to take [sth] in, to collect [*cahiers, devoirs*]; to collect [*ordures ménagères*]; to collect GB, to pick up [*écoliers*]; ③▶ (rassembler) to pick up [*objets, jouets*]; ④▶ (relever) to pick up [*enfant, ivrogne*]; ⑤▶ (recueillir) to collect GB, to take in [*personne, animal*]; ⑥▶ ᴼ(arrêter) [*police*] to nickᴼ sb

B▶ se ramasser *vpr* ①▶ (se replier) to huddle up, to shrink into oneself; (se pelotonner) to curl up; ②▶ ᴼ(échouer) to come a cropperᴼ

ramassis /ʀamasi/ *nm inv* pej (de vauriens) bunch; (d'idées, objets) jumble

rambarde /ʀɑ̃baʀd/ *nf* guardrail

rame /ʀam/ *nf* ①▶ Naut oar; **traversée à la ~** crossing in a rowing boat; ②▶ (de papier) ream; ③▶ (métro, train) train; **une ~ de métro** a metro train

(Idiome) **il n'en fiche pas une ~**ᴼ he doesn't do a strokeᴼ

rameau, *pl* **~x** /ʀamo/ *nm* gén branch; **~ d'olivier** olive branch

Rameaux /ʀamo/ *nmpl* **les ~** Palm Sunday

ramener /ʀamne/ [16]

A▶ *vtr* ①▶ (réduire) **~ l'inflation à 5%** to reduce inflation to 5 per cent; **~ qch à de justes proportions** *or* **à sa juste mesure** to get sth into proportion; ②▶ (faire revenir) to restore [*ordre, paix*]; **~ qn à la réalité** to bring sb back to reality; **~ qn à de meilleurs sentiments** to put sb into a better frame of mind; **~ qn sur terre** to bring sb down to earth; **~ qn à la vie** *or* **à soi** to bring sb round; **~ qn à la raison** to bring sb to his/her senses; **~ toujours tout à soi** always to relate everything to oneself; ③▶ (reconduire) to take [sb/sth] back; **~ qn en voiture** to give sb a lift GB *ou* ride US home; ④▶ (faire rentrer) to bring [sb/sth] back; ⑤▶ (rapporter) to bring back [*pain, photos, maladie*] (**de** from); to return [*objet prêté*]; to win [*médaille, titre*]; ⑥▶ (déplacer) **'~ les genoux vers le menton'** 'draw your knees up to your chin'; **~ ses cheveux en arrière** (avec un peigne) to comb one's hair back; (avec la main) to sweep one's hair back; **~ son manteau sur ses genoux** to pull one's coat over one's knees

B▶ se ramener *vpr* ①▶ (être réductible) **se ~ à** to come down to, to boil down to; ②▶ ᴼ(venir) to come over

(Idiome) **la ~**ᴼ (intervenir intempestivement) to stick one's oar inᴼ; (se vanter avec ostentation) to show offᴼ

ramequin /ʀamkɛ̃/ *nm* ramekin

ramer /ʀame/ [1] *vi* ①▶ Naut to row; ②▶ ᴼ(travailler dur) to work like a dogᴼ

rameur, -euse /ʀamœʀ, øz/ *nm,f* gén rower; Sport oarsman/oarswoman

rameuter /ʀamøte/ [1] *vtr* to round up

rami /ʀami/ ▸ p. 327 *nm* Jeux rummy

ramier /ʀamje/ *nm* woodpigeon

ramification /ʀamifikasjɔ̃/ *nf* ①▶ (de société secrète) network; (d'entreprise) several offshoots (*pl*); ②▶ (d'histoire, de complot) ramification; ③▶ (subdivision) subdivision; ④▶ Bot ramification

ramifier: se ramifier /ʀamifje/ [2] *vpr* ①▶ lit [*tronc, nerf, veine*] to branch (**en** into); [*branche*] to divide (**en** into); ②▶ fig **famille très ramifiée** family with many branches; **problème très ramifié** problem with many ramifications

ramolli, ~e /ʀamɔli/ *adj* ①▶ [*substance*] (devenu mou) soft; (rendu mou) softened; ②▶ ᴼ[*personne*] (avachi) limp; (apathique) spineless; **avoir le cerveau ~**ᴼ pej to be soft in the head

ramollir /ʀamɔliʀ/ [3]

A▶ *vtr* ①▶ (rendre mou) to soften [*matière*]; ②▶ (affaiblir) to make [sb] soft [*personne*]; to weaken [*volonté*]

B▶ se ramollir *vpr* ①▶ [*matière*] to become soft, to soften; ②▶ ᴼ(s'avachir) [*personne*] to get soft

ramollissement /ʀamɔlismɑ̃/ *nm* lit, fig softening

ramoner /ʀamɔne/ [1] *vtr* to sweep [*cheminée*]

ramoneur /ʀamɔnœʀ/ ▸ p. 372 *nm* chimney sweep

rampant, ~e /ʀɑ̃pɑ̃, ɑ̃t/ *adj* ①▶ [*animal*] crawling; [*tige*] prostrate; [*plante*] creeping; ②▶ (servile) [*manières, personne*] grovelling^GB; ③▶ (insidieux) [*idéologie, mal, inflation*] creeping; ④▶ ᴼAviat **personnel ~** ground staff; ⑤▶ Archit [*arc, voûte*] rampant

rampe /ʀɑ̃p/ *nf* ①▶ (d'escalier) (sur balustres) banister; (fixée au mur) hand-rail; ②▶ (plan incliné) ramp; ③▶ Théât **la ~** the footlights (*pl*)

(Composés) **~ d'accès** (d'autoroute) sliproad GB, entrance ramp US; (de bâtiment) ramp; **~ d'arrosage** irrigation line; **~ d'embarquement** embarcation ramp; **~ de lancement** launchpad

(Idiomes) **passer la ~** Théât [*dialogue*] to work; [*plaisanterie*] to come off; **tenir bon la ~**ᴼ to hold out; **lâcher la ~**ᴼ to kick the bucketᴼ

ramper /ʀɑ̃pe/ [1] *vi* ①▶ [*reptile, personne*] to crawl; [*chat, fauve*] to creep; **s'éloigner en rampant** to crawl away; ②▶ [*plante*] to creep; ③▶ fig (s'humilier) to grovel

ramure /ʀamyʀ/ *nf* ①▶ (d'arbre) branches (*pl*); ②▶ (de cerf) antlers (*pl*)

rancard⁰ /ʀɑ̃kaʀ/ nm [1] (rendez-vous) gén appointment; (amoureux) date; [2] (renseignement) tip

rancart⁰ /ʀɑ̃kaʀ/ nm **mettre au** ~ to scrap [objet, projet]; to shunt [sb] aside [personne]

rance /ʀɑ̃s/ adj [odeur, graisse] rancid

rancir /ʀɑ̃siʀ/ [3] vi [huile, graisse] to go rancid

rancœur /ʀɑ̃kœʀ/ nf (grief) resentment ¢

rançon /ʀɑ̃sɔ̃/ nf [1] (somme d'argent) ransom; [2] (contrepartie) **la** ~ **de la gloire** the price of fame

rançonner /ʀɑ̃sɔne/ [1] vtr (exiger de l'argent de) [brigand] to rob [voyageurs]; [racketteur] to extort money from [commerçants]

rancune /ʀɑ̃kyn/ nf (sentiment) resentment ¢; (grief) grudge; **sans** ~! no hard feelings; **garder** ~ **à qn** to bear a grudge against sb

rancunier, -ière /ʀɑ̃kynje, ɛʀ/ adj **être** ~ to be a person who holds grudges

randonnée /ʀɑ̃dɔne/ nf [1] (activité) (à pied) hiking; (de plusieurs jours) backpacking; **la** ~ **à cheval** pony-trekking; [2] (promenade) (à pied) hike; ~ **équestre** pony trek; **faire une** ~ (à pied) to go hiking

randonneur, -euse /ʀɑ̃dɔnœʀ, øz/ nm,f (à pied) hiker, rambler GB; (à bicyclette) cyclist

rang /ʀɑ̃/ nm [1] (rangée) (de personnes, chaises, légumes) row; (de collier) strand; **en** ~**s** in rows; **mettre les enfants en** ~**s** to make the children line up; **se mettre en** ~**s** [enfants] to get into (a) line; **(mettez-vous) en** ~**s par deux** line up in twos; [2] Mil rank; **rompre les** ~**s** (sur ordre) to fall out; (sans ordre) to break ranks; **sortir du** ~ Mil, fig to rise ou come up through the ranks; **serrer les** ~**s** Mil, fig to close ranks; **rentrer dans le** ~ lit to fall into line; fig to toe the line; **les** ~**s des mécontents** fig the ranks of the discontented; [3] (place) **arriver au 20ᵉ** ~ **mondial** to rank 20th in the world; **être au 5ᵉ** ~ **mondial des exportateurs** to be the 5th largest exporter in the world; **être sur les** ~**s pour un poste** to be in the running for a job; **acteur de second** ~ second-rate actor; [4] (ordre) order; **par** ~ **de taille** in order of height; [5] (dans une hiérarchie) rank; **accéder au** ~ **de** to rise to the rank of; **fonction de très haut** ~ high-ranking post; **des personnes de son** ~ people of one's own station; **tenir son** ~ to behave in a way appropriate to one's position; [6] (au tricot) row

rangé, -e¹ /ʀɑ̃ʒe/ adj (de bonne conduite) [vie] orderly; [personne] well-behaved

rangée² /ʀɑ̃ʒe/ nf row

rangement /ʀɑ̃ʒmɑ̃/ nm [1] (action) (de dossier, pièce) tidying up; (dans un meuble) putting away; **c'est un maniaque du** ~ he's obsessively tidy; [2] (meuble, espace) storage space ¢

ranger¹ /ʀɑ̃ʒe/ [13]

A vtr [1] (remettre à sa place) to put away; ~ **un livre sur une étagère** to put a book back on a shelf; **le dossier était mal rangé** the file had been put in the wrong place; **où ranges-tu tes verres?** where do you keep the glasses?; [2] (ordonner) (par classement) to arrange; (en ligne) to line up; ~ **qch dans l'ordre alphabétique** to put sth in alphabetical order; [3] (situer) ~ **un animal dans les mammifères** to class an animal as a mammal; [4] (mettre en ordre) to tidy [maison, meuble]; **tout est bien rangé** everything is nice and tidy

B **se ranger** vpr [1] (se mettre en rang) to line up; [2] (se mettre sur le côté) [véhicule, conducteur] to pull over; [cycliste] to pull in; [piéton] to step aside; [3] (se garer) [véhicule, conducteur] to park; **se** ~ **à quai** [navire] to dock; [4] (se placer) **se** ~ **parmi** or **au côté de** to side with; [5] (être mis à sa place) [vaisselle, livres] to be kept; **un couteau ça se range!** there's a place for knives!; [6] (s'assagir) to settle down

ranger² /ʀɑ̃dʒɛʀ/ nm (chaussure) heavy-duty boot

ranimer /ʀanime/ [1]

A vtr [1] (faire reprendre conscience à) to resuscitate [personne]; [2] (revigorer) [air, promenade] to revive [personne]; [3] (raviver) to rekindle [feu, ardeur, espoir, débat]; to stir up [querelle, inquiétude]; to restore [confiance]; to revive [marché financier, région]; to liven up [conversation]

B **se ranimer** vpr (se raviver) [feu] to flare up; [ardeur, flamme, débat] to be rekindled; [conversation] to liven up

rapace /ʀapas/

A adj [personne] rapacious

B nm Zool bird of prey

rapacité /ʀapasite/ nf [1] (d'animal) ferocity; [2] (de marchand) greed

rapatrié, -e /ʀapatʀije/ nm,f repatriate (**de** from)

rapatriement /ʀapatʀimɑ̃/ nm repatriation

rapatrier /ʀapatʀije/ [2] vtr to repatriate

râpe /ʀɑp/ nf Culin grater

râpé, -e /ʀɑpe/

A pp ▸ **râper**

B pp adj [carotte, fromage] grated; [vêtement] worn

C ⁰adj (loupé) **c'est** ~ it's off⁰

râper /ʀɑpe/ [1] vtr to grate [fromage, carotte]

rapetisser /ʀap(ə)tise/ [1]

A vtr lit **la distance rapetisse les objets** distance makes things look smaller

B vi to shrink

C **se rapetisser** vpr to shrink

râpeux, -euse /ʀɑpø, øz/ adj [langue, vin] rough; [voix] rasping

raphia /ʀafja/ nm (fibre) raffia

rapide /ʀapid/

A adj [1] (qui se déplace très vite) fast; **le plus** ~ the fastest; **le moins** ~ the slowest; **être** ~ **à la course** to be a fast runner; [2] (qui coule vite) [rivière, eau] fast-flowing; [courant] strong; [3] (fortement incliné) [pente, descente] steep; [4] (fait en peu de temps) [progrès, transformation, vieillissement] rapid; [moyen, victoire] quick; [livraison, succès, aggravation] quick, rapid; [réaction, intervention] quick, swift; [réponse, décision] prompt; [service] quick, speedy; **avec une machine c'est** ~ with a machine it's quick; [5] (au rythme soutenu) [mouvement, geste] quick; [allure] quick, rapid; [course] fast; [rythme, pouls] fast, rapid; [musique, danse] fast; **sa respiration était** ~ he/she was breathing rapidly; [6] (qui agit vite) [personne, esprit] quick; **à effet** ~ [médicament] quick-acting, fast-acting

B nm [1] (cours d'eau) rapids (pl); **descendre un** ~ to shoot the rapids; [2] Rail express

(Idiome) **être** ~ **comme l'éclair** to be as quick as lightning

rapidement /ʀapidmɑ̃/ adv [1] gén quickly; [2] Mus fast

rapidité /ʀapidite/ nf (promptitude) speed; **la** ~ **avec laquelle il a réagi m'a surpris** his quick reaction surprised me

rapiécer /ʀapjese/ [14] vtr to patch

rappel /ʀapɛl/ nm [1] (remise en mémoire) reminder (**de** of; **à** to); ~ **à l'ordre** call to order; [2] (avis de facturation) (lettre de) ~ reminder; '**dernier** ~' 'final demand'; ~ **d'impôts** tax adjustment; [3] (salaire différé) back pay; [4] (appel à revenir) (d'ambassadeur) recall; (de réservistes) call-up; (d'acteurs) curtain call; **battre** or **sonner le** ~ lit, fig to give the call to arms; [5] Méd (de vaccination) booster

rappeler /ʀaple/ [19]

A vtr [1] (remettre en mémoire) ~ **qch à qn** to remind sb of sth; ~ **(à qn) que** to remind (sb) that; ~ **le souvenir de qn** to evoke the memory of sb; ~ **le souvenir d'un événement** to recall an event; [2] (dire) to say; **rappelons-le** let's not forget; [3] (évoquer par ressemblance) to remind [sb] of; **vous me rappelez votre sœur** you remind me of your sister; [4] (par téléphone) to call back; [5] (appeler à revenir) to call [sb] back [personne]; Mil, Pol to recall [ambassadeur, réserviste]; to recall [product]; Théât to call back [acteur]; ~ **qn à l'ordre** to call to order

B **se rappeler** vpr (se souvenir de) to remember (**avoir fait** doing)

rappeur, -euse /ʀapœʀ, øz/ ▸ p. 372 nm,f rapper, rap artist

rappliquer⁰ /ʀaplike/ [1] vi (arriver) to turn up⁰; (revenir) to come back

rapport /ʀapɔʀ/

A nm [1] (lien) connection, link; **faire/établir le** ~ **entre** to make/to establish the connection ou the link between; **avoir** ~ **à qch** to have something to do with sth; **être sans** ~ **avec** to bear no relation to; **n'avoir aucun** ~ **avec** to have nothing to do with, to have no connection with; **les deux événements sont sans** ~ the two events are unrelated ou unconnected; **je ne vois pas le** ~! I don't see the connection!; **un emploi en** ~ **avec tes goûts** a job suited to ou that matches your interests; ~ **de cause à effet** relation of cause and effect; [2] (relations) ~**s** relations (**entre** between); **avoir** or **entretenir de bons/mauvais** ~**s avec qn** to be on good/bad terms with sb; **il a des** ~**s difficiles**

avec sa mère he has a difficult relationship with his mother; **3** (contact) **être/se mettre en ~ avec qn** to be/to get in touch with sb; **nous sommes en ~ avec d'autres entreprises** we have dealings with other companies; **mettre des gens en ~** to put people in touch with each other; **4** (point de vue) **sous tous les ~s** in every respect; **il est bien sous tous (les) ~s** he's a decent person in every way; **5** (compte rendu) report; **6** Mil daily briefing (with roll-call); **7** (rendement) return, yield; (de pari) **les ~s** the winnings (**de** on); **investissement d'un bon ~** investment that offers a good return ou yield; **être en plein ~** [arbres, terres] to be in full yield; **8** Math, Tech ratio; **le ~ hommes/femmes est de trois contre un** the ratio of men to women is three to one; **bon/mauvais ~ qualité prix** good/poor value for money

B par rapport à loc prép **1** (comparé à) compared with; **par ~ au dollar** against the dollar; **2** (en fonction de) **le nombre de voitures par ~ au nombre d'habitants** the number of cars per head of the population; **un changement par ~ à la position habituelle du parti** a departure from the usual party line; **3** (vis-à-vis de) with regard to, toward(s); **l'attitude de la population par ~ à l'immigration** people's attitudes (pl) to immigration

(Composés) **~ de force** (équilibre) balance of power; (lutte) power struggle; **~s sexuels** sexual relations; **avoir des ~s (sexuels)** to have intercourse ou sex

rapporter /ʀapɔʀte/ [1]
A vtr **1** (remettre en place) (ici) to bring back; (là-bas) to take back; (rendre) (ici) to bring back (**à** to), to return (**à** to); (là-bas) to take back (**à** to), to return (**à** to); **2** (ramener avec soi) to bring back [objet, cadeau, nouvelle] (**à** de from); **3** (procurer un bénéfice) to bring in [somme, revenu] (**à** to); **la vente de la maison leur a rapporté beaucoup d'argent** they made a lot of money on the sale of the house; **les obligations rapportent 10%** the bonds yield ou return 10%; **mes terres me rapportent beaucoup d'argent** my land brings me in a good income; **leurs investissements leur rapportent beaucoup d'argent** their investments give them a high return on their money; **ça ne rapporte rien** it doesn't pay; **qu'est-ce que ça va te ~ sinon des ennuis?** you'll get nothing out of it except trouble; **4** (relater) to report (**à** to); (citer) to quote [bon mot]; **je ne fais que ~ ses propos** I'm only repeating what he said; **on m'a rapporté que** I was told that; **5** ○(moucharder) to tell (tales) on sb
B vi **1** (procurer un bénéfice) to bring in money, to be lucrative; **un métier qui rapporte** a lucrative job; **2** ○(moucharder) to tell tales
C se rapporter vpr **1** (être en relation avec) **se ~ à** to relate to, to bear a relation to; **2** (faire confiance à) **s'en ~ à qn/qch** to rely on sb/sth

rapporteur○, **-euse** /ʀapɔʀtœʀ, øz/ nm,f (mouchard) telltale GB ou tattletale US

rapproché, **~e** /ʀapʀɔʃe/
A pp ▸ **rapprocher**
B pp adj **1** (dans l'espace) close together; **2** (dans le temps) close together; **à intervalles ~s** in quick succession

rapprochement /ʀapʀɔʃmɑ̃/ nm **1** Pol (entente) rapprochement; **2** (comparaison) connection

rapprocher /ʀapʀɔʃe/ [1]
A vtr **1** (rendre plus proche) to move [sth] closer [objet] (**de** to); **rapproche la chaise du mur** move the chair closer to the wall; **le courant nous rapproche de la côte** the current is taking us toward(s) the coast; **rapproche les deux vases** move the two vases closer together; **2** (dans le temps) to bring [sth] forward(s) [date, rendez-vous] (**de** to); **cette date nous rapproche trop des élections** that date brings us too close to the elections; **3** (disposer à l'entente) to bring [sb] (closer) together [personnes]; **leur passion pour la musique les rapproche** they are drawn together by their passion for music; **ses épreuves l'ont rapprochée des pauvres** having suffered herself, she feels for the poor; **ils ont réussi à ~ les deux pays** they managed to improve relations between the two countries; **4** (réunir) to bring together [personnes]; **5** (apparenter) to compare; **la situation est à ~ de ce qui s'est passé en 1951** the situation can be compared to that of 1951; **ses caractéristiques le rapprochent plus des mammifères** its characteristics make it closer to the mammals
B se rapprocher vpr **1** (devenir plus proche) to get closer, to get nearer (**de** to); **l'orage se rapproche** the storm is getting closer; **j'ai choisi ce travail pour me ~ d'elle** I took

this job so that I could be nearer to her; **2** (s'apparenter) **se ~ de** (processus) to get close to; (état) to be close to; **leurs peintures se rapprochent des fresques antiques** their paintings are similar to classical frescoes

rapt /ʀapt/ nm (enlèvement) kidnapping[GB], abduction

raquette /ʀakɛt/ nf **1** (de tennis, badminton) racket; (de tennis de table) bat GB, paddle US; **2** (pour marcher dans la neige) snowshoe

rare /ʀɑʀ/ adj **1** (peu commun) [personne, objet, animal, plante] rare; [denrée, main-d'œuvre, produit] scarce; [minerai] rare, scarce; **devenir** or **se faire ~** to be ou become scarce; **être l'un des ~s qui** to be one of the few (people) who; **2** (peu fréquent) [cas, mot, maladie] rare; [moment] rare; [visites] infrequent; [occasion] rare, unusual; [emploi, utilisation] uncommon; [voyages, trains] infrequent; [voitures, passants, clients, amis] few; **les clients sont ~s** there are very few customers; **vous voulez faites ~ ces temps-ci** you are not around much these days; **il est ~ de faire/qu'il fasse** it is unusual to do/for him to do; **cela n'a rien de ~** there's nothing unusual about it; **à de ~s exceptions près** with few exceptions; **3** (exceptionnel) [qualité, beauté, talent] rare; [maîtrise, intelligence, énergie, courage] exceptional; [bêtise, impudence, inconséquence] singular; **combat d'une ~ violence** exceptionally violent fight; **4** (clairsemé) [cheveux, barbe, végétation] sparse; [air] thin

raréfaction /ʀaʀefaksjɔ̃/ nf (de gaz, d'air) rarefaction

raréfier /ʀaʀefje/ [2]
A vtr **1** (rendre moins dense) to rarefy [air, gaz]; **2** (rendre rare) to make [sth] rare
B se raréfier vpr **1** [air] to become thinner; [gaz, atmosphère] to rarefy; [nourriture, denrée, argent] to become scarce; [espèce] to become rare

rarement /ʀaʀmɑ̃/ adv rarely, seldom

rareté /ʀaʀte/ nf **1** (d'argent, de crédit, denrées) shortage, scarcity; (d'édition, de médaille, mot) rarity; (d'offre, de demande) shortage; **la ~ des visiteurs** the small number of visitors; **2** (de phénomène, d'événement) rarity; (de lettres, d'appels) infrequency

rarissime /ʀaʀisim/ adj extremely rare

ras, **~e** /ʀɑ, ʀɑz/
A adj **1** (naturellement court) [poils, pelage] short; [végétation] low-growing; **à poil ~** [animal, fourrure] short-haired; **2** (coupé court) [barbe, gazon] short; [étoffe, tapis] short-piled; **en ~e campagne** in (the) open country; **3** [mesure] level; **à ~ bord** to the brim (**de** with)
B adv short; **couper (à) ~** to cut [sth] very short
C au ras de loc prép **au ~ de l'eau/des arbres** at water/tree level; **au ~ du sol** lit at ground level

(Idiomes) **être à ~ du sol** or **des pâquerettes**○ to be rather basic; **faire table ~e de** to make a clean sweep of

RAS /ɛʀɑɛs/ (abbr = rien à signaler) nothing to report

rasade /ʀazad/ nf (dans un verre) glassful; (au goulot) swig○

rasage /ʀazaʒ/ nm **1** (action) shaving; **2** (résultat) shave

rascasse /ʀaskas/ nf scorpion fish

ras-de-cou /ʀadku/, **ras-du-cou** /ʀadyku/ nm inv **1** (pull) crew-neck sweater; **2** (collier) choker

rasé, **~e** /ʀaze/
A pp ▸ **raser**
B pp adj **1** [poil, cheveux, tête] shaven; [menton] clean-shaven; [jambe] shaved; **2** (détruit) [quartier] demolished

rase-mottes /ʀazmɔt/ nm inv **le (vol en) ~** low flying; **faire du ~, voler en ~** to fly low

raser /ʀaze/ [1]
A vtr **1** to shave [personne, tête, joue, jambe] (**à** with); to shave off [cheveux, poils]; **~ de près** to give [sb] a close shave; **crème/mousse à ~** shaving cream/foam; **2** (abattre) [ouvriers] to demolish [bâtiment, quartier]; [soldats] to raze [sth] to the ground; **3** (effleurer) [projectile] to graze; [avion, oiseau] to skim; **4** ○(ennuyer) to bore [sb] stiff○
B se raser vpr **1** to shave (**à** with); **se ~ la barbe** to shave off one's beard

(Idiome) **~ les murs** to hug the walls

raseur○, **-euse** /ʀazœʀ, øz/ nm,f bore

ras-le-bol○ /ʀalbɔl/ nm inv discontent

rasoir /ʀazwaʀ/
A ○adj inv boring
B nm (objet) razor; **~ mécanique** or **de sûreté** safety razor; **~ électrique** electric shaver; **une coupure de ~** a nick with a razor; **coupe au ~** razor cut

r

rassasier /Rasazje/ [2]
A vtr [nourriture] to fill [sb] up; [personne] to stuff (**de** with); **être rassasié** (de nourriture) to have eaten one's fill (**de** of)
B **se rassasier** vpr to eat one's fill (**de** of)

rassemblement /Rasɑ̃bləmɑ̃/ nm **1** (manifestation) rally; (attroupement) gathering; (organisé) meeting; **2** (fait de se rassembler) gathering

rassembler /Rasɑ̃ble/ [1]
A vtr **1** (pour former un groupe) to gather [sb] together [personnes]; (pour mettre en contact) to bring [sb] together [personnes]; Mil to muster, to assemble [troupes]; to round up [moutons, troupeau]; **2** (autour d'une cause commune) to unite [citoyens, nation]; **3** (réunir) to gather [sth] together [effets personnels, documents]; to gather, to collect [informations, preuves]; ~ **ses forces** to summon up one's strength; ~ **ses idées** to collect one's thoughts
B **se rassembler** vpr [personnes] gén to gather; (dans un but précis) to assemble

rasseoir: **se rasseoir** /Raswar/ [41] vpr to sit down (again)

rasséréner /Raserene/ [14]
A vtr to calm [sb] down [personne]
B **se rasséréner** vpr [personne] to calm down; [visage] to clear

rassir /Rasir/ [3] vi, **se rassir** vpr to go stale

rassis, ~**e** /Rasi, iz/
A pp **1** ▸ **rasseoir**; **2** ▸ **rassir**
B pp adj [pain, gâteau] stale

rassurant, ~**e** /Rasyrɑ̃, ɑ̃t/ adj reassuring

rassurer /Rasyre/ [1]
A vtr to reassure; ~ **qn** to reassure sb, to put sb's mind at rest (**sur qch** about sth)
B **se rassurer** vpr to reassure oneself; **rassure-toi, tout va bien maintenant** don't worry, everything's all right now; **je suis rassuré de te savoir guéri** I'm relieved to hear you're better; **je n'étais pas très rassuré** I was quite worried

rat /Ra/ nm **1** Zool rat; **2** ○(terme d'affection) **mon petit** ~ my little darling; **3** (avare) pej skinflint, cheapskate○; **quel** ~○! he is so tight-fisted○

(Idiomes) **on est fait comme des** ~**s** we're caught like rats in a trap; **s'ennuyer comme un** ~ **mort**○ to be bored stiff○; **à bon chat bon** ~ Prov you/they etc have met your/their etc match

ratatiner: **se ratatiner** /Ratatine/ [1] vpr **1** [fruit] to shrivel; **2** [visage, personne] to become wizened

rate /Rat/ nf **1** Zool female rat; **2** Anat spleen

(Idiome) **se dilater la** ~○ to kill oneself laughing○

raté, ~**e** /Rate/
A pp ▸ **rater**
B pp adj **1** (pas réussi) [acteur, politicien, peintre] failed; **une vie** ~**e** a wasted life; **2** [occasion] missed
C nm,f (personne) failure
D ratés nmpl **1** (de négociations, système) hiccups; **2** Aut **avoir des** ~**s** to backfire, to misfire GB

râteau, pl ~**x** /Rato/ nm rake

râtelier /Ratəlje/ nm Agric hayrack

(Idiome) **manger à tous les** ~**s** to run with the hare and hunt with the hounds

rater /Rate/ [1]
A vtr **1** (ne pas réussir) to fail, to flunk○ US [examen]; **j'ai raté ma vie/ma photo** my life/my photo is a failure; **elle a raté son coup**○ she has failed; **2** (ne pas être présent pour) to miss [train, début de film, rendez-vous]; **3** (ne pas atteindre, ne pas voir) to miss [cible, objectif, marche, personne]
B vi [plan, opération] to fail, to flop○; **ça va tout faire** ~○ it'll spoil everything
C **se rater** vpr **1** (soi-même) to bungle one's suicide attempt; **2** (ne pas se voir) **nous nous sommes ratés** we missed each other

ratière /Ratjɛr/ nf rat trap

ratification /Ratifikasjɔ̃/ nf (action) ratification (**de** of; **par** by); (document) instrument of ratification

ratifier /Ratifje/ [2] vtr **1** Admin, Jur to ratify [traité, contrat]; **2** (confirmer) liter to confirm [projet, propos]

ration /Rasjɔ̃/ nf **1** (portion) ration; **2** fig share

rationaliser /Rasjɔnalize/ [1] vtr to rationalize

rationnel, -**elle** /Rasjɔnɛl/
A adj rational
B nm **1** Math rational number; **2** Philos **le** ~ the rational

rationnement /Rasjɔnmɑ̃/ nm rationing **C**; **ticket/carte de** ~ ration coupon/card

rationner /Rasjɔne/ [1]
A vtr Écon to ration [essence]; to impose rationing on [population]
B **se rationner** vpr to cut down (**en** on)

ratisser /Ratise/ [1] vtr **1** (égaliser) to rake over [allée]; (enlever) to rake up [feuilles mortes]; **2** (fouiller) to comb [région]; ~ **large**○ to cast one's net wide

raton /Ratɔ̃/ nm Zool young rat

(Composé) ~ **laveur** racoon

raton(n)ade /Ratɔnad/ nf racial attack (on Arabs or other minorities)

rattachement /Rataʃmɑ̃/ nm **1** (de territoire) unification (**à** with); **2** Admin (de personne) **demander son** ~ **à** to ask to be posted to

rattacher /Rataʃe/ [1]
A vtr **1** (faire dépendre) to attach [service, région] (**à** to); to link [devise] (**à** to); to post [employé] (**à** to); **2** (associer) to associate [œuvre, artiste] (**à** with); **3** (attacher de nouveau) to retie [lacets, poignets]; to fasten [sth] again [ceinture, collier]; to re-attach [remorque]; **4** (affectivement) **plus rien ne la rattache à Lyon** she no longer has any ties with Lyons
B **se rattacher** vpr [œuvre, artiste] to be linked (**à** to); [thème, problème] to relate (**à** to)

rattrapage /Ratrapaʒ/ nm **1** Comm, Écon (remise à jour) adjustment; (avec effet rétroactif) retroactive adjustment; **2** (de retard) catching up **C** (**de** with); Scol **cours/classe de** ~ remedial lesson/class

rattraper /Ratrape/ [1]
A vtr **1** (rejoindre) to catch up with [concurrent, passant, niveau]; **2** (capturer) to catch [fugitif, animal]; **3** (compenser) to make up for [absence, temps perdu, déficit, différence]; to make up [points, arriérés, temps de retard, distance] (**on** sur); ~ **son retard** to catch up; ~ **du sommeil en retard** to catch up on one's sleep; **4** (réparer) to make good [dommage, omission]; to put right [problème, tort, erreur]; to smooth over [paroles, gaffe verbale]; to get over [inconvénient]; to save [situation]; to pick up [maille]; ~ **le coup**○ to put things right; **5** (saisir) to catch [objet]; **6** ○Scol, Univ (permettre de passer) to let [sb] through; to let [sb] pass [élève, étudiant]
B **se rattraper** vpr **1** (se faire pardonner) to redeem oneself (**auprès de qn** with sb); **2** (compenser son désavantage) to make up for it; **3** Scol (atteindre le niveau requis) to catch up; **4** (compenser une perte) to make up one's losses (**avec** on); (compenser le temps perdu) to make up for lost time; **se** ~ **sur le dessert** to make up for it by eating a big dessert; **5** (éviter une catastrophe) **se** ~ **de justesse** to stop oneself just in time; **se** ~ **à une branche** to save oneself by catching hold of a branch

rature /RatyR/ nf crossing-out

raturer /Ratyre/ [1] vtr **1** (barrer) to cross out; **2** (corriger) to correct

rauque /Rok/ adj [voix] (naturellement) husky; (momentanément) hoarse

ravage /Ravaʒ/ nm **les** ~**s de la guerre/du temps** the ravages of war/time; **faire des** ~**s** [troupes, incendie, pollution] to wreak havoc; [épidémie] to take a terrible toll; **tu vas faire des** ~**s avec ta mini-jupe** hum you'll knock them dead in that mini-skirt

ravagé, ~**e** /Ravaʒe/ adj (fou) crazy

ravager /Ravaʒe/ [13] vtr **1** [incendie, guerre] to devastate, to ravage; **2** [maladie, alcool] to ravage [personne, visage]; [chagrin] to tear [sb] apart; [passions] to consume

ravageur, -**euse** /Ravaʒœr, øz/ adj **1** [désir, passion] all-consuming; [humour] crushing; [sourire] stunning; **2** [insecte, animal] destructive; [incendie] devastating

ravalement /Ravalmɑ̃/ nm **1** (de façades en pierre, brique) cleaning; (de façades crépies) refacing; **entreprise de** ~ firm specializing in renovating façades; **2** fig (amélioration) facelift

ravaler /Ravale/ [1] vtr **1** Constr to clean [façade en pierre, brique]; to reface [façade crépie]; to renovate [bâtiment]; **2** fig to revamp [image]; **3** to swallow [colère]; ~ **ses larmes** to hold back one's tears; **4** (déprécier) ~ **qch au rang de** to reduce sth to the level of

rave /ʀav/ nf turnip

ravi, ~e /ʀavi/
A pp ▸ **ravir**
B pp adj delighted (**de** with; **de faire** to do)

ravier /ʀavje/ nm small dish (for hors-d'oeuvre)

ravigoter⚬ /ʀavigɔte/ [1] vtr [air frais] to invigorate; [boisson] to perk [sb] up

ravin /ʀavɛ̃/ nm ravine

raviner /ʀavine/ [1] vtr **1** (creuser) to furrow [sol, terrain]; **collines ravinées** hillsides full of ravines; **2** (marquer) to line [visage]

ravir /ʀaviʀ/ [3] vtr **1** (plaire beaucoup) to delight; **le bleu lui va à ~** blue really suits him/her; **2** (dérober) fml to abduct [personne]; to steal [bien]

raviser: se raviser /ʀavize/ [1] vpr to change one's mind

ravissant, ~e /ʀavisɑ̃, ɑ̃t/ adj beautiful, delightful

ravissement /ʀavismɑ̃/ nm **1** (enchantement) rapture; **2** (rapt) abduction

ravisseur, -euse /ʀavisœʀ, øz/ nm,f abductor

ravitaillement /ʀavitajmɑ̃/ nm **1** (activité) (en vivres) provision of fresh supplies (**de qn** to sb); **aller au ~** to go and stock up; **2** (vivres) supplies (pl)

ravitailler /ʀavitaje/ [1]
A vtr (en vivres) to provide [sb] with fresh supplies [armée, ville] (**en qch** of sth); (en carburant) to refuel [avion, navire]
B se ravitailler vpr to obtain fresh supplies

raviver /ʀavive/ [1] vtr [personne] to rekindle [feu]; [produit] to revive [couleur]; [événement] to rekindle [colère, chagrin, passion, désir]; to bring back [mémoire, souvenir]; to revive [querelle, hostilité]; **~ une douleur** (physique) to bring the pain back; (mentale) to re-open an old wound

rayé, ~e /ʀeje/
A pp ▸ **rayer**
B pp adj [tissu] striped; **~ blanc et jaune** with white and yellow stripes

rayer /ʀeje/ [21] vtr **1** (barrer) to cross [sth] out; '**~ la mention inutile**' 'delete whichever does not apply'; **~ qch/qn d'une liste** to cross sth/sb's name off a list; **2** (supprimer) **la ville a été rayée de la carte** the town was wiped off the map; **3** (abîmer) to scratch [meuble, disque]

rayon /ʀejɔ̃/ nm **1** Math radius; **2** (limite) radius; **dans un ~ de 10 km** within a 10 km radius; **~ d'action** lit range; fig sphere of activity ou activities; **3** (de lumière, lune) ray; **un ~ de soleil** lit a ray of sunlight; fig (personne) a ray of sunshine; **4** Méd, Phys (radiation) ray; **les ~s X** X-rays; **~ laser** laser beam; **être traité** or **soigné aux ~s** to undergo radiation treatment; **5** (de roue) spoke; **6** (étagère) shelf; **~ de bibliothèque** (book)shelf; **7** Comm (dans un grand magasin) department; **au ~ (des) jouets** in the toy department; **en ~** on display; **8** ⚬(domaine) **c'est mon ~** (responsabilité) that's my department⚬; **ce n'est pas mon ~** (compétence) that's not (really) my line; **il en connaît un ~ à ce sujet** he knows a lot about it; **9** Zool **un ~ (de ruche)** a honeycomb

rayonnant, ~e /ʀejɔnɑ̃, ɑ̃t/ adj [air, personne, beauté, joie, visage] radiant; [sourire] beaming; **~ de** [personne] glowing with; [visage] shining ou radiant with

rayonne /ʀejɔn/ nf rayon

rayonnement /ʀejɔnmɑ̃/ nm **1** Phys (radiation) radiation; **2** (éclat) radiance; **3** (influence de pays, personne, pensée) influence

rayonner /ʀejɔne/ [1] vi **1** (se propager) [lumière, chaleur] to radiate (**de** from); **une chaleur qui rayonne** radiant heat; **2** (émettre de la lumière) liter [astre, étoile] to shine (forth); [mer] to glisten, to sparkle; **3** (resplendir) [personne] to glow (**de** with); **4** (manifester son influence) [personne, œuvre] to be an influence (**sur** on); [ville, pays] to exert its influence, to hold sway (**sur** over; **dans** throughout); **5** (se déplacer) [militaires, véhicule militaire] to patrol; [personnes, touristes] to tour around; [véhicule] to tour; **6** (être disposé en rayons) [avenues, lignes] to radiate out (**de** from)

rayure /ʀejyʀ/ nf **1** (motif) stripe; **à ~s** striped; **à ~s jaunes** with yellow stripes (épith, après n); **2** (éraflure) scratch

raz-de-marée /ʀadmaʀe/ nm inv lit, fig tidal wave; **~ électoral** electoral landslide

razzia /ʀazja/ nf raid

RDA /ɛʀdea/ nprf (abbr = **République démocratique allemande**) Hist German Democratic Republic, GDR

RDS /ɛʀdeɛs/ nm ▸ **remboursement**

ré /ʀe/ nm inv (note) D; (en solfiant) re

réabonner /ʀeabɔne/ [1] vtr **~ qn** (à une revue) to renew sb's subscription (**à** to); Théât to renew sb's season ticket

réaccoutumer /ʀeakutyme/ [1] vtr **~ qn à qch** to get sb used to sth again

réacteur /ʀeaktœʀ/ nm **1** **~ (nucléaire)** (nuclear) reactor; **2** Aviat jet engine; **3** Chimie reactor

réaction /ʀeaksjɔ̃/ nf **1** (en paroles, actions) reaction (**à** to; **contre** against); (corps posé, réfléchi) response; **en ~ à** in reaction to; **il est demeuré sans ~** he didn't react; **sans ~** [moteur, instrument] unresponsive; **sa ~ à la question fut de...** he/she responded to the question by...; **cela va provoquer des ~s** people are bound to react; **2** Chimie, Méd, Phys reaction; **moteur à ~** jet engine; **avion à ~** jet aircraft

réactionnaire /ʀeaksjɔnɛʀ/ adj, nmf reactionary

réactiver /ʀeaktive/ [1] vtr to rekindle [feu]; to reactivate [appareil]; to relaunch [négociations]; to increase [emploi]

réactualiser /ʀeaktɥalize/ [1] vtr gén to update; to relaunch [débat]

réadapter /ʀeadapte/ [1]
A vtr **~ qn à qch** to help sb to readjust to sth
B se réadapter vpr to readjust (**à qch** to sth)

réaffirmer /ʀeafiʀme/ [1] vtr to reaffirm, to reassert

réagir /ʀeaʒiʀ/ [3] vi **1** [personne, groupe] to react (**à** to; **contre** against); (de façon plus posée, réfléchie) to respond (**à** to); **2** (avoir des répercussions) **~ sur** to have an effect on; **3** Chimie to react (**à** to)

réajuster /ʀeaʒyste/ [1] vtr to readjust

réaligner /ʀealiɲe/ [1] vtr Fin, Pol to realign

réalisable /ʀealizabl/ adj [projet] feasible; [innovation] workable

réalisateur, -trice /ʀealizatœʀ, tʀis/ ▸ p. 372 nm,f Cin, Radio, TV director

réalisation /ʀealizasjɔ̃/ nf **1** (de rêve, d'ambition) (action, résultat) fulfilment^GB; **2** (d'étude, de sondage) carrying out; **conception et ~** (de meuble, satellite, hôtel) design and construction; **projet en cours de ~** project in progress; **amener un projet jusqu'à sa ~** (après sa conception) to get a project underway; (terminer) to bring a project to completion; **3** (ce qui est réalisé) achievement; **4** Cin, Radio, TV production; (film) film

réaliser /ʀealize/ [1]
A vtr **1** (rendre réel) to fulfil^GB [rêve, promesses]; to achieve [équilibre, idéal, exploit]; **~ des bénéfices** to make a profit; **elle a réalisé un exploit en faisant** it was no mean feat (for her) to do; **2** (exécuter, fabriquer) to make [maquette, meuble]; to carry out [sondage, projet, tâche]; **3** Radio, TV, Cin to direct; **4** (se rendre compte de) controv to realize
B se réaliser vpr **1** (devenir réel) [rêve] to come true; [promesses, prédictions] to be fulfilled^GB; **2** (s'épanouir) **se ~ (dans qch)** to find fulfilment^GB (in sth)

réalisme /ʀealism/ nm realism

réaliste /ʀealist/
A adj gén realistic; (en art) realist
B nmf realist

réalité /ʀealite/ nf **1** (réel) **la ~** reality; **en ~** in reality; **dans la ~, c'est impossible** in practice, it's impossible; **2** (caractère réel) **la ~ du problème/du marché** the real nature of the problem/of the market; **3** (fait réel) reality; **c'est déjà une ~** (nouvelle autoroute, chômage) it is already a reality; **tenir compte des ~s** to take the facts into consideration

[Composé] **~ virtuelle** virtual reality

réanimation /ʀeanimasjɔ̃/ nf **1** (service) intensive care; **service de ~** intensive care unit; **être en ~** to be in intensive care; **2** (technique) resuscitation

réanimer /ʀeanime/ [1] vtr ▸ **ranimer**

réapparaître /ʀeapaʀɛtʀ/ [73] vi [soleil] to come out again; [mot] to reappear; [phénomène] to recur

réapparition /ʀeapaʀisjɔ̃/ nf (de maladie, symptôme) recurrence; (de personne) reappearance

réapprovisionner /ʀeapʀɔvizjɔne/ [1]
A vtr to restock [magasin]
B se réapprovisionner vpr to stock up (**en** on)

réarmer /ReaRme/ [1] *vtr* **1** (munir d'armes) to rearm; **2** (mettre en ordre de marche) to reload [*fusil, appareil photo*]; **3** Naut (équiper) to refit [*navire*]

réassortiment /Reasɔrtimã/ *nm* (de stock) replenishment; (de marchandises) restocking

réassortir /Reasɔrtir/ [3]
A *vtr* **1** to match up [*tissu*] (**avec** with); **2** Comm to replenish [*stock*]
B se réassortir *vpr* to stock up (**en** on)

rébarbatif, -ive /Rebarbatif, iv/ *adj* [*travail*] off-putting; [*visage*] forbidding

rebâtir /R(ə)batir/ [3] *vtr* to rebuild

rebattre /R(ə)batr/ [61] *vtr* to reshuffle [*cartes à jouer*]
(Idiome) ~ **les oreilles de qn avec une histoire** to go on (and on) about something

rebattu, ~e /R(ə)baty/
A *pp* ▸ rebattre
B *pp adj* [*histoire*] hackneyed

rebelle /Rəbɛl/
A *adj* **1** Mil, Pol rebel (*épith*); **2** (refusant l'autorité) rebellious; **être ~ à** to be resistant to [*compromis*]; **3** [*mèche*] stray; [*tache*] stubborn; **4** Méd resistant
B *nmf* rebel

rebeller: se rebeller /Rəbɛle/ [1] *vpr* to rebel

rébellion /Rebɛljɔ̃/ *nf* **1** (action) rebellion; **2** (groupe de personnes) **la ~** the rebels (*pl*)

rebiffer○: se rebiffer /R(ə)bife/ [1] *vpr* to rebel

rebiquer○ /R(ə)bike/ [1] *vi* to stick up

reboiser /R(ə)bwaze/ [1] *vtr* to reafforest, to reforest

rebond /R(ə)bɔ̃/ *nm* **1** (de balle) bounce; **frapper la balle au ~** to hit the ball on the rebound; **2** (ressaisissement) recovery; (augmentation) increase

rebondi, ~e /R(ə)bɔ̃di/ *adj* **1** [*vase, cruche, forme*] round, rounded; [*joue*] chubby; [*visage*] plump; [*ventre*] fat; [*poitrine*] ample; [*fesses, hanches*] generously proportioned; [*cuisse, muscle*] bulging; **2** fig [*portefeuille*] bulging

rebondir /R(ə)bɔ̃dir/ [3] *vi* **1** [*balle, rayon, son, onde*] to bounce (**contre, sur** off); **fais ~ la balle par terre/contre le mur** bounce the ball on the ground/against the wall; **2** (repartir) [*conversation, polémique*] to start up again; [*économie, pays*] to pick up; [*procès, intrigue*] to take a new turn; **faire ~** to start [sth] up again [*conversation, débat*]; to give a new twist to [*procès*]

rebondissement /R(ə)bɔ̃dismã/ *nm* (de polémique) sudden revival (**de** of); (de procès, d'affaire) new development (**de** in); **les ~s de l'intrigue** the twists and turns of the plot

rebord /R(ə)bɔr/ *nm* **1** (partie en saillie) ledge; **2** (bord surélevé) gén raised edge; (d'objet rond) rim; **3** (bord arrondi) lip; **4** (bord) edge
(Composé) ~ **de fenêtre** windowsill; (plus large) (window) ledge

reboucher /R(ə)buʃe/ [1] *vtr* (avec un bouchon de liège) to recork [*bouteille*]; (avec un bouchon en verre) to replace the stopper of [*flacon*]; (avec un capuchon) to put the cap back on [*stylo*]; to put the top back on [*tube de dentifrice*]; ~ **un trou** to fill (up) a hole again

rebours: à rebours /aR(ə)buR/
A *loc adv* (compter, marcher) backward(s)
B à rebours de *loc prép* **à ~ de la tendance actuelle** contrary to the current trend; **aller à ~ de** to go against [*mode, tendance*]

rebouteux○, **-euse** /R(ə)butø, øz/ ▸ p. 372 *nm,f* bonesetter

reboutonner /R(ə)butɔne/ [1] *vtr* to button [sth] up again

rebrousse-poil: à rebrousse-poil /aR(ə)bRuspwal/ *loc adv* the wrong way; **caresser un chat à ~** to stroke a cat's fur the wrong way; **prendre qn à ~** fig to rub sb up the wrong way

rebrousser /R(ə)bRuse/ [1] *vtr* ~ **chemin** to turn back

rébus /Rebys/ *nm inv* rebus

rebut /R(ə)by/ *nm* **1** lit (déchet) rubbish ₵; **bon pour le ~** fit *ou* ready for the scrapheap; **mettre au ~** to throw [sth/sb] on the scrapheap; **le ~ de la société** fig the dregs (*pl*) of society; **2** Postes dead mail

rebutant, ~e /R(ə)bytã, ãt/ *adj* unpleasant

rebuter /R(ə)byte/ [1] *vtr* **1** (dégoûter) [*travail*] to disgust; [*personne*] to repel; **2** (décourager) to put [sb] off

récalcitrant, ~e /Rekalsitrã, ãt/ *adj* recalcitrant

recaler○ /R(ə)kale/ [1] *vtr* Scol, Univ to fail [*candidat*]; **être recalé à une épreuve** to fail a test

récapitulatif, -ive /Rekapitylatif, iv/
A *adj* **tableau ~** summary table
B *nm* (texte) summary of the main points

récapituler /Rekapityle/ [1] *vtr* to sum up

recaser○ /R(ə)kaze/ [1]
A *vtr* (dans un emploi) to find another job for [*personne*]
B se recaser *vpr* **1** (dans un emploi) to find another job; **2** (se remarier) [*femme*] to find a new husband; [*homme*] to find a new wife

receler /Rəs(ə)le, Rsəle/ [17] *vtr* **1** Jur to conceal [*criminel*]; ~ **des marchandises** (accepter) to receive stolen goods; (garder) to possess stolen goods; **2** (contenir) to contain; ~ **un trésor** to contain hidden treasure

receleur, -euse /Rəs(ə)lœr, Rsəlœr, øz/ *nm,f* (qui accepte) receiver of stolen goods, fence○; (qui garde) possessor of stolen goods

récemment /Resamã/ *adv* recently

recensement /R(ə)sãsmã/ *nm* **1** Sociol census; **2** (inventaire) inventory

recenser /R(ə)sãse/ [1] *vtr* **1** Sociol to take a census of [*population*]; **2** (inventorier) to list [*objets, problèmes*]

récent, ~e /Resã, ãt/ *adj* [*incident, nouvelle, découverte*] recent; [*maison*] new, newly built

recentrer /Rəsãtre/ [1] *vtr*, **se recentrer** *vpr* to refocus

récépissé /Resepise/ *nm* receipt

réceptacle /Resɛptakl/ *nm* **1** (récepteur) **c'est le ~ des eaux fluviales** it receives the fluvial waters; **le ~ des immondices de la ville** the town tip; **2** Géog catchment basin; **3** Bot receptacle; **4** (récipient) container

récepteur, -trice /Resɛptœr, tris/
A *adj* receiving
B *nm* **1** Biol receptor; **2** Radio, TV (appareil) receiver

réceptif, -ive /Resɛptif, iv/ *adj* receptive (**à** to)

réception /Resɛpsjɔ̃/ *nf* **1** (réunion) reception; **2** (manière d'accueillir) reception, welcome; **discours de ~** welcoming speech; **3** (bureau d'accueil) reception; **4** (de courrier, marchandises) receipt; **s'occuper de la ~ des marchandises** to take delivery of the goods; **5** Radio, TV (de signaux, d'ondes) reception; **6** Sport (après un saut) landing; (de ballon) catching

réceptionnaire /Resɛpsjɔnɛr/ ▸ p. 372 *nmf* **1** Comm receiving clerk; **2** (dans un hôtel) chief receptionist GB, head receptionist US

réceptionner /Resɛpsjɔne/ [1]
A *vtr* **1** Comm ~ **des marchandises** to take delivery of goods; **2** (accueillir) controv to welcome [*personne, voyageur*]; **3** Sport controv to catch [*ballon*]
B se réceptionner *vpr* to land

réceptionniste /Resɛpsjɔnist/ ▸ p. 372 *nmf* receptionist

récession /Resesjɔ̃/ *nf* recession

recette /R(ə)sɛt/ *nf* **1** Culin ~ **(de cuisine)** recipe; **livre de ~s** recipe book; **2** (méthode) formula, recipe; **3** Comm (argent encaissé) takings (*pl*); **faire ~** lit to bring in money; fig to be a success; **4** (rentrée d'argent) **les ~s et (les) dépenses** receipts and expenses; **5** (d'impôts) (bureau) tax collector's office, revenue office; (recouvrement) collection

recevable /Rəsvabl, R(ə)səvabl/ *adj* **1** gén [*excuse, offre*] acceptable; **2** Jur admissible

receveur, -euse /Rəs(ə)vœr, øz/ *nm,f* **1** ▸ p. 372 (d'autobus, de tramway) conductor; **2** Méd recipient
(Composés) ~ **des contributions** tax collector; ~ **des postes** postmaster

recevoir /Rəsvwar, R(ə)səvwar/ [5]
A *vtr* **1** (être le destinataire de) to receive, to get (**de** from); **nous avons bien reçu votre lettre** we acknowledge receipt of your letter; **il a reçu le ballon dans le visage** he was hit in the face by the ball; **j'ai reçu le marteau sur le pied** the hammer landed on my foot; **je n'ai d'ordre à ~ de personne** I don't take orders from anyone; **la mesure a reçu**

un accueil favorable de la part des enseignants the measure met with approval from teachers; **2** (accueillir) to welcome, to receive [invités, délégation]; **être bien/mal reçu** [proposition] to be well/badly received; [invités] to get a good/bad reception; **~ qn froidement** to give sb a cold reception; **demain nous les recevons à dîner** we're having them to dinner tomorrow; **ils reçoivent beaucoup** they do a lot of entertaining; **Laval reçoit Caen** Sport Laval is playing host to Caen; **il va se faire ~**○ he's going to get it○; **3** (pour consultation) to see [patients, clients]; **elle reçoit entre 14 et 17 heures** she's available for consultation between 2 and 5 pm; **4** Radio, TV (capter) to receive [signal, ondes]; **on reçoit mal cette chaîne** we get bad reception on that channel; **je vous reçois cinq sur cinq** Radio I'm receiving you loud and clear; **5** (contenir) [hôtel, refuge] to accommodate [personne]; [salle de spectacle, stade] to hold [spectateurs]; **6** (recueillir) to get [soleil, pluie]; **des bassins reçoivent l'eau de pluie** pools collect the rainwater; **7** Scol, Univ (admettre) to pass [élève, candidat]; **être reçu à un examen** to pass an exam; **il a été reçu premier au concours** he came first in the examination

B se recevoir *vpr* (après un saut, une chute) to land

rechange: **de rechange** /dəR(ə)ʃɑ̃ʒ/ *loc adj* [pièce, chemise] spare; [solution] alternative; **j'ai pris une chemise de ~** I have a change of shirt

réchapper /Reʃape/ [1] *vtr ind* **~ de** to come through [maladie, accident]; **personne n'en a** *or* **est réchappé** nobody came through it alive

recharge /R(ə)ʃaRʒ/ *nf* **1** (de briquet, stylo) refill; (d'arme) reload; **2** (processus) recharging

rechargeable /R(ə)ʃaRʒabl/ *adj* [briquet, stylo] refillable; [pile, appareil ménager] rechargeable

recharger /R(ə)ʃaRʒe/ [13]

A *vtr* **1** (avec cargaison) to reload [véhicule]; **2** (regarnir) to reload [arme, appareil photo]; to refill [stylo, briquet]; **3** to recharge [batterie]

B se recharger *vpr* **1** (qualité) [pile] to be rechargeable; [stylo] to be refillable; **2** (processus) [batterie, pile] to recharge

réchaud /Reʃo/ *nm* stove

(Composés) **~ à alcool** spirit stove; **~ électrique** electric ring GB, hotplate; **~ à gaz** (d'appartement) gas ring; (de camping) camping stove

réchauffé, ~e /Reʃofe/

A *pp* ▸ réchauffer

B *pp adj* (rebattu) [histoire, plaisanterie] hackneyed

C *nm* **c'est du ~** there's nothing new about it

réchauffement /Reʃofmɑ̃/ *nm* warming (up); **le ~ de la planète** global warming

réchauffer /Reʃofe/ [1]

A *vtr* **1** Culin to reheat, to heat [sth] up [plat, nourriture]; **2** (rendre chaud) to warm up [personne, pieds]; to heat up, to warm up [pièce]; **ça m'a réchauffé le cœur** fig it warmed my heart; **3** (détendre) **ses plaisanteries ont réchauffé l'atmosphère** his/her jokes relaxed the atmosphere

B *vi* Culin **faire ~ qch** to heat sth up, to reheat sth

C se réchauffer *vpr* **1** (soi-même) [personne] to warm oneself up; **2** (devenir chaud) [temps] to warm up; **les eaux du lac se sont réchauffées à cause de la pollution** the temperature of the water in the lake has risen because of pollution

rechausser /R(ə)ʃose/ [1] *vtr* **~ un enfant** to put a child's shoes back on; **~ ses skis** to put one's skis on again

rêche /Rɛʃ/ *adj* [mains, tissu] rough

recherche /R(ə)ʃɛRʃ/ *nf* **1** (étude) research **¢**; **travailler dans la ~** to work in research; **faire des ~s en biologie/sur le cancer** to do research in biology/into cancer; **2** (fouille) search; **après deux heures de ~** after a two-hour search; **tout le monde a participé aux ~s** everyone took part in the search; **être à la ~ de** to be looking for, to be in search of; **3** (volonté d'atteindre) **~ de** pursuit of; **être à la ~ d'un bonheur idéal** to be in pursuit of ideal happiness; **4** (soin) (raffinement) meticulousness; (affectation) pej affectation; **avec ~** [habillé, décoré, écrit] with meticulous care; **sans ~** (non affecté) without affectation; (négligé) carelessly

(Composé) **~ d'emploi** job-hunting

recherché, ~e /R(ə)ʃɛRʃe/

A *pp* ▸ rechercher

B *pp adj* **1** (rare) sought-after (pour for); **un livre très ~** a

much sought-after book; **2** (demandé) in demand (après n); **un mannequin très ~** a model very much in demand; **3** (soigné) [toilette] meticulous; péj affected; [style, écrit, expression] original, inventive; péj recherché; [décor] meticulously arranged (épith); **4** (visé) [but, effet] intended; **ce n'était pas le but ~** that wasn't the object of the exercise

rechercher /R(ə)ʃɛRʃe/ [1] *vtr* **1** (tâcher de trouver) to search out [objet convoité]; to look for [objet égaré]; to look for [logement, emploi, explication]; Ordinat to search for [donnée]; **~ les causes d'un accident** to look into the causes of an accident; **il est recherché par la police** he's wanted by the police; **'recherchons vendeuse qualifiée'** 'qualified sales assistant GB *ou* clerk US required'; **2** (tâcher d'obtenir) to seek [sécurité, bonheur, paix] (auprès de qn with sb); to seek, to look for [alliés, soutien]; to fish for [compliments]

rechigner /R(ə)ʃiɲe/ [1]

A rechigner à *vtr ind* **~ à qch/à faire** to balk at sth/at doing; **elle ne rechigne pas à la tâche** she's not afraid of hard work

B *vi* to grumble

rechute /Rəʃyt/ *nf* Méd, fig relapse

rechuter /R(ə)ʃyte/ [1] *vi* **1** Méd to have a relapse; fig to relapse (dans into); **2** Écon [prix, monnaie] to fall again; [ventes] to fall off again

récidive /Residiv/ *nf* **1** Jur second offence^GB; **il est accusé de vol avec ~** he has been charged with a second offence^GB of theft; **2** fig repetition; **3** Méd recurrence

récidiver /Residive/ [1] *vi* **1** Jur (la première fois) to commit a second offence^GB; (plusieurs fois) to commit subsequent offences; **2** (recommencer) fml to do it again; **3** Méd to recur

récidiviste /Residivist/ *nmf* **1** Jur (au second délit) second offender, recidivist; (après plusieurs délits) habitual offender, recidivist; **2** fig backslider

récif /Resif/ *nm* reef

récipient /Resipjɑ̃/ *nm* container (à for)

réciprocité /ResipRɔsite/ *nf* reciprocity

réciproque /ResipRɔk/

A *adj* **1** gén [aide, accord] reciprocal, mutual; [sentiment, confiance] mutual; **2** Ling, Math reciprocal

B *nf* **1** gén reverse; **2** Math reciprocal

réciproquement /ResipRɔkmɑ̃/ *adv* **se respecter ~** to respect one another; **et ~** and vice versa

récit /Resi/ *nm* **1** (narration) story; (genre) narrative; **un ~ d'aventures** an adventure story; **le ~ de mes aventures** the account of my adventures; **2** Théât narrative monologue

récital /Resital/ *nm* recital

récitatif /Resitatif/ *nm* recitative

récitation /Resitasjɔ̃/ *nf* **1** (texte littéraire) **apprendre une ~** to learn a text (off) by heart; **2** (matière) **être fort en ~** to be good at reciting (texts off by heart); **3** (action de réciter) reciting

réciter /Resite/ [1] *vtr* **1** lit to recite; **2** fig, pej to trot out○ [raisons, faits]

réclamation /Reklamasjɔ̃/ *nf* **1** (plainte) complaint; **2** (demande) claim (de for); **sur ~** on request

réclame /Reklam/ *nf* **1** (réputation) publicity; **2** †(annonce) advertisement; **3** (promotion) **'en ~'** 'on offer' GB, 'on sale'

réclamer /Reklame/ [1]

A *vtr* **1** (demander) to ask for [personne, chose, argent]; to call for [réforme, aide, silence, enquête]; to beg [indulgence]; to claim [dû, indemnité]; to demand [justice, augmentation]; **~ que** to demand that; **~ la parole** gén to ask to speak; (dans un débat) to ask to take the floor; **se voir ~ qch** to be asked for sth; **2** (en pleurant) [bébé] to cry for; **3** (nécessiter) to require [qualité]

B *vi* (se plaindre) to complain

C se réclamer *vpr* **1 se ~ de** (affirmer, représenter) [parti] to be an expression of [démocratie]; [organisation, personne] to claim to be representative of [parti, organisme, religion]; **2 se ~ de** (se fonder sur) [personne] to claim to follow [principe, idéologie, personne]

reclasser /Rəklase/ [1]

A *vtr* **1** (classer de nouveau) to reclassify [dossiers]; **2** (affecter à un nouveau poste) to redeploy (**dans** to); **3** (réajuster le salaire de) to regrade

B se reclasser *vpr* to find new employment

reclus, **~e** /Rəkly, yz/
A *adj* reclusive; **vivre ~** to live as a recluse
B *nm,f* recluse

réclusion /Reklyzjɔ̃/ *nf* **1** Jur imprisonment; **~ à perpétuité** *or* **à vie** life sentence; **2** Relig reclusion

recoiffer: se recoiffer /R(ə)kwafe/ [1] *vpr* to tidy one's hair

recoin /Rəkwɛ̃/ *nm* lit corner; fig recess; **tous les coins et les ~s** every nook and cranny (sg)

recoller /R(ə)kɔle/ [1] *vtr* to stick [sth] together again [*morceau*]; to reseal [*enveloppe*]

récolte /Rekɔlt/ *nf* Agric (activité) harvest; (produits récoltés) crop, harvest

récolter /Rekɔlte/ [1] *vtr* **1** Agric to harvest [*maïs, raisin*]; to dig up [*pommes de terre*]; **2** (ramasser) [*abeille*] to collect [*pollen*]; [*personne*] to win [*voix, points*]; to collect [*somme d'argent, informations*]; to reap [*avantage*]; **à l'aider, je n'ai récolté que des ennuis**○ I got nothing but trouble in return for helping him/her; **~ les fruits de son travail** *or* **de ses efforts** to reap the fruits of one's labour^{GB}

recommandable /Rəkɔmɑ̃dabl/ *adj* commendable; **un individu peu ~** a disreputable individual

recommandation /Rəkɔmɑ̃dasjɔ̃/ *nf* **1** (conseil) recommendation; **2** (parrainage) recommendation; **lettre de ~** letter of recommendation, reference; **3** Postes registration

recommandé, **~e** /Rəkɔmɑ̃de/
A *pp* ▸ **recommander**
B *pp adj* [*colis, lettre*] registered
C *nm* (lettre) registered letter; (colis) registered parcel; **en ~** [*envoyer*] by registered post GB *ou* mail

recommander /Rəkɔmɑ̃de/ [1]
A *vtr* **1** (conseiller fortement) to advise; **~ la prudence à qn**, **~ à qn d'être prudent** to advise sb to be cautious; **la vaccination est recommandée pour les séjours en Afrique** vaccination is recommended for visits to Africa; **il est ~ de faire** it is advisable to do, you are advised to do; **2** (formuler un avis) [*président, organisme international*] to recommend (**qch à qn** sth to sb); **3** (signaler pour sa qualité) to recommend [*film, médecin, méthode, restaurant*] (**à qn** to sb); **4** (parrainer) to recommend (**à, auprès de** to); **5** Postes to send [sth] by registered post GB *ou* mail
B se recommander *vpr* (invoquer l'appui de) **se ~ de qn** to give sb's name as a reference

recommencement /Rəkɔmɑ̃smɑ̃/ *nm* **la vie n'est qu'une suite de ~s** life is just a series of new beginnings; **l'histoire est un éternel ~** history is constantly repeating itself

recommencer /Rəkɔmɑ̃se/ [12]
A *vtr* **1** (complètement) to start [sth] again [*rapport, tâche*]; **tout est à ~** it will all have to be done again; **2** (après une pause) to start [sth] again; **~ à travailler/à vivre** to start working/living again; **3** (faire à nouveau) to do [sth] again [*rapport, action*]; to rewrite [*letter*]; **et ne recommence plus!** don't you ever do that again!
B *vi* to start again, to begin again

récompense /Rekɔ̃pɑ̃s/ *nf* (matérielle ou morale) reward; (honorifique) award; **en ~** as a reward

récompenser /Rekɔ̃pɑ̃se/ [1] *vtr* to reward (**de** for; **par** with)

recomposer /R(ə)kɔ̃poze/ [1]
A *vtr* gén to reconstruct [*scène*]; (en imprimerie) to reset [*page*]; **famille recomposée** reconstituted family; Télécom **~ un numéro** to dial a number again
B se recomposer *vpr* to re-form

recompter /R(ə)kɔ̃te/ [1] *vtr* to count [sth] again [*argent*]; to add up [sth] again [*addition*]

réconciliation /Rekɔ̃siljasjɔ̃/ *nf* reconciliation (**de X et de Y** of X with Y)

réconcilier /Rekɔ̃silje/ [2]
A *vtr* **~ Pierre et Paul**, **~ Pierre avec Paul** to bring Pierre and Paul back together; **~ la morale et la politique** to reconcile morality with politics
B se réconcilier *vpr* [*couple, amis*] to make up; [*nations*] to be reconciled

reconduction /R(ə)kɔ̃dyksjɔ̃/ *nf* renewal

reconduire /R(ə)kɔ̃dɥiR/ [69] *vtr* **1** (accompagner) (à la porte) to see [sb] out; **~ qn chez lui/à la gare** gén to take sb home/ to the station; (en voiture) to drive sb home/to the station; **la police l'a reconduit à la frontière** the police escorted him back to the border; **2** (prolonger) to extend [*grève, cessez-le-feu*]; (renouveler) to renew [*mandat, accord*]; **~ qn dans ses fonctions** to re-elect sb; **3** (piloter) to drive [sth] again

réconfort /Rekɔ̃fɔR/ *nm* comfort

réconforter /Rekɔ̃fɔRte/ [1]
A *vtr* **1** (consoler) to comfort; (rasséréner) **~ qn** to cheer sb up; **2** (revigorer) to fortify
B se réconforter *vpr* to restore one's strength

reconnaissable /R(ə)kɔnɛsabl/ *adj* recognizable

reconnaissance /R(ə)kɔnɛsɑ̃s/ *nf* **1** (gratitude) gratitude; **geste de ~** mark of gratitude; **en ~ de** in appreciation of [*aide, services*]; **avoir** *or* **éprouver de la ~ pour qn** to be *ou* feel grateful to sb; **2** (action d'identifier) recognition; **faire un signe de ~** to give a sign of recognition; **3** (fait d'admettre) (de torts, d'erreurs) admission, admitting; (de qualités, mérite) recognition, recognizing; **4** (de droit, d'indépendance, d'un État) recognition; **~ d'un enfant** legal recognition of a child; **5** (fait d'explorer) Mil reconnaissance, recon US; **aller** *or* **partir en ~** Mil to go on reconnaissance; fig to go and have a look around, to go and have a recce○

(Composé) **~ vocale** speech recognition

reconnaissant, **~e** /R(ə)kɔnɛsɑ̃, ɑ̃t/ *adj* grateful; **je vous serais ~ de bien vouloir faire** fml I should *ou* would be grateful if you would do

reconnaître /R(ə)kɔnɛtR/ [73]
A *vtr* **1** (retrouver) to recognize; (identifier) to identify; **je t'ai reconnu à ta voix** I recognized you by your voice; **je ne sais pas ~ les champignons** I can't identify different kinds of mushrooms; **je reconnais bien là leur grande générosité** it's just like them to be so generous; **2** (admettre) to admit [*faits, torts, erreurs*]; **il reconnaît avoir menti** *or* **qu'il a menti** he admits he lied; **~ qch comme une évidence** to accept sth as a fact; **~ qn comme le meilleur** to acknowledge sb to be the best; **~ qn coupable** to find sb guilty; **3** (considérer comme légitime ou valable) to recognize [*syndicat, régime, droit de grève, diplôme étranger*]; **~ un enfant** to recognize a child legally; **4** (explorer) **~ les lieux** Mil to reconnoitre^{GB} the area; fig to have a look round^{GB}
B se reconnaître *vpr* **1** (soi-même) to recognize oneself; **2** (l'un l'autre) to recognize each other; **3** (être identifiable) **se ~ à qch** to be recognizable by sth; **4** (s'orienter) to know where one is

reconnu, **~e** /R(ə)kɔny/
A *pp* ▸ **reconnaître**
B *pp adj* [*fait, diplôme, médecin*] recognized; **être ~ fiable** [*méthode, machine*] to be known to be reliable

reconquérir /R(ə)kɔ̃keRiR/ [35] *vtr* **1** Mil to reconquer, to recover [*territoire*]; **2** fig to regain [*dignité, estime, liberté*]; to win back [*personne, droit*]

reconquête /R(ə)kɔ̃kɛt/ *nf* **1** (de territoire) reconquest; **2** (de personne, droit) winning back; (de liberté) regaining

reconstituant, **~e** /R(ə)kɔ̃stitɥɑ̃, ɑ̃t/
A *adj* fortifying
B *nm* tonic

reconstituer /R(ə)kɔ̃stitɥe/ [1]
A *vtr* to re-form [*armée, association*]; to reconstruct [*crime, événement*]; to recreate [*époque, décor*]; to piece [sth] together again [*objet en morceaux*]; to build up again [*réserves, forces*]
B se reconstituer *vpr* to re-form

reconstitution /R(ə)kɔ̃stitysjɔ̃/ *nf* (d'armée, association) re-forming, reconstitution; (de crime, d'événement) reconstruction

reconstruction /R(ə)kɔ̃stRyksjɔ̃/ *nf* (d'édifice, de ville) reconstruction; (de pays, société) rebuilding

reconstruire /R(ə)kɔ̃stRɥiR/ [69] *vtr* to reconstruct [*édifice, ville*]; to rebuild [*pays, économie, société*]

reconversion /R(ə)kɔ̃vɛRsjɔ̃/ *nf* (de travailleur) redeployment; (de région) redevelopment; (d'économie) restructuring; (d'usine) conversion

reconvertir /R(ə)kɔ̃vɛRtiR/ [3]
A *vtr* to redeploy [*personnel*]; to redevelop [*région*]; to restructure [*économie, industrie*]; to convert [*usine, bâtiment*]; to adapt [*équipement*]
B se reconvertir *vpr* [*personnel*] to switch to a new type of

employment; [*entreprise*] to switch to a new type of production; **se ~ dans l'enseignement** to switch to teaching

recopier /ʀ(ə)kɔpje/ [2] *vtr* **1** (retranscrire) to copy out [*texte, citations*]; **2** (mettre au propre) to write up [*brouillon, devoir*]

record /ʀ(ə)kɔʀ/
A *adj inv* **en un temps ~** in record time
B *nm* Sport, fig record (**de** for)

recoucher: se recoucher /ʀ(ə)kuʃe/ [1] *vpr* to go back to bed

recoudre /ʀ(ə)kudʀ/ [76] *vtr* **1** to sew up [*ourlet, doublure*]; to sew [sth] back on [*bouton*]; **2** Méd to stitch up [*plaie, blessé*]

recoupement /ʀ(ə)kupmɑ̃/ *nm* (vérification) cross-check, cross-checking **₵**

recouper /ʀ(ə)kupe/ [1]
A *vtr* **1** (de nouveau) to cut [sth] again [*cheveux, haie*]; (davantage) to cut some more [*viande*]; to recut [*vêtement*]; **2** (comparer) to tie in, to tally with [*version, témoignage*]
B **se recouper** *vpr* (s'accorder) [*versions*] to tally; [*résultats*] to add up; (se couper) [*lignes*] to intersect

recourbé, ~e /ʀ(ə)kuʀbe/ *adj* [*bec, nez*] hooked; [*cils, ongles*] curved; [*tige de métal*] curved

recourir /ʀ(ə)kuʀiʀ/ [26] *vtr ind* **~ à** to use, to have recourse to [*remède, technique*]; to resort to [*expédient, stratagème, violence*]; to turn to [*parent, ami*]; to go to [*agence, expert*]; **~ à la justice** to go to court

recours /ʀ(ə)kuʀ/ *nm inv* **1** (moyen quelconque) recourse; (moyen extrême) resort; **sans autre ~ que** with no other way out but; **avoir ~ à** to have recourse to [*remède, technique*]; to resort to [*expédient, stratagème*]; to turn to [*parent, ami*]; to go to [*agence, expert*]; **en dernier ~** as a last resort; **2** Jur appeal; **~ en grâce** petition for reprieve

recouvrement /ʀ(ə)kuvʀəmɑ̃/ *nm* (d'impôt, de cotisation) collection; (de somme, dette) recovery

recouvrer /ʀ(ə)kuvʀe/ [1] *vtr* **1** to recover [*somme, créance*]; to collect [*impôt, cotisation*]; **2** (retrouver) to recover [*santé, forces*]; to regain [*liberté*]; **~ la raison** to regain one's sanity

recouvrir /ʀ(ə)kuvʀiʀ/ [32]
A *vtr* **1** (couvrir complètement) to cover (**de** with); **2** (couvrir de nouveau) to cover [sb] up again [*malade, enfant*]; to re-cover [*chaise, fauteuil*]; **3** (masquer) to hide, to conceal; **4** (inclure) **cela recouvre en partie ce que j'allais dire** this partly covers what I was about to say
B **se recouvrir** *vpr* **1** (devenir couvert) to become covered (**de** with); **2** (se chevaucher) [*tuiles*] to overlap; **3** (correspondre) [*concepts*] to overlap; **4** (remettre son chapeau) to put one's hat back on

récréatif, -ive /ʀekʀeatif, iv/ *adj* [*jeu, activité, film, soirée*] recreational; [*zone, parc*] recreation (*épith*)

récréation /ʀekʀeasjɔ̃/ *nf* **1** (à l'école primaire) playtime GB, recess US; (dans le secondaire) break GB, recess US; **2** (loisir) recreation

recréer /ʀ(ə)kʀee/ [11] *vtr* to recreate

récrier: se récrier /ʀekʀije/ [2] *vpr* to exclaim

récrimination /ʀekʀiminasjɔ̃/ *nf* recrimination

récriminer /ʀekʀimine/ [1] *vi* to rail *sout*

recroqueviller: se recroqueviller /ʀ(ə)kʀɔkvije/ [1] *vpr* **1** [*personne*] to huddle up; **2** [*objet, feuille*] to shrivel up

recru, ~e¹ /ʀəkʀy/ *adj liter* **~ (de fatigue)** exhausted

recrudescence /ʀ(ə)kʀydesɑ̃s/ *nf* (de violence, d'intérêt) fresh upsurge (**de** of); (de bombardements, peur, pessimisme, demandes, grèves) new wave (**de** of); (d'incendie, de combats) renewed outbreak (**de** of)

recrudescent, ~e /ʀ(ə)kʀydesɑ̃, ɑ̃t/ *adj* **être ~** to be on the increase

recrue² /ʀəkʀy/ *nf* recruit

recrutement /ʀ(ə)kʀytmɑ̃/ *nm* recruitment

recruter /ʀ(ə)kʀyte/ [1] *vtr* (engager) to recruit; **~ qn comme enseignant** to take sb on as a teacher

recruteur, -euse /ʀ(ə)kʀytœʀ, øz/
A *adj* [*officier, agent*] recruiting; [*bureau, agence*] recruitment (*épith*)
B *nm,f gén* recruitment specialist, recruiter US

rectangle /ʀɛktɑ̃gl/
A *adj* Math right-angled, right US
B *nm gén*, Math rectangle

rectangulaire /ʀɛktɑ̃gylɛʀ/ *adj* rectangular, oblong

recteur /ʀɛktœʀ/ *nm* Scol, Univ (d'académie) ≈ chief education officer GB, ≈ superintendent (of schools) US

rectificatif /ʀɛktifikatif/ *nm* **1** (dans un journal) correction; **2** (à une loi) amendment (**à** to)

rectification /ʀɛktifikasjɔ̃/ *nf* **1** (correction) (d'erreur) correction; (de contrat) rectification; (modification de chiffres) adjustment; **2** (de tracé, route) straightening; (de virage) straightening out; **3** (rectificatif) correction

rectifier /ʀɛktifje/ [2] *vtr* **1** (corriger) to correct, to rectify [*erreur*]; **2** (rendre conforme) to adjust [*position, chiffres*]; to rectify [*limites, contrat, ouvrage défectueux*]; to amend [*facture, document*]; **~ le tir** lit to adjust one's aim; fig to change one's approach; **3** (redresser) to straighten [*tracé, route*]; to straighten out [*virage*]

rectiligne /ʀɛktiliɲ/ *adj gén* straight; Math rectilinear

recto /ʀɛkto/ *nm* front; **~ verso** on both sides

rectorat /ʀɛktɔʀa/ *nm* **1** (administration) ≈ local education authority GB, ≈ board of education US; **2** (bureaux) local education offices (*pl*)

reçu, ~e /ʀ(ə)sy/
A *pp* ▸ **recevoir**
B *pp adj* **1** [*candidat*] successful; **2** [*usage*] accepted; **3** Radio **message ~** message received and understood
C *nm,f* Scol, Univ successful candidate
D *nm* (quittance) receipt

recueil /ʀ(ə)kœj/ *nm* (d'un auteur) collection; (de divers auteurs) anthology; (de documents, lois) compendium

recueillement /ʀəkœjmɑ̃/ *nm* **1** (méditation) contemplation; **2** (attitude respectueuse) reverence

recueilli, ~e /ʀəkœji/
A *pp* ▸ **recueillir**
B *pp adj* [*air, visage*] rapt; [*fidèle*] rapt in prayer (*épith, après n*); [*foule, silence*] reverential

recueillir /ʀəkœjiʀ/ [27]
A *vtr* **1** (rassembler) to collect [*dons, signatures, anecdotes*]; to gather, to collect [*témoignages, renseignements*]; **2** (obtenir) to get [*voix, nouvelles*]; to gain [*consensus*]; to achieve [*unanimité*]; to win [*louanges*]; **~ des applaudissements** [*personne, proposition*] to be greeted with applause; **3** (récupérer) to collect [*eau, résine*]; to gather [*miel*]; **cuvette pour ~ l'eau** bowl to catch the water; **4** (prendre avec soi) to take in [*orphelin*]; **5** (enregistrer) to record [*impression, opinions*]; (par écrit) to take down [*déposition*]; **6** (hériter) to inherit [*fortune*]; to receive [*héritage*]
B **se recueillir** *vpr* **1** (méditer) to commune with oneself; **2** (prier) to engage in private prayer

recul /ʀ(ə)kyl/ *nm* **1** (détachement) detachment; **avec le ~** with hindsight, in retrospect; **manquer de ~** to be incapable of being objective; **prendre du ~** to stand back; **2** (baisse) (d'investissements, de production, nombre) drop (**de** in), fall (**de** in); (de doctrine, maladie) decline (**de** in); **être en ~** [*investissements, exportations, ventes*] to be dropping *ou* falling; [*racisme, tendance*] to be on the decline; [*parti*] to be in decline; **un ~ de 5%** a 5% drop; **3** (dans l'espace) (d'armée) pulling *ou* drawing back; (des eaux, de la mer) recession; **avoir un mouvement de ~** to recoil; **feu de ~** Aut reversing light; **le ~ de la forêt amazonienne** the gradual disappearance of the Amazonian forest; **4** (de date, réunion) postponement; (d'âge de la retraite) raising

reculade /ʀəkylad/ *nf* climb-down

reculé, ~e /ʀəkyle/ *adj* **1** [*quartier, zone, village*] remote; **2** [*temps, époque*] distant, remote

reculer /ʀ(ə)kyle/ [1]
A *vtr* **1** (pousser) to move back [*vase, lampe*]; to move *ou* push back [*meuble*]; **~ les pendules d'une heure** to put the clocks back an hour; **2** (faisant marche arrière) to reverse GB, to back up; **3** (dans le temps) to put off [*moment du départ, événement, décision*]; to put back [*date*]
B *vi* **1** [*personne, groupe*] (aller en arrière) to move back; (pour mieux voir quelque chose, pour être vu) to stand back; [*chauffeur, voiture*] to reverse; **~ d'un pas** to step back; **~ de trois pas** to take three steps back(wards); **faire ~ un groupe de personnes** to move a group of people back; **~ d'une case** Jeux to go back a square; **c'est ~ pour mieux sauter** fig it's just putting off the inevitable; **2** [*armée*] to pull *ou* draw

back; **3)** [*falaise*] to be eroded; [*forêt*] to be gradually disappearing; [*eaux*] to go down; [*mer*] to recede; **4)** (régresser) [*monnaie, production, exportations*] to fall; [*doctrine, mouvement*] to decline; [*parti, politicien*] to suffer a drop in popularity; **faire ~** to cause a fall in [*euro, exportation*]; **faire ~ le chômage** to reduce unemployment; **~ de cinq places** [*élèves, sportif*] to fall back five places, to drop five places; **5)** (céder, se dérober) to back down; (hésiter) to shrink back; **cela m'a fait ~** it put me off; **~ devant une difficulté** to shrink from a difficulty; **ne ~ devant rien** to stop at nothing

reculons: **à reculons** /aʀ(ə)kylɔ̃/ *loc adv* **aller à ~** lit to go backward(s); fig to go reluctantly

récupérable /ʀekypeʀabl/ *adj* **1)** (réutilisable) [*matériau*] reusable; **2)** (réparable) [*objet, vêtement*] which can be made good again (*épith, après n*); **3)** (réformable) [*délinquant*] who can be rehabilitated (*épith, après n*)

récupération /ʀekypeʀasjɔ̃/ *nf* **1)** (de ferraille) salvage; (de chiffons) reclamation; **matériaux de ~** salvaged materials; **2)** (de l'organisme) recovery; **capacité de ~** recuperative power; **3)** (recouvrement) (d'argent, de prêt) recovery; **4)** (d'heures de travail) making up; **5)** Pol (de mouvement) taking over, hijacking; (d'idées) appropriation

récupérer /ʀekypeʀe/ [14]
A *vtr* **1)** (rentrer en possession de) to get back, to recover [*argent, objet, force*]; **2)** (aller chercher) to fetch [*enfant*]; **il a récupéré le ticket de caisse au fond de la poubelle** he retrieved the receipt from the bottom of the bin GB *ou* garbage can US; **3)** (ramasser pour réutiliser) to salvage [*ferraille*]; to reclaim [*chiffons, vieux journaux*]; **4)** (garder) to save [*timbres, boîtes*]; **5)** to make up [*journées, heures de travail*]; **6)** Pol to take over, to hijack [*mouvement, personne*]; to appropriate [*idées*]; **7)** (réinsérer) to rehabilitate [*délinquant*]
B *vi* (après un effort, une maladie) to recover (**de** from)

récurer /ʀekyʀe/ [1] *vtr* to scour [*casserole*]; to scrub [*lavabo*]; **poudre à ~** scouring powder

récurrence /ʀekyʀɑ̃s/ *nf* **1)** (répétition) recurrence; **2)** Math recursion

récurrent, ~e /ʀekyʀɑ̃, ɑ̃t/ *adj* gén, Anat, Méd recurrent

récusation /ʀekyzasjɔ̃/ *nf* challenging, challenge

récuser /ʀekyze/ [1]
A *vtr* to challenge, to object to [*juré, témoin*]
B **se récuser** *vpr* gén to declare oneself incompetent; Jur [*juge*] to decline to act in a case

recyclable /ʀ(ə)siklabl/ *adj* [*matériau*] recyclable; [*personne*] retrainable

recyclage /ʀ(ə)siklaʒ/ *nm* **1)** (de matériau) recycling; **2)** (de personnel) retraining; **3)** Fin (de capitaux) recycling; (de profits) reinvestment

recycler /ʀ(ə)sikle/ [1]
A *vtr* **1)** (pour réutiliser) to recycle [*matériau*]; **2)** **~ le personnel** (former de nouveau) to retrain the staff; (perfectionner) to provide refresher courses for the staff; **3)** (réinvestir) to recycle [*capitaux*]; to reinvest [*profits*]
B **se recycler** *vpr* **1)** (se perfectionner) to update one's skills; (faire un stage) to attend a refresher course; **2)** (se reconvertir) to retrain; (changer d'emploi) to change jobs

rédacteur, -trice /ʀedaktœʀ, tʀis/ ▸ p. 372 *nm,f* **1)** (de texte) author, writer; **2)** (de journal, magazine) editor

rédaction /ʀedaksjɔ̃/ *nf* **1)** (activité) (d'article, ouvrage) writing; (correction) editing; (de document, décret) drafting; **2)** (dans la presse) (bureaux) editorial offices; (personnel) editorial staff; **3)** Scol essay GB, theme US

rédactionnel, -elle /ʀedaksjɔnɛl/ *adj* editorial

reddition /ʀedisjɔ̃/ *nf* (capitulation) surrender

redemander /ʀədmɑ̃de, ʀ(ə)dəmɑ̃de/ [1] *vtr* **1)** (demander de nouveau) **~ qch à qn** to ask sb for sth again; **2)** (se faire rendre) **~ qch à qn** to ask sb for sth back; **3)** (demander davantage) **~ des fruits à qn** to ask sb for more fruit

redémarrer /ʀ(ə)demaʀe/ [1] *vi* **1)** Aut [*chauffeur*] to drive off again; **2)** Écon [*marché, économie*] to take off again; [*entreprise*] to relaunch itself; **3)** Ordinat to reboot

rédemption /ʀedɑ̃psjɔ̃/ *nf* redemption

redescendre /ʀ(ə)desɑ̃dʀ/ [6]
A *vtr* **1)** (transporter de nouveau) (en bas) to take [sb/sth] back down (**à** to); (à l'étage) to take [sb/sth] back downstairs; (d'en haut) gén to bring [sb/sth] back down (**de** from); (de l'étage) to bring [sb/sth] back downstairs; **je peux vous ~ au village** I can take you back down to the village; **2)** (remettre en bas)

to get [sth] back down [*valise, boîte*]; **3)** (rabaisser) to lower [*étagère, tableau, store*] (**de** by); to wind [sth] back down [*vitre de véhicule*]; **4)** (parcourir de nouveau) [*personne*] (en allant) to go back down [*pente, rue, étage*]; to go *ou* climb back down [*escalier, échelle*]; (en venant) to come back down [*rue, marches*]; [*voiture, automobiliste*] to drive back down [*route*]
B *vi* (descendre de nouveau) [*personne*] (en allant) gén to go back down, to go down again (**à** to); (de l'étage) to go back downstairs, to go downstairs again; (en venant) gén to come back down, to come down again (**de** from); (de l'étage) to come back downstairs, to come downstairs again; (après être remonté) (en allant) to go back down again; (en venant) to come back down again; [*ascenseur, avion*] (en allant) to go back down; (en venant) to come back down; [*oiseau*] to fly down again; [*prix, taux, monnaie*] to go down again; [*mer*] to go back out; [*température, baromètre*] to fall again, to go down again; **peux-tu ~ chercher mon sac?** can you go back downstairs and get my bag?; **~ de** gén did you walk back down?; **il est redescendu du col à bicyclette** he cycled back down from the pass; **~ de** to climb back down from [*mur*]; **~ de l'échelle** to climb back down the ladder; **il est redescendu du toit** [*enfant*] he's come back down off the roof; **on nous a fait ~ de l'avion** we were made to get out of the plane again; **~ à Marseille** (retourner) to go back down to Marseilles; **~ dans les sondages** [*politicien, parti*] to drop *ou* to move down in the opinion polls; **les cours sont redescendus de 20%** prices have dropped again by 20%

▢ Idiome **~ sur terre** to come down to earth

redevable /ʀədvabl, ʀ(ə)dəvabl/ *adj* **être ~ de qch à qn** to owe sth to sb, to be indebted to sb for sth; **être ~ de l'impôt** to be liable for tax

redevance /ʀədvɑ̃s, ʀ(ə)dəvɑ̃s/ *nf* **1)** (taxe) gén charge; (de télévision) licence GB *ou* license US fee; (de téléphone) rental charge; **2)** (droit d'exploitation) royalty

rédhibitoire /ʀedibitwaʀ/ *adj* [*coût*] prohibitive; [*obstacle*] insurmountable; [*condition*] unacceptable; [*timidité*] crippling

rediffuser /ʀ(ə)difyze/ [1] *vtr* to repeat GB, to rerun [*émission*]

rédiger /ʀediʒe/ [13] *vtr* (écrire) to write [*article, texte*]; (en développant ses notes) to write up [*notes, thèse*]; to draft [*décret, contrat*]

redingote /ʀ(ə)dɛ̃gɔt/ *nf* (d'homme) frock coat; (de femme) fitted coat

redire /ʀədiʀ/ [65] *vtr* to repeat; **~ qch à qn** (répéter) to tell sb sth again; **je le lui ai dit et redit** I've told him/her over and over again; **~ à qn de faire** to remind sb to do; **~ à qn que** to remind sb that; **avoir** *or* **trouver quelque chose à ~ à qch** to find fault with sth; **côté qualité, (il n'y a) rien à ~** from the point of view of quality, it can't be faulted

redistribuer /ʀ(ə)distʀibye/ [1] *vtr* to redistribute [*richesses*]; to reallocate [*tâches*]

redite /ʀ(ə)dit/ *nf* (needless) repetition

redondance /ʀ(ə)dɔ̃dɑ̃s/ *nf* **1)** (de style) verbosity; **2)** (terme superflu) superfluous term; **3)** Ling redundancy

redondant, ~e /ʀ(ə)dɔ̃dɑ̃, ɑ̃t/ *adj* **1)** [*style*] verbose; [*terme*] superfluous, redundant; **2)** Ling redundant

redonner /ʀ(ə)dɔne/ [1] *vtr* **1)** (donner de nouveau) **~ qch à qn** to give sb sth again, to give sth to sb again; **il m'a redonné de la soupe** he gave me some more soup; **2)** (rétablir) **~ confiance à qn** to restore sb's confidence; **~ espoir à qn** to give sb renewed hope; **~ des forces à qn** to restore sb's strength; **~ vie à un quartier** to breathe new life into an area; **3)** (rendre) to give [sth] back [*objet, argent*] (**à** to); **4)** (rediffuser) to show [sth] again [*film*]

redorer /ʀ(ə)dɔʀe/ [1] *vtr* to regild

▢ Idiome **~ son blason** [*personne*] to restore one's image; [*ville, groupe*] to restore its image

redoublant, ~e /ʀ(ə)dublɑ̃, ɑ̃t/ *nm,f* student repeating a year

redoublement /ʀ(ə)dubləmɑ̃/ *nm* **1)** Ling reduplication; **2)** (intensification) intensification

redoubler /ʀ(ə)duble/ [1]
A *vtr* **1)** Scol **~ une classe** to repeat a year; **2)** Ling to reduplicate [*consonne, syllabe*]
B **redoubler de** *vtr ind* **~ de prudence/d'égards** to be twice as careful/attentive; **~ d'efforts** to redouble one's efforts;

la tempête a redoublé de violence the storm has become even fiercer

C vi ⓵ Scol to repeat a year; ⓶ (s'intensifier) to intensify; **la pluie a redoublé** it's raining even harder

redoutable /R(ə)dutabl/ adj [arme, examen, concurrent] formidable; [mal] dreadful

redouter /R(ə)dute/ [1] vtr (craindre) to fear [ennemi, mort]; (appréhender) to dread [événement, avenir]

redressement /RədRɛsmã/ nm ⓵ (reprise) recovery; ⓶ (remise sur pied) re-establishment; **plan de** ~ recovery plan; ⓷ (remise en forme) straightening out; ⓸ (rééducation) **maison de** ~ reformatory

redresser /R(ə)dRese/ [1]
A vtr ⓵ (remettre d'aplomb) to straighten up [barrière, piquet]; (remettre debout) to put [sth] up again [barrière, piquet]; (détordre) to straighten [sth] out [barre de métal, pare-chocs]; to straighten [dent]; ~ **la tête** lit to lift one's head up; fig (tenir tête) to stand up for oneself; ⓶ (après une crise) to put [sth] back on its feet [économie]; to turn [sth] round GB ou around [entreprise]; ~ **la situation** to put the situation right; ⓷ (après une baisse) to aid the recovery of [monnaie]; to improve [marge de bénéfices]; ⓸ (après une manœuvre) to straighten up [voilier, planeur, volant]; ~ **la barre** lit to right the helm; fig to put things back on an even keel; ⓹ (corriger) to rectify [erreur]; to redress [injustices]; ~ **les torts** fml to right (all) wrongs

B se **redresser** vpr ⓵ [personne] (se mettre debout) to stand up; (s'asseoir) to sit up; (se mettre droit) (en position debout) to stand up straight; (en position assise) to sit up straight; ⓶ (reprendre de la vigueur) [industrie, économie, plante] to pick up again, to recover; [pays, compagnie] to get back on its feet

redresseur /RədRɛsœR/ nm ~ **de torts** redresser of wrongs

réductible /Redyktibl/ adj ⓵ (en diminuant) [frais] which can be reduced ou cut (après n); ⓶ Chimie, Math, Méd reducible

réduction /Redyksjõ/ nf ⓵ (remise) discount, reduction; (consentie à un groupe particulier) concession (**sur** on); ~ **de 5%** 5% reduction; **faire une** ~ **à qn** to give sb a discount; ~ **étudiants** concession GB ou special price for students; ⓶ (action de diminuer) (de dépenses, coût, subventions, production) cutting, reducing; (de délais) shortening, reducing; (d'armements, inégalités) reducing; ⓷ (diminution) (de dépenses, coût, d'armements) reduction, cut (**de** in); ~ **d'impôts** tax cut; ~**s d'effectifs** staff cuts; ⓸ Art (reproduction réduite) small replica; ⓹ Chimie, Culin, Math, Méd reduction

réduire /RedɥiR/ [68]
A vtr ⓵ (diminuer) to reduce; ~ **le personnel** to cut (down on) staff; ~ **un article de 3%** to reduce an article by 3%; ~ **les subventions de moitié** to cut subsidies by half; ~ **qch en taille** to make sth smaller, to reduce the size of sth; ~ **le nombre de succursales** to reduce the number of branches; **je dois** ~ **mes dépenses** I must cut down on my spending; ~ **l'écart entre** to narrow the gap between; ⓶ (en reproduisant) to reduce [photographie]; to scale down [dessin]; (en faisant des coupures) to cut [texte]; ⓷ (transformer) ~ **qch en poudre** to crush sth to powder; ~ **qch en bouillie** to reduce sth to a pulp; **être réduit en cendres** lit [ville] to be reduced to ashes; fig [espoirs, rêves] to turn to ashes; **être réduit à rien** ou **à néant** [efforts, travail, fortune] to be wiped out; ⓸ (en simplifiant) ~ **qch à** to reduce sth to; ⓹ (obliger) ~ **qn au silence** to reduce sb to silence; ⓺ (vaincre) to subdue [ennemi]; to silence [opposition]; to crush [émeute]; ⓻ Culin, Chimie to reduce [composé, sauce]; ⓼ Math to reduce [fraction]

B vi Culin [sauce] to reduce; [épinards] to shrink

C se **réduire** vpr ⓵ (diminuer) [coûts] to be reduced ou cut; [délais] to be reduced ou shortened; [importations] to be cut; [écart] to narrow; ⓶ (consister seulement en) **se** ~ **à** to consist merely of; **cela se réduit à bien peu de chose** it doesn't amount to very much

réduit, ~**e** /Redɥi, it/
A pp ▸ **réduire**

B pp adj ⓵ (diminué) [taux, cotisation, vitesse] reduced, lower; [délai] shorter; [activité] reduced; [main-d'œuvre] smaller, reduced; [groupe] smaller; **à vitesse** ~**e** at a lower speed; **billets à prix** ~ tickets at a reduced price; **avec un personnel** ~ with fewer staff; **à mobilité** ~**e** with restricted mobility; ⓶ (peu important) [moyens, choix] limited; [groupe]

small; ⓷ (petit) [taille] small; **de taille** ~**e** small; **en format** ~ [objet] in a scaled down ou reduced format

C nm (placard) cubbyhole

réécrire /ReekRiR/ [67] vtr to rewrite

rééditer /Reedite/ [1] vtr to reissue [livre]

réédition /Reedisjõ/ nf (de livre) reissue

rééducation /Reedykasjõ/ nf ⓵ Méd (des mouvements) physiotherapy, physical therapy US; (de handicapé) rehabilitation; ~ **de la parole** speech therapy; ⓶ (de délinquant) rehabilitation

rééduquer /Reedyke/ [1] vtr ⓵ Méd to restore normal functioning to [membre]; to rehabilitate [handicapé]; ~ **la parole** to treat speech disorder; ⓶ Jur to rehabilitate [délinquant]; ⓷ (éduquer différemment) to re-educate [personne]; to retrain [animal]

réel, réelle /Reɛl/
A adj ⓵ (non imaginaire) [besoin, risque, événement, être] real; (véritable) [cause, motif, coût] true, actual; [fait] true; ⓶ (grand) [émotion, difficultés, effort] real; ⓷ Fin [revenu] real; [taux d'intérêt] effective; ⓸ Math, Ordinat, Philos, Phys real

B nm Philos **le** ~ the real

réélection /Reelɛksjõ/ nf re-election

réélire /ReeliR/ [66] vtr to reelect

réellement /Reɛlmã/ adv really

réembaucher /Reãboʃe/ [1] vtr to take [sb] on again

réemployer /Reãplwaje/ [23] vtr to re-use [matériaux]; to reinvest [fonds]; to re-employ [personnel]

rééquilibrer /ReekilibRe/ [1] vtr ⓵ Tech to readjust [chargement]; ⓶ Aut to balance [wheels]; ⓷ Écon to balance [budget]; ~ **les pouvoirs** Pol to restore the balance of power

réessayer /Reeseje/ [21] vtr to try [sth] on again [robe]

réévaluer /Reevalɥe/ [1] vtr ⓵ (relever) to revalue [monnaie]; to revise [salaire, impôt]; ⓶ (estimer à nouveau) to reappraise, to re-evaluate [patrimoine, dépenses, forces, emploi]

réexaminer /Reegzamine/ [1] vtr to re-examine [dossier, budget]; to reconsider [décision, candidature]

réexpédier /Reekspedje/ [2] vtr ⓵ (faire suivre) to forward, to redirect; ⓶ (retourner) to send [sth] back

refaire /RəfɛR/ [10]
A vtr ⓵ (faire de nouveau) to do [sth] again, to redo [exercice, calcul, travail, vêtement]; to make [sth] again [voyage, erreur]; to repack [bagage]; ~ **le même chemin** (en sens inverse) to go back the same way; ~ **du cinéma** [ancien acteur] to get back into films GB ou movies US; **tout est à** ~ it will have to be done all over again; **'à** ~**'** (sur une copie d'élève) 'do it again'; ~ **un numéro de téléphone** to redial a number; **si c'était à** ~ if I had to do it all over again; **je vais** ~ **les rideaux de ta chambre** I'll make some new curtains for your bedroom; ⓶ (faire en plus) **je vais** ~ **de la soupe** I'll make some more soup; ⓷ (changer complètement) **vouloir** ~ **le monde** to want to change the world; **se faire** ~ **le nez** to have one's nose re-modelled^GB^; **on ne le refera pas** there's no changing him; ~ **sa vie** (avec quelqu'un d'autre) to start all over again (with somebody else); ⓸ (rénover) to redo [toit, gouttière, sol]; to redecorate [pièce]; to resurface [route]; **appartement refait à neuf** completely refurbished apartment

B se **refaire** vpr ⓵ (fabriquer pour soi) **se** ~ **une robe** to make oneself another dress; ⓶ (retrouver) **se** ~ **une santé** to recuperate; **se** ~ **une beauté** to redo one's make-up; ⓷ (se réhabituer) **se** ~ **à** to get used to [sth] again; ⓸ (changer) **on ne se refait pas** a person can't change

réfection /Refɛksjõ/ nf (de toiture, façade, bâtiment) repairing; (de route) mending; (de pièce, maison) redoing; **'en** ~**'** 'restoration work in progress'

réfectoire /RefɛktwaR/ nm (d'institution) refectory; Mil mess

référence /RefeRãs/
A nf ⓵ (renvoi) reference (**à** to); **en** or **par** ~ **à** in reference to; **faire** ~ **à** to refer to, to make reference to; ⓶ (modèle) (prime) example; **lui? ce n'est pas une** ~**!** who, him? well, he's not much of an example!; **date de** ~ date of reference; **livre de** ~ reference book; ⓷ (identification) reference; (numéro) reference number; ⓸ Ling reference

B **références** nfpl (pour emploi, location) references

r

référendum /ʀefeʀɛ̃dɔm/ nm referendum (**sur** on)

> ℹ️ **Référendum** A référendum may be called by the Président de la République on questions concerning the organization of the state, a matter which may change its nature, or proposed legislation affecting economic and social policy.

référentiel, -ielle /ʀefeʀɑ̃sjɛl/
A adj gén, Ling referential
B nm fml frame of reference

référer /ʀefeʀe/ [14]
A référer à vtr ind **1** **en ~ à** to consult; **2** Ling **~ à** to refer to
B se référer vpr se **~ à** (faire référence à) to refer to; (consulter) to consult

refermer /ʀ(ə)fɛʀme/ [1]
A vtr (fermer) to close; (de nouveau) to close [sth] again
B se refermer vpr [piège, porte] to close (**sur** on); [eau] to close (**sur** over); [blessure] to close up

réfléchi, ~e /ʀefleʃi/
A adj **1** (posé) [personne] reflective, thoughtful; [regard] thoughtful; **2** (mûri) [décision] considered; [action] well-considered; **tout bien ~** all things considered; **c'est tout ~** my mind is made up; **3** Phys reflected; **4** Ling reflexive
B nm Ling reflexive

réfléchir /ʀefleʃiʀ/ [3]
A vtr to reflect [onde, chaleur]
B réfléchir à vtr ind **~ à** to think about
C vi to think (**sur qch** about sth); **ça fait ~** it makes you think; **réfléchis et donne-moi ta réponse demain** think it over and give me your answer tomorrow; **mais réfléchis donc un peu!** use your brain!
D se réfléchir vpr [onde, image] to be reflected

réfléchissant, ~e /ʀefleʃisɑ̃, ɑ̃t/ adj reflective

réflecteur, -trice /ʀeflɛktœʀ, tʀis/
A adj reflecting
B nm reflector

reflet /ʀ(ə)flɛ/ nm **1** (image) lit, fig reflection; **être le ~ d'une époque** to reflect a period; **2** (lueur) glint; (plus délicat) shimmer **C**; **~s dorés** golden glints; **feuillage à ~s argentés** foliage with a silvery shimmer; **3** (nuance de couleur) sheen **C**; **les ~s du satin** the sheen of satin; **cheveux châtains aux ~s roux** brown hair with (natural) auburn highlights

refléter /ʀ(ə)flete/ [14]
A vtr to reflect; **son visage reflétait son émotion** his/her emotion showed in his/her face
B se refléter vpr lit, fig to be reflected (**dans** in)

refleurir /ʀ(ə)flœʀiʀ/ [3] vi **1** [fleur] to flower again; **2** [arts] to flourish again

réflexe /ʀeflɛks/
A adj reflex
B nm **1** (en physiologie) reflex; **2** (réaction, habitude) reaction; **manquer de ~** to be slow to react; **elle a eu le ~ de freiner** her instinctive reaction was to brake; **faire qch par ~** to do sth automatically

réflexif, -ive /ʀeflɛksif, iv/ adj reflexive

réflexion /ʀeflɛksjɔ̃/ nf **1** (pensée) thought, reflection; **2** (méditation) thinking, reflection; **cela demande ~** it needs thinking about; **sans ~** without thinking; **~ faite** or **à la ~, je n'irai pas** on reflection ou on second thoughts, I won't go; **donner matière à ~** to be food for thought; **3** (remarque) remark (**sur** about), comment (**sur** on); **s'attirer des ~s** to attract criticism ou adverse comment; **4** (étude) study (**sur** of); **document de ~** discussion paper; **5** Phys reflection

refluer /ʀ(ə)flɥe/ [1] vi [liquide] to flow back; [foule] to surge back; **faire ~** to push back [foule]

reflux /ʀ(ə)fly/ nm inv **1** (marée) ebb tide; **2** (de foule) surging away; (de chômage, devise) decline

refondre /ʀ(ə)fɔ̃dʀ/ [6] vtr lit to melt down again [métal]; to recast [objet]

refonte /ʀ(ə)fɔ̃t/ nf gén overhaul; (de contrat) rewriting

reforestation /ʀəfɔʀɛstasjɔ̃/ nf reafforestation

réformateur, -trice /ʀefɔʀmatœʀ, tʀis/
A adj [dirigeant, parti, idéologie] reforming; [milieu, courant, force] of reform (épith, après n)
B nm,f reformer

réforme /ʀefɔʀm/ nf **1** (modification) reform; **2** Mil discharge; **3** Relig **la Réforme** the Reformation

réformé, ~e /ʀefɔʀme/
A adj Relig Reformed
B nm Mil [appelé] person who has been declared unfit for service; [soldat] discharged soldier
C nm,f Relig Calvinist

reformer /ʀ(ə)fɔʀme/ [1]
A vtr to re-form; **~ les rangs** [soldats] to fall in again
B se reformer vpr [glace, équipe] to re-form; [soldats] to form up again; [peau] to renew itself

réformer /ʀefɔʀme/ [1]
A vtr **1** (changer) to reform; **2** Mil to declare [sb] unfit for service [appelé]; to discharge [soldat]
B se réformer vpr to mend one's ways

réformiste /ʀefɔʀmist/ adj, nmf reformist

refoulé, ~e /ʀ(ə)fule/ nm,f repressed person

refoulement /ʀ(ə)fulmɑ̃/ nm **1** Psych repression; **2** (expulsion) (d'ennemi) pushing back; (d'immigrant) turning back; (de la foule) driving back; (de liquide) forcing back

refouler /ʀ(ə)fule/ [1] vtr **1** (contenir) to suppress [émotion, souvenir]; to repress [tendance]; to hold back [larmes]; to stifle [sanglots]; **2** (repousser) to force [sth] back [liquide]; to push back [ennemi]; to turn back [immigrant]; to drive back [foule]

réfractaire /ʀefʀaktɛʀ/ adj **1** [personne] **~ à** resistant to [progrès, infection, influence]; impervious to [poésie, musique]; **2** [matériau] refractory

réfracter /ʀefʀakte/ [1]
A vtr to refract
B se réfracter vpr to be refracted

refrain /ʀ(ə)fʀɛ̃/ nm **1** (de chanson) chorus; **2** (rengaine) pej (old) refrain

réfréner /ʀefʀene/ [14] vtr to curb

réfrigérant, ~e /ʀefʀiʒeʀɑ̃, ɑ̃t/
A adj **1** lit [appareil] cooling; **2** fig [accueil] frosty
B nm (appareil) cooler

réfrigérateur /ʀefʀiʒeʀatœʀ/ nm refrigerator

réfrigérer /ʀefʀiʒeʀe/ [14] vtr to refrigerate [aliment]; to cool [local]

réfringent, ~e /ʀefʀɛ̃ʒɑ̃, ɑ̃t/ adj refractive

refroidir /ʀəfʀwadiʀ/ [3]
A vtr **1** lit to cool down [mélange, moteur]; to cool [atmosphère]; **2** fig to dampen [ardeur, enthousiasme]; **~ qn** to dampen sb's spirits
B vi (devenir moins chaud) to cool down; (devenir trop froid) to get cold
C se refroidir vpr [temps] to get colder; [muscle, articulation] to stiffen up; [personne] to get cold

refroidissement /ʀəfʀwadismɑ̃/ nm **1** Météo drop in temperature; **2** gén, Tech cooling; **tuyau de ~** cooling pipe; **liquide de ~** coolant; **3** Méd chill; **4** (de relations, sentiment) cooling

refroidisseur /ʀəfʀwadisœʀ/ nm coolant

refuge /ʀ(ə)fyʒ/
A nm **1** (abri, réconfort) refuge; **2** (en montagne) (mountain) refuge; **3** (pour animaux) sanctuary; **4** (de chaussée) traffic island; (de pont) refuge
B (-)refuge (in compounds) **monnaie ~** safe currency; **pays ~** country of refuge

réfugié, ~e /ʀefyʒje/ nm,f refugee

réfugier: se réfugier /ʀefyʒje/ [2] vpr lit, fig to take refuge

refus /ʀ(ə)fy/ nm inv refusal (**de qch** of sth; **de faire** to do); **ce n'est pas de ~** I wouldn't say no○

⬚ **Composés** **~ d'obéissance** Mil insubordination; Jur contempt of court; **~ d'obtempérer** refusal to comply; **~ de priorité** failure to give way

refuser /ʀ(ə)fyze/ [1]
A vtr **1** (ne pas accepter) to refuse [offre, don, invitation]; to turn down [poste]; **~ de faire qch** to refuse to do sth; **2** (ne pas accorder) to refuse [permission, crédit, entrée]; **~ qch à qn** to refuse sb sth; **se voir ~ qch** to be refused sth; **il a refusé qu'on vende la maison** he wouldn't allow the house to be sold; **~ sa porte à qn** to bar one's door to sb; **je lui refuse**

le droit de me juger he/she has no right to judge me; [3] (rejeter) to reject [*budget, manuscrit, racisme*]; to refuse to accept [*fait, évidence*]; to turn away [*spectateur, client*]; **~ un candidat** (à un poste) to turn down a candidate; (à un examen) to fail a candidate; **être refusé à un concours** to fail an examination

B se refuser *vpr* [1] (être décliné) **ça ne se refuse pas** (occasion) it's too good to pass up○ *ou* miss; (verre) I wouldn't say no○; [2] (se priver de) to deny oneself [*plaisir*]; **on ne se refuse rien**○! you're certainly not stinting yourself!; [3] (dire non) **se ~ à** to refuse to accept [*évidence*]; to refuse to adopt [*solution*]; **se ~ à faire** to refuse to do

réfuter /Refyte/ [1] *vtr* to refute

regagner /R(ə)gaɲe/ [1] *vtr* [1] (rejoindre) to get back to [*lieu, poste*]; **~ son domicile/sa place** to return home/to one's seat; [2] (recouvrer) to regain, to win back [*estime, confiance*]; to pick up [*point*]; **~ du terrain** Mil, fig to regain ground

regain /R(ə)gɛ̃/ *nm* [1] (reprise) (de marché) recovery (**de** of); (d'inflation, de chômage) rise (**de** in); **~ de la consommation** upturn in consumer spending; [2] (recrudescence) (d'intérêt) revival; (de violence, tension) resurgence, renewal; **connaître un ~ de popularité** to enjoy renewed popularity; [3] Agric second crop

régal /Regal/ *nm* [1] (mets savoureux) culinary delight; **c'est un (vrai) ~!** it's (absolutely) delicious!; [2] fig delight; **un ~ pour les yeux** a feast for the eyes

régalade /Regalad/ *nf* **boire à la ~** to drink without letting one's lips touch the bottle

régaler /Regale/ [1]
A *vtr* [*personne*] to treat [sb] to a delicious meal; **~ qn de** lit to treat sb to [*vin, mets*]; fig to regale sb with [*anecdotes*]
B se régaler *vpr* [1] (de nourriture) **je me régale** it's delicious; **les enfants se sont régalés avec ton dessert** the children really enjoyed your dessert; [2] fig **se ~ avec** to enjoy [sth] thoroughly [*film, personnage*]; **se ~ de** to love [*anecdote*]

regard /R(ə)gaR/
A *nm* [1] (action de regarder) look; **porter son ~ sur qch** to look at sth; **détourner le ~** to look away; **chercher qn du ~** to look around for sb; **interroger qn du ~** to look enquiringly GB *ou* inquiringly US at sb; **suivre qch/qn du ~** to follow sth/sb with one's eyes; **elle attire tous les ~s** everyone looks at her; **jeter un ~ rapide** *or* **sur qch** to glance at sth; **j'ai croisé son ~** our eyes met; **échanger des ~s** to exchange looks; **loin** *or* **à l'abri des ~s indiscrets** far from prying eyes; **soustraire qch aux ~s** to conceal sth from view; [2] (yeux) eyes (*pl*); **un ~ clair** light-coloured○○ eyes; [3] (expression) expression; **son ~ triste** his/her sad expression; **elle a un ~ intelligent** she looks intelligent; **sous le ~ amusé de qn** under the amused eye of sb; **jeter un ~ noir à qn** to give sb a black look; [4] (manière de juger) eye; **le ~ des autres** other people's opinion; **porter un ~ nouveau sur qch** to take a fresh look at sth
B au regard de *loc prép* fml with regard to; **au ~ du chômage** with regard to unemployment; **au ~ de la loi** in the eyes of the law
C en regard de *loc prép* fml compared with
D en regard *loc adv* **avec une carte en ~** with a map on the opposite page

regardant, ~e /R(ə)gaRdɑ̃, ɑ̃t/ *adj* **ne pas être très ~** (exigeant) not to be very particular *ou* fussy (**sur** about); (économe) not to care about what things cost; **être ~ (avec son argent)** to be careful with one's money

regarder /R(ə)gaRde/ [1]
A *vtr* [1] (diriger son regard vers) to look at; **~ qch par la fenêtre** to look out of the window at sth; **regarde qui vient!** look who's coming!; **~ qch méchamment** to glare at sth; **~ rapidement** to have a quick look at, to glance at [*bâtiment, paysage*]; to glance through [*document, livre*]; **~ qn en face** lit, fig to look sb in the face; **~ la réalité** *or* **les choses en face** to face facts; **~ qn de haut** fig to look down one's nose at sb; **~ qn de travers** fig to look askance at sb; [2] (fixer avec attention) to watch, to look at [*personne, scène*]; to look at [*tableau, paysage*]; to watch [*film, télévision*]; **~ qn faire** to watch sb doing; **regarde bien comment je fais** watch what I do carefully; **~ qch fixement** to stare at sth; **~ qn/qch longuement** to gaze at sb/sth; **~ qn dans les yeux** to look sb in the eye(s); [3] (pour vérifier, savoir) to look at [*montre, carte*]; to have a look at, to check [*pneus, niveau d'huile*]; **~ dans** to look up, to consult [*dictionnaire, annuaire*]; **~ si** to have a look to see if; [4] (examiner,

---

considérer) to look at [*pays, situation*]; **~ pourquoi/si/qui** to see why/if/who; [5] (constater) to look; **regarde-moi ça!** just look at that!; [6] ○(concerner) to concern [*personne*]; **ça ne vous regarde pas** that doesn't concern you; (moins poli) it's none of your business; **mêle-toi de ce qui te regarde!** mind your own business○!; [7] (prendre en compte, envisager) **elle ne regarde que ses intérêts** she thinks only of her own interests; **~ l'avenir avec confiance** to view the future with confidence; [8] (faire face à) [*maison*] to overlook [*baie, mer*]
B regarder à *vtr ind* to think about; **~ à la dépense** to watch what one spends; **ne pas ~ à la dépense** to spare no expense; **quand on y regarde de très près** when you look at it very closely; **tu devrais y ~ à deux fois avant de l'acheter** you should think twice before buying it
C *vi* [1] (diriger son regard) to look; **~ en l'air** to look up; **~ par terre** to look down; **regarde autour de toi** lit, fig look around; **regarde bien** have a good look; [2] (en cherchant) to look; [3] (faire attention) to look; **regarde où tu mets les pieds** look *ou* watch where you put your feet
D se regarder *vpr* [1] (soi-même) to look at oneself; [2] (l'un l'autre) to look at one another

regarnir /RəgaRniR/ [3] *vtr* to restock [*étalage, réfrigérateur*]; to refill [*trousse de secours*]

régate /Regat/ *nf* regatta

régence /Reʒɑ̃s/
A *adj inv* [*style*] French Regency; **~ anglais** Regency
B *nf* [1] Pol regency; [2] Hist **la Régence** the Regency

régénérer /ReʒeneRe/ [14]
A *vtr* [1] Biol, fig to regenerate; [2] Chimie to reactivate
B se régénérer *vpr* [1] Biol [*cellules*] to regenerate; [2] fig [*corps, personne*] to regain one's strength

régent, ~e /Reʒɑ̃, ɑ̃t/ *nm,f* Pol regent

régenter /Reʒɑ̃te/ [1] *vtr* (diriger) to rule, to regiment; (contrôler) to regulate

régie /Reʒi/ *nf* [1] (gestion) (par l'État) state control; (par la commune) local government control; [2] (entreprise) **~ d'État** state-owned company; [3] (de spectacle) Théât stage management; Cin, TV production department; (salle) central control room

regimber /R(ə)ʒɛ̃be/ [1] *vi* [1] [*personne*] to balk (**contre** at); [2] [*cheval, âne*] to jib

régime /Reʒim/ *nm* [1] (alimentation) diet; **être/se mettre au ~** to be/to go on a diet; **suivre un ~** to be on a diet; **produit de ~** dietary product; [2] Pol (mode de gouvernement) system (of government); (gouvernement) government; (totalitaire) regime; **~ parlementaire** parliamentary system; [3] (conditions) system, regime; **~ pénitentiaire** prison system; **~ de faveur** preferential treatment; [4] Admin (organisation) scheme; (règlement) regulations (*pl*); **~ de retraite** pension scheme; [5] Jur **~ matrimonial** marriage settlement; [6] (rythme) (de moteur) (running) speed; **tourner à plein ~** [*moteur*] to run at top speed; [*usine*] to work at full capacity; **à ce ~** fig at this rate; [7] Phys (débit) rate of flow; [8] Géog, Météo regime; [9] (de bananes) bunch; (de dattes) cluster; [10] Ling object

régiment /Reʒimɑ̃/ *nm* [1] Mil (unité) regiment; [2] ○(service militaire) military service; [3] ○(multitude) army

région /Reʒjɔ̃/ *nf* [1] Admin region; **la ~ parisienne** the Paris region; [2] Géog (territoire) region; (autour d'un lieu) area; **les ~s tropicales** tropical regions; **le Vésuve et sa ~** Vesuvius and the surrounding area; **le vin de la ~** the local wine; [3] Anat region; [4] Mil district

> **Région** The largest administrative unit in France, consisting of a number of *départements*. Each has its own *Conseil régional* (regional council) which has responsibilities in education and economic planning.

régional, ~e, *mpl* **-aux** /Reʒjɔnal, o/ *adj* regional

régionalisme /Reʒjɔnalism/ *nm* [1] Pol regionalism; [2] Ling regional expression, regionalism

régir /ReʒiR/ [3] *vtr* to govern

régisseur /ReʒisœR/ ▸ p. 372 *nm* [1] (de domaine) steward, manager; [2] Théât stage manager

(Composé) **~ de plateau** Cin studio manager; TV floor manager

registre /R(ə)ʒistR/ *nm* [1] (cahier) register; **~ des absences** Scol attendance register; **~ d'état civil** register of births, marriages and deaths; **les ~s de la police** police

Les régions

■ *Les indications ci-dessous valent pour les noms des états américains, des provinces canadiennes, des comtés anglais, des départements français, des provinces françaises, des régions administratives d'autres pays comme les cantons suisses ou les provinces belges, et même pour les noms de régions géographiques qui ne sont pas des entités politiques.*

Les noms de régions

■ *En général, l'anglais n'utilise pas l'article défini devant les noms de régions.*

aimer l'Alabama	= to like Alabama
aimer la Californie	= to like California
visiter le Nouveau-Mexique	= to visit New Mexico
visiter le Texas	= to visit Texas
le Lancashire	= Lancashire
la Bourgogne	= Burgundy
la Provence	= Provence
la Savoie	= Savoy

■ *Mais l'article est utilisé pour les noms de certaines provinces ou régions françaises, certains cantons suisses et beaucoup de départements français. En cas de doute, consulter le dictionnaire.*

le Berry	= the Berry
le Limousin	= the Limousin
le Valais	= the Valais
les Alpes-Maritimes	= the Alpes-Maritimes
l'Ardèche	= the Ardèche
les Landes	= the Landes
le Loir-et-Cher	= the Loir-et-Cher
le Loiret	= the Loiret
le Rhône	= the Rhône
le Var	= the Var

À, au, aux, dans, en

■ *À, au, aux, dans et en se traduisent par* to *avec les verbes de mouvement (par ex.* aller, se rendre *etc.) et par* in *avec les autres verbes (par ex.* être, habiter *etc.).*

vivre au Texas	**aller au Texas**
= to live in Texas	= to go to Texas
vivre en Californie	**aller en Californie**
= to live in California	= to go to California
vivre dans les Rocheuses	**aller dans les Rocheuses**
= to live in the Rockies	= to go to the Rockies

De avec les noms de régions

■ *Quelques noms de régions ont donné naissance à des adjectifs, mais il y en a beaucoup moins qu'en français. En cas de doute, consulter le dictionnaire.*

les habitants de la Californie
= Californian people

les vins de Californie
= Californian wines

■ *Ces adjectifs sont tous utilisables comme des noms.*

les habitants de la Californie
= Californians *ou* Californian people

■ *Lorsqu'il n'y a pas d'adjectif, on peut, la plupart du temps, utiliser le nom de la région en position d'adjectif.*

l'accent du Texas
= a Texas accent

le beurre de Normandie
= Normandy butter

les églises du Yorkshire
= Yorkshire churches

les paysages de la Californie
the California countryside

■ *Mais en cas de doute, il est plus sûr d'utiliser la tournure avec* of, *toujours possible.*

la frontière du Texas
= the border of Texas

les habitants de l'Auvergne
= the inhabitants of the Auvergne

les rivières du Dorset
= the rivers of Dorset

les villes du Languedoc
= the towns of Languedoc

Les adjectifs dérivés

■ *Les adjectifs dérivés des régions n'ont pas toujours d'équivalent en anglais. Plusieurs cas sont possibles mais on pourra presque toujours utiliser le nom de la région placé avant le nom qualifié:*

la région dauphinoise
= the Dauphiné region

■ *Pour souligner la provenance on choisira* from + *le nom de la région:*

l'équipe dauphinoise
= the team from the Dauphiné region

■ *Pour parler de l'environnement on optera pour* of + *le nom de la région:*

l'économie vendéenne
= the economy of the Vendée

■ *Pour situer on utilisera* in + *le nom de la région:*

mon séjour vendéen
= my stay in Vendée

---

records; **2** (de roman, film, discours) style; **3** (étendue) register; **cet acteur a un ~ limité** this actor has a limited range; **4** Ling, Ordinat, Tech register

réglable /ʀeglabl/ *adj* **1** [*hauteur, pression*] adjustable; **2** (payable) payable

réglage /ʀeglaʒ/ *nm* (mise au point) (de vitesse) regulating; (de compteur, thermostat) setting; (de moteur) tuning; (de pression, tir, volume, siège) adjustment; **avec ~ automatique** [*chauffage, four*] with a timing device

règle /ʀɛgl/

A *nf* **1** (instrument) ruler, rule; **à la ~** with a ruler; **2** (consigne) rule; **~ de grammaire** grammatical rule; **~ de conduite** rule of conduct; **~s de sécurité** safety regulations; **respecter les ~s du jeu** lit, fig to play the game according to the rules; **dans** *or* **selon les ~s de l'art**

by the rule book; **il se fait une ~** *or* **il a pour ~ de payer comptant** he makes it a rule to pay cash; **3** (usage établi) rule; **en ~ générale** as a (general) rule; **il est de ~ de répondre** *or* **qu'on réponde** it is customary to reply

B **règles** *nfpl* (menstruation) period (sg)

C **en règle** *loc adj* [*demande*] formal; [*papiers, comptes*] in order; **subir un interrogatoire en ~** to be given a thorough interrogation

D **en règle** *loc adv* **pour passer la frontière, il faut être en ~** to cross the frontier, your papers must be in order; **se mettre en ~ avec le fisc** to get one's tax affairs properly sorted out

réglé, ~e /ʀegle/ *adj* **1** (à lignes) [*papier*] ruled, lined; **2** (organisé) [*vie, maison*] well-ordered; [*défilé*] well-organized; **3** (décidé) **l'affaire est ~e** the matter is settled;

4 (pubère) [*adolescente*] who has started having periods (*épith, après n*)

(Idiome) **être ~ comme du papier à musique**○ *or* **comme une horloge** to be as regular as clockwork

règlement /ʀɛɡləmɑ̃/ *nm* **1** (règles) regulations (*pl*), rules (*pl*); **2** (paiement) payment; **mode de ~** method of payment; **3** (résolution) settlement; **~ à l'amiable** amicable settlement; Jur out-of-court settlement

(Composés) **~ de comptes** settling of scores; **~ direct** direct debit; **~ interne** rules and regulations (*pl*); **~ de sécurité** safety regulations (*pl*)

réglementaire /ʀɛɡləmɑ̃tɛʀ/ *adj* **1** (requis) [*tenue, taille*] regulation (*épith*); [*format*] prescribed; [*procédure*] statutory; **2** (de réglementation) [*pouvoir*] regulatory; **les textes ~s** rules and regulations

réglementation /ʀɛɡləmɑ̃tasjɔ̃/ *nf* **1** (règles) rules (*pl*), regulations (*pl*); **2** (contrôle) regulation, control

réglementer /ʀɛɡləmɑ̃te/ [1] *vtr* to regulate

régler /ʀeɡle/ [14] *vtr* **1** (payer) to settle [*compte, dette*]; to pay [*facture, montant, créancier, fournisseur*]; to pay for [*achat, travaux, fournitures*]; **réglons nos comptes** lit let's settle up; **avoir des comptes à ~ avec qn** fig to have a score *ou* account to settle with sb; **~ son compte à qn**○ to sort sb out; **2** (résoudre) to settle [*litige, problème*]; **~ ses affaires** to sort out one's affairs; **3** (mettre au point) to settle [*détails, modalités, ordre*]; to fix, to decide on [*programme, calendrier*]; to arrange [*mise en scène, chorégraphie*]; to organize [*défilé*]; **4** (ajuster) to adjust [*hauteur, micro, chauffage*]; to regulate, to adjust [*vitesse, mécanisme*]; to tune [*moteur*]; (fixer d'avance) to set [*allumage, pression*]; **5** (adapter) **~ sa conduite sur celle de qn** to model one's behaviour^GB on sb's; **~ sa montre sur celle de qn** to set one's watch by sb's; **6** (tracer des lignes) to rule (lines on) [*papier*]

réglette /ʀeɡlɛt/ *nf* (de règle à calcul) slide; (de balance) graduated beam

réglisse /ʀeɡlis/ *nf* liquorice GB, licorice US

régnant, ~e /ʀeɲɑ̃, ɑ̃t/ *adj* [*dynastie*] reigning; [*idéologie*] prevailing

règne /ʀɛɲ/ *nm* **1** Pol (de monarque) reign; (de président) rule; **2** fig (de qualité) reign; **3** Biol kingdom

régner /ʀeɲe/ [14] *vi* **1** Pol [*souverain*] to reign, to rule; **~ sur** to reign over, to rule; **2** (imposer sa domination) [*chef, personnalité*] to be in control; [*prédominer*] [*confusion, optimisme, harmonie*] to reign; [*ambiance*] to prevail; **la confiance règne!** iron there's trust for you!; **faire ~** to give rise to [*insécurité, injustice*]; to impose [*ordre*]; **l'inquiétude règne chez les jeunes** there is a lot of anxiety among young people

regonfler /ʀ(ə)ɡɔ̃fle/ [1] *vtr* **1** (gonfler de nouveau) to reinflate [*pneu*]; to blow [sth] up again [*ballon, bouée*]; **2** (gonfler davantage) to put more air into [*pneu, ballon*]; **3** ○fig to increase [*effectifs*]; to boost [*ventes, profits*]

regorger /ʀ(ə)ɡɔʀʒe/ [13] *vi* [*magasin, maison*] to be packed (**de** with); [*ville, région*] to have an abundance (**de** of); [*discours, film*] to be crammed (**de** with)

régresser /ʀeɡʀese/ [1] *vi* **1** (diminuer) [*eaux*] to recede; [*production*] to go down (**de** by); **faire ~ le chômage** to push down unemployment; (décliner) [*culture*] to be in decline; [*personnalité*] to lose ground; **il a régressé en maths** his work in maths GB *ou* math US has deteriorated; **3** (disparaître) [*épidémie*] to die out

régression /ʀeɡʀesjɔ̃/ *nf* gén decline; (en sciences) regression; **~ marine** marine regression; **de ~** [*courbe*] regression (*épith*)

regret /ʀəɡʀɛ/ *nm* **1** (remords) regret; **sans ~s** with no regrets; **je n'ai qu'un ~, c'est de ne pas l'avoir écouté** my only regret is that I didn't listen to him; **2** (insatisfaction) regret; **il a remarqué avec ~ que** he observed with regret that; **j'apprends avec ~ que** I'm sorry to hear that; **à ~** [*consentir*] with regret; **à mon grand ~** to my great regret; **j'ai le** *or* **je suis au ~ de vous annoncer** I regret to inform you; **j'ai le** *or* **je suis au ~ de ne pouvoir vous aider** I regret that I cannot help you

regrettable /ʀəɡʀɛtabl/ *adj* regrettable

regretter /ʀəɡʀete/ [1] *vtr* **1** (déplorer) to regret [*situation, agissement*]; **~ que qn fasse** to regret *ou* to be sorry that sb does; **je regrette de ne pas pouvoir t'aider** I'm sorry I can't help you; **nous regrettons de ne pouvoir donner suite à**

votre demande we regret to inform you that your application has been unsuccessful; **je regrette de partir** I'm sorry to be leaving; **j'ai beaucoup regretté leur départ** I was very sorry that they left; **'il n'y a pas de dialogue,' regrette un employé** 'there's no dialogue^GB,' complains one employee; **2** (se repentir de) to regret [*colère, erreur, décision*]; **~ son argent** to regret having spent one's money; **~ d'avoir fait** to regret doing, to be sorry for doing; **je ne regrette rien** I have no regrets; **3** (ressentir l'absence de) to miss [*passé, personne, lieu*]; **il a été beaucoup regretté** he was sorely *ou* greatly missed; **notre regretté collègue** fml our late lamented colleague; **4** (pour s'excuser) to be sorry; **je regrette, il est absent** I'm sorry but he's not here

regroupement /ʀ(ə)ɡʀupmɑ̃/ *nm* **1** (rassemblement) (de mots, services, d'usines) grouping; (d'intérêts) pooling; (de personnes, terrains) bringing together; (de provinces, terrains) grouping together, regrouping; **2** (fusion) merger; **3** (fait de remettre ensemble) (de personnes, pièces de collection) getting [sth] back together; (de troupes) rallying; (de troupeau) rounding up

regrouper /ʀ(ə)ɡʀupe/ [1]
A *vtr* **1** (mettre ensemble) to group [sth] together [*objets, mots, services, terrains*]; to bring [sth] together [*personnes*]; to pool [*intérêts*]; (amalgamer) to merge; **l'exposition regroupe vingt tableaux de Monet** the exhibition brings together twenty pictures by Monet; **~ deux chapitres en un seul** to merge two chapters into one; **2** (remettre ensemble) to reassemble [*élèves*]; to rally [*partisans, armée*]; to regroup [*parti*]; to round up [*animaux*]
B **se regrouper** *vpr* **1** (se mettre ensemble) [*groupes, entreprises*] to group together; [*mécontents*] to gather (together); **2** (se remettre ensemble) [*personnes*] to regroup; [*coureurs*] to bunch together again

régularisation /ʀeɡylaʀizasjɔ̃/ *nf* **1** (de situation) sorting out, regularization; **2** (de cours d'eau) regulation

régulariser /ʀeɡylaʀize/ [1] *vtr* **1** (rendre légal) to sort out, to regularize [*situation*]; to put [sth] in order [*papiers*]; **2** (ajuster) to regulate [*flux, fonctionnement*]; to stabilize [*cours, marché*]

régularité /ʀeɡylaʀite/ *nf* **1** (caractère répétitif) regularity; **2** (caractère constant) (de rythme, production, progrès) steadiness; (de traits du visage) regularity; (d'écriture) neatness; (de surface) evenness; (de qualité) consistency; **avec ~** [*progresser*] steadily; [*tracer*] evenly; **3** (légalité) legality, correctness

régulateur, -trice /ʀeɡylatœʀ, tʀis/
A *adj* regulating
B *nm* (mécanisme) regulator

régulation /ʀeɡylasjɔ̃/ *nf* regulation, control

(Composé) **~ des naissances** birth control

régulier, -ière /ʀeɡylje, ɛʀ/ *adj* **1** (en fréquence) [*versements, intervalles, battement*] regular; **être en contact ~ avec qn** to be regularly in touch with sb; (habituel) [*lecteur, client*] regular; [*train, ligne, service*] regular, scheduled; **vol ~** scheduled flight; **3** (de qualité constante) [*rythme, demande, hausse, effort, production*] steady; [*qualité, progrès*] consistent; [*épaisseur, surface, ligne*] even; [*écriture*] neat; [*vie*] (well-)ordered; **être ~ dans ses habitudes** to be regular in one's habits; **4** (symétrique) [*traits, polygone*] regular; [*façade*] symmetrical; **5** (honnête) [*affaire*] above board (*jamais épith*); [*personne*] honest; **6** (conforme) [*papiers, scrutin*] in order [*jamais épith*]; [*gouvernement*] legitimate; **il est en situation régulière** his official papers are in order; **7** Ling [*pluriel, vers*] regular; **8** Mil [*troupes*] regular; **9** Relig [*clergé*] regular

régulièrement /ʀeɡyljɛʀmɑ̃/ *adv* **1** (périodiquement, habituellement) [*expédier, rencontrer, se produire*] regularly; **2** (sans à-coups) [*progresser, couler*] steadily; **3** (en formant un motif répété) [*disposer, espacer*] evenly; **4** (selon les règles) [*inscrit*] properly, duly; [*effectué*] in the proper manner; **5** (en principe, d'habitude) normally

régurgiter /ʀeɡyʀʒite/ [1] *vtr* lit, fig to regurgitate

réhabilitation /ʀeabilitasjɔ̃/ *nf* **1** (de personne) rehabilitation; **2** (d'immeuble) renovation

réhabiliter /ʀeabilite/ [1]
A *vtr* **1** to rehabilitate [*personne*]; to redeem [*passé, institution*]; **2** to renovate [*immeuble, quartier*]
B **se réhabiliter** *vpr* [*personne*] to redeem oneself

réhabituer /ʀeabitɥe/ [1]
A *vtr* to reaccustom (**qn à qch** sb to sth; **qn à faire** sb to doing)
B **se réhabituer** *vpr* to become reaccustomed (**à** to)

r

rehausser /ʀəose/ [1] *vtr* **1** (surélever) to raise; **2** (accentuer) to enhance [*prestige, beauté*]; **3** (souligner) to set off [*contour, motif*]

réhydrater /ʀeidʀate/ [1] *vtr* to rehydrate [*plante, sol*]; to moisturize [*peau*]

réimplanter /ʀeɛ̃plɑ̃te/ [1]
A *vtr* **1** to re-establish [*usine, industrie*]; **2** to reimplant [*dent, cellule*]
B **se réimplanter** *vpr* [*usine, industrie*] to re-establish itself

réimpression /ʀeɛ̃pʀesjɔ̃/ *nf* **1** (activité) reprinting; **2** (ouvrage) reprint

réimprimer /ʀeɛ̃pʀime/ [1] *vtr* to reprint

rein /ʀɛ̃/ Anat
A *nm* (organe) kidney
B **reins** *nmpl* **les** ~**s** (bas du dos) the small of the back; **mal aux** ~**s** backache; **une serviette autour des** ~**s** a towel around the waist; **avoir les** ~**s solides**○ fig to be strong; **casser les** ~**s à qn**○ fig to break sb
(Composé) ~ **artificiel** kidney machine

réincarner: **se réincarner** /ʀeɛ̃kaʀne/ [1] *vpr* to be reincarnated

reine /ʀɛn/ *nf* **1** ▸ p. 590 Pol, Zool, Jeux queen; **2** fig **la** ~ **du bal** the belle of the ball; **être la** ~ **des imbéciles**○ to be a complete idiot
(Composés) ~ **de beauté** beauty queen; ~ **mère** queen mother

reine-claude, *pl* **reines-claudes** /ʀɛnklod/ *nf* greengage

reine-des-prés /ʀɛndepʀe/ *nf inv* Bot meadowsweet

reine-marguerite, *pl* **reines-marguerites** /ʀɛnmaʀgəʀit/ *nf* China aster

reinette /ʀɛnɛt/ *nf* rennet apple

réinscrire: **se réinscrire** /ʀeɛ̃skʀiʀ/ [67] *vpr* to re-enrol

réinsérer /ʀeɛ̃seʀe/ [14]
A *vtr* **1** to reintegrate [*personne*]; **2** to reinsert [*annonce, objet*]
B **se réinsérer** *vpr* [*personne*] to become reintegrated

réinstallation /ʀeɛ̃stalasjɔ̃/ *nf* **1** (dans un lieu) move, relocation; **2** (dans une fonction) reinstatement

réinstaller /ʀeɛ̃stale/ [1]
A *vtr* **1** (réaménager) to refit [*pièce*]; (changer de lieu) ~ **les bureaux au premier étage** to move the offices back to the first GB *ou* second US floor; **2** (rétablir) (dans une ville, une région) to resettle [*personne*] (**dans** to); (dans une maison) to move [sb] back [*personne*] (**dans** to); (à un poste) ~ **qn dans ses fonctions** to reinstate someone in his/her old job; (à un mandat) ~ **qn à la présidence** to re-elect sb as president
B **se réinstaller** *vpr* (dans un lieu) **se** ~ **dans un fauteuil** to settle (oneself) back into an armchair; **se** ~ **en banlieue** [*habitant*] to move back to the suburbs; [*compagnie, commerçant*] to set up business again in the suburbs

réintégration /ʀeɛ̃tegʀasjɔ̃/ *nf* (réadmission) (au travail) reinstatement (**de** of); (dans un système, un service) reintegration (**dans** into)

réintégrer /ʀeɛ̃tegʀe/ [14] *vtr* **1** (rejoindre) to return to [*lieu, groupe, système*]; **2** (rétablir) ~ **qn (dans ses fonctions)** to reinstate sb (in his/her job); ~ **qn dans la société** to reintegrate sb into society; ~ **qn dans ses droits** to restore sb's rights

réinventer /ʀeɛ̃vɑ̃te/ [1] *vtr* to reinvent

réitération /ʀeiteʀasjɔ̃/ *nf* reiteration, repetition

réitérer /ʀeiteʀe/ [14] *vtr* to repeat; **s'il réitère, ce sera la prison** if he re-offends, he will go to jail

rejaillir /ʀ(ə)ʒajiʀ/ [3] *vi* **1** [*liquide*] to splash back (**sur** onto); (sous pression) to spurt back (**sur** onto); [*lumière*] to be reflected (**sur** on); **2** fig ~ **sur qn** [*succès*] to reflect on sb; [*scandale*] to affect sb adversely

rejaillissement /ʀ(ə)ʒajismɑ̃/ *nm* (de liquide) splashing; (de scandale) adverse effect; (de succès) reflection

rejet /ʀ(ə)ʒɛ/ *nm* **1** (refus) gén rejection; Admin, Jur (de recours, plainte, charges) dismissal; (de motion) defeat; (de requête) denial; (de demande) rejection; **2** (exclusion) rejection; **le** ~ **d'un enfant** the rejection of a child; **3** (de déchets industriels) (production) discharge **C**; (évacuation) disposal; (déchets) ~**s** waste **C**; **les** ~**s en mer (de déchets)** dumping (of waste) at sea; **les** ~**s polluants** pollutants; **4** Méd (de greffon) rejection; **5** Agric ~ **de souche** shoot

rejeter /ʀəʒ(ə)te, ʀʒəte/ [20]
A *vtr* **1** (refuser) gén to reject [*théorie, initiative, alliance, conseil, pièce défectueuse, candidature*]; to turn down [*offre*]; Admin, Jur to dismiss [*plainte, charges, résolution*]; to defeat [*motion*]; to deny [*requête*]; to reject [*demande*]; to set aside [*décision, verdict*]; ~ **une proposition de paix** to reject a peace proposal; **2** (exclure) to reject [*enfant, marginal*]; **3** (renvoyer) ~ **qch sur qn** to shift sth onto sb [*tort, responsabilité*]; **4** (restituer) [*organisme*] to reject [*greffon*]; [*machine*] to reject [*jetons*]; **5** (produire) [*usine*] to discharge [*déchets*]; to eject [*fumée, gaz*]; [*volcan*] to spew out [*lave*]; **6** (se débarrasser de) [*personne, compagnie*] to dispose of [*déchets*]; [*pêcheur*] to throw [sth] back [*poisson*]; [*mer, marée*] to wash up [*corps, débris*]; ~ **des déchets en mer** to dump waste at sea; **7** (déplacer) ~ **un mot en fin de phrase** to put a word at the end of the sentence; **8** (chasser) [*armée*] to push *ou* drive back [*ennemi*] (**hors de** out of); **9** (bouger brutalement) [*personne*] to throw [*tête, cheveux, épaules*] (**en arrière** back)
B **se rejeter** *vpr* **1** (se reculer) **se** ~ **en arrière** to throw *ou* fling oneself back; **2** (se renvoyer) **se** ~ **la responsabilité de qch** to blame each other for sth

rejeton /ʀəʒ(ə)tɔ̃, ʀʒətɔ̃/ *nm* **1** ○(enfant) hum offspring (*inv*); **2** Bot, fig offshoot

rejoindre /ʀ(ə)ʒwɛ̃dʀ/ [56]
A *vtr* **1** (à un rendez-vous) to meet up with; **2** (rattraper) to catch up with; **3** (se joindre à) to join [*personne, groupe, mouvement*]; (de nouveau) to rejoin; **le sentier rejoint la route** the path joins the road; **4** (aller à) [*personne*] to get to [*endroit*]; (de nouveau) to get back to [*endroit*]; to return to [*domicile, caserne*]; ~ **son poste** to take up one's appointment; (de nouveau) to return to one's duties; **5** (s'accorder avec) [*personnes*] to concur with sb on sth; **ça rejoint ce qu'il a dit** it ties up with what he said
B **se rejoindre** *vpr* **1** (se rencontrer) [*personnes*] to meet up; [*routes*] to meet; **2** (s'accorder) [*personnes*] to be in agreement (**sur** on); [*opinions, goûts*] to be similar; **3** (se fondre) **la musique et la poésie se rejoignent** music and poetry merge

rejouer /ʀ(ə)ʒwe/ [1] *vtr* gén to play [sth] again; to replay [*match*]; ~ **une pièce** to perform a play again

réjoui, ~**e** /ʀeʒwi/ *adj* [*air, mine*] cheerful

réjouir /ʀeʒwiʀ/ [3]
A *vtr* **1** (faire plaisir à) to delight [*personne*]; to gladden [*cœur*]; **l'idée du départ me réjouit/ne me réjouit pas** I am delighted/less than delighted at the thought of leaving; **2** (divertir) to amuse
B **se réjouir** *vpr* to rejoice; **se** ~ **de qch** to be delighted at [*nouvelle*]; to be delighted with [*succès, projet*]; to delight in [*bonheur, malheur*]; **se** ~ **de faire** to be delighted to do; **se** ~ **à l'idée** *or* **à la pensée que** to be delighted at the thought that

réjouissance /ʀeʒwisɑ̃s/
A *nf* rejoicing
B **réjouissances** *nfpl* celebrations; **quel est le programme des** ~**s**○**?** hum what delights are in store for us?

réjouissant, ~**e** /ʀeʒwisɑ̃, ɑ̃t/ *adj* **1** (qui fait plaisir) heartening, delightful; **la nouvelle n'a rien de bien** ~ it's not exactly cheerful news; **c'est** ~**!** iron that's just wonderful!; **2** (divertissant) amusing

relâche /ʀ(ə)lɑʃ/ *nf* **1** Cin, Théât closure; (sur un panneau) '~' 'no performance'; **le jeudi est jour de** ~ it's closed on Thursdays; **faire** ~ to be closed; **2** (pause) break, rest; **sans** ~ relentlessly; **3** Naut port of call; **faire** ~ (dans un port) to put in

relâché, ~**e** /ʀ(ə)lɑʃe/ *adj* [*surveillance, discipline, morale, mœurs*] lax, slack; [*style*] slipshod

relâchement /ʀ(ə)lɑʃmɑ̃/ *nm* **1** (de discipline, zèle, d'attention, effort) slackening; (de morale, mœurs) loosening, relaxation; **il y a du** ~ **dans le travail** the work is slacking off; **2** (de muscle) slackening

relâcher /ʀ(ə)lɑʃe/ [1]
A *vtr* **1** (desserrer) to loosen [*étreinte, lien, muscle, ressort*]; **2** (libérer) to release [*personne, animal*]; to let [sth] go [*poisson*]; **3** (diminuer) to relax, to let up on [*discipline, surveillance*]; ~ **son attention** to let one's attention wander; ~ **ses efforts** to let up
B *vi* Naut (dans un port) to put in; (au large) to drop anchor
C **se relâcher** *vpr* **1** [*étreinte, lien, ressort*] to loosen; [*muscle*] to relax, to loosen up; **2** [*effort, discipline*] to slacken; [*zèle*] to flag; [*élève*] to grow slack

relais /ʀ(ə)lɛ/ *nm inv* **1** (intermédiaire) intermediary; **prendre le ~ (de qn/qch)** to take over (from sb/sth); **passer le ~ à** to hand over to; **2** Sport relay; **course de ~** relay race; **3** (restaurant) restaurant; (hôtel) hotel; **4** Tech, Télécom (dispositif) relay; **~ hertzien** radio relay station

relance /ʀ(ə)lɑ̃s/ *nf* **1** (reprise) (d'industrie, idée) revival; (d'économie) reflation; (impulsion donnée) boost (**de** to); (de débat, négociations) reopening; (recrudescence) (de terrorisme) upsurge; (d'inflation) rise; **mesures de ~** reflationary measures; **entraîner la ~ de** to give a boost to [construction, commerce]; to lead to an upsurge of [terrorisme]; to lead to a rise in [inflation]; **2** (au poker) **faire une ~** to raise the stakes

relancer /ʀ(ə)lɑ̃se/ [12]
A *vtr* **1** (lancer de nouveau) to throw [sth] again [balle]; (renvoyer) to throw [sth] back (again) [balle]; **2** (faire repartir) to restart [moteur]; to relaunch [compagnie, campagne]; to revive [idée, tradition]; to reopen [débat]; to boost [investissement, production]; to reflate [économie]; **~ la mode de...** to bring back the fashion for...; **3** (poursuivre) [créancier] to chase [sb] up; [importun] to pester
B *vi* (au poker) to raise the stakes (**de** by)

relaps, ~e /ʀəlaps/ *nm,f* (hérétique) relapsed heretic; (criminel) relapsed criminal

relater /ʀ(ə)late/ [1] *vtr fml* to recount

relatif, -ive /ʀ(ə)latif, iv/ *adj* **1** relative; **tout est ~** it's all relative; **le risque est très ~** the risk is relatively slight; **un confort très ~** limited comfort; **les lois relatives au divorce** the laws relating to divorce, divorce laws. **2** Ling relative

relation /ʀ(ə)lasjɔ̃/
A *nf* **1** (rapport) connection (**avec** with; **entre** between); **faire la ~ avec qch/qn** to make the connection with sth/sb; **un projet établi en ~ avec l'industrie** a project set up in partnership with industry; **2** (personne) acquaintance; **des ~s d'affaires** business acquaintances; **3** (personne puissante) connection; **avoir des ~s** to have connections; (lien) relationship (**avec** with; **entre** between); **avoir de bonnes ~s avec qn** to have a good relationship with sb; **être/ entrer en ~ avec qn** to be/to get in touch with sb; **être en ~ d'affaires avec qn** to have business dealings with sb; **5** Math relation
B relations *nfpl* (échanges) relations (**avec** with)
(Composés) **~s extérieures** Pol foreign affairs; **~s publiques** public relations

relationnel, -elle /ʀ(ə)lasjɔnɛl/ *adj* relational

relativement /ʀ(ə)lativmɑ̃/
A *adv* relatively
B relativement à *loc prép* in relation to, relative to

relativiser /ʀ(ə)lativize/ [1] *vtr* to put [sth] into perspective

relativisme /ʀəlativism/ *nm* relativism

relativité /ʀ(ə)lativite/ *nf* relativity

relaver /ʀ(ə)lave/ [1] *vtr* to wash [sth] again

relax○ /ʀəlaks/ *adj inv* [personne] relaxed, laid-back○; [tenue] casual; [soirée] informal

relaxant, ~e /ʀəlaksɑ̃, ɑ̃t/ *adj* [bain, vacances] relaxing; [médicament] relaxant

relaxer /ʀəlakse/ [1]
A *vtr* **1** (relâcher) to discharge [prévenu]; **2** (détendre) to relax [muscle, personne]
B se relaxer *vpr* to relax

relayer /ʀ(ə)leje/ [21]
A *vtr* **1** (remplacer) to take over from, to relieve; **2** Télécom, TV to relay [émission]
B se relayer *vpr* **1** gén to take turns (**pour faire** doing); **2** Sport gén to take over from each other

relecture /ʀ(ə)lɛktyʀ/ *nf* **1** (de livre) rereading; **2** (d'épreuves) proofreading; (de cassette) replaying

relégation /ʀ(ə)legasjɔ̃/ *nf* **1** Sport relegation GB; **2** (travaux forcés) transportation; (prison) imprisonment

reléguer /ʀ(ə)lege/ [14] *vtr* **1** fig (mettre à l'écart) to relegate [personne, question, équipe] (**à, dans, en** to); to banish, to consign [objet] (**à, dans** to); **2** Hist, Jur (bannir) to sentence [sb] to transportation

relent /ʀ(ə)lɑ̃/ *nm* **1** (puanteur) lingering odour^GB; **2** fig (trace) whiff

relevable /ʀələvabl/ *adj* [dossier] adjustable

relève /ʀ(ə)lɛv/ *nf* **1** (action) **la ~ de qn** relieving sb; **la ~ de la garde** the changing of the guard; **prendre** or

---

assurer la ~ lit, fig to take over; **2** (personne) relief; (équipe) relief team

relevé, ~e /ʀəlve, ʀləve/
A *adj* **1** Culin spicy; **2** (raffiné) [propos] refined
B *nm* **1** (action de noter) taking down, noting down; **faire le ~ de** to list [erreurs]; **faire le ~ du compteur** to read the meter; **2** (compte rendu) statement; **~ bancaire** bank statement; **~ de gaz** gas bill

relèvement /ʀ(ə)lɛvmɑ̃/ *nm* (hausse) (action) increasing; (résultat) increase

relever /ʀəl(ə)ve, ʀləve/ [16]
A *vtr* **1** (remettre debout) to pick up [personne tombée, tabouret]; to put [sth] back up (again) [statue, clôture]; **2** (mettre à la verticale) to raise [dossier de siège, manette]; **3** (bouger à nouveau) **~ la tête** (redresser) to raise one's head; (pour voir) to look up; (ne pas être vaincu) to refuse to accept defeat; **4** (mettre plus haut) to turn up [col]; to lift [jupe]; to wind up [vitre de voiture]; to raise [voile, store]; (à nouveau) to raise [sth] again; **~ ses cheveux** to put one's hair up; **5** (constater) to note, to notice [erreur, signe]; to notice [fait, absence]; (faire remarquer) to point out [erreur, contradiction]; **~ que** to note that; **6** (prendre note de) to take down, to note down [date, nom, dimensions, numéro]; to take [empreinte]; to note down [citation]; **~ le compteur** to read the meter; **7** (collecter) to take in [copies d'examen]; **8** (réagir à) to react to [remarque]; **~ le défi** to take up the challenge; '**il t'a encore critiqué'—'je n'ai pas relevé**' 'he criticized you again'—'I let it go'; **9** (reconstruire) to rebuild [mur]; to put [sth] back on its feet [pays, économie]; **10** (augmenter) to raise [niveau de vie, prix, productivité]; **11** (remplacer) to relieve [équipe]; **~ la garde** to change the guard, to relieve the guard; **12** (donner plus d'attrait à) **~ qch** to spice up [plat, récit]; **13** fml (libérer) **~ qn de** to release sb from [vœux, obligation]; **~ qn de ses fonctions** to relieve sb of their duties; **14** (en tricot) **~ une maille** to pick up a stitch
B relever de *vtr ind* **1** (dépendre de) **notre service relève du ministère de la Défense** our department comes under the Ministry of Defence; **2** (être de la compétence de) **l'affaire relève de la Cour européenne de justice** the case comes within the competence of the European Court of Justice; **cela ne relève pas de mes fonctions** this doesn't come within my duties; **3** (s'apparenter à) **cela relève de la gageure** this comes close to being impossible; **4** (se rétablir) **~ de** to be recovering from [maladie]
C se relever *vpr* **1** (après une chute) to pick oneself up; (après avoir été assis, couché) to get up again; **2** (être mis à la verticale) **se ~ facilement** [dossier] to be easy to raise; **3** (être remonté) [store] to be raised; **la vitre ne se relève plus** the window won't wind GB ou roll US up; **4** (se remettre) **se ~ de** to recover from [maladie, chagrin, crise]

relief /ʀəljɛf/
A *nm* **1** Géog relief ℂ; **le ~ sous-marin** the relief of the sea bed; **un ~ accidenté** a hilly landscape; **région au ~ accidenté** mountainous region; **2** (de surface, paroi) relief ℂ; (de médaille, monnaie) raised pattern; **en ~** [globe terrestre] in relief; [lettre, motif] raised; **cinéma en ~** three-dimensional cinema; **carte en ~** relief map; **mettre qch en ~** to accentuate sth, to throw sth into relief; **3** (profondeur) depth; **4** (caractère) **personnage qui manque de ~** one-dimensional ou flat character; **donner du ~ à un texte** to enliven a text
B reliefs† *nmpl* (de repas) leftovers

relier /ʀəlje/ [2] *vtr* **1** (réunir) to link up, to link [sb/sth] together [personnes, objets] (**à** to); to join up [points] (**à** to); **2** (faire communiquer) to link [ville, personne, organisme] (**à** to); to link (up ou together) [lieux]; **3** (rassembler) to link [idées, faits] (**à** to, with); to link [sth] together [mots, propositions] (**par** with); **4** to bind [livre]; **relié cuir** leather-bound

relieur, -ieuse /ʀəljœʀ, øz/ ▸ p. 372 *nm,f* (book)binder

religieuse¹ /ʀəliʒjøz/ *nf* Culin round éclair

religieusement /ʀəliʒjøzmɑ̃/ *adv* **1** (obéir) religiously; (écouter) with rapt attention; **2** (pieusement) [se marier] in church

religieux, -ieuse² /ʀəliʒjø, øz/
A *adj* **1** (culte, édifice, vie, personne, éducation, fête) religious; (école, mariage) (chrétien) church (épith); [musique] sacred; **l'habit ~** the monk's/nun's habit; **2** fig [silence] reverent; **avec un soin ~** most conscientiously
B *nm,f* monk/nun

religion /ʀ(ə)liʒjɔ̃/ *nf* **1** (croyance, culte) religion; (piété) religion, (religious) faith; **avoir de la ~** to be religious; **sa ~ est sincère** he is a sincere believer; **2** fig **avoir la ~ du progrès** to be a great believer in progress; **se faire une ~ de la ponctualité** to make a fetish of punctuality; **3** (vie monastique) **entrer en ~** to enter the Church

reliquaire /ʀ(ə)likɛʀ/ *nm* reliquary

reliquat /ʀ(ə)lika/ *nm* **1** (de somme) remainder; (de compte) balance; (de dette) outstanding amount; **2** (de maladie) after-effects (*pl*)

relique /ʀ(ə)lik/ *nf* Relig, fig relic

relire /ʀ(ə)liʀ/ *[66] vtr* **1** (de nouveau) to reread; **2** (pour corriger) to read [sth] over [*texte*]; **3** to proofread [*épreuves*]

reliure /ʀəljyʀ/ *nf* **1** (couverture) binding; **2** (travail) book-binding

reloger /ʀ(ə)lɔʒe/ *[13] vtr* to rehouse

reluire /ʀ(ə)lɥiʀ/ *[69] vi* [*bois, cuir*] to shine; [*surface mouillée*] to glisten; [*métal*] to shine; (au soleil) to glitter; **~ de propreté** to be sparkling clean

(Idiome) **il sait passer la brosse à ~** he's a real flatterer

reluisant, **~e** /ʀ(ə)lɥizɑ̃, ɑ̃t/ *adj* lit [*meuble*] shining, shiny; [*surface mouillée*] glistening; [*métal*] shiny; fig **peu ~** [*situation*] far from brilliant

remâcher /ʀ(ə)maʃe/ *[1] vtr* **1** [*ruminant*] to chew [sth] again; **2** ⁰(ressasser) to ruminate over [*problème, passé*]; to nurse [*rancœur, dépit*]

remailler /ʀəmaje/ *[1] vtr* to mend the mesh of [*filet*]; to mend a ladder GB *ou* run US in [*bas*]

rémanent, **~e** /ʀemanɑ̃, ɑ̃t/ *adj* [*magnétisme*] residual; [*odeur*] persistent; **image ~e** after-image

remaniement /ʀ(ə)manimɑ̃/ *nm* (de plan, projet) modification; (de manuscrit) revision; (radical) redrafting; (d'équipe) reorganization

(Composé) **~ ministériel** cabinet reshuffle

remanier /ʀ(ə)manje/ *[2] vtr* to modify [*plan, projet*]; to alter [*manuscrit*]; (radicalement) to redraft; to reorganize [*équipe*]; to reshuffle [*cabinet, ministère*]

remaquiller: **se remaquiller** /ʀ(ə)makije/ *[1] vpr* to redo one's make-up

remarier: **se remarier** /ʀ(ə)maʀje/ *[2] vpr* to remarry; **se ~ avec** to remarry

remarquable /ʀ(ə)maʀkabl/ *adj* **1** (exceptionnel) [*qualité, personne, œuvre, produit*] remarkable (**par** for); **d'une beauté ~** remarkably beautiful; **2** (frappant) [*caractère, trait*] striking; **il est ~ que** it is amazing that; **3** (méritant mention) [*événement, parole, produit*] noteworthy; **je n'ai rien vu de ~** I haven't seen anything of note

remarquablement /ʀ(ə)maʀkabləmɑ̃/ *adv* remarkably

remarque /ʀ(ə)maʀk/ *nf* **1** (propos) remark; **faire des ~s** to comment; **elle m'en a fait la ~** she commented on it to me; **2** (note) comment

remarqué, **~e** /ʀ(ə)maʀke/ *adj* [*initiative*] noteworthy; [*hausse*] noticeable; **leur entrée a été très ~e** their entrance attracted a lot of attention

remarquer /ʀ(ə)maʀke/ *[1]*

A *vtr* **1** (signaler) to point out; **faire ~ à qn que** to point out to sb that; **2** (dire) liter to observe (**que** that); **3** (voir) to notice [*personne, événement, objet*]; **remarque, ce n'est pas très important** mind you, it's not very important; **remarquons que ce n'est pas la première fois** let us note that it is not the first time; **se faire ~** to draw attention to oneself; **le film mérite d'être remarqué** the film is worthy of attention; **4** (distinguer) to spot

B **se remarquer** *vpr* **1** (attirer l'attention) [*personne, vêtement, caractéristique*] to attract attention; **2** (se voir) [*qualité, défaut, sentiment*] to show

remballer /ʀɑ̃bale/ *[1] vtr* **1** (emballer de nouveau) to pack [sth] up again; **2** ⁰(rabrouer) to send [sb] packing⁰

rembarrer⁰ /ʀɑ̃baʀe/ *[1] vtr* to send [sb] packing⁰

remblai /ʀɑ̃blɛ/ *nm* **1** (talus) embankment; **route en ~** raised road; (dans un marais) causeway; **2** (action) (de fossé) filling in; (de talus) banking up; **3** (matériau) **(terre de) ~** (pour rail, route) ballast; (pour fossé) fill; (pour excavation) backfill

remblayer /ʀɑ̃bleje/ *[21] vtr* to fill in [*fossé*]; to bank up [*route*]

rembobiner /ʀɑ̃bɔbine/ *[1] vtr* to rewind

remboîter /ʀɑ̃bwate/ *[1] vtr* **1** gén **~ qch dans qch** to fit sth back into sth; **2** Méd to relocate [*os*]

rembourrer /ʀɑ̃buʀe/ *[1] vtr* to stuff [*siège, coussin*]; (en couture) to pad [*épaules*]; **bien rembourré** hum [*personne*] well-padded

remboursable /ʀɑ̃buʀsabl/ *adj* [*emprunt, dette*] repayable; [*billet, médicament, soins*] refundable

remboursement /ʀɑ̃buʀsəmɑ̃/ *nm* **1** (de dette, d'emprunt) repayment; **2** (par un commerçant) refund; **3** (d'argent déboursé) reimbursement, refund; **faire une demande de ~** to claim for reimbursement *ou* a refund

(Composés) **~ de la dette sociale**, **RDS** tax on income designed to offset the social security budget deficit

rembourser /ʀɑ̃buʀse/ *[1]*

A *vtr* **1** (rendre de l'argent prêté par un organisme) to pay off, to repay [*emprunt, dette*]; **~ une dette sur 20 ans** to pay off a debt over 20 years; **2** (en reprenant des marchandises) to give a refund to [*client*]; to refund the price of [*article*]; **~ qch à qn** to give sb a refund on sth; **se faire ~ qch** to get a refund on sth; **3** (rendre de l'argent déboursé) to reimburse [*frais professionnels, employé*]; to reimburse *ou* refund the cost of [*opération, médicament*]; **~ qn de qch** to pay sb back for sth, to reimburse sb for sth; **~ les frais de qn** to reimburse sb; **~ un ami** to pay a friend back; **~ la différence** to refund the difference

B **se rembourser** *vpr* **je me suis remboursé en gardant sa montre** I kept his/her watch by way of payment

rembrunir: **se rembrunir** /ʀɑ̃bʀyniʀ/ *[3] vpr* [*visage*] to darken, to cloud over

remède /ʀ(ə)mɛd/ *nm* **1** (médicament) medicine; **un ~ universel** a panacea; **2** (solution) cure (**à**, **contre** for), remedy (**à**, **contre** for)

(Composés) **~ de bonne femme** old wives' remedy; **~ de cheval** strong medicine; **~ miracle** miracle cure

(Idiome) **aux grands maux les grands ~s** desperate times call for desperate measures

remédier /ʀ(ə)medje/ *[2] vtr ind* **à** to remedy

remembrement /ʀ(ə)mɑ̃bʀəmɑ̃/ *nm* regrouping of lands

remembrer /ʀ(ə)mɑ̃bʀe/ *[1] vtr* to regroup [*terres*]; to reconstitute [*domaine*]

remémorer: **se remémorer** /ʀ(ə)memɔʀe/ *[1] vpr* to recall, to recollect

remerciement /ʀ(ə)mɛʀsimɑ̃/ *nm* thanks (*pl*); **je n'ai pas eu un seul ~** I didn't get a word of thanks; **tous mes ~s** many thanks; **lettre de ~** thank you letter; **adresser ses ~s à qn** to thank sb

remercier /ʀ(ə)mɛʀsje/ *[2] vtr* **1** (dire merci à) to thank (**de**, **pour** for; **d'avoir fait** for doing); **je vous remercie** thank you; **tu peux me ~!** you have me to thank for that!; **remercions le ciel d'être encore en vie** thank God we are still alive; **nous vous remercions d'adresser votre courrier à...** please address your letters to...; **2** (congédier) iron to dismiss, to let [sb] go

remettre /ʀ(ə)mɛtʀ/ *[60]*

A *vtr* **1** (replacer) **~ qch dans/sur** to put sth back in/on; **remets ce livre là où tu l'as pris!** put that book back where you found it!; **~ qch à cuire** (sur la cuisinière) to put sth back on the ring; **~ la main sur qch** to put one's hands on sth again; **~ qch en mémoire à qn** to remind sb of sth; **2** (donner) **~ à qn** to hand [sth] over to sb [*clés, rançon*]; to hand [sth] in to sb [*lettre, rapport*]; to present [sth] to sb [*récompense, trophée*]; **~ sa démission** to hand in one's resignation (**à qn** to sb); **~ sa vie entre les mains de qn** to put one's life in sb's hands; **~ qn entre les mains de la justice** to hand sb over to the law; **3** (rétablir) **~ qch droit** *or* **d'aplomb** to put sth straight again; **~ qch à plat** to lay sth down again; **~ qch debout** to stand sth back up; **4** (différer) to postpone, to put off [*visite, voyage*]; to defer [*jugement*]; **~ qch à plus tard** to put sth off until later; **5** (faire fonctionner de nouveau) to put sth on again, to put [sth] back on [*gaz, chauffage*]; to play [sth] again [*disque, chanson*]; to turn [sth] on again [*contact*]; to switch on again [*essuie-glaces, phares*]; **6** (replacer) **~ un bouton à qch** to put a new button on sth; **~ une vis** to put a new screw in; **7** (ajouter) to add some more [*sel, bois, pl âtre*]; to add another [*bouton, clou*]; **~ de l'argent dans qch** to put some more money in sth; **8** (porter de nouveau) (ce que l'on vient d'enlever) to put [sth] back on [*chaussures, manteau, bijou*]; (ce que l'on portait dans le passé) **il va falloir ~ les bottes, c'est**

l'hiver we'll have to start wearing our boots again, it's winter; ⑨ Méd to put [sth] back in place [*épaule, cheville*]; ⑩ (réconforter) [*remontant, médicament*] to make [sb] feel better; ⑪ (se souvenir de) ~ **qn/le visage de qn** to remember sb/sb's face; ⑫ (faire grâce de) ~ **une dette à qn** to let sb off a debt; ~ **une peine à qn** to give sb remission; ⑬ ○(recommencer) ~ **ça** to start again; **on s'est bien amusé, quand est-ce qu'on remet ça?** that was fun, when are we going to do it again?

B **se remettre** *vpr* ① (retourner) **se** ~ **à un endroit** to go *ou* get back to a place; **se** ~ **en selle** to get back in the saddle; ② (s'appliquer à nouveau) **se** ~ **du rouge à lèvres** to put on some more lipstick; ③ (recommencer) **se** ~ **au travail** to go back to work; **se** ~ **au tennis** to start playing tennis again; **se** ~ **à faire** to start doing again; ④ (porter sur soi à nouveau) **se** ~ **en jean** to wear jeans again; ⑤ (se rétablir) **se** ~ **de** to recover from [*maladie, accident*]; to get over [*émotion, échec*]; **remets-toi vite!** get well soon!; ⑥ (faire confiance) **s'en** ~ **à qn** to leave it to sb; **s'en** ~ **à la décision de qn** to accept sb's decision; ⑦ (reprendre une vie de couple) **se** ~ **avec qn** to get back together with sb; ⑧ (se rappeler) **se** ~ **qn** to remember sb

réminiscence /ʀeminisɑ̃s/ *nf* ① (faculté de rappel) reminiscence; ② (souvenir) recollection; ③ (rappel) **il y a dans cette œuvre des** ~**s de Bach** this work is reminiscent of Bach

remise /ʀ(ə)miz/ *nf* ① (transmission) **attendre la** ~ **des clés** to wait for the keys to be handed over; **la date limite de** ~ **des rapports** the deadline for handing in the reports; ~ **des prix** prizegiving; ~ **des médailles** medals ceremony; ~ **des coupes** the presentation of the trophies; ② Comm (rabais) discount; ③ (de dette, péchés) remission; **une** ~ **de peine** a remission; ④ Fin remittance; ⑤ (bâtiment) shed

⟨Composé⟩ ~ **de cause** Jur adjournment (of hearing)

remiser /ʀ(ə)mize/ [1] *vtr* to put [sth] away (**dans** in)

rémission /ʀemisjɔ̃/ *nf* (de maladie, péchés) remission; **sans** ~ (sans indulgence) [*punir, condamner*] mercilessly; (sans interruption) [*pleuvoir, travailler*] without stopping

remmener /ʀɑ̃mne/ [16] *vtr* to take [sb] back

remodeler /ʀəmɔdle/ [17] *vtr* to restructure [*administration*]; to reshape [*nez, ébauche*]; to replan [*quartier*]

remontage /ʀ(ə)mɔ̃taʒ/ *nm* (de moteur, pièces) reassembly; (d'un tuyau) reconnection; (de mécanisme, montre) winding up

remontant /ʀ(ə)mɔ̃tɑ̃/ *nm* pick-me-up○, tonic

remontée /ʀ(ə)mɔ̃te/ *nf* ① (action de remonter) climb up; **la** ~ **de la Saône en péniche** going up the Saône by barge; ② (après une baisse) (d'influence, de prix, taux, parti) rise (**de** of); (de sportif, d'homme politique) recovery (**de** of); (de violence, d'incidents) increase (**de** in); **la** ~ **des eaux** the rise in the water levels

⟨Composé⟩ ~ **mécanique** Sport ski lift

remonte-pente, *pl* ~**s** /ʀ(ə)mɔ̃tpɑ̃t/ *nm* ski-tow

remonter /ʀəmɔ̃te/ [1]
A *vtr* (+ *v avoir*) ① (transporter de nouveau) ~ **qn/qch** (en haut) gén to take sb/sth back up (**à** to); (à l'étage) to take sb/sth back upstairs; (d'en bas) gén to bring sb/sth back up (**de** from); (de l'étage) to bring [sb/sth] back upstairs [*personne, objet*]; ~ **les bouteilles de la cave** to bring the bottles back up from the cellar; **je peux vous** ~ **au village** I can take you back up to the village; ② (replacer en haut) to put [sth] back up [*valise, boîte*]; ③ (relever) to raise [*étagère, store, tableau*] (de by); to wind [sth] back up [*vitre de véhicule*]; to roll up [*manches, jambes de pantalon*]; to hitch up [*jupe, pantalon*]; to turn up [*col*]; to pull up [*chaussettes*]; ④ (parcourir de nouveau) [*personne*] (en allant) to go back up [*pente, rue*]; to go ou climb back up [*escalier, échelle*]; (en venant) to drive back up [*pente, rue, échelle*]; [*voiture, automobiliste*] to drive back up [*pente*]; ~ **la colline à bicyclette** to cycle back up the hill; **il m'a fait** ~ **l'escalier en courant** he made me run back up the stairs; ⑤ (parcourir en sens inverse) [*bateau*] to sail up [*fleuve*]; [*poisson*] to swim up [*rivière*]; [*personne, voiture*] to go up [*rue*]; ~ **une rivière à la nage** to swim up a river; ~ **le flot de voyageurs** to walk against the flow of passengers; ~ **une filière** *or* **piste** fig to follow a trail (**jusqu'à qn** to sb); ~ **le temps par la pensée** to go back in time in one's imagination; ⑥ (rattraper un classement) [*cycliste*] to catch up with [*peloton, concurrent*]; ⑦ (réconforter) ~ **qn** *or* **le moral**

de qn to cheer sb up, to raise sb's spirits; ⑧ (assembler de nouveau) to put [sth] back together again [*armoire, jouet*]; to put [sth] back [*roue*]; ⑨ (retendre le ressort de) to wind [sth] up [*mécanisme, réveil*]; **être remonté à bloc**○ fig [*personne*] to be full of energy; ⑩ (remettre en scène) to revive [*pièce, spectacle*]

B *vi* (+ *être*) ① (monter de nouveau) [*personne*] (en allant) gén to go back up, to go up again (**à** to); (en venant) gén to come back up, to come up again (**de** from); (à l'étage) to go/to come back upstairs; (après être redescendu) to go/to come back up again; [*avion, hélicoptère*] to climb again; [*mer*] to come in again; [*prix, température, baromètre*] to rise again, to go up again; **reste ici, je remonte au grenier** stay here, I'm going back up to the attic; **peux-tu** ~ **chercher mon sac?** can you go back upstairs and get my bag?; **tu es remonté à pied?** did you walk back up?; ~ **à l'échelle** to climb back up the ladder; ~ **sur** [*personne*] to step back onto [*trottoir*]; to climb back onto [*mur*]; ~ **à la surface** lit [*plongeur*] to surface; [*huile, objet*] to rise to the surface; fig [*scandale*] to resurface; [*souvenirs*] to surface again; ~ **à cheval** to get back on a horse; ~ **à bord d'un avion** to board a plane again; ~ **dans les sondages** [*politicien, parti*] to move up in the opinion polls; ~ **de la quinzième à la troisième place** [*sportif, équipe*] to move up from fifteenth to third position; ~ **à Paris** (retourner) to go back up to Paris; **la criminalité remonte** crime is rising again; **faire** ~ **les cours** to put prices up again; **faire** ~ **la température** to raise the temperature; ② (pour retrouver l'origine) ~ **dans le temps** to go back in time; ~ **à** [*historien*] to go back to [*époque, date*]; [*événement, œuvre, tradition*] to date back to [*époque, date, personnage historique*]; [*habitude*] to be carried over from [*enfance, période*]; [*enquêteur, police*] to follow the trail back to [*personne, chef de gang*]; ~ **20 ans en arrière** [*historien*] to go back 20 years; **faire** ~ to trace (back) [*origines, ancêtres*] (**à** to); ③ (se retrousser) [*pull, jupe*] to ride up; ④ (se faire sentir) **les odeurs d'égout remontent dans la maison** the smell from the drains reaches our house; ⑤ Naut ~ **au** *or* **dans le vent** to sail into the wind

C **se remonter** *vpr* ① (se réconforter) **se** ~ **le moral** (seul) to cheer oneself up; (à plusieurs) to cheer each other up; ② (s'équiper de nouveau) **se** ~ **en meubles/draps** to get some new furniture/sheets

remontoir /ʀ(ə)mɔ̃twaʀ/ *nm* winder

remontrance /ʀəmɔ̃tʀɑ̃s/ *nf* (reproche) reprimand

remontrer /ʀəmɔ̃tʀe/ [1]
A *vtr* to show [sth] again
B *vi* **en** ~ **à qn** (lui donner une leçon) to teach sb a thing or two; (montrer sa supériorité) to prove one's superiority to sb

remords /ʀəmɔʀ/ *nm inv* remorse ₡; **plein de** ~ filled with remorse, remorseful; **avoir du** *or* **des** ~ to feel remorse

remorquage /ʀəmɔʀkaʒ/ *nm* towing

remorque /ʀəmɔʀk/ *nf* (vehicule) trailer; (câble) towrope; **prendre une voiture en** ~ to tow a car; **être à la** ~ fig to trail behind

remorquer /ʀəmɔʀke/ [1] *vtr* ① lit to tow [*véhicule*]; **se faire** ~ to be towed; ② fig to drag [sb] along

remorqueur /ʀəmɔʀkœʀ/ *nm* tug

rémoulade /ʀemulad/ *nf* mayonnaise-type dressing

rémouleur /ʀemulœʀ/ ▸ p. 372 *nm* grinder

remous /ʀ(ə)mu/ *nm inv* ① (dans l'eau, l'air) eddy; ② (sillage) backwash (*tjrs sg*); (contre la rive) wash (*tjrs sg*); ③ (agitation) (de sentiments, d'idées) turmoil ₡; (dans la foule) stir, movement; (dans l'opinion, l'auditoire) stir ₡

rempailler /ʀɑ̃paje/ [1] *vtr* to reseat [*chaise*]

rempailleur, -euse /ʀɑ̃pajœʀ, øz/ ▸ p. 372 *nm,f* repairer of rush seats

rempart /ʀɑ̃paʀ/ *nm* ① (mur) rampart; (de château-fort) battlements (*pl*); **les** ~**s de la ville** the city walls, the ramparts; ② (défense) defence^{GB} (**contre** against); **faire un** ~ **de son corps à qn** to shield sb with one's body

rempiler /ʀɑ̃pile/ [1]
A *vtr* to restack [*boîtes*]
B ○*vi* soldiers' slang to re-enlist

remplaçable /ʀɑ̃plasabl/ *adj* replaceable

remplaçant, ~e /ʀɑ̃plasɑ̃, ɑ̃t/ *nm,f* ① (provisoire) gén substitute, replacement; (professeur, instituteur) supply GB *ou* substitute US teacher; (acteur) stand-in; Sport substitute, reserve; ② (définitif) successor

r

remplacement /Rãplasmã/ *nm* [1] (de personne) replacement; **nommé en ~ de M. Robin** appointed as a replacement for Mr Robin; **assurer le ~ d'un collègue** to stand in for *ou* cover for a colleague; **faire des ~s** [*enseignant*] to do supply GB *ou* substitute US teaching; [*intérimaire*] to do temporary work, to do temping jobs○; [2] (de chose) replacement; **le ~ d'une pièce usée** the replacement of a worn part; **une télévision neuve en ~ de la vieille** a new television to replace the old one; **produit de ~** substitute

remplacer /Rãplase/ [12] *vtr* [1] (momentanément) to stand in for, to cover for [*collègue, docteur, acteur*]; **elle s'est fait ~ par un collègue** she got a colleague to stand in for her; [2] (succéder à) to replace [*personne, méthode, tradition, appareil*]; **M. Bon remplace Mme Roux à la direction** Mr Bon is replacing *ou* succeeds Mrs Roux as director; [3] (changer) to replace [*pièce, matériel, personne*] (**par** with); **~ un carreau** to replace a windowpane; [4] (tenir lieu de) to replace; **le pronom remplace le nom** the pronoun takes the place of *ou* replaces the noun; **on peut ~ le vinaigre par du jus de citron** you can use lemon juice as a substitute for vinegar

remplir /Rãplir/ [3]

A *vtr* [1] (dans l'espace) to fill (up) [*récipient*] (**de** with); (de nouveau) to refill [*récipient*]; to fill in *ou* out [*formulaire*]; **~ qch à moitié** to half fill sth; **un verre à moitié rempli** a half-filled glass; **~ qch aux deux tiers** to fill sth two thirds full; **sa vie est remplie de petites contrariétés** fig his/her life is full of small vexations; **~ qn de joie** fig to fill sb with joy; **une journée bien remplie** a busy day; **avoir le portefeuille bien rempli**○ to be well-heeled○, to be rich; [2] (s'acquitter de) [*personne*] to carry out, to perform [*rôle, mission*]; to fulfil^{GB} [*devoir, obligations, objectifs*]; to fulfil^{GB} [*engagements*]; [*objet, dispositif*] to fulfil^{GB} [*rôle, fonction*]; **~ les conditions** to fulfil^{GB} *ou* meet the conditions

B **se remplir** *vpr* to fill (up) (**de** with)

remplissage /Rãplisaʒ/ *nm* [1] (de récipient) filling; [2] pej (dans un texte, film) padding

remplumer: se remplumer /Rãplyme/ [1] *vpr* [1] ○[*personne*] (en argent) to get back on one's feet; (en poids) to put some weight back on; [2] [*oiseau*] to grow new feathers

rempocher /Rãpɔʃe/ [1] *vtr* to put [sth] back in one's pocket

remporter /Rãpɔrte/ [1] *vtr* [1] (gagner) to win [*épreuve, siège, titre, victoire*]; **la pièce a remporté un vif succès** the play was a great success; [2] (reprendre) to take [sth] away again

rempoter /Rãpɔte/ [1] *vtr* to repot

remuant, ~e /Rãmɥã, ãt/ *adj* [1] (agité) [*spectateur, adolescent, partisan*] rowdy; [2] (actif) [*enfant*] boisterous; [*adulte*] energetic

remue-ménage /Rãmymenaʒ/ *nm inv* [1] (désordre et confusion) commotion ¢; **faire du ~** to create a commotion; [2] (agitation) bustle ¢; [3] (changements) upheaval

remuer /Rãmɥe/ [1]

A *vtr* [1] (mouvoir) to move [*doigt, main, tête*]; to wiggle [*orteil, oreille, hanches*]; **le chien remuait la queue** the dog was wagging its tail; [2] (secouer) to shake [*objet*]; [3] (déplacer) to move [*objet*]; **il a tout remué dans le tiroir pour retrouver la clé** he turned the whole drawer upside down to find the key; [4] Culin to stir [*soupe, café, pâtes*]; to toss [*salade*]; [5] (brasser) lit to turn over [*terre*]; fig to poke [*cendres*]; fig to mull over [*pensées, chimères*]; to handle [*argent*]; [6] (évoquer) to rake up [*passé, vieille histoire*]; to stir up [*souvenirs*]; [7] (bouleverser) to upset [*personne*]; (émouvoir) to move

B *vi* (bouger) [*personne*] to move; [*enfant*] to fidget; [*feuilles*] to flutter; [*bateau*] to bob up and down

C **se remuer**○ *vpr* [1] (sortir de son apathie) to get a move on○; [2] (faire des efforts) **se ~ pour obtenir** to make an effort to get

rémunérateur, -trice /RemyneRatœR, tRis/ *adj* lucrative

rémunération /RemyneRasjõ/ *nf* (de travail) pay (**de** for); (de service) payment (**de** for)

rémunérer /RemyneRe/ [14] *vtr* to pay [*personne*]; to pay for [*service, travail*]

renâcler /R(ə)nakle/ [1] *vi* [1] [*personne*] to show reluctance; **~ à qch/à faire** to balk at sth/at doing; **sans ~** without complaining; [2] [*animal*] to snort

renaissance /R(ə)nɛsãs/ *nf* Relig rebirth; fig revival

Renaissance /R(ə)nɛsãs/ *nf* Hist Renaissance

renaître /R(ə)nɛtR/ [74] *vi* [1] [*personne, nature*] to come back to life; **faire ~ une région** to revive a region; **~ à la vie** to rediscover life; **~ de ses cendres** to rise from the ashes; [2] (réapparaître) [*désir, espoir*] to return; **faire ~ l'amour** to bring new love

rénal, ~e, *mpl* **-aux** /Renal, o/ *adj* [*artère, veine*] renal; [*infection*] kidney (*épith*)

renard /R(ə)naR/ *nm* [1] (animal, fourrure) fox; [2] (personne) cunning devil

renarde /R(ə)naRd/ *nf* vixen

renardeau, *pl* **~x** /R(ə)naRdo/ *nm* fox cub

renchérir /RãʃeRiR/ [3] *vi* [1] (ajouter) to add; **~ sur ce que dit qn** to add something to what sb says; [2] (aller plus loin) to go one step further; **il a renchéri en envoyant l'armée** he went one step further and sent in the army; [3] (dans une vente) to raise the bidding; **~ sur le prix de qch** to make a higher bid for sth

renchérissement /RãʃeRismã/ *nm* **le ~ des loyers** the increase in rents

rencontre /RãkõtR/ *nf* [1] (réunion) meeting (**avec** with; **entre** between); **aller/venir à la rencontre de qn** to go/to come to meet sb; **aller à la ~ de problèmes** to be heading for trouble; [2] (contact) meeting; (non prévu) encounter; **~ inattendue** unexpected encounter; **faire la ~ de qn** to meet sb; **au hasard des ~s** through chance meetings *ou* encounters; ▸ **mauvais**; [3] Sport (match) match GB, game US; (réunion) meeting GB, meet US; **~ d'athlétisme** athletics meeting GB, track meet US; [4] Mil encounter

(Composé) **~ au sommet** Pol summit meeting

rencontrer /Rãkõtre/ [1]

A *vtr* [1] (voir) to meet [*personne*]; **~ qn sur son chemin** to come across sb; [2] (faire connaissance avec) to meet [*personne*]; [3] (être en présence de) to meet with [*réaction, opposition*]; to encounter [*obstacle, problème*]; **ma main a rencontré la sienne** my hand met his/hers; [4] (trouver) [*personne*] to come across [*objet, personne, mot*]; [5] Sport to meet, to play [*joueur, équipe*]; to meet GB, to fight [*boxeur*]

B **se rencontrer** *vpr* [1] (se voir, faire connaissance) to meet; **leurs yeux se rencontrèrent** their eyes met; [2] (se trouver) [*qualité, objet, personne*] to be found; [3] Sport [*joueurs, équipes*] to meet, to play each other

rendement /Rãdmã/ *nm* [1] (production) (de terre, d'investissement) yield; (de machine, travailleur) output ¢; **tourner à plein ~** to run at full capacity; [2] (productivité) (d'usine) productivity ¢; (de machine, travailleur) efficiency ¢; [3] (résultat) (de sportif, d'élève) performance

rendez-vous /Rãdevu/ *nm inv* [1] (chez un médecin, coiffeur, avocat etc) appointment (**avec** with; **chez** at); **prendre ~ avec un spécialiste** to make an appointment with a specialist; [2] (avec des amis) **j'ai ~ avec un ami** I'm meeting a friend; **je leur ai donné ~ à minuit** I've arranged to meet them at midnight; **le soleil n'était pas au ~** the sun didn't shine; [3] (réunion professionnelle) meeting; [4] (rassemblement) gathering; (lieu) meeting place

rendormir: se rendormir /RãdɔRmiR/ [30] *vpr* to go back to sleep

rendre /RãdR/ [6]

A *vtr* [1] (retourner) (pour restituer) to give back, to return (**à** to); (pour refuser) to return, to give back [*cadeau*] (**à** to); to return [*article défectueux*] (**à** to); (pour s'acquitter de) to repay, to pay back [*somme*] (**à** to); to return [*salut, invitation*] (**à** to); **elle m'a rendu mon livre** she gave me back my book; **prête-moi 20 euros, je te les rendrai demain** lend me 20 euros, I'll pay you back tomorrow; **elle ne m'a pas rendu la monnaie** she didn't give me my change; **~ la pareille à qn** to pay sb back; [2] (redonner) **~ la santé/vue à qn** to restore sb's health/sight; **~ le sourire à qn** to put the smile back on sb's face; **~ son indépendance à un pays** to restore a country's independence; [3] (faire devenir) **~ qn heureux** to make sb happy; **~ qch possible** to make sth possible; **~ qn fou** to drive sb mad; [4] (remettre) [*élève, étudiant*] to hand in, to give in [*copie, devoir*] (**à** to); [5] (produire) [*terre, champ*] to yield [*récolte, quantité*]; [6] (exprimer, traduire) [*auteur, mots*] to convey [*pensée, atmosphère*]; to convey, to render [*nuance*]; [*traduction, tableau*] to convey [*atmosphère, style*]; **~ l'expression d'un visage** [*peintre, photographe*] to capture the expression on a face; **un poème chinois merveilleusement rendu en anglais** a Chinese poem beautifully translated *ou* rendered into English; **ça ne rendra rien en couleurs** it won't come out in colour^{GB};

7 ○(vomir) to bring up [*aliment, bile*]; **8** (prononcer) to pronounce [*jugement, sentence, arrêt*]; to return [*verdict*]; to pronounce [*oracle*]; **9** (émettre) [*instrument, objet creux*] to give off [*son*]; **10** (exsuder) **les tomates rendent de l'eau (à la cuisson)** tomatoes give out water during cooking; **11** Sport [*concurrent*] ~ **du poids** to have a weight handicap (**à** compared with); ~ **10 mètres à qn** to give sb a 10-metre^{GB} handicap

B vi **1** (produire) ~ **(bien)** [*terre*] to be productive; [*plante*] to produce a good crop; [*activité, commerce*] to be profitable; **2** ○(vomir) to be sick, to throw up○

C se rendre vpr **1** (aller) to go; **se** ~ **à Rome/en Chine** to go to Rome/to China; **se** ~ **chez des amis** to go to see friends; **2** (devenir) ~ **malade** to make oneself ill; **se** ~ **ridicule** to make a fool of oneself; **3** (capituler) [*criminel*] to give oneself up (**à** to); [*armée, ville*] to surrender (**à** to); **4** (se soumettre) ~ **à qch** to bow to [*argument, avis*]; to yield to [*prières, supplique*]; to answer [*appel*]

⸨Idiome⸩ ~ **l'âme** or **l'esprit** to pass away

rendu /R̃ɑdy/ *nm* **1** Art depiction; **2** Comm (objet rapporté) return, returned article

rêne /REn/ *nf* rein

renégat, ~**e** /Rənega, at/ *nm,f* Relig, fig renegade

renfermé, ~**e** /R̃afERme/
A *pp* ▸ **renfermer**
B *pp adj* [*personne*] withdrawn; [*sentiment*] hidden
C *nm* **ça sent le** ~ it smells musty

renfermer /R̃afERme/ [1]
A *vtr* (receler) to contain
B se renfermer *vpr* [*personne*] to become withdrawn

renflé, ~**e** /R̃afle/ *adj* [*vase*] rounded; [*dome*] bulbous; [*estomac*] bulging

renflement /R̃afləm̃a/ *nm* bulge

renflouer /R̃aflue/ [1] *vtr* **1** to raise [*navire*]; **2** to bail out [*personne, entreprise*]

renfoncement /R̃af̃osm̃a/ *nm* (de mur) recess; ~ **de porte** doorway

renforcer /R̃afORse/ [12]
A *vtr* **1** (rendre plus solide) to reinforce [*construction, vêtement*]; to strengthen [*muscles, tissus*]; **2** (accroître le nombre de) to strengthen [*équipe, effectifs*]; **3** (intensifier) to strengthen, to reinforce [*pouvoir, sanctions*]; to reinforce [*contrôle, déséquilibre*]; to step up [*surveillance*]
B se renforcer *vpr* [*pouvoir*] to increase; [*contrôle*] to become tighter; [*équipe, effectifs*] to grow; [*pays, secteur*] to grow stronger

renfort /R̃afOR/ *nm* **1** Mil reinforcement; **en** ~ as reinforcements; **2** gén support ₵; **en** ~ in support; **à grand** ~ **de qch** with a lot of sth; **annoncé à grand** ~ **de publicité** much heralded; **3** Sport substitute; **4** Tech support; **une pièce de** ~ a support piece

renfrogné, ~**e** /R̃afR̃oɲe/ *adj* [*visage, air, personne*] sullen

renfrogner: se renfrogner /R̃afR̃oɲe/ [1] *vpr* to become sullen

rengager /R̃ag̃aʒe/ [13]
A *vtr* **1** (embaucher de nouveau) to take [sb] on again [*employé*]; Mil to re-enlist [*soldat*]; **2** (reprendre) to renew [*hostilités*]; to reopen [*discussion*]
B se rengager *vpr* Mil to re-enlist, to sign up again

rengaine /R̃ag̃En/ *nf* (chanson) corny old song○; (air) corny old tune○; fig **c'est toujours la même** ~ fig it's the same old thing every time

rengainer /R̃ag̃Ene/ [1] *vtr* to sheathe [*épée, poignard*]; to put [sth] back in its holster [*pistolet*]

rengorger: se rengorger /R̃agORʒe/ [13] *vpr* [*oiseau*] to puff out its breast; [*personne*] to swell with conceit (**de qch** at sth)

reniement /R(ə)nim̃a/ *nm* **1** gén disavowal; **2** Relig denial

renier /Rəɲe/ [2]
A *vtr* to renounce [*religion, opinion*]; to disown [*enfant, œuvre*]; to disclaim [*obligation*]
B se renier *vpr* (désavouer ses opinions) to go back on one's opinions; (désavouer le passé) to go back on everything one has stood for

reniflement /R(ə)niflm̃a/ *nm* **1** (action) sniffing; **2** (bruit) sniff

renifler /R(ə)nifle/ [1]
A *vtr* [*personne, animal*] to sniff [*odeur, piste*]; [*cochon*] to sniff for [*truffes*]
B *vi* to sniff

renne /REn/ *nm* reindeer

renom /Rəño/ *nm* **1** (bonne réputation) fame, renown; **avoir du** ~ to be famous *ou* renowned; **de** *ou* **en** ~ famous (*épith*); **2** (réputation) reputation

renommé, ~**e**[1] /Rəñome/ *adj* famous, renowned

renommée[2] /Rəñome/ *nf* **1** (réputation) reputation; **2** (célébrité) fame; **faire la** ~ **de qn** to make sb famous

renoncement /R(ə)ñosm̃a/ *nm* renunciation

renoncer /R(ə)ñose/ [12] *vtr ind* **1** (après expérience) ~ **à** to give up [*poste, activité, lutte*]; **je renonce à chercher une maison** I'm giving up looking for a house; **elle a renoncé à lui** she has finished with him; **2** (avant de commencer) ~ **à** to abandon [*projet, objectif, principes*]; ~ **à faire** to abandon the idea of doing; **3** (abandonner) ~ **à** to relinquish [*pouvoir*]; to waive [*privilèges*]; to give up [*liberté*]; to renounce [*honneurs, couronne*]

renonciation /R(ə)ñosjasj̃o/ *nf* **1** Jur, gén (à une fonction) giving up; **2** liter renunciation

renouer /Rənwe/ [1]
A *vtr* **1** lit to retie [*lacets, ficelle*]; **2** fig to pick up the thread of [*conversation*]
B *vtr ind* ~ **avec** (après une dispute) to make up with [*personne*]; (après avoir perdu contact) to get back in touch with [*personne*]; to revive [*tradition*]; to re-establish [*pratique*]; to go back to [*passé*]

renouveau, *pl* ~**x** /Rənuvo/ *nm* **1** (renaissance) revival; **2** (regain) **un** ~ **d'intérêt** a renewal of interest

renouvelable /Rənuvlabl/ *adj* renewable

renouvelé, ~**e** /Rənuvle/
A *pp* ▸ **renouveler**
B *pp adj* **1** (neuf) [*joie, vitalité, ardeur, énergie*] renewed; **2** (changé) [*équipe, édition*] remodelled^{GB}; **3** (répété) **controverse maintes fois** ~**e** recurring controversy

renouveler /Rənuvle/ [19]
A *vtr* **1** (proroger) to renew [*passeport, abonnement*]; **2** (refaire) to renew, to repeat [*suggestion, expérience, promesse*]; **3** (remplacer) to replace [*matériel, équipe*]; to change [*eau*]; to renew [*stocks*]; ~ **l'air dans une chambre** to air a room; **4** (redonner) to renew [*soutien, prêt*]; **5** (rendre nouveau) to revitalize [*genre, style*]
B se renouveler *vpr* **1** (être remplacé) **une pièce où l'air ne se renouvelle pas** a room which isn't aired; **2** [*auteur, artiste*] to try out new ideas; **3** (se reproduire) [*exploit, expérience*] to happen again

renouvellement /RənuvElm̃a/ *nm* **1** (de passeport, d'abonnement) renewal; **2** (de matériel, d'équipe) replacement; **3** (de cellules, générations) renewal; **4** (de style, doctrine) revitalization

rénovateur, -trice /Rénovat̃œR, tRis/
A *adj* [*théorie, attitude*] reforming
B *nm,f* gén (de coutume) modernizer; (de science, religion) reformer

rénovation /Rénovasj̃o/ *nf* **1** Constr (de quartier) renovation; (de maison, d'immeuble) (pour gros travaux) renovation; (pour simples travaux) refurbishment; **2** fig (de politique) reform; (de secteur économique) revitalization

rénover /Rénove/ [1] *vtr* **1** Constr (avec de gros travaux) to renovate [*quartier, maison*]; (avec des travaux simples) to refurbish [*maison*]; to restore [*meuble*]; **2** (remettre à jour) to reform [*institution, politique*]; to revamp [*projet, procédure*]; to overhaul [*système*]

renseignement /R̃asEɲm̃a/ *nm*
A **1** (information) information ₵, piece of information; **des** ~**s** information; **prendre des** ~**s sur qch/qn** to find out about sth/sb; **demander des** ~**s à qn** to ask sb for information; **est-ce que je peux vous demander un** ~? can I ask you something?; **il est allé aux** ~**s** he went to find out (about it); ~**s pris, il semblerait que** upon investigation, it would appear that; **'pour tous** ~**s, s'adresser à...'** 'all inquiries to...'; **2** Mil intelligence
B renseignements *nmpl* (service, bureaux) information ₵; Télécom directory enquiries GB, information US, directory assistance US

renseigner /R̃asEɲe/ [1]
A *vtr* ~ **qn** to give information to sb (**sur** about); **être bien**

renseigné to be well-informed; **demandez au rayon accessoires, ils vous renseigneront** ask at the accessories department, they'll be able to help you

B se renseigner *vpr* (demander des informations) to find out, to enquire (**sur** about; **auprès de** from); (faire des recherches) to make enquiries (**sur** about; **auprès de** from); **se ~ sur les activités de qn** to make enquiries about *ou* to look into sb's activities

rentabilisation /Rɑ̃tabilizasjɔ̃/ *nf* **la ~ de l'entreprise est notre premier objectif** our primary aim is to make the company profitable

rentabiliser /Rɑ̃tabilize/ [1] *vtr* to secure a return on [*investissement*]; to make a profit on [*produit*]; to make [sth] profitable [*affaire*]; **l'isolation de ma maison sera vite rentabilisée** my home insulation will soon pay for itself

rentabilité /Rɑ̃tabilite/ *nf* **1** (caractère rentable) profitability; **2** (profit) return

rentable /Rɑ̃tabl/ *adj* profitable

rente /Rɑ̃t/ *nf* **1** (revenu personnel) private income; **2** (contrat financier) annuity; **~ viagère** life annuity; **~ mensuelle** monthly allowance; **3** Fin (emprunt d'État) government stock

rentier, -ière /Rɑ̃tje, ɛR/ *nm,f* person of independent means

rentré, ~e¹ /Rɑ̃tre/ *adj* **1** (retenu) [*colère*] suppressed; **2** (en retrait) [*joues, yeux*] sunken; [*ventre, fesses*] held in (*après n*)

rentrée² /Rɑ̃tre/ *nf* **1** (reprise d'activité) (general) return to work (*after the slack period of the summer break, in France*); (début d'année scolaire) start of the (new) school year; (début de trimestre) beginning of term; **des grèves sont prévues pour la ~** strikes are expected after the summer break; **mon livre sera publié à la ~** my book will be published in the autumn GB *ou* fall US; **2** (retour) return (to work); **3** (réapparition publique) comeback; **~ politique** political comeback; **4** (d'argent) (recette) receipts (*pl*); (revenu) **~ (d' argent)** income *₵*; (dans une caisse) takings (*pl*); **les ~s** receipts; **~s fiscales** (annuelles) tax revenue *₵*; (ponctuelles) tax revenues; **5** Astronaut, Mil (de vaisseau, capsule, missile) re-entry

(Composés) **~ des classes** start of the school year; **~ parlementaire** reassembly of Parliament; **~ scolaire = ~ des classes**; **~ universitaire** start of the academic year

> ⓘ **Rentrée** The week at the beginning of September when the new school year starts and around which much of French administrative life revolves. The preceding weeks see intensive advertising of associated merchandise, from books and stationery to clothes and sports equipment. Many stores and supermarkets have a range of special purchases at bargain prices. The concept of the *rentrée* also extends to literary, political and other activities which are resumed after the period of the *grandes vacances* in July and August when businesses can close for up to a month. *La rentrée littéraire* marks the start of the literary year and *la rentrée parlementaire* signals the reassembly of Parliament after the recess.

rentrer /Rɑ̃tre/ [1]

A *vtr* **1** (mettre à l'abri) gén to put [sth] in [*objet, animal*]; (en venant) to bring [sth] in [*objet, animal*]; (en allant) to take [sth] in [*objet, animal*]; **2** (rétracter) [*pilote*] to raise [*train d'atterrissage*]; [*félin*] to draw in [*griffes*]; **rentrez le ventre!** hold your stomach in!; **3** (faire pénétrer) to put [*clé*] (**dans** in, into); to tuck [*pan de chemise*] (**dans** into)

B *vi* (+ *v être*) **1** (pénétrer) (dans une pièce, une cabine téléphonique) to go in; (dans une voiture, un ascenseur) to get in; (tenir, s'adapter) to fit; **~ dans un arbre**○ to hit a tree; **2** (entrer de nouveau) (en allant) to go back in; (en venant) to come back in; **~ dans** (en allant) to go back into; (en venant) to come back into; **le satellite va ~ dans l'atmosphère** the satellite is about to re-enter the atmosphere; **3** (revenir) gén to get back, to come back, to return (**de** from); (chez soi) to come home (**de** from); **il ne va pas tarder à ~ du travail** he'll be back from work soon; **4** (repartir) gén to get back, to go back, to return; (chez soi) to go home (**de** from); **il fait trop froid, je rentre** (à l'intérieur) it's too cold, I'm going (back) inside; (de plus loin) it's too cold, I'm going (back) home; **se dépêcher de ~** (chez soi) to hurry home; **5** (récupérer) **~ dans son argent** to recoup one's money; **6** (être encaissé) [*argent, loyer, créance*] to come in; **faire ~ l'argent** to bring money

in; **7** (pouvoir trouver place) **mes chaussures ne rentrent pas dans ma valise** my shoes won't fit into my suitcase; **faire ~ qch dans la tête de qn** to get sth into sb's head; **~ dans la serrure** to fit the lock; **8** ○(être compris) **l'algèbre ça ne rentre pas!** I just can't understand *ou* get my head round○ algebra!

(Idiome) **je vais leur ~ dedans**❶ (physiquement, oralement) I'm going to lay into them○; **il m'est rentré dedans**❶ (en voiture) (légèrement) he bumped *ou* ran into me; (violemment) he crashed into me

renversant, ~e /Rɑ̃vɛRsɑ̃, ɑ̃t/ *adj* astounding, astonishing

renverse /Rɑ̃vɛRs/ *nf* **tomber à la ~** to fall flat on one's back; **il y a de quoi tomber à la ~!** it's absolutely astounding!

renversement /Rɑ̃vɛRsəmɑ̃/ *nm* **1** (inversion) (de situation, d'ordre) (d'image) inversion, reversal; **2** (de gouvernement, dirigeant) (par la force) overthrow; (par un vote) removal from office

renverser /Rɑ̃vɛRse/ [1]

A *vtr* **1** (faire tomber) to knock over [*personne, meuble, bouteille*]; [*automobiliste, véhicule*] to knock down [*piéton, cycliste*]; [*manifestants*] to topple [*statue*]; to overturn [*voiture*]; [*vague*] to overturn [*bateau*]; **2** (répandre) to spill [*liquide, contenu*]; **3** (mettre à l'envers) to turn [sth] upside down [*sablier, flacon*]; **4** (pencher) **~ la tête en arrière** to tip *ou* tilt one's head back; **~ le buste en arrière** to lean back; **5** (inverser) to reverse [*ordre, situation, rôles*]; Phys to invert, to reverse [*image*]; Électrotech to reverse [*courant*]; **6** Pol (mettre fin à) (par la force) to overthrow, to topple [*régime, dirigeant*]; (par un vote) to vote [sb/sth] out of office [*dirigeant, gouvernement*]; **7** ○(stupéfier) [*événement, nouvelle*] to stagger, to astound [*personne*]

B se renverser *vpr* [*véhicule*] to overturn; [*bateau*] to capsize; [*objet, bouteille*] to fall over; [*liquide, contenu*] to spill

renvoi /Rɑ̃vwa/ *nm* **1** (d'élève, immigré, de joueur) expulsion (**de** from); (d'employé, ambassadeur) dismissal (**de** from); **~ d'un élève pour trois jours** suspension of a pupil from school for three days; **~ des immigrés dans leur pays** repatriation of immigrants to their own country; **2** (retour à l'expéditeur) return; **~ d'un colis** return of a parcel; **3** Sport (au tennis, volley-ball) return; (au football, rugby) clearance; **4** (report) gén postponement; Jur, Pol (envoi) referral (**devant** to); (ajournement) adjournment (**à** until); **~ de l'affaire devant la Cour d'appel** referral of the case to the court of appeal; **~ à huitaine** adjournment for a week; **5** (référence) (dans un dictionnaire, livre, fichier) cross-reference (**à** to); **6** (éructation) belch, burp○; **avoir un ~** gén to burp○; [*bébé*] to burp○, to bring up wind

renvoyer /Rɑ̃vwaje/ [24] *vtr* **1** (relancer) to throw [sth] back [*projectile, ballon*]; (répercuter) to reflect [*lumière, chaleur*]; to echo [*son*]; **2** (réexpédier) to return [*courrier, marchandises*]; **3** (faire retourner) to send [sb] back [*personne*]; **~ qn dans son pays** to send sb back to his/her own country; **~ qn chez lui** *or* **dans ses foyers** to send sb home; **~ un projet de loi en commission** to send a bill to committee, to commit a bill US; **4** (expulser) to expel [*élève, immigré, joueur*] (**de** from); to dismiss [*employé, ambassadeur*] (**de** from); **5** (ajourner) to postpone [*débat, décision*] (**à** until); to adjourn [*affaire*] (**à** until); **6** (faire se reporter) **~ à** to refer to; **~ le lecteur à un livre** to refer the reader to a book

réorganisation /ReɔRganizasjɔ̃/ *nf* reorganization

réorganiser /ReɔRganize/ [1]

A *vtr* to reorganize

B se réorganiser *vpr* to reorganize oneself

réorienter /ReɔRjɑ̃te/ [1]

A *vtr* to reorientate [*élève, étudiant*] (**vers** toward(s)); to reshape [*politique*]; to reorientate [*fusée*]

B se réorienter *vpr* [*élève*] to transfer (**vers** to); [*étudiant*] to transfer (**vers** to) GB, to change majors US

réouverture /ReuvɛRtyR/ *nf* reopening

repaire /R(ə)pɛR/ *nm* (d'animal, de brigands) den; (de trafiquants, terroristes) hideout

repaître: se repaître /RəpɛtR/ [74] *vpr* **se ~ de** [*animal*] to feed on; [*personne*] to revel in

répandre /Repɑ̃dR/ [6]

A *vtr* **1** (mettre) to spread [*substance, matériau*] (**sur** on; **dans** in); to pour [*liquide*] (**sur** on; **dans** in); (accidentellement) to spill [*liquide*]; **~ un chargement** to empty a load; **2** (disperser) to scatter [*graines, farine, déchets*]; **3** (propager) to spread [*nouvelle, religion*] (**dans, à travers** throughout); to give off [*chaleur, fumée, odeur*] (**dans** into); ~ **la bonne parole** to spread the good word

B se répandre *vpr* [1] (se propager) [*nouvelle, religion, substance, odeur*] to spread (**dans, à travers** throughout); [2] (déverser) **se ~ en invectives** to let out a stream of abuse (**contre** at)

répandu, ~**e** /ʀepɑ̃dy/ *adj* (commun) widespread

réparable /ʀepaʀabl/ *adj* [1] [*objet*] repairable; [2] [*erreur*] which can be put right (*épith, après n*)

reparaître /ʀ(ə)paʀɛtʀ/ [73] *vi* [1] (apparaître de nouveau) = **réapparaître**; [2] (être publié à nouveau) [*journal*] to be back in print; [*œuvre, texte*] to be republished

réparateur, -trice /ʀepaʀatœʀ, tʀis/
A *adj* [*repos, sommeil*] refreshing
B ▸ p. 372 *nm,f* (d'appareil) engineer GB, fixer US

réparation /ʀepaʀasjɔ̃/
A *nf* [1] (de montre, machine) repairing, mending; (de véhicule, route, d'avarie) repairing; (de vêtement, chaussure) mending; **la ~ de la télévision m'a coûté 50 euros** it cost me 50 euros to get the television repaired; **être en ~** [*bâtiment, route*] to be under repair; **ma voiture est en ~** my car is being repaired; [2] Jur (de tort, préjudice) compensation (**de** for); **demander ~ de** to seek compensation for; [3] (d'injustice) redress (**de** for)
B réparations *nfpl* [1] (travaux) repairs, repair work ¢; [2] (dommages et intérêts) compensation ¢

réparer /ʀepaʀe/ [1] *vtr* [1] (remettre en état) to repair [*bâtiment, véhicule, route, maison*]; to repair, to mend, to fix US [*appareil, accroc, vêtement*]; ~ **sommairement qch** to patch sth up; [2] (compenser les effets de) to put [sth] right [*erreur, injustice*]; to make up for [*oubli*]; [3] Jur (dédommager) to compensate for [*dommage*]

reparler /ʀ(ə)paʀle/ [1] *vtr ind* [1] (après une interruption) ~ **de** to discuss [sth] again (**à qn, avec qn** with sb); **on reparle de l'affaire de l'hôpital** the hospital scandal is in the news again; [2] (après une dispute) ~ **à qn** to be back on speaking terms with sb

repartie /ʀepaʀti/ *nf* rejoinder *fml*; **elle a de la ~** she always has a ready reply; **avoir la ~ facile** *or* **l'esprit de ~** to have a quick wit

repartir /ʀ(ə)paʀtiʀ/ [30] *vi* [1] (quitter un endroit) to leave again; (regagner un lieu) to go back; **tu repars déjà?** you're leaving already?; [2] (après un arrêt) [*personne*] to set off again; [*machine*] to start again; [*bus*] to leave; [*emploi, secteur économique*] to pick up again; [3] (recommencer) ~ **sur de nouvelles bases** to start all over again; ~ **à zéro** to start again from scratch; **c'est reparti pour un tour**○! here we go again○!

répartir /ʀepaʀtiʀ/ [3]
A *vtr* [1] (distribuer) to share [sth] out [*somme, travail, objets*] (**entre** among, between); to split [*bénéfices, frais*] (**entre** among, between); to distribute [*poids, bagages*]; ~ **des gens dans des salles** to divide people into groups and put them in different rooms; ~ **les rôles** to distribute the roles; ~ **l'impôt** to spread taxes; [2] (étaler) to spread [*produit, crème*]
B se répartir *vpr* [1] (partager) to share out, to split [*travail, objets*]; [2] (être distribué) [*personnes*] to divide up; [*dépenses, travaux*] to be split *ou* shared; [*voix, votes*] to be split; **se ~ en** [*personnes, objets*] to divide (up) into, to split up into

répartition /ʀepaʀtisjɔ̃/ *nf* [1] (de biens, travail, rôles) sharing out (**entre** among, between; **en** into); (de personnes, terres, d'emplois) dividing up (**entre** among; **en** into); (de l'impôt) distribution (**de** of); [2] (résultat) distribution

repas /ʀ(ə)pɑ/ *nm inv* meal; ~ **de noces** wedding breakfast; ~ **d'affaires** (à midi) business lunch; (le soir) business dinner; '**téléphoner aux heures des ~**' 'please call at mealtimes'

repassage /ʀ(ə)pɑsaʒ/ *nm* ironing

repasser /ʀəpɑse/ [1]
A *vtr* [1] (avec un fer) to iron [*vêtement*]; '~ **à fer doux**' 'cool iron'; [2] (franchir de nouveau) to cross [sth] again [*fleuve, frontière*]; [3] (se soumettre de nouveau à) to take [sth] again [*permis de conduire, oral*]; to retake, to resit GB [*examen écrit*]; [4] (tenter de nouveau) to pass [sth] again [*outil, sel*] (**à qn** to sb); **je te repasse Jean** (au téléphone) I'll put you back on to Jean; ~ **qch dans son esprit** to think back over sth;

[5] ○(transmettre) to pass on [*virus*] (**à qn** to sb); to give [*rhume*] (**à qn** to sb)
B *vi* [1] (dans un même lieu) [*cyclistes, procession*] to go past again; ~ **devant qch** to go past sth again; **tu n'as pas besoin de ~ par Lyon** you don't have to go back through Lyons; **si tu repasses à Lyon, viens me voir** if you're ever back in Lyons, come and see me; **s'il croit que je vais accepter, il repassera**○ *or* **il peut toujours ~**○! if he thinks I'm going to agree, he's got another think coming○ GB *ou* he can think again!; [2] (être montré, diffusé) ~ **au cinéma/à Paris** [*film*] to be showing again at the cinema GB *ou* movies US/in Paris; [3] (pour terminer un travail) **quand elle fait la vaisselle, je dois ~ derrière elle** I always have to do the dishes again after she's done them

repayer /ʀ(ə)peje/ [21] *vtr* to pay [sth] again

repêchage /ʀ(ə)pɛʃaʒ/ *nm* [1] (dans l'eau) recovery (*from* water); [2] Scol, Univ **examen** *ou* **épreuve de** ~ resit GB, retest US; **question (de)** ~ supplementary question (*giving another chance to pass*)

repêcher /ʀ(ə)peʃe/ [1] *vtr* [1] (dans l'eau) to recover [*corps, véhicule*] (*from* water); to fish out [*objet*]; [2] Scol, Univ to award a discretionary pass to GB, to raise [sb] to a passing grade US [*candidat*]; Sport to allow [sb] to qualify [*personne*]

repeindre /ʀ(ə)pɛ̃dʀ/ [55] *vtr* to repaint

repenser /ʀ(ə)pɑ̃se/ [1]
A *vtr* to rethink [*théorie*]
B repenser à *vtr ind* ~ **à** to think back to [*enfance, vacances*]; to think again about [*discussion, anecdote*]

repenti, ~**e** /ʀ(ə)pɑ̃ti/
A *adj* repentant
B *nm,f* penitent

repentir[1]: **se repentir** /ʀ(ə)pɑ̃tiʀ/ [30] *vpr* [1] gén to regret (**de qch** sth); [2] Relig to repent (**de qch** of sth)

repentir[2] /ʀ(ə)pɑ̃tiʀ/ *nm* gén, Relig repentance

repérable /ʀ(ə)peʀabl/ *adj* gén that can be spotted (*épith, après n*)

repérage /ʀ(ə)peʀaʒ/ *nm* Aviat, Mil location (**de** of); Cin finding a location (**de** for)

répercussion /ʀepɛʀkysjɔ̃/ *nf* repercussion

répercuter /ʀepɛʀkyte/ [1]
A *vtr* [1] (transmettre) to pass [sth] on [*hausse, baisse*]; [2] Phys to send back [*son*]
B se répercuter *vpr* [1] [*son*] to echo; [*augmentation, baisse*] to be reflected (**sur** in); [2] [*sentiment*] to have repercussions (**sur** on)

repère /ʀ(ə)pɛʀ/ *nm* [1] (jalon) marker; (encoche, trait) (reference) mark; **la statue sert de** ~ the statue is a useful landmark; [2] (événement) landmark; (date) reference point; (référence) reference point, criterion

repérer /ʀ(ə)peʀe/ [14]
A *vtr* [1] ○(discerner) to spot [*personne, erreur, endroit*]; ~ **les lieux** to check out a place; **si tu ne veux pas te faire ~** if you don't want to get noticed; **se faire ~ par la police** to be spotted by the police; [2] (situer) to locate [*cible, ennemi*]
B se repérer○ *vpr* [1] lit, fig (dans un lieu) to get one's bearings; [2] (se remarquer) [*erreur*] to stand out

répertoire /ʀepɛʀtwaʀ/ *nm* [1] (carnet) notebook with thumb index; [2] (liste) ~ **téléphonique** (personnel) telephone book; ~ **d'adresses** (personnel) address book; [3] Mus, Théât repertoire; **une pièce du** ~ a stock play; **avoir tout un** ~ **d'anecdotes** *fig* to have an extensive repertoire of anecdotes

répertorier /ʀepɛʀtɔʀje/ [2] *vtr* [1] (faire la liste de) to list [*entreprises, informations*]; to index [*ouvrages*]; **non répertorié** unlisted; [2] (recenser) to identify [*espèces, cas, risques*]

répéter /ʀepete/ [14]
A *vtr* [1] (redire) to repeat; ~ **qch à qn** to say sth to sb again, to tell sb sth again; **je ne me le suis pas fait ~ deux fois!** I didn't need to be told twice!; **répète (un peu pour voir**○)! say that again!; **tu répètes toujours la même chose** you keep saying the same thing over and over again; [2] (rapporter) to tell; **ne le répète à personne** don't tell anyone; **elle répète tout ce qu'on lui dit** she repeats everything you tell her; [3] (refaire) to repeat [*expérience*]; [4] (rejouer) (pour harmoniser) to rehearse [*pièce*]; to rehearse for [*concert*]; (pour apprendre) to practise GB [*passage*]
B se répéter *vpr* [1] (redire) (en rabâchant) to repeat oneself; (pour se rappeler) to repeat [sth] to oneself [*phrase, conseil*]; **j'ai beau me ~ que** no matter how often I tell myself that;

2 (se reproduire) [*phénomène, événement*] to be repeated; **si ce genre d'accident se répète...** if this kind of accident happens again...

répétitif, -ive /ʀepetitif, iv/ *adj* repetitive

répétition /ʀepetisjɔ̃/ *nf* **1** (dans un texte) repetition; **2** (de geste, d'erreur) repetition; **3** Mus, Théât (mise au point) rehearsal

(Composé) **~ générale** Théât dress rehearsal; Mus final rehearsal

repeuplement /ʀ(ə)pœpləmɑ̃/ *nm* **1** Géog repopulation; **2** (de forêt) reforestation (**en** with); **3** (de rivière) restocking (**en** with)

repeupler /ʀ(ə)pœple/ [1]
A *vtr* **1** Géog to repopulate; **2** to restock [*étang, parc*] (**de** with); **3** Agric to reforest [*lieu*] (**en** with); **~ une forêt** to replant a forest
B se repeupler *vpr* Géog to become repopulated

repiquage /ʀ(ə)pikaʒ/ *nm* **1** (de riz) transplanting; (de salade, géranium) pricking out; **2** (de bande, disque) rerecording

repiquer /ʀ(ə)pike/ [1] *vtr* **1** to transplant [*riz*]; to prick out [*salade, géranium*]; **2** (piquer encore) [*insecte*] to bite again; **3** to rerecord [*bande, disque*]

répit /ʀepi/ *nm* respite; **travailler sans ~** to work ceaselessly *ou* without respite; **leur travail ne leur laisse aucun ~** they never get a break from work; **laisser un ~ de cinq jours à qn** to give sb five days' grace

replacer /ʀ(ə)plase/ [12]
A *vtr* **1** (placer à nouveau) to put [sth] back, to replace [*objet*]; **2** fig (situer) **~ qch dans son contexte** to set sth back in context
B se replacer *vpr* fig (s'imaginer) **se ~ dans un contexte** to imagine oneself back in a context

replanter /ʀ(ə)plɑ̃te/ [1] *vtr* **1** (changer de terre) to transplant [*rosier, arbre*]; **2** (après destruction) to replant [*arbre*]; **3** (reboiser) to replant [*parc, forêt*] (**en** with)

replâtrer /ʀ(ə)plɑtʀe/ [1] *vtr* **1** Constr to replaster [*mur*]; **2** fig to patch up [*groupe, union*]

replet, -ète /ʀəplɛ, ɛt/ *adj* [*personne*] plump; [*visage, joues*] plump, chubby

repli /ʀ(ə)pli/ *nm* **1** (double pli) double fold; **2** (pli profond) fold; **les ~s de sa conscience** fig the recesses of his/her conscience littér; **3** Mil (recul) **(mouvement de) ~** withdrawal (**sur** to); **4** Psych **~ sur soi(-même)** withdrawal

replier /ʀ(ə)plije/ [2]
A *vtr* **1** (plier à nouveau) to fold up [*dépliant, plan*]; **2** (rabattre) to fold [sth] back [*drap*] (**sur** over); **3** (refermer) to fold up [*siège, éventail*]; to close [*parapluie, canif*]; **4** (en place) **elle replia ses jambes** she tucked her legs under her; **~ ses ailes** [*oiseau*] to fold its wings
B se replier *vpr* **1** [*lame, canapé-lit*] to fold up; **2** [*troupe, armée*] to withdraw (**sur** to; **dans** into); **3** **se ~ sur soi-même** [*personne*] to become withdrawn; [*pays*] to shut itself off from the rest of the world

réplique /ʀeplik/ *nf* **1** (riposte verbale) retort, rejoinder; **faire qch en ~ à un discours** to do sth in response to a speech; **il a la ~ facile** he's never stuck for an answer; **2** (objection) **faire qch sans ~** to do sth without arguing; **argument sans ~** irrefutable argument; **3** Théât line; **donner la ~ à qn** (pour faire apprendre un rôle) to go through sb's lines with them; (dans une représentation) to play opposite sb; **les deux politiciens se sont donné la ~ pendant une heure** there was an hour-long sparring session between the two politicians; **4** (copie) Art replica; (personne) **elle est la ~ de sa mère** she is the image of her mother; **5** Géol aftershock

répliquer /ʀeplike/ [1]
A *vtr* (répondre) to retort
B répliquer à *vtr ind* **~ à qn** (en objectant) to argue with sb; **~ à** to respond to [*objections, critique, attaques*]
C *vi* **1** (verbalement) to answer back; **2** (par une action) to retaliate, to respond

répondant, ~e /ʀepɔ̃dɑ̃, ɑ̃t/ *nm,f* (d'une personne) referee; Fin, Jur (caution) surety, guarantor

(Idiome) **avoir du ~**° (de l'argent) to have money

répondeur /ʀepɔ̃dœʀ/ *nm* **~ (téléphonique)** (telephone) answering machine, answerphone GB

répondre /ʀepɔ̃dʀ/ [6]
A *vtr* to answer, to reply; **~ une bêtise** to give a silly answer

ou reply; **tu réponds n'importe quoi** you just give any answer that comes into your head; **je me suis vu ~ que, il m'a été répondu que** I was told that; **qu'as-tu à ~ (à cela)?** what's your answer (to that)?; **qu'est-ce qu'il t'a répondu?** what was his answer?

B répondre à *vtr ind* **1** (être conforme à) **~ à** to answer, to meet [*besoin, exigences*]; to fulfil [*souhait*]; to answer, to fit [*signalement*]; to come up to, to meet [*espérances*]; **2** (agir en retour) **~ à** to respond to [*avances, appel, attaque*]; to return [*affection, salut, politesse*]; **~ aux critiques de qn par le mépris** to treat sb's criticism with contempt; **~ à un sourire** to smile back; **~ à la violence par la violence** to meet violence with violence

C répondre de *vtr ind* (servir de caution) **~ de qn** to vouch for sb; Fin, Jur to stand surety for sb; **~ de ses actes** to answer for one's actions; **je me réponds plus de rien** it's out of his hands from now on; **ça sera fini, j'en** *or* **je vous en réponds**° it will be finished, take my word for it *ou* you can be sure of that

D *vi* **1** (donner une réponse) **~ à** to reply to, to answer [*personne, question, lettre*]; to reply to [*ultimatum*]; **~ à un questionnaire** to fill in a questionnaire; **~ par oui** *ou* **par non** to answer yes or no; **~ par un sourire** to answer with a smile; **2** (se manifester) **~ au téléphone/à la porte** to answer the phone/the door; **ça ne répond pas** there's no answer *ou* reply; **3** (être insolent) **~ à qn** to answer sb back GB, to talk back to sb; **4** (se nommer) liter **elle répond au nom de Flore** she answers to the name of Flore; **5** (réagir) [*mécanisme, organe, muscle*] to respond (**à** to)

réponse /ʀepɔ̃s/ *nf* **1** (à une question, lettre, objection) answer (**à** to), reply (**à** to); (à un questionnaire) reply; **en ~ à votre lettre** in reply to your letter; **ma lettre est restée sans ~** my letter remained unanswered; **2** (solution) answer (**à** to); **3** (réaction) response (**à** to); **temps de ~** response time; **la ~ du public a été favorable** the public has responded favourably[GB]

(Composé) **~ de Normand** noncommittal reply

(Idiome) **avoir ~ à tout** to have an answer for everything

report /ʀapɔʀ/ *nm* **1** (de procès) adjournment (**à** to); (de rendez-vous, départ) postponement (**à** to, until); (de jugement) deferment (**à** to, until); **2** (de dessin, d'image) transfer (**sur** onto); **3** (aux élections) transfer; **4** (de somme) carrying forward; (somme reportée) amount carried forward

reportage /ʀ(ə)pɔʀtaʒ/ *nm* **1** (dans les média) report (**sur** on); **2** (technique) reporting

reporter¹ /ʀ(ə)pɔʀte/ [1]
A *vtr* **1** (différer) to put back [*date*] (**à** to); to postpone, to put back [*rendez-vous, événement*] (**à** until); to postpone [*départ, match*] (**à** until); to defer [*jugement*] (**à** until); **~ son départ d'une semaine** to postpone one's departure by a week; **~ la réunion de lundi à vendredi** to postpone Monday's meeting until Friday; **2** (copier sur un autre support) to carry forward [*calcul, résultat*]; to copy out [*nom*]; **3** (déplacer) **~ un paragraphe en début d'un texte** to move a paragraph to the beginning of a text; **4** (aller remettre) to take [sth] back [*marchandise, objet*]; **5** (dans le passé) **cela nous reporte longtemps en arrière** that's going back a long time; **6** (transférer) to transfer [*affection*] (**sur** to); **~ des voix sur un autre candidat** to transfer votes to another candidate; **~ son agressivité sur qn** to take one's aggression out on sb
B se reporter *vpr* **1** (consulter) **se ~ à** to refer to; **2** (revenir en pensée) **se ~ à** to think back to; **3** (être transféré) [*voix*] to be transferred (**sur** to)

reporter² /ʀapɔʀtɛʀ/ ▸ p. 372 *nm* (journaliste) reporter; **un grand ~** a special correspondent

reporter-photographe, *pl* **reporters-photographes** /ʀ(ə)pɔʀtɛʀfɔtɔgʀaf/ ▸ p. 372 *nm* photojournalist

repos /ʀəpo/ *nm inv* **1** (inactivité, délassement) rest; **s'accorder du ~** to have a rest; **mon jour de ~** (sans travail) my day off; **ce n'est pas de tout ~** it's no easy task, it's no picnic°; **muscle au ~** relaxed muscle; **~!** Mil at ease!; **soldats au ~** soldiers standing at ease; **2** (absence de soucis) liter peace; **chercher le ~** to search for peace

reposant, -e /ʀəpozɑ̃, ɑ̃t/ *adj* [*occupation*] peaceful, restful; [*lumière*] soothing; [*position, lecture*] relaxing

reposé, ~e /ʀəpoze/
A *pp* ▸ reposer
B *pp adj* **avoir les traits ~s** to look rested; **lire qch à tête ~e** to read sth at one's leisure

repose-pied, pl ∼s /R(ə)pozpje/ nm footrest

reposer /Rəpoze/ [1]

A vtr **1** (d'une fatigue) to rest [jambes, esprit]; **cela me repose de mon travail habituel** it's a rest from my usual work; **2** (appuyer) ∼ **sa tête sur qch** to rest one's head on sth; **3** (placer) to put [sth] down [téléphone, verre]; (à nouveau) to put [sth] down again [bibelot]; **4** (soulever à nouveau) to ask [sth] again [question]; **cela repose le problème du chômage** this raises the problem of unemployment again

B vi **1** (être enterré) **qu'elle repose en paix** may she rest in peace; **où reposent de nombreux soldats** where many soldiers are buried; **'ici repose le Dr Grunard'** (sur une tombe) 'here lies Dr Grunard'; **2** (être inactif) **laisser** ∼ **la terre** to rest the land; **3** [navire, épave] to lie; **4** Culin **'laisser** ∼ **la pâte'** 'let the dough rest'; **5** ∼ **sur** [idée, expérience] to be based on; **la poutre repose sur...** the beam is supported by...; **tout repose sur elle** it all rests with her

C se **reposer** vpr **1** (d'une fatigue) to have a rest, to rest; **repose-toi bien** have a good rest; **2** (faire confiance à, avoir besoin de) **se** ∼ **sur qn** to rely on sb; **3** (à nouveau) **le problème va se** ∼ the problem will recur

repose-tête /Rəpoztɛt/ nm inv **1** gén head rest; **2** Aut head restraint

repoussant, ∼**e** /Rəpusã, ãt/ adj [laideur] hideous; [saleté, odeur] revolting; **être** ∼ **de laideur, être d'une laideur** ∼**e** to be hideously ugly

repousser /R(ə)puse/ [1]

A vtr **1** (remettre en place) to push [sth] back into [tiroir]; to push [sth] to [verrou, porte]; to push back [meuble, objet]; ∼ **la porte d'un coup de pied** to kick the door to ou shut; **2** (déplacer, éloigner) to push away [objets]; to push back [mèche de cheveux]; **3** (obliger à reculer) to push ou drive back [attaquant, foule]; **4** (s'opposer avec succès à) to repel [attaque]; **5** (rejeter) to dismiss [argument]; to decline [aide]; to turn down [demande]; ∼ **les avances de qn** to spurn sb's advances; **6** (dégoûter) [saleté] to revolt; **7** (différer) to postpone, to put [sth] back [départ, rendez-vous]; to put GB ou move [sth] back [date]; to postpone [événement]; ∼ **une réunion du lundi au vendredi** to postpone a Monday meeting until Friday

B vi [cheveux, barbe, herbe] (après une coupe) to grow again; (après disparition) to grow back; [feuille] to grow again; [dent] to come through

répréhensible /RepReãsibl/ adj reprehensible

reprendre /R(ə)pRãdR/ [52]

A vtr **1** (se resservir) ∼ **du pain/vin** to have some more bread/ wine; **j'en ai repris deux fois** I had three helpings; **2** (prendre de nouveau) to pick [sth] up again [objet, outil]; to take [sth] back [cadeau, objet prêté]; to recapture [ville, fugitif]; to go back on [parole, promesse]; (aller chercher) to pick [sb/sth] up, to collect [personne, voiture]; **tu passes me** ∼ **à quelle heure?** what time will you come back for me?; ∼ **sa place** (son siège) to go back to one's seat; **j'ai repris les kilos que j'avais perdus** I've put back on the weight I'd lost; ∼ **son nom de jeune fille** to revert to one's maiden name; **3** (accepter de nouveau) to take [sb] on again [employé]; Comm to take [sth] back [article]; (contre un nouvel achat) to take [sth] in part GB ou partial US exchange; **les marchandises ne sont ni reprises ni échangées** goods cannot be returned or exchanged; **4** (recommencer) to resume [promenade, récit, fonctions, études]; to pick up [sth] again, to go back to [journal, tricot]; to take up [sth] again [lutte]; to revive [pièce, tradition]; ∼ **le travail** (après un congé, une grève) to go back to work; **on quitte à midi et on reprend à 14 heures** we stop at 12 and start again at 2; **tu reprends le train à quelle heure?** what time is your train back?; ∼ **la parole** to start speaking again; ∼ **une histoire au début** to go back to the beginning of a story; ∼ **les arguments un à un** to go over the arguments one by one; **5** (acquérir) to take over [cabinet, commerce, entreprise]; **6** (surprendre de nouveau) **que je ne t'y reprenne plus!** don't let me catch you doing that again!; **on ne me reprendra plus à lui rendre service!** you won't catch me doing him/ her any favours[GB] again!; **7** (recouvrer) ∼ **confiance** to regain one's confidence; ∼ **ses vieilles habitudes** to get back into one's old ways; **la nature reprend ses droits** nature reasserts itself; **elle a repris sa liberté** she's a free woman again; **8** (retoucher) to alter [vêtement, couture]; ∼ **le travail de qn** to correct sb's work; **il y a tout à** ∼ **dans ce chapitre** the whole chapter needs re-writing; **9** (utiliser de nouveau) to take up [idée, politique]; **10** (répéter) to repeat [argument]; to take up [slogan, chant]; **reprenons à la vingtième mesure** Mus let's take it again from bar 20; ∼ **la leçon précédente** Scol to go over the previous lesson again; **tous les médias ont repris la nouvelle** the news was taken up by all the media; **11** (corriger) to correct [élève]; **12** (resurgir) **mon mal de dents m'a repris** my toothache has come back; **voilà que ça le reprend**○! there he goes again!

B vi **1** (retrouver sa vigueur) [commerce, affaires] to pick up again; [plante] to recover; **la vie reprend peu à peu** life is gradually getting back to normal; **2** (recommencer) [cours, bombardements] to start again; [négociations] to resume; **nos émissions reprendront à 7 heures** Radio, TV we shall be back on the air at 7 o'clock; **3** (continuer) **'c'est bien étrange,' reprit-il** 'it's very strange,' he continued

C se **reprendre** vpr **1** (se corriger) to correct oneself; **2** (se ressaisir) [personne] to pull oneself together; **3** (recommencer) **s'y** ∼ **à trois fois pour faire qch** to make three attempts to do ou at doing sth; **il se reprend à penser que c'est possible** he's gone back to thinking it might be possible

représailles /R(ə)pRezaj/ nfpl gén, Mil, Pol reprisals; (moins violentes) **Ⓒ**; **en** ∼ **in** retaliation

représentant, ∼**e** /R(ə)pRezãtã, ãt/ nmf **1** (délégué) representative (**de** of); ∼ **des forces de l'ordre** police officer; **2** ▸ p. 372 Comm ∼ (**de commerce**) sales representative, sales rep

représentatif, -ive /RəpRezãtatif, iv/ adj representative (**de** of)

représentation /RəpRezãtasjõ/ nf **1** (action de représenter) representation (**de** of); **2** Théât (séance) performance; **3** (rôle de mandataire, délégué) representation; (mandataires, délégation) representatives (pl); ∼ **proportionnelle** proportional representation; **4** Comm (activité) commercial travelling[GB]; ∼ **exclusive** sole agency; **faire de la** ∼ to be a sales representative ou rep

représenter /RəpRezãte/ [1]

A vtr **1** (figurer) [tableau, dessin] to depict, to show; [peintre] to depict [paysage, situation]; to portray [personne]; **le décor représente un jardin** Théât the scene shows a garden; **on l'a représenté comme un héros** he has been portrayed as a hero; **2** (exprimer) to represent; **que représente ce signe?** what does this sign represent?; **elle représente bien l'esprit de son époque** she typifies the spirit of her age; **3** (équivaloir à) to represent; (signifier) to mean; **le prix d'une voiture représente deux ans de salaire** a car represents two years' salary; **cela représente trop de sacrifices** it means too many sacrifices; **le vin représente 60% de la consommation d'alcool** wine accounts for 60% of alcohol consumption; **4** (être mandataire de) to represent; **5** Théât (jouer) to perform [pièce]; to put on [spectacle]

B se **représenter** vpr **1** (s'imaginer) to imagine [conséquences, scène, personne]; **on se la représente très bien en premier ministre** one can just see her as Prime Minister; **2** (survenir à nouveau) [occasion] to arise again; [problème] to crop up again; **3** (être à nouveau candidat) **se** ∼ **à un examen** to retake an examination; **se** ∼ **aux élections** to stand GB ou run US for election again

répressif, -ive /Represif, iv/ adj repressive

répression /Represjõ/ nf **1** Pol, Jur suppression (**de, contre** of); **2** Psych (d'élan, de pulsion) repression

réprimande /Reprimãd/ nf reprimand

réprimander /Reprimãde/ [1] vtr to reprimand

réprimer /Reprime/ [1] vtr to repress [envie, penchant]; to suppress [bâillement, sourire]; to suppress [révolte]; to crack down on [fraude, trafic]

repris /R(ə)pRi/ nm inv ∼ **de justice** ex-convict

reprise /RəpRiz/ nf **1** Jur (récupération) repossession; **2** (recommencement) (de travaux, cours, vols, dialogue, négociations, d'hostilités) resumption (**de** of); (de pièce, film) rerun; (d'émission) Radio, TV repeat; ∼ **du travail** resumption of work; (après une grève) return to work; **à deux** ∼**s** on two occasions; twice; **3** Écon, Fin (de demande, production) increase (**de** in); (de commerce) revival (**de** of); ∼ **de la Bourse** stock market rally; **on assiste à une** ∼ **de l'économie** we're seeing an upturn in the economy; **la** ∼ **de l'emploi** the increase ou rise in employment; **4** Comm (de marchandise) return, taking back; (contre un nouvel achat) trade-in, part exchange GB; Comm, Écon (d'entreprise, de commerce) takeover; **30 euros de** ∼ **sur votre vieille machine à laver contre achat d'une neuve** 30 euros for your old washing machine when you buy a new one; **5** (dans l'immobilier) key money; **6** Aut acceleration **Ⓒ**;

[7] (de tissu) mend; (de lainage) darn; **[8]** Sport (en boxe) round; (au football) start of second half; (en escrime) bout

repriser /ʀəpʀize/ [1] vtr to mend [vêtement, rideau, accroc]; to darn [chaussette]

réprobateur, -trice /ʀepʀɔbatœʀ, tʀis/ adj reproachful, disapproving

réprobation /ʀepʀɔbasjɔ̃/ nf gén disapproval, reprobation sout

reproche /ʀ(ə)pʀɔʃ/ nm reproach; **faire** or **adresser des ~s à qn** to reproach sb (**sur, au sujet de** for); **j'ai un ou deux ~s à vous faire** I've one or two criticisms to make; **un ton de ~** a reproachful tone; **sans ~** beyond reproach; **elle est toujours en train de lui faire des ~s** she's always finding fault with him/her

reprocher /ʀəpʀɔʃe/ [1]
A vtr **[1]** (parlant de personnes) **~ qch à qn** to criticize ou reproach sb for sth; **qu'est-ce que tu lui reproches?** what have you got against him/her?; **je ne vous reproche rien, mais...** I'm not criticizing ou reproaching you but...; **on ne peut rien lui ~** he's/she's beyond reproach; **je lui reproche de ne jamais tenir compte des autres** I hate the way he/she never considers other people; **elle me reproche de ne jamais lui écrire** she complains that I never write to her; **[2]** (parlant de choses) **ce que je reproche à cette voiture c'est...** what I don't like about this car is...; **tu ne peux pas me ~ les erreurs des autres** you can't blame me for other people's mistakes; **qu'est-ce que tu reproches à ma cravate?** what's wrong with my tie?; **les faits qui lui sont reprochés** the charges against him/her
B se reprocher vpr **se ~ qch** to blame ou reproach oneself for sth; **je n'ai rien à me ~** I've done nothing wrong

reproducteur, -trice /ʀəpʀɔdyktœʀ, tʀis/
A adj **[1]** Biol [organe, appareil, fonction] reproductive; **[2]** Agric [animal] breeding (épith)
B nm Agric breeding animal

reproduction /ʀ(ə)pʀɔdyksjɔ̃/ nf **[1]** Biol reproduction; **la ~ artificielle** assisted reproduction; **[2]** (action de copier) reproduction; (copie) reproduction, copy; **droit de ~** copyright; **droits de ~ réservés** all rights reserved; **~ interdite** no unauthorized reproduction ou copying

reproduire /ʀ(ə)pʀɔdɥiʀ/ [69]
A vtr **[1]** (répéter) to repeat [erreur, expérience]; to imitate, to copy [habitude, geste]; to recreate [condition, milieu]; to reproduce [son]; **[2]** (copier) to reproduce [tableau, motif, texte, déclaration]; to recreate [style, condition]; **sa déclaration sera reproduite dans les journaux** his/her declaration will be printed (in full) in the papers; **[3]** Tech (restituer) to reproduce [son]
B se reproduire vpr **[1]** Biol [homme, animal, plante] to reproduce; **[2]** (se répéter) [phénomène] to recur; **et que cela ne se reproduise plus!** and don't let it happen again!

réprouvé, ~e /ʀepʀuve/ nm,f outcast

réprouver /ʀepʀuve/ [1] vtr to condemn

reptile /ʀɛptil/ nm Zool reptile

repu, ~e /ʀəpy/
A pp ► repaître
B pp adj full (jamais épith)

républicain, ~e /ʀepyblikɛ̃, ɛn/ adj, nm,f republican

république /ʀepyblik/ nf republic; **après tout, on vit en ~** after all, it's a free country

répudier /ʀepydje/ [2] vtr **[1]** to repudiate [épouse]; **[2]** to renounce [droit, nationalité]; **[3]** (rejeter) liter to renege on [engagement]; to repudiate [idée, opinion]; to renounce [foi, croyance]

répugnance /ʀepyɲɑ̃s/ nf **[1]** (aversion) revulsion; **avoir** or **éprouver de la ~ pour** to loathe [aliment, idée, personne]; to find [sth] revolting ou disgusting [comportement, mensonge, violence]; to find [sth] disgusting [saleté]; **[2]** (hésitation) reluctance (**à faire** to do); **avec ~** reluctantly, with reluctance

répugnant, ~e /ʀepyɲɑ̃, ɑ̃t/ adj [personne, laideur, saleté] revolting; disgusting; [comportement, idée] loathsome; **d'une saleté ~e** disgustingly dirty

répugner /ʀepyɲe/ [1]
A vtr [nourriture, personne] to be repugnant to, to disgust [personne]; **vivre ici me répugne** I loathe ou detest living here
B répugner à vtr ind to be averse to [tâche, violence]; **~ à faire** to be reluctant to do, to be loath to do
C v impers **il me répugne de vous le dire, mais...** I hate to have to tell you, but...; **il me répugne de devoir faire** I am loath to do

répulsion /ʀepylsjɔ̃/ nf repulsion; **éprouver de la** or **un sentiment de ~ pour qn** to be repelled by sb; **il m'inspire de la ~** I find him repulsive

réputation /ʀepytasjɔ̃/ nf **[1]** (honorabilité) reputation; **[2]** (renom) reputation; **avoir bonne/mauvaise ~** to have a good/bad reputation; **se faire une ~** to make a name for oneself; **connaître qn de ~** to know sb by reputation; **sa ~ d'efficacité/de chanteur** his reputation for efficiency/as a singer; **avoir la ~ d'être honnête** to have a reputation for being honest

réputé, ~e /ʀepyte/ adj **[1]** (renommé) [compagnie, école] reputable; [écrivain, peintre] of repute; [produit] well-known; **~ pour qch** renowned for sth; **c'est l'avocat le plus ~ de Paris** he's/she's regarded as the best lawyer in Paris; **[2]** (tenu pour) **~ cher** reputed ou reckoned to be expensive

requérir /ʀəkeʀiʀ/ [35] vtr **[1]** (solliciter) to request [secours]; **[2]** (nécessiter) (au besoin) to call for [qualité]; (impérativement) to require [soin, compétences, unanimité, preuve]; **le maire peut ~ la force publique** the mayor can summon the police; **[3]** Jur to call for [peine]

requête /ʀəkɛt/ nf **[1]** (sollicitation) request; **à** or **sur la ~ de qn** at sb's request; **[2]** Jur petition; **adresser une ~ au juge** to petition the judge

requin /ʀ(ə)kɛ̃/ nm Zool, fig shark

requinquer○ /ʀ(ə)kɛ̃ke/ [1]
A vtr to buck [sb] up○; **ça (vous) requinque** [boisson] it peps you up○
B se requinquer vpr to perk up○

requis, ~e /ʀəki, iz/
A pp ► requérir
B pp adj (nécessaire) necessary; (exigé) required; **satisfaire aux conditions ~es** to meet the requirements

réquisition /ʀekizisjɔ̃/ nf Admin, Mil (de biens, locaux) (officiellement) requisitioning; (officieusement) commandeering; (de personnes) conscription (for forced labourGB)

réquisitionner /ʀekizisjɔne/ [1] vtr Admin, Mil (officiellement) to requisition; (officieusement) to commandeer [biens, locaux]; to conscript [ouvriers, civils]

réquisitoire /ʀekizitwaʀ/ nm **[1]** Jur (discours) closing speech for the prosecution (requesting a specific sentence); **[2]** (dénonciation) indictment (**contre** of)

RER /ɛʀəɛʀ/ nm: abbr ► réseau

rescapé, ~e /ʀɛskape/
A adj [personne] surviving
B nm,f survivor (de from)

rescousse: **à la rescousse** /alaʀɛskus/ loc adv **venir/ aller à la ~** to come/to go to sb's rescue; **appeler qn à la ~** to call to sb for help

réseau, pl ~x /ʀezo/ nm **[1]** Tech (de fils, conduits, routes) network; **sur l'ensemble du ~** throughout the network; **les abonnés du ~** Télécom telephone customers; **[2]** (de personnes) network; **~ d'espions/de trafiquants de drogue** spy/drugs ring; **[3]** Ordinat network; **~ local** local area network

‾‾‾‾‾
(Composés) **~ express régional**, **RER** rapid-transit rail system in the Paris region

réservation /ʀezɛʀvasjɔ̃/ nf reservation, booking GB

réserve /ʀezɛʀv/ nf **[1]** (restriction) reservation (**au sujet de, à l'égard de** about); **je me range sans ~ de votre côté** you have my unreserved support; **sous ~ de disponibilité/de changement** subject to availability/alteration; **'sous (toute) ~'** (dans un programme) 'to be confirmed'; **je vous le dis sous toutes ~s** I'm telling you for what it's worth; **[2]** (provision) stock; **faire des ~s de farine** to lay in a stock of flour; **~(s) d'argent** money in reserve; **j'ai toujours une bonne bouteille en ~** I always have a good bottle put by; **[3]** Écon **~s de charbon/pétrole** coal/oil reserves; **~s d'eau** water supply (sg); **[4]** (discrétion) reserve; **manquer de ~** to be too outspoken; **garder une certaine ~ avec qn** to keep a certain distance with sb; **[5]** (local de stockage) stockroom; **[6]** (section de bibliothèque) stacks (pl); (section de musée) storerooms (pl); **[7]** (territoire protégé) reserve; **~ naturelle/de chasse/de pêche** nature/game/fishing reserve; **[8]** (territoire alloué) reservation; **~ indienne** Indian reservation; **[9]** Mil (réservistes) **la ~** the reserves (pl); **officier de ~** reserve officer

réservé, ~e /ʀezɛʀve/
A pp ► réserver
B pp adj **[1]** (privé) [chasse, pêche] private; **[2]** (attribué) **~ à la**

clientèle (reserved) for patrons only; **voie ~e aux taxis** taxi lane; **'tous droits ~s'** Jur 'all rights reserved'; **3)** (réticent) [*personne, caractère*] reserved; [*attitude, propos*] reticent; **se montrer ~ sur** to be guarded about

réserver /RezɛRve/ [1]

A *vtr* **1)** (retenir à l'avance) to reserve [*chambre, place, billet*]; **2)** (mettre de côté) to put aside [*journal, marchandise*] (**pour** for); **~ qch pour les grandes occasions** to keep sth for special occasions; **3)** (garder pour plus tard) to set aside [*argent*]; to save [*énergie, explications*]; **est-ce que tu peux me ~ une heure cet après-midi?** can you set aside an hour for me this afternoon?; **4)** (destiner) **~ un bon accueil à qn** to give sb a warm welcome; **que nous réserve l'avenir?** what does the future hold?; **le (triste) sort qui lui était réservé** the sad fate that awaited him; **l'année passée m'a réservé bien des surprises** last year was full of surprises for me; **5)** (remettre à plus tard) **~ son jugement** to reserve judgement^{GB}; **~ son diagnostic** to defer diagnosis

B **se réserver** *vpr* elle se réserve quelques instants de repos après le déjeuner she sets aside a few minutes after lunch to relax; **se ~ les meilleurs morceaux** to save the best bits for oneself; **se ~ le droit de faire** to reserve the right to do; **se ~ pour le dessert** to save some room for dessert

réserviste /RezɛRvist/ *nmf* reservist

réservoir /RezɛRvwaR/ *nm* **1)** (cuve) gén tank; **~ à essence** petrol tank GB, gas tank US; **2)** (lac artificiel) reservoir; **3)** fig (source) **~ de main-d'œuvre** reservoir of labour^{GB}

résidant, ~e /Rezidã, ãt/ *adj* resident

résidence /Rezidãs/ *nf* **1)** (maison) residence; **2)** (domicile) place of residence; **en ~ surveillée** under house arrest; **3)** (groupe d'immeubles) block of flats GB, apartment complex US

(Composés) **~ principale/secondaire** main/second home; **~ universitaire** (university) hall of residence GB, residence hall US

résident, ~e /Rezidã, ãt/ *nm,f* **1)** (étranger) foreign resident, resident alien US; **2)** (diplomate) resident

résidentiel, -ielle /Rezidãsjɛl/ *adj* residential

résider /Rezide/ [1] *vi* **1)** (vivre) to reside sout, to live; **2)** (se trouver) **~ dans qch** to lie in sth

résidu /Rezidy/ *nm* **1)** (dépôt) residue **C**; **2)** (reste) remnant; (détritus) waste **C**

résiduel, -elle /Rezidɥɛl/ *adj* residual

résignation /Reziɲasjõ/ *nf* resignation (**à** to)

résigner: se résigner /Reziɲe/ [1] *vpr* to resign oneself (**à qch** to sth; **à faire** to doing); **dans la vie, il faut se ~** in life you have to learn to accept things

résiliation /Reziljasjõ/ *nf* (de contrat, bail) termination

résilier /Rezilje/ [2] *vtr* to terminate [*contrat, bail*]

résine /Rezin/ *nf* resin

résineux, -euse /Rezinø, øz/
A *adj* resinous
B *nm* conifer

résistance /Rezistãs/ *nf* **1)** (opposition) resistance (**à** to); **faire de la ~** to resist; **opposer** or **offrir une ~ à** to put up resistance to; **2)** (groupe de personnes) resistance; **la Résistance** Hist the Resistance; **3)** (fait de supporter physiquement) (de personne, microbe) resistance (**à** to); (de plante) hardiness; **manquer de ~** [*personne*] to lack stamina; **4)** (fait de supporter moralement) resilience (**à** to); **5)** Phys (de matériau, d'appareil) strength; **~ à la corrosion** resistance to corrosion; **~ au choc** shock-resistance; **~ de l'air** air ou wind resistance; **6)** Électrotech (propriété) resistance; (conducteur) resistance; (d'appareil ménager) element

résistant, ~e /Rezistã, ãt/
A *adj* **1)** [*personne, animal*] tough, resilient; [*plante*] hardy; **2)** (solide) [*matériau*] resistant; [*tissu, vêtement*] hard-wearing; **~ à** gén resistant to; **~ à l'eau/la chaleur** waterproof/heatproof
B *nm,f* Hist Resistance fighter

résister /Reziste/ [1] *vtr ind* **1)** (s'opposer par la force) **~ à** to resist [*agresseur, assaut, régime*]; **le voleur a tenté de ~** the thief tried to resist arrest; **2)** (supporter physiquement) **~ à** [*personne, organe, animal*] to stand [*effort*]; [*matériau, bateau*] to withstand [*force, poussée*]; [*bâtiment, bois, objet*] to resist [*intempéries*]; **l'appareil ne résistera pas longtemps à un tel traitement** the machine won't last long if you treat it like that; **tissu qui résiste à des lavages fréquents** material

that will stand frequent washing; **couleur qui résiste au soleil** colour^{GB} that won't fade in the sun; **le mur n'a pas résisté** the wall collapsed ou gave; **qui résiste à l'eau** waterproof; **qui résiste à la chaleur/rouille** heatproof/rustproof; **rien ne lui résiste, il casse tout** he breaks everything in sight, and I mean everything!; **3)** (supporter moralement) **~ à** to get through, to endure [*épreuve*]; **4)** (être plus fort que) **~ à** [*amour, amitié*] to withstand [*séparation*]; **~ au temps** or **à l'épreuve du temps** to stand the test of time; **théorie qui ne résiste pas à l'analyse** theory that doesn't stand up to ou bear analysis; **5)** (tenir tête) **~ à** to resist [*personne, pression, charme, tentation*]; **il ne supporte pas qu'on lui résiste** he doesn't like it when people stand up to him

résolu, ~e /Rezɔly/
A *pp* ▸ **résoudre**
B *pp adj* resolute, determined

résolument /Rezɔlymã/ *adv* [*opposé, favorable*] resolutely; [*confiant*] totally; [*croire*] firmly

résolution /Rezɔlysjõ/ *nf* **1)** (décision) resolution; **prendre la ~ de faire** to make a resolution to do, to resolve to do; **2)** Pol (proposition retenue) resolution; **voter une ~** to pass a resolution; **3)** (solution) resolution; **4)** (fermeté) resolve; **5)** Math, Mus, Méd, Ordinat resolution

résonance /Rezɔnãs/ *nf* **1)** gén, Électrotech, Phys, Télécom resonance; **2)** (de poème, musique) liter echo

résonner /Rezɔne/ [1] *vi* **1)** (faire du bruit) [*pas, rire, cloche*] to ring out; [*sonnerie*] to resound; [*cymbales*] to clash; **2)** (renvoyer un bruit) [*salle*] to echo; **~ de** to resound with

résorber /RezɔRbe/ [1]
A *vtr* **1)** fig to absorb [*excédent, déficit*]; to reduce [*inflation, chômage*]; **2)** Méd to resorb
B **se résorber** *vpr* **1)** fig [*excédent, déficit*] to be reduced; [*inflation, chômage*] to be coming down; **2)** Méd to be resorbed

résorption /RezɔRpsjõ/ *nf* **1)** Méd resorption (**de** of); **2)** fig (de chômage, d'inflation) reduction (**de** of)

résoudre /RezudR/ [75]
A *vtr* **1)** (trouver la solution à) to solve [*équation, mystère, problème*]; to resolve [*crise, conflits*]; **ce n'est pas résolu** it's unresolved; **2)** fml (décider) **~ de faire** to resolve ou decide to do
B **se résoudre** *vpr* **1)** (se décider) **se ~ à faire** to resolve ou make up one's mind to do; **être résolu à faire** to be determined to do; **2)** (se résigner) **je ne peux pas me ~ à la renvoyer** I can't bring myself to dismiss her

respect /Rɛspɛ/
A *nm* gén respect (**de, pour** for); **avoir peu/beaucoup de ~ pour** to have little/a lot of respect for; **avec tout le ~ qui leur est dû** with all the respect due to them; **malgré tout le ~ qu'on lui doit** with all due respect to him/her; **manquer de ~ à qn** to be disrespectful to ou toward(s) sb; **le ~ de soi** self-respect
B **respects** *nmpl* respects; **présenter ses ~s à qn** to pay one's respects to sb

(Idiomes) **sauf votre ~** with all due respect; **tenir qn en ~** to keep sb at bay

respectabilité /Rɛspɛktabilite/ *nf* respectability

respecter /Rɛspɛkte/ [1]
A *vtr* **1)** (considérer avec respect) to respect [*personne, mémoire*]; **il s'est toujours fait ~ par ses élèves** he has always commanded the respect of his pupils; **2)** (ne pas porter atteinte à) to respect, to have respect for [*opinion, action, nature, vie privée*]; to treat [sth] with respect [*objet, matériel*]; to respect [*promesse, loi, contrat*]; to honour^{GB} [*engagement*]; **en respectant l'ordre alphabétique** in alphabetical order; **faire ~ l'ordre** to enforce order; **respectez le sommeil des gens** remember people are sleeping
B **se respecter** *vpr* to respect oneself; **tout homme qui se respecte** any self-respecting man

respectif, -ive /Rɛspɛktif, iv/ *adj* respective

respectueusement /Rɛspɛktɥøzmã/ *adv* respectfully

respectueux, -euse /Rɛspɛktɥø, øz/ *adj* respectful (**envers** to, toward(s)); **se montrer peu ~ de qch** to show little respect for sth; **des propos peu ~** some rather disrespectful remarks; **~ de la loi** law-abiding; **salutations respectueuses** (dans une lettre) (à une personne non nommée) yours faithfully; (à une personne nommée) yours sincerely

respirable /RɛspiRabl/ *adj* **1)** lit [*air*] breathable; **2)** fig [*ambiance*] bearable

respiration /ʀɛspiʀasjɔ̃/ *nf* (fonction) breathing; (souffle) breath; ~ **artificielle** artificial respiration; **avoir une** ~ **difficile** to have breathing difficulties; **retenir sa** ~ to hold one's breath; **reprendre sa** ~ to get one's breath back

respiratoire /ʀɛspiʀatwaʀ/ *adj* respiratory

respirer /ʀɛspiʀe/ [1]
A *vtr* **1** (inhaler) to breathe in [*air, gaz, poussière*]; **2** (sentir) to smell [*parfum, odeur*]; **3** (exprimer) [*personne, endroit*] to exude; **il respire la santé** he's a picture of health
B *vi* **1** lit to breathe: **'respirez!'** 'breathe in!'; **'respirez bien fort'** 'take a deep breath'; ~ **avec difficulté** to have difficulty breathing; **2** fig (se reposer) to catch one's breath; **laisse-moi** ~ let me get my breath back; **3** (être soulagé) to breathe; **enfin je respire!** at last I can breathe again!

resplendir /ʀɛsplɑ̃diʀ/ [3] *vi* **1** (briller) [*lumière*] to shine brightly; [*neige*] to sparkle; [*surface métallique*] to gleam; **2** (rayonner) **la joie resplendissait sur son visage** his/her face was beaming with joy; ~ **de bonheur/santé** to be glowing with happiness/health

resplendissant, ~**e** /ʀɛsplɑ̃disɑ̃, ɑ̃t/ *adj* **1** (brillant) [*soleil, lumière*] brilliant; [*neige*] sparkling; [*surface métallique*] gleaming; **2** (rayonnant) [*santé, beauté, mine*] radiant

responsabiliser /ʀɛspɔ̃sabilize/ [1] *vtr* to give [sb] a sense of responsibility

responsabilité /ʀɛspɔ̃sabilite/ *nf* gén responsibility (de for); (légalement) liability; **avoir sa part de** ~ **dans qch** to share some of the responsibility for sth; **il en porte l'entière** ~ he bears full responsibility for it; **se renvoyer la** ~ to blame each other; **avoir la** ~ **de qch** to be responsible for sth; **un poste à** ~ a position of responsibility; **sous la** ~ **de qn** under the supervision of sb; **prendre ses** ~**s** to face up to one's responsibilities; **faute grave engageant la** ~ **de la société** serious mistake for which the company is liable

(Composé) ~ **civile** (assurance) personal liability

responsable /ʀɛspɔ̃sabl/
A *adj* **1** (coupable) [*personne, défaillance, erreur*] responsible (*après n*) (**de qch** for sth); **l'alcool est** ~ **de nombreux accidents** alcohol is responsible ou to blame for many accidents; **2** (devant répondre de ses actes) responsible, accountable (**de qch** for sth); (légalement) responsible, liable (**de qch** for sth); **3** (ayant la charge) **être** ~ **de qch/qn** to be responsible for sth/sb, to be in charge of sth/sb; **4** (raisonnable) [*personne, attitude, acte*] responsible; **un vote/ rapport** ~ a sensible vote/report
B *nmf* **1** (personne en charge) gén person in charge; (gérant, directeur) manager; (chef de parti) leader; (chef de service) head; (administrateur) official; **des** ~**s de la police** senior police officers; **2** (personne coupable) **les** ~**s de la catastrophe** the people responsible ou to blame for the catastrophe; **3** (cause) **le grand** ~ **c'est le tabac/le manque d'amour** smoking/lack of love is the main cause

(Composé) ~ **de classe** Scol form representative (*elected by the pupils*)

resquiller○ /ʀɛskije/ [1]
A *vtr* ~ **une place** to get in for free○
B *vi* (en train, métro) not to pay the fare; (au spectacle) to sneak in○, to get in for free; (dans une queue) to queue-jump GB, to cut in line US

resquilleur○, **-euse** /ʀɛskijœʀ, øz/ *nm,f* **1** (en train, métro) fare dodger; **2** (dans une queue) queue-jumper GB, person who cuts in line US

ressac /ʀəsak/ *nm* backwash

ressaisir /ʀ(ə)seziʀ/ [3]
A *vtr* [*peur, rire, envie, passion*] to take hold of [sb] again [*personne*]
B **se ressaisir** *vpr* [*personne, candidat, sportif*] to pull oneself together; [*équipe sportive, marché*] to recover; **appeler l'opinion à se** ~ to call on the public to come to their senses

ressasser /ʀ(ə)sase/ [1] *vtr* (ruminer) to brood over [*échec, pensées*]; to dwell on [*regrets, malheurs*]; (rabâcher) to keep trotting out○ [*griefs, conseils*] (**à qn** to sb); **théorie ressassée** hackneyed theory

ressemblance /ʀ(ə)sɑ̃blɑ̃s/ *nf* **1** (entre personnes) resemblance, likeness (**avec qn** to sb); **la** ~ **avec ton père est frappante** there's a striking resemblance between you and your father; **'toute** ~ **avec des personnes existant ou ayant existé...'** 'any similarity to persons living or dead...'; **2** (entre choses) similarity; **3** (de tableau, sculpture) likeness

(avec to); **un portrait d'une grande** ~ a portrait that is a very good likeness

ressemblant, ~**e** /ʀ(ə)sɑ̃blɑ̃, ɑ̃t/ *adj* **un portrait** ~/**peu** ~ a portrait which is a good likeness/isn't a very good likeness

ressembler /ʀ(ə)sɑ̃ble/ [1]
A **ressembler à** *vtr ind* **1** (en parlant de personnes) (physiquement) ~ **à** to look like, to resemble [*personne, animal*]; (psychologiquement) ~ **à** to be like [*personne*]; **tu as vu à quoi tu ressembles?** have you any idea what you look like?; **il ne ressemble pas à l'image que j'en avais** he's not how I imagined him; **cela ne te ressemble pas de perdre patience** it's not like you to get impatient; **2** (en parlant de choses) (par l'aspect) to look like; (par le contenu) to be like, to resemble; ~ **fort à qch** to be very like sth; **cela ne ressemble à rien** (spectacle, robe) it's like nothing on earth; (n'avoir aucun sens) it makes no sense; **à quoi ça ressemble de dire cela**○? what a thing to say!
B **se ressembler** *vpr* **1** [*personnes*] (physiquement) to look alike; (psychologiquement) to be alike; **2** [*choses*] to be alike

(Idiome) **les jours se suivent et ne se ressemblent pas** no two days are the same

ressemeler /ʀ(ə)səmle/ [19] *vtr* to resole

ressentiment /ʀ(ə)sɑ̃timɑ̃/ *nm* resentment; **éprouver du** ~ to feel resentful (**de** about)

ressentir /ʀ(ə)sɑ̃tiʀ/ [30]
A *vtr* to feel; **ressenti comme une urgence** felt to be an emergency
B **se ressentir** *vpr* **se** ~ **de** [*personne, pays*] to feel the effects of, to suffer from; [*travail, performances, qualité*] to show the effects of, to suffer from; **la qualité s'en ressent** the quality is suffering

resserrer /ʀ(ə)seʀe/ [1]
A *vtr* **1** (serrer de nouveau) to tighten [*nœud, vis, étreinte*]; **2** (rendre plus étroit) to narrow [*route*]; to take [sth] in [*vêtement*]; to tighten [*pores*]; **3** (renforcer) to strengthen [*amitié, relation*]; **4** (faire regrouper) to make [sb/sth] draw closer; **resserrez les rangs!** close up a bit!; **5** (rendre plus sévère) to tighten up on [*discipline, surveillance*]
B **se resserrer** *vpr* **1** (devenir plus étroit) [*vallée*] to narrow; **2** (devenir plus fort) [*amitié*] to become stronger; **3** (devenir plus serré) [*lien, nœud*] to tighten; **4** (se refermer) [*troupes*] to close in; [*étreinte, piège*] to tighten; [*écart*] to close; **5** (se regrouper) [*personnes, cercle*] to draw closer together; **6** (devenir plus sévère) [*discipline*] to become stricter

resservir /ʀ(ə)seʀviʀ/ [30]
A *vtr* **1** (servir de nouveau) to serve [sth] (up) again; ~ **qch à qn** to serve sb with sth again; **2** (à table) to give [sb] another helping; **3** ○(utiliser à nouveau) to trot○ [sth] out again [*thème*]
B *vi* [*objet, outil, vêtement*] to be used again; **cela peut toujours** ~ it may come in handy again
C **se resservir** *vpr* **1** (d'un plat) to take another helping; **se** ~ **du poulet** to help oneself to some more chicken; **2** (réutiliser) **se** ~ **de qch** to use sth again

ressort /ʀ(ə)sɔʀ/ *nm* **1** Tech spring; **un mécanisme à** ~ a spring mechanism; **un matelas à** ~ a sprung mattress; **2** (énergie) resilience; **avoir du/manquer de** ~ to have/to lack resilience; **3** (force agissante) impulse; **les** ~**s psychologiques du personnage** the character's psychological motivation; **4** (compétence) **être du** ~ **de qn** to be within sb's province; **l'affaire est du** ~ **de la Cour européenne** the case falls within the jurisdiction of the European court; **en premier/dernier** ~ in the first/last resort

ressortir /ʀ(ə)sɔʀtiʀ/ [30]
A *vtr* **1** (sortir à nouveau) to take [sth] out again, to get [sth] out again; **2** (ce qu'on ne sortait plus) to bring [sth] out again [*vieux vêtement*] (**de** from); to dig out○ [*affaire*] (**de** from); **3** ○(redire) **il nous ressort toujours les mêmes histoires** he's always coming out with the same stories; **4** (remettre sur le marché) to re-release [*disque, film*]
B *vi* **1** (sortir à nouveau) [*personne*] to go out again; **2** (après être entré) [*balle, tige*] to come out (**par** through); [*personne*] to come back out (**de** of); **3** (se distinguer nettement) to stand out; **cela ressort bien sur ce fond** it shows up very well against that background; **voici ce qui ressort de l'étude** the results of the study are as follows; **faire** ~ to bring to light [*contradiction*]; [*maquillage*] to bring out [*yeux*]; to set [sth] off well [*tableau*]; **faire** ~ **que** [*étude, rapport*] to bring out the fact that; **4** (être remis sur le marché) [*film, disque*] to be re-released; [*revue*] to be back in circulation

G *v impers* **il ressort que** it emerges that

ressortissant, ~e /ʀ(ə)sɔʀtisɑ̃, ɑ̃t/ *nm,f* national

ressouder /ʀ(ə)sude/ [1]
A *vtr* to solder [sth] again [*joint*]; to solder [sth] together again [*pièces*]
B **se ressouder** *vpr* [*os*] to knit (together); [*fracture*] to mend

ressource /ʀ(ə)suʀs/ *nf* [1] (richesse) resource; **les ~s énergétiques/forestières** energy/forest resources; [2] (option) option; **en dernière ~** as a last resort; **être à bout de ~** to be at one's wits' end; [3] (réserves) **avoir de la ~** to be resourceful; **puiser dans ses propres ~s** to fall back on one's inner resources; [4] (revenus) **~s** resources; **être sans ~s** to have no means of support; [5] (de lieu, technique) **~s** possibilities

ressourcer: se ressourcer /ʀ(ə)suʀse/ [12] *vpr* to recharge one's batteries

ressusciter /ʀesysite/ [1]
A *vtr* [1] (exhumer du passé) to revive [*tradition, passé, auteur*]; to rekindle [*haine, amour*]; [2] Relig to raise [sb] from the dead; *fig* to bring [sb] back to life
B *vi* [1] Relig [*mort*] to rise from the dead; [2] (revenir à la vie) [*nature, ville*] to come back to life; [*passé, souvenir*] to come alive again

restant, ~e /ʀɛstɑ̃, ɑ̃t/
A *adj* remaining; **avec les 10 euros ~s** with the remaining 10 euros
B *nm* [1] (ce qui est encore à venir) remainder; **mets-en trois ici et le ~ dans le jardin** put three here and the rest in the garden GB *ou* yard US; **passer le ~ de la journée à lire** to spend the rest of the day reading; [2] (ce qui subsiste) **un ~ de jambon** some left-over ham; **un ~ de clarté** a last glimmer of light

restaurant /ʀɛstɔʀɑ̃/ *nm* restaurant; **on mange** *or* **va souvent au ~** we often eat out
(Composés) **~ d'entreprise** staff canteen; **~ universitaire, RU** university canteen GB, cafeteria

restaurateur, -trice /ʀɛstɔʀatœʀ, tʀis/ *nm,f* [1] (hôtelier) restaurant owner; (de restaurant gastronomique) restaurateur; [2] ▸ p. 372 Art restorer

restauration /ʀɛstɔʀasjɔ̃/ *nf* [1] (hôtellerie) catering; [2] Art restoration; [3] (de monarchie, paix) restoration
(Composé) **~ rapide** fast-food industry

restaurer /ʀɛstɔʀe/ [1]
A *vtr* [1] (nourrir) to feed; [2] to restore [*tableau, monarchie, paix*]
B **se restaurer** *vpr* to have something to eat

reste /ʀɛst/
A *nm* [1] (ce qui subsiste) **le ~** *gén* the rest (**de** of); Math the remainder; **s'il y a un ~ de lait** if there is any milk left; **un ~ de tissu** some left-over material; **il a un ~ d'affection pour elle** he still feels a bit of affection for her; [2] (ce qui est encore à dire, faire etc) **le ~** the rest; **le loyer, les assurances et (tout) le ~** the rent, the insurance and everything else; **je te souhaite santé, bonheur et tout le ~** I wish you health, happiness and all the rest; **au ~, du ~** besides
B **restes** *nmpl* [1] (de fortune, bâtiment, d'armée) remains (**de** of); [2] (de repas) leftovers; **les ~s d'un gigot** the remains of a joint; [3] (cadavre) **les ~s de qn** the remains of sb
(Idiomes) **elle a encore de beaux ~s**[^o] hum she's still well preserved; **sans demander** *or* **attendre son ~** without further ado; **être** *or* **demeurer en ~ avec qn** to feel indebted to sb; **pour ne pas être en ~** so as not to be outdone

rester /ʀɛste/ [1] (+ *v être*)
A *vi* [1] (dans un lieu) to stay, to remain; **~ chez soi/en ville** to stay at home/in town; **les autres sont partis, mais elle est restée pour m'aider** the others left but she stayed behind to help me; **~ un moment à bavarder** to stay chatting for a while; **~ (à) dîner** to stay for dinner; **la clé est restée coincée dans la serrure** the key got stuck in the lock; **la bière est restée au soleil** the beer was left in the sun; **c'est resté dans ma mémoire** I still remember it; **cet enfant ne peut pas ~ en place!** the child can't keep still!; **que ça reste entre nous!** this is strictly between you and me!; **j'y suis, j'y reste** here I am and here I stay; [2] (dans une position, un état) to remain; **restez assis!** (par mesure de sécurité) remain seated!; (ne vous dérangez pas) don't get up!; **je suis resté debout pendant tout le voyage** I had to stand for the whole journey; **~ indécis** to remain undecided;

un auteur resté méconnu an author who went unrecognized; **~ sans manger** to go without food; **elle est restée très naturelle** she's stayed very natural; **~ paralysé** to be left paralyzed; **~ veuve/orphelin** to be widowed/orphaned; **~ les bras croisés** *fig* to stand idly by; [3] (subsister) to be left, to remain; **dis-moi ce qui reste à faire** tell me what there is left to do; **il reste 50 km à parcourir** there's still another 50 km to go; [4] (survivre) [*œuvre, souvenir*] to live on; **l'habitude est restée** the habit stuck; [5] (s'arrêter) **~ sur une bonne impression** to be left with a good impression; **leur refus m'est resté sur le cœur** their refusal still rankles; [6] (ne pas aller au-delà de) **en ~ à** to go no further than; **l'affaire aurait pu en ~ là** the matter needn't have gone any further; **je compte bien ne pas en ~ là** I won't let the matter rest there; **nous en sommes restés aux préliminaires** we didn't get beyond the preliminaries; **restons-en là pour le moment** let's leave it at that for now
B *v impers* **il reste encore quelques minutes** there are still a few minutes left; **il ne me reste plus que lui** he's all I've got left; **il me reste juste de quoi payer le loyer** I've just got enough left to pay the rent; **il me reste à peine le temps** I've barely got time; **il reste beaucoup à faire** there's still a lot to do *ou* to be done; **il ne te reste plus qu'à t'excuser** it only remains for you to apologize; **reste à résoudre le problème du logement** the housing problem remains to be solved; **il reste que, il n'en reste pas moins que** the fact remains that
(Idiome) **y ~**[^o] to meet one's end *ou* Maker

restituer /ʀɛstitɥe/ [1] *vtr* [1] (rendre) to restore (**à qn** to sb); [2] (rétablir, recréer) to reconstruct [*texte*]; to restore [*fresque*]; to reproduce [*son, image*]; to recreate [*ambiance*]

restitution /ʀɛstitysjɔ̃/ *nf* [1] (action de rendre) (de bien, terre) return; (de droit, qualité) restoration; [2] (de son, d'image) reproduction

restreindre /ʀɛstʀɛ̃dʀ/ [55]
A *vtr* to curb [*dépenses*]; to limit [*possibilités, choix*]; to restrict [*champ d'action, subventions, nombre*]
B **se restreindre** *vpr* [1] (devenir plus petit) [*champ d'action, possibilités*] to become restricted; [*influence*] to wane; [2] (se limiter) **se ~ (dans ses dépenses)** to cut back (on one's expenses)

restreint, ~e /ʀɛstʀɛ̃, ɛ̃t/ *adj* [*public, vocabulaire*] limited; [*équipe*] small; **être en nombre ~** to be few in number; **cela a été décidé en comité ~** it was decided by just a few people

restrictif, -ive /ʀɛstʀiktif, iv/ *adj* restrictive

restriction /ʀɛstʀiksjɔ̃/ *nf* [1] (limitation) restriction; **~s de crédit** credit restrictions; **~s salariales** wage restraints; **pendant les ~s** (de guerre) when there was rationing; **sans ~** [*voyager*] freely; [*commercialiser*] without restriction; [2] (réserve) qualification; **apporter une ~ à ce qui est dit** to qualify a statement; **sans ~** [*accepter, approuver*] without reservations; [*soutenir*] unreservedly

restructuration /ʀəstʀyktyʀasjɔ̃/ *nf* restructuring; (en urbanisme) redevelopment

restructurer /ʀəstʀyktyʀe/ [1] *vtr* to restructure [*service, organisation*]; to redevelop [*ville, quartier*]

résultat /ʀezylta/
A *nm* *gén* result; (de recherches) **~s** results (*pl*), findings (*pl*); (de négociations, d'enquête) result, outcome; **obtenir un ~** to get a result; **beau ~!** great work, well done!; **sans ~** without success; **avoir pour ~ de faire** to have the effect of doing
B **résultats** *nmpl* [1] (chiffres) (d'examen, entreprise, de compétition) results (*pl*); Scol, Univ (d'élève, de mois) marks GB, grades US; [2] Méd (d'analyse, examen) results

résulter /ʀezylte/ [1]
A **résulter de** *vtr ind* **~ de** to be the result of, to result from; **votre échec résulte d'un manque de travail** the reason for your failure is that you didn't do enough work; **la colère qui en résulte** the resulting anger
B *v impers* **il résulte de ce que vous venez de dire que** it follows from what you have just said that; **il en résulte que** as a result; **qu'en résultera-t-il?** what will be the result of this?

résumé /ʀezyme/ *nm* [1] (version courte) summary, résumé; **faire le ~ de qch** to summarize sth; **en ~** (pour finir) to sum up; (en bref) in brief; [2] (exposé succinct) rundown; **faire un ~ de qch (à qn)** to give (sb) a rundown of *ou* on sth

résumer /ʀezyme/ [1]
A *vtr* ① (raccourcir) to summarize [*texte, pensée*]; ② (récapituler) to sum up [*nouvelle, match, état d'esprit*]; **cette anecdote résume le personnage** this anecdote sums up the character
B **se résumer** *vpr* ① [*personne*] to sum up; ② **se ~ à** to come down to

résurgence /ʀezyʀʒɑ̃s/ *nf* ① (de rivière) re-emergence; ② (d'idéologie) resurgence; (de mode) revival

resurgir /ʀ(ə)syʀʒiʀ/ [3] *vi* [*rivière*] to re-emerge; [*idéologie, problème, personne*] to reappear; [*souvenir*] to come back

résurrection /ʀezyʀɛksjɔ̃/ *nf* ① (de mort) resurrection; ② (renaissance) (de cinéma, tradition) revival; (de personne) rebirth

rétablir /ʀetabliʀ/ [3]
A *vtr* ① (ramener) to restore [*électricité, ordre, confiance, régime, impôt*]; **~ la situation** to restore normality; **~ la circulation** to get the traffic moving again; ② (restituer) to re-establish [*vérité, faits*]; to restore [*texte*]; ③ (guérir) to restore [sb] to health [*malade*]; ④ (réintégrer) **~ qn dans ses fonctions** to reinstate sb in his/her job; **~ qn sur le trône** to restore sb to the throne
B **se rétablir** *vpr* ① lit, fig (s'améliorer) [*malade, monnaie, devise*] to recover; ② (être restauré) [*ordre, silence*] to be restored; [*calme*] to return; [*situation*] to return to normal

rétablissement /ʀetablismɑ̃/ *nm* ① (de malade, monnaie) recovery; ② Sport pull-up; **faire un ~** to pull oneself up

rétamer /ʀetame/ [1]
A *vtr* ① (réparer) to re-tin [*casseroles*]; ② ○(épuiser) to wear [sb] out○; (battre) to hammer○
B **se rétamer**○ *vpr* (tomber) to fall, to come a cropper○

retape○ /ʀ(ə)tap/ *nf* (recrutement) **faire de la ~ pour qch** to beat the drum for sth

retaper /ʀ(ə)tape/ [1] *vtr* ① ○(réparer) to do up [*maison, auto*]; ② ○(rétablir) [*traitement*] to put [sb] on his/her feet again; ③ (arranger) to straighten [*lit*]

retard /ʀ(ə)taʀ/ *nm* ① (absence de ponctualité) lateness; (temps écoulé) delay; **vos ~s répétés** your continual lateness (sg); **trois ~s en une semaine c'est trop!** being late three times in a week is too much!; **un ~ de dix minutes** a ten-minute delay; **avoir du ~** to be late; **avoir un ~ d'une heure, avoir une heure de ~** (avant échéance) to be one hour behind schedule; (après échéance) to be one hour late; **arriver en ~** to arrive late; **être/se mettre en ~** to be late; **avoir du ~ dans son travail** to be/to fall behind with one's work; **être en ~ sur l'emploi du temps** to be behind schedule; **prendre du ~** to fall *ou* get behind (**dans** with); **rattraper** *or* **combler son ~** to catch up; **être en ~ pour faire qch** to be late doing sth; **il lui a souhaité son anniversaire en ~** he wished him/her a belated happy birthday; **avoir du courrier/travail en ~** to have a backlog of mail/work; **après bien des ~s** after a lot of delay; **sans ~** without delay, straight away; ② (développement moins avancé) backwardness **Ȼ**; **~ industriel** industrial backwardness; **il a deux ans de ~** Scol he's two years behind at school; **être en ~ sur son temps** to be behind the times

retardataire /ʀ(ə)taʀdatɛʀ/
A *adj* ① (non ponctuel) **les élèves ~s** students who are late; ② (qui date) outdated
B *nmf* latecomer

retardé, **~e** /ʀətaʀde/ *adj* [*personne*] backward

retardement: **à retardement** /aʀ(ə)taʀdəmɑ̃/
A *loc adj* [*appareil photo, dispositif*] delayed-action (*épith*); **bombe à ~** time-bomb; **des applaudissements à ~** belated applause **Ȼ**
B *loc adv* [*se fâcher, agir*] after the event; **il comprend toujours à ~** he's slow on the uptake○

retarder /ʀ(ə)taʀde/
A *vtr* ① (par rapport à une heure convenue) to make [sb] late; **être retardé** [*train, avion*] to be delayed; ② (par rapport à un emploi du temps) to hold [sb] up; **il a été retardé par les embouteillages** he was held up by the traffic; **ça l'a retardé dans son travail** this held up his work; ③ (reporter) to put off, to postpone [*départ*]; ④ (reculer) to put back [*réveil*]
B *vi* ① (être en retard) [*réveil*] to be slow; **ma montre retarde de cinq minutes par jour** my watch loses five minutes a day; **je retarde de cinq minutes** my watch is five minutes slow; ② (être rétrograde) **~ sur son temps** *or* **son époque** to be behind the times; ③ (ne pas être au courant) to be out of touch

retéléphoner /ʀ(ə)telefɔne/ [1] *vi* to phone again

retendre /ʀ(ə)tɑ̃dʀ/ [6] *vtr* ① (de nouveau) to tighten up (again) [*corde*]; ② (davantage) to tighten up; **faire ~ les cordes** to have the strings tightened

retenir /ʀət(ə)niʀ, ʀtəniʀ/ [36]
A *vtr* ① (empêcher de partir) to keep [*personne*]; (retarder) to hold [sb] up, to detain [*personne*]; **il m'a retenu plus d'une heure avec ses bavardages** he kept me chatting for over an hour; **je ne vous retiens pas!** don't let me keep you!; **~ qn prisonnier** to hold sb captive *ou* prisoner; **~ qn à dîner** to ask sb to stay for dinner; ② (maintenir fixe) lit, fig to hold [*objet, attention*]; (en arrière) to hold back [*cheveux, volet, chien, personne, foule*]; to retain [*sol*]; (empêcher une chute) to stop [*personne*]; to rein in [*cheval*]; **~ sa langue** to hold one's tongue; **si je ne l'avais pas retenu, il aurait tout avoué** if I hadn't held him back, he would have confessed everything; **retenez-moi ou je fais un malheur**○! hold me down or I'll go berserk○!; **~ qn par la manche** to catch hold of sb's sleeve; **votre réclamation a retenu toute notre attention** your complaint is receiving our full attention; ③ (réprimer) to hold back [*larmes*]; to hold [*souffle*]; to stifle [*cri, rire, soupir*]; to bite back [*exclamation*]; to suppress [*sourire*]; to contain [*colère*]; to check [*geste*]; ④ (capturer) to retain [*chaleur, eau, odeur*]; to absorb [*lumière*]; ⑤ (réserver) to reserve [*table, place*]; to set [*date*]; ⑥ (confisquer) to withhold [*caution, bagages*]; to stop [*salaire*]; (prélever) to deduct [*somme, impôt*] (**sur** from); ⑦ (mémoriser) to remember [*nom, date*]; **retiens-bien ceci** remember this; **cet enfant ne retient rien** that child doesn't take anything in; **je retiens qu'on peut leur faire confiance** I've learned that they can be trusted; **toi, je te retiens**○! I won't forget this!; ⑧ (agréer) to accept [*argument, proposition*]; Jur to uphold [*chef d'accusation*]; (considérer favorablement) **votre candidature a été retenue** you're being considered for the post; **être retenu comme critère** to be used as a criterion; ⑨ Math to carry (over); **je pose 5 et je retiens 1** I put down 5 and carry 1
B **se retenir** *vpr* ① (se rattraper) to stop oneself; **se ~ à qch** to hang on to sth; ② (réprimer une envie psychique) to stop oneself; **je n'ai pas pu me ~ de pleurer** I couldn't hold back the tears; **il ne put se ~ de rire** he couldn't help laughing; **je me suis retenu de leur dire ce que je pensais** I refrained from telling them what I thought; **j'ai dû me ~ pour ne pas la gifler** it was all I could do not to slap her; ③ ○(réprimer un besoin physiologique) to control oneself

rétention /ʀetɑ̃sjɔ̃/ *nf* ① Méd retention; ② (refus de communiquer) withholding (**de** of)

retentir /ʀ(ə)tɑ̃tiʀ/ [3] *vi* ① (résonner) to ring out; (plus fort) to resound; **~ aux oreilles de qn** to ring in sb's ears; ② (affecter) **~ sur** [*fatigue, drogue, état*] to have an impact on; [*événement, situation*] to have repercussions on

retentissant, **~e** /ʀ(ə)tɑ̃tisɑ̃, ɑ̃t/ *adj* ① (éclatant) [*déclaration, échec, succès*] resounding; [*procès, film, découverte, discours*] sensational; ② (sonore) [*voix, bruit*] ringing; (plus fort) resounding

retentissement /ʀ(ə)tɑ̃tismɑ̃/ *nm* ① (répercussions) effect; (d'artiste, œuvre) impact; ② (succès) sensation; **avoir un (grand) ~** to cause a (great) sensation

retenue /ʀət(ə)ny/ *nf* ① (modération) restraint; **manquer de ~** to lack restraint; **perdre toute ~** to lose one's inhibitions; **n'avoir aucune ~ dans son langage** to use very immoderate language; **n'avoir aucune ~ dans sa conduite** to behave wildly; **sans ~** [*boire*] to excess; [*rire*] uproariously; ② (prélèvement) deduction (**sur** from); **faire une ~ de 10% sur le salaire de qn** to deduct 10% from sb's salary; ③ Scol detention; ④ Math **tu as oublié la ~ des dizaines** you forgot to carry over from the tens column; ⑤ (masse d'eau) reservoir; **ouvrage de ~** dam

réticence /ʀetisɑ̃s/ *nf* ① (répugnance) reluctance; **avec ~** reluctantly; **sans ~** [*parler*] openly; [*accepter*] unreservedly; ② liter (réserve) reticence **Ȼ**; **ses ~s en ce qui concerne le passé** his/her reticence about the past; ③ (chose omise) non-disclosure, omission

réticent, **~e** /ʀetisɑ̃, ɑ̃t/ *adj* (qui hésite) hesitant (**à faire** about doing); (qui rechigne) reluctant (**à faire** to do); **se montrer/être ~ à une idée** to seem/to be hostile to an idea

rétif, **-ive** /ʀetif, iv/ *adj* [*âne*] restive; [*personne, humeur*] rebellious

rétine /ʀetin/ *nf* retina

retiré, ~**e** /Rətiʀe/ adj (solitaire) [endroit, vie] secluded; (éloigné) [endroit] remote

retirer /Rətiʀe/ [1]

A vtr **1** (se débarrasser de) to take off [vêtement, bijou]; **2** (faire sortir) to take out, to remove (**de** from); ~ **une balle d'une blessure** to remove ou extract a bullet from a wound; ~ **les mains de ses poches** to take one's hands out of one's pockets; ~ **un enfant d'une école** to take a child away from a school, to remove a child from a school; ~ **qch de l'eau/des décombres** to pull sth out of the water/from ou out of the rubble; ~ **un gâteau d'un moule** to turn a cake out of a tin GB ou pan US; ~ **ses troupes d'un pays** to withdraw one's troops from a country; **3** (écarter) to withdraw [pied, main]; **retire ta main, tu vas te brûler** move your hand away, you'll burn yourself; **4** (supprimer, enlever) to withdraw [permission] (**à** from); to take away, to remove [droit, bien, objet] (**à** from); ~ **un produit de la vente** Comm to recall a product; ~ **la garde d'un enfant à qn** to withdraw custody of a child from sb; **on m'a retiré la garde de mon fils** I've lost custody of my son; **il s'est fait ~ son permis de conduire** he had his driver's licence^GB taken away from him; ~ **de la circulation** to withdraw [sth] from circulation [monnaie]; ~ **un livre du programme/de la table** to take a book off the syllabus/off the table; ~ **une pièce de l'affiche** to close a play; **5** (ne pas maintenir) to withdraw [plainte, offre]; ~ **sa candidature** (à un poste) to withdraw one's application; (à une élection) to stand down (**en faveur de** in favour^GB of); **je retire ce que j'ai dit** I take back what I said; **6** (rentrer en possession de) to collect, to pick up [billet, bagages, dossier]; to withdraw [argent]; **7** (recueillir) to get, to derive [bénéfice] (**de** from); **il en retire 3 000 euros par an** he gets 3,000 euros a year out of it; **je n'en ai retiré que des ennuis** I got nothing but trouble out of it; **8** (extraire) to extract [minerai, huile] (**de** from)

B **se retirer** vpr (partir) to withdraw, to leave; (aller se coucher)† to retire to bed; **se ~ dans son bureau** to withdraw to one's study; **se ~ sur ses terres** to retire to one's estate; **se ~ du monde** to withdraw from society; **un homme retiré de la politique** a man retired from political life; **se ~ du combat** to pull out; **se ~ sur la pointe des pieds** to tiptoe out ou away; **se ~ sans bruit** to slip away quietly; (reculer) [eaux de crue] to subside; [personne] to step back; (pour laisser passer) to step aside; **la mer se retire** the tide is going out

retombée /Rətɔ̃be/

A nf Archit springing

B **retombées** nfpl **1** (pluie) ~**s radioactives** radioactive fall-out **C**; **2** (conséquences) effects (pl), consequences (pl); **3** (d'une invention) spin-offs (pl)

retomber /Rətɔ̃be/ [1] vi **1** (faire une nouvelle chute) [personne, objet] to fall again; ~ **malade/amoureux** to fall ill/in love again; ~ **dans la misère/la facilité** to sink back into poverty/a state of complacency; ~ **en enfance** to regress to childhood; **2** (retourner au sol après s'être élevé) [personne, chat, projectile] to land; [ballon, capot] to come down; [brouillard] to set in again; ~ **sur ses pattes** [chat] to land on its feet; ~ **sur ses pieds** or **pattes**^○ fig to land on one's feet; **les fumées toxiques retombent en pluie acide** toxic fumes come down as acid rain; **ça va ~ sur le nez**^○ fig it'll come down on your head; **3** (s'affaisser) [personne] to fall back; [soufflé] to collapse; fig [intérêt] to wane; **4** (diminuer) [monnaie] to fall; [température] to go down, to fall; **le dollar est retombé à 90 centimes** the dollar has fallen to 90 cents; **5** (incomber à) ~ **sur qn** [responsabilité, ennui] to fall on sb; **tu fais des bêtises et c'est sur moi que ça retombe** you behave stupidly, and I'm the one who has to pay for it; **faire ~ la responsabilité sur qn** to pass the buck^○ to sb

retordre /R(ə)tɔʀdʀ/ [6] vtr **donner du fil à ~ à qn** to give sb a hard time

rétorquer /Retɔʀke/ [1] vtr (répliquer) to retort

retors, ~**e** /Rətɔʀ, ɔʀs/ adj pej [personne] crafty; [argument] devious

rétorsion /Retɔʀsjɔ̃/ nf retaliation; **mesure de ~** retaliatory measure

retouche /R(ə)tuʃ/ nf (de vêtement, texte) alteration; (de photo, tableau) retouch

retoucher /R(ə)tuʃe/ [1]

A vtr (modifier) to make alterations to [vêtement, texte]; to alter [col, manches]; to touch up [photographie]

B **retoucher à** vtr ind **il a juré qu'il ne retoucherait jamais à l'alcool** he vowed that he would never touch alcohol again

retour /R(ə)tuʀ/ nm **1** (trajet) return; (**billet de**) ~ return ticket GB, round trip (ticket) US; **au ~** on the way back; **être sur le chemin du ~** to be on one's way back; time ~ **s'est bien passé** we got back safely; **il pense déjà à son ~** he's already thinking about going back; **2** (au point de départ) return; **à mon ~ à Paris/de Paris** on my return to Paris/from Paris; **être de ~** to be back; **de ~ à la maison** back home; **à son ~, elle m'a téléphoné** when she got back, she phoned me; **partir sans espoir de ~** to leave for good; **3** (à un stade antérieur) return; ~ **à la normale** return to normal; **on attend le ~ au calme** people are waiting for things to calm down; ~ **à la terre** going back to the land; '~ **à la case départ**' 'back to square one'; **il connaît maintenant le succès et c'est un juste ~ des choses** he's successful now, and deservedly so; **4** (réapparition) return; **le ~ de la mode des années 60** the return of 60s fashions; **faire un ~ en force** [chanteur] to make a big comeback; [idéologie] to be back with a vengeance; [cycliste, coureur] to make a strong comeback; **5** (échange) **elle s'engage, en ~, à payer la facture** she undertakes for her part to pay the bill; **aimer sans ~** liter to suffer from unrequited love; **6** Comm (objet invendu) return; (de bouteille) return; '**sans ~ ni consigne**' 'no deposit or return'; **7** (renvoi) **par ~ du courrier** by return of post GB, by the next mail US

(Composés) ~ **d'âge** change of life; Cin, Littérat flashback; **ce serait un ~ en arrière** (non souhaitable) it would be a step backward(s); **un ~ en arrière s'impose** (souhaitable) we must go back to the previous state of affairs; ~ **de balancier** or **de bâton**^○ or **de manivelle**^○ backlash; ~ **de marée** undertow

(Idiome) **être sur le ~**^○ to be over the hill^○

retournement /R(ə)tuʀnəmɑ̃/ nm (de situation) reversal; **un ~ de l'opinion publique** a turn around in public opinion

retourner /R(ə)tuʀne/ [1]

A vtr (+ v avoir) **1** (changer de côté) to turn [sth] over [seau, steak]; to turn [matelas]; ~ **une carte à jouer** to turn over a playing card; **2** (mettre à l'envers) to turn [sth] inside out [vêtement, sac]; **3** (tourner à plusieurs reprises) to turn over [terre]; to toss [salade, foin]; ~ **une idée dans sa tête** fig to turn an idea over in one's mind; **4** (changer d'orientation) to return [compliment, critique]; ~ **la situation** to reverse the situation; **elle a retourné le pistolet contre elle-même** she then turned the gun on herself; **si tu retournes l'argument contre lui** if you turn his own argument against him; **5** (bouleverser) [personne] to turn [sth] upside down [maison]; [nouvelle, spectacle] to shake [personne]; **je suis encore tout retourné**^○ I'm still quite shaken; **6** (renvoyer) to send [sth] back, to return [colis, lettre]

B vi (+ v être) to go back (**à** to), to return (**à** to)

C **se retourner** vpr **1** (tourner la tête) to turn around; **partir sans se ~** lit, fig to leave without a backward glance; **elle est tellement grande que tout le monde se retourne sur son passage** she's so tall that everybody turns to look as she goes past; **2** to turn over; **se ~ sur le dos** to turn over onto one's back; **il n'a pas arrêté de se ~ (dans son lit)** he kept tossing and turning; **la voiture s'est retournée dans un fossé** the car overturned into a ditch; **3** (s'organiser) to get organized; **4** (prendre un tour inverse) **se ~ contre qn** [personne, animal] to turn against sb; [situation, agissements] to backfire on sb; **se ~ contre ses alliés** to turn on one's allies; **ses arguments se sont retournés contre lui** his arguments backfired on him; **5** (se tordre) **elle s'est retourné le doigt** she bent back her finger; **6** (repartir) **s'en ~** to go back; **s'en ~ chez soi** to go back home

D v impers **j'aimerais savoir de quoi il retourne** I'd like to know what's going on

(Idiome) ~ **qn comme une crêpe**^○ or **un gant**^○ to make sb change their mind completely

retracer /Rətʀase/ [12] vtr **1** (marquer) to redraw; **2** (narrer) to recount

rétractable /Retʀaktabl/ adj [pointe] retractable; [offre] revocable

rétracter /Retʀakte/ [1] vtr, **se rétracter** vpr to retract

retrait /R(ə)tʀɛ/

A nm **1** (de valise, commande, dossier) collection; (d'argent) withdrawal; [2] (d'autorisation, de soutien, monnaie) withdrawal (**de** of); Comm (d'article défectueux) recall (**de** of); **réclamer le ~ d'une mesure** to call for a measure to be lifted; **après le ~ de la candidature du maire sortant** after the outgoing mayor stood down; **~ du permis (de conduire)** disqualification from driving; [3] (départ) withdrawal; **le ~ des eaux a révélé l'ampleur du désastre** when the water went down *ou* subsided, the scale of the disaster became apparent

B en retrait *loc adv* (à l' écart) **maison (située) en ~ de** house set back from [*route*]; house a little way out of [*village*]; **se tenir en ~** lit to stand back; fig to occupy a back seat; **rester en ~** fig to stay in the background

retraite /ʀ(ə)tʀɛt/ *nf* [1] (cessation d'activité) retirement; **prendre sa ~** to retire; **mettre qn à la ~** to retire sb; **il a été mis à la ~ anticipée** he was made to take early retirement; **être en** *or* **à la ~** to be retired; **départ à la ~** retirement; [2] (pension) pension; [3] Mil retreat; **battre en ~** Mil to beat a retreat, to retreat; fig to beat a hasty retreat; [4] Relig retreat; [5] (lieu retiré) retreat; (de brigands) refuge

retraité, ~e /ʀətʀete/
A *adj* [*personne*] retired
B *nm,f* retired person; **les ~s** retired people (+ *v pl*)

retraiter /ʀətʀete/ [1] *vtr* to reprocess [*plutonium*]

retranché, ~e /ʀ(ə)tʀɑ̃ʃe/ *adj* [*village, cap, position*] entrenched

retranchement /ʀ(ə)tʀɑ̃ʃmɑ̃/ *nm* entrenchment; **pousser qn dans ses derniers ~s** fig to drive sb into a corner

retrancher /ʀ(ə)tʀɑ̃ʃe/ [1]
A *vtr* [1] (enlever) to cut out [*mot, phrase*] (**de** from); [2] (soustraire) to subtract, to take away [*montant*] (**de** from); to deduct [*frais*] (**de** from)
B se retrancher *vpr* [1] Mil (s'installer) to take up position; (pour être à l'abri) to entrench oneself; **être retranché dans un village** [*soldats*] to have taken up position in a village; [2] (se cacher) **se ~ derrière** to hide behind [*idéologie, loi*]; **il se retranche derrière le directeur** he says it's a matter for the manager; **se ~ dans** to take refuge in [*silence, rêve*]

retransmettre /ʀətʀɑ̃smɛtʀ/ [60] *vtr* [1] Radio, TV to broadcast [*émission*]; [2] (par relais) to relay; [3] Télécom, Radio to retransmit [*appel*]

retransmission /ʀətʀɑ̃smisjɔ̃/ *nf* [1] (d'émission) broadcast; [2] (relais) relay; **assurer la ~ d'un signal** to relay a signal; [3] (de message, d'appel) retransmission

retravailler /ʀətʀavaje/ [1]
A *vtr* to revise [*œuvre*]
B *vi* to start working again; (après des vacances, une maladie) to go back to work

rétrécir /ʀetʀesiʀ/ [3]
A *vtr* [1] [*lavage*] to shrink; [2] [*couturier*] to take in (**de** by); [3] to make [sth] narrower [*route, bague, orifice*]; to make [sth] smaller [*terrain, parc*]
B *vi* [*tissu*] to shrink (**de** by)
C se rétrécir *vpr* [1] [*route, champ d'investigation*] to narrow; [*groupe*] to shrink; [2] Anat [*pupille*] to contract; [3] [*pensée*] to become more restricted

rétrécissement /ʀetʀesismɑ̃/ *nm* [1] (après lavage) shrinkage; [2] (de route, vallée) narrowing; [3] (de pupille) contraction; (d'intestin) stricture

rétribuer /ʀetʀibɥe/ [1] *vtr* to remunerate [*personne, travail*]

rétribution /ʀetʀibysjɔ̃/ *nf* [1] (paiement) remuneration; [2] (récompense) reward (**de** for)

rétro /ʀetʀo/ *nm* [1] Archit, Art (style) nostalgic style; [2] (mode) retro fashions (*pl*)

rétroactif, -ive /ʀetʀoaktif, iv/ *adj* Admin, Jur retroactive; [*augmentation*] backdated

rétroaction /ʀetʀoaksjɔ̃/ *nf* [1] Admin, Jur retroactive effect; [2] Biol, Phys feedback

rétroactivité /ʀetʀoaktivite/ *nf* Admin, Jur retroactivity; (de jugement) ex post facto effect

rétrograde /ʀetʀoɡʀad/ *adj* [1] (réactionnaire) [*personne, gouvernement*] reactionary; [*loi, pensée*] retrograde; [2] (qui va en sens inverse) [*mouvement*] retrograde

rétrograder /ʀetʀoɡʀade/ [1]
A *vtr* [1] Mil, Admin to demote [*militaire, fonctionnaire*] (**à** to); [2] Sport to relegate [*sportif, cheval*]
B *vi* Aut to change down GB, to downshift US

rétrospectif, -ive¹ /ʀetʀɔspɛktif, iv/ *adj* retrospective

rétrospective² /ʀetʀɔspɛktiv/ *nf* Art retrospective; Cin festival

rétrospectivement /ʀetʀɔspɛktivmɑ̃/ *adv* [1] (après coup) [*avoir peur*] after the event; [2] (après réflexion) in retrospect

retroussé, ~e /ʀ(ə)tʀuse/ *adj* [*nez*] turned up; [*lèvre*] curling (*épith*)

retrousser /ʀ(ə)tʀuse/ [1] *vtr* to hitch up GB, to hike up US [*robe*]; to roll up [*pantalon*]; **~ ses manches** lit, fig to roll up one's sleeves; **le chien retroussa ses babines** the dog bared its teeth

retrouvailles /ʀətʀuvaj/ *nfpl* (après une séparation) reunion (**avec** with); (après une brouille) reconciliation (**avec** with)

retrouver /ʀətʀuve/ [1]
A *vtr* [1] (ce qui était perdu) to find [*sac, cadavre, fugitif*]; **~ son chemin** to find one's way; [2] (trouver à nouveau) to find [sth] again [*travail, objet*]; to come across [sth] again [*thème*]; [3] (redécouvrir) to rediscover [*technique, recette*]; [4] (récupérer) to get [sth] back [*assurance*]; to regain, to recover [*force, santé*]; **~ son sang-froid** to regain one's composure; **il a retrouvé le sourire** he's smiling again; **~ le sommeil** to be able to sleep again; [5] (se rappeler) to remember [*nom, air*]; [6] (revoir) to meet [sb] again [*connaissance*]; (regagner) to be back in [*lieu*]; [7] (reconnaître) to recognize [*personne, trait, style*]; **je retrouve sa mère en elle** I can see her mother in her; **on le retrouve dans cette œuvre** you can see his hand in this work; **quand tu souris, je te retrouve** that's more like you to be smiling; [8] (rejoindre) to join, to meet [*personne*]; **je te retrouverai!** (menace) I'll get my own back on you!
B se retrouver *vpr* [1] (se réunir) to meet; (se voir de nouveau) to meet again; **on se retrouvera devant le cinéma** let's meet (up) outside the cinema; **de temps en temps on se retrouve entre amis** we get together with a few friends once in a while; **on s'est retrouvé en famille** the family got together; [2] (être) to find oneself; **se ~ enceinte** to find oneself pregnant; **se ~ orphelin/sans argent/seul** to be left an orphan/penniless/on one's own; **se ~ confronté à** to be faced with; **se ~ à l'hôpital** to end up in hospital; **se ~ au même point** to be back to square one; [3] (s'orienter) **se** *or* **s'y ~ dans** lit to find one's way around in [*lieu, fichier*]; fig to follow [*explication*]; **tu t'y retrouves entre tous ces emplois/amants?** can you cope with all these jobs/lovers?; **il y a trop de changements, on ne s'y retrouve plus** there are too many changes, we don't know if we're coming or going; [4] ᴼ(rentrer dans ses frais) **s'y ~** to break even; (faire un bénéfice) to do well; [5] (être présent) [*personne, qualité*] to be found; [*problème*] to occur; **le même amour de la musique se retrouve chez les deux enfants** both children have the same love of music; [6] (se reconnaître) **se ~ dans qn/qch** to see *ou* recognize oneself in sb/sth

(Idiome) **un de perdu, dix de retrouvés** there are plenty more fish in the sea

rétroviseur /ʀetʀovizœʀ/ *nm* [1] (intérieur) rear-view mirror; [2] (extérieur) wing mirror GB, outside rear-view mirror US

réuni, ~e /ʀeyni/ *adj* [1] (mis ensemble) [*forces, qualités, salaires*] combined; [2] (assemblé) [*conseil, personnes*] assembled; [3] (remis ensemble) reunited; **les deux Berlin ~s** (a) reunited Berlin; [4] Comm (associés) associated

réunification /ʀeynifikasjɔ̃/ *nf* reunification

réunifier /ʀeynifje/ [2]
A *vtr* to reunify
B se réunifier *vpr* to be reunified, to reunite

réunion /ʀeynjɔ̃/ *nf* [1] (séance) meeting (**entre** between); **être en ~** [*personne*] to be at *ou* in a meeting; [*comité*] to be meeting; [2] (rencontre) gathering; **~ familiale** family gathering; [3] (retrouvailles) (après une séparation) reunion; (après une brouille) reconciliation; [4] (groupement) (de talents, volontés) combination; (d'œuvres) collection; [5] (rattachement) union (**à** with); (après séparation) reunification; (de sociétés) merger

Réunion /ʀeynjɔ̃/ ▸ p. 303 *nprf* **la ~** Reunion

réunir /ʀeyniʀ/ [3]
A *vtr* [1] (assembler) [*congrès*] to bring together [*participants*]; [*organisateur*] to get [sb] together [*participants*]; [2] (convoquer) to call [sb] together [*délégués*]; to convene [*assemblée*]; [3] (inviter) to have [sb] round GB *ou* over [*amis*]; [4] (rapprocher) to join [*bords*]; to bring [sb] together [*personnes*]; (après une brouille, une séparation) to reunite;

5) (fusionner) to merge [*sociétés*]; to unite [*provinces*] (**à** with); **6)** (cumuler) ~ **les qualités nécessaires** to have all the necessary qualifications; **7)** (recueillir) to raise [*fonds*]; to collect [*preuves, articles*]; **8)** (regrouper) to assemble [*éléments, preuves*]; to gather [sth] together [*documents*]; **9)** (relier) [*route, canal*] to connect [*lieux*]

B se réunir *vpr* **1)** (s'assembler) [*délégués, comité*] to meet; [*amis*] to get together; **2)** (se joindre) [*routes, fleuves*] to meet; **3)** (s'associer) [*sociétés*] to merge; [*nations*] to unite

réussi, ~**e** /ʀeysi/ *adj* **1)** (mené à bien) [*opération*] successful; **2)** (apprécié) [*soirée*] successful; **3)** (bien fait) [*œuvre*] accomplished; [*photo*] good

réussir /ʀeysiʀ/ [3]

A *vtr* to achieve [*unification, modernisation*]; to carry off [sth] successfully [*coup politique*]; to carry out [sth] successfully [*fabrication, opération*]; to make a success of [*vie, éducation*]; to win [*pari*]; to pass [*examen*]; ~ **l'impossible** to manage the impossible; ~ **son coup**○ to pull it off○

B réussir à *vtr ind* **1)** (parvenir à) ~ **à faire** to succeed in doing, to manage to do; ~ **à ne pas tomber** to manage not to fall; ~ **à un examen** to pass an exam; **2)** (être favorable à) ~ **à qn** [*vie, méthode*] to turn out well for sb; [*aliment, repos*] to do sb good; **le vin blanc ne me réussit pas** white wine doesn't agree with me

C *vi* **1)** (atteindre le but recherché) to succeed; **ça n'a pas réussi** it didn't work, it didn't come off; **2)** (être couronné de succès) [*opération chirurgicale, tentative*] to be successful; **3)** (obtenir un bon résultat) [*personne*] to do well (**en, dans** in)

réussite /ʀeysit/ *nf* **1)** gén success (**dans** in); ~ **sociale** social success; ~ **scolaire** success at school; ~ **à un examen** success in an examination; **2)** Jeux patience ¢ GB, solitaire ¢ US

revaloir /ʀ(ə)valwaʀ/ [45] *vtr* **je te revaudrai ça** (hostile) I'll get even with you for that; (reconnaissant) I'll return the favour^{GB}

revalorisation /ʀ(ə)valɔʀizasjɔ̃/ *nf* **1)** (augmentation) **une** ~ **des salaires de 3%** a 3% wage increase; **2)** (retour de l'estime) **la** ~ **des enseignants** the enhanced prestige of teachers; **3)** (amélioration) improvement (**de** in), enhancement (**de** of)

revaloriser /ʀ(ə)valɔʀize/ [1] *vtr* **1)** (augmenter) to increase, to raise [*salaire*]; to revalue [*monnaie*]; **2)** (rendre l'estime envers) to reassert the value of [*travail manuel, traditions*]; **3)** (remettre en état) to renovate [*bâtiment*]

revanche /ʀ(ə)vɑ̃ʃ/

A *nf* **1)** revenge; **désir de/esprit de** ~ desire for/spirit of revenge; **avoir sa** ~ to take one's revenge; **2)** Sport return match GB *ou* game US; Jeux return game

B en revanche *loc adv* on the other hand

(Idiome) **à charge de** ~ provided you'll let me return the favour^{GB}

rêvasser /ʀɛvase/ [1] *vi* to daydream

rêve /ʀɛv/ *nm* **1)** (de dormeur) (activité) dreaming; (résultat) dream; **faire un** ~ to have a dream; **fais de beaux** ~**s!** sweet dreams!; **j'ai l'impression de rêver** I feel as if I'm dreaming; **en** ~ in a dream; **2)** (fantasme) dream; ~ **de jeunesse** youthful dream; **avoir des** ~**s de grandeur** to dream of greatness; **une maison de** ~ a dream house; **3)** (idéal) **c'est le** ~ this is just perfect; **ce n'est pas le** ~ it's not ideal

(Composé) ~ **éveillé** daydream

rêvé, ~**e** /ʀɛve/ *adj* ideal, perfect

revêche /ʀəvɛʃ/ *adj* [*air, ton*] sour; [*personne*] crabby

réveil /ʀevɛj/ *nm* **1)** (après un somme) waking (up); **au** ~**/dès son** ~ when he wakes up/as soon as he wakes up; **2)** (après un malaise, une anesthésie) **j'ai eu des nausées au** ~ I felt nauseous when I came to; **3)** (de la nature, d'un sentiment) reawakening; (de nation, mouvement) resurgence; (de la foi) revival; (de douleurs) return, recurrence; (de la conscience) awakening; (de volcan) return to activity; **le** ~ **des minorités** the new activism of minorities; **4)** (retour à la réalité) awakening; **5)** Mil reveille; **en fanfare** fig rousing start to the day; **6)** (pendule) alarm clock

réveille-matin /ʀevɛjmatɛ̃/ *nm inv* alarm clock

réveiller /ʀeveje/ [1]

A *vtr* **1)** (tirer du sommeil, de rêverie, d'hypnose) to wake [sb] up, to wake; **être réveillé en sursaut** to wake up with a start; **être réveillé par l'orage** to be woken by the storm; **faire un bruit à** ~ **les morts**○ to make enough noise to wake the

dead; **2)** (ranimer) to revive [*malade*]; to bring some sensation back into [*membre ankylosé*]; to whet [*appétit*]; to awaken [*sentiment*]; to arouse [*crainte, curiosité, polémique*]; to bring out [*instinct*], to awaken, to stir up [*souvenir*]; ~ **la douleur** to bring back the pain

B se réveiller *vpr* **1)** (après un somme) to wake up; (après une rêverie, une hypnose) to awaken (**de** from); **se** ~ **en sursaut/en sueur** to wake up with a start/in a sweat; **2)** (après une anesthésie, un malaise) [*personne*] to come round GB, to regain consciousness; **3)** (après une période d'inertie) [*personne, peuple*] to wake up; [*nature*] to reawaken; [*volcan*] to become active again; **4)** (se raviver) [*douleur, appétit*] to come back; [*jalousie, souvenir*] to be reawakened

réveillon /ʀevɛjɔ̃/ *nm* ~ **de Noël/du Nouvel An** (fête) Christmas Eve/New Year's Eve party

réveillonner /ʀevɛjɔne/ [1] *vi* (pour le Nouvel An) to see the New Year in

révélateur, -trice /ʀevelatœʀ, tʀis/

A *adj* [*détail, fait*] revealing, telling

B *nm* **1)** Phot developer; **2)** (fait, détail) pointer (**de** to)

révélation /ʀevelasjɔ̃/ *nf* **1)** (découverte, aveu) revelation; **2)** (œuvre, auteur) discovery; **3)** Phot development

révéler /ʀevele/ [14]

A *vtr* **1)** (dévoiler) to reveal, to disclose [*fait, chiffres, nom*] (**à** to); to give away [*secret*] (**à** to); **2)** (indiquer) to show; **3)** (faire connaître) [*œuvre*] to make [sb] known [*auteur, acteur*] (**à** to); [*éditeur, imprésario*] to discover, to launch [*auteur, artiste*]; **cela l'a révélée à elle-même** it gave her a great deal of personal insight; **4)** Phot to develop

B se révéler *vpr* (être finalement) **se** ~ **faux** to turn out to be wrong; **se** ~ **comme un grand pianiste** to emerge as a great pianist

revenant, ~**e** /ʀəv(ə)nɑ̃, ɑ̃t/ *nm,f* ghost; **tiens, une** ~**e**○! hum long time no see○!

revendeur, -euse /ʀ(ə)vɑ̃dœʀ, øz/ ▸ p. 372 *nm,f* **1)** (détaillant) stockist; **un** ~ **de drogue** a drug dealer; **2)** (d'objets volés) seller (of stolen goods)

revendicatif, -ive /ʀ(ə)vɑ̃dikatif, iv/ *adj* [*action*] protest (épith); [*dossier*] of demands; **journée revendicative** day of protest

revendication /ʀ(ə)vɑ̃dikasjɔ̃/ *nf* (d'ouvrier, de catégorie sociale) demand; (de pays, population, d'héritier) claim (**sur, de** to)

revendiquer /ʀ(ə)vɑ̃dike/ [1] *vtr* **1)** (réclamer) to demand [*droit, augmentation*]; to claim [*héritage, trône, territoire*]; **2)** (s'affirmer l'auteur de) to claim responsibility for [*attentat*]; to claim authorship of [*livre*]; ~ **la paternité d'un enfant** to claim paternity of a child; ~ **la responsabilité de** to take (full) responsibility for; **3)** (affirmer avoir) to claim; **4)** (être fier de) to proclaim [*origines*]

revendre /ʀ(ə)vɑ̃dʀ/ [6]

A *vtr* **1)** (dévoiler au détail) to sell [sth] retail, to retail (**à** to); **2)** (vendre ce qui est à soi) to sell [*objet, maison*] (**à** to); to sell (off) [*actions, parts, or*]; (vendre des objets volés) to sell on; **avoir des crayons à** ~ fig to have pencils galore; **avoir de l'énergie à** ~ fig to have energy to spare

B se revendre *vpr* (se vendre d'occasion) to resell

revenez-y /ʀəvnezi, ʀvənezi/ *nm inv* **le gâteau a un petit goût de** ~ the cake is rather moreish○ GB, the cake is too good I'd like seconds

revenir /ʀəvniʀ, ʀvəniʀ/ [36]

A *vi* (+ *v être*) **1)** (fréquenter de nouveau) to come back; (venir une fois encore) to come again; **2)** (rentrer) [*personne, animal, véhicule*] to come back (**à** to; **de** from), to return (**à** to; **de** from); ~ **sur terre** fig to come down to earth; **partir pour ne jamais** ~ to leave never to return; ~ **de loin** lit to come back from far away; fig to have had a close shave; **en revenant du bureau** (en route) coming home from the office; (à l'arrivée) on getting home from the office; **je reviens tout de suite** I'll be back in a minute, I'll be right back○; **il en est revenu vivant** he got back in one piece; **elle est revenue en vitesse à la maison** she rushed back home; **mon chèque m'est revenu** my cheque GB *ou* check US was returned; **3)** (reprendre, retourner à) ~ **à** to return to, to come back to [*méthode, conception, histoire*]; **revenons à notre héros** let's return to our hero; ~ **à la normale/au pouvoir** to return to normal/to power; **le dollar est revenu à 95 centimes d'euro** the dollar has gone back to 95 cents; ~ **à la politique** to come back into politics; ~ **à ses habitudes/aux frontières d'avant la guerre** to revert to one's old habits/to pre-war borders; **pour (en)** ∼ **à ce que je disais** to get back to what I was saying; ∼ **à de meilleurs sentiments** to return to a better frame of mind; **4)** (réapparaître) [*tache, rhume, mode*] to come back; [*soleil*] to come out again; [*saison*] to return; [*date, fête*] to come round again GB, to come again US; [*idée, thème*] to recur; **cette idée me revenait souvent** the idea kept occurring to me; **le mot revient souvent sous sa plume** the word keeps cropping up in his/her writing; **le calme est revenu** calm has been restored, things have calmed down; **5)** (être recouvré) [*appétit, mémoire*] to come back; **l'appétit me revient** I'm getting my appetite back; **6)** (être remémoré) ∼ **à qn,** ∼ **à la mémoire** *or* **l'esprit de qn** to come back to sb; **ça me revient!** now I remember!, now it's coming back!; **7)** (coûter) ∼ **à 20 euros** to cost 20 euros, to cost 20 euros; **ça m'est revenu à 20 euros** it cost me 20 euros; **ça revient cher** it works out expensive; **8)** (équivaloir à) **ça revient au même** it amounts ou comes to the same thing; **ce qui revient à dire que** which amounts to saying that; **9)** (reconsidérer) ∼ **sur** to go back over [*question, passé*]; (changer d'avis) to go back on [*décision, promesse*]; to retract [*aveu*]; **10)** (sortir d'un état) ∼ **de** to get over [*maladie, surprise*]; to lose [*illusion*]; to abandon [*théorie*]; **la vie à la campagne, j'en suis revenu** as for life in the country, I've seen it for what it is; **être revenu de tout** to be blasé; **je n'en reviens pas**◦! I can't get over it!; **11)** (être rapporté) ∼ **à qn,** ∼ **aux oreilles de qn** [*propos*] to get back to sb, to reach sb's ears; **12)** (être attribué) ∼ **à qn** [*bien, titre*] to go to sb; [*honneur*] to fall to sb; (de droit) to be due to sb; **ce poste pourrait revenir à un écologiste** this post could go to an ecologist; **ça leur revient de droit** it's theirs by right; **les 10% qui me reviennent** the 10% that's coming to me; **la décision revient au rédacteur** it is the editor's decision; **13)** Culin **faire** ∼ to brown

B **s'en revenir** *vpr* liter to return (**de** from)

C *v impers* **1)** (incomber) **c'est à vous qu'il revient de trancher** it is for you to decide; **2)** (parvenir à la connaissance de) **il m'est revenu certains propos** certain remarks have reached my ears; **3)** (être remémoré) **il me revient que** I recall ou remember that

(Idiomes) ∼ **à soi** to come round GB, to come to; ∼ **à la vie** to come back to life; **il a une tête qui ne me revient pas** I don't like the look of him

revenu /Rəv(ə)ny, Rvəny/ *nm* (de personne) income; (de l'État) revenue ¢

(Composés) ∼ **minimum d'insertion, RMI** *minimum benefit paid to those with no other source of income*

> ⓘ **Revenu minimum d'insertion** Introduced in 1988, the *RMI* is an allowance designed to support the poorest members of society by bringing them above the poverty line, but also giving them rights of access to other allowances and social security benefits.

rêver /Reve/ [1]
A *vtr* **1)** (en dormant) to dream (**que** that); **2)** (imaginer) to dream of [*succès, vengeance*]

B *vi* **1)** [*dormeur*] to dream (**de** about); ∼ **tout éveillé** to be lost in a daydream; **on croit** ∼! you'd think you were dreaming!; **2)** (se faire des illusions) to dream; **3)** (rêvasser, aspirer à) to dream (**à** of)

réverbération /ReveRbeRasjɔ̃/ *nf* (de lumière) glare; (de chaleur) reflection; (de son) reverberation

réverbère /ReveRbɛR/ *nm* (lampadaire) street lamp

réverbérer /ReveRbeRe/ [14]
A *vtr* [*surface*] to reflect [*lumière, chaleur*]; to make [sth] reverberate [*son*]

B **se réverbérer** *vpr* [*lumière, chaleur*] to be reflected; [*son*] to reverberate

révérence /ReveRɑ̃s/ *nf* **1)** (salut) (de femme) curtsey; (d'homme) bow; **faire la** ∼ [*femme*] to curtsey (**à** to); [*homme*] to bow (**à** to); **2)** (respect) liter reverence; **traiter qn avec** ∼ to treat sb respectfully

(Idiome) **tirer sa** ∼◦ to take one's leave (**à qn** of sb)

révérencieux, -ieuse /ReveRɑ̃sjø, øz/ *adj* liter deferential (**envers** to); **attitude peu révérencieuse** irreverent attitude

révérend, ∼e /ReveRɑ̃, ɑ̃d/
A *adj* reverend
B ▸ p. 590 *nm,f* **1)** (dans un couvent) Father/Mother Superior; **2)** (pasteur) reverend

révérer /ReveRe/ [14] *vtr* to revere

rêverie /RɛvRi/ *nf* **1)** (activité) daydreaming, reverie; **se laisser aller à la** ∼ to drift off into a dream; **2)** (rêve éveillé) daydream

revérifier /R(ə)veRifje/ [2] *vtr* to double-check

revers /R(ə)vɛR/ *nm inv* **1)** (dos) (de feuille) back, reverse; (de tissu) wrong side; (de médaille) reverse; **d'un** ∼ **de la main** with the back of one's hand; **le** ∼ **de la médaille** fig the downside◦; **2)** (repli) (de veste) lapel; (de pantalon) turn-up GB, cuff US; (de manche) cuff; **3)** (au tennis) backhand (stroke); **faire un** ∼ to play a backhand (stroke); **4)** fig (échec) setback, reversal

(Composé) ∼ **de fortune** reversal of fortune

(Idiome) **toute médaille a son** ∼ Prov there is no rose without a thorn

reverser /R(ə)vɛRse/ [1] *vtr* **1)** Fin to transfer [*somme*] (**à** to); **2)** (une autre fois) ∼ **à boire à qn** to pour sb another drink

réversibilité /ReveRsibilite/ *nf* gén reversibility; Jur reversion

réversible /ReveRsibl/ *adj* gén reversible; Jur reversionary

revêtement /R(ə)vɛtmɑ̃/ *nm* **1)** (de route, terrain de sport) surface; ∼ **routier** road surface; **2)** (peinture, crépi, ciment) coating; (en vinyl, plastique) covering; **3)** (surface protectrice) skin

revêtir /R(ə)vetiR/ [33]
A *vtr* **1)** (avoir) to have [*caractère, intérêt*]; to assume [*gravité, solennité*]; to take on [*aspect, signification*]; to hold [*importance*]; to entail [*inconvénient*]; **la forme de** to take the form of; **2)** (mettre) to put on [*vêtement*]; **3)** (recouvrir) ∼ **qch de** to cover sth with [*moquette*]

B **se revêtir** *vpr* **se** ∼ **de** (se vêtir) to put on; (se recouvrir) to become covered with [*neige*]

rêveur, -euse /RɛvœR, øz/
A *adj* [*air, personne*] dreamy; **cela laisse** ∼ it makes you wonder
B *nm,f* dreamer

revient /R(ə)vjɛ̃/ *nm* **prix de** ∼ cost price; **calculer** or **établir le prix de** ∼ **de qch** to do the costing for sth

revigorer /R(ə)vigɔRe/ [1] *vtr* **1)** (physiquement) [*boisson*] to perk [sb] up, to revive; [*douche, air*] to revive; **2)** (moralement) to hearten

revirement /R(ə)viRmɑ̃/ *nm* (de situation, politique, d'opinion) turnaround (**de** in); ∼ **total** U-turn GB, flip-flop US

réviser /Revize/ [1] *vtr* **1)** (réexaminer) to revise [*position, contrat, tarifs*]; to review [*procès, Constitution*]; to redraw [*frontières*]; ∼ **qch à la hausse** to revise sth upward(s); **2)** (vérifier) to service, to overhaul [*machine, auto*]; to revise [*manuscrit*]; to audit [*comptes*]; **3)** Scol, Univ to revise GB, to review US

réviseur /RevizœR/ ▸ p. 372 *nm* (dans l'édition) proofreader

révision /Revizjɔ̃/ *nm* **1)** (de position, tarifs) revision; (de procès, frontière) review; (de frontière) redrawing; **2)** (de machine, voiture, chaudière) service; (de manuscrit) revision; (de comptes) audit; **3)** Scol, Univ revision ¢ GB, review ¢ US

révisionniste /Revizjɔnist/ *adj, nmf* revisionist

revitaliser /R(ə)vitalize/ [1] *vtr* to revitalize

revivifier /R(ə)vivifje/ [2] *vtr* liter to revive [*sentiment*]; to revivify [*personne*]

revivre /R(ə)vivR/ [63]
A *vtr* **1)** (se remémorer) to go over, to relive [*événement, passé*]; **faire** ∼ **qch à qn** to bring back memories of sth to sb; **2)** (connaître à nouveau) to live through [sth] again [*guerre*]
B *vi* **1)** (être ragaillardi) to come alive again; **2)** (être soulagé) to be able to breathe again; **3)** (renaître) [*idée, tradition*] to be reborn ou revived; **faire** ∼ to revive [*tradition*]; **4)** (être ressuscité) to live again (**dans, à travers** in); **faire** ∼ fig to bring [sth] back to life [*événement*]

révocation /Revɔkasjɔ̃/ *nf* (de testament, d'édit) revocation; (de personne) dismissal

revoici◦ /R(ə)vwasi/ *prép* **te** ∼! so you're back!; **nous** ∼ **au point de départ** we are back to ou at square one

revoilà /R(ə)vwala/ = **revoici**

revoir¹ /R(ə)vwaR/ [46]
A *vtr* **1)** (voir de nouveau) to see [sb/sth] again; **il ne l'avait pas revu depuis 10 ans** he hadn't seen him for 10 years; **2)** (en pensée) to see; **je la revois encore dans sa robe bleue** I can still see her in her blue dress; **3)** (réexaminer) to go over

devoir, épreuve]; to review [*méthode, action*]; to check through [*compte*]; **'à ~'** 'go over again'; **4** (corriger) to correct; **5** (réviser) Scol to revise GB, to review [*matière*]; to go over [*leçon*]

B se revoir *vpr* **1** (l'un l'autre) [*amis*] to see each other again; **2** (soi-même) **je me revois encore enfant** I can still see myself as a child

revoir²: au revoir /ɔʀ(ə)vwaʀ/ *loc nom* goodbye, bye○; **au ~ Monsieur/Madame** goodbye; **faire au ~ de la main** to wave goodbye

révolte /ʀevɔlt/ *nf* **1** (soulèvement) revolt; **la ~ gronde** there are murmurings of revolt; **2** (indignation, désobéissance) rebellion

révolté, ~e /ʀevɔlte/
A *adj* **1** (qui s'est soulevé) rebel (*épith*); **2** (qui refuse d'obéir) rebellious; **3** (indigné) appalled
B *nm,f* rebel

révolter /ʀevɔlte/ [1]
A *vtr* to appal^GB
B se révolter *vpr* **1** (se soulever, refuser d'obéir) to rebel; **2** (s'indigner) to be appalled (**contre, devant** by)

révolu, ~e /ʀevɔly/ *adj* **1** (passé) **ce temps est ~** those days are over *ou* past; **2** (achevé) **avoir 12 ans ~s** to be over 12 years of age; **après une année ~e** after a year has gone by

révolution /ʀevɔlysjɔ̃/ *nf* **1** (changement radical) revolution; **faire ~ dans** to revolutionize; **2** (effervescence) turmoil; **être en ~** to be in turmoil; **3** (de planète) revolution; **4** Math rotation

révolutionnaire /ʀevɔlysjɔnɛʀ/ *adj, nmf* revolutionary

révolutionner /ʀevɔlysjɔne/ [1] *vtr* **1** (transformer) to revolutionize [*sciences*] (**par** with); **2** ○(mettre en émoi) to upset; **3** (soulever) to revolutionize [*pays*]

revolver /ʀevɔlvɛʀ/ *nm* (à barillet) revolver; (arme de poing) handgun; **coup de ~** gunshot; **abattre qn à coups de ~** to shoot sb, to gun sb down

révoquer /ʀevɔke/ [1] *vtr* **1** to revoke [*testament*]; **2** to dismiss [*personne*]

revue /ʀ(ə)vy/ *nf* **1** (magazine) gén magazine; (spécialisé) journal; **2** Mil (parade) parade; (inspection) review; **passer en ~** to review [*troupes*]; to inspect [*équipement*]; **3** (spectacle) revue; **4** (examen) examination; **se livrer à une ~ minutieuse de ses papiers** to go through one's papers in minute detail; **passer qch en ~** to go over sth, to have a look at sth

(Composé) **~ de presse** TV, Radio review of the papers
(Idiome) **être de la ~**○ to miss out○

révulser /ʀevylse/ [1]
A *vtr* (indigner) to appal^GB
B se révulser *vpr* [*yeux*] to roll (upward(s)); [*visage*] to contort

rez-de-chaussée /ʀɛdʃose/ *nm inv* (niveau) ground floor GB, first floor US (**de** of); **au ~** on the ground GB *ou* first US floor

RF (*written abbr* = **République française**) French Republic

RFA /ɛʀefa/ *nprf* (*abbr* = **République fédérale d'Allemagne**) Hist Federal Republic of Germany, FRG

rhabiller: se rhabiller /ʀabije/ [1] *vpr* to get dressed again

(Idiome) **il peut aller se ~**⁰! he can go back where he came from!

rhapsodie /ʀapsɔdi/ *nf* rhapsody

rhénan, ~e /ʀenɑ̃, an/ ▸ p. 504 *adj* of the Rhineland

Rhénanie /ʀenani/ ▸ p. 504 *nprf* Rhineland

rhésus /ʀezys/ *nm inv* **1** Biol **facteur ~** rhesus factor; **~ positif** rhesus positive; **2** (macaque) **~** rhesus monkey

rhétorique /ʀetɔʀik/
A *adj* [*procédé, effet*] rhetorical
B *nf* rhetoric (**de** of)

Rhin /ʀɛ̃/ ▸ p. 259 *nprm* **le ~** the Rhine

rhinocéros /ʀinɔseʀɔs/ *nm inv* rhinoceros

rhino-pharyngite, *pl* **~s** /ʀinofaʀɛ̃ʒit/ ▸ p. 195 *nf* nasopharyngitis

rhodanien, -ienne /ʀɔdanjɛ̃, ɛn/ *adj* [*vallée, couloir*] Rhône (*épith*); [*capitale, club*] of the Rhône

rhododendron /ʀɔdɔdɛ̃dʀɔ̃/ *nm* rhododendron

rhubarbe /ʀybaʀb/ *nf* rhubarb; **confiture de ~** rhubarb jam

rhum /ʀɔm/ *nm* rum

rhumatismal, ~e, *mpl* **-aux** /ʀymatismal, o/ *adj* rheumatic

rhumatisme /ʀymatism/ ▸ p. 195 *nm* rheumatism **¢**

rhumatologie /ʀymatɔlɔʒi/ *nf* rheumatology

rhume /ʀym/ ▸ p. 195 *nm* cold; **un gros ~** a bad cold

(Composés) **~ de cerveau** head cold; **~ des foins** hay fever

riant, ~e /ʀijɑ̃, ɑ̃t/ *adj* [*visage*] happy; [*paysage*] pleasant

ribambelle○ /ʀibɑ̃bɛl/ *nf* (d'enfants) flock (**de** of); (d'amis) host (**de** of); (de noms) whole string (**de** of); (de procès) series (**de** of)

ricain○, **~e** /ʀikɛ̃, ɛn/ offensive *or* hum
A *adj* Yankee○
B *nm,f* Yank○

ricanement /ʀikanmɑ̃/ *nm* (rire moqueur) snigger; (rire sot) giggle; **des ~s** (de moquerie) sniggering **¢**; (de sottise) giggling **¢**

ricaner /ʀikane/ [1] *vi* (méchamment) to snigger; (bêtement) to giggle

richard○, **~e** /ʀiʃaʀ, aʀd/ *nm,f* pej well-heeled○ person

Richard /ʀiʃaʀ/ *npr* Richard

(Composé) **~ Cœur de Lion** Richard the Lionheart GB, Richard the Lion-hearted US

riche /ʀiʃ/
A *adj* **1** [*personne*] rich, wealthy, well-off; [*pays, ville*] rich; **~ à millions** extremely rich; **2** [*faune, collection, vocabulaire*] rich; [*bibliothèque*] well-stocked; **3** [*minerai, langue, aliment*] rich (**en** in); [*décor*] elaborate, rich; **4** [*bijoux, habit*] fine; [*étoffe*] rich; [*demeure*] sumptuous; [*cadeau*] magnificent; **une ~ idée** an excellent idea; **aliment ~ en fibres** food that is high *ou* rich in fibre^GB; **un pays ~ en uranium** a uranium-rich country; **~ de promesses** full of promise
B *nmf* rich man/woman; **les ~s** the rich (+ *v pl*), the wealthy (+ *v pl*)
(Idiome) **on ne prête qu'aux ~s** Prov unto those that have shall more be given

richement /ʀiʃmɑ̃/ *adv* [*meublé, vêtu, décoré, illustré*] richly, lavishly; **~ dotée** [*fille*] provided with a large dowry; [*tombola*] with big prizes

richesse /ʀiʃɛs/
A *nf* **1** (de personne, pays) wealth; **notre principale ~** our main source of wealth; **faire la ~ de** to bring wealth to; **c'est toute notre ~** it's all we have; **2** (de bijoux) magnificence; (d'étoffe, de vêtement) richness; (de mobilier, demeure) sumptuousness; **décoration d'une trop grande ~** over-elaborate decoration; **3** (teneur) richness (**en** in); **4** (de faune, vocabulaire, collection) richness; (de documentation) wealth
B **richesses** *nfpl* **1** (biens matériels) wealth **¢**; **2** (objets de grande valeur) treasures; **les ~s d'un musée** the treasures of a museum; **3** (ressources) resources; **~s naturelles** natural resources

richissime○ /ʀiʃisim/ *adj* fabulously rich *ou* wealthy

ricin /ʀisɛ̃/ *nf* castor-oil plant; **huile de ~** castor oil

ricocher /ʀikɔʃe/ [1] *vi* [*balle*] to ricochet (**sur** off); [*pierre*] (sur l'eau) to skim (**sur** on *ou* across); (sur un obstacle) to rebound (**sur** off)

ricochet /ʀikɔʃɛ/ *nm* (de balle) ricochet; (de pierre) (sur l'eau) bounce; (sur un obstacle) rebound; **faire des ~s** to skim stones (**sur** on *ou* across); **cela l'a touché par ~** (projectile) he was hit on the rebound; (chômage) he was indirectly affected

ric-rac○ /ʀikʀak/ *loc adv* **1** (de justesse) by the skin of one's teeth; **2** (rigoureusement) [*payer*] on the dot

rictus /ʀiktys/ *nm inv* (fixed) grin, rictus

ride /ʀid/ *nf* (de visage, fruit) wrinkle; (de lac) ripple; **ne pas avoir pris une ~** [*visage*] not to have aged; [*œuvre*] not to have dated

rideau, *pl* **~x** /ʀido/ *nm* **1** (dans une maison) curtain; (voilage) net curtain; **doubles ~x** curtains; **2** Théât curtain; **3** (de magasin, bâtiment) (plein) roller shutter; (grille) security grille; **4** (d'arbres, de brouillard) curtain; (de flammes) wall

(Composés) **~ de fer** Hist Iron Curtain; **~ de fumée** lit blanket of smoke; fig smokescreen

r

Idiomes tirer le ~ sur qch to draw a veil over sth; ~! Théât curtain!; fig (let's) drop it!; grimper aux ~x○ to go up the wall○

rider /ʀide/ [1]
A vtr [1] to wrinkle [peau]; [2] to ripple [surface, lac]
B se rider vpr [1] [peau] to wrinkle; [2] [lac] to ripple

ridicule /ʀidikyl/
A adj [1] (grotesque, insensé) ridiculous; [2] (insignifiant) [somme, salaire] ridiculously low, pathetic
B nm [1] (le grotesque) le ~ ridicule; **tourner qn en ~** to make sb look ridiculous; [2] (de situation) ridiculousness, absurdity; **il est d'un ~!** he looks so ridiculous!

Idiome le ~ ne tue pas Prov looking a fool never killed anyone

ridiculement /ʀidikylmɑ̃/ adv ridiculously

ridiculiser /ʀidikylize/ [1]
A vtr [personne] to ridicule [personne, théorie, propos] (**auprès de** in front of); to wipe the floor with [équipe, concurrent]; [comportement, situation] to make [sb] look ridiculous [personne]
B se ridiculiser vpr [personne] to make a fool of oneself

rien¹ /ʀjɛ̃/
A pron indéf [1] (nulle chose) ~ **n'est impossible** nothing is impossible; **un mois à ne ~ faire** a month doing nothing; **il n'y a ~ qui puisse la consoler** nothing can console her; **il n'y a plus ~** there's nothing left; **ce n'est ~** it's nothing; **elle n'est ~** she's a nobody; **il n'est ~ pour moi** he means ou is nothing to me; **il n'en est ~** it's nothing of the sort; **elle ne t'a ~ fait** she hasn't done anything to you; ~ **n'y fait!** nothing's any good!; **il n'a ~ d'un intrigant** there's nothing of the schemer about him; **elle n'a ~ de sa sœur** she's nothing like her sister; ~ **de bon** nothing good; ~ **d'autre** nothing else; **il n'y a ~ eu de cassé** nothing was broken; ~ **à déclarer** nothing to declare; **partir de** ~ to start from nothing; **pour** ~ (en vain) for nothing; (à bas prix) for next to nothing; **'pourquoi?'—'pour ~'** 'why?'—'no reason'; **parler pour** ~ to waste one's breath; **'merci'—'de** ~**'** 'thank you'—'you're welcome' ou 'not at all'; **en moins de** ~ in no time at all; **'que prends-tu?'—'~ du tout'** 'what are you having?'—'nothing at all'; **ça ou** ~, **c'est pareil** it makes no odds; **c'est trois fois** ~○ it's next to nothing; ~ **de** ~○ absolutely nothing; **faire qch comme** ~ (seulement) to do sth very easily; [2] (seulement) ~ **que la bouteille pèse deux kilos** the bottle alone weighs two kilos; **elle voudrait un bureau** ~ **qu'à elle**○ she would like an office all to herself; **la vérité,** ~ **que la vérité** the truth and nothing but the truth; ~ **que pour te plaire** just to please you; ~ **que ça**○? (en réponse) is that all?; **ils habitent un château,** ~ **que ça!** iron they live in a castle, no less! ou if you please!; [3] (quoi que ce soit) anything; **avant de** ~ **signer** before signing anything; **sans que j'en sache** ~ without my knowing anything about it; [4] Sport gén nil; (au tennis) love
B de rien (du tout) loc adj **fille de** ~ worthless girl; **un petit bleu de** ~ **(du tout)** a tiny bruise; **une affaire de** ~ **du tout** a trivial matter
C ○un rien loc adv a (tiny) bit; **un** ~ **pédant** a bit pedantic
D en rien loc adv at all, in any way

Idiomes ~ **à faire!** (c'est impossible) it's no good ou use!; (refus) no way!○; **on n'a** ~ **pour** ~ you get nothing for nothing; **ce n'est pas** ~! (exploit) it's quite something!; (tâche) it's no joke, it's not exactly a picnic○!; (somme) it's not exactly peanuts○!

rien² /ʀjɛ̃/ nm [1] (vétille) **un** ~ **le fâche** the slightest thing annoys him; **se disputer pour un** ~ to quarrel over nothing; **perdre son temps à des** ~**s** to waste one's time on trivial things; **les petits** ~**s qui rendent la vie agréable** the little things which make life pleasant; **faire qch comme un** ~○ to do sth very easily; [2] ○(petite quantité) **un** ~ **de** a touch of; **un** ~ **de cognac** a dash of brandy; **en un** ~ **de temps** in next to no time; [3] ○(personne) **un/une** ~ **du tout** (insignifiant) a nobody; (sans moralité) a no-good○, a worthless person

rieur, rieuse /ʀijœʀ, øz/ adj [personne] cheerful; [visage, yeux] laughing; [ton] cheerful

Idiome mettre les ~s de son côté to win the audience over

rififi◑ /ʀififi/ nm fight

rigide /ʀiʒid/ adj [1] [personne, règlement] rigid; [2] [matériau, support] rigid; [carton] stiff

rigidité /ʀiʒidite/ nf rigidity

rigolade○ /ʀiɡɔlad/ nf [1] (amusement) **quelle** ~! what a laugh○!, what fun!; **ça a été une partie de (franche)** ~ it was a really good laugh○; **prendre qch à la** ~ to make a joke of sth; **le moment n'est pas à la** ~ this is no time for laughter ou for fun and games; [2] (plaisanterie) joke; **la conférence a été une vaste** ~ the conference was one big joke; [3] (chose facile) **réparer ça, c'est de la** ~! repairing this is a piece of cake○ ou is dead easy○

rigole /ʀiɡɔl/ nf (conduit) channel; (écoulement) rivulet

rigoler○ /ʀiɡɔle/ [1] vi [1] (rire) to laugh; **on a bien rigolé** we had a good laugh; [2] (s'amuser) to have fun; **ça ne rigole pas tous les jours ici** it's not much fun here; [3] (plaisanter) to joke, to kid○; **il ne faut pas** ~ **avec la sécurité** you mustn't mess about ou fool around with security; **il a dit ça pour** ~ he said it as a joke

rigolo○, **-ote** /ʀiɡɔlo, ɔt/
A adj funny
B nm,f [1] (fumiste) joker; [2] (personne amusante) **c'est un petit** ~ he's quite a little comedian

rigoureusement /ʀiɡuʀøzmɑ̃/ adv [vrai, inexact] completely; [défendu, conforme] strictly; [punir, traiter] harshly; [obéir] scrupulously; [sélectionner, mesurer] carefully

rigoureux, -euse /ʀiɡuʀø, øz/ adj [1] [morale, discipline] strict, rigorous; [règlement, personne, application] strict; [2] [climat, hiver, conditions de travail] harsh, severe; [froid] severe; [3] [observations, recherches, démonstration] meticulous; [analyse, gestion, pensée, argumentation] rigorous

rigueur /ʀiɡœʀ/
A nf [1] (de sanction, loi, personne) strictness; (de répression) harshness; [2] (de climat, condition) harshness; [3] (d'observation, de recherche, style, démonstration) rigour^GB; **une analyse d'une grande** ~ a very rigorous analysis; **leur travail manque de** ~ their work is not rigorous enough; [4] Pol, Écon austerity; **plan de** ~ austerity measures (pl)
B rigueurs nfpl (de saison, climat) liter rigours^GB
C de rigueur loc adj obligatory; **les gants blancs sont de** ~ white gloves must be worn; **la prudence reste de** ~ **au ministère** caution is the order of the day at the ministry; **visite de** ~ obligatory social call
D à la rigueur loc adv **nous pouvons à la** ~ **emprunter à mes parents** if we absolutely have to we can borrow from my parents; **à la** ~ **je peux te prêter 20 euros** at a pinch GB ou in a pinch US I can lend you 20 euros; **je peux venir trois jours ou cinq à la** ~ I can come for three days or five at the very outside; **il est un peu excentrique à la** ~, **mais fou certainement pas** he may be a bit eccentric, but he's certainly not mad

Idiomes **tenir** ~ **à qn de qch** to bear sb a grudge for sth; **il ne t'en tiendra pas** ~ he won't hold it against you

rillettes /ʀijɛt/ nfpl ≈ potted meat **Ȼ**

rime /ʀim/ nf rhyme (**en** in)

rimer /ʀime/ [1] vi [1] (former une rime) to rhyme; [2] (signifier) **cela ne rime à rien** it makes no sense

rimmel® /ʀimɛl/ nm mascara

rinçage /ʀɛ̃saʒ/ nm (processus) rinsing; (de lave-linge, lave-vaisselle) rinse

rince-doigts /ʀɛ̃sdwa/ nm inv [1] (récipient) finger bowl; [2] (en papier) finger wipe

rincée◑ /ʀɛ̃se/ nf **prendre une** ~ (pluie) to get drenched; (coups) to get a thrashing○

rincer /ʀɛ̃se/ [12]
A vtr (ôter le savon) to rinse; (laver) to rinse [sth] out
B se rincer vpr **se** ~ **les mains** to rinse one's hands; **se** ~ **la bouche** to rinse one's mouth out

Idiome **se** ~ **l'œil**○ to get an eyeful

ringard, ~**e** /ʀɛ̃ɡaʀ, aʀd/
A ○adj [vêtement] dated; [politique] out of date; [personne] behind the times (jamais épith)
B nm,f (individu démodé) pej, gén fuddy-duddy○ péj; (artiste, politicien) has-been○ péj

ripaille /ʀipɑj/ nf blow-out○, feast

riper /ʀipe/ [1] vi [pied] to slip; [bicyclette] to skid

riposte /ʀipɔst/ nf [1] (verbale) reply, riposte; **prompt à la** ~ always ready with a reply; [2] (physique) response (**à** to); [3] Sport (en escrime) riposte; (en lutte, boxe) counter

riposter /ʀipɔste/ [1]
A vtr to retort (**que** that)
B vi [1] (verbalement) to retort; ~ **à qn/qch par** to counter

sb/sth with; **2** (par des coups) to respond (**à** to; **par** with; **en faisant** by doing); **3** Mil to return fire, to shoot back; **~ à qch par qch** to counter sth with sth; **4** (en sport) to ripost

riquiqui○ /ʀikiki/ *adj inv* [*vêtement*] ridiculously small; [*logement*] poky○

rire¹ /ʀiʀ/ [68]
A *vi* **1** (s'esclaffer) to laugh; **se mettre à ~** to burst out laughing; **tu nous feras toujours ~!** you're a real scream○!; **il n'y a pas de quoi ~!** that's not funny!, that's no laughing matter!; **il vaut mieux en ~** (qu'en pleurer) you might as well laugh as cry; **on a ri un bon coup**○ we had a good laugh; **2** (s'amuser) to have fun; **il faut bien ~ un peu** you need a bit of fun now and again; **fini de ~** the fun's over; **tu veux ~!** you must be joking *ou* kidding○!; **j'ai fait ça pour ~** I was joking; **c'était pour ~** it was a joke; **sans ~**○ seriously, honestly; **laisse-moi ~**○, **ne me fais pas ~**○ don't make me laugh; **3** (se moquer) **~ de qch/qn** to laugh at sth/sb; **4** (avoir une expression gaie) liter **elle a les yeux qui rient, ses yeux rient** she has laughing eyes
B se rire *vpr* **se ~ de qn** *fml* to laugh at sb; **se ~ des difficultés** *fml* to make light of difficulties

(Idiomes) **rira bien qui rira le dernier** Prov he who laughs last laughs longest Prov; **être mort** *or* **écroulé de ~**○ to be doubled up (with laughter)

rire² /ʀiʀ/ *nm* laughter; **un ~** a laugh; **avoir un ~ forcé** to give a forced laugh; **avoir le ~ facile** to laugh at the slightest thing; **il y eut des ~s dans le public** there was laughter in the audience; **il a eu un petit ~** he chuckled; **il éclata d'un gros ~** (bref) he let out a guffaw; (qui dure) he gave a hearty laugh

(Composé) **~s préenregistrés** Radio, TV canned laughter **ℂ**

ris /ʀi/ *nm inv* **1** Culin **~ (de veau)** calf's sweetbread; **2** Naut reef

risée /ʀize/ *nf* **1** (sujet de moquerie) **être la ~ de** to be the laughing stock of; **2** (vent) gust (of wind)

risette○ /ʀizɛt/ *nf* smile; **fais ~!** give me a smile!

risible /ʀizibl/ *adj* ridiculous, laughable

risque /ʀisk/ *nm* risk (**de** of; **à faire** in doing); **comporter** *or* **présenter un ~** [*processus*] to carry a risk; [*décision, action*] to involve some risk; **c'est sans ~** it's safe; **au ~ de faire** at the risk of doing; **à ~s** [*personne, prêt*] high-risk (épith)

(Composé) **les ~s du métier** occupational hazards

risqué, -e /ʀiske/ *adj* **1** (aléatoire) [*entreprise, comportement*] risky; [*investissement*] high-risk; **2** (osé) [*plaisanterie*] risqué; [*hypothèse*] daring

risquer /ʀiske/ [1]
A *vtr* **1** (être passible de) to face [*condamnation*]; **~ gros** to face a heavy sentence; **2** (s'exposer à) to risk [*mort, critique*]; **vas-y, tu ne risques rien** lit go ahead, you're safe; fig go ahead, you've got nothing to lose; **qu'est-ce qu'on risque?** lit what are the risks?; fig what have we got to lose?; **~ gros** to take a major risk; **tu risques qu'on t'abîme ta voiture** you run the risk of having your car damaged; **3** (mettre en danger) to risk [*vie, réputation, emploi*]; **~ sa peau**○ to risk one's neck○; **4** (oser) to venture [*regard, allusion, question*]; to risk [*geste*]; to attempt [*démarche, opération*]; **~ un œil** to venture a glance; **~ le coup**○ to risk it, to chance it
B risquer de *vtr ind* **1** (pouvoir) **tu risques de te brûler** you might burn yourself; **elle risque fort d'être déçue** she may well be disappointed; **ça ne risque pas de m'arriver!** there's no chance of that happening to me!; **2** (prendre le risque) **il ne veut pas ~ de perdre son travail** he doesn't want to risk losing his job
C se risquer *vpr* **1** (s'aventurer) to venture (**à faire** to do); **je ne m'y risquerais pas!** I wouldn't risk it; **2** (oser) **se ~ à dire** to dare to say
D *v impers* **il risque de pleuvoir** it might rain; **il risque d'y avoir du monde** there may well be a lot of people there

(Idiomes) **qui ne risque rien n'a rien** nothing ventured, nothing gained; **~ le tout pour le tout** to stake *ou* risk one's all

risque-tout /ʀiskətu/ *adj inv* daredevil

rissoler /ʀisɔle/ [1] *vtr, vi* Culin to brown

ristourne /ʀistuʀn/ *nf* discount, rebate

rite /ʀit/ *nm* lit, fig rite

ritournelle /ʀituʀnɛl/ *nf* **1** Mus ritornello; **2** ○fig harping on

rituel, -elle /ʀituɛl/ *adj, nm* ritual

rivage /ʀivaʒ/ *nm* shore

rival, ~e, *mpl* -aux /ʀival, o/ *adj, nm,f* rival

rivaliser /ʀivalize/ [1] *vi* **~ avec** to compete with [*personne*]; **~ avec qch** to rival sth; **~ d'adresse/d'esprit avec qn** to vie with sb in skill/wit

rivalité /ʀivalite/ *nf* rivalry (**entre** between; **avec** with)

rive /ʀiv/ *nf* **1** (de fleuve) bank; **2** (de mer, lac) shore

river /ʀive/ [1] *vtr* to clinch [*clou*]; to rivet [*plaques de tôle*]; to fasten [*prisonnier*] (**à** to); **être rivé à qch** fig to be tied to [*travail*]; to be glued to [*télévision*]; **avoir les yeux rivés sur** to have one's eyes riveted on

(Idiome) **~ son clou à qn**○ to leave sb speechless

riverain, ~e /ʀivʀɛ̃, ɛn/
A *adj* **1** (de voie) [*maison, propriété*] bordering the street *ou* road; **2** (de cours d'eau) riverside (épith); **3** (de lac) lakeside (épith)
B *nm,f* **1** (habitant) (de rue) resident; (de cours d'eau) riverside resident; (de bord de lac) lakeside resident; **2** (propriétaire) riparian

rivet /ʀivɛ/ *nm* rivet

rivière /ʀivjɛʀ/ *nf* **1** (cours d'eau) river; **2** (en équitation) water jump

(Composé) **~ de diamants** diamond necklace

(Idiome) **les petits ruisseaux font les grandes ~s** Prov great oaks from little acorns grow Prov

rixe /ʀiks/ *nf* brawl (**entre** between)

riz /ʀi/ *nm* rice

rizière /ʀizjɛʀ/ *nf* paddy field

RMI /ɛʀɛmi/ *nm: abbr* ▸ **revenu**

RMIste /ɛʀɛmist/ *nmf* person receiving minimum benefit payment ▸ **revenu**

RN /ɛʀɛn/ *nf* (abbr = **route nationale**) ≈ A road GB, highway US

robe /ʀɔb/ *nf* **1** (de femme) dress; **2** (d'avocat) gown; (de prêtre) robe; (de moine) frock; **la ~** the Robe; **3** (couleur) (de cheval) coat; (de vin) colour GB

(Composés) **~ de bal** ball gown; **~ de bure** habit; **~ bustier** (boned) strapless dress; **~ de chambre** dressing gown, robe US; **~ chasuble** pinafore dress, jumper US; **~ de grossesse** maternity dress *ou* smock; **~ d'intérieur** housecoat; **~ de mariée** wedding dress *ou* gown; **~ du soir** evening dress *ou* gown

Robin /ʀɔbɛ̃/ *npr* Robin

(Composé) **~ des bois** Robin Hood

robinet /ʀɔbinɛ/ *nm* (d'eau) tap GB, faucet US; (de gaz) tap GB, valve US

robinetterie /ʀɔbinɛtʀi/ *nf* (dispositif) plumbing fixtures (pl)

robinier /ʀɔbinje/ *nm* locust tree, false acacia

robot /ʀɔbo/ *nm* robot

(Composé) **~ ménager** food processor

robotique /ʀɔbɔtik/ *nf* robotics (+ *v sg*)

robotisation /ʀɔbɔtizasjɔ̃/ *nf* automation, robotization US

robotiser /ʀɔbɔtize/ [1] *vtr* to automate, to robotize US

robuste /ʀɔbyst/ *adj* [*personne, machine*] robust, sturdy; [*plante*] sturdy; [*constitution, santé*] robust, sound; [*appétit*] healthy; [*foi*] strong, firm

robustesse /ʀɔbystɛs/ *nf* robustness

roc /ʀɔk/ *nm* (roche, rocher) rock

rocade /ʀɔkad/ *nf* **1** (de dérivation) bypass; (circulaire) ring road, beltway US; **2** Mil transversal route

rocaille /ʀɔkaj/ *nf* **1** (pierres) loose stones (pl); **2** (terrain) rocky *ou* stony ground; **3** (décor de jardin) rockery, rock garden; **4** (pierre d'ornement) rocaille; **grotte en ~s** rockwork grotto

rocailleux, -euse /ʀɔkajø, øz/ *adj* **1** [*terrain*] rocky, stony; **2** [*voix, sonorités*] harsh, grating

rocambolesque /ʀɔkɑ̃bɔlɛsk/ *adj* fantastic, incredible

roche /ʀɔʃ/ *nf* rock

rocher /ʀɔʃe/ [1] *nm* **1** (pierre) rock; **2** (os) petrosal bone; **3** Culin praline chocolate

Rocheuses /ʀɔʃøz/ *nprfpl* **les ~** the Rocky Mountains, the Rockies

rocheux, **-euse** /ʁɔʃø, øz/ adj rocky; **paroi rocheuse** rock face

rock /ʁɔk/ nm [1] (musique) rock (music); [2] (danse) jive

Composés ~ **and roll**, ~**'n'roll** rock and roll, rock'n'roll

rocker = rockeur

rockeur, **-euse** /ʁɔkœʁ, øz/ nm,f (chanteur) rock singer; (musicien) rock musician; (amateur) rock fan

rococo /ʁɔkoko/
A adj inv [1] Art [art, style, objets] rococo; [2] (démodé) pej old-fashioned
B nm rococo

rodage /ʁɔdaʒ/ nm [1] (de véhicule, moteur) running in GB, breaking in US; [2] (de pièce, soupapes) grinding; **le spectacle/l'équipe est encore en ~** fig the show/the team is still getting into its stride

rodéo /ʁɔdeo/ nm rodeo; ~ **à la voiture volée** joyriding○

roder /ʁɔde/ [1] vtr [1] Aut to run in GB, to break in US [véhicule]; [2] Tech to grind [pièce, soupapes]; [3] (mettre au point) to bring [sth] up to scratch [spectacle, méthode]; ~ **qn à** ou **pour qch** Sport to train sb for sth; **être (bien) rodé** [personne] to have the hang of things; [service] to be running smoothly

rôder /ʁɔde/ [1] vi [1] (avec intention malfaisante) to prowl; ~ **autour de qn** to hang around sb; [2] (au hasard) to roam around, to wander about

rôdeur, **-euse** /ʁɔdœʁ, øz/ nm,f pej prowler

rogaton /ʁɔgatɔ̃/ nm [1] (reste de repas) ~**s** leftovers; [2] (objet de rebut) rubbish 𝄁, piece of junk

rogne○ /ʁɔɲ/ nf anger; **se mettre en ~** to get mad○

rogner /ʁɔɲe/ [1] vtr [1] (couper les bords de) to trim [bâton, angle]; to clip [griffes, ongles]; ~ **les ailes à qn** fig to clip sb's wings; [2] (prélever) ~ **sur** to cut down ou back on sth [budget]; to whittle away [économies]; [3] (découper) to trim [feuille]

rognon /ʁɔɲɔ̃/ nm Culin kidney

rognure /ʁɔɲyʁ/ nf (de papier) trimming; (d'ongles, or) clipping

rogue /ʁɔg/ adj haughty, contemptuous

roi /ʁwa/ nm [1] ▸ p. 590 (souverain) king; **mets de ~** dish fit for a king; [2] (sans rival en son genre) **le ~ des animaux** the king of beasts; **le ~ des imbéciles**○ a complete idiot; [3] (magnat) tycoon; [4] Jeux king

Composés **les ~s fainéants** Hist the last Merovingian kings; **les ~s mages** Bible the (three) wise men, the three kings, the Magi

Idiome **tirer les Rois** to eat Twelfth Night cake

roitelet /ʁwatlɛ/ nm [1] (oiseau) goldcrest; [2] (petit roi) kinglet

rôle /ʁol/ nm [1] (d'acteur) part, role; **premier ~** lead, leading role; **second ~** supporting part ou role; ~ **de composition** character part; **distribuer les ~s** to do the casting; [2] (fonction) gén role; (d'organe, de cœur, rein) function, role; **le comité a pour ~ de faire** the role of the committee is to do; **ils auront un ~ d'observateurs** they will act as observers; **faire qch à tour de ~** to take it in turns to do sth, to do sth in turn; [3] Jur (feuillet) roll; (registre) register

Idiome **avoir** or **tenir le beau ~**○ to have the easy job

rôle-titre, pl **rôles-titres** /ʁoltitʁ/ nm title role

roller /ʁɔlɛʁ/ ▸ p. 327 nm [1] (patin) rollerblade; [2] (activité) rollerblading

romain, **-e¹** /ʁɔmɛ̃, ɛn/ adj [1] (de Rome) Roman; [2] Relig **l'Église ~e** the Roman Catholic Church; [3] (en typographie) **caractères ~s** roman typeface 𝄁

romaine² /ʁɔmɛn/ nf [1] (salade) cos lettuce, romaine lettuce US; [2] (balance) steelyard

Idiome **être bon comme la ~**○ to be soft○ ou gullible

roman, **-e** /ʁɔmɑ̃, an/
A adj [1] Archit Romanesque; (en Angleterre) Norman; [2] Ling [langue] Romance (épith)
B nm [1] (œuvre en prose) novel; **sa vie est un vrai ~** his/her life is like something out of a novel; **ça n'existe que dans les ~s** that only happens in books; [2] (genre) **le ~** the novel; [3] (du Moyen Âge) romance; ~ **courtois** courtly romance; [4] Archit **le ~** the Romanesque; [5] Ling **le ~ (commun)** late vulgar Latin

Composés ~ **d'amour** love story, romance; ~ **d'analyse** psychological novel; ~ **d'anticipation** (œuvre) science fiction novel; (genre) science fiction; ~ **de cape et d'épée** swashbuckling historical romance; ~ **à clé** roman à clef; **le ~ d'évasion** escapist fiction; ~ **de gare** airport novel; ~ **de mœurs** novel of manners; ~ **noir** roman noir, crime novel; ~ **policier** detective story, whodunnit○; ~ **de série noire**® thriller; ~ **à thèse** philosophical novel; ~ **à tiroirs** episodic novel

romance /ʁɔmɑ̃s/ nf [1] (chanson) love song; [2] Littérat romance

romancer /ʁɔmɑ̃se/ [12] vtr [1] (déformer) to romanticize; [2] (présenter sous forme de roman) to fictionalize

romanche /ʁɔmɑ̃ʃ/ ▸ p. 336 nm, adj Ling Romans(c)h

romancier, **-ière** /ʁɔmɑ̃sje, ɛʁ/ ▸ p. 372 nm,f novelist

romand, **-e** /ʁɔmɑ̃, ɑ̃d/ adj [Suisse] French-speaking

romanesque /ʁɔmanɛsk/
A adj [1] [personne] romantic; [situation, histoire] like something out of a novel (après n); [2] [récit, texte] fictional; **c'est une œuvre ~** it's a work of fiction, it's a novel; **l'œuvre ~ de Balzac** Balzac's novels (pl)
B nm [1] (genre) **le ~** fiction; [2] (caractère) **le ~ d'une situation** the fantastical aspect of a situation

roman-feuilleton, pl **romans-feuilletons** /ʁɔmɑ̃fœjtɔ̃/ nm serial

roman-fleuve, pl **romans-fleuves** /ʁɔmɑ̃flœv/ nm roman-fleuve, saga

romanichel, **-elle** /ʁɔmaniʃɛl/ nm,f [1] (tzigane) offensive Romany, gypsy; [2] (vagabond) pej tramp

romanisant, **-e** /ʁɔmanizɑ̃, ɑ̃t/ adj [1] [église] Romanistic; [2] Ling [étudiant] specializing in Romance languages (épith, après n)

roman-photo, pl **romans-photos** /ʁɔmɑ̃foto/ nm photo-story

romantique /ʁɔmɑ̃tik/ adj, nmf romantic

romantisme /ʁɔmɑ̃tism/ nm [1] (genre) Romanticism; [2] (sentimentalisme) romanticism

romarin /ʁɔmaʁɛ̃/ nm rosemary

rombière❶ /ʁɔ̃bjɛʁ/ nf pej **une vieille ~** an old bag○

Rome /ʁɔm/ ▸ p. 621 npr Rome

Idiomes **tous les chemins mènent à ~** Prov all roads lead to Rome Prov; ~ **ne s'est pas faite en un jour** Prov Rome wasn't built in a day Prov

rompre /ʁɔ̃pʁ/ [53]
A vtr gén to break, to break off [fiançailles, relation]; to upset [équilibre]; to disrupt [harmonie]; to end [isolement]; to break up [unité]; to interrupt [uniformité]; to break through [ligne ennemie, barrage]; **rompez (les rangs)!** fall out!
B vi ~ **avec** to break with [habitude, tradition, doctrine]; to make a break from [passé]; to break away from [parti, milieu]; to break up with [fiancé]; **ils ont rompu** they've broken up
C se rompre vpr gén to break

rompu, **-e** /ʁɔ̃py/ adj [1] (habitué) ~ **à** well accustomed to; ~ **aux techniques modernes** well-versed in modern techniques; [2] (fatigué) ~ **(de fatigue)** worn-out

romsteck /ʁɔmstɛk/ nm rump steak

ronce /ʁɔ̃s/ nf [1] (plante, tige) bramble; [2] (nœud du bois) burr; ~ **de noyer** burr walnut

ronchon○, **-onne** /ʁɔ̃ʃɔ̃, ɔn/ adj grouchy○

ronchonner○ /ʁɔ̃ʃɔne/ [1] vi to grumble (**après** about), to grouse○ (**après** about)

rond, **-e¹** /ʁɔ̃, ʁɔ̃d/
A adj [1] (en forme de cercle) gén round; [bâtiment] circular; [2] (arrondi) gén rounded; [seins] full; [visage] round; [personne] tubby; **un bébé tout ~** a chubby baby; **elle se trouve trop ~e** euph she thinks she's too fat; [3] (net) [nombre] round; **un compte ~** a round sum; **ça fait 40 euros tout ~** that's 40 euros exactly; [4] ○(ivre) drunk
B nm (cercle) circle; **en ~** in a circle; **faire des ~s de fumée** to blow smoke rings; **faire des ~s dans l'eau** lit to make ripples in the water

Composés ~ **de jambe** (en danse) rond de jambe; **faire des ~s de jambe à qn** fig to be overly polite to sb; ~ **de serviette** napkin ring; ~ **de sorcière** fairy ring

Idiomes **être ~ en affaires**○ to be honest, to be on the level○; **ouvrir des yeux ~s** to be wide-eyed with astonishment; **être ~ comme une barrique** or **une queue de pelle** or

un petit pois○ to be blind drunk○

rond-de-cuir, pl **ronds-de-cuir** /ʀɔ̃dkɥiʀ/ nm pen-pusher GB, pencil pusher US

ronde² /ʀɔ̃d/
A nf [1] (danse) round dance; **faire une ~** to make ou form a circle; **entrer dans la ~** lit, fig to join the dance; (va-et-vient) **la ~ des voitures sur le circuit** the cars whirling round the circuit; [3] (de policiers) patrol; (de soldats, gardiens) watch; **faire sa ~** to be on patrol ou watch; [4] Mus (note) semibreve GB, whole note US; [5] (écriture) roundhand
B à la ronde loc adv around

rondelet○, **-ette** /ʀɔ̃dlɛ, ɛt/ adj [personne] plump, tubby○; [visage] chubby; **une somme rondelette** quite a tidy○ sum

rondelle /ʀɔ̃dɛl/ nf [1] (tranche) slice; [2] Tech washer

rondement /ʀɔ̃dmɑ̃/ adv promptly

rondeur /ʀɔ̃dœʀ/ nf [1] (de femme, bras) curve; [2] (de carac-tère) openness; **avec ~** (franchement) frankly

rondin /ʀɔ̃dɛ̃/ nm log; **cabane en ~s** log cabin

rondouillard○, **~e** /ʀɔ̃dujaʀ, aʀd/ adj tubby○

rond-point, pl **ronds-points** /ʀɔ̃pwɛ̃/ nm roundabout GB, traffic circle US

ronéoter○ /ʀɔneɔte/, **ronéotyper** /ʀɔneɔtipe/ [1] vtr to duplicate, to Roneo®

ronflant, **~e** /ʀɔ̃flɑ̃, ɑ̃t/ adj [1] [poêle] roaring; [2] [style] high-flown (épith); [discours] grandiloquent; [promesse] fine-sounding (épith)

ronflement /ʀɔ̃fləmɑ̃/ nm [1] (de dormeur) snore; [2] (de chaudière, poêle) roar ₵; (moins fort) purr ₵; (de moteur) purr ₵; (de petit avion) drone

ronfler /ʀɔ̃fle/ [1] vi [1] [dormeur] to snore; [poêle] to roar; [moteur] to purr; [2] ○(dormir) to be fast asleep

(Idiome) **~ comme une toupie** or **un orgue** or **un sonneur** to snore like a pig

ronfleur, **-euse** /ʀɔ̃flœʀ, øz/ nm,f [1] (personne) (qui ronfle) snorer; (qui aime dormir)○ great sleeper; [2] (de téléphone) elec-tric buzzer

ronger /ʀɔ̃ʒe/ [13]
A vtr [1] (grignoter) [souris, chien] to gnaw; [vers] to eat into [bois]; [chenille] to eat away [feuilles]; **rongé par les vers** worm-eaten; [2] (attaquer) [eau, acide, rouille] to erode, to eat away at; [3] fig [maladie] to wear down [personne]
B se ronger vpr **se ~ les ongles** to bite one's nails

(Idiome) **se ~ les sangs**○ to worry oneself sick

rongeur /ʀɔ̃ʒœʀ/ nm rodent

ronron /ʀɔ̃ʀɔ̃/ nm (also onomat) [1] (de chat) purr, purring ₵; **faire ~** to purr; [2] (de moteur) purring ₵; [3] (routine) le **~ de la vie quotidienne** the humdrum routine of daily life

ronronnement /ʀɔ̃ʀɔnmɑ̃/ nm (de chat, moteur) purring ₵

ronronner /ʀɔ̃ʀɔne/ [1] vi to purr

roque /ʀɔk/ nm castling; **grand/petit ~** castling long/short

roquer /ʀɔke/ [1] vi Jeux [1] (aux échecs) to castle; [2] (au croquet) to roquet

roquet /ʀɔkɛ/ nm [1] (chien) yappy little dog; [2] ○(personne) bad-tempered little runt○

roquette /ʀɔkɛt/ nf Mil rocket

rosace /ʀozas/ nf (figure géométrique) rosette; (vitrail) rose window; (au plafond) rose

rosaire /ʀozɛʀ/ nm (chapelet, prières) rosary

rosâtre /ʀozatʀ/ ▸ p. 140 adj pinkish

rosbif /ʀɔsbif/ nm [1] (viande) (crue) joint of beef GB, roast of beef US; (cuite) roast beef; [2] ○†(Anglais) offensive **les ~s** the English (+ v pl)

rose¹ /ʀoz/ ▸ p. 140
A adj gén pink; (de santé) rosy
B nm (couleur) pink

(Idiomes) **ce n'est pas (tout) ~** it's not all roses, it's not roses all the way; **la vie n'est pas ~** life isn't a bed of roses; **voir la vie en ~** to see life through rose-coloured GB spectacles

rose² /ʀoz/ nf [1] Bot rose; [2] (vitrail) rose window; [3] (en bijouterie) **diamant en ~** rose diamond

(Composés) **~ d'Inde** African marigold; **~ pompon** button rose; **~ des sables** gypsum flower; **~ trémière** hollyhock; **~ des vents** compass rose

---

(Idiomes) **il n'y a pas de ~ sans épines** Prov there is no rose without a thorn; **envoyer qn sur les ~s**○ to send sb pack-ing○; **découvrir le pot aux ~s**○ to find out what is going on

rosé, **~e¹** /ʀoze/
A ▸ p. 140 adj gén pinkish; [vin] rosé
B nm rosé

roseau, pl **~x** /ʀozo/ nm Bot reed

rosée² /ʀoze/ nf dew

roseraie /ʀozʀɛ/ nf rose garden

rosette /ʀozɛt/ nf [1] (insigne, ornement) rosette; (nœud) bow; [2] Bot rosette

rosier /ʀozje/ nm Bot rosebush, rose

rosière /ʀozjɛʀ/ nf: young girl recognized for her virtue

rosir /ʀoziʀ/ [3]
A vtr to turn [sth] pink
B vi [ciel, paysage] to turn pink; [visage] to go pink

rosse /ʀɔs/
A ○adj [professeur, critique] mean; [imitateur, humour] nasty
B nf [1] (cheval) nag○; [2] (personne) heel○, meanie○

rossée /ʀɔse/ nf thrashing○

rosser○ /ʀɔse/ [1] vtr [1] (battre) to give [sb] a good thrash-ing [personne]; to beat [animal]; [2] (vaincre) to thrash○ [équipe, armée]

rosserie /ʀɔsʀi/ nf [1] (parole) nasty remark; (action) mean trick; [2] (caractère) (de professeur) meanness; (d'imitateur) nas-tiness

rossignol /ʀɔsiɲɔl/ nm [1] (oiseau) nightingale; [2] ○(de cambrioleur) picklock; [3] ○(marchandise invendable) bit of junk

rot○ /ʀo/ nm burp○; **faire un ~** to burp○

rotatif, **-ive¹** /ʀɔtatif, iv/ adj rotary

rotation /ʀɔtasjɔ̃/ nf [1] (mouvement sur soi) rotation; **~ autour d'un axe** rotation about an axis; **mouvement de ~** rotational movement; **effectuer une ~ complète** to rotate fully; [2] (voyage) round trip; (fréquence des voyages) round trip service; Mil, Aviat, Naut turn round GB, turn-around; [3] (de locataire, stock) turnover; (d'équipe, de médecin) rotation; **système de ~** rota system; [4] Agric rotation; **~ des cultures** crop rotation

rotative² /ʀɔtativ/ nf rotary press

rotatoire /ʀɔtatwaʀ/ adj rotary

roter○ /ʀɔte/ [1] vtr to burp○, to belch

rôti, **~e¹** /ʀoti/
A adj [poulet, lapin] roast (épith)
B nm [1] (avant la cuisson) joint; [2] (après la cuisson) roast

rôtie² /ʀoti/ nf piece of toast

rotin /ʀɔtɛ̃/ nm (matériau) rattan

rôtir /ʀotiʀ/ [3]
A vtr to roast [viande]; to toast [pain]
B vi [1] Culin to roast; [2] ○(être exposé au soleil) to roast; **se faire ~ au soleil** to roast in the sun; [3] ○(subir une forte chaleur) [personne] to be roasting
C se rôtir vpr [personne] (au soleil) to roast (oneself); (devant un feu) to toast (oneself)

(Idiome) **il attend que ça lui tombe tout rôti dans le bec**○ he expects things to fall into his lap

rôtisseur, **-euse** /ʀotisœʀ, øz/ ▸ p. 372 nm,f seller of roast meat

rôtissoire /ʀotiswaʀ/ nf rotisserie, roasting spit

rotonde /ʀɔtɔ̃d/ nf [1] Archit (édifice) rotunda; [2] (dans un bus) back seat; [3] Rail roundhouse

rotondité /ʀɔtɔ̃dite/ nf (caractère) roundness

rotule /ʀɔtyl/ nf [1] Anat kneecap; [2] Tech ball-and-socket joint

(Idiomes) **être sur les ~s** to be on one's last legs; **mettre qn sur les ~s** to wear sb out○

roture /ʀɔtyʀ/ nf (condition) common birth

roturier, **-ière** /ʀɔtyʀje, ɛʀ/
A adj common
B nm,f Hist commoner

rouage /ʀwaʒ/ nm [1] (de machine) wheel; **les ~s** the parts ou works; [2] (d'administration) machinery ₵; **les ~s bureaucratiques** the wheels of bureaucracy; **être un ~ parmi d'autres** to be a cog in a machine

roublard○, **~e** /ʀublaʀ, aʀd/ adj crafty, cunning

roublardise○ /ʀublaʀdiz/ nf craftiness, cunning

rouble /Rubl/ ▸ p. 34 nm rouble

roucoulades /Rukulad/ nfpl (d'oiseau) cooing **¢**; (de chanteur) crooning**¢**; (d'amoureux) billing and cooing **¢**

roucoulement /Rukulmã/ nm 1 (d'oiseau) cooing **¢**; 2 ○(d'amoureux) billing and cooing **¢**; (mots tendres) murmuring **¢**

roucouler /Rukule/ [1]
A vtr to croon [chanson]; to coo [mots d'amour]
B vi 1 [oiseau] to coo; 2 [amoureux] to bill and coo

roue /Ru/ nf 1 (de véhicule, jeu) wheel; **être ~(s) à ~(s)** or **~ dans ~** to be neck and neck; **avoir une ~ à plat** to have a flat tyre GB ou tire US; ▸ **grand**; 2 (en gymnastique) cartwheel; 3 (de mécanisme) wheel; **~ dentée** cogwheel; 4 (supplice) wheel
(Composés) **~ à aube** paddle wheel; **~ libre** freewheel; **pédaler en ~ libre** to freewheel; **~ motrice** driving wheel; **véhicule à quatre ~s motrices** four-wheel-drive vehicle; **~ de secours** spare wheel GB ou tire US
(Idiomes) **être la cinquième ~ du carrosse** (inutile) to be superfluous; (de trop) to feel unwanted; **pousser qn à la ~** to be behind sb; **faire la ~** [paon] to spread its tail, to display; [personne] pej to strut around; (en gymnastique) to do a cartwheel

roué, ~e /Rwe/
A adj cunning
B nm,f (personne rusée) pej cunning devil

rouer /Rwe/ [1] vtr **~ qn de coups** to beat sb up

rouerie /RuRi/ nf 1 (caractère) cunning; 2 (action) cunning trick

rouet /Rwε/ nm (machine à filer) spinning wheel; **filer au ~** to spin

rouflaquettes○ /Ruflakεt/ nfpl sideburns

rouge /Ruʒ/ ▸ p. 140
A adj 1 gén red (**with**); (congestionné) red, flushed; **avoir le teint ~** to have a high colour^{GB}; 2 (roux) [cheveux, barbe] red, ginger; [pelage] ginger; 3 (incandescent) red-hot; **les braises sont encore ~s** the embers are still glowing; 4 (communiste) Red
B nmf Pol (communiste) Red
C adv **voter ~**○ to vote communist
D nm 1 (couleur) red; 2 (colorant) red; **les ~s organiques** natural red dyes; 3 **à joues** blusher, rouge; **~ à lèvres** lipstick; 4 (signal) red; **le feu est au ~** the (traffic) lights are red, the (traffic) light is red; **passer au ~** to jump the lights GB ou a red light; 5 (dû à l'incandescence) **chauffer** or **porter un fer au ~** to heat a piece of iron until it is red hot; **un fer porté au ~** a red-hot iron; 6 (coloration) **le ~ lui monta au visage** he/she went red in the face; 7 ○(vin) red (wine); **gros ~ (qui tache)**○ cheap red wine, red plonk○ GB; **un coup de ~**○ a glass of red wine; 8 (indicateur) red; **être dans le ~** (à la banque) to be in the red
(Composés) **~ brique** brick red; **~ sang** blood red
(Idiomes) **être ~ comme une tomate** or **un coq** or **une écrevisse** or **un coquelicot** (de timidité, honte) to be as red as a beetroot GB ou a beet US; (après avoir couru) to be red in the face; **voir ~** to see red

rougeâtre /RuʒatR/ ▸ p. 140 adj reddish

rougeaud, ~e /Ruʒo, od/ adj [personne] ruddy-faced, ruddy-cheeked; [visage, teint] ruddy

rouge-gorge, pl **rouges-gorges** /RuʒgɔRʒ/ nm robin (redbreast)

rougeoiement /Ruʒwamã/ nm red ou reddish glow

rougeole /Ruʒɔl/ ▸ p. 195 nf measles (+ v sg)

rougeoyant, ~e /Ruʒwajã, ãt/ adj [reflet] reddish, [ciel] reddening (épith), glowing red (jamais épith)

rougeoyer /Ruʒwaje/ [23] vi [ciel] to take on a red glow; [soleil couchant] to glow fiery red; [feu] to glow red

rouget /Ruʒε/ nm red mullet, goatfish US

rougeur /RuʒœR/ nf 1 (couleur, teinte) redness; 2 (congestion) redness, flushing; 3 (sur la peau) red blotch

rougir /RuʒiR/ [3]
A vtr 1 (teinter) gén to redden; **~ son eau** to put a little red wine in one's water; **~ la terre de son sang** to make the earth run red with one's blood; 2 (chauffer) to make [sth] red hot [métal]
B vi 1 [personne] (d'émotion, de honte) to blush (**de with**); (de colère) to flush (**de with**); (de chaleur) to go red; [peau, visage]

to go ou turn red; **~ jusqu'aux yeux** or **oreilles** to turn ou go as red as a beetroot GB ou a beet US; **il n'a pas à en ~** that's nothing for him to be ashamed of; **sans ~** without shame; **ne ~ de rien** to have no shame; 2 [fruit, feuille, forêt, ciel, crustacé, carapace] to turn red; 3 [métal, tison] to become red hot

rougissant, ~e /Ruʒisã, ãt/ adj [personne] blushing; [feuille, forêt, ciel] reddening

rouille /Ruj/
A ▸ p. 140 adj inv red-brown, rust(-coloured^{GB})
B nf 1 Chimie, Bot rust; 2 Culin rouille

rouillé, ~e /Ruje/ adj 1 lit [objet, fer] rusty, rusted; Bot rusty; 2 fig [athlète] out of practice; [corps, muscle, membre] stiff; [mémoire, personne, technique] rusty

rouiller /Ruje/ [1]
A vtr 1 lit to rust, to make [sth] go rusty [fer]; 2 fig to slow [sb] down; to dull [esprit]
B vi [fer] to rust, to go rusty
C se **rouiller** vpr [personne] to slow down; [sportif] to get out of shape; [muscle, corps] to lose tone; [mémoire, esprit, connaissances] to get rusty

roulade /Rulad/ nf 1 Culin (de viande) stuffed rolled meat, roulade; 2 Sport roll; 3 (de chanteur) roulade; (d'oiseau) trill, trilling **¢**

roulant, ~e /Rulã, ãt/ adj **table ~e** trolley GB, serving cart US; **matériel ~** Rail rolling stock; **personnel ~** (dans le train) train crew

roulé, ~e /Rule/
A adj 1 Culin **épaule ~e** rolled shoulder; 2 (en phonétique) **r ~** rolled r
B nm Culin roll; **~ au fromage** puff pastry filled with cheese

rouleau, pl **~x** /Rulo/ nm 1 (cylindre) roll; 2 (grosse vague) breaker, roller; 3 Agric, Tech roller; 4 (bigoudi) roller, curler; 5 Sport **~ ventral** straddle (roll); **~ dorsal** flop; **sauter en ~** (en ventral) to straddle; (en dorsal) to flop; 6 (pour peindre) roller
(Composés) **~ compresseur** Tech, fig steamroller; **~ à pâtisserie** Culin rolling pin; **~ de printemps** Culin spring roll
(Idiome) **être au bout du ~**○ (nerveusement) to be at the end of one's tether; (être mourant) to be at death's door

roulé-boulé, pl **roulés-boulés** /Rulebule/ nm roll

roulement /Rulmã/ nm 1 (bruit) (de train, tonnerre) rumble; (de tambour) roll; 2 Fin (de capital) circulation; 3 (alternance) rotation; **travailler par ~** to work (in) shifts; **faire** or **établir un ~** to draw up a rota GB ou schedule; 4 Tech bearing; **~ à billes** ball bearing

rouler /Rule/ [1]
A vtr 1 (entraîner) to roll [tonneau, pneu, boulette]; to wheel [charrette, brouette]; **le fleuve roule ses eaux boueuses** the muddy waters of the river swirl along; **les vagues roulent les galets** the waves shift the pebbles around; 2 (mettre en rouleau) to roll up [tapis, manche, col]; to roll [cigarette]; **~ qch en boule** to roll [sth] into a ball; 3 (faire bouger) **~ les** or **des épaules** to roll one's shoulders; **~ les** or **des hanches** to wiggle one's hips; **~ les** or **des yeux** to roll one's eyes; 4 (aplanir) to roll [champ, gazon]; to roll out [pâte à tarte]; 5 (en phonétique) **~ les r** to roll one's r's; 6 ○(tromper) **~ qn** to diddle○ GB ou cheat sb
B ▸ p. 624 vi 1 [boule, pièce, pierre, tronc, personne] to roll; **~ dans le ravin** to roll down into the ravine; **faire ~ les dés** to roll the dice; 2 [véhicule] to go; **ma voiture ne roule plus** my car won't go; **ma voiture n'a pas roulé depuis deux ans** my car hasn't been driven for two years; **les bus ne roulent pas le dimanche** buses don't run on Sundays; **~ à grande vitesse** [voiture, train] to travel at high speed; **~ au super**○ to run on 4-star GB ou premium US; **ça roule**○! fig (c'est entendu) it's a deal!; 3 (conduire) to drive; **~ à gauche** to drive on the left; **~ en Cadillac**® to drive a Cadillac®; 4 (bouger) [muscles] to ripple; **faire ~ ses épaules** to roll one's shoulders; **faire ~ ses biceps** to flex one's biceps; 5 [bateau] to roll; 6 [tonnerre, détonation] to rumble
C se **rouler** vpr 1 (se mettre) **se ~ dans** to roll in [boue]; **se ~ par terre** lit to roll (about) on the floor; fig (rire) to fall about laughing; **c'était à se ~ par terre** it was hilarious; **se ~ en boule** to curl up in a ball; 2 (s'envelopper) **se ~ dans** to wrap oneself in [couverture]
(Idiomes) **~ sous la table**○ to be under the table; **~ la caisse**○ or **des mécaniques**○ to swagger along

roulette /ʀulɛt/ nf **1** (petite roue) caster; **lit à ~s** bed on casters; **2** ▸ p. 327 Jeux roulette; **3** (de dentiste) (dentist's) drill; **4** Culin pastry wheel; **5** (en couture) tracing wheel; **6** (en reliure) fillet

Idiome **marcher comme sur des ~s**○ to go smoothly ou like a dream

rouleur, -euse /ʀulœʀ, øz/ nm,f cyclist

roulier /ʀulje/ nm **1** (navire) roll-on roll-off ship; **2** (personne) carter

roulis /ʀuli/ nm (de bateau) rolling; (de voiture, train) swaying

roulotte /ʀulɔt/ nf (horse-drawn) caravan GB, trailer US

roumain, ~e /ʀumɛ̃, ɛn/
A ▸ p. 392 adj Romanian
B ▸ p. 336 nm Ling Romanian

Roumanie /ʀumani/ ▸ p. 230 nprf Romania

roupie /ʀupi/ ▸ p. 34 nf rupee

Idiome **c'est de la ~ de sansonnet**○ it's a load of rubbish○

roupiller○ /ʀupije/ [1] vtr to sleep

roupillon○ /ʀupijɔ̃/ nm snooze○, nap

rouquin○, **~e** /ʀukɛ̃, in/
A adj [personne] red-haired; [cheveux] red
B nm,f redhead
C nm (vin) plonk○ GB, cheap red wine

rouspéter○ /ʀuspete/ [14] vi to grumble (**contre** about; **après** at)

rouspéteur○, **-euse** /ʀuspetœʀ, øz/ nm,f grumbler

roussâtre /ʀusatʀ/ ▸ p. 140 adj reddish

rousse /ʀus/ adj ▸ roux A, B

rousseur /ʀusœʀ/ nf (de cheveux, barbe, feuille) redness; (de teinte, ton) russet colourGB

roussi /ʀusi/ nm **ça sent le ~** lit it smells of burning; fig○ there's trouble brewing

roussir /ʀusiʀ/ [3]
A vtr **1** (colorer) liter to turn [sth] brown; **2** (brûler) [fer à repasser, soleil] to scorch; [flamme] to singe
B vi **1** (se colorer) to go brown; **2** Culin **faire ~** to brown

routage /ʀutaʒ/ nm **1** (de journaux, colis) sorting and mailing; **société de ~** mailing house; **2** Ordinat routing

routard○, **~e** /ʀutaʀ, aʀd/ nm,f backpacker

route /ʀut/ nf **1** (voie terrestre) road, highway US; **demain je prends la ~** tomorrow I take to the road; **tenir la ~** lit [voiture] to hold the road; fig○ [argument] to hold water; [équipement] to be well-made; **2** (moyen de transport) road; **par la ~** by road; **il y a six heures de ~** it's a six-hour drive; **je préfère prendre la ~** I prefer to go by road; **faire de la ~**○ to do a lot of mileage; **3** (itinéraire) route; **~s maritimes** sea routes; **s'éloigner** ou **dévier de sa ~** lit [avion, bateau] to go off course; [voiture, piéton] to go the wrong way; fig [personne] to stray from one's chosen path; **la ~ est toute tracée désormais** fig from now on, it's all plain sailing; **nos ~s se sont croisées** fig our paths crossed; **4** (parcours) lit, fig way; **la ~ sera longue** it will be a long journey; **être sur la ~ de qn** to be in sb's way; **rencontrer qch en ~** lit to meet sth on the way; fig to meet sth along the way; **j'ai changé d'avis en cours de ~** I changed my mind along the way; **je me suis arrêté en cours de ~** I stopped on the way; **finis ta phrase, ne t'arrête pas en (cours de) ~** finish your sentence, don't stop halfway through; **être en ~** [personne] to be on one's way; [plat] to be underway; **avoir qch en ~** to have sth underway; **remettre qn sur la bonne ~** to put sb right; **~ du succès** road to success; **faire ~ avec qn** to travel with sb; **faire ~ vers, être en ~ pour** [avion, passager] to be en route to; [bateau] to be sailing to; [voiture, train, piéton] to be heading for; **faire fausse ~** lit to go off course; fig to be mistaken; **se mettre en ~** to set off; **en ~!** let's go!; **bonne ~!** have a good journey GB ou a nice trip!; **mettre en ~** to start [machine, voiture]; to get [sth] going [projet, fabrication]; **la mise en ~ des négociations a été difficile** it was difficult to get the negotiations going; **5** (cyclisme) **géants** or **rois de la ~** road-cycling champions; **épreuve** ou **course sur ~** road race

Composés **~ départementale** secondary road (maintained by local authority); **~ des épices** Hist spice route; **~ à grande circulation** trunk road GB, highway US; **~ nationale** trunk road GB, ≈ A road GB, national highway US; **~ de navigation** shipping lane; **~ du rhum** Sport Rum route race; **~ secondaire** minor road; **~ de**

la soie Hist Silk Route ou Road; **~ du vin** wine trail

router /ʀute/ [1] vtr to sort [sth] for mailing [magazines, journaux]

routier, -ière[1] /ʀutje, ɛʀ/
A adj road (épith)
B nm **1** ▸ p. 372 (chauffeur) lorry driver GB, truck driver; **2** (restaurant) transport café GB, truck stop US; **3** (en cyclisme) road racer

routière[2] /ʀutjɛʀ/ nf **ma voiture n'est pas une très bonne ~** my car is not very good for long-distance driving

routine /ʀutin/ nf **1** (habitude) routine; **tomber dans la ~** to get into a rut; **2** Ordinat routine

routinier, -ière /ʀutinje, ɛʀ/ adj [personne] set in one's ways (jamais épith); [esprit, méthode, travail, vie] routine (épith)

rouvrir /ʀuvʀiʀ/ [32]
A vtr **1** to open [sth] again [porte, rideau, coffre, yeux]; to reopen [blessure]; to turn [sth] back on [gaz]; **2** (remettre en service) to reopen [magasin, route]; **3** (après arrêt) to resume [négociations, hostilités]; to reopen [débat, affaire]
B vi [magasin, école, route] to reopen
C se rouvrir vpr [porte, fenêtre] to open (again); [blessure, parapluie] to open up (again)

roux, rousse /ʀu, ʀus/ ▸ p. 140
A adj [couleur] russet; [cheveux, barbe] red; (plus clair) ginger; [feuilles] russet; [personne] red-haired (épith); [animal, pelage] ginger; **il est ~** he's a redhead
B nm,f red-haired person, redhead; **les ~** redheads

royal, ~e[1], mpl **-aux** /ʀwajal, o/ adj **1** (de souverain) royal; **2** (magnifique) [accueil] royal; [cadeau] fit for a king (après n); [salaire] princely; **3** (suprême) [indifférence] supreme; [mépris] majestic; [paix] blissful

royale[2] /ʀwajal/ nf **1** Culin royale (savoury egg custard); **2** Mil **la Royale** the French Navy; **3** (barbe) imperial

royalement /ʀwajalmɑ̃/ adv **1** (avec magnificence) [recevoir, traiter] royally, like royalty; [vivre] royally, like a king; **être payé ~** to be paid handsomely; **2** ○(complètement) **il se moque ~ de son travail** he really couldn't care less about his work

royaliste /ʀwajalist/ adj, nmf royalist

Idiome **être plus ~ que le roi** to be more Catholic than the pope

royaume /ʀwajom/ nm lit, fig kingdom

Idiome **au ~ des aveugles, les borgnes sont rois** Prov in the country of the blind, the one-eyed man is king Prov

Royaume-Uni /ʀwajomyni/ ▸ p. 230 nprm **~ de Grande-Bretagne et d'Irlande du Nord** United Kingdom of Great Britain and Northern Ireland; **le ~** the United Kingdom

royauté /ʀwajote/ nf **1** (dignité) kingship; **2** (régime) monarchy

RSVP (written abbr = **répondez s'il vous plaît**) RSVP

RTT /ɛʀtete/ nf (abbr = **réduction du temps de travail**) reduction in the number of working hours

RU /ʀy/ nm: abbr ▸ **restaurant**

ruade /ʀyad/ nf **1** (de cheval) buck; **2** fig (de personne) attack

ruban /ʀybɑ̃/ nm ribbon

Composés **~ d'acier** steel band ou strip; **~ adhésif** adhesive tape; **~ de chapeau** hat band; **~ perforé** Ordinat (punched) paper tape

rubéole /ʀybeɔl/ ▸ p. 195 nf German measles (+ v sg)

rubis /ʀybi/ nm inv **1** (pierre, bijou) ruby; **2** ▸ p. 140 (couleur) ruby; **3** (de montre) jewel

Idiome **payer ~ sur l'ongle**○ to pay cash on the nail

rubrique /ʀybʀik/ nf **1** (de journal) section; **tenir une ~ dans un journal** to have a column in a newspaper; **2** (catégorie) category; **classer des papiers sous la ~ 'à suivre'** to file papers under 'further action'; **3** Relig rubric

Composés **~ mondaine** social column; **~ nécrologique** obituary column

ruche /ʀyʃ/ nf **1** (habitation) beehive, hive; **2** fig hive of activity; **3** (en couture) ruche

rucher /ʀyʃe/ nm apiary

rude /ʀyd/ adj **1** [métier, journée, combat] hard, tough; [climat, hiver] harsh; [épreuve] severe; **2** [étoffe, barbe, peau] rough; **3** [voix, manières] harsh; [traits, personne] coarse;

4) [appétit] healthy; [montagnard, marin] rugged; **c'est un ~ gaillard** he's a strapping fellow; **5)** [adversaire] tough, formidable

Idiomes **en voir de ~s○** to have a hard ou tough time of it; **en faire voir de ~s○ à qn** to put sb through it

rudement /ʀydmɑ̃/ adv **1)** (sans ménagements) roughly, harshly; **2)** ○(très) really; **c'est ~ mieux!** it's a hell of a lot○ better!

rudesse /ʀydɛs/ nf **1)** (sévérité) harshness, severity; **2)** (manque de raffinement) coarseness

rudiment /ʀydimɑ̃/
A Anat rudiment; **un ~ de queue** a rudimentary tail
B **rudiments** nmpl rudiments; **avoir quelques ~s de** to have a rudimentary knowledge of

rudimentaire /ʀydimɑ̃tɛʀ/ adj **1)** (de base) basic; **2)** Anat rudimentary

rudoyer /ʀydwaje/ [23] vtr to bully

rue /ʀy/ nf **1)** (voie) street; **2)** (peuple) pej **la ~** the mob péj; **3)** Bot rue

Idiomes **ça ne court pas les ~s○** it's pretty thin on the ground; **être à la ~** to be on the street, to be down-and-out; **jeter/mettre qn à la ~** to throw/to put sb out on the street; **descendre dans la ~** to take to the street

ruée /ʀɥe/ nf rush; **~ vers l'or** gold rush

ruelle /ʀɥɛl/ nf alleyway, back street

ruer /ʀɥe/ [1]
A vi [cheval] to kick
B **se ruer** vpr to rush; **se ~ sur qn/qch** to pounce on sb/sth; **se ~ à l'assaut de qch** to launch an attack on sth; **les gens se ruent à l'assaut des magasins** there is a rush on the shops GB ou stores US

Idiome **~ dans les brancards** to kick over the traces, to rebel

rufian○ /ʀyfjɑ̃/ nm (aventurier) adventurer

rugby /ʀygbi/ ▸ p. 327 nm rugby; **~ à treize** rugby league; **~ à quinze** rugby union

rugbyman, pl **rugbymen** /ʀygbiman, mɛn/ ▸ p. 372 nm rugby player

rugir /ʀyʒiʀ/ [3]
A vtr to bellow (out), to growl
B vi [animal, moteur, mer] to roar; [personne, vent] to howl

rugissement /ʀyʒismɑ̃/ nm (d'animal, de personne) roar; (de vent) howling; **pousser un ~** or des **~s** to roar

rugosité /ʀygozite/ nf **1)** (état) roughness; **2)** (aspérité) rough patch

rugueux, **-euse** /ʀygø, øz/ adj rough

ruine /ʀɥin/ nf **1)** (destruction) (de bâtiment, pays, réputation, personne, d'entreprise) ruin; (de civilisation) collapse; (d'espoir) death; **en ~(s)** ruined (épith); **être/tomber en ~(s)** to be in ruins/to fall into ruin; **menacer ~** to be threatening to collapse; **c'est la ~○** fig it's exorbitant; **ce n'est pas la ~○** fig it's not that expensive; **les femmes seront sa ~** women will be the ruin of him/her; **être la ~ de** to ruin; **courir** or **aller à la ~** [personne, entreprise] to be heading for financial ruin; [civilisation] to be heading for collapse; **2)** (restes) (bâtiment) ruin; (personne) pej wreck

ruiner /ʀɥine/ [1]
A vtr **1)** (financièrement) to ruin [pays, personne, entreprise, économie]; **~ qn** to be a drain on sb's resources; **ça ne va pas le ~○** that's not going to break the bank; **2)** (physiquement) to destroy, to wreck [santé, forces]; [bombardement] to reduce [sth] to rubble [ville, bâtiment]; [éléments] to ruin [culture]; **3)** fig to ruin [vie, réputation]; to destroy [argument, théorie, bonheur]; to shatter [espérances, rêve]
B **se ruiner** vpr (perdre ses biens) to be ruined, to lose everything; (dépenser excessivement) to ruin oneself (**en faisant** doing); **se ~ pour une femme** to spend everything one has on a woman

ruineux, **-euse** /ʀɥinø, øz/ adj [entretien, dépense] exorbitant; [goût, plaisir, sortie] very expensive; [achat, guerre, affaire, objet] ruinously expensive

ruisseau, pl **~x** /ʀɥiso/ nm **1)** (cours d'eau) stream, brook; **2)** (flot) **~ de larmes/lave** stream of tears/lava; **3)** †(caniveau) gutter; **tirer** or **sortir qn du ~** fig to pull sb out of the gutter

ruisseler /ʀɥisle/ [19] vi **1)** (s'écouler) [eau, sang] to stream; [graisse] to drip; **2)** [personne, surface, objet] to be streaming

(de with); **~ de sueur** to be dripping with sweat; **~ de lumière** to be flooded with light

ruissellement /ʀɥisɛlmɑ̃/ nm (de pluie) streaming (**sur** down); (de produits toxiques) seepage

rumeur /ʀymœʀ/ nf **1)** (ouï-dire) rumourGB (**sur** about); **selon certaines ~s, il aurait quitté le pays** rumourGB has it that he may have left the country; **faire taire une ~** to put a stop to a rumourGB; **2)** (de voix, mer, vent) murmur

ruminant /ʀyminɑ̃/ nm ruminant

ruminer /ʀymine/ [1]
A vtr **1)** Zool to ruminate, to chew the cud; **2)** (penser constamment à) to brood on [malheur]; to chew over○ [idée, projet]
B vi **1)** Zool to ruminate, to chew the cud; **2)** [personne] to brood

rumsteck /ʀɔmstɛk/ nm rump steak

rupestre /ʀypɛstʀ/ adj **1)** [plante, flore] rock (épith); **2)** [peinture, art, dessin] cave (épith), rock (épith)

rupture /ʀyptyʀ/ nf **1)** (de relations, d'accord) breaking-off; **2)** (résultat) breakdown (**avec** in); **3)** (de couple, coalition, d'amis) break-up; **lettre de ~** letter ending a relationship; **4)** (opposition) **être en ~ avec** to be at odds with [hiérarchie, groupe]; to have broken away from [idéologie, tradition]; **5)** (cassure) gén break; (de barrage, digue) breaking; (de conduite) fracture; (de muscle, d'artère) rupture; (d'organe mécanique ou électrique) failure

Composés **~ d'anévrisme** ruptured aneurysm; **~ de charge** transshipment; **~ de contrat** breach of contract; **~ de stock** stock shortage; **être en ~ de stock** to be out of stock

rural, **~e**, mpl **-aux** /ʀyʀal, o/
A adj [exode, milieu] rural; [chemin, vie] country; **l'espace ~** the countryside
B nm,f **les ruraux** people who live in the country

ruse /ʀyz/ nf **1)** (procédé) trick, ruse; **c'est une ~ de guerre** hum it's a cunning stratagem; **c'est une ~ de Sioux** hum it's a crafty trick; **2)** (habileté) cunning, craftiness; **avec ~** cunningly

rusé, **~e** /ʀyze/
A adj cunning, crafty; **jouer au plus ~ avec qn** to try to outsmart sb
B nm,f **c'est une ~e** she's a crafty one

ruser /ʀyze/ [1] vi **1)** (être rusé) to be crafty; **2)** (être plus fin que) **~ avec** to trick [ennemi]; **3)** (vaincre) **~ avec** to find a way around [difficulté]

rush, pl **rushes** /ʀœʃ/
A nm **1)** Sport (à la course) final burst; (en sport collectif) attack; **2)** ○(ruée) rush
B **rushes** nmpl Cin rushes

russe /ʀys/ ▸ p. 336, p. 392 adj, nm Ling Russian

Russie /ʀysi/ ▸ p. 230 nprf Russia

russophone /ʀysɔfɔn/
A adj Russian-speaking
B nmf Russian speaker

rusticité /ʀystisite/ nf **1)** (de matériau, lieu) rustic character (**de** of); **2)** (de plante) hardiness (**de** of)

rustine® /ʀystin/ nf (puncture-repair) patch

rustique /ʀystik/
A adj **1)** (campagnard) rustic, country (épith); **2)** [plante] hardy (épith)
B nm **le ~** rustic style

rustre /ʀystʀ/
A adj uncouth
B nm **1)** (homme grossier) lout; **2)** †(paysan) peasant

rut /ʀyt/ nm rutting season; **être en ~** to be in rut

rutabaga /ʀytabaga/ nm swede GB, rutabaga US

rutilant, **~e** /ʀytilɑ̃, ɑ̃t/ adj [diamant] sparkling; [carrosserie, chrome] gleaming

rwandais, **~e** /ʀwɑ̃dɛ, ɛz/ ▸ p. 392 adj Rwandan

rythme /ʀitm/ nm **1)** Littérat, Mus rhythm; **au ~ de** to the rhythm of; **marquer le ~** to beat time; **avoir le ~ dans la peau○** to have a natural sense of rhythm; **2)** (d'accroissement, de production) rate; (de vie, film) pace; **changer au ~ des saisons** to change with the seasons; **la situation se dégrade à un ~ accéléré** the situation is deteriorating rapidly; **au ~ de** at a rate of; **3)** (mouvement régulier) rate; **~ cardiaque** heart rate

Composés **~ biologique** biorhythm; **~ de croissance** growth rate; **~s scolaires** school timetables

rythmé, **∼e** /ʀitme/ *adj* rhythmic; **la musique est très ∼e** the music has a very good rhythm

rythmer /ʀitme/ [1] *vtr* ① (scander) to put rhythm into [*phrase, poème*]; to give rhythm to [*tâche, marche*];

② (ponctuer) to regulate [*vie, journée, travail*]

rythmique /ʀitmik/
A *adj* rhythmic
B *nf* ① Ling rhythmics (+ *v sg*); ② Mus rhythm section

Ss

s, S /ɛs/ nm inv s, S

s' 1 ▸ se; 2 ▸ si¹

sa ▸ son¹

sabbat /saba/ nm 1 Relig Sabbath; 2 (des sorcières) witching hour

sabbatique /sabatik/ adj 1 Relig Sabbatical; 2 Univ, Admin [année] sabbatical

sabir /sabir/ nm 1 (charabia) mumbo-jumbo; 2 (mélange) pidgin

sable /sɑbl/
A ▸ p. 140 adj inv sand-coloured^GB
B nm sand; **bâtir sur le ~** fig to build on sand
C sables nmpl sands
(Composé) **~s mouvants** quicksands
(Idiome) **être sur le ~**^○ to be on one's beam ends

sablé, ~e /sable/
A adj 1 [route, allée] covered with sand; 2 Culin **pâte ~e** rich shortcrust pastry
B nm (biscuit) ≈ shortbread biscuit GB ou cookie US

sabler /sable/ [1] vtr 1 to grit [chaussée]; 2 Tech (pour nettoyer) to sandblast; (pour mouler) to sand-cast

sableuse¹ /sabløz/ nf 1 (pour la chaussée) gritter; 2 (pour décaper) sandblaster

sableux, -euse² /sablø, øz/ adj sandy

sablier /sablije/ nm hourglass; (pour cuire des œufs) egg timer

sablonneux, -euse /sablɔnø, øz/ adj sandy

sabord /sabɔr/ nm scuttle

sabordage /sabɔrdaʒ/ nm Naut scuttling

saborder /sabɔrde/ [1]
A vtr Naut, fig to scuttle
B se saborder vpr Naut to scuttle ou scupper one's/its etc own ship; fig to sink oneself/itself

sabot /sabo/ nm 1 (chaussure) clog; 2 Zool hoof; **donner un coup de ~** à qn to kick sb; 3 Aut shoe; 4 Tech (de pieu, poteau) shoe; (de pied de meuble) (metal) foot; 5 ^○(objet sans valeur) old contraption
(Composé) **~ de Denver**® wheel clamp
(Idiome) **jouer comme un ~**^○ to play very badly; **je te vois** or **t'entends venir avec tes gros ~s**^○ I can see it coming a mile off^○; **ne pas avoir les deux pieds dans le même ~** to be on one's toes

sabotage /sabɔtaʒ/ nm 1 (méthode) sabotage; 2 (acte) (act of) sabotage

saboter /sabɔte/ [1] vtr to sabotage; **~ un travail**^○ to botch^○ a job

saboteur, -euse /sabɔtœr, øz/ nm,f 1 (de matériel) saboteur; 2 (de travail) botcher

sabotier, -ière /sabɔtje, ɛr/ ▸ p. 372 nm,f (fabricant) clog maker; (commerçant) clog seller

sabre /sɑbr/ nm (à lame droite) sword; (à lame courbée) sabre^GB; **~ au clair** Mil with sword(s) drawn; **bruits de ~** fig sabre^GB rattling **€**
(Composés) **~ d'abattage** or **d'abattis** machete; **~ d'abordage** cutlass

sabrer /sabre/ [1] vtr 1 Mil to cut down; 2 ^○(écourter) to cut chunks out of [article, manuscrit]; (supprimer) to cut out [phrase, paragraphe]; to axe^GB [projet]; 3 ^○(critiquer) to tear [sb] to pieces [auteur]; to pan^○ [livre, film]; 4 ^○(recaler) to flunk^○ [étudiant]; (licencier) to fire, to sack^○ GB; 5 (rayer) to score [page, dessin] (**de** with); 6 ▸ ^○(bâcler) to rush through [travail]

sabreur /sabrœr/ nm 1 Mil, Sport swordsman; 2 (soldat) pej real fighter

sac /sak/ nm 1 (contenant) gén bag; (grossier, à usage commercial) sack; 2 (contenu) bag(ful), sack(ful); 3 Anat, Bot sac; 4 (pillage) sack; **mettre à ~** to sack [ville, région]; to ransack [boutique, maison]
(Composés) **~ à bandoulière** shoulder bag; **~ de congélation** freezer bag; **~ de couchage** sleeping bag; **~ à dos** rucksack, backpack; **~ d'embrouilles** can of worms; **~ isotherme** cool bag; **~ à main** handbag, purse US; **(de) marin** Naut kitbag GB, duffel bag US; **~ de nœuds** = **~ d'embrouilles**; **~ en plastique** (sans poignées) polythene bag; (avec poignées) carrier bag; **~ postal** mail sack; **~ poubelle** bin liner GB, trash bag US, trash-can liner US; **~ à provisions** shopping bag, carry-all US; **~ à puces**^○ fleabag^○ GB, flea-infested animal; **~ à vin**^○ (old) soak^○
(Idiomes) **l'affaire est dans le ~**^○ it's in the bag^○; **avoir plus d'un tour dans son ~** to have more than one trick up one's sleeve; **vider son ~**^○ to get it off one's chest; **se faire prendre la main dans le ~** to be caught red-handed; **mettre dans le même ~**^○ to lump [sth] together

saccade /sakad/ nf jerk

saccadé, ~e /sakade/ adj [mouvement, marche] jerky; [musique, rythme] staccato; [voix] clipped

saccage /sakaʒ/ nm (de région) devastation; (de bâtiment) vandalizing

saccager /sakaʒe/ [13] vtr 1 (abîmer) to wreck, to devastate [région, site, arbres]; to vandalize [bâtiment, tombe]; 2 (mettre à sac) to sack

saccharine /sakarin/ nf saccharin

SACEM /sasɛm/ nf (abbr = **Société des auteurs, compositeurs et éditeurs de musique**) association of composers and music publishers to protect copyright and royalties

sacerdoce /sasɛrdɔs/ nm 1 Relig priesthood; **30 ans de ~** 30 years in the priesthood; 2 fig vocation

sacerdotal, ~e, mpl -aux /sasɛrdɔtal, o/ adj priestly

sachet /saʃɛ/ nm (de poudre) packet; (d'aromates) sachet; (de confiseries) bag; **~ de thé** tea bag

sacoche /sakɔʃ/ nf 1 (gros sac) bag; 2 (contre la roue arrière d'un vélo, d'une moto) pannier GB, saddlebag US; 3 (d'écolier) (school)bag; (avec bretelles) satchel

sacquer^○ /sake/ [1] vtr 1 [employeur] to sack^○, to fire^○ [employé]; 2 [enseignant] to mark [sb] strictly; **se faire ~ en anglais** to get a really low mark in English
(Idiome) **je ne peux pas le ~** I can't stand the sight of him

sacraliser /sakralize/ [1] vtr 1 (rendre sacré) to make [sth] sacred; 2 (considérer comme sacré) to regard [sth] as sacred

sacre /sakr/ nm (de roi) coronation; (d'évêque) consecration; **le Sacre du Printemps** Mus The Rite of Spring

sacré, ~e /sakre/
A adj 1 Relig [art, objet, lieu] sacred; [cause] holy; 2 (à respecter) [règle, droit] sacred; 3 ^○(remarquable) **être un ~ menteur** to be a hell of^○ a liar; **il a un ~ courage** he's really courageous; 4 ^○(d'admiration, de surprise) **~ Paul, va!** Paul, you old devil!
B nm **le ~** the sacred
(Idiome) **avoir le feu ~** to be full of zeal ou enthusiasm

sacrement /sakʀəmɑ̃/ *nm* sacrament; **mourir muni des derniers ~s de l'Église** to die having received the last rites of the Church

sacrément○ /sakʀemɑ̃/ *adv* incredibly○

sacrer /sakʀe/ [1] *vtr* Relig to crown [*roi*]; to consecrate [*évêque*]

sacrifice /sakʀifis/ *nm* sacrifice

sacrifier /sakʀifje/ [1]
A *vtr* **1** (immoler) lit to sacrifice (**à** to); **2** (négliger) to sacrifice; **~ sa famille à son travail** to put one's work before one's family; **'prix sacrifiés'** Comm 'rock-bottom prices'
B **sacrifier à** *vtr ind* to conform to [*rite, coutume*]
C **se sacrifier** *vpr* **1** lit to sacrifice oneself (**pour qn** for sb); **2** ○fig (financièrement) to make sacrifices

sacrilège /sakʀilɛʒ/
A *adj* sacrilegious
B *nm* Relig sacrilege ¢; **un ~** an act of sacrilege

sacripant○ /sakʀipɑ̃/ *nm* tearaway○

sacristain /sakʀistɛ̃/ ▸ p. 372 *nm* sexton

sacristie /sakʀisti/ *nf* (d'église) sacristy; (de temple protestant) vestry

sacro-saint, **~e**, *mpl* **~s** /sakʀosɛ̃, ɛt/ *adj* sacrosanct

sadique /sadik/
A *adj* sadistic
B *nmf* sadist

sadisme /sadism/ *nm* sadism

sadomasochisme /sadomazɔʃism/ *nm* sadomasochism

sadomasochiste /sadomazɔʃist/
A *adj* sadomasochistic
B *nmf* sadomasochist

safran /safʀɑ̃/ ▸ p. 140
A *adj inv* saffron (yellow)
B *nm* **1** (épice) saffron; **riz au ~** saffron rice; **2** (couleur) saffron

sagace /sagas/ *adj* sagacious, shrewd

sagacité /sagasite/ *nf* sagacity, shrewdness

sagaie /sagɛ/ *nf* assegai

sage /saʒ/
A *adj* **1** (sensé) wise, sensible; **2** (docile) [*enfant, chien*] good, well-behaved; **sois ~!** be good!; **3** (modéré) [*goût, mode*] sober; [*prix*] moderate, reasonable; [*idées*] sensible; **4** (pudique) [*vêtement*] sober
B *nm* **1** (homme avisé) wise man; (dans l'antiquité) sage; **2** (conseiller) expert
(Idiome) **être ~ comme une image** to be as good as gold

sage-femme, *pl* **sages-femmes** /saʒfam/ ▸ p. 372 *nf* midwife; **un homme ~** a male midwife

sagement /saʒmɑ̃/ *adv* **1** (avec bon sens) wisely; **2** (avec docilité) quietly; **3** (avec décence) gén properly; [*s'habiller*] soberly; [*vivre*] quietly

sagesse /saʒɛs/ *nf* ▸**1** (de sage) wisdom; ▸ **crainte**; **2** (bon sens) (de personne) wisdom, common sense; (de parole, décision, d'action) wisdom; (de conseil) soundness; **faire preuve de ~** to show common sense; **3** (docilité) good behaviour^GB

Sagittaire /saʒitɛʀ/ ▸ p. 635 *nprm* Sagittarius

saharienne /saaʀjɛn/ *nf* (veste) safari jacket

saignant, **~e** /sɛɲɑ̃, ɑ̃t/ *adj* **1** [*viande*] rare; **2** ○fig [*critique*] savage; Sport [*rencontre*] bloody

saignée /sɛɲe/ *nf* **1** Méd bloodletting, bleeding; **2** (dans un budget) hole (**dans** in); **3** (entaille) cut

saignement /sɛɲ(ə)mɑ̃/ *nm* bleeding ¢

saigner /sɛɲe/ [1]
A *vtr* **1** Méd to bleed; **2** (tuer) to kill [*animal*] (by slitting its throat)
B *vi* to bleed; **~ du nez** to have a nosebleed
(Idiomes) **~ comme un bœuf**○ to bleed heavily; **~ qn à blanc** to bleed sb dry *ou* white; **se ~ (aux quatre veines) pour qn** to make big sacrifices for sb

saillant, **~e** /sajɑ̃, ɑ̃t/ *adj* **1** [*os*] prominent; [*muscle*] bulging; [*angle*] salient; **2** [*fait*] salient

saillie /saji/ *nf* **1** (avancée) projection; **en ~** projecting (épith); **faire ~** to project; **2** Zool covering, serving; **3** (pointe d'esprit) sally

saillir /sajiʀ/ [28] *vi* (avancer) to jut out; (ressortir) [*côtes, muscles*] to bulge

sain, **~e** /sɛ̃, sɛn/ *adj* **1** (en bonne santé) lit, fig [*personne, corps, plante*] healthy; [*dent*] sound, healthy; **~ d'esprit** sane; **~ de corps et d'esprit** sound in body and mind; **~ et sauf** [*revenir*] safe and sound; [*s'en tirer, s'en sortir*] unscathed; **2** (bénéfique) [*climat, vie*] healthy; [*affaire, entreprise*] sound; [*lecture*] wholesome; **3** (en bon état) [*fruit, maison*] sound; [*plaie*] clean; **4** (solide) [*jugement, bases*] sound; [*économie*] healthy

saindoux /sɛ̃du/ *nm inv* lard

sainement /sɛnmɑ̃/ *adv* **1** [*vivre*] healthily; **2** [*raisonner*] soundly

saint, **~e** /sɛ̃, sɛt/
A *adj* **1** (sacré) holy; **vendredi ~** Good Friday; **jeudi ~** Maundy Thursday; **2** (canonisé) **~ Paul** Saint Paul; **3** (vertueux) good, godly
B *nm,f* saint; **ce n'est pas une ~e!** she's no saint!; **se prendre pour un ~/une ~e** to think one is perfect; ▸ **vouer**
(Composés) **~e nitouche** pej goody-goody○ péj; **la Sainte Vierge** the Virgin Mary

Saint-Barthélémy /sɛ̃baʀtelemi/ *nf* **la ~** the St Bartholomew's Day massacre

saint-bernard /sɛ̃bɛʀnaʀ/ *nm inv* (chien) St Bernard; **c'est un vrai ~** fig he's/she's a real Good Samaritan

Saint-Cyr /sɛ̃siʀ/ *npr*: French military academy

Saint-Esprit /sɛ̃tɛspʀi/ *nprm* Holy Spirit; (en formule) Holy Ghost; **par l'opération du ~**○ by magic

sainteté /sɛ̃te/ *nf* (de personne) saintliness
(Idiome) **ne pas être en odeur de ~ (auprès de qn)** to be in sb's bad books

saint-frusquin○ /sɛ̃fʀyskɛ̃/ *nm inv* **tout le ~** the whole caboodle○

saint-glinglin○: **à la saint-glinglin** /alasɛ̃glɛ̃glɛ̃/ *loc adv* probably never; **rester/attendre jusqu'à la ~** to stay/to wait till the cows come home○

Saint-Guy /sɛ̃gi/ ▸ p. 195 *npr* **la danse de ~** Méd Saint Vitus's dance; fig the fidgets (*pl*)

saint-honoré /sɛ̃tɔnɔʀe/ *nm inv* Culin Saint-Honoré (cream-filled tart topped with choux and caramel)

Saint-Jacques /sɛ̃ʒak/ *npr* **coquille ~** scallop

Saint-Jean /sɛ̃ʒɑ̃/ *nf* **la ~** Midsummer Day; **feux de la ~** bonfires (*pl*) on Midsummer Night

Saint-Martin /sɛ̃maʀtɛ̃/ ▸ p. 155 *nf* **été de la ~** Indian summer

Saint-Sylvestre /sɛ̃silvɛstʀ/ *nf* **la ~** New Year's Eve

Saint-Valentin /sɛ̃valɑ̃tɛ̃/ ▸ p. 155 *nf* **la ~** St Valentine's Day, Valentine's Day

saisie /sezi/ *nf* **1** gén, Jur (confiscation) seizure; **2** Ordinat **~ (informatique)** keyboarding; **~ de données** data capture

saisir /seziʀ/ [3]
A *vtr* **1** (prendre fermement) to grab [*objet, personne, bras*]; **~ qn par le bras** to grab sb by the arm; **2** (attraper) [*animal*] to seize [*proie*]; (prendre) to snatch [sth] up [*clés*]; **~ au vol** lit to catch [*balle*]; fig to jump at [*affaire*]; **3** (profiter de) to seize [*occasion*]; **'affaire à ~'** 'amazing bargain'; **4** (comprendre) to understand; **tu saisis**○? do you get it○?; **5** (entendre) to catch [*bribes de conversation*]; **6** (s'emparer de) [*émotion, froid*] to grip [*personne*]; **7** (impressionner) to strike [*personne*]; **8** (confisquer) [*police, douane*] to seize [*drogue*]; **9** Jur to seize [*biens*]; **~ la justice d'une affaire** to refer a matter to a court; **10** Ordinat to capture [*données*]; to keyboard [*texte*]
B **se saisir** *vpr* **se ~ de** to catch

saisissable /sezisabl/ *adj* Jur [*biens*] distrainable; [*revenus*] attachable

saisissant, **~e** /sezisɑ̃, ɑ̃t/ *adj* **1** [*froid*] piercing; **2** (frappant) [*effet, ressemblance, coïncidence*] striking

saison /sɛzɔ̃/ ▸ p. 536 *nf* **1** (division de l'année) season; **en cette ~** at this time of year; **en toute ~** all (the) year round; **fruits de ~** seasonal fruits; **à la belle ~** in the summer months; **2** (période) season; **~ des pluies** rainy season; **~ des amours** mating season; **~ des foins** haymaking; **3** Tourisme, Sport, Théât season; **la haute/morte ~** the high/slack season; **prix hors ~** off-season prices

saisonnier, -ière /sɛzɔnje, ɛʀ/
A *adj* seasonal

Les saisons

■ *En anglais, on trouve quelquefois les noms des saisons avec des majuscules, mais les minuscules sont préférables.*

printemps	=	spring
été	=	summer
automne	=	autumn (*GB*) *ou* fall (*US*)
hiver	=	winter

■ *Dans les expressions suivantes, summer est pris comme exemple; les autres noms de saisons s'utilisent de la même façon.*

j'aime l'été
= I like the summer *ou* I like summer

l'été a été pluvieux
= the summer was wet *ou* summer was wet

un été pluvieux
= a rainy summer

l'été le plus chaud
= the warmest summer

....

Quand?

■ *L'anglais emploie souvent* in *devant les noms de saisons.*

en été
= in the summer *ou* in summer

au début de l'été
= in the early summer *ou* in early summer

à la fin de l'été
= in the late summer *ou* in late summer

à la mi-été
= in mid-summer

■ *Mais* in *peut être remplacé par une autre préposition, ou par* this, that, next, last *etc.*

pendant l'été
= during the summer

pendant tout l'été
= throughout the summer

tout au long de l'été
= all through the summer

avant l'été
= before the summer

jusqu'à l'été
= until the summer

un été sur deux
= every other summer *ou* every second summer

presque tous les étés
= most summers

cet été
= this summer

cet été-là
= that summer

l'été prochain
= next summer

l'été dernier
= last summer

tous les ans en été
= every summer

....

De avec les noms de saisons

■ *Les expressions françaises avec de se traduisent en anglais par l'emploi des noms de saisons en position d'adjectifs.*

la collection d'été
= the summer collection

une journée d'été
= a summer day

une pluie d'été
= a summer shower

un soir d'été
= a summer evening

■ *Enfin, comparer:*

un matin d'été
= one summer morning

par un matin d'été
= on a summer morning

le soleil d'été
= summer sunshine

les soldes d'été
= the summer sales

des vêtements d'été
= summer clothes

un temps d'été
= summer weather

un matin en été
= one morning in summer

B *nm,f* (ouvrier) seasonal worker

salace /salas/ *adj* salacious

salade /salad/ *nf* **1** (plante) lettuce; **2** (plat) salad; ~ **verte** green salad; ~ **de tomates/riz** tomato/rice salad; **3** ᴼ(embrouillamini) muddle; (mensonge) yarn; (boniment de vendeur) sales patter *ou* pitchᴼ; **raconter des ~s** to spin yarnsᴼ

saladier /saladje/ *nm* **1** (récipient) salad bowl; **2** (contenu) bowl

salaire /salɛʁ/ *nm* **1** (paie) salary; (à la journée, à l'heure, à la semaine) (taux) wage; (somme) wages (*pl*); ~ **annuel/mensuel** annual/monthly salary; ~ **brut/net** gross/take-home pay; ~ **de misère** *or* **famine** starvation wage; **2** *fig* (récompense) reward (**de** for); (châtiment) punishment (**de** for)

⟮Composés⟯ ~ **de base** basic salary GB, base pay US; ~ **d'embauche** starting salary; ~ **minimum interprofessionnel de croissance**, **SMIC** guaranteed minimum wage; ~ **unique** single income

⟮Idiome⟯ **toute peine mérite** ~ Prov hard work deserves a reward

salaison /salɛzɔ̃/ *nf* (viande) salt meat ℄; (poisson) salt fish ℄

salamandre /salamɑ̃dʀ/ *nf* Zool salamander

salami /salami/ *nm* salami GB, boloney US

salant /salɑ̃/ *adj m* **marais** ~ saltern

salarial, ~**e**, *mpl* **-iaux** /salaʀjal, o/ *adj* **1** (des salaires) [politique, augmentation] wage (épith); **2** (des salariés) **cotisation** ~**e** employee's contribution

salarié, ~**e** /salaʀje/
A *adj* [ouvrier, employé] wage-earning; [emploi, travail] salaried; **travailleur non** ~ non-wage-earning worker
B *nm,f* (ouvrier) wage earner; (employé) salaried employee

salaud❶ /salo/
A *adj m* rotten❶
B *nm* offensive bastard❶ injur

sale /sal/
A *adj* **1** (after *n*) (pas propre) dirty; (obscène) dirty; **2** ᴼ(before *n*) (désagréable) [individu] horrible; [bête, maladie, affaire, habitude] nasty; [temps] foul, horrible; [travail, endroit] rotten; offensive dirty; ~ **menteur!** you dirty liar!; **il a une** ~ **tête** (antipathique) he's got a nasty face; (maladif) he looks dreadful; **un** ~ **coup** lit, fig a very nasty blow; **jouer un** ~ **tour à qn** to play a dirty trick on sb; **un** ~ **caractère** a foul temper
B *nm* **mettre qch au** ~ to put sth in the wash

⟮Idiome⟯ **être** ~ **comme un peigne** *or* **un cochon** to be filthy dirty

salé, ~**e** /sale/
A *pp* ▸ **saler**
B *pp adj* **1** (contenant du sel) salt (épith); salty (jamais épith); **2** (additionné de sel) [beurre, eau, plat] salted; [mets, amusegueule] savouryᴳᴮ; (conservé avec du sel) [poisson, viande] salt (épith); **manger** ~ to eat savouryᴳᴮ things; **non** ~ unsalted; **trop** ~ too salty; **3** (de sel) salty; **goût** ~ salty taste
C *adj* (grivois) spicy; **propos** ~**s** spicy talk ℄

salement /salmɑ̃/ *adv* **1** (en salissant) **manger** ~ to be a messy eater; **2** (gravement) badly, seriously

saler /sale/ [1] *vtr* **1** (mettre du sel sur) to salt [mets]; **2** ᴼ(augmenter) to bump upᴼ [facture, note, prix]; **3** (en hiver) to grit GB, to salt US [route]

saleté /salte/ *nf* **1** (état) dirtiness; (crasse) dirt; **être d'une** ~ **repoussante** to be filthy; **vivre dans la** ~ to live in filth; **être couvert de** ~ to be covered with dirt; **2** (impureté) dirt ℄; **il y a une** ~ **sur l'objectif** there's dirt on the lens; **3** (ordure) **ramasser les** ~**s** to pick up the rubbish GB *ou* trash US; **faire des** ~**s** lit, euph to make a mess; **4** ᴼ(chose de mauvaise qualité) (objet) piece of junk; (aliment) junk food **𝄌**; **∼ d'ordinateur!** damn○ computer!; **c'est une vraie ∼ ce virus!** it's a rotten bug!

salière /saljɛʀ/ *nf* Culin saltcellar, saltshaker US

saligaud◑ /saligo/ *nm* offensive dirty bastard◑ injur

salir /saliʀ/ [3]

A *vtr* 1 (rendre sale) to dirty [*sol, assiette*]; to soil [*draps, lit*]; 2 (flétrir) to sully [*mémoire, amour, réputation*]; to corrupt [*artiste, imagination*]

B *vi* [*industrie, charbon*] to pollute

C se salir *vpr* (se couvrir de taches, de saleté) to get dirty, to dirty oneself

salissant, **∼e** /salisɑ̃, ɑ̃t/ *adj* 1 [*couleur, tissu*] which shows the dirt (*épith, après n*); 2 [*travail*] dirty

salissure /salisyʀ/ *nf* (dirty) mark

salive /saliv/ *nf* saliva

(Idiome) **perdre** *or* **dépenser inutilement sa ∼** to waste one's breath

saliver /salive/ [1] *vi* to salivate; **∼ devant qch** to drool over sth

salle /sal/ *nf* 1 (pièce) gén room; (de château, palais) hall; (de restaurant) (dining) room; (de cinéma, théâtre) auditorium; (de grotte) chamber; **cinéma à cinq ∼s** cinema with five screens; **faire ∼ comble** [*spectacle*] to be packed; [*acteur*] to fill the house; **en ∼** [*sport*] indoor; 2 (spectateurs) audience

(Composés) (entrepôt) armory; **∼ d'attente** waiting room; **∼ d'audience** Jur courtroom; **∼ de bains** bathroom; **∼ de cinéma** cinema GB, movie theater US; **∼ de classe** classroom; **∼ commune** (à l'hôpital) ward; **∼ de concert** concert hall; **∼ de conférences** (avec gradins) lecture theatre^GB, auditorium; **∼ d'eau** shower room; **∼ d'embarquement** Aviat departure lounge; **∼ d'études** Scol private study room GB, study hall US; **∼ des fêtes** (de village) village hall; (en ville) community centre^GB; **∼ de garde** (d'hôpital) staff room; **∼ de jeu(x)** (de casino) gaming room; (pour enfants) playroom; **∼ des machines** Naut engine room; **∼ à manger** (pièce) dining room; (mobilier) dining-room suite; **∼ omnisports** sports hall; **∼ d'opération** Méd operating theatre GB, operating room US; **∼ des pas perdus** waiting hall; **∼ polyvalente** multi-purpose hall; **∼ de séjour** living room; **∼ des ventes** auction room; **∼s obscures** cinemas GB, movie theaters US

saloir /salwaʀ/ *nm* salting tub

salon /salɔ̃/ *nm* 1 (pièce) gén lounge; (dans un château, palais) drawing room; **∼-salle à manger** living-cum-dining room; 2 (mobilier) living-room suite, sitting-room suite; **∼ de jardin** garden furniture; 3 (exposition) (pour professionnels) (trade) show; (pour grand public) fair; (artistique) exhibition; **le ∼ de l'auto** the car show; **∼ du livre** book fair; 4 (réunion mondaine, intellectuelle) salon; **faire ∼** to hold a salon

(Composés) **∼ de beauté** beauty salon; **∼ de coiffure** hairdressing salon; **∼ d'essayage** fitting room; **∼ de thé** tearoom

salope /salɔp/ *nf* offensive (garce) bitch◑ injur; (femme facile) tart○ injur, whore

saloper○ /salɔpe/ [1] *vtr* 1 (gâcher) to botch○ [*travail*]; 2 (salir) to muck up○ [*vêtement*]

saloperie◑ /salɔpʀi/ *nf* 1 (saleté) muck○ **𝄌**; fig (produit nocif, drogue) muck○ **𝄌**; 2 (microbe, maladie) bug○; 3 (nourriture) (infecte) muck○ **𝄌** GB, slop○; (malsaine) junk (food)○ **𝄌**; 4 (objet de rebut) junk○ **𝄌**; 5 (procédé) dirty trick

salopette /salɔpɛt/ *nf* (pour protéger) overalls (*pl*); (pour s'habiller) dungarees (*pl*) GB, overalls (*pl*) US

salpêtre /salpɛtʀ/ *nm* saltpetre^GB

salpingite /salpɛ̃ʒit/ ▸ p. 195 *nf* salpingitis

salsifis /salsifi/ *nm inv* salsify

saltimbanque /saltɛ̃bɑ̃k/ *nmf* 1 (bateleur) street acrobat; 2 (comédien) pej entertainer

salubre /salybʀ/ *adj* [*climat*] healthy; [*logement*] salubrious

salubrité /salybʀite/ *nf* (d'air, de climat) healthiness; (de logement) salubrity sout

(Composé) **∼ publique** public health

saluer /salɥe/ [1] *vtr* 1 (dire bonjour) to greet [*personne*]; **∼ qn de la main** to wave to *ou* at sb; **∼ qn de la tête** to nod to sb; **∼ qn de loin/en passant** to acknowledge sb from a

distance/in passing; **saluez-la de ma part** say hello to her from me; **∼ le public** to take a bow; 2 (dire au revoir) to say goodbye to [*personne*]; **je vous salue** I'll say goodbye; 3 (accueillir) to greet [*personne*]; 4 Mil to salute [*soldat, officier, drapeau, navire*]; 5 (accueillir avec satisfaction) to welcome [*décision, résultat*]; 6 (rendre hommage) to salute [*héros*]; to pay tribute to [*défunt*]; to praise [*travail, attitude*]; **je vous salue Marie** hail Mary

salut /saly/ *nm* 1 (salutation) greeting; **∼!** (bonjour) hello!, hi!; (au revoir) bye!; **∼ de la main** wave (of the hand); **∼ de la tête** nod; **∼ des acteurs** bow; 2 (geste) salute; 3 (secours) salvation (**dans** in); 4 Relig (rédemption) salvation; 5 (hommage) homage (**à** to)

salutaire /salytɛʀ/ *adj* (bénéfique) [*choc, expérience*] salutary; [*effet, environnement*] beneficial; [*air, habitude*] healthy; **cela leur a été ∼** it did them good

salutation /salytasjɔ̃/

A *nf* 1 gén greeting; 2 Relig salutation

B salutations *nfpl* **sincères ∼s** (à une personne nommée) yours sincerely; (à une personne non nommée) yours faithfully

salvateur, -trice /salvatœʀ, tʀis/ *adj* saving (*épith*)

salve /salv/ *nf* 1 (d'armes à feu) salvo; **tirer une ∼ d'honneur** to fire a salute; 2 (série) **∼ d'applaudissements** burst of applause; **∼ d'injures** volley of insults; 3 (attaque verbale) broadside

Samaritain, -e /samaʀitɛ̃, ɛn/ *nm,f* Samaritan; **jouer les ∼s** to act the good Samaritan

samedi /samdi/ ▸ p. 545 *nm* Saturday

sampler /sɑ̃ple/ [1] *vtr* Mus to sample

SAMU /samy/ *nm* (*abbr* = **Service d'assistance médicale d'urgence**) ≈ mobile accident unit GB, emergency medical service, EMS US

sanctifier /sɑ̃ktifje/ [1] *vtr* to sanctify

sanction /sɑ̃ksjɔ̃/ *nf* 1 (peine) Jur penalty, sanction; Admin disciplinary measure; Scol punishment; **prendre des ∼s contre qn** gén to discipline sb; Admin to take disciplinary action against sb; 2 (jugement) verdict

sanctionner /sɑ̃ksjɔne/ [1] *vtr* 1 (punir) to punish [*faute, coupable*]; 2 (consacrer) to give official recognition to [*études, formation*]

sanctuaire /sɑ̃ktɥɛʀ/ *nm* 1 (lieu saint) shrine; 2 (asile) sanctuary

sandale /sɑ̃dal/ *nf* sandal

sandalette /sɑ̃dalɛt/ *nf* light sandal

sandow® /sɑ̃do/ *nm* 1 (sangle) luggage elastic; 2 Aviat bungee

sandwich, *pl* **∼s** *ou* **∼es** /sɑ̃dwitʃ/ *nm* Culin sandwich; **(pris) en ∼** sandwiched

sang /sɑ̃/ *nm* 1 Biol blood; **donner son ∼** to give blood; **∼ contaminé** contaminated blood; **perte de ∼** loss of blood; **être en ∼** to be covered with blood; **couleur de ∼** blood-red; **taché de ∼** bloodstained; **mordre jusqu'au ∼** to bite through the skin; **animal à ∼ chaud/froid** warm-/cold-blooded animal; **avoir le ∼ qui monte au visage** to blush; **faire couler le ∼** fig to shed blood; **le ∼ a coulé** fig blood flowed; 2 (vie) **au prix du ∼** with loss of life; ▸ **pinte**; 3 (violence) bloodshed; **se terminer dans le ∼** to end in bloodshed; 4 (hérédité) blood; **de ∼** [*frère, liens*] blood (*épith*); **être du même ∼** to be kin

(Composés) **∼ bleu** blue blood; **∼ rouge** arterial blood

(Idiome) **avoir le ∼ chaud** (être sensuel) to be hot-blooded; (être coléreux) to be hotheaded; **avoir un coup de ∼** to have apoplexy; **il a ça dans le ∼** it's in his blood; **mettre qch à feu et à ∼** to put sth to fire and the sword; **mon ∼ n'a fait qu'un tour** (d'émotion) my heart missed a beat; (de colère) I saw red; **se faire du mauvais ∼**○ to worry; **bon ∼ (de bonsoir)!** for God's sake○!

sang-froid /sɑ̃fʀwa/ *nm inv* composure; **perdre son ∼** to lose one's composure; **garde ton ∼!** keep calm!; **faire qch de ∼** to do sth in cold blood

sanglant, -e /sɑ̃glɑ̃, ɑ̃t/ *adj* 1 (violent) [*affrontement, incident, répression, putsch, époque*] bloody; 2 (outrageant) [*affront, défaite*] cruel; 3 (couvert de sang) [*plaie, main*] bloody; [*couteau, vêtement*] bloodstained

sangle /sɑ̃gl/ *nf* 1 (pour attacher) strap; 2 (pour un cheval) girth; 3 (de siège, lit) webbing **𝄌**

(Composé) **∼ abdominale** Anat abdominal muscles (*pl*)

sangler /sɑ̃gle/ [1] *vtr* to girth [*cheval*]

sanglier /sɑ̃glije/ nm wild boar

sanglot /sɑ̃glo/ nm sob; **éclater en ~s** to burst out sobbing; **avec des ~s dans la voix** with a sob in one's voice

sangloter /sɑ̃glɔte/ [1] vi to sob

sangsue /sɑ̃sy/ nf leech

sanguin, ~e¹ /sɑ̃gɛ̃, in/
A adj **1** (de sang) blood; **examen/prélèvement ~** blood test/sample; **2** (rouge) [visage] ruddy; **3** (impétueux) impulsive
B nm,f **c'est un ~** he's hotheaded

sanguinaire /sɑ̃ginɛʀ/ adj [régime, bataille, crime] bloody; [personne] bloodthirsty

sanguine² /sɑ̃gin/
A adj f ▸ **sanguin**
B nf **1** (orange à pulpe rouge) blood orange; **2** Art (dessin) red chalk drawing; (crayon) red chalk

sanguinolent, ~e /sɑ̃ginɔlɑ̃, ɑ̃t/ adj [couteau, vêtement] blood-stained; [plaie] from which blood is oozing (épith, après n)

sanisette® /sanizɛt/ nf automatic public toilet

sanitaire /sanitɛʀ/
A adj [règlement, personnel] health (épith); [conditions] sanitary
B sanitaires nmpl **les ~s** (dans un bâtiment) the bathroom (sg); (dans un camping) the toilet block (sg)

sans /sɑ̃/

> ⚠ Lorsque sans marque l'absence, le manque ou la privation, il se traduit généralement par without. Lorsqu'il fait partie d'une expression figée comme sans concession, sans équivoque, sans emploi, sans intérêt la traduction est donnée respectivement sous concession, équivoque, emploi, intérêt etc.
> De même, quand il est associé à un verbe, compter sans, cela va sans dire etc, la traduction est donnée respectivement sous les verbes compter, dire¹ etc.
> La double négation non sans est traitée sous non. On trouvera ci-dessous d'autres exemples et les usages particuliers de sans.

A adv without; **faire ~** to do without
B prép **1** (absence, manque) without [personne, accord, permission]; **une maison ~ téléphone** a house without a telephone; **je suis ~ voiture aujourd'hui** I don't have a car today; **je bois mon thé ~ sucre** I don't take sugar in my tea; **du chocolat noir ~ sucre** sugar-free dark chocolate; **un visage ~ charme** an unattractive face; **un couple ~ enfant** a childless couple; **c'est un couple ~ enfant** they have no children; **une personne ~ fierté/scrupules** a person who has no pride/scruples; **~ cela** or **ça~** otherwise; **2** (pour écarter une circonstance) **il est resté trois mois ~ téléphoner** he didn't call for three months; **il est poli, ~ plus** he's polite, but that's as far as it goes; **~ plus tarder** without further delay; **3** (à l'exclusion de) **on sera douze ~ les enfants** there'll be twelve of us not counting the children; **500 euros ~ le voyage** 500 euros not including transport GB ou transportation US
C sans que loc conj without; **pars ~ qu'on te voie** leave without anyone seeing you

(Composés) **~ domicile fixe, SDF** of no fixed abode, NFA

sans-abri /sɑ̃zabʀi/ nmf inv **un ~** a homeless person; **les ~** the homeless

sans-cœur /sɑ̃kœʀ/ nmf inv heartless person

sans-emploi /sɑ̃zɑ̃plwa/ nmf inv unemployed person; **les ~** the unemployed (+ v pl), the jobless (+ v pl)

sans-faute /sɑ̃fot/ nm inv **1** (en équitation) clear round; **2** fig faultless performance

sans-gêne /sɑ̃ʒɛn/
A adj inv cheeky, bad-mannered (épith)
B nmf inv cheeky person, bad-mannered person
C nm **faire preuve de ~** to be cheeky ou bad-mannered

sans-logis /sɑ̃lɔʒi/ nmf inv homeless; **les ~** the homeless

santal /sɑ̃tal/ nm sandalwood

santé /sɑ̃te/ nf **1** (de personne, pays, d'organisation) health; **~ mentale** mental health; **être en bonne/mauvaise ~** to be in good/bad health; **avoir la ~** to enjoy good health; **il respire la ~** he's glowing with health; **avoir une ~ de fer** to have an iron constitution;

2 (en buvant) **à votre ~!** cheers!; **à la ~ de Janet!** here's to Janet!; **3** Admin health

santon /sɑ̃tɔ̃/ nm Christmas crib figure

saoudien, -ienne /saudjɛ̃, ɛn/ ▸ p. 392 adj Saudi (Arabian)

saoul, ~e ▸ **soûl**

sape /sap/ nf **travail de ~** Tech sap digging; fig sabotage

saper /sape/ [1]
A vtr (détruire) to undermine [mur, falaise, moral]
B °se saper vpr **1** (s'habiller) to dress; **être bien/mal sapé** to be well/badly dressed; **2** (s'habiller bien) to dress up to the nines°

sapeur /sapœʀ/ nm sapper

(Idiome) **fumer comme un ~** to smoke like a chimney

sapeur-pompier, pl sapeurs-pompiers /sapœʀpɔ̃pje/ nm fireman; **les sapeurs-pompiers de Paris** the Paris Fire Brigade

saphir /safiʀ/ nm **1** (pierre) sapphire; **2** (pointe de lecture) stylus

sapidité /sapidite/ nf sapidity; **agent de ~** flavouring^{GB} agent

sapin /sapɛ̃/ nm **1** fir tree; **2** (bois) deal

saquer° **= sacquer**

sarbacane /saʀbakan/ nf blowpipe

sarcasme /saʀkasm/ nm **1** (dérision) sarcasm; **2** (remarque) sarcastic remark

sarcastique /saʀkastik/ adj sarcastic

sarcler /saʀkle/ [1] vtr to hoe

sarcloir /saʀklwaʀ/ nm hoe

sarcophage /saʀkɔfaʒ/ nm sarcophagus

Sardaigne /saʀdɛɲ/ ▸ p. 303 nprf Sardinia

sarde /saʀd/ ▸ p. 336 adj, nm Sardinian

sardine /saʀdin/ nf **1** Zool sardine; **~ à l'huile** sardine in oil; **2** °(piquet de tente) tent peg

(Idiome) **être serrés comme des ~s°** to be crammed together like sardines

sardonique /saʀdɔnik/ adj sardonic

sarment /saʀmɑ̃/ nm **~ (de vigne)** vine shoot

sarrasin, ~e /saʀazɛ̃, in/
A adj Hist Saracen
B nm Bot, Culin buckwheat

Sarre /saʀ/ ▸ p. 259, p. 504 nprf (rivière, région) Saar

sas /sɑs/ nm inv **1** (pièce étanche) airlock; **2** (d'écluse) lock

satané°, ~e /satane/ adj damned°

satanique /satanik/ adj **1** (démoniaque) [sourire, ruse] fiendish; **2** (de Satan) [culte] Satanic

satelliser /satelize/ [1] vtr **1** Astronaut to put [sth] into orbit [engin]; **2** fig (assujettir) to turn [sth] into a satellite [pays, entreprise]

satellite /satelit/ nm **1** (astre, engin) satellite; **~ de transmission/météorologique** broadcasting/weather satellite; **2** Pol (pays) satellite

satello-opérateur, pl ~s /satelɔɔpeʀatœʀ/ nm satellite operator

satiété /sasjete/
A nf satiation, satiety
B à satiété loc adv **1** (jusqu'à satisfaction) **manger à ~** to eat one's fill; **il avait mangé à ~** he was replete; **2** (jusqu'à saturation) [répéter] ad nauseam

satin /satɛ̃/ nm satin; **une peau de ~** a satin-smooth skin

satiné, ~e /satine/ adj [étoffe] satiny (épith); [doublure] satin (épith); [peinture] satin-finish (épith)

satire /satiʀ/ nf satire

satirique /satiʀik/ adj satirical

satisfaction /satisfaksjɔ̃/ nf **1** (plaisir) satisfaction ¢; **à la ~ générale** to everyone's satisfaction; **motif de ~** reason to feel satisfied; **2** (contentement) satisfaction; **la ~ de nos besoins** the fulfilment^{GB} of our needs; **si le lave-vaisselle ne vous donne pas ~** if you are not entirely satisfied with the dishwasher; **3** (réparation) satisfaction; **obtenir ~ sur tout** to obtain complete satisfaction

satisfaire /satisfɛʀ/ [10]
A vtr (contenter) to satisfy [personne, demande, curiosité]; to please [électorat, client]; to meet [besoin]; to fulfil^{GB} [aspiration, exigence]; **~ les besoins d'un enfant** to meet the needs

of a child; **~ l'attente d'un client** to come up to a customer's expectations; **~ un besoin naturel** euph to answer a call of nature

B **satisfaire à** vtr ind to fulfil[GB] [obligation]; to meet [norme]

C **se satisfaire** vpr (se contenter) **se ~ de** [personne] to be satisfied with [explication, excuse]; to be content with [bas salaire]

satisfaisant, ~e /satisfəzɑ̃, ɑ̃t/ adj (adéquat) satisfactory; (gratifiant) satisfying

satisfait, ~e /satisfɛ, ɛt/ adj (contenté) [client, besoin] satisfied; [désir, envie] gratified; (content) [personne] happy; **être ~ de soi** to be pleased with oneself

saturation /satyʀasjɔ̃/ nf (de marché) saturation; (de trains, d'hôtels) overcrowding; (de réseau) overloading; **arriver à ~** [marché, réseau] to reach saturation point; [personne] to have had as much as one can take

saturé, ~e /satyʀe/ adj [1] (imprégné) saturated (**de** with); **terre ~e d'eau** waterlogged land; **atmosphère ~e d'humidité** saturated air; [2] (rassasié) **le public est ~ de publicité** the public has had its fill of advertising; [3] (surchargé) [marché] saturated; [profession] overcrowded; [système, équipement] overloaded; [région, transports] crowded out (**de** with); **le réseau est ~** Télécom all the lines are busy

saturer /satyʀe/ [1]
A vtr [1] (imprégner) to saturate (**de** with); [2] (gorger) **on nous sature de feuilletons** we're being inundated with soap operas
B ᴼvi **je sature** I've had it up to hereᴼ

satyre /satiʀ/ nm [1] Mythol satyr; [2] (homme) lecher

sauce /sos/ nf Culin sauce; **~ tomate/au vin** tomato/wine sauce; **viande/plat en ~** meat/dish with sauce; **allonger une ~** to thin a sauce; **(r)allonger la ~** fig to spin things out
(Idiomes) **mettre qch à toutes les ~s** to adapt sth to any purpose; **je me demande à quelle ~ on va me manger**ᴼ I wonder what's in store for me; **prendre la ~**ᴼ to get soaked ou drenched

saucer /sose/ [1] vtr [1] (éponger) to wipe [sth] with a piece of bread [assiette, plat]; [2] ᴼ(tremper) **se faire ~** to get soaked ou drenched

saucière /sosjɛʀ/ nf sauceboat

saucisse /sosis/ nf sausage; **chair à ~** sausage meat
(Composés) **~ de Francfort** frankfurter; **~ de Strasbourg** knackwurst **C**

saucisson /sosisɔ̃/ nm (slicing) sausage; **~ à l'ail** garlic sausage; **~ sec** ≈ salami, summer sausage US

sauf¹ /sof/
A prép [1] (excepté, hormis) except, but; **le film était bien ~ la fin** the film was good apart from the ending; [2] (sous réserve de) **~ contrordre** failing an order to the contrary; **~ avis contraire** unless otherwise stated; **~ imprévu** all things being equal, unless anything unforeseen happens; **~ dispositions contraires** Jur except as otherwise provided; **~ erreur de ma part** if I'm not mistaken
B **sauf si** loc conj unless
C **sauf que** loc conj except that

sauf², sauve /sof, sov/ adj [1] (sauvé) safe; **laisser la vie sauve à qn** to spare sb's life; [2] fig [honneur, réputation] intact

sauf-conduit, pl **~s** /sofkɔ̃dɥi/ nm safe-conduct; **accorder un ~ à qn** to issue sb with a safe-conduct

sauge /soʒ/ nf sage

saugrenu, ~e /sogʀəny/ adj crazy, pottyᴼ GB

saule /sol/ nm willow; **~ pleureur** weeping willow

saumâtre /somɑtʀ/ adj [eau] brackish; [goût] bitter and salty

saumon /somɔ̃/
A ▸ p. 140 adj inv salmon (pink)
B nm salmon; **~ fumé** smoked salmon

saumure /somyʀ/ nf brine

sauna /sona/ nm sauna

saupoudrer /supudʀe/ [1] vtr [1] lit to sprinkle (**de** with); [2] fig to give [sth] sparingly

saur /sɔʀ/ adj m **hareng ~** kipper, kippered herring

saut /so/ nm [1] (mouvement) jump; **faire un petit ~** to skip; **faire un ~ sur place** to leap in the air; **faire un ~ de 10 ans** to skip 10 years; **faire un ~ de 2%** to shoot up by 2%; **faire un ~ dans l'inconnu** to take a leap into the

unknown; **au ~ du lit** first thing in the morning; [2] ▸ p. 327 Sport (activité) **le ~** jumping; **être bon en ~** to be a good jumper; [3] ᴼ(visite) **faire un ~ à Paris** to make a flying visit to Paris; **faire un ~ chez qn** to pop in and see sb; **faire un ~ à la boulangerie** (de chez soi) to pop round to the baker's GB, to duck out to the bakery US; (en chemin) to pop in to the baker's; [4] Ordinat jump; **~ de page** page break

(Composés) **~ de l'ange** swallow dive GB, swan dive US; **~ à la corde** skipping; **~ à l'élastique** bungee jumping; **~ en hauteur** high jump; **~ d'obstacles** show jumping; **~ à la perche** pole vault; **~ périlleux** mid-air somersault

(Idiomes) **faire le ~** to take the plunge; **faire le grand ~** (se suicider) to kill oneself

saute /sot/ nf **~ de température** sudden change in temperature; **~ d'humeur** mood swing

sauté, ~e /sote/
A adj Culin sautéed
B nm Culin **~ de veau** sautéed veal

saute-mouton /sotmutɔ̃/ ▸ p. 327 nm inv **jouer à ~** to play leapfrog

sauter /sote/ [1]
A vtr [1] (franchir) to jump [distance, hauteur]; to jump over [ruisseau, barrière]; **~ quatre mètres en longueur** to do four metres[GB] in the long jump; [2] (omettre volontairement) to skip [étape, repas, période]; to leave out [détails]; [3] (omettre involontairement) to miss [mot, ligne]; **~ son tour** to miss one's turn; [4] Scol **~ une classe** to skip a year
B vi [1] (faire un saut) gén to jump; (vers le bas) to jump (down); (vers le haut) to jump (up); (vers l'extérieur) to jump (out); (vers l'intérieur) to jump (in); **~ sur le banc** to jump onto the bench; **~ du banc** to jump off the bench; **saute!** (de haut) jump (down)!; (dans une piscine) jump (in)!; **~ d'une branche à l'autre** to leap from branch to branch; **~ d'un pied sur l'autre** to hop from one foot to the other; **~ à pieds joints** lit to jump with one's feet together; **~ à pieds joints dans un piège** fig to fall straight into a trap; **~ dans le vide** to jump; **~ en hauteur/en longueur** to do the high/long jump; **~ à la perche** to pole vault; **~ en parachute** (une fois) to make a parachute jump; (régulièrement) to go parachute jumping; **~ à la corde** to skip; **faire ~ un enfant sur ses genoux** to dandle a child on one's knee; **~ dans l'inconnu** to take a leap into the unknown; **~ sur qn** to pounce on sb; **~ sur son téléphone/pistolet** to grab one's telephone/gun; **~ sur l'occasion/une offre** to jump at the chance/an offer; **~ à la gorge de qn** to go for sb's throat; **~ au cou de qn** to greet sb with a kiss; [2] (aller vivement) to jump; **~ du lit** to jump out of bed; **~ dans un taxi/dans un train** to jump into a taxi/onto a train; [3] (passer) **~ d'un sujet à l'autre** to skip from one subject to another; [4] ᴼ(être supprimé) **faire ~ un paragraphe** (délibérément) to take out a paragraph; (par erreur) to miss out GB ou miss a paragraph; **faire ~ une réunion** to cancel a meeting; **le poste va ~** the job is being axed; **faire ~ une contravention** to get out of paying a parking ticket; [5] (être délogé, instable) [courroie, chaîne de vélo] to come off; [images de télévision] to jump; **la troisième vitesse saute** the third gear keeps slipping; [6] (céder) **faire ~ une serrure** to force a lock; **faire ~ une maille** to drop a stitch; **faire ~ les boutons** to burst one's buttons; **faire ~ les barrières** fig to break down the barriers; [7] (exploser) [bombe, mine] to blow up, to go off; [pont, bâtiment] to be blown up, to go up; **faire ~ qch** to blow sth up; **faire ~ les plombs** to blow the fuses; [8] Culin **faire ~ des oignons** to sauté onions; **faire ~ une crêpe** to toss a pancake; **faire ~ les bouchons de champagne** to make the champagne corks pop

(Idiomes) **~ aux yeux** to be blindingly obvious; **et que ça saute**ᴼ! make it snappyᴼ!; **~ en l'air**ᴼ or **au plafond**ᴼ (de joie) to jump for joy; (de colère) to hit the roofᴼ; (de surprise) to be staggered

sauterelle /sotʀɛl/ nf grasshopper

sauterie† /sotʀi/ nf party, hop†

sauteur, -euse¹ /sotœʀ, øz/ nm Sport jumper; **~ en hauteur** high jumper; **~ en longueur** long jumper; **~ à la perche** pole vaulter

sauteuse² /sotøz/ nf [1] Culin (deep) frying pan; [2] (scie) jigsaw

sautillant, ~e /sotijɑ̃, ɑ̃t/ adj [démarche, rythme] bouncy; [oiseau] hopping

sautiller /sotije/ [1] *vi* **1** [*oiseau*] to hop; (d'un lieu à l'autre) to hop around; **2** [*enfant*] (en avançant) to skip along; (d'un pied sur l'autre) to hop from one foot to the other; (sur place) to jump up and down

sautoir /sotwaR/ *nm* (collier) long necklace

sauvage /sovaʒ/
A *adj* **1** (non apprivoisé) [*animal, plante, enfant, rire*] wild; [*tribu*] primitive; **2** (cruel) [*mœurs*] savage; [*lutte*] fierce; **3** (timide) unsociable; **4** (illégal) illegal
B *nmf* **1** (être primitif ou brutal) savage; **2** (être non sociable) unsociable person, loner

sauvageon, -onne /sovaʒɔ̃, ɔn/ *nm,f* (enfant) wild child

sauvagerie /sovaʒRi/ *nf* **1** (brutalité) savagery; **2** (insociabilité) unsociability

sauve ▸ **sauf²**

sauvegarde /sovgaRd/ *nf* (de patrimoine, paix, valeurs) maintenance; (de droits, libertés) protection; **assurer la ~ de** to safeguard

sauvegarder /sovgaRde/ [1] *vtr* **1** gén to safeguard; **2** Ordinat (provisoirement) to save; (recopier) to back [sth] up

sauve-qui-peut /sovkipø/ *nm inv* stampede

sauver /sove/ [1]
A *vtr* **1** (garder en vie) to save; (porter secours à) to rescue; **~ la vie à qn** to save sb's life; **~ qn de la noyade** to save sb from drowning; **~ sa peau**○ to save one's skin○; **elle est sauvée** [*malade*] she has pulled through○; **2** (sauvegarder) to save (**de** from); to salvage [*marchandises*] (**de** from); **3** (rendre acceptable) **ce qui le sauve à mes yeux, c'est sa générosité** his redeeming feature for me is his generosity
B **se sauver** *vpr* **1** (s'enfuir) (de prison, d'une cage) to escape (**de** from); (chez ses parents, de l'école) to run away (**de** from); (face à une situation difficile) to run away (**de** from); (face à un danger) to run; **se ~ en bateau/avion** to escape by boat/plane; **sauvez-vous!** run (for it)!; **2** ○(s'en aller) **il faut que je me sauve** I've got to rush off now

(Idiomes) **~ la situation** to save the day; **sauve qui peut!** (à terre) run for your life!; (en mer) it's every man for himself

sauvetage /sovtaʒ/ *nm* rescue

sauveteur /sovtœR/ ▸ p. 372 *nm* rescuer

sauvette: à la sauvette /alasovɛt/ *loc adv* **1** (en hâte) [*préparer, signer*] in a rush, hastily; **2** (à la dérobée) [*filmer, enregistrer*] on the sly; **3** (illégalement) **vendre qch à la ~** to sell sth illegally on the street

sauveur /sovœR/ *nm* Relig saviour^{GB}

savamment /savamɑ̃/ *adv* **1** (avec érudition) learnedly, eruditely; **2** (avec habileté) [*mené*] adroitly; [*construit, choisi*] skilfully^{GB}

savane /savan/ *nf* savannah

savant, ~e /savɑ̃, ɑ̃t/
A *adj* **1** [*personne*] learned (**en** in), erudite; [*assemblée*] learned, scholarly; **2** [*édition, étude, émission*] scholarly; [*calcul*] complicated, involved; **3** (habile) [*manœuvre, action*] clever; [*mise en scène*] skilful^{GB}; **4** [*animal*] performing
B *nm,f* (personne cultivée) scholar
C *nm* (scientifique) scientist

savate○ /savat/ *nf* (pantoufle) old slipper; (chaussure) old shoe

saveur /savœR/ *nf* (d'aliment, de boisson) flavour^{GB}; **plein de ~** [*fruit*] full of flavour^{GB}; [*plat cuisiné*] flavoursome^{GB}, tasty; [*remarque*] pungent

savoir¹ /savwaR/ [47]
A *vtr* **1** (connaître) to know [*vérité, réponse*]; **~ son texte** to know one's lines; **~ qch par cœur** to know sth by heart; **~ que** to know (that); **vous n'êtes pas sans ~ que** you are no doubt aware that; **elle ne sait plus ce qu'elle dit** she doesn't know what she's saying; **~ qch sur qn** to know sth about sb; **ne rien ~ de qch** to know nothing about sth; **elle en sait plus/moins que moi** she knows more/less about it than I do; **il n'en saura rien** he'll never know (about it); **va** *or* **allez ~!, qui sait!** who knows!; **on ne sait jamais** you never know; **est-ce que je sais, moi!** how should I know!; **elle n'a rien voulu ~** she just didn't want to know; **parler pour ne rien ~** to talk about things one knows nothing about; **sans le ~** without knowing (it); **pour autant que je sache** as far as I know; **pas que je sache** not as far as I know; **elle nous a fait ~ que** she informed us that; **comment l'as-tu su ?** how did you find out?; **je l'ai su par elle** she told me about it; **~ le chinois** to know Chinese; **on la savait riche** she was known to be rich; **reste à ~ si** it remains to be seen if *ou* whether; **ne ~ que faire pour...** to be at a loss as to how to...; **on croit ~ qu'elle est à Paris** she is understood *ou* thought to be in Paris; **sachant que** given that; **sache qu'il t'a menti** I'm telling you, he was lying; **la personne que vous savez, qui vous savez** you-know-who; **je ne sais quel journaliste** some journalist or other; **je ne sais qui** somebody or other; **tu viens ou pas, il faudrait ~!** are you coming or not? make your mind up!; **si tu savais** *or* **tu ne peux pas ~ comme je suis content!** you can't imagine how happy I am!; **tu en sais des choses!** you really know a thing or two!; **2** (être capable de) **~ faire** to be able to do, to know how to do; **~ comment faire** to know how to do; **je sais conduire/nager/taper à la machine** I can drive/swim/type; **il ne sait pas dire non** he can't say no; **~ écouter** to be a good listener; **elle sait bien expliquer** she's good at explaining things; **il a su nous parler** he was able to talk to us; **on ne saurait mieux dire** I couldn't have put it better myself; **elle sait y faire avec les enfants** she's good with children; **il pleurait tout ce qu'il savait** he cried and cried; **3** B (pouvoir) **je ne sais pas soulever la valise** I can't lift the suitcase
B **se savoir** *vpr* **1** (être connu) **ça se saurait** people would know about that; **tout se sait ici** people get to know everything in this place; **ça s'est su tout de suite** word immediately got around; **2** (être conscient d'être) **se savoir aimé** to know one is loved
C **à savoir** *loc adv* that is to say

(Idiome) **ne pas ~ où donner de la tête** not to know whether one is coming or going

savoir² /savwaR/ *nm* **1** (érudition) learning; **un grand ~** great learning; **2** (science) knowledge; **3** (culture) body of knowledge

savoir-faire /savwaRfɛR/ *nm inv* know-how

savoir-vivre /savwaRvivR/ *nm inv* manners (*pl*)

savon /savɔ̃/ *nm* **1** (produit) soap; **2** (morceau) (bar of) soap

(Composés) **~ de Marseille** household soap; **~ noir** soft soap

(Idiome) **passer un ~**○ **à qn** to give sb a telling-off

savonner /savɔne/ [1]
A *vtr* to rub soap on [*linge*]; to soap [sb] all over [*enfant*]
B **se savonner** *vpr* (pour se laver) to soap oneself all over; (pour se raser) to lather oneself

savonnette /savɔnɛt/ *nf* small cake of soap

savonneux, -euse /savɔnø, øz/ *adj* soapy

savourer /savuRe/ [1] *vtr* to savour^{GB} [*succès, instant*]

savoureux, -euse /savuRø, øz/ *adj* [*plat*] tasty; [*anecdote*] juicy

saxe /saks/ *nm* Dresden china **¢**

Saxe /saks/ ▸ p. 504 *nprf* Saxony

saxon, -onne /saksɔ̃, ɔn/
A *adj* Saxon
B *nm* Ling Saxon

saxophone /saksɔfɔn/ ▸ p. 389 *nm* **1** (instrument) saxophone; **2** (instrumentiste) saxophone player

saxophoniste /saksɔfɔnist/ ▸ p. 372 *nmf* saxophonist

saynète /sɛnɛt/ *nf* playlet

sbire /sbiR/ *nm* pej henchman péj

scabreux, -euse /skabRø, øz/ *adj* risqué

scalp /skalp/ *nm* scalp

scalper /skalpe/ [1] *vtr* to scalp

scandale /skɑ̃dal/ *nm* scandal; **~ boursier** scandal on the Stock Exchange; **faire éclater un ~** to cause a scandal to break; **étouffer un ~** to hush up a scandal; **faire un** *or* **du ~** (réprobation générale) to cause a scandal; (scène individuelle) to cause a fuss; **au grand ~ de** to the great disgust of; **un journal à ~** a scandal sheet; **la presse à ~** the gutter press; **c'est un ~!** it's scandalous, it's outrageous!

scandaleux, -euse /skɑ̃dalø, øz/ *adj* scandalous, outrageous

scandaliser /skɑ̃dalize/ [1]
A *vtr* to outrage, to scandalize [*personne*]; **être scandalisé par** to be outraged by
B **se scandaliser** *vpr* to be shocked (**de** by)

scander /skɑ̃de/ [1] *vtr* **1** Littérat (faire l'analyse métrique) to scan; **2** to chant [*slogan, nom*]

scandinave /skɑ̃dinav/ *adj* Scandinavian

Scandinavie /skɑ̃dinavi/ ▸ p. 504 *nprf* **la ~** Scandinavia

scanneur /skanœʀ/ *nm* (appareil) scanner

scaphandre /skafɑ̃dʀ/ *nm* **[1]** Naut deep-sea diving suit; **[2]** Astronaut spacesuit

scaphandrier /skafɑ̃dʀije/ ▸ p. 372 *nm* deep-sea diver

scarabée /skaʀabe/ *nm* **[1]** Zool beetle; **[2]** (bijou en archéologie) scarab

scarlatine /skaʀlatin/ ▸ p. 195 *nf* scarlet fever

scatologique /skatɔlɔʒik/ *adj* scatological

sceau, *pl* ~**x** /so/ *nm* **[1]** (objet, empreinte) seal; **sous le ~ du secret** in strictest secrecy; **[2]** (marque distinctive) stamp, hallmark

scélérat, ~**e** /seleʀa, at/ *liter*
A *adj* villainous
B *nm,f* villain

scellé /sele/ *nm* seal; **apposer les ~s** to affix seals

sceller /sele/ **[1]** *vtr* **[1]** (apposer un sceau) to seal [*document, acte*]; **[2]** (fixer solidement) to fix [sth] securely [*étagère, barreau*]; **[3]** (consacrer) to seal [*amitié, alliance, réconciliation*]

scénario /senaʀjo/ *nm* **[1]** Cin screenplay, script; **[2]** Théât scenario; **[3]** (déroulement) scenario

scénariste /senaʀist/ ▸ p. 372 *nmf* scriptwriter

scène /sɛn/ *nf* **[1]** Théât (plateau) stage; **'en ~!'** 'on stage!'; **entrer en ~** to come on; **entrée en ~** entrance; **sortir de ~** to go off; **le rideau de ~** the curtain; **[2]** (subdivision, action) scene; **la ~ se passe à Paris** the scene is set in Paris; **[3]** (activité théâtrale) stage; **quitter la ~** (métier) to give up the stage; **la ~ parisienne** Parisian theatre^GB; **musique de ~** music for the theatre^GB; **mettre 'Phèdre' en ~** [*troupe*] to stage 'Phèdre'; [*personne*] to direct 'Phèdre'; **mettre en ~ un film** to direct a film; **une excellente mise en ~** an excellent production; **à la ~ comme à la ville** on stage and off; **[4]** (actualité) scene; **occuper le devant de la ~** *fig* to be in the news; **[5]** (esclandre) **faire (toute) une ~ (à qn)** to throw a fit^○; **[6]** (épisode, spectacle) scene; **~s de chasse** hunting scenes; **~s de panique** scenes of panic

◯ *Composé* **~ de ménage** domestic dispute

scepticisme /sɛptisism/ *nm* gén, Philos (incrédulité) scepticism GB, skepticism US

sceptique /sɛptik/
A *adj* sceptical GB, skeptical US; **laisser qn ~** to leave sb unconvinced
B *nmf* gén, Philos sceptic GB, skeptic US

sceptre /sɛptʀ/ *nm* sceptre^GB

schéma /ʃema/ *nm* **[1]** (dessin) diagram; **[2]** (points principaux) outline; **[3]** (processus) pattern

schématique /ʃematik/ *adj* **[1]** (simplifié) [*vision, raisonnement*] simplistic; **[2]** (de schéma) schematic

schématiquement /ʃematikmɑ̃/ *adv* **[1]** (avec un schéma) [*représenter, reproduire*] in a diagram; **[2]** (en simplifiant) [*exposer, expliquer*] in broad outline

schématisation /ʃematizasjɔ̃/ *nf* simplification; (excessive) oversimplification

schématiser /ʃematize/ **[1]** *vtr* **[1]** (simplifier) to simplify; (à l'excès) to oversimplify; **[2]** (faire un schéma) to make *ou* draw a diagram

schilling /ʃiliŋ/ ▸ p. 34 *nm* schilling

schisme /ʃism/ *nm* schism

schizophrène /skizɔfʀɛn/ *adj, nmf* schizophrenic

schizophrénie /skizɔfʀeni/ ▸ p. 195 *nf* schizophrenia

sciatique /sjatik/
A *adj* **nerf ~** sciatic nerve
B ▸ p. 195 *nf* (douleur) sciatica

scie /si/ *nf* (outil) saw; **~ sauteuse** jigsaw

sciemment /sjamɑ̃/ *adv* knowingly

science /sjɑ̃s/ *nf* **[1]** (savoir) science; **dans l'état actuel de la ~** in the present state of science; **[2]** (domaine du savoir) science; **les ~s et les lettres** science and the arts; **[3]** (érudition) knowledge, erudition; **épater qn avec sa ~** to blind sb with science

◯ *Composés* **~s appliquées** applied sciences; **~s économiques** economics (+ *v sg*); **~s naturelles** ≈ biology (*sg*); **~s occultes** black arts; **~s politiques** political science (*sg*); **~s de la Terre** Earth sciences; **Sciences Po**^○ *Institute of Political Science*

◯ *Idiome* **être un puits de ~** to be a fount of knowledge

> **ⓘ** **Sciences Po** in Paris is a prestigious third-level institution offering courses in political science which have higher status than a university *licence*.
> ▸ **grande école**

science-fiction /sjɑ̃sfiksjɔ̃/ *nf* science fiction

scientifique /sjɑ̃tifik/
A *adj* scientific
B *nmf* scientist

scier /sje/ **[2]** *vtr* **[1]** to saw; **[2]** ^○(abasourdir) to stun

◯ *Idiome* **~ la branche sur laquelle on est assis** to shoot oneself in the foot

scierie /siʀi/ *nf* sawmill

scinder /sɛ̃de/ **[1]**
A *vtr* to split [*organisation, groupe*]; to break down [*problème, question*]
B **se scinder** *vpr* [*organisation, parti*] to split up

scintiller /sɛ̃tije/ **[1]** *vi* [*diamant*] to sparkle; [*regard, œil*] (de santé) to sparkle; (de malice) twinkle; [*étoile*] to twinkle; [*eau*] to glisten

scission /sisjɔ̃/ *nf* **[1]** (sécession) split, schism (**au sein de** within); **faire ~** to break away, to secede *sout*; **[2]** Biol, Phys fission

sciure /sjyʀ/ *nf* **~ (de bois)** sawdust

sclérosant, ~**e** /skleʀozɑ̃, ɑ̃t/ *adj* **[1]** Méd [*traitement, substance*] sclerosant; **[2]** *fig* [*mode de vie, travail*] mind-numbing

sclérose /skleʀoz/ *nf* **[1]** ▸ p. 195 Méd sclerosis; **[2]** (immobilisme) fossilization, ossification

◯ *Composé* **~ en plaques** multiple sclerosis, MS

scléroser /skleʀoze/ **[1]**
A *vtr* Méd to sclerose
B **se scléroser** *vpr* **[1]** *fig* (se figer) [*institution, personne*] to become fossilized; **[2]** Méd [*tissu, organe, veine*] to become hardened

scolaire /skɔlɛʀ/ *adj* [*vacances, programme, livre*] school (*épith*); [*réforme, publication*] educational; [*échec, réussite*] academic; **établissement ~** school

scolarisable /skɔlaʀizabl/ *adj* **[1]** (par l'âge) [*enfant*] ready to start school; **[2]** (ayant les capacités nécessaires) **il n'est pas ~** he needs special schooling

scolarisation /skɔlaʀizasjɔ̃/ *nf* schooling, education

scolariser /skɔlaʀize/ **[1]** *vtr* (envoyer à l'école) to send [sb] to school; **est-il scolarisé?** does he go to school?

scolarité /skɔlaʀite/ *nf* **[1]** (études) schooling; **durant ma ~** when I was at school; **après une ~ à** having been educated at; **arrêter sa ~ à 13 ans** to leave school at 13; **avoir une ~ difficile** not to do well at school; **la ~ obligatoire** compulsory education; **allonger la ~** to raise the school-leaving age; **[2]** Univ (service administratif) registrar's office

scoliose /skɔljoz/ *nf* scoliosis

scoop^○ /skup/ *nm* (en journalisme) scoop

scooter /skutœʀ/ *nm* (motor) scooter

◯ *Composés* **~ des mers** *or* **nautique** jetski; **~ des neiges** snowmobile

scorbut /skɔʀbyt/ ▸ p. 195 *nm* scurvy

score /skɔʀ/ *nm* **[1]** Scol, Sport score; **réaliser un bon/mauvais ~** to get a good/bad score; **~ nul** draw GB, tie US; **[2]** Pol result

scorie /skɔʀi/ *nf* **[1]** (géologique) scoria ¢; **[2]** (minière) slag ¢, scoria ¢

scorpion /skɔʀpjɔ̃/ *nm* Zool scorpion

Scorpion /skɔʀpjɔ̃/ ▸ p. 635 *nprm* Scorpio

scotch, *pl* ~**es** /skɔtʃ/ *nm* **[1]** (boisson) Scotch (whisky); **[2]** ®(ruban adhésif) Sellotape® GB, Scotch® tape US

scout, ~**e** /skut/
A *adj* scout (*épith*)
B *nm,f* (Catholic) boy scout/(Catholic) girl scout

scoutisme /skutism/ *nm* scouting

scribouillard^○, ~**e** /skʀibujaʀ, aʀd/ *nm,f* pen pusher^○ GB, pencil pusher US

script /skʀipt/ *nm* **[1]** (écriture) **écrire en ~** to print; **[2]** Cin, Radio, TV script

scripte /skʀipt/ *nmf* continuity man/girl

se

La traduction du pronom personnel *se* varie en fonction du verbe auquel il est associé et de son rôle ; il sera traité automatiquement avec le verbe pronominal auquel on aura tout intérêt à se reporter.

se complément d'objet direct ou indirect d'un verbe pronominal réfléchi

se blesser
= to hurt oneself

il se regarde
= he's looking at himself

elle se regarde
= she's looking at herself

ils se sont brûlés
= they burnt themselves

elles se sont brûlées
= they burnt themselves

le chien s'est brûlé
= the dog burnt itself

Mais attention, très souvent en anglais le pronom ne sera pas exprimé :

se laver
= to wash *ou* to have a wash

elle s'habille
= she's getting dressed

il se rase
= he's shaving

Avec les parties du corps

il se lave les pieds
= he's washing his feet

elles se coupent les ongles
= they're cutting their nails

se ronger les ongles
= to bite one's nails

le chat se lèche les moustaches
= the cat is cleaning its whiskers

ils se bouchent les oreilles
= they put their fingers in their ears

se pronom réciproque

ils se détestent
= they hate each other

On trouvera des exemples supplémentaires et des cas non envisagés ici dans l'article ci-dessous. En cas de doute, se reporter à l'article du verbe.

---

scrupule /skʀypyl/ *nm* scruple; **avoir des ~s à faire** to have scruples about doing; **être dénué de ~s** to be completely unscrupulous; **une personne sans ~s** an unscrupulous person

scrupuleusement /skʀypyløzmɑ̃/ *adv* gén [*respecter, appliquer*] scrupulously; **se comporter ~ en affaires** to be scrupulous in one's business dealings

scrupuleux, -euse /skʀypylø, øz/ *adj* scrupulous

scrutateur, -trice /skʀytatœʀ, tʀis/
A *adj* [*regard, air*] searching
B *nm,f* (de vote) scrutineer

scruter /skʀyte/ [1] *vtr* to scan [*mer, horizon, paysage*]; to scrutinize [*objet*]; to examine [*sol, personne, motif*]

scrutin /skʀytɛ̃/ *nm* ⓵ (vote) ballot; **par voie de ~** by ballot; **dépouiller le ~** to count the votes; ⓶ (élections) polls (*pl*); **jour du ~** polling day; **premier tour de ~** first ballot; **mode de ~** electoral system

Composés ~ **de liste** list system; ~ **majoritaire** election by majority vote; ~ **proportionnel** proportional representation, PR

sculpter /skylte/ [1] *vtr* ⓵ (réaliser) to sculpt, to carve [*statue*] (**dans** in); to carve [*ornements, meuble*] (**dans** out of); ⓶ (travailler) to sculpt, to carve [*pierre, marbre*]; to carve [*bois*]; ⓷ (éroder) to sculpt, to carve out [*roche*]

sculpteur /skyltœʀ/ ▸ p. 372 *nm* sculptor; **elle est ~** she's a sculptor

sculptural, ~e, *mpl* -**aux** /skyltyʀal, o/ *adj* [*art*] sculptural; [*forme, beauté, corps*] statuesque

sculpture /skyltyʀ/ *nf* sculpture; **faire de la ~** (comme passe-temps) to do sculpture; (comme travail) to be a sculptor; **la ~ sur bois** woodcarving

Scylla /sila/ *npr* Scylla; ▸ **Charybde**

SDF /ɛsdeɛf/ *nmf; abbr* ▸ **sans**

se (**s'** *before vowel or mute h*) /sə, s/ *pron pers* ⓵ (verbe à valeur intransitive) **elle ~ comporte honorablement** she behaves honourably; **la voiture s'est bien comportée** the car performed well; **l'écart ~ creuse** the gap is widening; ⓶ (verbe à valeur passive) **les exemples ~ comptent sur les doigts de la main** the examples can be counted on the fingers of your hand; **le médicament ~ vend sans ordonnance** the medicine is sold without a prescription; ⓷ (avec un verbe impersonnel) **comment ~ fait-il que...?** how come...?, how is it that...?; **il ~ produit une réaction chimique** there is a chemical reaction

séance /seɑ̃s/ *nf* ⓵ (réunion) (de tribunal, parlement, Bourse) session; (de comité, conseil municipal) meeting; ~ **d'ouverture** opening session; ~ **ordinaire/plénière** ordinary/plenary session; **tenir ~** to meet; ~ **tenante** immediately; ⓶ (période d'activité) session; **organiser une ~ de travail** to organize a workshop; ⓷ Cin show; **une ~ privée** a private screening

séant /seɑ̃/ *nm* **se mettre sur son ~** to sit up

seau, *pl* ~**x** /so/ *nm* (récipient) gén bucket, pail; (pour enfant) bucket; (contenu) bucket(ful)

Composés ~ **à champagne** champagne bucket; ~ **à charbon** coal scuttle; ~ **à glace** ice bucket; ~ **hygiénique** slop pail

Idiome **pleuvoir à ~x**° to rain buckets°, to pour

sébile /sebil/ *nf* begging bowl; **tendre la ~** to beg

sec, sèche¹ /sɛk, sɛʃ/
A *adj* ⓵ (sans humidité) [*temps, cheveux*] dry; [*fruit*] dried; **avoir la gorge sèche** to feel parched°; **à pied ~** without getting one's feet wet; ⓶ (pas doux) [*vin, cidre*] dry; (sans eau) **boire son gin ~** to like one's gin straight; ⓷ (austère) [*personne, communiqué*] terse; [*lettre, ton*] curt; [*style*] dry; **avoir un cœur ~** to be cold-hearted; ▸ **trique**; ⓸ (net) [*bruit*] sharp; **se briser d'un coup ~** to snap
B *nm* **être à ~** [*rivière, réservoir*] to have dried up; [*personne*] to have no money
C *adv* ⓵ (avec netteté) **se briser ~** to snap; ⓶ °(beaucoup) [*cogner, pleuvoir, boire*] a lot

Idiomes **aussi ~**° immediately; **rester ~**° to be unable to reply; **je l'ai eu ~**° I was pretty choked°

sécable /sekabl/ *adj* [*comprimé*] divisible

sécateur /sekatœʀ/ *nm* clippers (*pl*)

Composé ~ **à haie** shears (*pl*)

sécession /sesesjɔ̃/ *nf* secession ¢; **faire ~** to secede

sécessionniste /sesesjɔnist/ *adj, nmf* secessionist

sèche² /sɛʃ/
A *adj f* ▸ **sec A**
B °*nf* (cigarette) fag GB, cig°

sèche-cheveux /sɛʃʃəvø/ *nm inv* hairdrier GB, blow-dryer

sèche-linge /sɛʃlɛ̃ʒ/ *nm inv* tumble-drier GB, tumble-dryer

sèche-mains /sɛʃmɛ̃/ *nm inv* hand-drier GB, blower US

sèchement /sɛʃmɑ̃/ *adv* drily, coldly; **très ~** curtly

sécher /seʃe/ [14]
A *vtr* ⓵ gén to dry [*cheveux, fruit, larme, linge*]; ⓶ °(manquer) to skip [*cours*]
B *vi* ⓵ (devenir sec) [*linge, cheveux*] to dry; [*plaie, herbe, boue*] to

dry up; [*encre, peinture*] (normalement) to dry; (par négligence) to dry up; [*fleur*] to wither; [*jambon*] to get dried up; **fleur/ viande/boue séchée** dried flower/meat/mud; **mettre le linge à** ~ (dehors) to hang out the washing; **mettre des vêtements à** ~ (après un lavage) to hang clothes up to dry; (après la pluie) to dry out clothes; **mettre du bois à** ~ to leave wood to season; [2] ○(ne pas savoir répondre) to dry up

C **se sécher** *vpr* to dry oneself; **se** ~ **les cheveux** to dry one's hair

sécheresse /seʃʀɛs/ *nf* [1] (manque de pluie) drought; **une grave** ~ a severe drought; [2] (de climat) dryness **C**; [3] (austérité) (de personne) curt manner; (d'auteur, ouvrage) dryness; **la** ~ **de son ton** his/her curt tone

séchoir /seʃwaʀ/ *nm* (pour le linge) clothes airer, clothes horse; (machine) tumble-drier GB, tumble-dryer

second, ~e¹ /səɡɔ̃, ɔ̃d/
A *adj* [1] (dans une séquence) second; **chapitre** ~ chapter two; **en** ~**e lecture** at a second reading; **en** ~ **lieu** secondly; **dans un** ~ **temps, nous étudierons...** subsequently, we will study...; **c'est à prendre au** ~ **degré** it is not to be taken literally; [2] (dans une hiérarchie) second; **voyager en** ~**e classe** to travel second class; **de** ~ **ordre** second-rate; **politicien de** ~ **plan** minor politician; **de** ~ **choix** of inferior quality; **jouer un** ~ **rôle** Théât to play a supporting role; **jouer les** ~ **rôles** fig to play second fiddle
B *nm,f* **se** ~, **la** ~**e** gén the second one
C *nm* [1] (adjoint) second-in-command; [2] (étage) second floor GB, third floor US; [3] (dans un duel) second
D **en second** *loc adv* [arriver, partir] second; **passer en** ~ [*travail, amis*] to come second

secondaire /səɡɔ̃dɛʀ/
A *adj* [1] (en deuxième position) secondary; [2] (de moindre importance) [*personnage, route*] minor; [3] Scol **école** ~ secondary school GB, high school US; **j'ai fait mes études** ~**s à...** I was in secondary school GB *ou* high school US at...; [4] Méd **lésions** ~**s** secondary lesions; **syphilis** ~ the second stage of syphilis; **effets** ~**s** side effects; [5] (en géologie) **ère** ~ Mesozoic era; [6] Tech secondary
B *nm* [1] Scol secondary school GB *ou* high school US education; **les enseignants du** ~ secondary GB *ou* high US school teachers; [2] **le** ~ the Mesozoic

seconde² /səɡɔ̃d/
A *adj f* ▸ **second A**
B *nf* [1] ▸ p. 624 (unité de temps) second; **11 mètres par** ~ 11 metres^GB per *ou* a second; **à la** ~ **près** to the nearest second; [2] (court laps de temps) second; **en une fraction de** ~ in a split second; [3] Scol (classe) *fifth year of secondary school, age 15–16*; [4] (dans les transports en commun) **billet de** ~ second-class ticket; [5] Aut second gear; [6] Mus second

seconder /səɡɔ̃de/ [1] *vtr* [*personne*] to assist; [*circonstance*] to aid

secouer /səkwe/ [1]
A *vtr* [1] (agiter) to shake [*bouteille, branche, personne*]; to shake out [*nappe, tapis, parapluie*]; ~ **la tête** to shake one's head; **être un peu secoué** (dans une voiture, un avion) to have rather a bumpy ride; (sur un bateau) to have rather a rough trip; [2] (se débarrasser de) to shake off [*poussière, neige, joug*]; [3] (ébranler) [*crise*] to shake [*personne, pays*]; [4] ○(activer) to give [sb] a shaking-up○ [*personne*]
B **se secouer** *vpr* [1] (pour se dégager) [*personne*] to give oneself a shake; [2] (nerveusement) to jump about all over the place; [3] ○(contre le découragement) to pull oneself together; (contre l'inertie) to wake up, to get moving○

secourable /səkuʀabl/ *adj* [*personne*] helpful

secourir /səkuʀiʀ/ [26] *vtr* (aider) to help [*personne*]; (sauver) to rescue [*marin*]; (soigner) to give first aid to [*accidenté*]; (assister) to provide aid for [*réfugié*]

secourisme /səkuʀism/ *nm* first aid

secouriste /səkuʀist/ ▸ p. 372 *nmf* first-aid worker

secours /səkuʀ/
A *nm inv* (aide) help; **au** ~! help!; **appeler** *or* **crier au** ~ to shout for help; **appel au** ~ cry for help; **être d'un grand** ~ to be a great help; **il l'a appelée à son** ~ he got her to help him; **porter** ~ **à, se porter au** ~ **de** to help [*blessé, réfugié*]; to come to the aid of [*personne critiquée, entreprise*]; to rescue [*animal*]; **voler au** ~ **de qn** to rush to sb's aid; **le** ~ **en mer** sea rescue operations (*pl*); **de** ~ (de rechange) [*roue*] spare; (d'urgence) [*sortie*] emergency; (de soins) [*trousse*] first-aid; (de sauvetage) [*équipe*] rescue; (de sécurité) [*matériel*] back up
B *nmpl* [1] (personnes) (secouristes) rescuers, rescue team (*sg*);

(renforts) reinforcements; [2] (vivres, médicaments) relief supplies; ~ **humanitaires** humanitarian aid **C**; **premiers** ~, ~ **d'urgence** first aid **C**

secousse /səkus/ *nf* (mouvement brusque) jolt; **éviter les** ~**s** (en voiture, avion) to avoid the bumps; **avancer par** ~**s** [*voiture, train*] to jerk forward; Géog ~ **(sismique)** (earth) tremor

secret, -ète /səkʀɛ, ɛt/
A *adj* [1] (non divulgué) [*dossier, code, rite, société*] secret; **tenir qch** ~ to keep sth secret *ou* a secret; [2] (dissimulé) [*passage, mécanisme*] secret; [3] (intime, mystérieux) [*vie, sentiment, raisons*] secret; [4] (réservé) [*personne*] secretive
B *nm* [1] (ce qu'on cache) secret; **c'est un** ~ **entre nous** it's our secret; **ne pas avoir de** ~**s pour qn** to have no secrets from sb; **confier un** ~ **à qn** to let sb into GB *ou* in on a secret; **ce n'est un** ~ **pour personne** it's no secret (que that); [2] (ce qui est caché) secret; **livrer ses** ~**s** [*nature, tombe*] to yield up (its) secrets (à to); **la mécanique n'a plus de** ~**s pour elle** mechanics holds no secrets for her; [3] (discrétion) secrecy; **être tenu au** ~ to be sworn to secrecy; **dans le** ~ **de ton cœur** in your heart of hearts; **être dans le** ~ **(des dieux)** to be in on the secret; **mettre qn dans le** ~ to let sb into GB *ou* in on the secret; **garder le** ~ **sur qch** to keep sth a secret; **en** ~ in secret; [4] (recette) secret; **le** ~ **du bonheur** the secret of happiness; **avoir le** ~ **de qch** to know the secret of sth; **il a le** ~ **des solutions compliquées pour les problèmes simples** hum he has a knack of finding complicated answers to simple problems; [5] (prison) solitary confinement

(Composés) ~ **bancaire** Fin, Jur bank confidentiality; ~ **de fabrication** industrial secret; ~ **de Polichinelle** open secret; ~ **professionnel** Jur professional confidentiality

secrétaire /s(ə)kʀetɛʀ/ ▸ p. 372
A *nmf* (employé administratif) secretary
B *nm* [1] (cadre politique, diplomatique) secretary; [2] (meuble) secretaire GB, secretary US; [3] Zool secretary bird

(Composés) ~ **de direction** personal assistant; ~ **d'État** (en France) minister; (en Grande-Bretagne, aux États-Unis) Secretary of State; ~ **de rédaction** subeditor GB, copy-editor

secrétariat /s(ə)kʀetaʀja/ *nm* (travail) secretarial work; (lieu) secretariat

(Composés) ~ **d'État** ministry; ~ **d'État à l'emploi** ministry for employment; ~ **de rédaction** (activité) copy-editing; (bureau) copy-editors' room

secrètement /səkʀɛtmɑ̃/ *adv* secretly

sécréter /sekʀete/ [1] *vtr* to secrete [*sève, bile*]; [2] (exuder) to exude [*liquide*]; [3] fig to foster [*inégalités, idéologie*]; to hatch [*réforme*]

sécrétion /sekʀesjɔ̃/ *nf* secretion

sectaire /sɛktɛʀ/ *adj, nmf* sectarian

secte /sɛkt/ *nf* Relig sect; (clan) faction

secteur /sɛktœʀ/ *nm* [1] Écon (d'activités générales) sector; ~ **primaire/secondaire/tertiaire** primary/manufacturing/service sector; ~ **d'activité** sector; [2] Admin (subdivision) area, territory; Mil sector; [3] ○(parages) neighbourhood^GB; [4] Électrotech **le** ~ (réseau) the mains (*pl*); **appareil fonctionnant sur** ~ mains-operated appliance; **panne de** ~ power failure; [5] Math sector

section /sɛksjɔ̃/ *nf* [1] (division) Admin, Mil section; (de parti, syndicat) branch; (de route, chemin de fer) section; (de livre) part; [2] Scol (selon les niveaux) stream GB, track US; **choisir une** ~ **littéraire** to choose a literary option; [3] Univ department; [4] Math, Tech (coupe) section

(Composé) ~ **d'autobus** fare stage

sectionnement /sɛksjɔnmɑ̃/ *nm* (de tendon, membre) severing; (de territoire, service) division (**en** into)

sectionner /sɛksjɔne/ [1] *vtr* to sever [*membre, artère*]; to divide up [*service, administration*] (**en** into); to cut [*tuyau, câble, fil*]

sectoriel, -ielle /sɛktɔʀjɛl/ *adj* sectoral

sectorisation /sɛktɔʀizasjɔ̃/ *nf* division

sectoriser /sɛktɔʀize/ [1] *vtr* to divide [sth] into sectors

séculaire /sekylɛʀ/ *adj* [1] (vieux) [*tradition, arbre*] ancient; [2] (vieux de cent ans) [*arbre, maison*] hundred-year-old; [*personne*] centenarian; [3] (tous les cent ans) [*cérémonie*] centennial; [4] (en astronomie) secular

séculariser /sekylaʀize/ [1] *vtr* [1] (rendre séculier) to secularize [*personne, monastère*]; [2] (rendre laïque) to laicize [*personne*]; to secularize [*biens, fonctions*]

S

séculier, -ière /sekylje, ɛʀ/ adj secular

secundo /səgɔ̃do/ adv secondly

sécurisé, **~e** /sekyʀize/
A pp ▸ sécuriser
B pp adj Ordinat, Télécom secure; **une ligne ~e** a secure line

sécuriser /sekyʀize/ [1] vtr **1** gén (rassurer) to reassure; **2** Psych to make [sb] feel secure; **3** Mil to secure

securit® /sekyʀit/ nm **(verre)** ~ Triplex® (glass) GB, safety glass

sécurité /sekyʀite/ nf (absence de risques d'agression) security; (absence de danger fortuit) safety; ~ **de l'emploi** job security; **de** ~ [système, forces] security; [dispositif, zone] safety; [raisons, problème] of security (après n); **se sentir en ~** to feel secure ou safe

(Composés) ~ **routière** road safety; ~ **sociale** French national health and pensions organization

sédatif, -ive /sedatif, iv/
A adj [propriété] sedative; [potion, effet] soothing
B nm sedative

sédentaire /sedɑ̃tɛʀ/
A adj **1** gén [vie, travail, personne] sedentary; **2** [population] geographically stable; Mil [troupes] garrison(ed) (épith)
B nmf **1** (dans le travail) person with a sedentary ou desk job; (casanier) stay-at-home GB, homebody US; **2** **les ~s** the indigenous population (sg)

sédentariser /sedɑ̃taʀize/ [1] vtr to settle

sédiment /sedimɑ̃/ nm sediment

sédimentation /sedimɑ̃tasjɔ̃/ nf sedimentation

séditieux, -ieuse /sedisjø, øz/ adj **1** [personne] rebellious; **2** [écrit, esprit, propos] seditious

séducteur, -trice /sedyktœʀ, tʀis/
A adj seductive
B nm,f (trompeur) deceiver/seductress; (charmeur) charmer

séduction /sedyksjɔ̃/ nf (manœuvre) seduction; (charme naturel) charm; (de l'argent) lure; (du luxe) enticement; (des mots) seductive power

séduire /sedɥiʀ/ [1] vtr **1** (attirer) [personne] to captivate; **il aime** ~ he likes to charm people; **les qualités qui séduisent le plus chez un homme** the most attractive qualities in a man; **2** (plaire à) to appeal to [personne]; **3** (convaincre) [personne] to win over; **4** †(pour des relations sexuelles) to seduce

séduisant, **~e** /sedɥizɑ̃, ɑ̃t/ adj [personne, perspective] attractive; [projet, idée] appealing

segment /sɛgmɑ̃/ nm Ling, Math, Ordinat segment

segmenter /sɛgmɑ̃te/ [1] vtr, **se segmenter** vpr to segment

ségrégation /segʀegasjɔ̃/ nf segregation

seiche /sɛʃ/ nf cuttlefish

seigle /sɛgl/ nm rye; **farine de** ~ rye flour

seigneur /sɛɲœʀ/ nm **1** Hist (propriétaire, noble) lord; **être grand** ~ to be full of largesse; **2** fig (de la finance, l'industrie) heavyweight; (du sport) star
(Composé) ~ **de la guerre** warlord
(Idiome) **à tout** ~ **tout honneur** Prov credit where credit is due

Seigneur /sɛɲœʀ/
A nm Lord; **le** ~ **l'a rappelé à lui** euph he has gone to meet his Maker
B excl Good Lord!

seigneurial, **~e**, mpl **-iaux** /sɛɲœʀjal, o/ adj **1** [château, terres] (en France) seigneurial; (en Angleterre) manorial; **2** fig [demeure] stately; [manières] lordly

seigneurie /sɛɲœʀi/ nf **1** (terre) seigneury; **2** (autorité, droits) seigniory; **3** (titre) **votre** ~ your Lordship

sein /sɛ̃/ nm **1** Anat breast; **avoir les ~s nus** to be topless; **se faire refaire les ~s** to have plastic surgery on one's breasts; **nourrir au** ~ to breast-feed; **serrer qn contre** or **sur son** ~ to clasp sb to one's bosom; **2** (utérus) liter womb; **porter un enfant dans son** ~ to be carrying a child; **3** liter, fig bosom; **au** ~ **de** within; ▸ **faux¹**

seing /sɛ̃/ nm Jur signature; **acte sous** ~ **privé** private agreement

séisme /seism/ nm **1** lit earthquake, seism; **2** fig upheaval

seize /sɛz/ ▸ p. 398, p. 296, p. 155 adj inv, pron sixteen

seizième /sɛzjɛm/ ▸ p. 398, p. 155 adj sixteenth
(Composé) ~**s de finale** Sport round in competition with thirty-two competitors or teams

séjour /seʒuʀ/ nm **1** (période) stay; **il a fait plusieurs ~s en prison** he has been in prison several times; ~**s à l'étranger** (dans un CV) time spent abroad; **2** (pièce) living room; **3** (lieu) fml abode sout
(Composés) ~ **culturel** cultural holiday GB ou vacation; ~ **linguistique** language study holiday GB ou vacation

séjourner /seʒuʀne/ [1] vi to stay

sel /sɛl/
A nm **1** lit salt; **gros** ~ coarse salt; **régime sans** ~ salt-free diet; **pain sans** ~ unsalted bread; **2** fig (esprit) savour^GB; (piquant) piquancy
B sels nmpl smelling salts
(Composés) ~ **de cuisine** cooking salt; ~ **gemme** rock salt; ~ **marin** sea salt; ~**s de bain** bath salts

sélect○, **~e** /selɛkt/ adj [club, bar] exclusive; [clientèle] select

sélecteur, -trice /selɛktœʀ, tʀis/
A adj selective
B nm **1** Ordinat, Télécom, TV selector; **2** (de bicyclette, d'embrayage standard) gear lever, gearshift US; (de moto) gear change, gearshift US; (d'embrayage automatique) gearstick, gearshift US

sélectif, -ive /selɛktif, iv/ adj selective

sélection /selɛksjɔ̃/ nf **1** gén, Biol selection; (pour un emploi) selection process; ~ **à l'entrée** selective entry; **2** (choix) selection, choice; **3** Sport (choix) selection; (équipe) team; **épreuve de** ~ trial (**pour** for)

sélectionner /selɛksjɔne/ [1] vtr **1** (choisir) to select; ~ **des élèves pour un concours** to enter pupils for a competitive examination; **être sélectionné sur dossier** Univ, Scol to be selected on the basis of one's academic record; **2** Ordinat to highlight [texte]

sélectionneur, -euse /selɛksjɔnœʀ, øz/ nm,f Sport selector

self○ /sɛlf/ nm (restaurant) self-service restaurant

self-service, pl ~**s** /sɛlfsɛʀvis/ nm (restaurant) self-service restaurant

selle /sɛl/
A nf **1** (siège) saddle; **2** (de sculpteur) turntable; **3** †(chaise percée) commode; **aller à la** ~ euph to have a bowel movement
B selles nfpl Méd stools

seller /sele/ [1] vtr to saddle

sellerie /sɛlʀi/ nf **1** Comm (bourrellerie) saddlery; (maroquinerie) leatherwork

sellette /sɛlɛt/ nf **1** (pour plante, statue) stand; (de sculpteur) small turntable; **2** (d'ouvrier) cradle
(Idiome) **être sur la** ~ to be in the hot seat

sellier /selje/ ▸ p. 372 nm (bourrelier) saddler; (maroquinier) maker of fancy leather goods

selon /səlɔ̃/
A prép **1** gén according to; ~ **moi, il va pleuvoir** in my opinion, it's going to rain; ~ **les termes du président** in the President's words; ~ **la formule** as people ou they say; ~ **la loi** under the law; **l'idée** ~ **laquelle** the idea that; ~ **une pratique courante** in accordance with ou following a common practice; **dépenser** ~ **ses moyens** to spend according to one's pocket; **2** (en fonction de) depending on [heure, température, circonstances]; **la situation varie** ~ **les régions** the situation varies from region to region; **c'est** ~○ it all depends
B selon que loc conj depending on whether

Seltz /sɛlts/ npr **eau de** ~ seltzer water

semailles /səmaj/ nfpl (travail) sowing ₵; (époque) sowing season (sg); (graines semées) seeds

semaine /s(ə)mɛn/ ▸ p. 582 nf **1** (de calendrier) week; **2** (salaire hebdomadaire) week's wages (pl); (argent de poche) (weekly) pocket money
(Idiome) **vivre à la petite** ~ to live from day to day

semainier /səmɛnje/ nm (agenda) week-to-a-page diary

sémantique /semɑ̃tik/
A adj semantic
B nf semantics (+ v sg)

sémaphore /semafɔʀ/ nm Naut, Télécom semaphore

Les jours de la semaine

Les noms des jours

■ *L'anglais emploie la majuscule pour les noms de jours. Les abréviations sont courantes en anglais familier écrit, par ex. dans une lettre à un ami:* I'll see you on Mon 17 Sept.

		abréviation anglaise
dimanche	Sunday	Sun
lundi	Monday	Mon
mardi	Tuesday	Tue *ou* Tues
mercredi	Wednesday	Wed
jeudi	Thursday	Thur *ou* Thurs
vendredi	Friday	Fri
samedi	Saturday	Sat

■ *Noter que dans les pays anglophones on considère en général que la semaine commence le dimanche.*

■ *Dans les expressions suivantes,* Monday *est pris comme exemple; les autres noms de jours s'utilisent de la même façon.*

quel jour sommes-nous?
= what day is it?

nous sommes lundi
= it's Monday

c'est aujourd'hui lundi
= today is Monday

■ *Pour l'expression de la date* ► **p. 155**.

■ *L'anglais emploie normalement* on *devant les noms de jours, sauf lorsqu'il y a une autre préposition, ou un mot comme* this, that, next, last *etc.*

Lundi ou *le lundi*: un jour précis, passé ou futur

c'est arrivé lundi
= it happened on Monday

lundi matin
= on Monday morning

lundi après-midi
= on Monday afternoon

lundi matin de bonne heure
= early on Monday morning

lundi soir en fin de soirée
= late on Monday evening

lundi, on va au zoo
= on Monday, we're going to the zoo

lundi dernier
= last Monday

lundi dernier dans la soirée
= last Monday evening

lundi prochain
= next Monday

lundi en huit
= the Monday after next *ou* on Monday week

dans un mois lundi
= a month from Monday

dans un mois à dater de lundi dernier
= in a month from last Monday

à partir de lundi
= from Monday onwards

c'est arrivé le lundi
= it happened on the Monday

le lundi matin
= on the Monday morning

le lundi après-midi
= on the Monday afternoon

tard le lundi soir
= late on the Monday evening

tôt le lundi matin
= early on the Monday morning

elle est partie le lundi après-midi
= she left on the Monday afternoon

ce lundi
= this Monday

ce lundi-là
= that Monday

précisément ce lundi-là
= that very Monday

Le lundi: un même jour chaque semaine

quand est-ce que cela a lieu?
= when does it happen?

cela a lieu le lundi
= it happens on Mondays

le lundi, on va au zoo
= on Mondays, we go to the zoo

elle ne travaille jamais le lundi
= she never works on Mondays

le lundi après-midi, elle va à la piscine
= she goes swimming on Monday afternoons

tous les lundis
= every Monday

chaque lundi
= each Monday

un lundi sur deux
= every other Monday *ou* every second Monday

un lundi sur trois
= every third Monday

presque tous les lundis
= most Mondays

certains lundis
= some Mondays

un lundi de temps en temps
= on the occasional Monday

le deuxième lundi de chaque mois
= on the second Monday in the month

Un lundi: un jour quelconque

c'est arrivé un lundi
= it happened on a Monday *ou* it happened one Monday

un lundi matin
= on a Monday morning *ou* one Monday morning

un lundi après-midi
= on a Monday afternoon *ou* one Monday afternoon

☞ Voir page suivante

S

Les jours de la semaine *suite*

Du avec les noms des jours de la semaine

■ *Les expressions françaises avec du se traduisent normalement par l'emploi du nom de jour en position d'adjectif.*

les cours du lundi
= Monday classes

la fermeture du lundi
= Monday closing

les programmes de télévision du lundi
= Monday TV programmes

les trains du lundi
= Monday trains

le vol du lundi
= the Monday flight

Et comparer:

le journal du lundi
= the Monday paper

le journal de lundi
= Monday's paper

et de même the Monday classes *et* Monday's classes *etc*

---

semblable /sãblabl/
A *adj* [1] (comparable) similar (à to); **des résultats à peu près/tout à fait ~s** roughly/quite similar results; **ils sont ~s en tout** they are alike in all respects; **une journée ~ à tant d'autres** a day like any other; **j'en ai vu ~s** I've seen similar ones; [2] (identique) identical; [3] (tel) (*before n*) such; **~ proposition** such a proposal
B *nmf* fellow creature; **eux et leurs ~s** they and their kind

semblant /sãblã/ *nm* **un ~ de légalité** a semblance of legality; **faire ~ d'être triste** to pretend to be sad; **elle fait ~ de rien, mais elle t'a vu** she's seen you but she's not letting on○

sembler /sãble/ [1]
A *vi* to seem; **le temps m'a semblé long** the time seemed to me to pass slowly; **tout semble possible** it seems anything is possible
B *v impers* **il semble bon de faire** it seems appropriate to do; **faites comme bon vous semble** do whatever you think best; **le problème est réglé à ce qu'il me semble** the problem has been solved, or so it seems to me; **il me semble important de faire** I think it is important to do; **il me semble l'avoir déjà rencontrée** I think I've met her before; **elle a, semble-t-il, refusé** apparently, she has refused; **si bon me semble** if I feel like it

semelle /s(ə)mɛl/ *nf* [1] sole; **~ antidérapante** non-slip sole; [2] Tech (de fer à repasser) soleplate; (de machine) bedplate; (de rail) flange; (de ski) midsection
(Composés) **~ compensée** wedge heel; **~ intérieure** insole
(Idiomes) **être (dur comme) de la ~**○ to be as tough as old boots○ GB *ou* leather US; **ne pas quitter** *or* **lâcher qn d'une ~** to stick to sb like a leech

semence /s(ə)mãs/ *nf* seed

semer /s(ə)me/ [1] *vtr* [1] Agric to sow [*graines*]; **~ à la volée** to sow, to broadcast; [2] (apporter) to sow [*discorde, trouble*]; to spread [*confusion, panique*]; [*arme, ouragan*] to bring [*mort*]; **~ le doute** to sow doubt; [3] (parsemer) **~ des clous sur la route** to strew the road with nails; **mission semée de difficultés** mission bristling with difficulties; **copie semée de fautes** written work riddled with errors; **ciel semé d'étoiles** star-spangled sky; **on récolte ce qu'on a semé** as you sow so shall you reap; [4] ○(perdre) to drop; [5] ○(distancer) to shake off [*poursuivant, gêneur*]; to leave [sb] behind [*concurrent*]

semestre /s(ə)mɛstʀ/ ▸ p. 582 *nm* [1] (d'année civile) half-year; **tous les ~s** twice a year; [2] (d'année universitaire) semester; [3] (rente, pension) half-yearly payment

semestriel, -ielle /səmɛstʀijɛl/ *adj* [1] [*revue*] biannual; [*réunion, prévisions*] twice-yearly (épith); [*résultats*] half-yearly (épith); **la présidence semestrielle de la CEE** the six-month presidency of the EEC; [2] Univ [*examen*] end-of-semester (épith) GB, final US; [*cours*] one-semester (épith)

semeur, -euse /səmœʀ, øz/ *nmf* lit, fig sower; **~ de troubles** troublemaker

semi-circulaire, *pl* **~s** /səmisiʀkylɛʀ/ *adj* semicircular

semi-conserve, *pl* **~s** /səmikõsɛʀv/ *nf* Culin, Ind partially preserved product

semi-démocratique, *pl* **~s** /səmidemɔkʀatik/ *adj* relatively democratic

semi-désertique, *pl* **~s** /səmidezɛʀtik/ *adj* semidesert

semi-échec, *pl* **~s** /səmieʃɛk/ *nm* partial failure

semi-liberté, *pl* **~s** /səmilibɛʀte/ *nf* relative freedom

sémillant, ~e /semijã, ãt/ *adj* spirited; [*esprit*] sparkling

séminaire /seminɛʀ/ *nm* [1] (réunion) seminar; [2] (institution) seminary

séminal, ~e, *mpl* **-aux** /seminal, o/ *adj* seminal

séminariste /seminaʀist/ *nm* seminarist, seminarian

sémiologie /semjɔlɔʒi/ *nf* semiology

sémiotique /semjɔtik/
A *adj* semiotic
B *nf* semiotics (+ *v sg*)

semi-précieux, -ieuse /səmipʀesjø, øz/ *adj* [*pierre*] semiprecious

semi-remorque, *pl* **~s** /səmiʀəmɔʀk/ *nm* (camion) articulated lorry GB, tractor-trailer US

semis /s(ə)mi/ *nm inv* Agric (ensemencement) sowing; (jeune plant) seedling; (terrain) seedbed

semoir /səmwaʀ/ *nm* [1] (machine) seed drill; [2] †(sac) seedbag

semonce /səmõs/ *nf* reprimand; **coup de ~** lit, fig warning shot

semoule /səmul/ *nf* semolina; **sucre ~** caster sugar

sempiternel, -elle /sãpitɛʀnɛl/ *adj* perpetual, endless

sénat /sena/ *nm* senate

ⓘ **Sénat** The upper parliamentary chamber, with 321 *sénateurs*, elected for nine years. A third of the members are elected every three years by an electoral college within a *département*. The *président du Sénat* assumes the powers of the *Président de la République* in the event of the latter's incapacity.

sénateur /senatœʀ/ ▸ p. 590 *nm* senator

sénatorial, ~e, *mpl* **-iaux** /senatɔʀjal, o/ *adj* senatorial

séné /sene/ *nm* senna

sénile /senil/ *adj* senile

sénilité /senilite/ *nf* senility

senior /senjɔʀ/
A *adj* [1] Sport senior; [2] (âgé) [*personne*] senior; [*publication, mode*] for senior citizens
B *nmf* [1] Sport senior; [2] (personne âgée) senior citizen

sens /sãs/
A *nm* inv [1] (direction) lit, fig direction; **dans un ~** in both directions; **elle venait en ~ inverse** she was coming from the opposite direction; **mouvement en ~ contraire** backward movement; **en tous ~** in all directions; **dans le ~ Paris-Lyon** in the Paris to Lyons direction; **dans le ~ de la largeur** widthways, across; **dans le ~ de la longueur** lengthways, longways US; **être dans le bon/mauvais ~** to be the right/wrong way up; **des flèches dans tous les ~** arrows pointing in all directions; **retourner un problème dans tous les ~** to consider a

problem from every angle; **courir dans tous les** ~ to run all over the place; **dans le** ~ **de la marche** facing the engine; **dans le** ~ **des fils** (de tissu) with the grain; ~ **dessus dessous** /sɑ̃dəsydəsu/ (à l'envers) upside down; (en désordre) upside down; (très troublé) very upset; ~ **devant derrière** /sɑ̃dəvɑ̃dɛʀjɛʀ/ back to front; **aller dans le bon** ~ [réformes, mesures] to be a step in the right direction; **des mesures qui vont dans le** ~ **de notre rapport** measures which are in line with our report; **le pays va dans le** ~ **d'une plus grande indépendance** the country is moving toward(s) greater independence; **le** ~ **de l'histoire** the tide of history; **2** (signification) meaning; **le** ~ **figuré d'un mot** the figurative sense of a word; **employer un mot au** ~ **propre** to use a word literally; **au** ~ **fort du terme** in the fullest sense of the word; **cela n'a pas de** ~ gén it doesn't make sense; (idiot, ridicule) it's absurd; **3** (fonction physiologique) sense; **retrouver l'usage de ses** ~ to regain consciousness; **4** (intuition) sense; **avoir le** ~ **de l'orientation** to have a good sense of direction; **avoir le** ~ **pratique** to be practical; **ne pas avoir le** ~ **du ridicule** not to realize when one looks silly; **avoir le** ~ **des affaires** to have a flair for business; **ton** ~ **des affaires** your business sense; **ne pas avoir le** ~ **de la langue** to have no feeling for language; **n'avoir aucun** ~ **des réalités** to live in a dream world

B nmpl senses; **plaisirs des** ~ sensual pleasures

(Composés) ~ **giratoire** roundabout GB, traffic circle US; ~ **interdit** (panneau) no-entry sign; (rue) one-way street; ~ **obligatoire** (panneau) one-way sign; ~ **unique** (panneau) one-way sign; (rue) one-way street

(Idiome) **tomber sous le** ~ to be patently obvious

sensation /sɑ̃sasjɔ̃/ nf **1** lit, fig feeling, sensation; **cela ne procure pas les mêmes** ~s it doesn't have the same effect; **on a la** ~ **de flotter** you feel as if you're floating; **aimer les** ~s **fortes** to like one's thrills; **2** (réaction) sensation; **la décision a fait** ~ (a étonné) the decision caused a sensation; **reportages à** ~ keyhole journalism **¢**

sensationnel, -elle /sɑ̃sasjɔnɛl/ adj **1** ◦(formidable) fantastic◦; **2** (surprenant) sensational, astonishing; **3** (à sensation) sensational

sensé, ~e /sɑ̃se/ adj sensible

sensibilisation /sɑ̃sibilizasjɔ̃/ nf **1** **campagne de** ~ awareness campaign; **une** ~ **des médecins au problème** making doctors aware of the problem; **2** Méd, Phot sensitizing, sensitization

sensibiliser /sɑ̃sibilize/ [1] vtr **1** ~ **le public à un problème** to increase public awareness of an issue; **2** Chimie, Méd, Phot to sensitize

sensibilité /sɑ̃sibilite/ nf **1** (qualité) sensibility; **elle est d'une grande** ~ she is very sensitive; **2** Méd, Phot sensitivity

sensible /sɑ̃sibl/ **A** adj **1** gén sensitive; **être** ~ **aux compliments** to like compliments; **être** ~ **aux charmes de qn** to be susceptible to sb's charms; **j'ai été très** ~ **à votre gentille attention** I was most touched by your kindness; **je suis** ~ **au fait que** I am aware that; **avoir le cœur** ~ to be sensitive; **être** ~ **à un argument** to be swayed by an argument; **les natures** ~s pej the fainthearted; **avoir l'oreille** ~ to have keen hearing; **un être** ~ a sentient being; **je suis très** ~ **au froid** I really feel the cold; **2** [peau] sensitive; [peau cicatrisée] tender; [membre blessé] sore; **je suis** ~ **de la gorge, j'ai la gorge** ~ I often get a sore throat; **j'ai les pieds** ~s my feet are very sensitive; **3** (notable) [hausse, différence] appreciable; [effort] real; **4** (perceptible) **le monde** ~ the physical ou tangible world

B nmf sensitive person

sensiblement /sɑ̃siblǝmɑ̃/ adv **1** (considérablement) [réduire, augmenter] appreciably, noticeably; [différent] perceptibly; **2** (plus ou moins) [pareil] roughly

sensiblerie /sɑ̃siblǝʀi/ nf pej sentimentality péj

sensitif, -ive /sɑ̃sitif, iv/ adj sensory

sensoriel, -ielle /sɑ̃sɔʀjɛl/ adj sensory

sensualité /sɑ̃sɥalite/ nf sensuality

sensuel, -elle /sɑ̃sɥɛl/ adj sensual

sentence /sɑ̃tɑ̃s/ nf **1** (décision) sentence; **2** (propos) maxim

sentencieux, -ieuse /sɑ̃tɑ̃sjø, øz/ adj sententious

senteur /sɑ̃tœʀ/ nf liter scent

senti, ~**e** /sɑ̃ti/ adj **bien** ~ [remarques] well-chosen; [réponse] blunt; [discours] forthright

sentier /sɑ̃tje/ nm lit, fig path, track; **être sur le** ~ **de la guerre** fig to be on the warpath; **hors des** ~s **battus** off the beaten track

(Composés) ~ **de grande randonnée** long-distance footpath; ~ **de petite randonnée** footpath

sentiment /sɑ̃timɑ̃/ nm **1** gén feeling; **il est incapable de** ~ he's incapable of emotion; **agir par** ~ **plus que par raison** to be guided by one's feelings rather than by reason; **faire du** ~ to sentimentalize; **prendre qn par les** ~s to appeal to sb's better nature; **il ne fait pas de** ~ **en affaires** he doesn't let sentiment get in the way of business; **j'ai le** ~ **qu'il va pleuvoir** I've got a feeling it's going to rain; **donner le** ~ **de faire** to give the impression of doing; **2** (inclination) feeling, sentiment sout; **les beaux** or **bons** ~s fine sentiments; **être animé de mauvais** ~s to have bad intentions; **3** (dans les formules épistolaires) ~s **affectueux** or **amicaux** best wishes; **veuillez croire à mes** ~s **les meilleurs** (à une personne non nommée) yours faithfully; (à une personne nommée) yours sincerely

sentimental, ~e, mpl -aux /sɑ̃timɑ̃tal, o/ **A** adj **1** [attachement] sentimental; [vie] love (épith); [relations] romantic; **sur le plan** ~ (dans un horoscope) on the romance front; **2** (sensible) sentimental, romantic

B nm,f sentimental person

sentinelle /sɑ̃tinɛl/ nf **1** (soldat) sentry; **2** fig look-out; **faire la** ~ to stand guard, to keep watch

sentir /sɑ̃tiʀ/ [30] **A** vtr **1** (percevoir par l'odorat) to smell [parfum, fleur]; **on sent que tu fumes le cigare** one can tell that you smoke cigars by the smell; **2** (percevoir par le toucher, le corps, le goût) to feel; **j'ai marché trop longtemps, je ne sens plus mes pieds** I've been walking for too long, my feet are numb; **on sent qu'il y a du vin dans la sauce** tastes of wine; ~ **d'où vient le vent** lit, Naut to see how the wind blows ou lies; fig to see which way the wind is blowing; **3** (comprendre) to be conscious of [importance]; to feel [beauté, force]; to appreciate [difficulté]; to sense [danger, désapprobation]; ~ **que** (percevoir) to feel that; (avoir l'idée) to have a feeling that; **on sent que l'hiver approche** it feels wintry; **je te sens inquiet, je sens que tu es inquiet** I can tell you're worried; **je leur ai fait** ~ **mon désaccord** I made it clear to them that I didn't agree; **faire** ~ **le rythme d'un poème** to bring out the rhythm of a poem; **se faire** ~ [besoin, présence, absence] to be felt

B vi **1** (avoir une odeur) to smell; ~ **bon** to smell nice; **ça sent bon le café** there's a nice smell of coffee; **fleurs qui ne sentent rien** flowers which don't have a scent; **2** (puer) to smell; ~ **des pieds** to have smelly feet; **3** (révéler) to smack of; **ta douleur sent la comédie** your grief seems put on; **ciel nuageux qui sent l'orage** cloudy sky that heralds a storm

C se sentir vpr **1** to feel; **se** ~ **mieux** to feel better; **se** ~ **surveillé** to feel that one is being watched; **elle ne s'est pas sentie visée par ma remarque** she didn't feel that my remark was aimed at her; **ne plus se** ~◦ (de joie) to be overjoyed; (de vanité) to get above oneself; **2** (être perceptible) [phénomène, amélioration, effet] to be felt

(Idiomes) **je ne peux pas le** ~ I can't stand him; **je l'ai senti passer!** (piqûre, addition) it really hurt!; (réprimande) I really got it in the neck!

séparable /separabl/ adj separable (**de** from); **être difficilement** ~ **de** to be difficult to separate from

séparation /separasjɔ̃/ nf **1** gén, Pol, Jur separation; **la** ~ **des pouvoirs** Pol the separation of powers; **après la** ~ **des composants du mélange** after separating out the constituents of the mixture; **la** ~ **du pays en deux États** the division ou splitting of the country into two states; **après deux ans de** ~ after two years' separation; **2** (division) (entre des jardins) boundary; (entre des pièces) partition; fig boundary, dividing line; **mur de** ~ (extérieur) boundary wall; (intérieur) dividing wall; **établir une** ~ (nette) **entre sa vie privée et professionnelle** to keep one's private life (completely) separate from one's work

(Composés) ~ **de biens** Jur matrimonial division of property; ~ **de corps** Jur judicial separation; ~ **de fait** Jur de facto separation

séparatisme /separatism/ nm separatism

séparatiste /separatist/ adj, nmf separatist

S

séparé, ~e /separe/ adj [1] (sans contact) **vivre** ~ to live apart (**de** from); [2] (éloigné) **les deux villages sont** ~**s de quelques kilomètres** the two villages are a few kilometres^GB apart; [3] (distinct) separate

séparément /separemã/ adv separately

séparer /separe/ [1]
A vtr [1] (ne pas laisser ensemble) to separate [objets, rôles]; to separate out [composants]; ~ **l'aspect politique d'un problème de son aspect économique** to keep the political and economic aspects of a problem separate; **la mort les a séparés** they were parted by death; **la vie nous a séparés** we have gone our separate ways in life; [2] (distinguer) [personne] to distinguish between [concepts, domaines, problèmes]; **on ne peut** ~ **ces deux problèmes** one cannot dissociate these two problems; [3] (former une limite entre) to separate; **quelques kilomètres nous séparent de la mer** we are a few kilometres^GB away from the sea; **deux ans séparent les deux événements** there is a gap of two years between the two events; **le temps qui sépare le passage de deux véhicules** the time lapse between the passage of two vehicles; [4] (diviser) lit, fig to divide; **l'âge les séparait** the age difference between them was a problem; **les qualités qui séparent un bon musicien d'un virtuose** the qualities that distinguish a good musician from a virtuoso; **tout les sépare** they are worlds apart
B se séparer vpr [1] (se quitter) [invités] to part, to leave each other; [conjoints, amants] to split up; Jur to separate; [2] (quitter) se ~ **de** to leave [camarade, groupe, famille]; to split up with; Jur to separate from [mari, femme]; [3] (se disperser) [manifestants] to split (up); [assemblée] to break up; [4] (se passer de) **se** ~ **de** to let [sb] go [employé, collaborateur]; to part with [objet personnel]; **il ne se sépare jamais de son parapluie** he takes his umbrella everywhere; [5] (se diviser) to divide; **la route se sépare (en deux)** the road forks

sept /sɛt/ ▸ p. 398, p. 296, p. 155 adj inv, pron, nm inv seven
⬭Composé⬭ **les** ~ **Familles** Jeux Happy Families
⬭Idiome⬭ **tourne** ~ **fois ta langue dans ta bouche avant de parler** think before you speak

septante /sɛptãt/ ▸ p. 398, p. 155 adj inv, pron B, H seventy

septantième /sɛptãtjɛm/ ▸ p. 398 adj B, H seventieth

septembre /sɛptãbʀ/ ▸ p. 380 nm September

septennat /sɛptena/ nm seven-year term (of office)

septentrional, ~e, mpl **-aux** /sɛptãtʀijɔnal, o/ adj northern

septicémie /sɛptisemi/ ▸ p. 195 nf blood-poisoning, septicemia spéc

septième /sɛtjɛm/ ▸ p. 398, p. 155
A adj seventh
B nf Scol fifth year of primary school, age 10–11
⬭Composé⬭ **le** ~ **art** cinematography
⬭Idiome⬭ **être au** ~ **ciel** to be on cloud nine

septuagénaire /sɛptɥaʒenɛʀ/
A adj **être** ~ to be in one's seventies
B nm,f person in his/her seventies

septuor /sɛptɥɔʀ/ nm (œuvre, formation) septet

septupler /sɛptyple/ [1]
A vtr to increase [sth] sevenfold
B vi to increase sevenfold

sépulcral, ~e, mpl **-aux** /sepylkʀal, o/ adj [1] (funèbre) sepulchral; **silence** ~ deathly silence; [2] †(funéraire) [pierre, caveau] funerary

sépulcre /sepylkʀ/ nm sepulchre^GB

sépulture /sepyltyʀ/ nf [1] (tombe) grave; [2] (enterrement) burial

séquelle /sekɛl/ nf [1] Méd (d'accident, opération) after-effect; [2] (retombées) repercussion; (conséquence) consequence

séquence /sekãs/ nf [1] gén sequence; [2] Chimie (de polymère) block

séquestration /sekɛstʀasjõ/ nf [1] (détention) gén confinement; Jur ~ **(arbitraire)** illegal detention; [2] Jur, Chimie sequestration

séquestre /sekɛstʀ/ nm Jur sequestration; **biens (mis) sous** ~ sequestrated property 𝄌

séquestrer /sekɛstʀe/ [1] vtr [1] (détenir) gén to hold [otage]; Jur to confine [sb] illegally [personne]; [2] Jur (saisir) to sequestrate [biens]

sérail /seʀaj/ nm [1] Hist seraglio; [2] (entourage) innermost circle

séraphin /seʀafɛ̃/ nm (ange) seraph

serbe /sɛʀb/
A ▸ p. 504 adj Serbian
B ▸ p. 336 nm Ling Serbian

serbo-croate /sɛʀbokʀɔat/ ▸ p. 336 nm Serbo-Croatian

Sercq /sɛʀk/ ▸ p. 303 nprf Sark

serein, ~e /səʀɛ̃, ɛn/ adj [ciel, temps] clear; [personne, visage] serene; [jugement] dispassionate; [critique] objective

sereinement /səʀɛnmã/ adv [regarder] serenely; [réfléchir, parler] calmly; [voir l'avenir] with equanimity; [juger] dispassionately

sérénade /seʀenad/ nf [1] (concert) serenade; [2] ᴼ(tapage) racket^ᴼ

sérénissime /seʀenisim/ adj **son Altesse** ~ His/Her Serene Highness

sérénité /seʀenite/ nf [1] (de visage, d'esprit) serenity; (de personne) equanimity; [2] (de juge, jugement) impartiality; [3] (de ciel, temps) calmness

serf, serve /sɛʀ, sɛʀv/ nm,f serf

sergent /sɛʀʒã/ ▸ p. 283 nm Mil (de terre) ≈ sergeant; (de l'air) ≈ sergeant GB, ≈ staff sergeant US

sergent-chef, pl **sergents-chefs** /sɛʀʒãʃɛf/ ▸ p. 283 nm Mil (de terre) ≈ staff sergeant; (de l'air) ≈ flight sergeant GB, ≈ chief master sergeant US

série /seʀi/ nf [1] (suite) series (+ v sg); **catastrophes en** ~ a series of catastrophes; **avoir des problèmes en** ~, **avoir toute une** ~ **de problèmes** to have one problem after another; [2] (de production) **numéro de** ~ serial number; ~ **limitée** limited edition; **modèle de** ~ gén mass-produced model; (voiture) production model; **fabriqués** or **faits en** ~ mass-produced; **production en** ~ mass production; **voiture hors** ~ custom-built car; **numéro hors** ~ special issue; ▸ **grand**; [3] (collection) set; [4] TV series (+ v sg); [5] Cin (film de) ~ **B** B movie; [6] Sport (catégorie) division; (épreuve) heat; **tête de** ~ **numéro un** (au tennis) number one seed; [7] Chimie, Math, Mus series (sg); [8] Scol option
⬭Composé⬭ ~ **noire** Cin, Littérat thriller; fig (catastrophes) series of disasters (pl); (malchance) run of bad luck

sérieusement /seʀjøzmã/ adv [1] gén seriously; [2] (considérablement) seriously, considerably

sérieux, -ieuse /seʀjø, øz/
A adj [1] gén **être** ~ **dans son travail** [personne] to be serious about one's work; [2] (qui mérite considération) [affaire, menace] serious; [piste, indice] important; [annonce, proposition] genuine; **passer aux choses sérieuses** to move on to serious matters; **'pas** ~ **s'abstenir'** (dans une petite annonce) 'genuine inquiries only'; [3] (digne de confiance) reliable; (responsable) responsible; **cela ne fait pas très** ~ that doesn't make a very good impression; [4] (grave) serious; [5] (considérable) [effort, besoin] real; [progrès] considerable; [handicap] serious
B nm seriousness; **dire qch avec beaucoup de** ~ to say sth very seriously; **garder son** ~ to keep a straight face; **faire qch avec** ~ to do sth carefully; **il a fait preuve de beaucoup de** ~ **dans ses études** he's really worked hard (at his studies); **se prendre au** ~ to take oneself seriously

sérigraphie /seʀigʀafi/ nf [1] (procédé) silkscreen printing; [2] (œuvre) silkscreen print

serin /səʀɛ̃/ nm Zool canary

serinerᴼ /səʀine/ [1] vtr ~ **qch à qn** to drum sth into sb

seringa /səʀɛ̃ga/ nm syringa, mock orange

seringue /səʀɛ̃g/ nf syringe

serment /sɛʀmã/ nm [1] (devant une autorité) oath; **déclarer sous** ~ to declare under oath; **prêter** ~ to take the oath; [2] (promesse) liter vow
⬭Composé⬭ **le** ~ **d'Hippocrate** Méd the Hippocratic oath

sermon /sɛʀmõ/ nm [1] Littérat, Relig sermon; [2] (discours) pej lecture; (remontrance) pej talking-to

sermonner /sɛʀmɔne/ [1] vtr (conseiller) to lecture; (morigéner) to give [sb] a talking-to

séronégatif, -ive /seʀonegatif, iv/
A adj HIV-negative
B nm,f HIV-negative person

séropositif, -ive /seʀopozitif, iv/
A adj gén seropositive (**à** for); (dans le cas du sida) HIV positive
B nm,f HIV-positive person

séropositivité /seʀopozitivite/ nf (dans le cas du sida) (HIV antibody) seropositivity

sérosité /seʀozite/ nf serous fluid

serpe /seʀp/ nf billhook

serpent /seʀpã/ nm ① Zool snake; ② Bible serpent; ③ ▸ p. 389 Mus serpent
⸨Composés⸩ ~ **monétaire** Fin currency snake; ~ **à sonnette** rattlesnake

serpenter /seʀpãte/ [1] vi [route, fleuve] to wind

serpentin /seʀpãtɛ̃/ nm (de fête) streamer

serpette /seʀpɛt/ nf pruning knife

serpillière /seʀpijɛʀ/ nf floorcloth

serpolet /seʀpɔlɛ/ nm wild thyme

serre /seʀ/ nf ① (maison de verre) greenhouse; **mettre qch en** or **sous** ~ to put sth in a greenhouse; **effet de** ~ greenhouse effect; ② (de rapace) talon, claw

serré, ~e /seʀe/
A adj ① (ajusté) [vis, écrou] tight; [jupe, pantalon] tight; **je suis ~e dans ma veste** my jacket is too tight; **robe ~e à la taille** dress fitted at the waist; ② (dense) [herbe] thick; [écriture] cramped; **en rangs ~s** in serried rows; **il tombait une pluie fine et ~e** it was drizzling; ③ fig [délais, budget] tight; [virage] sharp; [contrôle, gestion] strict; [lutte] hard; [débat, négociation] heated; [partie, match] close; ④ (fort) [café] very strong
B adv [écrire] in a cramped hand; [tricoter] tightly; **il va falloir jouer ~ si…** we can't take any chances if…

serre-livres /seʀlivʀ/ nm inv book end

serrement /seʀmã/ nm ① lit ~ **de main** handshake; ② fig **avoir** or **ressentir un** ~ **de cœur** to feel a pang

serrer /seʀe/ [1]
A vtr ① (maintenir vigoureusement) [personne] to grip [volant, rame]; ~ **qn/qch dans ses bras** to hug sb/sth; ~ **qch entre ses dents** to clench sth between one's teeth; ~ **la main de qn** to shake hands with sb; ~ **les poings** to clench one's fists; **la peur me serrait la gorge** my throat was constricted with fear; **ça me serre le cœur de voir ça** it wrings my heart to see that; ② (ajuster) to tighten [nœud, corde]; **serre bien tes lacets** do your shoelaces up tight; **tu as trop serré ton nœud de cravate** your tie is too tight; **mon chignon n'est pas assez serré** my bun is (too) loose; ③ (tenir à l'étroit) [chaussures, vêtement] to be too tight; ④ (bloquer) to tighten [écrou, vis, boulon]; to turn [sth] off tightly [robinet]; **sans** ~ [fixer, visser] loosely; ⑤ (être près de) ~ **le trottoir** [automobiliste] to hug the kerb GB ou curb US; ~ **à droite** [véhicule] to get ou stay in the right-hand lane; ~ **qn de près** [concurrent] to be hot on sb's tail; ~ **un sujet de près** fig [to study a subject closely; ⑥ (rapprocher) to push [sth] closer together [livres, tables, objets]; to squeeze [personne]; **être serré** [livres, personnes] to be packed together; **nous sommes trop serrés dans la cuisine** there are too many of us in the kitchen; ~ **les rangs** lit, fig to close ranks; ⑦ (réduire) to cut [dépenses, prix]; ⑧ Naut to furl [voile]; ~ **le vent** to sail close to the wind; ⑨ (ranger) liter, dial to stow [sth] away [objet précieux, économies]
B **se serrer** vpr ① (se rapprocher de) [personnes] to squeeze up; **ils se sont serrés les uns contre les autres** they huddled together; ② (se comprimer) **se** ~ **dans une jupe** to squeeze oneself into a skirt; **nous nous sommes serré la main** we shook hands; ③ (se contracter) **avoir le cœur qui se serre** to feel deeply upset; **avoir la gorge qui se serre** (d'émotion) to have a lump in one's throat; (de peur) to have one's heart in one's mouth

serre-tête, pl ~**s** /seʀtɛt/ nm hairband

serrure /seʀyʀ/ nf lock; **trou de** ~ keyhole

serrurerie /seʀyʀʀi/ nf ① ▸ p. 372 (boutique) locksmith's; ② (corps de métier) locksmith's trade

serrurier /seʀyʀje/ ▸ p. 372 nm locksmith

sertir /seʀtiʀ/ [3] vtr (en joaillerie) to set [pierre]

sérum /seʀɔm/ nm serum; ~ **antirabique** anti-rabies serum; **un** ~ **antivenimeux** an antivenin; ~ **physiologique** saline solution; ~ **sanguin** blood serum; ~ **de vérité** truth drug

servage /seʀvaʒ/ nm Hist serfdom

servant /seʀvã/
A adj m **chevalier** ~ devoted admirer
B nm ① Relig server; ② Mil (au canon) member of a gun crew

servante /seʀvãt/ ▸ p. 372 nf (domestique) maidservant

serve ▸ **serf**

serveur, -euse /seʀvœʀ, øz/ ▸ p. 372
A nm,f (dans café, restaurant) waiter/waitress
B nm ① Sport server; ② (aux cartes) dealer; ③ Ordinat server

servi, ~e /seʀvi/ adj (à table) **'prends de la viande'—'merci je suis déjà ~'** 'have some meat'—'I already have some, thank you'; **nous voulions du soleil, nous sommes ~s**○ we wanted some sunshine and we've certainly got it

serviable /seʀvjabl/ adj obliging, helpful

service /seʀvis/
A nm ① (action serviable, faveur) **je peux te demander un** ~? (action serviable) can I ask you to do something for me?; (faveur) can I ask you a favour^GB?; **elle m'a rendu de nombreux** ~**s** she's been very helpful; **il est toujours prêt à rendre** ~ he is always ready to help; ② (liaison) service; ~ **de bus** bus service; ③ (fonctionnement) **être en** ~ [ascenseur] (en train de fonctionner) to be working; (en état de fonctionner) to be in working order; [autoroute] to be open; [ligne de métro, de bus] to be running; **être hors** ~ [ascenseur] to be out of order; **entrer en** ~ [ligne de métro, autoroute] to be opened, to come into service; **mettre en** ~ to bring [sth] into service [appareil, véhicule]; to open [gare, autoroute, ligne de bus]; ④ (aide) **rendre** ~ **à qn** [machine, appareil] to be a help to sb; [route, passage, magasin] to be convenient (for sb); **ça peut toujours rendre** ~ it might come in handy; ⑤ (action de servir) service; **être au** ~ **de son pays** to serve one's country; **je suis à leur** ~ (employé) I work for them; (dévoué) I'm at their disposal; **'à votre** ~**!'** (je vous en prie) 'don't mention it!', 'not at all!'; **'que puis-je faire or qu'y a-t-il pour votre** ~?' 'may I help you?'; ⑥ (à table) service; **12% pour le** ~ 12% service charge; **faire le** ~ (servir les plats) to serve; (desservir) to act as waiter; **manger au premier** ~ to go to the first sitting; ⑦ (des gens de maison) (domestic) service; **entrer au** ~ **de qn** to go to work for sb; **prendre qn à son** ~ to take sb on, to engage sb; **escalier de** ~ backstairs (pl); service stairs (pl); ⑧ (obligations professionnelles) service; **avoir 20 ans de** ~ **dans une entreprise** to have worked with a firm 20 years; **être de** or **en** ~ to be on duty; **assurer le** ~ **de qn** to cover for sb; **son** ~ **se termine à** he/she comes off duty at; **être en** ~ **commandé** [policier] to be acting under orders; **état de** ~(s) record of service, service record; **le** ~ **de nuit** night duty; **pharmacie de** ~ duty chemist; **être l'idiot de** ~ to be the house clown; ⑨ (section administrative) department; ~ **des urgences** casualty department GB, emergency room US; ~ **de réanimation** intensive care unit; **les** ~**s secrets** the secret service (sg); **les** ~**s d'espionnage** or **de renseignements** the intelligence services; ~ **de dépannage** breakdown service; **les** ~**s du Premier Ministre se refusent à tout commentaire** the Prime Minister's office has refused to comment; **chef de** ~ (dans une administration) section head; (dans un hôpital) senior consultant; ⑩ Mil ~ **(militaire)** military ou national service; ~ **national** national service; ~ **civil** non-military national service; **partir au** ~○ to go off to do one's military service; ~ **en temps de paix** peace time service; **être bon pour le** ~ lit to be passed fit for military service; fig hum to be passed fit; **reprendre du** ~ to re-enlist, to sign up again; ⑪ (vaisselle) set; **un** ~ **à thé** a tea set; ~ **de table** dinner service; ⑫ Relig service; ⑬ Sport service, serve; **être au** ~ to serve ou be serving
B **services** nmpl services; **se passer des** ~**s de qn** to dispense with sb's services
⸨Composés⸩ ~ **après-vente** (département) after-sales service department; (activité) after-sales service; ~ **minimum** reduced service; ~ **d'ordre** stewards (pl); ~ **de presse** (de ministère, parti, d'entreprise) press office; (de maison d'édition) press and publicity department; (livre) review copy

serviette /seʀvjɛt/ nf ① (en tissu) ~ **(de toilette)** towel; ~ **(de table)** (table) napkin; ② (cartable) briefcase
⸨Composé⸩ ~ **hygiénique** sanitary towel
⸨Idiome⸩ **il ne faut pas mélanger les torchons et les** ~**s**○ you've got to know what's what

serviette-éponge, pl **serviettes-éponges** /seʀvjɛtepɔ̃ʒ/ nf terry towel

S

servile /sɛʀvil/ *adj* **1** (soumis) [*personne, attitude*] servile; [*fidélité, obéissance*] slavish; **2** (peu original) [*adaptation*] slavish; [*traduction*] over-literal; **3** Hist (de serf) servile; (de domestique) menial

servilement /sɛʀvilmɑ̃/ *adv* [*obéir*] slavishly; [*flatter*] obsequiously; (sans originalité) [*imiter, copier*] slavishly

servilité /sɛʀvilite/ *nf* (soumission) servility

servir /sɛʀviʀ/ [30]

A *vtr* **1** gén to serve; **le boucher m'a mal servi aujourd'hui** the butcher didn't give me very good meat today; **~ qch à qn**, **~ qn en qch** to serve sb (with) sth; **qu'est-ce que je vous sers (à boire)?** what would you like to drink?; **tu as été bien servi en gâteau** you've been given a generous helping of cake; **'Madame est servie'** 'dinner is served Madam'; **au moment de ~** before serving; **'~ frais'** 'serve chilled'; **~ la messe** to serve mass; **2** fig (être utile à) [*situation*] to help [*personne, cause*]; to serve [*intérêt*]; [*personne*] to further [*ambition, intérêt*]; **3** ◦(donner) **~ qch comme excuse** to use sth as an excuse; **4** Jeux to deal [*cartes*]

B **servir à** *vtr ind* **1** lit **~ à qn** [*pièce, maison, salle*] to be used by sb; **cette casserole me sert pour faire des confitures** I use this pan for making jam; **~ à qch** to be used for sth; **les exercices m'ont servi à comprendre la règle** the exercises helped me to understand the rule; **2** fig to come in useful; **cela ne sert à rien** (objet) it's useless; (action) it's no good; **cela ne sert à rien de faire** there's no point in doing; **~ à quelque chose** to serve a useful purpose; **~ à faire** to be used for doing

C **servir de** *vtr ind* (avoir la fonction) **~ d'intermédiaire à qn** to act as an intermediary for sb; **~ d'arme** to be used as a weapon

D *vi* **1** Mil **~ dans** to serve in; **2** Sport to serve; **3** (être employé) **il a servi dix ans chez nous** he was in our service for ten years; **~ dans un café** gén to work as a waiter in a café; (au bar) to work as a barman; **4** (être utilisé) to be used

E **se servir** *vpr* **1** (à boire, à manger) to help oneself; **se ~ un verre de vin** to pour oneself a glass of wine; **sers-toi bien** take plenty; **2** (dans un magasin) to serve oneself; (faire ses courses) **se ~ chez le boucher du coin** to shop at the local butcher's; **3** (faire usage de) **se ~ de qch/qn** to use sth/sb; **se ~ d'une situation** to make use of a situation; **4** Culin to be served

F *v impers* **il ne sert à rien de crier** there's no point in shouting

⟨Idiome⟩ **on n'est jamais si bien servi que par soi-même** Prov if you want something done it's better to do it yourself

serviteur /sɛʀvitœʀ/ *nm* servant; **'votre ~!'** (à votre service) 'at your service, sir *ou* madam!'; **votre ~** (moi-même) yours truly

servitude /sɛʀvityd/ *nf* lit servitude; fig constraint

servofrein /sɛʀvofʀɛ̃/ *nm* power(-assisted) brakes (*pl*)

ses ▸ son¹

sésame /sezam/ *nm* sesame

⟨Idiome⟩ **Sésame ouvre-toi!** open sesame!

session /sesjɔ̃/ *nf* **1** (réunion) session; **2** Scol, Univ examination session; **~ de rattrapage** retakes (*pl*); **3** (stage) course

sesterce /sɛstɛʀs/ *nm* sestertium

set /sɛt/ *nm* Sport set

⟨Composé⟩ **~ de table** place mat

seuil /sœj/ *nm* **1** (dalle) **~ (de la porte)** doorstep; (entrée) doorway; **franchir le ~** to cross the threshold; **2** fig threshold; **au ~ de** (de saison, carrière) at the beginning of; (de la mort, l'adolescence) on the threshold of

⟨Composés⟩ **~ de pauvreté** poverty line; **~ de rentabilité** break-even point

seul, ~e /sœl/ *adj* **1** (sans compagnie) alone, on one's own; **elle est venue toute ~e** she came alone; **elle m'a laissé ~** she left me on my own; **vous êtes ~ dans la vie?** are you single?; **elle veut vous parler ~ à ~ ou ~ à ~(e)** she wants to speak to you alone *ou* in private; **parler tout ~** to talk to oneself; **2** (sans aide) by oneself, on one's own; **je peux le faire ~** I can do it by myself *ou* on my own; **elle a mené la révolution à elle ~e** she single-handedly led the revolution; **il a mangé un poulet à lui tout ~** he ate a whole chicken all by himself; **ça va tout ~** (c'est facile) it's really easy; (c'est sans problèmes) things are running smoothly; **3** (unique) only; **une ~e femme** only one woman; **un**

~ d'entre eux only one of them; **la ~e et unique personne** the one and only person; **pas un ~ client** not a single customer; **l'espion et l'ambassadeur sont une ~e et même personne** the spy and the ambassador are one and the same person; **d'une ~e pièce** in one piece; **pour cette ~e raison** for this reason alone; **dans le ~ but de faire** with the sole aim of doing; **à la ~e idée de faire** at the very idea of doing; **~ de son espèce** unique; **ils ont parlé d'une ~e voix** they were unanimous; **4** (solitaire) lonely; **5** (avec valeur adverbiale) only; **elle ~e pourrait vous le dire** only she could tell you; **l'offre est réservée à nos ~s employés** the offer is open only to our employees; **6** (avec valeur nominale) **le ~**, **la ~e** the only one; **j'ai été le ~ à aimer le spectacle** I was the only one who enjoyed the show; **ils sont les ~s à croire que** they're alone in thinking that; **il n'y en a pas un ~ qui se soit levé** not a single person stood up

seulement /sœlmɑ̃/ *adv* **1** gén only; **nous étions ~ deux** *or* **deux ~** there were only the two of us; **'nous étions dix'—'~?'** 'there were ten of us'—'is that all?'; **j'ai compris ~ plus tard** I only realized later; **elle revient ~ demain** she's not coming back until tomorrow; **il ne nous a pas ~ remerciés** he didn't even thank us; **2** (toutefois) only, but; **c'est possible, ~ je veux y réfléchir** it's possible, only *ou* but I'd like to think about it; **3** (au moins) **si ~** if only

sève /sɛv/ *nf* **1** Bot sap; **2** fig vigour^GB

sévère /sevɛʀ/ *adj* gén severe; [*personne, éducation*] strict; [*sélection*] rigorous; [*jugement*] harsh; [*défaite, pertes*] heavy

sévèrement /sevɛʀmɑ̃/ *adv* gén severely; [*punir*] harshly; [*réglementer*] strictly; [*regarder*] sternly

sévérité /severite/ *nf* (dureté) strictness, harshness; (austérité) sternness, severity

sévices /sevis/ *nmpl* physical abuse **⊄**

sévir /seviʀ/ [3] *vi* **1** (punir) to clamp down (**contre** on); **2** (causer des ravages) [*tempête, guerre*] to rage; [*épidémie, pauvreté*] to be rife; [*voyou*] to be running wild; **la sécheresse sévit dans le pays** drought is ravaging the country; **3** fig [*doctrine*] to hold sway; [*délation*] to be rife; **mon ancien professeur sévit toujours au lycée** hum my former teacher is still pegging away at the school

sevrage /səvʀaʒ/ *nm* weaning

sevrer /səvʀe/ [16] *vtr* **1** lit to wean [*enfant, animal*]; **2** (priver) hum **~ qn de qch** to deprive sb of sth

sexagénaire /sɛksaʒenɛʀ/

A *adj* **être ~** to be in one's sixties

B *nmf* person in his/her sixties

sexe /sɛks/ *nm* **1** Biol sex; **indépendamment du ~, de l'ethnie, de l'âge** irrespective of gender, race or age; **un bébé de ~ féminin** a female baby; **2** (organes génitaux) genitals (*pl*); **3** (sexualité) sex

sexiste /sɛksist/ *adj, nmf* sexist

sexologue /sɛksɔlɔg/ ▸ p. 372 *nmf* sex therapist

sextant /sɛkstɑ̃/ *nm* sextant

sextuor /sɛkstɥɔʀ/ *nm* (œuvre, formation) sextet

sextupler /sɛkstyple/ [1]

A *vtr* to multiply [sth] by six

B *vi* [*bénéfices*] to increase sixfold

sexualité /sɛksɥalite/ *nf* sexuality

sexué, ~e /sɛksɥe/ *adj* [*plante*] sexed; [*reproduction*] sexual

sexuel, -elle /sɛksɥɛl/ *adj* gén sexual; [*éducation, glande*] sex

seyant, ~e /sɛjɑ̃, ɑ̃t/ *adj* becoming

SF /ɛsɛf/ *nf* (abbr = **science-fiction**) sci-fi

SFP /ɛsɛfpe/ *nf* (abbr = **Société française de production et de création audiovisuelles**) television and video production company

shampooing /ʃɑ̃pwɛ̃/ *nm* shampoo

shampouiner /ʃɑ̃pwine/ [1] *vtr* to shampoo

shampouineur, -euse /ʃɑ̃pwinœʀ, øz/ ▸ p. 372 *nm,f*: trainee hairdresser (who washes hair)

shérif /ʃeʀif/ *nm* sheriff

shetland /ʃetlɑ̃d/ *nm* **1** (laine) Shetland wool; **2** (poney) Shetland pony

shoot /ʃut/ *nm* **1** Sport shot; **2** ◦(de drogue) fix◦

shooter /ʃute/ [1]

A *vi* to shoot

B se shooter○ *vpr* to shoot up○

short /ʃɔʀt/ *nm* shorts (*pl*)

si¹ /si/

> ⚠ *Si* adverbe de degré modifiant un adjectif a deux traductions en anglais selon que l'adjectif modifié est attribut: *la maison est si jolie* = the house is so pretty, ou épithète: *une si jolie maison* = such a pretty house.
> Dans le cas de l'épithète il existe une deuxième possibilité, assez rare et littéraire, citée pour information: = so pretty a house.

A *nm inv* if; **des ~ et des mais** ifs and buts

B *adv* **[1]** (marquant l'affirmation) yes; **'tu ne le veux pas?'—'~!'** 'don't you want it?'—'yes I do!'; **mais ~** yes, of course; **[2]** (marquant l'intensité) so; **de ~ bon matin** so early in the morning; **c'est un homme ~ agréable** he's such a pleasant man; **je suis heureux de visiter votre ~ jolie ville** I'm glad to visit your town, it's so pretty; **~ bien que** (par conséquent) so; (à tel point que) so much so that; **tant et ~ bien que** so much so that; **[3]** (pour marquer la comparaison) **rien n'est ~ beau qu'un coucher de soleil** there's nothing so beautiful as a sunset; **est-elle ~ bête qu'on le dit?** is she as stupid as people say (she is)?; **[4]** (pour marquer la concession) **~ peu que ce soit** however little it may be

C *conj* (**s'** *before il or ils*) **[1]** (marquant l'éventualité) if; **~ ce n'est (pas) toi, qui est-ce?** if it wasn't you, who was it?, if not you, who?; **il n'a rien pris avec lui ~ ce n'est un livre** he didn't take anything with him apart from a book; **à quoi servent ces réunions ~ ce n'est à nous faire perdre notre temps?** what purpose do these meetings serve other than to waste our time?; **~ tant est qu'une telle distinction ait un sens** if such a distinction makes any sense; **c'est un brave homme s'il en est** he's a brave man if ever there was one; **[2]** (marquant l'hypothèse) if; **~ j'étais riche** if I were rich; **~ j'avais su!** if only I'd known!; **vous pensez ~ j'étais content!** you can imagine how happy I was!; **~ j'ai envie de partir? ah ça oui!** leave? of course I want to leave!; **je me demande s'il viendra** I wonder if *ou* whether he'll come; **[3]** (quand) if; **enfant, ~ je lisais, je n'aimais pas être dérangé** when I was a child I used to hate being disturbed if *ou* when I was reading; **[4]** (introduit une suggestion) **~ tu venais avec moi?** how about coming with me?; **~ tu venais passer le week-end avec nous?** why don't you come and spend the weekend with us?; **et s'il décidait de ne pas venir?** and what if he decided not to come?; **[5]** (pour marquer l'opposition) whereas; **~ la France est favorable au projet, les autres pays y sont violemment opposés** whereas France is in favour^GB of the project, the other countries are violently opposed to it

si² /si/ *nm inv* (note) B; (en solfiant) ti

siamois, **~e** /sjamwa, az/
A *adj* **[1]** Zool [*chat*] Siamese; **[2]** Méd **des frères ~** male Siamese twins; **des sœurs ~es** female Siamese twins
B *nm inv* **[1]** Ling Siamese; **[2]** Zool Siamese cat

sibyllin, **~e** /sibilɛ̃, in/ *adj* lit, fig sibylline

SICAV /sikav/ *nf* (*abbr* = **société d'investissement à capital variable**) unit trust GB, mutual fund US

sicilien, **-ienne** /sisiljɛ̃, ɛn/ ▸ p. 504
A *adj* Sicilian
B ▸ p. 336 *nm* Ling Sicilian

sida /sida/ ▸ p. 195 *nm* (*abbr* = **syndrome immunodéficitaire acquis**) Aids (+ *v sg*)

side-car, *pl* **~s** /sidkaʀ/ *nm* **[1]** (caisse) sidecar; **[2]** (moto et caisse) motorcycle combination

sidéral, **~e**, *mpl* **-aux** /sideʀal, o/ *adj* sidereal

sidérer /sideʀe/ **[14]** *vtr* to stagger○, to astonish

sidérurgie /sideʀyʀʒi/ *nf* steel industry

sidérurgique /sideʀyʀʒik/ *adj* steel (*épith*)

siècle /sjɛkl/ ▸ p. 582 *nm* **[1]** (cent ans) century; **au Ve ~ après J.-C.** in the 5th century AD; **l'art du XVIIe ~** 17th-century art; **au ~ dernier** in the last century; **d'ici la fin du ~** by the turn of the century; **être né avec le ~** to be born at the turn of the century; **un ~ de photographie** one hundred years of photography; **il y a des ~s○ que je ne suis venu ici** I haven't been here for ages; **[2]** (époque) age; **le ~ de Louis XIV** the age of Louis XIV; **il est d'un autre ~** he belongs to another age; **il faut vivre avec son ~** one must move with the times; **[3]** Relig world; **dans** *or* **pour les ~s des ~s** forever and ever

siège /sjɛʒ/ *nm* **[1]** (pour s'asseoir) seat; **~ avant** front seat; **[2]** (d'entreprise) **~ (social)** head office; (d'organisation) headquarters (*pl*); (d'évêché) see; (de tribunal) seat; **[3]** Pol (d'élu) seat; **perdre son ~** to lose one's seat; **[4]** Mil (de ville, forteresse) siege; **faire le ~ d'une ville** to besiege a town; **[5]** Anat seat; **le bébé se présente par le ~** the baby is in the breech position

siéger /sjeʒe/ **[15]** *vi* **[1]** (être membre) to sit; **~ au sénat** to sit in the senate; **[2]** (tenir séance) to be in session; **[3]** (résider) to have its headquarters

sien, **sienne** /sjɛ̃, sjɛn/

> ⚠ En anglais, le choix du possessif de la troisième personne du singulier est déterminé par le genre du 'possesseur'. Sont du masculin: les personnes de sexe masculin et les animaux domestiques mâles; sont du féminin: les personnes de sexe féminin, les animaux domestiques femelles et souvent les navires; sont du neutre les animaux non domestiques et les non-animés. La forme masculine est *his*: *il m'a donné le sien/la sienne/les siens/les siennes* = he gave me his. La forme féminine est *hers*: *elle m'a donné le sien/la sienne/les siens/les siennes* = she gave me hers. Pour le neutre on répète le nom avec l'adjectif possessif *its*.

A *adj poss* **cette maison est sienne à présent** the house is now his/hers

B **le sien**, **la sienne**, **les siens**, **les siennes** *pron poss* his/hers/its; **celui-là, c'est le ~** that's his/hers; **être de retour parmi les ~s** (sa famille) to be back with one's family; (ses amis) to be back among one's own friends; **elle a encore fait des siennes!** she's been up to mischief again!

sieste /sjɛst/ *nf* nap, siesta

sifflant, **~e** /siflɑ̃, ɑ̃t/ *adj* **[1]** gén [*voix, son*] hissing; [*respiration, toux*] wheezing; **[2]** [*consonne*] sibilant

sifflement /sifləmɑ̃/ *nm* (de personne, train) whistle; (de bouilloire, vent) whistling ℂ; (d'oiseau, insecte) chirping ℂ; (de serpent) hissing ℂ

siffler /sifle/ **[1]**
A *vtr* **[1]** (avec la bouche) to whistle [*air, chanson*]; (appeler) to whistle for [*personne, chien*]; (interpeller) to whistle at [*personne*]; **se faire ~** [*femme*] to get wolf-whistles; **[2]** Sport [*arbitre*] to blow one's whistle for [*faute, fin*]; **[3]** (huer) to hiss, to boo [*vedette, politicien*]
B *vi* **[1]** gén to whistle; [*projectile*] to whistle through the air; [*oiseau*] to chirp; [*serpent*] to hiss; **[2]** (dans un sifflet) to blow one's whistle

sifflet /siflɛ/ *nm* **[1]** (instrument) whistle; **[2]** (sifflement) (de locomotive) whistle; (de désapprobation) hiss, boo, catcalls (*pl*); (de bouilloire) whistling ℂ

(Idiome) **couper le ~ à qn○** (faire taire) to shut sb up○; (interloquer) to take the wind out of sb's sails

siffleur, **-euse** /siflœʀ, øz/ *adj* [*oiseau*] chirping; [*serpent*] hissing

siffloter /siflɔte/ **[1]**
A *vtr* to whistle [sth] to oneself
B *vi* to whistle away to oneself

sigle /sigl/ *nm* acronym

signal, *pl* **-aux** /siɲal, o/ *nm* signal; **le ~ du départ** gén, Mil the signal to leave; Sport the starting signal

(Composés) **~ d'alarme** alarm signal; **tirer le ~ d'alarme** lit to pull the alarm; fig to raise the alarm; **~ d'appel** Télécom call waiting service; **~ de détresse** Aviat, Naut distress signal; Aut emergency signal; **~ sonore** (de répondeur) tone

signalement /siɲalmɑ̃/ *nm* description

signaler /siɲale/ **[1]**
A *vtr* **[1]** (faire remarquer) to point sth out to sb; (faire savoir) to inform sb of sth; **[2]** (rappeler) **~ à qn que** to remind sb that; **[3]** (indiquer) to indicate [*travaux, danger*]; **un virage mal/bien signalé** a badly/well signposted bend; **[4]** (rapporter) to report [*fait, événement*]
B **se signaler** *vpr* **se ~ par qch** to distinguish oneself by sth

signalétique /siɲaletik/ *adj* descriptive; **photo ~** identity photograph; **renseignement ~** detail of identity; **fiche ~** specification sheet

signalisation /siɲalizasjɔ̃/ *nf* **[1]** (système) signalling^GB; **[2]** (réseau) signals (*pl*)

S

Composés ~ **horizontale** road markings (*pl*); ~ **de piste** Aviat runway lights and markings (*pl*); ~ **routière** roadsigns and markings (*pl*); ~ **verticale** roadsigns (*pl*)

signaliser /sinalize/ [1] *vtr* to signpost [*route*]; to put up signals along [*voie ferrée*]; to mark out and light [*piste d'atterrissage*]

signataire /sinatɛʀ/ *nmf* signatory

signature /sinatyʀ/ *nf* ① (inscription) signature; **apposer sa** ~ to append one's signature; ② (droit de signer) **avoir la** ~ **de qn** to have the right to sign for sb; **avoir la** ~ **sur un compte** to be authorized to sign on an account; ③ (fait de signer) signing (**de** of); ④ (engagement) **il a donné sa** ~ he signed, he put his signature to it; ⑤ (caractéristique) hallmarks (*pl*)

signe /sin/ *nm* ① gén sign; ~ **précurseur** omen; **c'est** ~ **de pluie** it's a sign of rain; ~ **distinctif** *or* **particulier** distinguishing feature; **c'était un** ~ **du destin** it was fate; ② (symbole) gén sign; (d'écriture) mark; ~**s de ponctuation** punctuation marks; **marquer qch d'un** ~ to put a mark against sth; ~ **astral** star sign; **placé sous le** ~ **de** marked by [*violence, espoir*]; ③ (geste) sign; **faire** ~ **à qn** lit to wave to sb; (contacter) to get in touch with sb; **faire de grands** ~**s à qn** to gesticulate to sb; **faire** ~ **à qn de** to motion sb to [*parler, commencer*]; to beckon sb to [*avancer, reculer*]; **il m'a fait** ~ **de la tête** (pour que je vienne) he beckoned to me; (pour me saluer) he nodded to me; (pour désapprouver) he shook his head; **d'un** ~ **de la main, elle m'a montré la cuisine** she pointed to the kitchen; **faire** ~ **que oui/que non** to indicate agreement/disagreement; **faire comprendre par un** ~ **que** to indicate that; **échanger des** ~**s d'intelligence avec qn** (regards) to exchange knowing looks with sb; (gestes) to make meaningful signs at sb

Idiome **il n'a pas donné** ~ **de vie depuis six mois** there's been no sign of him for six months

signer /sine/ [1]

A *vtr* to sign; **il signe son troisième roman** he's written his third novel; **un parfum signé Fior** a perfume by Fior; **ça, c'est signé ta sœur**^O! that's your sister all over^O!; ~ **son arrêt de mort** to sign one's own death warrant; **le disque compact a signé la fin du 33 tours** the compact disc signalled^{GB} the end of the LP

B *vi* (s'exprimer en langage des signes) to sign, to use sign language

C **se signer** *vpr* to cross oneself

signet /sinɛ/ *nm* bookmark

signifiant, ~e /sinifjɑ̃, ɑ̃t/
A *adj* Ling significant, meaningful
B *nm* Ling signifier

significatif, -ive /sinifikatif, iv/ *adj* significant

signification /sinifikasjɔ̃/ *nf* ① (sens) gén meaning; Ling signification; ② (portée) importance; **avoir une** ~ **politique** to be politically significant; ③ Jur notification

signifié /sinifje/ *nm* Ling signified

signifier /sinifje/ [1] *vtr* ① to mean; **qu'est-ce que ça signifie?** (question normale) what does it mean?; (ton mécontent) what is the meaning of this?; ② (notifier) ~ **qch à qn** fml to inform sb of sth; Jur to notify sb of sth; ~ **son congé à qn** to give sb notice

silence /silɑ̃s/ *nm* ① (absence de bruit) silence; ② (fait de se taire) silence; '**un peu de** ~ **s'il vous plaît**' 'quiet please'; **en** ~ in silence; **garder le** ~ to keep silent; **réduire qn au** ~ (empêcher de s'exprimer) to reduce sb to silence; (tuer) to silence sb; **réduire un mouvement au** ~ to quell a movement; **passer qch sous** ~ to say nothing about sth; ③ Mus rest

silencieusement /silɑ̃sjøzmɑ̃/ *adv* silently

silencieux, -ieuse /silɑ̃sjø, øz/
A *adj* ① gén silent; ② (peu bruyant) [*aspirateur, moteur*] quiet
B *nm* ① (sur une arme) silencer; ② Aut (de pot d'échappement) silencer GB, muffler US

silex /silɛks/ *nm inv* (roche, objet) flint

silhouette /silwɛt/ *nf* (en contre-jour) silhouette; (dans l'obscurité) (de personne) figure; (d'objet) shape; (dans le lointain) outline

silice /silis/ *nf* silica

silicium /silisjɔm/ *nm* silicon

silicone /silikɔn/ *nf* silicone

sillage /sijaʒ/ *nm* ① (de navire) wake; (d'avion) (visible) vapour^{GB} trail; (invisible) slipstream; ② (de personne) wake; (de parfum) trail; ③ Phys wake

sillon /sijɔ̃/ *nm* ① Agric furrow; ② (rainure) line; ③ (ride profonde) furrow; ④ Anat, Zool fissure; ⑤ Audio (de disque) groove; ⑥ Géog line

sillonner /sijone/ [1] *vtr* ① (parcourir) [*personne, bicyclette, automobile*] to go up and down; [*aéronef*] to fly to and fro across; [*navire*] to sail to and fro across; [*réseau*] to crisscross; ② (creuser) to furrow

simagrée /simagʀe/ *nf* play-acting **¢**

simiesque /simjɛsk/ *adj* ape-like

similaire /similɛʀ/ *adj* similar (à to)

similicuir /similikɥiʀ/ *nm* imitation leather, Leatherette®

similitude /similityd/ *nf* gén, Math similarity

simple /sɛ̃pl/
A *adj* ① (facile) **c'est (bien)** ~, **il ne fait plus rien** he simply doesn't do anything any more; ② (sans prétention) [*repas, cérémonie, mariage, vie, goûts*] simple; [*décoration, intérieur*] plain; [*vêtement*] simple, plain; [*personne, air*] unaffected, unpretentious; **une jupe toute** ~ a very plain skirt; ③ (modeste) [*origines*] modest; **venir d'un milieu** ~ to come from a modest background; ④ (ordinaire) [*fonctionnaire, travailleur*] ordinary; **c'est une** ~ **question de bon sens** it's just common sense; **un** ~ **tour de clé suffit** just one turn of the key does it; **il est** ~ **garçon de café** he's just a waiter in a café; **même en hiver, il n'est vêtu que d'une** ~ **chemise** even in winter he only *ou* just wears a shirt; **pour la** ~ **raison que** for the simple reason that; **le** ~ **fait de poser la question** the mere fact of asking the question; **par** ~ **curiosité** out of pure curiosity; **sur** ~ **présentation du passeport** on presentation of one's passport; **ce ne sera qu'une** ~ **formalité/vérification** it will be a mere formality/a simple check; **réduire qch à sa plus** ~ **expression** to reduce sth to a minimum, to pare sth down to basics; ⑤ (peu intelligent) [*personne*] simple; ⑥ Chimie, Bot simple; ⑦ Ling [*passé, futur*] simple; ⑧ (non multiple) [*cornet de glace, nœud*] single
B *nm* ① (dans un calcul) **le prix varie du** ~ **au double** the price can turn out to be twice as high; ② Sport ~ **dames/ messieurs** ladies'/men's singles (*pl*)

simplement /sɛ̃pləmɑ̃/ *adv* ① (seulement) [*approuver, déclarer, rappeler*] just; **vas-y,** ~ **fais attention** you can go, only be careful; ② (sans sophistication) [*se vêtir, vivre*] simply; (absolument) simply; **tout** ~ quite simply; ③ (sans difficulté) easily

simplet, -ette /sɛ̃plɛ, ɛt/ *adj* simple-minded

simplicité /sɛ̃plisite/ *nf* ① (facilité) simplicity; **grâce à sa** ~ **d'utilisation** because it's so easy to use; ② (caractère) (de personne) unpretentiousness, lack of pretention; (de choses) simplicity; **recevoir qn en toute** ~ to entertain sb very unpretentiously; **avec** ~ simply

Composé ~ **d'esprit** simple-mindedness

simplifier /sɛ̃plifje/ [2]
A *vtr* ① gén to simplify; ② Math to reduce [*fraction*]
B **se simplifier** *vpr* **se** ~ **la vie** to make life easier for oneself

simpliste /sɛ̃plist/ *adj* simplistic

simulacre /simylakʀ/ *nm* liter ① (action simulée) pretence^{GB}; ~ **de procès** mock trial; ② (travesti) pej sham; ~ **de justice** travesty of justice; ~ **de bonheur** illusion of happiness

simulateur, -trice /simylatœʀ, tʀis/
A *nm,f* (personne qui feint) shammer, faker; (faux malade) malingerer
B *nm* Tech simulator; ~ **de vol** flight simulator

simulation /simylasjɔ̃/ *nf* ① gén, Méd simulation; (pour éviter une corvée) malingering **¢**; ② (en science) (méthode) simulation

simuler /simyle/ [1] *vtr* ① (feindre) to feign, to simulate [*attaque, émotion, sentiment*]; ② Ordinat, Tech (reproduire) to simulate

simultané, ~e /simyltane/ *adj* simultaneous

simultanéité /simyltaneite/ *nf* simultaneity

sincère /sɛ̃sɛʀ/ *adj* ① (dont on ne peut douter) [*personne, confession, regret, affection*] sincere; [*ami*] true (épith); (non feint) [*émotion, offre, soutien*] genuine; (franc) [*opinion, portrait*] honest; **sois** ~ **pour une fois!** be honest for once!; ② (en correspondance) ~**s condoléances** sincere *ou* heartfelt sympathy **¢**

sincèrement /sɛ̃sɛʀmɑ̃/ adv ⟨1⟩ (sans feindre) [regretter, croire] sincerely; [penser] really; [remercier, parler, s'exprimer] sincerely; **dis-moi ~ ce que tu en penses** tell me honestly what you think of it; **je suis ~ désolé** I'm truly sorry; ⟨2⟩ (franchement) frankly

sincérité /sɛ̃seʀite/ nf (de personne, paroles, d'affection) sincerity; (de réponse, d'opinion) honesty; (d'offre, de soutien) genuineness

sinécure /sinekyʀ/ nf sinecure

singe /sɛ̃ʒ/ nm ⟨1⟩ Zool monkey; (sans queue) ape; **les grands ~s** the apes, the large primates; ⟨2⟩ fig (imitateur) mimic; (personne agile) **c'est un vrai ~** he's very agile; **faire le ~** to clown about GB ou around

(Idiomes) **malin comme un ~** as cunning ou sly as a fox; **payer en monnaie de ~** to let sb whistle for his/her money; **ce n'est pas à un vieux ~ qu'on apprend à faire la grimace** Prov don't teach your grandmother to suck eggs

singer /sɛ̃ʒe/ [13] vtr to ape [personne, manière]; to feign, to fake [attitude, sentiment]

singeries /sɛ̃ʒʀi/ nfpl (grimaces) faces; (pitreries) antics; **faire des ~** to monkey about GB ou around

singulariser: se singulariser /sɛ̃gylaʀize/ [1] vpr to call attention to oneself; **se ~ par qch/en faisant qch** to distinguish oneself by sth/by doing sth

singularité /sɛ̃gylaʀite/ nf ⟨1⟩ (chose anormale) peculiarity, singularity; ⟨2⟩ (caractère unique) uniqueness; ⟨3⟩ Phys singularity

singulier, -ière /sɛ̃gylje, ɛʀ/
A adj ⟨1⟩ (insolite) peculiar; **un personnage ~** an unusual character; ⟨2⟩ (individuel) **combat ~** single combat
B nm ⟨1⟩ Ling singular; ⟨2⟩ (caractère étonnant) singularity

singulièrement /sɛ̃gyljɛʀmɑ̃/ adv ⟨1⟩ (curieusement) oddly; ⟨2⟩ (beaucoup) radically

sinistre /sinistʀ/
A adj ⟨1⟩ [personnage, projet] sinister; [bruit, lueur] sinister, ominous; [lieu, paysage, avenir] bleak; [soirée, invité] dreary; ⟨2⟩ (before n) **de ~s crétins**○/**crapules** absolute idiots/crooks
B nm (désastre) disaster; (accident) accident; (incendie) blaze

sinistré /sinistʀe/
A adj [personne, famille, pays] stricken (épith); **région ~e** disaster area
B nm,f disaster victim

sinon /sinɔ̃/
A conj ⟨1⟩ (autrement) otherwise, or else; **arrête ~ je crie/je me fâche!** stop or (else) I'll scream/I'll get cross!; ⟨2⟩ (à part) except, apart from; ⟨3⟩ (pour ne pas dire) not to say; **c'est devenu difficile ~ impossible** it has become difficult if not impossible
B sinon que loc conj except that, other than that

sinueux, -euse /sinɥø, øz/ adj [ligne] sinuous; [cours d'eau] winding, meandering; [sentier] winding; [approche] tortuous

sinus /sinys/ nm inv ⟨1⟩ Anat sinus; ⟨2⟩ Math sine

sinusite /sinyzit/ ▸ p. 195 nf sinusitis 𝒞

sionisme /sjɔnism/ nm Zionism

siphon /sifɔ̃/ nm ⟨1⟩ (tuyau) gén siphon; (d'évier, de lavabo) U-bend; ⟨2⟩ (bouteille) siphon (bottle)

siphonné○, **~e** /sifɔne/ adj nuts○, crazy○

sire /siʀ/ nm Hist Sire; **un triste ~** a disreputable character

sirène /siʀɛn/ nf ⟨1⟩ gén, Mil siren; (de bateau) foghorn; (d'usine) hooter GB, siren; **~ des pompiers** (dans la ville) fire siren; (sur un camion) fire engine siren; ⟨2⟩ (de mythologie) mermaid; (au chant fatal) siren

(Composé) **~ d'alarme** fire alarm

sirop /siʀo/ nm ⟨1⟩ Culin (pour dessert) syrup GB ou sirup US; (boisson) cordial; **~ d'érable** maple syrup GB ou sirup US; **~ de fraise** strawberry cordial; **~ de citron/d'orange** ≈ lemon/orange squash; ⟨2⟩ (médicament) syrup GB ou sirup US, mixture; **~ pectoral** cough mixture

siroter○ /siʀote/ [1] vtr to sip

sirupeux, -euse /siʀypø, øz/ adj lit, fig syrupy GB, sirupy US

sis, ~e /si, siz/ adj located

sismique /sismik/ adj seismic

sismologue /sismɔlɔg/ ▸ p. 372 nmf seismologist

site /sit/ nm ⟨1⟩ (lieu pittoresque) gén area; **~ touristique** or **pittoresque** place of interest; **visitez les ~s d'Égypte** visit Egypt's historic sites; **les merveilleux ~s de la Côte d'Azur** the splendours^GB of the Côte d'Azur; **~ archéologique** archeological site; **~ classé** conservation area; ⟨2⟩ Ind, Comm (lieu d'une implantation particulière) site

sitôt /sito/

⚠ *Sitôt* conjonction et préposition se traduit le plus souvent par *as soon as*. Mais attention au choix du temps: *sitôt rentré de voyage* (qu'il rentrera) = as soon as he gets back from his trip; (qu'il est rentré) = as soon as he got back from his trip; *sitôt la fin du mauvais temps* (dans le passé) = as soon as the bad weather was over; (dans l'avenir) = as soon as the bad weather is over.

A adv **~ après** (tout de suite) immediately after; (peu de temps) soon after; **elle est arrivée ~ après** she arrived soon afterwards; **nous partirons ~ après** we'll leave immediately afterwards; **je n'y retournerai pas de ~** I won't go back there in a hurry○
B conj **~ que** as soon as

(Idiome) **~ dit, ~ fait**† no sooner said than done

situation /sitɥasjɔ̃/ nf ⟨1⟩ (ensemble de conditions) situation; **une population en ~ d'extrême pauvreté** a population suffering extreme poverty; **~ financière** financial standing ou status; ⟨2⟩ (emploi) job, position; ⟨3⟩ (emplacement) location (de of)

(Composés) **~ de famille** marital status, family status; **~ militaire** status as regards military service

situer /sitɥe/ [1]
A vtr ⟨1⟩ (déterminer la position de) (dans l'espace) to locate [ville, pays]; (dans le temps) to place; **notre maison est située dans le nord d'Oxford** our house is on the north side of Oxford; **l'hôtel est bien situé** the hotel is in a good location; **~ un événement dans le temps** to situate an event historically; ⟨2⟩ (définir) to situate [écrivain, œuvre]; ⟨3⟩ (placer) **~ une histoire en 2001/à Palerme** to set a story in 2001/in Palermo
B se situer vpr ⟨1⟩ (se dérouler) **se ~ à Paris/à l'époque de la Révolution** to be set in Paris/at the time of the Revolution; ⟨2⟩ (être) **politiquement, je me situe plutôt à gauche/droite** politically I'm more to the left/right

six /sis, but before consonant si, and before vowel siz/ ▸ p. 398, p. 296, p. 155 adj inv, pron, nm inv six

sixième /sizjɛm/ ▸ p. 398, p. 155
A adj sixth
B nf Scol first year of secondary school, age 11–12

skaï® /skaj/ nm imitation leather, Leatherette®

skate-board, pl **~s** /skɛtbɔʀd/ ▸ p. 327 nm (objet) skateboard; (activité) skateboarding

sketch, pl **~es** /skɛtʃ/ nm (au théâtre) sketch

ski /ski/ ▸ p. 327 nm ⟨1⟩ (matériel) ski; **chausser des ~s** to put on skis; ⟨2⟩ (activité) **le ~** skiing; **faire du ~** to ski, to go skiing; **station de ~** ski resort

(Composés) **~ alpin** Alpine skiing; **~ de descente** = **~ de piste**; **~ de fond** (activité) cross-country skiing; (matériel) cross-country ski; **~ nautique** water skiing; **~ nordique** Nordic skiing; **~ de piste** (activité) downhill skiing; (matériel) downhill ski

skier /skje/ [2] vi to ski

skieur, -ieuse /skjœʀ, øz/ nm,f skier

slalom /slalɔm/ nm slalom; **faire du ~** lit to slalom

slalomer /slalɔme/ [1] vi ⟨1⟩ Sport to slalom (entre between); ⟨2⟩ fig to zigzag (entre between)

slave /slav/ adj Slavonic

slip /slip/ nm ⟨1⟩ (d'homme) underpants (pl) GB, undershorts (pl) US; (de femme) knickers (pl), pants (pl) GB, panties (pl) US; ⟨2⟩ Naut slipway

(Composé) **~ de bain** (d'homme) bathing trunks (pl)

slogan /slɔgɑ̃/ nm slogan

Slovaquie /slɔvaki/ ▸ p. 230 nprf Slovakia

Slovénie /slɔveni/ ▸ p. 230 nprf Slovenia

slow /slo/ nm slow dance; **danser un ~ avec qn** to dance a slow number with sb

smala○ /smala/ nf (famille) tribe○

smasher /smaʃe/ [1]
A vtr to smash [balle]

s

B *vi* to play a smash

SME /ɛsɛmə/ *nm: abbr* ▸ **système**

SMIC /smik/ *nm: abbr* ▸ **salaire**

smocks /smɔk/ *nmpl* smocking ₵

smoking /smɔkiŋ/ *nm* dinner jacket GB, tuxedo

SMS /ɛsɛmɛs/ *nm (abbr* = **short message service)** Télécom SMS

SNCF /ɛsɛnseɛf/ *nf (abbr* = **Société nationale des chemins de fer français)** *French national railway company*

> ⓘ SNCF The state-owned rail company, with access also to private finance, founded in 1937. Its remit covers the full range of rail transport services from small local trains to the high speed TGV.

snob /snɔb/

A *adj* [*personne*] stuck-up○; [*endroit, restaurant, soirée*] posh

B *nmf* snob; **c'est un ~** he's a snob

snober /snɔbe/ [1] *vtr* to snub [*personne*]

snobisme /snɔbism/ *nm* snobbery

sobre /sɔbʀ/ *adj* ① (qui mange et boit peu) abstemious; (qui ne boit jamais d'alcool) teetotal; (qui n'a pas trop bu) sober; **il est très ~ ce soir** he's being very abstemious tonight; **je suis ~, je peux conduire** I'm sober, so I can drive; ② (mesuré) [*personne*] temperate, sober, moderate; [*discours, récit, langage*] sober, low-key; [*vie*] simple; ③ (simple) [*style*] plain, sober; [*architecture, décoration, vêtement, mise en scène*] sober

sobrement /sɔbʀəmã/ *adv* ① (avec modération) [*manger, boire*] in moderation; ② (simplement) [*s'habiller*] plainly, soberly; [*dire*] soberly

sobriété /sɔbʀijete/ *nf* ① (fait de ne pas boire) temperance, sobriety sout; ② (réserve) (de personne) restraint, sobriety sout; (de discours, critique) moderation; ③ (de style, ligne, mise en scène, d'art) sobriety sout

sobriquet /sɔbʀikɛ/ *nm* nickname

soc /sɔk/ *nm* ploughshare GB, plowshare US

sociabilité /sɔsjabilite/ *nf* sociability

sociable /sɔsjabl/ *adj* ① gén [*personne, tempérament*] sociable; ② Sociol social

social, ~e, *mpl* **-iaux** /sɔsjal, o/

A *adj* ① (relatif à la vie en société) social; **sur le plan ~** in social terms; **mesures ~es** social policy measures; ② (propre à la société) social; **les origines ~es de qn, le milieu ~ de qn** sb's social background; ③ (relatif au travail) **conflit ~** industrial *ou* trade dispute

B *nm* **le ~** social issues (*pl*); **faire du ~** [*gouvernement*] to take a keen interest in social issues

social-démocratie /sɔsjaldemɔkʀasi/ *nf* social democracy

socialement /sɔsjalmã/ *adv* socially; **être ~ pris en charge** to be in the care of the social services

socialiser /sɔsjalize/ [1] *vtr* ① Sociol to socialize [*individus*]; ② Écon, Pol to collectivize

socialisme /sɔsjalism/ *nm* socialism

socialiste /sɔsjalist/ *adj, nmf* socialist

sociétaire /sɔsjetɛʀ/ *nmf* member

société /sɔsjete/ *nf* ① gén, Sociol society; ② (groupe spécifique) society; **~ de chasse** hunting club; ③ (entreprise) company; **~ de nettoyage** cleaning company; ④ (vie mondaine) society; **en ~** in society; **la bonne/haute ~** polite/ high society; (compagnie) fml company, society sout; **rechercher la ~ de qn** to seek sb's company

socioculturel, -elle /sɔsjokyltyʀɛl/ *adj* [*rapports*] sociocultural; **centre ~** recreation centre^{GB}

socio-démocrate, *pl* **~s** /sɔsjodemɔkʀat/

A *adj* social democratic

B *nmf* social democrat

socio-éducatif, -ive, *mpl* **~s** /sɔsjoedykatif, iv/ *adj* [*programme, système*] socioeducational

sociologie /sɔsjɔlɔʒi/ *nf* sociology

sociologique /sɔsjɔlɔʒik/ *adj* sociological

sociologue /sɔsjɔlɔg/ ▸ p. 372 *nmf* sociologist

socioprofessionnel, -elle /sɔsjopʀɔfɛsjɔnɛl/ *adj* social and occupational

socle /sɔkl/ *nm* ① (base) (de statue, pilier) pedestal, plinth; (de lampe, construction) base; (d'appareil) stand; ② fig (base) basis; ③ Géog platform

socquette /sɔkɛt/ *nf* ankle sock, anklet US

soda /sɔda/ *nm* (eau gazeuse) soda water; (boisson gazeuse sucrée) fizzy drink GB, soda US

sodium /sɔdjɔm/ *nm* sodium

sodomiser /sɔdɔmize/ [1] *vtr* to sodomize, to bugger

sœur /sœʀ/ *nf* ① (dans la famille) sister; **~ jumelle** twin sister; ② Relig sister; **une ~** a nun; **elle est allée à l'école chez les ~s** she went to a convent school

sœurette○ /sœʀɛt/ *nf* sis○, sister

soi /swa/ *pron pers* ① (personne) **autour de ~** around one; **pour une meilleure connaissance de ~** for better self-knowledge; **apprendre la maîtrise de ~** to learn self-control; **rester maître de ~** to keep one's self-control; **laisser la porte se refermer derrière ~** to let the door shut behind one; **développer sa confiance en ~** to build up one's self-confidence; **la haine de ~** self-loathing; **trouver en ~ les ressources nécessaires** to find the necessary inner resources; **garder qch pour ~** to keep sth to oneself; **malgré ~ on est ému** you can't help being moved; ② (objet, concept, idée) **un épisode banal en ~** an episode that is in itself commonplace; **la logique n'est pas un objectif en ~** logic is not an end in itself; **aller de ~** to go without saying; **ça devrait aller de ~** it should be obvious; **le parallèle allait de ~ entre...** there was an obvious parallel between...; **publier une œuvre de cette nature ne va pas de ~** publishing a work of this kind is a complicated business

soi-disant /swadizã/

A *adj inv* ① (qui prétend être) self-styled; ② (prétendu) controv [*démocratie, liberté, miracle*] so-called (*épith*)

B *adv* (prétendument) supposedly; **elle a ~ la migraine** she has a migraine, or so she says

soie /swa/ *nf* ① (tissu) silk; ② (poil) bristle; **une brosse à cheveux en ~s naturelles** a bristle hairbrush; ③ Bot awn; ④ Tech (de couteau) tang

soierie /swaʀi/ *nf* ① (étoffe) silk; ② Ind silk industry; ③ Comm silk trade

soif /swaf/ *nf* ① (besoin de boire) thirst; **avoir ~** to be thirsty; **mourir de ~** lit to die of thirst; fig to be dying of thirst; **boire jusqu'à plus ~** to drink one's fill; **donner ~** to make one thirsty; **il fait ~**○! hum it's thirsty work! hum; ② (désir) **~ de** thirst for [*justice, liberté, revanche, amour*]; hunger *ou* lust for [*pouvoir, richesses*]; **la ~ d'apprendre** the thirst for knowledge; **avoir ~ d'affection** to crave affection

(Idiome) **conserver une poire pour la ~** to save something for a rainy day

soignant, ~e /swaɲã, ãt/ *adj* [*personnel, équipe*] medical (*épith*); **médecin ~** doctor, GP

soigné, ~e /swaɲe/

A *pp* ▸ **soigner**

B *pp adj* ① (bien entretenu) [*mains, ongles*] well-manicured; [*coiffure, vêtements, tenue*] immaculate; **il est très ~ de sa personne** he's very well-groomed; **individu peu ~** unkempt person; ② (bien fait) [*catalogue, revue, édition*] carefully produced; [*emballage, maquette*] carefully done; [*conception, organisation, tactique*] carefully thought out; [*travail*] meticulous

soigner /swaɲe/ [1]

A *vtr* ① (chercher à guérir) to treat [*personne, animal, maladie*]; **faire ~ qn** to get sb treatment; **il faut te faire ~**○! hum you should have your head examined!; ② (s'occuper de) to look after [*personne, animal, client*]; ③ (faire attention à) to take care over [*tenue, présentation*]; to look after [*mains*]; **soignez votre écriture** take care over your writing

B se soigner *vpr* ① (chercher à se guérir) to treat oneself; **soigne-toi bien!** look after yourself!; ② (pouvoir être guéri) [*maladie*] to be treatable; **ça se soigne, tu sais!** hum (time to) get the men in white coats! hum; ③ (veiller à sa tenue) to take care over one's appearance; (veiller à son bien-être) to take care of oneself

soigneusement /swaɲøzmã/ *adv* [*ranger, laver, examiner, décrire, choisir, préparer, éviter*] carefully; [*travailler*] meticulously; [*écrire, colorier*] neatly

soigneux, -euse /swaɲø, øz/ *adj* ① (consciencieux) conscientious; (précautionneux) careful; ② (propre et ordonné) [*personne*] neat, tidy; ③ (bien fait) [*examen, recherche*] careful

soi-même /swamɛm/ *pron pers* oneself; **être ~** to be oneself; **la connaissance de ~** knowing oneself, self-knowledge; **le plaisir de faire ~ des confitures** the pleasure of making one's own jam

soin /swɛ̃/
A nm **1** (application) care; **avec ~** [choisir, préparer, travailler] carefully; **sans ~** carelessly; **prendre ~ de qch** to take care of sth; **prendre ~ de qn/sa santé** to look after sb/one's health; **nous avons pris ~ d'éviter toute confrontation** we were careful to avoid any confrontation; **prendre ~ de sa petite personne** to coddle oneself; **laisser à qn le ~ de faire** to leave it to sb to do; **2** (en cosmétique) (produit) product; **~ antipelliculaire** dandruff treatment
B soins nmpl **1** Méd (traitement) treatment **C**; (ensemble d'activités, service) care **C**; **recevoir des ~s** to receive treatment; **~s dentaires** dental care; **les premiers ~ à donner aux brûlés** first-aid treatment for burns; **~s à domicile** homecare **C**; **2** (en cosmétique) care **C**; **~s corporels** or **du corps** body care **C**; **~s du visage** skincare **C**; **3** (attention) care **C**; **'aux bons ~s de'** 'care of', 'c/o'; **publié par mes ~s** published by my good offices
(Idiome) **être aux petits ~s pour qn** to attend to sb's every need

soir /swaʀ/ nm **1** (fin du jour) evening; (partie de la nuit) night; **travailler le ~** to work in the evening, to work evenings; **le ~ du 3, le 3 au ~** on the evening of the 3rd; **par un beau ~ d'été** on a fine summer evening; **le ~ venu** when evening fell; **nous partirons samedi ~** we'll leave on Saturday evening; **il sort tous les samedis ~** he goes out every Saturday night; **6 heures du ~** 6 (o'clock) in the evening; (pour un horaire) 6 pm; **à ce ~!** see you tonight!; **2** (soirée) evening; **3** (déclin) liter twilight

soirée /swaʀe/ nf **1** (période) evening; **dans** or **pendant la ~**, **en ~** in the evening; **en début/fin de ~** at the beginning/end of the evening; **la pièce sera jouée en ~** there will be an evening performance of the play; **2** (réception) party; **aller dans une** or **en ~** to go to a party; **donner une ~** to give a party; **3** (spectacle) evening performance ou show

soit¹ /swa/
A ▸ **être¹**
B conj **1** (marque une alternative) **~, ~** either, or; **~ du fromage, ~ un gâteau** either cheese, or a cake; **elle suggère ~ que vous veniez chez nous, ~ qu'on aille au restaurant** she suggests that either you come to our place, or that we eat out; **c'est ~ l'un ~ l'autre, pas les deux** it's got to be one thing or the other, not both; **2** (à savoir) that is, ie; **toutes mes économies, ~ 200 euros** all my savings, ie ou that is, 200 euros; **3** Math **~ un triangle ABC** let ABC be a triangle.

⚠️ L'usage hésite, en mathématiques, entre la forme invariable de la conjonction et la forme verbale qui se met facultativement au pluriel (*soit* ou *soient* deux vecteurs), mais la traduction reste la même.

soit² /swat/ adv very well; **je me suis trompé, ~, mais là n'est pas la question** all right, so I was wrong, but that's not the point

soixantaine /swasɑ̃tɛn/ nf **avoir la ~** to be about sixty; **une ~ de kilomètres** about sixty kilometres^GB

soixante /swasɑ̃t/ ▸ p. 398, p. 155 adj inv, pron sixty

soixante-dix /swasɑ̃tdis/ ▸ p. 398, p. 155 adj inv, pron seventy

soixante-dixième /swasɑ̃tdizjɛm/ ▸ p. 398 adj seventieth

soixantième /swasɑ̃tjɛm/ ▸ p. 398 adj sixtieth

soja /sɔʒa/ nm soya bean GB, soybean US; **pâté de** or **au ~** soya GB ou soybean pâté; **sauce de ~** soy sauce; **salade de (pousses de) ~** bean sprout salad

sol /sɔl/ nm **1** (à l'extérieur) ground; (dans une maison) floor; **une maison au ~ en terre battue** a house with a trodden earth floor; **sentir le ~ se dérober sous ses pieds** lit to feel the ground giving way; fig to feel as if one is about to faint; **vitesse au ~ d'un avion** ground speed of an aeroplane; **la surface au ~ d'un bâtiment** the floor surface of a building; **exercices au ~** Sport floor exercises; **2** (territoire) soil; **le ~ africain** African soil; **3** (terrain) soil; **~ argileux** clay soil; **4** Mus (note) G; (en solfiant) soh; **5** (monnaie) sol

solaire /sɔlɛʀ/
A adj [calendrier, énergie] solar; [moteur, radio] solar-powered; [lumière, crème] sun (épith)
B nm (énergie) solar energy

soldat /sɔlda/ ▸ p. 283, p. 372 nm soldier, serviceman

solde¹ /sɔld/
A nm Fin balance; **faire le ~ d'un compte** to settle an account; **reçu pour ~ de tout compte** received in full and final payment
B en solde loc adv **acheter une veste en ~** to buy a jacket in a sale ou at sale price GB ou on sale US
C soldes nmpl sales; (écrit en vitrine) sale (sg)

solde² /sɔld/ nf Mil pay; **avoir qn à sa ~** fig to have sb in one's pay; **être à la ~ de l'ennemi** fig to be in the pay of the enemy ou the enemy's pay

solder /sɔlde/ [1]
A vtr **1** Comm to sell off, to clear [marchandises]; **2** to settle the balance of [compte]
B se solder vpr (finir) **se ~ par qch** to end in sth; **se ~ par un échec** [efforts] to end in failure

solderie /sɔldəʀi/ nf discount shop

soldeur, -euse /sɔldœʀ, øz/ ▸ p. 372 nm,f discount trader

soleil /sɔlɛj/ nm **1** gén sun; **~ de minuit** midnight sun; **au ~** in the sun; **se mettre au ~** [personne, animal] (s'exposer) to go into the sun; (rester) to sit in the sun; **le ~ se lève à l'est** the sun rises in the east; **en plein ~** [travailler, marcher, être assis] in hot sun; [laisser un produit, exposer] in direct sunlight; **la pièce était pleine de ~** the room was filled with sunlight; **nous avons eu deux jours de ~** we've had two sunny days; **quand il y a du ~** when it's sunny; **il fait ~** it's sunny; **attraper un coup** or **des coups de ~** to get sunburned
(Idiomes) **se faire une place au ~** to do well for oneself; **(il n'y a a) rien de nouveau sous le ~** there is nothing new under the sun; **le ~ brille pour tout le monde** Prov the sun shines upon all alike

solennel, -elle /sɔlanɛl/ adj **1** (empreint de gravité) solemn; **dire qch d'un ton ~** to say sth solemnly; **2** (officiel) [cérémonie] solemn; [appel, cadre] formal

solennité /sɔlanite/ nf solemnity; **chef d'État reçu avec ~** head of state given a ceremonious reception

solfège /sɔlfɛʒ/ nm music theory; **~ chanté** sol-fa

solfier /sɔlfje/ [2] vtr to sing using the tonic sol-fa system

solidaire /sɔlidɛʀ/ adj **1** (lié par des intérêts communs) [équipe, groupe] united; **ils forment un groupe très ~** they really stand together; **être ~ de qn** to be behind sb, to support sb; **se sentir ~ de qn** to feel solidarity with sb; **2** Tech [pièces] interdependent

solidariser: se solidariser /sɔlidaʀize/ [1] vpr **se ~ avec qch/qn** to stand by sth/sb

solidarité /sɔlidaʀite/ nf solidarity (**entre** between)

solide /sɔlid/
A adj **1** (consistant) solid; **2** (résistant) [maison, amitié, lien] solid; [chaussures, sac] sturdy; [lien, fixation, lame, mécanisme] strong; [position, base] firm; **la chaise n'est pas très ~** the chair is a bit rickety; **3** (vigoureux) [personne, constitution] strong; [poignée de main] firm; [cœur, poumons] strong, sound; **être ~ sur ses jambes** lit, fig to be steady on one's legs; **elle a les nerfs ~s** she's got nerves of steel; **avoir la tête ~** fig to have one's head screwed on; **4** (sérieux) [affaire, connaissances, expérience, raisons] sound; [garanties] firm; [qualités] solid; [partenaire] dependable; **ton rapport n'est pas assez ~** your report isn't very convincing; **5** (substantiel) hearty; **un ~ appétit** a hearty appetite
B nm **1** Math, Phys solid; **2** (fiable) **ce qu'il te dit, c'est du ~** what he says is sound; **3** (consistant) **manger du ~** to eat solids; **4** (durable) **les meubles anciens, c'est du ~** antique furniture is solidly built

solidement /sɔlidmɑ̃/ adv **1** (fermement) [lier, accrocher, soutenu] firmly; **2** (fortement) [s'établir, implanter, ancré] firmly; [barricadé] securely; [armé] heavily; **un rapport ~ documenté** a soundly-documented report; **elle a ~ établi sa réputation** she has established quite a reputation (**de, en tant que** as)

solidifier /sɔlidifje/ [2] vtr, **se solidifier** vpr to solidify

solidité /sɔlidite/ nf **1** (de construction) solidity; (de machine) strength; (de lien) firmness; (de vêtement) hard-wearing quality; **d'une grande ~** [construction] well-built; [machine] sturdy; [lien] strong; [vêtement] hard-wearing; **2** (de raisonnement) soundness

soliloque /sɔlilɔk/ nm soliloquy (**sur** on ou about)

soliloquer /sɔlilɔke/ [1] vi to soliloquize

soliste /sɔlist/ nmf soloist

solitaire /sɔlitɛʀ/
A adj **1** (sans compagnie) [*personne, vie, promenade*] solitary (*épith*); [*vieillesse, enfance*] lonely; **navigateur** ~ single-handed *ou* solo yachtsman; **2** (isolé) [*maison, hameau*] isolated
B nmf (personne) solitary person, loner; (ermite) hermit; **vivre en** ~ to live alone; **naviguer en** ~ to sail solo; **course en** ~ solo race
C nm **1** (diamant) solitaire; **2** (sanglier) rogue boar; **3** ▸ p. 327 Jeux solitaire

solitude /sɔlityd/ nf **1** (fait d'être seul) solitude; **aimer la** ~ to enjoy solitude, to enjoy being on one's own; **2** (sentiment) loneliness

solive /sɔliv/ nf joist

sollicitation /sɔlisitasjɔ̃/ nf **1** (requête) appeal, request; **2** (impulsion donnée) (à un cheval) prompting; (à une machine) touch

solliciter /sɔlisite/ [1] vtr **1** (demander) fml to seek [*entretien, poste, avis*]; to seek, to solicit sout [*contributions*]; to canvass, to solicit sout [*voix*]; **j'ai l'honneur de ~ de votre bienveillance l'autorisation de faire** I would respectfully request your permission to do; **son avis est très sollicité** his/her advice is much *ou* highly sought-after; **2** (démarcher) to approach, to call on *ou* upon [*personne, organisation*]; to canvass [*client, électeur*]; **être très sollicité** [*député, bienfaiteur*] to be assailed by requests; [*chanteur*] to be very much in demand; **3** (faire appel à) to attract [*intérêt, regard*]; to call upon [*mémoire*]

sollicitude /sɔlisityd/ nf concern, solicitude

solstice /sɔlstis/ nm solstice

soluble /sɔlybl/ adj **1** [*comprimé*] soluble; **2** [*problème*] solvable, soluble

solution /sɔlysjɔ̃/ nf **1** (action de résoudre) (de difficulté, mots croisés, d'énigme) solution (**de** of), solving (**de** of); (de crise, conflit) resolution (**de** of); **2** (réponse) solution (**de, à** to); **tenir la ~ de qch** to have the solution to sth; **une ~ de facilité** an easy way out; ~ **de compromis** compromise; **3** Chimie solution

solutionner /sɔlysjɔne/ [1] vtr controv to solve

solvabilité /sɔlvabilite/ nf (de débiteur) solvency; (de client, d'emprunteur) creditworthiness

solvable /sɔlvabl/ adj [*débiteur*] solvent; [*emprunteur, client*] creditworthy

solvant /sɔlvɑ̃/ nm solvent

somatique /sɔmatik/ adj Biol, Méd somatic

somatiser /sɔmatize/ [1] vtr to have a psychosomatic reaction to [*problème*]

sombre /sɔ̃bʀ/ adj **1** (obscur) dark; **vert/rouge** ~ dark green/red; **il fait** ~ it's dark; **2** (triste) [*pensée, avenir, période*] dark, black; [*tableau, conclusion*] depressing, grim; [*air, personne, visage*] solemn, sombre^GB; **d'un air** ~ [*annoncer*] in a sombre^GB tone; [*regarder*] gloomily; **3** (déplorable) (before n) [*crétin, brute*] absolute; [*affaire*] murky; **c'est une ~ histoire d'inceste** it's a grim story of incest

sombrer /sɔ̃bʀe/ [1] vi **1** (couler) [*navire*] to sink; **2** (s'engloutir) ~ **dans** [*personne*] to sink into [*désespoir, folie, oubli, débauche, alcoolisme*]; **le pays est en train de** ~ the country is going to the dogs

sommaire /sɔmmɛʀ/
A adj [*enquête*] perfunctory; [*examen, analyse, explication*] cursory; [*description*] rough; [*installation, éducation, repas*] rough and ready (*épith*); [*vision, conception*] shallow; [*toilette*] quick; [*compte rendu, jugement, procès, exécution*] summary
B nm **1** (table des matières) contents (*pl*); **au ~ de notre numéro de juillet** featured in our July issue; **2** (programme) **au ~: un débat sur le chômage** a debate on unemployment is on the programme^GB

sommairement /sɔmmɛʀmɑ̃/ adv [*exposer, juger, exécuter*] summarily

sommation /sɔmmasjɔ̃/ nf **1** Jur (acte d'huissier) notice; **2** (avertissement) (de policier) warning; (de sentinelle) challenge

somme¹ /sɔm/ nm nap, snooze°

somme² /sɔm/ nf **1** (argent) sum; **une ~!** it's quite a sum!; **2** (quantité) sum total; **la ~ de nos connaissances** the sum total of our knowledge; **en ~, ~ toute** all in all; **3** Math sum; **4** (œuvre) summa

sommeil /sɔmɛj/ nm **1** gén sleep ¢; **avoir** ~ to be *ou* feel sleepy; **nuit sans** ~ sleepless night; **avoir le** ~ **agité** to sleep fitfully; **avoir le** ~ **léger/lourd** to be a light/heavy sleeper; **tirer qn de son** ~ to wake sb up, to rouse sb sout; **2** (attente) **être en** ~ [*projet, activité, affaire*] to have been put on ice
(Idiome) **dormir d'un ~ de plomb** to sleep like a log°

sommeiller /sɔmeje/ [1] vi (somnoler) [*personne, animal*] to doze; [*nature, désir*] to lie dormant

sommelier, -ière /sɔmǝlje, ɛʀ/ ▸ p. 372 nm,f wine steward, sommelier

sommer /sɔmme/ [1] vtr ~ **qn de faire** to command sb to do; ~ **qn de comparaître** Jur to summons sb to appear

sommet /sɔmɛ/ nm **1** Géog (de montagne indéfinie) peak; (de montagne définie) summit; (montagne pointue) peak; **2** (d'arbre, de bâtiment, tour, mur, crâne, colline) top; (de vague) crest; (de courbe) peak; (de hiérarchie, d'organisation) top; (de carrière) summit; **3** (summum) (de gloire, réussite, bêtise) height; **atteindre un ~ or des ~s** [*prix, ventes*] to peak; **4** (rencontre) summit; **conférence au** ~ summit meeting; **se réunir au** ~ to meet at the summit; **5** Math (de triangle, d'angle) apex; (de cône, volume) vertex

sommier /sɔmje/ nm (de lit) (bed) base; ~ **tapissier** *or* **à ressorts** bed base GB, box spring US; ~ **à lattes** slatted bed base

sommité /sɔmmite/ nf (expert) leading expert (**en** in)

somnambule /sɔmnɑ̃byl/
A adj **être** ~ to sleepwalk
B nmf sleepwalker

somnifère /sɔmnifɛʀ/
A adj soporific
B nm (médicament) somnifacient; (comprimé) sleeping pill

somnolence /sɔmnɔlɑ̃s/ nf **1** lit drowsiness; **en état de** ~ in a drowsy state; **2** fig lethargy

somnolent, ~e /sɔmnɔlɑ̃, ɑ̃t/ adj **1** lit [*personne*] drowsy; **2** fig [*attention*] flagging; [*ville*] sleepy; [*industrie, pays, marché*] lethargic

somnoler /sɔmnɔle/ [1] vi **1** lit [*personne*] to drowse; **2** fig [*ville*] to be sleepy; [*marché, industrie, pays*] to be lethargic

somptuaire /sɔ̃ptɥɛʀ/ adj **1** Hist [*loi, édit*] sumptuary; **2** (excessif) controv [*dépense*] lavish

somptueux, -euse /sɔ̃ptɥø, øz/ adj sumptuous

somptuosité /sɔ̃ptɥozite/ nf liter sumptuousness

son¹, **sa**, pl **ses** /sɔ̃, sa, sɛ/ adj poss

> ⚠ En anglais, le choix du possessif de la troisième personne du singulier est déterminé par le genre du 'possesseur'. Sont du masculin: les personnes de sexe masculin et les animaux domestiques mâles; sont du féminin: les personnes de sexe féminin, les animaux domestiques femelles et souvent les navires; sont du neutre: les animaux non domestiques et les non-animés. La forme masculine est *his*: *sa femme/ moustache* = his wife/moustache; *son ordinateur* = his computer; *sa niche* = his kennel. La forme féminine est *her*: *son mari/ordinateur* = her husband/computer; *sa robe* = her dress; *sa niche* = her kennel. La forme neutre est *its*. Quand le 'possesseur' est indéterminé on peut dire *one's*: *faire ses devoirs* = to do one's homework. On ne répète pas le possessif coordonné: *sa robe et son manteau* = her dress and coat.

ses enfants à elle° her children; ~ **étourdie de sœur**° his/her absent-minded sister; **Sa Majesté** His/Her Majesty; **un de ses amis** a friend of his/hers; **elle** ~ **a lundi** (cette semaine) she's off on Monday; (toutes les semaines) she gets Mondays off

son² /sɔ̃/ nm **1** (bruit) sound; **le timbre et la hauteur d'un** ~ the tone and pitch of a sound; **2** (volume) volume; **baisser le** ~ to turn the volume down; **3** Radio, Mus, TV, Cin sound; **ingénieur du** ~ sound engineer; **4** (enveloppe du blé) bran; **des céréales au** ~ cereals with bran; **pain au** ~ bran loaf
(Idiome) **entendre plusieurs** ~s **de cloche** to hear several different versions (of the same thing)
(Composé) ~ **et lumière** son et lumière

sonate /sɔnat/ nf sonata

sondage /sɔ̃daʒ/ nm **1** (enquête) (pour opinion) poll; (pour étude) survey; ~ **d'opinion** opinion poll; **2** Méd (pour évacuer, introduire) catheterization; (pour examiner) probing; [3] Météo, Naut sounding

(Composé) **~ d'écoute** Radio, TV audience ratings poll

sonde /sɔ̃d/ *nf* [1] Méd (pour évacuer, introduire) catheter; (pour examiner) probe; [2] Naut (plomb) sounding lead; (ligne) sounding line; [3] Météo sonde; [4] (de roche) drill; [5] Ind (pour produits alimentaires) taster

(Composé) **~ spatiale** space probe

sonder /sɔ̃de/ [1] *vtr* [1] (enquêter) (pour opinion) to poll [*personne, groupe*]; (pour étude) to survey [*personne, groupe*]; (pour dévoiler) to sound [sb] out [*personne*]; to sound out [*intentions*]; [2] (fouiller) to probe [*ballot, couche de neige, mare*]; [3] Méd (pour évacuer, introduire dans) to catheterize [*organe*]; (pour examiner) to probe [*organe*]; [4] Météo to take soundings in [*atmosphère*]; [5] Naut to sound [*fond*]; [6] Tech to make test drills in [*couche*]

sondeur, -euse /sɔ̃dœR, øz/
A *nm,f* [1] ▸ p. 372 (enquêteur) pollster; [2] Naut (personne) sounder; [3] (de gisement) driller
B *nm* Météo, Naut (appareil) sounder; (de roche) driller

songe /sɔ̃ʒ/ *nm* liter dream

songer /sɔ̃ʒe/ [13]
A **songer à** *vtr ind* **~ à qch/qn** to think of sth/sb; **~ à faire** to think of doing; **~ que** to think that; **quand on** *or* **si l'on y songe** when you come to think of it; **il songe à changer de métier** he's contemplating a change of job; **tu n'y songes pas!** you can't be serious!; **songez-y** (n'oubliez pas) bear it in mind; (réfléchissez) think about it; **je n'y avais même pas songé** it hadn't even occurred to me; **songe à ton avenir** think of *ou* consider your future; **je songeais à lui pour ce poste** I was considering him for the post
B †*vi* liter to daydream

songeur, -euse /sɔ̃ʒœR, øz/ *adj* pensive

sonique /sɔnik/ *adj* [*barrière*] sound (*épith*)

sonnant, ~e /sɔnɑ̃, ɑ̃t/ *adj* **à trois heures ~es** on the stroke of three

(Idiome) **payer en espèces ~es et trébuchantes** to pay in cash

sonné, ~e /sɔne/
A *pp* ▸ sonner
B *pp adj* [1] (étourdi) (physiquement) groggy; (moralement) shattered; [2] (révolu) **elle a quarante ans bien ~s**○ she's well into her forties; [3] ○(fou) nuts○

sonner /sɔne/ [1]
A *vtr* [1] (faire tinter) to ring [*cloche*]; to strike [*heure*]; [*personne*] to sound [*charge, retraite, alarme*]; to ring out [*vêpres, angélus*]; [2] (faire venir) to ring for; **on ne t'a pas sonné**○! did anyone ask you?; [3] ○(faire vaciller) [*coup, boxeur*] to make [sb] dizzy [*personne*]; [*nouvelle, événement*] to stagger [*personne*]; [*vin, alcool*] to knock [sb] out [*personne*]
B **sonner de** *vtr ind* to sound [*cor, trompette*]; to play [*cornemuse*]
C *vi* [1] (se faire entendre) [*cloches, téléphone*] to ring; [*heure*] to strike; [*r éveil*] to go off; [*alerte, alarme, trompette*] to sound; **leur dernière heure a sonné** their last hour has come; **il fait ~ son réveil à 5 heures** he sets his alarm for 5 o'clock; [2] (rendre un son) [*mot, expression*] to sound; **ça sonne bien/mal** that sounds good/bad; [3] (actionner une sonnerie) to ring; **on a sonné à la porte** the doorbell has just rung; **va voir qui sonne** go and see who's at the door

sonnerie /sɔnRi/ *nf* [1] (son) ringing; (de carillon) chimes (*pl*); **je n'ai pas entendu la ~ du téléphone** I didn't hear the telephone ringing; [2] (de clairon, trompette) sounding

sonnet /sɔnɛ/ *nm* sonnet

sonnette /sɔnɛt/ *nf* (de bicyclette, d'intérieur) bell; (de porte) doorbell; **actionner la ~** to ring the bell; **tirer la ~ d'alarme** lit to pull the emergency cord; fig to sound the alarm

sonneur /sɔnœR/ *nm* (de cloches) bell-ringer; (d'autres instruments) player

(Idiome) **dormir** *or* **ronfler comme un ~**○ to sleep like a log

sonore /sɔnɔR/ *adj* [1] (éclatant) [*rire, baiser, gifle*] resounding; [*formules, paroles*] high-sounding; [2] (qui résonne) [*paroi*] resonant; [*pièce, couloir, voûte*] echoing; [*plancher*] hollow-sounding (*épith*); [3] (relatif au son) sound (*épith*); [4] Cin, Radio **effets ~s** sound effects; **un document ~** a recording; [5] (en phonétique) voiced

sonorisation /sɔnɔRizasjɔ̃/ *nf* [1] Tech (matériel) public address system, PA system; [2] Cin **la ~ d'un film** adding the soundtrack to a film

sonoriser /sɔnɔRize/ [1] *vtr* [1] (équiper d'une sonorisation) to install a public address system *ou* PA system in [*salle de conférences, rue*]; to install a sound system in [*salle de concert, cinéma*]; [2] Cin **~ un film** to add the soundtrack to a film; [3] (en phonétique) to voice

sonorité /sɔnɔRite/ *nf* [1] Mus (d'un instrument, d'une voix) tone (**de** of); **les ~s de l'italien** the sound of Italian; [2] Audio (d'une chaîne hi-fi) sound quality (**de** of); [3] (d'un plancher, mur) resonance (**de** of); [4] (en phonétique) voicing (**de** of)

sophisme /sɔfism/ *nm* sophism

sophistication /sɔfistikasjɔ̃/ *nf* sophistication

sophistiqué, ~e /sɔfistike/ *adj* (complexe) sophisticated; (artificiel) artificial, mannered

sophrologie /sɔfRɔlɔʒi/ *nf* relaxation therapy

soporifique /sɔpɔRifik/
A *adj* lit, fig soporific
B *nm* (médicament) somnifacient

soprano /sɔpRano/ ▸ p. 98
A *nm* (voix) soprano
B *nmf* (chanteur) (femme) soprano; (enfant) treble, soprano

sorbet /sɔRbɛ/ *nm* sorbet

Sorbonne : la Sorbonne /sɔRbɔn/ *nfpr* the Sorbonne

ℹ️ **La Sorbonne** Founded in 1253 by Robert de Sorbon as a theological college, the Sorbonne is the oldest and best-known university institution in France. It is located in the centre of Paris in the *Quartier Latin* and houses *l'Université Paris IV*.

sorcellerie /sɔRsɛlRi/ *nf* witchcraft; (maléfique) sorcery

sorcier /sɔRsje/
A ○*adj m* **ce n'est (pourtant) pas ~**! (but) it's dead○ easy!
B *nm* [1] (magicien) wizard; (maléfique) sorcerer; [2] (guérisseur) witch doctor

sorcière /sɔRsjɛR/ *nf* witch

sordide /sɔRdid/ *adj* [*habitation, quartier*] squalid, sordid; [*conditions de vie, crime, détails*] sordid; [*avarice, égoïsme*] base

sornettes /sɔRnɛt/ *nfpl* tall stories

sort /sɔR/ *nm* [1] (condition) lot; [2] (destin) fate **𝄴**; **remettre son ~ entre les mains de qn** to put one's fate in sb's hands; **c'est un coup du ~** it's just one of those things; **le ~ est contre moi** I'm ill-fated; **il a eu un ~ tragique** he came to a tragic end; **tirer au ~** to draw lots; **tirer qch au ~** to draw lots for sth; **faire un ~ à**○ **un plat** fig to polish off○ a dish

(Idiomes) **jeter un ~ à qn** to put a curse *ou* jinx on sb; **le ~ en est jeté** the die is cast

sortable /sɔRtabl/ *adj* **mon mari n'est pas ~** I can't take my husband anywhere

sorte /sɔRt/
A *nf* sort (**de** of), kind (**de** of); **d'aucune ~** of any sort *ou* kind *ou* type
B **de la sorte** *loc adv* [*agir, se comporter, mentir*] in this way; **je n'ai rien fait de la ~** I haven't done anything of the kind *ou* sort
C **de sorte que** *loc conj* [1] (de but) so that; [2] (de manière) **la toile est peinte de ~ que** the canvas is painted in such a way that; [3] (de conséquence) **de ~ que je n'ai pas pu venir** with the result that I couldn't come
D **en quelque sorte** *loc adv* in a way
E **en sorte de** *loc prép* **fais en ~ d'être à l'heure** try to be on time
F **en sorte que** *loc conj* [1] (de but) **fais en ~ que tout soit en ordre** make sure everything is tidy; [2] (de conséquence) so; **en ~ qu'il n'a rien compris** so he understood nothing

sortie /sɔRti/ *nf* [1] (lieu) exit; **je t'attendrai à la ~** I'll wait for you outside (the building); **prenez la première ~** (sur une route) take the first exit; **'~'** (sur un panneau) 'exit', 'way out' GB; **à la ~ de la ville** (extra-muros) on the outskirts of the town; (intra-muros) on the edge of the town; **surveiller la ~ des écoles** to patrol the school gates; [2] (moment) **à ma ~ du tribunal/de l'armée** when I left the court/the army; **sa femme l'attendait à sa ~ de prison** his wife was waiting for him when he came out of prison; **prendre ses enfants à la ~ de l'école** to pick the children up after school; **mendier à la ~ des églises** to beg outside churches; **à la ∼ de l'hiver** at the end of winter; **l'heure de la ∼** Scol home time; (du travail) knocking-off° time; **3⟩** (départ) **faire une ∼ fracassante** [*personne*] to make a dramatic exit; **je suis las de tes entrées et ∼s continuelles** I'm tired of your constant comings and goings; **∼ d'un navire** sailing of a boat; **la ∼ de la crise** the end of the crisis; **la ∼ de la livre hors du SME** the withdrawal of the pound from the ERM; **le droit à la libre ∼ du territoire** the right to travel freely abroad; **être interdit de ∼ (du territoire)** to be forbidden to leave the country; **4⟩** (activité) gén outing; **faire une ∼ avec l'école** to go on a school outing; **ce soir, c'est mon soir de ∼** tonight is my night out; **priver qn de ∼** to keep sb in; **première ∼ d'un convalescent** a convalescent's first time out; **5⟩** (commercialisation) (de nouveau modèle) launching ¢; (de film, disque) release; (de livre) publication; (de collection) showing; (de nouveau journal) publication; **le film a été interdit dès sa ∼** the film was banned as soon as it came out; **6⟩** ○(déclaration) remark; **7⟩** Électrotech, Ordinat output; **∼ sur imprimante** (processus) printing; **∼ laser** (processus) hardcopy laser output; (feuille imprimée) laser hardcopy

(Composés⟩ **∼ des artistes** Théât stage-door; **∼ d'autoroute** exit; **∼ de bain** bathrobe; **être en ∼ de bain** to be wearing a bathrobe; **∼ scolaire** (d'un jour) school outing; (de plus d'un jour) school trip

sortilège /sɔʀtilɛʒ/ *nm* spell

sortir¹ /sɔʀtiʀ/ [30]
A *vtr* **1⟩** (promener) to take [sb/sth] out [*personne, chien, cheval*]; **j'y vais moi-même, ça me sortira** I'll go myself, it'll give me a chance to get out; **2⟩** ○(inviter) to take [sb] out [*personne*]; **3⟩** ○(expulser) to throw [sb] out, to chuck° [sb] out [*personne*] (**de** of); to send [sb] out [*élève*]; **se faire ∼ en quart de finale** to be knocked out in the quarterfinal; **4⟩** (mettre à l'extérieur) to get [sb/sth] out (**de** of); **∼ qn du lit** to get sb out of bed; **∼ sa voiture en marche arrière** to reverse one's car out; **∼ les mains de ses poches** to take one's hands out of one's pockets; **∼ un revolver** to pull out a revolver; **∼ la poubelle** to put the bin out; **∼ sa langue** to stick one's tongue out; **∼ une carte** to bring out a card; **5⟩** (délivrer) **∼ qn de** to get sb out of; **∼ une entreprise de ses difficultés** to get a company out of difficulties; **∼ qn de sa léthargie** to shake sb out of his/her lethargy; **6⟩** (commercialiser) to bring out [*livre, disque, modèle*]; to release [*film*]; to show [*collection*]; **7⟩** (produire) to turn out [*livre, disque, film, produit*]; **8⟩** (imprimer) to bring [sth] out [*exemplaire, numéro, journal*]; **9⟩** ○(dire) to come out with° [*remarques*]; **∼ une blague** to crack a joke

B *vi* (+ *v être*) **1⟩** (aller dehors) [*personne, animal*] to go out; (venir dehors) [*personne, animal*] to come out (**de** of); **∼ par la fenêtre** to go out through the window; **∼ dans la rue/sur le balcon** to go out into the street/on the balcony; **∼ faire un tour** (à pied) to go out for a walk; **∼ faire des courses** to go out shopping; **∼ déjeuner** to go out for lunch; **être sorti** to be out; **∼ discrètement** to slip out (**de** of); **∼ en courant** to run out; **∼ en trombe de sa chambre** to burst out of one's room; **faire ∼ qn** to get sb outside; **laisser ∼ qn** to allow sb out; **empêcher de ∼** to keep [sb/sth] in; **∼ dans l'espace** to space-walk; **2⟩** (passer du temps dehors) to go out; **∼ au restaurant** to go out to a restaurant; **∼ avec qn** to go out with sb; **inviter qn à sortir** to ask sb out; **3⟩** (quitter un lieu) **∼ de** to leave; **∼ de chez qn** to leave sb's house; **∼ d'une réunion** to leave a meeting; **∼ du port** [*navire*] to leave port; **∼ du pays** [*personne, marchandise*] to leave the country; **∼ de chez soi** to go out; **∼ de la pièce** to walk out of the room; **sortez d'ici/de là!** get out of here/of there!; **∼ de la route** [*véhicule*] to leave the road; **∼ de la famille** [*bijou, tableau*] to go out of the family; **∼ tout chaud du four** to be hot from the oven; **4⟩** (venir d'un lieu) **∼ de** to come out of; **∼ de chez le médecin** to come out of the doctor's; **5⟩** (quitter un état, une situation) **∼ d'un profond sommeil** to wake up from a deep sleep; **∼ de son mutisme** *or* **silence** to break one's silence; **∼ de l'adolescence** to leave adolescence behind; **∼ de la récession** to pull out of the recession; **6⟩** (venir de quitter un état) **∼ à peine de l'enfance** to be just emerging from childhood; **∼ de maladie** to be recovering from an illness; **∼ d'une guerre** to emerge from a war; **7⟩** (émerger) to come out; **elle est sortie de sa dépression très affaiblie** after her depression she was a mere shadow of her former self; **8⟩** (s'échapper) [*eau, air, étincelle, fumée*] to come out (**de** of; **par** through); **faire ∼** to squeeze [sth] out [*pâte, colle, eau, jus*] (**de** of); to eject [*cassette*] (**de** from); **∼ en**

masse [*personnes*] to pour out; **9⟩** (pousser) [*bourgeon, insecte*] to come out; [*dent*] to come through; **∼ de terre** [*plante*] to come through; [*bâtiment*] to rise from the ground; **10⟩** (dépasser) to stick out; **il y a un clou qui sort** there's a nail sticking out; **11⟩** (être commercialisé) [*film, disque, livre, nouveau modèle*] to come out; **tous les jours** [*journal*] to be published daily; **12⟩** (provenir) [*personne, produit*] to come from; **∼ de Berkeley** Univ to have graduated from Berkeley; **d'où sors-tu à cette heure**°? where have you been?; **d'où il sort celui-là**°? where's he been living°?; **13⟩** (être en dehors) **∼ du sujet** [*personne*] to wander off the subject; [*remarque*] to be beside the point; **14⟩** (être tiré) [*numéro, sujet*] to come up; **15⟩** Ordinat to exit

C **se sortir** *vpr* **1⟩** (échapper) **se ∼ d'une situation difficile** to get out of a predicament; **se ∼ d'une** (situation difficile) to get out of it; (maladie) to get over it; **s'en ∼ vivant** to escape with one's life; **2⟩** (se débrouiller) **s'en ∼** gén to pull through; (financièrement) to cope; (intellectuellement, manuellement, physiquement) to manage; **tu t'en sors?** can you manage?; **s'en ∼ à peine** (financièrement) to scrape a living

sortir² /sɔʀtiʀ/ *nm* **au ∼ de** at the end of

SOS /ɛsoɛs/ *nm* **1⟩** (signal) SOS; **2⟩** (service) emergency service; **∼ médecins** emergency medical service; **3⟩** (ligne téléphonique) helpline

sosie /sɔzi/ *nm* double; **c'est ton ∼!** he/she's the spitting image of you!

sot, sotte /so, sɔt/ *adj* silly

(Idiome⟩ **il n'y a pas de ∼s métiers** Prov no profession is without merit

sottise /sɔtiz/ *nf* **1⟩** (manque de jugement) silliness, foolishness; **2⟩** (parole) silly *ou* foolish remark; **dire des ∼s** to talk rubbish; **3⟩** (acte) **c'est une ∼ de faire** it's silly to do; **faire une ∼** to do something silly; **faire des ∼s** [*enfants*] to be naughty

sou /su/ *nm* **1⟩** (petite monnaie) penny GB, cent US; **il est arrivé sans un ∼** he arrived without a penny; **être sans le ∼** to be penniless; **économiser ∼ par ∼** *or* **à ∼** to scrimp and save; **il est près de ses ∼s** he's a penny-pincher; **c'est une affaire de gros ∼s** there's big money involved; **un manteau de quatre ∼s** a cheap coat; **2⟩** (petite quantité) **il n'a pas un ∼ de bon sens** he hasn't got a scrap of common sense; **3⟩** Hist (pièce) sou

(Idiomes⟩ **un ∼ est un ∼** every penny counts; **être propre comme un ∼ neuf** to be clean as a new pin°; **s'ennuyer à cent ∼s de l'heure** to be bored to death

soubassement /subɑsmɑ̃/ *nm* **1⟩** Constr (de bâtiment) base, base course; (de colonne) base; **2⟩** (en géologie) bedrock

soubresaut /subʀəso/ *nm* (de personne, d'animal) start; (de véhicule) jolt; **les derniers ∼s** (de personne, d'animal, empire) the death throes

soubrette /subʀɛt/ *nf* maid

souche /suʃ/ *nf* **1⟩** (d'arbre) (tree) stump; (de vigne) stock; **2⟩** (origine) stock; **de ∼ paysanne** of peasant stock; **faire ∼** to establish a line; **3⟩** Biol strain; **4⟩** (de carnet, livret) stub

(Idiome⟩ **dormir comme une ∼** to sleep like a log

souci /susi/ *nm* **1⟩** (inquiétude) **se faire du ∼** to worry; **tu te fais du ∼ pour rien** there's nothing to worry about; **donner du ∼ à qn** to be a worry to sb; **2⟩** (problème) problem; **avoir des ∼s** to have problems; **j'ai d'autres ∼s (en tête)** I've got other things to worry about; **être sans ∼s** to have no worries; **leur unique ∼ est de faire** all they care about is doing; **3⟩** (soin) fml **avoir le ∼ de qch** to care about sth; **avoir le ∼ de faire** to be anxious to do; **leur ∼ du réalisme** their concern for realism; **dans le seul ∼ de plaire** with the sole intention of pleasing; **4⟩** Bot marigold

soucier: se soucier /susje/ [2] *vpr* to care (**de qch** about sth; **de faire** about doing); **il ne se soucie guère de son avenir** he cares little about his future; **sans se ∼ de qch/faire** without concerning oneself with sth/doing

soucieux, -ieuse /susjø, øz/ *adj* worried; **ça me rend ∼ de voir** it worries me to see; **être ∼ de** to be concerned about [*réputation, santé*]; to care about [*indépendance, qualité, avenir*]; **être peu ∼ de** to care little about; **être ∼ de faire** to be anxious to do

soucoupe /sukup/ *nf* saucer

(Composé⟩ **∼ volante** flying saucer

soudain, ∼e /sudɛ̃, ɛn/
A *adj* sudden, unexpected

B *adv* suddenly, all of a sudden

soudainement /sudɛnmɑ̃/ *adv* suddenly

soudaineté /sudɛnte/ *nf* suddenness

soudard /sudaʀ/ *nm* **1** (individu grossier) liter boor; **2** Hist soldier

soude /sud/ *nf* soda; ~ **caustique** caustic soda

souder /sude/ [1]
A *vtr* **1** Tech gén to weld [*pièces métalliques*]; (braser) to solder; **2** (réunir) to join [*bords, extrémités*] (**à** to); fig to bind [*sb*] together [*personnes*]
B se souder *vpr* **1** lit [*vertèbres*] to fuse; [*os*] to knit together; **2** fig [*équipe*] to become united; [*personnes*] to be brought closer together

soudoyer /sudwaje/ [23] *vtr* to bribe

soudure /sudyʀ/ *nf* Tech (joint) weld, join; (fil à souder) solder; (opération) gén welding; (brasage) soldering; ~ **à l'arc** arc welding

soufflant, ~**e** /suflɑ̃, ɑ̃t/ *adj* **1** Tech machine ~**e** blowing apparatus; **2** ○(étonnant) stunning

souffle /sufl/ *nm* **1** (respiration) breath; **couper le** ~ **à qn** lit to wind sb; fig to take sb's breath away; **à couper le** ~ [*beauté, vitesse*] breathtaking; [*beau*] breathtakingly; (**en**) **avoir le** ~ **coupé** lit to be winded; fig to be speechless; **être à bout de** ~ [*personne*] to be out of breath; [*pays, économie*] to be running out of steam; **dire qch dans un** ~ to say sth in a whisper; **retrouver un second** ~ (après un effort) to get one's second wind; (après un marasme, vieillissement) to get a new lease of GB *ou* on US life; **donner un second** *or* **nouveau** ~ **à qn/qch** to put new life into sb/sth; **avoir du** ~ lit [*trompettiste*] to have good lungs; [*acteur, chanteur*] to have a powerful voice; [*sportif*] to be fit; (avoir de l'endurance) [*personne*] to have staying power; (avoir de l'esprit) [*auteur, œuvre*] to be inspired; (avoir de l'audace)○ to have nerve; **2** (bruit de respiration) breathing; ~ **précipité** rapid breathing; (brise) breeze; **pas un** ~ (**de vent**) not a breath (of wind); **3** (force) inspiration; ~ **créateur** creative inspiration; **4** (esprit) spirit; ~ **de la révolte** spirit of rebellion; **5** (force) inspiration; ~ **créateur** creative inspiration; **6** (élément) touch; **7** Phys (d'explosion, de réacteur, ventilateur) blast; **8** Méd (en cardiologie) murmur; ~ **au cœur** heart murmur

soufflé, ~**e** /sufle/
A *pp* ▸ **souffler**
B *pp adj* **1** ○(stupéfait) flabbergasted; **2** Ind [*bitume, huile, pâte*] blown; **3** Culin [*omelette*] souffléed
C *nm* Culin soufflé

souffler /sufle/ [1]
A *vtr* **1** (éteindre) to blow out [*bougie, lampe*]; **2** (envoyer) to blow [*air, odeur, poussière*]; **3** (chuchoter) to whisper [*mots, texte*] (**à qn** to sb; **que** that); ~ **qch à l'oreille de qn** to whisper sth into sb's ear; ~ **la réplique à un acteur** to prompt an actor, to give an actor a prompt; **4** (suggérer) to suggest [*idée, nom*] (**à** to); **on lui a soufflé la réponse** he/she was prompted; **5** Ind to blow [*verre, bouteille*]; to blast [*métal*]; **6** (détruire) [*explosion, bombe*] to blow out [*vitre*]; to blow up [*construction*]; **7** Jeux (aux dames) to huff [*pièce*]; **8** ○(stupéfier) to flabbergast
B *vi* **1** Météo [*vent*] to blow; **le vent souffle fort** there's a strong wind; **ça souffle** it's windy; **2** (se propager) [*vent de révolte, liberté*] to blow; **un vent de folie souffle sur le stade** frenzy is sweeping through the stadium; **3** (reprendre sa respiration) to get one's breath back; [*cheval*] to get its wind back; fig [*personne, économie*] to take a breather○; **4** (respirer difficilement) to puff; **5** (produire un souffle) [*personne, animal*] to blow; ~ **dans une trompette** to blow a trumpet; ~ **sur une bougie** to blow out a candle; ~ **sur le feu** to blow on the fire; fig to inflame the situation; **6** (donner la réponse) to tell sb the answer; **on ne souffle pas!** no prompting!

(Idiome) ~ **comme un bœuf** *or* **un phoque** *or* **une locomotive** to puff and pant

soufflerie /sufləʀi/ *nf* **1** Tech (d'expérimentation) wind tunnel; **2** (d'orgue, de forge, four) bellows (*pl*); **3** (machine) blower; (lieu) blower house; **4** (de verre) (machine) glass-blower; (entreprise) glassblowing company

soufflet /suflɛ/ *nm* **1** Tech (de forge, d'orgue, appareil photo) bellows (*pl*); **2** (de wagon) concertina vestibule; **3** (de chaussure, poche) gusset; **4** †(gifle) slap

souffleur, -euse /suflœʀ, øz/ *nm,f* **1** ▸ p. 372 Théât prompter; **2** Ind ~ (**de verre**) glassblower

souffrance /sufʀɑ̃s/ *nf* suffering **₵**; **en** ~ [*projet, dossier*] pending; **colis en** ~ (non livré) parcel awaiting delivery; (non réclamé) unclaimed parcel

souffrant, ~**e** /sufʀɑ̃, ɑ̃t/ *adj* unwell

souffre-douleur /sufʀədulœʀ/ *nm inv* punch-bag GB, punching-bag US

souffreteux, -euse /sufʀətø, øz/ *adj* sickly

souffrir /sufʀiʀ/ [4]
A *vtr* **1** (supporter) ~ **tout de qn** to put up with anything from sb; **il ne souffre pas d'être contredit** he can't stand being contradicted; **elle ne peut plus le** ~ she can't stand him any more; **2** (permettre) **souffrez que je vous dise** allow me to tell you; **cette affaire ne peut** ~ **aucun retard** this matter brooks no delay
B *vi* **1** (physiquement) [*personne, animal*] to suffer; **faire** ~ **qn** to cause sb suffering; ~ **de qch** to suffer from [*diabète, malformation*]; ~ **du dos** to suffer from back problems; **ma cheville me fait** ~ my ankle hurts; **est-ce qu'il souffre?** is he in pain?; **2** (moralement) [*personne*] to suffer; **faire** ~ [*personne*] to make [sb] suffer; [*situation*] to upset; ~ **de** to suffer from [*trac*]; ~ **du racisme** to be a victim of racism; ~ **d'être rejeté** to suffer the pain of rejection; **ils souffrent de ne pas se voir** they find it painful to be separated; **elle souffre de voir que** it upsets her to see that; **3** (être endommagé) [*cultures, économie*] to be badly affected (**de** by); [*pays, ville*] to suffer (**de** from); **4** ○(peiner) [*personne, équipe*] to have a hard time (**pour faire** doing); **j'ai fini la course mais j'ai souffert!** I finished the race but it was tough!
C se souffrir *vpr* **ils ne peuvent pas se** ~ they can't stand each other

soufre /sufʀ/ *nm* sulphur^{GB}

soufrer /sufʀe/ [1] *vtr* to sulphurate^{GB} [*étoffe, laine*]; to sulphur^{GB} [*allumette*]; to treat [sth] with sulphur^{GB} [*vigne*]

souhait /swɛ/ *nm* wish; **répondre aux** ~**s de qn** [*proposition*] to suit sb; **à** ~ [*beau*] incredibly
(Idiome) **à vos** ~**s!** bless you!

souhaitable /swɛtabl/ *adj* desirable

souhaiter /swete/ [1] *vtr* **1** (espérer) to hope for; ~ **que** to hope that; **2** (exprimer) ~ **qch à qn** to wish sb sth; ~ **bonne chance à qn** to wish sb luck; **je vous souhaite une bonne et heureuse année** I wish you a happy New Year; ~ **la bienvenue à qn** to welcome sb; ~ **beaucoup de bonheur à qn** to wish sb every happiness; **je vous souhaite d'obtenir très bientôt votre diplôme** I hope you get your degree very soon; **3** (désirer) **il souhaite se rendre là-bas en voiture** he would like to go by car

souiller /suje/ [1] *vtr* **1** (salir, polluer) to soil, to make [sth] dirty; **2** (rendre impur) liter to defile [*lieu, personne*]; to sully [*mémoire, réputation*]

souillon /sujɔ̃/ *nf* slattern†

souillure /sujyʀ/ *nf* **1** (flétrissure morale) stain, taint; **2** (saleté) stain

souk /suk/ *nm* **1** (marché) souk; **2** ○(désordre) mess; (bruit) racket○

soûl, ~**e** /su, sul/
A *adj* drunk
B tout son soûl *loc adv* [*boire, manger*] one's fill; **dormir tout son** ~ to sleep as much as one wants

soulagement /sulaʒmɑ̃/ *nm* relief

soulager /sulaʒe/ [13]
A *vtr* **1** (décharger) to relieve [*personne, entreprise, étagère*] (**de** of); **2** (apaiser) to relieve [*personne*]; to relieve, to ease [*conscience, peine*]; ~ **qn d'un mal de tête** to relieve sb's headache; **pleure un bon coup, ça soulage** have a good cry, you'll feel better; **tu m'as soulagé d'un grand poids** you've taken a great weight off my shoulders; **3** ○fig (voler) to relieve (**de qch** of sth)
B se soulager *vpr* **1** ○(satisfaire un besoin naturel) euph to relieve oneself; **2** (s'apaiser) **elle m'a raconté tout cela pour se** ~ she told me the whole story to get it off her chest

soûlant○, ~**e** /sulɑ̃, ɑ̃t/ *adj* **elle est** ~**e!** she makes my head spin!

soûler○ /sule/ [1]
A *vtr* **1** (rendre ivre) [*personne*] to get [sb] drunk [*personne*]; [*alcool*] to make [sb] drunk [*personne*]; **2** (griser) [*odeur, parfum, grand air*] to intoxicate [*personne*]; **3** ○(étourdir) **tu me soûles avec tes histoires** give me a break, my head is spinning!
B se soûler *vpr* **1** (s'enivrer) to get drunk (**à, avec** on); **2** (se

griser) **se** ∼ **de** to become intoxicated with [*paroles, musique*]

soulèvement /sulɛvmɑ̃/ *nm* (insurrection) uprising

soulever /sulve/ [16]

A *vtr* **1** (déplacer vers le haut) [*personne*] to lift [*objet*]; [*vent, tourbillon, véhicule*] to whip up [*feuilles, poussière*]; ∼ **qn/qch de terre** [*personne*] to pick sb/sth up; [*vent*] to sweep sb/sth up into the air; **2** (entraîner) to arouse [*enthousiasme, colère, dégoût*]; to stir up [*foule, peuple, opinion*] (**contre** against); to raise [*problèmes, difficultés, obstacles*]; to give rise to [*protestations, applaudissements*]; **3** (faire considérer) to raise [*question, problème, interrogation*]

B **se soulever** *vpr* **1** (se dresser) to raise oneself up; **2** (se révolter) to rise up (**contre** against)

(Idiome) **ça me soulève le cœur** (odeur) it turns my stomach; (attitude) it makes me sick

soulier /sulje/ *nm* shoe

(Idiome) **être dans ses petits** ∼**s** to feel uncomfortable

souligner /suliɲe/ [1] *vtr* **1** (d'un trait) to underline [*mot, titre*]; to outline [*yeux*]; **2** (accentuer) to emphasize [*attitude, remarque*]; to set off [*teint, éclat*]

soumettre /sumɛtʀ/ [60]

A *vtr* **1** (vaincre) to bring [sb/sth] to heel [*personne, groupe, région*]; to subdue [*ennemi, rebelles, armée*]; **2** (assujettir) ∼ **qn/qch à** to subject sb/sth to; **3** (proposer) to submit (**à** to); ∼ **une proposition à qn** to put forward a proposal to sb; **4** (faire subir) ∼ **un produit à une température élevée** to subject a product to a high temperature

B **se soumettre** *vpr* **1** (se rendre) to submit; **2** (accepter) **se** ∼ **à** to accept [*règlement*]

soumis, ∼**e** /sumi, iz/ *adj* submissive

soumission /sumisjɔ̃/ *nf* **1** (assujettissement) submission (**à** to); **2** (reddition) submission (**à** to); **3** Admin, Comm tender

soumissionner /sumisjɔne/ [1] *vtr* to tender

soupape /supap/ *nf* valve

soupçon /supsɔ̃/ *nm* **1** (sur l'honnêteté, authenticité) suspicion; **avoir des** ∼**s sur qn/qch** to have one's suspicions about sb/sth; **2** (idée vague) **ne pas avoir** ∼ **de qch** to have no notion of sth; **3** ○(faible quantité) (de lait, vin) drop, spot○; (de cannelle, sel, d'herbes aromatiques) pinch; (dans un goût) hint

soupçonner /supsɔne/ [1] *vtr* **1** (suspecter) to suspect; ∼ **qn de qch/d'avoir fait** to suspect sb of sth/of having done; **2** (conjecturer) to suspect [*piège, coup bas*]

soupçonneux, **-euse** /supsɔnø, øz/ *adj* suspicious, mistrustful

soupe /sup/ *nf* **1** Culin soup; ∼ **de légumes/aux oignons** vegetable/onion soup; **à la** ∼○! hum grub up○!, come and get it!; **2** ○(neige) slush

(Composé) ∼ **populaire** soup kitchen

(Idiome) **par ici la bonne** ∼○! come on, cough up○!, come on, hand over the money!; **être** ∼ **au lait**○ to be quick-tempered; **cracher dans la** ∼○ to bite the hand that feeds you; **il me mange la** ∼ **sur la tête** he towers over me

soupente /supɑ̃t/ *nf* **1** (sous un toit) loft, garret; **2** (sous un escalier) cupboard under the stairs

souper¹ /supe/ [1] *vi* to have late dinner

(Idiome) **en avoir soupé de qch**○ to have had it up to here with sth○

souper² /supe/ *nm* late dinner, supper

soupeser /supəze/ [16] *vtr* **1** lit to heft, to feel the weight of [*objet*]; **2** fig to weigh up [*arguments*]

soupière /supjɛʀ/ *nf* soup tureen

soupir /supiʀ/ *nm* **1** (expiration) sigh (**de** of); **pousser un** ∼ to sigh ou heave a sigh; ∼ **de soulagement** sigh of relief; **2** (du vent) liter sighing; (d'amoureux) ∼**s** sighs; **3** Mus crotchet rest GB, quarter rest US

soupirail, *pl* **-aux** /supiʀaj, o/ *nm* cellar window

soupirer /supiʀe/ [1] *vi* [*personne, vent*] to sigh (**de** with); ∼ **pour qn** to pine for sb

souple /supl/ *adj* **1** (flexible) [*corps, animal*] supple; [*tige, lame*] flexible; [*cheveux, matière*] soft; **2** (aisé) [*démarche, geste, style*] flowing (*épith*); [*forme, contour*] smooth; **3** (adaptable) [*règlement, horaire*] flexible

souplesse /suplɛs/ *nf* **1** (de tige, lame, disque) flexibility; (de cheveux, matière) softness; (de corps, d'animal) suppleness; **2** (de démarche) litheness; (de geste) grace; (de voiture, conduite)

smoothness; (de style) fluidity; **3** (de règlement, d'esprit, horaire) flexibility; **en** ∼ smoothly; **4** Sport (en gymnastique) walk-over

source /suʀs/ *nf* **1** (d'eau) spring; **2** (de cours d'eau) source; **prendre sa** ∼ **dans** *or* **à** to rise in *ou* at; **3** (origine) source; **être à la** ∼ **de** to be at the root of; **être une** ∼ **de** to be a source of [*conflits, ennuis, profits*]; **4** (référence) source; **citer/vérifier ses** ∼**s** to give/to check one's sources

(Idiome) **ça coule de** ∼ it's obvious; **retour aux** ∼**s** return to basics

sourcil /suʀsi/ *nm* eyebrow; ∼**s épais** bushy eyebrows

sourcilier, **-ière** /suʀsilje, ɛʀ/ *adj* [*muscle*] superciliary

sourciller /suʀsije/ [1] *vi* to raise one's eyebrows; **sans** ∼ without batting an eyelid

sourd, ∼**e** /suʀ, suʀd/

A *adj* **1** Méd [*personne*] deaf; **être** ∼ **d'une oreille** to be deaf in one ear; **2** (insensible) deaf (**à** to); **3** (étouffé) [*bruit, explosion*] dull, muffled; [*voix*] muffled; [*plainte*] faint, muted; **4** (diffus) [*douleur*] dull; **5** (secret) [*lutte, machinations*] secret, hidden; **6** Ling voiceless, surd

B *nm,f* deaf person; **les** ∼**s** the deaf (+ *v pl*)

(Idiome) **faire la** ∼**e oreille** to turn a deaf ear; **mieux vaut entendre ça que d'être** ∼**!** hum what stupid things you hear!; **comme un** ∼ [*crier, taper, frapper*] like one possessed; **ce n'est pas tombé dans l'oreille d'un** ∼ it didn't go unheard

sourdine /suʀdin/ *nf* Mus mute; (de piano) soft pedal; **jouer en** ∼ to play softly; **mettre une** ∼ **à** fig to tone down [*critiques*]

sourd-muet, **sourde-muette**, *pl* **sourds-muets**, **sourdes-muettes** /suʀmɥɛ, suʀdmɥɛt/

A *adj* deaf and dumb

B *nm,f* deaf-mute

souriant, ∼**e**, /suʀjɑ̃, ɑ̃t/ *adj* smiling

souriceau, *pl* ∼**x** /suʀiso/ *nm* young mouse

souricière /suʀisjɛʀ/ *nf* **1** (pour souris) mousetrap; **2** (pour malfaiteur) trap

sourire¹ /suʀiʀ/ [68] *vi* **1** (adresser un sourire) to smile (**à qn** at sb); ∼ **jusqu'aux oreilles** to grin from ear to ear; **2** (être agréable) liter [*destin, fortune*] to smile; [*idée, projet*] to appeal to [*personne*]

(Idiome) ∼ **aux anges** to have a silly smile on one's face

sourire² /suʀiʀ/ *nm* smile; **un bon/large** ∼ a kindly/broad smile; **le** ∼ **aux lèvres** with a smile on one's face; **être tout** ∼ to be all smiles; **garder le** ∼ to keep smiling (through); **faire un** ∼ **à qn** to give sb a smile

souris /suʀi/ *nf inv* **1** Zool mouse; **2** Ordinat mouse; **3** ○(femme) bird○ GB, chick○ US

(Idiomes) **jouer au chat et à la** ∼ to play cat and mouse; **quand le chat n'est pas là les** ∼ **dansent** when the cat's away, the mice will play

sournois, ∼**e** /suʀnwa, az/

A *adj* [*personne, animal, air, regard*] sly; [*conduite, pensée, action*] underhand; [*douleur, mal*] insidious

B *nm,f* sly person, underhand person

sous /su/ *prép*

⚠ Lorsque *sous* indique une position dans l'espace il se traduit généralement par *under*: *sous la table/un arbre* = under the table/a tree.
   On trouvera ci-dessous exemples supplémentaires et exceptions.
   Lorsque *sous* a une valeur figurée comme dans *sous le choc*, *sous la menace*, *sous aucun prétexte* etc la traduction de *sous* sera fournie sous le deuxième élément, respectivement **choc**, **menace**, **prétexte** etc, auquel on se reportera.

1 (en dessous de) under, underneath, beneath sout; **un journal** ∼ **le bras** a newspaper under one's arm; **le jardin était** ∼ **la neige** the garden GB *ou* yard US was covered in snow; **le** ∼ **aux lèvres** the garden GB *ou* yard US was covered in snow; **le** ∼ **aux lèvres** under the water, underwater, below water; ∼ **la pluie** in the rain; **j'aurais voulu rentrer** ∼ **terre** fig I wished the ground would swallow me up; ∼ **étoile, herbe**; **2** (dans un classement) under; ∼ **le numéro 4757** under number 4757; **3** (pendant une période) during; ∼ **la présidence de Mitterrand** during Mitterrand's presidency; **4** (avant) within; ∼ **peu** before long; **5** (sous l'action de) ∼ **traitement** undergoing treatment; ∼ **antibiotiques** on antibiotics

sous-alimenté, ~e, mpl ~s /suzalimãte/ adj undernourished

sous-bois /subwɑ/ nm inv undergrowth ¢

sous-chef, pl ~s /suʃɛf/ nm gén second-in-command

souscripteur, -trice /suskʀiptœʀ, tʀis/ nm,f subscriber (de to)

souscription /suskʀipsjɔ̃/ nf [1] (à une publication, une œuvre charitable) subscription (à to); [2] (d'assurance) ~ d'un contrat d'assurances taking out an insurance policy; ~ **collective** collective underwriting; [3] Fin (à un emprunt, une émission) subscription (à to); ~ **d'actions** application for shares; **taux de** ~ take-up (of a rights issue)

souscrire /suskʀiʀ/ [67]
A vtr to take out [assurance, abonnement, plan d'épargne]; to sign [contrat, traite]; to subscribe [somme]
B souscrire à vtr ind [1] (en payant) ~ **à** to subscribe to [publication, emprunt, œuvre charitable]; [2] (adhérer) ~ **à** to subscribe to [propos, décision]; **j'y souscris entièrement** I go along with that completely

souscrit, ~e /suskʀi, it/
A pp ▸ souscrire
B pp adj [1] Fin subscribed; [2] (en imprimerie) [lettre] subscript

sous-cutané, ~e, mpl ~s /sukytane/ adj subcutaneous

sous-développé, ~e, mpl ~s /sudevlɔpe/ adj [pays, région, économie] underdeveloped

sous-directeur, -trice, mpl ~s /sudiʀɛktœʀ, tʀis/ nm,f assistant manager

sous-direction, pl ~s /sudiʀɛksjɔ̃/ nf division; ~ **des affaires économiques et financières** economic and financial affairs division

sous-effectif, pl ~s /suzefɛktif/ nm understaffing ¢; **ils sont en** ~ they're understaffed

sous-employer /suzɑ̃plwaje/ [23] vtr to underemploy

sous-entendre /suzɑ̃tɑ̃dʀ/ [6] vtr to imply

sous-entendu, ~e, mpl ~s /suzɑ̃tɑ̃dy/
A pp ▸ sous-entendre
B pp adj understood
C nm innuendo; **un sourire plein de** ~s a smile full of innuendo

sous-entraîné, ~e, mpl ~s /suzɑ̃tʀene/ adj ill-prepared

sous-équipé, ~e, mpl ~s /suzekipe/ adj under-equipped

sous-espèce, pl ~s /suzɛspɛs/ nf subspecies (+ v sg)

sous-estimer /suzɛstime/ [1] vtr to underestimate

sous-évaluer /suzevalɥe/ [1] vtr to underestimate [coût, problème]; to undervalue [maison, terrain]

sous-exposer /suzɛkspoze/ [1] vtr Phot to underexpose [photo]

sous-fifre○, pl ~s /sufifʀ/ nm underling

sous-jacent, ~e, mpl ~s /suʒasɑ̃, ɑ̃t/ adj [1] fig (latent) [idée, problème, tension] underlying; [2] (au-dessous) subjacent

sous-lieutenant, pl ~s /suljøtnɑ̃/ ▸ p. 283 nm (dans l'armée de terre) ≈ second lieutenant; (dans l'aviation) ≈ pilot officer GB, ≈ second lieutenant US

sous-louer /sulwe/ [1] vtr [1] (donner en location) to sublet, to sublease [appartement, pièce]; [2] (prendre en location) to sublease [appartement, pièce]

sous-main /sumɛ̃/
A nm inv desk blotter
B en sous-main loc adv under the table, secretly

sous-marin, ~e, mpl ~s /sumaʀɛ̃, in/
A adj [1] [relief, faune, flore] submarine, underwater; [2] [exploration, câble] underwater; [plongée] deep-sea
B nm [1] Naut submarine; [2] ○(espion) spy
(Composé) ~ **à propulsion nucléaire** nuclear-powered submarine

sous-marinier, pl ~s /sumaʀinje/ ▸ p. 372 nm submariner

sous-marque, pl ~s /sumaʀk/ nf sub-brand

sous-officier, pl ~s /suzɔfisje/ ▸ p. 283 nm non-commissioned officer

sous-ordre, pl ~s /suzɔʀdʀ/ nm suborder

sous-payer /supeje/ [21] vtr to underpay [employé]

sous-peuplé, ~e, mpl ~s /supœple/ adj [pays, région] underpopulated

sous-préfecture, pl ~s /supʀefɛktyʀ/ nf: administrative subdivision of a department in France

sous-préfet, pl ~s /supʀefɛ/ nm: permanent ministerial representative in a department in France

sous-produit, pl ~s /supʀɔdɥi/ nm [1] (produit secondaire) by-product; [2] (produit médiocre) second-rate product

sous-prolétariat, pl ~s /supʀɔletaʀja/ nm underclass

sous-pull, pl ~s /supyl/ nm thin polo-neck jumper

sous-secrétaire, pl ~s /sus(ə)kʀetɛʀ/ nmf ~ **d'État** Parliamentary Undersecretary of State

soussigné, ~e /susiɲe/
A adj undersigned
B nm,f les ~s the undersigned (+ v pl)

sous-sol, pl ~s /susɔl/ nm [1] Constr basement; [2] Géog subsoil ¢

sous-tasse, pl ~s /sutas/ nf saucer

sous-titrage, pl ~s /sutitʀaʒ/ nm subtitling

sous-titre, pl ~s /sutitʀ/ nm [1] (titre secondaire) subtitle; [2] Cin, TV, Mus (texte sous image) subtitle, caption

sous-titrer /sutitʀe/ [1] vtr Cin, TV, Mus to subtitle

soustractif, -ive /sustʀaktif, iv/ adj subtractive

soustraction /sustʀaksjɔ̃/ nf [1] Math (processus) subtraction ¢; (opération) subtraction; **faire une erreur de** ~ to make a mistake while subtracting; [2] Jur (vol) removal, taking away

soustraire /sustʀɛʀ/ [58]
A vtr [1] Math to subtract (de from); [2] (voler) to steal (à from); [3] (retirer) to take away [personne] (à from); ~ **qn/qch à la vue de qn** to hide sb/sth from sb; [4] (protéger) to shield [personne]; ~ **qn à la mort** to save sb's life
B se soustraire vpr [1] (éviter) **se** ~ **à** to escape from [tâche, ennui]; **se** ~ **à ses obligations** to shirk one's duties; [2] (échapper à) **se** ~ **à** to avoid [arrestation]; **se** ~ **à la justice** to escape justice

sous-traitance, pl ~s /sutʀɛtɑ̃s/ nf subcontracting; **travail donné en** ~ work contracted out

sous-verre /suvɛʀ/ nm inv [1] (encadrement) frame; [2] (œuvre) framed picture

sous-vêtement, pl ~s /suvɛtmɑ̃/ nm underwear ¢

soutane /sutan/ nf cassock; **porter la** ~ to be a priest

soute /sut/ nf Naut hold

soutenable /sutnabl/ adj [1] (supportable) bearable; **pas** ~ unbearable; [2] (défendable) [hypothèse] tenable

soutenance /sutnɑ̃s/ nf Univ (de mémoire, dossier) viva GB, orals (pl) US

soutènement /sutɛnmɑ̃/ nm gén retaining structure; (dans une mine) props (pl)

souteneur /sutnœʀ/ nm pimp○, procurer

soutenir /sutniʀ/ [36]
A vtr [1] (donner son appui) to support; ~ **une grève** to support a strike; ~ **à bout de bras** to keep [sb/sth] afloat [personne, projet]; ~ **qn contre qn** to side with sb against sb; [2] Écon, Fin to support [monnaie, marché, cours, économie]; [3] (affirmer) to maintain [contraire]; to defend [paradoxe]; to uphold [opinion]; ~ **que** to maintain that; [4] (servir de support) to support [personne, toit, monnaie]; **mur soutenu par des étais** wall supported by props; [5] (donner des forces) to keep [sb] going [personne]; [6] (réconforter) [personne] to support; [espoir] to sustain; ~ **le moral de qn** to keep sb's spirits up; [7] (faire durer) to keep [sth] alive [curiosité, intérêt]; to keep [sth] going [conversation]; to keep up, to sustain [effort, rythme]; [8] (résister) to withstand [choc, siège, assaut, regard]; to bear [comparaison]; [9] Univ ~ **sa thèse** to have one's viva GB ou defense US
B se soutenir vpr [1] (s'entraider) to support each other; [2] (être défendable) [argument, hypothèse] to be tenable, to hold oneself up

soutenu, ~e /sutny/
A pp ▸ soutenir
B pp adj [1] (intense) [activité, effort] sustained; [attention] close; [rythme] steady
C adj [1] gén [marché] firm; [couleur] deep; [style, langue] formal, elevated; [2] Mus (maintenu) [note, ton] sustained, long-drawn-out

souterrain, ~e /suteʀɛ̃, ɛn/
A adj [1] (sous terre) [lac, ouvrage, explosion] underground;

S

2 (secret) [menées, accord] secret; **économie ~e** black economy
B nm underground passage, tunnel

soutien /sutjɛ̃/ nm **1** (appui) support (à for); **le parti a manifesté son ~ à la majorité** the party showed its support for the majority; **~ en anglais** Scol extra help in English; **2** (agent) support; **3** (de voûte, plate-forme) support

soutien-gorge, pl **soutiens-gorge** /sutjɛ̃gɔrʒ/ nm bra

soutirer /sutire/ [1] vtr **1** (dérober) **~ à qn** to squeeze [sth] out of sb [argent]; to extract [sth] from sb [aveu]; **2** (clarifier) to rack [vin]

souvenance /suvnɑ̃s/ nf fml **à ma ~** as far as I recall; **avoir ~ de qch** to remember sth

souvenir¹ /suvnir/ [36]
A **se souvenir** vpr **se ~ de qn/qch** to remember sb/sth; **se ~ (d')avoir fait** to remember doing; **se ~ que** to remember that
B v impers **il me souvient que** liter I recollect that; **autant qu'il m'en souvienne** if my memory serves me right

souvenir² /suvnir/ nm **1** (pensée du passé) memory; **garder un bon/mauvais ~ de qch** to have happy/bad ou unhappy memories of sth; **le ~ que je garde de lui est encore très clair** I still remember him very clearly; **~s d'école** memories of schooldays; **~s d'enfance** childhood memories; **chercher dans ses ~s** to sift through one's memories; **avoir (le) ~ de qch** to remember sth; **ne pas avoir ~ de** to have no recollection of; **au ~ de** at the memory of; **2** (mémoire) memory; **3** (objet) (rappelant un lieu, un événement) souvenir (**de** of); (rappelant une personne) memento (**de** from); **en ~** gén as a souvenir; (avec valeur affective) as a memento; (cadeau ayant valeur affective) as a keepsake; **boutique de ~s** souvenir shop GB ou store US; **4** (salutation) **croyez à mon bon** or **fidèle** or **meilleur ~** yours ever; **mon bon ~ à** remember me to

souvent /suvɑ̃/ adv often; **le plus ~** more often than not

⌐Idiome⌐ **on a ~ besoin d'un plus petit que soi** Prov a mouse may help a lion

souverain, ~e /suvrɛ̃, ɛn/
A adj **1** (indépendant) [État, peuple, droit, pouvoir] sovereign; [décision, autorité] supreme; **2** (suprême) [bonheur, talent, mépris] supreme; **3** (infaillible) [remède, potion] sovereign; [conseil, vertu] sterling; **4** (hautain) [personne] haughty
B nmf sovereign, monarch
C nm (monnaie) sovereign

souverainement /suvrɛnmɑ̃/ adv **1** (sans appel) [décider, juger] without appeal; **2** (suprêmement) **votre attitude me déplaît ~** I dislike your attitude intensely

souveraineté /suvrɛnte/ nf sovereignty

soviétique /sɔvjetik/ adj Hist Soviet

soyeux, -euse /swajø, øz/
A adj silky
B ▸ p. 372 nm (fabricant) silk manufacturer

SPA /ɛspea/ nf (abbr = **Société protectrice des animaux**) society for the prevention of cruelty to animals

spacieux, -ieuse /spasjø, øz/ adj spacious

spaghetti /spageti/ nm inv spaghetti **¢**

sparadrap /sparadra/ nm **1** (bande adhésive) surgical ou adhesive tape; **2** (pansement) (sticking) plaster GB, Band-aid®

spartiate /sparsjat/ adj, nmf Spartan

spasme /spasm/ nm spasm

spasmophilie /spasmofili/ nf spasmophilia

spath /spat/ nm spar

spatial, ~e, mpl **-iaux** /spasjal, o/ adj **1** gén, Psych [repérage, perception, représentation] spatial; **2** (Astronaut) space (épith); **vaisseau ~** spaceship

spationaute /spasjonot/ ▸ p. 372 nmf astronaut

spatule /spatyl/ nf **1** Culin, Art spatula; (de plâtrier) filling-knife; **2** (de ski) tip; **3** Zool (poisson) paddlefish; (oiseau) spoonbill

speaker, speakerine /spikœr, spikrin/ ▸ p. 372 nm,f announcer

spécial, ~e, mpl **-iaux** /spesjal, o/ adj **1** (non général) [formation, tarif, statut] special; **2** (adapté) [appareil, chaussures, peigne] special; **3** (bizarre) [mentalité, personne] odd

spécialement /spesjalmɑ̃/ adv **1** (particulièrement) specially; **2** (très) especially; **pas ~** not especially

spécialisé, ~e /spesjalize/
A pp ▸ spécialiser
B pp adj **être ~ dans** or **en** [personne] to be a specialist in; [établissement, usine] to specialize in

spécialiser: se spécialiser /spesjalize/ [1] vpr to specialize (**en, dans** in)

spécialiste /spesjalist/ nmf specialist (**de, en** in)

spécialité /spesjalite/ nf **1** gén speciality GB, specialty US; **~ médicale** specialized medical field; **2** Culin speciality GB, specialty US

spécieux, -ieuse /spesjø, øz/ adj specious

spécificité /spesifisite/ nf **1** (de produit, maladie) specificity; **2** (caractéristique) characteristic; **3** (caractère unique) uniqueness

spécifier /spesifje/ [2] vtr to specify

spécifique /spesifik/ adj specific (**de** to)

spécimen /spesimɛn/ nm **1** (exemple) specimen; **2** (exemplaire) (free) sample; **3** °(personne) odd specimen°

spectacle /spektakl/
A nm **1** (vue) sight; (événement) sight; **au ~ de...** at the sight of...; **devant un tel ~** (affreux) at this awful sight; (merveilleux) at this amazing sight; **se donner en ~** pej to make an exhibition ou a spectacle of oneself; **2** (divertissement) **avoir le sens du ~** [metteur en scène] to have a real sense of theatre^GB; [politicien] to have an eye for effect; **3** Théât (représentation) show; **~ de marionnettes** puppet show; **'~s'** (rubrique) 'entertainment'; **film à grand ~** spectacular; **4** (activité professionnelle) **le ~, l'industrie du ~** show business
B **-spectacle** (in compounds) **1** péj **politique-~** showbiz° politics; **2** Théât **dîner-~** dinner and floor show

spectaculaire /spektakyler/ adj spectacular

spectateur, -trice /spektatœr, tris/ nm,f **1** (au théâtre, cinéma) member of the audience; (dans un stade, la rue) spectator; **les ~s** (au théâtre) the audience (sg); (dans un stade, la rue) the spectators, the crowd (sg); **2** (curieux) onlooker; **assister à une réunion en ~** to sit in on a meeting

spectral, ~e, mpl **-aux** /spektral, o/ adj **1** (de fantôme) liter spectral, ghostly; **2** Phys spectral

spectre /spektr/ nm **1** (fantôme) ghost; **2** (de guerre, famine, mort) spectre^GB (**de** of); **3** Phys spectrum

spectroscopie /spektrɔskɔpi/ nf spectroscopy

spéculateur, -trice /spekylatœr, tris/ nm,f speculator

spéculatif, -ive /spekylatif, iv/ adj speculative

spéculation /spekylasjɔ̃/ nf **1** Fin speculation; **~ sur** speculation in [actions, valeurs, or]; **2** gén, Philos speculation (**sur** on, about)

spéculer /spekyle/ [1] vi **1** Fin to speculate; **~ à la hausse/baisse** to bull/bear; **~ sur** to speculate in [valeurs, actions, or]; **2** Philos, gén to speculate (**sur** on, about)

spéléologie /speleɔlɔʒi/ nf **1** ▸ p. 327 (sport) potholing GB, caving, spelunking US; **2** (science) speleology

spéléologue /speleɔlɔg/ nmf **1** (sportif) potholer GB, caver, spelunker US; **2** ▸ p. 372 (scientifique) speleologist spéc

spermatozoïde /spɛrmatozɔid/ nm spermatozoon

sperme /spɛrm/ nm sperm

spermicide /spɛrmisid/
A adj [gelée] spermicidal
B nm spermicide

sphère /sfɛr/ nf **1** Math sphere; **2** (domaine) sphere; **les hautes ~s de la finance** the higher echelons of finance

sphérique /sferik/ adj spherical

sphincter /sfɛ̃ktɛr/ nm sphincter

sphinx /sfɛ̃ks/ nm inv **1** Mythol, Art Sphinx; **2** (papillon) hawkmoth

spinal, ~e, mpl **-aux** /spinal, o/ adj spinal

spirale /spiral/ nf **1** Math spiral; **monter/descendre en ~** to spiral up/down; **2** (amplification) spiral; **la ~ des prix et des salaires** the wage-price spiral

spire /spir/ nf Tech, Math turn

spiritisme /spiritism/ nm spiritualism

spiritualisme /spiritɥalism/ nm gén, Philos spiritualism

spiritualité /spiritɥalite/ nf spirituality

spirituel, -elle /spiʀitɥɛl/ adj ☐ (de l'esprit) spiritual; ☐ (amusant) witty

spiritueux, -euse /spiʀitɥø, øz/
A adj [vin] with a high alcohol content
B nm inv spirit; **vins et ~** wines and spirits

spleen /splin/ nm spleen; **avoir le ~** to feel despondent

splendeur /splɑ̃dœʀ/ nf (de paysage, site, jour) splendour^GB; (d'époque, de règne) glory; **cette église est une ~** this church is truly magnificent

splendide /splɑ̃did/ adj [objet, journée, victoire] splendid; [villa, pays] magnificent; [yeux, personne] stunning

spoliation /spɔljasjɔ̃/ nf fml despoliation sout

spolier /spɔlje/ [2] vtr fml to despoil sout (**de** of)

spongieux, -ieuse /spɔ̃ʒjø, øz/ adj spongy

sponsoriser /spɔ̃sɔʀize/ [1] vtr to sponsor

spontané, ~e /spɔ̃tane/ adj spontaneous; **candidature ~e** unsolicited application

spontanéité /spɔ̃taneite/ nf spontaneity

sporadique /spɔʀadik/ adj sporadic

spore /spɔʀ/ nf spore

sport /spɔʀ/ nm (activité générale) sport; (ensemble d'activités) sports (pl); **aimer le ~** to like sport; **vous faites du ~?** do you do any sports?; **je fais un peu de ~ tous les jours** I do some sport every day

(Composés) **~ automobile** motor sports (pl), car-racing; **~ cérébral** intellectual game; **~ de compétition** competitive sport; **~ d'équipe** team sport; **~ d'hiver** winter sport; **~ individuel** individual sport

(Idiomes) **ça c'est du ~**^○! this is no picnic^○!; **il va y avoir du ~**^○! this is going to be fun ou interesting!; **faire qch pour le ~** to do sth for fun

sportif, -ive /spɔʀtif, iv/
A adj ☐ lit [équipement, épreuve, journal, rencontre] sports (épith); **je ne suis pas ~** I'm not the sporty type; ☐ fig [allure] athletic, sporty^○; **conduite sportive** Aut speeding; ☐ (généreux) [personne, esprit, attitude] sporting; **faire preuve d'esprit ~** to be a good sport, to display sportsmanship
B nm,f sportsman/sportswoman

spot /spɔt/ nm ☐ (pour éclairer) spotlight, spot; ☐ (séquence) **~ (publicitaire)** commercial; ☐ Phys spot

squale /skwal/ nm shark

square /skwaʀ/ nm small public garden

squash /skwaʃ/ ▸ p. 327 nm squash

squatter /skwate/ [1], **squattériser** /skwateʀize/ [1] vtr to squat in [appartement]; to take over [escalier]

squelette /skəlɛt/ nm ☐ Anat skeleton; ☐ ^○(personne maigre) bag of bones^○, skeleton; ☐ (de bateau) framework; ☐ (d'une œuvre) outline

squelettique /skəlɛtik/ adj [personne, jambes] scrawny; Méd skeletal; fig [arbre] skeletal; [rapport, article] sketchy

SRAS /sʀas/ nm (abbr = **syndrome respiratoire aigu sévère**) SARS

stabilisateur, -trice /stabilizatœʀ, tʀis/
A adj stabilizing
B nm stabilizer

stabiliser /stabilize/ [1]
A vtr to stabilize [prix, marché, monnaie, pays, personnes, véhicule, gaz]; to consolidate [accotements]
B se stabiliser vpr [chômage, prix, taux] to stabilize; [personne] to become stable

stabilité /stabilite/ nf stability

stable /stabl/ adj stable

stade /stad/ nm ☐ Sport stadium; ☐ (étape) stage; **les ~s de la production** the stages of production

stage /staʒ/ nm ☐ (pour obtenir diplôme, titre) professional training; ☐ (pendant des études) work experience **C**; ☐ (pour le travail, le sport, les loisirs) course; **suivre un ~** to go on a course; **~ de formation** training course

stagiaire /staʒjɛʀ/ nmf gén trainee; (enseignant) student teacher; (infirmière) student nurse

stagnation /stagnasjɔ̃/ nf lit, fig stagnation

stagner /stagne/ [1] vi lit, fig to stagnate

stalactite /stalaktit/ nf stalactite

stalagmite /stalagmit/ nf stalagmite

stalle /stal/ nf ☐ (pour chevaux) stall; ☐ (d'église) stall

stand /stɑ̃d/ nm (d'exposition) stand; (de fête foraine) stall

(Composé) **~ de tir** (de club sportif) shooting range; (de fête foraine) shooting gallery

standard /stɑ̃daʀ/
A adj inv standard
B nm Télécom switchboard

standardisation /stɑ̃daʀdizasjɔ̃/ nf standardization

standardiste /stɑ̃daʀdist/ ▸ p. 372 nmf switchboard operator

standing /stɑ̃diŋ/ nm ☐ (confort) **de (grand) ~** [appartement] luxury (épith); ☐ (niveau de vie) standard of living

star /staʀ/ nf star

starlette /staʀlɛt/ nf starlet

starter /staʀtɛʀ/ nm Aut choke; **mettre le ~** to pull out the choke

station /stasjɔ̃/ nf ☐ (de métro) station; (de taxis) taxi-rank GB, taxi stand; **~ de métro** tube GB ou subway US station; ☐ Radio station; **~ de radio** radio station; ☐ (lieu de séjour) resort; **~ balnéaire** seaside resort; **~ de sports d'hiver** winter sports resort; **~ thermale** spa; ☐ (lieu d'observation scientifique) station; **~ météorologique** meteorological ou weather station; **~ orbitale** orbiting space station; **~ spatiale** space station; ☐ (position) posture; **~ debout** or **verticale** upright posture or position; ☐ (pause) stop, pause; ☐ ^○Aut (station-service) service station; **~ de lavage** car wash

(Composés) **~ d'épuration** sewage treatment plant; **~ de travail** workstation

stationnaire /stasjɔnɛʀ/ adj ☐ [planète, véhicule] stationary; ☐ [situation, production] stable; **être dans un état ~** [malade] to be in a stable condition

stationnement /stasjɔnmɑ̃/ nm ☐ Aut parking; **~ interdit** no parking; **~ payant** (dans la rue) metered parking; (dans un parking) pay and display parking; **~ à durée limitée** short-term parking; **'~ gênant'** 'no parking or waiting'; **une amende pour ~ gênant** a parking fine; **~ en épi** angle parking; **~ en bataille** perpendicular parking; ☐ C Aut car park GB, parking lot US; ☐ Mil (de troupes) stationing

stationner /stasjɔne/ [1] vi ☐ Aut to park; **~ en double file** to double-park; ☐ Mil to station

station-service, pl **stations-service** /stasjɔ̃sɛʀvis/ nf service station, filling station

statique /statik/ adj static

statistique /statistik/
A adj statistical
B nf (méthode) statistics (+ v sg); (donnée) statistic

statue /staty/ nf statue (**de** of)

(Idiome) **se changer en ~** to be frozen to the spot

statuer /statɥe/ [1] vi to give a ruling (**sur** on)

statuette /statɥɛt/ nf statuette

statu quo /statykwo/ nm inv status quo

stature /statyʀ/ nf ☐ lit (gabarit) stature; (sur une étiquette de vêtements) height; ☐ fig (envergure) calibre^GB

statut /staty/ nm ☐ (loi, règlement) statute; ☐ (situation) status; **avoir un ~ d'immigrant** to have immigrant status

statutaire /statytɛʀ/ adj statutory

steak /stɛk/ nm steak

(Composé) **~ haché** (cru) minced beef GB, ground beef US; (cuit) hamburger

stèle /stɛl/ nf stele

sténo^○ /steno/ ▸ **sténodactylo**

sténodactylo /stenodaktilo/
A ▸ p. 372 nmf (personne) shorthand typist GB, stenographer US
B nf (activité) shorthand typing GB, stenography US

sténodactylographie /stenodaktilɔgʀafi/ nf shorthand typing GB, stenography US

sténographier /stenɔgʀafje/ [2] vtr to take [sth] down in shorthand

sténotypie /stenɔtipi/ nf stenotypy

sténotypiste /stenɔtipist/ ▸ p. 372 nmf stenotypist

stentor /stɑ̃tɔʀ/ nm ☐ gén **voix de ~** stentorian voice; ☐ Zool stentor

steppe /stɛp/ nf steppe

S

stère /stɛʀ/ ▸ p. 628 nm stere

stéréo /steʀeo/
A adj inv (abbr = **stéréophonique**) stereo (épith)
B ○nf stereo

stéréophonie /steʀeɔfɔni/ nf stereophony; **en ~** [enregistrer] in stereo; [enregistrement] stereophonic (épith)

stéréophonique /steʀeɔfɔnik/ adj stereophonic

stéréotype /steʀeɔtip/ nm 1 (personne) stereotype; 2 (cliché) cliché

stérile /steʀil/ adj 1 [personne, animal, plante] sterile; [mariage] childless; [sol] barren; 2 [pansement, milieu] sterile; 3 fig [artiste] unproductive; [imagination] barren; [discussion] fruitless

stérilet /steʀilɛ/ nm coil, intrauterine device spéc

stériliser /steʀilize/ [1] vtr 1 lit to sterilize [personne, animal]; to make [sth] barren [sol]; 2 fig to stifle [créativité, artiste]; 3 (purifier) to sterilize [biberon, appareil, bocal, pansement]

stérilité /steʀilite/ nf 1 (de personne, d'animal) sterility; (de sol, région) barrenness; 2 fig (d'artiste) lack of creativity; (de travail) fruitlessness; 3 (de milieu) sterility

sterling /stɛʀliŋ/ adj inv sterling; **livre ~** pound sterling

sternum /stɛʀnɔm/ nm breastbone, sternum spéc

stéthoscope /stetɔskɔp/ nm stethoscope

steward /stjuwaʀd/ nm steward

stigmate /stigmat/
A nm 1 (trace sur la peau) scar; fig (de vice, guerre) mark; 2 Bot, Zool stigma
B stigmates nmpl Relig stigmata

stimulant, ~e /stimylɑ̃, ɑ̃t/
A adj (physiquement) [bain] invigorating; [air, climat] bracing; (mentalement) stimulating
B nm 1 (physique) (fortifiant) tonic; (excitant) stimulant; 2 (mental) stimulus

stimulation /stimylasjɔ̃/ nf stimulation

stimuler /stimyle/ [1]
A vtr 1 to stimulate [organe, fonction]; 2 (motiver) to spur [sb] on
B vi 1 [air, froid] to be bracing; 2 ○[récompense] to act as a spur

stipuler /stipyle/ [1] vtr to stipulate (**que** that)

stock /stɔk/ nm lit, fig stock; **avoir des ~s de**○ fig to have a whole stock of

stockage /stɔkaʒ/ nm 1 (mise en réserve) Comm stocking; (accumulation excessive) stockpiling; 2 (conservation) Comm, Ordinat storage

stocker /stɔke/ [1] vtr 1 Comm to stock; (à l'excès) to stockpile; 2 Ordinat to store [données]

stoïque /stɔik/
A adj stoical
B nmf stoic

stomacal, ~e, mpl **-aux** /stɔmakal, o/ adj stomach

stomatologie /stɔmatɔlɔʒi/ nf stomatology

stop /stɔp/
A nm 1 Aut (panneau) stop sign; (feu arrière) brake light; 2 ○(auto-stop) hitching○; **faire la France en ~** to hitch○ roundGB France; **prendre qn en ~** to give sb a lift GB ou ride US
B excl stop!

stopper /stɔpe/ [1]
A vtr 1 (arrêter) to stop [personne, voiture, attaque]; to halt [maladie, évolution]; 2 (en couture) to mend
B vi to stop

store /stɔʀ/ nm blind; (auvent) awning

strabisme /stʀabism/ nm squint, strabismus spéc

strapontin /stʀapɔ̃tɛ̃/ nm foldaway seat

strass /stʀas/ nm inv (verroterie) paste

stratagème /stʀataʒɛm/ nm stratagem

strate /stʀat/ nf lit, fig stratum

stratège /stʀatɛʒ/ nm strategist

stratégie /stʀateʒi/ nf strategy

stratégique /stʀateʒik/ adj strategic

stratifié, ~e /stʀatifje/
A adj 1 Biol, Sociol stratified; 2 Tech laminated
B nm (matériau) **du ~** laminate; **table en ~** laminated table

stratosphère /stʀatɔsfɛʀ/ nf stratosphere

stress /stʀɛs/ nm inv stress

stressant, ~e /stʀɛsɑ̃, ɑ̃t/ adj [journée] stressful; [incident] upsetting; [perspective] worrying

stresser /stʀɛse/ [1]
A vtr [perspective] to put [sb] on edge; [travail] to put [sb] under stress; **être stressé** (tendu) to be stressed; (irritable) to be on edge; (sous pression) to be under stress
B ○vi to get worked up

stretch /stʀɛtʃ/ nm stretch material

strict, ~e /stʀikt/ adj 1 (sévère) [discipline, morale, professeur] strict; **il est très ~ sur la propreté** he's very strict about cleanliness; 2 (complet) **au sens ~** in the strict sense of the word; **c'est la ~e vérité** it's the absolute truth; **le ~ nécessaire** what is strictly necessary; 3 (austère) [tenue, robe] severe, austere; [coiffure] severe

stricto sensu /stʀiktosɛ̃sy/ loc adv strictly speaking

strident, ~e /stʀidɑ̃, ɑ̃t/ adj 1 [bruit] piercing; [voix] strident; 2 Ling strident

strie /stʀi/ nf 1 (rayure) streak; 2 (sillon) gén groove; (de front, visage) furrow; Anat, Biol stria

strié, ~e /stʀije/ adj 1 (de couleur) streaked (**de** with); [muscle] striated; 2 (de sillons) [roche] striated; [colonne] fluted; [coquille, tige] grooved

strier /stʀije/ [2] vtr 1 (de couleur) to streak (**de** with); 2 (faire des sillons) to make grooves in; 3 (en géologie) to striate

strip-teaseur, -euse /stʀiptizœʀ, øz/ ▸ p. 372 nm,f stripper

stroboscope /stʀobɔskɔp/ nm stroboscope

strophe /stʀɔf/ nf 1 (de poème) stanza, verse; 2 (dans une tragédie grecque) strophe

structural, ~e, mpl **-aux** /stʀyktyʀal, o/ adj structural

structuralisme /stʀyktyʀalism/ nm structuralism

structure /stʀyktyʀ/ nf 1 (agencement) structure; 2 (organisme) organization; **~ d'accueil** shelter, refuge

structuré, ~e /stʀyktyʀe/ adj structured

structurel, -elle /stʀyktyʀɛl/ adj structural

structurer /stʀyktyʀe/ [1]
A vtr to structure
B se structurer vpr to be structured

stuc /styk/ nm stucco

studieux, -ieuse /stydjø, øz/ adj [élève] studious; [vacances] study (épith); [ambiance] industrious

studio /stydjo/ nm 1 (logement) studio flat GB, studio apartment US; 2 (atelier) studio; 3 Cin, Radio, TV studio; **tourné en ~** filmed ou shot in the studio

stupéfait, ~e /stypefɛ, ɛt/ adj astounded, dumbfounded; **rester ~ de qch/d'apprendre** to be astounded at sth/to hear

stupéfiant, ~e /stypefjɑ̃, ɑ̃t/
A adj 1 (étonnant) stunning, astounding; 2 Méd stupefying
B nm (drogue) drug, narcotic

stupéfier /stypefje/ [2] vtr 1 (étonner) to astound, to stun; 2 Méd (hébéter) to stupefy

stupeur /stypœʀ/ nf 1 (étonnement) astonishment; 2 Méd (torpeur) stupor

stupide /stypid/ adj stupid

stupidité /stypidite/ nf 1 (caractère) stupidity; 2 (remarque) stupid remark

style /stil/ nm 1 Art, Littérat, Sport style; **~ de vie** lifestyle; **avoir du ~** to have style; **elle veut se donner le ~ Marilyn Monroe** she's trying to cultivate the Marilyn Monroe look; **c'est bien (dans) ton ~ de faire** it's typical of you to do; **elle est du ~ à passer une nuit blanche pour finir un article** she's the kind that would stay up all night to finish an article; **il m'a répondu qch du ~ 'on vous téléphonera'** he told me they'd phone me, or something like that; 2 (de mobilier) period furniture; **meubles de ~** (anciens) period furniture; (copiés) reproduction period furniture; 3 Ling speech form; **~ direct/indirect** direct/indirect ou reported speech; 4 (tige de cadran solaire) style; 5 Bot, Zool style

styliser /stilize/ [1] vtr to stylize

styliste /stilist/ nmf ▸ p. 372 (de mode) fashion designer

stylistique /stilistik/
A adj stylistic
B nf stylistics (+ v sg)

stylo /stilo/ *nm* pen

⟨Composés⟩ ~ **(à) bille** ball-point pen; ~ **à encre** fountain pen; ~ **feutre** felt-tip pen; ~ **(à) plume** = ~ **à encre**

su /sy/ *nm* **au** ~ **de qn** liter to sb's knowledge; **au vu et au** ~ **de tous** openly, for all to see

suaire /sɥɛʀ/ *nm* shroud

suant, ~**e** /sɥɑ̃, ɑ̃t/ *adj* **1** (qui sue) sweaty; **2** °(ennuyeux) deadly dull

suave /sɥav/ *adj* liter [*parfum, sourire*] sweet; [*coloris, regard*] soft; [*contours*] smooth; [*voix*] mellifluous; [*plaisir*] exquisite; [*personne, manière*] suave

subalterne /sybaltɛʀn/
A *adj* [*poste*] junior; [*rôle*] subordinate; (au théâtre) minor
B *nmf* subordinate; Mil low-ranking officer

subconscient, ~**e** /sybkɔ̃sjɑ̃, ɑ̃t/
A *adj* subconscious
B *nm* subconscious

subdiviser /sybdivize/ [1]
A *vtr* to subdivide (**en** into)
B se subdiviser *vpr* to be subdivided (**en** into)

subdivision /sybdivizjɔ̃/ *nf* subdivision

subéquatorial, ~**e**, *mpl* -**iaux** /sybekwatɔʀjal, o/ *adj* subequatorial

subir /sybiʀ/ [3] *vtr* **1** (être victime de) to be subjected to [*mauvais traitements, violences, pressions*]; to suffer [*dégâts, discrimination, brimades*]; **faire** ~ **à qn** to subject sb to [*mauvais traitements*]; to inflict [sth] on sb [*défaite, pertes*]; **2** (être soumis à) to undergo, to be subjected to [*interrogatoire*]; to take [*examen scolaire*]; to have [*opération, examens médicaux*]; ~ **l'influence de qn** to be under sb's influence; **3** (supporter) to put up with [*personne, épreuve*]; **4** (être l'objet de) to undergo [*changements*]

subit, ~**e** /sybi, it/ *adj* sudden

subitement /sybitmɑ̃/ *adv* suddenly, all of a sudden

subjectif, -**ive** /sybʒɛktif, iv/ *adj* subjective

subjectivité /sybʒɛktivite/ *nf* subjectivity

subjonctif, -**ive** /sybʒɔ̃ktif, iv/
A *adj* subjunctive
B *nm* subjunctive; **au** ~ in the subjunctive

subjuguer /sybʒyge/ [1] *vtr* **1** (séduire) to captivate, to enthral^{GB}; **2** (asservir) liter to subjugate

sublime /syblim/ *adj* [*peinture, œuvre, acteur*] sublime; ~ **de générosité** extraordinarily generous

sublimer /syblime/ [1] *vtr*, *vi* to sublimate

subliminal, ~**e**, *mpl* -**aux** /sybliminal, o/ *adj* subliminal

submerger /sybmɛʀʒe/ [13] *vtr* **1** (inonder) lit to submerge [*terre, récif*]; fig to flood [*standard téléphonique, marché*] (**de** with); **2** (dominer) [*foule, ennemi, émotion*] to overwhelm [*personne, groupe*]; **3** (accabler) ~ **qn de travail** to inundate sb with work

submersible /sybmɛʀsibl/
A *adj* **1** Géog [*terre*] liable to flooding (*après n*); **2** Tech [*machine, navire*] submersible
B *nm* submersible

submersion /sybmɛʀsjɔ̃/ *nf* **1** Agric irrigation by flooding; **2** Naut (de sous-marin) submersion; (naufrage) sinking

subodorer /sybɔdɔʀe/ [1] *vtr* to detect [*piège*]

subordination /sybɔʀdinasjɔ̃/ *nf* **1** (dépendance) subordination (**à** to); **2** Ling subordination; **conjonction de** ~ subordinating conjunction

subordonné, ~**e**¹ /sybɔʀdɔne/ *nm,f* subordinate

subordonnée² /sybɔʀdɔne/ *nf* Ling subordinate clause; ~ **circonstancielle** adverbial clause

subordonner /sybɔʀdɔne/ [1] *vtr* **1** (dans une hiérarchie) **être subordonné à qn** [*soldat, fonctionnaire*] to be subordinate to sb; **2** (faire dépendre) **elle subordonne tout à son travail** everything else comes second to her job; **être subordonné à qch** [*réussite, réalisation*] to be subject to *ou* dependent on sth

suborner /sybɔʀne/ [1] *vtr* (corrompre) to bribe [*employé, garde*]; Jur to suborn [*témoin*]

subreptice /sybʀɛptis/ *adj* surreptitious

subside /sybsid/ *nm* (d'État, association) grant; (entre particuliers) allowance

subsidiaire /sybzidjɛʀ/ *adj* [*moyens*] ancillary; [*motif*] subsidiary; **question** ~ tiebreaker

subsistance /sybzistɑ̃s/ *nf* (de personne) subsistence; (de plante) sustenance; (moyens de survie) **(moyens de)** ~ means of support, livelihood; **frais de** ~ living expenses; **économie de** ~ subsistence economy; **assurer la** ~ **de sa famille** to support one's family

subsister /sybziste/ [1]
A *vi* **1** (durer) [*crainte, trace*] to remain; **2** (survivre) [*personne, coutume*] to survive; **3** (subvenir à ses besoins) [*personne*] to subsist; **ça leur suffit à peine pour** ~ it's barely enough for them to live on
B *v impers* **il subsistera toujours un doute** a doubt will always remain

substance /sypstɑ̃s/ *nf* substance; **en** ~ in substance; ~**s végétales** vegetable matter **₵**

substantiel, -**ielle** /sypstɑ̃sjɛl/ *adj* **1** (nourrissant) [*repas*] substantial; fig [*lecture*] solid; **2** (considérable) [*nombre, baisse*] substantial; [*progrès*] significant

substantif, -**ive** /sypstɑ̃tif, iv/
A *adj* [*proposition*] noun; [*style*] nominal; [*emploi*] nominal, substantival
B *nm* noun, substantive

substantiver /sypstɑ̃tive/ [1] *vtr* to substantivize

substituable /sypstitɥabl/ *adj* substitutable

substituer /sypstitɥe/ [1]
A *vtr* **1** ~ **A à B** to substitute A for B; **2** Jur ~ **un héritage** to entail an estate
B se substituer *vpr* **se** ~ **à** [*personne*] (pour représenter) to deputize for, to stand in for [*personne, groupe*]; (pour remplacer) to take the place of [*personne*]; [*chose*] to take the place of, to replace [*chose*]

substitut /sypstity/ *nm* **1** (magistrat) deputy public prosecutor; **2** (remplacement) substitute (**de** for); ~ **maternel** mother substitute

substitution /sypstitysjɔ̃/ *nf* (remplacement) substitution (**de qn/qch à** of sb/sth for); **produit de** ~ **du sucre/café** sugar/coffee substitute

subterfuge /s"yptɛʀfyʒ/ *nm* ploy, subterfuge **₵**

subtil, ~**e** /syptil/ *adj* [*personne, argument, nuance, parfum*] subtle; [*négociateur, manœuvre*] skilful^{GB}

subtiliser /syptilize/ [1] *vtr* (dérober) ~ **qch à qn** to steal sth from sb

subtilité /syptilite/ *nf* subtlety

subvenir /sybvəniʀ/ [36] *vtr ind* ~ **à** to meet [*dépenses, besoins*]; ~ **aux besoins de sa famille** to provide for one's family

subvention /sybvɑ̃sjɔ̃/ *nf* (allocation) grant; (pour que le public paie moins cher) subsidy

subventionner /sybvɑ̃sjɔne/ [1] *vtr* to subsidize

subversif, -**ive** /sybvɛʀsif, iv/ *adj* subversive

subversion /sybvɛʀsjɔ̃/ *nf* subversion (**de** of)

suc /syk/ *nm* **1** lit (de fruit, viande) juice; (de plante, fleur) sap; **2** fig essence **₵**

⟨Composé⟩ ~**s digestifs** *or* **gastriques** gastric juices

succédané /syksedane/ *nm* lit, fig substitute, ersatz (**de** for); (en pharmacie) succedaneum

succéder /syksede/ [14]
A succéder à *vtr ind* **1** (remplacer) ~ **à** [*personne*] to succeed [*personne*]; ~ **à qn à la tête d'une entreprise** to succeed sb as head of a company; **2** (suivre) ~ **à** [*chose*] to follow [*chose*]
B se succéder *vpr* (venir l'un après l'autre) [*personnes*] to succeed *ou* follow one another; [*choses*] to follow (one another); **les orages se succèdent sans interruption** there is storm after storm

succès /syksɛ/ *nm inv* success; **une série de** ~ a string of successes; **votre** ~ **aux élections/à l'école** your success in the elections/at school; **avoir du** ~, **être un** ~ [*produit, livre, opération*] to be a success (**auprès de** with); [*disque, chanson*] to be a hit (**auprès de** with); **avoir du** ~ [*artiste*] to be a success; **avoir du** ~ **auprès de qn** [*personne*] to be a hit with sb; **leur proposition n'a eu aucun** ~ their proposal got nowhere; **connaître un grand** ~ to be a great success; **faire le** ~ **de qn/qch** to make sb/sth successful; **à** ~ [*acteur, pièce, film*] successful; **auteur à** ~ best-selling author; **avec** ~ successfully

successeur /syksesœʀ/ *nm* successor

successif, -**ive** /syksesif, iv/ *adj* successive

s

succession /syksesjɔ̃/ nf **1** (série, suite) (de personnes, visiteurs) stream, succession; (d'événements) series (+ v sg), succession; (de jours, saisons) passage; (de nombres) series (+ v sg); (d'accidents, de malheurs) string, succession; **2** (transmission de pouvoir) succession; **prendre la ~ de** to succeed [roi]; to take over from [ministre, directeur]; **3** Jur (transmission) (de biens) succession; (de patrimoine) inheritance, estate

succinct, **~e** /syksɛ̃, ɛ̃t/ adj [écrit] succinct; [discours] brief

succion /syksjɔ̃/ nf **1** (avec appareil) suction; **2** (avec la bouche) sucking

succomber /sykɔ̃be/ [1] vi **1** (mourir) to die; **2** (fléchir) liter to give way, to yield; **~ sous le poids** to collapse under the weight; **~ sous le nombre** to be overwhelmed by numbers; **3** (s'abandonner) **~ à** to succumb to [charme, désespoir]; to yield to [tentation]

succulent, **~e** /sykylã, ãt/ adj **1** (savoureux) [repas, cuisine, fruit] delicious; **2** Bot **plante ~e** succulent

succursale /sykyʀsal/ nf branch, outlet

sucer /syse/ [12] vtr to suck

sucette /sysɛt/ nf **1** (bonbon) lollipop, lolly○; **2** (tétine) dummy GB, pacifier US

suçoter /sysɔte/ [1] vtr to suck

sucre /sykʀ/ nm **1** (substance) sugar; **je bois mon thé sans ~** I don't take sugar in my tea; **du chocolat noir sans ~** sugar-free dark chocolate; **2** (morceau) sugar lump; **combien de ~s dans ton café?** how many sugars in your coffee?

(Composés) **~ blanc** white sugar; **~ brun** dark brown sugar; **~ de canne** cane sugar; **~ cristallisé** granulated sugar; **~ glace** icing sugar GB, powdered sugar US; **~ d'orge** (substance) barley sugar; (bâton) stick of barley sugar, ≈ rock; **~ en poudre** caster sugar GB, superfine sugar US; **~ roux** brown sugar; **~ vanillé** vanilla sugar

(Idiomes) **être tout ~ tout miel** to be all sweetness and light; **casser du ~ sur le dos de qn** to run sb down, to badmouth sb○

sucré, **~e** /sykʀe/
A adj **1** lit [fruit, goût, vin, biscuit] sweet; [lait condensé, jus de fruit] sweetened; **2** fig [ton] honeyed
B nm (aliments) sweet food; **je n'aime pas le ~** I don't like sweet things

sucrer /sykʀe/ [1] vtr (rendre doux) [personne] to put sugar in [café, compote]; (en saupoudrant) to sprinkle sugar on [fraises]; [miel, saccharine] to sweeten

sucrerie /sykʀəʀi/
A nf (usine) sugar refinery
B sucreries nfpl sweets GB

sucrier, **-ière** /sykʀije, ɛʀ/
A adj [industrie] sugar; [région] sugar-producing
B nm (pot) sugar bowl; **~ verseur** sugar shaker

sud /syd/ ▸ p. 454
A adj inv [façade, versant, côté] south; [frontière, zone] southern
B nm **1** (point cardinal) south; **2** (région) south; **le ~ de la France** the south of France; **le ~ de l'Europe/du Japon** southern Europe/Japan; **3** Géog, Pol **le Sud** the South; **du Sud** [ville, accent] southern

(Composé) **le Sud Viêt Nam** Hist South Vietnam

sud-africain, **~e**, mpl **~s** /sydafʀikɛ̃, ɛn/ ▸ p. 392 adj South African

sudation /sydasjɔ̃/ nf sweating

sud-coréen, **-éenne**, mpl **~s** /sydkɔʀeɛ̃, ɛn/ ▸ p. 392 adj South Korean

sud-est /sydɛst/ ▸ p. 454
A adj inv [façade, versant] southeast; [frontière, zone] southeastern
B nm southeast; **le Sud-Est asiatique** South East Asia

sudiste /sydist/ adj, nmf Hist Confederate

sud-ouest /sydwɛst/ ▸ p. 454
A adj inv [façade, versant] southwest; [frontière, zone] southwestern
B nm southwest

Suède /sɥɛd/ ▸ p. 230 nprf Sweden

suédois, **~e** /sɥedwa, az/ ▸ p. 336, p. 392
A adj Swedish
B nm Ling Swedish

Suédois, **~e** /sɥedwa, az/ ▸ p. 392 nm,f Swede

suer /sɥe/ [1]
A vtr **1** (exsuder) [personne, peau] to sweat; [mur, roche] to ooze [eau, humidité]; **~ sang et eau** fig to sweat blood and tears (**pour faire** to do; **sur qch** over sth); **2** (dégager) [personne] to exude [bêtise, ennui, misère]
B vi **1** to sweat (**sur** over); **~ à grosses gouttes** to sweat buckets; **faire ~ qn**○ (embêter) to bore sb stiff○ (**avec** with)

sueur /sɥœʀ/ nf sweat; **se mettre en ~** to break into a sweat; **j'en avais des ~s froides** I was in a cold sweat about it; **gagner son pain à la ~ de son front** to earn one's living by the sweat of one's brow; **il avait le dos en ~** his back was covered in sweat

suffire /syfiʀ/ [64]
A vi (être suffisant) [somme, durée, quantité] to be enough; **quelques gouttes suffisent** a few drops are enough; **ma retraite suffit à mes besoins** my pension is enough to cover my needs; **deux heures suffisent amplement pour faire le trajet** two hours is ample time ou is easily enough for the journey; **un rien suffit à or pour le mettre en colère** it only takes the slightest thing to make him lose his temper
B se suffire vpr se ~ (à soi-même) [personne, pays] to be self-sufficient; **le film se suffit à lui-même** the film speaks for itself
C v impers **1** (être très simple) **il suffit de faire qch** all you have to do is do sth; **il suffit d'un coup de téléphone pour annuler son abonnement** it only takes one phone call to cancel your subscription; **2** (être suffisant) **il suffit d'une lampe pour éclairer la pièce** one lamp is enough to light the room; **il suffit d'une seconde d'inattention pour qu'un accident se produise** it only takes a second's carelessness to cause an accident; **3** (notion de cause à effet) **il suffit que je sorte sans parapluie pour qu'il pleuve!** every time I go out without my umbrella, it's guaranteed to rain; **4** (être satisfaisant) **ça suffit (comme ça)!, il suffit!** that's enough!; **il ne leur a pas suffi de nous cambrioler, il a fallu qu'ils saccagent la maison** they weren't satisfied with burgling GB ou burglarizing US us, they had to wreck the house as well

(Idiome) **à chaque jour suffit sa peine** Prov sufficient unto the day (is the evil thereof)

suffisamment /syfizamã/ adv enough; **~ intelligent pour** intelligent enough to; **nous avons ~ marché** we've walked enough; **il n'a pas ~ d'argent pour faire** he doesn't have enough money to do

suffisance /syfizãs/ nf (vanité) self-importance, arrogance; **il est plein de ~** he's very self-important

suffisant, **~e** /syfizã, ãt/ adj **1** (adéquat) sufficient; **deux heures, c'est ~ pour faire le trajet** two hours is enough for the journey; **l'éclairage n'est pas ~** the lighting is inadequate; **2** (vaniteux) [personne, ton, air] self-important

suffixe /syfiks/ nm suffix

suffocant, **~e** /syfɔkã, ãt/ adj **1** (étouffant) [chaleur, atmosphère] suffocating; **2** (stupéfiant) staggering

suffocation /syfɔkasjɔ̃/ nf (action) suffocation; (sensation) suffocating feeling; **crise de ~** fit of choking

suffoquer /syfɔke/ [1]
A vtr **1** (étouffer) [chaleur, fumée] to suffocate; **2** ○(stupéfier) **son aplomb m'a suffoqué** I was staggered by his/her cheek○
B vi **1** (étouffer) to suffocate; **on suffoque ici** it's suffocating in here; **2** (s'étrangler) to choke (**de** with)

suffrage /syfʀaʒ/ nm **1** Pol (système) suffrage; **~ universel** universal suffrage; **2** Pol (voix) vote; **~s exprimés** recorded votes; **remporter peu de ~s** to receive few votes; **3** fig (approbation) approval **₵**; **recueillir tous les ~s** to meet with universal approval

suggérer /sygʒeʀe/ [14] vtr to suggest (**à** to); **je suggère qu'on s'en aille** I suggest (that) we leave; **elle a suggéré à la commission de modifier le projet** she suggested to the commission that they should modify the project

suggestif, **-ive** /sygʒɛstif, iv/ adj [texte] evocative; [pose, photos] suggestive; [décolleté] provocative

suggestion /sygʒɛstjɔ̃/ nf suggestion

suicidaire /sɥisidɛʀ/
A adj lit, fig suicidal
B nmf person with suicidal tendencies

suicide /sɥisid/ nm lit, fig suicide; **c'est du or un ~** fig it's suicide

suicider: se suicider /sɥiside/ [1] vpr to commit suicide

suie /sɥi/ nf soot

suif /sɥif/ nm **1** (de chandelle) tallow; **2** Culin suet

suinter /sɥɛ̃te/ [1] vi **1** [eau] to seep (**de** through); [sang, sève] to ooze (**de** from); **2** [mur] to sweat; [plaie] to weep

suisse /sɥis/
A ▸ p. 392 adj Swiss; **∼ allemand** Swiss German; **∼ romand** French-speaking Swiss, of French-speaking Switzerland; **∼ italien** Italian-speaking Swiss, of Italian-speaking Switzerland
B nm **1** (au Vatican) Swiss Guard; **2** (d'église) verger
⌐Idiome⌐ **manger/boire en ∼** to eat/drink alone

Suisse /sɥis/
A ▸ p. 392 nm,f (habitant) Swiss; **∼ allemand** Swiss German; **∼ romand** French-speaking Swiss
B ▸ p. 230 nprf Switzerland; **∼ allemande/romande/italienne** German-speaking/French-speaking/Italian-speaking Switzerland

suite /sɥit/
A nf **1** (reste) rest; **je te raconterai la ∼ plus tard** I'll tell you the rest later; **la ∼ des événements** (à venir) what happens next; (déjà survenue) what happened next; **lis la ∼ pour comprendre** read on and you'll understand; **2** (partie suivante) (de récit) continuation; (de feuilleton) next instalment^GB; (de repas) next course; **∼ page 10/au prochain numéro** continued on page 10/in the next issue; **3** (nouveau film, roman) sequel (**à, de** to); (émission, article de suivi) follow-up (**à, de** to); **4** (résultat) **les ∼s** (d'acte, de décision) the consequences; (d'affaire, incident) the repercussions; (de maladie, d'opération) the after-effects; **mourir des ∼s d'une chute** to die as a result of a fall; **5** (réponse produite) **donner ∼ à** to follow up [plainte, affaire]; to pursue [projet]; to act on [requête]; to respond to [lettre]; Comm to deal with [commande]; **ne pas donner ∼ à une lettre** to fail to respond to a letter; **rester sans ∼** [demande] not to be followed up; [projet] to be dropped; **6** (indiquant la position) **faire ∼ à** to follow on from [paragraphe]; to follow upon [incident]; **la pièce qui fait ∼ au bureau** the room which leads off the study; **prendre la ∼ de qn** to take over from sb; **7** (cohérence) coherence; **avoir de la ∼ dans les idées** (savoir ce que l'on veut) to be single-minded; (être entêté) iron not to be easily deterred; **8** (série) (de sommets, d'incidents) series (+ v sg); (de malheurs, série) string, series (+ v sg); (de succès) run; **9** (dans un hôtel) suite; **10** (entourage) suite; **11** Math series (+ v sg); **12** Mus suite; **13** Ling string; **14** Jeux (aux cartes) run
B de suite loc adv **1** (d'affilée) in succession, in a row; **il a plu trois jours de ∼** it rained for three days running; **dormir dix heures de ∼** to sleep for ten hours solid; **sur dix pages de ∼** over ten consecutive pages; **et ainsi de ∼** and so on; **2** (immédiatement) straight ou right away
C par la suite loc adv (après) afterwards; (plus tard) later
D par suite loc adv consequently, as a result
E par suite de loc prép due to; **par ∼ d'encombrement, votre appel ne peut aboutir** all lines are engaged GB ou busy, please try later
F à la suite de loc prép **1** (en conséquence, après) following; **2** (derrière) behind; **à la ∼ les uns des autres, l'un à la ∼ de l'autre** one behind the other; **entraîner qn à sa ∼** (derrière soi) to drag sb along behind one; (dans une chute) lit, fig to drag sb down with one
G suite à loc prép **∼ à ma lettre** further to my letter; **∼ à votre lettre** with reference to your letter

suivant¹ /sɥivɑ̃/
A prép **1** (le long de) along [axe, pointillé]; **2** (conformément à) in accordance with [coutume, rituel]; **∼ leur habitude** (au présent) as they usually do; (au passé) as they usually did; **3** (en fonction de) depending on [temps, compétence, circonstances]; **4** (selon) according to; **∼ le plan/leurs instructions** according to the map/their instructions
B suivant que loc conj depending on whether

suivant², **∼e¹** /sɥivɑ̃, ɑ̃t/
A adj **1** (ci-après) following; **de la manière** or **façon ∼e** in the following manner; **2** (d'après) (dans le temps) following, next; (dans une série) next; **voir le chapitre ∼** see next chapter
B nm,f **le ∼** (dans le temps) the following one, the next one; (dans une série) the next one; **(au) ∼!** next!; **pas ce lundi, le ∼** not this Monday, the one after
C le suivant, la suivante loc adj as follows (jamais épith); **la situation est la ∼e** the situation is as follows

suivante² /sɥivɑ̃t/ nf **1** Théât, Littérat lady's maid; **2** †(dame de compagnie) companion

suivi, ∼e /sɥivi/
A pp ▸ **suivre**
B pp adj **1** (maintenu) [travail, demande] steady; [effort] sustained; [correspondance] regular; [habitudes] regular; [qualité] consistent; [relations] close; **2** Comm [article] in general production (après n), that is always in stock (épith, après n); **3** (apprécié) **la boxe est le sport le plus ∼** boxing is the most popular sport; **quelle est l'émission la plus ∼e?** which is the most popular programme^GB?; **c'est une mode peu ∼e** it's a fashion which hasn't really caught on; **4** (cohérent) [politique] consistent; [argumentation] coherent
C nm (de procédure) monitoring; Comm (de commande) follow-up; **le ∼ des malades** follow-up care for patients; **assurer le ∼ des jeunes délinquants** to follow up (on) young delinquents; **assurer le ∼ d'un produit** Comm to ensure the continued supply of a product

suivre /sɥivʀ/ [62]
A vtr **1** (aller derrière) to follow [personne, voiture]; (accompagner) to accompany [personne]; **faire ∼ qn** to have sb followed; **∼ qn dans le jardin** to follow sb into the garden GB ou yard US; **∼ qn de près/de loin** lit to follow sb closely/at a distance; **∼ de très près la voiture de tête** to be right behind the leading car; **il est mort en juin, et elle l'a suivi de près** he died in June and she followed not long after; **ta réputation t'a suivi jusqu'ici** your reputation has preceded you; **suivez le guide!** this way, please!; **2** (se situer après) to follow, to come after [période, incident, dynastie]; (succéder à) to follow; (résulter de) to follow; **le jour qui suivit** the next ou following day; **lis ce qui suit** read on; **'à ∼'** 'to be continued'; **3** (aller selon) [personne] to follow [flèche, sentier, itinéraire]; [police, chien] to follow [piste]; [bateau, route] to follow, to hug [côte]; [route] to run alongside [voie ferrée]; **indiquer (à qn) la route à ∼** to give (sb) directions; **quelle est la marche à ∼?** fig what is the best way to go about it?; **∼ le droit chemin** fig to keep to the straight and narrow; **lire en suivant (les lignes) du doigt dans son livre** to read with a finger under the line; **4** (se conformer à) to follow [coutume, exemple, instinct]; to obey [caprice, impulsion]; **décider de ∼ un régime** to decide to go on a diet; **5** (être attentif à) to follow [leçon, match, procès]; to follow the progress of [élève, malade]; **∼ l'actualité** to keep up with the news; **c'est une affaire à ∼** it's something worth watching; **être suivi** or **se faire ∼ par un spécialiste** Méd to be treated by a specialist; **elle ne suit jamais en classe** she never pays attention in class; **un de nos collègues, suivez mon regard**° hum one of our colleagues, not mentioning any names; **6** (assister à) **∼ un cours de cuisine** to do a cookery GB ou cooking US course; **7** (comprendre) to follow [explication, raisonnement]; **je vous suis** I'm with you; **8** fig (ne pas se laisser distancer) to keep pace with [personne]; **tu vas trop vite, je ne peux pas (te) ∼** you're going too fast, I can't keep up; **les prix augmentent, mais les salaires ne suivent pas** prices are going up but wages are not keeping pace; **9** Comm **∼ un article** to keep a line in stock; **10** Sport to follow [sth] through [ballon]
B vi **1** Postes **faire ∼ son courrier** to have one's mail forwarded; **(prière de) faire ∼** please forward; **2** Jeux (au poker) **je suis** I'm in
C se suivre vpr **1** (être placés dans un ordre) [numéros, pages] to be in order; Jeux [cartes] to be consecutive; **2** (se succéder) [incidents] to happen one after the other; **les deux frères se suivent de près** the two brothers are close in age
D v impers **il suit** it follows (**de** from); **comme suit** as follows

sujet, -ette /syʒɛ, ɛt/
A adj **être ∼ à** to be prone to [rhumes, migraine, vertige, accès de colère]; **∼ à caution** [information, témoignage] questionable
B nm **1** (question) subject; **traiter un ∼** to deal with a subject; **un ∼ de conversation** a topic of conversation; **leur vieille voiture est un ∼ de plaisanterie pour leurs amis** their friends joke about their old car; **un ∼ d'actualité** a topical issue; **je n'ai rien à dire à ce ∼** I've nothing to say on that subject ou matter; **c'est à quel ∼?** what is it about?; **au ∼ de** about; **2** (thème) subject; **3** Scol, Univ question; **un ∼ d'examen** an exam question; **quel est ton ∼ de thèse?** what's your thesis on?; **hors ∼** off the subject; **4** (raison) cause; **c'est un ∼ d'étonnement** it is amazing; **5** (individu) **les ∼s qui se sont soumis au test médical** those who have

La superficie

■ *Pour la prononciation des nombres, voir* **les nombres**
▸ **p. 398.**

Équivalences

1 sq in = 6,45 cm^2 1 acre = 40,47 ares *ou* 0,40 ha
1 sq ft = 929,03 cm^2 1 sq ml = 2,59 km^2
1 sq yd = 0,84 m^2

dire			dire
one square centimetre	1 cm^2	= 0.15 sq in	square inches
one square metre	1 m^2	= 10.76 sq ft 1.19 sq yds	square feet square yards
one square kilometre	1 km^2	= 0.38 sq mls	square miles
one are	1 are	= 119.6 sq yds	
one hectare	1 hectare	= 2.47 acres	acres

Pour l'écriture, noter:

– *l'anglais utilise un point là où le français a une virgule:* 0,15 *s'écrit* 0.15, *etc.*
– *on écrit* -metre *en anglais britannique et* -meter *en anglais américain.*
– *on peut écrire* sq *in ou* in^2, sq ft *ou* ft^2, *etc.*

il y a 10 000 centimètres carrés dans un mètre carré
= there are 10,000 square centimetres in a square metre

10 000 centimètres carrés font un mètre carré
= 10,000 square centimetres make one square metre

quelle est la superficie du jardin?
= what is the area of the garden?
  ou how big is the garden?

combien mesure le jardin?
= what size is the garden?
  ou what does the garden measure?

il fait 12 m^2
= it is 12 square metres

sa surface est de 12 m^2
= its area is 12 square metres

il a une surface de 12 m^2
= it is 12 square metres
  ou it is 12 square metres in area

il fait 20 m sur 10 m
= it is 20 metres by 10 metres

il fait à peu près 200 m^2
= it is about 200 square metres

presque 200 m^2
= almost 200 square metres

plus de 200 m^2
= more than 200 square metres

moins de 200 m^2
= less than 200 square metres

la superficie de A est égale à celle de B
= A is the same area as B

A et B ont la même surface
= A and B are the same area

■ *Noter l'ordre des mots dans l'adjectif composé anglais, et l'utilisation du trait d'union. Noter aussi que* metre, *employé comme adjectif, ne prend pas la marque du pluriel.*

un jardin de 200 m^2
= a 200-square-metre garden

On peut aussi dire: a garden 200 square metres in area.

6 mètres carrés de soie
= six square metres of silk

vendu au mètre carré
= sold by the square metre

---

had the medical; **c'est un brillant** ~ (étudiant) he's a brilliant student; **[6]▸** Ling, Philos subject; **[7]▸** (ressortissant d'un royaume) subject; **[8]▸** (d'expérience scientifique) subject

sujétion /syʒesjɔ̃/ *nf* **[1]** (servitude) subjection (**à** to); **être tenu en** ~ to be held in subjection; **[2]** (contrainte) constraint

sulfate /sylfat/ *nm* sulphate^{GB}

sulfite /sylfit/ *nm* sulphite^{GB}

sulfure /sylfyʀ/ *nm* **[1]** Chimie sulphide^{GB}; **[2]** Art (en verrerie) sulphide^{GB}; (presse-papier) glass paperweight

sulfuré, ~e /sylfyʀe/ *adj* sulphurated^{GB}; **hydrogène** ~ hydrogen sulphide^{GB}

sulfureux, -euse /sylfyʀø, øz/ *adj* **[1]** Chimie [*eau, vapeur*] sulphurous^{GB}; [*bain, source*] sulphur^{GB} (*épith*); [*odeur*] like sulphur^{GB} (*après n*); **[2]** fig [*personne, réputation, charme*] fiendish

sulfurisé, ~e /sylfyʀize/ *adj* **papier** ~ greaseproof paper

sultan /syltɑ̃/ *nm* sultan

summum /sɔm(m)ɔm/ *nm* height

sumo /sumo, symo/ ▸ p. 327 *nm inv* sumo wrestling

super^1 /sypɛʀ/ *préf* super

super^2 /sypɛʀ/
A ○*adj inv* great○
B *nm* (essence) four-star (petrol) GB, super, high-octane gasoline US
C ○*excl* great○!

superbe /sypɛʀb/
A *adj* [*fleurs, spectacle*] superb; [*personne*] superb-looking (*épith*); [*ville, pays*] magnificent
B *nf* liter haughtiness

superbement /sypɛʀbəmɑ̃/ *adv* gén [*décorer, cuisiner*] superbly; [*ignorer*] haughtily

supercarburant /sypɛʀkaʀbyʀɑ̃/ *nm* four-star *ou* high-octane petrol GB, super, high-octane gasoline US

supercherie /sypɛʀʃəʀi/ *nf* **[1]** (tromperie) deception; **[2]** (acte) hoax, act of deception; (faux) fake

supérette /sypeʀɛt/ *nf* minimarket, superette US

superficie /sypɛʀfisi/ *nf* **[1]** (aire) (de terrain, pays) area; (de pièce, bâtiment) floor area; **la** ~ **de la Terre** the surface area of the Earth; **[2]** (aspect superficiel) surface; **en** ~ fig superficially

superficiel, -ielle /sypɛʀfisjɛl/ *adj* **[1]** lit [*couche*] surface (*épith*); [*blessure*] superficial; **[2]** fig superficial, shallow

superflu, ~e /sypɛʀfly/
A *adj* (de trop) superfluous; (inutile) unnecessary
B *nm* (excédent) surplus; **s'offrir le** ~ to treat oneself to luxuries

supérieur, ~e /sypeʀjœʀ/
A *adj* **[1]** (situé en haut dans l'espace) [*mâchoire, membre, lèvre*] upper; [*niveau, étage*] upper, top; **dans le coin** ~ **droit** in the top right-hand corner; **[2]** (dans une hiérarchie) [*grades, classes sociales*] upper; **il a été promu au rang** ~ he was promoted to the next rank up; **[3]** (en valeur) [*vitesse, coût, salaire, nombre*] higher (**à** than); [*taille, dimensions*] bigger (**à** than); [*durée*] longer (**à** than); **mes notes sont** ~**es à la moyenne** my marks are above average; **être** ~ **en nombre** to be greater in number; **si a est** ~ **à b** if a is greater than b; **température** ~ **à 20°** temperature above 20°; **[4]** (de meilleure qualité) [*travail, qualité*] superior (**à** to); **leur ennemi leur était** ~ their enemy was better than them; **[5]** (hautain) [*air, ton, sourire*] superior
B *nm,f* **[1]** (chef) superior; **mon** ~ **hiérarchique** my immediate superior; **[2]** Relig Superior
C *nm* Univ higher education

supérieurement /sypeʀjœʀmɑ̃/ *adv* exceptionally

supériorité /sypeʀjɔʀite/ *nf* superiority; **avoir un sentiment de** ~ to feel superior

superlatif, -ive /sypɛʀlatif, iv/
A adj superlative
B nm superlative

supermarché /sypɛʀmaʀʃe/ nm supermarket

superposable /sypɛʀpozabl/ adj stackable

superposer /sypɛʀpoze/ [1] vtr **1** (l'un sur l'autre) to stack (up) [casiers, tabourets, caisses, briques, matelas]; **des lits superposés** bunk beds; **2** (faire coïncider) to superimpose [dessins, formes] (**à** on (top of)); to juxtapose [approches, théories] (**à** with)

superproduction /sypɛʀpʀɔdyksjɔ̃/ nf Cin block-buster○

superpuissance /sypɛʀpɥisɑ̃s/ nf superpower

supersonique /sypɛʀsɔnik/ adj supersonic

superstitieux, -ieuse /sypɛʀstisjø, øz/ adj superstitious

superstition /sypɛʀstisjɔ̃/ nf superstition

⬡Idiome **la ~ est fille de l'ignorance** Prov superstition is born of ignorance

superviser /sypɛʀvize/ [1] vtr to supervise

supplanter /syplɑ̃te/ [1] vtr to supplant (**dans** in)

suppléance /sypleɑ̃s/ nf gén temporary replacement post; Scol supply GB ou substitute US post; **être chargé d'une ~** gén to fill in for sb

suppléant, ~e /sypleɑ̃, ɑ̃t/ nm,f gén replacement; (de juge) deputy; (d'enseignant) supply GB ou substitute US teacher; (de médecin) stand-in (doctor); **un poste de ~** gén temporary replacement post; Scol supply GB ou substitute US post

suppléer /syplee/ [11] vtr ind **~ à** to make up for, to compensate for

supplément /syplemɑ̃/ nm **1** (somme d'argent) gén extra ou additional charge; (en voyage, à l'hôtel) supplement; **il y a un ~ à payer pour l'excédent de bagages** you have to pay a supplement ou you have to pay extra for excess baggage; **le vin est en ~** the wine is extra; **2** (complément) **~ d'informations** additional information; **3** (magazine) supplement (**à** to)

supplémentaire /syplemɑ̃tɛʀ/ adj additional, extra; **un obstacle ~** another obstacle; **un délai ~** another extension of the deadline; **train ~** relief train

suppliant, ~e /syplijɑ̃, ɑ̃t/ adj [voix] pleading; [air, regard] imploring

supplication /syplikasjɔ̃/ nf **1** gén plea; **2** Relig supplication

supplice /syplis/ nm torture; **les ~s au Moyen Âge** forms of torture in the Middle Ages; **subir un ~** lit to be tortured; fig to be in torment; **mettre qn au ~** fig to torture sb; **j'étais au ~** fig it was agony

supplicié, ~e /syplisje/ nm,f torture victim

supplicier /syplisje/ [2] vtr (torturer) to torture; (exécuter) to execute

supplier /syplije/ [2] vtr to beg, to beseech (**de faire** to do)

supplique /syplik/ nf liter petition; **présenter** or **adresser une ~ à qn** to petition sb; **céder aux ~s de qn** to give in to sb's entreaties

support /sypɔʀ/ nm **1** (soutien) support; **servir de ~ à qch** to serve as a support for sth; **2** (objet) (pour des bibelots) stand; (pour des tubes à essai) rack; **3** (aide) back-up; **utiliser des diapositives comme ~** to use slides as backup material; **~ audiovisuel** audio-visual aid; **4** Art support

supportable /sypɔʀtabl/ adj bearable

supporter¹ /sypɔʀte/ [1]
A vtr **1** (soutenir) [structure, colonne, pilier] to support, to bear the weight of [toiture, édifice]; **2** (prendre en charge) to bear [frais, dépenses]; **3** (endurer) to put up with, to endure [privations, malheur]; to put up with [personne, attitude, sarcasme]; to bear, to endure [souffrance, solitude]; [plante] to withstand [froid, chaleur]; **elle ne supporte pas d'attendre/la vue du sang** she can't stand waiting/the sight of blood; **il a mal supporté tes critiques** he found your criticisms hard to take; **elle supporte bien la chaleur** she can take ou stand the heat; **il a bien supporté son opération** he came through the operation well; **il a bien supporté le voyage** he stood the journey well; **il ne supporterait pas le voyage** the journey would be too much for him
B se supporter vpr **ils ne peuvent plus se ~** they can't stand each other any more

supporter² /sypɔʀtœʀ/ nmf supporter

supposer /sypoze/ [1] vtr **1** (comme base d'un raisonnement) gén to suppose; Math, Philos to postulate; **en supposant** or **à ~ que** supposing (that); **la chaleur est supposée constante** the heat is taken to be constant; **2** (tenir pour probable) to assume; **on peut ~ que** we can assume that; **3** (impliquer) to presuppose; **cela suppose que** this presupposes that

supposition /sypozisjɔ̃/ nf supposition, assumption

suppositoire /sypozitwaʀ/ nm suppository

suppôt /sypo/ nm liter pej **le ~ du dictateur** the dictator's henchman; **un dangereux ~ de la subversion/réaction** a dangerous subversive/reactionary

⬡Composé **~ de Satan** or **du diable** fiend

suppression /sypʀesjɔ̃/ nf (d'impôt) abolition; (de droit) revocation; (de sanction, contrôle) lifting; (d'avantages) withdrawal; (de preuves, faits) suppression; (de chômage, défauts) elimination; (de monopole) breaking; (de mot, ligne) deletion; **le ~ du train de 8 heures 50** the discontinuation of the 8.50 service; **~s d'emplois** job cuts; **il y a eu 20 ~s de postes** 20 posts have gone

supprimer /sypʀime/ [1]
A vtr **1** to cut [emploi, poste]; to stop [aide, vibration]; to abolish [impôt, rationnement, institution]; to lift [sanction, restriction]; to lift, to abolish [contrôle, censure]; to remove [effet, cause, obstacle, mur]; to do away with [examen, classe]; to put an end to [pauvreté]; to withdraw [avantage, subvention]; to break, to end [monopole]; to eliminate [nuisance, défaut]; to repeal [loi]; to cease to allow [dérogation]; to cut off [argent de poche]; to cut out [sucre, sel]; to delete [mot, ligne]; to take [sth] away [liberté]; **~ un train** (annuler) to cancel a train; (définitivement) to discontinue a service; **2** (tuer) euph to eliminate
B se supprimer vpr (se suicider) to do away with oneself

suppurer /sypyʀe/ [1] vi to suppurate

supputer /sypyte/ liter [1] vtr to calculate, to work out (**que** that); **~ ses chances de réussite** to weigh up one's chances of success

supranational, ~e, mpl -aux /sypʀanasjɔnal, o/ adj supranational

suprématie /sypʀemasi/ nf supremacy (**sur** over)

suprême /sypʀɛm/
A adj **1** (le plus élevé) [fonction, autorité] supreme; **2** (très grand) [élégance, habileté] supreme; [insolence] ultimate
B nm Culin **~ de foie gras** goose or duck liver pâté

suprêmement /sypʀɛmmɑ̃/ adv supremely

sur¹ /syʀ/ prép

⚠ Lorsque sur indique une position dans l'espace il se traduit généralement par on: sur la table/une chaise = on the table/a chair; sur la côte/le lac = on the coast/the lake.
On trouvera ci-dessous exemples supplémentaires et exceptions.
Lorsque sur a une valeur figurée comme dans régner sur, pleurer sur, sur l'honneur, sur place etc la traduction sera fournie dans l'article du deuxième élément, respectivement régner, pleurer, honneur, place etc.

1 (dessus) on; **prends un verre ~ la table** take a glass from the table; **appliquer la lotion ~ vos cheveux** apply the lotion to your hair; **la clé est ~ la porte** the key is in the door; **passer la main ~ une étoffe** to run one's hand over a fabric; **2** (au-dessus, sans contact) over; **un pont ~ la rivière** a bridge across ou over the river; **3** (étendue, surface) **~ 150 hectares** over an area of 150 hectares; **une table d'un mètre ~ deux** a table that measures one metre by two; **4** (direction) **se diriger ~ Valence** to head for Valence; **une voiture déboucha ~ la droite** a car pulled out on the right; **5** (support matériel) on; **écrire ~ du papier** to write on paper; **elle est ~ la photo** she's in the photograph; **dessiner ~ le sable** to draw in the sand; **6** (au sujet de) [débat, thèse] on; [étude, poème] about; **7** (objet d'un travail) **être ~ une affaire** to be involved in a business deal; **8** (indique un rapport de proportion) **une personne ~ dix** one person out of ten; **une semaine ~ trois** one week in three; **un mardi ~ deux** every other Tuesday; **9** (indique l'accumulation) lit upon; fig after; **faire proposition ~ proposition** to make one offer after another; **10** (juste après) **ils se sont quittés ~ ces mots** with these words, they parted; **~ le moment**

at the time; **~ ce** or **quoi** upon which; **~ ce, je vous laisse avec cela**, I must leave you; **11** (pendant) **on ne peut pas juger ~ une période aussi courte** you can't judge over ou in such a short period; **12** Radio, TV, Télécom on [radio, chaîne, ligne téléphonique]

sur², **~e** /syr/ adj (aigre) (slightly) sour

sûr, **~e** /syr/

A adj **1** (fiable) [information, service] reliable; [personne] reliable; [avis, base, investissement] sound; **avoir la main ~** to have a steady hand; **2** (sans danger) safe; **le voleur a été mis en lieu ~** euph the thief has been put in prison; **le plus ~ est de faire** the safest thing is to do; **peu ~** unsafe; **3** (garanti) certain; **une chose est ~e, tu t'es fait avoir**○ one thing's certain ou for sure, you've been had○; **ce n'est pas si ~** it's not that certain, I wouldn't be so sure; **c'est ~ et certain** it's definite; **à coup ~** definitely, for sure; **la victoire est ~e** victory is assured; **4** (convaincu) sure; **j'en suis ~ et certain** I'm positive (about it); **il est ~ de lui** (qualité) he's self-confident; (ponctuellement) he's sure of it; **être ~ de ses possibilités** to be confident of one's abilities; **être ~ de qn** to trust sb; **j'en étais ~!** I knew it!

B adv (sûrement) **bien ~ (que oui)** of course; **bien ~ que non** of course not

(Idiome) **être ~ de son coup**○ to be confident of success

surabondance /syrabɔ̃dɑ̃s/ nf overabundance

surabonder /syrabɔ̃de/ [1] vi **1** (être en nombre) to abound; **2** (être rempli) **~ de** ou **en** to abound in ou with

suraigu, -uë /syregy/ adj [son] very shrill

surajouter: se surajouter /syraʒute/ [1] vpr to be added on (**à** to)

suralimenter /syralimɑ̃te/ [1] vtr **1** to feed [sb] up [personne]; **2** to fatten [volaille, bétail]; **3** to supercharge, to boost [moteur]

suranné, **~e** /syrane/ adj [idées] outmoded; [style] outdated

surbaisser /syrbese/ [1] vtr **1** Archit to lower [plafond]; to surbase [arc]; **2** Aut to underslung

surcharge /syrʃarʒ/ nf (poids) excess load, overload; (fait d'être surchargé) overloading; **~ pondérale** excess weight; **un véhicule en ~** an overloaded vehicle; **une ~ de travail** an extra load of work

surchargé, **~e** /syrʃarʒe/ adj **1** (qui est trop chargé) [personne, animal, ascenseur, étagère] overloaded; **des voyageurs ~s de bagages** passengers weighed down ou overloaded with luggage; **décoration ~e** overabundant ou excessive decoration; **2** (aux activités trop nombreuses) [personne] overburdened; [journée, emploi du temps] overloaded, overfull; (aux effectifs trop nombreux) [classe] overcrowded

surcharger /syrʃarʒe/ [13] vtr **1** (charger à l'excès) to overload; **~ un texte de citations** to cram a text with quotations; **2** (accabler) to overburden (**de** with); **~ qn de travail** to overburden sb with work; **3** Ordinat to overload

surchauffe /syrʃof/ nf **1** lit superheating; **2** fig (de l'économie) overheating

surchauffer /syrʃofe/ [1]

A vtr **1** (chauffer) to overheat [maison, pièce]; **2** Phys, Tech to superheat [liquide]

B vi [voiture] to be overheating

surclasser /syrklase/ [1] vtr to outclass

surconsommation /syrkɔ̃sɔmasjɔ̃/ nf Écon overconsumption; **~ de médicaments** excessive drug consumption

surcroît /syrkrwa/ nm increase (**de** in); **un ~ de travail** extra work; **un ~ de prestige** increased prestige; **de ~** moreover

surdéveloppement /syrdevlɔpmɑ̃/ nm overdevelopment

surdité /syrdite/ nf deafness

surdoué, **~e** /syrdwe/

A adj [enfant] gifted; [pianiste, sportif] exceptionally gifted

B nm,f (enfant) gifted child; (pianiste) exceptionally gifted pianist

sureau, pl **~x** /syro/ nm elder (tree)

sureffectif /syrefɛktif/ nm (personnel) excess ou surplus staff **C**; (situation) (en usine) overmanning; (dans un bureau) overstaffing

surélever /syrelve/ [16] vtr to raise the height of [maison, route]

sûrement /syrmɑ̃/ adv **1** (très probablement) most probably; **elle est ~ malade** she must be ill; **elle sera ~ là demain** she should be there tomorrow; **2** (bien sûr) certainly; **~ pas** certainly not; **3** (sans risque) safely

surenchère /syrɑ̃ʃɛr/ nf **1** (enchère supérieure) higher bid; **faire une ~ sur qn** to bid higher than sb; **faire une ~ de 50 euros** to bid 50 euros more (**sur qn** than sb; **sur qch** for sth); **2** (exagération) escalation; **une ~ de violence** an escalation of violence; **faire de la ~** to try to go one better

surenchérir /syrɑ̃ʃerir/ [3] vi **1** (faire une offre plus élevée) to make a higher bid; **~ sur une offre** or **quelqu'un** to raise the bidding; **2** (ajouter) (après soi) to add; (après autrui) to chime in

surendetté, **~e** /syrɑ̃dete/ adj [personne, pays] deeply in debt (après n); [entreprise] overextended

surendettement /syrɑ̃dɛtmɑ̃/ nm excessive debt

suréquipement /syrekipmɑ̃/ nm (en matériel) overequipment; (d'hôtels) over-provision

surestimation /syrɛstimasjɔ̃/ nf (de bien, propriété) overvaluation; (de coût, capacité, d'importance) overestimation; (de qualité, mérite) overrating

surestimer /syrɛstime/ [1]

A vtr to overvalue [propriété, tableau]; to overestimate [coût, capacités, importance]; to overrate [qualités, mérites]

B se surestimer vpr to rate oneself too highly

sûreté /syrte/ nf **1** (sécurité) (d'équipement, de lieu, personne) safety; (d'investissement) soundness; (de pays) security; **être en ~** [bijou, argent, personne] to be in a safe place; **être en ~ à la banque** to be in safe keeping in the bank; **il se croyait en ~** he thought he was safe; **2** (assurance) (de jugement) soundness; (de geste) steadiness; (d'acteur, de musicien) confidence; **3** (dispositif de sécurité) (d'une arme) safety catch; (chaîne) safety chain; (serrure) safety lock

surévaluer /syrevalɥe/ [1] vtr to overvalue [monnaie]; to overestimate [coût]

surexciter /syrɛksite/ [1] vtr to overexcite [enfants]; **foule surexcitée** highly excited crowd

surexploiter /syrɛksplwate/ [1] vtr to overexploit

surexposer /syrɛkspoze/ [1] vtr to overexpose

surf /sœrf/ ▸ p. 327 nm surfing; **faire du ~** to go surfing

(Composé) **~ des neiges** Sport snowboarding; **faire du ~ des neiges** to snowboard

surface /syrfas/ nf **1** (partie externe) surface; **à la ~ de** lit, fig on the surface of; **en ~** (à l'extérieur) lit, fig on the surface; (au-dessus du sol) above ground; **de ~** lit [structure, tension] surface; [métro, installations] above ground (après n); fig [amabilité] superficial; **faire ~** lit, fig to surface; **refaire ~** lit, fig to resurface; **2** ▸ p. 568 (aire) surface area; **d'une ~ de** with a surface area of; **en ~** in area; **3** Sport (au football) area; (au tennis) surface

surfait, **~e** /syrfɛ, ɛt/ adj [personne, œuvre] overrated; [réputation] inflated

surfer /sœrfe/ vi to go surfing

surfiler /syrfile/ [1] vtr to oversew

surgelé, **~e** /syrʒəle/

A adj deep-frozen

B nm **le ~**, **les ~s** frozen food **C**

surgeler /syrʒəle/ [17] vtr to deep-freeze

surgénérateur /syrʒeneratœr/ nm fast-breeder reactor

surgir /syrʒir/ [3] vi [personne, animal] to appear suddenly (**de** from); [problème, difficulté] to crop up (**de** from); **faire ~** to conjure up [craintes, image]; **faire ~ la vérité** to bring the truth to light

surgras, -asse /syrgra, as/ adj oil-enriched

surhomme /syrɔm/ nm superman

surhumain, **~e** /syrymɛ̃, ɛn/ adj superhuman

surimpression /syrɛ̃presjɔ̃/ nf Phot double exposure; **en ~** superimposed (**à** on)

surinformation /syrɛ̃fɔrmasjɔ̃/ nf surfeit of information

surintendant /syrɛ̃tɑ̃dɑ̃/ nm superintendent

surjet /syrʒɛ/ nm oversewing

sur-le-champ /syrləʃɑ̃/ adv right away

surlendemain /syrlɑ̃d(ə)mɛ̃/ nm **le ~** two days later; **le lendemain et le ~** the next day and the day after that

surligner /syrliɲe/ [1] vtr to highlight

surligneur /syʀliɲœʀ/ nm highlighter (pen)

surmenage /syʀmənaʒ/ nm overwork

surmener /syʀmene/ [16]
A vtr to overwork
B se surmener vpr to push oneself too hard

surmontable /syʀmɔ̃tabl/ adj surmountable

surmonter /syʀmɔ̃te/ [1] vtr ① (dépasser) to overcome [obstacle, crise]; ~ l'épreuve de la séparation to get through the ordeal of separation; ② (être placé au-dessus de) être surmonté de qch to be topped by sth

surmultiplié, ~e /syʀmyltiplije/ adj vitesse ~e overdrive

surnager /syʀnaʒe/ [13] vi [pétrole, débris] to float

surnaturel, **-elle** /syʀnatyʀɛl/ adj ① (non naturel) supernatural; ② (extraordinaire) eerie

surnom /syʀnɔ̃/ nm nickname

surnombre /syʀnɔ̃bʀ/ nm en ~ [objets] surplus (épith); [employé] redundant; [personnel] excess (épith); [passager] extra (épith); deux d'entre nous étaient en ~ there were two too many of us

surnommer /syʀnɔme/ [1] vtr to nickname; X, surnommé Y X, known as ou dubbed Y

surnuméraire /syʀnymeʀɛʀ/ adj, nmf supernumerary

suroît /syʀwa/ nm Météo, Naut southwester

surpasser /syʀpase/ [1]
A vtr (faire mieux que) to surpass, to outdo [adversaire, concurrent]; ~ qn en habileté/érudition to surpass ou outdo sb in skill/erudition
B se surpasser vpr to surpass oneself

surpeuplé, ~e /syʀpœple/ adj [pays, région, ville] overpopulated; [local, train, rue] overcrowded

surpeuplement /syʀpœpləmɑ̃/ nm (de pays, région) overpopulation; (de ville, quartier) overcrowding

surpiquer /syʀpike/ [1] vtr to topstitch

surplace /syʀplas/ nm inv faire du ~ (dans un embouteillage) to be stuck; (dans un travail) to be getting nowhere; (en cyclisme) to do a track stand; (dans le ciel) to hover

surplis /syʀpli/ nm inv surplice

surplomb /syʀplɔ̃/ nm overhang; en ~ overhanging

surplomber /syʀplɔ̃be/ [1] vtr to overhang

surplus /syʀply/ nm inv surplus

surpopulation /syʀpɔpylasjɔ̃/ nf overpopulation

surprenant, ~e /syʀpʀənɑ̃, ɑ̃t/ adj [aspect, nombre, qualité, lieu] surprising; [personne] amazing; n'avoir rien de ~ to be hardly surprising; il serait ~ qu'il vienne it would be surprising if he came; il est ~ de voir comment/combien it is surprising how/how much; un enfant ~ d'intelligence an amazingly intelligent child

surprendre /syʀpʀɑ̃dʀ/ [52]
A vtr ① (étonner) to surprise; il sait ~ son monde he never fails to surprise; en ~ plus d'un to surprise more than a few; ② (prendre par surprise) [personne] to take [sb] by surprise [victime]; se laisser ~ par les événements to be caught out by events; se laisser ~ par la pluie to get caught in the rain; ③ (prendre sur le fait) to catch [malfaiteur] (à faire doing); ④ (être témoin de) to overhear [conversation]; to intercept [regard]
B vi [comportement] to be surprising; [spectacle] to surprise; [personne] to surprise people; avoir de quoi ~ to be somewhat surprising

surprise /syʀpʀiz/
A nf ① (événement étonnant) surprise; quelle ~! what a surprise!; être une ~ to come as a surprise; c'est la ~ de la journée that's a big surprise; créer la ~ to cause a stir; on veut leur faire une ~ we want it to be a surprise; ② (étonnement) surprise; à ma ~ to my surprise; il m'a fait la ~ de venir me voir he came to see me as a surprise; prendre qn par ~ to take sb by surprise; avoir la bonne ~/la mauvaise ~ d'apprendre que to be pleasantly surprised/unpleasantly surprised to hear that; discours sans ~ uneventful speech; l'élection a été sans ~ the election went as expected
B (-)surprise (in compounds) invité/visite ~ surprise guest/visit; voyage ~ unexpected trip; grève ~ lightning strike

surproduction /syʀpʀɔdyksjɔ̃/ nf overproduction

surpuissant, ~e /syʀpɥisɑ̃, ɑ̃t/ adj [moteur] high-powered

surqualifié, ~e /syʀkalifje/ adj overqualified

surréalisme /syʀ(ʀ)ealism/ nm surrealism

surréaliste /syʀ(ʀ)ealist/
A adj ① [œuvre, auteur] surrealist; ② [décor, paysage, vision] surreal
B nmf surrealist

surrégénérateur /syʀʀeʒeneʀatœʀ/ nm fast-breeder reactor

surrénal, ~e, mpl **-aux** /syʀ(ʀ)enal, o/ adj suprarenal

surréservation /syʀʀezɛʀvasjɔ̃/ nf overbooking

sursaut /syʀso/ nm ① lit (mouvement) start; en ~ with a start; ② fig (d'énergie, enthousiasme) sudden burst (de of); (d'orgueil, indignation) flash (de of); dans un dernier ~ in a final spurt of effort

sursauter /syʀsote/ [1] vi to jump, to start

surseoir /syʀswaʀ/ [41] vtr ind ~ à to postpone [décision]; to defer [versement]; to stay [exécution]

sursis /syʀsi/ nm inv ① (délai) respite; un ~ de trois mois a three-month respite; ② Jur suspended sentence; trois mois de prison dont deux avec ~ prison sentence of three months, with two months suspended; ③ Mil deferment of military service

sursitaire /syʀsitɛʀ/ nmf Mil person whose military service has been deferred

surtaxe /syʀtaks/ nf surcharge

surtaxer /syʀtakse/ [1] vtr to surcharge

surtitre /syʀtitʀ/ nm (de journal) subheading

surtout /syʀtu/ adv above all; j'ai ~ besoin de repos more than anything I need a rest; ~ quand/si/que especially when/if/as; ~ pas! certainly not!; ~ pas lui! especially not him!; ~ pas de chien dans la maison absolutely no dogs in the house

surveillance /syʀvɛjɑ̃s/ nf ① gén watch; (par la police) surveillance; exercer une ~ étroite sur qn/qch to keep a close watch over sb/sth; placer qn sous haute ~ to put sb under tight surveillance; déjouer la ~ de qn to escape detection by sb; ② Scol, Univ (d'examens, de récréation) supervision; assurer la ~ d'épreuves to supervise exams; ③ (contrôle) supervision; médicament à prendre sous ~ médicale drug to be taken under medical supervision; ④ Mil monitoring

surveillant, ~e /syʀvɛjɑ̃, ɑ̃t/ ▸ p. 372 nm,f ① Scol supervisor; ② Admin ~ de prison prison warder GB ou guard; ③ (dans un magasin) store detective

surveiller /syʀveje/ [1]
A vtr ① (veiller sur) to watch, to keep an eye on [enfants, cuisson, affaires]; to watch (over) [prisonnier, malade]; ~ du coin de l'œil to watch [sb/sth] out of the corner of one's eye; ② (exercer une surveillance sur) to keep watch on, to keep [sb/sth] under surveillance [adversaire, bâtiment]; c'est ton tour de ~ it's your turn to keep watch; ③ (contrôler) to supervise, to oversee [travail, projet]; to supervise [sortie d'école]; to monitor [cessez-le-feu, finances]; to man, to monitor [machine]; ~ les progrès d'un élève to monitor a pupil's progress; ④ Scol, Univ to supervise; ⑤ (veiller à) ~ son langage/sa ligne to watch one's language/one's figure; ~ sa santé to take care of one's health
B se surveiller vpr to watch oneself; avec eux, il faut sans cesse se ~ with them, you have to be on your best behaviour[GB]

survenir /syʀvəniʀ/ [36] vi [décès, orage] to occur; [difficulté, conflit] to arise; [personne] to arrive unexpectedly

survêtement /syʀvɛtmɑ̃/ nm tracksuit

survie /syʀvi/ nf lit, fig survival

survitrage /syʀvitʀaʒ/ nm secondary (double) glazing

survivance /syʀvivɑ̃s/ nf survival

survivant, ~e /syʀvivɑ̃, ɑ̃t/
A adj surviving
B nm,f survivor

survivre /syʀvivʀ/ [63]
A vtr ind ~ à to survive [événement, accident, blessures]; ~ à qn [personne] to outlive sb, to survive sb; [œuvre, influence] to outlast sb
B vi to survive

survol /syʀvɔl/ nm ① (en avion) flying over; effectuer le ~ de qch to fly over sth; ② (de sujet) synopsis (de of); (de magazine, livre) quick glance (de at)

S

survoler /syʀvɔle/ [1] vtr **1**▸ (en avion) [avion, pilote] to fly over [lieu]; **2**▸ (voir superficiellement) to skim through [livre, magazine]; to do a quick review of [problème]

survolté○, **~e** /syʀvɔlte/ adj [personne] overexcited; [ambiance] highly charged

survolter /syʀvɔlte/ [1] vtr to boost [circuit]

sus: en sus /ãsys/ loc adv **être en ~** to be extra; **en ~ de** on top of [salaire, location]; in addition to [choses, conseils]

susceptibilité /sysɛptibilite/ nf touchiness; **être d'une grande ~** to be very touchy; **pour ménager les ~s** so as not to upset anybody

susceptible /sysɛptibl/ adj **1**▸ (ombrageux) touchy; **2**▸ **~ de** likely to [influencer, intéresser]; **remarque ~ de plusieurs interprétations** remark open to several interpretations

susciter /sysite/ [1] vtr **1**▸ (provoquer) to spark off [réaction, débat]; **2**▸ (éveiller) to arouse [enthousiasme, intérêt]; **3**▸ (faire naître) to give rise to [réticences, vocation]; **4**▸ (créer) to create [problème] (à for)

susdit, **~e** /sysdi, it/ adj aforesaid

susnommé, **~e** /sysnɔme/ adj, nm,f aforementioned

suspect, **~e** /syspɛ, ɛkt/
A adj [mort, odeur, allure, objet] suspicious; [information, logique] dubious; [aliment, honnêteté, enthousiasme] suspect; [personne] suspicious-looking (épith)
B nm,f suspect; **le principal ~** the prime suspect

suspecter /syspɛkte/ [1] vtr to suspect [personne, groupe, institution] (**de qch** of sth; **de faire** of doing)

suspendre /syspɑ̃dʀ/ [6]
A vtr **1**▸ (pendre) to hang up; **~ qch à qch** to hang sth on sth; **~ qch/qn par** to hang sth/sb by; **2**▸ (interrompre) to suspend [émission, publication, relations, paiement]; to end [grève]; to adjourn [séance, réunion, enquête, procès]; to stop [diffusion]; **~ son souffle** to hold one's breath; **3**▸ (destituer) to suspend [fonctionnaire, médecin, sportif] (**de** from)
B se suspendre vpr [personne, animal] to hang; **se ~ à une corde** to hang from a rope; **se ~ par les bras** to hang by one's arms

suspendu, **~e** /syspɑ̃dy/ adj **1**▸ lit hanging (**à** from; **par** by); **2**▸ fig **être ~ aux lèvres de qn** to be hanging on sb's every word; **des maisons ~es au-dessus de la vallée** houses perched above the valley

suspens: en suspens /ãsyspɑ̃/ loc adv **1**▸ (en souffrance) [problème] outstanding (épith); **laisser un problème en ~** to leave a problem unresolved; **laisser des travaux en ~** to leave work unfinished; **2**▸ (dans l'expectative) in suspense; **tenir qn en ~** to keep sb in suspense; **3**▸ (en suspension) [fumée] hanging in the air

suspense /syspɛns/ nm suspense; **maintenir le ~** to maintain the suspense; **le ~ reste entier** everything still hangs in the balance; **film** or **roman à ~** thriller

suspension /syspɑ̃sjɔ̃/ nf **1**▸ (attache) suspension; **2**▸ Aut, Tech suspension; **3**▸ (interruption) (d'aide, de relations, travaux) suspension; (d'enquête, de procès) adjournment; **demander la ~ de la séance** to ask for the session to be adjourned; **4**▸ (sanction) suspension; **être condamné à deux ans de ~ du permis de conduire** to be disqualified GB ou suspended US from driving for two years; **5**▸ Chimie suspension; **en ~** [particules] in suspension; **6**▸ (éclairage) pendant
〈Composé〉 **~ d'armes** Mil cease-fire

suspensoir /syspɑ̃swaʀ/ nm Sport athletic support GB, athletic supporter US, jockstrap○

suspicieux, **-ieuse** /syspisjø, øz/ adj suspicious

suspicion /syspisjɔ̃/ nf suspicion; **faire peser la ~ sur qn** to bring suspicion to bear on sb; **avec ~** suspiciously

sustenter: se sustenter /systɑ̃te/ [1] vpr hum to have a little snack

susurrer /sysyʀe/ [1] vtr, vi to whisper

suture /sytyʀ/ nf suture; **point de ~** stitch

suzerain, **~e** /syzʀɛ̃, ɛn/ adj, nm,f suzerain

suzeraineté /syzʀɛnte/ nf suzerainty

svelte /svɛlt/ adj [personne, taille] slender

sveltesse /svɛltɛs/ nf slenderness

SVP (written abbr = **s'il vous plaît**) please

sycomore /sikɔmɔʀ/ nm sycamore

syllabe /sil(l)ab/ nf syllable

syllabique /sil(l)abik/ adj [écriture, vers] syllabic

syllogisme /silɔʒism/ nm syllogism

sylphide /silfid/ nf sylph

sylvestre /silvɛstʀ/ adj liter sylvan littér

sylvicole /silvikɔl/ adj silvicultural

sylviculture /silvikyltyʀ/ nf forestry

symbiose /sɛ̃bjoz/ nf symbiosis; **en ~** in symbiosis

symbole /sɛ̃bɔl/ nm **1**▸ gén, Ling symbol; **2**▸ Relig creed

symbolique /sɛ̃bɔlik/ adj **1**▸ (significatif) [œuvre, action, portée] symbolic; **2**▸ (pour la forme) [geste, salaire, augmentation] token (épith); [prix] nominal

symboliser /sɛ̃bɔlize/ [1] vtr to symbolize

symbolisme /sɛ̃bɔlism/ nm symbolism

symétrie /simetʀi/ nf symmetry (**par rapport à** in relation to)

symétrique /simetʀik/ adj **1**▸ (géométriquement) [dessin, visage, points] symmetrical; **2**▸ (en logique) [relation] symmetric

sympa○ /sɛ̃pa/ adj inv nice

sympathie /sɛ̃pati/ nf **1**▸ (amitié) **avoir** or **éprouver de la ~ pour qn** to like sb; **montrer** or **témoigner de la ~ à qn** to be friendly toward sb; **elle inspire la ~** she's very likeable; **2**▸ (d'un sympathisant) sympathy; **mes ~s vont aux...** my sympathies lie with...; **3**▸ (compassion) sympathy; **croyez à toute ma ~** you have my deepest sympathy

sympathique /sɛ̃patik/ adj [personne] nice, likeable; [endroit] nice, pleasant; [soirée] pleasant; [idée] nice

sympathisant, **~e** /sɛ̃patizɑ̃, ɑ̃t/ nm,f sympathizer

sympathiser /sɛ̃patize/ [1] vi to get on well (**avec qn** with sb)

symphonie /sɛ̃fɔni/ nf lit, fig symphony

symphonique /sɛ̃fɔnik/ adj symphonic

symposium /sɛ̃pozjɔm/ nm symposium (**sur** on)

symptomatique /sɛ̃ptɔmatik/ adj symptomatic

symptôme /sɛ̃ptom/ nm symptom (**de** of)

synagogue /sinagɔg/ nf synagogue

synchronique /sɛ̃kʀɔnik/ adj synchronic

synchronisation /sɛ̃kʀɔnizasjɔ̃/ nf synchronization

synchroniser /sɛ̃kʀɔnize/ [1] vtr to synchronize

syncope /sɛ̃kɔp/ nf **1**▸ fainting fit; **tomber en ~** to faint; **2**▸ Mus syncopation

syncopé, **~e** /sɛ̃kɔpe/ adj [rythme] syncopated

syndic /sɛ̃dik/ nm (d'immeuble) property manager

syndical, **~e**, mpl **-aux** /sɛ̃dikal, o/ adj (trade) union (épith); **droit ~** (trade) union law

syndicalisme /sɛ̃dikalism/ nm (fait social) trade unionism; (activité) union activities (pl)

syndicaliste /sɛ̃dikalist/
A adj (trade) union (épith)
B nmf union activist

syndicat /sɛ̃dika/ nm gén trade union; (d'employeurs) association
〈Composés〉 **~ du crime** underworld; **~ d'initiative** tourist information office; **~ professionnel** trade association

ⓘ **Syndicats** Although it plays a less central role than in the first half of the 20th century with only 10% of employees unionized, the trade union movement is still a significant actor in French public life and has considerable power and influence. The unions which have the broadest national base are the CGT (traditionally allied with the parti communiste), the CFDT (traditionally allied with the parti socialiste), FO, the CFTC, the CGC and the FEN. There is also an employers' association, the MEDEF.

syndiqué, **~e** /sɛ̃dike/
A adj **être ~** to be a union member; **main-d'œuvre non ~e** non-union labour[GB]
B nm,f union member

syndiquer /sɛ̃dike/ [1]
A vtr to unionize
B se syndiquer vpr [personne] to join a union

syndrome /sɛ̃dʀom/ nm syndrome
〈Composés〉 **~ immunodéficitaire acquis** acquired immunodeficiency syndrome; **~ respiratoire aigu sévère** severe acute respiratory syndrome

synergie /sinɛʀʒi/ *nf* synergy (**entre** between)

synode /sinɔd/ *nm* synod

synonyme /sinɔnim/
A *adj* synonymous (**de** with)
B *nm* synonym; **dictionnaire de** ~**s** ≈ thesaurus

synonymie /sinɔnimi/ *nf* synonymy

synopsis /sinɔpsis/ *nm inv* Cin synopsis

synovie /sinɔvi/ *nf* synovia; **avoir un épanchement de** ~ to have water on the knee

syntagme /sɛ̃tagm/ *nm* phrase, syntagm

syntaxe /sɛ̃taks/ *nf* syntax

syntaxique /sɛ̃taksik/ *adj* syntactic(al)

synthèse /sɛ̃tɛz/ *nf* ①⟩ (d'idées) synthesis; (résumé) summary; **faire la** ~ **de plusieurs documents** to extract the essential facts from several documents; **esprit de** ~ ability to synthesize; ②⟩ Chimie synthesis; **produit de** ~ synthetic product; ③⟩ Ordinat **images de** ~ computer generated images

synthétique /sɛ̃tetik/ *adj* ①⟩ Chimie, Tech synthetic; ②⟩ (non analytique) [*réflexion, vision*] global; [*ouvrage*] that gives a general picture (*épith, après n*); ③⟩ Mus synthetic

synthétiser /sɛ̃tetize/ [1] *vtr* to synthesize

syphilis /sifilis/ ▸ p. 195 *nf inv* syphilis

systématique /sistematik/ *adj* [*classification, refus*] systematic; [*aide, soutien*] unconditional

systématiser /sistematize/ [1]
A *vtr* to systematize
B **se systématiser** *vpr* to become the rule

système /sistɛm/ *nm* ①⟩ (ensemble organisé, doctrine) system; ②⟩ (dispositif, réunion d'éléments) system; ~ **de canaux** canal system *ou* network; ③⟩ (plan, méthode) system, scheme; ④⟩ (moyen) system, way; (combine) dodge◦; ⑤⟩ Anat system; ~ **cardio-vasculaire** cardio-vascular system; ~ **pileux** hair; ⑥⟩ Ordinat system; ~ **de gestion de bases de données** database (management) system; ⑦⟩ (en astronomie) ~ **solaire** solar system

(Composés) ~ **d'alarme** burglar alarm, alarm system; **le** ~ **D**◦ resourcefulness; ~ **d'exploitation** Ordinat operating system; ~ **monétaire européen, SME** European Monetary System, EMS

(Idiome) **taper** *or* **courir sur le** ~ **de qn**◦ to get on sb's nerves *ou* wick◦ GB

systémique /sistemik/
A *adj* systematic
B *nf* systematism

S

t, T /te/ *nm inv* t, T; **en (forme de) T** T-shaped

t' ▸ te

ta ▸ **ton¹**

tabac /taba/ *nm* 1 Bot, Ind tobacco; 2 ▸ p. 372 (magasin) tobacconist's GB, smoke shop US; 3 ᵒ(succès) **faire un** ∼ to be a big hit; 4 Naut **coup de** ∼ squall

(Composés) ∼ **blond** Virginia tobacco; ∼ **brun** dark tobacco; ∼ **à priser** snuff; ∼ **à rouler** rolling tobacco

(Idiome) **passer qn à** ∼ᵒ to beat sb up

tabagie /tabaʒi/ *nf* **c'est une vraie** ∼ **ici!** it's really smoky in here!

tabagisme /tabaʒism/ *nm* tobacco addiction

tabasser /tabase/ [1]
A *vtr* to give [sb] a beating; **se faire** ∼ to get a beating
B **se tabasser** *vpr* to lay into each otherᵒ

tabatière /tabatjɛʀ/ *nf* 1 (boîte à tabac) snuffbox; 2 (lucarne) skylight

table /tabl/ *nf* 1 (meuble) table; 2 (lieu du repas) table; **bien/mal se tenir à** ∼ to have good/bad table manners; **nous serons dix à** ∼ **ce midi** there'll be ten of us for lunch today; **nous étions toujours à** ∼ **quand...** we were still eating when...; **s'asseoir à** ∼ (pour manger) to sit down to eat; **passer** *or* **se mettre à** ∼ lit to sit down at the table; (avouer)ᵒ to spill the beansᵒ; 3 (nourriture) table; ∼ **remarquable** *or* **de roi** marvellousᴳᴮ spread; 4 (lieu de discussion) table; **s'asseoir autour d'une** ∼ to get round the table; 5 Math table

(Composés) ∼ **basse** coffee table; ∼ **de chevet** bedside table GB, night stand US; ∼ **de cuisson** hob; ∼ **à dessin** drawing board; ∼ **d'école** school desk; ∼ **d'écoute** wiretapping set; **être mis sur** ∼ **d'écoute** to have one's phone tapped; ∼ **des matières** (table of) contents; ∼ **de mixage** mixing desk; ∼ **de montage** editing bench *ou* table; ∼ **de nuit** = ∼ **de chevet**; ∼ **d'orientation** viewpoint diagram; ∼ **à repasser** ironing board; ∼ **roulante** trolley; ∼ **de toilette** washstand

(Idiome) **mettre les pieds sous la** ∼ to let others wait on you

tableau, *pl* ∼**x** /tablo/ *nm* 1 (œuvre d'art) gén picture; (peinture) painting; 2 (description) picture; **et pour achever le** ∼ and to cap it all; 3 (spectacle) picture; **en plus, il était ivre, tu vois un peu le** ∼ᵒ**!** on top of that he was drunk, you can just imagine!; 4 (présentation graphique) table, chart; **présenter qch sous forme de** ∼ to present sth in tabular form; 5 Scol blackboard; 6 (affichant des renseignements) gén board; Rail indicator board; ∼ **horaire** timetable; 7 (support mural) board; 8 Théât short scene

(Composés) ∼ **d'affichage** notice board; ∼ **de bord** Aut dashboard; Aviat, Rail instrument panel; ∼ **de chasse** (de chasseur) total number of kills; (de séducteur) list of conquests; ∼ **de commande** control panel; ∼ **d'honneur** honours board GB, honor roll US

(Idiomes) **jouer** *or* **miser sur les deux** ∼**x** to hedge one's bets; **gagner/perdre sur tous les** ∼**x** to win/to lose on all counts

tablée /table/ *nf* table; **une grande** ∼ a large party

tabler /table/ [1] *vi* ∼ **sur** to bankᵒ on

tablette /tablɛt/
A *nf* 1 (de chocolat) bar; (de chewing-gum) stick; 2 (étagère) shelf
B **tablettes** *nfpl* (archives) annals; **j'ai inscrit notre rendez-**

vous dans mes ∼**s** I've made a note of our meeting in my diary

tablier /tablije/ *nm* 1 (vêtement) apron; 2 (de pont) roadway

(Idiome) **rendre son** ∼ to give in GB *ou* give US one's notice

tabou /tabu/
A *adj* 1 (frappé d'interdit) taboo; (qu'on ne peut critiquer) untouchable, sacred; 2 Relig taboo
B *nm* taboo

tabouret /tabuʀɛ/ *nm* stool

tac /tak/ *nm* **répondre du** ∼ **au** ∼ to answer as quick as a flash

tache /taʃ/ *nf* 1 lit (salissure) stain; ∼ **d'encre** gén ink stain; (sur un manuscrit) ink blot; ∼ **d'humidité** damp patch; ∼ **de sang** bloodstain; **une** ∼ **sur la table** a mark on the table; **faire** ∼ fig to stick out like a sore thumb; 2 fig (souillure) stain, blot (**à** on); **sans** ∼ [*réputation*] spotless; 3 (altération) (sur un fruit) mark; (sur la peau) blotch, mark; 4 (note de couleur) (petite) spot; (plus grande) patch

(Composés) ∼ **de naissance** birthmark; ∼ **solaire** sunspot; ∼ **de vin** gén wine stain; Anat strawberry mark; ∼**s de rousseur** *or* **son** freckles

(Idiome) **faire** ∼ **d'huile** to spread like wildfire

tâche /taʃ/ *nf* task, job; **mener une** ∼ **à bien** to see a job through; **être à la hauteur de sa** ∼ to be up to the job; **les** ∼**s ménagères** household chores

tacher /taʃe/ [1]
A *vtr* 1 lit (salir) [*substance*] to stain; [*personne*] to get a stain on; **taché d'huile** oil-stained; 2 fig (souiller) to tarnish, to stain [*réputation*]; 3 (colorer) liter **pelage noir taché de blanc** black fur with white markings
B *vi* [*fruit, vin, produit*] to stain
C **se tacher** *vpr* 1 [*personne*] to get oneself dirty; 2 [*fruit*] to become blemished

tâcher /taʃe/ [1]
A *vtr* **tâchez que ce soit fini avant midi** (conseil) try and make sure it's finished before noon; (ordre) see to it that it's finished before noon
B **tâcher de** *vtr ind* ∼ **de faire** to try to do

tâcheron /taʃʀɔ̃/ *nm* pej (qui fait des tâches ingrates) drudge; (qui travaille beaucoup) hack; **un** ∼ **de la littérature** a literary hack

tacheter /taʃte/ [20] *vtr* to speckle, to spot [*pelage*]; to dot [*pré*]

tacite /tasit/ *adj* tacit

taciturne /tasityʀn/ *adj* taciturn

tacotᵒ /tako/ *nm* bangerᵒ GB, crateᵒ US

tact /takt/ *nm*; **avoir beaucoup de** ∼ to be very tactful; **manquer de** ∼ to be tactless; **avec** ∼ tactfully

tactique /taktik/
A *adj* gén, Mil tactical
B *nf* **une** ∼ **de vente** a sales tactic; **la** ∼ **de César/de notre entreprise est...** Caesar's/our firm's tactics are...; **la** ∼ (science militaire) tactics (+ *v sg*)

taie /tɛ/ *nf* 1 (enveloppe) ∼ (**d'oreiller**) pillowcase; ∼ **(de traversin)** bolstercase; 2 (sur l'œil) corneal opacity

taillader /tajade/ [1]
A *vtr* to slash [*poignets, rideaux*]; ∼ **une table** to make slashes on a table top
B **se taillader** *vpr* **se** ∼ **les poignets** to slash one's wrists; **se** ∼ **les mains** to cut one's hands badly

Les tailles

■ *Les tailles britanniques et américaines données dans les tableaux ci-dessous sont parfois arrondies aux tailles immédiatement supérieures: mieux vaut un vêtement un peu trop grand qu'un peu trop petit.*

Les chaussures d'homme		Les chaussures de femme		
en France	en GB et aux US	en France	en GB	aux US
39	6$^1/_2$	35	3	6
40	7	36	3$^1/_2$	6$^1/_2$
41	7$^1/_2$	37	4	7
42	8$^1/_2$	38	5	7$^1/_2$
43	9	39	6	8
44	10	40	7	8$^1/_2$
45	11	41	8	9
46	12			

Les vêtements d'homme		Les vêtements de femme*		
en France	en GB et aux US	en France	en GB	aux US
38	28	34	8	4
40	30	36	10	6
42	32	38	12	8
44	34	40	12	8
46	36	42	14	10
48	38	44	16	12
50	40	46	16	12
52	42	48	18	14
54	44	50	20	16
56	46			

* Ces tailles sont utilisées pour les robes, chemisiers, pantalons, etc.

Les chemises d'homme	
en France	en GB et aux US
36	14
37	14$^1/_2$
38	15
39	15$^1/_2$
40	16
41	16$^1/_2$
42	17
43	17$^1/_2$
44	18

■ *L'anglais emploie le mot size à la fois pour les vêtements et pour les chaussures.*

quelle taille faites-vous?
= what size are you?

quelle pointure faites-vous?
= what size are you?

faire du 85 de tour de poitrine
= to have a 34-inch bust

faire du 61 de tour de taille
= to have a 24-inch waist
ou to measure 24 inches round the waist

faire du 90 de tour de hanches
= to measure 36 inches round the hips

avez-vous une taille 40?
= have you got a size 7?

avez-vous du 39?
= have you got a size 6$^1/_2$?

je porte du 42
= I take a size 32

je fais du 52
= my size is 42

je chausse du 40
= my shoe size is 7

je cherche un 40
= I'm looking for a shirt with a size 16 collar

une paire de chaussures en 42
= a pair of shoes size 8$^1/_2$

une chemise taille 38
= a shirt size 15 *ou* a size 15 shirt

avez-vous ce modèle en 40?
= have you got the same thing in a 12?

avez-vous ce modèle en plus grand?
= have you got this in a larger size?

avez-vous ce modèle en plus petit?
= have you got the same thing in a smaller size?

---

taille /taj/ *nf* **1** ▸ p. 136 (partie du corps, de vêtement) waist, waistline; **avoir une ~ de guêpe** to have a very slim waist; **prendre qn par la ~** to put one's arm around sb's waist; **robe à ~ haute/basse** high-/low-waisted dress; **2** (volume) size; *fig* (importance) size; **de grande/petite ~** [*animal, entreprise, objet*] large/small; **entreprise de ~ moyenne** medium-sized company; **de la ~ de** the size of; **société de ~ européenne** company on a European scale; **de ~** [*problème, ambition, enjeu*] considerable, sizable; [*événement, question*] very important; **à la ~ de leurs ambitions/de l'entreprise** in keeping with their ambitions/the size of the company; **un partenaire à sa ~** a suitable partner; **l'entreprise est de ~!** it's no small undertaking!; **être de ~ à faire** to be up to *ou* capable of doing; **3** (dimension de vêtement) size; **~ 42** size 42; **'~ unique'** 'one size'; **essaie la ~ au-dessus/au-dessous** try the next size up/down; **avoir la ~ mannequin** to be a standard size; **rayon grandes ~s** outsize department; **rayon petites ~s** petite department; **4** (hauteur) height; **personne de petite/grande ~** short/tall person; **personne de ~ moyenne** person of average height; **se redresser de toute sa ~** to draw oneself up to one's full height; **5** (action de tailler) (d'arbre, buisson) pruning; (de haie) clipping, trimming; (de diamant, cristal) cutting; (de bois) carving; **6** (forme obtenue) (de diamant) cut; (de haie) shape; **7** *Hist* **la ~** tallage; **8** (tranchant de lame) edge

taillé, ~e /taje/
A *pp* ▸ **tailler**
B *pp adj* **1** (bâti) **~ en athlète** built like an athlete; **2** (apte)

être **~ pour faire** to be cut out to do; **3** (coupé) **cristal ~** cut glass

taille-crayons /tajkʀɛjɔ̃/ *nm inv* pencil sharpener

tailler /taje/ [1]
A *vtr* **1** (couper) to cut [*rubis, cristal, marbre*]; to carve [*bois*]; to sharpen [*crayon*]; to prune [*arbre*]; to cut, to clip [*haie*]; to trim [*cheveux, barbe*]; **~ une armée en pièces** to hack an army to pieces; **elle l'a taillé en pièces** *fig* she made mincemeat of him○; **bien taillé** [*moustache, haie*] neatly trimmed; [*veste*] well-cut; **taillé en pointe** [*crayon*] sharpened to a point; [*barbe*] trimmed to a point; **visage taillé à la serpe** craggy features (*pl*); **2** (découper) to cut [*steak*] (**dans** from); to carve [*sculpture*]; to cut out [*vêtement*]; **~ une robe dans de la soie** to make a dress out of silk; **~ un costume sur mesure** to make a suit to measure; **taillé sur mesure** [*vêtement*] made-to-measure GB, custom-made; *fig* [*rôle*] tailor-made
B *vi* **1** (faire des coupes dans) **~ dans les chairs** *or* **le vif** to cut into the flesh; **~ dans les programmes sociaux** to make cuts in the social programmes^GB; **2** (être coupé) **~ grand/petit** [*vêtement*] to be cut on the large/small side
C **se tailler** *vpr* **1** (se faire) to carve out [sth] for oneself [*carrière, empire*]; to make [sth] for oneself [*belle réputation*]; **se ~ une grande part du marché** to corner a large share of the market; **se ~ un vif succès** to be a great success; **2** ○(s'enfuir) to bolt○; **3** (se couper) **se ~ la moustache** to trim one's moustache GB *ou* mustache US

(Idiome) **ils sont tous taillés sur le même modèle** they are all exactly alike

tailleur /tajœʀ/ *nm* **1** (tenue) (woman's) suit; **2** ▸ p. 372 (personne) tailor; **s'asseoir/être assis en ~** to sit down/to be sitting cross-legged

(Composés) **~ pour dames** ladies' tailor; **~ de pierre** stone-cutter

taillis /taji/ *nm inv* (broussailles) undergrowth ¢; (sous-bois) coppice

tain /tɛ̃/ *nm* silvering; **glace** *or* **miroir sans ~** two-way mirror

taire /tɛʀ/ [59]

A *vtr* **1** (ne pas dire) not to reveal [*nom, secret*]; to hush up [*vérité*]; **dire ce qu'on aurait dû ~** to say what would have been better left unsaid; **2** (cacher) *liter* to keep [sth] to oneself [*tristesse, dépit*]

B **se taire** *vpr* **1** (ne pas parler) [*personne*] to be silent, to say nothing; [*nature, oiseaux*] to be silent; (ne pas dire qch) to remain silent; **se ~ sur qch** to keep quiet about sth; **2** (cesser de parler) [*personne*] to stop talking, to fall silent; [*oiseau*] to fall silent; (cesser de s'exprimer) [*journaliste, opposition*] to fall silent; **faire ~** to make [sb] be quiet [*élèves*]; to silence [*opposant, média*] ; to put a stop to [*rumeurs, sarcasmes*]; **faire ~ sa jalousie** to stifle one's jealousy; **fais ~ les enfants!** keep the children quiet!; **tais-toi!** (ne parle pas) be quiet!; (ne m'en parle pas) don't talk to me about that!; **3** (s'arrêter) [*musique*] to stop; [*canon, orchestre*] to fall silent

talc /talk/ *nm* **1** (poudre) talc, talcum powder; **2** (minéral) talc(um)

talent /talɑ̃/ *nm* **1** (aptitude) talent; **avoir du ~** to be talented, to have talent; **de ~** talented; **2** (personne douée) **chercher de nouveaux ~s** to look for new talent; **un jeune ~** a talented young person

talentueux, **-euse** /talɑ̃tɥø, øz/ *adj* talented, gifted

taliban /talibɑ̃/ *nm* Taliban

talion /taljɔ̃/ *nm* talion; **loi du ~** lex talionis; **appliquer la loi du ~** to demand 'an eye for an eye'

talkie-walkie, *pl* **talkies-walkies** /tokiwoki/ *nm* walkie-talkie

taloche○ /talɔʃ/ *nf* (gifle) clout○

talon /talɔ̃/ *nm* **1** (de pied, chaussure) heel; **2** (de carnet, chèque) stub; **3** (aux cartes) pile

(Composé) **~ aiguille** stiletto heel

(Idiomes) **tourner les ~s** to turn on one's heel and walk away; **être sur les ~s de qn** to be hard *ou* hot on sb's heels

talonner /talɔne/ [1] *vtr* **1** (suivre) **~ qn** to be hot on sb's heels; **2** (harceler) [*personne*] to badger [*personne*]; [*faim, inquiétude*] to torment [*personne*]; **3** Sport to spur [sth] on [*cheval*]; (au rugby) to heel [*ballon*]

talonnette /talɔnɛt/ *nf* (de chaussures) lift (in a shoe)

talus /taly/ *nm inv* (artificiel) embankment; (naturel) bank, slope

tamanoir /tamanwaʀ/ *nm* anteater

tambouille○ /tɑ̃buj/ *nf* grub○

tambour /tɑ̃buʀ/ *nm* **1** ▸ p. 389 (instrument) drum; **mener qch ~ battant** *fig* to deal with sth briskly; **2** ▸ p. 372 (personne) drummer; **3** (de lave-linge, frein) drum; **4** (de porte) tambour

tambourin /tɑ̃buʀɛ̃/ ▸ p. 389 *nm* tambourine

tambouriner /tɑ̃buʀine/ [1] *vi* **1** (frapper) **~ à la porte/fenêtre de qn** to hammer on sb's door/window; **2** (tapoter) **~ sur la table** to drum one's fingers on the table; **la pluie tambourine sur le toit** the rain is drumming on the roof

tamis /tami/ *nm inv* sieve; **passer au ~** to sieve, to sift

Tamise /tamiz/ ▸ p. 259 *nprf* **la ~** the Thames

tamiser /tamize/ [1] *vtr* to sieve, to sift [*sable, farine*]; to filter [*lumière, couleurs*]; **farine tamisée** sifted flour; **lumières tamisées** subdued lighting ¢

tampon /tɑ̃pɔ̃/

A *nm* **1** (de bureau) (marque) stamp; (objet gravé) stamp; (tissu encré) **~ (encreur)** (ink) pad; **mettre** *ou* **apposer un ~ sur un document** to stamp a document; **2** (pour éponger, frotter) *gén* pad; Méd swab; **3** (de wagon) buffer; **4** (pour boucher) plug

B **(-)tampon** (*in compounds*) buffer; **solution(-)~** Chimie buffer (solution); **mémoire(-)~** Ordinat buffer (storage)

(Composés) **~ hygiénique** tampon; **~ à récurer** scouring pad

(Idiome) **servir de ~** to act as a buffer

tamponner /tɑ̃pɔne/ [1] *vtr* **1** (éponger) to swab [*plaie*]; to mop [*front*]; **2** (timbrer) to stamp [*document*]; **3** (heurter) to crash into [*véhicule*]

tamponneuse /tɑ̃pɔnøz/ *adj f* **auto ~** bumper car, dodgem

tam-tam, *pl* **~s** /tamtam/ *nm* ▸ p. 389 tomtom

tancer /tɑ̃se/ [12] *vtr liter* to scold, to admonish *sout*; **elle s'est fait ~ vertement** *or* **d'importance** she was scolded sharply

tanche /tɑ̃ʃ/ *nf* tench

tandem /tɑ̃dɛm/ *nm* **1** (bicyclette) tandem; **2** *fig* (duo) duo; **travailler en ~** to work in tandem

tandis: **tandis que** /tɑ̃di(s)k(ə)/ *loc conj* while

tangage /tɑ̃gaʒ/ *nm* (de navire, d'avion) pitching

tangent, **~e**¹ /tɑ̃ʒɑ̃, ɑ̃t/ *adj* **1** Math tangent, tangential; **~ à** at a tangent to; **2** ○(de justesse) **elle passe en classe supérieure, mais c'est ~** she's moving up a year GB *ou* grade US, but only by the skin of her teeth○

tangente² /tɑ̃ʒɑ̃t/ *nf* Math tangent

(Idiome) **prendre la ~**○ to make oneself scarce○

tangible /tɑ̃ʒibl/ *adj* tangible

tanguer /tɑ̃ge/ [1] *vi* **1** [*navire, avion*] to pitch; **2** [*personne*] to be unsteady on one's feet

tanière /tanjɛʀ/ *nf* **1** (d'animal) den; **2** (retraite) lair; **3** (taudis) hovel

tank /tɑ̃k/ *nm* **1** (citerne) tank; **2** (char) tank

tannant, **~e** /tɑ̃nɑ̃, ɑ̃t/ *adj* **1** Tech [*produit*] tanning; **2** ○(lassant) [*personne*] infuriating

tanné, **~e** /tane/

A *pp* ▸ **tanner**

B *pp adj* **1** [*cuir*] tanned; **2** [*visage, peau*] leathery

tanner /tane/ [1] *vtr* **1** Tech to tan [*cuir, peaux*]; **2** (brunir) [*soleil*] to make [sth] leathery [*visage, peau*]; **3** ○(lasser) to badger○ [*personne*]

(Idiome) **~ le cuir à qn**○ to tan sb's hide○

tannerie /tanʀi/ *nf* **1** (établissement) tannery; **2** (métier) tanning

tanneur, **-euse** /tanœʀ, øz/ ▸ p. 372 *nm,f* tanner

tant /tɑ̃/ ▸ p. 483

A *adv* **1** (tellement) (modifiant un verbe) so much; (modifiant un participe passé) so much; **il y a ~ à faire que** there's so much to do that; **il quitta la pièce ~ il se sentait honteux** he was so ashamed that he left the room; **vous m'en direz ~**○! you don't say!; **il est vrai que...** since it's a well-known fact that...; **le moment ~ attendu** the long-awaited moment; **2** (autant) **~ ses films que ses romans** both his/her films and his/her novels *ou* his/her films as much as his/her novels; **ce n'est pas ~ une question d'argent qu'une question de principe** it's not so much a question of money as a question of principle; **n'aimer rien ~ que...** to like nothing so much as...; **tu peux protester ~ que tu voudras** you can protest as much as you like; **~ bien que mal** [*réparer, organiser, diriger*] after a fashion; [*se débrouiller*] more or less; **essayer ~ bien que mal de s'adapter** to be struggling to adapt; **3** (aussi longtemps) **~ que** as long as; **je ne partirai pas ~ qu'il ne m'aura pas accordé un rendez-vous** I won't leave until he's given me an appointment; **profites-en ~ que tu peux** make the most of it while you can; **~ que tu y es, balaye aussi la cuisine** while you're at it, sweep the kitchen as well; **traite-moi de menteur ~ que tu y es**○! go ahead and call me a liar!; **4** (remplaçant un nombre) **gagner/dépenser ~ par mois** to earn/to spend so much a month; **votre lettre datée du ~** your letter of such-and-such a date

B **tant de** *dét indéf* **1** (avec un nom dénombrable) so many; **et ~ d'autres** and so many others; **~ de meubles** so much furniture; **2** (avec un nom non dénombrable) so much; **~ d'argent** so much money; **je n'ai jamais vu ~ de monde** I've never seen so many people; **~ d'humilité force le respect** such humility commands respect

C (dans des locutions) **~ pis** too bad; **~ pis pour toi** too bad, that's your bad luck; **~ mieux** so much the better; **~ mieux pour toi** good for you; **~ et plus** *gén* a great deal; (avec un nom dénombrable) a great many; **~ et si bien que** so much so that; **il a fait ~ et si bien qu'il s'est fait renvoyer** he finally managed to get himself fired; **il est un ~ soit peu arrogant** he's a bit arrogant; **s'il avait un ~ soit peu de bon sens** if he had the slightest bit of common sense, if he had an ounce of common sense; **si tu étais (un) ~ soit peu inquiet** if you were in the least bit worried; **~ s'en faut** not by a long shot; **~ qu'à faire, autant repeindre toute la pièce** we may as well repaint the whole room while we're at it; **~ qu'à faire, je préférerais que ce soit lui qui l'achète** since somebody has to buy it, I'd rather it was him; **en ~ que** as; **en ~ que tel** as such; **si ~ est qu'il puisse y aller** that is if he can go at all; **~ que ça**? (avec un nom dénombrable) that many?; (avec un nom non dénombrable ou un verbe) that much?; **je ne l'aime pas ~ que ça** I don't like him/her all that much

Tantale /tɑ̃tal/ npr Tantalus; **supplice de ~** torment of Tantalus; **c'est un véritable supplice de ~** it's really tantalizing

tante /tɑ̃t/ nf aunt; **~ Julie** aunt Julie

tantinet○ /tɑ̃tinɛ/ nm **un ~** a trifle, a tiny bit; **un ~ de** (de whisky, sel) a dash of; (d'humour) a touch of

tantôt /tɑ̃to/ adv (parfois) sometimes

taon /tɑ̃/ nm horsefly

tapage /tapaʒ/ nm **1** (bruit) din, racket○; **faire du ~** to make a racket○; **2** (éclat) **la nouvelle a fait du ~** the news caused a furore GB ou furor US; **3** (battage) hype; **~ médiatique** media hype

(Composé) **~ nocturne** disturbance of the peace at night

tapageur, -euse /tapaʒœʀ, øz/ adj **1** (bruyant) [personne] rowdy; **2** (outrancier) [luxe, élégance] showy; (retentissant) [campagne] hyped-up; [propos] ostentatious

tapante /tapɑ̃t/ adj f **à trois heures ~s** at three o'clock sharp ou on the dot

tape /tap/ nf (amicale) pat; (plus forte) slap; **donner une petite ~ sur le dos de qn** (pour attirer l'attention) to give sb a little tap on the back

tape-à-l'œil○ /tapalœj/ adj inv [couleur] loud; [décoration, bijou, mobilier] garish

taper /tape/ [1]
A vtr **1** (frapper) to hit [personne, chien]; **2** (dactylographier) to type [lettre]; **lettre tapée à la machine** type-written letter; **3** ○(prendre) **je peux te ~ un euro?** can I scrounge○ a euro off you?
B **taper sur** vtr ind to hit [clou]; **~ sur l'épaule de qn** to tap sb on the shoulder; **~ sur qn**○ lit to thump ou belt○ sb; fig (critiquer) to badmouth○ sb; **~ sur la table** lit to bang (one's fist) on the table; **~ sur les nerfs de qn** to get on sb's nerves; **se faire ~ sur les doigts** fig to get one's knuckles rapped
C vi **1** (frapper) **~ des mains** (de joie) to clap one's hands; **~ des pieds** (de colère) to stamp one's feet; **~ du pied** (d'impatience) to tap one's foot; **~ à la porte** to knock at the door; **~ dans un ballon** to kick a ball around; **le soleil tape**○ **aujourd'hui** the sun is beating down today; **un vin qui tape**○ fig a wine that goes to one's head; **2** ○(se servir) **~ dans ses économies** to dip into one's savings; **3** (dactylographier) **~ (à la machine)** to type
D **se taper** vpr **1** ○(l'un l'autre) **se ~ dessus** to knock each other about; **2** (soi-même) **je me suis tapé sur le doigt** I hurt myself on the finger; **se ~ la tête contre le mur** to bang one's head against the wall; **c'est à se ~ la tête contre les murs** fig it's enough to drive you up the wall; **3** ○(endurer) to get stuck○ with [corvée, importun]; **j'ai dû me ~ le trajet à pied** I had to foot it○ all the way; **je me suis tapé la route sous la pluie** I ended up having to go all the way in the rain

(Idiomes) **~ comme un sourd**○ (à la porte) to thunder on the door; (au piano) to bash○ ou thump away; **ils se tapent sur le ventre**○ (soi-même) they are thick as thieves○; **c'est à s'en ~ le derrière par terre**○ it's hilarious, it's a riot○; **elle m'a tapé dans l'œil**○ I thought she was striking; **à côté** to be off target

tapette /tapɛt/ nf **1** ○(langue) **faire marcher sa ~** to chatter away endlessly; **2** (pour tapis) carpet beater; **3** (pour tuer les mouches) fly swatter; **4** (piège à souris) mousetrap; **5** (petite tape) pat

tapeur○**, -euse** /tapœʀ, øz/ nm,f scrounger○

tapinois: en tapinois /atapinwa/ loc adv furtively

tapir[1]**: se tapir** /tapiʀ/ [3] vpr [personne, animal] to hide; (en ramassant son corps) to crouch

tapir[2] /tapiʀ/ nm Zool tapir

tapis /tapi/ nm inv gén carpet, rug; (sur un meuble) cloth; (de salle de bains, sport) mat; **mettre qch sur le ~** fig to bring sth

up; **mettre** or **envoyer qn au ~** to throw sb

(Composés) **~ de bain(s)** bathmat; **~ roulant** (pour piétons) moving walkway; (pour bagages) carousel; (pour marchandises) conveyor belt; **~ vert** (sur table de conférence, de jeux) green baize; **~ volant** flying carpet

tapisser /tapise/ [1] vtr **1** (poser un revêtement) to decorate [pièce, mur]; to cover, to upholster [fauteuil]; Culin to line [moule] (de with); **2** (servir de revêtement) [mousse, neige] to carpet [sol]; to cover [mont, ruine]; [cellule, muqueuse] to line [organe, cavité]; [tentures, photos] to cover [mur, pièce]; [résidu, pâte] to line [fond]

tapisserie /tapisʀi/ nf **1** (tenture, broderie) tapestry; **2** (papier peint) wallpaper; **3** (art, technique) tapestry work

(Idiome) **faire ~** (au bal) to be a wallflower

tapissier, -ière /tapisje, ɛʀ/ ▸ p. 372 nm,f **1** (pour meubles) upholsterer; **2** (artiste) tapestry-maker

tapoter /tapɔte/ [1] vtr to tap [table, objet]; to pat [joues, dos]

taquin, ~e /takɛ̃, in/ adj [personne] teasing; **il est très ~** he's a great tease

taquiner /takine/ [1] vtr [personne] to tease; [histoire, douleur] to bother

taquinerie /takinʀi/ nf teasing **C**

tarabiscoté, ~e /taʀabiskɔte/ adj [motif] over-ornate; [écriture] over-elaborate; [esprit, style] convoluted

tarabuster○ /taʀabyste/ [1] vtr [ennuis, question] to bother; [personne] to badger

taratata○ /taʀatata/ excl nonsense!, rubbish○! GB

tard /taʀ/
A adv late; **plus ~** later; **au plus ~** at the latest; **~ dans la nuit** in the middle of the night; **il est un peu ~ pour changer de tactique** it's a bit late in the day to change tactics; **pas plus ~ qu'hier** only yesterday; **ce sera pour plus ~** (une autre fois) there'll be other times
B **sur le tard** loc adv [se marier] late in life; **déclarant sur le ~ que** announcing rather late in the day that

(Idiomes) **mieux vaut ~ que jamais** Prov better late than never Prov; **il n'est jamais trop ~ pour bien faire** Prov it's never too late to do the right thing

tarder /taʀde/ [1]
A vi **1** (à agir) **~ à faire** (être lent) to take a long time doing; (différer) to put off ou delay doing; **trop ~ à faire qch** to wait too long to do sth; **sans ~** immediately; **sans plus ~** without further delay; **elle n'a pas tardé à faire la même chose** she lost no time in doing the same thing; **il ne tardera pas à s'en rendre compte** he'll soon realize; **ne tardez pas!** don't delay!; **2** (à arriver, se manifester) **~ (à arriver)** [saison, réaction, réponse] to be a long time coming; [colis] to take a long time to come; **les enfants ne vont pas ~ (à arriver)** the children won't be long; **elle tarde à revenir** she's taking a long time; **ça ne va pas ~** it won't be long; **ça n'a pas tardé** it wasn't long coming
B v impers **il me tarde de la revoir/qu'elle parte** I'm longing to see her again/for her to go

tardif, -ive /taʀdif, iv/ adj [heure, floraison] late; [excuses, revirement] belated

tardivement /taʀdivmɑ̃/ adv [arriver] late; [réagir] rather belatedly; **ne découvrir qch que ~** to discover sth rather late in the day

tare /taʀ/ nf **1** (masse) tare; **2** Méd defect; **3** (grave défaut) defect; **être accusé d'avoir toutes les ~s** to be accused of every vice in the book

taré, ~e /taʀe/
A adj **1** Méd [personne, animal] with a defect (épith, après n); **2** ○(fou) offensive crazy○; **3** fig [société] sick
B ○nm,f offensive cretin péj

targette /taʀʒɛt/ nf bolt

targuer: se targuer /taʀge/ [1] vpr to claim (**de qch** sth; **de faire** to do), to boast (**de qch** sth); **il se targue d'avoir créé des emplois** he prides himself on having created jobs

tarif /taʀif/ nm **1** (prix) gén rate; (de transport) fare; (de consultation) fee; **payer plein ~** to pay full price; (en train, avion, bus) to pay full fare; **~ normal/économique** Postes ≈ first-class/second-class rate; **~ de nuit** Télécom night-time rate; **~ lettres** letter rate; **tu connais le ~**○, **c'est deux jours de renvoi** fig you know the penalty—two days' suspension; **2** (document) price list

tarification /taʀifikasjɔ̃/ nf (action) price setting; (résultat) tariff

tarir /taʀiʀ/ [23]

A vi ne pas ∼ sur qch/qn to talk endlessly about sth/sb; **ne pas ∼ d'éloges sur qch/qn** to be full of praise for sth/sb

B se tarir vpr lit, fig to dry up, to run dry

tartare /taʀtaʀ/ adj **1** Hist Tartar; **2** Culin **sauce** ∼ tartare sauce; **steak** ∼ steak tartare

tarte /taʀt/

A °adj (niais) [personne] daft° GB, daffy° US; [film, chanson, chapeau, robe] ridiculous

B nf **1** Culin tart; **2** °(gifle) wallop°

(Composé) ∼ **à la crème** (idée banale) stereotype; (gag) custard pie, slapstick

(Idiome) **c'est pas de la ∼⁹** it's no picnic°

tartelette /taʀtəlɛt/ nf tart

Tartempion° /taʀtɑ̃pjɔ̃/ npr **Monsieur et Madame** ∼ Mr and Mrs Whatnot; **demande donc à** ∼ go and ask what's-his-name°

tartine /taʀtin/ nf **1** (pain beurré) slice of bread and butter; **peux-tu me faire une ∼?** could you butter me a slice of bread?; **une** ∼ **de confiture** a slice of bread and jam; **2** °il en a écrit une ∼ he wrote reams about it; **il y en a une** ∼! there's reams of it!

tartiner /taʀtine/ [1] vtr to spread; **chocolat à** ∼ chocolate spread; **pâte à** ∼ sandwich spread

tartre /taʀtʀ/ nm (dans une bouilloire) scale, fur GB; (sur les dents) tartar; (de vin) tartar

tartufe /taʀtyf/ nm hypocrite

tas /ta/

A nm inv **1** lit heap, pile (**de** of); **en** ∼ **dans un coin** piled in a corner; ∼ **de fumier** manure heap; ∼ **de bois** (ordonné) woodpile; (désordonné) pile of wood; ∼ **de ferraille** lit scrap heap; fig (vieille voiture)° wreck; **2** °fig **un** ∼, **des** ∼ lots (**de** of), loads° (**de** of)

B dans le tas loc adv **taper dans le** ∼ to punch people indiscriminately; **foncer dans le** ∼ [personne] to fling oneself into the crowd; [police] to charge the crowd

C sur le tas loc adv **apprendre sur le** ∼ to learn on the job; **formation sur le** ∼ on-the-job training; **grève sur le** ∼ sit-down strike

tasse /tas/ nf **1** (récipient) cup; ∼ **à thé** teacup; **2** (contenu) cup

(Idiome) **boire la** ∼° to swallow a mouthful of water (when swimming)

tassé, ∼e /tase/

A pp ► **tasser**

B pp adj [terre] firmly packed; [neige] hard packed; **bien** ∼ [cigarette] hard; [neige] very hard packed; [whisky] stiff; **il y en a 4 kilos bien ∼s**° there's a good 4 kilos of it; **il a la cinquantaine bien ∼e**° he's well past fifty

tassement /tasmɑ̃/ nm (de l'emploi) contraction; ∼ **de vertèbres** compression of the vertebrae

tasser /tase/ [1]

A vtr to press down [terre]; to tamp down [tabac]; to pack down [paille]; to pack [habits, gens]; to cram [bagages]; **les passagers étaient tassés** the passengers were packed in tightly; **l'accident lui a tassé les vertèbres** the accident has given him/her compression of the vertebrae

B se tasser vpr **1** (s'affaisser) (avec l'âge) to shrink; (volontairement) to make oneself look smaller; **2** (se serrer) [personnes] to squash up; **3** °(se calmer) [conflit] to die down; **les choses se sont tassées** things settled down

tata° /tata/ nf auntie

tâter /tate/ [1]

A vtr **1** (palper) to feel; ∼ **le sol du pied** to test the ground; **2** (sonder) ∼ **l'opinion** to sound out public opinion

B tâter de vtr ind ∼ **de tous les métiers** to try one's hand at all kinds of jobs; ∼ **de la prison** to have a taste of prison

C se tâter vpr **je me tâte** I'm thinking about it

(Idiome) ∼ **le terrain** to put out feelers

tatillon, -onne /tatijɔ̃, ɔn/ adj nit-picking

tâtonnement /tatɔnmɑ̃/ nm ∼s **dans l'obscurité** groping around in the dark; **les** ∼s **des chercheurs** the tentative research ⊄; **après dix années de** ∼s fig after ten years of trial and error

tâtonner /tatɔne/ [1] vi to grope about ou around; **avancer en tâtonnant** lit, fig to grope one's way along; **on tâtonne** (dans des recherches) we're groping in the dark

tâtons: à tâtons /atatɔ̃/ loc adv **avancer à** ∼ lit, fig to feel one's way along

tatouage /tatwaʒ/ nm **1** (dessin) tattoo; **2** (procédé) tattooing

tatouer /tatwe/ [1] vtr to tattoo; **se faire** ∼ to get tattooed; **il s'est fait** ∼ **un aigle sur le dos** he has had an eagle tattooed on his back

tatoueur, -euse /tatwœʀ, øz/ ► p. 372 nm,f tattooist

taudis /todi/ nm inv (misérable) hovel; (mal tenu) pigsty

taule⁹ /tol/ nf (prison) prison, nick° GB; **faire de la** ∼ to do time°

taupe /top/ nf **1** Zool mole; **2** (peau) moleskin; **en** ∼ moleskin (épith); **3** °(femme désagréable) pej **une vieille** ∼ an old bag° péj; **4** °(espion) mole

taupinière /topinjɛʀ/ nf (monticule) molehill; (galeries) (mole) tunnels (pl)

(Idiome) **faire une montagne d'une** ∼ to make a mountain out of a molehill

taureau, pl ∼**x** /tɔʀo/ nm bull

(Idiome) **prendre le** ∼ **par les cornes** to take the bull by the horns

Taureau /tɔʀo/ ► p. 635 nprm Taurus

taurillon /tɔʀijɔ̃/ nm young bull

tauromachie /tɔʀɔmaʃi/ ► p. 327 nf bullfighting

taux /to/ nm inv **1** gén rate; ∼ **de chômage/croissance** unemployment/growth rate; **2** Méd (d'albumine, alcoolémie, de sucre) level; (de bactéries, spermatozoïdes) count

(Composés) ∼ **d'audience** audience ratings (pl); ∼ **de fréquentation** Cin, Théât audience figures (pl); ∼ **de natalité** birthrate; ∼ **de salaire horaire** hourly rate of pay

tavelé, ∼e /tavle/ adj [peau] spotted (**de** with); [fruit] blemished (**de** with)

taxation /taksasjɔ̃/ nf (imposition) taxation; (fixation) assessment

taxe /taks/ nf **1** Comm, Écon tax; **les** ∼s **sur les importations** import levies; **boutique hors** ∼s duty-free shop GB ou store US; **70 euros hors** ∼s 70 euros exclusive of tax; **toutes** ∼s **comprises, TTC** inclusive of tax; **2** Jur taxation

(Composés) ∼ **d'apprentissage** ≈ training levy; ∼ **de douane** customs duty; ∼ **foncière** property tax; ∼ **d'habitation** ≈ council tax (paid by residents to cover local services); ∼ **de raccordement** connection charge; ∼ **à la valeur ajoutée** value added tax

taxer /takse/ [1] vtr **1** Comm, Écon to tax; **2** (accuser) ∼ **qn de laxisme** to accuse sb of being lax

taxi /taksi/ nm **1** (véhicule) taxi, cab US; **chauffeur de** ∼ taxi driver; **station de** ∼s taxi rank GB, cab stand US; **2** °(chauffeur) taxi driver

taxidermiste /taksidɛʀmist/ ► p. 372 nmf taxidermist

Tchad /tʃad/ ► p. 333, p. 230 nprm Chad; **le lac** ∼ Lake Chad

tchador /tʃadɔʀ/ nm chador

tchao° /tʃao/ excl bye°!, see you°!

Tchécoslovaquie /tʃekɔslɔvaki/ nprf Hist Czechoslovakia

tchèque /tʃɛk/ ► p. 392, p. 230, p. 336 adj, nm Czech

Tchétchène /tʃetʃɛn/ ► p. 392 adj Chechen

Tchétchène /tʃetʃɛn/ ► p. 392 nmf Chechen

Tchétchénie /tʃetʃeni/ ► p. 230 nprf Chechnya

tchin(-tchin)° /tʃin(tʃin)/ excl cheers!

TD /tede/ nmpl: abbr ► **travail**

te (**t'** before vowel or mute h) /t(ə)/ pron pers **1** (objet direct) you; **2** (objet indirect) you; **3** (pronom réfléchi) yourself; **il faut que tu** ∼ **soignes** you must look after yourself; **va** ∼ **laver les mains** go and wash your hands

té /te/ nm (règle) T-square; **en** ∼ T-shaped

technicien, -ienne /tɛknisjɛ̃, ɛn/ ► p. 372 nm,f **1** (professionnel) technician; ∼ **supérieur** qualified technician; **2** (spécialiste) technical expert (**de** in); **c'est un très bon** ∼ he's technically very good; **3** (réparateur) engineer

(Composé) ∼ **de surface** cleaner

technique¹ /tɛknik/
A adj technical
B nm technical subjects (pl)
technique² /tɛknik/ nf ⟨1⟩ (méthode) technique; **il n'a pas la (bonne)** ∼○ he hasn't got the knack○; ⟨2⟩ (maîtrise) technique; ⟨3⟩ Écon, Ind technology ℂ; ⟨4⟩ Radio, TV **la** ∼ studio production
techno /tɛkno/ adj, nf Mus techno
technocrate /tɛknɔkʀat/ nmf technocrat
technologie /tɛknɔlɔʒi/ nf technology
teck /tɛk/ nm (arbre, bois) teak; **en** ∼ teak (épith)
teckel /tekɛl/ nm dachshund
tee-shirt, pl ∼**s** /tiʃœʀt/ nm T-shirt
teigne /tɛɲ/ nf ⟨1⟩ (mite) moth; ⟨2⟩ ○(personne hargneuse) nasty GB ou real US piece of work○; **être méchant comme une** ∼ to be a nasty GB ou real US piece of work
teigneux○, **-euse** /tɛɲø, øz/ adj (hargneux) cantankerous
teindre /tɛ̃dʀ/ [73]
A vtr to dye [cheveux, tissu, cuir]; to stain [bois, meuble]; ∼ **qch en vert** to dye sth green
B se teindre vpr [personne] to dye one's hair; **se** ∼ **les cheveux en roux** to dye one's hair red
teint, ∼**e¹** /tɛ̃, tɛ̃t/
A pp ▸ teindre
B pp adj [cheveux, étoffe, cuir] dyed; [bois, meuble] stained
C nm ⟨1⟩ (peau) complexion; **joli** ∼ lovely complexion; ⟨2⟩ (lié à la santé) **avoir le** ∼ **rose** or **frais** to have a healthy glow; **avoir le** ∼ **jaune** to be sallow-skinned; **avoir le** ∼ **pâle** to look pale
teinte² /tɛ̃t/ nf ⟨1⟩ (nuance de couleur) shade; ⟨2⟩ (couleur) colourᴳᴮ; ⟨3⟩ (d'envie, de supériorité) **une** ∼ **de** a tinge of
teinté, ∼**e** /tɛ̃te/
A pp ▸ teinter
B pp adj ⟨1⟩ [lunettes, verre, crème] tinted; [bois] stained; ∼ **jaune** yellow-tinted; ⟨2⟩ fig ∼ **de** [sentiment, couleur] tinged with
teinter /tɛ̃te/ [1]
A vtr ⟨1⟩ to tint [verre]; to stain [bois, meuble]; to dye [cuir]; ⟨2⟩ (nuancer) ∼ **qch de** to tinge sth with
B se teinter vpr liter **se** ∼ **de** to become tinged with
teinture /tɛ̃tyʀ/ nf ⟨1⟩ (produit) (pour cheveux, tissu, cuir) dye; (pour bois) stain; ∼ **d'iode** tincture of iodine; ⟨2⟩ (procédé) (de cheveux, tissu, cuir) dyeing; (de bois) staining; **se faire une** ∼ to dye one's hair; **se faire faire une** ∼ to have one's hair dyed
teinturerie /tɛ̃tyʀʀi/ nf ⟨1⟩ ▸ p. 372 (boutique de nettoyage) (dry-)cleaner's; ⟨2⟩ (industrie) (de la teinture) dyeing; (du nettoyage) (dry-)cleaning
teinturier, **-ière** /tɛ̃tyʀje, ɛʀ/ ▸ p. 372 nm,f (qui nettoie) dry-cleaner; (qui teint) dyer
tek /tɛk/ = teck
teknival, pl ∼**s** /tɛknival/ nm rave
tel, **telle** /tɛl/
A adj ⟨1⟩ (pareil) such; **un** ∼ **homme peut être dangereux** such a man can be dangerous, a man like that can be dangerous; **je n'ai jamais rien vu de** ∼ I've never seen anything like it; ⟨2⟩ (pareil à) like; ⟨3⟩ (ainsi) **telle est la vérité** that is the truth; ∼**s furent ses propos** those were his/her words; **il est honnête, du moins je le crois** ∼ he's honest, at least I believe him to be so; **comme** ∼, **en tant que** ∼ as such; **ce n'est pas sa fille mais il la considère comme telle** she's not his daughter but he treats her as if she were; ∼ **quel**, ∼ **que**○ controv (sans modification) as it is; **ses affaires étaient restées telles quelles** his/her things were left as they were; ∼ **que** (comme) as; **si cette maison est telle que tu le dis** if the house is as you say it is; ∼ **que je te connais** if I know you; ∼ **que vous le voyez il a 80 ans** you wouldn't believe it to look at him but he's 80; ⟨4⟩ (pour exprimer l'intensité) **avec un** ∼ **enthousiasme** with such enthusiasm; **il fait une telle chaleur** it is so hot; **il y avait un** ∼**bruit** there was so much noise; **de telle sorte** ou **façon** or **manière que** (accidentellement) in such a way that; (délibérément) so that; ⟨5⟩ (un certain) **admettons qu'il arrive** ∼ **jour, à telle heure** suppose that he arrives on such and such a day, at such and such a time; **que je prenne telle ou telle décision il critique toujours** no matter what decision I make, he criticizes it; **je me moque de ce que pense telle ou telle personne** I don't care what certain people think; ∼ **autre** others (pl); ∼**s autres** certain others

B pron indéf ∼ **voulait la guerre**, ∼ **voulait la paix** some wanted war, some wanted peace
télé○ /tele/
A adj inv TV; **programme** ∼ TV guide
B nf TV; **à la** ∼ on TV
télécabine /telekabin/ nm cable car
télécommande /telekɔmɑ̃d/ nf remote control
télécommander /telekɔmɑ̃de/ [1] vtr ⟨1⟩ Tech to operate [sth] by remote control; **voiture télécommandée** remote-controlled car; ⟨2⟩ fig (diriger) to mastermind
télécommunication /telekɔmynikasjɔ̃/ nf telecommunications (+ v sg)
téléconférence /telekɔ̃feʀɑ̃s/ nf ⟨1⟩ (séance) (audioconférence) conference call; (vidéoconférence) teleconference; ⟨2⟩ (principe) video-conferencing
télécopie /telekɔpi/ nf fax
télécopier /telekɔpje/ [2] vtr to fax
télécopieur /telekɔpjœʀ/ nm fax machine, fax
télédiffuser /teledifyze/ [1] vtr to broadcast
télé-enquêteur, **-trice** /teleɑ̃kɛtœʀ, tʀis/ ▸ p. 372 nm,f telemarketer
télé-enseignement, pl ∼**s** /teleɑ̃sɛɲəmɑ̃/ nm distance learning
téléfilm /telefilm/ nm TV film, TV movie
télégramme /telegʀam/ nm telegram, cable US
télégraphier /telegʀafje/ [1] vtr to telegraph, to send a telegram ou cable US
télégraphique /telegʀafik/ adj [poteau, message] telegraph; [style] telegraphic
téléguidage /telegidaʒ/ nm radio control
téléguider /telegide/ [1] vtr ⟨1⟩ lit to control [sth] by radio; **voiture téléguidée** radio-controlled car; ⟨2⟩ fig (diriger) to mastermind
télématique /telematik/
A adj [service, réseau] viewdata GB, videotex®
B nf telematics (+ v sg)
télémessage /telemesaʒ/ nm text message, text
téléobjectif /teleɔbʒɛktif/ nm telephoto lens
télépathie /telepati/ nf telepathy
téléphérique /teleferik/ nm cable car, téléphérique
téléphone /telefɔn/ nm (dispositif, appareil) phone; **avoir le** ∼ to be on the (tele)phone GB, to have a phone; **donner un coup de** ∼ to make a phone call; ∼ **à touches/pièces** push-button/coin-operated telephone; ∼ **à carte** card-phone

⟨Composés⟩ ∼ **arabe**○ (bouche-à-oreille) grapevine, bush telegraph; Jeux Chinese whispers (+ v sg); ∼ **portable** transmobile phone; ∼ **portatif** pocket car phone; ∼ **rose** erotic chat-line; **le** ∼ **rouge** the hot-line
téléphoner /telefɔne/ [1]
A vtr ∼ **qch à qn** to phone sb with sth
B vi (en général) to phone; (une fois) to make a phone call; ∼ **à qn** to phone sb, to call sb
C se téléphoner vpr to phone each other
téléphonique /telefɔnik/ adj (tele)phone (épith)
téléprospecteur, **-trice** /telepʀɔspɛktœʀ, tʀis/ ▸ p. 372 nm,f telemarketer
téléréalité /telerealite/ nf reality TV
téléreportage /teleʀəpɔʀtaʒ/ nm (activité) television reporting; (film) television report
télescopage /telɛskɔpaʒ/ nm lit collision; fig overlap
télescope /telɛskɔp/ nm telescope
télescoper /telɛskɔpe/ [1]
A vtr to collide with [voiture]
B se télescoper vpr lit [véhicules] to collide; fig [notions, tendances] to overlap
téléscripteur /teleskʀiptœʀ/ nm teleprinter GB, teletypewriter US
télésiège /telesjɛʒ/ nm chair lift
téléski /teleski/ nm ski tow
téléspectateur, **-trice** /telespɛktatœʀ, tʀis/ nm,f viewer
télésurveillance /telesyʀvɛjɑ̃s/ nf electronic surveillance
télétransmission /teletʀɑ̃smisjɔ̃/ nf transmission

télévente /televɑ̃t/ nf telesales pl

télévisé, **~e** /televize/ adj [programme, publicité] televi-sion (épith); [débat, retransmission] televised

téléviseur /televizœʀ/ nm television (set); **~ couleur** colourᴳᴮ television

télévision /televizjɔ̃/ nf television, TV; **travailler à la ~** to work in television

télex /telɛks/ nm inv telex; **par ~** by telex

télexer /telɛkse/ [1] vtr to telex

tellement /tɛlmɑ̃/ ▸ p. 483

A adv **1** (marquant l'intensité) (modifiant un adjectif ou un adverbe) so; (modifiant un verbe ou un comparatif) so much; **pas ~** not much; **il n'aime pas ~ lire** he doesn't like reading much; **'il y avait beaucoup de monde?'**—**'pas ~'** 'were there many people?'—'not really'; **ce n'est pas ~ que je sois fatigué mais...** it's not so much that I'm tired but...; **cela n'a plus ~ d'importance** it doesn't really matter any more; **je n'ai plus ~ envie d'y aller** I don't really want to go any more; **il n'est pas ~ plus jeune que moi** he's not that much younger than me; **il y avait ~ de gens que je me suis perdu** there were so many people that I got lost; **2** (si nombreux) **il y en a ~ qui aimeraient le faire** so many people would like to do it; **3** (introduisant une cause) **j'ai de la peine à suivre ~ c'est compliqué** it's so complicated that I find it hard to follow

B **tellement de** dét indéf **1** (avec un nom dénombrable) so many; **il y a ~ de choses à voir** there's so much to see; **2** (avec un nom non dénombrable) so much; **il a eu ~ de chance** he was so lucky; **j'ai vu ~ de monde** I saw so many people

tellurique /telyʀik/ adj **secousse ~** earth tremor

téméraire /temeʀɛʀ/ adj [personne, projet] reckless; [jugement] rash; **courageux mais pas ~** brave but not foolhardy

témérité /temeʀite/ nf (de personne, projet) recklessness; (de paroles) rashness; **avoir la ~ de faire** to have the temerity to do

témoignage /temwaɲaʒ/ nm **1** (histoire personnelle) story; (compte rendu) account; **recueillir les ~s des réfugiés** to get the refugees' stories; **apporter son ~** to give one's own account; **selon les ~s** according to (accounts given by); **2** (au cours d'une enquête) evidence ¢; (déposition) evidence ¢, testi-mony; **selon plusieurs ~s** according to several witnesses; **3** (marque) fml **~ d'amitié** (cadeau) token of friendship; (geste) expression of friendship; **~s de sympathie** expres-sions of sympathy; **donner des ~s de son amitié** to prove one's friendship

témoigner /temwaɲe/ [1]

A vtr **1** Jur to testify; **elle a témoigné l'avoir vu entrer** she testified to having seen him go in; **2** (montrer) **~ de l'affection** to show affection; **la confiance qu'elle m'a témoignée** the trust she placed in me; **les marques de sympathie qui leur ont été témoignées lors de...** the expressions of sympathy they received when...

B **témoigner de** vtr ind **1** (prouver) **~ de** to show; **comme en témoigne leur lettre** as their letter shows; **2** (se porter garant de) **~ du courage de qn** to vouch for sb's courage

C vi **1** Jur to give evidence; **être appelé à ~** to be called to give evidence; **2** (dire) **'il était toujours poli', témoignent les voisins** neighboursᴳᴮ say he was always polite

témoin /temwɛ̃/

A nm **1** (sur les lieux) witness; **~ oculaire** or **direct** eyewitness; **être (le) ~ de** to witness; **prendre qn à ~** to call sb to witness; **2** Jur witness; **3** (à un duel) second; **4** fig (d'une époque) **avoir été ~ de la naissance du IIIᵉ Reich** to have witnessed the birth of the Third Reich; **5** (preuve) **ils sont cruels, ~ le massacre** they are (certainly) cruel, as evi-denced by the massacre; **6** Tech (voyant) indicator ou warn-ing light; **~ d'huile** Aut oil warning light; **7** Sport baton

B (-)**témoin** (in compounds) control; **groupe(-)~** control group

(Idiome) **Dieu** or **le Ciel m'en est ~** as God is my witness

tempe /tɑ̃p/ ▸ p. 136 nf temple; **appuyer un pistolet sur la ~ de qn** to hold a gun to sb's head

tempérament /tɑ̃peʀamɑ̃/ nm **1** (caractère) disposition; **être un ~ calme** to have a calm disposition; **ce n'est pas dans mon ~ de me mettre en colère** I would never lose my temper; **elle devrait aller se plaindre, mais ce n'est pas dans son ~** she should go and complain, but she's not like that; **avoir du ~** (volontaire) to have a strong character;

2 Comm **à ~** by instalmentsᴳᴮ

température /tɑ̃peʀatyʀ/ nf **1** Méd, Phys temperature; **prendre la ~ de qn** to take sb's temperature; **2** (fièvre) temperature; **3** (humeur) **prendre la ~ du public** to sound out the public's mood

tempéré, **~e** /tɑ̃peʀe/ adj Géog temperate

tempérer /tɑ̃peʀe/ [14] vtr gén to temper; **~ ses ardeurs** to cool one's ardourᴳᴮ

tempête /tɑ̃pɛt/ nf **1** Météo (sans pluie) gale; (avec pluie) storm; **essuyer une ~** to weather a storm; **~ de neige** snowstorm; **~ de sable** sandstorm; **2** (agitation) uproar; **après la ~ boursière** after the upheaval on the stock exchange; **~ de protestations** wave of protest sg; **une ~ dans un verre d'eau** a storm in a teacup GB, a tempest in a teapot US

tempêter /tɑ̃pɛte/ [1] vi to rage (**contre** against)

temple /tɑ̃pl/ nm **1** Relig (non chrétien) temple; (protestant) church; **2** fig temple (**de** of)

tempo /tɛmpo/ nm **1** Mus tempo; **2** (de roman, film) pace

temporaire /tɑ̃pɔʀɛʀ/ adj temporary; **à titre ~** [employer, travailler] on a temporary basis; **délivrer un permis à titre ~** to issue a temporary permit

temporel, **-elle** /tɑ̃pɔʀɛl/ adj gén temporal; **biens ~s** worldly goods

temporisateur, **-trice** /tɑ̃pɔʀizatœʀ, tʀis/

A adj temporizing (épith)

B nm,f temporizer

temporiser /tɑ̃pɔʀize/ [1] vi to stall

temps /tɑ̃/ nm inv **1** Météo weather ¢; **un beau ~** fine weather; **un ~ de cochon**○ lousy○ weather; **le ~ est à la pluie** it looks like rain; **le ~ est à l'orage** there's going to be a storm; **par ~ clair** (de jour) on a clear day; (de nuit) on a clear night; **par ~ de pluie** when it rains; **2** (durée) time; **peu de ~ avant** shortly before; **dans peu de ~** shortly; **dans quelque ~** before long; **(pendant) quelque ~** or **un cer-tain ~** (assez courte période) for a while; (période plus longue) for some time; **pendant** or **pour un ~** for a while; **pendant ce ~(-là)** meanwhile; **en un rien de ~** in no time at all; **les trois quarts du ~** most of the time; **depuis le ~ que j'en parle!** I've been talking about it for long enough!; **depuis le ~ que ça existe, tu devrais être au courant** you should have known, it's been around for so long; **le ~ d'installa-tion a été plus long que prévu** it took longer than expect-ed to install; **ils sont restés le ~ de l'élection** they stayed just for the duration of the election; **il a souri le ~ de la photo** he smiled just long enough for the photo to be taken; **un an, le ~ d'écrire un roman** a year, just long enough to write a novel; **le ~ de me retourner, il avait disparu** by the time I turned round GB ou around, he had disappeared; **le ~ de ranger mes affaires et j'arrive** just let me put my things away and I'll be with you; **(j'ai) pas l'~**○! not now!; **avoir tout le ~** to have plenty of time; **avoir dix** or **cent fois le ~** to have all the time in the world; **vous avez combien de ~ pour le déjeuner?** how long do you have for lunch?; **nous avons du ~ devant nous** we have plenty of time; **plus de ~ que** longer than; **ne pas prendre beaucoup de ~** not to take long; **tu as mis combien de ~?** how long did it take you?; **ça a pris** or **mis un ~ fou**○ it took ages○; **tu y as mis le ~**!, **tu en as mis du ~**! you (certainly) took your time!; **j'y mettrai le ~ qu'il faudra, mais je le ferai** however long it takes, I'll get it done; **le ~ passe vite** time flies; **faire passer le ~** to while away the time (**en faisant** doing); **j'ai perdu un ~ fou**○ I've wasted loads○ of time; **avoir du ~ à perdre** to have time on one's hands; **faire qch à ~ perdu** to do sth in one's spare time; **le ~ presse!** time is short!; **j'ai trouvé le ~ long** (the) time seemed to drag; **nous sommes dans les ~** we've still got time; **finir dans les ~** to finish in time; **3** (moment) **de ~ en ~**, **de ~ à autre** from time to time; **il était ~**! (marquant l'impatience) (and) about time too!; (marquant le soulagement) just in the nick of time!; **il est ~** it's about time; **il est grand ~** it's high time (**de faire** to do); **il n'est plus ~ de faire** it's too late to do; **en ~ utile** in time; **en ~ voulu** (à venir) in due course; (quand il aurait fallu) at the right time; **que ne dure qu'un ~** to be short-lived; **4** (époque) time; **au ~ des dinosaures** in the age of the dinosaurs; **au** or **du ~ où** in the days when; **regretter le ~ où** to feel nostalgia for the days when; **le bon vieux ~** the good old days (pl); **c'était le bon ~**! those were the days!; **ces der-niers ~** recently; **ces ~-ci** lately; **de mon ~** in my day; **dans le ~, j'étais sportif** in my day, I did a bit of sport;

La température

■ *Dans les pays anglophones, la température se mesure traditionnellement en degrés Fahrenheit, mais les degrés Celsius sont de plus en plus utilisés, surtout en Grande-Bretagne. Le bulletin météo à la télévision britannique n'utilise que les degrés Celsius.*

Celsius (C)	Fahrenheit (F)	
100 °	212 °	boiling point (*point d'ébullition*)
90 °	194 °	
80 °	176 °	
70 °	158 °	
60 °	140 °	
50 °	122 °	
40 °	104 °	
37 °	98.4 °	
30 °	86 °	
20 °	68 °	
10 °	50 °	
0 °	32 °	freezing point (*point de congélation*)
−10 °	14 °	
−273.15 °	−459.67 °	absolute zero (*zéro absolu*)

* *Pour la prononciation des nombres* ▸ **p. 398**.

65°F
= 65°F (*sixty-five degrees Fahrenheit*)

−15°C
= −15°C (*minus fifteen degrees Celsius*)

environ 55°
= about 55° (*fifty-five degrees*)

presque 60°
= almost 60°

plus de 50°
= above 50° *ou* over 50°

moins de 60°
= below 60°

La température des choses

quelle est la température du lait?
= what temperature is the milk?

à quelle température est-il?
= what temperature is it?

il est à une température de 53°
= it is 53°

■ *Noter l'absence d'équivalent anglais de l'expression* à une température de.

A est plus chaud que B
= A is hotter than B

B est moins chaud que A
= B is cooler than A

B est plus froid que A
= B is colder than A

A est à la même température que B
= A is the same temperature as B

A et B sont à la même température
= A and B are the same temperature

■ *Noter que l'anglais n'a pas d'équivalent de la préposition* à *dans ces deux derniers exemples.*

à quelle température l'eau bout-elle?
= what temperature does water boil at?

elle bout à 100°
= it boils at 100°

La température du corps

quelle est sa température?
= what is his temperature?

sa température est de 38°C
= his temperature is 38°C

il a 38°C de fièvre
= he has a temperature of 38°C

le thermomètre indique 102°F
= the thermometer shows *ou* says 102°F

il a 39,5°
= his temperature is 39.5°

la température du corps est d'environ 37°
= body temperature is about 37°

Le temps

quelle température fait-il aujourd'hui?
= what is the temperature today?

25° au-dessous de zéro
= 25° below zero

il fait 12°
= it is 12°

il fait 40 degrés
= it is 40 degrees

il fait −15°
= it is −15° (*dire* minus fifteen degrees) *ou* it is −15° (minus fifteen)

il fait plus chaud à Nice qu'à Londres
= Nice is warmer than London

il fait la même température à Nice qu'à Londres
= it's the same temperature in Nice as in London

dans le ∼, on n'avait pas l'électricité in those days, we didn't have electricity; **depuis le** ∼, **les choses ont dû bien changer** since then things must have really changed; **il est loin le** ∼ **où** the days are long gone when; **en** ∼ **normal** usually; **en d'autres** ∼ at any other time; **en** ∼ **de paix** in peacetime; **être de son** ∼ to move with the times; **être en retard sur son** ∼ to be behind the times; **avoir fait son** ∼ [*prisonnier, militaire*] to have served one's time; [*fonctionnaire, diplomate*] to have put in one's time; [*personne usée*] to have outlived one's usefulness, to be past it○; [*produit à la mode, appareil, voiture*] to have had its day; ⑤ (phase) stage; **dans un premier** ∼ first; **dans un deuxième** ∼ subsequently; **dans un dernier** ∼ finally; ⑥ Ling (de verbe) tense; **adverbe de** ∼ adverb of time; ⑦ (de travail) time; **avoir un travail à** ∼ **partiel/plein** to have a part-/full-time job; ∼ **de travail quotidien** working day GB, workday US; ⑧ Sport time; **il a réalisé le meilleur** ∼ he

got the best time; **rester dans les** ∼ to be inside the time; ⑨ (de moteur) stroke; **moteur à quatre** ∼ four-stroke engine; ⑩ Mus time; **mesure à deux** ∼ two-four time

(Composés) ∼ **d'antenne** airtime; ∼ **d'attente** Ordinat latency; ∼ **fort** Mus forte; fig high point; ∼ **mort** Ordinat idle time; (d'activité) slack period; ∼ **de positionnement** *or* **de recherche** Ordinat seek time; ∼ **universel** Greenwich Mean Time, GMT, universal time

(Idiomes) **au** ∼ **pour moi!** my mistake!; **le** ∼ **perdu ne se rattrape jamais** Prov you can't make up for lost time; **par les** ∼ **qui courent** with things as they are; **prendre le** ∼ **comme il vient** to take things as they come; **prendre** *or* **se payer**○ **du bon** ∼ to have a whale of a time

tenable /tənabl/ *adj* ① (supportable) bearable; **la situation n'est pas** ∼ the situation is unbearable; ② Mil (défendable) tenable; ③ (discipliné) **les élèves ne sont pas** ∼**s**

La mesure du temps

une seconde
= a second

un jour†
= a day†

une année
= a year

une minute
= a minute

une semaine
= a week

un siècle
= a century

une heure
= an hour*

un mois
= a month‡

* Pour la façon de donner l'heure ▸ **p. 296**.

† Pour les expressions utilisant les noms de jours ▸ **p. 545**.

‡ Pour les expressions utilisant les noms de mois ▸ **p. 380**.

Les durées

Avec des verbes

combien de temps faut-il?
= how long does it take?

il faut trois heures
= it takes three hours

il faudra une année
= it'll take a year

il a fallu un quart d'heure
= it took a quarter of an hour

ça m'a pris une demi-heure
= it took me half an hour

j'ai mis trois heures à le faire
= it took me three hours to do it

la lettre a mis un mois pour arriver
= the letter took a month to arrive

■ *L'anglais traduit normalement* passer *par* spend:

passer une année à Paris
= to spend a year in Paris

■ *Mais avec les adjectifs évaluatifs on traduira par* have:

passer une bonne soirée
= to have a good evening

Avec des prépositions

en deux minutes
= in two minutes

en six mois
= in six months

en un an
= in a year

en l'espace de quelques minutes
= within minutes

Noter aussi:

dans deux minutes
= in two minutes

■ Pendant *et* pour *se traduisent par* for, *de même que* depuis *lorsqu'il exprime une durée:*

pendant une semaine
= for a week

pendant des heures et des heures
= for hours and hours

je suis ici pour deux semaines
= I'm here for two weeks

il travaille depuis un an
= he's been working for a year

depuis bientôt dix ans
= for going on ten years

■ *Noter aussi le temps du passé utilisé avec* for. *Voir d'autres exemples à l'article* for *dans le dictionnaire.*

il y a des années qu'ils sont mariés
= they have been married for years

■ *Noter l'ordre des mots et l'utilisation du trait d'union dans les adjectifs composés anglais qui indiquent une durée. Pour les noms anglais dénombrables* (wait, delay *etc.) on aura:*

une attente de six semaines
= a six-week wait

un retard de cinquante minutes
= a fifty-minute delay

une journée de huit heures
= an eight-hour day

■ Week, month, minute, hour *etc., employés comme adjectifs, ne prennent pas la marque du pluriel.*

■ *Mais pour les noms indénombrables* (leave, pay *etc.), il y a deux traductions possibles:*

quatre jours de congé
= four days' leave *ou* four days of leave

quatre semaines de salaire
= four weeks' pay *ou* four weeks of pay

vingt-cinq ans de bonheur
= twenty-five years' happiness
 ou twenty-five years of happiness

Un point dans le temps

Dans le passé

quand est-ce que cela s'est passé?
= when did it happen?

la semaine dernière
= last week

le mois dernier
= last month

l'année dernière
= last year

au cours des derniers mois
= over the last few months

■ *Noter l'ordre des mots avec* ago:

il y a deux ans
= two years ago

il y a des années
= years ago

il y aura un mois mardi
= it'll be a month ago on Tuesday

il y a huit jours hier
= a week ago yesterday *ou* a week past yesterday

il y aura huit jours demain
= a week ago tomorrow

il y a des années qu'il est mort
= he died years ago *ou* it's years since he died

un mois auparavant
= a month before

un mois plus tôt
= a month earlier

l'année d'avant
= the year before

l'année d'après
= the year after

☛ Voir page suivante

La mesure du temps *suite*

quelques années plus tard
= a few years later

au bout de quatre jours
= after four days

Dans le futur

quand est-ce que tu le verras?
= when will you see him?

la semaine prochaine
= next week

le mois prochain
= next month

l'année prochaine
= next year

■ Dans *se traduit souvent par* in (*comme en; voir ci-dessus*):

dans dix jours
= in ten days *ou* in ten days' time

dans quelques jours
= in a few days

Noter aussi:

dans un mois demain
= a month tomorrow

au cours de la semaine à venir
= this coming week

au cours des mois à venir
= over the coming months

Les fréquences

cela arrive tous les combien?
= how often does it happen?

tous les jeudis
= every Thursday

toutes les semaines
= every week

tous les deux jours
= every other day *ou* every second day

le dernier jeudi du mois
= the last Thursday of the month

jour après jour
= day after day

une fois tous les trois mois
= once every three months

deux fois par an
= twice a year

trois fois par jour
= three times a day

Les salaires

combien est-ce que tu gagnes de l'heure?
= how much do you get an hour?

je gagne 11 euros de l'heure
= I get 11 euros an hour

être payé 1 100 euros par mois
= to be paid 1,100 euros a month

30 000 euros par an
= 30,000 euros a year

Mais noter:

être payé à l'heure
= to be paid by the hour

---

aujourd'hui the pupils are being impossible today

tenace /tənas/ *adj* **1** [*tache, odeur, migraine*] stubborn; [*parfum*] long-lasting; [*brume, bronchite, toux*] persistent; [*rumeur, souvenir*] persistent; [*haine, croyance*] entrenched; **2** [*personne*] (obstiné) tenacious; (insistant) persistent; [*volonté*] tenacious

ténacité /tenasite/ *nf* **1** (de personne) (obstination) tenacity; (insistance) persistence; **2** (de souvenir, d'illusion) persistence

tenaille /tənaj/ *nf* pincers (*pl*)

tenailler /tənaje/ [1] *vtr* il était tenaillé par le remords he was racked with remorse; elle était tenaillée par la faim hunger gnawed at her

tenancier, -ière /tənɑ̃sje, ɛʀ/ ▸ p. 372 *nm,f* (de café) landlord/landlady; (d'hôtel, de casino) manager/manageress; tenancière de maison close madam

tenant, ~e /tənɑ̃, ɑ̃t/
A *nm,f* Jeux, Sport ~ du titre titleholder; ~ du trophée holder of the trophy
B *nm* **1** (adepte) advocate; **2** (morceau) d'un seul ~ all in one piece
(Idiome) les ~s et les aboutissants de qch the ins and outs of sth

tendance /tɑ̃dɑ̃s/
A °*adj inv* trendy, fashionable
1 *adj* trendy; c'est très ~ it's very trendy
C *nf* **1** (propension) tendency; avoir ~ à faire to tend to do; on a trop ~ à croire que we are too inclined to believe that; le marché a ~ à se stabiliser the market is becoming more stable; **2** (orientation) tendency; toutes ~s politiques confondues across party lines; **3** (école) trend; la ~ dominante the dominant trend; **4** (dynamique) trend; ~ à la baisse/hausse downward/upward trend

tendancieux, -ieuse /tɑ̃dɑ̃sjø, øz/ *adj* biased^GB, tendentious

tendeur /tɑ̃dœʀ/ *nm* **1** (de tente) guy rope; **2** (de porte-bagages, galerie) elastic strap; **3** (dispositif) gén tightener; Tech (pour clôture) slack adjuster

tendon /tɑ̃dɔ̃/ *nm* tendon

tendre¹ /tɑ̃dʀ/ [6]
A *vtr* **1** (étirer) to tighten [*corde, fil, câble*]; to stretch [*élastique, peau*]; to extend [*ressort*]; ~ le cou to crane one's neck; ~ les bras (allonger) to hold out one's arms; (étirer) to stretch one's arms out; jambes et pointes de pied tendues legs straight and toes pointed; ~ le bras (pour saisir, donner) to reach out; ~ le bras à qn (pour soutenir) to offer *ou* give one's arm to sb; ~ les bras à *or* vers qn (pour accueillir) to greet *ou* welcome sb with open arms; la victoire me tend les bras fig victory beckons; ~ la main (pour saisir, donner) to reach out; (pour mendier, serrer la main à qn) to hold out one's hand; ~ la main à qn (pour aider) lit to hold one's hand out to sb; fig to lend sb a helping hand; ~ la joue lit to offer one's cheek; ~ l'autre joue Bible to turn the other cheek; **2** (déployer) to spread [*toile, drap*] (sur over); **3** (disposer) to set [*piège*]; to put up [*fil à linge, filet*]; ~ un piège à qn fig to set a trap for sb; **4** (tapisser) ~ un mur de tissu to hang a wall with cloth; bureau tendu de toile de jute office hung with hessian; **5** (présenter) ~ qch à qn to hold sth out to sb; ~ une cigarette/du feu à qn to offer sb a cigarette/a light
B tendre ~ *vtr ind* **1** (viser à) ~ à un but to strive for a goal; **2** (avoir tendance à) ~ à faire to tend to do
C *vi* **1** (s'orienter) ~ vers to strive for; **2** (se rapprocher) ~ vers to approach [*valeur, chiffre*]; to tend to [*zéro, infini*]
D se tendre *vpr* (devenir tendu) to tighten; (devenir conflictuel) to become strained

tendre² /tɑ̃dʀ/
A *adj* **1** (non dur) [*roche, bois, fibre*] soft; [*chair, peau, légumes*] tender; **2** (jeune) [*pousse, herbe*] new; ~ enfance earliest childhood; **3** (pâle) [*rose, vert, bleu*] soft; des chaussettes

vert ~ pale green socks; **4)** (affectueux) [*personne*] loving; [*amour, sourire, paroles*] tender; [*tempérament*] gentle; **un cœur** ~ a loving heart; **poser un regard** ~ **sur qn** to look tenderly at sb; **être** ~ **avec qn** (affectueux) to be loving toward(s) sb; **ne pas être** ~ **avec qn/qch** to be hard on sb/sth; **leurs propos ne sont pas** ~**s pour le régime** they have some harsh words to say about the regime; **5)** (cher) [*ami, époux*] dear

B *nmf* soft-hearted person

tendrement /tɑ̃dʀəmɑ̃/ *adv* tenderly

tendresse /tɑ̃dʀɛs/ *nf* (donnée) tenderness; (reçue) affection; **avec une grande** ~ very tenderly; **éprouver de la** ~ **pour qn** to have tender feelings for sb; **chercher un peu de** ~ to be looking for affection

tendron /tɑ̃dʀɔ̃/ *nm* Culin (de bœuf) plate; (de veau) flank

tendu, **-e** /tɑ̃dy/
A *pp* ▸ **tendre¹**
B *pp adj* [*corde*] tight
C *adj* (crispé) [*personne, réunion*] tense; [*marché*] nervous

ténèbres /tenebʀ/ *nfpl* **les** ~ lit, fig darkness **¢**

ténébreux, **-euse** /tenebʀø, øz/ *adj* liter [*endroit*] dark; (mystérieux) obscure

teneur /tənœʀ/ *nf* **1)** (de solide) content; (de gaz, liquide) level; ~ **en sucre** sugar content; **boisson à faible** ~ **en alcool** low alcohol drink; **2)** (de rapport, discours, d'acte juridique) import

ténia /tenja/ *nm* tapeworm

tenir /təniʀ/ [36]
A *vtr* **1)** (serrer) to hold; **tiens-moi ça** hold this (for me); ~ **qn par la main** to hold sb's hand; ~ **la rampe** to hold onto the banisters; **tiens!** (voici) here you are!; (écoute-moi) look!; **tiens! c'est pour toi** (voici un cadeau) here, it's for you; (voici une gifle) take that!; **si je le tenais!** if I could get my hands on him!; **bien** ~ to hold on to; **2)** (avoir sous son contrôle) to keep [sb] under control; **il nous tient** he's got a hold on us; **3)** Mil to hold; **4)** (avoir attrapé) to hold; **je te tiens!** I've caught *ou* got you!; **pendant que je te tiens** fig whilst I've got you; ~ **une grippe**○ to have flu GB *ou* the flu US; **5)** (posséder) to have [*renseignements*]; **de qui tenez-vous ce renseignement?** where did you get that information?; **elle tient ses bijoux de sa mère** she inherited her jewels from her mother; **6)** (avoir la charge de) to hold [*emploi*]; to run [*boutique, maison, journal*]; to be in charge of [*standard, bureau d'accueil*]; **bien** ~ **sa maison** to keep one's house spick and span; ~ **la comptabilité** to keep the books; **7)** (garder) to keep; ~ **qn occupé** to keep sb busy; '~ **hors de portée des enfants**' 'keep out of reach of children'; ~ **une note** Mus to hold a note; **8)** (conserver une position) ~ **la tête droite** to hold one's head upright; ~ **les yeux baissés** to keep one's eyes lowered; **9)** (maintenir en place) to hold down [*chargement*]; to hold up [*pantalon, chaussettes*]; ~ **la porte fermée avec son pied** to hold the door shut with one's foot; **10)** (ne pas s'écarter de) to keep to [*trajectoire*]; **11)** (résister) ~ **la mer** [*navire*] to be seaworthy; ~ **le coup** (physiquement, moralement) to hold out; ~ **le choc** [*matériel*] to withstand the impact; [*personne*] to stand the strain; **12)** (contenir) to hold [*quantité, litres*]; **13)** (occuper) [*objet*] to take up [*espace, volume*]; [*personne*] to hold [*rôle, position*]; **14)** (considérer) ~ **qn/qch pour responsable** to hold sb/sth responsible; **je tiens mes renseignements pour exacts** I consider my information to be correct; ~ **qn pour mort** to give sb up for dead; ~ **pour certain que** to regard it as certain that

B *tenir à* **1)** (avoir de l'attachement pour) ~ **à** to be fond of, to like; ~ **à sa réputation/à la vie** to value one's reputation/one's life; **il tient à son argent** he can't bear to be parted from his money; ~ **à son indépendance** to like one's independence; **2)** (vouloir) **j'y tiens** I insist; ~ **à faire** to want to do; **je ne tiens pas à faire** I'd rather not do; ~ **à ce que qn fasse** to insist that sb should do; **je ne tiens pas à ce qu'elle y aille** I'd rather she didn't go; **je tiens beaucoup à la revoir** I'd really like to see her again; **nous tenons absolument à vous avoir à dîner bientôt** you really must come to dinner soon; **3)** (être dû à) ~ **à** to be due to

C *tenir de* *vtr ind* **1)** (ressembler à) ~ **de** to take after; **il a de qui** ~○ you can (just) see who he takes after *ou* where he gets it from; **de qui peut-elle** ~ **pour être si méchante?** where does she get her nastiness from?; **2)** (s'apparenter à) ~ **de** to border on

D *vi* **1)** (rester en place) [*attache, corde, étagère, barrage, soufflé*] to

hold; [*timbre, colle, sparadrap*] to stick (**à** to); [*assemblage, bandage*] to stay in place; [*coiffure*] to stay tidy; [*mise en plis*] to stay in; **ces chaussures ne me tiennent pas aux pieds** these shoes won't stay on my feet; **2)** (résister) ~ **(bon)** (surmonter les conditions) to hold out; (refuser de capituler) gén to hang on; Mil to hold out; (ne pas relâcher sa prise) [*personne*] to hang on; ~ **sans cigarettes jusqu'à la fin de la réunion** to last without cigarettes till the end of the meeting; **j'espère que ma voiture va** ~ **(bon)** I hope my car will last out; **il n'y a pas de télévision qui tienne**○ there's no question of watching television; **3)** (durer) **le plan tient-il toujours?** is the plan still on?; **la neige tient** the snow is settling; **les fleurs n'ont pas tenu** the flowers didn't last long; **la couleur n'a pas tenu** the colour^GB has faded; **4)** (rester valable) [*théorie, argument*] to hold good; [*alibi*] to stand up; **5)** (être contenu) [*personnes, objets*] to fit (**dans** into); **faire** ~ **six personnes dans une voiture** to fit six people into a car; **mon article tient en trois pages** my article takes up only three pages; ~ **en hauteur/largeur/longueur** to be short enough/narrow enough/short enough (**dans** for); ~ **en hauteur dans une pièce** to fit into a room (heightwise); **ne pas** ~ **en hauteur** to be too tall (**dans** for)

E *se tenir* *vpr* **1)** (soi-même) to hold; **se** ~ **la tête de douleur** to hold one's head in pain; **2)** (l'un l'autre) **se** ~ **par le bras** to be arm in arm; **ils se tenaient par la taille** they had their arms around each other's waists; **se** ~ **par la main** to hold hands; **3)** (s'accrocher) to hold on; **se** ~ **par les pieds** to hold on with one's feet; **tiens-toi** *or* **tenez-vous bien**○ fig prepare yourself for a shock; **4)** (demeurer) **se** ~ **accroupi/allongé** to be squatting/stretched out; **se** ~ **sans bouger** to stay still; **se** ~ **prêt** to be ready; **se** ~ **tranquille** (immobile) to keep still; (silencieux) to keep quiet; (dans la légalité) to behave oneself; **se** ~ **immobile** (debout) to stand still; **5)** (se comporter) to behave; **savoir se** ~ to know how to behave; **tiens-toi bien!** behave yourself!; **6)** (avoir une posture) **se** ~ **bien/mal** to have (a) good posture/(a) bad posture; **tiens-toi droit!** (debout) stand up straight!; (assis) sit straight!; **7)** (avoir lieu) [*manifestation, exposition*] to be held; **8)** (être liés) [*événements*] to fit together; (être cohérent) [*raisonnement, œuvre*] to hold together; **ça se tient** it makes sense; **10)** (se considérer) **se** ~ **pour** to consider oneself to be; **tenez-le pour dit**○! I don't want to have to tell you again!; **11)** (être fidèle) **s'en** ~ **à** to stand by; **12)** (se limiter) **s'en** ~ **à** to keep to; **s'en** ~ **aux ordres** to stick to orders; **s'en** ~ **là** to leave it there; **ne pas savoir à quoi s'en** ~ **avec** not to know what to make of

F *v impers* **il ne tient qu'à toi de partir** it's up to you to decide whether to leave; **qu'à cela ne tienne!** never mind!

G **tiens** *excl* oh!; **tiens (donc), vous voilà!** oh, there you are!; **tiens, vous croyez?** do you think so?; **tiens donc!** iron fancy that!; **tiens tiens (tiens)!** well, well!

tennis /tenis/
A ▸ p. 327 *nm inv* (activité) tennis; ~ **de table** table tennis
B *nm ou f inv* (chaussure) tennis shoe

tennisman, *pl* **tennismen** /tenisman, mɛn/ *nm* controv male tennis player

ténor /tenɔʀ/ *nm* **1)** ▸ p. 98 (chanteur, voix, instrument) tenor; **2)** (personnalité) (de sport) star; (de parti, profession) leading light

tensiomètre /tɑ̃sjɔmɛtʀ/ *nm* Tech tensiometer; Méd sphygmomanometer

tension /tɑ̃sjɔ̃/ *nf* **1)** (de câble, muscle) tension; **2)** Méd ~ **(artérielle)** blood pressure; **avoir de la** ~ to have high blood pressure; ~ **nerveuse** nervous tension; **être sous** ~ to be under stress; **3)** Électrotech tension, voltage; **4)** (discorde) tension; **la** ~ **entre les deux pays est telle que** relations between the two countries are so strained that

tentaculaire /tɑ̃takylɛʀ/ *adj* [*ville*] sprawling (épith); [*entreprise, organisation*] with far-reaching interests (après n); [*pouvoir*] far-reaching (épith)

tentacule /tɑ̃takyl/ *nm* tentacle

tentateur, **-trice** /tɑ̃tatœʀ, tʀis/ *nm,f* tempter/temptress

tentation /tɑ̃tasjɔ̃/ *nf* temptation **la** ~ **est forte de demander** plus it's very tempting to ask for more

tentative /tɑ̃tativ/ *nf* attempt; ~ **de meurtre** gén murder attempt; Jur attempted murder; **faire une** ~ **de meurtre contre qn** to attempt to murder sb; ~ **de coup d'État** attempted coup; **faire une** ~ **auprès de qn pour obtenir qch** to try to obtain sth from sb

tente /tɑ̃t/ nf tent; **dormir sous la** ~ gén to sleep under canvas; [nomades] to sleep in tents

(Composé) ~ **à oxygène** oxygen tent

tenter /tɑ̃te/ [1] vtr **1** (essayer) to attempt; **j'ai tout tenté pour l'en dissuader** I've tried everything to dissuade him/her; ~ **sa chance** to try one's luck; **je vais** ~ **l'expérience** I'll have a go; ~ **le tout pour le tout** to risk one's all; **2** (attirer) to tempt; **cela ne la tente guère** that doesn't appeal to her very much; **ça ne me tente qu'à moitié** I'm only half tempted by it; **se laisser** ~ **par** to let oneself be tempted by; **laisse-toi** ~**!** be a devil!; **3** (éprouver) to tempt; ~ **le diable** to court disaster

tenture /tɑ̃tyʀ/ nf **1** (grand rideau) curtain; ~**s** (décoratif) draperies; **2** (tendu aux murs) fabric wall covering

tenu, ~**e¹** /təny/

A pp ▸ **tenir**

B pp adj **1** (entretenu) **bien/mal** ~ [enfant] well/badly cared for; [maison] well/badly kept; [troupes] well/badly turned out; **chambre bien** ~**/mal** ~**e** tidy/untidy room; **2** (contraint) ~ **de faire** required to do; ~ **à** bound by

tenue² /təny/ nf **1** (vêtements) dress **C**, clothes (pl); **être en** ~ **décontractée** to wear casual clothes; ~ **d'hiver** gén winter clothes (pl); (de soldat, policier) winter uniform; **se mettre en** ~ to change; **être en petite** ~ to be scantily clad; **être en** ~ **légère** (peu vêtu) to be scantily dressed; (avec vêtements légers) to be in light clothing; **se mettre en grande** ~ gén to put on ceremonial dress; Mil to put on full dress uniform; **en** ~ uniformed; **avoir une** ~ **impeccable** to be impeccably dressed; **2** (manières) **avoir de la** ~ to have good manners; **ne pas avoir de** ~ to have bad manners; **un peu de** ~**!** mind your manners!; **3** (posture) posture **C**; **4** Fin (comportement) performance

(Composés) ~ **de campagne** Mil battle ou field dress; ~ **de cérémonie** ceremonial dress **C**; ~ **de route** Aut roadholding **C**; ~ **de travail** work(ing) clothes (pl); ~ **de ville** smart clothes (pl)

ter /tɛʀ/ adv **1** (dans une adresse) ter; **2** (indication) three times

térébenthine /teʀebɑ̃tin/ nf; **(essence de)** ~ turpentine

tergal® /tɛʀgal/ nm Terylene®

tergiversation /tɛʀʒivɛʀsasjɔ̃/ nf equivocation **C**

tergiverser /tɛʀʒivɛʀse/ [1] vi **1** (par indécision) to dither; **2** (discuter sans résultats) to shilly-shally

terme /tɛʀm/

A nm **1** (mot) term; **au sens premier du** ~ in the original sense of the word; **le** ~ **'quota' désigne** the term 'quota' designates; **en d'autres** ~**s** in other words; **dans tous les sens du** ~ in every sense of the word; **c'est en ces** ~**s que le ministre a décrit la situation** this was how the minister described the situation; **il a décrit les résultats en ces** ~**s** he described the results thus; **2** (fin) end; **toucher à son** ~ to come to an end; **arriver à** ~ [plan] to come to its appointed end; [période, contrat] to expire; **mener à** ~ to see [sth] through to completion [projet, opération]; **naître à** ~**/avant** ~ to be born at full term/before term; **accoucher avant** ~ to give birth prematurely; **enfant né avant** ~ premature baby; **3** (échéance) **passé ce** ~ **vous paierez des intérêts** after this date, you will pay interest; **à moyen** ~ [emprunt, stratégie] medium-term (épith); **4** Jur (date de paiement du loyer) due date; (période de location) rental period; (montant de la location) rent; **5** Math, Philos term; **trouver un moyen** ~ (équilibre) to find a happy medium; (compromis) to find a compromise

B **termes** nmpl **1** (clauses) terms; **2** (relations) terms; **en bons** ~**s** on good terms; **3** (dimension) **la question se pose aussi en** ~**s financiers** the issue is also a financial one

terminaison /tɛʀminɛzɔ̃/ nf Ling ending

terminal, ~**e¹,** mpl **-aux** /tɛʀminal, o/

A adj (année) final; **phase** ~**e** (d'une opération) concluding phase; (d'une maladie) terminal phase

B nm terminal

terminale² /tɛʀminal/ nf Scol final year (of secondary school)

terminer /tɛʀmine/ [1]

A vtr **1** (aller jusqu'au bout de) to finish; **termine ton déjeuner** finish your lunch; **2** (conclure) to end; ~ **son discours par une mise en garde** to end one's speech with a warning

B vi to finish; ~ **à la première place** to finish first; **en** ~ **avec** to be through with; **c'est terminé, je n'irai plus jamais!** that's that, I'm never going back!; **pour** ~ **je dirai que** in conclusion let me say that

C **se terminer** vpr **1** (dans le temps) to end; **le projet se termine** the project is coming to an end; **se** ~ **par** to end with; **se** ~ **bien/mal** [relation, événement] to end well/badly; [film, roman] to have a happy/sad ending; **se** ~ **tragiquement** [pièce] to end tragically; [excursion] to end in tragedy; **être terminé** to be over; **2** (dans l'espace) **se** ~ **par** [objet, mot, numéro] to end in; **un morceau de bois terminé par un crochet** a piece of wood with a hook at the end

terminologie /tɛʀminɔlɔʒi/ nf terminology

terminus /tɛʀminys/ nm inv (de train) end of the line; (de bus) terminus

ternaire /tɛʀnɛʀ/ adj Chimie, Math ternary; Mus compound

terne /tɛʀn/ adj [poil] dull; [couleur] drab; [blanc] dingy; [œil] lifeless; [personne, vie, événement] dull

ternir /tɛʀniʀ/ [3]

A vtr **1** to tarnish [métal]; to fade [tissu]; **2** to tarnish [image, réputation]; to detract from [exploit]

B **se ternir** vpr to tarnish

terrain /tɛʀɛ̃/ nm **1** (sol) ground **C**, soil **C**; (relief) ground **C**, terrain **C**; ~**s tertiaires/volcaniques** tertiary/volcanic formations; **avancer sur un** ~ **glissant** fig to be on slippery ground; **2** (parcelle) plot of land; ~ **à bâtir** building plot; **3** (étendue) land **C**; ~ **à bâtir** building land; **4** (de jeu, sport) (non aménagé) field; (avec les installations) gén ground; (au golf) course; **sortir du** ~ [joueur] to go off the field; [balle] (au football) to go out of play; (au rugby) to go into touch; **disputer un match sur** ~ **adverse/sur son propre** ~ to play an away game/a home game; **5** (sphère d'activité) **nous ne vous suivrons pas sur ce** ~ we won't go along with you there; **un** ~ **d'entente** fig common ground; **6** (champ de recherche) field; **travailler sur le** ~ to do fieldwork; **7** (état, milieu) Sociol environment; ~ **favorable** Méd predisposing factors (pl); Sociol favourable^GB environment; **offrir un** ~ **favorable à** (à une maladie, une idéologie) to provide a fertile breeding ground for; **les jeunes sont un** ~ **favorable** young people are easy targets; **8** Mil (lieu d'opérations) field; (en termes de relief) terrain; (en termes d'avance ou de recul) ground; **sur le** ~ in the field; **occuper le** ~ to hold the field; **être en** ~ **connu** or **familier** fig to be on familiar territory; **être sur son** ~, **avoir l'avantage du** ~ lit, fig to be on one's own ground; **déblayer le** ~ to clear the ground; **préparer le** ~ fig to pave the way; **tâter** or **sonder le** ~ fig to put out feelers

(Composés) ~ **d'atterrissage** landing strip; ~ **d'aviation** airfield; ~ **de camping** campsite; ~ **de jeu(x)** playground; ~ **de manœuvre** army training ground; ~ **de tir** firing range; ~ **de sport(s)** sports ground; ~ **vague** wasteland **C**

terrasse /tɛʀas/ nf **1** (le long d'un bâtiment) terrace; **s'installer à la** ~ **d'un café** to sit at a table outside a café; **2** (toiture) flat roof; (grand balcon) large balcony; **3** Agric **culture(s) en** ~**s** terrace cultivation **C**; **cultiver le riz en** ~**s** to grow rice on terraces

terrassement /tɛʀasmɑ̃/ nm excavation; **faire des travaux de** ~ to carry out excavation work

terrasser /tɛʀase/ [1] vtr **1** (jeter à terre) to knock down; **2** (priver de forces) [maladie] to strike down; **terrassé par** (par la chaleur, le chagrin) prostrated by

terrassier /tɛʀasje/ ▸ p. 372 nm building labourer

terre /tɛʀ/

A nf **1** (surface du sol) ground; **sous** ~ underground; **ne frappez jamais un adversaire à** ~ never hit a man when he's down; **mettre pied à** ~ [cavalier] to dismount; **2** (matière) gén earth; Agric soil; **sortir de** ~ lit [plante] to come up; [animal] to poke its head out of the ground; fig **une ville nouvelle est sortie de** ~ a new town has sprung up; **3** (campagne) land; **le retour à la** ~ the movement back to the land; **4** (terrain) land **C**; **se retirer sur ses** ~**s** to go and live on one's estate; **5** (région) land; **en** ~ **chrétienne** on Christian land; **leur pays a toujours été une** ~ **d'accueil** their country has always welcomed newcomers; **6** (opposé à mer) land; **aller à** ~ to go ashore; **'Terre!'** 'land ho!'; **s'enfoncer dans les** ~**s** to go deep inland; **7** (où vit l'humanité) earth; **il croit que la** ~ **entière est contre lui** he thinks the whole world is against him; **8** Art **de la ~ (glaise)** clay; **une pipe en ~** a clay pipe; **un pot de** or **en ~** an earthenware pot; **9** (en électricité) earth GB, ground US; **relier qch à la ~** to earth GB ou ground US sth

B **terre à terre** loc adj inv [question] basic; [conversation, personne] pedestrian

C **par terre** loc adv (dehors) on the ground; (dedans) on the floor; **se rouler par ~** (de rire) to fall about laughing; **c'est à se rouler par ~**○ it's hilarious; **se rouler par ~ de douleur** to roll on the ground with pain; **ça a fichu tous nos projets par ~**○ it messed up all our plans○

⸨Composés⸩ **~ d'asile** country of refuge; **~ battue** trodden earth; **sur ~ battue** [tennis] on a clay court; **~ de bruyère** ericaceous compost; **~ cuite** baked clay; Art terracotta; **~ de Sienne** sienna

⸨Idiomes⸩ **avoir les pieds sur ~**○ to have one's feet firmly planted on the ground; **garder les pieds sur ~**○ to keep one's feet on the ground; **ne pas avoir les pieds sur ~**○ to be a dreamer

Terre /tɛʀ/ nf Earth; **sur la ~** on Earth

⸨Composés⸩ **la ~ Adélie** Adelie land; **la ~ de Feu** Tierra del Fuego; **la ~ promise** the Promised Land; **la ~ Sainte** the Holy Land

terreau, pl **~x** /tɛʀo/ nm compost; **~ de feuilles** leaf mould

terre-neuve /tɛʀnøv/ nm inv Newfoundland (dog)

Terre-Neuve /tɛʀnøv/ ▸ p. 504 nprf Géog Newfoundland

terre-plein, pl **terres-pleins** /tɛʀplɛ̃/ nm **1** (de bâtiment) platform; **2** (de route) central reservation GB, median strip US; (de rond-point) central island; **3** Mil terre-plein

terrer: se terrer /tɛʀe/ [1] vpr **1** (dans son terrier) [lapin] to disappear into its burrow; [renard] to go to earth; **2** [fugitif] to hide; **ils se terrent chez eux** they're holed up in their house

terrestre /tɛʀɛstʀ/ adj **1** Géog (de la planète) of the Earth (après n); **2** [animaux] land (épith); **3** (au sol) [guerre, transport] land (épith); **la vie/le paradis ~** life/heaven on earth

terreur /tɛʀœʀ/ nf **1** (sentiment) terror; **vivre dans la ~** to live in fear; **2** (comme moyen politique) terror; **3** ○(personne) **c'est la ~ du quartier** he's the terror of the neighbourhood^GB; **jouer les ~s** to be a terror

terreux, -euse /tɛʀø, øz/ adj (semblable à la terre) earthy; **avoir le teint ~** fig to have a grey GB ou gray US complexion

terrible /tɛʀibl/ adj **1** (intense) gén terrible; [soif, envie] tremendous; **2** (épouvantable) terrible; **3** ○(pénible) terrible; **c'est ~ de devoir faire** it's awful ou terrible having to do; **il est ~, il ne veut jamais avoir tort** it's terrible the way he never wants to admit that he's wrong; **4** ○(remarquable) terrific○; **il n'est pas ~ ce film** that's not a great film

terriblement /tɛʀibləmã/ adv terribly; **il a ~ grandi** he's grown an awful lot

terrien, -ienne /tɛʀjɛ̃, ɛn/ adj **propriétaire ~** landowner

Terrien, -ienne /tɛʀjɛ̃, ɛn/ nm,f earthman/earthwoman

terrier /tɛʀje/ nm **1** (d'une bête) gén hole; **un ~ de renard** a fox's earth; **2** (chien) terrier

terrifiant, ~e /tɛʀifjã, ãt/ adj **1** (faisant peur) terrifying; **2** (hors du commun) [bêtise, changement] incredible

terrifier /tɛʀifje/ [2] vtr to terrify; **s'enfuir terrifié** to flee in terror

terrine /tɛʀin/ nf **1** Culin terrine; **2** (récipient) (allongé) terrine; (rond) earthenware bowl

territoire /tɛʀitwaʀ/ nm **1** (d'un pays) territory; **sur l'ensemble du ~** throughout the country; **2** (chez les animaux) territory

⸨Composés⸩ **~ d'outre-mer, TOM** French overseas (administrative) territory

territorial, ~e, mpl -iaux /tɛʀitɔʀjal, o/ adj **1** (d'un État) territorial; **2** [administration] (de subdivision) divisional; (de région) regional

terroir /tɛʀwaʀ/ nm land; **produits/vin du ~** local products/wine; **accent du ~** regional accent

terroriser /tɛʀɔʀize/ [1] vtr (user de terreur) to terrorize; (effrayer) [orage, mauvais rêve, adulte] to terrify

terrorisme /tɛʀɔʀism/ nm terrorism

terroriste /tɛʀɔʀist/ adj, nmf Pol terrorist

tertiaire /tɛʀsjɛʀ/

A adj **1** Écon [secteur, industrie] service (épith); **l'activité ~** activity in the service sector; **2** (en géologie) Tertiary

B nm Écon service sector; (en géologie) Tertiary

tertio /tɛʀsjo/ adv thirdly

tes ▸ **ton**¹

tesson /tesɔ̃/ nm **~ de bouteille** piece of glass; **des ~s de bouteille** broken glass ₡

test /tɛst/

A nm test

B -**test** (in compounds) match-**~** trial match; **rencontre-~** preliminary meeting; **région-~** pilot region

testament /tɛstamã/ nm Jur will; fig legacy; **ceci est mon ~** this is my last will and testament; **l'Ancien Testament** the Old Testament

testamentaire /tɛstamãtɛʀ/ adj of a will (après n)

tester /tɛste/ [1] vtr to test; **testé en laboratoire** laboratory-tested

testicule /tɛstikyl/ nm testicle

tétanos /tetanos/ ▸ p. 195 nm inv tetanus

têtard /tɛtaʀ/ nm **1** Zool tadpole; **2** (arbre) pollard

tête /tɛt/ ▸ p. 136 nf **1** gén head; **la ~ basse** (humblement) with one's head bowed; **la ~ haute** (dignement) with one's head held high; **~ baissée** [se lancer, foncer] headlong; **la ~ en bas** [être suspendu, se retrouver] upside down; **au-dessus de nos ~s** (en l'air) overhead; **sans ~** headless; **coup de ~** headbutt; **donner un coup de ~ à qn** to head-butt sb; **être tombé sur la ~**○ fig to have gone off one's rocker○; **2** (dessus du crâne) head; **se laver la ~** to wash one's hair; **j'ai la ~ toute mouillée** my hair's all wet; **3** (visage) face; **une bonne/sale ~** a nice/nasty face; **tu en fais une ~!** what a face!, why the long face?; **ne fais pas cette ~-là!** don't pull such a face!; **quelle ~ va-t-il faire?** how's he going to react?; **il (me) fait la ~** he's sulking; **ne fais pas ta mauvaise ~** don't be so difficult; **elle fait sa mauvaise ~** she's being difficult; **il a une ~ à tricher** he looks like a cheat; **tu as une ~ à faire peur, aujourd'hui!** you look dreadful today!; **4** (esprit) mind; **de ~** [citer, réciter] from memory; [calculer] in one's head; **tu n'as pas de ~!** you have a mind like a sieve!; **je n'ai pas la référence en ~** I can't recall the reference; **où avais-je la ~?** whatever was I thinking of?; **ça (ne) va pas, la ~?**○ are you out of your mind or what?; **j'avais la ~ ailleurs** I was thinking of something else; **avoir la ~ vide** to be empty-headed; **c'est lui qui t'a mis ça dans la ~!** you got that idea from him!; **mets-lui ça dans la ~** drum it into him/her; **se mettre dans la ~** or **en ~ de faire** to take it into one's head to do; **monter la ~ à Pierre contre Paul** to turn Pierre against Paul; **monter à la ~ de qn, faire tourner la ~ de qn** [alcool, succès] to go to sb's head; **elle t'a fait tourner la ~** she's turned your head; **il n'est pas bien dans sa ~**○ he isn't right in the head; **il a encore toute sa ~ (à lui)** he's still got all his faculties; **n'en faire qu'à sa ~** to go one's own way; **tenir ~ à qn** to stand up to sb; **sur un coup de ~** on an impulse; **5** (personne) face; **avoir ses ~s** to have one's favourites^GB; **en ~ à ~** [être, dîner] alone together; **rencontrer qn en ~ à ~** to have a meeting with sb in private; **un dîner en ~ à ~** an intimate dinner for two; **6** (mesure de longueur) head; **avoir une ~ de plus que qn** to be a head taller than sb; **gagner d'une courte ~** [personne] to win by a narrow margin; [cheval] to win by a short head; **avoir une ~ d'avance sur qn** to be a short length in front of sb; **7** (unité de troupeau) head (inv); **8** (individu) **par ~** gén a head, each; (dans des statistiques) per capita; **par ~ de pipe**○ each; **9** (vie) head; **vouloir la ~ de qn** (mort) to want sb's head; (disgrâce) to be after sb's head; **risquer sa ~** to risk one's neck○; **des ~s vont tomber** fig heads will roll; **10** (direction) **le groupe de ~** the leading group; **c'est lui la ~ pensante du mouvement** he's the brains behind the movement; **il restera à la ~ du groupe** he will stay on as head of the group; **prendre la ~ du parti** to become leader of the party; **prendre la ~ des opérations** to take charge of operations; **être à la ~ d'une immense fortune** to be the possessor of a huge fortune; **11** (premières places) top; **être en ~** (de liste, classement) to be at the top; (d'élection, de course, sondage) to be in the lead; **venir en ~** to come first; **marcher en ~** to walk at the front; **marcher en ~ d'un cortège** to walk in a procession; **le gouvernement, le premier ministre en ~, a décidé que...** the government, led by the Prime Minister, has decided that...; **des tas de gens viendront, ta femme en** ~ heaps of people are coming, your wife to begin with; **en** ~ **de phrase** at the beginning of a sentence; ⑫ (extrémité) (de train) front; (de convoi, cortège) head; (d'arbre, de mât) top; (de vis, rivet, clou) head; **une place en** ~ **de train** a seat at the front of the train; **en** ~ **de file** first in line; ⑬ Sport (au football) header; **faire une** ~ to head the ball; ⑭ Mil (d'engin) warhead; ⑮ (en électronique) (d'enregistrement, effacement) head; (d'électrophone) cartridge; ~ **de lecture** (de magnétophone, magnétoscope) head

(Composés) ~ **d'affiche** Cin, Théât top of the bill; ~ **en l'air** scatterbrain; **être** ~ **en l'air** to be scatterbrained; ~ **brûlée** daredevil; ~ **de chapitre** chapter heading; ~ **à claques**○ pain○; ~ **de cochon**○ = ~ **de lard**; ~ **d'épingle** lit, fig pinhead; ~ **de lard**○ (têtu) mule; (mauvais caractère) grouch; ~ **de linotte** = ~ **en l'air**; ~ **de liste** Pol chief candidate; ~ **de lit** bedhead GB, headboard; ~ **de mort** (crâne) skull; (symbole de mort) death's head; (emblème de pirates) skull and crossbones (+ *v sg*); ~ **de mule**○ mule; **être une vraie** ~ **de mule**○ to be as stubborn as a mule; ~ **d'oiseau**○ pej featherbrain; ~ **de pioche**○ = ~ **de mule**; ~ **de série** Sport seeded player; ~ **de série numéro deux** number two seed; ~ **de Turc**○ whipping boy

(Idiomes) **j'en mettrais ma** ~ **à couper** *or* **sur le billot** I'd swear to it; **en avoir par-dessus la** ~○ to be fed up to the back teeth○; **se prendre la** ~ **à deux mains**○ (pour réfléchir) to rack one's brains○; **prendre la** ~○ to be a drag○; **se prendre la** ~○ to do one's head in○; **te prends pas la** ~ **pour ça!** don't worry about it!

tête-à-queue /tɛtakø/ *nm inv* **faire un** ~ to slew round GB *ou* around; **à la suite d'un** ~ after the car slewed around

tête-à-tête /tɛtatɛt/ *nm inv* (d'amis, amants) tête-à-tête; (de politiciens) private meeting

tête-bêche /tɛtbɛʃ/ *adv* (pour des personnes) top-to-tail; (pour des objets) head-to-tail

tête-de-loup, *pl* **têtes-de-loup** /tɛtdəlu/ *nf* ceiling brush

tétée /tete/ *nf* ① (action) feeding; ② (repas) feed

téter /tete/
A *vtr* (bébé, animal) to suck at (sein, mamelle); to feed from (biberon); to suck (lait); ~ **sa mère** to suckle, to feed
B *vi* to suckle; **donner à** ~ (à un bébé) to feed; (à un animal) to suckle

tétine /tetin/ *nf* ① (de biberon) teat GB, nipple US; ② (sucette) dummy GB, pacifier US; ③ (mamelle) teat

téton /tetɔ̃/ *nm* ① (sein) tit○, breast; ② Tech lug

tétraplégie /tetrapleʒi/ *nf* quadriplegia

têtu, ~**e** /tety/ *adj* stubborn

(Idiome) **être** ~ **comme un âne**○ *or* **une mule**○ *or* **une bourrique**○ to be as stubborn as a mule

texte /tɛkst/ *nm* ① gén text; (livre) text; (passage) extract, text; **faire une explication de** ~ to do a commentary on a text; ~**s choisis de Montaigne** selected extracts from Montaigne; **en français dans le** ~ in French in the original text; '~ **intégral**' 'unabridged'; ② Cin, Théât (script) script; (rôle à apprendre) lines (*pl*), part; ③ Admin, Jur, Pol (libellé) wording, text

(Composé) ~ **de loi** (proposé) bill; (promulgué) law

textile /tɛkstil/
A *adj* textile; **le secteur** ~ the textile industry; **fibres** ~**s** fibres○; **matières** ~**s végétales** plant fibres○
B *nm* ① (secteur industriel) textile industry; **les ouvriers du** ~ textile workers; ② (avant tissage) fibre○; (tissu) textile; ~**s artificiels/synthétiques** artificial/synthetic fibres○

texto○ /tɛksto/ = **textuellement**

textuellement /tɛkstɥɛlmɑ̃/ *adv* (rapporter) word for word; **il m'a dit** ~, '**je m'en moque**' he told me in so many words, 'I couldn't care less'

texture /tɛkstyʀ/ *nf* ① (de matériau, peinture) texture; ② (de roman, pièce de théâtre) structure

TGV /teʒeve/ *nm* (*abbr* = **train à grande vitesse**) TGV, high-speed train

thé /te/ *nm* ① (feuilles, infusion) tea; ~ **à la bergamote** Earl Grey tea; **à l'heure du** ~ at teatime; **être invité à prendre le** ~ to be asked to tea; ② (réunion) tea party

théâtral, ~**e**, *mpl* **-aux** /teɑtral, o/ *adj* ① Théât (œuvre, langage) dramatic; (représentation) stage (*épith*); (saison,

compagnie) theatre GB (*épith*); ② (exagéré) pej (geste) histrionic; (ton) melodramatic

théâtre /teɑtr/ *nm* ① Littérat (genre) theatre GB; **le** ~ **de Racine** Racine's plays (*pl*); **le** ~ **antique** Greek classical drama; **de** ~ (acteur, directeur, billet) theatre GB (*épith*); (décor, costume, masque) stage (*épith*); fig (gestes) histrionic; **coup de** ~ lit coup de théâtre; fig dramatic turn of events; ② (art dramatique) **faire du** ~ (comme profession) to be an actor; (à l'école) to do drama; (en amateur) to be involved in amateur dramatics; **se destiner au** ~ to intend to go on stage; **adapter une nouvelle pour le** ~ to adapt a short story for the stage; **c'est du** ~ fig it's just a put-on○; ③ (lieu) theatre GB; **être le** ~ **d'émeutes** fig to be the scene of riots; **le** ~ **des opérations** Mil the theatre GB of operations

(Composés) ~ **de Boulevard** farce; ~ **de verdure** open-air theatre GB

théier /teje/ *nm* tea plant

théière /tejɛʀ/ *nf* teapot

thématique /tematik/
A *adj* thematic
B *nf* themes (*pl*)

thème /tɛm/ *nm* ① (de débat, d'émission) topic, subject; (de discours, film) theme; ~ **de réflexion** topic for thought; ② (traduction) prose; ③ Mus theme; ④ Ling (radical) stem; (topique) theme

(Composé) ~ **astral** birth chart

théologie /teɔlɔʒi/ *nf* theology

théorème /teɔʀɛm/ *nm* theorem

théoricien, **-ienne** /teɔʀisjɛ̃, ɛn/ *nm,f* theoretician

théorie /teɔʀi/ *nf* theory; **en** ~ in theory

théorique /teɔʀik/ *adj* theoretical

thérapeute /teʀapøt/ *nmf* therapist

thérapeutique /teʀapøtik/
A *adj* (effet) therapeutic; **choix** ~ choice of treatment
B *nf* ① (traitement) treatment; ② (science) therapeutics (+ *v sg*)

thérapie /teʀapi/ *nf* ① Méd treatment; ② Psych therapy

thermal, ~**e**, *mpl* **-aux** /tɛʀmal, o/ *adj* (source, eaux) thermal; **station** ~**e** spa

thermalisme /tɛʀmalism/ *nm* ① Méd balneology; ② (activité) hydrotherapy industry

thermes /tɛʀm/ *nmpl* ① (romains) thermae; ② (établissement thermal) thermal baths

thermique /tɛʀmik/ *adj* thermal

thermo /tɛʀmo/ *préf* ~**chimie** thermochemistry; ~**formé** thermally moulded; ~**gène** heat-generating; ~**nucléaire** thermonuclear; ~**résistant** heat-resistant

thermocollant, ~**e** /tɛʀmokɔlɑ̃, ɑ̃t/ *adj* (tissu, ruban) iron-on (*épith*)

thermomètre /tɛʀmomɛtr/ *nm* lit thermometer; fig barometer; **le** ~ **va chuter pendant le week-end** temperatures will drop over the weekend; **le** ~ **des tensions internationales** the barometer of international tensions

thermostat /tɛʀmosta/ *nm* thermostat

thésard○, ~**e** /tezaʀ, aʀd/ *nm,f* PhD student

thésauriser /tezoʀize/ (1)
A *vtr* to hoard (up)
B *vi* to hoard money

thésaurus /tezoʀys/ *nm inv* ① (de philologie, d'archéologie) lexicon; ② (répertoire) thesaurus

thèse /tɛz/ *nf* ① Univ (de doctorat) thesis GB, dissertation US; ② (point de vue) thesis, argument; **roman à** ~ novel with a message; ③ (supposition) theory; **avancer la** ~ **de l'accident** to put forward the theory that it was an accident

Thessalonique /tesalɔnik/ ▸ p. 621 *npr* Salonika

thibaude /tibod/ *nf* carpet underlay

thon /tɔ̃/ *nm* tuna

thonier, **-ière** /tɔnje, ɛʀ/
A *adj* tuna (*épith*)
B *nm* tuna boat

thoracique /tɔʀasik/ *adj* thoracic; **cage** ~ ribcage

thorax /tɔʀaks/ ▸ p. 136 *nm inv* thorax

thrombose /tʀɔ̃boz/ ▸ p. 195 *nf* thrombosis

THS /teaʃɛs/ *nm* ▸ **traitement**

Thurgovie /tyʀgɔvi/ ▸ p. 504 *nprf* **la** ~ the canton of Thurgau

t

thuriféraire /tyʀifeʀɛʀ/ *nm* [1] (admirateur) eulogist; [2] Relig thurifer

thuya /tyja/ *nm* thuja

thym /tɛ̃/ *nm* thyme

thyroïde /tiʀɔid/ *adj, nf* thyroid

tiare /tjaʀ/ *nf* tiara

tibétain, ~e /tibetɛ̃, ɛn/
A *adj* Tibetan
B ▸ p. 336 *nm* Ling Tibetan

tibia /tibja/ *nm* (os) shinbone, tibia spéc; **un coup de pied dans les ~s** a kick in the shins

tic /tik/ *nm* [1] (contraction) tic; **être plein de ~s** to be constantly twitching; [2] (geste habituel) habit; **~ de langage** verbal tic

ticket /tikɛ/ *nm* (de train, quai) ticket
(Composés) **~ de caisse** till receipt GB, sales slip US; **~ modérateur** *patient's contribution towards cost of medical treatment*

ticket-repas, *pl* **tickets-repas** /tikɛʀəpɑ/ *nm* luncheon voucher GB, meal ticket US

ticket-restaurant®, *pl* **tickets-restaurant** /tikɛ-ʀɛstɔʀɑ̃/ *nm* luncheon voucher GB, meal ticket US

tic-tac /tiktak/ *nm inv* (*also onomat*) ticktock; **faire ~** to tick

tie-break, *pl* **~s** /tajbʀɛk/ *nm* tiebreaker

tiède /tjɛd/
A *adj* [1] lit (désagréablement) [café, soupe] lukewarm; [bain] tepid; (agréablement) [eau, air, nuit] warm; [saison, température] mild; [2] fig (sans enthousiasme) lukewarm
B *nmf* (membre d'un parti, groupe) pej lukewarm *ou* half-hearted supporter; (adepte) pej half-hearted believer
C *adv* **servez ~** serve slightly warm; **dépêche-toi ou tu vas manger ~** hurry up or your food will get cold; **il fait ~** (dehors) it's mild; (dedans) it's nice and warm

tièdement /tjɛdmɑ̃/ *adv* fig half-heartedly

tiédeur /tjedœʀ/ *nf* [1] lit (de saison) mildness; (d'air, de nuit, pièce) warmth; [2] fig (de sentiment, partisan) half-heartedness

tiédir /tjediʀ/ [3]
A *vtr* to warm up [eau]
B *vi* [1] [liquide, air] (se réchauffer) to warm (up); (refroidir) to cool (down); **faire ~** to warm *ou* heat (up) [café]; **laisser ~** to allow [sth] to cool; [2] fig [sentiment] to cool; [enthousiasme] to wane

tien, tienne /tjɛ̃, tjɛn/
A *adj poss* **je suis tienne** I'm yours; **une tienne connaissance** liter an acquaintance of yours
B **le tien, la tienne, les tiens, les tiennes** *pron poss* yours; **un métier comme le ~** a job like yours; **à la tienne!** (à ta santé) cheers!; iron good luck to you!; **les ~s** (ta famille) your family (sg); **tu as encore fait des tiennes!** you've been up to mischief again!

tiens /tjɛ̃/ ▸ tenir

tierce¹ /tjɛʀs/
A *adj f* ▸ tiers A
B *nf* [1] (aux cartes) three card run, tierce; [2] Mus third

tiercé /tjɛʀse/ ▸ p. 327 *nm*: *system of betting on three placed horses;* **jouer au ~** to bet on the horses

tiers, tierce² /tjɛʀ, tjɛʀs/
A *adj* third; **un pays ~** gén another country; (par rapport à un groupe) a non-member country; **une tierce personne** a third party
B *nm inv* [1] Math third; **j'en suis aux deux ~** I'm two thirds of the way through; **la ville a été détruite aux deux ~** two thirds of the town has been destroyed; [2] (personne) (inconnu) outsider; Jur third party; **s'assurer au ~** to take out third-party insurance
(Composé) **le Tiers État** Hist the Third Estate

tiers-monde /tjɛʀmɔ̃d/ *nm* Pol Third World

tiers-mondisme /tjɛʀmɔ̃dism/ *nm* support for the Third World

tiers-mondiste /tjɛʀmɔ̃dist/
A *adj* [discours, politique] in support of the Third World (après n)
B *nmf* supporter of the Third World

tige /tiʒ/ *nf* [1] (de plante) gén stem, stalk; [2] (de botte) leg; [3] (baguette) rod; (partie allongée de clé, clou, rivet) shank; [4] (de plume) shaft

tignasse○ /tiɲas/ *nf* mop of hair

tigre /tigʀ/ *nm* [1] Zool (animal) tiger; (peau) tigerskin; [2] (personne cruelle) monster
(Idiome) **être jaloux comme un ~** to be insanely jealous

tigré, ~e /tigʀe/ *adj* [1] (rayé) striped; [2] (tacheté) spotted

tigresse /tigʀɛs/ *nf* Zool, fig tigress

tillac /tijak/ *nm* deck

tilleul /tijœl/ *nm* [1] (arbre) limetree; (bois) limewood; [2] ▸ p. 140 (couleur) **(vert) ~** lime green; [3] (tisane) lime-blossom tea

tilt /tilt/ *nm* Jeux tilt sign; **faire ~** [machine] to show tilt; [personne] to make the machine stop
(Idiomes) **ça a fait ~**○ **(dans mon esprit)** the penny dropped○; **ça a fait ~ entre nous**○ we clicked straight away

timbale /tɛ̃bal/ *nf* [1] (gobelet) metal (tumbler); [2] ▸ p. 389 Mus kettledrum; **~s** timpani; [3] (moule, mets) timbale

timbrage /tɛ̃bʀaʒ/ *nm* [1] (sur enveloppe) postmarking; **dispensé de ~** postage paid GB, post paid US; [2] (de document) stamping

timbre /tɛ̃bʀ/ *nm* [1] (vignette, marque, instrument) stamp; (cachet de la poste) postmark; [2] (de voix, d'instrument) tone, timbre; (de voyelle) timbre; **~ chaud/riche** warm/rich tone; **voix au ~ voilé** husky voice; **voix sans ~** toneless voice; [3] (sonnette) bell; [4] Méd patch
(Composés) **~ dateur** date stamp; **~ fiscal** stamp affixed to official document

timbré, ~e /tɛ̃bʀe/ *adj* **voix (bien) ~e** resonant voice

timbre-poste, *pl* **timbres-poste** /tɛ̃bʀəpɔst/ *nm* postage stamp

timbrer /tɛ̃bʀe/ [1] *vtr* to stamp, to put a stamp on

timide /timid/
A *adj* [personne, animal] shy, timid; [critique, réforme] timid; [succès, résultat] limited
B *nmf* shy person; **c'est un grand ~** he's terribly shy

timidement /timidmɑ̃/ *adv* (avec timidité) shyly; (craintivement) timidly; (sans conviction) half-heartedly

timidité /timidite/ *nf* shyness

timing /tajmiŋ/ *nm* [1] (calendrier) schedule; [2] Sport timing

timon /timɔ̃/ *nm* [1] Naut tiller; [2] (d'attelage) shaft

timonerie /timɔnʀi/ *nf* [1] Naut (abri) wheelhouse; (personnel) helmsmen (pl); [2] Aut, Aviat steering and braking systems (pl)

timonier /timɔnje/ ▸ p. 372 *nm* Naut helmsman

Timor /timɔʀ/ ▸ p. 230 *nprm* Timor; **~ oriental** East Timor

timoré, ~e /timɔʀe/ *adj* timorous

tinette /tinɛt/ *nf* latrine bucket

tintamarre /tɛ̃tamaʀ/ *nm* din; **faire du ~** to make a din

tintement /tɛ̃tmɑ̃/ *nm* (de cloche) chiming; (de clochette, grelot) tinkling; (de couverts, verres, monnaie) clinking; (de sonnette) ringing; (de clés) jingling
(Composé) **~ d'oreilles** Méd ringing in the ears, tinnitus spéc

tinter /tɛ̃te/ [1] *vi* [cloche] to chime; [sonnette] to ring; [clochette, grelot] to tinkle; [verre, monnaie, couvert] to clink; [bidon] to clang; [clé] to jingle; Mus [triangle] to ring; **faire ~** to ring [cloche, sonnette, clochette]; to clink [verre, monnaie, couvert]; to clang [bidon]; to jingle [clé]; Mus to strike [triangle]

tintinnabuler /tɛ̃tinabyle/ [1] *vi* to tinkle

tique /tik/ *nf* Zool tick

tiquer○ /tike/ [1] *vi* [personne] to wince; **sans ~** without batting an eyelid GB *ou* eyelash US

tir /tiʀ/ *nm* [1] (coups de feu) Mil fire ¢; **déclencher le ~** to open fire; [2] (discipline) Mil, Sport shooting ¢; (avec des armes lourdes) gunnery ¢; **exercices de ~** shooting practice ¢; [3] (action, manière de tirer) Mil firing ¢; **~ de grenades/missiles** grenade/missile firing; **~ continu** continuous firing; [4] (avec ballon, boule) shot; **~ au but** (au football) shot; [5] (à la chasse) shooting; **~ aux canards** duck shooting; [6] (stand) **~ forain** rifle range
(Composés) **~ à l'arbalète** crossbow archery; **~ à l'arc** archery; **~ d'élite** marksmanship; **~ aux pigeons d'argile** clay pigeon shooting

tirade /tiʀad/ *nf* **1** Littérat, Théât declamation; **2** (discours) pej tirade

tirage /tiʀaʒ/ *nm* **1** (à la loterie) ~ **(au sort)** draw; **désigner par ~ (au sort)** to draw [*nom, vainqueur*]; **2** (impression, réimpression) impression; (ensemble des exemplaires) edition; (nombre d'exemplaires) (d'un livre) run; (d'un journal) circulation; **troisième ~** third impression; **quotidien à grand ~** mass-circulation daily; **3** Ordinat (copie papier) hard copy; **4** Art, Cin, Phot (d'estampe, de négatif) (processus) printing ℂ; (résultat) print; **5** Constr (de cheminée) draught GB, draft US; **6** (désaccord) friction ℂ; **il y a du ~ entre eux** there's friction between them

tiraillement /tiʀajmɑ̃/ *nm* **1** (sur une corde) pulling ℂ, tugging ℂ; **2** (sensation) nagging pain; **~s d'estomac** hunger pangs; **3** (friction) friction ℂ

tirailler /tiʀaje/ [1]
A *vtr* **1** to tug (at), to pull (at) [*corde, manche, barbe*]; **2** fig **être tiraillé entre son travail et sa famille** to be torn between one's work and one's family
B *vi* [*soldat, tireur*] (au hasard) to fire *ou* shoot at random; (de temps en temps) to fire intermittently

tirailleur /tiʀajœʀ/ *nm* skirmisher; Hist colonial infantryman

tirant /tiʀɑ̃/ *nm* **1** (de chaussure) bootstrap; **2** (de charpente) tie beam
⌜Composés⌝ **~ d'air** (de pont) vertical clearance; **~ d'eau** Naut draught GB, draft US

tire○ /tiʀ/ *nf* (voiture) car

tire-au-flanc○ /tiʀoflɑ̃/ *nm inv* shirker, skiver○ GB

tire-botte, *pl* **~s** /tiʀbɔt/ *nm* bootjack

tire-bouchon, *pl* **~s** /tiʀbuʃɔ̃/ *nm* corkscrew; **en ~** [*queue*] curly; [*pantalon*] wrinkled

tire-bouchonner /tiʀbuʃɔne/ [1] *vi* [*manche, pantalon*] to be wrinkled

tire-d'aile: à tire-d'aile /atiʀdɛl/ *loc adv* lit in a flurry of wings; fig hurriedly

tirée○ /tiʀe/ *nf* (longue distance) long haul; (à pied) tidy walk○

tire-larigot○: à tire-larigot /atiʀlaʀigo/ *loc adv* [*boire*] non-stop

tire-ligne, *pl* **~s** /tiʀliɲ/ *nm* ruling pen

tirelire /tiʀliʀ/ *nf* piggy bank

tirer /tiʀe/ [1]
A *vtr* **1** (déplacer) to pull [*véhicule*]; to pull up [*chaise*]; to pull away [*tapis*]; **~ la tête en arrière** to toss one's head back; **2** (exercer une traction) (avec une force régulière) to pull [*cheveux*]; to pull on [*corde*]; (par à-coups) to tug at; **~ qn par le bras** to pull sb's arm; **3** (tendre) **~ ses bas** to pull up one's stockings; **~ sa chemise** to straighten one's shirt; **avoir les traits tirés** to look drawn; **4** (fermer) to draw [*verrou, rideau*]; to pull down [*store*]; to close [*porte, volet*]; **5** (avec une arme) to fire off [*balle, obus, grenade*]; to fire [*missile*]; to shoot [*flèche*]; **6** Sport (de ballon) **~ un corner/penalty** to take a corner/penalty; **7** (choisir au hasard) **~ (au sort)** to draw [*carte, loterie, nom*]; to draw for [*partenaire*]; **~ les cartes à qn** to tell the cards for sb; **se faire ~ les cartes** to have one's fortune told with cards; **8** (prendre) to draw [*vin, électricité, argent*] (**de, sur** from); **9** (sortir) **~ un stylo de son sac** to take a pen out of one's bag; **~ un enfant de l'eau** to pull a child out of the water; **~ qch de sa poche** to pull sth out of one's pocket; **10** (faire sortir) **~ le pays de la récession** to get the country out of recession; **tire-moi de là!** get me out of this!; **~ qn d'une maladie** to pull sb through an illness; **tu l'as tirée de son silence** you drew her out of her silence; **11** (obtenir) **~ de qn** to get [sth] from sb [*renseignement, aveu*]; **~ de qch** to draw [sth] from sth [*force, ressources*]; to derive [sth] from sth [*orgueil, satisfaction*]; to make [sth] out of sth [*argent*]; **tu ne tireras pas grand-chose de cette voiture** (comme argent) you won't get much for this car; (comme service) you won't get much out of this car; **~ le maximum de la situation** to make the most of the situation; **~ un son d'un instrument** to get a note out of an instrument; **12** (dériver) **le film est tiré du roman** the film is based on the novel; **la guillotine tire son nom de son inventeur** the guillotine gets its name from its inventor; **le mot est tiré de l'anglais** the word comes from the English; **13** (extraire) **texte tiré de Zola** text taken from Zola; **le médicament est tiré d'une plante** the drug

comes from a plant; **14** (faire un tirage) to print [*livre, négatif*]; to run off [*épreuve, exemplaire*]; **journal tiré à dix mille exemplaires** newspaper with a circulation of ten thousand; **tiré à part** [*texte*] off-printed; **15** (tracer) to draw [*ligne, trait*]; **~ un chèque** to draw a cheque GB *ou* check US; **~ des plans** fig to draw up plans; **16** ○(passer) **plus qu'une heure/semaine à ~** only one more hour/week to go; **~ quelques années en prison** to spend a few years in prison
B *vi* **1** (exercer une traction) to pull; **~ sur qch** to pull on sth; (d'un coup ou par à-coups) to tug at sth; **tire fort!** pull hard!; **2** (utiliser une arme) gén to shoot (**sur** at); (à feu) to fire (**sur** at); **~ à la carabine** to shoot with a rifle; **~ au fusil** to fire a gun; **elle lui a tiré dans la jambe** she shot him/her in the leg; **3** (au football) to shoot; (au handball, basket-ball) to take a shot; **4** (choisir au hasard) **~ (au sort)** to draw lots; **5** (prendre) **~ sur** to draw on; **~ sur son compte** to draw on one's account; **6** (aspirer) **la cheminée tire bien** the chimney draws well; **7** (être imprimé) **~ à mille exemplaires** [*périodique*] to have a circulation of one thousand; **8** (aller vers) **~ sur le jaune/l'orangé** [*couleur*] to be yellowish/orangy; **~ sur la cinquantaine** [*personne*] to be pushing fifty; **~ à gauche/droite** [*voiture*] to pull to the left/right
C **se tirer** *vpr* **1** (sortir) **se ~ de** to come through [*situation, difficultés*]; **2** ○(partir) to push off○; **3** (avec une arme) **se ~ une balle** to shoot oneself (**dans** in); **se ~ dessus** (l'un l'autre) lit to shoot at one another; **se ~**○ (se débrouiller) **s'en ~** to cope, to manage; **5** ○(échapper) **s'en ~** (à un accident) to escape; (à une maladie) to pull through; (à une punition) to get away with it○; **s'en ~ à bon prix** to get off lightly

tiret /tiʀɛ/ ▸ p. 413 *nm* dash

tirette /tiʀɛt/ *nf* Tech (rigide) pull tab; (souple) cord

tireur, -euse /tiʀœʀ, øz/ *nm,f* **1** Mil, Sport marksman/markswoman; **être (un) bon/mauvais ~** to be a good/poor shot; **2** (personne armée) gunman; **3** (au football) striker; (aux boules) thrower
⌜Composés⌝ **~ de cartes** fortune teller (*using cards*); **~ d'élite** expert marksman

tiroir /tiʀwaʀ/ *nm* (de meuble) drawer; **finir sa carrière dans le fond d'un ~** fig to end one's career in a second-rate job; **à ~s** fig [*pièce, roman*] episodic, à tiroirs spéc
⌜Idiome⌝ **racler les fonds de ~** to scrape some money together

tiroir-caisse, *pl* **tiroirs-caisses** /tiʀwaʀkɛs/ *nm* cash register

tisane /tizan/ *nf* herbal tea, tisane

tison /tizɔ̃/ *nm* (fire) brand

tisonner /tizɔne/ [1] *vtr* to poke

tisonnier /tizɔnje/ *nm* poker

tissage /tisaʒ/ *nm* **1** (fabrication) weaving ℂ; **faire du ~** to weave; **2** (texture) weave

tisser /tise/ [1] *vtr* **1** [*personne, machine*] to weave; **métier à ~** weaving loom; **tissé à la main** hand-woven; **récit tissé de mensonges** fig story riddled with lies; **2** [*araignée*] to spin [*toile*]

tisserand, ~e /tisʀɑ̃, ɑ̃d/ ▸ p. 372 *nm,f* weaver

tissu /tisy/ *nm* **1** (étoffe) material, fabric; **2** (cellules) **le ~ osseux** bone tissue; **3** (ensemble) (d'intrigues) web; (de mensonges) pack, tissue; (de calomnies, d'improbabilités, inepties) string; (de contradictions) mass; **~ social** social fabric; **~ industriel** industrial base

tissu-éponge, *pl* **tissus-éponges** /tisyepɔ̃ʒ/ *nm* (terry) towelling^GB, terry cloth US

tissulaire /tisylɛʀ/ *adj* tissue (épith)

titan /titɑ̃/ *nm* titan; **de ~** titanic

titane /titan/ *nm* titanium

titanesque /titanɛsk/ *adj* titanic

titi○ /titi/ *nm* **~ (parisien)** urchin, scamp

titiller /titije/ [1] *vtr* to titillate

titrage /titʀaʒ/ *nm* **1** (de film, livre, chanson) titling; **2** Chimie (de solution) titration; **3** (de minerai) assay

titre /titʀ/ *nm* **1** (d'œuvre) title; (de chapitre) heading; (dans un journal) headline; **avoir pour ~** to be entitled; **les ~s de l'actualité** the headlines; **2** (rang) title; **~ mondial** world title; **~ nobiliaire** or **de noblesse** title; **donner à qn le ~ de** to address sb as; **le ~ d'ingénieur** the status of qualified

Les titres de politesse

■ *On ne trouvera ici que quelques indications générales sur la façon de s'adresser à quelqu'un et de parler de quelqu'un en utilisant son titre. Pour les titres militaires, ▸ p. 283, et pour les autres titres, consulter les articles du dictionnaire.*

Comment s'adresser à quelqu'un

■ *Dans la plupart des circonstances ordinaires, l'anglais n'utilise pas d'équivalent de monsieur, madame etc.*

bonjour, madame
= good morning

bonsoir, mademoiselle
= good evening

bonjour, monsieur
= good afternoon

excusez-moi, madame
= excuse me

pardon, monsieur, pourriez-vous me dire ...
= excuse me, could you tell me ...

■ *Les mots Mr, Mrs, Miss et Ms sont toujours utilisés avec le nom de la personne; on ne les utilise jamais seuls.*

bonjour, madame
= good morning, Mrs Smith

au revoir, mademoiselle
= goodbye, Miss Smith

bonsoir, monsieur
= good evening, Mr Smith

■ *Attention: Ms (dire [mɪz] ou [məz]) permet de faire référence à une femme dont on connaît le nom sans préciser sa situation de famille. Il n'y a pas d'équivalent français:*

bonjour, madame ou bonjour, mademoiselle
= good morning, Ms Smith

■ *Les anglophones utilisent les prénoms beaucoup plus volontiers que les francophones. Lorsqu'en français on dit simplement bonjour, en anglais on précise souvent good morning, Paul ou good morning, Anne etc. De même, au début d'une lettre, un anglophone écrira facilement Dear Anne, Dear Paul etc., bien avant que le Français n'en vienne à utiliser le prénom.*

■ *Les mots Madam et Sir ne sont utilisés que par les vendeurs des magasins, les employés de restaurants,* d'hôtels etc. Ils sont toujours utilisés sans le nom propre:

bonjour, madame
= good morning, Madam

bonne nuit, monsieur
= good night, Sir

■ *En anglais, le titre de doctor est utilisé pour les docteurs de toutes disciplines. Mais on ne peut l'utiliser seul, sans nom propre, que pour un docteur en médecine.*

bonsoir, docteur
= good evening, doctor (*médecin*)

bonjour, docteur
= good morning, Doctor Smith (*en médecine ou d'une autre spécialité*)

Comment parler de quelqu'un

M. Dupont est arrivé
= Mr Dupont has arrived

Mme Dupont a téléphoné
= Mrs Dupont phoned *ou* Ms Dupont phoned

le rabbin Lévi est malade
= Rabbi Lévi is ill

■ *L'anglais n'utilise pas d'article défini devant les noms de titres lorsqu'ils sont suivis du nom propre.*

le roi Richard I
= King Richard I (*dire* King Richard the first)

l'inspecteur Hervet
= Inspector Hervet

le prince Charles
= Prince Charles

la princesse Anne
= Princess Anne

le pape Jean-Paul II
= Pope John-Paul II (*dire* Pope John-Paul the second)

■ *Mais si le titre est suivi du nom du pays, du peuple, de la ville etc., l'anglais utilise l'article défini.*

le roi des Belges
= the King of the Belgians

le prince de Galles
= the Prince of Wales

---

engineer; **en** ∼ [*professeur, directeur*] titular; [*fournisseur*] appointed; [*maître, rival*] official; **champion en** ∼ title holder; ∼**s universitaires** (diplômes) university qualifications; **③** (motif, qualité) **à juste** ∼ quite rightly; **à plus d'un** ∼ in many respects; **à** ∼ **de précaution** as a precaution; **à** ∼ **expérimental** by way of experiment; **à** ∼ **définitif** on a permanent basis; **à** ∼ **privé** in a private capacity; **à** ∼ **gracieux** *or* **gratuit** free; **à** ∼ **onéreux** for a fee; **à** ∼ **indicatif** as a rough guide; **à quel** ∼ **a-t-il été invité?** why was he invited?; **au même** ∼ **que vous** in the same capacity as yourself; **à** ∼ **de** on two counts; **au** ∼ **de l'aide économique** in economic aid; **perçu au** ∼ **de droits d'auteur** received as royalties; **④** Jur (document) deed; ∼ **de propriété** title deed; **⑤** (en Bourse) security; **⑥** Écon item; ∼ **budgétaire** budgetary item; **⑦** (de solution) titre^GB; (de vins et spiritueux) strength; (de métal précieux) fineness

(Composés) ∼ **de gloire** claim to fame; ∼ **de transport** ticket

titré , ∼**e** /titʀe/ *adj* **①** (noble) titled; **②** Chimie standard

titrer /titʀe/ [1] *vtr* **①** (dans un journal) **le journal du dimanche titrait...** the headlines in the Sunday paper read...; **le Temps titrait sur quatre colonnes 'la fin de la démocratie'** 'the end of democracy' announced 'le Temps' in a four-

column spread; **②** Chimie to titrate [*solution*]; to assay [*minerai*]

titubant , ∼**e** /titybã, ãt/ *adj* unsteady

tituber /titybe/ [1] *vi* to stagger; **ils sont sortis du pub en titubant** they staggered out of the pub

titulaire /titylɛʀ/

Ⓐ *adj* **①** gén permanent; Univ [*enseignant*] tenured; **②** Sport **joueur** ∼ full member of the team

Ⓑ *nmf* **①** (membre permanent) gén permanent staff member; Univ (enseignant) tenured lecturer GB *ou* professor US; **être** ∼ **d'un poste** (d'administration) to be a permanent staff member; (d'université) to have tenure; **②** (possesseur) holder; **être** ∼ **de** to hold [*diplôme, permis, chaire*]; to have [*nationalité, compte en banque, pension*]

titularisation /titylaʀizasjõ/ *nf* (action) gén confirmation in a post; Univ granting of tenure

titulariser /titylaʀize/ [1] *vtr* Admin to give permanent status to [*agent, personnel*]; Univ to grant tenure to [*professeur*]; Sport to make [sb] a full member of the team [*joueur*]

TMS /teɛmɛs/ *nm* ▸ **trouble**

toast /tost/ *nm* **①** (pain grillé) toast ¢; **trois** ∼**s** three pieces of toast; **②** (canapé) canapé; **③** (discours) toast; **porter un**

~ **en l'honneur de qn** to toast sb

toboggan /tɔbɔgɑ̃/ nm **1** (piste glissante) slide; **2** ®(viaduc) flyover GB, overpass US; **3** Tech (pour gravats) chute; **4** Sport (traîneau) toboggan

toc /tɔk/
A ○nm (faux) **c'est du ~** (ce collier) it's a fake; (ces colliers) they're fakes
B excl (also onomat); **~! ~!** knock! knock!; **tu vois, j'avais raison, et ~○!** you see, I was right, so there!

tocsin /tɔksɛ̃/ nm alarm (bell), tocsin littér; **sonner le ~** lit, fig to sound the alarm

toge /tɔʒ/ nf Univ gown; Jur robe; (antique) toga

tohu-bohu○ /tɔybɔy/ nm inv (confusion) confusion; (tumulte) commotion

toi /twa/ pron pers **1** (sujet, objet) you; **~, ne dis rien** don't say anything; **il les voit plus souvent que ~** (que tu ne les vois) he sees them more often than you do; (qu'il ne te voit) he sees them more often than you; **ce sont des amis à ~** they're YOUR friends; **une chambre à ~** a room of your own; **c'est à ~** (appartenance) it's yours; it belongs to you; (séquence) (it's) your turn; **c'est à ~ de choisir** (ton tour) it's your turn to choose; (ta responsabilité) it's up to you to choose; **2** (pronom réfléchi) yourself; **reprends-~** pull yourself together; (toi-même) yourself; **pense un peu à ~ aussi** think of yourself a little as well

toile /twal/ nf **1** (tissu) cloth; **~ de lin** linen (cloth); **des vêtements de ~** (heavy) cotton clothes; **de la grosse ~** canvas; **2** (de peintre) (support) canvas; (tableau) painting; **~ de maître** master painting; **3** Naut canvas
(Composés) **~ d'araignée** gén spider's web; (dans une maison) cobweb; **~ cirée** oilcloth; **~ de fond** Théât backcloth; fig backdrop; **~ goudronnée** tarpaulin; **~ de jute** hessian; **~ à matelas** ticking; **~ de tente** (tissu) canvas; (tente) tent

toilettage /twalɛtaʒ/ nm **1** (d'animal) grooming; **2** fig (de structure) cleaning up

toilette /twalɛt/
A nf **1** (soins corporels) **faire sa ~** [personne] to have a wash; [animal] to wash itself; **savon de ~** toilet soap; **faire la ~ d'un mort** to lay out a corpse; **faire la ~ d'un chien** to groom a dog; **faire la ~ de la ville** fig to give the town a face-lift; **2** (vêtements) outfit; **en belle** or **grande ~** all dressed up (jamais épith); **3** (meuble) (pour se laver) washstand; (coiffeuse) dressing table
B toilettes nfpl (chez soi) toilet (sg) GB, bathroom (sg) US; (dans un lieu public) toilets, restroom (sg) US

toiletter /twalete/ [1] vtr to groom [chien, chat, cheval]

toi-même /twamɛm/ pron pers yourself

toise /twaz/ nf **1** (instrument) height gauge; **passer à la ~** to be measured; **2** ▸ p. 347 (unité) toise (≈ 6 1/2 ft)

toiser /twaze/ [1] vtr to look [sb] up and down [personne]

toison /twazɔ̃/ nf **1** (de mouton) fleece; **2** (chevelure) mane; (poils abondants) abundant growth (of hair)
(Composé) **la Toison d'or** the Golden Fleece

toit /twa/ nm **1** lit roof; **habiter sous les ~s** to live in a garret; **2** fig (maison) roof; **se retrouver sans ~** to find oneself without a roof over one's head
(Composé) **~ ouvrant** sunroof
(Idiome) **crier qch sur (tous) les ~s** to shout sth from the rooftops

toiture /twatyʀ/ nf (structure) roof; (matériau) roofing

tôle /tol/ nf **1** (matière) sheet metal; (plaque) metal sheet ou plate; **2** ○(prison) = **taule**
(Composés) **~ ondulée** corrugated iron; **~ à tarte** tart tin

tolérable /tɔleʀabl/ adj (attente, douleur, situation) bearable; (attitude) tolerable, acceptable

tolérance /tɔleʀɑ̃s/ nf **1** (ouverture d'esprit) tolerance; (indulgence) indulgence; **être d'une grande ~ avec qn** to be very tolerant with sb; **2** (dérogation) **ce n'est pas un droit, c'est une ~** it isn't an entitlement, but it's something that is tolerated; **3** (à un médicament, au bruit) tolerance (à of)

tolérant, ~e /tɔleʀɑ̃, ɑ̃t/ adj tolerant

tolérer /tɔleʀe/ [14] vtr to tolerate

tôlerie /tolʀi/ nf (technique) sheet-metal working; (commerce) sheet-metal trade; (atelier) sheet-metal works (pl); (ensemble de tôles) metalwork; (de voiture) bodywork

tôlier, -ière /tolje, ɛʀ/ nm,f **1** Ind sheet-metal worker; Aut panel beater; **2** ○(patron d'hôtel) hotel boss

tollé /tɔle/ nm outcry, hue and cry

TOM /tɔm/ nm: abbr ▸ **territoire**

tomaison /tɔmɛzɔ̃/ nf volume numbering

tomate /tɔmat/ nf **1** (fruit) tomato; **2** (plante) tomato plant; **3** (apéritif) pastis with a dash of grenadine
(Idiome) **être rouge comme une ~** (à cause du soleil) to be as red as a lobster; (à cause de la gêne) to be as red as a beetroot

tombal, ~e, mpl **-aux** /tɔ̃bal, o/ adj **inscription ~e** gravestone inscription

tombant, ~e /tɔ̃bɑ̃, ɑ̃t/ adj [épaules] sloping; [moustaches, paupières] drooping (épith); [oreilles de chien] floppy; [poitrine] pej sagging

tombe /tɔ̃b/ nf (fosse) grave; (dalle) gravestone

tombeau, pl **~x** /tɔ̃bo/ nm **1** (monument) tomb; **mettre qn au ~** to lay sb in their grave; **la mise au ~** Art the Entombment; **2** (personne discrète) **c'est un ~** he/she will keep quiet; **3** (fin) death; **vivre avec qn jusqu'au ~** to live with sb till the grave
(Idiome) **rouler à ~ ouvert**○ to drive at breakneck speed

tombée /tɔ̃be/ nf **à la ~ du jour** at close of day littér; **(à) la ~ de la nuit** (at) nightfall

tomber¹ /tɔ̃be/ [1]
A vtr (+ v avoir) Sport to throw [lutteur]; fig to beat [équipe]
B vi (+ v être) **1** (faire une chute) gén to fall; (de sa propre hauteur) [personne, chaise] to fall over; [animal] to fall; [arbre, mur] to fall down; (d'une hauteur, d'un support) [personne, vase] to fall off; [fruits, feuilles, bombe] to fall; [cheveux, dents] to fall out; [plâtre, revêtement] to come off; **~ dans un trou** to fall down a hole; **j'ai fait ~ un vase** I knocked a vase over; **j'ai fait ~ le vase de l'étagère** I knocked the vase off the shelf; **le vent a fait ~ une tuile du toit** the wind blew a tile off the roof; **se laisser ~ dans un fauteuil** to flop into an armchair; **laisser ~ un gâteau sur le tapis** to drop a cake on the carpet; **le skieur s'est laissé ~ pour s'arrêter** the skier dropped to the ground to stop himself; **2** (venir d'en haut) [pluie, neige, foudre] to fall; [brouillard] to come down; [rayon, clarté] to fall; [rideau de théâtre] to fall, to drop; **il tombe des gouttes** it's spotting with rain; **qu' est-ce que ça tombe○!, ça tombe dru○!** (pluie) it's pouring down!; **la foudre est tombée sur un arbre** the lightning struck a tree; **une faible lueur tombait de la lucarne** there was a dim light coming through the skylight; **une pâle clarté tombait de la lune** the moon cast a pale light; **3** (faiblir, baisser) [valeur, prix, température] to fall; [ardeur, colère] to subside; [fièvre] to come down; [vent] to drop; [conversation] to draw to a close; [conversation] to die down; **faire ~** to bring down [prix, température]; to dampen [enthousiasme]; **il est tombé bien bas** (affectivement) he's in very low spirits; (moralement) he has sunk very low; **il est tombé bien bas dans mon estime** he has gone right down in my esteem ou estimation; **je tombe de sommeil** I can't keep my eyes open; **4** (être vaincu, renversé) [dictateur, régime, ville] to fall; (disparaître) [obstacle, objection] to vanish; [opposition] to subside; [préjugé] to die out; **le roi est tombé** (aux cartes) the king has been played; **faire ~** to bring down [régime, dictateur]; to break down [barrières]; **5** (s'affaisser) [poitrine] to sag; [épaules] to slope; **6** (pendre) [chevelure, mèche] to fall; **~ bien/mal** [vêtement, rideau] to hang well/badly; **sa jupe lui tombe (jusqu')aux chevilles** her skirt comes down to her ankles; **7** (se retrouver, se placer) **~ dans la vulgarité** to lapse into vulgarity; **vous tombez dans le paradoxe** you are being paradoxical; **~ sous le coup d'une loi** Jur to fall within the provisions of a law; **la conversation est tombée sur la politique** the conversation came around to politics; **8** (devenir) to fall; **~ malade/amoureux** to fall ill/in love; **9** (être donné) [décision] to be announced; [nouvelle] to break; [réponse] to be given; **~ sur les écrans** [nouvelle] to come through on screen; **dès que le journal tombe des presses** as soon as the newspaper comes off the press; **10** (rencontrer) **~ sur** gén to come across [inconnu, détail, objet]; to run into [ami]; (recevoir en partage) to get; (avoir de la chance dans ses recherches) to hit on the right page; **je suis tombé sur un examinateur sévère à l'examen** I got a harsh examiner in the exam; **je suis tombé par hasard sur ce que je cherchais** I found what I was looking for by chance; **si tu prends cette rue, tu tomberas sur la place** if you follow that street, you'll come to

the square; [11] (survenir) gén to come; **tu ne pouvais pas mieux ∼!** (au bon moment) you couldn't have come at a better time!; (avoir de la chance) you couldn't have done better!; **tu tombes bien/mal, j'allais partir** you're lucky/unlucky, I was just about to leave; **il faut toujours que ça tombe sur moi** or **que ça me tombe dessus**○† (décision, choix) why does it always have to be me?; (mésaventure) why does it always have to happen to me?; **∼ au milieu d'une** or **en pleine réunion** [personne] to walk right into a meeting; [annonce, nouvelle] to come right in the middle of a meeting; [12] (coïncider) [date] to fall on [jour, quantième]; [13] (abandonner) **laisser ∼** to give up [emploi, activité]; to drop [sujet, projet, habitude]; **laisse ∼!** (désintérêt, désabusement) forget it!; (irritation) give it a rest○!; **laisser ∼ qn** (pour se séparer) to drop sb; (pour ne plus aider) to let sb down; [14] (agresser) **∼ sur qn** (physiquement) [soldats, voyous] to fall on sb, to lay into sb○; [pillards, police] to descend on sb; (critiquer) to go for sb, to lay into sb○; [15] (mourir) euph to die

tomber² /tɔ̃be/ nm (de vêtement, tissu) hang ¢; **ce velours a un beau ∼** this velvet hangs well

tombereau, pl **∼x** /tɔ̃bʀo/ nm [1] (charrette) tip-up cart; (contenu) cartload; [2] (camion) dumper truck GB, dumptruck US; (contenu) truckload

tombeur○ /tɔ̃bœʀ/ nm [1] (séducteur) lady-killer, Casanova; [2] (vainqueur) **le ∼ d'une équipe** the one who brought a team down

tombola /tɔ̃bɔla/ nf tombola GB, lottery

tome /tom/ nm [1] (volume) volume; [2] (division) part, book

tommette /tɔmɛt/ nf hexagonal floor tile

ton¹, **ta**, pl **tes** /tɔ̃, ta, te/ adj poss

⚠ En anglais, on ne répète pas le possessif coordonné: *ta femme et tes enfants* = your wife and children.

your; **tes parents à toi**○ your parents; **à ∼ arrivée** (prochaine) when you arrive; (passée) when you arrived

ton² /tɔ̃/ nm [1] (de la voix) (hauteur) pitch; (inflexion) tone; (qualité) tone, voice; (expression) tone (of voice); **∼ grave/aigu** low/high pitch; **∼ criard/rauque** shrill/husky voice; **d'un ∼ dédaigneux** scornfully; **d'un ∼ sec** drily; **sur un ∼ solennel** in a solemn tone; **baisser le ∼** lit to lower one's voice; fig to moderate one's tone; **eh bien, si tu le prends sur ce ∼** well, if you're going to take it like that; **je le leur ai dit** or **répété sur tous les ∼s** I've told them a thousand times; [2] Ling tone; **langue à ∼s** tone language; [3] (style) tone; **donner le ∼** gén to set the tone; (pour une mode) to set the fashion; **être** or **se mettre dans le ∼** to fit in; **de bon ∼** in good taste, tasteful; **il est/serait de bon ∼ de faire** it is/it would be good form to do; [4] Mus (hauteur des notes) pitch; (tonalité) key; (intervalle) tone; (instrument) pitch pipe; [5] (couleur) shade, tone; **∼ sur ∼** in matching tones

tonal, **∼e** /tɔnal/ adj Ling, Mus tonal; **hauteur ∼e** pitch; **langue ∼e** tone language

tonalité /tɔnalite/ nf [1] Mus (ton) key; (échelle des sons) tonality; [2] (de voyelle, son) [3] (qualité) (de voix) tone; (de roman, film) tone; [4] (couleurs) tonality; [5] Télécom dialling tone GB, dial tone US

tondeur, **-euse¹** /tɔ̃dœʀ, øz/ ▸ p. 372 nm,f **∼ de chiens** dog groomer; **∼ de moutons** sheep shearer

tondeuse² /tɔ̃dœz/ nf [1] (pour chiens) clippers (pl); (pour moutons) shears (pl); [2] (de coiffeur) clippers (pl); [3] (de jardin) **∼ (à gazon)** lawnmower

tondre /tɔ̃dʀ/ [6] vtr [1] lit to shear [mouton, laine]; to clip [chien, poils]; to mow [gazon, pelouse]; **∼ qn** to shave sb's head; [2] ○(couper les cheveux à) **∼ qn** to cut sb's hair; [3] ○(voler) to fleece○

tondu, **∼e** /tɔ̃dy/
A adj [1] [mouton] shorn; [chien] clipped; [2] [cheveux] shorn; [crâne] shaven GB, shaved; [prisonnier] with a shaven head (après n)
B nm,f skinhead

tongs /tɔ̃g/ nfpl flip-flops, thongs US

tonicité /tɔnisite/ nf [1] (de climat, d'air) bracing effect; [2] (de muscle) tone

tonifiant, **∼e** /tɔnifjɑ̃, ɑ̃t/ adj [1] [climat, air] bracing; [promenade] invigorating; [2] (pour les muscles, la peau) [exercice, lotion] toning (épith)

tonifier /tɔnifje/ [2] vtr to tone up [muscles, épiderme]; **un climat qui tonifie** an invigorating climate

tonique¹ /tɔnik/
A adj [1] (stimulant) [boisson] tonic (épith); fig [air] invigorating; [lecture] stimulating; [2] (astringent) **lotion ∼** toning lotion; [3] Ling tonic
B nm [1] Méd, fig tonic; [2] (lotion) toning lotion

tonique² /tɔnik/ nf Mus tonic

tonitruant, **∼e** /tɔnitʀyɑ̃, ɑ̃t/ adj booming (épith)

tonitruer /tɔnitʀye/ [1] vi to thunder

tonnage /tɔnaʒ/ nm tonnage

tonnant, **∼e** /tɔnɑ̃, ɑ̃t/ adj [voix] booming; [colère] thunderous

tonne /tɔn/ nf ▸ p. 453 tonne, metric ton; **des ∼s de choses à faire**○ fig tons ou loads○ of things to do

tonneau, pl **∼x** /tɔno/ nm [1] (contenant, contenu) barrel; [2] (en voiture) somersault; **faire un ∼** to turn over, to somersault; [3] Naut ton; [4] Aviat barrel roll

(Idiome) **du même ∼**○ of the same kind

tonnelet /tɔnlɛ/ nm small barrel, keg

tonnelier /tɔnəlje/ ▸ p. 372 nm cooper

tonnelle /tɔnɛl/ nf arbour^GB

tonner /tɔne/ [1]
A vi [1] [personne] to thunder; **∼ contre** to inveigh against; [2] [artillerie] to thunder
B v impers to thunder; **il tonne** it's thundering

tonnerre /tɔnɛʀ/
A nm [1] Météo thunder; **coup de ∼** lit clap of thunder; fig thunderbolt; [2] (de canons, d'artillerie) thundering; **un ∼ d'applaudissements** thunderous applause; [3] ○(haute qualité) **du ∼** fabulous; **ça marche du ∼** it's going fantastically well
B excl blast!

tonte /tɔ̃t/ nf [1] (époque, action) **∼ (des moutons)** shearing; [2] (laine) fleece

tonton /tɔ̃tɔ̃/ nm uncle; **∼ Pierre** Uncle Pierre

tonus /tɔnys/ nm inv [1] (de personne) energy, dynamism; [2] (de muscle) tone, tonus

top /tɔp/
A ○adj top
B nm (signal sonore) pip, beep; **donner le ∼ de départ** (dans une course) to give the starting signal

topaze /tɔpaz/
A ▸ p. 140 adj inv (couleur) topaz-coloured^GB
B nf topaz

toper /tɔpe/ [1] vi **topons là!** let's shake on it!, done!

topinambour /tɔpinɑ̃buʀ/ nm Jerusalem artichoke

topo○ /tɔpo/ nm (oral) short talk; (écrit) short piece; **c'est toujours le même ∼** it's always the same old story○

topographie /tɔpɔgʀafi/ nf (science, relief) topography

toponyme /tɔpɔnim/ nm place name, toponym spéc

toquade○ /tɔkad/ nf [1] (pour une activité, un objet) passion; [2] (pour une personne) crush○ (**pour** on)

toque /tɔk/ nf (de femme) toque; (de cuisinier) chef's hat; (de juge) hat; (de jockey) cap; **∼ en fourrure** fur cap

toqué○, **∼e** /tɔke/ adj (fou) crazy○ (**about**)

toquer○; **se toquer** /tɔke/ [1] vpr **se ∼ de qch** to go crazy about sth; **se ∼ de qn** to fall for sb○, to become infatuated with sb

torche /tɔʀʃ/ nf (flambeau) torch; **∼ vivante** human torch; **parachute en ∼** candled parachute

(Composé) **∼ électrique** torch GB, flashlight

torcher○ /tɔʀʃe/ [1] vtr [1] (essuyer) to wipe; [2] (faire vite) to dash off○ [article, rapport]; (bâcler) to cobble [sth] together; **un article bien torché** a well-written article

torchère /tɔʀʃɛʀ/ nf [1] (candélabre) torchère; [2] (en pétrochimie) flare stack

torchis /tɔʀʃi/ nm inv cob (for walls)

torchon /tɔʀʃɔ̃/ nm [1] gén cloth; (pour la vaisselle) tea towel GB, dish towel US; **donner** or **passer un coup de ∼ sur** to give [sth] a wipe [vaisselle, meuble]; **coup de ∼**○ (épuration) purge, clean-up○; [2] ○(journal) pej rag○; [3] ○(travail mal présenté) messy piece of work

(Idiome) **le ∼ brûle (entre eux)**○ it's war (between them)

tordant○, **∼e** /tɔʀdɑ̃, ɑ̃t/ adj hilarious

tordre /tɔʀdʀ/ [6]

A vtr **1** (tourner violemment) to twist [bras]; to wring [cou]; **2** (déformer) to bend [clou, barre]; **3** (contracter) **la peur lui tordait le visage** his/her face was distorted with fear; **l'angoisse lui tordait l'estomac** fear was tying his/her stomach up in knots; **4** (enrouler) to twist [mouchoir]; **5** (essorer) to wring out [linge]

B **se tordre** vpr **1** [personne] **se ～ la cheville** to twist one's ankle; **se ～ de douleur** to writhe in pain; **se ～ de rire** to double up laughing; **2** [pare-chocs] to bend; [roue] to buckle

tordu, **～e** /tɔʀdy/ adj **1** (déformé) [nez, jambes, barre] crooked; [branches, ferraille] twisted; **2** fig [idée] weird, strange; [logique, esprit] twisted; **inventer un coup ～○** to come up with an underhand trick

tornade /tɔʀnad/ nf tornado

torpeur /tɔʀpœʀ/ nf torpor

torpille /tɔʀpij/ nf torpedo

torpilleur /tɔʀpijœʀ/ nm **1** (bateau) torpedo boat; **2** (marin) torpedo gunner

torréfacteur /tɔʀefaktœʀ/ nm **1** ▸ p. 372 (commerçant) coffee merchant; **2** (machine) roasting machine

torréfier /tɔʀefje/ [2] vtr to roast

torrent /tɔʀɑ̃/ nm lit, fig torrent; **des ～s de larmes** floods of tears; **pleuvoir à ～s** to rain very heavily

torrentiel, **-ielle** /tɔʀɑ̃sjɛl/ adj torrential

torride /tɔʀid/ adj [climat, région] torrid; [soleil, été, chaleur] scorching

tors, **torse¹** /tɔʀ, tɔʀs/ adj gén twisted; [jambes] crooked

torsade /tɔʀsad/ nf **1** gén twist, coil; **2** (point de tricot) cable stitch; **3** Archit cable moulding

torsader /tɔʀsade/ [1] vtr to twist [fils, soie]; **bougeoir torsadé** twisted candlestick; **colonne torsadée** cable column

torse² /tɔʀs/ nm **1** ▸ p. 136 gén chest; **se mettre ～ nu** to strip to the waist; **2** Anat, Art torso

torsion /tɔʀsjɔ̃/ nf **1** gén twisting; **2** Phys torsion

tort /tɔʀ/

A nm **1** (défaut de raison) **avoir ～** to be wrong; **tu n'as pas ～ de les laisser tomber!** I don't blame you for dropping them!; **j'aurais bien ～ de m'inquiéter!** it would be silly of me to worry!; **être en ～**, **être dans son ～** to be in the wrong; **donner ～ à qn** [arbitre, juge] to blame sb; [faits] to prove sb wrong; **2** (faute) fault; **les ～s sont partagés** there are faults on both sides; **prendre tous les ～s à son compte** to take all the blame ou all responsibility; **reconnaître ses ～s** to acknowledge that one has done wrong; **avoir des ～s envers qn** to have wronged sb; **le jugement a été prononcé à leurs ～s** Jur the case went against them; **3** (erreur) mistake; **mon ～, c'est d'être trop impulsif** my trouble is that I am too impulsive; **4** (préjudice) wrong; **demander réparation d'un ～** to demand compensation for a wrong; **faire du** or **porter ～ à qn/qch** to harm sb/sth

B **à tort** loc adv [accuser] wrongly; **à ～ ou à raison** rightly or wrongly; **à ～ et à travers** [dépenser] wildly; **parler à ～ et à travers** to talk a lot of nonsense

torticolis /tɔʀtikɔli/ ▸ p. 195 nm inv stiff neck

tortillard /tɔʀtijaʀ/ nm small local train

tortiller /tɔʀtije/ [1]

A vtr to twist [fibres]; to twiddle [mouchoir, moustache]

B **se tortiller** vpr to wriggle

(Idiome) **il n'y a pas à ～○** there's no wriggling out of it

tortillon /tɔʀtijɔ̃/ nm (de papier, tissu) twist

tortionnaire /tɔʀsjɔnɛʀ/ nmf torturer

tortue /tɔʀty/ nf **1** (reptile) (d'eau) turtle; (terrestre) tortoise, turtle US; **2** (personne lente) slowcoach○ GB, slowpoke○ US; **3** (papillon) tortoiseshell

(Idiome) **avancer comme une ～** to proceed at a snail's pace

tortueux, **-euse** /tɔʀtɥø, øz/ adj **1** lit [chemin, ruisseau] winding; **2** fig [manœuvres] devious; [langage] convoluted; [chemin, esprit] tortuous

torturant, **～e** /tɔʀtyʀɑ̃, ɑ̃t/ adj agonizing

torture /tɔʀtyʀ/ nf torture ¢; **sous la ～** under torture; **j'étais à la ～** fig it was torture

torturer /tɔʀtyʀe/ [1]

A vtr **1** [bourreau] to torture [personne]; **2** (faire souffrir)

[pensée, sentiment] to torment; **être torturé par la faim** to be starving; **3** (forcer le sens de) to distort [texte]; **style torturé** tortured style

B **se torturer** vpr fig to torment oneself; **se ～ l'esprit** (cherchant une solution) to rack one's brains

torve /tɔʀv/ adj [œil, regard] menacing, baleful

tôt /to/ adv **1** (de bonne heure) early; **～ le matin** early in the morning; **2** (bientôt, vite) soon, early; **le plus ～ serait le mieux** the sooner the better; **～ ou tard** sooner or later; **tu n'étais pas plus ～ parti qu'il est arrivé** no sooner had you left than he arrived; **j'aurai ～ fait de le réparer** it won't take me long to mend it, I'll soon have it mended; **on ne m'y reprendra pas de si ～** I won't do that again in a hurry; **tu as fini? ce n'est pas trop ～○!** you've finished? about time too○!

total, **～e**, mpl **-aux** /tɔtal, o/

A adj **1** (complet) complete, total; **2** (global) total

B nm total; **faire le ～ des dépenses** to work out the total expenditure; **il n'a pas fermé la porte à clé, ～○, il s'est tout fait voler** he didn't lock the door, the upshot was that he had everything stolen

C **au total** loc adv (dans un calcul) **au ～ cela fait 35 euros** altogether that comes to 35 euros

totalement /tɔtalmɑ̃/ adv totally, completely

totaliser /tɔtalize/ [1] vtr **1** (faire le total de) to total, to add up [bénéfices, souscriptions]; **2** (atteindre le total de) to have a total of [points, buts, votes]

totalitaire /tɔtalitɛʀ/ adj totalitarian

totalitarisme /tɔtalitaʀism/ nm totalitarianism

totalité /tɔtalite/ nf **la ～ du personnel** all the staff, the whole staff; **la ～ des dépenses** the total expenditure; **la presque ～ de ma fortune** almost all my fortune; **appréhender un problème dans sa ～** to look at a problem in its entirety; **financé en ～ par l'État** entirely ou completely state-financed; **rembourser en ～** to refund in full

totem /tɔtɛm/ nm (emblème) totem

toubib○ /tubib/ nm doctor, quack○ GB

touchant, **～e** /tuʃɑ̃, ɑ̃t/ adj (émouvant) moving; (attendrissant) touching; **～ de simplicité** touchingly simple

touche /tuʃ/ nf **1** Tech (commande manuelle) (de clavier) key; (de machine à laver, téléviseur) button; (d'instrument à cordes) fret; **2** Art (coup de pinceau) stroke; (style) touch; (tache de peinture) dash, touch; **3** Sport (ligne de) ～ sideline, touchline; **sortir en ～** to go into touch; **remise en ～** (au football) throw-in; (au rugby) line-out; **mettre qn sur la ～** fig to push sb aside fig; **4** (en escrime) hit; **5** (à la pêche) bite; **faire une ～** to get a bite

touche-à-tout /tuʃatu/ adj inv **être ～** [bébé] to be into everything; [esprit curieux] to be a jack of all trades

toucher¹ /tuʃe/ [1]

A vtr **1** (poser la main sur) **～ (de la main)** to touch [objet, surface, personne]; **～ du bois** (par superstition) to touch wood; **～ le front de qn** to feel sb's forehead; **～ qch du doigt** lit, fig to put one's finger on sth; **2** (être en contact avec) to be touching [mur, plafond, fond]; **～ le sol** [animal, sauteur, avion] to land; **3** (heurter) to hit [adversaire, voiture, trottoir]; **si tu recules encore tu vas ～ le mur** if you reverse any more, you'll hit the wall; **4** (attendrir) to touch [personne]; **ça me touche beaucoup** I am very touched; **5** (affecter) [changement, crise, loi] to affect [personne, secteur, pays]; [intempérie] to hit [région]; **6** (être contigu à) [pays, maison, usine] to be next to; **7** (encaisser) [personne] to get, to receive [argent]; to cash [chèque]; to get [retraite]; to win [lot]; **8** (joindre) **～ qn** to get hold of sb; **9** (atteindre) **～ trois millions d'auditeurs** or **de téléspectateurs** to have an audience of three million; **～ sept millions de lecteurs** to have a readership of seven million

B **toucher à** vtr ind **1** (poser la main sur) **～ à** to touch [objets]; **～ à tout** lit to be into everything; fig to be a jack of all trades; **il ne touche plus à un fusil** he won't go near a rifle anymore; **avec son air de ne pas y ～, c'est un malin○** he looks as if butter wouldn't melt in his mouth, but he's a sly one; **2** (concerner) **～ à** to concern; **la réforme touche à l'emploi des jeunes** the reform concerns youth employment; **3** (porter atteinte à) **～ à** to infringe on [droit, privilège]; **4** (modifier) **～ à** to change; **on ne peut ～ aux coutumes** tradition is sacrosanct; **5** (aborder) **vous touchez à un sujet délicat** you're getting on to a delicate subject

C **se toucher** vpr [maisons, jardins] to be next to each other

toucher² /tuʃe/ nm ① (sens) **le ~** touch, the sense of touch; **doux au ~** soft to the touch; ② Méd digital examination; ③ Mus (d'un pianiste) touch

touffe /tuf/ nf (de cheveux, d'herbe) tuft; (de genêts, d'arbres) clump

touffu, ~e /tufy/ adj ① [sourcils, barbe] bushy; [végétation, forêt] dense; [buisson] thick; [arbre] leafy; **au poil ~** [chien, chat] with thick fur; ② [texte, discours, style] dense

touiller° /tuje/ [1] vtr to stir [sauce]; to toss [salade]

toujours /tuʒuʀ/ adv ① (exprimant la continuité, la répétition) always; **j'en rêve depuis ~** I've always dreamed about it; **de ~** [ami] very old; [amitié] long-standing; **~ plus vite** faster and faster; **des frais ~ plus importants** ever-increasing costs; ② (encore) still; **c'est ~ aussi difficile** it's still just as hard; ③ (de toute façon) anyway; **viens ~** come anyway; **on peut ~ essayer** we can always try; **cela peut ~ servir** it might come in handy; **c'est ~ mieux que rien** it's still better than nothing; **c'est ~ ça de pris** or **de gagné** that's something at least; **~ est-il que** the fact remains that

toupet /tupɛ/ nm ① °(effronterie) cheek°, nerve°; **elle ne manque pas de ~!** she's got a cheek°!; ② (de cheveux) tuft; (sur le sommet de la tête) quiff GB, forelock US; **(faux) ~** toupee

toupie /tupi/ nf (jouet) top

tour¹ /tuʀ/ nm ① (mouvement rotatif) gén turn; (autour d'un axe) revolution; **donner un ~ de clé** to turn the key; **faire un ~ de manège** to have a go on the merry-go-round; **faire un ~ de valse** to waltz around the floor; **faire un ~ sur soi-même** [danseur] to spin around; [planète] to rotate; **un (disque) 33/45/78 ~s** an LP/a 45 or single/a 78; **fermer qch à double ~** to double-lock sth; **à ~ de bras°** [frapper] with a vengeance; [investir, racheter] left, right and centre°GB; ② (mouvement autour de) **faire le ~ de qch** gén to go around sth; (en voiture) to drive around sth; **faire le ~ du monde** to go around the world; **la nouvelle a vite fait le ~ du village** the news spread rapidly through the village; **~ de circuit** lap; ③ ▸ p. 347, p. 575 (pourtour) (bords) edges (pl); (circonférence) circumference; (mensuration) measurement; (mesure standard) size; **de 15 mètres de ~** 15 metresGB in circumference, 15 metresGB around; **~ de hanches** hip measurement; ④ (déplacement) (à pied) walk, stroll; (à bicyclette) ride; (en voiture) drive, spin; **faire un (petit) ~** (à pied) to go for a walk ou stroll; **je suis allé faire un ~ à Paris/en ville** I went to Paris/into GB ou down US town; **faire un ~ chez des amis** to go over to some friends; **faire des ~s et des détours** lit [route, rivière] to twist and turn; fig [personne] to beat about the bush; ⑤ (examen) look; **faire le ~ d'un problème** to have a look at a problem; **faire le ~ (rapide) d'horizon** to have a quick overall look; **faire le ~ de ses ennemis** to go through one's enemies; **on en a vite fait le ~°** pej there's not much to it/her/them etc; ⑥ (moment d'agir) gén turn; (de compétition, tournoi, coupe) round; **à qui le ~?** whose turn is it?; **il perd plus souvent qu'à son ~** (il regrette) he loses more often than he would like; (je critique) he loses more often than he should; **~ à ~** (alternativement) by turns; (à la suite) in turn; ⑦ (consultation électorale) **~ de scrutin** ballot, round of voting; **scrutin à deux ~s** two-round ballot; ⑧ (manœuvre, ruse) trick; **jouer un ~ à qn** to play a trick on sb; **le ~ est joué** (c'est fait) that's done the trick; (ce sera fait) that will do the trick; **ça te jouera des ~s** it's going to get you into trouble one of these days; **~ d'adresse** feat of skill; **~ de main** knack; **en un ~ de main** (habilement) deftly; (rapidement) in a flash; **~ de force** feat; (œuvre) tour de force; ⑨ (allure, aspect) turn; **~ (de phrase)** Ling turn of phrase; **le ~ qu'ont pris les événements** the turn events have taken; **donner un ~ nouveau à qch** to give a new twist to sth; ⑩ Tech (machine-outil) lathe

(Composés) **~ de chant** song recital; **~ de potier** potter's wheel; **~ de rein(s)** back strain

tour² /tuʀ/ nf ① Archit tower; (immeuble) tower block GB, high rise US; ② (aux échecs) rook, castle; ③ (machine de guerre) siege-tower

(Composé) **~ de forage** derrick

tourbe /tuʀb/ nf peat

tourbière /tuʀbjɛʀ/ nf peat bog

tourbillon /tuʀbijɔ̃/ nm ① (d'air) whirlwind; (d'eau) whirlpool; **~ de poussière** whirl of dust; ② fig (de souvenirs)

swirl; (de réformes) whirlwind, maelstrom; **le ~ de la vie** the merry-go-round of life

tourbillonnement /tuʀbijɔnmɑ̃/ nm (de neige, feuilles) swirling, whirling; (de danseurs) twirling

tourbillonner /tuʀbijɔne/ [1] vi ① lit [neige, feuilles] to swirl, to whirl; [danseurs] to twirl; ② fig [idées, souvenirs] to swirl around

tourelle /tuʀɛl/ nf ① Archit turret; ② (de char) turret; (de sous-marin) conning tower; ③ Phot **~ d'objectifs** lens turret

tourisme /tuʀism/ nm tourism; **l'industrie du ~** the tourist industry

(Composé) **~ vert** countryside holidays (pl) GB ou vacations (pl) US

touriste /tuʀist/ nmf tourist; **il suit les cours en ~** hum he goes to his lessons whenever he feels like it

touristique /tuʀistik/ adj [brochure, menu, saison] tourist (épith); [afflux] of tourists (épith, après n); [ville, région] which attracts tourists (épith, après n)

tourment /tuʀmɑ̃/ nm liter torment

tourmente /tuʀmɑ̃t/ nf liter ① (tempête) storm; ② fml (trouble) turmoil

tourmenté, ~e /tuʀmɑ̃te/ adj ① (inquiet) [personne, visage] tormented; [expression, esprit] tortured; ② (agité) liter [époque, histoire, mer, vie] turbulent; ③ (irrégulier) [paysage] rugged; [forme] contorted; ④ (tarabiscoté) [style] tortured; [parcours] tortuous

tourmenter /tuʀmɑ̃te/ [1]
A vtr ① (inquiéter) to worry; ② (faire souffrir) to torment; ③ (harceler) [créancier] to harass [débiteur]
B se tourmenter vpr to worry

tournage /tuʀnaʒ/ nm ① Cin (prise de vues) shooting ₵, filming ₵; (lieu de réalisation) set; **pendant le ~** during shooting; **entre deux ~s** between two films; ② Tech turning; **~ du bois** wood-turning

tournant, ~e /tuʀnɑ̃, ɑ̃t/
A adj ① (qui pivote) [siège, mécanisme] swivel; [jet] rotating; [porte] revolving; ② (qui fait des détours) [mouvement] turning; [service] mobile; ③ (qui alterne) [grève, mesure] staggered
B nm ① (virage) bend; ② (événement) turning point; ③ (charnière) turn; **au ~ du siècle** at the turn of the century; ④ (orientation) change of direction; **prendre un ~** to change tack

(Idiome) **je t'aurai au ~°!** I'll get my own back!

tournante /tuʀnɑ̃t/ nf gang rape

tourné, ~e¹ /tuʀne/ adj ① (orienté) **~ vers** [regard, yeux, personne] turned toward(s); [activité, opération, politique] oriented toward(s); [ouverture, maison, passage] facing (épith, après n); **~ vers le passé/l'avenir** backward-/forward-looking; **porte ~e vers la mer** gate facing the sea; ② (fait) **bien ~** [compliment, lettre] nicely phrased; [personne, taille] shapely; **expression bien ~e** well-turned phrase; **mal ~** [phrase] clumsy; ③ (aigri) [lait, sauce] off (jamais épith)

tournebroche /tuʀnəbʀɔʃ/ nm (rotating) spit

tourne-disque, pl **~s** /tuʀnədisk/ nm record player

tournée² /tuʀne/ nf ① (de facteur, livreur) round; (d'équipe, de chanteur, troupe) tour; ② °(au café) round

tournemain: en un tournemain /ɑ̃nœ̃tuʀnəmɛ̃/ loc adv in no time

tourner /tuʀne/ [1]
A vtr ① (faire pivoter) to turn [volant, clé, bouton, meuble]; **~ la tête vers** to turn to look at; **~ les yeux vers** to turn to look at; **le bruit m'a fait ~ la tête** I looked around at the noise; ② Cin to shoot [film, scène]; ③ (éluder) to get around [difficulté, loi]; ④ (formuler) to phrase [lettre, compliment, critique]; ⑤ Tech (façonner) to turn [bois, pièce]; to throw [pot]; ⑥ (transformer) **~ qn/qch en dérision** or **ridicule** to deride ou ridicule sb/sth; ⑦ (orienter) to turn [pensées, attention] (**vers** to); to direct [colère] (**contre** against); ⑧ (envisager) **~ et retourner qch dans son esprit** to mull sth over; **~ une proposition en tous sens** to look at a proposal from every angle; ⑨ (remuer) to stir [sauce]; to toss [salade]
B vi ① (pivoter) gén [clé, disque] to turn; [roue] to turn, to revolve; [planète, hélice] to rotate; [porte à gonds] to swing; [porte à tambour] to revolve; (rapidement) [toupie, danseur] to spin; **~ sur soi-même** to spin around; **faire ~ qch** to turn; (rapidement) to spin; **faire ~ les tables** (en spiritisme) to do table-turning; ② (graviter) **~ autour de** gén to turn around; [planète, étoile] to revolve around; [avion] to circle; ③ (aller

tout

Quand *tout* fait partie d'une locution comme *à tout hasard, de toute(s) part(s), tout compte fait, tout nu, tout neuf, tout plein, tout simplement* etc., la traduction sera donnée sous le terme principal.

....

Remarques sur l'adjectif

1 Lorsque *tout*, adjectif singulier, exprime la totalité, plusieurs traductions sont possibles mais non toujours interchangeables.

De manière générale:

on emploiera *all* lorsque le mot qualifié est non dénombrable:

tout le vin　　　　　**tout leur talent**
= all the wine　　　　　= all their talent

tout l'argent　　　　**c'est tout ce que je sais**
= all the money　　　　= that's all I know

tout ce bruit
= all that noise

on emploiera *whole* si *tout* peut être remplacé par *entier*:

tout le gâteau　　　　**tout un livre**
= the whole cake　　　　= a whole book

tout le groupe
= the whole group

Mais:

connaître tout Zola/le Japon
= to know the whole of Zola/Japan

lire tout 'Les Misérables'
= to read the whole of 'Les Misérables'

pendant tout mon séjour
= for the whole of my stay

2 *throughout* (ou *all through*) signifie *du début à la fin, d'un bout à l'autre*. On l'emploie souvent pour insister sur la durée ou l'étendue devant un terme singulier ou pluriel qui désigne l'espace de temps ou l'événement pendant lequel un fait a lieu, ou encore le territoire sur lequel il a lieu:

pendant tout le match
= throughout the match

pendant tous ces mois
= throughout those months

la rumeur se répandit dans toute la province
= the rumour spread throughout the province

faire tout le trajet debout
= to stand throughout the journey
ou to stand for the whole journey

il neige sur toute la France
= it's snowing throughout France
ou it's snowing all over France

Au pluriel, *tous, toutes* se traduiront par *all* pour exprimer la totalité, par *every* pour insister sur les composants d'un ensemble, ou encore par *any* pour indiquer l'absence de discrimination. On notera que *every* et *any* sont suivis du singulier.

---

et venir) ~ **(en rond)** [*personne*] to go around and around; [*automobiliste*] to drive around and around; ~ **en rond** fig [*discussion*] to go around in circles; **il tourne dans son bureau depuis une heure** he has been pacing up and down in his office for the last hour; [4] (virer) to turn (**vers** toward(s)); **tournez à gauche** turn left; **le chemin tourne entre les arbres** the path winds between the trees; [5] (se situer) ~ **autour de** [*effectifs, somme d'argent*] to be (somewhere) in the region of, to be round about○ GB, to be around; [6] (fonctionner) [*moteur, usine*] to run; ~ **rond** [*moteur*] to run smoothly; [*entreprise, affaires*] to be doing well; **les affaires tournent (bien)** business is good; **faire** ~ to run [*entreprise*]; **il y a quelque chose qui ne tourne pas rond dans cette histoire**○ there's something fishy○ about this business; **mon frère ne tourne pas rond**○ **depuis quelque temps** my brother has been acting strangely for some time; [7] (évoluer) **les choses ont bien/mal tourné pour lui** things turned out well/badly for him; **leur frère a mal tourné** their brother turned out badly; **leur réunion a mal tourné** their meeting went badly; ~ **à l'avantage de qn/au désavantage de qn** to swing in sb's favour○GB/against sb; **la réunion a tourné à la bagarre/en mascarade** the meeting turned into a brawl/into a farce; [8] Cin [*réalisateur*] to shoot, to film; ~ **(dans un film)** [*acteur*] to make a film GB *ou* movie US; **elle a tourné avec les plus grands acteurs** she's worked with top actors; [9] (faire une tournée) [*représentant, spectacle*] to tour; [10] (fermenter) [*lait, sauce, viande*] to go off; [11] (chercher à séduire) ~ **autour de qn** to hang around sb

C **se tourner** *vpr* [1] (se diriger, par intérêt ou besoin) **se** ~ **vers** *or* **du côté de qn/qch** to turn to sb/sth; **ne pas savoir vers qui se** ~/**de quel côté se** ~ not to know who to turn to/which way to turn; [2] (changer de position) **se** ~ **vers qn/qch** to turn toward(s) sb/sth; **tous les yeux se sont tournés vers elle** all eyes turned toward(s) her; [3] (faire demi-tour soi-même) ~ (to turn around; **tourne-toi un peu plus sur la** *or* **à gauche** just turn a little bit more to the left; **se** ~ **et se retourner dans son lit** to toss and turn

tournesol /tuʀnəsɔl/ *nm* [1] Bot sunflower; [2] Chimie **papier** ~ litmus paper

tourneur, -euse /tuʀnœʀ, øz/ ▸ p. 372 *nm,f* Tech turner; (sur machine industrielle) lathe operator

tournevis /tuʀnəvis/ *nm inv* screwdriver

tournicoter○ /tuʀnikɔte/ [1] *vi* ~ **autour de** to hang around

tourniquet /tuʀnikɛ/ *nm* [1] (barrière) turnstile; [2] (présentoir) revolving stand; [3] (d'arrosage) sprinkler; [4] (de chirurgie) tourniquet

tournoi /tuʀnwa/ *nm* gén tournament

tournoyer /tuʀnwaje/ [23] *vi* [1] [*feuilles, papiers*] to swirl around; [*vautours*] to wheel; [*moucherons*] to fly around in circles; [2] [*danseurs*] to whirl; **faire** ~ to spin [sb] around [*personne*]

tournure /tuʀnyʀ/ *nf* [1] (aspect) turn; **prendre bonne** ~ to take a turn for the better; **prendre** ~ [*projet*] to take shape; **cela donne à l'affaire une tout autre** ~ this puts a completely different complexion on things; [2] (formulation) turn of phrase; ~ **idiomatique** idiomatic expression
⬭ (Composé) ~ **d'esprit** frame of mind

tourte /tuʀt/ *nf* pie; ~ **à la viande** meat pie

tourteau, *pl* ~**x** /tuʀto/ *nm* [1] Culin, Zool crab; [2] Agric oil cake

tourtereau, *pl* ~**x** /tuʀtəʀo/
A *nm* Zool young turtle dove
B tourtereaux *nmpl* (amoureux) lovebirds

tourterelle /tuʀtəʀɛl/ *nf* turtle dove

tourtière /tuʀtjɛʀ/ *nf* pie dish

tous ▸ tout

Toussaint /tusɛ̃/ *nf* **la** ~ (jour) All Saints' Day; **à la** ~ (jour) on All Saints' Day; (période) at the end of October, at Halloween US

tousser /tuse/ [1] *vi* [*personne*] to cough; [*moteur*] to splutter

toussotement /tusɔtmɑ̃/ *nm* (de personne) (slight) cough; (de moteur) splutter

toussoter /tusɔte/ [1] *vi* [*personne*] to have a slight cough; [*moteur*] to splutter

tout /tu/, ~**e** /tut/, *mpl* **tous** /tu *adj*, tus *pron*/, *fpl* **toutes** /tut/
A *pron indéf* [1] **tout** (chaque chose) everything; (n'importe quoi) anything; (l'ensemble) all; ~ **est prêt** everything is ready;

~ **peut arriver** anything can happen; ~ **est prétexte à querelle(s)** any pretext will do to start a quarrel; ~ **n'est pas perdu** all is not lost; **en** ~ (au total) in all; (entièrement) in every respect; **en** ~ **et pour** ~ all told; ~ **bien compté** or **pesé** or **considéré** in all; ~ **est là** fig that's the whole point; **c'est** ~ **dire** I need say no more; **et** ~ **et** ~○ and all that sort of thing; **ce n'est pas** ~ **(que) de commencer un travail, il faut le finir** it's not enough ou it's all very well to start off a job, it's got to be finished; **avoir** ~ **d'un assassin** to look just like a murderer; **2)** **tous** /tus/, **toutes** (la totalité des êtres ou choses) all; (la totalité des éléments d'une catégorie, d'un groupe) all of them/us/you; **tous ensemble** all together; **tous ne sont pas d'accord** not all of them agree; ~**es tant qu'elles sont** all of them, each and every one of them; **est-ce que ça conviendra à tous?** will it suit everybody ou everyone?

B adj **1)** (exprimant la totalité) **bois** ~ **ton lait** drink all your milk, drink up your milk; ~ **le reste** everything else; **manger** ~ **un pain** to eat a whole loaf; ~ **Pompéi a été enseveli** the whole of Pompeii was buried; **je ne l'ai pas vu de** ~ **l'été** I haven't seen him all summer; ~ **le problème est là** that's where the problem lies; ~ **cela ne compte pas** none of that counts; ~ **le monde** everybody; **2)** (véritable) **c'est** ~ **un travail/événement** it's quite a job/an event; **3)** (devant ce qui/que/dont) (l'ensemble) all; (toutes les choses) everything; (sans discrimination) anything; ~ **ce dont j'ai besoin** all I need; **j'ai acheté** ~ **ce qui était sur la liste** I bought everything that was on the list; **il dit** ~ **ce qui lui passe par la tête** he says anything that comes into his head; ~ **ce qu'il dit n'est pas vrai** not all of what he says is true; **être** ~ **ce qu'il y a de plus serviable** to be most obliging; **c'est** ~ **ce qu'on fait de mieux** it's the best there is; **'tu en es sûr?'—'**~ **ce qu'il y a de plus sûr'** 'are you sure?'—'as sure as can be'; **4)** (n'importe quel) any; **à** ~ **âge** at any age; **à** ~ **moment** (n'importe quand) at any time; (sans cesse) constantly; ~**e publicité est interdite** all advertising is prohibited; **5)** (total) **en** ~**e innocence/franchise** in all innocence/honesty; **en** ~**e liberté** with complete freedom; **en** ~**e hâte** in a great hurry; **de** ~**e beauté** most beautiful; **6)** (unique, seul) **il a souri pour** ~**e réponse** his only reply was a smile, he smiled by way of a reply; **on lui donne quelques légumes pour tous gages** all that he gets in the way of wages is a few vegetables; **7)** **tous, toutes** (les uns et les autres sans distinction) all, every (+ sg); **en** ~**es choses** in all things, in everything; ~**es les pages sont déchirées** all the pages are torn, every page is torn; **tous les prétextes leur sont bons** they'll use any excuse (**pour** to); **meubles tous budgets** furniture to suit every pocket; **nous irons tous les deux** both of us will go, we'll both go; **je les prends tous les quatre** I'm taking all four (of them); **8)** (chaque) **tous/toutes les** every; **à tous les coins de rue** on every street corner; **tous les jours** every day; **tous les deux jours** every other day; **tous les combien?** how often?

C adv (normally invariable, but agrees in gender and in number with feminine adjective beginning with consonant or h-aspirate) **1)** (très, extrêmement) very, quite; (entièrement) all; ~ **doucement** very gently; ~ **étonnées/**~**es honteuses** very surprised/ashamed; ~ **enfant, elle aimait déjà dessiner** as a small child she already liked to draw; **c'est** ~ **naturel** it's quite natural; **des yeux** ~ **ronds de surprise** eyes wide with surprise; **être** ~ **mouillé/sale** to be all wet/dirty; **faire qch** ~ **seul** to do sth all by oneself; **c'est** ~ **autre chose, c'est une** ~ **autre histoire** it's a different matter altogether; **2)** (devant un nom) **c'est** ~ **le portrait de sa mère** she's the spitting ou very image of her mother; **c'est** ~ **l'inverse** or **le contraire** it's the very opposite; **ça m'en a** ~ **l'air** it looks very much like it to me; **tu as** ~ **le temps d'y réfléchir** you've got plenty of time to think it over; **avec toi, c'est** ~ **l'un ou** ~ **l'autre** you see everything in black and white; **3)** (tout à fait) **la** ~**e dernière ligne** the very last line; ~ **à côté de/contre/en haut** right by/against/at the top; **il les a mangés** ~ **crus** he ate them raw; **j'en sais** ~ **autant que lui** I know just as much as he does; **maison** ~ **en longueur** very long and narrow house; **ils étaient** ~ **en sang/en sueur** they were covered in blood/bathed in sweat; **être** ~ **en larmes** to be in floods of tears; **la colline est** ~ **en fleurs** the hill is a mass of flowers; **elle est** ~**(e) à son travail** she's totally absorbed in her work; **4)** (d'avance) ~ **prêt** ready-made; **des légumes** ~ **épluchés** ready-peeled vegetables; **5)** (en même temps) ~ **(e)** while; (bien que) although; **il lisait** ~ **en marchant** he was

reading as he walked; **elle le défendait** ~ **en le sachant coupable** she defended him although she knew he was guilty; **6)** (marquant la concession: quoique) ~ **aussi étrange que cela paraisse** however strange it may seem; ~ **malin/roi qu'il est, il...** he may be clever/a king, but he...; **7)** (rien d'autre que) **je suis** ~ **ouïe** hum I'm all ears; **veste** ~ **cuir** all leather jacket

D **du tout** loc adv **(pas) du** ~, **(point) du** ~ not at all; **sans savoir du** ~ without knowing at all

E nm (pl ~**s**) **1)** (ensemble) **former un** ~ to make up ou form a whole; **mon** ~ (charade) my whole, my all; **du** ~ **au** ~ completely; **2)** **le** ~ (la totalité) the whole lot, the lot; (l'essentiel) the main thing; **vendre le** ~ **pour 50 euros** to sell the (whole) lot for 50 euros; **le** ~ **est de réussir** the main ou most important thing is to succeed; **ce n'est pas le** ~○**!** this is no good!

F **Tout-** (in compounds) **le Tout-Paris/-Londres** the Paris/London smart set

(Composés) ~ **à coup** suddenly; ~ **d'un coup** (soudain) suddenly; (à la fois) all at once; ~ **à fait** (entièrement) quite, absolutely; **être** ~ **à fait pour/contre** to be totally for/against; ~ **à l'heure** (bientôt) in a moment; (peu avant) a little while ago, just now; **à** ~ **à l'heure!** see you later!; ~ **de même** (quand même) all the same, even so; (indigné) ~ **de même!** really!, honestly!; (vraiment) **c'est** ~ **de même bizarre que** it's quite strange that; ~ **de suite** at once, straight away

(Idiome) **être** ~ **yeux** ~ **oreilles** to be very attentive

tout-à-l'égout /tutalegu/ nm inv main drainage

toutefois /tutfwa/ adv however; **je viendrai demain, si** ~ **ça ne vous dérange pas** I'll come tomorrow, as long as that doesn't put you out

toute-puissance /tutpɥisɑ̃s/ nf (d'argent, de dictateur, Dieu) omnipotence; (de pays, d'entreprise) supremacy

toutou○ /tutu/ nm doggie○, dog

tout-petit, pl ~**s** /tup(ə)ti/ nm (nourrisson) baby; (très jeune enfant) toddler

tout-puissant, toute-puissante, pl ~**s**, **toutes-puissantes** /tupɥisɑ̃, tutpɥisɑ̃t/ adj all-powerful; **le** ~ **patron** the all-powerful boss

Tout-Puissant /tupɥisɑ̃/ nm Relig **le** ~ the Almighty, God Almighty

tout-venant /tuv(ə)nɑ̃/ nm inv gén (personnes) all and sundry; **il n'a pas choisi, il a pris le** ~ he did not choose, he just took whatever there was

toux /tu/ nf inv cough; **une** ~ **grasse** a loose cough; **médicament pour** or **contre la** ~ cough medicine; **avoir une quinte de** ~ to have a coughing fit

toxicité /tɔksisite/ nf toxicity

toxicodépendance /tɔksikodepɑ̃dɑ̃s/ nf drug dependency

toxicodépendant, ~**e** /tɔksikodepɑ̃dɑ̃, ɑ̃t/ nm,f drug addict

toxicologue /tɔksikɔlɔg/ ▸ p. 372 nmf toxicologist

toxicomane /tɔksikɔman/ nmf drug addict

toxicomanie /tɔksikɔmani/ nf drug addiction

toxine /tɔksin/ nf toxin

toxique /tɔksik/
A adj toxic, poisonous
B nm toxin, poison

TP /tepe/ nmpl; abbr ▸ **travail**

TPI nm (abbr = **tribunal pénal international**) International Criminal Tribunal, ICT

trac○ /tʀak/ nm (sur scène, devant une caméra) stage fright; (avant un examen, une conférence) nerves (pl); **avoir le** ~ gén to feel nervous; (sur scène) to have stage fright; **donner le** ~ **à qn** [situation, pensée, personne] to put the wind up sb○, to scare sb; **tout à** ~ out of the blue

traçabilité /tʀasabilite/ nf traceability

traçage /tʀasaʒ/ nm **1)** (dessin) Ind, Naut marking out; Constr laying-out; **2)** Ordinat tracing

traçant, ~e /tʀasɑ̃, ɑ̃t/ adj **1)** Ordinat **table** ~**e** graph plotter; **2)** Mil **balle** ~**e** tracer (bullet); **3)** Bot [racine] creeping

tracas /tʀaka/ nm inv **1)** (provoqué) trouble; **donner** or **valoir du** ~ **à qn** to put sb to a lot of trouble; **2)** (subi) problems

t

(*pl*); ~ **quotidiens** everyday problems; **3** (inquiétude) worries (*pl*); **se faire du ~ pour** *or* **au sujet de qn/qch** to worry about sb/sth

tracasser /tʀakase/ [1]
A *vtr* to bother [*personne*]
B se tracasser *vpr* (s'inquiéter) to worry (**pour** about)

tracasserie /tʀakasʀi/ *nf* **1** (ennui) hassle○ **ℂ**; **2** (harcèlement) harassment **ℂ**

trace /tʀas/ *nf* **1** (piste) trail; **perdre la ~ d'un animal** to lose an animal's tracks; **retrouver la ~ d'un voleur** to pick up the trail of a thief; **suivre qn à la ~** lit to track sb; fig to follow sb's trail; **2** (empreinte) ~**s** tracks; ~**s de pas** footprints, footmarks; **3** (marque) (de brûlure) mark; (cicatrice) scar; (de peinture) mark; (de sang, d'humidité) trace; ~**s de freinage** skidmarks; ~**s de doigts** fingermarks; ~**s de coups** (bleus) bruises; **l'aventure avait laissé des ~s profondes en lui** the experience had marked him deeply; **4** (indice) (d'activité) sign; (de passage, présence) trace; **des ~s d'effraction** signs of a break-in; **disparaître sans laisser de ~s** to disappear without trace; **5** (quantité infime) **des ~s de mercure** traces of mercury

tracé /tʀase/ *nm* **1** (plan de route, ville etc) layout; **2** (parcours) (de route, ligne ferroviaire) route; (de fleuve) course; (de frontière, côte) line; **3** (de courbe, croquis) line; **4** Ordinat inking

tracer /tʀase/ [12] *vtr* **1** (dessiner) to draw [*ligne, plan, rectangle, portrait*]; (sur un graphique) to plot [*courbe*]; (écrire) to write [*caractères, mot*]; to plan the route of [*autoroute, oléoduc*]; **dessin tracé à l'encre/à la craie** ink/chalk drawing; **2** (établir) ~ **un tableau pessimiste** to paint a pessimistic picture; **à 15 ans son avenir était déjà tout tracé** at 15, his/her future was already mapped out; ~ **les grandes lignes d'une action** to map out the main lines of action (to be taken); **3** (ouvrir) to open up [*piste, route*]; ~ **le chemin à qn** fig to show sb the way

trachée /tʀaʃe/ *nf* windpipe

trachée-artère, *pl* **trachées-artères** /tʀaʃeaʀtɛʀ/ *nf* windpipe, trachea

tract /tʀakt/ *nm* pamphlet, tract

tractation /tʀaktasjɔ̃/ *nf* negotiation

tracté, ~**e** /tʀakte/ *adj* [*remorque*] tractor-drawn

tracter /tʀakte/ [1] *vtr* [*véhicule*] to tow [*remorque*]; [*câble, remonte-pente*] to pull up [*funiculaire, skieur*]

tracteur /tʀaktœʀ/ *nm* tractor

traction /tʀaksjɔ̃/ *nf* **1** (mode d'entraînement) traction; **à ~ animale** drawn by animals; **2** Sport **faire des ~s** (à la barre, aux anneaux) to do pull-ups; (au sol) to do press-ups GB *ou* push-ups US; **3** Tech (effort mécanique) tension

(Composés) ~ **arrière** Aut rear-wheel drive; ~ **avant** Aut front-wheel drive

tradition /tʀadisjɔ̃/ *nf* **1** (coutume) tradition; **il est de ~ de** it's traditional to; **c'est la ~ que l'on fasse** *or* **de faire** it's traditional to do; **par ~** traditionally; **2** (légende) legend; **la ~ veut que...** legend has it that...

traditionnel, -elle /tʀadisjɔnɛl/ *adj* traditional

traducteur, -trice /tʀadyktœʀ, tʀis/ p. 372 *nm,f* translator

traduction /tʀadyksjɔ̃/ *nf* **1** (action) translation; **la ~ de ce texte m'a pris cinq heures** it took me five hours to translate this text; **la ~ en allemand** translating into German; **2** (texte) translation; **faire des ~s** to do translation work; **3** (de sentiments, d'idées) expression

(Composé) ~ **assistée par ordinateur** computer-aided translation

traduire /tʀadɥiʀ/ [69]
A *vtr* **1** (dans une langue différente) to translate; **2** (exprimer) [*mot, style*] to convey; [*violence*] to be the expression of; [*hausse, instabilité*] to be the result of; ~ **en actes** to put into practice; **3** Jur ~ **qn en justice** to bring sb to justice
B se traduire *vpr* **1** (être exprimé) [*joie, peur*] to show (**par** in); **2** (avoir pour résultat) [*crise, action*] to result (**par** in); [*mécontentement*] to find expression (**par** in); **se ~ par un échec** to result in failure

traduisible /tʀadɥizibl/ *adj* translatable

trafic /tʀafik/ *nm* **1** (commerce illicite) traffic (**de** in); ~ **d'armes** arms dealing; ~ **de drogue** drug trafficking; **faire du ~ de qch** to traffic *ou* deal in sth; **2** (circulation) ~ **(routier)** traffic; ~ **aérien** air traffic

(Idiome) **qu'est-ce-que c'est que ce ~**○? what's going on here?

trafiquant, ~**e** /tʀafikɑ̃, ɑ̃t/ *nm,f* trafficker, dealer (**de** in); ~ **de drogue** drugs dealer; ~ **d'armes** arms dealer, gunrunner; **petit ~** small-time dealer

trafiquer /tʀafike/ [1] *vtr* **1** (truquer) to fiddle with [*compteur, voiture*]; **2** ○(faire) pej **je me demande ce qu'il trafique** I wonder what he's up to

tragédie /tʀaʒedi/ *nf* tragedy

tragédien, -ienne /tʀaʒedjɛ̃, ɛn/ ▸ p. 372 *nm,f* tragic actor

tragi-comique, *pl* ~**s** /tʀaʒikɔmik/ *adj* tragicomic

tragique /tʀaʒik/
A *adj* tragic; **ce n'est pas ~** it's not the end of the world
B *nm* **1** Littérat, Théât (auteur) tragedian; (genre) **le ~** tragedy; (caractère) tragic elements (*pl*); **2** (gravité) tragedy; **tourner au ~** to take a tragic turn; **prendre qch au ~** to make a drama out of sth

trahir /tʀaiʀ/ [3]
A *vtr* **1** (manquer de fidélité à) to betray [*pays, ami, secret, confiance*]; to break [*promesse*]; **2** (révéler) to betray; **3** (rendre infidèle) [*traducteur, mots*] to misrepresent; **4** (faire défaut) [*jambes, forces*] to fail [*person*]
B se trahir *vpr* (se dévoiler) to give oneself away, to betray oneself

trahison /tʀaizɔ̃/ *nf* **1** (manquement à un engagement) treachery **ℂ**; ~ **de qch/qn** betrayal of sth/sb; **une ~** a betrayal, an act of treachery; **2** Mil, Pol treason **ℂ**; **haute ~** high treason

train /tʀɛ̃/
A *nm* **1** Rail train; **accompagner qn au ~**○ to see sb off at the station; **préférer le ~ à l'avion** to prefer train travel to flying; **2** (convoi) train; ~ **de péniches** series of barges; **3** (série) series (+ *v sg*); ~ **de mesures** series of measures; **4** (enchaînement) train; **le ~ des événements** the train of events; **5** (allure) pace; **accélérer/ralentir le ~** to speed up/to slow down; **aller bon ~** (marcher vite) to walk briskly; **aller bon ~** [*rumeurs*] to be flying around; [*ventes, affaires*] to be going well; [*conversation*] to flow easily; [*équipage, voiture*] to be going quite fast; **au ~ où l'on va/au train les choses** (at) the rate we're going/things are going; **aller son ~** [*affaire*] to be getting on all right; **aller son petit ~** [*personne, affaire, négociations*] to go peacefully along; **à fond de ~**○ at top speed; **6** Zool ~ **de derrière** hindquarters (*pl*); ~ **de devant** forequarters (*pl*); **7** ○(de personne) backside○; **8** Mil **le ~** corps of transport GB, transportation corps US
B en train *loc* **1** (en forme) **être en ~** to be full of energy; **ne pas être en ~** not to have much energy; **2** (en marche) **mettre en ~** to get [sth] started *ou* going [*processus, travail*]; **se mettre en ~** gén to get going; Sport to warm up; **3** (en cours) **être en ~ de faire** to be (busy) doing; **j'étais en ~ de dormir/lire** I was sleeping/reading

(Composés) ~ **d'atterrissage** undercarriage; ~ **électrique** electric train; (jeu avec accessoires) train set; ~ **de vie** lifestyle; **réduire son ~ de vie** to live more modestly

traînant, ~**e** /tʀɛnɑ̃, ɑ̃t/ *adj* shuffling; **voix ~e** drawl

traînard○, ~**e** /tʀɛnaʀ, aʀd/ *nm,f* (personne lente) slowcoach○ GB, slowpoke○ US; (qui reste en arrière) straggler

traînasser○ /tʀɛnase/ [1] *vi* **1** (perdre son temps) to loaf○ about; **2** (travailler lentement) to take ages

traîne /tʀɛn/ *nf* **1** (de robe) train; **2** (filet) seine (net)

(Idiome) **être à la ~** [*personne, pays*] to lag behind

traîneau, *pl* ~**x** /tʀɛno/ *nm* **1** (véhicule) sleigh; **2** (d'aspirateur) cylinder; **aspirateur ~** cylinder vacuum cleaner; **3** (de pêche) seine (net)

traînée /tʀɛne/ *nf* **1** (tache allongée) streak; ~ **de sang/peinture** streak of blood/paint; **2** (trace) trail

traîner /tʀɛne/ [1]
A *vtr* **1** (tirer) to drag [sth] (along) [*valise*]; to drag [sth] across the floor [*chaise*]; ~ **qn par les pieds** to drag sb (along) by the feet; **2** ○(être encombré) (en portant) to lug○ [sth] around [*objet*]; (en tirant) to drag [sth] around [*objet*]; (en subsistant) to drag [sb] along [*personne*]; **3** (forcer à aller) ~ **qn chez le médecin** to drag sb off to the doctor's; ~ **qn devant les tribunaux** to drag sb into court; **4** (supporter longtemps) **il traîne un rhume depuis deux semaines** for two weeks now he's had a cold that he can't shake off; **5** (utiliser avec lenteur) ~ **les pieds** lit, fig to drag one's feet

B *vi* **1** (perdre son temps) ~ **dans les rues/avec des voyous** to hang around on the streets/with yobbos; **'qu'est-ce que tu as fait aujourd'hui?'—'j'ai traîné'** 'what did you do today?'—'I loafed around°'; **j'ai traîné au lit** I had a lie-in GB, I slept in; **ne traîne pas, on doit terminer à 4 heures** get a move on°, we've got to finish at four; **ne traîne pas en rentrant de l'école** don't dawdle on your way back from school; ~ **(derrière)** to lag *ou* trail behind, to trail along in the rear; **ne traînez pas derrière!** keep up there at the back! **2** (ne pas se terminer) [*chantier, maladie*] to drag on; [*odeur*] to linger; **faire** *or* **laisser** ~ **(les choses)** to let things drag on; **un film qui traîne en longueur** a long-drawn-out film; **3** (être en contact avec) ~ **par terre** [*jupe*] to trail on the ground; [*rideaux*] to trail on the floor; **4** (être tiré) ~ **derrière qch** to be trailing behind sth; **5** (ne pas être rangé) [*vêtements, jouets*] to be lying about *ou* around; **6** (être très courant) **avec ces microbes qui traînent** with all the germs (that are) around

C **se traîner** *vpr* **1** (ramper) **se** ~ **par terre/jusqu'à la porte** to drag oneself along the ground/to the door; **2** (aller avec effort) **se** ~ **jusqu'à la cuisine** to drag oneself through to the kitchen; **3** (avancer lentement) [*voiture, escargot*] to crawl along

(Idiomes) ~ **la jambe** *or* **la patte** to limp; ~ **ses guêtres°** *or* **ses bottes°** to knock around°

train(-)train° /trɛ̃trɛ̃/ *nm inv* daily round

traire /trɛʀ/ [58] *vtr* to milk [*vache, chèvre, brebis*]; **machine à** ~ milking machine

trait /trɛ/
A *nm* **1** (ligne) *gén* line; (fait d'un seul mouvement) stroke; (de code morse) dash; **souligner un mot d'un** ~ **rouge** to underline a word in red; **exposer la situation à grands** ~**s** to explain the situation in broad outline; **d'un** ~ **de plume** *fig* with a stroke of the pen; ~ **pour** ~ [*réplique, copie*] line for line; [*reproduire*] line by line; **2** (particularité) (de chose) feature; (de personne) trait; ~ **dominant** *or* **essentiel** main feature; ~ **caractéristique** characteristic; ~ **particulier** particular feature; ~ **de caractère** *or* **personnalité** trait, characteristic; **le** ~ **commun entre cette méthode et l'autre** what the two methods have in common; **c'est un** ~ **commun entre ton fils et le mien** that's something our sons have in common; **3** (Ling) feature; **4** (pointe verbale) ~ **(mordant)** scathing remark; **diriger ses** ~**s contre qn** to be sarcastic at sb's expense; **5** (expression) ~ **d'humour** *or* **d'esprit** witticism; ~ **de génie** stroke of genius; **6** (rapport) **avoir** ~ **à** to relate to; **documents ayant** ~ **à la sécurité** documents relating to security; **7** (fois) **d'un (seul)** ~ *gén* at one go; **lire qch d'un** ~ to read sth straight through; **dire qch d'un** ~ to say sth straight out; **boire qch d'un** ~ to drink sth in one gulp; **boire à longs** *or* **grands** ~**s** to drink in long draughts GB *ou* drafts US; **8** (traction) **de** ~ [*animal*] draught GB *ou* draft US

B traits *nmpl* (visage) features; **avoir les** ~**s fatigués** *or* **tirés** to look drawn

(Composé) ~ **d'union** *Ling* hyphen; *fig* (intermédiaire) link; **s'écrire avec un** ~ **d'union** to be hyphenated, to have a hyphen

(Idiome) **tirer un** ~ **sur qch** to put sth firmly behind one

traitant /trɛtɑ̃/ *adj m* **médecin** ~ (généraliste) doctor, GP; (spécialiste) specialist

traite /trɛt/
A *nf* **1** Fin draft, bill; **2** (commerce) **la** ~ **des Blanches** the white slave trade; **la** ~ **des Noirs** Hist the slave trade; **3** Agric milking; **la** ~ **des vaches** milking cows; **l'heure de la** ~ milking time

B d'une traite *loc adv* **d'une (seule)** ~ [*réciter*] in one breath; [*boire*] in one go; **faire 500 km d'une (seule)** ~ to do 500 km non-stop *ou* at a stretch

traité /trɛte/ *nm* **1** Jur treaty; **le** ~ **de Maastricht** the Maastricht Treaty; ~ **commercial** trade agreement; **2** (ouvrage) treatise (**sur, de** on)

traitement /trɛtmɑ̃/ *nm* **1** Méd treatment **C**; **2** (salaire) salary; **3** (comportement envers) treatment; **c'est le** ~ **normal des prisonniers** it's the way prisoners are normally treated; **4** (manière d'aborder, de régler) handling; **il faut accélérer le** ~ **des demandes** applications must be dealt with *ou* processed more quickly; **5** Ordinat processing **C**; ~ **de l'information** data processing; **6** Tech (de minerai, d'eaux) processing **C**; (de bois, textile) treatment; **centre de** ~ **des eaux** water-processing plant

(Composés) ~ **de faveur** preferential *ou* special treatment; ~ **hormonal substitutif, THS** Méd hormone replacement therapy, HRT; ~ **de texte** Ordinat (processus) word-processing; (logiciel) word-processing package

traiter /trɛte/ [1]
A *vtr* **1** (agir envers) to treat [*personne, animal, objet*]; **la critique l'a traité durement** the critics gave him a rough ride; **2** Méd (soigner) to treat [*malade, affection, symptôme*]; **3** (développer) to deal with [*question, sujet*]; **4** (régler) to deal with [*problème, dossier, scandale, affaire*]; **5** (soumettre à une opération) to treat [*bois, textile, aliment, sang, récoltes*]; to process [*eaux usées*]; **non traité** [*bois, aliment*] untreated; **6** Ordinat to process [*données, information, image*]; **7** (qualifier) ~ **qn de qch** to call sb sth; ~ **qn de menteur** to call sb a liar; ~ **qn de paresseux** to call sb lazy; **elle m'a traité de tous les noms** she called me all sorts of names
B traiter de *vtr ind* ~ **de** to deal with [*sujet*]
C *vi* (négocier) to negotiate, to make GB *ou* make a deal

(Idiome) ~ **qn comme un chien** to treat sb very badly, to treat sb like dirt

traiteur /trɛtœʀ/ ▸ p. 372 *nm* caterer

traître, traîtresse /trɛtʀ, trɛtʀɛs/
A *adj* **1** treacherous; **2** °**pas un** ~ **mot** not a single word
B *nm,f* traitor (**à** to); *hum* traitor; **en** ~ in a treacherous *ou* underhand way; **prendre qn en** ~ to take sb by surprise

traîtrise /trɛtriz/ *nf* **1** (acte) act of treachery, (act of) betrayal; **par** ~ treacherously; **2** (de personne) treachery, treacherousness

trajectoire /traʒɛktwaʀ/ *nf* **1** (de projectile) trajectory; **2** (de planète, satellite, particule) path; **3** (carrière) career, path in life

trajet /traʒe/ *nm* **1** (voyage) journey; (par mer) crossing; **2** (parcours) route

trame /tram/ *nf* **1** (de tissu) weft, woof; **2** (d'histoire, de spectacle) framework; (de vie) fabric

tramer /trame/ [1]
A *vtr* **1** (tisser) to weave; **2** *fig* (ourdir) to hatch
B **se tramer** *vpr* [*complot*] to be hatched

tramway /tramwe/ *nm* (voiture) tram GB, streetcar US; (système) tramway GB, streetcar line US

tranchant, -e /trɑ̃ʃɑ̃, ɑ̃t/
A *adj* **1** *lit* sharp; **2** [*personne*] forthright; [*ton*] curt
B *nm* (de lame) sharp edge, cutting edge; **à double** ~ *lit, fig* double-edged

tranche /trɑ̃ʃ/ *nf* **1** (de pain, viande, fromage) slice; (de lard) rasher; **couper en** ~**s** to cut [sth] into slices; **2** (de temps) (d'opération, de travaux) phase; (dans l'emploi du temps) period, time slot; **3** (de livre, pièce de monnaie) edge

(Composés) ~ **d'âge** age bracket; ~ **d'imposition** tax bracket

(Idiome) **s'en payer une** ~° to have a whale of a time°, to have lots of fun

tranché, ~e¹ /trɑ̃ʃe/ *adj* **1** [*opinion, position, réponse, catégories*] clear-cut; [*inégalités*] marked; **2** [*couleurs*] bold, distinct

tranchée² /trɑ̃ʃe/ *nf* **1** Mil trench; **2** (chemin) cutting

trancher /trɑ̃ʃe/ [1]
A *vtr* **1** (couper) to slice, to cut [*pain, viande*]; to cut through, to slice through [*corde, nœud, peau*]; to cut [sth] off, to sever [*tête, membre*]; to slit [*gorge*]; **2** (régler) to settle, to resolve [*question, litige*]
B *vi* **1** (contraster) [*couleur, silhouette*] to stand out (**sur** against); ~ **avec** [*joie, état, décision*] to stand out in sharp contrast to, to contrast sharply with; **2** (décider) to come to a decision; **la justice a tranché en faveur de l'accusé** the court decided in favour GB of the accused; (arrêter une discussion) to break off, to stop short; **tranchons là!** let's leave it at that!

tranquille /trɑ̃kil/ *adj* **1** (calme) [*tempérament, voisins, classe*] quiet; [*allure, voix, assurance*] calm; **tiens-toi** ~! (ne bouge pas!) keep still!, stop fidgeting!; (tais-toi!) be quiet!; **2** (sans agitation) [*heure, jour*] quiet, calm; [*eau, ciel, nuit*] calm, tranquil *littér*; [*café, rue, vie, soirée, bonheur*] quiet; [*sommeil, vacances*] peaceful; **il s'est tenu** ~ **pendant quelques mois** he behaved himself for a few months; **c'est** ~, **ici!** it's peaceful here!; **3** (sans souci) **être** ~ to be *ou* feel easy in one's mind; **ne pas être** ~ to be *ou* feel uneasy, to be worried; **4** (en paix) **avoir l'esprit** ~ to be easy in one's mind; **j'ai la conscience** ～ my conscience is clear; **laisse ton frère** ～ leave your brother alone; **je te laisse** ～ I'll leave you in peace

tranquillement /tʀɑ̃kilmɑ̃/ adv **1** (dans le calme) **elle dort** ～ she's sleeping peacefully; **peut-on se voir** ～? (pour parler) could we have a quiet word?; **j'aimerais pouvoir travailler** ～ I wish I could work in peace; **2** (sans bruit) quietly; **il a réussi** ～ **à se faire un nom** he quietly made a name for himself; **3** (sans se presser) **nous avons marché** ～ we walked along at a leisurely pace; **elle a roulé** ～ she drove along unhurriedly; **je suis arrivé** ～ I wandered in; **4** (sereinement) **nous étions** ～ **en train de discuter** we were chatting away happily; **expliquer/affirmer qch** ～ to explain/to state sth calmly

tranquillisant, ～**e** /tʀɑ̃kilizɑ̃, ɑ̃t/
A adj reassuring, comforting
B nm tranquillizer

tranquilliser /tʀɑ̃kilize/ [1] vtr to reassure

tranquillité /tʀɑ̃kilite/ nf **1** (de tempérament, personne) calmness, serenity; (d'eau, de nuit) liter calmness, stillness; (de moment, lieu) calm, quiet; **pour une fois, j'ai pu travailler en toute** ～ for once I was able to work without being disturbed; **2** (absence d'inquiétude) ～ **(d'esprit)** peace of mind; **en toute** ～ with complete peace of mind, with an easy mind; **3** (vie paisible) **aspirer à la** ～ to long for peace and quiet; **je tiens à ma** ～ I value my peace and quiet

transaction /tʀɑ̃zaksjɔ̃/ nf transaction

transalpin, ～**e** /tʀɑ̃zalpɛ̃, in/ adj **1** (qui traverse les Alpes) transalpine; **2** (italien) Italian

transat[1]○ /tʀɑ̃zat/ nm deckchair; (pour bébé) baby chair

transat[2] /tʀɑ̃zat/ nf Sport transatlantic race

transatlantique /tʀɑ̃zatlɑ̃tik/ adj transatlantic

transborder /tʀɑ̃sbɔʀde/ [1] vtr to transship [marchandises]; to transfer [passagers]

transbordeur /tʀɑ̃sbɔʀdœʀ/ nm **1** (pont) transporter bridge; **2** Rail traverser; **3** Naut ferry

transcendant, ～**e** /tʀɑ̃sɑ̃dɑ̃, ɑ̃t/ adj **1** Philos transcendent; **2** ○(génial) wonderful; **3** Math transcendental

transcender /tʀɑ̃sɑ̃de/ [1] vtr to transcend

transcription /tʀɑ̃skʀipsjɔ̃/ nf **1** gén transcription; (discours transcrit) transcript; **2** Jur registration

transcrire /tʀɑ̃skʀiʀ/ [67] vtr **1** gén, Ling to transcribe [texte, mots]; **2** fig to translate [émotion, ambiance]; **3** Biol, Mus to transcribe

transe /tʀɑ̃s/ nf trance

transférer /tʀɑ̃sfeʀe/ [14] vtr **1** gén, Ordinat to transfer; to relocate [bureaux, usine]; to transfer [appel]; **faire** ～ to have [sth] transferred [contrat, appels]; **2** Jur to transfer [biens, propriétés]; to convey [droit] (**à** to); **3** Psych to transfer

transfert /tʀɑ̃sfɛʀ/ nm **1** gén (de personne, pouvoirs, siège social, données, d'argent) transfer; (de bureaux, d'usine) relocation; **faire** or **opérer un** ～ **de fonds** to transfer funds; ～ **de technologie** technological transfer; **il a demandé son** ～ **dans une autre agence** he asked to be transferred to another branch; **2** Jur (de biens, propriétés) transfer; (de droit) conveyance; **3** Psych transference

(Composé) ～ **d'appel** Télécom call diversion

transfigurer /tʀɑ̃sfigyʀe/ [1] vtr **1** Relig **être transfiguré** to be transfigured; **2** (transformer) to transform; **la joie l'a transfigurée** she is transformed by happiness

transformable /tʀɑ̃sfɔʀmabl/ adj [meuble] convertible

transformateur /tʀɑ̃sfɔʀmatœʀ/ nm transformer

transformation /tʀɑ̃sfɔʀmasjɔ̃/ nf **1** (modification) (de personne, pays) transformation; (de substance, d'énergie) conversion; **la maladie a opéré une profonde** ～ **en lui** the illness wrought a profound change in him; **2** Sport conversion; **3** Ling, Math transformation

transformer /tʀɑ̃sfɔʀme/ [1]
A vtr **1** (modifier) to alter [vêtement, façade]; to change, to alter [personne, attitude, paysage, société]; (profondément, en mieux) to transform; ～ **les mentalités** to alter people's thinking; (profondément) to transform people's thinking; **tout** ～ **dans le jardin** to change everything in the garden; **depuis qu'il ne boit plus, il est transformé** since he stopped drinking he's a different person; **2** (métamorphoser) ～ **en** gén to turn into; (en améliorant) to transform into; ～ **la maison en chantier** fig to turn the house into a building site; ～ **un garage en bureau** to convert a garage into an office;

3 Chimie to convert [substance] (**en** into); **4** Sport to convert [essai]; **5** Math to transform [figure]
B se transformer vpr (délibérément) to transform oneself; (passivement) to be transformed; **se** ～ **en** gén to turn into; (radicalement, en mieux) to be transformed into

transfrontalier, **-ière** /tʀɑ̃sfʀɔ̃talje, ɛʀ/ adj [travailleur] cross-border (épith)

transfuge /tʀɑ̃sfyʒ/
A nmf gén, Pol defector
B nm Mil deserter

transfuser /tʀɑ̃sfyze/ [1] vtr to give a blood transfusion to; ～ **du sang à** to give a blood transfusion to

transfusion /tʀɑ̃sfyzjɔ̃/ nf transfusion

transgénique /tʀɑ̃sʒenik/ adj transgenic

transgresser /tʀɑ̃sgʀese/ [1] vtr to contravene [ordre]; to break [loi, tabou]; to defy [interdiction]

transhumance /tʀɑ̃zymɑ̃s/ nf transhumance, seasonal migration of livestock to summer pastures

transi, ～**e** /tʀɑ̃zi/ adj chilled; ～ **de froid** chilled to the bone; ～ **de peur** paralysed with fear; **un amoureux** ～ a bashful lover

transiger /tʀɑ̃ziʒe/ [13] vi to compromise

transit /tʀɑ̃zit/ nm transit; **en** ～ in transit

transitaire /tʀɑ̃zitɛʀ/
A adj [commerce] transit (épith); **pays** ～ transit point
B nmf Comm forwarding agent

transiter /tʀɑ̃zite/ [1] vi ～ **par** [marchandises, passagers] to pass through, to go via; **les pays font** ～ **leur pétrole par** countries send their oil via

transitif, **-ive** /tʀɑ̃zitif, iv/ adj Ling, Math transitive

transition /tʀɑ̃zisjɔ̃/ nf transition (**entre** between; **vers** to); **passer sans** ～ **à** to move straight on to

transitoire /tʀɑ̃zitwaʀ/ adj (de transition) transitional

translucide /tʀɑ̃slysid/ adj translucent

transmanche /tʀɑ̃smɑ̃ʃ/ adj inv cross-Channel

transmetteur /tʀɑ̃smetœʀ/ nm transmitter

transmettre /tʀɑ̃smetʀ/ [60]
A vtr **1** (communiquer) to pass [sth] on, to convey [information, savoir, vœux, ordre, nouvelle] (**à** to); **envoyez votre candidature au journal qui transmettra** send your application to the newspaper which will then forward it; **transmets-leur mes amitiés** give them my regards; **2** Télécom to transmit; **3** Radio, TV (émettre) to broadcast; **4** (léguer) to pass [sth] on [récit, savoir, découverte]; to pass [sth] down, to hand [sth] down [secret, tradition, fortune] (**à** to); to hand [sth] on [propriété] (**à** to); **5** (passer) to hand over [pouvoir] (**à** to); **6** Méd to transmit, to pass [sth] on [maladie, microbe]; **7** Tech to transmit [vibration, chaleur]
B se transmettre vpr **1** (l'un à l'autre) to pass [sth] on to each other [information]; **2** Télécom [données] to be transmitted (**par** by); **3** [tradition, secret, culture, droit] to be handed down, to be passed down; [récit, savoir] to be passed on; **4** [maladie, microbe] to be transmitted, to be passed on; **une maladie qui se transmet sexuellement** a sexually transmitted disease

transmissible /tʀɑ̃smisibl/ adj transmissible, transmittable

transmission /tʀɑ̃smisjɔ̃/
A nf **1** (communication) transmission, passing on; **2** Phys, Télécom transmission; **3** Radio, TV broadcasting, transmission; **4** (de tradition, secret, culture) handing down, passing down; Jur (de fortune, bien, titre, d'héritage) transfer; **5** Aut transmission; **6** Méd transmission
B transmissions nfpl Mil signals

(Composé) ～ **de pensées** thought transference

transpalette /tʀɑ̃spalɛt/ nm forklift (truck)

transparaître /tʀɑ̃spaʀɛtʀ/ [73] vi [forme, lumière] to show through; [angoisse, embarras] to show; **laisser** ～ [visage, propos] to betray; [personne] to let [sth] show [émotions, sentiments]

transparence /tʀɑ̃spaʀɑ̃s/ nf **1** lit (de verre, diamant, tissu, cloison) transparency; (d'eau) clearness; **2** (de teint, peau) translucency; (de couleur) limpidity; **3** fig (de personne, d'allusions, intentions) transparency; (de gestion, transaction, débat) openness; **la** ～ Pol openness

transparent, ～**e** /tʀɑ̃spaʀɑ̃, ɑ̃t/
A adj **1** [verre, tissu, cloison] transparent; [eau] clear; **2** [teint]

translucent; [*regard, couleur*] limpid; **3** [*personne, allusion, intentions*] transparent

B *nm* (pour rétroprojecteur) transparency

transpercer /tʀɑ̃spɛʀse/ [12] *vtr* **1** [*flèche, lance*] to pierce [*corps*]; [*balle*] to go through; [*personne*] (avec une épée, flèche, lance) to pierce [*corps*]; to run [*sb*] through [*personne*]; ∼ **qn du regard** to give sb a piercing look; **2** [*douleur*] to shoot through; [*froid*] to go right through

transpiration /tʀɑ̃spiʀasjɔ̃/ *nf* **1** (phénomène) sweating, perspiration; **2** (sueur) sweat, perspiration; **3** Bot transpiration

transpirer /tʀɑ̃spiʀe/ [1] *vi* **1** lit to sweat, to perspire; ∼ **à grosses gouttes** to be dripping *ou* streaming with sweat; **2** ○(travailler dur) to sweat; **3** ○(être divulgué) [*information, secret*] to leak out; [*sentiment, opinion*] to come out

transplantation /tʀɑ̃splɑ̃tasjɔ̃/ *nf* **1** Méd transplant; ∼ **d'organes** organ transplants (*pl*); **2** Bot transplantation

transplanter /tʀɑ̃splɑ̃te/ [1] *vtr* to transplant

transport /tʀɑ̃spɔʀ/

A *nm* transport, transportation US; ∼ **ferroviaire et maritime** transport by rail and sea; ∼ **aérien** air transport; ∼ **par route** gén road transport; (de marchandises) road haulage; **endommagé pendant le** ∼ damaged in transit; **au cours de mon** ∼ **à l'hôpital** when I was being taken to hospital

B **transports** *nmpl* **1** gén transport **⊄**, transportation **⊄** US; ∼**s en commun** public transport *ou* transportation US; (effusion) liter transports; ∼**s de joie** transports of joy

transportable /tʀɑ̃spɔʀtabl/ *adj* [*objet*] transportable; **il n'est pas** ∼ (blessé) he cannot be moved

transporter /tʀɑ̃spɔʀte/ [1] *vtr* **1** (déplacer) (sur soi) to carry; (avec un véhicule) to transport; ∼ **qch sur son dos** to carry sth on one's back; **être transporté à l'hôpital** to be taken to hospital; **2** (transférer) to carry [*pollen, virus, maladie*]; **3** (en imagination) to transport; **être transporté dans un monde féerique** to be transported to a magical world; **4** (ravir) liter **être transporté de joie** to be beside oneself with joy

transporteur /tʀɑ̃spɔʀtœʀ/ *nm* **1** ▶ p. 372 (entreprise) carrier; ∼ **aérien** air carrier; ∼ **routier** road haulier GB, road haulage contractor GB, trucking company US; ∼ **maritime** (de marchandises) shipping company; (de personnes) shipping line; **2** (machine) conveyor

transposer /tʀɑ̃spoze/ [1] *vtr* to transpose

transsibérien, -ienne /tʀɑ̃sibeʀjɛ̃, ɛn/

A *adj* trans-Siberian

B *nm* **le Transsibérien** the Trans-Siberian Railway

transvaser /tʀɑ̃svaze/ [1] *vtr* to decant [*liquide*]

transversal, ∼e, *mpl* **-aux** /tʀɑ̃svɛʀsal, o/ *adj* [*muscle, disposition*] transverse; **coupe** ∼**e** cross-section; **poutre** ∼**e** cross-beam; **route/rue** ∼**e** side road/street

transversalement /tʀɑ̃svɛʀsalmɑ̃/ *adv* **1** gén crosswise; **2** Aut transversely

trapèze /tʀapɛz/ *nm* **1** Sport trapeze; **2** Math trapezium GB, trapezoid US; **3** Anat trapezium

trapéziste /tʀapezist/ ▶ p. 372 *nmf* trapeze artist

trappe /tʀap/ *nf* **1** gén (ouverture) trap door; **2** Théât trap door; **passer à la** ∼ fig to be whisked off; **3** (à la chasse) trap

trappeur /tʀapœʀ/ ▶ p. 372 *nm* trapper

trapu, ∼e /tʀapy/ *adj* (court et large) [*homme, silhouette*] stocky, thickset; [*bâtiment*] squat

traque /tʀak/ *nf* **1** (à la chasse) tracking; **2** fig (chasse à l'homme) hunt

traquenard /tʀaknaʀ/ *nm* lit, fig trap

traquer /tʀake/ [1] *vtr* **1** (poursuivre) to track down, to hunt [*sb*] down; (importuner) [*photographe*] to hound [*vedette*]; **2** (contrôler) to monitor [*dépenses, surplus*]; **3** (à la chasse) to track down, to stalk [*animal*]

traumatisant, ∼e /tʀomatizɑ̃, ɑ̃t/ *adj* traumatic

traumatiser /tʀomatize/ [1] *vtr* to traumatize

traumatisme /tʀomatism/ *nm* **1** Méd traumatism; ∼ **crânien** cranial traumatism; **2** Psych, fig trauma

travail, *pl* **-aux** /tʀavaj, o/

A *nm* **1** (contraire de repos) work; **être en plein** ∼ to be busy working; **2** (tâche faite, à faire) job; (ensemble des tâches, besogne) work **⊄**; **j'ai un** ∼ **fou** I'm up to my eyes in work,

I've got a lot of work on; **les gros travaux** the heavy work; **qu'est-ce que c'est que ce** ∼? what do you call this?; **et voilà le** ∼! that's that done!; **3** (fait d'exercer un emploi) work; (emploi rémunéré) work **⊄**, job; (lieu) work; **conditions de** ∼ working conditions; **4** Écon, Sociol (activité, population active) labour^GB **⊄**; **division du** ∼ division of labour^GB; **5** (résultat d'un fonctionnement) (de machine, d'organe) work **⊄**; **le** ∼ **musculaire** muscular effort; **6** (ouvrage érudit) work (**sur** on); **7** (façonnage) **le** ∼ **de** working with *ou* in [*métal, bois, pierre*]; **apprendre le** ∼ **du bois/métal** to learn woodwork/metalwork; **8** (technique, exécution) workmanship; **un** ∼ **superbe** a superb piece of workmanship; **9** Phys work; **10** (action) (d'eau, érosion) action (**de** of); fig (d'imagination, inconscient) workings (*pl*) (**de** of); **11** (altération) (de vin) fermentation, working; (de bois) warping; **12** Méd (pendant un accouchement) labour^GB

B **travaux** *nmpl* **1** (en chantier) work **⊄**; (sur une route) roadworks GB, roadwork US; **travaux de construction** construction work **⊄**; **travaux de terrassement** earthworks; **'fermé pour travaux'** (sur une devanture) 'closed for repairs *ou* alterations'; **'attention, travaux'** gén 'caution, work in progress'; (sur une route) 'caution, road under repair'; **2** (recherche, études) work **⊄** (**sur** on); **3** (débats) deliberations; **4** (opérations de même nature) **les travaux agricoles/de la ferme** agricultural/farm work **⊄**; **travaux de couture** needlework **⊄**

<u>Composés</u> ∼ **à la chaîne** assembly-line work; ∼ **au noir** gén *work for which no earnings are declared*; (exercice d'un second emploi non déclaré) moonlighting; **travaux dirigés, TD** Univ practical (sg); **travaux forcés** Jur hard labour^GB (sg); fig slave labour^GB **⊄**; **travaux manuels** Scol handicrafts; **travaux ménagers** housework **⊄**; **travaux pratiques, TP** Scol, Univ practical work **⊄**; (en laboratoire) lab work **⊄**; **travaux publics, TP** (travail) civil engineering **⊄**; (ouvrages) civil engineering works, public works

travaillé, ∼e /tʀavaje/

A *pp* ▶ **travailler**

B *pp adj* **1** (fignolé) [*bijou*] finely-worked; [*sculpture, dessin*] elaborate; [*or, argent*] wrought; [*métal*] chased; [*style, article*] polished; **2** (tourmenté) [*personne*] ∼ **par le doute** racked with doubt; **3** (non chômé) **heures** ∼**es** (à faire) hours of work; (faites) hours worked

travailler /tʀavaje/ [1]

A *vtr* **1** (pour perfectionner) to work on [*style, matière scolaire, voix, muscles*]; to practise^GB [*sport, instrument, chant*]; **2** (manipuler) to work [*bois, métal*]; Culin to knead [*pâte*]; Agric to work, to cultivate [*terre*]; to cultivate [*vigne*]; **3** (préoccuper) ∼ **qn** [*affaire, idée*] to be *ou* prey on sb's mind, to bother sb; [*tourmenter*] [*jalousie, douleur*] to plague sb; **un doute me travaillait** I had a nagging doubt; **ce sont ses dents qui le travaillent** (parlant d'un bébé) he is out of sorts because he's teething

B **travailler à** *vtr ind* ∼ **à** to work on [*projet, dissertation*]; to work toward(s) [*objectif*]; ∼ **à rétablir la paix** to endeavour^GB to restore peace

C *vi* **1** (faire un effort) [*personne, machine*] to work; [*muscles*] to work; **faire** ∼ **son cerveau** to apply one's mind; **ton imagination travaille trop** you have an overactive imagination; **2** (exercer un métier) to work; ∼ **en équipes/de nuit** to work shifts/nights; ∼ **au noir** gén *to work without declaring one's earnings*; (exercer un second emploi non déclaré) to moonlight; **3** Comm (faire des affaires) [*commerçant, magasin, hôtel*] to do business; **bien** ∼ to do good business; ∼ **avec l'étranger** to do business abroad; ∼ **pour l'exportation** to work in exports; **nous travaillons surtout l'été** most of our trade is in the summer; ∼ **à perte** [*entreprise, commerce*] to run at a loss; **4** (produire un revenu) **faire** ∼ **son argent** to make one's money work; **5** (œuvrer) **nous voulons la paix et c'est dans ce sens que nous travaillons** we want peace and we are working toward(s) it; **6** (s'entraîner) [*athlète*] to train; [*boxeur*] to train, to work out; [*musicien, danseur*] to practise^GB; **7** (se modifier) [*bois*] to warp; [*vin*] to ferment; **8** (se déformer) [*poutre*] to be in stress

travailleur, -euse /tʀavajœʀ, øz/

A *adj* **1** (appliqué) [*élève, employé*] hardworking; **2** Sociol [*classes, masses*] working

B *nm,f* worker

travailliste /tʀavajist/

A *adj* Labour; **congrès** ∼ Labour party congress; **être** ∼ (membre du parti) to be a member of the Labour party; (sympathisant) to be a Labour party supporter

B *nmf* (député) Labour MP; **le candidat des** ∿**s** the Labour candidate

travée /tʀave/ *nf* [1] (rangée) row; [2] Constr, Tech span

travelling /tʀavliŋ/ *nm* Cin (méthode) tracking; (plan) tracking shot; ∿ **avant/arrière** tracking in/out

travers /tʀavɛʀ/

A *nm inv* [1] (petit défaut) foible, quirk; (erreur) mistake; **tomber dans le** ∿ **de la sensiblerie** to lapse into sentimentality; [2] Naut (côté) beam; [3] Culin ∿ **de porc** sparerib

B **à travers** *loc* [1] (ponctuel) [*voir, regarder*] through; **passer à** ∿ **les mailles du filet** lit, fig to slip through the net; [2] (dans l'espace) [*voyager, marcher*] across; **voyager à** ∿ **le monde** to travel all over the world; **passer** *or* **aller** *or* **couper à** ∿ **champs** to cut across the fields; [3] (dans le temps) through; **voyager à** ∿ **le temps** to travel through time; **à** ∿ **l'histoire** throughout history; [4] (par l'intermédiaire de) through; **à** ∿ **ces informations** through this information

C **au travers** *loc* (en traversant) through; **passer au** ∿ **de** fig to escape [*contrôle, inspection*]; **il y a eu des licenciements, heureusement il est passé au** ∿ there have been redundancies, fortunately his job wasn't affected

D **de travers** *loc adv* [1] (dans une mauvaise position) askew; **il a mis son chapeau de** ∿ he has put his hat on askew; **ta veste est boutonnée de** ∿ your jacket is buttoned up wrongly; **il a le nez de** ∿ he has a twisted nose; **j'ai avalé de** ∿ lit it went down the wrong way; **regarder qn de** ∿ fig to give sb filthy looks, to glare at sb; [2] (de façon inexacte) wrong, wrongly; **tout va de** ∿ **aujourd'hui** everything's going wrong today; **elle prend tout de** ∿ she takes everything the wrong way; **comprendre de** ∿ to misunderstand

E **en travers** *loc* across; **un bus était en** ∿ **de la route** a bus was stuck across the road; **se mettre en** ∿ **de la route** [*personnes*] to stand in the middle of the road; **se mettre en** ∿ **du chemin de qn** fig to get in sb's way; **rester en** ∿ **de la gorge de qn**○ fig [*attitude*] to stick in sb's throat; [*propos*] to be hard to swallow

traverse /tʀavɛʀs/ *nf* [1] Rail sleeper GB, tie US; [2] (de fenêtre, grille, d'armoire) crosspiece, strut; (de porte) rail; [3] (rue) side street

traversée /tʀavɛʀse/ *nf* [1] (de mer, pont, pays, d'océan) crossing; **faire la** ∿ **du Vercors à pied** to cross the Vercors on foot; **la** ∿ **du désert** lit crossing the desert; fig (d'homme politique) the wilderness years (*pl*); (entreprise) a difficult period; [2] (de ville, tunnel) **évitez la** ∿ **de Paris** avoid going through Paris

traverser /tʀavɛʀse/ [1] *vtr* [1] (passer d'un côté à l'autre) to cross [*route, pont, frontière*]; to cross, to go across [*ville, montagne, océan, pays, pièce*]; (passer à travers) to go through, to pass through [*ville, pays, forêt, tunnel*]; to make one's way through [*groupe, foule*]; **il traversa le jardin en courant** he ran across the garden GB *ou* yard US; ∿ **le lac à la nage** to swim across the lake; [2] (franchir) [*rivière*] to run through, to flow through [*région, plaine*]; [*route, tunnel*] to go through [*ville, région, montagne*]; [*pont, rivière*] to cross [*voie ferrée, ville*]; [3] (transpercer) [*humidité, pluie*] to come through [*vêtement, mur*]; **la balle lui a traversé le bras** the bullet went *ou* passed right through his/her arm; [4] (passer par une période) to go through [*crise, difficulté*]; to live through, to go through [*guerre, occupation*]; [5] fig (se présenter de manière fugitive) [*douleur*] to shoot through; ∿ **l'esprit de qn** to cross sb's mind

traversin /tʀavɛʀsɛ̃/ *nm* bolster

travesti, ∿**e** /tʀavɛsti/

A *adj* (déguisé) in disguise; **rôle** ∿ role played by a member of the opposite sex

B *nm* [1] (personne) transvestite; [2] Théât (acteur) actor playing a female role; (dans un cabaret) drag artist○

travestir /tʀavɛstiʀ/ [3]

A *vtr* [1] (déguiser) to dress [sb] up [*personne*]; [2] (dénaturer) to distort [*vérité*]

B **se travestir** *vpr* [1] (se déguiser) to dress up; [2] (prendre l'apparence du sexe opposé) to cross-dress

travestissement /tʀavɛstismɑ̃/ *nm* [1] (action de se déguiser) dressing-up; [2] (déguisement) fancy dress, disguise; [3] (dénaturation) distortion, travesty; [4] Psych transvestism, cross-dressing

trébucher /tʀebyʃe/ [1] *vi* [1] lit to stumble (**sur** on; **contre** against); [2] fig [*candidat, adversaire*] to slip up; ∿ **sur un mot** to stumble over a word

trébuchet /tʀebyʃɛ/ *nm* [1] (piège) bird-trap; [2] (balance) assay balance

trèfle /tʀɛfl/ *nm* [1] Bot clover; ∿ **à quatre feuilles** four-leaf clover; [2] Jeux (carte) club; (couleur) clubs (*pl*); **avoir du** ∿ to be holding clubs; [3] ○(argent) dough○, bread○; [4] (symbole de l'Irlande) shamrock

tréfonds /tʀefɔ̃/ *nm inv* liter **le** ∿ **de** the very depths (*pl*) of

treillage /tʀejaʒ/ *nm* [1] (assemblage de lattes) trellis; ∿ **métallique** wire grille; [2] (clôture) lattice fence; [3] (pour vigne) trellis

treille /tʀɛj/ *nf* [1] (tonnelle) (vine) arbourGB; [2] (vigne) climbing vine

treillis /tʀeji/ *nm inv* [1] Mil (tenue) fatigues (*pl*); [2] (de textile) canvas; [3] (assemblage de lattes) trellis; ∿ **métallique** wire grille; [4] (de verrière, vitrail) lattice

treize /tʀɛz/ ▸ p. 398, p. 296, p. 155 *adj inv, pron* thirteen

treizième /tʀɛzjɛm/ ▸ p. 398, p. 155 *adj* thirteenth

tréma /tʀema/ ▸ p. 413 *nm* Ling diaeresis

tremblant, ∿**e** /tʀɑ̃blɑ̃, ɑ̃t/ *adj* [1] [*personne, animal, mains*] shaking, trembling; **être tout** ∿ to be shaking *ou* trembling all over; [2] [*voix*] trembling; [3] [*image, lueur*] flickering; [*son*] tremulous, quavering

tremble /tʀɑ̃bl/ *nm* aspen

tremblement /tʀɑ̃bləmɑ̃/ *nm* [1] (de personne, mains) shaking **C**, trembling **C**; (de lèvres) trembling **C**; **son corps était agité de** ∿**s** he/she was trembling *ou* shaking all over; [2] (de voix) tremor, trembling **C**; (de voix âgée) quavering **C**; (de son, note) wavering **C**; (de lueur, lumière) flickering **C**; [3] (de feuilles) quivering; (de vitres) rattling **C**

(Composé) ∿ **de terre** earthquake

trembler /tʀɑ̃ble/ [1] *vi* [1] [*personne, mains, jambes*] to shake, to tremble; [2] [*voix*] (de colère, joie) to tremble, to shake; (de vieillesse) to quaver; [*son, note*] to waver; [3] [*immeuble, plancher*] to shake; **la terre a encore tremblé en Californie** (légèrement) there have been tremors again in California; (tremblement de terre) there has been another earthquake in California; **faire** ∿ **qch** to shake sth, to make sth shake; [4] (avoir peur) to tremble; ∿ **pour qn** to fear for sb; [5] [*lumière, flamme, image*] to flicker; [6] [*feuilles*] to quiver; (mouvement très doux) to shiver

tremblotement /tʀɑ̃blɔtmɑ̃/ *nm* [1] (de personne, mains) trembling **C**, tremor **C**; (de voix) (émue, effrayée) tremor; (âgée) quaver; [3] (de lumière) flickering **C**

trembloter /tʀɑ̃blɔte/ [1] *vi* [1] [*personne, mains*] to tremble slightly; [2] [*voix*] (de joie, d'émotion) to tremble; (de vieillesse) to quaver; [3] [*lumière, flamme*] to flicker

trémolo /tʀemɔlo/ *nm* [1] (de voix) quaver; **avoir des** ∿**s dans la voix** to speak in a quavering voice; [2] (d'instrument) tremolo

trémousser: se trémousser /tʀemuse/ [1] *vpr* [1] (s'agiter) to fidget; [2] (danser) to wiggle around

trempe /tʀɑ̃p/ *nf* [1] (de personne) **avoir de la** ∿ to be made of stern stuff; **il faudrait quelqu'un de votre** ∿ we need someone of your calibreGB; **avoir la** ∿ **d'un dirigeant** to have the makings of a leader; [2] ○(coups) walloping○ **C**

trempé, ∿**e** /tʀɑ̃pe/

A *pp* ▸ **tremper**

B *pp adj* [1] [*personne, vêtements*] soaked (through), drenched; [*herbe*] sodden; [*linge*] soaking wet; **être** ∿ **de sueur** to be soaked in sweat, to be dripping with sweat; **avoir les cheveux** ∿**s** to have dripping wet hair; [2] Tech [*acier*] tempered; [*verre*] toughened

tremper /tʀɑ̃pe/ [1]

A *vtr* [1] (beaucoup) [*pluie, personne*] to soak [*personne, vêtement*]; [2] (rapidement) to dip; ∿ **son biscuit dans son thé** to dunk one's biscuit GB *ou* cookie US in one's tea; **j'ai juste trempé mes lèvres** I just had a sip; [3] (longuement) to soak [*mains, aliment*]; [4] Tech to temper [*acier, verre*]

B *vi* [1] (être dans un liquide) [*linge, légumes secs*] to soak; **faire** ∿ **qch** to soak sth; [2] (être impliqué) ∿ **dans qch** to be mixed up in sth

C **se tremper** *vpr* (dans la mer) to go for a dip; (dans un bain) to have a quick bath

tremplin /tʀɑ̃plɛ̃/ *nm* [1] Sport (de natation, gymnastique) springboard; (de ski) ski jump; (de ski nautique) water-ski jump; [2] fig springboard

trentaine /tʀɑ̃tɛn/ *nf* **avoir la** ∿ to be about thirty; **une** ∿ **de passagers** about thirty passengers

trente /tʀɑ̃t/ ▸ p. 398, p. 155 *adj inv, pron* thirty

trente(-)et(-)un /tʀɑ̃teœ̃/ ▸ p. 398, p. 155 *adj inv, pron* thirty-one

(Idiome) **être sur son trente et un**○ to be dressed up to the nines

trentenaire /tʀɑ̃tənɛʀ/ *adj* 1 (qui dure trente ans) thirty-year; 2 (qui a trente ans et plus) [*personne*] in his/her thirties (*après n*); [*arbre, construction*] around thirty years old (*après n*)

trente-six /tʀɑ̃tsis/ ▸ p. 398, p. 155 *adj inv, pron* thirty-six

(Idiome) **voir ~ chandelles**○ to see stars

trente-trois /tʀɑ̃ttʀwa/ ▸ p. 398, p. 155 *adj inv, pron* thirty-three

(Composé) **~ tours** LP

trentième /tʀɑ̃tjɛm/ ▸ p. 398 *adj* thirtieth

trépan /tʀepɑ̃/ *nm* 1 Tech trepan; 2 Méd trephine

trépaner /tʀepane/ [1] *vtr* to trephine

trépas† /tʀepɑ/ *nm inv* demise; **passer de vie à ~** to pass on GB, to pass away

trépasser /tʀepase/ [1] *vi* to pass away

trépidant, ~e /tʀepidɑ̃, ɑ̃t/ *adj* 1 [*moteur, machine*] vibrating; 2 [*allure, rythme*] pulsating; [*vie, activité*] hectic; [*histoire*] exciting

trépidation /tʀepidasjɔ̃/ *nf* vibration

trépied /tʀepje/ *nm gén* tripod; (pour chaudron) trivet

trépigner /tʀepiɲe/ [1] *vi* (de colère, d'impatience) to stamp one's feet (**de** with); (de joie, d'excitation) to jump up and down (**de** with)

très /tʀɛ/ *adv* 1 (modifiant un adjectif) very; **~ connu** very well-known; **le dîner était ~ réussi** the dinner went (off) very well; **~ disputé** [*match*] closely contested; **~ répandu** [*pratique*] very widespread; [*opinion*] widely held; **il est ~ aimé dans l'école** he is very well liked at school; **être ~ amoureux** to be very much in love; **à un prix ~ inférieur** at a very much lower price; **la grève a été ~ suivie** the strike was very well supported; 2 (modifiant une expression adjectivale) very; **~ en avance/au courant** very early/well-informed; **~ homme d'affaires** very much a businessman; 3 (modifiant un adverbe) very; **~ tôt/bien/loin** very early/well/far; **~ volontiers** gladly; **à ~ bientôt** see you very soon; **~ franchement, je ne sais pas** quite frankly, I don't know; **'tu vas bien?'—'non, pas ~'** 'are you well?'—'no, not terribly'; 4 (dans des locutions verbales) **j'ai ~ soif** I'm very thirsty; **elle a ~ envie de partir** she's dying○ to leave

trésor /tʀezɔʀ/ *nm* 1 (amas d'objets précieux) treasure ⊄; **découvrir un ~** to find some treasure; **chasse** *or* **course au ~** treasure hunt; 2 (objet précieux) treasure; **les ~s du cinéma français** the all-time greats of the French cinema; **les ~s de la mer** the riches of the sea; 3 (grande quantité) **déployer des ~s d'inventivité** to show infinite inventiveness; 4 (personne) treasure

trésorerie /tʀezɔʀʀi/ *nf* 1 (ressources disponibles) funds (*pl*); (somme en liquide) cash ⊄; **problèmes de ~** cash flow problems; 2 (comptabilité) accounts (*pl*); 3 Admin **la ~** (comptabilité) government finance

trésorier, -ière /tʀezɔʀje, ɛʀ/ *nm,f gén* treasurer; Admin paymaster

tressaillement /tʀesajmɑ̃/ *nm* 1 (de surprise, peur) start; (de plaisir, joie, d'espoir) quiver; (de douleur) wince; 2 (tremblement) (de personne, muscle, d'animal) twitch; (de machine, sol) vibration

tressaillir /tʀesajiʀ/ [28] *vi* 1 (de surprise, peur) to start (**de** with); (de plaisir, joie, d'espoir) to quiver; (de douleur) to wince; 2 (trembler) [*personne, animal, muscle*] to twitch; [*machine, sol, chose*] to vibrate

tressauter /tʀesote/ [1] *vi* 1 (sursauter) to start; 2 (être secoué) [*véhicule*] to jolt; [*personne*] to be jolted; [*objets*] to jump

tresse /tʀɛs/ *nf* 1 (de cheveux) plait, braid US; 2 (de fil, tissu, cuir) braid

tresser /tʀese/ [1] *vtr* 1 to plait, to braid US [*cheveux*]; 2 (pour faire un cordon) to plait [*paille, fil, corde, cuir*]; (tisser) to weave [*paille, corde, objet*]; **soulier tressé** latticework shoe

tréteau, *pl* **~x** /tʀeto/ *nm* trestle

treuil /tʀœj/ *nm* winch

trêve /tʀɛv/ *nf* 1 Mil truce; 2 (moment de répit) respite; **sans ~** unceasingly, without any let-up; **~ de plaisanteries/balivernes!** that's enough joking/nonsense!

tri /tʀi/ *nm* 1 (pour répartir) sorting; **faire le ~ de** to sort [*courrier*]; to sort out [*documents, vêtements*]; 2 (pour choisir) sorting out, selection; **faire le ~ de** to sort [sth] out [*photos, information*]; **faire un ~ parmi des choses/gens** to select among things/people; **opérer un ~ sévère** to be very selective; **fais le ~ dans ce qu'elle dit** don't believe everything she says

(Composés) **~ postal** sorting; **~ sélectif des ordures** household-waste sorting

triage /tʀijaʒ/ *nm* **procéder au ~ de qch** to sort sth out; **gare de ~** marshalling^{GB} yard

trial¹ /tʀijal/ *nm* (épreuve) scramble

trial² /tʀijal/ *nf* (moto) trial bike GB, dirt bike US

triangle /tʀijɑ̃gl/ *nm* 1 Math triangle; 2 (objet) triangle; **en ~** in a triangle; 3 ▸ p. 389 Mus triangle

triangulaire /tʀijɑ̃gylɛʀ/ *adj* 1 (en forme de triangle) triangular; 2 (entre trois personnes, pays) three-way

tribal, ~e, *mpl* **-aux** /tʀibal, o/ *adj* tribal

tribord /tʀibɔʀ/ *nm* starboard

tribu /tʀiby/ *nf* tribe; **le chef de ~** lit the head of the tribe; hum the Big Chief

tribun /tʀibœ̃/ *nm* 1 Hist tribune; 2 (orateur) great orator

tribunal, *pl* **-aux** /tʀibynal, o/ *nm* 1 Jur (lieu, magistrats) court; **porter une affaire devant les tribunaux** to bring *ou* take a case to court; **traîner qn devant les tribunaux** to take sb to court; 2 fig **le ~ de l'histoire/de l'humanité** the judgment of history/of humanity

(Composé) **T~ pénal international** International Criminal Tribunal

tribune /tʀibyn/ *nf* 1 (de stade, gymnase, champ de courses) stand; **la ~ officielle** *or* **d'honneur** the VIP stand; **les ~s du public** the stands; 2 (de salle de réunion, parlement) gallery; **la ~ de la presse** the press gallery; (estrade) platform; (pour une seule personne) rostrum; **monter à la ~** lit, fig to take the platform; **parler à la ~** to speak from the platform; **tenir la ~** to hold the floor; 4 (dans un journal) (rubrique) comments column; (lieu de débat) forum for debate; 5 Archit (de chapelle, d'église) gallery

tribut /tʀiby/ *nm* Hist tribute; **ils ont payé un lourd ~ à la guerre/aux accidents de la route** fig war has/road accidents have taken a heavy toll

tributaire /tʀibytɛʀ/ *adj* 1 gén **être ~ de qch** [*pays, personne, réalisation*] to depend *ou* be dependent on sth; **ils sont ~s les uns des autres** they're interdependent; 2 Géog **être ~ de qch** [*fleuve*] to be a tributary of sth, to flow into sth

tricentenaire /tʀisɑ̃tnɛʀ/ *adj* three-hundred-year-old (épith); **être ~** to be three hundred years old

triche○ /tʀiʃ/ *nf* **c'est de la ~** that's cheating

tricher /tʀiʃe/ [1] *vi* 1 (agir malhonnêtement) to cheat; **~ avec les chiffres** to doctor the figures; 2 (mentir) **~ sur qch** to lie about sth; **~ sur son âge** to lie about one's age; **~ sur la qualité d'un produit** to cut corners on product quality; **~ sur le poids** to give short measure; **~ sur les prix** to overcharge

tricherie /tʀiʃʀi/ *nf* 1 (action de tricher) cheating; 2 (acte trompeur) trick

tricheur, -euse /tʀiʃœʀ, øz/ *nm,f* cheat

tricolore /tʀikɔlɔʀ/ *adj* 1 (de trois couleurs) tricolour^{GB}, three-coloured^{GB} (épith); **feux ~s** traffic lights; 2 (bleu, blanc, rouge) [*écharpe, cocarde*] red, white and blue; **le drapeau ~** the tricolour^{GB}, the French flag; 3 ○(français) French; **l'équipe ~** the French team

tricorne /tʀikɔʀn/ *nm* tricorne

tricot /tʀiko/ *nm* 1 (activité) knitting; **faire du ~** to knit; **points de ~** knitting stitches; 2 (ouvrage) knitting ⊄; **mon ~** my knitting; **j'ai commencé un ~** I've started knitting something; 3 (étoffe) knitwear; **une robe en ~** a knitted dress; 4 †(pull) sweater, jumper GB; (cardigan) cardigan

(Composé) **~ de corps†** vest GB, undershirt US

tricoter /tʀikɔte/ [1]

A *vtr* to knit; **~ une écharpe à qn** to knit sb a scarf, to knit a scarf for sb; **un pull tricoté (à la) main** a handknit sweater; **robe tricotée** sweater dress, knitted dress

B *vi* to knit; **~ à la main** to hand-knit; **~ à la machine** to knit on a knitting machine; **aiguilles/machine à** ∼ knitting needles/machine

tricycle /tʀisikl/ nm tricycle

trident /tʀidɑ̃/ nm (objet) trident

tridimensionnel, -elle /tʀidimɑ̃sjɔnɛl/ adj three-dimensional

triennal, ∼e, mpl **-aux** /tʀijenal, o/ adj **1**̲ (pour trois ans) three-year (épith); **2**̲ (tous les trois ans) [exposition, vote] three-yearly (épith), triennial; [assolement] three-yearly (épith)

trier /tʀije/ [2] vtr **1**̲ (pour répartir) to sort [courrier]; **2**̲ (pour choisir) to sort [sth] out [photos, information]; to select [clientèle]

⬛Idiome ∼ **sur le volet** to handpick

trifouiller○ /tʀifuje/ [1] vi ∼ **dans** to rummage through [placard, affaires]; to tinker with [appareil, moteur]

trigonométrie /tʀigɔnɔmetʀi/ nf trigonometry

trijumeau, pl ∼**x** /tʀiʒymo/
Ⓐ adj m trigeminal
Ⓑ nm trigeminal nerve

trilingue /tʀilɛ̃g/ adj [texte, personne] trilingual

trille /tʀij/ nm **1**̲ Mus trill; **2**̲ (son) **les** ∼**s d'un oiseau** the trilling ⓒ of a bird

trillion /tʀiljɔ̃/ ▸ p. 398 nm trillion

trilogie /tʀilɔʒi/ nf trilogy

trimbal(l)er○ /tʀɛ̃bale/ [1]
Ⓐ vtr to lug [sth] around [valise, objet]; to drag [sb] around [personne]
Ⓑ **se trimbal(l)er** vpr to trail around

trimer○ /tʀime/ [1] vi to slave away; **faire** ∼ **qn** to keep sb slaving away

trimestre /tʀimɛstʀ/ nm **1**̲ Scol, Univ term; **2**̲ Fin, Pol, Écon quarter; **3**̲ (somme reçue) quarterly income; (somme payée) quarterly payment

trimestriel, -ielle /tʀimɛstʀijɛl/ adj **1**̲ Scol, Univ **examen** or **contrôle** ∼ end-of-term exam; **2**̲ [revue, numéro] quarterly; [cotisation, réunion] quarterly

trimoteur /tʀimɔtœʀ/
Ⓐ adj three-engined
Ⓑ nm three-engined plane

tringle /tʀɛ̃gl/ nf **1**̲ gén rail; ∼ **à rideaux** curtain rail, curtain rod US; ∼ **à vêtements** clothes rail, hanging rail; **2**̲ Tech rod

trinité /tʀinite/ nf (ensemble) trinity

Trinité /tʀinite/
Ⓐ nf Relig **la** ∼ the Trinity; (fête) Trinity Sunday
Ⓑ nprf ▸ p. 230, p. 303 (île) Trinidad; (État) ∼ **et Tobago** Trinidad and Tobago

⬛Idiome **à Pâques ou à la** ∼ when the cows come home

trinquer /tʀɛ̃ke/ [1] vi **1**̲ gén to clink glasses; ∼ **avec qn** lit to clink glasses with sb; fig to go drinking with sb; ∼ **à qch** to drink to sth; **trinquons à ta réussite!** let's drink to your success!; **2**̲ ○(boire avec excès) to booze○; **3**̲ ○(subir les conséquences de qch) to pay the price; (être puni) to take the rap○

trio /tʀi(j)o/ nm Mus, gén trio

triolet /tʀijɔlɛ/ nm **1**̲ Mus triplet; **2**̲ Littérat triolet

triomphal, ∼e, mpl **-aux** /tʀijɔ̃fal, o/ adj triumphant

triomphalisme /tʀijɔ̃falism/ nm triumphalism

triomphant, ∼e /tʀijɔ̃fɑ̃, ɑ̃t/ adj triumphant

triomphateur, -trice /tʀijɔ̃fatœʀ, tʀis/ nm,f triumphant victor

triomphe /tʀijɔ̃f/ nm triumph; **faire un** ∼ **à qn** to give sb a triumphal reception; **film qui remporte un** ∼ film which is having tremendous success; **avoir le** ∼ **modeste** to be modest about one's success

triompher /tʀijɔ̃fe/ [1]
Ⓐ **triompher de** vtr ind to triumph over [adversaire]; to overcome [résistance, crainte]; **la démocratie a triomphé du totalitarisme** democracy has triumphed over totalitarianism
Ⓑ vi **1**̲ (réussir) [combattant] to triumph; [artiste] to have a resounding success; [mensonge, vérité] to prevail; **2**̲ (manifester) [personne] to be triumphant ou exultant

tripartisme /tʀipaʀtism/ nm tripartite ou three-party system

tripatouiller○ /tʀipatuje/ [1] vtr **1**̲ (altérer) to fiddle about○ with, to tamper with [texte]; to fiddle○, to rig

[résultats électoraux]; **2**̲ (bricoler) to fiddle with○, to tinker with [moteur, machine]; **3**̲ (tripoter) to fiddle with○, to toy with [objet]; to paw○ [personne]

tripe /tʀip/
Ⓐ nf **1**̲ Culin tripe ⓒ; **2**̲ ○(sensibilité) **avoir la** ∼ **patriotique** to be a dyed-in-the-wool patriot; **prendre** or **saisir aux** ∼**s** to be gut-wrenching○; **chanter avec ses** ∼**s** to sing from the heart
Ⓑ **tripes** nfpl (entrailles) guts, innards; **rendre** ∼**s et boyaux**○ to be as sick as a dog, to spew up⬤

triperie /tʀipʀi/ ▸ p. 372 nf (boutique) tripe shop; (commerce) tripe trade

triphasé, -e /tʀifaze/ adj three-phase

triplace /tʀiplas/ adj three-seater

triple /tʀipl/
Ⓐ adj (before n) [rôle, objectif, détonation] triple (épith); **l'avantage est** ∼ the advantages are threefold; **en** ∼ **exemplaire** in triplicate; **avoir un livre/une photo en** ∼ to have three copies of a book/a photograph; ∼ **idiot**○! prize idiot○!
Ⓑ nm **coûter le** ∼ to cost three times as much; **son salaire est le** ∼ **du mien** he/she earns three times as much as I do

triplé, ∼e /tʀiple/
Ⓐ nm,f (enfant) triplet
Ⓑ nm Sport hat trick

triplement /tʀipləmɑ̃/
Ⓐ adv (pour trois raisons) in three respects
Ⓑ nm trebling, tripling (**de** of); ∼ **des effectifs/prix** threefold increase in staff/prices

tripler /tʀiple/ [1]
Ⓐ vtr **1**̲ (multiplier par trois) to treble [somme, quantité, prix]; to treble, to triple [épaisseur, dimension, volume]; **2**̲ (refaire à nouveau) ∼ **une classe** Scol to repeat a class GB ou grade US a second time
Ⓑ vi to treble, to increase threefold; ∼ **de** to treble in [valeur, poids, volume, taille]

triplex /tʀipleks/ nm inv **1**̲ ®(verre de sécurité) Triplex® GB, safety glass; **2**̲ (appartement) three-floor maisonette GB, triplex (apartment) US

triporteur /tʀipɔʀtœʀ/ nm delivery tricycle

tripot /tʀipo/ nm **1**̲ (maison de jeu) gambling joint○; **2**̲ (endroit mal famé) dive○

tripotée○ /tʀipɔte/ nf (ribambelle) **une** ∼ **de** hordes (pl) of, a whole slew of○ US

tripoter○ /tʀipɔte/ [1] vtr **1**̲ (caresser) pej to grope○ péj [femme, fesses]; **2**̲ (manier) (nerveusement) to fiddle with [objet, moustache]; (distraitement) to finger; **cesse de te** ∼ **le nez!** stop picking your nose!

triptyque /tʀiptik/ nm **1**̲ Art triptych; **2**̲ Littérat, Mus trilogy; **3**̲ Admin triptyque

trique /tʀik/ nf (gourdin) cudgel; **battre à coups de** ∼ to cudgel; **recevoir un coup de** ∼ to be cudgelled○ᴳᴮ

⬛Idiome **être maigre** or **sec comme un coup de** ∼ to be as thin as a rake, to be as skinny as a rail US

triréacteur /tʀiʀeaktœʀ/ nm tri-jet

trisaïeul, ∼e /tʀizajœl/ nm,f great-great-grandfather/grandmother; ∼**s** great-great-grandparents

trisannuel, -elle /tʀizanɥɛl/ adj triennial

trisomie /tʀizɔmi/ nf trisomy; ∼ **21** Down's Syndrome

trisomique /tʀizɔmik/
Ⓐ adj Méd [enfant] Down's syndrome (épith); **être** ∼ to have Down's syndrome
Ⓑ nmf Down's syndrome child

triste /tʀist/ adj **1**̲ (pas gai) [personne, visage] sad; [maison, ville, région] dreary, depressing; [ciel, temps, journée] gloomy; [histoire, livre, soirée, événement] sad, depressing; [couleur] drab, dreary; [existence] dreary; **avoir** ∼ **mine** or **faire** ∼ [personne] to look pitiful; **mon gâteau a bien** ∼ **mine** my cake is a sorry sight; **2**̲ (déplorable) [résultat, fin, affaire] dreadful; [conséquence] sad; [spectacle, état] sorry; **c'est la** ∼ **vérité** unfortunately, that's the truth of the matter; **détenir le** ∼ **record d'alcoolisme** to hold the record for heavy drinking, a dubious achievement; **faire la** ∼ **expérience de qch** to have learned about sth to one's sorrow; **se lamenter sur son** ∼ **sort** to lament one's fate; **3**̲ (méprisable) [personnage] unsavouryᴳᴮ, disreputable; [réputation] dreadful; **un** ∼ **imbécile** a despicable character; **un** ∼ **sire** a disreputable character

Idiomes ~ **comme la pluie** or **à mourir** desperately sad;
c'était pas ~○ it was quite something

tristement /tʀistəmɑ̃/ *adv* **1** (avec tristesse) [*sourire,
regarder*] sadly; [*s'habiller*] in drab colours^{GB}; **2** (de façon
regrettable) [*révélateur*] all too; **c'est ~ vrai** unfortunately, it's
only too true; **une vie ~ ordinaire** a drearily ordinary
life

tristesse /tʀistɛs/ *nf* (d'histoire, événement, de personne, musique)
sadness; (de lieu, maison, soirée) dreariness; (de ciel, temps,
journée) gloominess; **répondre/dire avec ~** to reply/to say
sadly; **c'est avec ~ que nous avons appris que** we have
learned with sorrow that; **M et Mme Vernet ont la ~ de
vous faire part du décès de leur fils Pierre** Mr and Mrs
Vernet have to inform you of the death of their son
Pierre

trithérapie /tʀiteʀapi/ *nf* triple-drug therapy

triturer /tʀityʀe/ [1] *vtr* **1** (tripoter) to twist [*mouchoir*]; to
fiddle with [*bouton*]; to knead [*pâte*]; **2** (broyer) to
grind up

Idiome **se ~ la cervelle**○ or **les méninges**○ to rack one's
brains○

trivial, ~e, *mpl* **-iaux** /tʀivjal, o/ *adj* **1** (grossier) [*manières, humour*] coarse, crude; **2** (banal) [*objet*] ordinary, everyday (épith); [*style*] mundane péj; **3** (simpliste) [*explication,
démonstration*] simplistic; **4** Math trivial

trivialité /tʀivjalite/ *nf* **1** (caractère vulgaire) coarseness,
crudeness; **2** (caractère banal) triteness, triviality; **3** (parole
banale) platitude; **4** (chose banale) triviality

troc /tʀɔk/ *nm* barter; **faire du ~** to barter; **faire un ~**○ to
do a swap○; **économie de ~** barter economy

troène /tʀɔɛn/ *nm* privet **₵**

troglodyte /tʀɔglɔdit/ *nm* **1** (homme) cave-dweller;
2 (oiseau) (winter) wren

trogne○ /tʀɔɲ/ *nf* mug○, face

trognon /tʀɔɲɔ̃/
A ○*adj inv* [*enfants*] sweet
B *nm* (de pomme, poire) core; (de salade, chou) stalk

trois /tʀwɑ/ ▸ p. 398, p. 296, p. 155 *adj inv, pron, nm inv*
three

Idiomes **être haut comme ~ pommes** to be kneehigh to a
grasshopper; **jamais deux sans ~** bad luck comes in
threes

trois-deux /tʀwɑdø/ *nm inv* Mus three-two time; **en ~** in
three-two time

trois-huit /tʀwɑɥit/ *nmpl* system (sg) of three eight-hour
shifts

troisième /tʀwazjɛm/ ▸ p. 398, p. 155
A *adj* third
B *nf* Scol fourth year of secondary school, age 14–15
Composé **le ~ âge** the elderly (+ *v pl*)

troisièmement /tʀwazjɛmmɑ̃/ *adv* thirdly

trois-mâts /tʀwɑmɑ/ *nm inv* three-master

trois-quarts /tʀwɑkaʀ/
A *adj inv* [*manches, veste*] three-quarter length
B *nm inv* **1** (manteau) three-quarter length coat; **2** (joueur de
rugby) three-quarter
C **de trois-quarts** *loc adj* [*portrait, photo*] three-quarter
length (épith)

trolleybus /tʀɔlɛbys/ *nm inv* trolley bus

trombe /tʀɔ̃b/ *nf* **1** (cyclone) waterspout; **partir en ~** to go
hurtling off; **traverser/passer en ~** to go hurtling across/
past; **2** (averse) **~s d'eau** downpour **₵**

trombine○ /tʀɔ̃bin/ *nf* mug○, face

trombone /tʀɔ̃bɔn/ *nm* **1** ▸ p. 389 (instrument) trombone;
~ à coulisse/à pistons slide/valve trombone; **2** ▸ p. 372
(musicien) trombonist, trombone player; **3** (de bureau)
paperclip

trompe /tʀɔ̃p/ *nf* **1** Zool (d'éléphant) trunk; (d'insecte, de
mollusque) proboscis; **2** ▸ p. 389 Mus horn
Composé **~ d'Eustache** Eustachian tube

trompe-la-mort /tʀɔ̃plamɔʀ/ *nmf inv* daredevil

trompe-l'œil /tʀɔ̃plœj/ *nm inv* **1** Art trompe l'oeil;
paysage/façade en ~ trompe l'oeil landscape/façade;
2 (ce qui fait illusion) smokescreen

tromper /tʀɔ̃pe/ [1]
A *vtr* **1** (duper) [*personne*] to deceive; **~ les électeurs** to mislead the voters; **il y a des signes** or **gestes qui ne trompent**

---

trop

trop, adverbe modifiant un verbe, se traduit par *too
much*. Il se traduit par *too* lorsqu'il modifie un adjectif,
un adverbe. Dans le cas d'expressions comme *avoir
soif/faim/chaud* traduites par *to be* + adjectif, il se
traduit par *too*:

j'ai trop froid, je rentre
= I'm too cold, I'm going home

Voir exemples supplémentaires et exceptions en **A**.

trop de, déterminant indéfini, se traduit par *too many*
lorsqu'il est suivi d'un nom dénombrable:

trop de livres   **trop d'idées**
= too many books   = too many ideas

et par *too much* lorsqu'il est suivi d'un nom non
dénombrable:

trop de travail
= too much work

Attention, certains mots dénombrables français ne le
sont pas en anglais et réciproquement:

trop de meubles   **trop de monde**
= too much furniture   = too many people

Voir exemples supplémentaires et exceptions en **B**.

---

pas there's no mistaking the signs; **~ l'ennemi** to deceive
ou trick the enemy; **2** (faire des infidélités à) to be unfaithful
to, to deceive [*mari, femme*]; **3** (échapper à) **~ la vigilance** or
surveillance de qn to slip past sb's guard; **~ la défense/le
gardien de but** to trick the defence^{GB}/the goalkeeper;
4 (faire diversion à) to stave off; **~ la faim** to stave off
hunger
B **se tromper** *vpr* **1** (mentalement) to be mistaken; **se ~ sur
qn** to be wrong about sb; **je me suis trompé sur leurs
intentions** I misunderstood their intentions; **si je ne me
trompe** if I'm not mistaken; **il ne faut pas s'y ~, qu'on ne
s'y trompe pas** make no mistake about it; **2** (concrètement)
to make a mistake; **se ~ de deux euros** to be two euros
out GB *ou* off US; **se ~ de bus** to take the wrong bus; **se
~ de jour** to get the day wrong; **se ~ de bâtiment** to get
the wrong building

tromperie /tʀɔ̃pʀi/ *nf* deceit **₵**

trompette¹ /tʀɔ̃pɛt/ ▸ p. 372 *nm* (dans un orchestre) trumpet
(player); (dans l'armée) bugler; (dans une fanfare) trumpeter

trompette² /tʀɔ̃pɛt/ ▸ p. 389 *nf* trumpet

trompettiste /tʀɔ̃petist/ ▸ p. 372 *nmf* trumpet (player)

trompeur, -euse /tʀɔ̃pœʀ, øz/ *adj* [*promesse, chiffre*] misleading; [*distance, apparence*] deceptive

tronc /tʀɔ̃/ *nm* **1** (fût) (d'arbre) trunk; (de colonne) shaft; **un
~ d'arbre** a tree-trunk; **2** (partie du corps) trunk, torso;
3 (dans une église) collection box
Composé **~ commun** (d'espèces, de langues) common origin;
(de disciplines) (common) core curriculum

tronche○ /tʀɔ̃ʃ/ *nf* mug○, face

tronçon /tʀɔ̃sɔ̃/ *nm* section

tronçonneuse /tʀɔ̃sɔnøz/ *nf* chain saw

trône /tʀon/ *nm* throne; **monter sur le ~** to come to the
throne

trôner /tʀone/ [1] *vi* **le professeur trônait au milieu de ses
étudiants** the professor was holding court among his/her
students; **~ sur** [*vase, photo*] to have pride of place on
[*cheminée*]

tronquer /tʀɔ̃ke/ [1] *vtr* to truncate [*texte, déclaration*]

trop /tʀo/ ▸ p. 483
A *adv* **1** (indiquant un excès) (modifiant un adjectif ou un adverbe) too;
(modifiant un verbe) too much; **j'ai ~ mangé/bu** I've had too
much to eat/to drink; **j'ai ~ dormi** I've slept too long; **tu
travailles ~** you work too hard; **ça c'est ~ fort**○! that's
(just) too much!; **nous sommes ~** there are too
many of us; **nous sommes ~ peu nombreux** there are too
few of us; **ce serait ~ beau!** I/you/we etc should be so
lucky!; **c'est ~ bête!** how stupid!; **~ enthousiaste** overenthusiastic; **on n'est jamais ~ prudent** you can't be too

careful; **tu en as ∼ dit** you've already said too much; **elle en fait (un peu) ∼** she overdoes it (a bit); **c'en est ∼!** that's the end!; **'tu aimes la viande?'—'pas ∼'** 'do you like meat?'—'not terribly' *ou* 'not very much'; **nous ne serons pas ∼ de deux** it'll take at least two of us; **je ne le connais que ∼** I know him only too well; **faire qch sans ∼ y croire** to do sth without really believing in it; **∼ c'est ∼!** enough is enough!; **2** (employé avec valeur de superlatif) **∼ mignon** too sweet *ou* cute○; **c'était ∼ drôle** it was so funny; **ça ne va pas ∼ mal, merci** not so bad, thanks; **je n'en sais ∼ rien**○ I don't really know; **ça ne me dit ∼ rien**○ I don't really feel like it; **3** ○(incroyable) **il est ∼, lui!** he's too much○!; **c'est ∼, ça!** that's incredible!

B **trop de** *dét indéf* **1** (avec nom dénombrable) too many; **il y a ∼ de choses à faire** there's too much to do; **2** (avec nom non dénombrable) too much; **∼ de pression** too much pressure; **∼ de monde** too many people

C **de trop, en trop** *loc adv* **il y a une assiette en ∼** there's one plate too many; **j'ai dix kilos de bagages en ∼** my luggage is ten kilos over the limit; **j'ai quelques kilos en ∼** I'm a few kilos overweight; **si tu as du tissu en ∼ tu peux faire un coussin** if you have some material left over, you can make a cushion; **il y a 12 euros de ∼** there's 12 euros too much; **sa remarque était de ∼** his/her remark was uncalled for; **se sentir de ∼** to feel one is in the way

D **par trop** *loc adv* = **trop**

trophée /tʀɔfe/ *nm* trophy

tropical, ∼e, *mpl* **-aux** /tʀɔpikal, o/ *adj* tropical

trop-perçu, *pl* **∼s** /tʀɔpɛʀsy/ *nm* **1** (d'argent) excess payment; **2** (d'impôts) overpayment of tax; **remboursement d'un ∼** tax refund

trop-plein, *pl* **∼s** /tʀɔplɛ̃/ *nm* **1** (excès) excess; **avoir un ∼ d'énergie** to have excess energy; **2** Tech (de lavabo, baignoire) overflow

troquer /tʀɔke/ [1] *vtr* **1** Comm to trade (**contre** for), to barter (**contre** for); **2** (échanger) **∼ qch contre** *or* **pour qch** to exchange *ou* swap sth for sth

troquet○ /tʀɔkɛ/ *nm* bar

trot /tʀo/ *nm* (de cheval) trot; **au ∼!** lit trot on!; fig at the double GB, on the double US

trotte○ /tʀɔt/ *nf* fair walk; **ça fait une ∼** it's a fair walk, it's quite a walk

trotter /tʀɔte/ [1] *vi* **1** (cheval, cavalier) to trot; **2** (aller à petits pas) (adulte, souris) to scurry (about); (enfant) to toddle along; **∼ dans la tête** (pensée) to go through one's mind; (musique) to go through one's head

trotteur /tʀɔtœʀ/ *nm* **1** (cheval) trotter; **2** (chaussure) shoe with a low, broad heel

trotteuse /tʀɔtøz/ *nf* (de montre, chronomètre) second hand

trottiner /tʀɔtine/ [1] *vi* **1** (cheval) to jog; **2** (personne, souris) to scurry along

trottinette /tʀɔtinɛt/ *nf* scooter

trottoir /tʀɔtwaʀ/ *nm* pavement GB, sidewalk US; **le bord du ∼** the kerb GB *ou* curb US

(Composé) **∼ roulant** moving pavement GB, moving sidewalk US

(Idiome) **faire le ∼**○ to be on the game○ GB, to be a hooker○

trou /tʀu/ *nm* **1** gén hole; **faire son ∼**○ (personne) to carve out a niche for oneself; **faire un ∼ à la perceuse** to drill a hole; **2** (lacune) gap; **j'ai un ∼ dans mon emploi du temps** gén I have a gap in my timetable; Scol I have a free period; **3** ○(déficit) deficit, shortfall; **un ∼ dans le budget** a budget deficit, a shortfall in the budget; **4** ○(petite localité) **∼ (perdu)** dump○, god-forsaken place; **il n'est jamais sorti de son ∼** he's never been out of his own backyard; **5** ◑(prison) prison, nick○

(Composés) **∼ d'air** air pocket; **∼ de mémoire** memory lapse; **∼ noir** black hole; **∼ normand** glass of spirits between courses to aid digestion; **∼ de serrure** keyhole; **∼ du souffleur** prompt box

(Idiome) **ne pas avoir les yeux en face des ∼s**○ not to be able to see straight

troublant, ∼e /tʀublɑ̃, ɑ̃t/ *adj* (problème, anecdote) disturbing; (coïncidence, fait) disconcerting; (décolleté) that stirs desire (après a)

trouble /tʀubl/
A *adj* **1** (pas transparent) (eau, vin) cloudy; (verres, vitres)

smudgy; **2** (flou) (image, photo) blurred; (contours) vague, blurred; **3** (équivoque) (sentiment) confused; (louche) (affaire, milieu) shady

B *adv* **je vois ∼** (temporaire) my eyes are blurred; (permanent) I have blurred vision

C *nm* **1** (insécurité) unrest; **2** (mésentente, malaise) **jeter le ∼** to stir up trouble; **jeter le ∼ dans les esprits** to sow confusion in people's minds; **3** (confusion) confusion; (gêne) embarrassment; **dominer son ∼** to overcome one's confusion; **4** (émoi) emotion; **ressentir un ∼** to feel an emotion; **5** Méd disorder; **de légers ∼s gastriques** minor gastric problems; **∼s de la mémoire** memory problems

D **troubles** *nmpl* Pol unrest **⊄**, disturbances; **∼s ethniques** ethnic unrest

(Composés) **∼ musculo-squelettique, TMS** Méd musculo-skeletal injury, MSI, RSI

trouble-fête /tʀublǝfɛt/ *nmf inv* spoilsport

troubler /tʀuble/ [1]
A *vtr* **1** (brouiller) to make [sth] cloudy, to cloud [eau, vin]; to blur [vue, image]; **2** (déranger) to disturb [silence, sommeil, personne]; to disrupt [réunion, spectacle]; **∼ l'ordre public** (individu) to cause a breach of the peace; [groupe d'insurgés] to disturb the peace; **en ces temps troublés** in these troubled times; **3** (déconcerter) to disconcert [accusé, candidat]; **quelque chose me trouble** (rendre perplexe) something's bothering *ou* puzzling me; **4** (mettre en émoi) liter to disturb euph [personne]

B **se troubler** *vpr* **1** (perdre contenance) [personne, accusé] to become flustered; **2** (devenir trouble) [liquide] to become cloudy, to cloud; **ma vue se troubla** my eyes became blurred

trouée /tʀue/ *nf* **1** (ouverture) gap, opening; **2** Mil breach

trouer /tʀue/ [1] *vtr* **1** (perforer) (d'un trou) to make a hole in; (de plusieurs trous) to make holes in; **∼ un drap avec une cigarette** to make *ou* burn a hole in a sheet with a cigarette; **j'ai troué mes chaussures** (à la longue) I've worn holes in my shoes; **chaussettes ∼es** socks with holes in them; **2** (transpercer) (lumière, cri) to pierce [nuit]

(Idiome) **∼ la peau à qn** to put a bullet in sb○

troufion○ /tʀufjɔ̃/ *nm* soldier

trouillard◑, **∼e** /tʀujaʀ, aʀd/
A *adj* cowardly
B *nm,f* chicken○, coward

trouille /tʀuj/ *nf* fear; **avoir la ∼** to be scared; **flanquer la ∼ à qn** to scare sb, to give sb a fright

troupe /tʀup/ *nf* **1** Mil troops (pl); **la ∼** (l'armée) the army; (les simples soldats) the rank and file, the troops (pl); **2** Théât company; (qui voyage) troupe; **3** (groupe) (d'éléphants, de cerfs) herd; (de moutons, d'oiseaux) flock; (de touristes) troop; (d'enfants) band

troupeau, *pl* **∼x** /tʀupo/ *nm* **1** (d'éléphants, de bisons, vaches, cerfs) herd; (de moutons, chèvres) flock; (d'oies) gaggle; **2** (de personnes) pej herd; **3** Relig flock

trousse /tʀus/ *nf* **1** (pochette) (little) case; **2** (contenu) kit

(Composés) **∼ d'écolier** pencil case; **∼ de maquillage** make-up bag; **∼ de médecin** doctor's bag; **∼ à outils** tool kit; **∼ de secours** first-aid kit; **∼ de toilette** toilet bag

(Idiome) **être aux ∼s de qn** to be hot on sb's heels

trousseau, *pl* **∼x** /tʀuso/ *nm* **1** (de clés) bunch; **2** (de mariée) trousseau; (d'enfant) clothes (pl)

trouvaille /tʀuvaj/ *nf* **1** (découverte) find; (invention) invention; **2** (idée originale) bright idea, brainwave

trouvé, ∼e /tʀuve/
A *pp* ▸ **trouver**
B *pp adj* **réplique bien ∼e** neat riposte; **tout ∼** [réponse, solution, prétexte] ready-made; [coupable, candidat] obvious; **vous êtes la personne toute ∼e pour ce travail** you're the very person we need for the job

trouver /tʀuve/ [1]
A *vtr* **1** (par hasard) to find; **c'est surprenant de vous ∼ ici!** I'm surprised to find you here!; **on trouve de tout ici** they have everything here; **∼ qch par hasard** to come across sth; **2** (en cherchant) to find; **veuillez ∼ ci-joint...** (dans une lettre) please find enclosed...; **j'ai trouvé!** I've got it!; **tu as trouvé ça tout seul?** iron did you work that all by yourself?; **si tu continues tu vas me ∼!**○ I don't push your luck○!; **il va ∼ à qui parler** he's going to be for it○; **∼ du**

plaisir à faire to get pleasure out of doing; **il ne nous reste plus qu'à ~ le financement** all we have to do now is get financial backing; **3)** (voir) to find; **~ qch dans un état lamentable** to find sth in an appalling state; **ils sont tous venus me ~ après le cours** they all came to see me after the class; **je vais aller ~ le responsable du rayon** I'm going to go and see the head of the department; **4)** (estimer) **~ qn gentil/pénible** to think sb is nice/tiresome; **je trouve ça bizarre/drôle** I think it's strange/funny, I find it strange/funny; **comment trouves-tu mon ami?** what do you think of my friend?, how do you like my friend?; **j'ai trouvé bon de vous prévenir** I thought it right to warn you; **~ un intérêt à qch** to find sth interesting; **elle ne me trouve que des défauts** she only sees my faults; **je me demande ce qu'elle lui trouve!** I wonder what she sees in him/her!; **elle m'a trouvé bonne mine** she thought I looked well; **je te trouve bien calme, qu'est-ce que tu as?** you're very quiet, what's the matter?; **tu trouves?** do you think so?; **5)** (imaginer) to come up with [raison, excuse, moyen, produit]; **~ à s'occuper** to find sth to do; **~ à redire** to find fault; **~ le moyen de faire** lit, iron to manage to do; **il n'a rien trouvé de mieux que de le leur répéter!** iron he would have to go and tell them!

B se trouver vpr **1)** (être situé) to be; **se ~ à Rome** to be in Rome; **le sommaire se trouve page 11** the table of contents is on page 11; **se ~ confronté à de grosses difficultés** to have run into major problems; **2)** (se sentir) to feel; **se ~ mal à l'aise quelque part** to feel uneasy somewhere; **se ~ bien quelque part** to be happy somewhere; **j'ai failli me ~ mal** I nearly passed out; **3)** (se considérer) **il se ~ beau** he thinks he's good-looking; **4)** (se procurer) to find [raison, excuse, motif]; **trouve-toi une occupation** find yourself something to do; **elle s'est trouvé un petit ami** she's found herself a boyfriend

C v impers **il se trouve que je le connais** I happen to know him; **il se trouve qu'elle ne leur avait rien dit** as it happened, she hadn't told them anything; **ça s'est trouvé comme ça**○ it just happened that way; **si ça se trouve**○ **ça te plaira** you might like it

truand /tʀyɑ̃/ nm **1)** (membre de la pègre) gangster, mobster; **2)** (escroc) crook

trublion /tʀyblijɔ̃/ nm troublemaker

truc /tʀyk/ nm **1)** ○(procédé) knack; **avoir un ~ pour gagner de l'argent** to know a good way of making money; **ça y est, j'ai pigé le ~** that's it, I've got it; **2)** ○(chose) thing; (dont on a oublié le nom) thingummy○, whatsit○; **passe-moi le ~ qui est sur la table** pass me the thingummy ou whatsit○ on the table; **3)** ○(fait quelconque) thing; **il y a un ~ qui ne va pas** there's something wrong; **je viens juste de penser à un ~** I've just thought of something; **le vélo, c'est pas mon ~**○ cycling's not my thing; **moi, mon ~ c'est les vacances à la campagne** what I love is a holiday GB ou vacation US in the country; **4)** (savoir-faire) trick; **un ~ du métier** a trick of the trade; **y a un ~**○ there's a trick to it; **5)** (personne) what's-his-name/what's-her-name, thingy○

trucage /tʀykaʒ/ nm **1)** Cin, Théât special effect; **2)** (de comptes, dossier) doctoring; (d'élections) rigging, fixing

truchement /tʀyʃmɑ̃/ nm (intermédiaire) liter **par le ~ de qch** through sth; **par le ~ de qn** through the intervention of sb

truculence /tʀykylɑ̃s/ nf earthiness

truculent, ~e /tʀykylɑ̃, ɑ̃t/ adj earthy

truelle /tʀyɛl/ nf trowel

truffe /tʀyf/ nf **1)** (champignon, chocolat) truffle; **2)** (de chien) nose

truffer /tʀyfe/ [1] vtr **1)** Culin to stuff [sth] with truffles [pâté, dinde]; **2)** (remplir) **il a truffé son discours de citations** he crammed his speech with quotations; **la pièce était truffée de micros** the room was full of bugging devices; **ta lettre est truffée de fautes** your letter is riddled with mistakes

truie /tʀɥi/ nf sow

truite /tʀɥit/ nf trout

truquage = trucage

truquer /tʀyke/ [1] vtr **1)** (altérer) to fiddle○ [comptes, résultats]; to doctor [dossier, déclaration]; **2)** Jeux to mark [cartes]; **3)** (fausser) to fix, to rig [enquête, élections, match]; **un combat truqué** a rigged fight

trust /tʀœst/ nm (groupement) trust; (entreprise puissante) trust, cartel; **loi anti-~** anti-trust law

tsar /tsaʀ/ nm tsar, czar

tsigane = tzigane

TTC written abbr ▸ **taxe**

tu /ty/ pron pers **1)** gén you; **~ es en retard** you're late; **2)** Relig you, thou‡

(Idiome) **être à ~ et à toi avec qn** to be on familiar terms with sb, to be pally○ with sb

tuant○, **~e** /tɥɑ̃, ɑ̃t/ adj exhausting

tuba /tyba/ nm **1)** ▸ p. 389 Mus tuba; **2)** Sport snorkel

tubage /tybaʒ/ nm **1)** Méd intubation; **2)** (de forage) (well) casing

tube /tyb/

A nm **1)** (objet cylindrique) tube; (tuyau) pipe; **2)** (contenant) tube; **3)** ○(chanson à succès) hit; **4)** (lampe) fluorescent light, lamp

B à pleins tubes○ loc adv **mettre le son à pleins ~s** to turn the sound right up○; **faire passer un disque à pleins ~s** to play a record at full blast; **déconner**○ **à pleins ~s** (faire des erreurs) to do really stupid things; (dire des bêtises) to talk a load of rubbish○

(Composés) **~ cathodique** cathode ray tube; **~ digestif** digestive tract; **~ à essai** test tube; **~ au néon** fluorescent light; **~ de rouge à lèvres** lipstick

tubercule /tybɛʀkyl/ nm **1)** Bot tuber; **2)** Anat tuberosity; **3)** Méd tubercle

tuberculeux, -euse /tybɛʀkylø, øz/

A adj [patient] tubercular

B nm,f TB ou tuberculosis sufferer

tuberculose /tybɛʀkyloz/ ▸ p. 195 nf tuberculosis, TB

tubulaire /tybylɛʀ/ adj tubular

tubulure /tybylyʀ/ nf **1)** Tech (ensemble des tubes) tubing; (orifice) connection piece, neck; **2)** (conduit) pipe

TUC /tyk/ nmpl (abbr = **travaux d'utilité collective**) paid community service (for the young unemployed)

tué /tɥe/ nm person killed; **sept ~s, cinq blessés** seven people killed, five injured

tuer /tɥe/ [1]

A vtr **1)** (faire périr) lit to kill [personne, animal, plante]; fig to kill [commerce, initiative]; **l'alcool tue** alcohol kills; **tu ne tueras point** Bible thou shalt not kill; **elle a été tuée d'une balle dans la tête** she was shot in the head and killed; **six personnes ont été tuées par balles** six people were shot dead; **~ qn à coups de bâton** to beat sb to death; **2)** ○(épuiser) **les enfants m'ont tuée ce matin** the children have worn me out ou run me ragged○ this morning; **tu sais, quelquefois tu me tues!** I think you'll be the death of me!

B se tuer vpr **1)** (trouver la mort) [personne] to be killed; **se ~ en voiture** to be killed in a car accident; **il s'est tué en tombant d'un toit** he fell to his death from a roof; **2)** (se suicider) to kill oneself; **3)** ○(s'épuiser) **se ~ au travail** or **à la tâche** to work oneself to death; **se ~ à faire** to kill oneself doing; **je me tue à te le dire** I've told you a thousand times

(Idiome) **~ le temps** to kill time

tuerie /tyʀi/ nf killings (pl)

tue-tête: à tue-tête /atytɛt/ loc adv [chanter, crier] at the top of one's voice

tueur, -euse /tɥœʀ, øz/

A adj [cellule] killer

B nm,f **1)** (assassin) killer; **2)** ▸ p. 372 (ouvrier d'abattoir) slaughterman/slaughterwoman

(Composés) **~ à gages** hired ou professional killer; **~ en série** serial killer

tuile /tɥil/ nf **1)** Constr tile; **2)** ○(événement fâcheux) blow; **tu parles d'une ~!** what a blow!

(Composé) **~ aux amandes** Culin almond biscuit

tulipe /tylip/ nf **1)** Bot tulip; **2)** (lampe) tulip-shaped lamp

tulipier /tylipje/ nm tulip tree

tuméfier /tymefje/ [2] vtr to make [sth] swell up [partie du corps]; **avoir les paupières tuméfiées** to have swollen eyelids

tumeur /tymœʀ/ nf tumour GB

tumulte /tymylt/ nm **1)** (désordre bruyant) uproar; **s'achever dans le ~** to end in uproar; **2)** (agitation) turmoil

tumultueux, -euse /tymyltɥø, øz/ adj [période, journée] turbulent; [vie, jeunesse] tempestuous; [relations, entrevue] stormy

tumulus /tymylys/ nm inv burial mound, tumulus spéc

tunique /tynik/ nf ① (vêtement) tunic; ② Anat tunic, tunica spéc

tunnel /tynɛl/ nm tunnel; **le ~ sous la Manche** the Channel Tunnel

(Idiome) **voir le bout du ~** to see light at the end of the tunnel

turban /tyʀbɑ̃/ nm turban

turbin○ /tyʀbɛ̃/ nm daily grind○, work; **aller au ~** to go to work

turbine /tyʀbin/ nf turbine

turboréacteur /tyʀboʀeaktœʀ/ nm turbojet (engine)

turbot /tyʀbo/ nm turbot

turbulence /tyʀbylɑ̃s/ nf ① (tourbillon) turbulence ¢; **zone de ~s** area of turbulence; ② (indiscipline) unruliness; (agitation) unrest ¢

turbulent, ~e /tyʀbylɑ̃, ɑ̃t/ adj [enfant] unruly; [classe] rowdy, unruly; [vie] tempestuous; [adolescent, région, ville] rebellious

turc, turque /tyʀk/ ▸ p. 336, p. 392

A adj Turkish; **toilettes** or **WC à la turque** hole-in-the-ground toilet

B nm Ling Turkish

turfiste /tœʀfist/ nmf racegoer, punter○ GB

turlupiner○ /tyʀlypine/ [1] vtr [idée, problème] to bother, to bug○

turpitude /tyʀpityd/ nf ① (caractère) turpitude sout, depravity; ② (acte) base act; (parole) low remark

turque ▸ **turc**

Turquie /tyʀki/ ▸ p. 230 nprf Turkey

turquoise /tyʀkwaz/ ▸ p. 140 adj inv, nf turquoise

tutelle /tytɛl/ nf ① Jur (d'enfant, adulte) guardianship, tutelage; **placer qn sous ~** to place sb in the care of a guardian; ② Admin ≈ supervision; **autorité de ~** supervision authority; ③ (en droit international) **(régime de) ~** trusteeship; **territoire sous ~** trust territory; ④ (dépendance) supervision, domination

tuteur, -trice /tytœʀ, tʀis/

A nmf ① Jur guardian; ② ▸ p. 372 Scol, Univ tutor

B nm Bot stake, support

tutoiement /tytwamɑ̃/ nm use of the form 'tu'

tutorat /tytɔʀa/ nm ① Scol, Univ tutorial system; ② Jur system of guardianship

tutoyer /tytwaje/ [23]

A vtr to address [sb] using the 'tu' form; fig to be on familiar terms with [auteurs classiques]

B **se tutoyer** vpr to address one another using the 'tu' form

tutu /tyty/ nm tutu

tuyau, pl **~x** /tɥijo/ nm ① Tech pipe; ② ○(information) tip○; **un ~ crevé** a lousy tip

(Composés) **~ d'arrosage** hose; **~ de cheminée** flue; **~ d'échappement** exhaust; **~ de poêle** stovepipe

tuyauterie /tɥijotʀi/ nf ① Tech piping ¢; ② Mus pipes (pl)

TVA /tevea/ nf (abbr = **taxe à la valeur ajoutée**) VAT

tympan /tɛ̃pɑ̃/ nm eardrum

type /tip/

A nm ① (genre) type, kind; **les emplois de ce ~ sont rares** jobs of this kind are rare; **un climat de ~ tropical** a tropical-type climate; ② (représentant) (classic) example; **elle est le ~ même de la femme d'affaires** she's the classic example of a business woman; ③ (modèle) type, kind; **un avion d'un ~ nouveau** a new type of plane; ④ (caractères physiques) type; **il a le ~ nordique** he is the Nordic type; **ce n'est pas mon ~** he's/she's not my type; ⑤ ○(homme) guy○, chap○; **quel sale ~!** what a swine○ ou bastard●!; **c'est un chic ~** he's a really nice guy○; **un brave ~** a nice chap○; **un pauvre ~** a pathetic individual

B **(-)type** (in compounds) typical, classic; **l'intellectuel(-)~** the typical intellectual; **l'exemple(-)~** the typical example; **un cas(-)~ de schizophrénie** a classic case of schizophrenia; **le formulaire(-)~** the standard application form

typer /tipe/ [1] vtr [auteur, dramaturge] to portray [sb] as a type [personnage]; [acteur] to play [sb] as a type [personnage]

typhoïde /tifɔid/ ▸ p. 195 nf typhoid fever

typhon /tifɔ̃/ nm typhoon

typhus /tifys/ ▸ p. 195 nm inv typhus

typique /tipik/ adj ① (caractéristique) typical; ② (pittoresque) controv [sculpture, village] typical

typiquement /tipikmɑ̃/ adv typically; **une famille ~ américaine** a typically American family

typographe /tipɔgʀaf/ ▸ p. 372 nmf typographer

typographie /tipɔgʀafi/ nf typography

typographique /tipɔgʀafik/ adj typographical; **erreur ~** typographical ou printer's error, misprint

typologie /tipɔlɔʒi/ nf typology

tyran /tiʀɑ̃/ nm tyrant; **~ domestique** domestic tyrant

tyrannie /tiʀani/ nf tyranny; **subir la ~ de qn/qch** to be tyrannized by sb/sth

tyrannique /tiʀanik/ adj tyrannical

tyranniser /tiʀanize/ [1] vtr to tyrannize

tzigane /dzigan, tsigan/

A adj, nmf gypsy

B ▸ p. 336 nm Ling Romany

t

Uu

u, U /y/ *nm inv* u, U; **en (forme de) U** U-shaped

ubiquité /ybikɥite/ *nf* ubiquity sout; **je n'ai pas le don d'~!** I can't be everywhere at once!

UDF /ydeɛf/ *nf* (*abbr* = **Union pour la démocratie française**) *French political party of the centre right*

UE /yə/ *nf* ▸ **union**

ukrainien, -ienne /ykʀɛnjɛ̃, ɛn/ ▸ p. 392, p. 336
A *adj* Ukrainian
B *nm* Ling Ukrainian

ulcère /ylsɛʀ/ ▸ p. 195 *nm* ulcer

ulcérer /ylseʀe/ [14] *vtr* **1** (outrer) [*propos, comportement*] to sicken; **2** Méd to ulcerate [*tissu, organe*]

ULM /yɛlɛm/ ▸ p. 327 *nm inv* (*abbr* = **ultraléger motorisé**) (engin) microlight; (sport) microlighting

ultérieur, ~e /ylteʀjœʀ/ *adj* subsequent; **une date ~e** a later date

ultérieurement /ylteʀjœʀmɑ̃/ *adv* **1** (par la suite) subsequently; **2** (plus tard) later

ultimatum /yltimatɔm/ *nm* ultimatum; **lancer un ~ à qn** to present sb with an ultimatum

ultime /yltim/ *adj* **1** (dernier d'une série) final; **2** (suprême) ultimate; **3** Ling ultimate

ultra /yltʀa/
A *adj* [*groupe*] extremist
B *nmf* **1** Pol extremist; **2** Hist ultraroyalist

ultraconfidentiel, -ielle /yltʀakɔ̃fidɑ̃sjɛl/ *adj* top secret

ultragauche /yltʀagoʃ/ *nf* Pol **l'~** the radical leftists (*pl*)

ultraléger, -ère /yltʀaleʒe, ɛʀ/ *adj* [*matériau, cigarette*] ultra light; [*équipement, tissu*] very light

ultramoderne /yltʀamɔdɛʀn/ *adj* [*maison*] ultra modern; [*technique, système, matériel*] state-of-the-art (*épith*)

ultrarapide /yltʀaʀapid/ *adj* high-speed (*épith*)

ultrasecret, -ète /yltʀasəkʀɛ, ɛt/ *adj* top secret

ultrasensible /yltʀasɑ̃sibl/ *adj* [*personne*] hypersensitive; [*appareil, film*] ultrasensitive; [*problème, donnée*] highly sensitive

ultrason /yltʀasɔ̃/ *nm* ultrasound ¢

ultraviolet /yltʀavjɔlɛ/ *nm* Phys ultraviolet ray; **séance d'~s** (en soins du corps) session on a sunbed

ululer /ylyle/ [1] *vi* to hoot

un, une¹ /œ̃(n), yn/ ▸ p. 398, p. 296
A *art indéf* (*pl* **des**) **1** (au singulier) a, an; **avec ~ sang-froid remarquable** with remarkable self-control; **il n'a pas dit ~ mot** he didn't say a *ou* one word; **il n'y avait pas ~ arbre** there wasn't a single tree; **~ chien est plus docile qu'~ chat** dogs are more docile than cats; **~ jour, je t'en parlerai** I'll tell you about it one day; **2** (au pluriel) **il y avait des mille-pattes et des scorpions** there were millipedes and scorpions; **il y a des gens qui ne comprennent jamais rien** there are some people who never understand anything; **les invités avaient déjà défait leur cravate** some guests had already loosened their ties; **3** (en emphase) **il fait ~ froid** *or* **~ de ces froids!** it's so cold!; **elle m'a donné une de ces gifles!** she gave me such a slap!
B *pron* (*pl* **uns, unes**) gén one; **(l')~ d'entre** *or* **de nous** one of us; **(l')~ des meilleurs** one of the best; **~ de ces jours** *or* **quatre°** one of these days; **les ~s pensent que...** some think that...
C *adj* one, a (*devant une consonne*), an (*devant une voyelle*);

---

un

Emploi et prononciation de *a* et *an*

On emploie a /ə/ devant les consonnes, les h aspirés et les semi-consonnes /j/, /w/ (dans *a university, a one-eyed man*), et an /ən/ devant les voyelles et h muets (*hour, honest, heir*).

un = pronom

L'emploi de *un* en corrélation avec *autre* est traité sous **autre**. Voir aussi **chose, comme**, ainsi que les verbes avec lesquels le pronom se substitue familièrement à un groupe nominal comme **coller** – *en coller un*, **placer** – *en placer une* etc.

un = adjectif numéral

En général, *un*, adjectif numéral, se traduit indifféremment par *a ou* one:

j'ai un garçon et deux filles
= I have a (*ou* one) boy and two girls

En revanche *un* se traduit par *one* quand on veut insister sur le nombre. Ainsi, on dira:

il ne reste qu'une pomme (*pas deux*)
= there's only one apple left

mais:

il ne reste qu'une pomme (*pas d'autres fruits*)
= there's only an apple left

j'ai un frère et deux sœurs (*nous sommes quatre enfants*)
= I have one brother and two sisters

mais:

j'ai un frère qui est informaticien (*j'ai d'autres frères*)
= I have a brother who is a computer scientist

ça coûte une livre
= it costs a pound *ou* it costs one pound

mais:

ça coûte une livre cinquante
= it costs one pound fifty

cela a pris une heure
= it took an hour *ou* it took one hour

mais:

il est une heure
= it is one o'clock

---

trente et une personnes ont été blessées thirty-one people were injured; **ici, il pleut ~ jour sur deux** it rains every other day here
D *nm,f* one; **il y en a ~ par personne** there's one each; **les deux villes n'en font plus qu'une** the two cities have merged into one; **~ à** *ou* **par ~** one by one
E °*adv* firstly, for one thing: **~, je fais ce que je veux et deux ça ne te regarde pas!** firstly, I do what I like and secondly it's none of your business!

F nm ① (nombre) one; ~, **deux, trois, partez!** one, two, three, go!; ② (valeur ordinale) **page/scène** ~ page/scene one; ③ fig **elle ne faisait qu'~ avec sa machine** she and her machine were as one

(Idiomes) **s'en jeter** ~ (derrière la cravate)○ to knock back a drink○; **il est menteur comme pas** ~ he's the biggest liar; ~ **pour tous et tous pour** ~ all for one and one for all; ▸ **dix**

unanime /ynanim/ adj unanimous (**à faire** in doing)

unanimement /ynanimmɑ̃/ adv ① (en politique) unanimously; ② fig universally; **il est** ~ **célébré comme un grand écrivain** he is universally hailed as a great writer

unanimité /ynanimite/ nf unanimity; **à l'~** unanimously; **il a été élu à l'~ moins deux voix** he was elected with only two votes against; **faire l'~** to have unanimous support ou backing (**parmi** from)

une² /yn/
A art indéf, pron, adj ▸ **un A, B, C, D**
B nf **la** ~ the front page; **être à la** ~ to be in the headlines, to be on the front page

UNESCO /ynesko/ nf (abbr = **United Nations Educational, Scientific and Cultural Organization**) UNESCO

uni, ~**e** /yni/
A pp ▸ **unir**
B pp adj [communauté, famille] close-knit; [amis, couple] close; [peuple, militants] united (**dans** in)
C adj ① (d'une teinte) [tissu, couleur] plain; ② (sans aspérité) [surface] smooth, even; [mer] calm
D nm **porter de l'~** to wear plain colours[GB]

unicellulaire /yniselylɛʁ/ adj unicellular

unicité /ynisite/ nf uniqueness

unidimensionnel, -**elle** /ynidimɑ̃sjɔnɛl/ adj unidimensional

unidirectionnel, -**elle** /ynidiʁɛksjɔnɛl/ adj Télécom [émetteur] unidirectional; [récepteur] one-way

unième /ynjɛm/ ▸ p. 398, p. 155 adj first; **vingt et** ~ twenty-first

unification /ynifikasjɔ̃/ nf unification

unifier /ynifje/ [2]
A vtr ① (rassembler) to unify [pays, forces,]; ② (homogénéiser) to standardize [procédure]
B s'**unifier** vpr [pays, groupes] to unite

uniforme /ynifɔʁm/
A adj [paysage, maisons, mouvement] uniform; [augmentation, réglementation] across-the-board (épith); [existence, journées] unchanging
B nm (costume) uniform

uniformément /ynifɔʁmemɑ̃/ adv uniformly

uniformiser /ynifɔʁmize/ [1] vtr to standardize [programmes, taux]; to make [sth] uniform [teinte]

uniformité /ynifɔʁmite/ nf (de goûts, résultats, paysage) uniformity; (de vie) monotony

unijambiste /yniʒɑ̃bist/
A adj **être** ~ to have only one leg
B nmf one-legged person

unilatéral, ~**e**, mpl -**aux** /ynilateʁal, o/ adj unilateral; **stationnement** ~ parking on one side only

unilingue /ynilɛ̃g/ adj unilingual, monolingual

uninominal, ~**e**, mpl -**aux** /yninominal, o/ adj Pol [scrutin] for a single candidate (épith, après n)

union /ynjɔ̃/ nf ① (alliance) union; ② (association) association; ~ **de consommateurs** consumers' association; ③ (mariage) union sout, marriage; ④ Math union
(Composés) ~ **douanière** customs union; ~ **libre** cohabitation; ~ **sacrée** united front; ~ **sportive, US** sports club; **Union européenne** European Union; **Union des Républiques socialistes soviétiques** Hist Union of Soviet Socialist Republics; **Union soviétique** Hist Soviet Union
(Idiome) **l'~ fait la force** Prov united we stand, divided we fall

unique /ynik/ adj ① (seul de son espèce) (before n) only; **il est l'~ témoin** he's the only witness; **parti** ~ single party; **système à parti** ~ one-party system; **'prix** ~' 'all at one price'; ③ (remarquable) unique; **c'est une occasion** ~ **de faire** it's a unique opportunity to do; ~ **au monde** [personne, objet, fait] unique in the world; ~ **en son genre** [personne, objet] one of a kind (jamais épith); [fait,

événement] one-off GB, one-shot (épith) US; ④ ○(singulier) **ce type est** ~! that guy's priceless○!; ⑤ (sans frère ni sœur) **être fille** or **fils** ~ to be an only child

uniquement /ynikmɑ̃/ adv ① (exclusivement) exclusively; **il pense** ~ **à sa famille/s'amuser** all he thinks about is his family/having fun; **en vente** ~ **par correspondance** available by mail order only; ② (seulement) only; **c'était** ~ **pour te taquiner** it was only to tease you; **nous ne sommes pas ici** ~ **pour travailler** we're not here just to work; ~ **dans un but commercial** purely for commercial ends

unir /yniʁ/ [3]
A vtr ① (rassembler) to unite [pays, territoire] (**à** to); [liens, intérêts, passion] to unite, bind [sb] together [personnes, groupes, pays]; **des hommes unis par les mêmes idées** men brought together by the same ideas; ② (combiner) to combine; **méthode qui unit simplicité et efficacité** method which combines simplicity with effectiveness; **unissons nos ressources** let us combine ou pool our resources; ③ (marier) to join [sb] in matrimony sout
B s'**unir** vpr ① (se rassembler) to unite (**à, avec** with); **contre** against); ② (se marier) to marry

unisexe /ynisɛks/ adj unisex

unisson /ynisɔ̃/ nm unison; **à l'~** Mus in unison; fig in accord

unitaire /ynitɛʁ/ adj ① Pol [manifestation, campagne, stratégie] common; ② Comm [prix, coût] unit (épith)

unité /ynite/ nf ① (cohésion) unity; ~ **d'action/de lieu** Théât unity of action/place; **réaliser l'~ d'un pays** to unify a country; **un film qui manque d'~** film lacking in cohesion; ② (élément) unit; **2 euros l'~** 2 euros each; **vendre qch à l'~** to sell sth singly; ③ (dans ensemble) unit; ~ **de production** production unit; ④ (étalon) unit; ~ **monétaire** unit of currency; ⑤ Math unit; **la colonne des** ~**s** the units column; ⑥ Mil (troupe) unit; (navire) craft; ⑦ Télécom unit; **télécarte 50** ~**s** 50-unit phonecard
(Composés) ~ **centrale (de traitement)** Ordinat central processing unit, CPU; ~ **de disque** Ordinat disk drive

univers /univɛʁ/ nm inv ① (en astronomie) universe; ② (humanité) whole world; ③ (monde) world; **l'~ de Kafka** Kafka's world

universaliser /ynivɛʁsalize/ [1] vtr to universalize

universalité /ynivɛʁsalite/ nf universality

universel, -**elle** /ynivɛʁsɛl/
A adj [langage, thème, méthode] universal; [histoire] world (épith); [remède] all-purpose (épith)
B nm Ling, Philos universal

universitaire /ynivɛʁsitɛʁ/
A adj [échange, ville, cursus] university (épith); [travail, niveau] academic
B nmf academic

université /ynivɛʁsite/ nf ① (établissement) university GB, college US; **être à l'~** to be at university GB, to be in college US; ② (enseignement supérieur) higher education
(Composé) ~ **d'été** Univ summer school; Pol party conference (assembling young members and potential members)

univoque /ynivɔk/ adj ① Ling univocal; ② [réalité, fait] unequivocal

uns pron ▸ **un B**

Untel, **Unetelle** /œtɛl, yntɛl/ nm,f **Monsieur** ~ Mr so-and-so; **Madame Unetelle** Mrs so-and-so

urbain, ~**e** /yʁbɛ̃, ɛn/ adj ① (de la ville) urban; **vie** ~**e** city life; ② fml (civil) urbane

urbanisation /yʁbanizasjɔ̃/ nf urbanization

urbanisé, ~**e** /yʁbanize/
A pp ▸ **urbaniser**
B pp adj [zone] built-up (épith)

urbaniser /yʁbanize/ [1] vtr to urbanize [région]

urbanisme /yʁbanism/ nm town planning GB, city planning US

urbaniste /yʁbanist/ ▸ p. 372 nmf town planner GB, city planner US

urée /yʁe/ nf urea

uretère /yʁtɛʁ/ nm ureter

urètre /yʁɛtʁ/ nm urethra

urgence /yʁʒɑ̃s/ nf ① (caractère) urgency; **il y a** ~ it's urgent; **d'**~ [agir, se réunir] immediately; **de toute** or **d'extrême** ~ as a matter of great urgency; **transporter qn d'**~ **à l'hôpital** to rush sb to hospital GB ou the hospital US;

convoquer qn d'~ to summon sb urgently; **appeler qn d'~** to call sb immediately; **opérer qn d'~** to give sb emergency surgery; **mesures d'~** emergency measures; **en ~** as a matter of urgency, immediately; ② (cas urgent) gén matter of urgency; Méd emergency; **le service des ~s, les ~s** the casualty department, casualty ¢

urgent, ~e /yrʒɑ̃, ɑ̃t/ adj urgent; **il est ~ de prendre des mesures** measures must be taken immediately

Uri /yri/ ► p. 504 npr **le canton d'~** the canton of Uri

urinaire /yrinɛr/ adj urinary

urinal, pl **-aux** /yrinal, o/ nm urinal

urine /yrin/ nf urine ¢; **une analyse des ~s** urinalysis

uriner /yrine/ [1] vi to urinate

urinoir /yrinwar/ nm ① (lieu) public urinal; ② (cuvette) urinal

urne /yrn/ nf ① (pour voter) **~ (électorale)** ballot box; **se rendre aux ~s** to go to the polls; **être appelé aux ~s** to be called upon to vote; ② (vase) urn; **~ cinéraire** or **funéraire** funeral urn

urologie /yrɔlɔʒi/ nf urology

URSS /yɛrɛsɛs, yrs/ nprf Hist (abbr = **Union des Républiques socialistes soviétiques**) USSR

urticaire /yrtikɛr/ ► p. 195 nf hives

(Idiome) **donner de l'~ à qn**○ to get on sb's nerves

us /ys/ nmpl **les ~ et coutumes** the ways and customs

US /yɛs/ nf: abbr ► **union**

USA /yesa/ nmpl (abbr = **United States of America**) USA

usage /yzaʒ/ nm ① (fait d'utiliser) use; **à l'~** [rétrécir, se distendre] with use; **par l'~** [sali, encrassé] with use; **en ~** in use; **disqualifié pour ~ d'anabolisants** disqualified for using anabolic steroids; **faire ~ de** to use; **faire ~ de son autorité** to exercise one's authority; **faire bon/mauvais ~ de qch** to put sth to good/bad use; **faire de l'~** [tissu, vêtement] to last; ② (possibilité d'utiliser) use; **'réservé à l'~ du personnel'** 'for staff use only'; **à ~ privé** for private use; **à ~ externe** for external use only; **à ~ multiples** [appareil] multipurpose (épith); **il a perdu l'~ d'un œil** he's lost the use of one eye; **hors d'~** [vêtement] unwearable; [machine] out of order; ③ Ling usage; **en ~** in usage; **les règles du bon ~** the rules of good usage; ④ (pratique courante) custom; **l'~ est de faire** (dans la vie courante) the custom is to do; (dans la vie professionnelle) it's usual practice to do; **comme le veut l'~** as is customary; **conformément aux ~s** in accordance with custom; **politesses d'~** customary courtesies; **précautions d'~** usual precautions

(Composé) **~ de faux** Jur use of false documents; **faux et ~ de faux** forgery and use of false documents

usagé, ~e /yzaʒe/ adj ① (usé) [vêtement] well-worn; [pneu] worn; ② (déjà utilisé) [vêtement, seringue] used

usager /yzaʒe/ nm (de service) user; (de langue) speaker; **~ de la route** road-user

usant, ~e /yzɑ̃, ɑ̃t/ adj [travail, vie] exhausting, wearing; [personne] wearing, tiresome

usé, ~e /yze/

A pp ► **user**

B pp adj [vêtement, chaussure, objet, pièce] worn; [personne] worn-down; [organisme, cœur, yeux] worn-out; [sujet, plaisanterie] hackneyed; **une veste complètement ~e** a threadbare jacket; **~ jusqu'à la corde** lit [vêtement, tapis] threadbare; [pneu] worn down to the tread; fig [plaisanterie] hackneyed

user /yze/ [1]

A vtr [personne, temps, frottement] to wear out [vêtement, chaussure, objet]; [travail, soucis, temps] to wear down [personne]; **les piles sont usées** the batteries have run down ou out; **~ ses vêtements jusqu'à la corde** to wear one's clothes out; **~ sa santé** to ruin one's health

B user de vtr ind to use [formule, termes, alcool]; to exercise [droit]; to exploit [possibilité]; to take [précautions]; **~ de**

diplomatie to be diplomatic; **~ et abuser de qch** to use and abuse sth; **il faut en ~ avec modération** it should be used in moderation

C s'user vpr ① [vêtement, chaussure] to wear out; ② [personne] **s'~ à la tâche** to wear oneself out with overwork; **s'~ la santé** to ruin one's health

usinage /yzinaʒ/ nm ① (fabrication avec une machine-outil) machining; ② (fabrication industrielle) manufacture

usine /yzin/ nf factory; **fabriqué en ~** factory-made; **c'est l'~, ici**○! fig it's like a production line here!

(Composés) **~ métallurgique** ironworks (pl); **~ sidérurgique** steelworks (pl)

usiner /yzine/ [1] vtr ① (avec machine-outil) to machine; ② (fabriquer) to manufacture

usité, ~e /yzite/ adj commonly used (jamais épith); **peu ~** rarely used (jamais épith)

ustensile /ystɑ̃sil/ nm utensil

usuel, -elle /yzɥɛl/

A adj [objet] everyday (épith); [mot, expression, appellation] common

B nm (livre) reference book (not for loan)

usufruit /yzyfrɥi/ nm Jur usufruct

usure /yzyr/ nf ① (détérioration) (de tissu, vêtement) wear and tear (de on); (de pneu, disque, machine) wear (de on); **résister à l'~** to wear well; ② (affaiblissement) (de forces, d'énergie, adversaire) wearing down; (d'idéologie) waning; (de régime) declining power; **l'~ du pouvoir** the erosion of power; ③ (action corrosive) **~ du temps** wearing effect of time; ④ Fin, Jur usury

usurier, -ière /yzyrje, ɛr/ nm,f usurer, loan shark○

usurpateur, -trice /yzyrpatœr, tris/ nm,f usurper

usurpation /yzyrpasjɔ̃/ nf usurpation

usurper /yzyrpe/ [1] vtr to usurp [titre, réputation]

ut /yt/ nm Mus C

utérin, ~e /yterɛ̃, in/ adj Anat, Jur uterine

utérus /yterys/ nm inv womb, uterus

utile /ytil/

A adj ① (d'utilité générale) useful; ② (d'utilité ponctuelle) **être ~** [personne, livre] to be helpful; [allumette, parapluie] to come in handy; **se rendre ~** to make oneself useful; **il est ~ de signaler** it's worth pointing out; **il n'a pas jugé ~ de me prévenir** he didn't think it necessary to let me know

B nm **joindre l'~ à l'agréable** to mix business with pleasure

utilement /ytilmɑ̃/ adv [combattre, intervenir] effectively; [s'occuper] usefully; [compléter] nicely

utilisable /ytilizabl/ adj usable

utilisateur, -trice /ytilizatœr, tris/ nm,f user

utilisation /ytilizasjɔ̃/ nf ① (fait d'utiliser) use; ② (utilité) use (de for)

utiliser /ytilize/ [1] vtr ① (se servir) to use [méthode, outil, produit]; to make use of [compétence]; **~ au mieux** to make the most of; **bien ~** to make good use of; ② (exploiter) to use, to exploit [personne]

utilitaire /ytilitɛr/ adj [conception, époque] utilitarian; [préoccupation, enseignement, rôle] practical; [objet] functional; [véhicule] commercial

utilité /ytilite/ nf ① (caractère utile) usefulness; **être d'une grande ~** [livre, appareil] to be very useful; [personne] to be very helpful; **d'aucune ~** of no use; **ne pas voir l'~ de faire** not to see the point of doing; ② (utilisation) use; **je n'en ai pas l'~** I have no use for it

utopie /ytɔpi/ nf Philos, Pol Utopia

utopique /ytɔpik/ adj [projet, idée] utopian

UV /yve/ nmpl (abbr = **ultraviolets**) Phys ultraviolet rays; **séance d'~** session on a sunbed

uvule /yvyl/ nf uvula

Vv

v, V /ve/ *nm inv* (lettre) v, V; **en (forme de) V** [*objet*] V-shaped; **encolure en V** V-neck; **pull en V** V-necked sweater; ▸ **vitesse**

va /va/ ▸ **aller¹**; ▸ **vat**

vacance /vakɑ̃s/
A *nf* (de charge, poste) vacancy
B **vacances** *nfpl* holiday GB, vacation US; **bonnes ~s!** have a good holiday GB *ou* vacation US!; **grandes ~s** Scol summer holidays GB, summer *ou* long vacation US

vacancier, -ière /vakɑ̃sje, ɛʀ/ *nm,f* holidaymaker GB, vacationer US

vacant, ~e /vakɑ̃, ɑ̃t/ *adj* vacant

vacarme /vakaʀm/ *nm* din, racket○

vacataire /vakatɛʀ/
A *adj* temporary
B *nmf* Admin temporary employee; Scol supply teacher GB, substitute teacher US

vaccin /vaksɛ̃/ *nm* Méd vaccine; **~ contre la grippe** flu vaccine

vaccination /vaksinasjɔ̃/ *nf* vaccination; **~ contre la polio/variole** polio/smallpox vaccination

vacciner /vaksine/ [1] *vtr* **1** lit to vaccinate (**contre** against); **se faire ~** to get vaccinated; **2** (endurcir) hum **~ qn contre** to put sb off; **plus d'affaires sentimentales, je suis vacciné○!** no more romance, I've learned my lesson!

vache /vaʃ/
A ○*adj* mean, nasty; **coup ~** mean *ou* dirty trick
B *nf* **1** (animal) cow; **2** (cuir) cowhide; **3** ○(personne méchante) (homme) bastard◑; (femme) bitch◑; **faire un coup en ~ à qn** to pull a mean *ou* dirty trick on sb
C ○**vache de** *loc adj* hell○ of; **on m'a offert un ~ de bouquin** I was given a hell○ of a good book
D ○**la vache** *excl* (admiration) wow!; (commisération) **oh la ~!** **il a dû se faire mal!** God! that must have hurt!; (agacement, douleur) hell!

〔Composés〕 **~ à eau** water bottle; **années de ~s grasses** prosperous years; **~ à lait** Agric dairy cow; fig milch cowɫ, money-spinner○; **~ laitière** dairy cow; **années de ~s maigres** lean years; **~ sacrée** Relig sacred cow

〔Idiome〕 **parler français comme une ~ espagnole**○ to speak very bad French

vachement○ /vaʃmɑ̃/ *adv* really; **il a ~ maigri** he lost a hell of a lot○ of weight

vacher /vaʃe/ ▸ p. 372 *nm* cowman

vachère /vaʃɛʀ/ ▸ p. 372 *nf* cowgirl

vacherie○ /vaʃʀi/ *nf* **1** (attitude) meanness, nastiness; **2** (propos) nasty *ou* bitchy◑ remark; **3** (sale coup) dirty trick; **4** (calamité) **c'est une vraie ~ ce virus** this virus is a bloody◑ GB *ou* damned○ nuisance

vachette /vaʃɛt/ *nf* **1** (animal) young cow; **2** (cuir) calfskin

vacillant, ~e /vasijɑ̃, ɑ̃t/ *adj* **1** (tremblant) [*jambes*] unsteady; [*personne*] unsteady on one's legs (jamais épith); [*lumière, flamme*] flickering; **2** (fragile) [*pouvoir, majorité*] shaky; [*santé, mémoire, raison*] failing

vacillement /vasijmɑ̃/ *nm* **1** (mouvement) (de chose) swaying ¢; (de flamme) flickering ¢; **2** (irrésolution) wavering ¢; **3** (affaiblissement) faltering ¢

vaciller /vasije/ [1] *vi* **1** (être chancelant) [*personne*] to be unsteady on one's legs; [*jambes*] to be unsteady; **2** (osciller)

[*personne, objet*] to sway; [*lumière, flamme*] to flicker; **3** (se détériorer) [*santé, mémoire, raison*] to fail; [*pouvoir, majorité*] to weaken

vadrouille○ /vadʀuj/ *nf* stroll; **être en ~** to be wandering about; **partir en ~** to wander off

vadrouiller○ /vadʀuje/ [1] *vi* to wander around

va-et-vient /vaevjɛ̃/ *nm inv* **1** (allées et venues) (de personnes, véhicules) comings and goings (*pl*); (de dossiers, d'idées) to-ing and fro-ing; **faire le ~** [*personne, bateau*] to go to and fro; [*dossier*] to go back and forth; **2** Électrotech two-way switch

vagabond, ~e /vagabɔ̃, ɔ̃d/
A *adj* [*personne*] wandering (épith); [*chien*] stray (épith); [*existence, esprit, imagination*] roving (épith); [*humeur*] ever-changing
B *nm,f* vagrant

vagabondage /vagabɔ̃daʒ/ *nm* **1** (errance) (de personne) wandering; (de pensée) wanderings *pl*; **2** Jur vagrancy ¢

vagabonder /vagabɔ̃de/ [1] *vi* **1** [*personne, animal*] to wander (**dans** through); **~ à travers le monde** to roam the world; **2** [*imagination*] to wander; [*pensées*] to stray

vagin /vaʒɛ̃/ *nm* vagina

vagir /vaʒiʀ/ [3] *vi* [*nouveau-né*] to wail

vagissement /vaʒismɑ̃/ *nm* wail

vague¹ /vag/
A *adj* (imprécis) vague; **d'un air ~** [*contempler*] vaguely; **ce sont de ~s parents** they're distant relatives
B *nm* **il regardait dans le ~** he was staring into space; **ton regard était perdu dans le ~** you had a faraway look in your eyes; **la direction est restée dans le ~ sur la question des salaires** management has remained vague as to the question of wages

〔Composé〕 **avoir du ~ à l'âme** to feel melancholic

vague² /vag/ *nf* **1** lit wave; **faire des ~s** [*vent*] to make ripples; fig [*démission, scandale*] to cause a stir, to make waves; **2** fig wave; **une ~ de violence** a wave of violence; **par ~s** [*arriver, attaquer*] in waves

〔Composés〕 **~ de chaleur** heatwave; **~ de froid** cold spell

〔Idiome〕 **être au creux de la ~** to be at a low ebb; **pas de ~s!** we don't want to stir up any trouble!

vaguement /vagmɑ̃/ *adv* (évoquer, indiquer) vaguely; [*honteux, embarrassé*] faintly; **on avait ~ décoré la pièce pour la circonstance** they had put up a few decorations for the occasion

vaillamment /vajamɑ̃/ *adv* courageously, valiantly *sout*

vaillance /vajɑ̃s/ *nf* courage; **avec ~** courageously

vaillant, ~e /vajɑ̃, ɑ̃t/ *adj* **1** (courageux) courageous; **2** (vigoureux) [*personne*] strong; [*vieillard*] hale and hearty

vain, ~e /vɛ̃, vɛn/
A *adj* **1** (inutile) [*effort, tentative*] vain, futile; [*regrets*] futile; [*démarche, discussion*] fruitless, futile; **mes efforts ont été ~s** my efforts were in vain; **avec lui, toute discussion serait ~e** talking to him would be futile; **2** (illusoire) [*promesses*] empty; [*espoirs*] vain; **3** (superficiel) [*plaisirs, mots*] vain, empty; **le pouvoir de la presse n'est pas un ~ mot** the power of the press is a very real thing; **4** (vaniteux) [*personne*] vain

en vain *loc adv* in vain

vaincre /vɛ̃kʀ/ [57]
A *vtr* to defeat [*adversaire, armée*]; to overcome [*préjugés, complexe, envie de dormir*]; to beat [*chômage, maladie*]

B *vi* to win

vaincu, **~e** /vɛ̃ky/
A *pp* ▸ **vaincre**
B *pp adj* defeated; **s'avouer ~** to admit defeat
C *nm,f* loser; **les ~s** Mil the defeated (+ *v pl*)

vainement /vɛnmɑ̃/ *adv* in vain

vainqueur /vɛ̃kœʀ/
A *adj m* victorious
B *nm* (de bataille) victor; (d'épreuve sportive, élections) winner (**de**, **devant** against); (de loterie, concours) prizewinner; (de désert, montagne) conqueror

vaisseau, *pl* **~x** /vɛso/ *nm* **1** Anat, Bot vessel; **2** Naut vessel; Mil, Naut warship; **3** Archit nave
(Composés) **~ amiral** lit, fig flagship; **~ sanguin** Anat blood vessel; **~ spatial** spaceship

vaisselier /vɛsəlje/ *nm* dresser

vaisselle /vɛsɛl/ *nf* **1** (pour manger) crockery, dishes (*pl*); **2** (à laver) dishes (*pl*); **laver** *or* **faire la ~** to do the dishes, to wash up GB, to do the washing-up GB

val, *pl* **~s** *or* **vaux** /val, vo/ *nm* valley
(Idiome) **être toujours par monts et par vaux** to be always on the move

valable○ /valabl/ *adj* **1** (acceptable) [*raison*] valid, [*solution*] viable; [*interlocuteur*] recognized; **2** (non périmé) valid; **ma proposition reste ~** my offer still holds; **3** ○(intéressant) [*œuvre, projet*] worthwhile

valdinguer○ /valdɛ̃ge/ [1] *vi* [*personne, objet*] to go flying○; **~ dans l'escalier** to go tumbling down the stairs; **envoyer ~** (faire tomber) to send [sb/sth] flying○

valet /valɛ/ ▸ p. 372 *nm* **1** (serviteur) manservant; **2** Jeux jack; **~ de pique** jack of spades
(Composés) **~ de chambre** valet; **~ de ferme** farm hand; **~ de nuit** valet; **~ de pied** footman

valeur /valœʀ/ *nf* **1** (prix) value; **prendre/perdre de la ~** to go up/to go down in value; **d'une ~ inestimable** [*bijou, meuble*] priceless; **avoir beaucoup de ~** to be very valuable; **n'avoir aucune ~** to have no value, to be worth nothing; **un vase de ~** a valuable vase; **les objets de ~** valuables; **mettre un terrain en ~** to develop a plot of land, to put a plot of land to good use; **2** (qualité) (de personne) worth; (d'œuvre) value, merit; (de méthode, découverte) value; **prouver sa ~** to show one's worth; **faire la ~ de qch** to give sth value; **attacher de la ~ à qch** to value sth; **sans ~** worthless; **un homme de ~** (moralement) a very estimable man; **attirer des candidats de ~** (en compétence) to attract high-quality candidates; **la ~ de l'écrivain a été reconnue** the author's talent has been recognized; **le mot garde toute sa ~** the word retains its full force; **mettre qch en ~** to emphasize, to highlight [*fait, talent, qualité*]; to set off [*yeux, teint, tableau*]; **mettre qn en ~** [*couleur, maquillage*] to suit sb; **se mettre en ~** [*coquette*] to make the best of oneself; [*candidat*] to show oneself to best advantage; **3** (validité) validity; **~ légale** legal validity; **avoir ~ de norme/symbole** to be the norm/a symbol; **ceci n'a pas ~ d'engagement** this does not constitute a commitment; **4** (principe moral) value; **nous n'avons pas les mêmes ~s** we don't share the same values; **5** (en Bourse) security; **~s** securities, stock ¢, stocks and shares; **le marché** *or* **la Bourse des ~s** the stock market; **6** (en comptabilité) asset; **~s disponibles** liquid assets; **7** (quantité) **ajouter la ~ de deux cuillerées à café** add the equivalent of two teaspoons; **8** Math value; **en ~ absolue/relative** fig in absolute/relative terms; **9** Jeux (de pion, carte) value; **10** †(courage) valour†GB
(Composés) **~ marchande** market value; **~ sûre** gilt-edged security GB, blue chip; fig safe bet; **~s mobilières** securities

valeureux, **-euse** /valøʀø, øz/ *adj* valorous†

validation /validasjɔ̃/ *nf* Jur, Univ validation; (dans les transports, dans un jeu) stamping

valide /valid/ *adj* **1** [*passeport, contrat*] valid; **non ~** invalid; **2** [*personne, population*] able-bodied; [*bras*] (épith); (en forme) fit; **je ne me sens pas encore bien ~** I don't feel very fit yet

valider /valide/ [1] *vtr* to stamp [*titre de transport*]; **faire ~** to have [sth] validated [*bulletin de loto*]; to have [sth] recognized [*diplôme*]

validité /validite/ *nf* validity

valise /valiz/ *nf* (bagage) suitcase; **faire/défaire ses ~s** to pack/to unpack; **s'il n'est pas content, il n'a qu'à faire ses ~s** if he doesn't like it, he can pack his bags
(Composé) **~ diplomatique** diplomatic bag GB *ou* pouch US
(Idiome) **avoir des ~s sous les yeux**○ to have bags under one's eyes

vallée /vale/ *nf* valley

vallon /valɔ̃/ *nm* dale, small valley

vallonné, **~e** /valɔne/ *adj* [*relief, paysage*] undulating; [*pays*] hilly

valoir /valwaʀ/ [45]
A *vtr* (procurer) **~ à qn** to earn sb [*châtiment, éloges, critiques*]; to win sb [*amitié, admiration*]; to bring sb sth [*ennuis*]; **ça ne m'a valu que des ennuis** it brought me nothing but trouble, I got nothing but trouble out of it; **cela lui a valu d'être élu** it got him elected; **que me vaut l'honneur de ta visite?** hum to what do I owe the honourGB (of this visit)?
B *vi* **1** (en termes monétaires) to be worth; **ça vaut bien 50 euros** (à peu près) it must be worth 50 euros; (largement) it's well worth 50 euros; **~ de l'or** fig to be very valuable; **2** (qualitativement) **que vaut ce film/vin?** what's that film/wine like?; **il ne vaut pas mieux que son frère** he's no better than his brother; **le film ne vaut pas grand-chose** the film isn't very good *ou* isn't up to much○; **il ne vaut pas cher** he is a worthless individual *ou* a bad lot○; **ne rien ~** [*matériau, produit, roman*] to be rubbish, to be no good; [*outil, traitement, méthode*] to be useless; [*argument*] to be worthless; **il ne vaut rien comme cuisinier** he's a useless cook; **le pneu ne vaut plus rien** the tyre has had it○; **la chaleur/le climat ne me vaut rien** the heat/the climate doesn't suit me; **l'alcool ne vaut rien pour le foie** alcohol doesn't do the liver much good; **le film vaut surtout par la qualité du dialogue** the principal merit of the film is the quality of the dialogueGB; **il ne me dit rien qui vaille** I've got misgivings about him; **ça ne me dit rien qui vaille** (projet, annonce) I don't like the sound of it; **elle valait mieux que cela!** she deserved better than that!; **3** (égaler) to be as good as; **ton travail vaut bien/largement le leur** your work is just as good/every bit as good as theirs; **rien ne vaut la soie** nothing beats silk; **le frère vaut la sœur** hum the brother is just as bad as the sister; **4** (équivaloir à) to be worth; **un ouvrier expérimenté vaut trois débutants** an experienced worker is worth three novices; **5** (mériter) to be worth; **ça vaut la peine que tu y ailles** it's worth your going; **ça en vaut la peine, ça vaut le coup**○ it's worth it; **6** (être valable) [*règle, critique*] to apply; **la règle vaut pour tout le monde** the rule applies to everybody; **7** (avec faire) **faire ~** (faire fructifier) to put [sth] to work [*argent*]; to farm [*terrain*]; to turn [sth] to good account [*bien*]; (mettre en avant) to point out [*mérite, nécessité*]; to emphasize, to highlight [*qualité, trait*]; to advance [*argument*]; to assert [*droit*]; to make [sth] known [*intention*]; **faire ~ que** to point out that, to argue that; **se faire ~** to push oneself forward, to get oneself noticed (**auprès de qn** by sb)
C *se valoir* *vpr* [*produit, œuvres*] to be the same; **les deux candidats se valent** there's nothing to choose between the two candidates
D *v impers* **il vaut mieux faire, mieux vaut faire** it's better to do; **mieux vaut** *or* **il vaut mieux une dispute qu'un malentendu** an argument is better than a misunderstanding, rather an argument than a misunderstanding; **il vaut mieux que tu y ailles** you'd better go; **il aurait mieux valu qu'il se taise** he would have done better to keep quiet; **cela vaut mieux**○ it's better like that *ou* that way

valorisation /valɔʀizasjɔ̃/ *nf* **1** (promotion) promotion; **~ d'un produit** promotion of a product; **2** (mise en valeur) development; **3** (hausse) (de monnaie) rise; (de terrains) rise in value

valoriser /valɔʀize/ [1] *vtr* **1** (promouvoir) to promote [*produit*]; to make [sth] attractive [*profession, études*]; **2** (mettre en valeur) to develop [*région, ressources*]; to put [sth] to good use [*diplôme, savoir-faire*]; **3** (faire fructifier) to put [sth] to work [*capital*]

valse /vals/ *nf* **1** (danse) waltz; **2** (changement fréquent) **~ des ministres** frequent cabinet reshuffles (*pl*); **~ des étiquettes** continual price rises (*pl*)

valse-hésitation, *pl* **valses-hésitations** /valsezitasjɔ̃/ *nf* shilly-shallying○ ¢

valser /valse/ [1] *vi* **1** (en danse) to waltz; **l'argent valse entre leurs mains**○ they spend money hand over fist;

envoyer ~ qn° (projeter) to send sb flying; (rembarrer) to send sb packing°; **2▶** °(changer) **faire ~ les étiquettes** to raise prices constantly; **il fait ~ les ministres** he keeps changing his ministers

valseur, -euse /valsœʀ, øz/ nm,f waltzer

valve /valv/ nf valve

vamp° /vɑ̃p/ nf vamp

vampire /vɑ̃piʀ/ nm **1▶** (revenant) vampire; **2▶** (personne avide) bloodsucker; **3▶** Zool vampire bat

vampiriser /vɑ̃piʀize/ [1] vtr **1▶** lit to suck the lifeblood from; **2▶** fig to cannibalize

van /vɑ̃/ nm **1▶** (fourgon) (pour chevaux) horsebox GB, horse-car US; (pour marchandises) van; **2▶** (panier) winnowing basket

vandale /vɑ̃dal/ nmf vandal

vandalisme /vɑ̃dalism/ nm vandalism

vanille /vanij/ nf vanilla; **à la ~** [glace] vanilla (épith); [crème] vanilla-flavoured^{GB} (épith)

vanillé, ~e /vanije/ adj [goût] vanilla (épith); [dessert] vanilla-flavoured^{GB}; **sucre ~** sugar containing vanilla

vanité /vanite/ nf **1▶** (orgueil) vanity; **sans ~** with all due modesty; **tirer ~ de qch** to pride oneself on sth; **flatter qn dans sa ~** to flatter sb's ego; **avoir la ~ de croire que** to be presumptuous enough to believe that; **2▶** (peu de valeur) (de richesses) vanity; (d'efforts) futility; (de promesse) hollowness; (d'entreprise) uselessness; **3▶** Art vanitas

vaniteux, -euse /vanitø øz/ adj vain, conceited

vanne /van/ nf **1▶** (de barrage) gate; (d'écluse, de moulin) sluice gate; **2▶** (propos) dig°; **envoyer une ~ or des ~s à qn** to have a dig at sb°

(Idiome) **ouvrir les ~s**° to make funds available; **fermer les ~s**° to cut funding

vanner /vane/ [1] vtr **1▶** Agric to winnow; **2▶** °(fatiguer) to tire [sb] out [personne]; **je suis vannée!** I'm tired out ou knackered[⌐] GB!

vannerie /vanʀi/ nf basket-making; **objets en ~** wickerwork

vantail, pl **-aux** /vɑ̃taj, o/ nm (de porte) leaf; (de fenêtre) casement; (de volet) shutter; (d'armoire) door; **porte à double ~** double-door

vantard, ~e /vɑ̃taʀ, aʀd/ nm,f boaster, braggart

vantardise /vɑ̃taʀdiz/ nf **1▶** (caractère) boastfulness; **2▶** (parole) boast

vanter /vɑ̃te/ [1]

A vtr to praise, to extol; **tant vanté** much vaunted; **~ les mérites de qn/qch** to speak highly of sb/sth

B se vanter vpr **1▶** (être un vantard) to brag (de about); **il n'y a pas de quoi se ~!** there's nothing to brag about!; **il a cassé le vase mais il ne s'en est pas vanté** he broke the vase but he kept quiet about it; **2▶** (s'enorgueillir) **se ~ de faire** to pride oneself on doing; **3▶** (prétendre) **se ~ de faire** to make out that one does

va-nu-pieds /vanypje/ nmf inv tramp, bum°

vapeur /vapœʀ/

A nf **1▶** (d'eau) steam; **à ~** [machine, bateau] steam (épith); **renverser la ~** Naut to go astern; fig to backpedal; **faire cuire à la ~** to steam; **la cuisine à la ~** steam cooking; **2▶** Phys vapour^{GB}

B vapeurs nfpl (émanations) fumes

vaporeux, -euse /vapoʀø, øz/ adj **1▶** (léger) [vêtement, matériau] diaphanous; **2▶** (brumeux) liter [paysage] misty

vaporisateur /vapoʀizatœʀ/ nm spray

vaporisation /vapoʀizasjɔ̃/ nf **1▶** (d'insecticide, de parfum) spraying; **2▶** Phys vaporization

vaporiser /vapoʀize/ [1]

A vtr (projeter) to spray

B se vaporiser vpr Phys to vaporize

vaquer /vake/ [1]

A vi (s'arrêter) [tribunal, assemblée] to be in recess; [cours] to stop

B vaquer à vtr ind **~ à ses occupations** to attend to one's business

varappe /vaʀap/ ▸ p. 327 nf rock-climbing

varappeur, -euse /vaʀapœʀ, øz/ nm,f rock-climber

varech /vaʀɛk/ nm kelp

vareuse /vaʀøz/ nf **1▶** (dans la marine) jersey; **2▶** Mil uniform jacket

variable /vaʀjabl/

A adj **1▶** (fluctuant) variable; **leurs sketches sont d'une durée ~** their sketches vary in length; **2▶** (changeant) [ciel, temps] changeable; [humeur] unpredictable; **vent ~ de faible à modéré** wind varying from weak to moderate; **ils ont des opinions ~s** they have shifting opinions; **3▶** (modifiable) [hauteur, focale] adjustable; **4▶** Math, Ordinat [quantité, nombre, données] variable; **5▶** Ling **un mot ~** a word which inflects

B nf variable

variante /vaʀjɑ̃t/ nf variant

variation /vaʀjasjɔ̃/ nf **1▶** (changement) variation; **~ de température** variation in temperature; **~ à la baisse/à la hausse** downward/upward movement; **~s de l'opinion publique** changes in public opinion; **connaître de fortes ~s** [prix, températures] to fluctuate considerably; **en données corrigées des ~s saisonnières** according to the seasonally adjusted figures; **2▶** Mus variation

varice /vaʀis/ nf varicose vein

varicelle /vaʀisɛl/ ▸ p. 195 nf chicken pox

varié, ~e /vaʀje/ adj **1▶** (diversifié) varied; **une expérience ~e** diverse ou varied experience; **plumage ~** variegated plumage; **2▶** (multiple) [instruments, exercices] various; **des activités aussi ~es que** activities as varied as; **une population d'origines ~es** a population of diverse origins; **'sandwichs ~s'** 'a selection of sandwiches'

varier /vaʀje/ [2]

A vtr to vary; **pour ~ les plaisirs** just for a (pleasant) change

B vi **1▶** (changer) to vary (**avec, en fonction de, au gré de** according to); **l'inflation varie de 4% à 6%** inflation fluctuates between 4% and 6%; **2▶** (changer d'opinion) **l'accusé ne varie pas** the accused is sticking to his story

(Idiome) **souvent femme varie, bien fol est qui s'y fie** Prov woman is fickle

variété /vaʀjete/

A nf **1▶** (diversité) variety; **manquer de ~** to be lacking in variety; **des menus d'une grande ~** very varied menus; **une grande ~ d'articles** a wide range of items; **2▶** Bot variety; **3▶** (type) sort; **différentes ~s de céréales** different sorts of cereals; **une ~ de grippe** a strain of flu; **4▶** Mus popular music; **la ~ française** French popular music

B variétés nfpl **spectacle de ~s** variety show; **la chanson de ~s** middle-of-the-road popular song; **les ~s italiennes** Italian popular music sg

> ⓘ **Variété française** Songs written in French for a French-speaking audience are known as *variété française*. This popular and productive musical genre is encouraged by a law which stipulates that a prescribed amount of air time be allocated to it on the French national radio. It is also celebrated at the annual *Francofolies* music festival in July in La Rochelle.

variole /vaʀjɔl/ ▸ p. 195 nf smallpox

Varsovie /vaʀsɔvi/ ▸ p. 621 npr Warsaw

vas /va/ ▸ **aller**[1]

vase[1] /vɑz/ nm (à fleurs, ornemental) vase

(Composé) **~s communicants** Phys connected vessels

(Idiomes) **vivre/être élevé en ~ clos** to live/to be brought up without any contact with the outside world; **c'est la goutte d'eau qui fait déborder le ~** it's the last straw

vase[2] /vɑz/ nf (boue) silt, sludge

vasectomie /vazɛktɔmi/ nf vasectomy

vaseux, -euse /vazø, øz/ adj **1▶** (boueux) muddy; **2▶** °(fatigué) **je me sens plutôt ~** I'm not really with it°; **3▶** °(peu cohérent) woolly

vasistas /vazistas/ nm inv (à lamelles) louvre^{GB} window; (dans une fenêtre) opening windowpane

vasque /vask/ nf **1▶** (de fontaine) basin; **2▶** (coupe) bowl

vassal, ~e, mpl **-aux** /vasal, o/

A adj vassal

B nm,f Hist vassal; fig slave

vaste /vast/ adj **1▶** (de grande étendue) [pièce, domaine, secteur, réseau] vast; [marché] huge; **la salle n'est pas très ~** the room is not very large; **le ~ monde** the wide world; **2▶** (nombreux) [public, choix, collection] large; [rassemblement] huge; **3▶** (de grande envergure) [programme, entreprise] massive; [campagne] extensive; [plaisanterie] huge; [débat, enquête] wide-ranging; [mouvement, offensive] large-scale;

[*réforme*] far-reaching; [*œuvre, sujet*] wide-ranging

vat: à Dieu va(t) /adjøva(t)/ *loc excl* come what may

va-t-en-guerre /vatɑ̃gɛʀ/ *nm inv* warmonger

va-tout /vatu/ *nm inv* **jouer/tenter son** ∼ to stake/to risk everything

vaudeville /vodvil/ *nm* light comedy; **tourner au** ∼ to turn into a farce

vaudou /vodu/ *adj inv, nm* voodoo

vaurien, -ienne /voʀjɛ̃, ɛn/ *nm,f* [1] (chenapan) rascal; [2] (crapule) *pej* lout, yobbo○ GB, hoodlum○

vautour /votuʀ/ *nm* Zool *fig* vulture

vautrer: **se vautrer** /votʀe/ [1] *vpr* [1] (s'étaler) to sprawl; [2] (s'affaler) to loll; **se** ∼ **dans un fauteuil** to loll in an armchair; [3] (se rouler) to wallow; **se** ∼ **dans la boue** to wallow in the mud

vauvert: **au diable vauvert** /odjabləvovɛʀ/ *loc adv* miles from anywhere

va-vite: **à la va-vite** /alavavit/ *loc adv* *pej* in a rush

veau, *pl* ∼**x** /vo/ *nm* [1] Zool calf; [2] Culin veal; **côte de** ∼ veal chop; **foie/pied de** ∼ calf's liver/foot; [3] (cuir) calf-skin

(Composés) ∼ **marin** Zool seal; **le** ∼ **d'or** Bible the golden calf; (les richesses) Mammon

(Idiomes) **pleurer comme un** ∼ to cry one's eyes out; **tuer le** ∼ **gras** to kill the fatted calf

vecteur /vɛktœʀ/ *nm* [1] (support) vehicle; [2] Math vector; [3] Biol (de maladie) carrier

vécu, ∼e /veky/
A *pp* ▸ **vivre**
B *pp adj* [1] (authentique) [*drame, histoire*] real-life (*épith*); [2] Philos (subjectif) [*durée, temps*] subjective
C *nm* [1] (expériences) personal experiences (*pl*); [2] (réalité) real life; **c'est du** ∼ [*film, roman*] it's real life

vedettariat /vədetaʀja/ *nm* stardom

vedette /vədet/
A *nf* [1] (célébrité) star; ∼ **de cinéma** film star; ∼ **de la politique** famous politician; **avoir la** ∼ [*acteur, orateur*] to have top billing; **tenir la** ∼ [*acteur, événement*] to be in the limelight; **se mettre en** ∼ to push oneself forward; **mettre qn/qch en** ∼ to turn the spotlight on sb/sth; [2] Naut launch
B (-)vedette (*in compounds*) **danseur** ∼ star; **enfant** ∼ child star; **élève** ∼ star pupil; **mannequin** ∼ top model; **match** ∼ big match GB *ou* game US

(Composés) ∼ **de combat** fast attack craft; ∼ **de croisière** cabin cruiser; ∼ **lance-torpilles** motor torpedo boat GB

végétal, ∼e, *mpl* **-aux** /veʒetal, o/
A *adj* (propre aux plantes) [*cellule, tissu*] plant (*épith*); (venant des plantes) [*huile, teinture*] vegetable (*épith*)
B *nm* vegetable, plant

végétalien, -ienne /veʒetaljɛ̃, ɛn/ *adj, nm,f* vegan

végétarien, -ienne /veʒetaʀjɛ̃, ɛn/ *adj, nm,f* vegetarian; **être** ∼ to be a vegetarian

végétation /veʒetasjɔ̃/
A *nf* Bot vegetation
B végétations *nfpl* Méd adenoids

végéter /veʒete/ [14] *vi* [*personne*] to vegetate; [*projet*] to stagnate

véhémence /veemɑ̃s/ *nf* vehemence; **avec** ∼ vehemently

véhément, ∼e /veemɑ̃, ɑ̃t/ *adj* [*personne, discours, propos*] passionate, vehement; [*orateur*] passionate

véhicule /veikyl/ *nm* [1] (moyen de transport) vehicle; ∼ **blindé** armoured○ GB vehicle; [2] (moyen d'expression) vehicle (de for)

(Composé) ∼ **de tourisme** private car

véhiculer /veikyle/ [1] *vtr* (transporter) to carry, to transport [*personnes, marchandises*]; (transmettre) to carry [*substance, message*]; ∼ **des rumeurs** to circulate *ou* spread rumours○ GB; ∼ **une image** to promote an image

veille /vɛj/ *nf* [1] (jour précédent) **la** ∼ the day before; **la** ∼ **au soir** the night *ou* evening before; **la** ∼ **de Noël** Christmas Eve; **en cette** ∼ **de Pâques 1951** the day before this Easter of 1951; **à la** ∼ **de** (juste avant) on the eve of [*guerre, élections*]; **être à la** ∼ **de faire** to be on the verge of doing; [2] (en physiologie) (état normal) waking; (état forcé) vigil; **une nuit de** ∼

an all-night vigil; **être en état de** ∼ to be awake; **ses longues heures de** ∼ **l'ont épuisée** the many hours without sleep have worn her out; [3] (garde) watch; **des heures de** ∼ hours on watch; [4] Tech standby

(Composé) ∼ **technologique** technology watch

veillée /veje/ *nf* [1] (soirée) evening; **à la** ∼ in the evening; [2] (auprès d'un malade) vigil

(Composé) ∼ **funèbre** *or* **mortuaire** wake

veiller /veje/ [1]
A *vtr* to watch over [*malade*]; to keep watch over [*mort*]
B *vtr ind* ∼ **au bon déroulement de qch** to see to it that sth goes smoothly; ∼ **à sa santé** to look after one's health; ∼ **à ce que** to make sure that, to see to it that; ∼ **sur un enfant** to watch over a child
C *vi* [1] (rester éveillé) to stay up; ∼ **au chevet** *or* **auprès de qn** to sit up at sb's bedside; [2] (monter la garde) to be on watch; [3] (être vigilant) to be watchful; **heureusement, la police veille** fortunately, the police are there

(Idiome) ∼ **au grain** to be on one's guard

veilleur, -euse[1] /vɛjœʀ, øz/ ▸ p. 372 *nm,f* (guetteur) lookout; ∼ **de nuit** night watchman

veilleuse[2] /vɛjøz/ *nf* [1] (lampe) night light; [2] (d'appareil à gaz) pilot light; [3] Aut side light GB, parking light US

veinard○, ∼e /venaʀ, aʀd/ *nm,f* lucky devil○

veine /vɛn/ *nf* [1] Anat vein; **ne pas avoir de sang dans les** ∼**s** *fig* to have no guts○; [2] Bot (nervure) vein; **les** ∼**s** (de chou, marbre) the veining **Ⓒ**; (de bois) the grain **Ⓒ**; [3] (mine) (de charbon) seam; (de métal) vein; [4] (inspiration) inspiration; **de** *or* **dans la même** ∼ in the same vein; **être en** ∼ **de générosité** to be in a generous mood; [5] ○(chance) luck; **il a de la** ∼ (en général) he's lucky; (cette fois) he's in luck; **il n'a pas de** ∼ (en général) he's unlucky; (cette fois) he's out of luck; **avoir une** ∼ **de pendu** *or* **cocu**○ to have the luck of the devil○; **coup de** ∼ stroke of luck; **c'est bien ma** ∼! that's just my luck!

veiné, ∼e /vene/ *adj* [*peau, main, marbre*] veined; [*bois*] grained; **pomme ∼e de rouge** apple streaked with red

veinure /venyʀ/ *nf* (du bois) grain **Ⓒ**; (du marbre) veining **Ⓒ**

vêler /vele/ [1] *vi* [*vache*] to calve

vélin /velɛ̃/ *nm* vellum

véliplanchiste /veliplɑ̃ʃist/ *nmf* windsurfer

velléitaire /vel(l)eitɛʀ/
A *adj* weak-willed
B *nmf* waverer

velléité /vel(l)eite/ *nf* (désir vague) vague desire; (tentative) vague attempt; **à la moindre** ∼ **de rébellion** at the slightest sign of rebellion

vélo○ /velo/ *nm* [1] (bicyclette) bike○; **aller en ville en** ∼ to cycle into town; [2] ▸ p. 327 (sport) cycling; **faire du** ∼ to cycle, to go cycling

(Composés) ∼ **d'appartement** exercise bike; ∼ **de course** racing bike; ∼ **tous chemins**, **VTC** hybrid bike; ∼ **tout terrain**, **VTT** mountain bike

vélocité /velosite/ *nf* (de pianiste) nimble-fingeredness; (de footballeur) speed; (d'animal) swiftness; **exercices de** ∼ Mus finger exercises

vélo-cross /velokʀɔs/ *nm inv* [1] ▸ p. 327 (sport) cyclo-cross; **faire du** ∼ to go cyclo-cross racing; [2] (vélo) cyclo-cross bike

vélodrome /velodʀom/ *nm* velodrome

vélomoteur /velomotœʀ/ *nm* moped

velours /vəluʀ/ *nm inv* (lisse) velvet; (à côtes) corduroy, cord; **rideau en** *or* **de** ∼ velvet curtain; **avoir une peau de** ∼ to have a velvety skin; **avoir des yeux de** ∼ to be doe-eyed

(Idiomes) **une main de fer dans un gant de** ∼ an iron fist in a velvet glove; **faire patte de** ∼ [*hypocrite*] to switch on the charm

velouté, ∼e /vəlute/
A *adj* (doux) [*peau*] velvety; [*pêche, son*] velvety; (suave) [*sauce, vin*] smooth; [*regard*] mellow
B *nm* [1] Culin (sauce) velouté sauce; (potage) ∼ **de champignons** cream of mushroom soup; [2] (douceur) (au toucher) softness; (au goût) smoothness; **le** ∼ **de sa peau** his/her velvety skin, his/her velvet skin

velu, ∼e /vəly/ *adj* [*personne, animal*] hairy; [*plantes*] villous

venaison /vənɛzɔ̃/ *nf* game; (daim) venison

venir

venir de + infinitif

venir verbe auxiliaire servant à former le passé immédiat:

venir de faire
= to have just done

elle vient (tout juste) de partir
= she's (only) just left

il venait de se marier
= he'd just got married

je viens de te le dire
= I've just told you

Attention aux exceptions du genre:

vient de paraître
= (*pour un livre*) 'just published!' (*mais pour un disque*) 'new release'

....

venir + infinitif

La traduction de la construction dépend du temps:

j'ai demandé au plombier de venir vérifier la chaudière
= I asked the plumber to come and check the boiler

le plombier viendra vérifier la chaudière
= the plumber will come and check the boiler

le plombier vient vérifier la chaudière aujourd'hui
= the plumber is coming to check the boiler today

te rappelles-tu quel jour le plombier est venu vérifier la chaudière?
= can you remember which day the plumber came to check the boiler?

il était venu vérifier la chaudière et il en a profité pour réparer le robinet de l'évier
= he had come to check the boiler and took the opportunity to mend the tap on the sink

viens voir
= come and see

Cependant, pour les activités sportives, on aura:

elle a décidé de venir nager
= she has decided to come swimming

elle a décidé de venir faire du cheval
= she has decided to come riding

On pourra aussi avoir:

viens déjeuner
= come for lunch (*lunch étant un nom*)

venez nous voir un de ces jours
= come over sometime *ou* (*GB*) come round sometime

Exemples supplémentaires et exceptions sont présentés ci-dessous aussi bien pour *venir* verbe auxiliaire **A**, que pour *venir* verbe intransitif **B**.

---

vénal, **~e**, *mpl* **-aux** /venal, o/ *adj* **1** (intéressé) [*personne*] venal; [*comportement*] mercenary; **2** Comm [*valeur*] monetary

vendable /vɑ̃dabl/ *adj* saleable^GB

vendange /vɑ̃dɑ̃ʒ/ *nf* grape harvest; **faire la ~** *or* **les ~s** [*vigneron*] to harvest the grapes; [*saisonnier*] to go grape-picking

vendanger /vɑ̃dɑ̃ʒe/ [13]
A *vtr* to harvest [*raisin*]; to pick the grapes from [*vigne*]; **machine à ~** mechanical grape harvester
B *vi* Agric (cueillir) to harvest the grapes

vendangeur, -euse[1] /vɑ̃dɑ̃ʒœʀ, øz/ *nm,f* grape-picker

vendangeuse[2] /vɑ̃dɑ̃ʒøz/ *nf* **1** (machine) mechanical grape harvester; **2** Bot aster

vendeur, -euse /vɑ̃dœʀ, øz/ *nm,f* **1** ▸ p. 372 (de magasin) shop assistant, salesclerk US, salesperson; **2** ▸ p. 372 (responsable des ventes) salesperson, salesman/saleswoman; **c'est un excellent ~** he's an excellent salesman; **3** (dans une transaction) seller; Jur vendor; **désolé mais je ne suis pas ~** sorry but I'm not selling
(Composés) **~ ambulant** Comm pedlar GB, peddler US; **~ de journaux** newsvendor GB, newsdealer US; **~ de rêve** pedlar of dreams

vendre /vɑ̃dʀ/ [6]
A *vtr* **1** gén to sell; **~ à crédit** to sell on credit; **~ en gros** to wholesale, to sell [sth] wholesale; **~ au détail** to retail; **ça fait ~** it boosts sales; **~ ses charmes** to sell one's charms; **'à ~'** 'for sale'; **ma voiture n'est pas à ~** my car is not for sale; **2** (trahir) to betray, to shop^○ GB [*personne, complice*] (à to)
B **se vendre** *vpr* **se ~ à la pièce/au poids** to be sold singly/by weight; **se ~ bien/mal** to sell well/badly; **se ~** [*personne*] to sell oneself; **se ~ à l'ennemi** to sell out to the enemy

vendredi /vɑ̃dʀədi/ ▸ p. 545 *nm* Friday; **~ saint** Good Friday

vendu, **~e** /vɑ̃dy/
A *pp* ▸ **vendre**
B *pp adj* (corrompu) [*juge, arbitre, fonctionnaire*] bribed; **~, l'arbitre!** the referee's a traitor!
C *nm,f* traitor; **c'est un ~!** he's sold out, he's a traitor

vénéneux, -euse /venenø, øz/ *adj* poisonous

vénérable /veneʀabl/ *adj* (respectable) [*personne*] venerable; [*arbre, objet*] ancient

vénération /veneʀasjɔ̃/ *nf* veneration

vénérer /venere/ [14] *vtr* **1** Relig to venerate; **2** (respecter) to revere [*personne*]; **~ la mémoire de qn** to venerate sb's memory

vénerie /vɛnʀi/ *nf* hunting, venery spéc

vénérien, -ienne /venerjɛ̃, ɛn/ *adj* venereal

vengeance /vɑ̃ʒɑ̃s/ *nf* revenge; **par ~** out of revenge; **un acte de ~** an act of revenge; **mettre sa ~ à exécution** to get one's revenge; **ma ~ sera terrible!** my vengeance will be terrible!

venger /vɑ̃ʒe/ [13]
A *vtr* to avenge
B **se venger** *vpr* to get *ou* take one's revenge (**de qn** on sb; **se ~ sur qn/qch** to take it out on sb/sth; **se ~ de qch** to get *ou* take one's revenge for sth; **il l'a fait pour se ~** he did it in revenge

vengeur, vengeresse /vɑ̃ʒœʀ, vɑ̃ʒʀɛs/
A *adj* [*personne, acte*] vengeful; [*bras, épée*] avenging; [*lettre*] vindictive
B *nm,f* avenger

véniel, -ielle /venjɛl/ *adj* **1** Relig [*péché*] venial; **2** (excusable) [*faute, oubli*] excusable, pardonable

venimeux, -euse /vənimø, øz/ *adj* venomous

venin /vənɛ̃/ *nm* venom; **~ de serpent** snake venom; **répandre son ~ contre qn** to make venomous *ou* poisonous remarks about sb

venir /vəniʀ/ [36]
A *v aux* **1** (marque l'occurrence) **~ aggraver la situation** to make the situation worse; **2** (marque le mouvement) **le ballon est venu rouler sous mes pieds** the ball rolled up to my feet; **3** (marque le développement) **s'il venait à pleuvoir** if it should rain; **s'il venait à l'apprendre** if he ever got to hear about it; **il en vint à la détester** he came to hate her
B *vi* **1** (dans l'espace) to come; **je viens** *or* **suis venu pour m'excuser** I've come to apologize; **il vient beaucoup de gens le samedi** lots of people come on Saturdays; **allez, viens!** come on!; **d'où viens-tu?** (reproche) where have you been?; **j'en viens** I've just been there; **je viens de sa part** he/she sent me to see you; **faire ~ qn** (demander) to send for sb, to get sb^○; (en le convainquant) to get sb to come; (attirer) to attract sb [*client*]; **faire ~ le médecin** to call the doctor;

faire ~ qch (commander) to order sth; (par la poste) to send for sth; **faire ~ ses chaussures d'Italie** to get one's shoes from Italy; **plantes venues d'ailleurs** plants from far-off places; **gens venus d'ailleurs** (de l'étranger) foreigners; (de l'extérieur) outsiders; **le nom ne me vient pas à l'esprit** the name escapes me; **les mots ne venaient pas** he/she etc couldn't find the words; **l'inspiration ne venait pas** inspiration failed him/her etc; **l'idée lui vint que** the idea occurred to him/her that; **ça ne m'est jamais venu à l'idée** or **l'esprit** it never crossed my mind ou occurred to me; **il lui est venu une idée bizarre** he/she had a weird idea; **2** (dans le temps) **il faut prendre les choses comme elles viennent** you must take things as they come; **ça vient, ça vient**○! it's coming!, it's on its way!; **dans les jours à ~** in the next few days; **le moment venu** (au futur) when the time comes; (au passé) when the time came; **la nuit va bientôt ~** it'll soon be dark; **dans l'heure qui vient** within the hour; **les difficultés à ~** future problems; **je préfère laisser** or **voir ~ (les choses)** I'd rather wait and see how things turn out; **comment êtes-vous venu à l'enseignement?** how did you come to take up teaching?; ~ **loin derrière** to trail a long way behind; **il est venu un moment où j'étais trop fatigué** I got to the point when I was too tired; **3** (marquant l'origine) ~ **d'une famille protestante** to come from a Protestant family; **cette bague me vient de ma tante** my aunt left me this ring; **le succès du roman vient de son style** the novel's success is due to its style; **ça vient de ce qu'ils ne se parlent pas** it's all because they don't talk to each other; **ça me vient naturellement** or **tout seul** that's just the way I am; **4** (dans une hiérarchie) ~ **après/avant** to come after/before; **5** **en ~ à** to come to; **j'en viens au problème qui vous préoccupe** I now come to your problem; **en ~ à abandonner ses études** to get to the point of dropping out of college; **s'il faut en ~ là** if it gets to that point, if it comes to that; **il en était venu à la faire suivre** he even had her followed; **venons-en à l'ordre du jour** let's get down to the agenda; **où veut-il en ~ (au juste)?** what's he driving at?; **en ~ aux mains** or **aux coups** to come to blows

vent /vɑ̃/ *nm* **1** Météo wind; ~ **du large** seaward wind; **grand** ~ gale, strong wind; ~ **de côté** crosswind; **il fait** or **il y a du** ~ it's windy, there's a wind blowing; **le ~ tourne** lit, fig the wind is turning; **coup** or **rafale de** ~ gust of wind; **cheveux au** ~ hair flying in the wind; **exposé à tous les** ~s exposed to all weathers; **en plein** ~ lit exposed to the wind; (dehors) in the open; **passer en coup de** ~ fig to rush through; **faire du** ~ (avec un éventail) to create a breeze; hum (en s'activant) to flap around; **2** Naut ~ **favorable, bon** ~ favourable^{GB} wind, fair wind; ~ **mauvais** unfavourable^{GB} wind; **avoir le** ~ **en poupe** lit to sail ou run before the wind; fig to have the wind in one's sails; ~ **frais** strong breeze; **coup de** ~ fresh gale; **3** (impulsion) **un** ~ **de liberté** a wind of freedom; **un** ~ **de folie soufflait sur le pays** a wave of madness swept through the country; **4** (flatulence) euph wind ₵

(Idiomes) **c'est du** ~! fig it's just hot air!; **du** ~○! (partez) get lost○!; **quel bon** ~ **vous amène?** to what do I ou we owe the pleasure (of your visit)?; **être dans le** ~ to be trendy; **avoir** ~ **de qch** to get wind of sth; **contre** ~s **et marées** [faire] come hell or high water; [avoir fait] against all odds

Vent /vɑ̃/ ▸ **p. 303** *nprm* **les îles du** ~ the Windward Islands

vente /vɑ̃t/ *nf* sale; **être en** ~ to be for sale; **en** ~ **chez votre marchand de journaux** available ou for sale at your newsagent's; **en** ~ **libre** gén freely available; [médicaments] available over the counter

(Composés) ~ **par correspondance** mail order selling; ~ **au détail** retailing; ~ **aux enchères** auction (sale); ~ **en gros** wholesaling

venter /vɑ̃te/ [1] *v impers* to blow; **il vente** the wind is blowing

venteux, -euse /vɑ̃tø, øz/ *adj* [journée, mois] windy; [région, pays] windswept

ventilateur /vɑ̃tilatœʀ/ *nm* gén fan; (aérateur) ventilator

ventilation /vɑ̃tilasjɔ̃/ *nf* **1** (aération) ventilation; (système) ventilation (system); **2** (répartition) ~ **du personnel** allocation of staff to different departments

ventiler /vɑ̃tile/ [1] *vtr* **1** (aérer) to ventilate; **2** Méd to ventilate [malade]; **3** (en comptabilité) to break down [dépenses, bénéfices]; **4** (diviser) to divide up [groupe, ensemble];

(répartir) to assign [personnel]; to allocate [tâches, matériaux]

ventouse /vɑ̃tuz/ *nf* **1** (d'adhésion) suction pad GB, suction cup US; **crochet à** ~ suction hook; **faire** ~ to stick; **2** (pour déboucher) plunger; **3** Bot, Zool sucker; (chez la grenouille) adhesive disc; **4** Méd cupping glass; **poser des** ~s **à qn** to cup sb

ventral, -e, *mpl* **-aux** /vɑ̃tʀal, o/ *adj* [nageoire] ventral; **parachute** ~ lap-pack parachute

ventre /vɑ̃tʀ/ ▸ **p. 136** *nm* **1** (abdomen, estomac) stomach, tummy○, belly; **s'allonger sur le** ~ to lie face down; **rentrer son** ~ to hold in one's stomach; **avoir mal au** ~ to have stomach-ache; **avoir le** ~ **creux/plein** to have an empty/a full stomach; **le de la terre** liter the bowels (pl) of the earth littér; ▸ **affamé; 2** (d'animal) (under)belly; **3** (utérus) womb; **4** (siège du courage) **ne rien avoir dans le** ~ to have no guts○; **avoir la rage/la peur au** ~ to feel sick with fury/fear; **je ne sais pas ce qu'il a dans le** ~○ I don't know what he's made of; **5** (partie renflée) (de marmite, bateau, d'avion) belly

(Idiomes) **courir** ~ **à terre** to run flat out; **tu as les yeux plus gros que le** ~ your eyes are bigger than your stomach

ventricule /vɑ̃tʀikyl/ *nm* Anat **1** (de cœur, d'encéphale) ventricle; **2** (d'oiseau) ventriculus

ventriloque /vɑ̃tʀilɔk/ ▸ **p. 372** *nmf* ventriloquist

ventripotent○, ~**e** /vɑ̃tʀipotɑ̃, ɑ̃t/ *adj* portly, fat-bellied péj

ventru, ~e /vɑ̃tʀy/ *adj* [homme] paunchy, pot-bellied; [marmite, meuble] rounded; [mur] bulging

venu, ~e¹ /vəny/

A *pp* ▸ **venir**

B *pp adj* **1** (à propos) **bien** ~ apt; **mal** ~ badly timed; **il serait mal** ~ **de le leur dire** it wouldn't be a good idea to tell them; **2** (réussi) **bien** ~ [œuvre, plaisanterie] clever

C *nm,f* **nouveau** ~ newcomer

venue² /vəny/ *nf* visit; **les raisons de sa** ~ **sont obscures** it's not clear why he/she came; ~ **au monde** birth; ~ **du Messie** coming of the Messiah

vêpres /vɛpʀ/ *nfpl* Relig vespers

ver /vɛʀ/ *nm* **1** Zool worm; (dans le bois) woodworm; (dans la nourriture) maggot, grub; **2** Méd (parasite) worm

(Composés) ~ **luisant** glowworm; ~ **de sable** sandworm; ~ **à soie** silkworm; ~ **solitaire** tapeworm; ~ **de terre** earthworm; ~ **de vase** bloodworm

(Idiomes) **être nu comme un** ~ to be stark naked; **tirer les** ~s **du nez à qn**○ to worm information out of sb

véracité /veʀasite/ *nf* truthfulness, veracity sout

véranda /veʀɑ̃da/ *nf* veranda; **sous la** ~ on the veranda

verbal, -e, *mpl* **-aux** /vɛʀbal, o/ *adj* **1** (oral) verbal; **2** (de langage) [attaque, violence] verbal; **3** Ling (de verbe) [groupe, adjectif] verbal; [catégorie, forme] verb (épith); **syntagme** ~ verb phrase

verbaliser /vɛʀbalize/ [1]

A *vtr* Psych to verbalize [sentiments]

B *vi* (dresser un procès-verbal) to record an offence^{GB}

verbe /vɛʀb/ *nm* **1** Ling verb; **2** (langage) language; **avoir le** ~ **facile** to be quick to talk; **avoir le** ~ **haut** to be arrogant in one's speech; **3** Relig **le Verbe** the Word

verbiage /vɛʀbjaʒ/ *nm* verbiage, verbosity

verdâtre /vɛʀdɑtʀ/ ▸ **p. 140** *adj* pej greenish

verdeur /vɛʀdœʀ/ *nf* **1** (truculence) rawness; **2** (vigueur) sprightliness; **3** (acidité) tartness, acidity

verdict /vɛʀdikt/ *nm* **1** Jur (décision de jury) verdict; **rendre un** ~ to return ou announce a verdict; ~ **d'acquittement** verdict of not guilty; **2** fig (appréciation) verdict, judgment; **un** ~ **sans appel** a verdict ou judgment without appeal

verdir /vɛʀdiʀ/ [3] *vi* **1** (devenir vert) gén to turn green; [cuivre] to tarnish; **2** (pâlir) to turn pale

verdoyant, ~e /vɛʀdwajɑ̃, ɑ̃t/ *adj* green, verdant littér

verdure /vɛʀdyʀ/ *nf* **1** (végétation) greenery; **2** (légumes verts) green vegetables (pl); **3** (couleurs) verdure littér, greenness

véreux, -euse /veʀø, øz/ *adj* **1** (contenant des vers) [fruit] worm-eaten; **2** (malhonnête) [politicien, avocat] bent○, crooked; [affaire, contrat] shady○, dubious

verge /vɛʀʒ/ *nf* **1** Anat penis; **2** (pour battre) switch, birch

vergé /vɛʀʒe/ *nm* laid paper

verger /vɛʀʒe/ *nm* orchard

vergeture /vɛʀʒətyʀ/ nf stretch mark

verglacé, **~e** /vɛʀglase/ adj icy

verglas /vɛʀgla/ nm inv black ice

vergogne: **sans vergogne** /sɑ̃vɛʀgɔɲ/
A loc adv **1** (sans honte) shamelessly; **2** (sans hésitation) straight out
B loc adj (sans scrupule) unscrupulous

vergue /vɛʀg/ nf Naut yard

véridique /veʀidik/ adj [détail, histoire, fait] true; [description, témoignage] truthful; **l'anecdote est ~** the story is true

vérifiable /veʀifjabl/ adj [histoire, source, méthode] verifiable sout; **être facilement ~** to be easy to check ou verify

vérificateur, **-trice** /veʀifikatœʀ, tʀis/ ▸ p. 372 nm,f controller

vérification /veʀifikasjɔ̃/ nf (d'appareil, expérience) check (de on); (d'alibi, de fait) verification; **une ~ d'identité** an identity check

vérifier /veʀifje/ [2]
A vtr **1** (tester) to check [appareil, instrument]; (contrôler) to check [identité, adresse, norme, calcul]; **2** (confirmer) to verify, to check [affirmation, témoignage]; to confirm [hypothèse]; to verify [fait]
B se **vérifier** vpr [hypothèse, théorie] to be borne out; **se ~ dans les faits** to be borne out by the facts

vérin /veʀɛ̃/ nm (screw) jack

véritable /veʀitabl/ adj **1** (authentique) [ami] true, genuine, real; [sentiment, discussion] true, real; [artiste] true; [cuir] real, genuine; [or, argent] real; **2** (réel) [nom, raison, responsable] real, actual; [colère] real; [joie] true; **3** (intensif) (before n) real, veritable; **la pièce est une ~ fournaise** the room is like an oven

véritablement /veʀitabləmɑ̃/ adv really, actually; **c'est ~ un scandale!** it really is a scandal!

vérité /veʀite/ nf **1** gén truth; **posséder** or **détenir la ~** to know everything; **le quart d'heure** or **la minute de ~** the moment of truth; **l'épreuve de ~** the acid test; **faire la ~ sur qch** to disclose the truth about sth; **à la ~** to tell the truth; **2** (affirmation vraie) truth; **énoncer des ~s premières** to state the obvious; **toute ~ n'est pas bonne à dire** some things are better left unsaid; **3** (authenticité) (de personnage, scène, reconstitution) realism; (de sentiment, d'expression) sincerity; **4** (nature profonde) true nature

Idiomes **à chacun sa ~** Prov each to his own; **la ~ sort de la bouche des enfants** Prov out of the mouths of (very) babes (and sucklings)

verlan /vɛʀlɑ̃/ nm: French slang formed by inverting the syllables

ⓘ Verlan is a form of French slang which reverses the order of syllables in many common words rendering them more or less incomprehensible to the uninitiated. For example, the term itself is derived from the word l'envers the syllables of which are reversed to create vers-l'en which in turn becomes verlan. Single syllable words are also converted so femme becomes meuf, mec becomes keum, etc. A recent coinage for énervé is vénère.

vermeil, **-eille** /vɛʀmɛj/
A ▸ p. 140 adj **1** (rouge vif) bright red; **teint ~** rosy complexion; **2** [vin] ruby
B nm (argent doré) vermeil

vermicelle /vɛʀmisɛl/ nm vermicelli ⓒ

vermifuge /vɛʀmifyʒ/
A adj worm (épith)
B nm wormer

vermillon /vɛʀmijɔ̃/ ▸ p. 140
A adj inv (rouge vif) bright red, vermilion
B nm **1** (couleur) bright red, vermilion; **2** (sulfure de mercure) vermilion

vermine /vɛʀmin/ nf **1** (parasites) vermin; **2** (personnes) scum, vermin

vermoulu, **~e** /vɛʀmuly/ adj **1** [planche, mobilier] worm-eaten; **2** [idéologie, institutions] moth-eaten

verni, **~e** /vɛʀni/
A pp ▸ vernir
B pp adj lit [bois, peinture] varnished; [chaussures] patent-leather (épith); [faïence] glazed
C °adj (chanceux) lucky; **il n'est pas ~** he's unlucky

vernir /vɛʀniʀ/ [3]
A vtr to varnish [planche, meuble]; to glaze [faïence, poterie]; to apply nail varnish GB ou nail polish to [ongles]
B se **vernir** vpr se ~ **les ongles** to varnish GB ou polish one's nails

vernis /vɛʀni/ nm inv **1** (sur bois) varnish; (sur céramique) glaze; **2** (apparence) veneer; **un ~ de culture** a veneer of culture; **si on gratte le ~, on voit que...** if you scratch the surface, you'll see that...

Composé **~ à ongles** nail varnish GB ou polish

vernissage /vɛʀnisaʒ/ nm **1** Art preview, private view; **2** (de bois) varnishing; (de céramique) glazing

vernissé, **~e** /vɛʀnise/ adj **1** [tuiles, carreaux] glazed; **2** [plumes, feuilles] glossy

véronique /veʀɔnik/ nf speedwell, veronica spéc

verre /vɛʀ/ nm **1** (matière) glass; **de** or **en ~** glass (épith); **travail du ~** glasswork; **des débris de ~** broken glass ⓒ; **2** (récipient) glass; **~s et couverts** glassware and cutlery; **lever son ~ à la santé de qn** to raise one's glass to sb; **3** (contenu) glass, glassful; **4** (boisson) drink; **un petit ~** a quick drink; **avoir bu un ~ de trop** to have had one too many; **boire le ~ de l'amitié** to toast one's friendship; **5** (plaque) glass; **mettre qch sous ~** to put sth under glass; [lentille] lens; **~s de lunettes** spectacle lenses; **~ grossissant** magnifying glass

Composés **~ antireflet** antiglare glass; **~ de contact** contact lens; **~ correcteur** corrective lens; **~ à dents** toothglass; **~ fumé** (pour lunettes) tinted lens; (pour vitrage) tinted glass; **~ gradué** measuring jug; **~ de lampe** lamp chimney; **~ à pied** stemmed glass; **~ progressif** varifocal lens

verrerie /vɛʀʀi/ nf **1** (fabrication) glassmaking; **2** (objets) glassware; **3** (usine) glassworks (pl), glass factory

verrier, **-ière¹** /vɛʀje, ɛʀ/
A adj glass (épith)
B ▸ p. 372 nm glassmaker, glass manufacturer

verrière² /vɛʀjɛʀ/ nf **1** (toit vitré) glass roof; **2** (grand vitrage) glass wall, glassed-in wall; **3** (de cockpit) canopy

verroterie /vɛʀɔtʀi/ nf glass jewellery GB ou jewelry US

verrou /vɛʀu/ nm gén bolt; (à bouton) deadbolt; (à clé) deadlock; **~ 3 points** multilock; **mettre le ~** to shoot the bolt

Idiome **être sous les ~s** to be under lock and key

verrouillage /vɛʀujaʒ/ nm (action) bolting; (d'arme à feu) locking; (dispositif) locking mechanism

Composé **~ central** or **centralisé (des portes)** Aut central locking

verrouiller /vɛʀuje/ [1] vtr gén to bolt [fenêtre, porte]; to lock [portière, arme]; to cordon off [quartier]; **~ une majorité parlementaire** to protect a parliamentary majority

verrue /vɛʀy/ nf Méd wart; **~ plantaire** verruca, plantar wart spéc

vers¹ /vɛʀ/ prép

⚠ Lorsque vers indique une direction, une tendance ou une orientation, il se traduit généralement par toward(s). On notera que towards est plus courant en anglais britannique et toward en anglais américain.
Lorsque vers fait partie d'une phrase du genre se tourner vers, tendre vers, départ vers etc la traduction est donnée respectivement à tourner, tendre, départ.
On trouvera ci-dessous des usages particuliers de vers.

1 (en direction de) toward(s); **il vint ~ moi** he came toward(s) me; **il n'a même pas tourné la tête ~ elle** he didn't even look in her direction; **se déplacer de la gauche ~ la droite** to move from left to right; **des migrations ~ le sud** migration to the south; **il habite plus ~ le nord** he lives further north; **2** (aux environs de) (lieu) near, around; (temps) about; (période) toward(s); **les rues sont toujours encombrées ~ le centre-ville** the streets are always congested around the town centre^GB; **~ cinq heures** about ou around five o'clock; **elle est tombée malade ~ l'âge de 25 ans** she became ill GB ou sick US when she was about 25

vers² /vɛʀ/
A nm inv (ligne de poésie) line (of verse); **le troisième ~** the third line; **poème en ~** poem in verse
B nmpl (poésie) poetry ⓒ

versant /vɛʀsɑ̃/ nm side

versatile /vɛʀsatil/ adj [personne] unpredictable, volatile

verse: **à verse** /avɛʀs/ loc adv **il pleut à** ~ it's pouring down

Verseau /vɛʀso/ ▸ p. 635 nprm Aquarius

versement /vɛʀsəmɑ̃/ nm [1] (de somme) payment; ~ **comptant** cash payment; [2] (échelonné) instalment^GB; [3] (dépôt) deposit; **faire un** ~ **sur son compte** to pay money into one's account

verser /vɛʀse/ [1]
A vtr [1] (servir) to pour [boisson]; (transvaser) to pour [liquide, sable]; (sans précautions) to tip [liquide, sable]; ~ **à boire à qn** to pour sb a drink; **attention, tu verses à côté** careful, you're spilling it; [2] (payer) to pay; **on leur verse une commission** they get a commission; [3] (répandre) to shed [larme, sang]; ~ **le sang** to shed blood; ~ **son sang pour la patrie** (mourir) to die fighting for one's country; [4] (ajouter) to add; ~ **une pièce à un dossier** to add a document to a file; [5] Mil (affecter) to assign (**dans** to)
B vi [1] (se renverser) to overturn; [2] (se laisser aller à) to lapse (**dans** into); [3] (laisser couler) [cruche] to pour

verset /vɛʀse/ nm [1] (de la Bible, du Coran) verse; [2] (prière) versicle; [3] Littérat verset

verseur, -euse /vɛʀsœʀ, øz/ adj pouring; **flacon** ~ bottle with a pouring spout

versifier /vɛʀsifje/ [2] vtr to put [sth] into verse

version /vɛʀsjɔ̃/ nf [1] (traduction) translation (into one's own language); [2] (interprétation) version; **la** ~ **officielle** the official version; [3] Cin, Littérat, Mus version; **en** ~ **espagnole** in the Spanish version; [4] Ind, Comm (modèle) model, version
(Composés) ~ **doublée** Cin dubbed version; ~ **originale, vo** Cin original version

verso /vɛʀso/ nm back; **voir au** ~ see over(leaf)

vert, ~**e** /vɛʀ, vɛʀt/
A ▸ p. 140 adj [1] gén green; [région, pays] green, verdant littér; **une banlieue** ~**e** a leafy suburb; **être** ~ **de peur** to be white with fear; [2] (non arrivé à maturité) [fruit, légume] green, unripe; [bois] green; [vin] immature; [3] (vigoureux) [vieillard] sprightly; [4] (before n) [semonce, réprimande] sharp, stiff
B ▸ p. 140 nm green; **le feu est passé au** ~ the light went ou turned green
C verts nmpl Pol **les** ~**s** the environmentalists, the ecologists GB; **les Verts** the French Green party
(Idiomes) **en dire de** ~**es** to tell spicy ou risqué stories; **avoir la main** ~**e** to have green fingers GB ou a green thumb US; **se mettre au** ~○ to take a break in the country

vert-de-gris /vɛʀdəgʀi/
A ▸ p. 140 adj inv blue-green
B nm inv Tech verdigris

vertébral, ~**e,** mpl **-aux** /vɛʀtebʀal, o/ adj vertebral

vertèbre /vɛʀtɛbʀ/ nf vertebra; **les** ~**s cervicales** cervical vertebrae; **se déplacer une** ~ to slip a disc

vertébré, ~**e** /vɛʀtebʀe/
A adj vertebrate
B nm vertebrate

vertement /vɛʀtəmɑ̃/ adv sharply

vertical, ~**e**[1], mpl **-aux** /vɛʀtikal, o/ adj [1] Math, gén [axe, plan, mouvement, position, décollage] vertical; [miroir, panneau] upright; **la station** ~**e** standing position; [2] (selon une hiérarchie) [intégration, organisation, croissance] vertical

verticale[2] /vɛʀtikal/ nf Math, Phys vertical; **mettre qch à la** ~ to put sth upright; **le rocher se dresse à la** ~ the rock rises sheer

verticalement /vɛʀtikalmɑ̃/ adv [1] gén vertically; [2] (dans les mots croisés) down

vertige /vɛʀtiʒ/ nm [1] (sensation) dizziness, giddiness; (dû à la hauteur) vertigo; **avoir le** ~ (habituellement) to suffer from vertigo; (ponctuellement) to feel dizzy ou giddy; [2] (malaise) **avoir des** ~**s** to have dizzy ou giddy spells; [3] (exaltation) ~ **de l'amour** intoxicating effect of love

vertigineux, -euse /vɛʀtiʒinø, øz/ adj [hauteur] dizzy, giddy; [profondeur, ascension, vitesse] breathtaking; [somme, chute, progression] staggering

vertu /vɛʀty/
A nf [1] (intégrité) (moral) virtue; [2] (chasteté) virtue, honour^GB; **de petite** ~ of easy virtue; [3] (qualité) quality, virtue;

[4] (propriété) (de plante, remède) property; (de choses abstraites) virtue
B **en vertu de** loc prép Jur by virtue of, pursuant to; gén in accordance with

vertueux, -euse /vɛʀtɥø, øz/ adj virtuous

verve /vɛʀv/ nf eloquence; **être (très) en** ~ to be in sparkling form

verveine /vɛʀvɛn/ nf [1] Bot verbena; [2] (liqueur) **(liqueur de)** ~ verbena liqueur; [3] (tisane) verbena tea

vésiculaire /vezikylɛʀ/ adj [1] Méd of the gall bladder (après n); [2] (en forme de vésicule) vesicular

vésicule /vezikyl/ nf [1] Anat, Bot vesicle; [2] Méd (cloque) blister
(Composés) ~ **biliaire** gall bladder; ~**s séminales** Anat seminal vesicles

vespasienne /vɛspazjɛn/ nf public urinal

vespéral, ~**e,** mpl **-aux** /vɛsperal, o/ adj liter evening (épith)

vessie /vesi/ nf bladder; ~ **gazeuse** or **natatoire** air ou swim bladder
(Idiomes) **prendre des** ~**s pour des lanternes**○ to think the moon is made of green cheese; **faire prendre des** ~**s pour des lanternes à qn** to pull the wool over sb's eyes

veste /vɛst/ nf jacket; ~ **de survêtement** Sport tracksuit top; **tomber la** ~○ to take off one's jacket
(Idiomes) **retourner sa** ~○ Pol to change sides, to sell out; **prendre une** ~○ to come a cropper○

vestiaire /vɛstjɛʀ/ nm [1] (salle) (dans un stade, gymnase) changing GB ou locker room; (dans un musée, un théâtre, une discothèque) cloakroom; **laisser sa fierté au** ~ fig to forget one's pride; [2] (meuble) locker

vestibule /vɛstibyl/ nm (d'édifice) hall; (d'hôtel, de théâtre) foyer GB, lobby

vestige /vɛstiʒ/ nm [1] (de construction, d'objet) relic; **des** ~**s archéologiques** archeological remains; [2] (d'époque, de civilisation) vestige

vestimentaire /vɛstimɑ̃tɛʀ/ adj tenue ~ way of dressing; **mode** ~ fashion; **élégance** ~ elegance in dress

veston /vɛstɔ̃/ nm (man's) jacket

vêtement /vɛtmɑ̃/ nm [1] (pièce d'habillement) item ou piece of clothing; **des** ~**s** clothes, clothing **₵**; ~**s de travail** workclothes; **ce** ~ **se vend très bien** this garment is selling very well; '~**s pour hommes**' 'menswear', 'men's fashions'; ~**s de sport** sportswear; [2] (secteur d'activité) clothing trade, garment industry US

vétéran /veterɑ̃/ nm veteran

vétérinaire /veteʀinɛʀ/
A adj veterinary
B ▸ p. 372 nmf vet, veterinary surgeon GB, veterinarian US

vétille /vetij/ nf trifle

vêtir /vetiʀ/ [33]
A vtr (habiller) to dress
B **se vêtir** vpr to dress (oneself), to get dressed

veto /veto/ nm veto; **mettre** or **opposer son** ~ **à qch** to veto sth

vêtu, ~**e** /vety/
A pp ▸ **vêtir**
B pp adj dressed; **être** ~ **de qch** to be dressed ou clad in sth, to be wearing sth

vétuste /vetyst/ adj (délabré) dilapidated; (obsolète) outdated

vétusté /vetyste/ nf (délabrement) dilapidation (**de** of), run-down state (**de** of); (ancienneté) (great) age (**de** of), outdated state (**de** of)

veuf, veuve /vœf, vœv/
A adj widowed; **être** ~/**veuve** to be a widower/widow
B nm,f widower/widow; **Mme Brun, veuve Dupont** Mrs Brun, the widow of Mr Dupont

veule /vøl/ adj weak, spineless

veuvage /vœvaʒ/ nm [1] (perte du conjoint) loss of one's husband/wife; [2] (état de veuf) (state of) being a widower; (état de veuve) widowhood

veuve ▸ **veuf**

vexant, ~**e** /vɛksɑ̃, ɑ̃t/ adj (blessant) hurtful (**pour** to); (contrariant) tiresome, vexing

vexation /vɛksasjɔ̃/ nf humiliation

vexer /vɛkse/ [1]
A *vtr* **1** (blesser) to offend, to upset; **être vexé par qch/par qn** to be upset at sth/by sb; **2** (contrarier) to annoy
B **se vexer** *vpr* to take offence^{GB}, to be upset

via /vja/ *prép* **1** (en passant par) via; **2** (par l'intermédiaire de) via, through

viabilisé, **~e** /vjabilize/ *adj* [*terrain*] with all mains services (*épith, après n*)

viabilité /vjabilite/ *nf* **1** (de fœtus) viability; **2** (de régime, d'entreprise) viability; **3** (de terrain) **assurer la ~ d'un terrain** to provide a building site *ou* plot with services; **4** (de route) suitability for vehicles

viable /vjabl/ *adj* **1** [*fœtus*] viable; **2** [*projet*] feasible; [*entreprise*] viable; [*situation*] bearable, tolerable

viaduc /vjadyk/ *nm* viaduct

viager, **-ère** /vjaʒe, ɛʁ/ *Jur*
A *adj* life (*épith*)
B *nm* (rente) life annuity; **acheter qch en ~** to buy sth by paying a life annuity; **vendre qch en ~** to sell sth for a life annuity

viande /vjɑ̃d/ *nf* Culin meat; **~ de bœuf/mouton** beef/mutton

vibrant, **~e** /vibʁɑ̃, ɑ̃t/ *adj* **1** (animé de vibrations) [*coussin, lame*] vibrating; **2** (ému) [*voix*] resonant; [*discours*] vibrant; [*hommage*] glowing; [*plaidoyer*] impassioned; [*foule*] excited, feverish; **~ d'excitation/de colère** quivering with excitement/with anger

vibration /vibʁasjɔ̃/ *nf* vibration; **traitement par ~s** vibromassage

vibratoire /vibʁatwaʁ/ *adj* vibratory

vibrer /vibʁe/ [1] *vi* **1** (osciller) gén, Phys [*lame, son*] to vibrate; **2** (frémir) [*voix*] to quiver (de with); [*cœur*] to thrill; **elle vibrait de tout son être** *liter* she felt a thrill go through her; **on vibre en les écoutant** your spine tingles when you listen to them; **faire ~ la corde patriotique** to rouse people's patriotism

vibreur /vibʁœʁ/ *nm* vibrator; **téléphone avec ~** telephone with a vibrate setting

vicaire /vikɛʁ/ *nm* curate
(Composés) **~ apostolique** vicar apostolic; **le ~ du Christ** the Vicar of Christ; **~ général** vicar general

vice /vis/ *nm* **1** (débauche) vice; **vivre dans le ~** to lead a dissolute life; **2** (mauvaise habitude) vice; **3** (défaut physique) fault, defect
(Composés) **~ caché** hidden defect *ou* fault; **~ de construction** structural defect; **~ de fabrication** manufacturing defect; **~ de procédure** legal irregularity

vice-amiral, *pl* **-aux** /visamiʁal, o/ ▸ p. 283 *nm* ≈ rear-admiral

vice-chancelier, *pl* **~s** /visʃɑ̃səlje/ ▸ p. 590 *nm* vice-chancellor

vice-présidence, *pl* **~s** /vispʁezidɑ̃s/ *nf* (d'État) vice-presidency; (de comité, d'entreprise) vice-chairmanship, vice-presidency US

vice-président, **~e**, *mpl* **~s** /vispʁezidɑ̃, ɑ̃t/ *nm,f* (d'État) vice-president; (de comité, d'entreprise) vice-chair(man), vice-president US

vice-roi, *pl* **~s** /visʁwa/ ▸ p. 590 *nm* viceroy

vice(-)versa /visvɛʁsa/ *adv* vice versa

vichy /viʃi/ *nm* **1** (tissu) gingham; **2** (eau) vichy water

vicier /visje/ [2]
A *vtr* (altérer) to pollute [*air*]; to contaminate [*sang*]
B **se vicier** *vpr* [*air*] to become polluted

vicieux, **-ieuse** /visjø, øz/
A *adj* **1** (dépravé) [*personne*] lecherous; **il faut être ~ pour aimer ça** you've got to be perverted to like that; **2** (sournois) [*personne*] sly; [*coup, attaque*] well-disguised; [*question*] trick (*épith*); [*argumentation*] deceitful; **3** (défectueux) [*locution, prononciation*] wrong; [*position*] abnormal; **un cercle ~** a vicious circle; **4** (indocile) [*cheval*] vicious
B *nm,f* pervert

vicinal, **~e**, *mpl* **-aux** /visinal, o/ *adj* Admin **chemin ~** byroad

vicissitudes /visisityd/ *nfpl* (épreuves) trials and tribulations; (changements) vicissitudes, ups and downs[○]

vicomte /vikɔ̃t/ ▸ p. 590 *nm* viscount

vicomtesse /vikɔ̃tɛs/ ▸ p. 590 *nf* viscountess

victime /viktim/ *nf* **1** (d'accident, de désastre, phénomène) victim, casualty; **être ~ d'un infarctus** to suffer a heart attack; **le joueur, ~ d'une blessure au genou...** the player, suffering from a knee injury...; **~ d'une panne, il a abandonné la course** hit by mechanical problems, he abandoned the race; **il a été ~ de son succès** his success has been his undoing; **2** Jur victim; **3** (créature offerte en sacrifice) sacrificial victim

victoire /viktwaʁ/ *nf* gén victory; Sport win, victory **crier** *or* **chanter ~** to claim victory; **(remporter) une ~ sur soi-même** (to win) a personal battle

victorieusement /viktɔʁjøzmɑ̃/ *adv* triumphantly

victorieux, **-ieuse** /viktɔʁjø, øz/ *adj* [*pays, armée*] victorious; [*athlète, équipe*] winning (*épith*); [*débuts, tir*] successful; [*sourire*] of victory (*épith, après n*)

victuailles /viktɥaj/ *nfpl* provisions, victuals

vidange /vidɑ̃ʒ/ *nf* **1** (de cuve, fosse, fossé) emptying; **2** Aut oil change; **faire la ~** to change the oil; **huile de ~** waste oil; **3** (tuyau d'évacuation) (de baignoire) drain; (de lave-linge) waste pipe

vidanger /vidɑ̃ʒe/ [13]
A *vtr* **1** to empty, to drain [*cuve, fosse*]; **2** to drain off [*liquide*]
B *vi* [*lave-linge*] to empty

vide /vid/
A *adj* **1** (sans contenu) [*boîte*] empty; [*cassette, page*] blank; **les mains ~s** fig empty-handed; **tu l'as loué ~ ou meublé?** are you renting it unfurnished or furnished?; **2** (dépeuplé, inoccupé) [*salle, rue, fauteuil*] empty; [*appartement*] empty, vacant; **3** (sans intérêt, substance, idées) [*vie, slogan, esprit*] empty; [*regard*] vacant; **j'ai la tête ~** my mind is a blank; **~ d'intérêt** devoid of any interest; **~ de sens** meaningless
B *nm* **1** (espace) space; **sauter** *or* **se jeter dans le ~** *lit* to jump into space; *fig* to leap into the unknown; **et au-dessous de lui, le ~** (alpiniste) and below him, a sheer drop; (acrobate) and nothing between him and the ground; **être attiré par le ~** to be drawn toward(s) the edge; **parler dans le ~** (sans auditeur) to talk to oneself; (sans sujet) to talk at random; **promettre dans le ~** *fig* to make empty promises; **2** Phys vacuum; **emballé sous ~** vacuum packed; **faire le ~ autour de soi** *fig* to drive everybody away; **j'ai besoin de faire le ~ dans ma tête** I need to forget about everything; **3** (absence à combler) vacuum, void; (absence douloureuse) void; **combler un ~** to fill a vacuum; **4** (vacuité) emptiness; **le ~ de l'existence** the emptiness of life; **5** (trou) (entre deux objets) gap, empty space; (dans un emploi du temps) gap; **combler un** *or* **le ~** *lit*, *fig* to fill a gap
C **à vide** *loc adv* (sans contenu) empty; (sans résultat) with no result; **la clé tourne à ~** the key is not catching; **camion à ~ truck** without a load

vidé, **~e** /vide/
A *pp* ▸ vider
B [○]*pp adj* (fatigué) worn out

vidéaste /videast/ ▸ p. 372 *nmf* video director

vide-greniers /vidgʁənje/ *nm inv* bric-a-brac sale

vidéo /video/ *adj inv, nf* video

vidéoclip /videoklip/ *nm* videoclip

vidéoclub /videoklœb/ *nm* video store, video shop GB

vidéoconférence /videokɔ̃feʁɑ̃s/ *nf* **1** (séance) video-conference; **2** (principe) video conferencing

vidéodisque /videodisk/ *nm* videodisc

vide-ordures /vidɔʁdyʁ/ *nm inv* rubbish GB *ou* garbage US chute

vidéothèque /videotɛk/ *nf* (de prêt) video library; (chez soi) video collection

vide-poches /vidpɔʃ/ *nm inv* (coupe) tidy

vider /vide/ [1]
A *vtr* **1** (débarrasser) to empty [*poche, boîte, pièce, verre*]; to empty, to drain [*cuve, étang, réservoir*]; (avaler) to down [*verre*]; to go through [*paquet de biscuits*]; **~ un coffre-fort** to clean out a safe; **2** (retirer) to empty [sth] (out) [*eau, ordures*]; **3** (rendre désert) to empty [*lieu*]; **4**[○] (expulser) to throw [sb] out[○], to kick [sb] out[○] [*intrus, indésirable*]; **5** (évider) to gut [*poisson*]; to draw [*volaille*]; to core [*pomme*]; to hollow out [*tomate*]; **6** (priver) **~ qch de son sens** to deprive sth of all meaning; **7** [○](épuiser) (physiquement) to wear [sb] out; (mentalement) to drain [*personne*]

B se **vider** *vpr* to empty; **en été, Paris se vide de ses habitants** in the summer all Parisians leave town

videur○, **-euse** /vidœʀ, øz/ ▸ p. 372 *nm,f* bouncer

vie /vi/ *nf* **1** gén, Biol life; **rendre la ~ à qn** to bring sb back to life; **sans ~** lifeless; **on l'a retrouvé sans ~** they found him dead; **donner la ~ à qn** to bring sb into the world; **2** (période) life; **pour la ~** for life; **vivre sa ~** to lead one's own life; **passer sa ~ à faire** gén to spend one's life doing; (tout le temps) to spend all one's time doing; **à ~** [*bannir, défigurer, marquer*] for life; [*bannissement, suspension*] lifetime (*épith*); [*emprisonnement, adhésion, président*] life (*épith*); **c'est la chance de ta ~** it's the chance of a lifetime; **3** (activité) life; **la ~ d'entreprise** corporate life; **la ~ est chère** the cost of living is high; **mode de ~** lifestyle; **apprendre la ~** to learn what life is all about; **notre ~ de couple** our relationship; ▸ **château**; **4** (vitalité) life; **prendre ~** to come to life; **donner de la ~ à une fête** to liven up a party; **manquant de ~, sans ~** [*personne, lieu*] lifeless; **5** (biographie) life; **écrire la ~ de qn** to write a life of sb; **6** Tech (durabilité) life; **~ d'une pile** life of a battery

(Idiomes) **ainsi va la ~** that's the way it goes; **c'est la belle ~!** this is the life!; **avoir la ~ dure** [*préjugés*] to be ingrained; **mener la ~ dure à qn** to make life hard for sb, to give sb a hard time; **faire la ~**○ [*enfants*] to have a wild time; [*adultes*] to live it up○; **à la ~, à la mort!** till death us do part!

vieil ▸ **vieux**

vieillard, ~e /vjɛjaʀ, aʀd/ *nm,f* old man/woman; **les ~s** old people

vieille ▸ **vieux**

vieillerie /vjɛjʀi/ *nf* (objet) old thing

vieillesse /vjɛjɛs/ *nf* **1** (de personne) old age; (de bâtiment, d'arbre) great age; **2** ○(personnes âgées) **la ~** the old (+ *v pl*)

vieilli, ~e /vjeji/

A *pp* ▸ **vieillir**

B *pp adj* **1** (usé) [*peau, tentures*] old-looking; **2** (démodé) [*équipement*] outdated; [*expression*] dated; **3** (bonifié) **vin ~ en fût** wine matured in the cask

vieillir /vjejiʀ/ [3]

A *vtr* **1** (en apparence) [*coiffure, robe*] to make [sb] look older; **2** (en estimation) **ne me vieillis pas, j'ai 59 ans!** don't make me out to be any older than I am, I'm only 59!; **3** (physiquement) [*maladie, pauvreté*] to age

B *vi* **1** (en âge) **je vieillis** I am getting old; **j'ai vieilli** I'm older; (en maturité) I have grown up; **je me sens ~** I feel my age; **pour bien ~, faites du sport** to stay young, take exercise; **je ne veux pas ~ ici** I don't want to be here till I die; **2** (se dégrader) [*corps, bâtiment*] to show signs of age; [*personne*] to age; **il vieillit mal** (apparence) he's losing his looks; **elle vieillit bien** she looks good for her age; **3** Sociol **notre population vieillit** we have an ageing population; **4** (pour un vin) to mature, to age; **5** (se démoder) [*œuvre, institution*] to become outdated

C se **vieillir** *vpr* **1** (en apparence) to make oneself look older; **2** (en estimation) to make oneself out to be older

vieillissant, ~e /vjejisã, ãt/ *adj* ageing

vieillissement /vjejismã/ *nm* (de personne, population, peau, vin) ageing; (d'institution) stultification

vieillot, -otte /vjejo, ɔt/ *adj* quaint; **cela te donne un air ~** it gives you a charming old-fashioned air

viennois, ~e /vjɛnwa, az/ ▸ p. 621 *adj* **1** (de Vienne) (en Autriche) Viennese; (en France) of Vienne; **2** Culin [*chocolat, café, pâtisserie, pain*] Viennese; **escalope ~e** Wiener schnitzel

viennoiserie /vjɛnwazʀi/ *nf* **1** (gâteau) Viennese pastry; **2** (ensemble des produits) Viennese pastries (*pl*)

vierge /vjɛʀʒ/

A *adj* **1** [*personne*] virgin (*épith*); **2** (non utilisé) [*cassette, feuille*] blank; [*cahier, pellicule*] unused; [*casier judiciaire*] clean; [*dossier, agenda*] empty; **3** (non exploré) [*terre, domaine*] virgin; **cimes ~s** unclimbed peaks; **4** (pur) [*laine*] new; [*cire, huile d'olive*] virgin; **5** (non souillé) liter [*neige*] virgin; [*réputation, vie*] unblemished; **~ de** free from, unsullied by; **6** (non fécondé) [*œuf, génisse*] unfertilized

B *nf* virgin

Vierge /vjɛʀʒ/

A *nf* **1** Relig **la (Sainte) ~** the (Blessed) Virgin; **Sainte ~!** Good Heavens!; **2** Art (représentation) madonna

B ▸ p. 635 *nprf* (en astronomie, en astrologie) Virgo

Viêt Nam /vjɛtnam/ ▸ p. 230 *nprm* Vietnam

vietnamien, -ienne /vjɛtnamjɛ̃, ɛn/ ▸ p. 392, p. 336

A *adj* Vietnamese

B *nm* Ling Vietnamese

vieux, (vieil *before vowel or mute h*), **vieille, mpl vieux** /vjø, vjɛj/

A *adj* old; **être ~ avant l'âge** to be old before one's time; **une institution vieille de 100 ans** a 100-year-old institution; **le ~ continent** the old world; **au bon ~ temps** in the good old days; **c'est de la vieille histoire** that's ancient history; **une vieille rivalité** a long-standing rivalry; **il est très vieille France** he's a gentleman of the old school

B *nm,f* **1** (personne âgée) old person; **un petit ~** a little old man; **une petite vieille** a little old woman; **les ~** old people; **mes ~**○ (parents) my parents; **2** ○(camarade) **salut, ~!** hello, mate○! GB, hi, pal○! US; **mon pauvre ~** you poor old thing; **ça va, ma vieille?** how are you, dear?

C *adv* **vivre ~** to live to a ripe old age; **il s'habille ~** he dresses like an old man; **ta sœur fait ~** your sister looks old

D *nm* (objets) **le ~** old things (*pl*); **prendre un coup de ~** to age; **faire du neuf avec du ~** to revamp things

(Composés) **vieille fille** old maid; **vieille peau** pej old bag○ péj; **~ beau** ageing Romeo; **~ clou**○ (véhicule) old crock○; **~ croûton**○ pej old duffer○; **~ garçon** old bachelor; **~ jeu** old-fashioned; **~ rose** dusty pink, old rose; **~ schnock**○ pej fuddy-duddy○

(Idiomes) **~ comme le monde, ~ comme Hérode** or **Mathusalem** as old as the hills; **c'est un ~ de la vieille**○ (vétéran) he's an old hand

vif, vive¹ /vif, viv/

A *adj* **1** (brillant) [*couleur, lumière*] bright; **2** (animé) [*personne*] lively, vivacious; [*imagination*] vivid; **3** (agressif) [*débat, protestations*] heated; [*opposition*] fierce; **répondre d'un ton ~** to answer sharply; **sa réaction a été un peu vive** he/she reacted rather strongly; **4** (important) [*contraste*] sharp; [*intérêt, désir*] keen; [*inquiétude*] deep; [*crainte, douleur*] acute; [*préoccupation*] serious; [*déception*] bitter; [*succès*] notable; **c'est avec un ~ plaisir que** it is with great pleasure that; **5** (rapide) [*rythme, geste*] brisk; **à vive allure** [*conduire, rouler*] at a fast speed; [*travailler, marcher*] at a brisk pace; **avoir l'esprit ~** to be very quick; **6** (perçant, tranchant) [*froid, vent*] keen; [*arête*] sharp; **air ~** fresh air; **l'air est ~** the air is bracing; **cuire à feu ~** to cook over a high heat; **7** (vivant) alive; **de vive voix** in person

B *nm* **1** gén **à ~** [*chair*] bared; [*genou*] raw; [*fil électrique*] exposed; **avoir les nerfs à ~** to be on edge; **la plaie est à ~** it's an open wound; **piquer** or **blesser qn au ~** to sting *ou* cut sb to the quick; **(pris) sur le ~** [*croquis*] thumbnail (*épith*); [*photo*] candid; [*notes*] taken on the spot (*jamais épith*); [*entretien*] live; **2** Jur **entre ~s** [*donation, partage*] inter vivos

vigie /viʒi/ *nf* **1** Naut (matelot) lookout; (poste) (sur le mât) crow's nest; (à la proue) lookout post; (balise) warning buoy; **2** Rail lookout box

vigilance /viʒilɑ̃s/ *nf* vigilance; **échapper à la ~ de qn** (de douanier, contrôleur) to escape sb's notice; (de mère, nourrice) to escape sb's attention

vigilant, ~e /viʒilã, ãt/ *adj* [*personne*] vigilant; [*œil*] watchful

vigile /viʒil/ *nm* **1** (veilleur de nuit) night watchman; (garde) security guard; **2** Hist watch

Vigipirate /viʒipiʀat/ *nm*: government public-security measures

> ⓘ **Vigipirate** is an emergency plan to reinforce police and military security, bringing an increased uniformed presence in public places at times of potential disorder, terrorist attacks, etc.

vigne /viɲ/ *nf* **1** (plant) vine; **2** (terrain planté) vineyard; **3** (travail) wine growing

(Composés) **~ mère** stock; **~ vierge** Virginia creeper

vigneron, -onne /viɲʀɔ̃, ɔn/ ▸ p. 372 *nm,f* winegrower

vignette /viɲɛt/ *nf* **1** (sur un médicament) detachable label on medicines for reimbursement by social security; **2** Aut tax disc GB; **3** Comm label; **4** (motif) vignette

vignoble /viɲɔbl/ *nm* vineyard; **le ~ hongrois/alsacien** the vineyards of Hungary/Alsace

vigoureux, -euse /viguʀø, øz/ *adj* **1** (physiquement) [*personne, poignée de main*] vigorous; [*athlète, corps*] strong,

Les villes

Les noms de villes

■ *Toute ville peut être désignée par les expressions* the town of… *ou* the city of… : town *s'applique en anglais britannique à toute agglomération d'une certaine importance, et en anglais américain à toute commune, même très peu peuplée. En Grande-Bretagne* city *désigne les très grandes villes, ainsi que les villes ayant une cathédrale.*

À avec les noms de ville

■ À *se traduit par* to *avec les verbes de mouvement (par ex.* aller, se rendre, *etc.).*

aller à Toulouse
= to go to Toulouse

se rendre à La Haye
= to travel to The Hague

■ À *se traduit par* in *avec les autres verbes (par ex.* être, habiter *etc.).*

vivre à Toulouse
= to live in Toulouse

■ *Lorsqu'une ville est une étape sur un itinéraire, à se traduira par* at.

s'arrêter à Dublin
= to stop at Dublin

Les noms des habitants

■ *L'anglais est moins friand que le français de noms d'habitants des villes. Pour les villes des îles britanniques, seuls quelques-uns sont assez courants, comme* Londoner, Dubliner, Liverpudlian *(de Liverpool),* Glaswegian *(de Glasgow),* Mancunian *(de Manchester) etc. Pour les villes américaines, on a* New Yorker, Philadelphian *etc. Pour les autres pays,* Parisian, Berliner, Roman *etc.*

■ *Pour traduire un nom d'habitant de ville, il est toujours possible d'utiliser* inhabitants *ou* people: *par ex., pour* les Toulousains, *on peut dire* the inhabitants of Toulouse, the people of Toulouse *etc.*

De avec les noms de villes

■ *Les expressions françaises avec de se traduisent le plus souvent par l'emploi du nom de ville en position d'adjectif.*

l'accent de Toulouse   **la région de Toulouse**
= a Toulouse accent   = the Toulouse area

l'aéroport de Toulouse   **les restaurants de Toulouse**
= Toulouse airport   = Toulouse restaurants

les cafés de Toulouse   **la route de Toulouse**
= Toulouse cafés   = the Toulouse road

l'équipe de Toulouse   **les rues de Toulouse**
= the Toulouse team   = Toulouse streets

les hivers de Toulouse   **le train de Toulouse**
= Toulouse winters   = the Toulouse train

les hôtels de Toulouse
= Toulouse hotels

Mais:

je suis de Toulouse   **le maire de Toulouse**
= I come from Toulouse   = the Mayor of Toulouse

une lettre de Toulouse   **un plan de Toulouse**
= a letter from Toulouse   = a map of Toulouse

Les adjectifs dérivés

■ *Les adjectifs dérivés des noms de villes n'ont pas toujours d'équivalent en anglais. Plusieurs cas sont possibles mais on pourra presque toujours utiliser le nom de la ville placé avant le nom qualifié:*

la région bordelaise
= the Bordeaux area

■ *Pour souligner la provenance on choisira* from + *le nom de la ville:*

l'équipe bordelaise
= the team from Bordeaux

■ *Pour parler de l'environnement on optera pour* of + *le nom de la ville:*

les rues bordelaises
= the streets of Bordeaux

■ *Et pour situer on utilisera* in + *le nom de la ville:*

mon séjour bordelais
= my stay in Bordeaux

---

powerful; [*plante*] sturdy; [*constitution, vieillard*] robust, sturdy; [*coup*] powerful; **2** (déterminé) [*résistance, mesure, style*] vigorous; [*croissance, sentiment*] strong; [*talent*] strong, robust; [*langage*] strong, forceful; **3** (net) [*dessin, contour*] strong, bold; [*coloris*] strong, striking

vigueur /vigœʀ/
A *nf* **1** (énergie) vigour^GB; **avec** ~ vigorously; **reprendre avec** ~ [*lutte*] to start again with renewed vigour^GB; **2** (force musculaire) strength; **frapper avec** ~ to bang; **3** (de plante) sturdiness; **4** (de trait, forme) vigour^GB
B en vigueur *loc adj* [*loi, dispositif*] in force; [*régime, conditions*] current; **cesser d'être en** ~ to cease to apply; **entrer en** ~ to come into force

VIH /veiaʃ/ *nm* (*abbr* = **virus immunodéficitaire humain**) HIV

vil, ~**e** /vil/ *adj liter* [*personne, âme*] base littér; [*action*] vile, base; [*besogne, tâche*] base littér

vilain, ~**e** /vilɛ̃, ɛn/
A *adj* **1** (laid) [*bâtiment, personne, animal*] ugly; **c'est vraiment** ~ **ce chapeau!** that hat looks awful!; **faire** ~ [*tableau, couleurs*] to look ugly; [*construction*] to be an eyesore; **2** ○(méchant) [*bête, microbe*] nasty; [*garçon, fille*] naughty; **jouer un** ~ **tour à qn** to play a nasty trick on sb; **la discussion a tourné au** ~ the discussion turned nasty○;

3 (répréhensible) [*affaire, bruits, rumeur*] nasty; [*défaut*] bad; [*mot*] dirty; **4** (inquiétant) [*toux, blessure*] nasty
B *nm,f* naughty boy/girl; **arrête de faire la** ~**e!** stop being naughty!
C *nm* Hist villein

(Idiome) **jeux de mains, jeux de** ~**s** Prov it will end in tears

vilebrequin /vilbʀəkɛ̃/ *nm* **1** (outil) brace and bit; **2** (de moteur) crankshaft

vilenie /vileni/ *nf liter* **1** (bassesse) baseness (**de** of); **2** (action vile) vile *ou* base act

villa /villa/ *nf* **1** (maison d'habitation) ≈ detached house; **2** (maison de plaisance) villa; **3** (dans l'antiquité) villa

village /vilaʒ/ *nm* village
(Composé) ~ **de toile** tent village

villageois, ~**e** /vilaʒwa, az/
A *adj* village (*épith*)
B *nm,f* villager

ville /vil/ *nf* **1** (agglomération, habitants) town, (de grande importance) city; **la** ~ **haute/basse** the upper/lower town; **une** ~ **d'art** a town of artistic interest; **de** ~ [*vêtements, chaussures*] town; **2** (administration) town *ou* city council
(Composés) ~ **d'eau(x)** spa town; ~ **franche** free city; ~ **libre** semiautonomous city

V

ville-dortoir, pl **villes-dortoirs** /vildɔʀtwaʀ/ nf dormitory town GB, bedroom community US

villégiature /vileʒjatyʀ/ nf (séjour) holiday GB, vacation US; **lieu de** ∼ holiday resort GB, vacation resort US

vin /vɛ̃/ nm wine; ∼ **rosé** rosé (wine); ∼ **demi-sec** medium-dry wine; **grand** ∼ fine wine; ∼ **de pays** or **de terroir** quality wine produced in a specific region; **ce** ∼ **a du corps** this wine is full-bodied; **couper son** ∼ (en mélanger deux) to blend one's wine; (mettre de l'eau) to add water to one's wine

⟨Composés⟩ ∼ **d'appellation d'origine contrôlée** appellation contrôlée wine (with a guarantee of origin); ∼ **chaud** mulled wine; ∼ **de coupage** blended wine; ∼ **cuit** wine which has undergone heating during maturation; ∼ **d'honneur** reception; **le** ∼ **nouveau** wine from the latest vintage; ∼ **de paille** wine made from dried grapes

⟨Idiomes⟩ **avoir le** ∼ **gai/triste** to get happy/maudlin after one has had a few drinks; **mettre de l'eau dans son** ∼ to mellow; **quand le** ∼ **est tiré, il faut le boire** Prov once you have started something, you have to see it through

vinaigre /vinɛgʀ/ nm vinegar

⟨Idiomes⟩ **tourner au** ∼ to turn sour; **on ne prend pas les mouches avec du** ∼ Prov it doesn't pay to take a hard line

vinaigrer /vinɛgʀe/ [1] vtr to season [sth] with vinegar

vinaigrette /vinɛgʀɛt/ nf vinaigrette, French dressing

vinasse° /vinas/ nf péj plonk° péj GB, cheap wine

vindicatif, -ive /vɛ̃dikatif, iv/ adj vindictive

vindicte /vɛ̃dikt/ nf condemnation

vineux, -euse /vinø, øz/ adj **1** ▸ p. 140 (couleur de vin rouge) [teint, visage] purplish; **2** (rappelant le vin) [odeur] of wine (après n); [fruit] tasting of wine; **3** (riche en alcool) [vin] full-bodied

vingt /vɛ̃, vɛ̃t/ ▸ p. 398, p. 296, p. 155

A adj inv twenty

B pron twenty; **j'ai eu** ∼ **sur** ∼ **à mon devoir d'histoire** ≈ I got full marks GB ou full credit US for my history paper

vingtaine /vɛ̃tɛn/ nf **avoir une** ∼ **d'années** to be about twenty; **nous étions plus d'une** ∼ there were more than twenty of us

vingt-deux /vɛ̃tdø/ ▸ p. 398, p. 296, p. 155

A adj inv, pron twenty-two

B °excl look out!; ∼**, v'là les flics!** look out! it's the cops°!

vingtième /vɛ̃tjɛm/ ▸ p. 398, p. 155 adj twentieth

vinicole /vinikɔl/ adj [activité, secteur, société, région] wine-producing (épith); [cave, commerce] wine (épith); [matériel, équipement] wine-making (épith)

vinification /vinifikasjɔ̃/ nf **1** (procédé) wine production; ∼ **en blanc/rouge** production of white/red wine; **2** (fermentation) vinification

vinyle /vinil/ nm **1** (matériau) vinyl; **2** (disque) vinyl

viol /vjɔl/ nm (de personne) rape; (de loi, temple) violation

violacé, ∼e /vjɔlase/ ▸ p. 140 adj purplish

violation /vjɔlasjɔ̃/ nf **1** (de loi, territoire, traité) violation; **2** (d'accord) breach; ∼ **du secret professionnel** breach of confidentiality

⟨Composés⟩ ∼ **de domicile** Jur forcible entry (into a person's home); ∼ **de sépulture** Jur desecration of a grave

violemment /vjɔlamɑ̃/ adv violently

violence /vjɔlɑ̃s/ nf **1** (de personne, sentiment, d'événement) violence; ∼ **verbale** verbal abuse; **d'une** ∼ **insoutenable** unbearably violent; **avec** ∼ violently; **avec une rare** ∼ with extreme violence; **par la** ∼ [imposer, soumettre] through violence; [répondre] with violence; **répliquer à la** ∼ **par la** ∼ to meet violence with violence; **faire** ∼ **à qn** to force sb (**pour qu'il fasse** to do); **se faire** ∼ to force oneself (**pour faire** to do); **2** (acte) act of violence; ∼**s à l'enfant** child abuse

violent, ∼e /vjɔlɑ̃, ɑ̃t/ adj [personne, réaction] violent; [couleur] harsh; [poison] powerful; [désir] overwhelming; **non** ∼ [mouvement, moyens] nonviolent; [manifestation] peaceful, nonviolent

violenter /vjɔlɑ̃te/ [1] vtr (agresser) to assault sexually; (violer) to rape

violer /vjɔle/ [1] vtr **1** to rape [personne]; **se faire** ∼ to be raped; **2** (profaner) to desecrate, to violate [tombe]; ∼ **l'intimité de qn** fig to invade sb's privacy; **3** (enfreindre) to infringe, to contravene [loi]

violet, -ette[1] /vjɔlɛ, ɛt/ ▸ p. 140

A adj purple

B nm (couleur) purple

violette[2] /vjɔlɛt/ nf (fleur) violet

violeur /vjɔlœʀ/ nm rapist

violon /vjɔlɔ̃/ ▸ p. 389 nm **1** (instrument) violin; **jouer du** ∼ to play the violin; **2** (musicien) violin; **3** °(prison) **au** ∼ in the nick° GB ou slammer° US ou can° US

⟨Composé⟩ ∼ **d'Ingres** hobby

⟨Idiomes⟩ **accorder ses** ∼**s** to reach an agreement; **autant pisser dans un** ∼°**!** it's just pissing° in the wind!; **payer les** ∼**s du bal** to foot the bill°

violoncelle /vjɔlɔ̃sɛl/ ▸ p. 389 nm (instrument) cello

violoncelliste /vjɔlɔ̃sɛlist/ ▸ p. 389, p. 372 nmf cellist

violoniste /vjɔlɔnist/ ▸ p. 389, p. 372 nmf violinist

vipère /vipɛʀ/ nf **1** Zool viper, adder; **2** (personne médisante) viper; **avoir** or **être une langue de** ∼ fig to have a wicked tongue

virage /viʀaʒ/ nm **1** (courbe) bend; ∼ **serré** sharp bend; **prendre un** ∼ **à la corde** to hug a bend; **rater un** ∼ to fail to negotiate a bend; **2** (changement d'orientation) change of direction; **parti qui amorce un** ∼ **à droite** party which takes a turn to the right ou shifts toward(s) the right; **3** Sport (en ski) turn

⟨Composé⟩ ∼ **à 180 degrés** fig U-turn

virée° /viʀe/ nf (voyage) trip; (promenade) (en voiture) drive, ride, spin; (à vélo, moto) ride; **une** ∼ **dans les bars de la ville** a tour of the bars in town

virement /viʀmɑ̃/ nm Fin transfer

⟨Composés⟩ ∼ **automatique** Fin standing order; ∼ **de bord** Naut tacking

virer /viʀe/ [1]

A vtr **1** Fin to transfer [argent, salaire] (**sur** to); **2** °(licencier) to fire, to sack° GB [employé]; **se faire** ∼ to get fired; **3** °(expulser) gén to throw [sb] out [importun]; (d'un cours) to send [sb] out [élève]; (du lycée) to expel [élève]; **4** °(enlever) to get rid of

B vi **1** (changer de direction) [véhicule] to turn; ∼ **à droite** [véhicule, parti politique] to turn ou shift to the right; ∼ **sur l'aile** to bank; **2** Naut [navire] to turn; ∼ **de bord** ou **vent devant** lit to go about; ∼ **de bord** fig to do a U-turn, to do a flip-flop US; **3** (changer de couleur) [étoffes, solution] to change colour°GB; [couleur] to change; **4** Phot [épreuve] to tone

C virer à vtr ind ∼ **au rouge** to turn red; ∼ **à l'aigre** to turn sour; ∼ **au conservatisme** to turn conservative

virevolter /viʀvɔlte/ [1] vi to twirl

virginité /viʀʒinite/ nf lit virginity

virgule /viʀgyl/ nf **1** Ling comma; **à la** ∼ **près** down to the last comma; **2** Math (decimal) point; **deux** ∼ **vingt-cinq** two point two five; **s'arrêter deux chiffres après la** ∼ to stop at two decimal places

viril, ∼e /viʀil/ adj [homme, force] manly, virile; [apparence] masculine, virile; **il est très** ∼ he's very masculine; **les amitiés** ∼**es** male friendships

virilité /viʀilite/ nf **1** (caractéristiques physiques) masculinity, virility; **2** (aptitude à engendrer) virility; **3** (attitude masculine) manliness; **manquer de** ∼ to be rather unmanly

virtualité /viʀtɥalite/ nf **1** Philos virtuality; **2** (aptitude) potentiality

virtuel, -elle /viʀtɥɛl/ adj **1** [succès, résultat, marché] potential; **à l'état** ∼ potentially; **2** Philos, Phys virtual; **3** Ordinat virtual

virtuellement /viʀtɥɛlmɑ̃/ adv **1** (pratiquement) virtually; **2** (en théorie) potentially

virtuose /viʀtɥoz/

A adj virtuoso (épith); [joueur] master; **être** ∼ **dans l'art de faire** to be a past master at doing

B nmf **1** Mus virtuoso; **2** (personne douée) master

virtuosité /viʀtɥozite/ nf **1** Mus virtuosity; **interpréter qch avec** ∼ to give a virtuoso performance of sth; **2** (habileté) brilliance

virulence /viʀylɑ̃s/ nf virulence; **avec** ∼ virulently

virulent, ∼e /viʀylɑ̃, ɑ̃t/ adj virulent

virus /viʀys/ nm inv **1** Méd virus; **2** (manie) bug°, craze; **le** ∼ **du cinéma** the film bug°; **3** Ordinat virus

vis /vis/ *nf inv* screw
(Composés) ~ **cruciforme** Phillips® screw; ~ **sans fin** worm, endless screw; ~ **platinées** Aut contact points
(Idiome) **serrer la** ~ **à qn** to tighten the screws on sb

visa /viza/ *nm* (sur un passeport) visa; ~ **de touriste** tourist visa
(Composé) ~ **de censure** Cin (censor's) certificate

visage /vizaʒ/ ▸ p. 136 *nm* lit, fig face; **à deux** ~**s** two-faced; **les deux** ~**s d'une politique** the two aspects of a policy; **sans** ~ faceless; **à** ~ **découvert** openly; **faire bon** ~ **à qn** to give sb a warm welcome
(Composé) ~ **pâle** Hist paleface

vis-à-vis /vizavi/
A *nm inv* **1** (bâtiment) **avoir la prison pour** ~ to live opposite the prison; **maison sans** ~ house with an open outlook; **2** (personne) (à table, dans le train) person opposite; (voisin d'en face) person who lives opposite; **3** (position) **assis en** ~ sitting opposite each other; **4** Sport opponent; **5** (rencontre face-à-face) meeting, encounter
B **vis-à-vis de** *loc prép* **1** (à l'égard de) ~ **de qch** in relation to sth; ~ **de qn** toward(s) sb; ~ **de soi-même** with oneself; **2** (comparé à) beside

viscéral, ~**e**, *mpl* **-aux** /viseʀal, o/ *adj* **1** (instinctif) [haine, émotion] deep-rooted; **réaction** ~**e** gut reaction; **2** Anat visceral

viscéralement /viseʀalmɑ̃/ *adv* violently, virulently

viscère /visɛʀ/ *nm* **1** Anat internal organ; **2** (de l'abdomen) **les** ~**s** viscera

visée /vize/ *nf* **1** (objectif) aim; (dessein) design; **une politique à** ~ **expansionniste** an expansionist policy; **avoir des** ~**s sur qn/qch** to have designs on sb/sth; ~**s agressives sur les États voisins** aggressive intentions toward(s) neighbouring^GB states; **ils ont des** ~**s sur le marché européen** they are aiming at the European market; **2** (avec un instrument) Géog sighting; Phot viewing; (avec une arme) aiming

viser /vize/ [1]
A *vtr* **1** (pointer son regard) to aim at [cible]; (vouloir atteindre) to aim for [cœur, centre]; **2** (aspirer à) to aim for [poste, résultats]; to aim at [marché]; ~ **la première place** to aim to be first; **3** (concerner) [loi, campagne] to be aimed at; [remarque, allusion] to be meant *ou* intended for; **les employés visés par la décision** the employees to whom the ruling applies; **se sentir visé** to feel one is being got at^○
B **viser à** *vtr ind* ~ **à qch/à faire** to aim at sth/to do
C *vi* **1** (avec un fusil, un appareil photo) to aim; **2** fig ~ **(trop) haut** to set one's sights (too) high

viseur /vizœʀ/ *nm* **1** Phot, Cin viewfinder; **2** (d'arme) sight

visibilité /vizibilite/ *nf* visibility

visible /vizibl/ *adj* **1** (perceptible) visible; **2** (manifeste) obvious; **son émotion était** ~ he/she was visibly moved; **elle va beaucoup mieux, c'est** ~ she's obviously a lot better; **3** (en état de recevoir) [personne] available; **4** (accessible au public) **les tableaux sont** ~**s jusqu'au 17 mai** the paintings can be seen until 17 May

visiblement /vizibləmɑ̃/ *adv* visibly

visière /vizjɛʀ/ *nf* **1** (de casquette) peak; **2** (sans couvre-chef) eyeshade, visor; **mettre la main en** ~ to shade one's eyes with one's hand

vision /vizjɔ̃/ *nf* **1** (faculté de voir) eyesight, vision; ~ **nocturne** night vision; **2** (conception) view; ~ **globale** global view; **3** (spectacle) sight; **une** ~ **d'horreur** a horrible sight; **4** (apparition) vision; **avoir des** ~**s** to see things, to have visions

visionnaire /vizjɔnɛʀ/ *adj, nmf* visionary

visionner /vizjɔne/ [1] *vtr* to view [film, diapositives]

visionneuse /vizjɔnøz/ *nf* viewer

visite /vizit/ *nf* visit; (rapide) call; ~ **de politesse** courtesy call; **rendre** ~ **à qn** to pay sb a call, to call on sb; **être en** ~ **chez qn** to be paying sb a visit; ~ **accompagnée** *or* **guidée** guided tour; **la** ~ **d'une maison** (avant de l'acheter) viewing a house; **avoir de la** ~ to have visitors *ou* company; **le médecin fait ses** ~**s** the doctor is making his/her (house) calls; ~**-éclair/-surprise** lightning/surprise visit
(Composés) ~ **de contrôle** Méd follow-up visit; ~ **médicale** (contrôle) medical (examination); (bilan) checkup

visiter /vizite/ [1] *vtr* **1** [touriste, curieux] to visit, to go round^GB [musée, ville, pays]; **faire** ~ **un lieu à qn** to show sb around a place; **le musée le plus visité** the museum that attracts the most visitors; **2** [client] to view [appartement]; **3** [médecin, prêtre] to visit [malade, prisonnier]

visiteur, -euse /vizitœʀ, øz/ *nm,f* visitor

vison /vizɔ̃/ *nm* **1** (animal, fourrure) mink; **2** (manteau) mink (coat)

visqueux, -euse /viskø, øz/ *adj* **1** [liquide, produit, consistance] viscous, viscid; **2** (poisseux) sticky, gooey^○

visser /vise/ [1] *vtr* **1** (fixer avec des vis) to screw on [serrure, boîtier]; (dans into; **sur** onto); ~ **qch à fond** to screw sth up tight; **2** (fermer) to screw [sth] on [couvercle, bouchon]; **3** (immobiliser) **être vissé sur sa chaise** to be glued to one's chair

visualisation /vizyalizasjɔ̃/ *nf* gén visualization; Ordinat display

visualiser /vizyalize/ [1] *vtr* **1** (mentalement) to visualize [image, mot]; **2** Ordinat to display

visuel, -elle /vizyɛl/
A *adj* visual
B *nm,f* person with a strong visual sense

vital, ~**e**, *mpl* **-aux** /vital, o/ *adj* vital

vitalité /vitalite/ *nf* (de personne) vitality, energy; (de marché, d'économie) vitality; **elle déborde de** ~ she's bursting with energy

vitamine /vitamin/ *nf* vitamin

vitaminé, ~**e** /vitamine/ *adj* with added vitamins (après n)

vite /vit/ *adv* **1** (rapidement) quickly; ~**!** quick!; **aller** ~, **faire** ~ to be quick; **ça ira** ~ (opération, traitement) it'll soon be over; (procédure, réparation) it won't take long; **faire qch** ~ **fait**^○ to do sth quickly; **on a pris un verre** ~ **fait**^○ we had a quick drink; **2** (peu après le début) soon; **c'est une affection bénigne, ça passera** ~ it's only a minor trouble, it'll soon get better; **3** (hâtivement) **j'ai parlé trop** ~ (sans réfléchir) I spoke too hastily; (sans tenir compte de tout) I spoke too soon; **c'est** ~ **dit!** that's easy to say!

vitesse /vitɛs/ *nf* **1** (rapidité) speed; ~ **de pointe** maximum speed; **il travaille à une** ~**!** he works so fast!; **partir à toute** ~ to rush away; **la voiture est passée à toute** ~ the car flashed past; **à deux** ~**s** [courrier, système] two-tier (épith); **faire de la** ~ [automobiliste] to drive fast; **gagner** *or* **prendre qn de** ~ lit, fig to outstrip sb; **en** ~ (vite) quickly; (trop vite) in a rush; **passer en** ~ [personne] to pop in^○; **nous avons mangé en** ~ we had a quick meal; **je vous écris en** ~ I'm writing you a quick note; **passer en** ~ ! tidy up your room, and be quick about it!; **(il s'enfuit) de toute la** ~ **de ses petites jambes** (he ran away) as fast as his little legs would carry him; **2** Tech (engrenage, rapport) gear; **boîte à cinq** ~**s** five-speed gearbox; **passer les** ~**s** to change gear GB, to shift gear US; **passer la** ~ **supérieure/inférieure** to change up/down a gear; **passer à la** ~ **supérieure** fig to speed things up; **passer ses** ~**s en douceur** to go smoothly through the gears; **faire grincer les** ~**s** to crunch the gears; **bicyclette à trois** ~**s** three-speed bicycle
(Composé) ~ **de sédimentation** Biol, Méd sedimentation rate
(Idiomes) **à la** ~ **grand V, en quatrième** ~ at top speed

viticole /vitikɔl/ *adj* [industrie, cave] wine (épith); [région, pays] wine-producing (épith)

viticulteur, -trice /vitikyltœʀ, tʀis/ ▸ p. 372 *nm,f* wine-grower, viticulturalist

viticulture /vitikyltyʀ/ *nf* wine-growing, viticulture

vitrage /vitʀaʒ/ *nm* (surfaces vitrées) windows (pl); **double** ~ double glazing

vitrail, *pl* **-aux** /vitʀaj, o/ *nm* stained glass window; **l'art du** ~ the art of stained glass

vitre /vitʀ/ *nf* **1** (de fenêtre) pane, windowpane; (fenêtre) window; (panneau) pane of glass; **2** (de voiture, train) window; ~ **arrière** rear window

vitré, ~**e** /vitʀe/ *adj* **1** (en vitres) glass (épith), glazed (épith); **bureaux** ~**s** glass-walled offices; **toiture** ~**e** glass roof; **2** Anat (de l'œil) vitreous

vitrer /vitʀe/ [1] *vtr* to glaze [panneau, fenêtre, serre]; ~ **une porte** to put windows in a door

La vitesse

La vitesse des véhicules

■ *En anglais, on mesure couramment la vitesse des trains, des avions et des automobiles en miles à l'heure, même si les compteurs indiquent aussi les kilomètres.*

> *30 miles à l'heure valent environ 50 km/h*
> *50 miles à l'heure valent environ 80 km/h*
> *80 miles à l'heure valent environ 130 km/h*
> *100 miles à l'heure valent environ 160 km/h*

■ *Noter qu'on écrit -metre en anglais britannique, et -meter en anglais américain.*

50 kilomètres à l'heure
= 50 kilometres an hour *ou* 50 kilometres per hour

100 km/h
= 100 kph (*dire* kilometres an hour; p *signifie* per = par)

100 miles à l'heure
= 100 mph (*dire* miles an hour),
= 160 km/h

à quelle vitesse la voiture roulait-elle?
= what speed was the car going at?
  ou how fast was the car going?

elle roulait à 150 km/h
= it was going at 150 kph

elle roulait à quatre-vingts à l'heure
= it was going at fifty (*50 miles à l'heure*), it was going at 80 kph

la voiture faisait du combien?
= what was the car doing?

elle faisait du 160 (km/h)
= it was doing a hundred (mph), it was doing 160 kph

faire du 160 à l'heure
= to do a hundred (mph) *ou* to do 160 kph

à une vitesse de 80 km/h
= at a speed of 50 mph, at a speed of 80 kph

■ *Noter l'absence d'équivalent anglais de la préposition française de avant le chiffre dans:*

la vitesse de la voiture était de 160 km/h
= the speed of the car was 100 mph,
  the speed of the car was 160 kph

à peu près 80 km/h
= about 50 mph, about 80 kph

presque 80 km/h
= almost 50 mph, almost 80 kph

plus de 70 km/h
= more than 45 mph, more than 70 kph

moins de 85 km/h
= less than 55 mph, less than 85 kph

A va plus vite que B
= A is faster than B

B roulait moins vite que A
= B was going slower than A

A va aussi vite que B
= A is as fast as B

A roulait à la même vitesse que B
= A was going at the same speed as B

A et B vont à la même vitesse
= A and B go at the same speed

La vitesse du son et de la lumière

le son se déplace à 330 m/s
= sound travels at 330 metres per second
  (*dire* three hundred and thirty metres per second)

la vitesse de la lumière est de 300 000 km/s
= the speed of light is 186,300 miles per second

---

vitrerie /vitRəRi/ ► p. 372 *nf* ① (magasin) glazier's; ② (fabrication) glasswork; (industrie) glass industry

vitreux, -euse /vitRø, øz/ *adj* [*regard*] glazed; [*éclat*] glassy; [*état, roche*] vitreous

vitrier /vitRije/ ► p. 372 *nm* glazier

vitrification /vitRifikasjɔ̃/ *nf* (de parquet) varnishing, sealing

vitrifier /vitRifje/ [2]
Ⓐ *vtr* ① (vernir) to varnish [*parquet*]; ② Tech (en verrerie) to vitrify; (en génie nucléaire) to vitrify
Ⓑ **se vitrifier** *vpr* to vitrify

vitrine /vitRin/ *nf* ① (de boutique) (shop *ou* store) window; **en ~** in the window; **faire les ~s** (regarder) to go window-shopping; ② (meuble) display cabinet GB, curio cabinet US; ③ (de musée) (show)case; ④ fig (mise en valeur) showcase

vitriol /vitRijɔl/ *nm* vitriol; **discours au ~** fig vitriolic speech

vitro ► **in vitro**

vitupérer /vitypeRe/ [14] *vi* to rail

vivable /vivabl/ *adj* bearable; **pas ~** unbearable; **ce n'est pas ~ ici** it is impossible to live here

vivace /vivas/ *adj* ① Bot **(plante) ~** perennial; ② (durable) enduring

vivacité /vivasite/ *nf* ① (fougue) (de personne) vivacity; (de sentiment, passion) intensity; ② (promptitude) (de mouvement) vivacity; (de repartie, d'intelligence) keenness; (de réaction) swiftness; **avec ~** [*se mouvoir, réagir*] swiftly; ③ (de souvenir, couleur, d'impression) vividness; (de regard) spark; (de lueur) brightness

vivant, ~e /vivɑ̃, ɑ̃t/
Ⓐ *adj* ① (en vie) living; **il est ~** he is alive; **un homard ~** a live lobster; **moi ~, jamais il ne l'épousera** he'll marry her over my dead body; ② (en chair et en os) [*exemple, symbole*] living; **d'après le modèle ~** from life; **ta mère, c'est un**

dictionnaire ~! your mother is a walking dictionary!; ③ (animé) [*personne, récit, style*] lively; [*description*] vivid; ④ (vivace) **être encore ~** [*coutume, souvenir*] to be still alive
Ⓑ *nm* **les ~s** the living; **de mon ~** in my lifetime; **du ~ de mon père** while my father was alive

vivats /viva/ *nmpl* cheers

vive² /viv/
Ⓐ *adj f* ► **vif A**
Ⓑ *nf* Zool weever

vivement /vivmɑ̃/ *adv* [*encourager, réagir*] strongly; [*inquiéter*] greatly; [*contraster*] sharply; [*émouvoir, regretter*] deeply; [*contester, attaquer*] fiercely; [*se lever*] swiftly; **je souhaite ~ vous rencontrer** I should very much like to meet you; **~ dimanche!/qu'elle s'en aille!** I can't wait for Sunday!/for her to go!

vivier /vivje/ *nm* (naturel) fishpond; (artificiel) fish-tank

vivifiant, ~e /vivifjɑ̃, ɑ̃t/ *adj* ① (revigorant) invigorating; ② (stimulant) stimulating

vivifier /vivifje/ [2] *vtr* to invigorate

vivisection /vivisɛksjɔ̃/ *nf* vivisection

vivoter /vivɔte/ [1] *vi* to struggle along

vivre /vivR/ [63]
Ⓐ *vtr* ① (connaître) to live through [*époque, période*]; to go through [*heures difficiles, enfer*]; to experience [*amour, passion*]; **être vécu comme un affront** to be taken as an insult; **~ sa vie** to lead one's own life; ② (ressentir) to cope with [*divorce, échec*]
Ⓑ *vi* ① Biol (être vivant) to live; **~ vieux/centenaire** to live to a great age/to be a hundred; **cesser de ~** euph to pass away; **vive le président!** long live the president!; **vive la vie!** life is wonderful!; **vive moi/nous!** three cheers for me/us!; **vive Paul!** hurray for Paul!; ② (habiter) to live; **être facile à**

~ [conjoint] to be easy to live with; [ami] to be easy to get on with; ~ **les uns sur les autres** to live on top of each other; **3** (exister) [personne] to live; ~ **avec son temps** to move with the times; **se laisser** ~ to take things easy; **apprendre à** ~ **à qn**○ to teach sb some manners○; **savoir** ~ (profiter de la vie) to know how to enjoy life; **4** (survivre) [personne] to live; **avoir de quoi** ~ to have enough to live on; ~ **de ses rentes** to have a private income; ~ **aux dépens de qn** to live off sb; **5** (durer) [relation, mode] to last; **avoir vécu** [personne] to have seen a great deal of life; (être usé) hum to have had its day; **6** (être animé) [ville, rue] to be full of life

(Idiomes) **le** ~ **et le couvert** board and lodging; ~ **de l'air du temps** to live on air; ~ **sur un grand pied** to live in great style; **qui vivra verra** what will be will be

vivres /vivʀ/ nmpl **1** (nourriture) food, supplies; **2** (moyens de subsistance) **couper les** ~ **à qn** to cut off sb's allowance

vizir /viziʀ/ nm vizier; **le Grand** ~ the Grand Vizier

vo /veo/ nf: abbr ▸ **version**

vocable /vɔkabl/ nm term

vocabulaire /vɔkabylɛʀ/ nm vocabulary

vocal, ~**e**, mpl **-aux** /vɔkal, o/ adj vocal

vocalement /vɔkalmɑ̃/ adv vocally

vocalise /vɔkaliz/ nf singing exercise

vocation /vɔkasjɔ̃/ nf **1** (de personne) vocation, calling; ~ **contrariée** frustrated calling; **se sentir une** ~ **de médecin** to feel that medicine is one's vocation; **il n'a pas la** ~ **de l'enseignement** he's not cut out to be a teacher; **2** (d'institution) purpose; **il assigne à l'école une double** ~ he thinks schools should serve a dual purpose; **l'association a pour** ~ **d'aider les malades** the association is intended to help the sick; **salles à** ~ **récréative** rooms intended for leisure activities; **région à** ~ **agricole** farming area

vocifération /vɔsiferasjɔ̃/ nf clamour^GB ¢

vociférer /vɔsifere/ [14] vtr, vi to shout (**contre** at)

vœu, pl ~**x** /vø/ nm **1** (souhait) wish; **les élèves doivent émettre des** ~**x d'orientation** pupils must indicate their preferred subject choices; **je fais des** ~**x pour que la paix revienne** I hope and pray that peace may return; **appeler qch de tous ses** ~**x** to hope and pray for sth; **former des** ~**x pour la santé de qn** to wish sb a speedy recovery; '**nos meilleurs** ~**x aux jeunes époux** ' 'our best wishes to the bride and groom'; **2** (de Nouvel An) New Year's greetings; **adresser ses** ~**x à qn** to wish sb a happy New Year; **3** (promesse) vow; **faire** ~ **de pauvreté** to take a vow of poverty; **faire** ~ **de fidélité** to vow to remain faithful

(Composé) ~ **pieux** wishful thinking ¢

vogue /vɔg/ nf (mode) fashion, vogue; **la** ~ **des cheveux longs** the fashion for long hair; **la** ~ **des Beatles** the Beatles craze○; **en** ~ [style, idée, personne] fashionable; [objet, vêtement] in fashion (jamais épith)

voguer /vɔge/ [1] vi liter **1** (naviguer) [navire] to sail; **2** fig [esprit, pensées] to wander

(Idiome) **et vogue la galère!** come what may!

voici /vwasi/

A prép ~ **un mois** a month ago; ~ **bientôt deux mois qu'elle travaille chez nous** she's been working with us for nearly two months

B présentatif ~ **mes clés** here are my keys; ~ **le docteur qui arrive** here comes ou here's the doctor; '**me'** ~ 'here I am'; ~ **ma fille** this is my daughter; **M. Bon que** ~ **est...** Mr Bon here is...; ~ **les résultats** here are the results, these are the results; ~ **le programme** the programme^GB is as follows; **le film raconte l'histoire que** ~ the film tells the following story; ~ **où je voulais en venir** that's the point I wanted to make; ~ **qui va vous amuser** here is ou this is something that you'll find amusing; ~ **enfin l'été** summer's here at last; ~ **venir l'hiver** here comes winter; **nous y** ~ (à la maison) here we are; (au cœur du sujet) now we're getting there

C voici que loc conj liter all of a sudden

voie /vwa/ nf **1** fig (chemin) way; **être sur la** ~ **d'un accord** to be on the way to an agreement; **montrer la** ~ **à qn** to show sb the way; **montrer la** ~ to lead the way; **ouvrir la** ~ **à** to pave the way for; **chercher sa** ~ to look for one's way in life; **s'engager dans une** ~ **dangereuse** to embark on a dangerous course; **être sur la bonne** ~ [personne] to be on the right track; **les travaux sont en bonne** ~ the

work is progressing; **la** ~ **royale vers le pouvoir** the fast track to power; **en** ~ **de faire** in the process of doing; **en** ~ **de désintégration** disintegrating (après n); **par** ~**s de conséquence** consequently; **espèce en** ~ **de disparition** endangered species; **pays en** ~ **de développement** developing country; **2** (intermédiaire) channels (pl); **par la** ~ **du référendum** by means of a referendum; **par** ~ **de presse** through the press; **par des** ~ **détournées** by roundabout means; **par** ~ **de mer** by sea; **3** (subdivision de route) lane; (route) road; (rue) street; **route à trois** ~**s** three-lane road; ~ **à sens unique** (en ville) one-way street; **4** (rails) track; '**défense de traverser les** ~**s**' 'keep off the tracks'; **le train entre en gare** ~ **2** the train is arriving at platform 2; **5** (mode d'administration) **par** ~ **intraveineuse** intravenously; **par** ~ **buccale** or **orale** orally

(Composés) ~ **aérienne** air route; ~ **express** expressway; ~ **ferrée** (infrastructure) railway track GB, railroad track US; (mode de transport, ligne) railway GB, railroad US; ~ **fluviale** (inland) waterway; ~ **de garage** siding; **mettre qn sur une** ~ **de garage** fig to shunt sb onto the sidelines; ~ **hiérarchique** Admin right channels (pl); **Voie lactée** Milky Way; ~ **maritime** sea route; ~ **navigable** waterway; ~ **privée** private road; ~ **publique** public highway; ~ **rapide** expressway; ~ **sans issue** lit, fig dead end; (sur panneau) no through road; ~ **souterraine** underpass; ~**s respiratoires** respiratory tract (sg); ~**s urinaires** urinary tract (sg)

voilà /vwala/

A prép ~ **un mois** a month ago; ~ **bientôt deux mois qu'elle travaille chez nous** she's been working with us for nearly two months

B présentatif **voici ton parapluie et** ~ **le mien** this is your umbrella and here's mine; **voici mon fils et** ~ **ma fille** this is my son and this is my daughter; ~ **ma mère** here's ou here comes my mother; **me** ~**!** (j'arrive) I'm coming!; (je suis là) here I am!; **ah! te** ~**!** ah, there you are!; ~ **tout** that's all; ~ **où nous en étions** that's where we were up to; ~ **ce que c'est de désobéir** that's what happens if you disobey; **je n'ai pas pu venir,** ~ **tout** (ne posez pas de questions) I couldn't come, that's all there is to it; ~ **qui ne va pas arranger vos affaires** well, that won't sort things out for you; ~ **le programme** the programme^GB is as follows; ~ **comment** (en introduction) this is how; (en conclusion) that's how; **seulement** ~ **je n'ai pas d'argent** the problem ou thing is I don't have any money; '**je voudrais la clé du trois'—'**~**, madame'** 'I'd like the key to number three'—'here you are, madam'; **nous y** ~ (à la maison) here we are; (au cœur du sujet) now we're getting there; **le** ~ **qui se remet à rire!** there he goes again laughing!; **te** ~ **content!** now you're happy!; **te** ~ **revenu!** you're back again!; ~ **bien les hommes!** that's men for you!; ~ **bien ta mauvaise foi!** so much for your dishonesty!

C en voilà loc **vous vouliez des explications? en** ~ you wanted more details! well, here you are (then); **en** ~ **pour deux euros** here's two euros worth; **en** ~ **un mal élevé!** what a badly brought up boy!; **mon dieu! en** ~ **des histoires!** good Lord! what a fuss!; **en** ~ **assez!** that's enough!; **en** ~ **un qui ne recommencera pas!** there's someone who won't do it again!

D voilà que○ loc **et** ~ **qu'une voiture arrive** and the next thing was a car arrived; ~ **qu'il se met à rire** all of a sudden he started laughing; **et** ~ **qu'elle refuse** and then she had to go and refuse

E excl ~**! j'arrive!** (I'm) coming!, (et) ~**! ils sont partis!** there you are, they've left!; (et) ~**! il remet ça!** there he goes again!

(Idiome) **il a de l'argent, en veux-tu en** ~**!** he has as much money as he could wish for!

voilage /vwalaʒ/ nm net curtain GB, sheer curtain US

voile¹ /vwal/ nm **1** (morceau d'étoffe) veil; **prendre le** ~ to take the veil; ~ **(islamique)** (Muslim) headscarf; **interdire le** ~ to ban the wearing of headscarfs; **2** (étoffe) voile; **3** (masque abstrait) veil; **on jeta un** ~ **(pudique) sur l'affaire** a veil was drawn over the affair; **lever le** ~ **sur qch** to bring sth out in the open; **soulever un coin du** ~ **sur qch** to gain a glimpse into sth; **4** Tech (dans un liquide) cloud; (sur une radiographie) shadow; Phot fog; **5** (écran) veil; **un** ~ **de larmes** a mist of tears

voile² /vwal/ nf Naut **1** (toile) sail; **faire** ~ **vers** to sail toward(s); **toutes** ~**s dehors** lit full sail ahead; fig using every possible means; **2** (activité) sailing; **il fait de la**

~ **depuis deux ans** he's been sailing for two years; **cours de** ~ sailing lessons

(Idiomes) **être à** ~ **et à vapeur**○ to be AC/DC○; **mettre les** ~**s**○ to clear off○ GB, to clear out○ US

voilé, ~**e** /vwale/ adj [1] [*personne, objet*] veiled; ~ **de noir** veiled in black; [2] [*soleil, ciel*] hazy; [*regard, yeux*] misty; [*voix*] with a catch in it (*épith, après n*); [*photo, film*] fogged; [*lune*] veiled (**de** in); [3] (*obscur*) [*allusion, menace, critique*] veiled; **des allusions à peine** ~**es** thinly veiled allusions; [4] (*déformé*) [*roue*] buckled; [*panneau*] warped

voiler /vwale/ [1]
A vtr [1] (*dissimuler*) to veil [*ciel, paysage, soleil*]; to conceal [*événement, fait*]; [2] (*déformer*) to buckle [*roue*]; [3] (*troubler*) to mist [*regard*]; **l'émotion voilait sa voix** his/her voice was choked with emotion; [4] (*couvrir d'étoffe*) to cover [*visage, nudité*]; to veil [*statue*]
B **se voiler** vpr [1] (*se troubler*) [*ciel*] to cloud over; [*soleil*] to become hazy; [*regard*] to become misty; [*voix*] to have a catch in it; [2] (*avec étoffe*) [*musulmane*] to wear the veil; **se** ~ **le visage** to veil one's face

(Idiome) **se** ~ **la face** to look the other way

voilette /vwalɛt/ nf veil

voilier /vwalje/ nm (*bateau*) sailing boat GB, sailboat US; (*grand navire*) yacht, sailing ship

voilure /vwalyʀ/ nf [1] Naut (*ensemble des voiles*) sails (*pl*); (*surface des voiles*) sail; **une** ~ **de 500m²** 500m² of sail; [2] (*d'avion*) wing surface; (*de parachute*) canopy

voir /vwaʀ/ [46]
A vtr [1] (*percevoir par les yeux*) to see [*personne, objet*]; **je n'y vois rien** I can't see a thing; **je les ai vus comme je te vois!** I saw them as plainly as I see you standing there!; **à la** ~ **si triste** when you see her so sad; **à le** ~, **on le prendrait pour un clochard** to look at him, you'd think he was a tramp; **faire** ~ **qch à qn** to show sb sth; **laisser** ~ **qch** to show sth; ~ **qch en rêve** to dream about sth; [2] (*être spectateur, témoin de*) [*personne*] to see [*film, incident*]; [*lieu*] to see [*événement, évolution*]; **la ville qui l'a vue naître** her native town; **le film est à** ~ the film is worth seeing; **c'est beau à** ~ it's beautiful to look at; **ce n'est pas beau à** ~ it's not a pretty sight; **je voudrais bien t'y** ~! I'd like to see how you'd get on!; **on n'a jamais vu ça!** it's unheard of!; **on aura tout vu!** could you ever have imagined such a thing!; **voyez-moi ça!** just look at that!; [3] (*se figurer*) to see; **j'ai vu le moment où il allait m'étrangler** I thought he was about to strangle me; **je vois ça d'ici** I can just imagine; [4] (*juger*) to see; **c'est ma façon de** ~ **(les choses)** that's the way I see things; **c'est à toi de** ~ it's up to you to decide; ~ **favorablement qch** to be favourably○ disposed toward(s) sth; **tu vas te faire mal** ~ **de Sophie** Sophie is going to think badly of you; [5] (*comprendre, déceler*) to see [*moyen, avantage*]; **je ne vois pas qui tu veux dire** I don't know who you mean; **si tu n'y vois pas d'inconvénient** if it's all right with you; **on voit bien qu'elle n'a jamais travaillé** you can tell she's never worked!; [6] (*constater, découvrir*) to see; ~ **si/pourquoi** to find out ou to see if/why; **on verra bien** well, we'll see; **'je ne paierai pas!'—'c'est ce que nous verrons!'** 'I won't pay!'—'we shall see about that!'; **c'est à** ~ that remains to be seen; **touches-y, pour** ~! (*menace*) you just touch it!; [7] (*examiner, étudier*) to see [*malade*]; to look at [*problème, dossier*]; [8] (*recevoir, se rendre chez*) to see [*client, médecin, ami*]; **je passerai la** ~ **demain** I'll call on her tomorrow; [9] (*visiter*) to see [*ville, monument*]; ~ **du pays** to see the world; [10] (*avoir un rapport avec*) **avoir quelque chose à** ~ **avec** to have something to do with
B **voir à** vtr ind (*veiller à*) to see to; **voyez à ce que tout soit prêt** see to it ou make sure that everything is ready
C vi [1] (*avec les yeux*) ~, **y** ~ to be able to see; **je** or **j'y vois à peine** I can hardly see; **je vois trouble** everything is a blur; [2] (*par l'esprit*) ~ **clair dans qch** to have a clear understanding of sth; ~ **loin** (*être prévoyant*) to look ahead; (*être perspicace*) to be far-sighted; ~ **grand** to think big; **elle a vu juste** she was right; **il faut** ~○ (*ça mérite réflexion*) we'll have to see; [3] (*rappel à l'ordre*) **voyons, sois sage!** come on now, behave yourself!
D **se voir** vpr [1] (*dans la glace, en imagination*) to see oneself; **il s'est vu sombrer dans la folie** he realized he was going mad; [2] (*se remarquer*) [*tache, défaut*] to show; **la tour se voit de loin** the tower can be seen from far away; **cela se voit tous les jours** it happens all the time ou every day; **ça ne s'est jamais vu!** it's unheard of!; [3] (*se trouver*) **se** ~ **obligé** or **dans l'obligation de faire qch** to find oneself forced to

do; [4] (*se fréquenter*) to see each other; **ils ne peuvent pas se** ~ **(en peinture**○**)** they can't stand each other

(Idiomes) **ne pas** ~ **plus loin que le bout de son nez** to see no further than the end of one's nose; **je préfère** ~ **venir** I would rather wait and see; **on t'a vu venir**○! they/we saw you coming○!; **je te vois venir**○ I can see what you're getting at GB ou where you're coming from○; **je t'ai assez vu** I've had enough of you; **en** ~ **de toutes les couleurs** to go through some hard times; **j'en ai vu d'autres** I've seen worse; **en faire** ~ **à qn** to give sb a hard time; **qu'il aille se faire** ~○! tell him to get lost○!; **il ferait beau** ~ **ça!** that would be the last straw!

voire /vwaʀ/ adv or even, not to say

voirie /vwaʀi/ nf road, rail and waterways network

voisin, ~**e** /vwazɛ̃, in/
A adj [1] (*de voisinage*) [*maison, ville*] neighbouring^{GB} (*épith*), nearby; [*rue, pays*] neighbouring^{GB} (*épith*); (*proche*) [*forêt, lac, hôpital*] nearby; (*d'à côté*) [*pièce, table, maison*] next (**de** to); **dans la maison** ~**e** in the house next door; fig [*date, résultat, pourcentage*] close (**de** to); **les régions** ~**es de la Manche** the regions bordering the English Channel; [2] (*similaire*) [*sentiments, idées*] similar; [*espèces*] (closely) related; ~ **de** [*théorie, idée*] akin to; [*espèce*] related to
B nm,f neighbour^{GB}; **ma** ~**e de palier** the woman across the landing; **mon** ~ **de table** the man ou person next to me at table; **dire du mal du** ~ fig to speak ill of others

voisinage /vwazinaʒ/ nm [1] (*voisins*) neighbourhood^{GB}, neighbours^{GB} (*pl*); **entretenir des rapports de bon** ~ lit, fig to maintain neighbourly^{GB} relations; [2] (*environs*) neighbourhood^{GB}; [3] (*proximité*) proximity; **vivre dans le** ~ **d'une usine** to live close to a factory

voiture /vwatyʀ/ nf [1] (*automobile*) car, automobile US; [2] (*wagon*) carriage GB, coach GB, car US; **en** ~! all aboard!

(Composés) ~ **à bras** hand-drawn cart; ~ **à cheval** horse-drawn carriage; ~ **d'enfant** pram GB, baby carriage US; ~ **de poste** stage coach; ~ **de tourisme** saloon (car) GB, sedan US

(Idiome) **à pied, à cheval, en** ~ by whatever means of transport

voiture-balai, pl **voitures-balais** /vwatyʀbalɛ/ nf support vehicle

voiture-lit, pl **voitures-lits** /vwatyʀli/ nf sleeper, sleeping car US

voix /vwa/ nf inv [1] (*en phonétique, physiologie*) voice; ~ **blanche** expressionless voice; **entendre des** ~**s** to hear voices; **à** ~ **haute** out loud; **à** ~ **basse** in a low voice; **donner de la** ~ [*chien*] to give tongue; **être/rester sans** ~ to be/to remain speechless; **à portée de** ~ within earshot; [2] (*expression*) voice; **la** ~ **de la sagesse/de la raison** the voice of wisdom/of reason; **c'est la** ~ **du sang qui parle** it's in the blood; [3] Mus voice; **avoir de la** ~ to have a loud voice; **poser** or **placer sa** ~ to place one's voice; [4] (*opinion*) voice; **faire entendre sa** ~ to make oneself heard; [5] Pol vote; **avoir** ~ **délibérative** to have the right to vote; [6] Ling voice

(Composé) ~ **off** Cin voice-over

vol /vɔl/
A nm [1] (*d'oiseau*) flight; **prendre son** ~ to take wing, to fly off; **à** ~ **d'oiseau** as the crow flies; [2] (*groupe*) (de canards, cigognes) flight; (d'insectes) cloud; **de haut** ~ fig [*diplomate*] high-flying; [*cambrioleur*] big-time; [*prostituée*] high-class; [3] (*d'avion, de fusée*) flight; **le** ~ **pour Paris** the Paris flight; **il y a trois heures de** ~ it's a three-hour flight; **avoir 1 000 heures de** ~ **à son actif** to have logged 1,000 flying hours; **en (plein)** ~ in flight; **de** ~ [*conditions*] flying; [*plan, simulateur*] flight; [4] (*délit*) theft; (*plus important*) robbery; **c'est du** ~ **(manifeste)!** it's daylight robbery!; **c'est du** ~ **organisé!** it's a racket!
B **au vol** loc adv **tirer un oiseau au** ~ to shoot a bird in flight; **attraper une balle au** ~ to catch a ball in mid-air; **saisir des bribes de conversations au** ~ to catch snatches of conversation

(Composés) ~ **à l'arraché** bag snatching; ~ **avec effraction** burglary; ~ **à l'étalage** shoplifting; ~ **libre** Sport hang gliding; ~ **à main armée** armed robbery; ~ **à la tire** pickpocketing; ~ **à voile** gliding

volage /vɔlaʒ/ adj fickle

volaille /vɔlɑj/ nf [1] (*ensemble*) poultry; [2] (*animal*) fowl

V

volant, ∼e /vɔlã, ãt/
A adj **1** (qui vole) flying; **2** (mobile) [camp, pont] flying; [personnel] mobile
B nm **1** (de voiture) steering wheel; **être au** ∼ to be at the wheel; **reprendre le** ∼ to get back behind the wheel; **donner un coup de** ∼ to turn the wheel sharply; **un as du** ∼ an ace driver; **la sécurité au** ∼ safe driving; **2** (de vêtement) flounce, tier; **à** ∼**s** flounced; **3** (réserve) margin, reserve; **4** (de badminton) shuttlecock

volatil, ∼e¹ /vɔlatil/ adj volatile

volatile² /vɔlatil/ nm **1** (volaille) fowl; **2** (oiseau) bird

volatiliser /vɔlatilize/ [1]
A vtr Chimie to volatilize
B se volatiliser vpr **1** Chimie to volatilize; **2** (disparaître) hum to vanish into thin air, to disappear

volcan /vɔlkã/ nm **1** (relief) volcano; **être assis sur un** ∼ fig to be sitting on a volcano; **2** (personne) spitfire

volcanique /vɔlkanik/ adj **1** [activité, région, roche] volcanic; **2** [tempérament] explosive

volée /vɔle/
A nf **1** (d'oiseaux) (action de voler) flight; (vol groupé) flock, flight; **une** ∼ **d'étourneaux** a flock ou flight of starlings; **une** ∼ **d'enfants** a swarm of children; **2** (de projectiles, coups) volley; **donner une** ∼ **à qn** lit to give sb a good thrashing; fig to thrash sb; **3** (d'escalier) flight (of stairs); **4** (sports de raquette, volley-ball) volley; **reprendre la balle de** ∼ to take the ball on the volley; **saisir la balle à la** ∼ fig to seize the opportunity
B à **toute volée** loc adv **lancer qch à toute** ∼ to hurl sth; **les cloches sonnaient à toute** ∼ to bells were pealing out
(Idiomes) **comme une** ∼ **de moineaux** like flies; **asséner une** ∼ **de bois vert à qn** to deliver a blistering critique of sb

voler /vɔle/ [1]
A vtr **1** (dérober) to steal (à qn from sb); **il s'est fait** ∼ **sa voiture** he's had his car stolen; **il s'est fait** ∼ **la victoire** fig he's been robbed of his victory; **tu ne l'as pas volé!** fig it serves you right!; **2** (léser) to rob; ∼ **le client** to rip the customer off○; ∼ **qn sur la quantité** to cheat sb over the quantity
B vi to fly; **au vent** to blow in the wind; ∼ **en éclats** [vitre] to shatter; fig [certitude] to be shattered; ∼ **au secours de qn** to rush to sb's aid
(Idiome) **ça vole bas!** that's pretty mindless stuff!

volet /vɔlɛ/ nm **1** (contrevent) shutter; **2** (de plan, politique, problème) constituent; **3** (de dépliant) (folding) section

voleter /vɔlte/ [20] vi [insecte, papier] to flutter

voleur, -euse /vɔlœʀ, øz/
A adj **être** ∼ [chat] to be a thief; [enfant] to be light-fingered; [commerçant] to be dishonest
B nm,f (malfaiteur) thief; (tricheur) swindler; **crier 'au** ∼**!'** to shout 'stop thief!'; **jouer au gendarme et au** ∼ to play cops and robbers
(Composé) ∼ **de grand chemin** Hist highwayman
(Idiomes) **être** ∼ **comme une pie** to be a real thieving magpie; **se sauver comme un** ∼ to slip away like a thief in the night; **entrer/sortir comme un** ∼ to slip in/out

volière /vɔljɛʀ/ nf aviary

volley(-ball) /vɔlɛ(bol)/ ▸ p. 327 nm volleyball

volontaire /vɔlɔ̃tɛʀ/
A adj **1** (délibéré) [départ, travail] voluntary; [abus] deliberate; **ce n'était pas** ∼ **de ma part** I didn't mean to; **2** (opiniâtre) [personne, air] determined
B nm,f volunteer; **se porter** ∼ **pour faire** to volunteer to do

volontairement /vɔlɔ̃tɛʀmã/ adv [se priver, renoncer, partir] voluntarily; [dissimuler, faire mal] deliberately

volontariat /vɔlɔ̃taʀja/ nm voluntary service

volontariste /vɔlɔ̃taʀist/ adj voluntarist

volonté /vɔlɔ̃te/
A nf **1** (disposition) will; **faire preuve de bonne/mauvaise** ∼ to show goodwill/ill-will; **elle y met de la mauvaise** ∼ she's doing it with bad grace or reluctantly; **aller contre la** ∼ **de qn** to go against sb's wishes; **manifester la** ∼ **de faire** to show one's willingness to do; ∼ **de puissance** desire for power; **faire appel aux bonnes** ∼**s** to appeal for volunteers; **2** (trait de caractère) willpower; **à force de** ∼ by sheer willpower; **avoir une** ∼ **de fer** to have an iron will
B à **volonté** loc adv (autant que l'on veut) **'vin/pain/crudités à** ∼**'** 'unlimited wine/bread/salad'; **2** (comme on veut) [modulable] as required

volontiers /vɔlɔ̃tje/ adv **1** (avec plaisir) gladly; **j'irais** ∼ **à Paris** I'd love to go to Paris; **'tu me le prêtes?'—'**∼**'** 'will you lend it to me?'—'certainly'; **2** (facilement) [imaginer] easily; [admettre] readily; **je le crois** ∼ I'm quite ready to believe him/it

volt /vɔlt/ nm volt

volte-face /vɔlt(ə)fas/ nf inv **1** lit **faire** ∼ to turn around; **2** fig volte-face, U-turn; **faire** ∼ to do a U-turn

voltige /vɔltiʒ/ nf **1** (au trapèze) **(haute)** ∼ acrobatics (+ v pl); **2** Aviat ∼ **(aérienne)** aerobatics (+ v pl)

voltiger /vɔltiʒe/ [13] vi **1** (doucement) [papiers, feuilles] to flutter; **2** (violemment) [classeur, objet] to fly, to go flying

volubile /vɔlybil/ adj **1** (personne) voluble; **2** Bot twining

volubilité /vɔlybilite/ nf volubility

volume /vɔlym/ nm **1** (grandeur) volume; **le** ∼ **d'un fleuve** the volume of a river's flow; **donner du** ∼ **à ses cheveux** to give one's hair body; [colis, bagages] to be bulky; **2** (tome) volume; **3** (intensité) volume; ∼ **sonore** sound level

volumineux, -euse /vɔlyminø, øz/ adj [livre, dossier] thick; [documentation, correspondance] voluminous; [objet, bagages] bulky; [seins, fesses] ample

volupté /vɔlypte/ nf **1** (sensuelle) voluptuousness; **avec** ∼ voluptuously; **2** (intellectuelle) exquisite pleasure

voluptueux, -euse /vɔlyptɥø, øz/ adj voluptuous

volute /vɔlyt/ nf **1** (de colonne) volute; (de violon) scroll; **des** ∼**s de fumée** curls of smoke; **2** Zool volute

vomi○ /vɔmi/ nm vomit

vomir /vɔmiʀ/ [3]
A vtr **1** (recracher) [personne] to bring up [repas, nourriture]; to vomit [bile, sang]; **2** (projeter) to spew out [lave, déchets]; to belch [feu, vapeur, fumée]; **3** (abhorrer) to loathe
B vi [personne] to be sick, to vomit; **je vais** ∼ I'm going to be sick; **avoir envie de** ∼ to feel sick; **donner envie de** ∼ lit to make [sb] feel sick; fig to make [sb] sick; **c'est à** ∼ fig it makes you sick, it makes you puke●

vomissement /vɔmismã/ nm (action) vomiting; (résultat) vomit; **être pris de** ∼**s** to start to vomit

vorace /vɔʀas/ adj lit, fig voracious

voracité /vɔʀasite/ nf voracity, voraciousness

vos ▸ votre

votant, ∼e /vɔtã, ãt/ nm,f voter

vote /vɔt/ nm **1** (action) voting, vote; **droit de** ∼ right to vote; ∼ **d'un budget** voting on a budget; ∼ **à main levée** vote by show of hands; ∼ **d'une loi** passing of a bill; ∼ **utile** tactical vote; **2** (opinion exprimée) vote

voter /vɔte/ [1]
A vtr to vote [budget, amendement]; to pass [projet de loi]; ∼ **les pleins pouvoirs à qn** to vote to give sb full powers
B vi to vote; ∼ **(pour) Durand** to vote for Durand; ∼ **à bulletin secret** to vote by secret ballot; ∼ **contre un projet de loi** to vote a bill down; ∼ **blanc** to cast a blank vote; ∼ **utile** to engage in tactical voting

votre, pl **vos** /vɔtʀ, vo/ adj poss

⚠️ En anglais, on ne répète pas le possessif coordonné: *votre nom et votre adresse* = your name and your address.

your; **c'est pour** ∼ **bien** it's for your own good; **un de vos amis** a friend of yours; ∼ **gentil collègue** (collègue absent) that nice colleague of yours; (collègue présent) your kind colleague; **j'ai fait vos courses** I've done the shopping for you; **à** ∼ **arrivée** when you arrive

vôtre /votʀ/
A adj poss **mes biens sont** ∼**s** all I have is yours; **'amicalement** ∼**'** 'best wishes'
B **le vôtre**, **la vôtre**, **les vôtres** pron poss yours; **ils ont des habitudes très différentes des** ∼**s** their habits are very different from your own; **à la** ∼○! (à votre santé) cheers!; **vous avez encore fait des** ∼**s!** you've been up to mischief again!

vouer /vwe/ [1]
A vtr **1** (porter) ∼ **un sentiment à qn** to nurse a feeling for sb; ∼ **une reconnaissance éternelle à qn** to be ou feel eternally grateful to sb; ∼ **un véritable culte à qn** to worship sb; **2** (destiner) to doom; **film voué à l'échec** film doomed to failure, film bound to fail; ∼ **qn à la vindicte publique** to expose sb to public condemnation; **3** (consacrer) ∼ **sa**

Le volume

■ *Pour les mesures en litres, décilitres, hectolitres etc.*
voir **la capacité ▸ p. 87.**
Pour la prononciation des nombres, voir **les nombres**
▸ p. 398.

Équivalences

1 cu in	=	16,38 cm^3	
1 cu ft	=	1728 cu in	= 0,03 m^3
1 cu yd	=	27 cu ft	= 0,76 m^3

dire   **dire**

one cubic   1 cm^3 = 0.061 cu in   *cubic inches*
  centimetre
one cubic   1 dm^3 = 0.035 cu ft   *cubic feet*
  decimetre
one cubic   1 m^3 = 35.315 cu ft
  metre   = 1.308 cu yd   *cubic yard*

■ *Pour l'écriture, noter:*

– *l'anglais utilise un point là où le français a une virgule.*

– *on écrit* -metre *en anglais britannique et* -meter *en*
  anglais américain.

– *on peut écrire* cu in *ou* in^3, cu ft *ou* ft^3, *etc.*

il y a 1 000 000 centimètres cubes dans un mètre cube
= there are a million cubic centimetres in a cubic metre

1 000 000 centimètres cubes font un mètre cube
= a million cubic centimetres make one cubic metre

quel est le volume de la caisse?
= what is the volume of the box?

elle fait 2 m^3
= it is 2 cubic metres

elle a un volume de 2 m^3
= its volume is 2 cubic metres

à peu près 3 m^3
= about 3 cubic metres

presque 3 m^3
= almost 3 cubic metres

plus de 2 m^3
= more than 2 cubic metres

moins de 3 m^3
= less than 3 cubic metres

le volume de A est supérieur à celui de B
= A has a greater volume than B

le volume de B est inférieur à celui de A
= B has a smaller volume than A

A et B ont le même volume
= A and B have the same volume

le volume de A est égal à celui de B
= A has the same volume as B

5 m^3 de terre
= five cubic metres of soil

vendu au mètre cube
= sold by the cubic metre

■ *Noter l'ordre des mots dans les adjectifs composés*
anglais, et l'utilisation du trait d'union. Noter aussi que
metre, *employé comme adjectif, ne prend pas la marque*
du pluriel.

un réservoir de 200 m^3
= a 200-cubic-metre tank

■ *On peut aussi dire* a tank 200 cubic metres in volume.

---

vie/son temps à to devote one's life/one's time to
B se vouer *vpr* **1** (se consacrer) **se ~ à** to devote oneself to;
2 (se porter) **ils se vouent une haine féroce** they hate each
other intensely
(Idiome) **je ne sais plus à quel saint me ~** I don't know
which way to turn
vouloir¹ /vulwaʀ/ [48]
A *vtr* **1** (exiger) to want; **qu'est-ce qu'ils nous veulent○**
encore? what do they want now?; **comme le veut la loi** as
the law demands; **le règlement voudrait que tu portes une**
cravate you're normally required to wear a tie; **2** (désirer,
souhaiter) **que veux-tu boire?** what do you want to drink?;
(plus poli) what would you like to drink?; **comme tu veux** as
you wish; **je voudrais un kilo de poires** I'd like a kilo of
pears; **je comprends très bien que tu ne veuilles pas**
répondre I can quite understand that you may not wish
to reply; **il ne suffit pas de ~, il faut encore pouvoir** wishing is not enough; **il suffisait de ~** all you needed was the
will to do it; **on dira ce qu'on voudra** they can say what
they like; **tu veux que je te dise , c'est un escroc** I hate to
say it, but he is a crook; **sans le ~** [bousculer, révéler] by
accident; [se retrouver] accidentally; **il m'a fait mal sans le**
~ he hurt me without meaning to; **'qu'est-ce qu'on fait**
ce soir?'—'comme tu veux *or* **voudras'** 'what shall we do
tonight?'—'whatever you like, it's up to you'; **que tu le**
veuilles ou non whether you like it or not; **elle fait ce**
qu'elle veut de son mari she twists her husband around
her little finger; **elle fait ce qu'elle veut de ses mains** she
can do anything with her hands; **je ne vous veux aucun**
mal I don't wish you any harm; **tu ne veux/voudrais pas**
me faire croire que you're not telling/trying to tell me
that; **après ce qu'il a fait, tu voudrais que je lui fasse con-**
fiance? do you expect me to trust him after what he's
done?; **comment veux-tu que je le sache?** how should I
know?; **pourquoi voudrais-tu qu'il refuse?** why should he
refuse?; **que veux-tu, on n'y peut rien!** what can you do,
it's hopeless!; **j'aurais voulu t'y voir○!** I'd like to have seen
you in the same position!; **tu l'auras voulu!** it'll be all your
own fault!; **3** (accepter) **voulez-vous fermer la fenêtre?**

would you mind closing the window?; **voudriez-vous**
avoir l'obligeance de faire fml would you be so kind as to
do; **on voudra bien se référer aux ouvrages suivants**
please refer to the following works; **voulez-vous répéter**
votre question, s'il vous plaît would you repeat your question please; **veuillez patienter** (au téléphone) please hold the
line; **si vous voulez bien me suivre** if you'd like to follow
me; **veux-tu te taire!** will you be quiet!; **ils ont bien voulu**
nous prêter leur voiture they were kind enough to lend us
their car; **elle n'a pas voulu signer** she would not sign; **le**
moteur ne veut pas partir the engine won't start; **elle veut**
bien prendre ce poste à condition d'être mieux payée she's
happy to take the job on condition that she's paid more;
je veux bien te croire I'm quite prepared to believe you; **si**
l'on veut bien se rappeler que if one remembers that; **je**
veux bien qu'il soit malade mais I know he's ill, but; **'ce**
n'est pas cher/difficile'—'si on veut!' 'it's not expensive/
difficult'—'or so you say!'; **4** (signifier) **~ dire** to mean;
qu'est-ce que ça veut dire? (signification) what does that
mean?; (attitude) what's all this about?; **tu ne veux pas dire**
qu'il est médecin? you don't mean to tell me he's a
doctor?; **5** (prétendre) **comme le veut la tradition** as tradition has it; **leur théorie veut que** according to their
theory; **on a voulu voir en lui un pionnier de l'architecture**
people tended to see him as a pioneering architect
B en vouloir *vtr ind* **1** ○(être déterminé) **il réussira, il en veut!**
he wants to get on, and he'll succeed!; **2** (garder rancune)
en ~ à qn to bear a grudge against sb; **je leur en veux de**
m'avoir trompé I hold it against them for not being
honest with me; **ne m'en veux pas** please forgive me;
3 (avoir des vues sur) **en ~ à qch** to be after sth
C se vouloir *vpr* **1** (prétendre être) [personne] to like to think
of oneself as; [ouvrage, théorie, méthode] to be meant to be;
2 (chercher à être) to try to be; **3** (se reprocher) **s'en ~** to be
cross with oneself; **s'en ~ de** to regret; **je m'en veux**
d'avoir été si dur avec elle I really regret being so hard on
her; **je m'en serais voulu de ne pas vous avoir prévenu** I
would never have forgiven myself if I hadn't warned you;
il ne faut pas vous en ~ you mustn't blame yourself

(Idiome) ~ **c'est pouvoir** Prov where there's a will there's a way

vouloir² /vulwaʀ/ nm Philos will; **bon** ~ goodwill; **attendre le bon** ~ **de qn** to wait on sb's pleasure sout

voulu, ~**e** /vuly/ adj **1** (requis) **les compétences** ~**es** the required skills; **avec toute la sévérité** ~**e** with due severity; **on n'obtient jamais les renseignements** ~**s** you never get the information you want; **en temps** ~ in time; **au moment** ~ at the right time; **2** (intentionnel) deliberate; **notre rencontre n'était pas** ~**e** our meeting was not planned

vous /vu/ pron pers **1** (sujet) you; **je sais que ce n'est pas** ~ I know it wasn't you; **c'est** ~ **qui avez gagné** you have won; ~ **aussi**, ~ **avez l'air malade** you don't look very well either; **2** (dans une comparaison) **elles travaillent plus que** ~ they work more than you (do); **3** (objet) **ils** ~ **ont trahis** they have betrayed you; **4** (après préposition) you; **après** ~ after you; **ce sont des amis à** ~**?** are they friends of yours?; **c'est à** ~ (appartenance) it's yours, it belongs to you; (séquence) it's your turn; **à** ~ (dans une séquence) your turn; **à** ~ **de choisir** (votre tour) it's your turn to choose; (votre responsabilité) it's up to you to choose; **5** (pronom réfléchi) (singulier) yourself; (pluriel) yourselves; **allez** ~ **laver les mains** go and wash your hands; **6** (vous-même) yourself; (vous-mêmes) yourselves; **prenez soin de** ~ look after yourself; **pensez à** ~ **deux** think of yourselves

vous-même, pl **vous-mêmes** /vumɛm/ pron pers **1** (de politesse) yourself; **vous me l'avez dit** ~ you told me yourself; **ne vous repliez pas sur** ~ don't turn in on yourself; **2** (vous tous) **allez-y** ~**s** go yourselves; **vous verrez par** ~**s** you'll see for yourselves

voûte /vut/ nf (plafond) vault; (de porche) archway; (de tunnel) roof; (de feuillage) arch; (ouvrage) vaulting **⊄**

(Composés) **la** ~ **céleste** gén the sky; littér the heavens (pl); ~ **crânienne** dome of the skull; ~ **du palais** roof of the mouth; ~ **plantaire** arch of the foot

voûté, ~**e** /vute/ adj **1** Archit vaulted, arched; **2** (courbé) [personne] stooping; [dos] bent; **il est** ~ he has a stoop

voûter /vute/ [1]
A vtr (courber) to give [sb] a stoop [personne]
B se voûter vpr [personne] to develop a stoop; [dos] to become bent

vouvoiement /vuvwamã/ nm using the 'vous' ou polite form

vouvoyer /vuvwaje/ [23]
A vtr to address [sb] using the 'vous' form
B se vouvoyer vpr to address one another using the 'vous' form

voyage /vwajaʒ/ nm (dans son ensemble) trip; (déplacement) journey; **le** ~ **aller** the outward journey; **faire un** ~ **en Italie** to go on a trip ou to travel to Italy; **aimer les** ~**s** to love travelling^GB

(Composés) ~ **d'études** study trip; ~ **de noces** honeymoon; ~ **organisé** package tour

(Idiome) **faire le grand** ~ to pass away

voyager /vwajaʒe/ [13] vi to travel; ~ **en train** to travel by train; **le vin ne voyage pas bien** this wine doesn't travel well; **les bagages ont voyagé par le train** the luggage went by train; **récit qui vous fait** ~ **dans le temps** story that takes you on a journey through time

voyageur, **-euse** /vwajaʒœʀ, øz/
A adj liter **être d'humeur voyageuse** to have itchy feet
B nmf **1** (passager) passenger; **'réservé aux** ~**s munis de billets'** 'ticketholders only'; **2** (aventurier) traveller^GB; **Marco Polo fut un grand** ~ Marco Polo was a great traveller^GB

(Composé) ~ **de commerce** travelling^GB salesman

voyagiste /vwajaʒist/ ▸ p. 372 nmf tour operator

voyance /vwajãs/ nf clairvoyance

voyant, ~**e** /vwajã, ãt/
A adj [couleur, robe] loud
B nmf **1** (extralucide) clairvoyant; **2** (qui y voit) sighted person
C nm light; ~ **d'huile** Aut oil warning light

voyelle /vwajɛl/ nf vowel

voyeur, **-euse** /vwajœʀ, øz/ nm,f voyeur

voyou /vwaju/ nm lout, yobbo^○ GB, hoodlum^○ US

vrac: **en vrac** /ãvʀak/ loc adv **1** (au détail) loose, unpackaged; (en gros) in bulk; **2** (pêle-mêle) **tout mettre en**

~ **dans un tiroir** to throw everything haphazardly into a drawer; **jeter ses idées en** ~ **sur le papier** to jot down one's ideas as they come

vrai, ~**e** /vʀɛ/
A adj **1** (conforme à la vérité) true; **c'est bien** ~**!** that's absolutely true!; **il n'en est pas moins** ~ **que...** it's nonetheless true that...; **il n'y a rien de** ~ **dans ses déclarations** there's no truth in his/her statements; **c'est bien toi qui l'as pris, pas** ~**?** you took it, didn't you?; **son film ne montre pas le** ~ **Napoléon** his/her film doesn't show the real Napoleon; **2** (réel) true; **une histoire** ~**e** a true story; **la** ~**e raison de mon départ** the real reason for my leaving; **3** (authentique) real, genuine; [jumeau] identical; **un** ~ **Rembrandt** a genuine Rembrandt; **une** ~**e blonde** a natural blonde; **4** (intensif) real, veritable; **c'est un** ~ **régal** it's a real delight; **la pièce est une** ~ **fournaise** the room is like an oven; **ma vie est un** ~ **roman** my life is like something out of a novel; **5** (naturel) (after n) [personnage, caractère] true to life; [sentiments, émotion] true; **plus** ~ **que nature** [tableau, scène] larger than life (après n)
B nm truth; **il y a du** ~ **dans ce que tu dis** there's some truth in what you say; **on ne distingue plus le** ~ **du faux dans leur histoire** one can't tell fact from fiction in their story; **être dans le** ~ to be in the right; **pour de** ~ for real; **à** ~ **dire**, **à dire** ~ to tell the truth
C adv faire ~ to look real; **parler** ~ to speak plainly; **son discours sonne** ~ his speech has the ring of truth

vraiment /vʀɛmã/ adv really

vraisemblable /vʀɛsãblabl/
A adj (qui paraît vrai) [excuse] convincing, plausible; [histoire, scénario] plausible; (probable) likely; **il est** ~ **que** it is likely ou probable that; **peu** ~ [excuse] not very convincing, quite unconvincing; [histoire] rather implausible; **ce qui me paraît peu** ~ **c'est** what strikes me as very unlikely is
B nm **nouvelles qui sont dans l'ordre du** ~ news which is within the bounds of probability; **rester dans le** ~ to keep within the bounds of credibility

vraisemblablement /vʀɛsãblabləmã/ adv probably; ~ **pas** probably not; **ils ne signeront** ~ **pas ce traité** it seems unlikely that they will sign this treaty

vraisemblance /vʀɛsãblãs/ nf **1** (d'hypothèse) likelihood; (de situation, d'intrigue) plausibility; (d'explication) plausibility, verisimilitude sout; **selon toute** ~ in all likelihood, in all probability; **2** Littérat, Théât verisimilitude sout

vrille /vʀij/ nf **1** (spirale) spiral; Sport spiral; Aviat tailspin, spiral; **descendre en** ~ [avion] to go into a spiral dive; **2** Bot tendril; **3** Tech gimlet

vrombir /vʀɔ̃biʀ/ [3] vi **1** [moteur] to roar; (en continu) to throb; **faire** ~ **un moteur** to rev up an engine; **2** [mouche] to buzz

VRP /veɛʀpe/ nm (abbr = **voyageur représentant placier**) representative, rep^○

VSL /veɛsɛl/ nm (abbr = **véhicule sanitaire léger**) PTS ambulance, patient transport service ambulance

VTC /vetese/ nm ▸ **vélo**

VTT /vetete/ nm: abbr ▸ **vélo**

vu, ~**e¹** /vy/
A adj **1** (considéré) **être bien** ~ [personne] to be well thought of; **être mal** ~ [personne] not to be well thought of; **c'est bien** ~ **de faire cela** it's good form to do that; **ce serait plutôt mal** ~ it wouldn't go down well; **2** (jugé) **bien** ~**!**, **c'est bien** ~**!** good point!; **c'est tout** ~ my mind is made up; **3** (compris) ~**?**, **c'est bien** ~**?** got it^○?
B prép in view of
C vu que loc conj in view of the fact that

(Idiomes) **ni** ~ **ni connu**^○! no-one will know!; **faire qch ni** ~ **ni connu**^○ to do sth without anybody knowing; **pas** ~ **pas pris** it can't hurt if nobody knows; **au** ~ **et au su de tous** openly and publicly

vue² /vy/ nf **1** (vision) eyesight; **les troubles de la** ~ eye trouble; **perdre/recouvrer la** ~ to lose/to regain one's sight; **don de double** ~ gift of second sight; **avoir la** ~ **basse** lit, fig to be short-sighted GB ou near-sighted US; **ça fatigue la** ~ it strains your eyes; **en** ~ [personnalité] prominent; **en** ~ **de la côte** within sight of the coast; **mettre une photo bien en** ~ to display a photo prominently; **c'est quelqu'un de très en** ~ he's/she's very much in the public eye; **2** (regard) sight; **à première** ~ at first sight; **ne perds pas cet enfant de** ~ don't let that child out of your sight; **perdre qn de** ~ fig to lose touch with sb; **le paysage**

qui s'offrait à la ~ the landscape before us; à ~ [tirer] on sight; [atterrir, piloter] without instruments; Fin [retrait] on demand; ③ (panorama) view; **chambre avec ~ sur la mer** room with sea view; **avoir ~ sur le lac** to look out onto the lake; **d'ici, on a une ~ plongeante sur la vallée** from here you get a bird's-eye view of the valley; ④ (spectacle) sight; **à ma ~, il s'enfuit** he took to his heels when he saw me *ou* on seeing me; ⑤ (dessin, photo) view; **~ de face/de côté** front/side view; ⑥ (façon de voir) view; **~s** views; **une ~ optimiste des choses** an optimistic view of things; ⑦ (projet) **~s** plans; (desseins) **avoir des ~s sur qn/qch** to have designs on sb/sth; **j'ai un terrain en ~** (je sais lequel conviendrait) I have a plot of land in mind; (je voudrais obtenir) I've got my eye on a piece of land; **en ~ de qch/de faire qch** with a view to sth/to doing sth

(Composés) **~ d'ensemble** overall view; **ce n'est qu'une ~ de l'esprit** it's entirely imaginary

(Idiomes) **à ~ d'œil** *or* **de nez**○ at a rough guess; **vouloir en mettre plein la ~ à qn** to try to dazzle sb

vulcanologue /vylkanɔlɔg/ ▸ p. 372 *nmf* volcanologist

vulgaire /vylgɛʀ/

A *adj* ① (grossier) [*personne, propos*] vulgar, coarse; ② (banal)

ordinary; **comme un ~ délinquant** like a common delinquent; **c'est un ~ employé** he's just a lowly employee; ③ (courant) [*plante, nom*] common; **la langue ~** the vernacular; **explication en langue ~** explanation in simple language; ④ [*esprit, opinion*] common

B *nm* (grossièreté) vulgarity

vulgairement /vylgɛʀmɑ̃/ *adv* ① (sans raffinement) [*s'habiller*] in a common way; [*s'exprimer*] coarsely; ② (dans la langue courante) [*appeler*] commonly

vulgarisation /vylgaʀizasjɔ̃/ *nf* popularization; **revue de ~ scientifique** scientific review for the general public

vulgariser /vylgaʀize/ [1]

A *vtr* (rendre accessible) to popularize [*science, technologie*]; to bring [sth] into general use [*expression*]

B **se vulgariser** *vpr* [*technologie*] to become generally accessible; [*expression*] to come into general use

vulgarité /vylgaʀite/ *nf* ① (grossièreté) vulgarity, coarseness; ② (banalité) ordinariness

vulnérabilité /vylneʀabilite/ *nf* vulnerability

vulnérable /vylneʀabl/ *adj* vulnerable

vulve /vylv/ *nf* vulva

Ww

w, W /dubləve/ *nm inv* ①► (lettre) w, W; ②► **W** (*written abbr =* **watt**) **60 W** 60 W

wagon /vagɔ̃/ *nm* ①► (pour matériel, animaux) wagon GB, car US; (pour personnes) carriage GB, car US; ②► (contenu) wagonload GB, carload US

Composés) ∼ **à bestiaux** cattle truck GB, cattle car US; ∼ **de marchandises** goods wagon GB, freight car US

wagon-citerne, *pl* **wagons-citernes** /vagɔ̃sitɛʀn/ *nm* Rail tanker

wagon-lit, *pl* **wagons-lits** /vagɔ̃li/ *nm* sleeper, sleeping car US

wagonnet /vagɔnɛ/ *nm* trolley GB, cart US

wagon-restaurant, *pl* **wagons-restaurants** /vagɔ̃ʀɛstɔʀɑ̃/ *nm* restaurant car GB, dining car US

wallon, -onne /walɔ̃, ɔn/ ► p. 336 *adj, nm* Walloon

Wallonie /walɔni/ ► p. 504 *nprf* Walloon area of Belgium

wassingue /vasɛ̃g/ *nf* floorcloth

waters○ /watɛʀ/ *nmpl* toilets

watt /wat/ *nm* watt

watt-heure, *pl* **watts-heures** /watœʀ/ *nm* watt-hour

WC /(dublə)vese/ *nmpl* toilet; **aller aux** ∼ to go to the toilet

webmestre /wɛbmɛstʀ/ ► p. 372 *nmf* webmaster

week-end, *pl* ∼**s** /wikɛnd/ *nm* weekend

whisky, *pl* **whiskies** /wiski/ *nm* (écossais) whisky, Scotch; (irlandais, américain) whiskey

winchester /winʃɛstɛʀ/ *nf* (fusil) Winchester® rifle

wishbone /wiʃbon/ *nm* Naut, Sport wishbone boom

wisigoth, ∼**e** /vizigo, ɔt/ *adj* Visigothic

w

x, **X** /iks/ *nm inv* ① (lettre) x, X; ② Math (inconnue) x; **il y a x temps que c'est fini** it's been over for ages; ③ (pour désigner un inconnu) **X, Monsieur X** X, Mr X; **porter plainte contre X** Jur to take an action against person or persons unknown; ④ Cin **film classé X** X-rated film GB *ou* movie

xénophobe /gzenɔfɔb/
A *adj* xenophobic
B *nmf* xenophobe

xénophobie /gzenɔfɔbi/ *nf* xenophobia

xérès /kseʀɛs/ *nm inv* sherry

xylographe /ksilɔgʀaf/ *nm* xylographer

xylophone /ksilofɔn/ ▸ p. 389 *nm* xylophone

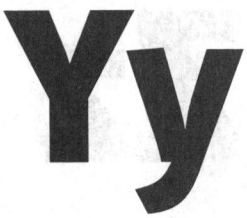

y¹, **Y** /igRɛk/ *nm inv* (lettre) y, Y

y² /i/ *pron*

> ⚠ Les expressions comme *y rester*, *il y a* sont trai-
> tées sous le verbe.
>
> Lorsque *y* met en relief un groupe exprimé, on ne
> le traduit pas: *tu y vas souvent, à Londres*○*?* = do you
> often go to London?; *je n'y comprends rien, moi, aux
> échecs*○ = I don't understand anything about chess.
> Lorsque *y* ne remplace aucun groupe identifiable,
> on ne le traduit pas: *c'est plus difficile qu'il n'y paraît*
> = it's harder than it seems; *je n'y vois rien* = I can't
> see a thing.

1 (à ça) **rien n'~ fait** it's no use; **elle n'~ peut rien** there's
nothing she can do about it; **j'~ viens** I'm coming to
that; **tu n'~ arriveras jamais** you'll never manage; **tu
~ crois?** do you believe it?; **je vais m'~ mettre demain** I'll
start tomorrow; **je n'~ comprends rien** I don't understand a thing; **il n'~ connaît rien** he knows nothing about
it; **j'~ pense parfois** I sometimes think about it; **tu
t'~ attendais?** were you expecting it?; **tu ~ as gagné** you
got the best deal; **2** (là) there; **n'~ va pas** don't go;
j'~ suis allé hier I went yesterday; **3** (avec le verbe avoir) **des
pommes? il n'y en a plus/pas** apples? there are none left/
none; **du vin? il n'y en a plus/pas** wine? there's none left/
none; **il n'~ a qu'à téléphoner** just phone

(Idiome) **~ mettre du sien** to work at it

ya(c)k /'jak/ *nm* yak

yaourt /'jauʀ(t)/ *nm* yoghurt; **~ nature/aromatisé/aux
fruits** natural/flavoured^{GB}/fruit yoghurt

yaourtière /'jauʀtjɛʀ/ *nf* yoghurt-maker

yéménite /'jemenit/ ▶ p. 392, p. 336 *adj* Yemeni

Yéménite /'jemenit/ ▶ p. 392 *nmf* Yemeni

yen /'jɛn/ ▶ p. 34 *nm* yen

yéti /'jeti/ *nm* yeti

yeux *nmpl* ▶ œil

yé-yé, *pl* **~s** /'jeje/ *nm* (musique) **le ~** *French version of rock 'n'
roll in the 60s*

yiddish /'jidiʃ/ ▶ p. 336 *adj inv*, *nm* Yiddish

yod /'jɔd/ *nm* Ling yod

yoga /'jɔga/ ▶ p. 327 *nm* yoga; **faire du ~** to do yoga

yoghourt /'jɔguʀ(t)/ *nm* = **yaourt**

yogi /'jɔgi/ *nm* yogi

yole /'jɔl/ *nf* skiff

yougoslave /'jugɔslav/ ▶ p. 392 *adj* Yugoslavian

youpi○ /'jupi/ *excl* yippee!

youyou /'juju/ *nm* **1** (cri) ululation *sout*; **2** (embarcation)
dinghy

yo-yo® /'jojo/ *nm inv* yoyo®

Zz

z, Z /zɛd/ nm inv z, Z

ZAC /zak/ nf: abbr ▸ **zone**

zapper /zape/ [1] vi (à la télévision) to flick through the channels

zapping○ /zapiŋ/ nm ① TV channel-hopping; ② fig brand-switching

zèbre /zebʀ/ nm ① zebra; ② ○fig bloke○ GB, guy○

zébré /zebʀe/ adj [tissu] zebra-striped; **~ de** streaked with

zébrure /zebʀyʀ/ nf stripe

zébu /zeby/ nm zebu

zèle /zɛl/ nm zeal, enthusiasm; **avec ~** enthusiastically, with zeal ou enthusiasm; **faire du ~** or **de l'excès de ~** to be overzealous, to overdo it

zélé, ~e /zele/ adj enthusiastic, zealous

zélote /zelɔt/ nm Hist Zealot

zen /zɛn/
Ⓐ adj inv ① lit zen; ② ○fig mellow, laid-back
Ⓑ nm zen

zénith /zenit/ nm lit, fig zenith; **à son ~** [soleil] in the ou at its zenith; [carrière] at its height; **être au ~ de qch** to be at the height of sth

ZEP /zɛp/ nf (abbr = **zone d'éducation prioritaire**) area earmarked for special educational assistance, cf Education Action Zone GB

> ⓘ **ZEP** The term ZEP refers to schools in deprived, usually urban, settings which are earmarked for special state support. The decision to categorize a school as a ZEP lies with the académie which can release additional funding to finance special-needs education. There is usually a high percentage of pupils with both learning difficulties and behavioural problems in attendance. Special educational needs ▸▸▸

include psychological support, speech therapy, psychomotor skills, and the additional work this represents for staff is remunerated.

zéphyr /zefiʀ/ nm liter zephyr

zéro /zeʀo/ ▸ p. 398
Ⓐ adj ① (avant nom) **~ heure** midnight, twenty-four hundred (hours); **il sera exactement ~ heure vingt minutes dix secondes** the time will be twelve twenty and ten seconds; **les enfants de ~ à six ans** children from nought to six years old; **j'ai eu ~ faute dans ma dictée** I didn't make a single mistake in my dictation; ② (après nom) zero; **niveau/croissance ~** zero level/growth
Ⓑ nm ① (chiffre) zero, nought GB; **le prix se termine par un ~** the price ends in a nought GB ou zero; ② (sur une échelle de valeurs) zero; **remettre un compteur à ~** to reset a counter to zero; **avoir le moral à ~** fig to be down in the dumps○; ③ (évaluation) zero, nought GB; **avoir un ~ en latin** to get zero ou nought in Latin; **c'est beau à regarder mais question goût c'est ~**○ it's nice to look at, but no marks for flavour GB; ④ (en sport) gén nil, nothing; (au tennis) love; **gagner trois (buts) à ~** to win three nil; **l'emporter par deux sets à ~** to win by two sets to love

⟮Composé⟯ **~ de conduite** bad mark for behaviour GB

⟮Idiomes⟯ **partir de ~** to start from scratch; **tout reprendre à ~** to start all over again; **avoir la boule à ~**○ to have a shaven head

zeste /zɛst/ nm (écorce) ¢; **un ~ de citron** the zest of a lemon; **un ~ de provocation** fig a touch of provocation

zêta /dzeta/ nm inv zeta

zézayer /zezeje/ [21] vi to lisp

zibeline /ziblin/ nf sable; **un manteau de ~** a sable coat

zieuter○ /zjøte/ [1] vtr to get a load of○, take a look at

zigomar○ /zigomaʀ/ nm pej guy○

zigoto○ /zigɔto/ nm guy○; **faire le ~** to clown around

Les signes du zodiaque

	signe			personnes	date
Bélier	=	Aries	['eəriːz]	Arians	Mar 21–Apr 20
Taureau	=	Taurus	['tɔːrəs]	Taureans	Apr 21–May 20
Gémeaux	=	Gemini	['dʒemɪnaɪ,-nɪː]	Geminis	May 21–Jun 21
Cancer	=	Cancer	['kænsə(r)]	Cancerians	Jun 22–July 22
Lion	=	Leo	['liːəʊ]	Leos	July 23–Aug 22
Vierge	=	Virgo	['vɜːgəʊ]	Virgos ou Virgoans	Aug 23–Sept 22
Balance	=	Libra	['liːbrə]	Libras	Sept 23–Oct 23
Scorpion	=	Scorpio	['skɔːpɪəʊ]	Scorpios	Oct 24–Nov 21
Sagittaire	=	Sagittarius	[,sædʒ'teərɪəs]	Sagittarians	Nov 22–Dec 21
Capricorne	=	Capricorn	['kæprɪ'kɔːn]	Capricorns	Dec 22–Jan 19
Verseau	=	Aquarius	[a'kweərɪəs]	Aquarians	Jan 20–Feb 18
Poissons	=	Pisces	['paɪsiːz]	Pisceans	Feb 19–Mar 20

■ *Dans les expressions suivantes, Lion est pris comme exemple; tous les autres signes s'utilisent de la même façon.*

je suis Lion
= I'm Leo ou I'm a Leo

je suis Gémeaux
= I'm a Gemini

né sous le signe du Lion
= born under the sign of Leo ou born in Leo

les Lions/Cancers sont très généreux
= Leos/Cancerians are very generous

que dit l'horoscope pour les Lions?
= what's the horoscope for Leo?

z

zigue○ /zig/ nm guy○

zigzag /zigzag/ nm zigzag; **une route en** ∼ a winding road; **faire des** ∼**s** to zigzag (**parmi** through); **partir en** ∼**s** to zigzag off

zinc /zɛ̃g/ nm ① zinc; **toiture de** or **en**∼ tin roofing; ② ○(comptoir) counter, bar; ③ ○(avion) plane

zingueur /zɛ̃gœR/ ▸ p. 372 nm roofer

zinzin○ /zɛ̃zɛ̃/
A adj inv cracked○
B nmf (personne) lunatic, nut○
C nm thingummy○ GB, thingamajig○

zip® /zip/ nm zip GB, zipper US

zippé, ∼**e** /zipe/ adj [sac, blouson] zip-up (épith)

zizanie /zizani/ nf ill-feeling, discord

zizi○ /zizi/ nm willy○ GB, wiener○ US, penis

zodiac® /zɔdjak/ nm Naut inflatable dinghy

zodiaque /zɔdjak/ nm zodiac

zombie /zɔ̃bi/ nm zombie

zona /zona/ ▸ p. 195 nm shingles ¢

zonard○, ∼**e** /zonaR, aRd/ nmf pej dropout○

zone /zon/ nf ① (secteur) zone, area; ∼ **interdite** no-go area GB, off-limits area; (sur un panneau) no entry; ② fig (domaine) area; ∼ **de recherche** area of research; ③ (banlieue pauvre) **la** ∼ the slum belt; **de seconde** ∼ second-rate

(Composés) ∼ **d'activités** business park; ∼ **d'aménagement concerté**, **ZAC** Admin integrated development zone; ∼ **artisanale** small industrial estate GB ou park; ∼ **bleue** Aut restricted parking zone; ∼ **d'environnement protégé** environmental protection zone; ∼ **euro** Euro Zone; ∼ **industrielle** industrial estate GB ou park; ∼ **libre** Hist unoccupied France; ∼ **de libre-échange** Écon free-trade area; ∼ **occupée** Hist occupied France; ∼ **sinistrée** Admin disaster area

zoner○ /zone/ [1] vi to hang about○ ou around○

zoo /zo/ nm zoo

zoologie /zɔɔlɔʒi/ nf zoology

zoologiste /zɔɔlɔʒist/ ▸ p. 372 nmf zoologist

zoom /zum/ nm ① Phot (objectif) zoom lens; ② Cin zoom; **un** ∼ **avant/arrière** a zoom in/out

zootechnicien, **-ienne** /zootɛknisjɛ̃, ɛn/ ▸ p. 372 nm,f animal technician

zouave /zwav/ nm ① ○(clown) clown, comedian; **faire le** ∼ to play the fool GB, to clown around○; ② (soldat) zouave

zozo○ /zozo/ nm ninny○ GB, jerk○

zozoter /zɔzɔte/ [1] vi to lisp

zut○ /zyt/ excl damn○!

zygomatique /zigɔmatik/ adj, nm zygomatic

z

Communication mode d'emploi
Guide to effective communication

La correspondance privée

Félicitations pour un mariage

Les Rosiers
22 Avenue des Epines
95100 Argenteuil
France

22/8/04

Dear Joe,

Thanks for your letter. I was delighted to hear that you two are getting married, and I'm sure you'll be very happy together. I will do my best to come to the wedding, it'd be such a shame to miss it.

I think your plans for a small wedding sound just the thing, and I feel honoured to be invited. I wonder if you have decided where you are going for your honeymoon yet? I look forward to seeing you both soon. Sarah sends her congratulations.

Best wishes,

Eric

Pour annoncer une naissance

26 James Street
Oxford
OX4 3AA

22 May 2004

Dear Charlie,

We wanted to let you know that early this morning Julia Claire was born. She weighs 7lbs 2oz, and she and Harriet are both very well. The birth took place at home, as planned.

It would be wonderful to see you, so feel free to come and visit and meet Julia Claire whenever you want. (It might be best to give us a ring first, though). It would be great to catch up on your news too. Give my regards to all your family, I haven't seen them for such a long time.

Looking forward to seeing you,

Nick

Vœux de Bonne Année

Flat 3, Alice House
44 Louis Gardens
London W5.

January 2nd 2004

Dear Arthur and Gwen,

Happy New Year! This is just a quick note to wish you all the best for the year 2004. I hope you had a good Christmas, and that you're both well. It seems like a long time since we last got together.

My New Year should be busy as I am trying to sell the flat. I want to buy a small house nearer my office and I'd like a change from the flat since I've been here nearly six years now. I'd very much like to see you, so why don't we get together for an evening next time you're in town? Do give me a ring so we can arrange a date.

With all good wishes from

Lance

Réponse à des vœux de Bonne Année

19 Wrekin Lane
Brighton
BN7 8QT

6th January 2005

My dear Renée,

Thank you so much for your letter and New Year's wishes. It was great to hear from you after all this time, and to get all your news from the past year. I'll write a "proper" reply later this month, when I've more time. I just wanted to tell you now how glad I am that we are in touch again, and to say that if you do come over in February I would love you to come and stay — I have plenty of room for you and Maurice.

All my love,

Helen

Personal and social correspondence

Congratulations on a wedding

Martigues, le 18 août 2004

Chers amis,

Nous nous réjouissons pour vous du mariage de votre fille et nous vous en félicitons de tout cœur. Paul sera certainement un excellent gendre pour vous et un beau-frère apprécié par vos enfants.

Nous vous chargeons de transmettre aux futurs époux nos meilleurs vœux de bonheur et serons enchantés de venir les embrasser le jour J.

Très amicalement,

Isabelle

Announcing the birth of a baby

Pierre et Marguerite partagent avec Adrien et Alice
la joie de vous annoncer la naissance de

Nathalie

Le 10 juillet 2004

Monsieur et Madame Bon
24, rue Basfroi
75011 PARIS

Good wishes for the New Year

Éliane Debard
25, rue des Alouettes
38180 Seyssins

le 15 décembre 2004

Je vous présente mes meilleurs vœux de bonheur et de réussite pour la nouvelle année. Que l'an deux mille cinq vous apporte tout ce que vous souhaitez, à vous, à votre famille et à tous ceux qui vous sont chers.

Éliane Debard

Thanks for New Year wishes

Fanny Cogne
7, avenue Calade
10000 Troyes

le 6 janvier 2005

Je vous remercie de vos vœux. Ma famille se joint à moi pour vous adresser, à notre tour, les nôtres les plus sincères.

Fanny Cogne

La correspondance privée

Invitation à une soirée

Ms L Hedley
2 Florence Drive, London SW1Z 9ZZ

Friday 13 July 2005

Dear Alex,

Would you be free to come to dinner with me when you are over in England next month? I know you'll be busy, but I would love to see you. Perhaps you could give me a ring when you get to London and we can arrange a date? Hope to see you then.

Best wishes,

Lena

Réponse à une invitation : acceptation (connaissances)

c/o 99 Henderson Drive
Inverness IV1 1SA

16/6/04.

Dear Mrs Mayhew,

It is very good of you to invite me to dinner and I shall be delighted to come on July 4th.

I am as yet uncertain as to where exactly I shall be staying in the south, but I will phone you as soon as I am settled in London in order to confirm the arrangements.

With renewed thanks and best wishes.

Yours sincerely,

Sophie Beauverie

Condoléances à une relation

Larch House
Hughes Lane
Sylvan Hill
Sussex

22 June 2005

Dear Mrs Robinson,

I would like to send you my deepest sympathies on your sad loss. It came as a great shock to hear of Dr Robinson's terrible illness, and he will be greatly missed by everybody who knew him, particularly those who, like me, had the good fortune to have him as a tutor. He was an inspiring teacher and a friend I am proud to have had. I can only guess at your feelings. If there is anything I can do, please do not hesitate to let me know.

With kindest regards,
Yours sincerely,

Malcolm Smith

Condoléances à un proche

18 Giles Road
Chester CH1 1ZZ
Tel: 01244 123341

May 21st 2005

My dearest Victoria,

I was so shocked to hear of Raza's death. He seemed so well and cheerful when I saw him at Christmas time. It is a terrible loss for all of us, and he will be missed very deeply. You and the children are constantly in my thoughts.

My recent operation prevented me from coming to the funeral and I am very sorry about this. I will try to come up to see you at the beginning of July, if you feel up to it. Is there anything I can do to help?

With much love to all of you
from

Penny

Invitation to a party

Paris, le 23 juin 2004

Cher Raymond,

Nous avons eu l'idée de réunir tous les copains de fac dans notre maison de Manosque le samedi 4 juillet pour arroser la thèse de Pierre. Même Albert a promis d'être là! Ce sera à la bonne franquette.

Rendez-vous aux environs de 21 heures. A bientôt.

Amicalement

Marie

Accepting an invitation: formal

Troyes, le 17 avril 2004

Chers amis,

Je vous remercie de votre aimable invitation au mariage de votre fille le samedi 12 juin, que j'accepte avec joie. J'arriverai par le train de vendredi soir, puisqu'il n'y a plus de train le samedi.

Dans l'attente du plaisir de vous revoir, je vous adresse mes meilleures salutations.

Thomas Lemaître

Condolences: formal

Jean et Eliane Pinchon
117, boulevard Lamartine
71000 Mâcon

Mâcon, le 27 novembre 2005

Monsieur,

Nous vous adressons nos condoléances les plus sincères à l'occasion de la disparition tragique de votre épouse. Sachez qu'elle restera dans notre souvenir comme une personne exceptionnelle, et que nous partageons votre peine.

Recevez, Monsieur, l'expression de notre douloureuse sympathie.

E. Pinchon

Condolences: informal

Belley, le 22 avril 2005

Chère Janine,

J'ai appris par Francette la triste nouvelle du décès de Paul.

Je te présente mes condoléances les plus sincères, et t'assure que je pense beaucoup à toi en ces moments difficiles.

Crois bien, ma chère Janine, à l'expression de ma profonde sympathie.

Richard

Remerciements après une invitation

75/9A Westgate
Wakefield
Yorks

30/9/04

Dear Mr and Mrs Frankel,

It was very kind of you to invite me to William's 21st birthday party and I am especially grateful to you for letting me stay the night. I enjoyed myself very much indeed, as did everyone else as far as I could tell.

In the hurry of packing to leave, I seem to have picked up a red and white striped T-shirt. If you let me know where to send it, I'll put it in the post at once. My apologies.

Many thanks once again.

Yours,

Julia (Robertson)

Remerciements pour un cadeau de mariage

Mill House
Mill Lane
Sandwich
Kent
CT13 0LZ

June 1st 2004

Dear Len and Sally,

We would like to thank you most warmly for the lovely book of photos of Scotland that you sent us as a wedding present. It reminds us so vividly of the time we spent there and of the friends we made.

It was also good to get all your news. Do come and see us next time you are back on leave - we have plenty of room for guests.

Once again many thanks, and best wishes for your trip to New Zealand.

Kindest regards from

Pierre and Francine

Phrases utiles

En-têtes

Quand vous écrivez à quelqu'un que vous connaissez bien, la formule la plus courante est *Dear…*

À des amis proches ou à des membres de votre famille :
• *My dearest Alexander*
• *Darling Katie*

À une famille ou à plusieurs personnes :
• *Dear all*

Expressions utiles

Thank you for your letter [inviting, offering, confirming]

I am very grateful to you for [letting me know, offering, writing]

It was so kind of you to [write, invite, send]

Many thanks for [sending, inviting, enclosing]

I am writing to tell you that …

I am writing to ask you if …

I am delighted to announce that …

I was delighted to hear that …

I am sorry to inform you that …

I was so sorry to hear that …

Formules de politesse

À des connaissances ou à des personnes qui exercent des fonctions officielles :
• *Best wishes*, ou *With best wishes*
• *Kindest regards*

À des amis proches ou à des membres de votre famille :
• *All my love*
• *All the best*
• *Love (from)*
• *Lots of love*
• *Much love*, or *With love*
• *Love from us both*
• *See you soon*
• *Once again many thanks*
• *I look forward to seeing you soon*
• *With love and best wishes*
• *With love to you all*
• *Paul sends his love to you both*
• *Do give my kindest regards to Sylvia*

Thanking for hospitality

Strasbourg, le 21 juin 2004

Chers madame et monsieur,

Je tiens à vous remercier de m'avoir invitée aux fiançailles d'Isolde, et je vous suis particulièrement reconnaissante de m'avoir offert de passer la nuit chez vous.

La fête a été très agréable et j'ai eu grand plaisir à vous revoir dans de si heureuses circonstances.

Encore merci pour tout. Bien à vous.

Anne

Thanking for a wedding gift

Brest, le 17 août 2005

Chère Anne

Je tenais à te remercier une fois encore pour le magnifique cadre en argent que tu nous as offert en cadeau de mariage. Nous l'avons déjà utilisé... pour exposer une photo du mariage!

Grosses bises

Isolde

Useful phrases

Letter openings

The standard opening greeting for personal correspondence is *Cher/Chère…*

Affectionate variations for very close friends and family:
- *Bonjour Paul,*
- *Ma chère Clarisse,*
- *Mes chers Emmanuel et Caroline,*
- *Très cher Sébastien,*

To a whole family or group:
- *Bonjour à tous,*
- *Chers tous,*
- *Chers amis,*

Useful phrases

Merci/Je te remercie [de ta lettre, de ton invitation, de ton petit cadeau, d'avoir pensé à …]

C'est avec un grand plaisir que j'ai reçu votre lettre m'informant de …

J'ai le plaisir de/je suis heureux/-euse de [t'annoncer que, t'inviter à, te confirmer que]

Je suis ravi(e) d'apprendre que …

Je me réjouis [d'apprendre que, de la nouvelle du]

Je t'écris pour te demander si …

J'ai le regret de [vous faire part de, vous apprendre que, ne pas pouvoir]

J'ai été bouleversé(e) [par la nouvelle du/d'apprendre le]

C'est avec une grande tristesse que j'ai appris le …

Closures

For acquaintances and formal situations:
- *Amitiés.*
- *Salutations distinguées.*
- *Croyez en nos sentiments les meilleurs.*
- *Recevez, [Madame/Monsieur, chère Madame, cher ami], mes meilleures salutations.*
- *Veuillez croire, [cher ami, cher confrère], à mon meilleur souvenir.*

Affectionate variations for close friends and family:
- *Salut.*
- *À (très) bientôt.*
- *Bises/Bisous/Grosses bises.*
- *Bien à toi/à vous.*
- *Je pense bien à toi/à vous.*
- *Je t'embrasse/Je vous embrasse.*
- *Amicalement/Très amicalement.*
- *Cordialement/Bien cordialement.*
- *Avec toute mon affection.*
- *Bonjour à la petite famille/à Véronique.*
- *J'espère avoir bientôt de tes nouvelles.*

Les vacances et l'organisation des voyages

Cartes postales

Having a wonderful time on and off the piste. Skiing conditions ideal and we've even tried snowboarding.

The local food and wine are delicious, especially the fondue.

See you soon,

Jo and Paul

Mr and Mrs S. Mitchell
The Old Forge
7 Wilson Street
CIRENCESTER
GLOS
GL12 9PZ
UNITED KINGDOM

Dear Jess,

The beaches here in Crete are great and the nightlife is brilliant! We've hired mopeds to get about locally, but hope to fit in a couple of day- trips to see some of the sights.

College and exams certainly seem very far away!

Lots of love,

Louise and Paul

Jessica Norton
45 Gibson Avenue
DURHAM
DH1 3NL
UNITED KINGDOM

Holidays and travel plans

Postcards

Chers amis,

Juste un petit bonjour de Palma
où nous passons de très
agréables vacances. Il fait un
temps splendide et les plages
sont superbes. Merci encore
d'avoir accepté de garder Félix
pendant notre absence. Nous
vous revaudrons cela à
l'occasion.

A très bientôt!

Emmanuel et Pierline

Monsieur et Madame Pierret
78 rue du Chemin vert
54000 Nancy
FRANCE

Soleil, pistes enneigées et soirées
raclette au coin du feu: on ne
pouvait rêver mieux.
Notre séjour s'annonce très bien et
nous espérons en profiter au
maximum.
Bons baisers de Courchevel et à
bientôt.
Frédéric et Josiane

Monsieur et Madame Gendre
56 rue Jean Jaurès
75018 Paris

Les vacances et l'organisation des voyages

Lettre à un correspondant : invitation

23 Av. Rostand
75018 Paris
France

5th June 2004

Dear Katrina,

I am writing to ask you if you would like to come and stay with my family here in Paris. We live in a pretty suburb, and my school is nearby. If you come we can go into the centre of Paris and do some sightseeing, as well as spending some time in my neighbourhood, which has a big outdoor swimming pool and a large shopping centre.

It would suit us best if you could come in August. If you say yes, my mother will write to your mother about details - it would be nice if you could stay about two weeks. I would be so happy if you could come.

Love from

Florence

À la famille d'un correspondant : renseignements

15 Durrer Place
Herne Bay
Kent CT6 2AA

Phone: (01227) 7685
jack_liz_holland@freeserve.co.uk

29-4-05

Dear Mrs Harrison,

It was good of you to invite Jane to go to Italy with you. She really is fond of Freda and is very excited at the thought of the holiday.

The dates you suggest would suit us perfectly. Could you let me know how much spending money you think Jane will need? Also, are there any special clothes she should bring?

Yours sincerely,

Lisa Holland

Pour proposer un échange de maisons

4 LONGSIDE DRIVE
KNOLEY
CAMBS
CB8 5RR
TEL: 01223 49586

May 13th 2004.

Dear Mr and Mrs Candiwell,

We found your names listed in the 2003 "Owners to Owners" handbook and would like to know if you are still taking part in the property exchange scheme.

We have a 3-bedroomed semi-detached house in a quiet village only 20 minutes' drive from Cambridge. We have two boys aged 8 and 13. If you are interested, and if three weeks in July or August would suit you, we would be happy to exchange references.

We look forward to hearing from you.

Yours sincerely,

John and Ella Valedict

John and Ella Valedict

Pour accepter un échange de maisons

Trout Villa
Burnpeat Road
Lochmahon
IZ99 9ZZ

(01463) 3456554

5/2/05

Dear Mr and Mrs Tamberley,

Further to our phone call, we would like to confirm our arrangement to exchange houses from August 2nd to August 16th inclusive. We enclose various leaflets about our area.

As we mentioned on the phone, you will be able to collect the keys from our neighbours the Brownes at 'Whitley House' (see enclosed plan).

We look forward to a mutually enjoyable exchange.

Yours sincerely,

Mr and Mrs R. Jones

Arranging an exchange visit

Dublin, le 2 avril 2004

Una et Dan Farrelly
28, Leeson Drive
Artane
Dublin 5
Irlande

Monsieur et Madame Pierre Beaufort
Chalet "Les Edelweiss"
Chemin des Rousses
74400 Chamonix

Chers Danièle et Pierre

Nous serions très heureux d'accueillir votre
fils chez nous entre le 10 et le 31 juillet et
d'envoyer en échange notre fils Kilian pendant
le mois d'août.

Kilian a 16 ans. Il fait du français depuis 4
ans. C'est un garçon sportif: il aime la randonnée, la natation et le tennis.

Merci de nous dire assez rapidement si cette idée
vous convient afin que nous puissions réserver
les places d'avion le plus tôt possible.

Croyez en nos sentiments les meilleurs.

U. Farrelly

U. Farrelly

Making travel plans

Rillieux-la-Pape, le 15 mai 2004

Monsieur et Madame Bernard Dubois
Villa les Etourneaux
132 bis, Passage du Réservoir
69140 Rillieux-la-Pape

Cher Monsieur, Chère Madame

Nous avons bien reçu votre lettre nous
confirmant que vous pourriez aller chercher
notre fille Lucy le 12 juillet au soir à
l'aéroport. Elle s'en réjouit car elle était un
peu inquiète à l'idée de prendre le bus toute
seule jusqu'à la gare. Nous vous
communiquerons, dès que nous l'aurons, le
numéro de son vol et l'heure exacte d'arrivée.

Lucy est facilement reconnaissable: elle
mesure 1 m 65 et elle a les cheveux roux. Nous
nous permettrons de vous appeler le soir même
afin de nous assurer qu'elle est bien arrivée.

Nous vous remercions de l'accueil que vous lui
réserverez et vous prions de croire, Cher
Monsieur, Chère Madame, en nos sentiments les
meilleurs

J. Smith

J. Smith

Offering a house exchange

Clermont, le 2 mai 2004

Pierre Clément
Résidence des Lacs d'Auvergne
Chalet n° 18
63610 Besse

Madame Perrin
2 rue de la Poste
14360 Trouville-sur-Mer

Chère Madame,

Vos amis, monsieur et madame Blanchet,
nous ont dit que vous seriez heureuse de
pouvoir échanger votre villa en Normandie
contre notre chalet qui est au bord du lac
des Corbeaux, en Auvergne. Nous serions
intéressés par cette idée pour la seconde
quinzaine d'août.

Si cette période vous convient, nous vous
adresserons une photo et un descriptif
détaillé du chalet.

Dans l'attente de vous lire, je vous
adresse, chère Madame, mes sentiments les
meilleurs.

P. Clément

P. Clément

Responding to an offer of a house exchange

le 1er mai 2004

L. Dury
Chalet des Pentes
38860 les Deux-Alpes

Madame J. Lemaire
Route de Châteauroux
36200 Argenton-sur-Creuse

Madame,

J'ai bien reçu votre offre d'échanger
votre ferme à la campagne et notre chalet
entre le 1er et le 30 juin prochains.
Nous sommes désolés, mais les dates que
vous proposez ne correspondent pas à celles
où nous envisageons de prendre nos
vacances. Peut-être l'année prochaine
cela sera-t-il possible? Nous reprendrons
contact avec vous en temps voulu.

Je vous souhaite bonne chance et vous
adresse, Madame, mes salutations
distinguées.

L. Dury

L. Dury

Les vacances et l'organisation des voyages

Pour offrir une maison de vacances en location

Mrs M Henderson
333a Sisters Avenue
Battersea
London SW3 0TR
Tel: 020-7344 5657

23/4/04

Dear Mr and Mrs Suchard,

Thank you for your letter of enquiry about our holiday home. The house is available for the dates you mention. It has three bedrooms, two bathrooms, a big lounge, a dining room, a large modern kitchen and a two-acre garden. It is five minutes' walk from the shops. Newick is a small village near the Sussex coast, and only one hour's drive from London.

The rent is £250 per week; 10% (non-refundable) of the total amount on booking, and the balance 4 weeks before arrival. Should you cancel the booking, after that, the balance is returnable only if the house is re-let. Enclosed is a photo of the house. We look forward to hearing from you soon.

Yours sincerely,

Margaret Henderson

Margaret Henderson

Pour louer une maison de vacances

23C TOLLWAY DRIVE
LYDDEN
KENT
CT33 9ER
(01304 399485)

4th June 2004

Dear Mr and Mrs Murchfield,

I am writing in response to the advertisement you placed in "Home Today" (May issue). I am very interested in renting your Cornish cottage for any two weeks between July 24th and August 28th. Please would you ring me to let me know which dates are available?

If all the dates are taken, perhaps you could let me know whether you are likely to be letting out the cottage next year, as this is an area I know well and want to return to.

I look forward to hearing from you.

Yours sincerely,

Michael Settle.

Pour louer un emplacement de caravane

10 Place Saint Jean
32340 Les Marais
France

25th April 2004

Mr and Mrs F. Wilde
Peniston House
Kendal
Cumbria
England

Dear Mr and Mrs Wilde,

I found your caravan site in the Tourist Board's brochure and would like to book in for three nights, from July 25th to 28th. I have a caravan with a tent extension and will be coming with my wife and two children. Please let me know if this is possible, and if you require a deposit. Would you also be good enough to send me instructions on how to reach you from the M6?

I look forward to hearing from you.

Yours sincerely,

John Winslow

Pour avoir des renseignements sur un camping

22 Daniel Avenue
Caldwood
Leeds LS8 7RR
Tel: 0113 9987676

3 March 2004

Dear Mr Vale,

Your campsite was recommended to me by a friend, James Dallas, who has spent several holidays there. I am hoping to come with my two boys aged 9 and 14 for three weeks this July.

Would you please send me details of the caravans for hire, including mobile homes, with prices and dates of availability for this summer. I would also appreciate some information on the area, and if you have any brochures you could send me this would be very helpful indeed.

Many thanks in advance.

Yours sincerely,

Frances Goodheart.

Letting your house

Bormes, le 4 avril 2004

Monsieur et Madame Léon Panisse
Résidence Le Bord de Mer
Rue des Pins
83230 Bormes-les-Mimosas

Monsieur Brun
8, place Colbert
69001 Lyon

Cher Monsieur,

La maison que nous mettons en location est une
villa de plain-pied, avec terrasse face à la
mer et accès direct à la plage. Elle est
située sur un terrain clos et boisé.

Elle se compose de deux chambres (couchage
pour 6 personnes en tout), un salon-salle à
manger, une kitchenette équipée, une salle de
bains avec douche et un WC indépendant. Le
montant de la location pour juillet est de
1700€ charges non comprises.

Souhaitant que cette offre vous convienne,
je vous prie d'agréer, cher Monsieur,
l'expression de mes sentiments distingués.

L. Panisse

Renting a holiday house

Paris, le 7 mai 2004

Monsieur C. Pernaudet
135, rue de la Gaîté-Montparnasse
75014 Paris

Agence "LES DUNES"
Promenade de l'Océan
33120 Arcachon

Messieurs,

Nous sommes à la recherche d'une location
pour le mois d'août prochain dans votre
région. Nous souhaitons trouver une maison
pour 6/8 personnes avec un terrain clos et
ombragé, même éloignée de la plage.

Pourriez-vous nous adresser le descriptif
détaillé, avec si possible une photo et les
tarifs de location, de ce que vous avez à
nous proposer?

Dans l'attente de votre réponse, je vous
prie d'agréer, Messieurs, l'expression de
mes sentiments distingués.

Booking a caravan site

Sarcelles, le 14 juin 2004

Monsieur C. Bonnet
235, Bd Lénine
95200 Sarcelles

Camping-Caravaning "LES EMBRUNS"
18, allée des Capucins
22116 Moëlan-sur-Mer

Madame,

Nous souhaitons à nouveau réserver, cette
année en août, l'emplacement de caravane que
nous avions loué en juillet dernier et qui se
trouvait dans la partie nord du camping
(numéro 12/B/224).

Acceptez-vous les animaux cette année? Nous
avons un tout petit chien que nous ne pouvons
laisser chez nous.

Dès que nous aurons confirmation de votre
part, nous vous adresserons le montant de la
réservation, que vous voudrez bien nous
indiquer.

Veuillez croire, Madame, en l'expression de
nos sentiments distingués.

Enquiry to a camp site

Fresnes, le 3 avril 2004

E. Aubin
3, bd du Maréchal Joffre
94260 Fresnes

Camping des Vagues
Bd de la Plage
44250 Saint-Brévin-les-Pins

Monsieur,

Nous avons eu votre adresse par le Syndicat
d'Initiative de Saint-Brévin, et nous aimerions avoir
quelques renseignements complémentaires sur votre
camping.

Pourriez-vous nous préciser si les emplacements
sont ombragés, si les animaux sont admis et s'il y a des
commerces à proximité? Nous aimerions également
connaître vos tarifs, ainsi que les délais pour réserver.

Vous remerciant par avance, je vous prie de
croire, Monsieur, en mes sentiments distingués.

E. Aubin

La vie quotidienne

Pour avoir des renseignements sur un club de tennis

101 Great George St
Leeds
LS1 3TT
Tel: 0113 567167

3 February 2004

Mr Giles Grant
Hon. Secretary
Lorley Tennis Club
Park Drive South
Leeds LS5 7ZZ

Dear Mr Grant,

I have just moved to this area and am interested in joining your tennis club. I understand that there is a waiting list for full membership and would be glad if you could let me have information on this.
A telephone call would do: I tried to phone you but without success. If you require references we can provide these from the tennis club we belonged to in Edinburgh.

Yours sincerely,

Leonard Jones

À une université

43 Wellington Vllas
York
YO6 93E

2.2.05

Dr T Benjamin,
Department of Fine Arts
University of Brighton
Falmer Campus
Brighton
BN3 2AA

Dear Dr Benjamin,

I have been advised by Dr Kate Rellen, my MA supervisor in York, to apply to pursue doctoral studies in your department.

I enclose details of my current research and also my tentative Ph.D proposal, along with my up-to-date curriculum vitae, and look forward to hearing from you. I very much hope that you will agree to supervise my Ph.D. If you do, I intend to apply to the Royal Academy for funding.

Yours sincerely,

Alice Nettle

Lettre de préavis (fin de location)

2 Grampian Close
HELENSBURGH
G84 7PP
30th June 2004

Scottish Property Services Ltd
3 Union Terrace
GLASGOW
G12 9PQ

Dear Sirs,

2 Grampian Close, Helensburgh

I wish to inform you of my intention to terminate the tenancy agreement for the above property signed on 1st April 2002. In accordance with the terms of the agreement, I am giving three months' notice of my proposed date of departure, October 1st 2004.
I would be very grateful if you could let me know the arrangements for checking the inventory, returning the keys and reclaiming my deposit.

Yours faithfully,

V. F. Cassels

V. F. Cassels

À une compagnie d'assurances

Flat 2
Grant House
Pillward Avenue
Chelmsford CM1 1SS

3rd January 2005

Park-Enfield Insurance Co
22 Rare Road
Chelmsford
Essex CM3 8AA

Dear Sirs,

On 2nd January my kitchen was damaged by a fire owing to a faulty gas cooker. Fortunately, I was there at the time and was able to call the fire brigade straight away, but the kitchen sustained considerable damage, from flames and smoke.

My policy number is 277488349/YPP. Please would you send me a claim form as soon as possible.

Yours faithfully,

Mark Good

Everyday life

Enquiry to the tennis club

le 15 juin 2005

Madame P. Martinez
23, clos des Martyrs
13006 Marseille

CLUB DE TENNIS
DES GARRIGUES
Chemin des Bruyères
13260 Cassis

Messieurs,

Future habitante de Cassis, je souhaiterais connaître les conditions d'inscription à votre club, et savoir si vous proposez des cours particuliers ou des stages. Pratiquez-vous des tarifs familiaux? En effet, mon mari et mon fils aîné, joueurs classés, souhaitent un entraînement intensif alors que mes deux plus jeunes enfants souhaiteraient débuter.

Par avance, je vous remercie des informations que vous voudrez bien me fournir et vous prie de croire, Messieurs, en mes sentiments les meilleurs.

P. Martinez

Enquiring about prices

le 18 février 2005

Association des Parents d'élèves
Groupe scolaire de la Ville basse
3, rue George Sand
87100 LIMOGES
Tél.: 05 55 22 78 04

RECREATOUR
25 avenue du Château
41000 BLOIS

Monsieur,

Nous souhaiterions organiser durant trois jours
- au moment du week-end du 1er mai - une visite
de la région bordelaise pour parents et enfants
denotre établissement.

J'aurais besoin d'une documentation complète,
ainsi que des tarifs :
- pour le voyage en car seulement,
- pour le voyage et l'hébergement,
- pour le voyage, l'hébergement et les repas en
demi-pension.

Vous remerciant par avance de votre réponse,
nous vous prions de croire, Monsieur, en nos
sentiments distingués.

Madame Petit
Présidente de l'Association

Giving written notice to a landlord

Sandrine Pulvar
24 rue des Arts
75011 Paris

Madame Solicot
35 boulevard Voltaire
75011 Paris

Le 24 mars 2004

Recommandé avec A.R.

Madame,

J'ai l'honneur de vous informer que je souhaite
résilier le bail signé le 4 avril 2002 pour la
location de l'appartement du 24 rue des Arts.

Je me tiens à votre disposition pour convenir
d'une date de remise des clés et établir avec
vous un état des lieux.

Je me permets de vous rappeler que vous
disposez d'un délai maximal de trois mois
après mon départ pour me restituer la somme de
500 Euros que je vous ai versée à titre de
dépôt de garantie.

Veuillez agréer, Madame, l'assurance de mes
sentiments distingués

S. Pulvar

To an insurance company about a claim

Paris, le 24 mars 2005

Monsieur Ramirez
86, rue de la Convention
75015 Paris

ASSURTOURIX
123, Rue Duranton
75449 Paris CEDEX 15

Lettre recommandée
Police n° 3400510F

Messieurs,

Par la police référencée ci-dessus en date du
24 janvier 1987, j'ai fait assurer mon
appartement situé rue de la Convention.

A la suite des très fortes bourrasques de la
nuit dernière, les stores de la terrasse nord,
ainsi que les volets, ont été arrachés et ont
gravement endommagé le balcon voisin. Puis-je
vous demander de m'envoyer un de vos experts le
plus tôt possible, afin de constater l'étendue
du sinistre et de chiffrer le montant des
dommages subis?

Avec mes remerciements, je vous prie de croire,
Messieurs, à l'assurance de mes sentiments
distingués.

A. Ramirez

Demande de remboursement à un tour-opérateur

```
                                    Flat 3,
                              Nesbit Lodge,
                         Goldsmith Crescent
                                       BATH
                                    BA7 2LR

                                    16/8/04

The Manager
Summersun Ltd
3 Travis Place
SOUTHAMPTON
SO19  6LP

Dear Sir,

Re: Holiday booking ref p142/7/2004

I am writing to express my dissatisfaction with the
self-catering accommodation provided for my family at
the Hellenos Holiday Village, Samos, Greece, from 1-14
August 2004.
On arrival, the accommodation had not been cleaned, the
refrigerator was not working and there was no hot water.
These problems were pointed out to your resort
representative Marie Finch, who was unable to resolve
them to our satisfaction. We were forced to accept a
lower standard of accommodation, despite having paid a
supplement for a terrace and sea view. This detracted
significantly from our enjoyment of the holiday.
I would appreciate it if you would look into this matter
at your earliest convenience with a view to refunding my
supplement and providing appropriate compensation for
the distress suffered.

     Yours faithfully,

                         Patrick Mahon
```

À la banque à propos de frais d'agence

23 St John Rd
London EC12 4AA

5th May 2005

The Manager
Black Horse Bank
Bow Rd
London EC10 5TG

Dear Sir,

I noticed on my recent statement, that you are charging me interest on an overdraft of £65. I assume this is a mistake, as I have certainly had no overdraft in the last quarter.

My account number is 0077-234-88. Please rectify this mistake immediately, and explain to me how this could have happened in the first place.

I look forward to your prompt reply,

Yours faithfully,

Dr J. M. Ramsbottom

À une entreprise pour se plaindre : retard

19 Colley Terrace
Bingley
Bradford

Tel: 01274 223447

4.5.05

Mr J Routledge
'Picture This'
13 High End Street
Bradford

Dear Mr Routledge,

I left a large oil portrait with you six weeks ago for framing. At the time you told me that it would be delivered to me within three weeks at the latest. Since the portrait has not yet arrived I wondered if there was some problem?

Would you please telephone to let me know what is happening, and when I can expect the delivery? I hope it will not be too long, as I am keen to see the results.

Yours faithfully,

Mrs. J J Escobado

À une entreprise pour se plaindre : travaux mal faits

112 Victoria Road
Chelmsford
Essex CM1 3FF

Tel: 01245 33433

Allan Deal Builders
35 Green St
Chelmsford
Essex CM3 4RT

ref. WL/45/LPO   13/6/2005

Dear Sirs,

I confirm my phone call, complaining that the work carried out by your firm on our patio last week is not up to standard. Large cracks have already appeared in the concrete area and several of the slabs in the paved part are unstable. Apart from anything else, the area is now dangerous to walk on.

Please send someone round this week to re-do the work. In the meantime I am of course withholding payment.

Yours faithfully,

W. Nicholas Cotton

To a tour operator: requesting a refund

Pierre Besson
20 rue de la Roquette
75011 Paris

Europ'air
Service clientèle
94542 Orly Aérogare Cedex

Ref. dossier: ORY EA 44564   Paris, le 10 août 2005

Monsieur,

Au débarquement de mon vol EA123 en provenance de Londres Heathrow et à destination d'Orly Sud le 5 août dernier, vol qui est arrivé à Paris avec plus de deux heures de retard, il s'est avéré que l'un de mes bagages avait été fortement endommagé. J'ai alors voulu faire état de cet incident au bureau des réclamations de votre compagnie aérienne à l'aéroport, mais ce bureau était fermé. Il m'a par conséquent été impossible de remettre le constat (ci-joint) établi par l'agent d'Aéroport de Paris.

Je suis indigné par le manque de sérieux dont votre compagnie a fait preuve durant mon voyage. Rien n'a été fait à Londres pour tenir les passagers de mon vol informés des raisons de notre retard. Il nous a fallu patienter deux heures en salle d'embarquement, sans avoir la possibilité de regagner le terminal pour acheter un journal ou une boisson. Enfin, j'ajouterais qu'il n'est pas normal de ne jamais pouvoir vous joindre par téléphone. Une telle attitude est intolérable, vous vous devez d'offrir à vos clients un service qui ne se limite pas à la vente de billets et au transport des passagers.

Je vous prie de bien vouloir faire le nécessaire pour que je sois dédommagé des dégâts infligés à mes bagages dans les plus brefs délais. En outre, le remboursement d'une partie du prix de mon billet m'encouragerait à ne pas faire appel aux services de vos concurrents pour mes prochains voyages.

Je vous remercie de votre diligence, et je vous prie d'agréer, Monsieur, l'expression de mes salutations distinguées,

Pierre Besson

To a bank: disputing bank charges

Jean-François Devert
3 rue des Lilas
92100 Boulogne

Monsieur Girard
Directeur d'agence
Banque MASSON
1 place Glacière
92100 Boulogne

Le 19 mars 2005

Monsieur,

Je reçois aujourd'hui même mon relevé bancaire et je constate avec étonnement que quatre jours d'agios ont été retenus sur mon compte.

Mon compte a effectivement été à découvert du 10 au 14 mars, mais à la suite d'une erreur de la part de vos services. Le 3 mars, j'ai en effet déposé un chèque de 650 euros qui a été égaré. Dès que je me suis aperçu que mon compte n'avait pas été crédité du montant du chèque, je l'ai signalé à l'un de vos employés, qui m'a assuré qu'il ne serait pas tenu compte de mon découvert.

Je trouve absolument anormal d'être pénalisé pour une erreur indépendante de ma volonté et me verrai dans l'obligation de clore définitivement mon compte courant et mon compte épargne si vous ne faites pas le nécessaire pour régler la situation au plus vite.

Veuillez agréer, Monsieur, l'expression de mes sentiments distingués.

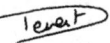

J.F. Devert

To the builders: complaining about delay

le 15 juin 2005

Monsieur Guy Moreau
12, rue Henri Gorjus
69004 Lyon

Entreprise Simon Associés
69006 Lyon
Lettre avec AR

Messieurs,

Lors de notre dernier rendez-vous de chantier, je vous avais dit mon inquiétude quant au retard qu'avaient pris les travaux que nous vous avons confiés. Vous m'aviez alors assuré que tout serait terminé pour le 1er juillet.

Il est évident aujourd'hui qu'il me sera impossible d'emménager à cette date, les travaux de plomberie n'ayant même pas commencé. Je vous rappelle que j'ai promis de libérer mon logement actuel pour le 30 juin et que les frais causés par un retard de votre part seront à votre charge.

Je vous prie d'agréer, Messieurs, l'expression de mes sentiments distingués.

G. Moreau

To the builders: complaining about quality of work

Mouthe, le 7 novembre 2004

M. Brunaud
25240 Mouthe
téléphone : 03.81.82.13.27

M. Pinet
Entreprise de bâtiment
Grand rue
25970 Epeugney

Monsieur,

Je vous ai fait poser des doubles vitrages en PVC dans ma résidence de Mouthe le mois dernier. Je suis au regret de vous dire que toutes les fenêtres de l'étage présentent le même défaut d'étanchéité, qui entraîne la présence de condensation entre les deux vitres. Ces travaux étant sous garantie, je vous demanderais de faire le nécessaire dans les plus brefs délais afin qu'une solution soit apportée avant l'hiver.

Veuillez agréer, Monsieur, l'expression de mes salutations distinguées.

M. Brunaud

La recherche d'un emploi et le monde du travail

Pour demander un stage (informaticien)

Rue du Lac, 989
CH-9878 Geneva
Switzerland

5th February 2005

Synapse & Bite Plc
3F Well Drive
Dolby Industrial Estate
Birmingham BH3 5FF

Dear Sirs,

As part of my advanced training relating to my current position as a junior systems trainee in Geneva, I have to work for a period of not less than two months over the summer in a computing firm in Britain or Ireland. Having heard of your firm from Mme Grenaille who worked there in 1998, I am writing to you in the hope that you will be able to offer me a placement for about eight weeks this summer.

I enclose my C.V. and a letter of recommendation.

Hoping you can help me, I remain,

Yours faithfully,

Madeleine Faure

Encls.

Candidature spontanée : enseignant

B.P. 3091
Pangaville
Panga

6th May 2004

Mrs J Allsop
Lingua School
23 Handle St
London SE3 4ZK

Dear Mrs Allsop,

My colleague Robert Martin, who used to work for you, tells me that you are planning to appoint extra staff this September. I am currently teaching French as a Foreign Language as part of the French Government's "cooperation" course in Panga which finishes in June.

You will see from my CV (enclosed) that I have appropriate qualifications and experience. I will be available for interview after the 22nd June, and may be contacted after that date at the following address:

c/o Lewis
Dexter Road
London NE2 6KQ
Tel: 020 7335 6978

Yours sincerely,

Jules Romains

Encl.

Réponse à une petite annonce

16 Andrew Road
Inverness IV90 OLL
Phone: 01463 34454

13th February 2005

The Personnel Manager
Pandy Industries PLC
Florence Building
Trump Estate
Bath BA55 3TT

Dear Sir or Madam,

I am interested in the post of Deputy Designer, advertised in the "Pioneer" of 12th February, and would be glad if you could send me further particulars and an application form.

I am currently nearing the end of a one-year contract with Bolney & Co, and have relevant experience and qualifications, including a BSc in Design Engineering and an MSc in Industrial Design.

Thanking you in anticipation, I remain,

Yours faithfully,

A Aziz

Pour demander un emploi de jeune fille au pair

2, Rue de la Gare
54550 Nancy
France

(33) 03 87 65 47 92

15 April 2004

Miss D Lynch
Home from Home Agency
3435 Pine Street
Cleveland, Ohio 442233

Dear Miss Lynch,

I am seeking summer employment as an au pair. I have experience of this type of work in Britain but would now like to work in the USA. I enclose my C.V. and copies of testimonials from three British families.

I would be able to stay from the end of June to the beginning of September. Please let me know if I need a work permit, and if so, whether you can get one for me.

Yours sincerely,

Alice Demeaulnes

Encls.

Seeking employment and the world of work

Looking for a placement in a computer company

Laurent PIGNON
14 bis, impasse des Aqueducs
69005 LYON
tél. : 04 78 47 98 54

Lyon, le 12 décembre 2004

Société Giudici
Z.I. des Pâquerettes
69575 DARDILLY CEDEX

à l'attention de Monsieur le Chef du Personnel

Monsieur,

Actuellement étudiant à l'École d'Informatique Générale de Lyon, je dois effectuer un stage d'une durée de quatre mois dans une entreprise d'informatique afin de mettre en pratique l'enseignement qui m'est dispensé.

Connaissant bien la réputation de votre entreprise dans la région, je souhaiterais vivement pouvoir faire ce stage d'informaticien chez vous. Je me tiens à votre entière disposition si vous désirez me rencontrer.

Vous remerciant par avance de l'attention que vous voudrez bien porter à ma candidature, je vous prie, Monsieur, d'agréer l'expression de mes sentiments respectueux.

L. Pignon

p.j.: un curriculum vitae

Enquiring about jobs

Valérie Giraud
Les Flots
Route de Deauville
14360 Trouville-sur-Mer
v.giraud@voodoocom.fr

Trouville, le 27 octobre 2004

A Monsieur le Directeur
Editions La Pensée Française
Paris

Monsieur,

Après un diplôme de sciences politiques (IEP Paris), j'ai entamé il y a quelques années une carrière de journaliste que je me vois contrainte d'abandonner pour des raisons familiales. J'aimerais dorénavant utiliser mes dons et mes compétences dans le domaine de l'édition ou de la traduction. Je parle trois des principales langues européennes, ainsi que l'indique le C.V. ci-joint, et je pense avoir de bonnes dispositions pour l'écriture.

Je suis prête à me rendre à un entretien si vous le jugez utile.

Recevez, Monsieur, l'expression de mes salutations distinguées.

V. Giraud

P.J. : un curriculum vitae

Replying to a job ad

MONSIEUR JEAN-LUC MORIN
12, AVENUE D'ANGLETERRE
62100 CALAIS

Calais, le 14 février 2004

A Monsieur le Directeur
Arts et Design Gadgeteria
27, rue Victor Hugo
59001 Lille

Monsieur,

L'annonce parue en page 2 de l'édition du 12 février du Courrier Picard concernant un poste de concepteur m'a vivement intéressé. Mon contrat à durée déterminée chez Solo and Co. touche à sa fin. Je pense posséder l'expérience et les qualifications requises pour vous donner toute satisfaction dans ce poste, comme vous pourrez le constater au vu de mon CV. Je me tiens à votre disposition pour un entretien éventuel, et vous prie d'agréer, Monsieur, l'expression de mes sentiments distingués.

J.L. Morin

P.J.: un CV avec photo

Applying for a job as an au pair

Sally Kendall
5, Tackley Place
Reading RG2 6RN
England

Reading, le 17 avril 2005

Madame et Monsieur,

Vos coordonnées m'ont été communiquées par l'agence "Au Pair International", qui m'a demandé de vous écrire directement. Je suis en effet intéressée par un emploi de jeune fille au pair pour une période de six mois au moins, à partir de l'automne prochain.

J'adore les enfants, quel que soit leur âge, et j'ai une grande expérience du baby-sitting, comme vous pourrez le constater au vu du CV ci-joint.

Dans l'espoir d'une réponse favorable, je vous prie d'agréer, Madame et Monsieur, l'expression de mes respectueuses salutations.

S. Kendall

P.J.: un CV

Pour demander une lettre de recommandation

8 Spring Close
Kelvindale
Glasgow GL2 0DS

Tel: 0141-357 6857

23rd February 2005

Dr M Mansion
Department of Civil Engineering
University of East Anglia

Dear Dr Mansion,

As you may remember, my job here at Longiron & Co is only temporary. I have just applied for a post as Senior Engineer with Bingley & Smith in Glasgow and have taken the liberty of giving your name as a referee.

I hope you will not mind sending a reference to this company should they contact you. With luck, I should find a permanent position in the near future, and I am very grateful for your help.

With best regards,

Yours sincerely,

Helen Lee.

Recommandation : favorable

University of Hull
South Park Drive
Hull HL5 9UU
Tel: 01482 934 5768
Fax:01482 934 5766

Your ref. DD/44/34/AW   5/3/04

Dear Sirs,

<u>Mary O'Donnel.   Date of birth 21-3-73</u>

I am glad to be able to write most warmly in support of Ms O'Donnel's application for the post of Designer with your company.

During her studies, Ms O'Donnel proved herself to be an outstanding student. Her ideas are original and exciting, and she carries them through - her MSc thesis was an excellent piece of work. She is a pleasant, hard-working and reliable person and I can recommend her without any reservations.

Yours faithfully,

Dr A A Jamal

Lettre de démission

3 Norton Gardens,
BRADFORD
BD7 4AU

30 May 2005

Regional Sales Director
Nortex and Co.
Cooper St.
LEEDS
LS5 2FH

Dear Mr Perrin,

I am writing to inform you of my decision to resign from my post of Sales Manager in the Bradford offices with effect from 1 July 2005. I am giving one month's notice as set out in my conditions of employment. I have for some time been considering a change of role and have been offered a post with a market research organization which I believe will meet my career aspirations.

I would like to take this opportunity to say how much I value the training and professional and personal support that I have received in my three years with Nortex and Co.

Yours sincerely,

Melinda MacPhee

Lettre de démission

Editorial Office

Modern Living Magazine
22 Salisbury Road, London W3 9TT
Tel: 020-7332 4343   Fax: 020-7332 4354

To: Ms Ella Fellows   6 June 2004
General Editor.

Dear Ella,

I am writing to you, with great regret, to resign my post as Commissioning Editor with effect from the end of August.

As you know, I have found the recent management changes increasingly difficult to cope with. It is with great reluctance that I have come to the conclusion that I can no longer offer my best work under this management.

I wish you all the best for the future,

Yours sincerely,

Elliot Ashford-Leigh

Asking for a reference

```
Craig McKenzie
15 Rowan Close
Torquay
Devon
TQ2 7QJ
```

Torquay, le 12 janvier 2005

Monsieur,

J'ai été votre étudiant en DEA pendant l'année 2001-2002.

Je constitue actuellement un dossier pour postuler un emploi à l'Université de St Andrews et je dois fournir deux lettres de recommandation. Accepteriez-vous d'en écrire une? Si votre réponse est oui, je vous serais très reconnaissant de faire parvenir cette lettre directement à l'université.

Avec mes remerciements, et l'expression de mes sentiments respectueux.

[signature]

```
P.J.: description de poste
      enveloppe timbrée
```

Giving a reference

🔔
UNIVERSITE DE CLERMONT-FERRAND 1
27, avenue Michelin
63567 Clermont-Ferrand Cedex 3
téléphone 04 73 40 60 31

Clermont-Ferrand, le 13 mars 2005

A QUI DE DROIT

Monsieur Louis Filard a été mon étudiant en classe de géométrie pendant l'année universitaire 2000-2002. Bien que la classe ait été fort nombreuse, je me souviens de lui comme d'un étudiant attentif, prompt à poser des questions très souvent pertinentes, et obtenant des résultats tout à fait honorables dans ses travaux écrits. Sérieux et appliqué, il a fait montre de qualités qui laissent bien augurer de son avenir. Je ne doute pas qu'il puisse donner entièrement satisfaction dans l'emploi qu'il postule.

[signature]

Madame Éliane Chapier
Maître de Conférences
Faculté de Mathématiques
Université de Clermont-Ferrand

Resigning from a post

Manuella Viera

27 rue des Epinettes

75017 Paris

M. Benoît Gance

Directeur Général

S.R.T.I.

Recommandé avec A.R.

Le 5 juin 2004

Monsieur,

J'ai l'honneur de vous présenter ma démission du poste d'assistante de direction que j'occupe dans votre entreprise depuis le 15 septembre 1999.

Mon préavis commencera le 6 juin 2004 et s'achèvera le 6 août 2004, date après laquelle je serai libre de tout engagement envers votre entreprise.

Veuillez agréer, Monsieur, toute ma considération.

[signature]

M. Viera

Resigning from a post

Frédéric Aubert
12, avenue de la Gare
07100 Annonay

M. Bedeau
Café-Bar des Anglais
Grand Place
07440 Alboussière

Annonay, le 12 septembre 2004

Monsieur,

Par cette lettre je vous prie de prendre note de ma décision de démissionner de mon emploi de garçon de café à dater du 12 octobre prochain. Pour des raisons familiales, je me vois en effet dans l'obligation de quitter la région.

Je vous remercie de la sympathie que vous m'avez exprimée au cours des dernières semaines, qui ont été particulièrement difficiles.

Je vous prie de croire à mes sentiments les meilleurs.

F. Aubert

Lettre de motivation

17 Roslyn Terrace,
London NW2 3SQ

15th October 2004

Ms R. Klein,
London Consultancy Group,
1 Canada Square,
Canary Wharf
LONDON E14 5BH

Dear Ms Klein,

Principal Consultant, E-business Strategy

I should like to apply for the above post, advertised in today's Sunday Times and have pleasure in enclosing my curriculum vitae for your attention.

MBA-qualified, I am a highly experienced information systems strategy consultant and have worked with a range of blue-chip clients, primarily in the financial services and retail sectors. In my most recent role, with Herriot Consulting, I have successfully led the development of a new electronic commerce practice.

I am now seeking an opportunity to fulfil my career aspirations with a major management consultancy, such as LCG, which has recognised the enormous potential of the e-business revolution. I believe I can offer LCG a combination of technical understanding, business insight and entrepreneurial flair.

I look forward to discussing this opportunity further with you at a future interview and look forward to hearing from you.

Yours sincerely,

J. O'Sullivan

encl: curriculum vitae.

Réponse à une offre d'entretien

2 Chalfont Close,
LONDON
W4 3BH

20 April 2005

C. Charles
Human Resources Manager
Phototex Ltd
2 Canal Street
LONDON
SW1 5TY

Dear Ms. Charles,

Thank you very much for your letter of 18 April 2005. I would be delighted to attend an interview on 25 April 2005 at 10.30 am.

As requested, I will bring with me a portfolio of my recent work to present to the interview panel.

Yours sincerely,

H. O'Neill

Helena O'Neill

Pour accepter une proposition d'emploi

16 Muddy Way
Wills
Oxon
OX23 9WD
Tel: 01865 76754

Your ref : TT/99/HH   4 July 2005

Mr M Flynn
Mark Building
Plews Drive
London
NW4 9PP

Dear Mr Flynn,

I was delighted to receive your letter offering me the post of Senior Designer, which I hereby accept.

I confirm that I will be able to start on 31 July but not, unfortunately, before that date. Can you please inform me where and when exactly I should report on that day? I very much look forward to becoming a part of your design team.

Yours sincerely,

Nicholas Marr

Pour refuser une proposition d'emploi

4 Manchester St
London
NW6 6RR
Tel: 020-8334
5343

Your ref : 099/PLK/001   9 July 2004

Ms F Jamieson
Vice-President
The Nona Company
98 Percy St
YORK
YO9 6PQ

Dear Ms Jamieson,

I am very grateful to you for offering me the post of Instructor. I shall have to decline this position, however, with much regret, as I have accepted a permanent post with my current firm.

I had believed that there was no possibility of my current position continuing after June, and the offer of a job, which happened only yesterday, came as a complete surprise to me. I apologize for the inconvenience to you.

Yours sincerely,

J D Salam

Covering letter for a CV

Chloé Dupuis
41 allée des peupliers
67000 Strasbourg

S.P.G. International
à l'attention de Madame Tesset
2 avenue du Général de Gaulle
67000 Strasbourg

Strasbourg, le 3 décembre 2004

Madame,

J'ai l'honneur de poser ma candidature pour le poste de gestionnaire de l'information de votre entreprise, dont j'ai appris qu'il était vacant par l'annonce publiée dans le journal Les Nouvelles. Je vous prie de bien vouloir trouver ci-joint un exemplaire de mon curriculum vitae.

Titulaire d'une maîtrise de gestion et d'un D.E.S.S. de gestion du développement des P.M.E., j'ai effectué au terme de mon année de D.E.S.S. un stage à Berlin dans une société d'envergure internationale. J'y ai mené à bien une mission marketing de mise en place d'un système de recherche de compétences à travers l'outil informatique. Ces emplois m'ont permis de mettre en œuvre les savoirs théoriques acquis pendant mes études, tout en élargissant le cadre de leur application. C'est dans cette perspective que je souhaite poursuivre ma carrière dans le domaine de la gestion de l'information pour l'entreprise. Organisée et volontaire, je saurai mettre mon expérience de terrain, mes connaissances techniques et mon sens des responsabilités au service de votre entreprise.

Je suis à votre disposition pour vous fournir tout renseignement supplémentaire.

Dans l'attente de votre réponse, je vous prie d'agréer, Madame, l'expression de mes sentiments respectueux,

Chloé Dupuis

Reply to an interview offer

Chloé Dupuis
41 allée des peupliers
67000 Strasbourg

S.P.G. International
à l'attention de Madame Tesset
Gestion des Ressources Humaines
2 avenue du Général de Gaulle
67000 Strasbourg

Strasbourg, le 15 décembre 2004

Madame,

Je vous remercie de votre lettre datée du 12 décembre dernier concernant ma candidature pour le poste de gestionnaire de l'information. Je suis très contente de pouvoir accepter votre offre d'entretien pour le 21 décembre 2004 à 14h, dans vos bureaux.

Dans cette attente, je vous prie d'agréer, Madame, l'expression de mes sentiments respectueux,

Chloé Dupuis.

Accepting a job

Gabriel Maréchal
11, rue Jules Ferry
85000 La Roche-sur-Yon

M. Ramirez
Ferme modèle du Grand Pré
14260 Aunay-sur-Odon

le 3 avril 2005

Monsieur,

C'est avec le plus grand plaisir que j'ai reçu votre courrier m'informant que j'avais été choisi pour le poste de pépiniériste auquel j'étais candidat. Je vous confirme par la présente que je serai en mesure de prendre ce poste à compter du 2 mai. J'arriverai dans la soirée du 1er, et me présenterai à vous dès 7 heures le lendemain matin.

Je vous prie de croire, Monsieur, à mes sentiments les meilleurs.

G. Maréchal

Turning down a job

René Perrot
13, rue Lamartine
38590 Brézins

Entreprise Bideau
Electricité générale
Quartier des Balmes
01370 Saint-André-de-Corcy

le 28 mars 2005

Monsieur,

Je vous suis reconnaissant de m'avoir offert un emploi d'électricien dans votre entreprise. Toutefois, ma situation personnelle a changé depuis notre dernier entretien. En effet, ma femme qui travaille dans l'Education nationale vient d'être nommée en Haute-Vienne. Je me vois donc dans l'obligation de refuser votre offre.

J'espère que vous ne me tiendrez pas rigueur de ce désistement, et vous prie d'agréer l'expression de mes meilleurs sentiments.

R. Perrot

CV : bachelière française

NAME:	Laurence BOUTON
ADDRESS:	18 Avenue Édouard Herriot 01000 Bourg-en-Bresse France Téléphone: 04 74 50 09 13
E-MAIL	lbouton@freestyle.fr
MARITAL STATUS:	Single

EDUCATION AND QUALIFICATIONS:

2000-2003	Lycée de Brou, Bourg-en-Bresse, France Baccalauréat, série L [this is the equivalent of A-levels in French and Languages]

PREVIOUS WORK EXPERIENCE:

2001-2003	Part-time: Private Tutor of English and French Language
2001 July	Camp counsellor, children's holiday camp, Nice. Duties included sports and games supervision, leisure co-ordination, general counselling of children aged 6-10 years
2001 March	One week exchange visit to German family in Bremen
2001 August	One month exchange visit to English family in Bournemouth

OTHER INFORMATION:	Love of children (I have 3 younger brothers and 2 sisters) Good spoken English and German 40 w.p.m Typing
INTERESTS:	Classical music Literature - especially modern poetry Museums and exhibitions Tap Dancing (participant in school competitions)
REFEREES:	M. Pierre Duval (Headmaster) Lycée de Brou 01000 Bourg-en-Bresse France Telephone: 04 74 39 84 73 Me Julie Huppert (Lawyer) 44 Rue Orange 01000 Bourg-en-Bresse France Telephone: 04 74 30 92 34

CV: English graduate

GRANTLEY Paul Alan

Adresse:
26 Countisbury Drive
BRIGHTON BN3 1RG
Grande-Bretagne
Tél.: 01273 53 49 50

Né le 22 mai 1978
Célibataire
Nationalité britannique

FORMATION

1997 – 2000
    King's College, Londres: B.Sc. (Licence) en Biochimie
    (2.1. = mention bien)

1996
    A Levels (Deuxième partie du Baccalauréat) options: Biologie,
    Chimie, Physique et Mathématiques.

1994
    GCSEs (Première partie du Baccalauréat) options :

    Mathématiques, Physique, Biologie, Chimie, Commerce, Anglais,
    Allemand et Sociologie.

1989 – 1996
    Brighton College Boys' School (Lycée)

EXPERIENCE PROFESSIONNELLE

Mars 1998
    une semaine comme "double" du Directeur Adjoint du Marketing
    chez EAA Technology (Sources d'énergie écologiques) à Didcot
    près d'Oxford.

Juillet 1997
    deux semaines chez Alford & Wilston Ltd (Produits chimiques),
    Warley, Midlands de l'Ouest.

CENTRES D'INTERET

Au Lycée
    Capitaine de l'équipe de rugby pendant deux ans.
    Membre du club d'échecs.

A l'Université
    Membre de l'équipe de rugby.
    Organisateur de la Semaine de Charité (1997).
    Délégué aux activités sportives dans l'association des
    étudiants.

DIVERS

    Bonne connaissance de l'outil informatique.
    Permis de conduire.
    Intérêt pour les voyages : tour du monde en 1996-1997, entre le
    Lycée et l'Université.

CV : jeune cadre belge

Name:	Jean-Baptiste LENOBLE
Date of Birth:	29/7/72
Nationality:	Belgian
Permanent Address:	
(After 3/8/04)	Rue des Frontières, 33 1234 Meuseville Belgium
Telephone:	(32) (88) 123.45.67
Temporary Address:	
(Until 3/8/04)	1642 West 195th St New York NY 23456 USA
Marital Status:	Single
E-mail	jblenoble@worldsurf.be

Education and Qualifications:

The qualifications described below do not have exact equivalents in the British system.
I enclose photocopies of my certificates with English translations.

1981-89:	Lycée Elisabeth, Meuseville, Belgium Qualification: School leaving certificate (Maths/Science option)
1989-92 1993-94	Université de Verviers: Department of Civil Engineering. Qualification: Diploma in Civil Engineering
2002-2004	Masters Program in Civil Engineering, New York Harbor University. (Results pending)

Work Experience

1990-1991	Summer work as volunteer at school for children with learning difficulties
1992-1993	Assistant civil engineer, Verviers Region, Belgium. Work on various road projects
1994-2002	Senior assistant civil engineer, Verviers Region

Other Skills & Interests

Languages: Fluent English,
Adequate spoken Dutch and German
(Native French speaker)
Clean Driving Licence
Squash: Regional finalist in University Squash team
I wish to expand my work experience in an English-speaking
country given the on-going changes in the European job market.

References:	Professeur H Vandecke Département de Génie Civil Université de Verviers B-1245 Verviers Belgium	Dr Jan C Waldermaker Managing Director Waldermaker Enterprises Inc 8822 West 214th St New York NY 24568 USA

CV : Female English middle-management

CURRICULUM VITAE

HUNT Mary Phyllis

16 Victoria Road
Brixton
LONDRES SW12 5HU
Tél.: 020 8675 7968
E-mail: m_p_hunt@Tonline.co.uk

Nationalité britannique

Née le 11 mars 1979

FORMATION ET DIPLOMES

2001 – 2002
Ecole de Commerce de l'Université d'Essex: Diplôme de Troisième
Cycle en Commerce-Gestion et Allemand.

1997 – 1999 et 2000 – 2002
London School of Economics (Grande Ecole en Sciences Economiques
de Londres), Département Commerce: BSc (Licence)
First Class Honours (distinction réservée aux meilleurs
étudiants) en Commerce et Economie.

1999 – 2000
Séjour d'une année à Bonn, Allemagne: étude de l'allemand
économique en cours du soir. Divers emplois de bureau en tant
qu'intérimaire.

1990 – 1997
Grammar School for Girls (Lycée de jeunes filles) : 7
disciplines à la première partie du Baccalauréat (O levels),et 4
à la deuxième partie (A levels): Mathématiques, Histoire,
Economie et Allemand

EXPERIENCE PROFESSIONNELLE

2002 – 2003
Formation de Directeur, Sainsway Foodstores plc (Grand magasin
d'alimentation), Londres.

2003 – 2004
Directrice adjointe, Sainsway Foodstores plc, Faversham, Kent.

2004 – 2005
Acheteuse adjointe, Delicatessen International, Paris

Depuis 2005
Sous-Directrice, Retail Outlets Division (Département des
Ventes au Détail), Delicatessen International, Londres.

CV : cadre supérieur français

NAME	Nathalie YVARD
ADDRESS	21 rue Saint-Jacques 75005 Paris France.
TELEPHONE	01 63 47 22 19
E-MAIL	nathalie_yvard@librenet.fr
DATE OF BIRTH	June 27th 1960
NATIONALITY	French
EDUCATION	
1970-1977	Lycée Camille Fontaine 15 rue D'Arcy 31000 Toulouse
June 1977	Baccalauréat, série C (equivalent of A-levels in Maths and Physics)
1984	HEC (Hautes Etudes Commerciales), University of Lyon
PREVIOUS EMPLOYMENT	
1986-1988	Marketing Director, American Express, Paris
1988-1991	Marketing & Publicity Director, Club Méditérranée, Paris
1991-2000	Marketing Director, Air Touraine, Paris
2000	Redundancy due to take-over of Air Touraine by British Airways
OTHER INFORMATION	
	Fluent in English and Italian
	Considerable experience in training recruits in the Marketing Dept., Air Touraine over the last 5 years
	Interests include travel and gardening
REFERENCES:	M. Jacques Clément Ms Polly Fitzgerald Directeur Général Deputy Director Club Méditérranée American Express 94 rue Dubois 55 Place Émile Zola 75010 Paris 75015 Paris

Phrases utiles

En-têtes

Quand vous écrivez à quelqu'un que vous connaissez peu ou pas du tout, la formule la plus courante est *Dear…*
- *Dear Sir*
- *Dear Madam*
- *Dear Sir or Madam*
- *Dear Sirs*
- *Dear Mr Dixon*
- *Dear Mrs Dixon*
- *Dear Ms Dixon*

Expressions utiles

I am writing in response to your advertisement in [publication]

I wish to enquire about the vacancy for a [job title]

Thank you for your letter of [date] offering me the post of …

I am delighted to accept the position of [job title]

I look forward to starting work with you.

Formules de politesse

Thank you for considering this application

I should be pleased to attend an interview

Please do not hesitate to contact me on the above number if you should require further information

I look forward to hearing from you

Si vous connaissez le nom de la personne :
- *Yours sincerely*

Si vous ne connaissez pas le nom de la personne :
- *Yours faithfully*

CV : Male English senior executive

```
Robert Charlton STEVENSON

                    21 Liston Road
                    Clapham Old Town
                    LONDON SW4 0DF
                    Royaume-Uni
Téléphone et télécopie: (44) (0)20 7622 2467

Nationalité britannique

Né le 27 juin 1960
```

FORMATION ET DIPLÔMES

1986	Maîtrise de Gestion (avec mention) à l'Armour Business School, Boston, Etats-Unis.
1984 – 1986	Deux années aux Etats-Unis.
1982	BSc (Licence) de Mécanique à l'Université du Dorset, Willingdon, Royaume-Uni.
1979 – 1982	Université du Dorset, Willingdon, Royaume-Uni.
1979	A level (Baccalauréat)

EXPÉRIENCE PROFESSIONNELLE

1998 – 2000	Directeur adjoint de Jermyn-Sawyers International, Londres.
1993 – 1998	Directeur pour l'Asie, Société Pharmaceutique Peterson, Hong Kong
1989 – 1993	Directeur, Kerry-Masterton Management Consultants (consultants en gestion des entreprises), Bonn.
1986 – 1989	Consultant, Masterton Management Consultants, Londres.
1982 – 1984	Stagiaire en gestion des entreprises, Jamieson Matthews Ltd, Crawley, Sussex.

DIVERS

Bilingue anglais-français.

Loisirs: ski, ski nautique, parapente, voile.

Useful phrases

Letter openings

The standard opening for formal correspondence is *Monsieur, Madame*, etc.

- *Mademoiselle,*
- *Messieurs,*
- *Mesdames,*
- *Madame, Monsieur,*
- *Maître/Cher Maître,* (to a lawyer)

Useful phrases

En réponse à l'annonce parue dans [journal] du [date].

J'ai l'honneur de poser ma candidature pour le poste de [emploi] dans votre société.

Je vous serais reconnaissant de bien vouloir m'envoyer un dossier de candidature.

Je vous remercie de la confiance que vous me témoignez en me proposant le poste de …

C'est avec enthousiasme que je rejoindrai votre équipe le [date].

Closures

Je vous remercie par avance de l'intérêt que vous voudrez bien porter à ma candidature.

Je serais très heureux/-euse de vous exposer mes motivations au cours d'un entretien.

Je me tiens à votre entière disposition pour vous rencontrer lors d'un entretien et pour tout renseignement complémentaire.

Dans la perspective d'une prochaine rencontre, je vous prie d'agréer, Madame, l'expression de mes sentiments respectueux. (Man to woman)

Je vous prie de croire, Madame/Monsieur, à l'expression de ma considération distinguée. (General)

La correspondance commerciale

Demande de catalogue

99 South Drive
London
WC4H 2YY

7 July 2004

Hemingway & Sons
Builders Merchants
11 Boley Way
London WC12

Dear Sirs,

Thank you for sending me your catalogue of timber building materials as requested. However, the catalogue you sent is last year's and there is no current price list.

I would be glad if you would send me the up-to-date catalogue plus this year's price list.

Yours faithfully,

Dr D Wisdom

Demande de devis : matériaux de construction

Eyer Shipyard
Old Wharf
Brighton
BN2 1AA
Tel 01273 45454
Fax 01273 45455

Our ref: TB/22/545

13 April 2004

Fankleman & Co. PLC
22 Mark Lane Estate,
Guildford,
Surrey
GU3 6AR.

Dear Sirs,

Timber Supplies

We would be glad if you could send us an estimate of the cost of supplying timber in the lengths and sizes specified on the enclosed list.

In general, we require large quantities for specific jobs at quite short notice and therefore need to be sure that you can supply us from current stock.

Thanking you in advance.

Yours faithfully,

(Ms) G N Northwood.
General Manager, Supplies.
Encl.

Demande d'échantillons

THE FRANK COMPANY
22 BLOOMING PLACE
LONDON SW12
TEL: 020-8669 7868
FAX: 020-8669 7866

5 June 2004

The Sales Director
June Office Supplies
55 Dewey Road
Wolverhampton
WV12 HRR

Dear Sir/Madam,

Thank you for sending us your brochures. We are particularly interested in the Dollis range, which would complement our existing stock.

Could you please arrange to send us samples of the whole range with the exception of items XC99 and XC100? We would be grateful if this could be done promptly, as we are hoping to place an order soon for the autumn.

Thanking you in advance,

Yours faithfully,

Mr T Jones
pp Mr F J Hart
Manager and Director
The Frank Company

Envoi de tarifs

Walter O'Neill & Co.
3 Eliot Mall
London NW12 9TH
Tel: 020-8998 990
Fax: 020-8998 000

Your ref: TRT/8/04
Our ref: DK/45/P

3 March 2004

Ms E Dickinson
Old Curiosity Inns
3 Haversham Street
London W6 6QF

Dear Ms Dickinson

Thank you for your letter of 22 April. We apologize for failing to send you the full price list which you will find enclosed. Please note that we have not increased our prices on any products available last year, and that we have managed to extend our range with new items still at very competitive rates.

Our usual discounts for large orders apply to you as a regular customer, and we are exceptionally doubling these to 10% on the 100/9 CPP range.

We look forward to receiving your order.

Yours sincerely,

E B Browning (Mrs)
Sales Director
Encl

Business correspondence

Asking for a catalogue

Thomas Lavant
3, rue des Epinettes
94170 Le Perreux

Besançon, le 12 janvier 2004

Entreprise J. Rossi SARL
Optique en gros
Z.I. des Hauts Fourneaux
25000 BESANÇON

Monsieur

Je vous serais reconnaissant de bien
vouloir m'envoyer le catalogue des jumelles et
longues-vues que vous commercialisez, avec la
liste des prix.

Recevez, Monsieur, l'assurance de mes
salutations distinguées.

T. Lavant

Asking for samples

le 18 avril 2004

Madame Bordoni
Couturière
2, impasse du Parc
50760 Barfleur
Téléphone: 02 45 45 22 34

Filatures Fouquet
185 route de Nantes
49300 Cholet

Madame, Monsieur,

J'ai bien reçu votre catalogue et je vous en remercie,
mais avant de passer ma commande, je souhaiterais
recevoir un lot d'échantillons des tissus qui figurent de la
page 248 à la page 322.

Je vous remercie de votre compréhension et vous
adresse, Madame, Monsieur, mes salutations distinguées.

G. Bordoni

Asking for an estimate

Monsieur et Madame Mercier
32, avenue des Marronniers
94500 Champigny sur Marne
Tél: 01 48 93 72 30

le 3 juin 2005

Cavanna & Fils
76, quai de la Marne
94170 Le Perreux

Messieurs,

Suite à notre conversation téléphonique de
ce jour, nous vous confirmons notre requête.

Propriétaires d'un petit pavillon, nous
souhaiterions procéder à quelques travaux
d'agrandissement, et en particulier faire
construire un jardin d'hiver dans le
prolongement de la salle de séjour. Nous
souhaiterions donc convenir d'un rendez-vous
afin que vous puissiez établir un devis.

Dans l'attente de votre réponse, nous vous
adressons nos sincères salutations.

C. Mercier

Sending details of prices

❦ **Société de location "Jardin et Maison"** ❧
157, route de Genas
69500 Bron
TELEPHONE : 04 78 54 65 77   TELECOPIE : 04 78 54 22 34
www.jardinsetmaisons.com

Bron, le 15 juin 2004

Monsieur Girardin
Résidence Martinon
27, rue Jules Ferry
69130 Ecully

Monsieur,

Vous trouverez ci-joint nos tarifs de
location pour l'outillage de jardin. Nous
attirons votre attention sur nos tarifs
dégressifs en cas de location de longue
durée et sur nos tarifs "fidélité" en cas de
location à intervalles réguliers.

Restant à votre disposition, nous vous
prions de croire, Monsieur, en nos
sentiments dévoués.

J.B.Roulet
Service commercial

La correspondance commerciale

Demande de réduction

Nielsen & Co
19 Westway Drive
Bradford BF8 9PP
Tel: 01274 998776
Fax: 01274 596969
www.nielsenco.com

Your ref: 4543/UIP   21 March 2005

Draft and Welling
15 Vine Street
London
NE22 2AA

Dear Sirs,

I acknowledge receipt of the goods listed in my order no. 1323YYY, but must query the total sum indicated on the invoice. I had understood that you were currently offering a discount of 15%, but no such deduction appears on the final invoice sheet.

I would be glad if you could give this matter your immediate attention.

Yours faithfully,

F. Nielsen

Frederick Nielsen
Associate Director, Procurement

Pour accepter une demande de réduction

GARRICK PAPER SUPPLIERS

108 Kingston Road
Oxford
OX3 7YY
Tel: 01865 9900
Fax: 01865 9908

28 April 2005

S Johnson & Co
Globe House
London W13 4RR

Dear Sir/Madam,

Thank you for your letter of 16 April in which you ask for a reduction on our normal prices, given the size of your order.

We are happy to agree to your request provided you, in return, make prompt payment of our account within two weeks of the delivery of your order. If that is agreeable to you, we can offer you a discount of 8%, instead of the usual 5%.

We hope to receive your acceptance of these terms and assure you of our very best attention.

Yours faithfully,

A. Rothwell

Ann Rothwell
Customer Relations Manager

Réclamation : retard de livraison

Duke & Ranger
45 High Street,
Stonebury.
SX6 0PP
Tel: 01667 98978

Your ref: 434/OP/9

9 August 2004

Do-Rite Furniture,
Block 5,
Entward Industrial Estate,
Wolverhampton.
WV6 9UP

Dear Sirs,

We are surprised not to have received delivery of the two dozen coffee tables from your "Lounge Lights" range (see our letter of 6 July) which you assured us by phone were being dispatched immediately.

Our sales are being considerably hampered by the fact that the coffee tables are missing from the range and it is now over three weeks since you promised that these items would be delivered. Please phone us immediately to state exactly when they will arrive.

Yours faithfully,

Jane Malvern

Jane Malvern
Manager

Réclamation : livraison non conforme à la commande

The Hough Company

23 Longacre Rd
London
SW3 5QT
Tel: 020-7886 7979
Fax: 020-7887 6954

5 October 2004

Dear Mrs Halliwell,

Order no. 54.77.PO

Further to our phone call, we are writing to complain about various items which are either missing or wrong in the above order.

I enclose a list of both categories of items and would remind you that we felt obliged to complain of mistakes in the two previous orders as well. We hesitate to change our supplier, particularly as we have no complaints as to the quality of the goods, but your errors are affecting our production schedules.

We hope that you will give this matter your immediate, urgent attention.

Yours sincerely,

J. Schott

Jane Schott
Manageress, Procurements

Encls
Mrs J Halliwell
Jessop & Jonson
23 High Street
Broadstairs
Kent CT10 1LA

Asking for discount

Société SOGEFOP
route de Pierrefeu
83170 Brignoles
téléphone : 04 42 27 86 13
télécopie: 04 42 27 00 01

Brignoles, le 14 novembre 2004

Confiseries du Port
2, place du Port
13500 Martigues

Messieurs,

Je souhaiterais offrir pour Noël à tout mon personnel un assortiment de fruits confits. Votre catalogue propose une présentation en paniers de 150 grammes au prix de 7,10€ pièce TTC sous la réf. 18/22. Je souhaiterais pouvoir vous en commander 1580.

Etant donné l'importance de cette commande, qui pourrait se renouveler chaque année, je vous demande une remise de 10%.

Par avance, je vous remercie de votre réponse et vous prie de croire, Messieurs, en mes sentiments distingués.

Monsieur Robert Ledoux
Président-directeur général

Agreeing to a discount

Société Levet
128 bis, Grande Rue
76190 Yvetot
téléphone: 02 35 89 27 68
télécopie: 02 35 89 99 99

le 16 février 2005

Garage des Sapins
27, Square des Sapins
33170 Gradignan

Référence RAD 00 35/22

Monsieur,

Nous avons bien reçu votre demande de réduction sur la commande du 12 janvier dernier, et nous avons le plaisir de vous faire savoir qu'à titre exceptionnel nous vous accordons une remise de 2,5 %. Votre facture est donc ramenée à 218390 €.

Veuillez agréer, Monsieur, l'expression de nos salutations distinguées.

R. Dormois
Directeur Commercial

Complaining about delivery: late arrival

le 30 mai 2005

M. F. Lorinet
89, impasse des Cordeliers
36100 Issoudun

Société Tout pour l'Eau
92, avenue de Paris
36000 Châteauroux

Objet: Commande 00/3/5302/127/VG

Monsieur,

Voilà plus de deux mois que j'attends la baignoire réf. 5302 couleur vert d'eau que je vous ai commandée le 15 mars dernier. Vous m'aviez assuré lors de la commande qu'elle me serait livrée sous trois semaines.

Je vous serais reconnaissant de me faire savoir dans les délais les plus brefs la date exacte où cet article me sera livré, faute de quoi je me verrai contraint d'annuler ma commande.

Dans l'attente de vous lire, je vous prie de croire, Monsieur, à mes sentiments distingués.

F. Lorinet

Complaining about delivery: wrong goods

"La Maison du Sous-Vêtement"

15, rue Magenta
42000 Saint-Etienne
Tél.: 04 77 42 17 82

le 12 septembre 2005

USINES LOIRETEXTILE
Confection - Vente en gros
Z.I. des Epis
42319 Roanne CEDEX

Référence commande n° 00/08/30-ZDX

Messieurs,

J'ai bien reçu votre livraison, mais je me vois dans l'obligation de vous retourner le colis, les tailles des articles ne correspondant pas à celles indiquées sur le bon de commande.

Je vous saurais gré de bien vouloir corriger votre erreur et de me faire parvenir les articles conformes à ma commande dans les plus brefs délais.

Veuillez agréer, Messieurs, l'expression de ma considération distinguée.

A. Hébert
Gérant

La correspondance commerciale

Réclamation : facture déjà payée

Old Forge Pottery
4 Money Lane
Falmouth
Cornwall TR11 3TT
Tel: 0326 66758
Fax: 0326 66774

19 September 2004

Oscar Goode & Co
3 Field Place
Truro
Cornwall
TR2 6TT

Dear Mr Last,

Re: Invoice no. 4562938

I refer to your reminder of 17 September, which we were rather surprised to receive.

We settled the above invoice in the usual manner by bank transfer on 23 August and our bank has confirmed that payment was indeed made. Coming after several delays in making recent deliveries, this does cast some doubt on the efficiency of your organization.

We hope that you will be able to resolve this matter speedily.

Yours sincerely,

Rupert Grant

Rupert Grant
Accounts Manager

Réclamation : facture trop élevée

The Round Place
2 Nighend High
Bristol
BS9 OUI
Tel: 117 66900
Fax: 117 55450

4 June 2004

Famous Gourmet
399 Old Green Road
Bristol
BS12 8TY

Dear Sirs,

Invoice no. B54/56/HP

We would be glad if you would amend your recent invoice (copy enclosed).

The quantities of the last three items are wrong, since they refer to "24 dozen" instead of the correct quantity of "14 dozen" in each case. In addition to this, our agreed discount of 4% has not been allowed.

Please check your records and issue a revised invoice, which we will then be happy to pay within the agreed time.

Yours faithfully,

M R Edwardson

M. R Edwardson
Chief Supplies Officer

Encl.

Avis de paiement insuffisant

T. Markham Ltd
34 Asquith Drive
London SW33
Tel: 020-8323 4343
Fax: 020-8323 4586

Our ref: 77877/99/PO

Mr Aidan Fadden
Fadden Enterprises PLC
234 Race Street
London NW8   20 March 2005

Dear Mr Fadden

Bill BQW 888R

We acknowledge receipt of your draft for £3,222.90. We must however point out that our February statement included a further sum of £1,998.13 which was still outstanding from the previous statement.

We would be glad if you would look into this matter and arrange for prompt payment of the sum outstanding.

Many thanks.

Yours faithfully,

J Roundwood

Mr J Roundwood - Chief Cashier

Relance pour facture impayée

ESTUARY SUPPLIES
45 Tully Street
YORK
YO3 9PO
Tel: 01904 59787
Fax: 01904 95757

Our ref: 998884/YT   9 September 2004

Ms T Blunt,
Crabbe and Long,
33-98 Grand Place,
YORK
YO8 6EF

Dear Ms Blunt,

I am writing to remind you that you have not yet settled our invoice no. 6TT 999, a copy of which I enclose.

We have never before had occasion to send you a reminder, so we assume that this matter is simply an oversight on your part. Perhaps you could arrange for payment to be made in the next few days.

Yours sincerely,

M Kington

pp M. Kington
Director

Disputing an invoice: already paid

le 21 décembre 2004

B. Conrad
Le Manoir aux Emaux
17108 Saintes

            Meubles Le Vieux Rustique
            Zone artisanale des Fougères
            D 939
            17030 La Rochelle

Monsieur,

Par lettre du 20 décembre, vous me demandez
de régler votre facture n° 721 de 7305,50 €
du 11 septembre concernant la livraison de
meubles divers. Or cette facture a déjà été
payée, par mandat postal daté du 7 octobre.
Je vous la renvoie donc, en vous demandant
de bien vouloir vérifier vos comptes.

Veuillez agréer, Monsieur, l'expression de
mes salutations distinguées.

                         B.Conrad

P.J.: votre facture

Disputing an invoice: too high

"Les Amis de la Spatule"
Association à but non lucratif Loi 1901
Téléphone 05 61 60 62 33

le 15 septembre 2004

Raoul Blanchard
Trésorier de l'Association
11, rue Juliette Lamber
24000 Périgueux

            "LA MERE LEGRAS"
            Hôtel Restaurant
            6, rue Ampère
            24200 Sarlat

Madame,

Je reçois votre facture n° 00/08/31/XYZ86
correspondant au banquet des Anciens de la
Spatule du 31 août dernier et je me permets d'en
contester le montant.

Nous étions convenus d'un prix d'environ 38 € par
personne pour le repas, apéritifs et digestifs
compris. Or votre facture fait apparaître un
prix de 45 € par personne, ce qui ramène le prix
du café (qui était en sus) à 6,50 €!

Pensant qu'il s'agit d'une erreur, je vous
demanderais de bien vouloir rectifier cette
facture en conséquence, et vous prie d'agréer,
Madame, l'expression de mes sentiments
distingués.

                         R. Blanchard

Wrong payment received

GARAGE SIMOUN
Place du Champ de Foire
91150 ETAMPES
téléphone: 01.60.14.91.49

        Etampes, le 25 octobre 2004

        Monsieur Dupuis
        25 ter, avenue du Stade
        14000 CAEN

Réf. facture 560/00/08/25789

Monsieur,

Nous avons bien reçu votre chèque bancaire n° 8
2563 114 du 19 octobre 2004 d'un montant de
230 €.

Le montant total de la facture qui vous a été
adressée étant de 298,30 €, vous nous êtes
redevable de la somme de 68,30 € que nous vous
remercions par avance de bien vouloir nous
régler dans les plus brefs délais.

Veuillez agréer, Monsieur, l'expression de nos
sentiments distingués.

                  B. Fournier
                  Gérant

Reminder of invoice outstanding

ENTREPRISE DE BATIMENT MAZZA
289, route Nationale
36000 Châteauroux
Tél.: 02 85 04 92 78

        Monsieur Jean-Louis Jacquet
        3, Place Albert Camus
        36100 Issoudun

        le 18 juillet 2005

Facture n° 94/126B72 du 22 avril 2000

Monsieur,

Nous vous rappelons que notre facture n° 00/126B72
du 22 avril 2005 dont le paiement était prévu au
deuxième trimestre 2005 reste impayée à ce jour.

Nous vous remercions par avance de bien vouloir
régulariser votre situation dans les plus brefs délais et
vous prions d'agréer, Monsieur, l'expression de nos
salutations distinguées.

                Luc Bayard
                Agent Comptable

Télécopie: entreprise

Swan Publishing
34 Paulton Street
London W2 9RW

FACSIMILE NUMBER: 020-7789 6544

Message for:	Charles Julien
Address:	25-30, rue d'Avignon, 75012 PARIS. France
Fax number:	00.33.4143 4555
From:	Emma Wallis, Swan Publishing
Date:	May 20, 2005
Number of pages including this one:	1

Thank you for your letter of 18 May 2005.

1. Please confirm meeting on June 6th at 10:00.

2. Two packages of brochures and two boxes of samples dispatched on March 23rd. Please confirm receipt.

3. Guidelines on government policy apparently to be issued next week. Will try and get copies for discussion at June 6th meeting.

Look forward to seeing you on June 6th.

Emma Wallis

Emma Wallis,
Marketing Director

Demande de renseignements : organisation d'une conférence

Herriot Consulting

18 Robert Adam Place   Tel: +44 (0) 131 339 8896 (direct line)
Edinburgh EH7 1AA   +44 (0) 131 339 8800 (switchboard)
United Kingdom   Fax: +44 (0) 131 339 8810
www.herriotconsulting.com

The Conference Manager
The Caledonia Thistle Hotel
George Grove
GLASGOW
G3 6DD

12th September 2004

Dear Sir or Madam,

I am currently organising a two-day residential staff-training event for 40 staff from our Scottish offices. In addition to accommodation and meals, our requirements would include a fully-equipped conference room, and four syndicate rooms suitable for workshop sessions.

I would be very grateful if you would forward me information on your conference and corporate hospitality facilities with room and meal rates and details of availability for early November.

I look forward to hearing from you,

Mike Hines

Professional Development Manager

Phrases utiles

En-têtes

Quand vous écrivez à quelqu'un que vous connaissez peu ou pas du tout, la formule la plus courante est *Dear…*
- *Dear Sir*
- *Dear Madam*
- *Dear Sir or Madam*
- *Dear Sirs*
- *Dear Mr Dixon*
- *Dear Mrs Dixon*
- *Dear Ms Dixon*

Expressions utiles

Thank you for your letter of [date] concerning …

Thank you for sending me a [catalogue, quotation]

Thank you for your enquiry of [date]

I refer to your letter of [date] concerning …

Further to our telephone conversation of [date], …

I am writing to confirm our telephone conversation of [date]

I would be grateful if you could forward me a [price list, catalogue]

As stated in your letter/ fax of [date] …

I wish to draw your attention to …

I wish to inform you that …

I am writing to inform you that …

I am writing to express my dissatisfaction with …

Please note that …

Please find enclosed …

Formules de politesse

I look forward to hearing from you …

I look forward to your response …

I would be most grateful if you would look into this matter as soon as possible …

Please let me know as soon as possible what action you propose to take …

I trust that you will give this matter your urgent attention …

Please do not hesitate to contact me should you require further information.

Si vous connaissez le nom de la personne:
- *Yours sincerely*

Si vous ne connaissez pas le nom de la personne:
- *Yours faithfully*

Fax: business

L.C. INFORMATIQUE
12, RUE CLAUDE BERNARD
86000 POITIERS
N° de téléphone: 05 49 41 54 67
N° de télécopie: 05 49 41 22 82
www.LCinformatique.fr

TRANSMISSION PAR TELECOPIE

Date: 12 août 2004

Veuillez remettre ce document à : Jean Briant

Numéro de télécopie : 19 44 705 82 31 54

De la part de : Stéphanie Langlois

Nombre de pages (y compris cette page) : 1

Message : Prière de me faire parvenir de toute
urgence, par Chronopost si possible,
l'original de vos billets d'avion et de train
pour que je puisse procéder à votre
remboursement.

J'aurai aussi besoin de vos notes d'hôtel et
de restaurant, mais c'est moins urgent.

Merci, et amitiés,

S. Langlois

Si vous ne recevez pas ce document au complet, veuillez nous en
aviser le plus rapidement possible par téléphone ou télécopie.

Enquiring about reproduction rights and costs

Julie Collins
Service des reproductions
Sandford Publishing Co.
Dalton Street
Wantage OX12 6DP
Grande-Bretagne

Service des Archives du film
Centre National de la Cinématographie

Le 13 février 2005

Madame, Monsieur,

Sandford Publishing Co s'apprête à publier un
ouvrage sur le cinéma européen des origines à nos
jours. Les auteurs souhaitant insérer dans le corps
du texte un certain nombre de clichés appartenant
à vos archives, je vous serais très reconnaissante
de bien vouloir me faire parvenir une
documentation sur les modalités et les coûts de
reproduction.

Veuillez agréer, Madame, Monsieur, l'expression
de ma considération distinguée.

Julie Collins

Useful phrases

Letter openings

The standard opening for formal correspondence is
Monsieur, Madame, etc.
- *Mademoiselle,*
- *Messieurs,*
- *Mesdames,*
- *Madame, Monsieur,*
- *Maître/Cher Maître, (to a lawyer)*

Useful phrases

*J'ai bien reçu votre [catalogue, réponse], et je vous en
remercie.*

J'ai bien reçu votre lettre du [date] concernant…

Je vous remercie de votre lettre et de vos suggestions sur…

*Pour faire suite à notre conversation téléphonique du
[date]…*

*Suite à notre entretien téléphonique de ce jour, je vous
envoie …*

*Je vous remercie par avance de bien vouloir me faire
parvenir [un catalogue, un dossier de candidature] à
l'adresse ci-dessus.*

Je vous serais reconnaissant de bien vouloir m'envoyer…

Comme vous le précisez dans votre lettre/fax du [date]…

Je vous informe par la présente de mon intention de…

*Je me permets de porter à votre connaissance les faits
suivants.*

*J'attire/Je me permets d'attirer votre attention [sur le fait
que, sur]…*

Je vous prie de trouver ci-joint, …

Closures

*Merci de me dire ce que vous comptez faire pour remédier à
ce problème.*

*Je vous demande de remédier à cette situation dans les
meilleurs délais.*

*Je vous prie de bien vouloir me répondre par retour de
courrier.*

*N'hésitez surtout pas à me contacter pour tout
renseignement complémentaire.*

*Dans l'attente de votre réponse, je vous prie d'agréer,
Madame, l'assurance de mes sentiments respectueux/de
mes hommages les plus respectueux.* (Man to woman)

*Recevez, Madame/Monsieur, l'expression de ma
considération distinguée.* (General)

*Veuillez croire, Madame/Monsieur, à l'assurance de mes
salutations distinguées.* (General)

Mots et expressions de liaison anglais

admittedly
Admittedly, revenge is not the character's only motive.

Certes, la vengeance n'est pas la seule motivation du héros.

again
Again, we have to consider the legal implications.

Une fois de plus, nous devons tenir compte des conséquences juridiques.

also
It is *also* interesting to ask to what extent the author has been influenced by his social background.

Aussi, il est intéressant de se demander à quel point l'auteur est influencé par son milieu social.

although
I doubt she approves of these changes, *although* she hasn't mentioned the subject.

Je doute qu'elle approuve ces changements, *bien qu'*elle n'ait rien dit à ce sujet.

as a result
They were directly involved in the conflict. *As a result*, their names have been changed to conceal their identity.

Ils ont directement pris part au conflit. *En conséquence*, leurs noms ont été changés pour préserver leur anonymat.

at any rate
At any rate it is the most credible hypothesis.

C'est *du moins* l'hypothèse la plus plausible.

besides
I haven't time to go and see this film — *besides*, it's had dreadful reviews.

Je n'ai pas le temps d'aller voir ce film. *De plus*, il a reçu de très mauvaises critiques.

be that as it may
Be that as it may, these measures will take time to have an effect.

Quoi qu'il en soit, ces mesures mettront du temps à produire leur effet.

but
But that doesn't justify resorting to violence.
But fate decided otherwise.

Mais cela ne justifie pas le recours à la violence.
Seulement, le destin en a décidé autrement.

consequently
Computers are more and more powerful. *Consequently*, home computers soon become obsolete.

Les ordinateurs sont de plus en plus performants. *En conséquence*, l'équipement des familles est vite dépassé.

despite
Despite his huge success, he has remained very unpretentious.

Malgré son immense succès, il est resté très simple.

finally
Finally, we will attempt to underline the points which the two poets have in common.
Finally, we will examine the future of the book in a world where information technology is becoming more important by the day.

Enfin, nous essaierons de souligner les points communs entre ces deux poètes.
Pour finir, nous nous interrogerons sur l'avenir du livre, dans un monde où le support informatique prend chaque jour plus d'importance.

first
First, we should recall the different stages of a child's development.

Avant toute chose, il convient de rappeler les différentes étapes de l'évolution de l'enfant.

French link words and expressions

To help you write in French, you will find below the most frequent link words and expressions, shown in context.

ainsi

Ainsi, il semble légitime de se demander si ces investissements sont justifiés.

Thus, it seems reasonable to wonder if these investments are justified.

à l'inverse

À l'inverse, on peut se demander si ce n'est pas un choix délibéré de l'auteur.

On the other hand, one may wonder if it is not a deliberate choice on the author's part.

alors

J'avais toujours mal, *alors* je suis allé voir un spécialiste.

It was still painful, *so* I went to see a specialist.

à savoir

Pendant la période d'incubation, *à savoir* deux semaines avant que la maladie ne se déclare, le sujet est très contagieux.

During the incubation period, *that is to say* for two weeks before the onset of symptoms, the subject is very infectious.

au contraire

On découvre, *au contraire*, que le personnage est coupable du crime.

On the contrary, we discover that the character is guilty of the crime.

aussi

Aussi faut-il tenir compte des bouleversements sociaux qu'a connu le XIXe siècle.

The social upheavals which took place during the nineteenth century must *also* be considered.

autant dire que

Autant dire qu'il faut se méfier des jugements hâtifs.

In other words we must be wary of hasty judgments.

autrement dit

Nous sommes en 1919, *autrement dit* au lendemain de la première guerre mondiale.

It is the year 1919, *in other words*, just after the end of the First World War.

avant tout/avant toute chose

Avant toute chose, il convient de rappeler les différentes étapes de l'évolution de l'enfant.

First, we should recall the different stages of a child's development.

bien que

Je doute qu'elle approuve ces changements, *bien qu'*elle n'ait rien dit à ce sujet.
*Bien qu'*ils ne disposent d'aucun soutien des syndicats, ils ont décidé de continuer la grève.

I doubt she approves of these changes, *although* she hasn't mentioned the subject.
Though they don't have any backing from the unions, they have decided to continue the strike.

cela dit

Cela dit, je n'ai pas d'objection.

That being said, I do not have any objections.

cependant

Il n'est *cependant* pas considéré comme un auteur majeur.

He is not, *however*, considered to be a major author.

certes

Certes, la vengeance n'est pas la seule motivation du héros.

Admittedly, revenge is not the character's only motive.

first of all

We shall see, *first of all*, how the author describes the unhappiness of the character.

Nous verrons, *d'abord*, comment l'auteur décrit la tristesse du personnage.

furthermore

Our survey only compares computers within the same power range. *Furthermore*, we limited ourselves to PCs.

Notre étude compare seulement des ordinateurs de même puissance. *De plus*, nous nous sommes limités aux PC.

hence

Hence the necessity for the child to identify with imaginary characters.

D'où la nécessité pour l'enfant de s'identifier à des personnages imaginaires.

however

He is not, *however*, considered to be a major author.

Il n'est *cependant* pas considéré comme un auteur majeur.

The racial problem is not, *however*, the only explanation.

Le problème racial ne constitue *pourtant* pas la seule explication.

in addition

In addition, the cat is known to have held an important place in ancient Egypt.

On sait, *par ailleurs*, que le chat tient une place importante dans l'Antiquité égyptienne.

in conclusion

In conclusion, we may regret that the author dealt with only one aspect of the problem.

En conclusion, on peut regretter que l'auteur n'ait abordé qu'un seul aspect du problème.

indeed

The author was well acquainted with the world of banking. *Indeed*, he had worked for a large Parisian bank for almost ten years.

L'auteur connaissait bien le milieu bancaire. Il avait, *en effet*, travaillé pour une grande banque parisienne pendant près de dix ans.

in fact

In fact we know nothing about the ties which bond them.

En fait, on ignore tout des liens qui les unissent.

in other words

In other words we must be wary of hasty judgments.

Autant dire qu'il faut se méfier des jugements hâtifs.

It is the year 1919, *in other words*, just after the end of the First World War.

Nous sommes en 1919, *autrement dit* au lendemain de la première guerre mondiale.

The child has difficulty in accepting the new baby. *In other words*, he is jealous.

L'enfant accepte mal l'arrivée d'un nouveau-né. *En d'autres termes*, il est jaloux.

in short

In short, it is an admission of failure.

En bref, il s'agit d'un constat d'échec.

in spite of

In spite of all his efforts, the envoy has been unable to obtain a peace agreement.

Malgré tous ses efforts, l'émissaire n'a pas obtenu d'accord de paix.

instead

Instead, students can enrol on a programming course.

À la place, les étudiants peuvent s'inscrire à un cours de programmation.

in the first place

In the first place, we must consider the economic situation of the country before the revolution.

Nous nous attacherons, *en premier lieu*, à rappeler la situation économique du pays avant la révolution.

moreover

Moreover, it must be stated that Verdi was an ardent supporter of Italian Unity.

En outre, il faut préciser que Verdi était un fervent partisan de l'unité italienne.

Moreover, close examination of the contract reveals several inconsistencies.

D'autre part, un examen attentif du contrat montre plusieurs incohérences.

Moreover, he is completely suited to the part.

De plus, ce rôle lui convient tout à fait.

nevertheless

The novel is *nevertheless* not entirely autobiographical.

Le roman n'est *toutefois* pas entièrement autobiographique.

French link words and expressions

c'est pourquoi

La lecture favorise l'ouverture d'esprit, *c'est pourquoi* un enfant qui lit aura moins de difficultés à comprendre le monde qui l'entoure.

Reading encourages one to be more open-minded. *That's why* a child who reads will find it easier to understand the world around him.

d'abord

Nous verrons, *d'abord*, comment l'auteur décrit la tristesse du personnage.

We shall see, *first of all*, how the author describes the unhappiness of the character.

d'autre part

D'autre part, un examen attentif du contrat montre plusieurs incohérences.

Moreover, close examination of the contract reveals several inconsistencies.

de la même manière

De la même manière, ils ont supprimé le traditionnel supplément du samedi.

Similarly, they have done away with the traditional Saturday supplement.

de plus

De plus, ce rôle lui convient tout à fait.
Notre étude compare des ordinateurs de même puissance. *De plus*, nous nous sommes limités aux PC.

Moreover, he is completely suited to the part.
Our survey compares computers within the same power range. *Furthermore*, we limited ourselves to PCs.

donc

Nous évoquerons *donc* les poètes contemporains de Verlaine.

We will, *therefore*, consider the poets who were Verlaine's contemporaries.

d'où

D'où la nécessité pour l'enfant de s'identifier à des personnages imaginaires.

Hence the necessity for the child to identify with imaginary characters.

du moins

C'est *du moins* l'hypothèse la plus plausible.

At any rate it is the most credible hypothesis.

en bref

En bref, il s'agit d'un constat d'échec.

In short, it is an admission of failure.

En conclusion

En conclusion, on peut regretter que l'auteur n'ait abordé qu'un seul aspect du problème.

In conclusion, we may regret that the author dealt with only one aspect of the problem.

en conséquence

Ils ont directement pris part au conflit. *En conséquence*, leurs noms ont été changés pour préserver leur anonymat.

They were directly involved in the conflict. *As a result*, their names have been changed to conceal their identity.

encore

Ces champignons ne sont, paraît-il, pas dangereux. *Encore* faut-il savoir les distinguer des autres.

These mushrooms are said not to be dangerous, but you *still* need to know how to tell them apart from the others.

en d'autres termes

L'enfant accepte mal l'arrivée d'un nouveau-né. *En d'autres termes*, il est jaloux.

The child has difficulty in accepting the new baby. *In other words*, he is jealous.

en dépit de

Il a accepté de publier ce roman, *en dépit du* manque d'enthousiasme du comité de lecture.

He agreed to publish this novel *despite* the lack of enthusiasm from the reading panel.

en effet

L'auteur connaissait bien le milieu bancaire. Il avait, *en effet*, travaillé pour une grande banque parisienne pendant près de dix ans.

The author was well acquainted with the world of banking. *Indeed*, he had worked for a large Parisian bank for almost ten years.

en fait

En fait, on ignore tout des liens qui les unissent.

In fact we know nothing about their bonds.

en outre

En outre, il faut préciser que Verdi était un fervent partisan de l'unité italienne.

Moreover, it must be stated that Verdi was an ardent supporter of Italian unity.

next

Next, we shall focus on the psychological approach.

Ensuite, nous allons nous intéresser à l'approche psychologique.

nonetheless

It must *nonetheless* be pointed out that he came from a very religious family.

Il faut *néanmoins* préciser qu'il a grandi au sein d'une famille très pratiquante.

on the contrary

On the contrary, we discover that the character is guilty of the crime.

On découvre, *au contraire*, que le personnage est coupable du crime.

on the other hand

On the other hand, one may wonder if it is not a deliberate choice on the author's part.

À *l'inverse*, on peut se demander si ce n'est pas un choix délibéré de l'auteur.

On the other hand, it is implausible that the author was unaware of Baudelaire's work.

En revanche, il est peu crédible que l'auteur ait ignoré l'œuvre de Baudelaire.

similarly

Similarly, they have done away with the traditional Saturday supplement.

De la même manière, ils ont supprimé le traditionnel supplément du samedi.

still

These mushrooms are said not to be dangerous, but you *still* need to know how to tell them apart from the others.

Ces champignons ne sont, paraît-il, pas dangereux. *Encore* faut-il savoir les distinguer des autres.

so

It was still painful, *so* I went to see a specialist.

J'avais toujours mal, *alors* je suis allé voir un spécialiste.

that is to say

During the incubation period, *that is to say* for two weeks before the onset of symptoms, the subject is very infectious.

Pendant la période d'incubation, *à savoir* deux semaines avant que la maladie ne se déclare, le sujet est très contagieux.

that's why

Reading encourages one to be more open-minded. *That's why* a child who reads will find it easier to understand the world around him.

La lecture favorise l'ouverture d'esprit, *c'est pourquoi* un enfant qui lit aura moins de difficultés à comprendre le monde qui l'entoure.

then

We will *then* talk about the problems of integration faced by immigrants.

Nous parlerons *ensuite* des problèmes d'insertion des immigrés.

therefore

We will, *therefore*, consider the poets who were Verlaine's contemporaries.

Nous évoquerons *donc* les poètes contemporains de Verlaine.

We must, *therefore*, take the historical context into account.

Il faut, *par conséquent*, tenir compte du contexte historique.

thus

Thus, it seems reasonable to wonder if these investments are justified.

Ainsi, il semble légitime de se demander si ces investissements sont justifiés.

to begin with

To begin with, one has to remember what happened that day.

Tout d'abord, il faut rappeler ce qui s'est passé ce jour-là.

to sum up

To sum up, one can say that television has taken part of the audience away from the cinema.

En résumé, on peut dire que la télévision a volé une partie des spectateurs du cinéma.

whereas

She was hardly worried about it, *whereas* he took this warning very seriously.

Cela ne l'a guère préoccupée, *alors que* lui a pris cet avertissement très au sérieux.

yet

She trained hard all year, *yet* still failed to reach her best form.

Elle s'est entraînée de façon intensive toute l'année, *mais* n'a toujours pas retrouvé le meilleur de sa forme.

en premier lieu

Nous nous attacherons, *en premier lieu*, à rappeler la situation économique du pays avant la révolution.

In the first place, we must consider the economic situation of the country before the revolution.

en résumé

En résumé, on peut dire que la télévision a volé une partie des spectateurs du cinéma.

To sum up, one can say that television has taken part of the audience away from the cinema.

en revanche

En revanche, il est peu crédible que l'auteur ait ignoré l'œuvre de Baudelaire.

On the other hand, it is implausible that the author was unaware of Baudelaire's work.

en somme

En somme, l'auteur se cantonne à réutiliser les recettes qui ont fait le succès de son roman précédent.

Basically, the author simply uses the same formula as the one which made his first novel such a success.

ensuite

Nous parlerons *ensuite* des problèmes d'insertion des immigrés.

We will *then* talk about the problems of integration faced by immigrants.

mais

Mais cela ne justifie pas le recours à la violence. Elle s'est entraînée de façon intensive toute l'année, *mais* n'a toujours pas retrouvé le meilleur de sa forme.

But that doesn't justify resorting to violence. She trained hard all year, *yet* still failed to reach her best form.

malgré

Malgré tous ses efforts, l'émissaire n'a pas obtenu d'accord de paix.

In spite of all his efforts, the envoy has been unable to obtain a peace agreement.

néanmoins

Il faut *néanmoins* préciser qu'il a grandi au sein d'une famille très pratiquante.

It must *nonetheless* be pointed out that he came from a very religious family.

or

Or l'auteur est lui-même d'origine slave.

Now the author is himself of Slav origin.

par ailleurs

On sait, *par ailleurs*, que le chat tient une place importante dans l'Antiquité égyptienne.

In addition, the cat is known to have held an important place in ancient Egypt.

par conséquent

Il faut, *par conséquent*, tenir compte du contexte historique.

We must, *therefore*, take the historical context into account.

pour commencer

Pour commencer, nous ferons un bref résumé de la situation.

To start with, we'll briefly sum up the situation.

pour finir

Pour finir, nous nous interrogerons sur l'avenir du livre, dans un monde où le support informatique prend chaque jour plus d'importance.

Finally, we will examine the future of the book in a world where information technology is becoming more important by the day.

pourtant

Le problème racial ne constitue *pourtant* pas la seule explication.

The racial problem is not, *however*, the only explanation.

quoi qu'il en soit

Quoi qu'il en soit, ces mesures mettront du temps à produire leur effet.

Be that as it may, these measures will take time to have an effect.

tout d'abord

Tout d'abord, il faut rappeler ce qui s'est passé ce jour-là.

To begin with, one has to remember what happened that day.

toutefois

Le roman n'est *toutefois* pas entièrement autobiographique.

The novel is *nevertheless* not entirely autobiographical.

Petites annonces anglaises

Emplois

JOBS

Female Student, 24 yrs, seeks p/t work as childminder/domestic help in Notting Hill area. Experienced, reliable, avail. mornings or afternoons and school hols, approx 15 h.p.w. Pay negotiable. 020 8 339 4857.

Secretary req'd for temp pos-ition in dynamic small company to cover maternity leave. 60 wpm typing, 90 wpm shorthand, wp experience essential, esp MS Office. Excellent verbal/ written communication skills. Competitive salary. Call Mrs Jones 020 8 338 4958

Handyman required for summer upkeep and repairs at Sutton sports ground. 3 month contract (Jun-Aug), approx 35 hrs pw. Hourly rate £6.35. Carpentry skills essential as is prev experience. Further details from Mr Ellison 020 8 3393283

French Language tuition offered. All levels in your own home, by exp native French speaker. School/univ exams, essays, journalism, business etc. £17 ph. Tel 01902 339449

French/English translators required by French Law firm for casual contract work. Must be native French speaker w/fluent English. German an advantage. For details Tel: 020 7 228 3854 ext. 6950

Au pair seeks position in family with 2-3 children in London. French female, 21yrs, non-smoker, clean driver's licence, excellent refs, good spoken Eng. Tel: 00 33 29930004

Experienced Au pair Wanted for 3 children aged 2,4,7 & some light hsewk in Shepherds Bush. Must be non-smoker, animal lover, driver, 21yrs+. Approx 40hpw, own flatlet & pocket money. Send CV + photo to PO Box 209.

Domestic Help wanted 3hrs 3 mornings pw for family home. Near bus route, £6 ph. Tel 01273 49586

Agent Wanted for 5 bed holiday home in Robin Hood's Bay. Duties incl. cleaning & gen upkeep betw. lets, showing families around, advice and emergency help. Salary neg. Suit retired person. Tel: 020 8 229 4848

Housesitter Wanted: for 4 bed holiday home in Cornwall, for 5 mo Nov-Mar. Rent-free in exch for care of 2 acre gdn, hse maintenance and bills. 6m nearest town. Tel 01273 48596

21yrs+ (21 years plus) ▸ plus de 21 ans
approx (approximately) ▸ approximativement
Aug (August) ▸ août
avail (available) ▸ libre
bed (bedroom) ▸ chambre
betw (between) ▸ entre
CV (Curriculum Vitae) ▸ CV
Eng (English) ▸ anglais
esp (especially) ▸ en particulier
etc (et cetera) ▸ etc
exch (exchange) ▸ échange
exp (experienced) ▸ expérimenté
ext. (extension) ▸ poste
gdn (garden) ▸ jardin
gen (general) ▸ général
hpw (hours per week) ▸ heures par semaine
hrs (hours) ▸ heures
hse (house) ▸ maison
hsewk (housework) ▸ ménage
incl. (include) ▸ comprennent
Jun (June) ▸ juin
m (miles) ▸ miles
mo (months) ▸ mois
Neg. (negotiable) ▸ négociable

Nov-Mar (November to March) ▸ de novembre à mars
ph (per hour) ▸ de l'heure
PO Box (Post Office Box) ▸ boîte postale
Prev (previous) ▸ antérieur
p/t (part time) ▸ temps partiel
pw (per week) ▸ par semaine
refs (references) ▸ références
school hols (school holidays) ▸ vacances scolaires
secretary req'd (secretary required) ▸ recherche secrétaire
temp (temporary) ▸ temporaire
univ (university) ▸ université
wp (word processing) ▸ traitement de texte
wpm (words per minute) ▸ mots à la minute
w/ (with) ▸ avec
yrs (years) ▸ ans

French advertisements

Jobs

Emplois Jne F., 23 ans, diplômée ESC. bil. Fr/Angl, tt txte, excel. présent. ch. empl. 1/2 tps, accept. déplcts. Ecr. jrnl Réf. OEZ98	Centre de vac. ch. H à tt faire du 1/7/05 au 31/8/05 pr petits trvx, surveill. enfts, sér. réf. exigées, logé, nourri, blanchi + 500€/ms. Ecr. jrnl réf. PLM258	J.F. nat. française, 20 ans, aimant enfts, sér. réf., souhaite trouver fam. anglophone, suivi trav. scol. poss., dispon. juil. août 05, écr. journ. ZOL150	Entr. TP ch. VRP multic., départ. 42, 74, 01. Envoy. CV + photo + prétent. à BATIDUR 285 cours Lafayette 69100 Villeurbanne
Pr remplt cong. mater. PME ch. hot. accueil, pet. secrét., tél., tt txte, CDD 5 mois à part. 15 oct. proch., voiture indisp., ts frs payés, possib. contr. long. dur. Ecr. jrnl PU322	Etud. prépa. donne cours anglais français ts niveaux tél: 01 27 42 31 86	URG fam. écossaise (avocat) rég. Glasgow, 2 enfts 3/5 ans cherche J.F. au pair, bon anglais, juillet-août 05, Ecrire Mme R. Burns 5 Menzies Crescent Fintry Stirlingshire G63 0YL	Ch. cple gardiens pr propriété isolée, 250 km sud Paris, petits travx jard., logt indpt, sal. intér., sér. réf. exigées. Se présent., Château du Lac 18100 Vierzon
	Rech. un/-e trad. spécial. bio-médical Ang/Alld et Alld/Ang. pr trad. simult congrès internat. Bruxelles du14/6 au 17/6/05. Pdre cont. Mme Roux en écriv. au jrnal qui transmettra	Ch. f. de mén. 2x4h/sem., a.m. préfér., sér. réf. exig., Tél Mme PIERRAT 01 42 59 17 23	

1/2 tps (mi-temps) ▶ half-time
2x4h/sem. (deux fois quatre heures par semaine) ▶ 4 hours twice a week
à part. (à partir de) ▶ from (date)
accept. déplcts (accepte les déplacements) ▶ will travel
angl (anglais) ▶ English
alld (allemand) ▶ German
a.m. préfér. (l'après-midi de préférence) ▶ preferably p.m.
bil. Fr/Angl (bilingue français/anglais) ▶ bilingual French/English
CDD (contrat à durée déterminée) ▶ fixed-term contract
ch. (cherche) ▶ seeks
cong. mater. (congé de maternité) ▶ maternity leave
contr. long. dur. (contrat de longue durée) ▶ long-term contract
cple (couple) ▶ couple
départ. (départements) ▶ departments (French districts)
dispon. (disponible) ▶ available
€/ms (euros par mois) ▶ euros per month
ESC (École Supérieure de Commerce) ▶ Business School
ecr. (écrire à) ▶ (please) write to
empl. (emploi) ▶ job
en écriv (en écrivant) ▶ by writing
enfts (enfants) ▶ children
entr. TP (entreprise de travaux publics) ▶ civil engineering firm
envoy. (envoyer) ▶ (please) send
étud. (étudiant(e)) ▶ student
excel. présent. (excellente présentation) ▶ very smart appearance
exig. (exigé) ▶ required, essential
f. de mén. (femme de ménage) ▶ cleaning lady
fam. (famille) ▶ family
H. à tt faire (homme à tout faire) ▶ odd-job man
h/sem. (heures par semaine) ▶ hours per week
hot. accueil (hôtesse d'accueil) ▶ receptionist
indisp. (indispensable)
internat. (international)
J.F., Jne F (jeune fille/femme) ▶ young woman
jrnl (journal) ▶ newspaper
logt indpt (logement indépendant) ▶ separate accommodation
nat. (nationalité) ▶ nationality
oct. (octobre) ▶ October
pdre cont. (prendre contact avec) ▶ contact
pet. secrét. (petit secrétariat) ▶ some secretarial duties
petits trvx (petits travaux) ▶ light (manual) work
PME (petite et/ou moyenne entreprise) ▶ small and/or medium-sized enterprise, SME
poss. (possible) ▶ possible
possib. (possibilité) ▶ possibility
pr (pour) ▶ for
prépa. (classe préparatoire) ▶ studies for entry to Grandes Écoles
prétent. (prétentions) ▶ salary expectation
proch. (prochain) ▶ next
rech. (recherche) ▶ seeking
réf. (référence) ▶ reference (number)
rég. (région) ▶ region
remplt (remplacement) ▶ replacement
sal. intér. (salaire intéressant) ▶ attractive salary
se présent. (se présenter) ▶ apply in person
sér. réf. (sérieuses références) ▶ excellent references
surveill. enfts (surveillance d'enfants) ▶ looking after children
tél. (téléphone) ▶ telephone
trad. simult. (traduction simultanée) ▶ simultaneous translation
trad. spécial. (traducteur/-trice spécialisé/-e) ▶ technical translator
trav. scol. (travail scolaire) ▶ homework
travx jard. (travaux de jardinage) ▶ gardening
ts (tous) ▶ all
ts frs payés (tous frais payés) ▶ all expenses paid
tt txte (traitement de texte) ▶ word processing
URG. (urgent) ▶ urgent
vac. (vacances) ▶ holidays
VRP multic. (voyageur représentant placier multicartes) ▶ sales representative for several different companies

Petites annonces anglaises

Ventes : divers

ARTICLES FOR SALE

Carpet for Sale: Brown wool twist, excel quality and cond. 12ft x 16ft. £80 ono. 01852 345679

Electric Hob, Siemens, brown, 4 rings & small elec oven. Vgc. Offers invited. Can deliver. 01321 4659634

Hotpoint Twin tub washing machine, perf working order, bargain at £100. 01273 495068. Will Deliver.

Hoover turbo power: brand new w/guarantee, still boxed, duplicate gift. Cost £209, will accept £175. Tel. 01865 456923

Pioneer Stereo: separate units, incl. digital tuner, graphics, amp, twin cassette, deck multiplay, cd, turntable. As new £475. tel. 01223 496590.

Hotpoint Larder Fridge. Sm freezer. 3yrs old. gwo. Offers? 01432 594058.

3-Piece Suite. Brown Draylon, 3-seater settee, 2 lge armchairs. £100 ovno. Buyer collects. Tel 020 8 669 4857 (eve/wkends)

Laptop IBM Thinkpad, Pentium 2 processor, 32MB Ram, 1.2 Gb hard drive, internal CD drive, Win 98, 33.3k modem, carrycase. £630 ono. Tel. 0141 338 5734.

Kenwood Chef Food Processor: w/attachments; mincer, dough, hood etc. Still guarant'd, hardly used. Tel: 01273 458695

Assorted Garden Tools: rake, hoe, shovel, wheelbarrow, broom. All gwo. £50 the lot, or indiv. offers accepted. Tel: 01432 458399

Bathroom wardrobe 6ft H, 4ft W, 20" D, dble doors w/centre mirror, buyer collects. Tel. 01865 556123.

18ct gold signet ring, cost over £250, will accept £100 ono, wd make a nice Xmas present. Tel. 01865 585561.

6ft H, 4ft W, 20" D (6 feet high, 4 feet wide, 20 inches deep) ▸ hauteur 1,80m, largeur 1,20m, profondeur 50cm
12ft x 16ft (12 feet by 16 feet) ▸ 3,65m x 4,90m
amp (amplifier) ▸ ampli(ficateur)
CD (compact disc) ▸ CD, disque compact
ct (carat) ▸ carat
cond (condition) ▸ condition
elec (electric) ▸ électrique
etc (et cetera) ▸ etc
eve (evenings) ▸ soir
excel (excellent) ▸ excellent
ft (feet) ▸ pieds
Gb (gigabyte) ▸ Go, gigaoctets
guarant'd (guaranteed) ▸ garanti
gwo (good working order) ▸ bon état de marche
HD (hard disk) ▸ disque dur
incl (including) ▸ comprenant

indiv (individual) ▸ individuel
lge (large) ▸ grand
MB (megabytes) ▸ Mo, mégaoctets
ono (or nearest offer) ▸ à débattre
ovno (or very near offer) ▸ à débattre
perf (perfect) ▸ parfait
RAM (RAM) ▸ RAM
sm (small) ▸ petit
tel (telephone) ▸ téléphone
vgc (very good condition) ▸ très bon état
w/ (with) ▸ avec
wd make (would make) ▸ ferait
Win/ (Windows) ▸ Windows
wkends (weekends) ▸ week-ends
yrs (years) ▸ ans
x (by) ▸ sur
Xmas (Christmas) ▸ Noël

Articles for sale

Ventes: divers

Tr. b. tap. persan, 125 x 230, frangé, fond bleu, impecc. 1250€, à sais.
T. 01 25 43 18 77

Cse dble empl., vds cuisinière mixte, 60 x 60, 4 feux électr., four à gaz, t. b. ét., tél. HR 01.39.50.71.23

Cède frigo Vedette 150 l, freezer 30 l, dim. 60 x 60 x 185, peu servi, intér. impecc., T 05 56 32 41 76

Offr. spéc. à sais., 1 lot de lav. ling. Miele, 5 kg, b. ét. mécan., px 50% nf, à emport.
ELECTROMENAGER, 152 rte de Limonest, dim. compris

---

vds sèch. linge Philips, modèle réc, état nf, 450€, tél 02 32 21 85 91

À vdre aspirat. Hoover traîneau, rouge, silencx, tire-fil, 220 v. tél 03.82.34.15.67

Vds fer à vap. Calor Pressing Plus, jam. servi, tél 05 58 32 14 97

À vdre chaîne hifi, dble K7, CD, 2 ampli. 25W, px à déb. T. 05.59.12.65.34

Suite cess. act. PME cède son outil inf.: ord. Philips P4000, disque mém. 120 millions, 3 écr., 1 impr. P2934/02, 1 log. compta. paie, gest. commerc., tt parf ét., val. ach. 45000€, px à déb 04.74.92.36.25 mat

---

URGT vds canapé 3 pl. + 2 chauff., imit. cuir fauv., parf. état 700€ tél 05.59 45 62 71

Cse dpt, cède sal. de jard. plast. blanc, 1 tble rde 6 pers. + chaises, 2 transat. et parasol assort., 450€, tél. ap. 19h 01 27 36 15 89

Cause démgnt, cède 2 paires dble ridx, 235 x 120 cm, coul. crème; 2 paires voilages; 1 bac fleur Riviera 1m/25cm. Tél 02 52 36 47 98

Compaq ordin.port., 2240 CDS nf, gar. 2a. 460mhz, mod. int. lect. CD, val. 1600€ vend. 1000€ 01 43 92 36 65

---

125 x 230 (125 sur 230) ▸ 125 by 230 (centimetres)

à déb. (à débattre) ▸ (price) to be discussed

à emport. (à emporter) ▸ for quick sale

à sais. (à saisir) ▸ bargain

à vdre (à vendre) ▸ for sale

ampli. (amplificateurs) ▸ amplifiers

ap. (après) ▸ after

aspirat. (aspirateur) ▸ vacuum cleaner

assort. (assortis) ▸ matching

b. ét. mécan. (bon état mécanique) ▸ good mechanical condition, good working order

cess. act. (cessation d'activité) ▸ going out of business, closing down

chauff. (chauffeuses) ▸ easy chairs (Note: also stands for chauffage)

compta. (comptabilité) ▸ accounts

coul. (couleur) ▸ colour

cse dble empl. (pour cause de double emploi) ▸ surplus to requirements

cse dpt (pour cause de départ) ▸ (as) owner leaving, moving house

dble K7 (double cassette) ▸ double-cassette deck

dble ridx (doubles rideaux) ▸ curtains

démgnt (déménagement) ▸ moving house/premises

dim. (dimensions) ▸ measurements

dim. comp. (dimanches compris) ▸ including Sundays

écr. (écrans) ▸ screens, monitors

électr. (électrique) ▸ electric

fauv. (fauve) ▸ fawn (colour)

frigo (réfrigérateur) ▸ fridge

gar. 2a (garanti 2 ans) ▸ 2 years guarantee

gest. commerc. (gestion commerciale) ▸ sales management

imit. (imitation) ▸ imitation

impecc. (impeccable) ▸ perfect condition, as new

impr. (imprimante) ▸ printer

inf. (informatique) ▸ computing (equipment)

intér. (intérieur) ▸ interior

jam. servi (jamais servi) ▸ never used

l (litre) ▸ litre

lav. ling. (lave-linge) ▸ washing machine

lect CD (lecteur CD-Rom) ▸ CD-ROM drive

log. (logiciel) ▸ software

mat. (matin) ▸ (in the) mornings

mém. (mémoire) ▸ memory

mhz (mégahertz) ▸ megahertz

mod. int. (modem intégré) ▸ built-in modem

nf (neuf) ▸ new

offr. spéc. (offre spéciale) ▸ special offer

ord. (ordinateur) ▸ computer

ordin. port (ordinateur portable) ▸ laptop

parf. ét. (parfait état) ▸ (in) perfect condition

pers. (personnes) ▸ people

pl. (places) ▸ seats

plast. (plastique) ▸ plastic

PME (petite et/ou moyenne entreprise) ▸ small and/or medium-sized enterprise/SME

px (prix) ▸ price

réc. (récent) ▸ recent

rte (route) ▸ road

sal. de jard. (salon de jardin) ▸ garden furniture

sèch. linge (sèche-linge) ▸ tumble dryer

silencx (silencieux) ▸ quiet

T. (téléphone) ▸ telephone

t. b. ét. (très bon état) ▸ very good condition

tap. (tapis) ▸ carpet

tble rde (table ronde) ▸ circular table

tél. HR (téléphoner aux heures des repas) ▸ phone at meal times (i.e. between 12 and 2 or between 7 and 9 p.m.)

transat (transatlantique) ▸ deckchair

tr. b. (très beau) ▸ very fine

tt (tout) ▸ all

urgt (urgent) ▸ urgent

v (volt) ▸ volt

val (valeur) ▸ worth

val. ach. (valeur à l'achat) ▸ cost when new

vap. (vapeur) ▸ steam

vds (vends) ▸ for sale

vend. (vendu) ▸ selling price

W (watt) ▸ watt

Échanges vacances

House/Apartment holiday exchanges

Exchange: Sml fam owned village hse nr Objat, slps 4-5, 1 bath, lounge, mod kit, sm gdn, for Seaside cott in Devon/Cornwall for 3 wks commenc. Jun 3rd 2005. Tel: 00 33 5 55 25 8899.

Room Exchange Wanted: lge rm in friendly non-smkg hse w/ 3 profs in Central Oxford for similar in Brixton area for 3 mos from Sept 05. Monthly rental £50 p.w. Pets welcome. Tel 01865 553389.

Caravan Exchange Wanted: comfortable 6 berth caravan on N. Cornish coast: running water, elec, camp shop. Padstow 2 m. For 3-4 berth caravan in S. Wales campsite for 3 wks July or Aug 05. Tel: 020 8 332 5454

Holiday Exchange: Clean, scenic, 6 pers Chalet in Provence (quiet town, 40 mins drive from St Tropez) offered in exch. for approx 4 pers cott on Sussex coast (pref nr. Newhaven) for 1 month beginning August 2005. Car exch poss. Tel: 00 33 249968504.

Trans-Atlantic Apartment Swap: Lux 2BR, 2ba apt in Evanston. Lake view frm balcony, prkg, fully a/c, cable, lndry, close to shops and trans to Chicago (20 mins). For 2 BR similar quality in Central London. Call Sarah: 00 1 312 866 7396.

Couple Seek Bedsit Exchange: beautiful roomy dble bedsit nr Camden Lock, 5 mins tube, great clubs nrby, in exch for similar in central Edinburgh for 3 wks of Festival. Pets, smokers welcome. Tel 020 8 223 4956

Vente de véhicules, deux-roues, bateaux

Vehicle sales

Ford Fiesta Zetec, 1999, M reg. 29,000 miles. Blue. Power steering, twin airbags, 4 mo MOT, VGC, 2 lady owners. £2,600 ono. Tel. 01224 572318

V.W Sharan, 1997, P Reg, silver. e/w, a/c, alloy wheels, taxed July 2004, excellent condition. One owner from new. £10,250 ono. Tel 01385 349450

Mini 1.3L, N Reg., limited edition, metallic green. Alarm, immobiliser, r/c, excellent condition, 40k miles. £2,900 ono. Tel. 07720 987142

Honda Civic hatchback. 1.6v, S Reg, 28,000 miles. Yellow. CD player, immobiliser, electric windows. 6 month's road tax. £5,500 ono. Tel. 020 8439 7783 (eve).

Bargain Boat! 32 ft Kitch Motor Sailer, 5 Berth, all navigation aids, 50hp diesel. Some work needed hence price, must sell: best offer over £18000. Call Jo 01273 495869

Bicycles for Sale: One Ladie's 5-spd, 27in wheels, 19 in frame. As new £75. One Boy's 10 spd racer, suit 10-12 yrs, PX if poss, otherwise £50. Phone 01223 4459305 after 6pm or wkend.

---

a/c (air conditioned) ▸ air conditionné
approx (approximately) ▸ approximativement
apt (apartment) ▸ appartement
ba (bathroom) ▸ salle de bains
bath (bathroom GB) ▸ salle de bains
BR (bedroom) ▸ chambre
car exch. (car exchange) ▸ échange de voiture
commenc. (commencing) ▸ à partir de
cott (cottage) ▸ petite maison (rustique)
dble bedsit (double bedsit) ▸ studio pour deux
elec (electricity) ▸ électricité
exch (exchange) ▸ échange
fam owned (family owned) ▸ familial
frm (from) ▸ depuis
hse (house) ▸ maison
lge rm (large room) ▸ grande chambre
lndry (laundry US) ▸ laverie
lux (luxury) ▸ luxueux
m (miles) ▸ miles
mod kit (modern kitchen) ▸ cuisine moderne
mos (months) ▸ mois
N. Cornish (North Cornish)
non-smkg (non-smoking) ▸ non-fumeur
nr (near) ▸ à proximité de
nrby (nearby) ▸ à proximité
pers (person) ▸ personne
pref (preferred) ▸ de préférence
prkg (parking) ▸ place de parking
profs (professionals) ▸ salariés
pw (per week) ▸ par semaine
slps (sleeps) ▸ peut loger
sm gdn (small garden) ▸ petit jardin
sml (small) ▸ petit
S.Wales (South Wales) ▸ au sud du Pays de Galles
trans (transport) ▸ transports en commun
w/ (with) ▸ avec
wks (weeks) ▸ semaines

1600c (1600 centilitres) ▸ 1600 centilitres
40k miles (40000 miles) ▸ 40000 miles
6pm (post meridiem) ▸ six heures du soir
a/c (air conditioning) ▸ climatisation
eve (evening) ▸ soir
e/w (electric windows) ▸ vitres électriques
ft (foot) ▸ pied
hp (horsepower) ▸ cv
in (inches) ▸ pouces
mo (months) ▸ mois
MOT (Ministry of Transport test) ▸ contrôle technique
ono (or nearest offer) ▸ à débattre
poss (possible) ▸ possible
PX (part exchange) ▸ reprise
r/c (radio-cassette) ▸ radiocassette
recon (reconditioned) ▸ remis à neuf
reg (registration) ▸ immatriculation
spd (speed) ▸ vitesse
tel (telephone) ▸ téléphone
vgc (very good condition) ▸ très bon état
wkend (weekend) ▸ week-end
yr(s) (year(s)) ▸ an(s)

House/Apartment holiday exchanges

Échanges vacances

Échange maison ds village Landes, 4/5 pers, sdb, cuis. équip., petit jard., avec maison ou appartement Alpes sud même caract. p. 3 sem. à part du 3 juin 2005.
Tél 01 45 20 16 38

VACANCES: éch t b maison Haute Provence (20 min. Draguignan), 6 pers., contre maison standing équiv. Sussex pour août 2005. Poss. éch. voit.
Tél. 01 43 54 09 53

Éch. bglw tt cft, 4/5 pers, PALAVAS LES FLOTS, contre logt équiv. Bret. sud, 14 juil/15 août. T. HR 02 98.72.41.68

Échange luxueux appt Paris Avenue Foch, 2ch, 2sdb, terrasse ombragée, tv câble, a/c, parking, contre appt similaire centre Londres pour avril mai juin 2005.
Tél. 01 45 27 98 12

La Ciotat, échange carav. Caravelair 4 pers. empl. ombragé ds camping 3 étoiles, prox. mer, centre com., animations, prise TV, contre standg ident. montagne ou camp. 1ère quinz. juil. Envoy. photo, descript. et propositions au jrnl, réf. EC 182

Vehicle Sales

Vente de véhicules, deux-roues, bateaux

VDS Opel Astra Bk
5 cv, gris métal, août 98 ttes opts, int. cuir, TBE, 49 000 kms, tél. dom. ap 19h
03 85 66 24 87

À vdre camping-car Ford ess., ann. 95, 3/4 pers., 120 000 kms, mot. ref. nf, intér. parf. ét., px à déb.
Tél. b.03 57.92.13.74

VW Fourg. Diesel
99, DA, ouv s/le côté, 40 000 kms, première main, CENTRAL AUTO St Priest
04.78.21.80.52

Part. vd
Suzuki Dk 650
05/98, 1re m., 5 200 km, accessoires.
Tél. 02.72.84.99.87. h.b.

Vélo femme, Peugeot 1/2 course, 10 vitesses, 2 plat., vert métal., t.b.ét., occas. à saisir, 180€ 01.42.51.36.10
Mme Millard

Vds dériveur 505, coque alu., voiles terg., av. remorque. A voir Port Leucate les w.e. Prendre r.v. 04 67 37 90 21

---

a/c (air conditionné) ▸ air conditioning
à part (à partir de) ▸ from (a date)
appt (appartement) ▸ flat
bglw (bungalow) ▸ holiday chalet
Bret. sud (Bretagne sud) ▸ southern Brittany
camp. (campagne) ▸ country
caract. (caractéristiques) ▸ features
carav. (caravane) ▸ caravan
centre com. (centre commercial) ▸ shopping centre
ch. (chambre) ▸ bedroom
cuis. équip. (cuisine équipée) ▸ fully fitted kitchen
descript. (description) ▸ description
ds (dans) ▸ in
éch. (échange) ▸ exchange (offered for)
empl. (emplacement) ▸ site (for caravan or tent)
envoy. (envoyer) ▸ (please) send
équiv. (équivalent) ▸ equivalent
HR (heures des repas) ▸ meal times (between 12 and 2 or between 7 and 9 p.m.)
jard. (jardin) ▸ garden
jrnl (journal) ▸ newspaper
logt équiv. (logement équivalent) ▸ equivalent accommodation
min (minutes) ▸ minutes
p (pour) ▸ for
pers. (personnes) ▸ people
poss. (possibilité) ▸ possibility
prox. mer (à proximité de la mer) ▸ close to the sea
quinz. juil. (quinzaine de juillet) ▸ fortnight in July
réf. (référence) ▸ reference number
sdb (salle de bains) ▸ bathroom
sem. (semaine) ▸ week
standg ident. (standing identique) ▸ comparable standard (of accommodation, fittings, etc.)
T (téléphoner) ▸ telephone
t b (très beau/belle) ▸ delightful
tél. (téléphoner) ▸ telephone
tt cft (tout confort) ▸ all mod cons
tv (télévision) ▸ television
voit. (voiture) ▸ car

1ère m. (première main) ▸ only one owner
à vdre (à vendre) ▸ for sale
alu. (aluminium) ▸ aluminium
ann. 95 (année 95) ▸ year (of manufacture) 1995
ap. (après) ▸ after
av. (avec) ▸ with
Bk (break) ▸ estate
cv (chevaux) ▸ horsepower
D.A. (direction assistée) ▸ power steering
ess. (à essence) ▸ petrol engine
fourg. (fourgonnette) ▸ small van
h.b. (heures de bureau) ▸ (in) office hours (i.e. between 8 and 12 or between 2 and 5)
int.cuir (intérieur en cuir) ▸ leather upholstery
intér (intérieur) ▸ interior
kms (kilomètres) ▸ kilometres
métal. (métallisé) ▸ metallic
mot. (moteur) ▸ engine
occas. (occasion) ▸ bargain
ouv. s/le côté (ouvrant sur le côté) ▸ side door
parf. ét. (parfait état) ▸ in perfect condition
part. (particulier) ▸ private sale
pers. (personnes) ▸ people
plat. (plateaux) ▸ gear wheels
px à déb. (prix à débattre) ▸ price to be discussed
ref. nf (refait à neuf) ▸ completely reconditioned
r.v. (rendez-vous) ▸ appointment
t.b.ét., TBE (très bon état) ▸ (in) excellent condition
tél. b. (téléphoner aux heures de bureau) ▸ phone in office hours (between 8 and 12 or between 2 and 5)
tél. dom. (téléphoner au domicile) ▸ phone home number
terg. (tergal) ▸ Terylene
ttes opts (toutes options) ▸ all extras
vd, vds (vend, vends) ▸ for sale
w.e. (weekend) ▸ weekend

Immobilier : ventes

Property
For Sale

For Sale: Lewes, Semi-det hse, BR 2 mins walk – 50 mins London. 1.5 baths, 4 beds, lge gdn, 2 recs, newly modernized kitchen, gch. £90,000. Tel: 01273 34790 eve/wkend.

Salcombe, Devon: Period Cott . Sea view, 2 acres gdn, 3 beds, 2 baths, lge fmly rm, wkg fireplaces, beams, fully renovated. OIRO £125,000 for quick sale. PO Box 41.

For Sale: 5 acres of land w/ Pl Permsn 3 stables/out-hses. Would make good paddock/ grazing. Easy road access, 3m from Maldon. Offers: 01622 859059.

Hereford £450,000: Stunning, spacious 19th century home in 3 acres gdn and woodland. Mstr suite + 4 BR, 3 ba, huge lounge w/patio, DR, Lge mod. kit, utility rm, bsmnt. 2 miles Hereford ctr. Dble Grge. Tel: 01432 273669

Development Potential: crumbling 18th cent Cotswold farmhouse in Bexley (Oxford 5m). Needs total refurbishment. Could bcome beautiful 3/4 bed country hse w/lge gdn in much sought-after area. Interested? Tel 01865 27768.

£180,000 Rottingdean. Purpose built apartment. Spacious dble bedrm, lounge, kit, bath, balcony, pking avail. Quiet residential area nr shops + golf course. Brighton 2m. Owner sale, call 01273 564789

Immobilier : locations

To Let

Wanted by non-smoking professional female: room in shared hse nr city ctr, w/ 2-3 other profs/grads. Rent up to £60 p.w + bills. Will provide refs and deposit if nec. Tel: Jane 01223 432675.

For Rent: Rehabbed grnd flr apt in divided semi-det hse, 2 mins walk Balham tube. Unfurn, 2 beds, sitting rm, sml kit w/washing mach, gch, use of garden. Quiet area. £155 p.w. + bills. 2 mo sec. dep + refs. No pets. Tel: 020 8 556 2310 after 6pm.

Alfriston: Lakeside bungalow for six mo lease. Fully furn, 2 bed, 1 bath, gch, sml gdn, all mod cons. Slps 4-5. Nr village center. Pking. £500 pcm, bills incl. except phone. Tel: 020 7 446 5090

Lavender Hill: Luxury Flat to let. 3rd flr, fully furn split-level w/roof gdn + spectacular view. 3 beds, 1 bath, spacious lounge w/skylights. Gch, security entry, semi-det Georgian building in quiet residential area. BR + Clapham common 5 mins walk. £900 pcm + bills. Tel: 020 8 224 3948.

To Let: Picturesque North Brittany Farmhouse for 3 mo from Jul 2005. Slps 6-8. Fully modernized. Level gdn l 9089 sq yds, outhouses & barn. Nearest town 2 m, good road. Tel: 00 33 2 96 437263

Wanted: Quiet prof. female to share small hse w/one other in central Chelmsford nr bus stn. Rent £60 p.w. Cat-lover pref. Tel: 01245 443228.

18th cent (18th century) ▸ (du) 18e siècle
avail (available) ▸ libre
ba (bathrooms US) ▸ salles de bains
baths (bathrooms GB) ▸ salles de bains
bed (bedroom) ▸ chambre
BR (bedroom US) ▸ chambre
BR (British Rail GB) ▸ gare
bsmnt (basement) ▸ sous-sol
cott (cottage) ▸ petite maison (rustique)
ctr (centre) ▸ centre
dble bedrm (double bedroom) ▸ chambre pour 2
dble grge (double garage) ▸ garage pour 2 voitures
DR (dining-room) ▸ salle à manger
eve (evening) ▸ soir
fam/fmly rm (family room) ▸ séjour
gch (gas central heating) ▸ chauffage central au gaz
gdn (garden) ▸ jardin
hse (house) ▸ maison
kit (kitchen) ▸ cuisine
lge (large) ▸ grand
m (miles) ▸ miles
mins (minutes) ▸ minutes
mod kit (modern kitchen) ▸ cuisine moderne
Mstr suite (master suite US) ▸ grande chambre avec salle de bains
nr (near) ▸ à proximité de
OIRO (offers in the region of) ▸ propositions de l'ordre de
outhses (outhouses) ▸ dépendances
Pl Permsn (planning permission) ▸ permis de construire
recs (reception rooms) ▸ pièces principales
semi-det hse (semi-detached house) ▸ maison jumelée
utility rm (utility room) ▸ buanderie
w/ (with) ▸ avec
wkend (weekend) ▸ week-end
wkg (working) ▸ en état de marche

3rd flr (third floor) ▸ 3e étage
all mod cons (modern conveniences) ▸ tout confort
apt (apartment) ▸ appartement
bed (bedroom(s)) ▸ chambre(s)
BR (British Rail GB) ▸ gare
bus stn (bus station) ▸ gare routière
ctr (centre) ▸ centre
dep (deposit) ▸ caution
furn (furnished) ▸ meublé
gch (gas central heating) ▸ chauffage central au gaz
grads (graduates) ▸ étudiants (après la licence)
grnd flr (ground floor) ▸ rez-de-chaussée
hse (house) ▸ maison
incl (including) ▸ comprenant
m (miles) ▸ miles
mach (machine) ▸ machine
mins (minutes) ▸ minutes
mo (months) ▸ mois
nec (necessary) ▸ nécessaire
nr (near) ▸ près de
pcm (per calendar month) ▸ par mois
pking (parking) ▸ place de parking
pref (preferred) ▸ de préférence
prof (professional) ▸ salarié
p.w. (per week) ▸ par semaine
refs (references) ▸ références
rehabbed (rehabilitated) ▸ refait
sec. dep (security deposit) ▸ caution
semi-det hse (semi-detached house) ▸ maison jumelée
sitting rm (sitting room) ▸ salon
slps (sleeps) ▸ peut loger
sml kit (small kitchen) ▸ petite cuisine
sq. yds (square yards) ▸ appr. mètres carrés
tel (telephone) ▸ téléphone
unfurn (unfurnished) ▸ non meublé
w/ (with) ▸ avec

Property: Sales and lets

Immobilier

Ventes

VDS mais. F4, 3 ch., 100 m²
env., 2 sdb, cuis. équip., gar.,
terr. clos, Exclus. Anse
Immobilier 04 74 77 01 13

Urgt cède cse mutation F3 ds
cft, t. b. état, ch. c. gaz indiv., ds
rés. stand., prest. lux., px à
déb., libre imméd.
Tél.HR 04.72.88.63.29

Part. vd F2 + mezz. ds mais.
mitoyenne, c.c. indiv. fuel, gar.,
jard. privat., quart. calme,
120 000€ ferme, libre 1/7/01.
Tél. 01 45 27 33 11

100 km nrd Lyon, autoroute
Tournus, mais. bressanne,
à rénov., 6 p., 350 m²
habitables, dépendances,
pré attenant 3500 m² convient
pour chevaux, px 50 000€.
S'adres. P. LALOY,
not. à Paris 01 45 05 79 88

Sologne, belle propriété XVᵉ,
cachet, 50 ha, étgs, bois,
poss. chasse, dépend., mais.
gard., excel. ét., px intér.
Écrire Maisons de France,
18 bd du Roi, 78000
Versailles

Prox. plage, vds Sanary,
villa 3/4 pers., 1 ch. + mezz.,
kitch. équip., ll, lv, park.
et jard. privat. 310 000 euros
Écr. jrnl réf.01zx007

A saisir, Villars les Dombes,
except. terr. arb., hors
lotissement, constructible,
1000m², calme, prox. golf.
04.74.83.65.12.

Feyzin le Haut, près église,
suite incendie, à vdre, épave
mais. bourgeoise, 400 m² sur
6600 m² terr. av. arbres,
px 35000€,
T. 04.78.15.62.03

Locations

Centr. ville Annecy, loue mais.
bourg., 8 p., récept. 45 m2,
gar., cave, jard. 300 m2,
ch.c. fuel, quartier résid.,
2100€/mens. cc,
LARAGENCE 05 56 32 48 79

Part. à part. ag. s'abst., loue
F3, 2ch., sdb, ds immeuble
centre Villeurbanne, esp. verts,
cave, b. état, 380€ CC
04 78 92 13 22 p. 249 hor. bur.

Part. loue ch. meublée pour
étudiant, 18 m2 dans tb villa
quartier univ., calme, av. douche,
poss. cuis., prise tél. et TV,
entrée séparée, lib. 27 sept.,
loyer 275€ cc,
tél : 04 78 49 26 76

A LOUER Hte Loire, rég.
Chambon sur Lignon, mais.
indiv. isolée, terr. expo. Sud,
tt conft, 7 pers maxi., juin juillet
septembre, mois, sem., quinz.
TEL HR 04 71 59 29 33

ag. s'abst. (agences s'abstenir) ► no agencies
à rénov. (à rénover) ► needs modernization
à vdre (à vendre) ► for sale
av. (avec) ► with
b. état bon état ► good condition
cc, CC (charges comprises) ► service charges included
c.c. (chauffage central) ► central heating (Also *charges comprises.* See Locations.)
ch. (chambre) ► bedroom
ch. c. (chauffage central) ► central heating
centr. ville (centre ville) ► city centre
cse mutation (pour cause de mutation) ► because of job transfer
cuis. équip. (cuisine équipée) ► fully fitted kitchen
dépend. (dépendances) ► outbuildings
ds (dans) ► in
écr. jrnl (écrire au journal) ► write to the newspaper
env. (environ) ► about
esp. verts (espaces verts) ► open spaces
étgs (étangs) ► ponds
excel. ét. (excellent état) ► (in) excellent condition
except. (exceptionnel) ► exceptional
exclus. (exclusivité) ► sole agents
expo. sud (exposé au sud) ► south facing
F4 (appartement quatre pièces) ► 3-bedroom flat
gar. (garage) ► garage
ha (hectare) ► hectare
hor. bur. (horaires de bureau) ► office hours

HR (heures des repas) ► (at) meal times (12am–2pm; 7–9pm)
Hte Loire (département de la Haute Loire) ► the department of the Haute Loire
imméd. (immédiatement) ► (available) immediately
indiv. (individuel) ► individual
jard. (jardin) ► garden
jard. privat. (jardin privatif) ► own garden
kitch. équip. (kitchenette équipée) ► fully fitted kitchenette
ll (lave-linge) ► washing machine
lib. (libre) ► free from
lv (lave-vaisselle) ► dishwasher
m² (mètres carrés) ► square metres
mais. (maison) ► house
mais. bourg. (maison bourgeoise) ► substantial family house
mais. indiv. (maison individuelle) ► detached house
mais. gard. (maison de gardien) ► caretaker's house
maxi (maximum) ► maximum
mens. (mensuels) ► per month
mezz. (mezzanine) ► mezzanine floor
not. (notaire) ► notary lawyer
nrd (nord) ► north
p. (pièce) ► room
p. 249 (poste 249) ► extension 249
park. (parking) ► parking space
part. (particulier) ► private individual (i.e. not an agency)
part. à part (particulier à particulier) ► private let
pers. (personnes) ► people
poss. chasse (possibilité de chasser) ► hunting possible
poss. cuis. (possibilité de faire la

cuisine) ► cooking facilities
prest. lux. (prestations luxueuses) ► luxuriously appointed
prox. (à proximité de) ► close to
px à déb. (prix à débattre) ► price to be discussed
px intér. (prix intéressant) ► attractive (i.e. low) price
quart. (quartier) ► neighbourhood
quartier résid. (quartier résidentiel) ► residential area
quartier univ. (quartier universitaire) ► university area
quinz. (quinzaine) ► fortnight(ly)
récept. (réception) ► reception room, living room
réf. (référence) ► reference (number)
rég. (région) ► region
rés. (résidence) ► apartment complex
s'adres. (s'adresser à) ► contact
sdb (salle de bains) ► bathroom
sem. (semaine) ► week(ly)
stand. (de bon standing) ► desirable
tb (très beau/belle) ► delightful
t. b. état (très bon état) ► (in) excellent condition
terr. (terrain) ► garden or plot
terr. arb. (terrain arboré) ► wooded land
terr. clos (terrain clos) ► fenced plot
tt cft (tout confort) ► all mod cons
urgt (urgent) ► urgent(ly)
vds/vd (vends) ► for sale
XVᵉ (quinzième siècle) ► 15th century

Le courrier électronique et l'Internet

Le courrier électronique

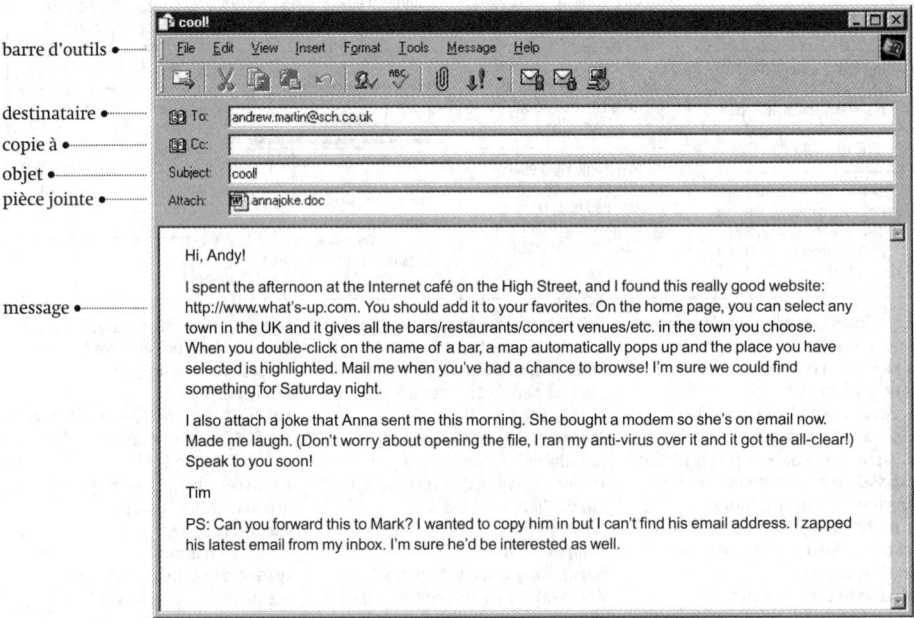

barre d'outils •

destinataire •

copie à •

objet •

pièce jointe •

message •

to be on email	être connecté
an email	un message électronique, un e-mail
an email address	une adresse électronique
an at sign	un arobase
an address book	un carnet d'adresses
a mailing list	une liste de diffusion
to send an email	envoyer un e-mail
to receive an email	recevoir un e-mail
to forward an email	faire suivre un message
to copy somebody in, to cc somebody	envoyer un message en copie à quelqu'un
c.c. (carbon copy)	copie
b.c.c. (blind carbon copy)	copie invisible
a file	un fichier
a signature file	un fichier signature
an emoticon, a smiley	un smiley/un émoticon
to attach a file	envoyer une annexe/ un attachement/une pièce jointe

to receive an attachment	recevoir une annexe/ un attachement/une pièce jointe
to open/run an attachment	ouvrir/lancer une annexe/ un attachement/une pièce jointe
to save a message on the desktop/hard disk	enregistrer un message sur le bureau/le disque dur
to delete a message	effacer/supprimer un message
to zap a message	effacer/supprimer un message
an inbox	une boîte de réception
an outbox	une boîte d'envoi
freemail	un service de courrier électronique gratuit
snail mail	le courrier postal
to send/get spam	envoyer/recevoir des messages non sollicités
spamming	le spamming
a mail bomb	une bombe (électronique)
a modem	un modem

Using email and the Internet

Email

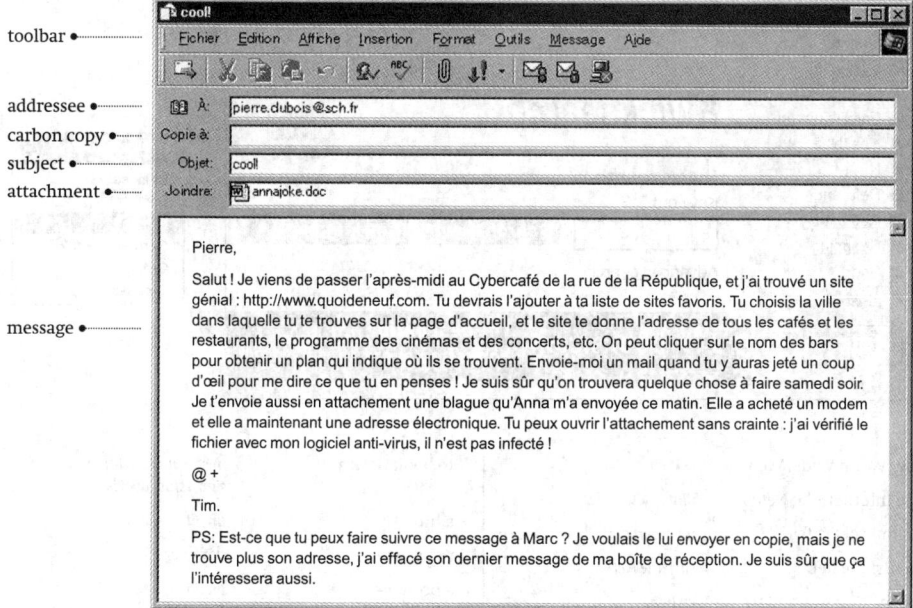

toolbar
addressee
carbon copy
subject
attachment

message

être connecté	to be on email
un message électronique, un e-mail	an email
une adresse électronique	an email address
un arobase	an at sign
un carnet d'adresses	an address book
une liste de diffusion	a mailing list
envoyer un e-mail	to send an email
recevoir un e-mail	to receive an email
faire suivre un message	to forward an email
envoyer un message en copie à quelqu'un	to copy somebody in, to cc somebody
copie	c.c. (carbon copy)
copie invisible	b.c.c. (blind carbon copy)
un fichier	a file
un fichier signature	a signature file
un smiley/un émoticon	an emoticon, a smiley
envoyer une annexe/ un attachement/ une pièce jointe	to attach a file

recevoir une annexe/ un attachement/ une pièce jointe	to receive an attachment
ouvrir/lancer une annexe/ un attachement/ une pièce jointe	to open/run an attachment
enregistrer un message sur le bureau/le disque dur	to save a message on the desktop/hard disk
effacer/supprimer un message	to delete a message
effacer/supprimer un message	to zap a message
une boîte de réception	an inbox
une boîte d'envoi	an outbox
un service de courrier gratuit électronique	freemail
le courrier postal	snail mail
envoyer/recevoir des messages non sollicités	to send/get spam
le spamming	spamming
une bombe (électronique)	a mail bomb
un modem	a modem

Internet

the (World Wide) Web	*le Web*	to bookmark a site	*mettre un site dans sa liste de signets/de favoris*
the Internet, the Net	*l'Internet, le Net*	a hit	*un hit*
an Internet café	*un cybercafé*	to browse	*naviguer*
to surf the net	*surfer le Net*	a browser	*un navigateur*
online	*en ligne*	a portal	*un portail*
to be online	*être en ligne*	a search engine	*un moteur de recherche*
an Internet Service Provider, ISP	*un fournisseur d'accès*	a web crawler	*un programme de recherche de sites (utilisé par les moteurs de recherche)*
an Online Service Provider, OSP	*un prestataire de services en ligne*	a keyword	*un mot-clef*
an access provider	*un fournisseur d'accès*	a quicksearch	*une recherche rapide*
FTP (File Transfer Protocol)	*FTP (protocole de transfert de fichiers)*	an advanced search	*une recherche avancée*
an intranet	*un réseau intranet*	exact match	*chercher l'expression exacte*
an extranet	*un réseau extranet*	match case	*respecter les majuscules/ minuscules*
a website	*un site web*	a dot-com	*une société Internet*
a web address	*une adresse Internet*	e-business	*le business électronique*
a URL (Uniform Resource Locator)	*une (adresse) URL (localisateur uniforme de ressources)*	e-commerce	*le commerce électronique*
a web page	*une page web*	a newsgroup	*un newsgroup/ un forum de discussion*
a webmaster	*un webmestre, un webmaster*	a chatgroup, a chatroom	*un forum de discussion/ un chat*
a home page	*une page d'accueil*	chat	*chat/tchatche*
home	*accueil*	a cookie	*un cookie*
a favorite	*un favori*	netiquette	*la nétiquette*
a bookmark	*un signet*		

Internet

le Web	the (World Wide) Web	mettre un site dans sa liste de signets/de favoris	to bookmark a site
l'Internet, le Net	the Internet, the Net		
un cybercafé	an Internet café	un hit	a hit
surfer le Net	to surf the net	naviguer	to browse
en ligne	online	un navigateur	a browser
être en ligne	to be online	un portail	a portal
un fournisseur d'accès	an Internet Service Provider, ISP	un moteur de recherche	a search engine
un prestataire de services en ligne	an Online Service Provider, OSP	un programme de recherche de sites (utilisé par les moteurs de recherche)	a web crawler
un fournisseur d'accès	an access provider	un mot-clef	a keyword
FTP (protocole de transfert de fichiers)	FTP (File Transfer Protocol)	une recherche rapide	a quicksearch
		une recherche avancée	an advanced search
un réseau intranet	an intranet	chercher l'expression exacte	exact match
un réseau extranet	an extranet	respecter les majuscules/ minuscules	match case
un site web	a website		
une adresse internet	a web address	une société internet	a dot-com
une (adresse) URL (localisateur uniforme de ressources)	a URL (Uniform Resource Locator)	le business électronique	e-business
		le commerce électronique	e-commerce
une page web	a web page	un newsgroup/ un forum de discussion	a newsgroup
un webmestre, un webmaster	a webmaster	un forum de discussion/ un chat	a chatgroup, a chatroom
une page d'accueil	a home page		
accueil	home	chat/tchatche	chat
un favori	a favorite	un cookie	a cookie
un signet	a bookmark	la nétiquette	netiquette

Internet

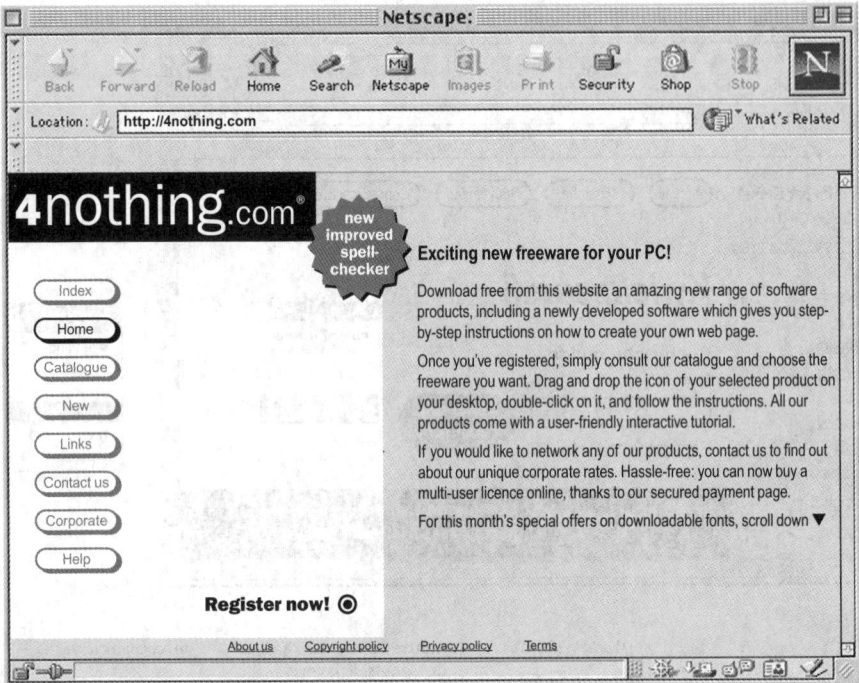

an icon	une icône
a desktop	un (dessus de) bureau
a dialog box	une boîte de dialogue
to highlight	sélectionner
to be highlighted	être en surbrillance
to click	cliquer
to double-click	double-cliquer/faire un double-clic
to drag and drop	glisser-déposer
to copy and paste	copier et coller
to scroll down/up	faire défiler vers le bas/le haut
a scrollbar	une barre de défilement
a drop-down menu	un menu déroulant
a pull-down menu	un menu déroulant
to pop up	apparaître à l'écran/s'afficher
a pop-up menu	un menu contextuel
a server	un serveur
a network	un réseau
to network	mettre en réseau
to download	télécharger

downloadable	téléchargeable
to upload	exporter/envoyer
uploadable	exportable
a font	une police de caractères
software	un/des logiciel(s)
freeware	un/des logiciel(s) gratuit(s)
shareware	un/des partagiciel(s)
a tutorial	un didacticiel
a multi-user licence	une licence multi-utilisateurs
a spellchecker	un correcteur d'orthographe
an anti-virus (software)	un logiciel anti-virus
a plug-in (application)	un module d'extension/un plug-in
a (hypertext) link	un lien (hypertexte)
a hot link	un lien
a secured page	une page sécurisée
an index	un index
a help page	une page d'aide
a help menu	un menu d'aide
user-friendly	convivial

Internet

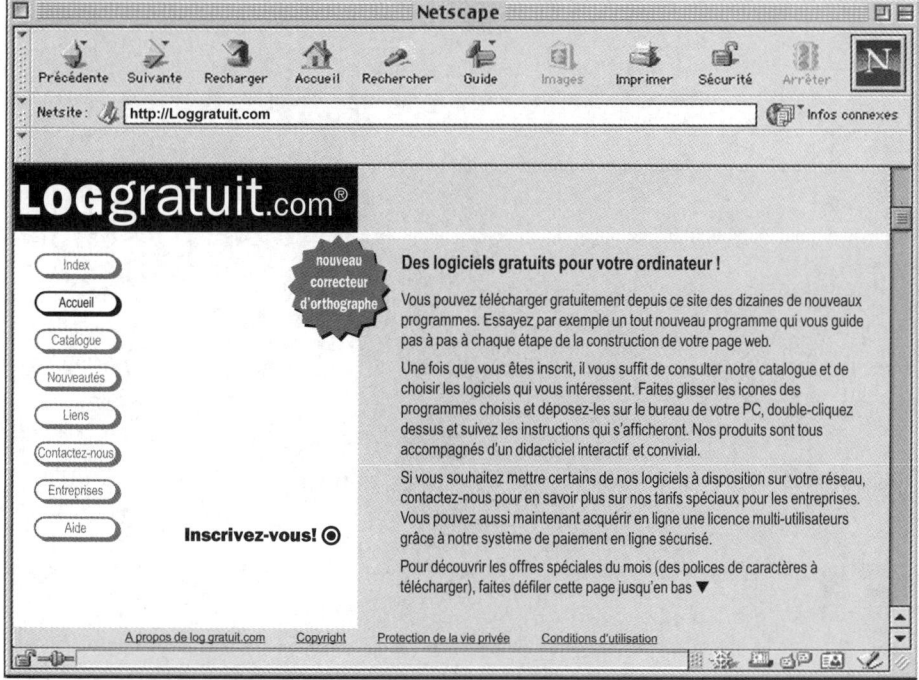

une icône	*an icon*	téléchargeable	*downloadable*
un (dessus de) bureau	*a desktop*	exporter/envoyer	*to upload*
une boîte de dialogue	*a dialog box*	exportable	*uploadable*
sélectionner	*to highlight*	une police de caractères	*a font*
être en surbrillance	*to be highlighted*	un/des logiciel(s)	*software*
cliquer	*to click*	un/des logiciel(s) gratuit(s)	*freeware*
double-cliquer/ faire un double-clic	*to double-click*	un/des partagiciel(s)	*shareware*
glisser/déposer	*to drag and drop*	un didacticiel	*a tutorial*
copier et coller	*to copy and paste*	une licence multi-utilisateurs	*a multi-user licence*
faire défiler vers le bas/le haut	*to scroll down/up*	un correcteur d'orthographe	*a spellchecker*
une barre de défilement	*a scrollbar*	un logiciel anti-virus	*an anti-virus (software)*
un menu déroulant	*a drop-down/pull-down menu*	un module d'extension/ un plug-in	*a plug-in (application)*
apparaître à l'écran/s'afficher	*to pop up*	un lien (hypertexte)	*a (hypertext) link*
un menu contextuel	*a pop-up menu*	un lien	*a hot link*
un serveur	*a server*	une page sécurisée	*a secured page*
un réseau	*a network*	un index	*an index*
mettre en réseau	*to network*	une page d'aide	*a help page*
télécharger	*to download*	un menu d'aide	*a help menu*
		convivial	*user-friendly*

a¹, A /eɪ/ n **1** (letter) a, A m; **the A to Z of cooking** la cuisine de A à Z; **2** Mus la m; **3** A (place) **to get from A to B** se rendre d'un endroit à un autre; **4** a (in house number) a; cf bis; **5** A GB (road) **the A7** la route A7

a² /ə, eɪ/ (avant voyelle ou 'h' muet **an** /æn, ən/) det un/une

AA n **1** GB Aut (abrév = **Automobile Association**) organisme m d'assistance pour les automobilistes; **2** abrév ▸ **Alcoholics Anonymous**

aback /ə'bæk/ adv **to be taken** ∼ être déconcerté

abacus /'æbəkəs/ n (pl **-cuses**) boulier m

abandon /ə'bændən/
A n abandon m; **with gay** ∼ avec une belle désinvolture
B vtr (leave) abandonner [person, hope]; (drop, stop) renoncer à [activity, attempt, claim]; arrêter [strike]

abandoned /ə'bændənd/ adj [person, animal] abandonné; [behaviour] dévergondé

abandonment /ə'bændənmənt/ n gen abandon m; (of strike) arrêt m

abashed /ə'bæʃt/ adj décontenancé

abate /ə'beɪt/
A vtr sout diminuer
B vi [flood, fever] baisser; [storm, rage] diminuer

abbess /'æbes/ n abbesse f

abbey /'æbɪ/ n abbaye f

abbot /'æbɪ/ n (père m) abbé m

abbreviate /ə'briːvɪeɪt/ vtr abréger (**to** en)

abbreviation /ə,briːvɪ'eɪʃn/ n (short form) abréviation f

ABC n **1** (alphabet) alphabet m; **2** (basics) **the** ∼ **of** le b.a. ba de; **3** US TV (abrév = **American Broadcasting Company**) chaîne de télévision américaine

abdicate /'æbdɪkeɪt/
A vtr renoncer à [right]; abdiquer [responsibility]
B vi abdiquer

abdication /,æbdɪ'keɪʃn/ n (royal) abdication f; (of responsibility) renonciation f (**of** à)

abdomen /'æbdəmən/ n abdomen m

abduct /əb'dʌkt/ vtr enlever

abduction /əb'dʌkʃn/ n enlèvement m

abductor /əb'dʌktə(r)/ n (kidnapper) ravisseur/-euse m/f

aberrant /ə'berənt/ adj [behaviour, nature] aberrant; [result] anormal

aberration /,æbə'reɪʃn/ n aberration f

abet /ə'bet/ vtr (p prés etc **-tt-**) ▸ **aid**

abeyance /ə'beɪəns/ n sout **in** ∼ [matter, situation] en suspens; **to hold sth in** ∼ garder qch vacant

abhor /əb'hɔː(r)/ vtr (p prés etc **-rr-**) abhorrer

abhorrence /əb'hɒrəns, US -'hɔːr-/ n horreur f

abhorrent /əb'hɒrənt, US -'hɔːr-/ adj odieux/-ieuse

abide /ə'baɪd/ (prét, pp **abode** ou ∼**d**)
A vtr **I can't** ∼ **sth/doing** je ne peux pas supporter qch/de faire
B vi **to** ∼ **by** respecter [rule, decision]

abiding /ə'baɪdɪŋ/ adj [image, memory] inoubliable

ability /ə'bɪlətɪ/
A n **1** (capability) capacité f (**to do** de faire); **to the best of one's** ∼ de son mieux; **2** (talent) talent m
B abilities npl (skills) compétences fpl; Sch (of pupils) aptitudes fpl

abject /'æbdʒekt/ adj [state] misérable; [failure] lamentable; [coward] abject; ∼ **poverty** misère f

---

a²

The determiner or indefinite article a or an is translated by un + masculine noun and by une + feminine noun:

a tree
= un arbre

a chair
= une chaise

There are, however, some cases where the article is not translated:

with professions and trades:

her mother is a teacher
= sa mère est professeur

with other nouns used in apposition:

he's a widower
= il est veuf

with *what a*:

what a pretty house!
= quelle jolie maison!

For translations of *a few, a little, a lot, a great many* see the entries **few, little, lot, many**.

When expressing prices in relation to weight, the definite article *le/la* is used in French:

ten francs a kilo
= dix francs le kilo

In other expressions where *a/an* means *per*, the French translation is usually *par*:

twice a day
= deux fois par jour

For translations of all other expressions using the indefinite article such as *to make a noise, to make a fortune, at a blow* etc. consult the appropriate noun entry (**noise, fortune, blow** etc.).

---

ablative /'æblətɪv/ n ablatif m

ablaze /ə'bleɪz/ adj en feu, en flammes; **to set sth** ∼ mettre le feu à qch; **the house was** ∼ la maison flambait; **his eyes were** ∼ **with anger** ses yeux brillaient de colère

able /'eɪbl/ adj

⚠ To be able to meaning can is usually translated by the verb *pouvoir*: I was not able to go = je ne pouvais pas y aller; I was not able to help him = je ne pouvais pas l'aider. The main exception to this occurs when *to be able to* implies the acquiring of a skill, when *savoir* is used: he's nine and he's still not able to read = il a neuf ans et il ne sait toujours pas lire. For more examples and other uses, see the entry below.

1 (having ability to) **to be** ∼ **to do** pouvoir faire; **she was** ∼ **to play the piano at the age of four** elle savait jouer du piano à quatre ans; **2** (skilled) [lawyer, teacher etc] compétent; (gifted) [child] doué

a

able: ~-bodied adj robuste, fort; **~ rating** n matelot m breveté; **~ seaman** n matelot m de deuxième classe

ably /'eɪblɪ/ adv [work, write] avec compétence

abnegation /ˌæbnɪ'geɪʃn/ n sout [1] (of rights, privileges) renoncement m (**of** à); [2] (also **self-~**) abnégation f

abnormal /æb'nɔːml/ adj anormal

abnormality /ˌæbnɔː'mælətɪ/ n (feature) anomalie f

abnormally /æb'nɔːməlɪ/ adv [high, difficult] anormalement; [behave] de façon anormale

aboard /ə'bɔːd/
A adv (on ship) à bord; **to go ~** monter à bord; **all ~!** tout le monde à bord!
B prep à bord de [plane]; dans [coach, train]

abode /ə'bəʊd/ n (home) sout demeure f; **of no fixed ~** sans domicile fixe

abolish /ə'bɒlɪʃ/ vtr abolir [law, right]; supprimer [service, allowance]

abolition /ˌæbə'lɪʃn/ n (of law, right) abolition f; (of service, allowance) suppression f

abominable /ə'bɒmɪnəbl/ adj abominable

abominably /ə'bɒmɪnəblɪ/ adv [behave] de manière odieuse; [perform] de manière abominable; [rude] abominablement

abominate /ə'bɒmɪneɪt, US -mən-/ vtr exécrer

aboriginal /ˌæbə'rɪdʒənl/
A n (native) indigène mf
B adj aborigène

Aborigine /ˌæbə'rɪdʒənɪ/ n aborigène mf (d'Australie)

abort /ə'bɔːt/
A vtr faire avorter [fœtus]; interrompre [launch, plan]; abandonner [computer program]
B vi [mother] avorter; fig [plan, launch] échouer

abortion /ə'bɔːʃn/
A n avortement m; **~ on demand** l'avortement libre; **to have an ~** se faire avorter
B noun modifier [law, debate] sur l'avortement

abortionist /ə'bɔːʃənɪst/ n avorteur/-euse m/f

abortive /ə'bɔːtɪv/ adj (épith) [attempt, project] avorté; [coup, raid] manqué

abound /ə'baʊnd/ vi abonder (**in, with** en)

about /ə'baʊt/

> ⚠ *About* is used after certain nouns, adjectives and verbs in English (*information about, a book about, curious about, worry about etc*). For translations, consult the appropriate entries (**information, book, curious, worry** etc).
> *about* often appears in British English as the second element of certain verb structures (*move about, jump about, lie about etc*). For translations, consult the relevant verb entries (**move, jump, lie** etc).

A adj [1] (expressing future intention) **to be ~ to do** être sur le point de faire; [2] (awake) **up and ~** debout
B adv [1] (approximately) environ, à peu près; **it's ~ the same as yesterday** c'est à peu près pareil qu'hier; **at ~ 6 pm** vers 18 h, à environ 18 h; [2] (almost) presque; **that seems ~ right** ça a l'air d'aller; **I've had just ~ enough of her!** j'en ai plus qu'assez d'elle!; [3] (in circulation) **there was no-one ~** il n'y avait personne; **there is a lot of flu ~** il y a beaucoup de grippes en ce moment; [4] (in the vicinity) **to be somewhere ~** être dans les parages
C prep [1] (concerning) **a book ~** un livre sur; **what's it ~?** (of book, film etc) ça parle de quoi?; **it's ~...** il s'agit de...; **it's ~ my son** c'est au sujet de mon fils; **~ your overdraft...** pour ce qui est de votre découvert...; [2] (in the nature of) **there's something weird ~ him** il a quelque chose de bizarre; **what I like ~ her is** ce que j'aime chez elle c'est; [3] (bound up with) **business is ~ profit** ce qui compte dans les affaires, ce sont les bénéfices; [4] (occupied with) **to know what one is ~** savoir ce qu'on fait; **while you're ~ it...** tant que tu y es..., par la même occasion...; **and be quick ~ it!** et fais vite!; [5] (around) **to wander ~ the streets** errer dans les rues; **strewn ~ the floor** éparpillés sur le sol; [6] (in invitations, suggestions) **how** ou **what ~ some tea?** et si on prenait un thé?; **how ~ it?** ça te dit?; [7] (when soliciting opinions) **what ~ the legal costs?** et les frais de justice?; **what ~ you?** et toi?; [8] sout (on) **hidden ~ one's person** [drugs, arms] caché sur soi

---

Idioms **it's ~ time (that)** il serait temps que (+ subj); **~ time too!** ce n'est pas trop tôt°!; **that's ~ it** (that's all) c'est tout

about-face, about-turn n GB fig volte-face f inv

above /ə'bʌv/
A pron **the ~** (people) les personnes susnommées
B prep [1] (vertically higher) au-dessus de; **the mountains ~ Monte Carlo** la montagne qui surplombe Monte-Carlo; **~ it** au-dessus; [2] (north of) au nord de; [3] (upstream of) en amont de; [4] (morally) **he's ~ such petty behaviour** il n'est pas capable d'un comportement aussi mesquin; **they're not ~ cheating** ils sont tout à fait capables de tricher; [5] (in preference to) par-dessus; **~ all others, ~ all else** par-dessus tout; [6] (superior in status, rank) au-dessus de; **he thinks he's ~ us** il se croit supérieur à nous; [7] (greater than) au-dessus de; **to rise ~** dépasser [limit, average]; [8] (beyond) au-dessus de tout soupçon; [9] (higher in pitch) au-dessus de; [10] (over) **~ the shouting** par-dessus les cris
C adj **the ~ items** les articles susmentionnés fml
D adv [1] (higher up) **the apartment ~** l'appartement du dessus; **the view from ~** la vue d'en haut; [2] (earlier in the text) ci-dessus; [3] (more) plus; **12 and ~** 12 ans et plus; [4] (in the sky) **to look up at the stars ~** lever les yeux vers les étoiles
E **above all** adv phr surtout

Idiom **to get ~ oneself** ne plus se sentir°

above: ~board adj régulier/-ière, correct; **~ground** adv au-dessus du sol, à la surface; **~-mentioned** adj susmentionné fml; **~-named** adj susnommé

abrasion /ə'breɪʒn/ n (on skin) écorchure f

abrasive /ə'breɪsɪv/ adj [person, manner, tone] mordant

abreast /ə'brest/ adv [1] (side by side) de front; **to be/come ~ of** être/venir à la hauteur de [vehicle, person]; [2] (in touch with) **to keep/keep sb ~ of** se tenir/tenir qn au courant de [developments]

abridge /ə'brɪdʒ/ vtr abréger

abridg(e)ment /ə'brɪdʒmənt/ n (version) version f abrégée

abroad /ə'brɔːd/ adv [1] [go, live] à l'étranger; **imported from ~** importé de l'étranger; [2] (in circulation) **there is a new spirit ~** il y a un nouvel état d'esprit général

abrupt /ə'brʌpt/ adj [1] (sudden) [end, change] brusque; **to come to an ~ end** se terminer brusquement; [2] (curt) [manner, person] brusque; [3] (steep) abrupt

abruptly /ə'brʌptlɪ/ adv [1] (suddenly) brusquement; [2] (curtly) avec brusquerie; [3] (steeply) à pic

ABS n, adj Aut (abrév = **anti-lock braking system**) ABS

abscess /'æbses/ n abcès m

abscond /əb'skɒnd/ vi s'enfuir (**from** de; **with** avec)

abseiling /'æbseɪlɪŋ/ n GB ▸ p. 881 GB descente f en rappel

absence /'æbsəns/ n (of person) absence f; (of thing) manque m; **in sb's ~** en l'absence de qn; **in the ~ of** (failing) faute de

Idiom **~ makes the heart grow fonder** Prov l'absence attise les grandes passions

absent
A /'æbsənt/ adj [1] (not there) [person, thing] absent (**from** de); [2] Mil **to be ~ without leave** être en absence illégale; [3] (preoccupied) [look] absent
B /əb'sent/ v refl sout **to ~ oneself** s'absenter

absentee /ˌæbsən'tiː/ n gen, Sch absent/-e m/f

absenteeism /ˌæbsən'tiːɪzəm/ n absentéisme m

absentee landlord n propriétaire mf absentéiste

absently /'æbsəntlɪ/ adv d'un air absent

absent: ~-minded adj distrait; **~-mindedly** adv [behave, speak] distraitement; [stare] d'un air absent; **~-mindedness** n distraction f

absolute /'æbsəluːt/
A n **the ~** l'absolu m
B adj [1] (complete) [monarch, minimum, majority] also Math, Philos absolu; **~ beginner** vrai débutant; [2] (emphatic) [chaos, idiot] véritable (before n); [3] Phys, Chem [humidity, scale] maximum; [zero] absolu; [4] Jur **decree ~** décret m irrévocable; [5] Ling [ablative] absolu

absolutely /'æbsəluːtlɪ/ adv (totally) gen absolument; [mad] complètement; **~ not!** pas du tout!

absolution /ˌæbsə'luːʃn/ n absolution f (**from** de)

absolve ▸ accommodation

absolve /əb'zɒlv/ *vtr* sout (clear) **to ~ sb of sth** décharger qn de qch

absorb /əb'zɔːb/ *vtr* lit, fig absorber

absorbed /əb'zɔːbd/ *adj* absorbé (**in** *ou* **by** par); **~ in one's work** plongé dans son travail; **to become ~ in sth** s'absorber dans qch

absorbency /əb'zɔːbənsɪ/ *n* pouvoir *m* absorbant

absorbent /əb'zɔːbənt/ *n*, *adj* absorbant (*m*)

absorbing /əb'zɔːbɪŋ/ *adj* passionnant

absorption /əb'zɔːpʃn/ *n* **1** lit absorption *f*; **2** fig (of costs) absorption *f*; **3** (in activity, book) concentration *f* (**in** sur)

abstain /əb'steɪn/ *vi* s'abstenir (**from** de)

abstemious /æb'stiːmɪəs/ *adj* [*person*] sobre; **you're being very ~!** tu es très raisonnable!

abstention /əb'stenʃn/ *n* Pol (from vote) abstention *f* (**from** de)

abstinence /'æbstɪnəns/ *n* abstinence *f* (**from** de)

abstract
A /'æbstrækt/ *n* **1** (theoretical) **in the ~** dans l'abstrait; **2** (summary) résumé *m*; **3** Fin, Jur extrait *m*; **4** Art œuvre *f* abstraite
B /'æbstrækt/ *adj* abstrait
C /əb'strækt/ *vtr* **1** (summarize) tirer (**from** de); **2** (theorize) extraire (**from** de)

abstracted /əb'stræktɪd/ *adj* [*gaze, expression*] distrait

abstraction /əb'strækʃn/ *n* abstraction *f*; **an air of ~** un air distrait

absurd /əb'sɜːd/
A *n* **the ~** Philos, Theat l'absurde *m*
B *adj* ridicule; **it is ~ that** il est absurde que (+ *subj*)

absurdity /əb'sɜːdətɪ/ *n* absurdité *f*

absurdly /əb'sɜːdlɪ/ *adv* [*expensive*] ridiculement

abundance /ə'bʌndəns/ *n* abondance *f* (**of** de); **in ~** en abondance, à profusion

abundant /ə'bʌndənt/ *adj* abondant

abundantly /ə'bʌndəntlɪ/ *adv* [*clear, obvious*] tout à fait

abuse
A /ə'bjuːs/ *n* **1** (maltreatment) mauvais traitement *m*; (sexual) sévices *mpl* (sexuels); **2** (misuse) abus *m*; **drug ~** usage *m* des stupéfiants; **alcohol ~** abus d'alcool; **3** (insults) injures *fpl*
B /ə'bjuːz/ *vtr* **1** (hurt) maltraiter; (sexually) abuser de [*woman*]; exercer des sévices sexuels sur [*child*]; **2** (misuse) abuser de [*position, power*]; **3** (insult) injurier

abusive /ə'bjuːsɪv/ *adj* [*person*] grossier/-ière; (insulting) [*words*] injurieux/-ieuse

abut /ə'bʌt/ *vi* (*p prés etc* **-tt-**) être contigu/-uë (**onto** à)

abysmal /ə'bɪzml/ *adj* épouvantable

abyss /ə'bɪs/ *n* lit, fig abîme *m*

a/c *n* (*abrév écrite* = **account**) compte *m*

academia /ˌækə'diːmɪə/ *n* l'université *f*

academic /ˌækə'demɪk/
A *n* universitaire *mf*
B *adj* **1** Univ [*career, post*] universitaire; [*year*] académique; **2** (scholarly) [*achievement, reputation*] intellectuel/-elle; **not very ~** [*person*] pas très doué pour les études; **3** (educational) [*book, publishing*] universitaire; **4** (theoretical) théorique; **that's ~** ça n'a aucun intérêt pratique; **5** Art [*painter*] académique

academician /əˌkædə'mɪʃn, US ˌækədə'mɪʃn/ *n* académicien/-ienne *m/f*

academy /ə'kædəmɪ/ *n* (place of learning) école *f*; (learned society) académie *f*

Academy Award *n* Cin Oscar *m*

ACAS /'eɪkæs/ *n* GB (*abrév* = **Advisory Conciliation and Arbitration Service**) comité qui traite des problèmes entre employeurs et employés

accede /ək'siːd/ *vi* sout accéder (**to** à); (to treaty) adhérer (**to** à); (to throne) monter (**to** sur)

accelerate /ək'seləreɪt/ *vi* **1** Aut accélérer; **to ~ away** partir en trombe (**from** de); **to ~ from 0–60 mph** monter de 0 à 100 km/h; **2** fig [*decline, growth*] s'accélérer

accelerated learning *n* apprentissage *m* accéléré

acceleration /əkˌselə'reɪʃn/ *n* accélération *f*

accelerator /ək'seləreɪtə(r)/ *n* accélérateur *m*

---

accent
A /'æksent, -sənt/ *n* accent *m*; **in** *ou* **with a French ~** avec l'accent français
B /æk'sent/ *vtr* Ling, Mus accentuer

accented /'æksentɪd, -sənt-/ *adj* [*speech*] avec un accent

accentuate /æk'sentʃʊeɪt/ *vtr* gen souligner; Mus accentuer

accept /ək'sept/
A *vtr* (receive, resign oneself to) accepter; (tolerate) admettre; (take on) assumer
B **accepted** *pp adj* admis; **in the ~ed sense of the word** dans le sens usuel du mot

acceptability /əkˌseptə'bɪlətɪ/ *n* admissibilité *f*

acceptable /ək'septəbl/ *adj* [*gift, money*] bienvenu; [*idea, behaviour, level*] acceptable

acceptance /ək'septəns/ *n* (of offer, invitation, bill, policy) acceptation *f*; (of plan, proposal) approbation *f* (**of** de)

access /'ækses/
A *n* **1** (means of entry) also Comput accès *m*; **wheelchair ~** accès pour les fauteuils roulants; **to gain ~ to sth** accéder à qch; **'No ~'** (on signs) 'accès interdit'; **2** (ability to obtain, use) accès *m* (**to** à); **open ~** libre accès; **3** Jur (right to visit) **to have ~ (to one's children)** avoir un droit de visite (auprès de ses enfants)
B *noun modifier* [*door, mode, point*] d'accès
C *vtr* accéder à [*database, information*]

accessible /ək'sesəbl/ *adj* (easy to reach, easy to understand) accessible (**to** à); (affordable) [*price*] abordable

accession /æk'seʃn/ *n* accession *f* (**to** à)

accessory /ək'sesərɪ/ *n* **1** accessoire *m*; (luxury item on car) extra *m*; **2** Jur complice *mf* (**to** de)

access: **~ provider** *n* Comput fournisseur *m* d'accès; **~ road** *n* (to building, site) route *f* d'accès; (to motorway) bretelle *f* d'accès; **~ time** *n* Comput temps *m* d'accès

accident /'æksɪdənt/
A *n* **1** (mishap) accident *m* (**with** avec); **by ~** accidentellement; **car/road ~** accident de voiture/de la route; **to have an ~** avoir un accident; **to meet with an ~** être victime d'un accident; **~ and emergency service** (in hospital) service des urgences; **2** (chance) hasard *m*; **by ~** par hasard; **it was more by ~ than design** c'était accidentel plutôt que délibéré
B *noun modifier* [*statistics*] se rapportant aux accidents; **~ victim** accidenté/-e *m/f*

accidental /ˌæksɪ'dentl/ *adj* [*death*] accidentel/-elle; [*meeting, mistake*] fortuit

accidentally /ˌæksɪ'dentəlɪ/ *adv* (by accident) accidentellement; (by chance) par hasard; **~ on purpose** iron malencontreusement iron

accident: **Accident and Emergency Unit** *n* (service *m* des) urgences *fpl*; **~-prone** *adj* sujet/-ette aux accidents

acclaim /ə'kleɪm/
A *n* (praise) louanges *fpl*; (cheering) acclamations *fpl*
B *vtr* **1** (praise) applaudir; **~ed by the critics** encensé par la critique; **2** (cheer) acclamer; fig **~ed as** acclamé comme; **3** (proclaim) **to ~ sb (as) sth** proclamer qn qch

acclimate /'æklɪmeɪt, ə'klaɪ-/ US = **acclimatize**

acclimation /ˌæklaɪ'meɪʃn/ US = **acclimatization**

acclimatization /əˌklaɪmətər'zeɪʃn, US -tɪ'z-/ *n* lit, fig acclimatation *f* (**to** à)

acclimatize /ə'klaɪmətaɪz/ *vtr* acclimater (**to** à); **to get** *ou* **become ~d** s'acclimater

accolade /'ækəleɪd, US -'leɪd/ *n* (from audience, in press) ovation *f*; (honour) honneur *m*; **the highest ~** la consécration suprême

accommodate /ə'kɒmədeɪt/ *vtr* **1** (put up) loger; **2** (hold) contenir; **3** (adapt to) s'adapter à [*idiosyncrasy, view*]; **4** (satisfy) satisfaire [*need*]; **to ~ sb with sth** accorder qch à qn [*loan, credit terms*]

accommodating /ə'kɒmədeɪtɪŋ/ *adj* accommodant

accommodation /əˌkɒmə'deɪʃn/ *n* (also **~s** US) (living quarters) logement *m*; **hotel/student ~** logement en hôtel/pour étudiants; **living ~** logement; **'~ to let'** GB 'location'; **office ~** bureaux *mpl*

accommodation: **~ bureau** GB, **~s bureau** US *n* agence *f* de logement; **~ officer** GB, **~s officer** US ▸ p. 1181 *n* responsable *mf* de l'hébergement

a

accompaniment /əˈkʌmpənɪmənt/ n accompagnement m; **as an ~ to sth** pour accompagner qch

accompanist /əˈkʌmpənɪst/ n accompagnateur/-trice m/f

accompany /əˈkʌmpəni/ vtr accompagner; **accompanied** accompagné (**by sb** par qn; **by sth** de qch; **on sth** Mus à qch)

accomplice /əˈkʌmplɪs, US əˈkɒm-/ n complice mf (**in, to** de)

accomplish /əˈkʌmplɪʃ, US əˈkɒm-/ vtr gen accomplir; réaliser [objective]

accomplished /əˈkʌmplɪʃt, US əˈkɒm-/ adj très compétent

accomplishment /əˈkʌmplɪʃmənt, US əˈkɒm-/ n ① (successful feat) réussite f; **that's quite an ~!** c'est remarquable!; ② (talent) talent m

accord /əˈkɔːd/
A n accord m; **of my own ~** de moi-même; **with one ~** d'un commun accord; **to reach an ~** se mettre d'accord
B vtr accorder (**sb sth** qch à qn)
C vi **to ~ with** concorder avec

accordance /əˈkɔːdəns/: **in accordance with** prep phr ① (in line with) [act] conformément à [rules, instructions]; [be] conforme à [law, agreement]; ② (depending on) selon

according /əˈkɔːdɪŋ/: **according to** prep phr ① (in line with) [act] selon [law, principles]; **~ to plan** comme prévu; ② (as described by or in) d'après [newspaper, person]

accordingly /əˈkɔːdɪŋli/ adv en conséquence

accordion /əˈkɔːdɪən/ ▸ **p. 1028** n accordéon m

accost /əˈkɒst/ vtr gen aborder; (for sexual purpose) accoster

account /əˈkaʊnt/
A n ① (in bank, post office) compte m (**at, with** à); **in my/his ~** sur mon/son compte; ② Comm (credit arrangement) compte m; **to charge sth to** ou **put sth on sb's ~** mettre qch sur le compte de qn; **on ~** (as part payment) d'acompte; **to settle an ~** (in shop) régler un compte; (in hotel) régler une note; ③ (in advertising) budget m (de publicité); ④ (bill) facture f; ⑤ (consideration) **to take sth into ~, to take ~ of sth** tenir compte de qch; ⑥ (description) compte-rendu m; (if contentious) version f; **by all ~s** manifestement; **by his own ~** tel qu'il le dit lui-même; ⑦ (impression) **to give a good ~ of oneself** faire bonne impression (**in** dans); ⑧ (indicating reason) **on ~ of sth** à cause de qch; **on this** ou **that ~** pour cette raison; **on no ~** sous aucun prétexte; **on my/his ~** (because of me/him) à cause de moi/lui; ⑨ (in matters concerning oneself) **she was worried on her own ~** elle s'inquiétait pour son (propre) sort; **to go into business on one's own ~** se mettre à son compte; ⑩ (importance) **it's of no ~ to them** peu leur importe
B accounts npl ① Fin (records) comptabilité f ¢, comptes mpl; ② (department) (service m) comptabilité f
C vtr sout **to ~ sb a genius** considérer qn comme un génie

⌖ (Phrasal verb)

■ **account for**: ▸ **~ for** [sth/sb] ① (explain) expliquer [events, fact, behaviour]; justifier [expense] (**to sb** auprès de qn); retrouver [missing people]; ② (represent) représenter [proportion, percentage]

accountability /əˌkaʊntəˈbɪləti/ n responsabilité f (**to** devant)

accountable /əˈkaʊntəbl/ adj responsable (**to** devant; **for** de)

accountancy /əˈkaʊntənsi/ n comptabilité f

accountant /əˈkaʊntənt/ ▸ **p. 1181** n comptable mf

account: **~ book** n livre m de comptes; **~ holder** n (with bank, credit company) titulaire mf

accounting /əˈkaʊntɪŋ/ n comptabilité f

accredit /əˈkredɪt/ vtr (appoint) accréditer; (approve) agréer

accreditation /əˌkredɪˈteɪʃn/ n accréditation f

accretion /əˈkriːʃn/ n accumulation f

accrue /əˈkruː/
A vi [advantages] revenir (**to** à); [power, money] s'accumuler
B accrued pp adj [interest] cumulé; [wealth] amassé

accumulate /əˈkjuːmjʊleɪt/
A vtr accumuler [possessions, debts]; amasser [wealth]; rassembler [evidence]
B vi s'accumuler
C accumulated pp adj [anger, tension] accumulé

accumulation /əˌkjuːmjʊˈleɪʃn/ n accumulation f; (of rubbish) entassement m

accumulator /əˈkjuːmjʊleɪtə(r)/ n Sport (bet) pari m avec report

accuracy /ˈækjərəsi/ n (of figures, watch) justesse f; (of map, aim) précision f; (of diagnosis, forecast) exactitude f

accurate /ˈækjərət/ adj [figures, watch, information] juste; [reports, map] précis; [diagnosis, forecast] exact; [assessment] correct

accurately /ˈækjərətli/ adv [calculate] exactement; [report] avec exactitude; [estimate, assess] précisément

accusation /ˌækjuːˈzeɪʃn/ n accusation f (**of** de; **against** contre; **that** selon laquelle); **to make an ~** porter une accusation

accusative /əˈkjuːzətɪv/ n Ling accusatif m

accuse /əˈkjuːz/ vtr accuser (**of** de; **of doing** d'avoir fait)

accused /əˈkjuːzd/ n **the ~** (one) l'accusé/-e m/f

accuser /əˈkjuːzə(r)/ n accusateur/-trice m/f

accusing /əˈkjuːzɪŋ/ adj accusateur/-trice

accusingly /əˈkjuːzɪŋli/ adv [say] d'un ton accusateur; [point] de façon accusatrice

accustom /əˈkʌstəm/ vtr **to ~ sb to sth/to doing** habituer qn à qch/à faire

accustomed /əˈkʌstəmd/ adj ① **to be ~ to sth/to doing** avoir l'habitude de qch/de faire; **to become ~ to sth/to doing** s'habituer à qch/à faire; ② [manner, route] habituel/-elle

ace /eɪs/
A n ① (in cards) as m; ② fig (trump) carte f maîtresse; ③ (in tennis) as m; ④ (expert) as m
B °adj (great) super°; **an ~ driver** un as du volant
⌖ (Idiom) **to hold all the ~s** avoir tout pouvoir

acerbic /əˈsɜːbɪk/ adj (all contexts) acerbe

acetate /ˈæsɪteɪt/ n acétate m

ache /eɪk/
A n (physical) douleur f (**in** à); **~s and pains** douleurs fpl
B vi ① (physically) [person] avoir mal; [limb, back] faire mal; **to ~ all over** avoir mal partout; ② littér (suffer emotionally) **to ~ with** mourir de [humiliation, despair]; ③ (yearn) brûler (**to do** de faire; **with** de)
⌖ (Idiom) **to laugh till one's sides ~** rire à se tenir les côtes

achieve /əˈtʃiːv/ vtr atteindre [aim]; atteindre à [perfection]; arriver à [consensus]; obtenir [success, result]; réaliser [ambition]; **to ~ nothing** ne rien accomplir

achievement /əˈtʃiːvmənt/ n ① (thing accomplished) réussite f (**in sth** dans le domaine de qch); ② (level of attainment) performance f; **academic ~** le succès universitaire; ③ (fulfilment) réalisation f (**de** of); **a sense of ~** un sentiment de satisfaction

achiever /əˈtʃiːvə(r)/ n (also **high ~**) personne f qui réussit

Achilles' heel /əˈkɪliːz hiːl/ n talon m d'Achille, point m faible

aching /ˈeɪkɪŋ/ adj [body, limbs] douloureux/-euse; **an ~ void** un grand vide

acid /ˈæsɪd/
A n ① Chem acide m; ② °(drug) acide° m
B adj ① (sour) acide; ② fig [tone] aigre; [remark] caustique

acid: **~ drop** n bonbon m acidulé; **~ green** n, adj vert (m) fluo° inv

acidic /əˈsɪdɪk/ adj acide

acidity /əˈsɪdəti/ n Chem acidité f

acid: **~ rain** n ¢ pluies fpl acides; **~ rock** n ≈ rock m psychédélique; **~ stomach** n Med acidité f gastrique; **~ test** n fig épreuve f de vérité (**of** de; **for** pour)

acknowledge /əkˈnɒlɪdʒ/
A vtr admettre [fact]; reconnaître [error, problem, authority]; répondre à [applause]; accuser réception de [letter]; citer [sources]; **to ~ sb** montrer qu'on a vu qn; **she didn't even ~ me** elle a fait semblant de ne pas me voir
B acknowledged pp adj [leader, champion, expert] incontesté; [writer, artist] renommé, reconnu

acknowledgement /əkˈnɒlɪdʒmənt/
A n ① (admission) reconnaissance f; (of error, guilt) aveu m; **in ~ of sth** en reconnaissance de qch; ② (confirmation of receipt) accusé m de réception; ③ (recognition of presence) signe m de reconnaissance

B **acknowledgements** *npl* (in book etc) remerciements *mpl*

acme /'ækmɪ/ *n* the ~ of le summum de

acne /'æknɪ/ ▸ p. 933 *n* acné *f*

acorn /'eɪkɔːn/ *n* gland *m*

acoustic /ə'kuːstɪk/ *adj* gen acoustique; [*tile, material*] insonorisant

acoustic guitar ▸ p. 1028 *n* guitare *f* sèche

acoustics /ə'kuːstɪks/ *n* the ~ are good l'acoustique est bonne

acquaint /ə'kweɪnt/ *vtr* to ~ sb with sth mettre qn au courant de qch; to be ~ed se connaître; to get *ou* become ~ed with sb faire la connaissance de qn; to get *ou* become ~ed with sth découvrir qch

acquaintance /ə'kweɪntəns/ *n* **1** (person) connaissance *f*; **2** (familiarity) connaissance *f* (with de); to improve on ~ gagner à être connu; to have a nodding ~ with sth avoir des notions de qch; **3** (friendly relationship) amitié *f*; to make sb's ~ faire la connaissance de qn

acquiesce /ˌækwɪ'es/ *vi* **1** (accept) accepter; **2** (collude) to ~ in sth donner son accord tacite à qch

acquiescence /ˌækwɪ'esns/ *n* **1** (agreement) accord *m*; **2** (collusion) connivence *f*

acquiescent /ˌækwɪ'esnt/ *adj* soumis

acquire /ə'kwaɪə(r)/ *vtr* acquérir [*expertise*]; obtenir [*information*]; faire l'acquisition de [*possessions*]; prendre [*meaning*]; acheter [*company*]; contracter [*habit*]; to ~ a taste for sth prendre goût à qch

acquired /ə'kwaɪəd/ *adj* [*characteristic*] acquis; it's an ~ taste c'est quelque chose qu'il faut apprendre à aimer

acquisition /ˌækwɪ'zɪʃn/ *n* (object, process) acquisition *f*; (company) achat *m*

acquisitive /ə'kwɪzətɪv/ *adj* [*society*] attaché aux biens de consommation; [*person*] rapace

acquit /ə'kwɪt/ (*p prés etc* **-tt-**)
A *vtr* Jur acquitter; to be ~ted être disculpé (of de)
B *v refl* to ~ oneself well in s'en tirer○ bien à [*interview*]

acquittal /ə'kwɪtl/ *n* Jur acquittement *m*

acre /'eɪkə(r)/ ▸ p. 1240
A *n* acre *f*, ≈ demi-hectare *m*
B **acres** *npl* ~s of des hectares *mpl* de [*woodland*]; ~s of room○ énormément d'espace

acreage /'eɪkərɪdʒ/ *n* superficie *f*

acrid /'ækrɪd/ *adj* âcre

acrimonious /ˌækrɪ'məʊnɪəs/ *adj* acrimonieux/-ieuse

acrimony /'ækrɪmənɪ, US -məʊnɪ/ *n* acrimonie *f*

acrobat /'ækrəbæt/ *n* acrobate *mf*

acrobatic /ˌækrə'bætɪk/ *adj* [*feat*] acrobatique; [*skill*] d'acrobate

acrobatics /ˌækrə'bætɪks/ *n* (+ *v pl*) acrobaties *fpl*

acronym /'ækrənɪm/ *n* acronyme *m*

across /ə'krɒs/

⚠ *Across* frequently occurs as the second element in certain verb combinations (*come across, run across, lean across* etc). For translations, look at the appropriate verb entry (**come, run, lean** etc).

A *prep* **1** (from one side to the other) to go *ou* travel ~ sth traverser qch; to travel ~ country traverser la campagne; (in car) prendre les petites routes; a journey ~ the desert un voyage à travers le désert; the bridge ~ the river le pont qui traverse la rivière; to be lying ~ the bed être couché en travers du lit; she leaned ~ the table elle s'est penchée au-dessus de la table; the scar ~ his face la cicatrice sur sa figure; **2** (to, on the other side of) de l'autre côté de; ~ the street/desk (from me) de l'autre côté de la rue/du bureau; to look ~ the lake regarder de l'autre côté du lac; **3** (all over, covering a wide range of) ~ the world partout dans le monde, à travers le monde; ~ the country dans tout le pays; scattered ~ the floor éparpillés sur le sol
B *adv* to be two miles ~ faire deux miles de large; to help sb ~ aider qn à traverser; to go ~ to sb aller vers qn; to look ~ at sb regarder vers qn
C **across from** *prep phr* en face de

across-the-board *adj, adv* à tous les niveaux

acrylic /ə'krɪlɪk/
A *n* acrylique *m*

B *noun modifier* [*garment*] en acrylique

act /ækt/
A *n* **1** (action, deed) acte *m*; an ~ of kindness un acte de bonté; **2** Jur, Pol (*also* **Act**) loi *f*; Act of Parliament/Congress loi votée par le Parlement/le Congrès; **3** Theat acte *m*; **4** (entertainment routine) numéro *m*; to put on an ~ fig jouer la comédie; to get in on the ~ s'y mettre
B *vtr* Theat jouer [*part, role*]
C *vi* **1** (take action) agir; we must ~ quickly il faut agir rapidement; to be ~ing for the best faire pour le mieux; to ~ for sb, to ~ on behalf of sb agir au nom de *or* pour le compte de qn; **2** (behave) agir, se comporter; **3** Theat jouer, faire du théâtre; fig (pretend) jouer la comédie, faire semblant; **4** (take effect) [*drug*] agir; **5** (serve) to ~ as [*person, object*] servir de

Ⓘ (Idioms) to be caught in the ~ être pris sur le fait *or* en flagrant délit; to get one's ~ together se prendre en main; it's a hard ~ to follow ça sera difficile à égaler

Ⓟ (Phrasal verbs)
■ **act out** jouer [*role, part*]; réaliser [*fantasy*]
■ **act up**○ (misbehave) se tenir mal; (malfunction) être détraqué

acting
A *n* Cin, Theat (performance) jeu *m*, interprétation *f*; (occupation) métier *m* d'acteur
B *adj* [*director etc*] intérimaire

action /'ækʃn/ *n* **1** Ⓒ gen action *f*; (to deal with situation) mesures *fpl*; to take ~ agir, prendre des mesures (against contre); drastic/immediate ~ des mesures draconiennes/immédiates; a man of ~ un homme d'action; to put a plan into ~ mettre un projet à exécution; to put sth out of ~ immobiliser qch; to be out of ~ [*machine*] être en panne; [*person*] être immobilisé; to be back in ~ être de retour; **2** (deed) acte *m*; ~s speak louder than words mieux vaut agir que parler; **3** (fighting) action *f*, combat *m*; to see (some) ~ combattre; to go into ~ aller au combat; killed in ~ tué au combat; **4** Cin, Theat action *f*; ~! moteur!; **5** ○(excitement) I don't want to miss out on the ~ je ne veux pas rater ce qui se passe; that's where the ~ is c'est là où ça bouge○; they want a piece of the ~ (want to be involved) ils ne veulent pas être en reste; (want some of the profits) ils veulent leur part du gâteau○; **6** Jur action *f*, procès *m*; to bring an ~ against sb intenter une action contre qn; **7** Tech (in machine, piano) mécanisme *m*

Ⓘ (Idiom) ~ stations! Mil, fig à vos postes!

action: ~ group *n* groupe *m* de pression; ~-packed *adj* [*film*] plein d'action; [*holiday*] bien rempli; ~ painting *n* peinture *f* gestuelle; ~ replay *n* GB TV répétition *f* d'une séquence

activate /'æktɪveɪt/ *vtr* faire démarrer [*machine, system*]; actionner [*switch*]; déclencher [*alarm*]; activer [*chemical*]

active /'æktɪv/ *adj* **1** [*person, life, member*] actif/-ive; [*campaign*] énergique; [*volcano*] en activité; to be ~ in doing s'employer (activement) à faire; to be ~ in doing s'employer (activement) à faire; to play an ~ role in sth jouer un rôle déterminant dans qch; to take an ~ interest in sth s'intéresser activement à qch; **2** Ling actif/-ive

active duty, active service *n* Mil service *m* actif

actively /'æktɪvlɪ/ *adv* activement; to be ~ considering doing penser sérieusement à faire

activist /'æktɪvɪst/ *n* activiste *mf*

activity /æk'tɪvətɪ/ *n* (all contexts) activité *f*

activity holiday *n* GB ≈ vacances *fpl* sportives

act of God *n* désastre *m* naturel

actor /'æktə(r)/ *n* acteur *m*, comédien *m*

actress /'æktrɪs/ *n* actrice *f*, comédienne *f*

actual /'æktʃʊəl/ *adj* **1** (real, exact) [*conditions, circumstances*] réel/réelle; I don't remember the ~ words je ne me rappelle pas les mots exacts; in ~ fact en fait; it has nothing to do with the ~ problem cela n'a rien à voir avec le problème lui-même; **2** (very) même (*after n*); this is the ~ room that Shakespeare worked in voici la pièce même où Shakespeare travaillait; **3** (as such) à proprement parler

actuality /ˌæktʃʊ'ælətɪ/ *n* réalité *f*

actually /'æktʃʊəlɪ/ *adv* **1** (contrary to expectation) en fait; their profits have ~ risen en fait, leurs bénéfices ont augmenté; **2** (in reality) vraiment; yes, it ~ happened! mais oui, c'est vraiment arrivé!; **3** (in fact) en fait; ~, I don't feel

a

like it à vrai dire je n'en ai pas envie; ⁴ (exactly) exactement; **what ~ happened?** qu'est-ce qui s'est passé exactement?; ⁵ (expressing indignation) carrément; **she ~ accused me of lying!** elle m'a carrément accusé de mentir!; ⁶ (expressing surprise) **she ~ thanked me** elle est allée jusqu'à me remercier

actuary /ˈæktʃʊərɪ, US -tʃʊrɪ/ ▸ p. 1181 *n* actuaire *mf*

acumen /ˈækjʊmən, əˈkjuːmən/ *n* sagacité *f*; **business ~** sens *m* des affaires

acupressure /ˈækjʊpreʃə(r)/ *n* digipuncture *f*

acupuncture /ˈækjʊpʌŋktʃə(r)/ *n* acupuncture *f*

acupuncturist /ˈækjʊpʌŋkʃərɪst/ ▸ p. 1181 *n* acupuncteur/-trice *m/f*

acute /əˈkjuːt/ *adj* ① (intense) [*anxiety*] vif/vive; [*boredom*] profond; **to cause sb ~ embarrassment** beaucoup embarrasser qn; ② Med [*condition, illness*] aigu/aiguë; ③ (grave) [*shortage, situation*] grave; ④ (keen) [*mind*] pénétrant

acute: **~ accent** *n* Ling accent *m* aigu; **~ angle** *n* angle *m* aigu

acutely /əˈkjuːtlɪ/ *adv* [*suffer*] vivement; [*embarrassed, sensitive*] excessivement

ad /æd/ *n* (*abrév* = **advertisement**) ① Journ (*also* **small ~**) petite annonce *f* (**for** pour); ② Radio, TV pub⁰ *f* (**for** pour)

AD (*abrév* = **Anno Domini**) ap J.-C

adage /ˈædɪdʒ/ *n* adage *m* (**that** selon lequel)

adamant /ˈædəmənt/ *adj* catégorique (**about** sur); **he is ~ that you are wrong** il maintient que tu as tort; **to remain ~** rester inébranlable

Adam's apple /ædəmz ˈæpl/ *n* pomme *f* d'Adam

adapt /əˈdæpt/
Ⓐ *vtr* adapter (**to** à; **for** pour; **from** de)
Ⓑ *vi* s'adapter (**to** à)

adaptability /ə,dæptəˈbɪlətɪ/ *n* (ability to change) adaptabilité *f* (**to** à)

adaptable /əˈdæptəbl/ *adj* [*person, organization*] souple

adapter, **adaptor** /əˈdæptə(r)/ *n* Elec adaptateur *m*

add /æd/ *vtr* ① gen ajouter, rajouter (**onto**, **to** à); **to ~ that...** ajouter que...; ② Math (*also* **~ together**) additionner; **to ~ sth to** ajouter qch à [*figure, total*]

⟨Phrasal verbs⟩
  ■ **add on**: ▸ **~ [sth] on**, **~ on [sth]** ajouter
  ■ **add up**: ▸ **~ up** [*facts, figures*] s'accorder; **it doesn't ~ up** fig cela ne tient pas debout⁰; **it all ~s up!** (makes sense) je comprends tout maintenant!; **to ~ up to** [*total*] s'élever à [*number*]; ▸ **~ up [sth]**, **~ [sth] up** additionner [*cost, numbers*]

added /ˈædɪd/ *adj* supplémentaire; **~ to which...** ajoutez à cela que...

adder /ˈædə(r)/ *n* ① (snake) vipère *f*; ② Comput additionneur *m*

addict /ˈædɪkt/ *n* ① (drug-user) toxicomane *mf*; ② fig (of TV, coffee) accro⁰ *mf* (**of** de)

addicted /əˈdɪktɪd/ *adj* **to be ~** lit avoir une dépendance (**to** à); fig être accro⁰ (**to** de)

addiction /əˈdɪkʃn/ *n* lit (to alcohol, drugs) dépendance *f* (**to** à); fig (to chocolate) passion *f* (**to** pour)

addictive /əˈdɪktɪv/ *adj* ① lit [*drug, substance*] qui crée une dépendance; ② fig **to be ~** [*chocolate, power*] être comme une drogue

add-in /ˈædɪn/ *n* Comput logiciel *m* complémentaire

adding machine *n* machine *f* à calculer

addition /əˈdɪʃn/
Ⓐ *n* (to list, house) ajout *m*; (to team, range) adjonction *f*; Math addition *f*
Ⓑ **in addition** *adv phr* en plus

additional /əˈdɪʃənl/ *adj* supplémentaire

additionally /əˈdɪʃənəlɪ/ *adv* (moreover) en outre; (also) en plus

additive /ˈædɪtɪv/ *n* additif *m*

addled /ˈædld/ *adj* [*thinking*] confus

add-on /ˈædɒn/ *adj* supplémentaire

address /əˈdres, US ˈædres/
Ⓐ *n* ① (place of residence) adresse *f*; **to change (one's) ~** changer d'adresse; ② (speech) discours *m* (**to** à); ③ (as étiquette) **form of ~** (**for sb**) formule *f* pour s'adresser à qn
Ⓑ *vtr* ① mettre l'adresse sur [*parcel, letter*]; **to ~ sth to sb**

adresser qch à qn; to be wrongly ~ed avoir un libellé incorrect; ② (speak to) s'adresser à [*group*]; ③ (aim) adresser [*remark, complaint*] (**to** à); ④ (tackle) aborder [*question*]; s'occuper de [*problem*]

address book *n* carnet *m* d'adresses

addressee /ædreˈsiː/ *n* destinataire *mf*

addressing /əˈdresɪŋ, US ˈædresɪŋ/ *n* Comput adressage *m*

adenoids /ˈædɪnɔɪdz, US -dən-/ *npl* végétations *fpl* (adénoïdes)

adept /əˈdept/ *adj* [*cook, gardener*] expert

adequate /ˈædɪkwət/ *adj* (sufficient) suffisant (**for** pour; **to do** pour faire); (satisfactory) satisfaisant

adequately /ˈædɪkwətlɪ/ *adv* [*prepared, equipped*] suffisamment; [*describe*] convenablement

ADHD *n* (*abrév* = **attention deficit hyperactivity disorder**) THADA *m*, trouble *m* d'hyperactivité avec déficit de l'attention

adhere /ədˈhɪə(r)/ *vi* lit adhérer (**to** à); **to ~ to** fig adhérer à [*belief*]; observer [*policy, plan, standard*]

adherence /ədˈhɪərəns/ *n* (to belief) adhésion *f* (**to** à); (to plan, policy) observation *f* (**to** de)

adherent /ədˈhɪərənt/ *n* (of cult) disciple *mf*; (of doctrine) adhérent/-e *m/f*; (of policy) tenant/-e *m/f*

adhesion /ədˈhiːʒn/ *n* adhérence *f*

adhesive /ədˈhiːsɪv/
Ⓐ *n* colle *f*, adhésif *m*
Ⓑ *adj* gen collant; **~ tape** papier *m* collant, Scotch® *m*; **self-~** auto-collant

ad hoc /,æd ˈhɒk/ *adj* [*arrangement*] improvisé; [*alliance*] temporaire; [*committee, legislation*] ad hoc *inv* (*after n*); **on an ~ basis** au coup par coup

adieu† /əˈdjuː, US əˈduː/ *n* (*pl* **~s** *ou* **~x**) adieu *m*; **to bid sb ~** faire ses adieux à qn

ad infinitum /,æd ,ɪnfɪˈnaɪtəm/ *adv* [*continue*] à n'en plus finir

adjacent /əˈdʒeɪsnt/ *adj* ① (touching) contigu-uë; **~ to sth** attenant à qch; ② (nearby) voisin (**to** de)

adjective /ˈædʒɪktɪv/ *n* adjectif *m*

adjoin /əˈdʒɔɪn/
Ⓐ *vtr* [*room*] être contigu-uë à; [*building, land*] être attenant à
Ⓑ **adjoining** *pres p adj* [*building, land*] attenant; [*room*] voisin

adjourn /əˈdʒɜːn/
Ⓐ *vtr* ajourner [*trial*] (**for** pour; **until** à); **the session was ~ed** la séance a été levée
Ⓑ *vi* ① (suspend proceedings) s'arrêter (**for** pour); **Parliament ~ed** (for break) la Chambre a interrompu les débats; (at end of debate) la Chambre a levé la séance; ② (retire) passer (**to** à)

adjournment /əˈdʒɜːnmənt/ *n* (of trial) ajournement *m*; (of session) suspension *f*

adjudge /əˈdʒʌdʒ/ *vtr* Jur ① (decree) déclarer (**that** que); ② (award) adjuger [*costs*]; allouer, accorder [*damages*]

adjudicate /əˈdʒuːdɪkeɪt/ *vtr* juger [*contest*]; examiner [*case, claim*]

adjudication /ə,dʒuːdɪˈkeɪʃn/ *n* ① (of contest) jugement *m*; ② Jur décision *f*; **under ~** en train d'être examiné

adjudicator /əˈdʒuːdɪkeɪtə(r)/ *n* juge *m*

adjunct /ˈædʒʌŋkt/ *n* ① (addition) annexe *f* (**of**, **to** de); ② (person) subalterne *mf* (**of**, **to** de)

adjust /əˈdʒʌst/
Ⓐ *vtr* régler [*level, position, speed*]; ajuster [*price, rate*]; rajuster [*clothing*]; modifier [*figures*]; **to ~ [sth] upwards/downwards** revoir [qch] à la hausse/baisse [*salary, sum*]
Ⓑ *vi* [*person*] s'adapter (**to** à); [*seat*] être réglable
Ⓒ **-adjusted** *combining form* **well-~ed** [*person*] équilibré

adjustable /əˈdʒʌstəbl/ *adj* gen [*appliance, position, seat*] réglable; [*rate*] ajustable

adjustable spanner, **adjustable wrench** *n* clé *f* à molette

adjustment /əˈdʒʌstmənt/ *n* (of rates, charges) rajustement *m* (**of** de); (of control, machine) réglage *m* (**of** de); (mental, physical) adaptation *f* (**to** à); **to make the ~ to** s'adapter à [*lifestyle*]

adjutant /ˈædʒʊtənt/ ▸ p. 1123 *n* Mil officier *m* adjoint

ad-lib /,æd ˈlɪb/
Ⓐ *n* (on stage) improvisation *f*; (witticism) bon mot *m*

B adj [comment] improvisé

C adv [speak] en improvisant

D vtr, vi (p prés etc **-bb-**) improviser

adman○ /'ædmæn/ n publicitaire m

admin○ /'ædmɪn/ GB n administration f

administer /əd'mɪnɪstə(r)/ vtr ① (also **administrate**) (manage) gérer [company, affairs, estate]; gouverner [territory]; ② (dispense) administrer [punishment]; exercer [justice]

administration /əd,mɪnɪ'streɪʃn/ n (of hospital, school, territory) administration f; (of justice) administration f; (paperwork) travail m administratif; **the ~** US le gouvernement

administration: **~ building**, **~ block** GB n bâtiment m administratif; **~ costs** n frais mpl de gestion

administrative /əd'mɪnɪstrətɪv, US -streɪtɪv/ adj administratif/-ive

administrator /əd'mɪnɪstreɪtə(r)/ ▸ p. 1181 n ① Comm administrateur/-trice m/f (**for, of** de); **sales ~** directeur/-trice m/f des ventes; ② (of hospital, school, theatre) administrateur m

admirable /'ædmərəbl/ adj admirable

admiral /'ædmərəl/ ▸ p. 1123 n Mil, Naut amiral m; **fleet ~** US, **~ of the fleet** GB amiral/

admiralty /'ædmərəltɪ/ n ① Mil (rank of admiral) amirauté f; ② GB Hist ≈ ministère m de la Marine

admiration /,ædmə'reɪʃn/ n admiration f (**for** pour); **to look at sb/sth with** ou **in ~** être en admiration devant qn/qch

admire /əd'maɪə(r)/ vtr admirer; **to be ~d by sb** être admiré de qn

admirer /əd'maɪərə(r)/ n ① admirateur/-trice m/f; ② (lover) soupirant m

admiring /əd'maɪərɪŋ/ adj admiratif/-ive

admiringly /əd'maɪərɪŋlɪ/ adv [look, say] avec admiration

admissible /əd'mɪsəbl/ adj recevable

admission /əd'mɪʃn/

A n ① (entry) entrée f, admission f (**to** dans); **'no ~'** 'entrée interdite'; ② (fee) (droit m d')entrée f; ③ (confession) aveu m

B **admissions** npl ① Univ inscriptions fpl; ② Med admissions fpl

admission: **~s office** n Univ service m d'inscriptions; **~s officer** ▸ p. 1181 n Univ agent m chargé des inscriptions

admit /əd'mɪt/ vtr (p prés etc **-tt-**) ① (accept) reconnaître, admettre [mistake, fact]; **to ~ that** reconnaître que; **to ~ to** reconnaître [error, mistake, fact]; **it is annoying, I** (**must** ou **have to**) **~** c'est embêtant, je dois l'avouer; **to ~ defeat** s'avouer vaincu; ② (confess) avouer [crime]; reconnaître [guilt]; ③ laisser entrer [person] (**into** dans); **'dogs not ~ted'** 'entrée interdite aux chiens'; **to be ~ted to hospital** être hospitalisé; ④ [club] admettre [person] (**to** à)

admittance /əd'mɪtns/ n accès m, entrée f; **'no ~'** 'accès interdit au public'

admittedly /əd'mɪtɪdlɪ/ adv il est vrai, il faut en convenir

admonish /əd'mɒnɪʃ/ vtr sout admonester fml

admonition /,ædmə'nɪʃn/ n sout (reprimand) admonition f fml; (warning) avertissement m

ad nauseam /,æd 'nɔːzɪæm/ adv [discuss, repeat] à n'en plus finir

ado /ə'duː/ n **without more** ou **further ~** sans plus de cérémonie f

(Idiom) **much ~ about nothing** beaucoup de bruit pour rien

adolescent /,ædə'lesnt/

A n adolescent/-e m/f

B adj ① (teenage) [crisis] d'adolescent; [problem] des adolescents; [years] de l'adolescence; ② pej puéril

adopt /ə'dɒpt/ vtr adopter [child, bill, attitude]; prendre [tone, identity]; choisir [candidate]

adopted /ə'dɒptɪd/ adj [child] adopté; [son, daughter] adoptif/-ive

adoption /ə'dɒpʃn/

A n (of child, bill, identity) adoption f

B noun modifier [papers, process] d'adoption

adoption agency n: service officiel chargé des questions d'adoption

adorable /ə'dɔːrəbl/ adj adorable

adoration /,ædə'reɪʃn/ n adoration f

adore /ə'dɔː(r)/ vtr adorer (**to do, doing** faire)

adoring /ə'dɔːrɪŋ/ adj [husband] épris; [fan] passionné

adoringly /ə'dɔːrɪŋlɪ/ adv avec adoration

adorn /ə'dɔːn/ littér vtr orner [building, room, walls] (**with** de); parer [body, hair] (**with** de)

adrenalin(e) /ə'drenəlɪn/ n adrénaline f

Adriatic (sea) /,eɪdrɪ'ætɪk/ ▸ p. 1049 pr n **the ~** la mer f Adriatique, l'Adriatique f

adrift /ə'drɪft/ adj, adv ① [person, boat] à la dérive; ② **to go ~** [plan] aller à vau-l'eau; ③ (loose) **to come ~** se détacher (**of, from** de)

adroit /ə'drɔɪt/ adj habile (**in, at** à; **in** ou **at doing** à faire)

adroitly /ə'drɔɪtlɪ/ adv habilement

ADSL n (abrév = **asymetrical digital subscriber line**) ADSL m

adspeak /'ædspiːk/ n jargon m publicitaire

adulation /,ædjʊ'leɪʃn, US ,ædʒʊ-/ n sout adulation f (**of** de); **in ~** avec adulation

adult /'ædʌlt/

A n adulte mf; **'~s only'** 'interdit aux moins de 18 ans'

B adj ① adulte; [life] d'adulte; ② euph [film, magazine] pour adultes

Adult Education n GB enseignement m pour adultes

adulterate /ə'dʌltəreɪt/ vtr frelater [wine]

adulterous /ə'dʌltərəs/ adj adultère

adultery /ə'dʌltərɪ/ n adultère m (**with** avec)

adulthood /'ædʌlthʊd/ n âge m adulte

adult literacy n GB **~ classes** cours m d'alphabétisation pour adultes

advance /əd'vɑːns, US -'væns/

A n ① (forward movement) avance f; fig (of civilization, in science) progrès m; ② (sum of money) avance f, acompte m (**on** sur); ③ (increase) **any ~ on £100?** (at auction etc) cent livres, qui dit mieux?

B **advances** npl (sexual) avances fpl; (other contexts) démarches fpl; **to make ~s to sb** (sexually) faire des avances à qn

C **in advance** adv phr à l'avance; **a month in ~** un mois à l'avance; **here's £30 in ~** voici 30 livres d'avance or d'acompte

D **in advance of** adv phr avant [person]

E vtr faire avancer [tape, clock]; avancer [sum of money, theory, troops]; faire avancer [career]; servir [cause, interests]

F vi ① (move forward) [person] avancer, s'avancer (**on, towards** vers); Mil [army] avancer (**on** sur); ② (progress) [civilization, knowledge] progresser, faire des progrès; **to ~ in one's career** progresser dans sa carrière

advance: **~ booking** n réservation f (faite à l'avance); **~ booking office** n service m des réservations

advanced /əd'vɑːnst, US -'vænst/ adj [course, class] supérieur; [student, stage] avancé; [level] élevé; [equipment, technology] de pointe, perfectionné; [research] poussé

advanced: **~ gas-cooled reactor, AGR** n réacteur m à gaz avancé or poussé, AGR m; **Advanced Level** n GB Sch = **A-level**

advancement /əd'vɑːnsmənt, US -'væns-/ n (of cause, minority) promotion f; (of science, person) avancement m

advance: **~ party** n Mil équipe f d'avant-garde; **~ payment** n Comm avance f; **~ warning** n préavis m

advantage /əd'vɑːntɪdʒ, US -'vænt-/ n ① avantage m; **there is an ~ in doing** il y a avantage à faire; **there is no ~ in doing** il n'est pas intéressant de faire; ② (asset) atout m; **their big ~ is to have...** leur grand atout, c'est d'avoir...; **'computing experience an ~'** (in job ad) 'une expérience en informatique serait un atout'; ③ (profit) **it is to his ~ to do** il est dans son intérêt de faire; **to turn a situation to one's ~** transformer une situation à son avantage; ④ (best effect) **to show sth to (best) ~** montrer qch sous un jour avantageux; ⑤ **to take ~ of** utiliser, profiter de [situation, offer]; (unfairly) exploiter [person]; ⑥ (in tennis) avantage m; ⑦ Sport **France's three-point ~** les trois points d'avance de la France

advantageous /,ædvən'teɪdʒəs/ adj avantageux/-euse; **it would be ~** ce serait une bonne chose

advent /'ædvent/ n gen apparition f (**of** de); **Advent** Relig l'Avent m

a

adventure /əd'ventʃə(r)/
A n aventure f
B noun modifier [story, film] d'aventures

adventure playground n GB aire f de jeux (aménagée)

adventurer /əd'ventʃərə(r)/ n **1** (daring person) aventurier/-ière m/f; **2** péj (schemer) aventurier m

adventuress /əd'ventʃərɪs/ n (pl **~es**) aventurière f

adventurous /əd'ventʃərəs/ adj [person, life] aventureux/-euse; **she doesn't have very ~ tastes** elle est très traditionnelle dans ses goûts

adverb /'ædvɜːb/ n adverbe m

adversary /'ædvəsərɪ, US -serɪ/ n adversaire mf

adverse /'ædvɜːs/ adj [reaction, conditions, publicity] défavorable; [effect, consequences] négatif/-ive

adversity /əd'vɜːsətɪ/ n adversité f

advert○ /'ædvɜːt/ n GB (in newspaper) annonce f; (in small ads) petite annonce f; (on TV) pub○ f, spot m publicitaire

advertise /'ædvətaɪz/
A vtr **1** (for publicity) faire de la publicité pour [product, service]; annoncer [price, rate]; **2** (for sale) mettre or passer une annonce pour [car, house]; **3** mettre or passer une annonce pour [job, vacancy]; **4** (make known) signaler [presence]; afficher [weakness]; **I wouldn't ~ the fact** à votre place, je n'en ferais pas état
B vi **1** (for sales, publicity) faire de la publicité; **2** (for staff) passer une annonce

advertisement /əd'vɜːtɪsmənt, US ˌædvər'taɪzmənt/ n **1** (for product, event) publicité f (**for** pour); **a good/bad ~ for** fig une bonne/mauvaise publicité pour; **2** (to sell house, get job etc) annonce f; (in small ads) petite annonce f

advertiser /'ædvətaɪzə(r)/ n (paying for ad) annonceur m

advertising /'ædvətaɪzɪŋ/ n (activity, advertisements) publicité f

advertising: **~ agency** n agence f de publicité; **~ agent** ▸ p. 1181 n publicitaire mf; **~ campaign** n campagne f publicitaire; **~ executive** ▸ p. 1181 n cadre m publicitaire; **~ industry** n publicité f; **~ man** ▸ p. 1181 n publicitaire m; **Advertising Standards Authority, ASA** n GB Admin, Comm bureau m de vérification de la publicité

advertorial /ˌædvɜː'tɔːrɪəl/ n publireportage m

advice /əd'vaɪs/ n **1** **₵** (informal) conseils mpl (**on** sur; **about** à propos de); **my ~ is to wait** je vous conseille d'attendre; **a word ou piece of ~** un conseil; **to do sth on sb's ~** suivre qch sur la recommandation de qn; **it was good ~** c'était un bon conseil; **if you want my ~** (opinion) si tu veux mon avis; **2** **₵** (professional) **to seek legal/medical ~** consulter un avocat/un médecin; **get expert ~** consultez un spécialiste; **3** Comm avis m; **~ of delivery** avis de réception

advisability /ədˌvaɪzə'bɪlətɪ/ n opportunité f (**of doing** de faire)

advisable /əd'vaɪzəbl/ adj **it is ~ to do** (speaking officially) il est recommandé de faire

advise /əd'vaɪz/
A vtr **1** (give advice to) conseiller, donner des conseils à (**about** sur); (give information to) renseigner (**about** sur); **to ~ sb against doing sth** déconseiller à qn de faire qch; **to ~ sb of** avertir qn contre [risk, danger]; **you are ~d to...** il est recommandé de...; **ill-~d** [course of action] malavisé; **2** (recommend) recommander [rest, course of action]; **3** sout (inform) aviser (**of** de)
B vi **to ~ on sth** (give advice) donner des conseils sur qch; (inform) donner des renseignements sur qch

advisedly /əd'vaɪzɪdlɪ/ adv [say] en toute connaissance de cause

adviser, advisor /əd'vaɪzə(r)/ n (in official capacity) conseiller/-ère m/f (**to** auprès de); (unofficially) collaborateur/-trice m/f

advisory /əd'vaɪzərɪ/ adj consultatif/-ive; **in an ~ capacity** à titre consultatif

advisory: **~ committee, ~ group** n comité m consultatif; **~ service** n service m d'aide et de conseil

advocacy /'ædvəkəsɪ/ n plaidoyer m (**of** en faveur de)

advocate
A /'ædvəkət/ n **1** ▸ p. 1181 Jur avocat/-e m/f; **2** (supporter) partisan m

B /'ædvəˌkeɪt/ vtr recommander (**doing** de faire)

Aegean /iː'dʒiːən/ ▸ p. 1049 pr n **the ~** la mer Égée

aegis /'iːdʒɪs/ n **under the ~ of** sous l'égide de

aeon, eon US /'iːən/ n **~s ago**○ fig il y a une éternité

aerate /'eəreɪt/ vtr aérer [soil]

aerial /'eərɪəl/ n antenne f

aerial: **~ camera** n appareil m de photo pour prises de vues aériennes; **~ warfare** n guerre f aérienne

aerie /'eərɪ/ US = eyrie

aerobatics /ˌeərə'bætɪks/ n (manoeuvres) (+ v pl) acrobaties fpl aériennes

aerobics /eə'rəʊbɪks/ ▸ p. 881
A n (+ v sg) aérobic m
B noun modifier [class, routine] d'aérobic

aerodynamics /ˌeərəʊdaɪ'næmɪks/ n **1** (science) (+ v sg) aérodynamique f; **2** (styling) (+ v sg) aérodynamisme m

aerogram(me) /'eərəgræm/ n aérogramme m

aeronautic(al) /ˌeərə'nɔːtɪk(l)/ adj [skill] aéronautique; [magazine, college] d'aéronautique

aeronautic: **~(al) engineer** ▸ p. 1181 n ingénieur m en aéronautique; **~(al) engineering** n aéronautique f

aeronautics /ˌeərə'nɔːtɪks/ n (+ v sg) aéronautique f

aeroplane /'eərəpleɪn/ n GB avion m

aerosol /'eərəsɒl, US -sɔːl/ n **1** (spray can) bombe f aérosol; **2** (system) aérosol m

aerospace /'eərəʊspeɪs/
A n (industry) industrie f aérospatiale
B noun modifier [engineer, company] de l'aérospatiale

aesthete /'iːsθiːt/, **esthete** /'esθiːt/ US = esthète mf

aesthetic, esthetic US /iːs'θetɪk/ adj **1** [sense, appeal] esthétique; **2** [design] harmonieux/-ieuse

aesthetically /iːs'θetɪklɪ/, **esthetically** /es'θetɪklɪ/ US adv [satisfying] esthétiquement; [restore] avec goût

aestheticism /iːs'θetɪsɪzəm/, **estheticism** /es'θetɪsɪzəm/ US n **1** (doctrine, quality) esthétisme m; **2** (taste) sens m du beau

aesthetics /iːs'θetɪks/, **esthetics** /es'θetɪks/ US n **1** (concept) (+ v sg) esthétique f; **2** (aspects of appearance) (+ v pl) esthétique f

afar /ə'fɑː(r)/ adv littér au loin, à distance; **from ~** de loin

affability /ˌæfə'bɪlətɪ/ n affabilité f

affable /'æfəbl/ adj affable

affair /ə'feə(r)/
A n **1** (event, incident, thing) affaire f; **the Haltrey ~** l'affaire Haltrey; **2** (matter) affaire f; **at first the conflict seemed a small ~** au début, le conflit ne paraissait pas grave; **state of ~s** situation f; **3** (relationship) liaison f (**with** avec); (casual) aventure f; **4** (concern) affaire f; **it's my ~** c'est mon affaire
B affairs npl **1** Pol, Journ affaires fpl; **foreign ~s** affaires étrangères; **~s of state** affaires d'état; **consumer ~s** la protection du consommateur; **2** (business) affaires fpl

affect /ə'fekt/ vtr **1** (have effect on) avoir une incidence sur [price, salary]; affecter, avoir des conséquences pour [career, future, environment]; affecter, toucher [region, population]; (influence) influer sur [decision, outcome]; **politics ~s all of us** la politique nous concerne tous; **countries ~ed by the famine** les pays touchés par la famine; **2** (emotionally) gen émouvoir; [news, discovery] affecter; **3** Med atteindre [person]; affecter [health, heart, lungs]; **4** sout (feign) feindre [surprise, ignorance]; prendre [accent]

affected /ə'fektɪd/ adj **1** (influenced) (by event, decision) (adversely) touché (**by** par); (concerned) concerné (**by** par); **2** (emotionally) ému (**by** par); (adversely) affecté (**by** par); **3** Med [part] infecté (**by** par); **4** péj (mannered) affecté; **5** péj (feigned) affecté

affection /ə'fekʃn/ n affection f (**for sb** pour qn)

affectionate /ə'fekʃənət/ adj [child, animal] affectueux/-euse; [memory] tendre; [picture, account] plein d'affection

affectionately /ə'fekʃənətlɪ/ adv affectueusement

affidavit /ˌæfɪ'deɪvɪt/ n déclaration f écrite sous serment

affiliate /ə'fɪlɪeɪt/
A vtr affilier (**to, with** à); **~d member** adhérent/-e m/f
B vi (combine) s'affilier (**with** à)

affiliation /əˌfɪlɪ'eɪʃn/ n (process, state) affiliation f; (link) attaches fpl

affinity /əˈfɪnətɪ/ n **1** (attraction) attirance f (**with, for** pour); **2** (resemblance) ressemblance f; **3** (relationship) rapport m (**between** entre)

affirm /əˈfɜːm/ vtr **1** (state positively) affirmer; **2** (confirm) confirmer [support, popularity]

affirmative /əˈfɜːmətɪv/
A n affirmatif m; **in the** ~ par l'affirmative
B adj [reply, nod, statement] affirmatif/-ive

affix
A /ˈæfɪks/ n Ling affixe m
B /əˈfɪks/ vtr sout coller [stamp]; apposer [signature]

afflict /əˈflɪkt/ vtr [poverty, disease] frapper; [grief] accabler; [illness] toucher; **to be ~ed by** souffrir de [illness]; être affligé de [stammer]

affliction /əˈflɪkʃn/ n (illness) affection f; (suffering) malheur m

affluence /ˈæflʊəns/ n **1** (wealthiness) richesse f; **2** (afflux) affluence f

affluent /ˈæflʊənt/ adj [person, area, society] riche

afford /əˈfɔːd/ vtr **1** (have money for) **to be able to** ~ **sth** avoir les moyens d'acheter qch; **if I can** ~ **it** si j'ai les moyens; **to be able to** ~ **to do sth** (as necessary expense) être en mesure de faire qch; (as chosen expense) pouvoir se permettre de faire qch; **how can he** ~ **to buy such expensive clothes?** comment est-ce qu'il fait pour acheter des vêtements aussi chers?; **2** (spare) **to be able to** ~ disposer de [space, time]; **3** (risk) **to be able to** ~ **sth/to do** se permettre qch/de faire; **he can ill** ~ **to wait** il ne peut guère se permettre d'attendre; **4** sout **to** ~ **sb sth** offrir qch à qn [protection]; fournir qch à qn [opportunity]; procurer qch à qn [satisfaction]

affordable /əˈfɔːdəbl/ adj [price] abordable

affranchise /əˈfræntʃaɪz/ vtr affranchir

affront /əˈfrʌnt/ n offense f

affronted /əˈfrʌntɪd/ adj blessé

Afghan /ˈæfgæn/ ▸ p. 1032, p. 969
A n **1** (also **Afghani**) (person) Afghan/-e m/f; **2** (also **Afghani**) (language) pachtou m; **3** (coat) afghan m
B adj (also **Afghani**) afghan

Afghan hound n lévrier m afghan

Afghanistan /æfˈgænɪstɑːn, -stæn/ ▸ p. 774 pr n Afghanistan m

aficionado /əˌfɪsjəˈnɑːdəʊ, əˌfɪʃj-/ n (pl ~**s**) passionné/-e m/f

afield /əˈfiːld/ **far afield** adv phr loin; **further** ~ plus loin; **from as far** ~ **as** d'aussi loin que

afire /əˈfaɪə(r)/ adj, adv littér en feu; **to be** ~ **with enthusiasm** déborder d'enthousiasme

aflame /əˈfleɪm/ adj, adv littér **to be** [cheek] être en feu; [sky] être embrasé; **to be** ~ **with desire** brûler de désir

AFL-CIO n US (abrév = **American Federation of Labor and Congress of Industrial Organizations**) AFL-CIO f

afloat /əˈfləʊt/ adj, adv **1** (in water) **to stay** ~ [person, object] rester à la surface (de l'eau); [boat] rester à flot; fig (financially) se maintenir à flot; **2** (at sea, on the water) sur l'eau; **a week** ~ une semaine sur l'eau

afoot /əˈfʊt/ adj (après n) **there is something** ~ il se prépare quelque chose; **there are changes** ~ il y a des changements dans l'air

afraid /əˈfreɪd/ adj **1** (frightened) **don't be** ~ n'aie pas peur; **to be** ~ avoir peur (**of** de; **to do, of doing** de faire); **2** (anxious) **to be** ~ craindre; **she was** ~ (**that) there would be an accident** elle craignait un accident; **I'm** ~ **it might rain** je crains qu'il (ne) pleuve; **3** (in expressions of regret) **I'm** ~ **I can't come** je suis désolé mais je ne peux pas venir; **'did they win?'—'I'm** ~ **not'** 'ont-ils gagné?'—'hélas, non'; **4** (as polite formula) **I'm** ~ **the house is in a mess** excusez le désordre dans la maison

afresh /əˈfreʃ/ adv à nouveau; **to start** ~ recommencer; (in life) repartir à zéro

Africa /ˈæfrɪkə/ pr n Afrique f; **to** ~ en Afrique

African /ˈæfrɪkən/
A n Africain/-e m/f
B adj africain; [elephant] d'Afrique

African(-)American /ˈæfrɪkənəˈmerɪkən/
A n Afro-américain/-e m/f
B adj afro-américain

ℹ️ African-American Expression employée aux États-Unis pour désigner les Noirs américains d'origine africaine. Cette dénomination est plus neutre que le mot *Black* qui fait explicitement référence à la couleur de la peau.

Afrikaans /ˌæfrɪˈkɑːns/ ▸ p. 969 n afrikaans m

Afrikaner /ˌæfrɪˈkɑːnə(r)/ ▸ p. 1032 n Afrikaner mf

Afro-American /ˌæfrəʊəˈmerɪkən/
A n Afro-américain/-e m/f
B adj afro-américain

Afro-Caribbean /ˌæfrəʊˌkærɪˈbiːən/ adj antillais

aft /ɑːft, US æft/ adv Naut, Aviat à l'arrière

after /ˈɑːftə(r), US ˈæftər/

⚠️ As both adverb and preposition, *after* is translated in most contexts by *après*: *after the meal* = après le repas; *H comes after G* = H vient après G; *day after day* = jour après jour; *just after 3 pm* = juste après 15 heures; *three weeks after* = trois semaines après.

When *after* is used as a conjunction it is translated by *après avoir (or être) + past participle* where the two verbs have the same subject: *after I finished my book, I cooked dinner* = après avoir fini mon livre j'ai préparé le dîner; *after he had consulted Bill or after consulting Bill, he decided to accept the offer* = après avoir consulté Bill, il a décidé d'accepter l'offre.

When the two verbs have different subjects the translation is *après que + indicative*: *I'll lend you the book after Fred has read it* = je te prêterai le livre après que Fred l'aura lu.

For more examples and particular usages see the entry below.

See also the usage note on time units ▸ p. 1267.

A adv **1** (following time or event) après; **soon** ou **not long** ~ peu après; **straight** ~ GB, **right** ~ US tout de suite après; **2** (following specific time) **the year** ~ l'année suivante or d'après; **the day** ~ le lendemain

B prep **1** (later in time than) après; **immediately/shortly** ~ **the strike** aussitôt/peu après la grève; ~ **that date** (in future) au-delà de cette date; (in past) après cette date; **it was** ~ **six o'clock** il était plus de six heures; ~ **that** après (cela); **the day** ~ **tomorrow** après-demain; **2** (given) après; ~ **all we did!** après tout ce que nous avons fait!; ~ **what she's been through?** malgré or après ce qu'elle a subi?; **3** (expressing contrast) après; **it's boring here** ~ **Paris** après Paris, on s'ennuie ici; **4** (behind) **to chase** ~ **sb/sth** courir après qn/qch; **to tidy up** ~ **sb** ranger derrière qn; **5** (following in sequence, rank) après; **the adjective comes** ~ **the noun** l'adjectif vient après le nom; ~ **you!** (letting someone pass ahead) après vous!; **6** (in the direction of) **to stare** ~ **sb** regarder qn s'éloigner; **'don't forget!' Mimi called** ~ **her** 'n'oublie pas!' lui a crié Mimi; **7** (in pursuit of) **that's the house they're** ~ c'est la maison qu'ils veulent acheter; **the police are** ~ **him** il est recherché par la police; **he'll come** ~ **me** il va essayer de me retrouver; **it's me he's** ~ (to settle score) c'est à moi qu'il en veut; **to be** ~ **sb** (sexually) s'intéresser à qn; **8** (beyond) après; **9** (stressing continuity) **generation** ~ **generation** génération après génération; **year** ~ **year** tous les ans; **it was one disaster** ~ **another** on a eu catastrophe sur catastrophe; **10** (about) **to ask** ~ **sb** demander des nouvelles de qn; **11** (in honour or memory of) **named** ~ [street, institution] portant le nom de; **we called her Kate** ~ **my mother** nous l'avons appelée Kate comme ma mère; **12** (in the manner of) **'** ~ **Millet'** 'd'après Millet'; **13** US (past) **it's twenty** ~ **eleven** il est onze heures vingt

C conj **1** (in sequence of events) après avoir or être (+ pp), après que (+ indic); ~ **we had left we realized that** après être partis nous nous sommes rendu compte que; **2** (once) ~ **you explained the situation they left** une fois que tu leur as expliqué la situation ils sont partis; **3** (in spite of the fact that) **why did he do that** ~ **we'd warned him?** pourquoi a-t-il fait ça alors que nous l'avions prévenu?

D afters○ npl GB dessert m

E after all adv, prep après tout

after: ~**birth** n placenta m; ~**care** n Med suivi m médical; ~**dinner speaker** n orateur/-trice m/f invité/-e; ~**effect** n Med contrecoup m; fig répercussion f; ~**life** n vie f après la mort

aftermath /'ɑːftəmæθ, -mɑːθ, US 'æf-/ n **¢** conséquences *fpl* (**of** de); **in the ~ of** à la suite de [*war, scandal, election*]

afternoon /ˌɑːftə'nuːn, US ˌæf-/ ▸ p. 745

A *n* après-midi *m or f inv*; **in the ~** (dans) l'après-midi; **at 2.30 in the ~** à 2 h 30 de l'après-midi; **in the early/late ~** en début/en fin d'après-midi; **earlier this ~** plus tôt dans l'après-midi; **the next ~** le lendemain après-midi; **the previous ~** l'après-midi d'avant

B ○*excl* (*also* **good ~**) bonjour!

afternoon tea *n* thé *m* (de cinq heures)

after: **~pains** *npl* tranchées *fpl* utérines; **~-shave** *n* après-rasage *m*; **~shock** *n* Geol réplique; fig retombées *fpl*; **~taste** *n* lit, fig arrière-goût *m*; **~-tax** *adj* [*profits, earnings*] après impôts

afterthought /'ɑːftəθɔːt, US 'æf-/ *n* pensée *f* après coup; **as an ~** après coup, en y repensant

afterwards /'ɑːftəwədz, US 'æf-/ GB, **afterward** /'ɑːftəwəd, US 'æf-/ US *adv* **1** (after) gen après; (in sequence of events) ensuite; **not long ~** peu après; **directly/straight ~** aussitôt/tout de suite après; **2** (later) plus tard; **it was only ~ that** ce n'est que plus tard que; **3** (subsequently) [*regret etc*] par la suite

again /ə'geɪn, ə'gen/

⚠ When used with a verb, *again* is often translated by adding the prefix *re* to the verb in French: *to start again* = recommencer; *to marry again* = se remarier; *I'd like to read that book again* = j'aimerais relire ce livre; *she never saw them again* = elle ne les a jamais revus. You can check *re*+ verbs by consulting the French side of the dictionary.
For other uses of *again* and for idiomatic expressions, see below.

adv encore; **sing it (once) ~!** chante-le encore (une fois)!; **yet ~ he refused** il a encore refusé; **when you are well ~** quand tu seras rétabli; **I'll never go there ~** je n'y retournerai jamais; **never ~!** jamais plus!; **not ~!** encore!; **~ and ~** à plusieurs reprises; **time and (time) ~** maintes fois; **~, you may think that** et là encore, vous pourriez penser que; **(and) then ~, he may not** mais il se peut aussi qu'il ne le fasse pas

against /ə'geɪnst, ə'genst/ *prep*

⚠ *Against* is translated by *contre* when it means *physically touching* or *in opposition to*: *against the wall* = contre le mur; *he's against independence* = il est contre l'indépendance; *the fight against inflation* = la lutte contre l'inflation.
If you have any doubts about how to translate a fixed phrase or expression beginning with *against* (*against the tide, against the clock, against the grain, against the odds etc*) you should consult the appropriate noun entry (**tide, grain, odds** etc).
against often appears in English with certain verbs (*turn against, compete against, discriminate against, stand out against etc*). For translations you should consult the appropriate verb entry (**turn, compete, discriminate, stand** etc).
against often appears in English after certain nouns and adjectives (*protection against, a law against, effective against etc*). For translations consult the appropriate noun or adjective entry (**protection, law, effective** etc). For particular usages see below.

1 (physically) contre; **~ the wall** contre le mur; **2** (objecting to) **I'm ~ it** je suis contre; **20 votes ~** 20 votes contre; **to be ~ the idea** s'opposer à l'idée; **to be ~ doing** être contre l'idée de faire; **3** (counter to) **to go** *ou* **be ~** aller à l'encontre de [*tradition, policy*]; [*conditions, decision*] ne pas être favorable à [*person*]; **4** (in opposition to) contre; **the fight ~ inflation** la lutte contre l'inflation; **5** (compared to) **the pound fell ~ the dollar** la livre a baissé par rapport au dollar; **the graph shows age ~ earnings** le graphique représente la courbe des salaires en fonction de l'âge; **6** (in contrast to) sur; **the blue looks pretty ~ the yellow** le bleu est joli sur le jaune; **~ a background of** sur un fond de; **~ the light** à contre-jour; **7** (in exchange for) contre, en échange de

Aga saga○ /'ɑːɡəˌsɑːɡə/ *n* GB *roman féminin populaire*

age /eɪdʒ/ ▸ p. 647

A *n* **1** (length of existence) âge *m*; **she's your ~** elle a ton âge; **to look one's ~** faire son âge; **to be of school ~** être en âge d'aller à l'école; **she's twice his ~** elle a le double de son âge; **they are of an ~** ils sont du même âge; **act** *ou* **be your ~!** ne fais pas l'enfant!; **men of retirement ~** les hommes en âge de la retraite; **to come of ~** atteindre la majorité; **to be under ~** Jur être mineur/-e; **~ of consent** Jur âge légal (for pour); **to feel one's ~** se sentir vieux/vieille; **2** (latter part of life) **with ~** avec l'âge; **3** (era) ère *f*, époque *f* (**of** de); **the video ~** l'ère de la vidéo; **in this day and ~** à notre époque; **4** ○(long time) **it's ~s since I've played golf** ça fait une éternité que je n'ai pas joué au golf; **for ~s** (long time) depuis une éternité; (for hours) depuis des heures; **it takes ~s** cela prend un temps fou

B *vtr* [*hairstyle, experiences etc*] vieillir [*person*]

C *vi* [*person*] vieillir; **to ~ well** bien vieillir

age bracket, age group *n* = **age range**

aged *adj* **1** /eɪdʒd/ (of an age) **~ between 20 and 25** âgé/-e de 20 à 25 ans; **a boy ~ 12** un garçon de 12 ans; **2** /'eɪdʒ-ɪd/ (old) [*person*] âgé

ageing /'eɪdʒɪŋ/

A *n* vieillissement *m*

B *adj* [*person, population*] vieillissant

ageism /'eɪdʒɪzəm/ *n* discrimination *f* en raison de l'âge

ageless /'eɪdʒlɪs/ *adj* **1** (of indeterminate age) sans âge; **2** (timeless) éternel/-elle

agency /'eɪdʒənsɪ/ *n* **1** (organization, office) agence *f*; **through an ~** par une agence; **aid ~** organisme *m* d'entraide; **2** GB Comm (representing firm) concessionnaire *m*; **3** (influence) intermédiaire *m*; **through an outside ~** par l'intermédiaire d'un tiers

agency: **~ fee** *n* commission *f* de gestion; **~ nurse** *n* infirmier/-ière *m/f* intérimaire

agenda /ə'dʒendə/ *n* **1** Admin ordre *m* du jour; **on the ~** à l'ordre du jour; **2** fig (list of priorities) programme *m*; **hidden ~** programme secret; **high on the political ~** prioritaire dans le monde politique

agent /'eɪdʒənt/ *n* **1** agent *m* (for sb de qn); **area/sole ~** agent régional/exclusif; **to go through an ~** passer par un intermédiaire; **to act as sb's ~** représenter qn; **2** Pol (spy) agent *m*; **3** (cause, means) also Chem agent *m*; **cleaning ~** agent nettoyant

(Idiom) **to be a free ~** être indépendant

age-old *adj* ancestral, très vieux/vieille

age range *n* tranche *f* d'âge

aggravate /'æɡrəveɪt/

A *vtr* (make worse) aggraver; (annoy) exaspérer

B aggravated *pp adj* Jur [*burglary, offence*] qualifié, aggravé

aggravating /'æɡrəveɪtɪŋ/ *adj* **1** Jur (worsening) aggravant; **2** ○(irritating) exaspérant

aggravation /ˌæɡrə'veɪʃn/ *n* **1** **¢** (annoyance) ennuis *mpl*; **2** (irritation) contrariété *f*; **3** (worsening) aggravation *f*

aggregate

A /'æɡrɪɡət/ *n* **1** gen, Econ ensemble *m*, total *m*; **in ~** dans l'ensemble; **2** Sport score *m* total; **on ~** GB au total

B /'æɡrɪɡət/ *adj* gen, Sport total; [*data*] d'ensemble

C /'æɡrɪɡeɪt/ *vtr* rassembler [*points*]; regrouper [*data*]

aggression /ə'ɡreʃn/ *n* gen agression *f*; (of person) agressivité *f*

aggressive /ə'ɡresɪv/ *adj* agressif/-ive

aggressor /ə'ɡresə(r)/ *n* agresseur *m*

aggrieved /ə'ɡriːvd/ *adj* **1** Jur lésé; **2** (resentful) mécontent (**at** de)

aggro○ /'æɡrəʊ/ *n* GB **1** (violence) violence *f*; **2** (hostility) hostilité *f*

aghast /ə'ɡɑːst, US ə'ɡæst/ *adj* horrifié (**at** par)

agile /'ædʒaɪl, US 'ædʒl/ *adj* agile

agility /ə'dʒɪlətɪ/ *n* (physical, mental) agilité *f*

agitate /'ædʒɪteɪt/

A *vtr* agiter [*liquid*]; troubler [*person*]

B *vi* (campaign) faire campagne (**for** pour)

agitated /'ædʒɪteɪtɪd/ *adj* agité, inquiet

agitation /ˌædʒɪ'teɪʃn/ *n* **1** (emotional) agitation *f*; **2** Pol (unrest) troubles *mpl*, agitation *f*; (campaigning) campagne *f* (**for** pour; **against** contre)

agitator /'ædʒɪteɪtə(r)/ *n* (person) agitateur/-trice *m/f*

AGM *n*: *abrév* ▸ **Annual General Meeting**

agnostic /æɡ'nɒstɪk/ *n, adj* agnostique (*mf*)

Age

■ *Note that where English says* to be X years old, *French says* avoir X ans (to have X years).

....

How old?

how old are you?
= quel âge as-tu?

what age is she?
= quel âge a-t-elle?

■ *The word* ans (*years*) *is never dropped:*

he is forty years old
or he is forty
or he is forty years of age
= il a quarante ans

she's eighty
= elle a quatre-vingts ans

the house is a hundred years old
= la maison a cent ans

a man of fifty
= un homme de cinquante ans

a child of eight and a half
= un enfant de huit ans et demi

I feel sixteen
= j'ai l'impression d'avoir seize ans

he looks sixteen
= on lui donnerait seize ans

■ *Note the use of* de *after* âgé *and* à l'âge:

a woman aged thirty
= une femme âgée de trente ans

at the age of forty
= à l'âge de quarante ans

Mrs Smith, aged forty
or Mrs Smith (40)
= Mme Smith, âgée de quarante ans

■ *Do not confuse* que *and* de *used with* plus *and* moins:

I'm older than you
= je suis plus âgé que toi

she's younger than him
= elle est plus jeune que lui

Anne's two years younger
= Anne a deux ans de moins

Margot's older than Suzanne by five years
= Margot a cinq ans de plus que Suzanne

Robert's younger than Thomas by six years
= Robert a six ans de moins que Thomas

X-year-old

a forty-year-old
= quelqu'un de quarante ans

a sixty-year-old woman
= une femme de soixante ans

an eighty-year-old pensioner
= un retraité de quatre-vingts ans

they've got an eight-year-old
= ils ont un enfant de huit ans

and a five-year-old
= et un autre de cinq ans

Approximate ages

■ *Note the various ways of saying these in French:*

he is about fifty
= il a environ cinquante ans
   or il a une cinquantaine d'années
   or (*less formally*) il a dans les cinquante ans

(*Other round numbers in* -aine *used to express age are* dizaine (*10*), vingtaine (*20*), trentaine (*30*), quarantaine (*40*), soixantaine (*60*) *and* centaine (*100*).)

she's just over sixty
= elle vient d'avoir soixante ans

she's just under seventy
= elle aura bientôt soixante-dix ans

she's in her sixties
= elle a entre soixante et soixante-dix ans

she's in her early sixties
= elle a entre soixante et soixante-cinq ans

she's in her late sixties
= elle va avoir soixante-dix ans
   or (*less formally*) elle va sur ses soixante-dix ans

she must be seventy
= elle doit avoir soixante-dix ans

he's in his mid forties
= il a entre quarante et cinquante ans
   or (*less formally*) il a dans les quarante-cinq ans

he's just ten
= il a tout juste dix ans

he's barely twelve
= il a à peine douze ans

games for the under twelves
= jeux pour les moins de douze ans

only for the over eighties
= seulement pour les plus de quatre-vingts ans

---

ago /əˈgəʊ/ *adv* three weeks ∼ il y a trois semaines; **some time/long** ∼ il y a quelque temps/longtemps; **how long** ∼**?** il y a combien de temps?; **not long** ∼ il y a peu de temps; **as long** ∼ **as 1986** dès 1986, déjà en 1986; **they got married forty years** ∼ **today** cela fait quarante ans aujourd'hui qu'ils sont mariés

agog /əˈgɒg/ *adj* ⓵ (excited) en émoi (**at** à cause de); ⓶ (eager) impatient (**to do** de faire)

agonize /ˈægənaɪz/ *vi* se tourmenter (**over, about** à propos de)

agonized /ˈægənaɪzd/ *adj* [*cry*] déchirant; [*expression*] angoissé

agonizing /ˈægənaɪzɪŋ/ *adj* [*pain*] atroce; [*decision*] déchirant

agony /ˈægənɪ/ *n* ⓵ (physical) douleur *f* atroce; ⓶ (mental) angoisse *f*; **it was** ∼**!** hum c'était l'horreur!

agony aunt, **agony uncle** *n* GB journaliste *mf* responsable du courrier du cœur

agoraphobia /ˌægərəˈfəʊbɪə/ *n* agoraphobie *f*

agoraphobic /ˌægərəˈfəʊbɪk/ *adj* agoraphobique

agree /əˈgriː/
A *vtr* (*prét*, *pp* **agreed**) ⓵ (concur) être d'accord (**that** sur le fait que); ⓶ (admit) convenir (**that** que); **I** ∼ **it sounds unlikely** ça a l'air peu probable, j'en conviens; **it's dangerous, don't you** ∼**?** c'est dangereux, tu ne crois pas?; ⓷ (consent) **to** ∼ **to do** accepter de faire; ⓸ (settle on, arrange) se mettre d'accord sur [*date, price, candidate, solution*]; **to** ∼ **to do** convenir de faire

B *vi* (*prét*, *pp* **agreed**) ⓵ (hold same opinion) être d'accord (**with** avec; **about, on** sur; **about doing** pour faire); **'I** ∼**!'** je suis bien d'accord!'; **I couldn't** ∼ **more!** je suis entièrement d'accord!; ⓶ (reach mutual understanding) se mettre d'accord, tomber d'accord (**about, on** sur); ⓷ (consent) accepter; **to** ∼ **to** consentir à [*plan, suggestion, terms*]; **they won't** ∼ **her going alone** ils ne consentiront pas à ce qu'elle y aille toute seule; ⓸ (hold with, approve) **to** ∼ **with** approuver [*belief, idea, practice*]; ⓹ (tally) [*stories, statements, figures*] concorder (with avec); **6** (suit) **to ~ with sb** [*climate, weather*] être bon pour qn; [*food*] réussir à qn; **7** Ling s'accorder (**with** avec; **in** en)

C agreed *pp adj* [*date, time, venue, amount, budget, rate, terms, signal*] convenu; **as ~d** comme convenu; **to be ~d on** être d'accord sur [*decision, statement, policy*]; **is that ~d?** c'est bien entendu?

agreeable /ə'griːəbl/ *adj* **1** (pleasant) [*experience, surroundings, person*] agréable; **2** sout (willing) **to be ~ to sth/to doing** être d'accord pour qch/pour faire

agreeably /ə'griːəblɪ/ *adv* (pleasantly) agréablement; (amicably) aimablement

agreement /ə'griːmənt/ *n* **1** gen, Pol, Comm accord *m* (**to do** pour faire); **to come to** *ou* **reach an ~** parvenir à un accord; **under an ~** en vertu d'un accord; **2** (undertaking) engagement *m* (**to do** à faire); **after an ~ by the union to end the strike** après que le syndicat s'est engagé à cesser la grève; **3** (mutual understanding) accord *m* (**about, on** sur); **to be in ~ with sb** être d'accord avec qn; **by ~ with sb** en accord avec qn; **to reach ~** se mettre d'accord; **to nod in ~** acquiescer d'un signe de tête; **4** Jur (contract) contrat *m*; **5** (consent) **~ to** acceptation *f* de [*reform, cease-fire*]; **6** Ling accord *m*

agricultural /ˌægrɪ'kʌltʃərəl/ *adj* [*land, worker*] agricole; [*expert*] agronome; [*college*] d'agriculture

agriculturalist /ˌægrɪ'kʌltʃərəlɪst/, **agriculturist** /ˌægrɪ'kʌltʃərɪst/ US ▸ p. 1181 *n* agronome *mf*

agricultural show *n* (rural) ≈ comices *mpl* agricoles; (trade fair) foire *f* agricole

agriculture /'ægrɪkʌltʃə(r)/ *n* agriculture *f*

agrochemical /ˌægrəʊ'kemɪkəl/
A *n* substance *f* agrochimique
B **agrochemicals** *npl* (+ v sg) (industry) agrochimie *f*
C *adj* agrochimique

agronomist /ə'grɒnəmɪst/ ▸ p. 1181 *n* agronome *mf*

aground /ə'graʊnd/ *adv* **to run ~** s'échouer

ah /ɑː/ *excl* ah!; **~ well!** (resignedly) eh bien voilà!

ahead /ə'hed/

⚠ *Ahead* is often used after verbs in English (*go ahead, plan ahead, think ahead* etc). For translations consult the appropriate verb entry (**go, plan, think** etc). For all other uses see the entry below

A *adv* **1** (spatially) [*go on, run*] en avant; **to send sb on ~** envoyer qn en éclaireur; **to send one's luggage on ~** faire envoyer ses bagages; **a few kilometres ~** à quelques kilomètres; **2** (in time) **in the months ~** pendant les mois à venir; **at least a year ~** [*apply*] au moins un an à l'avance; **who knows what lies ~?** qui sait ce que l'avenir nous réserve?; **3** fig (in leading position) **to be ~ in the polls** être en tête dans les sondages; **to be 30 points ~** avoir 30 points d'avance; **to be 3% ~** avoir une avance de 3%; **4** fig (more advanced) **to be ~ in** [*pupil, set*] être plus avancé en [*school subject*]

B **ahead of** *prep phr* **1** (in front of) devant [*person, vehicle*]; **to be three metres/seconds ~ of sb** avoir trois mètres/secondes d'avance sur qn; **~ of time** en avance; **to be ~ of one's time** en avance sur son temps; **to arrive ~ of sb** arriver avant qn; **2** (leading) **to be ~ of sb** (in polls, ratings) avoir un avantage sur qn; **3** fig (more advanced) **to be (way) ~ of the others** [*pupil*] être (bien) plus avancé que les autres; **to be ~ in the field** [*business*] devancer les autres

AI *n* (*abrév* = **artificial intelligence**) IA *f*

aid /eɪd/
A *n* **1** (help) aide *f*; **with the ~ of** à l'aide de [*tool etc*]; avec l'aide de [*person*]; **to come to sb's ~** venir en aide à qn; **2** (charitable support) aide *f* (**from** de; **to, for** à); **in ~ of** au profit de [*charity etc*]; **3** (equipment) aide *f*
B *noun modifier* [*programme etc*] d'entraide; **~ agency** organisation *f* humanitaire; **~ worker** employé/-e *m/f* d'une organisation humanitaire
C *vtr* aider [*person*] (**to do** à faire); faciliter [*digestion, recovery*]
D *vi* **1** **to ~ in** faciliter; **to ~ in doing sth** aider à faire; **2** Jur **charged with ~ing and abetting** accusé de complicité

aide /eɪd/ *n* aide *mf*, assistant/-e *m/f*

Aids /eɪdz/ *n* (*abrév* = **Acquired Immune Deficiency Syndrome**) sida *m*

Aids test *n* test *m* de dépistage du sida

ail /eɪl/
A *vtr* affliger [*society, economy*]
B *vi* **to be ~ing** [*person*] être souffrant; [*company*] être mal en point

ailment /'eɪlmənt/ *n* affection *f*, maladie *f*

aim /eɪm/
A *n* **1** (purpose) but *m*; **with the ~ of doing** dans le but de faire; **2** (with weapon) **to take ~ at sth/sb** viser qch/qn; **his ~ is bad** il vise mal
B *vtr* **1** **to be ~ed at sb** [*campaign, product, remark*] viser qn; **to be ~ed at doing** [*effort, action*] viser à faire; **2** braquer [*gun*] (**at** sur); lancer [*ball, stone*] (**at** sur); tenter de donner [*blow, kick*] (**at** à); **well-~ed** [*blow, kick*] bien placé
C *vi* **to ~ for sth, to ~ at sth** lit, fig viser qch; **to ~ at doing, to ~ to do** (try) s'efforcer de faire; (intend) avoir l'intention de faire; **to ~ high** fig viser haut

aimless /'eɪmlɪs/ *adj* [*person, wandering*] sans but; [*argument, gathering*] vain; [*violence*] sans objet

ain't /eɪnt/ = **am not, is not, are not, has not, have not**

air /eə(r)/
A *n* **1** (substance) air *m*; **in the open ~** en plein air, au grand air; **I need a change of ~** j'ai besoin de changer d'air; **to come up for ~** [*swimmer, animal*] remonter à la surface pour respirer; **to let the ~ out of sth** dégonfler qch; **2** (atmosphere, sky) air *m*; **he threw the ball up into the ~** il a jeté le ballon en l'air; **by ~** Post par avion; **Paris (seen) from the ~** Paris vu d'avion; **to clear the ~** lit [*storm*] rafraîchir l'air; fig apaiser les esprits; **3** Radio, TV **to be/go on the ~** [*broadcaster, interviewee*] être/passer à l'antenne; **still on the ~** encore en cours de diffusion; **off the ~, she confided that...** hors antenne, elle a confié que...; **to go off the ~** [*channel*] cesser d'émettre; **4** (manner) (of person) air *m*; (aura) (of place) aspect *m*, air *m*; **with an ~ of indifference** d'un air indifférent; **an ~ of mystery surrounds the project** le projet est entouré de mystère; **5** Mus air *m*
B *noun modifier* Aviat [*alert, base, corridor*] aérien/-ienne; [*pollution, pressure*] atmosphérique
C *vtr* **1** (dry) faire sécher; (freshen) aérer [*garment, room, bed*]; **that shirt hasn't been ~ed** cette chemise n'est pas complètement sèche; **2** (express) exprimer [*opinion, view*]; **to ~ one's grievances** exposer ses griefs

(Idioms) **there was trouble in the ~** il y avait de l'orage dans l'air fig; **there's a rumour in the ~ that...** le bruit court que...; **to put on ~s, to give oneself ~s** péj se donner de grands airs; **to be up in the ~** fig [*plans*] être très flou; **to be walking on ~** être aux anges; **to vanish into thin ~** se volatiliser

air: **~ ambulance** *n* avion *m* sanitaire; **~ bag** *n* Aut airbag *m*; **~ bed** *n* GB matelas *m* pneumatique

airborne /'eəbɔːn/ *adj* **1** Bot [*spore, seed*] porté par le vent; **2** Aviat, Mil [*troops, division*] aéroporté; **once the plane was ~** une fois que l'avion avait décollé

air: **~ brake** *n* Aut, Rail frein *m* à air comprimé; Aviat aérofrein *m*; **~brush** *n* aérographe *m*; **~ bubble** *n* (in liquid, plastic, wallpaper) bulle *f* d'air; (in glass, metal etc) soufflure *f*; **~-conditioned** *adj* climatisé; **~-conditioning** *n* climatisation *f*, air *m* conditionné; **~-cooled** *adj* [*engine*] à refroidissement par air; **~craft** *n* ℭ avion *m*, aéronef *m*; **~craft carrier** *n* porte-avions *m inv*; **~craft(s)man** ▸ p. 1123 *n* GB soldat *m* de deuxième classe (de l'armée de l'air); **~crew** *n* équipage *m* (d'un avion); **~ cushion** *n* (inflatable cushion) coussin *m* pneumatique; (of hovercraft) coussin *m* d'air; **~ disaster** *n* catastrophe *f* aérienne; **~drop** *n* parachutage *m*; **~ duct** *n* conduit *m* d'air; **~fare** *n* tarif *m* d'avion; **~field** *n* aérodrome *m*, terrain *m* d'aviation; **~flow** *n* gen, Aut, Aviat courant *m* atmosphérique; (in tunnel) écoulement *m* d'air; **~ force** *n* armée *f* de l'air, forces *fpl* aériennes

airfreight /'eəfreɪt/ *n* **1** (method of transport) transport *m* aérien; **2** (goods) fret *m* aérien; **3** (charge) tarif *m* aérien

air: **~-freshener** *n* désodorisant *m* d'atmosphère; **~ guitar** *n* guitare *f* imaginaire; **~ gun** *n* fusil *m* *or* carabine *f* à air comprimé; **~head** *n* péj évaporé/-e *m/f*; **~ hole** *n* trou *m* d'aération; **~ hostess** ▸ p. 1181 *n* hôtesse *f* de l'air

airing /'eərɪŋ/ *n* **1** (of linen) (drying) séchage *m*; (freshening) aération *f*; **2** fig (mention) **to give an idea an ~** mettre une idée sur le tapis

airing cupboard n GB placard qui contient la chaudière et où l'on range le linge

air: ∼ **kiss**○ n simulacre m de baiser sur la joue; ∼**less** adj [room] qui sent le renfermé; [evening] étouffant; ∼ **letter** n aérogramme m

airlift /'əəlɪft/ vtr évacuer [qn] par pont aérien [evacuees]; acheminer [qch] par pont aérien [supplies]

airline /'eəlaɪn/ n [1] Aviat (company) compagnie f aérienne; [2] (source of air) tuyau m d'air; (diver's) voie f d'air

air: ∼**liner** n avion m de ligne; ∼**lock** n gen poche f or bulle f d'air; (in spaceship) sas m

airmail /'eəmeɪl/
A n poste f aérienne; **by** ∼ par avion
B noun modifier [envelope, paper etc] par avion

air: ∼**man** n gen, Mil aviateur m; ∼**man basic** ► p. 1123 n US Mil Aviat soldat m (de l'armée de l'air américaine); ∼**man first class** ► p. 1123 n US Mil Aviat caporal m (de l'armée de l'air américaine); ∼ **marshal** ► p. 1123 n GB général m de corps aérien; ∼**plane** n US avion m; ∼ **pocket** n (in pipe, enclosed space) poche f d'air; Aviat trou m d'air; ∼**port** n aéroport m; ∼ **power** n puissance f aérienne; ∼ **pump** n pompe f à air, gonfleur m

air rage○ n cas m de violence parmi les passagers (durant un vol); ∼ **is on the increase** les cas de violence parmi les passagers sont de plus en plus nombreux

air: ∼ **raid** n attaque f aérienne, raid m (aérien); ∼**-raid shelter** n abri m antiaérien; ∼**-raid siren** n sirène f d'alerte aérienne; ∼**-raid warning** n alerte f aérienne; ∼ **rifle** n carabine f à air comprimé; ∼**-sea rescue** n opération f de sauvetage en mer (par hélicoptère); ∼ **shaft** n (in mine) puits m d'aérage; ∼**ship** n dirigeable m; ∼ **show** n (flying show) meeting m aérien; (trade exhibition) salon m de l'aéronautique; ∼**sickness** n mal m de l'air; ∼ **sock** n manche f à air; ∼**speed** n vitesse f propre, vitesse f par rapport à l'air; ∼**speed indicator** n Aviat badin m; ∼**stream** n gen, Meteorol courant m atmosphérique; ∼**strip** n piste f (d'atterrissage or de décollage); ∼ **terminal** n (at airport) aérogare f; (in town: terminus) terminal m; ∼**tight** adj étanche à l'air; ∼**time** n Radio, TV temps m d'antenne; ∼**-to-air** adj Mil [missile] air-air inv; [refuelling] en vol; ∼**-traffic controller** ► p. 1181 n contrôleur/-euse m/f aérien/-ienne, aiguilleur m du ciel; ∼ **valve** n gen soupape f d'air; (in central heating system) purgeur m d'air; ∼ **vent** n prise f d'air; ∼ **vice-marshal** n GB général m de division aérienne; ∼**waves** npl Radio, TV ondes fpl

airway /'eəweɪ/ n [1] Aviat (route) voie f aérienne; (airline) compagnie f aérienne; [2] (ventilating passage) galerie f d'aérage; [3] Anat voie f respiratoire

air: ∼**worthiness** n navigabilité f; ∼**worthy** adj en état de navigation

airy /'eərɪ/ adj [1] [room] clair/-e et spacieux/-ieuse; [2] (casual) [manner] désinvolte, insouciant

airy-fairy○ /ˌeərɪ'feərɪ/ adj GB [plan, person] farfelu○

aisle /aɪl/ n [1] (in church) (side passage) bas-côté m; (centre passage) allée f centrale; [2] (passageway) (in train, plane) couloir m; (in cinema, shop) allée f

ajar /ə'dʒɑː(r)/ adj, adv entrouvert, entrebaillé

AK US Post abrév écrite = **Alaska**

aka (abrév = **also known as**) alias

akin /ə'kɪn/ adj [1] (similar) **to be** ∼ **to** être semblable à; **to be more** ∼ **to** ressembler davantage à; [2] (tantamount) **to be** ∼ **to** (disapproving) équivalent à

AL US Post abrév écrite = **Alabama**

alabaster /'æləbɑːstə(r), US -bæs-/ n albâtre m

alacrity /ə'lækrɪtɪ/ n sout empressement m

alarm /ə'lɑːm/
A n [1] (feeling) frayeur f; (concern) inquiétude f; **in** ∼ avec inquiétude; (stronger) apeuré; **there is no cause for** ∼ inutile de s'inquiéter; [2] (warning signal, device) alarme f; **smoke** ∼ détecteur m de fumée; **to raise the** ∼ lit donner l'alarme; fig sonner l'alarme; [3] = **alarm clock**
B vtr (worry) inquiéter [person]

alarm bell n sonnette f d'alarme; **to set the** ∼**s ringing** GB fig tirer la sonnette d'alarme

alarm: ∼ **call** n Telecom réveil m par téléphone; ∼ **clock** n réveille-matin m, réveil m

alarmed /ə'lɑːmd/ adj effrayé; **don't be** ∼! rassurez-vous!

alarming /ə'lɑːmɪŋ/ adj alarmant

alarmist /ə'lɑːmɪst/ n, adj alarmiste (mf)

alas /ə'læs/ excl hélas

Albania /æl'beɪnɪə/ ► p. 774 pr n Albanie f

Albanian /æl'beɪnɪən/ ► p. 1032, p. 969
A n [1] (person) Albanais/-e m/f; [2] (language) albanais m
B adj albanais

albatross /'ælbətrɒs/ n albatros m (also in golf)

albeit /ˌɔːl'biːɪt/ conj sout quoique/bien que (+ subj)

albino /æl'biːnəʊ, US -baɪ-/ n, adj albinos (mf) inv

albumen /'ælbjʊmɪn/ n Biol, Bot albumen m

alcohol /'ælkəhɒl, US -hɔːl/
A n alcool m; ∼**-free** sans alcool
B noun modifier [abuse, level, consumption] d'alcool; [poisoning] par l'alcool; ∼ **content** teneur f en alcool

alcoholic /ˌælkə'hɒlɪk, US -hɔːl-/
A n alcoolique mf
B adj [drink etc] alcoolisé; [person, stupor] alcoolique

Alcoholics Anonymous, AA pr n Alcooliques Anonymes

alcopop /'ælkəʊpɒp/ n soda m alcoolisé

alcove /'ælkəʊv/ n renfoncement m

alder /'ɔːldə(r)/ n (tree, wood) aulne m

ale /eɪl/ n bière f; **brown/pale** ∼ bière brune/blonde

alert /ə'lɜːt/
A n alerte f; **to be on the** ∼ **for** se méfier de [danger]; **fire/bomb** ∼ alerte au feu/à la bombe; **security** ∼ alerte de sécurité
B adj [1] (lively) (child) éveillé; (old person) alerte; [2] (attentive) vigilant; **to be** ∼ **to** avoir conscience de [danger, risk, fact]
C vtr [1] (contact) alerter [authorities]; [2] **to** ∼ **sb to** mettre qn en garde contre [danger]; attirer l'attention de qn sur [fact, situation]

alertness /ə'lɜːtnɪs/ n (attentiveness) vigilance f; (liveliness) vivacité f

Aleutian Islands /ə'luːʃɪən/ ► p. 954 pr npl **the** ∼ les îles fpl Aléoutiennes

A level /'eɪlevl/ n GB Sch (abrév = **Advanced level**) ≈ baccalauréat m (dans une matière)

> ⓘ **A level** Examen dans une discipline préparé en deux ans après le *GCSE* au Royaume-Uni (sauf en Écosse). En général, les élèves choisissent trois ou quatre *A levels* (par exemple, *French, Maths, Chemistry, Biology*) et doivent obtenir une note comprise entre A et E pour être reçus à chacun. Les établissements d'enseignement supérieur sélectionnent les futurs étudiants en fonction des matières qu'ils ont réussies et de leurs notes. En Écosse, les *Highers* (*Highers grades*), que les élèves préparent en un an, représentent un niveau équivalent aux *A levels*.

alfalfa /æl'fælfə/ n luzerne f

alfresco /æl'freskəʊ/ adj, adv en plein air

algae /'ældʒiː, 'ælgaɪ/ npl algues fpl

algebra /'ældʒɪbrə/ n algèbre f

Algeria /æl'dʒɪərɪə/ ► p. 774 pr n Algérie f

Algerian /æl'dʒɪərɪən/ ► p. 1032
A n Algérien/-ienne m/f
B adj algérien/-ienne

Algiers /æl'dʒɪəz/ ► p. 1276 pr n Alger

ALGOL /'ælgɒl/ n (abrév = **algorithmic oriented language**) ALGOL m

algorithm /'ælgərɪðəm/ n Math, Comput algorithme m

alias /'eɪlɪəs/
A n [1] faux nom m; **under an** ∼ sous un faux nom; [2] Comput alias m
B prep alias

alibi /'ælɪbaɪ/ n [1] Jur alibi m; [2] (excuse) excuse f

alien /'eɪlɪən/
A n [1] gen, Jur étranger/-ère m/f (to à); [2] (from space) extraterrestre m
B adj **to be** ∼ **to sb/sth** être étranger/-ère à qn/qch

alienate /'eɪlɪəneɪt/ vtr (estrange) éloigner [supporters, colleagues]; Jur aliéner (**from** de); **they** ∼**d all their friends** ils se sont aliéné tous leurs amis

alienation /ˌeɪlɪə'neɪʃn/ n [1] gen (process) éloignement m (**of** de); (state) isolement m (**from** de); [2] Jur, Pol, Psych aliénation f

a

all

As a pronoun

When *all* is used to mean *everything*, it is translated by *tout*:

is that all?
= c'est tout?

all is well
= tout va bien

When *all* is followed by a *that* clause, *all that* is translated by *tout ce qui* when it is the subject of the verb and *tout ce que* when it is the object:

all that remains to be done
= tout ce qui reste à faire

that was all (that) he said
= c'est tout ce qu'il a dit

after all (that) we've done
= après tout ce que nous avons fait

we're doing all (that) we can
= nous faisons tout ce que nous pouvons

all that you need
= tout ce dont tu as besoin

When *all* is used to refer to a specified group of people or objects, the translation reflects the number and gender of the people or objects referred to; *tous* is used for a group of people or objects of masculine or mixed or unspecified gender and *toutes* for a group of feminine gender:

we were all delighted
= nous étions tous ravis

'where are the cups?' 'they're all in the kitchen'
= 'où sont les tasses?' 'elles sont toutes dans la cuisine'

For more examples and particular usages see the entry **all**.

As a determiner

In French, determiners agree in gender and number with the noun they precede. So *all* is translated by *tout* + masculine singular noun:

all the time
= tout le temps

by *toute* + feminine singular noun:

all the family
= toute la famille

by *tous* + masculine or mixed gender plural noun:

all men
= tous les hommes

all the books
= tous les livres

and by *toutes* + feminine plural noun:

all women
= toutes les femmes

all the chairs
= toutes les chaises

For more examples see the entry **all**.

As an adverb

When *all* is used as an adverb meaning *completely* it is generally translated by *tout*:

my coat's all dirty
= mon manteau est tout sale

he was all alone
= il était tout seul

they were all alone
= ils étaient tout seuls

the girls were all excited
= les filles étaient tout excitées

However, when the adjective that follows is in the feminine and begins with a consonant the translation is *toute/toutes*:

she was all alone
= elle était toute seule

the bill is all wrong
= la facture est toute fausse

the girls were all alone
= les filles étaient toutes seules

For more examples and particular usages see the entry **all**.

Phrases such as *all along*, *all but*, *at all*, *for all* and *of all* are each treated separately in the entry **all**.

---

alight /ə'laɪt/
A *adj* to be ~ [*fire*] être allumé; [*building*] être en feu; **to set sth** ~ mettre le feu à qch
B *vi* [*passenger*] descendre (**from** de); [*bird*] se poser (**on** sur); [*gaze*] s'arrêter (**on** sur)

align /ə'laɪn/ *vtr* aligner (**with** sur); **non-~ed** non-aligné

alignment /ə'laɪnmənt/ *n* ① gen, Pol alignement *m* (**with** sur); **to be in ~/out of** ~ être aligné/désaligné (**with** sur); ② Comput position *f*

alike /ə'laɪk/
A *adj* (identical) pareil/-eille; (similar) semblable; **to look** ~ se ressembler
B *adv* [*dress, think*] de la même façon; **for young and old** ~ pour les jeunes (tout) comme pour les personnes âgées

alimentary /ˌælɪ'mentərɪ/ *adj* [*system, process*] digestif/-ive; [*rules, laws*] alimentaire; ~ **canal** tube *m* digestif

alimony /'ælɪmənɪ, US -məʊnɪ/ *n* Jur pension *f* alimentaire

alive /ə'laɪv/ *adj* ① lit (living) vivant, en vie; **to keep sb/sth** ~ maintenir qn/qch en vie [*person, animal*]; **to stay** ~ rester en vie; **to bury sb** ~ enterrer qn vivant; **to be burnt** ~ être brûlé/-e vif/vive; ~ **and well**, ~ **and kicking** lit, fig bien vivant; ② (lively) **to be** ~ [*person*] être vivant; **to come**

~ [*party, place*] s'animer; [*history*] prendre vie; ③ (in existence) **to be** ~ [*art, tradition*] être vivant; [*interest, faith*] être vif/vive; **to keep** ~ préserver [*tradition etc*]; perpétuer [*memory*]; **it kept our hopes** ~ cela nous faisait garder espoir; ④ (teeming) ~ **with** grouillant de [*insects etc*]; ⑤ (aware) ~ **to** conscient de [*possibility etc*]

alkali /'ælkəlaɪ/ *n* alcali *m*

alkaline /'ælkəlaɪn/ *adj* alcalin

all /ɔːl/
A *pron* ① (everything) tout; **to risk** ~ tout risquer; ~ **is not lost** tout n'est pas perdu; ~ **was well** tout allait bien; ~ **will be revealed** hum vous saurez tout hum; **will that be** ~? ce sera tout?; **that's** ~ (all contexts) c'est tout; **500 in** ~ 500 en tout; ~ **in** ~ somme toute; **after** ~ **she's been through** après tout ce qu'elle a vécu; **it's not** ~ (that) it **should be** ça laisse à désirer; ~ **because he didn't write** tout ça parce qu'il n'a pas écrit; ② (the only thing) tout; **that's** ~ **I want** c'est tout ce que je veux; **she's** ~ **I have left** elle est tout ce qui me reste; **I know is that** tout ce que je sais c'est que; **that's** ~ **we need!** iron il ne manquait plus que ça!; ③ (everyone) tous; ~ **wish to participate** tous souhaitent participer; **thank you, one and** ~ merci à (vous) tous; '~ **welcome'** 'venez nombreux'; ④ (the whole amount) ~ **of our belongings** toutes nos affaires; **not** ~ **of the time** pas tout le temps; ⑤ (emphasizing entirety) **we** ~ **feel that**

nous avons tous l'impression que; **it** ~ **seems so point-less** tout cela paraît si futile; **I ate it** ~ j'ai tout mangé; **what's it** ~ **for?** (all contexts) à quoi ça sert (tout ça)?

B *det* **1** (each one of) tous/toutes; ~ **those who** tous ceux qui; **in** ~ **three films** dans les trois films; **2** (the whole of) tout/toute; ~ **his life** toute sa vie; ~ **year round** toute l'année; **you are** ~ **the family I have!** tu es toute la famille qui me reste!; **3** (total) **in** ~ **honesty** en toute franchise; **4** (any) **beyond** ~ **expectations** au-delà de toute attente; **to deny** ~ **knowledge of sth** nier avoir connaissance de qch

C *adv* **1** (emphatic: completely) tout; ~ **alone** tout seul; **to be** ~ **wet** être tout mouillé; ~ **in white** tout en blanc; ~ **along the canal** tout le long du canal; **to be** ~ **for sth** être tout à fait pour qch; **it's** ~ **about...** c'est l'histoire de...; **tell me** ~ **about it!** raconte-moi tout!; **he's forgotten** ~ **about us!** il nous a complètement oubliés!; **2** (emphatic: nothing but) **to be** ~ **smiles** (happy) être tout souriant; (two-faced) être tout sourire; **3** Sport **(they are)** ~ **six** (il y a) six partout

D *n* **to give one's** ~ tout sacrifier

E **all+** *combining form* (completely) ~**-concrete** tout en béton; ~**-digital**/**-electronic** entièrement numérique/ électronique; ~**-female**/**-male** [*group*] composé uniquement de femmes/d'hommes

F **all along** *adv phr* [*know etc*] depuis le début, toujours

G **all but** *adv phr* pratiquement, presque

H **all of** *adv phr* **to be** ~ **of 50** avoir au moins 50 ans

I **all that** *adv phr* **not** ~ **that strong** pas si fort que ça; **I don't know her** ~ **that well** je ne la connais pas si bien que ça

J **all the** *adv phr* ~ **the more** [*difficult, effective*] d'autant plus (before adj); **to laugh** ~ **the more** rire encore plus; ~ **the better!** tant mieux!

K **all too** *adv phr* [*accurate, easy, widespread, often*] bien trop; **she saw** ~ **too clearly that** elle a parfaitement bien vu que

L **and all** *adv phr* **1** **they moved books and** ~ ils ont tout déménagé y compris les livres; **2** ○GB **what with the heat and** ~ avec la chaleur et tout ça

M **at all** *adv phr* **not at** ~! (acknowledging thanks) de rien!; (answering query) pas du tout!; **it is not at** ~ **certain** ce n'est pas du tout certain; **if (it is) at** ~ **possible** si possible; **is it at** ~ **likely that...?** y a-t-il la moindre possibilité que...? (+ subj); **nothing at** ~ rien du tout; **if you knew anything at** ~ **about** si tu avais la moindre idée de

N **for all** *prep phr, adv phr* **1** (despite) **for** ~ **that** malgré tout, quand même; **2** (as regards) **for** ~ **I know** pour autant que je sache

O **of all** *prep phr* **1** (in rank) **the easiest of** ~ le plus facile; **first/last of** ~ pour commencer/finir; **2** (emphatic) **why today of** ~ **days?** pourquoi justement aujourd'hui?; **of** ~ **the nerve!** quel culot!

(Idioms) **he's not** ~ **there**○ il n'a pas toute sa tête; **it's** ~ **go**○ **here!** GB on s'active○ ici!; **it's** ~ **one to me** ça m'est égal; **it was** ~ **I could do not to laugh** il a fallu que je me retienne pour ne pas rire; **that's** ~ **very well, that's** ~ **well and good** tout ça c'est bien beau

all: ~**-American** *n* gen [*girl, boy, hero*] typiquement américain; Sport [*record, champion*] américain; ~**-around** *adj* US = **all-round**

allay /ə'leɪ/ *vtr* sout dissiper [*fear, suspicion, doubt*]

all clear *n* Mil signal *m* de fin d'alerte; **to give sb the** ~ fig donner le feu vert à qn (**to do** pour faire); [*doctor*] déclarer qn guéri

all: ~**-consuming** *adj* [*passion*] effréné; [*ambition*] démesuré; ~**-day** *adj* [*event*] qui dure toute la journée

allegation /ˌælɪ'geɪʃn/ *n* gen, Jur allégation *f* (**about** sur; **that** selon laquelle)

allege /ə'ledʒ/

A *vtr* **to** ~ **that** (claim) prétendre que (+ conditional); (publicly) déclarer que (+ conditional); **his** ~**d attempt to...** la tentative qu'il aurait faite de...; **it was** ~**d that...** il a été dit que...

B *alleged* *pp adj* [*attacker, crime*] présumé

allegedly /ə'ledʒɪdlɪ/ *adv* prétendument

allegiance /ə'liːdʒəns/ *n* gen, Jur allégeance *f*; **to swear** ~ **to** prêter serment *m* d'allégeance à

allegory /'ælɪgərɪ, US -gɔːrɪ/ *n* allégorie *f* (**of** de)

all-embracing *adj* global

allergic /ə'lɜːdʒɪk/ *adj* allergique (**to** à) also fig

---

allergist /'ælədʒɪst/ ▸ p. 1181 *n* allergologue *mf*

allergy /'ælədʒɪ/ *n* allergie *f* (**to** à) also fig

alleviate /ə'liːvɪeɪt/ *vtr* soulager [*boredom, pain*]; apaiser [*fears*]; réduire [*overcrowding, stress, unemployment*]

alley /'ælɪ/ *n* **1** (walkway) allée *f*; (for vehicles) ruelle *f*; **2** US (in tennis) couloir *m*

alleyway /'ælɪweɪ/ *n* = **alley 1**

all-found *adj* logé et nourri

alliance /ə'laɪəns/ *n* gen, Pol, Mil alliance *f* (**between** entre; **with** avec)

allied /'ælaɪd/ *adj* [*group*] allié; [*trades, subjects*] connexe

all: ~**-important** *adj* essentiel/-ielle; ~**-in** *adj* GB [*fee, price*] tout compris; ~ **in**○ *adj* GB crevé○, épuisé; ~**-inclusive** *adj* [*fee, price*] tout compris; ~**-in-one** *adj* [*garment*] d'une seule pièce; ~**-in wrestling** ▸ p. 881 *n* Sport catch *m*; ~**-night** *adj* [*party, meeting*] qui dure toute la nuit; [*service*] ouvert toute la nuit; [*radio station*] qui émet 24 heures sur 24

allocate /'æləkeɪt/ *vtr* affecter [*funds*] (**for, to** à); attribuer [*land*] (**to** à); accorder [*time*] (**to** à); assigner, attribuer [*tasks*] (**to** à)

allocation /ˌælə'keɪʃn/ *n* (amount) crédits *mpl*; (process) affectation *f*

all-or-nothing *adj* [*approach, policy*] extrémiste

allot /ə'lɒt/ *vtr* (*p prés etc* **-tt-**) attribuer [*money*] (**to** à); assigner [*task*] (**to** à); **in the** ~**ted time** dans le temps imparti

allotment /ə'lɒtmənt/ *n* **1** GB (garden) parcelle *f* de terre (loué pour en faire un jardin potager); **2** (allocation) attribution *f*

all-out /'ɔːlaʊt/

A *adj* [*strike*] total; [*attack*] en règle; [*effort*] acharné

B **all out** *adv* **to go all out for success** tout faire pour réussir

allover /'ɔːləʊvə(r)/ *adj* [*tan*] intégral

all over /ˌɔːl'əʊvə(r)/

A *adj* (finished) fini; **when it's** ~ quand tout sera fini

B *adv* **1** (everywhere) partout; **to be trembling** ~ trembler de partout; **2** ○(typically) **that's Mary** ~**!** c'est Mary tout craché!

C *prep* **1** partout dans [*room, town*]; ~ **China** partout en Chine; **2** ○fig (known in) **the news is** ~ **the village** la nouvelle s'est répandue dans tout le village; **3** (fawning over) **to be** ~ **sb** être aux petits soins pour qn; **they were** ~ **each other** ils n'arrêtaient pas de se bécoter○

allow /ə'laʊ/

A *vtr* **1** (authorize) autoriser [*person, organization*] (**to do** à faire); autoriser [*action, change*]; laisser [*choice, freedom*] (**to do de** faire); **to** ~ **sb in** autoriser qn à entrer; **she isn't** ~**ed alcohol** l'alcool lui est interdit; **2** (let) laisser; **he** ~**ed the situation to get worse** il a laissé la situation s'aggraver; **3** (enable) **to** ~ **sb/sth to do** permettre à qn/qch de faire; ~ **me!** permettez(-moi)!; **4** (allocate) prévoir; **to** ~ **two days for the job** prévoir deux jours pour faire le travail; **5** (concede) **to** ~ [*referee*] accorder [*goal*]; [*insurer*] agréer [*claim*]; [*supplier*] accorder, consentir [*discount*]; **6** (admit) [*club*] admettre [*non-member*]; **'no dogs** ~**ed'** 'interdit aux chiens'; **7** (condone) tolérer [*rudeness, swearing*]

B *v refl* **to** ~ **oneself 1** (grant) s'accorder [*drink, treat*]; **2** (allocate) prévoir; ~ **yourself two days** prévois deux jours; **3** (let) se laisser; **I** ~**ed myself to be persuaded** je me suis laissé persuader.

(Phrasal verb)

■ **allow for:** ▸ ~ **for** [sth] tenir compte de [*delays, wastage*]

allowable /ə'laʊəbl/ *adj* **1** (tax) déductible; **2** (permissible) gen admissible; Jur légitime

allowance /ə'laʊəns/ *n* **1** (grant) gen, Admin allocation *f*; (from employer) indemnité *f*; **2** (tax) abattement *m* fiscal; **3** (spending money) (for child) argent *m* de poche; (for student) argent *m* (pour vivre); (from trust, guardian) rente *f*; **4** (entitlement) **your baggage** ~ **is 40 kgs** vous avez droit à 40 kg de bagages; **5** Comm (discount) rabais *m*; US (trade-in payment) reprise *f*; **6** (concession) **to make** ~**(s) for sth** tenir compte de qch; **to make** ~**(s) for sb** essayer de comprendre qn

alloy /'ælɔɪ/ *n* alliage *m*

alloy: ~ **steel** *n* acier *m* allié; ~ **wheel** *n* roue *f* en alliage léger

all: ~ **points bulletin** *n* US alerte *f* générale; ~-**powerful** *adj* tout-puissant; ~-**purpose** *adj* [*building*] polyvalent; [*utensil*] multi-usages

all right, alright /ˌɔːlˈraɪt/

A *adj* **1** (expressing degree of satisfaction) [*film, garment etc*] pas mal°; **she's** ~ (pleasant) elle est plutôt sympa°; (attractive) elle n'est pas mal°; (competent) son travail est correct; '**how did the interview go?'—'~**' 'comment s'est passé ton entretien?'—'ça ne s'est pas trop mal passé' or 'ça a été°'; **sounds** ~ **to me**°! (acceptance) pourquoi pas!; **is my hair** ~? ça va mes cheveux?; **2** (well) **to feel** ~ aller bien; **3** (able to manage) **will you be** ~? est-ce que ça va aller?; **to be** ~ **for** avoir assez de [*money etc*]; **4** (acceptable) **is it** ~ **if...?** est-ce que ça va si...?; **would it be** ~ **to leave early?** est-ce que c'est gênant si on s'en va plus tôt?; **is that** ~ **with you?** ça ne te dérange pas?; **it's** ~ **for you** toi tu n'as pas à t'en faire; **that's (quite)** ~! ce n'est rien du tout!

B *adv* **1** [*function*] comme il faut; [*see*] bien; **she's doing** ~ (doing well) tout va bien pour elle; (managing to cope) elle s'en tire correctement; **2** (without doubt) **she knows** ~! bien sûr qu'elle sait!

C *particle* d'accord; ~ ~! **point taken!** ça va! j'ai compris!; ~, **let's move on to...** bien, passons à...

all: ~-**risk** *adj* [*policy, cover*] tous risques; ~-**round** *adj* [*athlete*] complet/-ète; [*improvement*] général

all-rounder /ˌɔːlˈraʊndə(r)/ *n* **to be a good** ~ être bon en tout

allspice /ˈɔːlspaɪs/ *n* piment *m* de la Jamaïque

all square *adj* **to be** ~ [*people*] être quitte; [*accounts*] être équilibré

all-time /ˈɔːltaɪm/ *adj* [*record*] absolu; **the** ~ **greats** (people) les grands *mpl*; ~ **high** record *m* absolu; **to be at an** ~ **low** [*person, morale*] être au plus bas; [*figures, shares*] n'avoir jamais été plus bas

all told *adv* en tout

allude /əˈluːd/ *vi* **to** ~ **to sth** faire allusion à qch

alluring /əˈlʊərɪŋ/ *adj* séduisant

allusion /əˈluːʒn/ *n* allusion *f* (**to** à)

all-weather *adj* [*pitch, track*] tous temps; ~ **court** (terrain *m* en) quick® *m*

ally /ˈælaɪ/

A *n* (*pl* **-ies**) gen, Mil allié/-e *m/f*

B /əˈlaɪ/ *v refl* **to** ~ **oneself with** s'allier avec

almighty /ɔːlˈmaɪti/ *adj* [*crash, row, explosion*] formidable

Almighty /ɔːlˈmaɪti/ *n* Relig **the** ~ le Tout-Puissant

almond /ˈɑːmənd/ *n* **1** (nut) amande *f*; **2** (*also* ~ **tree**) amandier *m*

almost /ˈɔːlməʊst/

> ⚠ When *almost* is used to mean *practically* it is translated by *presque*: *we're almost ready* = nous sommes presque prêts; *it's almost dark* = il fait presque nuit; *the room was almost empty* = la salle était presque vide.
> When *almost* is used with a verb in the past tense to describe something undesirable or unpleasant that nearly happened, it is translated using the verb *faillir* followed by an infinitive: *I almost forgot* = j'ai failli oublier; *he almost fell* = il a failli tomber.

adv **1** (practically) presque; ~ **any train** presque tous les trains; **we're** ~ **there** nous sommes presque arrivés; **2** (implying narrow escape) **he** ~ **died** il a failli mourir

almst† /ɑːmz/ *npl* aumône *f*

aloft /əˈlɒft, US əˈlɔːft/ *adv* **1** gen [*hold, soar*] en l'air; [*seated, perched*] en haut; **from** ~ d'en haut; **2** Naut dans la mâture

alone /əˈləʊn/

A *adj* (*épith*) **1** (on one's own) seul; **all** ~ tout seul; **to leave sb** ~ lit laisser qn seul; (in peace) laisser qn tranquille; **leave that bike** ~! ne touche pas à ce vélo!; **2** (isolated) seul; **I feel so** ~ je me sens si seul; **she is not** ~ **in thinking that...** elle n'est pas la seule à penser que...; **to stand** ~ [*building*] être isolé; [*person*] se tenir seul; fig être sans égal

B *adv* **1** (on one's own) [*work, live, travel*] seul; **2** (exclusively) **for this reason** ~ rien que pour cette raison; **this figure** ~ **shows** le chiffre à lui seul montre

(Idiom) **to go it** ~° faire cavalier seul

along /əˈlɒŋ, US əˈlɔːŋ/

> ⚠ When *along* is used as a preposition meaning *all along* it can usually be translated by *le long de*: *there were trees along the road* = il y avait des arbres le long de la route. For particular usages see the entry below.
> *along* is often used after verbs of movement. If the addition of *along* does not change the meaning of the verb, *along* will not be translated: *as he walked along* = tout en marchant.
> However, the addition of *along* often produces a completely new meaning. This is the case in expressions like *the project is coming along, how are they getting along?*. For translations consult the appropriate verb entry (**come, get** etc).

A *adv* **to push/pull sth** ~ pousser/tirer qch; **to be walking** ~ marcher; **I'll be** ~ **in a second** j'arrive tout de suite

B *prep* **1** (*also* ~**side**) (all along) le long de; **to run** ~ **the beach** [*path etc*] longer la plage; **there were chairs** ~ **the wall** il y avait des chaises contre le mur; **2** (the length of) **to walk** ~ **the beach** marcher sur la plage; **to look** ~ **the shelves** chercher dans les rayons; **3** (at a point along) **somewhere** ~ **the motorway** quelque part sur l'autoroute; **half-way** ~ **the path** à mi-chemin; **somewhere** ~ **the way** lit quelque part en chemin; fig quelque part

C **along with** *prep phr* (accompanied by) accompagné de; (at same time as) en même temps que

alongside /əˈlɒŋsaɪd, US əlɔːŋˈsaɪd/

A *prep* **1** (all along) = **along B 1**; **2** (next to) **to draw up** ~ **sb** [*vehicle*] s'arrêter à la hauteur de qn; **to learn to live** ~ **each other** [*groups*] apprendre à coexister

B *adv* **1** gen à côté; **2** Naut **to come** ~ accoster

aloof /əˈluːf/ *adj* distant; **to remain** ~ **from** se tenir à l'écart de

aloud /əˈlaʊd/ *adv* (audibly) [*say*] à haute voix; [*wonder*] tout haut

alpaca /ælˈpækə/ *n* (all contexts) alpaga *m*

alpha /ˈælfə/ *n* **1** (letter) alpha *m*; **2** GB Univ (grade) **to get an** ~ avoir un 20

alphabet /ˈælfəbet/ *n* alphabet *m*

alphabetical /ˌælfəˈbetɪkl/ *adj* alphabétique

alphabetically /ˌælfəˈbetɪklɪ/ *adv* [*list*] par ordre alphabétique

alpine /ˈælpaɪn/

A *n* plante *f* alpine

B *adj* (*also* **Alpine**) gen alpin

Alps /ælps/ *pr npl* **the** ~ les Alpes *fpl*

already /ɔːlˈredɪ/ *adv* déjà; **it's 10 o'clock** ~ il est déjà 10 heures; **he's** ~ **left** il est déjà parti; **I've told you twice** ~! je te l'ai déjà dit deux fois!; **it's June** ~ nous sommes déjà au mois de juin

(Idiom) **so come on** ~! US (indicating irritation) dépêche-toi à la fin!

alright = **all right**

Alsatian /ælˈseɪʃn/

A *n* **1** GB (dog) berger *m* allemand; **2** (native of Alsace) Alsacien/-ienne *m/f*

B *adj* alsacien/-ienne; ~ **wines** les vins d'Alsace

also /ˈɔːlsəʊ/ *adv* **1** (too, as well) aussi; ~ **available in red** existe aussi en rouge; **it is** ~ **worth remembering that** il serait bon aussi de ne pas oublier que; **2** (furthermore) ~, **he snores** en plus il ronfle

altar /ˈɔːltə(r)/ *n* autel *m*

altar: ~ **boy** *n* enfant *m* de chœur; ~ **cloth** *n* nappe *f* d'autel; ~ **piece** *n* retable *m*

alter /ˈɔːltə(r)/

A *vtr* **1** (change) changer [*opinion, lifestyle, person, rule, timetable*]; modifier [*amount, document*]; affecter [*speed, value, climate*]; transformer [*building*]; **that does not** ~ **the fact that** cela ne change rien au fait que; **to** ~ **the appearance of sth** changer l'aspect de qch; **2** (alter clothing) retoucher [*dress, shirt etc*]; (radically) transformer

B *vi* changer

alteration /ˌɔːltəˈreɪʃn/

A *n* **1** (act of altering) (of building) transformation *f*; (of text, law, process) modification *f*; (of timetable, route, circumstances) changement *m*; **2** (result of altering) modification *f* (**to, in** de); **3** (to garment) retouche *f*; (radical) transformation *f*

B alterations *npl* **1** (changes to building) transformations *fpl* (**to** à); **2** (building work) travaux *mpl*

altercation /ˌɔːltəˈkeɪʃn/ n sout altercation f (**about** ou **over** à propos de)

alternate

A /ɔːlˈtɜːnət/ n US (stand-in) remplaçant/-e m/f

B /ɔːlˈtɜːnət/ adj **1** (successive) [chapters, layers] en alternance; **2** (every other) **on ~ days** un jour sur deux; **3** US (other) autre; **4** Bot, Math alterne

C /ˈɔːltəneɪt/ vtr **to ~ sth and** ou **with sth** alterner qch et qch

D /ˈɔːltəneɪt/ vi [people] se relayer; [colours, patterns, seasons] alterner (**with** avec); **to ~ between hope and despair** passer de l'espoir au désespoir

alternately /ɔːlˈtɜːnətlɪ/ adv [move, bring, ask] alternative-ment; **they criticize and praise him ~** tantôt ils le critiquent, tantôt ils le félicitent

alternating current n courant m alternatif

alternative /ɔːlˈtɜːnətɪv/

A n **1** (specified option) (from two) alternative f, autre possibilité f; (from several) possibilité f; **one ~ is...** une des possibilités serait...; **the ~ is to do** l'autre possibilité serait de faire; **2** (possible option) choix m; **to have no ~** ne pas avoir le choix; **I chose the expensive ~** j'ai choisi la solution chère; **as an ~ to radiotherapy, you can choose...** outre la radiothérapie, vous pouvez choisir...

B adj **1** (other) [activity, career, date, flight, method, plan] autre; [accommodation, product] de remplacement; [solution] de rechange; **2** (unconventional) [comedian, bookshop] also Ecol alternatif/-ive

alternatively /ɔːlˈtɜːnətɪvlɪ/ adv sinon; **~, you can book by phone** vous avez aussi la possibilité de réserver par téléphone

alternative: **~ medicine** n **∅** médecines fpl parallèles or douces; **~ technology, AT** n technologie f alternative

alternator /ˈɔːltəneɪtə(r)/ n Elec alternateur m

although /ɔːlˈðəʊ/ conj **1** (in spite of the fact that) bien que (+ subj); **~ he claims to be shy** bien qu'il prétende être timide; **they're generous, ~ poor** ils sont généreux, quoique pauvres; **2** (but, however) mais; **you don't have to attend, ~ we advise it** vous n'êtes pas obligés de venir, mais nous vous le conseillons

altimeter /ˈæltɪmiːtə(r), US ˌælˈtɪmətər/ n altimètre m

altitude /ˈæltɪtjuːd, US -tuːd/ n altitude f; **at ~** en altitude

alto (pl **-tos**) /ˈæltəʊ/ n ▸ p. 1311 **1** (voice) (of female) contral-to m; (of male) haute-contre f; **2** (singer) (female) contralto f; (male) haute-contre m

altogether /ˌɔːltəˈgeðə(r)/ adv **1** (completely) complète-ment; **not ~ true** pas complètement vrai; **that's another matter ~** c'est une tout autre histoire; **2** (in total) en tout; **how much is that ~?** ça fait combien en tout?; **3** (all things considered) **~, it was a mistake** tout compte fait, c'était une erreur

altruistic /ˌæltruːˈɪstɪk/ adj altruiste

aluminium /ˌæljʊˈmɪnɪəm/ GB, **aluminum** /əˈluːmɪ-nəm/ US n aluminium m

aluminium foil n papier m aluminium

alumna /əˈlʌmnə/ n (pl **-nae**) US Sch, Univ (of school) ancienne élève f; (of college) ancienne étudiante f

alumnus /əˈlʌmnəs/ n (pl **-ni**) US Sch, Univ (of school) ancien élève m; (of college) ancien étudiant m

always /ˈɔːlweɪz/ adv toujours; **he's ~ complaining** il n'arrête pas de se plaindre

am¹ /æm/ ▸ **be**

am² /æm, eɪem/ ▸ p. 745 adv (abrév = **ante meridiem**) **three ~** trois heures (du matin)

AM n (abrév = **Assembly Member**) GB Pol membre m de l'Assemblée galloise

AMA n (abrév = **American Medical Association**) US Asso-ciation f médicale américaine

amalgam /əˈmælgəm/ n (all contexts) amalgame m

amalgamate /əˈmælgəmeɪt/

A vtr **1** (merge) fusionner [companies, schools] (**with** avec; **into** en); **2** amalgamer [metals] (**with** à)

B vi **1** [company, union] fusionner (**with** avec); **2** [metal] s'amalgamer (**with** à)

C amalgamated pp adj [school, association, trade union] unifié

amalgamation /əˌmælgəˈmeɪʃn/ n **1** (of companies) fusion f (**with** avec; **into** en); (of styles) mélange m; **2** (of metals) amalgamation f

amass /əˈmæs/ vtr accumuler [data]; amasser [fortune]

amateur /ˈæmətə(r)/

A n Sport, gen amateur m

B noun modifier [sportsperson, musician] amateur; [sport] en amateur; **~ dramatics** théâtre m amateur

amateurish /ˈæmətərɪʃ/ adj péj [work, attitude] d'amateur

amaze /əˈmeɪz/ vtr surprendre; (stronger) stupéfier

amazed /əˈmeɪzd/ adj [reaction, silence, look, person] stupé-fait; **I'm ~ (that)** ça m'étonne que (+ subj)

amazement /əˈmeɪzmənt/ n stupéfaction f; **in ~** avec stupéfaction; **to everyone's ~** à la stupéfaction générale; **to my/her etc ~** à ma/sa etc grande surprise

amazing /əˈmeɪzɪŋ/ adj extraordinaire

amazingly /əˈmeɪzɪŋlɪ/ adv incroyablement; **to be ~ clever** être d'une intelligence étonnante

Amazon /ˈæməzən, US -zɒn/ ▸ p. 1146

A pr n **1** (river) also Mythol Amazone m; **2** (also **amazon**) fig (strong woman) virago f pej

B noun modifier [basin, forest, tribe] amazonien/-ienne

ambassador /æmˈbæsədə(r)/ ▸ p. 869 n ambassa-deur m

ambassador-at-large n (pl **~s-at-large**) US ambas-sadeur m itinérant

amber /ˈæmbə(r)/ ▸ p. 752

A n **1** (resin, colour) ambre m; **2** GB (traffic signal) orange m; **to change** ou **turn to ~** passer à l'orange

B adj [eyes, fabric] couleur d'ambre inv; [light] ambré

ambidextrous /ˌæmbɪˈdekstrəs/ adj ambidextre

ambience /ˈæmbɪəns/ n sout ambiance f

ambient /ˈæmbɪənt/ adj [temperature, noise] ambiant

ambiguity /ˌæmbɪˈgjuːətɪ/ n ambiguïté f (**about** à propos de)

ambiguous /æmˈbɪgjʊəs/ adj gen, Ling ambigu/-uë

ambiguously /æmˈbɪgjʊəslɪ/ adv de façon ambiguë

ambition /æmˈbɪʃn/ n **1** (quality) ambition f (**to do** de faire); **2** (aim) rêve m (**to do** de faire); **it was his lifelong ~ to visit Japan** son rêve de toujours était de visiter le Japon; **3** (gén pl) (aspiration) ambition f (**to do, of doing** de faire); **political ~s** ambitions politiques

ambitious /æmˈbɪʃəs/ adj [person, scheme] ambitieux/-ieuse; **to be ~ to do** avoir l'ambition de faire

ambitiously /ˌæmˈbɪʃəslɪ/ adv ambitieusement

ambivalence /æmˈbɪvələns/ n ambivalence f

ambivalent /æmˈbɪvələnt/ adj ambivalent; **to be ~ about** avoir une attitude ambivalente à propos de

amble /ˈæmbl/ vi **1** (stroll) **to ~ off** partir tranquillement; **to ~ around the gardens** se promener tranquillement dans les jardins; **2** [horse] aller l'amble

ambulance /ˈæmbjʊləns/

A n ambulance f

B noun modifier [service, station] d'ambulances; **~ crew** équipe f d'ambulanciers/-ières

ambulance: **~man** ▸ p. 1181 n ambulancier m; **~woman** ▸ p. 1181 n ambulancière f

ambush /ˈæmbʊʃ/

A n **1** embuscade f; **to lie in ~** se tenir en embuscade

B vtr tendre une embuscade à [soldiers]; **to be ~ed** être pris en embuscade

ameba n US = amoeba

amen /ɑːmen, eɪ-/ excl amen; **~ to that!** assurément!

amenable /əˈmiːnəbl/ adj **1** (obliging) souple; **2** **~ to** [person] sensible à [reason etc]; [person, situation] soumis à [regulations]

amend /əˈmend/ vtr **1** (alter) amender [law]; modifier [document, plan]; **2** sout (correct) réformer fml [behaviour]

amendment /əˈmendmənt/ n (to law) amendement m (**to** à); (to contract) modification f (**to** à)

amends /əˈmendz/ npl **1** (reparation) **to make ~ for** réparer [damage, hurt]; **to make ~ to sb** (financially) dédommager qn; **2** **to make ~** (redeem oneself) se racheter

amenity /əˈmiːnətɪ, əˈmenətɪ/

A n sout (pleasantness) agrément m

B **amenities** npl (facilities) (of hotel, locality) équipements mpl; (of

a

house, sports club) installations *fpl*

America /ə'merɪkə/ ▸ p. 774 *pr n* Amérique *f*

American /ə'merɪkən/ ▸ p. 1032, p. 969
A *n* **1** (person) Américain/-e *m/f*; **2** (language) américain *m*
B *adj* américain

American Civil War *pr n* guerre *f* de Sécession

American dream *n* rêve *m* américain

> ⓘ **American dream** Cette expression désigne un
> principe américain selon lequel la réussite, en
> particulier financière et sociale, est accessible à qui-
> conque travaille avec acharnement. Pour les immi-
> grants, s'y ajoute le rêve de liberté et d'égalité.

American: ∼ **English** *n* américain *m*; ∼ **Indian**
▸ p. 1032 *n* Indien/-ienne *m/f* d'Amérique du Nord,
Amérindien/-ienne *m/f*

Americanism /ə'merɪkənɪzəm/ *n* américanisme *m*

American revolution *n* guerre *f* d'Indépendance
américaine

amethyst /'æmɪθɪst/ *n* (gem) améthyste *f*; ▸ p. 752 (colour)
violet *m* d'améthyste

Amex /'eɪmeks/ *n* (*abrév* = **American Stock Exchange**)
deuxième Bourse new-yorkaise

amiable /'eɪmɪəbl/ *adj* [*person*] aimable (**to** *ou* **towards**
avec); [*mood*] plaisant; [*chat*] amical

amicable /'æmɪkəbl/ *adj* **1** (friendly) [*manner, relationship*]
amical; **2** Jur **an** ∼ **settlement** un arrangement à
l'amiable

amicably /'æmɪkəblɪ/ *adv* [*behave*] de façon amicale;
[*settle, part*] à l'amiable

amid /ə'mɪd/, **amidst** /ə'mɪdst/ *prep* **1** au milieu de
[*laughter, applause*]; à la suite de [*allegations, reports,
rumours*]; ∼ **growing concern** alors qu'on s'inquiète de
plus en plus; **2** (surrounded by) parmi, au milieu de [*fields,
trees, wreckage*]

amino acid /ə,miːnəʊ 'æsɪd/ *n* acide *m* aminé

amiss /ə'mɪs/
A *adj* **there is something** ∼ il y a quelque chose qui ne
va pas
B *adv* **to take sth** ∼ prendre qch de travers; **a drink wouldn't
come** *ou* **go** ∼! un verre ne serait pas de refus

ammo⚪ /'æməʊ/ *n* ⓒ (*abrév* = **ammunition**) munitions *fpl*

ammonia /ə'məʊnɪə/ *n* (gas) ammoniac *m*; (solution) ammoniaque *f*

ammunition /,æmjʊ'nɪʃn/ *n* ⓒ Mil munitions *fpl*; fig
armes *fpl*

amnesia /æm'niːzɪə, US -niːʒə/ *n* amnésie *f*

amnesiac /æm'niːzɪæk, US -'niːʒɪæk/ *n*, *adj* amnésique
(*mf*)

amnesty /'æmnəstɪ/ *n* Pol, Jur (pardon, period) amnistie *f*;
under an ∼ dans le cadre de l'amnistie

amoeba /ə'miːbə/ *n* amibe *f*

amoebic /ə'miːbɪk/ *adj* [*dysentery etc*] amibien/-ienne

amok /ə'mɒk/ *adv* **to run** ∼ [*person, animal*] être pris de
folie furieuse; [*imagination*] se débrider

among /ə'mʌŋ/, **amongst** /ə'mʌŋst/ *prep* **1** (amidst)
parmi [*crowd, population*]; au milieu de, parmi [*trees, ruins*];
parmi, dans [*papers, belongings*]; ∼ **those present** parmi les
personnes présentes; **to be** ∼ **friends** être entre amis;
∼ **others** entre autres; **2** (affecting a particular group) chez;
unemployment ∼ **young people** le chômage chez les
jeunes; **3** (one of) ∼ **the world's poorest countries** un des
pays les plus pauvres du monde; **she was** ∼ **those who
survived** elle faisait partie des survivants; **to be** ∼ **the first**
être dans les premiers; **4** (between) entre; **divided** ∼ **his
heirs** partagé entre ses héritiers; **they can never agree**
∼ **themselves** ils n'arrivent jamais à se mettre d'accord;
one bottle ∼ **five** une bouteille pour cinq

amorality /eɪmə'rælɪtɪ/ *n* amoralité *f*

amorous /'æmərəs/ *adj* littér *ou* hum amoureux/-euse

amorphous /ə'mɔːfəs/ *adj* **1** Chem amorphe; **2** gen
[*shape, collection*] informe; [*ideas, plans*] confus

amount /ə'maʊnt/ *n* **1** gen (quantity) (of goods, food) quantité
f; (of people, objects) nombre *m*; **a considerable** ∼/**fair** ∼ **of**
beaucoup/pas mal de⚪; **a certain** ∼ **of imagination** une
certaine imagination; **I'm entitled to a certain** ∼ **of**

respect j'ai droit à un certain respect; **no** ∼ **of persuasion
will make him change his mind** on aura beau essayer de le
persuader, rien ne le fera changer d'avis; **2** (sum of money)
somme *f*; (bill) montant *m*; **the full** ∼ le montant total;
what is the outstanding ∼? combien reste-t-il à payer?;
∼ **paid (on account)** Comm acompte versé

⟮Phrasal verb⟯

■ **amount to**: ▸ ∼ **to [sth] 1** (add up to) [*cost*] s'élever à;
2 (be equivalent to) équivaloir à, revenir à [*confession, betrayal
etc*]; **it** ∼**s to the same thing** cela revient au même; **it** ∼**s to
blackmail!** ce n'est rien d'autre que du chantage!; **not to**
∼ **to much** [*accusation, report*] ne pas valoir grand-chose⚪

amp /æmp/ *n* **1** *abrév* ▸ **ampere**; **2** ⚪(*abrév* = **amplifier**)
ampli⚪ *m*

amperage /'æmpərɪdʒ/ *n* intensité *f* de courant, ampéra-
ge *m* controv

ampere /'æmpeə(r), US 'æmpɪə(r)/ *n* ampère *m*

ampersand /'æmpəsænd/ *n* esperluette *f*

amphibian /æm'fɪbɪən/ *n* **1** Zool amphibie *m*; **2** Aviat
appareil *m* amphibie; **3** Aut véhicule *m* amphibie; **4** Mil
(tank) char *m* amphibie

amphibious /æm'fɪbɪəs/ *adj* Zool, Mil amphibie

amphitheatre, amphitheater US /'æmfɪθɪətə(r)/ *n*
1 amphithéâtre *m*; **2** (natural) ∼ cirque *m*

ample /'æmpl/ *adj* **1** (plenty) [*provisions, resources*] largement suffisant (**for** pour); [*illustration*] ample; **there's**
∼ **room** il y a largement la place; **to have** ∼ **opportunity
to do** avoir largement la possibilité de faire; **he was given**
∼ **warning** il a été largement prévenu; **he's been given**
∼ **opportunity to apologize** on lui a donné toutes les
chances de s'excuser; **there is** ∼ **evidence that** il est
prouvé que; **2** (of generous size) [*proportions, bust*] généreux/
-euse; [*garment*] large

amplifier /'æmplɪfaɪə(r)/ *n* amplificateur *m*, ampli⚪ *m*

amplify /'æmplɪfaɪ/ *vtr* **1** Audio, Elec, Radio amplifier; **2** gen
développer [*account, statement, concept*]

amply /'æmplɪ/ *adv* [*compensated, fulfilled*] largement; [*demonstrated*] amplement

amputate /'æmpjʊteɪt/ *vtr* amputer; **to** ∼ **sb's leg** amputer qn de la jambe

amputee /,æmpjʊ'tiː/ *n* amputé/-e *m/f*

Amsterdam /,æmstə'dæm/ ▸ p. 1276 *pr n* Amsterdam

Amtrak /'æmtræk/ *n* US société de transports ferroviaires

amuse /ə'mjuːz/
A *vtr* **1** (cause laughter) amuser; **to be** ∼**d at** *ou* **by** s'amuser
de; **I'm not** ∼**d!** je ne trouve pas ça drôle!; **2** (entertain)
[*game, story*] amuser; **3** (occupy) [*activity, hobby*] occuper
B *v refl* **to** ∼ **oneself 1** (entertain) se distraire; **2** (occupy)
s'occuper

amusement /ə'mjuːzmənt/
A *n* **1** (mirth) amusement *m* (**at** face à); **a look of** ∼ un air
amusé; **to conceal one's** ∼ dissimuler son envie de rire;
2 (diversion) distraction *f*; **for** ∼ pour me/se etc distraire
B **amusements** *npl* (at fairground) attractions *fpl*

amusement: ∼ **arcade** *n* GB salle *f* de jeux électroniques; ∼ **park** *n* parc *m* d'attractions

amusing /ə'mjuːzɪŋ/ *adj* amusant

amyl: ∼ **alcohol** *n* alcool *m* amylique; ∼ **nitrate** *n*
nitrite *m* amylique

an /æn, ən/ ▸ a²

anabolic steroid /,ænə'bɒlɪk 'stɪərɔɪd/ *n* stéroïde *m*
anabolisant

anachronism /ə'nækrənɪzəm/ *n* anachronisme *m*; **to be
an** ∼ [*object, custom etc*] être un anachronisme

anaemia /ə'niːmɪə/ ▸ p. 933 *n* anémie *f*

anaemic /ə'niːmɪk/ *adj* **1** Med anémique; **to become** ∼
s'anémier; **2** fig [*performance, poem*] fade

anaerobic /,æneə'rəʊbɪk/ *adj* anaérobie

anaesthetic GB, **anesthetic** US /,ænɪs'θetɪk/ *n*, *adj*
anesthésique (*m*); **to be under** ∼ être sous anesthésie

anaesthetist /ə'niːsθətɪst/ ▸ p. 1181 *n* GB (médecin) anesthésiste *mf*

anaesthetize GB, **anesthetize** US /ə'niːsθətaɪz/ *vtr*
anesthésier

anagram /'ænəgræm/ *n* anagramme *f* (**of** de)

analgesic /,ænæl'dʒiːsɪk/ *n*, *adj* analgésique (*m*)

analogous /ə'næləgəs/ *adj* analogue (**to, with** à)

analogy /əˈnælədʒɪ/ n analogie f; **to draw an** ∼ faire une analogie (**between** entre; **with** avec)

analyse GB, **analyze** US /ˈænəlaɪz/ vtr [1] gen, Ling analyser; [2] GB Psych psychanalyser

analysis /əˈnælɪsɪs/ n [1] gen, Ling analyse f; **in the final** ou **last** ∼ en fin de compte; [2] Psych psychanalyse f; **to be in** ∼ être en analyse

analyst /ˈænəlɪst/ ▸ p. 1181 n analyste mf

analytic(al) /ˌænəˈlɪtɪk(l)/ adj analytique

anarchic(al) /əˈnɑːkɪk(l)/ adj anarchique

anarchist /ˈænəkɪst/ n, adj anarchiste (mf)

anarchy /ˈænəkɪ/ n anarchie f

anathema /əˈnæθəmə/ n (pl ∼**s**) Relig anathème m; fig abomination f; **history/cruelty is** ∼ **to him** il a l'histoire/la cruauté en horreur

anatomical /ˌænəˈtɒmɪkl/ adj anatomique

anatomy /əˈnætəmɪ/
A n [1] Med, Biol anatomie f; [2] fig (of subject, event) analyse f (détaillée) (**of** de)
B noun modifier [class, lesson] d'anatomie

ANC n (abrév = **African National Congress**) ANC f

ancestor /ˈænsestə(r)/ n lit, fig ancêtre mf

ancestral /ænˈsestrəl/ adj ancestral

ancestry /ˈænsestrɪ/ n [1] (lineage) ascendance f; [2] (ancestors collectively) ancêtres mpl, aïeux mpl

anchor /ˈæŋkə(r)/
A n [1] Naut ancre f; **to drop** ou **cast** ∼ jeter l'ancre; **to come to** ∼ mouiller; **to be** ou **lie at** ∼ être ancré; **to slip** ∼ filer par le bout; [2] fig point m d'ancrage; (person) soutien m
B vtr [1] ancrer [ship, balloon]; arrimer [tent, roof etc] (**to** à); [2] US Radio, TV présenter

anchorage /ˈæŋkərɪdʒ/ n gen, Naut ancrage m

anchorman /ˈæŋkəmæn/ ▸ p. 1181 n [1] Radio, TV présentateur m; (in network, organization) pivot m; [2] Sport relayeur m

anchorwoman /ˈæŋkəwʊmən/ ▸ p. 1181 n Radio, TV présentatrice f

anchovy /ˈæntʃəvɪ, US ˈæntʃəʊvɪ/ n anchois m

ancient /ˈeɪnʃənt/ adj [1] (dating from BC) antique; (very old) ancien/-ienne; ∼ **Greek** Ling grec ancien; ∼ **Greece** la Grèce antique; ∼ **history** (subject) histoire f ancienne; ∼ **monument** monument m historique; **in** ∼ **times** dans les temps anciens; [2] ○[person, car] très vieux/vieille

ancillary /ænˈsɪlərɪ, US ˈænsəlerɪ/ adj [service, staff, task, industry, equipment, role] auxiliaire; [cost] accessoire; [road] secondaire

and /ænd, unstressed ənd/

> ⚠ When used as a straightforward conjunction, and is translated by et: to shout and sing = crier et chanter; Tom and Linda = Tom et Linda; my friend and colleague = mon ami et collègue.
> and is sometimes used between two verbs in English to mean 'in order to' (wait and see, try and relax etc). To translate these expressions, look under the appropriate verb entry (wait, try etc).
> For examples and other uses, see the entry below.

conj [1] (joining words or clauses) et; **cups** ∼ **plates** des tasses et des assiettes; **he picked up his papers and went out** il a ramassé ses papiers et il est sorti; [2] (in numbers) **two hundred** ∼ **sixty-two** deux cent soixante-deux; [3] (with repetition) **faster** ∼ **faster** de plus en plus vite; **it got worse** ∼ **worse** c'est devenu de pire en pire; **I waited** ∼ **waited** j'ai attendu pendant des heures; **to talk on** ∼ **on** parler pendant des heures; **we laughed** ∼ **laughed!** qu'est-ce qu'on a ri!; [4] (for emphasis) **it's lovely** ∼ **warm** il fait bon; **come nice** ∼ **early** viens tôt; AND **he didn't even say thank you** et en plus il n'a même pas dit merci; [5] (in phrases) ∼ **all that** et tout le reste; ∼ **that**○ GB et tout ça; ∼ **so on** et ainsi de suite; ∼ **how**○! et comment!; ∼**?** et alors?; [6] (alike) **summer** ∼ **winter** été comme hiver; **day** ∼ **night** jour et nuit; [7] (with negative) **he doesn't like singing** ∼ **dancing** il n'aime ni chanter ni danser

Andean /ænˈdɪən/ adj andin, des Andes

Andes /ˈændiːz/ pr npl **the** ∼ les Andes fpl

Andorra /ænˈdɔːrə/ ▸ p. 774 pr n Andorre f

anecdotal /ˌænɪkˈdəʊtl/ adj [memoirs, account] anecdotique; [talk, lecture] plein d'anecdotes; **on the basis of** ∼ **evidence…** selon des sources non confirmées…

anemone /əˈnemənɪ/ n Bot anémone f

anesthesiologist /ˌænɪsˌθiːzɪˈɒlədʒɪst/ ▸ p. 1181 n US (médecin) anesthésiste mf

anesthetist /əˈniːsθətɪst/ ▸ p. 1181 n US infirmier/-ière m/f anesthésiste

anesthetize vtr US = **anaesthetize**

anew /əˈnjuː, US əˈnuː/ adv (once more) encore, de nouveau; (in a new way) à nouveau; **to begin** ∼ recommencer

angel /ˈeɪndʒl/ n lit, fig ange m; ∼ **of mercy** ange de miséricorde

> (Idiom) **to rush in where** ∼**s fear to tread** se lancer avec le courage de l'inconscience

angel: ∼ **cake** n gâteau m de Savoie (coloré en rose et blanc); ∼**fish** n scalaire m

angelic /ænˈdʒelɪk/ adj angélique

anger /ˈæŋɡə(r)/
A n colère f (**at** devant; **towards** contre); **in** ∼ sous le coup de la colère
B vtr [decision, remark] mettre [qn] en colère [person]

angina (pectoris) /ænˌdʒaɪnə (ˈpektərɪs)/ ▸ p. 933 n angine f de poitrine

angle /ˈæŋɡl/
A n [1] gen, Math angle m; ∼ **of descent** angle de chute; **camera** ∼ angle de vue; **to be at an** ∼ **to sth** [table] faire un angle avec [wall]; [tower] pencher par rapport à [ground]; **from every** ∼ sous tous les angles; **seen from this** ∼ d'ici; **at an** ∼ en biais; [2] (point of view) point m de vue (**on** sur); (perspective, slant) angle m; **seen from this** ∼ sous cet angle; [3] (corner) angle m (**of** de); [4] Sport gen angle m; (of shot, kick) angle m de tir
B vtr [1] (tilt) orienter [camera, light, table] (**towards** vers); incliner [racket, ball]; [2] Sport (hit) jouer [qch] près des lignes [ball, shot]; [3] fig (slant) orienter [programme]
C vi [1] (fish) pêcher (à la ligne); **to** ∼ **for salmon** pêcher le saumon; [2] ○fig (try to obtain) **to** ∼ **for sth** chercher à obtenir qch

angle bracket n Tech équerre f

Anglepoise® /ˈæŋɡlpɔɪz/ n ∼ **(lamp)** lampe f d'architecte

angler /ˈæŋɡlə(r)/ n pêcheur/-euse m/f (à la ligne)

anglicism /ˈæŋɡlɪsɪzəm/ n anglicisme m

anglicize /ˈæŋɡlɪsaɪz/ vtr angliciser

angling /ˈæŋɡlɪŋ/ ▸ p. 881 n pêche f (à la ligne)

Anglo+ /ˈæŋɡləʊ/ combining form anglo-

Anglo-American /ˌæŋɡləʊəˈmerɪkən/ ▸ p. 1032
A n Anglo-Américain/-e m/f
B adj anglo-américain

Anglo-French /ˌæŋɡləʊˈfrentʃ/ ▸ p. 1032, p. 969
A n Ling anglo-normand m
B adj anglo-français, franco-britannique

Anglophone /ˈæŋɡləʊfəʊn/ n, adj anglophone (mf)

Anglo-Saxon /ˌæŋɡləʊˈsæksn/ ▸ p. 1032, p. 969
A n [1] (person) Anglo-Saxon/-onne m/f; [2] (language) anglo-saxon m
B adj anglo-saxon/-onne

Angola /æŋˈɡəʊlə/ ▸ p. 774 pr n Angola m

angrily /ˈæŋɡrɪlɪ/ adv [react, speak] avec colère

angry /ˈæŋɡrɪ/ adj [1] [person, animal, reaction, tone, expression] furieux/-ieuse; [outburst, scene, words] de colère; **to look** ∼ avoir l'air en colère; **to be** ∼ **at** ou **with sb** être en colère contre qn; **I was** ∼ **at having to wait** j'étais en colère d'avoir à attendre; **to get** ou **grow** ∼ se fâcher; **to make sb** ∼ mettre qn en colère; [2] fig [sea, sky] littér menaçant; [wound, rash] vilain

anguish /ˈæŋɡwɪʃ/ n [1] (mental) souffrance f, douleur f; **to be in** ∼ être au supplice; [2] (physical) douleur f

anguished /ˈæŋɡwɪʃt/ adj [person] angoissé; [suffering] aigu/-uë

angular /ˈæŋɡjʊlə(r)/ adj [features, shape] anguleux/-euse; [person] au physique anguleux; [building] plein d'angles

animal /ˈænɪml/
A n [1] lit (creature, genus) animal m, bête f; [2] (brutish person) **to behave like** ∼**s** [people] se conduire comme des brutes; **to bring out the** ∼ **in sb** réveiller la bête qui est en qn; [3] fig **she is a political** ∼ elle a la politique dans le sang
B noun modifier [welfare, rights] des animaux; [feed] pour animaux; [behaviour, fat] animal

animal: ~ **activist** n militant/-e m/f pour les droits des animaux; ~ **experiment** n expérience f sur les animaux; ~ **husbandry** n élevage m; ~ **kingdom** n règne m animal; ~ **liberation front** n mouvement m pour la libération des animaux; ~ **lover** n ami/-e m/f des bêtes; ~ **product** n produit m d'origine animale; ~ **rights** npl droits mpl des animaux; ~ **sanctuary** n refuge m pour animaux; ~ **testing** n expérimentation f animale

animate

A /ˈænɪmət/ adj [person] vivant; [object] animé

B /ˈænɪmeɪt/ vtr animer

animated /ˈænɪmeɪtɪd/ adj (all contexts) animé

animatedly /ˈænɪmeɪtɪdlɪ/ adv avec animation

animator /ˈænɪmeɪtə(r)/ ▸ p. 1181 n (film cartoonist) animateur/-trice m/f; (director) réalisateur/-trice m/f de dessin animé

animosity /ˌænɪˈmɒsətɪ/ n animosité f (**towards** envers)

aniseed /ˈænɪsiːd/ n ⫶1⫶ (flavour) anis m; ⫶2⫶ (seed) graine f d'anis

ankle /ˈæŋkl/ ▸ p. 698 n cheville f

anklebone n astragale m

ankle-deep adj **to be ~ in mud** avoir de la boue jusqu'aux chevilles

ankle: ~**length** adj [dress] descendant jusqu'aux chevilles; ~ **sock** n socquette f

annals /ˈænlz/ npl annales fpl; **to go down in the ~ (of history)** figurer dans les annales

annex

A /ˈæneks/ n (also **annexe** GB) annexe f

B /əˈneks/ vtr annexer [territory, land, country] (**to** à)

annexation /ˌænɪkˈseɪʃn/ n (action) annexion f (**of** de); (land annexed) territoire m annexé

annihilate /əˈnaɪəleɪt/ vtr (all contexts) anéantir

anniversary /ˌænɪˈvɜːsərɪ/

A n anniversaire m (**of** de)

B noun modifier [festival, reunion] commémoratif/-ive

anno Domini, **Anno Domini** /ˌænəʊ ˈdɒmɪnaɪ/ adv après Jésus-Christ

annotate /ˈænəteɪt/ vtr annoter

announce /əˈnaʊns/

A vtr annoncer (**that** que)

B vi US annoncer sa candidature

announcement /əˈnaʊnsmənt/ n ⫶1⫶ (spoken) annonce f (**of** de; **that** indiquant que); ⫶2⫶ (written) avis m; (of birth, death) faire-part m inv

announcer /əˈnaʊnsə(r)/ n ⫶1⫶ (on TV) speaker/-erine m/f; **radio ~** présentateur/-trice m/f de radio; ⫶2⫶ (at rail station) annonceur/-euse m/f

annoy /əˈnɔɪ/ vtr [person] (by behaviour) agacer; (by opposing wishes) contrarier; [discomfort, noise] gêner; **what really ~s me is that** ce qui me contrarie, c'est que; **this man's ~ing me** cet homme m'embête

annoyance /əˈnɔɪəns/ n ⫶1⫶ (crossness) agacement m (**at** devant), contrariété f (**at** à); **a look of ~** un regard agacé; ⫶2⫶ (nuisance) désagrément m

annoyed /əˈnɔɪd/ adj contrarié (**at, by** par); (stronger) agacé, fâché (**at, by** par); ~ **with sb** fâché contre qn; **she was ~ with him for being late** elle était contrariée parce qu'il était en retard

annoying /əˈnɔɪɪŋ/ adj agaçant (**to do** de faire); **the ~ thing is that…** ce qui est agaçant or fâcheux, c'est que…

annual /ˈænjʊəl/

A n ⫶1⫶ (book) album m (annuel); ⫶2⫶ (plant) plante f annuelle

B adj annuel/-elle

Annual General Meeting, **AGM** n assemblée f générale annuelle

annually /ˈænjʊəlɪ/ adv [earn, produce] par an; [do, inspect] tous les ans

annuity /əˈnjuːətɪ, US -ˈnuː-/ n rente f

annul /əˈnʌl/ vtr (p prés etc **-ll-**) annuler [marriage, treaty, vote]; abroger [law]

annulment /əˈnʌlmənt/ n (of marriage) annulation f; (of legislation) abrogation f

Annunciation /əˌnʌnsɪˈeɪʃn/ n Annonciation f

anodyne /ˈænədaɪn/ adj (inoffensive) inoffensif/-ive; (bland) anodin

anoint /əˈnɔɪnt/ vtr ⫶1⫶ oindre; **to ~ with oil** oindre; ⫶2⫶ (appoint to office) sacrer

anomaly /əˈnɒməlɪ/ n anomalie f (**in** dans)

anon. /əˈnɒn/ abrév = **anonymous**

anonymity /ˌænəˈnɪmətɪ/ n anonymat m

anonymous /əˈnɒnɪməs/ adj anonyme; **to remain ~** garder l'anonymat

anonymously /əˈnɒnɪməslɪ/ adv [complain, write] anonymement; [inform, donate] de façon anonyme

anorak /ˈænəræk/ n anorak m

anorexia /ˌænəˈreksɪə/ n ⫶1⫶ (also ~ **nervosa**) anorexie f mentale; ⫶2⫶ (loss of appetite) anorexie f

anorexic /ˌænəˈreksɪk/ n, adj anorexique (mf)

another /əˈnʌðə(r)/

> ⚠️ When *another* is used as a determiner it is translated by *un autre* or *une autre* according to the gender of the noun that follows: *another ticket* = un autre billet; *another cup* = une autre tasse. However, when *another* means *an additional*, *encore* can also be used: *another cup of tea?* = une autre tasse de thé or encore une tasse de thé? For more examples and particular usages, see **A** below.
>
> When *another* is used as a pronoun it is translated by *un autre* or *une autre* according to the gender of the noun it refers to: *that cake was delicious, can I have another?* = ce gâteau était délicieux, est-ce que je peux en prendre un autre?; *I see you like the peaches—have another* = je vois que tu aimes les pêches—prends-en une autre. Note that *en* is always added in French when *un*/*une autre* are used as pronouns. For more examples and particular usages, see **B** below.

A det ⫶1⫶ (an additional) un/-e autre, encore un/-e; **would you like ~ drink?** est-ce que tu veux un autre verre?, encore un verre?; **yet ~ letter** encore une nouvelle lettre; **that will cost you ~ £5** cela vous coûtera 5 livres sterling de plus; **without ~ word** sans rien dire de plus; **in ~ five weeks** dans cinq semaines; **it was ~ ten years before they met again** dix ans se sont écoulés avant qu'ils se rencontrent de nouveau; **and ~ thing,…** et de plus,…; ⫶2⫶ (a different) un/-e autre; ~ **time** une autre fois; **he has ~ job now** il a un nouveau travail maintenant; **to put it ~ way…** en d'autres termes…; **that's quite ~ matter** ça c'est une autre histoire or question; ⫶3⫶ (new) ~ **Garbo** une nouvelle Garbo

B pron un/-e autre; **can I have ~?** est-ce que je peux en avoir un/-e autre?; ~ **of the witnesses said that** un autre témoin a dit que; **one after ~** l'un/l'une après l'autre; **of one kind or ~** d'une sorte ou d'une autre; **for one reason or ~** pour une raison ou une autre; **in one way or ~** d'une façon ou d'une autre

answer /ˈɑːnsə(r), US ˈænsər/

A n ⫶1⫶ (reply) réponse f (**to** à); **to get/give an ~** obtenir/donner une réponse; **there's no ~** (to door) il n'y a personne; (on phone) ça ne répond pas; **in ~ to sth** en réponse à qch; **I won't take no for an ~!** pas question de refuser!; **there's no ~ to that!** que voulez-vous répondre à ça?; **France's ~ to Marilyn Monroe** la version française de Marilyn Monroe; ⫶2⫶ (solution) (to difficulty, puzzle) solution f (**to** à); Sch, Univ réponse f (**to** à); **the right/wrong ~** la bonne/mauvaise réponse

B vtr ⫶1⫶ (reply to) répondre à [question, invitation, letter, person]; **to ~ that…** répondre que…; **to ~ the door** aller or venir ouvrir la porte; **to ~ the telephone** répondre au téléphone; **to ~ the call** lit, fig répondre à l'appel; ⫶2⫶ (respond) répondre à [criticism, accusation, allegation]; **to ~ a charge** répondre d'une accusation; ⫶3⫶ (meet) répondre à [need, demand]; **we saw nobody ~ing that description** nous n'avons vu personne qui réponde à cette description

C vi ⫶1⫶ (respond) répondre; **it's not ~ing** GB Telecom ça ne répond pas; **to ~ to the name of X** répondre au nom de X; ⫶2⫶ (correspond) **to ~ to** répondre or correspondre à [description]; ⫶3⫶ (account) **to ~ for sb** répondre de qn; **to ~ to sb** être responsable devant qn

(Phrasal verbs)

■ **answer back**: ▸ ~ **back** répondre; ▸ ~ **[sb] back** GB répondre; **don't ~ (me) back!** comment oses-tu (me) répondre?

■ **answer for**: ▸ ～ **for [sth]** (account for) répondre de [action]; **they have a lot to ～ for!** ils ont beaucoup de comptes à rendre!

answerable /'ɑːnsərəbl, US 'æns-/ adj **to be ～ to sb** être responsable devant qn; **to be ～ for** être responsable de [actions]; **they are ～ to no-one** ils n'ont de comptes à rendre à personne

answering: ～ **machine** n répondeur m (téléphonique); ～ **service** n permanence f téléphonique

answerphone /'ɑːnsəfəʊn, US 'æns-/ n répondeur m (téléphonique)

ant /ænt/ n fourmi f; **flying ～** fourmi volante

antacid /ænt'æsɪd/ n, adj alcalin (m)

antagonism /æn'tægənɪzəm/ n antagonisme m (**between** entre); ～ **to** ou **towards sb/sth** hostilité f à l'égard de qn/qch

antagonistic /æn,tægə'nɪstɪk/ adj (hostile) hostile (**to, towards** à); (mutually opposed) antagoniste

antagonize /æn'tægənaɪz/ vtr (annoy) contrarier (**with** avec); (stronger) éveiller l'hostilité de (**by doing** en faisant; **with** avec)

Antarctic /æn'tɑːktɪk/
A pr n **the ～** l'Antarctique m
B adj (also **antarctic**) antarctique

Antarctica /æn'tɑːktɪkə/ pr n Antarctique m

Antarctic: ～ **Circle** cercle m polaire antarctique; ～ **Ocean** ▸ p. 1049 n océan m Antarctique

anteater /'ænti:tə(r)/ n fourmilier m

antecedent /,æntɪ'si:dnt/
A n (precedent) antécédent m; (ancestor) ancêtre m
B adj antérieur (**to** à)

antedate /,æntɪ'deɪt/ vtr ① (put earlier date on) antidater [cheque, letter]; ② (predate) précéder (**by** de)

antediluvian /,æntɪdɪ'lu:vɪən/ adj antédiluvien/-ienne

antelope /'æntɪləʊp/ n antilope f

antenatal /,æntɪ'neɪtl/ GB
A n examen m prénatal
B adj prénatal

antenatal: ～ **class** n GB cours m de préparation à l'accouchement; ～ **clinic** n GB service m de consultation prénatale

antenna /æn'tenə/ n (pl **-ae** ou **-as**) antenne f

anterior /æn'tɪərɪə(r)/ adj antérieur

anteroom /'æntɪru:m, -rʊm/ n antichambre f

anthem /'ænθəm/ n (theme tune) hymne m; (motet) motet m

anthill /'ænthɪl/, **antheap** /'ænthi:p/ n fourmilière f

anthologist /æn'θɒlədʒɪst/ n anthologiste mf

anthology /æn'θɒlədʒɪ/ n anthologie f

anthracite /'ænθrəsaɪt/ n anthracite m

anthrax /'ænθræks/ ▸ p. 933 n (pl **-thraces**) (disease) charbon m; (pustule) anthrax m

anthropological /,ænθrəpə'lɒdʒɪkl/ adj anthropologique

anthropologist /,ænθrə'pɒlədʒɪst/ ▸ p. 1181 n anthropologue mf, anthropologiste mf

anthropology /,ænθrə'pɒlədʒɪ/ n anthropologie f

anti /'æntɪ/
A prep contre; **to be ～** être contre
B **anti+** combining form anti(-)

antiabortion /,æntɪə'bɔːʃn/ adj contre l'avortement

antiabortionist /,æntɪə'bɔːʃənɪst/ n adversaire mf de l'avortement

antiaircraft /,æntɪ'eəkrɑːft, US -kræft/ adj antiaérien/-ienne

antiapartheid /,æntɪə'pɑːteɪt, ,æntɪə'pɑːtaɪd/ adj anti-apartheid

antibacterial /'æntɪbæk'tɪərɪəl/ adj antibactérien/-ienne

antiballistic missile /,æntɪbəlɪstɪk 'mɪsaɪl, US 'mɪsl/ n missile m antimissile

antibiotic /,æntɪbaɪ'ɒtɪk/
A n antibiotique m; **on ～s** sous antibiotiques
B adj antibiotique

antibody /'æntɪbɒdɪ/ n anticorps m

anticipate /æn'tɪsɪpeɪt/
A vtr ① (expect, foresee) prévoir, s'attendre à [problem, delay];

to ～ that prévoir que; **as ～d** comme prévu; **we ～ meeting him soon** nous pensons le rencontrer bientôt; **I didn't ～ him doing that** je ne m'attendais pas à ce qu'il fasse ça; **long-～d** attendu depuis si longtemps; ② (guess in advance) anticiper [sb's needs, result]; ③ (preempt) devancer [person, act]; ④ (prefigure) préfigurer
B vi anticiper

anticipation /æn,tɪsɪ'peɪʃn/ n ① (excitement) excitation f; (pleasure in advance) plaisir m anticipé; **in ～ of sth** à l'idée de qch; **she smiled in ～** elle souriait en se réjouissant d'avance; ② (expectation) prévision f (**of** de); **in ～ of** en prévision de

anticlerical /,æntɪ'klerɪkl/ adj anticlérical

anticlimax /,æntɪ'klaɪmæks/ n déception f; **what an ～!** quelle déception!

anticlockwise /,æntɪ'klɒkwaɪz/ adj, adv GB dans le sens inverse des aiguilles d'une montre

antics /'æntɪks/ npl (comical) pitreries fpl; pej bouffonneries fpl

anticyclone /,æntɪ'saɪkləʊn/ n anticyclone m

antidepressant /,æntɪdɪ'presnt/ n, adj antidépresseur (m)

antidote /'æntɪdəʊt/ n Med, fig antidote m (**to, for** contre, à)

antiestablishment /,æntɪɪs'tæblɪʃmənt/ adj contestataire

antifreeze /'æntɪfriːz/ n antigel m

antiglare /,æntɪ'gleə(r)/ adj [screen] antireflet inv

anti-globalization /,æntɪgləʊbəlaɪ'zeɪʃən/ n antimondialisation f

antihistamine /,æntɪ'hɪstəmɪn/ n antihistaminique m

anti-inflation /,æntɪɪn'fleɪʃn/ adj (avant n) anti-inflation

anti-inflationary /,æntɪɪn'fleɪʃənərɪ, US -nerɪ/ adj anti-inflationniste

antilock /'æntɪlɒk/ adj antiblocage

antipathy /æn'tɪpəθɪ/ n antipathie f (**for, to, towards** envers; **between** entre)

antiperspirant /,æntɪ'pɜːspɪrənt/ n produit m anti-transpiration

antipodean /æn,tɪpə'di:ən/
A n: personne qui vient d'Australie ou de Nouvelle-Zélande
B adj d'Australie et Nouvelle-Zélande

Antipodes /æn'tɪpədi:z/ npl GB **the ～** l'Australie et la Nouvelle-Zélande

antiquarian /,æntɪ'kweərɪən/ ▸ p. 1181 n (dealer) antiquaire mf; (scholar) archéologue mf; (collector) collectionneur/-euse m/f d'antiquités

antiquarian bookshop n librairie f spécialisée dans le livre ancien

antiquated /'æntɪkweɪtɪd/ adj [machinery, idea] archaïque; [building] vétuste

antique /æn'ti:k/
A n ① (piece of furniture) meuble m ancien or d'époque; (other object) objet m ancien or d'époque; ② ○péj (person) vieux fossile m
B adj ① (old) ancien/-ienne; ② (old-style) à l'ancienne

antique: ～ **dealer** ▸ p. 1181, n antiquaire mf; ～**(s) fair** n foire f aux antiquités; ～ **shop** ▸ p. 1181 n magasin m d'antiquités

antiquity /æn'tɪkwətɪ/ n ① (ancient times) antiquité f; ② (great age) ancienneté f; **of great ～** très ancien/-ienne; ③ (relic) antiquité f

antiracism /,æntɪ'reɪsɪzəm/ n antiracisme m

anti-riot /,æntɪ'raɪət/ adj [police] antiémeutes inv

anti-rust /,æntɪ'rʌst/ adj antirouille inv

anti-Semitic /,æntɪsɪ'mɪtɪk/ adj antisémite

anti-Semitism /,æntɪ'semɪtɪzəm/ n antisémitisme m

antiseptic /,æntɪ'septɪk/ n, adj antiseptique (m)

anti-skid /,æntɪ'skɪd/ adj antidérapant

anti-smoking /,æntɪ'sməʊkɪŋ/ adj antitabac

antisocial /,æntɪ'səʊʃl/ adj ① ～ **behaviour** gen comportement m incorrect; (criminal behaviour) comportement m délinquant; ② (reclusive) sauvage

anti-terrorist /,æntɪ'terərɪst/ adj antiterroriste

anti-theft /,æntɪ'θeft/ adj [lock, device] antivol; [camera] de surveillance; ～ **steering lock** antivol de direction

a

antithesis /æn'tɪθəsɪs/ *n* (*pl* **-theses**) sout **1** (opposite) contraire *m* (**of** de); (in ideas) antithèse *f* (**of** de); **2** (contrast) contraste *m* (**between** entre); **3** Literat, Philos antithèse *f*

antithetic(al) /ˌæntɪ'θetɪk(l)/ *adj* antithétique; **to be ∼ to sth** aller à l'encontre de qch

antitrust /ˌæntɪ'trʌst/ *adj* antitrust *inv*

antivirus software /ˌæntɪ'vaɪərəs ˌsɒftweə(r), US sɔ:ft-/ *n* logiciel *m* antivirus

anti-vivisectionist /ˌæntɪˌvɪvɪ'sekʃənɪst/
A *n* militant/-e *m/f* contre la vivisection
B *adj* contre la vivisection

antlers /'æntləz/ *npl* (on stag) bois *mpl* de cerf

antonym /'æntənɪm/ *n* antonyme *m*

Antwerp /'æntwɜ:p/ ▸ p. 1276 *pr n* Anvers

anus /'eɪnəs/ *n* anus *m*

anvil /'ænvɪl/ *n* enclume *f* also Anat

anxiety /æŋ'zaɪətɪ/ *n* **1** (apprehension) grandes inquiétudes *fpl* (**about** à propos de; **for** pour); **she caused them great ∼** elle leur a causé beaucoup de soucis; **to be in a state of ∼** être angoissé; **2** (source of worry) souci *m*; **3** (eagerness) désir *m* ardent (**to do** de faire); **4** Psych anxiété *f*; **∼ attack** crise *f* d'angoisse

anxious /'æŋkʃəs/ *adj* **1** (worried) très inquiet/-iète (**about** à propos de; **for** pour); **to be ∼ about doing** s'inquiéter de faire; **to be very** *ou* **extremely ∼** être angoissé; **2** (causing worry) [*moment, time*] angoissant; **3** (eager) très désireux/-euse (**to do** de faire); **I am ∼ for him to know** *ou* **that he should know** je tiens beaucoup à ce qu'il sache; **to be ∼ for sth** avoir un fort désir de qch

anxiously /'æŋkʃəslɪ/ *adv* **1** (worriedly) avec inquiétude; **2** (eagerly) avec impatience

any /'enɪ/

⚠️ When *any* is used as a determiner in negative sentences it is not usually translated in French: *we don't have any money* = nous n'avons pas d'argent.
When *any* is used as a determiner in questions it is translated by *du, de l', de la* or *des* according to the gender and number of the noun that follows: *is there any soap?* = y a-t-il du savon?; *is there any flour?* = y a-t-il de la farine?; *are there any questions?* = est-ce qu'il y a des questions?
For examples and other determiner uses see **A** in the entry below.
When *any* is used as a pronoun in negative sentences and in questions it is translated by *en*: *we don't have any* = nous n'en avons pas; *have you got any?* = est-ce que vous en avez?
For more examples and other pronoun uses see **B** below.
For adverbial uses such as *any more, any longer, any better etc* see **C** below.

A *det* **1** (with negative, implied negative) **he hasn't got ∼ money** il n'a pas d'argent; **they never receive ∼ letters** ils ne reçoivent jamais de lettres; **they hardly ate ∼ cake** ils n'ont presque pas mangé de gâteau; **I don't want ∼ lunch** je ne veux pas de déjeuner; **I don't need ∼ advice** je n'ai pas besoin de conseils; **they couldn't get ∼ information** ils n'ont pas obtenu la moindre information; **he hasn't got ∼ common sense** il n'a aucun bon sens; **2** (in questions, conditional sentences) **is there ∼ tea?** est-ce qu'il y a du thé?; **if you have ∼ money** si vous avez de l'argent; **3** (no matter which) n'importe quel/quelle, tout; **you can have ∼ cup you like** vous pouvez prendre n'importe quelle tasse; **∼ information would be very useful** tout renseignement serait très utile; **∼ complaints should be addressed to Mr Cook** pour toute réclamation adressez-vous à M. Cook; **I'm ready to help in ∼ way I can** je suis prêt à faire tout ce que je peux pour aider; **I do not wish to restrict your freedom in ∼ way** je n'ai pas l'intention d'entraver votre liberté de quelque façon que ce soit; **he might return at ∼ time** il peut revenir d'un moment à l'autre; **if you should want to discuss this at ∼ time** si à un moment ou à un autre vous souhaitez discuter de cela; **come round and see me ∼ time** passe me voir quand tu veux; **I don't buy ∼ one brand in particular** je n'achète aucune marque en particulier

B *pron* **1** (with negative, implied negative) **he hasn't got ∼** il n'en a pas; **there is hardly ∼ left** il n'en reste presque pas; **she doesn't like ∼ of them** (people) elle n'aime aucun d'entre eux/elles; (things) elle n'en aime aucun/-e; **2** (in questions, conditional sentences) **I'd like some tea, if you have ∼** je voudrais du thé, si vous en avez; **have ∼ of you got a car?** est-ce que l'un/-e d'entre vous a une voiture?; **are ∼ of them blue?** y en a-t-il des bleus?; **3** (no matter which) n'importe lequel/laquelle; **'which colour would you like?'—'∼'** 'quelle couleur veux-tu?'—'n'importe laquelle'; **∼ of those pens** n'importe lequel de ces stylos; **∼ of them could do it** n'importe qui d'entre eux/elles pourrait le faire

C *adv* **1** (with comparatives) **is he feeling ∼ better?** est-ce qu'il se sent mieux?; **have you got ∼ more of these?** est-ce que vous en avez d'autres?; **do you want ∼ more wine?** voulez-vous encore du vin?; **I don't like him ∼ more than you do** je ne l'aime guère plus que toi; **I don't know ∼ more than that** c'est tout ce que je sais; **he doesn't live here ∼ more** *ou* **longer** il n'habite plus ici; **I won't put up with it ∼ longer** ça ne peut plus continuer ainsi; **if we stay here ∼ longer** si nous restons plus longtemps; **can't you walk ∼ faster?** tu ne peux pas marcher plus vite?; **I can't leave ∼ later than 6 o'clock** il faut que je parte à 6 heures au plus tard; **2** ○(at all) du tout; **that doesn't help me ∼** ça ne m'aide pas du tout

anybody /'enɪbɒdɪ/ *pron* **1** (with negative, implied negative) personne; **there wasn't ∼ in the house** il n'y avait personne dans la maison; **without ∼ knowing** sans que personne le sache; **I didn't have ∼ to talk to** il n'y avait personne avec qui j'aurais pu parler; **I don't like him and nor does ∼ else** je ne l'aime pas, d'ailleurs personne ne l'aime; **hardly ∼ came** il n'est venu presque personne; **2** (in questions, conditional sentences) quelqu'un; **is there ∼ in the house?** est-ce qu'il y a quelqu'un dans la maison?; **if ∼ asks, tell them I've gone out** si quelqu'un me cherche, dis que je suis sorti; **3** (no matter who) **∼ could do it** n'importe qui pourrait le faire; **but you/his boss would say yes** tout autre que toi/ton patron dirait oui; **'who shall I invite?'—'∼ but him'** 'qui vais-je inviter?'—'n'importe qui, sauf lui'; **∼ who wants to, can go** tous ceux qui le veulent, peuvent y aller; **∼ but you would have given it to him** n'importe qui d'autre que toi le lui aurait donné; **∼ can make a mistake** ça arrive à tout le monde de faire une erreur; **∼ would think you were deaf** c'est à croire que tu es sourd; **you can invite ∼ (you like)** tu peux inviter qui tu veux; **4** (somebody unimportant) **we can't ask just ∼ to do it** nous ne pouvons pas demander à n'importe qui de le faire; **5** (somebody important) **∼ who was ∼ was at the party** tous les gens importants étaient à la soirée

anyhow /'enɪhaʊ/ *adv* **1** (in any case) = **anyway**; **2** (in a careless way) n'importe comment

anyone /'enɪwʌn/ *pron* = **anybody**

anyplace○ /'enɪpleɪs/ *adv* US = **anywhere**

anything /'enɪθɪŋ/ *pron* **1** (with negative, implied negative) rien; **she didn't say/do ∼** elle n'a rien dit/fait; **he didn't have ∼ to do** il n'avait rien à faire; **don't believe ∼ he says** ne crois pas un mot de ce qu'il dit; **2** (in questions, conditional sentences) quelque chose; **if ∼ happens** *ou* **should happen to her** s'il lui arrive quoi que ce soit; **is there ∼ to be done?** peut-on faire quelque chose?; **is there ∼ in the rumour that...?** est-il vrai que...?; **3** (no matter what) tout; **∼ is possible** tout est possible; **I'd do** *ou* **give ∼ to get that job** je ferais tout pour obtenir cet emploi; **they'd do ∼ for you** ils sont toujours prêts à rendre service; **she likes ∼ sweet/to do with football** elle aime tout ce qui est sucré/qui a rapport au football; **to cost ∼ between £50 and £100** coûter de 50 à 100 livres sterling; **he was ∼ but happy/a liar** il n'était pas du tout heureux/menteur; **'was it interesting?'—'∼ but!'** 'est-ce que c'était intéressant?'—'tout sauf ça'; **he wasn't ∼ annoyed, if ∼, he was quite pleased** il n'était pas fâché, au contraire, il était content

⟨Idioms⟩ **∼ goes** tout est permis; **as easy/funny as ∼** facile/drôle comme tout; **to run/laugh/work like ∼** courir/rire/travailler comme un fou○

anytime /'enɪtaɪm/ *adv* (also **any time**) **1** (no matter when) n'importe quand; **∼ after 2 pm** n'importe quand à partir de 14 heures; **∼ you like** quand tu veux; **if at ∼ you feel lonely...** si jamais tu te sens seul...; **at ∼ of the day or night** à n'importe quelle heure du jour ou de la nuit; **2** (at any moment) à tout moment; **he could arrive ∼ now** il pourrait arriver d'un moment à l'autre

anyway /'enɪweɪ/ *adv* **1** (in any case, besides) de toute façon; **2** (nevertheless) quand même; **I don't really like hats, but I'll**

try it on ~ je n'aime pas vraiment les chapeaux, mais je vais quand même l'essayer; **thanks** ~ merci quand même; **3** (at least, at any rate) en tout cas; **we can't go out, not yet** ~ nous ne pouvons pas sortir, pas pour l'instant en tout cas; **4** (well: as sentence adverb) '~, **we arrived at the station...**' 'bon, nous sommes arrivés à la gare...'

anywhere /'enɪweə(r), US -hweər/ adv **1** (with negative, implied negative) **you can't go** ~ tu ne peux aller nulle part; **there isn't** ~ **to sit** il n'y a pas de place pour s'asseoir; **they didn't go** ~ **this weekend** ils ne sont allés nulle part ce week-end; **you won't get** ~ **if you don't pass your exams** fig tu n'arriveras à rien si tu ne réussis pas tes examens; **crying isn't going to get you** ~ fig ça ne t'avancera à rien de pleurer; **2** (in questions, conditional sentences) quelque part; **have you got a radio** ~? avez-vous une radio quelque part?; **did you go** ~ **nice?** est-ce que tu es allé dans un endroit agréable?; **we're going to Spain, if** ~ si on va quelque part, ce sera en Espagne; **3** (no matter where) ~ **you like** où tu veux; ~ **in the world/in England** partout dans le monde/en Angleterre; ~ **except** ou **but Bournemouth** partout sauf à Bournemouth; ~ **she goes, he follows her** il la suit partout où elle va; '**where do you want to go?**'—'~ **exotic/hot**' 'où veux-tu aller?'—'dans un endroit exotique/où il fait chaud'; ~ **between 50 and 100 people** entre 50 et 100 personnes

aorta /eɪ'ɔːtə/ n (pl **-tas**, **-tae**) aorte f

Aosta /æ'ɒstə/ n Aoste

apace /ə'peɪs/ adv littér rapidement

Apache /ə'pætʃɪ/ ▸ p. 1032, p. 969 n Apache mf

apart /ə'pɑːt/

⚠ *Apart* is used after certain verbs in English (*come apart, take apart, fall apart etc*). For translations consult the appropriate verb entry (**come, take, fall** etc).

A adj, adv **1** (at a distance in time or space) **the trees were planted 10 metres** ~ les arbres étaient plantés à 10 mètres d'intervalle; **the houses were far** ~ les maisons étaient éloignées les unes des autres; **he stood** ~ **(from the group)** il se tenait à l'écart (du groupe); **the posts need to be placed further** ~ les poteaux doivent être écartés davantage; **2** (separate from each other) séparé; **we hate being** ~ (of couple) nous détestons être séparés; **they need to be kept** ~ il faut les garder séparés; **3** (leaving aside) à part; **dogs** ~ **à part** les chiens; **4** (different) **a race/a world** ~ une race/un monde à part

B **apart from** prep phr **1** (separate from) à l'écart de; **it stands** ~ **from the other houses** elle est à l'écart des autres maisons; **he lives** ~ **from his wife** il vit séparé de sa femme; **2** (leaving aside) en dehors de, à part; ~ **from working in an office, he...** en plus de travailler dans un bureau, il...; ~ **from being illegal, it's also dangerous** (mis) à part que c'est illégal, c'est aussi dangereux

apartheid /ə'pɑːtheɪt, -aɪt/ n apartheid m

apartment /ə'pɑːtmənt/
A n (flat) appartement m
B **apartments** npl (suite of rooms) appartements mpl

apartment: ~ **block** n immeuble m; ~ **house** n US résidence f

apathetic /ˌæpə'θetɪk/ adj (by nature) amorphe; (from illness, depression) apathique; ~ **about sth/towards sb** indifférent à qch/envers qn

apathy /'æpəθɪ/ n apathie f

ape /eɪp/
A n grand singe m; **female** ~ guenon f
B vtr singer [speech, behaviour, manners]

Apennines /'æpənaɪnz/ pr npl **the** ~ les Apennins mpl

aperitif /ə'perətɪf, US ə,perə'tiːf/ n apéritif m

aperture /'æpətʃʊə(r)/ n **1** (in wall, door) ouverture f; (small) interstice m; **2** (in telescope, camera) ouverture f

apex /'eɪpeks/ n (pl **-exes**, **-ices**) Math, fig sommet m

aphid /'eɪfɪd/ n puceron m

aphrodisiac /ˌæfrə'dɪzɪæk/ n, adj aphrodisiaque (m)

apiary /'eɪpɪərɪ, US -ierɪ/ n rucher m

apiece /ə'piːs/ adv **1** (for each person) chacun/-e m/f; **an apple** ~ une pomme chacun/-e; **2** (each one) **one euro** ~ un euro la pièce

aplenty /ə'plentɪ/ adv en profusion

apocalypse /ə'pɒkəlɪps/ n **1** Bible **the Apocalypse** l'Apocalypse f; **2** (disaster, destruction) apocalypse f

apocalyptic /ə,pɒkə'lɪptɪk/ adj apocalyptique

apocryphal /ə'pɒkrɪfl/ adj apocryphe

apogee /'æpədʒiː/ n apogée m

apolitical /ˌeɪpə'lɪtɪkl/ adj apolitique

Apollo /ə'pɒləʊ/
A pr n Mythol Apollon m
B n (beautiful man) apollon m

apologetic /ə,pɒlə'dʒetɪk/ adj [gesture, letter] d'excuse; **to be** ~ **about sth** s'excuser de qch; **to be** ~ **about doing** ou **for having done** s'excuser d'avoir fait; **to look** ~ avoir l'air contrit

apologetically /ə,pɒlə'dʒetɪklɪ/ adv d'un ton or d'un air contrit

apologist /ə'pɒlədʒɪst/ n apologiste m; ~ **for sth/sb** défenseur de qch/qn

apologize /ə'pɒlədʒaɪz/ vi s'excuser (**to sb** auprès de qn; **for sth** de qch; **for doing** d'avoir fait)

apology /ə'pɒlədʒɪ/ n **1** (excuse) excuses fpl (**for sth** pour qch; **for doing** pour avoir fait); **to make an** ~ s'excuser; **to make/give one's apologies** faire/présenter ses excuses; **Mrs X sends her apologies** Mme X vous prie d'accepter ses excuses; **without** ~ sans excuse; **2** (poor substitute) **an** ~ **for sth** un semblant de qch

apoplectic /ˌæpə'plektɪk/ adj **1** (furious) furibond; **2** †Med [fit, attack] d'apoplexie

apoplexy /'æpəpleksɪ/ n **1** (rage) accès m de rage; **2** †Med apoplexie f

apostle /ə'pɒsl/ n Relig, fig apôtre m (**of** de)

apostrophe /ə'pɒstrəfɪ/ n apostrophe f

apostrophize /ə'pɒstrəfaɪz/ vtr lancer une apostrophe à

apotheosis /ə,pɒθɪ'əʊsɪs/ n (pl **-ses**) sout apothéose f

appal GB, **appall** US /ə'pɔːl/ vtr (GB p prés etc **-ll-**) (shock) scandaliser; (horrify, dismay) horrifier

Appalachians /ˌæpə'leɪtʃɪənz/ pr npl **the** ~ les Appalaches fpl

appalled /ə'pɔːld/ adj (horrified, dismayed) horrifié; (shocked) scandalisé

appalling /ə'pɔːlɪŋ/ adj **1** (shocking) [crime, conditions, bigotry] épouvantable; [injury] affreux/-euse; **it's** ~ **that** il est révoltant que (+ subj); **2** (very bad) [manners, joke, taste] exécrable; [noise, weather] épouvantable

appallingly /ə'pɔːlɪŋlɪ/ adv [behave, treat] de manière épouvantable; **unemployment figures are** ~ **high** le taux de chômage a atteint un niveau déplorable; **furnished in** ~ **bad taste** meublé avec un goût exécrable

apparatus /ˌæpə'reɪtəs, US -'rætəs/ n **1** (equipment) ⊄ gen équipement m; (in lab) instruments mpl; (in gym) agrès mpl; **2** (for specific purpose) appareil m

apparent /ə'pærənt/ adj **1** (seeming) [contradiction, willingness] apparent; **2** (clear) évident; **for no** ~ **reason** sans raison apparente

apparently /ə'pærəntlɪ/ adv apparemment

apparition /ˌæpə'rɪʃn/ n apparition f

appeal /ə'piːl/
A n **1** (call) appel m (**for** à); **an** ~ **for calm** un appel au calme; **2** (charity event) appel m (**on behalf of** en faveur de); **an** ~ **for** un appel au don de [food, blankets]; **3** Sport contestation f (**against** contre; **to** auprès de); **4** Jur appel m; **5** (attraction) charme m; (interest) intérêt m; **to have a certain** ~ avoir un certain charme; **it holds no** ~ **for me** ça ne m'intéresse pas
B vi **1** Jur faire appel (**against** de); **to** ~ **to** recourir à l'arbitrage de [tribunal, person]; faire appel à [high court]; **2** Sport **to** ~ **to** demander l'arbitrage de [referee]; **to** ~ **against** contester [decision]; **3** (call, request) **to** ~ **for** lancer un appel à [order, tolerance]; faire appel à [witnesses]; **to** ~ **to sb to do** (formal call) prier qn de faire; **to** ~ **to the public for help** demander de l'aide au public; **4** (attract, interest) **to** ~ **to sb** [idea] tenter qn; [person] plaire à qn; [place] attirer qn

appeal: ~(**s**) **court** n cour f d'appel; ~ **fund** n fonds m d'aide

appealing /ə'piːlɪŋ/ adj **1** (attractive) [child, kitten] attachant; [plan, theory] séduisant; [modesty] charmant; **2** (beseeching) suppliant

appealingly /ə'piːlɪŋlɪ/ adv **1** (beseechingly) d'un air suppliant; **2** (attractively) plaisamment

a

a

appear /ə'pɪə(r)/ vi **1** (become visible) apparaître; **2** (turn up) arriver; **to ~ on the scene** lit arriver sur les lieux; fig faire son apparition; **to ~ from nowhere** apparaître; **where did she ~ from**○? d'où est-ce qu'elle sort○? hum; **3** (seem) **to ~ to be/to do** [person] avoir l'air d'être/de faire; **to ~ depressed** avoir l'air déprimé; **it ~s that** il semble que; **there ~s to be, there would ~ to be** on dirait qu'il y a; **so it ~s, so it would ~** (according to rumour) à ce qu'il paraît; (this is visibly the case) on dirait bien; **4** [book, work, article] paraître; **5** (perform) **to ~ on stage** paraître en scène; **to ~ on TV** passer à la télévision; **to ~ as** jouer dans le rôle de; **6** Jur (be present) comparaître (**before** devant; **for** pour); **~ in court** comparaître devant le tribunal; **to ~ as a witness** comparaître comme témoin; **7** (be written) [name, score] paraître (**on** sur; **in** dans)

appearance /ə'pɪərəns/
A n **1** (arrival) (of person, vehicle) arrivée f; (of development, invention) apparition f; **2** Cin, Theat, TV passage m; **to make an ~ on television/on stage** passer à la télévision/à la scène; **cast in order of ~** Theat distribution par ordre d'entrée en scène; Cin distribution par ordre d'apparition (à l'écran); **3** (public, sporting) apparition f; **this is his first ~ for Ireland** il fait ses débuts pour l'équipe d'Irlande; **to put in an ~** faire acte de présence; **4** Jur (in court) comparution f (**in, before** devant); **5** (look) (of person) apparence f; (of district, object) aspect m; **to check one's ~** vérifier sa tenue; **6** (semblance) **to give the ~ of sth/of doing** donner l'apparence de qch/de faire; **it had all the ~s** ou **every ~ of** cela avait tout l'air de; **7** (of book, article) parution f
B **appearances** npl apparences fpl; **to judge** ou **go by ~s** se fier aux apparences; **for the sake of ~s, for ~s' sake** pour la forme

appease /ə'piːz/ vtr apaiser

appeasement /ə'piːzmənt/ n apaisement m; **a policy of ~** une politique de conciliation

append /ə'pend/ vtr sout ajouter (**to** à)

appendage /ə'pendɪdʒ/ n appendice m also fig

appendicitis /ə,pendɪ'saɪtɪs/ ▸ p. 933 n appendicite f

appendix /ə'pendɪks/ n (pl **-ixes, -ices**) **1** Anat appendice m; **to have one's ~ removed** se faire opérer de l'appendicite; **2** (to printed volume) appendice m; (to book, report) annexe f

appertain /,æpə'teɪn/ vi **to ~ to sth** se rapporter à qch

appetite /'æpɪtaɪt/ n appétit m; **he has a good/poor ~** il a bon appétit/il n'a pas d'appétit; **the walk has given me an ~** la promenade m'a donné de l'appétit; **it'll spoil your ~** ça va te couper l'appétit

appetite suppressant n coupe-faim m inv

appetizer /'æpɪtaɪzə(r)/ n (drink) apéritif m; (biscuit, olive etc) amuse-gueule m inv; (starter) hors-d'œuvre m

appetizing /'æpɪtaɪzɪŋ/ adj appétissant

applaud /ə'plɔːd/
A vtr **1** (clap) applaudir [performance]; **2** (approve of) applaudir à [choice, tactics]; applaudir [person]
B vi applaudir

applause /ə'plɔːz/ n ₵ applaudissements mpl; **there was a burst of ~** les applaudissements ont éclaté

apple /'æpl/
A n pomme f; **the (Big) Apple** New York
B noun modifier [juice, peel] de pomme; [tart] aux pommes
(Idiom) **he is the ~ of her eye** c'est la prunelle de ses yeux

apple-~core n trognon m de pomme; **~ orchard** n pommeraie f; **~ tree** n pommier m

applet /'æplɪt/ n Comput appliquette f, microprogramme m, applet m

appliance /ə'plaɪəns/ n appareil m; **electrical ~** appareil électrique; **household ~** appareil électroménager

applicable /'æplɪkəbl, ə'plɪkəbl/ adj [argument, excuse] valable; [law, rule] en vigueur; **if ~** le cas échéant; **to be ~ to** s'appliquer à, concerner

applicant /'æplɪkənt/ n **1** (for job, place) candidat/-e m/f (**for** à, de); **2** (for passport, benefit, loan, visa) demandeur/-euse m/f (**for** de); (for citizenship) postulant/-e m/f (**for** à); **3** (for membership) candidat/-e m/f; **4** (for shares) souscripteur/-trice m/f; **5** Jur (for divorce, patent) demandeur/-eresse m/f, requérant/-e m/f

application /,æplɪ'keɪʃn/ n **1** (request) (for job) candidature f (**for** à); (for membership, passport, loan, promotion, transfer) demande f (**for** de); (for shares) souscription f (**for** de); **to**

make an ~ for a job poser sa candidature à un poste; **to make an ~ for a university place** faire une demande d'inscription à une université; **a letter of ~** une lettre de candidature; **to fill out a job ~** remplir un formulaire de candidature; **on ~** sur demande; **2** (spreading) application f (**to** à); **one ~ is sufficient** une (seule) couche suffit; **3** (implementation) (of law, penalty, rule) application f; (of theory, training) application f; **4** (for divorce, patent, bankruptcy) demande f (**for** de)

application form n (for loan, credit card, passport) formulaire m de demande; (for job) formulaire m de candidature; (for membership) demande f d'inscription

applicator /'æplɪkeɪtə(r)/ n applicateur m

applied /ə'plaɪd/ adj [linguistics, maths] appliqué

appliqué /æ'pliːkeɪ, US ,æplɪ'keɪ/
A n application f
B noun modifier [motif, decoration] en application

apply /ə'plaɪ/
A vtr **1** (spread) appliquer [make-up, paint] (**to** sur); **2** (use) appliquer [theory, rule, method, heat] (**to** à); exercer [friction, pressure] (**to** sur); **3** (give) appliquer [label, term] (**to** à); **4** (affix) apposer [sticker] (**to** sur); appliquer [bandage, sequins] (**to** sur)
B vi **1** (request) faire une demande; **to ~ for** demander [divorce, citizenship]; faire une demande de [passport, loan, grant, visa]; **to ~ to do** demander à faire; **2** (seek work) poser sa candidature (**for** à); **to ~ for the job of** poser sa candidature au poste de; **'~ in writing to'** 'envoyez votre candidature par lettre manuscrite à'; **'~ within'** 'adressez-vous à l'intérieur'; **3** (seek entry) (to college) faire une demande d'inscription (**to** à); (to club, society) faire une demande d'adhésion (**to** à); **to ~ to join** demander à entrer dans [army, group]; **4** (be valid) [definition, term] s'appliquer (**to** à); [ban, rule, penalty] être en vigueur; **5** (contact) **to ~ to** s'adresser à
C v refl **to ~ oneself** s'appliquer

appoint /ə'pɔɪnt/
A vtr **1** (name) nommer [person] (**to sth** à qch; **to do** pour faire; **as** comme); fixer [date, place]; **2** (equip) aménager
B **appointed** pp adj [time, place] fixé

appointee /əpɔɪn'tiː/ n candidat/-e m/f retenu/-e

appointment /ə'pɔɪntmənt/ n **1** (meeting, consultation) rendez-vous m (**at** chez; **with** avec; **to do** pour faire); **business ~** rendez-vous m d'affaires; **by ~** sur rendez-vous; **to make an ~** prendre rendez-vous; **2** Admin, Pol (nomination) nomination f (**as** comme; **to sth** à qch; **to do** pour faire); **to take up an ~ (as sth)** prendre ses fonctions (comme qch); **3** (job) poste m (**as** de; **of** de); **'Appointments'** (in paper) 'Offres d'emploi'

apportion /ə'pɔːʃn/ vtr répartir (**among** parmi; **between** entre)

apposite /'æpəzɪt/ adj pertinent

apposition /,æpə'zɪʃn/ n apposition f

appraisal /ə'preɪzl/ n évaluation f; **to make an ~ of sth** (estimation) évaluer qch

appraise /ə'preɪz/ vtr **1** (examine critically) juger [painting, information]; **2** (evaluate) estimer [value]; évaluer [performance]

appreciable /ə'priːʃəbl/ adj [time, change, quantity] appréciable; [difference, reduction] sensible

appreciably /ə'priːʃəblɪ/ adv sensiblement

appreciate /ə'priːʃɪeɪt/
A vtr **1** (be grateful for) être sensible à [honour, favour]; être reconnaissant de [kindness, sympathy]; apprécier [help, effort]; **I'd ~ it if you could reply soon** je vous serais reconnaissant de répondre sans tarder; **I ~ being consulted** j'aime bien qu'on me consulte; **2** (realize) se rendre (bien) compte de, être conscient de; **to ~ that...** se rendre bien compte que...; **as you will ~** comme vous vous en rendrez bien compte; **3** (enjoy) apprécier [music, art, food]
B vi [object] prendre de la valeur; [value] monter

appreciation /ə,priːʃɪ'eɪʃn/ n **1** (gratitude) remerciement m (**for** pour); **in ~ of sth** en remerciement de qch; **to show one's ~** manifester sa gratitude; **2** (awareness) compréhension f (**of** de); **he has no ~ of how difficult it is to do** il ne se rend pas compte combien il est difficile de faire; **3** (enjoyment) appréciation f (**of** de); **4** (commentary) commentaire m; **5** Fin hausse f (**of, in** de)

appreciative /ə'priːʃətɪv/ *adj* **1** (grateful) reconnaissant (of de); **2** (admiring) admiratif/-ive; **3** (aware) sensible (of à)

apprehend /ˌæprɪ'hend/ *vtr* **1** (arrest) appréhender; **2** (comprehend) saisir

apprehension /ˌæprɪ'henʃn/ *n* **1** (fear) (specific) crainte *f*; (vague) inquiétude *f*; **2** (arrest) arrestation *f*

apprehensive /ˌæprɪ'hensɪv/ *adj* craintif/-ive; **to be ~** être inquiet/-iète; **to feel ~ about sth** (fearful) appréhender qch; (worried) avoir des inquiétudes au sujet de qch

apprehensively /ˌæprɪ'hensɪvlɪ/ *adv* avec appréhension

apprentice /ə'prentɪs/
A *n* **1** apprenti/-e *m/f* also fig (**to** de); **electrician's ~** apprenti/-e *m/f* électricien/-ienne
B *noun modifier* (trainee) [*baker, mechanic*] apprenti/-e (*before n*)
C *vtr* **to be ~d to sb** être en apprentissage chez qn

apprenticeship /ə'prentɪsʃɪp/ *n* apprentissage *m* also fig; **to serve one's ~** faire son apprentissage

apprise /ə'praɪz/ *vtr* sout **to ~ sb of sth** instruire qn de qch fml

approach /ə'prəʊtʃ/
A *n* **1** (route of access) (to town, island) voie *f* d'accès; Mil approche *f*; **2** (advance) (of person) approche *f*, arrivée *f*; (of season, old age) approche *f*; **3** (way of dealing) approche *f*; **an original ~ to the problem** une façon originale d'aborder le problème; **we need to try a different ~** nous devons essayer une méthode différente; **4** (overture) démarche *f*; (proposal to buy etc) proposition *f*; **to make ~s to sb** gen, Comm faire des démarches auprès de qn
B *vtr* **1** (draw near to) s'approcher de [*person, place*]; (verge on) approcher de; **it was ~ing dawn** l'aube approchait; **it was ~ing midnight** il était presque minuit; **he is ~ing sixty** il approche (de) la soixantaine; **gales ~ing speeds of 200 km per hour** des vents qui atteignaient presque 200 km à l'heure; **2** (deal with) aborder [*problem, topic, subject*]; **3** (make overtures to) s'adresser à; (more formally) faire des démarches auprès de; (with offer of job, remuneration) solliciter (**about** au sujet de); **she was ~ed by a man in the street** elle a été abordée par un homme dans la rue; **he has been ~ed by several publishers** il a reçu des propositions de plusieurs maisons d'édition
C *vi* [*person, car*] (s')approcher; [*event, season*] approcher

approachable /ə'prəʊtʃəbl/ *adj* abordable, d'un abord facile

approach: ~ lights *npl* Aviat balises *fpl*, balisage *m*; **~ path** *n* Aviat axe *m* d'approche; **~ road** *n* bretelle *f*, route *f* d'accès

appropriate
A /ə'prəʊprɪət/ *adj* **1** (suitable for occasion, situation) [*behaviour, choice, place*] approprié (**for** pour); [*dress, gift*] qui convient (*after n*) (**for** à); [*punishment*] juste (**for** à); [*remark*] de circonstance (*after n*); **~ to** approprié à [*needs, circumstances*]; **2** (apt) [*name, date*] bien choisi; **3** (relevant) [*authority*] compétent
B /ə'prəʊprɪeɪt/ *vtr* **1** (for own use) gen s'approprier; Jur affecter [*land*] (**for** à); **2** US Econ affecter [*funds*] (**for** à)

appropriately /ə'prəʊprɪətlɪ/ *adv* **1** (suitably) [*behave, dress, speak*] avec à-propos; [*dress*] convenablement; **2** (aptly) [*designed, chosen, sited*] judicieusement

appropriation /əˌprəʊprɪ'eɪʃn/ *n* **1** Jur (removal) appropriation *f*; **2** US Econ affectation *f* (**for** à)

approval /ə'pruːvl/ *n* **1** (favourable opinion) approbation *f* (of de); **to win sb's ~** gagner l'approbation de qn; **2** (authorization) approbation *f*; **subject to sb's ~** soumis à l'approbation de qn; **on ~** à l'essai

approve /ə'pruːv/
A *vtr* (authorize) approuver [*product, plan*]; accepter [*person*]
B *vi* (be in favour of) **to ~ of sth/sb** apprécier qch/qn; **(not) to ~ of sb doing** (ne pas) apprécier que qn fasse; **he doesn't ~ of drinking** il est contre l'alcool

approving /ə'pruːvɪŋ/ *adj* approbateur/-trice

approvingly /ə'pruːvɪŋlɪ/ *adv* d'un air *or* d'un ton approbateur

approximate
A /ə'prɒksɪmət/ *adj* approximatif/-ive; **~ to** proche de
B /ə'prɒksɪmeɪt/ *vtr* (come close to) se rapprocher de; (resemble) ressembler à
C /ə'prɒksɪmeɪt/ *vi* **to ~ to** (in quantity, size etc) être proche de, se rapprocher de; (in nature, quality etc) ressembler à

approximately /ə'prɒksɪmətlɪ/ *adv* **1** (about) environ; **at ~ four o'clock** vers quatre heures; **2** [*equal, correct*] à peu près

approximation /əˌprɒksɪ'meɪʃn/ *n* approximation *f*

Apr *abrév écrite* = **April**

apricot /'eɪprɪkɒt/ ▸ p. 752
A *n* **1** (fruit) abricot *m*; **2** (tree) abricotier *m*; **3** (colour) (couleur *f*) abricot *m*
B *noun modifier* [*stone*] d'abricot; [*jam*] d'abricots; [*sauce*] aux abricots
C *adj* abricot *inv*

April /'eɪprɪl/ ▸ p. 1020 *n* avril *m*

April: ~ Fools' Day *n* le premier avril; **~ showers** *npl* ≈ giboulées *fpl* de mars

apron /'eɪprən/ *n* **1** (garment) tablier *m*; **2** (for vehicles, planes) aire *f* de stationnement

(Idiom) **to be tied to sb's ~ strings** être pendu aux basques de qn

apropos /ˌæprə'pəʊ/ *adv* à propos (**of** de)

apse /æps/ *n* abside *f*

apt¹ /æpt/ *adj* **1** (suitable) [*choice, description*] heureux/-euse; [*title, style*] approprié (**to, for** à); **2** (inclined) **to be ~ to do** être enclin à faire

apt² *abrév écrite* = **apartment**

aptitude /'æptɪtjuːd, US -tuːd/ *n* aptitude *f*; **to have an ~ for maths** être doué pour les maths

aptly /'æptlɪ/ *adv* [*named, described*] avec justesse; [*chosen*] bien

aqualung /'ækwəlʌŋ/ *n* scaphandre *m* autonome

aquamarine /ˌækwəmə'riːn/ ▸ p. 752
A *n* (gem) aigue-marine *f*; (colour) bleu-vert *m*
B *adj* bleu-vert *inv*

aquaplane /'ækwəpleɪn/ *vi* Sport faire de l'aquaplane; GB Aut faire de l'aquaplanage

aquarium /ə'kweərɪəm/ *n* (*pl* **-iums, -ia**) aquarium *m*

Aquarius /ə'kweərɪəs/ ▸ p. 1350 *n* Verseau *m*

aquatic /ə'kwætɪk/ *adj* [*plant*] aquatique; [*sport*] nautique

aqueduct /'ækwɪdʌkt/ *n* aqueduc *m*

aquiline /'ækwɪlaɪn/ *adj* [*nose, features*] aquilin

AR US Post *abrév écrite* = **Arkansas**

Arab /'ærəb/ ▸ p. 1032
A *n* **1** [*person*] Arabe *mf*; **2** (horse) cheval *m* arabe; (mare) jument *f* arabe
B *adj* arabe

Arabia /ə'reɪbɪə/ *pr n* Arabie *f*

Arabian /ə'reɪbɪən/ *adj* [*desert, landscape*] d'Arabie; **the ~ Sea** la mer d'Arabie

Arabic /'ærəbɪk/ ▸ p. 969
A *n* arabe *m*
B *adj* arabe

Arab-Israeli /ˌærəbɪz'reɪlɪ/ *adj* israélo-arabe

arable /'ærəbl/ *adj* [*crop, land, sector*] arable

Aran sweater *n* pull *m* irlandais

arbiter /'ɑːbɪtə(r)/ *n* lit, fig arbitre *m* (**of** de)

arbitrary /'ɑːbɪtrərɪ, US 'ɑːrbɪtrerɪ/ *adj* arbitraire

arbitrate /'ɑːbɪtreɪt/
A *vtr* arbitrer [*dispute, claim*]
B *vi* arbitrer, jouer le rôle d'arbitre (**between** entre)

arbitration /ˌɑːbɪ'treɪʃn/ *n* arbitrage *m*; **to go to ~** ≈ aller aux prud'hommes

arbitrator /'ɑːbɪtreɪtə(r)/ *n* (mediator) médiateur/-trice *m/f* (**between** entre); **industrial ~** (conseiller/-ère *m/f*) prud'homme *m*

arbor US = **arbour**

arbour GB, **arbor** US /'ɑːbə(r)/ *n* charmille *f*

arc /ɑːk/ *n* gen, Geom arc *m*; Elec arc *m* (électrique)

arcade /ɑː'keɪd/ *n* arcade *f*; **shopping ~** galerie *f* marchande

arcane /ɑː'keɪn/ *adj* impénétrable, obscur

arch /ɑːtʃ/
A *n* **1** (dome) voûte *f*; (archway) arche *f*; (for bridge) arche *f*; (triumphal) arc *m*; **2** (of foot) voûte *f* plantaire; (of eyebrows) arc *m*
B *adj* **1** (mischievous) [*look, manner*] malicieux/-ieuse; **2** péj

(superior) [*person, voice, remark*] condescendant

C *vtr* arquer; **to ~ one's back** [*person*] cambrer le dos; [*cat*] faire le dos rond

D **arch+** *combining form* par excellence; **~-enemy** ennemi/-e *m/f* juré/-e; **~-rival** grand rival

archaeological GB, **archeological** US /ˌɑːkɪəˈlɒdʒɪkl/ *adj* archéologique

archaeologist GB, **archeologist** US /ˌɑːkɪˈɒlədʒɪst/ ▸ p. 1181 *n* archéologue *mf*

archaeology GB, **archeology** US /ˌɑːkɪˈɒlədʒɪ/ *n* archéologie *f*

archaic /ɑːˈkeɪɪk/ *adj* archaïque

archbishop /ˌɑːtʃˈbɪʃəp/ *n* archevêque *m*

arched /ɑːtʃd/ *adj* gen voûté; [*eyebrows*] arqué

archer /ˈɑːtʃə(r)/ *n* archer *m*

archery /ˈɑːtʃərɪ/ *n* tir *m* à l'arc

archetypal /ˌɑːkɪˈtaɪpl/ *adj* **the** *ou* **an ~ hero** l'archétype du héros

archetype /ˈɑːkɪtaɪp/ *n* archétype *m*

archipelago /ˌɑːkɪˈpeləɡəʊ/ *n* archipel *m*

architect /ˈɑːkɪtekt/ ▸ p. 1181 *n* **1** (as profession) architecte *mf*; **2** fig (of plan, policy) artisan *m*

architectural /ˌɑːkɪˈtektʃərəl/ *adj* [*design, style*] architectural; [*student*] en architecture; [*studies*] d'architecture

architecture /ˈɑːkɪtektʃə(r)/ *n* architecture *f*

archive /ˈɑːkaɪv/ *n* archive *f*

archly /ˈɑːtʃlɪ/ *adv* **1** (mischievously) malicieusement; **2** péj (condescendingly) avec condescendance

Arctic /ˈɑːktɪk/
A *pr n* **the ~** l'Arctique *m*; **to/in the ~** dans l'Arctique
B *adj* [*climate, animal*] arctique; [*expedition*] polaire; fig (icy) [*conditions, temperature*] glacial

Arctic Circle *n* cercle *m* polaire arctique

Arctic Ocean ▸ p. 1049 *n* océan *m* Arctique

arc: **~ welder** *n* soudeur *m* à l'arc; **~ welding** *n* soudage *m* à l'arc

ardent /ˈɑːdnt/ *adj* **1** (fervent) [*revolutionary, supporter*] fervent; [*defence, opposition*] passionné; **2** (passionate) passionné

ardently /ˈɑːdntlɪ/ *adv* [*look, worship*] ardemment; [*defend, speak*] avec ardeur; [*support*] passionnément

ardour GB, **ardor** US /ˈɑːdə(r)/ *n* ardeur *f*

arduous /ˈɑːdjʊəs, US -dʒʊ-/ *adj* ardu

arduously /ˈɑːdjʊəslɪ, US -dʒʊ-/ *adv* péniblement

are /ɑː(r)/ ▸ **be**

area /ˈeərɪə/
A *n* **1** (region) (of land) région *f*; (of sky) zone *f*; (of city) zone *f*; (district) quartier *m*; **in the London ~** dans la région de Londres; **residential ~** zone *f* résidentielle; **2** (part of building) **dining ~** coin *m* salle-à-manger; **no-smoking/smoking ~** zone *f* non-fumeurs/fumeurs; **reception ~** réception *f*; **waiting ~** salle *f* d'attente; **3** (sphere of knowledge) domaine *m*; (part of activity, business, economy) secteur *m*; **~ of interest** domaine d'intérêt; **~ of disagreement** sujet de désaccord; **4** Math (in geometry) aire *f*; (of land) superficie *f*
B *noun modifier* [*board, headquarters, manager, office*] régional

area code *n* Telecom indicatif *m* de zone

arena /əˈriːnə/ *n* arène *f* also fig

aren't /ɑːnt/ (= are not) ▸ **be**

Argentina /ˌɑːdʒənˈtiːnə/ ▸ p. 774 *pr n* Argentine *f*

Argentine /ˈɑːdʒəntaɪn/ ▸ p. 774
A *n* **1** **the ~ (Republic)** l'Argentine *f*; **2** (native, inhabitant) Argentin/-e *m/f*
B *adj* argentin

Argentinian /ˌɑːdʒənˈtɪnɪən/ ▸ p. 1032
A *n* Argentin/-e *m/f*
B *adj* argentin

arguable /ˈɑːɡjʊəbl/ *adj* discutable; **it's ~ that** on peut soutenir que

arguably /ˈɑːɡjʊəblɪ/ *adv* sans doute

argue /ˈɑːɡjuː/
A *vtr* **1** (debate) discuter (de), débattre (de); **to ~ the case for disarmament** exposer les raisons en faveur du désarmement; **it could be ~d that** on pourrait soutenir que; **well-~d** bien argumenté; **2** (maintain) soutenir
B *vi* **1** (quarrel) se disputer (**with** avec); **to ~ about** *ou* **over**

money se disputer pour des questions d'argent; **we ~d about who should pay** nous nous sommes disputés pour savoir qui devait payer; **don't ~ (with me)!** on ne discute pas!; **2** (debate) discuter, débattre; **to ~ about** discuter de, débattre de; **3** (put one's case) argumenter (**against** contre); **to ~ in favour of/against doing sth** exposer les raisons pour faire/pour ne pas faire qch; **to ~ for** *ou* **in favour of** parler en faveur de

argument /ˈɑːɡjʊmənt/ *n* **1** (quarrel) dispute *f* (**about** à propos de); **to have an ~** se disputer; **2** (discussion) débat *m*, discussion *f* (**about** à propos de); **there is a lot of ~ about this** c'est un sujet très discuté; **she won the ~** c'est elle qui a eu le dernier mot; **it's open to ~** c'est discutable; **one side of the ~** une version de l'affaire; **for ~'s sake** à titre d'exemple; **3** (case) argument *m* (**for** en faveur de; **against** contre); (line of reasoning) raisonnement *m*

argumentative /ˌɑːɡjʊˈmentətɪv/ *adj* [*person*] ergoteur/-euse

arid /ˈærɪd/ *adj* aride also fig

aridity /əˈrɪdətɪ/ *n* aridité *f* also fig

Aries /ˈeəriːz/ ▸ p. 1350 *n* Bélier *m*

arise /əˈraɪz/ *vi* (*prét* **arose**, *pp* **arisen**) **1** (occur) [*problem*] survenir (**out of** du fait de); [*question*] se poser; **to ~ from sth** émaner de qch; **if it ~s that** s'il se trouve que; **if the need ~s** si le besoin se fait sentir; **2** (be the result of) résulter (**from** de)

aristocracy /ˌærɪˈstɒkrəsɪ/ *n* aristocratie *f*

aristocrat /ˈærɪstəkræt, US əˈrɪst-/ *n* aristocrate *mf*

aristocratic /ˌærɪstəˈkrætɪk, US əˈrɪst-/ *adj* aristocratique

arithmetic /əˈrɪθmətɪk/ *n* (subject) arithmétique *f*

arithmetical /ˌærɪθˈmetɪkl/ *adj* arithmétique

ark /ɑːk/ *n* (boat, in synagogue) arche *f*

(Idiom) **to be out of the ~** être vieux/vieille comme tout

arm /ɑːm/ ▸ p. 698
A *n* **1** Anat, fig bras *m*; **~ in ~** bras dessus bras dessous; **to give sb one's ~** donner le bras à qn; **to take sb's ~** prendre le bras de qn; **to have sth over/under one's ~** avoir qch sur/sous le bras; **to fold one's ~s** croiser les bras; **within ~'s reach** à portée de la main; **2** (sleeve) manche *f*; **3** (influence) to have a long ~ avoir le bras long; **4** (of crane, robot, record player) bras *m*; **5** (of spectacles) branche *f*; **6** (of chair) accoudoir *m*; **7** (subsidiary) Pol branche *f*; Econ branche *f*, filiale *f*; **8** (of sea) bras *m*
B *n* **arms** *npl* **1** (weapons) armes *fpl*; **to take up ~s** lit prendre les armes; fig s'insurger (**against** contre); **to be up in ~s** (in revolt) être en rébellion (**against** contre); (angry) être furieux/-ieuse (**against** contre); **2** armes *fpl*, armoiries *fpl*; **coat of ~s** armoiries *fpl*
C *vtr* **1** (militarily) armer; **2** (equip) **to ~ sb with sth** lit, fig munir qn de qch
D *v refl* **to ~ oneself** Mil s'armer (**with** de)

(Idioms) **to cost an ~ and a leg**° coûter les yeux de la tête°; **to keep sb at ~'s length** tenir qn à distance; **to twist sb's ~** faire pression sur qn; **with open ~s** à bras ouverts

armadillo /ˌɑːməˈdɪləʊ/ *n* (*pl* **~s**) tatou *m*

armament /ˈɑːməmənt/ Mil
A *n* (loading of weapons) armement *m*
B **armaments** *npl* (system) armements *mpl*
C **armaments** *noun modifier* [*factory, firm, manufacturer*] d'armement; [*industry*] de l'armement

armband /ˈɑːmbænd/ *n* **1** (for swimmer) bracelet *m* de natation; **2** (for mourner) crêpe *m* de deuil

armchair /ˈɑːmtʃeə(r)/
A *n* fauteuil *m*
B *noun modifier* péj [*revolutionary, general*] de salon

armed /ɑːmd/ *adj* [*criminal, guard*] armé (**with** de); [*raid, robbery*] à main armée; [*missile*] muni d'une tête d'ogive

armed forces, **armed services** *npl* forces *fpl* armées; **to be in the ~** être dans l'armée

Armenia /ɑːˈmiːnɪə/ ▸ p. 774 *pr n* Arménie *f*

Armenian /ɑːˈmiːnɪən/ ▸ p. 1032, p. 969
A *n* **1** (person) Arménien/-ienne *m/f*; **2** (language) arménien *m*
B *adj* arménien/-ienne

arm: **~ful** *n* (*pl* **~s**) brassée *f*; **~hole** *n* emmanchure *f*

armistice /ˈɑːmɪstɪs/ *n* armistice *m*

Armistice Day n le jour de l'armistice, le onze novembre

armour GB, **armor** US /'ɑːmə(r)/ n **1** (clothing) **a suit of ~** une armure f (complète); **2** (on tank, ship etc) also Zool armure f; (on wire, cable) gaine f; fig (against criticism) cuirasse f

armour-clad /ˌɑːmə'klæd/ adj [vehicle] blindé; [ship] cuirassé

armoured GB, **armored** US /'ɑːməd/ adj blindé

armour: **~ plate**, **~ plating** n (on tank) blindage m; (on ship) cuirassage m; **~-plated** adj = armour-clad

armoury GB, **armory** US /'ɑːmərɪ/ n **1** Mil (store) arsenal m; (factory) manufacture f d'armes; **2** fig (resources) arsenal m (**of** de)

arm: **~pit** n aisselle f; **~rest** n accoudoir m; **~s control** n contrôle m des armements; **~s dealer** n négociant m d'armes; **~s dump** n dépôt m d'armes; **~s factory** n usine f d'armement; **~s limitation** n réduction f ou contrôle m des armements; **~s manufacturer** n fabricant m d'armes; **~s race** n course f aux armements; **~s treaty** n traité m sur le contrôle des armements; **~-twisting** n pressions fpl directes; **~ wrestling** ▸ p. 881 n bras-de-fer m

army /'ɑːmɪ/
A n **1** Mil armée f; **in the ~** dans l'armée; **to go into the ~** entrer dans l'armée; **to join the ~** s'engager; **2** fig armée f (**of** de)
B noun modifier [life, staff, uniform] militaire; [officer] de l'armée de terre

aroma /ə'rəʊmə/ n arôme m

aromatherapy /əˌrəʊmə'θerəpɪ/ n aromathérapie f

aromatic /ˌærə'mætɪk/ adj aromatique

arose /ə'rəʊz/ prét ▸ arise

around /ə'raʊnd/

> ⚠ *Around* often appears as the second element of certain verb structures (*come around*, *look around*, *turn around* etc). For translations, consult the appropriate verb entry (**come, look, turn** etc).
> *go around* and *get around* generate many idiomatic expressions. For translations see the entries **go** and **get**.

A adv **1** (approximately) environ, à peu près; **at ~ 3 pm** vers 15 heures; **2** (in the vicinity) **to be (somewhere) ~** être dans les parages; **are they ~?** est-ce qu'ils sont là?; **I just happened to be ~** je me trouvais là par hasard; **3** (in circulation) **CDs have been ~ for years** ça fait des années que les CD existent; **I wish I'd been ~ 50 years ago** j'aurais aimé être là il y a 50 ans; **she's been ~** fig elle a roulé sa bosse○, elle a vécu; **one of the most gifted musicians ~** un des musiciens les plus doués du moment; **4** (available) **to be ~** être là; **there are still some strawberries ~** on trouve encore des fraises; **5** (in all directions) **all ~** lit tout autour; (in general) partout; **to go all the way ~** faire tout le tour; **the only garage for miles ~** le seul garage à des kilomètres à la ronde; **6** (in circumference) **three metres ~** de trois mètres de circonférence; **7** (in different, opposite direction) **a way ~** lit un chemin pour contourner [obstacle]; **there is no way ~ the problem** il n'y a pas moyen de contourner le problème; **to go the long way ~** prendre le chemin le plus long; **to turn sth the other way ~** retourner qch; **to do it the other way ~** faire le contraire; **I didn't ask her, it was the other way ~** ce n'est pas moi qui lui ai demandé, c'est l'inverse; **the wrong/right way ~** dans le mauvais/bon sens; **to put one's skirt on the wrong way ~** mettre sa jupe à l'envers; (in specific place, home) **to ask sb (to come) ~** dire à qn de passer; **she's coming ~ today** elle passe aujourd'hui; **I'll be ~ in a minute** j'arrive
B prep **1** (on all sides of) autour de [fire, table, head]; **the villages ~ Dublin** les villages des environs de Dublin; **2** (throughout) **clothes scattered ~ the room** des vêtements éparpillés partout dans la pièce; **(all) ~ the world** partout dans le monde; **from ~ the world** venant du monde entier; **doctors ~ the world** les médecins à travers le monde; **to go ~ the world** faire le tour du monde; **to walk ~ the town** se promener dans la ville; **3** (in the vicinity of, near) **somewhere ~ the house/~ Paris** quelque part dans la maison/près de Paris; **I like having people ~ the house** j'aime avoir des gens à la maison; **the people ~ here** les gens d'ici; **4** (at) vers; **~ midnight/1980** vers minuit/ 1980; **5** (in order to circumvent) **to go ~** éviter [town centre]; contourner [obstacle]; **6** (to the other side of) **to go ~ the**

corner tourner au coin; **to go ~ a bend** prendre un virage; **~ the mountain** de l'autre côté de ou derrière la montagne; **7** (in sizes) **he's 90 cm ~ the chest** il fait 90 de tour de poitrine

arousal /ə'raʊzl/ n excitation f (**of** de)

arouse /ə'raʊz/ vtr **1** (excite) éveiller [interest, attention]; exciter [anger, jealousy]; **to be ~d by sth** être excité par qch; **2** (waken) **to ~ sb from sleep** tirer qn du sommeil

arpeggio /ɑː'pedʒɪəʊ/ n arpège m

arrange /ə'reɪndʒ/
A vtr **1** (put in position) disposer [chairs, ornaments]; arranger [room, hair, clothes]; arranger, disposer [flowers]; **2** (organize) organiser [party, meeting, holiday, schedule]; fixer [date, appointment]; **to ~ sth with sb** fixer ou organiser qch avec qn; **to ~ that** faire en sorte que (+ subj); **to ~ to do** s'arranger pour faire; **I'll ~ it** je ferai le nécessaire; **have you got anything ~d for this evening?** avez-vous quelque chose de prévu pour ce soir?; **3** (bring about agreement on) convenir de [loan, mortgage]; fixer [price]; **4** Mus arranger, adapter [piece]
B vi **to ~ for sth** prendre des dispositions pour qch; **to ~ for sb to do** prendre des dispositions pour que qn fasse; **to ~ with sb to do** décider avec qn de faire

arrangement /ə'reɪndʒmənt/ n **1** (of hair, jewellery) arrangement m; (of objects, chairs) disposition f; (of ideas: on page) organisation f; (of shells, flowers) composition f; **seating ~s** disposition des invités; **2** (agreement) entente f, accord m; **by ~ with sb** par un accord avec qn; **by ~** (par) entente préalable, sur demande; **to come to an ~** s'arranger; **3** (plan) dispositions fpl; (preparations) préparatifs mpl; (measures) mesures fpl; **to make ~s to do** s'arranger pour faire; **to make ~s with sb (for him to do)** prendre des dispositions avec qn (pour qu'il fasse); **to make ~s for doing** prendre des dispositions pour faire

array /ə'reɪ/
A n **1** (of goods, products) gamme f; **2** (of weaponry) panoplie f; **3** (of troops, people) déploiement m; **4** (of numbers) tableau m; **5** (clothes) habits mpl d'apparat; **6** (in electronics) réseau m
B vtr **1** **~ed in** (dressed in) paré de; **2** Jur établir la liste des [jurors]

arrears /ə'rɪəz/ npl arriéré m; **I am in ~ with my payments** j'ai du retard dans mes paiements; **to fall into ~** s'arriérer; **rent ~** arriéré de loyer

arrest /ə'rest/
A n arrestation f; **to be under ~** être en état d'arrestation; **to put sb under ~** arrêter qn
B vtr **1** [police] arrêter; **2** (halt) arrêter [decline, development, disease]

arresting /ə'restɪŋ/ adj (attractive) saisissant

arrival /ə'raɪvl/ n **1** (of person, transport) arrivée f; **on sb's/ sth's ~** à l'arrivée de qn/qch; **2** (of new character or phenomenon) apparition f; **3** (person arriving) arrivé/-e m/f; **late ~** (in theatre) retardataire mf; **new ~** (in community) nouveau/-elle venu/-e m/f; (baby) nouveau-né m

arrival: **~ lounge** n salon m d'arrivée; **~s board** n tableau m d'arrivée; **~ time** n heure f d'arrivée

arrive /ə'raɪv/ vi **1** (at destination) arriver (**at** à; **from** de); **'arriving Berlin 7.25 am'** (announcement) 'arrivée à Berlin 7 heures 25'; **to ~ on the scene** lit arriver (sur les lieux); fig apparaître; **2** (reach) **to ~ at** parvenir à [decision, solution]; **3** (be social success) arriver

arrogance /'ærəgəns/ n arrogance f

arrogant /'ærəgənt/ adj arrogant

arrogantly /'ærəgəntlɪ/ adv avec arrogance, arrogamment

arrow /'ærəʊ/ n **1** (weapon) flèche f; **to fire an ~** décocher une flèche; **2** (symbol) flèche f

arrow: **~head** n pointe f de flèche; **~root** n Bot marante f; Culin arrow-root m

arsenal /'ɑːsənl/ n lit, fig arsenal m

arsenic /'ɑːsnɪk/ n arsenic m

arson /'ɑːsn/ n incendie m criminel

arsonist /'ɑːsənɪst/ n pyromane mf

art /ɑːt/
A n **1** (creation, activity, representation) art m; **I'm bad at ~** je suis mauvais en dessin; **2** (skill) art m (**of doing** de faire)
B **arts** npl **1** (culture) **the ~s** les arts mpl; **2** Univ lettres fpl;

a

as

When *as* is used as a preposition or a conjunction to mean *like* it is translated by *comme*:

dressed as a sailor
= habillé comme un marin

as usual
= comme d'habitude

as often happens
= comme c'est souvent le cas

As a conjunction in time expressions, meaning *when* or *while*, *as* is translated by *comme*:

as she was coming down the stairs
= comme elle descendait l'escalier

However, where a gradual process is involved, *as* is translated by *au fur et à mesure que*:

as the day went on, he became more anxious
= au fur et à mesure que la journée avançait il devenait plus inquiet

As a conjunction meaning *because*, *as* is translated by *comme* or *puisque*:

as he is ill, he can't go out
= comme il est malade *or* puisqu'il est malade, il ne peut pas sortir

When used as an adverb in comparisons, *as...as* is translated by *aussi...que*:

he is as intelligent as his brother
= il est aussi intelligent que son frère

But see category **C** in the entry **as** for *as much as* and *as many as*.

Note also the standard translation used for fixed similes:

as strong as an ox
= fort comme un bœuf

as rich as Croesus
= riche comme Crésus

Such similes often have a cultural equivalent rather than a direct translation. To find translations for English similes, consult the entry for the second element.

When *as* is used as a preposition to indicate a person's profession or position, it is translated by *comme*:

he works as an engineer
= il travaille comme ingénieur

Note that the article *a/an* is not translated.

When *as* is used with a preposition to mean *in my/his capacity as*, it is translated by *en tant que*:

as a teacher I believe that ...
= en tant qu'enseignant je crois que...

For more examples, particular usages and phrases like *as for*, *as from*, *as to* etc. see the entry **as**.

---

3 ~s and crafts gen artisanat *m*; (school subject) travaux *mpl* manuels

art: ~ **collection** *n* (of paintings) collection *f* de tableaux; (of artworks) collection *f* d'œuvres d'art; ~ **collector** *n* collectionneur/-euse *m/f* d'œuvres d'art; (of paintings) collectionneur/-euse *m/f* de tableaux; ~ **college** *n* école *f* des beaux-arts; ~ **dealer** ► p. 1181 *n* marchand/-e *m/f* d'œuvres d'art; (of paintings) marchand/-e *m/f* de tableaux; ~ **deco** *n, adj* art déco (*m*) *inv*

artefact /'ɑːtɪfækt/ *n* objet *m* (fabriqué)

arterial /ɑːˈtɪərɪəl/ *adj* (avant *n*) **1** Anat artériel/-ielle; **2** ~ **road** grand axe *m*; ~ **line** Rail grande ligne *f*

artery /'ɑːtərɪ/ *n* **1** artère *f*; **2** (road) artère *f*; (railway) grande ligne *f*

art exhibition *n* (paintings) exposition *f* de tableaux; (sculpture) exposition *f* de sculpture

art form *n* lit forme *f* d'art; **to become an** ~ devenir un art

artful /'ɑːtfl/ *adj* (skilful) habile; (crafty) rusé

artfully /'ɑːtfəlɪ/ *adv* ingénieusement, astucieusement

art gallery *n* (museum) musée *m* d'art; (commercial) galerie *f* d'art

arthritic /ɑːˈθrɪtɪk/ *n, adj* arthritique (*mf*)

arthritis /ɑːˈθraɪtɪs/ ► p. 933 *n* arthrite *f*

artichoke /'ɑːtɪʃəʊk/
A *n* artichaut *m*
B noun modifier [heart] d'artichaut; [salad, soup] aux artichauts

article /'ɑːtɪkl/
A *n* **1** (object) objet *m*; ~ **of clothing** article *m* vestimentaire; **2** (written) article *m* (about, on sur); **3** Jur (clause) article *m*; **in** ou **under Article 12** à l'article 12; **4** Ling article *m*; **definite/indefinite/partitive** ~ article défini/indéfini/partitif
B **articles** *npl* Jur **to be in** ~s faire un stage chez un notaire

articulate
A /ɑːˈtɪkjʊlət/ *adj* [speaker] qui s'exprime bien; [document, speech] bien construit
B /ɑːˈtɪkjʊleɪt/ *vtr* (pronounce) articuler; (express) exprimer
C /ɑːˈtɪkjʊleɪt/ *vi* (pronounce) articuler

articulated lorry *n* GB semi-remorque *m*

articulately /ɑːˈtɪkjʊlətlɪ/ *adv* avec aisance (et clarté)

articulation /ɑːˌtɪkjʊˈleɪʃn/ *n* **1** (expression) articulation *f*; **2** (pronunciation) prononciation *f*; **3** Anat articulation *f*

artifact /'ɑːtɪfækt/ *n* = artefact

artifice /'ɑːtɪfɪs/ *n* **1** (trick) ruse *f*; **2** (cunning) astuce *f*

artificial /ˌɑːtɪˈfɪʃl/ *adj* artificiel/-ielle

artificial intelligence, AI *n* intelligence *f* artificielle

artificiality /ˌɑːtɪfɪʃɪˈælətɪ/ *n* pej (of person, manner) affectation *f*; (of situation) côté *m* artificiel

artificial limb *n* (appareil *m* de) prothèse *f*, membre *m* artificiel

artificial respiration *n* respiration *f* artificielle

artillery /ɑːˈtɪlərɪ/ *n* (guns, regiment) artillerie *f*

artisan /ˌɑːtɪˈzæn, US ˈɑːrtɪzn/ *n* artisan *m*

artist /'ɑːtɪst/ ► p. 1181 *n* Art, Theat artiste *mf*

artiste /ɑːˈtiːst/ *n* Theat artiste *mf*

artistic /ɑːˈtɪstɪk/ *adj* [talent, director, activity] artistique; [temperament, person] artiste

artistically /ɑːˈtɪstɪklɪ/ *adv* artistiquement

artistry /'ɑːtɪstrɪ/ *n* art *m*, talent *m* artistique

artless /'ɑːtlɪs/ *adj* naturel/-elle

artlessly /'ɑːtlɪslɪ/ *adv* [smile] avec naturel

art nouveau /ˌɑːt 'nuːvəʊ/ *n, adj* modern style (*m*), art (*m*) nouveau

art: ~ **school** *n* école *f* des beaux-arts; ~s **degree** *n* licence *f* ès lettres; ~s **funding** *n* (by state) subventions *fpl* accordées aux arts; (by sponsors) mécénat *m*; ~s **student** *n* étudiant/-e *m/f* en lettres; ~ **student** *n* étudiant/-e *m/f* des beaux-arts; ~**work** *n* travail *m* d'art

arty○ /'ɑːtɪ/ *adj* [person] du genre artiste; [district] bohème

Aryan /'eərɪən/
A *n* Aryen/-enne *m/f*
B *adj* aryen/-enne

as /æz, əz/
A *conj* **1** (in the manner that) comme; ~ **you know** comme vous le savez; ~ **usual** comme d'habitude; ~ **is usual in such cases** comme c'est l'usage en pareil cas; **do** ~ **I say** fais ce que je te dis; ~ **I see it** à mon avis; ~ **I understand it** autant que je puisse en juger; **knowing you** ~ **I do, it didn't surprise me** je te connais tellement bien que ça ne m'a pas étonné; **the street** ~ **it looked in the 1930s** la rue telle qu'elle était dans les années 30; ~ **often happens** comme c'est souvent le cas; **he lives abroad,** ~ **does his**

sister il vit à l'étranger, tout comme sa sœur; **leave it ∼ it is** laisse-le tel quel; **we're in enough trouble ∼ it is** nous avons déjà assez d'ennuis comme ça; **∼ one man to another** d'homme à homme; **∼ with so many people in the 1960s, she…** comme beaucoup de personnes dans les années 60, elle…; **∼ with so much in this country** comme beaucoup de choses dans ce pays; **2** (while, when) comme, alors que; (over more gradual period of time) au fur et à mesure que; **∼ she grew older** au fur et à mesure qu'elle vieillissait; **∼ a child, he…** (quand il était) enfant, il…; **3** (because, since) comme, puisque; **4** (although) strange **∼ it may seem** aussi curieux que cela puisse paraître; **comfortable ∼ the house is, it's still very expensive** aussi confortable que soit la maison, elle reste quand même très chère; **try ∼ he might, he could not forget it** il avait beau essayer, il ne pouvait pas oublier; **5** the same… **∼** le/la même… que; **I've got a jacket the same ∼ yours** j'ai la même veste que toi; **the same ∼ always** comme d'habitude; **6** (expressing purpose) **so ∼ to do** pour faire, afin de faire

B prep **1** (in order to appear to be) dressed **∼ a sailor** habillé en marin; **he is portrayed ∼ a victim** on le présente comme une victime; **2** (showing function, status) comme; **he works ∼ a pilot** il travaille comme pilote; **a job ∼ a teacher** un poste d'enseignant; **speaking ∼ his closest friend, I…** en tant que son meilleur ami, je voudrais dire que je…; **my rights ∼ a parent** mes droits en tant que parent; **with Lauren Bacall ∼ Vivien** Cin, Theat avec Lauren Bacall dans le rôle de Vivien; **3** to treat sb **∼ an equal** traiter qn en égal; **he was quoted ∼ saying that…** il aurait dit que…; **it came ∼ a shock** ça a été un véritable choc

C adv **1** (expressing degree, extent) **he is ∼ intelligent ∼ you** il est aussi intelligent que toi; **he's just ∼ intelligent ∼ you** il est tout aussi intelligent que toi; **she can't walk ∼ fast ∼ she used to** elle ne peut plus marcher aussi vite qu'avant; **∼ fast ∼ you can** aussi vite que possible; **∼ strong ∼ an ox** fort comme un bœuf; **he's twice ∼ strong ∼ me** il est deux fois plus fort que moi; **I paid ∼ much ∼ she did** j'ai payé autant qu'elle; **∼ much ∼ possible** autant que possible; **∼ little ∼ possible** le moins possible; **∼ soon ∼ possible** dès que possible; **not nearly ∼ much ∼** beaucoup moins que; **not ∼ often** moins souvent; **the population may increase by ∼ much ∼ 20%** l'augmentation de la population risque d'atteindre 20%; **∼ many ∼ 10,000 people attended the demonstration** il n'y avait pas moins de 10 000 personnes à la manifestation; **she can play the piano ∼ well ∼ her sister** elle joue du piano aussi bien que sa sœur; **he has a house in Nice ∼ well ∼ an apartment in Paris** il a une maison à Nice ainsi qu'un appartement à Paris; **2** (expressing similarity) comme; **∼ before** comme avant; **I thought ∼ much!** c'est ce qu'il me semblait!

D as against prep phr contre, comparé à

E as and when conj phr **∼ and when the passengers arrive** au fur et à mesure que les voyageurs arrivent; **∼ and when the need arises** quand il le faudra, quand le besoin s'en fera sentir

F as for prep phr quant à, pour ce qui est de

G as from, as of prep phr à partir de

H as if conj phr comme (si); **it's not ∼ if she hadn't been warned!** ce n'est pas comme si elle n'avait pas été prévenue!; **he looked at me ∼ if to say 'I told you so'** il m'a regardé avec l'air de dire 'je te l'avais bien dit'; **it looks ∼ if we've lost** on dirait que nous avons perdu; **∼ if by accident/magic** comme par hasard/magie

I as such prep phr en tant que tel

J as to prep phr sur, quant à

asbestos /əzˈbestɒs, æs-/ n amiante m

ascend /əˈsend/
A vtr gravir [steps, hill]
B vi [person] monter; [bird, soul, deity] s'élever

ascendancy /əˈsendənsɪ/ n ascendant m; **to gain the ∼ over sb** prendre l'ascendant sur qn

ascendant /əˈsendənt/ n (in astrology) ascendant m; **to be in the ∼** [star] être à l'ascendant; fig [person] avoir l'ascendant

Ascension /əˈsenʃn/ n Relig **the ∼** l'Ascension f

ascent /əˈsent/ n **1** (of smoke) montée f; (of soul, plane) ascension f; **2** (in cycling) montée f; (in mountaineering) ascension f

ascertain /ˌæsəˈteɪn/ vtr établir (**that** que)

ascetic /əˈsetɪk/
A n ascète mf
B adj ascétique

ascribable /əˈskraɪbəbl/ adj attribuable (**to** à); (laying blame) imputable (**to** à)

ascribe /əˈskraɪb/ vtr **to ∼ sth to sb** attribuer qch à qn [work, phrase]; imputer qch à qn [accident, mistake]; **the accident can be ∼d to human error** on peut mettre l'accident sur le compte d'une erreur humaine

aseptic /ˌeɪˈseptɪk, US əˈsep-/ adj aseptique

asexual /ˌeɪˈsekʃʊəl/ adj asexué also fig

ash /æʃ/
A n **1** (after burning) cendre f; **to be burned to ∼es** être réduit en cendres; **2** (tree, wood) frêne m
B ashes npl (remains) cendres fpl

ashamed /əˈʃeɪmd/ adj **to be** ou **feel ∼** avoir honte (**of** de; **to do** de faire); **to be ∼ that** avoir honte que (+ subj); **she was ∼ to be seen with him** elle avait honte de se montrer avec lui; **you ought to be ∼ of yourself** tu devrais avoir honte; **it's nothing to be ∼ of** il ne faut pas en avoir honte

ash: **∼bin**, **∼ can** n US poubelle f; **∼ blond** adj blond cendré inv

ashen /ˈæʃn/ adj [complexion] terreux/-euse

ashore /əˈʃɔː(r)/ adv **1** (towards seashore) vers le rivage; (towards lake shore, river bank) vers la rive; **he was swimming ∼** il nageait vers le rivage/la rive; **2** (arriving on shore) **to come/go ∼** débarquer; **to swim ∼** gagner le rivage/la rive à la nage; **washed ∼** rejeté sur le rivage; **3** (on land) à terre; **to spend a week ∼** [sailor] passer une semaine à terre; [tourist] faire une escale d'une semaine

ash: **∼tray** n cendrier m; **∼ tree** n frêne m; **Ash Wednesday** n mercredi m des Cendres

Asia /ˈeɪʃə, US ˈeɪʒə/ ▸ p. 774 pr n Asie f

Asia Minor /ˌeɪʃəˈmaɪnə(r), US ˌeɪʒə-/ pr n Asie f mineure

Asian /ˈeɪʃn, US ˈeɪʒn/
A n (from Far East) Asiatique mf; (in UK) personne f originaire du sous-continent indien
B adj [river, custom, politics, flu] asiatique

Asian: **∼ American** n Américain/-e m/f d'origine asiatique; **∼ Briton** n GB Britannique mf d'origine pakistanaise/indienne etc

Asiatic /ˌeɪʃɪˈætɪk, US ˌeɪʒɪ-/ adj [peoples, nations] asiatique

aside /əˈsaɪd/
A n gen, Theat, Cin aparté m; **to say sth as** ou **in an ∼** dire qch en aparté; (as digression) dire qch en passant
B adv **1** (to one side) **to stand** ou **step** ou **move ∼** s'écarter; **to turn ∼** se détourner; **to cast** ou **throw [sth] ∼** mettre [qch] au rebut [clothes, gift]; écarter [idea, theory]; **to set** ou **put** ou **lay [sth] ∼** (save) mettre [qch] de côté; (in shop) réserver; **to brush** ou **sweep [sth] ∼** écarter [objections, protests, worries]; **to lay** ou **put a book ∼** mettre un livre de côté; **to push** ou **move sb ∼** écarter qn; **to take sb ∼** prendre qn à part; **2** (apart) money **∼**, let's discuss accommodation laissons de côté la question d'argent et parlons du logement

C aside from prep phr à part

asinine /ˈæsɪnaɪn/ adj sot/sotte

ask /ɑːsk, US æsk/
A vtr **1** (enquire as to) demander [name, reason]; **to ∼ a question** poser une question; **to ∼ sb sth** demander qch à qn; **80% of those ∼ed said no** 80% des personnes interrogées ont répondu non; **I'm ∼ing you how you did it** je veux savoir comment tu l'as fait; **I wasn't ∼ing you** je ne t'ai rien demandé; **2** (request) demander [permission, tolerance]; **it's too much to ∼** c'est trop demander; **to ∼ to do** demander à faire; **to ∼ sb to do** demander à qn de faire; **to ∼ sth of** ou **from sb** demander qch à qn; **what price is she ∼ing for it?** combien elle le vend?; **3** (invite) inviter [person]; **to ∼ sb to** inviter qn à [concert, party]; **to ∼ sb to dinner** inviter qn à dîner; **to ∼ sb out** inviter qn à sortir; **to ∼ sb in** inviter qn à entrer; **we ∼ed him along** nous l'avons invité à se joindre à nous
B vi **1** (request) demander; **2** (make enquiries) se renseigner; **to ∼ about sb** s'informer au sujet de qn; **I'll ∼ around** je demanderai autour de moi
C v refl **to ∼ oneself** se demander [reason]

(Phrasal verbs)

■ **ask after**: ▶ ∼ **after [sb]** demander des nouvelles de [*person*]

■ **ask for**: ▶ ∼ **for [sth]** demander [*drink, money, help, restraint*]; **he was** ∼**ing for it**○, **he** ∼**ed for it**○! il l'a bien cherché!; ▶ ∼ **for [sb]** (on telephone) demander à parler à; (from sick bed) demander à voir

askance /əˈskæns/ *adv* **to look** ∼ **at sb/sth** considérer qn/qch avec méfiance

askew /əˈskjuː/ *adj, adv* de travers

asking price *n* prix *m* demandé

asleep /əˈsliːp/ *adj* **to be** ∼ dormir; **he's** ∼ il dort; **to fall** ∼ s'endormir; **they were found** ∼ on les a trouvés endormis; **to be half** ∼ (not yet awake) être à moitié endormi; (falling asleep) dormir à moitié; **to be sound** *ou* **fast** ∼ dormir à poings fermés

AS level /eɪˈeslevl/ *n* GB Sch (*abrév* = **Advanced Supplementary Level**) examen de fin d'études secondaires

> **ⓘ** AS level Examen dans une discipline qui se situe entre le niveau du *GCSE* et celui des *A levels*. Un *AS level* compte pour la moitié d'un *A level* dans les critères d'admission à l'université. De nombreux élèves préparent une combinaison de *AS levels* et de *A levels* à la fin de leurs études secondaires. ▸ **A level, GCSE**

asp /æsp/ *n* Zool aspic *m*

asparagus /əˈspærəgəs/
Ⓐ *n* asperge *f*
Ⓑ *noun modifier* [*sauce, soup*] aux asperges; ∼ **tip** pointe *f* d'asperge

aspect /ˈæspekt/ *n* ① (feature) also Ling aspect *m*; ② (angle) point *m* de vue; **to examine every** ∼ **of sth** examiner qch sous tous ses aspects; **seen from this** ∼ vu sous cet angle; ③ (orientation) orientation *f*; **house with a westerly** ∼ maison exposée à l'ouest; ④ (view) vue *f*

aspen /ˈæspən/ *n* tremble *m*

aspersions /əˈspɜːʃns, US -ʒnz/ *npl* sout **to cast** ∼ **on** dénigrer [*person*]; mettre [qch] en doute [*ability, capacity*]

asphalt /ˈæsfælt, US -fɔːlt/
Ⓐ *n* bitume *m*
Ⓑ *noun modifier* [*drive, playground*] bitumé
Ⓒ *vtr* bitumer

asphyxia /əsˈfɪksɪə, US æsˈf-/ *n* asphyxie *f*

asphyxiate /əsˈfɪksɪeɪt, US æsˈf-/
Ⓐ *vtr* asphyxier
Ⓑ *vi* s'asphyxier

asphyxiation /əsˌfɪksɪˈeɪʃn/ *n* asphyxie *f*; **to die of** *ou* **from** ∼ mourir asphyxié

aspic /ˈæspɪk/ *n* Culin aspic *m*; **salmon in** ∼ aspic de saumon

aspirate
Ⓐ /ˈæspərət/ *n* Ling aspirée *f*
Ⓑ /ˈæspərət/ *adj* aspiré
Ⓒ /ˈæspəreɪt/ *vtr* aspirer

aspiration /ˌæspɪˈreɪʃn/ *n* ① (desire) aspiration *f* (**to** à); **to have** ∼**s to do** aspirer à faire; ② Med, Ling aspiration *f*

aspire /əˈspaɪə(r)/ *vi* aspirer (**to** à; **to do** à faire); **it** ∼**s to be an exclusive restaurant** cela se veut un restaurant de luxe

aspirin /ˈæspərɪn/ *n* aspirine® *f*; **two** ∼**(s)** deux comprimés d'aspirine

aspiring /əˈspaɪərɪŋ/ *adj* ∼ **authors/journalists etc** ceux qui aspirent à devenir auteurs/journalistes etc

ass /æs/ *n* ① (donkey) âne *m*; ② ○(fool) idiot/-e *m/f*

assail /əˈseɪl/ *vtr* sout ① (attack) attaquer; ② (plague) assaillir; **to be** ∼**ed by worries/doubts** être assailli par les soucis/par le doute

assailant /əˈseɪlənt/ *n* agresseur *m*; Mil assaillant/-e *m/f*

assassin /əˈsæsɪn, US -sn/ *n* assassin *m*

assassinate /əˈsæsɪneɪt, US -sən-/ *vtr* assassiner

assassination /əˌsæsɪˈneɪʃn, US -səˈneɪʃn/ *n* assassinat *m*

assault /əˈsɔːlt/
Ⓐ *n* ① Jur (on person) agression *f* (**on** sur); (sexual) agression *f* sexuelle (**on** sur); **physical** ∼ agression *f*; **verbal** ∼ injures *fpl*; ② (attack) assaut *m* (**on** de); **air/ground** ∼ assaut aérien/terrestre; **to make an** ∼ **on** monter à l'assaut de

[*town*]; ③ fig (criticism) (on theory) attaque *f* (**on** de); (on person, reputation) atteinte *f* (**on** à)
Ⓑ *noun modifier* [*troops, weapon, ship*] d'assaut
Ⓒ *vtr* ① Jur agresser; **to be indecently** ∼**ed** être victime d'une agression sexuelle; ② Mil assaillir; ③ fig agresser [*ears, nerves*]

assault: ∼ **and battery** *n* Jur coups *mpl* et blessures *fpl*; ∼ **course** *n* Mil parcours *m* du combattant

assemblage /əˈsemblɪdʒ/ *n* ① (collection) collection *f*; ② Tech, Art assemblage *m*

assemble /əˈsembl/
Ⓐ *vtr* ① (gather) rassembler; ② (construct) assembler; **easy to** ∼ facile à monter
Ⓑ *vi* [*marchers, passengers, vehicles*] se rassembler; [*parliament, team, family*] se réunir
Ⓒ **assembled** *pp adj* [*reporters, delegates*] rassemblé; [*family, friends*] réuni

assembler /əˈsemblə(r)/ ▸ p. 1181 *n* ① (in factory) assembleur/-euse *m/f*; ② Comput assembleur *m*

assembly /əˈsemblɪ/ *n* ① (of people) assemblée *f*; ② Pol (institution) assemblée *f*; ③ Sch rassemblement *m*; ④ Pol (congregating) réunion *f*; **freedom of** ∼ liberté *f* de réunion; ⑤ (of components, machines) assemblage *m*; ∼ **instructions** instructions *fpl* de montage; ⑥ (device) assemblage *m*; **engine** ∼ bloc-moteur *m*

assembly line *n* chaîne *f* de montage

assent /əˈsent/
Ⓐ *n* assentiment *m* (**to** à); **by common** ∼ d'un commun accord
Ⓑ *vi* sout donner son assentiment (**to** à)

assert /əˈsɜːt/
Ⓐ *vtr* ① (state) affirmer (**that** que); (against opposition) soutenir (**that** que); **to** ∼ **one's authority** affirmer son autorité; ② (demand) revendiquer [*right, claim*]
Ⓑ *v refl* **to** ∼ **oneself** s'affirmer

assertion /əˈsɜːʃn/ *n* (statement) déclaration *f* (**that** selon laquelle); **it was an** ∼ **of her strength** c'était une manière d'affirmer son pouvoir

assertive /əˈsɜːtɪv/ *adj* assuré

assertiveness /əˈsɜːtɪvnɪs/ *n* affirmation *f* de soi; **lack of** ∼ manque *m* d'assurance; **I admire your** ∼ j'admire votre assurance

assess /əˈses/
Ⓐ *vtr* ① gen évaluer [*ability, effect, person, problem*]; ② (in insurance, law) estimer [*damage, value*]; ③ (for taxation) imposer [*person*]; fixer [*tax*]; ④ Sch contrôler [*pupil*]
Ⓑ *vi* évaluer

assessment /əˈsesmənt/ *n* ① gen appréciation *f* (**of** de); ② (in insurance, law) estimation *f* (**of** de); ③ (for taxation) imposition *f*; ④ Sch contrôle *m*

assessor /əˈsesə(r)/ ▸ p. 1181 *n* ① Fin contrôleur *m*; ② (in insurance) expert *m*; ③ Jur assesseur *m*

asset /ˈæset/
Ⓐ *n* ① Fin bien *m*; ② (advantage) atout *m*
Ⓑ **assets** *npl* (private) biens *mpl*, avoir *m* **Ⓒ**; Comm, Jur actif *m* **Ⓒ**; ∼**s and liabilities** actif et passif

asset stripping *n* dépeçage *m*

assiduity /ˌæsɪˈdjuːətɪ, US -duː-/ *n* assiduité *f*

assiduous /əˈsɪdjʊəs, US -dʒʊəs/ *adj* assidu

assign /əˈsaɪn/ *vtr* ① (allocate) assigner [*resources*] (**to** à); ② (delegate) **to** ∼ **a task to sb**, **to** ∼ **sb to a task** affecter qn à une tâche; **to** ∼ **sb to do** désigner qn pour faire; ③ (attribute) attribuer [*name, value*] (**to** à); ④ (appoint) nommer (**to** à); ⑤ Jur (transfer) céder

assignation /ˌæsɪɡˈneɪʃn/ *n* rendez-vous *m*

assignment /əˈsaɪnmənt/ *n* ① (diplomatic, military) poste *m*; (specific duty) mission *f*; ② (academic) devoir *m*; ③ (of duties, staff, funds) affectation *f*; ④ (of rights, contract) cession *f*

assimilate /əˈsɪmɪleɪt/
Ⓐ *vtr* assimiler (**to** à)
Ⓑ *vi* s'assimiler (**to** à)

assimilation /əˌsɪmɪˈleɪʃn/ *n* assimilation *f* (**to** à)

assist /əˈsɪst/
Ⓐ *vtr* ① (help) gen aider; (in organization) assister (**to do, in doing** à faire); **to** ∼ **one another** s'entraider; ② (facilitate) faciliter
Ⓑ *vi* ① (help) aider (**in doing** à faire); **to** ∼ **in** prendre part à [*operation, rescue*]; ② (attend) assister (**at** à)

C **-assisted** *combining form* **computer-~ed** assisté par ordinateur; **government-~ed scheme** projet financé par l'État

assistance /ə'sɪstəns/ *n* aide *f* (**to** à); (more formal) assistance *f* (**to** à); **to come to sb's ~** venir à l'aide de qn; **to give ~ to sb** prêter assistance à qn; **with the ~ of** avec l'aide de [*person*]; à l'aide de [*device*]; **can I be of ~?** puis-je aider *or* être utile?

assistant /ə'sɪstənt/ ▸ p. 1181

A *n* ① (helper) assistant/-e *m/f*; (in hierarchy) adjoint/-e *m/f*; ② GB Sch, Univ (**foreign language**) ~ (in school) assistant/-e *m/f*; (in university) lecteur/-trice *m/f*

B *noun modifier* [*editor, producer etc*] adjoint

assistant: **~ manager** ▸ p. 1181 *n* gérant/-e *m/f* adjoint/-e; **~ professor** ▸ p. 1181 *n* US Univ ≈ maître assistant *m*

assisted suicide *n* suicide *m* assisté

associate

A *n* /ə'səʊʃɪət/ *n* ① (colleague, partner) associé/-e *m/f also pej*; **an ~ in crime** un/une complice; ② (of society) associé/-e *m/f*; (of academic body) membre *m*; ③ US Univ ≈ DEUG *m*

B /ə'səʊʃɪət/ *adj* [*body, member*] associé

C /ə'səʊʃɪeɪt/ *vtr* ① associer [*idea, memory*] (**with** à); ② **to be ~d with** [*person*] faire partie de [*movement, group*]; *péj* être mêlé à [*shady business*]

D /ə'səʊʃɪeɪt/ *vi* **to ~ with sb** fréquenter qn

E **associated** *pp adj* ① [*idea, concept*] associé; ② (connected) [*member*] associé; [*benefits, expenses*] annexe; **the plan and its ~d problems** le projet et les problèmes qui en découlent

associate: **~ company** société *f* liée; **~ director** *n* Theat directeur/-trice *m/f* associé/-e; Comm directeur/-trice *m/f* adjoint/-e; **~ editor** ▸ p. 1181 *n* rédacteur/-trice *m/f* associé/-e; **~ member** *n* membre *m* associé; **~ membership** *n* adhésion *f* en tant que membre associé

association /ə,səʊsɪ'eɪʃn/ *n* ① (club, society) association *f*; ② (relationship) (between ideas) association *f*; (between organizations, people) relations *fpl* (**between** entre; **with** avec); (sexual) liaison *f* (**with** avec); ③ (mental evocation) (*gén pl*) souvenir *m*; **it has good/bad ~s for me** ça me rappelle de bons/mauvais souvenirs; **to have ~s with sth** évoquer qch

assorted /ə'sɔːtɪd/ *adj* [*objects, colours etc*] varié; [*foodstuffs*] assorti; [*group*] hétérogène; **ill ~** mal assorti; **in ~ sizes** dans toutes les tailles

assortment /ə'sɔːtmənt/ *n gen* assortiment *m* (**of** de); (of people) mélange *m* (**of** de); **in an ~ of colours** dans différentes couleurs

assuage /ə'sweɪdʒ/ *vtr litter* calmer

assume /ə'sjuːm, US ə'suːm/ *vtr* ① (suppose) supposer (**that** que); **I ~ she knows** je suppose qu'elle le sait; **it is ~d that** on suppose que; **let's ~** *ou* **assuming that's correct** supposons que cela soit exact; ② (take on) prendre [*control, identity, office*]; assumer [*responsibility*]; affecter [*expression, indifference*]; **under an ~d name** sous un nom d'emprunt

assumption /ə'sʌmpʃn/ *n* ① (supposition) supposition *f*; (belief) idée *f*; Philos hypothèse *f*; **the ~ that** l'idée selon laquelle; **to work on the ~ that** présumer que; **a false ~** une mauvaise hypothèse; ② (take on, power) prise *f* (**of** de)

Assumption /ə'sʌmpʃn/ *n* Relig Assomption *f*

assurance /ə'ʃɔːrəns, US ə'ʃʊərəns/ *n* ① (guarantee) assurance *f*, garantie *f*; **to give sb an** *ou* **every ~ that** donner à qn l'assurance que; **you have my ~ that** je peux vous assurer que; ② (self-confidence) assurance *f*; ③ GB (insurance) assurance *f*; **life ~** assurance-vie *f*

assure /ə'ʃɔː(r), US ə'ʃʊər/ *vtr* ① (state positively) assurer; **to ~ sb that** assurer à qn que; **to be ~d of sth** être sûr de qch; **rest ~d that** soyez assuré que; ② (ensure) assurer; ③ GB (insure) assurer

assured /ə'ʃɔːd, US ə'ʃʊərd/ *adj* ① (confident) [*voice, manner*] assuré; [*person*] plein d'assurance; ② (beyond doubt) assuré

Assyria /ə'sɪrɪə/ ▸ p. 774 *pr n* Assyrie *f*

asterisk /'æstərɪsk/ *n* astérisque *m*

astern /ə'stɜːn/ *adv* Naut à l'arrière (**of** de)

asteroid /'æstərɔɪd/ *n* astéroïde *m*

asthma /'æsmə, US 'æzmə/ ▸ p. 933 *n* asthme *m*; **~ sufferer** asthmatique *mf*

asthmatic /æs'mætɪk/ *n, adj* asthmatique (*mf*)

astigmatism /ə'stɪɡmətɪzəm/ *n* astigmatisme *m*

astonish /ə'stɒnɪʃ/ *vtr* surprendre, étonner; **it ~es me that** ce qui me surprend *or* m'étonne c'est que

astonished /ə'stɒnɪʃt/ *adj* surpris, étonné (**by, at** par; **to do** de faire); **to be ~ that** être vraiment étonné que (+ *subj*), trouver extraordinaire que (+ *subj*)

astonishing /ə'stɒnɪʃɪŋ/ *adj* [*skill, intelligence*] étonnant; [*career, performance*] extraordinaire; [*beauty, speed, success*] incroyable; **it is ~ that** il est incroyable que (+ *subj*)

astonishingly /ə'stɒnɪʃɪŋlɪ/ *adv* incroyablement

astonishment /ə'stɒnɪʃmənt/ *n* étonnement *m*; **to my ~** à ma grande surprise; **to look at sb/sth in ~** regarder qn/qch avec étonnement

astound /ə'staʊnd/ *vtr* stupéfier

astounding /ə'staʊndɪŋ/ *adj* incroyable

astrakhan /,æstrə'kæn, US 'æstrəkən/ *n* astrakan *m*

astray /ə'streɪ/ *adv* ① **to go astray** (go missing) se perdre; (go wrong) [*plan etc*] être contrarié; ② **to lead sb ~** (confuse) induire qn en erreur; (corrupt) détourner qn du droit chemin

astride /ə'straɪd/

A *adv lit* [*be, sit*] à califourchon

B *prep* à califourchon sur; *fig* **to stand** *ou* **sit ~ sth** [*building, company etc*] dominer qch

astringent /ə'strɪndʒənt/

A *n* astringent *m*

B *adj* ① Med astringent; ② *fig* [*remark, tone*] cinglant

astrologer /ə'strɒlədʒə(r)/ ▸ p. 1181 *n* astrologue *mf*

astrological /,æstrə'lɒdʒɪkl/ *adj* astrologique

astrology /ə'strɒlədʒɪ/ *n* astrologie *f*

astronaut /'æstrənɔːt/ ▸ p. 1181 *n* astronaute *mf*

astronomer /ə'strɒnəmə(r)/ ▸ p. 1181 *n* astronome *mf*

astronomic /,æstrə'nɒmɪk/, **astronomical** /,æstrə'nɒmɪkl/ *adj lit, fig* astronomique

astronomically /,æstrə'nɒmɪkəlɪ/ *adv* **prices are ~ high** les prix sont astronomiques; **~ expensive** incroyablement cher

astronomy /ə'strɒnəmɪ/ *n* astronomie *f*

astrophysicist /,æstrəʊ'fɪzɪsɪst/ ▸ p. 1181 *n* astrophysicien/-ienne *m/f*

astrophysics /,æstrəʊ'fɪzɪks/ *n* (+ *v sg*) astrophysique *f*

Astroturf® /'æstrəʊtɜːf/ *n* gazon *m* artificiel

astute /ə'stjuːt, US ə'stuːt/ *adj* astucieux/-ieuse

astutely /ə'stjuːtlɪ, US ə'stuːtlɪ/ *adv* astucieusement

astuteness /ə'stjuːtnɪs, US -'stuː-/ *n* astuce *f*

asylum /ə'saɪləm/ *n* asile *m*; **lunatic ~** asile de fous

asylum-seeker *n* demandeur/-euse *m/f* d'asile

asymmetric /,eɪsɪ'metrɪk/, **asymmetrical** /,eɪsɪ'metrɪkl/ *adj* asymétrique

at /æt, ət/ ▸ p. 668 *prep* ① (with place, time, age etc) à; ② (at the house etc of) chez; ③ (followed by superlative) **the garden is ~ its prettiest in June** juin est le mois où le jardin est le plus beau; **I'm ~ my best in the morning** c'est le matin que je me sens le mieux; **she was ~ her best at 50** (of musician, artist etc) à 50 ans elle était au sommet de son art; ④ ~ (harassing) **he's been (on) ~ me to buy a new car** il n'arrête pas de me casser les pieds pour que j'achète une nouvelle voiture○

Idioms **I don't know where he's ~**○ je ne le comprends pas du tout; **while we're ~ it**○ pendant qu'on y est○; **I've been (hard) ~ it all day** je n'ai pas arrêté de la journée

AT *n: abrév* ▸ **alternative technology**

atavistic /,ætə'vɪstɪk/ *adj* atavique

ate /eɪt/ *prét* ▸ **eat**

atheism /'eɪθɪɪzəm/ *n* athéisme *m*

atheist /'eɪθɪɪst/ *n, adj* athée (*mf*)

atheistic /,eɪθɪ'ɪstɪk/ *adj* athée

Athens /'æθɪnz/ ▸ p. 1276 *pr n* Athènes *f*

athlete /'æθliːt/ *n* athlète *mf*

athlete's foot /,æθliːts 'fʊt/ ▸ p. 933 *n* mycose *f*

athletic /æθ'letɪk/ *adj* ① [*event, club, coach*] d'athlétisme; ② [*person, body*] athlétique

athletics /æθ'letɪks/ ▸ p. 881

A *n* (+ *v sg*) GB athlétisme *m*; US sports *mpl*

B *noun modifier* [*club*] GB d'athlétisme; US sportif/-ive

Atlantic /ət'læntɪk/

A ▸ p. 1049 *pr n* **the ~** l'Atlantique *m*

a

at

When *at* is used as a straightforward preposition it is translated by *à*:

at the airport
= à l'aéroport

at midnight
= à minuit

at the age of 50
= à l'âge de 50 ans

Remember that *à + le* always becomes *au* and *à + les* always becomes *aux* (*au bureau, aux bureaux*).

When *at* means *at the house, shop*, etc. *of*, it is translated by *chez*:

at Amanda's
= chez Amanda

at the hairdresser's
= chez le coiffeur

If you have doubts about how to translate a phrase or idiom beginning with at (*at the top of, at home, at a guess* etc.) you should consult the appropriate noun entry (**top, home, guess** etc.). This dictionary contains usage notes on such topics as **age, the clock, length measurement, games and sports** etc. Many of these use the preposition *at*. For the index to these notes ▸ **p. 1354**.

at also often appears in English as the second element of a phrasal verb (*look at, aim at*, etc.). For translations, look at the appropriate verb entry (**look, aim** etc.).

at is used after certain nouns, adjectives and verbs in English (*her surprise at, an attempt at, annoyed at* etc.). For translations, consult the appropriate noun, adjective or verb entry (**surprise, attempt, annoy** etc.).

In the entry **at**, you will find particular usages and idiomatic expressions which do not appear elsewhere in the dictionary.

B *adj* gen de l'Atlantique; [*coast, current*] atlantique
Atlantic Ocean *n* océan *m* Atlantique
atlas /'ætləs/ *n* atlas *m*
Atlas Mountains *pr npl* (montagnes *fpl* de l')Atlas *m*
ATM *n*: *abrév* ▸ **automatic teller machine**
atmosphere /'ætməsfɪə(r)/ *n* **1** (air) atmosphère *f*; **2** (mood) gen ambiance *f*; (bad) atmosphère *f*; **there was a bit of an ~°** l'atmosphère était tendue
atmospheric /ˌætməs'ferɪk/
A **atmospherics** *npl* **1** Radio, TV (interference) parasites *mpl*, bruit *m* atmosphérique; Meteorol (disturbances) perturbations *fpl* atmosphériques; **2** (of song, film) ambiance *f*
B *adj* **1** [*conditions, pressure, pollution*] atmosphérique; **2** [*music*] d'ambiance; [*film*] évocateur/-trice
atom /'ætəm/ *n* Phys, fig atome *m*
atom bomb *n* bombe *f* atomique
atomic /ə'tɒmɪk/ *adj* [*explosion, power*] nucléaire, atomique
atomic: **~ power station** *n* centrale *f* atomique; **~ reactor** *n* réacteur *m* atomique; **~ scientist** ▸ p. 1181 *n* atomiste *mf*
atomize /'ætəmaɪz/ *vtr* atomiser
atomizer /'ætəmaɪzə(r)/ *n* atomiseur *m*
atone /ə'təʊn/ *vi* **to ~ for** expier [*sin, crime*]; racheter [*error*]
atonement /ə'təʊnmənt/ *n* rédemption *f*
atrocious /ə'trəʊʃəs/ *adj* (horrifying) atroce; (bad) épouvantable
atrociously /ə'trəʊʃəslɪ/ *adv* de façon atroce
atrocity /ə'trɒsətɪ/ *n* atrocité *f*
atrophy /'ætrəfɪ/
A *n* Med atrophie *f*

B *vi* Med, fig s'atrophier
at sign /'æt saɪn/ *n* arobase *m*
attach /ə'tætʃ/
A *vtr* **1** (fasten) attacher [*objet*] (**to** à); (to letter) joindre; **2** (to organization) **to be ~ed to sth** être attaché à qch; **3** (attribute) attacher (**to** à); **to ~ blame to sb for sth** reprocher qch à qn; **4** (in email) joindre, envoyer [*qch*] en pièce jointe [*document, file*]
B *v refl* **to ~ oneself to** lit, fig s'attacher à
attaché /ə'tæʃeɪ, US ˌætə'ʃeɪ/ *n* attaché/-e *m/f*
attaché case *n* attaché-case *m*
attached /ə'tætʃt/ *adj* **1** (fond) **~ to sb/sth** attaché à qn/qch; **to grow ~ to sb/sth** s'attacher à qn/qch; **2** [*document*] ci-joint
attachment /ə'tætʃmənt/ *n* **1** (affection) attachement *m*; **to form an ~ to sb** s'attacher à qn; **2** (device) accessoire *m*; **3** (placement) **to be on ~** gen, Mil être en détachement à; **4** (act of fastening) fixation *f*; **5** (in email) pièce *f* jointe
attack /ə'tæk/
A *n* **1** gen, Mil, Sport attaque *f* (**on** contre); (criminal) agression *f* (**against, on** contre); (terrorist) attentat *m*; **to come under ~** Mil être attaqué (**from** par); fig être l'objet de critiques virulentes (**from** de la part de); **to leave oneself open to ~** fig s'exposer à la critique; **to mount ou launch an ~ on sth** lit attaquer qch; fig s'attaquer à qch; **2** Med (of chronic illness) crise *f* (**of** de); **to have an ~ of flu** attraper la grippe
B *vtr* **1** gen, Med, Mil, Sport attaquer; (criminally) agresser [*victim*]; fig attaquer [*book, idea*]; **2** (tackle) s'attaquer à [*task, problem*]
attacker /ə'tækə(r)/ *n* gen agresseur *m*; Mil, Sport attaquant/-e *m/f*
attain /ə'teɪn/ *vtr* atteindre [*position, objective, level*]; réaliser [*ambition*]; acquérir [*knowledge*]; parvenir à [*happiness*]
attainable /ə'teɪnəbl/ *adj* réalisable
attainment /ə'teɪnmənt/ *n* **1** (achieving) (of knowledge) acquisition *f*; (of goal) réalisation *f*; **2** (success) réussite *f*
attempt /ə'tempt/
A *n* **1** tentative *f* (**to do** de faire); **to make an ~ to do** *ou* **at doing** tenter de faire; **in an ~ to do** pour essayer de faire; **on his first ~** dès sa première tentative; **~ to escape, escape ~** tentative d'évasion; **he made no ~ to apologize** il n'a même pas tenté de s'excuser; **good ~!** bien essayé!; **2** (attack) attentat *m*; **~ on sb's life** attentat contre la vie de qn
B *vtr* tenter (**to do** de faire); s'attaquer à [*exam question*]; **to ~ suicide** tenter de se suicider; **~ed murder** tentative de meurtre
attend /ə'tend/
A *vtr* **1** (go to) assister à [*ceremony, meeting, performance*]; aller à [*church, school*]; suivre [*class, course*]; **the event was well/poorly ~ed** beaucoup de/peu de monde assistait à l'événement; **2** (accompany) accompagner; **3** (take care of) soigner
B *vi* **1** (be present) être présent; **2** sout (pay attention) être attentif/-ive (**to** à)

(Phrasal verb)

■ **attend to**: ▸ **~ to [sb/sth]** s'occuper de [*person, problem*]
attendance: **~ record** *n* taux *m* de présence; **~ register** *n* Sch registre *m* des absences
attendant /ə'tendənt/
A ▸ p. 1181 *n* (in cloakroom, museum, car park) gardien/-ienne *m/f*; (in cinema) ouvreuse *f*; (at petrol station) pompiste *mf*; (at swimming pool) surveillant/-e *m/f*; **medical ~** membre *m* du personnel médical
B *adj* sout **1** (associated) [*cost, danger, issue*] associé; [*symptom*] concomitant; **2** (attending) [*aide, bodyguard*] attaché à sa personne
attention /ə'tenʃn/
A *n* **1** (notice, interest) attention *f*; **to attract ~** attirer l'attention; **to be the centre** *ou* **focus of ~** être le centre d'attention; **to draw ~ to sth** attirer l'attention sur qch; **to seek** *ou* **demand ~** [*child*] chercher à attirer l'attention; **to give one's full ~ to sth** prêter toute son attention à qch; **to pay ~** faire attention; **to bring sth to sb's ~** porter qch à l'attention de qn; **it has come to my ~ that…** j'ai appris que…; **~ please!** votre attention s'il vous plaît!; **pay ~!** écoutez!; **2** (treatment, care) gen attention *f*; Med assistance *f*; **~ to detail** le souci du détail; **to give some ~ to sth** s'occuper de qch; **the car needs ~** il faut s'occuper de la

voiture; **for the ~ of** à l'attention de; **3** Mil **to stand to** ou **at ~** être au garde-à-vous
B *excl* garde-à-vous!

attention-seeking
A *n* besoin *m* d'attirer l'attention
B *adj* [*person*] cherchant à attirer l'attention

attention span *n* he has a very short **~** il n'arrive pas à se concentrer très longtemps

attentive /ə'tentɪv/ *adj* (alert) attentif/-ive; (solicitous) attentionné (**to** à)

attentively /ə'tentɪvlɪ/ *adv* (alertly) attentivement; (solicitously) avec attention

attentiveness /ə'tentɪvnɪs/ *n* **1** (concentration) attention *f*; **2** (solicitude) prévenance *f*

attenuate /ə'tenjʊeɪt/ *vtr* modérer

attest /ə'test/ sout
A *vtr* **1** (prove) confirmer; **an ~ed fact** un fait reconnu; **2** (declare) attester (**that** que); **3** (authenticate) légaliser [*will*]
B *vi* **1** **to ~ to** (prove) témoigner de; **2** (affirm) attester

attic /'ætɪk/ *n* grenier *m*; **in the ~** au grenier

Attica /'ætɪkə/ *pr n* Attique *f*

attic: **~ room** *n* mansarde *f*; **~ window** *n* lucarne *f*

attire† /ə'taɪə(r)/
A *n* vêtements *mpl*
B *vtr* vêtir; **~d in** vêtu de

attitude /'ætɪtjuːd, US -tuːd/
A *n* **1** attitude *f* (**to, towards** GB à l'égard de); **her ~ to life/ the world** sa façon de voir la vie/le monde; **2** ○(assertiveness, dynamism) **to have ~** avoir de l'allure
B **attitudes** *npl* (of social group etc) **young people's ~s towards religion** l'attitude *f* des jeunes envers la religion

attorney /ə'tɜːnɪ/ ▸ **p. 1181** *n* US (lawyer) avocat *m*; **power of ~** procuration *f*

Attorney General, AG *n* (*pl* **Attorneys General**) Attorney *m* General, ministre *m* de la justice des États-Unis

attract /ə'trækt/ *vtr* attirer; **to ~ attention** attirer l'attention; **he was very ~ed to her** elle l'attirait beaucoup

attraction /ə'trækʃn/ *n* **1** (favourable feature) attrait *m* (**of sth** de qch; **of doing** de faire; **for** pour); **I can't see the ~ of (doing)** je ne vois pas l'intérêt de (faire); **2** (entertainment, sight) attraction *f*; **3** (instinctive allure) attirance *f* (**to** à pour); **her ~ to him** son attirance pour lui; **4** Phys attraction *f*

attractive /ə'træktɪv/ *adj* [*person*] séduisant; [*child*] charmant; [*place, feature*] attrayant; [*offer, idea*] séduisant; [*plant*] joli

attractively /ə'træktɪvlɪ/ *adv* [*furnished, arranged*] de manière attrayante; [*dressed*] coquettement

attractiveness /ə'træktɪvnɪs/ *n* (of person, place) charme *m*; (of investment) attrait *m*; (of proposal) intérêt *m*

attributable /ə'trɪbjʊtəbl/ *adj* **to be ~ to** [*change, profit, success etc*] être dû à; [*error, fall, loss etc*] être imputable à

attribute
A /'ætrɪbjuːt/ *n* gen attribut *m*; Ling épithète *f*
B /ə'trɪbjuːt/ *vtr* attribuer (**to** à)

attribution /ˌætrɪ'bjuːʃn/ *n* attribution *f* (**of** de; **to** à)

attributive /ə'trɪbjʊtɪv/ *adj* Ling épithète

attrition /ə'trɪʃn/ *n* (all contexts) usure *f*

attune /ə'tjuːn, US ə'tuːn/ *vtr* **to be ~d to** (accustomed to) être habitué à; (aware of) être sensible à

aubergine /'əʊbəʒiːn/ *n* GB aubergine *f*

auburn /'ɔːbən/ ▸ **p. 752** *adj* auburn *inv*

auction /'ɔːkʃn, 'ɒkʃn/
A *n* enchère *f* (*gen pl*); **at ~** aux enchères; **to put sth up for ~** mettre qch aux enchères
B *vtr* (*also* **~ off**) vendre [qch] aux enchères

auctioneer /ˌɔːkʃə'nɪə(r)/ ▸ **p. 1181** *n* commissaire-priseur *m*

auction: **~ house** *n* US société *f* de commissaires-priseurs; **~ room(s)** *n*(*pl*) salle *f* de vente aux enchères; **~ sale** *n* vente *f* aux enchères

audacious /ɔː'deɪʃəs/ *adj* audacieux/-ieuse

audacity /ɔː'dæsətɪ/ *n* audace *f*

audible /'ɔːdəbl/ *adj* audible

audibly /'ɔːdəblɪ/ *adv* distinctement

audience /'ɔːdɪəns/ *n* **1** (in cinema, concert, theatre) public *m*, salle *f*; Radio auditeurs *mpl*; TV téléspectateurs *mpl*; **2** (for books) lecteurs *mpl*; (for ideas) public *m*; **3** (meeting) audience *f* (**with sb** auprès de qn)

audience: **~ participation** *n* participation *f* du public; **~ ratings** *npl* indice *m* d'écoute; **~ research** *n* sondages *mpl* du public

audio /'ɔːdɪəʊ/ *adj* audio *inv*

audio: **~book** *n* livre-cassette *m*; **~ cassette** *n* audio-cassette *f*

audiotyping /'ɔːdɪəʊtaɪpɪŋ/ *n* audiotypie *f*

audiotypist /'ɔːdɪəʊtaɪpɪst/ ▸ **p. 1181** *n* audiotypiste *mf*

audiovisual, AV /ˌɔːdɪəʊ'vɪʒʊəl/ *adj* audiovisuel/-elle

audit /'ɔːdɪt/
A *n* audit *m*
B *vtr* auditer, vérifier

auditing /'ɔːdɪtɪŋ/ *n* audit *m*

audition /ɔː'dɪʃn/
A *n* audition *f* (**for** pour); **to go for an ~** passer une audition
B *vtr*, *vi* auditionner (**for** pour)

auditor /'ɔːdɪtə(r)/ ▸ **p. 1181** *n* **1** commissaire *m* aux comptes; **2** US (student) auditeur/-trice *m/f*

auditorium /ˌɔːdɪ'tɔːrɪəm/ *n* (*pl* **-iums** ou **-ia**) **1** Theat salle *f*; **2** US (for meetings) salle *f* de conférences; Sch, Univ amphithéâtre *m*; (concert hall) salle *f* de spectacle; (stadium) stade *m*

auditory /'ɔːdɪtrɪ, US -tɔːrɪ/ *adj* auditif/-ive

Aug *abrév écrite* = **August**

augment /ɔːg'ment/ *vtr*, *vi* augmenter

augmentation /ˌɔːgmen'teɪʃn/ *n* gen, Mus augmentation *f*

augur /'ɔːgə(r)/ *vi* **to ~ well/ill** être de bon/mauvais augure (**for** pour)

august /ɔː'gʌst/ *adj* sout imposant, auguste fml

August /'ɔːgəst/ ▸ **p. 1020** *n* août *m*

auk /ɔːk/ *n* **great ~** grand pingouin *m*; **little ~** mergule *m* nain

aunt /ɑːnt, US ænt/ *n* tante *f*; **no, Aunt** non, ma tante

auntie, aunty○ /'ɑːntɪ, US 'æntɪ/ *n* tantine○ *f*, tata○ *f*

au pair /ˌəʊ 'peə(r)/ *n* (jeune) fille *f* au pair

aura /'ɔːrə/ *n* (*pl* **-ras** ou **-rae**) (of place) atmosphère *f*; (of person) aura *f*

aural /'ɔːrəl, aʊrəl/
A *n* Sch exercice *m* de compréhension et d'expression orales; Mus ≈ dictée *f* musicale
B *adj* **1** gen auditif/-ive; **2** Med auriculaire; [*test*] auditif; **3** Sch [*comprehension, test*] oral

aurora /ɔː'rɔːrə/ *n* (*pl* **-ras** ou **-rae**) **~ australis/borealis** aurore *f* australe/boréale

auspicious /ɔː'spɪʃəs/ *adj* prometteur/-euse

Aussie○ /'ɒzɪ/ *n*, *adj* = **Australian**

austere /ɒ'stɪə(r), ɔː'stɪə(r)/ *adj* austère

austerity /ɒ'sterətɪ, ɔː'sterətɪ/ *n* austérité *f*

Australasia /ˌɒstrə'leɪʒɪə, ˌɔːs-/ *pr n* Australasie *f*

Australia /ɒ'streɪlɪə, ɔː's-/ ▸ **p. 774** *pr n* Australie *f*

Australian /ɒ'streɪlɪən, ɔː's-/ ▸ **p. 1032**
A *n* Australien/-ienne *m/f*
B *adj* australien/-ienne

Austria /'ɒstrɪə, 'ɔːstrɪə/ ▸ **p. 774** *pr n* Autriche *f*

Austrian /'ɒstrɪən, 'ɔːstrɪən/ ▸ **p. 1032**
A *n* Autrichien/-ienne *m/f*
B *adj* autrichien/-ienne

Austro-Hungarian /'ɒstrəʊ hʌŋ'geərɪən/ *adj* austro-hongrois

autarchy /'ɔːtɑːkɪ/ *n* autocratie *f*

authentic /ɔː'θentɪk/ *adj* authentique

authenticate /ɔː'θentɪkeɪt/ *vtr* authentifier

authenticity /ˌɔːθen'tɪsətɪ/ *n* authenticité *f*

author /'ɔːθə(r)/ ▸ **p. 1181** *n* **1** (of book, play, report) auteur *m*; **2** (by profession) écrivain *m*; **3** (of scheme) auteur *m*

authoritarian /ɔːˌθɒrɪ'teərɪən/ *adj* pej autoritaire

authoritarianism /ɔːˌθɒrɪ'teərɪənɪzəm/ *n* pej autoritarisme *m*

a

authoritative /ɔː'θɒrətətɪv, US -teɪtɪv/ adj [1] (forceful) autoritaire; [2] (reliable) [work] qui fait autorité; [source] bien informé

authority /ɔː'θɒrətɪ/
A n [1] (power) autorité f (over sur); **to have the ~ to do** être habilité à faire; **to be in ~** occuper un poste de responsabilité; **he will be reported to those in ~** son cas sera référé à qui de droit; **who's in ~ here?** qui commande ici?; **to do sth on sb's ~** faire qch sous les ordres de qn; [2] (forcefulness, confidence) autorité f; [3] (permission) autorisation f; **to give sb (the) ~ to do** autoriser qn à faire; [4] (organization) autorité f; [5] (expert) (person) autorité f, expert m (on en matière de); (book, film) œuvre f de référence; [6] (source of information) source f; **I have it on good ~ that** je sais de source sûre que
B authorities npl gen, Admin, Pol autorités fpl; **the school/hospital authorities** la direction de l'école/de l'hôpital

authorization /,ɔː:θəraɪ'zeɪʃn/ n (authority, document) autorisation f; **to give** ou **grant ~ to do** accorder l'autorisation de faire

authorize /'ɔː:θəraɪz/ vtr autoriser (**to do** à faire); **~d** [signature, version] autorisé; [dealer] agréé

autism /'ɔː:tɪzəm/ n autisme m

autistic /ɔː:'tɪstɪk/ adj [person] autiste; [response etc] autistique

auto° /'ɔː:təʊ/ US
A n auto f
B noun modifier [industry] automobile; [workers] de l'industrie automobile

autobiographical /,ɔː:təʊbaɪə'græfɪkl/ adj autobiographique

autobiography /,ɔː:təʊbaɪ'ɒgrəfɪ/ n autobiographie f

autocrat /'ɔː:təkræt/ n autocrate mf

autocratic /,ɔː:tə'krætɪk/ adj autocratique

autocue /'ɔː:təʊkjuː/ n TV prompteur m

autograph /'ɔː:təgrɑːf, US -græf/
A n autographe m
B noun modifier [album, hunter] d'autographes
C vtr dédicacer [book, record]; signer [memento]

autoimmune /ˌɔː:təʊɪ'mjuːn/ adj [disease] auto-immun; [system] autoimmunitaire

automate /'ɔː:təmeɪt/ vtr automatiser [factory, process]

automatic /,ɔː:tə'mætɪk/
A n [1] (washing machine) machine f à laver automatique; [2] (car) voiture f (à changement de vitesse) automatique; [3] (gun) automatique m; [4] (setting) **to be on ~** [machine] être en position automatique
B adj automatique

automatically /,ɔː:tə'mætɪklɪ/ adv automatiquement

automatic pilot n (device) pilote m automatique; (system) lit, fig pilotage m automatique; **to be on ~** Aviat être sur pilote automatique

automatic teller machine, ATM n guichet m automatique

automation /,ɔː:tə'meɪʃn/ n automatisation f; **office ~** bureautique f; **industrial ~** robotique f

automaton /ɔː:'tɒmətən, US -tɒn/ n (pl **-s, automata**) automate m

automobile /'ɔː:təməbiːl, ,ɔː:təmə'biːl/ n US, GB† automobile f

automotive /,ɔː:tə'məʊtɪv/ adj [1] [design, industry] automobile; [2] (self-propelling) automoteur/-trice

autonomous /ɔː:'tɒnəməs/ adj autonome

autonomy /ɔː:'tɒnəmɪ/ n autonomie f

autopilot /'ɔː:təʊpaɪlət/ n Aviat, fig pilote m automatique, bloc m de pilotage

autopsy /'ɔː:tɒpsɪ/ n autopsie f also fig

autosuggestion /,ɔː:təʊ sə'dʒestʃən/ n autosuggestion f

autumn /'ɔː:təm/ ▶ p. 1166 n surtout GB automne m

autumnal /ɔː:'tʌmnəl/ adj d'automne

auxiliary /ɔː:g'zɪlɪərɪ/
A n (person) auxiliaire mf; Ling auxiliaire m
B adj [equipment, staff] auxiliaire

auxiliary: ~ nurse ▶ p. 1181 n aide-soignant/-e m/f; **~ verb** n (verbe m) auxiliaire m

avail /ə'veɪl/ sout
A n **to be of no ~** ne servir à rien; **to no ~, without ~** en vain
B v refl **to ~ oneself of** profiter de [opportunity]; accepter [offer]

availability /ə,veɪlə'bɪlətɪ/ n (of option, service) existence f; (of drugs) présence f (sur le marché); **subject to ~** (of holidays, rooms, theatre seats etc) dans la limite des places disponibles

available /ə'veɪləbl/ adj disponible (**for** pour; **to** à); **to make sth ~ to sb** mettre qch à la disposition de qn; **to be ~ from** [product] être disponible dans [shop]; [service] être fourni par [organization]; **by every ~ means** par tous les moyens possibles; **to make oneself ~ for sth/sb** se libérer pour qch/qn

avalanche /'ævəlɑːnʃ, US -læntʃ/ n avalanche f

avant-garde /,ævɒŋ'gɑːd/
A n avant-garde f
B adj d'avant-garde

avarice /'ævərɪs/ n cupidité f

avaricious /,ævə'rɪʃəs/ adj cupide

Ave abrév écrite = **Avenue**

avenge /ə'vendʒ/
A vtr venger [person, death, defeat]
B v refl **to ~ oneself on sb** se venger de qn

avenger /ə'vendʒə(r)/ n vengeur/-eresse m/f

avenging /ə'vendʒɪŋ/ adj vengeur/-eresse

avenue /'ævənjuː, US -nuː/ n [1] (street, road) avenue f; (path, driveway) allée f; [2] fig (possibility) possibilité f

average /'ævərɪdʒ/
A n moyenne f (**of** de); **on (the) ~** en moyenne; **above/below (the) ~** au-dessus de/au-dessous de la moyenne; **to work out an ~** faire une moyenne; **the law of ~s** la loi des probabilités; **Mr Average** Monsieur Tout-le-Monde
B adj gen, Math moyen/-enne; **on an ~ day I work seven hours** en moyenne, je travaille sept heures par jour
C vtr faire en moyenne [distance, quantity, time]; **we ~d 95 km/h** nous avons fait une moyenne de 95 km/h

averse /ə'vɜːs/ adj opposé (**to** à); **to be ~ to doing** répugner à faire

aversion /ə'vɜːʃn, US ə'vɜːrʒn/ n aversion f (**to** pour); **to have an ~ to doing** avoir horreur de faire

avert /ə'vɜːt/ vtr [1] (avoid, prevent) éviter; [2] (turn away) **to ~ one's eyes/gaze from sth** détourner les yeux/le regard de qch

aviary /'eɪvɪərɪ, US -vɪerɪ/ n volière f

aviation /,eɪvɪ'eɪʃn/ n aviation f

aviation: ~ fuel n kérosène m; **~ industry** n industrie f aéronautique

aviator /'eɪvɪeɪtə(r)/ ▶ p. 1181 n aviateur/-trice m/f

avid /'ævɪd/ adj [collector, reader] passionné; [enthusiast, supporter] fervent; **to be ~ for sth** être avide de qch

avidity /ə'vɪdɪtɪ/ n avidité f (**for** de)

avidly /'ævɪdlɪ/ adv [read, collect] avec avidité; [support] avec ferveur

avocado /,ævə'kɑːdəʊ/
A n [1] (fruit) avocat m; [2] (plant) avocatier m
B noun modifier [salad, mousse] à l'avocat

avoid /ə'vɔɪd/ vtr [1] (prevent) éviter; **to ~ doing** éviter de faire; **it is to be ~ed** c'est à éviter; [2] (keep away from) éviter [person, location, gaze, nuisance]; esquiver [issue, question]

avoidable /ə'vɔɪdəbl/ adj évitable

avoidance /ə'vɔɪdəns/ n (of injuries, expenditure, delay) prévention f (**of** de); (of responsibility) refus m (**of** de); (of subject, problem) fuite f (**of** devant)

avowed /ə'vaʊd/ adj (admitted) avoué; (declared) déclaré

avuncular /ə'vʌŋkjʊlə(r)/ adj bienveillant

await /ə'weɪt/ vtr attendre; **long-~ed** longuement attendu; **eagerly ~ed** attendu avec impatience

awake /ə'weɪk/
A adj (not yet asleep) éveillé; (after sleeping) réveillé; **wide ~** bien réveillé; **half ~** mal réveillé; **to lie ~** rester au lit sans dormir; **I was still ~** je ne dormais pas; **the noise kept me ~** le bruit m'a empêché de dormir
B vtr (prét **awoke** ou **awaked** littér, pp **awoken** ou **awaked** littér) [1] (from sleep) réveiller; [2] fig éveiller [fear, suspicion]
C vi (prét **awoke** ou **awaked** littér, pp **awoken** ou **awaked** littér) (from sleep) se réveiller; **to ~ from a deep sleep** sortir d'un sommeil profond

awaken /əˈweɪkən/ (*prét* **awoke** *ou* **awakened** littér, *pp* **awoken** *ou* **awakened** littér)
A vtr **1** (from sleep) réveiller; **2** (generate) faire naître [*fear, interest*]; éveiller [*suspicions*]
B vi (*prét* **awoke** *ou* **awakened** littér, *pp* **awoken** *ou* **awakened** littér) (from sleep) se réveiller

awakening /əˈweɪkənɪŋ/
A n lit (from sleep) réveil m; fig (of emotion, interest) éveil m (**of** de); (of awareness) prise f de conscience (**to** de); **rude** ∼ lit réveil brutal; fig rappel m brutal à la réalité
B adj lit qui se réveille; fig naissant

award /əˈwɔːd/
A n **1** (prize) prix m; (medal, certificate) distinction f honorifique; **the** ∼ **for the best actor** le prix du meilleur acteur; **2** (grant) bourse f; **3** (decision to give) (of prize, grant) attribution f
B vtr décerner [*prize*]; attribuer [*grant*]; accorder [*points, penalty*]

award: ∼ **ceremony** n cérémonie f de remise de prix; ∼ **winner** n lauréat/-e m/f; ∼**-winning** adj [*book, film, design*] primé; [*writer, architect*] lauréat

aware /əˈweə(r)/ adj **1** (conscious) conscient (**of** de); (informed) au courant (**of** de); **to become** ∼ **that** prendre conscience que; **to make sb** ∼ **of/that** rendre qn conscient de/que; **I'm well** ∼ **of that** j'ai bien conscience de cela; **to be** ∼ **that** savoir que, se rendre compte que; **as far as I'm** ∼ à ma connaissance; **2** (well-informed) averti; **to be environmentally** ∼ être au courant des questions d'environnement

awareness /əˈweənɪs/ n conscience f (**of** de; **that** que); **public** ∼ **of this problem has increased** l'opinion publique a de plus en plus pris conscience de ce problème

away /əˈweɪ/

⚠️ *Away* often appears in English as the second element of a verb (*run away, put away, get away, give away* etc). For translations, look at the appropriate verb entry (**run, put, get, give** etc).
away often appears after a verb in English to show that an action is continuous or intense. If *away* does not change the basic meaning of the verb only the verb is translated: *he was snoring away* = il ronflait. If *away* does change the basic meaning of the verb (*he's grinding away at his maths*), consult the appropriate verb entry.
This dictionary contains usage notes on such topics as distance. For the index to these Notes see ▸ p. 1354.

A adj Sport [*goal, match, win*] à l'extérieur; **the** ∼ **team** les visiteurs mpl
B adv **1** (not present, gone) **to be** ∼ gen, Sch être absent (**from** de); (on business trip) être en déplacement; **I'll be** ∼ **(for) two weeks** je serai absent pendant deux semaines; **to be** ∼ **on business** être en voyage d'affaires or en déplacement; **to be** ∼ **from home** ne pas être chez soi, être absent de chez soi; **I'll have to be** ∼ **by 10** il faut que je sois parti avant 10 heures; **she's** ∼ **in Paris** elle est à Paris; **2** (distant in space) **3 km/50 m** ∼ à 3 km/50 m; **10 cm** ∼ **from the edge** à 10 cm du bord; **3** (distant in time) **London is two hours** ∼ Londres est à deux heures d'ici; **my birthday is two months** ∼ mon anniversaire est dans deux mois; **4** (in the opposite direction) **to shuffle/crawl** ∼ partir en traînant les pieds/en rampant; **5** (for emphasis) ∼ **back in 1920** en 1920; ∼ **over the other side of the lake** de l'autre côté du lac; **6** Sport [*play*] à l'extérieur

awe /ɔː/
A n crainte f mêlée d'admiration; (less fearful) respect m; **to watch/listen in** ∼ regarder/écouter impressionné; **to be in** ∼ **of sb** avoir peur de qn
B vtr **to be** ∼**ed by sth** être impressionné par qch

awe-inspiring /ˈɔːɪnspaɪərɪŋ/ adj impressionnant

awesome /ˈɔːsəm/ adj **1** (impressive) redoutable; **2** ○(stunningly good) extra○, genial○

awful /ˈɔːfl/ adj **1** (bad) affreux/-euse; (stronger) exécrable; **it was** ∼ **to have to...** ça a été horrible d'être obligé de...; **2** (horrifying, tragic) horrible, atroce; **3** (unwell) **I feel** ∼ je ne me sens pas bien du tout; **you look** ∼ tu n'as pas l'air bien du tout; **4** (guilty) ennuyé; **5** ○(emphasizing) **an** ∼ **lot (of)** énormément (de)

awfully /ˈɔːflɪ/ adv extrêmement; **he's** ∼ **late** il est terriblement en retard; **thanks** ∼ mille mercis

awkward /ˈɔːkwəd/ adj **1** (not practical) [*tool*] peu commode; [*shape, design*] difficile; **2** (clumsy) maladroit; **3** (complicated, inconvenient) [*arrangement, issue*] compliqué, difficile; [*choice*] difficile; [*moment, day*] mal choisi; **at an** ∼ **time** au mauvais moment; **to make life** ∼ **for sb** compliquer la vie à qn; **it's a bit** ∼ c'est difficile; **4** (embarrassing) [*question*] embarrassant; [*situation*] délicat; [*silence*] gêné; **5** (embarrassed) mal à l'aise, gêné; **to feel** ∼ **about doing** se sentir gêné de faire; **6** (uncooperative) [*person*] difficile (**about** à propos de); **the** ∼ **age** l'âge ingrat

awkwardly /ˈɔːkwədlɪ/ adv **1** (inconveniently) ∼ **placed/designed** mal placé/conçu; **2** (clumsily) [*move, express oneself*] maladroitement; [*fall, land*] lourdement; **3** (with embarrassment) [*speak, apologize*] d'un ton gêné; [*behave*] d'une manière embarrassée

awkwardness /ˈɔːkwədnɪs/ n **1** (clumsiness) maladresse f; **2** (delicacy) (of situation) côté m gênant; **3** (inconvenience) caractère m mal commode; **4** (embarrassment) malaise m

awl /ɔːl/ n (for leather) alène f; (for wood etc) poinçon m

awning /ˈɔːnɪŋ/ n (on shop) banne f, auvent m; (on tent, caravan, house, restaurant) auvent m; (on market stall) bâche f

awoke /əˈwəʊk/ prét ▸ **awake**

awoken /əˈwəʊkən/ pp ▸ **awake**

AWOL /ˈeɪwɒl/ adj, adv Mil, hum (abrév = **absent without leave**) **to be** ou **go** ∼ Mil être en absence illégale; hum disparaître

awry /əˈraɪ/
A adj de travers inv
B adv **to go** ∼ [*plan*] mal tourner; [*economy*] péricliter

axe, ax US /æks/
A n hache f; **to get the** ∼○ [*employee*] se faire virer○
B vtr virer○ [*employee*]; supprimer [*jobs*]; abandonner [*plan*]
(Idiom) **to have an** ∼ **to grind** servir un intérêt

axiom /ˈæksɪəm/ n axiome m (**that** selon lequel)

axiomatic /ˌæksɪəˈmætɪk/ adj axiomatique; **it is** ∼ **that...** il est évident que...

axis /ˈæksɪs/ n (pl **axes**) gen, Math axe m

axle /ˈæksl/ n essieu m; **front/rear** ∼ essieu avant/arrière

aye /aɪ/
A particle GB dial oui
B n (in voting) **the** ∼**s** les oui, les voix pour

AZ US Post abrév écrite = **Arizona**

Azerbaijan /ˌæzəbaɪˈdʒɑːn/ ▸ p. 774 pr n Azerbaïdjan m

Azerbaijani /ˌæzəbaɪˈdʒɑːnɪ/ ▸ p. 1032, p. 969
A n **1** (person) Azéri mf; **2** (language) azéri m, azerbaïdjanais m
B adj azerbaïdjanais

Azores /əˈzɔːz/ ▸ p. 954 pr n **the** ∼ les Açores fpl

AZT n (abrév = **azidothymidine**) AZT f

Aztec /ˈæztek/ ▸ p. 1032, p. 969
A n **1** (person) Aztèque mf; **2** (language) aztèque m
B adj aztèque

azure /ˈæʒə(r), -zjə(r)/ ▸ p. 752
A n azur m
B adj [*sea, sky, eyes*] d'azur; [*fabric*] azur inv

b, B /biː/ n **1** (letter) b, B m; **2** **B** Mus si m; **3** **b** abrév écrite = **born**

BA n (abrév = **Bachelor of Arts**) diplôme m universitaire en lettres et sciences humaines

baa /bɑː/
A vi (3ᵉ pers sg prés **~s**, prét, pp **~ed**) bêler
B excl bê!

BAA n: abrév ▸ **British Airports Authority**

babble /ˈbæbl/
A n murmure m confus
B vtr bafouiller [words, excuse]
C vi [baby] babiller; [stream] murmurer

babe /beɪb/ n **1** littér bébé m; **a ~ in arms** lit un enfant au berceau; fig un jeunot○; **2** ○(woman) minette○ f; (form of address) ma belle○

baboon /bəˈbuːn/ n babouin m

baby /ˈbeɪbɪ/
A n **1** (child) bébé m; **Baby Jesus** le petit Jésus; **she's the ~ of the family** c'est la petite dernière; **don't be such a ~**○! ne fais pas le bébé!; **2** ○ (of team, group) benjamin/-e m/f; **3** ○(pet project) **the show/project is his ~**○ il a la responsabilité du spectacle/projet; **4** (as address) chéri/-e m/f○
B noun modifier [brother, sister, son etc] petit; [animal] bébé-; [vegetable] nain; [clothes, food] pour bébés

(Idioms) **I was left holding the ~** on m'a refilé le bébé○; **to throw the ~ out with the bathwater** jeter le bébé avec l'eau du bain

baby: **~ bird** n oisillon m; **~ blue** ▸ p. 752 adj bleu clair inv; **~ boom** n baby boom m; **~ boomer** n personne f née pendant les années du baby-boom; **~ buggy** n GB poussette f; **~ carriage** n US landau m; **~ carrier** n porte-bébé m inv (dorsal); **~-faced** adj fig au visage innocent; **Babygro**® n grenouillère f, pyjama m de bébé

babyish /ˈbeɪbɪɪʃ/ adj enfantin; péj puéril

baby-sit /ˈbeɪbɪsɪt/ (prét, pp **-sat**)
A vtr garder
B vi faire du baby-sitting, garder des enfants

baby: **~-sitter** n baby-sitter mf; **~-sitting** n baby-sitting m; **~ talk** n langage m enfantin; **~ tooth** n dent f de lait; **~ walker** n trotteur m; **~wear** n vêtements mpl pour bébés; **~ wipe** n lingette f (pour bébé)

baccalaureate /ˌbækəˈlɔːrɪət/ n **1** US Univ (diploma) ≈ licence f; **2** Sch **European/International Baccalaureate** baccalauréat m européen/international

bachelor /ˈbætʃələ(r)/ n **1** (single man) célibataire m; **2** Univ **Bachelor of Arts/Law** ≈ diplôme m universitaire de lettres/droit

bachelor: **~ apartment**, **~ flat** GB n garçonnière f; **~hood** n célibat m

bacillus /bəˈsɪləs/ n (pl **-li**) bacille m

back /bæk/ ▸ p. 698
A n **1** Anat, Zool dos m; **to be (flat) on one's ~** lit être (à plat) sur le dos; fig être au bout du rouleau; **to turn one's ~ on sb/sth** lit, fig tourner le dos à qn/qch; **to do sth behind sb's ~** lit, fig faire qch dans le dos de qn; **I was glad to see the ~ of him** j'étais content de le voir partir; **2** (reverse side) (of page, cheque, hand, fork, envelope) dos m; (of fabric) envers m; (of medal, coin) revers m; **3** (rear-facing part) (of vehicle, head) arrière m; (of electrical appliance) face f arrière; (of shirt, coat) dos m; (of chair,

sofa) dossier m; **on the ~ of the door/head** derrière la porte/tête; **the shelves are oak but the ~ is plywood** les étagères sont en chêne mais le fond est en contreplaqué; **4** (area behind building) **to be out ~**, **to be in the ~** US être dans le jardin or la cour; **there's a small garden out ~** ou **round the ~** il y a un petit jardin derrière (la maison); **the steps at the ~ of the building** l'escalier à l'arrière de l'immeuble; **5** (of car, plane) arrière m; **6** (of cupboard, drawer, fridge, bus, stage) fond m; **at ou in the ~ of the drawer** au fond du tiroir; **those at the ~ couldn't see** ceux qui étaient derrière ne pouvaient pas voir; **7** Sport arrière m; **left ~** arrière gauche; **8** (end) fin f; **at the ~ of the book** à la fin du livre

B adj **1** (at the rear) [leg, paw, edge, wheel] arrière; [bedroom] du fond; [page] dernier/-ière (before n); [garden, gate] de derrière; **2** (isolated) [road] petit (before n); **~ alley** ou **lane** ruelle f; **3** Fin, Comm **~ interest/rent/tax** arriérés mpl d'intérêts/de loyer/d'impôts

C adv **1** (after absence) **to be ~** être de retour; **I'll be ~ in five minutes** je reviens dans cinq minutes; **to arrive ou come ~** rentrer (from de); **he's ~ at work** il a repris le travail; **she's ~ in (the) hospital** elle est retournée à l'hôpital; **when is he due ~?** quand doit-il rentrer?; **the mini-skirt is ~ (in fashion)** les mini-jupes sont de nouveau à la mode; **2** (in return) **to call ou phone ~** rappeler; **I'll write ~ (to him)** je lui répondrai; **to punch sb ~** rendre son coup à qn; **to smile ~ at sb** rendre son sourire à qn; **3** (backwards) [glance, jump, step, lean] en arrière; **4** (away) **we overtook him 20 km ~** nous l'avons doublé il y a 20 km; **ten lines ~** dix lignes plus haut; **ten pages ~** dix pages (avant or plus tôt); **5** (ago) **25 years ~** il y a 25 ans; **a week/five minutes ~** il y a une semaine/cinq minutes; **6** (a long time ago) **~ in April** en avril; **~ in the days when** du temps où; **it was obvious as far ~ as last year that** déjà l'année dernière il était évident que; **7** (once again) **she's ~ in power** elle a repris le pouvoir; **8** (expressing a return to a former location) **to travel to London and ~** faire l'aller-retour à Londres; **we walked there and took the train ~** nous y sommes allés à pied et nous avons pris le train pour rentrer; **9** (in a different location) **meanwhile, ~ in France, he...** pendant ce temps, en France, il...; **I'll see you ~ at the house** je te verrai à la maison

D **back and forth** adv phr **to go ou travel ~ and forth** (commute) [person, bus] faire la navette (**between** entre); **to walk ou go ~ and forth** faire des allées et venues (**between** entre); **to swing ~ and forth** [pendulum] osciller; **the film cuts ou moves ~ and forth between New York and Paris** le film se passe entre New York et Paris

E vtr **1** (support) soutenir [party, person, bid, bill, strike, action]; appuyer [application]; apporter son soutien à [enterprise, project]; **2** (finance) financer [project, undertaking]; **3** (endorse) garantir [currency]; **to ~ a bill** Comm, Fin endosser ou avaliser une traite; **4** (substantiate) justifier [argument, claim] (**with** à l'aide de); **5** (reverse) **to ~ the car into the garage** rentrer la voiture au garage en marche arrière; **to ~ sb into sth** faire reculer qn dans qch; **6** (bet on) parier sur [horse, favourite, winner]; **7** (stiffen, line) consolider, renforcer [structure]; endosser [book]; renforcer [map]; maroufler [painting]; doubler [fabric]

F **-backed** combining form **1** (of furniture) **a high-/low-~ed chair** une chaise avec un dossier haut/bas; **2** (lined, stiffened) **canvas-/foam-~ed** doublé de toile/de mousse; **3** (supported) **UN-~ed** soutenu par l'ONU; **4** (financed) **government-~ed** financé par l'État

(Idioms) **to put one's ~ into it** travailler dur; **he's always on my ~**○ il est toujours sur mon dos; **to be at the ~ of sth** être à l'origine de qch; **to put sb's ~ up** offenser qn; **to live off sb's ~** vivre aux crochets de qn; **to break the ~ of a journey/task** faire le plus gros du voyage/travail

(Phrasal verbs)
■ **back away** reculer; **to ~ away from** lit s'éloigner de [*person*]; fig prendre ses distances par rapport à [*issue, problem*]; chercher à éviter [*confrontation*]
■ **back down**: ▶ ~ **down** (give way) céder; **to ~ down on** *ou* **over** reconsidérer [*sanctions, proposal, allegations*]
■ **back off** 1 (move away) reculer; 2 fig (climb down) se montrer plus coopérant
■ **back onto**: ▶ ~ **onto** [*sth*] [*house*] donner sur [qch] à l'arrière
■ **back out**: ▶ ~ **out** 1 lit [*person*] sortir à reculons; [*car, driver*] sortir en marche arrière; 2 fig se désister; **to ~ out of** lit [*person*] sortir de [qch] en reculant [*room*]; [*car, driver*] sortir de [qch] en marche arrière; fig annuler [*deal, contract*]; [*competitor*] se retirer de [*event*]; ▶ ~ [*sth*] **out** faire sortir [qch] en marche arrière [*vehicle*]
■ **back up**: ▶ ~ **up** 1 Aut reculer, faire marche arrière; 2 US (block) [*drains*] s'obstruer; [*traffic*] se bloquer; ▶ ~ [*sth*] **up**, ~ **up** [*sth*] 1 (support) [*facts, evidence*] confirmer [*claims, case, theory*]; 2 Comput sauvegarder; ▶ ~ [*sb*] **up** soutenir [*person*]

backache /'bækeɪk/ *n* mal *m* de dos; **to have ~** GB, **to have a ~** US avoir mal au dos

back bacon *n* Culin bacon *m* maigre

backbench /ˌbæk'bentʃ/ *n* (*also* ~**es**) GB Pol 1 (area of the House) banc *m* des députés; 2 ₵ (MPs) députés *mpl*

back: ~**bencher** *n* GB Pol député *m*; ~**biting** *n* médisance *f*; ~**board** *n* (in basketball) panneau *m*; ~**boiler** *n* chaudière *f* (*située derrière le foyer d'une cheminée*)

backbone /'bækbəʊn/ *n* 1 (spine) (of person, animal) colonne *f* vertébrale; (of fish) grande arête *f*; 2 fig (strong feature) ossature *f*; **to be the ~ of** [*people, players*] constituer l'ossature de [*group, team*]; [*person, concept*] être le pilier de [*organization, project*]; 3 fig (courage) cran○ *m*; **he has no ~** c'est une larve

back: ~**-breaking** *adj* éreintant; ~**chat** *n* GB insolence *f*; ~**cloth** *n* Theat, fig toile *f* de fond

backcomb /'bækkəʊm/ *vtr* **to ~ one's hair** se crêper les cheveux

back: ~ **copy** *n* ancien numéro *m*; ~ **cover** *n* gen dos *m*; quatrième *f* de couverture

backdate /'bækdeɪt/ *vtr* antidater [*cheque, letter*]; **to be ~d to 1 April** être antidaté avec effet rétroactif au 1er avril

back door *n* (of car) portière *f* arrière; (of building) porte *f* de derrière

backdrop /'bækdrɒp/ *n* Theat, fig toile *f* de fond

back-end /ˌbæk'end/ *n* 1 (rear) arrière *m*; 2 Comput terminal *m*

backer /'bækə(r)/ *n* 1 (supporter) allié/-e *m/f*; 2 Fin (of project, event) commanditaire *m*; (of business) bailleur *m* de fonds

backfire /'bækfaɪə(r)/ *vi* 1 [*scheme, tactics*] avoir l'effet inverse; **to ~ on sb** se retourner contre qn; 2 [*car*] pétarader

back: ~ **flip** *n* saut *m* périlleux (en planche) arrière; ~**gammon** ▸ p. 881 *n* jaquet *m*

background /'bækgraʊnd/
A *n* 1 (of person) (social) milieu *m*; (personal, family) origines *fpl*; (professional) formation *f*; **to come from a poor ~** être issu d'un milieu pauvre; **a ~ in law/linguistics** une formation juridique/en linguistique; 2 (context) contexte *m*; **against a ~ of violence** sur un climat de violence; **what's the ~ to the situation?** qu'est-ce qui est à l'origine de la situation?; 3 (of painting, photo, scene) arrière-plan *m*; **in the ~** à l'arrière-plan; **against a ~ of** sur un fond *ou* un arrière-plan de; 4 (not upfront) **in the ~** au second plan; **ill-feeling was always there in the ~** la rancune était toujours là dans l'ombre; 5 (of sound, music) **voices/music in the ~** des voix/de la musique en bruit de fond
B *noun modifier* 1 [*information, knowledge*] concernant les origines de la situation; 2 [*music, lighting*] d'ambiance

background: ~ **noise** *n* bruit *m* de fond; ~ **radiation** *n* radiation *f* naturelle; ~ **reading** *n* lectures *fpl* complémentaires

backhand /'bækhænd/
A *n* 1 Sport revers *m*; 2 (writing) écriture *f* penchée à gauche
B *adj* 1 Sport [*volley*] de revers; ~ **drive** coup *m* droit de dos; 2 [*writing*] penché à gauche

back: ~**handed** *adj* [*compliment*] équivoque; ~**hander** *n* (bribe) pot-de-vin *m*

backing /'bækɪŋ/
A *n* 1 (reverse layer) revêtement *m* intérieur; 2 Fin, fig (support) soutien *m*; 3 Mus accompagnement *m*
B *noun modifier* Mus [*singer, group, track*] d'accompagnement; ~ **vocals** chœurs *mpl*, choristes *mfpl*

back issue *n* ancien numéro *m*

backlash /'bæklæʃ/ *n* retour *m* de bâton; **a ~ against sth** une réaction violente contre qch

back: ~**less** *adj* [*dress*] dos-nu *inv*; ~**list** *n* liste *f* des ouvrages disponibles

backlog /'bæklɒg/ *n* retard *m*; **I've got a huge ~ (of work)** j'ai plein de travail en retard; **a ~ of orders** une accumulation de commandes en souffrance

back: ~ **marker** *n* Sport dernier/-ière *m/f*; ~ **number** *n* ancien numéro *m*; ~**pack** *n* sac *m* à dos; ~**packer** *n* routard/-e *m/f*

backpacking /'bækpækɪŋ/ *n* **to go ~** partir en voyage avec son sac à dos

back: ~ **passage** *n* Anat rectum *m*; ~ **pay** *n* rappel *m* de salaire; ~**pedal** *vi* (*p prés etc* -**ll**- GB, -**l**- US) lit rétropédaler; fig faire marche arrière; ~ **rest** *n* dossier *m*; ~ **room** *n* chambre *f* du fond; ~ **room boys** *npl*: *experts qui travaillent dans l'ombre*; ~**scratcher** *n* gratte-dos *m inv*

back seat *n* siège *m* arrière; **to take a ~** fig s'effacer

back: ~**seat driver** *n*: *passager qui donne sans arrêt des conseils au conducteur*; ~**side**○ *n* derrière *m*, fesses *fpl*; ~**slang** *n* GB argot *qui consiste à prononcer les mots à l'envers*, ≈ verlan *m*; ~**slash** *n* Print barre *f* oblique inverse, antislash *m*; ~**space** *n* Comput retour *m* arrière

backspin /'bækspɪn/ *n* Sport **to put ~ on a ball** donner de l'effet à une balle

backstage /'bæksteɪdʒ/ *adv* **he's ~** il est en coulisse; [*work, go*] dans les coulisses

backstairs /'bæksteəz/
A *npl* escalier *m* de service
B *adj* [*gossip, connivance*] de coulisses

backstitch /'bækstɪtʃ/
A *n* point *m* arrière
B *vi* coudre en point arrière

back: ~**stop** *n* Sport (fielder) receveur *m*; ~ **straight** *n* Sport ligne *f* droite de retour

backstreet /'bækstriːt/
A *n* petite rue *f*
B *noun modifier* [*loanshark, abortionist*] clandestin

back: ~**stroke** *n* dos *m* crawlé; ~**talk** *n* US = back-chat

back to back *adv* 1 (with backs touching) **to stand ~** [*two people*] se mettre dos à dos; 2 (consecutively) de suite

back to front *adj, adv* (facing the wrong way) à l'envers; **you've got it all ~** fig tu as tout compris de travers

back: ~**track** *vi* lit rebrousser chemin; fig faire marche arrière; ~ **translation** *n* Ling rétro-traduction *f*

backup /'bækʌp/
A *n* 1 (support) soutien *m*; 2 Mil (reinforcements) renforts *mpl*; 3 (replacement) **to keep a battery as a ~** garder une batterie de secours
B *noun modifier* (replacement) [*plan, system, vehicle*] de secours

backup light *n* US Aut feu *m* de recul

backward /'bækwəd/
A *adj* 1 (towards the rear) [*look, step*] en arrière; ~ **roll** roulade *f* arrière; ~ **somersault** saut *m* périlleux (groupé); 2 (retarded) [*child, nation, society, economy*] arriéré
B *adv* US = backwards

(Idiom) **she isn't ~ in coming forward** hum elle n'hésite pas à se mettre en avant

backward-looking *adj* passéiste

backwards /'bækwədz/ *adv* 1 (in a reverse direction) [*walk, crawl*] à reculons; [*lean, step, fall*] en arrière; **to face ~** [*person*] tourner le dos; **to move ~** reculer; **to travel ~ and forwards** faire la navette (**between** entre); **to walk ~ and**

b

forwards faire des allées et venues; ▸ **bend**; [2] (starting from the end) [count] à rebours; [play, wind] à l'envers; [3] (the wrong way round) **to put sth on ∼** mettre qch à l'envers; **you've got it all ∼!** tu as tout mélangé!; [4] (thoroughly) **to know sth ∼** connaître qch par cœur

backwater /ˈbækwɔːtə(r)/ n [1] lit (of pool, river) eaux fpl mortes; [2] fig (isolated area) gen village m tranquille; péj village m tranquille; péj trou° m pej; **cultural ∼** désert m culturel

backyard /ˌbækˈjɑːd/ n [1] GB (courtyard) arrière-cour f; [2] US (back garden) jardin m de derrière; [3] fig **in one's ∼** (in a nearby area) près de chez soi; (in nearby country) près de ses frontières

bacon /ˈbeɪkən/ n ≈ lard m; **a rasher of ∼** une tranche de bacon; **streaky/smoked ∼** lard maigre/fumé; **∼ and egg(s)** des œufs au bacon

(Idioms) **to bring home the ∼**° faire bouillir la marmite°; **to save sb's ∼**° tirer qn d'affaire°

bacon-slicer n coupe-jambon m inv

bacteria /bækˈtɪərɪə/ npl bactéries fpl

bacterial /bækˈtɪərɪəl/ adj bactérien/-ienne

bacteriology /bækˌtɪərɪˈɒlədʒɪ/ n bactériologie f

bad /bæd/
A n [1] (evil) **there is good and ∼ in everyone** il y a du bon et du mauvais dans chacun; **she only sees the ∼ in him** elle ne voit que ses mauvais côtés; [2] (unpleasantness, unfavourableness) **the good and the ∼** le bon et le mauvais
B adj (comparative **worse**; superlative **worst**) [1] (poor, inferior, incompetent, unacceptable) [book, eyesight, cook, idea] mauvais (before n); [joke] stupide; **to have ∼ hearing** ne pas très bien entendre; **to have ∼ teeth/∼ legs** avoir de mauvaises dents/de vilaines jambes; **to be ∼ at** être mauvais en [subject]; **to be ∼ at doing** (to do badly) ne pas être doué pour faire; **not ∼**° pas mauvais, pas mal°; [2] (unfavourable) [news, day, moment, smell, dream, result, omen, mood] mauvais (before n); **it's ∼ enough having to wait, but...** c'est déjà assez pénible de devoir attendre, mais...; **it looks ∼** ou **things look ∼** cela s'annonce mal (**for** pour); **the journey/exam wasn't ∼ at all** le voyage/l'examen s'est plutôt bien passé; **it's a ∼ time to buy a house** ce n'est pas le bon moment pour acheter une maison; **too ∼°!** (sympathetic) pas de chance!; (hard luck) tant pis!; [3] (morally or socially unacceptable) [person, behaviour, reputation] mauvais (before n); [language, word] grossier/-ière; **∼ dog!** vilain!; **you ∼ girl!** vilaine!; **it is ∼ to do** c'est mal de faire; **it is ∼ of sb to do** ce n'est pas bien de la part de qn de faire; **it is ∼ that** il est regrettable que (+ subj); **it will look ∼** cela fera mauvais effet; **to feel ∼** avoir mauvaise conscience (**about** à propos de); [4] (severe, serious) [accident, attack, injury, mistake] grave; **a ∼ cold** un gros rhume; **how ∼ is it?** c'est grave?; [5] (harmful) **∼ for** mauvais pour; **smoking is ∼ for you** ou **your health** fumer est mauvais pour la santé; **it's ∼ for you to eat that** tu ne devrais pas manger ça; **it's ∼ for industry** c'est néfaste pour l'industrie; **it will be ∼ for mothers** cela fera du tort aux mères; [6] (ill, injured) **to have a ∼ back** souffrir du dos; **to have a ∼ chest** être malade des poumons; **to have a ∼ heart** être cardiaque; **to have a ∼ leg** avoir mal à la jambe; **my back is ∼ today** j'ai très mal au dos aujourd'hui; **she was very ∼ in the night** elle a été très malade pendant la nuit; **to feel ∼** se sentir mal; **'how are you?'—'not so ∼'** 'comment vas-tu?'—'pas trop mal'; **to be in a ∼ way** aller très mal; [7] Fin [money, note] faux/fausse; [loan, debt] douteux/-euse; [8] (rotten) [fruit] pourri; **to go ∼** pourrir; [9] °(good) terrible°
C adv° surtout US [need, want] méchamment°; **it hurts ∼** ça fait sérieusement mal; **he's/she's got it ∼** il/elle est vraiment mordu/-e°

(Idioms) **to be in ∼** US avoir des ennuis; **to be in ∼ with sth** US être en froid avec qn; **he's ∼ news** il faut se méfier de lui; **he's having a ∼ hair day**° ce n'est pas son jour

bad blood n **there is ∼ between them** ils sont à couteaux tirés

bad: **∼ boy** n enfant m terrible; **∼ breath** n mauvaise haleine f; **∼ cheque** n chèque m sans provision

baddie°, **baddy**° /ˈbædɪ/ n méchant/-e m/f

badge /bædʒ/ n [1] (sew-on, pin-on, adhesive) badge m; [2] (coat of arms) insigne m; [3] (symbol) symbole m, insigne m liter; **∼ of office** insigne m de fonction

badger /ˈbædʒə(r)/
A n Zool blaireau m
B vtr harceler

badly /ˈbædlɪ/ adv (comparative **worse**; superlative **worst**)
[1] (not well) [begin, behave, sleep] mal; [educated, fed, made, worded] mal; **to go ∼** [exam, interview, meeting] mal se passer; **to do ∼** [candidate, company] obtenir de mauvais résultats; **to take sth ∼** mal prendre qch; **he didn't do too ∼** il ne s'est pas mal débrouillé°; **to do ∼ by sb** ne pas être correct avec qn; **please don't think ∼ of me** s'il vous plaît, ne m'en veuillez pas; [2] (seriously) [suffer] beaucoup; [beat] brutalement; [disrupt, affect] sérieusement; [burnt, hurt, damaged] gravement; **∼ hit** fig durement touché; **our plans went ∼ wrong** nos projets ont très mal tourné; **I was ∼ mistaken** je me suis lourdement trompé; [3] (urgently) **to want/need sth ∼** avoir très envie de/grand besoin de qch

badly behaved adj désobéissant

badly off (poor) pauvre; **to be ∼ for space/clothes** manquer d'espace/de vêtements

bad-mannered adj qui a de mauvaises manières

badminton /ˈbædmɪnt(ə)n/ ▸ p. 881 n badminton m

bad-tempered adj (temporarily) irrité; (habitually) irritable

baffle /ˈbæfl/ vtr rendre [qn] perplexe, confondre

baffled /ˈbæfld/ adj perplexe (**by** devant), confondu (**by** par)

baffling /ˈbæflɪŋ/ adj déroutant

bag /bæg/
A n (container) sac m (**of** de); **20 pence a ∼** 20 pence le sac
B bags npl [1] (baggage) bagages mpl; **to pack one's ∼s** lit faire ses bagages; fig faire ses valises; [2] °GB (lots) **∼s of** plein de [money, time]
C vtr (p prés etc **-gg-**) [1] °†(save) retenir [seat, table]; empocher [medal]; [2] (put in bags) = **bag up**

(Idioms) **a mixed ∼** un mélange hétérogène; **∼s** |°†, **∼s me**° GB à moi; **it's in the ∼**° c'est dans la poche°; **it's not my ∼**° US ce n'est pas mon truc°; **to have ∼s under one's eyes** avoir des valises sous les yeux°

(Phrasal verb)

■ **bag up**: ▸ **∼ [sth] up**, **∼ up [sth]** mettre [qch] en sac, ensacher

bagel /ˈbeɪgl/ n petit pain m (en couronne)

baggage /ˈbægɪdʒ/ n [1] (luggage) ₵ bagages mpl; [2] fig (legacy) **to carry a lot of emotional ∼** avoir trop de problèmes personnels

(Idiom) **bag and ∼** avec armes et bagages°

baggage: **∼ allowance** n franchise f de bagages; **∼ car** n fourgon m; **∼ carousel** n tapis m roulant (pour bagages); **∼ check** n US bulletin m de consigne; **∼ hall** n = **baggage reclaim**; **∼ handler** ▸ p. 1181 n bagagiste mf; **∼ locker** n US consigne f automatique; **∼ reclaim** n réception f des bagages

baggy /ˈbægɪ/ adj [garment] large; **to go ∼ at the knees** [garment] faire des poches aux genoux

Baghdad /ˌbægˈdæd/ ▸ p. 1276 pr n Bagdad

bag: **∼ lady**° n clocharde f; **∼ person**° n clochard/-e m/f; **∼ pipes** ▸ p. 1028 n cornemuse f; **∼ snatcher** n voleur/-euse m/f de sacs à main

Bahamas /bəˈhɑːməz/ ▸ p. 774 pr n **the ∼** les Bahamas fpl

Bahrain, Bahrein /bɑːˈreɪn/ ▸ p. 774 pr n Bahreïn m

bail /beɪl/
A n [1] Jur caution f; **to be (out) on ∼** être libéré sous caution; **to jump ∼** ne pas comparaître (devant un tribunal); [2] Sport (in cricket) bâtonnet m
B vtr Jur mettre [qn] en liberté provisoire

(Phrasal verb)

■ **bail out**: ▸ **∼ out** [1] Naut écoper; [2] (jump from plane) sauter; ▸ **∼ out [sb/sth]**, **∼ [sb/sth] out** [1] Naut écoper [water]; vider [boat]; [2] (get out of trouble) tirer [qn] d'affaire [person]; Fin renflouer [company]; [3] Jur payer la caution pour [person]

bail bond n US Jur caution f

bailiff /ˈbeɪlɪf/ ▸ p. 1181 n [1] Jur (also for evictions) huissier m; [2] GB (on estate) intendant/-e m/f

bait /beɪt/
A n lit, fig appât m; **to rise to** ou **swallow the ∼** lit, fig mordre à l'hameçon
B vtr [1] (put bait on) appâter [trap, hook] (**with** avec); [2] (tease) taquiner [person]

baize /beɪz/ n drap m de billard

bake /beɪk/
A n (dish) **fish/vegetable** ~ ≈ gratin m de poisson/de légumes
B vtr Culin faire cuire [qch] au four [dish, vegetable]; faire [bread, cake]
C vi **1** (make bread) [person] faire du pain; (make cakes) faire de la pâtisserie; **2** (cook) [food] cuire; **3** (in sun) [town, land] cuire; [person] lézarder
D **baked** pp adj [salmon, apple] au four

bake: ~**d beans** n Culin haricots mpl blancs à la sauce tomate; ~**d potato** n Culin pomme f de terre en robe des champs (au four)

baker /'beɪkə(r)/ ▸ p. 1181 n **1** (who makes bread) boulanger/-ère m/f; (who makes bread and cakes) boulanger-pâtissier/boulangère-pâtissière m/f; **2** (shop) ~**'s (shop)** boulangerie f, boulangerie-pâtisserie f

bakery /'beɪkərɪ/ ▸ p. 1181 n boulangerie f, boulangerie-pâtisserie f

baking○ /'beɪkɪŋ/ adj (hot) [place, day] brûlant; **I'm absolutely ~!** je crève○ de chaud!

baking: ~ **powder** n Culin levure f chimique; ~ **soda** n Culin bicarbonate m de soude

balaclava /ˌbælə'klɑːvə/ n (also ~ **helmet**) cagoule f

balance /'bæləns/
A n **1** (stable position) lit, fig équilibre m (**between** entre); **to lose one's** ~ perdre l'équilibre; **to keep one's** ~ garder son équilibre; **to catch sb off** ~ fig prendre qn au dépourvu; **to throw sb off** ~ fig perturber qn; **the right** ~ le juste milieu; **the** ~ **of nature** l'équilibre naturel; **the** ~ **of power** l'équilibre des forces; **2** (scales) lit, fig balance f; **to be in the** ~ fig être dans la balance; **to hang in the** ~ fig être en jeu; **on** ~ tout compte fait; **3** Comm (in account) solde m; **to pay the** ~ verser le surplus; **4** (remainder) restant m
B vtr **1** fig (compensate for) (also ~ **out**) compenser, équilibrer; **2** (counterbalance) contrebalancer [weights, design, elements]; **3** (perch) mettre [qch] en équilibre (**on** sur); **to be** ~**d on sth** être en équilibre sur qch; **4** (adjust) équilibrer [diet, activity]; **5** (weigh up, compare) peser; **to** ~ **sth against sth** mesurer qch en fonction de qch; **6** Comm équilibrer [account, economy]
C vi **1** lit [one person] se tenir en équilibre (**on** sur); [one thing] tenir en équilibre (**on** sur); [two things, persons] s'équilibrer; **2** Comm [books, figures, budget] être en équilibre; **to make sth** ~, **to get sth to** ~ équilibrer qch
D **balanced** pp adj [person, behaviour, view, diet, budget] équilibré; [article, report] objectif/-ive

balance: ~ **of payments** n balance f des paiements; ~ **of power** n Pol équilibre m des forces, rapport m de force; ~ **of trade** n balance f du commerce extérieur; ~ **sheet** n bilan m

balancing act n lit numéro m d'équilibriste; **to do a** ~ fig tenter d'atteindre un compromis

balcony /'bælkənɪ/ n **1** (in house, hotel) balcon m; **on the** ~ (seen from below) au balcon; (seen from interior) sur le balcon; **2** (of theatre) deuxième balcon m

bald /bɔːld/ adj **1** [man, head] chauve; **to go** ~ devenir chauve; **2** [lawn, carpet, terrain] pelé; **3** Aut [tyre] lisse; **4** (blunt) [statement, question] abrupt; [fact] brut; [style] dépouillé

balding /'bɔːldɪŋ/ adj **he's slightly** ~ il commence à perdre ses cheveux

baldly /'bɔːldlɪ/ adv [state, remark] sans détours

baldness /'bɔːldnɪs/ n (of person) calvitie f

bale /beɪl/
A n balle f
B vtr mettre [qch] en balles [hay, cotton, paper]

Balearic Islands /ˌbælɪˌærɪk 'aɪləndz/ ▸ p. 954 pr npl (also **Balearics**) (îles fpl) Baléares fpl

baleful /'beɪlfʊl/ adj littér [influence, presence] maléfique liter; [glance, eye] torve

balk /bɔːk/
A vtr contrecarrer [plan, intention]
B vi [person] regarder à deux fois; **to** ~ **at** reculer devant [risk, cost, prospect]; **she** ~**ed at spending so much** elle rechignait à dépenser autant d'argent; **he** ~**ed at the idea** l'idée lui répugnait

Balkan /'bɔːlkən/
A Balkans pr npl **the** ~**s** les Balkans mpl

B adj [state, peninsula, peoples] balkanique

ball /bɔːl/
A n **1** Sport, Tech (sphere) (in tennis, golf, cricket) balle f; (in football, rugby) ballon m; (in croquet) boule f; (in billiards) bille f; (for children) balle f, ballon m; Mil, Tech balle f; **2** (rolled-up object) (of dough, clay) boule f (**of** de); (of wool, string) pelote f (**of** de); **to curl up into a** ~ [person, cat] se rouler en boule; **to wind sth into a** ~ pelotonner qch; **3** Anat **the** ~**s of one's feet** les demi-pointes fpl (des pieds); **4** (dance) bal m
B vtr (clench) serrer [fist]
C vi [fist] se serrer

(Idioms) **the** ~ **is in your/his court** la balle est dans ton/son camp; **to be on the** ~○ gen être efficace; (old person) avoir toute sa tête; **to play** ~○ coopérer (**with** avec); **to set the** ~ **rolling** (for conversation) lancer la conversation; (for activity) démarrer; **to have a** ~○ s'amuser comme un fou/une folle○; **that's the way the** ~ **bounces!** US c'est la vie!; **to carry the** ~○ US prendre la responsabilité

ballad /'bæləd/ n ballade f

ball: ~ **and chain** n lit, fig boulet m; ~**-and-socket joint** n Anat articulation f mobile

ballast /'bæləst/ n **1** (in balloon, ship) lest m; **2** (on rail, road) ballast m

ball: ~ **bearing** n (ball) bille f de roulement; (bearing) roulement m à billes; ~**boy** n (in tennis) ramasseur m de balles; ~ **cock** n Tech robinet m à flotteur; ~ **control** n contrôle m du ballon; ~ **dress** n robe f de bal

ballerina /ˌbælə'riːnə/ ▸ p. 1181 n danseuse f de ballet, ballerine f

ballet /'bæleɪ/ n ballet m

ballet: ~ **dancer** n danseur/-euse m/f de ballet; ~ **dress** n tutu m; ~ **shoe** n chausson m (de danse)

ballgame /'bɔːlgeɪm/ n **1** gen jeu m de balle or ballon; **2** US match m

(Idiom) **that's a whole new** ou **completely different** ~○ c'est tout une autre histoire

ball: ~ **girl** n (in tennis) ramasseuse f de balles; ~ **gown** n robe f de bal

ballistic /bə'lɪstɪk/ adj [missile] balistique

(Idiom) **to go** ~○ devenir fou furieux/folle furieuse

balloon /bə'luːn/
A n **1** Aviat gen ballon m; **2** (hot air) ~ montgolfière f; **3** (for cartoon speech) bulle f
B vi **1** Aviat **to go** ~**ing** faire de la montgolfière; **2** (also ~ **out**) (swell) [sail, skirt] se gonfler; **3** (increase quickly) [deficit, debt] galoper

(Idiom) **to go down** GB ou **go over** US **like a lead** ~ tomber à plat

balloonist /bə'luːnɪst/ n aéronaute mf

ballot /'bælət/
A n **1** (process) scrutin m; **by** ~ au scrutin; **2** (vote) vote m (à bulletins secrets) (**of** de; **on** sur); **the first/second** ~ le premier/second tour de scrutin; **3** (also ~ **paper**) bulletin m de vote
B vtr consulter [qn] (par vote) (**on** sur)

ballot box n **1** lit urne f (électorale); **2** fig (system) urnes fpl; **at the** ~ aux urnes

ball: ~**park figure** n chiffre m approximatif; ~**point (pen)** n stylo m (à) bille; ~**room** n salle f de danse; ~**room dancing** n danse f de salon

balm /bɑːm/ n **1** (oily) baume m; **2** littér (peace) baume m; **3** Bot (also **lemon** ~) citronnelle f

balmy /'bɑːmɪ/ adj [air, evening, weather] doux/douce

balsam /'bɔːlsəm/ n **1** (oily) baume m; **2** (tree) baumier m

Baltic /'bɔːltɪk/
A pr n **the** ~ la Baltique
B adj balte; **the** ~ **Sea** la mer f Baltique

balustrade /ˌbælə'streɪd/ n balustrade f

bamboo /bæm'buː/ n bambou m

bamboozle○ /bæm'buːzl/ vtr **1** (trick) emboîner○; **to** ~ **sb into doing** emboîner○ qn pour qu'il fasse; **to** ~ **sb out of** refaire○ qn de [money]; **2** (mystify) déboussoler○, désorienter

ban /bæn/
A n interdiction f (**on sth** de qch; **on doing** de faire)
B vtr (p prés etc **-nn-**) interdire [author, group, activity, book,

drug]; suspendre [athlete]; **to ~ sb from** exclure qn de [sport, event]; **to ~ sb from driving** interdire à qn de conduire

banal /bə'nɑːl, US 'beɪnl/ adj banal

banality /bə'næləti/ n banalité f

banana /bə'nɑːnə/
A n **1** (fruit) banane f; **2** (also ~ **palm**) bananier m
B noun modifier [yoghurt, ice cream] à la banane

banana: ~ **republic** n péj république f bananière pej; ~ **skin** n peau f de banane

band /bænd/ n **1** Mus (rock) groupe m (de rock); (army) clique f; (municipal) fanfare f; **2** (with common aim) groupe m (of de); **3** (of light, colour, land) bande f; **4** Radio bande f; **5** GB (of age, income tax) tranche f; **6** (for binding) (for hair, hat) ruban m; (around waist) ceinture f; (around neck) col m; (around arm) brassard m; (around head) bandeau m; **7** Tech (metal) ruban m (métallique); (rubber) courroie f; **8** (ring) anneau m

(Phrasal verb)

■ **band together** se réunir (**to do** pour faire)

bandage /'bændɪdʒ/
A n bandage m; **he has a ~ round his head** il a à la tête bandée
B vtr bander [head, limb, wound]

Band-Aid® /'bændeɪd/ n Med (plaster) pansement m (adhésif)

B and B, b and b /ˌbi: ən 'bi:/ n GB abrév ► **bed and breakfast**

bandit /'bændɪt/ n bandit m

band: ~ **leader** n chef m d'orchestre; ~**master** n (of military band) chef m de musique; (of brass band) chef m de fanfare; ~ **saw** n scie f à ruban; ~**sman** n (pl **-men**) gen, Mil musicien m; ~**stand** n kiosque m (à musique)

bandwagon /'bændwægən/ n

(Idiom) **to jump** ou **climb on the ~** prendre le train en marche

bandy /'bændɪ/
A adj arqué
B vtr **to ~ words with sb** avoir des mots avec qn

(Phrasal verb)

■ **bandy about, bandy around**: ► ~ **[sth]** about ou around avancer [names, information, statistics]

bane /beɪn/ n fléau m (**of** de); **she/it is the ~ of my life!** elle/ça m'empoisonne la vie!

bang /bæŋ/
A n (noise) (of explosion) détonation f, boum m; (of door, window) claquement m
B bangs npl US frange f
C adv○ ~ **in the middle** en plein centre; **to arrive ~ on time** arriver à l'heure pile
D excl (imitating gun) pan!; (imitating explosion) boum!, bang!
E vtr **1** (place noisily) **to ~ sth down on** poser bruyamment qch sur; **2** (causing pain) **to ~ one's head** se cogner la tête (**on** contre); **3** (strike) taper sur [drum, saucepan]; **to ~ one's fist on the table** taper du poing sur la table; **4** (slam) claquer [door, window]
F vi **1** (strike) **to ~ on** cogner à [wall, door]; **2** (make noise) [door, shutter] claquer

(Idioms) ~ **goes**○ **my holiday/my promotion** je peux dire adieu à mes vacances/mon avancement; **to go out with a ~** quitter la scène avec panache

(Phrasal verbs)

■ **bang in**: ► ~ **[sth]** in, ~ **in [sth]** enfoncer [nail, peg, tack] (**with** à coups de)
■ **bang into**: ► ~ **into [sb/sth]** heurter

banger /'bæŋə(r)/ n **1** ○(car) guimbarde○ f; **2** (firework) pétard m; **3** ○GB (sausage) saucisse f

Bangladesh /ˌbæŋglə'deʃ/ ► p. 774 pr n Bangladesh m

bangle /'bæŋgl/ n bracelet m, jonc m

banish /'bænɪʃ/ vtr bannir (**from** de)

banishment /'bænɪʃmənt/ n bannissement m

banister, bannister GB /'bænɪstə(r)/ n (also ~s) rampe f (d'escalier)

banjo /'bændʒəʊ/ ► p. 1028 n (pl **-jos** ou **-joes**) banjo m

bank /bæŋk/
A n **1** Fin, Games banque f; **it won't break the ~**○ fig ça ne ruinera personne; **2** (border) (of river, lake) rive f; (of major river)

bord m; (of canal) berge f; **3** (mound) (of earth, mud) talus m; (of snow) congère f; (by road, railway track) talus m; (by racetrack) virage m incliné; (by mineshaft) carreau m; **4** (mass) (of flowers) massif m; (of fog, mist) banc m; **5** (series) (of switches, oars, keys, floodlights) rangée f
B vtr **1** Fin déposer [qch] à la banque [cheque, money]; **2** (border) border [track, road]
C vi Fin **to ~ with X** avoir un compte (bancaire) à la X

(Idiom) **to be as safe as the Bank of England** être à toute épreuve

(Phrasal verbs)

■ **bank on**: ► ~ **on [sb/sth]** compter sur [qn/qch] (**to do** pour faire); **to ~ on doing** escompter faire
■ **bank up**: ► ~ **up** [snow, earth] s'amonceler; ► ~ **[sth]** up, ~ **up [sth]** **1** (pile up) entasser [snow, earth]; **2** (cover with fuel) charger [fire]

bank: ~ **account** n compte m bancaire; ~ **balance** n Fin solde m bancaire; ~**book** n livret m bancaire; ~ **card** n carte f bancaire; ~ **charges** npl Fin frais mpl bancaires; ~ **clerk** ► p. 1181 n employé/-e m/f de banque

banker /'bæŋkə(r)/ ► p. 1181 n Fin (owner) banquier/-ière m/f; (executive) cadre mf de banque

banker: ~'s **draft** n Fin traite f bancaire; ~'s **order** n virement m bancaire

bank: **Bank Giro Credit, BGC** n GB Fin crédit m par virement bancaire; ~ **holiday** n GB jour m férié; US jour m de fermeture des banques

banking /'bæŋkɪŋ/
A n Fin **1** (business) opérations fpl bancaires; **2** (profession) la banque; **to study ~** faire des études bancaires
B noun modifier [group, sector, system, facilities] bancaire; ~ **business** affaires fpl bancaires

banking hours n heures fpl d'ouverture des banques

bank: ~ **manager** ► p. 1181 n directeur/-trice m/f d'agence bancaire; ~**note** n billet m de banque; ~ **raid** n hold-up m; ~ **robber** n cambrioleur/-euse m/f de banque; ~ **robbery** n cambriolage m de banque

bankroll /'bæŋkrəʊl/
A n fonds mpl
B ○vtr financer [person, party]

bankrupt /'bæŋkrʌpt/
A adj Fin [person] ruiné; [business, economy] en faillite; ~ **stock** articles mpl de saisie; **to go ~** faire faillite
B vtr mettre [qn/qch] en faillite [person, company]

bankruptcy /'bæŋkrʌpsi/ n Fin faillite f

bankruptcy: ~ **court** n ≈ tribunal m de commerce; ~ **proceedings** npl procédure f de faillite

bank: ~ **statement** n relevé m de compte; ~ **transfer** n virement m bancaire

banner /'bænə(r)/ n **1** (in protest, festival) banderole f; **under the ~ of** sous la bannière de; **2** Hist (ensign) étendard m; **3** (also ~ **advert**) (Internet advert) bandeau m publicitaire

banner headline n gros titre m

bannister n GB = **banister**

banns /bænz/ npl Relig bans mpl

banquet /'bæŋkwɪt/
A n banquet m
B vi banqueter

bantam /'bæntəm/ n poule f naine; ~ **cock** coq m nain; ~ **hen** poule f naine

banter /'bæntə(r)/
A n ₵ plaisanteries fpl
B vi badiner (**with** avec)

baptism /'bæptɪzəm/ n **1** Relig baptême m; **2** fig (initiation) débuts mpl

Baptist /'bæptɪst/ n, adj baptiste (mf)

baptize /bæp'taɪz/ vtr baptiser

bar /bɑː(r)/
A n **1** (strip of metal, wood) barre f; (on cage, cell, window) barreau m; **behind ~s** derrière les barreaux; **2** (place for drinking) bar m; (counter) comptoir m; **I'll go to the ~** je vais chercher les boissons; **3** (block) (of soap, gold, chocolate) barre f; **4** (obstacle) obstacle m; **5** Jur (profession) **the ~** le barreau; **to be called to the ~** entrer au barreau; **6** Jur (in court) barre f;

7) Sport barre *f*; **8)** Mus mesure *f*; **9)** (in electric fire) résistance *f*; **10)** Mil GB (to medal) barrette *f*; US (on uniform) galon *m*

B *prep* sauf; **all ~ one** tous sauf un seul; **~ none** sans exception

C *vtr* (*p prés etc* **-rr-**) **1)** (block) barrer [*way, path*]; **to ~ sb's way** barrer le passage à qn; **2)** (ban) exclure [*person*] **(from sth** de qch); interdire [*activity*]; **to ~ sb from doing** interdire à qn de faire; **3)** (fasten) mettre la barre à [*gate, shutter*]

(Idiom) **a no holds ~red contest** une lutte où tous les coups sont permis

barb /bɑːb/ *n* **1)** lit barbe *f*; **2)** fig (remark) pique *f*

Barbados /bɑːˈbeɪdɒs/ ▸ **p. 774, p. 954** *pr n* Barbade *f*

barbarian /bɑːˈbeərɪən/ *n, adj* barbare (*mf*)

barbaric /bɑːˈbærɪk/ *adj* barbare

barbarism /ˈbɑːbərɪzəm/ *n* **1)** (brutality, primitiveness) barbarie *f*; **2)** littér (error) barbarisme *m*

barbarity /bɑːˈbærəti/ *n* **1)** *Ȼ* (brutality, primitiveness) barbarie *f*; **2) C** (brutal act) atrocité *f*

barbarous /ˈbɑːbərəs/ *adj* barbare

barbecue /ˈbɑːbɪkjuː/
A *n* barbecue *m*
B *vtr* **1)** (on charcoal etc) faire [qch] au barbecue; **2)** (cook in spicy sauce) faire [qch] façon barbecue

barbed /ˈbɑːbd/ *adj* **1)** [*hook, arrow*] à barbes; **2)** [*comment, criticism*] acerbe; [*wit*] mordant

barbed wire, **barbwire** US *n* (fil *m* de fer) barbelé *m*

barber /ˈbɑːbə(r)/ ▸ **p. 1181** *n* coiffeur *m* (pour hommes)

barber's shop GB, **barbershop** US ▸ **p. 000** *n* salon *m* de coiffure (pour hommes)

barbital /ˈbɑːbɪtl/ US = **barbitone**

barbitone /ˈbɑːbɪtəʊn/ *n* GB barbital *m*

barbiturate /bɑːˈbɪtjʊrət/ *n* barbiturique *m*

barbwire *n* US = **barbed wire**

Barcelona /ˌbɑːsɪˈləʊnə/ ▸ **p. 1276** *pr n* Barcelone

bar: **~ chart** *n* histogramme *m*; **~ code** *n* code *m* (à barres; **~-coded** *adj* à code barres

bard /bɑːd/ *n* littér (poet) chantre *m*

bare /beə(r)/
A *adj* **1)** (naked) [*flesh, leg, boards, wall*] nu; **to sit in the sun with one's head ~** s'asseoir au soleil la tête nue *ou* nu-tête (*inv*); **with one's ~ hands** à mains nues; **2)** (empty) [*cupboard, house, room*] vide; **to strip sth ~** vider qch; **3)** (stark) [*branch, mountain, rock*] nu; [*earth, landscape*] dénudé; **~ of** dépourvu de [*leaves, flowers*]; **4)** (mere) **a ~ 3%/20 dollars** à peine 3%/20 dollars; **5)** (absolute) strict (*before n*); **6)** (unembellished) [*facts, statistics*] brut
B *vtr* **to ~ one's chest** se découvrir la poitrine; **to ~ one's teeth** montrer les dents; **to ~ one's head** se découvrir; **to ~ one's soul** ouvrir son âme à

bareback *adv* [*ride*] à cru

bare bones /ˌbeəˈbəʊnz/ *npl* **the ~** l'essentiel *m*

barefaced /ˈbeəfeɪst/ *adj* [*lie*] éhonté; [*cheek, nerve*] effronté

barefoot /ˈbeəfʊt/
A *adj* **to be ~** être nu-pieds
B *adv* [*run, walk*] pieds nus

barely /ˈbeəli/ *adv* **1)** [*audible, capable, conscious, disguised*] à peine, tout juste; **to be ~ able to walk** pouvoir à peine *ou* tout juste marcher; **~ 12 hours later** à peine 12 heures plus tard; **2)** [*furnished*] pauvrement

bareness /ˈbeənɪs/ *n* nudité *f*

bargain /ˈbɑːgɪn/
A *n* **1)** (deal) marché *m* (**between** entre); **to drive a hard ~** négocier ferme *or* serré; **2)** (good buy) affaire *f*; **to get a ~** faire une affaire
B *noun modifier* [*price*] avantageux/-euse
C *vi* **1)** (for deal) négocier (**with** avec); **2)** (over price) marchander (**with** avec)
(Phrasal verb)
■ **bargain for**, **bargain on**: ▸ **~ for**, **~ on sth** s'attendre à qch; **we got more than we ~ed for** nous ne nous attendions pas à ça

bargain basement *n* coin *m* des affaires

bargaining /ˈbɑːgɪnɪŋ/
A *n* (over pay) négociations *fpl*

B *noun modifier* [*position, power, rights*] de négociation

bargaining chip *n* atout *m* dans les négociations

barge /bɑːdʒ/
A *n* **1)** péniche *f*; (freight only) chaland *m*; **2)** (for ceremony) barque *f* d'apparat; **3)** (in navy) vedette *f*
B *vtr* (shove) bousculer [*player, runner*]
C *vi* (move roughly) **to ~ past sb** passer devant qn en le bousculant
(Phrasal verbs)
■ **barge in** (enter noisily) faire irruption; (interrupt) interrompre brutalement
■ **barge into** faire irruption dans [*room, house*]; bousculer [*person*]

bargepole /ˈbɑːdʒpəʊl/ *n*:
(Idiom) **I wouldn't touch him/it with a ~** je ne voudrais de lui/cela pour rien au monde

baritone /ˈbærɪtəʊn/ ▸ **p. 1311** *n* baryton *m*

bark /bɑːk/
A *n* **1)** (of tree) écorce *f*; **2)** (of dog) aboiement *m*; **3)** littér (boat) barque *f*
B *vi* [*dog, person*] fig aboyer (**at sb/sth** après qn/qch)
(Idioms) **his ~ is worse than his bite** il fait plus de bruit que de mal; **to be ~ing up the wrong tree** faire fausse route

barking /ˈbɑːkɪŋ/
A *n* aboiements *mpl*
B *adj* [*dog*] qui aboie; [*cough, laugh*] aboyant
(Idiom) **to be ~ mad**○ GB être complètement fou/folle

barley /ˈbɑːli/ *n* orge *f*

barley: **~corn** *n* grain *m* d'orge; **~ sugar** *n* sucre *m* d'orge; **~ water** *n* GB sirop *m* d'orgeat; **~ wine** *n* GB ≈ bière *f* (très forte)

bar: **~maid** ▸ **p. 1181** *n* serveuse *f* de bar; **~man** ▸ **p. 1181** *n* (*pl* **~men**) barman *m*

bar mitzvah /ˌbɑː ˈmɪtsvə/ *n* **1)** (*also* **Bar Mitzvah**) (ceremony) bar-mitsva *f*; **2)** (boy) bar-mitsva *m*

barmy○ /ˈbɑːmɪ/ *adj* GB [*person*] maboul○; [*plan, idea, outfit*] loufoque○; **to go ~** (get angry) piquer une crise○; (get excited) devenir dingue○

barn /bɑːn/ *n* (for crops) grange *f*; (for cattle) étable *f*; (for horses) écurie *f*

barnacle /ˈbɑːnəkl/ *n* bernacle *f*

barn dance *n* soirée *f* de danses villageoises

barn: **~ owl** *n* (chouette *f*) effraie *f*; **~storming** *adj* tonitruant; **~yard** *n* basse-cour *f*

barometer /bəˈrɒmɪtə(r)/ *n* Meteorol baromètre *m*

barometric /ˌbærəˈmetrɪk/ *adj* barométrique

baron /ˈbærən/ *n* **1)** (noble) baron *m*; **2)** (tycoon) baron *m*; **drugs ~** baron *m* de la drogue; **media ~** magnat *m* des médias; **industrial ~** gros industriel *m*

baroness /ˈbærənɪs/ *n* baronne *f*

baronial /bəˈrəʊnɪəl/ *adj* baronnial

baroque /bəˈrɒk/, US bəˈrəʊk/ *n, adj* baroque (*m*)

barrack /ˈbærək/ *vtr* GB (heckle) conspuer

barracking /ˈbærəkɪŋ/ *n* huées *fpl*

barrack room
A *n* chambrée *f*
B *noun modifier* péj [*joke*] de corps de garde; [*language*] grossier/-ière

barrack-room lawyer GB, **barracks lawyer** US *n* péj chicaneur/-euse *m/f*

barracks /ˈbærəks/ *n* Mil, gen caserne *f*

barrage /ˈbærɑːʒ, US bəˈrɑːʒ/ *n* **1)** Constr barrage *m*; **2)** Mil tir *m* de barrage; **3)** fig (of questions, criticism) barrage *m*; (of complaints) déluge *m*

barrage balloon *n* ballon *m* de barrage

barrel /ˈbærəl/ *n* **1)** (container) (for beer, wine, olives etc) tonneau *m*, fût *m*; (for herring) caque *f*; (for tar) gonne *f*; (for petroleum) baril *m*; **2)** (cylinder) (of cannon) tube *m*; (of firearm) canon *m*; (of pen) corps *m*
(Idioms) **it was a ~ of laughs** *ou* **fun**○ iron ce n'était pas très marrant○; **to have sb over a ~**○ avoir qn à sa merci; **he bought the farm lock, stock and ~** il a acheté la ferme et tout ce qui allait avec; **to scrape the bottom of the ~** gratter les fonds de tiroir

barrel: ∼**-chested** adj [person] baraqué○; ∼ **organ** n orgue m de Barbarie

barren /'bærən/ adj **1** [land] aride; **2** (unrewarding) [effort, activity] stérile; [style] sec/sèche

barricade /ˌbærɪˈkeɪd/
A n barricade f
B vtr barricader

barrier /'bærɪə(r)/ n lit, fig barrière f; **(ticket)** ∼ Rail guichet m (de quai); **language/trade** ∼ barrière f linguistique/douanière

barrier: ∼ **cream** n crème f protectrice; ∼ **method** n Med méthode f de contraception locale; ∼ **nursing** n ≈ traitement m d'isolement préventif; ∼ **reef** n barrière f corallienne

barring /'bɑːrɪŋ/ prep à moins de

barrister /'bærɪstə(r)/ ▸ **p. 1181** n GB avocat/-e m/f

barrow /'bærəʊ/ n **1** (for garden, building) brouette f; **2** GB (in market) voiture f de quatre saisons

barrow boy ▸ **p. 1181** n GB marchand m de quatre saisons

bar: ∼ **school** n institution f où l'on prépare le certificat d'aptitude à la profession d'avocat; ∼ **stool** n tabouret m de bar; ∼**tender** n US barman/barmaid m/f

barter /'bɑːtə(r)/
A n troc m
B vtr troquer **(for** contre)
C vi **1** (exchange) faire du troc; **2** (haggle) marchander

base /beɪs/
A n **1** gen, Mil (centre of operations) base f; **to return to** ∼ Mil rentrer à sa base; **2** (bottom part) (of object, spine, mountain, structure) base f; (of tree, cliff, lamp) pied m; (of tail) point m d'attache; (of sculpture, statue) socle m; fig (for assumption, theory) base f; **3** Chem, Culin base f; **4** Math base f; **5** Sport base f
B adj (contemptible) [act, motive, emotion] ignoble
C vtr **1** (take as foundation) fonder [calculation, assumption, decision, research, character] **(on** sur); **the film is** ∼**d on a true story** le film est tiré d'une histoire vraie; **2** (have as operations centre) (gén au passif) baser; **to be** ∼**d in London/Paris** [person, company] être basé à Londres/Paris
D **-based** combining form **computer/pupil-**∼**d** [method, policy] basé sur les ordinateurs/les élèves

base: ∼**ball** ▸ **p. 881** n base-ball m; ∼**ball boot** n basket m; ∼ **camp** n lit, fig camp m de base; ∼ **form** n Ling base f

Basel /'bɑːzl/, **Basle** /bɑːl/ ▸ **p. 1276** pr n Bâle m

base: ∼ **lending rate** n taux m de base bancaire; ∼**less** adj sans fondement

baseline /'beɪslaɪn/ n **1** (in tennis) ligne f de fond; **2** fig base f; **3** (in advertising) signature f

basement /'beɪsmənt/
A n sous-sol m; **in the** ∼ au sous-sol
B noun modifier [flat, apartment, kitchen] en sous-sol

base: ∼ **metal** n métal m non précieux; ∼ **period** n (statistics) période f de base; ∼ **rate** n taux m de base; ∼ **year** n Fin année f de référence

bash○ /bæʃ/
A n (pl **-es**) **1** (blow) coup m; **2** (accident) **I had a** ∼ **in my car** j'ai eu un accident de voiture; **3** (attempt) tentative f; **to have a** ∼ **at sth, to give sth a** ∼ s'essayer à qch; **4** (party) grande fête f; **5** US (good time) **to have a** ∼ bien s'amuser
B vtr cogner [person]; rentrer dans [tree, wall, kerb]; **she** ∼**ed her head on** ou **against the shelf** elle s'est cogné la tête contre l'étagère; **to** ∼ **sb on** ou **over the head** frapper qn à la tête

(Phrasal verbs)
■ **bash in**: ▸ ∼ **[sth] in**, ∼ **in [sth]** défoncer [door, part of car]
■ **bash into**: ▸ ∼ **into [sth]** rentrer dans
■ **bash on** persévérer.
■ **bash out**: ▸ ∼ **out [sth]**, ∼ **[sth] out** expédier [work]; jouer [tune]

bashful /'bæʃfl/ adj timide; **to be** ∼ **about doing** hésiter à faire

bashfully /'bæʃfəlɪ/ adv timidement

bashing○ /'bæʃɪŋ/ n **1** (beating, defeat) raclée○ f; **to take a** ∼ ramasser une raclée○; **2** fig (criticism) dénigration f systématique

basic /'beɪsɪk/
A **basics** npl essentiel m: (of knowledge, study) principes mpl

fondamentaux; (food) denrées fpl de première nécessité; **to get down to** ∼**s** aborder l'essentiel
B adj **1** (fundamental) [aim, arrangement, fact, need, quality] essentiel/-ielle; [belief, research, problem, principle] fondamental; [theme] principal; **2** (elementary) [education, skill, rule] élémentaire; **3** (rudimentary) [accommodation, meal, supplies] de base; **the accommodation was rather** ∼ péj le logement était un peu rudimentaire; **4** (before additions) [pay, wage, hours] de base; **5** Chem basique

basically /'beɪsɪklɪ/ adv **1** (fundamentally) fondamentalement; **2** (for emphasis) ∼**, I don't like him very much** en fait, je ne l'aime pas beaucoup; ∼**, life's been good** dans l'ensemble, on a eu de la chance

basic: ∼ **law** n Pol, Jur ≈ Constitution f; ∼ **rate** n gen taux m de base; (in tax) taux m de base d'imposition; ∼ **training** n Mil formation f militaire de base

basil /'bæzl/ n basilic m

basilica /bəˈzɪlɪkə/ n basilique f

basin /'beɪsn/ n **1** Culin bol m; (for mixing) terrine f; **2** (for washing) lavabo m; (for washing up) cuvette f; **3** Geog bassin m; **4** (of port, fountain) bassin m

basinful /'beɪsɪnfʊl/ n pleine cuvette f

basis /'beɪsɪs/ n (pl **-ses**) (for action, negotiation) base f **(for, of** de); (of discussion) cadre m; (of theory) point m de départ; (for belief, argument) fondements mpl **(for** de); **on the** ∼ **of** sur la base de; **on that** ∼ ceci étant; **on the same** ∼ dans les mêmes conditions

bask /bɑːsk, US bæsk/ vi **to** ∼ **in** se prélasser à [sunshine, warmth]; jouir de [approval, affection]

basket /'bɑːskɪt, US 'bæskɪt/ n **1** panier m, corbeille f; (carried on back) hotte f; (for game, fish) bourriche f; ∼ **of currencies** Fin panier m de devises; **2** Sport (in basketball) panier m; (in fencing) coquille f

basket: ∼**ball** ▸ **p. 881** n (game) basket(-ball) m; (ball) ballon m de basket; ∼ **chair** n fauteuil m en osier; ∼ **maker** ▸ **p. 1181** n vannier/-ière m/f; ∼**work** n (craft, objects) vannerie f

Basle /bɑːl/ ▸ **p. 1276** pr n = **Basel**

basque /bæsk/ n (on jacket etc) basques fpl

Basque /bæsk, bɑːsk/ ▸ **p. 1032, p. 969**
A n **1** (person) Basque mf; **2** (language) basque m
B adj basque

bass¹ /beɪs/ ▸ **p. 1311, p. 1028**
A n Mus, Audio basse f
B noun modifier **1** Mus [voice, part, line, range, solo] de basse; [aria] pour basse; [instrument] basse; **2** Audio [controls, sound, notes] grave

bass² /bæs/ n Zool (freshwater) perche f; (sea) Zool bar m; Culin loup m (de mer)

bass beɪs: ∼**-baritone** ▸ **p. 1311** n baryton-basse m; ∼ **clef** n clé f de fa; ∼ **drum** ▸ **p. 1028** n grosse caisse f

basset /'bæsɪt/ n (also ∼ **hound**) (chien m) basset m

bassist /'beɪsɪst/ ▸ **p. 1028** n bassiste mf

bassoon /bə'suːn/ ▸ **p. 1028** n basson m

bastard /'bɑːstəd, US 'bæs-/
A n **1** ◐(term of abuse) salaud◑ m; **2** †(illegitimate child) bâtard/-e m/f
B adj **1** [child] bâtard; **2** fig (hybrid) bâtard, corrompu

bastardized /'bɑːstədaɪzd, US 'bæs-/ adj [language] abâtardi; [style of architecture] dégradé; [race] dégénéré

baste /beɪst/ vtr **1** Culin arroser; **2** (in sewing) bâtir, faufiler

bastion /'bæstɪən/ n lit, fig bastion m **(of** de)

bat /bæt/
A n **1** Sport batte f; **table tennis** ∼ raquette f de tennis de table; **2** Zool chauve-souris f
B vtr (p prés etc **-tt-**) frapper
C vi (p prés etc **-tt-**) Sport (be batsman) être le batteur; (handle a bat) manier la batte

(Idioms) **to be blind as a** ∼ être myope comme une taupe; **to do sth off one's own** ∼○ faire qch de sa propre initiative; **like a** ∼ **out of hell**○ comme un possédé; **without** ∼**ting an eyelid** GB ou **eye(lash)** US sans sourciller

batch /bætʃ/ n **1** (of loaves, cakes) fournée f; (of cement) gâchée f; (of eggs, fish) arrivage m; (of letters) tas m, liasse f; (of books, text, goods, orders) lot m; (of candidates, prisoners etc) groupe m; Comput lot m

batch: ~ **file** n Comput fichier m séquentiel; ~ **mode** n Comput mode m différé; ~ **processing** n Comput traitement m séquentiel

bated /'beɪtɪd/ adj with ~ **breath** en retenant son souffle

bath /bɑːθ, US bæθ/
A n **1** (wash, washing water) bain m; **2** GB (tub) baignoire f; **I was in the** ~ j'étais dans mon bain; **3** US (bathroom) salle f de bains; **4** Chem, Phot, Tech bain m
B **baths** npl **1** (for swimming) piscine f; **2** (in spa) thermes mpl; **3** †(municipal) bains mpl publics
C vtr GB baigner
D vi GB prendre un bain

bathe /beɪð/
A vtr laver [wound] (**in** dans; **with** à); **to** ~ **one's feet** prendre un bain de pieds
B vi **1** (swim) [person] se baigner; **2** US (take bath) prendre un bain; **3** **to be** ~**ed** in ruisseler de [sweat]; être inondé de [light]; être baigné de [tears]

bather /'beɪðə(r)/ n baigneur/-euse m/f

bathing /'beɪðɪŋ/ n baignade f

bathing: ~ **cap** n bonnet m de bain; ~ **costume**† n costume m de bain; ~ **hut** n cabine f de bain; ~ **suit**† n = **bathing costume**; ~ **trunks** n slip m de bain

bath: ~ **mat** n tapis m de bain; ~ **oil** n huile f de bain

bathos /'beɪθɒs/ n bathos m, chute f du sublime au trivial

bathrobe /'bɑːθrəʊb/ n sortie f de bain

bathroom /'bɑːθruːm, -rʊm/ n **1** (for washing) salle f de bains; **2** US (lavatory) (public) toilettes fpl; (at home) salle f de bains

bathroom: ~ **cabinet** n armoire f de toilette; ~ **fittings** npl accessoires mpl de salle de bains; ~ **scales** npl pèse-personne m

bath: ~ **salts** npl sels mpl de bain; ~ **towel** n serviette f de bain; ~**tub** n baignoire f

baton /'bætn, 'bætɒn, US bə'tɒn/ n GB (policeman's) matraque f; Mil, Mus baguette f; Sport (in relay race) témoin m; (used by French traffic policeman, majorette) bâton m

baton: ~ **charge** n GB charge f à la matraque; ~ **round** n GB balle f en caoutchouc

batsman /'bætsmən/ n Sport batteur m

battalion /bə'tælɪən/ n Mil, fig bataillon m

batten /'bætn/
A n **1** Constr (for door, floor) latte f; (in roofing) volige f; **2** Naut latte f; **3** Theat herse f
B vtr latter [door, floor]; voliger [roof]

batter /'bætə(r)/
A n Culin gen pâte f; (for frying) pâte f à frire; **fish in** ~ beignets mpl de poisson
B vtr [person] battre [person]; [storm, bombs] ravager; [waves] battre

battered /'bætəd/ adj [kettle, hat] cabossé; [book, suitcase etc] très abîmé; [person] battu; [pride] meurtri

battering /'bætərɪŋ/ n **1** (from person) raclée○ f; **2** **to take** ou **get a** ~ (from bombs, storm, waves) être ravagé (**from** par); (from opponents) Sport prendre une raclée○; (from critics) se faire descendre (**by** par); (emotionally) en prendre un coup○

battering-ram n bélier m

battery /'bætərɪ/ n **1** Elec pile f; Aut batterie f; **2** Mil batterie f; **3** Agric (for hens) batterie f; **4** fig (large number) (of objects, tests) batterie f; (of questions) feu m nourri; **5** Jur coups mpl et blessures fpl

battery: ~ **acid** n solution f acide pour piles; ~ **charger** n chargeur m de batteries; ~ **chicken** n poulet m d'élevage industriel; ~ **controlled** adj à piles; ~ **farming** n élevage m en batterie; ~ **fire** n tir m par salves; ~ **hen** n = **battery chicken**; ~ **operated**, ~ **powered** adj à piles

battle /'bætl/
A n **1** Mil bataille f (**for** pour, **against** contre, **between** entre); **to die in** ~ mourir au combat; **to fight a** ~ combattre; **to go into** ~ engager le combat; **2** fig lutte f (**for** pour, **against** contre, **over** à propos de); **political** ~ lutte f politique; **legal** ~ bataille f légale; **it's a** ~ **of wills between them** c'est à qui l'emportera entre eux; **a** ~ **of words** un échange acerbe; **to fight one's own** ~**s** se défendre tout seul; **to fight sb's** ~**s** se battre pour le compte de qn

B noun modifier Mil [formation, zone] de combat
C vi Mil, fig combattre (**with sb** contre qn); **to** ~ **for sth/to do** lutter pour qch/pour faire; **to** ~ **one's way through sth** vaincre qch de haute lutte
(Idiom) **that's half the** ~ c'est déjà un grand pas de fait
(Phrasal verbs)
■ **battle on** persévérer
■ **battle out**: **to** ~ **it out** lutter avec acharnement (**for** pour)

battle-axe /'bætlæks/ n **1** ○fig péj (woman) virago○ f; **2** lit hache f d'armes

battle: ~ **cry** n lit, fig cri m de ralliement; ~**dress** n tenue f de campagne; ~ **drill** n Mil **C** manœuvres fpl; ~**field** n lit, fig champ m de bataille; ~**ground** n lit champ m de bataille; fig sujet m de discussion; ~ **lines** npl Mil lignes fpl de combat; fig stratégie f

battlements /'bætlmənts/ npl lit, fig remparts mpl

battle: ~ **order** n lit, fig ordre m de bataille; ~**-scarred** adj lit marqué par la guerre; fig marqué par la vie; ~**ship** n cuirassé m

batty○ /'bætɪ/ adj cinglé○, fou/folle

bauble /'bɔːbl/ n (ornament) babiole f; pej (item of jewellery) colifichet m

Bavaria /bə'veərɪə/ pr n Bavière f

bawdiness /'bɔːdɪnɪs/ n (of story, song) grivoiserie f; (of person) paillardise f

bawdy /'bɔːdɪ/ adj [song] grivois; [person] paillard

bawl /bɔːl/ vi (weep) brailler; (shout) hurler

bay /beɪ/
A n **1** Geog baie f; **2** Bot (also ~ **tree**) laurier(-sauce) m; **3** (parking area) aire f de stationnement; **loading** ~ aire de chargement; **4** Archit (section of building) travée f; (recess) renfoncement m; (window) fenêtre f en saillie; **5** Aviat, Naut (compartment) soute f; **6** (horse) cheval m bai
B adj [horse] bai
C vi [dog] aboyer (**at** contre, après); **to** ~ **for sb's blood** fig réclamer la tête de qn
(Idiom) **to hold** ou **keep at** ~ fig tenir [qn] à distance [attacker, opponent]; stopper [famine]; enrayer [unemployment, inflation etc]

bay leaf n feuille f de laurier

bayonet /'beɪənɪt/ n Mil, Elec baïonnette f

bay: ~ **rum** n lotion f capillaire (au piment de la Jamaïque); ~ **window** n fenêtre f en saillie

bazaar /bə'zɑː(r)/ n bazar m

bazooka /bə'zuːkə/ n bazooka m, lance-roquettes m inv antichar

B & B n: abrév ▸ **bed and breakfast**

BBC (abrév = **British Broadcasting Corporation**) BBC f

BC (abrév = **Before Christ**) av. J.-C

BDS n GB (abrév = **Bachelor of Dental Surgery**) diplôme m de chirurgie dentaire

be /biː, bɪ/ vi (p prés **being**; 3e pers sg prés **is**, prét **was**, pp **been**) **1** gen être; **it's me, it's I** c'est moi; **he's a good pupil** c'est un bon élève; **2** (in probability) **if Henri were here** si Henri était là; **were it not that...** ne serait-ce que...; **were they to know** s'ils savaient; **if I were you** à ta place; **had it not been for Frank, I'd have missed the train** sans Frank j'aurais raté le train; **3** (phrases) **so** ~ **it** d'accord; **that as it may** quoi qu'il en soit; **as it were** pour ainsi dire; **even if it were so** même si c'était le cas; **I preferred it as it was** je l'aimais mieux avant; **leave it as it is** ne changez rien; **let** ou **leave him** ~ laisse-le tranquille ▸ p. 680

BE n: abrév ▸ **bill of exchange**

beach /biːtʃ/
A n plage f
B vtr échouer [boat]; ~**ed whale** lit baleine f échouée; fig (building, object, person) mastodonte m

beach: ~ **ball** n ballon m de plage; ~ **buggy** n buggy m; ~**comber** n: personne qui récupère les objets échoués ou oubliés sur la plage; ~**head** n tête f de pont; ~ **hut** n cabine f de plage; ~**robe** n serviette-cabine f; ~**wear** n tenues fpl de plage

beacon /'biːkən/ n **1** Aviat balise f, phare m; (lighthouse) phare m; (lantern) fanal m; (signalling buoy) balise f; fig (guide) phare m; **2** (also **radio** ~) (transmitter) radiobalise f; **3** Hist

be

The direct French equivalent of the verb *to be* in subject + to be + predicate sentences is *être*:

I am tired
= je suis fatigué

Caroline is French
= Caroline est française

the children are in the garden
= les enfants sont dans le jardin

It functions in very much the same way as *to be* does in English and it is safe to assume it will work as a translation in the great majority of cases.

Note, however, that when you are specifying a person's profession or trade, *a/an* is not translated:

she's a doctor
= elle est médecin

Claudie is still a student
= Claudie est toujours étudiante

This is true of any noun used in apposition when the subject is a person:

he's a widower
= il est veuf

But

Lyons is a beautiful city
= Lyon est une belle ville

For more information or expressions involving professions and trades consult the usage note ▸ **p. 1181**.

For the conjugation of the verb *être* see the French verb tables.

Grammatical functions

The passive

être is used to form the passive in French just as *to be* is used in English. Note, however, that the past participle agrees in gender and number with the subject:

the rabbit was killed by a fox
= le lapin a été tué par un renard

the window had been broken
= la fenêtre avait été cassée

their books will be sold
= leurs livres seront vendus

our doors have been repainted red
= nos portes ont été repeintes en rouge

In spoken language, French native speakers find the passive cumbersome and will avoid it where possible by using the impersonal *on* where a person or people are clearly involved: *on a repeint nos portes en rouge.*

Progressive tenses

In French the idea of something happening over a period of time cannot be expressed using the verb *être* in the way that *to be* is used as an auxiliary verb in English.

The present

French uses simply the present tense where English uses the progressive form with *to be*:

I am working
= je travaille

Ben is reading a book
= Ben lit un livre

In order to accentuate duration *être en train de* is used: *je suis en train de travailler; Ben est en train de lire un livre.*

The future

French also uses the present tense where English uses the progressive form with *to be*:

we are going to London tomorrow
= nous allons à Londres demain

I'm (just) coming!
= j'arrive!

I'm (just) going!
= j'y vais!

The past

To express the distinction between *she read a newspaper* and *she was reading a newspaper* French uses the perfect and the imperfect tenses: *elle a lu un journal/elle lisait un journal:*

he wrote to his mother
= il a écrit à sa mère

he was writing to his mother
= il écrivait à sa mère

However, in order to accentuate the notion of describing an activity which went on over a period of time, the phrase *être en train de* (= *to be in the process of*) is often used:

'what was he doing when you arrived?'
'he was cooking the dinner'
= 'qu'est-ce qu'il faisait quand tu es arrivé?' 'il était en train de préparer le dîner'

she was just finishing her essay when ...
= elle était juste en train de finir sa dissertation quand ...

The compound past

Compound past tenses in the progressive form in English are generally translated by the imperfect in French:

I've been looking for you
= je te cherchais

For progressive forms + *for* and *since* (*I've been waiting for an hour, I had been waiting for an hour, I've been waiting since Monday* etc.) see the entries **for** and **since**.

Obligation

When *to be* is used as an auxiliary verb with another verb in the infinitive (*to be to do*) expressing obligation, a fixed arrangement or destiny, *devoir* is used:

she's to do it at once
= elle doit le faire tout de suite

what am I to do?
= qu'est-ce que je dois faire?

he was to arrive last Monday
= il devait arriver lundi dernier

she was never to see him again
= elle ne devait plus le revoir.

In tag questions

French has no direct equivalent of tag questions like *isn't he?* or *wasn't it?* There is a general tag question *n'est-ce pas?* (literally *isn't it so?*) which will work in many cases:

their house is lovely, isn't it?
= leur maison est très belle, n'est-ce pas?

he's a doctor, isn't he?
= il est médecin, n'est-ce pas?

it was a very good meal, wasn't it?
= c'était un très bon repas, n'est-ce pas?

☞ See next page

be *continued*

However, *n'est-ce pas* can very rarely be used for positive tag questions and some other way will be found to express the extra meaning contained in the tag: *par hasard* (*by any chance*) can be very useful as a translation:

'I can't find my glasses' 'they're not in the kitchen, are they?'
= 'je ne trouve pas mes lunettes' 'elles ne sont pas dans la cuisine, par hasard?'

you haven't seen Gaby, have you?
= tu n'as pas vu Gaby, par hasard?

In cases where an opinion is being sought, *si?* meaning more or less *or is it?* or *was it?* etc. can be useful:

it's not broken, is it?
= ce n'est pas cassé, si?

he wasn't serious, was he?
= il n'était pas sérieux, si?

In many other cases the tag question is simply not translated at all and the speaker's intonation will convey the implied question.

In short answers

Again, there is no direct equivalent for short answers like *yes I am*, *no he's not* etc. Where the answer *yes* is given to contradict a negative question or statement, the most useful translation is *si:*

'you're not going out tonight' 'yes I am'
= 'tu ne sors pas ce soir' 'si'

In reply to a standard enquiry the tag will not be translated:

'are you a doctor?' 'yes I am'
= 'êtes-vous médecin?' 'oui'

'was it raining?' 'yes it was'
= 'est-ce qu'il pleuvait?' 'oui'

Probability

For expressions of probability and supposition (*if I were you* etc.) see the entry **be**.

Other functions

Expressing sensations and feelings

In expressing physical and mental sensations, the verb used in French is *avoir*:

to be cold	*to be hungry*
= avoir froid	= avoir faim
to be hot	*to be ashamed*
= avoir chaud	= avoir honte
I'm cold	*my hands are cold*
= j'ai froid	= j'ai froid aux mains
to be thirsty	
= avoir soif	

If, however, you are in doubt as to which verb to use in such expressions, you should consult the entry for the appropriate adjective.

Discussing health and how people are

In expressions of health and polite enquiries about how people are, *aller* is used:

how are you?
= comment allez-vous?
(*more informally*) comment vas-tu?
(*very informally as a greeting*) ça va?

are you well?
= vous allez bien?

how is your daughter?
= comment va votre fille?

my father is better today
= mon père va mieux aujourd'hui

Discussing weather and temperature

In expressions of weather and temperature *faire* is generally used:

it's cold	*it's windy*
= il fait froid	= il fait du vent

If in doubt, consult the appropriate adjective entry.

Visiting somewhere

When *to be* is used in the present perfect tense to mean *go*, *visit* etc., French will generally use the verbs *venir*, *aller* etc. rather than *être*:

I've never been to Sweden
= je ne suis jamais allé en Suède

have you been to the Louvre?
= est-ce que tu es déjà allé au Louvre?
or est-ce que tu as déjà visité le Louvre?

Paul has been to see us three times
= Paul est venu nous voir trois fois

Note too:

has the postman been?
= est-ce que le facteur est passé?

For *here is*, *here are*, *there is*, *there are* see the entries **here** and **there**.

The translation for an expression or idiom containing the verb *to be* will be found in the dictionary at the entry for another word in the expression: for *to be in danger* see **danger**, for *it would be best to* ... see **best** etc.

This dictionary contains usage notes on topics such as **the clock**, **time units**, **age**, **weight measurement**, **days of the week**, and **shops, trades and professions**, many of which include translations of particular uses of *to be*. For the index to these notes ▸ **p. 1354**.

(on hill etc) feu *m* (*pour donner l'alarme*)

bead /biːd/ *n* **1** (jewellery) perle *f*; **(string of)** ∼s collier *m*; **2** (drop) (of sweat, dew) goutte *f*, perle *f*

beaded /'biːdɪd/ *adj* [*dress, blouse*] garni de perles

beady-eyed /,biːdɪ'aɪd/ *adj* aux yeux perçants

beagle /'biːgl/ *n* beagle *m*

beak /biːk/ *n* bec *m*

beaker /'biːkə(r)/ *n* gen gobelet *m*; Chem vase *m* à bec

beam /biːm/

A *n* **1** (of light, torch, laser) rayon *m*; (of car lights, lighthouse) also Phys faisceau *m*; **on full** GB *ou* **high** US ∼ Aut en (pleins) phares;

on low ∼ US Aut en code; **2** (piece of wood) poutre *f*; **3** (central shaft) (of weighing scales) fléau *m*; (in mechanics) balancier *m*; **4** Aviat, Naut (radio or radar course) faisceau *m* de guidage; **to be off** ∼ GB, **to be off the** ∼ US lit être sorti du faisceau; fig être à côté de la plaque○; **5** Naut (cross-member) traverse *f*; (greatest width) largeur *f*; **6** (smile) grand sourire *m*

B *vtr* [*radio, satellite*] transmettre [*programme, signal*]

C *vi* lit, fig rayonner

(Idiom) **to be broad in the** ∼○ être fort des hanches

beam: ∼ **balance** *n* balance *f* à fléau; ∼ **compass** *n* compas *m* à verge

beaming /'biːmɪŋ/ *adj* (all contexts) rayonnant

bean /biːn/ n haricot m

(Idioms) **to be full of ~s**○ GB (be lively) être en pleine forme; US (be wrong) se gourer○ complètement; **it's not worth a ~**○ ça ne vaut rien

bean: **~ bag** n (seat) fauteuil m poire; (for throwing) sac m de haricots; **~ curd** n fromage m de soja; **~feast**○ n gueuleton○ m; **~pole** n espalier m; fig (thin person) perche f; **~sprout** n germe m de soja

bear /beə(r)/

A n **1** Zool ours m; **2** ○péj (man) ours m (mal léché); **3** Fin baissier m

B vtr (prét **bore**, pp **borne**) **1** (carry) [person, animal] porter [load]; **2** (bring) [person] apporter [gift, message]; [wind, water] porter [seed, sound]; **3** (show, have) porter [address, inscription, name]; **he still ~s the scars** fig il en reste marqué; **to ~ a resemblance to** ressembler à; **to ~ no relation to** n'avoir aucun rapport avec; **to ~ witness to** témoigner de; **4** (keep) **to ~ sth in mind** tenir compte de [suggestion, factor, information]; **to ~ in mind that** ne pas oublier que; **5** (support) **to ~ the weight of** [structure, platform] supporter le poids de [person, object]; **6** fig (endure, tolerate) supporter [illness, suspense, smell, person]; **I can't ~ to watch** je ne veux pas voir ça; **7** (accept) encourir [cost, responsibility]; **8** (stand up to) résister à [scrutiny, inspection]; **it doesn't ~ thinking about** il vaut mieux ne pas y penser; **9** (nurture) porter [love]; **10** (yield) donner [fruit, blossom, crop]; Fin [account, investment] rapporter [interest]; **to ~ fruit** [tree] donner des fruits; fig [idea, investment] porter ses fruits; **11** † ou littér (pp actif **borne**, pp passif **born**) (give birth to) [woman] donner naissance à; [animal] mettre bas; **to ~ sb a child** donner un enfant à qn

C vi (prét **bore**, pp **borne**) **1** **to ~ left/right** [person] prendre à gauche/à droite; **to ~ east/west** [person] aller à l'est/ à l'ouest; [road] obliquer vers l'est/l'ouest; **2** (weigh) **~ heavily/hardest on sb** [tax, price increase] peser lourdement/le plus durement sur qn; **to bring pressure to ~ on** exercer une pression sur [person, system]

D v refl (prét **bore**, pp **borne**) **to ~ oneself** (behave) se comporter

(Phrasal verbs)
■ **bear along**: ▸ **~ [sb/sth] along**, **~ along [sb/sth]** entraîner
■ **bear away**: ▸ **~ [sb/sth] away**, **~ away [sb/sth]** [person] enlever [person]; [wind, water] emporter [person, boat]
■ **bear down** **1** gen appuyer (fort) (**on** sur); **2** (approach) **to ~ down on** se ruer sur [person, group]; **3** (in childbirth) pousser
■ **bear off = bear away**
■ **bear on**: ▸ **~ on [sb/sth]** avoir un effet sur; (stronger) peser sur
■ **bear out**: ▸ **~ out [sth]** confirmer [theory, claim, story]; ▸ **~ [sb] out** appuyer
■ **bear up**: ▸ **~ up** [person] tenir le coup; [structure] résister
■ **bear upon = bear on**
■ **bear with**: ▸ **~ with [sb]** être indulgent avec; **please ~ with me for a minute** pardonnez-moi un instant; **to ~ with it** être patient

bearable /'beərəbl/ adj supportable

bear: **~baiting** n combat m d'ours et de chiens; **~ cub** n ourson m

beard /'bɪəd/

A n **1** (on man) barbe f; **to grow a ~** se faire pousser la barbe; **the man with the ~** l'homme qui a une barbe; **2** (tuft, barbel) (on dog, goat) barbiche f; (on fish) barbes fpl; (on bird, wheat) barbe f

B vtr affronter

bearded /'bɪədɪd/ adj barbu

bearer /'beərə(r)/

A n (of news, gift, letter, cheque) porteur/-euse m/f; (of passport) titulaire mf

B noun modifier Fin [bond, cheque] au porteur

bearing /'beərɪŋ/

A n **1** (posture) allure f; **his dignified ~** son port digne; **2** (relevance) **to have no/little ~ on sth** n'avoir aucun rapport/avoir peu de rapport avec qch; **3** Naut relèvement m au compas; **to take the ship's ~s** faire le point; **4** Tech palier m

B bearings npl **1** (orientation) **to get** ou **find one's ~s** se repé-

rer; **to lose one's ~s** lit être désorienté; fig perdre le nord; **2** Aut, Tech palier m

bear: **~ market** n Fin marché m à la baisse; **~ pit** n fosse f aux ours; **~skin** n (pelt) peau f d'ours; (hat) bonnet m à poil

beast /biːst/ n **1** (animal) bête f; **the Beast** Bible l'antéchrist m; **2** ○pej (annoying) chameau○ m; (brutal) brute f; **to bring out the ~ in sb** (make lustful, brutal) réveiller la bête qui sommeille en qn

(Idiom) **it's in the nature of the ~** hum c'est dans l'ordre des choses

beastly○ /'biːstlɪ/ adj **1** (unpleasant) [person, behaviour] rosse○; [trick] sale (before n); [weather] moche○; **2** (bestial) bestial

beat /biːt/

A n **1** (repeated sound) (of drum, feet) battement m; **to the ~ of the drum** au son du tambour; **2** Mus (rhythm) rythme m; (in a bar) temps m; (in verse) accentuation f; **3** (pulsation) (of heart) battement m, pulsation f; **80 ~s per minute** 80 pulsations à la minute; **4** Phys, Elec (pulse) battement m; **5** (in police force) (area) secteur m de surveillance; (route) ronde f

B noun modifier Literat [poet, writer, philosophy] de la Beat Generation

C ○adj (tired) claqué○

D vtr (prét **beat**, pp **beaten**) **1** (strike) [person] battre [person, animal, metal, ground, drum]; [person] marteler [door] (**with** avec); [wing] battre [air, ground]; **to ~ sb with a stick/whip** donner des coups de bâton/de fouet à qn; **to ~ sth into sb** inculquer qch à qn; **he beat the dust out of the carpet** il a battu le tapis pour le dépoussiérer; **to ~ sth into shape** façonner qch; **you'll have to ~ the truth out of him** il te faudra lui arracher la vérité; **to ~ sb into submission** faire obéir qn par la manière forte; **to ~ sb black and blue**○ rouer qn de coups; **to ~ the hell**○ **out of sb** tabasser○ qn; **to ~ time** Mus battre la mesure; **to ~ its wings** [bird] battre des ailes; **2** Culin (mix vigorously) battre [mixture, eggs]; **to ~ sth into sth** incorporer qch à qch en battant; **3** (make escape) **to ~ one's way/a path through** se frayer un chemin/un passage à travers [crowd, obstacles]; **to ~ a retreat** gen, Mil battre en retraite; **~ it!** fiche le camp○!; **4** (defeat) battre [opponent, team] (**at** à); vaincre [inflation, drug abuse]; surmonter [illness]; mettre fin à [child abuse, rape]; **5** (confound) **it ~s me how/why** je n'arrive pas à comprendre comment/pourquoi; **we admit to being beaten** nous nous avouons vaincus; **'~s me○!'**, **'it's got me beaten'** 'ça me dépasse!'; **6** (arrive earlier) éviter [rush, crowds]; devancer [person]; **she beat me to it** elle a été plus rapide que moi; **7** (outdo) gen, Sport battre [score]; dépasser [target]; surclasser [product]; **it ~s working** c'est toujours mieux que de travailler; **you can't ~ Italian shoes** rien ne vaut les chaussures italiennes; **our prices are difficult to ~** nos prix sont imbattables; **~ that (if you can)**○! qui dit mieux!

E vi (prét **beat**, pp **beaten**) [waves, rain] battre (**against** contre); [person] cogner (**at, on** à); [heart, drum, wings] battre

(Idioms) **a rod** ou **stick to ~ sb with** une arme contre qn; **if you can't ~ 'em, join 'em**○ il faut savoir hurler avec les loups

(Phrasal verbs)
■ **beat back**: ▸ **~ [sth] back**, **~ back [sth]** repousser [group, flames]
■ **beat down**: ▸ **~ down** [rain, hail] tomber à verse (**on** sur); [sun] taper (**on** sur); ▸ **~ [sth] down**, **~ down [sth]** **1** (flatten) [rain, wind] coucher [crop, grass]; **2** (break open) [person] enfoncer [door]
■ **beat in**: ▸ **~ [sth] in**, **~ in [sth]** défoncer [skull]○
■ **beat off**: ▸ **~ [sb/sth] off**, **~ off [sb/sth]** repousser [attack, attackers]; chasser [insects]
■ **beat out**: ▸ **~ [sth] out**, **~ out [sth]** marteler [metal]; rythmer [tune]; battre [rhythm] (**on** sur); étouffer [flames]
■ **beat up**: ▸ **~ [sb] up**, **~ up [sb]** tabasser○

beaten /'biːtn/

A pp ▸ **beat**

B adj battu

(Idiom) **to go off the ~ track** quitter les sentiers battus

beatify /brˈætɪfaɪ/ vtr béatifier

beating /'biːtɪŋ/ n **1** (punishment) lit raclée○ f, correction f; **to get a ~** recevoir une raclée○; **to take a ~** fig [speaker, politician] être malmené; [toy, car] en voir de dures○;

2 (sound) (of drum, heart, wings) battement *m*; **3** (of metal, carpet) battage *m*

beating-up° /ˌbiːtɪŋ ˈʌp/ *n* tabassage° *m*

beat-up° /ˈbiːtʌp/ *adj* |*car*| déglingué

beau /bəʊ/ *n* (*pl* **beaux**) littér *ou* hum (suitor) galant *m*

Beaufort scale /ˌbəʊfət ˈskeɪl/ *n* échelle *f* de Beaufort

beautician /bjuːˈtɪʃn/ ▸ p. 1181 *n* **1** (beauty specialist) esthéticien/-ienne *m/f*; **2** US (hairdresser) coiffeur/ -euse *m/f*

beautiful /ˈbjuːtɪfl/ *adj* |*woman, house, car, landscape*| beau/ belle (*before n*); |*day, holiday, feeling, experience*| merveilleux/ -euse; |*weather, goal, shot*| superbe.

⚠ The irregular form *bel* of the adjective *beau* is used before masculine nouns beginning with a vowel or a mute 'h'

beautifully /ˈbjuːtɪfəlɪ/ *adv* **1** (perfectly) |*play, write, function*| admirablement (bien); |*written, designed etc*| admirablement; **2** (attractively) |*displayed, furnished, situated*| magnifiquement; **~ dressed** habillé avec beaucoup de goût; **3** (emphatic) |*empty, quiet, soft, warm, accurate*| merveilleusement

beautiful people *n* the **~** le beau monde

beautify /ˈbjuːtɪfaɪ/ *vtr* embellir

beauty /ˈbjuːtɪ/
A *n* beauté *f*; **the ~ of the system is that...** ce qu'il y a de bien dans ce système, c'est que...
B *noun modifier* |*contest, product, treatment*| de beauté

(Idioms) **age before ~** ≈ c'est le bénéfice de l'âge; **~ is in the eye of the beholder** Prov rien n'est laid pour celui qui aime

beauty: **~ editor** *n* rédacteur/-trice *m/f* de la rubrique 'beauté'; **~ parlour**†, **~ shop**, **~ salon** US ▸ p. 1181 *n* salon *m* de beauté; **~ queen** *n* reine *f* de beauté

beauty sleep *n* hum **to need one's ~** avoir besoin de ménager sa santé

beauty spot *n* **1** (on skin) grain *m* de beauté; (fake) mouche *f*; **2** Tourism gen coin *m* superbe; (official) site *m* pittoresque

beaver /ˈbiːvə(r)/ *n* castor *m*

(Phrasal verb)
■ **beaver away** travailler d'arrache-pied (**at** à)

becalmed /bɪˈkɑːmd/ *adj* encalminé

became /bɪˈkeɪm/ *prét* ▸ become

because /bɪˈkɒz, US *also* -kɔːz/
A *conj* parce que; **just ~ you're older doesn't mean you're right** ce n'est pas parce que tu es plus âgé que tu as raison
B **because of** *prep phr* à cause de; **~ of the rain** à cause de la pluie

beck /bek/ *n* **to be at sb's ~ and call** être à la disposition de qn

beckon /ˈbekən/
A *vtr* faire signe à; **to ~ sb in** faire signe à qn d'entrer
B *vi* faire signe (**to** à)

become /bɪˈkʌm/ (*prét* **became**; *pp* **become**)
A *vtr* sout |*colour, dress*| aller bien à |*person*|; |*attitude, modesty*| convenir à |*person*|
B *vi* devenir; **to ~ fat** devenir gros, grossir; **to ~ law** devenir loi; **to ~ ill** tomber malade
C *v impers* **what has ~ of your brother?** qu'est-ce que ton frère est devenu?

becoming /bɪˈkʌmɪŋ/ *adj* |*behaviour*| convenable; |*garment, hair cut*| seyant

bed /bed/
A *n* **1** lit *m*; **to get into ~** se mettre au lit; **to get out of ~** sortir du lit; **to go to ~** aller au lit; **to go to ~ with** coucher avec; **to put sb to ~** mettre qn au lit; **to be in ~** être au lit, être couché; **to take to one's ~**† s'aliter; **a 40 ~ ward/hotel** une salle/un hôtel de 40 lits; **to give sb a ~ for the night** héberger qn pour une nuit; **2** (of flowers) parterre *m*; (of compost) lit *m*; (of produce) carré *m*; **3** (of sea) fond *m*; (of river) lit *m*; (in geology) couche *f*; **4** **to put a newspaper to ~** boucler un journal
B *vtr* (*p prés etc* **-dd-**) (*also* **~ out**) repiquer |*seedlings*|; dépoter |*plants*|

(Idioms) **to get out of ~ on the wrong side** se lever du pied gauche; **life is not a ~ of roses** tout n'est pas rose dans la vie; **you've made your ~, lie in it** Prov comme on fait son lit, on se couche Prov

(Phrasal verb)
■ **bed down**: ▸ **~ down** se coucher

BEd /ˌbiːˈed/ *n* (*abrév* = **bachelor of education**) diplôme *m* universitaire de pédagogie

bed and board *n* le gîte et le couvert *m*

bed and breakfast, B and B /ˌbed ən ˈbrekfəst/ *n* (type of accommodation) chambre *f* avec petit déjeuner, ≈ chambre *f* d'hôte; **to run a ~** avoir des chambres d'hôte

bed: **~ base** *n* sommier *m*; **~ bath** *n* toilette *f* au lit; **~bug** *n* punaise *f* de lit; **~chamber**† *n* chambre *f* à coucher; **~clothes** *npl* couvertures *fpl*

bedding /ˈbedɪŋ/ *n* (for humans) literie *f*; (for animals) litière *f*

bedeck /bɪˈdek/ *vtr* orner (**with** de)

bedevil /bɪˈdevl/ *vtr* (*p prés etc* **-ll-, -l-** US) (plague) tracasser |*person*|; contrarier |*plans*|; (confuse) embrouiller |*situation*|

bedfellow /ˈbedfeləʊ/ *n* fig **to make strange ~s** former un tandem bizarre

bed: **~head** *n* tête *f* de lit; **~ jacket** *n* liseuse *f*

bedlam /ˈbedləm/ *n* chahut° *m*; **it's ~ in here!** quel cirque° ici!

bed: **~ linen** *n* draps *mpl*; **~ pad** *n* alaise *f*; **~pan** *n* Med bassin *m*

bedraggled /bɪˈdrægld/ *adj* |*person, clothes*| dépenaillé; |*hair*| embroussaillé

bedridden /ˈbedrɪdn/ *adj* alité, cloué au lit

bedrock /ˈbedrɒk/ *n* lit substrat *m* rocheux; fig fondement *m*

bedroom /ˈbedruːm, -rʊm/
A *n* chambre *f* (à coucher); **a two ~ flat** GB *ou* **apartment** un trois pièces
B *noun modifier* **1** |*carpet, furniture, window*| de chambre; **2** |*secrets*| intime; |*scene*| d'amour

bedroom: **~ farce** *n* Theat vaudeville *m*; **~ slipper** *n* pantoufle *f*; **~ suburb** *n* US banlieue-dortoir *f*

Beds *n* GB Post *abrév écrite* = **Bedfordshire**

bed-settee /ˌbedsəˈtiː/ *n* canapé-lit *m*

bedside /ˈbedsaɪd/
A *n* chevet *m*
B *noun modifier* |*book, lamp, table*| de chevet

bedside manner *n* **to have a good ~** être gentil/-ille avec les malades

bed: **~sit**°, **~sitter** *n* GB chambre *f* meublée; **~sock** *n* chausson *m* de nuit; **~sore** *n* escarre *f*; **~spread** *n* dessus *m* de lit; **~stead** *n* cadre *m* de lit

bedtime /ˈbedtaɪm/
A *n* **it's ~** c'est l'heure d'aller se coucher
B *noun modifier* |*story, drink*| avant de s'endormir; **~ reading** lecture *f* pour l'oreiller

bedwetting /ˈbedˌwetɪŋ/ *n* énurésie *f*

bee /biː/ *n* (insect) abeille *f*

(Idioms) **to think one is the ~'s knees**° se prendre pour un crack°; **the birds and the ~s** hum ≈ les cigognes et les choux hum; **to be as busy as a ~** s'activer comme une abeille

beech /biːtʃ/ *n* (tree) hêtre *m*; (*also* **~ wood**) (bois *m* de) hêtre

beef /biːf/ *n* bœuf *m*

(Phrasal verb)
■ **beef up**: ▸ **~ up [sth]** étoffer |*content, resources*|

beef: **~burger** *n* hamburger *m*; **~eater** *n* gardien *m* de la Tour de Londres; **~steak** *n* steak *m* (de bœuf); **~steak tomato** *n* grosse tomate *f*; **~ stew** *n* pot-au-feu *m inv*; **~ tea** *n* bouillon *m* de bœuf

beefy /ˈbiːfɪ/ *adj* **1** |*flavour*| de bœuf; **2** °|*man*| mastoc°

bee: **~hive** *n* (for bees) ruche *f*; (hairstyle) chignon *m* en hauteur; **~keeper** ▸ p. 1181 *n* apiculteur/-trice *m/f*

before

When *before* is used as a preposition in expressions of time or order of sequence or importance, it is translated by *avant*:

before the meeting
= avant la réunion

she left before me
= elle est partie avant moi

For more examples and particular usages, see **A 1, 2, 3** in the entry **before**.

When *before* is used as a preposition meaning *in front of* (when you are talking about physical space) or *in the presence of*, it is translated by *devant*:

before our eyes
= devant nos yeux

he declared before his mother that ...
= il a déclaré devant sa mère que ...

When *before* is used as an adjective after a noun, it is translated by *précédent/-e*:

the time before
= la fois précédente

the one before is translated by *le précédent* or *la précédente*:

no, I'm not talking about that meeting but the one before
= non, je ne parle pas de cette réunion-là mais de la précédente

For particular usages see **B** in the entry **before**.

When *before* is used as an adverb meaning *beforehand*, it is translated by *avant* in statements about the present or future;

I'll try to talk to her before
= j'essaierai de lui en parler avant

you could have told me before
= tu aurais pu me le dire avant

When *before* means *previously* in statements about the past, it is translated by *auparavant*:

I had met her two or three times before
= je l'avais rencontrée deux ou trois fois auparavant

When *before* means *already* it is translated by *déjà*:

I've met her before
= je l'ai déjà rencontrée

you've asked me that question before
= tu m'as déjà posé cette question

In negative sentences *before* is often used in English simply to reinforce the negative. In such cases it is not translated at all:

I'd never eaten snails before
= je n'avais jamais mangé d'escargots

you've never told me that before
= tu ne m'as jamais dit ça

For particular usages see **C** in the entry **before**.

When *before* is used as a conjunction, it is translated by *avant de* + infinitive where the two verbs have the same subject:

before he saw her he recognized her voice
= il a reconnu sa voix avant de la voir

before I cook dinner I'm going to phone my mother
= avant de préparer le dîner je vais appeler ma mère

Where the two verbs have different subjects, the translation is *avant que* + subjunctive:

Tom wants to see her before she leaves
= Tom veut la voir avant qu'elle parte

Some speakers and writers add *ne* before the verb: *Tom veut la voir avant qu'elle ne parte*, but this is simply a slightly precious effect of style and is never obligatory. For particular usages see **D** in the entry **before**.

---

beeline /'biːlaɪn/ *n*:
(Idiom) **to make a ~ for** se diriger tout droit vers

been /biːn, US bɪn/ *pp* ▸ **be**

beep /biːp/
A *n* (of electronic device) bip *m*; (of car) coup *m* de klaxon®; Radio top *m* sonore
B *vtr* appeler [qn] au bip, biper
C *vi* [*device*] faire bip *or* bip-bip; [*car*] klaxonner

beeper /'biːpə(r)/ *n* bip(-bip) *m*

beer /bɪə(r)/
A *n* bière *f*
B *noun modifier* [*barrel, bottle*] de bière

beer: ~ **belly** *n* bedaine *f* (de buveur de bière); ~ **bottle** *n* bouteille *f* de bière; ~ **can** *n* canette *f* de bière; ~ **garden** *n* GB jardin *m* de pub; (in Germany) ≈ guinguette *f*; ~ **mat** *n* dessous *m* de verre; ~**swilling** *adj* péj se soûlant à la bière

bee: ~ **sting** *n* piqûre *f* d'abeille; ~**swax** *n* cire *f* d'abeille

beet /biːt/ *n* betterave *f*

beetle /'biːtl/
A *n* ① Zool (insect) scarabée *m*; (genus) coléoptère *m*; ② ○Aut coccinelle○ *f* (*modèle de Volkswagen*)
B *vi*○ **to ~ in** entrer précipitamment; **to ~ off** filer○

beetroot /'biːtruːt/ *n* GB betterave *f*
(Idiom) **to turn as red as a ~** devenir rouge comme une tomate

befall /bɪ'fɔːl/ (*prét* **befell**, *pp* **befallen**) littér (*s'emploie uniquement à l'infinitif et à la troisième personne*)
A *vtr* arriver à, échoir à
B *vi* advenir

befit /bɪ'fɪt/ *v impers* (*p prés etc* **-tt-**) sout convenir à

befitting /bɪ'fɪtɪŋ/ *adj* sout [*modesty, honesty*] approprié
before /bɪ'fɔː(r)/
A *prep* ① (earlier than) avant; **the day ~ yesterday** avant-hier; **the day ~ the exam** la veille de l'examen; **I was there the week ~ last** j'y étais il y a deux semaines; **six weeks ~ then** six semaines avant *or* auparavant; **~ long it will be winter** ce sera bientôt l'hiver; **not ~ time!** ce n'est pas trop tôt!; ② (in order, sequence) avant; **G comes ~ H in the alphabet** dans l'alphabet le G est avant le H; **the page ~ this one** la page précédente; ③ (in importance, priority) avant; **for him, work comes ~ everything else** pour lui le travail passe avant tout; ④ (this side of) avant; **turn left ~ the crossroads** tournez à gauche avant le carrefour; ⑤ ▸ p. 745 US (in time expressions) **ten ~ six** six heures moins dix; ⑥ (in front of) devant; **she appeared ~ them** elle est apparue devant eux; **~ our very eyes** sous nos propres yeux; **to appear ~ a court** comparaître devant un tribunal; **to bring a bill ~ parliament** présenter un projet de loi au parlement; ⑦ (confronting) face à; **these are the alternatives ~ us** voici les choix qui s'offrent à nous; **the task ~ us** la tâche qui nous attend
B *adj* précédent; **the day ~** la veille; **the week/year ~** la semaine/l'année précédente
C *adv* (at an earlier time) avant; **long ~** bien avant; **two months ~** deux mois auparavant; **have you been to India ~?** est-ce que tu es déjà allé en Inde?; **I've never been there ~** je n'y suis jamais allé; **I've never seen him ~ in my life** c'est la première fois que je le vois
D *conj* ① (in time) **~ I go, I would like to say that** avant de partir, je voudrais dire que; **~ he goes, I must remind him that** avant qu'il parte, il faut que je lui rappelle que; **it was some time ~ she was able to walk again** il lui a fallu un certain temps pour pouvoir marcher de nouveau; **oh, ~ I forget...** avant que j'oublie...; ② (rather than) plutôt que; **he would die ~ betraying that secret** il mourrait plutôt

que de révéler ce secret; **3)** (or else) **get out of here ~ I call the police!** sortez d'ici ou j'appelle la police!; **4)** (as necessary condition) pour que (+ *subj*); **you have to show your ticket ~ they'll let you in** il faut que tu montres ton ticket pour qu'ils te laissent entrer

(Idioms) **~ you could say Jack Robinson** en moins de deux○; **~ you know where you are…** on n'a pas le temps de dire ouf que…

beforehand /bɪ'fɔːhænd/ *adv* **1)** (ahead of time) à l'avance; **be there one hour ~** sois là une heure à l'avance; **let me know ~** prévenez-moi; **2)** (earlier) auparavant, avant; **we had seen them five minutes ~** nous les avions vus cinq minutes auparavant *ou* plus tôt

before tax *adj* [*income*] brut; [*profit*] avant impôts

befriend /bɪ'frend/ *vtr* (look after) prendre [qn] sous son aile; (make friends with) se lier d'amitié avec

befuddle /bɪ'fʌdl/ *vtr* embrouiller [*mind*]

beg /beg/

A *vtr* (*p prés etc* **-gg-**) demander [*food, money, favour*] (**from** à); **to ~ sb for sth** demander qch à qn; **I ~ged his forgiveness** je lui ai demandé de me pardonner; **I ~ your pardon** je vous demande pardon; **'stop, I ~ (of) you!'** 'arrêtez, je vous en supplie!'

B *vi* (*p prés etc* **-gg-**) [*person*] mendier (**from** à); [*dog*] faire le beau; **to ~ for** mendier [*money, food*]; **to ~ for help** demander de l'aide; **to ~ to be forgiven** implorer le pardon

(Idioms) **these apples are going ~ging** personne ne veut de ces pommes; **to ~ the question** laisser de côté le problème de fond

(Phrasal verb)

■ **beg off** s'excuser de ne pas pouvoir venir

began /bɪ'gæn/ *prét* ▸ **begin**

beggar /'begə(r)/

A *n* **1)** (pauper) mendiant/-e *m/f*; **2)** ○GB (man) **you lucky ~!** espèce de veinard○!

B *vtr* ruiner [*person, company*]

(Idiom) **~s can't be choosers** Prov faute de grives on mange des merles Prov

beggarly /'begəlɪ/ *adj* [*existence, meal*] misérable; [*wage*] dérisoire

beggar-my-neighbour /ˌbegəmər'neɪbə(r)/ ▸ p. 881 *n* ≈ bataille f

beg: ~ging bowl *n* sébile *f*; **~ging letter** *n* lettre *f* de sollicitation

begin /bɪ'gɪn/

A **to begin with** *adv phr* (at first) au début, au départ; (firstly) d'abord, premièrement; **I wish I hadn't told her to ~ with** pour commencer, je n'aurais jamais dû lui en parler

B *vtr* (*p prés* **-nn-**; *prét* **began**; *pp* **begun**) **1)** (start) commencer [*journey, list, meeting, job, game, meal*] (**with** par, avec); aller à [*school*]; provoquer [*debate, dispute*]; lancer [*campaign, trend*]; commencer [*tradition*]; déclencher [*war*]; fonder [*dynasty*]; **it's ~ning to rain** il commence à pleuvoir; **to ~ doing** commencer à faire; **to ~ a conversation with** engager la conversation avec; **he began life as a sailor** il a débuté comme marin; **2)** (start to use) entamer [*bottle, packet*]; commencer [*page*]; **3)** (come first in) marquer le commencement de [*series, collection, festival*]

C *vi* (*p prés* **-nn-**; *prét* **began**; *pp* **begun**) gen commencer; [*river*] prendre sa source; **let's ~** commençons; **to ~ with** commencer par; **the week ~ning the 25th** la semaine qui commence le 25; **your problems have only just begun!** tes problèmes ne font que commencer!; **to ~ well/badly** bien/mal commencer; **to ~ again** recommencer

beginner /bɪ'gɪnə(r)/ *n* débutant/-e *m/f*; **~s' class** cours *m* pour débutants

beginning /bɪ'gɪnɪŋ/

A *n* début *m*, commencement *m*; **in** *ou* **at the ~** au départ, au début; **at the ~ of September** au début du mois de septembre, début septembre; **from ~ to end** du début jusqu'à la fin; **to go back to the ~** reprendre au début

B **beginnings** *npl* (origins) (of person, business) débuts *mpl*; (of theory, movement) origines *fpl*

begonia /bɪ'gəʊnɪə/ *n* bégonia *m*

begrudge /bɪ'grʌdʒ/ *vtr* = **grudge B**

beguile /bɪ'gaɪl/ *vtr* **1)** (entice, trick) leurrer; **to be ~d** se laisser leurrer (**with** par); **2)** (charm) captiver

beguiling /bɪ'gaɪlɪŋ/ *adj* captivant

begun /bɪ'gʌn/ *pp* ▸ **begin**

behalf /bɪ'hɑːf, US -'hæf/: **on ~ of** GB, **in ~ of** US *prep phr* [*act, speak, accept award etc*] au nom de, pour; [*phone, write*] de la part de; [*campaign, plead*] en faveur de, pour; [*negotiate*] pour le compte de

behave /bɪ'heɪv/

A *vi* [*person, group, animal*] gen se comporter (**towards** envers); [*machine, device*] se comporter; (in given circumstances) se conduire (**towards** avec, envers); **he ~d badly towards her** il s'est mal conduit envers elle

B *v refl* **to ~ oneself** [*person*] bien se comporter; **~ yourself!** tiens-toi bien!

behaviour GB, **behavior** US /bɪ'heɪvjə(r)/ *n* gen comportement *m* (**towards** envers); (in given set of circumstances) conduite *f*; (of device, machine) fonctionnement *m*; **for good/bad ~** pour bonne/mauvaise conduite

(Idiom) **to be on one's best ~** bien se tenir

behavioural GB, **behavioral** US /bɪ'heɪvjərəl/ *adj* [*change, disorder, problem*] de comportement; [*theory, science*] du comportement

behaviourist GB, **behaviorist** US /bɪ'heɪvjərɪst/ *n, adj* behavioriste (*mf*)

behead /bɪ'hed/ *vtr* décapiter

beheld /bɪ'held/ *prét, pp* ▸ **behold**

behind /bɪ'haɪnd/

⚠ When used as a preposition to talk about the physical position of something, *behind* is translated by *derrière*: *behind the house* = derrière la maison.

behind is sometimes used in verb combinations (*fall behind, lag behind etc*). For translations, consult the appropriate verb entry (**fall, lag** etc).

For adverbial uses and figurative prepositional uses see the entry below.

A ○*n* derrière○ *m*

B *adj* **to be ~ with** avoir du retard dans [*studies, work*]; **to be too far ~** avoir trop de retard

C *adv* [*follow on, trail*] derrière; [*look, glance*] en arrière; **the car ~** la voiture de derrière

D *prep* **1)** derrière; **~ my back** fig derrière mon dos; **he has three years' experience ~ him** il a trois ans d'expérience derrière lui; **I've put all that ~ me now** j'ai oublié tout ça; **the real story ~ the news** la véritable histoire que les médias n'ont pas révélée; **to be ~ the others** [*pupil*] être en retard par rapport aux autres; **2)** fig (motivating) **the reasons ~ his declaration** les raisons qui motivent/motivaient sa déclaration; **who is ~ this proposal?** qui est à l'origine de cette proposition?; **3)** fig (supporting) **to be (solidly) ~ sb** soutenir qn (à fond)

behindhand /bɪ'haɪndhænd/ *adv* **to be** *ou* **get ~ with** être en retard dans [*work, studies*]

behold /bɪ'həʊld/ *vtr* (*prét, pp* **beheld**) littér *ou* hum voir; **it was a wonder to ~** c'était un spectacle merveilleux

beholder /bɪ'həʊldə(r)/ *n*:

(Idiom) **beauty is in the eye of the ~** Prov ≈ ce qu'on aime est toujours beau Prov

beige /beɪʒ/ ▸ p. 752 *n, adj* beige (*m*)

Beijing /beɪ'dʒɪŋ/ ▸ p. 1276 *pr n* Pékin, Bei-jing

being /'biːɪŋ/ *n* **1)** (human) **~** être *m* (humain); **with my whole ~** de tout mon être; **2)** (existence) **to bring sth into ~** faire de qch une réalité; **to come into ~** prendre naissance

Beirut /'beɪruːt, ˌbeɪ'ruːt/ ▸ p. 1276 *pr n* Beyrouth

bejewelled GB, **bejeweled** US /bɪ'dʒuːəld/ *adj* paré de bijoux

belated /bɪ'leɪtɪd/ *adj* tardif/-ive

belch /beltʃ/

A *n* renvoi *m*, rot *m*

B *vi* roter○, avoir un renvoi

(Phrasal verb)

■ **belch out**: ▸ **~ [sth] out, ~ out [sth]** vomir, cracher [*smoke, flames*]

beleaguered /bɪ'liːgəd/ *adj* **1)** [*city, troops*] assiégé; **2)** fig [*person*] débordé; [*company*] menacé

Belfast /ˌbel'fɑːst/ ▸ p. 1276 *pr n* Belfast

belfry /'belfrɪ/ *n* beffroi *m*, clocher *m*

(Idiom) **to have bats in the ~**○ avoir une araignée au plafond○

Belgian /'beldʒən/ ▸ p. 1032
A n Belge mf
B adj belge

Belgium /'beldʒəm/ ▸ p. 774 pr n Belgique f

Belgrade /ˌbel'greid/ ▸ p. 1276 pr n Belgrade

belie /bɪ'laɪ/ vtr contredire [hopes, promises]; tromper sur [appearances, feelings, facts]

belief /bɪ'li:f/ n **1** (conviction, opinion) conviction f (**about** sur, à propos de); **in the ~ that** convaincu que; **contrary to popular ~** contrairement à ce qu'on pense généralement; **2** (confidence) confiance f, foi f; **her ~ in democracy** sa foi or confiance dans la démocratie; **~ in oneself** confiance en soi; **3** Relig (faith) foi f; (article of faith) croyance f

believable /bɪ'li:vəbl/ adj crédible

believe /bɪ'li:v/
A vtr **1** croire [evidence, statement, person]; **~ (you) me!** croyez-moi!; **~ it or not** croyez-le ou pas; **it has to be seen to be ~d** il faut le voir pour le croire; **I can't ~ (that) he did that** je n'arrive pas à croire qu'il ait fait cela; **I can ~ that of her!** ça ne m'étonne pas d'elle!; **don't you ~ it!** n'en croyez rien!; **I don't ~ you!** ce n'est pas vrai!; **I can well ~ it** je suis prêt à le croire; **I don't ~ a word of it!** je n'en crois pas un mot!; **if he's to be ~d** à l'en croire; **2** (think, be of the opinion) croire, estimer; **I ~ (that) she is right, I ~ her to be right** je crois or j'estime qu'elle a raison; **she is ~d to be a spy** on pense que c'est une espionne; **to let sb ~ (that)** laisser croire à qn que; **I ~ so** je crois que oui; **I ~ not** je crois que non
B vi **1** **to ~ in** croire à [promises, discipline, exercise etc]; **to ~ in sb** avoir confiance en qn; **to ~ in doing** croire or estimer qu'il est bon de faire; **2** Relig avoir la foi; **to ~ in God** croire en Dieu

(Idiom) **seeing is believing** il faut le voir pour le croire

believer /bɪ'li:və(r)/ n Relig croyant/-e m/f; gen (in hard work, progress, liberty) adepte mf (**in** de)

belittle /bɪ'lɪtl/ vtr rabaisser [person, achievement]; déprécier [efforts]; **to feel ~d** se sentir déprécié

belittling /bɪ'lɪtlɪŋ/ adj [comment] désobligeant

Belize /be'li:z/ ▸ p. 774 pr n Bélize m

bell /bel/ n **1** (in church) cloche f; (on sheep, goat) clochette f; (on toy, cat) grelot m; (on bicycle) sonnette f; (for servant) clochette f; **door ~** sonnette f; **to ring the ~s** faire sonner les cloches; **2** (warning device) sonnerie f; **3** ○GB (phone call) **to give sb a ~** passer un coup de fil à qn; **4** Naut coup m de cloche

(Idioms) **that name/number rings a ~** ce nom/numéro me dit quelque chose; **to be as sound as a ~** être en parfaite santé; **saved by the ~** sauvé par le gong

bell: **~-bottoms** npl pantalon m à pattes d'éléphant; **~boy** ▸ p. 1181 n US groom m; **~ buoy** n bouée f à cloche

belle /bel/ n belle f, beauté f

bellhop ▸ p. 1181 n US groom m

belligerence /bɪ'lɪdʒərəns/ n gen agressivité f; Pol belligérance f

belligerent /bɪ'lɪdʒərənt/
A n Pol (country) belligérant m
B adj **1** gen agressif/-ive; **2** Pol (at war) belligérant

bell jar n cloche f en verre

bellow /'beləʊ/
A n (of bull) mugissement m; (of person) hurlement m
B vi [bull] mugir (**with** de); [person] hurler, beugler○
C vtr (also ~ out) brailler [command]

bellows /'beləʊz/ npl (for fire, in forge) soufflet m; (of organ) soufflerie f

bell: **~-pull** n (rope) cordon m de sonnette; **~-push** n bouton m de sonnette; **~-ringer** n carillonneur m, sonneur m

bell-ringing n to go ~ aller carillonner

bell: **~-shaped** adj en forme de cloche; **~ tower** n clocher m

belly /'belɪ/ n **1** ○(stomach) ventre m; (paunch) bedaine○ f; **2** (of animal) ventre m; **3** (abdomen) ventre m; **4** **~ of pork** Culin poitrine f de porc

(Phrasal verb)
■ **belly out:** ▸ **~ out** [sail] se gonfler; **~ [sth] out** gonfler

bellyache○ /'belɪeɪk/
A n mal m au ventre
B vi (p prés **-aching**) râler○ (**about** contre)

belly: **~button**○ n nombril m; **~ dancer** n danseuse f du ventre; **~ flop**○ n (in swimming) plat m

bellyful /'belɪfʊl/ n:
(Idiom) **to have a ~ of sth** en avoir sa claque○ de qch

belong /bɪ'lɒŋ, US -'lɔ:ŋ/ vi **1** (be property of) **to ~ to** appartenir à; **the house ~s to his mother** la maison appartient à sa mère or est à sa mère; **2** (be member of) **to ~ to** appartenir à [family, generation, party]; faire partie de [club, society, set]; être inscrit à [library]; **3** (of object) aller; **where do these books ~?** où vont ces livres?; **put it back where it ~s** remets-le à sa place

belongings /bɪ'lɒŋɪŋz, US -'lɔ:ŋ-/ npl affaires fpl; **personal ~** effets mpl personnels

beloved /bɪ'lʌvɪd/
A n littér ou hum bien-aimé/-e m/f
B adj bien-aimé

below /bɪ'ləʊ/

⚠ When below is used as a preposition to talk about the physical position of something, it is most often translated by au-dessous de: the apartment below mine = l'appartement au-dessous du mien; below the knee = au-dessous du genou.
The most notable exceptions are for the expressions below the ground and below the surface, when sous is used: sous le sol, sous la surface.
For other prepositional uses of below and for adverbial uses see the entry below.

A prep **1** (under) en dessous de; **~ the waist** au-dessous de la taille; **~ sea level** au-dessous du niveau de la mer; **~ the castle** en contrebas du château; **the valley ~ them/you etc** la vallée en contrebas; **2** (less than) en dessous de, inférieur à; **~ 10%** en dessous de or inférieur à 10%; **3** (in rank) **those ~ the rank of Major** Mil les militaires qui sont au-dessous du grade de major; **4** (south of) au sud de, au-dessous de; (downstream from) en aval de; **5** (unworthy of) ▸ **beneath A 2**
B adv **100 metres ~** 100 mètres plus bas; **the village ~** le village en contrebas; **the people/cars (down) ~** les gens/voitures en bas; **the apartment ~** l'appartement en dessous; **seen from ~** vu d'en bas; **see ~** (on page) voir ci-dessous

belt /belt/
A n **1** (for garment) also Aut, Aviat ceinture f; **safety ou seat ~** ceinture de sécurité; **2** (area) gen, Meteorol zone f; **mountain/earthquake ~** zone f de montagnes/de séisme; **3** Tech courroie f; **4** Sport (in boxing, judo) ceinture f; **to be a black ~** être ceinture noire; **5** ○(blow) beigne○ f, coup m de poing; **6** (for punishing) lanière f de cuir
B vtr **1** ○(hit) flanquer une beigne à○, gifler [person]; **2** (as punishment) donner une correction à
C vi **to ~ in/out etc**○ entrer/sortir etc à toute vitesse

(Idioms) **to tighten one's ~** se serrer la ceinture; **that remark was a bit below the ~** cette remarque était un coup bas; **she has 15 years' experience under her ~** elle a 15 ans d'expérience à son actif

(Phrasal verbs)
■ **belt off**○ filer à toute vitesse
■ **belt out:** ▸ **~ out [sth]**, **~ [sth] out** chanter [qch] à pleins poumons [song]
■ **belt up** **1** ○GB (shut up) la fermer○, se taire; **~ up!** ferme-la!○; **2** Aut attacher sa ceinture de sécurité

beltway /'beltweɪ/ n US Aut périphérique m

bemoan /bɪ'məʊn/ vtr sout déplorer

bemused /bɪ'mju:zd/ adj perplexe

bench /bentʃ/ n **1** gen, Sport (seat) banc m; **2** GB Pol banc m; **to be on the opposition ~es** siéger dans l'opposition; **3** Jur (also **Bench**) (judges collectively) magistrature f (assise); (judge or judges in one case) Cour f; **4** Tech (workbench) établi m

benchmark /'bentʃmɑ:k/ n **1** gen point m de référence; **2** Fin (price) prix m de référence; **3** Comput test m de performance

bend /bend/
A n gen (in road) tournant m, virage m; (in pipe) coude m; (in river) courbe f; (of elbow, knee) pli m; **there's a ~ in the road** la route fait un virage

B bends ▸ p. 933 *npl* Med (+ *v sg ou pl*) maladie *f* des caissons

C *vtr* (*prét, pp* **bent**) plier [*knee, arm, leg*]; courber, pencher [*head*]; courber [*back*]; faire un coude à [*pipe, bar*]; plier [*wire*]; (by mistake) tordre [*pipe, nail*]; **to ~ the rules** gen contourner la loi (*or* le règlement); (make exception) faire une exception

D *vi* (*prét, pp* **bent**) **1** [*road, path*] tourner; [*river*] (once) s'incurver; (several times) faire des méandres; [*branch*] ployer; [*nail, mudguard*] se tordre; **2** [*person*] se courber, se pencher; **to ~ forward/backwards** se pencher en avant/en arrière

(Idioms) **to drive sb (a)round the ~**○ rendre qn fou/folle; **to ~ over backwards for sb/to do** se mettre en quatre pour qn/pour faire

(Phrasal verbs)
■ **bend back:** ▸ **~ back** [*person*] se pencher en arrière; ▸ **to ~ sth back into shape** redresser qch
■ **bend down, bend over** [*person*] se pencher, se courber

beneath /bɪˈniːθ/

⚠ When used as a preposition (= under), *beneath* is translated by *au-dessous de*: *beneath his feet* = au-dessous de ses pieds. When used as an adverb (the trees beneath), *beneath* is translated by *en dessous*: *the trees beneath* = les arbres en dessous. For particular and figurative usages see below

A *prep* **1** sous; **~ the table** sous la table; **the valley ~ them/you etc** la vallée en contrebas; **2** **it is ~ you to do** c'est indigne de toi de faire

B *adv* en dessous; **the apartment ~** l'appartement en dessous; **the valley ~** la vallée en contrebas

Benedictine /ˌbenɪˈdɪktɪn/
A *n* Relig bénédictin/-e *m/f*
B *adj* bénédictin

benediction /ˌbenɪˈdɪkʃn/ *n* bénédiction *f*

benefactor /ˈbenɪfæktə(r)/ *n* bienfaiteur *m*

beneficial /ˌbenɪˈfɪʃl/ *adj* [*effect, influence*] bénéfique; [*change*] salutaire; [*outcome*] favorable; **to be ~ to the health** être bon/bonne pour la santé

beneficiary /ˌbenɪˈfɪʃərɪ, US -fɪʃɪerɪ/ *n* Jur bénéficiaire *mf*

benefit /ˈbenɪfɪt/
A *n* **1** avantage *m* (from de); **to be of ~ to** profiter à; **to feel the ~ of** ressentir l'effet favorable de [*change, holiday*]; **to give sb the ~ of** faire profiter qn de [*experience, knowledge*]; **the ~s of modern technology** les avantages de la technologie moderne; **to have the ~ of** bénéficier de [*education*]; **to be to sb's ~** être à l'avantage de qn; **it's for your own ~** c'est pour ton propre bien; **'salary £20,000 plus ~s'** 'salaire de 20 000 livres sterling plus avantages sociaux'; **2** (financial aid) allocation *f*; **to be on ~(s)** GB toucher les allocations

B *noun modifier* [*concert, match*] de bienfaisance; [*claim*] d'allocation

C *vtr* (*p prés etc* **-t-**) profiter à [*person*]; être avantageux/-euse pour [*group, nation*]

D *vi* (*p prés etc* **-t-**) profiter; **to ~ from** *ou* **by** tirer profit de; **to ~ from** *ou* **by doing** gagner à faire

(Idiom) **to give sb the ~ of the doubt** accorder à qn le bénéfice du doute

Benelux /ˈbenɪlʌks/
A *n* Bénélux *m*
B *noun modifier* [*countries, organization*] du Bénélux

benevolence /bɪˈnevələns/ *n* (kindness) bienveillance *f*; (generosity) générosité *f*

benevolent /bɪˈnevələnt/ *adj* **1** [*person, smile*] bienveillant (**to, towards** envers); [*dictator*] éclairé; **2** (charitable) [*organization, fund*] de bienfaisance

Bengal /beŋˈgɔːl/ *pr n* Bengale *m*

benighted /bɪˈnaɪtɪd/ *adj* littér arriéré, primitif/-ive

benign /bɪˈnaɪn/ *adj* **1** [*person, smile*] bienveillant; [*conditions*] propice; [*influence*] bénéfique; **2** Med bénin/-igne

Benin /beˈniːn/ ▸ p. 774 *pr n* Bénin *m*

bent /bent/
A *prét, pp* ▸ **bend**
B *n* (flair) dispositions *fpl* (**for** pour); (liking) goût *m*, penchant *m* (**for, towards** pour)

C *adj* **1** [*nail, wire, stick*] tordu; [*old person*] (stooped) courbé; **2** **to be ~ on doing sth** vouloir à tout prix faire qch

benzene /ˈbenziːn/ *n* benzène *m*

benzine /ˈbenziːn/ *n* benzine *f*

bequeath /bɪˈkwiːð/ *vtr* Jur, fig léguer (**to** à)

bequest /bɪˈkwest/ *n* Jur, fig legs *m* (**to** à)

berate /bɪˈreɪt/ *vtr* sout admonester fml, réprimander (**for** pour)

bereaved /bɪˈriːvd/
A *n* **the ~** (+ *v pl*) la famille endeuillée
B *adj* [*person, family*] endeuillé, en deuil

bereavement /bɪˈriːvmənt/ *n* (state, event, period of mourning) deuil *m*; (sorrow) chagrin *m*

bereft /bɪˈreft/ *adj* sout **1** **~ of** privé de [*love, friendship*]; dépourvu de [*contents, ideas*]; **2** (forlorn) abandonné

beret /ˈbereɪ, US bəˈreɪ/ *n* béret *m*

bergamot /ˈbɜːgəmɒt/ *n* (fruit) bergamote *f*; (tree) bergamotier *m*; (herb) monarde *f*

Berks *n* GB Post abrév écrite = **Berkshire**

Berlin /bɜːˈlɪn/ ▸ p. 1276 *pr n* Berlin

Berliner /bɜːˈlɪnə(r)/ *n* Berlinois/-e *m/f*

Bermuda /bəˈmjuːdə/ ▸ p. 774 *pr n* les Bermudes *fpl*

Bermudas /bəˈmjuːdəz/, **Bermuda shorts** *npl* bermuda *m*

berry /ˈberɪ/ *n* baie *f*

(Idiom) **to be as brown as a ~** être tout bronzé

berserk /bəˈsɜːk/ *adj* fou furieux/folle furieuse; **to go ~** être pris/prise de folie furieuse

berth /bɜːθ/
A *n* **1** Naut, Rail (for sleeping) couchette *f*; **2** Naut (for ship) mouillage *m*; **at ~** au mouillage
B *vtr* faire mouiller; **to be ~ed at** être mouillé à

(Idiom) **to give sb/sth a wide ~**○ éviter qn/qch

beseech /bɪˈsiːtʃ/ *vtr* (*prét, pp* **beseeched** *ou* **besought**) sout implorer [*forgiveness*]; solliciter [*favour*]; **to ~ sb to do** supplier qn de faire

beseeching /bɪˈsiːtʃɪŋ/ *adj* sout implorant, suppliant

beset /bɪˈset/ *vtr* (*prét, pp* **beset**) (*gén au passif*) assaillir (**with** de); Mil assiéger; **a country ~ by strikes** un pays en proie aux grèves

beside /bɪˈsaɪd/ *prep* **1** (next to) à côté de; **~ you** à côté de toi; **~ the sea** au bord de la mer; **2** (in comparison with) par rapport à; **my problems seem rather minor ~ yours** mes problèmes semblent assez insignifiants par rapport aux tiens *or* à côté des tiens

(Idiom) **to be ~ oneself (with anger)** être hors de soi; **~ oneself (with excitement)** être surexcité; **to be ~ oneself with happiness** être fou/folle de joie

besides /bɪˈsaɪdz/
A *adv* **1** (moreover) d'ailleurs; **2** (in addition) en plus, aussi; **she has a car and a motorbike ~** elle a une voiture et en plus *or* aussi une moto; **and much else ~** et bien d'autres choses encore

B *prep* (apart from) en plus de, à part; **~ John they're all teachers** à part John ils sont tous professeurs; **~ being an artist, she's also a poet** en plus d'être une artiste, elle est aussi poète; **everyone ~ me/you** tout le monde sauf moi/toi

besiege /bɪˈsiːdʒ/ *vtr* Mil assiéger; fig assaillir

besotted /bɪˈsɒtɪd/ *adj* follement épris (**with** de)

bespatter /bɪˈspætə(r)/ *vtr* éclabousser (**with** de)

bespectacled /bɪˈspektəkld/ *adj* à lunettes

bespoke /bɪˈspəʊk/ *adj* GB [*suit, jacket*] (fait) sur mesure; [*tailor*] à façon

best /best/
A *n* **1** **the ~** le/la meilleur/-e *m/f*; **it's the ~ of his novels** c'est son meilleur roman; **we've had the ~ of the day** le beau temps est fini pour aujourd'hui; **to sound the ~** avoir le meilleur son, sonner le mieux; **the ~ of its kind** le meilleur du genre; **it's not her ~** (of book, play) ce n'est pas le/la meilleur/-e qu'elle ait écrit/-e; **only the ~ is good enough for me/my son** je veux ce qu'il y a de mieux pour moi/mon fils; **she is the ~ at physics/at tennis** c'est la meilleure en physique/au tennis; **who's the ~ at drawing?** qui dessine le mieux?; **it's the ~ I've got** c'est le meilleur que j'aie; **it's for the ~** (recommending course of action) c'est la meilleure solution; (of something done) c'est tant

b

mieux; **it was not in the ～ of taste** ce n'était pas du meilleur goût; **the ～ of friends** les meilleurs amis du monde; **2** (most favourable) **the ～ we can hope for** le mieux qu'on puisse espérer; **at ～** au mieux; **he's a difficult man at the ～ of times** déjà en temps ordinaire il est difficile à vivre; **to make the ～ of sth** s'accommoder de qch; **to get the ～ of** avoir la part du lion dans [*deal, bargain*]; gagner dans [*arrangement*]; **3** (peak, apogee) **the city is at its ～ in autumn** c'est en automne que la ville est la plus belle; **Balzac at his ～** c'est Balzac dans ce qu'il a fait de meilleur; **to be at one's ～** être au mieux de sa forme; **4** (greatest personal effort) **to do one's ～ to do** faire de son mieux *or* faire (tout) son possible pour faire; **is that the ～ you can do?** c'est le mieux que tu puisses faire?; **to get the ～ out of** obtenir le meilleur de [*pupil, worker*]; **bring out the ～ in sb** [*crisis, suffering*] inciter qn à donner le meilleur de lui-même; **5** (good wishes) **all the ～!** (good luck) bonne chance!; (cheers) à ta santé!; **all the ～, Ellie** (in letter) amitiés, Ellie; **wishing you all the ～ on your retirement** meilleurs vœux de bonheur pour votre retraite

B *adj* (*superl of* **good**) **1** (most excellent) meilleur; **the ～ idea she's had all day** la meilleure idée qu'elle ait eue de la journée; **the ～ thing about sth/about doing** ce qu'il y a de mieux dans qch/lorsqu'on fait; **to taste ～** avoir le meilleur goût; **she looks ～ in black** c'est en noir qu'elle est le mieux; **she speaks the ～ French** c'est elle qui parle le mieux français; **my ～ dress** ma plus belle robe; **'～ before end May'** 'à consommer de préférence avant fin mai'; **2** (most competent) [*teacher, poet, actor*] meilleur; **who is the ～ swimmer?** qui nage le mieux?; **to be ～ at** être le/la meilleur/-e en [*subject*]; être le/la meilleur/-e à [*instrument, game, sport*]; **may the ～ man win!** que le meilleur gagne!; **3** (most suitable) [*tool, way, time, idea*] meilleur; **the ～ person for the job** la personne qui convient le mieux pour ce travail; **the ～ thing to do** la meilleure chose à faire; **the ～ thing would be to do, it would be ～ to do** le mieux serait de faire

C *adv* (*superl of* **well**) le mieux; **to behave/fit ～** se comporter/aller le mieux; **the ～ organized person** la personne la mieux organisée; **the ～ loved woman** la femme la plus aimée; **to like sth ～** aimer qch le mieux *or* le plus; **～ of all** mieux que tout; **to do ～** réussir le mieux; **such advice ～ ignored** il vaut mieux ignorer de tels conseils; **you know ～** c'est toi le meilleur juge

D *vtr* littér (in argument) avoir le dessus sur [*person*]; (in struggle) vaincre [*opponent*]

(Idiom) **it happens to the ～ of us** ça arrive à tout le monde

best friend *n* meilleur/-e ami/-e *m/f*

bestial /'bestɪəl, US 'bestʃəl/ *adj* lit, fig bestial

bestiality /ˌbestɪ'ælətɪ, US ˌbestʃɪ-/ *n* lit, fig bestialité *f*

best man *n* témoin *m* (de mariage)

bestow /bɪ'stəʊ/ *vtr* sout gen accorder (**on** à); conférer [*title*] (**on** à); octroyer [*gift*] (**on** à)

bestseller /ˌbest'selə(r)/ *n* (book) bestseller *m*, livre *m* à succès; (writer) auteur *m* de bestsellers, auteur à succès

best-selling /ˌbest'selɪŋ/ *adj* [*product*] le/la plus vendu/-e; **the ～ novelist of 1992** le romancier qui s'est vendu le plus en 1992

bet /bet/

A *n* **1** (gamble) pari *m*; **to place** *ou* **put** *ou* **lay a ～ on** parier *or* faire un pari sur [*horse, dog*]; miser sur [*number, colour*]; **to make a ～ that** faire le pari que; **'place your ～s!'** (in roulette) 'faites vos jeux!'; **a good** *ou* **safe ～** fig une valeur sûre; **2** (guess) **my ～ is that** moi je pense que; **3** (stake) gen pari *m*; (in casino) mise *f*

B *vtr* (*p prés etc* **-tt-**; *prét, pp* **bet** *ou* **～ted**) gen parier (**on** sur); (in gambling) parier, miser; **I ～ you 100 dollars (that) I win** je te parie 100 dollars que je gagne; **～ you can/can't!** (between children) chiche!

C *vi* (*p prés etc* **-tt-**; *prét, pp* **bet** *ou* **～ted**) gen parier (**on** sur) gen parier; (in casino) miser; **to ～ on a horse/race** parier sur un cheval/dans une course; **to ～ on sth happening** parier que qch va se produire; **something will go wrong, you can ～ on it** il y a forcément quelque chose qui va aller de travers, tu peux en être sûr; **I wouldn't ～ on it!** je n'y compterais pas trop!; **you ～!** tu parles!, et comment!

beta /'bi:tə, US 'beɪtə/ *n* béta *m*; **～blocker** bétabloquant *m*

betray /bɪ'treɪ/ *vtr* gen trahir; tromper [*lover*]; manquer à [*promise*]; fig révéler [*interest, nature*]; trahir [*curiosity, presence*]

betrayal /bɪ'treɪəl/ *n* gen trahison *f*; (of secret, plan) révélation *f*; **～ of trust** abus *m* de confiance

betrothal‡ /bɪ'trəʊðl/ *n* fiançailles *fpl* (**to** avec)

betrothed‡ /bɪ'trəʊðd/
A *n* (*pl* **～**) fiancé/-e *m/f*
B *adj* **to be ～** être fiancé

better /'betə(r)/

⚠ When *better* is used as an adjective it is translated by *meilleur* or *mieux* depending on the context (see below, and note that *meilleur* is the comparative form of *bon*, *mieux* the comparative form of *bien*). The translation of the construction *to be better than* varies depending on whether *bon* or *bien* works originally with the noun collocate: *their wine is better than our wine* = leur vin est meilleur que le nôtre; *her new apartment is better than her old one* = son nouvel appartement est mieux que l'ancien; *his new film is better than his last one* = son nouveau film est mieux *or* meilleur que le précédent (both *bon* and *bien* work with the collocate in this last example). Other constructions may be translated as follows: *this is a better bag/car* = ce sac/cette voiture est mieux; *it is better to do* = il vaut mieux faire *or* il est mieux de faire.

As an adverb, *better* can almost always be translated by *mieux*. For more examples and particular usages, see the entry below.

A *n* **1** **the ～ of the two** le/la meilleur/-e *or* le/la mieux des deux; **2** (more desirable state of affairs) **to deserve/hope for ～** mériter/espérer mieux; **so much the ～, all the ～** tant mieux; **to change for the ～** s'améliorer; **3** (superior person) **one's ～s** ses supérieurs *mfpl*

B *adj* (*compar de* **good**) meilleur; **to get ～** gen s'améliorer; [*ill person*] aller mieux; **the weather is no ～** le temps n'est pas meilleur *or* ne s'est pas amélioré; **things are getting ～** ça va mieux; **to taste ～** être meilleur, avoir un meilleur goût; **she looks ～ in red** elle est mieux en rouge; **that's ～!** voilà qui est mieux!; **to be ～** [*patient, cold, headache*] aller mieux; **to feel all the ～ for** se sentir mieux après [*rest, meal*]; **if it makes you feel any ～** (less worried) si ça peut te rassurer; (less sad) si ça peut te consoler; **to feel ～ about doing** (less nervous) se sentir à même de faire; (less worried, guilty) avoir moins de scrupules à faire; **they sent him to a ～ school** ils l'ont mis dans une meilleure école; **I sold the car and bought a ～ one** j'ai vendu la voiture et j'en ai acheté une mieux; **to be no ～ than a thief** être un voleur ni plus ni moins; **to be a ～ swimmer than sb** nager mieux que qn; **to be ～ at** être meilleur en [*subject, sport*]; **he's no ～ at driving than she is** il ne conduit pas mieux qu'elle; **to be ～ than nothing** être mieux que rien; **the bigger/sooner the ～** le plus grand/vite possible; **the less said about that the ～** mieux vaut ne pas parler de ça; **who ～ to play the part?** qui mieux pourrait jouer le rôle?; **fish is ～ for you than meat** le poisson est meilleur pour la santé que la viande

C *adv* (*compar de* **well**) mieux; **to fit/behave ～ than** aller/se comporter mieux que; **made/organized than** mieux fait/organisé que; **to think ～ of sb** avoir une meilleure opinion de qn; **～ behaved/educated** plus sage/cultivé; **to do ～** (in career, life) réussir mieux; (in exam, essay) faire mieux; (in health) aller mieux; **the ～ to see/hear** pour mieux voir/entendre; **it couldn't have been ～ timed** ça n'aurait pas pu mieux tomber; **the money would be ～ spent on a holiday** il vaudrait mieux garder cet argent pour les vacances; **you had ～ do, you'd ～ do** (advising) tu ferais mieux de faire; (warning) tu as intérêt à faire; **I'd ～ go** je ferais mieux de m'en aller; **'will she come?'—'she'd ～!'** 'est-ce qu'elle viendra?'—'elle a intérêt!'; **～ still,...** ou mieux,...

D *vtr* améliorer [*one's performance, achievement*]; faire mieux que [*rival's performance, achievement*]

(Idioms) **for ～ (or) for worse** gen advienne que pourra; (in wedding vow) pour le meilleur et pour le pire; **to get the ～ of** [*person*] triompher de [*enemy, problem*]; **his curiosity got the ～ of him** sa curiosité a pris le dessus; **to feel ～ encore mieux** (**than** que); **to think ～ of it** changer d'avis

better off /ˌbetər'ɒf/
A *n* **the better-off** (+ *v pl*) les riches *mpl*

B *adj* **1)** (more wealthy) plus riche (**than** que); **our better-off neighbours** nos voisins plus riches; **2)** (in better situation) mieux; **you'd be ~ in hospital** tu serais mieux à l'hôpital; **you're ~ without him** tu es mieux sans lui

betting /'betɪŋ/ *n* (activity) paris *mpl*; (odds) côte *f*; **what's the ~ that...?** quelles sont les chances que...? (+ *subj*)

betting shop *n* GB bureau *m* de PMU

between /bɪ'twiːn/

⚠ When *between* is used as a preposition expressing physical location (*between the lines*), time (*between 8 am and 11 am*), position in a range (*between 30 and 40 kilometres*), relationship (*link between*, *difference between*) it is translated by *entre*. For particular usages, see the entry below

A *prep* **1)** (in time, space etc) entre; **the wall ~ the two gardens** le mur entre les deux jardins; **flights ~ London and Paris** les vols entre Londres et Paris; **~ the ages of 12 and 18** entre l'âge de 12 ans et l'âge de 18 ans *or* entre 12 et 18 ans; **~ now and next year** d'ici à l'année prochaine; **it costs ~ £10 and £20** cela coûte entre dix et vingt livres sterling; **it's ~ 50 and 60 kilometres away** c'est à environ 50 ou 60 kilomètres d'ici; **nothing now stands ~ us and success** rien ne peut plus faire obstacle à notre réussite maintenant; **we mustn't allow this to come ~ us** il ne faut pas que cela crée des problèmes entre nous; **2)** (together, in combination) **the couples have seven children ~ them** à eux tous, les couples ont sept enfants; **they drank the whole bottle ~ (the two of) them** ils ont bu toute la bouteille à eux deux; **~ them, they collected £200** en tout, ils ont réuni 200 livres sterling

B *adv* (*also* **in ~**) (in space) au milieu, entre les deux; (in time) dans l'intervalle, entre les deux; **the two main roads and the streets (in) ~** les deux rues principales et les petites rues situées entre elles *or* et les petites rues au milieu

(Idioms) **~ ourselves, ~ you and me (and the gatepost)** entre nous

betweentimes /bɪ'twiːntaɪmz/, **betweenwhiles** /bɪ'twiːnwaɪlz US -hwaɪlz/ *adv* entre-temps

betwixt /bɪ'twɪkst/ *adv* **~ and between** entre les deux

bevel /'bevl/
A *n* (edge) biseau *m*; (larger) surface *f* oblique; (tool) fausse équerre *f*
B *vtr* tailler [qch] en biseau [*mirror, edge*]

beverage /'bevərɪdʒ/ *n* boisson *f*, breuvage *m*

bevy /'bevɪ/ *n* (of quails) volée *f*; fig (of people) troupeau *m*

beware /bɪ'weə(r)/
A *excl* prenez garde!, attention!
B *vi* **1)** se méfier (**of** de); **to ~ of doing** faire attention à ne pas faire, se garder de faire fml; **2)** (on sign) **'~ of pickpockets'** 'attention aux pickpockets'; **'~ of the dog'** 'attention chien méchant'

bewilder /bɪ'wɪldə(r)/ *vtr* déconcerter

bewildered /bɪ'wɪldəd/ *adj* [*person*] déconcerté (**at, by** par); [*look, curiosity*] perplexe

bewildering /bɪ'wɪldərɪŋ/ *adj* déconcertant

bewilderment /bɪ'wɪldəmənt/ *n* stupéfaction *f*

bewitch /bɪ'wɪtʃ/ *vtr* lit, fig ensorceler

beyond /bɪ'jɒnd/

⚠ *Beyond* is often used with a noun to produce expressions like *beyond doubt*, *beyond a joke*, *beyond the bounds of* etc. For translations of these and similar expressions where *beyond* means *outside the range of*, consult the appropriate noun entry (**doubt, joke, bound** etc). See also **A 3** below

A *prep* **1)** (in space, time) au-delà de; **~ the city walls** au-delà des murs de la ville; **just ~ the tower** juste après la tour; **well ~ midnight** bien au-delà de minuit; **~ the age of 10** au-delà de l'âge de 10 ans; **to go ~ a deadline** dépasser un délai; **2)** (outside the range of) **~ one's means** au-dessus de ses moyens; **~ all hope** au-delà de toute espérance; **~ one's control** hors de son contrôle; **he is ~ help** on ne peut rien faire pour lui; **to be wise ~ one's years** être très mûr pour son âge; **to be ~ sb's ability** [*task, activity*] être au-dessus des capacités de qn; **to be ~ sb** [*activity, task, subject*] dépasser qn; **it's ~ me how she manages** je ne sais pas comment elle s'en sort–ça me dépasse; **3)** (other than) en dehors de, à part; **we know little about it ~ the fact that** nous savons très peu de choses là-dessus en dehors du fait que *or* à part que

B *adv* **1)** (in space) **in the room ~** dans la pièce d'après; **~ there was a garden** plus loin il y avait un jardin; **as far as London and ~** jusqu'à Londres et au-delà; **2)** (in time) au-delà; **up to the year 2000 and ~** jusqu'à l'an 2000 et au-delà

C *conj* à part (+ *infinitive*); **there was little I could do ~ telling him that** je ne pouvais pas faire grand-chose à part lui dire que

(Idiom) **to be in the back of ~** être au bout du monde

bezique /bɪ'ziːk/ ▸ p. 881 *n* bésigue *m*

B film, B movie *n* film *m* de série B

BGC *n: abrév* ▸ **Bank Giro Credit**

Bhutan /buː'tɑːn/ ▸ p. 774 *pr n* Bhoutan *m*

bias /'baɪəs/
A *n* (*pl* **-es**) **1)** (prejudice) parti *m* pris; **to display ~** faire preuve de parti pris; **political ~** parti pris politique; **2)** (tendency) tendance *f* (**in favour of, towards** pour); **an American ~** une tendance pro-américaine; **a female ~** un préjugé favorable envers les femmes; **3)** (in sewing) biais *m*
B *vtr* (*p prés etc* **-s-** *ou* **-ss-**) influer sur [*person, decision, result*]; **to ~ sb against/in favour of** prévenir qn contre/en faveur de

bias binding, bias tape US *n* (in sewing) (ruban *m* de) biais *m*

biased, biassed /'baɪəst/ *adj* [*decision, opinion, person*] partial; [*system, report*] manquant d'objectivité (*after n*); **to be ~** [*person*] avoir des partis pris; **to be ~ against/in favour of** avoir un préjugé défavorable/favorable envers

bib /bɪb/ *n* **1)** (baby's) bavoir *m*; **2)** (of apron, dungarees) bavette *f*

Bible /'baɪbl/ *n* Bible *f*; **it's his ~** fig c'est sa bible

Bible Belt *n: région du sud des États-Unis caractérisée par son fondamentalisme*

biblical /'bɪblɪkl/ *adj* biblique

bibliographic(al) /ˌbɪblɪə'græfɪk(l)/ *adj* bibliographique

bibliography /ˌbɪblɪ'ɒgrəfɪ/ *n* bibliographie *f*

bicarbonate of soda *n* bicarbonate *m* de soude

bicentenary /ˌbaɪsen'tiːnərɪ, US -'sentənərɪ/, **bicentennial** /ˌbaɪsen'tenɪəl/
A *n* bicentenaire *m*
B *noun modifier* [*celebration, year*] du bicentenaire

biceps /'baɪseps/ *n* (*pl* **~**) biceps *m*

bicker /'bɪkə(r)/ *vi* se chamailler (**about** au sujet de)

bickering /'bɪkərɪŋ/ *n* ⊄ chamailleries *fpl*

bicycle /'baɪsɪkl/
A *n* bicyclette *f*, vélo○ *m*; **on a/by ~** à bicyclette; **to ride a ~** faire de la bicyclette
B *noun modifier* [*pump*] à bicyclette; [*bell, chain, lamp*] de bicyclette; [*hire, repair*] de bicyclette; [*race*] cycliste
C *vi* aller à bicyclette

bicycle: ~ clip *n* pince *f* à vélo; **~ lane** *n* piste *f* cyclable; **~ rack** *n* (in yard) parc *m* à bicyclettes; (on car) galerie *f*

bid /bɪd/
A *n* **1)** (at auction) enchère *f* (**for** sur; **of** de); **the opening ~** la première enchère; **to raise one's ~ by £200** surenchérir de 200 livres sterling; **2)** (for contract) soumission *f* (**for** pour; **of** de); (for company) offre *f* (**for** pour; **of** de); **3)** (attempt) tentative *f* (**to do** pour faire); **escape/suicide ~** tentative *f* d'évasion/de suicide; **to make a ~ for power** tenter d'accéder au pouvoir; **4)** (in bridge) (first) annonce *f*; (subsequent) enchère *f*; **it's your ~** c'est à toi de déclarer
B *vtr* (*p prés* **-dd-**; *prét* **bade** *ou* **bid**; *pp* **bidden** *ou* **bid**) **1)** Comm, Fin offrir [*money*] (**for** pour); **what am I bid for this painting?** à combien est-ce que j'estime ce tableau?; **2)** (say) **to ~ sb good morning** dire bonjour à qn; **to ~ sb farewell** faire ses adieux à qn; **to ~ sb welcome** souhaiter la bienvenue à qn; **3)** (in bridge) annoncer
C *vi* (*p prés* **-dd-**; *prét* **bade** *ou* **bid**; *pp* **bidden** *ou* **bid**) **1)** Comm, Fin (at auction) mettre une enchère, enchérir (**for** sur); (for contract) soumissionner (**for** pour); (for company) faire une offre (**for** pour); **to ~ against sb** (at auction) renchérir sur qn; **2)** (in bridge) faire une annonce, parler

bidden /'bɪdn/ *pp* ▸ **bid**

b

bidder /'bɪdə(r)/ n **1** (at auction) enchérisseur/-euse m/f (**for** pour); **to go to the highest ~** être adjugé au plus offrant; **successful ~** adjudicataire mf; **2** Comm (for contract) soumissionnaire m (**for** pour)

bidding /'bɪdɪŋ/ n **1** ¢ (at auction) enchères fpl; **the ~ closed at £50,000** l'adjudication s'est faite à 50 000 livres sterling; **2** (command) **he did my ~** il a fait ce que je lui ai dit; **3** ¢ (in bridge) annonces fpl

bide‡ /baɪd/ vi:
(Idiom) **to ~ one's time** attendre le bon moment

bidet /'biːdeɪ, US biː'deɪ/ n bidet m

biennial /baɪ'enɪəl/ adj [plant] bisannuel/-elle; [event] biennal

bier /bɪə(r)/ n (coffin) bière f; (stand) catafalque m

bifocals /baɪ'fəʊklz/ npl verres mpl à double foyer

big /bɪg/ adj **1** (tall) grand (before n); (strong) grand et fort, costaud○; euph (heavy) fort; **to get ~(ger)** (taller) grandir; (fatter) grossir; (in pregnancy) s'arrondir; **2** (in size) [bed, room, building, garden, lake, town] grand (before n); [animal, car, boat, parcel, box] gros/grosse (before n), grand (before n); **a ~ book** (thick) un gros livre; (large-format) un grand livre; **to have ~ hands** avoir de grandes mains; **3** (in age) grand (before n); **his ~ brother** son grand frère, son frère aîné; **4** (in extent) [family, crowd, class, party] grand (before n); [collection, organization, company] gros/grosse (before n), grand (before n); [meal] copieux/-ieuse; **to be a ~ eater** être un gros mangeur; **5** (important) [question, problem, decision, change, moment, event] grand (before n); **it makes a ~ difference** ça fait une grande différence; **a ~ mistake** une grave erreur; **I think we're on to something ~**○ je sens qu'on est sur un gros coup○; **6** (emphatic) **you ~ baby!** espèce de bébé!; **~ bully!** espèce de grande brute!; **to be ~ in the music business**○ être très connu dans le monde de la musique; **to be in ~ trouble** être dans le pétrin○; **he gave me a ~ smile** il m'a fait un grand sourire; **the ~ moment** le grand moment; **he fell for her in a ~ way** il est tombé follement amoureux d'elle; **7** ○US (enthusiastic) **to be ~ on** être fanatique or fana○ de [activity]; **8** (generous) [person] généreux/-euse; **to have a ~ heart** être très généreux; **9** gen, Pol **the Big Four/Five** les Quatre/Cinq Grands
(Idioms) **to be** ou **go over ~**○ faire fureur, faire un tabac (**in** à, en); **to have a ~ head** péj avoir la grosse tête○; **to have a ~ mouth** avoir la langue trop longue○; **why can't you keep your ~ mouth shut**○? tu n'aurais pas pu la fermer○?; **to have ~ ideas, think ~**○ voir grand○; **what's the ~ idea?** qu'est-ce qui te prend?; **to make it ~**○ avoir beaucoup de succès

bigamist /'bɪgəmɪst/ n bigame mf

bigamous /'bɪgəməs/ adj [person, marriage] bigame

bigamy /'bɪgəmɪ/ n bigamie f

big bang n (in astronomy) big bang m

big business n **1** ¢ les grandes entreprises fpl; **2** **to be ~** rapporter gros

big: **~ cat** n grand félin m; **~ dipper** n GB (at fair) montagnes fpl russes; **Big Dipper** n US (stars) Grande Ourse f, Grand Chariot m

big fish○ n:
(Idiom) **to be a ~ in a small pond** GB ou **sea** US briller dans un petit groupe

big: **~ game** n gros gibier m; **~ game hunting** n chasse f au gros gibier; **~head**○ n péj crâneur/-euse m/f; **~headed**○ adj péj crâneur/-euse, prétentieux/-ieuse; **~-hearted** adj généreux/-euse

bigmouth○ /'bɪgmaʊθ/ n péj **1** (indiscreet person) **he's such a ~**○! il a la langue trop longue!; **2** (loudmouth) grande gueule○ f pej

big name n (in music, art) grand nom m; (in film, sport) star f; **to be a ~** être connu (**in** dans le monde de)

big noise○ n gros bonnet○ m, huile○ f pej

bigot /'bɪgət/ n **he's a ~** il est sectaire or intolérant

bigoted /'bɪgətɪd/ adj intolérant, sectaire

bigotry /'bɪgətrɪ/ n intolérance f, sectarisme m

big: **~ screen** n grand écran m; **~ shot**○ n gros bonnet○ m; **Big Smoke**○ n GB hum Londres

big time○ /'bɪgtaɪm/
A n **to make** ou **hit the ~**○ percer, réussir
B big-time noun modifier [crook] de grande envergure; **~ gambler** flambeur○ m

big: **~ toe** n gros orteil m; **~ top** n (tent) grand chapiteau m; fig (circus) cirque m; **~wig**○ n péj grosse légume○ f, huile○ f pej

bike /baɪk/ n (cycle) vélo m; (motorbike) moto f; **to ride a ~** (cycle) faire du vélo

biker○ /'baɪkə(r)/ n motard○ m; **~('s) jacket** veste f de moto

bikini /bɪ'kiːnɪ/ n bikini® m

bilateral /ˌbaɪ'lætərəl/ adj bilatéral

bilberry /'bɪlbrɪ, US -berɪ/ n (fruit, bush) myrtille f

bile /baɪl/ n lit bile f; fig fiel m

bilge /bɪldʒ/ n **1** Naut bouchain m; **2** (nonsense)○† inepties fpl

bilingual /ˌbaɪ'lɪŋgwəl/ adj bilingue

bilingualism /ˌbaɪ'lɪŋgwəlɪzəm/ n bilinguisme m

bilious /'bɪlɪəs/ adj Med bilieux; fig [colour] repoussant; **~ attack** crise f de foie

bill /bɪl/
A n **1** Comm (in restaurant) addition f; (for maintenance, electricity etc) facture f; (from hotel, doctor, dentist) note f; **gas/telephone ~** facture f de gaz/de téléphone; **a ~ for £10** une note or facture de 10 livres; **2** Jur, Pol (law) (also **Bill**) projet m de loi; **3** (poster) affiche f; **to top the ~** Theat être en tête d'affiche; **'stick no ~s'** 'défense d'afficher'; **4** US (banknote) billet m (de banque); **5** Zool (beak) bec m
B vtr **1** gen, Comm faire une facture à [person, company]; **to ~ sb for sth** facturer qch à qn; **2** gen, Theat (advertise) **to be ~ed as...** [event, meeting] être annoncé comme étant...; **he is ~ed to appear as Othello** il est à l'affiche dans le rôle d'Othello
(Idioms) **to fit** ou **fill the ~** faire l'affaire; **to give sb/sth a clean ~ of health** lit trouver qn/qch en parfait état de santé; fig blanchir qn/qch

billboard /'bɪlbɔːd/ n panneau m d'affichage

billet /'bɪlɪt/
A n Mil cantonnement m
B vtr cantonner [soldier, refugee] (**on, with** chez)

bill: **~fold** n US portefeuille m; **~ hook** n serpe f

billiard /'bɪlɪəd/ ▸ p. 881
A **billiards** n (+ v sg) billard m
B noun modifier [ball, cue, table] de billard

billing /'bɪlɪŋ/ n **1** **to get top ~** Theat tenir le haut de l'affiche; **2** Comm facturation f

billion /'bɪlɪən/ ▸ p. 1044
A n (a thousand million) milliard m; GB (a million million) billion m; **~s of** des tonnes○ fpl of○
B adj **a ~ people** un milliard de personnes

billionaire /ˌbɪlɪə'neə(r)/ n milliardaire mf

bill: **~ of exchange**, BE n Comm, Fin lettre f de change; **~ of fare** n menu m; **~ of rights** n gen, Pol déclaration f des droits (d'un peuple); **~ of sale** n acte m de vente

billow /'bɪləʊ/
A n (of smoke, steam) tourbillons mpl
B vi [clouds, smoke] s'élever en tourbillons
(Phrasal verb)
■ **billow out** [skirt, sail] se gonfler; [steam] s'élever

billposter /'bɪlpəʊstə(r)/, **billsticker** /'bɪlstɪkə(r)/ ▸ p. 1181 n colleur m d'affiches

billy /'bɪlɪ/ n **1** Austral, GB (also **~can**) gamelle f; **2** US (truncheon) matraque f

billy goat n bouc m

bimbo○ /'bɪmbəʊ/ n péj ravissante idiote f

bin /bɪn/ n **1** GB (for rubbish) poubelle f; **2** (for storage) casier m; (for wine) casier m (à bouteilles)

binary /'baɪnərɪ/ adj (all contexts) binaire

bind /baɪnd/
A ○ n corvée f; **what a ~!** quelle corvée!
B vtr (prét, pp **bound**) **1** (tie up) attacher [person, hands, feet] (**to** à); panser [wound]; **2** **to ~ sb to do** [law, oath] imposer à qn de faire; **to be bound by** être tenu par [law, oath]; **3** (unite) (also **~ together**) unir [people, community]; **4** (in sewing) poser un biais sur; **5** (in bookbinding) relier [book]; **6** Culin lier (**with** avec)
C vi (prét, pp **bound**) Culin [mixture] lier
(Idiom) **to be in a ~**○ être dans le pétrin○

(Phrasal verbs)

■ **bind over**: ▶ ~ **[sb] over** Jur relâcher [qn] sous condition

■ **bind up**: ▶ ~ **up [sth]**, ~ **[sth] up** bander [*wound*]; attacher [*bundle*]

binder /'baɪndə(r)/ n ① (for papers) classeur m; ② Agric lieuse f; ③ Constr, Ind (for cement, paint) liant m

binding /'baɪndɪŋ/
Ⓐ n ① (of book) reliure f; ② (in sewing) (bias) biais m; (for hem, seam) extrafort m
Ⓑ adj [*agreement, contract, rule*] qui lie, qui engage

bindweed /'baɪndwiːd/ n liseron m

binge○ /bɪndʒ/ n (drinking) beuverie f; (festive eating) gueuleton○ m; **to go on a** ~ aller faire la noce

bingo /'bɪŋɡəʊ/ ▸ p. 881
Ⓐ n bingo m
Ⓑ noun modifier [*card, game, hall*] de bingo

bin liner n GB sac m poubelle

binoculars /bɪ'nɒkjʊləz/ npl jumelles fpl

biochemist /ˌbaɪəʊ'kemɪst/ ▸ p. 1181 n biochimiste mf

biochemistry /ˌbaɪəʊ'kemɪstrɪ/ n biochimie f

biodegradable /ˌbaɪəʊdɪ'ɡreɪdəbl/ adj biodégradable

biodiversity /ˌbaɪəʊdaɪ'vɜːsətɪ/ n diversité f biologique

bioengineering /ˌbaɪəʊˌendʒɪ'nɪərɪŋ/ n génie m biologique

bioethics /baɪəʊ'eθɪks/ n (+ v sg) bioéthique f

biographer /baɪ'ɒɡrəfə(r)/ ▸ p. 1181 n biographe mf

biographical /ˌbaɪə'ɡræfɪkl/ adj biographique

biography /baɪ'ɒɡrəfɪ/ n biographie f

biological /ˌbaɪə'lɒdʒɪkl/ adj biologique

biological clock n horloge f biologique

biologically /ˌbaɪə'lɒdʒɪklɪ/ adv biologiquement

biological: ~ **powder** n lessive f avec enzyme; ~ **shield** n bouclier m biologique; ~ **warfare** n guerre f biologique

biologist /baɪ'ɒlədʒɪst/ ▸ p. 1181 n biologiste mf

biology /baɪ'ɒlədʒɪ/ n biologie f

bionic /baɪ'ɒnɪk/ adj bionique

biopic○ /baɪ'ɒpɪk/ n Cin biographie f romancée

biopsy /'baɪɒpsɪ/ n biopsie f

biorhythm /'baɪəʊrɪðəm/ n biorythme m

bioterrorism /'baɪəʊˌterərɪzəm/ n bioterrorisme m

bipartisan /baɪˌpɑː'tɪzæn, baɪ'pɑːtɪzn/ adj Pol bipartite

bipartite /baɪ'pɑːtaɪt/ adj bipartite

birch /bɜːtʃ/
Ⓐ n ① (tree, wood) bouleau m; ② (also ~ **rod**) Hist fouet m
Ⓑ vtr Hist fouetter [*offender*]

bird /bɜːd/ n ① Zool oiseau m; ② ○GB (girl) nana○ f

(Idioms) **a little** ~ **told me**○ mon petit doigt m'a dit; **to tell sb about the** ~**s and the bees** expliquer à qn comment naissent les enfants; **to kill two** ~**s with one stone** faire d'une pierre deux coups

bird: ~**brain** n cervelle f d'oiseau○; ~ **call** n cri m d'oiseau

birdie /'bɜːdɪ/ n (in golf) birdie m

bird: ~**like** adj semblable à un oiseau; ~ **of paradise** n oiseau m de paradis; ~ **of prey** n oiseau m de proie; ~ **sanctuary** n réserve f ornithologique; ~**seed** n Ⓒ graines fpl (pour les oiseaux); ~**'s eye view** n vue f d'ensemble; ~**'s nest** n nid m d'oiseau; ~**'s nest soup** n soupe f aux nids d'hirondelle; ~**song** n chant m des oiseaux; ~**table** n perchoir m; ~**watcher** n ornithologue mf amateur

bird-watching /'bɜːdwɒtʃɪŋ/ n **to go** ~ observer les oiseaux

biro® /'baɪərəʊ/ n GB (pl ~**s**) stylo-bille m, bic® m

birth /bɜːθ/ n gen, lit, fig naissance f (**of** de); Med (process of giving birth) accouchement m; **to give** ~ **to** [*woman*] accoucher de; [*animal*] mettre bas; **from** ~ **he had lived in Paris** depuis sa naissance il vivait à Paris; **blind from** ~ aveugle de naissance; **of high** ~ de haute naissance; **of low** ~ d'origine modeste; **of French** ~ né/née français/-e

birth: ~ **certificate** n certificat m de naissance; ~ **control** n (in society) contrôle m des naissances; (by couple) contraception f

birthday /'bɜːθdeɪ/
Ⓐ n anniversaire m; **to wish sb (a) happy** ~ souhaiter à qn un bon or joyeux anniversaire
Ⓑ noun modifier [*cake, card, greetings, guest, present*] d'anniversaire

(Idiom) **in one's** ~ **suit**○ hum, euph en costume d'Adam or d'Ève

birthday party n (for child) goûter d'anniversaire; (for adult) soirée f d'anniversaire

birth: ~**ing pool** n Med piscine f d'accouchement; ~**ing stool** n Med chaise f d'accouchement; ~**mark** n tache f de naissance; ~**place** n lit lieu m de naissance; fig berceau m (**of** de); ~**rate** n taux m de natalité; ~**right** n gen droit m (acquis à la naissance); (of first-born) droit m d'aînesse; ~**s column** n (in newspaper) rubrique f des naissances; ~ **sign** n signe m du zodiaque; ~**s, marriages, and deaths** npl (in newspaper) carnet m du jour; ~**stone** n pierre f porte-bonheur

biscuit /'bɪskɪt/
Ⓐ n ① GB biscuit m, petit gâteau m; ② US pain m au lait
Ⓑ ▸ p. 752 adj (also ~**-coloured**) de couleur bise inv

(Idiom) **that takes the** ~○! ça, c'est le pompon!

biscuit barrel, **biscuit tin** n boîte f à biscuits

bisect /baɪ'sekt/ vtr diviser [qch] en deux parties égales

bisexual /baɪ'sekʃʊəl/ n, adj ① [*person*] bisexuel/-elle (m/f); ② Bot, Zool bisexué

bishop /'bɪʃəp/ n ① Relig évêque m; ② (in chess) fou m

bistro /'biːstrəʊ/ n ≈ bistrot m

bit /bɪt/
Ⓐ prét ▸ **bite**
Ⓑ n ① (of food, substance, wood) morceau m (**of** de); (of paper, string, garden, land) bout m (**of** de); **every** ~ **of dirt** la moindre petite saleté; **to take sth to** ~**s** démonter qch; ② ○(small amount) **a** ~ un peu; **would you like a** ~ **more?** tu en veux encore?; **a** ~ **of** un peu de [*time, money etc*]; **a** ~ **of difficulty/information** quelques difficultés/informations; **a** ~ **of advice** un petit conseil; **with a** ~ **of luck** avec un peu de chance; **to do a** ~ **of shopping** faire quelques courses; **it won't do a** ~ **of good** ça ne servira à rien; **wait a** ~! attends un peu!; **after a** ~ un peu après; **quite a** ~ **of, a good** ~ **of** pas mal de [*time, money etc*]; **quite a** ~ **ou a good** ~ **bigger** bien plus grand; ③ ○(section) passage m; **listen, this** ~ **is brilliant!** écoute, ce passage est génial○!; **the** ~ **where Hamlet dies** le moment où Hamlet meurt; ④ †(coin) pièce f; ⑤ (for horse) mors m; ⑥ Comput bit m; ⑦ Tech (also **drill** ~) mèche f
Ⓒ ○**a bit** adv phr (rather) un peu; **a** ~ **deaf/cold** un peu sourd/froid; **a** ~ **early** un peu trop tôt; **it's asking a** ~ **much** c'est un peu trop demander; **she isn't a** ~ **like me** elle ne me ressemble pas du tout; **it's a** ~ **of a surprise** c'est un peu surprenant; **he's a** ~ **of a brute** il a un côté brute; **a** ~ **of a problem** un petit problème

(Idioms) ~ **by** ~ petit à petit; ~**s and bobs**○ affaires fpl; ~**s and pieces** (fragments) morceaux m; (belongings) affaires fpl; **every** ~ **as good/clever** tout aussi bon/intelligent; **not a** ~ **of it!** pas du tout!; **to do one's** ~ faire sa part (de boulot○); **to take the** ~ **between one's teeth** prendre le mors aux dents

bitch /bɪtʃ/
Ⓐ n ① (dog) chienne f; ② ○pej (woman) garce○ f, salope○ f; **life's a** ~○! la vie n'est pas un cadeau○!
Ⓑ ○vi ① (gossip spitefully) dire du mal (**about** de); ② US (complain) pester○ (**about** contre)

bitchy○ /'bɪtʃɪ/ adj [*person, comment*] malveillant

bite /baɪt/
Ⓐ n ① (mouthful) bouchée f; **in one** ~ en une bouchée; **to have ou take a** ~ **of sth** prendre une bouchée de qch; ② (from insect) piqûre f; (from dog, snake) morsure f; fig (of wind, cold) morsure f; (of performance, film) mordant m; ③ (in fishing) touche f; **to have a** ~ lit avoir une touche; fig trouver amateur
Ⓑ vtr (prét **bit**; pp **bitten**) [*person, animal*] mordre; [*insect*] piquer; **to** ~ **one's nails** se ronger les ongles
Ⓒ vi (prét **bit**; pp **bitten**) [*fish*] mordre

(Idioms) **he won't** ~ **you**○! il ne va pas te manger○!; **to** ~ **one's lip** se mordre les lèvres; **to** ~ **the hand that feeds you** cracher dans la soupe; **to be bitten by the DIY bug**○ attraper le virus du bricolage

(Phrasal verbs)

■ **bite into**: ▸ ~ **into [sth]** lit mordre dans [*fruit, sandwich etc*]; fig avoir un effet sur [*finances*]

■ **bite off**: ▸ ~ **off [sth]**, ~ **[sth] off** arracher [qch] d'un coup de dent

■ **bite through**: ▸ ~ **through [sth]** percer [qch] avec ses dents

biting /'baɪtɪŋ/ *adj* [*wind*] cinglant; [*cold*] pénétrant; fig [*comment, irony*] mordant

bit part *n* Theat petit rôle *m*

bitten /'bɪtn/ *pp* ▸ **bite**

(Idiom) **once ~ twice shy** Prov chat échaudé craint l'eau froide Prov

bitter /'bɪtə(r)/

A *n* GB (beer) bière *f* (légèrement amère)

B *adj* **1** (sour) amer/-ère; **2** (resentful) [*person, memory, comment*] amer/-ère; **she felt ~ about the way they had treated her** la façon dont ils l'avaient traitée la remplissait d'amertume; **3** (fierce) [*critic*] acerbe; [*hatred*] profond; [*attack, battle*] féroce; [*argument, feud*] violent; **they are ~ enemies** ce sont des ennemis jurés; **4** [*weather, wind*] glacial; **5** (severe) [*disappointment, truth*] cruel/-elle; [*blow*] dur

(Idioms) **it's a ~ pill to swallow** la pilule est dure à avaler; **to the ~ end** jusqu'au bout

bitter: ~ **almond** *n* amande *f* amère; ~ **aloes** *n* aloès *m* médicinal; ~ **lemon** *n* Schweppes® *m* (citron)

bitterly /'bɪtəlɪ/ *adv* [*complain, laugh, speak*] amèrement; [*disappointed*] cruellement; [*regret*] profondément; [*fight*] farouchement; [*weep*] amèrement

bitterness /'bɪtənɪs/ *n* lit, fig amertume *f*

bitter: ~ **orange** *n* Bot, Culin bigarade *f*; ~ **sweet** *adj* lit aigre-doux/aigre-douce; fig doux-amer/douce-amère

bitty /'bɪtɪ/ *adj* [*account*] fragmentaire

bitumen /'bɪtjʊmɪn, US bə'tuːmən/ *n* bitume *m*

bivouac /'bɪvʊæk/

A *n* bivouac *m*

B *vi* bivouaquer

bizarre /bɪ'zɑː(r)/ *adj* bizarre

blab° /blæb/ (*p prés etc* **-bb-**)

A *vtr* (*also* ~ **out**) aller raconter

B *vi* **1** (reveal secret) vendre la mèche°; **2** US (talk idly) jacasser

black /blæk/ ▸ **p. 752**

A *n* **1** (colour) noir *m*; **2** (*also* **Black**) (person) Noir/-e *m/f*; **3** Fin **to be in the ~** être créditeur/-trice; **4** (in chess, draughts) noirs *mpl*; (in roulette) noir *m*; (snooker or pool ball) (bille *f*) noire *f*

B *adj* **1** gen noir; [*night*] obscur; **to paint sth ~** peindre qch en noir; **to turn ~** noircir; **2** (*also* **Black**) [*skin, community, culture*] noir; [*school*] pour les Noirs; **3** [*coffee*] noir; [*tea*] nature; **4** (dirty) [*face, mark, towel*] noir; **5** (macabre) [*comedy, humour*] noir; **6** (gloomy) [*mood, picture, thoughts*] noir; [*despair*] profond; [*future*] sombre; [*day*] mauvais; **7** (angry) [*look*] meurtrier/-ière; [*mood*] massacrant; **8** (evil) [*deed, magic*] noir

C *vtr* **1** (put black onto) noircir [*sb's face, hands*]; cirer [*boots*]; **2** GB (boycott) boycotter

(Phrasal verb)

■ **black out**: ▸ ~ **out** [*person*] s'évanouir; ▸ ~ **[sth] out**, ~ **out [sth]** **1** (darken) faire le black-out dans [*house*]; faire l'obscurité sur [*stage*]; **2** (cut power) couper le courant dans [*area*]

black: **Black Africa** *pr n* Geog Afrique *f* noire; ~ **American** *n* noir/-e *m/f* américain/-e

black and white ▸ **p. 752**

A *n* Cin, Phot noir et blanc *m*

B *adj* [*TV, camera film*] noir et blanc (inv); [*movie, photography*] (en) noir et blanc (inv); fig [*matter, situation*] nettement défini

(Idiom) **he sees everything in ~** pour lui c'est tout noir ou tout blanc

black: ~ **arts** *npl* sciences *fpl* occultes; ~ **ball** *vtr* black-bouler (**from** de)

black belt *n* ceinture *f* noire (**in** de)

blackberry /'blækbrɪ, -berɪ/

A *n* mûre *f*

B *noun modifier* [*pie*] aux mûres; [*jam*] de mûres

blackberry bush *n* Bot ronce *f*

blackbird /'blækbɜːd/ *n* merle *m*

blackboard /'blækbɔːd/ *n* tableau *m* (noir); **on the ~** au tableau

black: ~ **box** *n* Aviat, Comput boîte *f* noire; ~ **bread** *n* pain *m* noir, pumpernickel *m*

blackcurrant /ˌblæk'kʌrənt/ Bot, Culin

A *n* cassis *m*

B *noun modifier* [*tart*] aux cassis; [*jam*] de cassis

Black Death *n* peste *f* noire

blacken /'blækən/ *vtr* [*actor*] se barbouiller [qch] de noir [*face*]; [*smoke*] noircir [*brick, wood*]; [*frost*] brûler [*plant*]; [*dirt*] salir [*towel*]; fig ternir [*reputation, name*]

black eye /ˌblæk'aɪ/ *n* œil *m* poché, œil *m* au beurre noir°; **to give sb a ~** pocher l'œil à qn

black: **Black Forest gateau** GB, **Black Forest cake** US *n* Culin Forêt-Noire *f*; ~ **gold**° *n* or *m* noir°, pétrole *m*; ~ **guard** *n* ‡ *ou* hum canaille *f*; ~ **head** *n* Med point *m* noir; ~ **headed gull** *n* mouette *f* rieuse; ~ **ice** *n* verglas *m*

blacking /'blækɪŋ/ *n* **1** GB (boycotting) boycottage *m* (**of** de); **2** †(polish) cirage *m* noir

blackish /'blækɪʃ/ ▸ **p. 752** *adj* tirant sur le noir, noirâtre pej

blackjack /'blækdʒæk/ ▸ **p. 881** *n* Games black jack *m*

blacklist /'blæklɪst/

A *n* liste *f* noire

B *vtr* mettre [qn] à l'index

blackmail /'blækmeɪl/

A *n* chantage *m*

B *vtr* faire chanter; **to ~ sb into doing** lit faire chanter qn pour qu'il/elle fasse; fig, hum soudoyer qn pour qu'il/elle fasse

black: ~ **mailer** *n* maître-chanteur *m*; ~ **mark** *n* fig mauvais point *m*

black market *n* **on the ~** au marché noir

black: ~ **marketeer** *n* personne *f* qui vend au marché noir; ~ **mass** *n* messe *f* noire

blackness /'blæknɪs/ *n* (darkness) obscurité *f*; (dark colour) (of hair, ink) noir *m*; fig (gloominess) caractère *m* sombre; (evilness) (of heart, thoughts) noirceur *f*

blackout /'blækaʊt/ *n* **1** (power cut) panne *f* de courant; (in wartime) black-out *m*; **2** Radio, TV interruption *f* des émissions; (in newspapers) black-out *m*; **3** (faint) étourdissement *m*; (loss of memory) trou *m* de mémoire

black: ~ **pepper** *n* poivre *m* noir; ~ **pudding** *n* GB Culin boudin *m* noir; **Black Sea** *pr n* Geog mer *f* Noire; ~ **sheep** *n* fig brebis *f* galeuse; **Blackshirt** *n* Hist Chemise *f* noire; ~ **smith** ▸ **p. 1181** *n* forgeron *m*

blackspot /'blækspɒt/ *n* fig point *m* noir

black: ~ **swan** *n* Zool cygne *m* noir; ~ **thorn** *n* prunellier *m*

black tie *n* (on invitation) '~' 'tenue *f* de soirée'

black widow (spider) *n* Zool veuve *f* noire

bladder /'blædə(r)/ *n* Anat vessie *f*; Bot vésicule *f*

blade /bleɪd/ *n* **1** (of knife, sword, axe) lame *f*; (of fan, propeller, oar) pale *f*; (of turbine) aube *f*; (of windscreen wiper) balai *m*; **2** Bot (of grass) brin *m*; **3** Ling (of tongue) plat *m*

Blairite /'bleəraɪt/ GB Pol

A *n* supporter *mf* de Tony Blair

B *adj* [*policies, ideas*] de Tony Blair

blame /bleɪm/

A *n* **1** (responsibility) responsabilité *f* (**for** de); **to take** *ou* **bear the ~** prendre *or* assumer la responsabilité; **to put** *ou* **lay the ~ for sth on sb** attribuer la responsabilité de qch à qn; **why do I always get the ~?** pourquoi est-ce toujours moi qu'on accuse?; **2** (criticism) reproches *mpl*

B *vtr* en vouloir à [*person, group*]; accuser [*weather, recession, system*]; **she has always ~d me** elle m'en a toujours voulu; **to ~ sb for sth** reprocher qch à qn; **to ~ sth on sb** attribuer la responsabilité de qch à qn; **to be to ~ for sth** être responsable de qch

C *v refl* **to ~ oneself for sth** se sentir responsable de qch; **you mustn't ~ yourself** tu n'as rien à te reprocher; **you've only yourself to ~** tu ne peux t'en prendre qu'à toi-même

blameless /'bleɪmlɪs/ *adj* irréprochable

blameworthy /'bleɪmwɜːðɪ/ *adj* [*person*] responsable; [*conduct*] répréhensible

blanch /blɑːntʃ, US blæntʃ/
A *vtr* (all contexts) blanchir
B *vi* sout [*person*] blêmir

blancmange /blə'mɒnʒ/ *n* blanc-manger *m*

bland /blænd/ *adj* [*food, flavour*] fade; [*person*] terne; [*account*] insipide

blandly /'blændlɪ/ *adv* platement

blank /blæŋk/
A *n* **1** (empty space) blanc *m*; **to fill in the ~s** remplir les blancs; **my mind's a ~** j'ai la tête vide; **2** US (clean form) fiche *f* vierge; **3** (dummy bullet) balle *f* à blanc; **4** Ind pièce *f* brute
B *adj* **1** (without writing, pictures) [*paper, page*] blanc/blanche; [*screen*] vide; [*form, canvas*] vierge; **2** (unused) [*cassette, disk*] vierge; **3** (expressionless) **a ~ look** un air absent; **a row of ~ faces** des visages à l'air absent; **4** (uncomprehending) [*look, expression*] ébahi; **to look ~** avoir l'air ébahi; **5** (without memory) **my mind went ~** j'ai eu un trou de mémoire; **6** (absolute) [*refusal, rejection*] catégorique
(Idiom) **to draw a ~** faire chou blanc
(Phrasal verb)
■ **blank out**: ▸ **~ out** [*person*] avoir un trou de mémoire; ▸ **~** [*sth*] **out, ~ out** [*sth*] rayer [qch] de sa mémoire

blank cheque GB, **blank check** US *n* **1** Fin chèque *m* en blanc; **2** fig carte *f* blanche

blanket /'blæŋkɪt/
A *n* **1** (bedcover) couverture *f*; **electric ~** couverture chauffante; **2** (layer) (of snow, ash) couche *f*; (of cloud, fog) nappe *f*; (of smoke) nuage *m*; (of flowers, weeds) tapis *m*
B *noun modifier* (global) [*ban, policy*] global; [*use*] excessif/-ive
(Idiom) **to be a wet ~** être un/-e rabat-joie

blanket: ~ box, ~ chest *n* GB coffre *m* à linge; **~ cover** *n* fig couverture *f* globale; **~ coverage** *n* reportage *m* intégral; **~ stitch** *n* point *m* de feston

blankly /'blæŋklɪ/ *adv* **1** (uncomprehendingly) d'un air ébahi; **2** (without expression) d'un air absent

blank verse *n* vers *mpl* blancs *or* non rimés

blare /bleə(r)/ *n* beuglement *m*
(Phrasal verb)
■ **blare out**: ▸ **~ out** [*music, radio*] jouer à plein volume; ▸ **~ out** [*sth*] déverser [*music*]

blarney° /'blɑːnɪ/ *n* baratin° *m*

blaspheme /blæs'fiːm/ *vtr, vi* blasphémer

blasphemous /'blæsfəməs/ *adj* [*person*] blasphémateur/-trice; [*statement*] blasphématoire

blasphemy /'blæsfəmɪ/ *n* blasphème *m*

blast /blɑːst, US blæst/
A *n* **1** (explosion) explosion *f*; **2** (gust) rafale *f*; **3** (air current from explosion) souffle *m* (**from** de); **4** (noise) (on trumpet) sonnerie *f*; (on whistle, car horn) coup *m*; **to give a ~ on** faire sonner [*trumpet*]; donner un coup de [*whistle, car horn*]; **he plays his records at full ~** il écoute ses disques à plein volume
B °*excl* zut°!
C *vtr* **1** (blow up) faire sauter [*building*]; dynamiter [*rockface*]; **to ~ a hole in a wall** percer un mur à l'explosif; **2** (damage) [*wind*] endommager [*tree*]; [*frost, disease*] détruire [*crop*]; **3** °(criticize) descendre [qn/qch] en flammes°
D *vi* **1** (in mining) utiliser des explosifs; **to ~ through sth** faire sauter qch à l'explosif; **2** (make a noise) [*trumpets*] retentir
(Phrasal verbs)
■ **blast away**: ▸ **~ away** mitrailler; **to ~ away at** mitrailler [*target*]
■ **blast off** [*rocket*] décoller
■ **blast out**: ▸ **~ out** [*music*] retentir; ▸ **~** [*sth*] **out, ~ out** [*sth*] [*radio*] cracher° [*music*]

blasted /'blɑːstɪd, US 'blæst-/ *adj* **1** (withered) flétri; **2** °(for emphasis) fichu; **some ~ idiot** une espèce d'idiot

blast furnace *n* haut-fourneau *m*

blasting /'blɑːstɪŋ, US 'blæst-/ *n* travail *m* à l'explosif

blast-off /'blɑːstɒf, US 'blæst-/ *n* lancement *m*

blatant /'bleɪtnt/ *adj* [*lie, bias, disregard*] éhonté; [*example, abuse*] flagrant; **to be ~ about** [*person*] être direct à propos de

blatantly /'bleɪtntlɪ/ *adv* [*copy, disregard*] ouvertement; **to be ~ obvious** être l'évidence même

blather° /'blæðə(r)/ *vi* dire n'importe quoi

blaze /bleɪz/
A *n* **1** (fire) (in hearth) feu *m*, flambée *f*; (accidental) incendie *m*; **2** (sudden burst) (of flames) embrasement *m*; **she left in a ~ of publicity** elle est partie sous les feux des médias; **3** (on horse) liste *f*; **4** (cut in tree) encoche *f*
B **blazes**°† *npl* **what the ~s are you up to?** qu'est-ce que tu fabriques°?; **how the ~s did he do it?** comment diable a-t-il fait ça?; **to run like ~s** courir comme un dératé/une dératée
C *vtr* (mark) griffer [*tree*]; **to ~ a trail** lit baliser une voie; fig faire œuvre de pionnier
D *vi* **1** (also **~ away**) (burn) [*fire*] brûler, flamber; [*house, car*] brûler; **2** (also **~ away**) (give out light) [*lights*] briller; **3** (shoot) [*gun*] pétarader
E **blazing** *pres p adj* **1** (violent) [*argument*] violent; [*heat*] accablant; [*fire*] ronflant; [*building, car*] embrasé; [*sunshine*] plein (**before** *n*); **2** °(furious) fou/folle de rage

blazer /'bleɪzə(r)/ *n* blazer *m*

bleach /bliːtʃ/
A *n* **1** (also **household ~**) (disinfectant) ≈ eau *f* de javel; **2** (for hair) décolorant *m*
B *vtr* décolorer [*hair*]; blanchir [*linen*]; faire disparaître [*colour, stain*]

bleak /bliːk/ *adj* **1** (cold, raw) [*landscape*] désolé; [*weather, season*] maussade; **2** (miserable) [*outlook, future*] sombre; [*world, surroundings*] sinistre

bleakly /'bliːklɪ/ *adv* [*stare, say*] sombrement

bleakness /'bliːknɪs/ *n* **1** (of weather, surroundings) sévérité *f*; **2** (of prospects, future) noirceur *f*

bleary /'blɪərɪ/ *adj* [*eyes*] bouffi; **to be ~-eyed** avoir les yeux bouffis; **to feel ~** se sentir vaseux/-euse

bleat /bliːt/
A *n* bêlement *m*
B *vi* **1** [*sheep, goat*] bêler; **2** péj [*person*] se lamenter

bled /bled/ *pp* ▸ **bleed**

bleed /bliːd/ (*prét, pp* **bled**)
A *vtr* **1** †Med saigner; **2** fig **to ~ sb for sth** soutirer qch à qn; **to ~ sb dry** saigner qn à blanc; **3** Tech purger [*radiator*]
B *vi* **1** saigner; **my finger's ~ing** j'ai le doigt qui saigne; **he was ~ing from the head** il saignait d'une blessure à la tête; **he bled to death** il est mort d'une hémorragie; **2** fig **my heart ~s for the baby's mother** mon cœur saigne pour la mère du bébé; **3** [*colour, dye*] déteindre

bleeding /'bliːdɪŋ/
A *n* gen saignement *m*; (heavy) hémorragie *f*; (deliberate) saignée *f*
B *adj* [*wound*] saignant; [*corpse*] ensanglanté; [*hand, leg*] qui saigne

bleeding heart *n* fig péj cœur *m* sensible péj

bleep /bliːp/
A *n* **1** (signal) bip *m*, bip-bip *m*; Radio, TV top *m*; **2** GB = **bleeper**
B *vtr* **1** GB **to ~ sb** appeler qn (au bip), biper qn; **2** Radio, TV censurer par un bip [*word, person*]
C *vi* émettre un signal sonore *or* des signaux sonores

bleeper /'bliːpə(r)/ *n* GB (for doctor) bip *m*

blemish /'blemɪʃ/
A *n* imperfection *f*; (on fruit) tache *f*; (pimple) bouton *m*, défaut *m* (**on** dans); (on reputation) tache *f* (**on** à)
B *vtr* tacher [*fruit*]; ternir [*beauty*]; entacher [*reputation*]

blend /blend/
A *n* **1** (fusion) (of sounds, smells) mélange *m* (**of** de); (of styles, colours, ideas) mariage *m* (**of** de); (of qualities, skills) combinaison *f* (**of** de); **2** (of coffees, teas, whiskies) mélange *m*; (of wines) coupage *m*
B *vtr* mélanger [*foods, colours, styles*]; allier [*ideas*]
C *vi* **to ~ (together)** [*colours, tastes, styles*] se fondre ensemble; **to ~ with** [*colours, tastes, sounds*] se marier à; [*smells, visual effects*] se mêler à; [*buildings, styles, ideas*] s'accorder à
(Phrasal verb)
■ **blend in**: ▸ **~ in** s'harmoniser (**with** avec); ▸ **~ in** [*sth*], **~** [*sth*] **in** incorporer

blender /'blendə(r)/ *n* **1** (device) mixeur *m*, mixer *m*; **2** (person) (of coffee) torréfacteur *m*

blending /'blendɪŋ/ *n* (of coffees) torréfaction *f*; (of wines) coupage *m*; (of whiskies) mélange *m*

b

bless /bles/
A vtr **1** Relig bénir; **God ~ you** que Dieu vous bénisse; **goodbye, God ~!** au revoir!; **2** ○(affectionately) **~ her** ou **~ her heart!** c'est un ange!; **~ you!** (after sneeze) à vos souhaits!; **3** ○†(in surprise) **~ me!** ou **~ my soul!** ou **well I'm ~ed!** ça alors!; **4** (favour) **to ~ sb with** doter qn de; **to be ~ed with** jouir de [health, beauty]; **5** (be grateful to) **~ you for answering so quickly** merci d'avoir répondu si vite
B v refl **to ~ oneself** se signer

blessed /'blesɪd/
A n Relig **the ~** (+ v pl) les bienheureux
B adj **1** (holy) [place] béni; **the Blessed Sacrament** le saint sacrement; **the Blessed Virgin** la Sainte Vierge; **2** (beatified) bienheureux/-euse (before n); **3** (welcome) [warmth, quiet] bienfaisant; [relief] heureux/-euse; **4** ○(damned) fichu○

blessedly /'blesɪdlɪ/ adv [warm, quiet] délicieusement

blessing /'blesɪŋ/ n **1** (asset, favour) bienfait m; **it is a ~ (for him) that he is healthy** heureusement, il est en bonne santé; **dishwashers are a ~ for busy people** les lave-vaisselle sont une bénédiction pour les personnes actives; **a ~ in disguise** un bienfait caché; **2** (relief) soulagement m; **it is a ~ to know (that) he's safe** c'est un soulagement de savoir qu'il est sauf; **3** (approval) **with the ~ of sb, with sb's ~** avec la bénédiction de qn; **to give one's ~ to sth** approuver qch sans réserve; **4** Relig bénédiction f; **to give sb one's ~** donner sa bénédiction à qn; **to say a ~ over sth** bénir qch

blew /blu:/ prét ▸ **blow B, C**

blight /blaɪt/
A n **1** Bot rouille f; **potato ~** mildiou m (de la pomme de terre); **2** fig (on society) plaie f (on de); **urban ~, inner city ~** délabrement m urbain
B vtr attaquer [crop]; fig gâcher [childhood, chances]

blighter†○ /'blaɪtə(r)/ n GB andouille○ f; **poor ~** pauvre andouille○; **you lucky ~!** sacré veinard○!

blimey† /'blaɪmɪ/ excl GB mince alors○!

blind /blaɪnd/
A n **1** (unsighted) **the ~** (+ v pl) les aveugles mpl voir note; **2** (at window) store m; **3** (front) façade f; (subterfuge) feinte f; **4** US (hide) affût m
B adj **1** lit [person] aveugle voir note; **to go ~** perdre la vue; **to be ~ in one eye** être borgne; **2** (unaware) [person, rage, obedience] aveugle; **to be ~ to** être aveugle à [fault]; être insensible à [quality]; être inconscient de [danger]; **3** (from which one can't see) [corner] sans visibilité; **on my ~ side** dans mon angle mort; (without looking) [tasting] en aveugle; **5** (blank) [wall, façade] aveugle
C adv [fly] sans visibilité; [taste] en aveugle; [bake] à blanc
D vtr **1** lit [injury, accident] rendre aveugle; **to be ~ed in one eye** perdre un œil; **2** (dazzle) [sun, light] éblouir; **3** (mislead) [pride, love] aveugler
(Idioms) **it's a case of the ~ leading the ~** ils n'en savent pas plus long l'un que l'autre; **to turn a ~ eye** fermer les yeux (**to** sur).

⚠️ Ce mot peut être perçu comme injurieux dans cette acception. Lui préférer visually handicapped ou visually impaired

blind alley n lit, fig voie f sans issue
blind date n rendez-vous m avec un/-e inconnu/-e
blind drunk /ˌblaɪn'drʌŋk/ adj complètement bourré○
blindfold /'blaɪndfəʊld/
A n bandeau m
B adj (also **~ed**) aux yeux bandés; **to be ~** avoir les yeux bandés
C adv (also **~ed**) [find way] les yeux fermés
D vtr bander les yeux à [person]

blinding /'blaɪndɪŋ/ adj [light] aveuglant; [headache] atroce
blindingly /'blaɪndɪŋlɪ/ adv [shine] d'un éclat aveuglant; **to be ~ obvious** sauter aux yeux
blindly /'blaɪndlɪ/ adv **1** fig [obey, follow] aveuglément; **2** lit [advance, grope] à l'aveuglette
blind man's buff n Games colin-maillard m
blindness /'blaɪndnɪs/ n **1** Med cécité f; **2** fig aveuglement m
blind spot n **1** (in eye) point m aveugle; **2** (in car, on hill) angle m mort; **3** fig (point of ignorance) ignorance f **₵**

blink /blɪŋk/
A n battement m des paupières
B vi [person] cligner des yeux; [light] clignoter; **without ~ing** sans ciller
(Idiom) **on the ~**○ [television, microwave] détraqué○
(Phrasal verb)
■ **blink away: to ~ away one's tears** battre des paupières pour s'arrêter de pleurer

blinker /'blɪŋkə(r)/ n **1** Aut clignotant m; US (at crossing) (feu m) clignotant m; **2** (on horse) œillère f
blinkered /'blɪŋkə(r)d/ adj [attitude, approach] borné
blinking /'blɪŋkɪŋ/ n **₵** (of eye) battement m des paupières; (of light) clignotement m
blip /blɪp/ n **1** (on screen) spot m; (on graph, line) accident m (d'une courbe); **2** (sound) bip m; **3** (hitch) contretemps m
bliss /blɪs/ n **1** Relig, littér béatitude f; **2** ○fig délice m
blissful /'blɪsfl/ adj **1** (wonderful) délicieux/-ieuse; **2** Relig bienheureux/-euse
blissfully /'blɪsfəlɪ/ adv voluptueusement; **to be ~ happy** être au comble du bonheur; **to be ~ unaware of/that** être à cent lieues de se douter de/que; **~ ignorant** dans la plus parfaite ignorance
blister /'blɪstə(r)/
A n (on skin) ampoule f; (on paint) cloque f; (in glass, on metal) soufflure f
B vtr faire peler [skin]; faire cloquer [paint]
C vi [skin, paint] cloquer; [person] peler; **my feet ~ easily** j'ai facilement des ampoules aux pieds
blistering /'blɪstərɪŋ/
A n (of skin) formation f d'ampoules; (of paint) formation f de cloques
B adj [heat] caniculaire; [sun] torride; [attack, criticism] féroce; [reply] cinglant
blister pack n blister m, habillage m transparent
blithe /blaɪð/ adj (nonchalant) insouciant; (cheerful) allègre
blithely /'blaɪðlɪ/ adv (nonchalantly) avec insouciance; (cheerfully) allègrement; **~ ignorant of sth** parfaitement inconscient de qch
blitz /blɪts/
A n **1** Mil Aviat bombardement m aérien; **the Blitz** GB Hist le Blitz; **2** fig **to have a ~ on sth** s'attaquer à qch
B vtr lit, fig bombarder
blitzkrieg /'blɪtskri:g/ n guerre f éclair inv
blizzard /'blɪzəd/ n tempête f de neige; (in Arctic regions) blizzard m
bloated /'bləʊtɪd/ adj **1** lit [face, body] bouffi; [stomach] ballonné; **to feel ~** se sentir ballonné; **2** fig [estimate] gonflé; [style] ampoulé
blob /blɒb/ n **1** (drop) grosse goutte f; **2** (shape) forme f floue
bloc /blɒk/ n Pol bloc m; **en ~** en bloc
block /blɒk/
A n **1** (slab) bloc m; **2** (building) **~ of flats** immeuble m (d'habitation); **office ~** immeuble de bureaux; **administration ~** bâtiment m administratif; **3** (group of buildings) pâté m de maisons; **to drive round the ~** faire le tour du pâté de maisons; **he lives three ~s away** il habite à trois rues d'ici; **4** (for butcher, executioner) billot m; **to put one's head on the ~** fig donner sa tête à couper; **5** (group) (of seats, tickets) groupe m; (of shares) paquet m, tranche f; **a ~ of three lessons** trois cours d'affilée; **6** (obstruction) **to be a ~ to** être un obstacle à [reform, agreement]; **to put a ~ on** bloquer [price, sale]; entraver [initiative]; Sport obstruction f
B **blocks** npl (shoes) chaussons mpl à pointes
C vtr **1** (obstruct) bloquer [exit, road]; boucher [drain, hole, artery]; gêner [traffic]; **to ~ sb's way** ou **path** barrer le passage à qn; **to have a ~ed nose** avoir le nez bouché; **2** (impede) faire obstacle à [advance, escape, progress]; faire opposition à [bill]; **you're ~ing my light** tu me caches la lumière; **3** Fin bloquer [assets]
(Phrasal verbs)
■ **block in:** ▸ **~ [sb/sth] in** (when parking) bloquer [car, driver]
■ **block off:** ▸ **~ [sth] off, ~ off [sth]** (seal off) barrer [road, path]
■ **block out:** ▸ **~ [sth] out, ~ [sth] out 1** (hide) boucher [view]; cacher [light, sun]; **2** (suppress) refouler [memory, problem]
■ **block up:** ▸ **~ up [sth], ~ [sth] up** boucher

blockade /blɒˈkeɪd/
A n Mil blocus m
B vtr bloquer, faire le blocus de [port]

blockage /ˈblɒkɪdʒ/ n (in artery) obstruction f; (in pipe, drain, distribution) blocage m; (in river) engorgement m

block: ∼ **and tackle** n moufle f; ∼**board** n latté m; ∼**book** vtr louer [qch] en groupe [seats]; ∼**-booking** n location f de groupe

blockbuster○ /ˈblɒkbʌstə(r)/ n **1** (book) livre m à succès, bestseller m; **2** (film) superproduction f; **3** Mil bombe f de très grande puissance

block capital n majuscule f d'imprimerie; **in** ∼**s** (on form) en caractères mpl or capitales fpl d'imprimerie

block: ∼**head**○ n péj âne○ m, imbécile○ mf; ∼**house** n Mil blockhaus m; US Hist (fort) fortin m

blocking software /ˈblɒkɪŋ ˌsɒftweə(r), US sɔːft-/ n Comput logiciel m de filtrage

block: ∼ **letter** n = block capital; ∼ **printing** n impression f sur cliché bois; ∼ **release course** n cours m de formation continue; ∼ **vote** n vote m groupé; ∼ **voting** n système m du vote groupé

bloke○ /bləʊk/ n GB type○ m, mec○ m

blond /blɒnd/ ▸ p. 752 adj [person, hair] blond; [wood] clair

blonde /blɒnd/ ▸ p. 752
A n blonde f
B adj blond

blood /blʌd/ n **1** Biol sang m; **to give** ∼ donner son sang; **the** ∼ **rushed to his cheeks** il a rougi; **to kill sb in cold** ∼ tuer qn de sang-froid; **to do** ∼ **tests** faire des analyses de sang; **2** (breeding) sang m; **music is in her** ∼ elle a la musique dans le sang; **3** (anger) **his** ∼ **is up** il est furieux; **4** (vigour) **new** ou **fresh** ou **young** ∼ sang m neuf

Idioms ∼ **is thicker than water** la voix du sang est la plus forte; **he's after my** ∼○! il veut ma peau○!; **it's like getting** ∼ **out of a stone** autant essayer de faire parler un muet

blood: ∼**-and-thunder** adj [novel, film] d'aventures; ∼ **bank** n banque f du sang; ∼**bath** n bain m de sang; ∼ **blister** n pinçon m; ∼ **brother** n frère m de sang; ∼ **cell**, ∼ **corpuscle** n globule m (du sang); ∼ **count** n numération f globulaire; ∼ **curdling** adj à vous figer le sang dans les veines; ∼ **donor** n donneur/-euse m/f de sang; ∼ **group** n groupe m sanguin; ∼**hound** n limier m

bloodless /ˈblʌdlɪs/ adj **1** (peaceful) [revolution, coup] sans effusion de sang; **2** (pale) blême; **3** (drained of blood) exsangue

blood: ∼**letting** n Med saignée f; (killing) massacre m; ∼ **lust** n soif f de sang; ∼ **money** n argent m versé pour un meurtre; ∼ **orange** n orange f sanguine; ∼ **poisoning** n septicémie f

blood pressure n Med tension f artérielle; **high** ∼ hypertension f; **low** ∼ hypotension f

blood: ∼**-red** ▸ p. 752 n, adj rouge (m) sang inv; ∼ **rela-tion**, ∼ **relative** n parent/-e m/f par le sang; ∼**shed** n effusion f de sang; ∼**shot** adj injecté de sang; ∼ **sport** n sport m sanguinaire; ∼**stained** adj taché de sang; ∼**stock** n (+ v sg ou pl) bêtes fpl de race; ∼**stream** n courant m sanguin; ∼**sucker** n lit, fig sangsue f; ∼ **test** n analyse f de sang; ∼**thirsty** adj sanguinaire; ∼ **transfusion** n transfusion f sanguine; ∼ **type** n groupe m sanguin; ∼ **vessel** n vaisseau m sanguin

bloody /ˈblʌdɪ/
A adj **1** (covered in blood) ensanglanté; **to have a** ∼ **nose** avoir le nez en sang; **to give sb a** ∼ **nose** lit faire saigner le nez de qn; fig faire souffrir qn; **2** (violent) [battle, deed] sanglant; [regime, tyrant] sanguinaire; **3** ○GB (expressing anger) sacré○; ∼ **fool!** espèce d'idiot○!; **4** (red) rouge sang (inv)
B ○adv GB (for emphasis) [dangerous, expensive] sacrément○; ∼ **awful** absolument nul○; **a** ∼ **good film** un super○ film; **what a** ∼ **stupid idea!** quelle idée débile○!

bloody-minded○ /ˌblʌdɪˈmaɪndɪd/ adj GB **don't be so** ∼ ne fais pas ta tête de mule; **he's just being** ∼ il fait ça pour embêter le monde

bloom /bluːm/
A n **1** (flower) fleur f; **2** (flowering) floraison f; **in** ∼ en fleur; **to come into** ∼ fleurir; **3** (on skin, fruit) velouté m
B vi (be in flower) être fleuri; (come into flower) fleurir

bloomer /ˈbluːmə(r)/ n **1** ○†(mistake) GB bévue f; **2** GB Culin gros pain m

bloomers /ˈbluːməz/ npl culotte f bouffante

blooming /ˈbluːmɪŋ/ adj **1** (healthy) [person] resplendis-sant (**with** de); [plant] magnifique; [friendship] florissant; **2** ○†(for emphasis) GB fichu○

blossom /ˈblɒsəm/
A n **1** (flowers) fleurs fpl; **in** ∼ en fleur(s); **in full** ∼ en pleine floraison; **to come into** ∼ fleurir; **2** (flower) fleur f
B vi fleurir; fig **to** ∼ **(out)** s'épanouir

blot /blɒt/
A n gen tache f; (of ink) pâté m; fig ombre f
B vtr (p prés etc **-tt-**) **1** (dry) sécher [qch] au buvard; **2** (stain) tacher; fig ternir; **3** = blot out

Idioms **to** ∼ **one's copybook** se faire mal voir; **to be a** ∼ **on the landscape** lit gâter le paysage; fig faire une ombre au tableau

Phrasal verb
■ **blot out**: ▸ ∼ **out [sth]** [person] effacer; [mist, rain] masquer

blotch /blɒtʃ/
A n (on skin) plaque f rouge; (of ink, colour) tache f
B vtr barbouiller [paper, face]
C vi [pen] faire des taches

blotchy /ˈblɒtʃɪ/ adj [skin] marbré; [leaf, paper] tacheté

blotter /ˈblɒtə(r)/ n **1** (for ink) (small) tampon m buvard; (on desk) sous-main m inv; **2** US (police, commercial) registre m

blotting paper n papier m buvard

blotto○ /ˈblɒtəʊ/ adj cuité○

blouse /blaʊz, US blaʊs/ ▸ p. 1191 n (woman's) chemisier m; US Mil vareuse f

blow /bləʊ/
A n **1** (stroke) coup m; **killed by a** ∼ **to the back of the head** tué d'un coup derrière la tête; **to come to** ∼**s** en venir aux mains (**over** au sujet de); **to strike a** ∼ **for** fig frapper un grand coup pour [freedom, rights]; **2** fig (shock, knock) coup m; **to be a** ∼ être un coup terrible (**to sth** porté à qch; **to, for sb** pour qn); **3** **to give one's nose a** ∼ se moucher
B vtr (prét blew; pp blown) **1** [wind] **to** ∼ **sth out of** faire voler qch par [window]; **the wind blew the door shut** un coup de vent a fermé la porte; **to be blown off course/onto the rocks** être dévié/poussé sur les rochers par le vent; **it's** ∼**ing a gale** il y a de la tempête; **2** faire [bubble, smoke ring]; souffler [glass]; **to** ∼ **sb a kiss** envoyer un baiser à qn; **3** **to** ∼ **one's nose** se moucher; **4** gen, Mus souffler dans [trumpet, whistle]; **5** [explosion] provoquer [hole] (**in** dans); **to be blown to pieces** ou **bits by** être réduit en poussière par; **6** Elec, Tech faire sauter [fuse, gasket]; griller [lightbulb]; **7** ○(spend) claquer○ [money] (**on** dans); **8** ○(expose) faire tomber [cover]; **9** ○(make a mess of) **to** ∼ **it** tout ficher en l'air○; **to** ∼ **one's chances** ficher ses chan-ces en l'air○
C vi (prét blew; pp blown) **1** [wind] souffler; **2** (move with wind) **to** ∼ **in the wind** [leaves, clothes] voler au vent; **3** [person] souffler (**into** dans; **on** sur); **4** (sound) [whistle] retentir; [trumpet] sonner, retentir; [foghorn] rugir; **5** (break, explode) [fuse, gasket] sauter; [bulb] griller; [tyre] éclater

Idioms **to** ∼ **a fuse**○ ou **a gasket**○ ou **one's top**○ piquer une crise○; **it really blew my mind**○ ou **blew me away**○! j'en suis resté baba○

Phrasal verbs
■ **blow around, blow about** GB: ▸ ∼ **around** voler dans tous les sens; ▸ ∼ **[sth] around**, ∼ **around [sth]** faire voler [qch] dans tous les sens
■ **blow away**: ▸ ∼ **away** s'envoler; ▸ ∼ **[sth] away**, ∼ **away [sth]** [wind] emporter [object]; ▸ ∼ **[sb] away**○ (kill) descendre○ [person]
■ **blow down**: ▸ ∼ **down** [tree, fence] tomber (à cause du vent); ▸ ∼ **[sth] down**, ∼ **down [sth]** [wind] faire tomber [tree]
■ **blow in**: ▸ ∼ **in 1** [snow, rain] entrer; **2** (in explosion) [door, window] être enfoncé; ▸ ∼ **[sth] in**, ∼ **in [sth] 1** [wind] faire entrer [snow, rain]; **2** [explosion] enfoncer [door, window]
■ **blow off**: ▸ ∼ **off** [hat] s'envoler; ▸ ∼ **[sth] off**, ∼ **off [sth]** [wind] emporter [hat]; [explosion] emporter [limb, roof]; **to** ∼ **the leaves off the trees** [wind] faire tomber les feuilles des arbres

b

■ **blow out**: ▶ ~ **out** [1] [*flame*] s'éteindre; [2] [*oil well*] laisser échapper du pétrole; ▶ ~ **[sth] out, ~ out [sth]** [1] (extinguish) souffler [*candle*]; éteindre [*flames*]; [2] (inflate) **to ~ one's cheeks out** gonfler les or ses joues; **to ~ itself out** [*storm*] tomber

■ **blow over**: ▶ ~ **over** [1] (die down) [*storm*] tomber; [*affair*] être oublié; [*discontent, protest*] se calmer; [*anger*] passer; [2] (topple) [*fence, tree*] tomber; ▶ ~ **[sb/sth] over** [*wind*] renverser [*person, tree*]

■ **blow up**: ▶ ~ **up** [1] (in explosion) [*building*] sauter; [*bomb*] exploser; [2] [*storm*] se lever; [3] [*problem, affair*] éclater; [4] ○(become angry) s'emporter; [5] (inflate) **it ~s up** c'est gonflable; ▶ ~ **[sth/sb] up, ~ up [sb/sth]** faire sauter [*building, person*]; faire exploser [*bomb*]; ▶ ~ **[sth] up, ~ up [sth]** [1] (inflate) gonfler [*tyre*]; [2] Phot (enlarge) agrandir; [3] (exaggerate) exagérer

blow-by-blow *adj* [*account*] par le menu

blow-dry /'bləʊdraɪ/
A *n* brushing *m*
B *vtr* **to ~ sb's hair** faire un brushing à qn

blowhole /'bləʊhəʊl/ *n* (of whale) évent *m*; (in ice) trou *m* d'air

blown /bləʊn/ *pp* ▸ **blow B, C**

blowout /'bləʊaʊt/ *n* [1] Elec court-circuit *m*; [2] Aut (of tyre) crevaison *f*; [3] (in oil or gas well) jaillissement *m*; [4] ○(meal) gueuleton○ *m*

blow: ~**pipe** *n* sarbacane *f*; ~**torch** /'bləʊtɔːtʃ/ *n* lampe *f* à souder

blow-up /'bləʊʌp/
A *n* Phot agrandissement *m*
B *adj* (inflatable) [*doll, toy, dinghy*] gonflable

blowy○ /'bləʊɪ/ *adj* venteux/-euse, venté

blowzy /'blaʊzɪ/ *adj* péj [*woman*] à l'aspect négligé

blubber /'blʌbə(r)/
A *n* [1] (of whale) graisse *f* de baleine; [2] ○fig (of person) graisse *f*
B ○*vi* pleurer comme un veau

blubbery /'blʌbərɪ/ *adj* adipeux/-euse

bludgeon /'blʌdʒən/
A *n* matraque *f*
B *vtr* matraquer; **to ~ sb to death** tuer qn à coups de matraque

blue /bluː/ ▸ p. 752
A *n* [1] (colour) bleu *m*; **to go** ou **turn ~** devenir bleu; [2] (sky) littér **the ~** l'azur *m* litér; [3] GB Univ **to be an Oxford ~** être membre d'une équipe sportive d'Oxford; [4] ○GB Pol **a true ~** un partisan ardent du parti Conservateur
B **blues** *npl* [1] Mus **the ~s** le blues *m*; [2] ○(depression) **to have the ~s** avoir le cafard○
C *adj* [1] (in colour) bleu; fig ~ **from** ou **with the cold** bleu de froid; [2] (depressed) **to feel ~** avoir le cafard○; [3] ○(smutty) [*film*] porno○; [*joke*] osé, cochon/-onne○; [4] ○GB Pol conservateur/-trice

(Idioms) **to say sth out of the ~** dire qch à brûle-pourpoint; **to appear/happen out of the ~** apparaître/se passer à l'improviste; **to vanish into the ~** s'évanouir dans la nature; **black and ~** couvert de bleus; **to beat sb black and ~**○ battre qn comme plâtre; **to tell sb sth until one is ~ in the face** se tuer à dire qch à qn

blue: **Bluebeard** *pr n* Barbe-bleue *m*; ~**bell** *n* Bot jacinthe *f* des bois; ~**berry** *n* US Bot myrtille *f*; ~**black** ▸ p. 752 *n, adj* bleu-noir (*m*) *inv*; ~ **blood** *n* sang *m* bleu or noble; ~**blooded** *adj* de sang bleu or noble; ~**bottle** *n* mouche *f* bleue; ~ **cheese** *n* (fromage *m*) bleu *m*

blue chip
A *n* [1] Fin valeur *f* vedette; [2] Games (in poker) jeton *m* de grande valeur
B *noun modifier* Fin [*company*] de premier ordre; ~ **(share)** valeur *f* de premier ordre; ~ **investment** placement *m* sûr or de tout repos

blue collar *adj* ~ **worker** ouvrier *m*, col *m* bleu

blue-eyed /'bluːaɪd/ *adj* aux yeux bleus; ~ **boy** GB fig chouchou○ *m*

blue: **Blue Helmets**, **Blue Berets** *npl* Mil Casques *mpl* bleus; ~ **jay** *n* geai *m* bleu; ~ **jeans** *npl* jean *m*; ~ **light** *n* (on emergency vehicles) gyrophare *m*

blueness /'bluːnɪs/ *n* bleu *m* ¢

blue pencil *n* **to go through sth with the ~** (edit) corriger qch; (censor) censurer qch

blueprint /'bluːprɪnt/ *n* [1] Archit, Tech bleu *m*; [2] fig (plan) projet *m*, propositions *fpl* (**for** pour; **for doing** pour faire); **it's a ~ for disaster** cela mène tout droit à la catastrophe

blue: ~ **rinse** *n* rinçage *m* à reflets argentés; ~ **rinse brigade** *n* GB hum péj vieilles bourgeoises *fpl* bien-pensantes péj; ~**stocking** *n* péj bas-bleu *m* péj; ~ **tit** *n* mésange *f* bleue; ~ **whale** *n* baleine *f* bleue

bluff /blʌf/
A *n* [1] (ruse) bluff *m*; [2] (cliff) falaise *f*
B *adj* [*person, manner*] carré
C *vtr* bluffer○; **to ~ sb into thinking sth** faire croire qch à qn; **to ~ one's way out of a situation** se tirer d'une situation en bluffant
D *vi* bluffer○ (also in cards)

(Idioms) **to call sb's ~** prendre qn au mot (*sachant qu'il bluffe*); **it's time we called his ~** il est temps qu'on le mette au pied du mur; **to ~ it (out)** s'en tirer en bluffant or au bluff

blunder /'blʌndə(r)/
A *n* bourde *f*
B *vi* [1] (make mistake) faire une bourde; [2] (move clumsily) **to ~ into the table** se cogner à la table; **to ~ about in the dark** avancer dans l'obscurité en se cognant

blundering /'blʌndərɪŋ/ *adj* balourd

blunt /blʌnt/
A *adj* [1] [*knife, scissors*] émoussé; [*pencil*] mal taillé; [*instrument*] contondant; [*needle*] épointé; **this knife is ~** ce couteau ne coupe plus; [2] (frank) [*person, manner*] abrupt; [*refusal*] catégorique; [*criticism*] direct; **to be ~ with you** pour être tout à fait franc avec toi
B *vtr* émousser [*knife*]; épointer [*pencil, needle*]; émousser [*intelligence*]; tempérer [*enthusiasm*]

bluntly /'blʌntlɪ/ *adv* franchement

bluntness /'blʌntnɪs/ *n* (of person) franc-parler *m*; (of manner) rudesse *f*

blur /blɜː(r)/
A *n* image *f* floue; **after that it's a ~** après ça, je ne me rappelle plus rien; **her memories are just a ~** ses souvenirs sont extrêmement confus
B *vtr* (*p prés etc* **-rr-**) brouiller
C *vi* (*p prés etc* **-rr-**) se brouiller

blurb /blɜːb/ *n* gen descriptif *m* (promotionnel); (on book cover) texte *m* de présentation (*sur la couverture*); péj baratin *m*

blurred /blɜːd/ *adj* indistinct; [*image, idea*] flou; [*memory*] confus; **to have ~ vision** avoir des troubles de la vue; **to become ~** [*eyes*] se voiler

blurt /blɜːt/ *vtr* ▸ **blurt out**

(Phrasal verb)

■ **blurt out**: ▶ ~ **[sth] out, ~ out [sth]** laisser échapper

blush /blʌʃ/
A *n* rougeur *f*; **without a ~** sans scrupules; **to spare sb's ~es** ménager (la modestie de) qn
B *vi* rougir (**at** devant; **with** de); **to ~ for sb** avoir honte pour qn

blusher /'blʌʃə(r)/ *n* fard *m* à joues

blushing /'blʌʃɪŋ/
A *n* rougissement *m*
B *adj* [*person*] rougissant

bluster /'blʌstə(r)/
A *n* fig (angry) fulminations *fpl*; (boasting) fanfaronnades *fpl*
B *vi* [1] [*wind*] souffler en bourrasques; [2] fig [*person*] (angrily) fulminer (**at** contre); (boastfully) fanfaronner

blustering /'blʌstərɪŋ/
A *n* (boasting) fanfaronnades *fpl*; (rage) fulminations *fpl*
B *adj* (boastful) fanfaron/-onne; (angry) braillard

blustery /'blʌstərɪ/ *adj* ~ **wind** bourrasque *f*; **it's a ~ day** le vent souffle en bourrasques

B movie /'biː muːvɪ/ *n* film *m* de série B

BO○ *n* (*abrév* = **body odour**) odeur *f* corporelle

boa /'bəʊə/ *n* [1] (snake) boa *m*; [2] (feather) ~ boa *m*

boa constrictor *n* (boa) constricteur *m*

boar /bɔː(r)/ *n* [1] (wild) sanglier *m*; [2] (pig) verrat *m*

board /bɔːd/
A *n* [1] (plank) planche *f*; [2] Admin conseil *m*; ~ **of directors**

conseil d'administration; ~ **of inquiry** commission *f* d'enquête; ~ **of governors** comité *m* de gestion d'une école; **3**⟩ (playing surface) tableau *m*; **4**⟩ Sch tableau *m* (noir); **5**⟩ (notice board) (for information) panneau *m* d'affichage; (to advertise) panneau *m*; **6**⟩ Comput, Elec plaquette *f*; **7**⟩ (accommodation) **full** ~ pension *f* complète; **half** ~ demi-pension *f*; ~ **and lodging, room and** ~ le gîte et le couvert

B **boards** *npl* **1**⟩ (floor) plancher *m*; **bare** ~**s** plancher nu; **2**⟩ Theat estrade *f*; **to tread the** ~**s** faire du théâtre

C *noun modifier* Admin [*meeting, member*] du conseil d'administration

D **on board** *adv phr* **to be on** ~ *ou* **on** ~ **ship** être à bord; **to go on** ~ embarquer, monter à bord; **to get on** ~ monter dans [*bus, train*]; monter à bord de [*plane, ship*]; **to take sth on** ~ lit embarquer [*cargo, passengers*]; fig prendre [qch] en compte [*changes, facts*]; adopter [*proposal*]

E *vtr* **1**⟩ (get on) monter à bord de [*boat, plane*]; monter dans [*bus, train*]; **2**⟩ Naut [*customs officer*] arraisonner [*vessel*]; [*pirates, marines*] aborder [*vessel*]

F *vi* être en pension (**with** chez); Sch [*pupil*] être interne

(Idioms) **above** ~ légal; **across the** ~ à tous les niveaux; **to go by the** ~ tomber à l'eau; **to sweep the** ~ tout gagner, tout rafler○

(Phrasal verbs)

■ **board out**: ▸ ~ **[sb] out**, ~ **out [sb]** mettre [qn] en pension

■ **board up**: ▸ ~ **[sth] up**, ~ **up [sth]** boucher [qch] avec des planches [*window*]; barricader [qch] avec des planches [*house*]

boarder /'bɔːdə(r)/ *n* **1**⟩ (lodger) pensionnaire *m*; **2**⟩ Sch interne *mf*

board game *n* jeu *m* de société (à damier)

boarding /'bɔːdɪŋ/ *n* **1**⟩ Aviat, Naut embarquement *m*; **2**⟩ Naut (by customs officer) arraisonnement *m*; **3**⟩ Mil abordage *m*

boarding: ~ **card** *n* carte *f* d'embarquement; ~ **house** *n* pension *f*; ~ **party** *n* groupe *m* d'abordage; ~ **school** *n* école *f* privée avec internat

board: ~**room** *n* salle *f* du conseil; ~**walk** *n* US chemin *m* fait de planches

boast /bəʊst/

A *n* vantardise *f*; **it is his** ~ **that he is never late** il se vante de ne jamais être en retard; **it was an empty** *ou* **idle** ~ c'était du bluff

B *vtr* **the town** ~**s a beautiful church** la ville s'enorgueillit d'une belle église; **the computer** ~**s two disk drives** l'ordinateur est équipé de deux lecteurs de disquettes

C *vi* se vanter (**about** de); **nothing to** ~ **about** (sth good) rien de bien extraordinaire; (sth bad) pas de quoi se vanter

boaster /'bəʊstə(r)/ *n* vantard/-e *m/f*

boastful /'bəʊstfl/ *adj* [*person*] vantard; **without being** ~ sans se vanter

boastfully /'bəʊstfəlɪ/ *adv* en se vantant

boasting /'bəʊstɪŋ/ *n* vantardise *f*

boat /bəʊt/

A *n* (vessel, ferry) bateau *m*; (sailing) voilier *m*; (rowing) barque *f*; (liner) paquebot *m*; **he crossed the lake in a** ~ il a traversé le lac en bateau

B *noun modifier* [*trip*] en bateau; [*hire*] de bateaux

(Idioms) **to be in the same** ~○ être tous dans la même galère; **to miss the** ~ manquer le coche; **to push the** ~ **out**○ GB faire les choses en grand; **to rock the** ~○ jouer les trouble-fête○

boater /'bəʊtə(r)/ *n* **1**⟩ (hat) canotier *m*; **2**⟩ US (person) canoteur *m*

boat: ~**hook** *n* gaffe *f*; ~**house** *n* abri *m* à bateaux

boating /'bəʊtɪŋ/

A *n* navigation *f* de plaisance; (rowing) canotage *m*

B *noun modifier* [*accident, enthusiast*] de bateau; [*trip*] en bateau

boatload /'bəʊtləʊd/ *n* (of goods) cargaison *f*; ~**s of tourists** des bateaux pleins de touristes

boat: ~**swain** *n* maître *m* d'équipage; ~**yard** *n* chantier *m* de construction de bateaux

bob /bɒb/

A *n* **1**⟩ (haircut) coupe *f* au carré; **2**⟩ (nod) **a** ~ **of the head** un signe de tête; **3**⟩ (curtsy) petite révérence *f*; **4**⟩ (weight) (on plumb line) plomb *m*; (on pendulum) poids *m*; (on fishing line) bouchon *m*; **5**⟩ (tail) queue *f* écourtée; **6**⟩ ○GB (money) (*pl* ~)

shilling *m*; **to cost a** ~ **or two** coûter une fortune; **7**⟩ Sport bobsleigh *m*

B *vtr* (*p prés etc* **-bb-**) **1**⟩ (cut) couper [qch] au carré [*hair*]; couper [qch] court [*tail*]; **2**⟩ (nod) **to** ~ **one's head** faire un signe de tête; **3**⟩ **to** ~ **a curtsy** faire une petite révérence (**to à**)

C *vi* (*p prés etc* **-bb-**) [*boat, float*] danser; **to** ~ **down** [*person*] se baisser subitement; **to** ~ **up and down** [*person, boat*] s'agiter; [*heads*] apparaître et disparaître

D **bobbed** *pp adj* [*hair, tail*] coupé court

bobbin /'bɒbɪn/ *n* bobine *f*; (for lace-making) fuseau *m*

bobble /'bɒbl/ *n* pompon *m*; ~ **hat** bonnet à pompon

bobby○† /'bɒbɪ/ GB *n* agent *m* (de police)

bobcat /'bɒbkæt/ *n* lynx *m* roux

bobsled /'bɒbsled/, **bobsleigh** /'bɒbsleɪ/ ▸ p. 881

A *n* bobsleigh *m*

B *vi* faire du bobsleigh

bode /bəʊd/ *vi* **to** ~ **well/ill** être de bon/mauvais augure

bodge GB = **botch**

bodice /'bɒdɪs/ *n* (of dress) corsage *m*

bodily /'bɒdɪlɪ/

A *adj* [*function*] physiologique; [*fluid*] organique; [*need, well-being*] physique; [*injury*] corporel/-elle

B *adv* [*carry, pick up*] à bras-le-corps

bodkin /'bɒdkɪn/ *n* (for piercing) poinçon *m*

body /'bɒdɪ/

A *n* **1**⟩ (of person, animal) corps *m*; ~ **and soul** corps et âme; **just enough to keep** ~ **and soul together** juste assez pour survivre; **to sell one's** ~ se prostituer; **2**⟩ (corpse) corps *m*, cadavre *m*; **3**⟩ (main section) (of car) carrosserie *f*; (of boat) coque *f*; (of aircraft) fuselage *m*; (of camera) boîtier *m*; (of violin, guitar) caisse *f* de résonance; (of dress) corsage *m*; **4**⟩ (large quantity) (of water) étendue *f*; (of laws) recueil *m or* corps *m* (de lois); **a large** ~ **of evidence** un vaste faisceau de preuves; **5**⟩ (group) (of troops, students) corps *m*; **the student** ~ la masse des étudiants; **the main** ~ **of demonstrators** le gros des manifestants; **6**⟩ (organization) organisme *m*; **disciplinary** ~ commission *f* disciplinaire; **7**⟩ Phys corps *m*; **8**⟩ (fullness) (of wine) corps *m*; (of hair) volume *m*; **9**⟩ (garment) body *m*

B *noun modifier* [*lotion*] pour le corps; [*care, paint*] corporel/-elle

(Idiom) **over my dead** ~! plutôt mourir!

body: ~ **armour** GB, ~ **armor** US *n* tenue *f* pare-balles; ~ **bag** *n* housse *f* mortuaire

body blow *n* lit coup *m* porté au corps; **to deal a** ~ **to** fig porter un coup sérieux à

body: ~**builder** *n* culturiste *mf*; ~**building** *n* culturisme *m*; ~**guard** *n* (individual) garde *m* du corps; (group) protection *f* rapprochée; ~ **heat** *n* chaleur *f* corporelle; ~ **language** *n* langage *m* corporel; ~ **odour** GB, ~ **odor** US, **BO**○ *n* odeur *f* corporelle; ~ **politic** *n* corps *m* social; ~ **shop** *n* Aut atelier *m* de carrosserie; ~ **snatching** *n* vol *m* de cadavres; ~ **stocking**, ~ **suit** *n* body *m*, justaucorps *m*; ~ **warmer** *n* gilet *m* matelassé; ~ **weight** *n* poids *m*; ~**work** *n* carrosserie *f*

boffin○ /'bɒfɪn/ *n* GB expert *m*

bog /bɒg/ *n* **1**⟩ (marshy ground) marais *m*; **2**⟩ (also **peat** ~) tourbière *f*

(Idiom) **to get** ~**ged down in sth** s'enliser dans qch

bogey /'bəʊgɪ/ *n* **1**⟩ (evil spirit) (also ~**man**) croquemitaine *m*; **2**⟩ (to frighten people) épouvantail *m*; **3**⟩ (in golf) bogey *m*

boggle /'bɒgl/ *vi* **the mind** *ou* **imagination** ~**s at the idea** on a du mal à imaginer ça

boggy /'bɒgɪ/ *adj* (swampy) marécageux/-euse; (muddy) bourbeux/-euse; (peaty) tourbeux/-euse

bogus /'bəʊgəs/ *adj* [*official, doctor, document*] faux/fausse (*before n*); [*claim*] bidon○; [*company*] factice

bohemia /bəʊ'hiːmɪə/ *n* (community) bohème *f*; (district) quartier *m* bohème

bohemian /bəʊ'hiːmɪən/ *adj* [*lifestyle*] de bohème; [*person*] bohème *inv*

boil /bɔɪl/

A *n* **1**⟩ **to be on the** ~ GB lit, fig être en ébullition; **to bring sth to the** ~ porter qch à ébullition; **to go off the** ~ GB [*water*] cesser de bouillir; **2**⟩ Med furoncle *m*

B *vtr* **1**⟩ (also ~ **up**) faire bouillir, porter [qch] à ébullition [*liquid*]; **2**⟩ (cook) faire bouillir, faire cuire [qch] à l'eau; **to**

b

The human body

■ *When it is clear who owns the part of the body mentioned, French tends to use the definite article where English uses a possessive adjective:*

he raised his hand
= il a levé la main

she closed her eyes
= elle a fermé les yeux

■ *Note, for instance, the use of* la *and* mon *here:*

she ran her hand over my forehead
= elle a passé la main sur mon front

■ *For expressions such as* he hurt his foot *or* she hit her head on the beam, *where the owner of the body part is the subject of the verb, i.e. the person doing the action, use a reflexive verb in French:*

she has broken her leg
= elle s'est cassé la jambe

(*literally* she has broken to herself the leg – *there is no past participle agreement because the preceding reflexive pronoun* se *is the indirect object*).

he was rubbing his hands
= il se frottait les mains

she was holding her head
= elle se tenait la tête

■ *Note also the following:*

she broke his leg
= elle lui a cassé la jambe

(*literally* she broke to him the leg)

the stone split his lip
= le caillou lui a fendu la lèvre

(*literally* the stone split to him the lip)

....

Describing people

■ *For ways of saying how tall someone is* ▸ **p. 977**, *of stating someone's weight* ▸ **p. 1323**, *and of talking about the colour of hair and eyes* ▸ **p. 752**.

■ *Here are some ways of describing people in French:*

his hair is long
= il a les cheveux longs

he has long hair
= il a les cheveux longs

a boy with long hair
= un garçon aux cheveux longs

a long-haired boy
= un garçon aux cheveux longs

the boy with long hair
= le garçon aux cheveux longs

her eyes are blue
= elle a les yeux bleus

she has blue eyes
= elle a les yeux bleus

she is blue-eyed
= elle a les yeux bleus

the girl with blue eyes
= la fille aux yeux bleus

a blue-eyed girl
= une fille aux yeux bleus

his nose is red
= il a le nez rouge

he has a red nose
= il a le nez rouge

a man with a red nose
= un homme au nez rouge

a red-nosed man
= un homme au nez rouge

■ *When referring to a temporary state, the following phrases are useful:*

his leg is broken
= il a la jambe cassée

the man with the broken leg
= l'homme à la jambe cassée

but note

a man with a broken leg
= un homme avec une jambe cassée

~ an egg faire cuire un œuf
C *vi* **1** [*water, vegetables etc*] bouillir; **the kettle is ~ing** l'eau bout (dans la bouilloire); **the saucepan ~ed dry** toute l'eau de la casserole s'est évaporée; **2** *fig* [*sea*] bouillonner; [*person*] bouillir (**with** de); **to make sb's blood ~** faire sortir qn de ses gonds
D **boiled** *pp adj* **~ed chicken** poule *f* au pot; **~ed egg** œuf *m* à la coque
(Phrasal verbs)
■ **boil away** (evaporate) s'évaporer
■ **boil down**: ▸ **~ down** Culin se réaliser (par ébullition); ▸ **~ down to** *fig* se ramener *or* se résumer à; ▸ **~ down [sth]**, **~ [sth] down** **1** Culin faire réduire [qch] [*sauce*]; **2** *fig* réduire [*text*] (**to** à)
■ **boil over** *lit* [*liquid*] déborder; *fig* [*anger, tension*] déborder

boiler /'bɔɪlə(r)/ *n* (in heating system, steam generator) chaudière *f*; (for storing water) chauffe-eau *m inv*; (chicken) poule *f* (*à faire au pot*)

boiler: **~ house** *n* bâtiment *m* des chaudières; **~maker** ▸ **p. 1181** *n* chaudronnier *m*; **~ room** *n* salle *f* des chaudières; **~ suit** *n* GB (workman's) bleu *m* de travail *or* de chauffe; (woman's) combinaison *f*

boiling /'bɔɪlɪŋ/ *adj* **1** (at boiling point) bouillant; **2** °*fig* **it's ~ in here**°! il fait une chaleur infernale ici!; **3** (for cooking) (*épith*) [*fowl*] à faire au pot

boiling: **~ hot**° *adj* [*day*] torride; [*liquid*] bouillant°; **~ point** *n lit* point *m* d'ébullition; *fig* point *m* limite

boisterous /'bɔɪstərəs/ *adj* **1** [*adult*] bruyant; [*child*] turbulent; [*meeting, game*] bruyant; **2** (tempestuous) [*sea*] houleux/-euse

bold /bəʊld/
A *n* GB (in printing) (*also* **boldface** US) caractères *mpl* gras; **in ~** en (caractères) gras
B *adj* **1** (daring) [*person*] intrépide; [*attempt, plan*] audacieux/-ieuse; **2** (cheeky) [*person, look*] effronté; [*behaviour*] hardi; **3** (strong) [*colour*] vif/vive; [*design*] voyant; [*handwriting*] assuré; [*outline*] net/nette; **4** (of typeface) gras/grasse
(Idiom) **to be as ~ as brass** avoir un culot monstre°

boldly /'bəʊldlɪ/ *adv* **1** (daringly) hardiment; (cheekily) avec effronterie; **2** [*designed*] de manière voyante; [*outlined*] nettement; **~ coloured** aux couleurs vives

boldness /'bəʊldnɪs/ *n* **1** (intrepidity) hardiesse *f*; (cheek) effronterie *f*; **2** (of design, colour) netteté *f*

Bolivia /bə'lɪvɪə/ ▸ **p. 774** *pr n* Bolivie *f*

bollard /'bɒlɑːd/ *n* **1** (on quay, ship) bollard *m*; **2** (in road) balise *f*

Bollywood /'bɒlɪwʊd/ *pr n* Bollywood, le Hollywood de Bombay

Bolognese /ˌbɒlə'neɪz/
A *n* (*pl* **~**) Bolognais/-aise *m/f*
B *adj* **~ sauce** sauce *f* bolognaise; **spaghetti ~** spaghettis *mpl* (à la) bolognaise

boloney° /bə'ləʊnɪ/ *n* **C** balivernes *fpl*

Bolshevik /'bɒlʃəvɪk/, US *also* 'bəʊl-/
A *n* bolchevique *mf*

b *adj* bolchevique

bolshy○ GB /'bɒlʃɪ/ *adj* **1** (on one occasion) [*child*] buté; [*adult*] pas commode; **to get** ∼ se braquer; **2** (by temperament) **he's/she's** ∼ c'est un râleur○/une râleuse○

bolster /'bəʊlstə(r)/
A *n* traversin *m*
B *vtr* (*also* ∼ **up**) **1** (boost) renforcer [*confidence*]; **to** ∼ **sb's ego** donner de l'assurance à qn; **2** (shore up) soutenir [*economy*]; appuyer [*argument*]

bolt /bəʊlt/
A *n* **1** (lock) verrou *m*; **2** (screw) boulon *m*; **3** ∼ **of lightning** coup *m* de foudre; **4** (of cloth) rouleau *m* (de tissu); **5** (for crossbow) carreau *m*; **6** (for rifle) culasse *f* mobile; **7** (in mountaineering) piton *m* à expansion; **8** (dash) départ *m* précipité; **to make a** ∼ **for it** décamper○
B **bolt upright** *adj phr* droit comme un i
C *vtr* **1** (lock) verrouiller; **to be** ∼**ed shut** être fermé au verrou; **2** Constr boulonner; **3** (*also* ∼ **down**) (swallow) engloutir [*food*]
D *vi* [*horse*] s'emballer; [*rabbit, person*] détaler○; **to** ∼ **out/off** sortir/partir à toute allure

(Idiom) **a** ∼ **from** *ou* **out of the blue** un coup de tonnerre

bolt hole *n* GB lit, fig refuge *m*

bomb /bɒm/
A *n* **1** (explosive device) bombe *f*; **2** ○GB (large amount of money) **to cost a** ∼ coûter un argent fou○; **3** ○(flop) fiasco *m*
B *vtr* bombarder [*town, house*]
C ○*vi* **1** (move fast) **to** ∼ **up the road** remonter la rue à fond de train○; **2** (fail) échouer

(Phrasal verb)
∎ **bomb out: we were** ∼**ed out** nous avons été forcés de quitter notre maison à cause des bombardements

bombard /bɒm'bɑːd/ *vtr* bombarder (**with** de)

bombardment /bɒm'bɑːdmənt/ *n* bombardement *m*

bombastic /ˌbɒm'bæstɪk/ *adj* ampoulé, grandiloquent

bomb: ∼ **attack** *n* attentat *m* à la bombe; ∼ **blast** *n* explosion *f*; ∼ **disposal** *n* déminage *m*; ∼ **disposal expert** ▸ p. 1181 *n* démineur *m*; ∼ **disposal squad** *n* équipe *f* de déminage

bomber /'bɒmə(r)/
A *n* **1** Mil, Aviat bombardier *m*; **2** (terrorist) poseur/-euse *m/f* de bombes
B *noun modifier* [*pilot*] de bombardier; [*raid, squadron*] de bombardiers

bomber jacket *n* blouson *m* d'aviateur

bombing /'bɒmɪŋ/ *n* Mil bombardement *m*; (by terrorists) attentat *m* à la bombe

bomb: ∼**proof** *adj* à l'épreuve des bombes; ∼ **scare** *n* alerte *f* à la bombe

bombshell /'bɒmʃel/ *n* fig bombe *f*

bomb shelter *n* abri *m* antiaérien

bombsite /'bɒmsaɪt/ *n* **1** lit zone *f* touchée par une explosion; **2** fig (mess) champ *m* de bataille

Bomb Squad /'bɒmskwɒd/ *n* brigade *f* antiterroriste

bona fide /ˌbəʊnə 'faɪdɪ/ *adj* [*attempt*] sincère; [*member, refugee*] vrai (*before n*); [*offer*] sérieux/-ieuse; [*contract*] de bonne foi

bonanza /bə'nænzə/ *n* **1** (windfall) pactole *f*, filon *m*; **2** (performance, festival etc) événement *m* exceptionnel; **3** (in mining) riche filon *m*

bond /bɒnd/
A *n* **1** (link) lien(s) *m(pl)* (**of** de; **between** entre); **to strengthen a** ∼ resserrer des liens; **to feel a strong** ∼ **with sb** se sentir très proche de qn; **2** (fetter) lit lien *m*; fig chaîne *f* (**of** de); **3** Fin obligation *f*; **government** ∼ obligation d'État; **savings** ∼ bon *m* d'épargne; **4** (adhesion) adhérence *f*; **5** Chem liaison *f*; **6** Jur (guarantee) engagement *m* écrit; (deposit) caution *f*; **7** (at customs) **in** ∼ en dépôt de douane
B *vtr* (*also* ∼ **together**) **1** [*glue*] faire adhérer [*surfaces*]; enlier [*bricks*]; **2** [*suffering*] créer des liens entre [*people*]
C *vi* **1** gen, Psych s'attacher (**with** à); **2** [*materials*] adhérer (**with** à); **3** Chem [*atoms*] s'associer (**with** à)

bondage /'bɒndɪdʒ/ *n* lit, fig esclavage *m*

bonding /'bɒndɪŋ/ *n* **1** (between mother and baby) (process) formation *f* des liens maternels; **2** (between people) (process) formation *f* du lien affectif (**between** entre); **male** ∼ amitié *f* virile

bone /bəʊn/
A *n* **1** (of human, animal) os *m*; (of fish) arête *f*; **made of** ∼ en os; **chicken on/off the** ∼ poulet à l'os/désossé; **to break every** ∼ **in one's body** se rompre les os; **2** (in corset etc) baleine *f*
B **bones** *npl* **1** (animal skeleton) ossements *mpl*; **2** (human remains) (in archeology) ossements *mpl* humains; **to lay sb's** ∼**s to rest** enterrer la dépouille de qn
C *vtr* Culin désosser [*joint, chicken*]; enlever les arêtes de [*fish*]

(Idioms) ∼ **of contention** sujet *m* de dispute, pomme *f* de discorde; **close to the** ∼ (wounding) blessant; (racy) osé; **to cut sth to the** ∼ réduire qch au minimum; **to feel sth in one's** ∼**s** avoir le pressentiment de qch; **to have a** ∼ **to pick with sb** avoir un compte à régler avec qn; **to make no** ∼**s about sth** ne pas cacher qch; **sticks and stones may break my** ∼**s (but words will never harm me)** ≈ les chiens aboient, la caravane passe; **to work one's fingers to the** ∼ se crever à la tâche○

(Phrasal verb)
∎ **bone up on**○: ▸ ∼ **up on [sth]** potasser○ [*subject*]

bone china *n* porcelaine *f* tendre *or* à l'os

boned /bəʊnd/ *adj* **1** [*joint, leg, chicken*] désossé; [*fish*] sans arête; **2** [*corset, bodice*] à armature

bone: ∼ **dry** *adj* complètement desséché; ∼**head**○ *n* abruti-e○ *m/f*; ∼ **idle**○ *adj* flemmard○

boneless /'bəʊnlɪs/ *adj* [*chicken breast*] sans os; [*fish*] sans arête

bone: ∼ **marrow** *n* moelle *f* osseuse; ∼**-marrow transplant** *n* greffe *f* de moelle osseuse

bonemeal /'bəʊnmiːl/ *n* **1** (fertilizer) engrais *m* phosphaté; **2** (feed) fourrage *m* phosphaté (*de cendres d'os*)

bonfire /'bɒnfaɪə(r)/ *n* (of rubbish) feu *m* de jardin; (for celebration) feu *m* de joie

Bonfire Night *n* GB la soirée du 5 novembre (*fêtée avec feux de joie et feux d'artifice*)

bonkers○ /'bɒŋkəz/ *adj* dingue○

bonnet /'bɒnɪt/ *n* **1** (hat) bonnet *m*; **2** GB Aut capot *m*

(Idiom) **to have a bee in one's** ∼ avoir une idée fixe

bonus /'bəʊnəs/ *n* **1** (payment) prime *f*; **no claims** ∼ GB bonus *m*; **cash** ∼ prime *f*; **2** (advantage) avantage *m* (**of being** d'être)

bonus point *n* bonus *m* d'un point; **five** ∼**s** un bonus de cinq points

bony /'bəʊnɪ/ *adj* **1** [*person, body, shoulders, face*] anguleux/-euse; [*finger, arm, knee*] osseux/-euse; **2** [*fish*] plein d'arêtes

boo /buː/
A *n* (jeer) huée *f*
B *excl* (to give sb a fright) hou!; (to jeer) hou! hou!
C *vtr* (3e *pers sg prés* **boos**, *prét, pp* **booed**) huer [*actor, speaker*]; **to be** ∼**ed off the stage** quitter la scène sous les huées
D *vi* (3e *pers sg prés* **boos**, *prét, pp* **booed**) pousser des huées

boob○ /buːb/ *n* **1** GB (mistake) bêtise *f*; **2** (breast) nichon○ *m*

boo-boo○ /'buːbuː/ *n* boulette○ *f*

booby prize *n* prix *m* de consolation (*décerné au dernier*)

booby trap
A *n* **1** Mil mécanisme *m* piégé; **2** (joke) traquenard *m*
B *vtr* (*p prés etc* **-pp-**) Mil piéger

boogie○ /'buːgɪ/ *vi* danser

booing /'buːɪŋ/ *n* **∅** huées *fpl*

book /bʊk/
A *n* **1** (reading matter) livre *m*, bouquin○ *m* (**about** sur; **of** de); **history** ∼ livre d'histoire; **'Carlton Books'** 'Éditions *fpl* Carlton'; **2** (part) (of novel, trilogy) livre *m*, tome *m*; (of poem, epic, bible) livre *m*; **3** Fin (for recording deposits, withdrawals) livret *m* bancaire; **4** (exercise book) cahier *m*; **drawing** ∼ cahier de dessin; **5** (of cheques, tickets, vouchers, stamps) carnet *m*; ∼ **of matches** pochette *f* d'allumettes; **6** (in betting) **to make a** ∼ **on** prendre des paris sur; **to open** *ou* **start a** ∼ **on** ouvrir les paris sur; **7** (directory) annuaire *m*; **8** (rulebook) règlement *m*; **to do things by the** ∼ fig suivre le règlement; **9** (opera libretto) livret *m*
B **books** *npl* **1** (accounts) livres *mpl* de comptes, comptabilité *f* **∅**; **to keep the** ∼**s** tenir les comptes, s'occuper de la

comptabilité; **2** (records) registre *m*; **to be on the ～s of** être inscrit à [*organization*]

C *vtr* **1** (reserve) réserver [*table, room, taxi, ticket*]; faire les réservations pour [*holiday*]; engager [*babysitter, entertainer*]; **to ～ sth for sb, to ～ sb sth** réserver qch pour qn; **to ～ sb into a hotel** réserver une chambre dans un hôtel pour qn; **to be fully ～ed** être complet/-ète; **my Tuesday afternoons are ～ed** je suis pris le mardi après-midi; **2** (charge) [*policeman*] dresser un procès-verbal *or* un P.V.○ à [*motorist, offender*]; US (arrest) arrêter [*suspect*]; **he was ～ed for speeding** il a été poursuivi pour excès de vitesse; **3** GB Sport [*referee*] donner un carton jaune à [*player*]; **to be ～ed** recevoir un carton jaune

D *vi* réserver; **you are advised to ～** il est conseillé de réserver

(Idioms) **I can read her like a ～** elle ne peut rien me cacher; **his past is an open ～** il n'a rien à cacher sur son passé; **economics is a closed ～ to me** je ne connais rien à l'économie; **to throw the ～ at sb** (reprimand) passer un savon○ à qn; (accuse) n'omettre aucun chef d'accusation (*quand on arrête qn*); (punish *or* sentence) donner le maximum à qn; **to be in sb's good ～s** être dans les petits papiers de qn○; **to be in sb's bad ～s** ne pas avoir la cote avec qn; **in my ～**○ à mon avis

(Phrasal verbs)
■ **book in**: ▸ **～ in** GB (check in) se présenter à la réception; (reserve) réserver une chambre; ▸ **～ [sb] in** réserver une chambre pour
■ **book up**: **to be ～ed up** être complet/-ète

book: **～binder** ▸ p. 1181 *n* relieur/-euse *m/f*; **～binding** *n* reliure *f*; **～-burning** *n* autodafé *m*; **～case** *n* bibliothèque *f*; **～ club** *n* club *m* du livre; **～end** *n* serre-livres *m inv*; **～ fair** *n* salon *m* du livre

bookie○ /'bʊkɪ/ *n* bookmaker *m*

booking /'bʊkɪŋ/ *n* **1** GB (reservation) réservation *f*; **to make a ～** faire une réservation; **2** (for performance) engagement *m*; **3** GB (from referee) **to get a ～** recevoir un carton jaune

booking: **～ clerk** ▸ p. 1181 *n* GB préposé/-e *m/f* aux réservations; **～ form** *n* GB bon *m* de réservation; **～ office** *n* GB bureau *m* de location

bookish /'bʊkɪʃ/ *adj* [*person*] studieux/-ieuse

book: **～ jacket** *n* jaquette *f*; **～keeper** ▸ p. 1181 *n* comptable *mf*; **～keeping** *n* comptabilité *f*

booklet /'bʊklɪt/ *n* brochure *f*

book: **～list** *n* liste *f* de livres; **～ lover** *n* bibliophile *mf*; **～maker** ▸ p. 1181 *n* bookmaker *m*

bookmark /'bʊkmɑːk/
A *n* **1** (for books) marque-page *m*, signet *m*; **2** (for website) signet *m*
B *vtr* marquer [*qch*] d'un signet, mettre [*qch*] dans la liste des favoris [*website*]

book: **～plate** *n* ex-libris *m*; **～rest** *n* lutrin *m*; **～seller** ▸ p. 1181 *n* (person) libraire *mf*; (shop) librairie *f*; **～shelf** *n* (single) étagère *f*; (in bookcase) rayon *m*; **～shop** ▸ p. 1181 *n* librairie *f*; **～stall** *n* (in market) étalage *m* de livres; (GB) (station) kiosque *m* à journaux; **～store** ▸ p. 1181 *n* US librairie *f*; **～ token** *n* GB chèque-livre *m*; **～worm** *n* mordu/-e○ *m/f* de la lecture

boom /buːm/
A *n* **1** (noise) (of voices, cannon, thunder) grondement *m*; (of waves) mugissement *m*; (of drum) boum *m*; (of explosion) détonation *f*; **2** (onomat) badaboum!; **3** (period of prosperity) boom *m*, période *f* de forte expansion; (in demand, prices, sales etc) explosion *f* (**in** de); **export/consumer ～** boom des exportations/de la consommation; **property ～** boom immobilier; **4** (increase in popularity) boom *m* (**in** de); **5** Naut (spar) bôme *f*; (barrage) estacade *f*; **6** (on crane) gui *m*; **7** Cin, Radio, TV perche *f*
B *noun modifier* [*industry, town*] en pleine expansion; [*period, year*] de croissance; [*share*] à la hausse
C *vi* **1** (make a noise) [*cannon, thunder*] gronder; [*bell, voice*] retentir; [*sea*] mugir; **2** (prosper) [*economy, trade*] prospérer; [*exports, sales*] monter en flèche; [*industry*] être en plein essor; [*hobby, sport*] être en plein boom; **business is ～ing** les affaires vont bien

(Phrasal verb)
■ **boom out**: ▸ **～ out** [*music, sound*] retentir; ▸ **～ [sth] out, ～ out [sth]** [*person*] brailler [*speech*]; [*loudspeaker*] faire retentir [*announcement*]; [*drum*] faire retentir [*rhythm*]

boomerang /'buːməræŋ/
A *n* boomerang *m*; **～ effect** effet boomerang
B *vi* [*plan*] faire boomerang

booming /'buːmɪŋ/ *adj* **1** (loud) [*sound*] retentissant; [*voice*] tonitruant; **2** (flourishing) [*economy*] en plein essor; [*demand, exports, sales*] en forte progression

boom microphone *n* micro *m* à perche

boon /buːn/ *n* **1** (advantage) avantage *m*; **2** (asset) aide *f* précieuse (**to** à); **to be a great ～ to sb** apporter une aide précieuse à qn; **3** (stroke of luck) aubaine *f* (**for** pour)

boor /'bʊə(r), bɔː(r)/ *n* grossier personnage *m*, malotru *m*

boorish /'bʊərɪʃ, bɔː-/ *adj* grossier/-ière

boost /buːst/
A *n* **1** (stimulus) coup *m* de fouet (**to** à); **to give sth a ～** stimuler qch; **2** (encouragement) encouragement *m*; **to give sb a ～** encourager qn; **3** (publicity) publicité *f*; **to give sth a ～** faire du battage pour qch
B *vtr* **1** (stimulate) stimuler [*economy, productivity, sales*]; encourager [*investment, lending*]; augmenter [*capacity, number, pay, profit, value*]; relancer [*interest*]; **to ～ sb's confidence** redonner confiance à qn; **to ～ morale** remonter le moral; **2** (enhance) améliorer [*image, performance*]; **3** (promote) faire la promotion de, promouvoir [*product*]; **4** Elec, Telecom amplifier [*signal, voltage*]; **5** Aut rendre [qch] plus puissant [*engine*]; **6** (push up) propulser [*rocket*]

booster /'buːstə(r)/
A *n* **1** Radio, Telecom amplificateur *m*; **2** Elec survolteur *m*; **3** Aut compresseur *m*; **4** Med vaccin *m* de rappel
B *noun modifier* [*dose, injection*] de rappel; **～ rocket** fusée *f* d'appoint

boot /buːt/ ▸ p. 1191
A *n* **1** (footwear) botte *f*; (for workman, soldier) brodequin *m*; **climbing/hiking ～** chaussure *f* de montagne/randonnée; **football ～** GB chaussure *f* de football; **to put the ～ in** lit rouer qn de coups de pied; fig y aller fort; **2** GB Aut coffre *m*; **3** (dismissal) **to get the ～** se faire virer; **4** ○(kick) coup *m* de pied; **～ up the backside** un bon coup de pied au derrière also fig; **5** US (wheel clamp) sabot *m* de Denver
B *vtr* **1** ○(kick) envoyer un coup de pied à [*person*]; donner un coup de pied dans [*ball*]; **2** Comput = **boot up**

(Idioms) **the ～ is on the other foot** GB les rôles sont renversés; **to be/get too big for one's ～s** GB avoir/prendre la grosse tête; **to ～** par dessus le marché; **to lick sb's ～s** lécher les bottes à qn

(Phrasal verbs)
■ **boot out**: ▸ **～ [sb] out, ～ out [sb]** (from institution) renvoyer; (from company, house) mettre [qn] à la porte
■ **boot up** Comput: ▸ **～ [sth] up, ～ up [sth]** amorcer [*computer*]

boot: **～black** *n* cireur *m* de chaussures; **～ drive** *n* Comput unité *f* d'initialisation

bootee /buː'tiː/ *n* **1** (knitted) chausson *m*; **2** (leather) bottine *f*

booth /buːð, US buː'θ/ *n* (in language lab) cabine *f*; (in restaurant) alcôve *f*; (at fair) baraque *f*; **polling ～** isoloir *m*; **telephone ～** cabine *f* (téléphonique)

boot: **～jack** *n* tire-botte *m*; **～lace** *n* lacet *m* (de chaussure); **～legger** *n* US bootlegger *m*; **～licker** *n* lèche-bottes *mf inv*; **～maker** ▸ p. 1181 *n* bottier *m*; **～polish** *n* cirage *m*; **～ sale** *n* GB brocante *f* (*d'objets apportés dans le coffre de sa voiture*); **～ scraper** *n* décrottoir *m*

bootstrap /'buːtstræp/ *n* **1** (on boot) tirant *m* de botte; **2** Comput programme *m* d'amorce

(Idiom) **to pull oneself up by one's ～s** se faire tout seul

booty /'buːtɪ/ *n* butin *m*

booze○ /buːz/
A *n* bibine○ *f*; (wine only) pinard○ *m*
B *vi* picoler○

booze cruise○ *n* expédition *f* alcool à gogo, aller-retour *m* en ferry pour acheter de l'alcool à bas prix à l'étranger

boozer○ /'buːzə(r)/ *n* (person) poivrot/-ote○ *m/f*; (pub) GB bistro *m*

booze-up○ /'buːzʌp/ *n* GB beuverie *f*

boozy○ /'buːzɪ/ *adj* [*meal*] bien arrosé; [*laughter*] aviné

bop /bɒp/
A *n* **1** ○(blow) coup *m*; **2** ○(dancing) **to go for a ～** aller en boîte○

B ○*vtr* (*p prés etc* **-pp-**) cogner
C ○*vi* (*p prés etc* **-pp-**) GB danser
Bordeaux /bɔː'dəʊ/ *n* (wine) bordeaux *m*
border /'bɔːdə(r)/ ▸ **p. 1132**
A *n* **1** (frontier) frontière *f*; **France's ~ with Spain** la frontière entre la France et l'Espagne; **on the Swiss ~** sur la frontière suisse; **to cross the ~** passer la frontière; **to escape over ou across the ~** s'échapper en passant la frontière; **our allies across the ~** nos alliés de l'autre côté de la frontière; **2** (edge) (of forest) lisière *f*; (of estate, lake, road) bord *m*; **3** (decorative edge) (on crockery, paper) liseré *m*; (on picture, cloth) bordure *f*; **4** (flowerbed) plate-bande *f*; **5** (hypothetical limit) frontière *f* (**between** entre); **6** Comput (of window) bordure *f*
B *noun modifier* [*control*] aux frontières; [*crossing, patrol, state*] frontalier/-ière; [*area, post, town, zone*] frontière (*after n, inv*); [*police*] des frontières; [*incident*] de frontière
C *vtr* **1** (lie alongside) [*road, land*] longer [*lake, forest*]; [*country*] border [*ocean*]; **France ~s Italy** la France a une frontière commune avec l'Italie; **2** (surround) border; **to be ~ed by trees** être bordé d'arbres.

(Phrasal verb)
■ **border on:** ▸ **~ on [sth]** **1** (have a frontier with) [*country*] avoir une frontière commune avec; [*garden, land*] toucher; **2** (verge on) friser

border: ~ dispute *n* différend *m* frontalier; **~ guard** *n* garde-frontière *m*
borderline /'bɔːdəlaɪn/ *n* frontière *f*, limite *f* (**between** entre); **a ~ case** un cas limite
border raid *n* incursion *f* armée
bore /bɔː(r)/
A *prét* ▸ **bear**
B *n* **1** (person) raseur○/-euse *m/f*; **2** (situation) **what a ~!** quelle barbe!; **3** (*also* **~hole**) trou *m* de forage; **4** (of gun barrel, pipe) calibre *m*; **12-~ shotgun** fusil *m* de calibre 12
C *vtr* **1** (annoy) ennuyer; **2** (drill) percer [*hole*]; creuser [*well, tunnel*]
D *vi* **to ~ into/through** forer dans/à travers; **her eyes ~d into me** elle me perçait de son regard

(Idiom) **to ~ sb stiff** *ou* **to death** *ou* **to tears** faire mourir qn d'ennui

bored /bɔːd/ *adj* [*person*] qui s'ennuie; [*expression, voice*] ennuyé; **to get** *ou* **be ~** s'ennuyer (**with** de); **to look ~** avoir l'air de s'ennuyer
boredom /'bɔːdəm/ *n* **1** (feeling) ennui *m* (**with** devant); **2** (of activity, job, lifestyle) monotonie *f*
boring /'bɔːrɪŋ/
A *n* (drilling) (in wood) perforation *f*; (in rock) forage *m*
B *adj* [*person, place, activity, event*] ennuyeux/-euse; [*colour, food*] fade; **it's ~ being/doing** c'est assommant d'être/de faire
born /bɔːn/
A *adj* [*person, animal*] né (**of** de; **to do** pour faire; **with** avec); **to be ~** naître; **when the baby is ~** quand le bébé sera né; **~ a Catholic** d'origine catholique; **to be ~ blind** être aveugle de naissance; **to be a ~ leader** être un chef né; **a ~ liar** un parfait menteur; **to be ~ (out) of sth** [*idea, group*] naître de qch
B **-born** *combining form* **London-/Irish-~** né à Londres/en Irlande, originaire de Londres/d'Irlande

(Idioms) **in all my ~ days** de toute ma vie; **I wasn't ~ yesterday** je ne suis pas né de la dernière pluie; **there's one ~ every minute**○! quel idiot/quelle idiote!

born-again /ˌbɔːnə'geɪn/ *adj* [*Christian*] régénéré
borne /bɔːn/ *pp* ▸ **bear**
borough /'bʌrə, US -rəʊ/ *n* arrondissement *m* urbain
borough council *n* GB conseil *m* municipal
borrow /'bɒrəʊ/
A *vtr* emprunter (**from** à)
B *vi* Fin faire un emprunt (**from** à)

(Idiom) **he/she is living on ~ed time** ses jours sont comptés

borrower /'bɒrəʊə(r)/ *n* emprunteur/-euse *m/f*
borrowing /'bɒrəʊɪŋ/ *n* **1** Fin **¢** emprunt *m*; **increase in ~** augmentation des emprunts; **~ costs** le coût de l'emprunt; **2** Ling, Literat emprunt *m* (**from** à)
borstal† /'bɔːstəl/ *n* GB maison *f* de correction
Bosnia /ˌbɒznɪə/ ▸ **p. 774** *pr n* Bosnie *f*

Bosnia-Herzegovina /ˌbɒznɪə ˌhɜːtsəgəʊ'viːnə/ ▸ **p. 774** *pr n* Bosnie-Herzégovine *f*
bosom /'bʊzəm/ *n* littér **1** (chest) poitrine *f*; **to hug sb to one's ~** serrer qn contre sa poitrine; **2** (breasts) **to have a large ~** avoir beaucoup de poitrine; **3** fig (heart, soul) cœur *m*; **in the ~ of one's family** au sein de sa famille
bosom buddy○, **bosom friend** *n* ami/-e *m/f* intime
boss /bɒs/ *n* **1** ○(person in charge) gen patron/-onne *m/f*; (in politics, underworld) chef *m*; **you're the ~** iron c'est toi le patron; **we'll show them who's ~** on va leur montrer qui commande ici; **2** (on shield) umbo *m*; (on ceiling) bossage *m*; (on wheel) tourteau *m*

(Phrasal verb)
■ **boss about**○, **boss around**○: ▸ **~ [sb] about** mener [qn] par le bout du nez

bossy○ /'bɒsɪ/ *adj* autoritaire
bosun *n* = boatswain
botanic(al) /bə'tænɪk(l)/ *adj* [*studies, drawing, term*] botanique; [*name*] latin; **~ gardens** jardin *m* botanique
botanist /'bɒtənɪst/ ▸ **p. 1181** *n* botaniste *mf*
botany /'bɒtənɪ/ *n* botanique *f*
botany wool *n* laine *f* mérinos
botch /bɒtʃ/
A *n* (*also* **~-up**) **to make a ~ of sth** saboter qch
B *vtr* bâcler
both /bəʊθ/
A *adj* **~ sides of the road** les deux côtés de la rue; **~ her eyes/parents** ses deux yeux/parents; **~ their faces/lives** leurs visages/vies; **~ children came** les enfants sont venus tous les deux
B *conj* **~ you and I saw him** tu l'as vu comme moi; **~ here and abroad** ici comme à l'étranger; **to show ~ firmness and tact** faire preuve à la fois de fermeté et de tact; **~ Paris and London have their advantages** aussi bien Paris que Londres a ses avantages
C *pron* (+ *v pl*) (of things) les deux; (of people) tous les deux; **let's do ~** faisons les deux; **~ are young, they are ~ young** ils sont jeunes tous les deux
D **both of** *pron phr* (+ *v pl*) **let's take ~ of them** prenons les deux; **~ of you are wrong** vous avez tort tous les deux
bother /'bɒðə(r)/
A *n* **1** (inconvenience) ennui *m*, embêtement○ *m*; **to do sth without any ~** faire qch sans aucune difficulté; **it's too much ~** c'est trop de tracas; **to have the ~ of doing** avoir le tracas de faire; **to go to the ~ of doing** se donner le mal de faire; **it's no ~** ce n'est pas un problème; **2** ○**¢** GB (trouble) ennuis *mpl*; **to be in a bit** *ou* **spot of ~** avoir des ennuis; **3** (person) casse-pieds○ *mf inv*, enquiquineur/-euse○ *m/f*
B ○*excl* zut alors!
C *vtr* **1** (worry) tracasser; **don't let it ~ you** ne te tracasse pas avec ça; **to be ~ed by noise** être dérangé par le bruit; **it ~s me that** cela m'ennuie que (+ *subj*); **they won't be ~ing you again** ils ne t'embêteront plus; **2** (inconvenience) déranger; **oh stop ~ing me**○! mais arrête de m'embêter à la fin○!; **to ~ sb with** ennuyer qn avec [*details, problems*]; **3** (hurt) faire souffrir
D *vi* **1** (take trouble) s'en faire; **please don't ~** s'il te plaît, ne te dérange pas; **why ~?** pourquoi se tracasser?; **I don't think I'll ~** je ne vais pas m'embêter avec ça; **I wouldn't ~** ce n'est pas la peine; **to ~ doing** *ou* **to do** prendre la peine de faire; **don't** *ou* **you needn't ~ doing** ce n'est pas la peine de faire; **to ~ about** se tracasser au sujet de; **I don't know why I ~** je ne sais pas pourquoi je me tracasse; **don't** *ou* **you needn't ~ coming back!** ce n'est pas la peine de revenir!; **2** (worry) **to ~ about** se soucier de; **it's not worth ~ing about** ça ne vaut pas la peine qu'on s'en occupe
E **bothered** *pp adj* (concerned) **to be ~ed that** être ennuyé que (+ *subj*); **to be ~ed with** s'embêter avec [*detail, problem*]; **he's not ~ed about money** ça ne l'intéresse pas d'avoir de l'argent; **I'm not ~ed** GB ça m'est égal; **you just couldn't be ~ed** to turn up! tu ne t'es même pas donné la peine de venir!
Botswana /bɒt'swɑːnə/ ▸ **p. 774** *pr n* Botswana *m*
bottle /'bɒtl/
A *n* **1** (container) (for drinks) bouteille *f*; (for perfume, medicine) flacon *m*; (for baby) biberon *m*; (for gas) bouteille *f*; **milk ~** bouteille *f* de lait; **2** ○fig (alcohol) **to hit the ~, to be on the ~** caresser la bouteille○; **3** ○GB (courage) courage *m*, cran○ *m*

B *vtr* **1** (put in bottles) embouteiller, mettre [qch] en bouteilles [*milk, wine*]; **2** GB (preserve) mettre [qch] en bocal *or* en conserve [*fruit*]

C bottled *pp adj* [*beer, gas*] en bouteille; **~d water** eau *f* minérale

Phrasal verbs

■ **bottle out**○ GB se dégonfler○

■ **bottle up**: ▸ ~ [**sth**] **up**, ~ **up** [**sth**] étouffer [*anger, grief*]

bottle: ~ **bank** *n* réceptacle *m* à verre; ~ **feed** *vtr* nourrir [qn] au biberon; ~ **feeding** *n* alimentation *f* au biberon; ~ **green** ▸ p. 752 *n, adj* vert (*m*) bouteille *inv*

bottleneck /'bɒtlnek/ *n* **1** (traffic jam) embouteillage *m*; **2** (narrow part of road) rétrécissement *m* de la chaussée; **3** (hold-up) goulet *m* d'étranglement

bottle: ~**-opener** *n* décapsuleur *m*; ~ **top** *n* capsule *f* (de bouteille)

bottlewasher /'bɒtlwɒʃə(r)/ *n* **chief cook and** ~ hum factotum *m*

bottom /'bɒtəm/

A *n* **1** (base) (of hill, pile, steps, wall) pied *m*; (of page) bas *m*; (of bag, bottle, hole, river, sea) fond *m*; **to sink** *ou* **go to the** ~ [*ship*] couler; **from the** ~ **of one's heart** du fond du cœur; **the** ~ **has fallen** *ou* **dropped out of the market** le marché s'est effondré; **2** (underside) (of boat) œuvres *fpl* vives, carène *f*; (of vase, box) dessous *m*; **3** (lowest position) (of list) bas *m*; (of league) dernière place *f*; (of hierarchy) dernier rang *m*, bas *m*; **at the** ~ **of the heap** *ou* **pile** fig au bas de l'échelle; **to be** *ou* **come** ~ **of the class** être dernier/-ière de la classe; **to hit rock** ~ fig toucher le fond; **4** (far end) (of garden, field) fond *m*; (of street) bout *m*; **5** ○(buttocks) derrière○ *m*; **6** fig (root) fond *m*; **to get to the** ~ **of a matter** découvrir le fin fond d'une affaire

B ○**bottoms** *npl* **pyjama** ~**s** pantalon *m* de pyjama; **bikini** ~**s** bas *m* de maillot de bain

C *adj* **1** (lowest) [*rung, shelf*] du bas; [*sheet*] de dessous; [*apartment*] du rez-de-chaussée; [*bunk*] inférieur; [*division, half, part*] dernier/-ière; ~ **of the range** bas de gamme; **2** (last) [*place, team*] dernier/-ière; [*score*] le plus bas

Idiom ~**s up**○! (drink up) cul sec○!; (cheers) santé!

Phrasal verb

■ **bottom out** [*recession*] atteindre son point le plus bas

bottom drawer *n* lit tiroir *m* du bas; fig trousseau *m* de mariée

bottom end *n* **1** lit (far end) (of street) bout *m*; **2** fig (of league, division) partie *f* inférieure; (of market) bas *m* de gamme

bottom: ~ **gear** *n* GB Aut première *f*; ~**less** *adj* sans fond

bottom line *n* **1** Fin dernière ligne *f* du bilan; **2** (decisive factor) **the** ~ **is that** la vérité c'est que; **that's the** ~ ça c'est le vrai problème

botulism /'bɒtjʊlɪzəm/ ▸ p. 933 *n* botulisme *m*

bouffant /'buːfɑːn/ *adj* [*hair, hairstyle*] crêpé; [*sleeve*] bouffant

bough /baʊ/ *n* branche *f*

bought /bɔːt/ *prét, pp* ▸ **buy**

boulder /'bəʊldə(r)/ *n* rocher *m*

bounce /baʊns/

A *n* **1** (rebound of ball) rebond *m*; **2** (of mattress, material) élasticité *f*; (of hair) souplesse *f*; **3** fig (vigour) allant *m*; **4** (in email) retour *m* à l'expéditeur

B *vtr* **1** faire rebondir [*ball*]; retransmettre [*signal*]; **2** ○**to** ~ **a cheque** [*bank*] GB refuser d'honorer un chèque; [*person*] US faire un chèque sans provision; **3** Comput renvoyer [qch] à l'expéditeur [*email*]

C *vi* **1** [*ball, object*] rebondir (**off** sur; **over** au-dessus de); [*person*] (on trampoline, bed) faire des bonds, sauter; **to** ~ **up and down on sth** faire des bonds *or* sauter sur qch; **2** fig (move energetically) **to** ~ **in/along** entrer/marcher énergiquement; **3** ○[*cheque*] être sans provision; **4** Comput [*email*] revenir à l'expéditeur

Phrasal verb

■ **bounce back** (after illness) se remettre; (in career) faire un retour en force

bouncer○ /'baʊnsə(r)/ *n* videur *m*

bouncy /'baʊnsɪ/ *adj* **1** [*ball*] qui rebondit bien; [*mattress*] élastique; [*walk*] sautillant; **2** fig [*person*] dynamique

bound /baʊnd/

A *prét, pp* ▸ **bind**

B *n* bond *m*; **in a** ~, **with one** ~ d'un bond

C bounds *npl* lit, fig limites *fpl*; **to be out of** ~**s** [*place*] être interdit d'accès; Sport être hors du terrain; **to be within/beyond the** ~**s of sth** fig rester dans/dépasser les limites de qch; **it's not beyond the** ~**s of possibility** ce n'est pas impossible; **there are no** ~**s to her curiosity** il n'y a pas de limites à sa curiosité

D *adj* **1** (certain) **to be** ~ **to do sth** aller sûrement faire qch; **she's** ~ **to know** elle doit sûrement savoir; **it was** ~ **to happen** cela devait arriver; **2** (obliged) (by promise, rules, terms) tenu (**by** par; **to do** de faire); **I am** ~ **to say that...** je dois dire que...; **3** [*book*] relié; **leather-**~ relié en cuir; **4** (heading for) ~ **for** [*person, bus, train*] en route pour; [*aeroplane*] à destination de; **5** (connected) **to be** ~ **up with sth** être lié à qch

E *vtr* (border) borner; ~**ed by** lit, fig borné par

F *vi* bondir; **to** ~ **into the room** entrer dans la pièce en coup de vent

G -bound *combining form* **1** (heading for) **London-**~ à destination de Londres; **2** (confined) **fog-/strike-**~ immobilisé par le brouillard/la grève

boundary /'baʊndrɪ/ *n* **1** gen, Geog limite *f* (**between** entre); **city** ~ limites de la ville; **national** ~ frontières *fpl* du pays; **2** fig (defining) limite *f*; (dividing) ligne *f*; **3** Sport limites *fpl* du terrain

boundless /'baʊndlɪs/ *adj* [*terrain, space*] infini; [*enthusiasm, energy, ambition*] sans bornes

bounty /'baʊntɪ/ *n* **1** (generosity) générosité *f*; **2** (gift) don *m*; **3** (reward) prime *f*; ~ **hunter** chasseur *m* de primes

bouquet /bʊ'keɪ/ *n* bouquet *m*

bourbon /'bɜːbən/ *n* bourbon *m*

bourgeois /'bɔːʒwɑː, US ˌbʊər'ʒwɑː/

A *n* bourgeois/-e *m/f*

B *adj* bourgeois; **a** ~ **woman** une bourgeoise

bourgeoisie /ˌbɔːʒwɑː'ziː, US ˌbʊəʒwɑː'ziː/ *n* bourgeoisie *f*

bout /baʊt/ *n* **1** (attack) (of fever, malaria) accès *m*; (of insomnia) crise *f*; **a** ~ **of coughing** une quinte de toux; **drinking** ~ soûlerie *f*; **to have a** ~ **of flu** avoir une grippe; **2** Sport combat *m*; **3** (outbreak) crise *f*; **4** (period of activity) période *f*

boutique /buː'tiːk/ ▸ p. 1181 *n* boutique *f*; **fashion** ~ boutique de mode

bovine /'bəʊvaɪn/ *adj* lit, fig bovin

bow[1] /bəʊ/ *n* **1** (weapon) arc *m*; **2** Mus archet *m*; **3** (knot) nœud *m*; **to tie a** ~ faire un nœud

Idiom **to have more than one string to one's** ~ avoir plus d'une corde à son arc

bow[2] /baʊ/

A *n* **1** (movement) salut *m*; **to take a** ~ Theat saluer; **2** Naut avant *m*, proue *f*; **on the starboard** ~ par tribord devant

B *vtr* baisser [*head*]; courber [*branch*]; incliner [*tree*]

C *vi* **1** (bend forward) saluer; **to** ~ **to** saluer; **2** (give way) **to** ~ **to** s'incliner devant [*wisdom, necessity*]; **to** ~ **to pressure** céder à la pression; **3** (sag) [*plant, shelf*] se courber (**under** sous)

D bowed *pp adj* [*head*] penché; [*back*] courbé

Idioms **to** ~ **and scrape** fig faire des courbettes (**to** devant); **to fire a shot across sb's** ~**s** fig tirer un coup de semonce à qn

Phrasal verbs

■ **bow down**: ▸ ~ **down** lit se prosterner (**before** devant); fig se soumettre (**before** devant); ▸ ~ [**sth**] **down** [*wind*] courber [*tree*]

■ **bow out** (resign) prendre congé, tirer sa révérence○

bowel /'baʊəl/

A *n* intestin *m*; ~ **cancer** cancer de l'intestin

B bowels *npl* **1** Med intestins *mpl*; **2** fig (inner depths) profondeurs *fpl*

bowel movement *n* selles *fpl*

bower /'baʊə(r)/ *n* **1** (in garden) tonnelle *f*; **2** littér (chamber) boudoir *m*

bowl /bəʊl/

A *n* **1** (for food) bol *m*; (large) saladier *m*; (for soup) assiette *f* creuse; (for washing) cuvette *f*; (of lavatory) cuvette *f*; **a** ~**(ful) of milk** un bol de lait; **2** Sport boule *f* (en bois)

B *vtr* **1** (roll) faire rouler [*hoop, ball*]; **2** (throw) lancer [*ball*]

C *vi* **1** Sport lancer; **to ~ to sb** lancer la balle à qn; **2** US (go bowling) aller au bowling; **3** (move fast) **to ~ along** [*vehicle*] rouler à toute vitesse

(Phrasal verb)

■ **bowl over**: ▸ **~ [sb] over 1** (knock down) renverser [*person*]; **2** (impress) stupéfier [*person*]; **to be ~ed over** être sidéré

bowlegged /ˌbəʊˈlegɪd/ *adj* [*person*] aux jambes arquées; **to be ~** avoir les jambes arquées

bowler /ˈbəʊlə(r)/ *n* **1** Sport (in cricket) lanceur *m*; (in bowls) joueur/-euse *m/f* de boules (*sur gazon*); **2** (hat) = **bowler hat**

bowler hat *n* chapeau *m* melon

bowling /ˈbəʊlɪŋ/ ▸ p. 881 *n* Sport **1** (ten-pin) bowling *m*; **2** (on grass) jeu *m* de boules (*sur gazon*); **3** (in cricket) service *m*

bowling: **~ alley** *n* bowling *m*; **~ green** *n* terrain *m* de boules (*sur gazon*)

bowls /bəʊlz/ ▸ p. 881 *n* (+ *v sg*) jeu *m* de boules (*sur gazon*)

bow bəʊ: **~string** *n* corde *f* d'arc; **~ tie** *n* nœud-papillon *m*; **~ window** *n* fenêtre *f* en saillie

box /bɒks/

A *n* **1** (small, cardboard) boîte *f*; (larger, crate) caisse *f*; **~ of matches/of chocolates** boîte d'allumettes/de chocolats; **2** (on page) case *f*; **put a tick in the ~** cocher la case; **3** (seating area) Theat loge *f*; Sport tribune *f*; **4** (in stable) box *m*; **5** GB Sport (for protection) coquille *f*; **6** ○(television) **the ~** la télé; **7** Sport (in soccer) surface *f* de réparation; **8** (in gymnastics) cheval *m* de saut; **9** Post (*also* **Box**) boîte *f* postale; **(P.O.) Box 20** BP 20; **10** (for gears) boîte *f*; **11** (slap) **a ~ on the ear** une gifle; **12** Bot buis *m*

B *vtr* **1** (pack) mettre [qch] en caisse, encaisser; **2** (fight) boxer; **3** (strike) **to ~ sb's ears** gifler qn

C *vi* Sport boxer

D **boxed** *pp adj* [*note, information*] en encadré; **~ed set** coffret *m*; **~ed advertisement** encadré *m*

(Phrasal verb)

■ **box in**: ▸ **~ in** [*sth/sb*], **~ [sth/sb] in** coincer○ [*runner, car*]; **to be ~ed in** [*person*] être coincé○; **to feel ~ed in** se sentir enfermé

boxer /ˈbɒksə(r)/ ▸ p. 1181 *n* **1** Sport boxeur *m*; **2** (dog) boxer *m*

boxer shorts *npl* caleçon *m* (court)

boxing /ˈbɒksɪŋ/ ▸ p. 881

A *n* boxe *f*; **to take up ~** se mettre à la boxe

B *noun modifier* [*champion, glove, match*] de boxe; **~ ring** ring *m*

Boxing Day /ˈbɒksɪŋ deɪ/ *n* GB lendemain *m* de Noël

box: **~ junction** *n* GB milieu *m* d'intersection (*délimité par des bandes jaunes*); **~ number** *n* numéro *m* de boîte postale

box office

A *n* lit guichet *m*; fig **to do well/badly at the ~** être bien/mal accueilli au box office

B *noun modifier* [*failure, success*] au box office; **~ takings** recettes *fpl* des guichets; **to be a ~ attraction** attirer les foules

box: **~ room** *n* GB petite chambre *f* (*servant de débarras*); **~wood** *n* (bois *m* de) buis *m*

boy /bɔɪ/

A *n* **1** (young male) garçon *m*; **the ~s' toilet** les toilettes des garçons; **a ~'s bike** un vélo pour garçon; **come here ~!** viens ici, mon garçon!; **a new ~** fig, Sch un nouveau; **there's a good ~!** voilà, c'est bien mon petit!; **look ~s and girls** regardez, les enfants; **2** (son) fils *m*; **3** ○GB (man) gars○ *m*; **to be one of the ~s** faire partie de la bande; **to have a drink with the ~s** boire un coup avec les copains○; **an old ~** Sch un ancien élève; (old man) un vieillard; **4** (male animal) **down ~!** doucement, mon vieux!

B ○**boys** *npl* **1** (experts) gars○ *mpl*; **the legal ~s** les gars○ du service juridique; **2** (soldiers) gars○ *mpl*

C *noun modifier* [*detective, genius, soprano*] jeune (*before n*)

D ○*excl* **~, it's cold here!** bon sang○! ce qu'il fait froid ici!

boy band *n* boys band *m*

boycott /ˈbɔɪkɒt/

A *n* boycottage *m*, boycott *m* (**against, of, on** de)

B *vtr* boycotter

boy: **~friend** *n* (petit) copain *m* or ami *m*; **~hood** *n* enfance *f*

boyish /ˈbɔɪɪʃ/ *adj* **1** (youthful) [*figure, looks*] d'adolescent; **2** (endearingly young) [*grin, charm*] enfantin

boy: **~ racer**○ *n* jeune chauffard○ *m*; **~ toy**○ *n* gadget *m* pour gamin

BR *n*: *abrév* ▸ **British Rail**

bra /brɑː/ ▸ p. 1191 *n* soutien-gorge *m*

brace /breɪs/

A *n* **1** (for teeth) appareil *m* dentaire; **2** Med (for broken limb) attelle *f*; (permanent support) appareil *m* orthopédique; **3** Constr support *m*; **4** (pair) (of birds, animals) couple *m* (**of** de); (of pistols) paire *f* (**of** de); **5** (tool) vilebrequin *m*

B *vtr* **1** [*person*] arc-bouter [*body, back*] (**against** contre); **to ~ one's legs/feet against sth** appuyer les jambes/pieds contre qch; **2** Constr renforcer, consolider [*wall, structure*]

C **braces** *npl* GB (for trousers) bretelles *fpl*

D *v refl* **to ~ oneself** (physically) s'arc-bouter (**for** en prévision de); fig se préparer (**for** à; **to do** à faire)

bracelet /ˈbreɪslɪt/ *n* **1** (jewellery) bracelet *m*; **2** (watch-strap) bracelet *m* (de montre)

bracing /ˈbreɪsɪŋ/ *adj* vivifiant, tonifiant

bracken /ˈbrækən/ *n* fougère *f*

bracket /ˈbrækɪt/

A *n* **1** (in typography) (round) parenthèse *f*; (square) crochet *m*; **in ~s** entre parenthèses *or* crochets; **2** (support) (for shelf) équerre *f*; (for lamp) applique *f*; **3** (category) tranche *f*, catégorie *f*; **age ~** tranche d'âge; **price ~** catégorie de prix

B *vtr* **1** (put in brackets) (round) mettre [qch] entre parenthèses; (square) mettre [qch] entre crochets; **2** (put in category) accoler [*names, items*]; mettre [qn] dans le même groupe [*people*]

brackish /ˈbrækɪʃ/ *adj* saumâtre

bradawl /ˈbrædɔːl/ *n* poinçon *m*

brag /bræg/

A *n* **1** (boast) fanfaronnade *f*; **2** (card game) ≈ poker *m*

B *vi* (*p prés etc* **-gg-**) se vanter (**to** auprès de; **about** de)

bragging /ˈbrægɪŋ/ *n* fanfaronnade *f* (**about** au sujet de)

Brahmin /ˈbrɑːmɪn/ *n* **1** Relig brahmane *m*; **2** fig mandarin *m*

braid /breɪd/

A *n* **1** (of hair) tresse *f*, natte *f*; **2** (trimming) galon *m*

B *vtr* **1** tresser [*hair*]; **2** galonner [*cushion, uniform*]

brain /breɪn/

A *n* **1** (living organ) cerveau *m*; **2** (*also* **~s**) (substance) **~s** cervelle *f*; **to blow one's ~s out** se faire sauter la cervelle○; **3** Culin cervelle *f*; **calves' ~s** cervelle de veau; **4** (mind) **to have a good ~** être intelligent; **to have football on the ~**○ ne penser qu'au football

B **brains** (intelligence) intelligence *f*; **to have ~s** être intelligent; **he's the ~s of the family** c'est lui le cerveau de la famille; **to use one's ~s** faire marcher ses cellules grises

C *noun modifier* [*cell, tissue*] du cerveau, cérébral; [*tumour*] au cerveau; [*haemorrhage, fever*] cérébral

D ○*vtr* (knock out) assommer, estourbir○

(Idiom)

■ **to pick sb's ~s** avoir recours aux lumières de qn

brain: **~child** *n* grande idée *f*; **~ damage** *n* **C** lésions *fpl* cérébrales; **~ dead** *adj* Med dans un coma dépassé; **~ death** *n* mort *f* cérébrale; **~ drain** *n* fuite *f* des cerveaux; **~less** *adj* idiot; **~ scan** *n* scanographie *f* du cerveau; **~ scanner** *n* scanographe *m*; **~storm** *n* Med, fig coup *m* de folie; **~storming** *n* remue-méninges *m inv*; **~s trust** GB, **~ trust** US *n* brain-trust *m*, comité *m* d'experts; **~ surgeon** ▸ p. 1181 *n* neurochirurgien/-ienne *m/f*; **~ surgery** *n* neurochirurgie *f*; **~ teaser** *n* casse-tête *m inv*

brainwash /ˈbreɪnwɒʃ/ *vtr* faire subir un lavage de cerveau à; **they were ~ed into thinking that...** on a fini par leur faire croire que...

brain: **~washing** *n* (of prisoners) lavage *m* de cerveau; fig (of public) bourrage○ *m* de crâne; **~wave** *n* idée *f* géniale, illumination *f*

brainy /ˈbreɪnɪ/ *adj* doué

braise /breɪz/ *vtr* braiser

brake /breɪk/

A *n* lit, fig frein *m*; **to apply the ~(s)** freiner

B *vi* lit, fig freiner

brake: ~ **block** n patin m de frein; ~ **disc** n disque m de frein; ~ **drum** n tambour m de frein; ~ **fluid** n liquide m de frein; ~ **light** n feu m stop; ~ **lining** n garniture f de frein; ~ **pad** n plaquette f de frein; ~ **pedal** n pédale f de frein

braking /'breɪkɪŋ/ n freinage m

bramble /'bræmbl/
A n ①. (plant) ronce f; ②. GB (berry) mûre f
B noun modifier GB [jam, jelly] de mûres; [tart] aux mûres

bran /bræn/ n Bot, Culin son m

branch /brɑːntʃ, US bræntʃ/
A n ①. (of tree) branche f; fig (of pipe, road, railway) embranchement m; (of river) bras m; (of candlestick) branche f; (of antlers) ramure f; (of family, language) rameau m; (of study, subject) domaine m; ②. Comm, Admin (of shop) succursale f; (of bank) agence f; (of company) filiale f; (of organization) division f, secteur m; (of union) section f
B vi [tree, river] se ramifier; [road, railway] se diviser

(Phrasal verbs)
■ **branch off**: ▸ ~ **off** [road, river, railway] bifurquer; ▸ ~ **off (from)** se séparer de [road, railway]; fig dévier de [topic]
■ **branch out**: ▸ ~ **out** [business] se diversifier; **to** ~ **out into** [business, person] se lancer dans [new area]

branch: ~ **line** n ligne f secondaire; ~ **manager** n (of shop) directeur m de succursale; (of company) directeur m de filiale; (of bank) directeur m d'agence; ~ **office** n agence f

brand /brænd/
A n ①. (make) marque f; ②. (type) (of humour) type m; (of belief) conception f; (of art, of music) genre m; ③. (for identification) (on animal) marque f (au fer rouge); (on prisoner) marque f; ④. littér (in fire) tison m
B vtr ①. (mark) lit marquer (au fer) [animal]; ②. fig marquer [person]; **to** ~ **sb as sth** désigner qn comme qch

branded /'brændɪd/ adj [article, goods] de marque inv

brandish /'brændɪʃ/ vtr brandir

brand: ~ **leader** n leader m du marché; ~ **name** n marque f déposée; ~**-new** adj tout neuf/toute neuve

brandy /'brændɪ/ n ①. (from grape) cognac m; ②. (from other fruit) eau-de-vie f

brash /bræʃ/ adj ①. (self-confident) bravache; ②. (garish) tape-à-l'œil (inv); ③. (harsh) agressif/-ive

brass /brɑːs, US bræs/
A n ①. (metal) laiton m, cuivre m jaune; ②. (fittings, objects) cuivres mpl; ③. Mus (also ~ **section**) cuivres mpl; ④. (in church) plaque f commémorative; ⑤. ᵒ(money) GB pognon⁰ m; ⑥. ᵒ(nerve) culot⁰ m; ⑦. ᵒMil (+ v pl) **the top** ~ les galonnés
B noun modifier [button, plaque] en cuivre jaune

(Idioms) **to get down to** ~ **tacks** passer aux choses sérieuses; **to be as bold as** ~ avoir un drôle de culot⁰

brass band n orchestre m de cuivres, fanfare f

brassière† /'bræzɪə(r), US brə'zɪər/ n soutien-gorge m

brass: ~ **instrument** ▸ p. 1028 n Mus cuivre m; ~ **neck**⁰ n GB culot⁰ m; ~ **rubbing** n Art (activity) estampage m de plaques en laiton; (impression) estampe f d'une plaque en laiton

brassy /'brɑːsɪ, US 'bræsɪ/ adj ①. ▸ p. 752 (shiny) cuivré; ②. péj [appearance, woman] provocant

brat /bræt/ n péj marmot⁰ m, môme⁰ mf

bravado /brə'vɑːdəʊ/ n bravade f

brave /breɪv/
A n ①. (Indian) brave m; ②. **the** ~ (+ v pl) les courageux
B adj ①. (courageous) [person, effort] courageux/-euse; [smile] brave; **be** ~! courage!; ②. (fine) littér beau/belle (before n)
C vtr braver

(Idiom) **to put on a** ~ **face** faire bonne contenance

bravely /'breɪvlɪ/ adv courageusement; hum vaillamment

bravery /'breɪvərɪ/ n courage m, bravoure f

bravura /brə'vʊərə/ n bravoure f

brawl /brɔːl/
A n bagarre f
B vi se bagarrer (**with** avec)

brawn /brɔːn/ n ①. Culin fromage m de tête; ②. (muscle) muscles mpl

brawny /'brɔːnɪ/ adj musclé

bray /breɪ/
A n (of donkey) braiment m; péj (of person) braillement m
B vi [donkey] braire; péj [person] brailler

brazen /'breɪzn/ adj éhonté

(Phrasal verb)
■ **brazen out**: ▸ ~ **it out** payer d'audace

brazier /'breɪzɪə(r)/ n brasero m

Brazil /brə'zɪl/ ▸ p. 774 pr n Brésil m

Brazil nut n noix f du Brésil

breach /briːtʃ/
A n ①. (infringement) (by breaking rule) infraction f (**of** à); (by failure to comply) manquement m (**of** à); (of copyright, privilege) violation f; **security** ~ (of official secret) atteinte f à la sûreté nationale; **to be in** ~ **of** enfreindre [law]; violer [agreement]; ②. Mil brèche f also fig; ③. (in relationship) rupture f
B vtr faire une brèche dans [defence]; ne pas respecter [rule]

(Idiom) **to step into the** ~ faire un remplacement au pied levé

breach: ~ **of contract** n Jur rupture f de contrat; ~ **of promise** n rupture f de promesse de mariage; ~ **of the peace** n Jur atteinte f à l'ordre public; ~ **of trust** n Jur abus m de confiance

bread /bred/
A n ①. Culin pain m; **a loaf/slice of** ~ une miche/tranche de pain; ②. ᵒ(money) fric⁰ m, argent m; ③. (livelihood) **to earn one's (daily)** ~ gagner sa vie
B noun modifier [oven, plate] à pain; [sauce] au pain
C vtr Culin paner; ~**ed cutlets** côtelettes panées

(Idiom) **to know which side one's** ~ **is buttered on** savoir où est son intérêt

bread and butter
A n tartine f de pain beurré; fig gagne-pain m
B **bread-and-butter** adj [work] de tous les jours

bread: ~**basket** n lit corbeille f à pain; fig grenier m; ~**bin** n GB boîte f or huche f à pain; ~**board** n planche f à pain

breadcrumb /'bredkrʌm/
A n miette f de pain
B **breadcrumbs** npl Culin chapelure f

bread: ~**fruit** n fruit m de l'arbre à pain; ~**knife** n couteau m à pain

breadline /'bredlaɪn/ n **to be on the** ~ être au seuil de l'indigence

bread: ~ **roll** n Culin petit pain m; ~**stick** n longuet m

breadth /bretθ/ ▸ p. 977 n ①. lit largeur f; **the length and** ~ **of** d'un bout à l'autre de; ②. fig (of experience, knowledge, provisions, regulations) étendue f (**of** de); (of mind, opinions, vision) largeur f (de de)

(Idiom) **to be** ou **come within a hair's** ~ **of** être à deux doigts de

breadwinner /'bredwɪnə(r)/ n soutien m de famille

break /breɪk/
A n ①. (fracture) fracture f; ②. (crack) fêlure f; ③. (gap) (in wall) brèche f; (in row, line) espace m; (in circuit, chain) rupture f; (in conversation, match) pause f; (in performance) entracte m; (in traffic) trou m, espace m; **a** ~ **in the clouds** une éclaircie; **a** ~ **in transmission** une interruption dans la retransmission; ④. Radio, TV page f de publicité; ⑤. (pause) gen pause f; Sch récréation f; **to take a** ~ faire une pause; **to work for six hours without a** ~ travailler pendant six heures sans s'arrêter; **to take** ou **have a** ~ **from working** ne plus travailler pendant un temps; **I often give her a** ~ **from looking after the kids** je m'occupe souvent des enfants pour qu'elle se repose; (from job) il est temps de passer à autre chose; ⑥. (holiday) vacances fpl; **the Christmas** ~ les vacances de Noël; ⑦. fig (departure) rupture f (**with** avec); **a** ~ **with tradition** une rupture avec la tradition; **it's time to make a** ou **the** ~ (from family) il est temps de voler de ses propres ailes; (from job) il est temps de passer à autre chose; ⑧. ᵒ(opportunity) chance f; **her big** ~ **came in 1973** 1973 a été l'année de sa veine⁰; **he gave me a** ~ il m'a donné ma chance; ⑨. (dawn) **at the** ~ **of day** au lever du jour, à l'aube f; ⑩. (escape bid) **to make a** ~ **for it**⁰ (from prison) se faire la belle⁰; **to make a** ~ **for the door** se précipiter vers la porte; ⑪. Sport (in tennis) break m; (in snooker, pool) **it's your** ~ c'est à toi de casser; **to make a 50 point** ~ marquer une série de 50 points
B vtr (prét **broke**; pp **broken**) ①. (damage) casser [chair, eggs,

rope, stick, toy]; casser [*plate, window*]; **to ∼ a tooth/a bone** se casser une dent/un os; **to ∼ one's leg** se casser la jambe; **to ∼ one's neck** lit avoir une rupture des vertèbres cervicales; fig se casser la figure; **2)** (rupture) briser [*seal*]; **the skin is not broken** il n'y a pas de plaie; **the river broke its banks** la rivière a débordé; **3)** (interrupt) [*person*] rompre [*silence*]; [*shout, siren*] déchirer [*silence*]; couper [*circuit*]; rompre [*monotony, spell, ties, links*] (**with** avec); **to ∼ one's silence** sortir de son silence (**on** à propos de); **we broke our journey in Milan** nous avons fait un arrêt à Milan; **4)** (disobey) enfreindre [*law*]; ne pas respecter [*embargo, terms*]; violer [*treaty*]; désobéir à [*rule*]; briser [*strike*]; rompre [*vow*]; manquer [*appointment*]; **to ∼ one's word/ promise** manquer à sa parole/promesse; **5)** (exceed, surpass) dépasser [*speed limit, bounds*]; battre [*record*]; franchir [*speed barrier*]; **6)** (lessen the impact of) couper [*wind*]; [*branches*] freiner [*fall*]; [*hay*] amortir [*fall*]; **7)** fig (destroy) troops briser [*rebellion*]; briser [*person, resistance, will*]; **to ∼ sb's spirit** saper le moral de qn; **to ∼ a habit** se défaire d'une habitude; **8)** (ruin) ruiner [*person*]; **9)** (tame) débourrer [*young horse*]; **10)** (in tennis) **to ∼ sb's serve** faire le break; **11)** (decipher) déchiffrer [*code*]; **12)** (leave) **to ∼ camp** lever le camp; **13)** (announce) annoncer [*news*]; révéler [*truth*]; **to ∼ the news to sb** apprendre la nouvelle à qn

◖C◗ vi (*prét* **broke**; *pp* **broken**) **1)** (be damaged) [*branch, chair, egg, string*] se casser; [*plate, window*] se casser; [*arm, bone, leg*] se fracturer; [*bag*] se déchirer; **to ∼ in two** se casser en deux; **the sound of ∼ing glass** le bruit de verre brisé; **2)** (separate) [*clouds*] se disperser; [*waves*] se briser; **3)** (stop for a rest) faire une pause; **4)** (change) [*good weather*] se gâter; [*heatwave*] cesser; **5)** (begin) [*day*] se lever; [*storm*] éclater; [*scandal, story*] éclater; **6)** (discontinue) **to ∼ with sb** rompre les relations avec qn; **to ∼ with tradition** rompre avec la tradition; **7)** (weaken) **their spirit never broke** leur moral n'a jamais faibli; **to ∼ under torture** céder sous la torture; **8)** (change tone) [*boy's voice*] muer; **in a voice ∼ing with emotion** d'une voix brisée par l'émotion

(Phrasal verbs)

■ **break away**: ▶ ∼ **away 1)** (become detached) se détacher (**from** de); **to ∼ away from** rompre avec [*family, organization*]; se détacher de [*herd*]; rompre [*moorings*]; **2)** (escape) échapper (**from** à); **3)** Sport [*runner, cyclist*] se détacher (**from** de); ▶ ∼ **away** [**sth**], ∼ [**sth**] **away** enlever

■ **break down**: ▶ ∼ **down 1)** (stop functioning) [*machine*] tomber en panne; **2)** (collapse) fig [*alliance*] éclater; [*negotiations*] échouer; [*communication*] cesser; [*law and order*] se dégrader; [*argument*] ne pas tenir debout; [*system*] s'effondrer; [*person*] s'effondrer, craquer; **3)** (cry) fondre en larmes; **4)** (be classified) se décomposer (**into** en); **5)** (decompose) se décomposer (**into** en); **6)** (confess) céder; ▶ ∼ [**sth**] **down**, ∼ **down** [**sth**] **1)** (demolish) enfoncer [*door*]; démolir [*fence*]; fig faire tomber [*barriers*]; vaincre [*resistance*]; **2)** (analyse) ventiler [*cost, statistics*]; décomposer [*data, findings*] (**into** par); **3)** (cause to decompose) décomposer [*compound*] (**into** en); dissoudre [*protein, starch*]

■ **break even** rentrer dans ses frais

■ **break free**: ▶ ∼ **free** [*prisoner*] s'évader; **to ∼ free of** se couper de [*family*]; échapper à [*captor*]

■ **break in 1)** (enter forcibly) [*thief*] entrer (par effraction); [*police*] entrer de force; **2)** (interrupt) interrompre; ▶ ∼ [**sth**] **in** débourrer [*young horse*]; assouplir [*shoe*]; ▶ ∼ [**sb**] **in** accoutumer [qn] au travail

■ **break into**: ▶ ∼ **into** [**sth**] **1)** (enter by force) entrer dans [qch] (par effraction) [*building*]; forcer la portière de [*car*]; forcer [*safe*]; **her car was broken into** sa voiture a été cambriolée; **2)** (start to use) entamer [*new packet*]; **3)** (encroach on) empiéter sur [*leisure time*]; couper [*morning*]; **4)** (begin to do) **to ∼ into song/cheers** se mettre à chanter/acclamer; **to ∼ into a run** se mettre à courir; **5)** (make headway) [*company*] s'implanter sur [*market*]; percer dans [*show business*]

■ **break off**: ▶ ∼ **off 1)** (snap off) [*end, mast*] se casser; [*handle, piece*] se détacher; **2)** (stop speaking) s'interrompre; **3)** (pause) faire une pause; ▶ ∼ **off** [**sth**], ∼ [**sth**] **off 1)** (snap) casser; **2)** (terminate) rompre [*engagement, negotiations*]; interrompre [*conversation*]

■ **break out**: ▶ ∼ **out 1)** (erupt) [*epidemic, fire*] se déclarer; [*fight, riot, storm*] éclater; [*rash*] apparaître; **to ∼ out in a rash** [*person*] avoir une éruption de boutons; **to ∼ out in a sweat** se mettre à transpirer; **2)** (escape) [*prisoner*] s'évader; **to ∼ out of** s'échapper de [*prison*]; sortir de [*routine*]; se libérer de [*chains*]

■ **break through**: ▶ ∼ **through** [*army*] faire une percée;

▶ ∼ **through** [**sth**] percer [*defences, reserve*]; franchir [*barrier*]; traverser [*mur*]; [*sun*] percer [*clouds*]

■ **break up**: ▶ ∼ **up 1)** (disintegrate) lit [*wreck*] se désagréger; fig [*empire*] s'effondrer; [*alliance*] éclater; [*family, couple*] se séparer; **2)** (disperse) [*crowd*] se disperser; [*cloud, slick*] se disperser; [*meeting*] se terminer; **3)** GB Sch **schools ∼ up on Friday** les cours finissent vendredi; ▶ ∼ [**sth**] **up**, ∼ **up** [**sth**] disperser [*demonstrators*]; démanteler [*drugs ring*]; séparer [*team, couple*]; désunir [*family*]; briser [*alliance, marriage*]; démembrer [*empire*]; morceler [*land*]; [*diagrams*] aérer [*text*]; mettre fin à [*party, demonstration*]

breakable /'breɪkəbl/
◖A◗ breakables npl objets mpl fragiles
◖B◗ adj fragile

breakage /'breɪkɪdʒ/ n (damage) casse f; (broken item) article m cassé

breakaway /'breɪkəweɪ/
◖A◗ n **1)** (from organization) séparation f (**from** de); (from person) rupture f (**from** avec); **2)** Sport échappée f
◖B◗ noun modifier Pol (épith) [*faction, group, state*] séparatiste

breakdown /'breɪkdaʊn/
◖A◗ n **1)** Aut, Tech panne f (**in, of** de); **in the event of a ∼** en cas de panne; **he had a ∼** il est tombé en panne; **2)** (collapse) (of communications, negotiations) rupture f; (of discipline, order) dégradation f; (of alliance) éclatement m; (of plan) échec m; **3)** Med dépression f; **to have a (nervous) ∼** faire une dépression (nerveuse); **4)** (detailed account) (of figures, statistics) ventilation f; (of argument) décomposition f; **a ∼ of the voters according to sex/age** une répartition de l'ensemble des électeurs par sexe/tranche d'âge; **5)** Biol, Chem décomposition f
◖B◗ noun modifier [*vehicle, truck*] de dépannage

breaker /'breɪkə(r)/ n **1)** (wave) brisant m; **2)** ▸ p. 1181 (scrap merchant) casseur m; **3)** (CB radio user) cibiste mf

breaker's yard n Aut casse f

break: **∼-even** n seuil m de rentabilité; **∼-even point** n point m mort

breakfast /'brekfəst/
◖A◗ n petit déjeuner m
◖B◗ vi prendre le petit déjeuner

breakfast: **∼ bar** n bar m de cuisine; **∼ bowl** n assiette f creuse; **∼ cereals** npl céréales fpl (pour le petit déjeuner); **∼ television** n télévision f à l'heure du petit déjeuner

break-in /'breɪkɪn/ n cambriolage m

breaking /'breɪkɪŋ/ n **1)** (smashing) lit (of bone) fracture f; (of rope, chain) rupture f; (of glass, seal) bris m; fig (of waves) déferlement m; **2)** (of promise) manquement m (**of** à); (of law, treaty) violation f (**of** de); (of contract) rupture f (**of** de); (of link, sequence, tie) rupture f (**of** de); **3)** (of horse) débourrage m; **4)** (of voice) mue f

breaking and entering n Jur effraction f

breaking point n **1)** Tech point m de rupture; **2)** fig **to be at ∼** être à bout

break: **∼neck** adj [*pace, speed*] fou/folle, insensé; **∼-out** n évasion f; **∼point** n Sport balle f de break; **∼through** n Mil percée f; (in science, medicine, career) percée f; (in negotiations, investigation) progrès m; **∼-up** n (of empire) démembrement m; (of alliance, relationship) rupture f; (of political party, family, group) éclatement m; (of marriage) échec m; (of a company) morcellement m; **∼water** n brise-lames m inv

bream /briːm/ n (pl ∼) (freshwater) brème f

breast /brest/
◖A◗ n **1)** Anat (woman's) sein m; (chest) poitrine f; **2)** Culin (of poultry) blanc m, filet m; (of lamb) poitrine f; (of veal) tendron m; (of duck, pigeon) filet m, magret m
◖B◗ vtr affronter [*wave*]; atteindre le sommet de [*hill*]
(Idiom) **to make a clean ∼ of sth** soulager sa conscience en avouant qch

breast-feed /'brestfiːd/ vtr, vi (prét, pp **-fed**) allaiter; **breast-fed** nourri au sein

breast: **∼-feeding** n allaitement m maternel; **∼ pocket** n poche f de poitrine; **∼ stroke** n brasse f

breath /breθ/ n **1)** (air taken into lungs) souffle m; **to stop ou pause for ∼** s'arrêter pour reprendre son souffle; **to get one's ∼ back** reprendre son souffle; **out of ∼** à bout de souffle; **to be short of ∼** avoir le souffle court; **to hold one's ∼** lit retenir sa respiration; fig retenir son souffle;

b

2 (air in or leaving mouth) (with smell) haleine f; (visible) respiration f; **sb's hot** ∼ le souffle chaud de qn; **to have bad** ∼ avoir (une) mauvaise haleine; **I could smell alcohol on his** ∼ je sentais à son haleine qu'il avait bu; **3** (single act) respiration f; **to take a deep** ∼ respirer profondément or à fond; **take a deep** ∼**!** fig assieds-toi○! ; **in a single** ∼ sans respirer; **in the same** ∼ dans la foulée; **4** (of air, wind) a ∼ **of** un souffle de; **to go out for a** ∼ **of (fresh) air** sortir prendre l'air; **sb/sth is like a** ∼ **of fresh air** qn/qch est une vraie bouffée de fraîcheur; **5** (word) **a** ∼ **of** un soupçon de [*scandal*]

Idioms **to take sb's** ∼ **away** couper le souffle à qn; **save your** ∼○ ne gaspille pas ta salive○; **to say sth under one's** ∼ dire qch à voix basse

breathalyse GB, **breathalyze** US /'breθəlaɪz/ vtr faire subir un alcootest à [*driver*]; **to be** ∼**d** subir un alcootest

Breathalyzer® /'breθəlaɪzə(r)/ n alcootest m

breathe /briːð/

A vtr **1** (inhale, respire) respirer [*air, oxygen, gas, scent*]; **to** ∼ **one's last** rendre son dernier soupir; **2** (exhale, blow) souffler [*air, smoke, germs*] **(on** sur); cracher [*fire, vapour*]; **3** (whisper) murmurer (*to* à); **don't** ∼ **a word!** pas un mot!; **4** (inspire with) **to** ∼ **hope into sb** redonner de l'espoir à qn; **to** ∼ **(some) life into sth** animer qch

B vi **1** (respire) respirer; **to** ∼ **hard** *ou* **heavily** souffler fort, haleter; **to** ∼ **more easily** fig respirer; **2** (exhale, blow) **to** ∼ **over sb/on sth** souffler sur qn/sur qch; **3** (wine) s'aérer

Idioms **to** ∼ **down sb's neck**○ (watch closely) être sur le dos de qn○; (be close behind) être sur les talons de qn○; **to** ∼ **fire** fulminer

Phrasal verbs

■ **breathe in**: ▶ ∼ **in** inspirer; ▶ ∼ **in [sth]**, ∼ **[sth] in** inhaler

■ **breathe out**: ▶ ∼ **out** expirer; ▶ ∼ **out [sth]**, ∼ **[sth] out** exhaler

breather /'briːðə(r)/ n **1** (from work) pause f; **to have** *ou* **take a** ∼ faire une pause; **2** (from pressure) répit m

breathing /'briːðɪŋ/ n respiration f

breathing apparatus n masque m à oxygène

breathing space n **1** (respite) répit m; **to give oneself a** ∼ s'accorder un répit; **2** (postponement) délai m

breathless /'breθlɪs/ adj **1** (out of breath) [*person, runner*] à bout de souffle; [*asthmatic*] haletant; **to make** *ou* **leave sb** ∼ essouffler qn; **2** (excited) [*hush, fascination*] extasié; **to be** ∼ **with** avoir le souffle coupé par; **3** (fast) **at a** ∼ **pace** à toute allure

breathlessly /'breθlɪslɪ/ adv d'une voix haletante

breathlessness /'breθlɪsnɪs/ n essoufflement m

breathtaking /'breθteɪkɪŋ/ adj [*feat, pace, skill*] stupéfiant; [*scenery, view*] à vous couper le souffle

breathtakingly /'breθteɪkɪŋlɪ/ adv ∼ **beautiful** d'une beauté à vous couper le souffle; ∼ **audacious** d'une audace stupéfiante

breath test

A n alcootest m

B vtr faire subir un alcootest à [*driver*]; **to be** ∼**ed** subir un alcootest

bred /bred/ prét, pp ▸ **breed**

breech /briːtʃ/ n **1** Med (also ∼ **birth**, ∼ **delivery**) accouchement m par le siège; **2** (of gun) culasse f

breeches /'brɪtʃɪz/ npl **1** (also **knee** ∼) culotte f; **a pair of** ∼ une culotte; **2** (also **riding** ∼) culotte f (de cheval); **3** ○US pantalon m

breed /briːd/

A n **1** Zool race f; **2** (type of person, thing) type m

B vtr (prét, pp **bred**) élever [*animals*]; produire [*plants*]; fig engendrer [*disease, unrest*]; produire [*person*]

C vi (prét, pp **bred**) [*animals*] se reproduire; [*organisms*] se multiplier

D bred pp adj **ill-/well-**∼ mal/bien élevé

breeder /'briːdə(r)/ n **1** Agric, Zool (of animals) éleveur m; (of plants) producteur m; **2** (nuclear) (also ∼ **reactor**) surgénérateur m

breeding /'briːdɪŋ/ n **1** Agric, Zool reproduction f; **2** (good manners) bonnes manières fpl

breeding ground n **1** Zool lieu m de reproduction (**for** de); **2** fig foyer m (**for** de)

breeding: ∼ **period**, ∼ **season** n saison f de reproduction; ∼ **stock** n Agric ₵ reproducteurs mpl

breeze /briːz/

A n brise f; **sea** ∼ brise de mer; **in the** ∼ dans la brise

B vi **to** ∼ **in/out** entrer/sortir d'un air dégagé; **to** ∼ **through life** traverser la vie avec insouciance; **to** ∼ **through an exam** réussir un examen sans difficulté

breeze block /'briːzblɒk/ n GB parpaing m, moellon m

breezily /'briːzɪlɪ/ adv **1** (casually) de façon désinvolte; **2** (cheerfully) jovialement; **3** (confidently) avec assurance

breezy /'briːzɪ/ adj **1** [*place*] exposé au vent; **it will be** ∼ il y aura de la brise; **it's a** ∼ **morning** il y a une bonne brise ce matin; **2** (cheerful) jovial; (confident) qui a de l'aplomb; **bright and** ∼ enjoué

brethren /'breðrən/ npl **1** Hist, Relig, hum frères mpl; **2** (in trades union) hum camarades mpl

brevity /'brevɪtɪ/ n (of event) brièveté f; (of speech) concision f

brew /bruː/

A n **1** (beer) bière f; **2** (tea) thé m, infusion f; **3** (unpleasant mixture) mixture f

B vtr brasser [*beer*]; préparer [*tea, mixture*]; fig préparer, mijoter○ [*plot, scandal*]; **freshly** ∼**ed coffee** café fraîchement passé

C vi **1** lit [*beer*] fermenter; [*tea*] infuser; [*brewer*] brasser; **2** fig [*storm, crisis*] se préparer; [*quarrel, revolt*] se tramer; **there's trouble** ∼**ing** il y a de l'orage dans l'air

brewer /'bruːə(r)/ ▸ **p. 1181** n brasseur m

brewery /'bruːərɪ/ n brasserie f

brewing /'bruːɪŋ/

A n brasserie f

B noun modifier [*group, company*] qui fabrique de la bière; [*business, industry, magnate*] de la bière; [*method*] de brassage

brew-up○ /'bruːʌp/ n GB thé m

briar /'braɪə(r)/ n **1** (also ∼ **rose**) églantier m; **2** (heather) bruyère f; **3** (also ∼ **pipe**) pipe f en bruyère; **4** **briars** (thorns) ronces fpl

bribe /braɪb/

A n pot-de-vin m; **to give sb a** ∼ graisser la patte○ à qn

B vtr **1** (large-scale) soudoyer [*police*] (**with** avec; **to do** de faire); suborner [*witness*] (**to do** de faire); acheter [*voter*]; **2** (small-scale) graisser la patte à○ [*official*]

bribery /'braɪbərɪ/ n corruption f; (de témoin) subornation f

brick /brɪk/

A n **1** Constr brique f; **made of** ∼ en brique; **2** GB (child's toy) cube m

B noun modifier [*wall*] de briques; [*building*] en briques

Idioms **it's like banging one's head against** *ou* **talking to a** ∼ **wall** autant parler à un mur; **to run up against** *ou* **run into a** ∼ **wall** se heurter à un mur

Phrasal verb

■ **brick up**: ▶ ∼ **[sth] up**, ∼ **up [sth]** murer, boucher

brick: ∼**bat** n fig violente critique f; ∼**-built** adj en briques; ∼**layer** ▸ **p. 1181** n maçon m; ∼**laying** n maçonnerie f; ∼ **red** ▸ **p. 752** n, adj rouge (m) brique inv; ∼**work** n briquetage m; ∼**works** n briqueterie f

bridal /'braɪdl/ adj [*dress etc*] de mariée; [*car, procession, bed, chamber*] des mariés; [*feast*] de noce

bridal: ∼ **party** n (+ v sg ou pl) proches mpl de la mariée; ∼ **suite** n suite f nuptiale; ∼ **wear** n robes fpl de mariée

bride /braɪd/ n **1** (jeune) mariée f; **his** ∼ (after wedding) son épouse f; (before wedding) sa future épouse f; **the** ∼ **and (bride)groom** les (jeunes) mariés mpl; **2** (also ∼**-to-be**) future mariée f

bride: ∼**groom** n jeune marié m; (before wedding) futur marié m; ∼**smaid** n demoiselle f d'honneur

bridge /brɪdʒ/

A n **1** Constr pont m (**over** sur; **across** au-dessus de); **2** fig (link) rapprochement m; **to build** ∼ établir des relations (**between** entre); **3** (intermediate stage) (transitional) passerelle f (**between** entre); (springboard) tremplin m (**to** vers); **4** (on ship) passerelle f; **5** (of nose) arête f; **6** (of spectacles) arcade f; **7** (on guitar, violin) chevalet m; **8** (for teeth) bridge m; **9** ▸ **p. 881** Games bridge m

B vtr **1** lit construire un pont sur [*river*]; **2** fig **to** ∼ **the gap between two adversaries** effectuer un rapprochement entre *or* rapprocher deux adversaires; **to ~ a gap in [sth]** combler un vide dans [*conversation*]; combler un trou dans [*budget*]; combler une lacune dans [*knowledge*]; **3** (span) enjamber [*two eras*]

Idioms **a lot of water has flowed under the ~** beaucoup d'eau a coulé sous les ponts; **it's all water under the ~** c'est du passé; **we'll cross that ~ when we come to it** on s'occupera de ce problème en temps voulu

bridge-building *n* Mil installation *f* de ponts provisoires; fig médiation *f* (**between** entre)

bridging loan *n* GB Fin prêt *m* relais

bridle /'braɪdl/
A *n* (for horse) bride *f*; fig frein *m*
B *vtr* (restrain) brider [*temper*]; brider [*horse*]
C *vi* (in anger) se cabrer (**at** contre; **with** sous l'effet de)

bridle path, **bridle track**, **bridleway** *n* piste *f* cavalière

brief /briːf/ ▸ p. 1191
A *n* **1** GB (remit) attributions *fpl*; (role) tâche *f*; **it is your ~** *ou* **your ~ is to do** votre tâche consiste à faire; **with a ~ for** chargé de [*environment, immigration*]; **2** Jur dossier *m*; **3** GB (instructions) directives *fpl*; **designer's ~** directives du concepteur
B **briefs** *npl* (undergarment) slip *m*
C *adj* **1** (concise) [*event, summary, speech*] bref/brève; [*reply*] laconique; **to be ~** je serai bref; **in ~** en bref; **the news in ~** les brèves; **2** (short) [*skirt*] court
D *vtr* informer [*politician, worker*] (**on** de); donner des instructions à [*police, troops*] (**on** sur); donner des directives à [*artist, designer*] (**on** sur); confier une cause à [*lawyer*]; **to be well-~ed** être bien au courant

Idiom **to hold a watching ~ on sb** tenir qn à l'œil

briefcase /'briːfkeɪs/ *n* serviette *f*; (without handle) porte-documents *m inv*

briefing /'briːfɪŋ/ *n* briefing *m* (**on** sur), réunion *f* d'information (**on** sur); **press ~** briefing *m* de presse

briefly /'briːflɪ/ *adv* **1** (concisely) [*describe, speak*] brièvement; [*reply, say*] laconiquement; **2** (for short time) [*affect, look, pause*] un bref instant; [*work, meet*] brièvement; **3** (in short) en bref

brigade /brɪ'geɪd/ *n* brigade *f*; **cavalry ~** brigade de cavalerie; **the anti-smoking ~** la brigade anti-tabac

brigadier /ˌbrɪgə'dɪə(r)/ ▸ p. 1123 *n* général *m* de brigade

bright /braɪt/
A *adj* **1** (vivid) [*blue, red*] vif/vive; [*garment, carpet, wallpaper*] (of one colour) de couleur vive; (of several colours) aux couleurs vives; **he went ~ red** il est devenu tout rouge; **2** (clear) [*sunshine*] éclatant; [*room, day*] clair; [*weather*] radieux/-ieuse; [*sky*] lumineux/-euse; **~ spell** éclaircie *f*; **3** (shiny) [*star, eye, coin, metal*] brillant; [*jewel*] étincelant; **4** (clever) intelligent; **a ~ idea** une idée lumineuse; **5** (cheerful) [*person, mood*] joyeux/-euse; [*smile, face*] radieux/-ieuse; **to look on the ~ side** voir le bon côté des choses; **6** (promising) [*future*] brillant; **one of our ~est hopes** l'un de nos meilleurs espoirs
B *adv* [*shine, burn*] d'un vif éclat

brighten /'braɪtn/ *v*
■ **brighten up**: ▸ **1** (become cheerful) [*person, mood*] s'égayer (**at** à); [*face*] s'illuminer (**at** à); [*eyes*] s'allumer (**at** à; **with** de); **2** (improve) [*situation*] s'améliorer; [*weather, sky*] s'éclaircir; ▸ **~ up [sth]**, **~ [sth] up** **1** (make colourful, cheerful) égayer; **2** (illuminate) éclairer; **3** (improve) rendre [qch] plus réjouissant [*prospects*]

bright-eyed /ˌbraɪt'aɪd/ *adj* aux yeux brillants

Idiom **~ and bushy-tailed** frais et dispos

brightly /'braɪtlɪ/ *adv* **1** (vividly) [*dressed*] de couleurs vives; **~ coloured** (several colours) aux couleurs vives; (of one colour) de couleur vive; **~ painted** aux couleurs vives; **2** (of sun, fire) [*shine, burn*] d'un éclat vif; (of eyes, metal) [*shine, sparkle*] intensément; **3** (intensely) [*lit*] brillamment; **4** (cheerfully) joyeusement

brightness /'braɪtnɪs/ *n* **1** (of colour, light, smile) éclat *m*; **2** (of room) clarté *f*; **3** (of metal, eyes) brillant *m*; **4** (cheerfulness) vivacité *f*; **5** TV luminosité *f*

bright sparkᴼ *n* GB petit/-e futé/-eᴼ *m/f*

bright young thing *n* GB **the ~s** la jeunesse dorée

brill /'brɪl/
A *n* Zool barbue *f*, sandre *f*

B ᴼ*adj*, *excl* GB (*abrév* = **brilliant**) superᴼ

brilliance /'brɪlɪəns/ *n* (of light, music) éclat *m*; (of person) génie *m*

brilliant /'brɪlɪənt/
A *n* (diamond) brillant *m*
B *adj* **1** (successful) [*student, career, success*] brillant; **2** (bright) éclatant; **3** GB ᴼ(fantastic) génialᴼ; **we had a ~ time** c'était génial; **to be ~ at sth** être doué en qch; **to be ~ at doing** avoir le don de faire
C *excl* superᴼ! also iron

brilliantly /'brɪlɪəntlɪ/ *adv* **1** (very well) brillamment; **2** (particularly) [*witty, clever*] extrêmement; **3** (very brightly) [*shine*] avec éclat; [*illuminated*] vivement; **~ coloured**, **~ colourful** aux couleurs éclatantes

Brillo pad® /'brɪləʊ pæd/ *n* tampon *m* Jex®

brim /brɪm/
A *n* bord *m*; **a hat with a wide ~** un chapeau à large bord; **to fill sth to the ~** remplir qch à ras bord; **filled to the ~ with** rempli jusqu'au bord de [*liquid, objects*]
B *vi* (*p prés etc* **-mm-**) **to ~ with** lit [*receptacle*] être plein à ras bord de; fig déborder de; **his eyes ~med with tears** ses yeux se remplirent de larmes

Phrasal verb
■ **brim over** lit, fig déborder (**with** de)

brine /braɪn/ *n* **1** (sea water) eau *f* de mer; **2** Culin saumure *f*

bring /brɪŋ/ (*prét, pp* **brought**)
A *vtr* **1** (convey, carry) apporter; **wait and see what tomorrow ~s** attends de voir ce que demain nous apportera; **to ~ flowers** apporter des fleurs à qn; **the case has brought him publicity** l'affaire lui a fait de la publicité; **to ~ sb wealth/fame** rendre qn riche/célèbre; **to ~ sth to** (contribute) apporter qch à [*school, work, area*]; **to ~ one's experience to sth** faire bénéficier qch de son expérience; **that ~s the total to 100** cela fait un total de 100; **to ~ a smile to sb's face** faire sourire qn; **to ~ sth into** faire entrer qch dans [*room*]; introduire qch dans [*conversation*]; **to ~ sth into existence** créer qch; **the wind brought the tree down** le vent a fait tomber l'arbre; **don't forget to ~ it home** n'oublie pas de le rapporter; **to ~ shame/disgrace on sb** attirer la honte/le déshonneur sur qn; **to ~ sth on** *ou* **upon oneself** attirer qch; **you brought it on yourself** tu l'as cherché; **2** (come with) amener [*friend, relative, dog*]; **to ~ sb with one** amener qn (avec soi); **to ~ sb to** amener qn à; **3** (lead, draw) **the path ~s you to the church** le chemin te conduit jusqu'à l'église; **the Games brought people to the city** les Jeux ont attiré du monde vers la ville; **I brought him to the ground** je l'ai fait tomber; **that ~s me to the question of** ceci m'amène à la question de; **to ~ sb to do sth** faire faire qch à qn; **to ~ sb/a dog into the country** faire entrer *or* introduire qn/un chien dans le pays; **to ~ sb into contact with sb** mettre qn en contact avec qn; **to ~ sb home** (transport home) raccompagner qn, ramener qn; (to meet family) amener qn à la maison; **4** TV, Radio **the game will be brought to you live** le match sera retransmis en direct; **we ~ you all the latest news** on vous donne les dernières nouvelles; **5** Jur, Admin **to ~ a case before the court** porter une affaire devant le tribunal; **to ~ sb before the court** faire comparaître qn devant le tribunal; **to ~ a matter before the committee** soumettre une question au comité
B *v refl* **to ~ oneself to do** se décider à faire; **I couldn't ~ myself to get up/to tell him** je n'ai pas pu me lever/le lui dire

Phrasal verbs
■ **bring about**: ▸ **~ about [sth]**, **~ [sth] about** provoquer [*change, disaster, death*]; amener [*settlement, reconciliation*]; entraîner [*success, failure, defeat*]
■ **bring along**: ▸ **~ along [sth]**, **~ [sth] along** apporter [*object*]; ▸ **~ along [sb]**, **~ [sb] along** amener, venir avec [*friend, partner*]
■ **bring back**: ▸ **~ back [sth]**, **~ [sth] back** **1** (return with) rapporter [*souvenir*] (**from** de); **to ~ sb back sth** rapporter qch à qn; **2** (restore) redonner [*colour, shine*]; **to ~ sb's memory back** rendre la mémoire à qn; **3** (reintroduce) rétablir [*custom*]; restaurer [*monarchy*]; **4** (restore memory of) rappeler [*night, occasion*]; **seeing her brought it all back to me** tout m'est revenu lorsque je l'ai vue; **to ~ back memories** ranimer des souvenirs
■ **bring down**: ▸ **~ down [sth]**, **~ [sth] down** **1** (cause

collapse of) renverser [*government*]; **2** (reduce) réduire [*inflation, expenditure*]; faire baisser [*rate, level, price, temperature*]; diminuer [*cost of living*]; **3** (shoot down) abattre; ▸ ~ **[sb] down**⚬ déprimer [*person*]

■ **bring forth**: ▸ ~ **forth [sth]**, ~ **[sth] forth** **1** (provoke) susciter; **2** littér (produce) produire [*object, fruit*]; faire jaillir [*water*]; donner naissance à [*child*]

■ **bring forward**: ▸ ~ **forward [sth]**, ~ **[sth] forward** **1** (make sooner) avancer (**by** de); **2** (propose) avancer [*proposals*]; proposer [*bill*]

■ **bring in**: ▸ ~ **in [sth]** rapporter [*amount, money, interest*]; introduire [*custom*]; ▸ ~ **in [sth]**, ~ **[sth] in** **1** (introduce) introduire [*legislation, measure*]; **2** Agric rentrer [*harvest*]; récolter [*wheat*]; ▸ ~ **in [sb]**, ~ **[sb] in** **1** (involve) faire appel à [*expert, army*] (**from** de; **as** pour être); **2** (to police station) amener [qn] (au poste)

■ **bring into**: ▸ ~ **[sb] into** faire participer [qn] à [*conversation, organization*].

■ **bring off**: ▸ ~ **off [sth]**, ~ **[sth] off** réussir [*feat*]; conclure [*deal*]; décrocher [*victory*].

■ **bring on**: ▸ ~ **on [sth]**, ~ **[sth] on** (provoke) provoquer [*attack, migraine*]; être à l'origine de [*bronchitis, rheumatism*]; ▸ ~ **on [sb]**, ~ **[sb] on** (to stage, field) faire entrer [*dancer, substitute*]

■ **bring out**: ▸ ~ **out [sth]**, ~ **[sth] out** **1** sortir [*gun etc*]; **2** Comm sortir [*edition, new model*]; **3** (highlight) faire ressortir [*flavour, meaning*]; ▸ ~ **out [sb]**, ~ **[sb] out** **1** (on strike) mettre [qn] en grève [*workers*]; **2** **to ~ sb out in spots** donner des boutons à qn

■ **bring round**: ▸ ~ **[sb] round** **1** (revive) faire revenir [qn] à soi; **2** (convince) convaincre

■ **bring together**: ▸ ~ **together [sth/sb]**, ~ **[sth/sb] together** **1** (assemble) réunir; **2** (create bond between) rapprocher

■ **bring up**: ▸ ~ **up [sth]**, ~ **[sth] up** **1** (mention) aborder, parler de; **2** (vomit) vomir, rendre; ▸ ~ **up [sb]**, ~ **[sb] up** élever; **to ~ sb up to do** apprendre à [qn] à faire; **to be brought up as a Catholic** recevoir une éducation catholique; **well/badly brought up** bien/mal élevé

bring and buy sale n GB vente f de charité

brink /brɪŋk/ n lit, fig bord m; **on the ~ of doing** sur le point de faire; **on the ~ of disaster** à deux doigts du désastre

brinkmanship /'brɪŋkmənʃɪp/ n art m d'aller jusqu'aux limites du possible

brisk /brɪsk/ adj **1** (efficient) [*manner, tone, gesture*] vif/vive; [*person*] efficace; **2** (energetic) [*pace, trot, movements*] rapide; [*debate*] animé; **to go for a ~ walk/swim** faire une bonne marche/quelques longueurs; **at a ~ pace** à vive allure; **3** (good) [*business, trade*] florissant; **business/betting was ~** les affaires/les paris marchaient bien; **we've been doing a ~ trade in suitcases** nos valises se sont bien vendues; **4** (invigorating) [*air*] vivifiant; [*wind*] vif/vive

brisket /'brɪskɪt/ n Culin poitrine f

briskly /'brɪsklɪ/ adv **1** (efficiently) [*say*] vivement; [*work*] rapidement; [*resolve, deal with*] de façon efficace; **she moved ~ to the next point** elle s'est attaquée sans tarder au point suivant; **2** (quickly) [*walk*] d'un bon pas; [*sell*] très vite

bristle /'brɪsl/

A n **1** (single hair) (on brush, chin, animal) poil m; (on pig) soie f; **2** (material) (on brush, mat) (real) soies fpl; (synthetic) poils mpl

B vi **1** lit [*fur*] se hérisser; [*hairs*] se dresser; **2** (react angrily) se hérisser (**at** à; **with** de)

(Phrasal verb)

■ **bristle with**: ▸ ~ **with [sth]** être hérissé de [*spikes, pins, problems*]; grouiller de [*police, soldiers*]

bristly /'brɪslɪ/ adj [*beard, fibres*] dru; [*surface*] couvert de poils durs

Britain /'brɪtn/ pr n (also **Great ~**) Grande-Bretagne f

Britannia /brɪ'tænjə/ pr n Britannia

ⓘ **Britannia** Nom romain de la Grande-Bretagne, *Britannia* est aussi la représentation symbolique de ce pays sous les traits d'une femme casquée qui tient un trident et un bouclier. Son effigie est reproduite sur les pièces de *50 pence. Rule, Britannia!* est un air patriotique que l'on chante traditionnellement au cours de la soirée de clôture des *Proms.* ▸ **Proms**

British /'brɪtɪʃ/ ▸ p. 1032

A npl **the ~** les Britanniques mpl

B adj britannique; **the ~ embassy/ambassador** l'ambassade f/l'ambassadeur m de Grande-Bretagne

British: ~ **Airports Authority**, **BAA** n administration f des aéroports britanniques; ~ **Broadcasting Corporation**, **BBC** n BBC f; ~ **Columbia**, **BC** n Colombie f britannique

Britisher /'brɪtɪʃə(r)/ n US Britannique mf

British: ~ **Gas** n GB société f de distribution de gaz britannique

British Isles npl îles fpl britanniques

ⓘ **British Isles** Les Îles britanniques comprennent la Grande-Bretagne, l'Irlande (République d'Irlande et Irlande du Nord) et toutes les petites îles qui les entourent : *the Shetland Islands*, *the Orkney Islands*, *the Hebrides*, *the Isle of Man*, *the Scilly Isles*, *the Channel Islands*.

British: ~ **Rail**, **BR** n société f nationale des chemins de fer britanniques; ~ **Telecom**, **BT** n GB société f britannique de télécommunications

Briton /'brɪtn/ n Britannique mf; Hist Breton/-onne m/f

brittle /'brɪtl/ adj **1** lit [*twig*] cassant; [*nails, hair*] fragile; **2** fig [*relationship, confidence*] fragile; [*tone, laughter*] cassant

brittle bones, **brittle-bone disease** n décalcification f

broach /brəʊtʃ/ vtr aborder [*subject*]; entamer [*bottle*]

broad /brɔːd/ ▸ p. 977 adj **1** (wide) large; **to have a ~ back** lit, fig avoir le dos large; **2** (extensive) [*area, expanse*] vaste; **3** (wide-ranging) [*choice, range*] grand; [*introduction, syllabus, consensus, implication*] général; [*alliance*] large; **4** (general) [*meaning, term*] large; [*base, outline, principle*] général; **5** (liberal) [*view*] large; **to have a ~ mind** avoir l'esprit large; **6** (unsubtle) [*wink*] bien visible; **to drop ~ hints about** faire des allusions évidentes à; **7** (pronounced) [*accent*] fort (*before n*); **8** (complete) **in ~ daylight** en plein jour; **9** (vulgar) grossier/-ière

(Idiom) **it's as ~ as it's long** c'est du pareil au même⚬

B road n GB route f secondaire

broadband /'brɔːdbænd/

A adj (connection) à haut débit

B n ADSL m, haut débit m; **have you got ~?** tu as l'ADSL?

broad: ~**-based** adj [*approach, campaign*] global; [*education*] généralisé; [*coalition*] d'origine très variée; [*consensus*] général; ~ **bean** n Bot, Culin fève f

broadcast /'brɔːdkɑːst, US -kæst/

A n émission f; **TV/radio ~** émission télévisée/radiophonique; **news ~** bulletin m d'informations

B vtr (*prét, pp ~ ou ~ed*) **1** Radio, TV diffuser (**to** à); **2** (tell) péj raconter

C vi (*prét, pp ~ ou ~ed*) **1** [*station, channel*] émettre (**on** sur); **2** [*person*] faire une émission; **to ~ on gardening** faire des émissions sur le jardinage

D pp adj (on TV) télévisé; (on radio) radiodiffusé; (on both) radiotélévisé

broadcaster /'brɔːdkɑːstə(r), US -kæst-/ ▸ p. 1181 n animateur/-trice m/f; **news ~** journaliste mf de radio or télévision

broadcasting /'brɔːdkɑːstɪŋ, US -kæst-/

A n (field) communication f audiovisuelle; (action) diffusion f; **to work in ~** travailler dans l'audiovisuel; **children's ~** programmes mpl pour les enfants

B noun modifier [*authorities, union*] de la communication audiovisuelle; ~ **ban** interdiction f d'antenne

broad-chested adj au torse large

broaden /'brɔːdn/

A vtr **1** (extend) étendre [*appeal, scope*]; élargir [*horizons, knowledge*]; **travel ~s the mind** les voyages ouvrent l'esprit; **2** (widen) élargir [*road*]

B vi **1** (expand) [*appeal, horizons, scope*] s'élargir; **2** (also ~ **out**) (widen) [*river, road, pipe, smile*] s'élargir; [*skirt*] s'évaser; [*conversation*] s'étendre

broadly /'brɔːdlɪ/ adv **1** (in general) [*agree, correspond*] en gros; [*similar, true*] globalement; ~ **speaking** en règle générale; **2** (widely) [*smile*] largement

broad: ~**minded** adj [*person*] large d'esprit; [*attitude*] libéral; ~**ness** n largeur f; ~**sheet** n journal m de grand format; ~**-shouldered** adj large d'épaules

broadside /'brɔːdsaɪd/
A n **1** (criticism) attaque f cinglante (**at** contre); **2** Naut (of ship) flanc m; (enemy fire) bordée f; **to deliver a ~** lâcher une bordée
B adv (also **~ on**) par le travers

Broadway /'brɔːdweɪ/ pr n Theat Broadway; **on ~** à Broadway; **an off-~ production** pièce donnée dans une salle à proximité de Broadway

ⓘ **Broadway** Grande avenue de New York, célèbre pour son animation, ses salles de spectacle et ses cinémas. Lieu des grandes créations théâtrales, *Broadway* est devenu le symbole de l'industrie du spectacle. L'expression *Off-Broadway* désigne les théâtres new-yorkais qui ne sont pas situés dans le quartier de *Broadway*, ainsi que leurs productions d'avant-garde ou moins commerciales. *Off-off-Broadway* désigne le théâtre expérimental ou d'avant-garde mis en scène dans des petites salles à New York.

brocade /brə'keɪd/ n brocart m
broccoli /'brɒkəlɪ/ n ¢ Bot brocoli m; Culin brocolis mpl
brochure /'brəʊʃə(r), US brəʊ'ʃʊər/ n (booklet) brochure f; (larger) catalogue m; (leaflet) dépliant m; (for hotel) prospectus m
brogue /brəʊg/ n **1** (shoe) richelieu m; **2** (accent) accent m du terroir
broil /brɔɪl/
A vtr US Culin faire griller [meat]
B vi Culin, fig griller
broiler /'brɔɪlə(r)/ n **1** (also **~ chicken**) poulet m d'élevage; **2** US (grill) gril m
broke /brəʊk/
A prét ▸ break
B adj (insolvent) [person] fauché°; [company, Treasury] insolvable; **to go ~** [company] faire faillite
broken /'brəʊkən/
A pp ▸ break
B adj **1** (damaged) [glass, window] brisé; [fingernail, tooth, bone, leg] cassé; [bottle, chair, handle, toy] cassé; [radio, machine] détraqué; **2** (interrupted) [circle, line] brisé; [voice] brisé; **3** (irregular) [coastline] découpé; [ground] accidenté; **4** (depressed) [man, woman] brisé; [spirit] abattu; **5** (not honoured) [contract, engagement, promise] rompu; **6** (flawed) (épith) [French] mauvais (before n); [sentence] maladroit
broken-down /ˌbrəʊkən'daʊn/ adj (épith) **1** (non-functional) [machine] en panne; **2** (damaged) [wall] délabré
broken heart /ˌbrəʊkən 'hɑːt/ n cœur m brisé; **to die of a ~** mourir de chagrin
broken-hearted /ˌbrəʊkən'hɑːtɪd/ adj [person] au cœur brisé; **to be ~** avoir le cœur brisé
broken home n famille f désunie
brokenly /'brəʊkənlɪ/ adv [say] d'une voix brisée
broken marriage n foyer m désuni
broker /'brəʊkə(r)/ ▸ p. 1181
A n Fin, Comm courtier m; (on stock exchange) courtier m en Bourse; Naut courtier m maritime; **insurance ~** courtier m d'assurance; **real-estate ~** US agent m immobilier; **power ~** négociateur/-trice m/f influent/-e
B vtr Pol négocier
C vi agir en médiateur (**between** entre)
brokerage /'brəʊkərɪdʒ/ n (fee, business) courtage m
broking /'brəʊkɪŋ/ GB, **brokering** /'brəʊkərɪŋ/ US n courtage m
brolly° /'brɒlɪ/ n GB hum pépin° m, parapluie m
bromide /'brəʊmaɪd/ n **1** (in pharmacy, printing) bromure m; **2** fig (comment) platitude f (lénifiante)
bronchial /'brɒŋkɪəl/ adj [infection] des bronches; [asthma] bronchique; [wheeze, cough] bronchitique; **~ pneumonia** broncho-pneumonie f
bronchitis /brɒŋ'kaɪtɪs/ ▸ p. 933 n bronchite f; **to have ~** avoir une bronchite; **~ sufferer** bronchitique mf
bronze /brɒnz/
A n **1** (statue, metal) bronze m; **2** (colour) (couleur f de) bronze m
B noun modifier [coin, ornament] en bronze
C vtr, vi (all contexts) bronzer
Bronze Age n âge m du bronze
brooch /brəʊtʃ/ n broche f

brood /bruːd/
A n **1** Zool (of birds) couvée f, nichée f; (of mammals) nichée f; **2** hum (of children) nichée f, progéniture f hum
B vi **1** (ponder) broyer du noir; **to ~ about** ou **on** ou **over** ressasser, ruminer [problem, disappointment]; **2** Zool [bird] couver
brooding /'bruːdɪŋ/ adj [landscape] menaçant; [person, face] sombre
broody /'bruːdɪ/ adj **1** (depressed) mélancolique; **2** a **~ hen** une poule qui cherche à couver; **3** °GB **to feel ~** [woman] désirer avoir un enfant
brook /brʊk/
A n ruisseau m
B vtr sout tolérer [argument, refusal]
broom /bruːm, brʊm/ n **1** (for sweeping) balai m; **2** Bot genêt m
(Idiom) **a new ~ sweeps clean** Prov nouveau chef, nouvelles méthodes
broom: **~ cupboard** n GB lit cagibi° m; **~ handle** n GB manche m à balai; **~stick** n manche m à balai
Bros. npl Comm (abrév écrite = **Brothers**) Frères
broth /brɒθ, US brɔːθ/ n bouillon m
(Idiom) **too many cooks spoil the ~** Prov on n'arrive à rien quand tout le monde s'en mêle
brothel /'brɒθl/ n maison f close
brother /'brʌðə(r)/ n **1** (relative) frère m; **2** (trade unionist) camarade m; **3** (fellow man) frère m; **~s in arms** frères d'armes; **4** Relig frère m
brotherhood /'brʌðəhʊd/ n **1** (bond) fraternité f; **2** (organization) (of idealists) confrérie f; (trade-union) association f; (of monks) communauté f
brother-in-law n (pl **brothers-in-law**) beau-frère m
brotherly /'brʌðəlɪ/ adj (all contexts) fraternel/-elle
brought /brɔːt/ prét, pp ▸ bring
brow /braʊ/ n **1** (forehead) front m; **2** (eyebrow) sourcil m; **to knit** ou **furrow one's ~s** froncer les sourcils; **3** (of hill) sommet m
browbeat /'braʊbiːt/ vtr (prét **-beat**; pp **-beaten**) intimider; **to ~ sb into doing** forcer qn à faire; **to ~ sb into silence** réduire qn au silence
brown /braʊn/ ▸ p. 752
A n (colour) (of object) marron m; (of hair, skin, eyes) brun m; **in ~** en marron
B adj **1** (in colour) [shoes, leaves, paint, eyes] marron inv; [hair] châtain inv; **to go** ou **turn ~** devenir marron; **to paint sth ~** peindre qch en marron; **to turn the water ~** rendre l'eau marron; **2** (tanned) bronzé; **to go ~** bronzer; **3** (as racial feature) basané
C vtr **1** (in cooking) faire roussir [sauce]; faire dorer [meat, onions]; **2** (tan) brunir
D vi [meat, potatoes] dorer
brown: **~ ale** n GB bière f brune; **~ bear** n ours m brun; **~ bread** n pain m complet
browned-off° /ˌbraʊnd'ɒf/ adj GB **to be ~** en avoir marre°
brown envelope n enveloppe f kraft
brownfield site /'braʊnfiːld saɪt/ n zone f industrielle urbaine destinée à être réaménagée
brownie /'braʊnɪ/
A n **1** US (cake) brownie m (petit gâteau au chocolat et aux noix); **2** (elf) lutin m
B Brownie n jeannette f
brownie point° n hum bon point m
brownish /'braʊnɪʃ/ ▸ p. 752 adj tirant sur le brun, brunâtre pej
brown: **~out** n US black-out m partiel; **~ owl** n chathuant m; **~ paper** n papier m kraft; **~ rice** n riz m complet; **~-skinned** adj basané, brun de peau; **~stone** n US maison f à façade de grès rouge; **~ sugar** n Culin sucre m brun, cassonade f; **~ trout** n truite f de mer
browse /braʊz/
A n **to have a ~ in a bookshop** flâner dans une librairie; **to have a ~ through a book** feuilleter un livre
B vtr Comput naviguer sur, consulter [Web]
C vi **1** (potter, stroll around) flâner; (look at objects in shop) regarder; **2** (graze) brouter

b

browser /ˈbraʊzə(r)/ n Comput (also **Web** ◯) navigateur m, fureteur m Can

bruise /bruːz/
A n (on skin) bleu m, ecchymose f spec (on sur); (on fruit) tache f, talure f (on sur); **covered in** ◯s [skin, limb] couvert de bleus; **cuts and** ◯s des blessures légères
B vtr **1** meurtrir [person]; **to** ◯ **one's knee/arm** se meurtrir le genou/bras; **2** (damage) taler, abîmer [fruit]; **3** (emotionally) meurtrir, blesser
C vi [person] se faire facilement des bleus; [arm, skin] se meurtrir; [fruit] se taler or s'abîmer facilement

bruised /bruːzd/ adj **1** (physically) [knee, elbow] contusionné; [eye, cheek, ribs] meurtri; [fruit] talé, abîmé; **badly** ◯ sérieusement contusionné; **2** (emotionally) [ego, spirit] blessé; [heart] meurtri, blessé

bruiser◯ /ˈbruːzə(r)/ n malabar◯ m, balèze◯ m

bruising /ˈbruːzɪŋ/
A n contusions fpl, ecchymoses fpl
B adj **1** (emotionally) [campaign, encounter] violent; [remark] blessant; [defeat] écrasant; **2** (physically) [game, encounter] acharné

brunch /brʌntʃ/ n brunch m (petit déjeuner tardif et copieux remplaçant le déjeuner)

Brunei /bruːˈnaɪ/ ▸ p. 774 pr n Brunei m

brunette /bruːˈnet/ n (person) brune f

brunt /brʌnt/ n **to bear** ou **take the** ◯ **of** être le plus touché par [disaster, unemployment]; subir tout le poids de [anger]

brush /brʌʃ/
A n **1** (implement) (for hair, clothes, shoes etc) brosse f; (small, for sweeping up) balayette f; (broom) balai m; (for paint) pinceau m; (chimney sweep's) hérisson m; **2** (act of brushing) coup m de brosse; **to give one's teeth a quick** ◯ se brosser rapidement les dents; **3** (encounter) (confrontation with person) accrochage m (**with** avec); (contact with person, celebrity) contact m (**with** avec); **to have a** ◯ **with the police** avoir des démêlés avec la police; **4** (light touch) frôlement m; **5** (vegetation or twigs) broussailles fpl; **6** (fox's tail) queue f de renard; **7** (in motor) balai m
B vtr **1** (sweep, clean) brosser [carpet, clothes]; **to** ◯ **one's hair/teeth** se brosser les cheveux/les dents; **2** (touch lightly) effleurer (**with** avec); **3** Culin **to** ◯ **sth with** badigeonner qch avec [milk, egg]
C vi **to** ◯ **against** frôler; **to** ◯ **past sb** frôler qn en passant
D brushed pp adj [fabric] gratté

(Phrasal verbs)
■ **brush aside**: ▸ ◯ **aside** [sth/sb], ◯ [sb/sth] **aside** **1** (dismiss) repousser [idea, criticism, person]; **2** (move away) écarter
■ **brush away**: ▸ ◯ **away** [sth], ◯ [sth] **away** enlever [crumbs]; essuyer [tear]
■ **brush back**: ▸ ◯ **back** [sth], ◯ [sth] **back** brosser [qch] en arrière
■ **brush down**: ▸ ◯ **down** [sth], ◯ [sth] **down** brosser [suit, horse]
■ **brush off**: ▸ ◯ **off** [sth/sb], ◯ [sth/sb] **off** repousser [person, offer, allegation, challenge]; écarter [threat, incident]
■ **brush up**: ▸ ◯ **up** [sth], ◯ [sth] **up** se remettre à [skill, subject]

brush-off◯ /ˈbrʌʃɒf/ n **to give sb the** ◯ rembarrer◯ qn

brushstroke /ˈbrʌʃstrəʊk/ n coup m de pinceau

brushup /ˈbrʌʃʌp/ n GB **to have a (wash and)** ◯ se rafraîchir

brushwork n Art facture f

brusque /bruːsk, US brʌsk/ adj brusque (**with** avec)

brusquely /ˈbruːsklɪ, US ˈbrʌsklɪ/ adv avec brusquerie

Brussels /ˈbrʌslz/ ▸ p. 1276 pr n Bruxelles

Brussels sprout n chou m de Bruxelles

brutal /ˈbruːtl/ adj [dictator, reply] brutal; [murderer, régime] cruel/-elle; [attack] sauvage; [film] violent

brutality /bruːˈtælətɪ/ n brutalité f (**of** de)

brutalize /ˈbruːtəlaɪz/ vtr **1** (make brutal) rendre [qn] brutal; **2** (treat brutally) brutaliser

brutally /ˈbruːtəlɪ/ adv [murder, treat] sauvagement; [say] brutalement; ◯ **honest** d'une honnêteté brutale

brute /bruːt/
A n **1** (man) brute f; **2** (animal) bête f
B adj **1** (physical) [strength] simple (before n); **by (sheer)** ◯ **force** par la force; **2** (animal-like) bestial

brutish /ˈbruːtɪʃ/ adj bestial

BS n US Univ (abrév = **Bachelor of Science**) ≈ (degree) diplôme m universitaire de sciences; (person) diplômé/-e m/f en sciences

BSc n GB Univ (abrév = **Bachelor of Science**) diplôme m universitaire en sciences

BSE n (abrév = **Bovine Spongiform Encephalopathy**) ESB f, encéphalopathie f spongiforme bovine

B side /ˈbiːsaɪd/ n (of record) face f B

BST n (abrév = **British Summer Time**) heure d'été britannique

bubble /ˈbʌbl/
A n **1** (in air, liquid, glass) bulle f (**in** dans); **to blow** ◯s faire des bulles; **2** Comm prix m gonflé; **3** (germ-free chamber) chambre f stérile
B vi **1** (form bubbles) gen faire des bulles; [fizzy drink] pétiller; [boiling liquid] bouillonner; **2** fig (boil) **to** ◯ **beneath the surface** bouillonner sous la surface; **3** (be lively, happy) être très animé; **to** ◯ **with** déborder de [enthusiasm, ideas]; **4** (make bubbling sound) glouglouter

(Phrasal verbs)
■ **bubble over** d éborder (**with** de)
■ **bubble up** [boiling liquid] bouillonner; [spring water] jaillir en bouillonnant

bubble: ◯ **bath** n bain m moussant; ◯ **car** n GB œuf◯ m (voiture monoplace des années 60); ◯**gum** n bubble-gum m; ◯ **memory** n mémoire f à bulles; ◯ **pack** n GB (for small item) blister m; (for pills) emballage m pelliculé; ◯**wrap** n bulle-pack® m

bubbling /ˈbʌblɪŋ/
A n (sound) glouglou m, gargouillis m
B adj bouillonnant

bubbly /ˈbʌblɪ/
A ◯n champagne m
B adj **1** [personality] pétillant de vitalité; **2** [liquid] pétillant

bubonic plague /bjuːˌbɒnɪk ˈpleɪɡ/ ▸ p. 933 n peste f bubonique

buccaneer /ˌbʌkəˈnɪə(r)/ n boucanier m

Bucharest /ˌbjuːkəˈrest/ ▸ p. 1276 pr n Bucarest

buck /bʌk/
A n **1** US◯ (dollar) dollar m; **2** ◯(money) fric◯ m; **to make a fast** ou **quick** ◯ se faire du fric facile◯; **3** Zool mâle m; **4** (of lively horse) ruade f
B vtr **1** (throw) [horse] désarçonner [rider]; **2** (go against) aller contre [trend, market]
C vi **1** [horse] ruer; **2** (oppose) **to** ◯ **at** ou **against sth** regimber devant or contre [changes, rule]

(Idioms) **to** ◯ **up one's ideas** se secouer◯; **the** ◯ **stops here** c'est moi qui ai la responsabilité finale; **to pass the** ◯ refiler◯ la responsabilité à quelqu'un d'autre

(Phrasal verb)
■ **buck up**: ▸ ◯ **up** **1** (cheer up) se dérider; ◯ **up!** courage! **2** ◯(hurry up) se grouiller◯; ▸ ◯ [sb] **up** (cheer up) remonter le moral à [person]

bucket /ˈbʌkɪt/
A n **1** gen seau m (**of** de); **2** Tech (of scoop, dredger, waterwheel) godet m; (of pump) piston m
B ◯ **buckets** npl **to rain** ◯s pleuvoir à seaux; **to cry** ◯s pleurer comme une Madeleine◯; **to sweat** ◯s suer à grosses gouttes
C ◯vi GB (also ◯ **down**) pleuvoir à seaux

(Idiom) **to kick the** ◯ mourir, casser sa pipe◯

bucket: ◯**ful** n seau m (**of** de); ◯ **seat** n Aut, Aviat siège-baquet m; ◯ **shop**◯ n GB Tourism agence f de voyage (proposant des billets d'avion à prix réduit)

bucking bronco /ˌbʌkɪŋ ˈbrɒŋkəʊ/ n cheval m de rodéo

buckle /ˈbʌkl/
A n **1** (clasp) boucle f; **2** (dent) (in metal) gondolage m
B vtr **1** (fasten) attacher, boucler [belt, shoe, strap]; ◯**d** bien attaché; **to** ◯ **sb into sth** attacher qn dans qch; **2** (damage) gondoler [material, surface]
C vi **1** (give way) lit [metal, surface] se gondoler; [wheel] se voiler; [pillar, wall] se déformer; [knees, legs] céder; fig [person] céder; **2** (fasten) [belt, shoe, strap] s'attacher, se boucler

(Phrasal verb)
■ **buckle down** se mettre au boulot◯

buckram /'bʌkrəm/ n bougran m

Bucks n GB Post abrév écrite = **Buckinghamshire**

buck: **~shot** n chevrotine f; **~skin** n daim m; **~ teeth** npl péj dents fpl de lapin pej; **~wheat** n sarrasin m, blé m noir

bucolic /bju:'kɒlɪk/ n, adj bucolique (f)

bud /bʌd/

A n **1** Bot (of leaf) bourgeon m; (of flower) bouton m; **in ~** [leaf] en bourgeon; [flower] en bouton; **2** Biol bourgeon m

B vi (p prés etc **-dd-**) **1** Bot (develop leaf buds) bourgeonner; (develop flower buds) boutonner; **2** (develop) [flower, breast] pointer

(Idiom) **to nip sth in the ~** tuer qch dans l'œuf

Buddha /'bʊdə/ pr n (god) Bouddha m

Buddhism /'bʊdɪzəm/ n bouddhisme m

Buddhist /'bʊdɪst/

A n bouddhiste mf

B adj [monk, temple] bouddhiste; [art] bouddhique

budding /'bʌdɪŋ/ adj **1** Bot (into leaf) bourgeonnant; (into flower) boutonnant; **2** fig [athlete, champion] en herbe; [talent, career, romance] naissant

buddy○ /'bʌdɪ/ n **1** (friend) copain m, pote○ m; **2** US (form of address) mec○ m; **3** (in Aids care) volontaire mf (attaché à un sidéen)

budge /bʌdʒ/

A vtr **1** lit bouger; **2** fig faire changer d'avis à

B vi lit bouger (**from, off** de); fig changer d'avis (**on** sur); **she would not ~ an inch** fig elle était inflexible

(Phrasal verb)

■ **budge over**○, **budge up**○ se pousser

budgerigar /'bʌdʒərɪɡɑ:(r)/ n perruche f

budget /'bʌdʒɪt/

A n **1** (personal, commercial) budget m (**for** pour); **education ~** budget de l'éducation; **to go over/stay within ~** dépasser/ ne pas dépasser le budget; **2** GB Pol (also **Budget**) Budget m

B noun modifier **1** [cut, deficit] budgétaire; [constraints, increase] du budget; **2** (cheap) [holiday, price] pour petits budgets; **a low-/high-~ film** un film à petit budget/à gros budget

C vtr budgétiser [money]; US budgétiser [time]

D vi **to ~ for** [company, government] budgétiser ses dépenses en fonction de [increase, needs]; **I hadn't ~ed for a new car** je n'avais pas prévu d'acheter une nouvelle voiture

budget account n GB (with bank, shop) compte-crédit m

budgetary /'bʌdʒɪtərɪ, US -terɪ/ adj budgétaire

budget: **~ day** n GB Pol jour m de la présentation du Budget; **~ heading** n Fin, Comm poste m budgétaire

budgeting /'bʌdʒɪtɪŋ/ n **as a result of careful ~, I have paid off my debts** en gérant soigneusement mon budget, j'ai réussi à rembourser mes dettes

budgie○ /'bʌdʒɪ/ n = **budgerigar**

buff /bʌf/

A n **1** ○(enthusiast) mordu/-e m/f; **2** (colour) chamois m; **3** (leather) peau m de buffle

B adj chamois

C vtr lustrer [shoes]; polir [fingernails, metal]

buffalo /'bʌfələʊ/ n (pl **-oes** or collective **~**) buffle m; US bison m

buffer /'bʌfə(r)/

A n **1** fig (protection) tampon m; **2** (for polishing) polissoir m

B buffers npl Rail (on line) butoir m; (on train) tampon m

(Idiom) **to run into the ~s** finir en queue de poisson

buffer: **~ state** n État m tampon; **~ zone** n zone f tampon

buffet¹ /'bʊfeɪ, US bə'feɪ/ n buffet m

buffet² /'bʌfɪt/ vtr [wind, sea] secouer; fig [misfortune] frapper

buffet car n GB Rail voiture-buffet f

buffoon /bə'fu:n/ n bouffon/-onne m/f

bug /bʌɡ/

A n **1** ○(any insect) bestiole f; **2** (bedbug) punaise f; **3** ○(also **stomach ~** ou **tummy ~**) ennuis mpl gastriques; **4** (germ) microbe m; **5** (fault) gen défaut m; Comput bogue f or m, bug m; **6** (hidden microphone) micro m caché; **7** ○(craze) virus m, manie f; **8** ○US (enthusiast) mordu/ -e m/f

B vtr (p prés etc **-gg-**) **1** (hide microphones in) poser des micros dans [room, building]; **the room is ~ged** il y a un micro (caché) dans la pièce; **2** ○(annoy) embêter○ [person]

bugaboo /'bʌɡəbu:/ n (pl **~s**) croquemitaine m

bugbear /'bʌɡbeə(r)/ n (problem, annoyance) plaie f

bugging /'bʌɡɪŋ/ n pose f de micros

bugging device n micro m d'écoute

buggy /'bʌɡɪ/ n **1** GB (pushchair) poussette f; **2** US (pram) landau m; **3** Hist (carriage) boghei m

bugle /'bju:ɡl/ ▸ p. 1028 n clairon m (instrument)

bugler /'bju:ɡlə(r)/ n clairon m (joueur)

build /bɪld/

A n carrure f; **of average ~** de carrure moyenne; **she is slender in ~** elle est mince

B vtr (prét, pp **built**) **1** (construct) construire [factory, city, railway]; édifier [church, monument]; **to ~ an extension onto a house** agrandir une maison; **2** (assemble) construire [engine, ship]; **3** Comput créer [software, interface]; **4** (establish) bâtir [career, future]; établir [relations, relationship]; fonder [empire]; créer [prosperity]; former [team]; **to ~ one's hopes on sth** fonder ses espoirs sur qch; **5** Games former [sequence, set, word]

C vi (prét, pp **built**) **1** (construct) construire; **2** fig (use as a foundation) **to ~ on** tirer parti de [popularity, success]; se développer à partir de [base]

(Phrasal verbs)

■ **build in**: ▸ **~ [sth] in**, **~ in [sth]** **1** (construct) encastrer; **2** (incorporate) introduire [clause, guarantee]

■ **build up**: ▸ **~ up** [gas, deposits] s'accumuler; [traffic] s'intensifier; [business, trade] se développer; [tension, excitement] monter; ▸ **~ up [sth]**, **~ [sth] up** **1** (accumulate) accumuler; **2** (boost) établir [trust]; gonfler [morale]; **don't ~ your hopes up too high** ne te fais pas d'illusions; **3** (establish) constituer [collection]; créer [business]; constituer [army]; établir [picture, profile]; créer [database]; se faire [reputation]; ▸ **~ [sth/sb] up**, **~ up [sth/sb]** **1** (strengthen) affirmer [muscles]; **to ~ oneself up** prendre des forces; **2** (promote) **they built him up to be a star** ils l'ont présenté comme si c'était une vedette

builder /'bɪldə(r)/ ▸ p. 1181 n (contractor) entrepreneur m en bâtiment; (worker) ouvrier/-ière m/f du bâtiment; **a firm of ~s** une entreprise de bâtiment

builder: **~'s labourer** ▸ p. 1181 n ouvrier/-ière m/f du bâtiment; **~'s merchant** ▸ p. 1181 n fournisseur m de matériaux de construction

building /'bɪldɪŋ/ n **1** (structure) bâtiment m; (with offices, apartments) immeuble m; (palace, church) édifice m; **school ~** bâtiment m d'école; **2** (industry) bâtiment m; **3** (action) construction f

building: **~ block** n (child's toy) cube m; (basic element) élément m de base; **~ contractor** ▸ p. 1181 n entrepreneur m en bâtiment; **~ land** n terrain m à bâtir; **~ materials** npl matériaux mpl de construction; **~ permit** n permis m de construire; **~ plot** n terrain m à bâtir; **~ site** n lit, fig chantier m (de construction); **~ society** n GB société f d'investissement et de crédit immobilier; **~ trade** n bâtiment m; **~ worker** ▸ p. 1181 n GB ouvrier/-ière m/f du bâtiment

build-up /'bɪldʌp/ n **1** (increase) accumulation f (**of** de); (in traffic, pressure) intensification f (**of** de); (in weapons, stocks) accumulation f (**of** de); (in tension, excitement) accroissement m (**of** de); (of levels) augmentation f (**of** de); **2** (publicity) **C the ~ to sth** les préparatifs de qch; **to give sth a good ~** faire du battage○ autour de qch

built /bɪlt/

A prét, pp ▸ **build**

B adj **1** (made) **he's powerfully ~** il a une puissante carrure; **he's slightly ~** il est fluet; **2** (designed) **to be ~ for** être conçu pour [efficiency, speed]; **~ to last** construit pour durer

C -**built** combining form **Russian-~** de construction russe; **stone-~** en pierre

built-in /,bɪlt'ɪn/ adj **1** [wardrobe] encastré; **2** [guarantee] intégré

built-up /,bɪlt'ʌp/ adj [region] urbanisé; **the centre of the town has become very ~** on a beaucoup construit dans le centre de la ville; **~ area** n agglomération f

bulb /bʌlb/ n **1** Elec ampoule f (électrique); **2** Bot bulbe m; **3** (of thermometer) réservoir m

bulbous /'bʌlbəs/ adj bulbeux/-euse; **a ~ nose** un gros nez

Bulgaria /bʌl'geərɪə/ ▸ **p. 774** n Bulgarie f

bulge /bʌldʒ/

A n **1** (swelling) (in clothing, carpet) bosse f; (in vase, column, pipe, tube) renflement m; (in tyre) hernie f; (in wall) bombement m; (in plaster) boursouflure f; (in cheek) gonflement m; **2** (in statistics) poussée f; **3** (increase) augmentation f (**in** de)

B vi [bag, pocket] être gonflé; [wallet] être bourré; [surface] se boursoufler; [stomach] ballonner; [cheeks] être gonflé; **his eyes were bulging** les yeux lui sortaient de la tête; **to be bulging with** [bag, vehicle] être bourré de; [book, building] être rempli de

bulging○ /'bʌldʒɪŋ/ adj [eye] exorbité; [cheek, stomach, vein] gonflé; [muscle] saillant; [surface, wall] bombé; [bag] plein à craquer○ (**after** n)

bulimia (nervosa) /bjuː'lɪmɪə nɜː'vəʊsə/ n boulimie f

bulimic /bjuː'lɪmɪk/ n, adj boulimique (mf)

bulk /bʌlk/

A n **1** (large size) (of package, correspondence, writings) volume m; (of building, vehicle) masse f; **2** (large body) corps m massif; **3** (large quantity) **in ~** [buy, sell] en gros; [transport] en vrac; **4** (majority) **the ~ of** la majeure partie de [imports, research, applications]; le plus gros de [army, workforce]; la plupart des [workers, voters]; **5** (dietary fibre) fibre f

B noun modifier **1** Comm [order, sale] en gros; [mailing] en nombre; **2** Naut [cargo, shipment] en vrac

bulk: **~-buy** vtr, vi [company] acheter en gros; **~-buying** n achat m en gros; **~ carrier** n cargo m, vraquier m; **~head** n Naut, Aviat cloison f

bulky /'bʌlkɪ/ adj [person] corpulent; [package, equipment, item] volumineux/-euse; [book] épais/-aisse

bull /bʊl/

A n **1** (animal) taureau m; **2** (large man) mâle m; **3** (in zodiac) **the Bull** le Taureau; **4** Fin spéculateur m à la hausse; **5** GB abrév ▸ **bull's-eye**

B noun modifier [elephant, whale] mâle m

C adj [market] à la hausse

D vi [speculator] spéculer à la hausse; [shares] être en hausse

(Idiom) **to go at sb/sth like a ~ at a gate** foncer tête baissée sur qn/qch

bulldog /'bʊldɒg/ n bouledogue m

bulldog clip n pince f à dessin

bulldoze /'bʊldəʊz/ vtr **1** lit (knock down) détruire [qch] au bulldozer [building]; (clear) nettoyer [qch] au bulldozer [site]; **2** fig (force) forcer (**into doing** à faire)

bulldozer /'bʊldəʊzə(r)/ n bulldozer m, bouteur m

bullet /'bʊlɪt/

A n balle f

B noun modifier [wound] par balle; [hole, mark] de balle

bulletin /'bʊlətɪn/ n bulletin m; **news ~** bulletin d'informations; **weather ~** bulletin météorologique

bulletin board n tableau m d'affichage; Comput messagerie f

bullet point n Print puce f

bulletproof /'bʊlɪtpruːf/

A adj [glass, vehicle, door] blindé; **~ vest** ou **jacket** gilet m pare-balles inv

B vtr blinder [glass, vehicle]

bull: **~fight** n corrida f; **~fighter** ▸ p. 1181 n torero m; **~fighting** n gen corridas fpl; (art) tauromachie f; **~frog** n grenouille f taureau; **~horn** n US mégaphone m

bullion /'bʊlɪən/ n ₵ lingots mpl

bullish /'bʊlɪʃ/ adj **1** Fin [market, shares, stocks] en hausse, haussier/-ière; [trend] à la hausse; **2** (optimistic) franchement optimiste

bullock /'bʊlək/ n (young) bouvillon m; (mature) bœuf m

bullring n (arena) arène f; (building) arènes fpl

bull's-eye /'bʊlzaɪ/ n (on a target) mille m

bully /'bʊlɪ/

A n **1** (child) petite brute f; (adult) tyran m; **the class ~** la terreur de la classe; **2** ○†(also **~ beef**) singe○ m

B ○excl **~ for you!** tant mieux pour toi!

C vtr [person, child] maltraiter; [country] intimider; **to ~ sb into doing sth** forcer qn à faire qch

bullying /'bʊlɪɪŋ/

A n (of person, child) mauvais traitements mpl; (of country) intimidation f

B adj [behaviour] brutal; [tactics] d'intimidation

bulrush /'bʊlrʌʃ/ n jonc m (des chaisiers)

bulwark /'bʊlwək/ n Mil, fig rempart m; Naut bastingage m; (breakwater) brise-lames m inv

bum○ /bʌm/

A n **1** GB (buttocks) derrière m; **2** US (vagrant) clochard m; **3** (lazy person) fainéant/-e m/f; **4** US **to be on the ~** vivre de la manche○

B vtr (p prés etc **-mm-**) (scrounge) taper○ [cigarette, money] (**off, from** à); **to ~ a ride, to ~ a lift** se faire emmener en voiture

C vi (p prés etc **-mm-**) vivre de la manche○

(Phrasal verb)

■ **bum around** **1** (travel aimlessly) vadrouiller○; **2** (be lazy) traînasser

bumbag /'bʌmbæg/ n GB (sacoche f) banane f

bumble /'bʌmbl/ vi (also **~ on**) (mumble) marmonner

bumblebee /'bʌmblbiː/ n bourdon m

bumbler○ /'bʌmblə(r)/ n cafouilleur/-euse m/f

bumbling○ /'bʌmblɪŋ/ adj **1** (incompetent) [person] empoté○; [attempt] maladroit○; **2** (mumbling) [person] radoteur/-euse; [speech] cafouilleux/-euse○

bumf○, **bumph**○ /'bʌmf/ n GB (documents) paperasserie○ f; (toilet paper) papier m hygiénique

bump /bʌmp/

A n **1** (lump) (on body) bosse f (**on** à); (on road surface) bosse f (**on, in** sur); **2** (jolt) secousse f; **3** (sound of fall) bruit m sourd; **4** onomat boum; **to go ~** faire boum; **5** ○(of pregnant woman) ventre m

B vtr **1** (knock) cogner (**against, on** contre); **to ~ one's head** se cogner la tête; **2** ○US (remove) **to ~ sb from** virer○ qn de [list, job]; **3** ○US (promote) **to ~ sb to** catapulter○ qn au poste de

C vi **1** (knock) **to ~ against** buter contre; **2** (move jerkily) **to ~ along** [vehicle] brinquebaler sur [road]; **to ~ over** [vehicle] cahoter sur [road]

(Idiom) **to come down to earth with a ~** être ramené à la dure réalité

(Phrasal verbs)

■ **bump into**: ▸ **~ into [sb/sth]** (collide) rentrer dans [person, object]; ▸ **~ into [sb]** (meet) tomber sur○ qn

■ **bump off**○: ▸ **~ off [sb],** **~ [sb] off** liquider○

■ **bump up**○: ▸ **~ up [sth]** faire grimper○ [price, tax]

bumper /'bʌmpə(r)/

A n **1** Aut pare-chocs m; **~ to ~** pare-chocs contre pare-chocs; **2** US Rail butoir m

B adj (épith) [crop, sales, year] record inv; [edition] exceptionnel/-elle

bumper: **~ car** n auto f tamponneuse; **~ sticker** n autocollant m

bumpkin○ /'bʌmpkɪn/ n pej (also **country ~**) péquenaud/-e○ m/f

bumptious /'bʌmpʃəs/ adj fat

bumpy /'bʌmpɪ/ adj lit [road surface] accidenté; [wall, ceiling] irrégulier/-ière; [flight, landing] agité

(Idiom) **to be in for a ~ ride** entrer dans une mauvaise passe

bun /bʌn/ n **1** Culin (roll) petit pain m; (cake) petit cake m; **2** (hairstyle) chignon m; **to put/wear one's hair in a ~** se faire/avoir un chignon

bunch /bʌntʃ/

A n **1** ○(of people) groupe m; pej bande f; **a mixed ~** un groupe hétéroclite; **2** (of flowers) bouquet m (**of** de); **3** (of vegetables) botte f; (of bananas) régime m; **4** (of objects) **a ~ of feathers** une touffe de plumes; **a ~ of keys** un trousseau de clés; **a ~ of wires** un faisceau de fils; **5** ○(lot) tas○ m (**of** de); **a whole ~ of things** tout un tas○ de choses; **the best** ou **pick of the ~** le meilleur du lot; **6** GB (of hair) couette f; **7** Sport peloton m

B vtr mettre [qch] en bottes [vegetables]; mettre [qch] en bouquets [flowers]

bundle /'bʌndl/

A n **1** (collection) (of objects) ballot m; (of clothes, cloth) balluchon m; (of papers, banknotes) liasse f; (of books) paquet m; (of straw) botte f; **2** (baby, person) **~ of joy** petit ange m; iron petit trésor m; **~ of nerves** boule f de nerfs

B ○vtr **to ~ sb/sth into** fourrer○ qn/qch dans; **to ~ sb outside** ou **through the door** pousser qn dehors sans ménagement

C ○*vi* **to ~ into a car** se ruer dans une voiture

(Idioms) **I don't go a ~ on jazz** GB le jazz ne me botte pas○; **to make a ~**○ gagner un paquet○

(Phrasal verbs)
- **bundle off**; ▸ **~ [sb] off** faire sortir [qn] sans ménagement; [*police*] embarquer○
- **bundle up**: ▸ **~ [sth] up, ~ up [sth]** mettre [qch] en paquet [*papers*]; faire un ballot de [*clothes*]; mettre [qch] en liasse [*banknotes*]

bundled software /ˌbʌndld ˈsɒftweə(r), US ˈsɔːft-/ *n* Comput ensemble *m* de logiciels, bundle *m*

bung /bʌŋ/
A *n* tampon *m*, bouchon *m*
B *vtr* **1** (stop up) boucher; **2** ○GB (put, throw) balancer○

(Phrasal verbs)
- **bung in**○ GB: ▸ **~ [sth] in, ~ in [sth]** donner [qch] en prime
- **bung up**○ GB: ▸ **~ [sth] up, ~ up [sth]** boucher [*drain, nose*]

bungalow /ˈbʌŋgələʊ/ *n* pavillon *m* (sans étage)

bungee jumping /ˈbʌndʒiː dʒʌmpɪŋ/ ▸ p. 881 *n* saut *m* à l'élastique

bungle /ˈbʌŋgl/
A *n* gaffe *f*
B *vtr* rater○ [*attempt, burglary*]
C *vi* rater son coup○

bungling /ˈbʌŋglɪŋ/ *adj* maladroit

bunion /ˈbʌnjən/ *n* Med oignon *m*

bunk /bʌŋk/
A *n* **1** Naut, Rail couchette *f*; **2** gen (*also* **~ bed**) (whole unit) lits *mpl* superposés; **the top/lower ~** le lit du haut/du bas
B ○*vi* (*also* **~ down**) dormir

(Idiom) **to do a ~**○ prendre le large○

(Phrasal verb)
- **bunk off**○ s'éclipser; **to ~ off school** sécher l'école

bunk bed *n* = **bunk A 2**

bunker /ˈbʌŋkə(r)/ *n* **1** (shelter) (for commander) bunker *m*; (for gun) blockhaus *m*; (beneath building) abri *m*; **2** (in golf) bunker *m*; **3** (container) soute *f*

bunny /ˈbʌnɪ/ *n* **1** (*also* **~ rabbit**) (Jeannot) lapin *m*; **2** (*also* **~ girl**) hôtesse *f* (*du club Playboy®, déguisée en lapin*)

Bunsen (burner) /ˈbʌnsn/ *n* (bec *m*) Bunsen *m*

bunting /ˈbʌntɪŋ/ *n* **1** (flags) guirlandes *fpl*; **2** Zool bruant *m*

buoy /bɔɪ/
A *n* gen bouée *f*; (for marking) balise *f* (flottante)
B *vtr* **1** (*also* **~ up**) (make cheerful) revigorer (**by** par); **2** (*also* **~ up**) Fin stimuler [*share prices*] (**by** par); **3** (*also* **~ up**) lit (keep afloat) maintenir à flot

buoyancy /ˈbɔɪənsɪ/ *n* **1** (of floating object) flottabilité *f*; (of medium) poussée *f*; **2** (cheerfulness) entrain *m*; **3** (of exports, market) fermeté *f*

buoyancy aid *n* bouée *f*

buoyant /ˈbɔɪənt/ *adj* **1** [*object*] qui flotte; **2** (cheerful) [*person*] vif/vive; [*mood, spirits*] enjoué; [*step*] allègre; **3** Econ gen soutenu; [*economy*] en expansion

buoyantly /ˈbɔɪəntlɪ/ *adv* **1** (cheerfully) [*speak*] avec enjouement; [*walk*] d'un pas allègre; **2** (lightly) [*rise, float*] vivement

burble /ˈbɜːbl/
A *n* = **burbling**
B *vi* **1** [*stream*] glouglouter; **2** [*person*] marmonner; **to ~ (on) about sth** radoter à propos de qch

burbling /ˈbɜːblɪŋ/
A *n* **1** (of stream, voices) gargouillis *m*; **2** (rambling talk) galimatias *m*
B *adj* [*stream, voice*] qui gargouille

burden /ˈbɜːdn/
A *n* **1** (responsibility) fardeau *m* (**to sb** pour qn); **the ~ of guilt/responsibility** le poids de la culpabilité/responsabilité; **the ~ of taxation** la pression fiscale; **to ease the ~ on sb** alléger le fardeau qui pèse sur qn; **the ~ of proof** Jur la charge de la preuve; **2** lit (load) fardeau *m*
B *vtr* (*also* **~ down**) fig ennuyer (**with** de); lit encombrer (**with** de)
C *v refl* **to ~ oneself with sth** se charger de qch

bureau /ˈbjʊərəʊ, US -ˈrəʊ/ *n* (*pl* **~s** *ou* **~x**) **1** (agency) agence *f*; (local office) bureau *m*; **information ~** bureau *m* de renseignements; **2** surtout US (government department) service *m*; **3** GB (writing desk) secrétaire *m*; **4** US (chest of drawers) commode *f*

bureaucracy /bjʊəˈrɒkrəsɪ/ *n* bureaucratie *f*

bureaucrat /ˈbjʊərəkræt/ *n* bureaucrate *mf*

bureaucratic /ˌbjʊərəˈkrætɪk/ *adj* bureaucratique

burgeon /ˈbɜːdʒən/ *vi* sout **1** fig (grow) croître; (multiply) se multiplier; **2** fig (flourish) fleurir; **3** lit [*plant*] bourgeonner

burgeoning /ˈbɜːdʒənɪŋ/ *adj* **1** (growing) [*talent, love, industry, crime*] croissant; [*population, industries*] en plein essor; **2** (flourishing) florissant; **3** [*plant*] bourgeonnant

burger /ˈbɜːgə(r)/ *n* hamburger *m*; **beef~** beefburger *m*

burger bar *n* fast-food *m*

burglar /ˈbɜːglə(r)/ *n* cambrioleur/-euse *m/f*

burglar alarm *n* sonnerie *f* d'alarme

burglarize /ˈbɜːgləraɪz/ *vtr* US cambrioler

burglar-proof /ˈbɜːgləpruːf/ *adj* [*house*] protégé contre les cambrioleurs; [*safe*] inviolable; [*lock*] incrochetable

burglary /ˈbɜːglərɪ/ *n* gen cambriolage *m*; Jur vol *m* avec effraction

burgle /ˈbɜːgl/ *vtr* cambrioler

burgundy /ˈbɜːgəndɪ/ ▸ p. 873, p. 752
A Burgundy *pr n* Bourgogne *f*; **in ~** en Bourgogne
B *n* **1** (*also* **Burgundy**) (wine) bourgogne *m*; **2** (colour) (couleur *f*) bordeaux *m*
C *adj* (colour) bordeaux *inv*

burial /ˈberɪəl/
A *n* **1** (ceremony) enterrement *m*; **2** (of body) inhumation *f*; (of object, waste) ensevelissement *m*
B *noun modifier* [*site*] de sépulture; [*rites*] funéraire

burka /ˈbɜːkə/ *n* burqua *f*

burlesque /bɜːˈlesk/
A *n* **1** (piece of writing) parodie *f*; (genre) (genre *m*) burlesque *m*; **2** (sham) parodie *f*; **3** †US (show) burlesque *m*
B *adj* **1** [*style, show*] burlesque; **2** (sham) caricatural
C *vtr* parodier

burly /ˈbɜːlɪ/ *adj* [*person*] solidement charpenté; [*build*] imposant

Burma /ˈbɜːmə/ ▸ p. 774 *pr n* Birmanie *f*

burn /bɜːn/
A *n* brûlure *f*
B *vtr* (*prét, pp* **burned** *ou* **burnt** GB) **1** (damage by heat or fire) brûler [*papers, rubbish*]; incendier, faire brûler [*building*]; [*sun*] brûler; [*acid*] ronger, brûler; [*alcohol, food*] brûler [*mouth*]; laisser brûler [*food*]; brûler [*pan*]; **to be ~ed to the ground** *ou* **to ashes** être détruit par le feu; **to be ~ed alive** être brûlé vif; **to be ~ed to death** mourir carbonisé; **to ~ one's finger** se brûler le doigt; **2** (use) **to ~ coal/gas** [*boiler*] marcher au charbon/au gaz; **3** Comput graver [*CD*]
C *vi* (*prét, pp* **burned** *ou* **burnt** GB) **1** (be consumed by fire) [*wood*] brûler; (be turned on) [*light*] être allumé; **2** (be painful) [*blister, wound*] cuire; (from sun) brûler; **he has the kind of skin that ~s easily** il y a attrape facilement des coups de soleil; **his cheeks were ~ing** il était rouge de honte; **4** Culin [*toast, meat*] brûler; [*sauce*] prendre au fond; **5** fig (be eager) **to be ~ing with desire** brûler de désir
D *v refl* (*prét, pp* **burned** *ou* **burnt** GB) **to ~ oneself** se brûler

(Idiom) **to ~ one's boats** brûler ses vaisseaux

(Phrasal verbs)
- **burn away** [*candle, log*] se consumer
- **burn down**: ▸ **~ down 1** [*house*] brûler complètement, être réduit en cendres; **2** [*candle, fire*] baisser; ▸ **~ down [sth], ~ [sth] down** incendier, réduire [qch] en cendres [*house etc*]
- **burn off**: ▸ **~ off** [*alcohol*] s'évaporer; ▸ **~ off [sth], ~ [sth] off** décaper [qch] au chalumeau [*paint*]; fig dépenser [*energy*]
- **burn out**: ▸ **~ out** [*candle, fire*] s'éteindre; [*light bulb*] griller; [*fuse*] sauter; fig [*person*] (through overwork) s'user; ▸ **~ out [sth], ~ [sth] out** (destroy by fire) incendier [*building, vehicle*]; Aut, Tech griller [*clutch, motor*]; ▸ **~ out [sb], ~ [sb] out** gen, Mil forcer [qn] à sortir par l'incendie
- **burn up**: ▸ **~ up 1** [*fire, flames*] flamber; **2** [*satellite, meteorite*] se volatiliser; ▸ **~ up [sth], ~ [sth] up** brûler [*calories, fuel, waste*]; dépenser [*energy*]

b

burned-out *adj* = burnt-out

burner /'bɜːnə(r)/ *n* (on gas cooker) brûleur *m*; (of lamp) bec *m* (de gaz)

(Idiom) **to put sth on the back ~** mettre qch en veilleuse

burning /'bɜːnɪŋ/
A *n* **1** there's a smell of ~ ça sent le brûlé; **I can smell ~!** je sens une odeur de brûlé!; **2** (setting on fire) incendie *m*
B *adj* **1** (on fire) en flammes, en feu; (alight) [*candle, lamp, fire*] allumé; [*ember, coal*] embrasé, ardent; fig (very hot) brûlant; **a ~ sensation** une sensation de brûlure; **2** fig (intense) [*fever, desire*] brûlant; [*passion*] ardent; **a ~ question** une question brûlante

burnish /'bɜːnɪʃ/ littér
A *vtr* brunir
B **burnished** *pp adj* [*copper, skin, leaves*] bruni

burn: **~-out** *n* surmenage *m*, épuisement *m*; **~s unit** *n* Med service *m* des grands brûlés

burnt /bɜːnt/
A *prét, pp* ▸ **burn**
B *adj* gen [*smell, taste*] de brûlé, de roussi

burnt: **~ orange** ▸ p. 752 *n* orange *m* foncé; **~-out** *adj* lit [*building, car*] calciné; fig [*person*] usé (par le travail)

burp○ /bɜːp/
A *n* rot○ *m*, renvoi *m*
B *vtr* faire faire son rot○ à [*baby*]
C *vi* [*person*] roter○; [*baby*] faire son rot○

burr /bɜː(r)/ *n* **1** Bot *partie de certaines plantes qui s'accroche aux vêtements, au pelage des animaux*; **2** Ling grasseyement *m*

burrow /'bʌrəʊ/
A *n* terrier *m*
B *vtr* [*animal*] creuser [*hole, tunnel*]; **to ~ one's way into sth** [*animal, person*] se creuser un chemin dans qch
C *vi* [*animal*] creuser un terrier; **to ~ into/under sth** (in ground) creuser dans/sous qch

bursar /'bɜːsə(r)/ ▸ p. 1181 *n* Sch, Univ intendant/-e *m/f*

bursary /'bɜːsərɪ/ *n* GB Sch, Univ **1** (grant) bourse *f* (d'études); **2** (office) bureau *m* de l'intendant

burst /bɜːst/
A *n* (of flame) jaillissement *m*, jet *m*; (of bomb, shell) éclatement *m*; (of gunfire) rafale *f*; (of activity, energy, enthusiasm) accès *m*; **a ~ of growth** une poussée; **a ~ of laughter** un éclat de rire; **a ~ of anger** un accès de colère; **a ~ of applause** un tonnerre d'applaudissements; **to put on a ~ of speed** Aut faire une pointe de vitesse
B *vtr* (*prét, pp* **burst**) crever [*balloon, bubble, tyre*]; rompre [*blood vessel*]; **the river burst its banks** le fleuve a débordé; **a burst pipe** un tuyau qui a éclaté
C *vi* (*prét, pp* **burst**) **1** [*balloon, bubble, tyre*] crever; [*pipe, boiler*] éclater; [*dam*] rompre; [*bomb, firework*] éclater; **to be ~ing at the seams** [*bag, room, building*] être plein à craquer; **to be ~ing to do** mourir d'envie de faire; **to be ~ing with health/pride** déborder de santé/de fierté; **2** (emerge suddenly) [*people*] surgir; [*water*] jaillir; **to ~ onto the rock scene** faire irruption dans le monde du rock

(Phrasal verbs)

■ **burst in:** ▸ ~ **in** faire irruption, entrer en trombe; **to ~ in on a meeting** interrompre brusquement une réunion

■ **burst into:** ▸ ~ **into** [sth] **1** faire irruption dans [*room, meeting*]; **2** **to ~ into blossom** ou **bloom** s'épanouir; **to ~ into flames** s'enflammer; **to ~ into song** se mettre à chanter; **to ~ into tears** fondre en larmes; **to ~ into laughter** éclater de rire

■ **burst open:** ▸ ~ **open** [*door*] s'ouvrir violemment; [*sack*] crever; ▸ ~ **open** [sth], ~ [sth] **open** ouvrir [qch] violemment

■ **burst out** **1** (come out) **to ~ out of a room** sortir en trombe d'une pièce; **he was ~ing out of his waistcoat** il était boudiné dans son gilet; **2** (start) **to ~ out laughing** éclater de rire; **to ~ out crying** fondre en larmes; **to ~ out singing** se mettre à chanter; **3** (exclaim) s'écrier, s'exclamer

■ **burst through:** ▸ ~ **through** [sth] rompre [*barricade*]; **to ~ through the door** entrer violemment ou brusquement

Burundi /bəˈrʊndɪ/ ▸ p. 774 *pr n* Burundi *m*

bury /'berɪ/ *vtr* **1** (after death) enterrer, inhumer [*person*]; enterrer [*animal*]; **2** [*avalanche etc*] ensevelir [*person, building, town*]; **to be buried alive** être enterré vivant; **3** (hide)

enterrer, enfouir [*treasure, bone*]; **to ~ oneself in the countryside** aller s'enterrer à la campagne; **to ~ one's face in one's hands** se cacher le visage dans ses mains; **4** (suppress) enterrer [*differences, hatred, memories*]; **5** (engross) **to be buried in** être plongé dans [*book, work*]; **6** (plunge) enfoncer [*dagger, teeth, hands*] (**in** dans)

bus /bʌs/
A *n* (*pl* **buses**) **1** (vehicle) autobus *m*, bus *m*; (long-distance) autocar *m*, car *m*; **by ~** [*come, go, travel*] en (auto)bus, par le bus; **on the ~** dans le bus; **2** Comput (*also* **~bar**) bus *m*
B *noun modifier* [*depot, service, stop, ticket*] d'autobus
C *vtr* (*p prés etc* **-ss-** GB, **-s-** US) acheminer [qn] par or en bus

busby /'bʌzbɪ/ *n* bonnet *m* à poil (de soldat)

bus: **~ conductor** ▸ p. 1181 *n* receveur *m* d'autobus; **~ conductress** ▸ p. 1181 *n* receveuse *f* d'autobus; **~ driver** ▸ p. 1181 *n* conducteur/-trice *m/f* d'autobus

bush /bʊʃ/ *n* **1** (shrub) buisson *m*; **a ~ of hair** fig une épaisse tignasse; **2** (in Australia, Africa) **the ~** la brousse *f*

(Idiom) **don't beat about the ~** cessez de tourner autour du pot

bushed○ /bʊʃt/ *adj* (tired) crevé○

bushel /'bʊʃl/ *n* boisseau *m*; **~s of**○ US des quantités de

(Idiom) **to hide one's light under a ~** être trop modeste

bush: **~fighting** *n* Mil combat *m* de brousse; **~fire** *n* feu *m* de brousse; **~ telegraph** *n* lit téléphone *m* de brousse; fig hum téléphone *m* arabe

bushy /'bʊʃɪ/ *adj* **1** [*hair, tail*] touffu; [*beard*] épais/-aisse; [*eyebrows*] broussailleux/-euse; **2** [*garden*] broussailleux/-euse

busily /'bɪzɪlɪ/ *adv* **to be ~ doing** être occupé à faire

business /'bɪznɪs/
A *n* **1** ¢ (commerce) affaires *fpl*; **to be in ~** être dans les affaires; **to go into ~** se lancer dans les affaires; **to set up in ~** s'établir à son compte; **the firm is no longer in ~** l'entreprise a fermé; **to do ~ with sb** faire des affaires avec qn; **they're in ~ together** ils sont associés; **he is a man I can do ~ with** c'est un homme avec qui je peux travailler; **to go out of ~** faire faillite; **they're back in ~** Comm ils ont repris leurs activités; **she's gone to Brussels on ~** elle est allée à Bruxelles pour affaires or en voyage d'affaires; **the recession has put them out of ~** la récession les a obligés à cesser leurs activités; **it's good/bad for ~** ça fait marcher/ne fait pas marcher les affaires; **to talk ~** parler affaires; **are you in London for ~ or pleasure?** êtes-vous à Londres pour affaires ou pour le plaisir?; **to mix ~ with pleasure** joindre l'utile à l'agréable; **'~ as usual'** 'nous restons ouverts pendant les travaux'; **it is/it was ~ as usual** fig c'est/c'était comme à l'habitude; **2** (custom, trade) **to lose ~** perdre de la clientèle; **how's ~** comment vont les affaires?; **~ is slow at the moment** les affaires marchent au ralenti en ce moment; **most of our ~ comes from tourists** la plupart de nos clients sont des touristes; **we are doing twice as much ~ as last summer** notre chiffre d'affaires a doublé par rapport à l'été dernier; **3** (trade, profession) métier *m*; **what (line of) ~ are you in?** qu'est-ce que vous faites dans la vie?; **he's in the insurance ~** il travaille dans les assurances; **4** (company, firm) affaire *f*, entreprise *f*; (shop) commerce *m*, boutique *f*; **small ~es** les petites entreprises; **a small mail-order ~** une petite affaire de vente par correspondance; **5** ¢ (important matters) questions *fpl* importantes; (duties, tasks) devoirs *mpl*, occupations *fpl*; **let's get down to ~** passons aux choses sérieuses; **can we get down to ~?** on peut s'y mettre?; **to go about one's ~** vaquer à ses occupations; **we still have some unfinished ~ to discuss** nous avons encore des choses à discuter; **he got on with the ~ of letterwriting** il s'est mis à faire la correspondance; **'any other ~'** (on agenda) 'questions diverses'; **6** (concern) **that's her ~** ça la regarde; **it's none of your ~!** ça ne te regarde pas!; **to make it one's ~ to do** se charger de faire; **mind your own ~**○! occupe-toi or mêle-toi de tes affaires○!; **he had no ~ telling her!** ce n'était pas à lui de le lui dire!; **7** (affair) histoire *f*, affaire *f*; **it's a bad** ou **sorry ~** c'est une triste affaire; **what a dreadful ~!** quelle histoire horrible!; **a nasty ~** une sale affaire; **8** (bother, nuisance) histoire *f*
B *noun modifier* [*address, letter, transaction*] commercial; [*pages*] affaires; [*meeting, consortium*] d'affaires; **~ people** hommes

mpl d'affaires; **the ~ community** le monde des affaires

(Idioms) **now we're in ~!** maintenant nous sommes prêts!; **to be in the ~ of doing** avoir pour habitude de faire; **she can play the piano like nobody's ~**○ elle joue du piano comme personne; **to work like nobody's ~**○ travailler d'arrache-pied; **she means ~!** elle ne plaisante pas!

business: **~ activity** *n* activité *f* industrielle et commerciale; **~ analyst** ▸ p. 1181 *n* analyste *mf* financier/-ière; **~ associate** *n* associé/-e *m/f*; **~ call** *n* (visit) visite *f* d'affaires; (phone call) communication *f* d'affaires; **~ card** *n* carte *f* de visite; **~ centre** GB, **~ center** US *n* centre *m* d'affaires; **~ class** *n* Aviat classe *f* affaires; **~ college** *n* école *f* de commerce; **~ contact** *n* relation *f* d'affaires; **~ cycle** *n* cycle *m* économique; **~ deal** *n* affaire *f*; **~ expenses** *npl* frais *mpl* professionnels; **~ failures** *npl* faillites *fpl* d'entreprises; **~ hours** *npl* gen heures *fpl* ouvrables; (in office) heures *fpl* de bureau; (of shop) heures *fpl* d'ouverture

businesslike /'bɪznɪslaɪk/ *adj* [person, manner] sérieux/-ieuse; [transaction] régulier/-ière, sérieux/-ieuse; fig hum [knife, tool] sérieux/-ieuse

business: **~ lunch** *n* déjeuner *m* d'affaires; **~ machine** *n* machine *f* de bureau

businessman /'bɪznɪsmən/ ▸ p. 1181 *n* (*pl* **-men**) homme *m* d'affaires; **big ~** brasseur *m* d'affaires, affairiste *m* pej; **he's a good ~** il a le sens des affaires

business: **~ park** *n* parc *m* d'affaires or d'activités; **~ plan** *n* projet *m* commercial; **~ premises** *npl* locaux *mpl* commerciaux; **~ proposition** *n* proposition *f*; **~ reply envelope** *n* enveloppe *f* préaffranchie, enveloppe-réponse *f*; **~ school** *n* école *f* de commerce; **~ software** *n* logiciel *m* de gestion; **~ studies** *npl* études *fpl* commerciales or de commerce; **~ suit** *n* costume *m* de ville, complet *m*; **~-to-~** *adj* interentreprise; **~ trip** *n* voyage *m* d'affaires; **~woman** *n* femme *f* d'affaires

busk /bʌsk/ *vi* GB [musician] jouer dans la rue; [singer] chanter dans la rue

busker /'bʌskə(r)/ *n* GB (musician) musicien-ienne *m/f* ambulant/-e; (singer) chanteur/-euse *m/f* ambulant/-e

bus lane *n* couloir *m* d'autobus

busload /'bʌsləʊd/ *n* car *m*; **a ~ of tourists** un car plein de voyageurs; **by the ~, by ~s** par cars entiers

busman /'bʌsmən/ *n* employé *m* des autobus

(Idiom) **a ~'s holiday** GB vacances *fpl* qui n'en sont pas vraiment

bus: **~ pass** *n* carte *f* de bus; **~ route** *n* ligne *f* d'autobus; **~ shelter** *n* abribus® *m*; **~ station** *n* gare *f* routière

bussing /'bʌsɪŋ/ *n* US ramassage *m* scolaire (*surtout pour abolir la ségrégation raciale aux États-Unis*)

> ⓘ **Bussing** Ce système, instauré aux États-Unis en 1971, consiste à organiser le transport en car scolaire d'élèves de couleur dans une école à majorité blanche et inversement, afin de favoriser un plus grand mixage ethnique. Cette réglementation fut assouplie par la Cour suprême en 1992 qui déclara que l'équilibre racial n'était pas le seul critère à prendre en considération pour réussir un processus d'intégration.

bust /bʌst/

A *n* [1] (breasts) poitrine *f*; [2] Art buste *m*; [3] ○US (binge) **to go on the ~** faire la bringue○; [4]○ (failure) (person) raté/-e *m/f*; (business, career) échec *m*; Econ effondrement *m*; [5] ○(police raid) rafle *f*; (arrest) arrestation *f*

B *noun modifier* **~ size, ~ measurement** tour *m* de poitrine

C *adj*○ [1] (broken) fichu○; [2] (bankrupt) **to go ~** faire faillite

D ○*vtr* (*prét, pp* **~** *ou* **~ed**) [1] (break) bousiller○; [2] (break up) démanteler [drugs ring]; (raid) faire une descente dans [premises]; (arrest) épingler○ [suspect]; [3] (financially) ruiner [person, firm]; [4] ○US (demote) rétrograder [soldier, policeman] (**to au rang de**)

E ○*vi* (*prét, pp* **~** *ou* **~ed**) = **burst** C

(Idiom) **to ~ a gut doing**○ se donner un mal de chien○ pour faire

(Phrasal verb)

■ **bust up**○: ▸ **~ up** [couple] rompre; [friends] se brouiller; ▸ **~ [sth] up, ~ up [sth]** flanquer [qch] en l'air○ [party, relationship]

buster○ /'bʌstə(r)/ *n* US **move over, ~!** pousse-toi de là, mon pote○!

bustle /'bʌsl/

A *n* [1] (activity) affairement *m* (**of** de); **hustle and ~** grande animation *f*; [2] Hist (on dress) faux cul○ *m*, tournure *f*

B *vi* [person, crowd] (*also* **~ about**) s'affairer; **to ~ in/out** entrer/sortir d'un air affairé

bustling /'bʌslɪŋ/ *adj* [street, shop, town] animé; [person] affairé

bust-up○ /'bʌstʌp/ *n* engueulade○ *f*

busy /'bɪzi/

A *adj* [1] [person] occupé (**with** avec; **doing** à faire); **to look ~** avoir l'air occupé; **to keep oneself/sb ~** trouver de quoi s'occuper/occuper qn; **that should keep them ~!** cela devrait les occuper!; [2] [shop] où il y a beaucoup de monde; [junction, airport] où le trafic est intense; [road] très fréquenté; [street, town] animé; [day, week] chargé; **were the shops ~?** est-ce qu'il y avait beaucoup de monde dans les magasins?; [3] (engaged) [line] occupé

B *v refl* **to ~ oneself doing** s'occuper à faire

busybody○ *n* **he's a real ~** il se mêle de tout

but /bʌt, bət/

A *adv* (only, just) **if I had ~ known** si seulement j'avais su; **these are ~ two of the possibilities** ce ne sont que deux possibilités; **I can ~ try** je peux toujours essayer; **one can't help ~ admire her** on ne peut pas s'empêcher de l'admirer

B *prep* **anything ~ that** tout, sauf ça; **anybody ~ him** n'importe qui sauf lui; **anywhere ~ Australia** n'importe où sauf en Australie; **everybody ~ Paul** tout le monde sauf Paul; **nobody ~ me knows how to do it** il n'y a que moi qui sache le faire; **he's nothing ~ a coward** ce n'est qu'un lâche; **to do nothing ~ disturb people** ne rien faire d'autre que déranger les gens; **there's nothing for it ~ to leave** il n'y a plus qu'une solution, c'est de partir; **where ~ in France?** où sinon en France?; **and whom should I meet ~ Steven!** et devine qui j'ai rencontré, Steven!; **the last ~ one** l'avant-dernier; **the next road ~ one** la deuxième rue

C **but for** *prep phr* **~ for you, I would have died** sans toi je serais mort; **he would have gone ~ for me** si je n'avais pas été là il serait parti

D *conj* [1] (expressing contrast, contradiction) mais; **it's not an asset ~ a disadvantage** ce n'est pas un atout mais un désavantage; **I'll do it, ~ not yet** je le ferai, mais pas tout de suite; [2] (yet) mais; **cheap ~ nourishing** bon marché mais nourrissant; [3] (expressing reluctance, protest, surprise) **~ that's wonderful!** mais c'est formidable!; **~ we can't afford it!** mais c'est trop cher pour nous!; [4] (except that) **never a day passes ~ she visits him** elle ne laisse pas passer un jour sans aller le voir; [5] (in apologies) mais; **excuse me, ~** excusez-moi, mais; [6] (for emphasis) **not twice, ~ three times** pas deux mais trois fois; [7] (adding to the discussion) **~ to continue...** mais, pour continuer...; **~ first** mais tout d'abord

(Idiom) **no ~s (about it)** il n'y a pas de 'mais' qui tienne, pas de discussion

butane /'bju:teɪn/ *n* butane *m*

butch /bʊtʃ/ *adj* [woman] injur hommasse○; [man] macho○

butcher /'bʊtʃə(r)/ ▸ p. 1181

A *n* (person) lit, fig boucher *m*; **~'s (shop)** boucherie *f*

B *vtr* abattre [animal]; débiter [meat]; fig massacrer

butchery /'bʊtʃərɪ/ *n* [1] (trade) boucherie *f*; [2] (slaughter) massacre *m*

butler /'bʌtlə(r)/ ▸ p. 1181 *n* maître *m* d'hôtel, majordome *m*

butt /bʌt/

A *n* [1] (end) gen bout *m*; (of rifle) crosse *f*; (of cigarette) mégot○ *m*; [2] ○US (buttocks) derrière○ *m*; [3] (barrel) (gros) tonneau *m*; [4] (person: target) **to be the ~ of sb's jokes** être la cible des blagues de qn; [5] (blow) (by person) coup *m* de tête; (by animal) coup *m* de corne

B *vtr* [person] donner un coup de tête à; [animal] donner un coup de corne à

(Phrasal verb)

■ **butt in** (on conversation) interrompre; (during meeting) intervenir; **he kept ~ing in on our conversation** il n'arrêtait pas de mettre son grain de sel○

butter /ˈbʌtə(r)/
A n beurre m
B vtr beurrer [bread]
(Idioms) **it's her bread and ~** c'est son gagne-pain; **~ wouldn't melt in her mouth** on lui donnerait le bon Dieu sans confession
(Phrasal verb)
■ **butter up**○: ▸ **~ [sb] up**, **~ up [sb]** passer de la pommade à○

butter: **~bean** n haricot m de Lima, pois m de sept ans; **~cup** n Bot bouton d'or m; **~ dish** n beurrier m; **~fingered** adj maladroit, empoté; **~fingers** n empoté/-e m/f

butterfly /ˈbʌtəflaɪ/ n **1** Zool (pl **-ies**) papillon m; **she's a bit of a social ~** elle papillonne en société; **2** Sport = **butterfly stroke**
(Idiom) **to have butterflies (in one's stomach)** avoir le trac○

butterfly: **~ net** n filet m à papillons; **~ nut** n papillon m, écrou m à ailettes; **~ stroke** n brasse f papillon

butter: **~milk** n babeurre m; **~ muslin** n étamine f

butterscotch /ˈbʌtəskɒtʃ/
A n (sweet) caramel m dur; (flavour) caramel m
B noun modifier [ice cream, sauce] au caramel

buttock /ˈbʌtək/ n fesse f

button /ˈbʌtn/
A n **1** (on coat, switch) bouton m; **to do up/undo a ~** boutonner/déboutonner un bouton; **2** US (badge) insigne m, badge m; **3** Comput bouton m
B vi [dress, etc] se boutonner
(Idiom) **as bright as a ~** [child] très éveillé/-e
(Phrasal verb)
■ **button up**: ▸ **~ [sth] up**, **~ up [sth]** boutonner [garment]

button-down adj [collar] à pointes boutonnées; [shirt] avec col à pointes boutonnées

buttonhole /ˈbʌtnhəʊl/
A n **1** (in sewing) boutonnière f; **2** GB (flower) fleur f (portée à la boutonnière)
B ○vtr (accost) accrocher○

button: **~hook** n tire-bouton m; **~ mushroom** n (petit) champignon m de Paris

buttress /ˈbʌtrɪs/
A n **1** gen contrefort m; fig soutien m; **2** (also **flying ~**) arc-boutant m
B vtr lit, fig étayer

buxom /ˈbʌksəm/ adj plantureux/-euse

buy /baɪ/
A n **1** (bargain) **a good/bad ~** une bonne/mauvaise affaire; **2** (purchase) acquisition f
B vtr (prét, pp **bought**) **1** (purchase) acheter [food, car, shares, house] (**from sb** à qn); **to ~ sth from the supermarket/from the baker's** acheter qch au supermarché/chez le boulanger; **to ~ sb sth** acheter qch à qn; **the best that money can ~** ce qui se fait de mieux; **2** (obtain with money) acheter [fame, freedom, friends]; **to ~ some time** gagner du temps; **3** (bribe) acheter [loyalty, silence, person]; **she can't be bought** elle est incorruptible; **4** ○(believe) avaler○, croire
C v refl (prét, pp **bought**) **to ~ oneself sth** s'acheter qch
(Phrasal verbs)
■ **buy in** GB: ▸ **~ [sth] in**, **~ in [sth]** s'approvisionner en
■ **buy into**: ▸ **~ into [sth]** Comm acheter or acquérir une part dans
■ **buy off**: ▸ **~ [sb] off**, **~ off [sb]** acheter [person, witness]
■ **buy out**: ▸ **~ [sb] out**, **~ out [sb]** Comm racheter la part de [co-owner]; **to ~ oneself out of** racheter son engagement dans [army]
■ **buy up**: ▸ **~ up [sth]**, **~ [sth] up** acheter systématiquement [shares, property]

buyer /ˈbaɪə(r)/ ▸ p. 1181 n acheteur/-euse m/f; **~'s market** marché m d'acheteurs, marché m où la demande est faible

buying /ˈbaɪɪŋ/ n achat m

buyout /ˈbaɪaʊt/ n Comm rachat m d'entreprise

---

by

When by is used with a passive verb, it is translated by par:

he was killed by a tiger
= il a été tué par un tigre

she was horrified by the news
= elle a été horrifiée par la nouvelle

For particular usages, see the entry **by**.

When by is used with a present participle to mean by means of, it is translated by en:

she learned French by listening to the radio
= elle a appris le français en écoutant la radio

For particular usages, see the entry **by**.

When by is used with a noun to mean by means of or using, it is translated by par:

by telephone
= par téléphone

to hold something by the handle
= tenir quelque chose par la poignée

Note, however:

to travel by bus/train/plane
= voyager en bus/train/avion

In time expressions by is translated by avant:

it must be finished by Friday
= il faut que ce soit fini avant vendredi

For particular usages, see the entry **by**.

by often appears as the second element in phrasal verbs (get by, put by, stand by etc.). For translations, consult the appropriate verb entry (**get**, **put**, **stand** etc.).

For translations of fixed phrases and expressions such as to learn something by heart, to deliver something by hand etc. consult the appropriate noun entry (**heart**, **hand** etc.).

For all other uses of by see the entry **by**.

---

buzz /bʌz/
A n **1** (of insect, conversation) bourdonnement m; **2** ○(phone call) **to give sb a ~** passer un coup de fil à qn; **3** ○(thrill) **it gives me a ~** (from alcohol) ça me fait planer○; **to get a ~ out of doing** prendre son pied○ en faisant
B vtr **1** (call) **to ~ sb** appeler qn au bip, biper; **2** [plane] raser [crowd, building]; frôler [other plane]
C vi [bee, fly] bourdonner; [buzzer] sonner; **~ if you know the answer** appuyez sur la sonnette si vous connaissez la réponse; **her head ~ed with thoughts** les idées se bousculaient dans son esprit; **the house was ~ing with activity** tout le monde s'affairait dans la maison
(Phrasal verb)
■ **buzz off**○ s'en aller; **~ off!** dégage○!

buzzard /ˈbʌzəd/ n Zool buse f

buzzer /ˈbʌzə(r)/ n gen sonnerie f; (on pocket) bip m

buzzing /ˈbʌzɪŋ/
A n (of insects) bourdonnement m; (of buzzer) vibration f
B ○adj (lively) [town] animé; [party, atmosphere] planant○

buzz: **~ saw** n scie f circulaire; **~word** n mot m à la mode

by /baɪ/
A prep **1** (showing agent, result) par; **he was bitten ~ a snake** il a été mordu par un serpent; **designed ~ an architect** conçu par un architecte; **destroyed ~ fire** détruit par le feu; **~ working extra hours** en faisant des heures supplémentaires; **to begin ~ saying that** commencer par dire que; **2** (through the means of) **to travel ~ bus/train** voyager en bus/train; **~ bicycle** à bicyclette, en vélo; **to pay ~ cheque** payer par chèque; **~ candlelight** [dine] aux chandelles; [read] à la bougie; **I know her ~ sight** je la connais de vue; **I took him ~ the hand** je l'ai pris par la main; **he has two children ~ his first wife** il a deux

enfants de sa première femme; **3‣** (according to, from evidence of) à; **~ my watch it is three o'clock** à ma montre, il est trois heures; **I could tell ~ the look on her face that she was angry** rien qu'à la regarder je savais qu'elle était fâchée; **I knew him ~ his walk** je l'ai reconnu à sa démarche; **it's all right ~ me** ça me va; **4‣** (via, passing through) par; **~ the back door** par la porte de derrière; **to travel to Rome ~ Venice and Florence** aller à Rome en passant par Venise et Florence; **5‣** (near, beside) à côté de, près de; **~ the bed/the window** à côté du lit/de la fenêtre; **~ the sea** au bord de la mer; **6‣** (past) **to go** ou **pass ~ sb** passer devant qn; **they passed us ~ in their car** ils nous ont dépassés dans leur voiture; **let us get ~** laissez-nous passer; **7‣** (showing authorship) de; **a film ~ Claude Chabrol** un film de Claude Chabrol; **who is it ~?** c'est de qui?; **8‣** (before, not later than) avant; **~ four o'clock/next Thursday** avant quatre heures/jeudi prochain; **~ this time next week** d'ici la semaine prochaine; **~ the time she had got downstairs he was gone** le temps qu'elle descende, il était parti; **he ought to be here ~ now** il devrait être déjà là; **~ now it was clear that they were going to win** à ce moment-là il était clair qu'ils allaient gagner; **9‣** (during) **~ day as well as ~ night** de jour comme de nuit; **~ daylight** au jour; **~ moonlight** au clair de lune; **10‣** (according to) **forbidden ~ law** interdit par la loi; **to play ~ the rules** jouer selon les règles; **it seems primitive ~ western standards** cela a l'air primitif selon ou d'après les critères occidentaux; **11‣** (to the extent or degree of) de; **prices have risen ~ 20%** les prix ont augmenté de 20%; **he's taller than me ~ two centimetres** il fait deux centimètres de plus que moi, il est plus grand que moi de deux centimètres; **~ far** de loin; **it's better ~ far** c'est beaucoup mieux; **12‣** (in measurements) sur; **a room 20 metres ~ 10 metres** une pièce de 20 mètres sur 10; **13‣** (in multiplication, division) par; **10 multiplied ~ 5 is 50** 10 multiplié par 5 égale 50; **14‣** (showing rate, quantity) à; **to be paid ~ the hour** être payé à l'heure; **~ the dozen** à la douzaine; **15‣** (in successive degrees, units) **little ~ little** peu à peu; **day ~ day** jour après jour; **one ~ one** un par un, un à un; **16‣** (with regard to) de; **he is an architect ~ profession** ou **trade** il est architecte de son métier; **~ birth** de naissance; **17‣** (as a result of) par; **~ accident/ mistake** par accident/erreur; **~ chance** par hasard; **18‣** (used with reflexive pronouns) **he did it all ~ himself** il l'a fait tout seul; **19‣** Naut (in compass directions) quart; **south ~ south-west** sud quart sud-ouest

B *adv* **1‣** (past) **to go ~** passer; **the people walking ~** les gens mpl qui passent/passaient, les passants mpl; **a lot of time has gone ~ since then** il s'est écoulé beaucoup de temps depuis lors; **as time goes ~** avec le temps; **2‣** (near) près; **he lives close ~** il habite tout près; **3‣** (aside, in reserve) **to put money ~** mettre de l'argent de côté; **4‣** (to one's house) **come ~ for a drink** passe prendre un verre

⬚(Idioms)⬚ **~ and ~** bientôt, en peu de temps; **~ the ~**, **~ the bye** à propos; **but that's ~ the ~** mais ça c'est un détail, mais ça c'est autre chose

bye /baɪ/
A *n* **1‣** GB Sport **to have** ou **get a ~** gagner par défaut
B ○*excl* au revoir!; **~ for now!** à bientôt!

bye-bye○ /'baɪbaɪ, bə'baɪ/
A *excl* au revoir!
B *adv* **to go ~** US partir; **to go ~s** GB lang enfantin aller au lit

byelaw *n* = bylaw

by(e)-election /'baɪɪlekʃn/ *n* GB élection *f* partielle

Byelorussia /ˌbjeləʊ'rʊʃə/ ▸ p. 774 *pr n* Biélorussie *f*

bygone /'baɪɡɒn/ *adj* [*days, years, scene, etc*] d'antan; **a ~ age** ou **era** une époque révolue
⬚(Idiom)⬚ **to let ~s be ~s** enterrer le passé

bylaw /'baɪlɔː/ *n* arrêté *m* municipal

by-line /'baɪlaɪn/ *n* **1‣** (in newspaper) nom *m* de journaliste (*en tête d'un article*); **2‣** Sport ligne *f* de touche

bypass /'baɪpɑːs/
A *n* **1‣** Aut rocade *f*; **2‣** (pipe, channel) by-pass *m inv*; **3‣** Elec dérivation *f*; **4‣** Med pontage *m*
B *vtr* Aut contourner [*town, city*]; fig éviter [*issue, question*]; contourner [*law*]; éviter de passer par [*manager, chief*]

bypass operation *n* Med pontage *m*

by-product *n* Biol, Ind dérivé *m*; fig effet *m* secondaire

by: **~road** *n* petite route *f*, petit chemin *m*; **~stander** *n* spectateur/-trice *m/f*

byte /baɪt/ *n* Comput octet *m*

byway /'baɪweɪ/ *n* lit petite route *f*, petit chemin *m*; fig périphérie *f*

byword /'baɪwɜːd/ *n* **to be a ~ for fanaticism** être synonyme de fanatisme

by-your-leave *n* **without so much as a ~** sans même demander la permission

Byzantine /baɪ'zæntaɪn, 'bɪzəntaɪn/
A *n* Byzantin/-e *m/f*
B *adj* [*art, empire*] byzantin; [*emperor*] de Byzance

Cc

c, C /siː/ n **1** (letter) c, C m; **2** C Mus do m, ut m; **3** (abrév écrite) **century**) **c19th, C19th** XIXᵉ siècle; **4** c (abrév écrite = **circa**) vers; **c1890** vers 1890; **5** c abrév écrite = **carat**; **6** c US abrév écrite = **cent(s)**; **7** C GB Sch (grade) ≈ note f de 12 sur 20; **8** C abrév ▸ **Celsius, centigrade**

CA 1 US Post abrév écrite = **California**; **2** abrév ▸ **Central America**; **3** GB Fin abrév ▸ **chartered accountant**

CAA n GB abrév ▸ **Civil Aviation Authority**

cab /kæb/ n **1** (taxi) taxi m; **2** (for driver) cabine f

CAB n **1** GB abrév ▸ **Citizens' Advice Bureau**; **2** US abrév ▸ **Civil Aeronautics Board**

cabal /kə'bæl/ n cabale f

cabana /kə'bɑːnə/ n US (hut) cabine f de plage

cabaret /'kæbəreɪ, US ,kæbə'reɪ/ n cabaret m

cabbage /'kæbɪdʒ/ n **1** Bot, Culin chou m; **2** ○GB injur (person) personne réduite à l'état végétatif

cabby○ /'kæbɪ/ n chauffeur m de taxi

cab-driver /'kæbdraɪvə(r)/ n chauffeur m de taxi

cabin /'kæbɪn/ n **1** (hut) cabane f; (in holiday camp) chalet m; **2** Naut cabine f; **3** Aviat (for passengers) cabine f; (cockpit) cabine f de pilotage; **4** (in rocket) habitacle m; **5** GB (driver's compartment) cabine f

cabin: ~ **boy** n Hist mousse m; ~ **crew** n Aviat personnel m de bord; ~ **cruiser** n cruiser m

cabinet /'kæbɪnɪt/

A n **1** (cupboard) petit placard m; (glass-fronted) vitrine f; (decorative, on legs) cabinet m; **2** GB Pol cabinet m; cf Conseil m des ministres

B noun modifier [decision, post] ministériel/-ielle

cabinet: ~**maker** ▸ p. 1181 n ébéniste m; ~**making** n ébénisterie f; ~ **meeting** n GB cf Conseil des ministres; ~ **minister** n GB ministre m (faisant partie du Cabinet du premier ministre); ~ **reshuffle** n GB remaniement m ministériel

cable /'keɪbl/

A n **1** (rope, wire) câble m; **brake** ~ câble de frein; **to lay a** ~ poser un câble; **power** ~ câble électrique; **2** (television) câble m; **3** (telegram) câble m

B vtr (all contexts) câbler

C noun modifier [channel, network] câblé

cable: ~ **car** n téléphérique m; ~**gram** n câblogramme m; ~**-knit** adj [sweater] à torsades; ~ **railway** n funiculaire m; ~ **television**, ~ **TV** n télévision f par câble; ~**way** n téléphérique m

caboodle○ /kə'buːdl/ n **the whole** ~ tout le bazar○ or bataclan○

cab-rank, cab stand n station f de taxis

cache /kæʃ/ n **1** (hoard) cache f; **2** (place) cachette f

cache memory n Comput antémémoire f

cachet /'kæʃeɪ, US kæ'ʃeɪ/ n cachet m

cackle /'kækl/

A n (of hen) caquet m; (of person) ricanement m; **cut the** ~○! arrêtez de jacasser!

B vi [hen] caqueter; [person] (talk) caqueter; (laugh) ricaner

cacophony /kə'kɒfənɪ/ n sout cacophonie f

cactus /'kæktəs/ n (pl **-ti**) cactus m

CAD n: abrév ▸ **computer-aided design**

cadaver /kə'dɑːvə(r), -'deɪv-, US kə'dævər/ n sout cadavre m

cadaverous /kə'dævərəs/ adj cadavérique

CADCAM /'kædkæm/ n Comput (abrév = **computer-aided design and computer-aided manufacture**) CFAO f

caddie, caddy /'kædɪ/ n caddie m

caddy /'kædɪ/ n **1** US (shopping trolley) chariot m, caddie m; **2** GB (also **tea** ~) boîte f à thé; **3** Sport = **caddie**

cadence /'keɪdns/ n (intonation) inflexion f; (rhythm) cadence f

cadet /kə'det/ n Mil (also **officer** ~) élève mf officier; (in police force) élève mf agent de police

cadet: ~ **corps** n Mil unité f de préparation militaire (jusqu'à 18 ans); ~ **school** n école f militaire

cadge○ /kædʒ/ vtr péj **to** ~ sth off ou from sb taper○ qn de qch [sum]; taper○ qch à qn [cigarette, money]; **to** ~ **a meal/a lift** se faire inviter/emmener en voiture

cadger○ /'kædʒə(r)/ n péj gen parasite m; (of money) tapeur/-euse○ m/f; (of meals) pique-assiette○ mf inv

cadre /'kɑːdə(r), US 'kædrɪ/ n **1** (group) Mil cadre m; Admin, Pol noyau m (d'hommes); **2** Pol (person) cadre m

CAE n Comput (abrév = **computer-aided engineering**) IAO f

Caesarean, Caesarian /sɪ'zeərɪən/ n (also ~ **section**) césarienne f

café /'kæfeɪ, US kæ'feɪ/ n **1** gen ≈ snack-bar m (ne vendant pas de boissons alcoolisées); **pavement** ~, **sidewalk** ~ café m; **2** US (restaurant) bistro m

cafeteria /,kæfə'tɪərɪə/ n gen cafétéria f; Sch cantine f; Univ restaurant m universitaire

caffein(e) /'kæfiːn/ n caféine f; ~**-free** décaféiné

cage /keɪdʒ/

A n **1** (for bird, animal) cage f; (of lift) cabine f; (in mine) cage f; **2** ○(in ice-hockey) cage f (de buts)

B vtr mettre [qch] en cage [animal]; **a** ~**d animal** un animal en cage

cagebird /'keɪdʒbɜːd/ n oiseau m d'appartement

cagey○, **cagy**○ /'keɪdʒɪ/ adj **1** (wary) réticent/-e; **to be** ~ **about doing** hésiter à faire; **she's very** ~ **about her family** elle n'aime pas beaucoup parler de sa famille; **2** US (shrewd) astucieux/-ieuse

cagoule /kə'guːl/ n GB K-way® m

cahoots /kə'huːts/ npl **to be in** ~ être de mèche○

Cain /keɪn/ pr n Caïn

Idiom **to raise** ~○ (make a noise) faire du boucan○

cairn /keən/ n (of stones) cairn m

Cairo /'kaɪərəʊ/ ▸ p. 1276 pr n Le Caire

cajole /kə'dʒəʊl/ vtr cajoler; **to** ~ **sb into doing sth** amener qn à faire qch par la cajolerie

Cajun /'keɪdʒən/ ▸ p. 1032, p. 969 adj acadien/-ienne

cake /keɪk/

A n **1** Culin gâteau m; (sponge) génoise f; **2** (of soap, wax) pain m; **3** (of fish, potato) croquette f

B vi [mud, blood] former une croûte (on sur)

Idioms **it's a piece of** ~○ c'est du gâteau○; **to get a** ou **one's slice** ou **share of the** ~ avoir sa part du gâteau; **you can't have your** ~ **and eat it** on ne peut pas avoir le beurre et l'argent du beurre; ▸ **hot cake**

cake: ~ **mix** n préparation f or mélange m pour gâteau; ~ **pan** n US = **cake tin**; ~ **shop** n ≈ pâtisserie f; ~ **tin** n (for baking) moule m à gâteaux; (for storing) boîte f à gâteaux

CAL n: abrév ▸ **computer-aided learning**

calabrese /ˌkæləˈbreɪzɪ/ n broccoli m

calamine /ˈkæləmaɪn/ n calamine f; ~ **lotion** lotion f calmante à la calamine

calamitous /kəˈlæmɪtəs/ adj catastrophique, désastreux/-euse

calamity /kəˈlæmətɪ/ n calamité f

calcify /ˈkælsɪfaɪ/ vi se calcifier

calcium /ˈkælsɪəm/ n calcium m

calculate /ˈkælkjʊleɪt/ vtr **1** (work out) calculer [cost, distance, price]; **2** (estimate) évaluer [effect, probability]; **3** (intend) **to be ~d to do** avoir été conçu pour faire

calculated /ˈkælkjʊleɪtɪd/ adj [crime] prémédité; [attempt, decision, insult] délibéré; [risk] calculé

calculating /ˈkælkjʊleɪtɪŋ/ adj **1** (scheming) [manner, person] calculateur/-trice; **2** (shrewd) [policy] prudent

calculating machine n machine f à calculer

calculation /ˌkælkjʊˈleɪʃn/ n **1** (operation) calcul m; **to make** ou **do ~s** faire des calculs; **to get one's ~s wrong** se tromper dans ses calculs; **2** (scheming) préméditation f

calculator /ˈkælkjʊleɪtə(r)/ n calculatrice f, calculette f

calculus /ˈkælkjʊləs/ n Math, Med calcul m

calendar /ˈkælɪndə(r)/ n calendrier m

calendar: ~ **month** n mois m calendaire; ~ **year** n année f civile

calf /kɑːf, US kæf/ n (pl **calves**) **1** Zool (cow) veau m; (deer) faon m; (buffalo) buffletin m; (elephant) éléphanteau m; (whale) baleineau m; **to be in ~** être pleine; **calves' liver** Culin foie m de veau; **2** (leather) vachette f; **3** (part of leg) mollet m

calf: ~ **love** n amour m juvénile; ~**skin** n vachette f

caliber n US = **calibre**

calibrate /ˈkælɪbreɪt/ vtr étalonner [scales]; calibrer [instrument]

calibre GB, **caliber** US /ˈkælɪbə(r)/ n calibre m

California /ˌkælɪˈfɔːnɪə/ ▸ p. 1222 pr n Californie f

caliper n US = **calliper**

calisthenics n = **callisthenics**

call /kɔːl/

A n **1** Telecom appel m (téléphonique) (**from** de); **(tele)phone** ~ appel m (téléphonique); **to make a** ~ téléphoner; **to make a ~ to Italy** appeler l'Italie, téléphoner en Italie; **to give sb a** ~ appeler qn; **to return sb's** ~ rappeler qn; **2** (cry) (human) appel m (**for** à); (animal) cri m; **to give sb a** ~ appeler qn; **3** (summons) appel m; **to put out a** ~ **for sb** (over public address) faire appeler qn; (over radio) lancer un appel à qn; **4** (visit) visite f; **social** ~ visite f de courtoisie; **to make** ou **pay a** ~ lit rendre visite (**on** à); **5** (demand) demande f (**for** de); **there were ~s for his resignation** sa démission a été réclamée; **she has many ~s on her time** elle est très sollicitée; **we don't get much ~ for that** nous n'avons guère de demande pour cela; **to have first ~ on sth** avoir la priorité sur qch; **6** (need) **there's no ~ for sth/to do** il n'y a pas de raison pour qch/de faire; **there was no ~ for her to say that** elle n'avait aucune raison or aucun besoin de dire cela; **7** (allure) appel m (**of** de); **8** Sport décision f; **9** (for repayment) demande f de remboursement; **a ~ for capital/tenders** un appel de fonds/ d'offres; **10** (duty) **to be on** ~ [doctor] être de garde; [engineer] être de service; **11** Relig (vocation) vocation f

B vtr **1** (also ~ **out**) (say loudly) appeler [name, number]; crier [answer, instructions]; annoncer [result, flight]; Sch faire l'appel; **he ~ed (out) 'Goodbye'** il a crié 'au revoir'; **2** (summon) appeler [lift]; (by shouting) appeler [person, animal]; (by phone) appeler; (by letter) convoquer; **the boss ~ed me into his office** le chef m'a fait venir dans son bureau; **the police were ~ed to the scene** la police a été appelée sur les lieux; **3** (telephone) (also ~ **up**) appeler (**at** à; **from** de); **4** (give a name) appeler [person, baby, animal, place, product] (**by** par); intituler [book, film, music, play]; **5** (arrange) organiser [strike]; convoquer [meeting, rehearsal]; fixer [election]; **6** (waken) réveiller [person]; **7** (describe as) **to ~ sb stupid/a liar** traiter qn d'imbécile/de menteur/-euse; **I wouldn't ~ it spacious** je ne dirais pas que c'est spacieux; **it's not what you'd ~ an exciting film** on ne peut pas dire que ce film soit passionnant; **it's what you might ~ a delicate situation** c'est ce qui s'appelle une situation délicate; ~ **it what you will** appelle ça comme tu veux; **parapsychology or whatever they** ou **you ~ it**○ la métapsychologie ou quelque chose dans ce goût-là○; **(let's) ~ it £5** disons cinq livres sterling; **he hasn't a place to ~ his own**

il n'a pas de chez-lui; **8** Sport [referee] déclarer; **9** Comput appeler [file]

C vi **1** (also ~ **out**) (cry out) [person, animal] appeler; (louder) crier; [bird] crier; **London ~ing** Radio ici Londres; **2** (telephone) appeler; **thank you for ~ing** merci d'avoir appelé; **please ~ back in an hour** rappelez dans une heure s'il vous plaît; **who's ~ing?** qui est à l'appareil?; **3** (visit) passer; **to ~ at** passer chez [person, shop]; passer à [bank, library]; [train] s'arrêter à [town, station]; [ship] faire escale à [port]; **the London train ~ing at Reading and Slough** le train à destination de Londres desservant les gares de Reading et Slough; **4** (tossing coins) parier

D v refl **to ~ oneself** se faire appeler [Smith, Bob]; (claim to be) se dire, se prétendre [poet, designer]; **I am proud to ~ myself European** je suis fier d'être européen

(Phrasal verbs)

■ **call away**: ▸ ~ **[sb] away** appeler; **to be ~ed away** être obligé de s'absenter

■ **call back**: ▸ ~ **back 1** (on phone) rappeler; **2** (return) repasser; ▸ ~ **[sb] back** rappeler [person]

■ **call by** passer

■ **call for** [sth] **1** (shout) appeler à [help]; appeler [ambulance, doctor]; **2** (demand) demander [food, equipment]; réclamer [changes]; **3** (require) exiger [treatment, skill]; nécessiter [change, intervention]; **this ~s for a celebration!** ça se fête!; **4** (collect) passer prendre [person]; passer chercher [object]

■ **call in**: ▸ ~ **in 1** (visit) passer; **2** (telephone) appeler; **to ~ in sick** [employee] appeler pour dire qu'on est malade; ▸ ~ **in [sb], ~ [sb] in** faire entrer [client, patient]; faire appel à [expert, engineer]; ▸ ~ **in [sth], ~ [sth] in** (recall) retirer [qch] du commerce [product]; demander le remboursement de [loan]

■ **call off**: ▸ ~ **off [sth], ~ [sth] off 1** lit rappeler [dog]; **2** fig (halt) abandonner [search]; (cancel) annuler [deal, wedding]; **to ~ off one's engagement** rompre ses fiançailles; **let's ~ the whole thing off** laissons tomber

■ **call on**: ▸ ~ **on [sb/sth] 1** (visit) (also ~ **in on**) rendre visite à [relative, friend]; visiter [patient, client]; **2** (invite) demander à [speaker] (**to do** de faire); **3** (urge) demander à (**to do** de faire); **4** (appeal to, resort to) s'adresser à [person]; avoir recours à [services]; faire appel à [moral quality]

■ **call out**: ▸ ~ **out** (cry aloud) appeler; (louder) crier; ▸ ~ **out [sb], ~ [sb] out** (summon outside) appeler; **the teacher ~ed me out to the front of the class** le professeur m'a fait venir devant le reste de la classe; **2** (send for) appeler [doctor, repairman, troops]; **3** Ind [union] lancer un ordre de grève à [members]; ▸ ~ **[sth] out, ~ out [sth]** appeler [name, number]

■ **call over**: ▸ ~ **[sb] over** appeler

■ **call round** (visit) venir

■ **call up**: ▸ ~ **up** appeler; ▸ ~ **up [sb/sth], ~ [sb/sth] up 1** (on phone) appeler; **2** (summon) appeler [qn] sous les drapeaux [soldier]; invoquer [spirit]; **3** (evoke) rappeler [memory]; **4** Comput appeler (à l'écran), afficher [file]; **5** Sport sélectionner [player]

CALL n: abrév ▸ **computer-aided language learning**

call: ~**back facility** n Telecom rappel m automatique; ~ **box** n GB cabine f téléphonique; US poste m téléphonique; ~ **centre** GB, ~ **center** US n centre m d'appel

caller /ˈkɔːlə(r)/ n **1** Telecom personne f qui appelle; **we've had 15 ~s today** nous avons reçu 15 appels aujourd'hui; **2** (visitor) visiteur/-euse m/f

call girl n call-girl f

calligrapher /kəˈlɪɡrəfə(r)/, **calligraphist** /kəˈlɪɡrəfɪst/ ▸ p. 1181 n calligraphe mf

calligraphy /kəˈlɪɡrəfɪ/ n calligraphie f

calling /ˈkɔːlɪŋ/ n **1** (vocation) vocation f; **2** (profession) métier m

calliper GB, **caliper** US /ˈkælɪpə(r)/ n **1** (leg support) appareil m orthopédique; **2** (for measuring) compas m d'épaisseur

callisthenics /ˌkælɪsˈθenɪks/ n (+ v sg) gymnastique f suédoise

callous /ˈkæləs/ adj [person] inhumain, insensible; [attitude, brutality, crime] inhumain

callously /ˈkæləslɪ/ adv [act, speak] durement; [suggest] cyniquement

callousness /ˈkæləsnɪs/ n dureté f, inhumanité f

call: ~**-out** n dépannage m; ~**-out charge** n frais mpl de déplacement

callow ▸ can

callow /ˈkæləʊ/ *adj* gauche

call: ~ **sign** *n* Radio indicatif *m*; ~**-up** *n* Mil appel *m*; (of reservists) rappel *m*; ~**-up papers** *npl* Mil ordre *m* d'appel

callused /ˈkæləst/ *adj* calleux/-euse

calm /kɑːm, US *also* kɑːlm/
A *n* **1** (of place, atmosphere) tranquillité *f*, calme *m*; **2** (of person) calme *m*; (in adversity) sang-froid *m*; **to keep one's** ~ garder son sang-froid; **3** Naut calme *m*
B *adj* calme; **keep** ~**!** du calme!
C *vtr* calmer
(Idiom) **the** ~ **before the storm** le calme avant la tempête
(Phrasal verb)
■ **calm down**: ▸ ~ **down** se calmer; ▸ ~ **[sth/sb] down**, ~ **down [sth/sb]** calmer

calming /ˈkɑːmɪŋ, US *also* ˈkɑːlm-/ *adj* apaisant

calmly /ˈkɑːmlɪ, US *also* ˈkɑːlmlɪ/ *adv* [*act, speak*] calmement; [*sleep, smoke*] tranquillement

calmness /ˈkɑːmnɪs, US *also* ˈkɑːlm-/ *n* calme *m*

Calor gas® /ˈkælə gæs/ *n* GB butane *m*

calorie /ˈkælərɪ/ *n* calorie *f*; **low-**~ **diet/drink** régime/boisson à basses calories; **to be** ~**-conscious** faire attention aux calories

calorific /ˌkæləˈrɪfɪk/ *adj* calorifique

calvary /ˈkælvərɪ/
A *n* calvaire *m*
B **Calvary** *pr n* le Calvaire

calve /kɑːv, US kæv/ *vi* mettre bas

calves /kɑːvz/ *npl* ▸ **calf**

Calvinistic /ˌkælvɪˈnɪstɪk/ *adj* calviniste

cam /kæm/ *n* Tech came *f*

camaraderie /ˌkæməˈrɑːdərɪ, US -ˈræd-/ *n* camaraderie *f*

camber /ˈkæmbə(r)/ *n* (of road) bombement *m*

Cambodia /kæmˈbəʊdɪə/ ▸ **p. 774** *pr n* Cambodge *m*

Cambs *n* GB Post *abrév écrite* = **Cambridgeshire**

camcorder /ˈkæmkɔːdə(r)/ *n* caméscope® *m*

came /keɪm/ *prét* ▸ **come**

camel /ˈkæml/ ▸ **p. 752** *n* **1** chameau *m*; (female) chamelle *f*; (for racing) méhari *m*; ~ **train** caravane *f* de chameaux; ~ **driver** chamelier *m*; **2** (colour) couleur *f* caramel

camel hair *n* poil *m* de chameau; ~ **coat** manteau *m* en poil de chameau

camellia /kəˈmiːlɪə/ *n* camélia *m*

cameo /ˈkæmɪəʊ/ *n* **1** camée *m*; **2** Theat, Cin **a** ~ **role** un camée

camera /ˈkæmərə/ *n* **1** Phot appareil *m* photo; Cin, TV caméra *f*; **2** Jur **in** ~ à huis clos

camera: ~ **crew** *n* équipe *f* de télévision; ~**man** ▸ **p. 1181** *n* cadreur *m*, cameraman *m*

Cameroon /ˌkæməˈruːn/ ▸ **p. 774** *pr n* Cameroun *m*

camisole /ˈkæmɪsəʊl/ *n* caraco *m*

camomile /ˈkæməmaɪl/ *n* camomille *f*

camouflage /ˈkæməflɑːʒ/
A *n* camouflage *m*
B *vtr* camoufler (**with** avec)

camp /kæmp/
A *n* **1** (of tents) camp *m*; (of nomads) campement *m*; **to make** *ou* **pitch** ~ planter son camp; **to strike** ~ lever le camp; **2** fig (group) camp *m*; **to go over to the other** ~ changer de camp; **to have a foot in both** ~**s** avoir un pied dans chaque camp; **3** ᵒpéj (mannered style) cabotinageᵒ *m*
B *adj* péj **1** (exaggerated) [*person*] cabotinᵒ; [*gesture, performance*] théâtral; **2** (effeminate) efféminé
C *vi* camper; **to go** ~**ing** faire du camping
(Idiom) **to** ~ **it up**ᵒ (overact) cabotinerᵒ; (act effeminately) forcer dans le genre efféminé
(Phrasal verb)
■ **camp out** camper

campaign /kæmˈpeɪn/
A *n* campagne *f*
B *vi* faire campagne (**for** pour; **against** contre)

campaigner /kæmˈpeɪnə(r)/ *n* gen militant/-e *m/f* (**for** pour; **against** contre); Pol candidat/-e *m/f* en campagne (électorale); **old** ~ Mil vétéran *m*

---

can¹

can and *could* are usually translated by the verb *pouvoir*. For the conjugation of *pouvoir*, see the French verb tables.

he can wait until tomorrow
= il peut attendre jusqu'à demain

you can go out now
= vous pouvez sortir maintenant

The two notable exceptions to this are as follows:

When *can* or *could* is used to mean *know how to*, the verb *savoir* is used:

she can speak French
= elle sait parler français

he could read at the age of four
= à l'âge de quatre ans il savait lire

When *can* or *could* is used with a verb of perception such as *see*, *hear* or *feel* it is not translated at all:

I can't see her
= je ne la vois pas

she couldn't feel anything
= elle ne sentait rien

In requests *can* is translated by the present tense of *pouvoir* and the more polite *could* by the conditional tense of *pouvoir*:

can you help me?
= peux-tu m'aider?

could you help me?
= pourrais-tu m'aider?

For particular usages of *could* when it is not simply the preterite or conditional of *can* see **13**, **15**, **16** in the entry **can¹**.

See also the entry **able**.

---

campaign: ~ **literature** *n* ¢ tracts *mpl*; ~ **medal** *n* médaille *f* militaire

campaign trail *n* **on the** ~ en tournée électorale

campaign worker *n* GB Pol membre *m* de l'état-major

camp: ~ **bed** *n* lit *m* de camp; ~ **chair** *n* US chaise *f* pliante; ~ **commandant** *n* commandant *m* de camp

camper /ˈkæmpə(r)/ *n* **1** (person) campeur/-euse *m/f*; **2** (*also* ~ **van**) camping-car *m*; **3** US (folding caravan) caravane *f* pliante

campfire /ˈkæmpfaɪə(r)/ *n* feu *m* de camp

camphor /ˈkæmfə(r)/ *n* camphre *m*

camping /ˈkæmpɪŋ/ *n* camping *m*; **to go** ~ faire du camping

camping: ~ **equipment** *n* matériel *m* de camping; ~ **gas** *n* camping-gaz® *m*; ~ **ground** *n* = **campsite**; ~ **holiday** *n* vacances *fpl* sous la tente; ~ **site** *n* = **campsite**; ~ **stool** *n* GB pliant *m*; ~ **stove** *n* réchaud *m*

camp: ~**site** *n* (official) terrain *m* de camping, camping *m*; ~ **stool** *n* pliant *m*

campus /ˈkæmpəs/ (*pl* ~**es** /ˈkæmpəsɪz/) *n* campus *m*

camshaft /ˈkæmʃɑːft, US -ʃæft/ *n* arbre *m* à cames

can¹ /kæn/ *modal aux* (*prét, conditional* **could**; *nég au prés* **cannot, can't**) **1** (expressing possibility) **we** ~ **rent a house** nous pouvons louer une maison; **it** ~ **also be used to dry clothes** on peut aussi s'en servir pour sécher le linge; **you can't have forgotten!** tu ne peux pas avoir oublié!; **it cannot be explained logically** ça n'a pas d'explication logique; **it could be that...** il se peut que... (+ *subj*); **could be**ᵒ peut-être; **it could be a trap** c'est peut-être un piège, ça pourrait être un piège; **I could be wrong** je me trompe peut-être, il se peut que j'aie tort; **you could have been electrocuted!** tu aurais pu t'électrocuter!; **'did she**

know?'—'no, how could she?' est-ce qu'elle était au courant?'—'non, comment est-ce qu'elle aurait pu l'être?'; **the computer couldn't** *ou* **can't have made an error** l'ordinateur n'a pas pu faire d'erreur, il est impossible que l'ordinateur ait fait une erreur; **nothing could be simpler** il n'y a rien de plus simple; **2** (expressing permission) **you ~ turn right here** vous pouvez tourner à droite ici; **I can't leave yet** je ne peux pas partir pour le moment; **could I interrupt?** puis-je vous interrompre?; **3** (when making requests) **~ you leave us a message?** est-ce que tu peux nous laisser un message?; **~ I ask you a question?** puis-je vous poser une question?; **4** (when making permission) **I give you a hand?** est-ce que je peux te donner un coup de main?; **what ~ I do for you?** (in shop) qu'y a-t-il pour votre service?; **5** (when making suggestions) **you ~ always exchange it** tu peux toujours l'échanger; **we could try and phone him** nous pourrions essayer de lui téléphoner; **6** (have skill, knowledge to) **she can't read yet** elle ne sait pas encore lire; **~ he type?** est-ce qu'il sait taper à la machine?; **7** (have ability, power to) **computers ~ process data rapidly** les ordinateurs peuvent traiter rapidement les données; **to do all one ~** faire tout ce qu'on peut *or* tout son possible; **he couldn't sleep for weeks** il n'a pas pu dormir pendant des semaines; **I wish I could have been there** j'aurais aimé (pouvoir) être là; **8** (have ability, using senses, to) **~ you see it?** est-ce que tu le vois?; **I can't hear anything** je n'entends rien; **I could feel my heart beating** je sentais mon cœur battre; **9** (indicating capability, tendency) **she could be quite abrupt** elle pouvait être assez brusque; **10** (expressing likelihood, assumption) **it can't be as bad as that!** ça ne peut pas être aussi terrible que ça!; **he couldn't be more than 10 years old** (now) il ne peut pas avoir plus de 10 ans; **11** (expressing willingness to act) **we ~ take you home** nous pouvons te déposer chez toi; **I couldn't leave the children** (didn't want to) je ne pouvais pas laisser les enfants; (wouldn't want to) je ne pourrais pas laisser les enfants; **12** (be in a position to) **they ~ hardly refuse** ils peuvent difficilement refuser; **I couldn't possibly accept the money** je ne peux vraiment pas accepter cet argent; **13** (expressing a reproach) **they could have warned us** ils auraient pu nous prévenir; **you could at least say sorry!** tu pourrais au moins t'excuser!; **how could you!** comment as -tu pu faire une chose pareille!; **14** (expressing surprise) **what ~ she possibly want from me?** est-ce qu'elle peut bien me vouloir?; **who could it be?** qui est-ce que ça peut bien être?; **you can't** *ou* **cannot be serious!** tu veux rire°!; **~ you believe it!** tu te rends compte?; **15** (for emphasis) **I couldn't agree more!** je suis entièrement d'accord!; **they couldn't have been nicer** ils ont été extrêmement gentils; **you couldn't be more mistaken** tu te trompes complètement; **16** (expressing exasperation) **I was so mad I could have screamed!** j'aurais crié tellement j'étais en colère!; **I could murder him**°! je le tuerais°!; **17** (expressing obligation) **she ~ ask me herself** elle peut venir me le demander elle-même; **you ~ get lost**°! va te faire fiche°!; **18** (avoiding repetition of verb) '**~ we borrow it?'—'you ~'** 'est-ce que nous pouvons l'emprunter?' —'bien sûr'; **leave as soon as you ~** partez dès que vous le pourrez; '**~ anyone give me a lift home?'—'we ~'** 'est-ce que quelqu'un peut me déposer chez moi?'—'oui, nous'

(Idioms) **as happy/excited as ~** *ou* **could be** très heureux/excité; **no ~ do**° non, je ne peux pas

can² /kæn/
A *n* (of food) boîte *f*; (aerosol) bombe *f*; (for petrol) bidon *m*; (of drink) cannette *f*
B *vtr* (*p prés etc* **-nn-**) Culin mettre [qch] en conserve
C **canned** *pp adj* **1** [*food*] en boîte; **2** °[*laughter*] enregistré

(Idioms) **a ~ of worms** une affaire dans laquelle il vaut mieux ne pas trop fouiller; **in the ~**° Cin (of film) dans la boîte; (of negotiations) dans la poche; **to carry the ~ for sb**° porter le chapeau à la place de qn°

Canada /'kænədə/ ▸ **p. 774** *pr n* Canada *m*

Canadian /kə'neɪdɪən/ ▸ **p. 1032**
A *n* Canadien/-ienne
B *adj* canadien/-ienne; **to speak ~ French** parler le français du Canada

canal /kə'næl/ *n* **1** (waterway) canal *m*; **2** Anat (in ear) conduit *m*

canal boat, **canal barge** *n* péniche *f*

canapé /'kænəpɪ, US ˌkænə'peɪ/ *n* canapé *m*

Canaries /kə'neərɪz/ ▸ **p. 954** *pr npl* (*also* **Canary Islands**) **the ~** les Canaries *fpl*

canary /kə'neərɪ/ *n* canari *m*, serin *m*

cancel /'kænsl/ (*p prés etc* **-ll-, -l-** US)
A *vtr* **1** (call off) annuler; **2** (nullify) résilier [*contract*]; annuler [*debt*]; mettre une opposition à [*cheque, credit card*]; **3** Jur lever [*order*]; révoquer [*decree*]; **4** Post oblitérer [*stamp*]
B *vi* (from meal, function, meeting) se décommander; (after booking) annuler

(Phrasal verb)
■ **cancel out**: ▸ **~ out** [*arguments, figures*] s'annuler; ▸ **~ out [sth]** neutraliser [*emotion, effect*]

cancellation /ˌkænsə'leɪʃn/ *n* **1** (of event, order, booking, train, flight) annulation *f*; **2** (of contract, policy) résiliation *f*; (of debt, loan) annulation *f*; **3** (of order, decree) levée *f*

cancer /'kænsə(r)/ ▸ **p. 933** *n* Med, fig cancer *m*; **to have ~** avoir un cancer; **lung ~** cancer du poumon; **a ~ sufferer** un/-e cancéreux/-euse *m/f*

Cancer /'kænsə(r)/ ▸ **p. 1350** *n* **1** (in zodiac) Cancer *m*; **2** Geog **tropic of ~** tropique *m* du Cancer

cancerous /'kænsərəs/ *adj* cancéreux/-euse

cancer: **~ patient** *n* cancéreux/-euse *m/f*; **~ research** *n* cancérologie *f*

candelabra /ˌkændɪ'lɑːbrə/ *n* (*pl* **~** *ou* **~s**) candélabre *m*

candid /'kændɪd/ *adj* franc/franche; **~ camera** caméra *f* invisible

candidacy /'kændɪdəsɪ/, **candidature** /'kændɪdətʃə/ *n* GB candidature *f*

candidate /'kændɪdət, US -deɪt/ *n* **1** Pol candidat/-e *m/f*; **the ~ for mayor/for Oxford** le candidat à la mairie/pour Oxford; **the Conservative ~** le candidat du parti conservateur; **to stand as a ~** (in an election) se porter candidat (à une élection); **2** (for job) candidat/-e *m/f*, postulant/-e *m/f*; **to be a likely ~** (**for the job**) être bien placé (pour obtenir le poste); **the successful ~** (in ad) le candidat retenu; **3** (in exam, for admission) candidat/-e *m/f*; **4** fig **to be a ~ for** être candidat potentiel à

candidature *n* GB = **candidacy**

candidly /'kændɪdlɪ/ *adv* franchement

candied /'kændɪd/ *adj* confit; **~ peel** écorce *f* d'orange et de citron confite

candle /'kændl/ *n* bougie *f*; (in church) cierge *m*

(Idioms) **to burn the ~ at both ends** brûler la chandelle par les deux bouts; **the game's not worth the ~** le jeu n'en vaut pas la chandelle; **he can't hold a ~ to his sister** il n'arrive pas à la cheville de sa sœur

candlelight /'kændllaɪt/ *n* lueur *f* de bougie; **by ~** à la lueur d'une bougie *or* des bougies

candle: **~lit dinner** *n* dîner *m* aux chandelles; **Candlemas** *n* la Chandeleur; **~stick** *n* bougeoir *m*; (more ornate) chandelier *m*

candlewick /'kændlwɪk/ *n* **~ bedspread** couvre-lit *m* en tuft

candour GB, **candor** US /'kændə(r)/ *n* franchise *f*

candy /'kændɪ/ *n* US **1** (sweets) bonbons *mpl*; **2** (sweet) bonbon *m*

candy: **~ floss** *n* GB barbe *f* à papa; **~ striped** *adj* (pink) à rayures rose bonbon; (blue) à rayures bleu pâle

cane /keɪn/
A *n* **1** (material) rotin *m*; **~ furniture** meubles en rotin; **2** (of sugar, bamboo) canne *f*; **3** (for walking) canne *f*; (for plant) tuteur *m*; (officer's) badine *f*; GB (for punishment) badine *f*
B *vtr* **1** canner [*chair*]; **2** donner des coups de badine à [*pupil*]

cane sugar *n* sucre *m* de canne

canine /'keɪnaɪn/
A *n* **1** (tooth) canine *f*; **2** (animal) canidé *m*
B *adj* **1** [*species*] canin; **2** **a ~ tooth** une canine

canister /'kænɪstə(r)/ *n* boîte *f* métallique; **a ~ of tear gas, a tear gas ~** une bombe lacrymogène

cannabis /'kænəbɪs/ *n* cannabis *m*; **~ resin** résine *f* de cannabis

cannibal /'kænɪbl/ *n* cannibale *mf*, anthropophage *mf*

cannibalism /'kænɪbəlɪzəm/ *n* cannibalisme *m*, anthropophagie *f*

cannibalize /'kænɪbəlaɪz/ *vtr* cannibaliser

canning /'kænɪŋ/ n mise f en conserve

cannon /'kænən/
A n (pl ∼ ou ∼**s**) Mil Hist canon m
B vi **to ∼ into sb/sth** se heurter contre qn/qch

cannonball /'kænənbɔːl/ n **1** (missile) boulet m de canon; **2** (dive) **to do a ∼** faire la bombe; **3** (also **∼ serve**) (in tennis) service m canon

cannon fodder n chair f à canon

cannot /'kænɒt/ ▸ **can¹**

canoe /kə'nuː/ ▸ p. 881
A n gen canoë m; (African) pirogue f; Sport canoë-kayac m
B vi faire du canoë; **they ∼d down the river** ils ont descendu la rivière en canoë

canoeing /kə'nuːɪŋ/ ▸ p. 881 n **to go ∼** faire du canoë-kayac

canoeist /kə'nuːɪst/ n canoéiste mf

canon /'kænən/ ▸ p. 869 n **1** (rule) gen critère m; (of church) canon m; **2** Relig chanoine m; **3** Literat (complete works) œuvre m; **4** Mus canon m

canonize /'kænənaɪz/ vtr canoniser

canoodle○ /kə'nuːdl/ vi se faire des mamours○

can-opener n ouvre-boîtes m inv

canopy /'kænəpɪ/ n **1** (for bed) baldaquin m; (for throne, altar) dais m; (for hammock) toit m; **2** Aviat (cockpit) verrière f; (for parachute) voilure f; fig (sky, leaves) voûte f; **3** Ecol (forest) canopée f

cant /kænt/ n **1** (false words) paroles fpl creuses; (ideas) notions fpl creuses; **2** (prisoners', thieves') argot m; (lawyers') jargon m; **3** (sloping surface) (of road) déclivité f

can't /kɑːnt/ abrév = **cannot**

cantankerous /kæn'tæŋkərəs/ adj acariâtre

canteen /kæn'tiːn/ n **1** GB (dining room) cantine f; **in the ∼** à la cantine; **2** Mil (flask) bidon m; (mess tin) gamelle f; **3** a **∼ of cutlery** une ménagère

canter /'kæntə(r)/
A n gen petit galop m; **at a ∼** au petit galop; **to go for a ∼** aller faire une promenade à cheval
B vi [rider] faire un petit galop; [horse] galoper

Canterbury /'kæntəbərɪ/ ▸ p. 1276 pr n Cantorbéry; **the ∼ Tales** les Contes de Cantorbéry

cantilever /'kæntɪliːvə(r)/ n cantilever m, porte-à-faux m inv

cantonal /'kæntənl, kæn'tɒnl/ adj cantonal

canvas /'kænvəs/
A n **1** (fabric) toile f; (for tapestry) canevas m; **under ∼** (in a tent) sous la tente; (under sail) sous voiles; **2** Art toile f; **3** (in boxing) tapis m
B noun modifier [shoes, bag, chair] en toile

canvass /'kænvəs/
A vtr **1** Pol **to ∼ voters** faire du démarchage électoral auprès des électeurs; **to ∼ people for their votes** solliciter les voix des électeurs; **2** (in survey) sonder [public]; **to ∼ opinion** ou **views on sth** sonder l'opinion au sujet de qch; Comm prospecter [area]; **to ∼ door to door** faire du démarchage
B vi **1** Pol faire du démarchage électoral (**for** pour); **2** Comm faire du démarchage (**for** pour)

canvasser /'kænvəsə(r)/ n (for party) agent m électoral

canvassing /'kænvəsɪŋ/ n (door to door) démarchage m; **∼ for votes** démarchage électoral; **∼ of opinion** sondage m d'opinion

canyon /'kænjən/ n cañon m

canyoning /'kænjənɪŋ/ ▸ p. 881 n canyoning m

cap /kæp/
A n **1** (headgear) (peaked) casquette f; (of nurse) coiffe f; **baseball ∼** casquette de baseball; **2** GB Sport **he's got his Scottish ∼** il a été selectionné pour l'équipe écossaise; **3** (cover) (of pen, valve) capuchon m; (of bottle) capsule f; (for camera lens) bouchon m; **4** (of mushroom) chapeau m; **5** (for toy gun) amorce f; **6** (for tooth) couronne f; **7** GB (also **Dutch ∼**) diaphragme m (contraceptif)
B vtr (p prétérit etc -**pp-**) **1** Admin imposer une limite budgétaire à [local authority]; plafonner [budget]; **2** couronner [tooth]; **3** GB Sport sélectionner [qn] pour l'équipe nationale [footballer]; **4** (cover) couronner (**with** de)
⌐Idioms⌐ **to ∼ it all** pour couronner le tout; **to go to sb ∼ in hand** se présenter à qn chapeau bas, aller voir qn la main tendue

cap. /kæp/ n (abrév = **capital letter**) maj

CAP n: abrév ▸ **Common Agricultural Policy**

capability /ˌkeɪpə'bɪlətɪ/ n **1** (capacity) (of intellect, machine, system) capacité f (**to do** de faire); **2** (potential strength) capacité f (**to do** de faire); **nuclear ∼** capacité nucléaire; **3** (aptitude) aptitude f (**for** à); **management ∼** aptitude à la gestion; **within/outside my capabilities** dans/au-delà de mes compétences

capable /'keɪpəbl/ adj **1** (competent) compétent; **in the ∼ hands of** entre les mains expertes de; **2** (able) capable (**of** de); **to be ∼ of doing** (have potential to) être capable de faire; (be in danger of) risquer de faire

capably /'keɪpəblɪ/ adv avec compétence

capacious /kə'peɪʃəs/ adj [pocket, car boot] vaste

capacity /kə'pæsətɪ/ n **1** (ability to hold) (of box, bottle) contenance f; (of barrel) capacité f (**of** de); (of building) capacité f d'accueil; (of road) capacité f; **seating/storage ∼** capacité d'accueil ou de stockage; **packed** ou **full to ∼** comble; **2** (of factory) capacité f de production; **to operate at full ∼** opérer au maximum de ses capacités; **the plant is stretched to ∼** l'usine tourne au maximum de ses capacités de production; **3** (role) **in my ∼ as a doctor** en ma qualité de médecin; **in an advisory ∼** à titre consultatif; **4** (ability) **to have a ∼ for** avoir de la facilité pour [learning, maths]; **a ∼ for doing** une aptitude à faire; **a great ∼ for hard work** une grande capacité de travail; **to have the ∼ to do** avoir les moyens de faire; **the task is well within your capacities** vous êtes parfaitement capable de faire ce travail; **5** Aut cylindrée f; **6** Elec capacité f; **7** Jur capacité f

cape /keɪp/ n **1** (for rainwear, fashion) cape f; (for child, policeman) pèlerine f; **2** Geog promontoire m, cap m

cape: **Cape Coloureds** npl (in South Africa) métis mpl sud-africains; **Cape of Good Hope** pr n cap m de Bonne-Espérance; **Cape Province** n province f du Cap

caper /'keɪpə(r)/
A n **1** (playful leap) cabriole f; **to cut a ∼**† faire des cabrioles; **2** ○ (funny film) comédie f; **3** ○ (dishonest scheme) combine○ f; **4** Bot, Culin (tree) câprier m; (berry) câpre f; **5** ○GB (hassle) **what a ∼!** quel bazar○!; **and all that ∼** et tout le bazar○
B capers npl (antics) aventures fpl
C vi (also **∼ about**, **∼ around**) gambader

Cape Town ▸ p. 1276 pr n Le Cap

cap: **∼ful** n (contenu m d'un) bouchon-mesure m; **∼ gun** n pistolet m à amorces

capillary /kə'pɪlərɪ, US 'kæpɪlərɪ/ n, adj capillaire (m)

capital /'kæpɪtl/
A n **1** (letter) majuscule f; **2** (also **∼ city**) capitale f; **3** ¢ gen (wealth) capital m; (funds) capitaux mpl, capital m; **to make ∼ out of sth** fig tirer parti de qch
B noun modifier [loss, outlay, turnover] de capital
C adj [letter] majuscule; **∼ A** A majuscule; **crazy with a ∼ C**○ dingue avec un D majuscule ou un grand D○; **2** Jur [offence] capital; **3** (essential) capital; **4** ○† GB (excellent) épatant

capital: **∼ account**, **C/A** n compte m capital; **∼ allowances** npl déduction f fiscale pour amortissement; **∼ assets** npl actif m immobilisé; **∼ city** n capitale f; **∼ cost** n coût m d'investissement; **∼ expenditure** n dépenses fpl d'investissement; (personal) apport m personnel (en capital); **∼ gains tax** n impôt m sur les plus-values des capitaux; **∼ goods** n biens mpl d'équipement; **∼-intensive industry** n industrie f de capitaux; **∼ investment** n dépenses fpl d'investissement

capitalism /'kæpɪtəlɪzəm/ n capitalisme m

capitalist /'kæpɪtəlɪst/ n, adj capitaliste (m)

capitalization /ˌkæpɪtəlaɪ'zeɪʃn, US -lɪ'z-/ n **1** (market value) capitalisation f; **2** Ling emploi m de lettres majuscules

capitalize /'kæpɪtəlaɪz/
A vtr **1** capitaliser [assets]; **2** Ling écrire [qch] en majuscules
B vi **to ∼ on** tirer parti de [situation, advantage]

capital: **∼ punishment** n peine f capitale; **∼ reserves** npl réserves fpl de capitaux; **∼ spending** n dépenses fpl d'investissement; **∼ sum** n gen capital m; (of loan) principal m; **∼ taxation** n impôt m sur le capital

Capacity measurement

■ *For cubic measurements* ► **p. 1311**.

British liquid measurements

20 fl oz = 0,57l (*litre*)
1 qt = 1,13l* (*litres*)
1 pt = 0,57l
1 gal = 4,54l

* There are three ways of saying 1,13l, and other measurements like it: un virgule treize litres, or (less formally) un litre virgule treize, or un litre treize. For more details on how to say numbers ► **p. 1044**.

American liquid measurements

16 fl oz = 0,47l
1 qt = 0,94l
1 pt = 0,47l
1 gal = 3,78l

Phrases

what does the tank hold?
= combien le réservoir contient-il?

what's its capacity?
= quelle est sa contenance?

it's 200 litres
= il fait 200 litres

its capacity is 200 litres
= il fait 200 litres

my car does 28 miles to the gallon
= ma voiture fait dix litres aux cent† or ma voiture fait du dix litres aux cent

they use 20,000 litres a day
= ils utilisent 20 000 litres par jour

† *Note that the French calculate petrol consumption in litres per 100 km. To convert miles per gallon to litres per 100 km and vice versa simply divide the factor 280 by the known figure.*

A holds more than B
= A contient plus que B

B holds less than A
= B contient moins que A

A has a greater capacity than B
= A a une plus grande contenance que B

B has a smaller capacity than A
= B a une moins grande contenance que A

A and B have the same capacity
= A et B ont la même contenance

20 litres of wine
= 20 litres de vin

it's sold by the litre
= cela se vend au litre

■ *Note the French construction with* de, *coming after the noun it describes:*

a 200-litre tank
= un réservoir de 200 litres

Capitol Hill *n* US **1** (hill) colline *f* du Capitole; **2** (congress) congrès *m* américain
capitulate /kə'pɪtʃʊleɪt/ *vi* gen, Mil capituler (**to** devant)
caplet® /'kæplɪt/ *n* comprimé *m* (allongé)
capon /'keɪpən, -ɒn/ *n* chapon *m*
caprice /kə'priːs/ *n* (whim) caprice *m*
capricious /kə'prɪʃəs/ *adj* capricieux/-ieuse
Capricorn /'kæprɪkɔːn/ ► **p. 1350** *n* **1** (in zodiac) Capricorne *m*; **2** Geog **tropic of** ~ tropique *m* du Capricorne
caps (*abrév* = **capital letters**) majuscules *fpl*
capsicum /'kæpsɪkəm/ *n* poivron *m*
capsize /kæp'saɪz, US 'kæpsaɪz/
A *vtr* faire chavirer
B *vi* chavirer
cap sleeve *n* mancheron *m*
caps lock *n* (*abrév* = **capitals lock**) verr *m* maj
capstan /'kæpstən/ *n* cabestan *m*
capsule /'kæpsjuːl, US 'kæpsl/ *n* capsule *f*
Capt Mil *abrév écrite* = **Captain**
captain /'kæptɪn/ ► **p. 1123**
A *n* gen, Mil, Sport capitaine *m*; US (precinct commander) (in police) commissaire *m* de quartier; (in fire service) capitaine *m* des pompiers; **naval/army** ~ capitaine de vaisseau/de l'armée de terre; ~ **of industry** fig capitaine d'industrie
B *vtr* être le capitaine de [*team*]; commander [*ship, platoon*]
caption /'kæpʃn/
A *n* **1** (under photo) légende *f* (**to, for** accompagnant); **2** TV, Cin (subtitle) sous-titre *m*
B *vtr* mettre une légende à [*photo*]; sous-titrer [*film*]
captious /'kæpʃəs/ *adj* [*remark*] critique
captivate /'kæptɪveɪt/ *vtr* captiver, fasciner; **he was** ~**d by her** elle le fascinait
captivating /'kæptɪveɪtɪŋ/ *adj* fascinant
captive /'kæptɪv/
A *n* captif/-ive *m/f*; **to hold sb** ~ garder qn en captivité; **to take sb** ~ faire qn prisonnier
B *adj* captif/-ive; ~ **audience** public captif

captivity /kæp'tɪvəti/ *n* captivité *f*; **in** ~ en captivité
captor /'kæptə(r)/ *n* (of person) geôlier/-ière *m/f*
capture /'kæptʃə(r)/
A *n* gen capture *f*; (of stronghold) prise *f*
B *vtr* **1** lit capturer [*person, animal*]; prendre [*stronghold*]; Comm s'emparer de [*market*]; **2** fig saisir [*moment, likeness*]; rendre [*feeling, beauty*]
car /kɑː(r)/
A *n* **1** Aut voiture *f*; **2** Rail wagon *m*, voiture *f*; **restaurant** ~ wagon-restaurant *m*; **3** US (also **street**~) tramway *m*
B *noun modifier* Aut [*industry, insurance*] automobile; [*journey, chase*] en voiture; [*accident*] de voiture; ~ **allowance** indemnité *f* de déplacement
carafe /kə'ræf/ *n* carafe *f*
caramel /'kærəmel/ *n* (toffee, sugar) caramel *m*; ~ **dessert** dessert au caramel
carat /'kærət/ *n* carat *m*; **18** ~ **gold** or 18 carats
caravan /'kærəvæn/
A *n* gen caravane *f*; (for circus, gypsies) roulotte *f*
B *noun modifier* GB [*holiday*] en caravane; [*site, park*] pour caravanes
C *vi* (*p prés etc* -**nn**-) **to go** ~**ning** GB faire du caravanage
caraway /'kærəweɪ/ *n* (plant) carvi *m*
carbohydrate /ˌkɑːbə'haɪdreɪt/
A *n* hydrate *m* de carbone
B *noun modifier* **low-/high-**~ **diet** alimentation *f* pauvre/riche en hydrates de carbone
carbolic /kɑː'bɒlɪk/ *adj* [*soap*] phéniqué
car bomb *n* bombe *f* dissimulée dans une voiture
carbon /'kɑːbən/
A *n* carbone *m*
B *noun modifier* [*atom, compound*] de carbone
carbonate /'kɑːbəneɪt/
A *n* carbonate *m*
B *vtr* carbonater
carbonated /'kɑːbəneɪtɪd/ *adj* [*drink*] gazéifié
carbon: ~ **copy** *n* lit copie *f* carbone; fig réplique *f* exacte; ~**-date** *vtr* dater [qch] au carbone 14;

~ dating n datation f au carbone 14; **~ dioxide** n dioxyde m de carbone; **~ filter** n filtre m au carbone

carbonize /'kɑːbənaɪz/ vtr carboniser also hum

carbon: **~ monoxide** n monoxyde m de carbone; **~ paper** n (papier m) carbone m

car boot sale n GB brocante f (d'objets apportés dans le coffre de sa voiture)

carbuncle /'kɑːbʌŋkl/ n **1** Med anthrax m; **2** (gem) escarboucle f

carburettor /ˌkɑːbə'retə(r)/ GB, **carburetor** /'kɑːrbər-eɪtər/ US n carburateur m

carcass /'kɑːkəs/ n carcasse f

carcinogen /kɑːˈsɪnədʒən/ n substance f cancérigène

carcinogenic /ˌkɑːsɪnə'dʒenɪk/ adj cancérigène

carcinoma /ˌkɑːsɪ'nəʊmə/ n carcinome m

card /kɑːd/ n **1** (for correspondence, greetings) carte f; (for indexing) fiche f; (at races) programme m; (in golf) carte f (de parcours); **2** Games carte f (à jouer); **to play ~s** jouer aux cartes; **one's strongest ~** fig sa carte maîtresse; **3** °†GB (person) original/-e m/f

Idioms **a ~ up one's sleeve** un atout dans sa manche; **it is on** GB ou **in** US **the ~s that** il est bien possible que (+ subj); **an election is on** ou **in the ~s** il y a de fortes chances pour qu'il y ait une élection; **to get** ou **be given one's ~s** °† GB être renvoyé; **to hold all the ~s** avoir tous les atouts; **to play one's ~s right** bien jouer son jeu°

cardboard /'kɑːdbɔːd/
A n carton m
B noun modifier [cut-out] en carton; **~ box** (boîte f en) carton m

card: **~board city** n: zone urbaine où les sans-abri logent dans des cartons; **~ catalogue**, **~ catalog** US n fichier m; **~ game** n (type of game) jeu m de cartes; (as activity) partie f de cartes; **~holder** n titulaire mf d'une carte

cardiac /'kɑːdɪæk/ adj cardiaque; **~ arrest** arrêt m du cœur

cardigan /'kɑːdɪgən/ ▸ p. 1191 n cardigan m

cardinal /'kɑːdɪnl/
A n Relig cardinal m
B adj [sin] capital; [principle] fondamental; [number] cardinal

card index n fichier n

cardiologist /ˌkɑːdɪ'ɒlədʒɪst/ ▸ p. 1181 n cardiologue mf

cardiology /ˌkɑːdɪ'ɒlədʒɪ/ n cardiologie f

cardiovascular /ˌkɑːdɪəʊ'væskjʊlə(r)/ adj cardiovasculaire

card: **~ key** n carte f magnétique; **~phone** n téléphone m à carte; **~sharp(er)** n tricheur/-euse m/f (professionnel-elle); **~ trick** n tour m de cartes

care /keə(r)/
A n **1** (attention) attention f, soin m; **to take ~ to do** prendre soin de faire; **to take ~ not to do** faire attention de ne pas faire; **to take ~ when doing** faire attention en faisant; **to take ~ that** faire attention que (+ subj); **he took (great) ~ over** ou **with his work** il a fait son travail avec (le plus grand) soin; **to take ~ in doing sth** faire qch avec soin; **'take ~!'** 'fais attention!'; (expression of farewell) 'à bientôt!'; **with ~** avec soin, en faisant attention; **'handle with ~'** 'fragile'; **to exercise due ~** Jur prendre les précautions nécessaires; **2** (looking after) (of person, animal) soins mpl; (of car, plant, clothes) entretien m (of de); **to take ~ of** (deal with) gen s'occuper de [child, client]; Med soigner [patient]; (be responsible for) s'occuper de [garden, details]; (be careful with) prendre soin de [machine, car]; (keep in good condition) entretenir [car, teeth]; (look after) garder [shop, watch]; **to take good ~ of sb/sth** prendre soin de qn/qch; **customer ~** service m auprès des clients; **to put** ou **leave sb/sth in sb's ~** confier qn/qch à qn; **in his/your ~** à sa/ta garde; **the pupils/patients in my ~** les élèves/malades dont j'ai la responsabilité; **in the ~ of his father** à la garde de son père; **John Smith, ~ of Mrs L. Smith** (on letter) John Smith, chez or aux bons soins de Mme L. Smith; **to take ~ of oneself** (look after oneself) prendre soin de soi; (cope) se débrouiller tout seul; (defend oneself) se défendre; **that takes ~ of that** c'est réglé; **3** Med, Psych soins mpl; **~ in the community** soins en dehors du milieu hospitalier; **4** GB (for child at risk) **to be in ~** être (placé) en garde; **to take** ou **put a child into ~** placer un enfant sous la garde des services sociaux; **5** (worry)

souci m; **without a ~ in the world** parfaitement insouciant

B vtr **if you ~ to examine the report** si vous voulez avoir l'obligeance d'examiner le rapport; (as polite formula) **would you ~ to sit down?** voulez-vous vous asseoir?; **he has more money than he ~s to admit** il a plus d'argent qu'il ne veut bien le dire

C vi **1** (feel concerned) **she really ~s** elle prend ça à cœur; **to ~ about** s'intéresser à [art, culture, money, environment]; se soucier du bien-être de [pupils, the elderly]; **I don't ~!** ça m'est égal!; **what do I ~ if...?** qu'est-ce que ça peut me faire que... (+ subj)?; **as if he ~d!** comme si ça lui faisait quelque chose!; **he couldn't ~ less!** ça lui est complètement égal!; **she couldn't ~ less about...** elle se moque or se fiche° complètement de...; **I couldn't ~ less who wins** je me moque or me fiche° de savoir qui va gagner; **they could all have died, for all he ~d** ils auraient pu mourir tous, cela lui était égal; **I don't ~ who he marries** il peut épouser qui il veut, ça m'est égal; **I'm past caring** je m'en moque; **who ~s?** qu'est-ce que ça peut faire?; **2** (love) **to ~ about sb** aimer qn

Idiom **he doesn't ~ a fig** ou **a damn**° il s'en fiche° complètement

Phrasal verb
■ **care for**: ▸ **~ for [sth] 1** (like) aimer; **I don't ~ for chocolate** je n'aime pas le chocolat; **would you ~ for a drink?** voulez-vous boire quelque chose?; **2** (maintain) entretenir [car, garden]; prendre soin de [skin, plant]; ▸ **~ for [sb/sth]** s'occuper de [child, animal]; soigner [patient, wounded animal]

care: **~ assistant** ▸ p. 1181 n GB Med aide-soignant/-e m/f; **~ attendant** ▸ p. 1181 n GB aide f familiale

career /kə'rɪə(r)/
A n carrière f; **political ~** carrière politique; **a ~ in television/in teaching** une carrière à la télévision/dans l'enseignement; **a ~ as a journalist** une carrière de journaliste; **school ~** scolarité f
B noun modifier [diplomat] de carrière; [soldier] de métier
C vi **to ~ in/out** entrer/sortir à toute vitesse; **to ~ off the road** quitter la route; **to ~ out of control** s'emballer

career break n interruption f de carrière

career: **~ move** n pas m en avant dans son évolution professionnelle; **~s adviser** GB, **~ advisor** US ▸ p. 1181 n conseiller/-ère m/f d'orientation; **~s guidance** n orientation f professionnelle; **~s library** n centre m d'information et d'orientation professionnelle; **~s office** n service m d'orientation professionnelle; **~s officer** n GB = careers adviser; **~s service** GB, **~ service** US n service m d'orientation professionnelle

carefree /'keəfriː/ adj [person, smile, life] insouciant

careful /'keəfl/ adj [person, driving] prudent; [planning, preparation] minutieux/-ieuse; [research, monitoring, examination] méticuleux/-euse; **to be ~ to do** ou **about doing** prendre soin de faire; **to be ~ that** faire attention que (+ subj); **to be ~ of sth** faire attention à qch; **to be ~ with sth** faire attention à qch; **to be ~ (when) doing** faire attention en faisant; **to be ~ what one says** faire attention à ce qu'on dit; **be ~!** (fais) attention!; **be ~ how you open it** fais attention en l'ouvrant; **you can't be too ~!** on n'est jamais trop prudent!

carefully /'keəfəlɪ/ adv [go, walk, drive] prudemment; [say] avec circonspection; [open, remove, handle] prudemment, avec précaution; [write, choose words, organize, wash] soigneusement, avec soin; [listen, read, look] attentivement; **drive** ou **go ~!** soyez prudent! **listen/think ~!** écoutez/réfléchissez bien!

careless /'keəlɪs/ adj (negligent) [person] négligent, imprudent; [work] bâclé; [writing] négligé; [driving, handling] négligent; [talk] imprudent; **~ mistake** faute d'étourderie or d'inattention; **it was ~ of me to do** ça a été de la négligence de ma part de faire; **to be ~ about sth/about doing** négliger qch/de faire; **to be ~ with** ne pas prendre soin de [books, clothes]; **to be ~ of one's appearance** se négliger

carelessly /'keəlɪslɪ/ adv **1** (negligently) [do, act] avec négligence; [make, repair, write] sans soin; [drive] avec négligence; [break, lose] par manque d'attention; [dressed, arranged] avec négligence; **2** (in carefree way) avec insouciance

carelessness /'keəlɪsnɪs/ n (negligence) négligence f

carer /'keərə(r)/ ▸ p. 1181 n GB (relative) *personne ayant un parent handicapé ou malade à charge*; (professional) aide *f* familiale

caress /kə'res/
A n caresse *f*
B vtr caresser

caretaker /'keəteɪkə(r)/ ▸ p. 1181
A n GB (at school, club) concierge *mf*; (in apartments) gardien/-ienne *m/f*, concierge *mf*
B noun modifier [administration] intérimaire; [president] par intérim

care: ~ **worker** ▸ p. 1181 n GB assistant/-e *m/f* social/-e; ~**worn** adj [face] marqué par les soucis

car ferry n ferry *m*

cargo /'kɑːgəʊ/ n (pl ~**es** ou ~**s**) gen chargement *m*; Naut cargaison *f*, chargement *m*

cargo: ~ **plane** n avion *m* cargo; ~ **ship** n cargo *m*

car: ~ **hire** n location *f* de voitures; ~ **hire company** n société *f* de location de voitures

Caribbean /ˌkærɪ'biːən/ ▸ p. 1049
A n **1** (sea) mer *f* des Antilles; **2** (person) habitant/-e *m/f* des Caraïbes
B noun modifier [climate, cookery] des Caraïbes; [carnival] des Antilles

Caribbean Islands ▸ p. 954 pr npl petites Antilles *fpl*

caricature /'kærɪkətʃʊə(r)/
A n caricature *f*
B vtr caricaturer

caricaturist /'kærɪkətʃʊərɪst/ ▸ p. 1181 n caricaturiste *mf*

caring /'keərɪŋ/
A n travail *m* social
B noun modifier Med, Sociol [profession] paramédical; ~ **professionals** le personnel paramédical
C adj **1** (loving) [parent] affectueux/-euse; [environment, home] chaleureux/-euse; **2** (compassionate) [person, attitude] compréhensif/-ive; [society] humain

carjacking /'kɑːdʒakɪŋ/ n vol *m* de voiture (avec agression du conducteur)

carload /'kɑːləʊd/ n a ~ **of people** une voiture pleine de gens

carnage /'kɑːnɪdʒ/ n carnage *m* also fig

carnal /'kɑːnl/ adj [pleasure, desire] charnel/-elle

carnation /kɑː'neɪʃn/ n œillet *m*

carnation: ~ **pink** ▸ p. 752 n rose *m* incarnat; ~ **red** ▸ p. 752 n rouge *m* incarnat

carnival /'kɑːnɪvl/ n **1** GB (procession) carnaval *m*; **2** US (funfair) fête *f* foraine

carnivore /'kɑːnɪvɔː(r)/ n carnivore *m*

carnivorous /kɑː'nɪvərəs/ adj carnivore

carob /'kærəb/ n (tree) caroubier *m*; (pod) caroube *f*

carol /'kærəl/ n chant *m* de Noël

carotene /'kærətiːn/, **carotin** /'kærətɪn/ n carotène *m*

carotid /kə'rɒtɪd/
A n carotide *f*
B adj carotidien/-ienne

carouse /kə'raʊz/ vi faire la noce

carousel /ˌkærə'sel/ n **1** (merry-go-round) manège *m*; **2** (for luggage) carrousel *m*; **3** (for slides) carrousel *m*

carp /kɑːp/
A n (fish) carpe *f*
B ○vi maugréer (**about** contre)

car park n GB parc *m* de stationnement

carpenter /'kɑːpəntə(r)/ ▸ p. 1181 n (joiner) menuisier *m*; (on building site) charpentier *m*

carpentry /'kɑːpəntrɪ/ n gen menuiserie *f*; (structural) charpenterie *f*

carpet /'kɑːpɪt/
A n **1** (fitted) moquette *f*; (loose) tapis *m*; **2** fig tapis *m*; ~ **of flowers** tapis de fleurs
B noun modifier [showroom] de tapis; [shampoo] pour tapis
C vtr **1** lit mettre de la moquette dans [room]; **to ~ the living-room floor** mettre de la moquette dans le séjour; ~**ed with flowers** fig, littér tapissé de fleurs; **2** fig (reprimand) passer un savon à
Idiom **to brush** ou **sweep sth under the** ~ enterrer or étouffer qch

carpetbagger /'kɑːpɪtbægə(r)/ n **1** US Hist carpetbagger *m*; **2** Pol candidat *m* parachuté

carpet: ~ **fitter** ▸ p. 1181 n poseur *m* de moquette; ~ **slipper** n charentaise *f*; ~ **sweeper** n balai *m* mécanique; ~ **tile** n dalle *f* de moquette

car: ~**phone** n radiotéléphone *m* de voiture; ~ **phone** n téléphone *m* de voiture

carping /'kɑːpɪŋ/
A n **ℂ** chicaneries *fpl*
B adj [criticism, person] malveillant

car: ~ **radio** n autoradio *m*; ~ **rental** n ▸ car hire

carriage /'kærɪdʒ/ n **1** (vehicle) (ceremonial) carrosse *m*; (for transport) attelage *m*; **2** (of train) wagon *m*, voiture *f*; **3** **ℂ** (of goods, passengers) transport *m*; ~ **free/forward** port *m* gratuit/dû; ~ **paid** port *m* payé; **4** (of typewriter) chariot *m*; **5** (bearing) maintien *m*

carriage: ~ **clock** n pendulette *f*; ~**way** n chaussée *f*

carrier /'kærɪə(r)/ n **1** (transport company) transporteur *m*; (airline) compagnie *f* aérienne; **to send sth by** ~ expédier qch; **2** (of disease) porteur/-euse *m/f*; **3** GB (also ~ **bag**) sac *m* (en plastique)

carrier pigeon n pigeon *m* voyageur

carrion /'kærɪən/ n (also ~ **flesh**) charogne *f*

carrot /'kærət/ n carotte *f* also fig

carroty○ /'kærətɪ/ adj [hair] rouquin○

carry /'kærɪ/
A n (range) portée *f*
B vtr **1** porter [bag, shopping, load, news, message] (**in** dans; **on** sur); **to ~ sth up/down** porter qch en haut/en bas; **to ~ sth in/out** apporter/emporter qch; **to ~ a child across the road** porter un enfant pour lui faire traverser la route; **to ~ cash/a gun** avoir de l'argent liquide/un revolver sur soi; **to ~ a picture in one's mind** avoir une image toujours en tête; **to ~ sth too far** fig pousser qch trop loin; **2** [vehicle, pipe, wire, vein] transporter; [wind, tide, current, stream] emporter; **to be carried on the wind** être porté or transporté par le vent; **his quest carried him to India** sa quête l'a amené en Inde; **3** (feature) comporter [warning, guarantee, report]; porter [symbol, label]; publier [advert]; **4** (entail) comporter [risk]; être passible de [penalty]; **to ~ conviction** être convaincant; **5** (bear, support) [bridge, road] supporter [load, traffic]; **6** (win) l'emporter dans [state, constituency]; remporter [battle, match]; **the motion was carried by 20 votes to 13** la motion l'a emporté par 20 votes contre 13; **to ~ all before one** l'emporter haut la main; **7** Med être porteur de [disease]; **8** (be pregnant with) [woman] être enceinte de [girl, twins]; [animal] porter [young]; **I am ~ing his child** je porte son enfant; **9** Comm (stock, sell) faire [item, brand]; **we ~ a wide range of** nous offrons un grand choix de; **10** (hold, bear) porter (permanently) [tail, head]; **11** Math retenir [one, two]
C vi [sound, voice] porter; **to ~ well** porter bien
D v refl **to ~ oneself** se tenir
Idiom **to get carried away**○ s'emballer○, se laisser emporter

Phrasal verbs
■ **carry back**: ▸ ~ **back** [sth], ~ [sth] **back** rapporter [object]; ▸ ~ [sb] **back** (in memory) ramener [person] (**to** à)
■ **carry forward**: ▸ ~ **forward** [sth], ~ [sth] **forward** reporter [balance, total]
■ **carry off**: ▸ ~ **off** [sth] lit emporter; fig remporter [prize, medal]; **to ~ it off**○ (succeed) réussir, y arriver; ▸ ~ **off** [sb], ~ [sb] **off** [illness, disease] emporter [person, animal]; (lead away) emmener
■ **carry on**: ▸ ~ **on** **1** (continue) continuer (**doing** à faire); ~ **on down** ou **along the road** (in car) continuer la route; (on foot) poursuivre son chemin; **to ~ on with sth** continuer or poursuivre qch; **2** ○(behave) se conduire; **3** ○(have affair) avoir une liaison; ▸ ~ **on** [sth] **1** (conduct) conduire [business]; entretenir [correspondence]; mener [conversation]; **2** (continue) maintenir [tradition]; poursuivre [activity, discussion]
■ **carry out**: ▸ ~ **out** [sth], ~ [sth] **out** réaliser [study]; effectuer [experiment, reform, attack, operation, repairs]; exécuter [plan, orders, punishment]; mener [investigation, campaign]; accomplir [mission]; remplir [duties]; mettre [qch] à exécution [threat]; tenir [promise]
■ **carry over**: ▸ ~ **over into** [problem, rivalry] s'étendre à

[*personal life*]; ▶ ~ **sth over into** transférer qch dans [*private life, area of activity, adulthood*]; ▶ ~ **over** [sth], ~ [sth] **over** reporter [*debt*]
■ **carry through**: ▶ ~ **through** [sth], ~ [sth] **through** mener [qch] à bien [*reform, policy, task*]; ▶ ~ [sb] **through** [*humour*] soutenir [*person*]

carry: ~**all** *n* US fourre-tout *m inv*; ~**cot** *n* GB porte-bébé *m*; ~**ing-on**○ *n* (*pl* carryings-on) incartade *f*; ~**on**○ *n* cirque○ *m*; ~**out** *n* GB (food) repas *m* à emporter

car seat *n* siège-auto *m*

carsick /'kɑːsɪk/ *adj* **to be** ~ avoir le mal de la route

cart /kɑːt/
A *n* (for goods) charrette *f*; (for passengers) carriole *f*
B *vtr* ①○gen (*also* ~ **around**, ~ **about**) (drag) trimballer○ [*bags, shopping*]; ② Agric charrier [*hay*]
(Idiom) **to put the** ~ **before the horse** mettre la charrue avant les bœufs
(Phrasal verb)
■ **cart off**○: ▶ ~ [sb] **off** emmener [qn] de force

cartel /kɑː'tel/ *n* cartel *m*; **drug** ~ cartel *m* de la drogue

carthorse /'kɑːθɔːs/ *n* cheval *m* de trait

cartilage /'kɑːtɪlɪdʒ/ *n* cartilage *m*

cartload /'kɑːtləʊd/ *n* charretée *f*

cartographer /kɑː'tɒɡrəfə(r)/ ▸ p. 1181 *n* cartographe *mf*

cartography /kɑː'tɒɡrəfɪ/ *n* cartographie *f*

carton /'kɑːtn/ *n* (small) boîte *f*; (of yoghurt, cream) pot *m*; (of juice, milk, ice cream) carton *m*, brique *f*; (of cigarettes) cartouche *f*; US (for house removals) carton *m*

cartoon /kɑː'tuːn/ *n* ① Cin dessin *m* animé; ② (drawing) dessin *m* humoristique; (in comic) bande *f* dessinée; ③ Art carton *m*

cartoonist /kɑː'tuːnɪst/ ▸ p. 1181 *n* (in newspaper) dessinateur/-trice *mf* humoristique; (of strip cartoons) dessinateur/-trice *m/f* de bandes dessinées

cartridge /'kɑːtrɪdʒ/ *n* ① (for pen, gun) cartouche *f*; ② (for video, typewriter etc) cartouche *f*; ③ (for camera) chargeur *m*

cartridge: ~ **belt** *n* cartouchière *f*; ~ **paper** *n* Art papier *m* à dessin; ~ **pen** *n* stylo *m* à cartouche

cart-track /'kɑːttræk/ *n* chemin *m* charretier

cartwheel /'kɑːtwiːl, US -hwiːl/ *n* ① (in gymnastics) roue *f*; **to do** ou **turn a** ~ faire la roue; ② lit roue *f* de charrette

carve /kɑːv/
A *vtr* ① (sculpt) tailler, sculpter [*wood, stone, figure*]; creuser [*channel*] (**out of**, **from** dans); **to** ~ **sth into** creuser qch en forme de; ② (inscribe) graver (**onto** sur; **in** dans); ③ Culin découper
B *vi* découper
(Phrasal verbs)
■ **carve out**: ▶ ~ **out** [sth], ~ [sth] **out** ① fig se faire [*niche, name*]; se tailler [*reputation, market*]; se construire [*career*]; ② lit creuser [*gorge, channel*]
■ **carve up**: ▶ ~ **up** [sth], ~ [sth] **up** ① ○(divide) partager [*proceeds*]; morceler [*estate, territory*]; ② Culin découper; ▶ ~ **up** [sb]○ ① (with knife) tailladers; ② Aut faire une queue de poisson à

carving /'kɑːvɪŋ/ *n* ① (figure, sculpture) sculpture *f*; ② (technique) (of object) sculpture *f*; (of motif) gravure *f*; ③ Culin découpage *m*; ~ **knife** couteau *m* à découper

car: ~ **wash** *n* lavage *m* automatique; ~ **worker** ▸ p. 1181 *n* ouvrier/-ière *m/f* de l'industrie automobile

cascade /kæ'skeɪd/
A *n* ① (of water) cascade *f*; (of hair, silk) flot *m*; ② Comput cascade *f*
B *vi* tomber en cascade

case¹ /keɪs/
A *n* ① (instance, example) cas *m*; **on a** ~ **by** ~ **basis** au cas par cas; **in which** ~, **in that** ~ en ce cas, dans ce cas-là; **in such** ou **these** ~**s** dans un cas pareil; **in 7 out of 10** ~**s** 7 fois sur 10, dans 7 cas sur 10; **a** ~ **in point** un cas d'espèce, un exemple typique; **it's a** ~ **of substituting X for Y** il s'agit de substituer X à Y; **this being the** ~ en ce cas, dans ce cas-là; **such** ou **this being the** ~ ou if this is the ~ s'il c'est le cas; ③ Jur the ~ **for the Crown** GB, the ~ **for the State** US l'accusation *f*; the ~ **for the defence** la défense *f*; **to state the** ~ exposer les faits; **the** ~ **against Foster** les faits

qui sont reprochés à Foster; **the** ~ **is closed** Jur, fig l'affaire ou la cause est entendue; ④ (convincing argument) arguments *mpl*; **to make a good** ~ **for sth** donner des arguments convaincants en faveur de qch; **to argue the** ~ **for sth** donner des arguments en faveur de qch; **there's a strong** ~ **for/against doing** il y a de bonnes raisons pour/pour ne pas faire; ⑤ (trial) affaire *f*, procès *m*; **criminal** ~ affaire criminelle; **divorce/murder** ~ procès en divorce/pour meurtre; **to win one's** ~ gagner son procès; **his** ~ **comes up next week** il passe en jugement la semaine prochaine; **famous** ~**s** causes *fpl* célèbres; ⑥ (criminal investigation) **the Burgess** ~ l'affaire Burgess; **to work** ou **be on a** ~ enquêter sur une affaire; **a blackmail** ~ une affaire de chantage; **the** ~**s of Sherlock Holmes** les enquêtes de Sherlock Holmes; ⑦ Med (instance of disease) cas *m*; (patient) malade *mf*; ⑧ (client) cas *m*; ⑨ ○(person) **he's a real** ~! c'est vraiment un cas!; **a hopeless** ~ un cas désespéré; **a hard** ~ un dur; ▸ **head case**; ⑩ Ling cas *m*; **in the accusative** ~ à l'accusatif
B **in any case** *adv phr* (besides, anyway) de toute façon; (at any rate) en tout cas
C **in case** *conj phr* au cas où (+ *conditional*); **in** ~ **it rains** au cas où il pleuvrait; **take the map just in** ~ prends le plan au cas où
D **in case of** *prep phr* en cas de

case² /keɪs/
A *n* ① (suitcase) valise *f*; ② (crate, chest) caisse *f*; ③ (display cabinet) vitrine *f*; ④ (for spectacles, binoculars, cartridge, weapon) étui *m*; (for jewels) écrin *m*; (of camera, watch) boîtier *m*; (of piano, clock) caisse *f*
B ○*vtr* (reconnoitre) **to** ~ **the joint** faire du repérage

CASE /keɪs/ *n* (abrév = **computer-aided software engineering**) CPAO *f*

case history *n* ① Med antécédents *mpl*; ② (study) = **case study**

caseload /'keɪsləʊd/ *n* nombre *m* de cas à traiter; **to have a heavy** ~ avoir une clientèle nombreuse

casement window /'keɪsmənt/ *n* fenêtre *f* à battants

case keɪs: ~ **notes** *npl* dossier *m*; ~ **study** *n* étude *f* de cas; ~ **system** *n* Ling système *m* casuel

casework /'keɪswɜːk/ *n* **to be involved in** ou **to do** ~ s'occuper des cas sociaux

caseworker ▸ p. 1181 *n* ≈ assistant/-e *m/f* social/-e

cash /kæʃ/
A *n* ① (notes and coin) espèces *fpl*, argent *m* liquide; **to pay in** ~ payer en espèces; **£3,000 (in)** ~ 3 000 livres sterling en espèces; **to be paid in** ~ **in hand** être payé en espèces; **I haven't got any** ~ **on me** je n'ai pas d'argent liquide; ② (money in general) argent *m*; ③ (immediate payment) comptant *m*; **discount for** ~ remise *f* pour paiement comptant; **£50** ~ **in hand** ou ~ **down** 50 livres sterling en liquide
B *noun modifier* [*advance, book*] de caisse; [*offer, sale, discount, transaction*] au comptant; [*alternative, deposit, sum, refund, prize*] en espèces; [*price*] comptant
C *vtr* encaisser [*cheque*]
(Phrasal verb)
■ **cash in**: ▶ ~ **in** en profiter; **to** ~ **in on** tirer profit de, profiter de; ▶ ~ **in** [sth], ~ [sth] **in** se faire rembourser, réaliser [*bond, policy*]; US encaisser [*check*]; encaisser [*gambling chips*]

cash: ~-**and-carry** *n* libre-service *m* de vente en gros; ~ **box** *n* caisse *f*; ~ **card** *n* carte *f* de retrait; ~ **crop** *n* culture *f* commerciale; ~ **desk** *n* caisse *f*; ~ **dispenser** *n* distributeur *m* automatique de billets de banque, billetterie *f*

cash-back /'kæʃbæk/ *n* (in shops when paying by credit card) **would you like** ~? voulez-vous retirer de l'argent?

cashew /'kæʃuː/ *n* (also ~ **nut**) cajou *m*

cash flow *n* marge *f* brute d'auto-financement, MBA *f*

cashier /kæ'ʃɪə(r)/ ▸ p. 1181
A *n* caissier/-ière *m/f*
B *vtr* Mil casser [*officer*]; gen congédier [*employee*]

cash limit *n* limite *f* budgétaire

cashmere /ˌkæʃ'mɪə(r)/ *n* (lainage *m* en) cachemire *m*; ~ **sweater** pullover en cachemire

cash: ~ **on delivery, COD** *n* envoi *m* contre remboursement; ~**point** *n* = **cash dispenser**; ~**point card** *n* = **cash card**; ~ **register** *n* caisse *f* enregistreuse; ~ **reserves** *npl* trésorerie *f*

casing /ˈkeɪsɪŋ/ n (of bomb, machinery) revêtement m; (of gearbox) carter m; (of tyre) enveloppe f extérieure

casino /kəˈsiːnəʊ/ n casino m

cask /kɑːsk, US kæsk/ n fût m, tonneau m

casket /ˈkɑːskɪt, US ˈkæskɪt/ n (box) coffret m; (coffin) cercueil m

cassava /kəˈsɑːvə/ n Bot manioc m; Culin farine f de manioc

casserole /ˈkæsərəʊl/
A n Culin **1** (container) daubière f, cocotte f; **2** GB (food) ragoût m cuit au four
B vtr cuire [qch] à four doux

cassette /kəˈset/ n cassette f; **to record on ~** enregistrer sur cassette; **available on ~** disponible en cassette

cassette: ~ **deck** n platine f à cassettes; ~ **player** n lecteur m de cassettes; ~ **recorder** n magnétophone m à cassettes; ~ **tape** n cassette f audio

cassock /ˈkæsək/ n soutane f

cast /kɑːst, US kæst/
A n **1** Cin, Theat, TV (list of actors) distribution f; (actors) acteurs mpl; **the members of the ~** les acteurs; ~ **of characters** (in play, novel) liste f des personnages; **2** (mould) moule m; (moulded object) moulage m; **3** (arrangement) ~ **of mind** tournure f d'esprit; **4** (in fishing) lancer m; **5** (squint) strabisme m; **to have a ~ in one eye** avoir un œil qui louche; **6** Med (also **plaster ~**) plâtre m; **to have one's arm in a ~** avoir un bras dans le plâtre
B vtr (prét, pp **cast**) **1** (throw) jeter, lancer [stone, net, fishing line]; jeter [dice]; projeter [light, shadow]; **to ~ doubt on** émettre des doutes sur; **to ~ light on** éclairer; **to ~ (a) new light on** éclairer [qch] d'un jour nouveau; **to ~ a spell on** jeter un sort à; **2** (direct) jeter [glance, look] (**at** sur); **her eyes were cast downwards** elle avait les yeux baissés; **to ~ one's eyes around the room/over a letter** parcourir la pièce/une lettre des yeux; **to ~ one's mind back over sth** se remémorer qch; **if you ~ your mind back to last week** si tu te rappelles ce qui s'est passé la semaine dernière; **3** Cin, Theat, TV distribuer les rôles de [play, film]; **she was cast in the role of** ou **as Blanche** elle a joué Blanche; **4** (shed) se dépouiller de [leaves, feathers]; **the snake ~s its skin** le serpent mue; **5** Art, Tech couler; **6** Pol **to ~ one's vote** voter

(Phrasal verbs)
■ **cast about** GB, **cast around**: ▸ ~ **about for** chercher [excuse]
■ **cast down**: ▸ ~ **down** [sth], ~ [sth] **down** lit jeter [qch] par terre [object]; déposer [weapons]; baisser [eyes, head]; **to be cast down** littér être abattu
■ **cast off**: ▸ ~ **off** **1** Naut larguer les amarres; **2** (in knitting) rabattre les mailles restantes; ▸ ~ **off** [sth], ~ [sth] **off** **1** (discard) ôter, enlever [garment]; se libérer de [chains]; abandonner [lover]; **2** Naut larguer les amarres de; **3** (in knitting) rabattre [stitches]
■ **cast on**: ▸ ~ **on** monter les mailles; ▸ ~ **on** [sth] monter [stitch]
■ **cast out**: ▸ ~ **out** [sth/sb], ~ [sth/sb] **out** littér chasser

castanets /ˌkæstəˈnets/ ▸ p. 1028 npl castagnettes fpl

castaway /ˈkɑːstəweɪ, US ˈkæst-/ n naufragé/-e m/f

caste /kɑːst/ n caste f; **the ~ system** le système des castes

caster /ˈkɑːstə(r), US ˈkæstər/ n **1** (shaker) saupoudreuse f; **2** (wheel) roulette f

caster sugar n GB sucre m en poudre

casting /ˈkɑːstɪŋ, US ˈkæst-/ n **1** (throwing) lancement m; **2** (in metallurgy) coulée f, moulage m; **3** Art moulage m; **4** Cin, Theat, TV distribution f

casting: ~ **director** ▸ p. 1181 n directeur/-trice m/f de la distribution; ~ **vote** n voix f prépondérante

cast iron
A n fonte f
B cast-iron noun modifier lit [object] de ou en fonte; fig [alibi] en béton○

castle /ˈkɑːsl, US ˈkæsl/ n **1** Archit château m; **2** (in chess) tour f

(Idiom) ~**s in the air** ou **in Spain** US des châteaux en Espagne

cast-offs /ˈkɑːstɒf, US ˈkæst-/ npl (clothes) vêtements mpl dont on n'a plus besoin, vieux vêtements; **society's ~s** fig

les laissés mpl pour compte de la société

castor /ˈkɑːstə(r), US ˈkæs-/ n (wheel) (also **caster**) roulette f

castor oil n huile f de ricin

castrate /kæˈstreɪt, US ˈkæstreɪt/ vtr castrer [man, animal]; fig expurger [book, article]

casual /ˈkæʒʊəl/
A n (temporary worker) travailleur/-euse m/f temporaire; (occasional worker) travailleur/-euse m/f occasionnel/-elle
B casuals npl (clothes) vêtements mpl sport
C adj **1** (informal) décontracté; **to have a ~ chat** bavarder, causer○; **2** (occasional) [acquaintance, relationship] de passage; ~ **sex** relations fpl sexuelles non suivies; **3** (nonchalant) désinvolte; **4** péj [cruelty, violence] ordinaire; [remark, assumption] désinvolte; **5** [glance, onlooker] superficiel/-ielle; **to the ~ eye it seems that** l'observateur superficiel dirait que; **6** (chance) [encounter] fortuit; **7** [worker, labour] (temporary) temporaire; (occasional) occasionnel/-elle

casually /ˈkæʒʊəlɪ/ adv **1** [inquire, remark] d'un air détaché; [stroll, greet] nonchalamment; [glance, leaf through] superficiellement; **2** [dressed] simplement; **3** [offend] sans y penser; **4** [employed] temporairement

casualness /ˈkæʒʊəlnɪs/ n **1** (of manner, tone, remark) désinvolture f; **2** (of clothes, dress) décontraction f

casualty /ˈkæʒʊəltɪ/
A n **1** gen (person) victime f; **2** (part of hospital) urgences fpl; **in ~** aux urgences; **3** fig (person, plan) victime f; **to be a ~ of sth** être victime de qch
B casualties npl (soldiers) pertes fpl; (civilians) victimes fpl
C noun modifier [department, nurse GB] des urgences; [ward GB] d'urgence; Mil [list] des victimes

cat /kæt/
A n **1** (domestic) chat m; (female) chatte f; **2** (feline) félin m; **3** ○péj (woman) chipie f
B noun modifier [basket] pour chat; [litter, food] pour chats; **the ~ family** les félins mpl

(Idioms) **to be like a ~ on a hot tin roof** ou **on hot bricks** être sur les charbons ardents; **to fight like ~ and dog** se battre comme des chiffonniers; **to let the ~ out of the bag** vendre la mèche; **to rain ~s and dogs** pleuvoir des cordes; **to think one is the ~'s whiskers** GB ou **pajamas** US ou **meow** US se croire sorti de la cuisse de Jupiter; **when the ~'s away, the mice will play** quand le chat n'est pas là, les souris dansent; **to play ~ and mouse with sb** jouer au chat et à la souris avec qn

CAT n **1** GB (abrév = **College of Advanced Technology**) ≈ IUT; **2** Comput (abrév = **computer-assisted teaching**) enseignement m assisté par ordinateur; **3** Comput (abrév = **computer-assisted training**) formation f assistée par ordinateur

cataclysm /ˈkætəklɪzəm/ n lit, fig cataclysme m

catacombs /ˈkætəkuːmz, US -kəʊmz/ npl catacombes fpl

Catalan /ˈkætəlæn/ ▸ p. 1032, p. 969 n, adj catalan (m)

catalogue, catalog US /ˈkætəlɒg, US -lɔːg/
A n **1** (of goods, books etc) catalogue m; **2** (series) série (**of** de); **3** (also **catalog** US Univ brochure f (universitaire)
B vtr dresser un catalogue de

catalyst /ˈkætəlɪst/ n Chem, fig catalyseur m

catalytic /ˌkætəˈlɪtɪk/ adj catalytique; ~ **converter** pot m catalytique

catapult /ˈkætəpʌlt/
A n **1** GB lance-pierres m inv; **2** Mil, Aviat (also ~ **launcher**) catapulte f; **3** Mil, Hist catapulte f
B vtr projeter; fig **to be ~ed to** être catapulté vers [power]

cataract /ˈkætərækt/ n **1** Med cataracte f; **2** (waterfall) cataracte f

catarrh /kəˈtɑː(r)/ n catarrhe m

catastrophe /kəˈtæstrəfɪ/ n catastrophe f

catastrophic /ˌkætəˈstrɒfɪk/ adj catastrophique

cat burglar n GB monte-en-l'air m inv

catcall /ˈkætkɔːl/ n sifflet m

catch /kætʃ/
A n **1** (fastening) (on purse, brooch) fermoir m, fermeture f; (on window, door) fermeture f; **2** (drawback) piège m fig; **what's the ~?** où est le piège?; **3** (break in voice) **with a ~ in his voice** d'une voix émue; **4** (act of catching) prise f; **to take a ~** GB, **to make a ~** US Sport prendre la balle; **to play ~** jouer à la balle; **5** (haul) pêche f; (one fish) prise f; **6** (marriage partner) **a good ~** un beau parti

B vtr (prét, pp **caught**) **1** (hold and retain) [person] attraper [ball, fish]; [container] recueillir [water, dust]; (by running) [person] attraper [person]; **I managed to ~ her in** (at home) j'ai réussi à la trouver chez elle; **2** (take by surprise) prendre, attraper; **to ~ sb doing** surprendre qn en train de faire; **to be** ou **get caught** se faire prendre; **to ~ sb in the act, to ~ sb at it**○ prendre qn sur le fait; **you wouldn't ~ me smoking!** ce n'est pas moi qui fumerais!; **we got caught in the rain** nous avons été surpris par la pluie; **you've caught me at an awkward moment** vous tombez mal; **3** (be in time for) prendre [bus, train, plane]; avoir [last post]; **4** (manage to see) voir [programme]; aller voir [show]; **5** (grasp) prendre [hand, arm]; agripper [branch, rope]; captiver, éveiller [interest, imagination]; **to ~ hold of sth** attraper qch; **to ~ sb's attention** ou **eye** attirer l'attention de qn; **to ~ the chairman's eye** Admin obtenir la parole; **6** (hear) saisir○, comprendre; **7** (perceive) discerner [sound]; surprendre [look]; **to ~ sight of sb/sth** surprendre qn/qch; **8** (get stuck) **to ~ one's fingers in** se prendre les doigts dans [drawer, door]; **to ~ one's shirt on** accrocher sa chemise à [nail]; **to get caught in** [person] se prendre dans [net, thorns]; **9** Med attraper [disease, virus, flu]; **10** (hit, knock) heurter [object, person]; **11** (have an effect on) [light] faire briller [object]; [wind] emporter [paper, bag]; **to ~ one's breath** retenir son souffle; **12** (be affected by) **you've caught the sun** on voit bien que tu es resté au soleil; **to ~ fire** ou **light** prendre feu, s'enflammer; **to ~ the light** refléter la lumière; **13** (capture) rendre [atmosphere, spirit]; **14** Sport ▸ **catch out**, **15** (trick) ▸ **catch out**, **16** (manage to reach) ▸ **catch up**

C vi (prét, pp **caught**) **1** (become stuck) **to ~ on** [shirt, sleeve] s'accrocher à [nail]; [wheel] frotter contre [frame]; **2** (start to burn) [wood, fire] prendre

(Idiom) **you'll ~ it**○! tu vas en prendre une○!

(Phrasal verbs)

■ **catch on 1** (become popular) devenir populaire (**with** auprès de); **2** (understand) comprendre, saisir; **to ~ on to sth** comprendre qch

■ **catch out**: ▸ **~ [sb] out 1** (take by surprise) prendre [qn] de court; (doing something wrong) prendre [qn] sur le fait; **2** (trick) attraper, jouer un tour à; **3** (in cricket, baseball) éliminer [batsman]

■ **catch up**: ▸ **~ up** (in race) regagner du terrain; (in work) rattraper son retard; **to ~ up with** rattraper; **to ~ up on** rattraper [work, sleep]; se remettre au courant de [news, gossip]; ▸ **~ [sb/sth] up 1** (manage to reach) rattraper; **2 to ~ sth up in** (tangle) prendre [qch] dans [thorns, chain]; **to get one's feet caught up in sth** se prendre les pieds dans qch; **to get caught up in** se laisser entraîner par [excitement]; se trouver pris dans [traffic]; se trouver mêlé à [scandal, argument]

catch: **~-22 situation** n situation f inextricable; **~-all** adj [term] passe-partout inv; [clause] couvrant tous les cas de figure

catcher /'kætʃə(r)/ n Sport receveur m

catching /'kætʃɪŋ/ adj Med, fig contagieux/-ieuse

catchment area n secteur m desservi

catch: **~phrase** n formule f favorite, rengaine f; **~up** n = ketchup; **~word** n mot m d'ordre

catchy /'kætʃɪ/ adj [tune] entraînant; [slogan] accrocheur/-euse

catechism /'kætəkɪzəm/ n catéchisme m

categorical /ˌkætə'gɒrɪkl, US -'gɔːr-/, **categoric** /ˌkætə'gɒrɪk, US -'gɔːr-/ adj catégorique

categorically /ˌkætə'gɒrɪklɪ, US -'gɔːr-/ adv catégoriquement

categorize /'kætəgəraɪz/ vtr classer (**by** d'après)

category /'kætəgərɪ, US -gɔːrɪ/ n catégorie f

cater /'keɪtə(r)/ vi **1** (supply food etc) organiser des réceptions; **2 to ~ for** GB ou **to** US (accommodate) accueillir [children, guests]; pourvoir à [needs, tastes]; (aim at) [newspaper, programme] s'adresser à; **3** (fulfil) **to ~ to** satisfaire [whim, taste]

caterer /'keɪtərə(r)/ ▸ p. 1181 n traiteur m

catering /'keɪtərɪŋ/

A n (provision) approvisionnement m; (trade, industry, career) restauration f

B noun modifier [company, staff] de restauration; **~ course** études fpl spécialisées dans la restauration

caterpillar /'kætəpɪlə(r)/ n Zool, Tech chenille f

Caterpillar® /'kætəpɪlə(r)/ n engin m à chenilles

caterwaul /'kætəwɔːl/ vi miauler

caterwauling /'kætəwɔːlɪŋ/ n **C** miaulements mpl

cat: **~fish** n poisson-chat m; **~flap** n chattière f; **~ food** n aliments mpl pour chats; **~gut** n boyau m (de chat), catgut m

cathedral /kə'θiːdrəl/ n cathédrale f

Catherine wheel /'kæθrɪn wiːl, US -hwiːl/ n soleil m (feu d'artifice)

catheter /'kæθɪtə(r)/ n cathéter m

cathode /'kæθəʊd/ n sonde f, cathode f; **~-ray tube** tube m cathodique

catholic /'kæθəlɪk/ adj éclectique

Catholic /'kæθəlɪk/ n, adj catholique (mf)

Catholicism /kə'θɒlɪsɪzəm/ n catholicisme m

catkin /'kætkɪn/ n chaton m

catlike /'kætlaɪk/ adj félin

cat litter n litière f pour chats

catnap /'kætnæp/

A n somme m

B vi (p prés etc **-pp-**) faire un somme, sommeiller

cat: **~-o'-nine-tails** n (pl **~**) martinet m; **Catseye**® n GB plot m rétroréfléchissant; **~'s paw** n dupe f; **~suit** n combinaison-pantalon f

catsup /'kætsəp/ n US = ketchup

cattery /'kætərɪ/ n pension f pour chats

cattiness /'kætɪnɪs/ n méchanceté f

cattle /'kætl/

A n (+ v pl) bovins mpl

B noun modifier [breeder, raising, rustler] de bétail

cattle grid GB, **cattle guard** US n grille f (au sol qui empêche le passage du bétail)

cattle: **~ market** n lit marché m aux bestiaux; fig○ (for sexual encounters) lieu m de drague○; **~ shed** n étable f; **~ truck** n Aut fourgon m à bestiaux

catty /'kætɪ/ adj méchant (**about** envers)

catwalk /'kætwɔːk/ n **1** (walkway) passerelle f; **2** (at fashion show) podium m; **~ show** défilé m de mode

Caucasian /kɔː'keɪʒn, -'keɪzɪən/

A n **1** (white person) personne f de race blanche; **2** Geog (inhabitant) Caucasien/-ienne m/f

B adj **1** [race, man] blanc/blanche; **2** Geog caucasien/-ienne

caucus /'kɔːkəs/ n (pl **-es**) **1** (meeting) réunion f des instances dirigeantes; **2** (faction) groupe m

caught /kɔːt/ prét, pp ▸ **catch**

cauldron /'kɔːldrən/ n chaudron m

cauliflower /'kɒlɪflaʊə(r), US 'kɔːlɪ-/ n chou-fleur m; **to have a ~ ear**○ fig avoir l'oreille en chou-fleur○

cauliflower cheese n gratin m de chou-fleur

causal /'kɔːzl/ adj causal

causality /kɔː'zælətɪ/, **causation** /kɔː'zeɪʃn/ n causalité f

cause /kɔːz/

A n **1** (reason) cause f, raison f (**of** de); **there is/he has ~ for concern/optimism** il y a/il a des raisons de s'inquiéter/d'être optimiste; **to give sb ~ to do** donner à qn des raisons de faire; **to have ~ to do** avoir des raisons de faire; **to give ~ for concern** susciter des inquiétudes; **the immediate ~** la cause directe; **with good ~** à juste titre; **without good ~** sans motif valable; **2** (objective) cause f; **a lost ~** une cause perdue; **all in a good ~** pour la bonne cause; **in the ~ of equality** pour la cause de l'égalité; **3** Jur (grounds) cause f; **4** Jur (court action) action f

B vtr causer, occasionner [damage, grief, problem]; provoquer [chaos, delay, controversy, reaction]; susciter [excitement, surprise]; entraîner [suffering]; amener [dismay, confusion]; **to ~ sb to cry/leave** faire pleurer/partir qn; **to ~ sb problems** causer des problèmes à qn; **to ~ trouble** créer des problèmes; **to ~ cancer/migraine** donner or provoquer un cancer/la migraine

causeway /'kɔːzweɪ/ n chaussée f (vers une île)

caustic /'kɔːstɪk/ adj Chem, fig caustique; **~ soda** soude f caustique

cauterize /'kɔːtəraɪz/ vtr cautériser

caution /'kɔːʃn/

A n **1** (care) prudence f; **to err on the side of ~** pécher par excès de prudence; ~ **should be exercised** la prudence est de mise; ② (wariness) circonspection *f*; ③ (warning) avertissement *m*; **a word of** ~ un petit conseil; **'Caution! Drive slowly!'** 'Attention! Conduire lentement!'; ④ GB Jur (given to suspect) **to be under** ~ faire l'objet d'une mise en garde; ⑤ Jur (admonition) avertissement *m*

B *vtr* ① (warn) avertir (that que); **'he's dangerous,'** she ~ed 'il est dangereux,' dit-elle à titre de mise en garde; **to** ~ **sb against doing** avertir qn de ne pas faire; **to** ~ **sb against** *ou* **about** mettre qn en garde contre [*danger*]; ② Jur [*policeman*] informer [qn] de ses droits [*suspect*]; ③ Jur (admonish) réprimander; ④ Sport donner un avertissement à [*player*]

(Idiom) **to throw** *ou* **cast** ~ **to the wind(s)** oublier toute prudence

cautionary /'kɔːʃənərɪ, US -nerɪ/ *adj* (*épith*) [*look, gesture*] d'avertissement; **a** ~ **word** *ou* **comment** un avertissement; **a** ~ **tale** un conte moral

cautious /'kɔːʃəs/ *adj* ① (careful) prudent; ② (wary) [*person, reception, response*] réservé; [*optimism*] prudent; **to be** ~ **about doing** ne pas aimer faire

cautiously /'kɔːʃəslɪ/ *adv* ① (carefully) prudemment; ② (warily) avec circonspection; [*optimistic, confident*] raisonnablement

cavalcade /ˌkævl'keɪd/ *n* (on horseback) cavalcade *f*; (motorized) cortège *m*

cavalier /ˌkævə'lɪə(r)/
A Cavalier *pr n* GB Hist cavalier *m* (*partisan de Charles Premier*)
B *adj* cavalier/-ière

cavalry /'kævlrɪ/ *n* cavalerie *f*

cave /keɪv/ *n* grotte *f*
(Phrasal verb)
■ **cave in**: ▸ ~ **in** ① lit [*tunnel, roof, building*] s'effondrer; ② fig [*person*] céder

caveat /'kævɪæt, US 'keɪvɪæt/ *n* mise *f* en garde

cave: ~ **dweller** *n* troglodyte *m*; ~**-in** *n* effondrement *m*; ~**man** *n* (*pl* **-men**) homme *m* des cavernes; ~ **painting** *n* peinture *f* rupestre

caver /'keɪvə(r)/ *n* spéléologue *mf*

cavern /'kævən/ *n* caverne *f*

cavernous /'kævənəs/ *adj* [*groan, voice, room*] caverneux/-euse; [*mouth, yawn*] énorme; [*eyes*] cave

caviar(e) /'kævɪɑː(r), ˌkævɪ'ɑː(r)/ *n* caviar *m*

cavil /'kævl/ *vi* (*p prés etc* **-ll-, -l-** US) ergoter (**about, at** sur)

caving /'keɪvɪŋ/ *n* spéléologie *f*; **to go** ~ faire de la spéléologie

cavity /'kævətɪ/ *n* cavité *f*

cavity: ~ **block** *n* GB moellon *m* creux; ~ **wall insulation** *n* isolation *f* des murs creux

cavort /kə'vɔːt/ *vi* (*also* ~ **about**, ~ **around**) faire des cabrioles *fpl*

caw /'kɔː/
A *n* ① (noise) croassement *m*; ② (cry) croa!
B *vi* croasser

cayenne (pepper) /keɪ'en/ *n* poivre *m* de Cayenne

CB (*abrév* = **Citizens' Band**)
A *n* bande *f* CB
B *noun modifier* [*equipment, radio, wavelength*] CB; ~ **user** cibiste *mf*

CBI *n* GB (*abrév* = **Confederation of British Industry**) patronat britannique; *cf* CNPF

cc ▸ p. 1311 *n* (*abrév* = **cubic centimetre**) cm³

CC *n* GB *abrév* ▸ **County Council**

CCT *n*: *abrév* ▸ **closed-circuit television**

CD *n* ① (*abrév* = **compact disc**) (disque *m*) compact *m*; **on** ~ sur (disque) compact; ② (*abrév* = **corps diplomatique**) CD; ③ Mil *abrév* ▸ **Civil Defence**; ④ US *abrév* ▸ **Congressional District**

CD burner *n* Comput graveur *m* de CD

CDI *n* (*abrév* = **compact disc interactive**) CD-I *m*, disque *m* compact interactif

CD player, **CD system** *n* platine *f* laser

Cdr *n* Mil (*abrév écrite* = **Commander**) *cf* capitaine *m* de frégate

CD-R *n* Comput CD-R *m*

CD-ROM /ˌsiːdiː'rɒm/ *n* CD-ROM *m*, cédérom *m*; **on** ~ sur CD-ROM

CD-RW *n* Comput CD-RW *m*

cease /siːs/
A *n* **without** ~ sans cesse
B *vtr* cesser; **you never** ~ **to amaze me!** tu m'étonneras toujours!; **to** ~ **fire** cesser le feu
C *vi* cesser

cease-fire /'siːsfaɪə(r)/
A *n* cessez-le-feu *m inv*
B *noun modifier* [*agreement*] de cessez-le-feu; [*call*] au cessez-le-feu

ceaseless /'siːslɪs/ *adj* incessant

ceaselessly /'siːslɪslɪ/ *adv* [*labour, talk*] sans cesse; [*active, vigilant*] continuellement

cedar /'siːdə(r)/ *n* cèdre *m*

cede /siːd/ *vtr*, *vi* céder (**to** à)

cedilla /sɪ'dɪlə/ *n* cédille *f*

ceiling /'siːlɪŋ/ *n* lit, fig plafond *m*; **to set a** ~ fixer un plafond
(Idiom) **to hit the** ~ US sortir de ses gonds

ceiling: ~ **light** *n* plafonnier *m*; ~ **price** *n* Comm, Econ prix *m* plafond

celebrate /'selɪbreɪt/
A *vtr* ① fêter [*occasion*]; (more formally) célébrer; **there's nothing/there's something to** ~ il n'y a pas de quoi/il y a de quoi se réjouir; ② Relig célébrer [*mass, Easter*]; ③ (pay tribute to) célébrer
B *vi* faire la fête; **let's** ~! il faut fêter ça!

celebrated /'selɪbreɪtɪd/ *adj* célèbre

celebration /ˌselɪ'breɪʃn/ *n* ① ₡ (action of celebrating) célébration *f*; ② (party) fête *f*; **to have a** ~ faire une fête; ③ (public festivities) ~**s** cérémonies *fpl*; ④ (tribute) hommage *m* (**of** à); ⑤ Relig célébration *f*

celebratory /ˌselɪ'breɪtərɪ, US -tɔːrɪ/ *adj* [*air, mood*] de fête; **a** ~ **drink** un verre pour célébrer

celebrity /sɪ'lebrətɪ/
A *n* célébrité *f*
B *noun modifier* [*guest*] célèbre; [*panel*] de célébrités

celeriac /sɪ'lerɪæk/ *n* céleri-rave *m*

celery /'selərɪ/ *n* céleri *m*; **a stick/head of** ~ une côte/un pied de céleri; **braised** ~ céleris *mpl* braisés

celestial /sɪ'lestɪəl/ *adj* céleste

celibacy /'selɪbəsɪ/ *n* (unmarried) célibat *m*; (abstaining) chasteté *f*

celibate /'selɪbət/
A *n* (unmarried) célibataire *mf*; (chaste) personne *f* chaste
B *adj* (unmarried) célibataire; (chaste) chaste

cell /sel/ *n* ① (for prisoner, monk) cellule *f*; ② Biol, Bot cellule *f*; ③ Elec, Chem élément *m*; ④ Pol cellule *f*; ⑤ Telecom cellule *f*

cellar /'selə(r)/ *n* cave *f*

cellist /'tʃelɪst/ ▸ p. 1181, p. 1028 *n* violoncelliste *mf*

cello /'tʃeləʊ/ ▸ p. 1028 *n* violoncelle *m*

cellphone /'selfəʊn/ *n* radiotéléphone *m*

cellular /'seljʊlə(r)/ *adj* Biol cellulaire

cellular phone, **cellular telephone** *n* radiotéléphone *m*

cellulite /'seljʊlaɪt/ *n* cellulite *f*, peau *f* d'orange○

celluloid® /'seljʊlɔɪd/ *n* celluloïd® *m*

cellulose /'seljʊləʊs/ *n* cellulose *f*

Celsius /'selsɪəs/ *adj* Celsius *inv*

Celt /kelt, US selt/ *n* Celte *mf*

Celtic /'keltɪk, US 'seltɪk/ *adj* celtique, celte

cement /sɪ'ment/
A *n* ① Constr ciment *m*; (for tiles) mastic *m*; ② (in dentistry) amalgame *m*; ③ fig ciment *m*
B *vtr* ① lit, fig cimenter; ② [*dentist*] obturer

cement mixer *n* bétonnière *f*

cemetery /'semətrɪ, US -terɪ/ *n* cimetière *m*

cenotaph /'senətɑːf, US -tæf/ *n* cénotaphe *m*

censor /'sensə(r)/
A *n* censeur *m*
B *vtr* censurer

censorious /sen'sɔːrɪəs/ *adj* sévère (**of** envers)

censorship /ˈsensəʃɪp/ n (all contexts) censure f

censure /ˈsenʃə(r)/
A n censure f; **vote of** ∼ vote m de censure
B vtr critiquer

census /ˈsensəs/ n recensement m; **traffic** ∼ étude f chiffrée de la circulation

cent /sent/ ▶ p. 782 n (of dollar) cent m; (of euro) centime m (d'euro); Belg cent m; **I haven't got a** ∼ je n'ai pas un sou

centenarian /ˌsentɪˈneərɪən/ n, adj centenaire (mf)

centenary /senˈtiːnərɪ/ n centenaire m

centennial /senˈtenɪəl/
A n US centenaire m
B adj (every 100 years) séculaire; (lasting 100 years) centenaire

center n US = **centre**

centigrade /ˈsentɪɡreɪd/ adj [thermometer] Celsius; **in degrees** ∼ en degrés Celsius

centilitre GB, **centiliter** US /ˈsentɪliːtə(r)/ ▶ p. 1311 n centilitre m

centimetre GB, **centimeter** US /ˈsentɪmiːtə(r)/ ▶ p. 977 n centimètre m

centipede /ˈsentɪpiːd/ n mille-pattes m inv

central /ˈsentrəl/
A Central pr n (also **Central Region**) (Hist: in Scotland) la région Central
B adj **1** (in the middle) central; ∼ **London** le centre de Londres; **2** (in the town centre) situé en centre-ville; **3** (key) principal; ∼ **to** essentiel à; **4** Admin, Pol central

central: **Central African Republic** pr n République f centrafricaine; **Central America** pr n Amérique f centrale; **Central American** adj d'Amérique centrale; **Central Europe** pr n Europe f centrale; **Central European** adj d'Europe centrale; ∼ **heating** n chauffage m central

centralization /ˌsentrəlaɪˈzeɪʃn, US -lɪˈz-/ n centralisation f

centralize /ˈsentrəlaɪz/ vtr centraliser

central locking n Aut verrouillage m central or centralisé

centrally /ˈsentrəlɪ/ adv [live, work] en centre-ville; [situated] en centre-ville; [funded, managed] de façon centralisée; ∼ **heated** [flat] avec chauffage central; ∼ **planned** n planification centralisée

central: ∼ **nervous system** n système m nerveux central; ∼ **processing unit**, CPU, ∼ **processor** n Comput unité f centrale; ∼ **reservation** n GB (on motorway) terre-plein m central

centre GB, **center** US /ˈsentə(r)/
A n **1** (middle) centre m; **in the** ∼ au centre; **the** ∼ **of London** le centre de Londres; **town** ∼, **city** ∼ centre-ville m; **sweets with soft** ∼s bonbons mpl fourrés; **2** (focus) centre m; **to be at the** ∼ **of a row** être au centre d'une dispute; **the** ∼ **of attention** le centre de l'attention; **3** (seat) siège m; **4** (area) centre m; **business** ∼ quartier m des affaires; **shopping/sports/leisure** ∼ centre m commercial/sportif/ de loisirs; **5** Pol centre m; **to be left of** ∼ être à gauche du centre; **a** ∼**-left party** un parti du centre gauche; **6** Sport centre m; ▶ **left**
B noun modifier gen central; [parting] au milieu
C vtr, vi Comput, Sport, Tech centrer; **child-centred** centré sur l'enfant

⸨Phrasal verb⸩

■ **centre around**, **centre on**: ▶ ∼ around [sth] [activities, person] se concentrer sur; [people, industry] se situer autour de [town]; [life, thoughts] être centré sur [person, work]; [demands] viser [pay]

centre-fold /ˈsentəfəʊld/ n (pin-up) (picture) photo f de pin-up (sur double page); (model) pin-up f

centre-forward /ˌsentəˈfɔːwəd/ n Sport avant-centre m

centre ground n centre m; **to occupy the** ∼ être au centre

centre: ∼**-half** n Sport demi-centre m; ∼ **of gravity** GB, **center of gravity** US, **cg** n centre m de gravité; ∼**-piece** n (of table) décoration f centrale; (of exhibition) clou m; ∼ **spread** n double page f du milieu

centre-stage /ˌsentəˈsteɪdʒ/
A n **1** Theat centre m de la scène; **2** fig (prime position) **to take/ occupy** ∼ devenir/être le point de mire
B adv **to stand** ∼ se tenir au centre de la scène

centrifugal /ˌsentrɪˈfjuːɡl, senˈtrɪfjʊɡl/ adj centrifuge

centrifuge /ˈsentrɪfjuːdʒ/ n centrifugeuse f

century /ˈsentʃərɪ/ ▶ p. 1267 n siècle m; **in the 20th** ∼ au XXᵉ siècle; **at the turn of the** ∼ au début du siècle; **half a** ∼ un demi-siècle; **centuries-old** séculaire

ceramic /sɪˈræmɪk/
A n céramique f
B adj [tile, pot] en céramique; [hob] en vitro-céramique; [design, art] de la céramique

ceramics /sɪˈræmɪks/ n **1** (+ v sg) (study) la céramique; **2** (+ v pl) (artefacts) céramiques fpl

cereal /ˈsɪərɪəl/
A n céréale f; (for breakfast) céréales fpl; **breakfast** ∼ céréales pour le petit déjeuner
B adj [harvest, imports] de céréales; [crop, production] céréalier/ -ière

cerebral /ˈserɪbrəl, US səˈriːbrəl/ adj Med cérébral; fig intellectuel/-elle

cerebral palsy /ˌserɪbrəl ˈpɔːlzɪ, US səˈriːbrəl/ ▶ p. 933 n paralysie f motrice centrale

ceremonial /ˌserɪˈməʊnɪəl/
A n cérémonial m; (religious) rites mpl
B adj **1** [dress] de cérémonie; **2** (ritual) cérémoniel/-ielle; (solemn) solennel/-elle; (official) officiel/-ielle

ceremonially /ˌserɪˈməʊnɪəlɪ/ adv selon le cérémonial d'usage

ceremoniously /ˌserɪˈməʊnɪəslɪ/ adv avec cérémonie

ceremony /ˈserɪmənɪ, US -məʊnɪ/ n **1** (event) cérémonie f; **marriage** ∼ cérémonie f du mariage; **2** ¢ (protocol) cérémonies fpl; **to stand on** ∼ faire des cérémonies

cert /sɜːt/ n GB it's a (dead) ∼! ça ne fait pas un pli!

certain /ˈsɜːtn/
A pron ∼ **of our members/friends** certains de nos adhérents/amis
B adj **1** (sure, definite) certain, sûr (**about, of** de); **I'm** ∼ **of it** ou **that** j'en suis certain or sûr; **of that you can be** ∼ tu peux en être sûr; **absolutely** ∼ sûr et certain; **I'm** ∼ **that I checked** je suis sûr d'avoir vérifié; **I'm** ∼ **that he refused** je suis sûr qu'il a refusé; **she's not** ∼ **that you'll be able to do it** elle n'est pas sûre que tu sois capable de le faire; **to make** ∼ s'en assurer, vérifier; **to make** ∼ **of** s'assurer de [cooperation, support]; vérifier [facts, details]; **to make** ∼ **to do** faire bien attention de faire; **to make** ∼ **that** (ascertain) vérifier que; (ensure) faire en sorte que (+ subj); **he's** ∼ **to be there** il y sera certainement or sûrement; **the strike seems** ∼ **to continue** il est presque certain que la grève continuera; **I know for** ∼ **that** je sais de façon sûre que; **be** ∼ **to tell him that** n'oublie pas de lui dire que; **nobody knows for** ∼ personne ne sait au juste; **I can't say for** ∼ je ne sais pas au juste; **2** (assured, guaranteed) [death, defeat] certain (after n); **to be** ∼ **of doing** être sûr de faire; **he's** ∼ **to agree** il sera d'accord, il n'y a aucun doute là-dessus; **the changes are** ∼ **to provoke anger** ces changements provoqueront sûrement des réactions violentes; **to my** ∼ **knowledge** à ma connaissance; **in the** ∼ **knowledge that he would fail** tout en sachant très bien qu'il allait échouer; **3** (specific) [amount, number] certain (before n); ∼ **people** certains mpl; **4** (slight) [shyness, difficulty] certain (before n); **to a** ∼ **extent** ou **degree** dans une certaine mesure; **a** ∼ **amount of time** un certain temps

certainly /ˈsɜːtnlɪ/ adv (without doubt) certainement; (indicating assent) certainement, bien sûr; ∼ **not!** certainement pas!; **it's** ∼ **possible that** il est tout à fait possible que (+ subj); **this exercise is** ∼ **very difficult** cet exercice est vraiment très difficile; **we shall** ∼ **attend the meeting** nous serons à la réunion sans faute; **he** ∼ **got his revenge!** iron c'est sûr qu'il a pris sa revanche!; **'are you annoyed?'—'I most** ∼ **am!'** 'tu es fâché?'—'ah! ça, oui alors!'

certainty /ˈsɜːtntɪ/ n **1** (sure thing) certitude f (**about** quant à); **for a** ∼ à coup sûr; **it's by no means a** ∼ ce n'est pas du tout sûr (**that** que + subj); **this candidate is a** ∼ **for election** ce candidat est sûr d'être élu; **she is a** ∼ **to play** elle est sûre de jouer; **2** ¢ (guarantee) certitude f (**of** de); **we have no** ∼ **of success** nous ne sommes pas certains de réussir

certifiable /ˌsɜːtɪˈfaɪəbl/ adj **1** (mad) dont l'état justifie l'internement; **2** (verifiable) [statement, evidence] vérifiable

certificate /səˈtɪfɪkət/ n **1** (academic) certificat m; (more advanced) diplôme m; **2** (for electrician, instructor, first-aider etc) brevet m; **3** (of child's proficiency in sth) brevet m; **4** (of safety, building standards etc) certificat *m*; **test** ~, **MOT** ~ GB certificat *m* de contrôle technique; **5** Admin (of birth, death, marriage) acte *m*; **6** Comm (of authenticity, quality) certificat *m*; **7** Cin **18-**~ **film** film interdit aux moins de 18 ans

certification /ˌsɜːtɪfɪ'keɪʃn/ *n* **1** Jur (of document) authentification *f*; (of ship) certification *f*; (of ownership) certificat *m*; **2** (document) certificat *m*; **3** (of mental patient) mandat *m* d'internement psychiatrique

certified: ~ **bankrupt** *n* débiteur *m* (failli); ~ **public accountant**, **CPA** *n* US expert-comptable *m* agréé

certify /'sɜːtɪfaɪ/
A *vtr* **1** (confirm) certifier, constater [*death*]; **to** ~ **sth a true copy** certifier qch pour copie conforme; **to** ~ **sb insane** certifier que qn est atteint d'aliénation mentale; **2** (authenticate) authentifier; **3** (issue certificate to) délivrer un certificat d'aptitude professionnelle à; **4** Comm garantir [*goods*]
B **certified** *pp adj* certifié; [*teacher*] US Sch qualifié; **to send by certified mail** US envoyer en recommandé

certitude /'sɜːtɪtjuːd, US -tuːd/ *n* certitude *f*, conviction *f*

cervical /'sɜːvɪkl/ *adj* cervical; ~ **cancer** ▸ p. 933 cancer *m* du col de l'utérus; ~ **smear** frottis *m* vaginal

cervix /'sɜːvɪks/ *n* col *m* de l'utérus

cesspit /'sespɪt/, **cesspool** /'sespuːl/ *n* fosse *f* d'aisances

Ceylon /sɪ'lɒn/
A *pr n* Hist Ceylan *m*
B *noun modifier* ~ **tea** thé *m* de Ceylan

CFC *n* Ecol (abrév = **chlorofluorocarbon**) CFC *m*; **'contains no** ~**s'** 'sans CFC'

CFE *n* GB (abrév = **College of Further Education**) ≈ centre *m* de formation continue

cg **1** (abrév = **centigram**) cg; **2** abrév ▸ **centre of gravity**

Chad /tʃæd/ ▸ p. 774 *pr n* Tchad *m*

chafe /tʃeɪf/
A *vtr* (rub) irriter; (restore circulation) frictionner
B *vi* (rub) frotter (**on**, **against** sur)
(Idiom) **to** ~ **at the bit** ronger son frein

chaff /tʃɑːf, tʃæf, US tʃæf/
A *n* Agric (husks) balle *f*; (fodder) menue paille *f*
B *vtr* plaisanter (**about** sur)

chaffinch /'tʃæfɪntʃ/ *n* pinson *m*

chagrin /'ʃægrɪn, US ʃə'griːn/ *n* dépit *m*; **(much) to his** ~ à son grand dépit

chain /tʃeɪn/
A *n* **1** (metal links) chaîne *f*; **a length of** ~ une chaîne; **to put** *ou* **keep sb in** ~**s** enchaîner qn; **to keep a dog on a** ~ tenir un chien à la chaîne; **2** (on lavatory) chasse *f* (d'eau); **3** (on door) chaîne *f* de sûreté; **4** Comm chaîne *f* (**of** de); **supermarket/hotel** ~ chaîne *f* de supermarchés/d'hôtels; **5** (series) (of events) série *f*; (of ideas) enchaînement *m*; ~ **of causation** rapport *m* or relation *f* de cause à effet; **a link in the** ~ un maillon de la chaîne; **to make** *ou* **form a (human)** ~ faire la chaîne, faire une chaîne humaine; **6** Biol, Geog, Phys chaîne *f*; **7** (measurement) = 20,12 m
B *vtr* enchaîner [*person*]; **to** ~ **sb's wrists** attacher les poignets de qn avec des chaînes; **to** ~ **a bicycle to sth** attacher une bicyclette à qch avec une chaîne; **to be** ~**ed to one's desk/the kitchen sink** fig être esclave de son travail/ ses casseroles

chain: ~ **gang** *n* chaîne *f* de forçats; ~ **letter** *n* (lettre *f* de) chaîne *f*; ~ **mail** *n* cotte *f* de mailles; ~ **of command** *n* hiérarchie *f*; ~ **reaction** *n* réaction *f* en chaîne; ~ **saw** *n* tronçonneuse *f*; ~**-smoke** *vi* fumer comme un sapeur○, fumer sans arrêt; ~**-smoker** *n* gros fumeur/grosse fumeuse *m/f*; ~ **store** *n* (single shop) magasin *m* faisant partie d'une chaîne; (retail group) magasin *m* à succursales multiples

chair /tʃeə(r)/
A *n* **1** (seat) (wooden) chaise *f*; (upholstered) fauteuil *m*; **to take a** ~ s'asseoir; **2** (chairperson) président/-e *m/f*; **to take** *ou* **be in the** ~ présider; **3** (professorship) chaire *f* (**of**, **in** de); **to hold the** ~ **of...** être titulaire de la chaire de...; **4** US (also **electric** ~) **to go to the** ~ passer sur la chaise électrique
B *vtr* présider [*meeting*]

chair lift *n* télésiège *m*

chairman /'tʃeəmən/ ▸ p. 869 *n* président/-e *m/f*; **Mr Chairman** monsieur le Président; **Madam Chairman** madame la Présidente

⚠ L'usage moderne préfère *chairperson*

chairmanship /'tʃeəmənʃɪp/ *n* présidence *f*

chairperson /'tʃeəpɜːsn/ *n* président/-e *m/f*

chairwoman /'tʃeəwʊmən/ ▸ p. 869 *n* présidente *f*

chalet /'ʃæleɪ/ *n* (mountain) chalet *m*; (in holiday camp) bungalow *m*

chalice /'tʃælɪs/ *n* calice *m*

chalk /tʃɔːk/
A *n* craie *f*; **a piece of** ~ un bâton de craie
B *noun modifier* **1** gen, Art [*drawing*] à la craie; ~ **mark** (on blackboard) trace *f* de craie; (in sewing) repère *m* à la craie; **2** [*cliff, landscape*] de craie
C *vtr* **1** (write) écrire [qch] à la craie; **2** (apply chalk to) frotter [qch] avec de la craie
(Idioms) **not by a long** ~○! loin de là○!; **white as** ~ blanc comme un linge
(Phrasal verbs)
■ **chalk out**: ▸ ~ **out** [sth], ~ [sth] **out** tracer [qch] à la craie
■ **chalk up**: ▸ ~ [sth] **up**, ~ **up** [sth] lit, fig marquer [*score, points*]; ~ **it up to experience** la prochaine fois vous saurez

chalkboard /'tʃɔːkbɔːd/ *n* US tableau *m* (noir)

chalky /'tʃɔːkɪ/ *adj* [*soil*] crayeux/-euse; [*hands*] couvert de craie

challenge /'tʃælɪndʒ/
A *n* **1** (provocation) défi *m*; **to put out** *ou* **issue a** ~ lancer un défi; **to take up a** ~ relever un défi; **2** (situation or opportunity) (stimulating) challenge *m*; (considered difficult) épreuve *f*; **to present a** ~ représenter un challenge; **to rise to** *ou* **meet the** ~ relever le challenge; **to face a** ~ affronter une épreuve; **unemployment is a** ~ **for us** le chômage nous met à l'épreuve; **I'm looking for a** ~ je cherche un défi à relever; **the** ~ **of new ideas** la stimulation des idées nouvelles; **3** (contest) **to make a** ~ **for** essayer de s'emparer de [*title*]; entrer dans la course à [*presidency*]; **leadership** ~ Pol tentative *f* pour s'emparer de la direction du parti; **4** (questioning) (of claim, authority) contestation *f* (**to** de); **5** Sport attaque *f*
B *vtr* **1** (invite to justify) défier [*person*] (**to** à; **to do** de faire); **to** ~ **sb to a duel** provoquer qn en duel; **2** (question) débattre [*ideas*]; contester [*statement, authority*]; [*sentry*] faire une sommation à; **3** (test) mettre à l'épreuve [*skill, person*]

challenger /'tʃælɪndʒə(r)/ *n* challenger *m* (**for** de)

challenging /'tʃælɪndʒɪŋ/ *adj* **1** (stimulating) [*ideas, career*] stimulant; [*task*] qui représente un challenge; [*work*] difficile mais motivant; [*book*] d'un abord difficile; **2** (confrontational) provocateur/-trice

chamber /'tʃeɪmbə(r)/ *n* **1** gen, Tech chambre *f*; **council** ~ GB salle *f* de réunion; **2** GB Pol **the upper/lower** ~ la Chambre des lords/des communes; **3** Anat (of heart) cavité *f*; (of eye) chambre *f*; **4** (cave) salle *f*; **5** **chambers** *npl* Jur cabinet *m*

chamber: ~**maid** ▸ p. 1181 *n* femme *f* de chambre; ~ **music** *n* musique *f* de chambre; **Chamber of Commerce**, **C of C** *n* chambre *f* de commerce et d'industrie; ~ **orchestra** *n* orchestre *m* de chambre; ~ **pot** *n* pot *m* de chambre

chameleon /kə'miːlɪən/ *n* caméléon *m* also fig

chamois /'ʃæmwɑː, US 'ʃæmɪ/ *n* (*pl* ~) Zool chamois *m*

chamois cloth US, **chamois leather** *n* peau *f* de chamois

champ /tʃæmp/
A *vtr* mâchonner
B *vi* **to** ~ **at the bit** [*horse*] piaffer d'impatience; [*person*] fig ronger son frein

champagne /ʃæm'peɪn/ *n, adj* champagne (*m*) inv

champagne glass *n* (tall) flûte *f* à champagne; (open) coupe *f* à champagne

champion /'tʃæmpɪən/
A *n* champion/-ionne *m/f*; **world** ~ champion/-ionne *m/f* du monde; ~ **boxer**, **boxing** ~ champion *m* de boxe
B *vtr* se faire le champion de [*cause*]; prendre fait et cause pour [*person*]

championship /'tʃæmpɪənʃɪp/ *n* championnat *m*

chance /tʃɑːns, US tʃæns/

A n **1** (opportunity) occasion f; **to have** ou **get the ∼ to do** avoir l'occasion de faire; **give me a ∼ to explain** laisse-moi t'expliquer; **to take one's ∼** saisir l'occasion; **you've missed your ∼** tu as laissé passer l'occasion; **now's your ∼!** c'est l'occasion ou jamais!; **I haven't had a ∼ yet** je n'en ai pas encore eu l'occasion; **this is your big ∼** c'est l'occasion ou jamais; **if you get a** ou **the ∼, can you…?** quand tu auras le temps est-ce que tu pourras…?; **2** (likelihood) chance f; **there's little ∼ of sb doing** il y a peu de chances que qn fasse; **the ∼s of catching the thief are slim** il y a peu de chances qu'on attrape le voleur; **there is a ∼ that sb will do** il y a des chances que qn fasse; **the ∼s are that** il y a de grandes chances que (+ *subj*); **the ∼s of sb doing are poor** il y a peu de chances que qn fasse; **she has a good ∼** elle a de bonnes chances; **what are his ∼s of recovery?** a-t-il des chances de s'en tirer?; **any ∼ of a coffee**○? est-ce que c'est possible d'avoir un café?; **3** (luck) hasard m; **a game of ∼** un jeu de hasard; **by ∼** par hasard; **4** (risk) risque m; **to take a ∼** prendre un risque; **it's a ∼ I'm willing to take** c'est un risque à prendre; **5** (possibility) chance f; **not to stand a ∼** n'avoir aucune chance; **do you have his address by any ∼?** auriez-vous, par hasard, son adresse?

B noun modifier [encounter, occurrence] fortuit; [discovery] accidentel/-elle

C vtr **1** **to ∼ doing** courir le risque de faire; **to ∼ one's arm, to ∼ it** tenter sa chance; **I wouldn't ∼ it** je ne risquerais pas le coup; **2** (happen to do) **I ∼d to see it** je l'ai vu par hasard

(Idiom) **no ∼**○! pas question○!

(Phrasal verb)

■ **chance upon, chance on**: ▸ **∼ upon [sb]** rencontrer [qn] par hasard; ▸ **∼ upon [sth]** trouver [qch] par hasard

chancel /ˈtʃɑːnsl, US tʃænsl/ n Archit chœur m

chancellor /ˈtʃɑːnsələ(r), US ˈtʃæns-/ n **1** (head of government) chancelier m; **2** Univ ≈ président m

Chancellor of the Exchequer n GB Pol Chancelier m de l'Échiquier

chancy○ /ˈtʃɑːnsɪ, US ˈtʃænsɪ/ adj risqué

chandelier /ˌʃændəˈlɪə(r)/ n lustre m

chandler /ˈtʃɑːndlə(r), US ˈtʃæn-/ ▸ **p. 1181** n (also **ship's ∼**) vendeur m de matériel pour bateaux

change /tʃeɪndʒ/

A n **1** (alteration) (by replacement) changement m; (by adjustment) modification f; **the ∼ in the schedule** la modification du programme; **∼ of plan** changement de programme; **∼ for the better/worse** un changement en mieux/pire; **social ∼** changements sociaux; **to make a ∼ in sth** changer qch; **to make ∼s in** apporter des changements à [text]; faire des changements dans [room, company]; **there will have to be a ∼ in your attitude** il va falloir que vous changiez d'attitude; **people opposed to ∼** les personnes qui sont contre le progrès; **2** (substitution, replacement) changement m (of de); **costume ∼** Theat changement de costume; **∼ of government** Pol changement de gouvernement; **3** (fresh, different experience) changement m; **it makes a ∼ from television/from staying at home** cela change un peu de la télévision/de rester chez soi; **that makes a nice** ou **refreshing ∼** ça change agréablement; **she needs a ∼** elle a besoin de se changer les idées; **to need a ∼ of air** avoir besoin de changer d'air; **for a ∼** pour changer; **to ring the ∼s** fig introduire des changements; **4** (of clothes) **∼ of clothes** des vêtements de rechange; **5** (cash) monnaie f; **small ∼** petite monnaie; **she gave me 6p ∼** elle m'a rendu 6 pence; **have you got ∼ for £10?** pouvez-vous me changer un billet de 10 livres?; **60p in ∼** 60 pence en petite monnaie; **'no ∼ given'** (on machine) 'ne rend pas la monnaie'; **'exact ∼ please'** 'faites l'appoint, s'il vous plaît'; **you won't get much ∼ out of £20**○ tu vas payer près de 20 livres

B vtr **1** (alter) (completely) changer; (in part) modifier; **we have ∼d the look of the town** nous avons modifié l'aspect de la ville; **to ∼ X into Y** transformer X en Y; **to ∼ one's mind** changer d'avis (about à propos de); **to ∼ one's mind about doing** abandonner l'idée de faire; **to ∼ sb's mind** faire changer qn d'avis; **to ∼ one's ways** changer de mode de vie; **that won't ∼ anything** ça n'y changera rien; **2** (exchange for sth different) gen changer de [clothes, name, car]; (in shop) échanger [item] (for pour); **can I ∼ it for a size 12?**

est-ce que je peux l'échanger contre une taille 12?; **if it's too big, we'll ∼ it for you** s'il est trop grand, nous vous l'échangerons; **to ∼ colour** changer de couleur; **hurry up and get ∼d!** dépêche-toi de te changer!; **to ∼ sth from X to Y** (of numbers, letters, words) remplacer X par Y; (of building, area etc) transformer X en Y; **they ∼d their car for a smaller one** ils ont remplacé leur voiture par un modèle plus petit; **3** (replace sth dirty, old, broken) changer; **to ∼ a bed** changer les draps; **4** (exchange with sb) échanger [clothes, seats]; **to ∼ places** changer de place (with avec); fig (roles) intervertir les rôles; **I wouldn't ∼ places with the Queen** je ne voudrais pas être à la place de la Reine; **5** (actively switch) changer de [side, job, direction, TV channel, doctor]; **to ∼ hands** fig [property, object] changer de propriétaire; **no money ∼d hands** il n'y a pas eu d'échange d'argent; **6** (alter character) changer; **to ∼ sb/sth into** changer qn/qch en [frog, prince]; **sugar is ∼d into alcohol** le sucre se transforme en alcool; **7** (replace nappy of) changer [baby]; **8** (convert) changer [cheque, currency] (**into, for** en)

C vi **1** (alter) gen changer; [wind] tourner; **to ∼ from X to Y** passer de X à Y; **2** (into different clothes) se changer; **to ∼ into** passer [different garment]; **to ∼ out of** ôter, enlever [garment]; **3** (from bus, train) changer; **'∼ at Tours for Paris'** 'correspondance à Tours pour Paris'; **all ∼!** tout le monde descend!; **4** (become transformed) se métamorphoser

D **changed** pp adj [man, woman] autre (before n)

(Phrasal verbs)

■ **change down** GB Aut rétrograder

■ **change over**: ▸ **∼ over** (swap) [drivers] changer; **to ∼ over from sth to sth** passer de qch à qch; ▸ **∼ over [sth/sb]**, **∼ [sth/sb] over** intervertir

■ **change round**: ▸ **∼ round** GB changer de place; ▸ **∼ [sth/sb] round**, **∼ round [sth/sb]** déplacer [large objects]; changer [qn/qch] de place [workers, objects, words]

■ **change up** GB Aut passer à une vitesse supérieure

changeable /ˈtʃeɪndʒəbl/ adj [condition, behaviour, opinion, weather] changeant; [price, rate] variable; **∼ moods** sautes d'humeur

changeless /ˈtʃeɪndʒlɪs/ adj [law, routine] immuable; [appearance] inaltérable; [character] constant

change: **∼ machine** n distributeur m de monnaie; **∼ of address** n changement m d'adresse; **∼ of life** n retour m d'âge

changeover /ˈtʃeɪndʒəʊvə(r)/ n **1** (time period) phase f de changement; **2** (transition) passage m (**to** à); **3** (of leaders) remaniement m; (of employees, guards) relève f; **4** Sport (of ends) changement m; (in relay) passage m du témoin

changing /ˈtʃeɪndʒɪŋ/

A n changement m

B adj [colours, environment] changeant; [attitude, world] en évolution

changing-room /ˈtʃeɪndʒɪŋ ruːm, rʊm/ n Sport vestiaire m; US (fitting room) cabine f d'essayage

channel /ˈtʃænl/

A n **1** (passage for liquid) canal m; **2** (navigable water) chenal m; **3** (diplomatic, commercial) canal m; **to do sth through the proper** ou **usual** ou **normal ∼s** faire qch par la voie normale; **to go through official ∼s** passer par la voie officielle; **diplomatic/legal ∼s** voie f diplomatique/légale; **∼s of communication** un réseau de communication; **4** TV chaîne f; **to change ∼s** changer de chaîne; **to flick ∼s**○ zapper; **∼ one** la première chaîne; **5** Radio canal m; **6** Archit cannelure f; **7** (groove) rainure f

B vtr (p prés etc **-ll-**, **-l-** US) **1** (carry) acheminer, canaliser [liquid] (**to, into** dans; **through** par l'intermédiaire de); **2** fig (direct) concentrer, canaliser [efforts, energy] (**into** dans; **into doing** pour faire); affecter [funds] (**into** à); **3** (cut) creuser

Channel /ˈtʃænl/ ▸ **p. 1049**

A pr n (also **English ∼**) **the ∼** la Manche

B noun modifier [crossing, port] de la Manche

channel: **∼ ferry** n ferry m trans-Manche; **∼-flick**○, **∼-hop** (p prés etc **-pp-**) vi zapper; **Channel Islander** n habitant/-e m/f des îles Anglo-Normandes; **Channel Islands** ▸ **p. 954** pr npl îles fpl Anglo-Normandes; **Channel Tunnel** pr n tunnel m sous la Manche

chant /tʃɑːnt, US tʃænt/

A n **1** gen chant m scandé; **2** Mus, Relig mélopée f

B vtr scander [name, slogan]; chanter [psalm]; psalmodier [liturgy, schoolwork]

C vi [crowd] scander des slogans; Mus, Relig psalmodier

chaos /'keɪɒs/ n **1** (on roads, at home, at work) pagaille○ f; (political) confusion f, désordre m; (economic) chaos m; **in a state of ~** [house, room] sens dessus dessous; [country] en plein chaos; **to cause ~** semer la pagaille; **2** (cosmic) chaos m; **~ theory** théorie f du chaos

chaotic /keɪˈɒtɪk/ adj désordonné; **it's absolutely ~**○ c'est la pagaille○

chap /tʃæp/
A ○n GB gen type○ m; (boy) garçon m; (young man) gars○ m; **a nice ~** un chouette type; **an old ~** un vieux; **old ~...** mon vieux...
B vtr (p prés etc **-pp-**) gercer; **~ped lips** lèvres gercées

chapel /'tʃæpl/ n chapelle f

chaperone /'ʃæpərəʊn/
A n chaperon m
B vtr chaperonner

chaplain /'tʃæplɪn/ n gen aumônier m; (to a person) chapelain m

chapter /'tʃæptə(r)/ n **1** (in book) chapitre m; **in ~ 3** au chapitre 3; **2** fig (stage) chapitre m; **a new ~ in** un nouveau chapitre de
(Idioms) **a ~ of accidents** une série d'accidents; **to give ~ and verse** donner la référence exacte

char /tʃɑː(r)/
A ○n GB (cleaner) femme f de ménage
B vtr (p prés etc **-rr-**) carboniser
C vi (p prés etc **-rr-**) se carboniser

character /'kærəktə(r)/ n **1** (personality) caractère m; **to have a pleasant ~** être d'un caractère agréable; **to act in/out of ~** agir de façon habituelle/surprenante; **his remarks are totally in ~/out of ~** ces remarques ne me surprennent pas/me surprennent de sa part; **2** (reputation) réputation f; **a person of good ~** une personne d'une bonne réputation; **3** Literat, Theat, TV personnage m (from de); **to play the ~ of Romeo** jouer le rôle de Roméo; **4** (person) individu m; **a real ~** un sacré numéro○; **a local ~** une figure locale; **5** Comput caractère m (also in printing)

character: **~ actor** n acteur m de genre; **~ assassination** n dénigrement m

characteristic /ˌkærəktəˈrɪstɪk/
A n (of person) trait m de caractère; (of place, work) caractéristique f
B adj caractéristique (**of** de); **it was ~ of them to do** c'était typique de leur part de faire

characteristically /ˌkærəktəˈrɪstɪklɪ/ adv typiquement

characterize /'kærəktəraɪz/ vtr **1** (depict) dépeindre (**as** comme); **2** (typify) caractériser; **to be ~d by** se caractériser par; **3** (sum up) représenter [era, place]; faire le portrait de [person]

characterless /'kærəktəlɪs/ adj sans caractère

character: **~ reference** n références fpl; **~ sketch** n portrait m rapide

charade /ʃəˈrɑːd, US ʃəˈreɪd/ n **1** (in game) charade f mimée; **to play ~s** jouer aux charades; **2** pej (pretence) comédie f

charbroiled /'tʃɑːbrɔɪld/ adj US = **char-grilled**

charcoal /'tʃɑːkəʊl/
A n **1** (fuel) charbon m de bois; **2** Art fusain m; **3** (colour) gris m anthracite
B ▶ p. 752 adj (also **~ grey**) (gris) anthracite inv

charge /tʃɑːdʒ/
A n **1** (fee) frais mpl; **delivery/handling ~** frais de livraison/manutention; **additional ~** supplément m; **small** ou **token ~** participation f; **there's a ~ of £2 for postage** il y a 2 livres de frais de port; **there's no ~ for installation** l'installation est gratuite; **free of ~** gratuitement; **at no extra ~** sans supplément; **2** Jur inculpation f; **murder ~** inculpation d'assassinat; **criminal ~s** poursuites fpl criminelles; **to bring ~s** porter plainte; **to prefer** ou **press ~s against sth** engager des poursuites contre qch; **to drop (the) ~s** abandonner les poursuites; **3** (accusation) accusation f (**of** de); **this leaves you open to ~s of** cela laisse la porte ouverte aux accusations de [nepotism]; **4** (attack) charge f (**against** contre); **5** (control) **to be in ~** gen être responsable (**of** de); Mil commander; **the person in ~** le/la responsable; **to put sb in ~ of sth** confier la charge de qch à qn [company, plane, project]; **to take ~ of** assumer la charge de; **to have ~ of** être chargé de; **the pupils in my ~** les élèves à

ma charge; **to take ~** prendre les choses en main; **I've left Paul in ~** c'est Paul qui sera responsable; **6** (person in one's care) (child) enfant mf dont on s'occupe; (pupil) élève mf; (patient) malade mf; **7** (explosive) charge f; **8** Elec, Phys charge f

B vtr **1** Comm faire payer [customer]; prélever [commission]; percevoir [interest] (**on** sur); **to ~ sb for sth** faire payer qch à qn; **how much do you ~?** vous prenez combien?; **I ~ £20 an hour** je prends 20 livres de l'heure; **interest is ~d at 2% a month** l'intérêt perçu sera de 2% par mois; **labour is ~d at £25 per hour** il faut compter 25 livres de l'heure pour la main-d'œuvre; **what do you ~ for doing...?** combien faut-il compter pour faire...?; **2** (pay on account) **to ~ sth to** mettre qch sur [account]; **3** Jur [police] inculper [suspect] (**with** de); **4** (accuse) accuser (**with** de); **5** (rush at) charger [enemy]; [bull] foncer sur [person]; **6** Elec, Phys charger

C vi **1** (demand payment) **to ~ for** faire payer [delivery, admission]; **2** (rush at) **to ~ at** charger [enemy]; [bull] foncer sur [person]; **~!** à l'attaque!; **3** (run) se précipiter (**into** dans; **out of** de); **to ~ across** ou **through** traverser [qch] à toute vitesse [room]; **to ~ up/down** monter/descendre [qch] à toute vitesse [stairs]

charge: **~ account** n US Comm compte-client m; **~ card** n (credit card) carte f de crédit; (store card) carte f d'achat

charged /tʃɑːdʒd/ adj **1** Phys chargé; **2** (intense) [atmosphere] très tendu; **emotionally ~** chargé d'émotion

charge: **~ hand** ▶ p. 1181 n sous-chef m d'équipe; **~ nurse** ▶ p. 1181 n infirmier/-ière m/f en chef

char-grilled /'tʃɑːgrɪld/ adj grillé au charbon de bois

chariot /'tʃærɪət/ n char m

charisma /kəˈrɪzmə/ n gen, Relig charisme m

charismatic /ˌkærɪzˈmætɪk/ adj charismatique

charitable /'tʃærɪtəbl/ adj [person, act, explanation] charitable (**to** envers); [organization] caritatif/-ive; **a company having ~ status** ≈ une association reconnue d'utilité publique; **~ trust** fondation f d'utilité publique; **~ work** bonnes œuvres fpl

charitably /'tʃærɪtəblɪ/ adv charitablement

charity /'tʃærɪtɪ/
A n **1** (virtue) charité f; **out of ~** par charité; **2** (aid, aid organizations) **to give to/collect money for ~** donner à/collecter des fonds pour des œuvres de bienfaisance; **to accept/refuse ~** accepter/refuser l'aumône f; **3** (individual organization) organisation f caritative
B noun modifier [sale, event] au profit d'œuvres de bienfaisance
(Idiom) **~ begins at home** Prov charité bien ordonnée commence par soi-même Prov

charity: **~ box** n (in church) tronc m; **~ shop** n magasin m d'articles d'occasion (vendus au profit d'une œuvre de bienfaisance); **~ work** n travail m bénévole (au profit d'une œuvre de bienfaisance)

charlady† /'tʃɑːleɪdɪ/ ▶ p. 1181 n GB femme f de ménage

charm /tʃɑːm/
A n **1** (capacity to please) charme m; **to turn on the ~** péj se mettre à faire du charme; **2** (jewellery) amulette f; **~ bracelet** bracelet m à breloques; **lucky ~** porte-bonheur m inv; **3** (magic words) charme m
B vtr charmer; **he ~ed his way into Head Office** il usa de tout son charme pour parvenir jusqu'à la direction; **the ~ed (inner) circle** les initiés mpl
(Idioms) **to lead a ~ed life** être béni des dieux; **to work like a ~** faire merveille

charmer /'tʃɑːmə(r)/ n **he is a real ~** il est adorable

charming /'tʃɑːmɪŋ/ adj [person, place] charmant; [child, animal] adorable

chart /tʃɑːt/
A n **1** (graph) graphique m; **temperature ~** Med feuille f de température; **2** (table) tableau m; **3** (map) carte f; **weather ~** carte du temps; **4** Mus **the ~s** le hit-parade; **number one in the ~s** numéro un au hit-parade
B vtr **1** (on map) porter [qch] sur la carte [feature]; tracer [route]; **2** (record) enregistrer [changes, progress]

charter /'tʃɑːtə(r)/
A n **1** gen, Pol charte f; (for company) acte m constitutif; **2** (hiring) affrètement m; **on ~ to** sous contrat d'affrètement avec

B vtr affréter [plane]

C **chartered** pp adj [professional] agréé; [corporation] à charte

charter: **~ed accountant**, CA ▸ p. 1181 n GB ≈ expert-comptable m; **~ed surveyor** ▸ p. 1181 n GB expert m immobilier; **~ flight** n GB vol m charter; **~ plane** n GB charter m

chary /'tʃeərɪ/ adj méfiant; **to be ~** se méfier

chase /tʃeɪs/
A n **1** (pursuit) poursuite f (after de); **car/police ~** poursuite f en voiture/par la police; **to give ~ to sb** se lancer à la poursuite de qn; **2** (race) course f (for à)
B vtr **1** (also **~ after**) (pursue) pourchasser [person, animal]; courir après [contract, job]; **to ~ sb/sth up** ou **down the street** courir après qn/qch dans la rue; **2** (also **~ after**) (make advances) courir après; **3** ᴼ(also **~ after**) (try to win) viser [title]; **4** (remove) **to ~ sb/sth from** chasser qn/qch de [room]; **5** (engrave) ciseler
(Idiom) **to ~ one's (own) tail** tourner en rond
(Phrasal verbs)
▪ **chase about**, **chase around**: ▸ **~ about** courir en tous sens; ▸ **~ around**ᴼ **[sth]** parcourir [qch] dans tous les sens [building, town]; ▸ **~ [sb] around** poursuivre
▪ **chase away**: ▸ **~ [sb/sth] away**, **~ away [sb/sth]** lit, fig chasser
▪ **chase down** US = **chase up**
▪ **chase off** = **chase away**
▪ **chase up** GB: ▸ **~ up [sth]** retrouver [details, statistics]; ▸ **~ [sb] up**, **~ up [sb]** activer [person]

chaserᴼ /'tʃeɪsə(r)/ n petit coup m entre deux verresᴼ

chasm /'kæzəm/ n gouffre m; (deeper) abîme m; fig abîme m

chassis /'ʃæsɪ/ n (pl **~**) châssis m

chaste /tʃeɪst/ adj **1** (celibate) chaste; **2** (innocent) [relationship] innocent; [kiss] chaste; **3** (sober) [style] sobre

chasten /'tʃeɪsn/
A †vtr réprimander
B **chastened** pp adj assagi; **they were suitably ~ed** comme il se doit cela les a fait réfléchir

chastening /'tʃeɪstnɪŋ/ adj humiliant

chastise /tʃæ'staɪz/ vtr châtier

chastity /'tʃæstətɪ/ n chasteté f

chat /tʃæt/
A n conversation f; **to have a ~** bavarder (**with** avec; **about** sur); **I must have a ~ with her about her work** il faut que je lui parle de son travail
B vi (p prés etc **-tt**) bavarder (**with, to** avec); (on Internet) chatter
(Phrasal verb)
▪ **chat up**ᴼ: ▸ **~ up [sb]**, **~ [sb] up** GB (flirtatiously) draguerᴼ; (to obtain sth) baratinerᴼ

chat: **~line** n GB gen réseau m téléphonique; (for sexual encounters etc) cf téléphone m rose; **~room** n salle f de causette, salle f de bavardage; **~ show** n GB talk-show m

chattel /'tʃætl/ n Jur bien m, possession f; **goods and ~s** biens et effets

chatter /'tʃætə(r)/
A n (of person) bavardage m; (of crowd, audience) bourdonnement m; (of birds) gen gazouillis m; (of magpies) jacassement m; (of machine) cliquetis m
B vi (also **~ away**, **~ on**) [person] bavarder; [birds] gazouiller; [magpies] jacasser; [machine] cliqueter; **her teeth were ~ing** elle claquait des dents

chatterbox /'tʃætəbɒks/ n moulin m à parolesᴼ

chatty /'tʃætɪ/ adj [person] ouvert; [letter, style] vivant

chauffeur /'ʃəʊfə(r), US ʃəʊ'fɜːr/ ▸ p. 1181
A n chauffeur m; **a ~-driven car** une voiture avec chauffeur
B vtr conduire

chauvinism /'ʃəʊvɪnɪzəm/ n **1** gen chauvinisme m; **2** (also **male ~**) machisme m

chauvinist /'ʃəʊvɪnɪst/ n, adj **1** gen chauvin/-e (m/f); **2** (also **male ~**) macho (m)

chauvinistic /ˌʃəʊvɪ'nɪstɪk/ adj chauvin

cheap /tʃiːp/
A adj **1** (not expensive) bon marché inv; **to be ~** être bon marché, ne pas coûter cher inv; **it's ~ to produce** cela ne

revient pas cher de le/la produire; **it works out ~er to take the train** cela revient moins cher de prendre le train; **the ~ seats** les places moins chères; **it's ~ at the price** c'est une occasion à ce prix-là; **~ and cheerful** sans prétentions; **life is ~** la vie est sans importance; **to hold sth ~** ne pas respecter qch; **2** péj (shoddy) de mauvaise qualité; **it's ~ and nasty** c'est de la camelote; **3** péj (easy) [joke, gimmick] facile; **a ~ thrill** une sensation forte; **talk is ~** bavarder est facile; **4** péj (mean) [trick, liar] sale (before n); **a ~ shot** un coup bas
B advᴼ [buy, get, sell] pour rien; **they're going ~** ils sont au rabais
C **on the cheap** adv phr [buy, sell] au rabais; **to do things on the ~** péj y aller à l'économieᴼ

cheapen /'tʃiːpən/ vtr rendre [qch] moins cher [process]; dévaloriser [life, liberty]

cheaply /'tʃiːplɪ/ adv [produce, do, sell] à bas prix; [available, accessible] à un prix raisonnable; **to eat ~** manger pour pas cher

cheapness /'tʃiːpnɪs/ n **1** (low cost) bas prix m; **2** (of joke, trick) bassesse f

cheap rate adj, adv Telecom à tarif réduit; **to cost 25 pence a minute ~** coûter 25 pence la minute au tarif réduit

cheat /tʃiːt/
A n tricheur/-euse m/f
B vtr tromper [person, company]; **to feel ~ed** se sentir lésé; **to ~ sb (out) of** dépouiller qn de
C vi tricher; **to ~ in** tricher à [exam, test]; **to ~ at cards** tricher aux cartes; **to ~ on** tromper [person]

Chechen /'tʃetʃen/ ▸ p. 1032
A n Tchétchène mf
B adj tchétchène

Chechnya /ˌtʃetʃ'njɑː/ ▸ p. 774 pr n Tchétchénie f

check /tʃek/
A n **1** (inspection) (for quality, security) contrôle m (**on** sur); **security ~** contrôle de sécurité; **to carry out ~s** exercer des contrôles; **to give sth a ~** vérifier qch; **to keep a (close) ~ on sb/sth** surveiller qn/qch (de près); **2** Med examen m; **eye ~** examen des yeux; **3** (restraint) frein m (**on** à); **to put ou place a ~ on** mettre un frein à [production, growth]; **to hold ou keep sb/sth in ~** contrôler qn/qch; **to hold oneself in ~** se maîtriser; **4** (in chess) **in ~** en échec; **to put the king in ~** faire échec au roi; **your king is in ~** échec au roi; **5** (fabric) tissu m à carreaux; (pattern) carreaux mpl; **6** US (cheque) chèque m; **7** US (bill) addition f; **to pick up the ~** payer l'addition; **8** US (receipt) ticket m; **9** US (tick) croix f (pour cocher)
B noun modifier [fabric, garment etc] à carreaux
C vtr **1** (for security) vérifier [vehicle, mechanism, fuse]; contrôler [person, product, ticket, area]; **to ~ that/whether** vérifier que/si; **they ~ed the hotel for bombs** ils se sont assurés qu'il n'y avait pas de bombe dans l'hôtel; **2** (for accuracy, reliability) vérifier [bill, spelling, data, signature, banknote]; contrôler [accounts, invoice, output, work]; corriger [proofs]; **to ~ sth for defects** contrôler la qualité de qch; **to ~ that/whether** vérifier que/si; **to ~ sth against** vérifier qch par rapport à [data, inventory]; comparer qch avec [signature]; **3** (for health, progress) prendre [temperature, blood pressure]; tester [reflexes]; examiner [eyesight]; **to ~ that/whether** vérifier que/si; **4** (inspect) examiner [watch, map, pocket]; **5** (find out) vérifier [times, details]; **6** (curb) contrôler [price rises, inflation]; freiner [increase, growth, progress]; réduire [abuse, emigration, influence]; démentir [rumour]; déjouer [plans]; **7** (restrain, keep in) maîtriser [emotions]; retenir [tears]; **8** (stop) arrêter [person, enemy, rebellion]; **9** (in chess) faire échec à; **10** US (for safekeeping) mettre [qch] au vestiaire [coat]; mettre [qch] à la consigne [baggage]; **11** US (register) enregistrer [baggage]; **12** US (tick) to ~ = **check off**
D vi **1** (verify) vérifier; **to ~ with sb** demander à qn; **2** (examine) **to ~ for** dépister [problems, disease]; chercher [leaks, flaws]; **3** (register) **to ~ into** arriver à [hotel]; **4** US (tally) [accounts] être exact
E v refl (restrain) **to ~ oneself** se retenir
F excl **1** (in chess) **~!** échec au roi!; **2** ᴼUS (in agreement) d'accord
G **checked** pp adj [fabric, garment] à carreaux
(Phrasal verbs)
▪ **check in**: ▸ **~ in** (at airport) enregistrer; (at hotel) remplir la fiche (**at** à); US (clock in) pointer (à l'entrée); ▸ **~ [sb/sth] in**, **~ in [sb/sth]** **1** Aviat, Tourism enregistrer [baggage, passengers]; accueillir [hotel guest]; **2** US (for safekeeping) mettre

[qch] à la consigne [*baggage*]; mettre [qch] au vestiaire [*coat*]
■ **check off:** ▶ ~ **off [sth]**, ~ **[sth] off** cocher [*items*]
■ **check on:** ▶ ~ **on [sb/sth]** ① (observe) surveiller [*person*]; **to ~ on sb's progress** vérifier les progrès de qn; ② (investigate) faire une enquête sur [*person*]; **to ~ on how/whether** voir comment/si
■ **check out:** ▶ ~ **out** ① (leave) partir; **to ~ out of** quitter [*hotel*]; ② (be correct) être correct; ③ US (clock out) pointer (à la sortie); ▶ ~ **out [sth]**, ~ **[sth] out** ① (investigate) vérifier [*information*]; examiner [*package, building*]; se renseigner sur [*club, scheme*]; ② ○(try) essayer; ③ US (remove) (from library) emprunter; (from cloakroom, left luggage) retirer; ▶ ~ **[sb] out**, ~ **out [sb]** faire une enquête sur [*person*]
■ **check over:** ▶ ~ **[sth] over** vérifier [*document, wiring, machine*]; ▶ ~ **[sb] over** Med faire un examen médical à [*person*]
■ **check through:** ▶ ~ **[sth] through** ① vérifier [*work*]; ② US Aviat enregistrer [*luggage*] (**to** pour)
■ **check up:** ▶ ~ **up** vérifier (**that** que); **to ~ up on** (observe) surveiller [*person*]; (investigate) faire une enquête sur [*person*]; vérifier [*story, details*]

checkbook /'tʃekbʊk/ n US carnet m de chèques, chéquier m

checker /'tʃekə(r)/ ▸ **p. 1181**
A n ① (employee) vérificateur/-trice m/f; ② US (cashier) caissier/-ière m/f; ③ US (in fabric) carreau m; ④ US Games (piece) pion m
B checkers npl ▸ **p. 881** jeu m de dames; **to play ~s** jouer aux dames

checkerboard /'tʃekəbɔːd/ n US damier m

checkered adj US = **chequered**

check-in /'tʃekɪn/
A n ① (also ~ **desk**) enregistrement m; ② (procedure) enregistrement m
B noun modifier [*counter*] d'enregistrement; ~ **time** enregistrement m

checking /'tʃekɪŋ/ n vérification f

checking account n US compte m courant

checklist /'tʃeklɪst/ n liste f de contrôle

checkmate /'tʃekmeɪt/
A n échec m et mat; fig échec m
B vtr faire échec à [*opponent*]; fig battre [qn] à plates coutures○

checkout /'tʃekaʊt/ n caisse f; **on the ~** à la caisse

checkout assistant, **checkout operator** n GB caissier/-ière m/f

checkpoint /'tʃekpɔɪnt/ n poste m de contrôle

checkroom /'tʃekruːm, -rʊm/ n US ① (cloakroom) vestiaire m; ② (for baggage) consigne f

checkup /'tʃekʌp/ n ① Med examen m médical, bilan m de santé; **to go for/have a ~** passer/se faire faire un examen médical; ② (at the dentist's) visite f de routine

cheddar /tʃedə(r)/ n cheddar m (*fromage*)

cheek /tʃiːk/
A n ① (of face) joue f; ~ **to** ~ joue contre joue; ② (impudence) culot○ m; **what a ~!** quel culot○!
B vtr○ GB être insolent envers [*person*]

⟨Idiom⟩ **to turn the other ~** tendre l'autre joue

cheekbone /'tʃiːkbəʊn/ n pommette f

cheekily /'tʃiːkɪlɪ/ adv [*say*] effrontément; [*perched*] crânement

cheeky /'tʃiːkɪ/ adj ① (impudent) [*person*] effronté, insolent; [*question*] impoli; ② (pert) [*grin*] espiègle, coquin

cheer /'tʃɪə(r)/
A n acclamation f; **to give a ~** pousser une acclamation or un hourra; **to get a ~** être acclamé; **to give three ~s for** faire un ban à; **three ~s!** un ban!, hourra!
B cheers excl ① (toast) à la vôtre○!; (to close friend) à la tienne○!; ② ○GB (thanks) merci!; ③ ○GB (goodbye) salut!
C vtr, vi applaudir

⟨Phrasal verbs⟩
■ **cheer on:** ▶ ~ **on [sb]**, ~ **[sb] on** encourager [*person*]
■ **cheer up:** ▶ ~ **up** reprendre courage; ~ **up!** courage!; ▶ ~ **[sb] up** remonter le moral à [*person*]; ▶ ~ **up [sth]**, ~ **[sth] up** égayer [*room*]

cheerful /'tʃɪəfl/ adj [*person, smile, mood, music*] joyeux/-euse; [*news*] réjouissant; [*remark, tone*] enjoué; [*colour*] gai; [*optimism*] inébranlable; **to be ~ about** se réjouir de

cheerfully /'tʃɪəfəlɪ/ adv (joyfully) joyeusement; (blithely) allégrement

cheerfulness /'tʃɪəflnɪs/ n gaieté f

cheerily /'tʃɪərɪlɪ/ adv joyeusement, gaiement

cheering /'tʃɪərɪŋ/
A n **C** acclamations fpl
B adj [*message, news, words*] réconfortant, réjouissant

cheerio○ /ˌtʃɪərɪ'əʊ/ excl salut○

cheerleader /'tʃɪəliːdə(r)/ n majorette f

cheerless /'tʃɪəlɪs/ adj [*place*] triste, morne; [*outlook*] sombre

cheery /'tʃɪərɪ/ adj joyeux/-euse, gai

cheese /tʃiːz/ n fromage m; ~ **sandwich** sandwich au fromage

⟨Idioms⟩ **they are as different as chalk and ~** c'est le jour et la nuit; **say ~!** (for photo) souriez!

⟨Phrasal verb⟩
■ **cheese off**○: **to be ~d off with** en avoir marre○ de

cheese: ~**board** n (object) plateau m à fromage; (selection) plateau m de fromages; ~**burger** n hamburger m au fromage; ~**cake** n Culin cheesecake m; ~**cloth** n étamine f; ~ **counter** n fromagerie f; ~**paring** n économies fpl de bouts de chandelle

cheesy /'tʃiːzɪ/ adj ① [*smell*] de fromage; ② [*grin*] large

cheetah /'tʃiːtə/ n guépard m

chef /ʃef/ ▸ **p. 1181** n chef m cuisinier

chemical /'kemɪkl/
A n produit m chimique
B adj [*process, reaction, industry, formula, warfare, waste*] chimique; [*equipment, experiment*] de chimie

chemical engineer ▸ **p. 1181** n ingénieur m chimiste

chemise /ʃə'miːz/ n (dress) robe-combinaison f; (undergarment) chemise f

chemist /'kemɪst/ ▸ **p. 1181** n ① GB (person) pharmacien/-ienne m/f; ~**'s (shop)** pharmacie f; ② (scientist) chimiste mf

chemistry /'kemɪstrɪ/ n ① (science) chimie f; ② (structure, properties) propriétés fpl chimiques; ③ fig (rapport) affinités fpl

chemotherapy /ˌkiːməʊ'θerəpɪ/ n chimiothérapie f

cheque GB, **check** US /tʃek/ n chèque m; **by** ~ par chèque; **to make out ou write a ~ for £20** faire un chèque de 20 livres sterling

⟨Idiom⟩ **to give sb a blank ~** fig donner carte blanche à qn

cheque: ~**book** GB, **checkbook** US n chéquier m, carnet m de chèques; ~ **card** n carte f de garantie bancaire

chequer GB, **checker** US /'tʃekə(r)/ n ① Games pion m; ② (square) carreau m; (pattern) damier m

chequered GB, **checkered** US /'tʃekəd/ adj ① (patterned) à damiers; ② fig [*career, history*] en dents de scie

chequers GB, **checkers** US /'tʃekəz/ ▸ **p. 881** n (+ v sg) dames fpl

cherish /'tʃerɪʃ/ vtr ① (nurture) caresser [*hope, ambition*]; chérir [*memory, idea*]; **her most ~ed ambition** son ambition la plus chère; ② †(love) chérir

cherry /'tʃerɪ/ ▸ **p. 752**
A n ① (fruit) cerise f; ② (tree, wood) cerisier m
B adj (also ~-**red**) rouge cerise inv

⟨Idiom⟩ **life is not a bowl of cherries** la vie n'est pas rose

cherry: ~ **brandy** n cherry m; ~ **orchard** n cerisaie f; ~ **tomato** n tomate f cerise; ~ **tree** n cerisier m

cherub /'tʃerəb/ n (angel) chérubin m; (child) angelot m

cherubic /tʃɪ'ruːbɪk/ adj [*face*] de chérubin; [*child*] angélique

chervil /'tʃɜːvɪl/ n cerfeuil m

chess /tʃes/ ▸ **p. 881** n échecs mpl; **a game of ~** une partie d'échecs

chess: ~**board** n échiquier m; ~**man**, ~**piece** n pièce f (de jeu d'échecs); ~ **set** n jeu m d'échecs

chest /tʃest/
A n ① Anat poitrine f; ② (furniture) coffre m; ③ (crate) caisse f
B noun modifier [*pains*] de poitrine; [*infection, specialist*] des voies respiratoires; [*X-ray*] des poumons

C

C

Idioms **to get something off one's ~**◦ vider son sac◦; **to hold ou keep one's cards close to one's ~** ne pas jouer cartes sur table

chest: **~ freezer** *n* congélateur *m* coffre; **~ measurement** ▸ p. 1191 *n* tour *m* de poitrine

chestnut /'tʃɛsnʌt/
A *n* **1** (*also* **~ tree**) (horse) marronnier *m* (d'Inde); (sweet) châtaignier *m*; **2** (timber) châtaignier *m*; **3** (nut) marron *m*, châtaigne *f*; **4** (horse) alezan *m*; **5** fig (joke) **an old ~** une plaisanterie éculée
B *noun modifier* [*cream, puree*] de marrons; [*stuffing*] aux marrons
C *adj* [*hair*] châtain; **a ~ horse** un (cheval) alezan

chest of drawers *n* commode *f*

chesty◦ /'tʃɛstɪ/ *adj* [*person*] fragile des bronches; [*cough*] de poitrine

chew /tʃuː/
A *n* **1** (act) mâchement *m*; **2** (sweet) bonbon *m*
B *vtr* **1** [*person*] mâcher [*food, gum*]; mordiller [*pencil etc*]; **to ~ a hole in sth** faire un trou dans qch (en rongeant); **2** [*animal*] ronger [*bone*]; mordiller [*carpet etc*]
C *vi* mâcher

Idiom **to bite off more than one can ~** être trop ambitieux/-ieuse

Phrasal verb
■ **chew over**◦: ▸ **~ over [sth]**, **~ [sth] over**◦ cogiter sur◦ [*problem*]

chewing gum /'tʃuːɪŋ ɡʌm/ *n* chewing-gum *m*

chewy /'tʃuːɪ/ *adj* difficile à mâcher

chiaroscuro /kɪˌɑːrəˈskʊərəʊ/ *n* clair-obscur *m*

chic /ʃiːk/
A *n* chic *m*; **to have ~** avoir du chic
B *adj* chic *inv*

chick /tʃɪk/ *n* **1** (fledgling) oisillon *m*; (of fowl) poussin *m*; **2** ◦(young woman) nana◦ *f*

chicken /'tʃɪkɪn/
A *n* **1** (fowl) poulet *m*, poule *f*; **2** Culin poulet *m*; **3** ◦(coward) poule *f* mouillée
B *noun modifier* [*wing, stock*] de poulet; [*sandwich, soup*] au poulet

Idioms **it's a ~ and egg situation** c'est l'histoire de l'œuf et de la poule; **to count one's ~s (before they are hatched)** vendre la peau de l'ours avant de l'avoir tué

Phrasal verb
■ **chicken out**◦ se dégonfler◦

chicken: **~ breast** *n* filet *m* de poulet; **~ curry** *n* poulet *m* au curry; **~ drumstick** *n* pilon *m*; **~ farmer** ▸ p. 1181 *n* éleveur *m* de volailles

chicken feed *n* **C** **1** Agric nourriture *f* pour volaille; **2** ◦(paltry sum) bagatelle *f*, somme *f* dérisoire

chicken: **~ livers** *npl* foies *mpl* de volaille; **~ noodle soup** *n* soupe *f* de poulet au vermicelle; **~ pox** ▸ p. 933 *n* varicelle *f*; **~ run** *n* basse-cour *f*; **~ wire** *n* grillage *m* (à mailles fines)

chickpea *n* pois *m* chiche

chicory /'tʃɪkərɪ/ *n* **1** (vegetable) endive *f*; **2** (in coffee) chicorée *f*

chief /tʃiːf/
A *n* **1** (leader) gen chef *m*; **party ~** Pol dirigeant/-e *m/f* de parti; **defence ~s** Pol responsables *mpl* de la défense; **2** ◦(boss) chef◦ *m*, patron◦ *m*
B *adj* **1** (primary) principal *m*; **2** (highest in rank) en chef
C **-in-chief** *combining form* en chef

chief: **~ accountant** *n* chef comptable *m*; **~ constable** *n* GB ≈ directeur *m* de police

chief executive *n* **1** Admin, Comm directeur *m* général; **2** US Pol Chef *m* de l'Exécutif (le Président)

chief inspector *n* gen inspecteur/-trice *m/f* principal/-e; GB (of police) inspecteur *m* de police divisionnaire

chiefly /'tʃiːflɪ/ *adv* notamment, surtout

chief: **~ of police** *n* ≈ préfet *m* de police; **Chief of Staff**, **C of S** ▸ p. 1123 *n* Mil chef *m* d'état-major; (of White House) secrétaire *m* général; **~ of state** *n* US chef *m* d'État; **~ petty officer**, **CPO** ▸ p. 1123 *n* premier maître *m*; **Chief Rabbi** *n* Grand Rabbin *m*; **~ superintendent** *n* GB ≈ commissaire *m* divisionnaire

chieftain /'tʃiːftən/ *n* chef *m* (de clan ou de tribu)

chiffon /'ʃɪfɒn, US ʃɪ'fɒn/
A *n* mousseline *f*
B *noun modifier* [*dress, scarf*] en mousseline

chilblain /'tʃɪlbleɪn/ *n* engelure *f*

child /tʃaɪld/ *n* (*pl* **children**) enfant *mf*; **when I was a ~** quand j'étais enfant; **~ star/prodigy** enfant vedette/prodige; fig **~ of nature** fig enfant de la nature

Idiom **it's ~'s play** c'est un jeu d'enfant

child abuse *n* gen mauvais traitements *mpl* infligés à un enfant; (sexual) sévices *mpl* sexuels exercés sur l'enfant

childbearing /'tʃaɪldbeərɪŋ/ *n* maternité *f*; **of ~ age** en âge d'avoir des enfants, nubile

child benefit *n* GB ≈ allocations *fpl* familiales

childbirth /'tʃaɪldbɜːθ/ *n* accouchement *m*; **in ~** en couches

child: **~care** *n* (nurseries etc) structures *fpl* d'accueil pour les enfants d'âge préscolaire; (bringing up children) éducation *f* des enfants; **~care facilities** *npl* crèche *f*; **~ guidance** *n* GB assistance *f* sociopsychologique de l'enfance

childhood /'tʃaɪldhʊd/
A *n* enfance *f*; **in (his) early ~** dans sa prime enfance
B *noun modifier* [*friend, memory*] d'enfance; [*illness*] infantile; [*event*] survenu dans mon/son etc enfance

childish /'tʃaɪldɪʃ/ *adj* **1** (of child) d'enfant; **2** péj (immature) puéril

childishly /'tʃaɪldɪʃlɪ/ *adv* comme un enfant

childishness /'tʃaɪldɪʃnɪs/ *n* puérilité *f*

childless /'tʃaɪldlɪs/ *adj* sans enfants

childlike /'tʃaɪldlaɪk/ *adj* enfantin

child: **~minder** ▸ p. 1181 *n* GB nourrice *f*; **~ molester** *n* agresseur *m* d'enfants; **~-proof** *adj* [*container, lock*] de sécurité (à l'épreuve des enfants)

children /'tʃɪldrən/ *pl* ▸ **child**

children's home *n* maison *f* d'enfants

Chile /'tʃɪlɪ/ ▸ p. 774 *pr n* Chili *m*

chill /tʃɪl/
A *n* **1** (coldness) fraîcheur *f*; **there is a ~ in the air** le fond de l'air est frais; **2** (illness) coup *m* de froid; **to catch a ~** prendre *or* attraper un coup de froid; **3** fig frisson *m*; **to send a ~ down sb's spine** donner des frissons à qn
B *adj* **1** lit [*wind*] frais/fraîche; **2** fig [*reminder, words*] brutal
C *vtr* **1** Culin (make cool) mettre [qch] à refroidir [*dessert, soup*]; rafraîchir [*wine*]; (keep cool) réfrigérer; **2** (make cold) faire frissonner [*person*]; **3** fig (cause to fear) faire frissonner [*person*]; **to ~ sb's** *ou* **the blood** glacer le sang à qn
D *vi* [*dessert*] refroidir; [*wine*] rafraîchir
E **chilled** *pp adj* [*wine*] bien frais; [*food*] réfrigéré

Phrasal verb
■ **chill out**◦ décompresser◦; **~ out!** laisse faire!

chilli, **chili** /'tʃɪlɪ/ *n* **1** (pod) (*also* **~ pepper**) piment *m* rouge; (powder) chili *m*; **2** (*also* **~ con carne**) chili *m* con carne

chilling /'tʃɪlɪŋ/ *adj* [*story, thought, look*] effrayant

chilly /'tʃɪlɪ/ *adj* lit, fig froid; **it's ~** il fait froid

chime /tʃaɪm/
A *n* (of clock, church bell) carillon *m*; **the ~s of the clock** (sound) le carillon de l'horloge
B *vi* (strike) sonner; (play a tune) carillonner; **the clock ~d three** la pendule a sonné trois heures

Phrasal verb
■ **chime in** interrompre

chimera /kaɪ'mɪərə/ *n* littér (beast, idea) chimère *f*

chimeric /kaɪ'merɪk/ *adj* chimérique

chimney /'tʃɪmnɪ/ *n* (*pl* **-neys**) cheminée *f*; (in mountaineering) cheminée *f*; **in the ~ corner** au coin du feu

chimney: **~breast** *n* manteau *m* de cheminée; **~pot** *n* mitron *m* (sur cheminée); **~stack** *n* cheminée *f*; **~ sweep** ▸ p. 1181 *n* ramoneur *m*

chimp /tʃɪmp/ *n* = **chimpanzee**

chimpanzee /ˌtʃɪmpænˈziː, ˌtʃɪmpænˈziː/ *n* chimpanzé *m*

chin /tʃɪn/ *n* menton *m*; **weak ~** menton fuyant

Idioms **to keep one's ~ up**◦ tenir le coup◦; **~ up!** tiens bon!; **to take it on the ~**◦ encaisser◦ bravement

china /'tʃaɪnə/
A n **C** porcelaine f; **a piece of** ~ une porcelaine; **rare** ~ porcelaines fpl rares
B noun modifier [cup, plate] en porcelaine
(Idiom) **like a bull in a** ~ **shop** comme un éléphant dans un magasin de porcelaine

China /'tʃaɪnə/ ▸ p. 774 pr n Chine f
(Idiom) **not for all the tea in** ~ pour rien au monde

china cabinet n vitrine f (meuble)

China: ~ **Sea** pr n mer f de Chine; ~ **tea** n thé m de Chine; ~**town** n le quartier chinois

Chinese /tʃaɪ'niːz/ ▸ p. 1032, p. 969
A n **1** (person) Chinois/-oise m/f; **2** (language) chinois m
B adj chinois/-oise; **to eat** ~ manger chinois

Chinese: ~ **cabbage** n US = **Chinese leaves**; ~ **gooseberry** n kiwi m; ~ **leaves** npl GB chou m de Chine; ~ **puzzle** n lit, fig casse-tête m inv chinois

chink /tʃɪŋk/
A n **1** (slit) (in wall) fente f; (in door, curtain) entrebâillement m; **2** (sound) tintement m
B vi [glasses, coins] tinter
(Idiom) **it's the** ~ **in his armour** c'est le défaut de sa cuirasse

chinos /'tʃiːnəʊs/ npl chino® m; pantalon m kaki; **a pair of** ~ un chino®

chintz /tʃɪnts/ n chintz m

chip /tʃɪp/
A n **1** (fragment) gen fragment m (**of** de); (of wood) copeau m; (of glass) éclat m; **2** (in wood, china, glass) ébréchure f; **3** GB Culin (fried potato) frite f; **4** US (potato crisp) chips f; **5** Comput puce f (électronique); (in gambling) plaque f; (smaller) jeton m
B vtr (p prés etc **-pp-**) **1** (damage) ébrécher [glass, plate]; écorner [precious stone]; écailler [paint]; **to** ~ **a tooth** se casser une dent; **2** (carve) tailler
C vi (p prés etc **-pp-**) [plate, glass] s'ébrécher; [paint] s'écailler; [tooth] se casser; [gem] s'écorner
(Idioms) **to have a** ~ **on one's shoulder** être amer/-ère; **to be a** ~ **off the old block** être bien le fils de son père/la fille de sa mère; **when the** ~**s are down** dans les moments difficiles; **he's had his** ~**s**○ GB il est cuit○
(Phrasal verbs)
■ **chip away:** ▸ ~ **away** [paint, plaster] s'écailler; **to** ~ **away at** tailler [stone]; fig affaiblir [qch] progressivement [authority]; miner [confidence]; ▸ ~ **away** [sth], ~ [sth] **away** enlever [qch] petit à petit [plaster]
■ **chip in** GB○ **1** (in conversation) gen interrompre; (officiously) mettre son grain de sel○; **2** (contribute money) donner un peu d'argent
■ **chip off:** ▸ ~ **off** [paint, plaster] s'écailler; ▸ ~ **off** [sth], ~ [sth] **off** écailler [plaster] (**from** de)

chipboard n aggloméré m

chipmunk /'tʃɪpmʌŋk/ n tamia m

chip: ~ **pan** n friteuse f; ~**ped potatoes** npl frites fpl

chippings /'tʃɪpɪŋz/ npl gravillons mpl; **'loose** ~**!'** 'danger: gravillons!'

chippy○ /'tʃɪpɪ/ n GB marchand m de frites

chip shop ▸ p. 1181 n marchand m de frites

chiropodist /kɪ'rɒpədɪst/ ▸ p. 1181 n pédicure mf

chiropody /kɪ'rɒpədɪ/ n podologie f

chiropractor /'kaɪərəʊpræktə(r)/ ▸ p. 1181 n chiropraticien/-ienne m/f, chiropracteur m

chirp /tʃɜːp/
A n pépiement m
B vi [bird] pépier

chirpy○ /'tʃɜːpɪ/ adj pétillant

chisel /'tʃɪzl/
A n ciseau m
B vtr **1** (p prés etc **-ll-**, US **-l-**) (shape) tailler au ciseau; (finely) ciseler; **finely** ~**led features** traits finement ciselés; **2** ○US rouler○ (**out of** de)

chit /tʃɪt/ n **1** GB (voucher) bon m; (bill, note, memo) note f; **2** ○péj **a** ~ **of a girl** une gamine

chitchat○ /'tʃɪttʃæt/ n bavardage m; **to spend one's time in idle** ~ perdre son temps en bavardages

chivalrous /'ʃɪvəlrəs/ adj **1** (heroic) [deeds, conduct] chevaleresque; **2** (polite) galant

chivalry /'ʃɪvəlrɪ/ n **1** **C** (qualities, system of values) chevalerie f; **2** (courtesy) galanterie f

chive /tʃaɪv/ n (gén pl) ciboulette f

chivvy○, US **chivy** /'tʃɪvɪ/ vtr harceler; **to** ~ **sb into doing** harceler qn jusqu'à ce qu'il fasse

chloride /'klɔːraɪd/ n chlorure m

chlorinate /'klɔːrɪneɪt/ vtr **1** Chem chlorer; **2** (disinfect) javelliser [water, swimming pool]

chlorine /'klɔːriːn/ n chlore m

chlorofluorocarbon, CFC /ˌklɔːrəˌflʊəʊ'kɑːbən/ n chlorofluorocarbone m, CFC m

chloroform /'klɒrəfɔːm, US 'klɔːr-/
A n chloroforme m
B vtr chloroformer

chlorophyll /'klɒrəfɪl/ n chlorophylle f

choc-ice /'tʃɒkaɪs/ n GB esquimau m

chock /tʃɒk/ n cale f; **to put sth on** ~**s** mettre qch sur cales; ~**s away!** enlevez les cales!

chock-a-block /ˌtʃɒkə'blɒk/ adj plein à craquer

chock-full /ˌtʃɒk'fʊl/ adj archiplein (**of** de)

chocolate /'tʃɒklət/ ▸ p. 752
A n **1** (substance) chocolat m; **cooking** ~ chocolat m de ménage; **2** (sweet) chocolat m; **3** (drink) chocolat m; **hot** ~ chocolat m chaud; **4** (colour) chocolat m; **dark** ~ tête-de-nègre m
B noun modifier [eggs, sweets] en chocolat; [biscuit, cake, ice cream] au chocolat

chocolate-coated adj enrobé de chocolat

choice /tʃɔɪs/
A n **1** (selection) choix m; **to make a** ~ faire un choix, choisir; **it was my** ~ **to do** c'est moi qui ai choisi de faire; **it's your** ~ c'est à toi de choisir; **2** **C** (right to select) choix m; **to have the** ~ avoir le choix; **to have a free** ~ être libre de choisir; **3** (option) choix m (**between, of** entre); **you have a** ~ **of three colours** tu as le choix entre trois couleurs; **to have no** ~ **but to do** se voir contraint de faire; **you have two** ~**s open to you** vous avez deux possibilités; **4** (range of options) choix m; **a wide** ~ un grand choix; **a narrow** ~ un choix limité; **to be spoilt for** ~ avoir l'embarras du choix; **5** **C** (preference) choix m; **a car of my** ~ une voiture de mon choix; **out of** ou **from** ~ par choix
B adj **1** (quality) [example, steak] de choix; **2** (well-chosen) bien choisi

choir /'kwaɪə(r)/ n **1** Mus (of church, school) chorale f; (professional) chœur m; (of boys at cathedral) maîtrise f; **to be** ou **sing in the** ~ faire partie de la chorale; **2** Archit chœur m

choir: ~**boy** n petit chanteur m, jeune choriste m; ~**girl** n jeune choriste f; ~**master** n chef m des chœurs; (in church) maître m de chapelle; ~ **school** n GB maîtrise f, manécanterie f; ~ **screen** n grille f de chœur; ~**stall** n stalle f

choke /tʃəʊk/
A n starter m; **to pull out/use the** ~ tirer/mettre le starter
B vtr **1** (throttle) étrangler [person]; **2** (impede breathing) [fumes, smoke] étouffer; **3** (render speechless) ~**d with** [voice] étranglé par [emotion]; **4** (block) = **choke up**
C vi s'étouffer; **to** ~ **on a fish bone/on a drink** s'étouffer avec une arête/en buvant; **to** ~ **to death** mourir étouffé; **to** ~ **with** emotion étouffer de [rage]
D choked○ pp adj **1** (angry) furieux/-ieuse (**about** au sujet de); **2** (upset) affecté (**over, about** par)
(Phrasal verbs)
■ **choke back:** ▸ ~ **back** [sth] étouffer [cough, sob]; **to** ~ **back one's tears** retenir ses larmes
■ **choke off:** ▸ ~ **off** [sth] stopper [lending, growth]; faire taire [opposition, protest]
■ **choke up:** ▸ ~ [sth] **up**, ~ **up** [sth] (block) boucher [drain, road]; [weeds] étouffer [garden]; ~**d up with traffic** embouteillé

choker /'tʃəʊkə(r)/ n collier m ras de cou

choking /'tʃəʊkɪŋ/ adj [gas, fumes] asphyxiant; [sensation] d'étouffement

cholera /'kɒlərə/ ▸ p. 933
A n choléra m
B noun modifier [victim, epidemic] de choléra

choleric /'kɒlərɪk/ adj colérique, coléreux/-euse

cholesterol /kə'lestərɒl/ n cholestérol m

cholesterol count, cholesterol level *n* taux *m* de cholestérol

chomp○ /tʃɒmp/
A *vtr* mâcher bruyamment
B *vi* mâcher bruyamment; **to ~ on sth** ronger qch

choose /tʃuːz/
A *vtr* (*prét* **chose**; *pp* **chosen**) **1** (select) choisir [*book, person, option*] (**from** parmi); **to ~ sb as** choisir qn comme [*adviser, friend*]; élire qn [*leader*]; **2** (decide) décider (**to do** de faire)
B *vi* (*prét* **chose**; *pp* **chosen**) **1** (select) choisir (**between** entre); **there are many models to ~ from** il y a un grand choix de modèles; **there's not much to ~ from** il y a très peu de choix; **there's nothing to ~ between X and Y** il y a très peu de différence entre X et Y; **2** (prefer) vouloir; **to ~ to do** préférer faire

choosy /tʃuːzɪ/ *adj* difficile (**about** en ce qui concerne)

chop /tʃɒp/
A *n* **1** (blow) coup *m*; **2** Culin côtelette *f*; **pork ~** côtelette *f* de porc
B **chops**○ *npl* gueule● *f*; **to lick one's ~s** (at food) se lécher les babines; (at idea) se frotter les mains
C *vtr* (*p prés etc* **-pp-**) **1** (cut up) couper [*wood*]; couper, émincer [*vegetable, meat*]; hacher [*parsley, onion*]; **to ~ sth into cubes** couper qch en cubes; **to ~ sth to pieces** *ou* **bits** couper qch en morceaux; **to ~ sth finely** hacher qch; **2** fig (cut, reduce) réduire [*service, deficit*]; (cut out) couper [*quote, footage*]
D **chopped** *pp adj* [*parsley, nuts, meat*] haché

(Idioms) **~ ~!** GB et que ça saute○!; **to ~ and change** [*person*] changer d'avis comme de chemise; [*situation*] évoluer par à-coups; **to get the ~**○ GB [*person*] se faire saquer○; [*scheme, service*] être supprimé

(Phrasal verbs)
■ **chop down**: ▸ **~ down** [sth], **~** [sth] **down** abattre
■ **chop off**: ▸ **~ off** [sth], **~** [sth] **off** couper [*branch, end*]; trancher [*head, hand, finger*]
■ **chop up**: ▸ **~ up** [sth], **~** [sth] **up** couper [*wood, log*]; émincer [*meat, onion*] (**into** en)

chopper /tʃɒpə(r)/
A *n* **1** (axe) hache *f*; (for kitchen) hachoir *m*; **2** ○(helicopter) hélico○ *m*
B **choppers**○ *npl* (real) dents *fpl*; (false) râtelier○ *m*, dentier *m*

chopping block *n* billot *m*

(Idiom) **to put one's head on the ~** prendre des risques

chopping: **~ board** *n* planche *f* à découper; **~ knife** *n* couteau *m* de cuisine

choppy /tʃɒpɪ/ *adj* [*sea, water*] agité; [*wind*] instable

chopstick /tʃɒpstɪk/ *n* baguette *f* (chinoise)

choral /kɔːral/ *adj* choral; **~ society** chorale *f*

chord /kɔːd/ *n* **1** Mus accord *m*; **2** fig (response) **it struck a ~ in** *ou* **with him/his listeners** cela a trouvé un écho en lui/chez ses auditeurs; **to strike the right ~** toucher la corde sensible; **3** (of harp) corde *f*

chore /tʃɔː(r)/ *n* **1** (routine task) tâche *f*; **the (household) ~s** les tâches ménagères; **to do the ~s** faire le ménage; **2** (unpleasant task) corvée *f*

choreograph /kɒrɪəɡrɑːf, -ɡræf, US -ɡræf/ *vtr* lit chorégraphier; fig orchestrer

choreographer /ˌkɒrɪˈɒɡrəfə(r)/ ▸ p. 1181 *n* chorégraphe *mf*

choreography /ˌkɒrɪˈɒɡrəfɪ/ *n* chorégraphie *f*

chorister /kɒrɪstə(r), US kɔːr-/ *n* choriste *mf*

chortle /tʃɔːtl/
A *n* gloussement *m*
B *vi* glousser, rire; **to ~ at** *ou* **about** *ou* **over sth** rire de qch

chorus /kɔːrəs/
A *n* **1** (people) (singers) chœur *m*; (dancers, actors) troupe *f*; (of town etc) chorale *f*; **2** (piece of music) chœur *m*; **3** (refrain) refrain *m*; (in jazz) chorus *m*; **to join in the ~** (one person) reprendre le refrain; (several people) reprendre le refrain en chœur; **4** (of bird song, yells) concert *m*; **a ~ of protest** une tempête de protestations; **in ~** en chœur; **5** Theat chœur *m*
B *vtr* (utter in unison) crier [qch] à l'unisson

chorus girl *n* danseuse *f* de revue

chose /tʃəʊz/ *prét* ▸ **choose**

chosen /tʃəʊzn/
A *pp* ▸ **choose**
B *adj* élu; **the ~ few** les privilégiés; **the Chosen People** le peuple élu

chowder /tʃaʊdə(r)/ *n*: soupe épaisse à base de fruits de mer

chow mein /ˌtʃaʊ ˈmeɪn/ *n* ✪ nouilles *fpl* frites

Christ /kraɪst/ *n* le Christ, Jésus-Christ; **the ~ child** l'enfant *m* Jésus

christen /krɪsn/ *vtr* Relig, Naut baptiser; fig (name, nickname) baptiser, nommer [*person, pet, place*]; **I was ~ed John** mon nom de baptême est John; **they ~ed the dog Max** ils ont baptisé le chien du nom de Max

christening /krɪsnɪŋ/ *n* baptême *m*

Christian /krɪstʃən/
A *n* chrétien/-ienne *m/f*; **to become a ~** se faire chrétien
B *adj* **1** Relig chrétien/-ienne; **2** [*attitude*] charitable; **a ~ burial** un enterrement convenable

Christianity /ˌkrɪstɪˈænətɪ/ *n* **1** (religion) christianisme *m*; **2** (fact of being a Christian) fait *m* d'être chrétien, qualité *f* de chrétien

Christian: **~ name** *n* nom *m* de baptême; **~ Science** *n* science *f* chrétienne; **~ Scientist** *n* scientiste *mf* chrétien/-ienne.

Christmas /krɪsməs/
A *n* (day) Noël *m*; (period) période *f* de Noël; **at ~** à Noël; **over ~** pendant la période de Noël; **Merry ~, Happy ~!** Joyeux Noël!
B *noun modifier* [*cake, card, present*] de Noël

Christmas: **~ box** *n* GB étrennes *fpl*; **~ carol** *n* (song) chant *m* de Noël; Relig cantique *m* de Noël; **~ cracker** *n* GB diablotin *m*; **~ day** *n* jour *m* de Noël; **~ eve** *n* veille *f* de Noël; **~ stocking** *n* bas *m* de Noël (contenant de petits cadeaux)

Christmastime /krɪsməstaɪm/ *n* période *f* de Noël

chrome /krəʊm/
A *n* chrome *m*
B *noun modifier* [*article*] chromé, en chrome

chrome: **~ steel** *n* acier *m* chromé; **~ yellow** ▸ p. 752 *n* jaune *m* de chrome

chromium /krəʊmɪəm/ *n* chrome *m*

chromium-plated *adj* chromé, en chrome

chromosome /krəʊməsəʊm/ *n* chromosome *m*

chronic /krɒnɪk/ *adj* **1** Med [*illness*] chronique; **2** fig [*liar*] invétéré; [*problem, shortage*] chronique; **3** ○GB (bad) nul/nulle○

chronically /krɒnɪklɪ/ *adv* **1** Med **to be ~ ill** souffrir d'une maladie chronique; **the ~ sick** ceux qui sont atteints d'une affection chronique; **2** fig [*jealous, underfunded*] extrêmement

chronicle /krɒnɪkl/
A *n* (tale) chronique *f*; **a ~ of misfortunes** fig une suite de mésaventures
B *vtr* [*person*] écrire une chronique de; [*book*] être une chronique de

chronological /ˌkrɒnəˈlɒdʒɪkl/ *adj* chronologique

chronologically /ˌkrɒnəˈlɒdʒɪklɪ/ *adv* chronologiquement, par ordre chronologique

chronology /krəˈnɒlədʒɪ/ *n* chronologie *f*

chrysalis /krɪsəlɪs/ *n* chrysalide *f*

chrysanthemum /krɪˈsænθəməm/ *n* chrysanthème *m*

chubby /tʃʌbɪ/ *adj* [*child, finger*] potelé; [*cheek*] rebondi; [*face, cherub*] joufflu; [*adult*] rondelet/-ette

chuck /tʃʌk/
A *n* **1** (stroke) caresse *f* (sous le menton); **2** Culin (also **~ steak**) macreuse *f*; **3** Tech mandrin *m*
B *vtr* **1** ○(throw) balancer○, jeter (**to** à); **2** ○(get rid of) larguer○ [*boyfriend, girlfriend*]; **3** (stroke) **to ~ sb under the chin** caresser qn sous le menton

(Phrasal verbs)
■ **chuck away**○: ▸ **~** [sth] **away**, **~ away** [sth] **1** (discard) balancer○ [rubbish], jeter; **2** (squander) gâcher [*chance, life*]; gaspiller [*money*]
■ **chuck down**○: **it's ~ing it down** il pleut à verse
■ **chuck in**○: ▸ **~** [sth] **in**, **~ in** [sth] laisser tomber
■ **chuck out**○: ▸ **~** [sth] **out**, **~ out** [sth] balancer○, jeter [*rubbish*]; ▸ **~** [sb] **out**, **~ out** [sb] vider, éjecter

chuckle /'tʃʌkl/
A *n* gloussement *m*, petit rire *m*
B *vi* glousser, rire; **to ~ at** *ou* **over sth** rire de qch; **to ~ with pleasure** glousser *or* rire de plaisir; **to ~ to oneself** rire sous cape

chuffed○ /tʃʌft/ *adj* GB vachement○ content (**about, at, with** de)

chug /tʃʌg/
A *n* halètement *m*, teuf-teuf *m*
B *vi* (*prés etc* **-gg-**) [*train*] haleter, faire teuf-teuf; **the train ~ged into/out of the station** le train est entré en gare/est sorti de la gare en haletant

(Phrasal verb)
■ **chug along** [*train, car*] avancer en haletant *or* en faisant teuf-teuf; [*project*] suivre son cours

chum○† /tʃʌm/ *n* copain/copine○ *m/f*, pote○ *m*

chummy○† /'tʃʌmɪ/ *adj* [*person*] sociable; **to be ~ with sb** être intime *or* très lié avec qn; **they're very ~** ils sont très copains○

chump /tʃʌmp/ *n* ① ○† idiot/-e *m/f*; ② Culin selle *f* d'agneau; **~ chop** tranche *f* de selle

chunk /tʃʌŋk/ *n* ① (piece) (of meat, fruit) morceau *m*; (of wood) tronçon *m*; (of bread) quignon *m*; **pineapple ~s** ananas *m* en morceaux; ② (portion) (of population, text, day) partie *f*; **a fair ~** une bonne partie

chunky /'tʃʌŋkɪ/ *adj* [*sweater, jewellery*] gros/grosse; [*person*] costaud○, trapu

Chunnel○ /'tʃʌnl/ *n* GB tunnel *m* sous la Manche

church /tʃɜːtʃ/
A *n* (*pl* **~es**) ① (building) (Catholic, Anglican) église *f*; (Protestant) temple *m*; ② (*also* **Church**) (religious body) Église *f*; **the Church of England** l'Église d'Angleterre; **to go into the ~** entrer dans les ordres; ③ (service) office *m*; (Catholic) messe *f*
B *noun modifier* [*bell, choir, clock, steeple*] d'église; [*land*] ecclésiastique; [*fête*] paroissial; [*wedding*] religieux/-ieuse

church: **~goer** *n* pratiquant/-e *m/f*; **~ hall** *n* salle *f* paroissiale; **~ school** *n* école *f* religieuse; **~ service** *n* gen office *m*; (Catholic) messe *f*

churchyard /'tʃɜːtʃjɑːd/ *n* cimetière *m*

churlish /'tʃɜːlɪʃ/ *adj* (surly) revêche; (rude) grossier/-ière

churn /tʃɜːn/
A *n* ① (for butter) baratte *f*; ② GB (container) bidon *m*
B *vtr* ① **to ~ butter** baratter; ② fig faire tourbillonner [*water, air*]
C *vi* [*ideas*] tourbillonner; **my stomach was ~ing** (with nausea) mon cœur se soulevait; (with nerves) j'avais l'estomac noué

(Phrasal verbs)
■ **churn out**: ▸ **~ [sth] out, ~ out [sth]** pondre [qch] en série [*novels*]; produire [qch] en série [*goods*]
■ **churn up**: ▸ **~ [sth] up, ~ up [sth]** faire des remous dans [*water*]; labourer [*earth*]

chute /ʃuːt/ *n* ① (slide) toboggan *m*; ② (for rubbish) vide-ordures *m inv*; ③ (for toboggan) piste *f* de toboggan; ④ ○(parachute) parachute *m*

chutney /'tʃʌtnɪ/ *n*: condiment aigre-doux

CI *n*: abrév écrite ▸ **Channel Islands**

cicada /sɪ'kɑːdə, US -'keɪdə/ *n* cigale *f*

CID *n* GB (abrév = **Criminal Investigation Department**) police *f* criminelle

cider /'saɪdə(r)/ *n* cidre *m*

cider: **~ apple** *n* pomme *f* à cidre; **~ vinegar** *n* vinaigre *m* de cidre

cigar /sɪ'gɑː(r)/
A *n* cigare *m*
B *noun modifier* [*box, case*] à cigares; [*smoker*] de cigares; **~ cutter** coupe-cigare *m*

cigarette /ˌsɪgə'ret, US 'sɪgərət/
A *n* cigarette *f*
B *noun modifier* [*ash, smoke*] de cigarette; [*case, paper*] à cigarettes

cigarette: **~ butt, ~ end** *n* mégot *m*; **~ holder** *n* fume-cigarette *m inv*; **~ lighter** *n* (portable) briquet *m*; (in car) allume-cigares *m inv*

cigar: **~ holder** *n* fume-cigare *m inv*; **~-shaped** *adj* oblong/oblongue

C-in-C /ˌsiː ɪn 'siː/ *n* (abrév = **Commander in Chief**) commandant *m* en chef

cinch○ /sɪntʃ/ *n* **doing sth was a ~** faire qch a été facile comme bonjour; **it's a ~** c'est du gâteau○

cinder /'sɪndə(r)/ *n* (glowing) braise *f*; (ash) cendre *f*; **to burn sth to a ~** réduire qch en cendres; **~ track** (piste *f*) cendrée *f*

Cinderella /ˌsɪndə'relə/ *pr n* Cendrillon

cine: **~camera** *n* caméra *f* (d'amateur); **~ club** *n* ciné-club *m*; **~ film** *n* pellicule *f* cinématographique

cinema /'sɪnəmɑː, 'sɪnəmə/ *n* cinéma *m*

cinema: **~ complex** *n* complexe *m* multisalles; **~goer** *n* (regular) cinéphile *mf*, amateur *m* de cinéma; (spectator) spectateur/-trice *m/f*

cinematic /ˌsɪnə'mætɪk/ *adj* cinématographique

cinematographer /ˌsɪnəmə'tɒgrəfə(r)/ ▸ p. 1181 *n* directeur *m* de la photo, cameraman *m*

cinematography /ˌsɪnəmə'tɒgrəfɪ/ *n* technique *f* cinématographique

cinnamon /'sɪnəmən/
A *n* ① Culin cannelle *f*; ② (tree) cannelier *m*; ③ ▸ p. 752 (colour) (couleur *f*) cannelle *f*
B *adj* ① Culin [*cake, cookie*] à la cannelle; [*stick*] de cannelle; ② (colour) cannelle *inv*

cipher /'saɪfə(r)/ *n* ① (code) chiffre *m*; **in ~** en chiffre, en code; ② Math zéro *m*; ③ (Arabic numeral) chiffre *m* (arabe); ④ (monogram) chiffre *m*

circa /'sɜːkə/ *prep* environ

circle /'sɜːkl/
A *n* ① (shape) cercle *m*; (of spectators, trees, chairs) cercle *m*; (of fabric, paper, colour) rond *m*; **to form a ~** [*objects*] former un cercle; [*people*] faire un cercle; **to sit in a ~** s'asseoir en cercle; **to go round in ~s** lit, fig tourner en rond; **to have ~s under one's eyes** avoir les yeux cernés; ② (group) cercle *m*, groupe *m*; **his ~ of friends** le cercle de ses amis; **in business ~s** dans les milieux d'affaires; **literary ~s** le monde littéraire; **fashionable ~s** le beau monde; ③ Theat balcon *m*; **in the ~** au balcon
B *vtr* ① (move round) [*plane*] tourner autour de [*airport*]; [*satellite*] graviter autour de [*planet*]; [*person, animal, vehicle*] faire le tour de [*building*]; tourner autour de [*person, animal*]; ② (encircle) encercler
C *vi* tourner en rond (**around** autour de)

(Idioms) **to come full ~** [*person*] boucler la boucle; [*situation*] revenir à son point de départ; **the wheel has come full ~** la boucle est bouclée

circuit /'sɜːkɪt/
A *n* ① (track) (for vehicles) circuit *m*; (for athletes) piste *f*; ② (lap) tour *m*; **to do 15 ~s of the track** faire 15 tours de circuit; ③ (regular round) circuit *m*; **the tennis ~** le circuit du tennis; ④ (round trip) circuit *m*; ⑤ Elec circuit *m*
B *vtr* faire le circuit de [*course, town*]

circuit: **~ board** *n* carte *f* de circuit imprimé; **~ breaker** *n* disjoncteur *m*; **~ diagram** *n* schéma *m* de circuit; **~ judge** ▸ p. 1181 *n* Jur juge *m* itinérant

circuitous /sɜː'kjuːɪtəs/ *adj* [*route, means*] indirect; [*argument*] tortueux/-euse; [*procedure*] compliqué

circuitry /'sɜːkɪtrɪ/ *n* ensemble *m* de circuits

circular /'sɜːkjʊlə(r)/
A *n* (newsletter) circulaire *f*; (advertisement) prospectus *m*
B *adj* [*object*] rond; [*argument*] circulaire

circular: **~ letter** *n* circulaire *f*; **~ saw** *n* scie *f* circulaire

circulate /'sɜːkjʊleɪt/
A *vtr* ① (spread) (to limited circle) faire circuler; (widely) diffuser (**to entre**); **the report was ~d to the members** le rapport a été transmis aux membres; ② faire circuler [*blood, water*]
B *vi* gen circuler; **let's ~** (at party) on va aller faire connaissance

circulation /ˌsɜːkjʊ'leɪʃn/ *n* ① (of blood, air, water, fuel) circulation *f*; ② (distribution) (of newspaper) tirage *m*; **a ~ of 2 million** un tirage de 2 millions d'exemplaires; ③ (of coins, books) circulation *f*; ④ (of document, information) circulation *f*; ⑤ (to wide public) diffusion *f*; (social group) **she's back in ~** elle est de nouveau dans le circuit

circulation: **~ figures** *npl* chiffres *mpl* de tirage; **~ manager** *n* responsable *mf* du service de distribution

circulatory /ˌsɜːkjʊ'leɪtərɪ, US 'sɜːkjələtɔːrɪ/ *adj* circulatoire

circumcise /'sɜːkəmsaɪz/ *vtr* circoncire [*boy*]; exciser [*girl*]

circumcision /ˌsɜːkəm'sɪʒn/ *n* (of boy) circoncision *f*; (of girl) excision *f*

circumference /sə'kʌmfərəns/ *n* circonférence *f*; **to be 4 km in ~** avoir une circonférence de 4 km

circumflex /'sɜːkəmfleks/
A *n* accent *m* circonflexe (**on, over** sur)
B *adj* circonflexe; **e ~ e** e accent circonflexe

circumlocution /ˌsɜːkəmlə'kjuːʃn/ *n* circonlocution *f*, périphrase *f*

circumnavigate /ˌsɜːkəm'nævɪgeɪt/ *vtr* faire le tour de [*world*]; passer [qch] au large [*cape*]

circumscribe /'sɜːkəmskraɪb/ *vtr* sout **1▸** (define) circonscrire; **2▸** (limit) limiter

circumspect /'sɜːkəmspekt/ *adj* circonspect (**about** quant à); **to be ~ about doing** ne pas vouloir faire

circumstance /'sɜːkəmstəns/
A *n* circonstance *f*
B **circumstances** *npl* **1▸** (state of affairs) circonstances *fpl*; **in ou under the ~s** dans ces circonstances; **under no ~s** en aucun cas; **due to ~s beyond our control** pour des raisons indépendantes de notre volonté; **2▸** (conditions of life) situation *f*

circumstantial /ˌsɜːkəm'stænʃl/ *adj* **1▸** Jur [*evidence*] indirect; **2▸** (detailed) circonstancié

circumvent /ˌsɜːkəm'vent/ *vtr* sout (avoid) contourner [*law, problem*]; circonvenir [*official*]

circus /'sɜːkəs/ *n* cirque *m*

cirrhosis /sɪ'rəʊsɪs/ ▸ p. 933 *n* cirrhose *f*

CIS *n* (abrév = **Commonwealth of Independent States**) CEI *f*

cissy *n*, *adj* = **sissy**

cistern /'sɪstən/ *n* (of lavatory) réservoir *m* de chasse d'eau; (in loft or underground) citerne *f*

citadel /'sɪtədəl/ *n* citadelle *f*

cite /saɪt/ *vtr* **1▸** (quote) citer; (adduce) avancer; **2▸** Mil (commend) citer (**for** pour); **3▸** Jur citer

citizen /'sɪtɪzn/ *n* **1▸** (of state) citoyen/-enne *m/f*; (when abroad) ressortissant/-e *m/f*; **2▸** (of town) habitant/-e *m/f*

citizen: **Citizens' Advice Bureau, CAB** *n* service *m* bénévole d'assistance sur des problèmes juridiques; **~'s arrest** *n* arrestation *f* par un particulier; **~'s band, CB** *n* Radio (bande *f*) CB *f*, citizen's band *f*; **~ship** nationalité *f*

citric /'sɪtrɪk/ *adj* citrique

citrus /'sɪtrəs/
A *n* (*pl* **-ruses**) (tree) citrus *m*; (fruit) agrume *m*
B *adj* [*colour*] acidulé; **~ trees** les citrus *mpl*

citrus fruit *n* (individual) agrume *m*; (collectively) agrumes *mpl*

city /'sɪtɪ/ *n* **1▸** (town) (grande) ville *f*; **the medieval ~** la cité médiévale; **~ life** la vie citadine; **2▸** GB **the City** la City

> **ⓘ** The **City** Quartier londonien des affaires et de la finance, la *City* est le siège des grandes banques, des compagnies d'assurance et de la plupart des sociétés d'agents de change. 500 000 personnes viennent y travailler chaque jour.

city: **City and Guilds certificate** *n* ≈ certificat *m* d'aptitude professionnelle; **~ centre** GB, **~ center** US *n* centre-ville *m*; **~ council** *n* conseil *m* municipal; **~ councillor** *n* GB conseiller/-ère *m/f* municipal/-e; **~ dweller** *n* citadin/-e *m/f*

city hall *n* US **1▸** (building) (in large town) hôtel *m* de ville; (in small town) mairie *f*; **2▸** Admin administration *f* municipale

city: **~ manager** *n* US personne *f* chargée d'administrer une municipalité; **~ news** *n* GB rubrique *f* financière; **~ planner** ▸ p. 1181 *n* urbaniste *mf*; **~scape** *n* paysage *m* urbain; **~ slicker°** *n* citadin/-e *m/f* branché/-e; **~ state** *n* Hist cité *f*; **~ technology college, CTC** *n* ≈ collège *m* technique

civic /'sɪvɪk/ *adj* [*administration, official*] municipal; [*pride, responsibility*] civique

civic centre GB, **civic center** US *n* centre *m* municipal (culturel et administratif)

civics /'sɪvɪks/ *n* (+ *v sg*) instruction *f* civique

civil /'sɪvl/ *adj* **1▸** (civic, not military) civil; **2▸** Jur [*case, court, offence*] civil; [*claim*] au civil; **3▸** (polite) courtois

Idiom **to keep a ~ tongue in one's head** mesurer ses paroles

civil: **Civil Aeronautics Board, CAB** *n* US administration *f* de l'aviation civile; **Civil Aviation Authority, CAA** *n* GB administration *f* de l'aviation civile; **~ defence, ~ defense** US *n* défense *f* passive; **~ disobedience** *n* résistance *f* passive; **~ engineer** ▸ p. 1181 *n* ingénieur *m* des travaux publics; **~ engineering** *n* génie *m* civil

civilian /sɪ'vɪlɪən/
A *n* civil/-e *m/f*
B *adj* civil

civility /sɪ'vɪlətɪ/ *n* **1▸** (manners) courtoisie *f*, politesse *f*; **2▸** (forms) civilité *f*, politesse *f*

civilization /ˌsɪvəlaɪ'zeɪʃn, US -əlɪ'z-/ *n* civilisation *f*

civilize /'sɪvəlaɪz/ *vtr* civiliser, rendre [qn/qch] plus civilisé [*manners, person*]

civilized /'sɪvəlaɪzd/ *adj* civilisé; **to become ~** se civiliser

civil: **~ law** *n* droit *m* civil; **~ liability** *n* Jur responsabilité *f* civile; **~ liberty** *n* libertés *fpl* individuelles

civil rights
A *npl* droits *mpl* civils
B *noun modifier* [*march, activist*] pour les droits civils

civil: **~ servant** ▸ p. 1181 *n* fonctionnaire *mf*; **~ service** *n* fonction *f* publique; **~ war** *n* guerre *f* civile; **~ wedding** *n* mariage *m* civil

civvies° /'sɪvɪz/ *npl* **to be in ~** être en civil

cl *n* (abrév écrite = **centilitre(s)**) cl

clad /klæd/ *adj* **~ in** habillé en, vêtu de

cladding /'klædɪŋ/ *n* revêtement *m*

claim /kleɪm/
A *n* **1▸** (demand) revendication *f*; **to make ~s ou lay ~ to** prétendre à [*throne*]; revendiquer [*right, land, title*]; **wage ~** revendications *fpl* salariales; **there are too many ~s on her generosity** on abuse de sa générosité; **there are many ~s on my time** je suis très pris; **to have first ~ on sth** avoir la priorité sur qch; **2▸** (in insurance) (against a person) réclamation *f*; (for fire, theft) demande *f* d'indemnisation; **to make ou put in a ~** faire une demande d'indemnisation; **3▸** (for welfare benefit) demande *f* d'allocation; **to make ou put in a ~** faire une demande d'allocation; **4▸** (refund request) demande *f* de remboursement; **travel ~** demande *f* de remboursement des frais de déplacement; **5▸** (assertion) affirmation *f* (**about** au sujet de; **by** de la part de; **of** de); **his ~ that he is innocent** ses protestations d'innocence; **her ~(s) to be able to do** ses affirmations selon lesquelles elle peut faire; **some extraordinary ~s have been made for this drug** on a affirmé des choses extraordinaires sur ce médicament; **my ~ to fame** ma prétention à la gloire; **6▸** (piece of land) concession *f*
B *vtr* **1▸** (assert) **to ~ to be able to do** prétendre pouvoir faire; **to ~ to be innocent** prétendre être innocent; **to ~ responsibility for an attack** revendiquer un attentat; **2▸** (assert right to) revendiquer [*money, property*]; **3▸** (apply for) faire une demande de [*benefit*]; faire une demande de remboursement de [*expenses*]; **4▸** (cause) **the accident ~ed 50 lives** l'accident a fait 50 victimes *or* morts
C *vi* **1▸** Jur **to ~ for damages** faire une demande pour dommages et intérêts; **2▸** (apply for benefit) faire une demande d'allocation

Phrasal verb
■ **claim back**: ▸ **~ back [sth], ~ [sth] back** se faire rembourser [*cost*]; **to ~ one's money back** se faire rembourser

claimant /'kleɪmənt/ *n* **1▸** (for benefit, grant, compensation) demandeur/-euse *m/f* (**to** à); **2▸** (to title, estate) prétendant/-e *m/f* (**to** à)

claim form *n* déclaration *f* de sinistre

clairvoyance /kleə'vɔɪəns/ *n* voyance *f*

clairvoyant /kleə'vɔɪənt/
A *n* voyant/-e *m/f*, extralucide *mf*
B *adj* [*person*] doué de seconde vue; [*powers*] de voyance

clam /klæm/ *n* Zool, Culin palourde *f*

Phrasal verb
■ **clam up** ne plus piper mot (**on sb** à qn)

clamber /'klæmbə(r)/ *vi* grimper, se hisser (péniblement); **to ∼ over/up/across** escalader

clam chowder *n* soupe *f* aux palourdes

clammy /'klæmɪ/ *adj* [*skin, hand*] moite (**with** de); [*surface*] collant; [*weather*] moite

clamorous /'klæmərəs/ *adj* [*crowd*] vociférant; [*protest*] violent, bruyant; [*demand*] impérieux/-ieuse

clamour GB, **clamor** US /'klæmə(r)/
A *n* **1** (loud shouting) clameur *f*; **2** (demands) réclamations *fpl*
B *vi* **1** (demand) **to ∼ for sth** réclamer qch; **to ∼ for sb to do** réclamer à qn de faire; **2** (rush, fight) se bousculer (**for** pour avoir; **to do** pour faire); **3** (shout together) pousser des cris

clamp /klæmp/
A *n* **1** Tech (on bench) valet *m*; (unattached) presse *f*; Chem, Med pince *f*; **2** fig frein *m* (**on** à); **to put a ∼ on sth** freiner; **3** Aut (*also* **wheel∼**) sabot *m* de Denver
B *vtr* **1** Tech cramponner [*two parts*]; (at bench) fixer [qch] à l'aide d'un valet (**onto** à); **2** (clench) serrer [*jaw, teeth*]; **his jaws were ∼ed shut** il serrait les mâchoires; **3** Aut (*also* **wheel∼**) mettre un sabot de Denver à [*car*]
(Phrasal verb)
■ **clamp down**: ▶ **∼ down** prendre des mesures; **to ∼ down on** faire de la répression contre [*crime*]; mettre un frein à [*extravagance*]

clampdown /'klæmpdaʊn/ *n* mesures *fpl* de répression (**on sb** contre qn; **on sth** de qch)

clan /klæn/ *n* lit, fig clan *m*

clandestine /klæn'destɪn/ *adj* clandestin

clang /klæŋ/
A *n* fracas *m*, bruit *m* métallique
B *vtr* faire sonner [qch] à toute volée [*bell*]
C *vi* [*gate*] claquer avec un son métallique; [*bell*] retentir

clanger° /'klæŋə(r)/ *n* GB boulette° *f*, gaffe *f*

clanging /'klæŋɪŋ/ *n* bruit *m* métallique, fracas *m*

clank /klæŋk/
A *n* bruit *m* métallique
B *vi* [*heavy object*] cliqueter; [*chains*] s'entrechoquer

clannish /'klænɪʃ/ *adj* péj [*family, profession*] fermé; [*person*] qui a l'esprit de clan

clap /klæp/
A *n* (of hands) battement *m* de mains; (round of applause) applaudissements *mpl*; (friendly slap) tape *f*; **to give sb a ∼** applaudir qn; **a ∼ of thunder** un coup de tonnerre
B *vtr* (*p prés etc* **-pp-**) **1** **to ∼ one's hands** battre *or* taper des mains, frapper dans ses mains; **to ∼ one's hand over sb's mouth** mettre *or* plaquer la main sur la bouche de qn; **to ∼ sb on the back** taper qn dans le dos; **to ∼ sth shut** fermer qch d'un coup sec; **2** (applaud) applaudir; **3** °(put) **to ∼ sb in irons** mettre qn aux fers
C *vi* (*p prés etc* **-pp-**) applaudir
(Idiom) **to ∼ eyes on** voir, poser les yeux sur
(Phrasal verb)
■ **clap on**: **to ∼ on one's hat** enfoncer son chapeau sur sa tête; **to ∼ on the brakes**° Aut freiner brusquement, piler°

clapboard /'klæpbɔːd/
A *n* planche *f* en clin
B *noun modifier* [*house*] en bois

clapped-out° /ˌklæpt'aʊt/ *adj* [*car*] pourri; [*machine*] mort°; [*horse*] claqué°; [*person*] (exhausted) crevé°; (past it) fichu°, fini

clapping /'klæpɪŋ/ *n* ¢ applaudissements *mpl*

claptrap° /'klæptræp/ *n* ¢ âneries *fpl*

claret /'klærət/ ▸ p. 752 *n* **1** (wine) bordeaux *m* (rouge); **2** (colour) bordeaux *m*

clarification /ˌklærɪfɪ'keɪʃn/ *n* éclaircissement *m*, clarification *f*

clarify /'klærɪfaɪ/
A *vtr* **1** (explain) éclaircir, clarifier [*point*]; **2** Culin clarifier [*butter, stock*]; coller [*wine*]
B *vi* [*person*] s'expliquer

clarinet /ˌklærə'net/ ▸ p. 1028 *n* clarinette *f*

clarinettist /ˌklærə'netɪst/ ▸ p. 1028, p. 1181 *n* clarinettiste *mf*

clarity /'klærətɪ/ *n* clarté *f*

clash /klæʃ/
A *n* **1** (confrontation) affrontement *m*; fig (disagreement) querelle *f*; **2** (contest) affrontement *m*; **3** (contradiction) conflit *m*, incompatibilité *f*; **a ∼ of cultures** un conflit de cultures; **a personality ∼** un conflit de personnalités; **4** (inconvenient coincidence) **there's a ∼ of meetings** les réunions ont lieu en même temps; **5** (noise) (of swords) cliquetis *m*; **a ∼ of cymbals** un coup de cymbales
B *vtr* entrechoquer [*bin lids*]; frapper [*cymbals*]
C *vi* **1** (meet and fight) [*armies, groups*] s'affronter; fig (disagree) s'affronter; **to ∼ with sb** (fight) se heurter à qn; (disagree) se quereller avec qn (**on, over** au sujet de); **2** (be in conflict) [*interests, beliefs*] être incompatibles; **3** (coincide) [*meetings*] avoir lieu en même temps (**with** que); **4** (not match) [*colours*] jurer

clasp /klɑːsp, US klæsp/
A *n* **1** (on bracelet, bag, purse) fermoir *m*; (on belt) boucle *f*; **2** (grip) étreinte *f*
B *vtr* **1** (hold) serrer [qch] dans la main [*purse, knife*]; **he ∼ed her hand** il lui a serré la main; **2** (embrace) étreindre; **to ∼ sb to one's breast** prendre qn dans ses bras

class /klɑːs, US klæs/
A *n* **1** Sociol classe *f*; **2** (group of students) classe *f*; (lesson) cours *m* (**in** de); **in ∼** en cours *or* classe; **to give a ∼** assurer un cours; **to take a ∼** GB assurer un cours; US suivre un cours; **3** (year group) promotion *f*, classe *f*; **4** (category) classe *f*, catégorie *f*; **to be in a ∼ of one's own** être hors catégorie; **she's in a different ∼ from him** il n'y a aucune comparaison possible entre elle et lui; **he's not in the same ∼ as her** il n'arrive pas à sa cheville; **5** °(elegance) classe *f*; **6** Tourism classe *f*; **to travel first/second** voyager en première/deuxième classe; **a first ∼ seat** une place de première classe; **7** GB Univ ≈ mention *f*; **a first-/second-∼ degree** ≈ licence avec mention très bien/bien; **8** Biol, Math classe *f*
B *vtr* classer; **to ∼ sb/sth as** assimiler qn/qch à

class: ∼ conscious *adj* soucieux/-ieuse des distinctions sociales; **∼ consciousness** *n* sentiment *m* de classe

classic /'klæsɪk/
A *n* **1** (literary, sporting) classique *m*; **2** °(hilarious example) **it was a real ∼!** (of gaffe) c'était un chef-d'œuvre du genre!; (of comment, situation) c'était trop drôle!
B *adj* classique

classical /'klæsɪkl/ *adj* gen classique; **∼ scholar** philologue *mf*

classically /'klæsɪklɪ/ *adv* dans un style classique

classicism /'klæsɪsɪzəm/ *n* classicisme *m*

classicist /'klæsɪsɪst/ *n* (student) étudiant/-e *m/f* en lettres classiques; (scholar) spécialiste *mf* de lettres classiques, philologue *mf*

classics /'klæsɪks/ *n* (+ *v sg*) lettres *fpl* classiques

classification /ˌklæsɪfɪ'keɪʃn/ *n* **1** (category) classification *f*, catégorie *f*; **2** (categorization) classement *m*

classified /'klæsɪfaɪd/
A *n* (*also* **∼ ad**) petite annonce *f*
B *adj* **1** (categorized) classifié; **2** (secret) confidentiel/-ielle

classified: ∼ ad *n* petite annonce *f*; **∼ section** *n* rubrique *f* des petites annonces

classify /'klæsɪfaɪ/ *vtr* **1** (file) classer; **2** (declare secret) classer [qch] confidentiel/-ielle

classless /'klɑːslɪs, US 'klæs-/ *adj* [*society*] sans classes; [*accent*] neutre

class: ∼ mark *n* cote *f*; **∼mate** *n* camarade *mf* de classe; **∼room** *n* salle *f* de classe; **∼ struggle** *n* lutte *f* des classes; **∼ system** *n* système *m* de classes; **∼ war(fare)** *n* guerre *f* des classes

classy° /'klɑːsɪ, US 'klæsɪ/ *adj* [*person, dress*] qui a de la classe; [*car, hotel*] de luxe; [*actor, performance*] de grande classe

clatter /'klætə(r)/
A *n* cliquetis *m*; (loud) fracas *m*
B *vi* [*typewriter*] cliqueter; [*dishes*] s'entrechoquer; [*vehicle*] rouler avec fracas

clause /klɔːz/ *n* **1** Ling proposition *f*; **2** Jur, Pol clause *f*; (in will, act of Parliament) disposition *f*

claustrophobia /ˌklɔːstrə'fəʊbɪə/ *n* claustrophobie *f*

claustrophobic /ˌklɔːstrə'fəʊbɪk/
A *n* claustrophobe *mf*

B adj [person] claustrophobe; [feeling] de claustrophobie; **it's ~ in here** il y a une atmosphère oppressante ici; **to get ~** avoir une sensation de claustrophobie

clavichord /'klævɪkɔːd/ ▸ p. 1028 n clavicorde m

clavicle /'klævɪkl/ n clavicule f

claw /klɔː/
A n **1** Zool (of animal) griffe f; (of bird of prey) serre f; (of crab, lobster) pince f; **2** ºfig (hand) patte º f; **to get one's ~s into sb** mettre le grappin sur qn; **3** (on hammer) arrache-clou m, pied-de-biche m
B vtr (scratch) griffer; **to ~ sb's eyes out** arracher les yeux de qn; fig **he ~ed his way to the top** il est arrivé en employant tous les moyens

(Phrasal verb)
■ **claw back**: ▸ ~ **[sth] back**, ~ **back [sth]** **1** Fin récupérer; **2** Comm, Sport regagner péniblement [position]

clay /kleɪ/
A n **1** (for sculpture) argile f, terre f glaise; **2** (soil) argile f; **3** (in tennis) terre f battue
B noun modifier **1** [pot, pipe] en terre; **2** Sport [court] en terre battue

(Idiom) **to have feet of** ~ avoir des pieds d'argile

clay pigeon shooting ▸ p. 881 n ball-trap m, tir m aux pigeons d'argile

clean /kliːn/
A n **to give sth a** ~ nettoyer qch
B adj **1** (not dirty) [clothes, dishes, floor] propre; [air, water] pur; [syringe] désinfecté; **she keeps her house** ~ elle tient sa maison propre; **my hands are** ~ lit, fig j'ai les mains propres; ~ **and tidy** impeccable de propreté; **a** ~ **sheet of paper** une feuille blanche; **to rinse sth** ~ rincer qch; **keep your shoes** ~ ne salis pas tes chaussures; **2** (with no pollution) [fuel] propre; **3** (not obscene) [joke] anodin; **keep it** ~! restons décents!; **4** (unsullied) [reputation] sans tache; [record, licence] vierge; **5** (no longer addicted) désintoxiqué; **6** º(without illicit property) **he's** ~ il n'a rien; **the room is** ~ on n'a rien trouvé dans la pièce; **7** Sport [tackle] sans faute; [hit] précis; **keep it** ~ (in match) pas de bavures; **8** (neat) [lines, profile] pur; [edge] net/nette; ~ **break** Med fracture f simple; **to make a** ~ **break with the past** fig rompre définitivement avec le passé
C adv **the bullet went** ~ **through his shoulder** la balle lui a littéralement traversé l'épaule; **to jump** ~ **over the wall** sauter par-dessus le mur sans le toucher; **we're** ~ **out of bread** on n'a plus de pain
D vtr **1** nettoyer [room, shoes, gun]; effacer [blackboard]; ~ **sth from** ou **off** enlever qch de [hands, car]; **to have sth ~ed** donner qch à nettoyer; **to** ~ **one's teeth** se brosser les dents; **2** Culin vider [fish]
E vi (do housework) faire le ménage
F v refl **to** ~ **itself** [animal] faire sa toilette

(Idioms) **to** ~ **up one's act** [person] devenir plus sérieux; **I'll have to come** ~ º il va falloir que je dise la vérité

(Phrasal verbs)
■ **clean down**: ▸ ~ **[sth] down**, ~ **down [sth]** nettoyer [qch] à fond
■ **clean off**: ▸ ~ **off** [stain] partir; ▸ ~ **[sth] off**, ~ **off [sth]** enlever [stain, graffiti]; **to** ~ **sth off** effacer qch de [blackboard]; enlever qch de [car, wall]
■ **clean out**: ▸ ~ **[sth] out**, ~ **out [sth]** nettoyer [qch] à fond; ▸ ~ **[sb/sth] out**, ~ **out [sb/sth]** (leave empty, penniless) [thief] mettre [qch] à sac [house]; [thief, holiday] mettre [qn] à sec [person]
■ **clean up**: ▸ ~ **up** **1** (remove dirt) tout nettoyer; **2** (tidy) tout remettre en ordre (**after sb** derrière qn); **3** (wash oneself) se débarbouiller; **4** º(make profit) [dealer] faire son beurre º (**on** avec); [gambler] rafler la mise º; ▸ ~ **[sb] up** faire la toilette de [patient]; ▸ ~ **[sth] up**, ~ **up [sth]** **1** (remove dirt) nettoyer; **that rubbish up off** ou **from the floor** débarrasse le sol de ces saletés; **2** fig (remove crime) nettoyer º [street, city]; (make less obscene) expurger [comedy act]

clean-cut adj [image, person] soigné

cleaner /'kliːnə(r)/ ▸ p. 1181 n **1** (person) (in workplace) agent m de nettoyage; (in home) (woman) femme f de ménage; (man) agent m de nettoyage; **2** (machine) nettoyeur m; **carpet** ~ shampouineuse f (de tapis); **3** (detergent) produit m de nettoyage; **suede** ~ produit m pour nettoyer le daim; **4** (shop) (also **cleaner's**) pressing m

(Idiom) **to take sb to the** ~**s** º (swindle) plumer qnº; (leave penniless) nettoyer

cleaning /'kliːnɪŋ/ n (domestic) ménage m; (commercial) nettoyage m, entretien m; **to do the** ~ faire le ménage

cleaning: ~ **lady** ▸ p. 1181 n femme f de ménage; ~ **product** n produit m d'entretien

cleanliness /'klenlɪnɪs/ n propreté f

clean-living /ˌkliːn'lɪvɪŋ/
A n vie f saine
B adj [person] aux habitudes saines

cleanly /'kliːnlɪ/ adv [cut] bien, franchement; [catch, hit] avec précision; **to break off** ~ se casser net

clean-out º /'kliːnaʊt/ n nettoyage m à fond

cleanse /klenz/ vtr **1** lit nettoyer [skin, wound]; **2** fig laver, purifier [person, mind]; nettoyer [society]

cleanser /'klenzə(r)/ n **1** (for face) démaquillant m; **2** (household) produit m d'entretien

clean-shaven /ˌkliːn'ʃeɪvn/ adj **he's** ~ il n'a ni barbe ni moustache

clean sheet n fig (record) casier m vierge

cleansing /'klenzɪŋ/ n nettoyage m

cleansing department n GB Admin (service m de la) voirie f

cleanup /'kliːnʌp/ n **to give sth a** ~ º nettoyer qch

clear /klɪə(r)/
A adj **1** (transparent) [glass, liquid] transparent; [blue] limpide; [lens, varnish] incolore; **2** (distinct) [image, outline] net/nette; [writing] lisible; [sound, voice] clair; **he had a** ~ **view of the man** il voyait très bien l'homme; **3** (comprehensibly plain) [description, instruction] clair; **to make sth** ~ **to sb** faire comprendre qch à qn; **I wish to make it** ~ **that** je tiens à préciser que; **is that** ~?, **do I make myself** ~? est-ce que c'est clair?; **to make one's views** ~ exprimer clairement ses opinions; **let's get this** ~ que les choses soient claires; **4** (obvious) [need, sign] évident; [advantage, lead] net/nette; [example] beau/belle (before n); [majority] large (before n); **it is** ~ **that** il est clair que; **5** (not confused) [idea, memory] clair; [plan] précis; **to keep a** ~ **head** garder les idées claires; **a** ~ **thinker** un esprit lucide; **I'm not** ~ **what to do** je ne sais pas très bien quoi faire; **6** (empty) [road, view] dégagé; [table] débarrassé; [space] libre; **7** (not guilty) [conscience] tranquille; **8** (unblemished) [skin] net/nette; **9** Med [X-ray, scan] normal; **10** (cloudless) [sky] sans nuage; [day, night] clair; **on a** ~ **day** par temps clair; **11** (frank) [gaze] franc/franche; **12** (pure) [tone, voice] clair; **13** Culin [honey] liquide; ~ **soup** consommé m; **14** (exempt from) **to be** ~ **of** être libre de [debt]; être exempt de [blame]; être lavé de [suspicion]; **15** (free) [day, diary] libre; **keep Monday** ~ ne prévois rien d'autre lundi; **16** (whole) [week, day] entier/-ière; **17** (net) [gain, profit] net inv (after n)
B adv (away from) **to jump** ~ sauter sur le côté; **to jump** ~ **of** (jump out of) sauter hors de [vehicle]; (avoid) **to pull sb** ~ **of** extraire qn de [wreckage]; **to stay** ou **steer** ~ **of** éviter [town centre]; éviter [alcohol, troublemakers]; **stand** ~ **of the gates!** éloignez-vous des portes!; **to get** ~ **of** sortir de [traffic, town]
C vtr **1** (remove) abattre [trees]; arracher [weeds]; enlever [debris, papers, mines]; dégager [snow] (**from, off** de); **to** ~ **the streets of demonstrators** débarrasser les rues des manifestants; **2** (free from obstruction) déboucher [drains]; dégager [road]; débarrasser [table, surface]; déblayer [site]; défricher [land]; **to** ~ **the road of obstacles** dégager la route de obstacles; **to** ~ **sth out of the way** (from table, seat) enlever qch; (from floor) enlever qch du passage; **to** ~ **the way for sth/sb** lit libérer le passage pour qch/qn; fig ouvrir la voie pour [developments]; fig laisser la place à [person]; **3** (freshen) **to** ~ **the air** lit aérer; fig apaiser les tensions; **4** (empty) vider [desk] (**of** de); débarrasser [room, surface] (**of** de); évacuer [area, building]; **5** (create) faire [space]; **to** ~ **a path through sth** se frayer un chemin à travers qch; **6** (disperse) dissiper [fog, smoke]; disperser [crowd]; **7** (unblock) dégager [nose]; **to** ~ **one's throat** se racler la gorge; **the fresh air will** ~ **your head** un peu d'air frais t'éclaircira les idées; **8** (eliminate) faire disparaître [dandruff, spots]; **9** Comput effacer [screen]; **10** (dispose of) liquider [stock]; **'reduced to** ~**'** 'solde'; **11** (pay off) s'acquitter de [debt]; **12** Fin [bank] compenser [cheque]; **13** (free from blame) innocenter [accused] (**of** de); **to be** ~**ed of suspicion** être lavé de tout soupçon; **to** ~ **one's name** blanchir son nom; **14** (vet) mener une enquête administrative sur [employee]; **15** (officially approve)

approuver [*request*]; **to ~ sth with sb** obtenir l'accord de qn pour qch; **16)** (jump over) franchir [*hurdle, wall*]; **17)** (pass through) passer sous [*bridge*]; **to ~ customs** passer à la douane

D *vi* **1)** (become unclouded) [*liquid, sky*] s'éclaircir; **2)** (disappear) [*smoke, fog, cloud*] se dissiper; **3)** (become pure) [*air*] se purifier; **4)** (go away) [*rash*] disparaître; **5)** Fin [*cheque*] être compensé

Idioms the coast is ~ fig le champ est libre; **to be in the ~** (safe) être hors de danger; (free from suspicion) être lavé de tout soupçon

Phrasal verbs
■ **clear away**: ▸ ~ **away** débarrasser; ▸ ~ **[sth] away**, ~ **away [sth]** balayer [*leaves*]; enlever [*rubbish*]; ranger [*papers, toys*]
■ **clear off**: ▸ ~ **off**○ GB (run away) filer○; (go away) ficher le camp○
■ **clear out**: ▸ ~ **out** (run away) filer○, se sauver; ▸ ~ **[sth] out**, ~ **out [sth]** **1)** (tidy) ranger [*room*]; faire le tri dans [*drawer*]; **2)** (empty) vider [*room*]; **3)** (throw away) jeter
■ **clear up**: ▸ ~ **up** **1)** (tidy up) faire du rangement; **2)** (improve) [*weather*] s'éclaircir; [*infection*] disparaître; ▸ ~ **up [sth]**, ~ **[sth] up** **1)** (tidy) ranger [*mess, room, toys*]; ramasser [*litter*]; **2)** (resolve) résoudre [*problem*]; dissiper [*misunderstanding*]; tirer [qch] au clair [*mystery*]

clearance /'klɪərəns/ *n* **1)** (permission) autorisation *f*; ~ **for take-off** autorisation de décoller; **to have ~ to do** être autorisé à faire; **2)** (customs certificate) déclaration *f* en douane; **3)** Admin, Mil habilitation *f* sécuritaire; **4)** (removal) (of trees) abattage *m*; (of buildings) démolition *f*; (of vegetation) défrichage *m*; **5)** Comm liquidation *f*; **6)** (gap) **a 10 cm ~** un espace de 10 cm; **7)** Fin compensation *f*

clearance sale *n* Comm (total) liquidation *f*; (partial) soldes *mpl*

clear-cut /ˌklɪə'kʌt/ *adj* [*plan, division*] précis; [*difference, outline*] net/nette; [*problem, rule*] clair; **the matter is not so ~** l'affaire n'est pas si simple

clear-headed *adj* lucide

clearing /'klɪərɪŋ/ *n* **1)** (glade) clairière *f*; **2)** (removal) (of obstacles) enlèvement *m*; (of road, mines, debris) déblaiement *m*; **3)** (levelling) (of forest) abattage *m*; (of land) défrichage *m*; **4)** Fin compensation *f*

clearing: ~ **bank** *n* GB Fin banque *f* affiliée à une chambre de compensation; ~ **house** *n* Fin chambre *f* de compensation; Admin bureau *m* central; **~-up** *n* rangement *m*

clearly /'klɪəlɪ/ *adv* **1)** (distinctly) [*speak, hear, write*] clairement; [*audible*] nettement; [*visible*] bien; [*see*] lit bien; fig clairement; [*labelled*] clairement; **2)** (intelligibly) [*describe*] clairement; **3)** (lucidly) [*think*] clairement; **4)** (obviously) manifestement

clearness /'klɪənɪs/ *n* **1)** (of glass, water) transparence *f*; **2)** (of day, sky) clarté *f*; **3)** (purity) (of air) pureté *f*; (of note, voice) clarté *f*; **4)** (of image, writing) netteté *f*; (of memory) précision *f*; **5)** (intelligibility) clarté *f*

clear-out○ /'klɪəraʊt/ *n* GB **to have a ~** faire du rangement

clear: ~ **round** *n* parcours *m* sans faute; **~-sighted** *adj* perspicace; **~way** *n* route *f* à stationnement interdit

cleavage /'kli:vɪdʒ/ *n* **1)** (of breasts) décolleté *m*; **to show a lot of ~** avoir un décolleté plongeant; **2)** (of opinion) clivage *m*, division *f*

cleave /kli:v/ *vtr* (*prét* **clove** *ou* **cleaved**; *pp* **cleft** *ou* **cleaved**) fendre

cleaver /'kli:və(r)/ *n* fendoir *m*

clef /klef/ *n* clef *f*; **in the treble ~** en clef de fa

cleft /kleft/
A *n* fente *f*
B *adj* [*chin*] marqué d'un sillon; [*palate*] fendu

clemency /'klemənsɪ/ *n* **1)** (mercy) clémence *f* (**towards** envers, à l'égard de); **2)** (of weather) clémence *f*

clement /'klemənt/ *adj* [*weather, judge*] clément

clench /klentʃ/ *vtr* serrer; **to ~ one's fist** serrer le poing; **to ~ one's teeth** serrer les dents; **to say sth between ~ed teeth** dire qch sans desserrer les dents; **~ed-fist salute** salut *m* le poing levé

clergy /'klɜːdʒɪ/ *n* clergé *m*

clergyman /'klɜːdʒɪmən/ ▸ p. 1181 *n* (*pl* **-men**) ecclésiastique *m*

cleric /'klerɪk/ *n* ecclésiastique *m*

clerical /'klerɪkl/ *adj* (avant n) **1)** Relig [*matters, faction*] clérical; [*control, influence*] du clergé; **2)** [*staff, worker*] de bureau; ~ **work** travail *m* de bureau; ~ **error** erreur *f* d'écriture (*dans les comptes*)

clerical: ~ **assistant** ▸ p. 1181 *n* commis *m*; ~ **collar** *n* (Catholic) col *m* romain; (Protestant) col *m* de clergyman

clerk /klɑːk, US klɜːrk/ ▸ p. 1181 *n* **1)** (in office, bank etc) employé/-e *m/f*; **booking** ~ employé/-e *m/f* aux réservations; **head** ~ Admin chef *m* de bureau; Comm premier commis *m*; **2)** (in UK) (to lawyer) ≈ clerc *m*; (in court) greffier/ -ière *m/f*; **3)** US (in hotel) réceptionniste *mf*; (in shop) vendeur/-euse *m/f*

clever /'klevə(r)/ *adj* **1)** (intelligent) [*person*] intelligent; **to be ~ at sth/at doing** être doué pour qch/pour faire; **to be ~ with figures** être doué pour le calcul; **that wasn't very ~!** ce n'était pas malin!; **2)** (ingenious) [*solution, gadget, person*] astucieux/-ieuse, futé; **how ~ of you!** félicitations!; **how ~ of you to find the solution** je te félicite d'avoir trouvé la solution; **3)** (shrewd) astucieux/-ieuse; **4)** (skilful) habile, adroit; **to be ~ at doing** être habile à faire; **he's ~ with his hands** il est adroit de ses mains; **5)** (persuasive) [*argument, advertisement*] astucieux/-ieuse; [*lawyer, salesperson*] malin/-igne; **6)** (cunning) **to be too ~ for sb** être trop malin/-igne pour qn; **to be too ~ by half** être beaucoup trop intelligent

cleverly /'klevəlɪ/ *adv* (intelligently) intelligemment; (astutely) astucieusement; (dextrously) adroitement

cleverness /'klevənɪs/ *n* (intelligence) intelligence *f*; (ingenuity) ingéniosité *f*; (dexterity) adresse *f*, habileté *f*

cliché /'kli:ʃeɪ, US kli:'ʃeɪ/ *n* cliché *m*, lieu *m* commun

clichéd /'kli:ʃeɪd, US kli:'ʃeɪd/ *adj* [*expression*] rebattu; [*idea, technique*] éculé; [*art, music*] bourré○ de clichés

click /klɪk/
A *n* **1)** (of metal, china) petit bruit *m* sec; (of machine) déclic *m*; (of fingers, heels, tongue) claquement *m*; **2)** Comput clic *m*
B *vtr* **to ~ one's fingers/tongue** faire claquer ses doigts/sa langue; **to ~ one's heels** claquer des talons; **to ~ sth shut** fermer qch avec un bruit sec
C *vi* **1)** [*camera, lock*] faire un déclic; [*door*] faire un petit bruit sec; **2)** ○(become clear) **suddenly something ~ed** tout d'un coup ça a fait tilt○; **3)** (work out perfectly) **everything ~ed for them** tout a bien marché pour eux○; **4)** ○(strike a rapport) **we just ~ed** on a sympathisé du premier coup; **5)** Comput cliquer (**on** sur)

clickable /'klɪkəbl/ *adj* [*image*] cliquable, sensible

clicking /'klɪkɪŋ/ *n* (of machine, cameras) cliquetis *m*; ~ **noise** cliquetis *m*

client /'klaɪənt/ *n* client/-e *m/f*

clientele /ˌkli:ən'tel, US ˌklaɪən'tel/ *n* clientèle *f*

cliff /klɪf/ *n* (by sea) falaise *f*; (inland) escarpement *m*

cliffhanger○ /'klɪfhæŋə(r)/ *n* (film) film *m* à suspense; (story) récit *m* à suspense; (situation) situation *f* à suspense

climactic /klaɪ'mæktɪk/ *adj* [*event, moment*] crucial

climate /'klaɪmɪt/ *n* **1)** Meteorol climat *m*; **2)** fig (surroundings) atmosphère *f*; **3)** Econ, Pol climat *m*

climatic /klaɪ'mætɪk/ *adj* climatique

climax /'klaɪmæks/
A *n* (of career) apogée *m*; (of war) paroxysme *m*; (of plot, speech, play) point *m* culminant; **to reach its ~** [*battle*] atteindre son paroxysme; [*contest, performance*] atteindre son point culminant; **it's a fitting ~ to a long career** c'est le couronnement d'une longue carrière
B *vi* (reach a high point) atteindre son grand moment

climb /klaɪm/
A *n* **1)** (ascent) (of hill) escalade *f* (**up** de; **to** jusqu'à); (of tower) montée *f*; (of mountain, rockface) ascension *f* (**up** de; **to** jusqu'à); **it's a steep ~ to the top of the tower** il y a une montée raide jusqu'en haut de la tour; **2)** (steep hill) montée *f*; **to stall on the ~** caler dans la montée; **3)** Aviat montée *f*; **4)** fig (rise) ascension *f*
B *vtr* **1)** [*car, person*] grimper [*hill*]; faire l'ascension de [*cliff, mountain*]; escalader [*lamppost, mast, wall*]; grimper à [*ladder, rope, tree*]; monter [*staircase*]; **2)** [*plant*] grimper à [*trellis*]
C *vi* **1)** (scale) gen grimper (**along** le long de, **to** jusqu'à); Sport

faire de l'escalade; **to ~ down** descendre [*rockface*]; **to ~ into** monter dans [*car*]; **to ~ into bed** se mettre au lit; **to ~ over** enjamber [*log, stile*]; passer par-dessus [*fence, wall*]; escalader [*debris, rocks*]; **to ~ up** grimper à [*ladder, tree*]; monter [*steps*]; **②** (rise) [*sun*] se lever; [*aircraft*] monter; **③** (slope up) [*path, road*] monter; **④** (increase) monter

(Phrasal verb)

■ **climb down** revenir sur sa décision

climber /'klaɪmə(r)/ n **①** (mountaineer) grimpeur/-euse m/f, alpiniste mf; (rock-climber) varappeur/-euse m/f; **②** (plant) plante f grimpante

climbing /'klaɪmɪŋ/ ▸ p. 881 n escalade f

climbing: **~ boot** n chaussure f de randonnée; **~ expedition** n expédition f en montagne; **~ frame** n cage f à poules

clinch /klɪntʃ/
A n **①** (in boxing) corps-à-corps m; **②** ○(embrace) **in a ~** enlacé
B vtr **①** (secure) décrocher [*victory, market, order*]; **to ~ a deal** Comm conclure une affaire; Pol conclure un accord; **②** (resolve) décider de [*argument*]; **what ~ed it was...** ce qui a été décisif c'est...

clincher○ /'klɪntʃə(r)/ n (act, remark) facteur m décisif; (argument) argument m décisif

cling /klɪŋ/ (*prét, pp* **clung**) vi **①** (physically) **to ~ (on)** to se cramponner à; **to ~ together** se cramponner l'un à l'autre; **to ~ on to sth for dear life** se cramponner de toutes ses forces à qch; **②** (emotionally) **to ~ to** se cramponner à [*parent, beliefs, hope*]; **③** (adhere) [*leaf, moss*] coller (**to** à); [*smell*] résister

(Phrasal verb)

■ **cling on** [*custom, myth*] survivre obstinément

clingfilm /'klɪŋfɪlm/ n GB scellofrais® m

clinging /'klɪŋɪŋ/ adj [*plant*] à crampons; [*person*] fig collant

clinic /'klɪnɪk/ n **①** (treatment centre) centre m médical; **Dr X's ~** le service du Dr X; **②** GB (nursing-home) clinique f; **③** (advice or teaching session) clinique f

clinical /'klɪnɪkl/ adj **①** Med clinique; **②** (scientific) [*approach*] objectif/-ive; [*precision*] clinique; **③** (unfeeling) froid

clinically /'klɪnɪklɪ/ adv **①** (medically) cliniquement; **②** (unemotionally) avec une précision clinique

clinical: **~ psychologist** ▸ p. 1181 n psychologue mf clinicien/-ienne; **~ psychology** n psychologie f clinique

clink /klɪŋk/
A n **①** (noise) tintement m; **②** ○(prison) taule○ f, trou○ m
B vtr faire tinter [*glass, keys*]; **to ~ glasses with** trinquer avec
C vi [*glass, keys*] tinter

clip /klɪp/
A n **①** (on clipboard) pince f; (on earring, bow tie) clip m; (for hair) barrette f; (on pen) agrafe f; (jewellery) clip(s) m; **②** (for wire) cavalier m; **③** TV, Cin (excerpt) extrait m; **④** Mil (also **cartridge ~**) chargeur m
B vtr (*p prés etc* **-pp-**) **①** (cut, trim) tailler [*hedge*]; couper [*nails, hair, moustache*]; tondre [*dog, sheep*]; rogner [*wing*]; **to ~ an article out of the paper** découper un article dans un journal; **②** (by hooking) accrocher [*pen, microphone*] (**to** à); (by securing) fixer [*brooch*] (**to** à); **③** GB poinçonner [*ticket*]; **④** (hit) heurter
C vi (*p prés etc* **-pp-**) (by hooking) s'accrocher (**to** à); (by fastening) se fixer (**to** à)

(Idioms) **to ~ sb's wings** rogner les ailes à qn; **to give sb a ~ on the ear**○ flanquer une taloche à qn○

clip: **~ art** n Comput images fpl clipart, clipart m; **~board** n gen porte-bloc m inv à pince; Comput presse-papiers m inv; **~-clop** n bruit m de sabots; **~ frame** n sous-verre m inv

clip-on /'klɪpɒn/
A n **clip-ons** npl (earrings) clips mpl
B adj [*bow tie*] agrafable; **~ microphone** micro-cravate m

clipped /klɪpt/ adj [*speech*] haché

clipper /'klɪpə(r)/
A n Aviat, Naut clipper m
B n **clippers** npl (for nails) coupe-ongles m inv; (for hair, hedge) tondeuse f

clipping /'klɪpɪŋ/
A n (from paper) coupure f de presse
B n **clippings** npl (hair) cheveux mpl coupés; (nails) bouts mpl d'ongles

clique /kli:k/ n clique f péj, bande f

cliquey, **cliquish** /'kli:kɪ/ adj [*profession, group*] fermé; [*atmosphere*] exclusif/-ive

Cllr GB abrév écrite = **councillor**

cloak /kləʊk/
A n **①** (garment) cape f; (long, worn by men) houppelande f; **②** fig (front, cover) **to be a ~ for** servir de couverture à [*operation etc*]; **a ~ of respectability** un voile de respectabilité
B vtr **①** (surround) **to ~ sth in** ou **with** entourer qch de [*anonymity, secrecy*]; **to ~ sth in respectability** jeter un voile de respectabilité sur qch; **~ed in** enveloppé dans [*darkness*]; enveloppé de [*ambiguity, secrecy*]; **②** (hide, disguise) masquer

cloak-and-dagger adj clandestin

cloakroom /'kləʊkrʊm/ n **①** (for coats) vestiaire m; **②** GB (lavatory) toilettes fpl

cloak: **~room attendant** ▸ p. 1181 n (in hotel) préposé/-e m/f au vestiaire; GB (at toilets) préposé/-e m/f à l'entretien des toilettes; **~room ticket** n ticket m de vestiaire

clobber○ /'klɒbə(r)/
A n GB attirail○ m, barda○ m
B vtr **①** (hit) tabasser○; **②** (defeat) démolir○

cloche /klɒʃ/ n **①** (in garden) cloche f; **②** (also **~ hat**) chapeau m cloche

clock /klɒk/ ▸ p. 745
A n **①** (timepiece) (large) horloge f; (small) pendule f; **to set a ~** mettre une pendule à l'heure; **to put the ~s forward/back one hour** avancer/reculer les pendules d'une heure; **he does everything by the ~** tout est minuté chez lui; **to work around the ~** travailler 24 heures sur 24; **to work against the ~** faire une course contre la montre; **②** (timer) (in computer) horloge f (interne); (for central heating system) horloge f (incorporée); **③** ○Aut compteur m; **40,000 kilometres on the ~** 40 000 kilomètres au compteur; **④** Sport chronomètre m
B vtr **①** (hit) flanquer un marron○ à qn; **②** (achieve) **to ~ 9.6 seconds in the 100 metres** faire le 100 mètres en 9,6 secondes

(Idiom) **to turn the ~ back 200 years** revenir 200 ans en arrière

(Phrasal verbs)

■ **clock off** GB pointer (à la sortie)
■ **clock on** GB pointer
■ **clock up**: **~ up [sth]** **①** faire [*distance*]; **②** [*worker*] travailler [*hours*]

clock: **~ face** n cadran m; **~maker** ▸ p. 1181 n horloger/-ère m/f; **~ radio** n radio-réveil m; **~ tower** n beffroi m; **~-watch** vi regarder tout le temps l'heure; **~wise** adj, adv dans le sens des aiguilles d'une montre

clockwork /'klɒkwɜːk/
A n (in clock) mécanisme m or mouvement m d'horloge; (in toy) mécanisme m
B adj [*toy*] mécanique

(Idioms) **to be as regular as ~** être réglé comme une horloge; **to go like ~** aller comme sur des roulettes

clod /klɒd/ n **①** (of earth) motte f (de terre); **②** ○(fool) plouc○ m

clog /klɒg/ n sabot m

(Idiom) **to pop one's ~s**○ casser sa pipe○

(Phrasal verb)

■ **clog up**: ▸ **~ up** se boucher; ▸ **~ up [sth]**, **~ [sth] up** boucher; **to be ~ged up with traffic** être embouteillé

cloister /'klɔɪstə(r)/
A n cloître m
B vtr cloîtrer; **to lead a ~ed existence** mener une vie très protégée

clone /kləʊn/
A n Biol, Comput, fig clone m
B vtr cloner

cloning /'kləʊnɪŋ/ n clonage m

close[1] /kləʊs/
A n **①** (road) passage m; **②** (of cathedral) enceinte f
B adj **①** (with close links) [*relative*] proche; [*resemblance*] frap-

The clock

What time is it?

It is...	Il est...	say...
4 o'clock	4 heures or 4 h	quatre heures
4 o'clock in the morning or 4 am	4 h 00	quatre heures du matin
4 o'clock in the afternoon or 4 pm	16 h 00	quatre heures de l'après-midi or seize heures*
0400	4 h 00	quatre heures
4.02	4 h 02	quatre heures deux
two minutes past four	4 h 02	or quatre heures deux minutes†
4.05	4 h 05	quatre heures cinq
five past four	4 h 05	quatre heures cinq
4.10	4 h 10	quatre heures dix
ten past four	4 h 10	quatre heures dix
4.15	4 h 15	quatre heures quinze‡
a quarter past four	4 h 15	quatre heures et quart‡
4.20	4 h 20	quatre heures vingt
4.25	4 h 25	quatre heures vingt-cinq
4.30	4 h 30	quatre heures trente‡
half past four	4 h 30	quatre heures et demie§
4.35	4 h 35	quatre heures trente-cinq
twenty-five to five	4 h 35	cinq heures moins vingt-cinq
4.37	4 h 37	quatre heures trente-sept
twenty-three minutes to five	4 h 37	quatre heures trente-sept
4.40	4 h 40	quatre heures quarante
twenty to five	4 h 40	cinq heures moins vingt
4.45	4 h 45	cinq heures moins le quart
4.50	4 h 50	quatre heures cinquante
ten to five	4 h 50	cinq heures moins dix
4.55	4 h 55	quatre heures cinquante cinq
five to five	4 h 55	cinq heures moins cinq
5 o'clock	5 h	cinq heures
16.15	16 h 15	seize heures quinze
16.25	16 h 25	seize heures vingt-cinq
8 o'clock in the evening	8 h du soir	huit heures du soir
8 pm	20 h 00	vingt heures
12.00	12 h 00	douze heures
noon or 12 noon	12 h 00	midi
midnight or 12 midnight	24 h 00	minuit

* In timetables etc., the twenty-four hour clock is used, so that 4 pm is seize heures. In ordinary usage, one says quatre heures (de l'après-midi).

what time is it?
= quelle heure est-il?

my watch says five o'clock
= il est cinq heures à ma montre

could you tell me the time?
= pouvez-vous me donner l'heure?

it's exactly four o'clock
= il est quatre heures juste
  or il est exactement quatre heures

it's about four
= il est environ quatre heures

it's almost three o'clock
= il est presque trois heures

it's just before six o'clock
= il va être six heures

it's just after five o'clock
= il est à peine plus de cinq heures

it's gone five
= il est cinq heures passées

When?

■ French never drops the word heures: at five is à cinq heures and so on.

■ French always uses à, whether or not English includes the word at. The only exception is when there is another preposition present, as in vers cinq heures (towards five o'clock), avant cinq heures (before five o'clock) etc.

what time did it happen?
= à quelle heure cela s'est-il passé?

what time will he come at?
= à quelle heure va-t-il venir?

it happened at two o'clock
= c'est arrivé à deux heures

he'll come at four
= il viendra à quatre heures

at ten past four
= à quatre heures dix

at half past eight
= à huit heures et demie

at three o'clock exactly
= à trois heures précises

at about five
= vers cinq heures or à cinq heures environ

at five at the latest
= à cinq heures au plus tard

a little after nine
= un peu après neuf heures

it must be ready by ten
= il faut que ce soit prêt avant dix heures

I'll be here until 6 pm
= je serai là jusqu'à six heures du soir

I won't be here until 6 pm
= je ne serai pas là avant six heures du soir

it lasts from seven till nine
= cela dure de sept à neuf heures

closed from 1 to 2 pm
= fermé entre treize et quatorze heures

every hour on the hour
= toutes les heures à l'heure juste

at ten past every hour
= toutes les heures à dix

† This fuller form is possible in all similar cases in this list. It is used only in 'official' styles.

‡ Quatre heures et quart sounds less official than quatre heures quinze (and similarly et demie and moins le quart are the less official forms). The demie and quart forms are not used with the 24-hour clock.

§ Demi agrees when it follows its noun, but not when it comes before the noun to which it is hyphenated, e.g. quatre heures et demie but les demi-heures etc. Note that midi and minuit are masculine, so midi et demi and minuit et demi.

C

pant; **to bear a ~ resemblance to sb/sth** ressembler beaucoup à qn/qch; **~ links with** liens *mpl* étroits avec [*country*]; liens *mpl* d'amitié avec [*group*]; **in ~ contact with** en contact permanent avec; [2] (intimate) [*friend*] proche (**to** de); **they have a ~ friendship** ils sont très bons amis; [3] (almost equal) [*contest, result*] serré; **'is it the same?'—'no but it's ~'** 'c'est le même?'—'non mais c'est proche'; [4] (careful, rigorous) [*scrutiny*] minutieux/-ieuse; [*supervision*] étroit; **to pay ~ attention to sth** faire une attention toute particulière à qch; **to keep a ~ watch ou eye on sb/sth** surveiller étroitement qn/qch; [5] (compact) [*texture*] dense; [*print, formation*] serré; [6] (stuffy) [*weather*] lourd; **it's ~ il fait lourd**; [7] ◦(secretive) **she's been very ~ about it** elle n'a rien voulu dire

C *adv* [1] (nearby) **to live quite ~ (by)** habiter tout près; **they look ~er than they are** ils semblent plus près qu'ils ne le sont; **how ~ is the town?** est-ce que la ville est loin?; **it's ~, I can hear it** il ne doit pas être loin, je l'entends; **the closer he came** plus il approchait; **to bring sth closer** approcher qch; **to follow ~ behind** suivre de près; **to hold sb ~** serrer qn; **~ together** serrés les uns contre les autres; [2] (close temporally) **the time is ~ when** dans peu de temps; **how ~ are they in age?** combien ont-ils de différence d'âge?; **Christmas is ~** Noël approche; [3] (almost) **that's closer to the truth** ça c'est plus proche de la vérité; **'is the answer three?'—'~!'** 'est-ce que la réponse est trois?'—'tu y es presque'

D **close enough** *adv phr* **that's ~ enough** (no nearer) tu es assez près; (acceptable) ça ira; **20 yachts or ~ enough** à peu près 20 yachts

E **close** *prep phr, adv phr* [1] (near) près de [*place, person, object*]; **how ~ are we to…?** à quelle distance sommes-nous de…?; [2] (on point of) au bord de [*tears, hysteria*]; **to be ~ to doing** être sur le point de faire; [3] (almost at) **closer to 50 than 40** plus proche *or* plus près de 40 ans que de 30; **to come closest to** s'approcher le plus de [*ideal, conception*]; **to come ~ to doing** faillir faire; **how ~ are you to completing…?** est-ce que vous êtes sur le point de finir…?; **to the time when** à peu près au moment où; **it's coming ~ to the time when we must decide** l'heure de nous décider approche; [4] (also ~ **on**◦) (approximately) près de, presque

F **close by** *prep phr, adv phr* près de [*wall, bridge*]; **the ambulance is ~ by** l'ambulance n'est pas loin

(Idioms) **(from) ~ to**◦, **(from) ~ up** de près; **it was a ~ call**◦ *ou* **shave**◦ *ou* **thing** je l'ai/tu l'as etc échappé belle

close² /kləʊz/

A *n* [1] gen, Sport fin *f*; **to bring sth to a ~** mettre fin à qch; **to draw to a ~** tirer à sa fin; **to come to a ~** se terminer; **at the ~ of day** littér à la tombée du jour liter; [2] Fin **~ (of trading)** clôture *f*

B *vtr* [1] (shut) fermer; [2] (block) fermer [*border, port*]; boucher [*pipe, opening*]; barrer [*road*]; interdire l'accès à [*area of town*]; [3] (bring to an end) mettre fin à [*meeting, case*]; fermer [*account*]; **the subject is now ~d** le sujet est clos; [4] (reduce) **to ~ the gap** réduire l'écart; [5] (agree) conclure [*deal, contract*]

C *vi* [1] (shut) [*airport, polls, shop*] fermer; [*door, container, eyes, mouth*] se fermer; [2] (cease to operate) [*business, mine*] fermer définitivement; [3] (end) [*meeting, play*] prendre fin; **to ~ with** se terminer par [*song*]; [4] Fin [*currency, index*] clôturer (**at** à); **the market ~d down/up** le marché a clôturé en baisse/en hausse; [5] (get smaller) se réduire; [6] (get closer) se rapprocher (**on** de)

D **closed** *pp adj* [1] (shut) fermé; **'~d'** (sign in shop) 'fermé'; **'~d for lunch/for repairs'** 'fermé pour le déjeuner/pour cause de réparations'; **'road ~d'** 'route barrée'; **'~d to the public'** 'interdit au public'; **'~d to traffic'** 'circulation interdite'; **behind ~d doors** fig à huis clos; [2] (restricted) [*community, meeting*] fermé; **to have a ~d mind** avoir l'esprit fermé

(Phrasal verbs)

■ **close down:** ▸ ~ **down** [*shop, business*] fermer définitivement; ▸ ~ **down** [sth], ~ [sth] **down** fermer [qch] définitivement [*business, factory*]

■ **close in** [*pursuers*] se rapprocher (**on** de); [*winter*] approcher; [*fog*] descendre (**on** sur); **the nights are closing in** les jours commencent à raccourcir

■ **close off:** ▸ ~ **off** [sth], ~ [sth] **off** fermer [qch] au public

■ **close up:** ▸ ~ **up** [1] [*flower, wound*] se refermer; [*group*] se serrer; [2] [*shopkeeper*] fermer; ▸ ~ **up** [sth], ~ [sth] **up** [1] fermer [*shop*]; [2] boucher [*hole*]

■ **close with:** ▸ ~ **with** [sb] [1] Comm tomber d'accord avec [*trader*]; [2] Mil engager le combat avec [*enemy*]; ▸ ~ **with** [sth] Fin accepter [*deal*]

close /kləʊs/ **~ combat** *n* corps-à-corps *m*; **~-cropped** *adj* [*hair*] coupé ras

closed-circuit television, **CCTV** *n* télévision *f* en circuit fermé

closedown /kləʊzdaʊn/ *n* [1] Comm, Ind fermeture *f* (définitive); [2] GB Radio, TV fin *f* des émissions

closed season *n* période *f* de fermeture de la chasse et de la pêche

closed shop *n*: industrie employant exclusivement les membres des syndicats

close /kləʊs/ **~-fitting** *adj* [*garment*] ajusté, près du corps; **~-knit** *adj* fig [*family, group*] très uni

closely /ˈkləʊslɪ/ *adv* [1] (in close proximity) [*follow, look*] lit, fig de près; **to work ~ together** travailler en étroite collaboration; **~ written** écrit très serré; **to be ~ packed** être entassés; [2] (not distantly) [*resemble*] beaucoup; [*identify*] tellement; [*conform*] tout à fait; [*coordinated*] bien; **to be ~ akin to sth** ressembler beaucoup à qch; **to be ~ related** gen être étroitement lié (**to** à); (of people) être proches parents; [3] (rigorously) [*study, monitor*] de près; [*listen*] attentivement; [*question*] avec attention; **~ guarded secret** secret bien gardé; [4] (evenly) **~ contested ou fought** serré

closeness /ˈkləʊsnɪs/ *n* [1] (emotionally) intimité *f*; [2] (in mutual understanding) bonnes relations *fpl*; **the ~ of their alliance** les liens *mpl* étroits qui les unissent; [3] (rapport) rapport *m* (**to** à); [4] (proximity) (of place) proximité *f*; (of event) approche *f*; [5] (of atmosphere) (inside) manque *m* d'air; (outside) **the ~ of the weather** le temps lourd; [6] (accuracy) (of copy) fidélité *f*

close /kləʊs/ **~-run** *adj* très serré; **~-set** *adj* très rapproché

closet /ˈklɒzɪt/

A *n* [1] US (cupboard) placard *m*; (for clothes) penderie *f*; **linen ~** placard *m* à linge; [2] (room) cabinet *m*

B *noun modifier* (secret) [*alcoholic, fascist*] inavoué, qui s'en cache

C *vtr* enfermer; **to be ~ed with sb** être en tête-à-tête avec qn

close-up /ˈkləʊsʌp/

A *n* gros plan *m*; **in ~** en gros plan

B **close up** /kləʊˈsʌp/ *adv* (**from**) ~ de près

closing /ˈkləʊzɪŋ/

A *n* fermeture *f*; **Sunday ~** fermeture *f* dominicale (des magasins)

B *adj* [*minutes, months, days, words*] dernier/-ière; [*scene, pages, stage*] final; [*speech*] de clôture

closing: ~ date *n* date *f* limite (**for** de); **~-down sale**, **~-out sale** US *n* liquidation *f*; **~ price** *n* Fin prix *m* de clôture; **~ time** *n* heure *f* de fermeture

closure /ˈkləʊʒə(r)/ *n* [1] (of road, lane, factory) fermeture *f*; [2] Pol clôture *f*; [3] (fastening) fermeture *f*

clot /klɒt/

A *n* [1] (in blood, milk) caillot *m*; **~ in an artery** caillot obstruant une artère; **~ on the lung/on the brain** embolie *f* pulmonaire/cérébrale; [2] ◦GB (idiot) balourd/-e *m/f*, empoté/-e◦ *m/f*

B *vtr, vi* (*p prés etc* **-tt-**) coaguler, cailler

cloth /klɒθ, US klɔ:θ/

A *n* [1] (fabric) tissu *m*; **wool ~** tissu *m* de laine; [2] (piece of fabric) (for polishing, dusting) chiffon *m*; (for floor) serpillière *f*; (for drying dishes) torchon *m*; (for table) nappe *f*; **damp ~** (for cleaning) chiffon *m* humide; (for ironing) pattemouille *f*; [3] Relig **a man of the ~** un ecclésiastique

B *noun modifier* [*cover, blind*] en tissu; **hey ~ ears**◦! alors, tu es sourd?; **~ cap** casquette *f* de drap

clothe /kləʊð/

A *vtr* habiller, vêtir; **~d in** habillé en *or* vêtu de; **fully ~d** tout habillé

B *v refl* **to ~ oneself** s'habiller, se vêtir

clothes /kləʊðz, US kləʊz/

A *npl* [1] (garments) vêtements *mpl*; **to put on/take off one's ~** s'habiller/se déshabiller; **without any ~ on** tout nu; [2] (washing) linge *m*

B *noun modifier* [*basket, line, peg, pin*] à linge

clothes: ~ airer *n* séchoir *m* à linge; **~ brush** *n* brosse *f* à habits; **~ drier** *n* (machine) sèche-linge *m inv*;

(airer) séchoir *m* à linge; **∼hanger** *n* cintre *m*; **∼ horse** *n* lit séchoir *m* à linge; **∼ moth** *n* mite *f*; **∼ shop** *n* GB magasin *m* de vêtements; **∼ tree** *n* US portemanteau *m*

clothing /'kləʊðɪŋ/ *n* Ȼ vêtements *mpl*; **an item** *ou* **article of** ∼ un vêtement; **∼ trade** habillement *m*, confection *f*

clotted cream *n* GB ≈ crème *f* fraîche épaisse

cloud /klaʊd/
A *n* **1** C (in sky) nuage *m*, nuée *f* liter; **2** Ȼ Meteorol nuages *mpl*; **some patches of** ∼ quelques nuages; **there's a lot of** ∼ **about** il fait un temps très nuageux; **3** (mass) (of insects, smoke, dust, gas) nuage *m*; **4** fig (negative feature) **a** ∼ **of gloom** un voile de tristesse; **to cast a** ∼ **over sth** jeter une ombre sur qch; **5** (blur) (in liquid, marble, gem) nuage *m*; (in glass, on mirror) buée *f*
B *vtr* **1** (blur) [*steam, breath*] embuer [*mirror*]; [*tears*] brouiller [*vision*]; **∼ed with tears** [*eyes*] voilé *or* brouillé de larmes; **2** (confuse) obscurcir [*judgment*]; brouiller [*memory*]; **to** ∼ **the issue** brouiller les cartes; **3** (blight) assombrir [*occasion*]
Idioms **to be living in** ∼**-cuckoo-land** croire au père Noël; **to have one's head in the** ∼**s** avoir la tête dans les nuages; **to be on** ∼ **nine**○ être aux anges; **to leave under a** ∼ partir en état de disgrâce
Phrasal verb
■ **cloud over** [*sky*] se couvrir (de nuages); [*face*] s'assombrir

cloudburst *n* violente averse *f*

cloudless /'klaʊdlɪs/ *adj* sans nuages, limpide

cloudy /'klaʊdɪ/ *adj* **1** [*weather*] couvert; **it's** ∼ le temps est couvert; **2** [*liquid*] trouble; [*glass*] (misted) embué; (opaque) terni

clout /klaʊt/
A *n* **1** (blow) claque *f*, coup *m*; **2** fig (weight) influence *f* (**with** auprès de, sur); **to have** *ou* **carry a great deal of** ∼ avoir beaucoup d'influence, avoir du poids
B ○*vtr* donner un coup *or* une claque à [*person*]

clove /kləʊv/
A *prét* ▸ **cleave**
B *n* Culin **1** (spice) clou *m* de girofle; **oil of** ∼**s** essence *f* de girofle; **2** (of garlic) gousse *f*

cloven /'kləʊvn/ *pp* ▸ **cleave**

cloven foot, cloven hoof *n* (of animal) sabot *m* fendu; (of devil) pied *m* fourchu

clover /'kləʊvə(r)/ *n* trèfle *m*
Idiom **to be/live in** ∼ être/vivre comme un coq en pâte

clown /klaʊn/ *n* **1** (in circus) clown *m*; **2** péj (fool) clown *m*, pitre *m*
Phrasal verb
■ **clown around** GB faire le clown *or* le pitre

cloy /klɔɪ/ *vi* [*food*] finir par lasser; [*pleasure*] perdre son charme

cloying /'klɔɪɪŋ/ *adj* mièvre, mielleux/-euse

club /klʌb/
A *n* ▸ p. 881 **1** (society) (+ *v sg ou pl*) club *m*; **tennis** ∼ club *m* de tennis; **book** ∼ club *m* de livres; **to be in a** ∼ faire partie d'un club; **2** ○(nightclub) boîte *f* de nuit○; **3** Sport club *m*; **football** ∼ club *m* de football; **4** (stick) massue *f*; (for golf) club *m*; **5** (at cards) trèfle *m*; **the ace of** ∼**s** l'as de trèfle
B *noun modifier* [*captain, member*] du club; [*DJ*] de boîte de nuit○
C *vtr* (*p prés etc* **-bb-**) frapper [*qn/qch*] à coups de massue; **to** ∼ **sb with sth** frapper qn avec qch
Idiom **join the** ∼○! tu n'es pas le seul/la seule!
Phrasal verb
■ **club together** cotiser (**for** pour; **to do** pour faire)

club: ∼ **car** *n* US wagon-bar *m* de première classe; ∼ **class** *n* classe *f* club *or* affaires

club foot *n* pied *m* bot; **to have a** ∼ être pied-bot

club: ∼**house** *n* (for changing) US vestiaire *m*; (for socializing) maison *f* de club, club-house *m*; ∼ **sandwich** *n* sandwich *m* mixte, club sandwich *m*; ∼ **soda** *n* US eau *f* de seltz

cluck /klʌk/
A *n* gloussement *m*; **to give a** ∼ glousser
B *vtr* **to** ∼ **one's tongue** claquer de la langue
C *vi* **1** [*hen*] glousser; **2** fig **to** ∼ **over** (fuss) s'affairer

comme une mère poule autour de

clue /kluː/ *n* **1** (in investigation) indice *m* (**to** quant à); **2** (hint) indication *f* (**to, as to** quant à); **I'll give you a** ∼ je vais vous mettre sur la piste; **give me a** ∼ aide-moi; **I haven't (got) a** ∼ je n'ai aucune idée; **they haven't (got) a** ∼ (incompetent) ils n'(en) ont pas la moindre idée; (unsuspecting) ils ne se doutent de rien; **he hasn't (got) a** ∼ **about history** il ne connaît rien de rien à l'histoire; **4** (to crossword) définition *f*

clued-up ○ /ˌkluːˈdʌp/ GB *adj* calé○ (**about** sur)

clueless ○ /'kluːlɪs/ *adj* GB nul/nulle○ (**about** en)

clump /klʌmp/
A *n* **1** (of flowers, grass) touffe *f*; (of trees) massif *m*; (of earth) motte *f*; **2** (thud) bruit *m* sourd
B *vtr* (*also* ∼ **together**) gen grouper; planter [qch] en groupes [*plants*]
Phrasal verb
■ **clump about, clump around** marcher d'un pas lourd

clumsily /'klʌmzɪlɪ/ *adv* [*move*] gauchement; [*painted, expressed*] de façon maladroite

clumsiness /'klʌmzɪnɪs/ *n* (carelessness) maladresse *f*; (awkwardness) gaucherie *f*; (of style) lourdeur *f*; (of system) côté *m* peu pratique

clumsy /'klʌmzɪ/ *adj* [*person, attempt*] maladroit; [*object*] grossier/-ière; [*animal*] pataud; [*tool*] peu maniable; [*style*] lourd; **to be** ∼ **at tennis** ne pas être très adroit au tennis; **to be** ∼ **with one's hands** ne pas être très adroit de ses mains

clung /klʌŋ/ *prét, pp* ▸ **cling**

cluster /'klʌstə(r)/
A *n* (of flowers, berries) grappe *f*; (of people, islands, insects, trees) groupe *m*; (of houses) ensemble *m*; (of ideas) ensemble *m*; (of diamonds) entourage *m*; (of stars) amas *m*
B *vi* [*people*] se rassembler (**around** autour de); **the trees were** ∼**ed around the church** les arbres étaient groupés tout autour de l'église

clutch /klʌtʃ/
A *n* **1** Aut embrayage *m*; **to let in the** ∼ débrayer; **to let out the** ∼ embrayer; **2** (cluster) (of eggs, chicks) couvée *f*; fig (of books, awards) ensemble *m*; (of people) groupe *m*
B *clutches npl* **to fall into the** ∼**es of** tomber sous les griffes *or* la patte○ de
C *vtr* tenir fermement [*object, child*]; **to** ∼ **sb/sth to** serrer qn/qch contre [*chest*]
Phrasal verb
■ **clutch at**: ▸ ∼ **at** [*sth/sb*] tenter d'attraper [*branch, rail, person*]; saisir [*arm*]; fig s'accrocher à [*hope*]; sauter sur [*opportunity, excuse*]

clutch: ∼ **bag** *n* pochette *f*; ∼ **cable** *n* câble *m* de commande d'embrayage

clutter /'klʌtə(r)/ *n* **1** (mess) fatras *m*; **in a** ∼ en désordre; **2** Ȼ (on radar) échos *mpl* fixes *or* parasites
Phrasal verb
■ **clutter up**: ▸ ∼ **up** [*sth*], ∼ [*sth*] **up** encombrer

cluttered /'klʌtəd/ *adj* encombré (**with** de)

cm (*abrév écrite* = **centimetre**) cm

Cmdr *n* Mil *abrév écrite* = **Commander**

CND (*abrév* = **Campaign for Nuclear Disarmament**) mouvement *m* pour le désarmement nucléaire

c/o Post (*abrév écrite* = **care of**) chez

Co *n* **1** Comm (*abrév* = **company**) Cie; **...and co ...**et Cie; hum et compagnie; **2** Geog (*abrév* = **county**) comté *m*

CO *n* **1** Mil *abrév* ▸ **commanding officer**; **2** *abrév écrite* = **Colorado**

coach /kəʊtʃ/
A *n* **1** (bus) (auto)car *m*; **by** ∼ en (auto)car; **2** GB (of train) wagon *m*; **3** Sport entraîneur/-euse *m*/*f*; **4** (for drama, voice) répétiteur/-trice *m*/*f*; **5** (tutor) professeur *m* particulier; **6** (horsedrawn) (for royalty) carrosse *m*; (for passengers) diligence *f*
B *noun modifier* [*holiday, journey, travel*] en (auto)car
C *vtr* **1** Sport entraîner [*team*]; être entraîneur/-euse de [*sport*]; **2** (teach) **to** ∼ **sb** donner des leçons particulières à qn (**in** en); **to** ∼ **sb for an exam/for a rôle** préparer qn à un examen/pour un rôle

coaching /'kəʊtʃɪŋ/ *n* Ȼ **1** (in sport) entraînement *m*; **2** (lessons) cours *mpl* particuliers

coach: ~**man** n cocher m; ~ **party** n GB groupe m voyageant en autocar; ~ **station** n GB gare f routière; ~ **trip** n excursion f en autocar; ~**work** n GB carrosserie f

coagulate /kəʊˈægjʊleɪt/ vtr, vi coaguler

coagulation /ˌkəʊægjʊˈleɪʃn/ n coagulation f

coal /kəʊl/
A n **1** ¢ (mineral) charbon m; **2** C (piece) charbon m; **hot** ou **live** ~**s** charbons mpl ardents
B noun modifier [cellar, shed, shovel] à charbon
(Idioms) **as black as** ~ noir comme du charbon; **to carry** ~**s to Newcastle** porter de l'eau à la rivière; **to haul sb over the** ~**s**○ passer un savon à qn○

coal-burning adj à charbon

coalesce /ˌkəʊəˈles/ vi [groups of people, ideas] fusionner; [substances] se mélanger

coal: ~**face** n front m de taille or d'abattage; ~**field** n bassin m houiller; ~ **fire** n GB cheminée f (où brûle un feu de charbon); ~-**fired** adj à charbon; ~ **industry** n industrie f minière

coalition /ˌkəʊəˈlɪʃn/
A n **1** Pol coalition f (**between** entre; **with** avec); **2** gen mélange m
B noun modifier [government, party] de coalition

coal: ~ **man**, ~ **merchant** ▸ p. 1181 n charbonnier m, marchand m de charbon; ~**mine** n mine f de charbon; ~**miner** ▸ p. 1181 n mineur m

coalmining /ˈkəʊlmaɪnɪŋ/
A n extraction f du charbon
B noun modifier [family, region, town] de mineurs

coal: ~ **pit** n mine f de charbon; ~ **scuttle** n seau m à charbon; ~ **seam** n gisement m houiller

coarse /kɔːs/ adj **1** [texture, fibre] grossier/-ière; [skin] épais/-aisse; [hair, grass] dru; [sand, salt] gros/grosse (before n); [sandpaper] à gros grains; **2** (not refined) [laugh, manners] grossier/-ière; [accent] vulgaire; ~ **features** traits mpl grossiers; **3** (indecent) [language, joke] cru; **4** [food, wine] ordinaire

coarse-grained adj (of texture) à gros grains

coarsely /ˈkɔːslɪ/ adv [speak] grossièrement; ~ **woven** à tissage grossier; ~ **ground** à grosse mouture

coarsen /ˈkɔːsn/
A vtr rendre [qch] rêche [skin]; rendre [qn] grossier [person]
B vi [speech] se dégrader; [features] devenir lourd

coarseness /ˈkɔːsnɪs/ n **1** (of manners) grossièreté f; **2** (of sand, salt) grosseur f; (of cloth) grossièreté f

coast /kəʊst/
A n côte f; **off the** ~ près de la côte; **the east** ~ la côte est; **from** ~ **to** ~ dans tout le pays; **the** ~ **is clear** fig la voie est libre
B noun modifier [road, path] côtier/-ière
C vi **1** (freewheel) **to** ~ **downhill** descendre en roue libre; **2** (travel) **to** ~ **along at 50 mph** rouler à une vitesse de croisière de 80 km/h; **3** Naut caboter

coastal /ˈkəʊstl/ adj côtier/-ière

coaster /ˈkəʊstə(r)/ n **1** (mat) dessous-de-verre m inv; **2** (boat) caboteur m

coastguard /ˈkəʊstɡɑːd/ ▸ p. 1181 n **1** (organization) gendarmerie f maritime; **2** (person) garde-côte m

coastguard: ~ **station** n poste m de la gendarmerie maritime; ~ **vessel** n (vedette f) garde-côte m

coastline n littoral m

coat /kəʊt/ ▸ p. 1191
A n **1** (garment) manteau m; (for men) pardessus m; (jacket) veste f; **2** Zool (of dog) poil m, pelage m; (of cat) fourrure f, pelage m; (of horse, leopard) robe f; **3** (layer) couche f
B vtr **1** gen, Tech **to** ~ **sth with** enduire qch de [paint, adhesive]; revêtir qch de [rubber]; couvrir qch de [dust, oil]; **2** Culin **to** ~ **sth in** ou **with** enrober qch de [breadcrumbs, chocolate, sauce]; dorer qch à [egg]; ~**ed with sugar** [sweet] glacé; [pill] dragéifié

coat hanger n cintre m

coating /ˈkəʊtɪŋ/ n (edible) enrobage m; Ind revêtement m; **protective** ~ enduit m protecteur

coat: ~ **of arms** n blason m, armoiries fpl; ~ **of mail** n Hist cotte f de mailles; ~**rack** n portemanteau m; ~**room** n US vestiaire m

coat-tails /ˈkəʊtteɪlz/ npl queue f d'un habit
(Idioms) **to be always hanging on sb's** ~ être toujours pendu aux basques de qn○; **to ride on sb's** ~ profiter des efforts de qn

coat tree n US portemanteau m

coax /kəʊks/ vtr cajoler [person]; attirer [qch] par la ruse [animal]; **to** ~ **sb to do** ou **into doing sth** persuader qn (gentiment) de faire qch; **to** ~ **sth out of sb** réussir à tirer qch de qn; **to** ~ **a car into starting** bichonner une voiture pour qu'elle démarre

coaxial /kəʊˈæksɪəl/ adj coaxial

coaxing /ˈkəʊksɪŋ/ n efforts mpl de persuasion; **no amount of** ~ **would make him drink it** rien ne l'amènerait à le boire

cob /kɒb/ n **1** (horse) cob m; **2** (swan) cygne m mâle; **3** (of maize) épi m de maïs; **4** GB (nut) noisette f; **5** GB Tech torchis m

cobble /ˈkɒbl/
A cobbles npl pavés mpl
B vtr **1** paver [road]; ~**d street** rue pavée; **2** faire [shoes]
(Phrasal verb)
■ **cobble together**: ▸ ~ [sth] **together**, ~ **together** [sth] concocter [qch] à la hâte

cobbler /ˈkɒblə(r)/ ▸ p. 1181 n cordonnier m

cobblestones /ˈkɒblstəʊnz/ npl pavés mpl

cobra /ˈkəʊbrə/ n cobra m; (Indian) serpent m à lunettes

cobweb /ˈkɒbweb/ n toile f d'araignée; **that will blow away the** ~**s** fig ça me/te etc rafraîchira les idées

cobwebbed /ˈkɒbwebd/, **cobwebby** /ˈkɒbwebɪ/ adj couvert de toiles d'araignée

cocaine /kəʊˈkeɪn/
A n cocaïne f
B noun modifier [dealer, dealing] de cocaïne; ~ **addict** cocaïnomane mf; ~ **addiction** cocaïnomanie f

coccyx /ˈkɒksɪks/ n (pl -**yxes** ou -**yges**) coccyx m

cochair /kəʊtʃeə(r)/ n coprésident/-e m/f

cochairman /kəʊtʃeəmən/ n (pl -**men**) coprésident m

cochineal /ˌkɒtʃɪˈniːl/ n **1** Culin carmin m; **2** Zool cochenille f

cock /kɒk/
A n **1** (rooster) coq m; **2** Zool (male bird) (oiseau m) mâle m; **3** (of hay, straw) meulon m; **4** (weathervane) girouette f; **5** (of gun) chien m de fusil; **at full/half** ~ au cran d'armé/de repos
B noun modifier [pheasant, sparrow] mâle; ~ **bird** mâle m
C vtr **1** (raise) **to** ~ **an eyebrow** hausser les sourcils; **to** ~ **a leg** [dog] lever la patte; **to** ~ **an ear** dresser l'oreille; **to keep an ear** ~**ed** dresser l'oreille; **2** (tilt) pencher; **3** Mil armer [gun]
(Idioms) **to be** ~ **of the walk** être le roi de la basse-cour; **to go off at half** ~○ (get angry) prendre la mouche; (be hasty) être impulsif/-ive; **to live like fighting** ~**s** vivre comme des coqs en pâte

cockade /kɒˈkeɪd/ n cocarde f

cock-a-doodle-doo /ˌkɒkəˌduːdlˈduː/ n cocorico m; **to go** ~ pousser son cocorico

cock-a-hoop○ /ˌkɒkəˈhuːp/ adj fier/fière comme Artaban

cock-and-bull story n histoire f abracadabrante or à dormir debout

cockatoo /ˌkɒkəˈtuː/ n cacatoès m

cockcrow /ˈkɒkkrəʊ/ n **at** ~ au chant du coq

cocked hat n (two points) bicorne m; (three points) tricorne m
(Idiom) **to knock sb/sth into a** ~○ (defeat) enfoncer○ qn/qch

cocker (spaniel) /ˈkɒkə(r)/ n cocker m

cockerel /ˈkɒkərəl/ n jeune coq m

cockfighting /ˈkɒkfaɪtɪŋ/ n combats mpl de coqs

cockily /ˈkɒkɪlɪ/ adv effrontément

cockiness /ˈkɒkɪnɪs/ n impudence f

cockle /ˈkɒkl/ n (mollusc) coque f

cockleshell /ˈkɒklʃel/ n coquille f de coque

cockney /ˈkɒknɪ/
A n cockney mf
B adj cockney inv

ℹ **Cockney** Le mot désigne deux réalités: les personnes nées dans l'est de Londres, 'à portée du son des cloches de l'église de St Mary-le-Bow', et l'anglais parlé par ces personnes dont l'argot (*rhyming slang*) est caractéristique. ► **Rhyming slang**

cock: ∼**pit** n Aviat cockpit m, poste m de pilotage; Naut, Aut cockpit m; ∼**roach** n cafard m

cocksure /ˌkɒkˈʃɔː(r), US ˌkɒkˈʃʊər/ adj péj [*person, manner, attitude*] présomptueux/-euse

cocktail /ˈkɒkteɪl/ n **1** (drink) cocktail m; **gin** ∼ cocktail à base de gin; **to have** ∼**s** prendre l'apéritif; **2** (mixture) **fruit** ∼ salade f de fruits; **seafood** ∼ cocktail m de fruits de mer; **3** fig (of elements, ideas, drugs) cocktail m

cocktail: ∼ **bar**, ∼ **lounge** n bar m; ∼ **cabinet** n GB bar m (*meuble*); ∼ **dress** n robe f de cocktail; ∼ **party** n cocktail m; ∼ **shaker** n shaker m; ∼ **stick** n pique f (à apéritif)

cocky /ˈkɒkɪ/ adj impudent

cocoa /ˈkəʊkəʊ/
A n **1** (substance) cacao m; **2** (drink) chocolat m
B noun modifier ∼ **powder** cacao en poudre; ∼ **butter** beurre m de cacao

coconut /ˈkəʊkənʌt/
A n noix f de coco
B noun modifier [*milk, oil, butter*] de coco; [*ice cream*] à la noix de coco

coconut: ∼ **matting** n natte f en coco; ∼ **palm** n cocotier m; ∼ **shy** n GB jeu m de massacre

cocoon /kəˈkuːn/
A n Zool, fig cocon m
B vtr envelopper douillettement; **a** ∼**ed existence** une existence surprotégée

cod /ˈkɒd/
A n **1** Zool (also ∼**fish**) (pl ∼) morue f; **2** Culin cabillaud m
B adj péj [*psychology*] de cuisine; [*theatre*] de second ordre

COD (abrév = **cash on delivery**, **collect on delivery** US) envoi m contre remboursement

coddle /ˈkɒdl/ vtr **1** gen dorloter; **2** Culin ∼**d eggs** œufs mpl mollets

code /kəʊd/
A n **1** (laws, rules) code m; **safety** ∼ règlement m de sécurité; ∼ **of practice** Med déontologie f (médicale); (in advertising) code m de bonne conduite; (in banking) conditions fpl générales; ∼ **of ethics** moralité f; **2** (of behaviour) code m de conduite; ∼ **of conduct** code m de conduite; ∼ **of honour** code m d'honneur; **3** (cipher) code m; **in** ∼ en code; **4** Telecom (dialling) ∼ indicatif m; **5** Comput code m
B vtr gen, Comput coder

codeine /ˈkəʊdiːn/ n codéine f

code name n nom m de code

codeword /ˈkəʊdwɜːd/ n lit (name) nom m de code; (password) mot m de passe; fig expression f codifiée

codify /ˈkəʊdɪfaɪ, US ˈkɒd-/ vtr codifier [*laws*]

cod-liver oil n huile f de foie de morue

co-driver /kəʊˈdraɪvə(r)/ n copilote mf

Co Durham n: abrév écrite = **County Durham**

coed /ˌkəʊˈed/ adj: abrév = **coeducational**

coeducational /ˌkəʊedʒuˈkeɪʃənl/ adj mixte

coefficient /ˌkəʊɪˈfɪʃnt/ n coefficient m

coerce /kəʊˈɜːs/ vtr exercer des pressions sur [*person*]; **to** ∼ **sb into doing** contraindre qn à faire

coercion /kəʊˈɜːʃn, US -ʒn/ n coercition f

coercive /kəʊˈɜːsɪv/ adj coercitif/-ive

coexist /ˌkəʊɪɡˈzɪst/ vi coexister (**with** avec)

C of E (abrév = **Church of England**) Église f d'Angleterre

coffee /ˈkɒfɪ, US ˈkɔːfɪ/
A n **1** (commodity, liquid) café m; **a cup of** ∼ une tasse de café; **2** (cup of coffee) café m; **a black/white** ∼ un café (noir)/au lait
B noun modifier [*cake, dessert*] au café; [*crop, drinker*] de café; [*cup, filter, grinder, spoon*] à café

coffee: ∼ **bag** n sachet m de café moulu; ∼ **bar** n café m

coffee bean n grain m de café; **a kilo of** ∼**s** un kilo de café en grains

coffee: ∼ **break** n pause(-)café f; ∼**-coloured** GB, ∼**-colored** US adj café-au-lait (*inv*); ∼ **grounds** n marc m de café; ∼ **house** n café m; ∼ **machine** n (in café) percolateur m; (domestic) cafetière f électrique; (vending machine) machine f à café; ∼ **maker**, ∼ **percolator** n (electric) cafetière f électrique; (on stove) cafetière f; ∼ **morning** n GB réunion entre amies pour boire le café et discuter; ∼ **pot** n cafetière f; ∼ **service**, ∼ **set** service m à café; ∼ **shop** ► p. 1181 n (merchant's) brûlerie f; (café) café m; ∼ **table** n table f basse; ∼**-table book** n beau livre m (sorti en grand format)

coffer /ˈkɒfə(r)/ n coffre m, caisse f

coffin /ˈkɒfɪn/ n cercueil m

cog /ˈkɒɡ/ n Tech (tooth) dent f d'engrenage; (wheel) pignon m; **a (tiny)** ∼ **in the machine** fig un (simple) rouage de la machine

cogency /ˈkəʊdʒənsɪ/ n puissance f

cogent /ˈkəʊdʒənt/ adj convaincant

cogently /ˈkəʊdʒəntlɪ/ adv de façon convaincante

cogitate /ˈkɒdʒɪteɪt/ vi réfléchir (**about, on** à)

cogitation /ˌkɒdʒɪˈteɪʃn/ n réflexion f

cognitive /ˈkɒɡnɪtɪv/ adj cognitif/-ive

cognizance /ˈkɒɡnɪzəns/ n connaissance f

cognoscenti /ˌkɒɡnəˈʃentɪ/ npl connaisseurs mpl

cohabit /kəʊˈhæbɪt/ vi cohabiter (**with** avec)

cohere /kəʊˈhɪə(r)/ vi être cohérent

coherence /kəʊˈhɪərəns/ n (of thought) cohérence f; (of artistic approach) harmonie f; **to give** ∼ **to sth** apporter une cohérence à qch

coherent /kəʊˈhɪərənt/ adj [*argument, plan*] cohérent; **he was barely** ∼ on avait peine à le comprendre

coherently /kəʊˈhɪərəntlɪ/ adv de façon cohérente

cohesion /kəʊˈhiːʒn/ n cohésion f

cohesive /kəʊˈhiːsɪv/ adj [*group*] uni; [*force*] cohésif/-ive

cohort /ˈkəʊhɔːt/ n cohorte f

coil /kɔɪl/
A n **1** (of rope, barbed wire) rouleau m; (of electric wire) bobine f; (of smoke) volute f; (of hair) boucle f; (of snake) anneau m; **2** (contraceptive) stérilet m
B vtr (also ∼ **up**) enrouler [*hair, rope, wire*]
C vi [*river, procession*] serpenter
D v refl to ∼ **itself** gen s'enrouler; [*snake*] se lover

coin /kɔɪn/
A n **1** pièce f (de monnaie); **a gold** ∼ une pièce d'or; **a pound** ∼ une pièce d'une livre; **2** ¢ (coinage) monnaie f
B vtr **1** frapper [*coins*]; **she's really** ∼**ing it in**○ elle fait des affaires en or○; **2** fig forger [*word, term*]; **to** ∼ **a phrase** comme on dit

Ⓘ**dioms** **two sides of the same** ∼ les deux facettes d'un même problème; **the other side of the** ∼ **is that** (sth negative) le revers de la médaille, c'est que; (sth positive) le bon côté de la chose, c'est que

coinage /ˈkɔɪnɪdʒ/ n **1** ¢ (coins, currency) monnaie f; **2** (word, phrase) création f; **a recent** ∼ un néologisme

coin box n **1** (pay phone) cabine f (téléphonique) à pièces; **2** (pay phone, in laundromat) caisse f

coincide /ˌkəʊɪnˈsaɪd/ vi coïncider (**with** avec)

coincidence /kəʊˈɪnsɪdəns/ n coïncidence f, hasard m; **it is a** ∼ **that** c'est par coïncidence que; **a happy** ∼ un heureux hasard; **by** ∼ par hasard

coincidental /kəʊˌɪnsɪˈdentl/ adj fortuit

coincidentally /kəʊˌɪnsɪˈdentəlɪ/ adv tout à fait par hasard

coin operated adj qui marche avec des pièces

coke /kəʊk/ n **1** (fuel) coke m; **2** ○(cocaine) coke○ f, cocaïne f

Col abrév écrite = **Colonel**; **Col X** (on envelope) le Colonel X

cola /ˈkəʊlə/ n **1** Bot cola f, colatier m; **2** (drink) coca m

colander /ˈkʌləndə(r)/ n passoire f

cold /kəʊld/
A n **1** ¢ (chilliness) froid m; **to feel the** ∼ être sensible au froid, être frileux/-euse; **to come in from** ou **out of the** ∼ lit se mettre à l'abri du froid; fig rentrer en grâce; **to be left out in the** ∼ fig être isolé; **2** C Med rhume m; **to have a** ∼ être enrhumé, avoir un rhume; **to catch a** ∼ attraper un rhume; **a bad** ∼ un gros rhume; **a** ∼ **in the head** un rhume de cerveau

B *adj* **1** (chilly) froid; fig [*colour, light*] froid; **to be** *ou* **feel ~** [*person*] avoir froid; **the room was ~** il faisait froid dans la pièce; **it's** *ou* **the weather's ~** il fait froid; **to go ~** [*food, water*] se refroidir; **don't let the baby get ~** ne laisse pas le bébé prendre froid; **to keep sth ~** tenir [qch] au frais [*food*]; **2** (unemotional) [*manner, logic*] froid; **to be ~ to** *ou* **towards sb** être froid avec qn; **to leave sb ~** laisser qn froid; **3** (unconscious) **to be out ~** être sans connaissance; **to knock sb out ~** assommer qn, mettre qn KO

C *adv* **1** ○(without preparation) [*speak, perform*] à froid○; **2** US (thoroughly) [*learn, know*] par cœur

(Idioms) **to have** *ou* **get ~ feet** avoir les jetons○; **in ~ blood** de sang-froid; **my blood runs ~** mon sang se fige; **in the ~ light of day** à tête reposée; **to be as ~ as ice** [*feet*] être gelé; [*room*] être glacial; **to pour ~ water on sth** descendre qch en flammes

cold-blooded /ˌkəʊld'blʌdɪd/ *adj* **1** lit [*animal*] à sang froid; **2** fig [*killer*] sans pitié; [*crime*] commis de sang-froid

cold: **~-bloodedly** *adv* de sang-froid; **~ calling** *n* Comm démarchage *m* par téléphone; **~ comfort** *n* piètre consolation *f* (**for** pour); **~ cuts** *npl* assiette *f* anglaise; **~ frame** *n* châssis *m*; **~-hearted** *adj* impitoyable

coldly /'kəʊldlɪ/ *adv* [*say*] froidement; [*receive, stare*] avec froideur; **~ polite** d'une politesse glaciale

coldness /'kəʊldnɪs/ *n* lit, fig froideur *f*

cold shoulder *n* **to give sb the ~** snober qn, battre froid à qn

cold: **~ snap** *n* brève vague *f* de froid; **~ sore** *n* bouton *m* de fièvre

cold storage *n* (process) gén conservation *f* par le froid; Chem conservation *f* cryogénique

cold store *n* chambre *f* froide *or* frigorifique

cold sweat *n* sueurs *fpl* froides; **to bring sb out in a ~** donner des sueurs froides à qn

cold: **~ table** *n* buffet *m* froid; **~ tap** *n* robinet *m* d'eau froide

cold turkey○ *n* (treatment) sevrage *m*; (reaction) réaction *f* de manque; **to go ~** s'abstenir (**on** de); **to be ~** être en manque

Cold War *n* guerre *f* froide

coleslaw /'kəʊlslɔː/ *n* salade *f* à base de chou cru

colic /'kɒlɪk/ *n* ¢ coliques *fpl*

colicky /'kɒlɪkɪ/ *adj* [*baby*] qui souffre de coliques

collaborate /kə'læbəreɪt/ *vi* collaborer (**on, in** à; **with** avec)

collaboration /kəˌlæbə'reɪʃn/ *n* collaboration *f* (**between** entre; **with** avec; **in** à)

collaborative /kə'læbərətɪv/ *adj* [*project, task*] en collaboration; [*approach*] de collaboration

collaborator /kə'læbəreɪtə(r)/ *n* collaborateur/-trice *m/f*

collage /'kɒlɑːʒ, US kə'lɑːʒ/ *n* **1** Art collage *m*; **2** (film) montage *m*

collapse /kə'læps/

A *n* **1** (of regime, system, bank, economy, market, hopes) effondrement *m* (**of, in** de); **to be on the point of ~** être sur le point de s'effondrer; **2** (of deals, talks, relationship) échec *m*; **3** (of company) faillite *f* (**of** de); **4** (of person) (physical) écroulement *m*; (mental) effondrement *m*; **to be close to ~** être sur le point de s'écrouler; **5** (of building, bridge) effondrement *m*; (of tunnel, wall) écroulement *m*; (of chair, bed) affaissement *m*; **6** Med (of lung) collapsus *m*

B *vtr* **1** (fold) plier; **2** (combine) synthétiser

C *vi* **1** (founder) [*regime, system, hopes, plan*] s'effondrer; [*case, deal, talks*] échouer; **2** (go bankrupt) [*company*] faire faillite (**through** à cause de); **3** (slump) [*person*] s'écrouler; **to ~ onto the bed** s'effondrer sur le lit; **to ~ and die** mourir subitement; **to ~ in tears** s'effondrer en larmes; **4** (fall down) [*building, bridge*] s'effondrer; [*tunnel, wall*] s'écrouler; [*chair*] s'affaisser (**under** sous); **5** (deflate) [*balloon*] se dégonfler; [*soufflé*] tomber; **6** Med [*lung*] se dégonfler; **7** (fold) [*bike*] se plier

collapsible /kə'læpsəbl/ *adj* pliant

collar /'kɒlə(r)/ ▸ p. 1191

A *n* **1** (on garment) col *m*; **to grab sb by the ~** prendre qn au collet; **2** (for animal) collier *m*; **3** Tech (ring) bague *f* d'arrêt

B ○*vtr* alpaguer● [*thief*]; (in conversation) coincer○

(Idiom) **to get hot under the ~** se mettre en rogne○

collar: **~bone** *n* clavicule *f*; **~ size** ▸ p. 1191 *n* encolure *f*; **~ stud** *n* bouton *m* de col

collate /kə'leɪt/ *vtr* collationner

collateral /kə'lætərəl/

A *n* nantissement *m*; **to put up ~** offrir une garantie supplémentaire

B *adj* **1** Jur (relative) collatéral; (subordinate) secondaire; **2** Mil **~ damage** dommages *mpl* collatéraux, dégâts *mpl* parmi la population civile; **3** Fin **~ loan** prêt *m* nanti

colleague /'kɒliːg/ *n* collègue *mf*

collect /kə'lekt/

A *adv* US Telecom **to call sb ~** appeler qn en PCV

B *vtr* **1** (gather) ramasser [*wood, litter, eggs*]; rassembler [*information, documents*]; recueillir [*signatures*]; **to ~ one's wits** rassembler ses esprits; **to ~ one's strength** rassembler *or* ramasser ses forces; **to ~ one's thoughts** se recueillir; **2** (as hobby) collectionner, faire collection de [*stamps, coins*]; **3** (receive, contain) (intentionally) recueillir [*rain water*]; (accidentally) [*objects*] prendre, ramasser [*dust*]; **4** (obtain) percevoir [*rent*]; encaisser [*fares, money*]; recouvrer [*debt*]; toucher [*pension*]; Admin percevoir [*tax, fine*]; remporter [*prize*]; **to ~ money for charity** collecter de l'argent pour les bonnes œuvres; **5** (take away) ramasser [*rubbish*]; faire la levée de [*mail, post*]; **6** (pick up) aller chercher [*person*]; récupérer [*keys, book etc*]; **to ~ a suit from the cleaners** passer prendre un costume chez le teinturier

C *vi* **1** (accumulate) [*dust, leaves*] s'accumuler; [*crowd*] se rassembler, se réunir; **2** (raise money) **to ~ for charity** faire la quête pour des bonnes œuvres

D **collected** *pp adj* **1** [*person*] calme; **2** (assembled) **the ~ed works of Dickens** les œuvres complètes de Dickens; **the ~ed poems of W. B. Yeats** la collection complète des poèmes de W. B. Yeats

collect call *n* US Telecom appel *m* en PCV

collection /kə'lekʃn/ *n* **1** ¢ (collecting) (of objects) ramassage *m*; (of old clothes, newspapers etc) collecte *f*; (of information, facts) rassemblement *m*; (of rent) encaissement *m*; (of debt) recouvrement *m*; (of tax) perception *f*; Post levée *f*; **your suit is ready for ~** votre costume est prêt; **refuse ~** ramassage *m* des ordures; **2** (set of collected items) (of coins, records etc) collection *f*; (anthology) recueil *m*; **art ~** collection *f* (de tableaux); **an odd ~ of people** un mélange curieux de gens; **spring ~** (clothes) collection de printemps; **3** (sum of money collected) gén collecte *f* (**for** pour); (in church) quête *f*; **to make** *ou* **organize a ~** faire la quête, organiser une collecte

collective /kə'lektɪv/

A *n* entreprise *f* collective

B *adj* collectif/-ive

collective: **~ bargaining** *n*: négociations entre le syndicat et le patronat; **~ farm** *n* ferme *f* collective

collectively /kə'lektɪvlɪ/ *adv* collectivement; **~ owned** en copropriété

collective: **~ noun** *n* Ling (nom *m*) collectif *m*; **~ ownership** *n* copropriété *f*

collector /kə'lektə(r)/ *n* **1** (of coins etc) collectionneur/-euse *m/f*; **to be a stamp ~** collectionner les timbres; **2** (official) (of taxes) percepteur *m*; (of rent, debts) encaisseur *m*; (of funds) quêteur/-euse *m/f*

collector's item *n* pièce *f* de collection

college /'kɒlɪdʒ/ *n* **1** (place of tertiary education) établissement *m* d'enseignement supérieur; (school, part of university) collège *m*; US Univ faculté *f*; **to go to ~**, **to be at** *ou* **in** US **~** faire des études supérieures; **2** (body) (of arms, cardinals) collège *m*; (of surgeons) académie *f*; (of midwives, nurses) association *f*

ⓘ **Colleges** Aux États-Unis, on emploie ce terme pour divers types d'établissements d'enseignement supérieur qui proposent des études en deux ans (*community college*, *technical college*, *junior college*), ou en quatre ans (*four-year college*, *university*) qui préparent au *Bachelor's Degree* puis à un diplôme de troisième cycle. L'admission dans ces établissements se fait en fonction du dossier scolaire des élèves, des matières qu'ils ont étudiées en *high school*, et de leurs résultats aux examens de fin d'études secondaires. ▸ **High school**

college education n études fpl supérieures; **to have a** ~ faire des études supérieures

college: ~ **of advanced technology, CAT** n GB ≈ Institut m Universitaire de Technologie; ~ **of agriculture** n institut m agronomique; ~ **of education** n GB ≈ École f normale; ~ **of further education, CFE** n GB école ouverte aux adultes et aux jeunes pour terminer un cycle d'études secondaires

collide /kə'laɪd/ vi [vehicle] entrer en collision; **I** ~**d with a tree** j'ai heurté un arbre; **we** ~**d in the corridor** nous nous sommes heurtés dans le couloir

collie /'kɒlɪ/ n colley m

collier /'kɒlɪə(r)/ ▸ p. 1181 n (worker) mineur m

colliery /'kɒljərɪ/ n houillère f

collision /kə'lɪʒn/ n 1 (crash) collision f; **to come into** ~ **with** entrer en collision avec; 2 (clash) affrontement m (**between** entre)

collision course n **the planes were on a** ~ les avions allaient se percuter; fig **to be on a** ~ [people] aller droit à l'affrontement

colloquial /kə'ləʊkwɪəl/ adj familier/-ière; ~ **English** anglais parlé

colloquialism /kə'ləʊkwɪəlɪzəm/ n expression f familière

colloquially /kə'ləʊkwɪəlɪ/ adv familièrement

colloquium /kə'ləʊkwɪəm/ n (pl ~**s** ou **-quia**) colloque m

collude /kə'luːd/ vi comploter (**with** avec)

collusion /kə'luːʒn/ n connivence f; **in** ~ **with** de connivence avec

cologne /kə'ləʊn/ n eau f de Cologne

Colombia /kə'lɒmbɪə/ ▸ p. 774 pr n Colombie f

colon /'kəʊlən/ n 1 Anat côlon m; 2 Ling deux points mpl

colonel /'kɜːnl/ ▸ p. 1123 n colonel m

colonial /kə'ləʊnɪəl/
A n colonial/-e m/f
B adj colonial; US Archit en style colonial

colonialist /kə'ləʊnɪəlɪst/ n, adj colonialiste (mf)

colonization /ˌkɒlənaɪ'zeɪʃn, US -nɪ'z-/ n colonisation f

colonize /'kɒlənaɪz/ vtr coloniser also fig

colonizer /'kɒlənaɪzə(r)/ n colon m

colony /'kɒlənɪ/ n colonie f

color US n, vtr, vi = **colour**

Colorado beetle /ˌkɒlə'rɑːdəʊ 'biːtl/ n doryphore m

color line n US discrimination f raciale

colossal /kə'lɒsl/ adj colossal

colour GB, **color** US /'kʌlə(r)/ ▸ p. 752
A n 1 (hue) couleur f; **what** ~ **is it?** de quelle couleur est-il?; **the sky was the** ~ **of lead** le ciel était de la couleur du plomb; **in** ~ Cin, TV en couleur; **to give** ~ **to sth** colorer qch; **to paint sth in glowing** ~**s** fig brosser un tableau brillant de qch; **'available in 12** ~**s'** 'existe en 12 coloris'; 2 (in writing, description) couleur f; 3 (dye) (for food) colorant m; (for hair) teinture f; 4 (make-up) **eye** ~ fard m à paupières; **lip** ~ rouge m à lèvres; 5 (pigmentation) couleur f de peau; **people of all races and** ~**s** des gens de toutes races et de toutes couleurs; 6 (complexion) couleur f; **to lose (one's)** ~ perdre ses couleurs; **to put** ~ **into sb's cheeks** redonner des couleurs à qn; **he's getting his** ~ **back** il reprend des couleurs
B **colours** npl Mil, Sport couleurs fpl; Naut pavillon m; **racing** ~**s** couleurs de l'écurie; **under false** ~**s** fig sous un faux jour; **to get one's football** ~**s** GB être sélectionné pour l'équipe de football
C noun modifier 1 Phot, TV [photo, photography] (en) couleur; [copier, printer] couleur; ~ **film** (for camera) pellicule f couleur; Cin film m en couleur; 2 Sociol [prejudice, problem] racial
D vtr 1 lit (with paints, crayons) colorier; (with commercial paints) peindre; (with food dye) colorer; (with hair dye) teindre; **to** ~ **sth blue** colorier or teindre qch en bleu; 2 fig (prejudice) fausser [judgment]; 3 fig (enhance) enjoliver [account]
E vi [person] (also ~ **up**) rougir
(Idioms) **to be off** ~ ne pas être en forme; **to pass with flying** ~**s** réussir haut la main; **to show one's true** ~**s** se montrer sous son vrai jour

colour: ~ **bar** n GB discrimination f raciale; ~ **blind** adj daltonien/-ienne; ~ **blindness** n daltonisme m

colour code GB, **color code** US vtr classer [qch] par couleurs [files]

coloured GB, **colored** US /'kʌləd/
A n 1 (in GB, US) injur personne f de couleur; 2 (in South Africa) métis/-isse m/f
B **coloureds** npl (laundry) couleurs fpl
C adj 1 lit [pen, paper, bead] de couleur; [picture] en couleur; [light, glass] coloré; **brightly** ~ aux couleurs vives; 2 (non-white) injur GB, US de couleur; (in South Africa) métis/-isse
D **-coloured** combining form **a raspberry-**~ **dress** une robe (couleur) framboise; **copper-**~ couleur cuivre; **a highly-**~ **account** un récit très enjolivé

colour: ~**-fast** adj grand teint inv; ~ **filter** n Phot filtre m coloré

colourful GB, **colorful** US /'kʌləfl/ adj 1 lit aux couleurs vives; 2 fig [story, life] haut en couleur; [character] pittoresque

colourfully GB, **colorfully** US /'kʌləfəlɪ/ adv en couleurs vives

colouring GB, **coloring** US /'kʌlərɪŋ/ n 1 (hue) (of plant, animal) couleurs fpl; (complexion) teint m; 2 ₵ Art coloriage m; ~ **book** album m à colorier; 3 (dye) (for food) colorant m; (for hair) teinture f

colourless GB, **colorless** US /'kʌləlɪs/ adj 1 lit [liquid, gas] incolore; 2 fig (bland) terne

colour: ~ **scheme** n couleurs fpl, coloris m; ~ **sense** n sens m des couleurs; ~ **supplement** n supplément m illustré; ~ **television** n télévision f (en) couleur; ~**way** n coloris m

colt /kəʊlt/ n Zool poulain m

Columbus /kə'lʌmbəs/ pr n Christophe Colomb

column /'kɒləm/ n 1 gen, Archit colonne f; 2 (in newspaper) rubrique f; **sports/political** ~ rubrique sportive/politique; **letters** ~ courrier m des lecteurs

columnist /'kɒləmnɪst/ n journaliste mf

coma /'kəʊmə/ n coma m; **in a** ~ dans le coma; **to go into a** ~ entrer dans le coma

comatose /'kəʊmətəʊs/ adj 1 Med comateux/-euse; 2 fig abruti

comb /kəʊm/
A n 1 (for hair) peigne m; **to run a** ~ **through one's hair, to give one's hair a (quick)** ~ se donner un coup de peigne; 2 (in weaving) carde f; 3 (honeycomb) rayon m; 4 (cock's crest) crête f
B vtr 1 **to** ~ **sb's hair** peigner qn; **to** ~ **one's hair** se peigner; 2 (search) **to** ~ **a place** passer un lieu au peigne fin; 3 (in weaving) carder

(Phrasal verbs)
■ **comb out**: ▸ ~ **out [sth], ~ [sth] out** démêler
■ **comb through**: ▸ ~ **through [sth]** passer [qch] au peigne fin (**for sth** à la recherche de qch)

combat /'kɒmbæt/
A n combat m; **in** ~ au combat; **close/single** ~ combat rapproché/singulier
B noun modifier [aircraft, troops, zone] de combat
C vtr (p prés etc **-tt-**) lutter contre, combattre

combatant /'kɒmbətənt/ n combattant/-e m/f

combative /'kɒmbətɪv/ adj combatif/-ive

combat jacket n veste f de treillis

combination /ˌkɒmbɪ'neɪʃn/ n 1 (mixture) gen combinaison f (**of** de); (of factors, events) conjonction f; 2 (mixing) mélange m (**of** de); **in** ~ **with** en association avec; 3 (of numbers, chemicals) combinaison f; ~ **lock** serrure f à combinaison

combine
A /'kɒmbaɪn/ n 1 Comm groupe m; 2 Agric = **combine harvester**
B vtr 1 /kəm'baɪn/ (pair up, link) combiner [activities, colours, items, elements] (**with** avec); associer [ideas, aims] (**with** à); **to** ~ **two companies** regrouper deux sociétés; **to** ~ **fantasy with realism** allier la fantaisie au réalisme; **to** ~ **forces** [countries, people] (merge) s'allier; (cooperate) collaborer; 2 /kəm'baɪn/ Culin mélanger (**with** avec); 3 /'kɒmbaɪn/ (on farm) moissonner, battre [crops]
C /kəm'baɪn/ vi 1 (go together) [activities, colours, elements] se combiner; 2 (join) [people, groups] s'associer; [institutions, firms] fusionner

Colours

■ *Not all English colour terms have a single exact equivalent in French: for instance, in some circumstances* brown *is* marron, *in others* brun. *If in doubt, look the word up in the dictionary.*

Colour terms

what colour is it?
= c'est de quelle couleur?
  or (more formally) de quelle couleur est-il?

it's green
= il est vert *or* elle est verte

to paint sth green
= peindre qch en vert

to dye sth green
= teindre qch en vert

to wear green
= porter du vert

dressed in green
= habillé de vert

■ *Colour nouns are all masculine in French:*

I like green
= j'aime le vert

I prefer blue
= je préfère le bleu

red suits her
= le rouge lui va bien

it's a pretty yellow!
= c'est un joli jaune!

have you got it in white?
= est-ce que vous l'avez en blanc?

a pretty shade of blue
= un joli ton de bleu

it was a dreadful green
= c'était un vert affreux

a range of greens
= une gamme de verts

■ *Most adjectives of colour agree with the noun they modify:*

a blue coat
= un manteau bleu

a blue dress
= une robe bleue

blue clothes
= des vêtements bleus

■ *Some that don't agree are explained below.*

Words that are not true adjectives

■ *Some words that translate English adjectives are really nouns in French, and so don't show agreement:*

a brown shoe
= une chaussure marron

orange tablecloths
= des nappes *fpl* orange

hazel eyes
= des yeux *mpl* noisette

■ *Other French words like this include:* cerise (*cherry-red*), chocolat (*chocolate-brown*) *and* émeraude (*emerald-green*).

Shades of colour

■ *Expressions like* pale blue, dark green *or* light yellow *are also invariable in French and show no agreement:*

a pale blue shirt
= une chemise bleu pâle

dark green blankets
= des couvertures *fpl* vert foncé

a light yellow tie
= une cravate jaune clair

bright yellow socks
= des chaussettes *fpl* jaune vif

■ *French can also use the colour nouns here: instead of* une chemise bleu pâle *you could say* une chemise d'un bleu pâle; *and similarly* des couvertures d'un vert foncé (*etc*). *The nouns in French are normally used to translate English adjectives of this type ending in* -er *and* -est:

a darker blue
= un bleu plus foncé

the dress was a darker blue
= la robe était d'un bleu plus foncé

Similarly:

a lighter blue
= un bleu plus clair (*etc*)

■ *In the following examples,* blue *stands for most basic colour terms:*

pale blue	**dark blue**
= bleu pâle	= bleu foncé
light blue	**deep blue**
= bleu clair	= bleu profond
bright blue	**strong blue**
= bleu vif	= bleu soutenu

■ *Other types of compound in French are also invariable, and do not agree with their nouns:*

a navy-blue jacket
= une veste bleu marine

■ *These compounds include:* bleu ciel (*sky-blue*), vert pomme (*apple-green*), bleu nuit (*midnight-blue*), rouge sang (*blood-red*) *etc. However, all English compounds do not translate directly into French. If in doubt, check in the dictionary.*

■ *French compounds consisting of two colour terms linked with a hyphen are also invariable:*

a blue-black material
= une étoffe bleu-noir

a greenish-blue cup
= une tasse bleu-vert

a greeny-yellow dress
= une robe vert-jaune

■ *English uses the ending* -ish, *or sometimes* -y, *to show that something is approximately a certain colour, e.g.* a reddish hat *or* a greenish paint. *The French equivalent is* -âtre:

blue-ish	**greenish** *or* **greeny**
= bleuâtre	= verdâtre
greyish	**reddish**
= grisâtre	= rougeâtre
yellowish *or* **yellowy**	
= jaunâtre	
etc.	

☞ See next page

Colours *continued*

■ *Other similar French words are* rosâtre, noirâtre *and* blanchâtre. *Note however that these words are often rather negative in French. It is better not to use them if you want to be complimentary about something. Use instead* tirant sur le rouge/jaune *etc.*

■ *To describe a special colour, English can add* -coloured *to a noun such as* raspberry (framboise) *or* flesh (chair). *Note how this is said in French, where the two-word compound with* couleur *is invariable, and, unlike English, never has a hyphen:*

a chocolate-coloured skirt
= une jupe couleur chocolat

raspberry-coloured fabric
= du tissu couleur framboise

flesh-coloured tights
= un collant couleur chair

Colour verbs

■ *English makes some colour verbs by adding* -en (e.g. blacken). *Similarly French has some verbs in* -ir *made from colour terms:*

to blacken
= noircir

to redden
= rougir

to whiten
= blanchir

■ *The other French colour terms that behave like this are:* bleu (bleuir), jaune (jaunir), rose (rosir) *and* vert (verdir). *It is always safe, however, to use* devenir, *thus:*

to turn purple
= devenir violet

Describing people

■ *Note the use of the definite article in the following:*

to have black hair
= avoir les cheveux noirs

to have blue eyes
= avoir les yeux bleus

Note the use of à *in the following:*

a girl with blue eyes
= une jeune fille aux yeux bleus

the man with black hair
= l'homme aux cheveux noirs

■ *Not all colours have direct equivalents in French. The following words are used for describing the colour of someone's hair (note that* les cheveux *is plural in French):*

fair	**red**
= blond	= roux
dark	**black**
= brun	= noir
blonde *or* **blond**	**grey**
= blond	= gris
brown	**white**
= châtain *inv*	= blanc

■ *Check other terms such as* yellow, ginger, auburn, mousey *etc. in the dictionary.*

■ *Note these nouns in French:*

a fair-haired man	**a dark-haired man**
= un blond	= un brun
a fair-haired woman	**a dark-haired woman**
= une blonde	= une brune

■ *The following words are useful for describing the colour of someone's eyes:*

blue	**green**
= bleu	= vert
light blue	**grey**
= bleu clair *inv*	= gris
light brown	**greyish-green**
= marron clair *inv*	= gris-vert *inv*
brown	**dark**
= marron *inv*	= noir
hazel	
= noisette *inv*	

---

combined /kəmˈbaɪnd/ *adj* **1** (joint) ~ **operation** collaboration *f*; **a** ~ **effort** une collaboration; **2** (total) [*salary, age*] total; **3** (put together) [*effects*] combiné; [*forces*] conjoint; ~ **with** combiné avec; **more than all the rest** ~ plus que tous les autres réunis

combined pill *n* pilule *f* combinée

combine harvester *n* moissonneuse-batteuse *f*

combustible /kəmˈbʌstəbl/ *adj* combustible

combustion /kəmˈbʌstʃn/ *n* combustion *f*; **internal** ~ **engine** moteur *m* à combustion interne

come /kʌm/
A *excl* ~ **(now)**! allons!; ~, ~! allons, allons!
B *vtr* (*prét* **came**; *pp* **come**) (travel) faire; **to** ~ **100 km to see** faire 100 km pour voir
C *vi* (*prét* **came**; *pp* **come**) **1** (arrive) [*person, day, success, fame*] venir; [*bus, letter, news, rains, winter, war*] arriver; **to** ~ **after sb** poursuivre qn; **to** ~ **by** (take) prendre [*bus, taxi, plane*]; **I came on foot/by bike** je suis venu à pied/à bicyclette; **to** ~ **down** descendre [*stairs, street*]; **to** ~ **up** monter [*stairs, street*]; **to** ~ **from** venir de [*airport, hospital*]; **to** ~ **into** entrer dans [*house, room*]; **to** ~ **past** [*car, person*] passer; **to** ~ **through** [*person*] passer par [*town centre, tunnel*]; [*water, object*] traverser [*window etc*]; **to** ~ **to** venir à [*school, telephone*]; **to** ~ **to the door** venir ouvrir; **to** ~ **running** arriver en courant; **to** ~ **limping down the street** descendre la rue en boitant; **when the time** ~**s** lorsque le moment sera venu; **the time has come to do** le moment est venu de faire; **I'm coming!** j'arrive!; **to** ~ **and go** aller et venir; **you can** ~ **and go as you please** tu es libre de tes mouvements; **fashions** ~ **and go** les modes vont et viennent; ~ **next year** l'année prochaine; ~ **Christmas/summer** à Noël/en été; **for some time to** ~ encore quelque temps; **there's still the speech to** ~ il y a encore le discours; **2** (approach) s'approcher; **to** ~ **and see/help sb** venir voir/aider qn; **to** ~ **to sb for** venir demander [qch] à qn [*money, advice*]; **I could see it coming** (of accident) je le voyais venir; **don't** ~ **any closer** ne vous approchez pas (plus); **to** ~ **close** *ou* **near to doing** faillir faire; **3** (call, visit) [*dustman, postman*] passer; [*cleaner*] venir; **I've come to do** je viens faire; **I've come for the keys** je viens chercher les clés; **my brother is coming for me at 10 am** mon frère passe me prendre à 10 heures; **4** (attend) venir; **to** ~ **to** venir à [*meeting, party*]; **5** (reach) **to** ~ **to**, **to** ~ **up/down to** [*water*] venir jusqu'à; [*dress, curtain*] arriver à; **6** (happen) **how did you** ~ **to do?** comment as-tu fait pour faire?; **that's what** ~**s of doing** voilà ce qui arrive quand on fait; **how** ~**?** comment ça se fait?; ~ **what may** advienne que pourra; **to take things as they** ~ prendre les choses comme elles viennent; ~ **to think of it** en fait; **7** (begin) **to** ~ **to believe/hate** finir par croire/détester; **8** (originate) **to** ~ **from** [*person*] être originaire de, venir de [*city, country*]; [*word, legend*] venir de [*country, language*]; [*substance*] provenir de [*raw material*]; [*coins, stamps*] provenir de [*place*]; [*smell, sound*] venir de [*place*]; **to** ~ **from France** [*fruit, painting*] provenir de France; [*person*] être français/-e; **9** (be available) **to** ~ **in** exister en [*sizes, colours*]; **to** ~ **with chips** être servi

avec des frites; **to ~ with matching napkins** être vendu avec les serviettes assorties; [10] (tackle) **to ~ to** aborder [*problem, subject*]; **I'll ~ to that in a moment** je reviendrai sur ce point dans un moment; [11] (develop) **it ~s with practice** cela s'apprend avec la pratique; **wisdom ~s with age** la sagesse vient en vieillissant; [12] (be situated) venir; **to ~ after** suivre, venir après; **to ~ before** (in time, list, queue) précéder; (in importance) passer avant; **to ~ first/last** arriver premier/dernier; **where did you ~?** tu es arrivé combien°?; **my family ~s first** ma famille passe avant tout; **don't let this ~ between us** on ne va pas se fâcher pour ça; **to ~ between two people** s'interposer entre deux personnes; [13] (be due) **the house ~s to me when they die** la maison me reviendra quand ils mourront; **he had it coming (to him)**° ça lui pendait au nez; **they got what was coming to them**° ils ont fini par avoir ce qu'ils méritaient; [14] (be a question of) **when it ~s to sth/to doing** lorsqu'il s'agit de qch/de faire

(Idioms) **~ again**°? pardon?; **I don't know if I'm coming or going** je ne sais plus où j'en suis; **he's as stupid as they ~** il n'y a pas plus stupide que lui; **~ to that** ou **if it ~s to that, you may be right** en fait, tu as peut-être raison; **to ~ as a shock** être un choc

(Phrasal verbs)

■ **come about** [*problems, reforms*] survenir; [*situation, change*] se produire

■ **come across**: ► **~ across** [*meaning, message*] passer; [*feelings*] transparaître; **she ~s across well on TV** elle passe bien à la télé; **~ across as** donner l'impression d'être [*liar, expert*]; paraître [*enthusiastic, honest*]; ► **~ across [sth]** tomber sur [*article, example*]; ► **~ across [sb]** rencontrer [*person*]

■ **come along** [1] (arrive) [*bus, person*] arriver; [*opportunity*] se présenter; [2] (hurry up) **~ along!** dépêche-toi!; [3] (attend) venir; **to ~ along to** venir à [*lecture, party*]; [4] (make progress) [*pupil*] faire des progrès; [*book, work, project*] avancer; [*painting, tennis*] progresser; [*seedling*] pousser; **your Spanish is coming along** votre espagnol a progressé

■ **come apart** [1] (accidentally) [*book, box*] se déchirer; [*toy, camera*] se casser; **the toy came apart in my hands** le jouet m'est resté dans les mains; [2] (intentionally) [*components*] se séparer; [*machine*] se démonter

■ **come around** US = **come round**

■ **come at**: ► **~ at [sb]** (attack) [*person*] attaquer; [*bull*] foncer sur

■ **come away** [1] (leave) partir; **to ~ away from** quitter [*cinema, match*]; sortir de [*meeting*]; **to ~ away with the feeling that** rester sur l'impression que; [2] (move away) s'éloigner; [3] (detach) se détacher (**from** de)

■ **come back** [1] (return) gen revenir (**from** de; **to** à); (to one's house) rentrer; **to ~ running back** revenir en courant; **to ~ back to** revenir à [*topic, problem*]; **to ~ back with sb** raccompagner qn; **to ~ back with** (return) revenir avec [*present, idea, flu*]; (reply) répondre par [*offer, suggestion*]; **can I ~ back to you on that?** est-ce que nous pourrions en reparler?; **it's all coming back to me now** tout me revient maintenant; [2] (become popular) [*law, system*] être rétabli; [*trend*] revenir à la mode

■ **come by**: ► **~ by** [*person*] passer; ► **~ by [sth]** trouver [*book, job, money*]

■ **come down** [1] (move lower) [*person, lift, blind*] descendre; [*curtain*] tomber; **he's really come down in the world** fig il est vraiment tombé bas; [2] (drop) [*price, inflation, temperature*] baisser (**from** de; **to** à); [*cost*] diminuer; **cars are coming down in price** le prix des voitures baisse; [3] [*snow, rain*] tomber; [4] (land) [*helicopter*] se poser; [*aircraft*] atterrir; [5] (crash) [*plane*] s'écraser; [6] (fall) [*ceiling, wall*] s'écrouler; [*hem*] se défaire; [7] fig (be resumed by) se ramener à [*problem, fact*]; [8] (catch) **to ~ down with** attraper [*flu*]

■ **come forward** [1] (step forward) s'avancer; [2] (volunteer) se présenter; **to ~ forward with** présenter [*proof*]; offrir [*help, money, suggestions*]

■ **come in** [1] (enter) [*person, rain*] entrer (**through** par); [2] (return) rentrer (**from** de); [3] (come inland) [*tide*] monter; [4] (arrive) arriver; **we've got £2,000 a month coming in** nous avons une rentrée de 2 000 livres sterling par mois; [5] (become current) [*trend, invention*] faire son apparition; [6] Radio **~ in, Delta Bravo!** c'est à vous, Delta Bravo!; [7] (serve a particular purpose) **where do I ~ in?** à quel moment est-ce que j'interviens?; **to ~ in useful** ou **handy** être utile; [8] (receive) **to ~ in for criticism** [*person*] être critiqué; [*plan*] faire l'objet de nombreuses critiques

■ **come into**: ► **~ into [sth]** [1] (inherit) hériter de [*money*]; entrer en possession de [*inheritance*]; [2] (be relevant) **to ~ into it** [*age, experience*] entrer en ligne de compte, jouer; **luck doesn't ~ into it** ce n'est pas une question de hasard

■ **come off**: ► **~ off** [1] (become detached) (accidentally) [*button, label, handle*] se détacher; [*lid*] s'enlever; [*paint*] s'écailler; (intentionally) [*handle, panel, lid*] s'enlever; [2] (fall) [*rider*] tomber; [3] (wash, rub off) [*ink*] s'effacer; [*stain*] partir; [4] (take place) [*deal*] se réaliser; [*merger, trip*] avoir lieu; [5] (succeed) [*plan, trick*] réussir; [6] (fare) **she came off well** (in deal) elle s'en est très bien tirée; **who came off worst?** (in fight) lequel des deux a été le plus touché?; ► **~ off [sth]** [1] (stop using) arrêter [*tablet, heroin*]; [2] (fall off) tomber de [*bicycle, horse*]

■ **come on** [1] (follow) **I'll ~ on later** je vous rejoindrai plus tard; [2] (exhortation) **~ on!** allez!; [3] (make progress) [*person, patient*] faire des progrès; [*bridge, novel*] avancer; [*plant*] pousser; [4] (begin) [*attack, headache*] commencer; [*programme*] commencer; [*rain*] se mettre à tomber; [5] (start to work) [*light*] s'allumer; [*heating, fan*] se mettre en route; **the power came on again** le courant est revenu; [6] Theat [*actor*] entrer en scène

■ **come out** [1] (emerge) [*person, animal, vehicle*] sortir (**of** de); [*star*] apparaître; [*sun, moon*] se montrer; **he came out of it rather well** fig il ne s'en est pas mal tiré; [2] (originate) **to ~ out of** [*person*] être originaire de; [*song*] venir de; [*news report*] provenir de; **the money will have to ~ out of your savings** il faudra prendre l'argent sur tes économies; [3] (result) **something good came out of the disaster** il est sorti quelque chose de bon du désastre; [4] (strike) faire la grève; **to ~ out on strike** faire la grève; [5] (fall out) [*contact lens, tooth*] tomber; [*contents*] sortir; [*cork*] s'enlever; **his hair is coming out** il commence à perdre ses cheveux; [6] (be emitted) [*water, smoke*] sortir (**through** par); [7] (wash out) [*stain*] s'en aller, partir; [8] (be published, issued) [*magazine, novel*] paraître; [*album, film, product*] sortir; [9] (become known) [*feelings*] se manifester; [*details, facts*] être révélé; [*results*] être connu; **it came out that** on a appris que; **the truth is bound to ~ out** la vérité finira forcément par se savoir; [10] Phot [*photo, photocopy*] être réussi; [11] (end up) **to ~ out at 200 dollars** [*cost, bill*] s'élever à 200 dollars; **the jumper came out too big** le pull était trop grand; [12] (say) **to ~ out with** sortir [*excuse*]; raconter [*nonsense*]; **whatever will she ~ out with next?** qu'est-ce qu'elle va encore nous sortir°?; **to ~ straight out with it** le dire franchement

■ **come over** [1] (drop in) venir; **~ over for a drink** venez prendre un verre; **to ~ over to do** venir faire; [2] (travel) venir; [3] (convey impression) [*message*] passer; [*feelings, love*] transparaître; **to ~ over very well** [*person*] donner une très bonne impression; **to ~ over as** donner l'impression d'être [*lazy, honest*]; [4] ° (suddenly become) **to ~ over all embarrassed** se sentir gêné tout à coup; **to ~ over all faint** être pris de vertige tout d'un coup; ► **~ over [sb]** [*feeling*] envahir; **what's come over you?** qu'est-ce qui te prend?

■ **come round** GB, **come around** US [1] (regain consciousness) reprendre connaissance; [2] (circulate) [*waitress*] passer; [3] (visit) venir; [4] (occur) [*event*] avoir lieu; [5] (change one's mind) changer d'avis; **to ~ round to my way of thinking** se rallier à mon point de vue

■ **come through**: ► **~ through** [1] (survive) s'en tirer; [2] (penetrate) [*heat, ink*] traverser; [*light*] passer; [3] (arrive) **my posting has just come through** je viens de recevoir ma mutation; [4] (emerge) apparaître; ► **~ through [sth]** [1] (survive) se tirer de [*crisis*]; se sortir de [*recession*]; survivre à [*operation, ordeal*]; [2] (penetrate) [*ink*] traverser; [*light*] passer au travers de

■ **come to**: ► **~ to** [1] (regain consciousness) (from faint) reprendre connaissance; (from trance) se réveiller; ► **~ to [sth]** [1] (total) [*shopping*] revenir à; [*bill, total*] s'élever à; **that ~s to £40** cela fait 40 livres sterling; [2] (result in) **all her plans came to nothing** aucun de ses projets ne s'est réalisé; **I never thought it would ~ to this** je n'aurais jamais imaginé que les choses en arriveraient là; **it may not ~ to that** nous n'en arriverons peut-être pas là

■ **come under**: ► **~ under [sth]** [1] (be subjected to) **to ~ under scrutiny** faire l'objet d'un examen minutieux; **to ~ under suspicion/threat** être soupçonné/menacé; [2] (be classified under) (in library, shop) être classé dans le rayon [*reference, history*]

■ **come up** ⓵ (arise) [*problem, issue*] être soulevé; [*name*] être mentionné; **to ~ up in conversation** [*subject*] être abordé dans la conversation; ⓶ (be due) **to ~ up for re-election** se représenter aux élections; **my salary ~s up for review in April** mon salaire sera révisé en avril; ⓷ (occur) [*opportunity*] se présenter; **something urgent has come up** j'ai quelque chose d'urgent à faire; **a vacancy has come up** une place s'est libérée; ⓸ (rise) [*sun, moon*] sortir; [*tide*] monter; [*daffodils, beans*] sortir; ⓹ Jur [*case, hearing*] passer au tribunal; [*person*] comparaître devant; ⓺ **to ~ up against** se heurter à [*problem*]; ⓻ (find) **to ~ up with** trouver

■ **come upon**: ▸ **~ upon [sth]** tomber sur [*book, reference*]; trouver [*idea*]

comeback /'kʌmbæk/
Ⓐ *n* ⓵ (of musician, actor, boxer) come-back *m*; (of politician) rentrée *f*; **to make** *ou* **stage a ~** [*person*] faire un come-back *or* une rentrée; [*style*] revenir à la mode; ⓶ (redress) recours *m*
Ⓑ *noun modifier* [*album*] de come-back; **~ bid** (of singer, actor) come-back *m*; (of politician) rentrée *f*

comedian /kə'miːdɪən/ ▸ p. 1181 *n* ⓵ (actor) (male) comique *m*; (female) actrice *f* comique; ⓶ (joker) pitre *m*

comedienne /kə‚miːdɪ'en/ ▸ p. 1181 *n* actrice *f* comique

comedown○ /'kʌmdaʊn/ *n* déchéance *f*; **it's quite a ~ for her to have to do** elle trouve humiliant d'avoir à faire

comedy /'kɒmədɪ/ *n* ⓵ (genre) comédie *f*; **black/light ~** comédie *f* macabre/légère; ⓶ (play) comédie *f*; ⓷ (funny aspect) comique *m*

comer /'kʌmə(r)/ *n* **to take on all ~s** se battre contre tous les challengeurs; **open to all ~s** ouvert à tout le monde

comet /'kɒmɪt/ *n* comète *f*

comeuppance○ /kʌm'ʌpəns/ *n* **to get one's ~** avoir ce qu'on mérite

comfort /'kʌmfət/
Ⓐ *n* ⓵ (well-being) confort *m*; (wealth) aisance *f*; **to live in ~** vivre dans l'aisance; ⓶ (amenity) confort *m*; **every modern ~** tout le confort moderne; **home ~s** le confort du foyer; ⓷ (consolation) réconfort *m*, consolation *f*; (relief from pain) soulagement *m*; **it's a ~ to know that** il est consolant de savoir que; **to be a great ~ to sb** [*person*] être un grand réconfort pour qn; [*knowledge, belief*] apporter beaucoup de réconfort à qn; **to take ~ from** trouver un réconfort dans; **we can take ~ from the fact that** nous pouvons nous consoler à l'idée que; **if it's any ~ to you** si cela peut vous réconforter *or* consoler; **to be small ~ for sb** n'être qu'une maigre consolation pour qn
Ⓑ *vtr* consoler; (stronger) réconforter

(Idiom) **it's (a bit) too close for ~** (of where sb is, lives) ça fait un peu trop près; (of fighting, war) c'est dangereusement proche, ça devient inquiétant

comfortable /'kʌmftəbl, US -fərt-/ *adj* ⓵ [*room, chair, clothes, journey*] confortable; [*temperature*] agréable; ⓶ (relaxed) [*person*] à l'aise; **to make oneself ~** (in chair) s'installer confortablement; (at ease) se mettre à son aise; **to make sb feel ~** mettre qn à l'aise; **the patient's condition is described as ~** l'état du malade est jugé satisfaisant; ⓷ (financially) [*person*] aisé; [*income*] conséquent; ⓸ (reassuring) [*idea, thought*] sécurisant; [*majority, lead*] confortable; ⓹ (happy) **I don't feel ~ doing** ça m'embête○ de faire; **I would feel more ~ about leaving if...** je partirais plus volontiers si...

comfortably /'kʌmftəblɪ, US -fərt-/ *adv* ⓵ (physically) confortablement; ⓶ (financially) [*live*] confortablement; **~ off** à l'aise; ⓷ (easily) facilement, aisément

comforter /'kʌmfətə(r)/ *n* ⓵ †(scarf) cache-nez *m inv*; ⓶ (person) consolateur/-trice *m/f*; ⓷ US (quilt) édredon *m*

comforting /'kʌmfətɪŋ/ *adj* réconfortant

comfort station *n* US toilettes *fpl*

comfy○ /'kʌmfɪ/ *adj* confortable

comic /'kɒmɪk/ ▸ p. 1181
Ⓐ *n* ⓵ (man) comique *m*; (woman) actrice *f* comique; ⓶ (magazine etc) bande *f* dessinée
Ⓑ *adj* comique

comical /'kɒmɪkl/ *adj* cocasse, comique

comic: **~ book** *n* bande *f* dessinée; **~ opera** *n* opéra *m* comique

comic relief *n* **to provide some ~** Theat, fig détendre l'atmosphère

comic strip *n* bande *f* dessinée

coming /'kʌmɪŋ/
Ⓐ *n* ⓵ (arrival) arrivée *f*; **~ and going** va-et-vient *m inv*; **~s and goings** allées et venues *fpl*; ⓶ (approach) (of winter, old age) approche *f*; (of new era, event) arrivée *f*; ⓷ Relig avènement *m*
Ⓑ *adj* election, event] prochain (*before n*); [*war, campaign*] qui se prépare (*after n*); [*months, weeks*] à venir (*after n*); **this ~ Monday** (ce) lundi

comma /'kɒmə/ *n* virgule *f*

command /kə'mɑːnd, US -'mænd/
Ⓐ *n* ⓵ (order) ordre *m*; **to carry out/give a ~** exécuter/donner un ordre; ⓶ (military control) commandement *m*; **to give sb ~ of sth** confier le commandement de qch à qn; **to be in ~** commander; **to be under the ~ of sb** [*person*] être sous les ordres de qn; [*regiment*] être sous les ordres *or* sous le commandement de qn; **I'm in ~ of the troops** les troupes sont sous mes ordres; **~ of the air** maîtrise *f* du ciel; ⓷ (mastery) maîtrise *f*; **to have full ~ of one's faculties** maîtriser parfaitement ses facultés; **an excellent ~ of Russian** une excellente maîtrise du russe; **to be in ~ of the situation** avoir la situation en main; **to have sth at one's ~** avoir qch à sa disposition; ⓸ Comput commande *f*
Ⓑ *vtr* ⓵ (order) ordonner à [*person*] (**to do** de faire); **to ~ that** ordonner que (+ *subj*); ⓶ (obtain as one's due) inspirer [*affection, respect*]; **to ~ a good price** se vendre cher; ⓷ (dispose of) disposer de [*funds, support, majority*]; ⓸ (dominate) dominer [*valley*]; **to ~ a view of** avoir vue sur; ⓹ Mil commander [*regiment*]; maîtriser [*air, sea*]
Ⓒ *vi* commander

commandant /‚kɒmən'dænt/ *n* Mil commandant *m*

commandeer /‚kɒmən'dɪə(r)/ *vtr* Mil réquisitionner

commander /kə'mɑːndə(r), US -mæn-/ ▸ p. 1123 *n* gen chef *m*; Mil commandant *m*; Mil Naut *cf* capitaine *m* de frégate; **~ in chief** commandant en chef

commanding /kə'mɑːndɪŋ, US -mæn-/ *adj* ⓵ (authoritative) [*look, manner, voice*] impérieux/-ieuse; [*presence*] imposant; ⓶ (dominant) [*position*] dominant; **to have a ~ lead in the polls** être en tête des sondages; ⓷ (elevated) [*position*] surélevé

commanding officer, CO ▸ p. 1123 *n* commandant *m*

commandment /kə'mɑːndmənt, US -mæn-/ *n* ⓵ (order) injonction *f*; ⓶ Relig commandement *m*

commando /kə'mɑːndəʊ, US -mæn-/ *n* (*pl* **-os, -oes**) commando *m*

command: **~ performance** *n* GB Theat représentation *f* de gala (*donnée en présence d'un membre de la famille royale*); **~ post, CP** *n* Mil poste *m* de commandement

commemorate /kə'meməreɪt/ *vtr* commémorer

commemorative /kə'memərətɪv, US -'meməreɪt-/ *adj* commémoratif/-ive

commend /kə'mend/
Ⓐ *vtr* ⓵ (praise) louer (**for, on** pour); ⓶ (recommend) **to have much to ~ it** avoir de grandes qualités; ⓷ (entrust) confier
Ⓑ *v refl* **to ~ itself** être acceptable (**to** à)

commendable /kə'mendəbl/ *adj* louable; **highly ~** très louable

commendably /kə'mendəblɪ/ *adv* **~ quick/restrained** avec une louable promptitude/retenue

commendation /‚kɒmen'deɪʃn/ *n* ⓵ (praise, award) éloge *m*; ⓶ (medal, citation) citation *f*

commensurate /kə'menʃərət/ *adj* sout ⓵ (proportionate) proportionné (**with** à); ⓶ (appropriate) **to be ~ with** être à la mesure de

comment /'kɒment/
Ⓐ *n* ⓵ (remark) (public) commentaire *m* (**on** sur); (in conversation) remarque *f* (**on** sur); (written) annotation *f*; ⓶ Ⓒ (discussion) commentaires *mpl* (**about** portant sur); **without ~** [*listen*]

sans commentaire; [*occur*] sans susciter des commentaires; **'no ~'** 'je n'ai pas de déclaration à faire'; **3** (criticism) **to be a ~** on en dire long sur

B *vtr* (orally) remarquer; (in writing) constater

C *vi* **1** (remark) faire des commentaires *mpl*; **to ~ on sth/sb** faire des commentaires sur qch/qn; **2** (discuss) **to ~ on** commenter [*text etc*]

commentary /'kɒməntrɪ, US -terɪ/ *n* gen, Literat commentaire *m* (**on** de)

commentate /'kɒmənteɪt/
A *vtr* commenter
B *vi* faire le commentaire; **to ~ on** commenter [*sporting event*]

commentator /'kɒmənteɪtə(r)/ ▸ p. 1181 *n* (sports) commentateur/-trice *m/f*; (current affairs) journaliste *mf*

commerce /'kɒmɜːs/ *n* commerce *m*; **in ~** dans les affaires

commercial /kə'mɜːʃl/
A *n* annonce *f* publicitaire, publicité *f*; **TV ~** annonce publicitaire à la télé; **beer ~** annonce publicitaire pour de la bière
B *adj* **1** [*airline, sector, radio, product*] commercial; **2** (profitable) commercial *pej*; qui se vend bien; **3** (large-scale) industriel/-ielle

commercial: **~ artist** *n* graphiste *mf*; **~ break** *n* publicité *f*

commercialism /kə'mɜːʃəlɪzəm/ *n* **1** péj mercantilisme *m* péj; **2** (principles of commerce) esprit *m* commercial

commercialization /kə,mɜːʃəlaɪ'zeɪʃn, US -lɪ'z-/ *n* péj commercialisation *f*

commercialize /kə'mɜːʃəlaɪz/ *vtr* commercialiser

commercial law *n* droit *m* commercial

commercially /kə'mɜːʃəlɪ/ *adv* commercialement

commercial: **~ traveller** ▸ p. 1181 *n* voyageur *m* de commerce; **~ vehicle** *n* véhicule *m* utilitaire

commiserate /kə'mɪzəreɪt/ *vi* compatir (**with** avec; **about, over** à propos de)

commissar /'kɒmɪsɑː(r)/ *n* commissaire *m*

commissariat /kɒmɪ'seərɪət/ *n* **1** Mil intendance *f*; **2** Pol Hist (in USSR) commissariat *m*

commission /kə'mɪʃn/
A *n* **1** (for goods sold) commission *f*; **to get a 5% ~** recevoir *or* toucher une commission de 5%; **to work on ~** travailler à la commission; **2** (fee) commission *f*; **we charge 1% ~ on travellers' cheques** nous prenons 1% de commission sur les chèques de voyage; **3** (advance order) commande *f* (**for** de); **to give sb a ~** passer une commande à qn; **to work to ~** travailler sur commande; **4** (committee) commission *f* (**on** sur); **~ of inquiry** commission d'enquête; **5** Mil ≈ brevet *m*; **to get one's ~** être nommé officier; **to resign one's ~** démissionner; **6** (of crime, sin) perpétration *f*; **7** (operation) **in ~** en service; **out of ~** hors service
B *vtr* **1** (order) commander (**from** à); **a ~ed portrait** un portrait sur commande; **2** (instruct) **to ~ sb to do** charger qn de faire; **3** Mil **a ~ed officer** un officier; **4** (prepare for service) armer [*ship*]; mettre [qch] en service [*plane, equipment, weapon system*]

commissionaire /kə,mɪʃə'neə(r)/ ▸ p. 1181 *n* GB portier *m*

commissioner /kə'mɪʃənə(r)/ *n* **1** Admin membre *m* d'une commission; **2** GB (in police) ≈ préfet *m* de police; **3** (in the EC Commission) membre *m* de la Commission européenne

Commissioner for Oaths *n* GB Jur *officier habilité à enregistrer les déclarations sous serment*

commit /kə'mɪt/ (*p prés etc* **-tt-**)
A *vtr* **1** (perpetrate) commettre [*crime, error*]; **to ~ adultery** commettre un adultère; **2** (engage) engager [*person*] (**to do** à faire); **3** (assign) consacrer [*money, time*] (**to** à); Jur **to ~ sb for trial** mettre qn en accusation; **to ~ sb to jail/to a psychiatric hospital** faire incarcérer/interner qn; **5** (consign) sout confier (**to** à; **to sb's care** à la garde de qn); **to ~ sth to paper** consigner qch; **to ~ sth to memory** mémoriser qch
B *v refl* **to ~ oneself** s'engager (**to** à); **I can't** *ou* **I won't ~ myself** je ne peux rien promettre (**as to** quant à)

commitment /kə'mɪtmənt/ *n* **1** (obligation) engagement *m* (**to do** à faire); **a previous ~** un engagement antérieur; **to meet one's ~s** honorer ses engagements; **to give a firm ~ that** s'engager fermement à ce que (+ *subj*); **family ~s** obligations *fpl* familiales; **2** (sense of duty) attachement *m* (**to** à); **to have a strong ~ to doing** être particulièrement attaché à faire; **the job demands complete ~** ce travail exige un total don de soi

committal /kə'mɪtl/ *n* **1** Jur (to prison) incarcération *f*; (to psychiatric hospital) internement *m*; (to court) renvoi *m* devant un tribunal; **2** (consigning) **the ~ of X to Y's care** la remise de X aux soins de Y

committed /kə'mɪtɪd/ *adj* **1** (devoted) [*parent, teacher*] dévoué; [*Christian, Socialist*] fervent; **to be ~ to/to doing** se consacrer à/à faire; **to be politically ~** être engagé politiquement; **2** (with commitments) pris (**to doing** pour faire); **I am heavily ~** (timewise) je suis très pris; (financially) j'ai de lourds engagements

committee /kə'mɪtɪ/ *n* gen comité *m*; (to investigate, report) commission *f*; **in ~** en comité

committee: **~ meeting** *n* réunion *f* du comité; **~ stage** *n*: *phase pendant laquelle une commission discute un projet de loi*

commodious /kə'məʊdɪəs/ *adj* spacieux/-ieuse

commodity /kə'mɒdətɪ/ *n* **1** Comm, gen article *m*; (food) denrée *f*; **a rare ~** fig une denrée rare; **2** (on stock market) matière *f* première

commodore /'kɒmədɔː(r)/ ▸ p. 1123 *n* contre-amiral *m*

common /'kɒmən/
A *n* (land) terrain *m* communal
B *npl* **1** (the people) **the ~s** le peuple; **2** Pol (also **Commons**) **the ~s** les Communes *fpl*
C *adj* **1** (frequent) courant, fréquent; **in ~ use** d'un usage courant; **in ~ parlance** dans le langage courant; **it is ~ for sb to do** il est courant que qn fasse; **to be ~ among** être répandu chez [*children, mammals etc*]; **2** (shared) commun (**to** à); **in ~** en commun; **for the ~ good** pour le bien commun; **it is ~ property** c'est la propriété de tous; **it is ~ knowledge** c'est de notoriété publique; **3** (ordinary) [*man*] du peuple (*after n*); **the ~ people** le peuple; **the ~ herd** péj la masse; **a ~ criminal** péj un criminel ordinaire; **4** péj (low-class) commun; **it looks/sounds ~** ça fait commun; **5** [*courtesy, decency*] le/la plus élémentaire; **6** Zool, Bot commun

⏺ (idioms) **to be as ~ as muck** *ou* **dirt**⃝ (vulgar) être d'une vulgarité crasse⃝; **they are as ~ as muck**⃝ (widespread) on en ramasse à la pelle; **to have the ~ touch** avoir de la simplicité

common: **Common Agricultural Policy, CAP** *n* politique *f* agricole commune; **~ cold** ▸ p. 933 *n* rhume *m* de cerveau

commoner /'kɒmənə(r)/ *n* roturier/-ière *m/f*

common: **~ ground** *n* fig terrain *m* d'entente; **~-law husband** *n* concubin *m*; **~-law marriage** *n* concubinage *m*; **~-law wife** *n* concubine *f*

commonly /'kɒmənlɪ/ *adv* communément; **~ known as** communément appelé

common market, Common Market *n* Marché *m* commun

common: **~ noun** *n* nom *m* commun; **~-or-garden** *adj* ordinaire

commonplace /'kɒmənpleɪs/
A *n* lieu *m* commun
B *adj* (widespread) commun; (banal, trite) banal

common room *n* salle *f* de détente

common sense
A *n* bon sens *m*, sens *m* commun
B **commonsense** *adj* (also **commonsensical**) plein de bon sens

Commonwealth /'kɒmənwelθ/
A *n* **1** GB Pol (the (British) ~ (of Nations)) le Commonwealth; **2** GB Hist **the ~** le Commonwealth, la République de Cromwell
B *noun modifier* [*country, Games*] du Commonwealth; [*leader*] d'un pays du Commonwealth; [*summit*] des pays du Commonwealth

ⓘ Commonwealth Le *British Commonwealth of Nations* est une association de 54 nations indépendantes, pour la plupart d'anciennes colonies, présidée par le souverain britannique. Leurs Premiers ministres se rencontrent tous les deux ans lors de la *Commonwealth Conference* pour décider d'une politique d'aide et de coopération dans les domaines de la culture, de l'économie et de l'éducation. Des championnats d'athlétisme (*Commonwealth Games*) se déroulent tous les quatre ans entre les pays membres. Le mot *Commonwealth* figure aussi dans le nom officiel de certains États américains (*Kentucky, Virginia, Pennsylvania, Massachusetts*).

Commonwealth of Independent States *pr n* Communauté *f* des États indépendants

commotion /kə'məʊʃn/ *n* ① (noise) vacarme *m*, brouhaha *m*; **to make a ~** faire du vacarme; ② (disturbance) émoi *m*, agitation *f*; **to cause a ~** causer un grand émoi; **to be in a state of ~** [*crowd*] être agité; [*town*] être en émoi

communal /'kɒmjʊnl, kə'mju:nl/ *adj* [*property, area, showers*] commun; [*garden*] collectif/-ive; [*facilities*] commun, collectif/-ive; **~ ownership** copropriété *f*; [*prayer*] collectif/-ive; [*life*] communautaire

communally /'kɒmjʊnəlɪ, kə'mju:nəlɪ/ *adv* en commun, collectivement

commune
Ⓐ /'kɒmju:n/ *n* ① (group of people) communauté *f*; **to live in a ~** vivre en communauté; ② Admin (in continental Europe) commune *f*
Ⓑ /kə'mju:n/ *vi* **to ~ with** communier avec, être en communion avec [*nature*]; converser intimement avec [*person*]

communicable /kə'mju:nɪkəbl/ *adj* Med contagieux/-ieuse

communicant /kə'mju:nɪkənt/ *n* Relig communiant/-e *m/f*

communicate /kə'mju:nɪkeɪt/
Ⓐ *vtr* ① (convey) communiquer [*ideas, feelings*] (**to** à); transmettre [*information*] (**to** à); **his anxiety ~s itself to others** son angoisse est communicative; ② (transmit) transmettre [*disease*]
Ⓑ *vi* ① (relate) communiquer (**by** par; **through** au moyen de; **with** avec); ② (be in contact) communiquer (**with** avec; **by** par); **we no longer ~** nous avons perdu tout contact; ③ (connect) **to ~ with** communiquer avec

communicating door *n* porte *f* de communication

communication /kə,mju:nɪ'keɪʃn/
Ⓐ *n* ① (of information) transmission *f*; (of ideas, feelings) communication *f*; ② (contact) communication *f*; **the lines of ~** les voies *fpl* de communication; **to be in ~ with sb** être en communication *or* en contact avec qn; ③ (message) communication *f*
Ⓑ **communications** *npl* communications *fpl*, liaison *f*

communication: **~ cord** *n* GB sonnette *f* d'alarme; **~s company** *n* société *f* de communications; **~s link** *n* liaison *f*; **~s satellite** *n* satellite *m* de communication; **~ studies** *n* études *fpl* en communication

communicative /kə'mju:nɪkətɪv, US -keɪtɪv/ *adj* (talkative) expansif/-ive (**about** au sujet de)

communicator /kə'mju:nɪkeɪtə(r)/ *n* **to be a good ~** avoir le sens de la communication

communion /kə'mju:nɪən/ *n* littér (with nature, fellow man etc) communion *f*

Communion /kə'mju:nɪən/ *n* (*also* **Holy ~**) (sainte) communion *f*, Eucharistie *f*; **to make one's First ~** faire sa première communion; **to take ~** communier

communiqué /kə'mju:nɪkeɪ, US kə,mju:nə'keɪ/ *n* communiqué *m*

Communism, communism /'kɒmjʊnɪzəm/ *n* communisme *m*

Communist, communist /'kɒmjʊnɪst/ *n, adj* communiste (*mf*)

Communist Party, CP *n* parti *m* communiste

communitarianism /kə,mju:nɪ'teərɪənɪzəm/ *n* communautarisme *m*

community /kə'mju:nətɪ/
Ⓐ *n* ① (social, cultural grouping) communauté *f*; **the student/Italian ~** la communauté estudiantine/italienne; **the business ~** le monde des affaires; **research ~** communauté *f* des chercheurs; **relations between the police and**

the **~** (at local level) les relations entre la police et les habitants; (at national level) les relations entre la police et le public; **sense of ~** esprit *m* communautaire; ② Relig communauté *f*; ③ Jur communauté *f*; ④ (on the Internet) communauté *f*
Ⓑ **Community** *pr n* **the (European) Community** Hist la Communauté (Européenne)
Ⓒ **Community** *noun modifier* Hist communautaire, de la Communauté

community: **~ care** *n*: soins en dehors du milieu hospitalier; **~ centre** *n* maison *f* de quartier; **~ chest** *n* US fonds *m* de secours; **~ education** *n* GB cours ouverts à tous organisés par la municipalité; **~ health centre** *n* centre *m* médico-social; **~ life** *n* vie *f* associative; **~ medicine** *n* médecine *f* générale; **~ policeman** ▸ p. 1181 *n* ≈ îlotier *m*; **~ policing** *n* ≈ îlotage *m*; **~ service** *n* travail *m* d'intérêt public; **~ spirit** *n* esprit *m* communautaire; **~ worker** *n* animateur/-trice *m/f* socio-culturel/-elle

commute /kə'mju:t/
Ⓐ *n* US trajet *m* journalier
Ⓑ *vtr* Fin convertir; Jur commuer (**to** en)
Ⓒ *vi* **to ~ between Oxford and London** faire le trajet entre Oxford et Londres tous les jours; **she ~s to Glasgow** elle se rend à Glasgow tous les jours

commuter /kə'mju:tə(r)/ *n* navetteur/-euse *m/f*, migrant/-e *m/f* journalier/-ière

commuter: **~ belt** *n* grande banlieue *f*; **~ train** *n* train *m* de banlieue

Comoros /'kɒmərəʊz/ ▸ p. 774 *pr n* (îles *fpl*) Comores *fpl*

compact
Ⓐ /'kɒmpækt/ *n* ① (agreement) (written) accord *m*, contrat *m*, convention *f*; (verbal) entente *f*; ② (for powder) poudrier *m*
Ⓑ /kəm'pækt/ *adj* ① (compressed) [*snow, mass*] compact, dense; [*style, sentence*] concis, ramassé; ② (neatly constructed) compact
Ⓒ /kəm'pækt/ *vtr* comprimer [*waste, rubbish*]; tasser [*soil, snow*]

compact: **~ disc, CD** *n* disque *m* compact; **~ disc player** *n* platine *f* laser

compactly /kəm'pæktlɪ/ *adj* **~ built** [*person*] trapu; **~ designed** compact

companion /kəm'pænɪən/ *n* ① (friend) compagnon/compagne *m/f*; **to be sb's constant ~** [*hunger, fear*] être le perpétuel compagnon de qn; ② (*also* **paid ~**) dame *f* de compagnie; ③ (item of matching pair) pendant *m* (**to** de); ④ (book) guide *m* (**to** de); ⑤ Naut capot *m*

companionable /kəm'pænɪənəbl/ *adj* [*person*] sociable; [*chat, meal*] amical; [*silence*] sympathique

companionship /kəm'pænɪənʃɪp/ *n* compagnie *f*; **I have a dog for ~** j'ai un chien pour me tenir compagnie

companion: **~ volume** *n* pendant *m*; **~way** *n* Naut escalier *m*

company /'kʌmpənɪ/
Ⓐ *n* ① Comm, Jur société *f*; **airline ~** compagnie *f* aérienne; ② Mus, Theat troupe *f*, compagnie *f*; **theatre ~** troupe *f* de théâtre, compagnie *f* théâtrale; ③ Mil compagnie *f*; ④ (companionship) compagnie *f*; **to keep sb ~** tenir compagnie à qn; **to be good ~** être d'une compagnie agréable; **I have a cat for ~** j'ai un chat pour me tenir compagnie; **in sb's ~** *ou* **in ~ with sb** en compagnie de qn; **to part ~ with** [*person*] hum se séparer de [*person, bike*]; **on political matters they part ~** en ce qui concerne la politique, ils divergent complètement; **to keep bad ~** avoir de mauvaises fréquentations; **to be fit ~ for sb** être une fréquentation pour qn; **to keep ~ with sb** fréquenter qn; ⑤ (visitors) visiteurs *mpl*; **to have ~** avoir du monde; ⑥ (society) **in ~** en société; **in mixed ~** quand les dames sont présentes; **Lisa and ~** Lisa et compagnie○; ⑦ (similar circumstances) **you're in good ~** tu n'es pas le seul; ⑧ (gathering) compagnie *f*; **the assembled ~** l'assemblée; ⑨ Naut équipage *m*
Ⓑ *noun modifier* gen [*law, profits, records*] des sociétés; (of one business) [*accountant, headquarters*] de la société

company: **~ car** *n* voiture *f* de fonction; **~ director** ▸ p. 1181 *n* directeur/-trice *m/f* général/-e; **~ doctor** *n* redresseur *m* d'entreprise; **~ name** *n* Jur raison *f* sociale; **~ pension scheme** *n* régime *m* de retraite de l'entreprise; **~ policy** *n* ℂ politique *f* de l'entreprise; **~ secretary** ▸ p. 1181 *n* secrétaire *mf* général/-e;

∼ sergeant major, CSM ▸ p. 1123 *n* Mil adjudant *m* de compagnie; **∼ tax** *n* impôt *m* sur les sociétés

comparability /ˌkɒmpərəˈbɪləti/ *n* ① (comparison) comparabilité *f*; ② (equivalence) harmonisation *f*; **pay ∼** harmonisation des salaires

comparable /ˈkɒmpərəbl/ *adj* comparable (**to, with** à)

comparative /kəmˈpærətɪv/
A *n* Ling comparatif *m*; **in the ∼** au comparatif
B *adj* ① Ling comparatif/-ive; ② (relative) relatif/-ive; **in ∼ terms** en termes relatifs; ③ (based on comparison) [*method, study*] comparatif/-ive; [*literature, religion*] comparé

comparatively /kəmˈpærətɪvli/ *adv* ① (relatively) relativement; **∼ speaking** en termes relatifs; ② (by comparison) comparativement

compare /kəmˈpeə(r)/
A *n* **a beauty beyond ∼** une beauté incomparable; **to be brave beyond ∼** être incomparablement courageux/-euse
B *vtr* comparer; **to ∼ sb/sth with** *ou* **to** comparer qn/qch à *or* avec; **to ∼ notes with sb** fig échanger ses impressions avec qn
C **compared with** *prep phr* **∼d with sb/sth** par rapport à qn/qch
D *vi* être comparable (**with** à); **to ∼ favourably with** soutenir la comparaison avec; **how do they ∼?** et si on les compare?; **how does this job ∼ with your last one?** comment trouvez-vous cet emploi par rapport au précédent?
E *v refl* **to ∼ oneself with** *ou* **to** se comparer à

comparison /kəmˈpærɪsn/ *n* comparaison *f*; **beyond ∼** sans comparaison; **to draw a ∼ between sth and sth** comparer qch avec qch; **for** *ou* **by** à titre de comparaison; **in** *ou* **by ∼ with** par rapport à

compartment /kəmˈpɑːtmənt/ *n* compartiment *m*

compartmentalize /ˌkɒmpɑːtˈmentəlaɪz/ *vtr* compartimenter

compass /ˈkʌmpəs/
A *n* ① gen boussole *f*; Naut compas *m*; **the points of the ∼** les points *mpl* cardinaux; ② (extent) étendue *f*; (scope) portée *f*, rayon *m*
B **compasses** *npl* **a pair of ∼es** un compas

compassion /kəmˈpæʃn/ *n* compassion *f* (**for** pour)

compassionate /kəmˈpæʃənət/ *adj* compatissant; **on ∼ grounds** pour raisons *fpl* personnelles; **∼ leave** Mil permission *f* exceptionnelle

compatibility /kəmˌpætəˈbɪləti/ *n* gen, Comput compatibilité *f*

compatible /kəmˈpætəbl/ *adj* compatible (**with** avec); **X-∼** Comput compatible X

compatriot /kəmˈpætrɪət, US -ˈpeɪt-/ *n* compatriote *mf*

compel /kəmˈpel/ *vtr* (*p prés etc* **-ll-**) ① (force) contraindre (**to do** à faire), obliger (**to do** de faire); ② (win) imposer [*respect*]; retenir [*attention*]

compelling /kəmˈpelɪŋ/ *adj* [*reason, argument*] convaincant; [*performance, film, speaker*] fascinant

compellingly /kəmˈpelɪŋli/ *adv* [*argue*] de façon convaincante; [*speak, write*] de manière fascinante

compendium /kəmˈpendɪəm/ *n* (*pl* **-diums** *ou* **-dia**) ① (handbook) manuel *m*; ② GB (box of games) mallette *f* de jeux

compensate /ˈkɒmpenseɪt/
A *vtr* ① (financially) dédommager, indemniser [*person*]; **to ∼ sb for** dédommager qn de; ② (offset) compenser
B *vi* compenser; **to ∼ for** compenser [*loss, difficulty*]

compensation /ˌkɒmpenˈseɪʃn/ *n* ① gen compensation *f*; **to be no ∼ for sth** ne pas compenser qch; **as** *ou* **by way of ∼** en compensation (**for** de); ② Jur indemnisation *f*

compère /ˈkɒmpeə(r)/ *n* GB
A *n* animateur/-trice *m/f*
B *vtr* présenter

compete /kəmˈpiːt/
A *vi* ① (for prominence, job, prize) rivaliser; **to ∼ against** *ou* **with** rivaliser avec (**for** pour obtenir); **they were competing for the same job** ils se disputaient le même emploi; **I just can't ∼ (with her)** je ne peux pas lui faire concurrence; ② Comm [*companies*] se faire concurrence; **to ∼ against** *ou* **with** faire concurrence à (**for** pour obtenir); ③ Sport être en compétition (**against, with** avec); **to ∼ in** participer à [*Olympics, race*]
B **competing** *pres p adj* rival

competence /ˈkɒmpɪtəns/ *n* ① (ability) compétence *f*; **to have the ∼ to do** avoir la compétence voulue pour faire; **I doubt his ∼ to do** je doute qu'il soit capable de faire; ② (skill) compétences *fpl*; **her ∼ as an accountant** ses compétences de comptable; **∼ in word-processing** connaissances *fpl* en traitement de texte; **∼ in Spanish** une bonne connaissance de l'espagnol; ③ Jur compétence *f* (**to do** pour faire); **to be within the ∼ of the court** relever de la compétence du tribunal

competent /ˈkɒmpɪtənt/ *adj* ① (capable) compétent, capable; (trained) qualifié; **to be ∼ to do** être compétent *or* qualifié pour faire, être capable de faire; ② (adequate) [*performance*] honorable; [*knowledge*] suffisant; [*answer*] satisfaisant; ③ Jur compétent

competently /ˈkɒmpɪtəntli/ *adv* d'une manière compétente

competition /ˌkɒmpəˈtɪʃn/ *n* ① **𝒞** gen, Comm concurrence *f*, compétition *f* (**between** entre); **in ∼ with** en concurrence *or* comptabilité *or* compétition avec (**for** pour); ② **C** (contest) (for prize, award, job) concours *m*; (race) compétition *f*; ③ (competitors) concurrence *f*, compétition *f*

competitive /kəmˈpetɪtɪv/ *adj* ① (enjoying rivalry) [*person*] qui a l'esprit de compétition; [*environment*] compétitif/-ive; ② Comm [*company, price, product*] compétitif/-ive; **∼ edge** avantage *m* concurrentiel; **∼ tender** appel *m* d'offres; ③ (decided by competition) [*sport*] de compétition; **by ∼ examination** sur concours

competitively /kəmˈpetɪtɪvli/ *adv* [*play*] dans un esprit de compétition; [*operate*] compétitivement; **∼ priced** à des prix compétitifs

competitor /kəmˈpetɪtə(r)/ *n* concurrent/-e *m/f*

compilation /ˌkɒmpɪˈleɪʃn/ *n* ① (collection) compilation *f*; ② (act of compiling) (of reference book) rédaction *f*; (of dossier) constitution *f*

compile /kəmˈpaɪl/ *vtr* ① (draw up) dresser [*list, catalogue*]; établir [*report*]; rédiger [*reference book, entry*]; ② Comput compiler

compiler /kəmˈpaɪlə(r)/ *n* compilateur/-trice *m/f*

complacency /kəmˈpleɪsnsi/ *n* suffisance *f*, assurance *f* excessive

complacent /kəmˈpleɪsnt/ *adj* suffisant, trop confiant; **to be ∼ about** être trop confiant de [*success, future*]; **to grow ∼ about** perdre sa vigilance en ce qui concerne [*danger, threat*]

complacently /kəmˈpleɪsntli/ *adv* avec suffisance, avec une confiance excessive

complain /kəmˈpleɪn/ *vi* gen se plaindre (**to** à; **about** de); (officially) se plaindre (**to** auprès de), faire une réclamation (**to** à); (of illness, symptom) se plaindre (**of** de); **to ∼ that** se plaindre parce que; **I can't ∼** je n'ai pas à me plaindre

complaint /kəmˈpleɪnt/ *n* ① (protest, objection) gen plainte *f* (**about** concernant, au sujet de); (official) réclamation *f* (**about** concernant, au sujet de); **there have been ∼s about the noise** on s'est plaint du bruit; **there have been ∼s that the service is slow** on s'est plaint de la lenteur du service; **tiredness is a common ∼** les gens se plaignent souvent de fatigue; **in case of ∼**, contact the management en cas de réclamation, adressez-vous à la direction; **to have grounds** *ou* **cause for ∼** avoir lieu de se plaindre; **to file a ∼** déposer une plainte *or* porter plainte contre qn; **to make a ∼** se plaindre, faire une réclamation; **I've no ∼s** je n'ai rien à redire; **I've no ∼s about the service** je n'ai pas à me plaindre du service; ② Med maladie *f*

complement /ˈkɒmplɪmənt/
A *n* gen, Math, Ling complément *m* (**to** à); **with a full ∼ of staff** avec le personnel au complet
B *vtr* compléter; **to ∼ one another** se compléter; **wine ∼s cheese** le vin accompagne bien le fromage

complementary /ˌkɒmplɪˈmentri/ *adj* (all contexts) complémentaire (**to** de)

complementary medicine *n* médecine *f* parallèle

complete /kəmˈpliːt/
A *adj* ① (total, utter) (épith) [*chaos, darkness*] complet/-ète, total; **he's a ∼ fool** il est complètement idiot; **it's the ∼ opposite** c'est tout à fait le contraire; **with ∼ confidence** avec une confiance totale; **∼ and utter** total; **it's ∼ and utter rubbish** c'est complètement absurde; ② (finished) achevé; ③ (entire, full) [*collection, works, set*] complet/-ète; **∼ with** avec; **to make my happiness ∼** pour que rien ne manque

à mon bonheur; **4** (consummate) [*artist, star*] complet/-ète; [*gentleman*] parfait (*before n*)

B *vtr* **1** (finish) terminer [*building, course, exercise*]; achever [*task, journey*]; **half ~d** inachevé; **2** (make whole) compléter [*collection, group, phrase*]; **3** (fill in) remplir [*form*]

completely /kəm'pliːtlɪ/ *adv* complètement

completion /kəm'pliːʃn/ *n* **1** (finishing) achèvement *m* (of de); **on ~ (of the works)** à l'achèvement des travaux; **nearing ~** près d'être achevé; **2** (of house sale) signature *f* de la vente

complex /'kɒmpleks, US kəm'pleks/

A *n* **1** (development) complexe *m*; **sports/leisure ~** complexe *m* sportif/de loisirs; **housing ~** complexe *m* résidentiel; **2** Med, Psych complexe *m*; **he's got a ~ about his weight** son poids lui donne un complexe

B *adj* complexe

complexion /kəm'plekʃn/ *n* **1** (skin colour) teint *m*; **to have a clear/bad ~** avoir une peau nette/à problèmes; **to have a fair/dark ~** avoir un teint clair/mat; **2** (nature) aspect *m*; **to put a new ~ on sth** présenter qch sous un jour nouveau

complexity /kəm'pleksətɪ/ *n* complexité *f*

compliance /kəm'plaɪəns/ *n* **1** (conformity) conformité *f* (with à); **in ~ with the law** conformément à la loi; **2** (yielding disposition) caractère *m* conciliant

compliant /kəm'plaɪənt/ *adj* conciliant

complicate /'kɒmplɪkeɪt/ *vtr* compliquer; **to ~ matters** *ou* **life** compliquer les choses

complication /ˌkɒmplɪ'keɪʃn/ *n* **1** (problem) inconvénient *m*, problème *m*; **2** Med complication *f*

complicity /kəm'plɪsətɪ/ *n* complicité *f*

compliment /'kɒmplɪmənt/

A *n* compliment *m*; **to pay sb a ~** faire un compliment à qn; **to return the ~** lit retourner le compliment; fig répondre de la même façon

B **compliments** *npl* **1** (in expressions of praise) compliments *mpl* (to à); **to give sb one's ~s** faire ses compliments à qn; **2** (in expressions of politeness) 'with ~s' (on transmission slip) 'avec tous nos compliments'; **'with the ~s of the author'** 'avec les hommages de l'auteur'; **3** (in greetings) **'with the ~s of the season'** (on Christmas cards) 'meilleurs vœux'

C *vtr* complimenter, faire des compliments à

complimentary /ˌkɒmplɪ'mentrɪ/ *adj* **1** (flattering) flatteur/-euse; **he wasn't very ~ about my poems** il s'est montré plutôt critique à l'égard de mes poèmes; **she was very ~ about my work** elle m'a fait des compliments sur mon travail; **2** (free) gratuit, à titre gracieux; **~ copy** exemplaire *m* donné en hommage

compliments slip *n* carte *f* avec les compliments de l'expéditeur

comply /kəm'plaɪ/ *vi* s'exécuter; **to ~ with** se plier à [*sb's wishes*]; accéder à [*request*]; se conformer à [*orders, regulations*]; respecter, observer [*rules*]; **failure to ~ with the rules** le non-respect des règles

component /kəm'pəʊnənt/ *n* gen, Math composante *f*; Aut, Tech pièce *f*; Elec composant *m*; Chem constituant *m*; **~ part** élément *m*

compose /kəm'pəʊz/

A *vtr* **1** (write) gen, Literat, Mus composer; **2** (arrange) composer [*painting*]; agencer [*elements of work*]; **3** (order) composer [*features*]; rassembler [*thoughts*]; **4** (constitute) composer; **~d of** composé de; **5** (in printing) composer

B *vi* (all contexts) composer

C *v refl* **to ~ oneself** se ressaisir

composed /kəm'pəʊzd/ *adj* [*person, features*] calme

composer /kəm'pəʊzə(r)/ ▸ **p. 1181** *n* Mus compositeur/-trice *m/f* (of de)

composite /'kɒmpəzɪt/

A *n* **1** (substance) composite *m*; **2** (character, photo, word) composite *m* (of de); **3** Comm entreprise *f* diversifiée

B *adj* **1** Chem, Phot composite; **2** Math composé; **3** Comm diversifié

composition /ˌkɒmpə'zɪʃn/ *n* **1** (make-up) composition *f* (of de); **metallic in ~** d'une composition métallique; **2** Mus, Literat composition *f* (of de); **this is my own ~** cela est ma propre composition; **of my/her own ~** de ma/sa composition; **3** Sch rédaction *f* (about, on sur); **4** Art composition *f*

compositor /kəm'pɒzɪtə(r)/ ▸ **p. 1181** *n* compositeur/-trice *m/f*

compos mentis /ˌkɒmpəs 'mentɪs/ *adj* **to be ~** être en possession de toutes ses facultés

compost /'kɒmpɒst/ *n* compost *m*, terreau *m*

composure /kəm'pəʊʒə(r)/ *n* calme *m*; **to lose/regain one's ~** perdre/retrouver son calme

compound

A /'kɒmpaʊnd/ *n* **1** (enclosure) enceinte *f*; **prison ~** enceinte *f* de prison; **workers' ~** quartier *m* de travailleurs; **2** Chem composé *m* (of de); **3** (word) mot *m* composé; **4** (mixture) composé *m* (of de)

B /'kɒmpaʊnd/ *adj* **1** gen, Biol, Bot, Chem composé; **2** Ling [*tense, noun*] composé; [*sentence*] complexe; **3** Med [*fracture*] multiple; **4** Fin [*interest*] composé

C /kəm'paʊnd/ *vtr* **1** (exacerbate) aggraver [*error, offence, problem*] (by par; by doing en faisant); **2** (combine) combiner (with à); **~ed of** composé de

comprehend /ˌkɒmprɪ'hend/ *vtr* comprendre, saisir

comprehensible /ˌkɒmprɪ'hensəbl/ *adj* compréhensible, intelligible

comprehension /ˌkɒmprɪ'henʃn/ *n* **1** (understanding) compréhension *f*, entendement *m*; **that is beyond my ~** cela dépasse mon entendement; **2** Sch, Univ exercice *m* de compréhension

comprehensive /ˌkɒmprɪ'hensɪv/

A *n* GB Sch école *f* (publique) secondaire

B *adj* **1** (all-embracing) [*report, list*] complet/-ète, détaillé; [*knowledge*] vaste; [*planning*] global; [*coverage, training*] complet/-ète; [*measures*] d'ensemble; **~ insurance policy** assurance *f* tous risques; **2** GB Sch **a ~ school** école *f* (publique) secondaire

compress

A /'kɒmpres/ *n* compresse *f*

B /kəm'pres/ *vtr* **1** (condense) comprimer; **~ed air** air comprimé; **2** to ~ one's lips pincer les lèvres; **3** fig (shorten) condenser [*text*]; réduire [*time*]

compression /kəm'preʃn/ *n* **1** gen, Phys compression *f*; **2** (condensing) of book, chapters) réduction *f*; **3** (of data) condensation *f*, compression *f*

compressor /kəm'presə(r)/ *n* compresseur *m*

comprise /kəm'praɪz/ *vtr* (include) comprendre; (consist of) être composé de

compromise /'kɒmprəmaɪz/

A *n* compromis *m*; **to come to** *ou* **reach a ~** arriver *or* aboutir à un compromis

B *noun modifier* [*agreement, solution*] de compromis

C *vtr* **1** (threaten) compromettre; **2** US (settle) régler [*disagreement*]

D *vi* transiger, arriver à un compromis; **to ~ on sth** trouver un compromis sur qch

E *v refl* **to ~ oneself** se compromettre

compromising /'kɒmprəmaɪzɪŋ/ *adj* compromettant

compulsion /kəm'pʌlʃn/ *n* **1** (urge) compulsion *f*; **to feel a ~ to do** avoir une envie irrésistible de faire; **2** (force) force *f*; **there is no ~ on you to do** tu n'es pas obligé de faire; **to act under ~** agir sous la contrainte

compulsive /kəm'pʌlsɪv/ *adj* **1** (inveterate) invétéré; Psych compulsif/-ive; **~ eater** boulimique *mf*; **2** (fascinating) fascinant; **to be ~ viewing** être fascinant

compulsively /kəm'pʌlsɪvlɪ/ *adv* Psych de façon compulsive

compulsory /kəm'pʌlsərɪ/ *adj* [*subject, attendance, education*] obligatoire; **to be forced to take ~ redundancy** être mis au chômage d'office

compulsory purchase *n* GB expropriation *f* (*pour cause d'utilité publique*)

compunction /kəm'pʌŋkʃn/ *n* **∅** **to have no ~ about doing** n'avoir aucun scrupule à faire

computation /ˌkɒmpjuː'teɪʃn/ *n* calcul *m*

compute /kəm'pjuːt/ *vtr* calculer

computer /kəm'pjuːtə(r)/ *n* ordinateur *m*; **by ~/on a ~** par/sur ordinateur; **to have sth on ~** avoir qch sur ordinateur; **the ~ is up/down** l'ordinateur fonctionne/est en panne

computer: **~-aided** *adj* assisté par ordinateur; **~-aided design**, **CAD** *n* conception *f* assistée par ordinateur, CAO *f*; **~-aided language learning**,

CALL n apprentissage m des langues assisté par ordinateur; **~-aided learning**, **CAL** n enseignement m assisté par ordinateur, EAO m; **~ animation** n imagerie f de synthèse; **~ code** n code m informatique; **~ dating service** n club m de rencontres (utilisant un ordinateur); **~ engineer** ▸ p. 1181 n technicien/-ienne m/f en informatique; **~ error** n erreur f informatique; **~ game** n jeu m informatique; **~ graphics** n (+ v sg) infographie f; **~ hacker** n pirate m informatique; **~ hacking** n piratage m informatique

computerization /kəm,pju:təraɪ'zeɪʃn, US -rɪ'z-/ n (of records, accounts) mise f sur ordinateur; (of work, workplace) informatisation f

computerize /kəm'pju:təraɪz/ vtr (store) mettre [qch] sur ordinateur [records, accounts]; (treat by computer) informatiser [list]

computer: **~ keyboard** n clavier m d'ordinateur; **~ keyboarder** n claviste mf, opérateur/-trice m/f de saisie; **~ language** n langage m de programmation; **~ literacy** n maîtrise f de l'outil informatique

computer-literate adj [person] avec une bonne maîtrise de l'outil informatique; **to be ~** avoir une bonne maîtrise de l'outil informatique

computer: **~ operator** ▸ p. 1181 n opérateur/-trice m/f sur ordinateur; **~ program** n programme m informatique; **~ programmer** ▸ p. 1181 n programmeur/-euse m/f; **~ programming** n programmation f; **~ science** n informatique f; **~ scientist** ▸ p. 1181 n informaticien/-ienne m/f; **~ studies** n Sch, Univ informatique f; **~ virus** n virus m informatique

computing /kəm'pju:tɪŋ/ n informatique f

comrade /'kɒmreɪd, US -ræd/ n † ou Pol camarade mf; **~-in-arms** compagnon m d'armes

con /kɒn/
A n escroquerie f, arnaque◐ f
B◐vtr (p prés etc **-nn-**) (swindle) rouler◯, escroquer; (dupe) emboîner◯, duper; **to ~ sb into doing sth**◯ amener qn à faire qch en abusant de sa crédulité; **to ~ sb out of sth**◯ obtenir qch de qn par la ruse; **I was ~ned out of £5** on m'a eu◯ de 5 livres sterling

con artist n = con man

concave /'kɒnkeɪv/ adj concave

conceal /kən'si:l/
A vtr dissimuler (**from** à)
B concealed pp adj [entrance, camera] caché

concealment /kən'si:lmənt/ n dissimulation f; **place of ~** cache f

concede /kən'si:d/
A vtr **1** (admit) concéder [point]; **to ~ that** reconnaître que; **2** (surrender) accorder [right] (**to** à); céder [territory] (**to** à); **3** Sport concéder [point, goal] (**to** à); **4** Pol **to ~ an election** concéder la victoire électorale (**to** à)
B vi **1** gen céder; **2** Pol reconnaître une défaite électorale

conceit /kən'si:t/ n **1** (vanity) suffisance f; **2** (affectation) afféterie f liter

conceited /kən'si:tɪd/ adj [person] vaniteux/-euse; [remark] suffisant; [expression] de suffisance

conceitedly /kən'si:tɪdlɪ/ adv avec vanité

conceivable /kən'si:vəbl/ adj concevable, imaginable; **it is ~ that** il est concevable que (+ subj)

conceivably /kən'si:vəblɪ/ adv **it might just ~ cost more than £100** cela est concevable que cela coûte plus de 100 livres; **it could ~ be true** il est concevable que ce soit vrai; **I can't ~ eat all that** je ne vois pas comment je pourrai manger tout ça

conceive /kən'si:v/
A vtr **1** concevoir [child]; **2** (develop) concevoir [hatred, idea]; **3** (believe) concevoir
B vi **1** (become pregnant) concevoir, devenir enceinte; **2** (imagine) **to ~ of sth** imaginer or concevoir qch

concentrate /'kɒnsntreɪt/
A n Chem, Culin concentré m; **tomato ~** concentré de tomates
B vtr concentrer [effort] (**on** sur; **on doing** pour faire); employer [resources] (**on** sur; **on doing** à faire); centrer [attention] (**on** sur); **fear ~s the mind** la peur fait réfléchir
C vi **1** (pay attention) [person] se concentrer (**on** sur); **to ~ on**

doing s'appliquer à faire; **2** (focus) **to ~ on** [film, journalist] s'intéresser surtout à; **3** (congregate) se concentrer

concentration /,kɒnsn'treɪʃn/ n **1** (attention) concentration f (**on** sur); **my powers of ~** mon pouvoir de concentration; **to lose one's ~** se déconcentrer; **2** (specialization) spécialisation f; **~ on sales** spécialisation dans le domaine de la vente; **3** Chem concentration f; **high/low ~** forte/faible concentration; **4** (accumulation) concentration f

concentration camp n camp m de concentration

concentric /kən'sentrɪk/ adj concentrique

concept /'kɒnsept/ n concept m

conception /kən'sepʃn/ n Med, fig conception f (**of** de); **you can have no ~ of** tu ne peux pas imaginer

concern /kən'sɜːn/
A n **1** (worry) inquiétude f (**about, over** à propos de); **there is growing ~ about crime** la criminalité suscite de plus en plus d'inquiétude; **there is ~ for her safety** on s'inquiète pour sa sécurité; **to cause ~** être inquiétant; **there is no cause for ~** il n'y a pas lieu d'être inquiet; **he expressed ~ at my results/for my health** il m'a fait part de son inquiétude quant à mes résultats/ma santé; **2** (preoccupation) préoccupation f; **environmental ~s** des préoccupations écologiques; **3** (care) (for person) prévenance f; **out of ~ for him** par égard pour lui; **you have no ~ for safety** tu ne te préoccupes pas de la sécurité; **4** (company) entreprise f; **a going ~** une affaire rentable; **5** (personal business) **that's her ~** cela la regarde; **your private life is no ~ of mine** ta vie privée ne me regarde pas
B vtr **1** (worry) inquiéter; **2** (affect, interest) concerner, intéresser; **to whom it may ~** à qui de droit; (in letter) Monsieur; **as far as the pay is ~ed** en ce qui concerne le salaire; **3** (involve) **to be ~ed with** s'occuper de [security, publicity]; **to be ~ed in** être impliqué dans [scandal]; **4** (be about) [book, programme] traiter de; [fax, letter] concerner
C v refl **to ~ oneself with sth/with doing** s'occuper de qch/de faire

concerned /kən'sɜːnd/ adj **1** (anxious) inquiet/-ète (**about** à propos de); **to be ~ at the news** trouver la nouvelle inquiétante; **to be ~ that sb might do** être inquiet/-iète à l'idée que qn fasse; **to be ~ for sb** se faire du souci pour qn; **2** (involved) concerné; **all (those) ~** toutes les personnes concernées

concerning /kən'sɜːnɪŋ/ prep concernant

concert /'kɒnsət/
A n **1** Mus concert m; **in ~ at/with** en concert à/avec; **2** (cooperation) concert m; **in ~** de concert, d'un commun accord
B noun modifier [music, ticket, pianist] de concert

concerted /kən'sɜːtɪd/ adj [action, campaign] concerté; **to make a ~ effort to do** faire un sérieux effort pour faire

concert: **~goer** n habitué/-e m/f des concerts; **~ hall** n salle f de concert

concertina /,kɒnsə'ti:nə/ ▸ p. 1028
A n concertina m
B vi GB [part of vehicle] se plier en accordéon; [carriages] se télescoper

concerto /kən'tʃeətəʊ, -'tʃɜːt-/ n concerto m

concert: **~ performer** n concertiste mf; **~ tour** n tournée f

concession /kən'seʃn/ n **1** (compromise) concession f (**on** sur; **to** à); **as a ~** à titre de concession; **2** (discount) réduction f; **'~s'** 'tarif réduit'; **3** (property rights) concession f; **4** (marketing rights) **to run a perfume ~** être concessionnaire de parfumerie

concessionary /kən'seʃənərɪ/ adj [fare, price, rate] réduit

conciliate /kən'sɪlɪeɪt/ vtr apaiser

conciliation /kən,sɪlɪ'eɪʃn/ n conciliation f; **~ service** commission f de conciliation

conciliator /kən'sɪlɪeɪtə(r)/ n médiateur/-trice m/f

conciliatory /kən'sɪlɪətərɪ, US -tɔːrɪ/ adj [gesture, mood, terms] conciliant; [measures, speech] conciliatoire

concise /kən'saɪs/ adj **1** (succinct) concis; **2** (abridged) **A Concise History of Celtic Art** Précis m d'histoire de l'art celte

concisely /kən'saɪslɪ/ adv avec concision

conclude /kən'klu:d/
A vtr **1** (finish) conclure, terminer; **'finally...,' he ~d**

'enfin...,' dit-il pour conclure; **'to be ∼d'** (on TV) 'suite et fin au prochain épisode'; (in magazine) 'suite et fin au prochain numéro'; **2**▸ (settle) conclure [*treaty*]; **3**▸ (deduce) conclure (**from** de)

B *vi* [*story, event*] se terminer (**with** par, sur); [*speaker*] conclure (**with** par); **he ∼d by saying that** il a conclu en disant que

concluding /kən'kluːdɪŋ/ *adj* final

conclusion /kən'kluːʒn/ *n* **1**▸ (end) fin *f*; **in ∼** en conclusion, pour terminer; **2**▸ (opinion, resolution) conclusion *f*; **to come to** *ou* **to reach a ∼** arriver à une conclusion; **to draw a ∼ from sth** tirer une conclusion de qch; **this leads us to the ∼ that** ceci nous amène à conclure que; **he jumped** *ou* **leapt to the ∼ that she was dead** il a conclu un peu trop hâtivement qu'elle était morte; **don't jump** *ou* **leap to ∼s!** ne tire pas de conclusions hâtives!; **3**▸ (outcome) conclusion *f*; **taken to its logical ∼, this would mean that** si on va jusqu'au bout, ceci signifierait que

conclusive /kən'kluːsɪv/ *adj* concluant

concoct /kən'kɒkt/ *vtr* concocter

concoction /kən'kɒkʃn/ *n* **1**▸ (drink) breuvage *m*; (dish) mélange *m*; **2**▸ fig (style, effect) mélange *m*

concord /'kɒŋkɔːd/ *n* concorde *f*

concordance /kən'kɔːdəns/ *n* **1**▸ sout (agreement) accord *m*; **to be in ∼ with** s'accorder avec; **2**▸ (index) concordance *f*

concourse /'kɒŋkɔːs/ *n* (interior area) hall *m*

concrete /'kɒŋkriːt/
A *n* béton *m*
B *adj* **1**▸ Constr [*block*] de béton; [*base*] en béton; **2**▸ fig concret/-ète; **in ∼ terms** concrètement

(Phrasal verb)

■ **concrete over**: ▸ **∼ over [sth]** recouvrir [qch] de béton, bétonner

concrete: **∼ jungle** *n* univers *m* de béton; **∼ mixer** *n* bétonnière *f*

concur /kən'kɜː(r)/ (*p prés etc* **-rr-**)
A *vtr* convenir (**that** que)
B *vi* **1**▸ (agree) être d'accord (**with** avec); **2**▸ (act together) **to ∼ in** participer à [*action, measure, decision*]; **to ∼ with sb in condemning** se joindre à qn pour condamner; **3**▸ (tally) [*data, views*] concorder (**with** avec); **4**▸ (combine) **to ∼ to do** contribuer à faire

concurrent /kən'kʌrənt/ *adj* **1**▸ (simultaneous) simultané; **2**▸ sout (in agreement) **to be ∼ with** [*views*] concorder avec

concurrently /kən'kʌrəntlɪ/ *adv* simultanément

concussion /kən'kʌʃn/ *n* Med commotion *f* cérébrale

condemn /kən'dem/
A *vtr* **1**▸ (censure) condamner (**for doing** pour avoir fait); **to ∼ sth as pointless/provocative** condamner la futilité/l'aspect provocateur de qch; **to ∼ sb as an opportunist** dénoncer l'opportunisme de qn; **2**▸ Jur (sentence) **to ∼ sb to death/life imprisonment** condamner qn à mort/à perpétuité; **3**▸ (doom) **to be ∼ed to do** être condamné à faire; **to ∼ sb to condamner** qn à [*poverty*]; **4**▸ (declare unsafe) déclarer [qch] inhabitable [*building*]
B **condemned** *pp adj* **1**▸ [*cell*] des condamnés à mort; **∼ed man/woman** condamné/-e *m/f* à mort; **2**▸ [*building*] déclaré inhabitable

condemnation /ˌkɒndem'neɪʃn/ *n* **1**▸ (censure) condamnation *f*; **2**▸ (indictment) **to be a ∼ of sb/sth** remettre qn/qch en question

condemnatory /ˌkɒndem'neɪtərɪ/ *adj* dénonciateur/-trice

condensation /ˌkɒnden'seɪʃn/ *n* **1**▸ (droplets) (on walls) condensation *f*; (on windows) buée *f*; **2**▸ Chem (process) condensation *f*

condense /kən'dens/
A *vtr* condenser (**into** en)
B *vi* Chem se condenser

condensed milk *n* lait *m* concentré sucré *or* condensé

condenser /kən'densə(r)/ *n* condenseur *m*

condescend /ˌkɒndɪ'send/
A *vtr* (deign) **to ∼ to do** condescendre à faire
B *vi* **to ∼ to sb** être condescendant envers qn

condescending /ˌkɒndɪ'sendɪŋ/ *adj* condescendant

condescension /ˌkɒndɪ'senʃn/ *n* condescendance *f*

condition /kən'dɪʃn/
A *n* **1**▸ (stipulation) condition *f*; **to meet** *ou* **satisfy the ∼s** remplir les conditions; **under certain ∼s** sous certaines conditions; **on ∼ that** à condition que (+ *subj*); **I agree, on one ∼, namely that you pay in cash** je suis d'accord, mais à une condition, que vous payiez en liquide; **2**▸ (state) état *m*, condition *f*; **to be in good/bad ∼** [*house, car etc*] être en bon/mauvais état; **he's in good ∼** il est en bonne santé; **to be in a critical ∼** être dans un état critique; **her ∼ is serious** elle est dans un état grave; **to be in no ∼ to do** ne pas être en état de faire; **3**▸ (disease) maladie *f*; **a heart/skin ∼** une maladie cardiaque/de la peau; **4**▸ (fitness) forme *f*; **to be out of ∼** ne pas être en forme; **to get one's body into ∼** se mettre en forme; **5**▸ (situation) condition *f*; **the human ∼** la condition humaine
B **conditions** *npl* conditions *fpl*; **to work under difficult ∼s** travailler dans des conditions difficiles; **housing/living ∼s** conditions de logement/de vie; **weather ∼s** conditions météorologiques
C *vtr* **1**▸ Psych conditionner; **2**▸ (treat) traiter [*hair*]

conditional /kən'dɪʃənl/
A *n* Ling conditionnel *m*; **in the ∼** au conditionnel
B *adj* **1**▸ conditionnel/-elle; **the offer is ∼ on** *ou* **upon the name of the donor remaining secret** l'offre a pour condition que le nom du donateur demeure (*subj*) secret; **to make sth ∼ on** *ou* **upon sth** faire dépendre qch de qch; **2**▸ [*clause, sentence*] conditionnel/-elle; **in the ∼ tense** au conditionnel

conditionally /kən'dɪʃənəlɪ/ *adv* sous conditions

conditioner /kən'dɪʃənə(r)/ *n* (for hair) après-shampooing *m*, démêlant *m*; (for laundry) assouplisseur *m*

conditioning /kən'dɪʃənɪŋ/
A *n* **1**▸ Psych conditionnement *m*; **2**▸ (of hair) traitement *m*
B *adj* [*shampoo, lotion etc*] démêlant

condole /kən'dəʊl/ *vi* **to ∼ with** présenter ses condoléances à

condolence /kən'dəʊləns/
A *n* **letter of ∼** lettre *f* de condoléance
B **condolences** *npl* condoléances *fpl*

condom /'kɒndɒm/ *n* préservatif *m*

condominium /ˌkɒndə'mɪnɪəm/ *n* US **1**▸ (also **∼ unit**) appartement *m* (dans une copropriété); **2**▸ (complex) (immeuble *m* en) copropriété *f*

condone /kən'dəʊn/ *vtr* tolérer

conducive /kən'djuːsɪv, US -'duː-/ *adj* **to be ∼ to** être favorable à

conduct
A /'kɒndʌkt/ *n* **1**▸ (behaviour) conduite *f* (**towards** envers); **2**▸ (handling) conduite *f* (**of** de)
B /kən'dʌkt/ *vtr* **1**▸ (lead) conduire [*visitor, group*]; **she ∼ed us around the house** elle nous a fait faire le tour de la maison; **∼ed tour** *ou* **visit** visite guidée; **2**▸ (manage) mener [*life, business*]; **3**▸ (carry out) mener [*experiment, inquiry*]; faire [*poll*]; célébrer [*ceremony*]; **4**▸ Mus diriger [*orchestra*]; **5**▸ Elec, Phys conduire
C /kən'dʌkt/ *vi* Mus diriger
D /kən'dʌkt/ *v refl* **to ∼ oneself** se comporter

conduction /kən'dʌkʃn/ *n* conduction *f*

conductor /kən'dʌktə(r)/ ▸ p. 1181 *n* **1**▸ Mus chef *m* d'orchestre; **2**▸ (on bus) receveur *m*; Rail chef *m* de train; **3**▸ Elec, Phys conducteur *m*

conductress /kən'dʌktrɪs/ ▸ p. 1181 *n* receveuse *f*

conduit /'kɒndɪt, 'kɒndjuːɪt, US 'kɒndwɪt/ *n* conduit *m*

cone /kəʊn/ *n* **1**▸ Math, gen cône *m*; **paper ∼** cornet *m* (en papier); **2**▸ (also **ice-cream ∼**) cornet *m*; **3**▸ (for traffic) balise *f*

(Phrasal verb)

■ **cone off**: ▸ **∼ [sth] off**, **∼ off [sth]** baliser

confection /kən'fekʃn/ *n* **1**▸ Culin (cake) pâtisserie *f*, gâteau *m*; (dessert) dessert *m*; **2**▸ (combination) **a ∼ of** une savante combinaison de; **3**▸ (process) confection *f*

confectioner /kən'fekʃənə(r)/ *n* (making sweets) confiseur/-euse *m/f*; (making cakes) pâtissier-confiseur *m*; **∼'s custard** crème *f* pâtissière; **∼'s (shop)** pâtisserie-confiserie *f*; **∼'s sugar** US sucre *m* glace

confectionery /kən'fekʃənərɪ, US -ʃənerɪ/ *n* **C** (sweets) gen sucreries *fpl*; (high quality) confiserie *f*; (cakes) pâtisserie *f*

confederacy /kən'fedərəsɪ/ *n* Pol confédération *f*

confederate

A /kən'fedərət/ n **1** (in conspiracy) complice *mf*; **2** Pol confédéré/-e *m/f*

B /kən'fedərət/ *adj* Pol confédéré

C /kən'fedəreit/ *vi* (unite) se confédérer (**with** avec)

confederation /kən,fedə'reiʃn/ *n* confédération *f*

confer /kən'fɜː(r)/

A *vtr* (*p prés etc* **-rr-**) conférer (**on, upon** à)

B *vi* (*p prés etc* **-rr-**) conférer (**about** de)

conference /'kɒnfərəns/

A *n* conférence *f*; Pol congrès *m*; **peace ~** conférence pour la paix

B *noun modifier* [*room, centre*] de conférences; **~ member** participant/-e *m/f*; **~ table** lit table *f* de conférence; fig table *f* de négociation

confess /kən'fes/

A *vtr* **1** avouer, confesser [*crime, truth, mistake*]; avouer, reconnaître [*liking, weakness*]; **to ~ that** avouer que; **2** Relig confesser

B *vi* **1** (admit) avouer; **to ~ to a crime** avouer (avoir commis) un crime; **2** Relig se confesser

confession /kən'feʃn/ *n* **1** gen, Jur aveu *m* (**of** de); **to make a full ~** faire des aveux complets; **2** Relig confession *f*; **to go to ~, to make one's ~** se confesser; **to hear sb's ~** confesser qn

confessional /kən'feʃənl/ *n* confessionnal *m*

confessor /kən'fesə(r)/ *n* confesseur *m*

confetti /kən'feti/ *n* **C** confettis *mpl*

confide /kən'faid/

A *vtr* confier [*secret*] (**to** à)

B *vi* **to ~ in** se confier à [*person*]

confidence /'kɒnfidəns/ *n* **1** (faith) confiance *f* (**in** en); **to have (every) ~ in sb/sth** avoir (pleine) confiance en qn/qch; **to put one's ~ in sb** mettre sa confiance en qn; **2** Pol **vote of ~** vote *m* de confiance; **motion of no ~** motion *f* de censure; **3** (self-assurance) assurance *f*, confiance *f* en soi; **4** (certainty) assurance *f*; **I can say with ~ that** je suis sûr que; **5** (confidentiality) **to take sb into one's ~** se confier à qn; **to tell sb sth in (strict) ~** dire qch à qn (tout à fait) confidentiellement; **6** (secret) confidence *f*

confidence: **~ man**, **~ trickster** *n* GB escroc *m*; **~ trick** *n* escroquerie *f*

confident /'kɒnfidənt/ *adj* **1** (sure) sûr, confiant; **to be ~ that** être sûr *or* persuadé que; **to be ~ of success** *ou* **of succeeding** avoir la certitude de réussir; **to feel ~ about the future** avoir confiance en l'avenir; **2** (self-assured) assuré, sûr de soi

confidential /,kɒnfi'denʃl/ *adj* confidentiel/-ielle *m/f*; **~ secretary** secrétaire *mf* privé/-e

confidentiality /,kɒnfiden'ʃi'æləti/ *n* confidentialité *f*

confidentially /,kɒnfi'denʃəli/ *adv* confidentiellement

confidently /'kɒnfidəntli/ *adv* [*speak, behave*] avec assurance; [*expect, predict*] en toute confiance

confiding /kən'faidiŋ/ *adj* confiant

confine /kən'fain/

A *vtr* **1** (shut up) confiner [*person*] (**in, to** dans); enfermer [*animal*] (**in** dans); **to be ~d to bed** être alité; **to be ~d to the house** être obligé de rester à la maison; **~d to barracks** Mil consigné au quartier; **2** (limit) limiter [*comments etc*] (**to** à); **the problem is not ~d to old people** le problème ne concerne pas uniquement les personnes âgées

B *v refl* **to ~ oneself to/to doing** se contenter de/de faire

confined /kən'faind/ *adj* [*area*] confiné; [*space*] restreint

confinement /kən'fainmənt/ *n* **1** (detention) (in cell) détention *f* (**in, to** dans); Jur réclusion *f*; **2** Med (labour) couches *fpl*; (birth) accouchement *m*

confines /'kɒnfainz/ *npl* contraintes *fpl*; **within the ~ of** dans le cadre de [*regulations*]; dans l'enceinte de [*building*]

confirm /kən'fɜːm/ *vtr* **1** (state as true, validate) confirmer; **two people were ~ed dead** on a confirmé que deux personnes ont trouvé la mort; **to ~ receipt of sth** accuser réception de qch; **2** Admin approuver [*appointment*]; **3** (justify) **to ~ sb in** conforter qn dans [*belief, opinion*]; **4** Relig confirmer

confirmation /,kɒnfə'meiʃn/ *n* **1** (of belief, statement, news, fear) confirmation *f*; (of appointment, booking) confirmation *f*; **2** Relig confirmation *f*

confirmed /kən'fɜːmd/ *adj* [*alcoholic, smoker, liar, habit*] invétéré; [*bachelor, sinner*] endurci

confiscate /'kɒnfiskeit/ *vtr* confisquer (**from** à)

confiscation /,kɒnfi'skeiʃn/ *n* confiscation *f*

conflate /kən'fleit/ *vtr* regrouper

conflict

A /'kɒnflikt/ *n* conflit *m*; **to be in/come into ~** lit, fig être/entrer en conflit (**with** avec); **~ of interests** conflit d'intérêts; **to have a ~ of loyalties** être déchiré par des loyautés contradictoires

B /kən'flikt/ *vi* (contradict) être en contradiction (**with** avec); (clash) tomber au même moment (**with** que)

conflicting /kən'fliktiŋ/ *adj* **1** (incompatible) [*views, feelings*] contradictoire; **2** (coinciding) **two ~ engagements** deux rendez-vous qui tombent en même temps

confluence /'kɒnfluəns/ *n* (of rivers) confluent *m*; fig confluence *f*

conform /kən'fɔːm/

A *vtr* conformer (**to** à)

B *vi* **1** (to rules, standards) [*person*] se conformer (**with, to** à); [*model, machine etc*] être conforme (**to** à); **to ~ to type** se conformer à la norme; **2** (correspond) [*ideas, beliefs*] se conformer (**with, to** à); [*situation*] être conforme (**with, to** à)

conformist /kən'fɔːmist/ *n, adj* conformiste (*mf*)

conformity /kən'fɔːməti/ *n* **1** conformité *f* (**to** à); **in ~ with** conformément à; **2** Relig conformisme *m*

confound /kən'faund/ *vtr* **1** (perplex) déconcerter; **2** (discredit) donner tort à [*critics*]

confront /kən'frʌnt/ *vtr* **1** (face) affronter [*danger, enemy*]; faire face à [*problem*]; **to ~ the truth** voir la réalité en face; **to be ~ed by sth** être confronté à qch; **to be ~ed by the police** se retrouver face à la police; **the task which ~ed us** le travail qui se présentait à nous; **2** (bring together) **to ~ sb with sth/sb** mettre qn en présence de qch/qn

confrontation /,kɒnfrʌn'teiʃn/ *n* affrontement *m*

confrontational /,kɒnfrən'teiʃənəl/ *adj* provocateur/-trice

confuse /kən'fjuːz/ *vtr* **1** (bewilder) troubler [*person*]; **to ~ the enemy troops** semer la confusion dans les troupes ennemies; **2** (fail to distinguish) confondre (**with** avec); **3** (complicate) compliquer [*argument*]; **to ~ the issue** compliquer les choses

confused /kən'fjuːzd/ *adj* **1** [*person*] troublé; [*thoughts, mind*] confus; **to get ~** s'embrouiller; **he was ~ about the instructions** il ne comprenait pas bien le mode d'emploi; **I'm ~ about what to do** je ne sais pas trop ce que je dois faire; **2** (muddled) [*account, reasoning*] confus; [*memories, sounds*] indistinct; [*voices*] indistinct; [*impression*] vague

confusedly /kən'fjuːzidli/ *adv* **1** (in bewilderment) confusément; **2** (unclearly) [*speak*] de façon confuse

confusing /kən'fjuːziŋ/ *adj* déroutant, peu clair

confusion /kən'fjuːʒn/ *n* confusion *f*; **to create ~** jeter la confusion (dans les esprits); **I was in a state of total ~** j'étais complètement embrouillé; **to avoid ~** pour éviter toute confusion; **to throw sb/sth into ~** plonger qn/qch dans la confusion

congeal /kən'dʒiːl/ *vi* [*fat*] se figer; [*blood*] se coaguler

congenial /kən'dʒiːniəl/ *adj* sympathique, agréable

congenital /kən'dʒenitl/ *adj* **1** Med congénital; **2** fig [*fear, dislike*] congénital; [*liar*] invétéré

congenitally /kən'dʒenitəli/ *adv* **1** Med **to be ~ deformed** avoir une malformation congénitale; **2** fig [*dishonest, lazy*] congénitalement

congested /kən'dʒestid/ *adj* **1** [*road*] embouteillé; [*pavement, passage*] encombré; [*district*] surpeuplé; **2** Med congestionné

congestion /kən'dʒestʃn/ *n* **1** (of district) surpeuplement *m*; (of road) encombrement *m*; **traffic ~** embouteillages *mpl*; **~ charge** péage *m* urbain; **2** Med congestion *f*

conglomerate

A /kən'glɒmərət/ *n* conglomérat *m*

B /kən'glɒməreit/ *vi* s'agglomérer

congratulate /kən'grætʃuleit/

A *vtr* féliciter (**on** de; **on doing** d'avoir fait); **may we ~ you on your success/engagement?** permettez-nous de vous féliciter de votre succès/à l'occasion de vos fiançailles

B *v refl* **to ~ oneself** se féliciter (**on** de)

congratulations /kən‚grætʃʊ'leɪʃns/ npl félicitations fpl; ~ **on your success/on the birth of your new baby** (toutes mes *or* nos) félicitations pour votre succès/à l'occasion de la naissance de votre bébé; **to offer one's ~ to sb** adresser ses félicitations à qn

congregate /'kɒŋgrɪgeɪt/
A vtr rassembler
B vi se rassembler (**around** autour de)

congregation /‚kɒŋgrɪ'geɪʃn/ n (+ v sg ou pl) (in church) assemblée f des fidèles; (of clergy) congrégation f

congregational /‚kɒŋgrɪ'geɪʃənl/ adj [prayer, singing] des fidèles; **the Congregational Church** l'Église congrégationaliste

congress /'kɒŋgres, US 'kɒŋgrəs/ n congrès m (**on** sur)

Congress /'kɒŋgres, US 'kɒŋgrəs/ n Pol Congrès m; **in ~** au Congrès

> ℹ️ **Congress** Le Congrès est le corps législatif des États-Unis. Il est composé de la Chambre des représentants (*House of Representatives*) qui compte 435 membres élus pour un mandat de deux ans, et du Sénat (*Senate*) qui compte 100 sénateurs, deux par État, élus pour six ans. Un tiers des sénateurs est renouvelé tous les deux ans. Pour devenir loi (*act*), un projet de loi (*bill*) doit être examiné puis approuvé par les deux chambres, et ratifié par le président. Le Congrès siège au Capitole, situé sur *Capitol Hill* à Washington DC. Par métonymie, *the Capitol* ou *the Hill* font donc référence au Congrès. ▸ **Washington DC**

Congressional /kən'greʃənl/ adj US [candidate] au Congrès; [committee] du Congrès

Congressional District, **CD** n US circonscription f d'un membre du Congrès

congress: **~man** n (pl **-men**) US membre m du Congrès; **~woman** n (pl **-women**) US membre m du Congrès

conical /'kɒnɪkl/ adj conique

conifer /'kɒnɪfə(r), 'kəʊn-/ n conifère m

coniferous /kə'nɪfərəs, US kəʊ'n-/ adj [tree] conifère; [forest] de conifères

conjecture /kən'dʒektʃə(r)/
A n hypothèse f; **to be a matter for ~** être hypothétique
B vi faire des conjectures (**about** sur)

conjugal /'kɒndʒʊgl/ adj conjugal

conjugate /'kɒndʒʊgeɪt/
A vtr conjuguer
B vi se conjuguer [verb]

conjugation /‚kɒndʒʊ'geɪʃn/ n conjugaison f

conjunction /kən'dʒʌŋkʃn/ n **1** (of events) concours m; **in ~** ensemble; **in ~ with** conjointement avec; **2** Ling conjonction f

conjunctivitis /kən‚dʒʌŋktɪ'vaɪtɪs/ ▸ p. 933 n conjonctivite f

conjure /'kʌndʒə(r)/ vi faire des tours de prestidigitation; **a name to ~ with** fig un nom qu'on évoque avec respect

<u>Phrasal verb</u>
■ **conjure up**: ▸ **~ up** [sth] faire apparaître [qch] comme par magie; **to ~ up an image of sth** évoquer qch

conjuring /'kʌndʒərɪŋ/ n prestidigitation f

conjuring trick n tour m de prestidigitation

conjuror /'kʌndʒərə(r)/ n prestidigitateur/-trice m/f

conk /kɒŋk/ v
■ **conk out**° [person] s'endormir; [car, machine] tomber en panne

conker° /'kɒŋkə(r)/ n GB **1** marron m; **2** **conkers** jeu de marrons

con man n arnaqueur❶ m, escroc m

connect /kə'nekt/
A vtr **1** (attach) raccorder [end, hose] (**to** à); accrocher [wagon, coach] (**to** à); **to ~ two tubes** raccorder deux tubes; **2** (link) [road, bridge, railway] relier [place, road] (**to, with** à); **I always ~ rain with Oxford** j'associe toujours la pluie à Oxford; **3** (to mains) brancher [appliance] (**to** à); brancher [qch] sur le secteur [household]; **4** Telecom raccorder [phone, subscriber]; **to ~ sb to** passer [qn] à qn [department]
B vi **1** [room] communiquer (**with** avec); **2** [service, bus] assurer la correspondance (**with** avec)

<u>Phrasal verb</u>
■ **connect up**: ▸ **~ up** [sth], **~** [sth] **up** faire les branchements de [video, computer]; **to ~ sth up to** brancher qch sur; **to ~ two machines up** connecter deux machines

connected /kə'nektɪd/ adj **1** (related) [idea, event] lié (**to, with** à); **everything ~ with music** tout ce qui se rapporte à la musique; **2** (in family) apparenté (**to** à); **to be well ~** (through family) être de bonne famille; (having influence) avoir des relations; **3** (linked) [road, town] relié (**to, with** à); [pipe] raccordé (**to, with** à); **4** (electrically) branché; **5** Comput connecté; **to be ~ to the Internet** être connecté à Internet

connecting /kə'nektɪŋ/ adj **1** [flight] de correspondance; **2** [room] attenant

connection, **connexion**† GB /kə'nekʃn/ n **1** (logical link) rapport m; **to have no ~ with** n'avoir aucun rapport *or* n'avoir rien à voir avec; **to make the ~** faire le rapprochement; **in ~ with** au sujet de, à propos de; **in this ~...** à ce sujet...; **2** (personal link) lien m (**between** entre; **with** avec); **3** (person) (contact) relation f; **to have useful ~s** avoir des relations; **4** (connecting up) (to mains) branchement m; (of pipes, tubes) raccord m; (of wires) câblage m; **5** Telecom (to network) raccordement m; (to number) mise f en communication (**to** avec); **bad ~** mauvaise communication f; **6** (in travel) correspondance f; **7** Comput connexion f; **Internet ~** connexion à Internet

connivance /kə'naɪvəns/ n connivence f

connive /kə'naɪv/
A vi **to ~ at** contribuer délibérément à; **to ~ (with sb) to do sth** être de connivence *or* de mèche° (avec qn) pour faire qch
B **conniving** pres p adj [person] fourbe; **a conniving glance** un regard de connivence

connoisseur /‚kɒnə'sɜː(r)/ n connaisseur/-euse m/f

connotation /‚kɒnə'teɪʃn/ n connotation f (**of** de)

connote /kə'nəʊt/ vtr **1** (summon up) évoquer; **2** Ling connoter

conquer /'kɒŋkə(r)/
A vtr conquérir [territory, people]; vaincre [enemy, unemployment, disease]; surmonter [habit, fear]; maîtriser [skill, technology]
B **conquering** pres p adj victorieux/-ieuse

conqueror /'kɒŋkərə(r)/ n gen vainqueur m; Sport gagnant/-e m/f; Mil conquérant/-e m/f

conquest /'kɒŋkwest/ n **1** Ⓒ (of country, mountain) conquête f; (of disease) éradication f; (of person) hum conquête f; **2** (territory) terre f conquise; (person) hum conquête f

conscience /'kɒnʃəns/ n conscience f; **in all ~** en mon/son etc âme et conscience; **they have no ~** ils n'ont aucun sens moral; **the ~ of the nation** la voix de la conscience nationale; **to have a guilty** ou **bad ~** avoir mauvaise conscience; **to have a clear ~** avoir la conscience tranquille; **to do sth with a clear ~** faire qch la conscience tranquille

conscience-stricken adj bourrelé de remords

conscientious /‚kɒnʃɪ'enʃəs/ adj consciencieux/-ieuse

conscientiously /‚kɒnʃɪ'enʃəslɪ/ adv consciencieusement

conscientiousness /‚kɒnʃɪ'enʃəsnɪs/ n application f, soin m

conscientious objector, **CO** n objecteur m de conscience

conscious /'kɒnʃəs/
A n Psych **the ~** le conscient
B adj **1** (aware) conscient (**of** de; **that** du fait que); **politically ~** politisé; **to be environmentally ~** avoir une conscience écologique; **2** (deliberate) [decision] réfléchi; [effort] consciencieux; **3** Med conscient

consciously /'kɒnʃəslɪ/ adv consciemment

consciousness /'kɒnʃəsnɪs/ n **1** (awareness) conscience f (**of** de); (undefined) sentiment m (**of** de); **2** Med **to lose/regain ~** perdre/reprendre connaissance

consciousness raising n sensibilisation f

conscript
A /'kɒnskrɪpt/ n appelé m
B /kən'skrɪpt/ vtr appeler [soldier]; enrôler [qn] de force [worker]

conscription /kən'skrɪpʃn/ n **1** (system) conscription f; **2** (process) incorporation f (**into** dans)

consecrate /'kɒnsɪkreɪt/ vtr consacrer

consecration /ˌkɒnsɪˈkreɪʃn/ n consécration f

consecutive /kənˈsekjʊtɪv/ adj consécutif/-ive

consecutively /kənˈsekjʊtɪvlɪ/ adv consécutivement

consensus /kənˈsensəs/ n consensus m (**among** au sein de; **about, as to** quant à; **for** en faveur de; **on** sur); **what's the ∼?** quelle est l'opinion générale?

consent /kənˈsent/
A n **1** (permission) (by person in authority) consentement m; (other) accord m; **age of ∼** âge m légal; **2** (agreement) **by common** ou **mutual ∼** d'un commun accord
B vtr **to ∼ to do** consentir à faire
C vi consentir (**to** à); **to ∼ to sb doing** consentir à ce que qn fasse; **∼ing adults** adultes consentants

consequence /ˈkɒnsɪkwəns, US -kwens/ n **1** (result) conséquence f; **as a ∼ of** du fait de [change, process]; à la suite de [event]; **in ∼** par conséquent; **to face the ∼s** accepter les conséquences; **to suffer the ∼s** subir les conséquences; **2** (importance) importance f; **he is a man of no ∼** c'est quelqu'un sans importance; **it's of no ∼ to me** cela m'est complètement indifférent

consequent /ˈkɒnsɪkwənt, US -kwent/ adj **the strike and the ∼ redundancies** la grève et les licenciements qu'elle a entraînés; **∼ upon** (because of) en raison de; **to be ∼ upon sth** (the result of) être la conséquence de qch

consequently /ˈkɒnsɪkwəntlɪ/ adv par conséquent

conservation /ˌkɒnsəˈveɪʃn/
A n **1** (of nature, natural resources) protection f (**of** de); **energy ∼** maîtrise f de l'énergie; **2** (of heritage) conservation f; **3** Phys conservation f
B noun modifier [group, measure] de protection; **∼ area** zone f protégée

conservationist /ˌkɒnsəˈveɪʃənɪst/ n défenseur m des ressources naturelles

conservatism /kənˈsɜːvətɪzəm/ n conservatisme m

conservative /kənˈsɜːvətɪv/
A n Pol conservateur/-trice m/f
B adj **1** Pol conservateur/-trice; **2** (cautious) prudent; **at a ∼ estimate** au bas mot; **3** [taste, style] classique

Conservative /kənˈsɜːvətɪv/ GB Pol
A n Conservateur/-trice m/f
B adj conservateur/-trice; **to vote ∼** voter pour le parti conservateur

conservatory /kənˈsɜːvətrɪ, US -tɔːrɪ/ n **1** (for plants) jardin m d'hiver; **2** US Mus conservatoire m

conserve /kənˈsɜːv/
A n (jam) confiture f
B vtr **1** (protect) protéger [forest]; sauvegarder [wildlife]; conserver [remains, ruins]; **2** (save up) économiser [resources]; garder [moisture]; ménager [energy]

consider /kənˈsɪdə(r)/
A vtr **1** (give thought to, study) considérer [options, facts]; examiner [evidence, problem]; étudier [offer]; **to ∼ how** réfléchir à la façon dont; **to ∼ why** examiner les raisons pour lesquelles; **to ∼ whether** décider si; **the jury is ∼ing its verdict** le jury délibère; **2** (take into account) prendre [qch] en considération [risk, cost]; songer à [person]; faire attention à [person's feelings]; **when you ∼ that** quand on songe que; **all things ∼ed** tout compte fait; **3** (envisage) envisager [course of action]; **to ∼ doing** envisager de faire; **to ∼ sb for a role** penser à qn pour un rôle; **to ∼ sb/sth as sth** penser à qn/qch comme qch; **4** (regard) **to ∼ that** considérer or estimer que; **to ∼ sb/sth favourably** voir qn/qch sous un jour favorable; **the matter closed** considérez que l'affaire est close; **∼ it done** tiens-le pour fait
B vi réfléchir
C considered pp adj [answer, view] réfléchi; **in my ∼ed opinion** selon ma conviction
D v refl **to ∼ oneself (to be)** a writer/genius se prendre pour pej or se considérer comme un écrivain/génie

considerable /kənˈsɪdərəbl/ adj considérable; **to a ∼ degree** ou **extent** dans une large mesure

considerably /kənˈsɪdərəblɪ/ adv considérablement

considerate /kənˈsɪdərət/ adj [person, nature] attentionné; [behaviour, motorist] courtois; **to be ∼ towards sb** avoir des égards pour qn; **it was ∼ of you to wait** c'est aimable à vous d'avoir attendu

considerately /kənˈsɪdərətlɪ/ adv [act] de manière attentionnée; **to behave ∼ towards sb** avoir des égards pour qn

consideration /kənˌsɪdəˈreɪʃn/ n **1** (thought) considération f, réflexion f; **after careful ∼** après mûre réflexion; **to give ∼ to sth** réfléchir à qch; **to give sth careful ∼** réfléchir longuement à qch; **∼ is being given to...** on examine actuellement...; **to take sth into ∼** prendre qch en considération; **to be under ∼** [matter] être à l'étude; **she's under ∼ for the job** on est en train d'étudier sa candidature; **2** (thoughtfulness, care) considération f (**for** envers); **out of ∼** par considération; **3** (factor, thing to be considered) considération f; (concern) (objet m de) souci m; **safety is the overriding ∼** la sécurité constitue le souci dominant; **4** (fee) **for a ∼** moyennant finance

considering /kənˈsɪdərɪŋ/
A prep, conj étant donné, compte tenu de; **∼ (that) he was tired** étant donné sa fatigue
B adv tout compte fait

consign /kənˈsaɪn/ vtr **1** (get rid of) reléguer (**to** à); **to ∼ sth to the flames** livrer qch aux flammes; **2** (entrust) **to ∼ sth to sb's care** confier qch aux soins de qn; **3** (send) expédier [goods] (**to** à)

consignment /kənˈsaɪnmənt/ n (sending) expédition f; (goods) lot m, livraison f; **for ∼** à expédier

consist /kənˈsɪst/ vi **to ∼ of** se composer de; **to ∼ in** résider dans; **to ∼ in doing** consister à faire

consistency /kənˈsɪstənsɪ/ n **1** (texture) consistance f; **2** (of view, policy) cohérence f; (of achievement) qualité f suivie

consistent /kənˈsɪstənt/ adj **1** [growth, level, quality] régulier/-ière; [kindness, help] constant; [sportsman, playing] régulier/-ière; **2** (repeated) [attempts, demands] répété; **3** (logical) cohérent; **4** **∼ with** en accord avec [account, belief]; **injuries ∼ with a fall** des blessures correspondant à une chute

consistently /kənˈsɪstəntlɪ/ adv (invariably) systématiquement, invariablement; (repeatedly) à maintes reprises

consolation /ˌkɒnsəˈleɪʃn/ n consolation f (**to** à); **∼ prize** lit, fig prix m de consolation

console
A /ˈkɒnsəʊl/ n **1** (controls) console f; **2** (cabinet) meuble m hi-fi (ou vidéo etc); **3** (table) console f
B /kənˈsəʊl/ vtr consoler (**for, on** de; **with** avec)
C /kənˈsəʊl/ v refl **to ∼ oneself** se consoler

consolidate /kənˈsɒlɪdeɪt/
A vtr **1** consolider [knowledge, position]; **2** Comm réunir [resources]; fusionner [companies]
B vi **1** (become stronger) s'affermir; **2** (unite) [companies] fusionner

consolidation /kənˌsɒlɪˈdeɪʃn/ n **1** (of knowledge, position) consolidation f; **2** (of companies) fusion f

consoling /kənˈsəʊlɪŋ/ adj consolant

consonant /ˈkɒnsənənt/ n consonne f

consortium /kənˈsɔːtɪəm/ n (pl **-tiums** ou **-tia**) consortium m

conspicuous /kənˈspɪkjʊəs/ adj **1** (to the eye) [feature, sign] visible; [garment] voyant; **to be ∼** se remarquer (**for** à cause de); **to make oneself ∼** se faire remarquer; **I feel ∼** j'ai l'impression que tout le monde me regarde; **to be ∼ by one's absence** iron briller par son absence; **in a ∼ position** bien en évidence; **2** (unusual) [success] remarquable; [failure] flagrant; [lack] total; **to be ∼ for** être remarquable pour

conspicuously /kənˈspɪkjʊəslɪ/ adv [placed] bien en évidence; [dressed] de façon voyante; [silent, empty] remarquablement; **to be ∼ absent** iron briller par son absence

conspiracy /kənˈspɪrəsɪ/ n conspiration f (**against** contre; **to do** en vue de faire); **a ∼ of silence** une conspiration du silence

conspirator /kənˈspɪrətə(r)/ n conspirateur/-trice m/f

conspiratorial /kənˌspɪrəˈtɔːrɪəl/ adj entendu

conspire /kənˈspaɪə(r)/ vi conspirer; **to ∼ to do** [people] conspirer en vue de faire; [events] conspirer à faire

constable /ˈkʌnstəbl, US ˈkɒn-/ ▶ p. 869 n GB agent m (de police)

constabulary /kənˈstæbjʊlərɪ, US -lerɪ/ n GB police f

constancy /ˈkɒnstənsɪ/ n constance f (**to** envers)

constant /ˈkɒnstənt/
A n constante f
B adj [problem, reminder, threat] permanent; [care, temperature]

constant; [disputes, questions] incessant; [attempts] répété; [companion] éternel/-elle

constantly /'kɒnstəntlɪ/ adv constamment

constellation /ˌkɒnstə'leɪʃn/ n constellation f

consternation /ˌkɒnstə'neɪʃn/ n consternation f; **in** ∼ frappé de consternation; **to my/his etc** ∼ à ma/sa etc grande consternation

constipated /'kɒnstɪpeɪtɪd/ adj constipé

constipation /ˌkɒnstɪ'peɪʃn/ ▸ p. 933 n constipation f; **to have** ∼ être constipé

constituency /kən'stɪtjʊənsɪ/ n (district) circonscription f électorale; (voters) électeurs mpl; ∼ **party** GB section f locale du parti

constituent /kən'stɪtjʊənt/
A n **1** Pol électeur/-trice m/f; **2** (of character) trait m; (of event, work of art) élément m; **3** Chem composant m
B adj [element, part] constitutif/-ive; Pol constituant

constitute /'kɒnstɪtjuːt/ vtr **1** (represent) constituer; **2** (set up) créer

constitution /ˌkɒnstɪ'tjuːʃn, US -'tuːʃn/ n (all contexts) Constitution f

constitutional /ˌkɒnstɪ'tjuːʃənl, US -'tuː-/
A †n promenade f
B adj **1** Pol constitutionnel/-elle; **2** (innate) inné

constitutionally /ˌkɒnstɪ'tjuːʃənəlɪ, US -'tuː-/ adv **1** Pol constitutionnellement; **2** (innately) par nature

constrain /kən'streɪn/ vtr sout **1** (compel) contraindre (**to do** à faire); **2** (limit) entraver; ∼ed [smile] contraint; [silence] gêné; [atmosphere] de gêne

constraint /kən'streɪnt/ n sout **1** (compulsion) contrainte f; **to put a** ∼ **on** imposer une contrainte à; **under** ∼ sous la contrainte; **you are under no** ∼ vous n'êtes en rien obligé; **2** (uneasiness) contrainte f

constrict /kən'strɪkt/
A vtr comprimer [flow, blood vessel]; gêner [breathing, movement]; ∼ing clothes vêtements serrés
B constricted pp adj [voice] étranglé; [breathing] gêné; [space] restreint; [life] étriqué

constriction /kən'strɪkʃn/ n **1** (constraint) contrainte f; **2** (of chest, throat) resserrement m; (of blood vessel) constriction f; **3** (by snake) étranglement m

construct
A /'kɒnstrʌkt/ n gen construction f; Psych concept m
B /kən'strʌkt/ vtr construire (**of** avec; **in** en)

construction /kən'strʌkʃn/
A n **1** (composition) construction f; **under** ∼ en construction; **2** ⊄ (also ∼ **industry**) bâtiment m; **3** (interpretation) **to put the wrong** ∼ **on sth** interpréter mal qch; **4** Ling construction f
B noun modifier [work, toy] de construction

construction: ∼ **engineer** ▸ p. 1181 n ingénieur m en génie civil; ∼ **site** n chantier m; ∼ **worker** ▸ p. 1181 n ouvrier/-ière m/f du bâtiment

constructive /kən'strʌktɪv/ adj constructif/-ive

constructively /kən'strʌktɪvlɪ/ adv de manière constructive

construe /kən'struː/ vtr interpréter (**as sth** comme qch); **wrongly** ∼d mal interprété

consul /'kɒnsl/ n consul m; **the French** ∼ le consul de France

consular /'kɒnsjʊlə(r), US -səl-/ adj consulaire

consulate /'kɒnsjʊlət, US -səl-/ n consulat m

consult /kən'sʌlt/
A vtr consulter (**about** sur)
B vi (also ∼ **together**) s'entretenir (**about** sur)

consultancy /kən'sʌltənsɪ/
A n **1** (also ∼ **firm**) cabinet-conseil m; **2** ⊄ (advice) conseils mpl; **to work in** ∼ travailler comme consultant; **3** GB Med (job) poste m de spécialiste (dans un hôpital)
B noun modifier [fees, service, work] de conseil

consultant /kən'sʌltənt/ ▸ p. 1181 n **1** (expert) consultant/-e m/f, conseiller/-ère m/f (**on, in** en; **to** de); **beauty** ∼ esthéticienne-conseil f; **2** GB Med spécialiste mf (attaché à un hôpital); ∼ **obstetrician** chef m du service d'obstétrique

consultation /ˌkɒnsl'teɪʃn/ n **1** (meeting) (for advice) consultation f (**about** sur); (for discussion) entretien m (**about** sur); **to have a** ∼ ou ∼s **with sb** (for advice) conférer avec qn;

(for discussion) s'entretenir avec qn; **2** (process) consultation f; **after** ∼ **with** après avoir consulté

consultative /kən'sʌltətɪv/ adj consultatif/-ive

consult: ∼**ing hours** npl Med heures fpl de consultation; ∼**ing room** n Med cabinet m

consumables /kən'sjuːməblz, US -'suːm-/ npl consommables mpl

consume /kən'sjuːm, US -'suːm-/ vtr **1** manger [food]; boire [drink]; **2** (use up) consommer [fuel, food, drink]; absorber [time]; **3** (destroy) [flames] consumer; **4** (overwhelm) **to be** ∼**d by** ou **with** être dévoré par [envy]; brûler de [desire]; être rongé par [guilt]

consumer /kən'sjuːmə(r), US -'suːm-/ n gen consommateur/-trice m/f; (of electricity, gas etc) abonné/-e m/f

consumer: ∼ **advice** n conseils mpl au consommateurs; ∼ **durables** npl biens mpl durables; ∼ **goods** npl biens mpl de consommation

consumerism /kən'sjuːmərɪzəm, US -'suːm-/ n consumérisme m

consumerist /kən'sjuːmərɪst, US -'suːm-/ péj adj [society, culture] de consommation

consumer: ∼ **products** npl produits mpl de consommation; ∼ **protection** n défense f du consommateur; ∼ **society** n société f de consommation

consuming /kən'sjuːmɪŋ, US -suːm-/ adj [passion] dévorant; [urge, desire] brûlant; [hatred] insatiable

consummate
A /kən'sʌmət/ adj sout parfait
B /'kɒnsəmeɪt/ vtr sout consommer fml [marriage]

consumption /kən'sʌmpʃn/ ▸ p. 933 n **1** (of food, fuel, goods) consommation f; **electricity** ∼ la consommation d'électricité; **unfit for human** ∼ impropre à la consommation; **2** ‡(tuberculosis) tuberculose f (pulmonaire)

cont. abrév écrite = **continued**

contact
A /'kɒntækt/ n **1** (touch) lit ou fig contact m (**between** entre; **with** avec); **to be in/come in(to)/make** ∼ être en/entrer en/se mettre en contact; **to get in(to)** ∼ prendre contact; **to maintain/lose** ∼ garder/perdre contact; **to be in constant** ∼ être en rapports constants; **sporting** ∼s relations fpl sportives; **2** (by radar, radio) contact m; **to make/ lose** ∼ établir/perdre contact; **in** ∼ en contact; **3** (acquaintance) gen connaissance f; (professional) contact m; (for drugs, spy) contact m; **4** Elec contact m; **5** Med personne ayant approché un malade contagieux
B /kən'tækt, 'kɒntækt/ vtr contacter, se mettre en rapport avec

contactable /kən'tæktəbl, 'kɒn-/ adj she is/is not ∼ on peut/ne peut pas la joindre

contact lens n lentille f ou verre m de contact

contagious /kən'teɪdʒəs/ adj contagieux/-ieuse

contain /kən'teɪn/
A vtr **1** (hold) contenir [amount, ingredients]; contenir, comporter [information, mistakes]; **2** (curb) maîtriser [blaze]; enrayer [epidemic]; limiter [costs, problem]; canaliser [strike]; **3** (within boundary) endiguer [river]; retenir [flood]; **4** (control) contenir [joy]; contenir [enemy]
B v refl **to** ∼ **oneself** se contenir

container /kən'teɪnə(r)/ n (for food, liquids) récipient m; (for plants) bac m; (skip, for waste) conteneur m; (for transporting) conteneur m

container: ∼ **port** n terminal m à conteneurs; ∼ **ship** n porte-conteneurs m inv; ∼ **truck** n porte-conteneur m

contaminate /kən'tæmɪneɪt/ vtr contaminer

contamination /kənˌtæmɪ'neɪʃn/ n gen, Ling contamination f

contd abrév écrite = **continued**

contemplate /'kɒntəmpleɪt/
A vtr **1** (consider deeply) réfléchir sur, contempler; **2** (envisage) envisager (**doing** de faire); **3** (look at) contempler
B vi méditer

contemplation /ˌkɒntem'pleɪʃn/ n contemplation f

contemplative /kən'templətɪv, 'kɒntempleɪtɪv/ adj songeur/-euse; Relig contemplatif/-ive

contemporaneous /kənˌtempə'reɪnɪəs/ adj contemporain (**with** de)

contemporaneously /kənˌtempəˈreɪnɪəslɪ/ adv en même temps (**with** que)

contemporary /kənˈtemprərɪ, US -pərerɪ/

A n contemporain/-e m/f; **he was a ~ at university** nous étions à l'université à la même époque; **our contemporaries** les gens de notre âge

B adj **1** (present-day) contemporain; (up-to-date) moderne; **2** (of same period) de l'époque; **to be ~ with** [event] coïncider avec

contempt /kənˈtempt/ n mépris m (**for** de); **to feel ~ for sb/sth**, **to hold sb/sth in ~** mépriser qn/qch; **to be beneath ~** être en-dessous de tout; **~ of court** Jur outrage m à magistrat

contemptible /kənˈtemptəbl/ adj méprisable

contemptuous /kənˈtemptjʊəs/ adj méprisant; **to be ~ of sth/sb** mépriser qch/qn

contemptuously /kənˈtemptjʊəslɪ/ adv [smile, say, treat] avec mépris; [behave] de façon méprisante

contend /kənˈtend/

A vtr soutenir (**that** que)

B vi **1** **to ~ with** affronter; **he's got a lot to ~ with** il a beaucoup de problèmes; **2** (compete) **she was ~ing with him for first place** elle lui disputait la première place

contender /kənˈtendə(r)/ n **1** Sport concurrent/-e m/f; **to be a ~ for first place** être bien placé pour gagner; **2** (for post) candidat/-e m/f (**for** à)

content

A n **1** /ˈkɒntent/ (relative quantity) teneur f; **the fat ~** la teneur en matières grasses; **low/high lead ~** faible/forte teneur en plomb; **to have a low/high fat ~** être pauvre/riche en matières grasses; **2** /ˈkɒntent/ (meaning) fond m; **form and ~** le fond et la forme; **3** /kənˈtent/ (happiness) contentement m

B **contents** /ˈkɒntents/ npl en gen contenu m; (of house, for insurance) biens mpl mobiliers; **he emptied the drawer of its ~s** il a vidé le tiroir de tout ce qu'il contenait; **list** ou **table of ~s** table f des matières

C /kənˈtent/ adj satisfait (**with** de); **to be ~ to do se** contenter de faire; **not ~ with doing** non content de faire; **he's ~ with what he has** il se contente de ce qu'il a; **I'm quite ~ here** je suis bien ici

D /kənˈtent/ v refl **to ~ oneself with sth/with doing** se contenter de qch/de faire

contented /kənˈtentɪd/ adj [person] content (**with** de); [feeling] de bien-être; **a ~ child** un enfant heureux

contentedly /kənˈtentɪdlɪ/ adv de bien-être

contention /kənˈtenʃn/ n **1** (opinion) assertion f; **it is my ~ that** je soutiens que; **2** (dispute) dispute f (**about** au sujet de); **point of ~** sujet m de dispute; **3** (competition) compétition f; **in ~** en compétition

contentious /kənˈtenʃəs/ adj **1** [subject] controversé; [view] discutable; **2** [person, group] discuteur/-euse

contentment /kənˈtentmənt/ n contentement m; **with ~** [sigh] de bien-être; **there was a look of ~ on his face** il avait l'air satisfait

contest

A /ˈkɒntest/ n **1** (competition) concours m; **fishing ~** concours m de pêche; **sports ~** rencontre f sportive; **it's no ~** c'est couru° d'avance; **2** (struggle) lutte f; **the presidential ~** la course à la présidence

B /kənˈtest/ vtr **1** (object to) contester; **2** (compete for) Sport disputer [match]; **strongly ~ed** Pol âprement disputé; **to ~ an election** Pol se présenter à une élection

contestant /kənˈtestənt/ n (in competition, game) concurrent/-e m/f; (in fight) adversaire mf; (for job, in election) candidat/-e m/f

context /ˈkɒntekst/ n contexte m; **in ~** [study, understand] dans son contexte; **out of ~** [quote, examine] hors contexte; **to put sth into ~** replacer qch dans son contexte

continent /ˈkɒntɪnənt/ n (land mass) continent m; **the Continent** GB l'Europe f continentale; **on the Continent** GB en Europe continentale

continental /ˌkɒntɪˈnentl/

A n Européen/-éenne m/f du continent

B noun modifier [vegetation, climate] continental; [universities, philosophy] d'Europe continentale; [holiday] en Europe continentale

continental: **~ breakfast** n petit déjeuner m (avec café, pain, beurre et confiture); **~ quilt** GB n couette f

contingency /kənˈtɪndʒənsɪ/ n **1** gen imprévu m; **to provide for all contingencies** parer à toute éventualité; **2** Philos contingence f

contingency: **~ fund** n fonds m de secours; **~ plan** n plan m de réserve

contingent /kənˈtɪndʒənt/ adj contingent; **to be ~ on** ou **upon** dépendre de

continual /kənˈtɪnjʊəl/ adj continuel/-elle

continually /kənˈtɪnjʊəlɪ/ adv continuellement

continuation /kənˌtɪnjʊˈeɪʃn/ n **1** (of situation, process) continuation f; **2** (resumption) continuation f, reprise f; **3** (in book) suite f; (of route) prolongement m

continue /kənˈtɪnjuː/

A vtr **1** continuer, poursuivre [career, studies, enquiry, TV series]; **2** (resume) continuer; **'to be ~d'** (in film) 'à suivre'; **'~d overleaf'** 'suite page suivante'; **'what's more,' she ~d** 'de plus,' reprit-elle; **3** continuer, poursuivre [journey]; **4** (preserve) maintenir

B vi **1** [noise, debate, strike, film] se poursuivre; **2** (keep on) continuer (**doing, to do** à or de faire); **3** [person, route] continuer; **he ~d across/down the street** il a continué de traverser/descendre la rue; **4** (in career, role) rester (**in** dans); **she will ~ as minister** elle restera ministre; **5** (in speech) poursuivre; **6** **to ~ with** continuer, poursuivre [task, treatment]; **to ~ with the ironing** continuer de repasser

C **continuing** pres p adj continuel/-elle

continuity /ˌkɒntɪˈnjuːɪtɪ/ n continuité f

continuity: **~ announcer** ▸ p. 1181 n speaker/speakerine m/f; **~ girl** ▸ p. 1181 n scripte f

continuous /kənˈtɪnjʊəs/ adj **1** [growth, flow, decline] continu; [love, care] constant; [line, surface] ininterrompu; [noise] continu; **~ assessment** GB Sch, Univ contrôle m continu; **2** Ling [tense] progressif/-ive; **in the present ~** au présent progressif

continuously /kənˈtɪnjʊəslɪ/ adv (without a break) sans interruption; (repeatedly) continuellement

continuum /kənˈtɪnjʊəm/ n (pl **-nuums** ou **-nua**) continuum m

contort /kənˈtɔːt/

A vtr tordre [limbs]; **to ~ one's body** se contortionner; **his features were ~ed with rage** ses traits étaient déformés par la colère

B vi [face, features, mouth] se crisper

contortion /kənˈtɔːʃn/ n contorsion f

contour /ˈkɒntʊə(r)/ n **1** (outline) contour m; **2** (also **~ line**) Geog courbe f hypsométrique or de niveau

contraband /ˈkɒntrəbænd/ n contrebande f

contraception /ˌkɒntrəˈsepʃn/ n contraception f

contraceptive /ˌkɒntrəˈseptɪv/

A n contraceptif m

B adj [method] contraceptif/-ive; **~ device** contraceptif m

contract

A /ˈkɒntrækt/ n **1** (agreement) contrat m (**for** pour; **with** avec); **employment ~**, **~ of employment** contrat m de travail; **to enter into a ~ with** passer un contrat avec; **to be on a ~** être sous contrat; **to be under ~ to** travailler sous contrat avec; **2** (tender) contrat m; **to win/lose a ~** remporter/perdre un contrat; **to award a ~** octroyer un contrat à; **to place a ~ for sth** octroyer un contrat pour qch à; **to put work out to ~** donner un travail en sous-traitance; **3** °(of assassination) **there's a ~ out on him** un tueur a été engagé pour l'abattre

B /ˈkɒntrækt/ noun modifier [labour] contractuel/-elle

C /kənˈtrækt/ vtr **1** (develop) contracter [disease] (**from** par le contact avec); **2** (arrange) contracter [marriage, debt, loan]; **to be ~ed to do** être tenu par contrat de faire; **3** (tighten) contracter

D /kənˈtrækt/ vi **1** (undertake) **to ~ to do** s'engager par contrat à faire; **2** (shrink) [metal] se contracter; [support, market] diminuer; **3** Med se contracter

(Phrasal verbs)

■ **contract into** GB: ▸ **~ into** [sth] souscrire à

■ **contract out** GB: ▸ **~ out** renoncer par contrat; **to ~ out of** se retirer de [scheme]; ▸ **~ out** [sth], **~ [sth] out** donner [qch] en sous-traitance (**to** à)

contraction /kənˈtrækʃn/ n gen, Med contraction f

contract killer n tueur/-euse m/f à gages

contractor /kən'træktə(r)/ ▸ p. 1181 *n* ① (business) entrepreneur/-euse *m/f*; ② (worker) contractuel/-elle *m/f*

contractual /kən'træktʃʊəl/ *adj* contractuel/-elle

contract: ~ **work** *n* prestation *f* de service; ~ **worker** *n* contractuel/-elle *m/f*

contradict /ˌkɒntrə'dɪkt/ *vtr*, *vi* contredire

contradiction /ˌkɒntrə'dɪkʃn/ *n* contradiction *f*; **in** ~ **with** en contradiction avec; **it's a** ~ **in terms** c'est une contradiction criante

contradictory /ˌkɒntrə'dɪktərɪ/ *adj* contradictoire (**to** à)

contraflow /'kɒntrəfləʊ/ GB *n* circulation *f* à sens alterné

contraindication /ˌkɒntrəɪndɪ'keɪʃn/ *n* contre-indication *f*

contralto /kən'træltəʊ/ ▸ p. 1311 *n* (*pl* **-tos** *ou* **-ti**) (voice) contralto *m*; (singer) contralto *f*

contraption /kən'træpʃn/ *n* (machine) engin○ *m*; (device) machin○ *m*

contrariness /'kɒntreərɪnɪs/ *n* esprit *m* de contrariété

contrariwise /'kɒntrərɪwaɪz/, US -trerɪ/ *adv* ① (conversely) inversement; ② (in the opposite direction) en sens inverse

contrary /'kɒntrərɪ/, US -trerɪ/
A *n* contraire *m*; **quite the** ~ bien au contraire; **on the** ~ (bien) au contraire; **despite views/claims to the** ~ contrairement à ce que certains pensent/disent; **evidence to the** ~ une preuve du contraire; **unless you hear anything to the** ~ sauf contrordre
B *adj* ① [*idea, view*] contraire; **to be** ~ **to** [*activity, proposal, opinion, measure*] être contraire à; ② [*direction, movement*] contraire (**to** à); ③ /kən'treərɪ/ [*person*] contrariant
C **contrary to** *prep phr* contrairement à; ~ **to popular belief/to rumours** contrairement à ce que l'on peut croire/à la rumeur; ~ **to expectations** contre toute attente

contrast
A /'kɒntrɑːst, US -træst/ *n* ① (difference) contraste *m*; **in** ~ **to sth, by** ~ **with sth** par contraste avec qch; **in** ~ **to sb** à la différence de qn; **to be a** ~ **to** *ou* **with** présenter un contraste avec; **by** *ou* **in** ~ par contre; ② Phot, TV contraste *m*
B /kən'trɑːst, US -'træst/ *vtr* **to** ~ **X with Y** faire ressortir le contraste (qui existe) entre X et Y
C *vi* contraster (**with** avec)
D **contrasting** *adj* [*examples*] opposé; [*colour, material*] contrasté; [*views, opinions*] très différents

contravene /ˌkɒntrə'viːn/ *vtr* enfreindre

contravention /ˌkɒntrə'venʃn/ *n* sout infraction *f* (**of** à); **in** ~ **of** en violation de [*rule, law*]

contribute /kən'trɪbjuːt/
A *vtr* ① (pay) verser [*sum, percentage*] (**to** à); financer [*costs, expenses*]; ② (to gift, charity) donner (**to** à; **towards** pour); ③ (put up) contribuer; **to** ~ **£5m** contribuer pour 5 millions de livres; ④ (to project, undertaking, magazine) apporter [*ideas*] (**to** à); écrire [*article, column*] (**to** pour)
B *vi* ① (be a factor in) **to** ~ **to** *ou* **towards** contribuer à [*change, awareness, decline*]; ② (to community life, company expansion, research) participer (**to** à); ③ (pay into) **to** ~ **to** cotiser à [*pension fund*]; ④ (to charity) donner (de l'argent) (**to** à); (to programme, magazine) collaborer à

contribution /ˌkɒntrɪ'bjuːʃn/ *n* ① (to tax, pension) contribution *f* (**towards** à); ② (to charity, campaign) don *m*; **to make a** ~ faire un don (**to** à); **'~s gratefully received'** 'merci d'avance pour vos dons'; ③ (role played) **sb's** ~ **to** le rôle que qn a joué dans [*success, undertaking*]; ce que qn a apporté à [*science, sport*]; **his outstanding** ~ **to politics** sa participation marquante à la vie politique; ④ (to profits, costs) contribution *f*; ⑤ Radio, TV participation *f*; (to magazine) article *m*; **with** ~**s from** avec la collaboration de

contributor /kən'trɪbjʊtə(r)/ *n* ① (to charity) donateur/-trice *m/f*; (in discussion) participant/-e *m/f*; (to magazine, book) collaborateur/-trice *m/f*

contributory /kən'trɪbjʊtərɪ/, US -tɔːrɪ/ *adj* **to be** ~ **to** contribuer à; **to be a** ~ **cause** être partiellement responsable (**of** de); **a** ~ **factor in** un facteur de

con trick○ *n* escroquerie *f*, duperie *f*

contrite /'kɒntraɪt/ *adj* contrit

contrivance /kən'traɪvəns/ *n* dispositif *m*, appareil *m*

contrive /kən'traɪv/ *vtr* ① (arrange) organiser; **to** ~ **to do** parvenir à faire, trouver moyen de faire; ② (invent) fabriquer [*device*]; inventer [*plot*]

contrived /kən'traɪvd/ *adj* pej ① [*incident, meeting*] non fortuit; ② (forced) [*plot, ending*] tiré par les cheveux; [*style, effect*] étudié

control /kən'trəʊl/
A *n* ① *C* (domination) (of animals, children, crowd, country, organization) contrôle *m* (**of** de); (of operation, project) direction *f* (**of** de); (of life, fate) maîtrise *f* (**of, over** de); (of disease, pests, social problem) lutte *f* (**of** contre); **to be in** ~ **of** contrôler [*territory*]; diriger [*operation, organization*]; maîtriser [*problem*]; **to have** ~ **over** contrôler [*territory*]; maîtriser [*fate, life*]; **to take** ~ **of** prendre le contrôle de [*territory*]; prendre la direction de [*organization, project*]; prendre [qch] en main [*situation*]; **to be under sb's** ~ [*person*] être sous la direction de qn; [*organization, party*] être sous le contrôle de qn; **to be under** ~ [*fire, problem, riot*] être maîtrisé; **everything's under** ~ tout va bien; **to bring** *ou* **get** *ou* **keep** [sth] **under** ~ maîtriser; **to be out of** ~ [*crowd, riot*] être déchaîné; [*fire*] ne plus être maîtrisable; **the situation is out of** ~ la situation est devenue incontrôlable; **to lose** ~ **of sth** perdre le contrôle de qch; **to be beyond** *ou* **outside sb's** ~ échapper au contrôle de qn; **due to circumstances beyond our** ~ pour des raisons indépendantes de notre volonté; ② *C* (restraint) (of self, appetite, emotion, urge) maîtrise *f*; **to have** ~ **over sth** maîtriser qch; **to keep** ~ **of oneself, to be in** ~ **of oneself** se maîtriser; **to lose** ~ **(of oneself)** perdre le contrôle (de soi); ③ *C* (physical mastery) (of vehicle, machine, ball) contrôle *m*; (of body, process, system) maîtrise *f*; **to be in** ~ **of** avoir le contrôle de; **to keep/lose** ~ **of a car** garder/perdre le contrôle d'une voiture; **to take** ~ (of plane) prendre les commandes; **his car went out of** ~ il a perdu le contrôle de son véhicule; ④ *C* (lever, switch) (on vehicle, equipment) commande *f*; (on TV) bouton *m* de réglage; **volume** ~ TV bouton de réglage du son; **to be at the** ~**s** être aux commandes; ⑤ (regulation) contrôle *m* (**on** de); ⑥ (in experiment) contrôle *m*
B *noun modifier* [*knob*] de commande; [*group*] témoin
C *vtr* (*p prés etc* **-ll-**) ① (dominate) dominer [*market, situation*]; contrôler [*territory*]; diriger [*traffic, project*]; s'emparer de [*mind*]; Fin être majoritaire dans [*company*]; ② (discipline) maîtriser [*person, animal, temper, inflation, riot, fire*]; endiguer [*epidemic*]; dominer [*emotion*]; retenir [*laughter*]; commander à [*limbs*]; ③ (operate) commander [*machine, process*]; manœuvrer [*boat, vehicle*]; piloter [*plane*]; contrôler [*ball*]; ④ (regulate) régler [*speed, temperature*]; contrôler [*immigration, prices*]; ⑤ (check) contrôler [*quality*]; vérifier [*accounts*]
D *v refl* (*p prés etc* **-ll-**) **to** ~ **oneself** se contrôler

control: ~ **column** *n* Aviat manche *m* à balai; ~ **freak**○ *n* maniaque *mf* qui veut tout contrôler; ~ **key** *n* Comput touche *f* de contrôle

controlled /kən'trəʊld/
A *adj* lit [*explosion, landing*] contrôlé; [*person, voice*] calme; [*economy*] dirigé; [*performance*] maîtrisé; **electronically** ~ contrôlé électroniquement; **under** ~ **conditions** sous contrôle
B **-controlled** *combining form* **Labour-**~ dominé par les Travaillistes; **computer-**~ commandé par ordinateur

controller /kən'trəʊlə(r)/ *n* ① gen, Radio, TV directeur/-trice *m/f*; ② Fin planificateur/-trice *m/f*

controlling /kən'trəʊlɪŋ/ *adj* [*group, organization*] de contrôle; ~ **interest** majorité *f* de contrôle

control: ~ **panel** *n* (for plane) tableau *m* de bord; (on machine) tableau *m* de contrôle; (on TV) (panneau *m* de) commandes *fpl*; ~ **room** *n* gen poste *m* de commande; Radio, TV (salle *f* de) régie *f*; ~ **tower** *n* tour *f* de contrôle

controversial /ˌkɒntrə'vɜːʃl/ *adj* ① [*decision, plan, film*] (criticized) controversé; (open to criticism) discutable; ② [*person, group*] (much discussed) controversé; (dubious) douteux/-euse

controversially /ˌkɒntrə'vɜːʃəlɪ/ *adv* de façon controversée

controversy /'kɒntrəvɜːsɪ, kən'trɒvəsɪ/ *n* controverse *f*; **to be the subject of much** ~ soulever de nombreuses controverses

conundrum /kə'nʌndrəm/ *n* énigme *f*

conurbation /ˌkɒnɜː'beɪʃn/ *n* conurbation *f*

convalesce /ˌkɒnvə'les/ *vi* se remettre; **he's convalescing** il est en convalescence

convalescence /ˌkɒnvə'lesns/ *n* convalescence *f*

convalescent /ˌkɒnvəˈlesnt/
A *n* convalescent/-e *m/f*
B *adj* [*person*] convalescent; [*leave, home*] de convalescence
convection /kənˈvekʃn/ *n* convection *f*
convector (heater) /kənˈvektə (ˈhiːtə)/ *n* convecteur *m*
convene /kənˈviːn/
A *vtr* organiser [*meeting*]; convoquer [*group*]
B *vi* se réunir
convener /kənˈviːnə(r)/ *n* ① (organizer) organisateur/-trice *m/f* (d'une réunion); ② (chair) président/-e *m/f*
convenience /kənˈviːnɪəns/ *n* ① **₡** (advantage) avantage *m* (**of doing** de faire); **the ~ of** les avantages de [*practice, method*]; la commodité de [*instant food, device, shop*]; **for (the sake of) ~** pour raisons de commodité; **for his/our ~** pour sa/notre convenance; **at your ~** quand cela vous conviendra; **at your earliest ~** dès que cela vous sera possible; ② GB (toilet) toilettes *fpl*
convenience: **~ foods** *npl* plats *mpl* (tout) préparés; **~ store** *n* épicerie *f* (ouverte tard le soir)
convenient /kənˈviːnɪənt/ *adj* ① (suitable) [*place, time*] commode; **now is not a very ~ time** ce n'est pas vraiment le moment maintenant; **to be ~ for sb** convenir à qn; **to be ~ for sb to do** convenir à qn de faire; **a ~ place for sth** un endroit approprié pour qch; ② (useful, practical) pratique, commode (**that** que + *subj*; **to do** de faire); ③ (in location) [*shops, amenities*] situé tout près; [*chair, table*] à portée de main; **to be ~ for** GB, **to be ~ to** US ne pas être loin de [*station, shops*]; ④ iron, péj (expedient) [*excuse, explanation*] commode; **it's ~ for them** ça les arrange
conveniently /kənˈviːnɪəntlɪ/ *adv* ① [*arrange*] de façon commode; **the conference was ~ timed to coincide with** la date de la conférence était bien choisie pour coïncider avec; **~ situated,** **~ located** bien situé, bien placé; ② iron (expediently) comme par hasard
convenor = convener
convent /ˈkɒnvənt, US -vent/ *n* couvent *m*; **to enter a ~** entrer au couvent
convention /kənˈvenʃn/ *n* ① (meeting) (of party, profession, union) convention *f*, congrès *m*; (of society, fans) assemblée *f*; ② **₡** (social norms) convenances *fpl*; **to flout** *ou* **defy ~** braver les convenances; ③ (usual practice) convention *f*; ④ (agreement) convention *f* (**on** sur)
conventional /kənˈvenʃənl/ *adj* ① (conformist) [*person*] conformiste; [*idea, role*] conventionnel/-elle; ② (traditionally accepted) [*approach, method*] conventionnel/-elle; [*medicine, agriculture*] traditionnel/-elle; **the ~ wisdom about sth** ce qui est communément admis au sujet de qch; ③ Mil [*weapons*] conventionnel/-elle
conventionally /kənˈvenʃənəlɪ/ *adv* [*dress, behave*] de façon conventionnelle
convent school *n* école *f* de religieuses
converge /kənˈvɜːdʒ/ *vi* converger (**at** à); **to ~ on** [*people*] converger sur [*place*]; [*rays, paths*] converger vers [*point*]
convergence /kənˈvɜːdʒəns/ *n* convergence *f*
conversant /kənˈvɜːsnt/ *adj* **to be ~ with sth** être versé dans qch
conversation /ˌkɒnvəˈseɪʃn/ *n* conversation *f*; **to have** *ou* **hold a ~** avoir une conversation; **to make ~** faire la conversation; **in ~** en conversation
conversational /ˌkɒnvəˈseɪʃnl/ *adj* [*ability, skill, class, exercise*] de conversation
conversationalist /ˌkɒnvəˈseɪʃənəlɪst/ *n* personne *f* qui excelle dans l'art de la conversation
converse
A /ˈkɒnvɜːs/ *n* ① gen contraire *m*; ② Math, Philos converse *f*
B /ˈkɒnvɜːs/ *adj* contraire
C /kənˈvɜːs/ *vi* converser (**with** avec; **in** en)
conversely /ˈkɒnvɜːslɪ/ *adv* inversement
conversion /kənˈvɜːʃn, US kənˈvɜːrʒn/ *n* ① (transformation) transformation *f* (**from** de; **to, into** en); ② (of currency, measurement) conversion *f* (**from** de; **into** en); ③ (of building) aménagement *m* (**to, into** en); **barn ~** grange *f* aménagée; ④ Relig, Pol conversion *f* (**from** de; **to** à); **to undergo a ~** se convertir; ⑤ (in rugby) transformation *f*
conversion: **~ rate** *n* taux *m* de change; **~ table** *n* table *f* de conversion
convert
A /ˈkɒnvɜːt/ *n* converti/-e *m/f* (**to** à); **to become a ~** se con-

vertir; **to win** *ou* **make ~s** faire des adeptes
B /kənˈvɜːt/ *vtr* ① (change into sth else) transformer; ② (modify) adapter; ③ convertir [*currency, measurement*] (**from** de; **to, into** en); ④ Archit aménager [*building, loft*] (**to, into** en); ⑤ Relig, Pol convertir (**to** à; **from** de); ⑥ (in rugby) transformer [*try*]
C /kənˈvɜːt/ *vi* ① (change) **to ~ to sth** passer à qch; ② (be convertible) être convertible (**into** en); ③ Relig, Pol se convertir (**to** à; **from** de); ④ (in rugby) transformer
converter /kənˈvɜːtə(r)/ *n* convertisseur *m*
convertible /kənˈvɜːtəbl/
A *n* Aut décapotable *f*
B *adj* convertible; [*car*] décapotable
convertor /kənˈvɜːtə(r)/ *n* = converter
convex /ˈkɒnveks/ *adj* convexe
convey /kənˈveɪ/ *vtr* ① (transmit) [*person*] transmettre [*message, information*] (**to** à); exprimer [*condolences, feeling, idea*] (**to** à); **to ~ to sb that/how** faire savoir à qn que/comment; **to ~ the impression of/that** donner l'impression de/que; ② (communicate) [*words, images*] traduire [*mood, impression*]; ③ (transport) [*vehicle*] transporter; [*pipes, network*] amener
conveyance /kənˈveɪəns/ *n* ① (of goods, passengers) transport *m*, acheminement *m*; ② †(vehicle) véhicule *m*
conveyancing /kənˈveɪənsɪŋ/ *n* rédaction *f* des actes de propriété
conveyor /kənˈveɪə(r)/ *n* ① (also **~ belt**) (in factory) transporteur *m* à bande *or* à courroie; (for luggage) tapis *m* roulant; ② (of goods, persons) transporteur *m*
convict
A /ˈkɒnvɪkt/ *n* (imprisoned criminal) détenu/-e *m/f*; (deported criminal) bagnard *m*; **ex-~** ancien détenu; **escaped ~** détenu évadé
B /kənˈvɪkt/ *vtr* reconnaître *ou* déclarer [qn] coupable (**of** de; **of doing** d'avoir fait); [*evidence*] condamner; **a ~ed murderer** (in prison) un condamné pour meurtre; (now released) un ancien condamné pour meurtre
conviction /kənˈvɪkʃn/ *n* ① Jur condamnation *f* (**for** pour); ② (belief) conviction *f* (**that** que); **to lack ~** manquer de conviction
convince /kənˈvɪns/
A *vtr* ① (gain credibility of) convaincre [*person, jury, reader*] (**of** de; **that** que; **about** au sujet de); ② (persuade) persuader [*voter, consumer*] (**to do** de faire); **~d** convaincu, persuadé
B *v refl* **to ~ oneself** se convaincre
convincing /kənˈvɪnsɪŋ/ *adj* [*account, evidence, proof, theory*] convaincant; [*victory, lead, win*] indiscutable
convincingly /kənˈvɪnsɪŋlɪ/ *adv* [*argue, claim, demonstrate, portray*] de façon convaincante; [*win, beat*] de façon indiscutable
convivial /kənˈvɪvɪəl/ *adj* ① [*atmosphere, evening*] cordial; ② [*person*] chaleureux/-euse
convocation /ˌkɒnvəˈkeɪʃn/ *n* convocation *f*
convoke /kənˈvəʊk/ *vtr* convoquer
convoluted /ˈkɒnvəluːtɪd/ *adj* ① [*argument, style*] alambiqué; ② [*vine, tendril*] convoluté; [*design*] vrillé
convoy /ˈkɒnvɔɪ/ *n* convoi *m*; **in ~** en convoi
convulse /kənˈvʌls/ *vtr* ① [*pain, sobs, laughter*] convulser [*person, body*]; [*joke, comic*] faire tordre de rire [*person*]; **~d with pain** convulsé de douleur; ② [*riots, unrest*] secouer [*country*]
convulsion /kənˈvʌlʃn/ *n* convulsion *f*; **to go into ~s** entrer en convulsions; **to be in ~s** fig se tordre de rire
convulsive /kənˈvʌlsɪv/ *adj* convulsif/-ive
convulsively /kənˈvʌlsɪvlɪ/ *adv* convulsivement
coo /kuː/
A *n* (of dove) roucoulement *m*
B *vi* [*lover, dove*] roucouler; **to ~ over** s'extasier devant [*baby*]
cooing /ˈkuːɪŋ/ *n* roucoulement *m*, roucoulade *f*
cook /kʊk/ ▶ p. 1181
A *n* cuisinier/-ière *m/f*; **he's a good ~** c'est un bon cuisinier
B *vtr* ① Culin faire cuire [*vegetables, pasta, eggs*]; préparer [*meal*] (**for** pour); ② ○(falsify) trafiquer○, falsifier [*data*]; **to ~ the books** trafiquer○ la comptabilité
C *vi* ① [*person*] cuisiner, faire la cuisine; [*vegetable, meat, meal*] cuire; **the carrots are ~ing** les carottes sont en train de cuire; **there's something ~ing**○ fig il y a quelque chose qui se mijote○

D **cooked** *pp adj* cuit; **lightly** ~**ed** à peine cuit.
(Phrasal verb)
■ **cook up**○: ▶ ~ **up [sth]** préparer [*dish, meal*]; inventer [*excuse, story*]; mijoter○ [*scheme*]

cook: ~**book** *n* livre *m* de cuisine; ~**-chill foods** *npl* plats *mpl* préparés; ~**ed meats** *npl* ≈ charcuterie *f*

cooker /'kʊkə(r)/ *n* GB cuisinière *f*

cookery /'kʊkərɪ/ *n* GB cuisine *f*; ~ **book** livre de cuisine

cookie /'kʊkɪ/ *n* **1** gâteau *m* sec, biscuit *m* (sec); **2** Comput mouchard *m*, cookie *m*

cooking /'kʊkɪŋ/ *n* cuisine *f*; **to do the** ~ faire la cuisine; **to be good at** ~ bien cuisiner; **Chinese** ~ cuisine chinoise

cooking: ~ **apple** *n* pomme *f* à cuire; ~ **chocolate** *n* chocolat *m* pâtissier; ~ **foil** *n* papier *m* aluminium; ~ **salt** *n* gros sel *m*

cook: ~**out** *n* US barbecue *m*; ~**ware** *n* ustensiles *mpl* de cuisine

cool /kuːl/
A *n* **1** (coldness) fraîcheur *f*; **2** ○(calm) sang-froid *m*; **to keep one's** ~ (stay calm) garder son sang-froid; (not get angry) ne pas s'énerver; **to lose one's** ~ (get angry) s'énerver; (panic) perdre son sang-froid

B *adj* **1** [*day, drink, water, weather*] frais/fraîche; [*dress*] léger/-ère; [*colour*] froid; **it's** ~ **today** il fait frais aujourd'hui; **to feel** ~ [*surface, wine*] être frais/fraîche; **I feel** ~**er now** j'ai moins chaud maintenant; **it's getting** ~, **let's go in** il commence à faire frais, rentrons; **2** (calm) [*approach, handling*] calme; **to stay** ~ garder son sang-froid; **to keep a** ~ **head** garder la tête froide; **keep** ~! reste calme; **3** (unemotional) [*manner*] détaché; [*logic*] froid; **4** (unfriendly) froid; **to be** ~ **with** *ou* **towards sb** être froid avec qn; **5** (casual) décontracté, cool○; **he's a** ~ **customer** il n'a pas froid aux yeux; **6** (for emphasis) **a** ~ **million dollars** la coquette somme d'un million de dollars○; **7** ○(sophisticated) branché○; **he thinks it's** ~ **to smoke** il pense que ça fait bien de fumer; **it's not** ~ ça fait nul○; **8** ○US (great) super○!

C *vtr* **1** (lower the temperature of) refroidir [*soup, pan*]; rafraîchir [*wine, room*]; **to** ~ **one's hands** se rafraîchir les mains; **2** *fig* calmer [*anger, ardour*]

D *vi* **1** (get colder) refroidir; **2** (subside) [*passion*] tiédir; [*enthusiasm*] faiblir; [*friendship*] se dégrader; **wait until tempers have** ~**ed** attends que les esprits se calment

(Idioms) ~ **it**○! ne t'énerve pas!; **to play it** ~○ rester calme
(Phrasal verbs)
■ **cool down**: ▶ ~ **down** [*engine, water*] refroidir; *fig* [*person, situation*] se calmer; ▶ ~ **[sth] down** refroidir [*mixture*]; rafraîchir [*wine*]; ▶ ~ **[sb] down** rafraîchir; *fig* calmer [*person*]
■ **cool off** (get colder) se rafraîchir; *fig* (calm down) se calmer

cool: ~ **bag** *n* GB sac *m* isotherme; ~ **box** *n* GB glacière *f*; ~**-headed** *adj* [*person*] qui garde la tête froide; [*decision, approach*] réfléchi

cooling /'kuːlɪŋ/
A *n* refroidissement *m*
B *adj* [*drink, swim*] rafraîchissant; [*agent*] réfrigérant; [*system, tower*] de refroidissement

cooling-off period *n* (in industrial relations) délai *m* de conciliation; Comm délai *m* de réflexion

coolly /'kuːlɪ/ *adv* **1** (lightly) [*dressed*] légèrement; **2** (without warmth) [*greet, say*] froidement; **3** (calmly) calmement; **4** (boldly) sans la moindre gêne

coolness /'kuːlnɪs/ *n* **1** (coldness) fraîcheur *f*; **2** (unfriendliness) froideur *f*; **3** (calmness) calme *m*

coop /kuːp/ *n* (*also* **chicken** ~, **hen** ~) poulailler *m*
(Phrasal verb)
■ **coop up**: ▶ ~ **[sb/sth] up** enfermer, cloîtrer

co-op /'kəʊɒp/ *n* = **cooperative A 1**

cooper /'kuːpə(r)/ ▸ p. 1181 *n* tonnelier *m*

cooperate /kəʊ'ɒpəreɪt/ *vi* coopérer (**with** avec; **in** à; **in doing** pour faire)

cooperation /kəʊ,ɒpə'reɪʃn/ *n* coopération *f* (**on** à); **in** (**close**) ~ en (étroite) coopération

cooperative /kəʊ'ɒpərətɪv/
A *n* **1** (organisation) coopérative *f*; **workers'** ~ coopérative

ouvrière; **2** US (apartment house) immeuble *m* en copropriété

B *adj* **1** (joint) conjoint; **to take** ~ **action** agir conjointement; **2** (helpful) coopératif/-ive; **3** Comm, Pol [*movement, society*] coopératif/-ive; **4** US [*apartment, building*] en copropriété

cooperatively /kəʊ'ɒpərətɪvlɪ/ *adv* [*work*] en coopération; **to act** ~ se montrer coopératif/-ive

cooperative society *n* coopérative *f*

co-opt /kəʊ'ɒpt/ *vtr* **1** (onto committee) coopter [*person*] (**onto** dans); **2** (commandeer) utiliser [*celebrity*] (**to** pour soutenir)

coordinate
A /kəʊ'ɔːdɪnət/ *n* coordonnée *f*
B **coordinates** *npl* (clothes) ensemble *m*
C **coordinating** *pres p adj* **1** [*clothes, garment*] assorti, coordonné; **2** [*committee*] de coordination
D /kəʊ'ɔːdɪneɪt/ *vtr* coordonner (**with** avec)
E /kəʊ'ɔːdɪneɪt/ *vi* agir en coordination (**with** avec)

coordinated /kəʊ'ɔːdɪneɪtɪd/ *adj* coordonné

coordination /kəʊ'ɔːdɪ'neɪʃn/ *n* coordination *f*

coordinator /kəʊ'ɔːdɪneɪtə(r)/ *n* coordinateur/-trice *m/f*

co-owner /kəʊ'əʊnə(r)/ *n* copropriétaire *mf*

cop○ /kɒp/
A *n* **1** (police officer) flic *m*; **to play** ~**s and robbers** jouer aux gendarmes et aux voleurs; **2** GB (arrest) **it's a fair** ~! bien joué, je me rends○!; **3** GB (use) **to be not much** ~ ne pas valoir grand-chose
B *vtr* (*p prés etc* **-pp-**) **1** (receive) écoper de○ [*punch, punishment*]; **to** ~ **it** trinquer○; **2** (*also* ~ **hold of**) (catch) attraper; ~ **hold of the rope** attrape la corde
(Phrasal verb)
■ **cop out**○ se dégonfler○; **to** ~ **out of doing** se défiler○ au moment de faire

cope /kəʊp/ *vi* **1** (manage practically) [*person*] s'en sortir○, se débrouiller; [*police, services, system*] faire face; **to** ~ **with** [*person*] s'occuper de [*person, correspondence, work*]; [*government, police, system*] faire face à [*demand, disaster, inquiries*]; **to learn to** ~ **alone** apprendre à se débrouiller tout seul; **it's more than I can** ~ **with** je ne m'en sors plus; **the organization can't** ~ l'organisation ne s'en sort plus *ou* ne peut pas faire face; **2** (manage financially) s'en sortir; **to** ~ **on £60 a week** s'en sortir avec 60 livres sterling par semaine; **to** ~ **with a loan** arriver à rembourser un prêt; **3** (manage emotionally) **to** ~ **with** supporter [*bereavement, depression*]; **to** ~ **with sb** supporter qn; **if you left me, I couldn't** ~ si tu me quittais, je ne pourrais pas le supporter

Copenhagen /,kəʊpn'heɪgən/ ▸ p. 1276 *pr n* Copenhague

copier /'kɒpɪə(r)/ *n* photocopieuse *f*

co-pilot /,kəʊ'paɪlət/ *n* copilote *mf*

copious /'kəʊpɪəs/ *adj* **1** (plentiful) [*crop, supply, tears*] abondant; ~ **notes** une quantité abondante de notes; **2** (generous) [*quantity, serving*] copieux/-ieuse

copiously /'kəʊpɪəslɪ/ *adv* abondamment

cop-out○ /'kɒpaʊt/ *n* (excuse) excuse *f* bidon○; (evasive act) échappatoire *f*

copper /'kɒpə(r)/ ▸ p. 752
A *n* **1** Chem cuivre *m*; **2** ○(policeman) flic○ *m*; **3** ○GB (coin) petite monnaie *f* **¢**; **a few** ~**s** quelques sous *mpl*; **4** GB Hist (for washing) lessiveuse *f*; **5** (colour) couleur *f* cuivre
B *noun modifier* [*alloy, mine, ore*] de cuivre; [*bracelet, coin, pipe, wire*] de *ou* en cuivre; [*kettle, pan*] en cuivre
C *adj* [*hair, leaf, lipstick*] couleur cuivre *inv*

copper: ~**-bottomed** *adj* sûr; ~**-coloured** GB, **-colored** US ▸ p. 752 *adj* [*hair*] cuivré; [*leaf, metal*] couleur cuivre *inv*; ~**plate** *n* écriture *f* ronde

coppery /'kɒpərɪ/ ▸ p. 752 *adj* [*colour*] cuivré

co-property /kəʊ'prɒpətɪ/ *n* copropriété *f*

copse /kɒps/ *n* taillis *m*

copulate /'kɒpjʊleɪt/ *vi* s'accoupler, copuler

copy /'kɒpɪ/
A *n* **1** (reproduction, imitation) copie *f*; **certified** ~ copie *f* certifiée conforme; **2** (edition) (of book, newspaper, report) exemplaire *m*; **3** (journalist's, advertiser's text) copie *f*; **to be** *ou* **make good** ~ être un bon sujet d'article; **to file (one's)** ~ présenter sa copie

c

B *vtr* ⚊ (imitate) copier [*person, design*] (**from** sur); ⚋ (duplicate) copier [*document, disk*]; **to ~ sth onto a disk** copier qch sur disquette; **to have sth copied** faire faire une copie de qch

C *vi* copier (**from** sur); **to ~ in a test** copier à un examen

(Phrasal verbs)

■ **copy down**: ▸ **~ down** [sth], **~** [sth] **down** recopier (**into** sur)

■ **copy out**: ▸ **~ out** [sth], **~** [sth] **out** recopier

copybook /'kɒpɪbʊk/ *n* cahier *m* d'écriture

(Idiom) **to blot one's ~** faire des bêtises

copycat○ /'kɒpɪkæt/

A *n* péj copieur/-ieuse *m/f*

B *adj* [*crime, murder*] inspiré par un autre (*after n*)

copy: ~ editor *n* (on newspaper) secrétaire *mf* de rédaction; **~ing machine** *n* photocopieuse *f*

copyist /'kɒpɪɪst/ *n* ⚊ (of old texts) copiste *mf*; ⚋ (forger) faussaire *mf*

copyread *vtr* (*prét, pp* **-read**) US corriger (*pour la publication*)

copyright /'kɒpɪraɪt/

A *n* copyright *m*, droit *m* d'auteur; **to have** *ou* **hold the ~** détenir le copyright *or* les droits; **the ~ of** *ou* **on sth** le copyright de qch, les droits sur qch; **to be in ~** être protégé par copyright

B *adj* [*book, work*] protégé par un copyright

C *vtr* déposer [*work*]

copy: ~ typist ▸ p. 1181 *n* dactylo *mf*; **~writer** ▸ p. 1181 *n* rédacteur/-trice *m/f* publicitaire

coquetry /'kɒkɪtrɪ/ *n* coquetterie *f*

coquettish /kɒ'ketɪʃ/ *adj* [*person*] coquet/-ette; [*smile, look, manner*] aguichant

coral /'kɒrəl, US 'kɔːrəl/ *n* corail *m*

coral: ~ island *n* île *f* corallienne; **~ pink** ▸ p. 752 *n, adj* (rouge *m*) corail (*m*) *inv*; **~ reef** *n* récif *m* corallien *or* de corail

cord /kɔːd/

A *n* ⚊ (of dressing gown, curtains) cordon *m*; **sash ~** corde *f* (de fenêtre à guillotine); ⚋ Elec fil *m*, cordon *m*; ⚌ ○(abrév = **corduroy**) velours *m* côtelé

B *npl* **cords**○ pantalon *m* en velours (côtelé)

cordial /'kɔːdɪəl, US 'kɔːrdʒəl/

A *n* ⚊ (fruit) sirop *m* de fruits; ⚋ US (liqueur) liqueur *m*

B *adj* cordial (**to, with** avec)

cordless /'kɔːdlɪs/ *adj* sans fil, sans cordon; **~ telephone** téléphone *m* sans fil

cordon /'kɔːdn/ *n* (all contexts) cordon *m*; **police ~** cordon *m* de police

(Phrasal verb)

■ **cordon off**: ▸ **~ off** [sth], **~** [sth] **off** boucler [*street, area*]; contenir [*crowd*]

corduroy /'kɔːdərɔɪ/ *n* velours *m* côtelé; **~s** un pantalon *m* en velours (côtelé)

core /kɔː(r)/

A *n* ⚊ (of apple) trognon *m*; ⚋ fig (of problem) cœur *m*; ⚌ (inner being) **rotten to the ~** pourri jusqu'à l'os; **English to the ~** anglais jusqu'au bout des ongles; **it shook me to the ~** cela m'a remué jusqu'au fond de l'âme; ⚍ (nuclear) cœur *m*; ⚎ (small group) noyau *m*

B *vtr* Culin évider [*apple*]

core curriculum /ˌkɔːkə'rɪkjʊləm/ *n* Sch, Univ tronc *m* commun

co-respondent /ˌkəʊrɪ'spɒndənt/ *n* Jur complice *mf* d'adultère

core subject *n* Sch, Univ matière *f* du tronc commun

Corfu /kɔː'fuː/ ▸ p. 954 *pr n* Corfou *f*

cork /kɔːk/

A *n* ⚊ (substance) liège *m*; ⚋ (object) bouchon *m*

B *vtr* boucher [*bottle*]

corkage /'kɔːkɪdʒ/ *n* droit *m* de bouchon

corked /kɔːkt/ *adj* [*wine*] bouchonné

corker○† /'kɔːkə(r)/ *n* GB (story) histoire *f* épatante○; (stroke, shot) coup *m* de maître

cork: ~screw *n* tire-bouchon *m*; **~screw curls** *npl* anglaises *fpl*

corn /kɔːn/ *n* ⚊ GB (wheat) blé *m*; ⚋ US (maize) maïs *m*; ⚌ (for sowing) grain *m* (de céréale); ⚍ Med (on foot) cor *m*

corn: ~cob *n* épi *m* de maïs; **~ dolly** GB *n* poupée *f* de paille

cornea /'kɔːnɪə/ *n* (*pl* **~s** *ou* **-neae**) cornée *f*

corneal /'kɔːnɪəl/ *adj* cornéen/-éenne

corner /'kɔːnə(r)/

A *n* ⚊ lit (in geometry) angle *m*; (of street, building) angle *m*, coin *m*; (of table, field, room) coin *m*; Aut (bend) virage *m*; **the house on the ~** la maison qui fait l'angle; **at the ~ of the street** au coin de la rue; **to turn** *ou* **go round the ~** tourner au coin de la rue; **to turn down the ~ of a page** corner une page; **just around the ~** (nearby) tout près; (around the bend) juste après le coin; **she disappeared round the ~** elle a disparu au coin de la rue; **spring is just around the ~** le printemps approche; ⚋ (of eye, mouth) coin *m*; **out of the ~ of one's eye** du coin de l'œil; ⚌ (place) coin *m*; **a remote ~ of India** une région reculée de l'Inde; **to search every ~ of the house** chercher partout dans la maison; ⚍ Sport (in boxing) coin *m* (de repos); (in football, hockey) corner *m*; **to take a ~** tirer un corner

B *vtr* ⚊ (trap) lit acculer [*animal, enemy*]; fig coincer○ [*person*]; ⚋ (monopolize) accaparer [*market*]

C *vi* Aut [*car*] prendre un virage

(Idioms) **to be in a tight ~** être dans une impasse; **to hold one's ~** se défendre; **to cut ~s** (financially) faire des économies; (in a procedure) simplifier les choses

corner: ~ cupboard *n* meuble *m* d'angle; **~ing** *n* Aut tenue *f* de route (dans les virages); **~ shop** *n* petite épicerie *f*; **~stone** *n* Archit, fig pierre *f* angulaire; **~ways, ~wise** *adj, adv* en diagonale

cornet /'kɔːnɪt/ *n* ⚊ (instrument) cornet *m* (à pistons); ⚋ GB (for ice cream) cornet *m*

corn: ~field *n* champ *m* de blé; (sweetcorn) champ *m* de maïs; **~flour** *n* farine *f* de maïs; **~flower** *n* bleuet *m*, barbeau *m*

cornice /'kɔːnɪs/ *n* (all contexts) corniche *f*

Cornish pasty /ˌkɔːnɪʃ'pæstɪ/ *n*: petit pâté de viande et légumes

corn: ~ oil *n* huile *f* de maïs; **~ on the cob** *n* maïs *m* en épi; **~ plaster** *n* pansement *m* pour cors; **~ salad** *n* mâche *f*; **~ starch** *n* US = **cornflour**

cornucopia /ˌkɔːnjʊ'kəʊpɪə/ *n* corne *f* d'abondance

Cornwall /'kɔːnwɔːl/ ▸ p. 1132 *pr n* (comté *m* de) Cornouailles *f*

corny○ /'kɔːnɪ/ *adj* péj [*joke*] (old) éculé; (feeble) faiblard○; [*film, story*] à la guimauve

corollary /kə'rɒlərɪ, US 'kɒrəlerɪ/ *n* corollaire *m* (**to** de)

coronary /'kɒrənrɪ, US 'kɔːrənerɪ/ *n* Med infarctus *m*

coronary: ~ care unit *n* unité *f* de soins intensifs cardiologiques; **~ thrombosis** *n* infarctus *m* du myocarde

coronation /ˌkɒrə'neɪʃn, US ˌkɔːr-/ *n* couronnement *m*

coroner /'kɒrənə(r), US 'kɔːr-/ *n* coroner *m*

coronet /'kɒrənet, US 'kɔːr-/ *n* couronne *f*

corp *n* US abrév ▸ **corporation**

corporal /'kɔːpərəl/ ▸ p. 1123 *n* ⚊ (in infantry, air force) caporal-chef *m*; (in cavalry, artillery) brigadier-chef *m*

corporal punishment *n* châtiment *m* corporel

corporate /'kɔːpərət/ *adj* ⚊ Comm [*accounts, funds*] appartenant à une société; [*clients, employees*] d'une société (or de sociétés); ⚋ (collective) [*action*] commun; [*ownership*] en commun; [*decision*] collectif/-ive

corporate: ~ advertising *n* publicité *f* institutionnelle; **~ culture** *n* culture *f* d'entreprise; **~ identity**, **~ image** *n* image *f* de marque (d'une société); **~ law** *n* US Jur droit *m* des sociétés; **~ lawyer** *n* US Jur (in a firm) avocat/-e *m/f* d'entreprise; (business law expert) juriste *mf* d'entreprise; **~ name** *n* raison *f* sociale; **~ planning** *n* planification *f* d'entreprise; **~ raider** *n* raider *m* (organisateur d'OPA)

corporation /ˌkɔːpə'reɪʃn/ *n* ⚊ Comm (grande) société *f*; ⚋ GB (town council) conseil *m* municipal

corporation tax *n* GB impôt *m* sur les sociétés

corps /kɔː(r)/ *n* Mil corps *m*; **~ de ballet** corps de ballet

corpse /kɔːps/ *n* cadavre *m*

corpus /'kɔːpəs/ *n* (*pl* **-pora**) Ling corpus *m*

corpuscle /'kɔːpʌsl/ *n* (blood) **~** globule *m* sanguin; **red/white (blood) ~** globule *m* rouge/blanc

correct /kə'rekt/
A adj ⒈ (right) [amount, answer, decision, method, order] correct, bon/bonne; [figure] exact; **that is** ~ c'est exact; **the** ~ **time** l'heure exacte; **you are quite** ~ tu as parfaitement raison; **to prove** ~ s'avérer juste; ⒉ (proper) correct, convenable
B vtr corriger; ~ **me if I'm wrong, but...** arrêtez-moi si je me trompe, mais...; **I stand** ~**ed** je reconnais mon erreur
C v refl **to** ~ **oneself** se reprendre

correcting fluid n liquide m correcteur

correction /kə'rekʃn/ n correction f; (in dictation) rectification f

corrective /kə'rektɪv/
A n correctif m; **this is a** ~ **to the idea that** ceci apporte un démenti à l'idée que
B adj gen [action, lens] correcteur/-trice; [measure] de redressement; ~ **surgery** chirurgie f réparatrice

correctly /kə'rektlɪ/ adv (all contexts) correctement

correlate /'kɒrəleɪt, US 'kɔːr-/
A vtr corréler
B vi être en corrélation (**with** avec)

correlation /ˌkɒrə'leɪʃn/ n corrélation f

correspond /ˌkɒrɪ'spɒnd, US ˌkɔːr-/ vi ⒈ (match up) concorder, correspondre (**with** à); ⒉ (be equivalent) être équivalent (**to** à); ⒊ (exchange letters) correspondre (**with** avec; **about** au sujet de)

correspondence /ˌkɒrɪ'spɒndəns, US ˌkɔːr-/ n (link, exchange of letters) correspondance f; **to be in** ~ **with sb** correspondre avec qn; **to enter into** ~ engager une correspondance (**about** au sujet de)

correspondence: ~ **column** n courrier m des lecteurs; ~ **course** n cours m par correspondance

correspondent /ˌkɒrɪ'spɒndənt, US ˌkɔːr-/ ▸ p. 1181 n ⒈ (journalist) journaliste mf; (abroad) correspondant/-e m/f; **political** ~ commentateur/-trice m/f politique; ⒉ (letter writer) correspondant/-e m/f

corresponding /ˌkɒrɪ'spɒndɪŋ, US ˌkɔːr-/ adj (matching) correspondant; (similar) équivalent

correspondingly /ˌkɒrɪ'spɒndɪŋlɪ, US ˌkɔːr-/ adv ⒈ (consequently) par conséquent; ⒉ (proportionally) proportionnellement

corridor /'kɒrɪdɔː(r), US 'kɔːr-/ n (in building, train) couloir m; (in international politics) corridor m; **the** ~**s of power** fig les hautes sphères fpl du pouvoir

corroborate /kə'rɒbəreɪt/ vtr corroborer

corrode /kə'rəʊd/
A vtr lit, fig corroder
B vi se corroder

corrosion /kə'rəʊʒn/ n corrosion f

corrosive /kə'rəʊsɪv/ adj corrosif/-ive

corrugated: ~ **cardboard** n carton m ondulé; ~ **iron** n tôle f ondulée

corrupt /kə'rʌpt/
A adj corrompu; (character) dépravé
B vtr corrompre [person, text]; **to** ~ **sb's morals** dépraver qn
C vi [lifestyle, power] corrompre

corruption /kə'rʌpʃn/ n corruption f; (of computer data) altération f

corsage /kɔː'sɑːʒ/ n ⒈ (flowers) petit bouquet m de fleurs (porté au corsage); ⒉ (bodice) corsage m

Corsica /'kɔːsɪkə/ ▸ p. 954, p. 873 pr n Corse f

cosh /kɒʃ/ GB
A n matraque f
B vtr matraquer

cosignatory /ˌkəʊ'sɪgnətərɪ, US -tɔːrɪ/ n cosignataire mf (**to, of** de)

cosily /'kəʊzɪlɪ/ adv [sit, lie] confortablement

cosiness /'kəʊzɪnɪs/ n ⒈ (of room) atmosphère f douillette; ⒉ (intimacy) intimité f

cos lettuce /ˌkɒz 'letɪs/ n (salade f) romaine f

cosmetic /kɒz'metɪk/
A n produit m de beauté
B adj ⒈ lit cosmétique; ⒉ fig superficiel/-ielle

cosmetic surgery n chirurgie f esthétique

cosmic /'kɒzmɪk/ adj [ray] cosmique; [dust] interstellaire; [event, struggle] prodigieux/-ieuse

cosmonaut /'kɒzmənɔːt/ ▸ p. 1181 n cosmonaute mf

cosmopolitan /ˌkɒzmə'pɒlɪtn/ n, adj cosmopolite (mf)

Cossack /'kɒsæk/ n, adj cosaque (m)

cosset /'kɒsɪt/ vtr choyer [person]; protéger [industry, group]

cost /kɒst, US kɔːst/
A n ⒈ (price) coût m, prix m (**of** de); (expense incurred) frais mpl; **at a** ~ **of £100** au prix de 100 livres; **at** ~ au prix coûtant; **you'll bear the** ~ les frais seront à votre charge; **the** ~ **is quite high** ça revient assez cher; **at no extra** ~ sans frais supplémentaires; **at great** ~ à grands frais; **to count the** ~ **of** lit estimer le coût de; fig mesurer les conséquences de; ⒉ fig prix m; **at all** ~**s** à tout prix; **he knows to his** ~ **that** il a appris à ses dépens que; **the** ~ **in human lives was great** beaucoup de vies ont été perdues; **whatever the** ~ coûte que coûte
B **costs** npl ⒈ Jur **to pay** ~**s** être condamné aux dépens; **to be awarded** ~**s** se voir accorder le remboursement des frais; ⒉ Comm frais mpl; **transport** ~**s** frais de transport; **to cut** ~**s** réduire les coûts
C vtr ⒈ (prét, pp **cost**) coûter; **how much does it** ~? combien ça coûte?; **the TV will** ~ **£100 to repair** cela coûtera 100 livres de faire réparer la télé; **to** ~ **money** coûter cher; ⒉ (prét, pp **cost**) fig **that decision cost him his job** cette décision lui a coûté son travail; **politeness** ~**s nothing** ça ne coûte rien d'être poli; ⒊ (prét, pp ~**ed**) Comm (also ~ **out**) calculer le prix de revient de [product]; calculer le coût de [project, work]

co-star /'kəʊstɑː(r)/ Cin, Theat
A n co-vedette f
B vtr (p prés etc **-rr-**) **a film** ~**ring X and Y** un film avec X et Y
C vi (p prés etc **-rr-**) **to** ~ **with sb** partager la vedette avec qn

Costa Rica /ˌkɒstə'riːkə/ ▸ p. 774 pr n Costa Rica m

cost-cutting /'kɒstkʌtɪŋ, US 'kɔːst-/ n réduction f des frais; **as a** ~ **exercise** pour réduire les frais

cost: ~**-effective** adj rentable; ~**-effectiveness** n rentabilité f

costing /'kɒstɪŋ, US 'kɔːstɪŋ/ n ⒈ (discipline) ¢ comptabilité f analytique ou d'exploitation; ⒉ (process) (for project) établissement m des coûts; (for product) établissement m des coûts de production

costly /'kɒstlɪ, US 'kɔːstlɪ/ adj [scheme, exercise] coûteux/-euse; [error] fâcheux/-euse; **the decision proved to be** ~ la décision lui/leur etc a coûté beaucoup

cost: ~ **of living** n coût m de la vie; ~ **of living allowance** n indemnité f de vie chère; ~ **of living index** n indice m du coût de la vie

cost price n Comm (for producer) prix m de revient; (for consumer) prix m coûtant; **at** ~ au prix coûtant

costume /'kɒstjuːm, US -tuːm/ n ⒈ (clothes) costume m; **in** ~ costumé; ⒉ GB (swimsuit) (also **swimming** ~) maillot m de bain

costume: ~ **drama** n (play) pièce f en costume d'époque; ~ **jewellery** n ¢ bijoux mpl fantaisie

cosy GB, **cozy** US /'kəʊzɪ/ adj ⒈ (comfortable) [chair, room, atmosphere] douillet/-ette; **to feel** ~ [person] être confortablement installé; **it's** ~ **here** on est bien ici; ⒉ (intimate) intime; ⒊ fig [situation, belief] rassurant

cot /kɒt/ n ⒈ GB (for baby) lit m de bébé; ⒉ US (bed) lit m de camp

cot death n GB mort f subite du nourrisson

cottage /'kɒtɪdʒ/ n maisonnette f; (thatched) chaumière f; **weekend** ~ maison f de campagne

cottage: ~ **cheese** n fromage m blanc à gros grains; ~ **hospital** n GB ≈ polyclinique f; ~ **industry** n travail m artisanal à domicile; ~ **loaf** n GB miche f de pain; ~ **pie** n GB hachis m Parmentier

cotton /'kɒtn/
A n ⒈ (raw material) coton m; ⒉ (thread) fil m de coton

B noun modifier [clothing, fabric, field] de coton; [industry, town] cotonnier/-ière

cotton: ~ **bud** n Coton-Tige® m; ~ **candy** n US barbe f à papa; ~ **mill** n filature f de coton; ~ **reel** n bobine f de coton; ~**tail** n US lapin m

cotton wool n ouate f (de coton)

(Idiom) **to wrap sb in** ~ élever qn dans du coton

couch /kaʊtʃ/
A n **1** (sofa) canapé m; **2** (doctor's) lit m; (psychoanalyst's) divan m
B vtr formuler [idea, response]

couchette /kuːˈʃet/ n couchette f

cougar /ˈkuːɡə(r)/ n puma m

cough /kɒf, US kɔːf/
A n toux f; **to have a** ~ tousser; **she has a bad** ~ elle a une mauvaise toux
B vi tousser

(Phrasal verb)
■ **cough up**: ▸ ~ **up [sth]** **1** lit cracher [blood]; **2** °fig cracher° [information]; **to** ~ **up (the money)** cracher°

coughing /ˈkɒfɪŋ, US ˈkɔːfɪŋ/ n toux f; ~ **fit** accès m de toux; **there was a lot of** ~ il y avait des gens qui toussaient

could /kʊd/ ▸ **can¹**

couldn't /ˈkʊdnt/ = **could not**

could've /ˈkʊdəv/ = **could have**

council /ˈkaʊnsl/
A n conseil m; **the Council of Europe** le Conseil de l'Europe; **in** ~ en assemblée
B noun modifier [employee, workman] municipal; [grant] de la municipalité

council: ~ **chamber** n salle f du conseil; ~ **estate** n lotissement m de logements sociaux; ~ **house** n habitation f à loyer modéré; ~ **housing** n logements mpl sociaux

councillor /ˈkaʊnsələ(r)/ n conseiller/-ère m/f

council tax n GB ≈ impôts mpl locaux

counsel /ˈkaʊnsl/
A n **1** sout (advice) conseil m; **to keep one's own** ~ être circonspect; **2** Jur avocat/-e m/f; ~ **for the defence** avocat/-e m/f de la défense; ~ **for the prosecution** procureur m
B vtr **1** (advise) conseiller [person] (**about, on** sur); **2** sout (recommend) conseiller [prudence]

counselling, counseling US /ˈkaʊnsəlɪŋ/
A n **1** (psychological advice) aide f psychosociale; **2** (practical advice) assistance f; **careers** ~ orientation f professionnelle; **3** Sch orientation f scolaire
B noun modifier [group, centre, service] d'aide psychosociale, d'assistance

counsellor, counselor US /ˈkaʊnsələ(r)/ ▸ p. 1181 n **1** (adviser) conseiller/-ère m/f; **2** US (in holiday camp) moniteur/-trice m/f

count /kaʊnt/ ▸ p. 869
A n **1** (numerical record) gen décompte m; Pol (at election) dépouillement m; **at the last** ~ au dernier décompte; **to lose** ~ lit ne plus savoir où on en est dans ses calculs; **I've lost** ~ **of the number of complaints I've received** je ne compte plus le nombre de plaintes que j'ai reçues; **2** (level) taux m; **cholesterol** ~ taux de cholestérol; **3** (figure) chiffre m; **4** Jur chef m d'accusation; **on three** ~**s** pour trois chefs d'accusation; **5** (in boxing) **to be out for the** ~° être KO° also fig; **7** (also **Count**) (nobleman) comte m
B vtr **1** (add up) compter; vérifier [one's change]; énumérer [reasons, causes]; **to** ~ **the votes** Pol dépouiller le scrutin; gen compter les votes; ~**ing the children** en comptant les enfants; **not** ~**ing my sister** sans compter ma sœur; **to** ~ **the cost of sth** fig faire le bilan de qch; **2** (consider) **to** ~ **sb as sth** considérer qn comme qch
C vi **1** gen, Math compter; **to** ~ **(up) to 50** compter jusqu'à 50; **2** (be of importance) compter; **to** ~ **for little** compter peu; **to** ~ **for nothing** ne pas compter; **3** (be considered) être considéré

(Idioms) **to** ~ **sheep** compter les moutons; **to** ~ **the pennies** regarder à la dépense; **to** ~ **oneself lucky** s'estimer heureux; **it's the thought that** ~**s** c'est l'intention qui compte;

to stand up and be ~**ed** se faire entendre

(Phrasal verbs)
■ **count against**: ▸ ~ **against [sb]** jouer contre
■ **count in**: ▸ ~ **[sb] in** (include) ~ **me in!** j'en suis!
■ **count on**: ▸ ~ **on [sb/sth]** compter sur [person, event]; **don't** ~ **on it!** ne comptez pas (trop) dessus!
■ **count out**: ▸ ~ **out [sth]** **he** ~**ed out the money** il a compté l'argent (pièce par pièce or billet par billet): ▸ ~ **[sb] out** **1** (exclude) ~ **me out!** ne compte pas sur moi!; **2** Sport **the ref** ~**ed him out** il est allé au tapis
■ **count up**: ▸ ~ **up [sth]** calculer [cost, hours]; compter [money, boxes]

countable /ˈkaʊntəbl/ adj Ling comptable

countdown /ˈkaʊntdaʊn/ n lit, fig compte m à rebours (**to** avant)

counter /ˈkaʊntə(r)/
A n **1** (service area) (in shop, snack bar) comptoir m; (in bank, post office) guichet m; (in pub, bar) bar m; **the girl at** ou **behind the** ~ (in shop) la vendeuse; (in bank, post office) la caissière; **available over the** ~ [medicine] vendu sans ordonnance; **under the** ~ en sous-main; **2** (section of a shop) rayon m; **perfume** ~ rayon parfumerie; **cheese** ~ fromagerie f, rayon m fromagerie; **3** (token) jeton m
B **counter to** prep phr [be, go, run] à l'encontre de; [act, behave] contrairement à
C vtr répondre à [accusation, threat]; neutraliser [effet]; parer [blow]; enrayer [inflation]
D vi (retaliate) riposter (**with sth** par qch)
E **counter+** combining form contre-

counteract /ˌkaʊntəˈrækt/ vtr contrebalancer [influence]; contrecarrer [negative publicity]

counter-attack /ˈkaʊntərətæk/
A n contre-attaque f (**against** sur)
B vi contre-attaquer

counterbalance
A /ˈkaʊntəbæləns/ n contrepoids m
B /ˌkaʊntəˈbæləns/ vtr contrebalancer

counter cheque GB, **counter check** US n chèque-guichet m

counter-claim /ˈkaʊntəkleɪm/ n rétorsion f

counter clerk ▸ p. 1181 n US caissier/-ière m/f

counter-clockwise /ˌkaʊntəˈklɒkwaɪz/ adj, adv US dans le sens inverse des aiguilles d'une montre

counter-espionage /ˌkaʊntərˈespɪənɑːʒ/ n contre-espionnage m

counterfeit /ˈkaʊntəfɪt/
A adj [signature, note] contrefait; ~ **money** fausse monnaie f
B vtr contrefaire

counterfoil /ˈkaʊntəfɔɪl/ n talon m, souche f

counter-inflationary /ˌkaʊntərɪnˈfleɪʃnrɪ, US -nerɪ/ adj anti-inflationniste

counter-insurgency /ˌkaʊntərɪnˈsɜːdʒənsɪ/ n contre-insurrection f

counter-intelligence /ˌkaʊntərɪnˈtelɪdʒəns/ n contre-espionnage m

countermand /ˌkaʊntəˈmɑːnd, US -ˈmænd/ vtr annuler [order, decision]

counter-measure /ˈkaʊntəmeʒə(r)/ n contre-mesure f

counter-offensive /ˌkaʊntərˈfensɪv/ n contre-offensive f (**against** sur)

counterpane /ˈkaʊntəpeɪn/ n couvre-lit m

counterpart /ˈkaʊntəpɑːt/ n (of person) homologue mf; (of company, institution etc) équivalent m (**of, to** de)

counterpoint /ˈkaʊntəpɔɪnt/ n contrepoint m

counter-productive /ˌkaʊntəprəˈdʌktɪv/ adj contre-productif/-ive

counter-revolution /ˌkaʊntəˌrevəˈluːʃn/ n contre-révolution f

countersign /ˈkaʊntəsaɪn/ vtr contresigner

counter staff n caissiers/-ières mpl/fpl

counter-tenor /ˌkaʊntəˈtenə(r)/ ▸ p. 1311 n (person) haute-contre m; (voice) haute-contre f

counter-terrorism /ˌkaʊntəˈterərɪzəm/ *n* contre-terrorisme *m*

countess /ˈkaʊntɪs/ ▸ p. 869 *n* (*also* **Countess**) comtesse *f*

counting /ˈkaʊntɪŋ/ *n* gen calcul *m*; **the ∼ of votes** le dépouillement du scrutin

countless /ˈkaʊntlɪs/ *adj* ∼ **letters** un nombre incalculable de lettres; **on ∼ occasions** je ne sais combien de fois; ∼ **millions of** des millions et des millions de

countrified /ˈkʌntrɪfaɪd/ *adj* rustique; pej rustaud

country /ˈkʌntrɪ/
A *n* ▸ p. 774 **1** (nation, people) pays *m*; **to go to the ∼** GB Pol appeler le pays aux urnes; **2** (native land) patrie *f*; **the old ∼** le pays natal; **3** (*also* ∼**side**) (out of town) campagne *f*; **in the ∼** à la campagne; **open ∼** rase campagne; **4** **⊄** région *f*; **walking ∼** une région bonne pour la marche; **Brontë ∼** le pays des Brontë; **5** (*also* ∼ **music**) country (music) *f*
B *adj* [*road*] de campagne; [*scene*] campagnard; ∼ **life** la vie à la campagne

(Idioms) **it's a free ∼!** on est en république!, on est libre de faire ce qu'on veut!; **it's my line of ∼** ça me connaît; **it's not really my line of ∼** ce n'est pas vraiment mon fort

country: ∼ **and western** *n* musique *f* country et western; ∼ **bumpkin** *n* péj plouc⁰ *mf*; ∼ **club** *n* club *m* de loisirs; ∼ **cousin** *n* pej campagnard/-e *m/f*; ∼ **dancing** *n* danse *f* folklorique; ∼ **house** *n* manoir *m*; ∼**man** (*also* **fellow** ∼) compatriote *m*; ∼ **music** *n* country music *f*; ∼ **seat** *n* domaine *m*

countryside /ˈkʌntrɪsaɪd/ *n* campagne *f*; **there is some lovely ∼ around here** il y a de beaux paysages par ici

countrywide *adj, adv* dans tout le pays

county /ˈkaʊntɪ/
A *n* comté *m*
B *adj* GB [*boundary, team*] du comté; [*accent*] ≈ d'aristocrate; **he's very ∼** il fait très gentleman-farmer

county: ∼ **council, CC** *n* GB Pol ≈ conseil *m* régional; ∼ **court** *n* GB Jur ≈ tribunal *m* d'instance

coup /ku:/ *n* (*also* ∼ **d'état**) coup *m* d'État; fig **to pull off/score a ∼** réussir/faire un beau coup

couple /ˈkʌpl/
A *n* **1** couple *m*; **young (married) ∼** jeune couple; **2** **a ∼ of** (two) deux; (a few) deux ou trois; **a ∼ of times** deux ou trois fois
B *vtr* **1** Rail atteler; **2** ∼**d with** s'ajoutant à
C *vi* [*person, animal*] s'accoupler

coupon /ˈkuːpɒn/ *n* **1** (for goods) bon *m*; **petrol ∼** bon d'essence; **2** (cut-out in ad) coupon *m*; **reply ∼** coupon-réponse *m*; **3** (for pools) grille *f* de paris

courage /ˈkʌrɪdʒ/ *n* courage *m*; **to have the ∼ of one's convictions** avoir le courage de ses opinions; **to pluck up the ∼ to do** trouver le courage de faire; **it takes ∼** il faut du courage; **to take ∼ from the fact that** trouver du réconfort dans le fait que

courageous /kəˈreɪdʒəs/ *adj* courageux/-euse; **it was ∼ of him** c'était courageux de sa part

courier /ˈkʊrɪə(r)/ ▸ p. 1181 *n* **1** (*also* **travel** ∼) accompagnateur/-trice *m/f*; **2** (for parcels, documents) coursier *m*; (for drugs) transporteur *m*

course /kɔːs/
A *n* **1** (progression) (of time, event, history) cours *m* (**of** de); **in the ∼ of** au cours de; **in (the) ∼ of time** avec le temps; **in the normal ∼ of events** normalement; **in ∼ of restoration** en cours de restauration; **to run** *ou* **take its ∼** suivre son cours; **in due ∼** en temps utile; **2** (route) cours *m*; (of boat, plane) cap *m*; **to be on ∼** Aviat, Naut tenir le cap; **the economy is back on ∼** l'économie s'est restabilisée; **to go off ∼** [*ship, government*] dévier de son cap; **to change ∼** gen, lit changer de direction; Aviat, Naut, fig changer de cap; ∼ **of action** conduite *f*; **to take a ∼ of action** adopter une certaine conduite; **3** Sch, Univ cours *m* (**in** en; **of** de); **French ∼** cours *m* de français; **beginners' ∼** cours *m* pour débutants; **a ∼ of study** Sch programme *m* scolaire; Univ cursus *m* universitaire; **to go on** *ou* **be on a ∼** (aller) suivre un cours; **4** Med **a ∼ of treatment** un traitement; **5** Sport (in golf, athletics) parcours *m*; (in racing) cours *m*; **to stay the ∼** lit finir la course; fig tenir bon; **6** (part of meal) plat *m*; **the cheese ∼** le plateau de fromages; **five-∼ meal** repas *m* de cinq plats
B *vi* **1** (gush) couler; **2** Sport **to go coursing** chasser

---

C of course *adv phr* bien sûr, évidemment; **of ∼ I do!** (confirming suggestion) bien sûr que oui!; (refuting allegation) bien sûr que si!; **of ∼ he doesn't!** bien sûr que non!; **'did you lock the door?'—'of ∼ I did!'** 'tu as fermé la porte à clé?'—'mais oui, enfin!'; **'you didn't believe him?'—'of ∼ not!'** 'tu ne l'as pas cru?'—'mais non, voyons!'

course: ∼ **book** *n* méthode *f*; ∼ **material** *n* support *m* de cours; ∼**ware** *n* logiciel *m* d'enseignement à distance; ∼**work** *n* Sch, Univ devoirs *mpl* (de contrôle continu)

court /kɔːt/
A *n* **1** Jur cour *f*, tribunal *m*; **to go to ∼** aller devant les tribunaux (**over** pour); **to take sb to ∼** poursuivre qn en justice; **2** Sport (for tennis, squash) court *m*; (for basketball) terrain *m*; **to be on ∼** jouer; **3** (of sovereign) cour *f*
B *noun modifier* Jur [*case*] judiciaire; [*ruling*] du tribunal; ∼ **appearance** comparution *f* en justice
C *vtr* **1** (woo) courtiser [*woman, voters*]; **2** **to ∼ disaster** courir au désastre
D †*vi* [*couple*] se fréquenter; **he's ∼ing** il a une petite amie; **in our ∼ing days** avant notre mariage

(Idioms) **to get laughed out of ∼** se rendre complètement ridicule; **to pay ∼ to sb** faire la cour à qn

court circular *n* bulletin *m* quotidien de la cour

courteous /ˈkɜːtɪəs/ *adj* courtois (**to** envers)

courteously /ˈkɜːtɪəslɪ/ *adv* courtoisement

courtesy /ˈkɜːtəsɪ/ *n* **1** courtoisie *f*; **it is only common ∼** c'est la moindre des politesses; **2** **(by) ∼ of** (with permission from) avec la gracieuse permission de; (with funds from) grâce à la générosité de; (thanks to) grâce à; **a free trip ∼ of the airline** un voyage gratuit offert par la compagnie aérienne

courtesy call *n* visite *f* de courtoisie

courthouse /ˈkɔːthaʊs/ *n* **1** Jur palais *m* de justice; **2** US ≈ préfecture *f* (*d'un comté*)

courtier /ˈkɔːtɪə(r)/ *n* courtisan/dame de (la) cour *m/f*

courtly /ˈkɔːtlɪ/ *adj* (polite) courtois; ∼ **love** amour *m* courtois

court-martial /ˌkɔːtˈmɑːʃl/
A *n* (*pl* **courts-martial**) cour *f* martiale
B *vtr* (*p prés etc* **-ll-**) faire passer [qn] en cour martiale [*soldier*]; **to be ∼led** passer en cour martiale

court: ∼ **of inquiry** *n* commission *f* d'enquête; ∼ **of law** *n* Jur cour *f* de justice; ∼ **order** *n* Jur décision *f* judiciaire; ∼**room** *n* Jur salle *f* d'audience

courtship /ˈkɔːtʃɪp/ *n* **1** (period of courting) fréquentation *f*; **2** (act of courting) cour *f*

courtyard *n* cour *f*

cousin /ˈkʌzn/ *n* cousin/-e *m/f*

cove /kəʊv/ *n* **1** (bay) anse *f*; **2** ⁰†(man) type⁰ *m*

covenant /ˈkʌvənənt/ *n* (agreement) convention *f*; (payment agreement) engagement *m*

Coventry /ˈkɒvəntrɪ/ *pr n*:
(Idiom) **to send sb to ∼** mettre qn en quarantaine

cover /ˈkʌvə(r)/
A *n* **1** (protective lid, sheath) couverture *f*; (for duvet, typewriter, cushion) housse *f*; (for umbrella, blade, knife) fourreau *m*; **2** (blanket) couverture *f*; **3** (of book, magazine) couverture *f*; (of record) pochette *f*; **on the ∼** (of book) sur la couverture; (of magazine) en couverture; **from ∼ to ∼** de la première à la dernière page; **4** (shelter) abri *m*; **take ∼!** aux abris!; **under ∼** à l'abri; **under ∼ of darkness** à la faveur de la nuit; **5** (for spy, crime) couverture *f* (**for** pour); **to blow sb's ∼**⁰ griller⁰ qn; **6** Mil couverture *f*; **air ∼** couverture aérienne; **to give sb ∼** couvrir qn; **7** (replacement) (for teacher, doctor) remplacement *m*; **to provide emergency ∼** offrir un service d'urgence; **8** (insurance) assurance *f* (**for** pour; **against** contre); **to give** *or* **provide ∼ against** garantir contre
B *vtr* **1** (conceal or protect) couvrir (**with** avec); recouvrir [*cushion, sofa, corpse*] (**with** de); **2** (coat) recouvrir [*ground, surface, person, cake*] (**with** de); **to be ∼ed in glory** être couvert de gloire; **3** (be all over) [*litter, graffiti, bruises*] couvrir; ∼**ed in spots/litter** couvert de boutons/papiers; **4** (travel over) parcourir [*distance, area*]; (extend over) s'étendre sur [*area*]; **to ∼ a lot of miles** faire beaucoup de kilomètres; **5** (deal with, include) [*article, speaker*] traiter; [*term*] englober; [*teacher*] faire; [*rule, law*] s'appliquer à; [*department*] s'occuper de;

c

Countries and continents

■ *Most countries and all continents are used with the definite article in French:*

France is a beautiful country
= la France est un beau pays

I like Canada
= j'aime le Canada

to visit the United States
= visiter les États-Unis

to know Iran
= connaître l'Iran

A very few countries do not:

to visit Israel
= visiter Israël

■ *When in doubt, check in the dictionary.*

■ *All the continent names are feminine in French. Most names of countries are feminine e.g.* la France, *but some are masculine e.g.* le Canada.

■ *Most names of countries are singular in French, but some are plural (usually, but not always, those that are plural in English) e.g.* les États-Unis *mpl (the United States), and* les Philippines *fpl (the Philippines). Note, however, the plural verb* sont:

the Philippines is a lovely country
= les Philippines sont un beau pays

In, to and from somewhere

■ *With continent names, feminine singular names of countries and masculine singular names of countries beginning with a vowel, for* in *and* to, *use* en, *and for* from, *use* de:

to live in Europe   **to go to Europe**
= vivre en Europe   = aller en Europe

to come from Europe   **to live in France**
= venir d'Europe   = vivre en France

to go to France   **to come from France**
= aller en France   = venir de France

to live in Afghanistan   **to go to Afghanistan**
= vivre en Afghanistan   = aller en Afghanistan

to come from Afghanistan
= venir d'Afghanistan

■ *Note that names of countries and continents that include* North, South, East, *or* West *work in the same way:*

to live in North Korea   **to go to North Korea**
= vivre en Corée du Nord   = aller en Corée du Nord

to come from North Korea
= venir de Corée du Nord

■ *With masculine countries beginning with a consonant, and with plurals, use* au *or* aux *for* in *and* to, *and* du *or* des *for* from:

to live in Canada
= vivre au Canada

to go to Canada
= aller au Canada

to come from Canada
= venir du Canada

to live in the United States
= vivre aux États-Unis

to go to the United States
= aller aux États-Unis

to come from the United States
= venir des États-Unis

to live in the Philippines
= vivre aux Philippines

to go to the Philippines
= aller aux Philippines

to come from the Philippines
= venir des Philippines

Adjective uses: *français* or *de France* or *de la France?*

■ *For* French, *the translation* français *is usually safe; here are some typical examples:*

the French army   **French literature**
= l'armée française   = la littérature française

the French coast   **French money**
= la côte française   = l'argent français

French cooking   **the French nation**
= la cuisine française   = le peuple français

French currency   **French politics**
= la monnaie française   = la politique française

the French Customs   **a French town**
= la douane française   = une ville française

the French government   **French traditions**
= le gouvernement français   = les traditions françaises

the French language
= la langue française

■ *Some nouns, however, occur more commonly with* de France *(usually, but not always, their English equivalents can have* of France *as well as* French):

the Ambassador of France or **the French Ambassador**
= l'ambassadeur de France

the French Embassy
= l'ambassade de France

the history of France or **French history**
= l'histoire de France

the King of France or **the French king**
= le roi de France

the rivers of France
= les fleuves et rivières de France

the French team
= l'équipe de France

but note:

the capital of France or **the French capital**
= la capitale de la France

■ *Note that many geopolitical adjectives like* French *can also refer to nationality, e.g.* a French tourist ▶ **p. 1032**, *or to the language, e.g.* a French word ▶ **p. 969**.

[rep] couvrir; **6** (report on) [journalist] couvrir; ~**ed live on BBC1** diffusé en direct par BBC1; **7** (pay for) couvrir [costs]; combler [loss]; **£20 should** ~ **it** 20 livres sterling devraient suffire; **to** ~ **one's costs** rentrer dans ses frais; **8** (insure) assurer, couvrir [person, possession] (**for, against** contre; **for doing** pour faire); **9** Mil, Sport couvrir; **I've got you** ~**ed!** (threat) ne bougez pas ou je tire!; **to** ~ **one's back** fig se couvrir; **10** (conceal) cacher [ignorance]; masquer [smell]
C v refl **to** ~ **oneself** se protéger (**against** contre)
D -**covered**: **snow-**~**ed** couvert de neige; **chocolate-**~**ed** enrobé de chocolat
E **covered** pp adj [market, porch] couvert; [dish] à couvercle

■ **cover for**: ▸ ~ **for [sb]** (replace) remplacer [*employee*]; (conceal error) '~ **for me!**' 'trouve-moi une excuse!'

■ **cover over**: ▸ ~ **over [sth]**, ~ **[sth] over** couvrir [*yard, pool*] (**with** avec); recouvrir [*mark*] (**with** de)

■ **cover up**: ▸ ~ **up** ① (put clothes on) se couvrir (**with** de); ② **to** ~ **up for** couvrir [*friend*]; **they're** ~**ing up for each other** ils se couvrent l'un l'autre; ▸ ~ **up [sth]**, ~ **[sth] up** fig dissimuler [*mistake, truth*]; étouffer [*scandal*]

coverage /'kʌvərɪdʒ/ n ① (in media) couverture f; **television/newspaper** ~ couverture par la télévision/les journaux; **live** ~ reportage m en direct; ② (in book, programme) traitement m; **its** ~ **of the period is good/poor** il couvre bien/mal cette période

covered: ~ **market** n marché m couvert; ~ **wagon** n chariot m bâché

covering /'kʌvərɪŋ/ n ① (for wall, floor) revêtement m; ② (layer of snow, moss) couche f

covering ~ **fire** n tir m de couverture; ~ **letter** n lettre f d'accompagnement

cover: ~ **note** n (from insurance company) attestation f d'assurance; ~ **story** n (in paper) article m annoncé en couverture

cover sheet n (for fax) page f de garde

covert
Ⓐ /'kʌvə(r)/ n (thicket) fourré m
Ⓑ /'kʌvət, US 'kəʊvɜːrt/ adj [*operation*] secret/-ète; [*glance*] furtif/-ive; [*threat*] voilé

covertly /'kʌvətlɪ, US 'kəʊvɜːrtlɪ/ adv secrètement

cover: ~**-up** n opération f de camouflage; ~ **version** n Mus version f

covet /'kʌvɪt/ vtr convoiter

covetous /'kʌvɪtəs/ adj cupide

covetously /'kʌvɪtəslɪ/ adv avec convoitise

cow /kaʊ/ n (cattle) vache f; (other animal) femelle f

(Idiom) **till the** ~**s come home** jusqu'à la saint-glinglin○

coward /'kaʊəd/ n lâche mf

cowardice /'kaʊədɪs/ n lâcheté f

cowardly /'kaʊədlɪ/ adj lâche

cowbell n sonnaille f

cowboy /'kaʊbɔɪ/
Ⓐ n ① ▸ p. 1181 US cowboy m; **to play** ~**s and indians** jouer aux cowboys et aux indiens; ② (incompetent worker) péj fumiste m
Ⓑ noun modifier ① [*hat, film*] de cowboy; ② péj [*workman*] fumiste; [*outfit*] pas sérieux/-ieuse

cowed /kaʊd/ adj apeuré

cower /'kaʊə(r)/ vi se recroqueviller (de peur)

cow: ~**herd** ▸ p. 1181 n vacher/-ère m/f; ~**hide** n (leather) peau f de vache

cowl /kaʊl/ n capuchon m

cowlick○ /'kaʊlɪk/ n mèche f (de cheveux)

cowl neck /,kaʊl 'nek/ n col m boule

cow: ~**pat** n bouse f de vache; ~**shed** n étable f

cox /kɒks/ Sport
Ⓐ n barreur m
Ⓑ vtr, vi barrer

coxswain /'kɒksn/ n (on ship) ≈ capitaine m en second; (in rowing) barreur m

coy /kɔɪ/ adj [*smile, look*] de fausse modestie; ② (reticent) réservé (**about** à propos de)

coyly /'kɔɪlɪ/ adv avec fausse modestie; (flirtatiously) avec coquetterie

coypu /'kɔɪpuː/ n (pl ~**s** ou ~) ragondin m

cozy adj US = **cosy**

CPU n Comput abrév ▸ **central processing unit**

cr Comm abrév écrite = **credit A 5**

crab /kræb/ n Zool, Culin crabe m

(Idiom) **to catch a** ~ (in rowing) plonger la rame trop profond, aller à la pêche○

crab apple n (tree) pommier m sauvage; (fruit) pomme f sauvage

crack /kræk/
Ⓐ n ① (in varnish, ground) craquelure f (**in** dans); (single line in wall, cup, mirror, ground, bone) fêlure f (**in** dans); ② (in door) entrebâillement m; (in curtains) fente f; (in rock) fissure f; ③ (drug)

(*also* ~ **cocaine**) crack m; ④ (noise) craquement m; ⑤ ○(attempt) essai m, tentative f; **to have a** ~ **at doing** essayer de faire; **to have a** ~ **at** essayer de remporter [*title*]; essayer de battre [*record*]; ⑥ plaisanterie f (**about** à propos de); **a cheap** ~ une plaisanterie facile
Ⓑ adj (tjrs épith) [*player*] de première; [*troops, shot*] d'élite
Ⓒ vtr ① (make a crack in) fêler [*mirror, bone, wall, cup*]; (make fine cracks in) fendiller, faire craqueler [*varnish*]; ② (break) casser [*nut, egg, casing*]; **to** ~ **a safe** fracturer un coffre-fort; **to** ~ **sth open** ouvrir qch; **to** ~ **one's head open** se fendre le crâne; ③ (solve) résoudre [*problem*]; déchiffrer [*code*]; **I've** ~**ed it**○ j'ai pigé○ or compris; ④ faire claquer [*whip*]; faire craquer [*knuckles*]; **to** ~ **sb on the head** asséner un coup sur la tête de qn; **to** ~ **one's head on sth** se cogner la tête sur qch; **to** ~ **the whip** fig agiter le fouet; ⑤ (overcome) faire craquer [*defences*]; ⑥ **to** ~ **a joke** sortir une blague○
Ⓓ vi ① (develop crack(s)) se fêler; [*varnish*] se craqueler; [*skin*] se crevasser; [*ground*] se fendre; ② (cease to resist) [*person*] craquer; **to** ~ **under pressure** ne pas tenir le coup; ③ (make sound) [*knuckles, twig*] craquer; [*whip*] claquer; ④ [*voice*] se casser

(Idioms) **not all** ou **not as good as it's** ~**ed up to be**○ pas aussi bon qu'on le prétend; **to get** ~**ing**○ s'y mettre; **go on, get** ~**ing**○! vas-y, remue-toi○!; **to have a fair** ~ **of the whip** avoir sa chance; **to give sb a fair** ~ **of the whip** donner sa chance à qn

(Phrasal verbs)
■ **crack down** prendre des mesures énergiques, sévir (**on** contre)
■ **crack up**○: ▸ ~ **up** ① (have breakdown) craquer; ② (laugh) rire; ▸ ~ **[sb] up** faire rire qn

crack-brained○ /'krækbreɪnd/ adj saugrenu

crackdown /'krækdaʊn/ n mesure f sévère (**on** contre); **the** ~ **on drugs** l'action f anti-drogue

cracker /'krækə(r)/ n ① (biscuit) cracker m, biscuit m salé; ② (for Christmas) diablotin m

crackers○ /'krækəz/ adj GB cinglé○

cracking /'krækɪŋ/
Ⓐ ○adj GB [*game, start*] excellent; **at a** ~ **pace** à toute vitesse
Ⓑ ○†adv GB **a** ~ **good shot** un coup formidablement bien joué; **it was a** ~ **good lunch** on a formidablement bien déjeuné

crackle /'krækl/
Ⓐ n (sound) crépitement m
Ⓑ vtr faire crisser [*foil, paper*]
Ⓒ vi [*twig, fire, radio*] crépiter; [*hot fat, burning wood*] grésiller

crackling /'kræklɪŋ/ n ① (of fire) crépitement m; (of foil, cellophane) crissement m; (on radio) friture○ f; ② (crisp pork) couenne f grillée

crackpot○ n, adj cinglé/-e○ (m/f)

cradle /'kreɪdl/
Ⓐ n ① (for baby) berceau m also fig; **from the** ~ **to the grave** du berceau à la tombe; ② (platform) nacelle f
Ⓑ vtr bercer [*baby*]; tenir [qch] délicatement [*object*]

cradlesnatcher○ /'kreɪdlsnætʃə(r)/ n **he's/she's a** ~ il/elle les prend au berceau○

craft /krɑːft, US kræft/
Ⓐ n ① (skill) (art-related) art m; (job-related) métier m; ② (handiwork) artisanat m; **arts and** ~**s** artisanat (d'art); ③ (boat) embarcation f
Ⓑ noun modifier [*exhibition, guild*] artisanal

craft: ~**sman** n (manual) artisan m; (artist) artiste m; ~**smanship** n (manual) dextérité f; (artistic) art m

crafty /'krɑːftɪ, US 'kræftɪ/ adj astucieux/-ieuse

crag /kræg/ n rocher m escarpé

craggy /'krægɪ/ adj ① [*mountain*] escarpé; ② [*features*] taillé à coups de serpe

cram /kræm/ (p prés etc **-mm-**)
Ⓐ vtr **to** ~ **sth into** enfoncer or fourrer○ qch dans [*bag, car*]; **to** ~ **sb into** entasser qn dans [*room*]; **to** ~ **a lot into one day** faire beaucoup de choses dans une seule journée; **to** ~ **three meetings into a morning** caser○ trois rendez-vous dans la matinée; ~**med full** plein à craquer
Ⓑ vi Sch bachoter (**for** pour)
Ⓒ v refl **to** ~ **oneself with** se bourrer de [*sweets*]

crammer○ /'kræmə(r)/ n GB (school) ≈ boîte f à bac○

cramp /kræmp/ n (pain) crampe f; **to have ~** GB ou **a ~** US avoir une crampe; **writer's ~** crampe de l'écrivain

Idiom **to ~ sb's style** faire perdre ses moyens à qn

cramped /kræmpt/ adj 1 [cell, house, office] exigu/-uë; **~ conditions** conditions d'exiguïté; **we're very ~ in here** nous sommes très à l'étroit ici; 2 [handwriting] en pattes de mouche

cranberry /'krænbəri, US -beri/ n canneberge f; **~ sauce** sauce f à la canneberge

crane /kreɪn/
A n Constr grue f
B vtr **to ~ one's neck** tendre le cou

cranium /'kreɪnɪəm/ n (pl **~s, -ia**) crâne m, boîte f crânienne

crank /kræŋk/ n 1 ᴼ(freak) fanatique mf, fana ᴼ mf; 2 Tech manivelle f

Phrasal verb
■ **crank up**: ▶ **~ up [sth], ~ [sth] up** lit remonter (à la manivelle)

cranky ᴼ /'kræŋkɪ/ adj 1 US (grumpy) grincheux/-euse; 2 (eccentric) loufoque ᴼ; 3 [machine] déglingué

cranny /'krænɪ/ n petite fente f

crapᴼ /kræp/
A n 1 (nonsense) conneries● fpl; 2 (of film, book etc) foutaise ᴼ f; 3 (faeces) merde● f; **to have a ~** chier●
B vi (p prés etc **-pp-**) chier●

crappyᴼ /'kræpɪ/ adj merdique ᴼ, nul/nulle ᴼ

crash /kræʃ/
A n 1 (noise) fracas m; 2 (accident) accident m; **car ~** accident de voiture; **train/air ~** catastrophe f ferroviaire/aérienne; **to have a ~** avoir un accident; 3 (of stock market) krach m; 4 Comput plantage ᴼ m
B vtr 1 (involve in accident) **to ~ the car** avoir un accident de voiture; **to ~ one's car into a bus** rentrer dans ou percuter un bus; 2 ᴼ(gatecrash) **to ~ a party** s'introduire dans une fête sans y être invité
C vi 1 (have accident) [car, plane] s'écraser; (collide) [vehicles, planes] se rentrer dedans, se percuter; **to ~ into sth** rentrer dans or percuter qch; 2 [share prices] s'effondrer; 3 (move loudly) faire du boucan ᴼ; 4 (fall) **to ~ to the ground** [cup, picture] se fracasser sur le sol; [tree] s'abattre; 5 ᴼComput [computer, system] planter ᴼ

Phrasal verb
■ **crash out** ᴼ (go to sleep) pioncer ᴼ; (collapse) s'écrouler ᴼ

crash barrier n glissière f de sécurité

crash: ~ course n cours m intensif; **~ diet** n régime m d'amaigrissement intensif; **~ helmet** n casque m

crashing /'kræʃɪŋ/ adj **to be a ~ bore** [person] être un/une sacré-e raseur/-euse m/f; [event] être barbant ᴼ à mourir

crash-land /ˌkræʃ'lænd/
A vtr **to ~ a plane** poser un avion en catastrophe
B vi atterrir en catastrophe

crash landing n atterrissage m en catastrophe

crass /kræs/ adj gen grossier/-ière; **~ ignorance** ignorance f crasse

crate /kreɪt/ n 1 (for bottles, china) caisse f; (for fruit, vegetables) cageot m; 2 ᴼ†(car) caisse ᴼ f; (plane) zinc ᴼ m

crater /'kreɪtə(r)/ n cratère m; (caused by explosion) entonnoir m

cravat /krə'væt/ n foulard m (pour homme)

crave /kreɪv/ vtr 1 (also **~ for**) avoir un besoin maladif de [drug]; avoir soif de [affection]; avoir envie de [food]; 2 sout solliciter [permission]

craving /'kreɪvɪŋ/ n (for drug) besoin m maladif (**for** de); (for fame, love) soif f (**for** de); (for food) envie f (**for** de)

crawl /krɔːl/
A n 1 Sport crawl m; 2 (slow pace) **at a ~** au pas; **to go at a ~** [vehicle] rouler au pas
B vi 1 [insect, snake, person] ramper; **to ~ in/out** entrer/sortir en rampant; **to ~ into bed** se traîner au lit; 2 (on all fours) [baby] marcher à quatre pattes; 3 (move slowly) [vehicle] rouler au pas; **to ~ along** avancer au pas; **to ~ down/up sth** descendre/monter lentement qch; 4 (pass slowly) [time] se traîner; 5 (seethe) **to be ~ing with** fourmiller de [insects, tourists]; 6 ᴼ(flatter) faire du lèche-bottes (**to** à)

Idiom **to make sb's skin** or **flesh ~** donner la chair de poule à qn ᴼ

crayfish /'kreɪfɪʃ/ n 1 (freshwater) écrevisse f; 2 (spiny lobster) langouste f

crayon /'kreɪən/
A n (wax) craie f grasse; (pencil) crayon m de couleur
B vtr colorier

craze /kreɪz/
A n vogue f; (passing) engouement m; **it's just a ~** c'est une toquade or une folie passagère; **to be the latest ~** faire fureur
B vi (also **~ over**) [china, glaze] se craqueler

crazed /kreɪzd/ adj 1 (mad) [animal, person] fou/folle; **power-~** ivre de pouvoir; 2 [china, glaze] craquelé

crazily /'kreɪzɪlɪ/ adv [veer] follement

crazy /'kreɪzɪ/
A adj 1 [person, scheme, price, speed] fou/folle; [behaviour, idea] insensé; **to go ~** devenir fou/folle; **~ with** fou/folle de [grief]; 2 (infatuated) **~ about** fou/folle de [person]; passionné de [activity]
B **like crazy** adv phr [shout, laugh, run] comme un fou/une folle; **they used to fight like ~** ils n'arrêtaient pas de se bagarrer

crazy: ~ golf ▶ p. 881 n GB mini-golf m; **~ paving** n GB pavage avec des pierres de forme irrégulière

creak /kriːk/
A n (of hinge) grincement m; (of floorboard) craquement m
B vi [hinge] grincer; [floorboard] craquer; **the door ~ed open** la porte s'ouvrit en grinçant

creaking /'kriːkɪŋ/
A n = creak A
B adj (épith) 1 lit [hinge, lift] grinçant; [floorboard] qui craque; 2 fig [regime, structure] déliquescent

creaky /'kriːkɪ/ adj 1 [door, hinge] grinçant; [leather] qui crisse; [joint, bone, floorboard] qui craque; 2 fig [alibi, policy] bancal ᴼ

cream /kriːm/ ▶ p. 752
A n (all contexts) crème f; **the ~ of society** fig la fine fleur de la société; **sun/shoe ~** crème solaire/à chaussures; **orange ~** chocolat fourré à l'orange
B noun modifier Culin [cake, bun] à la crème
C adj (colour) crème inv
D vtr Culin travailler [ingredients]; **~ed potatoes** purée f de pommes de terre

Idiom **to look like the cat that's got the ~** avoir l'air très content de soi

Phrasal verb
■ **cream off**: ▶ **~ off [sth], ~ [sth] off** prélever [best pupils]; ramasser [profits]

cream: ~ cheese n fromage m à tartiner; **~ cracker** n GB cracker m; **~ puff** n chou m à la crème; **~ soda** n soda m parfumé à la vanille; **~ tea** n GB thé m complet (accompagné de scones avec de la crème fraîche et de la confiture)

creamy /'kriːmɪ/ adj [texture] crémeux/-euse; [colour] (couleur) crème inv; [complexion] laiteux/-euse

crease /kriːs/
A n (intentional) pli m; (accidental) faux pli m
B vtr (crumple) froisser [paper, cloth]
C vi 1 [cloth] se froisser; 2 **her face ~d into a smile** son visage se dérida

creased /kriːst/ adj [cloth, paper] froissé; [brow] (with anxiety) inquiet

crease-resistant /'kriːsrɪsɪstənt/ adj infroissable

create /kriː'eɪt/
A vtr gen créer; lancer [fashion]; provoquer [interest, scandal, repercussion]; poser [problem]; faire [good impression]
B ᴼvi GB faire une scène

creation /kriː'eɪʃn/ n (all contexts) création f; **job/wealth ~** création d'emplois/de richesses

creative /kriː'eɪtɪv/ adj 1 (inventive) [person, solution] créatif/-ive; 2 (which creates) [process, imagination] créateur/-trice

creative writing n (school subject) ≈ composition f

creativity /ˌkriːeɪ'tɪvətɪ/ n créativité f

creator /kriː'eɪtə(r)/ n créateur/-trice m/f (**of** de)

creature /'kriːtʃə(r)/ n 1 (living being) créature f; **(the) poor ~!** le/la pauvre!; 2 (animal) animal m

creature comforts npl confort m matériel **Ȼ**; **to like one's ~** aimer son confort

crèche /kreʃ, kreɪʃ/ n GB (nursery) crèche f; (in shop etc) garderie f; **workplace** ~ crèche f d'entreprise

credence /'kriːdns/ n sout crédit m; **to give** ~ **to sth** (believe) accorder du crédit à qch; **to lend** ~ **to sth** donner du crédit à qch

credentials /krɪ'denʃlz/ npl **1** (qualifications) qualifications fpl; **to establish one's** ~ **as a writer** s'affirmer comme écrivain; **2** pièce f d'identité

credibility /ˌkredə'bɪlətɪ/ n crédibilité f; ~ **gap** écart m entre les apparences et la réalité

credible /'kredəbl/ adj (all contexts) crédible

credit /'kredɪt/

A n **1** (resultant praise) mérite m (**for** de); **to get/take the** ~ se voir attribuer/s'attribuer le mérite (**for** de); **2** (subject of pride) **to be a** ~ **to sb/sth** faire honneur à qn/qch; **it does you** ~ c'est tout à votre honneur; **she has two medals to her** ~ elle a deux médailles à son actif; **3** (recognition) **he is more intelligent than he is given** ~ **for** il est plus intelligent qu'on ne le croit généralement; ~ **where** ~ **is due** il faut en convenir; **4** (credence) crédit m; **5** Comm crédit m; **on** ~ à crédit; **to live on** ~ vivre de crédits; **to give sb** ~ faire crédit à qn; **her** ~ **is good** elle a une réputation de bonne payeuse; **to be £25 in** ~ être créditeur de 25 livres sterling

B **credits** npl Cin, TV générique m

C vtr **1** **to** ~ **sb with** attribuer à qn [achievement]; **to** ~ **sb with a little intelligence** ne pas prendre qn pour un imbécile; **2** créditer [account] (**with** de); **to** ~ **sth to an account** porter qch sur un compte; **3** (believe) croire; **would you** ~ **it!** le croirais-tu!

creditable /'kredɪtəbl/ adj honorable

credit: ~ **account**, **C/A** n Comm compte m personnel; ~ **balance** n solde m créditeur; ~ **card** n Comm carte f de crédit; ~ **control** n encadrement m du crédit; ~ **facilities** npl facilités fpl de crédit; ~ **freeze** n Econ gel m des crédits; ~ **limit** n limite f de crédit; ~ **line** n Comm ligne f de crédit; ~ **note** n Comm avoir m

creditor /'kredɪtə(r)/ n Comm créancier/-ière m/f

credit side n **on the** ~... le bon côté des choses, c'est que...

credit: ~ **squeeze** n Econ restrictions fpl de crédits; ~ **terms** npl Comm conditions fpl de crédit; ~ **transfer** n virement m

creditworthiness /'kredɪtwɜːðmɪs/ n solvabilité f

creditworthy /'kredɪtwɜːðɪ/ adj Fin solvable

credulity /krɪ'djuːlətɪ, US -'duː-/ n crédulité f; **to strain sb's** ~ aller trop loin

credulous /'kredjʊləs, US -dʒə-/ adj crédule, naïf/naïve

creed /kriːd/ n (religious persuasion) croyance f; (opinions) principes mpl, credo m

creek /kriːk, US also krɪk/ n **1** GB (from sea) bras m de mer; (from river) bras m mort; **2** (stream) ruisseau m

⌜Idiom⌝ **to be up the** ~ **(without a paddle)**⁰ être mal barré⁰

creep /kriːp/

A n⁰ **1** GB (flatterer) lèche-bottes mf inv; **2** (repellent person) raclure⁰ f

B vi (prét, pp **crept**) **1** (furtively) **to** ~ **in/out** entrer/sortir à pas de loup; **to** ~ **under sth** se glisser sous qch; **2** (slowly) **to** ~ **forward** ou **along** [vehicle] avancer lentement; [insect, cat] ramper; **3** [plant] (horizontally) ramper; (climb) grimper

⌜Idiom⌝ **to give sb the** ~**s**⁰ donner la chair de poule à qn⁰

⌜Phrasal verbs⌝

  ■ **creep in** **1** [error] se glisser; **2** [feeling] intervenir
  ■ **creep up** [inflation, unemployment] grimper; **to** ~ **up on sb** lit s'approcher de qn à pas de loup; fig prendre qn par surprise

creeper /'kriːpə(r)/ n (in jungle) liane f; (climbing plant) plante f grimpante; **the** ~ les plantes grimpantes

creeping /'kriːpɪŋ/ adj [change, menace] insidieux/-ieuse; [plant, animal] rampant

creepy⁰ /'kriːpɪ/ adj [film] glaçant; [feeling] déplaisant; [person] affreux/-euse⁰

creepy-crawly⁰ /ˌkriːpɪ'krɔːlɪ/ n bestiole⁰ f

cremate /krɪ'meɪt/ vtr incinérer

cremation /krɪ'meɪʃn/ n (ceremony) crémation f; (practice) incinération f

crematorium /ˌkremə'tɔːrɪəm/ GB n crématorium m

crepe, **crêpe** /kreɪp/ n (all contexts) crêpe m

crepe: ~ **bandage** n bande f Velpeau®; ~ **paper** n papier m crépon; ~ **soles** npl semelles fpl de crêpe

crept /krept/ prét, pp ▸ **creep**

crescendo /krɪ'ʃendəʊ/ n Mus crescendo m inv; fig **to reach a** ~ [campaign] atteindre son apogée; [noise, protest] atteindre son paroxysme

crescent /'kresnt/ n **1** (shape) croissant m; **2** rangée de maisons en arc de cercle

crescent moon n croissant m de (la) lune

cress /kres/ n cresson m

crest /krest/ n **1** (ridge) crête f; **2** (coat of arms) armoiries fpl

⌜Idiom⌝ **to be on the** ~ **of a wave** être en période de réussite

crested /krestɪd/ adj [bird] huppé; [stationery] armorié

crestfallen /'krestfɔːlən/ adj déconfit

Crete /kriːt/ ▸ p. 954 pr n Crète f

crevice /'krevɪs/ n fissure f

crew /kruː/

A prét ▸ **crow**

B n **1** Aviat, Naut équipage m; **2** (rowing) équipe f; **3** Cin, TV équipe f; **4** ⁰péj ou hum (gang) bande f

C vi Naut **to** ~ **for sb** être l'équipier de qn

crewcut n coupe f (de cheveux) en brosse

crew neck sweater n pull m ras du cou

crib /krɪb/

A n **1** (cot) lit m d'enfant; **2** GB (Nativity) crèche f; **3** (borrowing) emprunt m; **4** Sch (illicit aid) antisèche⁰ f; (translation) traduction f

B vi (p prés etc **-bb-**) gen faire des emprunts; Sch copier (**from** sur)

cribbage /'krɪbɪdʒ/ n: jeu de cartes

crick /krɪk/

A n a ~ **in one's back** un tour de reins; **a** ~ **in one's neck** un torticolis

B vtr **to** ~ **one's back** se faire un tour de reins; **to** ~ **one's neck** attraper un torticolis

cricket /'krɪkɪt/ ▸ p. 881 n **1** Zool grillon m; **2** Sport cricket m

⌜Idiom⌝ **it's not** ~ ce n'est pas franc-jeu

cricketer /'krɪkɪtə(r)/ n joueur m de cricket

crime /kraɪm/

A n **1** (offence) (minor) délit m; (serious) crime m (**against** contre); **the** ~ **of murder/theft** le meurtre/vol; **a** ~ **of violence** un crime violent; **2** Ȼ (criminal activity) criminalité f; **3** fig **it's a** ~ **to waste food** c'est un crime de gaspiller la nourriture

B noun modifier [fiction, novel, writing] policier/-ière; [wave, rate] de criminalité

crime: ~ **of passion** n crime m passionnel; ~ **prevention** n lutte f contre le crime

criminal /'krɪmɪnl/

A n criminel/-elle m/f

B adj **1** criminel/-elle; **2** fig **it's** ~! c'est un crime!

criminal charges npl charges fpl; **to face** ~ être sous le coup d'une inculpation

criminal: ~ **inquiry** n enquête f criminelle; **Criminal Investigation Department**, **CID** n GB ≈ police f judiciaire; ~ **justice** n justice f pénale; ~ **law** n droit m pénal

criminally insane adj dément; **to be** ~ être en état de démence

criminal: ~ **offence** n délit m; ~ **proceedings** npl poursuites fpl judiciaires

criminal record n casier m judiciaire; **to have a/no** ~ avoir un casier judiciaire chargé/vierge

criminology /ˌkrɪmɪ'nɒlədʒɪ/ n criminologie f

crimp /krɪmp/ vtr friser [hair]; pincer [pastry]; plisser [fabric]

crimson /'krɪmzn/ ▸ p. 752

A n cramoisi m

B adj pourpre; **to go** ou **blush** ~ devenir cramoisi

cringe /krɪndʒ/
A vi **1** (physically) avoir un mouvement de recul; **2** (with embarrassment) avoir envie de rentrer sous terre; **3** (grovel) se comporter de manière servile; **4** (in disgust) **it makes me** ∼ ça me hérisse
B cringing pres p adj servile

crinkle /'krɪŋkl/
A n pli m
B vi [fabric] se froisser; [paper] se plisser

crinkly /'krɪŋklɪ/ adj [hair] frisé; [paper, material] gaufré

cripple /'krɪpl/
A n **1** (lame) injur impotent/-e m/f; **2** (inadequate) **emotional** ∼ personne f bloquée sur le plan émotionnel
B vtr **1** (physically) estropier; ∼**d for life** infirme à vie; **2** fig paralyser [country, industry]; désemparer [ship]; mettre [qch] hors d'usage [vehicle]

crippled /'krɪpld/ adj **1** (physically) [person] impotent; **to be** ∼ **with sth** être perclus de qch; **2** fig (by debt) écrasé (**by** par); [country, industry] paralysé (**by** par); [vehicle] hors d'usage; [ship] désemparé

crippling /'krɪplɪŋ/ adj [disease] invalidant; [taxes, debts] écrasant; [strike, effect] paralysant

crisis /'kraɪsɪs/ n (pl **-ses**) crise f (**in** dans; **over** à cause de); **cabinet/cash** ∼ crise au sein du gouvernement/de trésorerie; **midlife** ∼ crise des cinquante ans; **to have reached a** ∼ [people] être en crise; **to reach a** ∼ [situation] devenir critique; **at** ∼ **level** à un niveau critique

crisp /krɪsp/
A n GB (also **potato** ∼) chip f
B adj [batter, biscuit] croustillant; [fruit] croquant; [garment] frais/fraîche; [banknote, snow] craquant; [air] vif/vive; [morning] froid et piquant; [order, words] bref/brève; [manner] brusque

(Idiom) **to be burnt to a** ∼○ être carbonisé

crispbread /'krɪspbred/ n GB pain m grillé suédois

crisply /'krɪsplɪ/ adv [ironed] fraîchement; [speak] brusquement

crispy /'krɪspɪ/ adj croustillant

crisscross /'krɪskrɒs, US -krɔːs/
A adj en croisillons
B adv en croisillons; **to run** ∼ s'entrecroiser
C vtr sillonner

criteria /kraɪ'tɪərɪə/ npl ▸ **criterion**

criterion /kraɪ'tɪərɪən/ n (pl **-ia**) critère m (**for** de)

critic /'krɪtɪk/ ▸ p. 1181 n (reviewer) critique m; (opponent) détracteur/-trice m/f

critical /'krɪtɪkl/ adj [point, condition, remark] critique; [stage] crucial; [moment] décisif/-ive; [acclaim] de la critique; **to be** ∼ **of sb/sth** critiquer qn/qch; **the film was a** ∼ **success** le film a été acclamé par la critique; **to take a** ∼ **look at sth** examiner qch d'un œil critique

critically /'krɪtɪklɪ/ adv **1** (using judgment) [compare, examine] d'un œil critique; **2** (with disapproval) [view] sévèrement; [speak] avec animosité (**of, about** de); **3** (seriously) [ill] très gravement; ∼ **important** capital; ∼ **flawed** profondément vicié

criticism /'krɪtɪsɪzəm/ n **1** C (remark, reproach) critique f; **2** C (study) étude f critique (**of** sur); **3** ₵ (analysis) critique f; **literary** ∼ critique f littéraire

criticize /'krɪtɪsaɪz/ vtr **1** (find fault) critiquer; **to** ∼ **sb for sth** reprocher qch à qn; **to** ∼ **sb for doing** reprocher à qn de faire; **2** critiquer [poem etc]

croak /krəʊk/
A n (of frog) coassement m
B vtr dire [qch] d'une voix rauque
C vi **1** (frog) coasser; **2** ◐(die) crever◐

Croatia /krəʊ'eɪʃə/ ▸ p. 774 pr n Croatie f

crochet /'krəʊʃeɪ, US krəʊ'ʃeɪ/
A n (art) crochet m
B vtr faire [qch] au crochet; **a** ∼(**ed**) **sweater** un pull au crochet
C vi faire du crochet

crock /krɒk/ n **1** ○(car) tacot○ m; (person) croulant/-e○ m/f; **2** (shard) tesson m

crockery /'krɒkərɪ/ n vaisselle f

crocodile /'krɒkədaɪl/
A n **1** (animal, leather) crocodile m; **2** GB (line) rang m par deux
B noun modifier [bag] en crocodile, en croco○

(Idiom) **to shed** ∼ **tears** verser des larmes de crocodile

croft /krɒft, US krɔːft/ n petite ferme f (en Écosse)

crone /krəʊn/ n péj vieille bique f péj

crony /'krəʊnɪ/ n péj (petit/-e) copain/copine m/f

crook /krʊk/ n (rogue) escroc m; (of arm) creux m; (shepherd's) houlette f; (bishop's) crosse f

(Idioms) **by hook or by** ∼ coûte que coûte; **to** ∼ **one's little finger** lever le petit doigt

crooked /'krʊkɪd/
A adj **1** (with a bend) [line] brisé; [limb] tors; [back] difforme; [stick, finger] crochu; **a** ∼ **smile** un sourire en coin; **2** (off-centre) de travers; [house] de guingois inv; **3** ○(dishonest) malhonnête
B adv de travers

croon /kruːn/ vtr, vi chantonner

crop /krɒp/
A n **1** (type of produce) culture f; **a cereal** ∼ une culture céréalière; **2** (growing in field) (souvent pl) culture f; **the** ∼**s will fail** les cultures seront perdues; **3** (harvest) récolte f; **the rice** ∼ la récolte de riz; **4** fig (of medals) moisson f; (of students, films) cuvée f; **the cream of the** ∼ les meilleurs du lot; **5** fig hum (of weeds, spots) paquet○ m; **6** (haircut) coupe f courte; **7** (whip) cravache f
B vtr (p prés etc **-pp-**) couper [qch] court [hair]; brouter [grass]; rogner [photograph]

(Phrasal verb)

■ **crop up** [matter, problem] surgir; [name] être mentionné; [opportunity] se présenter; **something's** ∼**ped up** il y a un contretemps

cropped /krɒpt/ adj [hair] coupé court; [top] court

crop: ∼ **rotation** n rotation f des cultures; ∼ **spraying** n pulvérisation f de pesticides

croquet /'krəʊkeɪ, US krəʊ'keɪ/ ▸ p. 881 n croquet m

cross /krɒs, US krɔːs/
A n **1** (shape) croix f; **the Cross** Relig la Croix; **to put a** ∼ **against** cocher [name, item]; **'put a** ∼ **in the box'** 'faites une croix dans la case', 'cochez la case'; **2** (hybrid) croisement m (**between** entre); **a** ∼ **between X and Y** fig un mélange de X et de Y; **3** (in sewing) **on the** ∼ dans le biais
B adj **1** (angry) fâché; **to be** ∼ **with sb** être fâché contre qn; **to be** ∼ **about sth** être agacé par qch; **to get** ∼ se fâcher (**with** contre); **to make sb** ∼ mettre qn en colère, agacer qn; **2** (contrary to general direction) [breeze] contraire
C vtr **1** (go across by moving) lit traverser [road, room]; traverser, passer [river]; franchir [border, line, mountains]; (span) [bridge] franchir, enjamber; (have route across) [road, railway line, river] traverser; fig dépasser [limit, boundary]; **it** ∼**ed his mind that** il lui est venu à l'esprit or l'idée que; **to** ∼ **the class divide** surmonter la barrière des classes; **to** ∼ **the bounds of decency** dépasser les limites de la décence; **2** (intersect with) couper; **to** ∼ **each other** se couper; **3** (place in shape of a cross) croiser; **to** ∼ **one's legs/arms** croiser les jambes/bras; **4** Biol, Bot, Zool croiser (**with** avec); **5** (oppose) contrarier [person]; **6** (draw line across) barrer [cheque]
D vi **1** (also ∼ **over**) **to** ∼ **to North America** aller en Amérique; **to** ∼ **into Italy** passer en Italie; **2** (intersect) se croiser; [lines] se couper; **3** [letters] se croiser
E v refl **to** ∼ **oneself** faire le signe de la croix
F crossed pp adj Telecom [line] brouillé

(Idioms) **we seem to have got our wires** ∼**ed** il semble y avoir un malentendu (quelque part); **to have a** ou **one's** ∼ **to bear** porter sa croix

(Phrasal verbs)

■ **cross off**: ▸ ∼ [sth/sb] **off**, ∼ **off** [sth/sb] barrer, rayer [name, thing]

■ **cross out**: ▸ ∼ **out** [sth], ∼ [sth] **out** rayer, barrer [qch]

cross: ∼**bar** n gen barre f; ∼**-border** adj transfrontalier/-ière m; ∼**bow** n arbalète f; ∼**bred** n, adj hybride (m)

crossbreed /'krɒsbriːd, US 'krɔːs-/
A n (animal) hybride m; (person) injur métis/-isse m/f
B vtr (prét, pp **-bred**) croiser [animals]; hybrider [plants]

cross-Channel adj trans-Manche

cross-check
A /'krɒtʃek, US 'krɔːs-/ n revérification f
B /ˌkrɒs'tʃek, US ˌkrɔːs-/ vtr, vi revérifier
cross-country /ˌkrɒs'kʌntrɪ, US ˌkrɔːs-/
A ▸ p. 881 n Sport (in running) cross m; (in skiing) ski m de fond
B adj **1** Sport (running) [race, champion] de cross; [runner] de fond; (skiing) [skiing, skier] de fond; **2** (across fields) [hike, run] à travers champs; **3** (across a country) [route] qui traverse le pays
C adv [walk, hike] à travers champs
cross: ~**-court** adj Sport [shot, volley] droit croisé;
~**-cultural** adj inter-culturel/-elle; ~**current** n contre-courant m; ~**-curricular** adj multidiscipli-naire; ~**-dresser** n travesti/-e m/f; ~**-examination** n contre-interrogatoire m
cross-examine /ˌkrɒsɪg'zæmɪn, US ˌkrɔːs-/ vtr Jur faire subir un contre-interrogatoire à; gen interroger
cross-eyed /'krɒsaɪd, US 'krɔːs-/ adj [person] atteint de strabisme; **to be** ~ loucher, avoir un strabisme
crossfire /'krɒsfaɪə(r), US 'krɔːs-/ n feux mpl croisés; **to be** ou **get caught in the** ~ lit, fig être pris entre deux feux
crossing /'krɒsɪŋ, US 'krɔːsɪŋ/ n **1** (journey over water) tra-versée f; **2** (area of road) passage m (pour) piétons, passage m clouté; (level crossing) passage m à niveau
crossing-out /ˌkrɒsɪŋ'aʊt, US ˌkrɔːs-/ n (pl ~**s-out**) rature f
cross-legged /ˌkrɒs'legɪd, US ˌkrɔːs-/
A adj assis en tailleur
B adv [sit] en tailleur
crossly /'krɒslɪ, US 'krɔːslɪ/ adv avec humeur
crossover /'krɒsəʊvə(r), US 'krɔːs-/ adj [straps] croisé
cross: ~**-party** adj Pol [initiative] commun à plusieurs partis; [group] comprenant des membres de différents partis; ~**patch**○ n grognon○ mf
cross-purposes /ˌkrɒs'pɜːpəsɪz, US ˌkrɔːs-/ npl **we are at** ~ il y a un malentendu; (disagreement) nous sommes en désaccord; **to be at** ~ se comprendre mal
cross-question /ˌkrɒs'kwestʃən, US ˌkrɔːs-/ vtr faire subir un interrogatoire à [person]
cross-reference /ˌkrɒs'refrəns, US ˌkrɔːs-/
A n renvoi m (**to** à)
B vtr mettre un renvoi sous [entry, item] (**to** à)
crossroads /'krɒsrəʊdz, US 'krɔːs-/ n carrefour m
cross-section /ˌkrɒs'sekʃn, US ˌkrɔːs-/ n **1** lit coupe f transversale; **2** fig (selection) échantillon m (**of** de)
cross: ~**-town** adj US qui traverse la ville; ~**wind** n vent m de travers
crosswise /'krɒswaɪz, US 'krɔːs-/ adj, adv en diagonale
crossword /'krɒswɜːd, US 'krɔːs-/ n (also ~ **puzzle**) mots mpl croisés
crotch /krɒtʃ/ n **1** Anat entrecuisse m; **2** (in trousers) entre-jambe m
crotchet /'krɒtʃɪt/ n GB Mus noire f
crotchety /'krɒtʃɪtɪ/ adj grincheux/-euse
crouch /kraʊtʃ/ vi (also ~ **down**) [person] s'accroupir; [person, animal] (in order to hide) se tapir; (for attack) se ramasser
croupier /'kruːpɪə(r)/ ▸ p. 1181 n croupier m
crouton /'kruːtɒn/ n croûton m
crow /krəʊ/
A n corbeau m
B vi **1** (exult) exulter; **it's nothing to** ~ **about** il n'y a pas de quoi exulter; **2** [baby] gazouiller; **3** (prét **crowed** ou **crew**†) [cock] chanter
(Idiom) **as the** ~ **flies** à vol d'oiseau
crowbar /'krəʊbɑː(r)/ n pince-monseigneur f
crowd /kraʊd/
A n **1** (mass of people) gen foule f; Sport spectateurs mpl; (audi-ence) public m; **a** ~ **of 10,000** gen une foule de 10 000 per-sonnes; Sport une foule de 10 000 spectateurs; ~**s of people** une foule de gens; **a** ~ **gathered at the scene** un attroupement s'est formé sur les lieux; **we are hoping for a big** ~ nous espérons que le public viendra nombreux; **2** ○(group) bande f; **the usual** ~ toujours la même bande
B vtr **1** (fill) se presser sur [pavement, platform]; s'entasser sur [beach]; **tourists** ~**ed the bars** les bars étaient pleins de

touristes; **2** (squash) entasser [people, furniture] (**into** dans); **to** ~ **as much as possible into a visit to Paris** voir le plus de choses possible quand on est à Paris; **3** (fill to excess) encombrer [room, house] (**with** de); **4** ○(put pressure on) har-celer; **don't** ~ **me!** arrête de me harceler!
C vi lit **to** ~ **into** s'entasser dans [room, lift, vehicle]; **to** ~ **onto** s'entasser dans [bus, train]; **to** ~ (**up**) **against** se presser contre [barrier]
(Phrasal verbs)
■ **crowd around, crowd round**: ▸ ~ **around** s'attrou-per; ▸ ~ **around [sth]** se presser autour de
■ **crowd in**: ▸ ~ **in** [people, animals] s'entasser; [thoughts, memories] se presser
crowd control n contrôle m de la foule
crowded /'kraʊdɪd/ adj **1** (place) plein de monde; (jam-packed) bondé; **to be** ~ **with** être plein de [people, cars]; **2** (busy) [schedule] chargé
crowd: ~**-puller** n (event) grosse attraction f; ~ **scene** n Cin, Theat scène f de foule
crowing /'krəʊɪŋ/ n **1** (of cock) cocoricos mpl; **2** (boasting) vantardises fpl
crown /kraʊn/
A n **1** (of monarch) couronne f; **the Crown** la Couronne f; **2** (top) (of hill) crête f; (of hat) fond m; (of head) crâne m; **3** (on tooth) couronne f; **4** GB (old coin) ancienne pièce de monnaie
B vtr **1** couronner; **to** ~ **sb emperor** couronner qn empe-reur; **2** (bring to worthy end) couronner; **to** ~ **it all** pour couronner le tout; **3** couronner [tooth]
crown: ~ **colony** n GB Pol colonie f britannique; **Crown court** n GB Jur ≈ cour f d'assises; ~**ed head** n Pol tête f couronnée
crowning /'kraʊnɪŋ/
A n couronnement m
B adj [irony] suprême; [moment] grand; ~ **achievement** (of artist etc) chef d'œuvre m
crowning glory n **1** (achievement) couronnement m; **2** (hair) **her hair is her** ~ sa chevelure la rend resplen-dissante
crown: ~ **jewels** npl joyaux mpl de la Couronne; ~ **prince** n prince m héritier
crow: ~**'s feet** npl (on face) pattes-d'oie fpl; ~**'s nest** n nid m de pie
crucial /'kruːʃl/ adj crucial; **it is** ~ **that** il est essentiel que (+ subj)
crucially /'kruːʃəlɪ/ adv ~ **important** d'une importance cruciale
crucifix /'kruːsɪfɪks/ n crucifix m
crucifixion /ˌkruːsɪ'fɪkʃn/ n crucifixion f
crucify /'kruːsɪfaɪ/ vtr **1** (execute) crucifier; **2** ○(criticize, defeat) démolir○
crude /kruːd/
A n (oil) pétrole m brut
B adj **1** (rough) [method] rudimentaire; [estimate] approximatif/-ive; **2** (coarse) [person, manners] fruste; [attempt, expression] grossier/-ière; **3** (vulgar, rude) [language, joke] grossier/-ière; [person] vulgaire; **4** (unprocessed) [rubber, statistic] brut; ~ **oil** pétrole m brut
crudely /'kruːdlɪ/ adv **1** (simply) [describe, express] de manière schématique; ~ **speaking,...** grosso modo...; **2** (roughly) [painted, made] grossièrement; [assembled] som-mairement
crudity /'kruːdɪtɪ/ n (vulgarity) grossièreté f
cruel /'kruːəl/ adj cruel/-elle; [winter, climate] rigoureux/-euse; **a** ~ **blow** un coup très dur
(Idiom) **you have to be** ~ **to be kind** qui aime bien châtie bien Prov
cruelly /'kruːəlɪ/ adv cruellement
cruelty /'kruːəltɪ/ n cruauté f (**to** envers)
cruet /'kruːɪt/ n GB (also ~ **stand**) service m à condi-ments
cruise /kruːz/
A n croisière f; **to go on a** ~ faire une croisière
B vtr **1** (by boat) [tourist] faire une croisière sur le Nil/en Méditerranée; **2** [driver, taxi] par-courir [street, city]
C vi **1** [liner, tourist] faire une croisière (**in** en; **on** sur; **along** le long de; **around** aux abords de); **2** [plane] **to** ~ **at 10,000 metres** voler à une altitude de croisière de 10 000

mètres; **3** [car] **to ∼ at 80 km/h** rouler à une vitesse de croisière de 80 km/h; **4** °**to ∼ to victory** triompher sans peine

cruise: ∼ liner n paquebot m; **∼ missile** n missile m de croisière

cruiser /'kru:zə(r)/ n petit bateau m de croisière

cruising speed n vitesse f de croisière

crumb /krʌm/ n **1** (of food) miette f; **2** (tiny amount) **a ∼ of** une bribe de [information, conversation]; **a ∼ of comfort** une maigre consolation

crumble /'krʌmbl/
A vtr (also **∼ up**) émietter [bread]; réduire [qch] en poussière [soil]
B vi **1** lit [rock, façade] s'effriter; [building] se délabrer; [cliff] s'ébouler; **2** fig [relationship, economy] se désagréger; [empire] s'écrouler; [opposition] s'effondrer

crumbling /'krʌmblɪŋ/ adj **1** lit [building, façade] délabré; **2** [economy, empire] qui s'effondre

crumbly /'krʌmblɪ/ adj [bread, cheese] qui s'émiette facilement; [pastry, earth] friable

crummy° /'krʌmɪ/ adj **1** (substandard) minable°; **2** US (unwell) **to feel ∼** se sentir patraque°

crumpet /'krʌmpɪt/ n Culin petit pain spongieux à griller

crumple /'krʌmpl/
A vtr froisser [paper]; **to ∼ sth into a ball** rouler qch en boule
B vi **1** (crush up) [paper, garment] se froisser; **his face ∼d** ses traits se sont décomposés; **the car ∼s on impact** la voiture se plie sous le choc; **2** (collapse) [opposition, resistance] s'effondrer

(Phrasal verb)
■ **crumple up**: ▸ ∼ **[sth] up**, ∼ **up [sth]** froisser

crunch /krʌntʃ/
A n **1** (sound) (of footsteps) crissement m; (of gears, bone) craquement m; **2** US Econ (squeeze) crise f
B vtr **1** (eat) croquer [apple, biscuit]; **2** (making noise) **she ∼ed her way across the gravel** le gravier crissait sous ses pas

(Idioms) **when** ou **if it comes to the ∼** au moment crucial; **the ∼ came when** le moment critique est arrivé lorsque

crunchy /'krʌntʃɪ/ adj [vegetables, biscuits] croquant

crusade /kru:'seɪd/
A n **1** (also **Crusade**) Hist croisade f; **2** (campaign) croisade f
B vi (campaign) être en croisade

crusader /kru:'seɪdə(r)/ n **1** Hist croisé m; **2** (campaigner) militant/-e m/f (**for** pour)

crusading /kru:'seɪdɪŋ/ adj combatif/-ive

crush /krʌʃ/
A n **1** (crowd) bousculade f; **2** GB (drink) **orange/lemon ∼** boisson f à l'orange/au citron
B vtr **1** fig écraser [enemy, uprising]; étouffer [protest]; anéantir [hopes]; (by ridicule) anéantir [person]; **to be ∼ed by** être accablé par [sorrow, defeat]; **2** (squash) écraser [can, fruit, person, vehicle] (**against** contre); broyer [part of body]; **to be ∼ed to death** (by vehicle) se faire écraser; (by masonry) être écrasé sous les décombres; **3** (crease) chiffonner [garment, fabric]

crushing /'krʌʃɪŋ/ adj [defeat, weight] écrasant; [blow] percutant; **a ∼ setback** un revers cuisant

crust /krʌst/ n croûte f; **the earth's ∼** l'écorce f terrestre; **he'd share his last ∼** il donnerait sa chemise

crustacean /krʌ'steɪʃn/ n crustacé m

crusty /'krʌstɪ/ adj **1** [bread] croustillant; **2** (irritable) grincheux/-euse

crutch /krʌtʃ/ n **1** (prop) lit, fig béquille f; **to be on ∼es** marcher avec des béquilles; **2** GB (crotch) Anat entrecuisse m; (in trousers) entrejambe m

crux /krʌks/ n **the ∼ of the matter** ou **problem** le point crucial

cry /kraɪ/
A n **1** (of person, bird) cri m; **nobody heard his cries for help** personne ne l'a entendu crier au secours; **a ∼ for help** un appel à l'aide; **there were cries of 'shame!'** les gens criaient au scandale; **there have been cries for reprisals** on a réclamé des représailles; **2** (of hounds) **to be in full ∼**

[pack] donner de la voix; **the press were in full ∼** fig la presse était sur la brèche
B vtr **1** (shout) **'no!' he cried** 'non!' cria-t-il; **2** verser [larmes]
C vi **1** (weep) pleurer (**about** à cause de; **with** de); **he was ∼ing for his mother** il réclamait sa mère en pleurant; **to ∼ with laughter** rire aux larmes; **2** (call out) = **cry out**

(Idioms) **it's a far ∼ from the days when** il est loin le temps où; **this house is a far ∼ from our last one** cette maison est sans comparaison avec celle que nous avions avant; **to ∼ one's eyes** ou **heart out** pleurer à chaudes larmes

(Phrasal verbs)
■ **cry off** GB: (cancel) se décommander
■ **cry out** (with pain, grief) pousser un cri or des cris; (call) crier, s'écrier; **to ∼ out to sb** interpeller qn; **to ∼ out for** (need) avoir grand besoin de [help, reform]

crying /'kraɪɪŋ/
A n **¢** pleurs mpl
B adj (blatant) [need] urgent; **it's a ∼ shame!** c'est une honte!

crypt /krɪpt/ n crypte f

cryptic /'krɪptɪk/ adj (mysterious) énigmatique

cryptically /'krɪptɪklɪ/ adv [say, speak] de façon énigmatique; **∼ worded** en termes sibyllins

crystal /'krɪstl/ n cristal m; (watchface) verre m

(Idiom) **as clear as ∼** [sound] cristallin; [explanation] clair comme de l'eau de roche

crystal ball n boule f de cristal; **to look into one's ∼** fig essayer de deviner l'avenir

crystal clear adj **1** [water, sound] cristallin; **2** [explanation] clair comme de l'eau de roche; **let me make it ∼** que cela soit bien clair

crystal gazing n tentatives fpl pour prévoir l'avenir

crystallize /'krɪstəlaɪz/
A vtr fig déterminer [attitude]; cristalliser [divisions]
B vi **1** lit se cristalliser; **2** fig [ideas] se concrétiser
C **crystallized** pp adj [fruit, ginger] confit

CS gas n GB gaz m lacrymogène

CT US Post abrév écrite = **Connecticut**

cub /kʌb/ n Zool petit m

Cuba /'kju:bə/ ▸ p. 774 pr n Cuba f (never with article)

cubby-hole° /'kʌbɪhəʊl/ n **1** (cramped space) réduit m; (snug room) piaule° f; **2** (storage space) cagibi° m

cube /kju:b/
A n cube m; **sugar ∼** sucre m; **ice ∼** glaçon m
B vtr **1** Math élever [qch] au cube; **2** Culin couper [qch] en cubes

cubic /'kju:bɪk/ ▸ p. 1311, p. 723 adj **1** (form) cubique; **2** (measurement) [metre, centimetre] cube inv

cubicle /'kju:bɪkl/ n (in changing room) cabine f; (in public toilets) cabinet m

cubism /'kju:bɪzəm/ n cubisme m

cubist /'kju:bɪst/ n, adj cubiste (mf)

cub reporter ▸ p. 1181 n journaliste mf stagiaire

cuckoo /'kuku:/ n coucou m

cuckoo clock n pendule f à coucou

cucumber /'kju:kʌmbə(r)/ n concombre m

(Idiom) **to be as cool as a ∼** être d'un calme absolu

cud /kʌd/ n **to chew the ∼** lit, fig ruminer

cuddle /'kʌdl/
A n câlin m; **to give sb a ∼** faire un câlin à qn
B vtr câliner

(Phrasal verb)
■ **cuddle up** se blottir (**against** contre)

cuddly /'kʌdlɪ/ adj (sweet) adorable; (soft) doux/douce

cuddly toy n GB peluche f

cue /kju:/ n **1** lit Theat (line) réplique f précédente; (action) signal m; TV, Radio, Cin signal m; **on ∼** (after word) après la réplique; (after action) après le signal; **to take one's ∼ from sb** fig faire comme qn; **2** Sport queue f de billard

cuff /kʌf/
A n **1** (at wrist) gen poignet m; (on shirt) manchette f; **2** US (on trousers) revers m; **3** (blow) tape f
B vtr (on head) calotter°

(Idiom) **to speak off the ∼** faire un discours au pied levé; **an off-the-∼ remark** une remarque impromptue

cuff link n bouton m de manchette

cuisine /kwɪˈziːn/ n cuisine f; **haute** ~ la grande cuisine

cul-de-sac /ˈkʌldəsæk/ n (street) impasse f, cul-de-sac m; (on roadsign) voie f sans issue

culinary /ˈkʌlɪnərɪ, US -nerɪ/ adj culinaire

cull /kʌl/ vtr **1** (kill) massacrer [seal, whale]; **2** (gather) puiser [information] (**from sth** dans qch)

culminate /ˈkʌlmɪneɪt/ vtr aboutir (**in** à)

culmination /ˌkʌlmɪˈneɪʃn/ n couronnement m (**of** de)

culottes /kjuːˈlɒts/ npl jupe-culotte f

culpable /ˈkʌlpəbl/ adj coupable (**for** de)

culpable homicide n Jur homicide m volontaire

culprit /ˈkʌlprɪt/ n **1** (guilty person) coupable mf; **2** (main cause) principal/-e responsable mf

cult /kʌlt/
A n culte m; (contemporary religion) secte f
B noun modifier **a** ~ **band/film** un groupe-/film-culte; **to be a** ~ **figure** faire l'objet d'un culte

cultivate /ˈkʌltɪveɪt/ vtr **1** lit cultiver; **2** fig **to** ~ **one's image** cultiver son image; **to** ~ **one's mind** se cultiver l'esprit; **to** ~ **the right people** cultiver de bonnes relations

cultivation /ˌkʌltɪˈveɪʃn/ n Agric culture f

cultural /ˈkʌltʃərəl/ adj culturel/-elle

cultural attaché ▸ p. 1181 n attaché/-e m/f culturel/-elle

culturally /ˈkʌltʃərəlɪ/ adv [similar, different] culturellement; ~ **diverse** qui présente une variété de cultures

culture /ˈkʌltʃə(r)/ n **1** **C** (art and thought) culture f; **to bring** ~ **to the masses** mettre la culture à la portée de tous; **2** (way of life) culture f; **street** ~ culture qui vient de la rue; **drug** ~ l'univers m de la drogue; **3** (cultivation) culture f; **4** (of bacteria) culture f (bactérienne)

culture-bound /ˈkʌltʃəbaʊnd/ adj culturel/-elle

cultured /ˈkʌltʃəd/ adj cultivé

cultured pearl n perle f de culture

culture: ~ **shock** n choc m culturel; ~ **vulture**° n fana mf de culture°

culvert /ˈkʌlvət/ n conduite f souterraine

-cum- /kʌm/ combining form **garage~workshop** garage-atelier m; **gardener~handyman** jardinier-homme m à tout faire

cumbersome /ˈkʌmbəsəm/ adj [luggage, furniture] encombrant; [method, phrase] lourd

cummerbund /ˈkʌməbʌnd/ n large ceinture f (d'habit de soirée ou de costume hindou)

cumulative /ˈkjuːmjʊlətɪv, US -leɪtɪv/ adj cumulatif/-ive

cunning /ˈkʌnɪŋ/
A n **1** péj (of person) ruse f; (nastier) fourberie f; (of animal) ruse f; **native** ~ débrouillardise f naturelle
B adj **1** péj [person] rusé; (nastier) fourbe; [animal] rusé; **he's a** ~ **old fox** c'est un vieux renard; **2** (clever) [trick, plot] habile; [device] astucieux/-ieuse

cunningly /ˈkʌnɪŋlɪ/ adv [devised] astucieusement; [fashioned] ingénieusement

cup /kʌp/
A n **1** (object, contents) tasse f; **a** ~ **of tea** une tasse de thé; **2** Sport coupe f; **3** (in bra) bonnet m; **4** (of flower) corolle f
B vtr (p prés etc -pp-) **to** ~ **sth in one's hands** prendre qch dans le creux de ses mains [butterfly, water]; **to** ~ **one's hands around** entourer [qch] de ses mains [insect]; mettre ses mains en paravent autour de [flame, match]; **to** ~ **one's hand over** couvrir [qch] de sa main [receiver]; **in one's** ~**ped hand** dans le creux de sa main

cupboard /ˈkʌbəd/ n placard m
(Idiom) **the** ~ **is bare** les caisses sont vides

cupboard love n GB hum amour m intéressé

cupboard space n espace m de rangement

cupful /ˈkʌpfʊl/ n tasse f (**of** de)

cupid /ˈkjuːpɪd/ n Art amour m

Cupid /ˈkjuːpɪd/ pr n Cupidon

cupola /ˈkjuːpələ/ n Archit coupole f

cup tie n GB match m de coupe

cur /kɜː(r)/ n péj (dog) corniaud m

curable /ˈkjʊərəbl/ adj guérissable

curate /ˈkjʊərət/ n vicaire m
(Idiom) **it's like the** ~**'s egg** tout n'est pas mauvais

curator /kjʊəˈreɪtə(r), US also ˈkjʊərətər/ ▸ p. 1181 n (of museum, gallery) conservateur/-trice m/f

curb /kɜːb/
A n **1** (control) restriction f (**on** à); **2** US (sidewalk) bord m du trottoir
B vtr **1** (control) refréner [desires]; limiter [powers, influence]; juguler [spending]; restreindre [consumption]; **to** ~ **one's temper** se dominer; **2** US ~ **your dog!** apprenez le caniveau à votre chien!

curd cheese n fromage m blanc (lait caillé égoutté)

curdle /ˈkɜːdl/ vi [milk] se cailler; [sauce] tourner

cure /ˈkjʊə(r)/
A n (remedy) remède m (**for** à); (for illness) traitement m (**for** pour)
B vtr **1** guérir [disease, patient] (**of** de); **2** fig guérir [bad habit, person] (**of** de); remédier à [inflation]; **3** Culin (dry) sécher; (salt) saler; (smoke) fumer

cure-all /ˈkjʊərɔːl/ n panacée f (**for** contre)

curfew /ˈkɜːfjuː/ n couvre-feu m; **ten o'clock** ~ couvre-feu à partir de dix heures

curing /ˈkjʊərɪŋ/ n Culin (drying) séchage m; (salting) salaison f; (smoking) fumage m

curio /ˈkjʊərɪəʊ/ n curiosité f, objet m rare

curiosity /ˌkjʊərɪˈɒsətɪ/ n **1** (desire to know, nosiness) curiosité f (**about** sur, au sujet de); **out of (idle)** ~ par (simple) curiosité; **2** (person) original/-e m/f; **3** (object) curiosité f
(Idiom) ~ **killed the cat** Prov la curiosité est un vilain défaut

curious /ˈkjʊərɪəs/ adj **1** (interested, nosy) curieux/-ieuse; ~ **to know** curieux de savoir; **to be** ~ **about sth** éprouver de la curiosité au sujet de qch; **I'm just** ~**!** j'aurais aimé savoir, c'est tout!; **2** (odd) [person, case, effect] curieux/-ieuse; [place, phenomenon] étrange

curiously /ˈkjʊərɪəslɪ/ adv **1** (oddly) [silent, detached] étrangement; ~ **shaped** d'une forme bizarre; ~ **enough,...** chose assez curieuse,...; **2** [ask] avec curiosité

curl /kɜːl/
A n **1** (of hair) boucle f; **2** (of smoke) volute f; **with a** ~ **of one's lip** avec une moue dédaigneuse
B vtr **1** friser [hair]; **2** (wind, coil) **to** ~ **one's fingers around sth** [person] saisir qch; **to** ~ **itself around sth** [snake, caterpillar] s'enrouler autour de qch; **to** ~ **one's lip** [person] faire une moue dédaigneuse
C vi [hair] friser; [paper] (se) gondoler; [edges, corner, leaf] se racornir; **smoke** ~**ed upwards** la fumée montait en volutes
(Idiom) **to make sb's hair** ~° (in shock) faire dresser les cheveux sur la tête de qn
(Phrasal verb)
■ **curl up** [person] se pelotonner; [cat] se mettre en rond; [paper] se gondoler; [edges, corner, leaf] se racornir; **to** ~ **up in bed** se blottir dans son lit; **to** ~ **up into a ball** [person] se recroqueviller; [hedgehog] se mettre en boule; **to** ~ **up at the edges** [photo, paper] (se) gondoler

curler /ˈkɜːlə(r)/ n (roller) bigoudi m

curling /ˈkɜːlɪŋ/ ▸ p. 881 n Sport curling m

curly /ˈkɜːlɪ/ adj [hair] (tight curls) frisé; (loose curls) bouclé; [tail, eyelashes] recourbé

curly-haired /ˌkɜːlɪˈheəd/, **curly-headed** /ˌkɜːlɪˈhedɪd/ adj (tight curls) frisé; (loose curls) bouclé

currant /ˈkʌrənt/
A n raisin m de Corinthe
B noun modifier ~ **bun** ≈ brioche f aux raisins; ~ **loaf** ≈ pain m brioché aux raisins

currency /ˈkʌrənsɪ/ ▸ p. 782 n **1** Fin monnaie f, devise f; **the** ~ **of Poland** la monnaie polonaise; **to buy foreign** ~ acheter des devises étrangères; **have you any German** ~**?** avez-vous de l'argent allemand?; ~ **market** marché m monétaire; **2** (of term) fréquence f; (of idea) crédibilité f; **to gain** ~ [term] devenir courant; [idea, opinion] se répandre

current /ˈkʌrənt/
A n (of electricity, water) courant m; (of air) flux m; (trend) tendance f
B adj **1** (present) [leader, crisis, situation, policy, value] actuel/-elle; [developments, year, research] en cours; **2** (in common use)

C

Currencies and money

■ *For how to say numbers in French* ▸ *p. 1044.*

French money

write	say
0,25 €	vingt-cinq centimes
1 €*	un euro
1,50† €	un euro cinquante
	or un euro cinquante centimes
2 €	deux euros
2,75 €	deux euros soixante-quinze
20 €	vingt euros
100 €	cent euros
1 000 €	mille euros
1 000 000 €	un million d'euros

* *Note that French normally puts the abbreviation after the amount, unlike British (£1) or American ($1) English. However, in some official documents amounts may be given as* € *10 000 etc.*

† *French uses a comma to separate units (e.g. 2,75 €), where English normally has a period (e.g. £5.50).*

there are 100 cents in one euro
= il y a 100 centimes dans un euro

a hundred-euro note
= un billet de cent euros

a twenty-euro note
= un billet de vingt euros

a two-euro coin
= une pièce de deux euros

a 50-cent piece
= une pièce de cinquante centimes

British money

write	say
1p	un penny [pɛnɪ]
25p	vingt-cinq pence [pɛns]
	or vingt-cinq pennies [pɛnɪ]
50p	cinquante pence *or* cinquante pennies
£1	une livre
£1.50	une livre cinquante
	or une livre cinquante pence
£2.00	deux livres

a five-pound note
= un billet de cinq livres

a pound coin
= une pièce d'une livre

a 50p piece
= une pièce de cinquante pence

American money

write	say
12c	douze cents [sɛnts]
$1	un dollar
$1.50	un dollar cinquante
	or un dollar cinquante cents

a ten-dollar bill
= un billet de dix dollars

a dollar bill
= un billet d'un dollar

a dollar coin
= une pièce d'un dollar

How much?

how much is it? or how much does it cost?
= combien est-ce que cela coûte?

it's 15 euros
= cela coûte 15 euros

the price of the book is 30 euros
= le prix du livre est de§ 30 euros

the car costs 15,000 euros
= la voiture coûte 15 000 euros

it costs over 500 euros
= ça coûte plus de 500 euros

just under 1,000 euros
= un peu moins de 1 000 euros

more than 200 euros
= plus de 200 euros

less than 200 euros
= moins de 200 euros

it costs 15 euros a metre
= cela coûte 15 euros le mètre

another ten pounds
= encore dix livres

§ *The de is obligatory here.*

■ *In the following examples, note the use of à in French to introduce the amount that something costs:*

a two-euro stamp
= un timbre à deux euros

a £10 ticket
= un billet à 10 livres

■ *and the use of de to introduce the amount that something consists of:*

a £500 cheque
= un chèque de 500 livres

a two-thousand-pound grant
= une bourse de deux mille livres

Handling money

200 euros in cash
= 200 euros en liquide

a cheque for 500 euros
= un chèque de 500 euros

to change a 100-euro note
= faire la monnaie d'un billet de 100 euros

a dollar travellers' check
= un chèque de voyage en dollars

a sterling travellers' cheque
= un chèque de voyage en livres

a £100 travellers' cheque
= un chèque de voyage de 100 livres

there are 1.12 euros to the dollar
= le dollar vaut 1,12 euros

to pay in pounds
= payer en livres

to make a transaction in euros
= faire une transaction en euros

[*term, word*] usité; **in ~ use** usité

current: **~ account** n GB compte m courant; **~ affairs** n (+ v sg) actualité f

currently /ˈkʌrəntlɪ/ adv actuellement, en ce moment

curriculum /kəˈrɪkjʊləm/ n (pl **-lums** ou **-la**) Sch programme m; **in the ~** au programme

curriculum: ~ **development** n Sch développement m des programmes; ~ **vitae, CV** n curriculum vitae m, CV m

curry /'kʌrɪ/
A n curry m; **chicken** ~ curry de poulet
B vtr faire un curry de [meat]
(Idiom) **to** ~ **favour** chercher à se faire bien voir (**with sb** de qn)

curry powder n curry m

curse /kɜːs/
A n [1] (scourge) fléau m; [2] (swearword) juron m; [3] (spell) malédiction f; **to put a** ~ **on** appeler la malédiction sur
B vtr maudire
C vi jurer (**at** après); **to** ~ **and swear** jurer comme un charretier
D **cursed** pp adj [1] /'kɜːsɪd, kɜːst/ maudit; [2] /kɜːst/ **to be** ~**d with** être affligé de

cursor /'kɜːsə(r)/ n curseur m

cursorily /'kɜːsərəlɪ/ adv rapidement

cursory /'kɜːsərɪ/ adj rapide; **to give sth a** ~ **glance** jeter un coup d'œil rapide à qch

curt /kɜːt/ adj sec/sèche

curtail /kɜːˈteɪl/ vtr [1] (restrict) mettre une entrave à; [2] (cut back) réduire; [3] (cut short) écourter

curtailment /kɜːˈteɪlmənt/ n [1] (of rights, freedom) limitation f; [2] (of expenditure, service) réduction f; [3] (of holiday) interruption f

curtain /'kɜːtn/
A n [1] (drape) rideau m; [2] Theat rideau m; **after the final** ~ après la chute du rideau
B noun modifier [hook, ring] de rideau; [rail] à rideaux
C vtr mettre des rideaux à [room, window]
(Phrasal verb)
  ■ **curtain off**: ▸ ~ **[sth] off,** ~ **off [sth]** fermer [qch] par un rideau; **to be** ~**ed off from sth** être séparé de qch par un rideau

curtain call n Theat rappel m

curtly /'kɜːtlɪ/ adv sèchement

curtsey /'kɜːtsɪ/
A n (pl **-eys** or **-ies**) révérence f
B vi (prét, pp **-seyed** or **-sied**) faire la révérence

curvaceous /kɜːˈveɪʃəs/ adj bien faite

curve /kɜːv/
A n courbe f
B vtr gen courber
C vi [line, wall, arch] s'incurver; [edge] se recourber; [road, railway] faire une courbe

curved /kɜːvd/ adj [line, surface] courbe, incurvé; [wall, flowerbed] courbe; [staircase, blade] incurvé; [edge] arrondi; [arch] cintré; [beak] crochu

curvy /'kɜːvɪ/ adj [woman] bien faite

cushion /'kʊʃn/
A n lit [1] coussin m; [2] fig (protection, reserve) garantie f (**against** contre)
B vtr amortir
C **cushioned** pp adj (padded) matelassé; (pampered) hyperprotégé

cushion cover n housse f de coussin

cushy○ /'kʊʃɪ/ adj peinard○

custard /'kʌstəd/ n GB (creamy) ≈ crème f anglaise; (set, baked) flan m

custard: ~ **cream** n GB biscuit m fourré; ~ **pie** n tarte f à la crème; ~ **tart** n tarte f à la crème

custodial /kʌˈstəʊdɪəl/ adj ~ **sentence** peine f de prison

custodian /kʌˈstəʊdɪən/ ▸ p. 1181 n (of building, collection) gardien/-ienne m/f; (in museum) conservateur/-trice m/f

custody /'kʌstədɪ/ n [1] Jur (detention) détention f; **in** ~ en détention; **to take sb into** ~ arrêter qn; [2] (of child) garde f; **to award** ~ accorder la garde; [3] **in the** ~ **of** à la garde de; **in safe** ~ en mains sûres

custom /'kʌstəm/ n [1] (personal habit) coutume f, habitude f; **it was her** ~ **to do** elle avait l'habitude de faire; [2] (convention) coutume f, usage m; **it is the** ~ c'est la coutume; ~ **requires that** l'usage veut que (+ subj); [3] Comm (patronage) clientèle f; **they've lost a lot of** ~ ils ont perdu beaucoup de clients; **I shall take my** ~ **elsewhere** j'irai me faire servir ailleurs

customary /'kʌstəmərɪ, US -merɪ/ adj gen habituel/-elle; (more formal) coutumier/-ière f; **as is/was** ~ comme de coutume

custom: ~**-built** adj [house] fait sur plans; ~ **car** n voiture f personnalisée

customer /'kʌstəmə(r)/ n [1] Comm client/-e m/f; '~ **services'** 'service m clientèle'; [2] ○(person) type○ m; **a nasty** ~ un sale type○; **he's a cool** ~ il est imperturbable

customer careline /'kʌstəmə'kɛəlaɪn/ n Comm service m d'assistance téléphonique

customize /'kʌstəmaɪz/ vtr personnaliser

custom-made /ˌkʌstəm'meɪd/ adj fait sur mesure

customs /'kʌstəmz/ n douane f; **at** ~ à la douane; **to go through** ~ passer à la douane

customs: **Customs and Excise** n GB douane f (britannique); ~ **clearance** n dédouanement m; ~ **declaration** n déclaration f en douane; ~ **duties** npl droits mpl de douane; ~ **hall** n douane f; ~ **officer**, ~ **official** ▸ p. 1181 n douanier/-ière m/f; ~ **union** n union f douanière

cut /kʌt/
A n [1] (incision) gen entaille f; (in surgery) incision f; [2] (wound) coupure f; [3] (hairstyle) coupe f; **a** ~ **and blow-dry** une coupe-brushing; [4] ○(share) part f; [5] (reduction) réduction f (**in** de); **a price** ~ une baisse des prix; **a** ~ **in the unemployment rate** une baisse du taux de chômage; **job** ~**s** suppression f d'emplois; **to take a** ~ **in salary** accepter une baisse de salaire; [6] (trim) **to give [sth] a** ~ couper [hair, grass]; [7] Culin morceau m; [8] (of diamond) taille f; [9] (of suit, jacket) coupe f; [10] Cin (removal of footage) coupure f; (shot) plan m de raccord (**from** de; **to** à); [11] (in editing) coupure f; [12] Mus (track) morceau m
B vtr (p prés **-tt-**; prét, pp **cut**) [1] (with knife, scissors etc) couper [bread, fabric, wood]; faire [hole, slit]; **to** ~ **sth out of** couper qch dans [fabric]; découper qch dans [magazine]; **to** ~ **sth in half** couper qch en deux; [2] (sever) couper [rope, corn, flower]; ouvrir [vein]; fig rompre [ties]; [3] (carve out) faire [notch]; creuser [channel, tunnel]; graver [initials] (**in** dans); **to** ~ **sth open** ouvrir qch; [4] (draw blood) couper; fig [remark] blesser; **to** ~ **one's finger** se couper le doigt; [5] (trim) couper [grass, hair]; tailler [hedge]; **to** ~ **one's fringe** se couper la frange; **to have one's hair cut** se faire couper les cheveux; [6] (shape, fashion) tailler [gem, suit, marble]; [locksmith] faire [key]; [7] (liberate) **to** ~ **sb from sth** dégager qn de [wreckage]; **to** ~ **sb free** ou **loose** libérer qn (**from** de); [8] (edit) couper [article, film]; supprimer [scene]; [9] (reduce) réduire; (grow) **to** ~ **a tooth** percer une dent; **to** ~ **one's teeth** faire ses dents; [11] (record) faire, graver [album]; [12] Comput couper [paragraph]; ~ **and paste** couper-coller; [13] Games couper [cards]; [14] (intersect) [line] couper; [15] ○(stop) ~ **the cackle** arrête de jacasser; ~ **the flattery/sarcasm!** assez de flatteries/sarcasme!; [16] ○(fail to attend) sécher○ [class, lesson]; ne pas aller à [meeting]; [17] (snub) ignorer, snober; **to** ~ **sb dead** ignorer complètement qn
C vi (p prés **-tt-**; prét, pp **cut**) [1] (slice, make an incision) couper; **to** ~ **into** entamer [cake, pie]; couper [fabric, paper]; inciser [flesh]; [2] (move, go) couper; **to** ~ **down a side street** couper par une petite rue; **to** ~ **in front of sb** (in a queue) passer devant qn; (in a car) faire une queue de poisson à qn; [3] Cin **to** ~ **from A to B** passer sans transition de A à B; [4] Games couper; [5] fig **to** ~ **into** (impinge on) empiéter sur [leisure time]
D v refl (p prés **-tt-**; prét, pp **cut**) **to** ~ **oneself** se couper
E **cut** pp adj [1] (sliced, sawn) coupé; [2] (shaped) [gem, stone] taillé; **a well-cut jacket** une veste bien coupée; [3] (bleeding) [lip] coupé; **to have a cut finger** avoir une coupure au doigt; [4] [hay] fauché; [grass, flowers] coupé; [5] (edited) avec coupures (**after** n)
(Idioms) **a** ~ **above** supérieur; **to** ~ **and run** fig fuir, partir en courant; **to** ~ **both ways** être à double tranchant; **to have one's work cut out** avoir du travail en perspective
(Phrasal verbs)
  ■ **cut across**: ▸ ~ **across [sth]** [1] (bisect) traverser; [2] (transcend) dépasser [class barriers, distinctions]
  ■ **cut back**: ▸ ~ **back** faire des économies; ▸ ~ **back [sth],** ~ **[sth] back** [1] (reduce) réduire [production, spending] (**to** à); [2] (prune) tailler
  ■ **cut down**: ▸ ~ **down** réduire sa consommation; **to** ~ **down on smoking** fumer moins; **to** ~ **down on alcohol** réduire sa consommation d'alcool; ▸ ~ **down [sth],**

∼ **[sth] down** ⟦1⟧ (chop down) abattre; ⟦2⟧ (reduce) réduire; ⟦3⟧ (make smaller, shorter) couper; **to ∼ sb down to size** rabattre le caquet à qn

■ **cut in:** ▶ ∼ **in** ⟦1⟧ (in conversation) intervenir; **to ∼ in on sb** interrompre qn; ⟦2⟧ (in vehicle) **to ∼ in in front of sb** faire une queue de poisson à qn

■ **cut off:** ▶ ∼ **off [sth]**, ∼ **[sth] off** ⟦1⟧ (remove) couper [hair, piece, corner]; enlever [excess, crusts]; **to ∼ off one's finger** se couper le doigt; **to ∼ off sb's head** couper la tête à qn; ⟦2⟧ (reduce) **to ∼ 20 minutes off the journey** raccourcir le trajet de 20 minutes; ⟦3⟧ (disconnect) couper [mains service]; ▶ ∼ **off [sth]** ⟦1⟧ (discontinue) supprimer [grant]; suspendre [aid]; ⟦2⟧ (isolate) [tide, army] couper; ⟦3⟧ (block) bloquer [exit]; ▶ ∼ **[sb] off** ⟦1⟧ Telecom couper qn; ⟦2⟧ (disinherit) déshériter qn; **he cut me off without a penny** il m'a déshérité; ⟦3⟧ (interrupt) interrompre qn; ▶ ∼ **[sb] off**, ∼ **off [sb]** (isolate) couper; **to feel cut off** se sentir isolé; **to ∼ oneself off** s'isoler

■ **cut out:** ▶ ∼ **out** [engine, fan] s'arrêter; ▶ ∼ **out [sth]** (eliminate) supprimer; ▶ ∼ **[sth] out, ∼ out [sth]** ⟦1⟧ (snip out) découper (**from** dans); ⟦2⟧ (remove) enlever [tumour]; supprimer [scene, chapter]; éliminer [draught, noise]; ⟦3⟧ ○(stop) ∼ **it out!** ça suffit!; ▶ ∼ **[sb] out** ⟦1⟧ (isolate) exclure qn; **to ∼ sb out of one's will** déshériter qn; ⟦2⟧ **to be cut out for teaching** être fait pour être professeur

■ **cut short:** ▶ ∼ **short [sth]**, ∼ **[sth] short** abréger [holiday, discussion]; ▶ ∼ **[sb] short** interrompre

■ **cut through:** ▶ ∼ **through [sth]** [boat] fendre [water]; [person] éviter [red tape]

■ **cut up:** ▶ ∼ **[sth] up**, ∼ **up [sth]** gen couper (**into** en) [food]; disséquer [specimen]; **to be very cut up** être très affecté (**about, by** par)

cut-and-dried adj [answer, solution] tout fait; **I like everything to be ∼** j'aime que tout soit fin prêt

cut and paste n Comput couper-coller m

cut and thrust n **the ∼ of debate** les échanges mpl animés du débat

cutback /'kʌtbæk/ n réduction f; **∼s in** réductions dans le budget de [defence, health, education]; **government ∼s** réductions budgétaires du gouvernement

cute○ /kjuːt/ adj surtout US ⟦1⟧ (sweet, attractive) mignon/-onne; (sickly sweet) mièvre; ⟦2⟧ (clever) précoce; pej malin/-igne; **to get ∼** faire le malin; **to get ∼ with sb** répondre avec insolence à qn

cut glass n verre m taillé

cutlery /'kʌtlərɪ/ n ₵ couverts mpl; **a set of ∼** (for one) un couvert; (complete suite) ménagère f

cutlet /'kʌtlɪt/ n côtelette f

cut-off /'kʌtɒf/

Ⓐ n (upper limit) limite f

Ⓑ **cut-offs** npl jean m coupé

cut: ∼-off date n date-limite f; **∼-off point** n gen limite f; Comm plafond m

cut-out /'kʌtaʊt/ n (outline) silhouette f

cut-price /ˌkʌt'praɪs/ adj, adv GB à prix réduit

cut-rate adj US = **cut-price**

cutter /'kʌtə(r)/ n ⟦1⟧ (tool) couteau m, cutter m; ⟦2⟧ (ship) cotre m

cut-throat /'kʌtθrəʊt/

Ⓐ n assassin

Ⓑ adj [competition] acharné; **a ∼ business** un milieu très dur

cut-throat razor n GB rasoir m (à lame), coupe-choux○ m inv

cutting /'kʌtɪŋ/

Ⓐ n ⟦1⟧ (newspaper extract) coupure f (**from** de); ⟦2⟧ (of plant) bou-

ture f; ⟦3⟧ (by rail track) tranchée f; ⟦4⟧ Cin montage m; ⟦5⟧ Comput **∼ and pasting** coupé-collé m

Ⓑ **cuttings** npl grass **∼s** herbe f coupée

Ⓒ adj [tone] cassant; [remark] désobligeant

cutting edge n ⟦1⟧ (blade) tranchant m; ⟦2⟧ fig avant-garde f; **to be at the ∼** être à l'avant-garde

cuttingly /'kʌtɪŋlɪ/ adv [speak] d'un ton cassant

cutting room n Cin salle f de montage; **to end up on the ∼ floor** être coupé au montage

CV, cv (abrév = **curriculum vitae**) cv, CV

cwt abrév écrite = **hundredweight**

cyanide /'saɪənaɪd/ n cyanure m

cybercrime /'saɪbəkraɪm/ n cybercriminalité f

cybernaut /'saɪbənɔːt/ n internaute mf

cybernetics /ˌsaɪbə'netɪks/ n (+ v sg) cybernétique f

cyberpunk /'saɪbəpʌŋk/ n ⟦1⟧ Comput pirate m informatique; ⟦2⟧ (sci-fi genre) science-fiction f cyberpunk

cybersquatting /'saɪbəskwɒtɪŋ/ n accaparement m de nom de domaine

cycle /'saɪkl/

Ⓐ n ⟦1⟧ (series) cycle m; **wash ∼** cycle m de lavage; ⟦2⟧ (bicycle) vélo m

Ⓑ vtr **to ∼ 15 miles** parcourir or faire 24 km à vélo

Ⓒ vi aller à vélo; **to go cycling** faire du vélo; **she ∼s to work** elle va au travail à vélo

cycle: ∼ clip n pince f à vélo; **∼ lane** n piste f cyclable; **∼ race** n course f cycliste; **∼ rack** n parking m à vélos; **∼ track** n piste f cyclable

cyclic(al) /'saɪklɪk(l)/ adj cyclique

cycling /'saɪklɪŋ/ ▸ p. 881 n cyclisme m; **to do a lot of ∼** gen faire beaucoup de vélo

cycling holiday GB n vacances fpl à vélo; **to go on a ∼** faire du cyclotourisme

cycling shorts npl Sport cuissard m

cyclist /'saɪklɪst/ n gen cycliste mf; Sport coureur/-euse m/f cycliste

cyclo-cross /'saɪkləkrɒs/ ▸ p. 881 n cyclo-cross m

cyclone /'saɪkləʊn/ n cyclone m; **∼ fence** US barrière f en grillage

cygnet /'sɪgnɪt/ n jeune cygne m

cylinder /'sɪlɪndə(r)/ n ⟦1⟧ Tech cylindre m; **four-∼** à quatre cylindres; ⟦2⟧ (of revolver) barillet m; ⟦3⟧ GB (also **hot water ∼**) ballon m d'eau chaude

(Idiom) **to be firing on all ∼s**○ être au meilleur de sa forme

cylindrical /sɪ'lɪndrɪkl/ adj cylindrique

cymbal /'sɪmbl/ ▸ p. 1028 n cymbale f

cynic /'sɪnɪk/

Ⓐ n cynique mf

Ⓑ adj (all contexts) cynique

cynical /'sɪnɪkl/ adj cynique (**about** en ce qui concerne)

cynicism /'sɪnɪsɪzəm/ n cynisme m

cypher n, vtr = **cipher**

cypress (tree) /'saɪprəs/ n cyprès m

Cyprus /'saɪprəs/ ▸ p. 954, p. 774 pr n Chypre f

Cyrillic /sɪ'rɪlɪk/ adj cyrillique

cyst /sɪst/ n Med, Biol kyste m

czar, Czar /zɑː(r)/ ▸ p. 869 n tsar m; **Czar Nicolas** le tsar Nicolas

Czech /tʃek/ ▸ p. 1032, p. 969

Ⓐ n ⟦1⟧ (person) Tchèque mf; ⟦2⟧ (language) tchèque m

Ⓑ adj tchèque

Czech Republic ▸ p. 774 pr n République f tchèque

Dd

d, D /diː/ *n* ① (letter) d, D *m*; ② D Mus ré *m*; ③ d *abrév écrite* = **died**

DA *n* US Jur *abrév* ▸ **District Attorney**

dab /dæb/
A *n* (of paint) touche *f*; (of butter) petit morceau *m*
B *vtr* se tamponner [*one's eyes, mouth*]; tamponner [*wound, stain*] (**with** de); **to ~ sth on** appliquer qch par petites touches; **to ~ sth off** enlever qch en tamponnant

dabble /'dæbl/ *vtr* **to ~ one's toes in sth** tremper ses orteils dans qch
(Phrasal verb)
■ **dabble in:** ▸ **~ in [sth]** faire [qch] en amateur [*painting, writing, politics*]; flirter avec⁰ [*ideology*]; **to ~ in the Stock Exchange** boursicoter⁰

Dacca /'dækə/ ▸ **p. 1276** *pr n* Dhaka

dachshund /'dækshʊnd/ *n* teckel *m*

dad⁰, **Dad**⁰ /dæd/ *n* (child speaker) papa *m*; (adult speaker) père *m*; (old man) hum pépé⁰ *m*

daddy⁰, **Daddy**⁰ /'dædɪ/ *n* papa *m*

daddy-long-legs /,dædɪ'lɒŋlegz/ *n* (*pl* **~**) GB tipule *f*; US faucheux *m*

daffodil /'dæfədɪl/ *n* jonquille *f*

daffodil yellow *n, adj* jaune (*m*) vif *inv*

daft⁰ /dɑːft, US dæft/ *adj* (silly) bête

dagger /'dægə(r)/ *n* poignard *m*
(Idioms) **to be at ~s drawn** être à couteaux tirés (**with** avec); **to look ~s at sb** fusiller qn du regard

Dail Éireann /dɔɪl 'eɪrən/ *n* Pol ≈ Chambre *f* des Députés (*du parlement irlandais*)

daily /'deɪlɪ/
A *n* (*pl* **dailies**) ① (newspaper) quotidien *m*; **the national dailies** les grands quotidiens; ② GB (*also* **~ help, ~ maid**) femme *f* de ménage
B *adj* (each day) quotidien/-ienne; (per day) [*wage, rate, intake*] journalier/-ière; **~ newspaper** (journal *m*) quotidien *m*; **on a ~ basis** tous les jours; **to be paid on a ~ basis** être payé à la journée
C *adv* quotidiennement, tous les jours; **twice ~** deux fois par jour

daintily /'deɪntɪlɪ/ *adv* délicatement

dainty /'deɪntɪ/ *adj* [*porcelain, handkerchief, dish*] délicat; [*shoe, hand, foot*] mignon/-onne; [*figure*] menu

dairy /'deərɪ/
A *n* ① (on farm etc) laiterie *f*; (shop) crémerie *f*; ② Comm (company) société *f* laitière
B *noun modifier* [*butter*] fermier/-ière; [*cow, farm, product, cream*] laitier/-ière

dairyman /'deərɪmən/ *n* (on farm) ouvrier *m* de laiterie; US (farmer) éleveur *m* de vaches laitières

dais /'deɪɪs/ *n* estrade *f*

daisy /'deɪzɪ/ *n* (common) pâquerette *f*; (garden) marguerite *f*
(Idioms) **to be as fresh as a ~** être frais/fraîche comme une rose; **to be pushing up (the) daisies**⁰ manger les pissenlits par la racine

daisy wheel
A *n* Comput marguerite *f*
B *noun modifier* [*printer, terminal*] à marguerite

dale /deɪl/ *n* vallée *f*, val *m* liter

dally /'dælɪ/ *vi* ① **to ~ with** fig caresser, jouer avec [*idea*]; flirter avec [*political party*]; ② (linger) traîner

dam /dæm/
A *n* (construction) barrage *m*; (to prevent flooding) digue *f*
B *vtr* Constr construire un barrage sur [*river, lake*]; (to prevent flooding) endiguer
(Phrasal verb)
■ **dam up:** ▸ **~ up [sth], ~ [sth] up** bloquer, obstruer [*river, canal*]

damage /'dæmɪdʒ/
A *n* Ⓒ ① (physical) (to goods, environment) dégâts *mpl* (**to** causés à; **from** causés par); **£300-worth of ~** pour 300 livres sterling de dégâts; **storm ~** dégâts dûs aux intempéries; **water ~** dégâts des eaux; **~ to property** dégâts matériels; ② (medical) lésions *fpl*; **to cause ~ to** abîmer [*health, part of body*]; **brain ~** lésions *fpl* cérébrales; ③ fig **to do sth ~** porter atteinte à [*cause, reputation, trade*]; **the ~ is done** le mal est fait
B **damages** *npl* Jur dommages-intérêts *mpl*; **to be liable for ~** être civilement responsable
C *vtr* ① (physically) endommager [*building, machine, furniture*]; abîmer [*health, part of body*]; nuire à [*environment, crop*]; ② fig porter atteinte à [*reputation, relationship, negotiations*]

damaging /'dæmɪdʒɪŋ/ *adj* ① (to reputation, career, person) préjudiciable (**to** à, pour); [*effect*] préjudiciable; [*consequences*] désastreux/-euse; ② (to health, environment) nuisible (**to** pour)

damask /'dæməsk/
A *n* (fabric) damas *m*
B *noun modifier* [*cloth*] damassé *inv*

dammit⁰ /'dæmɪt/ *excl* zut⁰!; **(or) as near as ~**⁰ GB ou quelque chose dans ce goût-là

damn /dæm/
A *n* **not to give a ~ about sb/sth** se ficher⁰ de qn/qch
B *adj* [*object*] fichu⁰; **your ~ husband** ton fichu⁰ mari
C *adv* franchement; **I should ~ well hope so!** j'espère bien!
D *excl* zut⁰!
E *vtr* ① ⁰(curse) **~ you!** tu m'énerves!; **...and ~ the consequences!** et tant pis pour le reste!; **I'll be ~ed!** ça alors!; **~ it!** merde⁰!, zut⁰!; ② damner [*sinner*]; **to ~ sb with faint praise** déguiser le blâme sous le voile de la louange

damnation /dæm'neɪʃn/
A *n* damnation *f*
B *excl*⁰ zut⁰!

damned /dæmd/
A *n, adj* Relig damné⁰; ② ⁰ ▸ **damn B**
B *adv* ▸ **damn C**

damnedest⁰ /'dæmdɪst/ *n* ① (hardest) **to do** *ou* **try one's ~ (to do)** faire tout son possible (pour faire); ② (surprising) **it was the ~ thing** c'était incroyable

damning /'dæmɪŋ/ *adj* accablant

damp /dæmp/
A *n* humidité *f*
B *adj* gen humide; [*skin*] moite
C *vtr* ① = **dampen**; ② = **damp down**
(Phrasal verb)
■ **damp down:** ▸ **~ [sth] down, ~ down [sth]** couvrir [*fire*]; étouffer [*flames*]

dampen /'dæmpən/ *vtr* ① humecter [*cloth, sponge, ironing*]; ② fig refroidir [*enthusiasm, ardour*]; amenuiser [*hopes, resolve*]; **to ~ sb's spirits** décourager qn

damper /'dæmpə(r)/ n

(Idiom) **the news put a ~ on the evening**○ la nouvelle a jeté un froid dans l'assistance

damson /'dæmzn/ n (fruit) prune f de Damas

dance /dɑːns, US dæns/
A n gen danse f; (social occasion) soirée f dansante
B noun modifier de danse
C vtr **1** danser [steps, dance]; **2** (dandle) faire danser
D vi lit, fig danser (**with** avec); [eyes] briller (**with** de); **to ~ for joy** danser de joie

(Idioms) **to ~ the night away** danser jusqu'à l'aube; **to lead sb a merry ~** donner du fil à retordre à qn

(Phrasal verb)

■ **~ about**, **~ up and down** sautiller sur place

dance hall n dancing m

dancer /'dɑːnsə(r), US 'dænsə(r)/ n danseur/-euse m/f

dancing /'dɑːnsɪŋ, US 'dænsɪŋ/
A ▸ p. 881 n danse f
B noun modifier de danse
C adj [waves, sunbeams] dansant

dandle /'dændl/ vtr **to ~ a baby on one's knee** faire sauter un bébé sur ses genoux

dandruff /'dændrʌf/ n ¢ pellicules fpl; **anti-~ shampoo** shampooing m antipelliculaire

danger /'deɪndʒə(r)/ n danger m (**of** de; **to** pour); (from different sources) dangers mpl; **to be in ~** être en danger; **to be in ~ of doing** risquer de faire; **the ~ is that** le danger est que (+ subj); **there is a ~ that** il y a un risque que (+ subj); **there is a ~ that they may change their minds** ils risquent de changer d'avis; **there's no ~ of that!** ça ne risque pas○!; **out of ~** hors de danger

danger list n **on the ~** Med dans un état critique

danger money n prime f de risque

dangerous /'deɪndʒərəs/ adj dangereux/-euse (**for** pour; **to do** de faire)

(Idiom) **to be on ~ ground** être sur un terrain miné

dangerously /'deɪndʒərəslɪ/ adv gen dangereusement; [ill] gravement; **to live ~** prendre des risques

danger signal n lit, fig signal m de danger

dangle /'dæŋgl/
A vtr balancer [puppet, keys]; laisser pendre [legs]; fig faire miroiter [prospect] (**before, in front of** à)
B vi [puppet, keys] se balancer (**from** à); [earrings] pendiller; **with legs dangling** les jambes ballantes

Danish /'deɪnɪʃ/ ▸ p. 1032, p. 969
A n (language) danois m
B adj danois

Danish pastry n feuilleté m sucré (aux fruits)

dank /dæŋk/ adj froid et humide

dapper /'dæpə(r)/ adj soigné

dapple /'dæpl/
A vtr tacheter
B **dappled** pp adj [grey, horse, sky] pommelé; [shade, surface] tacheté de lumière

dare /deə(r)/
A n défi m; **to do sth for a ~** faire qch pour répondre à un défi
B modal aux **1** (to have the courage to) oser; **to ~ to do sth** avoir le courage de faire qch; **they don't ~ ou daren't** GB ils n'osent pas; **I ~ say it** il faut bien le dire; **I ~ say, I daresay** GB je pense; (sarcastically) certes!; **I ~ say ou I daresay** GB **that…** je suppose que…; **2** (expressing anger, indignation) oser (do faire); **they wouldn't ~!** ils n'oseraient pas!; **don't (you) ~ speak to me like that!** je t'interdis de me parler sur ce ton!; **don't you ~!** (warning) ne t'avise pas de faire ça!
C vtr **to ~ sb to do** défier qn de faire; **go on, I ~ you!** chiche que tu ne le fais pas○!

daredevil /'deədevl/ n, adj casse-cou (mf) inv

daren't /deənt/ (= dare not) ▸ dare

daresay GB ▸ dare B 1

daring /'deərɪŋ/
A n audace f
B adj (courageous, innovative) audacieux/-ieuse; (shocking) [suggestion, dress] osé

dark /dɑːk/
A n **the ~** le noir, l'obscurité f; **in the ~** dans le noir or l'obscurité; **before/until ~** avant/jusqu'à la (tombée de la)

nuit; **after ~** après la tombée de la nuit
B adj **1** (lacking in light) sombre; **it is getting ~** il commence à faire noir or nuit; **it's ~** il fait noir or nuit; **2** (in colour) [colour, suit] sombre; **~ blue** bleu foncé inv; **3** (physically) [hair, eyes, skin] brun; **she's ~** elle est brune, elle a les cheveux bruns; **4** (gloomy) [time, days, mood] sombre; **5** (sinister) [secret, thought] noir (before n); [threat, warning] sombre; **the ~ side of** le côté sinistre de; **6** (evil) [force, power] maléfique

(Idioms) **to be in the ~** être dans le noir; **I was completely in the ~** j'étais dans le noir le plus complet; **to leave sb in the ~** laisser qn dans l'ignorance; **to keep sb in the ~ about sth** cacher qch à qn; **a shot in the ~** (guess) un coup pour voir

dark: **Dark Ages** n Hist Haut Moyen-Âge m; **~ chocolate** n chocolat m noir

darken /'dɑːkən/
A vtr **1** (reduce light in) obscurcir [sky, landscape]; assombrir [house, room]; **2** (in colour) foncer [colour]; brunir [complexion]; **3** fig assombrir
B vi **1** (lose light) s'obscurcir; **2** (in colour) foncer; [skin] brunir; **3** (show anger) [eyes, face] se rembrunir; **4** (become gloomy) s'assombrir
C **darkened** pp adj [room, house] sombre

(Idiom) **never ~ my door again!** ne remettez plus les pieds ici!

dark: **~-eyed** adj [person] aux yeux sombres or noirs; **~ glasses** npl lunettes fpl noires

dark horse n **1** ○GB (enigmatic person) mystère m; **2** (in sports) outsider m

darkly /'dɑːklɪ/ adv (grimly) [mutter, hint] sombrement

darkness /'dɑːknɪs/ n (blackness) obscurité f; **in ~** dans l'obscurité; **as ~ fell** à la tombée de la nuit

dark: **~room** n chambre f noire; **~-skinned** adj [person] basané

darling /'dɑːlɪŋ/
A n **1** (term of address) (to loved one) chéri/-e m/f; (to child) mon chou○; (affectedly: to acquaintance) mon cher/ma chère m/f; **~ Rosie** ma Rosie chérie; **2** (kind, lovable person) amour m, ange m; **be a ~** sois un ange; **3** (favourite) (of circle, public) coqueluche f; (of family, parent, teacher) chouchou/-te m/f
B adj **1** (expressing attachment) chéri; **2** (expressing delight) **a ~ little baby** un amour de bébé

darn /dɑːn/
A n raccommodage m (**in** à)
B ○adj (also **darned**) sacré○ (before n)
C ○adv sacrément○; **~ good** super○
D ○excl zut○!
E vtr repriser, raccommoder

darning /'dɑːnɪŋ/ n (all contexts) raccommodage m

dart /dɑːt/
A n **1** ▸ p. 881 Sport fléchette f; **to play ~s** jouer aux fléchettes; **2** (arrow) lit, fig flèche f; **3** (in garment) pince f
B vi **to ~ in/away** entrer/filer comme une flèche

dartboard /'dɑːtbɔːd/ n cible f

dash /dæʃ/
A n **1** (rush) course f folle; **it has been a mad ~ on** a dû se presser; **to make a ~ for it** (run off) s'enfuir; **to make a ~ for the train** courir pour attraper le train; **2** (small amount) (of liquid) goutte f; (of powder) pincée f; (of colour) touche f; **3** (flair) panache m; **4** (punctuation) tiret m; **5** (in morse code) trait m
B vtr **1** (smash) **to ~ sb/sth against** projeter qn/qch contre [rocks]; **to ~ sth to the ground** lancer violemment qch par terre; **2** fig (crush) anéantir [hope]
C vi (hurry) se précipiter (**into** dans); **to ~ out of** sortir en courant de; **I must ~!** je me sauve!

(Idiom) **to cut a ~** avoir grande allure

(Phrasal verb)

■ **dash off**: ▸ **~ off** se sauver; ▸ **~ off [sth]**, **~ [sth] off** écrire [qch] en vitesse

dashboard /'dæʃbɔːd/ n tableau m de bord

dashing /'dæʃɪŋ/ adj [person] fringant; [outfit] superbe

data /'deɪtə/
A npl gen, Comput données fpl
B noun modifier [acquisition, analysis, base, bank, dictionary, management, structure, type] de données

data: **~ base** n base f de données; **~base management system**, **DBMS** n système m de gestion de données, SGBD; ~ **capture** n saisie f de données; ~ **carrier** n support m d'information; ~ **collection** n collecte f de données; ~ **communications** npl transmission f de données; ~ **directory** n répertoire m de données; ~ **disk** n disque m enregistré; ~ **entry** n introduction f de données; ~ **file** n fichier m de données; ~ **handling** n manipulation f de données; ~ **input** n introduction f de données; ~ **item** n donnée f élémentaire; ~ **link** n liaison f de données; ~ **processing** n (procedure) traitement m des données; (career) informatique f; (department) service m informatique; ~ **protection** n protection f de l'information; ~ **protection act** n Jur loi f sur l'informatique et les libertés; ~ **retrieval** n extraction f de données; ~ **security** n sécurité f des données; ~ **storage** n (process) stockage m des données; (medium) support m d'information; ~ **transmission, DT** n transmission f de données

date /deɪt/ ▸ p. 788

A n ① (day of the month) date f; ~ **of birth** date de naissance; **what ~ is your birthday?** quelle est la date de ton anniversaire?; **what's the ~ today?** on est le combien aujourd'hui?; **there's no ~ on the letter** la lettre n'est pas datée; **to set a ~** fixer une date; **at a later ~, at some future ~** plus tard; ② (year: of event) date f; (on coin) millésime m; ③ (meeting) rendez-vous m; **to have a lunch ~** être pris à déjeuner; **to make a ~ for Monday** prendre rendez-vous pour lundi; ④ (person one is going out with) **who's your ~ for tonight?** avec qui sors-tu ce soir?; ⑤ (fruit) datte f

B **to date** adv phr à ce jour, jusqu'ici

C vtr ① (person) dater; (machine) imprimer la date sur; ~**d March 21st** daté du 21 mars; **a statuette ~d 1875** une statuette portant la date 1875; ② (identify age of) dater (skeleton, building, object); ③ (reveal age of) **that hairstyle ~s her** sa coiffure trahit son âge; ④ (go out with) sortir avec (person)

D vi ① (originate) **to ~ from** ou **back to** (building) dater de; (problem, custom, friendship) remonter à; ② (become dated) se démoder

dated /ˈdeɪtɪd/ adj (clothes, style) démodé; (idea, convention, custom) dépassé; (expression, language) vieilli; **the film seems ~ now** le film a mal vieilli

dateline /ˈdeɪtlaɪn/ n (when travelling) **the international ~** la ligne de changement de date

date: ~ **rape** n viol m par un familier; ~ **stamp** n (mark) cachet m, tampon m

dating agency /ˈdeɪtɪŋ/ n club m de rencontres

dative /ˈdeɪtɪv/
A n datif m; **in the ~** au datif
B adj (case) datif/-ive; (ending, noun) au datif

daub /dɔːb/
A On péj (painting) croûte○ f pej
B vtr **to ~ paint on a wall** maculer un mur de peinture

daughter /ˈdɔːtə(r)/ n lit, fig fille f

daughter-in-law n (pl **daughters-in-law**) belle-fille f, bru f

daunt /dɔːnt/ vtr décourager; **nothing ~ed** imperturbable

daunting /ˈdɔːntɪŋ/ adj (task, prospect) décourageant; (person) intimidant; **it can be (quite) ~** c'est un pas difficile; **I'm faced with a ~ amount of work** j'ai devant moi une quantité effrayante de travail

dawdle /ˈdɔːdl/ vi flâner, traînasser○; **he ~d over breakfast** il a pris son petit déjeuner en traînassant; **he ~d along the road** il a traînassé sur la route

dawn /dɔːn/
A n ① lit aube f, aurore f liter; **at ~** à l'aube; **before** ou **by ~** avant l'aube; **at the crack of ~** lit, fig à l'aube; ~ **broke** le jour se leva; **from ~ till dusk** du matin au soir; ② fig (beginning) aube f; **the ~ of socialism** la naissance du socialisme
B vi ① (become light) (day) se lever; **the day ~ed sunny and warm** le jour s'annonçait chaud et ensoleillé; ② (become apparent) **it ~ed on me that** je me suis rendu compte que; **it suddenly ~ed on him why** il a compris soudain pourquoi

dawn: ~ **chorus** n concert m matinal des oiseaux; ~ **raid** n descente f de police très tôt le matin

day /deɪ/ ▸ p. 1267

A n ① (24-hour period) jour m; **one summer's ~** un jour d'été; **what ~ is it today?** quel jour sommes-nous aujourd'hui?; ~ **after ~, ~ in ~ out** jour après jour; **every ~** tous les jours; **every other ~** tous les deux jours; **from ~ to ~** d'un jour à l'autre; **from one ~ to the next** d'un jour à l'autre; **from that ~ to this** depuis ce jour-là; **any ~ now** d'un jour à l'autre; **one ~, some ~** un jour; **within ~s** en quelques jours; **the ~ when** ou **that** le jour où; **it's ~s since I've seen him** ça fait des jours que je ne l'ai pas vu, je ne l'ai pas vu depuis des jours; **it's 15 years to the ~ since...** ça fait 15 ans jour pour jour que...; **to come on the wrong ~** se tromper de jour; **it had to happen today of all ~s!** il fallait que cela arrive ou que ça tombe○ aujourd'hui; **to this ~** aujourd'hui encore; **the ~ after** le lendemain; **the ~ before** la veille; **the ~ before yesterday** avant-hier; **the ~ after tomorrow** après-demain; **two ~s after/two ~s before the wedding** le surlendemain/l'avant-veille du mariage; **from that ~ onwards** dès lors; ② (until evening) journée f; **working ~** journée de travail; **a hard ~** une journée difficile; **an enjoyable ~'s golf** une agréable journée de golf; **all ~** toute la journée; **all that ~** tout au long de cette journée; **before the ~ was out** avant la fin de la journée; **during/for the ~** pendant/pour la journée; **paid by the ~** payé à la journée; **to take all ~ doing** mettre toute une journée à faire; **pleased with their ~'s work** contents de leur journée; **we haven't got all ~!** nous n'avons pas la journée devant nous!; **it was a hot ~** il faisait chaud; **have a nice ~!** bonne journée!; ③ (as opposed to night) jour m; **it's almost ~** il fait presque jour; **to be on ~s** être ou travailler de jour; **by ~** de jour; ④ (specific) jour m; **decision ~** le jour décisif; **the ~ of judgment** le jour du jugement dernier; **to her dying ~** jusqu'à son dernier jour; **it's not your ~ is it?** décidément c'est ton jour! iron; **I never thought I'd see the ~** je n'aurais jamais cru; ⑤ (as historical period) (gén pl) époque f; **in those ~s** à cette époque; **in his/my ~** (at that time) de son/mon temps; (at height of success, vitality) dans le temps; **his dancing ~s** sa carrière de danseur; **these ~s** ces temps-ci

B noun modifier (job, nurse) de jour

(Idioms) **in ~s gone by** autrefois; **it's all in a ~'s work** c'est du quotidien; **not to give sb the time of ~** ignorer qn superbement; **to pass the time of ~** bavarder; **it's one of those ~s!** il y a des jours comme ça!; **those were the ~s** c'était le bon temps; **to be a bit late in the ~** être un peu tard; **that'll be the ~!** je voudrais voir ça!; **to call it a ~** s'arrêter là; **to win the ~** avoir le dessus; **to have an off ~** ne pas être dans son assiette; **to have had its ~** avoir fait son temps; **to have seen better ~s** avoir connu des jours meilleurs; **he's 50 if he's a ~** il a 50 ans bien tassés○!; **to make a ~ of it** profiter de la journée; **to save the ~** sauver la situation; **to see the ~** apparaître au grand jour; **to take one ~ at a time** prendre les choses comme elles se présentent; **your ~ will come** ton heure arrivera

day: ~**boy** n GB Sch externe m; ~**break** n aube f; ~**-care** n (for young children) service m de garderie; ~ **centre** GB, ~ **center** US n centre m d'accueil

daydream /ˈdeɪdriːm/
A n rêves mpl
B vi rêver (about de; about doing de faire); pej rêvasser

daygirl n Sch externe f

daylight /ˈdeɪlaɪt/
A n ① (light) jour m, lumière f du jour; **it was still ~** il faisait encore jour; **we have two hours of ~ left** on a encore deux heures avant la tombée de la nuit; **in (the) ~** (by day) de jour; (in natural light) à la lumière du jour; ② (dawn) lever m du jour, point m du jour
B noun modifier de jour; **during ~ hours** pendant qu'il fait jour

daylight robbery○ n **it's ~!** c'est de l'arnaque○!

daylight saving time, DST n heure f d'été

day: ~ **nursery** n garderie f; ~ **pass** n forfait m pour la journée; ~ **patient** n patient/-e m/f ambulatoire; ~ **release** n formation f en alternance; ~ **return (ticket)** n GB aller-retour m valable une journée; ~ **school** n externat m; ~ **surgery** n chirurgie f ambulatoire

daytime /ˈdeɪtaɪm/ n journée f

day-to-day /ˌdeɪtəˈdeɪ/ adj quotidien/-ienne; **on a ~ basis** au jour le jour

day: ~**-trip** n excursion f pour la journée; ~**-tripper** n excursionniste mf

Date

■ *Where English has several ways of writing dates, such as* May 10, 10 May, 10th May *etc. French has only one generally accepted way:* le 10 mai, *(say* le dix mai*). However, as in English, dates in French may be written informally:* 10.5.68 *or* 31/7/65 *etc.*

■ *The general pattern in French is:*

le   cardinal number   month   year
le   10   mai   1901

■ *But if the date is the first of the month, use* premier, *abbreviated as* 1er:

May 1st 1901
= le 1er mai 1901

■ *Note that French does not use capital letters for months, or for days of the week ▸ **p. 1020** and ▸ **p. 1322**; also French does not usually abbreviate the names of the months:*

Sept 10
= le 10 septembre *etc.*

■ *If the day of the week is included, put it after the* le:

Monday, May 1st 1901
= le lundi 1er mai 1901

Monday the 25th
= lundi 25 (*say* lundi vingt-cinq)

Saying and writing dates

what's the date?
= quel jour sommes-nous?

it's the tenth
= nous sommes le dix *or* (*less formally*) on est le dix

it's the tenth of May
= nous sommes le dix mai *or* (*less formally*) on est le dix mai

	Write	Say
May 1	le 1er mai	le premier mai
May 2	le 2 mai	le deux mai
May 11	le 11 mai	le onze mai
May 21	le 21 mai	le vingt et un mai
May 30	le 30 mai	le trente mai
May 6 1968	le 6 mai 1968	le six mai mille neuf cent soixante-huit
Monday	le lundi 6	le lundi six mai
May 6 1968	mai 1968	mille neuf cent soixante-huit
16.5.68 GB *or*		
5.16.68 US	16.5.68	le seize cinq soixante-huit
AD 230	230 apr. J.-C.	deux cent trente après Jésus-Christ
2500 BC	2500 av. J.-C.	deux mille cinq cents ans avant Jésus-Christ*
the 16th century	le XVIe siècle†	le seizième siècle

* (*i*) *There are two ways of saying hundreds and thousands in dates:*

1968
= mille neuf cent soixante-huit
  or dix-neuf cent soixante-huit

(*ii*) *The spelling* mil *is used in legal French, otherwise* mille *is used in dates, except when a round number of thousands is involved, in which case the words* l'an *are added:*

1900   **2000**
= mille neuf cents   = l'an deux mille

† *French prefers Roman numerals for centuries:*

the 16th century
= le XVIe

Saying *on*

■ *French uses only the definite article, without any word for* on:

it happened on 6th March
= c'est arrivé le 6 mars (*say* le six mars)

he came on the 21st
= il est arrivé le 21 (*say* le vingt et un)

see you on the 6th
= on se voit le 6 (*say* le six)

on the 2nd of every month
= le 2 de chaque mois (*say* le deux ...)

he'll be here on the 3rd
= il sera là le 3 (*say* le trois)

Saying *in*

■ *French normally uses* en *for years but prefers* en l'an *for out-of-the-ordinary dates:*

in 1968
= en 1968 (*say* en mille neuf cent soixante-huit
  or en dix-neuf cent ...)

in 1896
= en 1896 (*say* en mille huit cent quatre-vingt-seize
  or en dix-huit cent ...)

in the year 2000
= en l'an deux mille

in AD 27
= en l'an 27 (*say* l'an vingt-sept) de notre ère

in 132 BC
= en l'an 132 (*say* l'an cent trente-deux) avant Jésus-Christ

■ *With names of months,* in *is translated by* en *or* au mois de:

in May 1970
= en mai mille neuf cent soixante-dix
  or au mois de mai mille neuf cent soixante-dix

■ *With centuries, French uses* au:

in the seventeenth century
= au dix-septième siècle

■ *The word* siècle *is often omitted in colloquial French:*

in the eighteenth century
= au dix-huitième siècle
  or (*less formally*) au dix-huitième

■ *Note also:*

in the early 12th century
= au début du XIIe siècle (*say* du douzième siècle)

in the late 14th century
= à *or* vers la fin du XIVe siècle (*say* du quatorzième siècle)

☛ See next page

Date *continued*

Phrases

■ Remember that the date in French always has the definite article, so, in combined forms, au and du are required:

from the 10th onwards
= à partir du 10 (*say* du dix)

stay until the 14th
= reste jusqu'au 14 (*say* au quatorze)

from 21st to 30th May
= du 21 au 30 mai (*say* du vingt et un au trente mai)

around 16th May
= le 16 mai environ/vers le 16 mai (*say* le seize mai) *or* aux environs du 16 mai (*say* du seize mai)

not until 1999
= pas avant 1999 (*say* mille neuf cent quatre-vingt-dix-neuf)

Shakespeare (1564–1616)
= Shakespeare (1564–1616) (*say* Shakespeare, quinze cent soixante-quatre – seize cent seize)

Shakespeare b. 1564 d.1616
= Shakespeare, né en 1564, mort en 1616 (*say* Shakespeare, né en quinze cent soixante-quatre, mort en seize cent seize).

■ Note that French has no abbreviations for né and mort.

in May '45
= en mai 45 (*say* en mai quarante-cinq)

in the 1980s
= dans les années 80 (*say* dans les années quatre-vingts)

in the early sixties
= au début des années 60 (*say* des années soixante)

in the late seventies
= à la fin des années 70 (*say* des années soixante-dix)

the riots of '68
= les émeutes de 68 (*say* de soixante-huit)

the 14–18 war
= la guerre de 14
or de 14–18 (*say* de quatorze *or* de quatorze-dix-huit)

the 1912 uprising
= le soulèvement de 1912 (*say* de mille neuf cent douze)

---

daze /deɪz/ n **in a ~** (from blow) étourdi; (from drug) hébété; (from news) ahuri; (feeling vague) abruti

dazed /deɪzd/ adj (by blow) abasourdi; (by news) ahuri

dazzle /'dæzl/
A n (of sunlight, headlights) lumière f aveuglante
B vtr [sun, torch] éblouir; **to ~ sb with** fig éblouir qn par

dazzling /'dæzlɪŋ/ adj éblouissant

DBMS n Comput abrév ► **database management system**

DC Geog abrév = **District of Columbia**

D-day /'diː deɪ/ n ⊡ (important day) jour m J; ⊠ Mil Hist le 6 juin 1944 (*jour du débarquement des Alliés en Normandie*)

DDP n: abrév ► **distributed data processing**

DE US Post abrév écrite = **Delaware**

dead /ded/
A n ⊡ **the ~** (+ v pl) (people) les morts mpl; ⊠ fig (depths) **at ~ of night** en pleine nuit; **in the ~ of winter** en plein hiver
B adj ⊡ (no longer living) mort; **the ~ man/woman** le mort/la morte; **a ~ body** un cadavre; **to drop (down) ~** tomber raide mort; **to play ~** faire le mort/la morte; **to shoot sb ~** abattre qn; **~ and buried** lit, fig mort et enterré; **they're ~ and gone** ils nous ont quittés; **to give sb up for ~** tenir qn pour mort; **I'm absolutely ~**○! (exhausted) je suis mort○!; ⊠ (extinct) [language] mort; [custom] désuet/-ète; [issue] dépassé; [fire] mort; ⊡ (dull, not lively) [place] mort; [audience] apathique; **the ~ season** la morte-saison; ⊡ (not functioning, idle) [battery] à plat; [capital] inactif/-ive; **the phone went ~** tout d'un coup, plus rien (sur la ligne); ⊡ (impervious) insensible (**to** à); ⊡ (numb) [limb] engourdi; ⊡ (absolute) **~ silence** un silence de mort; **to come to a ~ stop** s'arrêter net
C adv surtout GB (absolutely, completely) absolument; **~ certain** absolument sûr; **~ level** parfaitement plat; **~ on time** pile○ à l'heure; **~ on six o'clock** à six heures pile○; **~ easy**○ simple comme bonjour○; **~ on target** parfaitement calculé; **they were ~ lucky**○! ils ont eu du pot○!; **~ drunk**○ ivre mort; **~ tired**○ crevé, claqué○! **I was ~ scared**○! j'avais une trouille bleue○!; **you're ~ right**○! tu as parfaitement raison!; **'~ slow'** Aut 'roulez au pas'; **~ straight** tout à fait droit; **to be ~ against** être totalement opposé à [idea, plan]; **to be ~ set on doing** être tout à fait décidé à faire; **to stop ~** s'arrêter net

Idioms **to be ~ to the world** dormir comme une souche; **I wouldn't be seen ~ in a place like that!** pour rien au monde je ne voudrais être vu dans un endroit pareil!

deaden /'dedn/ vtr calmer [pain]; amortir [blow]; assourdir [sound]

dead end /ˌded'end/
A n lit, fig impasse f
B **dead-end** noun modifier [job] sans perspectives

deadening /'dednɪŋ/ adj [effect] lit anesthésiant; fig abrutissant

deadhead /'dedhed/
A n péj (stupid person) nullité f
B vtr enlever les fleurs fanées de [plant]

dead heat n (in athletics) arrivée f ex-aequo; (in horseracing) dead-heat m inv; **it was a ~** ils ont fini ex-aequo

deadline /'dedlaɪn/ n date f or heure f limite, délai m; **to meet a ~** respecter un délai; **to work to very tight ~s** travailler dans des délais très serrés; **the ~ for applications is the 15th** les candidatures doivent être déposées avant le 15

deadlock /'dedlɒk/ n ⊡ (impasse) impasse f; **to reach (a) ~** aboutir à une impasse; **to break the ~** sortir de l'impasse; ⊠ (lock) verrou m haute sécurité

deadlocked /'dedlɒkt/ adj dans l'impasse

dead loss n ○péj **to be a ~** être nul/nulle○

deadly /'dedlɪ/
A adj ⊡ [poison, disease, enemy] mortel/-elle; [hatred, weapon] meurtrier/-ière; [rivalry] acharné; ⊠ (absolute) **in ~ earnest** avec le plus grand sérieux; **with ~ accuracy** avec la plus grande précision; ⊡ ○(dull, boring) [person, event] mortel/-elle○, rasant○
B adv (dull, boring) terriblement; **~ pale** pâle comme la mort; **to be ~ serious** être des plus sérieux

dead: ~ on arrival, DOA adj Med mort avant d'arriver à l'hôpital; **~pan** adj [humour] pince-sans-rire inv; [expression] de marbre

dead ringer○ n **to be a ~ for sb** être le sosie de qn

Dead Sea pr n mer f Morte

dead set n GB **to make a ~ at sb** jeter son dévolu sur qn○

dead: ~ weight n lit poids m mort; fig (burden) poids m; **~ wood** n lit bois m mort; GB fig personnel m inutile

deaf /def/
A n **the ~** (+ v pl) les sourds mpl, les malentendants mpl voir note
B adj ⊡ sourd voir note; **to go ~** devenir sourd; **to be ~ in one ear** être sourd d'une oreille; **that's his ~ ear** il n'entend pas de cette oreille; ⊠ fig **to be ~ to** être sourd à; **to turn a ~ ear to** faire la sourde oreille à, rester sourd à; **to fall on ~ ears** [request, advice] ne pas trouver d'écho

Idiom **to be as ~ as a post**○ être sourd comme un pot○.

⚠ Ce mot peut être perçu comme injurieux dans cette acception. Lui préférer *hearing-impaired*

deaf: ~ **aid** n GB prothèse f auditive; ~**-and-dumb** n, adj injur = **deaf without speech**

deafen /'defn/ vtr assourdir, rendre [qn] sourd

deafening /'defnɪŋ/ adj assourdissant

deaf-mute /ˌdef'mjuːt/ n, adj sourd-muet/sourde-muette (m/f)

deafness /'defnɪs/ n surdité f

deaf without speech n (+ v pl) the ~ les sourds-muets mpl

deal /diːl/
A n **1** (agreement) gen accord m; (in commerce, finance) affaire f; (with friend, criminal) marché m; **the pay** ~ l'accord salarial; **to make a** ~ **with** faire un marché avec [friend, criminal]; négocier une affaire avec [client, company]; **it's a** ~! marché conclu!; **the** ~**'s off** le marché ne tient pas; **let's do a** ~ je vous propose un marché; **a good** ~ une bonne affaire; **it's all part of the** ~ (part of the arrangement) ça fait partie du marché; (part of the price, package) c'est inclus dans le reste; **to be in on the** ~ être dans le coup○; **2** (sale) vente f; **3** (special offer, bargain) **the best** ~(s) **in electrical goods** les meilleurs prix en électroménager; **4** (amount) **a great** ou **good** ~ beaucoup (of de); **a great** ~ **in common** beaucoup de choses en commun; **she means a great** ~ **to me** je l'aime beaucoup; **it means a great** ~ **to me** cela compte beaucoup pour moi; **5** (treatment) **he got a raw** ~ il s'est fait avoir○; **6** (in cards) donne f; **it's my** ~ c'est à moi de donner

B vtr (prét, pp **dealt**) **1** porter [blow] (**to** à); **2** distribuer [cards]; donner [hand]

C vi (prét, pp **dealt**) Comm (carry on business) [person, firm] être en activité; (operate on stock exchange) faire des opérations boursières; **to** ~ **in** être dans le commerce de [commodity, shares]

(Idioms) **big** ~○! iron la belle affaire! iron; **it's no big** ~○ (not hard) ce n'est rien du tout; **to make a big** ~ **out of sth** faire tout un plat○ de qch

(Phrasal verbs)
■ **deal out**: ▸ ~ **out** [sth], ~ [sth] **out** (mete out) administrer [punishment, fine]
■ **deal with**: ▸ ~ **with** [sth] **1** s'occuper de [complaint, emergency, matter]; faire face à [vandalism, unemployment]; **2** (discuss) traiter de [issue]; ▸ ~ **with** [sb] **1** (attend to) s'occuper de; **2** (do business with) traiter avec

dealer /'diːlə(r)/ ▸ p. 1181 n **1** Comm marchand/-e m/f; (on a large scale) négociant/-e m/f; (for a specific product) concessionnaire m; **art** ~ marchand/-e m/f de tableaux; **authorized** ~ revendeur m agréé; **2** (on stock exchange) opérateur/-trice m/f; **3** (in drugs) revendeur/-euse m/f de drogue, dealer○ m

dealership /'diːləʃɪp/ n Comm concession f (**for** de)

dealing /'diːlɪŋ/
A n **1** Comm vente f; **foreign exchange** ~ opérations fpl de change; ~ **resumed this morning** les transactions ont repris ce matin; **share** ~ transactions fpl boursières; **2** (trafficking) trafic m; **drug** ~ le trafic de drogue
B dealings npl gen relations fpl (**with** avec); Comm relations fpl commerciales (**with** avec); **to have** ~s **with sb** traiter avec qn

dealt /delt/ prét, pp ▸ **deal**

dean /diːn/ n doyen m

dear /dɪə(r)/
A n (term of address) (affectionate) mon chéri/ma chérie m/f; (more formal) mon cher/ma chère m/f; (to woman shopper) ma petite dame○; **you poor** ~ (to adult) mon pauvre/ma pauvre m/f; **he's a** ~ il est adorable; **be a** ~ sois gentil; (more affectionate) sois un amour
B adj **1** (expressing attachment) [friend, mother] cher/chère; **she's a very** ~ **friend of mine** c'est une très bonne amie à moi; **he's my** ~**est friend** c'est mon meilleur ami; ~ **old Richard** ce bon vieux Richard; **the project is** ~ **to his heart** le projet lui tient vraiment à cœur; **her** ~**est wish** son vœu le plus cher; **2** (expressing admiration) **a** ~ **little house** une jolie petite maison; **a** ~ **old lady** une vieille dame adorable; **3** (in letter) cher/chère; **Dear Sir/Madam** Monsieur, Madame; **Dear Sirs** Messieurs; **Dear Mr Jones** Cher Monsieur; **Dear Mr and Mrs Jones** Cher Monsieur, Chère Madame; **Dear Anne and Paul** Chers Anne et Paul; **4** (expensive) cher/chère; **to get** ~**er** augmenter
C adv fig [cost] cher
D excl **oh** ~! (dismay, surprise) oh mon Dieu!; (less serious) aïe!, oh là là!; ~ **me, no!** certainement pas!

dearly /'dɪəlɪ/ adv **1** (very much) **to love sb** ~ aimer tendrement qn; **they would** ~ **love to see you fail** ils seraient ravis de te voir échouer; **I would** ~ **love to know** je payerais cher pour savoir; **2** fig [pay] chèrement; ~ **bought** chèrement payé

death /deθ/ n (of person) mort f, décès m; fig anéantissement m; **at (the time of) his** ~ à sa mort; **a** ~ **in the family** un décès dans la famille; ~ **by drowning** mort par noyade; **to put sb to** ~ exécuter qn; **to the** ~ à mort; **to drink/work oneself to** ~ se tuer en buvant/au travail; **she fell to her** ~ elle s'est tuée en tombant; **he met his** ~ **in a skiing accident** il a trouvé la mort dans un accident de ski; **to die a violent** ~ mourir de mort violente; **'Deaths'** (newspaper column) 'Nécrologie'; **a fall would mean** ~ une chute serait fatale

(Idioms) **to die a** ou **the** ~ [fashion] disparaître complètement; [entertainer, play] faire un bide○; **he'll be the** ~ **of me!** il me tuera!; **it's a matter of life or** ~ c'est une question de vie ou de mort; **to look like** ~ **warmed up** avoir l'air d'un cadavre ambulant; **to be at** ~**'s door** être à (l'article de) la mort; **to be worried/frightened to** ~○ être mort d'inquiétude/de peur; **to frighten sb to** ~ faire une peur bleue à qn○; **to be bored to** ~○ s'ennuyer à mourir; **I'm sick to** ~○ **of this!** j'en ai par-dessus la tête○!; **you'll catch your** ~ **(of cold)**○ tu vas attraper la crève○

death: ~**bed** n lit m de mort; ~ **camp** n camp m de la mort; ~ **certificate** n Jur acte m de décès; ~ **duties** npl droits mpl de succession

death knell /'deθnel/ n lit, fig glas m

death list n liste f noire

deathly /'deθlɪ/
A adj [pallor] cadavérique; [calm, silence] de mort
B adv ~ **pale** d'une pâleur cadavérique; **it was** ~ **quiet** il y avait un silence de mort

death: ~ **mask** n masque m mortuaire; ~ **penalty** n peine f de mort; ~ **rate** n taux m de mortalité; ~ **ray** n rayon m mortel; ~ **row** n US quartier m des condamnés à mort; ~ **sentence** n lit, fig condamnation f à mort; ~ **threat** n menaces fpl de mort

death throes npl lit, fig agonie f

death toll n nombre m de morts

death trap n **to be a** ~ être très dangereux/-euse

death: ~ **warrant** n ordre m d'exécution; ~ **wish** n pulsion f de mort

debacle /deɪ'bɑːkl/ n fiasco m, débâcle f

debar /dɪ'bɑː(r)/ vtr (p prés etc **-rr-**) exclure; **to be** ~ed **from doing** ne pas avoir le droit de faire

debase /dɪ'beɪs/
A vtr dégrader [emotion, ideal]; déprécier [currency]; rabaisser [person]
B debased pp adj [language] appauvri

debatable /dɪ'beɪtəbl/ adj discutable; **that's** ~! cela se discute!; **it is** ~ **whether** on peut se demander si

debate /dɪ'beɪt/
A n (formal, about an issue) débat m (**on, about** sur); (informal discussion) discussion f (**about** à propos de); **to hold a** ~ **on** débattre de [issue]
B vtr gen, Pol (formally) débattre de [issue, bill]; (informally) discuter de [question]; **I am debating whether to leave** je me demande si je dois partir
C vi **to** ~ **about sth** discuter de qch (**with** avec)

debauch /dɪ'bɔːtʃ/ vtr dépraver

debauchery /dɪ'bɔːtʃərɪ/ n débauche f

debenture: ~ **bond** n certificat m d'obligation; ~ **stock** n obligations fpl non garanties

debilitating /dɪ'bɪlɪteɪtɪŋ/ adj [disease] débilitant

debit /'debɪt/ Fin
A n débit m
B noun modifier [account, balance] débiteur/-trice; ~ **entries** sommes fpl inscrites au débit
C vtr débiter [account] (**with** de)

debonair /ˌdebə'neə(r)/ adj [person] élégant et plein d'assurance

debrief /ˌdiː'briːf/ vtr interroger; **to be** ~ed [diplomat, agent] rendre compte (oralement) d'une mission; [defector, freed hostage] être interrogé

debriefing /ˌdiːˈbriːfɪŋ/ n [1] 𝒞 (of freed hostage, defector) interrogation f; **the soldiers will remain here for** ~ les soldats resteront ici pour rendre compte de leur mission; [2] **C** (report) compte-rendu m (oral), critique f

debris /ˈdeɪbriː, ˈde-, US dəˈbriː/ n (of plane) débris mpl; (of building) décombres mpl; (rubbish) déchets mpl

debt /det/
A n [1] Fin dette f (**to** envers); **bad** ~s créances fpl douteuses; **to get into** ~ s'endetter; **to be in** ~ avoir des dettes; **she is $2,000 in** ~ elle a 2 000 dollars de dettes; **to get out of** ~ acquitter ses dettes; **to pay off one's** ~s rembourser ses dettes; [2] (obligation) dette f (**to** envers); **to acknowledge one's** ~ **to sb** reconnaître qu'on doit beaucoup à qn
B noun modifier Fin [collection, recovery, relief] des créances; [capacity, level, ratio] d'endettement

debt collector n agent m de recouvrement

debtor /ˈdetə(r)/ Fin n débiteur/-trice m/f

debug /ˌdiːˈbʌg/ vtr (p prés etc **-gg-**) [1] Comput déboguer; [2] enlever les micros cachés dans [room]

debunk /ˌdiːˈbʌŋk/ vtr démystifier [theory]; briser [myth]

debut /ˈdeɪbjuː, US dɪˈbjuː/
A n (artistic, sporting) débuts mpl; **to make one's** ~ **as** (in unfamiliar activity) faire ses débuts comme [director]; (in particular role) débuter dans le rôle de
B noun modifier [album, concert, role] premier/-ière

Dec abrév écrite = **December**

decade /ˈdekeɪd, dɪˈkeɪd, US dɪˈkeɪd/ n décennie f

decadent /ˈdekədənt/ adj décadent

decaffeinated /ˌdiːˈkæfɪneɪtɪd/ adj décaféiné

decalitre GB, **decaliter** US /ˈdekəliːtə(r)/ ▸ p. 723 n décalitre m

decametre GB, **decameter** US /ˈdekəmiːtə(r)/ ▸ p. 977 n décamètre m

decamp /dɪˈkæmp/ vi (leave) partir; **to** ~ **with sth** s'éclipser en emportant qch

decant /dɪˈkænt/ vtr lit décanter [wine]; transvaser [other liquid]

decanter /dɪˈkæntə(r)/ n (for wine, port) carafe f (à décanter); (for whisky) flacon m à whisky

decapitate /dɪˈkæpɪteɪt/ vtr décapiter

decathlon /dɪˈkæθlɒn/ n décathlon m

decay /dɪˈkeɪ/
A n [1] (rot) (of timber, vegetation) pourriture f; (of house, area) délabrement m; **to fall into** ~ [building] se délabrer; [2] (dental) carie f; [3] fig (of culture) déclin m; (of institution, industry) déclin m; (of civilization) décadence f; **moral** ~ déchéance morale
B vi [1] (rot) [timber, vegetation, food] pourrir; [corpse] se décomposer; [tooth] se carier; [bone] se détériorer; [2] (disintegrate) [building] se détériorer; [3] fig (decline) [civilization] décliner

deceased /dɪˈsiːst/
A n **the** ~ (dead person) le défunt/la défunte; (collectively) les défunts mpl
B adj décédé, défunt

deceit /dɪˈsiːt/ n malhonnêteté f

deceitful /dɪˈsiːtfl/ adj malhonnête

deceive /dɪˈsiːv/
A vtr [1] (lie to and mislead) tromper, duper [friend]; **to be** ~d (fooled) être dupe; **don't be** ~d **by his air of calm** ne te laisse pas abuser par son calme; [2] (be unfaithful to) tromper [spouse, lover]
B v refl **to** ~ **oneself** se faire des illusions

December /dɪˈsembə(r)/ ▸ p. 1020 n décembre m

decency /ˈdiːsnsɪ/ n [1] (good manners) politesse f; **common** ~ la simple politesse; **you can't in all** ~... tu ne peux décemment pas...; [2] (morality) **he hasn't an ounce of** ~ il n'a pas le moindre sens moral; [3] (propriety) convenances fpl; (in sexual matters) décence f; **he has no sense of** ~ il n'a aucun sens des convenances

decent /ˈdiːsnt/ adj [1] (respectable) [family, man, woman] comme il faut, bien inv; **no** ~ **person would do a thing like that** quelqu'un de normal ne ferait jamais ça; **a** ~ **burial** un enterrement convenable; **after a** ~ **interval** après une période convenable; **to do the** ~ **thing** faire la chose qu'il faut/fallait; [2] (pleasant) sympathique, bien° inv; **it's** ~ **of him** c'est très gentil à lui; [3] (adequate) [housing, wages, level, facilities] convenable; [4] (not shabby) [garment] correct; **I've nothing** ~ **to wear** je n'ai rien de mettable; [5] (good)

[camera, education, result] bon/bonne (before n); [profit] appréciable; **to make a** ~ **living** bien gagner sa vie; **a** ~ **night's sleep** une bonne nuit de sommeil; **they do a** ~ **fish soup** leur soupe de poisson n'est pas mauvaise; [6] (not indecent) décent, correct; **are you** ~? es-tu habillé?

decently /ˈdiːsntlɪ/ adv [1] (fairly) [paid, treated, housed] convenablement; [2] (respectably) [behave] convenablement; [3] (politely) **we left as soon as we** ~ **could** nous sommes partis dès que nous l'avons décemment pu

decentralize /diːˈsentrəlaɪz/ vtr décentraliser

decent-sized adj assez grand

deception /dɪˈsepʃn/ n [1] 𝒞 (deceiving) **is she capable of such** ~? est-elle capable d'une telle duplicité?; **to obtain sth by** ~ obtenir qch par fraude; [2] (trick) supercherie f; (to gain money, property) escroquerie f

deceptive /dɪˈseptɪv/ adj [appearance] trompeur/-euse

deceptively /dɪˈseptɪvlɪ/ adv **it's** ~ **easy** c'est plus difficile qu'il n'y paraît

decide /dɪˈsaɪd/
A vtr [1] (reach a decision) **to** ~ **to do** décider de faire; (after much thought) se décider à faire; **I** ~d **to do it** j'ai décidé de le faire; **I finally** ~d **to do it** je me suis décidé à le faire; **I** ~d **that I would leave** j'ai décidé de partir; **he hasn't** ~d **whether to resign** il n'a pas encore décidé s'il va démissionner; [2] (settle) régler [matter]; décider de [fate, outcome]; **the goal** ~d **the match** le but a été décisif; [3] (persuade) **to** ~ **sb to do** décider qn à faire
B vi décider; **let her** ~ laisse-la décider or prendre la décision; **it's up to him to** ~ c'est à lui de décider; **I can't** ~ je n'arrive pas à me décider; **have you** ~d? as-tu pris une décision?; **to** ~ **against doing** décider de ne pas faire; **to** ~ **against** ne pas adopter [plan, idea]; rejeter [candidate]; **to** ~ **against sth** (choose not to buy) décider de ne pas acheter qch; **to** ~ **between** choisir, faire un choix entre [applicants, books]; **to** ~ **in favour of doing** décider de faire; **to** ~ **in favour of** choisir [candidate, applicant]

⬡ (Phrasal verb)

■ **decide on:** ▸ ~ **on [sth]** [1] (choose) se décider pour [hat, wallpaper]; fixer [date]; **to** ~ **on a career in law** se diriger vers le droit; [2] (come to a decision on) décider de [course of action, size, budget]; ▸ ~ **on [sb]** choisir [member, applicant]; sélectionner [team]

decided /dɪˈsaɪdɪd/ adj [1] (appreciable) net/nette; [2] (determined) [manner, tone] décidé, résolu; [views] arrêté

decidedly /dɪˈsaɪdɪdlɪ/ adv (distinctly) [smaller, better, happier] nettement; [unwell, violent, odd] franchement

decider /dɪˈsaɪdə(r)/ n (point) point m décisif; (goal) but m décisif; **the** ~ (game) la belle

deciding /dɪˈsaɪdɪŋ/ adj décisif/-ive

deciduous /dɪˈsɪdjʊəs, dɪˈsɪdʒʊəs/ adj [tree] à feuilles caduques

decigram(me) /ˈdesɪgræm/ ▸ p. 1323 n décigramme m

decilitre GB, **deciliter** US /ˈdesɪliːtə(r)/ ▸ p. 723 n décilitre m

decimal /ˈdesɪml/
A n décimale f
B adj [system, currency] décimal; ~ **point** virgule f; **to calculate to two** ~ **places** calculer à deux décimales; **to go** ~ adopter le système décimal

decimate /ˈdesɪmeɪt/ vtr lit, fig décimer

decimetre GB, **decimeter** US /ˈdesɪmiːtə(r)/ ▸ p. 977 n décimètre m

decipher /dɪˈsaɪfə(r)/ vtr déchiffrer

decision /dɪˈsɪʒn/ n décision f; **my** ~ **to leave** la décision que j'ai prise de partir; **to make** ou **take a** ~ prendre une décision; **to reach** or **come to a** ~ se décider; **the right/wrong** ~ la bonne/mauvaise décision; **the judges'** ~ **is final** la décision du jury est sans appel

decision-making
A n **to be good/bad at** ~ savoir/ne pas savoir prendre des décisions
B noun modifier ~ **skills** compétences fpl en matière de décision; **the** ~ **processes** les processus décisionnels

decisive /dɪˈsaɪsɪv/ adj [1] (firm) [manner, tone] ferme; **a more** ~ **leader** un dirigeant plus ferme; [2] (conclusive) [battle, factor] décisif/-ive; [argument] concluant

decisively /dɪˈsaɪsɪvlɪ/ adv avec fermeté

deck /dek/
A n [1] (on ship) pont m; **car** ~ pont des voitures; **on** ~ sur le

pont; **below** ∼**(s)** sur le pont inférieur; **2**▸ US (terrace) terrasse f; **3**▸ (on bus) étage m; **4**▸ ∼ **of cards** jeu m de cartes

B vtr (decorate) orner [building, table] (**with** de); décorer [tree] (**with** de)

(Idioms) **all hands on** ∼! tout le monde sur le pont!; **to clear the** ∼**s** déblayer le terrain; **to hit the** ∼○ tomber par terre

deckchair n chaise f longue, transat○ m

decking /'dekɪŋ/ n terrasse f en bois

declaration /,deklə'reɪʃn/ n déclaration f; **the Declaration of Independence** la Déclaration d'indépendance des États-Unis d'Amérique; **a customs** ∼ une déclaration en douane; ∼ **of intent** déclaration f de principe

> ⓘ **Declaration of Independence** Document rédigé en 1776 par Thomas Jefferson pour affirmer l'indépendance des treize colonies américaines vis-à-vis de la Grande-Bretagne. Y sont déjà posés le principe d'égalité entre les hommes ainsi que 'le droit à la vie, à la liberté et à la poursuite du bonheur'. ▸ Independence Day

declare /dɪ'kleə(r)/
A vtr **1**▸ (state firmly) déclarer (**that** que); (state openly) annoncer [intention, support]; **2**▸ (proclaim) déclarer [war]; proclamer [independence]; **to** ∼ **war on** déclarer la guerre à; **to** ∼ **a state of emergency** déclarer l'état d'urgence; **3**▸ (officially) déclarer [income]; communiquer [dividend]
B vi **1**▸ (come out in favour) se déclarer (**for** pour); **2**▸ US Pol annoncer sa candidature (à la présidence)

declassify /,di:'klæsɪfaɪ/ vtr rendre [qch] accessible [document, information]

declension /dɪ'klenʃn/ n déclinaison f

decline /dɪ'klaɪn/
A n **1**▸ (waning) déclin m (**of** de); **to be in** ∼ être en déclin; **to go into** ou **fall into** ∼ tomber en déclin; **2**▸ (drop) baisse f (**in, of** de); **to be on the** ou **in** ∼ être en baisse; **3**▸ (of health, person) déclin m (**in, of** de); **to go/fall into (a)** ∼ dépérir
B vtr décliner
C vi **1**▸ (drop) baisser (**by** de); [support] être en baisse; [business] ralentir; **2**▸ (wane) être sur le déclin; **3**▸ (refuse) refuser
D declining pres p adj **1**▸ (getting fewer, less) **a declining birth rate** un taux de natalité en baisse; **declining sales** la baisse des ventes; **2**▸ (in decline) [industry, influence] en déclin; **3**▸ (getting worse) [health] déclinant

declutch /,di:'klʌtʃ/ vi GB débrayer

decode /,di:'kəʊd/ vtr décoder [code, message, signal]

decoding /,di:'kəʊdɪŋ/ n (all contexts) décodage m

décolleté /deɪ'kɒlteɪ, US -kʊl'teɪ/ n, adj décolleté (m)

decompose /,di:kəm'pəʊz/ vi se décomposer

decomposition /,di:kɒmpə'zɪʃn/ n décomposition f

decompress /,di:kəm'pres/ vtr Comput décompacter

decompression /,di:kəm'preʃn/ n décompression f

decontamination /,di:kən,tæmɪ'neɪʃn/ n décontamination f

decor /'deɪkɔ:(r), US deɪ'kɔ:r/ n (specific style) décoration f, décor m; (of house) décoration f; Theat décor m

decorate /'dekəreɪt/
A vtr **1**▸ (adorn) décorer (**with** de, avec); **2**▸ (paint and paper) gen refaire; (paint only) peindre; (paper only) tapisser; **the whole house needs to be** ∼**d** il faudra refaire toute la décoration de la maison; **to** ∼ **the kitchen** (with paint) refaire les peintures dans la cuisine; (with paper) tapisser la cuisine; **3**▸ Mil décorer (**for** pour)
B vi (in house) faire des travaux de décoration

decorating /'dekəreɪtɪŋ/ n (of room, house) travaux mpl de décoration

decoration /,dekə'reɪʃn/ n **1**▸ (object) décoration f; **to put up/take down** ∼**s** mettre/enlever les décorations; **2**▸ (trimming on clothes) **with embroidered** ∼ orné de broderies; **3**▸ (act or result) (for festivities) décoration f; (by painter) travaux mpl de décoration; **only for** ∼ purement ornemental; **4**▸ Mil décoration f

decorative /'dekərətɪv, US 'dekəreɪtɪv/ adj [border, frill] décoratif/-ive; [sculpture, design] ornemental

decorator /'dekəreɪtə(r)/ n peintre m, décorateur/-trice m/f

decorum /dɪ'kɔ:rəm/ n **with** ∼ en respectant les convenances; **a sense of** ∼ un sens des convenances or du décorum

decoy
A /'di:kɔɪ/ n (person, vehicle) leurre m; (for hunting) appeau m, leurre m
B /dɪ'kɔɪ/ vtr attirer [qn] dans un piège

decrease
A /'di:kri:s/ n gen diminution f (**in** de); (in price) baisse f (**in** de)
B /dɪ'kri:s/ vtr diminuer, réduire
C /dɪ'kri:s/ vi [population] diminuer; [price] baisser; [popularity, rate] baisser, diminuer

decreasing /dɪ'kri:sɪŋ/ adj [population, proportion] décroissant; [strength] déclinant; [price] en baisse

decreasingly /dɪ'kri:sɪŋlɪ/ adv de moins en moins

decree /dɪ'kri:/
A n **1**▸ (order) décret m; **2**▸ (judgment) jugement m, arrêt m; ∼ **absolute/nisi** (in divorce) jugement définitif/provisoire (de divorce)
B vtr **1**▸ gen décréter; **2**▸ Jur ordonner

(Idiom) **fate had** ∼**d otherwise** le sort en avait décidé autrement

decrepit /dɪ'krepɪt/ adj [chair, table] en mauvais état; [building] délabré; [horse, old person] décrépit

decrypt /di:'krɪpt/ vtr décoder, déchiffrer

decryption /di:'krɪpʃn/ n décodage m, déchiffrement m

dedicate /'dedɪkeɪt/ vtr **1**▸ (devote) consacrer, dédier [life, time] (**to** à); dédier [book, performance] (**to** à); **2**▸ Relig consacrer [church, shrine] (**to** à)

dedicated /'dedɪkeɪtɪd/ adj **1**▸ (keen, devoted) [teacher, mother, fan] dévoué; [worker, secretary] zélé; [disciple] enthousiaste; [socialist] convaincu; [musician, attitude] sérieux/-ieuse; **we only want people who are really** ∼ nous ne voulons que des gens sérieux; **he is** ∼ **to social reform** il consacre tous ses efforts aux réformes sociales; **2**▸ Comput spécialisé

dedication /,dedɪ'keɪʃn/ n **1**▸ (devoted attitude) dévouement m (**to** à); **her** ∼ **to duty** son dévouement; **2**▸ (in a book, on music programme) dédicace f; **3**▸ (act of dedicating) dédicace f

deduce /dɪ'dju:s, US -'dus/ vtr déduire

deduct /dɪ'dʌkt/ vtr prélever [subscription, tax] (**from** sur); déduire [sum, expenses] (**from** de)

deductible /dɪ'dʌktəbl/ adj Comm déductible

deduction /dɪ'dʌkʃn/ n **1**▸ (on wages) retenue f; (of tax) prélèvement m; (on bill) déduction f; **after** ∼**s** une fois les retenues effectuées; **a** ∼ **from** une déduction or une retenue or un prélèvement sur; **2**▸ (conclusion) déduction f, conclusion f; **to make a** ∼ tirer une conclusion (**from** de); **3**▸ (reasoning) déduction f

deed /di:d/ n **1**▸ (action) acte m; **to do one's good** ∼ **for the day** faire sa bonne action; **2**▸ (for property) acte m de propriété

deed: ∼ **box** n coffre m à documents; ∼ **of covenant** n Jur acte m de donation

deed poll n (pl **deeds poll**) **to change one's name by** ∼ changer légalement son nom

deem /di:m/ vtr considérer; **it was** ∼**ed necessary/appropriate to do** on a jugé nécessaire/convenable de faire

deep /di:p/ ▸ p. 977
A n littér **the** ∼ l'océan m
B adj **1**▸ (from top to bottom) gen profond; [mud, snow, carpet] épais/épaisse; [container, drawer, saucepan, grass] haut; **a** ∼**-pile carpet** une moquette de haute laine; **how** ∼ **is the lake?** quelle est la profondeur du lac?; **the lake is 13 m** ∼ le lac a 13 m de profondeur; **a hole 5 cm** ∼ un trou de 5 cm; **2**▸ (in width) [band, strip] large; **3**▸ (from front to back) [shelf, alcove, stage] profond; **a shelf 30 cm** ∼ une étagère de 30 cm de profondeur; **4**▸ fig (intense) [grief, desire, need] grand; **to be in** ∼ **trouble**○ avoir de sérieux ennuis; **5**▸ (impenetrable) gen profond; [secret] grand; [person] réservé; **in** ∼**est Wales** hum au fin fond du pays de Galles; **you're a** ∼ **one**○! tu caches bien ton jeu○!; **6**▸ (intellectually profound) gen profond; [knowledge] approfondi; **at a** ∼**er level** plus en profondeur; **7**▸ (dark) [colour] intense; [tan] prononcé; ∼ **blue eyes** des yeux d'un bleu profond; **8**▸ (low) [voice] profond; [note, sound] grave; **9**▸ (involved, absorbed) ∼ **in** absorbé dans [thought, entertainment]; plongé dans [book,

conversation]; **~ in debt** endetté jusqu'au cou; ⑩ (long) [*shot, serve*] en profondeur

C *adv* ① (a long way down) [*dig, bury, cut*] profondément; **~ beneath the earth's surface** à une grande profondeur sous la surface de la terre; **to sink ~er** s'enfoncer plus profondément; **to dig ~er into an affair** fig creuser (plus loin) une affaire; **to sink ~er into debt** fig s'endetter davantage; ② (a long way in) **~ in** *ou* **into** au cœur de [*region*]; **~ in my heart** tout au fond de moi-même; **to be ~ in thought** être plongé dans ses pensées; **~ into the night** jusque tard dans la nuit; ③ fig (emotionally, in psyche) **~ down** *ou* **inside** dans mon/ton etc for intérieur; **to go ~** [*faith, loyalty*] être profond; **it goes ~er than that** c'est plus sérieux que ça; **to run ~** [*belief, feeling, prejudice*] être bien enraciné; ④ Sport [*kick, serve*] en profondeur

(Idioms) **to be in ~**○ y être jusqu'au cou○; **to be in ~ water** être dans de beaux draps○

deepen /ˈdiːpən/
A *vtr* ① (make deeper) creuser [*channel, hollow*]; ② fig (intensify) augmenter [*admiration, concern, love*]; ③ (make lower) rendre [qch] plus grave [*voice, tone*]; ④ (make darker) foncer [*colour*]
B *vi* ① [*water*] devenir plus profond; [*snow, mud*] s'épaissir; [*wrinkle*] se creuser; ② fig (intensify) [*admiration, concern, love*] augmenter; [*knowledge*] s'approfondir; [*crisis*] s'aggraver; [*mystery*] s'épaissir; [*silence*] se faire plus profond; [*rift*] s'élargir; ③ (grow lower) [*voice, pitch, tone*] devenir plus grave; ④ (grow darker) [*colour*] foncer
C **deepening** *pres p adj* ① fig (intensifying) [*mystery, need, rift*] croissant; [*crisis*] de plus en plus grave; [*awareness*] de plus en plus approfondi; [*confusion*] de plus en plus grand; [*conviction*] de plus en plus profond; ② lit [*water*] de plus en plus haut; [*snow*] de plus en plus épais/épaisse; ③ (of a voice) de plus en plus grave; ④ (becoming darker) [*colour*] de plus en plus foncé

deep end /ˈdiːpɛnd/ *n* grand bassin *m*

(Idioms) **to go off the ~**○ sortir de ses gonds○; **to jump in at the ~** fig prendre le taureau par les cornes; **to throw sb in at the ~** fig forcer qn à prendre le taureau par les cornes

deep-felt /ˌdiːpˈfɛlt/ *adj* [*admiration*] sincère; [*loathing*] profond

deep-freeze /ˌdiːpˈfriːz/
A *n* congélateur *m*
B *vtr* (*prét* **-froze**, *pp* **-frozen**) congeler

deep: **~-fried** *adj* frit; **~-frozen** *adj* congelé; **~-fry** *vtr* faire frire; **~-(fat-)fryer** *n* friteuse *f*

deeply /ˈdiːplɪ/ *adv* [*felt, moving*] profondément; [*involved*] à fond; **our most ~ held convictions** nos convictions les plus solides; [*think*] profondément; **to go ~ into sth** analyser qch en profondeur; [*breathe, sigh, sleep*] profondément; [*dig, cut, thrust*] profondément; [*drink*] à grands traits; [*tanned*] extrêmement

deep: **~-rooted** *adj* [*anxiety, prejudice, problem*] profondément enraciné; [*habit*] ancré; **~-sea** *adj* [*exploration, diver, diving*] sous-marin/-e; [*fisherman, fishing*] hauturier/-ière; **~-seated** *adj* = **deep-rooted**; **~-set** *adj* (très) enfoncé; **~ South** *n* US Sud *m* profond; **~ space** *n* espace *m* lointain

deer /dɪə(r)/ *n* (red) cerf *m*; (roe) chevreuil *m*; (fallow) daim *m*; (female of all species) biche *f*

de-escalate /ˌdiːˈɛskəleɪt/
A *vtr* faire baisser [*tension, violence*]; désamorcer [*crisis*]
B *vi* [*tension, violence*] baisser; [*arms race*] ralentir; [*crisis*] se désamorcer

deface /dɪˈfeɪs/ *vtr* abîmer [*wall, door*]; dégrader, couvrir [qch] d'inscriptions [*painting, monument*]; **to ~ sth with** barbouiller qch de

default /dɪˈfɔːlt/
A *n* (failure to keep up payments) non-remboursement *m*; (failure to pay fine, debt) non-paiement *m*; **the company is in ~** la compagnie manque à ses engagements
B *vi* (fail to make payments) ne pas régler ses échéances; **to ~ on payments** *ou* **on a loan** ne pas régler ses échéances d'un emprunt
C **by default** *adv phr* par défaut; **to win by ~** gagner par forfait; **to be elected by ~** être élu à défaut de concurrents
D **in default of** *prep phr* en l'absence de

defeat /dɪˈfiːt/
A *n* ① (getting beaten) défaite *f*; **to suffer a ~** essuyer une

défaite; **England's 3–2** ~ la défaite de l'Angleterre 2–3; ② (of proposal, bill) rejet *m* (**of** de); ③ (personal failure) échec *m*; **an admission of ~** un aveu d'échec; **to admit ~** avouer son échec
B *vtr* ① (beat) vaincre [*enemy*]; battre [*team, opposition, candidate*]; faire subir une défaite à [*government*]; **the government was ~ed** le gouvernement a été mis en échec; ② (overthrow) rejeter [*bill, proposal*]; ③ (thwart) faire échouer [*take-over bid*]; vaincre [*inflation*]; **it ~s the whole purpose!** ça ne sert plus à rien!

defeated /dɪˈfiːtɪd/ *adj* [*army, party*] vaincu; [*candidate, opponent*] malheureux/-euse

defeatist /dɪˈfiːtɪst/
A *n* défaitiste *mf*
B *adj* défaitiste

defect
A /ˈdiːfɛkt/ *n* ① (flaw) défaut *m*; (minor) imperfection *f*; **mechanical ~** faute *f* mécanique; **structural ~** vice *m* de construction; ② (disability) **a speech ~** un défaut d'élocution
B /dɪˈfɛkt/ *vi* faire défection; **to ~ from** s'enfuir de [*country*]; **to ~ to the West** passer à l'Ouest

defection /dɪˈfɛkʃn/ *n* **~ from** défection *f* de; **~ to** passage *m* à

defective /dɪˈfɛktɪv/ *adj* (faulty) gen défectueux/-euse; (sight etc) déficient; **~ workmanship** malfaçons *fpl*

defector /dɪˈfɛktə(r)/ *n* transfuge *mf* (**from** de)

defence GB, **defense** US /dɪˈfɛns/
A *n* ① (act of protecting) défense *f*; **to put up a spirited ~** se défendre vaillamment; **in ~ of the right to strike** pour le droit de grève; **in the ~ of freedom** pour défendre la liberté; ② (means of protection) défense *f* (**against** contre); **a ~ against** un moyen de lutter contre [*anxiety, boredom*]; ③ (support) défense *f*; **in my own ~ I must say that...** je dois dire pour ma propre défense que...; **an article in ~ of monetarism** un article défendant le monétarisme; ④ Jur **the ~** (representatives of the accused, case, argument) la défense; **the case for the ~** la défense; **in her ~** à sa décharge; ⑤ Sport défense *f*; **to play in ~** jouer en défense; ⑥ Univ soutenance *f* (de thèse)
B **defences** *npl* gen, Mil défenses *fpl*
C *noun modifier* ① Mil gen de la défense; [*contract*] pour la défense; [*policy, forces*] de défense; [*cuts*] dans la défense; ② Jur [*counsel, lawyer*] pour la défense; [*witness*] à décharge

Defence Department GB, **Defense Ministry** US *n* ministère *m* de la Défense nationale

defenceless GB, **defenseless** US /dɪˈfɛnslɪs/ *adj* [*person, animal*] sans défense; [*town, country*] sans défenses

Defence Minister GB, **Defense Secretary** US *n* ministre *m* de la défense nationale

defend /dɪˈfɛnd/
A *vtr* défendre [*fort, freedom, interests, client, title, belief*]; justifier [*behaviour, decision*]; **to ~ a thesis** soutenir une thèse
B *vi* Sport défendre
C *v refl* **to ~ oneself** (protect oneself) lit, fig se défendre
D **defending** *pres p adj* [*counsel*] de la défense; **the ~ing champion** le tenant du titre

defendant /dɪˈfɛndənt/ *n* gen défendeur/-eresse *m/f*

defender /dɪˈfɛndə(r)/ *n* gen, Sport défenseur *m*

defense *n* US = **defence**

defensive /dɪˈfɛnsɪv/
A *n* gen, Sport, Mil défensive *f*
B *adj* [*weapon*] défensif/-ive; [*reaction, behaviour*] de défense; **to be (very) ~** être sur la défensive

defer /dɪˈfɜː(r)/
A *vtr* (*p prés etc* **-rr-**) gen reporter (**until** à); suspendre [*judgment*]; remettre [qch] à plus tard [*departure, journey*]; différer [*payment*]
B *vi* (*p prés etc* **-rr-**) **to ~ to sb** s'incliner devant qn
C **deferred** *pp adj* [*departure, purchase*] différé; [*annuity, interest*] différé; [*sale*] à tempérament, à crédit

deference /ˈdefərəns/ *n* déférence *f*; **in ~ to** par déférence pour

deferential /ˌdefəˈrenʃl/ *adj* déférent

deferment /dɪˈfɜːmənt/, **deferral** /dɪˈfɜːrəl/ *n* (postponement) prorogation *f*

defiance /dɪˈfaɪəns/ *n* ∅ défi *m* (**of** à); **in ~ of logic/all the evidence** contre la logique/toute évidence

defiant /dɪˈfaɪənt/ adj [person] rebelle; [behaviour] provocant

defiantly /dɪˈfaɪəntlɪ/ adv [say] avec défi

deficiency /dɪˈfɪʃənsɪ/ n **1** (shortage) insuffisance f (of, in de); Med carence f (of en); **2** (weakness) **his deficiencies as a poet** ses faiblesses fpl en tant que poète; **3** Med défaut m

deficient /dɪˈfɪʃnt/ adj (inadequate) insuffisant; (faulty, flawed) déficient (in en)

deficit /ˈdefɪsɪt/ n Comm déficit m; **in** ~ en déficit

defile /dɪˈfaɪl/ vtr **1** (pollute) lit, fig souiller; **2** Relig profaner

define /dɪˈfaɪn/ vtr **1** définir [term, limits] (**as** comme); **2** (pinpoint) déterminer [problem]; **3** **to be** ~d **against** se détacher nettement sur [sky]

definite /ˈdefɪnɪt/ adj **1** (not vague) [plan, criteria, amount] précis; [impression] net/nette; **a** ~ **answer** une réponse claire et nette; ~ **evidence** preuves fpl formelles; **nothing is** ~ **yet** rien n'est encore sûr; **2** (firm) [contract, agreement, decision, intention] ferme; [refusal] catégorique; **3** (obvious) [change, improvement, increase] net/nette; [advantage] certain, évident; [smell] très net/nette; **4** **to be** ~ [person] (sure) être certain (**about** de); (unyielding) être formel/-elle (**about** sur)

definite article n Ling article m défini

definitely /ˈdefɪnɪtlɪ/ adv **1** (certainly) sans aucun doute; **he** ~ **said he wasn't coming** il a bien dit qu'il ne viendrait pas; **she's** ~ **not there** elle n'est pas là, c'est sûr; **I'm** ~ **not going** c'est décidé, je n'y vais pas; **it's** ~ **colder today** il fait nettement plus froid aujourd'hui; **this one is** ~ **the best** celui-ci est sans conteste le meilleur; **this** ~ **isn't going to work** manifestement ça ne va pas marcher; **'**~**!'** 'absolument!'; **2** (categorically) [commit oneself] formellement

definition /ˌdefɪˈnɪʃn/ n gen, TV définition f

definitive /dɪˈfɪnətɪv/ adj définitif/-ive

definitively /dɪˈfɪnətɪvlɪ/ adv gen définitivement; [answer] de manière définitive

deflate /dɪˈfleɪt/
A vtr **1** lit dégonfler; **2** fig **to** ~ **sb's ego** remettre qn à sa place
B vi [tyre, balloon] se dégonfler

deflation /dɪˈfleɪʃn/ n Econ déflation f

deflationary /ˌdiːˈfleɪʃənərɪ, US -nerɪ/ adj déflationniste

deflect /dɪˈflekt/ vtr **1** défléchir, dévier [missile]; **2** fig détourner [blame, criticism, attention]

deflection /dɪˈflekʃn/ n (of missile) déviation f; Phys (of air) déflexion f; (of light) déviation f

deform /dɪˈfɔːm/
A vtr déformer
B deformed pp adj **1** Med déformé; (from birth) difforme; **2** [metal, structure] déformé

defraud /dɪˈfrɔːd/ vtr escroquer [client, employer]; frauder [tax authority]; **to** ~ **sb of sth** escroquer qch à qn

defrost /ˌdiːˈfrɒst/
A vtr décongeler [food]; dégivrer [refrigerator]
B vi [refrigerator] dégivrer; [food] décongeler

deft /deft/ adj adroit de ses mains, habile

deftly /ˈdeftlɪ/ adv adroitement

defunct /dɪˈfʌŋkt/ adj [organization, person] défunt

defuse /ˌdiːˈfjuːz/ vtr désamorcer

defy /dɪˈfaɪ/ vtr **1** (disobey) défier [authority, law, death, gravity, person]; **2** (challenge) **to** ~ **sb to do** mettre qn au défi de faire; **3** (elude, resist) défier [description, logic, analysis]

degenerate
A /dɪˈdʒenərət/ n dégénéré/-e m/f
B /dɪˈdʒenərət/ adj gen dégénéré; [life] dépravé
C /dɪˈdʒenəreɪt/ vi dégénérer (**into** en)

degeneration /dɪˌdʒenəˈreɪʃn/ n dégénérescence f

degradation /ˌdegrəˈdeɪʃn/ n **1** (squalor) décrépitude f; **2** (debasement) déchéance f; (of culture) dégradation f

degrade /dɪˈɡreɪd/ vtr **1** (humiliate) humilier [person]; **2** (damage) dégrader [environment]

degrading /dɪˈɡreɪdɪŋ/ adj [conditions, film] dégradant; [job] avilissant; [treatment] humiliant

degree /dɪˈɡriː/ n **1** Geog, Math, Phys degré m; **40** ~**s to the vertical** 40 degrés par rapport à la verticale; **ten** ~**s of** latitude/longitude 10 degrés de latitude/longitude; **30** ~**s centigrade** 30 degrés centigrades; **a temperature of 104** ~**s** 39 de fièvre; **2** Univ diplôme m universitaire; **first** ou **bachelor's** ~ ≈ licence f; **to get a** ~ obtenir un diplôme (universitaire); **to have a** ~ être diplômé; **3** (amount) degré m; **a high** ~ **of efficiency** beaucoup de compétence; **to such a** ~ **that** à un tel point que; **to a** ~, **to some** ~ dans une certaine mesure; **to a lesser** ~ dans une moindre mesure; **not in the slightest** ~ pas le moins du monde; **by** ~**s** petit à petit; **with varying** ~**s of success** avec un succès variable; **4** US Jur **first** ~ **murder** homicide m volontaire avec préméditation

degree: ~ **ceremony** n GB Univ cérémonie f de remise des diplômes; ~ **course** n GB Univ programme m d'études universitaires

dehydrate /ˌdiːˈhaɪdreɪt/ vtr déshydrater

dehydrated /ˌdiːˈhaɪdreɪtɪd/ adj gen déshydraté; [milk] en poudre; **to become** ~ se déshydrater

dehydration /ˌdiːhaɪˈdreɪʃn/ n déshydratation f

de-icer /ˌdiːˈaɪsə(r)/ n Aut dégivrant m

deign /deɪn/ vtr **to** ~ **to do** condescendre à faire

deity /ˈdiːətɪ/ n divinité f; **the Deity** Dieu

dejected /dɪˈdʒektɪd/ adj découragé

delay /dɪˈleɪ/
A n **1** (of train, plane, post) retard m (**of** de; **to, on** sur); **a few minutes'** ~ un délai de quelques minutes; **2** (slowness) **without (further)** ~ sans (plus) tarder; **3** (time lapse) délai m (**of** de; **between** entre)
B vtr **1** (postpone) différer [decision, publication]; **to** ~ **doing** attendre pour faire; **2** (hold up) retarder [train, arrival, post]; **flights were** ~**ed by up to 12 hours** les vols ont eu jusqu'à 12 heures de retard
C delayed pp adj [passenger] en retard; **to have a** ~**ed reaction** réagir après coup (**to** à)
D delaying pres p adj [action, tactic] dilatoire

delayed action /dɪˈleɪd/ adj à retardement

delegate
A /ˈdelɪgət/ n délégué/-e m/f
B /ˈdelɪgeɪt/ vtr déléguer

delete /dɪˈliːt/ vtr gen supprimer (**from** de); (with pen) barrer; Comput effacer; ~ **where inapplicable** rayer les mentions inutiles

deletion /dɪˈliːʃn/ n (word, line taken out) suppression f; (word, line crossed out) rature f

deliberate
A /dɪˈlɪbərət/ adj **1** (intentional) délibéré; **it was** ~ il/elle l'a fait etc exprès; **2** (measured) mesuré
B /dɪˈlɪbərət/ vi délibérer (**over, about** sur)

deliberately /dɪˈlɪbərətlɪ/ adv **1** (intentionally) [do, say] exprès; [sarcastic, provocative] délibérément; **2** (slowly and carefully) [speak] posément; [walk] délibérément

deliberation /dɪˌlɪbəˈreɪʃn/ n **1** **after careful** ~ après mûre réflexion; **2** **with** ~ posément

delicacy /ˈdelɪkəsɪ/ n **1** (of colour, workmanship, touch) délicatesse f; **2** (of mechanism) sensibilité f; **3** (of situation, subject) délicatesse f; **a matter of great** ~ une affaire très délicate; **4** Culin (savoury) mets m raffiné; (sweet) friandise f

delicate /ˈdelɪkət/ adj [fabric, shade, health, mechanism, operation, situation, subject] délicat; [features] fin; [touch] léger; [china] fragile

delicately /ˈdelɪkətlɪ/ adv **1** [crafted, flavoured] délicatement; **2** [handle, phrase] avec délicatesse

delicatessen /ˌdelɪkəˈtesn/ n **1** (shop) épicerie f fine; **2** US (eating-place) restaurant-traiteur m

delicious /dɪˈlɪʃəs/ adj délicieux/-ieuse

deliciously /dɪˈlɪʃəslɪ/ adv délicieusement

delight /dɪˈlaɪt/
A n joie f, plaisir m; **to take** ~ **in sth/in doing** prendre un malin plaisir à qch/à faire; **a cry of** ~ un cri de joie; **it is a** ~ **to do** c'est un plaisir (que) de faire; **(much) to my** ~ à ma plus grande joie
B vtr ravir [person] (**with** par)

delighted /dɪˈlaɪtɪd/ adj ravi (**about, at, by, with** de; **at doing, to do** de faire); **to be** ~ **with sb** être très content de qn; ~ **to meet you** enchanté

delightedly /dɪˈlaɪtɪdlɪ/ adv [announce, smile] d'un air ravi; [laugh, applaud] avec ravissement

delightful /dɪˈlaɪtfl/ adj merveilleux/-euse

delightfully /dɪˈlaɪtfəlɪ/ adv [warm, peaceful] agréablement; [eccentric, shy] délicieusement

delineate /dɪˈlɪnɪeɪt/ vtr **1** déterminer [concerns, strategy, terms]; décrire [aspects, character]; **2** lit, fig délimiter [area, space]

delineation /dɪˌlɪnɪˈeɪʃn/ n (of problem, plan) présentation f; (of character) portrait m (psychological)

delinquency /dɪˈlɪŋkwənsɪ/ n (behaviour) délinquance f

delinquent /dɪˈlɪŋkwənt/
A n délinquant/-e m/f
B adj **1** [behaviour, child, youth] délinquant; [act] de délinquance; **2** US Fin [tax] non payé; [debtor] défaillant

delirious /dɪˈlɪrɪəs/ adj Med, fig délirant; **to become ~** être pris de délire

deliriously /dɪˈlɪrɪəslɪ/ adv fig follement

delirium /dɪˈlɪrɪəm/ n Med, fig délire m

deliver /dɪˈlɪvə(r)/
A vtr **1** (take to address) livrer (**to** à); (to several houses) distribuer; (to an individual) apporter (**to** à); remettre [note, written message]; '**~ed to your door**' 'livraison à domicile'; **2** mettre au monde [baby, baby animal]; **3** (utter) faire [speech, sermon, reprimand]; donner [ultimatum, decision]; rendre [verdict]; réciter [lines]; **4** (hand over) céder [property] (**over to, up to** à); livrer [town] (**over to, up to** à); **5** (rescue) délivrer (**from** de)
B vi [tradesman] livrer; [postman] distribuer le courrier
(Idiom) **to ~ the goods**° tenir ses engagements

delivery /dɪˈlɪvərɪ/ n
A n **1** (of goods, milk) livraison f; (of mail) distribution f; **on ~** à la livraison; **2** (way of speaking) élocution f; **3** (of baby) accouchement m; **4** Sport lancer m; **5** (handing over of property) remise f
B noun modifier [cost, date, note, order, service, vehicle] de livraison

delivery: **~ address** n adresse f du destinataire; **~ man** n livreur m; **~ room** n Med salle f d'accouchement

delta /ˈdeltə/ n (all contexts) delta m

delude /dɪˈluːd/
A vtr tromper (**with** par)
B v refl **to ~ oneself** se faire des illusions

deluge /ˈdeljuːdʒ/
A n lit, fig déluge m
B vtr lit, fig submerger (**with** de)

delusion /dɪˈluːʒn/ n gen illusion f; **~s of grandeur** la folie des grandeurs

de luxe /dəˈlʌks, ˈlʊks/ adj [model, version, edition] de luxe; [accommodation] luxueux/-euse

delve /delv/ vi **to ~ into** fouiller dans [pocket, records, past]; creuser [subject]; examiner [motive]

demand /dɪˈmɑːnd, US dɪˈmænd/
A n **1** (request) demande f; **on ~** [divorce, access] à la demande; [payable] à vue; **2** (pressure) exigence f; **I have many ~s on my time** mon temps est très pris; **3** Econ demande f (**for** de); **4** (favour) **to be in ~** être très demandé
B vtr **1** (request) demander [reform, release]; (forcefully) exiger [attention, ransom]; réclamer [inquiry]; **2** (require) demander [skill, time] (**of sb** de qn); (more imperatively) exiger [punctuality, qualities]

demanding /dɪˈmɑːndɪŋ, US -ˈmænd-/ adj **1** [person] exigeant; **2** [work, course] ardu; [schedule] chargé

demanning /ˌdiːˈmænɪŋ/ n GB réduction f de main-d'œuvre

demarcation /ˌdiːmɑːˈkeɪʃn/ n **1** (physical) (action, boundary) démarcation f; **2** Jur, Admin délimitation f

demarcation dispute n querelle f de compétence (entre syndicats)

demean /dɪˈmiːn/ v refl **to ~ oneself** s'abaisser

demeaning /dɪˈmiːnɪŋ/ adj humiliant

demeanour GB, **demeanor** US /dɪˈmiːnə(r)/ n (behaviour) comportement m; (bearing) maintien m

demented /dɪˈmentɪd/ adj fou/folle

dementia /dɪˈmenʃə/ n démence f; ▶ **senile dementia**

demerara (sugar) /ˌdeməˈreərə/ n sucre m roux cristallisé

demilitarize /ˌdiːˈmɪlɪtəraɪz/ vtr démilitariser

demise /dɪˈmaɪz/ n **1** (of institution, movement) disparition f; (of aspirations) mort f; **2** (death) disparition f

demisemiquaver /ˌdemɪˈsemɪkweɪvə(r)/ n GB triple croche f

demister /ˌdiːˈmɪstə(r)/ GB n dispositif m antibuée

demo° /ˈdeməʊ/
A n (abrév = **demonstration**) Pol manif° f
B noun modifier [tape, model] de démonstration

demobilize /diːˈməʊbɪlaɪz/ vtr démobiliser

democracy /dɪˈmɒkrəsɪ/ n démocratie f

democrat /ˈdeməkræt/ n démocrate mf

Democrat /ˈdeməkræt/ n Pol Démocrate mf

democratic /ˌdeməˈkrætɪk/ adj démocratique

Democratic /ˌdeməˈkrætɪk/ adj US Pol démocrate

demolish /dɪˈmɒlɪʃ/ vtr **1** démolir [building, argument, person]; **2** °hum engloutir [food]; **3** °battre [qn] à plates coutures [team]

demolition /ˌdeməˈlɪʃn/ n lit, fig démolition f

demon /ˈdiːmən/ n Relig, fig démon m

demonic /dɪˈmɒnɪk/ adj [aspect, power] diabolique; [noise] infernal

demonstrable /ˈdemɒnstrəbl, US dɪˈmɒnstrəbl/ adj démontrable

demonstrably /ˈdemɒnʃtrəblɪ, dɪˈmɒnstrəblɪ/ adv manifestement

demonstrate /ˈdemənstreɪt/
A vtr **1** (illustrate, prove) démontrer [theory, truth]; **2** (show, reveal) manifester [emotion, concern, support]; montrer [skill]; **3** (display) faire la démonstration de [machine, product]; **to ~ how to do** montrer comment faire
B vi Pol manifester (**for** en faveur de; **against** contre)

demonstration /ˌdemənˈstreɪʃn/ n **1** Pol manifestation f (**against** contre; **for** en faveur de); **2** (of emotion, support) manifestation f; **3** (of machine, theory) démonstration f; **to give a ~** faire une démonstration

demonstrative /dɪˈmɒnstrətɪv/ adj démonstratif/-ive

demonstrator /ˈdemənstreɪtə(r)/ n **1** Pol manifestant/-e m/f; **2** Comm démonstrateur/-trice m/f

demoralize /dɪˈmɒrəlaɪz, US -ˈmɔːr-/ vtr démoraliser

demote /diːˈməʊt/ vtr rétrograder [person]; ramener [qch] au deuxième plan [idea, policy]

demur /dɪˈmɜː(r)/ sout
A n **without ~** sans objection(s)
B vi (p prés etc **-rr-**) **1** (disagree) soulever des objections (**at** contre); **2** (complain) rechigner

demure /dɪˈmjʊə(r)/ adj [behaviour, dress] discret/-ète; [girl] sage et modeste

den /den/ n **1** (of lion) antre m; (of fox) tanière f; **2** (room) tanière f

denationalize /ˌdiːˈnæʃənəlaɪz/ vtr dénationaliser

denial /dɪˈnaɪəl/ n (of accusation, rumour) démenti m; (of guilt, doctrine, rights) négation f; (of request) rejet m

denier /ˈdenɪə(r)/ n denier m

denigration /ˌdenɪˈɡreɪʃn/ n dénigrement m (**of** de)

denim /ˈdenɪm/
A n jean m; **~s** (trousers) jean m
B noun modifier [jacket] en jean; **~ jeans** jean m

Denmark /ˈdenmɑːk/ ▶ p. 774 pr n Danemark m

denomination /dɪˌnɒmɪˈneɪʃn/ n **1** (name) dénomination f; **2** Relig confession f; **3** Fin valeur f; **high ~ bank-note** grosse coupure

denote /dɪˈnəʊt/ vtr (stand for) indiquer; [word, notice] signifier

denounce /dɪˈnaʊns/ vtr **1** (inform on) dénoncer (**to** à); **2** (criticize) dénoncer; **3** (accuse) accuser

dense /dens/ adj dense

densely /ˈdenslɪ/ adv **~ populated/wooded** très peuplé/boisé

density /ˈdensətɪ/ n densité f

dent /dent/
A n (in wood) entaille f; (in metal) bosse f
B vtr faire une entaille dans [wood]; cabosser [car]; entamer [pride]

dental /ˈdentl/
A n Ling dentale f

d

French departments

■ *The names of French departments usually have the definite article, except when used after the preposition en.*

In, to and from somewhere

■ *For in and to, use dans le or dans les for masculine and plural names of departments:*

to live in the Loiret
= vivre dans le Loiret

to go to the Loiret
= aller dans le Loiret

to live in the Landes
= vivre dans les Landes

to go to the Landes
= aller dans les Landes

to live in the Loir-et-Cher
= vivre dans le Loir-et-Cher

to go to the Loir-et-Cher
= aller dans le Loir-et-Cher

■ *For in and to, use en for feminine names of departments:*

to live in Savoy
= vivre en Savoie

to go to Savoy
= aller en Savoie

to live in Seine-et-Marne
= vivre en Seine-et-Marne

to go to Seine-et-Marne
= aller en Seine-et-Marne

■ *For from, use du (or de l' before a vowel) for masculine and des for plural names of departments:*

to come from the Loiret
= venir du Loiret

to come from the Landes
= venir des Landes

to come from the Loir-et-Cher
= venir du Loir-et-Cher

■ *For from, use de without the definite article for feminine names of departments:*

to come from Savoy
= venir de Savoie

to come from Seine-et-Marne
= venir de Seine-et-Marne

Uses with nouns

■ *Use de with the definite article in most cases:*

a Cantal accent
= un accent du Cantal

the Var area
= la région du Var

the Creuse countryside
= les paysages de la Creuse

Loiret people
= les gens du Loiret

Yonne representatives
= les représentants de l'Yonne

Landes restaurants
= les restaurants des Landes

the Calvados team
= l'équipe du Calvados

Ardennes towns
= les villes des Ardennes

■ *but use de without the definite article with feminine names that include et:*

Seine-et-Marne hotels
= les hôtels de Seine-et-Marne

Some cases are undecided:

Savoy roads
= les routes de Savoie *or* de la Savoie

B *adj* gen dentaire; Ling dental

dental: ∼ **appointment** n rendez-vous m chez le dentiste; ∼ **clinic** n centre m de soins dentaires; ∼ **floss** n fil m dentaire; ∼ **plate** n dentier m; ∼ **surgeon** ▸ p. 1181 n chirurgien-dentiste m; ∼ **surgery** n GB (premises) cabinet m dentaire; (treatment) chirurgie f dentaire

dentist /'dentist/ ▸ p. 1181 n dentiste mf

dentistry /'dentistri/ n médecine f dentaire

denture /'dentʃə(r)/
A n (prosthesis) prothèse f dentaire
B **dentures** npl dentier m (sg)

denunciation /dɪˌnʌnsɪ'eɪʃn/ n dénonciation f (**of** de)

deny /dɪ'naɪ/ vtr ① démentir [*rumour*]; nier [*accusation*]; **to ∼ that...** nier que...; **she denies that this is true** elle nie que cela soit vrai; **to ∼ doing** ou **having done** nier avoir fait; ② (refuse) **to ∼ sb sth** refuser qch à qn; **to ∼ sb admittance to a building** refuser l'accès d'un bâtiment à qn; **to ∼ oneself sth** se priver de qch; ③ (renounce) renier [*God*]

deodorant /di:'əʊdərənt/ n (personal) déodorant m; (for room) désodorisant m; **roll-on/spray ∼** déodorant à bille/en bombe

deodorize /di:'əʊdəraɪz/ vtr désodoriser

depart /dɪ'pɑːt/ vi ① sout partir (**from** de; **for** pour); **the train now ∼ing from platform one** le train au départ du quai numéro un; ② (deviate) **to ∼ from** s'éloigner de [*position, truth*]; abandonner [*practice*]

departed /dɪ'pɑːtɪd/ adj euph (dead) défunt

departing /dɪ'pɑːtɪŋ/ adj [*chairman*] sortant

department /dɪ'pɑːtmənt/ n ① Comm (section) service m; **personnel ∼** service du personnel; ② (governmental) ministère m; (administrative) service m; **social services ∼** services sociaux; ③ (in store) rayon m; **electrical ∼** rayon m électricité; ④ (in hospital) service m; **X ray ∼** radiologie f; ⑤ (in university) département m; cf UFR f; ⑥ Sch section f (regroupement des professeurs par matière); ⑦ Admin, Geog (district) département m; ⑧ °(area) domaine m

departmental /ˌdiːpɑːt'mentl/ adj ① Pol [*colleague, meeting*] de ministère; ② Admin [*head, meeting*] de service, de département

department: **Department for Culture, Media and Sport, DCMS** n GB ministère m de la Culture, des Médias et des Sports; **Department for Education and Skills, DfES** n GB ministère m de l'Éducation et de la Formation professionnelle

department head n ① Admin, Comm chef m de service, directeur/-trice m/f du service; ② Univ directeur/-trice m/f de département

department: ∼ **manager** n (of business) chef m de service, directeur/-trice m/f du service; (of store) chef m de rayon; **Department of Defense, DOD** n US ministère m de la Défense; **Department of Energy, DOE** n US ministère m de l'Énergie; **Department of the Environment, Transport and the Regions, DETR** n GB ministère m de l'Environnement, du Transport et des Régions; **Department of Health, DOH** GB, **Department of Health and Human Services** US n ministère m de la Santé; **Department of Social Security, DSS** n GB ministère *m* des Affaires sociales; **Department of Trade and Industry, DTI** *n* GB ministère *m* du Commerce et de l'industrie; **~ store** *n* grand magasin *m*

departure /dɪˈpɑːtʃə(r)/ *n* **1** (of person, train) départ *m* (**from** de; **for** pour); **2** fig (start) **a new ~ in physics** un nouveau départ en physique; **3** (from truth, regulation) entorse *f* (**from** à); (from policy, tradition) rupture *f* (**from** par rapport à); **to be a total ~ from** s'éloigner totalement de

departure: **~ gate** *n* porte *f* de départ; **~ platform** *n* Rail quai *m* de départ; **~s board** *n* tableau *m* des départs

depend /dɪˈpend/ *vi* **1** (rely) **to ~ on** dépendre de, compter sur (**for** pour); **to ~ on sb/sth to do** compter sur qn/qch pour faire; **you can't ~ on the bus arriving on time** tu ne peux pas être sûr que le bus sera à l'heure; **the temperature varies ~ing on the season** la température varie suivant la saison; **2** (financially) **to ~ on sb** vivre à la charge de qn

dependability /dɪ,pendəˈbɪlətɪ/ *n* (of equipment) fiabilité *f*

dependable /dɪˈpendəbl/ *adj* [*person*] digne de confiance; [*machine*] fiable; [*forecast, news, source*] sûr

dependant /dɪˈpendənt/ *n* personne *f* à charge

dependence, dependance US /dɪˈpendəns/ *n* **1** (reliance) dépendance *f* (**on** vis-à-vis de); **2** (addiction) dépendance *f* (**on** à)

dependency /dɪˈpendənsɪ/ *n* **1** Pol (territory) territoire *m* dépendant; **2** (reliance) dépendance *f* (**on sb** vis-à-vis de qn; **on sth** à qch)

dependent /dɪˈpendənt/ *adj* **1** (reliant) [*relative*] à charge; **to be ~ (up)on** gen dépendre de; (financially) vivre à la charge de

depict /dɪˈpɪkt/ *vtr* Art représenter; (in writing) dépeindre (**as** comme)

depiction /dɪˈpɪkʃn/ *n* peinture *f*, représentation *f*

depilatory /dɪˈpɪlətrɪ, US -tɔːrɪ/ *n, adj* dépilatoire (*m*)

deplete /dɪˈpliːt/ *vtr* réduire [*reserves, numbers*]

depletion /dɪˈpliːʃn/ *n* (of resources, funds) baisse *f*

deplorable /dɪˈplɔːrəbl/ *adj* déplorable

deplore /dɪˈplɔː(r)/ *vtr* déplorer

deploy /dɪˈplɔɪ/ *vtr* gen, Mil déployer

deployment /dɪˈplɔɪmənt/ *n* déploiement *m*

depopulation /diːˌpɒpjʊˈleɪʃn/ *n* dépeuplement *m*

deport /dɪˈpɔːt/ *vtr* Jur expulser (**to** vers); Hist déporter

deportation /ˌdiːpɔːˈteɪʃn/ *n* Jur expulsion *f*; Hist déportation *f*

deportee /ˌdiːpɔːˈtiː/ *n* déporté/-e *m/f*

deportment /dɪˈpɔːtmənt/ *n* sout maintien *m*

depose /dɪˈpəʊz/ *vtr* Pol, Jur déposer

deposit /dɪˈpɒzɪt/
A *n* **1** (to bank account) dépôt *m*; **on ~** en dépôt; **2** (part payment) (on house, hire purchase goods) versement *m* initial (**on** sur); (on holiday, goods) acompte *m*, arrhes *fpl* (**on** sur); **3** (to secure goods, hotel room) arrhes *fpl*, acompte *m*; **4** (paid by hirer, tenant) caution *f*; **5** (on bottle) consigne *f*; **6** GB Pol cautionnement *m*; **7** (of silt, mud) dépôt *m*; (of coal, mineral) gisement *m*; **8** (sediment) dépôt *m*
B *vtr* (put down) [*object*]; **2** (entrust) déposer [*money*]; **to ~ sth with sb** confier qch à qn

deposit account *n* GB Fin compte *m* de dépôt

depositor /dɪˈpɒzɪtə(r)/ *n* Fin déposant/-e *m/f*

deposit slip *n* bordereau *m* de versement

depot /ˈdepəʊ, US ˈdiːpəʊ/ *n* **1** (for storage) dépôt *m*; **2** (terminus, garage) **bus ~** dépôt *m* d'autobus; **3** US (station) (bus) gare *f* routière; (rail) gare *f* ferroviaire

deprave /dɪˈpreɪv/ *vtr* dépraver

depravity /dɪˈprævətɪ/ *n* dépravation *f*

deprecating /ˈdeprɪkeɪtɪŋ/ *adj* (disapproving) désapprobateur/-trice

deprecatingly /ˈdeprɪkeɪtɪŋlɪ/ *adv* (about oneself) avec modestie; (about sb else) avec condescendance

deprecatory /ˌdeprɪˈkeɪtərɪ, US -tɔːrɪ/ *adj* **1** (disapproving) désapprobateur/-trice; **2** (apologetic) d'excuse

depreciate /dɪˈpriːʃɪeɪt/ *vi* se déprécier (**against** par rapport à)

depress /dɪˈpres/ *vtr* **1** gen déprimer; **2** Comm, Fin faire baisser [*prices*]; affaiblir [*trading*]

depressed /dɪˈprest/ *adj* **1** déprimé; **I got ~ about it** cela m'a déprimé; **2** [*region, market, industry*] en déclin; [*sales, prices*] très bas/basse

depressing /dɪˈpresɪŋ/ *adj* déprimant

depression /dɪˈpreʃn/ *n* **1** Med, Psych dépression *f*; **to suffer from ~** être dépressif/-ive; **2** (slump) récession *f*, crise *f* (**in** de); **3** (hollow) creux *m*; **4** Meteorol dépression *f*

depressive /dɪˈpresɪv/ *n, adj* dépressif/-ive (*m/f*)

depressurize /ˌdiːˈpreʃəraɪz/ *vi* se dépressuriser

deprivation /ˌdeprɪˈveɪʃn/ *n* **1** (poverty) (of person) privations *fpl*; (of society) dénuement *m*; **2** Psych carence *f* affective; **3** (of right, privilege) privation *f*

deprive /dɪˈpraɪv/ *vtr* priver (**of** de)

deprived /dɪˈpraɪvd/ *adj* [*area, family*] démuni; [*childhood*] malheureux/-euse

dept *abrév écrite* = **department**

depth /depθ/ *n* **1** (measurement) (of hole, water) profondeur *f*; (of layer) épaisseur *f*; **at a ~ of 30 m** à 30 m de profondeur; **12 m in ~** profond de 12 m; **to be out of one's ~** (in water) ne plus avoir pied; fig être complètement perdu; **in the ~s of the countryside** en pleine campagne; **2** (of colour, emotion) intensité *f*; (of crisis, recession) gravité *f*; (of ignorance) étendue *f*; (of despair) fond *m*; **3** (of knowledge) étendue *f*; (of analysis, hero, novel) profondeur *f*; **to examine sth in ~** examiner qch en détail; **4** Cin, Phot **~ of focus** distance *f* focale; **~ of field** profondeur *f* de champ

deputation /ˌdepjʊˈteɪʃn/ *n* délégation *f*

depute /dɪˈpjuːt/ *vtr* sout charger [*person*]

deputize /ˈdepjʊtaɪz/ *vi* **to ~ for sb** remplacer qn

deputy /ˈdepjʊtɪ/
A *n* **1** (aide) adjoint/-e *m/f* (**to sb** de qn); (replacement) remplaçant/-e *m/f*; **2** (politician) député *m*; **3** US (also **~ sheriff**) shérif *m* adjoint
B *noun modifier* [*director, editor, head, manager, mayor*] adjoint

deputy: **~ chairman** *n* vice-président *m*; **~ leader** *n* GB Pol vice-président *m*; **~ premier, ~ prime minister** *n* Pol vice-premier ministre *m*; **~ president** *n* gen, Pol vice-président *m*

derail /dɪˈreɪl/ *vtr* faire dérailler

derailleur gears /dəˈreɪljə(r)/ *npl* dérailleur *m*

derailment /dɪˈreɪlmənt/ *n* déraillement *m*

derange /dɪˈreɪndʒ/ *vtr* déranger

deregulate /ˌdiːˈregjʊleɪt/ *vtr* Fin libérer [*prices*]; déréguler [*market*]

derelict /ˈderəlɪkt/
A *n* (tramp) clochard/-e *m/f*
B *adj* (abandoned) abandonné; (ruined) en ruines

deride /dɪˈraɪd/ *vtr* ridiculiser

derision /dɪˈrɪʒn/ *n* ⊄ moqueries *fpl*

derisory /dɪˈraɪsərɪ/ *adj* dérisoire

derivative /dəˈrɪvətɪv/
A *n* dérivé *m*
B *adj* **1** dérivé; **2** péj [*style*] sans originalité

derive /dɪˈraɪv/
A *vtr* tirer [*benefit, income*] (**from** de); retirer [*satisfaction*] (**from** de)
B *vi* **to ~ from** [*power*] découler de; [*custom*] provenir de

dermatitis /ˌdɜːməˈtaɪtɪs/ ▸ p. 933 *n* dermatite *f*

derogatory /dɪˈrɒgətrɪ, US -tɔːrɪ/ *adj* [*remark, person*] désobligeant (**about** envers); [*term*] péjoratif/-ive

descaler /ˌdiːˈskeɪlə(r)/ GB *n* détartrant *m*

descant /ˈdeskænt/ *n* déchant *m*

descant recorder *n* flûte *f* à bec soprano

descend /dɪˈsend/
A *vtr* descendre [*steps, slope, path*]
B *vi* **1** (go down) [*person, plane*] descendre (**from** de); **2** (fall) [*rain, darkness, mist*] tomber (**on, over** sur); [*gloom, exhaustion*] s'abattre (**on** sur); [*peace*] s'étendre (**on** sur); **4** (arrive) arriver, débarquer°; **5** (be related to) **to be ~ed from** descendre de; **6** (sink) **to ~ to doing** s'abaisser à faire

descendant /dɪˈsendənt/ *n* descendant/-e *m/f* (**of** de)

descent /dɪˈsent/ *n* **1** (downward motion) descente *f* (**on, upon** sur); **to make one's ~** faire sa descente; **2** (extraction) descendance *f*; **to claim ~ from** prétendre descendre de; **a British citizen by ~** un citoyen britannique par filiation

d

descrambler /diːˈskræmblə(r)/ n Telecom, TV désembrouilleur m

describe /dɪˈskraɪb/ vtr ① (give details of) décrire [person, event, object]; ② (characterize) qualifier; **to ~ sb as an idiot/ sth as useless** qualifier qn d'idiot/qch d'inutile; **he's ~d as generous** on dit de lui qu'il est généreux; **it could be ~d as pretty** on pourrait dire que c'est joli; ③ Math, Tech décrire

description /dɪˈskrɪpʃn/ n ① gen description f (**of** de; **as** comme étant); (for police) signalement m (**of** de); **to be beyond ~** être indescriptible; ② (type, kind) genre m; **of every ~** de toutes sortes

descriptive /dɪˈskrɪptɪv/ adj descriptif/-ive

desecrate /ˈdesɪkreɪt/ vtr ① gen défigurer; ② Relig profaner [altar, shrine]

desecration /ˌdesɪˈkreɪʃn/ n ① (of area, landscape) enlaidissement m; ② Relig (of altar, shrine) profanation f

desegregate /diːˈsegrɪgeɪt/ vtr **to ~ a school** abolir la ségrégation dans une école

deselect /ˌdiːsɪˈlekt/ vtr GB **to be ~ed** perdre l'investiture du parti

desensitize /ˌdiːˈsensɪtaɪz/ vtr désensibiliser (**to** à)

desert

A /ˈdezət/ n (all contexts) désert m

B /dɪˈzɜːt/ vtr gen, hum abandonner (**for** pour); déserter [cause]; abandonner [post]

C /dɪˈzɜːt/ vi [soldier] déserter; [politician] faire défection

deserted /dɪˈzɜːtɪd/ adj ① (empty) désert; ② [person] abandonné

deserter /dɪˈzɜːtə(r)/ n déserteur m (**from** de)

desertion /dɪˈzɜːʃn/ n ① gen, Mil désertion f; ② Jur abandon m du domicile conjugal

desert island n île f déserte

deserts /dɪˈzɜːts/ npl **to get one's (just) ~** avoir ce qu'on mérite

deserve /dɪˈzɜːv/ vtr mériter (**to do** de faire); **she ~s to be remembered as...** elle mérite que l'on se souvienne d'elle comme...

deservedly /dɪˈzɜːvɪdlɪ/ adv à juste titre

deserving /dɪˈzɜːvɪŋ/ adj ① [winner] méritant; [cause] louable; ② **to be ~ of** sout être digne de [respect]

desiccated /ˈdesɪkeɪtɪd/ adj ① Culin séché; ② péj (dried up) desséché

design /dɪˈzaɪn/

A n ① (idea, conception) conception f; ② (planning, development) (of object, appliance) conception f; (of building, room) agencement m; (of clothing) création f; ③ (drawing, plan) (detailed) plan m (**for** de); (sketch) croquis m (**for** de); ④ (model, completed object) modèle m; ⑤ (art of designing) gen design m; (fashion) stylisme m; ⑥ (decorative pattern) motif m; **a leaf ~** un motif de feuilles; ⑦ Art, Univ arts mpl appliqués; ⑧ (intention) dessein m (**to do** de faire); **by ~** à dessein; **to have ~s on** avoir des vues fpl sur; **to have evil ~s on** être mal intentionné envers

B vtr ① (conceive, plan out) concevoir; ② (intend) **to be ~ed for sth/to do** (destined for) être destiné à qch/à faire; (made for) être conçu pour qch/pour faire; ③ (draw plan for) [draughtsman] dessiner le patron de [garment]; [designer] créer [costume, garment]; dessiner [building, appliance]

designate

A /ˈdezɪgnət, -neɪt/ adj [president, director] en titre

B /ˈdezɪgneɪt/ vtr [word] désigner; **to ~ sb (as) sth** désigner qn (comme) qch; **to ~ sth (as) sth** classer qch (comme) qch; **to ~ sth for** destiner qch à

designated driver n US (at a party) conducteur/-trice m/f qui ne boit pas (pour une sortie)

designation /ˌdezɪgˈneɪʃn/ n désignation f; **the ~ of sth as** le classement de qch comme [reserve, non-smoking area]

design: **~ centre** n (for exhibiting) salon m permanent; (for planning, conception) bureau m d'études; **~ consultant** n conseiller/-ère m/f en aménagement

designer /dɪˈzaɪnə(r)/ ▸ p. 1181

A n gen concepteur/-trice m/f; (of furniture, in fashion) créateur/ -trice m/f; (of sets) décorateur/-trice m/f; **costume ~** Theat, Cin costumier/-ière m/f

B noun modifier [drink, cocktail, hi-fi, sunglasses] de dernière mode; **~ clothes, ~ labels** (made to order) vêtements mpl de haute couture; (available in various outlets) vêtements mpl griffés; **~ label** griffe f

design: **~ fault** n faute f de conception, vice m caché; **~ feature** n caractéristique f (nominale)

designing /dɪˈzaɪnɪŋ/ adj péj intrigant

design specification n spécification f du modèle

desirability /dɪˌzaɪərəˈbɪlətɪ/ n gen avantages mpl; (sexual) charmes mpl

desirable /dɪˈzaɪərəbl/ adj ① [outcome, solution] souhaitable; [area, position] convoité; [job, gift] séduisant, tentant; **~ residence, ~ property** (in ad) maison f de standing; ② (sexually) désirable

desire /dɪˈzaɪə(r)/

A n ① gen désir m (**for** de; **to do** de faire); **to have no ~ to do** n'avoir aucune envie de faire; ② (sexual) désir m

B vtr gen avoir envie de, désirer; (sexually) désirer; **to ~ to do** désirer faire; **it leaves a lot to be ~d** cela laisse beaucoup à désirer

desist /dɪˈzɪst/ vi cesser (**from doing** de faire)

desk /desk/ n ① (furniture) bureau m; Mus pupitre m; **writing ~** secrétaire m; ② Sch (pupil's) table f; (old-fashioned) pupitre m; (teacher's) bureau m; ③ (in public building) **reception ~** réception f; **information ~** bureau m de renseignements; **cash ~** caisse f; ④ (in newspaper office) **the ~** la rédaction; **news ~** service m des informations; ⑤ (in organization, government office) (department) département m

desk: **~bound** adj [job] sédentaire; **~ clerk** n US réceptionniste mf; **~ pad** n (blotter) sous-main m; (notebook) bloc-notes m

desktop /ˈdesktɒp/ n ① (dessus m de) bureau m; ② (also **~ computer, ~ PC**) ordinateur m de bureau

desktop publishing, **DTP** n micro-édition f, PAO

desolate

A /ˈdesələt/ adj ① (deserted) [landscape] désolé; [house] abandonné; ② (devastated) dévasté; ③ (forlorn) [cry] désolé; [life] désespérément triste; ④ (grief-stricken) affligé

B /ˈdesəleɪt/ vtr dévaster [town, country]; affliger [person]

desolation /ˌdesəˈleɪʃn/ n ① (of landscape) aspect m désolé; (of person) désolation f; ② (misery) affliction f; ③ (devastation) dévastation f

despair /dɪˈspeə(r)/

A n (emotion) désespoir m; **to be in ~ about** ou **over** être désespéré par; **to do sth in** ou **out of ~** faire qch par désespoir

B vi désespérer (**of** de; **of doing** de faire)

despairing /dɪˈspeərɪŋ/ adj désespéré

desperate /ˈdespərət/ adj ① [person, plea, situation] désespéré; [criminal] prêt à tout; **to be ~ to do** avoir très envie de faire; **to be ~ for** avoir désespérément besoin de [affection, help]; attendre désespérément [news]; **to do something ~** commettre un acte de désespoir; ② ○(terrible) affreux/ -euse

desperately /ˈdespərətlɪ/ adv ① [plead, look, fight] désespérément; **to need sth ~** avoir très besoin de qch; ② [poor] terriblement; [ill] très gravement; **~ in love** éperdument amoureux

desperation /ˌdespəˈreɪʃn/ n désespoir m; **in (sheer) ~ she...** en désespoir de cause elle...; **her ~ to win** son désir intense de gagner

despicable /dɪˈspɪkəbl, ˈdespɪkəbl/ adj méprisable

despicably /dɪˈspɪkəblɪ, ˈdespɪkəblɪ/ adv ignoblement

despise /dɪˈspaɪz/ vtr mépriser

despite /dɪˈspaɪt/ prep malgré; **~ the fact that** bien que (+ subj)

despoil /dɪˈspɔɪl/ vtr sout, littér dévaster

despondency /dɪˈspɒndənsɪ/ n découragement m

despondent /dɪˈspɒndənt/ adj découragé, abattu

despot /ˈdespɒt/ n despote m

despotism /ˈdespətɪzəm/ n despotisme m

des res○ /dez ˈrez/ n (abrév = **desirable residence**) maison f de standing

dessert /dɪˈzɜːt/ n dessert m

dessert: **~ apple** n pomme f à couteau; **~spoon** n cuillère f à dessert; **~ wine** n vin m doux

destabilize /ˌdiːˈsteɪbəlaɪz/ vtr déstabiliser

destination /ˌdestɪˈneɪʃn/ n destination f

destine /ˈdestɪn/ vtr destiner (**for** à)

destined /ˈdestɪnd/ adj ① (preordained) destiné (**for, to** à; **to do** à faire); **it was ~ to happen** cela devait arriver; ② Post, Rail **~ for Paris** à destination de Paris

destiny /'destɪnɪ/ n destin m, destinée f

destitute /'destɪtjuːt, US -tuːt/
A n the ~ (+ v pl) les indigents mpl
B adj [person, community] sans ressources; **to leave sb ~** laisser qn dans le dénuement

destitution /ˌdestɪ'tjuːʃn, US -tuːt-/ n indigence f

de-stress /diː'stres/ vtr déstresser

destroy /dɪ'strɔɪ/ vtr **1** détruire [building, landscape, evidence, hopes, career]; anéantir [person]; faire exploser [bomb, package]; **2** (kill) abattre [animal]; détruire, anéantir [population, enemy]; **3** ○(defeat) écraser [opponent]

destroyer /dɪ'strɔɪə(r)/ n Naut contre-torpilleur m

destruct /dɪ'strʌkt/ vi s'autodétruire

destruction /dɪ'strʌkʃn/ n (of building, population, evidence, enemy) destruction f; (of hopes, reputation) ruine f

destructive /dɪ'strʌktɪv/ adj **1** (causing destruction) destructeur/-trice; **2** (having potential to destroy) [weapon, capacity] destructif/-ive; [urge, emotion, criticism] destructeur/-trice

desultory /'desəltrɪ, US -tɔːrɪ/ adj [conversation] décousu; [attempt] sporadique; [friendship] épisodique

detach /dɪ'tætʃ/ vtr détacher (**from** de); **to ~ oneself** se détacher (**from** de)

detachable /dɪ'tætʃəbl/ adj [coupon, section, strap] détachable; [lever, collar] amovible; Phot [lens] mobile

detached /dɪ'tætʃt/ adj **1** (separate) détaché; **2** [person, view, manner] détaché; [observer] indépendant

detached: **~ garage** n garage m indépendant; **~ house** n maison f (individuelle); **~ retina** n Med rétine f décollée

detachment /dɪ'tætʃmənt/ n **1** (separation) séparation f (**from** de); **2** (emotional, intellectual) détachement m; **3** Mil détachement m

detail /'diːteɪl, US dɪ'teɪl/
A n **1** gen, Art détail m; **in (more** ou **greater) ~** (plus) en détail; **to go into ~s** entrer dans les détails; **to have an eye for ~** prêter attention aux détails; **for further ~s...** pour de plus amples renseignements...; **2** Mil détachement m
B vtr **1** (list) exposer [qch] en détail [plans]; énumérer [items]; **2** **to ~ sb to** affecter qn à

detail drawing n épure f

detain /dɪ'teɪn/ vtr **1** (delay) retenir; **2** (keep in custody) placer [qn] en détention; **to be ~ed for questioning** être placé en garde à vue pour être interrogé; **3** (in hospital) garder

detainee /ˌdiːteɪ'niː/ n (general) détenu/-e m/f; (political) prisonnier/-ière m/f (politique)

detect /dɪ'tekt/ vtr **1** (find) déceler [error, traces, change]; détecter [crime, leak, plane]; **2** (sense) détecter [sound]; sentir [mood]

detectable /dɪ'tektəbl/ adj discernable

detection /dɪ'tekʃn/ n (of disease, error) détection f; **crime ~** la lutte contre la criminalité; **to escape ~** [criminal] ne pas être découvert; [error] ne pas être décelé

detective /dɪ'tektɪv/ n ≈ inspecteur/-trice m/f (de police); (private) détective m; **store ~** inspecteur/-trice m/f

detective: **~ constable** n GB ≈ enquêteur m; **~ inspector, DI** n GB ≈ inspecteur m principal; **~ story** n roman m policier, polar○ m; **~ work** n enquêtes fpl also fig

detector /dɪ'tektə(r)/ n détecteur m

detention /dɪ'tenʃn/ n **1** (confinement) détention f; **2** (prison sentence) détention f criminelle; (awaiting trial) détention f provisoire; **3** Sch retenue f, colle○ f

deter /dɪ'tɜː(r)/ vtr (p prés etc **-rr-**) **1** (dissuade) dissuader; **a scheme to ~ vandalism** un projet pour décourager le vandalisme; **2** (prevent) empêcher (**from doing** de faire)

detergent /dɪ'tɜːdʒənt/ n, adj détergent (m)

deteriorate /dɪ'tɪərɪəreɪt/ vi [weather, health, situation, wood] se détériorer; [economy, sales] décliner; [work, building] se dégrader; **to ~ into** dégénérer en

deterioration /dɪˌtɪərɪə'reɪʃn/ n (in weather, of building) dégradation f (**in** de); (in health, situation) détérioration f (**in** de); (in work, performance) baisse f de qualité (**in** de)

determination /dɪˌtɜːmɪ'neɪʃn/ n gen détermination f; Jur, Admin décision f

determine /dɪ'tɜːmɪn/ vtr **1** (find out) déterminer; **to ~ how** établir comment; **2** (decide) déterminer, fixer [price]; **to ~ to do** résoudre de faire; **3** (control) [factor] déterminer

determined /dɪ'tɜːmɪnd/ adj [person] fermement décidé (**to do** à faire); [air] résolu; [attempt] ferme

determining /dɪ'tɜːmɪnɪŋ/ adj (épith) déterminant

deterrent /dɪ'terənt, US -'tɜː-/
A n gen moyen m de dissuasion; Mil force f de dissuasion; **to be a ~ to sb** dissuader qn
B adj [effect] dissuasif/-ive; [measure] de dissuasion

detest /dɪ'test/ vtr détester (**doing** faire)

detonate /'detəneɪt/
A vtr faire exploser
B vi exploser

detonation /ˌdetə'neɪʃn/ n détonation f, explosion f

detonator /'detəneɪtə(r)/ n détonateur m

detour /'diːtʊə(r), US dɪ'tʊər/ n détour m

detoxify /ˌdiː'tɒksɪfaɪ/ vtr désintoxiquer

DETR n: abrév GB ▸ **Department of the Environment, Transport and the Regions**

detract /dɪ'trækt/ vi **to ~ from** porter atteinte à [success, value]; nuire à, porter atteinte à [harmony, image]; diminuer [pleasure]

detractor /dɪ'træktə(r)/ n détracteur/-trice m/f

detriment /'detrɪmənt/ n **to the ~ of** au détriment de; **to the great ~ of** au grand dommage de

detrimental /ˌdetrɪ'mentl/ adj nuisible (**to** à)

detritus /dɪ'traɪtəs/ n détritus mpl

deuce /djuːs, US duːs/ n **1** Sport ~! égalité!; **2** (in cards) deux m

devaluation /ˌdiːvæljʊ'eɪʃn/ n **1** (of currency) dévaluation f; (of shares) baisse f; **2** gen dévalorisation f

devalue /ˌdiː'væljuː/
A vtr **1** Fin dévaluer (**against** contre); **~d by 6%** dévalué de 6%; **2** (underestimate) dévaloriser
B vi [currency] être dévalué (**against** par rapport à); [property] baisser; [shares] dévaloriser

devastate /'devəsteɪt/ vtr ravager [land, town]; anéantir [person]

devastating /'devəsteɪtɪŋ/ adj **1** (stunning) lit dévastateur/-trice; fig ravageur/-euse; **2** (crushing) [news, loss, criticism] accablant; [argument] écrasant

devastation /ˌdevə'steɪʃn/ n lit dévastation f; fig anéantissement m

develop /dɪ'veləp/
A vtr **1** (acquire) acquérir [knowledge]; attraper [illness]; prendre [habit]; présenter [symptom]; **to ~ an awareness of** prendre conscience de; **to ~ cancer** développer un cancer; **2** (evolve) élaborer [plan, project]; mettre au point [technique, invention]; exposer [theory]; développer [argument]; **3** (create) créer [market]; établir [links]; **4** (expand, build up) développer [mind, physique, business, market]; **5** (improve) mettre en valeur [land, site]; aménager [city centre]; **6** Phot développer
B vi **1** (evolve) [child, society, country, plot, play] se développer; [intelligence] s'épanouir; [skills] s'améliorer; **to ~ into** devenir; **2** (come into being) [friendship, difficulty] naître; [crack, hole] se former; [illness] se déclarer; **3** (progress, advance) [friendship] se développer; [difficulty] s'aggraver; [crack, fault] s'accentuer; [war, illness] s'aggraver; [game, story] se dérouler; [in size, extent] [town, business] se développer

developer /dɪ'veləpə(r)/ n **1** (also **property ~**) promoteur m (immobilier); **2** Phot révélateur m; **3** Psych, Sch **early ~** enfant m précoce

developing: **~ bath** n Phot bain m révélateur; **~ country** n pays m en voie de développement; **~ tank** n Phot cuve f à développement

development /dɪ'veləpmənt/
A n **1** (creation) (of product) mise f au point; (of housing, industry) création f; **2** (evolution, growth) développement m; **3** (of land) mise f en valeur; (of site, city centre etc) aménagement m; **4** (land developed) **housing ~** ensemble m d'habitation; (individual houses) lotissement m; **commercial ~** (ensemble m de) commerces et bureaux à bâtir; **5** (innovation) progrès m; **major ~s** des découvertes fpl majeures (**in** dans le domaine de); **6** (event) changement m; **recent ~s in Europe** les derniers événements en Europe; **to await ~s**

attendre la suite des événements; [7] (of idea, theme) développement *m*

B *noun modifier* [*area, planning*] d'aménagement; [*costs, bank*] de développement

development company *n* groupe *m* immobilier

deviant /'di:vɪənt/ *adj* déviant

deviate /'di:vɪeɪt/ *vi* [1] (from norm) s'écarter (**from** de); [2] (from course) dévier (**from** de)

deviation /ˌdi:vɪ'eɪʃn/ *n* [1] (from course, party line, policy) déviation *f* (**from** par rapport à); [2] (from norm) écart *m* (**from** par rapport à); [3] (sexual) déviance *f*

device /dɪ'vaɪs/ *n* [1] (household) appareil *m*; **labour-saving** ∼ appareil *m* électroménager; [2] Tech dispositif *m*; [3] (system) système *m*; **security** ∼ système *m* de sécurité; [4] (*also* **explosive** ∼, **incendiary** ∼) engin *m* explosif; [5] (means) gen moyen *m* (**for doing, to do** de *or* pour faire); Econ mesure *f* (**for doing, to do** pour faire); [6] Literat procédé *m*

⌐Idiom⌐ **to be left to one's own** ∼**s** être laissé à soi-même

devil /'devl/

A *n* [1] (*also* **Devil**) Relig **the** ∼ le Diable; [2] (evil spirit) démon *m*; [3] ○(for emphasis) **we'll have a** ∼ **of a job doing** ça va être sacrément○ dur de faire; [4] ○(expressing affection, sympathy) **a lucky** ∼ un sacré veinard○

B **devilled** GB, **deviled** US *adj* Culin à la diable

⌐Idioms⌐ **be a** ∼○**!** allez, laisse-toi tenter!; **to be caught between the** ∼ **and the deep blue sea** être pris entre l'enclume et le marteau; **to have the luck of the** ∼○ GB avoir une veine de cocu○; **like the** ∼○ comme un fou○; **speak of the** ∼**!** quand on parle du loup (on en voit la queue)○!

devilish /'devəlɪʃ/ *adj* (all contexts) diabolique

devilishly /'devəlɪʃlɪ/ *adv* [1] (horribly) ∼ **cruel** d'une cruauté diabolique; [2] ○fig sacrément○

devil-may-care /ˌdevlmeɪ'keə(r)/ *adj* insouciant

devilment /'devlmənt/ *n* GB malice *f*

devil: ∼**'s advocate** *n* avocat *m* du diable; ∼ **worship** *n* satanisme *m*

devious /'di:vɪəs/ *adj* [1] (sly) [*person, mind, plan*] retors; [*method*] détourné; [2] (winding) [*road, path*] tortueux/-euse

deviously /'di:vɪəslɪ/ *adv* de façon retorse

devise /dɪ'vaɪz/ *vtr* [1] (invent) concevoir [*scheme, course*]; inventer [*product, machine*]; [2] Theat écrire [qch] en groupe

deviser /dɪ'vaɪzə(r)/ *n* inventeur *m*

devoid /dɪ'vɔɪd/: **devoid of** *prep phr* dépourvu de

devolution /ˌdi:və'lu:ʃn, US ˌdev-/ *n* [1] (transfer) transfert *m* (**from** de; **to** à); [2] Pol régionalisation *f*

ⓘ **Devolution** Au Royaume-Uni, ce terme désigne le transfert du pouvoir politique de Londres vers de nouvelles structures parlementaires en Écosse, au pays de Galles et en Irlande du Nord. Le Parlement d'Écosse et l'Assemblée du Pays de Galles furent institués après consultation des populations concernées par référendum (1997). En Irlande du Nord, c'est le *Good Friday Agreement* (1998) conclu entre le gouvernement britannique et les chefs politiques irlandais, puis approuvé par la population des deux parties de l'île, qui a conduit à la création d'une assemblée parlementaire (*Northern Ireland Assembly*).

---

devolve /dɪ'vɒlv/

A *vtr* déléguer

B *vi* [1] [*responsibility, duty*] incomber (**on** à); [2] Jur passer (**on, to** à)

devote /dɪ'vəʊt/ *vtr* consacrer (**to** à; **to doing** à faire); **to** ∼ **oneself** se consacrer (**to** à; **to doing** à faire)

devoted /dɪ'vəʊtɪd/ *adj* dévoué (**to** à); [*friendship, service*] loyal; [*fan*] fervent; **they're** ∼ **to each other** ils sont très attachés l'un à l'autre

devotee /ˌdevə'ti:/ *n* (of music) passionné/-e *m/f* (**of** de); (of cause) partisan/-e *m/f* (**of** de); (of person) admirateur/-trice *m/f* (**of** de); (of sect) adepte *mf*

devotion /dɪ'vəʊʃn/ *n* (to person, work, homeland) dévouement *m* (**to** à); (to doctrine, cause) attachement *m* (**to** à); (to God) dévotion *f* (**to** à)

devour /dɪ'vaʊə(r)/ *vtr* [1] (consume) lit, fig dévorer [*food, book*]; consommer beaucoup de [*petrol, resources*]; [2] (destroy) dévorer

devout /dɪ'vaʊt/ *adj* [1] [*Catholic, prayer*] fervent; [*act, person*] pieux/pieuse; [2] (sincere) ardent

devoutly /dɪ'vaʊtlɪ/ *adv* Relig pieusement; (sincerely) ardemment

dew /dju:, US du:/ *n* rosée *f*

dewy /'dju:, US 'du:-/ *adj* humide de rosée

dewy-eyed /ˌdju:ɪ'aɪd, US ˌdu:-/ *adj* (moved) ému; (naive) ingénu

dexterity /dek'sterətɪ/ *n* dextérité *f*

dexterous /'dekstrəs/ *adj* [*person, movement*] adroit; [*hand*] habile; [*mind*] agile

dexterously /'dekstrəslɪ/ *adv* [*move*] (of person) adroitement; (of animal) agilement; [*manage*] habilement

DfES *n*: *abrév* GB ▸ **Department for Education and Skills**

dg *n* (*abrév écrite* = **decigram**) dg *m*

DG *n*: *abrév* ▸ **director general**

diabetes /ˌdaɪə'bi:ti:z/ ▸ **p. 933** *n* diabète *m*

diabetic /ˌdaɪə'betɪk/ *n, adj* diabétique (*mf*)

diabolical /ˌdaɪə'bɒlɪkl/ *adj* [1] ○[*food*] infect; [*behaviour*] lamentable; [2] (evil) diabolique

diabolically /ˌdaɪə'bɒlɪklɪ/ *adv* [1] ○(badly) [*perform*] de façon épouvantable; [*behave*] de façon odieuse; [2] (wickedly) de façon diabolique

diacritic /ˌdaɪə'krɪtɪk/ *adj* (*also* **diacritical**) Ling diacritique

diaeresis GB, **dieresis** US /daɪ'erəsɪs/ *n* (*pl* **-ses**) tréma *m*

diagnose /'daɪəgnəʊz, US ˌdaɪəg'nəʊs/ *vtr* [1] Med diagnostiquer; **the illness was** ∼**d as cancer** les médecins ont diagnostiqué un cancer; [2] gen identifier

diagnosis /ˌdaɪəg'nəʊsɪs/ *n* (*pl* **-ses**) diagnostic *m*

diagnostic /ˌdaɪəg'nɒstɪk/ *adj* diagnostique

diagnostics /ˌdaɪəg'nɒstɪks/ *n* [1] Med diagnose *f*; [2] Comput (+ *v pl*) diagnostic *m*

diagonal /daɪ'ægənl/

A *n* (all contexts) diagonale *f*

B *adj* [*line, stripe*] diagonal; **our street is** ∼ **to the main road** notre rue part en biais de la rue principale

diagonally /daɪ'ægənəlɪ/ *adv* en diagonale

diagram /'daɪəgræm/ *n* gen schéma *m*; Math figure *f*

dial /'daɪəl/

A *n* cadran *m*

B *vtr* (*p prés etc* **-ll-** GB, **-l-** US) faire; (more formal) composer [*number*]; appeler [*person, country*]; **to** ∼ **999** ≈ (for police, ambulance) appeler police secours; (for fire brigade) appeler les pompiers

dialect /'daɪəlekt/ *n* dialecte *m*

dialectic /ˌdaɪə'lektɪk/ *n, adj* dialectique (*f*)

dialectics /ˌdaɪə'lektɪks/ *n* (+ *v sg*) dialectique *f*

dialling GB, **dialing** US /'daɪəlɪŋ/ *n* **abbreviated** ∼ utilisation *f* de numéros abrégés; **direct** ∼ appel *m* direct

dialling: ∼ **code** *n* GB indicatif *m*; ∼ **tone** *n* GB tonalité *f*

dialogue /'daɪəlɒg, US -lɔ:g/

A *n* dialogue *m*

B *vi* dialoguer (**with** avec)

dial: ∼ **tone** *n* US tonalité *f*; ∼**-up** *adj* [*network*] commuté; [*connection*] par ligne téléphonique

dialysis /daɪ'ælɪsɪs/ *n* (*pl* **-lyses**) (kidney) ∼ dialyse *f*

dialysis machine *n* rein *m* artificiel

diamanté /ˌdaɪə'mæntɪ, dɪə'mɒnteɪ/ *n* (decorative trim, jewellery, material) strass *m*; (fabric) tissu *m* pailleté

diameter /daɪ'æmɪtə(r)/ *n* diamètre *m*; **to be 2 m in** ∼ avoir 2 m de diamètre

diametrically /ˌdaɪə'metrɪklɪ/ *adv* diamétralement

diamond /'daɪəmənd/ ▸ **p. 881**

A *n* [1] (stone) diamant *m*; [2] (shape) losange *m*; [3] (in cards) carreau *m*; [4] (in baseball) terrain *m* (de baseball)

B *noun modifier* [*cutter, ring*] de diamants

diamond: ∼ **jubilee** *n* soixantième anniversaire *m*; ∼**-shaped** *adj* en (forme de) losange; ∼ **wedding**

(anniversary) n noces fpl de diamant

diaper /'daɪəpə(r), (US) 'daɪpər/ US

A n couche f (pour bébé)

B vtr changer la couche de [baby]

diaphanous /daɪ'æfənəs/ adj diaphane

diaphragm /'daɪəfræm/ n (all contexts) diaphragme m

diarist /'daɪərɪst/ n **1** (author) auteur m d'un journal (intime); **2** (journalist) chroniqueur/-euse m/f

diarrhoea GB, **diarrhea** US /ˌdaɪə'rɪə/ n diarrhée f

diary /'daɪərɪ/ n **1** (for appointments) agenda m; **to put sth in one's ~** noter qch dans son agenda; **2** (journal) journal m intime; **3** (in newspaper) chronique f

diatribe /'daɪətraɪb/ n diatribe f (**against** contre)

dice /daɪs/

A n (pl **~**) (object) dé m; (game) dés mpl; **to throw the ~** jeter le dé or les dés; **no ~!** (refusal) pas question!; (no luck) pas de chance!

B vtr Culin couper [qch] en cubes

(Idioms) **to ~ with death** risquer sa vie; **the ~ are loaded** les dés sont pipés

dicey○ /'daɪsɪ/ adj **1** (risky) risqué; **2** (uncertain, unreliable) douteux/-euse

dichotomy /daɪ'kɒtəmɪ/ n dichotomie f

dichromatic /ˌdaɪkrəʊ'mætɪk/ adj dichromatique

dicky /'dɪkɪ/

A n faux plastron m

B ○adj GB [heart] qui flanche; [condition] précaire

dicta /'dɪktə/ pl ▸ **dictum**

dictate

A /'dɪkteɪt/ n (decree) ordre m

B /dɪk'teɪt, US 'dɪkteɪt/ vtr **1** Sch, Comm dicter; **2** (prescribe) imposer [terms] (**to** à); déterminer [outcome]; régenter [policy]; **to ~ how** prescrire comment

C /dɪk'teɪt, US 'dɪkteɪt/ vi **1** (out loud) **to ~ to one's secretary** dicter une lettre (or un texte etc) à sa secrétaire; **2** **to ~ to sb** imposer sa volonté à qn

dictation /dɪk'teɪʃn/ n Sch, Comm dictée f; **to take ~** écrire sous la dictée

dictator /dɪk'teɪtə(r), US 'dɪkteɪtər/ n Pol dictateur m; fig tyran m

dictatorial /ˌdɪktə'tɔːrɪəl/ adj [person] tyrannique; [regime, powers] dictatorial

dictatorship /dɪk'teɪtəʃɪp, US 'dɪkt-/ n Pol dictature f; fig tyrannie f

diction /'dɪkʃn/ n (articulation) diction f; (choice of words) langage m

dictionary /'dɪkʃənrɪ, US -nerɪ/ n dictionnaire m

dictionary entry n entrée f de dictionnaire

dictum /'dɪktəm/ n (pl **-ums** ou **-a**) phrase f célèbre

did /dɪd/ prét ▸ **do**

diddle○ /'dɪdl/ vtr (swindle) rouler○, escroquer

didn't /'dɪd(ə)nt/ = **did not**

die /daɪ/

A n Games (pl **dice**) dé m (à jouer)

B vtr (p prés **dying**; prét, pp **died**) **to ~ a violent death** mourir de mort violente; **to ~ a hero's death** mourir en héros

C vi (p prés **dying**; prét, pp **died**) **1** (expire) mourir; **he was dying** il était en train de mourir; **she ~d a year ago** elle est morte il y a un an; **as she lay dying** alors qu'elle se mourait; **to be left to ~** être abandonné à la mort; **to ~ young** mourir jeune; **to ~ of** ou **from** mourir de [starvation, disease]; **2** (be killed) mourir, périr liter (**doing** en faisant); **to ~ in action** mourir au combat; **he' d sooner** ou **rather ~ than do** il mourrait plutôt que de faire; **I'd sooner ~!** plutôt mourir!; **to ~ for** mourir pour [beliefs, person]; **3** (wither) [plant, crop] crever; **4** fig (of boredom etc) mourir (**of** de); **5** ○(long) **to be dying to do** mourir d'envie de faire; **to be dying for** avoir une envie folle de; **clothes to ~ for**○ des vêtements à craquer○; **6** (go out) [light, flame] s'éteindre; **7** (fade) [emotion, memory, fame] s'éteindre; [enthusiasm] tomber; **8** ○ (cease functioning) [machine, engine] s'arrêter; **9** ○(on stage) faire un bide○

(Idioms) **never say ~!** il ne faut jamais baisser les bras!; **to ~ hard** avoir la vie dure

(Phrasal verbs)

■ **die down** **1** (in intensity) [emotion, row] s'apaiser; [scandal, opposition, publicity] disparaître; [fighting] s'achever;

[tremors, storm] se calmer; **2** (in volume) [laughter] diminuer; [applause] se calmer; **3** [plant] se flétrir

■ **die out** **1** (become extinct) disparaître; **2** (ease off) s'arrêter

diehard /'daɪhɑːd/ n **1** Pol (in party) réactionnaire mf; **2** péj (conservative) ultraconservateur/-trice m/f; **3** (stubborn person) irréductible mf

dieresis US ▸ **diaeresis**

diesel /'diːzl/ n (also **~ fuel**, **~ oil**) gazole m; (also **~ car**) diesel m

diesel: ~ engine n (in train) motrice f Diesel; (in car) moteur m Diesel; **~ train** n train m Diesel

diet /'daɪət/

A n **1** (of person) alimentation f (**of** à base de); (of animal) nourriture f (**of** à base de); **2** Med (limiting food) régime m; **to go on a ~** se mettre au régime; **3** fig cure f (**of** de); **4** Hist, Pol diète f

B vi être au régime

dietary /'daɪətrɪ, US -terɪ/ adj [habit] alimentaire; [method] diététique

dietary: ~ fibre GB, **~ fiber** US n fibres fpl alimentaires; **~ supplement** n complément m vitaminique

dietician, dietitian /ˌdaɪə'tɪʃn/ ▸ p. 1181 n diététicien/-ienne m/f

differ /'dɪfə(r)/ vi **1** (be different) différer (**from** de; **in** par); **to ~ widely** être complètement différent; **2** (disagree) différer (d'opinion) (**on** sur; **from sb** de qn); **I beg to ~** permettez-moi d'être d'un avis différent

difference /'dɪfrəns/ n **1** (dissimilarity) différence f (**in, of** de); **to tell the ~ between** faire la différence entre; **it won't make any ~** ça ne changera rien; **what ~ does it make if...?** qu'est-ce que ça change si...?; **it makes no ~ to me** cela m'est égal; **as near as makes no ~** peu s'en faut; **a vacation with a ~** des vacances pas comme les autres; **2** (disagreement) différend m (**between** entre; **over** à propos de; **with** avec); **a ~ of opinion** une divergence d'opinion

different /'dɪfrənt/ adj **1** (dissimilar) différent (**from, to** GB, **than** US de); **they are ~ in this respect** ils diffèrent à cet égard; **it's very ~** c'est complètement différent; **2** (other) autre; **to be a ~ person** être une tout autre personne; **that's ~** c'est autre chose; **it would have been a ~ story if...** cela aurait été tout autre chose si...; **3** (distinct) différent; **4** (unusual) différent; **he has to be ~** il faut qu'il se distingue

differential /ˌdɪfə'renʃl/

A n **1** (in price, rate etc) écart m; **pay ~s** écart des salaires; **2** Math différentielle f; **3** Aut différentiel m

B adj (all contexts) différentiel/-ielle

differentiate /ˌdɪfə'renʃɪeɪt/

A vtr **1** (tell the difference) différencier (**from** de); **2** (make the difference) différencier (**from** de); **3** Math calculer la différentielle de

B vi **1** (tell the difference) faire la différence (**between** entre); **2** (show the difference) faire la distinction (**between** entre); **3** (discriminate) faire des différences (**between** entre)

differentiation /ˌdɪfərenʃɪ'eɪʃn/ n **1** (distinction) différenciation f; **2** Math différentiation f

differently /'dɪfrəntlɪ/ adv **1** (in another way) autrement (**from** que); **2** (in different ways) différemment (**from** de); **it affects men and women ~** cela touche les hommes et les femmes différemment

difficult /'dɪfɪkəlt/ adj **1** (hard, not easy to do) difficile; **it will be ~ for me to decide** il me sera difficile de décider; **to find it ~ to do** avoir du mal à faire; **2** (complex, inaccessible) [author, concept] difficile; **3** (awkward) [age, position, personality] difficile; **to get on with** difficile à vivre

difficulty /'dɪfɪkəltɪ/ n **1** (of task, situation) difficulté f; **to have ~ (in) doing** avoir du mal à faire; **I have ~ with that idea** cette idée me pose un problème; **2** (problem) difficulté f, problème m; **the difficulties of living here** les difficultés de la vie ici; **3** (trouble) **in ~** en difficulté

diffidence /'dɪfɪdəns/ n manque m d'assurance

diffident /'dɪfɪdənt/ adj [person] qui manque d'assurance; [smile, gesture] timide; **to be ~ about doing** hésiter à faire

diffidently /'dɪfɪdəntlɪ/ adv d'un air or d'un ton mal assuré

diffuse

A /dɪ'fjuːs/ adj (all contexts) diffus

B /dɪ'fjuːz/ vtr diffuser (**in** dans)

d

C /dɪˈfjuːz/ vi se diffuser (**into** dans)

diffuseness /dɪˈfjuːsnɪs/ n ① (of argument) prolixité f; ② (of organization) éparpillement m

dig /dɪg/

A n ① (with elbow) coup m de coude (**in** dans); ② ⚬(jibe) pique⚬ f (**at à**); **to get in a ~ at sb** lancer une pique⚬ à qn; ③ (in archaeology) fouilles fpl; **to go on a ~** aller faire des fouilles; ④ (when gardening) coup m de bêche

B **digs** npl GB chambre f (meublée) (chez des particuliers)

C vtr (p prés **-gg-**; prét, pp **dug**) ① (excavate) creuser (**in** dans); ② bêcher [garden, plot]; fouiller [site]; ③ (extract) arracher [root crops]; extraire [coal, turf] (**out of** de); ④ (embed) enfoncer [knife, needle etc] (**into** dans); ⑤ ⚬ (like) **she really ~s that guy** ce mec la botte⚬

D vi (p prés **-gg-**; prét, pp **dug**) ① (excavate) gen creuser (**into** dans; **for** pour trouver); (in garden) bêcher; (in archaeology) fouiller; ② (search) **to ~ in** ou **into** fouiller dans (**for** pour trouver) [sb's past]; ③ **to ~ into** [springs, thorns] s'enfoncer dans

(Phrasal verbs)

■ **dig in:** ▸ **~ in** Mil, fig se retrancher; ▸ **~ in [sth]**, **~ [sth] in** enterrer [compost]; enfoncer [teeth, weapon]

■ **dig out:** ▸ **~ out [sth]**, **~ [sth] out** déterrer [animal] (**of** de); arracher [root, weed] (**of** de); enlever [splinter] (**of** de); dénicher⚬ [book, information] (**of** dans)

■ **dig up:** ▸ **~ up [sth]**, **~ [sth] up** (unearth) déterrer [body, treasure]; arracher [roots]; excaver [road]; (turn over) retourner [soil]; bêcher [garden]; fig dénicher⚬ [information]; déterrer [scandal]

digest

A /ˈdaɪdʒest/ n ① (periodical) digest m; ② (summary) résumé m

B /daɪˈdʒest, dɪ-/ vtr digérer [food]; assimiler [facts]

digestible /dɪˈdʒestəbl/ adj digeste

digestion /daɪˈdʒestʃn, dɪ-/ n digestion f

digestive /dɪˈdʒestɪv, daɪ-/

A n GB Culin ≈ biscuit m (sablé)

B adj digestif/-ive

digestive: **~ biscuit** n GB ≈ biscuit m (sablé); **~ system** n système m digestif; **~ tract** n appareil m digestif

digger /ˈdɪgə(r)/ n (excavator) excavateur m

digging /ˈdɪgɪŋ/

A n ① (in garden) bêchage m; **to do some ~** bêcher; ② Constr creusement m; ③ (in mining) forage m (**for** pour trouver)

B **diggings** npl (in archaeology) fouilles fpl; (from mine) déblais mpl

digit /ˈdɪdʒɪt/ n ① (number) chiffre m; ② (finger) doigt m; (toe) orteil m

digital /ˈdɪdʒɪtl/ adj ① [display, recording, camera, TV] numérique; [clock, watch] à affichage numérique; ② Anat digital

digital: **~ access lock**, **~ lock** n digicode® m; **~ audio tape**, **DAT** n cassette f audionumérique, DAT f; **~ computer** n calculateur m numérique; **~ signature** n Comput signature f électronique

digitizer /ˈdɪdʒɪtaɪzə(r)/ n Comput numériseur m

dignified /ˈdɪgnɪfaɪd/ adj [person] digne; [manner] empreint de dignité

dignify /ˈdɪgnɪfaɪ/ vtr donner du faste à [occasion, building]

dignitary /ˈdɪgnɪtərɪ/ n dignitaire m

dignity /ˈdɪgnətɪ/ n (of person, occasion) dignité f; **to stand on one's ~** prendre de grands airs

digress /daɪˈgres/ vi faire une digression

digression /daɪˈgreʃn/ n digression f

dike n ▸ **dyke 1**

dilapidated /dɪˈlæpɪdeɪtɪd/ adj délabré

dilapidation /dɪˌlæpɪˈdeɪʃn/ n délabrement m

dilate /daɪˈleɪt/

A vtr dilater

B vi ① (widen) se dilater; ② (discuss at length) **to ~ on a subject** s'étendre sur un sujet

dilatory /ˈdɪlətərɪ, US -tɔːrɪ/ adj sout ① (slow) lent; ② (time-wasting) dilatoire also Jur

dilemma /daɪˈlemə, dɪ-/ n dilemme m (**about**, **over** à propos de); **in a ~** devant un dilemme

diligence /ˈdɪlɪdʒəns/ n zèle m (**in** dans; **in doing** à faire)

diligent /ˈdɪlɪdʒənt/ adj appliqué; **to be ~ in doing sth** faire qch avec application

diligently /ˈdɪlɪdʒəntlɪ/ adv [work] avec zèle

dill /dɪl/ n aneth m

dill pickle n concombres mpl au vinaigre et à l'aneth

dillydally⚬ /ˈdɪlɪdælɪ/ vi ① (dawdle) lambiner⚬; ② (be indecisive) tergiverser

dilute /daɪˈljuːt, US -ˈluːt/ vtr ① lit diluer [liquid] (**with** avec); éclaircir [colour]; ② fig diluer

dilution /daɪˈljuːʃn, US -ˈluːt-/ n lit, fig dilution f (**of** de)

dim /dɪm/

A adj ① (badly lit) sombre; ② (weak) faible; **to grow ~** s'affaiblir; ③ (hard to see) vague; ④ (vague) vague; ⑤ ⚬(stupid) bouché⚬; ⑥ (not favourable) sombre

B vtr (p prés etc **-mm-**) baisser [light]; mettre [qch] en veilleuse [lamp]; US baisser [headlights]

C vi (p prés etc **-mm-**) [lights, lamp] baisser; [memory] s'estomper; [sight] s'affaiblir; [colour, beauty, hope] se ternir

(Idiom) **to take a ~ view of sth** n'apprécier guère qch

dime /daɪm/ n US (pièce f de) dix cents mpl

(Idioms) **they're a ~ a dozen**⚬ on en trouve à la pelle⚬; **to stop on a ~**⚬ s'arrêter pile

dimension /daɪˈmenʃn/ n ① (aspect) dimension f; ② (scope) **~s** étendue f (**of** de); ③ (measurement) gen dimension f; Archit, Math, Tech cote f

-dimensional /-dɪˈmenʃənl/ combining form **three-~** à trois dimensions

dime store n US bazar m

diminish /dɪˈmɪnɪʃ/

A vtr ① (reduce) diminuer; ② (weaken) amoindrir [influence, strength]; diminuer [emotion]; ③ (denigrate) dénigrer; ④ Mus diminuer

B vi ① (decrease) diminuer; ② (weaken) [emotion] s'amenuiser; [influence, strength] s'amoindrir

diminished /dɪˈmɪnɪʃd/ adj ① [amount, enthusiasm, level] réduit; [awareness, support] amoindri; ② Jur **on grounds of ~ responsibility** pour raisons de responsabilité atténuée; ③ Mus diminué

diminution /ˌdɪmɪˈnjuːʃn, US -ˈnuːʃn/ n (of size, quantity) diminution f; (of intensity, power) affaiblissement m

diminutive /dɪˈmɪnjʊtɪv/

A n Ling diminutif m

B adj [object] minuscule; [person] tout petit

dimly /ˈdɪmlɪ/ adv ① [lit] faiblement; ② [perceive, recall, sense] vaguement

dimmer /ˈdɪmə(r)/ n (also **~ switch**) variateur m d'ambiance

dimming /ˈdɪmɪŋ/ n (of lights) atténuation f; (of hope etc) ternissement m

dimple /ˈdɪmpl/ n (in flesh) fossette f; (on water) ride f

dim: **~wit**⚬ n andouille⚬ f; **~-witted**⚬ adj bouché⚬

din /dɪn/ n (of machine) vacarme m; (of people) chahut m

(Idiom) **to ~ sth into sb**⚬ enfoncer qch dans la tête de qn⚬

dine /daɪn/ vi dîner; ▸ **wine**

(Phrasal verbs)

■ **dine in** dîner à la maison

■ **dine off**, **dine on:** ▸ **~ off [sth]** dîner de qch

■ **dine out** dîner dehors; **to ~ out on** fig resservir [story, anecdote]

diner /ˈdaɪnə(r)/ n ① (person) dîneur/-euse m/f; ② US (restaurant) café-restaurant m; ③ (in train) wagon-restaurant m

dinette /daɪˈnet/ n US ① (room) coin-repas m; ② (also **~ set**) table f et chaises fpl de cuisine

dingdong⚬ /ˈdɪŋdɒŋ/ n ① GB (quarrel) échange m vif de mots; ② onomat ding dong

dinghy /ˈdɪŋgɪ/ n ① (also **sailing ~**) dériveur m; ② (inflatable) canot m

dingy /ˈdɪndʒɪ/ adj [colour] défraîchi; [place] minable

dining: **~ car** n wagon-restaurant m; **~ hall** n réfectoire m; **~ room** n gen salle f à manger; (in hotel) salle f de restaurant

dink /dɪŋk/ n Sport amorti m

dinky⚬ /ˈdɪŋkɪ/ adj ① GB (sweet) mignon/-onne; ② (small) petit

dinner /ˈdɪnə(r)/ n ① (meal) (evening) dîner m; (midday) déjeuner m; **at ~** au dîner or déjeuner; **to go out to ~** dîner dehors; **to have** ~ **dîner; to have chicken for** ~ manger du poulet au dîner; **to give the dog its** ~ donner à manger au chien; ② (banquet) dîner *m* (**for** en l'honneur de)

dinner: ~ **dance** *n* dîner-dansant *m;* ~ **fork** *n* grande fourchette *f;* ~ **hour** *n* GB Sch heure *f* du déjeuner; ~ **jacket, DJ** *n* smoking *m;* ~ **knife** *n* grand couteau *m;* ~ **money** *n* GB Sch argent *m* pour la cantine; ~ **party** *n* dîner *m;* ~ **plate** *n* grande assiette *f;* ~ **service,** ~ **set** *n* service *m* de table; ~**time** *n* heure *f* du dîner; ~**ware** *n* US vaisselle *f*

dinosaur /'daɪnəsɔː(r)/ *n* lit, fig dinosaure *m*

dint /dɪnt/: **by dint of** *prep phr* grâce à

diocesan /daɪˈɒsɪsn/ *n, adj* diocésain (*m*)

diocese /'daɪəsɪs/ *n* diocèse *m*

dioxide /daɪˈɒksaɪd/ *n* dioxyde *m*

dip /dɪp/
A *n* ① (bathe) baignade *f;* **to have a quick** ~ se baigner rapidement; ② (in ground, road) déclivité *f;* ③ (of plane, head) inclinaison *f;* ④ fig (in prices, rate, sales) (mouvement *m* de) baisse *f* (**in** dans); ⑤ Culin sauce *f* froide (*pour crudités*); ⑥ (also **sheep** ~) bain *m* parasiticide
B *vtr* (*p prés etc* **-pp-**) ① (put partially) tremper (**in, into** dans); ② (immerse) plonger [*garment*]; tremper [*food*]; baigner [*sheep*]; ③ GB Aut baisser [*headlights*]; ~**ped headlights** codes *mpl;* **to drive with** ~**ped headlights** rouler en code
C *vi* (*p prés etc* **-pp-**) ① (move downwards) piquer; **to** ~ **below the horizon** [*sun*] disparaître derrière l'horizon; ② (slope downwards) être en pente; ③ fig (decrease) [*price, value, speed, rate*] descendre; ④ (put hand) **to** ~ **into one's bag for sth** chercher qch dans son sac; fig **to** ~ **into one's savings** puiser dans ses économies; ⑤ (read a little) **to** ~ **into** parcourir

Dip *n: abrév écrite* = **diploma**

diphthong /'dɪfθɒŋ, US -θɔːŋ/ *n* diphtongue *f*

diploma /dɪˈpləʊmə/ *n* diplôme *m* (**in** en)

diplomacy /dɪˈpləʊməsɪ/ *n* gen, Pol diplomatie *f*

diplomat /'dɪpləmæt/ ▸ **p. 1181** *n* diplomate *mf*

diplomatic /ˌdɪpləˈmætɪk/ *adj* ① Pol diplomatique; ② (astute) [*person*] diplomate; [*behaviour*] diplomatique; ③ (tactful) **to be** ~ avoir du tact

diplomatic bag GB, **diplomatic pouch** US *n* valise *f* diplomatique

diplomatist /dɪˈpləʊmətɪst/ *n* diplomate *mf*

dippy○ /'dɪpɪ/ *adj* farfelu○

dipstick /'dɪpstɪk/ *n* Aut jauge *f* de niveau d'huile

dip switch *n* interrupteur *m* à positions multiples

diptych /'dɪptɪk/ *n* diptyque *m*

dire /'daɪə(r)/ *adj* ① (terrible) [*consequence*] terrible; [*situation*] désespéré; **in** ~ **straits** dans une situation désespérée; ② ○(awful) affreux/-euse

direct /daɪˈrekt, dɪ-/
A *adj* ① (without intermediary) direct; **in** ~ **contact with** (touching) en contact direct avec; (communicating) directement en contact avec; ② (without detour) direct; **to be a** ~ **descendant of** descendre en droite ligne de; ③ (clear) [*cause, influence, reference, threat*] direct; [*contrast, evidence*] flagrant; **to be the** ~ **opposite of** être tout le contraire de; ④ (straightforward) [*answer, method*] direct; [*person*] franc/franche
B *adv* ① (without intermediary) directement; ② (without detour) directement (**from** de)
C *vtr* ① (address, aim) adresser [*appeal, criticism*] (**at** à; **against** contre); cibler [*campaign*] (**at** sur); orienter [*effort, resource*] (**to, towards** vers); **to** ~ **one's attention to** concentrer son attention sur; **to** ~ **sb's attention to** attirer l'attention de qn sur; ② (control) diriger [*company, project*]; régler [*traffic*]; ③ diriger [*attack, light, car*]; pointer [*gun*] (**at** vers); ④ Cin, Radio, TV réaliser; Theat mettre [qch] en scène [*play*]; diriger [*actor, opera*]; ⑤ (instruct) **to** ~ **sb to do** gen ordonner à qn de faire; **he did it as** ~**ed** il l'a fait comme on le lui avait indiqué; **'to be taken as** ~**ed'** 'à consommer selon la prescription médicale'; ⑥ (show route) **to** ~ **sb to sth** indiquer le chemin de qch à qn
D *vi* Cin, Radio, TV faire de la réalisation; Theat faire de la mise en scène

direct: ~ **access** *n* Comput accès *m* direct; ~ **access device** *n* unité *f* à accès direct; ~ **current, DC** *n* Elec courant *m* continu; ~ **debit** *n* prélèvement *m* automatique; ~ **discourse** *n* US = **direct speech;** ~ **hit** *n* Mil coup *m* au but

Street directions

How do I get there?

En sortant de la gare, allez tout droit, traversez la place où attendent les taxis, puis le parking. Vous déboucherez dans la Grand-Rue. Continuez dans la même direction sur plusieurs centaines de mètres. Vous passerez trois feux rouges. Tournez à droite au troisième, et vous vous trouverez dans la rue Maginot. Prenez la troisième rue à gauche (il y a une banque qui fait l'angle) et continuez jusqu'au bout de cette rue. Vous verrez le théâtre en face de vous. Empruntez le passage à gauche du théâtre, descendez les escaliers et vous vous retrouverez dans l'avenue des Marronniers. Prenez-la sur votre gauche en marchant sur le trottoir de gauche. Vous verrez une boucherie chevaline sur la droite de la rue juste avant le deuxième carrefour. Traversez le carrefour en diagonale. Vous apercevrez une sorte de terrain vague sur votre droite après le carrefour. Le dernier magasin, juste avant le terrain vague, est celui d'un tailleur, et il y a un café dans une cour derrière. Je vous y attendrai avec la valise et toutes les instructions. Mais attention: pas un mot à qui que ce soit!

direction /daɪˈrekʃn, dɪ-/
A *n* ① (left, right, north, south) direction *f;* **in the right/wrong** ~ dans la bonne/mauvaise direction; **to go in the opposite** ~ aller en sens inverse; **from all** ~**s** de tous les côtés; ② (taken by company, government, career) orientation *f;* **the right/ wrong** ~ **for sb** la bonne/mauvaise option pour qn; **to lack** ~ manquer d'objectifs; ③ Cin, Radio, TV réalisation *f;* Theat mise *f* en scène; Mus direction *f;* ④ (control) direction *f;* (guidance) conseils *mpl*
B directions *npl* ① (for route) indications *fpl;* **to ask for** ~**s** demander son chemin (**from** à); ② (for use) instructions *fpl* (**as to, about** sur); ~**s for use** mode *m* d'emploi

directional /daɪˈrekʃənl, dɪ-/ *adj* directionnel/-elle

directive /daɪˈrektɪv, dɪ-/
A *n* Admin, Comput directive *f* (**on** relative à)
B *adj* directif/-ive

directly /daɪˈrektlɪ, dɪ-/
A *adv* ① (without a detour) [*connect, challenge, go, refer*] directement; [*aim, point*] droit; [*move*] tout droit; **to look** ~ **at sb** regarder qn droit dans les yeux; ② (exactly) [*above*] juste; [*contradict*] totalement; ③ (at once) ~ **after** aussitôt après; ~ **before** juste avant; ④ (very soon) d'ici peu; ⑤ (frankly) [*speak*] franchement; [*deny*] catégoriquement
B *conj* GB (as soon as) dès que

direct mail *n* mailing *m*, publipostage *m*

directness /daɪˈrektnɪs, dɪ-/ *n* ① (of person, attitude) franchise *f;* ② (of play, work, writing) authenticité *f*

direct object *n* objet *m* direct

director /daɪˈrektə(r), dɪ-/ *n* ① Admin, Comm (of company, programme) (sole) directeur/-trice *m/f;* (one of board) administrateur/-trice *m/f;* ② gen (of project, investigation) responsable *mf;* ③ (of play, film) metteur *m* en scène; (of orchestra) chef *m* d'orchestre; (of choir) chef *m* des chœurs; ④ Sch, Univ ~ **of studies** directeur/-trice *m/f* des études; ~ **of admissions** responsable *mf* du service des inscriptions

directorate /daɪˈrektərət, dɪ-/ *n* (board) conseil *m* d'administration

director general, DG *n* directeur *m* général

directorial /ˌdaɪrekˈtɔːrɪəl, ˌdɪ-/ *adj* ① Admin [*duties*] de directeur/-trice; ② Theat [*debut*] de metteur en scène; [*style*] de direction

Director of Public Prosecutions, DPP *n* GB ≈ procureur *m* général

directorship /daɪˈrektəʃɪp, dɪ-/ *n* (in organization, institution) direction *f;* (in company) poste *m* d'administrateur

directory /daɪˈrektərɪ, dɪ-/ *n* ① Telecom annuaire *m;* ② Comm répertoire *m* d'adresses; **street** ~ répertoire *m* des rues; ③ Comput répertoire *m*

directory: ∼ **assistance** n US = directory enquiries; ∼ **enquiries** npl GB (service m des) renseignements mpl

direct: ∼ **primary** n US élection f primaire directe; ∼ **rule** n Pol gouvernement m direct; ∼ **speech** n style m direct; ∼ **transfer** n virement m automatique

dirt /dɜːt/ n **1** (mess) (on clothing, in room) saleté f; (on body, cooker) crasse f; (in carpet, engine, filter) saletés fpl; **to show the** ∼ être salissant; **2** (soil) terre f; (mud) boue f; **3** °péj (gossip) ragots mpl; **4** euph (obscenity) obscénités fpl; (excrement) excréments mpl

(Idiom) it's ∼ cheap° c'est donné

dirtiness /ˈdɜːtɪnɪs/ n (of person etc) saleté f

dirt track n **1** Sport cendrée f; **2** (road) chemin m de terre battue

dirty /ˈdɜːtɪ/
A adj **1** (messy, soiled) [face, clothing, street] sale; [work] salissant; **to get** ∼ se salir; **to get** ou **make sth** ∼ salir qch; **2** (not sterile) [needle] qui a déjà servi; [wound] infecté; **3** °(obscene) [book, joke] cochon/-onne°; [mind] mal tourné; **4** °(dishonest) [contest, fighter] déloyal; [cheat] sale; [lie] grossier/-ière; **5** [colour] sale
B °adv **1** (dishonestly) **to play** ou **fight** ∼ donner des coups en traître; **2** (obscenely) grossièrement
C vtr lit, fig salir

(Idioms) **to do the** ∼ **on°** faire une crasse° à; **to give sb a** ∼ **look°** regarder qn d'un sale œil

dirty: ∼**-minded°** adj à l'esprit mal tourné; ∼ **tricks** npl Pol diffamation f; ∼ **weekend°** n week-end m de débauche

disability /ˌdɪsəˈbɪlətɪ/
A n Med infirmité f; **mental/physical** ∼ handicap m mental/ physique; **partial** ∼ incapacité f partielle
B noun modifier [benefit, pension] d'invalidité

disable /dɪsˈeɪbl/ vtr **1** [accident] rendre [qn] infirme; **to be** ∼**d by arthritis** être handicapé par l'arthrite; **2** (make useless) immobiliser [machine]; avarier [ship]; **3** Mil mettre [qch] hors d'action; **4** Comput désactiver

disabled /dɪsˈeɪbld/
A n **the** ∼ les handicapés mpl
B adj handicapé

disabled: ∼ **access** n voie f d'accès pour handicapés; ∼ **driver** n conducteur/-trice m/f invalide; ∼ **person** n invalide mf

disabuse /ˌdɪsəˈbjuːz/ vtr sout détromper (**of** de)

disadvantage /ˌdɪsədˈvɑːntɪdʒ, US -ˈvæn-/
A n **1** (drawback) inconvénient m; **2** (position of weakness) **to be at a** ∼ être désavantagé; **to get sb at a** ∼ avoir l'avantage sur qn; **3** (discrimination) inégalité f
B vtr désavantager

disadvantaged /ˌdɪsədˈvɑːntɪdʒd, US -ˈvæn-/ adj défavorisé

disadvantageous /ˌdɪsˌædvɑːnˈteɪdʒəs, US -væn-/ adj défavorable (**to** à)

disaffected /ˌdɪsəˈfektɪd/ adj mécontent (**with** de)

disagree /ˌdɪsəˈɡriː/ vi **1** (differ) ne pas être d'accord (**with** avec; **on, about** sur); **we often** ∼ nous avons souvent des avis différents; **2** (oppose) **to** ∼ **with** s'opposer à; **3** (conflict) être en désaccord (**with** avec); **4** **to** ∼ **with sb** [food] ne pas réussir à qn; [weather] ne pas convenir à qn

disagreeable /ˌdɪsəˈɡriːəbl/ adj [person, reaction, appearance] désagréable; [remark] désobligeant

disagreeably /ˌdɪsəˈɡriːəblɪ/ adv désagréablement

disagreement /ˌdɪsəˈɡriːmənt/ n **1** (difference of opinion) désaccord m (**about, on** sur; **as to** quant à); **there is some** ∼ **as to our aims** les avis divergent quant à nos objectifs; **2** (argument) différend m (**about, over** sur); **3** (inconsistency) divergence f (**between** entre)

disallow /ˌdɪsəˈlaʊ/ vtr **1** Sport refuser; **2** gen, Admin, Jur rejeter

disappear /ˌdɪsəˈpɪə(r)/ vi (all contexts) disparaître; **to be fast** ∼**ing** être en voie de disparition

disappearance /ˌdɪsəˈpɪərəns/ n disparition f (**of** de)

disappoint /ˌdɪsəˈpɔɪnt/ vtr **1** (let down) décevoir [person]; **2** (upset) décevoir [hopes, dream]; contrecarrer [plan]

disappointed /ˌdɪsəˈpɔɪntɪd/ adj **1** (let down) déçu (**about, at, by, with sth** par qch); **I am** ∼ **in you** tu me déçois; **2** (unfulfilled) déçu

disappointing /ˌdɪsəˈpɔɪntɪŋ/ adj décevant

disappointment /ˌdɪsəˈpɔɪntmənt/ n **1** (feeling) déception f; **2** (source of upset) **to be a** ∼ **to sb** décevoir qn

disapproval /ˌdɪsəˈpruːvl/ n désapprobation f (**of** de)

disapprove /ˌdɪsəˈpruːv/ vi ne pas être d'accord; **to** ∼ **of** désapprouver [person, behaviour, lifestyle]; être contre [smoking, hunting]

disapproving /ˌdɪsəˈpruːvɪŋ/ adj [look, gesture] désapprobateur/-trice; **to be** ∼ être contre

disarm /dɪsˈɑːm/ vtr, vi désarmer

disarmament /dɪsˈɑːməmənt/ n désarmement m

disarming /dɪsˈɑːmɪŋ/ adj désarmant

disarrange /ˌdɪsəˈreɪndʒ/ vtr déranger [objects]; défaire [clothing]

disarray /ˌdɪsəˈreɪ/ n **1** (confusion) confusion f; **in total** ∼ dans une confusion totale; **2** (disorder) désordre m

disaster /dɪˈzɑːstə(r), US -zæs-/ n gen catastrophe f; (long-term) désastre m; **rail** ∼ catastrophe ferroviaire; ∼ **struck** le malheur a frappé

disaster: ∼ **area** n lit région f sinistrée; fig catastrophe f; ∼ **fund** n fonds m de soutien; ∼ **victim** n sinistré/ -e m/f

disastrous /dɪˈzɑːstrəs, US -zæs-/ adj catastrophique

disastrously /dɪˈzɑːstrəslɪ, US -zæs-/ adv [end, turn out] d'une manière désastreuse; [fail] lamentablement; **to go** ∼ **wrong** tourner à la catastrophe

disband /dɪsˈbænd/
A vtr gen dissoudre; Mil licencier
B vi se disperser

disbelief /ˌdɪsbɪˈliːf/ n incrédulité f

disbelieve /ˌdɪsbɪˈliːv/ vtr ne pas croire

disc /dɪsk/ n **1** gen, Mus disque m; **2** Anat disque m (intervertébral); **a slipped** ∼ une hernie discale; **3** gen, Mil **identity** ∼ plaque f d'identité; **4** Aut **tax** ∼ vignette f (automobile)

discard /dɪsˈkɑːd/
A vtr **1** (get rid of) se débarrasser de [possessions]; jeter [qch] par terre [litter]; mettre [qch] au rebut [furniture]; Culin jeter [stalks, bones]; **2** (drop) abandonner [plan, policy]; laisser tomber [person]; **3** (take off) enlever [garment]; **4** (in cards) se défausser de
B vi (in cards) se défausser (d'une carte)

disc brakes npl Aut freins mpl à disques

discern /dɪˈsɜːn/ vtr sout (see) discerner; (deduce) percevoir

discernible /dɪˈsɜːnəbl/ adj perceptible

discerning /dɪˈsɜːnɪŋ/ adj perspicace

discharge
A /ˈdɪstʃɑːdʒ/ n **1** (release) renvoi m au foyer; **to get one's** ∼ [soldier] être libéré; **2** (pouring out) (of gas) émission f; (of liquid) écoulement m; Med (of pus) suppuration f; (of blood) perte f; **3** (emptying out) (of waste) déversement m; **4** (substance released) (waste) déchets mpl; Med (from eye, wound etc) sécrétions fpl; **5** Fin (of debt) règlement m; **6** Elec décharge f; **7** (performance) exercice m; **8** (firing) décharge f; **9** (unloading) déchargement m
B /dɪsˈtʃɑːdʒ/ vtr **1** (release) renvoyer [patient]; donner son congé à [soldier]; décharger [accused]; **to be** ∼**d from hospital** être autorisé à quitter l'hôpital; **he has** ∼**d himself** il a quitté l'hôpital; **to be** ∼**d from the army** être libéré de l'armée; **2** (dismiss) renvoyer [employee]; **to** ∼ **sb from his duties** démettre qn de ses fonctions; **3** (give off) émettre [gas]; déverser [sewage, waste]; **4** Med **to** ∼ **pus** suppurer; **5** Fin s'acquitter de [debt]; réhabiliter [bankrupt]; **6** (perform) s'acquitter de [duty]; remplir [obligation]; **7** (unload) décharger [cargo]; débarquer [passengers]; **8** (fire) décharger [rifle]

disciple /dɪˈsaɪpl/ n gen, Bible disciple mf

disciplinarian /ˌdɪsɪplɪˈneərɪən/ n **to be a** ∼ être strict en matière de discipline

disciplinary /ˈdɪsɪplɪnərɪ, US -nerɪ/ adj disciplinaire

discipline /ˈdɪsɪplɪn/
A n **1** (controlled behaviour) discipline f; **2** (academic subject) discipline f
B vtr (control) discipliner; (punish) punir

disciplined /ˈdɪsɪplɪnd/ adj [person, group, manner] discipliné; [approach] méthodique

disclaim /dɪsˈkleɪm/ vtr nier

disclaimer /dɪsˈkleɪmə(r)/ n démenti m

disclose /dɪsˈkləʊz/ vtr laisser voir [sight]; révéler [information]

disclosure /dɪsˈkləʊʒə(r)/ n révélation f (**of** de)

disco /ˈdɪskəʊ/ n (event) soirée f disco; (club) discothèque f

discoloration /ˌdɪskʌləˈreɪʃn/ n décoloration f

discomfort /dɪsˈkʌmfət/ n [1] (physical) sensation f pénible; **to be in** ~, **to suffer** ~ avoir mal; [2] (embarrassment) sentiment m de gêne

disconcerting /ˌdɪskənˈsɜːtɪŋ/ adj (worrying) troublant; (unnerving) déconcertant

disconnect /ˌdɪskəˈnekt/
A vtr débrancher [pipe, appliance]; couper [telephone, gas etc]; décrocher [carriage]
B vi Comput se déconnecter

disconnected /ˌdɪskəˈnektɪd/ adj [remarks] décousu

disconsolately /dɪsˈkɒnsələtlɪ/ adv d'un air désespéré

discontent /ˌdɪskənˈtent/ n mécontentement m

discontented /ˌdɪskənˈtentɪd/ adj mécontent

discontinue /ˌdɪskənˈtɪnjuː/ vtr supprimer [service]; arrêter [production]; cesser [visits]; **'~d line'** Comm 'fin de série'

discord /ˈdɪskɔːd/ n [1] ₵ dissensions fpl; **a note of** ~ une note de discorde; [2] Mus discordance f

discordant /dɪsˈkɔːdənt/ adj gen, Mus discordant

discount
A /ˈdɪskaʊnt/ n Comm remise f (**on** sur); (on minor purchase) rabais m (**on** sur); Fin escompte m; **to give sb a** ~ faire une remise à qn; ~ **for cash** escompte de caisse (pour paiement au comptant); **at a** ~ [purchase] au rabais; [shares] avec une décote
B /dɪsˈkaʊnt, US ˈdɪskaʊnt/ vtr [1] (reject) écarter [idea, claim, possibility], ne pas tenir compte de [advice, report]; [2] /ˈdɪskaʊnt/ Comm solder [goods]; faire une remise de [sum of money]

discount flight n vol m à tarif réduit

discourage /dɪsˈkʌrɪdʒ/ vtr [1] (dishearten) décourager; [2] (deter) décourager

discouragement /dɪsˈkʌrɪdʒmənt/ n [1] (despondency) découragement m; [2] (disincentive) **it's more of a** ~ **than an incentive** cela décourage plutôt que cela ne motive

discourteous /dɪsˈkɜːtɪəs/ adj peu courtois

discover /dɪsˈkʌvə(r)/ vtr (all contexts) découvrir

discovery /dɪˈskʌvərɪ/ n gen découverte f; **a voyage of** ~ un voyage d'exploration

discredit /dɪsˈkredɪt/
A n discrédit m
B vtr discréditer [person, organization]; mettre en doute [report, theory]

discreet /dɪˈskriːt/ adj [behaviour, colour] discret/-ète

discrepancy /dɪsˈkrepənsɪ/ n divergence f

discretion /dɪˈskreʃn/ n [1] (authority) discrétion f; **to use one's** ~ agir à sa discrétion; **I have** ~ **over that decision** cette décision est à ma discrétion; [2] (tact) discrétion f

discriminate /dɪˈskrɪmɪneɪt/ vi [1] (act with prejudice) établir une discrimination (**against** envers; **in favour of** en faveur de); [2] (distinguish) **to** ~ **between** faire une or la distinction entre

discriminating /dɪˈskrɪmɪneɪtɪŋ/ adj plein de discernement

discrimination /dɪˌskrɪmɪˈneɪʃn/ n [1] (prejudice) discrimination f; [2] (taste) discernement m; [3] (ability to differentiate) capacité f d'établir des distinctions

discus /ˈdɪskəs/ n (object) disque m; (event) lancer m du disque

discuss /dɪˈskʌs/ vtr (talk about) discuter de; (in writing) examiner

discussion /dɪˈskʌʃn/ n gen discussion f; (in public) débat m; (in text) analyse f; **under** ~ en discussion; **to bring sth up for** ~ soumettre qch à la discussion; **to be open to** ~ être à discuter

discussion document, **discussion paper** n avant-projet m

disdain /dɪsˈdeɪn/
A n dédain m (**for** pour)
B vtr dédaigner; **to** ~ **to do** ne pas daigner faire

disdainful /dɪsˈdeɪnfl/ adj dédaigneux/-euse

disease /dɪˈziːz/ n [1] (specific illness) maladie f; [2] ₵ (range of infections) maladies fpl

diseased /dɪˈziːzd/ adj lit, fig malade

disembark /ˌdɪsɪmˈbɑːk/ vtr, vi débarquer

disembodied /ˌdɪsɪmˈbɒdɪd/ adj désincarné

disenchanted /ˌdɪsɪnˈtʃɑːntɪd, US -ˈtʃænt-/ adj désabusé; **to become** ~ **with sth** perdre ses illusions sur qch

disenfranchise /ˌdɪsɪnˈfræntʃaɪz/ vtr priver [qn] du droit de vote

disengage /ˌdɪsɪnˈgeɪdʒ/
A vtr gen dégager (**from** de); **to** ~ **the clutch** Aut débrayer
B vi [1] Mil cesser le combat; [2] gen, Mil **to** ~ **from** se retirer de

disentangle /ˌdɪsɪnˈtæŋgl/ vtr lit, fig démêler

disfavour GB, **disfavor** US /dɪsˈfeɪvə(r)/ n désapprobation f; **to fall into** ~ tomber en disgrâce

disfigure /dɪsˈfɪgə(r), US dɪsˈfɪgjər/ vtr défigurer

disgorge /dɪsˈgɔːdʒ/ vtr déverser [crowd, liquid]

disgrace /dɪsˈgreɪs/
A n (shame) honte f; **to bring** ~ **on sb** déshonorer qn; **to be in** ~ (officially) être en disgrâce; **it's an absolute** ~! c'est scandaleux!
B vtr déshonorer [team, family]; **he** ~**d himself** il s'est mal conduit
C **disgraced** pp adj [leader, player] disgracié

disgraceful /dɪsˈgreɪsfl/ adj [conduct, situation] scandaleux/-euse

disgruntled /dɪsˈgrʌntld/ adj mécontent

disguise /dɪsˈgaɪz/
A n déguisement m; **in** ~ déguisé
B vtr déguiser [person, voice]; camoufler [blemish]; cacher [emotion, fact]; **there's no disguising the fact that** on ne peut pas cacher le fait que
(Idiom) **it's a blessing in** ~ c'est une bonne chose, même si ça n'en a pas l'air

disgust /dɪsˈgʌst/
A n (physical) dégoût m; (moral) écœurement m (**at** devant); **in** ~ dégoûté, écœuré
B vtr (physically) dégoûter; (morally) écœurer

disgusting /dɪsˈgʌstɪŋ/ adj (morally) écœurant; (physically) répugnant

disgustingly /dɪsˈgʌstɪŋlɪ/ adv **to be** ~ **dirty/fat** être d'une saleté/obésité répugnante

dish /dɪʃ/
A n [1] (plate) (for eating) assiette f; (for serving) plat m; [2] Culin (food) plat m; **side** ~ garniture f; [3] TV (also **satellite** ~) antenne f parabolique; [4] ᴼ(person) (male) beau mecᴼ m, (female) belle fille f
B **dishes** npl vaisselle f; **to do the** ~**es** faire la vaisselle
(Phrasal verbs)
  ■ **dish out:** ▸ ~ **out [sth]** distribuer [advice, compliments, money]; servir [food]
  ■ **dish up:** ▸ ~ **up [sth]** servir [meal]

dishcloth /ˈdɪʃklɒθ/ n (for washing) lavette f; (for drying) torchon m (à vaisselle)

dishearten /dɪsˈhɑːtn/ vtr décourager, démoraliser

dishevelled /dɪˈʃevld/ adj [person] débraillé; [hair] décoiffé; [clothes] en désordre

dishonest /dɪsˈɒnɪst/ adj malhonnête

dishonesty /dɪsˈɒnɪstɪ/ n (lack of honesty) (financial) malhonnêteté f; (moral, intellectual) mauvaise foi f

dishonour GB, **dishonor** US /dɪsˈɒnə(r)/ n déshonneur m; **to bring** ~ **on sb** déshonorer qn

dishonourable GB, **dishonorable** US /dɪsˈɒnərəbl/ adj [act] déshonorant

dish: ~**pan** n US cuvette f; ~**rag** n US lavette f; ~**towel** n torchon m

dishwasher /ˈdɪʃˌwɒʃə/
A n (machine) lave-vaisselle m inv; (person) plongeur/-euse m/f
B noun modifier [powder, detergent, salt] pour lave-vaisselle

dishwater /ˈdɪʃwɔːtə(r)/ n eau f de vaisselle; **as dull as** ~ US ennuyeux/-euse comme la pluie

dishyᴼ /ˈdɪʃɪ/ adj GB séduisant, beau/belle (before n)

disillusion /ˌdɪsɪˈluːʒn/ vtr **to** ~ **sb** désabuser qn

disillusioned /ˌdɪsɪˈluːʒnd/ adj désabusé; **to be** ~ **with sth/sb** perdre ses illusions sur qch/qn

disillusionment /ˌdɪsɪˈluːʒnmənt/ n désillusion f

disincentive /ˌdɪsɪnˈsentɪv/ n démotivation f

disinclined /ˌdɪsɪnˈklaɪnd/ adj ~ **to do** peu disposé à faire

disinfect /ˌdɪsɪnˈfekt/ vtr désinfecter

disinfectant /ˌdɪsɪnˈfektənt/ n désinfectant m

disingenuous /ˌdɪsɪnˈdʒenjʊəs/ adj [comment] peu sincère; [smile] faux/fausse

disinherit /ˌdɪsɪnˈherɪt/ vtr déshériter

disintegrate /dɪsˈɪntɪɡreɪt/ vi gen se desagréger; [aircraft] se désintégrer

disinterested /dɪsˈɪntrəstɪd/ adj **1** (impartial) [observer, party, stance, advice] impartial; **2** (uninterested) usage critiqué: voir note indifférent (**in** à).

⚠️ Dans ce sens, utiliser de préférence uninterested

disjointed /dɪsˈdʒɔɪntɪd/ adj [programme, speech, report] décousu; [organization, effort] incohérent

disk /dɪsk/ n **1** Comput disque m; **on** ~ sur disque; **2** US = **disc**

disk: ~ **directory** n répertoire m disques; ~ **drive (unit)** n unité f de disques; ~ **management** n gestion f disques; ~ **operating system, DOS** n système m d'exploitation à disques, DOS m

dislike /dɪsˈlaɪk/

A n aversion f (**of** pour); **to take a** ~ **to sb/sth** prendre qn/qch en grippe, (stronger) prendre qn/qch en aversion; **we all have our likes and** ~**s** chacun a ses préférences

B vtr ne pas aimer (**doing** faire); **I have always** ~**d him** il m'a toujours été antipathique; **I** ~ **her intensely** je la déteste cordialement; **I don't** ~ **city life** je n'ai rien contre la vie urbaine

dislocate /ˈdɪsləkeɪt, US ˈdɪsləʊkeɪt/ vtr **1** Med **to** ~ **one's shoulder** se démettre l'épaule; **2** (disrupt) désorganiser [system]; bouleverser [economy, social structure]; disperser [population]

dislocation /ˌdɪsləˈkeɪʃn, US ˌdɪsləʊˈkeɪʃn/ n (of hip, knee) luxation f

dislodge /dɪsˈlɒdʒ/ vtr déplacer [rock, tile, obstacle]; déloger [foreign body, sniper]

disloyal /dɪsˈlɔɪəl/ adj déloyal (**to** envers)

dismal /ˈdɪzməl/ adj **1** [place, sight] lugubre; **2** ○[failure, attempt] lamentable

dismantle /dɪsˈmæntl/ vtr **1** (take apart) démonter [construction]; **2** (phase out) démanteler [organization, service]

dismantling /dɪsˈmæntlɪŋ/ n (of machine) démontage m; (of system) démantèlement m

dismay /dɪsˈmeɪ/ n consternation f (**at** devant)

dismayed /dɪsˈmeɪd/ adj consterné

dismember /dɪsˈmembə(r)/ vtr **1** démembrer [corpse]; **2** fig démembrer [country]; démanteler [organization]

dismiss /dɪsˈmɪs/ vtr **1** (reject) écarter [idea, suggestion]; exclure [possibility]; **to** ~ **sth as insignificant** écarter qch d'emblée; **2** (put out of mind) chasser [thought, worry]; **3** (sack) licencier [employee, worker]; renvoyer [servant]; révoquer [civil servant]; démettre [qn] de ses fonctions [director, official]; **4** (end interview with) congédier [person]; (send out) [teacher] laisser sortir [class]; **5** Jur rejeter [appeal]; **the case was** ~**ed** il y a eu non-lieu

dismissal /dɪsˈmɪsl/ n **1** (of employee, worker) licenciement m; (of servant) renvoi m; (of civil servant) révocation f; (of manager, minister) destitution f; **unfair** ~, **wrongful** ~ licenciement abusif; **2** (of idea, threat) refus m de prendre qch en considération; **3** Jur (of appeal, claim) rejet m

dismissive /dɪsˈmɪsɪv/ adj [person, attitude] dédaigneux/-euse; [gesture] de dédain; **to be** ~ **of** faire peu de cas de

dismount /dɪsˈmaʊnt/ vi mettre pied à terre; **to** ~ **from** descendre de [horse, bicycle]

disobedient /ˌdɪsəˈbiːdɪənt/ adj [child] désobéissant

disobey /ˌdɪsəˈbeɪ/

A vtr désobéir à [person]; enfreindre [law]

B vi désobéir

disorder /dɪsˈɔːdə(r)/ n **1** ¢ (lack of order) désordre m; **to retreat in** ~ Mil être mis en déroute; **2** ¢ gen, Pol (disturbances) émeutes fpl; **3** **C** Med, Psych (malfunction) troubles mpl; (disease) maladie f; **eating** ~ troubles de l'alimentation

disordered /dɪsˈɔːdəd/ adj [life] désordonné; Med [mind] déséquilibré

disorderly /dɪsˈɔːdəlɪ/ adj **1** [room] en désordre; **2** (disorganized) désordonné; [crowd, meeting] turbulent

disorderly behaviour, disorderly conduct n Jur perturbation f de l'ordre public

disorganized /dɪsˈɔːɡənaɪzd/ adj désorganisé

disorientate /dɪsˈɔːrɪənteɪt/ vtr désorienter

disown /dɪsˈəʊn/ vtr gen désavouer; renier [person]

disparaging /dɪsˈpærɪdʒɪŋ/ adj désobligeant

disparate /ˈdɪspərət/ adj **1** (different) [group] hétérogène; **2** (incompatible) incompatible

dispassionate /dɪsˈpæʃənət/ adj **1** (impartial) objectif/-ive (**about** au sujet de); **2** (unemotional) froid

dispatch /dɪˈspætʃ/

A n **1** (report) dépêche f; **mentioned in** ~**es** Mil cité à l'ordre du jour; **2** (sending) expédition f; **date of** ~ date d'expédition

B vtr **1** (send) envoyer [person] (**to** à); expédier [letter, parcel] (**to** à); **2** hum (consume) expédier [plateful]; descendre [drink]; **3** (complete) expédier [work]; régler [problem]

dispatch box n **1** valise f diplomatique; **2** **Dispatch Box** GB Pol tribune f (d'où parlent les membres du gouvernement)

dispel /dɪˈspel/ vtr (p prés etc **-ll-**) **1** chasser [doubt, fear]; dissiper [myth, notion]; **2** sout dissiper [mist]

dispensable /dɪˈspensəbl/ adj **to be** ~ [thing, idea] être superflu; [person] être une quantité négligeable

dispensary /dɪˈspensərɪ/ n GB (in hospital) pharmacie f; (in chemist's) officine f

dispense /dɪˈspens/ vtr **1** [machine] distribuer [drinks, money]; **2** sout exercer [justice]; faire [charity]; prodiguer [advice]; attribuer [funds]; **3** préparer [medicine, prescription]; **4** (exempt) dispenser

(Phrasal verb)

■ **dispense with** (manage without) se passer de [services, formalities]; (get rid of) abandonner [policy, regulations etc]; (make unnecessary) rendre inutile [resource, facility]

dispenser /dɪˈspensə(r)/ n distributeur m

dispensing: ~ **chemist** n GB pharmacien/-ienne m/f; ~ **optician** n GB opticien/-ienne m/f

dispersal /dɪˈspɜːsl/ n (of fumes) dispersion f; (of seeds, installations) dissémination f

disperse /dɪˈspɜːs/

A vtr (scatter) disperser; (distribute) disséminer; Chem décomposer [particle]

B vi **1** [crowd] se disperser; **2** [mist] se dissiper

dispersion /dɪˈspɜːʃn, US dɪˈspɜːrʒn/ n gen dispersion f; (of light) décomposition f

dispirited /dɪˈspɪrɪtɪd/ adj [look, air] découragé; [mood] abattu

displace /dɪsˈpleɪs/ vtr **1** (replace) supplanter [competitor]; déplacer [worker]; **2** (expel) chasser [person]

displaced person /dɪsˈpleɪst/ n personne f déplacée

displacement /dɪsˈpleɪsmənt/ n déplacement m

display /dɪsˈpleɪ/

A n **1** Comm (for sale) étalage m; (of larger objects) exposition f; **window** ~ vitrine f; **to be on** ~ être exposé; **to put sth on** ~ exposer qch; **2** (for decoration, to look at) **what a lovely** ~ **of flowers** quel bel arrangement de fleurs; **3** (demonstration) (of art, craft) démonstration f; (of dance, sport) exhibition f; **air** ~ fête f aéronautique; **4** (of emotion, failing, quality) démonstration f; (of strength) déploiement m; (of wealth) étalage m; **in a** ~ **of** dans un geste de [anger, impatience]; **5** Aut, Aviat, Comput écran m; **6** (of advert) **full page** ~ page f entière de publicité; **7** Zool parade f

B vtr **1** gen, Comm, Comput (show, set out) afficher [information, poster]; exposer [object]; **2** (reveal) faire preuve de [intelligence, interest, skill]; révéler [emotion, vice, virtue]; **3** péj (flaunt) faire étalage de [beauty, knowledge, wealth]; exhiber [legs, chest]

C vi gen parader; [peacock] faire la roue

display: ~ **advertisement** n grande annonce f; ~ **artist** ▸ p. 1181 n Comm étalagiste mf; ~ **cabinet**, ~ **case** n (in house) vitrine f; (in museum) vitrine f d'exposition; ~ **panel** n écran m d'affichage; ~ **rack** n présentoir m; ~ **window** n vitrine f

displeased /dɪsˈpliːzd/ adj mécontent (**with, at** de)

displeasure /dɪsˈpleʒə(r)/ n mécontentement m

disposable /dɪ'spəʊzəbl/ adj 1️⃣ (throwaway) jetable; 2️⃣ (available) disponible

disposal /dɪ'spəʊzl/ n 1️⃣ (removal) (of waste product) élimination f; **for** ~ à jeter; 2️⃣ (sale) (of company, property) vente f; (of deeds, securities) cession f; 3️⃣ (completion) exécution f; 4️⃣ (for use, access) **to be at sb's** ~ être à la disposition de qn; **all the means at my** ~ tous les moyens dont je dispose; 5️⃣ (arrangement) disposition f

dispose /dɪ'spəʊz/ vtr 1️⃣ (arrange) disposer [furniture, troops]; 2️⃣ (encourage) **to** ~ **sb to sth/to do** disposer qn à qch/à faire

(Phrasal verb)

■ **dispose of**: ▸ ~ **of [sth/sb]** 1️⃣ se débarrasser de [body, rival, rubbish]; détruire [evidence]; désarmer [bomb]; 2️⃣ Comm écouler [stock]; (sell) vendre [car, shares]; 3️⃣ (deal with) expédier [business, problem, theory]

disposition /ˌdɪspə'zɪʃn/ n 1️⃣ (temperament) tempérament m; **to be of a nervous** ~ avoir un tempérament nerveux; **to have a cheerful** ~ être d'un naturel gai; 2️⃣ (tendency) tendance f; **to have a** ~ **to do** avoir tendance à faire; 3️⃣ (arrangement) disposition f

dispossessed /ˌdɪspə'zest/ adj [family] exproprié; [son] déshérité

disproportionate /ˌdɪsprə'pɔːʃənət/ adj disproportionné (**to** par rapport à)

disproportionately /ˌdɪsprə'pɔːʃənətlɪ/ adv [affect] de façon disproportionnée; ~ **high** [costs, expectations] disproportionné

disprove /dɪs'pruːv/ vtr réfuter

dispute /dɪ'spjuːt/

🅐 n 1️⃣ (quarrel) (between individuals) dispute f; (between groups) conflit m (**over, about** à propos de); **to have a** ~ **with** se disputer avec; 2️⃣ 🇨 (controversy) controverse f (**over, about** sur); **to be/not to be in** ~ [fact] être/ne pas être controversé; **beyond** ~ incontestable; **without** ~ sans conteste; **to be open to** ~ être contestable

🅑 vtr 1️⃣ (question truth of) contester [claim, figures]; **I** ~ **that!** je m'inscris en faux!; 2️⃣ (claim possession of) se disputer [property, title]

disqualification /dɪsˌkwɒlɪfɪ'keɪʃn/ n 1️⃣ gen (from post) exclusion f (**from** de); 2️⃣ Sport disqualification f; 3️⃣ GB Jur suspension f; 4️⃣ (also **driving** ~) Aut retrait m du permis de conduire

disqualify /dɪs'kwɒlɪfaɪ/ vtr 1️⃣ gen (from post, career) exclure; **to** ~ **sb from doing** interdire à qn de faire; 2️⃣ Sport [regulation] disqualifier; [physical condition] empêcher (**from doing** de faire); 3️⃣ GB Aut, Jur **to** ~ **sb from driving** retirer à qn son permis de conduire

disquiet /dɪs'kwaɪət/ sout n inquiétude f

disquieting /dɪs'kwaɪətɪŋ/ adj troublant

disregard /ˌdɪsrɪ'gɑːd/

🅐 n (for problem, feelings, person) indifférence f (**for sth** à qch; **for sb** envers qn); (for danger, convention, life, law, right) mépris m (**for** de)

🅑 vtr 1️⃣ (discount) ne pas tenir compte de [irrelevance, problem, evidence, remark]; fermer les yeux sur [fault]; mépriser [danger]; 2️⃣ ne pas respecter [law, instruction]

disrepair /ˌdɪsrɪ'peə(r)/ n délabrement m; **to fall into** ~ se délabrer

disreputable /dɪs'repjʊtəbl/ adj 1️⃣ (unsavoury) [person] peu recommandable; [place] mal famé; [behaviour] déshonorant; 2️⃣ (tatty) [clothes] miteux/-euse; 3️⃣ (discredited) [method] douteux/-euse

disrepute /ˌdɪsrɪ'pjuːt/ n **to be held in** ~ être discrédité; **to bring into** ~ jeter le discrédit sur

disrespect /ˌdɪsrɪ'spekt/ n manque m de respect (**for** envers); **to show** ~ **to sb** manquer de respect envers qn; **no** ~ **(to him/her)** avec tout le respect que je lui dois

disrespectful /ˌdɪsrɪ'spektfl/ adj [person] irrespectueux/-euse (**to, towards** envers); [remark, behaviour] irrévérencieux/-ieuse

disrupt /dɪs'rʌpt/ vtr perturber [traffic, trade, meeting]; bouleverser [lifestyle, schedule, routine]; interrompre [power supply]

disruption /dɪs'rʌpʃn/ n 1️⃣ 🇨 (disorder) perturbations fpl (**in** dans); **to cause** ~ **to sth** perturber qch; 2️⃣ (disrupting) (of service, meeting) perturbation f; (of schedule) bouleversement m; Elec interruption f

disruptive /dɪs'rʌptɪv/ adj perturbateur/-trice

dissatisfaction /dɪˌsætɪs'fækʃn/ n mécontentement m

dissatisfied /dɪ'sætɪsfaɪd/ adj mécontent

dissect /dɪ'sekt/ vtr 1️⃣ (cut up) disséquer [cadaver, plant]; 2️⃣ péj disséquer [performance, relationship]; éplucher [book, play]

dissemble /dɪ'sembl/ vtr, vi sout dissimuler

disseminate /dɪ'semɪneɪt/ vtr diffuser [information, products]; propager [ideas, views]

dissension /dɪ'senʃn/ n (discord) discorde f, dissensions fpl

dissent /dɪ'sent/

🅐 n 🇨 gen, Pol contestation f, dissensions fpl sout; Sport contestation f

🅑 vi gen, Jur (disagree) contester; **to** ~ **from sth** contester qch

🅒 **dissenting** pres p adj gen, Pol [group, opinion, voice] contestataire

dissertation /ˌdɪsə'teɪʃn/ n 1️⃣ GB Univ mémoire m (**on** sur); 2️⃣ US Univ thèse f (**on** sur)

disservice /dɪs'sɜːvɪs/ n **to do a** ~ **to sb, to do sb a** ~ rendre un mauvais service à qn

dissident /'dɪsɪdənt/ n, adj dissident/-e (m/f)

dissimilar /dɪ'sɪmɪlə(r)/ adj dissemblable; ~ **to** différent de

dissimilarity /ˌdɪsɪmɪ'lærətɪ/ n 1️⃣ 🇨 (lack of similarity) dissemblance f (**in** de; **between** entre); 2️⃣ (difference) différence f (**in** de)

dissipate /'dɪsɪpeɪt/ sout

🅐 vtr gen dissiper; anéantir [hope, enthusiasm]

🅑 vi (all contexts) se dissiper

dissipated /'dɪsɪpeɪtɪd/ adj dissolu

dissociate /dɪ'səʊʃɪeɪt/ vtr gen, Chem dissocier

dissociation /dɪˌsəʊʃɪ'eɪʃn/ n dissociation f

dissolute /'dɪsəluːt/ adj [lifestyle] dissolu

dissolve /dɪ'zɒlv/

🅐 n Cin fondu m enchaîné

🅑 vtr 1️⃣ [acid, water] dissoudre [solid, grease]; 2️⃣ faire dissoudre [tablet, powder] (**in** dans); 3️⃣ (break up) dissoudre [assembly, parliament, partnership]

🅒 vi 1️⃣ (liquefy) se dissoudre (**in** dans; **into** en); 2️⃣ (fade) [hope, feeling, opposition] s'évanouir; [outline, image] disparaître; 3️⃣ (collapse) **to** ~ **into tears** fondre en larmes; 4️⃣ (break up) [assembly] être dissous/-oute

dissonant /'dɪsənənt/ adj 1️⃣ Mus dissonant; 2️⃣ sout [sounds etc] discordant

dissuade /dɪ'sweɪd/ vtr dissuader

distance /'dɪstəns/ ▸ p. 977

🅐 n lit, fig distance f (**between** entre; **from** de; **to** à); **at a** ou **some** ~ **from** à bonne distance de; **at a safe/an equal** ~ à bonne/égale distance; **a long/short** ~ **away** loin/pas loin; **to keep sb at a** ~ tenir qn à distance; **to keep one's** ~ lit, fig garder ses distances (**from** avec); **to go the** ~ Sport, fig tenir la distance; **from a/in the** ~ de/au loin; **it's no** ~ c'est tout près; **it's within walking** ~ on peut y aller à pied; **he's within shouting** ~ il est assez près pour pouvoir t'entendre; **at a** ~ **it's easy to see that I made mistakes** avec du recul je vois très bien que j'ai commis des erreurs

🅑 noun modifier [runner, race] de fond

🅒 vtr (outdistance) créer une distance entre [two people]; 2️⃣ (outdistance) distancier [rival]

🅓 v refl **to** ~ **oneself** (dissociate oneself) se distancier (**from** de); (stand back) prendre du recul (**from** par rapport à)

distant /'dɪstənt/ adj 1️⃣ (remote) éloigné; **the** ~ **sound of sth** le bruit de qch dans le lointain; ~ **from** loin de; **40 km** ~ **from** à 40 km; **in the not too** ~ **future** dans un avenir assez proche; 2️⃣ (faint) [memory, prospect, hope, similarity] lointain; 3️⃣ (cool) [person, manner] distant

distantly /'dɪstəntlɪ/ adv vaguement

distaste /dɪs'teɪst/ n déplaisir m; (marked) dégoût m; ~ **for** répugnance f pour

distasteful /dɪs'teɪstfl/ adj déplaisant; (markedly) répugnant; **I find the remark** ~ je trouve cette réflexion de mauvais goût

distemper /dɪ'stempə(r)/ n 1️⃣ (in dogs) maladie f de Carré; (in horses) angine f des chevaux; 2️⃣ (paint) (on wall) badigeon m; (in art) détrempe f

distend /dɪ'stend/ vtr distendre

distil GB, **distill** US /dɪˈstɪl/ vtr (p prés etc **-ll-** GB) ❶ (purify) distiller [liquid]; **to ~ sth from sth** extraire qch par distillation de qch; ❷ (make) distiller [alcohol] (**from** à partir de)

distillation /ˌdɪstɪˈleɪʃn/ n (of liquids) distillation f; fig condensé m

distinct /dɪˈstɪŋkt/ adj ❶ [image] (not blurred) net/nette; (easily visible) distinct; ❷ (definite) [resemblance, preference, progress, impression] net/nette; [advantage] indéniable; **it's a ~ possibility** c'est fort possible; ❸ (separable) distinct (**from** de); ❹ (different) différent (**from** de); **as ~ from** par opposition à

distinction /dɪˈstɪŋkʃn/ n ❶ (differentiation) distinction f; ❷ (difference) différence f (**between** entre); ❸ (preeminence) mérite m; **of ~** réputé; **to have the ~ of doing** (have the honour) avoir le mérite de faire; (be the only one) avoir la particularité de faire; ❹ (elegance) distinction f; ❺ (specific honour) distinction f; ❻ Mus, Sch, Univ mention f très bien

distinctive /dɪˈstɪŋktɪv/ adj caractéristique (**of** de)

distinctly /dɪˈstɪŋktlɪ/ adv ❶ [speak, hear, see] distinctement; [remember] nettement; [say, tell] explicitement; ❷ [possible, embarrassing, odd] vraiment

distinguish /dɪˈstɪŋgwɪʃ/
Ⓐ vtr distinguer; **to be ~ed from** se distinguer de; **to be ~ed by** se caractériser par
Ⓑ **distinguishing** pres p adj [factor, feature, mark] distinctif/-ive; **~ing marks** (on passport) signes mpl particuliers

distinguishable /dɪˈstɪŋgwɪʃəbl/ adj ❶ **the two cars are not easily ~** il est difficile de distinguer les deux voitures; ❷ (visible) visible; ❸ (audible) perceptible

distinguished /dɪˈstɪŋgwɪʃt/ adj ❶ (elegant) distingué; ❷ (famous) éminent

distort /dɪˈstɔːt/ vtr ❶ (misrepresent) dénaturer [statement, opinion, fact]; déformer [truth]; fausser [assessment, figures]; falsifier [history]; ❷ déformer [features, sound, metal]

distortion /dɪˈstɔːʃn/ n (of truth) déformation f; (of metal) déformation f; (of sound, features, figures) distorsion f

distract /dɪˈstrækt/ vtr ❶ **to ~ sb from doing** empêcher qn de faire; **I was ~ed by the noise** le bruit m'a empêché de me concentrer; **to ~ attention** détourner l'attention (**from** de)

distracting /dɪˈstræktɪŋ/ adj [sound, presence, flicker] gênant; **I found the noise too ~** le bruit m'empêchait de me concentrer

distraction /dɪˈstrækʃn/ n ❶ (from concentration) distraction f; **I don't want any ~s** (environmental) je ne veux pas être distrait; (human) je ne veux pas qu'on me dérange; **a moment's ~** un moment d'inattention; ❷ (diversion) diversion f; **to be a ~ from** détourner l'attention de [problem, priority]; ❸ (entertainment) distraction f; ❹ (madness) **to drive sb to ~** rendre qn fou/folle

distraught /dɪˈstrɔːt/ adj [person] éperdu (**with** de); **to be ~ at** ou **over sth** être bouleversé par qch

distress /dɪˈstres/
Ⓐ n ❶ (anguish) désarroi m; **in ~** complètement bouleversé; (stronger) dans un grand désarroi; **to cause sb ~** faire de la peine à qn; **to my/his ~, they...** à mon/son grand chagrin, ils...; ❷ (physical trouble) souffrance(s) f(pl); **she seems to be in ~** ça n'a pas l'air d'aller du tout; ❸ (poverty) détresse f; ❹ Naut **in ~** en détresse
Ⓑ noun modifier [call, rocket, signal] de détresse
Ⓒ vtr faire de la peine à [person]; (stronger) bouleverser [person]
(**to do** de faire)
Ⓓ v refl **to ~ oneself** s'inquiéter

distressed /dɪˈstrest/ adj ❶ (upset) [person] peiné (**at, by** par); (stronger) bouleversé (**at, by** par)

distressing /dɪˈstresɪŋ/ adj [case, event, idea] pénible; [news] navrant; [sight] affligeant; **it is ~ that** il est pénible que (+ subj)

distribute /dɪˈstrɪbjuːt/ vtr ❶ (share out) distribuer [information, documents, supplies, money] (**to** à; **among** entre); ❷ Comm distribuer [goods, books, films]; ❸ (spread out) répartir [weight, load, tax burden]; ❹ (disperse) **to be ~d** [flora, fauna, mineral deposits] être réparti

distribute: **~d data processing**, **DDP** n informatique f répartie; **~d system** n système m d'information répartie

distribution /ˌdɪstrɪˈbjuːʃn/ n ❶ gen, Cin, Comm distribution f; ❷ (spread) répartition f

distributor /dɪˈstrɪbjuːtə(r)/ n ❶ Comm, Cin distributeur m (**for sth** de qch); **sole ~ for** concessionnaire m exclusif de; ❷ Aut distributeur m

district /ˈdɪstrɪkt/ n ❶ (in country) région f; ❷ (in city) quartier m; ❸ (sector) (administrative) district m; US (electoral) circonscription f électorale; (postal) secteur m postal

district attorney n US représentant m du ministère public

district: **~ council** n GB ≈ conseil m général; **~ court** n US cour f fédérale; **~ manager** n directeur/-trice m/f régional/-e; **~ nurse** n GB infirmière f visiteuse

distrust /dɪsˈtrʌst/
Ⓐ n méfiance f (**of** à l'égard de)
Ⓑ vtr se méfier de [person, motive, government]

disturb /dɪˈstɜːb/ vtr ❶ (interrupt) déranger [person, work]; troubler [silence, sleep]; ❷ (upset) troubler [person]; (concern) inquiéter [person]; **to ~ the peace** Jur troubler l'ordre public; ❸ (disarrange) déranger [papers, bedclothes]; troubler [surface of water]; remuer [sediment]

disturbance /dɪˈstɜːbəns/ n ❶ (interruption, inconvenience) dérangement m; ❷ (riot) troubles mpl; (fight) altercation f; ❸ Meteorol perturbation f; ❹ Psych trouble m; (more serious) perturbation f

disturbed /dɪˈstɜːbd/ adj ❶ Psych perturbé; **emotionally ~** qui a des troubles psychologiques; **to be mentally ~** avoir l'esprit dérangé; ❷ (concerned) **I am ~ by the news** cette nouvelle m'inquiète; ❸ (restless) [sleep] agité

disturbing /dɪˈstɜːbɪŋ/ adj (unsettling) [portrayal] troublant; [book, film] perturbant; (worrying) [report, increase] inquiétant; (stronger) alarmant

disuse /dɪsˈjuːs/ n (of machinery) abandon m; **to fall into ~** [plant, building] être laissé à l'abandon; [practice, tradition] tomber en désuétude

disused /dɪsˈjuːzd/ adj abandonné, désaffecté

ditch /dɪtʃ/
Ⓐ n fossé m
Ⓑ ○vtr ❶ (get rid of) laisser tomber [friend, ally]; abandonner [system, agreement, machine]; plaquer○ [girlfriend, boyfriend]; ❷ US (evade) échapper à [police]; ❸ (crash-land) **to ~ a plane** faire un amerrissage forcé; ❹ US (crash) emboutir○ [voiture]

ditchwater /ˈdɪtʃwɔːtə(r)/ n:
(Idiom) **as dull as ~** ennuyeux comme la pluie

dither /ˈdɪðə(r)/
Ⓐ ○n **in a ~, all of a ~** dans tous ses états
Ⓑ vi tergiverser (**about, over** sur)

ditto○ /ˈdɪtəʊ/ adv idem; **the food is awful and ~ the nightlife** la nourriture est affreuse la vie nocturne idem; **'I'm fed up'○—'~'** 'j'en ai marre○'—'moi aussi'

ditto marks npl guillemets mpl de répétition

dive /daɪv/
Ⓐ n ❶ gen, Sport (plunge) plongeon m; ❷ (swimming under sea) plongée f sous-marine; ❸ (descent) (of plane, bird) piqué m; **to take a ~** fig [prices] chuter; ❹ (lunge) **to make a ~ for sth** foncer vers qch; ❺ ○péj (bar) tripot○ m
Ⓑ vi (prét **~d** GB, **dove** US) ❶ gen, Sport plonger (**off, from** de; **down to** jusqu'à); ❷ [plane, bird] plonger; ❸ (as hobby) faire de la plongée; (as job) être plongeur; ❹ (throw oneself) **to ~ under the bed** plonger sous le lit; **to ~ into** s'engouffrer dans [bar, shop]
(Phrasal verbs)
▪ **dive for**: ▸ **~ for [sth]** ❶ [diver] pêcher [pearls]; ❷ [player] plonger sur [ball]; ❸ [person] foncer vers [exit]; **to ~ for cover** foncer à l'abri
▪ **dive in** ❶ lit plonger; ❷ fig se lancer○

dive-bomb vtr Mil bombarder [qch] en piqué

diver /ˈdaɪvə(r)/ ▸ p. 1181 n gen plongeur/-euse m/f; (deep-sea) scaphandrier m

diverge /daɪˈvɜːdʒ/ vi [interests, opinions, paths] diverger; **to ~ from** s'écarter de [truth, norm, belief]; [railway line, road] se séparer de

diverse /daɪˈvɜːs/ adj ❶ (varied) divers; ❷ (different) différent

diversion /daɪˈvɜːʃn, US daɪˈvɜːrʒn/ n ❶ (of watercourse, money) détournement m; (of traffic) déviation f; ❷ (distraction) diversion f (**from** à); ❸ GB (detour) déviation f; ❹ †(entertainment) divertissement m

diversionary /daɪ'vɜːʃənərɪ, US daɪ'vɜːrʒəneɪrɪ/ *adj* [*tactic, attack*] de diversion

divert /daɪ'vɜːt/
A *vtr* **1** (redirect) détourner [*water, flow*]; dévier [*traffic*] (**onto** vers; **through** par); dérouter [*flight, plane*] (**to** sur); détourner [*resources, supplies, funds, manpower*] (**from** de; **to** au profit de); **2** (distract) détourner [*attention, efforts, conversation, person*]
B *vi* **to** ~ **to** se détourner sur

divest /daɪ'vest/ *sout vtr* **to** ~ **sb of sth** (of power, rights etc) dépouiller qn de qch; (of robes, regalia) ôter qch à qn

divide /dɪ'vaɪd/
A *n* **1** (split) division *f* (**between** entre); **the North-South** ~ l'opposition *f* Nord-Sud; **2** (watershed) *fig* démarcation *f* (**between** entre)
B *vtr* **1** (split into parts) partager [*food, money, time, work*]; diviser [*class, house, room*] (**into** en); **he** ~**d the pupils into boys and girls** il a séparé les garçons des filles; **2** (share) partager [*time*] (**between** entre); **3** (separate) séparer (**from** de); **4** (cause disagreement) diviser [*friends, management, group*]; **5** GB Pol faire voter [*House*]; **6** Math diviser [*number*]; **to** ~ **2 into 14** diviser 14 par 2
C *vi* **1** *lit* [*road*] bifurquer; [*river, train*] se séparer en deux; [*group*] (into two) se séparer en deux; [*cell, organism*] se diviser; **2** GB Pol [*House*] voter; **3** Math être divisible

(Phrasal verbs)

■ **divide out**: ▸ ~ [sth] **out**, ~ **out** [sth] distribuer
■ **divide up**: ▸ ~ [sth] **up**, ~ **up** [sth] partager (**among** entre)

dividend /'dɪvɪdend/ *n* **1** Fin (share) dividende *m*; **final** ~ dividende *m* annuel; **to pay** ~**s** *lit, fig* rapporter; **2** *fig* (bonus) avantage *m*; **peace** ~ Pol dividendes *mpl* de la paix

divider /dɪ'vaɪdə(r)/ *n* (in room) cloison *f*; (in file) intercalaire *m*

dividers /dɪ'vaɪdəz/ *npl* compas *m* à pointes sèches

dividing /dɪ'vaɪdɪŋ/ *adj* [*wall, fence*] mitoyen/-enne

dividing line *n* ligne *f* de démarcation

divine /dɪ'vaɪn/
A *adj* divin
B *vtr* **1** *littér* (intuit) deviner; **2** (dowse) découvrir [qch] par la radiesthésie

divinely /dɪ'vaɪnlɪ/ *adv* **1** [*revealed*] divinement; **2** ○[*dance, smile*] divinement

diving /'daɪvɪŋ/ *n* (from board) plongeon *m*; (under sea) plongée *f* sous-marine

diving: ~ **board** *n* plongeoir *m*; ~ **suit** *n* scaphandre *m*

divinity /dɪ'vɪnətɪ/ *n* (deity) divinité *f*; (theology) théologie *f*

divisible /dɪ'vɪzəbl/ *adj* divisible (**by** par)

division /dɪ'vɪʒn/ *n* **1** (splitting) *gen*, Biol, Bot, Math division *f* (**into** en); **2** (sharing) (of one thing) répartition *f*; (of several things) distribution *f*; **3** Mil, Naut division *f*; Admin circonscription *f*; **4** Comm (branch, sector) division *f*; (department, team) service *m*; **5** (in football) division *f*; **to be in** ~ **one** être en première division; **6** (dissent) désaccord *m* (**between** entre); **7** (in container) compartiment *m*; **8** GB Pol vote *m*; **9** US Univ faculté *f*

divisional /dɪ'vɪʒənl/ *adj* [*commander, officer*] Mil divisionnaire; [*championship*] Sport de division

divisive /dɪ'vaɪsɪv/ *adj* [*policy*] qui sème la discorde; **to be socially** ~ créer des inégalités sociales

divorce /dɪ'vɔːs/
A *n* *lit, fig* divorce *m* (**from** avec; **between** entre); **to ask for a** ~ demander le divorce; **to file for** ~, **to sue for** ~ Jur intenter une action en divorce
B *vtr* **1** *lit* **to** ~ **sb** divorcer de or d'avec [*husband, wife*]; **2** *fig* dissocier (**from** de)

divorcee /dɪ,vɔː'siː/ *n* divorcé/-e *m/f*

divulge /daɪ'vʌldʒ/ *vtr* divulguer (**that** que; **to** à)

Dixie /'dɪksɪ/ *pr n* (*also* ~**land**) États *mpl* du sud des États-Unis

DIY GB *n*: *abrév* ▸ **do-it-yourself**

dizzy /'dɪzɪ/ *adj* **1** pris de vertige; **to make sb** ~ donner le vertige à qn; **to suffer from** ~ **spells** avoir des vertiges; **to feel** ~ avoir la tête qui tourne; ~ **with** ivre de [*delight*,

surprise]; **2** [*height, spell*] vertigineux/-euse; **3** (scatterbrained) écervelé

DJ *n* **1** (*abrév* = **disc jockey**) DJ *mf*; **2** GB *abrév* ▸ **dinner jacket**

DNA
A *n* (*abrév* = **deoxyribonucleic acid**) ADN *m*
B *noun modifier* [*testing*] de l'empreinte *f* génétique

DNA fingerprinting, DNA profiling *n* identification *f* génétique

do¹ /duː, də/ ▸ 810
A *vtr* (3e pers sg prés **does**; *prét* **did**; *pp* **done**) **1** (be busy) faire [*washing, ironing etc*]; **to** ~ **sth again** refaire qch; **she's been** ~**ing too much lately** elle en fait trop ces derniers temps; **will you** ~ **something for me?** peux-tu me rendre un service?; **2** (make smart) **to** ~ **sb's hair** coiffer qn; **to** ~ **one's teeth** se brosser les dents; **to** ~ **the living room in pink** peindre le salon en rose; **3** (complete) faire [*military service, period of time*]; **4** (finish) **have you done**○ **complaining?** tu as fini de te plaindre?; **tell him now and have done with it** dis-le lui maintenant, ce sera fait; **it's as good as done** c'est comme si c'était fait (task successfully completed) ça y est; (expressing dismay) il ne manquait plus que ça; **5** (complete through study) faire [*subject, degree, homework*]; **6** (write) faire [*translation, critique*]; **7** (effect change) faire; **what have you done to your hair?** qu'est-ce que vous avez fait à vos cheveux?; **I haven't done anything with your pen!** je n'ai pas touché à ton stylo!; **that hat does a lot for her** ce chapeau lui va bien; **8** (hurt) faire; **to** ~ **sth to one's arm** se faire mal au bras; **9** ○(deal with) **they don't** ~ **theatre tickets** ils ne vendent pas de billets de théâtre; **to** ~ **breakfasts** servir le petit déjeuner; **10** (cook) faire [*sausages, spaghetti etc*]; **well done** [*meat*] bien cuit; **11** (prepare) préparer [*vegetables*]; **12** (produce) monter [*play*]; faire [*film, programme*]; **13** (imitate) imiter [*celebrity, mannerism*]; **14** (travel at) faire; **to** ~ **60** faire du 60 à l'heure; **15** (cover distance of) faire [*30 km etc*]; **16** ○(satisfy needs of) **will this** ~ **you?** ça vous ira?; **17** ○(cheat) **we've been done on** s'est fait avoir; **to** ~ **sb out of £5** refaire○ qn de 5 livres sterling; **18** ○(rob) **to** ~ **a bank** faire un casse○ dans une banque; **19** ○(arrest, convict) **to get done for** se faire prendre pour [*illegal parking etc*]
B *vi* (3e pers sg prés **does**; *prét* **did**; *pp* **done**) **1** (behave) faire; ~ **as you're told** (by me) fais ce que je te dis; (by others) fais ce qu'on te dit; **2** (serve purpose) **that box will** ~ cette boîte fera l'affaire; **3** (be acceptable) **this really won't** ~! (as reprimand) ça ne peut pas continuer comme ça!; **4** (be sufficient) [*amount of money*] suffire; **5** (finish) finir; **6** (get on) [*person*] s'en sortir; [*business*] marcher; **7** (in health) **mother and baby are both** ~**ing well** la mère et l'enfant se portent bien; **the patient is** ~**ing well** l'état de santé du patient s'améliore rapidement
C *v aux* (3e pers sg prés **does**; *prét* **did**; *pp* **done**) **1** (with questions, negatives) **own up, did you or didn't you take my pen?** avoue, est-ce que c'est toi qui as pris mon stylo ou pas?; **didn't he look wonderful!** est-ce qu'il n'était pas merveilleux!; **2** (for emphasis) **so you** ~ **want to go after all!** alors tu veux vraiment y aller finalement!; **I** ~ **wish you'd let me help you** j'aimerais tant que tu me laisses t'aider; **3** (referring back to verb) **he said he'd tell her and he did** il a dit qu'il le lui dirait et il l'a fait; **you draw better than I** ~ tu dessines mieux que moi; **4** (in requests, imperatives) ~ **sit down** asseyez-vous, je vous en prie; ~ **shut up!** tais-toi veux-tu!; **don't you tell me what to do!** je n'ai pas de leçons à recevoir de toi; **5** (in tag questions and responses) **he lives in France, doesn't he?** il habite en France, n'est-ce pas?; **'who wrote it?'—'I did'** 'qui l'a écrit?'—'moi'; **'shall I tell him?'—'no don't'** 'est-ce que je le lui dis?'—'non surtout pas'; **'he knows the President'—'does he?'** 'il connaît le Président'—'vraiment?'; **so/neither does he** lui aussi/ non plus
D ○*n* GB fête *f*; **his leaving** ~ son pot○ de départ

(Idioms) ~ **as you would be done by** ne faites pas ce que vous ne voudriez pas qu'on vous fasse; **how** ~ **you** ~ enchanté; **it doesn't** ~ **to be** ce n'est pas une bonne chose d'être; **it's a poor** ~○ if c'est vraiment grave si; **it was all I could** ~ **not to...** je me suis retenu pour ne pas...; **nothing** ~**ing!** (no way) pas question!; **well done!** bravo!; **what are you** ~**ing with yourself these days?** qu'est-ce que tu deviens?; **what are you going to** ~ **for money?** où vas-tu trouver l'argent?; **all the** ~**s and don'ts** tout ce qu'il faut/ fallait faire et ne pas faire

do¹

The direct French equivalent of the verb *to do* in *subject + to do + object* sentences is *faire*:

she's doing her homework
= elle fait ses devoirs

what are you doing?
= qu'est-ce que tu fais?

what has he done with the newspaper?
= qu'est-ce qu'il a fait du journal?

faire functions in very much the same way as *to do* does in English and it is safe to assume it will work in the great majority of cases. For the conjugation of the verb *faire*, see the French verb tables.

....

Grammatical functions

In questions

In French there is no use of an auxiliary verb in questions equivalent to the use of *do* in English.

When the subject is a pronoun, the question is formed in French either by inverting the subject and verb and putting a hyphen between the two (*veux-tu?*) or by prefacing the *subject + verb* by *est-ce que* (literally *is it that*):

do you like Mozart?
= aimes-tu Mozart? *or* est-ce que tu aimes Mozart?

did you put the glasses in the cupboard?
= as-tu mis les verres dans le placard?
or est-ce que tu as mis les verres dans le placard?

When the subject is a noun there are again two possibilities:

did your sister ring?
= est-ce que ta sœur a téléphoné?
or ta sœur a-t-elle téléphoné?

did Max find his keys?
= est-ce que Max a trouvé ses clés?
or Max a-t-il trouvé ses clés?

In negatives

Equally, auxiliaries are not used in negatives in French:

I don't like Mozart
= je n'aime pas Mozart

you didn't feed the cat
= tu n'as pas donné à manger au chat

don't do that!
= ne fais pas ça!

In emphatic uses

There is no verbal equivalent for the use of *do* in such expressions as *I DO like your dress*. A French speaker will find another way, according to the context, of expressing the force of the English *do*. Here are a few useful examples:

I DO like your dress
= j'aime beaucoup ta robe

I DO hope she remembers
= j'espère qu'elle n'oubliera pas

I DO think you should see a doctor
= je crois vraiment que tu devrais voir un médecin

When referring back to another verb

In this case the verb *to do* is not translated at all:

I don't like him any more than you do
= je ne l'aime pas plus que toi

I live in Oxford and so does Lily
= j'habite à Oxford et Lily aussi

she gets paid more than I do
= elle est payée plus que moi

I haven't written as much as I ought to have done
= je n'ai pas écrit autant que j'aurais dû

'I love strawberries' 'so do I'
= 'j'adore les fraises' 'moi aussi'

In polite requests

In polite requests the phrase *je vous en prie* can often be used to render the meaning of *do*:

do sit down
= asseyez-vous, je vous en prie

do have a piece of cake
= prenez un morceau de gâteau, je vous en prie

'may I take a peach?' 'yes, do'
= 'puis-je prendre une pêche?' 'je vous en prie'

In imperatives

In French there is no use of an auxiliary verb in imperatives:

don't shut the door　　**do be quiet!**
= ne ferme pas la porte　= tais-toi!

don't tell her anything
= ne lui dis rien

In tag questions

French has no direct equivalent of tag questions like *doesn't he?* or *didn't it?* There is a general tag question *n'est-ce pas?* (literally *isn't it so?*) which will work in many cases:

you like fish, don't you?
= tu aimes le poisson, n'est-ce pas?

he lives in London, doesn't he?
= il habite à Londres, n'est-ce pas?

However, *n'est-ce pas* can very rarely be used for positive tag questions and some other way will be found to express the meaning contained in the tag: *par hasard* can often be useful as a translation:

Lola didn't phone, did she?
= Lola n'a pas téléphoné par hasard?

Paul doesn't work here, does he?
= Paul ne travaille pas ici par hasard?

In many cases the tag is not translated at all and the speaker's intonation will convey what is implied:

you didn't tidy your room, did you? (*i.e. you ought to have done*)
= tu n'as pas rangé ta chambre?

In short answers

Again, there is no direct French equivalent for short answers like *yes I do*, *no he doesn't* etc. Where the answer *yes* is given to contradict a negative question or statement, the most useful translation is *si*:

'Marion didn't say that' 'yes she did'
= 'Marion n'a pas dit ça' 'si'

'they don't sell vegetables at the baker's' 'yes they do'
= 'ils ne vendent pas les légumes à la boulangerie' 'si'

In response to a standard enquiry the tag will not be translated:

'do you like strawberries?' 'yes I do'
= 'aimez-vous les fraises?' 'oui '

For more examples and particular usages, see the entry **do¹**.

(Phrasal verbs)

■ **do away with**: ▶ ~ **away with [sth]** se débarrasser de [*procedure, custom, rule, feature*]; supprimer [*bus service etc*]; démolir [*building*]; ▶ ~ **away with [sb]**◯ (kill) se débarrasser de [*person*]

■ **do in**◯: ▶ ~ **[sb] in** ① (kill) tuer; ② (exhaust) épuiser

■ **do out**◯: ▶ ~ **[sth] out**, ~ **out [sth]** faire *or* nettoyer à fond [*room*]

■ **do up**: ▶ ~ **up** [*dress, coat*] se fermer; ▶ ~ **[sth] up**, ~ **up [sth]** ① (fasten) nouer [*laces*]; remonter [*zip*]; ~ **up your buttons** boutonne-toi; ② (wrap) faire [*parcel*]; ③ (renovate) restaurer [*house, furniture*]; ▶ ~ **oneself up** se faire beau/belle

■ **do with**: ▶ ~ **with [sth/sb]** ① (involve) **it has something to** ~ **with** ça a quelque chose à voir avec; **what's it (got) to** ~ **with you?** en quoi est-ce que ça te regarde?; (concern) **it has nothing to** ~ **with you** cela ne vous concerne pas; ② (tolerate) supporter; **I can't** ~ **with all these changes** je ne supporte pas tous ces changements; ③ (need) **I could** ~ **with a holiday** j'aurais bien besoin de partir en vacances; ④ (finish) **it's all over and done with** c'est bien fini; **have you done with my pen?** tu n'as plus besoin de mon stylo?

■ **do without**: ▶ ~ **without [sb/sth]** se passer de [*person, advice etc*]

do² /dəʊ/ *n* Mus = **doh**

d.o.b. *abrév écrite* = **date of birth**

docile /'dəʊsaɪl, US 'dɒsl/ *adj* docile

dock /dɒk/

A *n* ① Naut, Ind dock *m*, bassin *m*; (for repairing ship) cale *f*; **to be in** ~ (for repairs) être en réparation; ② US (wharf) appontement *m*; ③ GB Jur banc *m* des accusés; ④ US (also **loading** ~) zone *f* de chargement; ⑤ Bot patience *f*

B *noun modifier* (also ~**s**) Naut, Ind [*area*] des docks; [*strike*] des dockers

C *vtr* ① Naut mettre [qch] à quai [*ship*]; ② GB (reduce) faire une retenue sur [*wages*]; enlever [*marks*]; ③ [*spacecraft*] amarrer; ④ écourter [*tail*]

D *vi* ① Naut (come into dock) arriver au port; (moor) accoster; ② Aerosp s'arrimer

docket /'dɒkɪt/

A *n* ① Comm, Admin (label) étiquette *f* de reconnaissance; (customs certificate) récépissé *m* de douane; ② US (list) gen registre *m*

B *vtr* Comm étiqueter [*parcel, package*]

docking /'dɒkɪŋ/ *n* Naut, Aerosp amarrage *m*

dock: ~**worker** *n* docker *m*; ~**yard** *n* chantier *m* naval

doctor /'dɒktə(r)/ ▸ p. 1181, p. 869

A *n* ① Med médecin *m*, docteur *m*; **to train as a** ~ faire des études de médecine; **to be under a** ~ GB être suivi par un médecin; ② Univ docteur *m*

B *vtr* ① (tamper with) frelater [*food, wine*]; falsifier [*figures*]; altérer [*document*]; ② GB châtrer [*animal*]

(Idiom) **that's just what the** ~ **ordered!** c'est exactement ce qu'il me/te etc fallait!

doctorate /'dɒktərət/ *n* doctorat *m*

doctor: **Doctor of Philosophy**, **PhD**, **DPhil** *n* ≈ titulaire *mf* d'un doctorat d'État; ~**'s note** *n* certificat *m* médical

doctrine /'dɒktrɪn/ *n* doctrine *f*

document /'dɒkjʊmənt/

A *n* gen document *m*; Jur acte *m*; **travel/insurance** ~**s** papiers *mpl* de voyage/d'assurance; **policy** ~ Pol déclaration *f* de politique générale

B *vtr* ① (give account of, record) décrire [*development, events*]; **this period is not well** ~**ed** on sait peu de choses sur cette période; ② (support or prove with documents) documenter [*case, claim*]

documentary /,dɒkjʊ'mentrɪ, US -terɪ/

A *n* documentaire *m* (**about, on** sur)

B *adj* [*film, realism, technique, source*] documentaire; ~ **evidence** Jur preuves *fpl* écrites; (in historical research) documents *mpl* de l'époque

documentation /,dɒkjʊmen'teɪʃn/ *n* **⊄** (documents) gen documentation *f*; Comm documents *mpl*

document: ~ **case**, ~ **holder** *n* porte-documents *m inv*; ~ **retrieval** *n* Comput recherche *f* documentaire; ~ **wallet** *n* chemise *f* (en carton)

docusoap /'dɒkjʊsəʊp/ *n* TV feuilleton *m* documentaire

dodder /'dɒdə(r)/ *vi* tituber

doddering /'dɒdərɪŋ/, **doddery** /'dɒdərɪ/ *adj* ① (unsteady) branlant; ② (senile) gâteux/-euse◯

doddle◯ /'dɒdl/ *n* GB **it's a** ~ c'est simple comme bonjour!

dodge /dɒdʒ/

A *n* ① (movement) gen mouvement *m* de côté; Sport esquive *f*; ② ◯GB (trick) combine◯ *f*

B *vtr* esquiver [*bullet, blow, difficult question*]; échapper à [*pursuers*]; se dérober à [*confrontation, accusation*]; éviter de payer [*tax*]; éviter [*person*]; **to** ~ **the issue** éluder la question

dodgem (car) /'dɒdʒəm/ *n* GB auto *f* tamponneuse

dodgy◯ /'dɒdʒɪ/ *adj* GB ① (untrustworthy) [*person, business, establishment, method*] louche◯; ② (risky, dangerous) [*decision, plan, investment*] risqué; [*situation, moment*] délicat; [*finances*] précaire; [*weather*] instable

doe /dəʊ/ *n* (deer) biche *f*; (rabbit) lapine *f*; (hare) hase *f*

DOE *n* ① GB *abrév* ▸ **Department of the Environment**; ② US *abrév* ▸ **Department of Energy**

does /dʌz/ (3ᵉ pers sg prés) ▸ **do**

doesn't /'dʌznt/ (= **does not**) ▸ **do**

dog /dɒg, US dɔːg/

A *n* ① Zool chien *m*; (female) chienne *f*; ② (male fox, wolf, etc) mâle *m*; ③ ◯(person) **you lucky** ~! sacré veinard◯!

B ~**dogs** *npl* the ~**s** les courses *fpl* de lévriers

C *noun modifier* [*biscuit, basket*] pour chien; [*food*] pour chiens

D *vtr* (*p prés etc* -**gg**-) ① **to** ~ **sb's footsteps** être sur les talons de qn; ② ~**ged by** poursuivi par [*misfortune*]

(Idioms) **it's** ~ **eat** ~ c'est chacun pour soi, c'est la foire d'empoigne; **every** ~ **has its day** à chacun vient sa chance; **give a** ~ **a bad name (and hang him)** Prov qui veut noyer son chien l'accuse de la rage Prov; **love me, love my** ~ aime-moi tel que je suis; **to go and see a man about a** ~ euph (relieve oneself) aller se soulager; (go on unspecified business) aller voir le pape hum; **they don't have a** ~**'s chance** ils n'ont pas la moindre chance *or* l'ombre d'une chance; **to go to the** ~**s**◯ [*company, country*] aller à vau-l'eau; **it's a real** ~**'s breakfast**◯! c'est n'importe quoi!

dog breeder ▸ p. 1181 *n* éleveur/-euse *m*/*f* de chiens

dog collar *n* ① lit collier *m* de chien; ② ◯hum (clergyman's collar) col *m* romain

dog: ~ **days** *npl* (warm weather) canicule *f*; fig période *f* creuse; ~**-eared** *adj* écorné; ~**-end**◯ *n* mégot◯ *m*; ~**fight** *n* lit bagarre *f* de chiens; Mil Aviat combat *m* aérien

dogged /'dɒgɪd, US 'dɔːgɪd/ *adj* [*attempt*] obstiné; [*person, persistence, refusal*] tenace; [*resistance*] opiniâtre

doggy: ~ **bag** *n*: petit sac pour emporter les restes d'un repas; ~ **paddle**◯ *n* = **dog paddle**

dog handler ▸ p. 1181 *n* maître-chien *m*

doghouse /'dɒghaʊs, US 'dɔːg-/ *n* US niche *f* (à chien)

(Idiom) **to be in the** ~◯ être tombé en disgrâce

dogma /'dɒgmə, US 'dɔːgmə/ *n* dogme *m*

dogmatic /dɒg'mætɪk, US dɔːg-/ *adj* dogmatique (**about** sur)

do-gooder◯ /duː'gʊdə(r)/ *n* péj bonne âme *f*

dog: ~ **paddle** *n* nage *f* à la manière d'un chien; ~**sbody**◯ *n* GB (also **general** ~) bonne *f* à tout faire; ~ **tag** *n* US Mil plaque *f* d'identification (*portée par le personnel militaire américain*); ~**-tooth check** *n*, *adj* pied-de-poule (*m*) *inv*

doh /dəʊ/ *n* Mus do *m*, ut *m*

doing /'duːɪŋ/

A *p prés* ▸ **do**

B *n* **this is her** ~ c'est son ouvrage; **it's none of my** ~ ce n'est pas moi qui l'ai fait; **it takes some** ~! ce n'est pas facile du tout!

C **doings** *npl* (actions) faits et gestes *mpl*; (events) événements *mpl*

do-it-yourself /,duːɪtjɔː'self/, **DIY** *n* bricolage *m*

doldrums /'dɒldrəmz/ *npl* fig **to be in the** ~ [*person*] être en pleine déprime; [*economy, company*] être en plein marasme

dole◯ /dəʊl/ *n* GB allocation *f* de chômage; **on the** ~ au chômage

d

d

Phrasal verb
■ **dole out**○: ▸ ~ **out [sth]**, ~ **[sth] out** distribuer

doleful /ˈdəʊlfl/ adj dolent, triste

dole queue n GB ① lit ≈ file f d'attente à l'agence pour l'emploi; ② fig nombre m de chômeurs

doll /dɒl, US dɔːl/ n ① poupée f; **to play with one's ~s** jouer à la poupée; ② ○(pretty girl) jolie nana○ f

Phrasal verb
■ **doll up**: ▸ ~ **up [sb/sth]**○, ~ **[sb/sth] up**○ pomponner○ [person]; bichonner○ [room, house]

dollar /ˈdɒlə(r)/ ▸ p. 782 n dollar m

Idiom **the 64 thousand ~ question** la question à mille francs

dollar: ~ **bill** n billet m d'un dollar; ~ **diplomacy** n diplomatie f qui s'appuie sur le pouvoir financier; ~ **sign** n symbole m du dollar

dollop○ /ˈdɒləp/ n lit cuillerée f; fig bonne dose f

dolly /ˈdɒlɪ, US ˈdɔːlɪ/ n ① ○(doll) poupée f; ② (mobile platform) plate-forme f (de manutention); Cin, TV dolly m; ③ US Rail diabolo m

dolphin /ˈdɒlfɪn/ n dauphin m

domain /dəʊˈmeɪn/ n (all contexts) domaine m (**of** de)

domain name n Comput nom m de domaine

dome /dəʊm/ n gen dôme m; Archit coupole f

domed /dəʊmd/ adj [skyline, tower, city] à coupoles; [roof, ceiling] en dôme; [forehead, helmet] bombé

domestic /dəˈmestɪk/ adj ① Pol (home) [market, affairs, flight, price] intérieur; [consumer] du pays; [crisis, issue] de politique intérieure; ② (of house) [activity, animal] domestique; ③ (family) [life, situation, harmony] familial; [dispute] conjugal

domestically /dəˈmestɪklɪ/ adv [produced, sold] à l'intérieur du pays

domestic appliance n appareil m électroménager

domesticate /dəˈmestɪkeɪt/ vtr domestiquer [animal]; **to be ~d** [person] aimer s'occuper de la maison

domestic help n aide f ménagère

domesticity /ˌdɒməˈstɪsətɪ, ˌdəʊ-/ n ① (home life) vie f de famille; ② (household duties) tâches fpl ménagères

domiciliary /ˌdɒmɪˈsɪlɪərɪ, US -erɪ/ adj [visit, care] à domicile; [rights, information] relatif/-ive au domicile

dominance /ˈdɒmɪnəns/ n ① (domination) domination f (**of** de); Biol, Zool dominance f; ② (numerical strength) prépondérance f (**of** de)

dominant /ˈdɒmɪnənt/ adj gen, Biol dominant; Mus [chord, key] de dominante

dominate /ˈdɒmɪneɪt/
A vtr dominer [person, region, town]; dominer dans [industry, market]; **an area ~d by factories/shops** une zone très industrielle/commerçante
B vi [person] dominer; [issue, question] prédominer

domineering /ˌdɒmɪˈnɪərɪŋ/ adj [person, behaviour] despotique; [ways] de despote; [tone] autoritaire

Dominican Republic ▸ p. 774 pr n République f Dominicaine

dominion /dəˈmɪnɪən/ n ① (authority) domination f (**over** sur); ② (area ruled) territoire m

domino /ˈdɒmɪnəʊ/ ▸ p. 881 n ① Games (piece) domino m; ② Hist (cloak) domino m; (eye-mask) loup m

don /dɒn/ n GB Univ professeur m d'université

donate /dəʊˈneɪt, US ˈdəʊneɪt/ vtr faire don de

donation /dəʊˈneɪʃn/ n don m (**of** de; **à** to)

done /dʌn/
A pp ▸ do
B excl (making deal) marché conclu!
Idiom **it's not the ~ thing** ça ne se fait pas

donkey /ˈdɒŋkɪ/ n Zool âne m

Idioms **she could talk the hind leg off a ~**! c'est un vrai moulin à paroles○!; **I've known him for ~'s years**○ je le connais depuis des années or une éternité

donkey: ~ **jacket** n grosse veste f de travail; ~ **work** n travail m pénible

donor /ˈdəʊnə(r)/ n (of organ) donneur/-euse m/f; (of money) donateur/-trice m/f

donor card n carte f de donneur d'organes

don't /dəʊnt/ (= do not) ▸ do

don't know n (in survey) sans opinion mf inv

doodle /ˈduːdl/ vi gribouiller (**on** sur)

doom /duːm/
A n (death) mort f; (unhappy destiny) (of person) perte f; (of country, group) catastrophe f
B vtr condamner [person, project] (**to** à); **~ed from the start** voué à l'échec avant même de commencer

doomsday /ˈduːmzdeɪ/ n fin f du monde

doomwatch /ˈduːmwɒtʃ/ n Ecol catastrophisme m

door /dɔː(r)/
A n ① gen porte f (**to** de); **a few ~s down** quelques maisons plus bas; **behind closed ~s** à huis clos; **to shut** ou **close the ~ on sth** fig fermer la porte à qch; **to slam the ~ in sb's face** fig envoyer promener qn; ② Aut, Rail porte f, portière f; ③ (entrance) entrée f
B noun modifier [handle, chime] de porte
Idioms **to be at death's ~** être à l'article de la mort; **to get a foot in the ~** mettre un pied dans la place; **to lay sth at sb's ~** imputer qch à qn; **to show sb the ~** mettre qn à la porte

door: ~ **bell** n sonnette f; ~**man** n (at hotel) portier m; (at cinema) contrôleur m; ~**mat** n lit, fig paillasson m; ~ **plate** n (of doctor etc) plaque f (de porte)

doorstep /ˈdɔːstep/ n ① (step) pas m de porte; ② (threshold) seuil m; **on the ~** ou **one's ~** (nearby) tout près; (unpleasantly close) juste à côté

doorstop /ˈdɔː(r)stɒp/ n butoir m (de porte)

door-to-door /ˌdɔːtəˈdɔː/
A adj [canvassing] à domicile; ~ **selling** porte à porte m inv
B door to door adv phr [sell] à domicile; **it's 90 minutes ~** le trajet prend 90 minutes de porte à porte

doorway /ˈdɔːweɪ/ n ① (frame) embrasure f; ② (entrance) porte f, entrée f; **in a shop ~** à l'entrée d'une boutique

dope /dəʊp/
A n ① ○cannabis m; ② ○ (fool) andouille○ f; ③ ○(information) tuyaux○ mpl (**on** sur); ④ (varnish) enduit m
B vtr ① (give drug to) Sport doper [horse, athlete]; gen droguer [person]; ② (put drug in) mettre un somnifère dans [food, drink]

dope test n Sport contrôle m antidopage

dopey○ /ˈdəʊpɪ/ adj (not fully awake) groggy○

dormant /ˈdɔːmənt/ adj ① [emotion, talent] latent; **to lie ~** sommeiller; ② [volcano] en repos

dormer /ˈdɔːmə(r)/ n (also ~ **window**) lucarne f

dormitory /ˈdɔːmɪtrɪ, US -tɔːrɪ/
A n ① GB dortoir m; ② US Univ résidence f, foyer m
B noun modifier [suburb, town] dortoir inv

dormouse /ˈdɔːmaʊs/ n (pl **dormice**) Zool muscardin m

dosage /ˈdəʊsɪdʒ/ n posologie f

dose /dəʊs/
A n Med, fig dose f (**of** de); **a ~ of flu** une bonne grippe
B vtr **to ~ sb with medicine** bourrer○ qn de médicaments
Idiom **like a ~ of salts** à la vitesse grand V

doss○ /dɒs/ n GB **it's a ~!** facile!

Phrasal verb
■ **doss down**○ dormir

dot /dɒt/
A n gen point m; (on fabric, wallpaper) pois m; **'~, ~, ~'** 'points de suspension'
B vtr (p prés etc **-tt-**) ① (in writing) mettre un point sur [letter]; ② Culin parsemer [chicken, joint] (**with** de); ③ (be scattered along) **the coast is ~ted with fishing villages** il y a des ports de pêche éparpillés le long de la côte
Idioms **since the year ~**○ depuis des siècles; **at ten on the ~** à dix heures pile

dotage /ˈdəʊtɪdʒ/ n **to be in one's ~** être dans ses vieux jours pej

dot-com /dɒtˈkɒm/
A n (Internet company) société f en ligne, société f point com
B modif [millionaire, revolution] de l'Internet; [era] Internet; [society] en ligne; [shares] des sociétés en ligne

dote /dəʊt/ vi **to ~ on sb/sth** adorer qn/qch

dot matrix printer n imprimante f matricielle

dotted /ˈdɒtɪd/ adj ① [fabric] à pois; ② Mus [note] pointé

dotted line n pointillé m; **'tear along** ∿ 'découpez suivant le pointillé'; **to sign on the** ∿ lit signer à l'endroit indiqué

dotty○ /'dɒtɪ/ adj GB farfelu○

double /'dʌbl/

A n **1** **a** ∿ **please** (drink) un double, s'il vous plaît; **2** (of person) sosie m; Cin, Theat doublure f; **3** Games (in bridge) contre m; (in dominoes, darts) double m

B **doubles** npl (in tennis) double m; **ladies'/mixed** ∿s double dames/mixte

C adj **1** (twice as much) [portion, dose] double (before n); **2** (when spelling, giving number) **Anne is spelt** GB ou **spelled** US **with a** ∿ **'n'** Anne s'écrit avec deux 'n'; **two** ∿ **four (244)** deux cent quarante-quatre; **3** (dual, twofold) double; **with a** ∿ **meaning** à double sens; **4** (intended for two people or things) [sheet, garage etc] double; [ticket, invitation] pour deux

D adv **1** (twice) deux fois; **2** [fold, bend] en deux; **to see** ∿ voir double

E vtr **1** (increase twofold) doubler [amount, rent, dose etc]; multiplier [qch] par deux [number]; **2** (also ∿ **over**) (fold) plier [qch] en deux [blanket etc]; **3** (in spelling) doubler [letter]; **4** (in bridge) contrer

F vi **1** [sales, prices, salaries etc] doubler; **2** **to** ∿ **for sb** Cin, Theat doubler qn; **3** (serve dual purpose) **the sofa** ∿**s as a bed** le canapé fait aussi lit

(Idioms) **on** ou **at the** ∿ fig au plus vite; Mil au pas redoublé; ∿ **or quits!** quitte ou double!

(Phrasal verbs)

■ **double back** [person, animal] rebrousser chemin; [road etc] former un demi-tour

■ **double up** **1** (bend one's body) se plier en deux; **to** ∿ **up with laughter** être plié en deux de rire; **2** (share sleeping accommodation) partager la même chambre

double act n Theat, fig duo m

double-barrelled GB, **double-barreled** US /ˌdʌbl-'bærəld/ adj [gun] à deux coups; ∿ **name** GB ≈ nom à particule

double: ∿ **bass** ▸ p. 1028 n (instrument) contrebasse f; ∿ **bed** n lit m double, grand lit; ∿ **bend** n Aut virage m en S; ∿ **bill** n Theat représentation f avec deux œuvres au programme; Cin séance f avec deux films à la suite; ∿ **bluff** n: fait de dire la vérité à quelqu'un en faisant croire que c'est un mensonge; ∿ **boiler** n US ≈ bain-marie m

double-book

A vtr **to** ∿ **a room/seat etc** réserver la même chambre/place etc pour deux personnes

B vi [hotel, airline, company] (as practice) surbooker

double-breasted adj [jacket] croisé

double check

A n deuxième ou nouveau contrôle m

B **double-check** vtr vérifier [qch] à nouveau [detail]

double: ∿ **chin** n double menton m; ∿ **cream** n GB Culin ≈ crème f fraîche

double-click /dʌbl'klɪk/ Comput

A n double-clic m

B vi cliquer deux fois, double-cliquer (**on** sur)

double-cross○

A n trahison f

B vtr doubler, trahir [person]

double cuff n poignet m mousquetaire

double-dealing

A n fourberie f

B adj hypocrite, fourbe

double-decker n **1** GB (bus) autobus m à impériale or à deux étages; **2** (sandwich) sandwich m double

double door(s) n(pl) porte f à deux battants

double Dutch○ n baragouinage○ m

double-edged adj lit, fig à double tranchant

double entendre /ˌduːbl ɑːn'tɑːndrə/ n (word, phrase) sous-entendu m (grivois)

double: ∿ **entry** n comptabilité f en partie double; ∿ **exposure** n Phot (process) surimpression f; ∿ **fault** n double faute f; ∿ **feature** n Cin séance f avec deux films à la suite

double figures npl **to go into** ∿ [inflation] passer la barre des 10%

double: ∿-**fronted** adj [house] avec une fenêtre de part et d'autre de la porte; ∿ **glazing** n double vitrage m; ∿-**jointed** adj [person, limb, finger] souple; ∿ **knitting**

(wool) n grosse laine f; ∿ **lock** vtr fermer [qch] à double tour

double-park

A vtr garer [qch] en double file [vehicle]

B vi se garer en double file

double-quick

A adj **in** ∿ **time** en un rien de temps

B adv en vitesse, le plus vite possible

double: ∿ **room** n chambre f pour deux personnes; ∿ **saucepan** n GB ≈ bain-marie m inv; ∿ **spacing** n double interligne m; ∿ **spread** n Journ article m (or publicité f) sur double page

double standard n **to have** ∿s faire deux poids deux mesures

double take n **to do a** ∿ avoir une réaction à retardement

double talk n péj langue f de bois

double time n **1** **to be paid** ∿ être payé double; **2** US Mil pas m redoublé

double vision n **to have** ∿ voir double

double: ∿ **whammy**○ n double coup m de malchance; ∿ **yellow line(s)** n(pl) GB Aut marquage au sol interdisant le stationnement

doubling /'dʌblɪŋ/ n (of salary, amount, size, strength) doublement m; (of number, letter) (re)doublement m

doubly /'dʌblɪ/ adv [deprived, disappointed] doublement; [difficult, confident] deux fois plus (before n); **I made** ∿ **sure that** j'ai bien vérifié que

doubt /daʊt/

A n doute m; **there is no** ∿ **(that)** il ne fait aucun doute que; **there is little** ∿ **(that)** il est presque certain que; **there is some** ∿ **about its authenticity** son authenticité est mise en doute; **there's (some)** ∿ **as to whether he will be able to come** on ne sait pas s'il pourra venir; **there is no** ∿ **in my mind that I'm right** je suis convaincu d'avoir raison; **to have one's** ∿s **about doing** hésiter à faire; **no** ∿ **the police will want to speak to you** la police voudra sans doute vous parler; **to leave sb in no** ∿ **about sth** ne laisser à qn aucun doute quant à qch; **to be in** ∿ [outcome, project] être incertain; [honesty, innocence, guilt] gen être douteux/-euse; (on particular occasion) être mis en doute; [person] être dans le doute; **the election result is not in any** ∿ le résultat de l'élection ne fait aucun ou ne fait pas l'ombre d'un doute; **if** ou **when in** ∿ dans le doute; **to be open to** ∿ [evidence, testimony] être sujet à caution; **without (a)** ∿ sans aucun doute; **to prove sth beyond (all)** ∿ prouver qch de façon indubitable

B vtr douter de [fact, value, ability, honesty, person]; **I** ∿ **it!** j'en doute!; **to** ∿ **(if** ou **that** ou **whether)** douter que (+ subj)

C vi douter

doubtful /'daʊtfl/ adj **1** (unsure) incertain; **it is** ∿ **if** ou **that** ou **whether** il n'est pas certain que (+ subj); **to be** ∿ **about doing** hésiter à faire; **to be** ∿ **about** ou **as to** être peu convaincu par [idea, explanation, plan]; avoir des doutes sur [job, object, purchase]; **2** (questionable) [character, past, activity, taste] douteux/-euse

doubtfully /'daʊtfəlɪ/ adv (hesitantly) d'un air or d'un ton hésitant; (with disbelief) d'un air or d'un ton sceptique

doubtless /'daʊtlɪs/ adv sans doute

douche /duːʃ/

A n gen Med douche f

B vtr gen, Med doucher

dough /dəʊ/ n **1** Culin pâte f; **pizza** ∿ pâte à pizza; **2** ○(money) fric○ m, argent m

doughnut, donut US /'dəʊnʌt/ n beignet m

dour /dʊə(r)/ adj [person, expression] renfrogné; [landscape] morne; [mood] maussade; [building] austère

douse, dowse /daʊs/ vtr tremper [person, room]; éteindre [flame]; **to** ∿ **sb/sth with water** tremper qn/qch

dove

A /dʌv/ n Zool, Pol colombe f

B /dəʊv/ US prét ▸ **dive**

dovecot(e) /'dʌvkɒt, 'dʌvkəʊt/ n pigeonnier m

Dover /'dəʊvə(r)/ ▸ p. 1276 pr n Douvres; **the Straits of** ∿ le Pas de Calais

dovetail /'dʌvteɪl/

A vtr **1** fig faire concorder [plans, policies, research, arguments] (**with** avec); **2** Constr assembler [qch] à queue-d'aronde [pieces]

d

d

B vi fig (also ~ **together**) bien cadrer ensemble

dowdy /'daʊdɪ/ adj [woman] sans élégance; [clothes] vieux jeu inv; [image] vieillotte○

down¹ /daʊn/

> ⚠ *Down* often occurs as the second element in verb combinations in English (*go down, fall down, get down, keep down, put down* etc). For translations, consult the appropriate verb entry (**go, fall, get, keep, put** etc).
>
> When used to indicate vague direction, *down* often has no explicit translation in French: *to go down to London* = aller à Londres; *down in Brighton* = à Brighton.
>
> For examples and further usages, see the entry below.

A adv ① (from higher to lower level) **to go** ou **come** ~ descendre; **to fall** ~ tomber; **to sit** ~ **on the floor** s'asseoir par terre; **to pull** ~ **a blind** baisser un store; **I'm on my way** ~ je descends; ~! (to dog) couché!; '~' (in crossword) 'verticalement'; **read** ~ **to the end of the paragraph** lire jusqu'à la fin du paragraphe; ② (indicating position at lower level) ~ **below** en bas; (when looking down from height) en contrebas; **two floors** ~ deux étages plus bas; **it's on the second shelf** ~ c'est au deuxième rayon en partant du haut; ~ **at the bottom of the lake** tout au fond du lac; **the telephone lines are** ~ les lignes téléphoniques sont coupées; ③ (from upstairs) **is Tim** ~ **yet?** est-ce que Tim est déjà descendu?; ④ (indicating direction) **to go** ~ **to London** aller à Londres; ~ **in Brighton** à Brighton; **they've gone** ~ **to the country** ils sont allés à la campagne; **they moved** ~ **here from Scotland** ils ont quitté l'Écosse pour venir s'installer ici; **they live** ~ **south**○ ils habitent dans le sud; ⑤ (in a range, scale, hierarchy) **children from the age of 10** ~ les enfants de moins de dix ans; **everybody from the Prime Minister** ~ tout le monde depuis le Premier ministre; ⑥ (indicating loss of money etc) **bookings are** ~ **by a half** les réservations ont baissé de moitié; **profits are well** ~ **on last year's** les bénéfices sont nettement inférieurs à ceux de l'année dernière; **I'm £10** ~ il me manque 10 livres sterling; ⑦ (indicating reduction) **to get one's weight** ~ maigrir; **to get the price** ~ faire baisser le prix; **I'm** ~ **to my last cigarette** il ne me reste plus qu'une cigarette; **that's seven** ~, **three to go!** en voilà sept de faits, il n'en reste plus que trois à faire!; ⑧ (on list, schedule) **you're** ~ **to speak next** c'est toi qui es le prochain à intervenir; **I've got you** ~ **for next Thursday** (in appointment book) vous avez rendez-vous jeudi prochain; ⑨ (incapacitated) **to be** ~ **with the flu** avoir la grippe; ⑩ Sport (behind) **to be two sets** ~ [tennis player] avoir deux sets de retard; ⑪ (as deposit) **to pay £40** ~ payer 40 livres sterling comptant; ⑫ (downwards) **face** ~ (of person) le visage face au sol

B prep ① (from higher to lower point) **to run** ~ **the hill** descendre la colline en courant; **did you enjoy the journey** ~? est-ce que tu as fait bon voyage?; ~ **town** en ville; ② (at lower part of) **they live** ~ **the road** ils habitent un peu plus loin dans la rue; **a few miles** ~ **the river from here** à quelques kilomètres en aval de la rivière; ③ (along) **to go** ~ **the street** descendre la rue; **with buttons all** ~ **the front** boutonné sur le devant; **he looked** ~ **her throat** il a regardé au fond de sa gorge; ④ (throughout) ~ **the ages** ou **centuries** à travers les siècles

C adj ① ○**to feel** ~ être déprimé; ② [escalator] qui descend; [train] descendant; ③ Comput en panne

D ○vtr ① abattre [person]; descendre [plane]; ② descendre○ [drink]

(Idioms) **to have a** ~ **on sb** en vouloir à qn; **it's** ~ **to you to do it** c'est à toi de le faire; ~ **with tyrants!** à bas les tyrans!

down² /daʊn/ n (feathers) (all contexts) duvet m

down-and-out /ˌdaʊnən'aʊt/ n clochard/-e m/f

downbeat /'daʊnbiːt/ adj ① (pessimistic) [view] pessimiste; ② (laidback) décontracté

downcast /'daʊnkɑːst, US -kæst/ adj ① (dejected) découragé; ② [eyes] baissé

downfall /'daʊnfɔːl/ n chute f; **drink proved to be his** ~ c'est la boisson qui a causé sa perte

downgrade /'daʊnɡreɪd/ vtr ① (demote) rétrograder [employee]; **the hotel has been** ~**d to a guest house** l'hôtel a été déclassé et c'est maintenant une pension de famille; ② (degrade) dévaloriser [task]

downhearted adj abattu

downhill /ˌdaʊn'hɪl/
A adj [path, road] qui descend
B adv **to go** ~ [path, person, vehicle] descendre; fig [person] être sur le déclin; **from now on it's** ~ **all the way** fig (easy) à partir de maintenant il ne devrait plus y avoir de problèmes; (disastrous) à partir de maintenant c'est le déclin

downhill ski(ing) n ski m de descente

Downing Street /ˌdaʊnɪŋ'striːt/ n GB Downing Street

down daʊn: ~**-in-the-mouth** ○ adj abattu; ~**load** vtr Comput transférer, télécharger; ~**loadable** adj Comput téléchargeable; ~**market** adj [products, hotel, restaurant] bas de gamme inv; [area] populaire; [newspaper, programme] grand public inv; ~ **payment** n acompte m; ~**pipe** n GB gouttière f

downpour /'daʊnpɔːr/ n averse f

downright /'daʊnraɪt/
A adj [insult] véritable (before n); [refusal] catégorique; [liar] fieffé (before n)
B adv [stupid, rude] carrément

downs /daʊnz/ npl GB (hills) collines fpl

downshift /'daʊnʃɪft/ vi (change lifestyle) opter pour un mode de vie plus simple

downshifter /'daʊnʃɪftə(r)/ n personne qui choisit de vivre plus modestement (en changeant d'emploi notamment)

downside○ /'daʊnsaɪd/
A n gen inconvénient m
B **downside up** adj phr, adv phr US sens dessus dessous

Down's syndrome /'daʊnz sɪndrəʊm/ n trisomie f 21

downstairs /ˌdaʊn'steəz/
A n rez-de-chaussée m inv
B adj [room] gen en bas; (on ground-floor) du rez-de-chaussée; **the** ~ **flat** GB ou **apartment** US l'appartement du rez-de-chaussée
C adv en bas; **to go** ou **come** ~ descendre (l'escalier)

downstream /'daʊnstriːm/ adj, adv lit, fig en aval (**of** de); **to go** ~ descendre le courant

down-to-earth /ˌdaʊntə'ɜːθ/ adj [person, approach] pratique; **she's very** ~ (practical) elle a les pieds sur terre; (unpretentious) elle est très simple

downtown /'daʊntaʊn/ adj surtout US du centre ville; ~ **New York** le centre de New York

down daʊn: ~**trodden** adj [person, country] tyrannisé; ~**turn** n (in economy, career) déclin m (**in** de); (in demand, profits, spending) chute f (**in** de); ~ **under** ○ adv en Australie

downward /'daʊnwəd/ adj [movement, glance, stroke] vers le bas

downwards /'daʊnwədz/ adv [look, gesture] vers le bas; **to slope** ~ être en pente (**to** vers); **read the list from the top** ~ lire la liste de haut en bas; **he was floating face** ~ il flottait le visage dans l'eau; **everybody from the boss** ~ tout le monde depuis le patron

downwind /ˌdaʊn'wɪnd/ adv dans le sens du vent

dowse /daʊz/
A vtr = **douse**
B vi (for water) faire de la rhabdomancie; (for minerals) faire de la radiesthésie

doz abrév écrite = **dozen**

doze /dəʊz/
A n somme m
B vi [person, cat] somnoler.
(Phrasal verb)
■ **doze off** (momentarily) s'assoupir; (to sleep) s'endormir

dozen /'dʌzn/ n ① (twelve) douzaine f; **by the** ~ à la douzaine; ② (several) **I've told you a** ~ **times!** je te l'ai déjà dit cent fois!; ~**s of** des dizaines de [people, things, times]

DPhil n: abrév ▸ **Doctor of Philosophy**

DPP n GB abrév ▸ **Director of Public Prosecutions**

Dr n ① abrév écrite = **Doctor**; ② abrév écrite = **Drive**

drab /dræb/ adj [colour, life] terne; [building] triste

draft /drɑːft, US dræft/
A n ① (of letter, speech) brouillon m; (of novel, play) ébauche f; (of contract, law) avant-projet m; ② Fin traite f (**on** sur); **to make a** ~ **on a bank** tirer sur une banque; ③ US Mil (conscription) service m militaire; ④ US = **draught**
B noun modifier [agreement, version] préliminaire
C vtr ① faire le brouillon de [letter, speech]; faire l'avant-

projet de [contract, law]; **2)** US (conscript) incorporer (**into** dans); **3)** GB (transfer) détacher (**to** auprès de; **from** de); **4)** Sport sélectionner; **5)** US (choose) **to ~ sb to do** charger qn de faire

(Phrasal verb)

■ **draft in** GB: ▸ **~ in** [sb], **~** [sb] **in** faire venir

draft: **~ board** n US Mil conseil m de révision; **~ card** n US Mil ordre m d'incorporation; **~ dodger** n US Mil insoumis m

drafty US = draughty

drag /dræg/

A n **1)** ○(person) raseur/-euse m/f; **what a ~!** quelle barbe○!; **2)** (women's clothes worn by men) vêtements mpl de travesti

B noun modifier **1)** Theat [artist, show] de travesti; **2)** Aut Sport [race, racing] de dragsters

C vtr (p prés etc -**gg**-) **1)** (pull) tirer (**to, up to** jusqu'à; **towards** vers); **to ~ sth along the ground** faire traîner qch par terre; **to ~ sb from** arracher qn de [chair, bed]; **to ~ sb to** traîner qn à [place]; traîner qn chez [person]; **don't ~ my mother into this** ne mêle pas ma mère à ça; **2)** (search) draguer [river, lake]; **3)** Comput déplacer; **4)** (trail) traîner; **to ~ one's feet** ou **heels** lit traîner les pieds; fig faire preuve de mauvaise volonté (**on** quant à)

D vi (p prés etc -**gg**-) **1)** (go slowly) [hours, days] traîner; [story, plot] traîner en longueur; **2)** (trail) **to ~ in** [hem, belt] traîner dans [mud]; **3)** (inhale) **to ~ on** tirer une bouffée de [cigarette]

E v refl **to ~ oneself to** se traîner jusqu'à

(Phrasal verbs)

■ **drag along**: ▸ **~** [sth] **along** traîner
■ **drag away**: ▸ **~** [sb] **away** emmener [qn] de force; **to ~ sb away from** arracher qn à; ▸ **~** [oneself] **away from** [sth] partir à regret de
■ **drag in**: ▸ **~** [sth] **in**, **~ in** [sth] mentionner
■ **drag on** traîner en longueur
■ **drag out**: ▸ **~** [sth] **out** faire traîner; ▸ **~** [sth] **out of sb** arracher [qch] à qn
■ **drag up**: ▸ **~** [sth] **up**, **~ up** [sth] déterrer [secret]

drag: **~ and drop** n glisser-déposer m; **~ lift** n Sport tire-fesses○ m inv

dragon /'drægən/ n dragon m

drain /dreɪn/

A n **1)** lit (in street) canalisation f; (in building) canalisation f d'évacuation; (pipe) descente f d'eau; (ditch) fossé m d'écoulement; **2)** fig (of people, skills, money) hémorragie f; **to be a ~ on sb's resources** épuiser les ressources de qn

B vtr **1)** lit drainer [land, lake]; purger [radiator, boiler]; **2)** fig épuiser [resources]; **3)** vider [glass]; boire [qch] jusqu'à la dernière goutte [drink]; **4)** [river] collecter les eaux de [area, basin]

C vi **1)** [liquid] s'écouler (**out of, from** de); [bath, sink] se vider; **to ~ into** s'écouler dans [sea, gutter]; s'infiltrer dans [soil]; **the blood** ou **colour ~ed from her face** le sang reflua de son visage; **2)** [dishes, food] s'égoutter

(Idioms) **to go down the ~**○ fig tomber à l'eau○; **that's £100 down the ~**○ ça fait 100 livres sterling de fichues en l'air○

(Phrasal verbs)

■ **drain away** lit s'écouler; fig s'épuiser
■ **drain off**, **drain out**: ▸ **~ off** s'écouler; ▸ **~** [sth] **off**, **~ off** [sth] vider [fluid, water]

drainage /'dreɪnɪdʒ/ n (of land) drainage m; (system of pipes, ditches) tout-à-l'égout m inv

draining board n égouttoir m

drainpipe /'dreɪnpaɪp/ n descente f

drake /dreɪk/ n canard m (mâle)

drama /'drɑːmə/

A n (genre) gen théâtre m; TV, Radio (as opposed to documentary programmes) fiction f; (acting, directing) art m dramatique; (play, dramatic event) drame m; TV, Radio dramatique f; **to make a ~ out of sth** faire tout un drame de qch

B noun modifier [school, course, student] d'art dramatique; **~ critic** critique m dramatique; **~ documentary** TV reportage m fiction

dramatic /drə'mætɪk/ adj **1)** [literature, art, irony, effect] dramatique; [gesture, entrance, exit] théâtral; **2)** (tense, exciting) [situation, event] dramatique; **3)** (sudden) [change, impact, landscape] spectaculaire

dramatically /drə'mætɪklɪ/ adv (radically) radicalement; (causing excitement) de façon spectaculaire; Literat, Theat du point de vue théâtral; [gesture, pause] de façon théâtrale

dramatics /drə'mætɪks/ npl art m dramatique; péj cinéma m pej

dramatist /'dræmətɪst/ n auteur m dramatique

dramatization /ˌdræmətaɪ'zeɪʃn, US -tɪ'z-/ n **1)** (version) version f théâtrale; **2)** (technique) (for stage) adaptation f pour la scène; (for screen) adaptation f pour l'écran; **3)** (exaggeration) dramatisation f

dramatize /'dræmətaɪz/ vtr **1)** (adapt) Theat adapter [qch] pour la scène; Cin, TV adapter [qch] pour l'écran; Radio adapter [qch] pour la radio; **2)** (depict) dépeindre; **3)** (make dramatic) donner un caractère dramatique à; pej dramatiser

drank /dræŋk/ prét ▸ drink

drape /dreɪp/

A n US (curtain) rideau m

B vtr **to ~ sth with sth**, **to ~ sth over sth** draper qch de qch; **~d in sth** enveloppé dans qch

drastic /'dræstɪk/ adj [policy, measure] draconien/-ienne; [reduction, remedy] drastique; [effect] catastrophique; [change] radical

drastically /'dræstɪklɪ/ adv [change, reduce] radicalement; [reduce, limit] sévèrement

draught GB, **draft** US /drɑːft, US dræft/

A n **1)** (cold air) courant m d'air; **2)** (in fireplace) tirage m; **3) on ~** [beer etc] à la pression; **4)** (of liquid, air) trait m; **5)** GB Games pion m (de jeu de dames)

B noun modifier [beer, cider] (à la) pression

(Idiom) **to feel the ~**○ en ressentir les effets

draughtproof GB, **draftproof** US /'drɑːftpruːf, US 'dræft-/

A adj calfeutré

B vtr calfeutrer

draughts /drɑːfts, US dræfts/ ▸ p. 881 n GB (jeu m de) dames fpl

draughty GB, **drafty** US /'drɑːftɪ, US 'dræftɪ/ adj plein de courants d'air

draw /drɔː/

A n **1)** Games tirage m (au sort); **2)** Sport match m nul; **it was a ~** (in race) ils sont arrivés ex aequo; **3)** (attraction) attraction f

B vtr (prét **drew**; pp **drawn**) **1)** lit faire [picture, plan]; dessiner [person, object]; tracer [line]; **2)** fig dépeindre [character, picture]; faire [comparison]; **3)** (pull) [animal, engine] tirer; [machine, suction] aspirer; **he drew the child towards him** il a attiré l'enfant vers lui; **he drew his finger along the shelf** il a passé un doigt sur l'étagère; **to ~ blood** provoquer un saignement; **4)** (derive) tirer [conclusion] (**from** de); **I drew comfort from the fact that** cela m'a un peu réconforté de savoir que; **he drew hope from this** cela lui a donné de l'espoir; **to be drawn from** [energy, information] provenir de; **5)** (cause to talk) faire parler [person] (**about, on** de); **to ~ sth from** ou **out of sb** obtenir qch de qn [information]; arracher qch à qn [truth, smile]; **6)** (attract) attirer [crowd] (**to** vers); **his speech drew great applause** son discours a soulevé des applaudissements; **to ~ sb into** mêler qn à [conversation]; entraîner qn dans [argument, battle]; **they were drawn together by their love of animals** leur amour des animaux les a rapprochés; **to ~ the enemy fire** offrir une cible au feu ennemi; **7)** Fin retirer [money] (**from** de); tirer [cheque] (**on** sur); toucher [wages, pension]; **8)** Games, Sport tirer [qch] au sort [ticket]; **to ~ a match** faire match nul; **9)** (remove) retirer [cork] (**from** de); sortir [sword, knife, gun]; tirer [card]

C vi (prét **drew**; pp **drawn**) **1)** (make picture) dessiner; **2)** (move) **to ~ ahead (of sth/sb)** lit gagner du terrain (sur qch/qn); fig prendre de l'avance (sur qch/qn); **to ~ alongside** [boat] accoster; **the car drew alongside the lorry** la voiture s'est mise à côté du camion; **to ~ close** ou **near** [time] approcher; **they drew nearer to listen** ils se sont rapprochés pour écouter; **to ~ into** [bus] arriver à [station]; **the train drew into the station** le train est entré en gare; **to ~ level** se retrouver au même niveau; **to ~ over** [vehicle] (stop) se ranger; (still moving) se rabattre vers le bas-côté; **to ~ round** ou **around** se rassembler; **to ~ to a halt** s'arrêter; **to ~ to a close** ou **an end** [day, event] toucher à sa fin; **3)** (in match) faire match nul; **4)** (choose at random) **to ~ for sth** tirer qch (au sort); **5)** [tea] infuser

to be quick/slow on the ~° (in understanding) avoir l'esprit vif/lent; (in replying) avoir/ne pas avoir la repartie facile; [*cowboy*] dégainer/ne pas dégainer vite; **to ▸ the line** fixer des limites

(Phrasal verbs)

■ **draw apart** se séparer
■ **draw aside**: ▸ **~ [sth] aside**, **~ aside [sth]** écarter; ▸ **~ [sb] aside** prendre [qn] à part
■ **draw away**: ▸ **~ away** (move off) s'éloigner (**from** de); (move ahead) prendre de l'avance (**from** sur); (recoil) avoir un mouvement de recul; ▸ **~ [sth/sb] away**, **~ away [sth/sb]** retirer [*hand, foot*]; éloigner [*person, object*]; distraire [qn] de [*book, task*]
■ **draw back**: ▸ **~ back** reculer; ▸ **~ [sth] back**, **~ back [sth]** ouvrir [*curtains*]; retirer [*hand, foot*]; ▸ **~ [sb] back**, **~ back [sb]** faire revenir
■ **draw down**: ▸ **~ [sth] down**, **~ down [sth]** baisser
■ **draw in**: ▸ **~ in** ① [*days, nights*] raccourcir; ② (arrive) [*bus*] arriver; [*train*] entrer en gare; ▸ **~ [sth] in**, **~ in [sth]** ① (in picture) ajouter; ② tirer sur [*rope*]; rentrer [*stomach, claws*]; ③ (suck in) [*person*] aspirer [*air*]; [*pump, machine*] aspirer [*air, liquid, gas*]; **to ~ in one's breath** inspirer; ④ (attract) attirer
■ **draw off**: ▸ **~ off** [*vehicle, train*] partir; ▸ **~ [sth] off**, **~ off [sth]** tirer [*beer, water*]; retirer [*gloves*]; Med évacuer [*fluid*]
■ **draw on**: ▸ **~ on** (approach) approcher; (pass) [*time*] passer; [*evening, day, season*] (s')avancer; ▸ **~ on [sth]** exploiter [*skills, reserves*]; **the report ~s on information from...** le rapport tire des informations de...; **to ~ on one's experience** faire appel à son expérience
■ **draw out**: ▸ **~ out** ① [*train, bus*] partir; **the train drew out of the station** le train a quitté la station; **a car drew out in front of me** une voiture a déboîté devant moi; ② [*day, night*] rallonger; ▸ **~ [sth] out**, **~ out [sth]** ① gen tirer [*handkerchief, purse, knife*] (**from, out of** de); retirer [*nail, cork*] (**from, out of** de); aspirer [*liquid, air*]; ② Fin retirer [*cash, money*]; ③ (cause to last longer) faire durer [*event*]; (unnecessarily) faire traîner; ④ obtenir [*information, confession*]; (using force) soutirer; ▸ **~ [sb] out** faire sortir [qn] de sa coquille
■ **draw up**: ▸ **~ up** s'arrêter; ▸ **~ up [sth]**, **~ [sth] up** ① établir [*contract, programme, proposals*]; dresser, établir [*list, plan, report*]; ② (pull) hisser [*bucket*]; approcher [*chair*] (**to** de); ③ tirer sur [*thread*]; ▸ **~ oneself up** se redresser

drawback /'drɔːbæk/ *n* inconvénient *m*
drawer /'drɔː(r)/ *n* ① tiroir *m*; ② Fin tireur/-euse *m/f*
drawing /'drɔːɪŋ/
Ⓐ *n* dessin *m*
Ⓑ *noun modifier* [*class, teacher, tools*] de dessin; [*paper, pen*] à dessin
drawing board *n* (board) planche *f* à dessin; **we'll have to go back to the ~** fig il faudra tout recommencer; **the project never got off the ~** fig le projet n'a jamais dépassé le stade de l'étude
drawing: **~ pin** *n* punaise *f*; **~ room** *n* salon *m*
drawl /drɔːl/
Ⓐ *n* voix *f* traînante
Ⓑ *vi* parler d'une voix traînante
drawn /drɔːn/
Ⓐ *pp* ▸ **draw**
Ⓑ *adj* ① [*features*] tiré; **to look ~** avoir les traits tirés; ② [*game, match*] nul/nulle
dread /dred/
Ⓐ *n* terreur *f*; **to have a ~ of sth** être terrifié par qch; (weaker) avoir horreur de qch
Ⓑ *vtr* appréhender; (stronger) redouter; **I ~ to think!** je préfère ne pas y penser!
dreadful /'dredfl/ *adj* [*weather, person*] affreux/-euse; [*day, accident*] épouvantable; [*film, book, meal*] lamentable; **I had a ~ time trying to convince him** j'ai eu toutes les peines du monde à le convaincre; **to feel ~** ne pas se sentir bien du tout; **to feel ~ about sth** avoir honte de qch
dreadfully /'dredfəli/ *adv* [*disappointed, cross, short of money*] terriblement; [*suffer*] affreusement; [*behave*] abominablement; **I'm ~ sorry** je suis navré
dream /driːm/
Ⓐ *n* rêve *m*; **I had a ~ about sth/about doing** j'ai rêvé de qch/que je faisais; **to be in a ~** être dans les nuages; **to make sb's ~ come true** faire que le rêve de qn devienne réalité; **it worked like a ~** ça a marché à merveille

Ⓑ *noun modifier* [*house, car, vacation*] de rêve
Ⓒ *vtr* (*prét, pp* **dreamt** /dremt/, **~ed**) ① (while asleep) rêver (**that** que); ② (imagine) **I never dreamt (that)** je n'aurais jamais pensé que
Ⓓ *vi* (*prét, pp* **dreamt** /dremt/, **~ed**) rêver; **he dreamt about** *ou* **of sth/doing** il a rêvé de qch/qu'il faisait; **you must be ~ing if you think...** tu te fais des illusions si tu crois que...; **I wouldn't ~ of doing** il ne me viendrait jamais à l'esprit de faire

(Phrasal verb)

■ **dream up**: ▸ **~ up [sth]** concevoir [*idea*]; imaginer [*character, plot*]

dreamer /'driːmə(r)/ *n* (inattentive person) rêveur/-euse *m/f*; (idealist) idéaliste *mf*
dreamworld /'driːmwɜːld/ *n* monde *m* de rêves
dreamy /'driːmɪ/ *adj* ① (distracted) rêveur/-euse; [*sound, music*] doux/douce; ② °(attractive) [*person*] séduisant; [*object*] ravissant
dreary /'drɪərɪ/ *adj* [*weather, landscape*] morne; [*person*] ennuyeux/-euse; [*life, routine*] monotone
dredge /dredʒ/ *vtr* ① draguer [*river*]; ② Culin saupoudrer (**with** de)

(Phrasal verb)

■ **dredge up**: ▸ **~ up [sth]**, **~ [sth] up** lit remonter qch (à la drague); fig exhumer [*incidents*]

dregs /dregz/ *npl* (of wine) lie *f*; (of coffee) marc *m*; **the ~ of society** la lie de la société
drench /drentʃ/ *vtr* (in rain, sweat) tremper (**in** de); (in perfume) asperger (**in** de); **~ed to the skin** trempé jusqu'aux os
dress /dres/ ▸ p. 1191
Ⓐ *n* ① robe *f*; ② Ⓒ tenue *f*; **his style of ~** son style vestimentaire
Ⓑ *noun modifier* [*material, design*] de robe
Ⓒ *vtr* ① habiller [*person*]; **to get ~ed** s'habiller; ② Culin assaisonner [*salad*]; préparer [*meat, fish*]; ③ Med panser [*wound*]
Ⓓ *vi* s'habiller; **to ~ in a suit** mettre un costume
Ⓔ *v refl* **to ~ oneself** s'habiller

(Idiom) **~ed to kill** habillé de façon irrésistible

(Phrasal verbs)

■ **dress down**: ▸ **~ down** s'habiller 'décontracté'
■ **dress up**: ▸ **~ up** (smartly) s'habiller; (in fancy dress) se déguiser (**as** en); ▸ **~ [sb] up**, **~ up [sb]** déguiser; ▸ **~ [sth] up**, **~ up [sth]** agrémenter

dress: **~ circle** *n* Theat premier balcon *m*; **~ designer** ▸ p. 1181 *n* modéliste *mf*
dresser /'dresə(r)/ *n* ① **to be a sloppy/stylish ~** s'habiller mal/avec chic; ② (for dishes) buffet *m*; US (for clothes) commode-coiffeuse *f*
dressing /'dresɪŋ/ *n* ① Med pansement *m*; ② (sauce) sauce *f*; ③ US (stuffing) farce *f*
dressing: **~ gown** *n* robe *f* de chambre; **~ room** *n* Theat loge *f*; (in house) dressing *m*; **~ table** *n* coiffeuse *f*
dress: **~maker** ▸ p. 1181 *n* couturière *f*; **~making** *n* couture *f*; **~ rehearsal** *n* (répétition *f*) générale *f*
dress sense *n* **to have ~** s'habiller avec goût
dressy° /'dresɪ/ *adj* habillé
drew /druː/ *prét* ▸ **draw**
dribble /'drɪbl/
Ⓐ *n* ① (of liquid) filet *m*; (of saliva) bave *f*; ② Sport drible *m*
Ⓑ *vtr* ① laisser dégouliner [*liquid*] (**on, onto** sur); ② Sport dribbler
Ⓒ *vi* ① [*liquid*] dégouliner (**on, onto** sur; **from** de); [*person*] baver; ② Sport dribbler
dried /draɪd/
Ⓐ *prét, pp* ▸ **dry**
Ⓑ *adj* [*fruit, herb, pulse*] sec/sèche; [*flower, vegetable*] séché; [*milk, egg*] en poudre
drier /'draɪə(r)/ *n* (clothes, hair) séchoir *m*; (helmet type) casque *m*
drift /drɪft/
Ⓐ *n* ① (flow, movement) **the ~ of the current** le sens du courant; **the ~ of events** fig le cours des événements; **the ~ from the land** l'exode *m* rural; **the slow ~ of strikers back to work** le lent retour des grévistes au travail; ② (of snow) congère *f*; (of leaves, sand) tas *m*; (of smoke, mist) nuage *m*; ③ (general meaning) sens *m* (général); **to catch the ~ of sb's argument** comprendre où quelqu'un veut en venir

B *vi* **1)** (be carried by current) dériver; (by wind) [*balloon*] voler à la dérive; [*smoke, fog*] flotter; **2)** (pile up) [*snow*] former des congères *fpl*; [*leaves*] s'amonceler; **3) to ~ along** [*person*] lit flâner; fig se laisser aller; **to ~ from job to job** passer d'un emploi à un autre

(Phrasal verbs)

■ **drift apart** se détacher progressivement (**from** de)
■ **drift off** (doze off) s'assoupir; (leave) s'en aller lentement

drill /drɪl/

A *n* **1)** (tool) (for wood, metal, masonry) perceuse *f*; (for oil) trépan *m*; (for mining) foreuse *f*; (for teeth) roulette *f*; **power ~** perceuse *f* électrique; **2)** Mil exercice *m*; **3) fire ~** exercice *m* d'évacuation en cas d'incendie

B *vtr* **1)** gen percer; passer la roulette à [*tooth*]; **2)** Mil entraîner; **3) to ~ sb in sth** former (intensivement) qn à qch

C *vi* **1)** (in wood, metal, masonry) percer un trou (**into** dans); **to ~ for sth** faire des forages pour trouver qch; **2)** Mil faire de l'exercice; **3)** fig **to ~ sth into sb** faire entrer qch dans la tête de qn

drilling /'drɪlɪŋ/ *n* (for oil, gas, water) forage *m* (**for** pour trouver); (in wood, metal, masonry) perçage *m*

drink /drɪŋk/

A *n* **1)** (nonalcoholic) boisson *f*; **to have a ~** boire quelque chose; **2)** (alcoholic) verre *m*; **3)** (act of drinking) **to take** *ou* **have a ~ of sth** boire une gorgée de qch; **4) ₵** (collectively) boisson *f*; (alcoholic) alcool *m*

B *vtr* (*prét* **drank**; *pp* **drunk**) boire (**from sth** dans qch)

C *vi* (*prét* **drank**; *pp* **drunk**) boire (**from, out of** dans); **don't ~ and drive** ne conduisez pas si vous avez bu; **2)** (as toast) **to ~ to the bride** boire à la mariée

(Idioms) **to drive sb to ~** pousser qn à la boisson; **I'll ~ to that!** excellente idée!

(Phrasal verbs)

■ **drink in:** ▸ **~ in** [sth] respirer [*air*]; s'imbiber de [*atmosphere*]; [*roots*] absorber [*water*]
■ **drink up:** ▸ **~ up** finir son verre; ▸ **~ up** [sth], **~** [sth] **up** finir

drinkable /'drɪŋkəbl/ *adj* (safe) potable; (nice) buvable

drink-driving *n* GB conduite *f* en état d'ivresse

drinker /'drɪŋkə(r)/ *n* **1)** gen buveur/-euse *m/f*; **2)** (of alcohol) **to be a ~** boire

drinking /'drɪŋkɪŋ/

A *n* (of alcohol) consommation *f* d'alcool; **~ and driving** l'alcool au volant

B *noun modifier* [*laws*] sur l'alcool; [*companion*] de beuverie

drinking: **~ chocolate** *n* GB chocolat *m* en poudre; **~ water** *n* eau *f* potable

drink: **~ problem** *n* GB penchant *m* pour la boisson; **~s cupboard** *n* GB bar *m*; **~s dispenser** *n* GB distributeur *m* de boissons; **~s machine** *n* GB machine *f* à boissons; **~s party** *n* GB cocktail *m*

drip /drɪp/

A *n* **1)** goutte *f* (qui tombe); **the constant ~ of a tap** le bruit continuel d'un robinet qui goutte; **2)** GB Med (device) goutte-à-goutte *m inv*; (solution) sérum *m*; **to be on a ~** être sous perfusion

B *vtr* (*p prés etc* **-pp-**) [*object*] laisser tomber [qch] goutte à goutte [*liquid*]; [*person*] dégouliner de [*sweat, blood*]; **to ~ sth onto** *ou* **down sth** faire goutter qch sur qch

C *vi* (*p prés etc* **-pp-**) **1)** [*liquid*] tomber goutte à goutte; **to ~ from** *ou* **off** dégouliner de; **2)** [*tap, branches*] goutter; [*washing*] s'égoutter; [*engine*] fuir; **to be ~ping with** dégouliner de [*liquid*]; ruisseler de [*sweat*]

drip-dry

A *adj* qui se lave et s'étend sans essorage

B *vtr* **'wash and ~'** 'laver et étendre sans essorer'

drip feed /'drɪp fiːd/ *n* alimentation *f* par perfusion

dripping /'drɪpɪŋ/

A *n* Culin graisse *f* de rôti

B *adj* [*tap*] qui goutte; [*trees*] ruisselant; [*washing*] trempé; **~ wet** trempé

drive /draɪv/

A *n* **1)** (in car) **to go for a ~** aller faire un tour (en voiture); **it's only five minutes' ~ from here** ce n'est qu'à cinq minutes d'ici en voiture; **it's a 40 km ~** il y a 40 km de route; **2)** (campaign) campagne *f* (**against** contre; **for, towards** pour; **to do** pour faire); **3)** (motivation) dynamisme *m*;

m; **the ~ to win** la volonté de vaincre; **4)** Comput entraînement *m* de disques; **5)** Aut transmission *f*; **6)** (path) allée *f*; **7)** Sport drive *m*

B *noun modifier* Aut [*mechanism*] de transmission

C *vtr* (*prét* **drove**; *pp* **driven**) **1)** conduire [*vehicle, passenger*]; piloter [*racing car*]; transporter [*cargo, load*]; parcourir [qch] (en voiture) [*distance*]; **I ~ 15 km every day** je fais 15 km en voiture chaque jour; **to ~ sth into** rentrer qch dans [*garage, space*]; **2)** (compel) pousser (**to do** à faire); **to be driven out of business** être conduit à la faillite; **3)** (chase or herd) conduire; **he was driven from** *ou* **out of the country** il a été chassé du pays; **4)** (power, propel) actionner; **the generator is driven by steam** le générateur fonctionne à la vapeur; **5)** (force, push) lit, fig pousser [*boat, person*]; enfoncer [*nail*]; faire passer [*road*]; **6)** Sport (in golf) envoyer [*ball*]; (in tennis) envoyer [qch] d'un coup droit [*ball*]

D *vi* (*prét* **drove**; *pp* **driven**) **1)** Aut conduire; **to ~ along** rouler; **you can't ~ along the High Street** on n'a pas le droit de circuler dans la grand-rue; **to ~ to work** aller au travail en voiture; **to ~ into** entrer dans [*garage, space*]; rentrer dans [*tree, lamppost*]; **to ~ up/down a hill** monter/ descendre une côte; **to ~ past** passer; **2)** Sport (in golf) driver; (in tennis) faire un drive

E *v refl* **to ~ oneself 1)** Aut conduire soi-même; **2) to ~ one-self to do** se forcer à faire; **to ~ oneself too hard** se surmener

(Phrasal verbs)

■ **drive away:** ▸ **~ away** démarrer; ▸ **~ away** [sth/sb], **~** [sth/sb] **away 1)** Aut faire démarrer; **2)** faire partir [*animals, persons*]; chasser [*fear, cares*]
■ **drive at: what are you driving at?** où veux-tu en venir?
■ **drive back:** ▸ **~ back** rentrer; **to ~ there and back** faire l'aller-retour; ▸ **~ back** [sth/sb], **~** [sth/sb] **back 1)** (repel) repousser [*people, animals*]; **2)** Aut ramener
■ **drive off** Aut démarrer
■ **drive on:** ▸ **~ on** (continue) poursuivre sa route; (set off again) repartir; ▸ **~** [sb] **on** pousser
■ **drive out:** ▸ **~ out** [sth/sb], **~** [sth/sb] **out** chasser

drivel○ /'drɪvl/ *n* ₵ bêtises *fpl*

driven /'drɪvn/

A *pp* ▸ **drive**

B *adj* passionné, motivé

C **-driven** *combining form* **petrol-/motor-~** à essence/moteur; **market-~** déterminé par le marché

driver /'draɪvə(r)/ *n* **1)** gen conducteur/-trice *m/f*; (chauffeur) chauffeur *m*; **~s** (motorists) automobilistes *mfpl*; **2)** (mechanical) actionneur *m*; **3)** Comput pilote *m*, gestionnaire *m* de périphérique

driver: **~'s license** *n* US = driving licence; **~'s seat** *n* = driving seat

drive: **~-through** *n* US comptoir *m* de vente à l'extérieur; **~way** *n* allée *f*

driving /'draɪvɪŋ/

A *n* conduite *f*; **his ~ has improved** il conduit mieux qu'avant

B *noun modifier* [*skills, offence*] de conduite

C *adj* [*rain*] battant; [*wind, hail*] cinglant

driving: **~ force** *n* (person) force *f* agissante (**behind** de); (money, ambition, belief) moteur *m* (**behind** de); **~ instructor** ▸ p. 1181 *n* moniteur/-trice *m/f* d'auto-école; **~ lesson** *n* cours *m* de conduite; **~ licence** GB *n* permis *m* de conduire; **~ mirror** *n* rétroviseur *m*; **~ school** *n* auto-école *f*

driving seat *n* place *f* du conducteur

(Idiom) **to be in the ~** être aux commandes

driving test *n* examen *m* du permis de conduire

drizzle /'drɪzl/

A *n* bruine *f*

B *vi* bruiner

droll /drəʊl/ *adj* drôle

drone /drəʊn/

A *n* (of engine) ronronnement *m*; (of insects) bourdonnement *m*

B *vi* [*engine*] ronronner; [*insect*] bourdonner

(Phrasal verb)

■ **drone on** péj faire de longs discours rasants○

drool /druːl/ *vi* lit baver; ○fig baver (d'envie); **to ~ over sth/ sb** s'extasier

droop /druːp/
A n affaissement m
B vi [eyelids, head] tomber; [branch, shoulders, wings] s'affaisser; [flower, plant] commencer à se faner

drop /drɒp/
A n **1** gen, Med goutte f; **~ by ~** goutte à goutte; **2** (decrease) gen diminution f (**in** de); (in temperature) baisse f (**in** de); **a 5% ~ in sth** une baisse de 5% de qch; **3** (vertical distance) **there's a ~ of 100 m from the top** il y a une hauteur de 100 m du sommet; **there was a steep ~ on either side** il y avait une pente abrupte de chaque côté; **4** (delivery) (from aircraft) largage m; (from lorry, van) livraison f; (parachute jump) saut m en parachute
B vtr (p prés etc **-pp-**) **1** (allow to fall) (by accident) laisser tomber; (on purpose) mettre, lâcher; **2** (deliver) [aircraft] parachuter [person, supplies, equipment]; larguer [bomb]; **3** (leave) (also ~ **off**) déposer [person, object]; **4** (lower) baisser [level, price]; **to ~ one's eyes** baisser les yeux; **5** **to ~ a hint about sth** faire allusion à qch; **to ~ sb a note** envoyer un mot à qn; **6** (exclude) (deliberately) supprimer [article, episode]; écarter [player]; (by mistake) omettre [figure, letter, item on list]; ne pas prononcer [sound]; **7** (abandon) laisser tomber [friend, school subject]; renoncer à [habit, idea]; abandonner [conversation, matter]; retirer [accusation]; **to ~ everything** tout laisser tomber; **can we ~ that subject, please?** on ne pourrait pas parler d'autre chose?; **8** gen, Sport (lose) perdre [point, game]
C vi (p prés etc **-pp-**) **1** (fall) [object] tomber; [person] (deliberately) se laisser tomber; (by accident) tomber; **we ~ped to the ground as the plane flew over** nous nous sommes jetés à terre quand l'avion est passé au-dessus de nous; **the plane ~ped to an altitude of 1,000 m** l'avion est descendu à une altitude de 1 000 m; **2** (fall away) **the cliff ~s into the sea** la falaise tombe dans la mer; **the road ~s steeply down the mountain** la route descend abruptement le long de la montagne; ► **drop away**; **3** (decrease) baisser; **to ~ (from sth) to sth** tomber (de qch) à qch; **she ~ped to third place** elle est descendue à la troisième place

Idioms **to ~ a brick**° ou **clanger**° faire une gaffe°; **a ~ in the bucket** ou **ocean** une goutte d'eau dans la mer; **to ~ sb in it**° mettre qn dans le pétrin°; **to be ready** ou **fit to ~** tomber de fatigue

Phrasal verbs
■ **drop away** **1** (diminish) diminuer; **2** (fall steeply) descendre brusquement
■ **drop back** (deliberately) rester en arrière; (unable to keep up) prendre du retard
■ **drop by** passer
■ **drop in**: ► **~ in** [person] passer; ► **~ [sth] in**, **~ in [sth]** I'll **~ it in** (to you) later je passerai te le donner plus tard
■ **drop off**: ► **~ off** **1** (fall off) tomber; **2** **~ off (to sleep)** s'endormir; **3** (become smaller) diminuer; ► **~ [sth/sb] off**, **~ off [sth/sb]** = **drop B 3**
■ **drop out** **1** (fall out) tomber (**of** de); **2** (from race) se désister; (from project) se retirer; (from school, university) abandonner ses études; (from society) se marginaliser
■ **drop over** = **drop round**
■ **drop round**: ► **~ round** [person] passer; ► **~ [sth] round**, **~ round [sth]** I'll **~ your books round** je passerai te donner tes livres

drop: **~ goal** n drop m; **~ handlebars** npl guidon m de course; **~ kick** n coup m de pied tombé

dropout /'drɒpaʊt/ n (from society) marginal/-e m/f; (from school) étudiant/-e m/f qui abandonne ses études

droppings /'drɒpɪŋz/ npl (of mouse, rabbit, sheep) crottes fpl; (of horse) crottin m; (of bird) fiente f

drop shot n Sport amorti m

drop zone, **dropping zone** n (for supplies etc) zone f de largage; (for parachutist) zone f de saut

drought /draʊt/ n sécheresse f

drove /drəʊv/
A prét ► **drive**
B n **~s of people** des foules fpl de gens

drown /draʊn/
A vtr lit, fig noyer [person, animal, food]; couvrir [sound]
B vi se noyer
C v refl **to ~ oneself** se noyer

Idiom **to ~ one's sorrows** noyer son chagrin dans l'alcool

■ **drown out**: ► **~ [sth] out**, **~ out [sth]** couvrir [sound]; ► **~ [sb] out** couvrir la voix de [person]

drowning /'draʊnɪŋ/
A n noyade f
B adj [person] qui se noie

drowse /draʊz/ vi (be half asleep) être à moitié endormi; (sleep lightly) somnoler

drowsiness /'draʊzɪnɪs/ n somnolence f

drowsy /'draʊzɪ/ adj à moitié endormi; **to feel ~** avoir envie de dormir

drug /drʌg/
A n **1** Med médicament m; **to be on ~s** prendre des médicaments; **2** (narcotic) drogue f; **to be on** ou **to take ~s** gen se droguer; Sport se doper
B noun modifier **1** (narcotic) [problem, shipment, smuggler, trafficking] de drogue; [culture, use] de la drogue; **2** Med [company, industry] pharmaceutique
C vtr (p prés etc **-gg-**) **1** (sedate) [kidnapper] administrer des somnifères à [victim]; [vet] endormir [animal]; **2** (dope) mettre un somnifère dans [drink]; Sport doper [horse]

drug: ~ abuse n consommation f de stupéfiants; **~ addict** n toxicomane mf; **~ addiction** n toxicomanie f

drugged /drʌgd/ adj [person] drogué; [state] d'abrutissement; [drink] additionné d'un narcotique

drug rape n **to be a victim of ~** être victime d'un viol après avoir été drogué/-e

drug: ~-related adj lié à la drogue; **~s charges** npl **to be arrested on ~s charges** être arrêté pour infraction f à la législation sur les stupéfiants; **Drug Squad** n GB brigade f des stupéfiants; **~s raid** n opération f antidrogue; **~s ring** n réseau m de trafiquants de drogue; **~store** n US drugstore m; **~-taking** n gen usage m de stupéfiants; Sport dopage m; **~ test** n Med Sport contrôle m antidopage; **~ user** n toxicomane mf

drum /drʌm/
A n ► p. 1028 **1** Mus tambour m; **2** Ind, Comm bidon m; (larger) baril m; **3** Aut tambour m
B **drums** npl batterie f
C vtr (p prés etc **-mm-**) **to ~ one's fingers** tambouriner des doigts (**on** sur); **to ~ sth into sb** fig enfoncer qch dans le crâne de qn°
D vi (p prés etc **-mm-**) **1** (beat drum) jouer du tambour; **2** (make drumming sound) [rain] tambouriner

Phrasal verbs
■ **drum home**: ► **~ [sth] home** réussir à faire comprendre [lesson, point]
■ **drum out**: ► **~ [sb] out** expulser [person]
■ **drum up**: ► **~ up [sth]** trouver [business, custom]; ► **~ up [sb]** racoler; **to ~ up sb's support for** obtenir le soutien de qn en faveur de

drum kit n batterie f

drummer /'drʌmə(r)/ ► p. 1181, p. 1028 n Mil tambour m; (jazz or pop) batteur m; (classical) percussionniste mf

drumstick /'drʌmstɪk/ n **1** Mus baguette f de tambour; **2** Culin pilon m

drunk /drʌŋk/
A pp ► **drink**
B n ivrogne/-esse m/f
C adj lit, fig; **to get ~** s'enivrer (**on** de); **to get sb ~** faire boire qn

drunkard /'drʌŋkəd/ n ivrogne/-esse m/f

drunken /'drʌŋkən/ adj [person] ivre; [party] bien arrosé; [sleep] éthylique; [state] d'ivresse

drunkenly /'drʌŋkənlɪ/ adv lit [shout, laugh] d'une voix avinée; [walk] en titubant

dry /draɪ/
A adj **1** gen sec/sèche; **to run ~** se tarir; **to keep sth ~** tenir qch au sec; **to get ~** se sécher; **to get sth ~** (faire) sécher qch; **to wipe sth ~** essuyer qch; **on ~ land** sur la terre ferme; **a ~ day** un jour sans pluie; **2** fig [wit, person, remark] pince-sans-rire inv; [book, subject matter] aride; (forbidding alcohol) [state] qui interdit la vente de boissons alcoolisées
B vtr faire sécher [clothes, washing]; sécher [meat, produce]; **to ~ the dishes** essuyer la vaisselle; **to ~ one's hands** se sécher les mains
C vi sécher
D v refl **to ~ oneself** se sécher

(Idiom) **(as)** ~ **as dust** ennuyeux/-euse comme la pluie

(Phrasal verbs)
■ **dry off:** ▶ ~ **off** [*material, object*] sécher; [*person*] se sécher; ▶ ~ **off** [**sb/sth**], ~ [**sb/sth**] **off** sécher [*person, object*]

■ **dry out** ① sécher; ② ○[*alcoholic*] se faire désintoxiquer

■ **dry up:** ▶ ~ **up** ① [*river, well*] s'assécher; ② fig (run out) se tarir; ③ (wipe crockery) essuyer la vaisselle; ▶ ~ **up** [**sth**], ~ [**sth**] **up** assécher [*puddle, river*]; essuyer [*crockery*]

dry cell *n* pile *f* sèche

dry-clean *vtr* nettoyer [qch] à sec; **to have sth ~ed** faire nettoyer qch (chez le teinturier)

dry: ~**-cleaner's** ▸ p. 1181 *n* teinturerie *f*; ~**-cleaning** *n* nettoyage *m* à sec

dryer /'draɪə(r)/ *n* = **drier**

dry ice *n* neige *f* carbonique

drying-up /ˌdraɪɪŋ'ʌp/ *n* GB **to do the** ~ essuyer la vaisselle

dryness /'draɪnɪs/ *n* sécheresse *f*; fig causticité *f*

dry rot *n* pourriture *f* sèche (*du bois*)

DSS *n* GB (abrév = **Department of Social Security**) ① (ministry) ministère *m* des Affaires sociales; ② (local office) *service social responsable des chômeurs*

DT *n*: abrév ▶ **data transmission**

DTI *n* GB abrév ▶ **Department of Trade and Industry**

DTP *n* (abrév = **desktop publishing**) PAO *f*

dual /'dju:əl, US 'du:əl/ *adj* double

dual: ~ **carriageway** *n* GB route *f* à quatre voies; ~**-purpose** *adj* à double usage

dub /dʌb/ *vtr* (*p prés etc* **-bb-**) (into foreign language) doubler (**into** en); (add soundtrack) postsynchroniser [*film*]; mixer [*sound effect*] (**onto** à)

dubbing /'dʌbɪŋ/ *n* (into foreign language) doublage *m*; (adding soundtrack) postsynchronisation *f*; (sound mixing) mixage *m*

dubious /'dju:bɪəs, US 'du:-/ *adj* [*translation, reputation, answer*] douteux/-euse; [*motive, claim*] suspect; [*distinction*] discutable; [*person*] **to be** ~ **(about sth)** avoir des doutes (en ce qui concerne qch)

dubiously /'dju:bɪəslɪ, US 'du:-/ *adv* [*say*] dubitativement; [*look at*] d'un air incertain

duchess /'dʌtʃɪs/ ▸ p. 869 *n* duchesse *f*

duck /dʌk/
A *n* (*pl* ~**s**, *collective* ~) Zool, Culin canard *m*; (female) cane *f*
B *vtr* ① (dodge) baisser la tête; ② (dodge) lit, fig esquiver; se dérober à [*responsibility*]
C *vi* baisser la tête; [*boxer*] esquiver un coup; **to** ~ **behind sth** se cacher derrière qch

(Idioms) **he took to it like a** ~ **to water** il s'y est mis comme s'il avait fait ça toute sa vie; **it's like water off a** ~**'s back** ça ne le/la etc touche absolument pas

duct /dʌkt/ *n* (for air, water) conduit *m*; (for wiring) canalisation *f*; Med conduit *m*

dud○ /dʌd/
A *n* **to be a** ~ [*banknote*] être faux/fausse; [*machine*] être détraqué; [*film*] être nul/nulle○
B *adj* [*banknote*] faux/fausse; [*cheque*] en bois○; [*machine*] détraqué; [*book, movie*] nul/nulle○

due /dju:, US du:/
A *n* dû *m*; **I must give her her** ~**, she...** il faut lui rendre cette justice, elle...
B *dues* *npl* (for membership) cotisation *f*; (for import, taxes etc) droits *mpl*
C *adj* ① (payable) **to be/fall** ~ arriver/venir à échéance; **when** ~ à l'échéance; **the rent is** ~ **on the 6th** le loyer doit être payé le 6; **the balance** ~ le solde dû; ② (entitled to) **they should pay him what is** ~ **to him** on devrait lui payer l'argent auquel il a droit; ③ (about to be paid, given) **I'm** ~ **some back pay** on me doit des arriérés; **we are** ~ **(for) a wage increase soon** nos salaires doivent bientôt être augmentés; ④ (appropriate) **with** ~ **solemnity** avec toute la solennité qui s'impose/s'imposait etc; **after** ~ **consideration** après mûre réflexion; **you will receive a letter in** ~ **course** vous recevrez une lettre en temps utile; **in** ~ **course it transpired that** à la longue il est apparu que; ⑤ (expected) **to be** ~ **to do** devoir faire; **we are** ~ **to leave in the evening** nous devons partir le soir; **to be** ~ **(in)** ou

~ **to arrive** [*train, bus*] être attendu; [*person*] devoir arriver

D *adv* (directly) ~ **north** [*building*] être orienté plein nord; **to go** ~ **south** aller droit vers le sud

E **due to** *prep phr* en raison de; **he resigned** ~ **to the fact that** il a démissionné parce que; **to be** ~ **to** [*delay, cancellation*] être dû/due à; ~ **to unforeseen circumstances** pour des raisons indépendantes de notre volonté; **it's all** ~ **to you** c'est uniquement grâce à toi

duel /'dju:əl, US 'du:əl/ *n* lit, fig duel *m*

duet /dju:'et, US du:-/ *n* (composition) duo *m* also fig

dug /dʌg/ *prét, pp* ▶ **dig C, D**

duke /dju:k, US du:k/ ▸ p. 869 *n* duc *m*

dull /dʌl/
A *adj* ① (uninteresting) [*person, play, book*] ennuyeux/-euse; [*life, journey*] monotone; [*music*] sans intérêt; [*food*] médiocre; [*appearance, outfit*] triste; ② (not bright) [*eye, colour*] éteint; [*weather, day*] maussade; [*complexion*] terne; ③ (muffled) [*explosion*] sourd; ④ (not sharp) [*pain*] sourd; ⑤ Fin [*market*] terne
B *vtr* ternir [*shine*]; émousser [*blade, senses, pain*]

dullness /'dʌlnɪs/ *n* (of life) ennui *m*; (of routine) monotonie *f*; (of company, conversation) manque *m* d'intérêt

dully /'dʌlɪ/ *adv* [*say, repeat*] d'un ton morne; [*gleam*] faiblement; [*move, trail*] lourdement

duly /'dju:lɪ, US 'du:-/ *adv* (in proper fashion) gen, Jur dûment; (as expected, as arranged) comme prévu

dumb /dʌm/ *adj* ① (handicapped) muet/muette *voir note*; ~ **animals** les bêtes *fpl*; **to be struck** ~ rester muet/muette; ② ○(stupid) [*person*] bête; [*question, idea*] idiot

(Phrasal verb)
■ **dumb down:** ▶ ~ [**sth**] **down**, ~ **down** [**sth**] baisser le niveau de [*course, TV programmes, news coverage*].

⚠ Ce mot peut être perçu comme injurieux dans cette acception. Lui préférer *speech-impaired*

dumbfounded /dʌm'faʊndɪd/ *adj* abasourdi

dummy /'dʌmɪ/
A *n* ① (model) mannequin *m*; ② GB (for baby) tétine *f*; ③ (in bridge) (player) mort *m*
B *noun modifier* [*furniture, drawer*] factice; [*document*] faux/fausse; [*bullet*] à blanc; [*bomb*] d'exercice

dummy run *n* gen (trial) essai *m*; Mil attaque *f* simulée

dump /dʌmp/
A *n* ① (public) décharge *f* publique; (rubbish heap) tas *m* d'ordures; ② Mil **arms/munitions** ~ dépôt *m* d'armes/de munitions; ③ ○péj (town, village) trou○ *m*; (house) baraque○ *f* minable; ④ Comput vidage *m*; **screen** ~ recopie *f* d'écran
B *vtr* ① jeter [*refuse*]; ensevelir [*nuclear waste*]; déverser [*waste, sewage*]; ② ○(get rid of) plaquer○ [*boyfriend*]; se débarrasser de [*car, shopping*]; ③ ○(put down) poser○ [*car, shopping*]; ④ Comput faire un vidage de [*data*]

(Idiom) **to be down in the** ~**s** avoir le cafard○

dumper /'dʌmpə(r)/ *n* ① (small) motobasculeur *m*; ② (large truck) tombereau *m*, dumper *m*

dumping /'dʌmpɪŋ/ *n* ① déversement *m*; **'no** ~**'** 'interdiction de déposer des ordures'; ② Fin dumping *m*

dumpy /'dʌmpɪ/ *adj* (plump) boulot/-otte

dunce /dʌns/ *n* péj cancre *m* (**at, in** en)

dune /dju:n, US du:n/ *n* dune *f*

dung /dʌŋ/ *n* 𝗖 excrément *m*; (for manure) fumier *m*

dungarees /ˌdʌŋgə'ri:z/ *npl* (fashionwear) salopette *f*; (workwear) bleu *m* de travail

Dunkirk /dʌn'kɜːk/ ▸ p. 1276 *pr n* Dunkerque *f*

dunno○ /də'nəʊ/ = **don't know**

duo /'dju:əʊ, US 'du:əʊ/ *n* Theat, Mus, fig duo *m*

dupe /dju:p, US du:p/
A *n* dupe *f*
B *vtr* duper

duplicate
A /'dju:plɪkət, 'du:pləkət/ *n* ① (copy) (of document) double *m* (**of** de); (of painting, cassette) copie *f*; **in** ~ en deux exemplaires; ② (photocopy) photocopie *f*
B /'dju:plɪkət, 'du:pləkət/ *adj* ① (copied) [*cheque, receipt*] en duplicata; **a** ~ **key/document** un double de clé/de document; ② (in two parts) [*form, invoice*] en deux exemplaires
C /'dju:plɪkeɪt, US 'du:pləkeɪt/ *vtr* ① (copy) faire un double

de [document]; copier [painting, cassette]; **2** (photocopy) photocopier; **3** (repeat) refaire [qch] inutilement [work]; répéter [action, performance]

duplicity /dju:'plɪsətɪ, US du:-/ n duplicité f

durable /'djʊərəbl, US 'dʊərəbl/ adj [material] résistant; [equipment] solide; [friendship, tradition, goods] durable

duration /djʊ'reɪʃn, US dʊ'reɪʃn/ n durée f

(Idiom) **for the ~**○ pour une durée indéterminée

during /'djʊərɪŋ/ prep pendant, au cours de

dusk /dʌsk/ n (twilight) nuit f tombante, crépuscule m

dusky /'dʌskɪ/ adj [complexion] mat

dust /dʌst/

A n **1** (grime) poussière f; **thick with ~** couvert de poussière; **to allow the ~ to settle** lit laisser retomber la poussière; fig laisser les choses se calmer; **2** (fine powder) poudre f

B vtr épousseter [furniture]; saupoudrer [cake] (**with** de, avec); poudrer [face] (**with** de, avec)

C vi épousseter

(Idiom) **to bite the ~** [person] mordre la poussière; [plan, idea] tomber à l'eau

(Phrasal verbs)

■ **dust down**: ▸ **~** [sth] **down**, **~ down** [sth] épousseter

■ **dust off**: ▸ **~** [sth] **off**, **~ off** [sth] épousseter [surface]; brosser [crumbs, powder] (**from** de)

dust: **~bin** n GB poubelle f; **~bin man** n GB éboueur m; **~ cover** n (on book) jaquette f; (on furniture) housse f (de protection)

duster /'dʌstə(r)/ n chiffon m (à poussière)

dusting /'dʌstɪŋ/ n (cleaning) époussetage m; (of snow) fine couche f; Culin saupoudrage m

dust: **~ jacket** n jaquette f; **~man** n GB éboueur m

dustpan /'dʌstpæn/ n pelle f (à poussière); **a ~ and brush** une pelle (à poussière) et une balayette

dust sheet n housse f (de protection)

dusty /'dʌstɪ/ adj [house, table, road] poussiéreux/-euse; [climb, journey] dans la poussière (after n)

(Idiom) **to give sb a ~ answer** envoyer qn sur les roses○

Dutch /dʌtʃ/ ▸ p. 1032, p. 969

A n **1** (language) néerlandais m; **2** (people) **the ~** les Néerlandais mpl

B adj [culture, food, football, politics] néerlandais; [teacher, lesson, textbook] de néerlandais

(Idioms) **to go ~**○ payer chacun sa part; **to go ~ with sb**○ faire fifty-fifty avec qn○

Dutch: **~ cap** n diaphragme m (contraceptif); **~ courage** n courage m puisé dans l'alcool; **~woman** n Néerlandaise f

dutiable /'dju:tɪəbl, US 'du:-/ adj taxable; (at customs) passible de droits de douane

dutiful /'dju:tɪfl, US 'du:-/ adj (obedient) [person] dévoué; [smile] poli; (conscientious) [person] consciencieux/-ieuse

duty /'dju:tɪ, US 'du:tɪ/

A n **1** (obligation) devoir m (**to** envers); **to have a ~ to do** avoir le devoir de faire; **in the course of ~** Mil en service; gen dans l'exercice de ses fonctions; **to feel ~ bound to do** se sentir tenu de faire; **out of a sense of ~** par devoir; **2** (task) (gén pl) fonction f; **to take up one's duties** prendre ses fonctions; **to perform** ou **carry out one's duties** remplir

ses fonctions (**as** de); **3** **¢** (work) service m; **to be on/off ~** Mil, Med être/ne pas être de service; Sch être/ne pas être de surveillance; **to go on/off ~** commencer/finir son service; **4** (tax) taxe f; **customs duties** droits mpl de douane; **to pay ~ on sth** payer des droits de douane sur qch

B noun modifier [nurse, security guard] (during the day) de service; (outside hours) de permanence

duty chemist n pharmacien/-ienne m/f de garde

duty: **~-free** adj, adv hors taxes inv; **~-free allowance** n quantité f autorisée de marchandises hors taxes; **~ roster**, **~ rota** n Admin tableau m de service

duvet /'du:veɪ/ n GB couette f

duvet cover n GB housse f de couette

DVD n (abrév = Digital Video Disc, Digital Versatile Disc) DVD m

DVD: **~ audio** n DVD-audio m; **~-ROM** n DVD-ROM m; **~ video** n DVD-vidéo m

dwarf /dwɔ:f/

A n, adj (all contexts) nain/naine (m/f)

B vtr gen faire paraître [qn/qch] tout petit; éclipser [achievement, issue]

dwell /dwel/ vi (prét, pp **dwelt**) demeurer liter

(Phrasal verb)

■ **dwell on**: ▸ **~ on** [sth] (talk about) s'étendre sur; (think about) s'attarder sur

dweller /'dwelə(r)/ n habitant/-e m/f; **city** or **town ~** citadin/-e m/f

dwelling /'dwelɪŋ/ n littér ou Admin habitation f

dwelt /dwelt/ prét, pp ▸ **dwell**

dwindle /'dwɪndl/ vi [numbers, resources] diminuer; [interest] tomber; [health] décliner

dwindling /'dwɪndlɪŋ/ adj [resources, audience, interest] en baisse; [strength, health] déclinant

dye /daɪ/

A n teinture f; **vegetable ~** colorant m végétal

B vtr teindre; **to ~ sth red** teindre qch en rouge

C vi [fabric] se teindre

D dyed pp adj [hair, fabric] teint

dyed-in-the-wool /ˌdaɪdɪnðə'wʊl/ adj invétéré

dying /'daɪɪŋ/

A p prés ▸ **die**

B n **1** (people) **the ~** les agonisants mpl; **2** (death) mort f

C adj **1** mourant; **to his ~ day** jusqu'à sa dernière heure; **with her ~ breath** dans son dernier souffle; **2** fig [art, tradition] en voie de disparition; [community] moribond; **3** (final) [moments] dernier/-ière; **4** [light, fire] mourant

dyke /daɪk/ n **1** (US **dike**) (to prevent flooding) digue f; (beside ditch) remblai m; **2** GB (ditch) fossé m

dynamic /daɪ'næmɪk/

A n, adj dynamique (f)

B dynamics npl dynamique f

dynamism /'daɪnəmɪzəm/ n dynamisme m

dynamite /'daɪnəmaɪt/ n dynamite f; **political ~** fig une bombe politique

dynamo /'daɪnəməʊ/ n **1** Elec dynamo f; **2** ○fig (person) **he's a real ~** il déborde d'énergie

dysentery /'dɪsəntrɪ, US -terɪ/ ▸ p. 933 n dysenterie f

dyslexic /dɪs'leksɪk/ n, adj dyslexique (mf)

e, **E** /iː/ n **1** (letter) e, E m; **2** E Mus mi m; **3** E Geog (abrév = **east**) E

e+ (dans composés) ~**-book**/**text**/**catalogue** livre m/texte m/catalogue m électronique; ~**-shopping** les achats m en ligne

each /iːtʃ/

> ⚠ When used as a determiner each is translated by chaque when an object or person is singled out: each document was examined = chaque document a été examiné. Tout/toute and tous les/toutes les are also used to express each and every: each passport must be checked = chaque passeport or tout passeport doit être contrôlé.
> When used as a pronoun each (= each one) is almost always translated by chacun/chacune. For examples and exceptions see below.

A det [person, group, object] chaque inv; ~ **time I do** chaque fois que je fais; ~ **morning** chaque matin, tous les matins; ~ **person will receive** chaque personne or tout le monde recevra; ~ **and every day** tous les jours sans exception; **he lifted** ~ **box in turn, ~ one heavier than the last** il soulevait des boîtes de plus en plus lourdes
B pron chacun/-e m/f; ~ **will receive** chacun recevra; **we** ~ **want something different** chacun de nous veut une chose différente; ~ **of you** chacun de vous, chacun d'entre vous; **three bundles of ten notes** ~ trois liasses de dix billets chacune; **I'll try a little of** ~ je prendrais bien un peu de chaque; **oranges at 30p** ~ des oranges à 30 pence pièce

each other /ˌiːtʃ ˈʌðə(r)/

> ⚠ Each other is very often translated by using a reflexive pronoun (nous, vous, se).
> For examples and particular usages see the entry below.

pron (also **one another**) **they know** ~ ils se connaissent; **to help** ~ s'entraider; **they wear** ~**'s clothes** ils se prêtent leurs vêtements; **to worry about** ~ s'inquiéter l'un pour l'autre; **kept apart from** ~ séparés l'un de l'autre

each way /ˌiːtʃ ˈweɪ/ adj, adv GB **to place an** ~ **bet on a horse, to bet on a horse** ~ jouer un cheval gagnant et placé

eager /ˈiːgə(r)/ adj [person, acceptance] enthousiaste; [face] où se lit l'enthousiasme; [anticipation] impatient; [student] plein d'enthousiasme; ~ **to do** (keen) désireux/-euse de faire; (impatient) pressé de faire; **to be** ~ **to please** chercher à faire plaisir; **to be** ~ **for sb to do** tenir vraiment à ce que qn fasse

eager beaver° n **to be an** ~ être zélé

eagerly /ˈiːgəlɪ/ adv gen avec enthousiasme; [listen] avidement; [wait] impatiemment

eagerness /ˈiːgənɪs/ n (keenness) empressement m (**to do** à faire); (impatience) impatience f (**to do** de faire); (enthusiasm) enthousiasme m

eagle /ˈiːgl/ n Zool aigle m; (emblem) aigle f

eagle-eyed adj (sharp-eyed) à l'œil m perçant; (vigilant) vigilant

ear /ɪə(r)/ ▸ p. 698
A n **1** oreille f; **inner**/**middle** ~ oreille f interne/moyenne; **to play (music) by** ~ jouer de la musique à l'oreille; **to have a good** ~ **for languages** avoir une bonne oreille pour les langues; **2** Bot (of wheat, corn) épi m

B noun modifier [infection, operation] (of one ear) de l'oreille; (of both ears) des oreilles

> Idioms **around one's** ~**s** tout autour de soi; **my** ~**s are burning** j'ai les oreilles qui sifflent; **to be all** ~**s**° être tout ouïe; **to be out on one's** ~° (from job) avoir été mis à la porte°; (from home) être à la rue; **to be up to one's** ~**s in debt** être endetté jusqu'au cou; **he's wet behind the** ~**s** c'est un petit jeunot; **to get a thick** ~° recevoir une baffe°; **to have a word in sb's** ~ parler à qn en privé; **to have** ou **keep one's** ~ **to the ground** garder l'œil ouvert; **to listen with (only) half an** ~ n'écouter que d'une oreille; **to play it by** ~ fig improviser

earache /ˈɪəreɪk/ n **to have** ~ GB ou **an** ~ avoir une otite
eardrum /ˈɪədrʌm/ n tympan m
earl /ɜːl/ n comte m
earlobe /ˈɪələʊb/ n lobe m de l'oreille
early /ˈɜːlɪ/

A adj **1** (one of the first) [attempt, role, years, novel, play] premier/-ière; ~ **man** les premiers hommes; **2** (sooner than usual) [death] prématuré; [delivery, settlement] rapide; [vegetable, fruit] précoce; **to have an** ~ **lunch**/**night** déjeuner/se coucher tôt; **to take** ~ **retirement** partir en préretraite; **at the earliest possible opportunity** le plus tôt possible; **at your earliest convenience** sout à votre convenance fml; **3** (in period of time) **in** ~ **childhood** dans la petite ou première enfance; **at an** ~ **age** à un très jeune âge; **to be in one's** ~ **thirties** avoir entre 30 et 35 ans; **to make an** ~ **start** partir tôt; **to take the** ~ **train** prendre le premier train; **at the earliest** au plus tôt; **the earliest I can manage is Monday** je ne peux rien faire avant lundi; **at an** ~ **hour** très tôt; **in the** ~ **hours** au petit matin; **in the** ~ **spring** au début du printemps; **in the** ~ **afternoon** en début d'après-midi; **an earlier attempt** une tentative précédente
B adv **1** (in period of time) tôt; **it's too** ~ **to say** il est trop tôt pour le dire; **can you make it earlier?** (arranging time) pouvez-vous plus tôt?; **as** ~ **as 1983** dès 1983; ~ **next year** au début de l'année prochaine; ~ **in the afternoon** en début d'après-midi; **(very)** ~ **on** dès le début; **as I said earlier** comme je l'ai déjà dit; **2** (before expected, too soon) en avance; **I'm a bit** ~ je suis un peu en avance; **to do sth two days**/**three weeks** ~ faire qch avec deux jours/trois semaines d'avance; **to retire** ~ partir en préretraite

> Idioms **it's** ~ **days yet** ce n'est que le début; **it's the** ~ **bird that catches the worm** Prov l'avenir appartient à ceux qui se lèvent tôt; **to be an** ~ **bird** être un/-e lève-tôt

early warning n **to be** ou **come as an** ~ **of sth** être le signe avant-coureur de qch
early warning system n Mil système m d'alerte avancée
earmark /ˈɪəmɑːk/
A n caractéristique f
B vtr (set aside) désigner [money, site] (**for** pour)
earmuffs /ˈɪəmʌfs/ npl cache-oreilles m inv
earn /ɜːn/ vtr **1** (bring in) [person] gagner [money]; toucher [salary]; [investment] rapporter [interest]; **to** ~ **a** ou **one's living** gagner sa vie; **2** (win) **to** ~ **sb's respect** se faire respecter de qn; **well-**~**ed** bien mérité

earned income n revenus mpl professionnels
earner /ˈɜːnə(r)/ n **1** (person) salarié/-e m/f; **2** GB **the main (revenue)** ~ la principale source de revenus; **a nice little** ~ une petite source de revenus
earnest /ˈɜːnɪst/
A n **in** ~ [speak] sérieusement; [begin, start] vraiment, pour

de bon; **to be in** ∼ être sérieux/-ieuse

B adj [person] sérieux/-ieuse; [intention] ferme; [promise, wish] sincère; [plea] fervent

earning power n capacité f de gain

earnings /'ɜːnɪŋz/ npl (of person) salaire m, revenu m (**from** de); (of company) gains mpl (**from** de); Fin (from shares) (taux m de) rendement m; **export** ∼ gains mpl à l'exportation

ear: ∼ **nose and throat department**, **ENT department** n service m d'oto-rhino-laryngologie, service m ORL; ∼**phones** npl (over ears) casque m; (in ears) écouteurs mpl; ∼**plug** n (for noise) boule f Quiès®; (for water) bouchon m d'oreille; ∼**ring** n boucle f d'oreille

earshot /'ɪəʃɒt/ n **within/out of** ∼ à portée de/hors de portée de voix

earsplitting /'ɪəsplɪtɪŋ/ adj [scream, shout] strident

earth /ɜːθ/

A n **1** (also **Earth**) (planet) Terre f; (soil) terre f; **the** ∼**'s atmosphere** l'atmosphère terrestre; **to the ends of the** ∼ jusqu'au bout du monde; **to come down to** ∼ lit, fig revenir sur terre; **to go to** ∼ lit, fig se terrer; **2** ○(as intensifier) **how/ where/who on** ∼...? comment/où/qui donc or diable○...?; **nothing on** ∼ **would persuade me to do** pour rien au monde je ne ferais; **3** GB Elec terre f; **4** ○(huge amount) **to cost the** ∼ coûter les yeux de la tête○; **to expect the** ∼ demander la lune

B noun modifier GB Elec [cable, wire] de terre

C vtr GB Elec mettre [qch] à la terre

(Idioms) **did the** ∼ **move for you**○? tu as pris ton pied○?; **to look like nothing on** ∼ ressembler à un épouvantail; **to run sb/sth to** ∼ dénicher qn/qch

earthenware /'ɜːθnweə(r)/

A n faïence f

B noun modifier [crockery] en faïence

earthly /'ɜːθlɪ/ adj **1** terrestre; **2** **it's no** ∼ **use** ça ne sert à rien du tout; **there's no** ∼ **reason** il n'y a aucune raison

earth: ∼**quake** n tremblement m de terre; ∼ **science** n science f de la Terre; ∼**shaking**○ adj bouleversant; ∼ **tremor** n secousse f sismique; ∼**work** n (pl ∼ ou ∼s) (embankment) rempart m; (excavation work) terrassement m; ∼**worm** n ver m de terre

earthy /'ɜːθɪ/ adj **1** [humour] truculent; [person] naturel/ -elle; [common sense] robuste; **2** [taste, smell] de terre; [tone] ocre

ear: ∼**wax** n cérumen m; ∼**wig** n perce-oreille m; ∼**-witness** n témoin m auditif

ease /iːz/

A n **1** (lack of difficulty) facilité f; **for** ∼ **of** pour faciliter; **2** (freedom from anxiety) **at** ∼ gen à l'aise; **at** ∼! Mil repos!; **to put sb at their** ∼ mettre qn à son aise; **to take one's** ∼ se détendre; **to put sb's mind at** ∼ rassurer qn (**about** à propos de); **3** (confidence of manner) aisance f; **4** (affluence) aisance f

B vtr **1** (lessen) gen atténuer; réduire [congestion]; diminuer [burden]; **2** (make easier) détendre [situation]; faciliter [communication, transition]; **3** (move carefully) **to** ∼ **sth into** introduire qch délicatement dans; **to** ∼ **sth out of** sortir qch délicatement de

C vi [tension, problem, pain, pressure] s'atténuer; [congestion, rain, rate] diminuer; [situation] se détendre; [price] être en légère baisse

(Phrasal verbs)
  ■ **ease off**: ▸ ∼ **off** [business] se ralentir; [demand, congestion] se réduire; [traffic, rain] diminuer; [person] relâcher son effort; ▸ ∼ [sth] **off**, ∼ **off** [sth] ôter délicatement
  ■ **ease up** [tense person, storm, traffic] se calmer; [worker, team] relâcher ses efforts; [authorities] relâcher la discipline; **to** ∼ **up on sb/on sth** être moins sévère envers qn/pour qch

easel /'iːzl/ n chevalet m

easily /'iːzɪlɪ/ adv **1** (with no difficulty) facilement; **to be** ∼ **forgotten** être facile à oublier; **2** (comfortably) [breathe] bien; [talk] à l'aise; **3** (unquestionably) de loin; **it's** ∼ **80 kilometres** ça fait facilement 80 kilomètres; **4** (probably) **she could** ∼ **die** elle pourrait bien mourir

east /iːst/ ▸ p. 1089

A n est m

B n Geog **the** ∼ (Orient) l'Orient m; (of country) l'Est m

C adj [side, face, coast, door] est inv; [wind] d'est

D adv [live, lie] à l'est (**of** de); [move] vers l'est

east: **East Africa** pr n Afrique f de l'Est; **East Berlin** pr n Pol Hist Berlin-Est

eastbound /'iːstbaʊnd/ adj [carriageway, traffic] en direction de l'est; **the** ∼ **train** GB la rame direction est

East End pr n quartiers mpl est de Londres

Easter /'iːstə(r)/

A n (festival) Pâques m; **at** ∼ à Pâques; (in greetings) pâques fpl; **Happy** ∼ joyeuses pâques

B noun modifier [Sunday, Monday, bunny, egg] de Pâques

easterly /'iːstəlɪ/

A n vent m d'est

B adj [wind] d'est; [point] à l'est; [area] de l'est

eastern /'iːstən/ ▸ p. 1089 adj **1** [coast, border] est; [town, custom, accent] de l'est; [Europe, United States] de l'Est; ∼ **France** l'est de la France; **2** (also **Eastern**) (oriental) oriental

Eastern bloc n Pol Hist **the** ∼ le bloc des pays de l'Est

East German ▸ p. 1032 Pol Hist

A n Allemand/-e m/f de l'Est

B adj est-allemand

east: **East Germany** ▸ p. 774 pr n Pol Hist Allemagne f de l'Est; **East Indies** pr npl Indes fpl orientales

eastward /'iːstwəd/ ▸ p. 1089

A adj [route, movement] vers l'est; **in an** ∼ **direction** en direction de l'est

B adv (also ∼s) vers l'est

easy /'iːzɪ/

A adj **1** (not difficult) [job, question, victory, life, victim] facile; **that's** ∼ **to fix** c'est facile à réparer; **it's not** ∼ **to talk to him** ce n'est pas facile de lui parler; **it's an** ∼ **walk from here** c'est facilement accessible à pied d'ici; **within** ∼ **reach** tout près (**of** de); **to make it** ou **things easier** faciliter les choses (**for** pour); **to make life too** ∼ **for** être trop complaisant avec [criminal, regime]; **to take the** ∼ **way out** choisir la solution de facilité; **2** (relaxed) [smile, grace] décontracté; [style] plein d'aisance; **at an** ∼ **pace** d'un pas tranquille; **to feel** ∼ (**in one's mind**) **about** ne pas se faire de souci à propos de; **3** ○péj (promiscuous) facile○; **4** ○**I'm** ∼ ça m'est égal

B adv **1** (in a relaxed way) **to take it** ou **things** ∼ ne pas s'en faire; **stand** ∼! Mil repos!; **2** ○**to go** ∼ **on** ou **with** y aller doucement avec

(Idioms) **as** ∼ **as pie** ou **falling off a log** facile comme tout, simple comme bonjour; ∼ **on the eye** agréable à regarder; ∼ **come,** ∼ **go** ça se remplace facilement; ∼ **does it** doucement; **he's** ∼ **game** c'est une proie facile

easy: ∼**care** adj d'entretien facile; ∼ **chair** n fauteuil m; ∼**going** adj [person] accommodant; [manner, attitude] souple; ∼ **money** n argent m vite gagné; ∼ **terms** n facilités fpl de paiement

eat /iːt/

A vtr (prét **ate**; pp **eaten**) (consume) gen manger; prendre [meal]; **to** ∼ (**one's**) **lunch/dinner** déjeuner/dîner; **she looks good enough to** ∼! elle est belle à croquer○!; **to** ∼ **sb/sth alive** [mosquitoes] dévorer qn/qch; **to** ∼ **one's words** ravaler ses paroles

B vi (prét **ate**; pp **eaten**) manger; **to** ∼ **from** ou **out of** manger dans; **I'll have him** ∼**ing out of my hand** fig j'en ferai ce que je voudrai; **we** ∼ **at six** nous dînons à 18 heures

(Phrasal verbs)
  ■ **eat away**: ▸ ∼ [sth] **away**, ∼ **away** [sth] ronger; ▸ ∼ **away at** [sth] lit ronger; fig manger
  ■ **eat into**: ▸ ∼ **into** [sth] lit faire un trou dans; fig [duties, interruptions] empiéter sur; [bills, fees] entamer
  ■ **eat out** aller au restaurant
  ■ **eat up**: ▸ ∼ **up** finir de manger; ∼ **up!** finis ce que tu as dans ton assiette!; ▸ ∼ [sth] **up**, ∼ **up** [sth] finir [food]; [car] dévorer [miles]; consommer [petrol]; engloutir [savings]; fig **to be** ∼**en up with** être dévoré de [curiosity, desire, envy]

eatable /'iːtəbl/ adj = edible

eaten /'iːtn/ pp ▸ eat

eater /'iːtə(r)/ n mangeur/-euse m/f; **he's a fast** ∼ il mange vite

eating /'iːtɪŋ/ n **healthy** ∼ **is essential** il est essentiel de manger sainement

eating: ~ **apple** n pomme f à couteau; ~ **disorder** n trouble m du comportement alimentaire; ~ **habits** npl habitudes fpl alimentaires

eavesdrop /ˈiːvzdrɒp/ vi (p prés etc **-pp-**) écouter aux portes

ebb /eb/
A n reflux m; **the ~ and flow** le flux et le reflux also fig
B vi lit descendre; fig décliner; **to ~ and flow** monter et descendre
(Idiom) **to be at a low ~** être au plus bas
(Phrasal verb)
■ **ebb away** [strength, enthusiasm, support] décliner

Ebonics /eˈbɒnɪks/ n US Ébonique m

ⓘ **Ebonics** Formé des mots Ebony (ébène) et phonics (phonique), l'Ébonique est une variante simplifiée de l'anglais parlé par certains Afro-Américains. Ce langage considéré comme argotique est cependant reconnu par certains comme une langue à part entière avec son propre vocabulaire et sa propre syntaxe. Des écoles américaines l'acceptent comme langue de communication et dans les travaux écrits de leurs élèves, mais beaucoup d'entre eux ont renoncé à l'utiliser afin de ne pas gâcher leurs chances professionnelles.

ebony /ˈebənɪ/ n ①（wood）ébène f; ② ▸ p. 752 (colour) noir m d'ébène

ebullient /ɪˈbʌlɪənt, ɪˈbʊlɪənt/ adj exubérant

e-business /ˈiːbɪznɪs/ n cyber-business m

EC n (abrév = **European Community**) CE f

eccentric /ɪkˈsentrɪk/ n, adj excentrique (mf)

eccentricity /ˌeksenˈtrɪsətɪ/ n excentricité f

ECG n (abrév = **electrocardiogram, electrocardiograph**) ECG m

echo /ˈekəʊ/
A n (pl **~es**) écho m; **to have ~es of sth** fig rappeler qch
B vtr lit répercuter; reprendre [idea, opinion]; rappeler [artist, style]
C vi retentir, résonner (**to, with** de; **around** dans)

echoing /ˈekəʊɪŋ/ adj sonore

eclipse /ɪˈklɪps/
A n éclipse f (**of** de)
B vtr éclipser

eco+ /ˈiːkəʊ-/ combining form éco+

eco: ~**-friendly** adj qui ne nuit pas à l'environnement; ~**-labelling** n étiquetage m écologique

ecological /ˌiːkəˈlɒdʒɪkl/ adj écologique

ecologist /iːˈkɒlədʒɪst/ n, adj écologiste (mf)

ecology /ɪˈkɒlədʒɪ/
A n écologie f
B noun modifier Pol [movement, issue] écologique

e-commerce /ˈiːkɒmɜːs/ n commerce m électronique, commerce m en ligne, cyber-business m

economic /ˌiːkəˈnɒmɪk, ˌek-/ adj ① (financial) économique; ② (profitable) [proposition, business] rentable

economical /ˌiːkəˈnɒmɪkl, ˌek-/ adj ① [machine, method] économique; **to be ~ on petrol** consommer peu d'essence; ② [person] économe; ③ fig [style, writer] concis; **to be ~ with the truth** iron ne pas dire toute la vérité

economically /ˌiːkəˈnɒmɪklɪ, ek-/ adv (financially) sur le plan économique; [operate] de façon économique; [write] avec concision

economic: ~ **analyst** ▸ p. 1181 n analyste mf économique; ~ **and monetary union, EMU** n Union f économique et monétaire; ~ **history** n histoire f de l'économie; ~ **indicator** n indicateur m économique or de conjoncture; ~ **management** n gestion f de l'économie

economics /ˌiːkəˈnɒmɪks, ˌek-/
A n (science) (+ v sg) économie f; (subject of study) (+ v sg) sciences fpl économiques; (financial aspects) (+ v pl) aspects mpl économiques (**of** de)
B noun modifier [degree, textbook, faculty] de sciences économiques; [editor, expert] en économie

economist /ɪˈkɒnəmɪst, ˌek-/ ▸ p. 1181 n économiste mf; **business ~** économiste mf d'entreprise

economize /ɪˈkɒnəmaɪz/ vtr, vi économiser

economy /ɪˈkɒnəmɪ/ n (all contexts) économie f; **the ~** l'économie du pays

economy: ~ **class** n Aviat classe f économique; ~ **drive** n campagne f de restriction; ~ **pack**, ~ **size** n paquet m économique

ecotourism /ˈiːkəʊtʊərɪzəm, -tɔːr-/ n tourisme m vert, écotourisme m

eco-warrior /ˈiːkəʊwɒrɪə(r), US -wɔːr-/ n éco-guerrier/-ière m/f, écologiste mf ultra

ecstasy /ˈekstəsɪ/ n ① extase f; ② (drug) ecstasy m

ecstatic /ɪkˈstætɪk/ adj [person] enchanté (**about** par); [state] extatique; [reception, crowd] enthousiaste

ecstatically /ɪkˈstætɪklɪ/ adv [applaud, welcomed] avec un enthousiasme délirant; ~ **happy** radieux/-ieuse

ectopic pregnancy /ekˌtɒpɪk ˈpregnənsɪ/ n grossesse f extra-utérine

ecu, ECU /eɪˈkuː/ ▸ p. 782
A n (abrév = **European Currency Unit**) écu m, ÉCU m; **hard ~** écu m dur
B noun modifier [value] en écus

Ecuador /ˈekwədɔː(r)/ ▸ p. 774 pr n Équateur m

ecumenical /ˌiːkjuːˈmenɪkl, ˈek-/ adj œcuménique

eczema /ˈeksɪmə, US ɪɡˈziːmə/ ▸ p. 933 n eczéma m

Ed.B n US Univ (abrév = **Bachelor of Education**) diplôme m universitaire de pédagogie

eddy /ˈedɪ/
A n tourbillon m
B vi [water] faire des tourbillons; [smoke, crowd] tournoyer

Eden /ˈiːdn/ pr n Éden m, paradis m terrestre

edge /edʒ/
A n ① (outer limit) gen bord m; (of wood, clearing) lisière f; **on the ~ of the city** en bordure de la ville; **the film had us on the ~ of our seats** fig le film nous a tenus en haleine; ② (of blade) tranchant m; **with a sharp ~** bien aiguisé; ③ (of book, plank) tranche f; ④ fig **to give an ~ to** aiguiser [appetite]; **to take the ~ off** gâter [pleasure]; calmer [anger, appetite]; **there was an ~ to his voice** sa voix avait quelque chose de tendu; **to lose one's ~** [writing, style] perdre sa vivacité; [person] perdre sa vigueur; ⑤ (advantage) **to have the ~ over** ou **on** avoir l'avantage sur; **to have a slight ~** avoir une légère avance (**over** sur); ⑥ (touchy) **to be on ~** [person] être énervé; **that sets my teeth on ~** cela me fait grincer des dents; ⑦ fig (extremity) **to live on the ~** vivre dangereusement; **the news pushed him over the ~** cette nouvelle l'a achevé
B vtr ① (move slowly) **to ~ sth towards** approcher qch de; **to ~ one's way along** longer la bordure de [cliff, parapet]; ② (trim) border
C vi (advance) **to ~ forward** avancer doucement; **to ~ closer to** se rapprocher de; **to ~ towards** s'approcher à petits pas de
(Phrasal verbs)
■ **edge out**: ▸ ~ **out** [car, driver] (of space) se dégager petit à petit (**of** de); ▸ ~ **sb out of** évincer qn de [job]; **we've ~d our competitors out of the market** nous avons éliminé tous nos concurrents du marché
■ **edge up** ① [prices, figure] augmenter lentement; ② **to ~ up to sb/sth** s'approcher doucement de qn/qch

edgeways /ˈedʒweɪz/, **edgewise** /ˈedʒwaɪz/ adv [move] latéralement; [lay, put] sur le côté
(Idiom) **I can't get a word in ~** je n'arrive pas à placer un mot

edgily /ˈedʒɪlɪ/ adv nerveusement

edging /ˈedʒɪŋ/ n bordure f

edgy /ˈedʒɪ/ adj énervé, anxieux/-ieuse

edible /ˈedɪbl/ adj [fruit, plant, mushroom, snail] comestible; [meal] mangeable

edict /ˈiːdɪkt/ n ① Hist édit m; ② Jur, Pol décret m

edifice /ˈedɪfɪs/ n édifice m also fig

edifying /ˈedɪfaɪɪŋ/ adj édifiant

Edinburgh /ˈedɪnbərə/ ▸ p. 1276 pr n Édimbourg

edit /ˈedɪt/
A n (of film) montage m; (for publication) mise f au point
B vtr ① (in publishing) (check) réviser; (annotate, select) éditer; (cut down) couper; ② (in journalism) être le rédacteur/la rédactrice m/f en chef de [newspaper]; être le rédacteur/la rédactrice m/f de [page]; ③ TV, Cin monter [film, programme]
(Phrasal verb)
■ **edit out**: ▸ ~ **out** [sth], ~ **[sth] out** Cin couper [qch] au montage; Audio, Radio couper [qch]

editing /'edɪtɪŋ/ n [1] (tidying for publication) mise f au point; [2] (annotation, choice) édition f; [3] (of film) montage m; [4] (of newspaper) rédaction f

edition /ɪ'dɪʃn/ n (of book, newspaper) édition f; (of news programme) édition f; (of documentary) émission f

editor /'edɪtə(r)/ ▸ p. 1181 n (of newspaper) rédacteur/-trice m/f en chef (of de); (of book, manuscript) correcteur/-trice m/f; (of writer, works, anthology) éditeur/-trice m/f; (of dictionary) rédacteur/-trice m/f; (of film) monteur/-euse m/f

editorial /,edɪ'tɔːrɪəl/
A n éditorial m (on sur)
B adj [1] (in journalism) [staff, office] de la rédaction; **to have ~ control** avoir la direction de la rédaction; [2] (in publishing) [policy, decision] éditorial; **to have ~ control** avoir le contrôle du texte

educate /'edʒʊkeɪt/ vtr [1] (teach) instruire; [2] (provide education for) assurer l'instruction de; **to ~ one's children privately** mettre ses enfants dans une école privée; **to be ~d in Paris** faire ses études à Paris; [3] (inform) informer [public, smokers, drivers] (about, in sur); éduquer [palate, tastes, mind]

educated /'edʒʊkeɪtɪd/
A n the ~ (having education) les gens mpl instruits; (cultivated) les gens mpl cultivés
B adj [person] (having an education) instruit; (cultivated) cultivé; [taste] raffiné; [accent] élégant; [classes] instruit
(Idiom) ~ **guess** opinion fondée (sur l'expérience)

education /,edʒʊ'keɪʃn/
A n [1] (training) gen éducation f, instruction f; (in health, road safety) information f; [2] (formal schooling) études fpl; **a university** ou **college ~** des études supérieures; **to get a good ~** faire de solides études; [3] (national system) enseignement m; **government spending on ~** le budget de l'éducation; [4] Univ (field of study) sciences fpl de l'éducation
B noun modifier [budget, spending, crisis] de l'enseignement; [method] Sch, Univ d'enseignement; [Minister, Ministry] Admin de l'éducation; ~ **standards** Sch niveau m scolaire; Univ niveau m universitaire; **the ~ system** le système éducatif

educational /,edʒʊ'keɪʃənl/ adj [1] [establishment, method, system] d'enseignement; [developments] de l'enseignement; [standards, supplies] Sch scolaire; Univ universitaire; [2] (instructive) [game, programme, value] éducatif/-ive; [experience, talk] instructif/-ive

educationalist /,edʒʊ'keɪʃənəlɪst/ n spécialiste mf des sciences de l'éducation

educationally /,edʒʊ'keɪʃənəli/ adv [useless, useful] pédagogiquement; [disadvantaged, privileged] sur le plan scolaire

educationally subnormal, ESN
A n the ~ les arriérés mpl
B adj arriéré

educational: ~ **psychology** n psychologie f scolaire; ~ **television, ETV** US télévision f scolaire

education: ~ **authority** n GB administration locale qui gère les affaires scolaires; ~ **committee** n GB comité gérant les affaires scolaires d'une région

education department n [1] GB (also **Department of Education and Skills**) ministère m de l'éducation; [2] GB (in local government) service m chargé des affaires d'enseignement; [3] (in university) département m des sciences de l'éducation

educative /'edʒʊkətɪv/ adj éducatif/-ive

educator /'edʒʊkeɪtə(r)/ n éducateur/-trice m/f

edutainment /,edjʊ'teɪnmənt/ n logiciel m ludoéducatif

Edwardian /ed'wɔːdɪən/
A n contemporain/-e m/f d'Édouard VII
B adj de l'époque d'Édouard VII

EEC
A n (abrév ▸ **European Economic Community**) CEE f
B noun modifier [policy, directive, country] de la CEE

eel /iːl/ n anguille f

eerie /'ɪəri/ adj [silence, place] étrange et inquiétant

efface /ɪ'feɪs/ vtr effacer also fig

effect /ɪ'fekt/
A n [1] (net result) effet m (of de; on sur); **to have the ~ of doing** avoir pour effet de faire; **the ~ of advertising is to increase demand** la publicité a pour effet d'accroître la demande; **the film had quite an ~ on me** ce film m'a fait forte impression; **to use sth to good ~** employer qch avec succès; **to use sth to dramatic ~** obtenir un effet spectaculaire en utilisant qch; [2] (repercussions) répercussions fpl (of de; on sur); [3] (power, efficacy) efficacité f; **of no ~** sans effet; **to little ~** sans grand résultat; **to no ~** en vain; **to take ~** [price increases] prendre effet; [ruling] entrer en vigueur; [pills, anaesthetic] commencer à agir; **to come into ~** Jur, Admin entrer en vigueur; **to put policies into ~** appliquer des directives; **with ~ from January 1** à dater du 1er janvier; [4] (theme) **the ~ of what he is saying is that** il veut dire par là que; **a note to the ~ that** un mot pour dire que; **a remark to that ~** une remarque en ce sens; **or words to that ~** ou quelque chose de ce genre; [5] (impression) effet m; **the overall ~** l'effet d'ensemble; **to achieve an ~** obtenir un effet; **he paused for ~** il a fait une pause théâtrale; **she dresses like that for ~** elle s'habille comme ça pour faire de l'effet
B effects npl Jur (belongings) effets mpl
C in effect adv phr dans le fond
D vtr effectuer [repair, sale, change]; apporter [improvement]; parvenir à [reconciliation]

effective /ɪ'fektɪv/ adj [1] (successful) efficace (against contre; in doing pour faire); [2] [legislation] en vigueur; **to become ~** entrer en vigueur; [3] [speech, contrast, demonstration] percutant; [4] (actual) Econ [rate, income] réel/réelle; [control] effectif/-ive

effectively /ɪ'fektɪvli/ adv [1] (efficiently) efficacement; [2] (in effect) en réalité; [3] (impressively) **the statistics ~ demonstrate** les statistiques démontrent avec force

effectiveness /ɪ'fektɪvnɪs/ n efficacité f (of de)

effeminate /ɪ'femɪnət/ adj efféminé

effervescent /,efə'vesnt/ adj lit effervescent; fig exubérant

effete /ɪ'fiːt/ adj pej [person] mou/molle; [civilization] déliquescent

efficacious /,efɪ'keɪʃəs/ adj efficace (in doing pour faire)

efficacy /'efɪkəsi/ n efficacité f (of de)

efficiency /ɪ'fɪʃnsi/ n (of person, method, organization) efficacité f (in doing à faire); (of machine) rendement m; **to produce electricity at 50% ~** produire de l'électricité avec un rendement de 50%

efficient /ɪ'fɪʃnt/ adj [1] [person, management] efficace (at doing pour ce qui est de faire); **to make ~ use of energy** faire une utilisation rationnelle de l'énergie; [2] [machine] économique; **to be 40% ~** avoir un rendement de 40%

efficiently /ɪ'fɪʃntli/ adv [work, deal with, carry out] de façon efficace; **the machine operates ~** la machine a un bon rendement

effigy /'efɪdʒi/ n (all contexts) effigie f

effluent /'eflʊənt/
A n effluent m
B noun modifier [treatment, management] des effluents

effort /'efət/ n [1] (energy) efforts mpl; **to put a lot of ~ into sth/into doing** se donner beaucoup de peine pour qch/pour faire; **to put all one's ~(s) into doing** consacrer tous ses efforts à faire; **to spare no ~** ne pas ménager ses efforts; **it's a waste of ~** c'est du travail pour rien; **to be worth the ~** en valoir la peine; [2] [physical, mental] **it is an ~ to do** il est pénible de faire; [3] (attempt) **to make the ~** faire l'effort; **he made no ~ to apologize** il n'a fait aucun effort pour s'excuser; **his ~s at doing** ses tentatives pour faire; **to make every ~** faire tout son possible; **in an ~ to do** pour essayer de faire; **joint ~** initiative f commune; **this is my first ~** c'est ma toute première œuvre; **not a bad ~** pas mal; [4] (initiative) initiative f; **war ~** effort m de guerre; [5] fig (exercise) effort m; **an ~ of will** un effort de volonté

effortless /'efətlɪs/ adj (easy) aisé; (innate) naturel/-elle

effortlessly /'efətlɪsli/ adv sans effort, sans peine

effrontery /ɪ'frʌntəri/ n effronterie f

effusion /ɪ'fjuːʒn/ n fig (enthusiasm) débordements mpl; (emotional outpouring) effusion f; (written) épanchement m

effusive /ɪ'fjuːsɪv/ adj [person, style] expansif/-ive; [thanks] très chaleureux/-euse

effusively /ɪ'fjuːsɪvli/ adv [speak] avec effusion; [welcome, thank] très chaleureusement

EFL
A n (abrév = **English as a Foreign Language**) anglais m langue étrangère
B noun modifier [teacher, course] d'anglais langue étrangère
EFT n: abrév ▸ **electronic funds transfer**
EFTA /'eftə/ n (abrév = **European Free Trade Association**) AELE f
eg (abrév = **exempli gratia**) par ex
egalitarian /ɪˌɡælɪ'teərɪən/ adj [person] égalitariste; [principles, tradition] égalitaire
egg /eɡ/
A n œuf m
B noun modifier [sandwich] à l'œuf; [collector] d'œufs; [farm] producteur/-trice d'œufs; [noodles, sauce] aux œufs
(Idioms) **to have ~ on one's face**○ avoir l'air fin○; **as sure as ~s is ~s** aussi vrai que deux et deux font quatre
(Phrasal verb)
■ **egg on**: ▸ **~ [sb] on** pousser fig

egg: **~ box** n (pl **~es**) boîte f à œufs; **~cup** n coquetier m; **~ custard** n flan m aux œufs; **~head**○ n péj grosse tête○ f; **~nog** n (with milk) lait m de poule; (with alcohol) flip m; **~plant** n US aubergine f; **~-shaped** adj ovoïde; **~shell** n coquille f d'œuf; **~ timer** n sablier m; **~ whisk** n fouet m à œufs; **~ white** n blanc m d'œuf; **~ yolk** n jaune m d'œuf
ego /'eɡəʊ, 'iːɡəʊ, US 'iːɡəʊ/ n **1** gen amour-propre m; **to be on an ~ trip** se faire mousser○; **2** Psych moi m, ego m
egocentric /ˌeɡəʊ'sentrɪk, 'iːɡəʊ-, US 'iːɡ-/ adj égocentrique
egoism /'eɡəʊɪzəm, 'iːɡ-, US 'iːɡ-/ n égoïsme m
egoist /'eɡəʊɪst, 'iːɡ-, US 'iːɡ-/ n égoïste mf
egoistic(al) /ˌeɡəʊ'ɪstɪk(l), ˌiːɡ-, US ˌiːɡ-/ adj égoïste
egotism /'eɡəʊtɪzəm, 'iːɡ-, US 'iːɡ-/ n égotisme m
egotist /'eɡəʊtɪst, 'iːɡ-, US 'iːɡ-/ n égotiste mf
Egypt /'iːdʒɪpt/ ▸ p. 774 pr n Égypte f
Egyptian /ɪ'dʒɪpʃn/ ▸ p. 1032, p. 969
A n Égyptien/-ienne m/f
B adj égyptien/-ienne
eiderdown /'aɪdədaʊn/ n (quilt) édredon m
eight /eɪt/ ▸ p. 1044 n, adj huit (m) inv; **~-hour day** journée f de huit heures; **to work ~-hour shifts** faire les trois-huit
(Idiom) **to be one over the ~**○ avoir un verre dans le nez○
eighteen /eɪ'tiːn/ ▸ p. 1044 n, adj dix-huit (m) inv
eighteenth /eɪ'tiːnθ/ ▸ p. 1044, p. 788
A n (in order) dix-huitième mf; (of month) dix-huit m; (fraction) dix-huitième m
B adj, adv dix-huitième
eighth /eɪtθ/ ▸ p. 1044, p. 788
A n (in order) huitième mf; (of month) huit m inv; (fraction) huitième m; Mus octave f
B adj, adv huitième
eighth note n US Mus croche f
eightieth /'eɪtɪəθ/ ▸ p. 1044
A n **1** (in order) quatre-vingtième mf; **2** (fraction) quatre-vingtième m
B adj, adv quatre-vingtième
eighty /'eɪtɪ/ ▸ p. 1044, p. 647
A n quatre-vingts m
B adj quatre-vingts inv
eighty-one ▸ p. 1044 n, adj quatre-vingt-un (m)
Éire /'eərə/ ▸ p. 774 pr n Éire f, République f d'Irlande
either /'aɪðər, US 'iːðər/
A pron **1** (one or other) l'un/l'une ou l'autre; **without ~ (of them)** sans l'un ni l'autre; **there was no sound from ~ of the rooms** aucun bruit ne provenait ni d'une chambre ni de l'autre; **~ or both of you can do it** vous pouvez le faire seul ou tous les deux; **2** (both) **~ of the two is possible** les deux sont possibles; **~ of us could win** nous avons tous les deux les mêmes chances de gagner; **'which book do you want?'–'~'** 'quel livre veux-tu?'–'n'importe'
B det **1** (one or the other) n'importe lequel/laquelle; (in the negative) **I can't see ~ child** je ne vois aucun des deux enfants; **2** (both) **~ one of the solutions is acceptable** les deux solutions sont acceptables; **in ~ case** dans les deux cas; **~ way, you win** vous gagnez dans les deux cas; **~ way, it will be difficult** de toute manière, ce sera difficile; **I don't**

e

have strong views **~ way** je ne suis ni pour ni contre
C adv non plus; **I can't do it ~** je ne peux pas le faire non plus
D conj **1** (as alternatives) **I was expecting him ~ Tuesday or Wednesday** je l'attendais soit mardi, soit mercredi; **it's ~ him or me** c'est lui ou moi; **2** (in the negative) **I wouldn't reward ~ Patrick or Emily** je ne donnerais de récompense ni à Patrick ni à Emily; **you're not being ~ truthful or fair** tu n'es ni honnête ni juste; **3** (as an ultimatum) **~ you finish your work or you will be punished!** ou tu finis ton travail ou je te punis!; **put the gun down, ~ that or I call the police** pose ton arme sinon j'appelle la police

ejaculate /ɪ'dʒækjʊleɪt/
A vtr (exclaim) s'exclamer
B vi éjaculer
ejaculation /ɪˌdʒækjʊ'leɪʃn/ n **1** exclamation f; **2** éjaculation f
eject /ɪ'dʒekt/
A vtr **1** (give out) [machine, system] rejeter [waste]; [volcano] cracher [lava]; **2** Audio faire sortir [cassette]; **3** (throw out) expulser [troublemaker]
B vi [pilot] s'éjecter
ejection /ɪ'dʒekʃn/ n (of gases, waste) rejet m; (of lava) éruption f; (of troublemaker) expulsion f; Aviat éjection f
eke /iːk/ v
■ **eke out**: ▸ **~ out [sth]**, **~ [sth] out** faire durer [income, supplies] (by à force de; by doing en faisant); **to ~ out a living** ou **an existence** essayer de joindre les deux bouts
elaborate
A /ɪ'læbərət/ adj gen compliqué; [system, network, plan] complexe; [design] travaillé; [painting, sculpture] ouvragé; [costume] recherché; [precaution, preparation] minutieux/-ieuse
B /ɪ'læbəreɪt/ vtr élaborer [theory, scheme]; développer [point, statement, idea]
C /ɪ'læbəreɪt/ vi entrer dans les détails; **to ~ on** s'étendre sur [proposal]; développer [remark]
elaborately /ɪ'læbərətlɪ/ adv [decorated, dressed] de manière recherchée; [defined, constructed] minutieusement
elaboration /ɪˌlæbə'reɪʃn/ n (of plan, theory) élaboration f (of de)
elapse /ɪ'læps/ vi s'écouler
elastane /ɪ'læsteɪn/ n élasthanne m
elastic /ɪ'læstɪk/ n, adj élastique (m)
elasticated /ɪ'læstɪkeɪtɪd/ adj [waistband, bandage] élastique
elastic band n élastique m
elated /ɪ'leɪtɪd/ adj transporté de joie; **I was ~ at having won** j'exultais d'avoir gagné
elation /ɪ'leɪʃn/ n joie f, allégresse f
Elba /'elbə/ ▸ p. 954 pr n île f d'Elbe
elbow /'elbəʊ/
A n (all contexts) coude m; **to lean on one's ~s** être accoudé; **at sb's ~** à portée de main; **to wear sth through at the ~s** percer or trouer qch aux coudes
B vtr **to ~ sb aside** écarter qn du coude; **to ~ one's way through a crowd** se frayer un passage à travers la foule (en jouant des coudes)
(Idioms) **more power to your ~** GB je te souhaite bien du courage○; **out at (the) ~(s)** [person] loqueteux; [garment] miteux; **to be up to the ~s in sth** être dans qch jusqu'au cou; **to give sb the ~** se débarrasser de qn; **to rub ~s with sb**○ US fréquenter qn
elbow grease n huile f de coude○
elbowroom /'elbəʊruːm/ n (room to move) espace m vital; fig marge f de manœuvre; **there isn't much ~ in this kitchen** on est un peu à l'étroit dans cette cuisine
elder /'eldə(r)/
A n **1** (older person) aîné/-e m/f; (of tribe, group) ancien m; **2** Bot sureau m
B adj aîné; **the ~ girl** l'aînée f, la fille aînée
elderberry n baie f de sureau; **~ wine** vin m de sureau
elderly /'eldəlɪ/
A n **the ~** (+ v pl) les personnes fpl âgées
B adj [person, population] âgé; [vehicle] vieux/vieille; **her ~ father** son vieux père
elder statesman n (pl **-men**) (all contexts) doyen m

eldest /'eldɪst/
A n aîné/-e m/f; **my ~** mon aîné/-e
B adj aîné; **the ~ child** l'aîné/-e
elect /ɪ'lekt/
A n **the ~** les élus mpl
B vtr **1** (by vote) élire (**from, from among** parmi); **to be ~ed to a post** être élu à un poste; **to ~ sb (as) president** élire qn président; **2** (choose) choisir
C adj (after n) futur; **the president ~** le président élu (n'ayant pas encore pris ses fonctions)
election /ɪ'lekʃn/
A n **1** (ballot) élection f, scrutin m; **in** ou **at the ~** aux élections; **to win/lose an ~** gagner/perdre aux élections; **2** (appointment) élection f (**to** à); **to stand for ~** se porter candidat aux élections
B noun modifier [manifesto] électoral; [day, results] du scrutin
electioneering /ɪ,lekʃə'nɪərɪŋ/ n (campaigning) campagne f électorale; pej électoralisme m
elective /ɪ'lektɪv/ adj **1** (elected) [office, official] électif/-ive, élu; (empowered to elect) [assembly, body] électoral; **2** Sch, Univ [course] facultatif/-ive
elector /ɪ'lektə(r)/ n **1** (voter) électeur/-trice m/f; **2** US Pol membre m du collège électoral
electoral /ɪ'lektərəl/ adj électoral
electoral: **~ register**, **~ roll** n listes fpl électorales; **~ vote** n US vote m des grands électeurs
electorate /ɪ'lektərət/ n électorat m, électeurs mpl
electric /ɪ'lektrɪk/
A ○**electrics** npl GB Aut circuits mpl électriques (d'une voiture)
B adj électrique also fig
electrical /ɪ'lektrɪkl/ adj électrique
electric: **~ blanket** n couverture f chauffante; **~ eye** n cellule f photoélectrique
electrician /ɪ,lek'trɪʃn/ ▸ ▸ p. 1181 n électricien/-ienne m/f
electricity /ɪ,lek'trɪsəti/
A n lit, fig électricité f; **to turn off/on the ~** couper/rétablir le courant (électrique)
B noun modifier [generator, cable] électrique; [bill, charges] d'électricité
electricity: **~ board** n GB compagnie f d'électricité; **~ supply** n alimentation f en électricité
electric shock n décharge f électrique; **to get an ~** recevoir une décharge
electric: **~ storm** n orage m; **~ window** n lève-glaces m électrique
electrify /ɪ'lektrɪfaɪ/ vtr gen électrifier; fig électriser
electrifying /ɪ'lektrɪfaɪɪŋ/ adj [speech] électrisant
electro+ /ɪ'lektrəʊ/ combining form électro+
electrocute /ɪ'lektrəkjuːt/ vtr électrocuter; **to be ~d** (accidentally) s'électrocuter
electrocution /ɪ,lektrə'kjuːʃn/ n électrocution f
electrode /ɪ'lektrəʊd/ n électrode f
electrolysis /ɪ,lek'trɒləsɪs/ n **1** Chem électrolyse f; **2** (hair removal) épilation f électrique
electron /ɪ'lektrɒn/ n électron m
electronic /ɪ,lek'trɒnɪk/ adj (all contexts) électronique
electronic: **~ engineer** ▸ p. 1181 n électronicien/-ienne m/f; **~ engineering** n électronique f; **~ eye** n cellule f photoélectrique; **~ funds transfer, EFT** n transfert m électronique de fonds; **~ mail** n messagerie f électronique; **~ organizer** n (diary, address book) agenda m électronique; (pocket PC) ordinateur m de poche; **~ publishing** n édition f électronique, éditique f
electronics /ɪ,lek'trɒnɪks/ n (+ v sg) électronique f
electronic tag n bracelet m électronique
electroshock therapy, electroshock treatment, EST /ɪ,lektrəʊ'ʃɒk/ n électroconvulsivothérapie f, électrochocs mpl
elegance /'elɪgəns/ n élégance f
elegant /'elɪgənt/ adj [person, clothes, gesture] élégant; [manners] distingué; [restaurant] chic (inv)
elegantly /'elɪgəntli/ adv [dress, write] avec élégance; [dressed, furnished] élégamment
elegy /'elədʒi/ n élégie f (**for** à)

element /'elɪmənt/ n **1** (constituent) élément m; **the key ~ in his success** l'élément clé de son succès; **the poor salary was just one ~ in my dissatisfaction** le salaire médiocre n'expliquait que partiellement mon mécontentement; **2** (factor) facteur m; **the time ~** le facteur temps; **3** (small part) part f; **an ~ of luck/risk** une part de chance/risque; **4** (rudiment) (of courtesy, diplomacy) élément m; (of grammar, mathematics etc) base f; **5** (constituent group) élément m; **6** (air, water etc) **the ~s** (weather) les éléments; **exposed to the ~s** exposé aux intempéries; **7** Chem, Math, Radio élément m; **8** Elec résistance f
(idiom) **to be in/out of one's ~** être/ne pas être dans son élément
elementary /,elɪ'mentrɪ/ adj **1** (basic, simple) élémentaire; **2** [school] primaire; [teacher] de primaire
elephant /'elɪfənt/ n éléphant m; **baby ~** éléphanteau m
elephantine /,elɪ'fæntaɪn/ adj [person] éléphantesque; [task] gigantesque
elevate /'elɪveɪt/ vtr élever (**to** au rang de)
elevated /'elɪveɪtɪd/ adj gen élevé; [railway, canal] sur-élevé
elevated railroad n US métro m aérien
elevation /,elɪ'veɪʃn/ n **1** gen élévation f (**to** au rang de); **2** Archit élévation f; **front ~** élévation de la façade; **3** (height) altitude f
elevator /'elɪveɪtə(r)/ n **1** US (in building) ascenseur m; **2** (hoist) élévateur m; **3** US (for grain) silo m à grain
eleven /ɪ'levn/
A n **1** onze m inv; **2** Sport **the football ~** le onze; **a football ~** une équipe de football
B adj onze inv
eleven plus n ≈ examen m d'entrée en sixième
elevenses○ /ɪ'levnzɪz/ n GB pause-café f (dans la matinée)
eleventh /ɪ'levnθ/ ▸ p. 1044, p. 788
A n **1** (in order) onzième mf; **2** (of month) onze m inv; **3** (fraction) onzième m
B adj, adv onzième
eleventh hour n **at the ~** à la toute dernière minute
elf /elf/ n (pl **elves**) lutin m
elicit /ɪ'lɪsɪt/ vtr obtenir [opinion]; provoquer [reaction, response]; tirer [explanation]
eligibility /,elɪdʒə'bɪləti/ n droit m (**for** à; **to do** de faire)
eligible /'elɪdʒəbl/ adj (qualifying) **to be ~ for** avoir droit à [allowance, benefit, membership]; **to be ~ for appointment** remplir les conditions pour être nommé; **to be ~ to do** être en droit de faire; **the ~ candidates** les candidats qui remplissent les conditions requises; **an ~ bachelor** un beau ou bon parti
eliminate /ɪ'lɪmɪneɪt/ vtr gen éliminer; écarter [suspect]
elimination /ɪ,lɪmɪneɪʃn/ n élimination f; **by a process of ~** en procédant par élimination
élite /eɪ'liːt/
A n élite f
B adj [group, minority] élitaire; [restaurant, club] réservé à l'élite; [troop, team, squad] d'élite
elliptic(al) /ɪ'lɪptɪk(l)/ adj (all contexts) elliptique
elm /elm/ n orme m
elocution /,elə'kjuːʃn/ n élocution f, diction f
elongate /'iːlɒŋgeɪt, US ɪ'lɔːŋ-/
A vtr (lengthen) allonger; (stretch) étirer
B vi s'allonger
elope /ɪ'ləʊp/ vi [couple] s'enfuir ensemble; [man, woman] s'enfuir (**with** avec)
elopement /ɪ'ləʊpmənt/ n fugue f amoureuse
eloquence /'eləkwəns/ n éloquence f
eloquent /'eləkwənt/ adj [orator, speech, gesture] éloquent
El Salvador /,el 'sælvədɔː(r)/ ▸ p. 774 pr n Salvador m; **in ~** au Salvador
else /els/
A adv d'autre; **somebody/nothing ~** quelqu'un/rien d'autre; **something ~** autre chose; **somewhere** ou **someplace** US **~** ailleurs; **how ~ can we do it?** comment le faire autrement?; **what ~ would you like?** qu'est-ce que tu voudrais d'autre?; **there's not much ~ to do** il n'y a pas grand-chose d'autre à faire; **he talks of little ~** il ne parle presque que de ça; **everyone ~ but me went to the football**

match tout le monde est allé voir le match de football sauf moi; **was anyone ∼ there?** y avait-il quelqu'un d'autre?; **anyone ∼ would go to bed early, but you...** à ta place n'importe qui irait se coucher tôt, mais toi, tu...; **anywhere ∼ it wouldn't matter** en tout autre lieu ça n'aurait aucune importance; **he didn't see anybody ∼** il n'a vu personne d'autre; **if nothing ∼ he's polite** à défaut d'autre chose il est poli; **she's something ∼**○! (very nice) elle est géniale!; (unusual) elle est spéciale!; **'is that you, David?'—'who ∼?'** 'c'est toi, David?'—'qui veux-tu que ce soit?'

B **or else** conj phr sinon, ou; **eat this or ∼ you'll be hungry** mange ça ou or sinon tu vas avoir faim; **stop that now, or ∼...**○! arrête tout de suite, sinon...

elsewhere /ˌels'weə(r), US ˌels'hweər/ adv ailleurs; **from ∼** venu/-e d'ailleurs

ELT n: abrév ▸ **English Language Teaching**

elucidate /ɪˈluːsɪdeɪt/ vtr élucider [mystery, problem]; expliquer [text, concept]

elude /ɪˈluːd/ vtr échapper à [pursuer, attention, memory, person]; se dérober à [police]; esquiver [blow]

elusive /ɪˈluːsɪv/ adj [person, animal, happiness] insaisissable; [prize, victory] hors d'atteinte; [scent, memory] fugace

'em○ /əm/ = **them**

emaciated /ɪˈmeɪʃɪeɪtɪd/ adj [person, feature] émacié; [limb, body] décharné; [animal] étique

email, e-mail /ˈiːmeɪl/

A **①** (medium) courrier m électronique, messagerie f électronique, courriel m Can; **to be on ∼** avoir une adresse électronique; **②** (mail item) message m électronique, e-mail m; **to send sb an ∼** envoyer un message électronique à qn; **③** (on letterhead, business card) mél m, courriel m Can

B modif [address, message] électronique

C vtr envoyer un message électronique à [person]; envoyer [document]; **to ∼ sth to sb** envoyer qch à qn par courrier électronique

emanate /ˈeməneɪt/

A vtr émettre, dégager [radiation]

B vi lit, fig émaner (**from** de)

emancipate /ɪˈmænsɪpeɪt/ vtr émanciper; **to become ∼d** [woman] s'émanciper

emancipation /ɪˌmænsɪˈpeɪʃn/ n émancipation f

emasculate /ɪˈmæskjʊleɪt/ vtr lit, fig émasculer

embalm /ɪmˈbɑːm, US -bɑːlm/ vtr lit, fig embaumer

embankment /ɪmˈbæŋkmənt/ n **①** (to carry railway, road) remblai m; **②** (to hold back water) quai m, digue f

embargo /ɪmˈbɑːɡəʊ/

A n embargo m (**on** sur; **against** contre); **trade ∼** embargo commercial; **arms ∼** embargo sur les livraisons d'armes; **to impose/lift an ∼** instaurer/lever un embargo

B vtr instaurer un embargo sur [trade]

embark /ɪmˈbɑːk/

A vtr Naut embarquer

B vi **①** Naut s'embarquer (**for** pour); **②** **to ∼ on** entreprendre [journey]; se lancer dans [campaign, career, relationship, process, project]; pej s'engager dans [dubious path]; s'embarquer dans [dubious process]

embarkation /ˌembɑːˈkeɪʃn/ n embarquement m

embarrass /ɪmˈbærəs/ vtr plonger [qn] dans l'embarras; **to be/feel ∼ed** être/se sentir gêné; **to be ∼ed by** être gêné par [situation, remark]; avoir honte de [person, ignorance]; **I feel ∼ed about doing** ça me gêne de faire; **to be financially ∼ed** avoir des embarras d'argent

embarrassing /ɪmˈbærəsɪŋ/ adj gen embarrassant; **my uncle is ∼** mon oncle me fait honte; **to put sb in an ∼ position** mettre qn dans l'embarras

embarrassingly /ɪmˈbærəsɪŋlɪ/ adv [behave] de façon gênante; **∼ frank** d'une franchise embarrassante

embarrassment /ɪmˈbærəsmənt/ n **①** (feeling) confusion f, gêne f (**about, at** devant); **to cause sb ∼** mettre qn dans l'embarras; **to my ∼** à ma grande confusion; **②** (person, action, event) **to be an ∼ to sb** [person] faire honte à qn; **his past is an ∼ to him** il a honte de son passé; **③** (superfluity) sout embarras m; **an ∼ of riches** l'embarras du choix

embassy /ˈembəsɪ/ n ambassade f

embed /ɪmˈbed/ vtr (p prés etc **-dd-**) **①** lit **∼ded in** [sharp object, rock] enfoncé dans; [plant] ancré dans; [plaque] encastré dans; **②** fig **to be ∼ded in** être ancré dans;

③ Comput incorporer (**in** dans)

embellish /ɪmˈbelɪʃ/ vtr lit, fig embellir

ember /ˈembə(r)/ n **the ∼s** les braises fpl

embezzle /ɪmˈbezl/ vtr détourner [funds] (**from** de)

embezzlement /ɪmˈbezlmənt/ n détournement m de fonds

embitter /ɪmˈbɪtə(r)/ vtr aigrir, remplir [qn] d'amertume [person]; **to become ∼ed** s'aigrir

emblem /ˈembləm/ n emblème m

emblematic /ˌembləˈmætɪk/ adj emblématique

embodiment /ɪmˈbɒdɪmənt/ n (incarnation of quality, idea) incarnation f

embody /ɪmˈbɒdɪ/ vtr **①** (incarnate) incarner [virtue, evil, ideal]; **to be embodied in** s'incarner dans; **②** (express) donner corps à [theory, philosophy]; **③** (legally) incorporer (**in** dans)

embolism /ˈembəlɪzəm/ n Med embolie f

emboss /ɪmˈbɒs/ vtr gaufrer [fabric, paper]; estamper [leather]; repousser, travailler [qch] en relief [metal]

embrace /ɪmˈbreɪs/

A n étreinte f; **to hold sb in a fond ∼** étreindre qn affectueusement

B vtr **①** (hug) étreindre; **②** (adopt) embrasser [religion, ideology]; épouser [cause]; s'engager dans [policy]; adopter [principle, technology, method]; **③** (include) comprendre [subject areas]; englober [cultures, beliefs]

C vi s'étreindre

embroider /ɪmˈbrɔɪdə(r)/

A vtr lit broder (**with** de); fig broder sur [fact]; embellir [story, truth]

B vi broder, faire de la broderie

embroidery /ɪmˈbrɔɪdərɪ/

A n broderie f

B noun modifier [frame, silk, thread] à broder

embroil /ɪmˈbrɔɪl/ vtr entraîner (**in** dans)

embryo /ˈembrɪəʊ/

A n Biol, fig embryon m

B adj = **embryonic**

embryonic /ˌembrɪˈɒnɪk/ adj Biol, fig embryonnaire

emend /ɪˈmend/ vtr corriger

emerald /ˈemərəld/

A n **①** (stone) émeraude f; **②** ▸ p. 752 (colour) émeraude m

B adj **①** [ring, necklace] d'émeraudes; **②** (colour) émeraude inv

emerge /ɪˈmɜːdʒ/

A vi **①** [person, animal] sortir (**from** de); **②** [issue, news, problem, result] se faire jour; [trend, pattern] se dégager; [truth] apparaître; [talent] voir le jour; [evidence, message] ressortir; [new nation, ideology] naître; **to ∼ victorious** ressortir vainqueur; **it ∼ed that** il est apparu que

B **emerging** pres p adj [market] naissant, émergent; [democracy] qui émerge; [opportunity] qui apparaît; [writer, artist] qui devient connu; [nation] émergent

emergence /ɪˈmɜːdʒəns/ n apparition f

emergency /ɪˈmɜːdʒənsɪ/

A n gen cas m d'urgence; Med urgence f; **in an ∼, in case of ∼** en cas d'urgence; **in times of ∼** en temps de crise; **state of ∼** Pol état m d'urgence

B noun modifier [plan, measures, operation, repairs, aid, call, stop] d'urgence; Pol [meeting, session] extraordinaire; Aut [brakes, vehicle] de secours

emergency: **∼ ambulance service** n service m ambulancier de secours d'urgence; cf SAMU; **∼ case** n Med urgence f; **∼ centre** GB, **∼ center** US n (for refugees etc) centre m d'accueil (pour sinistrés); Med poste m de secours; Aut poste m de dépannage; **∼ exit** n sortie f de secours; **∼ landing** n Aviat atterrissage m d'urgence; **∼ laws** npl Pol lois fpl d'exception; **∼ medical service**, **EMS** n US service m ambulancier de secours d'urgence; cf SAMU; **∼ number** n numéro m des urgences; **∼ powers** npl Pol ≈ pleins pouvoirs mpl; **∼ rations** npl vivres mpl de secours; **∼ room** n US = **emergency ward**; **∼ service** n Med service m de garde; Aut service m de dépannage; **∼ services** npl (police) police f secours; (ambulance) service m d'aide médicale d'urgence; (fire brigade) (sapeurs-)pompiers mpl

emergency surgery n **to undergo ∼** être opéré d'urgence

emergency: ~ **ward** n salle f des urgences; ~ **worker** n secouriste mf

emergent /ɪ'mɜːdʒənt/ adj [industry, nation] jeune; [power, artist, genre] naissant

emery /'eməri/ n émeri m

emery: ~ **board** n lime f à ongles; ~ **paper** n papier-émeri m

emigrant /'emɪgrənt/
A n (about to leave) émigrant/-e m/f; (settled elsewhere) émigré/-e m/f
B noun modifier [worker] émigré; [family] d'émigrés

emigrate /'emɪgreɪt/ vi émigrer

emigration /,emɪ'greɪʃn/ n émigration f

eminence /'emɪnəns/ n **1** (fame) renommée; **2** (honour) distinction f; **3** littér (hill) éminence f

eminent /'emɪnənt/ adj éminent

eminently /'emɪnəntlɪ/ adv [respectable] éminemment; [capable, suitable] parfaitement; [desirable] hautement

emirate /'emɪəreɪt/ n émirat m

emissary /'emɪsərɪ/ n émissaire m (**to** auprès de)

emission /ɪ'mɪʃn/ n (all contexts) émission f (**from** provenant de)

emit /ɪ'mɪt/ vtr (discharge) émettre [gas, heat, sound, signal]; dégager [smell, vapour]; lancer [spark]; laisser échapper [cry]

Emmy /'emɪ/ n: récompense décernée par la télévision américaine

emollient /ɪ'mɒlɪənt/ n, adj émollient (m)

emoticon /ɪ'məʊtɪkɒn, -'mɒtɪ-/ n Comput frimousse f, binette f Can

emotion /ɪ'məʊʃn/ n émotion f

emotional /ɪ'məʊʃənl/ adj [development, problem] émotif/-ive; [reaction, state] émotionnel/-elle; [tie, response] affectif/-ive; [film] émouvant; [speech] passionné; [occasion] chargé d'émotion; **to feel** ~ se sentir ému (**about** par); **she's rather** ~ elle est facilement émue; ~ **health** équilibre m mental

emotionally /ɪ'məʊʃənəlɪ/ adv [speak, react] avec émotion; [drained, involved] émotionnellement; [immature] sur le plan affectif; ~ **charged** [relationship] intense; [atmosphere] chargée d'émotion; ~ **deprived** privé d'affection; ~ **disturbed** caractériel/-ielle

emotionless /ɪ'məʊʃnlɪs/ adj impassible

emotive /ɪ'məʊtɪv/ adj [issue] brûlant, qui soulève les passions; [word] chargé de connotations

empathize /'empəθaɪz/ vi **to** ~ **with** s'identifier à [person]

empathy /'empəθɪ/ n empathie f

emperor /'empərə(r)/ n empereur m

emphasis /'emfəsɪs/ n (pl **-ses**) accent m; **the new** ~ **on training** l'importance récemment accordée à la formation; **to put special** ~ **on sth** insister sur l'importance de qch

emphasize /'emfəsaɪz/ vtr mettre l'accent sur [policy, need]; mettre [qch] en valeur [eyes]; **to** ~ **that** insister sur le fait que; **to** ~ **the importance of sth** insister sur l'importance de qch

emphatic /ɪm'fætɪk/ adj [statement] catégorique; [voice, manner] énergique; [tone, style] vigoureux/-euse; **to be** ~ **about/that** insister sur/pour que

emphatically /ɪm'fætɪklɪ/ adv gen énergiquement; [insist] avec force; **and I say this most** ~ et je ne saurais trop insister là-dessus; **he is most** ~ **not a genius** il n'a vraiment rien d'un génie

empire /'empaɪə(r)/ n lit, fig empire m

empirical /ɪm'pɪrɪkl/ adj empirique

employ /ɪm'plɔɪ/
A n sout **in his** ~ à son service
B vtr **1** employer [person, company] (**as** en qualité de); **2** (use) utiliser [machine, tool]; employer [method, tactics, technique, expression]; recourir à [measures]; **to be** ~**ed in doing** (busy) être en train de faire

employable /ɪm'plɔɪəbl/ adj [person] capable de faire un travail

employed /ɪm'plɔɪd/
A n **the** ~ les actifs mpl
B adj (in work) qui a un emploi; (an employee) salarié

employee /,emplɔɪ'iː, ɪm'plɔɪi:/ n salarié/-e m/f

employer /ɪm'plɔɪə(r)/ n employeur/-euse m/f; ~**s' organizations** associations fpl patronales

employment /ɪm'plɔɪmənt/ n travail m, emploi m; **to take up** ~ commencer un travail; **to seek/find** ~ chercher/trouver du travail; **to be in** ~ avoir un emploi; **without** ~ sans emploi; **people in** ~ les actifs mpl; **conditions of** ~ conditions fpl d'emploi; **place of** ~ lieu m de travail

employment: ~ **agency** n bureau m de recrutement; ~ **contract** n contrat m de travail; ~ **exchange** n agence f pour l'emploi; **Employment Minister**, **Employment Secretary** n ministre m du Travail

emporium /ɪm'pɔːrɪəm/ n (pl ~**s** ou **-ria**) sout ou hum grand magasin m

empower /ɪm'paʊə(r)/ vtr (legally) **to** ~ **sb to do** autoriser qn à faire; (politically) donner à qn le pouvoir de faire; **the police are** ~**ed to do** la police a pleins pouvoirs pour faire

empress /'emprɪs/ n impératrice f

emptiness /'emptɪnɪs/ n (of space, house, life) vide m

empty /'emptɪ/
A adj **1** [street] désert; [desk] libre; [container] vide; [page] vierge; **to stand** ~ être inoccupé; **2** fig [promise, threat] en l'air; [dream, rhetoric] creux/creuse; [gesture] vide de sens; [life] vide
B vtr, vi = **empty out**

(Phrasal verb)
■ **empty out**: ▸ ~ **out** [building, container] se vider; [contents] se répandre; ▸ ~ **[sth] out**, ~ **out [sth]** gen vider; verser [liquid]

empty: ~**-handed** adj [arrive, leave] les mains vides; [return] bredouille inv; ~**-headed** adj écervelé

EMS n **1** (abrév = **European Monetary System**) SME m; **2** abrév ▸ **emergency medical service**

emulate /'emjʊleɪt/ vtr sout **1** (imitate) imiter; (rival) rivaliser avec; **2** Comput émuler

emulsify /ɪ'mʌlsɪfaɪ/
A vtr émulsionner, émulsifier
B vi être émulsionné or émulsifié

emulsion /ɪ'mʌlʃn/ n (all contexts) émulsion f

enable /ɪ'neɪbl/ vtr **1** **to** ~ **sb to do** permettre à qn de faire; **2** (facilitate) faciliter [growth]; favoriser [learning]

enact /ɪ'nækt/ vtr **1** (perform) jouer; **2** Jur Pol (pass) voter; (bring into effect) promulguer

enamel /ɪ'næml/
A n émail m
B noun modifier [pan] en émail; [ring] en émaux
C vtr émailler
D **enamelled**, **enameled** US pp adj [glass, pottery] émaillé; [ornament] en émaux

enamelling, **enameling** US /ɪ'næmlɪŋ/ n (process) émaillage m; (art) émaillerie f

enamoured GB, **enamored** US /ɪ'næməd/ adj **to be** ~ **of** être épris/-e or amoureux/-euse de

enc. abrév = **encl.**

encampment /ɪn'kæmpmənt/ n gen campement m; Mil cantonnement m

encapsulate /ɪn'kæpsjʊleɪt/ vtr (summarize) résumer; (include) contenir

encase /ɪn'keɪs/ vtr revêtir, recouvrir (**in** de); ~**d in** pris dans [concrete]; serré dans [plaster]

encash /ɪn'kæʃ/ n GB encaisser

encephalogram /en'kefələgræm/ n encéphalogramme m

enchant /ɪn'tʃɑːnt, US -tʃænt/
A vtr (all contexts) enchanter
B **enchanted** pp adj [garden, wood] enchanté

enchanting /ɪn'tʃɑːntɪŋ, US -tʃænt-/ adj [vision] enchanteur/-eresse; [smile] ravissant

enchantment /ɪn'tʃɑːntmənt, US -tʃænt-/ n (all contexts) enchantement m

encircle /ɪn'sɜːkl/ vtr [troops, police] encercler; [fence, wall] entourer; [belt, bracelet] enserrer

encl.
A n (abrév = **enclosure**) PJ f
B adj (abrév = **enclosed**) ci-joint

enclose /ɪn'kləʊz/ vtr gen entourer (**with, by** de); (with fence, wall) clôturer (**with, by** avec); (in outer casing) enfermer (**in** dans); (in brackets) insérer (**in** dans); (in letter) joindre (**with, in** à); **please find ~d a cheque for £10** veuillez trouver ci-joint un chèque de dix livres; **a letter enclosing a cheque** une lettre accompagnée d'un chèque

enclosed /ɪn'kləʊzd/ adj [garden, space] clos; [sea, harbour] fermé; [letter] ci-joint

enclosure /ɪn'kləʊʒə(r)/ n ①▸ (space) (for animals) enclos m; (for race-horses) paddock m; (for officials) enceinte f; ②▸ (fence) clôture f

encode /ɪn'kəʊd/ vtr gen coder, chiffrer; Comput, Ling encoder

encoder /ɪn'kəʊdə(r)/ n Comput, Ling encodeur m

encompass /ɪn'kʌmpəs/ vtr inclure, comprendre [people, ideas, territories, area]

encore /'ɒŋkɔ:(r)/ Theat
A n bis m; **to give** ou **play an ~** jouer un bis; **to get an ~** être bissé
B excl ~! bis!

encounter /ɪn'kaʊntə(r)/
A n gen rencontre f (**with** avec); Mil affrontement m; **his frequent ~s with the law** ses démêlés mpl fréquents avec la police
B vtr rencontrer [opponent, resistance, problem]; essuyer [setback]; croiser [person]

encourage /ɪn'kʌrɪdʒ/ vtr ①▸ (support) encourager; (reassure) rassurer; **to ~ sb to do** encourager qn à faire; **these observations ~d him in his belief that** ces observations l'ont conforté dans l'idée que; ②▸ (foster) stimuler [investment]; favoriser [rise, growth]

encouragement /ɪn'kʌrɪdʒmənt/ n (support) encouragement m (**to** pour); (inducement) incitation f (**to** à); **she needs no ~ to do** elle ne se fait pas prier pour faire; **to give ~ to sb, to be an ~ to sb** encourager qn; **without ~ from sb** sans mon soutien

encouraging /ɪn'kʌrɪdʒɪŋ/ adj encourageant

encroach /ɪn'krəʊtʃ/ vi **to ~ on** [sea, vegetation] gagner du terrain sur; [person] empiéter sur; **to ~ on sb's privacy** violer l'intimité de qn

encrust /ɪn'krʌst/ vtr **to be ~ed with** être recouvert de [ice]; être incrusté de [jewels]

encrypt /en'krɪpt/ vtr encrypter

encryption /en'krɪpʃən/ n Telecom cryptage m

encumber /ɪn'kʌmbə(r)/ vtr encombrer (**with** de)

encumbrance /ɪn'kʌmbrəns/ n (hindrance) entrave f (**to** à); (burden) (person) charge f (**to** pour); (possession) embarras m (**to** pour)

encyclop(a)edia /ɪn,saɪklə'pi:dɪə/ n encyclopédie f

end /end/
A n ①▸ (final part) fin f; **'The End'** (of film, book etc) 'Fin'; **at the ~ of** à la fin de [year, story]; **at the ~ of May** fin mai; **by the ~ of** à la fin de [year, journey, game]; **to put an ~ to sth, to bring sth to an ~** mettre fin à qch; **to get to the ~ of** arriver à la fin de [holiday]; arriver au bout de [story, work]; **to come to an ~** se terminer; **in the ~ I went home** finalement je suis rentré chez moi; **in the ~, at the ~ of the day** (all things considered) en fin de compte; **it's the ~ of the line** ou **road for the project** le projet arrive en fin de course; **for days on ~** pendant des jours et des jours; **there is no ~ to his talent** son talent n'a pas de limites; **no ~ of°** trouble énormément de problèmes; **that really is the ~°!** c'est vraiment le comble°!; **you really are the ~°!** tu exagères!; ②▸ (extremity) bout m, extrémité f; **at the ~ of, on the ~ of** au bout de; **at the ~ of the garden** au fond du jardin; **from one ~ to another** d'un bout à l'autre; **from ~ to ~** de bout en bout; **to lay sth ~ to ~** poser qch bout à bout; **the lower ~ of the street** le bas de la rue; **the third from the ~** le/la troisième avant la fin; **to stand sth on (its) ~** mettre qch debout; ③▸ (side of conversation, transaction) côté m; **things are fine at my** ou **this ~** de mon côté tout va bien; **to keep one's ~ up** tenir bon; **there was silence at the other ~** c'était le silence au bout du fil; ④▸ (of scale, spectrum) extrémité f; **at the lower ~ of the scale** au plus bas de l'échelle; **this suit is from the cheaper** ou **bottom ~ of the range** ce costume est un des moins chers de la gamme; ⑤▸ (aim) but m; **to this** ou **that ~** dans ce but; **a means to an ~** un moyen d'arriver à ses fins; ⑥▸ Sport côté m, camp m; **to change ~s** changer de côté; ⑦▸ (scrap) (of rope, string) bout m; (of loaf, joint of meat) reste m; ⑧▸ (death) mort f; **to meet**

one's **~** trouver la mort; **to be nearing one's ~** sentir sa fin proche; **to come to a bad ~** mal finir
B noun modifier [house] du bout; [carriage] de queue
C vtr gen mettre fin à; rompre [marriage]; **to ~ sth with** terminer qch par; **he ~ed his days in hospital** il a fini ses jours à l'hôpital; **to ~ it all** en finir avec la vie; **the sale to ~ all sales** ce qu'il y a de mieux comme soldes
D vi gen se terminer (**in, with** par); [contract, agreement] expirer; **where will it all ~?** comment tout cela finira-t-il?
Idiom **all's well that ~s well** tout est bien qui finit bien
Phrasal verb
■ **end up:** ▸ finir par devenir [president]; finir par être [rich]; **to ~ up (by) doing** finir par faire; **to ~ up in Paris** se retrouver à Paris

endanger /ɪn'deɪndʒə(r)/ vtr mettre [qch] en danger [health, life]; constituer une menace pour [environment, species]; compromettre [reputation, career, prospects]; **~ed species** espèce f menacée

endear /ɪn'dɪə(r)/
A vtr **to ~ sb to** faire aimer qn de
B v refl **to ~ oneself to sb** se faire aimer or apprécier de qn

endearing /ɪn'dɪərɪŋ/ adj [person, habit] attachant; [remark] touchant; [smile] engageant

endearingly /ɪn'dɪərɪŋlɪ/ adv [smile] de manière touchante; **~ honest** d'une honnêteté touchante

endearment /ɪn'dɪəmənt/ n terme m d'affection; **terms of ~** termes mpl d'affection

endeavour, endeavor US /ɪn'devə(r)/
A n (attempt) tentative f (**to do** de faire); (industriousness) effort m
B vtr **to ~ to do** (do one's best) faire tout son possible pour faire; (find a means) trouver un moyen de faire

endemic /en'demɪk/
A n endémie f
B adj endémique (**in, to** dans)

ending /'endɪŋ/ n gen fin f, dénouement m; Ling terminaison f

endive /'endɪv, US -daɪv/ n GB (lettuce) chicorée f; US (chicory) endive f

endless /'endlɪs/ adj (unlimited) gen infini; [supply, stock] inépuisable; (interminable) interminable

endlessly /'endlɪslɪ/ adv ①▸ (unlimitedly) infiniment; ②▸ (without stopping) [talk, cry, argue] sans s'arrêter; [search, play, try] inlassablement; ③▸ (to infinity) [stretch, extend] à perte de vue

endo+ /'endəʊ/ combining form endo+

endocrinology /,endəʊkrɪ'nɒlədʒɪ/ n endocrinologie f

endorse /ɪn'dɔ:s/ vtr ①▸ donner son aval à [view, policy]; appuyer [candidate, decision]; approuver [product, claim]; endosser [cheque, bill]; ②▸ GB Aut **to have one's licence ~d** ≈ perdre des points sur son permis de conduire

endorsement /ɪn'dɔ:smənt/ n ①▸ (of opinion, claim) approbation f (**of** de); (of candidate) appui m (**of** à); (of decision) sanction f (**of** à propos de); (of cheque) endossement m; ②▸ GB Aut **he has had two ~s for speeding** ≈ il a perdu des points pour excès de vitesse

endow /ɪn'daʊ/ vtr (with money) doter [hospital, charity, person] (**with** de); fonder [academic post]

endowment /ɪn'daʊmənt/ n ①▸ (action) (of hospital, school) dotation f; (of prize, academic post) fondation f; (money given) dotation f; ②▸ (talent) don m

endowment insurance n assurance f à capital différé

end: **~paper** n page f de garde; **~ product** n produit m fini; **~ result** n résultat m final

endurable /ɪn'djʊərəbl, US -'dʊər-/ adj supportable

endurance /ɪn'djʊərəns, US -dʊə-/ n (physical) endurance f; (moral) courage m; (of cold) résistance f; **past** ou **beyond ~** intolérable; **to provoke sb beyond ~** pousser qn à bout

endurance test n Sport, Mil épreuve f d'endurance

endure /ɪn'djʊə(r), US -'dʊər/
A vtr endurer [personal experience, hardship]; supporter [behaviour, sight, person]; subir [attack, defeat, imprisonment]
B vi durer

enduring /ɪn'djʊərɪŋ, US -'dʊə-/ adj [influence, fame] durable; [grudge] tenace; [ability] constant; [government] stable; [charm] éternel

end user n Comm, Comput utilisateur m final

enema /'enɪmə/ n Med lavement m

enemy /'enəmɪ/

A n (pl **-mies**) gen, fig, Mil ennemi/-e m/f; **to make enemies** se faire des ennemis; **to be one's own worst ~** être son pire ennemi; **to go over to the ~** passer à l'ennemi

B noun modifier [forces, aircraft, propaganda, territory] ennemi; [agent] de l'ennemi; **~ alien** ressortissant/-e m/f d'un pays ennemi; **killed by ~ action** tombé sous le feu de l'ennemi; **under ~ occupation** occupé par l'ennemi

energetic /ˌenə'dʒetɪk/ adj (full of life) gen énergique; [exercise] vigoureux/-euse; [debate] animé

energetically /ˌenə'dʒetɪklɪ/ adv [work, exercise] avec vigueur; [deny] vigoureusement; [speak, promote, publicize] avec force

energize /'enədʒaɪz/ vtr gen stimuler; Elec alimenter [qch] en courant

energizing /'enədʒaɪzɪŋ/ adj [influence] stimulant

energy /'enədʒɪ/ n ① (vitality) énergie f; **it would be a waste of ~** ce serait se donner du mal pour rien; ② (power, fuel) énergie f; **nuclear ~** énergie f nucléaire

energy: **~ efficiency** n économies fpl d'énergie; **~ resources** npl ressources fpl énergétiques

energy saving

A n économies fpl d'énergie

B **energy-saving** adj [device] qui permet de faire des économies d'énergie; [measure] destiné à économiser l'énergie

enervate /'enəveɪt/ vtr débiliter

enfold /ɪn'fəʊld/ vtr envelopper

enforce /ɪn'fɔːs/ vtr ① (impose) appliquer [rule, policy, decision]; faire respecter [law, court order]; faire valoir [legal rights]; imposer [silence, discipline]; exiger [payment]; faire exécuter [contract]; ② (strengthen) renforcer [opinion, hypothesis]; appuyer [argument, theory]

enforced /ɪn'fɔːst/ adj [abstinence, redundancy] forcé

enforcement /ɪn'fɔːsmənt/ n gen application f; (of discipline) imposition f

engage /ɪn'ɡeɪdʒ/

A vtr ① (attract) retenir [attention]; éveiller [interest, sympathy]; séduire [imagination]; ② (involve) **to be ~d in** se livrer à [activity]; **to be ~d in discussions/negotiations** être en discussion/négociations; **to ~ sb in conversation** engager la conversation avec qn; **to be otherwise ~d** être pris ailleurs; **to be ~d in doing** être en train de faire; ③ (employ) prendre [lawyer]; engager [secretary, interpreter]; ④ Aut passer [gear]; **to ~ the clutch** embrayer; ⑤ Mil engager le combat avec [enemy]

B vi sout **to ~ in** se livrer à [activity]; se lancer dans [research]; engager [dialogue, negotiations, combat]

engaged /ɪn'ɡeɪdʒd/ adj ① (before marriage) **to be ~** être fiancé (**to** à); **to get ~d** se fiancer (**to** à); ② [WC, phone] occupé; [taxi] pris

engaged tone n GB tonalité f 'occupé'

engagement /ɪn'ɡeɪdʒmənt/ n ① (appointment) rendezvous m inv; (for performer, artist) engagement m; **official ou public ~** obligation f officielle; **social ou prior ~** obligation f sociale; **I have a dinner ~ tomorrow** j'ai un dîner demain; ② (before marriage) fiançailles fpl

engagement: **~ book** n agenda m; **~ ring** n bague f de fiançailles

engaging /ɪn'ɡeɪdʒɪŋ/ adj [character] attachant; [person, laugh, tale] charmant; [smile] engageant

engender /ɪn'dʒendə(r)/ vtr engendrer, causer

engine /'endʒɪn/ n ① (in car, train, aeroplane, boat) moteur m; (in jet) réacteur m; (in ship) machines fpl; **jet ~** moteur à réaction; ② Rail (locomotive) locomotive f; **diesel/steam ~** locomotive diesel/à vapeur; **to sit facing the ~** être assis dans le sens de la marche

engine driver ► p. 1181 n mécanicien m

engineer /ˌendʒɪ'nɪə(r)/ ► p. 1181

A n (graduate) ingénieur m; (in factory) mécanicien m monteur; (repairer) technicien m; (on ship) mécanicien m; US Rail mécanicien m; **heating ~** chauffagiste m; **telephone ~** technicien m des télécommunications; ► **civil engineer etc**

B vtr ① (plot) manigancer; ② (build) construire

engineering /ˌendʒɪ'nɪərɪŋ/ n ① (subject, science) gen ingénierie f; **civil ~** génie m civil; ② (industry) industrie f mécanique; **light ~** génie m léger

engineering: **~ company** n société f de constructions mécaniques; **~ department** n Univ département

m d'ingénierie; **~ factory**, **~ works** n usine f de constructions mécaniques; **~ industry** n industrie f mécanique; **~ science** n Univ ingénierie f

engine: **~ failure** n gen panne f de moteur; (in jet) panne f de réacteur; **~ oil** n huile f; **~ room** n salle f des machines; **~ shed** n Rail dépôt m

England /'ɪŋɡlənd/ ► p. 774 pr n Angleterre f

English /'ɪŋɡlɪʃ/ ► p. 1032, p. 969

A n ① (language) anglais m; **the Queen's ~** l'anglais correct; ② (people) **the ~** les Anglais mpl

B adj [language, history] anglais; [lesson, teacher] d'anglais

English: **~ as a Foreign Language**, **EFL** n anglais m langue étrangère; **~ as a Second Language**, **ESL** n anglais m deuxième langue

English Channel n **the ~** la Manche

English: **~ for Special Purposes**, **ESP** n anglais m de spécialités; **~ Language Teaching**, **ELT** n enseignement m de l'anglais

Englishman /'ɪŋɡlɪʃmən/ n (pl **-men**) Anglais m

Idiom **an ~'s home is his castle** Prov ≈ charbonnier est maître dans sa maison Prov

English: **~ rose** n jeune fille f au teint frais; **~ speaker** n anglophone mf; **~-speaking** adj anglophone; **~woman** n (pl **-women**) Anglaise f

engrave /ɪn'ɡreɪv/ vtr graver

engraving /ɪn'ɡreɪvɪŋ/ n gravure f

engross /ɪn'ɡrəʊs/ vtr **~ed in** absorbé or plongé dans

engrossing /ɪn'ɡrəʊsɪŋ/ adj absorbant

engulf /ɪn'ɡʌlf/ vtr [sea, waves, fire] engloutir; [silence] envelopper; [panic] s'emparer de

enhance /ɪn'hɑːns, US -hæns/ vtr améliorer [prospects, status]; accroître [rights, power]; rehausser [public image]; mettre [qch] en valeur [appearance, qualities]; augmenter [value]; majorer [pension, salary]

enigma /ɪ'nɪɡmə/ n énigme f

enigmatic /ˌenɪɡ'mætɪk/ adj énigmatique

enjoy /ɪn'dʒɔɪ/

A vtr ① (get pleasure from) aimer; **I ~ looking after Paul** j'aime bien m'occuper de Paul; **he knows how to ~ life** il sait vivre; **I ~ed my day in London** j'ai passé une bonne journée à Londres; **I didn't ~ the party** je ne me suis pas bien amusé à la soirée; **the tourists are ~ing the good weather** les touristes profitent du beau temps; **~ your meal!** bon appétit!; ② (benefit from) jouir de

B v refl **to ~ oneself** s'amuser (**doing** à faire); **~ yourselves!** amusez-vous bien!

enjoyable /ɪn'dʒɔɪəbl/ adj agréable

enjoyment /ɪn'dʒɔɪmənt/ n (pleasure) plaisir m; (of privileges, rights) jouissance f (**of** de); **to get ~ from chess** prendre plaisir à jouer aux échecs; **to read for ~** lire pour le plaisir

enlarge /ɪn'lɑːdʒ/

A vtr agrandir [space, photograph]; développer [business]; augmenter [capacity]

B vi ① (get bigger) [space] s'agrandir; [majority] s'accroître; ② [pupil, pores] se dilater; [tonsils] enfler; ③ **to ~ on** s'étendre sur [subject]; développer [idea]

C **enlarged** pp adj Med [pupil] dilaté; [tonsils, joint] enflé; [heart, liver] hypertrophié

enlargement /ɪn'lɑːdʒmənt/ n ① (of space, photograph, document) agrandissement m; (of territory) élargissement m; (of business) accroissement m; (of index) augmentation f; ② Med (of pupil) dilatation f; (of heart, liver) hypertrophie f

enlarger /ɪn'lɑːdʒə(r)/ n Phot agrandisseur m

enlighten /ɪn'laɪtn/ vtr éclairer (**on** sur)

enlightened /ɪn'laɪtnd/ adj éclairé

enlightening /ɪn'laɪtnɪŋ/ adj instructif/-ive

enlightenment /ɪn'laɪtnmənt/ n (edification) instruction f; (clarification) éclaircissement m; **(the Age of) the Enlightenment** le Siècle des lumières

enlist /ɪn'lɪst/

A vtr Mil, fig recruter; **to ~ sb's help** s'assurer l'aide de qn

B vi Mil s'enrôler, s'engager

enmesh /ɪn'meʃ/ vtr **to become ~ed in** s'empêtrer dans

enmity /'enmətɪ/ n inimitié f (**towards** envers)

ennoble /ɪ'nəʊbl/ vtr lit anoblir; fig ennoblir

enormity /ɪ'nɔːmətɪ/ n énormité f

enormous /ɪ'nɔːməs/ adj gen énorme; [effort] prodigieux/-ieuse; **an ~ amount of** énormément de; **an ~ number of people** un monde fou

enormously /ɪ'nɔːməslɪ/ adv [change, enjoy, vary] énormément; [big, long, complex, impressed] extrêmement

enough /ɪ'nʌf/

> ⚠ When *enough* is used as an adverb or a pronoun, it is most frequently translated by *assez*: *is the house big enough?* = est-ce que la maison est assez grande? (Note that *assez* comes before the adjective); *will there be enough?* = est-ce qu'il y en aura assez? (Note that if the sentence does not specify what it is enough of, the pronoun *en*, meaning *of it/of them*, must be added before the verb in French.)
> When used as a determiner, *enough* is generally translated by *assez de*: *we haven't bought enough meat* = nous n'avons pas acheté assez de viande; *there's enough meat for two meals/six people* = il y a assez de viande pour deux repas/six personnes; *have you got enough chairs?* = avez-vous assez de chaises? For more examples and particular usages, see the entry below.

adv, det, pron assez; **big ~ for us** assez grand pour nous; **big ~ to hold 50 people** assez grand pour contenir 50 personnes; **quite big ~** bien assez grand **(for** pour; **to do** pour faire); **just wide ~** juste assez large **(for** pour; **to do** pour faire); **to eat ~** manger assez; **have you had ~ to eat?** avez-vous assez mangé?; **~ money/seats** d'argent/de sièges; **there's more than ~ for everybody** il y en a plus qu'assez *or* largement assez pour tout le monde; **is there ~?** y en a-t-il assez?; **is he old ~ to vote?** a-t-il l'âge de voter?; **you're not trying hard ~** tu ne fais pas assez d'efforts; **curiously ~, I like her** aussi bizarre que cela puisse paraître, je l'aime bien; **will that be ~ (money)?** est-ce que ça suffira?; **I've had ~ of him** j'en ai assez de lui; **I've had ~ of working for one day** j'ai assez travaillé pour aujourd'hui; **I've got ~ to worry about** j'ai assez de soucis (comme ça); **I think you have said ~** je crois que vous en avez dit assez; **once was ~ for me!** une fois m'a suffi!; **that's ~ (from you)!** assez!; **~ said!** j'ai compris!; **she's a nice ~ woman** elle n'est pas désagréable; **~'s ~** ça suffit (comme ça); **and sure ~...!** et ça n'a pas manqué...!

(Idiom) **~ is as good as a feast** Prov ≈ il ne faut pas abuser des bonnes choses

enquire vtr, vi = inquire

enquiry n = inquiry

enrage /ɪn'reɪdʒ/ vtr mettre [qn] en rage, rendre [qn] furieux/-ieuse

enraged /ɪn'reɪdʒd/ adj furieux/-ieuse

enrich /ɪn'rɪtʃ/ vtr (all contexts) enrichir

enrol, enroll US /ɪn'rəʊl/ (p prés etc **-ll-**)
A vtr gen inscrire; Mil enrôler
B vi gen s'inscrire; Mil s'engager (**in** dans); **to ~ on a course** s'inscrire à un cours

enrolment, enrollment US /ɪn'rəʊlmənt/ n gen inscription f (**in, on** à); Mil enrôlement m

ensconce /ɪn'skɒns/ vtr **~d in** bien installé dans

ensign /'ensən/ n (flag) pavillon m; (officer) enseigne m

ensuing /ɪn'sjuːɪŋ, US -'suː-/ adj [period] qui suivit; [event] qui s'ensuivit

en suite /,ɒn 'swiːt/ adj attenant

ensure /ɪn'ʃɔː(r), US ɪn'ʃʊər/ vtr garantir; **to ~ that...** s'assurer que...

ENT n (abrév = Ear, Nose and Throat) ORL f

entail /ɪn'teɪl/ vtr impliquer [travel, action, work]; exiger [patience, discretion]; entraîner [change, expense, responsibility, study]; nécessiter [effort, time, journey, modification]; **to ~ that...** impliquer que... (+ subj)

entangle /ɪn'tæŋgl/ vtr ⊡ lit **to become ~d** s'enchevêtrer (**in** dans); **to be ~d in sth** être pris dans qch; ⊡ fig **to be ~d with** être étroitement lié à [ideology]; (sexually) se compromettre avec

entanglement /ɪn'tæŋglmənt/ n ⊡ (complicated situation) imbroglio m; ⊡ (involvement) liaison f (**with** avec)

enter /'entə(r)/
A vtr ⊡ (go into) entrer dans, pénétrer dans; ⊡ (commence) entrer dans [phase, period]; entamer [new term, final year];

the country is ~ing a recession le pays s'engage dans la récession; ⊡ (join) entrer dans [profession, firm, army]; participer à [race, competition]; entrer à [institution, parliament, party, EC]; **to ~ the war** entrer en guerre; **to ~ the Church** entrer en religion; ⊡ (put forward) inscrire [competitor, candidate] (**for** à); engager [horse] (**for** dans); présenter [poem, picture] (**for** à); ⊡ (record) inscrire [figure, fact] (**in** dans); (in diary) noter [fact, appointment] (**in** dans); **to ~ an item in the books** (in bookkeeping) porter un article (sur le livre de comptes); ⊡ fig (come into) venir à l'idée *or* à l'esprit de qn; ⊡ Comput entrer [data]
B vi ⊡ (come in) entrer; ⊡ (enrol) **to ~ for** s'inscrire à [exam]; s'inscrire pour [race]

(Phrasal verbs)

■ **enter into:** ▸ **~ into** [sth] ⊡ (embark on) entrer en [correspondence, conversation]; entamer [negotiations, argument]; se lancer dans [explanations]; conclure [deal]; passer [agreement, contract]; **to ~ into detail** entrer dans les détails; **to ~ into the spirit of the game** entrer dans le jeu; ⊡ (be part of) faire partie de [plans]; **that doesn't ~ into it** c'est sans rapport

■ **enter on = enter upon**

■ **enter up:** ▸ **~ up** [sth], **~** [sth] **up** inscrire [figure, total]

■ **enter upon:** ▸ **~ upon** [sth] s'engager dans

enteritis /,entə'raɪtɪs/ ▸ p. 933 n entérite f

enterprise /'entəpraɪz/ n ⊡ (undertaking) entreprise f; (venture) aventure f; **business ~** affaire f commerciale; ⊡ (initiative) esprit m d'initiative; ⊡ Econ entreprise f; **private ~** entreprise privée

enterprising /'entəpraɪzɪŋ/ adj [person] entreprenant; [plan] audacieux/-ieuse; **it was very ~ of you** vous avez fait preuve de beaucoup d'initiative

enterprisingly /'entəpraɪzɪŋlɪ/ adv de sa propre initiative

entertain /,entə'teɪn/
A vtr ⊡ (keep amused) divertir; (make laugh) amuser; (keep occupied) distraire, occuper; ⊡ (play host to) recevoir; ⊡ entretenir [ideal]; nourrir [doubt, ambition, illusion]
B vi recevoir

entertainer /,entə'teɪnə(r)/ ▸ p. 1181 n (comic) comique mf; (performer, raconteur) amuseur/-euse m/f

entertaining /,entə'teɪnɪŋ/
A adj divertissant
B n art m de recevoir; **they do a lot of ~** ils reçoivent beaucoup

entertainment /,entə'teɪnmənt/
A n ⊡ ¢ divertissement m, distractions fpl; **for sb's ~** pour le divertissement de qn; **the world of ~** le monde du spectacle; ⊡ (event) spectacle m
B noun modifier [allowance, expenses] de représentation; [industry] du spectacle

enthralling /ɪn'θrɔːlɪŋ/ adj [novel, performance] captivant

enthuse /ɪn'θjuːz, US -θuːz/ vi s'extasier (**about, over** devant)

enthusiasm /ɪn'θjuːzɪæzəm, US -'θuːz-/ n ⊡ ¢ enthousiasme m (**for** pour); ⊡ (hobby) passion f

enthusiast /ɪn'θjuːzɪæst, US -'θuːz-/ n (for sport, DIY) passionné/-e m/f; (for music, composer) fervent/-e m/f

enthusiastic /ɪn,θjuːzɪ'æstɪk, US -,θuːz-/ adj [crowd, response] enthousiaste; [discussion] exalté; [worker, gardener] passionné; [member] fervent; **to be ~ about sth** (present or future event) être enthousiasmé par qch; (past event) parler de qch avec enthousiasme; **he's not very ~ about his work** il ne montre pas beaucoup d'enthousiasme pour son travail

enthusiastically /ɪn,θjuːzɪ'æstɪklɪ, US -,θuːz-/ adv avec enthousiasme

entice /ɪn'taɪs/ vtr (with offer, charms, prospects) attirer; (with food, money) appâter; **to ~ sb to do** persuader qn de faire

(Phrasal verb)

■ **entice away:** ▸ **~** [sb] **away** détourner

enticing /ɪn'taɪsɪŋ/ adj [prospect, offer] attrayant; [person] séduisant; [food, smell] appétissant

entire /ɪn'taɪə(r)/ adj entier/-ière; **the ~ family** toute la famille, la famille (tout) entière; **throughout her ~ career** pendant toute sa carrière; **our ~ support** notre soutien absolu; **the ~ length of the street** toute la longueur de la rue; **the ~ 50,000 dollars** les 50 000 dollars dans leur totalité; **we are in ~ agreement** nous sommes entièrement d'accord

entirely /ɪnˈtaɪəlɪ/ adv [destroy, escape] entièrement; [reject] totalement; [innocent, different, unnecessary] complètement; **that changes things ~** ça change tout; **not ~** pas tout à fait

entirety /ɪnˈtaɪərətɪ/ n ensemble m, totalité f; **in its ~** dans son ensemble

entitle /ɪnˈtaɪtl/ vtr **1** (authorize) **to ~ sb to sth** donner droit à qch à qn; **to ~ sb to do** autoriser qn à faire; **to be ~d to sth** avoir droit à qch; **to be ~d to do** avoir le droit de faire; **everyone's ~d to their own opinion** à chacun ses opinions; **2** (call) intituler [text, music]; donner un titre à [work of art]; **the poem is ~d 'Love'** le poème s'intitule 'L'amour'

entitlement /ɪnˈtaɪtlmənt/ n droit m (**to sth** à qch; **to do** de faire)

entity /ˈentətɪ/ n entité f

entomology /ˌentəˈmɒlədʒɪ/ n entomologie f

entrance
A /ˈentrəns/ n **1** (door, act of entering) entrée f; **to make an ~** Theat, fig faire son entrée; **2** (admission) admission f; **to gain ~ to** être admis à or dans [club, university]; **to deny** ou **refuse sb ~** refuser de laisser entrer qn
B /ɪnˈtrɑːns, US -ˈtræns/ vtr transporter, ravir

entrance: ~ examination n GB Sch, Univ examen m d'entrée; (for civil service) concours m d'entrée; **~ fee** n droit m d'entrée; **~ hall** n (in house) vestibule m; (in public building) hall m; **~ requirements** npl diplômes mpl requis; **~ ticket** n billet m d'entrée

entrancing /ɪnˈtrɑːnsɪŋ, US -ˈtræns-/ adj ravissant

entrant /ˈentrənt/ n (in race, competition) participant/-e m/f; (in exam) candidat/-e m/f

entreat /ɪnˈtriːt/ vtr implorer, supplier (**to do** de faire)

entreatingly /ɪnˈtriːtɪŋlɪ/ adv [beg, ask] d'une voix suppliante or implorante; [gaze] d'un air suppliant or implorant

entreaty /ɪnˈtriːtɪ/ n prière f, supplication f

entrée /ˈɒntreɪ/ n **1** Culin GB entrée f; US plat m principal; **2** (into society) **her wealth gave her an ~ into high society** sa fortune lui a ouvert les portes de la haute société

entrenched /ɪnˈtrentʃt/ adj **1** Mil retranché; **2** fig [opinion] inébranlable; [idea] bien arrêté; [tradition, rights] bien établi

entrepreneur /ˌɒntrəprəˈnɜː(r)/ n entrepreneur/-euse m/f

entrepreneurial /ˌɒntrəprəˈnɜːrɪəl/ adj **to have ~ spirit/skills** avoir le sens/le don des affaires

entrust /ɪnˈtrʌst/ vtr confier; **to ~ sb with sth, to ~ sth to sb** confier qch à qn

entry /ˈentrɪ/ n **1** (door, act of entering) entrée f; **to gain ~ to** ou **into** s'introduire dans [building]; (to computer file); **to force ~ to** ou **into** s'introduire de force dans; **2** (admission) gen admission f; (to country) entrée f; **'no ~'** (on door) 'défense d'entrer'; (in one way street) 'sens interdit'; **3** (recorded item) (in dictionary, log) entrée f; (in encyclopedia) article m; (in diary) note f; (in register) inscription f; (in ledger, accounts book) écriture f; **to make an ~ in one's diary** écrire or noter quelque chose dans son journal; **4** (for competition) œuvre f présent ée à un concours; (for song contest) titre m; **send your ~ to...** envoyez votre réponse à...

entry: ~ fee n droit m d'entrée; **~ form** n fiche f d'inscription; **~-level** adj [product] entrée de gamme; **~ permit** n visa m d'entrée; **~ phone** n interphone m; **~ requirements** npl diplômes mpl requis; **~ word** n US entrée f

entwine /ɪnˈtwaɪn/
A vtr lit entrelacer; fig mêler (**with** à)
B v lit s'entrelacer; fig s'entremêler

E number n GB (number) numéro d'additif alimentaire (approuvé par la UE); (additive) additif m alimentaire

enumerate /ɪˈnjuːməreɪt, US -ˈnuː-/ vtr sout énumérer

enumeration /ɪˌnjuːməˈreɪʃn, US -ˌnuː-/ n sout (list) énumération f; (counting) dénombrement m

enunciate /ɪˈnʌnsɪeɪt/ vtr articuler [words, lines]; énoncer [truth, clause]; exposer [principle, policy]

enunciation /ɪˌnʌnsɪˈeɪʃn/ n (of word) articulation f; (of facts) énonciation f; (of principle) exposé m

envelop /ɪnˈveləp/ vtr envelopper

envelope /ˈenvələʊp, ˈɒn-/ n enveloppe f; **to put sth in an ~** mettre qch sous enveloppe

Idiom **to push the ~** faire œuvre nouvelle, innover

enviable /ˈenvɪəbl/ adj enviable

enviably /ˈenvɪəblɪ/ adv **he was ~ slim/rich** sa minceur/richesse faisait envie

envious /ˈenvɪəs/ adj [person] envieux/-ieuse; [look] d'envie, envieux/-ieuse; **to be ~ of sb/sth** envier qn/qch; **to make sb ~** rendre qn jaloux/-ouse

enviously /ˈenvɪəslɪ/ adv avec envie

environment /ɪnˈvaɪərənmənt/ n (physical, cultural) environnement m; (social) milieu m; **friendly ~** ambiance f amicale; **working ~** conditions fpl de travail

environmental /ɪnˌvaɪərənˈmentl/ adj [conditions, changes] du milieu; [concern, issue] lié à l'environnement, écologique; [damage, protection, pollution] de l'environnement; **~ effect** conséquences fpl sur l'environnement; **~ group** groupe m écologiste; **~ disaster** catastrophe f écologique

environmental health n hygiène f publique

environmentalist /ɪnˌvaɪərənˈmentəlɪst/ n Pol, Ecol écologiste mf

environmentally /ɪnˌvaɪərənˈmentəlɪ/ adv **~ safe**, **~ sound** qui ne nuit pas à l'environnement; **~ speaking** en ce qui concerne l'environnement; **~ friendly product** produit qui respecte l'environnement

environmental: ~ scientist n écologiste mf; **Environmental Studies** npl GB Sch études fpl géographiques et biologiques de l'environnement

envisage /ɪnˈvɪzɪdʒ/ vtr (anticipate) prévoir (**doing** de faire); (visualize) envisager (**doing** de faire)

envy /ˈenvɪ/
A n (brief) envie f; (long-term) jalousie f; **out of ~** par jalousie; **in ~** par envie; **to be the ~ of sb** faire envie à qn
B vtr envier; **to ~ sb sth** envier qch à qn

enzyme /ˈenzaɪm/ n enzyme f

EOC n GB abrév ► **Equal Opportunities Commission**

ephemeral /ɪˈfemərəl/ adj (all contexts) éphémère

epic /ˈepɪk/
A n gen épopée f; (film) film m à grand spectacle; (novel) roman-fleuve m
B adj épique

epicentre GB, **epicenter** US /ˈepɪsentə(r)/ n épicentre m

epidemic /ˌepɪˈdemɪk/
A n lit, fig épidémie f
B adj épidémique

epidermis /ˌepɪˈdɜːmɪs/ n épiderme m

epidural /ˌepɪˈdjʊərəl/
A n Med (anaesthetic) péridurale f
B adj épidural; Med [anaesthetic] péridural

epigram /ˈepɪgræm/ n épigramme f

epilepsy /ˈepɪlepsɪ/ **► p. 933** n épilepsie f

epileptic /ˌepɪˈleptɪk/ n, adj épileptique (mf)

Epiphany /ɪˈpɪfənɪ/ n Épiphanie f, jour m des Rois

episode /ˈepɪsəʊd/ n (all contexts) épisode m

episodic /ˌepɪˈsɒdɪk/ adj épisodique

epistle /ɪˈpɪsl/ n épître f also hum

epitaph /ˈepɪtɑːf, US -tæf/ n épitaphe f also fig

epithet /ˈepɪθet/ n épithète f

epitome /ɪˈpɪtəmɪ/ n (abstract) épitomé m; fig **the ~ of kindness** la bonté incarnée

epitomize /ɪˈpɪtəmaɪz/ vtr (embody) personnifier, incarner

epoch /ˈiːpɒk, US ˈepək/ n époque f

epoch-making adj [invention, event] marquant

eponymous /ɪˈpɒnɪməs/ adj éponyme

equable /ˈekwəbl/ adj [climate] tempéré; [temperament] égal

equably /ˈekwəblɪ/ adv calmement

equal /ˈiːkwəl/
A n égal/-e m/f
B adj **1** (same number, status, type) égal (**to** à); **'~ work ~ pay'** 'à

travail égal salaire égal'; **to fight for ∼ pay** lutter pour l'égalité des salaires; **they're about ∼** [*candidates*] ils se valent à peu près; **on ∼ terms** [*fight, compete*] à armes égales; [*judge, place*] sur un pied d'égalité; **2** (up to) to **be/feel ∼ to** être/se sentir à la hauteur de; **to feel ∼ to doing** se sentir à même de faire
C *adv* Sport [*finish*] à égalité
D *vtr* égaler
(Idiom) **all things being ∼** sauf imprévu

equality /ɪˈkwɒlətɪ/ *n* égalité *f*; **sexual ∼** égalité des sexes

equalize /ˈiːkwəlaɪz/ *vtr, vi* égaliser

equalizer /ˈiːkwəlaɪzə(r)/ *n* **1** Sport but *m* égalisateur; **2** Audio correcteur *m* de fréquence

equally /ˈiːkwəlɪ/ *adv* [*divide, share*] en parts égales; **∼ difficult/pretty** tout aussi difficile/joli; **∼, we might say that...** de même, on pourrait dire que...

Equal Opportunities Commission, **EOC** *n* GB Commission *f* de l'égalité de traitement

equal opportunity
A **equal opportunities** *npl* égalité *f* des chances
B *noun modifier* [*employer*] appliquant la non-discrimination; [*legislation*] qui assure l'égalité d'accès

equal: **∼ rights** *npl* égalité *f* des droits; **∼s sign** GB, **∼ sign** US *n* signe *m* égal

equanimity /ˌekwəˈnɪmətɪ/ *n* sérénité *f*

equate /ɪˈkweɪt/ *vtr* (identify) assimiler (**with, to** à); (compare) comparer (**with, to** à)

equation /ɪˈkweɪʒn/ *n* Math équation *f*; fig **the other side of the ∼** l'autre aspect du problème

equator /ɪˈkweɪtə(r)/ *n* équateur *m*

equatorial /ˌekwəˈtɔːrɪəl/ *adj* équatorial

Equatorial Guinea *pr n* Guinée *f* équatoriale

equestrian /ɪˈkwestrɪən/ *adj* [*statue, portrait*] équestre; [*competition*] hippique

equidistant /ˌiːkwɪˈdɪstənt/ *adj* gen à égale distance (**from** de)

equilateral /ˌiːkwɪˈlætərəl/ *adj* équilatéral

equilibrium /ˌiːkwɪˈlɪbrɪəm/ *n* (*pl* **-riums** *ou* **-ria**) (all contexts) équilibre *m*; **in ∼** en équilibre

equine /ˈekwaɪn/ *adj* [*disease*] équin; [*species, features*] chevalin

equinox /ˈiːkwɪnɒks, ˈek-/ *n* équinoxe *m*

equip /ɪˈkwɪp/ *vtr* (*p prés etc* **-pp-**) **1** lit équiper (**for** pour); **well ∼ped with sth** bien pourvu en qch; **fully ∼ped kitchen** cuisine équipée; **2** fig (psychologically) préparer; **we were well ∼ped to answer their questions** nous étions à même de répondre à leurs questions

equipment /ɪˈkwɪpmənt/ *n* Ind, Mil, Sport équipement *m*; (office, electrical, photographic) matériel *m*; **a piece** *ou* **item of ∼** un article

equitable /ˈekwɪtəbl/ *adj* équitable

equity /ˈekwɪtɪ/
A *n* (fairness) équité *f*; Fin participation *f*
B **equities** *npl* Fin actions *fpl* ordinaires
C **Equity** *pr n* Theat syndicat *m* des acteurs

equity: **∼ capital** *n* Fin capital *m* en actions; **∼ financing** *n* Fin financement *m* par émission d'actions; **∼ market** *n* Fin marché *m* des actions

equivalent /ɪˈkwɪvələnt/
A *n* équivalent *m*
B *adj* équivalent; **∼ to sth** équivalent à qch

equivocal /ɪˈkwɪvəkl/ *adj* [*words, attitude*] équivoque; [*result*] incertain; [*behaviour, circumstances*] suspect

equivocate /ɪˈkwɪvəkeɪt/ *vi* user de faux-fuyants

equivocation /ɪˌkwɪvəˈkeɪʃn/ *n* faux-fuyants *mpl*

era /ˈɪərə/ *n* gen ère *f*; (in politics, fashion etc) époque *f*

eradicate /ɪˈrædɪkeɪt/ *vtr* gen éliminer; éradiquer [*disease*]

eradication /ɪˌrædɪˈkeɪʃn/ *n* gen élimination *f*; (of disease) éradication *f*

erase /ɪˈreɪz, US ɪˈreɪs/ *vtr* **1** lit, Audio, Comput effacer; **2** fig éliminer [*poverty*]; effacer [*memory*]

erase head *n* Audio, Comput tête *f* d'effacement

eraser /ɪˈreɪzə(r), US -sər/ *n* (for paper) gomme *f*; (for blackboard) brosse *f* feutrée

eraser head *n* = **erase head**

erasure /ɪˈreɪʒə(r)/ *n* (act) effacement *m*; (result) rature *f*

erect /ɪˈrekt/
A *adj* [*posture*] droit; [*tail, ears*] dressé; [*construction*] debout; [*penis*] en érection; **with head ∼** la tête haute; **to hold oneself ∼** se tenir droit
B *vtr* ériger [*building*]; monter [*scaffolding, tent, sign, screen*]; fig ériger [*system*]

erection /ɪˈrekʃn/ *n* **1** (of monument) érection *f*; (of building, bridge) construction *f*; (of tent) montage *m*; (of sign) mise *f* en place; (of penis) érection *f*; **2** (edifice) édifice *m*

ergonomics /ˌɜːgəˈnɒmɪks/ *n* (+ *v sg*) ergonomie *f*

Erie /ˈɪərɪ/ *pr n* **Lake ∼** le lac Érié

Eritrea /erɪˈtreɪə/ ▸ p. 774 *pr n* Érythrée *f*

ERM *n*: *abrév* ▸ **Exchange Rate Mechanism**

ermine /ˈɜːmɪn/ *n* (animal, fur) hermine *f*

erode /ɪˈrəʊd/ *vtr* lit éroder; fig saper

erogenous /ɪˈrɒdʒənəs/ *adj* érogène

erosion /ɪˈrəʊʒn/ *n* lit, fig érosion *f*

erotic /ɪˈrɒtɪk/ *adj* érotique

erotica /ɪˈrɒtɪkə/ *npl* Literat littérature *f* érotique; Cin films *mpl* érotiques; Art art *m* érotique

eroticism /ɪˈrɒtɪsɪzəm/ *n* érotisme *m*

err /ɜː(r)/ *vi* **1** (make mistake) faire une erreur; **to ∼ in one's judgment** faire une erreur de jugement; **2** (stray) pécher; **to ∼ on the side of caution** pécher par excès de prudence
(Idiom) **to ∼ is human** Prov l'erreur est humaine

errand /ˈerənd/ *n* commission *f*, course *f*; **to go on** *ou* **to run an ∼ for sb** aller faire une commission pour qn; **to send sb on an ∼** envoyer qn faire une commission; **∼ of mercy** mission *f* de charité

errant /ˈerənt/ *adj* [*husband, wife*] infidèle

erratic /ɪˈrætɪk/ *adj* [*behaviour, person, driver*] imprévisible; [*performance*] inégal; [*moods*] changeant; [*movements*] désordonné; [*timetable*] fantaisiste; [*deliveries*] irrégulier/-ière

erroneous /ɪˈrəʊnɪəs/ *adj* erroné, faux/fausse

erroneously /ɪˈrəʊnɪəslɪ/ *adv* à tort

error /ˈerə(r)/ *n* (in spelling, grammar, typing) faute *f*; Math, Comput erreur *f*; **in ∼** par erreur; **∼ of 10%, 10% ∼** erreur de 10%; **margin of ∼** marge *f* d'erreur
(Idiom) **to see the ∼ of one's ways** revenir de ses erreurs

ersatz /ˈeəzæts, ˈɜːsɑːts/
A *n* ersatz *m*, succédané *m*
B *adj* **it's ∼ tobacco** c'est de l'ersatz de tabac

erudite /ˈeruːdaɪt/ *adj* [*person*] érudit; [*book, discussion*] savant

erudition /ˌeruːˈdɪʃn/ *n* érudition *f*

erupt /ɪˈrʌpt/ *vi* **1** lit entrer en éruption; Med apparaître; **2** fig éclater

eruption /ɪˈrʌpʃn/ *n* **1** (of volcano, rash) éruption *f*; **2** fig (of violence, anger) explosion *f*; (of laughter) éclat *m*; (of political movement) apparition *f*

escalate /ˈeskəleɪt/
A *vtr* intensifier [*war, problem, efforts*]; aggraver [*inflation*]
B *vi* [*conflict, violence*] s'intensifier; [*prices*] monter en flèche; [*unemployment*] augmenter rapidement

escalation /ˌeskəˈleɪʃn/ *n* (of violence, war) intensification *f*; (of prices, inflation) montée *f* en flèche

escalator /ˈeskəleɪtə(r)/ *n* escalier *m* mécanique, escalator® *m*

escapade /ˈeskəpeɪd, ˌeskəˈpeɪd/ *n* frasque *f*

escape /ɪˈskeɪp/
A *n* **1** (of person) lit évasion *f*, fuite *f* (**from de**; **to** vers); fig fuite *f*; **to make good one's ∼** réussir son évasion; **to make an** *ou* **one's ∼** s'évader; **to have a narrow** *ou* **lucky ∼** l'échapper belle; **2** (leak) fuite *f* (**from** de)
B *vtr* **1** (avoid) **to ∼ death/danger** échapper à la mort/au danger; **to ∼ defeat** éviter une la défaite; **to ∼ detection** [*person*] échapper aux recherches (de la police); [*fault*] ne pas être détecté; **we cannot ∼ the fact that** on ne peut pas ignorer le fait que; **2** (elude) [*name, fact*] échapper à [*person*]
C *vi* **1** (get away) lit [*person*] s'enfuir, s'évader; [*animal*] s'échapper (**from** de); fig s'évader; **to ∼ unharmed** s'en sortir indemne; **to ∼ with one's life** s'en sortir vivant; **2** (leak) fuir

escape: ∼ **chute** n Aviat toboggan m; ∼ **clause** n Jur Comm clause f dérogatoire

escapee /ɪˌskeɪˈpiː/ n évadé/-e m/f

escape: ∼ **hatch** n Naut sas m de secours; ∼ **road** n voie f de ralentissement d'urgence; ∼ **route** n (in case of fire etc) plan m d'évacuation; (for fugitives) itinéraire m d'évasion

escapism /ɪˈskeɪpɪzəm/ n péj (in literature, cinema etc) évasion f (du réel); (of person) refus m d'affronter la réalité

escapologist /ˌeskəˈpɒlədʒɪst/ ▸ p. 1181 n: artiste dont la spécialité est de se libérer de liens

escarpment /ɪˈskɑːpmənt/ n escarpement m

eschew /ɪsˈtʃuː/ vtr sout éviter [discussion, temptation]; rejeter [violence]

escort
A /ˈeskɔːt/ n **1** Mil, Naut escorte f; **police** ∼ escorte de police; **armed** ∼ escorte de soldats; **to put under** ∼ placer sous escorte; **2** (companion) compagnon/compagne m/f; (to a dance) cavalier/-ière m/f; (in agency) hôtesse f
B /ˈeskɔːt/ noun modifier [duty, vessel] Naut, Mil d'escorte; ∼ **agency** agence f d'hôtesses
C /ɪˈskɔːt/ vtr **1** Mil escorter; **to** ∼ **sb in/out** faire entrer/sortir qn sous escorte; **2** (to a function) accompagner; (home) raccompagner

Eskimo /ˈeskɪməʊ/ ▸ p. 1032, p. 969
A n **1** (person) Esquimau/-aude m/f; **2** (language) esquimau m
B adj esquimau/-aude

ESL n: abrév ▸ **English as a Second Language**

esophagus n US = **oesophagus**

esoteric /ˌiːsəʊˈterɪk, ˌe-/ ésotérique

esp abrév écrite = **especially**

ESP n **1** abrév ▸ **extrasensory perception**; **2** abrév ▸ **English for Special Purposes**

especial /ɪˈspeʃl/ adj sout exceptionnel/-elle; [benefit] particulier/-ière

especially /ɪˈspeʃəlɪ/ adv **1** (above all) surtout, en particulier; **him** ∼ lui en particulier; ∼ **as** d'autant plus que; **2** (on purpose) exprès, spécialement; **3** (unusually) particulièrement

espionage /ˈespɪənɑːʒ/ n espionnage m

espouse /ɪˈspaʊz/ vtr embrasser [cause]

espresso /eˈspresəʊ/ n (pl ∼s) express m inv

Esq GB (abrév écrite = **esquire**) (on letter) M

essay /ˈeseɪ/ n Sch rédaction f (**on, about** sur); (extended) dissertation f (**on** sur); Literat essai m (**on** sur)

essence /ˈesns/
A n essence f; **it's the** ∼ **of stupidity** c'est la stupidité même; **time is of the** ∼ la vitesse s'impose
B **in** ∼ adv phr essentiellement

essential /ɪˈsenʃl/
A n (quality) qualité f essentielle; (object) objet m indispensable
B **essentials** npl **the** ∼**s** l'essentiel m
C adj **1** (vital) [services] de base; [role] essentiel/-ielle; [maintenance, ingredient] indispensable; ∼ **goods** produits de première nécessité; **it is** ∼ il est indispensable (**that** que (+ subj); **for sth** à qch; **to do** de faire); **2** (basic) [feature, element] essentiel/-ielle; [difference] fondamental; [reading] indispensable; [goodness, humility] intrinsèque

essentially /ɪˈsenʃəlɪ/ adv **1** (basically) essentiellement; ∼, **it's an old argument** en fait, c'est une vieille discussion; **2** (emphatic) (above all) avant tout; **3** (more or less) [correct, true] en gros

est abrév écrite = **established**

establish /ɪˈstæblɪʃ/
A vtr gen établir; déterminer [cause]; fonder [company]; **to** ∼ **that/whether** montrer que/si; **to** ∼ **a reputation for oneself as** se faire connaître en tant que [singer, actor]
B v refl **to** ∼ **oneself as a butcher** s'installer boucher; **to** ∼ **oneself as a market leader** s'imposer comme leader du marché

established /ɪˈstæblɪʃt/ adj établi; **a well** ∼ **fact** un fait bien établi; **the** ∼ **church** l'église d'État

establishment /ɪˈstæblɪʃmənt/
A n **1** (process) instauration f; **2** (institution, organization) établissement m; **3** (shop, business) maison f
B **Establishment** n GB **the Establishment** (ruling group) classe f dominante, establishment m; (social order) ordre m établi; **to become part of the Establishment** s'embourgeoiser; **the literary** ∼ l'establishment littéraire; **the legal** ∼ les institutions fpl judiciaires

estate /ɪˈsteɪt/ n **1** (stately home and park) domaine m, propriété f; **2** = **housing estate**; **3** (assets) biens mpl; **a large** ∼ une grande fortune; **4** GB = **estate car**

estate: ∼ **agency** n GB agence f immobilière; ∼ **agent** n GB agent m immobilier; ∼ **car** n GB break m; ∼ **duty** n GB droits mpl de succession

esteem /ɪˈstiːm/ n estime f; **to go up/down in sb's** ∼ remonter/baisser dans l'estime de qn

esthete n US = **aesthete**

estimate
A /ˈestɪmət/ n **1** (assessment of size, quantity etc) estimation f; **the original** ∼ l'estimation de départ; **at a rough** ∼ très approximativement; **at a conservative** ∼ sans exagération; **2** Comm (quote) devis m; **to put in an** ∼ établir un devis
B /ˈestɪmeɪt/ vtr évaluer [value, size, distance]; **to** ∼ **that** estimer que
C **estimated** pp adj [cost, figure] approximatif/-ive; **an** ∼ **300 people** environ 300 personnes

estimated time of arrival, ETA n heure f d'arrivée prévue

estimation /ˌestɪˈmeɪʃn/ n **1** (esteem) estime f; **to go up/down in sb's** ∼ remonter/baisser dans l'estime de qn; **2** (judgment) opinion f; **in her** ∼ à son avis

Estonia /ɪˈstəʊnɪə/ ▸ p. 774 pr n Estonie f

estrange /ɪˈstreɪndʒ/
A vtr brouiller (**from** avec)
B **estranged** pp adj ∼**d from sb** séparé de qn; **her** ∼**d husband** son mari dont elle est/était séparée

estrogen n US = **oestrogen**

estuary /ˈestʃʊərɪ, US -ʊerɪ/ n estuaire m

Estuary English n GB mélange d'accent londonien et standard parlé dans le sud

E Sussex n: abrév écrite = **East Sussex**

ETA abrév ▸ **estimated time of arrival**

e-tailer /ˈiːteɪlə(r)/ n cyber-vendeur/cyber-vendeuse m/f

e-tailing /ˈiːteɪlɪŋ/ n vente f en ligne

et al (abrév = **et alii**) et autres; hum et tutti quanti

et cetera, etcetera /ɪt ˈsetərə, et-/ adv et cætera, et cetera

etch /etʃ/ vtr graver [qch] à l'eau-forte; ∼**ed on her memory** fig gravé dans sa mémoire

etching /ˈetʃɪŋ/ n (picture) eau-forte f

eternal /ɪˈtɜːnl/ adj [life, salvation] éternel/-elle; [chatter, optimist] perpétuel/-elle; [recriminations] sempiternel/-elle pej (before n)

eternal triangle n triangle m classique, ≈ ménage m à trois

eternity /ɪˈtɜːnətɪ/ n éternité f; **it seemed an** ∼ **before he answered** il a mis une éternité à répondre

ether /ˈiːθə(r)/ n éther m

ethereal /ɪˈθɪərɪəl/ adj aérien/-ienne

ethic /ˈeθɪk/ n éthique f

ethical /ˈeθɪkl/ adj [problem, objection] moral; [fund, investment] éthique; ∼ **code** code m déontologique

ethics /ˈeθɪks/ n **1** (+ v sg) Philos éthique f; **2** (+ v pl) (code of behaviour) moralité f; **professional** ∼ déontologie f; **medical** ∼ déontologie f médicale

Ethiopia /ˌiːθɪˈəʊpɪə/ ▸ p. 774 pr n Éthiopie f

ethnic /ˈeθnɪk/ adj [group, minority] ethnique; [food, music] exotique; [clothes] inspiré du folklore (indien, africain etc)

ethnically /ˈeθnɪklɪ/ adv sur le plan ethnique

ethnic cleansing n purification f ethnique, nettoyage m ethnique

ethnology /eθˈnɒlədʒɪ/ n ethnologie f

ethos /ˈiːθɒs/ n (approach) philosophie f; **company** ∼ philosophie f de l'entreprise

etiquette /ˈetɪket, -kət/ n **1** (social) bienséance f, étiquette f; **2** (professional, diplomatic) protocole m

Etruscan /ɪˈtrʌskən/
A n (person) Étrusque mf
B adj étrusque

etymology /ˌetɪˈmɒlədʒɪ/ n étymologie f

EU (abrév = **European Union**) UE f

eugenics /juːˈdʒenɪks/ n (+ v sg) eugénisme m

eulogize /ˈjuːlədʒʌɪz/
A vtr faire le panégyrique de
B vi **to ~ over sth** faire le panégyrique de qch

eulogy /ˈjuːlədʒɪ/ n gen panégyrique m; Relig éloge m funèbre

eunuch /ˈjuːnək/ n eunuque m

euphemism /ˈjuːfəmɪzəm/ n euphémisme m

euphemistic /ˌjuːfəˈmɪstɪk/ adj euphémique

euphoria /juːˈfɔːrɪə/ n euphorie f

euphoric /juːˈfɒrɪk, US -ˈfɔːr-/ adj euphorique

Eurasian /jʊəˈreɪʒn/
A n Eurasien/-ienne m/f
B adj [people, region] eurasien/-ienne; [continent] eurasiatique

EURATOM /ˈjʊərətɒm/ n (abrév = **European Atomic Energy Community**) EURATOM f

eurhythmics GB, **eurythmics** US /juːˈrɪðmɪks/ n (+ v sg) gymnastique f rythmique

euro /ˈjʊərəʊ/ ▸ p. 782 n euro m

Euro+ /ˈjʊərəʊ-/ combining form euro+

eurobond /ˈjʊərəʊbɒnd/ n euro-obligation f

eurocheque /ˈjʊərəʊtʃek/ n Eurochèque m; **~ card** carte f Eurochèque

eurocurrency /ˈjʊərəʊkʌrənsɪ/ n eurodevise f, euro-monnaie f; **~ market** marché m des eurodevises

eurodollar /ˈjʊərəʊdɒlə(r)/ n eurodollar m

Euroland /ˈjʊərəʊlænd/ n euroland m

euromarket /ˈjʊərəʊmɑːkɪt/ n marché m européen; **in the ~** au sein du marché européen

Euro-MP /ˌjʊərəʊemˈpiː/ n député m européen

Europe /ˈjʊərəp/ ▸ p. 774 pr n Europe f; (EEC) le Marché commun

European /ˌjʊərəˈpɪən/
A n Européen/-éenne m/f
B adj européen/-éenne

European: **~ Atomic Energy Community**, **EAEC** n Communauté f Européenne de l'Énergie Atomique, CEEA; **~ Bank for Reconstruction and Development**, **EBRD** n Banque f européenne pour la reconstruction et le développement, BERD f; **~ Central Bank** n Banque f centrale européenne, BCE f; **~ Commission** n Commission f européenne; **~ Court of Human Rights** n Cour f européenne des droits de l'homme; **~ Court of Justice** n Cour f européenne de justice, Cour f de justice des communautés européennes; **~ Cup** n Sport Coupe f d'Europe; **~ currency unit**, **ecu** n Hist écu m; **~ Economic Community**, **EEC** n Hist Communauté f économique européenne f, CEE; **~ Free Trade Association**, **EFTA** n Association f européenne de libre-échange, AELE; **~ Monetary System**, **EMS** système m monétaire européen, SME m; **~ Monetary Union** n Union f monétaire européenne; **~ Parliament** n Parlement m européen; **~ Union**, **EU** Union f européenne, UE f

eurosceptic /ˈjʊərəʊskeptɪk/ n GB eurosceptique mf

Eurostar® /ˈjʊərəʊstɑː(r)/ n Transp Eurostar® m

Euro zone n zone f euro, euroland m

eurythmics n US = **eurhythmics**

euthanasia /ˌjuːθəˈneɪzɪə, US -ˈneɪʒə/ n euthanasie f

evacuate /ɪˈvækjʊeɪt/ vtr évacuer

evacuation /ɪˌvækjʊˈeɪʃn/ n évacuation f

evacuee /ɪˌvækjuːˈiː/ n évacué/-e m/f

evade /ɪˈveɪd/ vtr esquiver [blow]; éluder [question, problem]; fuir [responsibility]; échapper à [pursuer]

evaluate /ɪˈvæljʊeɪt/ vtr gen évaluer; mesurer [progress]

evaluation /ɪˌvæljʊˈeɪʃn/ n (all contexts) évaluation f

evangelical /ˌiːvænˈdʒelɪkl/ adj évangélique

evangelist /ɪˈvændʒəlɪst/ n (preacher) évangélisateur/ -trice m/f

evaporate /ɪˈvæpəreɪt/ vi **1** [liquid] s'évaporer; **2** fig [hopes, confidence] s'évaporer; [anger] se dissiper

evaporated milk n lait m condensé non sucré

evasion /ɪˈveɪʒn/ n **1** (of responsibility) dérobade f (**of** à); **tax ~** évasion f fiscale; **2** (excuse) faux-fuyant m

evasive /ɪˈveɪsɪv/ adj gen évasif/-ive; [look] fuyant; **to take ~ action** lit changer de cap pour éviter un accident; fig esquiver la difficulté

eve /iːv/ n veille f; **on the ~ of** à la veille de

even¹ /ˈiːvn/

> ⚠ Even can always be translated by même when it is used to express surprise or for emphasis. For examples and other uses, see below

A adv **1** (showing surprise) même; **he didn't ~ try** il n'a même pas essayé; **without ~ apologizing** sans même s'excuser; **2** (emphasizing point) même; **I can't ~ swim, never mind dive** je ne sais même pas nager, encore moins plonger; **don't tell anyone, not ~ Bob** ne dis rien à personne, pas même à Bob; **~ if/when/now** même si/quand/maintenant; **3** (with comparative) encore; **~ colder** encore plus froid; **4** sout **~ as I watched** alors même que je regardais
B **even so** adv phr quand même; **it was interesting ~ so** c'était quand même intéressant
C **even then** adv phr (at that time) même à ce moment-là; (all the same) de toute façon
D **even though** conj phr bien que (+ subj)

even² /ˈiːvn/ adj [surface, voice, temper, contest] égal; [teeth, hemline] régulier/-ière; [temperature] constant; [distribution] équitable; [number] pair; **we're ~** nous sommes quittes; **to get ~ with sb** rendre à qn la monnaie de sa pièce; **to be ~** [competitors] être à égalité; **I'll give you ~ odds ou money that** il y a une chance sur deux que (+ subj)

Phrasal verbs
■ **even out:** ▸ **~ out** [differences] s'atténuer; ▸ **~ [sth] out**, **~ out [sth]** répartir [distribution]; réduire [inequalities]
■ **even up:** ▸ **~ [sth] up**, **~ up [sth]** équilibrer [contest]; **it will ~ things up** ce sera plus équilibré

even-handed adj impartial

evening /ˈiːvnɪŋ/ ▸ p. 745
A n **1** soir m; (with emphasis on duration) soirée f; **in the ~** le soir; **during the ~** pendant la soirée; **6 o'clock in the ~** six heures du soir; **this ~** ce soir; **later this ~** plus tard dans la soirée; **tomorrow/yesterday ~** demain/hier soir; **on the ~ of the 14th** le 14 au soir; **on Friday ~** vendredi soir; **on the following ou next ~** le lendemain soir; **the previous ~**, **the ~ before** la veille au soir; **every ~** tous les soirs; **every Thursday ~** tous les jeudis soir; **all ~** toute la soirée; **what do you do in the ~s?** qu'est-ce que tu fais le soir?; **let's have an ~ in** passons la soirée à la maison; **to work ~s** travailler le soir; **to be on ~s** être du soir; **2** musical **~** soirée musicale
B noun modifier [bag, shoe] habillé; [meal, newspaper, walk] du soir

evening class n cours m du soir

evening dress n **1** (formal clothes) tenue f de soirée; **2** (gown) robe f de soirée

evening: **~ performance** n représentation f en soirée; **~ primrose** n onagre f; **~ shift** n équipe f du soir; **~ star** n étoile f du berger

evenly /ˈiːvnlɪ/ adv **1** [spread, apply] uniformément; [breathe] régulièrement; [divide] en parts égales; **~ matched** de force égale; **2** (placidly) [say] posément

event /ɪˈvent/ n **1** (incident) événement m; **unable to control ~s** incapable de contrôler la situation; **in the normal course of ~s** si tout va bien; **2** (eventuality) cas m; **in the ~ of** en cas de; **in the unlikely ~ that** au cas improbable où; **in either ~** en tout cas; **in the ~** GB (as things turned out) en l'occurrence; **in any ~**, **at all ~s** de toute façon; **3** (occasion) social **~** événement m mondain; **quite an ~** un événement; **4** (in athletics) épreuve f; **field/track ~** épreuve f d'athlétisme/de vitesse

even-tempered adj d'une humeur égale

eventful /ɪˈventfl/ adj mouvementé

eventing /ɪˈventɪŋ/ n GB concours m complet

eventual /ɪˈventʃʊəl/ adj [aim, hope] à long terme; [outcome, decision, success] final

eventuality /ɪˌventʃʊˈælətɪ/ n éventualité f

eventually /ɪˈventʃʊəlɪ/ adv finalement; **to do sth ~** finir par faire qch

ever /ˈevə(r)/
A adv **1** (at any time) **nothing was ~ said** rien n'a jamais été

dit; **no-one will ~ forget** personne n'oubliera jamais; **I can't say I ~ noticed it** je ne l'ai jamais remarqué; **rarely, if ~** rarement sinon jamais; **hardly ~** rarement, presque jamais; **something I would never ~ do** quelque chose que je ne ferais jamais de ma vie; **has he ~ lived abroad?** est-ce qu'il a déjà vécu à l'étranger?; **do you ~ make mistakes?** est-ce qu'il t'arrive de te tromper?; **if ~** si jamais; **she's a liar if ~ I saw one** *ou* **if ~ there was one!** c'est une menteuse ou je ne m'y connais pas!; **2⟩** (when making comparisons) **more beautiful than ~** plus beau/belle que jamais; **it's windier than ~ today** il y a encore plus de vent aujourd'hui; **more than ~ before** plus que jamais; **there are more working women than ~ before** les femmes n'ont jamais été aussi nombreuses à travailler; **he's happier than he's ~ been** il n'a jamais été aussi heureux; **the worst mistake I ~ made** la pire erreur que j'aie jamais faite; **the last time anyone ~ saw him** la dernière fois qu'on l'a vu; **the first ~** le tout premier; **3⟩** (at all times, always) toujours; **~ hopeful** toujours plein d'espérance; **as cheerful as ~** toujours aussi gai; **the same as ~** toujours le même; **they lived happily ~ after** ils vécurent toujours heureux; **~ the diplomat** l'éternel diplomate; **yours ~** (in letter) bien à toi *ou* à vous; **4⟩** (expressing anger, irritation) **don't (you) ~ do that again!** ne refais jamais ça!; **if you ~ speak to me like that again** si jamais tu me reparles sur ce ton; **do you ~ think about anyone else?** ça ne t'arrive jamais de penser à quelqu'un d'autre?; **that's the last time he ~ comes here!** c'est la dernière fois qu'il vient ici!; **have you ~ heard/seen anything like it?** as-tu jamais entendu/vu rien de pareil?; **that's all he ~ does!** c'est tout ce qu'il sait faire!; **5⟩** (expressing surprise) **why ~ not?** GB pourquoi pas?; **who ~ would have guessed?** qui donc aurait deviné?; **6⟩** GB (very) **~ so** si; **~ so glad** si heureux/-euse; **~ so slightly damp** très légèrement humide; **thanks ~ so much!** merci mille fois!; **he's ~ so much better** il va beaucoup mieux; **it's ~ such a shame!** c'est vraiment dommage!; **7⟩** ○(in exclamations) **is he ~ dumb!** ce qu'il peut être bête!; **am I ~ glad to see you!** qu'est-ce que je suis content de te voir!; **do I ~!** (emphatic yes) et comment!
B **ever-** *combining form* **~-growing** *ou* **-increasing** toujours croissant; **~-present** toujours présent; **~-changing** qui évolue sans cesse
C **as ever** *adv* comme toujours
D **ever more** *adv phr* de plus en plus
E **ever since** *adv phr, conj phr* depuis; **~ since we arrived** depuis notre arrivée

evergreen /ˈevəɡriːn/
A *n* **1⟩** (tree) arbre *m* à feuilles persistantes; **2⟩** (song) chanson *f* de toujours
B *adj* (épith) **1⟩** [*tree*] à feuilles persistantes; **2⟩** (popular) [*song, programme*] toujours populaire

everlasting /ˌevəˈlɑːstɪŋ, US -ˈlæst-/ *adj* éternel/-elle

every /ˈevrɪ/

⚠ *Every* is most frequently translated by *tous les/toutes les* + plural noun: *every day* = tous les jours. When *every* is emphasized to mean *every single*, it can also be translated by *chaque*. For examples and exceptions, see the entry below

A *det* **1⟩** (each) **~ house in the street** toutes les maisons de la rue; **~ time I go there** chaque fois que j'y vais; **I've read ~ one of her books** j'ai lu tous ses livres; **that goes for ~ one of you!** c'est valable pour tout le monde!; **I enjoyed ~ minute of it** chaque minute a été un plaisir; **he spent ~ last penny** il a dépensé jusqu'au dernier sou; **~ second day** tous les deux jours; **there are three women for ~ ten men** il y a trois femmes pour dix hommes; **from ~ side de** toutes parts; **in ~ way** (from every point of view) à tous les égards; (using every method) par tous les moyens; **2⟩** (emphatic) **there is ~ chance that** il y a toutes les chances que; **~ right to complain** tous les droits de se plaindre; **I wish you ~ success** je vous souhaite beaucoup de succès; **~ bit as much as** tout autant que; **3⟩** (indicating frequency) **~ day/Thursday** tous les jours/jeudis; **once ~ few days** tous les deux ou trois jours; **~ 20 kilometres** tous les 20 kilomètres
B **every other** *adj phr* (alternate) **~ other day** tous les deux jours; **~ other Sunday** un dimanche sur deux
(Idioms) **~ now and then, ~ now and again, ~ so often, ~ once in a while** de temps en temps; **~ man for himself!** (in fight to succeed) chacun pour soi!; (abandoning ship etc) sauve qui peut!; **~ which way** dans tous les sens

everybody /ˈevrɪbɒdɪ/ *pron* tout le monde; **~ else** tous les autres; **~ knows that** tout le monde le sait; **~ who is anybody** tous les gens importants

everyday /ˈevrɪdeɪ/ *adj* [*activity, routine*] quotidien/-ienne; [*clothes*] de tous les jours; **in ~ use** d'usage courant

everyone /ˈevrɪwʌn/ *pron* = **everybody**

everyplace○ /ˈevrɪpleɪs/ *adv* US = **everywhere**

everything /ˈevrɪθɪŋ/

⚠ *Everything* is almost always translated by *tout*. For examples and particular usages, see below

pron tout; **is ~ all right?** est-ce que tout va bien?; **don't believe ~ you hear** il ne faut pas croire tout ce que tu entends; **~ else** tout le reste; **money isn't ~** l'argent n'est pas tout; **he's got ~ going for him** il a tout pour lui; **she meant ~ to him** elle était tout pour lui; **have you got your papers and ~?** est-ce que vous avez vos papiers et tout le reste?

everywhere /ˈevrɪweə(r), US -hweər/ *adv* partout; **~ else** partout ailleurs; **~ I go** partout où je vais; **she's been ~** elle a voyagé partout

evict /ɪˈvɪkt/ *vtr* expulser (**from** de)

eviction /ɪˈvɪkʃn/ *n* expulsion *f* (**from** de)

evidence /ˈevɪdəns/ *n* **1⟩** (proof) ⊄ preuves *fpl* (**that** que; **of, for** de; **against** contre); **a piece of ~** une preuve; **there is no ~ that** rien ne prouve que; **all the ~ suggests that…** tout indique que…; **the ~ of one's own eyes** ce qu'on a vu de ses propres yeux; **2⟩** (testimony) témoignage *m* (**from** de); **convicted on the ~ of sb** condamné sur le témoignage de qn; **to be used in ~ against sb** servir de témoignage contre qn; **to give ~** témoigner, déposer (**for sb** en faveur de qn; **against sb** contre qn); **3⟩** (trace) trace *f* (**of** de); **to be (much) in ~** être (bien) visible

evident /ˈevɪdənt/ *adj* [*anger, relief*] manifeste; **it is ~ that** il est évident que

evidently /ˈevɪdəntlɪ/ *adv* **1⟩** (apparently) apparemment; **2⟩** (patently) manifestement

evil /ˈiːvl/
A *n* **1⟩** ⊄ **~** le mal; **2⟩** (bad thing) mal *m*; **the ~s of racism** les maux du racisme
B *adj* [*person, forces, genius*] malfaisant; [*act, intent*] diabolique; [*spirit*] maléfique; [*smell*] nauséabond
(Idioms) **to give sb the ~ eye** jeter le mauvais œil à qn; **the lesser of two ~s** le moindre mal; **money is the root of all ~** l'argent est la source de tous les maux; **to put off the ~ hour** *ou* **day** repousser le moment fatidique

evil-smelling *adj* nauséabond

evocative /ɪˈvɒkətɪv/ *adj* évocateur/-trice

evoke /ɪˈvəʊk/ *vtr* **1⟩** évoquer [*memory*]; **2⟩** susciter [*response*]

evolution /ˌiːvəˈluːʃn/ *n* évolution *f* (**from** à partir de)

evolutionary /ˌiːvəˈluːʃənərɪ, US -nerɪ/ *adj* évolutionniste

evolve /ɪˈvɒlv/
A *vtr* élaborer [*system, policy*]
B *vi* évoluer; **to ~ from** [*theory*] se développer à partir de; [*species*] descendre de

ewe /juː/ *n* brebis *f*; **~ lamb** agnelle *f*

ex /eks/
A ○*n* (former partner) ex○ *mf*
B *prep* Comm **~ works/factory** [*price*] départ usine
C **ex+** *combining form* **~-wife/-husband** ex-mari/-femme

exacerbate /ɪɡˈzæsəbeɪt/ *vtr* aggraver

exact /ɪɡˈzækt/
A *adj* gen exact; [*moment*] précis; **it's the ~ opposite** c'est exactement le contraire; **tell me your ~ whereabouts** dis-moi où tu te trouves exactement; **those were her ~ words** voilà exactement ce qu'elle a dit; **it was in the summer, July to be ~** c'était en été, plus précisément en juillet
B *vtr* exiger (**from** de)

exacting /ɪɡˈzæktɪŋ/ *adj* astreignant

exactly /ɪɡˈzæktlɪ/ *adv* exactement; **my sentiments ~!** exactement!; **what ~ were you doing?** que faisais-tu au juste?; **she wasn't ~ overjoyed** iron elle n'était pas précisément ravie

exaggerate /ɪɡˈzædʒəreɪt/
A *vtr* gen exagérer; (in one's own mind) s'exagérer [*problem, effect*]

B vi exagérer

exaggerated /ɪgˈzædʒəreɪtɪd/ adj exagéré; **he has an ~ sense of his own importance** il se fait une idée exagérée de son importance

exaggeration /ɪg,zædʒəˈreɪʃn/ n exagération f; **it's no ~ to say that…** on peut dire sans exagération que…

exalted /ɪgˈzɔːltɪd/ adj sout **1** (elevated) [rank, position] élevé, haut; [person] haut placé; **2** (jubilant) exalté

exam /ɪgˈzæm/ n examen m; ▸ **examination A 1, B**

examination /ɪg,zæmɪˈneɪʃn/

A n **1** examen m (**in** de); **French ~** examen m de français; **to take/pass an ~** passer/réussir un examen; **2** (inspection) examen m; **on ~** après examen; **under ~** à l'examen; **to have an ~** Med passer un examen médical; **3** (of accused, witness) interrogatoire m

B noun modifier [question, results] d'examen; [candidate] à un examen

examination paper n sujets mpl d'examen

examine /ɪgˈzæmɪn/ vtr **1** (intellectually) considérer [facts]; examiner [evidence]; étudier [question]; **2** (visually) gen examiner; fouiller [luggage]; **3** Sch, Univ **to be ~d in maths** passer un examen en math; **4** interroger [prisoner]

(Idiom) **you need your head ~d**○! tu devrais te faire soigner○!

examinee /ɪg,zæmɪˈniː/ n candidat/-e m/f

examiner /ɪgˈzæmɪnə(r)/ n examinateur/-trice m/f

example /ɪgˈzɑːmpl, US -ˈzæmpl/ n exemple m; **for ~** par exemple; **to set a good ~** donner l'exemple; **he's an ~ to us all** c'est notre modèle à tous; **you're setting a bad ~** tu ne donnes pas le bon exemple; **to make an ~ of sb** punir qn pour l'exemple

exasperate /ɪgˈzæspəreɪt/ vtr exaspérer; **to get ~d** s'énerver

exasperation /ɪg,zæspəˈreɪʃn/ n exaspération f

excavate /ˈekskəveɪt/
A vtr fouiller [site]; creuser [tunnel]
B vi faire des fouilles

excavation /,ekskəˈveɪʃn/
A n excavation f
B excavations npl fouilles fpl

excavator /ˈekskəveɪtə(r)/ n (machine) excavateur m; (person) fouilleur/-euse m/f

exceed /ɪkˈsiːd/ vtr outrepasser [functions, authority]; dépasser [speed limit, credit limit] (**by** de); **to ~ all expectations** dépasser toute attente; **do not ~ the speed limit** respecter les limitations de vitesse

exceedingly /ɪkˈsiːdɪŋlɪ/ adv extrêmement

excel /ɪkˈsel/
A vi exceller (**at, in** en; **at** ou **in doing** à faire)
B v refl **to ~ oneself** se surpasser also iron

excellence /ˈeksələns/ n excellence f

Excellency /ˈeksələnsɪ/ n Excellence f

excellent /ˈeksələnt/
A adj excellent
B excl parfait!

except /ɪkˈsept/

> ⚠ There are four frequently used translations for
> _except_ when used as a preposition. By far the
> most frequent of these is _sauf_, the others are _excepté_,
> _à l'exception de_ and _hormis_. Note, however, that in
> _what/where/who_ questions, _except_ is translated by
> _sinon_. For examples and the phrase _except for_ see
> below

A prep **everybody ~ Lisa** tout le monde sauf Lisa, tout le monde à l'exception de or excepté or hormis Lisa; **nothing ~** rien d'autre que; **nobody ~** personne d'autre que; **~ if/when** sauf si/quand; **~ that** sauf que, si ce n'est que; **who could have done it ~ him?** qui aurait pu le faire sinon lui?

B **except for** prep phr à part, à l'exception de

C vtr excepter; **~ing** à l'exception de; **present company ~ed** exception faite des personnes présentes

exception /ɪkˈsepʃn/ n **1** (special case) exception f (**for** pour); **with the (possible) ~ of** à l'exception (peut-être) de; **the only ~ being** à la seule exception de; **with some** ou **certain ~s** à quelques exceptions près; **to make an ~** faire une exception; **there can be no ~s** il n'y aura pas d'exception; **the ~ proves the rule** c'est l'exception qui confirme

la règle; **2** **to take ~ to** (be offended by) s'offusquer de

exceptional /ɪkˈsepʃənl/ adj exceptionnel/-elle

excerpt /ˈeksɜːpt/ n extrait m

excess /ɪkˈses/

A n **1** gen excès m (**of** de); **to eat to ~** faire des excès de table, trop manger; **carried to ~** poussé à l'excès; **to be (far) in ~ of** dépasser (largement); **2** GB (insurance) franchise f

B adj **~ alcohol/weight** excès m d'alcool/de poids; **drain off the ~ water** égoutter l'excédent d'eau

excess baggage n excédent m de bagages

excessive /ɪkˈsesɪv/ adj excessif/-ive

excess: **~ luggage** n GB = **excess baggage**; **~ postage** n surtaxe f postale; **~ profits** npl superbénéfices mpl

exchange /ɪksˈtʃeɪndʒ/

A n **1** (swap) échange m; **in ~** en échange (**for** de); **2** Comm, Fin change m; **the rate of ~** le taux de change; **bill of ~** lettre f de change; **3** (discussion) discussion f; (in parliament) débat m; **a heated ~** une discussion houleuse; **4** (visit) échange m; **~ visit** voyage m d'échange; **5** Telecom (also **telephone ~**) central m (téléphonique)

B vtr échanger (**for** contre; **with** avec); **to ~ contracts** Comm, Jur ≈ signer le contrat de vente; **they ~d hostages** ils ont échangé leurs otages

exchangeable: **~ disk** n Comput disque m amovible; **~ disk storage, EDS** n Comput unité f de disques à chargeur

exchange: **~ control** n contrôle m des changes; **~ controls** npl mesures fpl de contrôle des changes; **~ rate** n taux m de change; **Exchange Rate Mechanism, ERM** n système m monétaire européen

Exchequer /ɪksˈtʃekə(r)/ pr n GB Pol **the ~** l'Échiquier m, le ministère des finances

excise

A /ˈeksaɪz/ n (also **excise duty**) excise f, taxe f

B /ɪkˈsaɪz/ vtr **1** Med exciser; **2** (from text) supprimer

excitable /ɪkˈsaɪtəbl/ adj nerveux/-euse

excite /ɪkˈsaɪt/ vtr **1** gen exciter; (fire with enthusiasm) enthousiasmer; **2** (give rise to) susciter [interest, controversy]; éveiller [curiosity, suspicion]; faire naître [envy]

excited /ɪkˈsaɪtɪd/ adj [person, crowd, animal] excité; [voice, conversation] animé; **to be ~ about sth** (enthusiastic) s'enthousiasmer pour qch; (in anticipation) être emballé○ à l'idée de qch; **to get ~** s'exciter; **don't get ~!** (cross) ne t'énerve pas!

excitedly /ɪkˈsaɪtɪdlɪ/ adv avec animation

excitement /ɪkˈsaɪtmənt/ n (emotion) excitation f; **what ~!** quelle émotion!; **in the ~** dans l'agitation générale; **to cause great ~** faire sensation; **he was in a state of great ~** il était tout excité

exciting /ɪkˈsaɪtɪŋ/ adj gen passionnant; **an ~ new acting talent** un acteur qui promet

excl. abrév = **excluding**

exclaim /ɪkˈskleɪm/ vtr s'exclamer

exclamation /,ekskləˈmeɪʃn/ n exclamation f

exclamation mark, exclamation point US n point m d'exclamation

exclude /ɪkˈskluːd/ vtr exclure [person, group] (**from** de); ne pas inclure [name] (**from** dans); exclure [issue, possibility] (**from** de); exclure temporairement [pupil]

excluding /ɪkˈskluːdɪŋ/ prep à l'exclusion de; **~ VAT** TVA non compris

exclusion /ɪkˈskluːʒn/ n **1** exclusion f (**from** de); **2** Scol exclusion f temporaire

exclusion zone n zone f interdite

exclusive /ɪkˈskluːsɪv/

A n (report) exclusivité f

B adj **1** [club, social circle] fermé; [hotel] de luxe; [school, district] huppé; **2** [story, coverage, rights] exclusif/-ive; [interview] en exclusivité; **~ to Harrods** en exclusivité; **to have ~ use of** avoir l'usage exclusif de; **to be mutually ~** s'exclure mutuellement; **~ of meals** les repas non compris

exclusively /ɪkˈskluːsɪvlɪ/ adv exclusivement

excommunicate /,ekskəˈmjuːnɪkeɪt/ vtr excommunier

excrement /ˈekskrɪmənt/ n excrément m

e

excrete /ɪkˈskriːt/ vtr [animal, human] excréter; [plant] exsuder

excretion /ɪkˈskriːʃn/ n (of animal, human) excrétion f; (of plant) exsudation f

excruciating /ɪkˈskruːʃɪeɪtɪŋ/ adj ① [pain] atroce; ② ○(awful) exécrable

excruciatingly○ /ɪkˈskruːʃɪeɪtɪŋlɪ/ adv [boring] mortellement; ~ **funny** à mourir de rire

excursion /ɪkˈskɜːʃn/ n (organized) excursion f; (casual) promenade f

excuse
Ⓐ /ɪkˈskjuːs/ n (self-justification) excuse f; (pretext) prétexte m (for sth à qch; for doing pour faire; to do pour faire); to make ~s trouver des excuses; to be an ~ to do ou for doing servir de prétexte pour faire; I have a good ~ j'ai une bonne excuse; an ~ to leave early un bon prétexte pour partir tôt; is that the best ~ you can come up with? c'est tout ce que tu as trouvé comme excuse?; any ~ will do! toutes les excuses sont bonnes!; there's no ~ for such behaviour ce genre de conduite est inexcusable; that's no ~ ce n'est pas une excuse or une raison
Ⓑ /ɪkˈskjuːz/ vtr ① (forgive) excuser [person] (for doing de faire, d'avoir fait); ~ me! (bumping into sb) excusez-moi!, pardon!; (beginning an inquiry, making polite correction) excusez-moi; (making angry correction) je regrette, mais; (not hearing properly) pardon?; may I be ~d? GB euph est-ce que je peux aller aux toilettes?; ② (justify) justifier [intervention, procedure]; excuser [person]; ③ (exempt) dispenser (from sth de qch; from doing de faire)

ex-directory /ˌeksdaɪˈrektərɪ, -dɪ-/ adj GB sur la liste rouge

exec○ /ɪkˈzek/ n US (abrév = **executive**) cadre m

execrable /ˈeksɪkrəbl/ adj sout exécrable

execute /ˈeksɪkjuːt/ vtr exécuter

execution /ˌeksɪˈkjuːʃn/ n ① (killing) exécution f (by par); ② (of plan, task) exécution f; (by musician) interprétation f; in the ~ of his duty dans l'exercice m de ses fonctions; ③ Comput exécution f

executioner /ˌeksɪˈkjuːʃənə(r)/ n bourreau m

executive
Ⓐ n ① (administrator) Comm cadre m; (in Civil Service) cadre m administratif; sales ~ cadre m commercial; top ~ cadre m dirigeant; ② (committee) exécutif m, comité m exécutif; party/trade union ~ bureau m du parti/du syndicat; ③ US the ~ le pouvoir exécutif
Ⓑ adj ① (administrative) [power, committee] exécutif/-ive; [status] de cadre; ② (luxury) [chair] directorial
executive: ~ **council** n (of company) conseil m de direction; (of trade union, political party) commission f exécutive; ~ **director** n directeur/-trice m/f exécutif/-ive; ~ **jet** n jet m privé; ~ **producer** n Cin producteur m en chef or exécutif; ~ **program** n Comput superviseur m; ~ **secretary** n Admin secrétaire m exécutif; (manager's secretary) secrétaire mf de direction; ~ **session** n séance f parlementaire à huis clos; ~ **toy** n gadget m antistress

executor /ɪgˈzekjʊtə(r)/ n Jur exécuteur m testamentaire

exemplary /ɪgˈzemplərɪ, US -lerɪ/ adj [behaviour, life] exemplaire; [student] modèle

exemplify /ɪgˈzemplɪfaɪ/ vtr illustrer, exemplifier

exempt /ɪgˈzempt/
Ⓐ adj exempt (from de)
Ⓑ vtr exempter [person] (from sth de qch)

exemption /ɪgˈzempʃn/ n exemption f (from de); (from exam) dispense f (from de); tax ~ dégrèvement m d'impôts

exercise /ˈeksəsaɪz/
Ⓐ n ① (planned activity) opération f; (long-term or large-scale) stratégie f; it was an academic ~ c'était pour la beauté de la chose; public relations ~ campagne f de relations publiques; an ~ in diplomacy un exercice de diplomatie; ② Ⓒ (exertion) exercice m; ③ (training task) exercice m; maths ~ exercice de maths; ④ (of duties, rights, power) exercice m (of de); ⑤ Mil manœuvres fpl; to go on an ~ ou on ~s partir en manœuvres
Ⓑ vtr ① (apply) faire preuve de [caution, control, restraint]; exercer [power, right]; ② (train) exercer [body, mind]; faire travailler [limb, muscles]; promener [dog]; sortir [horse]; ③ (worry) préoccuper
Ⓒ vi faire de l'exercice

exercise: ~ **bicycle** n (in gym) vélo m d'entraînement; (at home) vélo m d'appartement; ~ **book** n cahier m

exert /ɪgˈzɜːt/
Ⓐ vtr exercer [pressure, influence] (on sur); employer [force]
Ⓑ v refl to ~ oneself se fatiguer

exertion /ɪgˈzɜːʃn/ n (physical effort) effort m

ex gratia /ˌeks ˈgreɪʃə/ adj [award, payment] à titre gracieux

exhale /eksˈheɪl/
Ⓐ vtr [person] expirer; [chimney] dégager
Ⓑ vi [person] expirer

exhaust /ɪgˈzɔːst/
Ⓐ n Aut ① (pipe) pot m d'échappement; ② (fumes) gaz mpl d'échappement
Ⓑ noun modifier [fumes, pipe, system] d'échappement
Ⓒ vtr épuiser; ~ed épuisé

exhaustion /ɪgˈzɔːstʃn/ n épuisement m

exhaustive /ɪgˈzɔːstɪv/ adj [bibliography, list] exhaustif/-ive; [analysis, description, coverage] très détaillé; [investigation, research] approfondi

exhibit /ɪgˈzɪbɪt/
Ⓐ n ① œuvre f exposée; ② US (exhibition) exposition f; a Gauguin ~ une exposition Gauguin; ③ Jur pièce f à conviction; ~ A pièce à conviction numéro un
Ⓑ vtr (display) exposer [work of art]; manifester [preference, sign]

exhibition /ˌeksɪˈbɪʃn/
Ⓐ n ① (of art, goods) exposition f; art ~ exposition; the Picasso ~ l'exposition Picasso; to be on ~ être exposé; to make an ~ of oneself péj se donner en spectacle; ② (of skill) démonstration f; ③ GB Univ bourse f d'études
Ⓑ noun modifier [catalogue, hall, stand] d'exposition

exhibition centre GB, **exhibition center** US n palais m des expositions

exhibitionist /ˌeksɪˈbɪʃənɪst/ n, adj exhibitionniste (mf)

exhibitor /ɪgˈzɪbɪtə(r)/ n exposant/-e m/f

exhilarate /ɪgˈzɪləreɪt/ vtr [atmosphere, music, speed] griser; to feel ~d être tout joyeux/toute joyeuse

exhilarating /ɪgˈzɪləreɪtɪŋ/ adj [game] stimulant; [experience] exaltant; [music] grisant; [speed] enivrant

exhilaration /ɪgˌzɪləˈreɪʃn/ n joie f intense

exhume /eksˈhjuːm, US ɪgˈzuːm/ vtr exhumer

exile /ˈeksaɪl/
Ⓐ n ① (person) exilé/-e m/f; ② (expulsion) exil m (from de); in ~ en exil; to go into ~ partir en exil
Ⓑ vtr exiler (de from); to ~ for life exiler à vie

exist /ɪgˈzɪst/ vi ① (be) exister; ② (survive) survivre; ③ (live) vivre; to ~ on a diet of potatoes ne vivre que de pommes de terre

existence /ɪgˈzɪstəns/ n existence f (of de); the largest plane in ~ le plus grand avion qui existe; I wasn't aware of its ~ je ne connaissais pas son existence; to come into ~ naître

existential /ˌegzɪˈstenʃl/ adj existentiel/-ielle

existentialism /ˌegzɪˈstenʃəlɪzəm/ n existentialisme m

existing /ɪgˈzɪstɪŋ/ adj [laws, order] existant; [policy, management, leadership] actuel/-elle

exit /ˈeksɪt/
Ⓐ n sortie f; 'no ~' 'interdit'; to make a quick ou hasty ~ s'éclipser
Ⓑ vi sortir

exit: ~ **point** n Comput point m de sortie; ~ **poll** n Pol sondage m fait à la sortie des urnes; ~ **sign** n panneau m (de) sortie; ~ **visa** n visa m de sortie

exodus /ˈeksədəs/ n exode m

ex officio /ˌeks əˈfɪʃɪəʊ/ adj [member] de droit

exonerate /ɪgˈzɒnəreɪt/ vtr disculper

exorbitant /ɪgˈzɔːbɪtənt/ adj exorbitant

exorbitantly /ɪgˈzɔːbɪtəntlɪ/ adv [tax] de façon excessive; [expensive] excessivement

exorcism /ˈeksɔːsɪzəm/ n exorcisme m

exorcist /ˈeksɔːsɪst/ n exorciste mf

exorcize /ˈeksɔːsaɪz/ vtr exorciser [demon, memory]

exotic /ɪgˈzɒtɪk/ adj exotique

exotica /ɪgˈzɒtɪkə/ n objets mpl exotiques

expand /ɪkˈspænd/
Ⓐ vtr ① gen développer; élargir [horizon, knowledge]; accroître

[*production, workforce*]; étendre [*empire*]; gonfler [*lungs*]; **2**] Math, Comput développer

B *vi* gen se développer; [*population, production*] s'accroître; [*universe, market, economy*] être en expansion; [*metal*] se dilater; [*institution*] s'agrandir; [*chest*] se gonfler; **the company is ~ing into overseas markets** la société commence à s'implanter sur les marchés étrangers

C **expanded** *pp adj* [*programme*] élargi

(Phrasal verb)

■ **expand on**: ▸ ~ **(up)on [sth]** s'étendre sur [*plans*]

expanding /ɪk'spændɪŋ/ *adj* **1**] (growing) [*population, sector*] en expansion; **2**] [*file, bracelet*] extensible

expanse /ɪk'spæns/ *n* (of land, water) étendue *f*; (of flesh) étalage *m*

expansion /ɪk'spænʃn/ *n* gen développement *m* (**in** de; **into** dans); (of economy) expansion *f*; (of population, borrowing) accroissement *m*; (of site) agrandissement *m*; (of sales) progression *f*; (of metal) dilatation *f*; **rate of ~** taux d'accroissement

expansion board, **expansion card** *n* Comput carte *f* d'extension

expansionist /ɪk'spænʃənɪst/ *n, adj* Econ, Pol expansionniste (*mf*)

expansion: ~ **programme**, ~ **scheme** *n* Comm programme *m* de développement; ~ **slot** *n* Comput emplacement *m* libre (pour extension)

expansive /ɪk'spænsɪv/ *adj* (effusive) [*person, mood*] expansif/-ive; (grand) [*ambitions*] grandiose

expansively /ɪk'spænsɪvlɪ/ *adv* (effusively) [*smile, say*] avec effusion

expatriate /ˌeks'pætrɪət/ *n, adj* expatrié/-e (*m/f*)

expect /ɪk'spekt/

A *vtr* **1**] (anticipate) s'attendre à [*event, victory, defeat, trouble*]; **to ~ the worst** s'attendre au pire; **what did you ~?** qu'est-ce que tu croyais?; **I ~ed as much** je m'y attendais; **you knew what to ~** tu savais à quoi t'attendre; **to ~ sb to do** s'attendre à ce que qn fasse; **she is ~ed to win** on s'attend à ce qu'elle gagne; **he is ~ed to arrive at six** on l'attend pour six heures; **to ~ that...** s'attendre à ce que... (+ *subj*) **I ~ (that) I'll lose** je m'attends à perdre; **it is only to be ~ed that he should go** c'est bien naturel qu'il y aille; **it was hardly to be ~ed that** on ne pouvait guère s'attendre à ce que (+ *subj*); **more/worse than ~ed** plus/pire que prévu; **2**] (rely on) s'attendre à [*sympathy, help*] (**from** de la part de); **3**] (await) attendre [*baby, guest, company*]; ~ **me when you see me** GB je ne sais pas à quelle heure j'arriverai; **4**] (require) demander, attendre [*commitment, hard work*] (**from** de); **I ~ you to be punctual** je vous demande d'être ponctuel; **I can't be ~ed to know everything** je ne peux pas tout savoir; **it's too much to ~** c'est trop demander; **5**] GB (suppose) **I ~ so** je pense que oui; **I don't ~ so** je ne pense pas; **I ~ he's tired** il doit être fatigué

B *vi* **1**] (anticipate) **to ~ to do** s'attendre à faire; **I was ~ing to do better** je comptais faire mieux; **2**] (require) **I ~ to see you there** je compte bien vous y voir; **3**] (be pregnant) **to be ~ing** attendre un enfant

expectancy /ɪk'spektənsɪ/ *n* **to have an air of ~** avoir l'air d'attendre quelque chose; **a feeling of ~** un sentiment d'attente

expectant /ɪk'spektənt/ *adj* **1**] [*look*] plein d'attente; **2**] [*mother*] futur (*before n*)

expectantly /ɪk'spektəntlɪ/ *adv* avec l'air d'attendre quelque chose

expectation /ˌekspek'teɪʃn/ *n* **1**] (assumption, prediction) prévision *f*; **it is my ~ that** je m'attends à ce que (+ *subj*); **against all ~(s)** à l'encontre des prévisions générales; **2**] (aspiration, hope) aspiration *f*, attente *f*; **to live up to sb's ~s** répondre à l'attente de qn; **I don't want to raise their ~s** je ne veux pas trop leur promettre; **3**] (requirement, demand) exigence *f*; **to have certain ~s of** attendre *or* demander certaines choses de [*police, employee*]

expediency /ɪk'spiːdɪənsɪ/ *n* **1**] (appropriateness) opportunité *f*; **2**] (self-interest) opportunisme *m*

expedient /ɪk'spiːdɪənt/

A *n* expédient *m*

B *adj* **1**] (appropriate) opportun; **2**] (advantageous) politique

expedite /'ekspɪdaɪt/ *vtr* sout (speed up) accélérer [*operation, process*]; faciliter [*work*]

expedition /ˌekspɪ'dɪʃn/ *n* **1**] (exploration) expédition *f*; **to go on an ~** partir en expédition; **2**] (for leisure) **climbing ~** expédition *f* en montagne; **hunting ~** partie *f* de chasse; **sightseeing ~** visite *f* touristique; **to go on a shopping ~** aller faire des courses

expeditionary force *n* corps *m* expéditionnaire

expel /ɪk'spel/ *vtr* (*p prés etc* **-ll-**) **1**] expulser [*alien, diplomat*]; renvoyer [*pupil*]; **2**] expulser [*air, water*]

expend /ɪk'spend/ *vtr* consacrer [*effort, time*]; dépenser [*energy*]

expendable /ɪk'spendəbl/ *adj* [*troops, equipment*] sacrifiable; [*worker*] licenciable à tout moment; [*goods*] non durables

expenditure /ɪk'spendɪtʃə(r)/ *n* **1**] (amount spent) dépenses *fpl*; **defence ~** dépenses *fpl* militaires; **capital ~** dépenses *fpl* d'investissement; **public ~** dépense *f* publique; **2**] (in bookkeeping) sortie *f*; **3**] (output) (of energy, time, money) dépense *f*

expense /ɪk'spens/

A *n* **1**] (cost) frais *mpl*; **at one's own ~** à ses propres frais; **to go to some ~** faire des frais; **to go to great ~** dépenser beaucoup d'argent (**to do** pour faire); **to put sb to ~** faire faire des frais à qn; **to spare no ~** ne pas regarder à la dépense; **2**] (cause for expenditure) dépense *f*; **a wedding is a big ~** un mariage revient cher; **3**] **at the ~ of** (prejudicing sth) au détriment de [*health, public, safety*]; **at sb's ~** [*laugh, joke*] aux dépens de qn

B **expenses** *npl* Comm frais *mpl*; **to cover sb's ~s** [*sum*] couvrir les frais de qn; **all ~s paid** tous frais payés

expense account *n* frais *mpl* de représentation

expensive /ɪk'spensɪv/ *adj* gen cher/chère; (onerous) coûteux/-euse; [*taste*] de luxe; ~ **to maintain** cher à entretenir

expensively /ɪk'spensɪvlɪ/ *adv* ~ **furnished** luxueusement meublé; **to be ~ dressed** porter des toilettes chères

experience /ɪk'spɪərɪəns/

A *n* **1**] (expertise) expérience *f*; **management ~** expérience *f* de la gestion; **from my own ~** d'après mon expérience; **in my ~** autant que je puisse dire; **to have ~ with children/computers** avoir de l'expérience avec les enfants/en informatique; **to know from ~** savoir d'expérience; **2**] (incident) expérience *f*; **a new ~** une nouvelle expérience; **the ~ of a lifetime** une expérience unique

B *vtr* connaître [*loss, problem*]; éprouver [*emotion*]; ressentir [*physical pleasure*]

experienced /ɪk'spɪərɪənst/ *adj* gen expérimenté; [*eye*] entraîné

experiment /ɪk'sperɪmənt/

A *n* expérience *f* (**in** en; **on** sur); **to conduct** *ou* **carry out an ~** faire *or* effectuer une expérience; **as an ~** à titre d'expérience

B *vi* expérimenter, faire des essais; **to ~ with drugs** goûter à la drogue

experimental /ɪkˌsperɪ'mentl/ *adj* expérimental; [*novelist, writing*] d'avant-garde; ~ **model** prototype *m*; **on an ~ basis** à titre d'expérience

experimentally /ɪkˌsperɪ'mentəlɪ/ *adv* [*establish*] expérimentalement; [*introduce, try*] à titre d'expérience

experimentation /ɪkˌsperɪmen'teɪʃn/ *n* expériences *fpl*

expert /'ekspɜːt/

A *n* spécialiste *mf* (**in** en, de), expert *m* (**in** en); **an ~ at doing** un expert dans l'art de faire; **computer ~** spécialiste *mf* en informatique; **you're the ~!** c'est toi qui t'y connais!

B *adj* [*knowledge*] spécialisé; [*opinion, advice*] autorisé; [*witness*] expert; [*eye*] exercé; **an ~ cook** un cordon bleu

expertise /ˌekspɜː'tiːz/ *n* compétences *fpl*; (very specialized) expertise *f* (**in** dans le domaine de); **to have the ~ to do** avoir les compétences requises pour faire

expertly /'ekspɜːtlɪ/ *adv* magistralement

expiate /'ekspɪeɪt/ *vtr* expier [*crime, sin*]; effacer [*guilt*]

expiration /ˌekspɪ'reɪʃn/ *n* (end, exhalation) expiration *f*

expiration date *n* US = expiry date

expire /ɪk'spaɪə(r)/ *vi* **1**] (end) [*deadline, offer*] expirer; [*period*] arriver à terme; **my passport has ~d** mon passeport est périmé; **2**] (die) hum rendre l'âme

expiry /ɪk'spaɪərɪ/ *n* gen expiration *f*; (of deadline, mandate) terme *m*

expiry date n GB (of credit card, permit) date f d'expiration; (of contract) terme m; (of loan) date f d'échéance

explain /ɪk'spleɪn/
A vtr (all contexts) expliquer (**that** que; **to** à); **I can't ~** je ne peux pas dire pourquoi; **that ~s it!** ça explique tout!
B v refl **to ~ oneself** s'expliquer

(Phrasal verb)
■ **explain away**: ▸ **~ away [sth]**, **~ [sth] away** trouver des justifications à [discrepancy]

explanation /ˌeksplə'neɪʃn/ n explication f (**of** de; **for** à); **by way of ~**, **in ~** en guise d'explication; **it needs no ~** c'est clair

explanatory /ɪk'splænətrɪ, US -tɔːrɪ/ adj [leaflet, diagram] explicatif/-ive

expletive /ɪk'spliːtɪv, US 'eksplətɪv/ sout n (swearword) juron m

explicit /ɪk'splɪsɪt/ adj **1** (precise) explicite; **2** (overt) gen formel/-elle; [aim] avoué; **sexually ~** sexuellement explicite

explode /ɪk'spləʊd/
A vtr faire exploser [bomb]; fig pulvériser [theory, rumour, myth]
B vi **1** lit [bomb] exploser; [boiler, building, ship] sauter; **2** fig [person] (with anger) exploser; [affair] éclater; [population] exploser; **to ~ with laughter** éclater de rire; **they ~d onto the rock music scene** ils ont fait irruption dans le monde du rock

exploit
A /'eksplɔɪt/ n exploit m
B /ɪk'splɔɪt/ vtr exploiter

exploitation /ˌeksplɔɪ'teɪʃn/ n exploitation f

exploitative /ɪk'splɔɪtətɪv/ adj [system] fondé sur l'exploitation des individus; **an ~ attitude** une mentalité d'exploiteur

exploration /ˌeksplə'reɪʃn/ n exploration f; **oil ~** prospection f pétrolière

exploratory /ɪk'splɒrətrɪ, US -tɔːrɪ/ adj [talks] exploratoire; [surgery] explorateur/-trice

explore /ɪk'splɔː(r)/
A vtr **1** gen, Med explorer; **2** (investigate) étudier [idea, opportunity]; **to ~ ways and means of doing** explorer tous les moyens de faire; **to ~ every avenue** examiner toutes les possibilités
B vi **to go exploring** [explorer] partir en exploration; **to ~ for oil** chercher du pétrole

explorer /ɪk'splɔːrə(r)/ n explorateur/-trice m/f

explosion /ɪk'spləʊʒn/ n **1** lit explosion f; **to hear an ~** entendre une détonation; **2** fig (of mirth, rage) explosion f; **pay/population ~** explosion f salariale/démographique

explosive /ɪk'spləʊsɪv/
A n explosif m
B adj gen explosif/-ive; [substance] explosible

exponent /ɪk'spəʊnənt/ n (of policy, theory) avocat/-e m/f, défenseur m; (of technique, art) interprète mf

exponential /ˌekspəʊ'nenʃl/ adj exponentiel/-ielle

export
A /'ekspɔːt/ n (process) exportation f (**of** de); (product) produit m d'exportation; **'for ~ only'** (on product) 'exportation'
B /ɪk'spɔːt/ vtr (all contexts) exporter; **to ~ sth to France/Japan** exporter qch en France/au Japon
C /ɪk'spɔːt/ vi exporter (**to** vers)

export: **~ agent** n agent m exportateur; **~ control** n contrôle m des exportations; **~ drive** n campagne f d'exportation; **~ duty** n droit m à l'exportation; **~ earnings** npl gains mpl à l'exportation

exporter /ɪk'spɔːtə(r)/ n exportateur/-trice m/f (**of** de)

export: **~ finance** n financement m des exportations; **~-import company** n société f d'import-export; **~ licence** GB, **~ license** US n licence f d'exportation; **~ trade** n exportations fpl

expose /ɪk'spəʊz/
A vtr **1** (display) exposer [skin]; **to ~ one's ignorance** étaler son ignorance; **2** (make public) révéler [identity]; dénoncer [injustice, person, scandal]; **3** (uncover) exposer [inside, dirt]; [excavations] mettre à jour [fossil, remains]; **4** (make vulnerable) **to ~ sb/sth to** exposer qn/qch à [infection, light]; livrer qn/qch à [ridicule, temptation]; **5** Phot exposer [film]
B v refl **1** **to ~ oneself** Jur commettre un outrage à la

pudeur; **2** **to ~ oneself to** (make oneself vulnerable) s'exposer à [risk, danger]

C **exposed** pp adj [area, film] exposé; [beam] apparent

exposé /ek'spəʊzeɪ, US ˌekspə'zeɪ/ n (about scandal) révélations fpl (**of** sth sur qch)

exposition /ˌekspə'zɪʃn/ n (of facts) présentation f

expostulation /ɪkˌspɒstjʊ'leɪʃn/ n sout remontrances fpl

exposure /ɪk'spəʊʒə(r)/ n **1** (of secret, crime) révélation f; **to fear ~** craindre d'être démasqué; **to threaten sb with ~** menacer qn de dénonciation; **2** (to light, sun, radiation) exposition f (**to** à); fig (to art, ideas, politics) contact m (**to** avec); **3** (to cold, weather) **to die of ~** mourir de froid; **4** (in media) couverture f médiatique; **5** (orientation) exposition f; **6** Phot (aperture and shutter speed) temps m de pose; (picture) pose f; **a 24 ~ film** une pellicule de 24 poses

exposure: **~ meter** n Phot posemètre m; **~ time** n Phot temps m de pose

expound /ɪk'spaʊnd/
A vtr exposer [theory, opinion]
B vi **~ on** disserter sur

express /ɪk'spres/
A n rapide m
B adj **1** (rapid) [letter, parcel] exprès; [delivery, train] rapide; **2** (explicit) [order, promise] formel/-elle; **on the ~ condition that** à la condition expresse que (+ subj); **with the ~ aim** dans le but précis
C adv **to send sth ~** envoyer qch en exprès
D vtr **1** (show) gen exprimer; **2** Math exprimer [number, quantity]; **to ~ sth as a percentage** exprimer qch en pourcentage; **3** (squeeze out) faire sortir [fluid]
E v refl **to ~ oneself** s'exprimer (**in** en; **through** à travers)

expression /ɪk'spreʃn/ n **1** (phrase) expression f; **2** (look) expression f; **3** ₵ (utterance) expression f; **freedom of ~** liberté f d'expression; **to give ~ to** exprimer; **4** (of friendship, gratitude) témoignage m; **as an ~ of** en témoignage de

expressionism /ɪk'spreʃənɪzəm/ n expressionnisme m

expressionless /ɪk'spreʃnlɪs/ adj [eyes, face] inexpressif/-ive; [tone, voice] monocorde; [playing] plat

expressive /ɪk'spresɪv/ adj expressif/-ive

expressively /ɪk'spresɪvlɪ/ adv de manière significative

expressly /ɪk'spreslɪ/ adv **1** (explicitly) gen expressément; [forbid] formellement; **2** (specifically) [designed, intended] spécialement

expulsion /ɪk'spʌlʃn/ n (of pupil) renvoi m; (of diplomat) expulsion f; (of member) exclusion f

exquisite /'ekskwɪzɪt, ɪk'skwɪzɪt/ adj gen exquis; [setting] charmant; [tact, precision] parfait; [pleasure] vif/vive; **she has ~ taste** elle a un goût exquis

exquisitely /ek'skwɪzɪtlɪ/ adv [dressed, written] d'une façon exquise; **~ beautiful** d'une beauté exquise

ex-serviceman /ˌeks'sɜːvɪsmən/ n ancien militaire m

ex-servicewoman /ˌeks'sɜːvɪswʊmən/ n ancienne combattante f

extant /ek'stænt, US 'ekstənt/ adj existant

extemporize /ɪk'stempəraɪz/ vi improviser

extend /ɪk'stend/
A vtr **1** (enlarge) agrandir [house]; prolonger [runway]; élargir [range, vocabulary]; **2** (prolong) prolonger [visit, visa, show]; proroger [loan, contract]; **the deadline was ~ed by six months** un délai supplémentaire de six mois a été accordé; **3** (stretch) étendre; **to ~ one's hand in greeting** tendre la main; **4** (offer) sout présenter [congratulations]; accorder [credit, loan]; faire [invitation]
B vi **1** (stretch) (over an area) s'étendre; (from one point to another) aller; **2** (reach) **to ~ beyond** dépasser; **3** fig (go as far as) **to ~ to doing** aller jusqu'à faire
C **extended** pp adj [stay] prolongé; [contract, leave, sentence] de longue durée; [area, family] étendu; [premises] agrandi; [credit] à long terme

extendable /ɪk'stendəbl/ adj **1** (of adjustable length) [cable] extensible; [ladder] coulissant; **2** (renewable) renouvelable

extension /ɪk'stenʃn/ n **1** (extra section) (of cable, table) rallonge f; (of road) prolongement m; (of house) addition f; **2** (phone) poste m supplémentaire; (number) (numéro m de) poste m; **3** (prolongation) (of visa, loan) prorogation f; (of deadline) délai m supplémentaire; **4** (widening) (of powers, services) extension *f*; (of knowledge) élargissement *m*; (of business) développement *m*; **by ~** (logically) par extension; **5** (hair) tresse *f* artificielle; **6** Comput extension *f*

extension: **~ ladder** *n* échelle *f* coulissante; **~ lead** *n* Elec rallonge *f*

extensive /ɪkˈstensɪv/ *adj* **1** (wide-ranging) [*network, programme*] vaste (*before n*); [*list*] long/longue (*before n*); [*tests*] approfondi; [*changes*] important; [*training*] complet; [*powers*] étendu; **2** (substantial) [*forest*] vaste (*before n*); [*investment*] considérable; [*damage, loss*] grave, considérable; [*flooding*] important; [*burns*] grave; **to make ~ use of** utiliser beaucoup

extensively /ɪkˈstensɪvlɪ/ *adv* [*correct*] considérablement; [*quote*] abondamment; [*read*] énormément

extent /ɪkˈstent/ *n* **1** (size) (of park, problem) étendue *f*; **to its full ~** complètement; **2** (amount) (of damage) ampleur *f*; (of knowledge, influence) étendue *f*; (of involvement) importance *f*; **3** (degree) mesure *f*; **to what ~...?** dans quelle mesure...?; **to a certain/great ~** dans une certaine/large mesure; **to the ~ that** dans la mesure où; **not to any great ~** très peu

extenuating /ɪkˈstenjʊeɪtɪŋ/ *adj* atténuant

exterior /ɪkˈstɪərɪə(r)/
A *n* extérieur *m* (of de); **on the ~** à l'extérieur
B *adj* gen extérieur (**to** à); **~ decorating** peintures *fpl* extérieures; **for ~ use** (paint) pour extérieurs

exterminate /ɪkˈstɜːmɪneɪt/ *vtr* éliminer [*vermin*]; exterminer [*people, race*]

extermination /ɪkˌstɜːmɪˈneɪʃn/ *n* (of vermin) élimination *f*; (of people, race) extermination *f*

external /ɪkˈstɜːnl/ *adj* **1** (outer) [*appearance, reality*] extérieur (**to** à); [*surface, injury*] externe; **'for ~ use only'** 'usage externe'; **2** (from outside) [*examiner*] externe; [*influence, mail, call*] extérieur; **3** (foreign) extérieur; **4** Comput externe

externalize /ɪkˈstɜːnəlaɪz/ *vtr* extérioriser

externally /ɪkˈstɜːnəlɪ/ *adv* (on the outside) [*calm, healthy*] en apparence; **in good condition ~** en bon état extérieurement

externals /ɪkˈstɜːnlz/ *npl* apparences *fpl*

extinct /ɪkˈstɪŋkt/ *adj* [*species, animal, plant*] disparu; [*volcano, passion*] éteint; **to become ~** [*species, animal, plant*] disparaître; [*volcano*] s'éteindre

extinction /ɪkˈstɪŋkʃn/ *n* extinction *f*

extinguish /ɪkˈstɪŋgwɪʃ/ *vtr* gen éteindre; anéantir [*hope*]

extinguisher /ɪkˈstɪŋgwɪʃə(r)/ *n* extincteur *m*

extol GB, **extoll** US /ɪkˈstəʊl/ *vtr* (*p prés* **-ll-**) louer [*predecessor, rights*]; prôner [*system*]; **to ~ the virtues of** chanter les louanges de

extort /ɪkˈstɔːt/ *vtr* extorquer [*money, promise, signature*] (**from** à); arracher [*confession*] (**from** à)

extortion /ɪkˈstɔːʃn/ *n* gen, Jur extorsion *f*

extortionate /ɪkˈstɔːʃənət/ *adj* exorbitant

extra /ˈekstrə/
A *n* **1** (charge) supplément *m*; **there are no hidden ~s** il n'y a pas de faux frais *mpl*; **2** (feature) option *f*; **the sunroof is an ~** le toit ouvrant est en option; **the little ~s in life** (luxuries) les petits agréments *mpl* de l'existence; **3** Cin, Theat figurant/-e *m/f*
B *adj* supplémentaire; **an ~ £1,000** 1 000 livres de plus; **postage is ~** les frais de port sont en supplément *or* en sus
C *adv* **~ careful** encore plus prudent (que d'habitude); **you have to pay ~** il faut payer un supplément; **that model costs ~** ce modèle coûte plus cher

extra charge *n* supplément *m*; **at no ~** sans supplément

extract
A /ˈekstrækt/ *n* (all contexts) extrait *m* (**from** de); **meat ~** extrait de viande
B /ɪkˈstrækt/ *vtr* **1** (pull out) gen sortir (**from** de); extraire [*tooth, bullet*] (**from** de); **2** (obtain) arracher [*confession, promise*] (**from** à); tirer [*money, energy, heat*] (**from** sth de qch); dégager [*sense*]; **3** Ind extraire [*mineral, oil*] (**from** de)

extraction /ɪkˈstrækʃn/ *n* **1** (process) extraction *f*; **2** (origin) of French **~** d'origine française

extractor /ɪkˈstræktə(r)/ *n* gen extracteur *m*

extractor fan *n* ventilateur *m* d'extraction

extra-curricular /ˌekstrəkəˈrɪkjʊlə(r)/ *adj* parascolaire

extradite /ˈekstrədaɪt/ *vtr* extrader (**from** de; **to** vers)

extradition /ˌekstrəˈdɪʃn/ *n* extradition *f* (**from** de; **to** vers)

extra: **~-dry** *adj* [*sherry, wine*] extra-sec; [*champagne*] brut; **~-fast** *adj* ultrarapide; **~-fine** *adj* extra-fin

extra-large /ˌekstrəˈlɑːdʒ/ *adj* [*pullover, shirt*] extra-large; [*coat*] de grande taille

extramarital /ˌekstrəˈmærɪtl/ *adj* extraconjugal

extra-mural /ˌekstrəˈmjʊərəl/ *adj* **1** GB Univ [*course, lecture*] ouvert à tous et assuré par un universitaire; **2** US Sch **~ sports** matchs *mpl* inter-établissements

extraneous /ɪkˈstreɪnɪəs/ *adj* (not essential) [*issue, detail, information*] superflu; [*considerations*] sans rapport avec la question

extranet /ˈekstrənet/ *n* Comput extranet *m*

extraordinary /ɪkˈstrɔːdnrɪ, US -dənerɪ/ *adj* (all contexts) extraordinaire; **to go to ~ lengths** se donner un mal extraordinaire; **there's nothing ~ about it** cela n'a rien d'extraordinaire; **to find it ~ that** trouver extraordinaire que (+ *subj*)

extrapolate /ɪkˈstræpəleɪt/ *vtr* extrapoler (**from** de)

extrasensory perception, **ESP** *n* perception *f* extrasensorielle

extra: **~-special** *adj* exceptionnel/-elle; **~-strong** *adj* [*coffee*] très serré; [*paper*] extra-strong; [*thread*] extra-solide; [*disinfectant, weed killer*] super-puissant

extraterrestrial /ˌekstrətəˈrestrɪəl/ *n, adj* extraterrestre (*mf*)

extra time *n* Sport prolongation *f*; **to go into** *ou* **play ~** jouer les prolongations

extravagance /ɪkˈstrævəgəns/ *n* **1** ¢ (prodigality) prodigalité *f*; **2** C (luxury) luxe *m*; **3** ¢ (of behaviour, claim) extravagance *f*

extravagant /ɪkˈstrævəgənt/ *adj* **1** [*person*] dépensier/-ière; [*way of life*] dispendieux/-ieuse; **to be ~ with sth** gaspiller qch; **2** (luxurious) [*dish*] luxueux/-euse; **3** (exaggerated) extravagant

extravagantly /ɪkˈstrævəgəntlɪ/ *adv* **1** [*furnished*] luxueusement; **2** [*praise, claim*] à outrance

extravaganza /ɪkˌstrævəˈgænzə/ *n* spectacle *m* somptueux

extreme /ɪkˈstriːm/
A *n* (all contexts) extrême *m*; **to go from one ~ to the other** passer d'un extrême à l'autre; **~s of temperature** écarts *mpl* extrêmes de température; **to take/carry sth to ~s** pousser/porter qch à l'extrême; **to go to ~s** pousser les choses à l'extrême; **to be driven to ~s** être poussé à bout; **to go to any ~** ne s'arrêter devant rien; **naïve in the ~** naïf à l'extrême
B *adj* [*example, case, heat, edge*] extrême; [*view, measure, reaction*] extrémiste; **fashion at its most ~** la mode poussée à l'extrême; **on the ~ right/left** à l'extrême droite/gauche; **to go to ~ lengths** ne reculer devant rien; **to be ~ in one's views** avoir des opinions extrémistes; **to have ~ difficulty doing** avoir énormément de difficulté à faire

extremely /ɪkˈstriːmlɪ/ *adv* extrêmement; **he did ~ well** il s'est bien débrouillé

extreme sport *n* sport *m* extrême

extremism /ɪkˈstriːmɪzəm/ *n* extrémisme *m*

extremity /ɪkˈstremətɪ/ *n* **1** (of place) extrémité *f* (**of** de); **extremities** (of body) extrémités *f*; **2** (dire situation) situation *f* désespérée; **to do sth in ~** faire qch en dernier recours; **to be reduced to extremities** être à bout; **3** (extremeness) degré *m* extrême (**of** de)

extricate /ˈekstrɪkeɪt/
A *vtr* (from trap, net) dégager (**from** de); (from situation) sortir (**from** de)
B *v refl* **to ~ oneself from** s'extirper de [*place*]; se dégager de [*embrace*]; se sortir de [*situation*]

extrovert /ˈekstrəvɜːt/ *n, adj* extraverti/-e (*m/f*)

exuberance /ɪgˈzjuːbərəns, US -ˈzuː-/ *n* exubérance *f*

exuberant /ɪgˈzjuːbərənt, US -ˈzuː-/ *adj* exubérant

exude /ɪgˈzjuːd, US -ˈzuːd/ *vtr* **1** (radiate) respirer [*charm*]; **2** (give off) exsuder [*sap*]; exhaler [*smell*]

exult /ɪgˈzʌlt/ *vi* **to ~ at** *ou* **in sth** se réjouir de qch

exultant /ɪgˈzʌltənt/ *adj* gen triomphant; [*cry*] de triomphe; **to be ~** exulter

exultantly /ɪgˈzʌltəntlɪ/ *adv* triomphalement
ex-works /ˌeksˈwɜːks/ *adj* [*price, value*] départ-usine
eye /aɪ/ ▸ p. 698

A *n* ① Anat œil *m*; **with blue ~s** aux yeux bleus; **to lower one's ~s** baisser les yeux; **in front of** *ou* **before your (very) ~s** sous vos yeux; **to the untrained ~** pour un œil non exercé; **to see sth with one's own ~s** voir qch de ses propres yeux; **keep your ~s on the road!** c'est la route qu'il faut regarder!; **to keep an ~ on sth/sb** surveiller qch/qn; **under the watchful ~ of sb** sous le regard vigilant de qn; **to have one's ~ on sb/sth** (watch) surveiller qn/qch; (want) avoir envie de [*house*]; (lust after) loucher◦ sur [*person*]; (aim for) viser [*job*]; **with an ~ to doing** en vue de faire; **to keep one** *ou* **half an ~ on sth/sb** garder un œil sur qch/qn; **to run one's ~ over sth** parcourir qch du regard; **to catch sb's ~** attirer l'attention de qn; **to close** *ou* **shut one's ~s** fermer les yeux; **to close** *ou* **shut one's ~s to sth** fig se refuser à reconnaître qch; **to open one's ~s** ouvrir les yeux; **to open sb's ~s to sth** fig ouvrir les yeux de qn sur qch; **to do sth with one's ~s open** fig faire qch en toute connaissance de cause; **to go around with one's ~s shut** fig vivre sans rien voir; **to keep an ~ out** *ou* **one's ~s open for sb/sth** essayer de repérer qn/qch; **as far as the ~ can see** à perte de vue; **I've got ~s in my head!** j'ai des yeux pour voir!; **use your ~s!** tu es aveugle?; **she couldn't take her ~s off him** elle ne le quittait pas des yeux; ② (opinion) **in the ~s of the law** aux yeux de la loi; **in his ~s…** à ses yeux…; ③ (flair) **to have a good ~** avoir un bon coup d'œil; **to have an ~ for** avoir le sens de [*detail, colour*]; s'y connaître en [*antiques*]; ④ (hole in needle) chas *m*; (to attach hook to) œillet *m*; ⑤ (on potato) œil *m*; ⑥ (on peacock's tail) œil *m*, ocelle *m*; ⑦ (of storm) œil *m*; **the ~ of the storm** fig l'œil de la tempête

B *noun modifier* [*operation*] de l'œil; [*muscle, tissue*] de l'œil, oculaire; [*ointment, lotion*] pour les yeux; **~ trouble** troubles *mpl* oculaires

C -eyed *combining form* **blue-~d** aux yeux bleus

D *vtr* ① (look at) regarder [*person, object*]; **to ~ sth with envy** regarder qch avec envie; ② ◦(ogle at) ▸ **eye up**

(Idioms) **to be all ~s** être tout yeux; **to be up to one's ~s in** être submergé de [*mail, work*]; **to be up to one's ~s in debt** être endetté jusqu'au cou; **an ~ for an ~** œil pour œil; **it was one in the ~ for him** c'était bien fait pour lui iron; **to have ~s in the back of one's head** avoir des yeux dans le dos; **to make ~s at sb** faire les yeux doux à qn; **to give sb the glad ~** faire de l'œil à qn; **to see ~ to ~ with sb (about sth)** partager le point de vue de qn (au sujet de qch)

(Phrasal verbs)
■ **eye up**◦: ▸ **~ [sb] up, ~ up [sb]** lorgner◦, reluquer◦
■ **eye up and down**: ▸ **~ [sb] up and down** (suspiciously) toiser [qn]; (appreciatively) dévorer [qn] des yeux

eyeball /ˈaɪbɔːl/ *n* Anat globe *m* oculaire; **to be ~ to ~ with sb** être nez à nez avec qn

eye: ~ bank *n* banque *f* des yeux; **~bath** *n* œillère *f*

eyebrow /ˈaɪbraʊ/ *n* sourcil *m*; **to raise one's** *ou* **an ~** (in surprise) hausser les sourcils; (in disapproval) froncer les sourcils; **to raise a few ~s** provoquer quelques froncements de sourcils

eye: ~brow pencil *n* crayon *m* à sourcils; **~-catching** *adj* [*design, poster*] attrayant; [*advertisement, headline*] accrocheur/-euse

eye candy◦ *n* ① Comput image *f* fractale; ② (man) beau mâle *m*; ③ (woman) belle fille *f*

eye contact *n* échange *m* de regards; **to make ~ with sb** croiser le regard de qn

eyedrops /ˈaɪdrɒps/ *npl* gouttes *fpl* pour les yeux

eyeful /ˈaɪfʊl/ *n* ① (amount) **to get an ~ of** avoir [qch] plein les yeux [*dust, sand*]; ② ◦(good look) **to get an ~ (of sth)** se rincer l'œil◦ (au spectacle de qch)

eye: ~glass *n* (monocle) monocle *m*; **~glasses** *npl* US lunettes *fpl* (de vue); **~ hospital** *n* hôpital *m* ophtalmologique; **~lash** *n* cil *m*

eye level /ˈaɪ levl/
A *n* **at ~** à hauteur des yeux
B **eye-level** *adj* [*grill, shelf*] à hauteur des yeux

eye: ~lid *n* paupière *f*; **~ make-up** *n* maquillage *m* pour les yeux; **~-opener**◦ *n* révélation *f*; **~patch** *n* bandeau *m*; **~shade** *n* visière *f*; **~ shadow** *n* fard *m* à paupières; **~sight** *n* vue *f*

eyesore /ˈaɪsɔː(r)/ *n* **to be an ~** choquer la vue

eye: ~ strain *n* fatigue *f* oculaire; **~ test** *n* examen *m* de la vue

eyetooth /ˈaɪtuːθ/ *n* (*pl* **-teeth**) canine *f* supérieure

(Idiom) **I'd give my eyeteeth for that job** je donnerais n'importe quoi pour obtenir ce poste

eye: ~wash *n* collyre *m*; fig (nonsense) poudre *f* aux yeux; **~witness** *n* témoin *m* oculaire

eyrie /ˈeərɪ, ˈaɪərɪ/ *n* aire *f*, nid *m* d'aigle

f, F /ef/ n [1] (letter) f, F m; [2] **F** Mus (note, key) fa m

fa /fɑː/ n Mus fa m

FA n GB (abrév = **Football Association**) fédération f britannique de football; cf FFF

FAA n US (abrév = **Federal Aviation Association**) direction f générale de l'aviation civile américaine

fable /'feɪbl/ n fable f

fabric /'fæbrɪk/ n (cloth) tissu m; (of building) structure f; fig (basis) **the ~ of society** le tissu social

fabricate /'fæbrɪkeɪt/ vtr [1] inventer [qch] de toutes pièces [story, evidence]; [2] fabriquer [document]

fabrication /ˌfæbrɪ'keɪʃn/ n [1] (lie) fabrication f; **that's pure ou complete ~** c'est de l'invention pure et simple; [2] (of document) fabrication f

fabric conditioner, **fabric softener** n (produit m) assouplissant m

fabulous /'fæbjʊləs/

A adj gen fabuleux/-euse; (wonderful) sensationnel/-elle

B excl génial!

fabulously /'fæbjʊləslɪ/ adv fabuleusement; **to be ~ successful** avoir un succès fou

face /feɪs/

A n [1] (of person) visage m, figure f; (of animal) face f; **to slam the door/laugh in sb's ~** claquer la porte/rire au nez de qn; **I told him to his ~ that he was lazy** je lui ai dit en face qu'il était paresseux; **to be ~ up/down** [person] être sur le dos/ventre; [2] (expression) air m; **to pull ou make a ~** faire la grimace; **you should have seen their ~s!** tu aurais vu la tête qu'ils ont fait; [3] fig (outward appearance) **to change the ~ of** changer le visage de [industry]; **the changing ~ of Europe** la face changeante de l'Europe; **the acceptable ~ of capitalism** le bon côté du capitalisme; [4] (dignity) **to lose ~** perdre la face; **to save ~** sauver la face; [5] (surface) (of clock, watch) cadran m; (of gem, dice) face f; (of coin) côté m; (of planet) surface f; (of cliff, mountain) face f; (of rock) paroi f; (of playing card) face f; (of document) recto m; **to disappear ou vanish off the ~ of the earth** disparaître de la circulation; **~ up/down** à l'endroit/l'envers

B vtr [1] (look towards) [person] faire face à; [building, room] donner sur; **to ~ north/south** [person] regarder au nord/sud; [building] être orienté au nord/sud; **facing our house, there is...** en face de notre maison, il y a...; [2] (confront) se trouver face à [challenge, crisis]; se voir contraint de payer [fine]; se trouver menacé de [defeat, redundancy]; être contraint de faire [choice]; affronter [attacker, rival, team]; **to be ~d with** se trouver confronté à [problem, decision]; **~d with the prospect of having to resign** devant la perspective d'avoir à démissionner; **to ~ sb with** confronter qn à [truth, evidence]; [3] (acknowledge) **the facts, you're finished!** regarde la réalité en face, tu es fini!; **let's ~ it, nobody's perfect** admettons-le, personne n'est parfait; [4] (tolerate prospect) **I can't ~ doing** je n'ai pas le courage de faire; **he couldn't ~ the thought of walking/eating** l'idée de marcher/manger lui était insupportable; [5] (run the risk of) risquer [fine, suspension]; [6] Constr revêtir [façade, wall] (**with de**); [7] (in printing) [photo etc] être face à [page]

C vi [1] **to ~ towards** [person, chair] être tourné vers; [building, house] être en face de; **to ~ forward** regarder devant soi; **to ~ backwards** [person] tourner le dos; **to be facing forward** [person] être de face; [2] Mil **about ~!** demi-tour!; **left ~!** à gauche!

D **in the face of** prep phr [1] (despite) en dépit de [difficulties]; [2] (in confrontation with) face à, devant [opposition, enemy, danger]

(Idiom) **to set one's ~ against** s'élever contre

(Phrasal verb)

■ **face up to**: ► **~ up to [sth]** faire face à [problem, responsibilities]; ► **~ up to [sb]** affronter

faceless /'feɪslɪs/ adj anonyme

face-lift /'feɪslɪft/ n gen lifting m; fig rénovation f; **to give sth a ~** rénover qch [building]; réaménager qch [town centre]

face: **~-pack** n masque m de beauté; **~ paint** n maquillage m (pour déguisement); **~ powder** n poudre f (de riz)

face-saving /'feɪseɪvɪŋ/ adj [plan, solution] qui permet de sauver la face (after n)

facet /'fæsɪt/ n (of gemstone, of personality) facette f; (of question, problem) aspect m

facetious /fə'siːʃəs/ adj [remark] facétieux/-ieuse

facetiousness /fə'siːʃəsnɪs/ n gouaillerie f

face-to-face /ˌfeɪstə'feɪs/

A adj **a ~ discussion ou interview ou meeting** un face-à-face inv

B **face to face** adv [be seated] face à face; **to come ~ with** se retrouver face à; **to meet sb ~** rencontrer qn en face-à-face; **to talk to sb ~** parler à qn en personne

face value n valeur f nominale; fig **to take sth at ~** prendre qch au pied de la lettre [claim]; prendre qch pour argent comptant [compliment]; **to take sb at ~** juger qn sur les apparences

facial /'feɪʃl/

A n soin m (complet) du visage

B adj [hair] du visage; [injury] au visage; [angle, muscle, nerve] facial; **~ expression** expression f

facile /'fæsaɪl, US 'fæsl/ adj [1] (glib) spécieux/-ieuse, facile; [2] (easy) facile

facilitate /fə'sɪlɪteɪt/ vtr faciliter [progress, talks]; favoriser [development]

facility /fə'sɪlətɪ/

A n [1] (building) complexe m, installation f; **manufacturing ~** complexe industriel; **computer ~** installation informatique; [2] (ease) facilité f; [3] (ability) talent m; **to have a ~ for** être doué pour; [4] (feature) fonction f; **a pause ~** une fonction pause; [5] Admin, Comm facilités fpl; **'fax facilities available'** 'télécopieur disponible'

B **facilities** npl [1] (equipment) équipement m; **facilities for the disabled** installations fpl pour les handicapés; **to have cooking and washing facilities** être équipé d'une cuisine et d'une laverie; [2] (infrastructure) infrastructure f; **harbour facilities** installations fpl portuaires; **sporting facilities** infrastructure sportive; **postal facilities** service m postal; [3] (area) **changing facilities** vestiaire m; **parking facilities** (aire f de) parking m

facing /'feɪsɪŋ/ n [1] Archit revêtement m; [2] (in sewing) entoilage m; [3] (in fashion) revers m

facsimile /fæk'sɪməlɪ/ n [1] gen fac-similé m; [2] (sculpture) reproduction f

fact /fækt/ n fait m; **it is a ~ that** c'est un fait que; **to know for a ~ that** savoir de source sûre que; **owing ou due to the ~ that** étant donné que; **in ~**, **as a matter of ~** en fait; **the ~ remains (that)** toujours est-il que; **the ~s and figures** les faits et les chiffres; **the story was presented as ~** l'histoire a été présentée comme véridique; **to be based on ~** être fondé sur des faits réels; **space travel is now a ~** les voyages dans l'espace sont désormais une réalité

(Idioms) **to know the ~s of life** (sex) savoir comment les enfants viennent au monde; **the ~s of life** (unpalatable truths) les réalités de la vie

fact-finding /'fæktfaɪndɪŋ/ adj [mission, tour, trip] d'information

faction /'fækʃn/ n ① (group) faction f; ② (discord) dissension f; ③ Theat, TV docudrame m

factional /'fækʃənl/ adj [leader, activity] de faction; [fighting, arguments] entre factions

factor /'fæktə(r)/ n gen, Math facteur m; **common ~** gen point m commun; Math facteur commun; **human ~** élément m humain; **protection ~** (of suntan lotion) indice m de protection

factory /'fæktərɪ/ n usine f; **tobacco ~** manufacture f de tabac; **bomb ~** atelier m clandestin (de fabrication de bombes)

factory: **~ farming** n élevage m industriel; **~ floor** n (place) ateliers mpl; (workers) ouvriers/-ières mpl/fpl; **~ inspector** ▸ p. 1181 n inspecteur/-trice m/f du travail; **~-made** adj fabriqué en usine; **~ outlet** n magasin m d'usine; **~ ship** n navire-usine m; **~ shop** n = factory outlet; **~ unit** n unité f de production; **~ worker** ▸ p. 1181 n ouvrier/-ière m/f (d'usine)

fact sheet n bulletin m d'informations

factual /'fæktʃʊəl/ adj [evidence] factuel/-elle; [account, description] basé sur les faits; **~ error** erreur de fait; **~ programme** GB TV, Radio reportage m

factually /'fæktʃʊəlɪ/ adv [incorrect] dans les faits

faculty /'fæklti/ n (pl **-ties**) ① (ability) faculté f (**of** de; **for** de; **for doing** de faire); **critical faculties** esprit m critique; ② GB Univ faculté f; ③ US Univ, Sch (staff) corps m enseignant

fad /fæd/ n (craze) engouement m (**for** pour); (whim) (petite) manie f

faddish /'fædɪʃ/, **faddy** /'fædɪ/ adj GB difficile (**about** pour)

fade /feɪd/
A vtr faner
B vi ① (get lighter) [fabric] se décolorer, se faner; [colour] passer; [lettering, typescript] s'effacer; **to ~ in the wash** [garment, fabric] se décolorer au lavage; [colour] passer au lavage; ② (wither) [flowers] se faner; ③ (disappear) [image, drawing] s'estomper; [sound] s'affaiblir; [smile, memory] s'effacer; [interest, excitement, hope] s'évanouir; [hearing, light] baisser; **to ~ into the background** se fondre dans l'arrière-plan

(Phrasal verbs)
■ **fade away** [sound] s'éteindre; [sick person] dépérir.
■ **fade in**: ▸ **~ [sth] in** monter progressivement [sound, voice]; faire apparaître [qch] en fondu [image]; ouvrir [qch] en fondu [scene].
■ **fade out**: ▸ **~ out** [speaker, scene] disparaître en fondu; ▸ **~ [sth] out** Cin faire disparaître [qch] en fondu [picture, scene]

faded /'feɪdɪd/ adj [clothing, carpet] décoloré; [colour, glory] passé; [jeans] délavé; [drawing] estompé; [photo, wallpaper] jauni; [flower, beauty] fané; [writing, lettering] à demi effacé

fade: **~-in** n Cin, Radio, TV fondu m; **~-out** n Cin, Radio, TV fondu m

faeces, feces US /'fiːsiːz/ npl matières fpl fécales

fag /fæg/ n ① ○(cigarette) clope○ f; ② ○GB (nuisance) corvée f

fag end n ① ○(cigarette) mégot○ m; ② (of material) restant m; (of day, decade, conversation) fin f

faggot /'fægət/ n ① (meatball) boulette f de viande; ② (firewood) fagot m

fah /fɑː/ n Mus fa m

fail /feɪl/
A n Sch, Univ échec m
B without fail adv phr [arrive, do] sans faute; [happen] à coup sûr
C vtr ① Sch, Univ échouer à [exam, driving test]; échouer en or être collé○ en [subject]; coller○ [candidate, pupil]; ② (omit) **to ~ to do** manquer de faire; **to ~ to keep one's word** manquer à ses promesses; **it never ~s to work** ça marche à tous les coups; **not to ~ to mention that...** omettre de signaler que...; ③ (be unable) **to ~ to do** ne pas réussir à faire; **one could hardly ~ to notice that...** il était évident que...; **I**

~ to understand why je n'arrive pas à comprendre pourquoi; ④ (let down) laisser tomber [friend]; manquer à ses engagements envers [dependant, supporter]; [courage] manquer à [person]; [memory] faire défaut à [person]

D vi ① (be unsuccessful) [exam candidate] échouer, être collé○; [attempt, plan] échouer; **to ~ in one's duty** manquer or faillir à son devoir; **if all else ~s** en dernier recours; ② (weaken) [eyesight, hearing, light] baisser; [health, person] décliner; ③ (not function) [brakes] lâcher; [engine] tomber en panne; [power, water supply] être coupé; Agric [crop] être mauvais; ⑤ (go bankrupt) faire faillite; ⑥ Med [heart] lâcher; **his liver ~ed** il a eu une défaillance du foie

E failed pp adj [actor, writer] raté○

failing /'feɪlɪŋ/
A n défaut m
B pres p adj **to have ~ eyesight** avoir la vue qui baisse; **to be in ~ health** être en mauvaise santé
C prep **~ that, ~ this** sinon

fail-safe adj [device, system] à sécurité intégrée

failure /'feɪljə(r)/ n ① (lack of success) gen échec m (**in** à); (of business) faillite f; **his ~ to understand the problem** son incapacité f à comprendre le problème; ② (unsuccessful person) raté-e○ m/f; (unsuccessful venture or event) échec m; **he was a ~ as a teacher** comme professeur il ne valait rien; ③ (breakdown) (of engine, machine, power) panne f; Med (of organ) défaillance f; **crop ~** perte f de récolte; **power ~** panne de courant; **due to a mechanical ~** dû à une défaillance mécanique; ④ (omission) **~ to keep a promise** manquement m à une promesse; **~ to comply with the rules** non-respect m de la réglementation; **~ to pay** non-paiement m

faint /feɪnt/
A n évanouissement m
B adj ① (slight) [smell, accent, breeze] léger/-ère; [sound, voice, protest] faible; [markings] à peine visible; [recollection] vague; [chance] minime; **I haven't the ~est idea** je n'en ai pas la moindre idée; ② (dizzy) **to feel ~** se sentir mal, défaillir
C vi s'évanouir (**from** sous l'effet de)

fainthearted /ˌfeɪnt'hɑːtɪd/
A n **the ~** (+ v pl) (cowardly) les timorés mpl; (over-sensitive) les natures fpl sensibles
B adj [attempt] timide

fainting fit /ˌfeɪntɪŋ/ n évanouissement m

faintly /'feɪntlɪ/ adv [glisten, breathe, smile] faiblement; [coloured, disappointed] légèrement

faintness /'feɪntnɪs/ n faiblesse f

fair /feə(r)/
A n (funfair, market) foire f; (for charity) kermesse f; **book ~** gen foire f du livre; (in Paris, Montreal) salon m du livre
B adj ① (just, reasonable) [arrangement, person, trial, wage] équitable (**to** envers); [comment, decision, point] juste; **it's only ~ that she should be first** ce n'est que justice qu'elle soit la première; **to give sb a ~ deal** ou **shake** US être tout à fait honnête envers qn; **that's a ~ question** c'est une question raisonnable; **a ~ sample** un échantillon représentatif; **to be ~ he did try to pay** il faut dire à sa décharge qu'il a essayé de payer; **it (just) isn't ~!** ce n'est pas juste!; **~ enough!** bon d'accord!; ② (moderately good) [chance, condition, performance] assez bon/bonne; Sch passable; ③ (quite large) **a ~ number** of un bon nombre de; **to go at a ~ pace** ou **speed** aller bon train; **he's had a ~ amount of luck** il a eu pas mal de chance; **the house was a ~ size** la maison était de bonne taille; **to be a ~ way off** être à bonne distance; ④ Meteorol (fine) [weather] beau/belle; [forecast] bon/bonne; [wind] favorable; ⑤ (light-coloured) [hair] blond; [complexion, skin] clair; ⑥ littér (beautiful) [lady, city] beau/belle; **with her own ~ hands** hum de ses belles mains; **the ~ sex** hum le beau sexe
C adv [play] franc jeu

(Idioms) **to be ~ game for sb** être une proie rêvée pour qn; **~ and square** indiscutablement; **to win ~ and square** remporter une victoire indiscutable

fair: **~ copy** n version f au propre; **~ground** n champ m de foire

fairly /'feəlɪ/ adv ① (quite, rather) assez; [sure] pratiquement; ② (justly) [obtain, win] honnêtement; [say] à juste titre

fair-minded /ˌfeə'maɪndɪd/ adj impartial

fairness /'feənɪs/ n ① (justness) (of person) équité f; (of judgment) impartialité f; **in all ~** en toute justice; **in ~ to him, he did phone** il faut dire à sa décharge qu'il a téléphoné;

2) (lightness) (of complexion) blancheur *f*; (of hair) blondeur *f*

fair play *n* **to have a sense of** ∼ jouer franc jeu, être fair-play; **to ensure** ∼ faire respecter les règles du jeu

fair: ∼**-sized** *adj* assez grand; ∼**-skinned** *adj* à la peau claire

fair trade *n* **1)** Econ commerce *m* équitable; **2)** US régime *m* des prix imposés

fairway /'feəweɪ/ *n* **1)** (in golf) parcours *m* normal; **2)** Naut chenal *m*

fair-weather friend *n* péj **he's a** ∼ dès qu'on a des ennuis, il n'est plus votre ami

fairy /'feərɪ/ *n* (magical being) fée *f*

fairy: ∼ **godmother** *n* bonne fée *f*; ∼ **lights** GB guirlande *f* électrique; ∼ **story** *n* conte *m* de fées

fairy tale

A *n* (story) conte *m* de fées; (lie) histoire *f* à dormir debout

B (also **fairy-tale**, **fairytale**) *noun modifier* [*romance, princess*] de conte de fées

faith /feɪθ/ *n* **1)** (confidence) confiance *f*; **he has no** ∼ **in socialism** il ne croit pas au socialisme; **I have no** ∼ **in her** elle ne m'inspire pas confiance; **in good** ∼ en toute bonne foi; **2)** (belief) foi *f* (**in** en); **the Muslim** ∼ la foi musulmane; **people of all** ∼**s** les gens de toutes confessions

faithful /'feɪθfl/

A *n* **the** ∼ (+ *v pl*) les fidèles *mpl*

B *adj* (all contexts) fidèle (**to** à)

faithfully /'feɪθfəlɪ/ *adv* **1)** (loyally, accurately) fidèlement; **2)** (in letter writing) **yours** ∼ veuillez agréer, Monsieur/Madame, mes/nos salutations distinguées

faithfulness /'feɪθflnɪs/ *n* fidélité *f*

faith: ∼ **healer** *n* guérisseur *m*; ∼ **healing** *n* guérison *f* par la foi

faithless /'feɪθlɪs/ *adj* littér [*friend, husband*] infidèle; [*servant*] déloyal

fake /feɪk/

A *n* **1)** (jewel, work of art etc) faux *m*; **2)** (person) imposteur *m*

B *adj* [*fur, gem, passport*] faux/fausse; [*flower*] artificiel/-ielle; [*smile*] feint; **it's** ∼ **wood/granite** c'est de l'imitation bois/granit

C *vtr* **1)** contrefaire [*signature, document*]; falsifier [*results*]; feindre [*emotion, illness*]; **2)** US Sport **to** ∼ **a pass** feindre une passe

falcon /'fɔːlkən, US 'fælkən/ *n* faucon *m*

Falklands /'fɔːkləndz/ ▸ p. 954 *pr npl* (also **Falkland Islands**) **the** ∼ les îles *fpl* Malouines

fall /fɔːl/ ▸ p. 1166

A *n* **1)** lit gen chute *f* (**from** de); (of snow, hail) chutes *fpl*; (of earth, soot) éboulement *m*; (of axe, hammer, dice) coup *m*; **a heavy** ∼ **of rain** une grosse averse; **to have a** ∼ faire une chute, tomber; **2)** (in temperature, shares, production, quality, popularity) baisse *f* (**in** de); (more drastic) chute *f* (**in** de); **a** ∼ **in value** une dépréciation; **3)** (of leader, regime, town) chute *f*; (of monarchy) renversement *m*; (of seat) perte *f*; **the government's** ∼ **from power** la chute du gouvernement; **4)** ∼ **from grace** *ou* **favour** disgrâce *f*; **5)** US (autumn) automne *m*; **6)** (in pitch, intonation) descente *f*; **7)** (in wrestling) tombé *m*; (in judo) chute *f*

B **falls** *npl* chutes *fpl*

C *vi* (*prét* **fell**; *pp* **fallen**) **1)** (come down) tomber; **to** ∼ **10 metres** tomber de 10 mètres; **to** ∼ **from** *ou* **out of** tomber de [*boat, nest, bag, hands*]; **to** ∼ **off** *ou* **from** tomber de [*chair, table, roof, bike, wall*]; **to** ∼ **on** tomber sur [*person, town*]; **to** ∼ **in** *ou* **into** tomber dans [*bath, river*]; **to** ∼ **down** tomber dans [*hole, stairs*]; **to** ∼ **under** tomber sous [*table*]; passer sous [*bus, train*]; **to** ∼ **through** passer à travers [*ceiling, hole*]; **to** ∼ **through the air** tomber dans le vide; **to** ∼ **to the floor** *ou* **to the ground** tomber par terre; **to** ∼ **on the floor** tomber par terre; **2)** (drop) [*quality, standard, level*] diminuer; [*temperature, price, production, number, attendance, morale*] baisser; **to** ∼ **(by)** baisser de; **to** ∼ **to** descendre à; **to** ∼ **from** descendre de; **to** ∼ **below zero/5%** descendre au-dessous de zéro/5%; **3)** (yield position) tomber; **to** ∼ **from power** tomber; **to** ∼ **to** tomber aux mains de [*enemy, allies*]; **the seat fell to Labour** le siège a été perdu au profit des travaillistes; **4)** euph (die) tomber; **5)** fig (descend) [*night, silence, gaze*] tomber (**on** sur); [*blame*] retomber (**on** sur); [*shadow*] se projeter (**over** sur); **suspicion fell on her husband** les soupçons se sont portés sur son mari; **6)** (occur) [*stress*] tomber (**on** sur); **Christmas** ∼**s on a Monday** Noël

tombe un lundi; **to** ∼ **into/outside a category** rentrer/ne pas rentrer dans une catégorie; **7)** (be incumbent on) **it** ∼**s to sb to do** c'est à qn de faire; **8)** (throw oneself) **to** ∼ **into bed** se laisser tomber sur son lit; **to** ∼ **to** *ou* **on one's knees** tomber à genoux; **to** ∼ **at sb's feet/on sb's neck** se jeter aux pieds/au cou de qn

[Idioms] **did he** ∼ **or was he pushed?** hum est-ce qu'il est parti de lui-même ou est-ce qu'on l'a forcé?; **the bigger you are** *ou* **the higher you climb, the harder you** ∼ plus dure sera la chute; **to stand or** ∼ **on sth** reposer sur qch, dépendre de qch

[Phrasal verbs]

■ **fall about**⁰ GB: **to** ∼ **about (laughing** *ou* **with laughter)** se tordre⁰ de rire

■ **fall apart** [*bike, table*] être délabré; [*shoes*] être usé; [*car, house, hotel*] tomber en ruine; [*organization*] se désagréger

■ **fall away** **1)** [*paint, plaster*] se détacher (**from** de); **2)** [*ground*] descendre en pente (**to** vers); **3)** [*demand, support*] diminuer

■ **fall back** gen reculer; Mil se replier (**to** sur)

■ **fall back on**: ▸ ∼ **back on [sth]** avoir recours à [*savings, parents*]; **to have something to** ∼ **back on** avoir quelque chose sur quoi se rabattre

■ **fall behind**: ▸ ∼ **behind** [*country, student*] se laisser distancer; [*work, studies*] prendre du retard; **to** ∼ **behind with** GB *ou* **in** US prendre du retard dans [*work, project*]; être en retard pour [*payments, rent*]; ▸ ∼ **behind [sth/sb]** se laisser devancer par

■ **fall down** **1)** lit [*person, poster*] tomber; [*tent, scaffolding*] s'effondrer; **2)** GB fig [*argument, comparison*] faiblir; **to** ∼ **down on** échouer à cause de [*detail, question, obstacle*]

■ **fall for**: ▸ ∼ **for [sth]** se laisser prendre à [*trick, story*]; ▸ ∼ **for [sb]** tomber amoureux/-euse de

■ **fall in** **1)** [*walls, roof*] s'écrouler, s'effondrer; **2)** Mil [*soldier*] rentrer dans les rangs; [*soldiers*] former les rangs

■ **fall in with**: ▸ ∼ **in with [sth/sb]** **1)** (get involved with) faire la connaissance de [*group*]; **2)** (go along with) se conformer à [*plans, action*]; **3)** (be consistent with) être conforme à [*expectations*]

■ **fall off** **1)** lit [*person, hat, label*] tomber; **2)** fig [*attendance, sales, output*] diminuer; [*enthusiasm, quality*] baisser; [*support*] retomber; [*curve on graph*] décroître

■ **fall on**: ▸ ∼ **on [sth]** se jeter sur [*food, treasure*]; ▸ ∼ **on [sb]** tomber sur [*person*]

■ **fall open** [*book*] tomber ouvert; [*robe*] s'entrebâiller

■ **fall out** **1)** [*tooth, contact lens, page*] tomber; **his hair is** ∼**ing out** il perd ses cheveux; **2)** Mil [*soldiers*] rompre les rangs; **3)** ⁰(quarrel) se brouiller (**over** à propos de); **to** ∼ **out with sb** GB (quarrel) se brouiller avec qn; US (have fight) se disputer avec qn; **4)** GB (turn out) se passer.

■ **fall over**: ▸ ∼ **over** [*person*] tomber (par terre); [*object*] se renverser; ▸ ∼ **over [sth]** trébucher sur [*object*]; **people were** ∼**ing over themselves to buy shares** c'était à qui achèterait les actions

■ **fall through** [*plans, deal*] échouer

■ **fall to**: ▸ ∼ **to** attaquer; ▸ ∼ **to doing** se mettre à faire

■ **fall upon = fall on**

fallacious /fə'leɪʃəs/ *adj* fallacieux/-ieuse

fallacy /'fæləsɪ/ *n* (belief) erreur *f*; (argument) faux raisonnement *m*

fallen /'fɔːlən/

A *pp* ▸ **fall**

B *n* **the** ∼ (+ *v pl*) les morts *mpl* au champ d'honneur

C *pp adj* [*leaf, soldier*] mort; [*tree*] abattu

fallibility /ˌfæləˈbɪlətɪ/ *n* faillibilité *f*

fallible /'fæləbl/ *adj* faillible

falling-off /ˌfɔːlɪŋˈɒf/ *n* (also **falloff**) diminution *f*

Fallopian tube /fəˈləʊpɪən/ *n* trompe *f* de Fallope

fall: ∼**out** *n* ⊄ retombées *fpl*; ∼**out shelter** *n* abri *m* antiatomique

fallow /'fæləʊ/ *adj* [*land*] en jachère

fallow deer *n* daim *m*

false /fɔːls/ *adj* faux/fausse; **to prove** ∼ s'avérer sans fondement; **a** ∼ **sense of security** une fausse impression de sécurité; **to give** ∼ **evidence** Jur faire un faux témoignage

false: ∼ **alarm** *n* fausse alerte *f*; ∼ **bottom** *n* (in bag, box) double fond *m*; ∼ **economy** *n* fausse économie *f*

falsehood /'fɔːlshʊd/ *n* (lie) mensonge *m*

falsely /ˈfɔːlslɪ/ adv **1** (wrongly) faussement; (mistakenly) à tort; **2** [*smile, laugh*] avec affectation

false: ∼ **memory syndrome** n Psych syndrome m du faux souvenir; ∼ **move** n fausse manœuvre f

falseness /ˈfɔːlsnɪs/ n fausseté f

false note n gen couac○ m; (in film, novel) son m discordant; **to strike a** ∼ [*person*] faire une gaffe

false pretences npl (on ou under ∼ gen en utilisant un subterfuge; Jur (by an action) par des moyens frauduleux

false: ∼ **start** n faux départ m; ∼ **step** n faux pas m; ∼ **teeth** npl dentier m

falsetto /fɔːlˈsetəʊ/
A n (voice) voix f de fausset; (singer) fausset m
B adj de fausset

falsification /ˌfɔːlsɪfɪˈkeɪʃn/ n (of document, of figures) falsification f; (of the truth, of facts) déformation f

falsify /ˈfɔːlsɪfaɪ/ vtr falsifier [*documents, accounts*]; déformer [*facts*]

falsity /ˈfɔːlsətɪ/ n fausseté f

falter /ˈfɔːltə(r)/
A vtr (also ∼ **out**) balbutier [*word, phrase*]
B vi **1** [*demand, economy*] fléchir; [*person, courage*] faiblir; **2** (when speaking) [*person*] bafouiller; [*voice*] trembloter; **to speak without** ∼**ing** parler avec assurance; **3** (when walking) [*person*] chanceler; [*footstep*] hésiter; **to walk without** ∼**ing** marcher d'un pas assuré

faltering /ˈfɔːltərɪŋ/ adj [*economy, demand*] en déclin; [*footsteps, voice*] hésitant

fame /feɪm/ n renommée f (as en tant que); ∼ **and fortune** la gloire et la fortune

famed /feɪmd/ adj célèbre (for pour; as en tant que)

familiar /fəˈmɪlɪə(r)/
A n (animal spirit) démon m familier
B adj gen familier/-ière (to à); (customary) habituel; **her face looked** ∼ **to me** son visage m'était familier; **that name has a** ∼ **ring to it**, **that name sounds** ∼ ce nom me dit quelque chose; **it's a** ∼ **story** c'est un scénario connu; **to be on** ∼ **ground** être en terrain connu; **to be** ∼ **with sb/sth** bien connaître qn/qch; **to make oneself** ∼ **with sth** se familiariser avec qch

familiarity /fəˌmɪlɪˈærətɪ/ n gen familiarité f (with avec); (of surroundings, place) caractère m familier

familiarize /fəˈmɪlɪəraɪz/
A vtr **to** ∼ **sb with** familiariser qn avec [*job, procedure*]; habituer qn à [*environment, person*]
B v refl **to** ∼ **oneself with** se familiariser avec [*system, work*]; s'habituer à [*person, place*]

familiarly /fəˈmɪlɪəlɪ/ adv avec familiarité

family /ˈfæməlɪ/
A n famille f; **to run in the** ∼ tenir de famille; **to be one of the** ∼ faire partie de la famille; **to start a** ∼ avoir un (premier) enfant
B noun modifier [*home*] de famille; [*friend*] de la famille; **for** ∼ **reasons** pour raisons familiales

family: **Family Allowance** n GB Admin ≈ allocations fpl familiales; ∼ **business** n entreprise f familiale; ∼ **butcher** n boucher m de quartier

family circle n **1** (group) cercle m familial; **2** US Theat deuxième balcon m

family: ∼ **court** n US Jur tribunal m des affaires familiales; **Family Credit** n GB Admin ≈ Complément m Familial; ∼ **man** n bon père m de famille; ∼ **name** n nom m de famille; ∼**-owned** adj [*business*] familial; ∼ **planning** n planning m familial

family practice n US **to have a** ∼ être médecin m généraliste

family: ∼ **room** n US salle f de jeu; ∼**-size(d)** adj familial; ∼ **tree** n arbre m généalogique; ∼ **unit** n Sociol cellule f familiale; ∼ **viewing** n émission f pour les petits et les grands

famine /ˈfæmɪn/ n famine f

famished○ /ˈfæmɪʃt/ adj **I'm** ∼ je meurs de faim

famous /ˈfeɪməs/ adj gen célèbre (for pour); [*school, university*] réputé (for pour); **a** ∼ **victory** une grande victoire

famously /ˈfeɪməslɪ/ adv **1** (wonderfully) à merveille; **2** Churchill is ∼ quoted as saying... tout le monde connaît les célèbres mots de Churchill...

fan /fæn/
A n **1** (of football, jazz etc) mordu/-e○ m/f; (of star, actor etc) fan○ m/f; (of politician, artist) admirateur/-trice m/f; Sport (of team) supporter m; **I'm a** ∼ **of American TV** j'adore la télé américaine; **2** (for cooling) gen, Aut (mechanical) ventilateur m; (hand-held) éventail m
B vtr (p prés etc **-nn-**) **1** (stimulate) attiser [*fire, hatred, passion*]; **2** (cool) [*breeze*] rafraîchir [*face*]; **to** ∼ **one's face** s'éventer le visage
C v refl (p prés etc **-nn-**) **to** ∼ **oneself** s'éventer

(Phrasal verb)

■ **fan out**: ▸ ∼ **out** [*police, troops*] se déployer (en éventail); [*lines, railway lines*] se diviser et partir dans toutes les directions; ▸ ∼ **[sth] out**, ∼ **out [sth]** ouvrir [qch] en éventail [*cards, papers*]

fanatic /fəˈnætɪk/ n fanatique mf

fanatical /fəˈnætɪkl/ adj fanatique

fanaticism /fəˈnætɪsɪzəm/ n fanatisme m

fan belt n Aut courroie f de ventilateur

fanciful /ˈfænsɪfl/ adj [*person*] fantasque; [*idea, name*] extravagant; [*explanation*] fantaisiste; [*building*] orné

fancy /ˈfænsɪ/
A n **1** (liking) **to catch** ou **take sb's** ∼ [*object*] faire envie à qn; **he had taken her** ∼ (sexually) il lui avait tapé dans l'œil○; gen il lui plaisait bien; **to take a** ∼ **to sb** (sexually) GB s'enticher de qn; gen s'attacher à qn; **I've taken a** ∼ **to that car** cette voiture m'a tapé dans l'œil○; **2** (whim) caprice m; **as/when the** ∼ **takes me** comme/quand ça me prend; **3** (fantasy) imagination f; **a flight of** ∼ une lubie
B adj **1** (elaborate) [*lighting, equipment*] sophistiqué; [*food*] de luxe; [*paper, box*] fantaisie inv; Zool [*breed*] d'agrément; **nothing** ∼ (meal) rien de spécial; **2** ○péj (pretentious) [*hotel, restaurant*] de luxe; [*price*] exorbitant; [*name*] tordu; [*clothes*] chic
C vtr **1** ○(want) avoir (bien) envie de [*food, drink, object*]; **what do you** ∼ **for lunch?** qu'est-ce qui te plairait pour le déjeuner?; **do you** ∼ **going to the cinema?** ça te dirait○ d'aller au cinéma?; **I don't** ∼ **the idea of sharing a flat** l'idée de partager un appartement ne me dit rien; **2** ○GB (feel attracted to) **she fancies him** elle s'est entichée de lui; **3** (expressing surprise) ∼ **her remembering my name!** figure-toi qu'elle se souvenait de mon nom!; ∼ **seeing you here**○! tiens donc, toi ici?; ∼ **that**○! pas possible○!; **4** †(believe) croire; (imagine) s'imaginer; **5** Sport voir [qn/qch] gagnant [*athlete, horse*]
D v refl ○péj **he fancies himself** il ne se prend pas pour rien; **she fancies herself in that hat** elle n'arrête pas de frimer○ avec ce chapeau; **he fancies himself as James Bond** il se prend pour James Bond
E **fancied** pp adj Sport [*contender*] favori

fancy dress
A n ₵ GB déguisement m; **in** ∼ déguisé
B (also **fancy-dress**) noun modifier [*party*] costumé; [*competition*] de déguisement

fanfare /ˈfænfeə(r)/ n fanfare f

fang /fæŋ/ n (of dog, wolf) croc m; (of snake) crochet m (à venin)

fan: ∼ **heater** n radiateur m soufflant; ∼ **mail** n ₵ lettres fpl envoyées par des admirateurs

fantasize /ˈfæntəsaɪz/
A vtr **to** ∼ **that** rêver que
B vi fantasmer (about sur); **to** ∼ **about doing** rêver de faire

fantastic /fænˈtæstɪk/ adj **1** ○(wonderful) merveilleux, super○; **2** (unrealistic) invraisemblable; **3** ○(huge) [*profit*] fabuleux/-euse; [*speed, increase*] vertigineux/-euse; **4** (magical) fantastique

fantastically /fænˈtæstɪklɪ/ adv **1** ○[*wealthy*] immensément; [*expensive*] terriblement; **2** ○[*increase*] de façon vertigineuse; [*perform*] incroyablement; **3** [*coloured, portrayed*] fabuleusement

fantasy /ˈfæntəsɪ/ n **1** gen rêve m; Psych fantasme m; (untruth) idée f fantaisiste; **2** (genre) fantastique m

FAO
A n (abrév = **Food and Agriculture Organization**) FAO f
B prep phr (abrév écrite = **for the attention of**) à l'attention de

FAQ npl (abrév = **frequently asked questions**) FAQ f, foire f aux questions

far /fɑː(r)/
A adv **1** (in space) loin; **have you come** ∼? est-ce que vous

venez de loin?; **is it ∼ to York?** est-ce que York est loin d'ici?; ∼ **off**, ∼ **away** au loin; **to be ∼ from home** être loin de chez soi; ∼ **beyond the city** bien au-delà de la ville; **how ∼ is it to Leeds?** combien y a-t-il (de kilomètres) jusqu'à Leeds?; **how ∼ is Glasgow from London?** Glasgow est à quelle distance de Londres?; **as ∼ as** jusqu'à; ②- (in time) ∼ **back in the past** loin dans le passé; **as ∼ back as 1965** déjà en 1965; **as ∼ back as he can remember** d'aussi loin qu'il s'en souvienne; **the holidays are not ∼ off** c'est bientôt les vacances; **he's not ∼ off 70** il n'a pas loin de 70 ans; **he worked ∼ into the night** il a travaillé tard dans la nuit; ③- (to a great degree, very much) bien; ∼ **better** bien mieux; ∼ **too fast** bien trop vite; ∼ **too much money** bien trop d'argent; ∼ **more** bien plus; ∼ **above the average** bien au-dessus de la moyenne; ④- (to what extent, to the extent that) **how ∼ is it possible to...?** dans quelle mesure est-il possible de...?; **how ∼ have they got?** où en sont-ils?; **as** ou **so ∼ as we can**, **as** ou **so ∼ as possible** autant que possible, dans la mesure du possible; **as** ou **so ∼ as we know** pour autant que nous le sachions; **as** ou **so ∼ as I am concerned** quant à moi; ⑤- (to extreme degree) loin; **to go too ∼** aller trop loin; **she took** ou **carried the joke too ∼** elle a poussé la plaisanterie un peu loin; **to push sb too ∼** pousser qn à bout
B adj ①- (remote) **the ∼ north/south (of)** l'extrême nord/sud (de); **the ∼ east/west (of)** tout à fait à l'est/l'ouest (de); ②- (further away, other) autre; **at the ∼ end of the room** à l'autre bout de la salle; **on the ∼ side of the wall** de l'autre côté du mur; ③- Pol **the ∼ right/left** l'extrême droite/gauche
C by far adv phr de loin
D far and away adv phr de loin
E far from prep phr loin de; ∼ **from satisfied** loin d'être satisfait
F so far adv phr ①- (up till now) jusqu'ici; **so ∼**, **so good** pour l'instant tout va bien; ②- (up to a point) **they will only compromise so ∼** ils sont prêts à transiger jusqu'à un certain point seulement; **you can only trust him so ∼** tu ne peux pas lui faire entièrement confiance
⌐Idioms⌐ **not to be ∼ off** ou **out** ou **wrong** ne pas être loin du compte; ∼ **and wide**, ∼ **and near** partout; ∼ **be it from me to do sth** loin de moi l'idée de faire; **to be a ∼ cry from** être bien loin de; **she will go ∼** elle ira loin; **this wine/food won't go very ∼** on ne va pas aller loin avec ce vin/ce qu'on a à manger

faraway /'fɑːrəweɪ/ adj (épith) lit, fig lointain

farce /fɑːs/ n Theat, fig farce f

farcical /'fɑːsɪkl/ adj ridicule

far-distant /ˌfɑːˈdɪstənt/ adj lointain

fare /feə(r)/
A n ①- (cost of travelling) (on bus, underground) prix m du ticket; (on train, plane) prix du billet; **taxi ∼** prix m de la course; **child/ adult ∼** tarif m enfants/adultes; **half/full ∼** demi-plein tarif m; **return ∼** prix m d'un aller-retour; **∼s are going up** les tarifs augmentent; ②- (taxi passenger) client/-e m/f (d'un taxi); ③- †(food) nourriture f; **prison ∼** régime m de prison
B vi (get on) **how did you ∼?** comment ça s'est passé?; **the company is faring well despite the recession** la société se porte bien malgré la récession

far: **Far East** pr n Extrême-Orient m; **Far Eastern** adj [affairs, influence, markets] de l'Extrême-Orient

farewell /ˌfeəˈwel/
A n, excl adieu m; **to say one's ∼s** faire ses adieux
B noun modifier [party, speech] d'adieu

far-fetched /ˌfɑːˈfetʃt/ adj tiré par les cheveux◦

far-flung /ˌfɑːˈflʌŋ/ adj ①- (remote) [country] lointain; ②- (widely distributed) [towns] éloignés les uns des autres

farm /fɑːm/
A n ferme f; **chicken/pig ∼** élevage m de poulets/de porcs
B noun modifier [building, animal] de ferme
C vtr cultiver, exploiter [land]
D vi être fermier
E farmed pp adj [fish] élevé dans une pisciculture
⌐Phrasal verb⌐
■ **farm out**: ▸ ∼ **out [sth]** sous-traiter [work] (**to** à)

farmer /'fɑːmə(r)/ ▸ p. 1181 n (in general) fermier m; (in official terminology) agriculteur m; (arable) cultivateur m; **pig ∼** éleveur m de porcs; **∼'s wife** fermière f

farm: ∼ **hand** ▸ p. 1181 n = farm worker; **∼house** n (where farmer lives) habitation f du fermier; (house in country) ferme f

farming /'fɑːmɪŋ/
A n (profession) agriculture f; (of land) exploitation f; **sheep ∼** élevage m de moutons
B noun modifier [community] rural; [method] de culture; [subsidy] à l'agriculture

farm: ∼ **labourer** n = farm worker; **∼land** n C (for cultivation) terres fpl arables; ∼ **produce** n C produits mpl de la ferme; ∼ **worker** ▸ p. 1181 n ouvrier/-ière m/f agricole; **∼yard** n cour f de ferme

Faroes /'feərəʊz/ pr npl (also **Faroe Islands**) **the ∼** les îles fpl Féroé

far-off /'fɑːrɒf/ adj (épith) lointain

farrago /fəˈrɑːgəʊ/ n ramassis m

far-reaching /ˌfɑːˈriːtʃɪŋ/ adj [effect, implication] considérable; [change, reform] radical; [programme, plan, proposal] d'une portée considérable

farrier /'færɪə(r)/ n GB maréchal-ferrant m

far-sighted /ˌfɑːˈsaɪtɪd/ adj ①- (prudent) [person, policy] prévoyant; ②- US Med [person] presbyte

farther /'fɑːðə(r)/ (comparative of **far**)
A adv ▸ **further A 1, 2**
B adj ▸ **further B 2**.

⚠ Au sens littéral on préférera farther et au sens figuré further

farthest /'fɑːðɪst/ adj, adv (superlative of **far**) ▸ **furthest**.

⚠ Au sens littéral on préférera farthest et au sens figuré furthest

fascia /'feɪʃə/ n GB (dashboard) tableau m de bord; (over shop) panneau m

fascinate /'fæsɪneɪt/ vtr (interest) passionner; (stronger) fasciner

fascinated /'fæsɪneɪtɪd/ adj (by spectacle) captivé; (by person) fasciné; (by subject) passionné

fascinating /'fæsɪneɪtɪŋ/ adj [book, discussion] passionnant; [person] fascinant

fascination /ˌfæsɪˈneɪʃn/ n ①- (interest) passion f (**with, for** pour); **in ∼** captivé; (stronger) fasciné; ②- (power) (pouvoir m de) fascination f

fascism /'fæʃɪzəm/ n fascisme m

fascist /'fæʃɪst/ n, adj fasciste (mf) also pej

fashion /'fæʃn/
A n ①- (manner) façon f, manière f; **in my own ∼** à ma manière; **in the Chinese ∼** à la chinoise; **after a ∼** plus ou moins bien; ②- (vogue, trend) mode f (**for** de); **in ∼** à la mode; **out of ∼** démodé; **to go out of ∼** se démoder, passer de mode
B noun modifier [accessory] de mode; [jewellery] fantaisie inv
C fashions npl **ladies' ∼s** vêtements mpl pour femmes; **Paris ∼s** la mode parisienne
D vtr façonner [clay, wood] (**into** en); fabriquer [object] (**out of, from** de)

fashionable /'fæʃnəbl/ adj [garment, name] à la mode (**among, with** parmi); [resort, restaurant] chic inv (**among, with** parmi); [pastime, topic] en vogue (**among, with** parmi); **it's no longer ∼ to smoke** cela ne se fait plus de fumer

fashionably /'fæʃnəblɪ/ adv à la mode

fashion: ∼ **designer** ▸ p. 1181 n gen modéliste mf; (world-famous) grand couturier m; ∼ **house** n maison f de couture; ∼ **model** ▸ p. 1181 n mannequin m; ∼ **show** n présentation f de collection

fast /fɑːst, US fæst/
A n jeûne m
B adj ①- (speedy) also Phot rapide; **a ∼ train** un express; **a ∼ time** Sport un bon temps; **to be a ∼ walker/reader** marcher/lire vite; ②- Sport [court, pitch, track] rapide; ③- (ahead of time) **my watch is ∼** ma montre avance; **you're five minutes ∼** ta montre avance de cinq minutes; ④- (firm) [jammis épith) [door, lid] bien fermé; [rope] bien attaché; **to make [sth] ∼** amarrer [boat]; attacher [rope]; ⑤- (loyal) [friend] fidèle; [friendship] solide; ⑥- (permanent) ∼ **dye** grand teint m
C adv ①- (rapidly) vite, rapidement; **how ∼ can you knit/read?** est-ce que tu tricotes/lis vite?; **I need help ∼** j'ai besoin d'aide tout de suite; **I ran as ∼ as my legs would carry me**

je me suis sauvé à toutes jambes; [2] (firmly) [hold] ferme; [stuck] bel et bien (before pp); [shut] bien; **to be ~ asleep** dormir à poings fermés

D vi (abstain from food) jeûner

(idioms) **to pull a ~ one on sb** rouler qn○; **to play ~ and loose** faire les quatre cents coups○

fast: **~back** n GB Aut voiture f à l'arrière profilé; **~ breeder reactor** n Tech surgénérateur m

fasten /'fɑːsn, US 'fæsn/
A vtr [1] (close) fermer [lid, case]; attacher [belt, necklace]; boutonner [coat]; boucler [buckle]; [2] (attach) fixer [notice, shelf] (**to** à; **onto** sur); attacher [lead, rope] (**to** à); **his eyes ~ed on me** son regard s'est fixé sur moi
B vi [box] se fermer; [necklace, skirt] s'attacher

(Phrasal verbs)
■ **fasten down**: ▸ ~ **down** [sth], ~ [sth] **down** fermer [hatch, lid]
■ **fasten on**: ▸ ~ **on** [lid, handle] s'attacher; ▸ ~ [sth] **on** attacher [lid, handle]; ▸ ~ **on** [sth] fig se mettre [qch] dans la tête [idea]
■ **fasten up**: ▸ ~ **up** [sth], ~ [sth] **up** boutonner [coat]

fastener /'fɑːsnə(r), US 'fæsnə(r)/ n gen attache f; (hook) agrafe f; (clasp) fermoir m

fast food /ˌfɑːst 'fuːd, US ˌfæst-/
A n nourriture f de fast-food
B noun modifier [chain] de restauration rapide ou de fast-food; [industry] de la restauration rapide or du fast-food; **a ~ restaurant** un fast-food

fast-forward /ˌfɑːstˈfɔːwəd, US ˌfæst-/
A n Audio avance f rapide
B vtr noun modifier [key, button] d'avance rapide (after n)
C vtr faire avancer rapidement

fast-growing /ˌfɑːstˈɡrəʊɪŋ, US ˌfæst-/ adj en pleine expansion

fastidious /fæˈstɪdɪəs/ adj [1] (extremely careful) [person] méticuleux/-euse (**about** sur); [work] minutieux/-ieuse; [2] (fussy) pointilleux

fast lane /ˈfɑːst leɪn, US 'fæst-/ n Aut voie f de dépassement; **life in the ~** fig la vie à cent à l'heure

fast-talking adj [salesperson] baratineur/-euse○

fat /fæt/
A n [1] (in diet) matières fpl grasses; **animal ~s** graisses fpl animales; [2] (on meat) gras m; **you can leave the ~** tu peux laisser le gras; [3] (for cooking) gen matière f grasse; (from meat) graisse f; [4] (in body) graisse f; **body ~** tissu adipeux
B adj [1] (overweight) [person, animal, body, bottom, etc] gros/grosse; (of child) [cheek] rebondi; [thigh, finger] dodu; **to get ~** grossir; [2] (full) [wallet, envelope] rebondi; [file, magazine] épais/épaisse; [3] (remunerative) [profit, cheque] gros/grosse

(idioms) **the ~'s in the fire** ○ ça va faire des étincelles○; **to live off the ~ of the land** vivre grassement

fatal /'feɪtl/ adj [accident, injury, blow] mortel/-elle (**to** pour); [flaw, mistake] fatal; [decision] funeste; [day, hour] fatidique; **to be ~ to sb/sth** porter un coup fatal à qn/qch; **it would be ~ to do** ce serait une grave erreur de faire

fatalist /'feɪtəlɪst/ n fataliste mf

fatalistic /ˌfeɪtəˈlɪstɪk/ adj fataliste

fatality /fəˈtælətɪ/ n (person killed) mort m; **road fatalities** accidents mpl mortels de la route

fatally /'feɪtəlɪ/ adv [1] [injured, wounded] mortellement; **to be ~ ill** être condamné; [2] fig [flawed, compromised] irrémédiablement

fate /feɪt/ n sort m; **a (cruel) twist of ~** un (cruel) caprice du sort

fated /'feɪtɪd/ adj ~ **to do** destiné à faire; **it was ~** c'était écrit

fateful /'feɪtfl/ adj [decision] fatal; [day] fatidique

fat-free adj sans matières grasses

father /'fɑːðə(r)/
A n père m; **to be like a ~ to sb** être un vrai père pour qn; **like ~ like son** tel père tel fils; **land of our ~s** patrie de nos pères or aïeux
B vtr engendrer [child]

Father /'fɑːðə(r)/ ▸ p. 869 n [1] Relig (God) Père m; **the Our ~** le Notre Père; **God the ~** Dieu le Père; [2] (title for priest) père m; **~ Smith** le père Smith

father: **Father Christmas** GB n le père Noël; **~ confessor** n Relig confesseur m; fig directeur m de conscience; **~ figure** n image f du père

fatherhood /'fɑːðəhʊd/ n paternité f

father: **~-in-law** n (pl **~s-in-law**) beau-père m; **~land** n patrie f

fatherless /'fɑːðəlɪs/ adj sans père

fatherly /'fɑːðəlɪ/ adj paternel/-elle

fathom /'fæðəm/
A n Naut brasse f anglaise (= 1,83 m)
B vtr [1] Naut sonder; [2] (also GB ~ **out**) (understand) comprendre

fatigue /fəˈtiːɡ/
A n [1] (of person) épuisement m; [2] Tech metal ~ fatigue f du métal; [3] US Mil corvée f
B fatigues npl Mil [1] (uniform) treillis m; **camouflage ~s** tenue f de camouflage; [2] (duties) corvée f

fatness /'fætnɪs/ n corpulence f

fatten /'fætn/
A vtr = fatten up
B vi [animal] engraisser

(Phrasal verb)
■ **fatten up**: ▸ ~ [sb/sth] **up**, ~ **up** [sb/sth] engraisser [animal]; faire grossir [person]

fattening /'fætnɪŋ/ adj [food, drink] qui fait grossir (after n)

fatty /'fætɪ/ adj [tissue, deposit] graisseux/-euse; [food, meat] gras/grasse; **~ acid** acide m gras

fatuous /'fætʃʊəs/ adj [comment, smile] stupide; [activity] futile

faucet /'fɔːsɪt/ n US robinet m

fault /fɔːlt/
A n [1] (flaw) défaut m (**in** dans); (electrical failure) panne f; **structural/design ~** défaut structurel/de conception; **he's always finding ~** il trouve toujours quelque chose à redire; [2] (responsibility) faute f; **to be sb's ~, to be the ~ of sb** être la faute de qn; **to be sb's ~ that** être à cause de qn que; **it's my own ~** c'est de ma faute; **whose ~ was it?** à qui la faute?; **the ~ lies with him** c'est lui qui est entièrement responsable; **to be at ~** être en tort; [3] Sport (call) faute!; **to serve a ~** faire une faute au service; [4] (in earth) faille f; [5] Jur faute f
B vtr prendre [qch/qn] en défaut; **it cannot be ~ed** c'est irréprochable

fault-finding /'fɔːltfaɪndɪŋ/
A n [1] Tech localisation f du défaut or de la panne; [2] (of person) habitude f de tout critiquer
B adj [person] qui critique tout; [attitude] négatif/-ive

faultless /'fɔːltlɪs/ adj [performance, manners] impeccable; [taste] irréprochable

faulty /'fɔːltɪ/ adj [wiring, machine] défectueux/-euse; [logic, argument] erroné

faun /fɔːn/ n faune m

fauna /'fɔːnə/ n (pl **~s** ou **-ae**) faune f

faux pas /ˌfəʊ 'pɑː/ n (pl **~**) impair m

favour GB, **favor** US /'feɪvə(r)/
A n [1] (approval) **to regard sb/sth with ~** considérer qn/qch avec bienveillance; **to win/lose ~ with sb** s'attirer/perdre les bonnes grâces de qn; **to find ~ with sb** trouver grâce aux yeux de qn; **to be out of ~ with sb** [person] ne plus être dans les bonnes grâces de qn; [idea, method] ne plus être en vogue auprès de qn; **to fall** ou **go out of ~** [idea, method] passer de mode; [2] (kindness) service m; **to do sb a ~** rendre service à qn; **they're not doing themselves any ~s** ils desservent leur (propre) cause (**by doing** en faisant); **as a (special) ~** à titre de service exceptionnel; **to ask a ~ of sb, to ask sb a ~** demander un service à qn; **to return a ~** lit, **to return the ~** iron rendre la pareille (**by doing** en faisant); [3] (advantage) **to be in sb's ~** [situation] être avantageux pour qn; [financial rates, wind] être favorable à qn; **to have sth in one's ~** avoir qch pour soi; **the plan has a lot in its ~** le projet présente beaucoup d'avantages
B favours npl euph (sexual) faveurs fpl
C vtr [1] (prefer) être pour [method, solution]; préférer [clothing, colour]; être partisan de [political party, course of action]; **to ~ sb** gen montrer une préférence pour qn; (unfairly) accorder un traitement de faveur à qn; [2] (benefit) [plans, circumstances] favoriser; [law, balance of power] privilégier

D **favoured** pp adj gen favori/-ite; (most likely) [date, plan, view] privilégié

E **in favour of** prep phr **1** (on the side of) en faveur de; **to be in ~ of sb/sth** être pour qn/qch; **to speak in ~ of** soutenir [motion]; **to speak in sb's ~** se prononcer en faveur de qn; **to come out in ~ of** exprimer son soutien à [plan, person]; **2** (to the advantage of) **to work in ~ of sb** avantager qn; **to decide in sb's ~** gen donner raison à qn; Jur donner gain de cause à qn; **3** (out of preference for) [reject] au profit de

favourable GB, **favorable** US /ˈfeɪvərəbl/ adj gen favorable (**to** à); [result, sign] bon/bonne (before n); **to have a ~ reception** être bien reçu

favourably GB, **favorably** US /ˈfeɪvərəbli/ adv [speak, write] en termes favorables; [look on, consider] d'un œil favorable; **to compare ~ with sth** soutenir la comparaison avec qch

favourite GB, **favorite** US /ˈfeɪvərɪt/
A n **1** préféré/-e m/f; **to be a great ~ with sb** avoir beaucoup de succès auprès de qn; **2** Sport favori/-ite m/f
B adj préféré, favori/-ite

favouritism GB, **favoritism** US /ˈfeɪvərɪtɪzəm/ n favoritisme m

fawn /fɔːn/ ▸ p. 752
A n **1** Zool faon m; **2** (colour) beige m foncé
B adj beige foncé inv
C vi **to ~ on sb** [dog] faire la fête à qn; [person] péj flagorner qn

fawning /ˈfɔːnɪŋ/ adj servile

fax /fæks/
A n (pl ~es) **1** (also ~ **message**) télécopie f, fax m; **2** (also ~ **machine**) télécopieur m, fax m
B vtr télécopier, faxer [document]; envoyer une télécopie or un fax à [person]

fax number n numéro m de télécopie or de fax

faze○ /feɪz/ vtr dérouter

FBI n US (abrév = **Federal Bureau of Investigation**) Police f judiciaire fédérale

FCO n GB (abrév = **Foreign and Commonwealth Office**) ministère m des Affaires étrangères et du Commonwealth

FDA n US (abrév = **Food and Drug Administration**) organisme gouvernemental de contrôle pharmaceutique et alimentaire

fear /fɪə(r)/
A n **1** (fright) peur f; **he accepted out of ~** c'est la peur qui l'a fait accepter; **to live** ou **go in ~ of one's life** craindre pour sa vie; **the news struck ~ into his heart** la nouvelle l'a rempli d'effroi; **2** (apprehension) crainte f (**for** pour); **my ~s proved groundless** mes craintes se sont révélées injustifiées; **the future/the operation holds no ~s for her** elle n'a pas peur de l'avenir/de l'opération; **3** (possibility) **there's no ~ of him** ou **his being late** il n'y a pas de danger qu'il soit en retard
B vtr craindre; **I ~ (that) she may be dead** j'ai (bien) peur or je crains qu'elle (ne) soit morte; **it is ~ed (that)** on craint que (+ subj); **a ruler who was greatly ~ed** un chef qui inspirait la crainte; **she's a woman to be ~ed** c'est une femme redoutable; **to ~ the worst** craindre le pire, s'attendre au pire; **I ~ not** je crains (bien) que non; **I ~ so** (to positive question) je crains bien que oui; (to negative question) j'ai bien peur que si
C vi **to ~ for sth/sb** craindre pour qch/qn; **I ~ for her life** je crains pour sa vie

(Idioms) **without ~ or favour** de façon impartiale; **in ~ and trembling** tremblant de peur

fearful /ˈfɪəfl/ adj **1** (afraid) craintif/-ive; **to be ~ of sth/of doing** avoir peur de qch/de faire; **2** (dreadful) affreux/-euse

fearless /ˈfɪələs/ adj sans peur, intrépide

fearsome /ˈfɪəsəm/ adj (frightening) effroyable; (formidable) redoutable

feasibility /ˌfiːzəˈbɪlətɪ/ n **1** (of idea, plan, proposal) faisabilité f (**of** de); **the ~ of doing** la possibilité de faire; **2** (of claim, story) vraisemblance f (**of** de)

feasible /ˈfiːzəbl/ adj **1** (possible) [project] réalisable; **it is ~ that** il est possible que (+ subj); **to be ~ to do sth** être possible de faire qch; **2** [excuse, explanation] plausible

feast /fiːst/
A n gen festin m; Relig fête f; **~ day** jour m de fête; **wedding ~**

banquet de mariage; fig (delight for the senses) régal m (**to, for** pour)
B vtr régaler [person] (**on, with** de)
C vi se régaler (**on** de)

feat /fiːt/ n exploit m; **it was no mean ~** cela n'a pas été une mince affaire; **a ~ of engineering** une prouesse technologique

feather /ˈfeðə(r)/
A n plume f
B noun modifier [mattress, bed] de plumes
(Idioms) **as light as a ~** léger comme une plume; **birds of a ~ (flock together)** Prov qui se ressemble s'assemble Prov; **that's a ~ in his cap** c'est un bon point pour lui; **you could have knocked me down with a ~** j'en avais le souffle coupé

feather: **~-brained** adj écervelé; **~ duster** n plumeau m

feathered /ˈfeðə(r)d/ adj [garment] à plumes

featherweight n poids m plume

feature /ˈfiːtʃə(r)/
A n **1** (distinctive characteristic) trait m, caractéristique f; **a ~ of those times** une caractéristique de cette époque; **2** (aspect) aspect m, côté m; **to have no redeeming ~s** n'avoir rien pour soi; **3** (of face) trait m; **with sharp ~s** aux traits anguleux; **4** (of car, computer, product) accessoire m; **built-in safety ~s** équipement m de sécurité intégré; **5** (film) long métrage m; **6** (in newspaper) article m de fond (**on** sur); **she does a ~ in the Times** elle est chroniqueuse au 'Times'; **7** TV, Radio reportage m (**on** sur); **8** Ling trait m
B vtr **1** (present) [film, magazine] présenter [story, photo, star]; [advert, poster] représenter [person, scene]; **to be ~d in** figurer dans; **2** (highlight) être équipé de [accessory]
C vi **1** (figure) figurer; **2** TV, Cin [performer] jouer

feature: **~ article** n article m de fond; **~ film** n long métrage m; **~-length** adj long métrage inv (after n)

featureless /ˈfiːtʃəlɪs/ adj sans caractère

Feb /feb/ n: abrév écrite = **February**

February /ˈfebrʊərɪ, US -ʊrɪ/ ▸ p. 1020 n février m

feckless /ˈfeklɪs/ adj **1** (improvident) irresponsable; **2** (helpless) incapable; **3** (inept) maladroit

fecund /ˈfiːkənd, ˈfekənd/ adj littér fécond

fed /fed/ prét, pp ▸ **feed**

Fed /fed/ abrév ▸ **federal**, **federation**

federal /ˈfedərəl/
A **Federal** pr n US Hist (party supporter) Fédéraliste mf; (soldier) nordiste m
B adj Admin, Pol [court, judge, police] fédéral; **the ~ government** US le gouvernement fédéral
(Idiom) **to make a ~ case out of sth** US faire toute une histoire de qch○

federalist /ˈfedərəlɪst/ n, adj fédéraliste (mf)

federally /ˈfedərəlɪ/ adv **1** [elect, govern] à un niveau fédéral; **2** US [funded, built] par le gouvernement fédéral

federal: **Federal Republic of Germany** n République f fédérale d'Allemagne; **Federal Reserve Bank** n US banque f régionale des États-Unis

federate /ˈfedəreɪt/
A adj fédéré
B vtr fédérer
C vi se fédérer

federation /ˌfedəˈreɪʃn/ n fédération f

fed up○ /ˌfed ˈʌp/ adj **to be ~** en avoir marre○

fee /fiː/ n **1** (for professional, artistic service) honoraires mpl; **school ~s** frais mpl de scolarité; **he charged us a ~ of $200** il nous a fait payer 200 dollars; **he will do it for a ~** il le fera s'il est payé; **2** (for admission) droit m d'entrée; (for membership) cotisation f; **registration ~** frais mpl d'inscription

feeble /ˈfiːbl/ adj [person, institution, sound, light, movement] faible; [argument, excuse] peu convaincant; [joke, attempt] médiocre

feeble-minded /ˌfiːblˈmaɪndɪd/ adj imbécile; euph (handicapped) faible d'esprit

feebleness /ˈfiːblnɪs/ n faiblesse f

feebly /ˈfiːblɪ/ adv [smile, wave] faiblement; [protest] mollement

feed /fiːd/

A n **1** (meal) (for animal) ration f de nourriture; (for baby) (breast) tétée f; (bottle) biberon m; **2** Agric (also ~ **stuffs**) aliments mpl pour animaux; **3** Ind, Tech (material) alimentation f; (mechanism) mécanisme m d'alimentation

B vtr (prét, pp **fed**) **1** (supply with food) nourrir [animal, plant, person] (on de); donner à manger à [pet]; ravitailler [army]; **to ~ a baby** (on breast) donner le sein à un bébé; (on bottle) donner le biberon à un bébé; **I shall have ten to ~** je ferai la cuisine pour dix; **2** (supply) alimenter [lake, machine]; mettre des pièces dans [meter]; fournir [information] (**to** à); **to ~ sth into** mettre or introduire qch dans; **3** fig (fuel) alimenter [ambition, prejudice]; **4** Sport faire passer [ball] (**to** à); **5** Theat donner la réplique à [comedian]

C vi (prét, pp **fed**) **1** (eat) manger; **to ~ on** lit se nourrir de; fig être alimenté par; **2** (enter) **to ~ into** [paper, tape] s'introduire dans [machine]

D v refl **to ~ oneself** [child, invalid] manger tout seul

(Phrasal verb)

■ **feed up** GB: ▸ ~ **[sth/sb] up** bien nourrir [child, invalid]; engraisser [animal]

feedback /ˈfiːdbæk/ n **1** ⊄ gen (from people) remarques fpl (**on** sur; **from** de la part de); **I'd like some ~** j'aimerais avoir vos impressions; **we haven't had any ~** il n'y a pas eu de réactions; **2** Comput feed-back m inv; **3** Audio (on hifi) réaction f parasite

feeder /ˈfiːdə(r)/ n **1** (also ~ **bib**) GB bavette f; **2** (also ~ **road** GB) bretelle f de raccordement; **3** (for printer, photocopier) chargeur m

feeding /ˈfiːdɪŋ/ n alimentation f

feeding: ~ **bottle** n GB biberon m; ~ **time** n heure f de nourrir les animaux

feel /fiːl/

A n **1** (atmosphere, impression created) atmosphère f; **there was a relaxed ~ about it** il régnait une atmosphère détendue; **it has the ~ of a country cottage** cela a l'allure d'une maison de campagne; **2** (sensation to the touch) sensation f; **to have an oily ~** être huileux au toucher; **I like the ~ of leather** j'aime le contact du cuir; **3** (act of touching, feeling) **to have a ~ of sth** tâter qch; **let me have a ~** (touch) laisse-moi toucher; (hold, weigh) laisse-moi soupeser; **4** (familiarity, understanding) **to get the ~ of** se faire à [controls, system]; **to get the ~ of doing** s'habituer à faire; **5** (flair) don m (**for** pour); **to have a ~ for language** bien savoir manier la langue

B vtr (prét, pp **felt**) **1** (experience) éprouver [affection, desire, pride]; ressentir [hostility, obligation, effects]; **to ~ a sense of isolation** éprouver un sentiment de solitude; **I no longer ~ anything for her** je n'éprouve plus rien pour elle; **the effects will be felt throughout the country** les effets se feront sentir dans tout le pays; **to ~ sb's loss very deeply** être très affecté par la perte de qn; **2** (believe) **to ~ (that)** estimer que; **I ~ I should warn you** je me sens dans l'obligation de vous prévenir; **I ~ he's hiding something** j'ai l'impression qu'il cache quelque chose; **I ~ deeply ou strongly that they are wrong** j'ai la profonde conviction qu'ils ont tort; **3** (physically) sentir [blow, draught, heat]; ressentir [ache, stiffness, effects]; **she ~s/doesn't ~ the cold** elle est/n'est pas frileuse; **4** (touch deliberately) tâter [texture, washing, cloth]; palper [patient, body part, parcel]; **to ~ the weight of sth** soupeser qch; **to ~ one's breasts for lumps** se palper les seins pour voir si on a des grosseurs; **to ~ one's way** lit avancer à tâtons; fig tâter le terrain; **5** (sense) percevoir [presence, tension, seriousness, irony]; **I could ~ her frustration** je ressentais sa frustration

C vi (prét, pp **felt**) **1** (emotionally) se sentir [sad, happy, nervous, safe]; être [sure, surprised]; avoir l'impression d'être [trapped, betrayed]; **to ~ afraid/ashamed** avoir peur/honte; **to ~ as if ou as though** avoir l'impression que; **how do you ~?** que ressens-tu?; **how do you ~ about marriage?** qu'est-ce que tu penses du mariage?; **how does it ~ ou what does it ~ like to be a dad?** qu'est-ce que ça fait d'être papa?; ▸ **feel for**; **2** (physically) se sentir [ill, better, tired]; **to ~ hot/thirsty** avoir chaud/soif; **it felt as if I was floating** j'avais l'impression de flotter; **she isn't ~ing herself today** elle n'est pas dans son assiette aujourd'hui°; **3** (create certain sensation) être [cold, smooth]; avoir l'air [eerie]; **the house ~s empty** la maison fait vide; **something doesn't ~ right** il y a quelque chose qui ne va pas; **it ~s strange living alone** ça me fait tout drôle de vivre seul; **it ~s like leather** on dirait du cuir; **it ~s like (a) Sunday** on se croirait un dimanche; **the bone ~s as if it's broken** on dirait que l'os est cassé; **4** (want) **to ~ like sth** avoir envie de qch; **I ~ like a drink** je prendrais bien un verre; **I don't ~ like it** je n'en ai pas envie; **5** (touch, grope) **to ~ in** fouiller dans [bag, pocket, drawer]; **to ~ along** tâtonner le long de [edge, wall]; ▸ **feel around, feel for**

D v refl **to ~ oneself doing** se sentir faire; **she felt herself losing her temper** elle sentait la colère la gagner

(Phrasal verbs)

■ **feel about** = **feel around**

■ **feel around**: ▸ ~ **around** tâtonner; **to ~ around in** fouiller dans [bag, drawer]; **to ~ around for** chercher [qch] à tâtons

■ **feel for**: ▸ ~ **for** [sth] chercher; ▸ ~ **for** [sb] plaindre

■ **feel out** US: ▸ ~ **out** [sb], ~ **[sb] out** tester [person]

■ **feel up to**: ▸ ~ **up to (doing) sth** se sentir d'attaque° or assez bien pour (faire) qch

feeler /ˈfiːlə(r)/ n gen antenne f; (of snail) corne f

(Idiom) **to put out ~s** tâter le terrain, lancer un ballon d'essai

feelgood /ˈfiːlɡʊd/ adj péj faussement rassurant; **to play on the ~ factor** essayer de créer un sentiment de bien-être illusoire

feeling /ˈfiːlɪŋ/

A n **1** (emotion) sentiment m; **it is a strange ~ to be** c'est une sensation étrange que d'être; **to put one's ~s into words** trouver des mots pour dire ce que l'on ressent; **to spare sb's ~s** ménager qn; **to hurt sb's ~s** blesser qn; **2** (opinion, belief) sentiment m; **I have strong ~s about it** c'est quelque chose qui me tient à cœur; **~s are running high** les esprits s'échauffent; **3** (sensitivity) sensibilité f; **have you no ~?** n'as-tu pas de cœur?; **to speak with great ~** parler avec beaucoup de passion; **4** (impression) impression f; **I had a ~ you'd say that** je sentais que tu allais dire ça; **I've got a bad ~ about this** j'ai le pressentiment que cela va mal se passer; **I've got a bad ~ about her** je me méfie d'elle; **5** (physical sensation) sensation f; **a dizzy ~** une sensation de vertige; **6** (atmosphere) ambiance f; **there was a general ~ of tension** l'ambiance était tendue; **7** (instinct) don m (**for** pour)

B adj [person] sensible; [gesture] sympathique

feelingly /ˈfiːlɪŋlɪ/ adv [write, speak] avec passion; [say] avec compassion

fee-paying /ˈfiːpeɪɪŋ/

A n paiement m des frais de scolarité

B adj [school] payant; [parent, pupil] qui paie les frais de scolarité

feet /fiːt/ pl ▸ **foot**

feign /feɪn/ vtr sout feindre [innocence, surprise]; simuler [illness, sleep]

feint /feɪnt/

A n **1** Sport, Mil feinte f; **2** (in printing) réglure f fine

B vi Sport, Mil feinter

feisty° /ˈfaɪstɪ/ adj **1** (lively) fougueux/-euse; **2** US (quarrelsome) bagarreur/-euse°

felicitous /fəˈlɪsɪtəs/ adj sout heureux/-euse

feline /ˈfiːlaɪn/

A n félin m

B adj lit, fig félin

fell /fel/

A prét ▸ **fall**

B n montagne f (dans le Nord de l'Angleterre)

C vtr abattre [tree]; assommer [person]

(Idioms) **in one ~ swoop** d'un seul coup

fellow /ˈfeləʊ/

A n **1** °(man) type° m, homme m; **poor little ~** brave petit bonhomme; **what do you ~s think?** qu'est-ce que vous en pensez, vous autres?; **2** (of society, association) (also in titles) membre m (**of** de); **3** GB Univ (lecturer) membre du corps enseignant d'un collège universitaire; (governor) membre du comité de direction d'un collège universitaire; **4** US (researcher) universitaire mf titulaire d'une bourse de recherche

B noun modifier **her ~ lawyers/teachers** ses collègues avocats/professeurs; **he and his ~ students/sufferers** lui et les autres étudiants/malades

fellow: ~ **citizen** n concitoyen/-enne m/f; ~ **countryman** n compatriote m; ~ **feeling** n (understanding) compréhension f; (solidarity) solidarité f;

~ human being, **~ man** *n* semblable *mf*

fellowship /'feləʊʃɪp/ *n* **1** (companionship) gen camaraderie *f*; Relig fraternité *f*; **2** (association) gen association *f*; Relig confrérie *f*; **3** Univ (post) poste *m* de recherche et d'enseignement universitaire

fellow traveller GB, **fellow traveler** US *n* lit compagnon/compagne *m/f* de voyage; fig Pol compagnon *m* de route

felon /'felən/ *n* Hist, Jur criminel *m*

felony /'felənɪ/ *n* Hist, Jur crime *m*

felt /felt/
A *prét, pp* ▸ **feel**
B *n* (cloth) feutre *m*; (thinner) feutrine *f*
C *noun modifier* [*cloth, cover*] en feutre; (thinner) en feutrine; **~ hat** feutre *m*

felt-tip (pen) *n* feutre *m*

female /'fiːmeɪl/
A *n* **1** Biol, Zool femelle *f*; **2** (woman) femme *f*; pej bonne femme○ *f*
B *adj* **1** Bot, Zool femelle; **~ rabbit** lapine *f*; **2** (relating to women) [*population, role, trait, condom*] féminin; [*voice*] de femme; **~ student** étudiante *f*; **3** Elec femelle

female circumcision *n* excision *f*

feminine /'femənɪn/
A *n* Ling féminin *m*; **in the ~** au féminin
B *adj* gen, Ling féminin

femininity /ˌfemə'nɪnətɪ/ *n* féminité *f*

feminist /'femɪnɪst/ *n, adj* féministe (*mf*)

fen /fen/ *n* marais *m*

fence /fens/
A *n* **1** (barrier) clôture *f*; **2** (in showjumping) obstacle *m*; (in horseracing) haie *f*; **3** ○(receiver of stolen goods) receleur/-euse *m/f*
B *vtr* **1** (enclose) clôturer [*area, garden*]; **2** ○(sell stolen goods) fourguer○ [*stolen goods*]
C *vi* **1** Sport faire de l'escrime; **2** (be evasive) se dérober
(Idioms) **to mend ~s** se raccommoder (**with** avec); **to sit on the ~** ne pas prendre position
(Phrasal verbs)
■ **fence in**: ▸ **~ [sth] in**, **~ in [sth]** entourer [qch] d'une clôture [*area, garden*]; parquer [*animals*]; ▸ **~ [sb] in** fig étouffer
■ **fence off**: ▸ **~ [sth] off**, **~ off [sth]** clôturer [qch]

fencing /'fensɪŋ/ ▸ p. 881 *n* **1** Sport escrime *f*; **2** (fences) enceinte *f*

fend /fend/ *v*
(Phrasal verbs)
■ **fend for**: ▸ **~ for oneself** se débrouiller (tout seul)
■ **fend off**: ▸ **~ off [sb/sth]**, **~ [sb/sth] off** repousser [*attacker*]; parer [*blow*]; écarter [*question*]

fender /'fendə(r)/ *n* **1** (for fire) garde-cendre *m*; **2** US Aut aile *f*

feng shui /ˌfɛŋ'ʃuːɪ, ˌfʌŋ'ʃweɪ/ *n* feng shui *m*

fennel /'fenl/ *n* fenouil *m*

feral /'fɪərəl, US 'ferəl/ *adj* sauvage

ferment
A /'fɜːment/ *n* (unrest) agitation *f*
B /fə'ment/ *vtr* faire fermenter [*beer, wine*]; fig fomenter [*trouble*]
C /fə'ment/ *vi* [*beer, yeast*] fermenter

fermentation /ˌfɜːmen'teɪʃn/ *n* fermentation *f*

fern /fɜːn/ *n* fougère *f*

ferocious /fə'rəʊʃəs/ *adj* [*animal*] féroce; [*attack*] sauvage; [*wind*] violent; [*heat*] accablant; [*climate*] rude

ferociously /fə'rəʊʃəslɪ/ *adv* [*attack*] violemment; (verbally) violemment; (physically) férocement; [*bark*] avec férocité

ferocity /fə'rɒsətɪ/ *n* férocité *f*

ferret /'ferɪt/ *n* Zool furet *m*
(Phrasal verbs)
■ **ferret about** fureter, fouiller (**in** dans)
■ **ferret out**○: ▸ **~ [sth] out**, **~ out [sth]** dégoter○ [*bargain*]; découvrir [*truth, information*]; ▸ **~ [sb] out** dénicher [*agent, thief*]

ferrous /'ferəs/ *adj* ferreux/-euse

ferry /'ferɪ/
A *n* (long-distance) ferry *m*; (over short distances) bac *m*

B *vtr* transporter [*passenger, goods*]; **to ~ sb to** emmener qn à [*school, station*]

ferryman /'ferɪmæn/ *n* passeur *m*

fertile /'fɜːtaɪl, US 'fɜːrtl/ *adj* lit [*land, soil*] fertile; [*human, animal, egg*] fécond; fig [*imagination, mind, environment*] fertile

fertility /fə'tɪlətɪ/
A *n* **1** lit (of land) fertilité *f*, fécondité *f*; (of human, animal, egg) fécondité *f*; **2** fig (of mind, imagination) fertilité *f*
B *noun modifier* [*symbol, rite*] de fertilité

fertility drug *n* médicament *m* contre la stérilité

fertilization /ˌfɜːtɪlaɪ'zeɪʃn, US -lɪ'z-/ *n* (of land) fertilisation *f*; (of animal, plant, egg) fécondation *f*

fertilize /'fɜːtɪlaɪz/ *vtr* fertiliser [*land*]; féconder [*animal, plant, egg*]

fertilizer /'fɜːtɪlaɪzə(r)/ *n* engrais *m*

fervent /'fɜːvənt/ *adj* [*admirer*] fervent; [*support*] inconditionnel

fervently /'fɜːvəntlɪ/ *adv* [*declare*] avec ferveur; [*hope*] vivement

fervour GB, **fervor** US /'fɜːvə(r)/ *n* ferveur *f*

fester /'festə(r)/ *vi* [*wound, sore*] suppurer; [*situation*] pourrir; [*feeling*] s'envenimer

festival /'festɪvl/ *n* gen fête *f*; (arts event) festival *m*

festive /'festɪv/ *adj* [*occasion, person*] joyeux/-euse; **the ~ season** la saison des fêtes

festivity /fe'stɪvətɪ/ *n* réjouissance *f*

festoon /fe'stuːn/
A *n* guirlande *f*
B *vtr* orner (**with** de)

fetch /fetʃ/ *vtr* **1** (bring) gen aller chercher; **to ~ sth for sb** aller chercher qch pour qn; (carry back) (r)apporter qch à qn; **~ him a chair please** apporte-lui une chaise s'il te plaît; **~!** (to dog) rapporte!; **2** (bring financially) [*goods*] rapporter; **to ~ a good price** rapporter un bon prix; **these vases can ~ up to £600** le prix de ces vases peut atteindre 600 livres
(Idiom) **to ~ and carry for sb** faire les quatre volontés de qn

fetching /'fetʃɪŋ/ *adj* [*child, habit, photo*] charmant; [*outfit, hat*] ravissant

fete /feɪt/
A *n* (church, village) kermesse *f* (paroissiale); **charity ~** fête *f* de bienfaisance
B *vtr* fêter [*celebrity, hero*]

fetid, foetid /'fetɪd, US 'fiːtɪd/ *adj* fétide, nauséabond

fetish /'fetɪʃ/ *n* **1** (object) fétiche *m*; **2** (obsessive interest) passion *f* fétichiste (**for** pour)

fetlock /'fetlɒk/ *n* **1** (joint) boulet *m*; **2** (tuft of hair) fanon *m*

fetter /'fetə(r)/
A *fetters* *npl* lit fers *m*; **the ~s of authority** fig les entraves de l'autorité
B *vtr* lit mettre [qn] aux fers; fig entraver l'influence de [*party*]

fettle /'fetl/ *n*
(Idiom) **in fine** ou **good ~** en excellente forme

fetus *n* US = **foetus**

feud /fjuːd/
A *n* querelle *f* (**with** avec; **between** entre)
B *vi* se quereller (**with** avec; **about** au sujet de)

feudal /'fjuːdl/ *adj* féodal

feuding /'fjuːdɪŋ/ *adj* [*factions, families*] en conflit

fever /'fiːvə(r)/ *n* lit, fig fièvre *f*; **to have a ~** lit avoir de la fièvre; **gold ~** la fièvre de l'or

fevered /'fiːvəd/ *adj* [*brow*] fiévreux/-euse; [*imagination*] fébrile

feverish /'fiːvərɪʃ/ *adj* [*person, eyes*] fiévreux/-euse; [*dreams*] délirant; [*excitement, activity*] fébrile

feverishly /'fiːvərɪʃlɪ/ *adv* lit fiévreusement; fig fébrilement

fever pitch *n* **to bring a crowd to ~** déchaîner une foule; **our excitement had reached ~** notre excitation était à son comble

few /fjuː/ (*comparative* **fewer**; *superlative* **fewest**)

⚠ When *few* is used as a quantifier to indicate the smallness or insufficiency of a given number or quantity (*few houses*, *few people*, *few shops*) it is translated by *peu de*: *peu de maisons*, *peu de gens*, *peu de magasins*. Equally *the few* is translated by *le peu de*: *the few people who knew her* le peu de gens qui la connaissaient. For examples and particular usages see **A 1** in the entry.

When *few* is used as a quantifier in certain expressions to mean *several*, translations vary according to the expression: see **A 2** in the entry.

When *a few* is used as a quantifier (*a few books*), it can often be translated by *quelques*: *quelques livres*; however, for expressions such as *quite a few books*, *a good few books*, see **B** in the entry.

For translations of *few* used as a pronoun (*few of us succeeded*, *I only need a few*) see **B**, **C** in the entry.

For translations of *the few* used as a noun (*the few who voted for him*) see **C** in the entry.

A *quantif* **1** (not many) peu de; ~ **visitors/letters** peu de visiteurs/lettres; **one of my** ~ **pleasures** un de mes rares plaisirs; **their needs are** ~ ils ont peu de besoins; **to be** ~ **in number** être peu nombreux; **too** ~ **women** trop peu de femmes; **with** ~ **exceptions** à quelques exceptions près; **2** (some, several) **every** ~ **days** tous les deux ou trois jours; **over the next** ~ **days/weeks** (in past) dans les jours/semaines qui ont suivi; (in future) dans les jours/semaines à venir; **these past** ~ **days** ces derniers jours; **the first** ~ **weeks** les premières semaines; **the** ~ **books she possessed** les quelques livres qu'elle possédait

B **a few** *quantif*, *pron* quelques; **a** ~ **people/houses** quelques personnes/maisons; **I would like a** ~ **more** j'en voudrais quelques-unes/quelques-uns de plus; **quite a** ~ **people/ houses** pas mal○ de gens/maisons, un bon nombre de personnes/maisons; **a good** ~ **years** un bon nombre d'années; **a** ~ **of the soldiers/countries** quelques-uns *or* certains des soldats/pays; **a** ~ **of us** un certain nombre d'entre nous; **there were only a** ~ **of them** il n'y en avait que quelques-uns/quelques-unes; **quite a** ~ *ou* **a good** ~ **of the tourists come from Germany** un bon nombre des touristes viennent d'Allemagne; **there are only a very** ~ **left** il n'en reste que très peu

C *pron* (not many) peu; ~ **of us succeeded** peu d'entre nous ont réussi; **there are so** ~ **of them that** il y en a tellement peu que; **there are four too** ~ il en manque quatre; **as** ~ **as four people turned up** quatre personnes seulement sont venues; **the** ~ **who voted for him** les rares personnes qui ont voté pour lui

(Idioms) **they are** ~ **and far between** ils sont rarissimes; **to have had a** ~ **(too many)**○ avoir bu quelques verres (de trop)

fewer /'fjuːə(r)/ (*comparative of* **few**)
A *adj* moins de; ~ **and** ~ **pupils** de moins en moins d'élèves
B *pron* moins; ~ **than 50 people** moins de 50 personnes; **no** ~ **than** pas moins de; **they were** ~ **than before** ils étaient moins nombreux qu'avant

fewest /'fjuːɪst/ (*superlative of* **few**)
A *adj* le moins de
B *pron* le moins

fey /feɪ/ *adj* **1** (clairvoyant) extralucide; **2** (whimsical) loufoque○

fez /fez/ *n* (*pl* ~**zes**) fez *m*

ff (*abrév écrite* = **following**) et les lignes (*ou* pages) qui suivent

fiancé /fɪ'ɒnseɪ, US ,fiːɑːn'seɪ/ *n* fiancé *m*

fiancée /fɪ'ɒnseɪ, US ,fiːɑːn'seɪ/ *n* fiancée *f*

fiasco /fɪ'æskəʊ/ *n* fiasco *m*

fib○ /fɪb/
A *n* bobard○ *m*, mensonge *m*
B *vi* (*p prés etc* **-bb-**) raconter des bobards○, mentir

fibber○ /'fɪbə(r)/ *n* menteur/-euse *m/f*

fibre GB, **fiber** US /'faɪbə(r)/ *n* **1** (strand) (of thread, wood) fibre *f*; **2** (material) fibre *f*; **3** (in diet) fibres *fpl*; **a high** ~ **diet** une alimentation riche en fibres; **4** Biol, Bot (cell) fibre *f*; **5** fig (strength) courage *m*

fibre: ~**glass** GB, **fiberglass** US *n* **℄** fibres *fpl* de verre; ~ **optic** GB, **fiber optic** US *adj* [*cable*] à fibres optiques; [*link*] par fibres optiques; ~**optics** GB, **fiberoptics** US *n* (*v sg ou pl*) fibres *fpl* optiques

fibroid /'faɪbrɔɪd/
A *n* fibrome *m*
B *adj* fibreux/-euse

fibrous /'faɪbrəs/ *adj* fibreux/-euse

fibula /'fɪbjʊlə/ *n* (*pl* ~**s** *ou* **-ae**) Anat péroné *m*

fiche /fiːʃ/ *n* microfiche *f*

fickle /'fɪkl/ *adj* [*lover, friend*] inconstant; [*fate, public opinion*] changeant; [*weather*] capricieux/-ieuse

fickleness /'fɪklnɪs/ *n* (of person) inconstance *f*; (of behaviour) instabilité *f*; (of weather) caprices *mpl*; (of fortune, of stock market) fluctuations *fpl*

fiction /'fɪkʃn/ *n* **1** (literary genre) le roman; **2** (books) romans *mpl*; **in** ~ dans les romans; **3** (delusion) illusion *f*; **4** (untruth) histoire *f*; **5** (creation of the imagination) fiction *f*; **6** (pretence) **they keep up the** ~ **that** ils font croire à tout le monde que

fictional /'fɪkʃənl/ *adj* [*character, event*] imaginaire

fictionalize /'fɪkʃənəlaɪz/ *vtr* romancer

fictitious /fɪk'tɪʃəs/ *adj* **1** (false) [*name, address*] fictif/-ive; [*justification, report*] fallacieux/-ieuse; **2** (imaginary) imaginaire

fiddle /'fɪdl/
A *n* **1** ○(dishonest scheme) magouille○ *f* **℄**; **tax** ~ fraude *f* fiscale; **to be on the** ~ traficoter○; **2** ▸ **p. 1028** (violin) violon *m*
B *vtr*○ (illegally) falsifier [*tax return, figures*]
C *vi* **1** (fidget) **to** ~ **with sth** tripoter qch; **2** (adjust) **to** ~ **with** tourner [*knobs, controls*]

(Idioms) **to be as fit as a** ~ être en santé; **to** ~ **while Rome burns** se ficher de tout comme de l'an 40○; **to play second** ~ **to sb** être le sous-fifre○ de qn

(Phrasal verb)
■ **fiddle around with**: ▸ ~ **around with [sth]** (readjust) bricoler [*engine*]; (fidget) jouer avec [*object*]

fiddly /'fɪdlɪ/ *adj* [*job, task*] délicat; [*clasp, fastening*] pas pratique; ~ **to open** difficile à ouvrir

fidelity /fɪ'delətɪ/ *n* gen, Telecom fidélité *f* (of de; to à)

fidget /'fɪdʒɪt/
A *n* **they're real** ~**s** ils n'arrêtent pas de gigoter○
B *vi* (move about) ne pas tenir en place

fidgety /'fɪdʒɪtɪ/ *adj* (child) remuant; (adult) agité

fief /fiːf/, **fiefdom** /'fiːfdəm/ *n* fief *m*

field /fiːld/
A *n* **1** Agric, Geog, gen champ *m* (of de); **2** Sport (ground) terrain *m*; **football** ~ terrain de football; **3** **℄** Sport (competitors) (athletes) concurrents *mpl*; (horses) partants *mpl*; **to lead** *ou* **be ahead of the** ~ Sport mener le peloton; fig être en tête; **4** (area of knowledge) domaine *m* (of de); **5** Ling champ *m* sémantique; **6** (real environment) **to test sth in the** ~ faire des essais de qch sur le terrain; **7** Mil **the** ~ **of battle** le champ de bataille; **to take the** ~ se mettre en campagne; **to hold the** ~ se maintenir sur ses positions; fig [*theory*] dominer; **8** (range) champ *m*; ~ **of fire** Mil secteur *m* de tir; **9** Comput, Math, Phys champ *m*
B *noun modifier* **1** [*hospital*] de campagne; **2** (in real environment) [*test, study*] sur le terrain
C *vtr* **1** Sport réceptionner [*ball*]; **2** Sport, gen (select) faire jouer [*team, player*]; présenter [*candidate*]; **3** (respond to) répondre à [*questions*]
D *vi* Sport jouer dans l'équipe de défense

(Idiom) **to play the** ~ sortir avec tout le monde

field day *n* **1** Sch, Univ sortie *f* (éducative); **2** US (sports day) journée *f* sportive

(Idiom) **to have a** ~ [*press, critics*] jubiler; (make money) [*shopkeepers*] faire d'excellentes affaires; **to have a** ~ **with sth** exploiter qch à fond

fielder /'fiːldə(r)/ *n* Sport homme *m* de champ, défenseur *m*

field: ~ **event** *n* Sport épreuve *f* sportive (*de saut et de lancer*); ~ **hand** *n* US ouvrier/-ière *m/f* agricole; ~ **hockey** ▸ **p. 881** *n* US Sport hockey *m* sur gazon; ~ **label** *n* Ling marqueur *m* de champ sémantique; ~ **marshal, FM** ▸ **p. 1123** *n* Mil maréchal *m*; ~**mouse** *n* Zool mulot *m*; ~**sman** *n* US Sport = **fielder**; ~ **sports** *npl* Sport sports *mpl* de plein air; ~ **trip** *n* Sch, Univ (one day) sortie *f* éducative; (longer) voyage *m* d'études; ~**work** *n* travail *m* de terrain; ~**worker** ▸ **p. 1181** *n* personne *f* qui travaille sur le terrain

fiend /fiːnd/ n **1** (evil spirit) démon m; **2** ○(mischievous person) petit monstre m; **3** ○(fanatic) **he's a racing/football** ~ c'est un fana○ des courses/du football

fiendish /ˈfiːndɪʃ/ adj **1** (cruel) [tyrant, cruelty] monstrueux/-euse; [expression, glee] diabolique; **2** (ingenious) [plan, gadget] diabolique

fiendishly /ˈfiːndɪʃlɪ/ adv **1** (wickedly) diaboliquement; **2** (extremely) extrêmement

fierce /fɪəs/ adj [animal, expression, person] féroce; [battle, storm, hatred] violent; [determination, loyalty] farouche; [supporter] fervent; [criticism, speech] virulent; [competition] acharné; [flames, heat] intense; **he has a** ~ **temper** c'est un caractère explosif

fiercely /ˈfɪəslɪ/ adv [defend, hit, oppose] avec acharnement; [fight] sauvagement; [stare] férocement; [shout, speak] violemment; [burn] avec intensité; [competitive, critical] extrêmement; [determined, loyal] farouchement

fierceness /ˈfɪəsnɪs/ n (ferocity) (of animal) férocité f; (of person, expression, storm, battle) violence f

fiery /ˈfaɪərɪ/ adj [person, wound, gas] enflammé; [speech, performance] passionné; [sky] embrasé; [eyes] ardent; [heat] brûlant; ~ **red/orange** rouge/orange feu inv

fiesta /fɪˈestə/ n fête f

fife /faɪf/ ▸ p. 1028 n fifre m

fifteen /ˌfɪfˈtiːn/ ▸ p. 1044, p. 745 n, adj quinze (m) inv

fifteenth /ˌfɪfˈtiːnθ/ ▸ p. 1044, p. 788
A n **1** (in order) quinzième mf; **2** (of month) quinze m inv; **3** (fraction) quinzième m
B adj, adv quinzième

fifth /fɪfθ/ ▸ p. 1044, p. 788
A n **1** (in order) cinquième mf; **2** (of month) cinq m; **3** (fraction) cinquième m; **4** Mus quinte f; **5** (also ~ **gear**) Aut cinquième f; **6** US (unit of measurement) ≈ 75 cl
B adj, adv cinquième

fifth: **Fifth Amendment** n US Jur cinquième amendement m; ~ **columnist** n élément m subversif

fiftieth /ˈfɪftɪəθ/ ▸ p. 1044
A n **1** (in order) cinquantième mf; **2** (fraction) cinquantième m
B adj, adv cinquantième

fifty /ˈfɪftɪ/ ▸ p. 1044 n, adj cinquante (m) inv

fifty-fifty /ˌfɪftɪˈfɪftɪ/
A adj **to have a** ~ **chance** avoir une chance sur deux (**of doing** de faire)
B adv **to split** ou **share sth** ~ partager qch moitié-moitié; **to go** ~ faire moitié-moitié

fig /fɪg/
A n (fruit) figue f
B adj (abrév = **figurative**) figuré

fig. n (abrév écrite = **figure**) fig.; **see** ~ **3** voir fig. 3

fight /faɪt/
A n **1** fig (struggle) lutte f (**against** contre; **for** pour; **to do** pour faire); **to keep up the** ~ continuer le combat; **to put up a** ~ se défendre (**against** contre); **2** (outbreak of fighting) (between civilians) bagarre f (**between** entre; **over** pour); Mil bataille f (**between** entre; **for** pour); (between animals, in boxing) combat m (**between** entre); **to get into** ou **have a** ~ **with sb** se bagarrer contre ou avec qn; **3** (argument) dispute f (**over** au sujet de; **with** avec); **to have a** ~ **with sb** se disputer avec qn; **4** (combative spirit) (physical) envie f de se battre; (psychological) envie f de lutter
B vtr (prét, pp **fought**) **1** lit se battre contre [person]; fig lutter contre [disease, evil, opponent, emotion, proposal]; combattre [fire]; mener [campaign, war] (**against** contre); **to** ~ **one's way through** se frayer un passage dans [crowd]; **2** Pol [candidate] disputer [seat, election]; **3** Jur défendre [case, cause]
C vi (prét, pp **fought**) **1** fig (campaign) lutter; **2** lit, Mil se battre; **to** ~ **for breath** suffoquer; **3** (squabble) se quereller (**over** à propos de)

○ (Idiom) **to** ~ **the good** ~ se battre pour la bonne cause
⌐ (Phrasal verbs)
■ **fight back**: ▸ ~ **back** (physically, tactically) se défendre (**against** contre); (emotionally) ne pas se laisser faire; ▸ ~ **back [sth]** refréner [tears, fear, anger]
■ **fight off**: ▸ ~ **off [sth]**, ~ **[sth] off** lit se libérer de [attacker]; vaincre [troops]; repousser [attack]; ▸ ~ **off [sth]** fig lutter contre [illness, despair]; rejeter [challenge, criticism, proposal]

■ **fight on** poursuivre la lutte
■ **fight out**: **leave them to** ~ **it out** laissez-les régler cela entre eux

fighter /ˈfaɪtə(r)/ n **1** (determined person) lutteur/-euse m/f; **2** (also ~ **plane**) avion m de chasse

fighter: ~ **bomber** n Aviat chasseur-bombardier m; ~ **pilot** ▸ p. 1181 n pilote m de chasse

fighting /ˈfaɪtɪŋ/
A n **1** Mil combat m; ~ **has broken out** la bataille a éclaté; **2** gen bagarre f
B adj **1** Mil [unit, force] de combat; **2** (aggressive) [talk, words] agressif/-ive

fighting chance n **to have a** ~ avoir de bonnes chances

fighting fit adj **to be** ~ être en pleine forme○

fig leaf n Bot feuille f de figuier

figment /ˈfɪgmənt/ n **a** ~ **of the/of your imagination** un produit de l'imagination/de ton imagination

fig tree n figuier m

figurative /ˈfɪgərətɪv/ adj **1** Ling figuré; **2** Art figuratif/-ive

figuratively /ˈfɪgərətɪvlɪ/ adv [speak, mean] au (sens) figuré; ~ **speaking,...** métaphoriquement parlant,...

figure /ˈfɪgə(r), US ˈfɪgjər/
A n **1** (number, amount) chiffre m; **a four-/six-**~ **sum** un montant de quatre/six chiffres; **in double** ~s à deux chiffres; **to have a head for** ~s, **to be good with** ~s être doué pour le calcul; **2** (person) personnalité f; **well-known** ~ personnalité célèbre; **3** (human form) gen personnage m; Art figure f; **a familiar** ~ un personnage familier; **reclining** ~ Art figure allongée; **4** (symbol) **father** ~ image f du père; **authority** ~ symbole m de l'autorité; **5** (body shape) ligne f; **to lose one's** ~ prendre de l'embonpoint; **to have a great** ~○ avoir une silhouette sensationnelle○; **6** (geometric or other shape) figure f; **7** (diagram) figure f; **see** ~ **4** voir figure 4
B vtr **1** ○(suppose) **to** ~ **(that)** penser ou se dire que; **2** Literat (express) symboliser
C vi **1** (appear) figurer (**in** dans); **2** ○(make sense) se comprendre
⌐ (Phrasal verbs)
■ **figure on**○: ~ **on [sth]** s'attendre à; **to** ~ **on doing** compter faire
■ **figure out**: ▸ ~ **out [sth]**, ~ **[sth] out** trouver [answer, reason]; ~ **to** ~ **out who/why etc** arriver à comprendre qui/pourquoi etc

figurehead /ˈfɪgəhed, US ˈfɪgjər-/ n **1** (symbolic leader) personnalité f de prestige; **2** (of ship) figure f de proue

figure: ~ **of speech** n Literat, Ling figure f de rhétorique; ~ **skater** n patineur/-euse m/f artistique; ~ **skating** ▸ p. 881 n patinage m artistique

figurine /ˌfɪgəˈriːn, US ˌfɪgjəˈriːn/ n figurine f

Fiji /ˌfiːˈdʒiː/ ▸ p. 774, p. 954 pr n (also ~ **Islands**) (îles fpl) Fidji fpl

filament /ˈfɪləmənt/ n **1** Elec filament m; **2** (of fibre) fil m

filch○ /fɪltʃ/ vtr chiper○, voler (**from** à)

file /faɪl/
A n **1** (for papers etc) gen dossier m; (cardboard) chemise f; (ring binder) classeur m; (card tray) fichier m; **2** (record) dossier m (**on** sur); **to be on** ~ être classé; **3** Comput fichier m; **4** (tool) lime f; **5** (line) file f; **in single** ~ en file indienne
B vtr **1** Admin classer [invoice, letter, record] (**under** sous); **2** Jur déposer [application, complaint] (**with** auprès de); **to** ~ **a lawsuit (against sb)** intenter ou faire un procès (à qn); **3** Journ envoyer [report]; **4** limer [wood, metal]; **to** ~ **one's nails** se limer les ongles
C vi **1** (walk) **they** ~**d into/out of the classroom** ils sont entrés dans/sortis de la salle l'un après l'autre; **2** Jur **to** ~ **for (a) divorce** demander le divorce

file: ~ **cabinet** n US = **filing cabinet**; ~ **card** n US = **filing card**; ~ **clerk** n US = **filing clerk**; ~ **copy** n copie f de classement; ~ **manager** n Comput gestionnaire m de fichiers

filial /ˈfɪlɪəl/ adj filial

filibuster /ˈfɪlɪbʌstə(r)/ n obstruction f parlementaire

filigree /ˈfɪlɪgriː/ n filigrane m

filing /ˈfaɪlɪŋ/ n classement m

filing: ∼ **cabinet** *n* classeur *m* à tiroirs; ∼ **card** *n* fiche *f*; ∼ **clerk** ▸ p. 1181 *n* employé-e *m/f* de bureau chargé/-e du classement; ∼ **system** *n* système *m* de classement

Filipino /ˌfɪlɪˈpiːnəʊ/ ▸ p. 1032
A *n* Philippin-e *m/f*
B *adj* [*culture, food*] philippin; [*embassy, captial*] des Philippines

fill /fɪl/
A *n* **to eat/drink one's** ∼ manger/boire tout son content; **to have had one's** ∼ en avoir assez
B *vtr* [1] (make full) remplir [*container*] (**with** de); **tears** ∼**ed his eyes** ses yeux se sont remplis de larmes; [2] (occupy) [*crowd, sound*] remplir [*room, street, train*]; [*smoke, gas, light, protesters*] envahir [*building, room*]; remplir [*page, chapter, volumes, tape*] (**with** de); occuper [*time, day, hours*]; [*emotion, thought*] remplir [*heart, mind, person*] (**with** de); (plug) lit, fig boucher [*crack, hole, void*] (**with** avec); [4] (fulfil) répondre à [*need*]; [5] (appoint for) [*company, university*] pourvoir [*post, vacancy*]; [6] (perform duties of) [*applicant*] occuper [*post, vacancy*]; [7] (put filling in) garnir [*cushion, pie, sandwich*] (**with** de); [8] [*dentist*] plomber [*tooth, cavity*]; [9] Naut [*wind*] gonfler [*sail*]
C *vi* [1] [*bath, theatre, streets, eyes*] se remplir (**with** de); [2] Naut [*sail*] se gonfler
D *-filled combining form* rempli de; **smoke-/book-**∼**ed room** pièce remplie de fumée/de livres

(Phrasal verbs)

■ **fill in**: ▸ ∼ **in** [*person*] faire un remplacement; **to** ∼ **in for sb** remplacer qn; ▸ ∼ **in** [*sth*] passer [*time, hour*]; ▸ ∼ **in** [*sth/sb*], ∼ [*sth/sb*] **in** [1] (complete) remplir [*form, section*]; [2] (plug) boucher [*hole, crack*] (**with** avec); [3] (supply) donner [*detail, name, date*]; [4] (inform) mettre [qn] au courant (**on** de); [5] (colour in) remplir [*shape, panel*]
■ **fill out**: ▸ ∼ **out** [*person*] prendre du poids; [*face*] s'arrondir; ▸ ∼ **out** [*sth*], ∼ [*sth*] **out** remplir [*form, application*]; faire [*certificate, prescription*]
■ **fill up**: ▸ ∼ **up** [*bath, theatre, bus*] se remplir (**with** de); **to** ∼ **up on sth** [*person*] se bourrer° de [*bread, sweets*]; ▸ ∼ **up** [*sth*], ∼ [*sth*] **up** remplir [*kettle, box, room*] (**with** de); ▸ ∼ **up** [*sb*], ∼ [*sb*] **up** bourrer° qn (**with** de)

filler /ˈfɪlə(r)/ *n* [1] (for wood) bouche-pores *m inv*; (for car body) mastic *m*; (for wall) reboucheur *m*; [2] Journ, TV bouche-trou *m*

fillet /ˈfɪlɪt/
A *n* filet *m*
B *vtr* enlever les arêtes de, fileter [*fish*]

fillet steak *n* filet *m* de bœuf

fill-in° /ˈfɪlɪn/ *n* remplaçant-e *m/f*

filling /ˈfɪlɪŋ/
A *n* [1] Culin (of sandwich, baked potato) garniture *f*; (stuffing for vegetable, meat, pancake) farce *f*; **pie with blackberry/meat** ∼ tourte *f* fourrée aux mûres/à la viande; [2] (for tooth) plombage *m*; [3] (of quilt, cushion) garnissage *m*; (of bed, mattress) garniture *f*
B *adj* [*food, dish*] bourratif/-ive°

filling station *n* station-service *f*

fillip /ˈfɪlɪp/ *n* coup *m* de fouet fig

filly /ˈfɪlɪ/ *n* pouliche *f*

film /fɪlm/
A *n* [1] Cin (movie) film *m*; **to be** *ou* **work in** ∼**s** travailler dans le cinéma; **short** ∼ court métrage *m*; [2] Phot (for snapshots) pellicule *f*; (for movies) film *m*; [3] (layer) pellicule *f*; [4] Culin scellofrais® *m*
B *vtr* [*person*] filmer [*event, programme*]; enregistrer [*action, scene*]
C *vi* [*camera man, crew*] tourner

film: ∼ **archive** *n* archives *fpl* cinématographiques; ∼ **award** *n* prix *m* de cinéma; ∼ **buff**° *n* mordu-e° *m/f* de cinéma; ∼ **camera** *n* caméra *f*; ∼ **club** *n* ciné-club *m*; ∼ **director** ▸ p. 1181 *n* réalisateur/-trice *m/f*, metteur *m* en scène; ∼ **festival** *n* festival *m* de cinéma; ∼**goer** *n* cinéphile *mf*; ∼ **industry** *n* industrie *f* cinématographique

filming /ˈfɪlmɪŋ/ *n* Cin tournage *m*

film: ∼ **laboratory** *n* laboratoire *m* cinématographique; ∼ **library** *n* cinémathèque *f*; ∼**-maker** ▸ p. 1181 *n* cinéaste *mf*; ∼**-making** *n* cinéma *m*; ∼ **rights** *mpl* cinématographiques; ∼**set** *n* Cin plateau *m* de tournage; ∼ **show** *n* présentation *f* de films; ∼ **star**

▸ p. 1181 *n* vedette *f* de cinéma; ∼ **studio** *n* studio *m* de cinéma

filmy /ˈfɪlmɪ/ *adj* [1] (thin) [*dress*] très léger/-ère; [*fabric, screen*] transparent; [*cloud, layer*] léger/-ère; [2] (cloudy) [*glass, lens*] sale

filter /ˈfɪltə(r)/
A *n* [1] Audio, Phot, Tech, Telecom filtre *m*; **sun** ∼ filtre solaire; [2] GB (also ∼ **lane**) voie *f* réservée aux véhicules qui tournent; [3] GB (also ∼ **arrow**) flèche *f* (directionnelle)
B *vtr* filtrer [*liquid, gas*]; faire passer [*coffee*]
C *vi* [1] (also ∼ **off**) GB **to** ∼ **off to the left** [*vehicle*] passer sur la voie de gauche pour tourner; [2] (trickle) **to** ∼ **into** [*light, sound, water*] pénétrer dans [*area*]

(Phrasal verbs)

■ **filter out**: ▸ ∼ **out** [*news*] filtrer; ∼ **out** [*sth*], ∼ [*sth*] **out** éliminer [*applicants, impurities, light*]
■ **filter through** [*details, light, sound*] filtrer (**to** jusqu'à)

filter: ∼ **cigarette** *n* cigarette *f* (à bout) filtre; ∼ **coffee** *n* (cup of coffee) café *m* (filtre); (ground coffee) café *m* moulu pour filtres; ∼ **paper** *n* papier-filtre *m*; ∼ **tip** *n* (cigarette) filtre *m*; ∼**-tipped** *adj* [*cigarette*] (à bout) filtre *inv*

filth /fɪlθ/ *n* [1] (dirt) crasse *f*; [2] (vulgarity) obscénités *fpl*; (swearing) grossièretés *fpl*

filthy /ˈfɪlθɪ/ *adj* [1] (dirty) crasseux/-euse; (revolting) répugnant; **that's a** ∼ **habit** c'est dégoûtant; [2] (vulgar) [*language*] ordurier/-ière; [*mind*] mal tourné; [3] GB (unpleasant) [*weather*] épouvantable; [*look*] noir

filthy rich° *adj* plein aux as°

fin /fɪn/ *n* [1] Zool (of fish, seal) nageoire *f*; (of shark) aileron *m*; [2] Aerosp empennage *m*; [3] Tech, Aut ailette *f*; [4] Naut dérive *f*

final /ˈfaɪnl/
A *n* [1] Sport finale *f*; [2] (newspaper edition) dernière édition *f*
B *adj* [1] (last) (*épith*) dernier/-ière [*day, question, book, meeting*]; ∼ **examinations** GB Univ examens *mpl* de fin d'études; US Univ examens *mpl* de fin de semestre; [2] (definitive) [*decision, invoice*] définitif/-ive; [*result*] final; [*judgment*] irrévocable; **she has the** ∼ **say** c'est à elle de décider

final approach *n* Aviat approche *f*

finale /fɪˈnɑːlɪ, US -næli/ *n* Mus, Theat, gen finale *f*

finalist /ˈfaɪnəlɪst/ *n* finaliste *mf*

finality /faɪˈnælətɪ/ *n* irrévocabilité *f*

finalize /ˈfaɪnəlaɪz/ *vtr* conclure [*letter, purchase, contract*]; arrêter [*plan, decision, details*]; faire la dernière mise au point de [*article, report*]; boucler [*team*]; fixer [*timetable, route*]; prononcer [*divorce*]

finally /ˈfaɪnəlɪ/ *adv* [1] (eventually) [*decide, accept, arrive, happen*] finalement, enfin; [2] (lastly) finalement, pour finir; [3] (definitively) [*settle, decide*] définitivement

finals /ˈfaɪnlz/ *npl* [1] GB Univ examens *mpl* de fin d'études; US Univ examens *mpl* de fin de semestre; [2] Sport (last few games) phase *f* finale; (last game) finale *f*

finance /ˈfaɪnæns, fɪˈnæns/
A *n* [1] (banking, money systems) finance *f*; [2] (funds) fonds *mpl* (**for** pour; **from** auprès de); [3] (credit) crédit *m*
B **finances** *npl* (financial situation) situation *f* financière
C *noun modifier* [*minister, ministry*] des Finances; [*committee, director, correspondent*] financier/-ière
D *vtr* financer [*project*]

finance company, **finance house** *n* société *f* de financement

financial /faɪˈnænʃl, fɪ-/ *adj* financier/-ière

financially /faɪˈnænʃəlɪ, fɪ-/ *adv* financièrement

financial year *n* GB exercice *m*, année *f* budgétaire

financing /ˈfaɪnænsɪŋ, fɪˈnænsɪŋ/ *n* financement *m*

finch /fɪntʃ/ *n* fringillidé *m*

find /faɪnd/
A *n* (discovery) gen découverte *f*; (lucky purchase) trouvaille *f*
B *vtr* (*prét, pp* **found**) [1] (discover by chance) trouver [*thing, person*]; **to leave sth as one found it** laisser qch dans l'état où on l'a trouvé; **to** ∼ **sb doing** trouver qn en train de faire; **to** ∼ **that** constater que; [2] (discover by looking) trouver, retrouver [*thing, person*]; **to** ∼ **one's way out of** arriver à sortir de [*building, forest, city*]; **to** ∼ **one's own way home** se débrouiller tout seul pour rentrer chez soi; [3] (discover desired thing) trouver [*job, car, seat, solution*]; avoir assez de [*time, energy, money*]; **to** ∼ **sth for sb, to** ∼ **sb sth** trouver

qch pour qn; **to ~ oneself sth** se trouver qch; **4** (encounter) trouver [*word, term, species*]; **it is to be found in the Louvre** on peut le voir au Louvre; **5** (judge, consider) trouver (**that** que); **to ~ sb a bore** trouver qn ennuyeux; **to ~ sb/sth to be** trouver que qn/qch est; **to ~ sth easy to do** trouver qch facile à faire; **to ~ it easy to do** trouver facile de faire; **to ~ it incredible that** trouver incroyable que (+ *subj*); **6** (experience) éprouver [*pleasure, satisfaction*] (in dans); trouver [*comfort*] (in dans); **7** (reach) **to ~ its mark/its target** toucher son but/sa cible; **to ~ its way to/into** arriver dans [*bin, pocket, area*]; **8** Jur **to ~ that** conclure que; **to ~ sb guilty** déclarer qn coupable; **9** (arrive to find) [*letter, card, day*] trouver [*person*]; **the next day found him feeling ill** le lendemain il se sentait malade; **10** Comput rechercher

C *vi* (*prét, pp* **found**) Jur **to ~ for/against sb** se prononcer en faveur de/contre qn

D *v refl* (*prét, pp* **found**) **to ~ oneself** **1** (discover suddenly) se retrouver; **to ~ oneself unable to do** se sentir incapable de faire; **to ~ oneself doing** se surprendre à faire; **2** (discover one's vocation) se découvrir

Idioms **to ~ one's feet** [*person*] prendre ses marques; [*company*] prendre pied; **to take sb as one ~s him/her** prendre qn comme il/elle est

Phrasal verb

■ **find out**: ▸ **~ out** (get information) se renseigner; **if he ever ~s out** si jamais il l'apprend; ▸ **~ out [sth]**, **~ [sth] out** découvrir [*fact, answer, name, cause, truth*]; ▸ **~ out who/why/where etc** trouver qui/pourquoi/où etc; ▸ **~ out that** découvrir *or* apprendre que; ▸ **~ [sb] out** découvrir [*person*]; ▸ **~ out about [sth]** **1** (learn by chance) découvrir [*plan, affair, breakage*]; **2** (research) faire des recherches sur [*subject*]

finder /ˈfaɪndə(r)/ *n*:

Idiom **~s keepers (losers weepers)** celui qui le trouve le garde

finding /ˈfaɪndɪŋ/ *n* (conclusion) conclusion *f*

fine /faɪn/
A *n* gen amende *f*; (for traffic offence) contravention *f* (**for** pour)
B *adj* **1** (very good) [*performance, writer, example, quality*] excellent; **2** (satisfactory) [*holiday, meal, arrangement*] bien; **that's ~** très bien; '**~, thanks**' 'très bien, merci'; '**we'll go now, OK?'—'~**' 'on y va maintenant?'—'d'accord'; **that's ~ by** *ou* **with me** je n'y vois pas d'inconvénient; ○iron **a ~ friend you are!** en voilà un ami!; **you're/she's etc a ~ one to talk!** c'est bien à toi/elle etc de dire ça!; **4** (nice) [*weather, morning, day*] beau/belle; **it's** *ou* **the weather's ~** il fait beau; **5** (delicate) [*hair, thread, line, feature, fabric, mist, layer*] fin; [*sieve, net*] à mailles fines; [*china, lace, linen, wine*] fin; **6** (small-grained) [*powder, soil*] fin; **7** (subtle) [*adjustment, detail, distinction, judgment*] subtil; **8** (refined) [*lady, clothes, manners*] beau/belle; **9** (commendable) [*person*] merveilleux/-euse; **10** (pure) [*gold, silver*] pur
C *adv* (well) [*get along, come along, do*] très bien
D *vtr* gen condamner [qn] à une amende [*offender*] (**for** pour; **for doing** pour avoir fait); (for traffic offence) donner une contravention à [*offender*]

Idioms **not to put too ~ a point on it** bref; **chance would be a ~ thing**○! ça serait trop beau○!; **you are cutting it a bit ~** ce sera un peu juste; **there is a ~ line between X and Y** il y a une distinction subtile entre X et Y

fine art *n* beaux-arts *mpl*

Idiom **she's got cheating down to a ~** elle est passée maître dans l'art de tricher

finely /ˈfaɪnlɪ/ *adv* **1** (not coarsely) [*chopped, grated*] finement; **2** (carefully) [*balanced, judged*] soigneusement; **3** (very well) [*written, painted, executed*] splendidement

finery /ˈfaɪnərɪ/ *n* parure *f*; **in all her ~** dans ses plus beaux atours

finespun /ˈfaɪnspʌn/ *adj* [*notion, argument*] très subtil

finesse /fɪˈnes/ ▸ p. 881
A *n* finesse *f*
B *vtr* (handle adroitly) manipuler adroitement [*situation, person*]; contourner [*objections*]

fine-tooth(ed) comb /ˌfaɪnˈtuːθ kəʊm/ *n* peigne *m* fin

Idiom **to go over** *ou* **through sth with a ~** passer qch au peigne fin

fine: **~-tune** *vtr* ajuster; **~ tuning** *n* ajustement *m*

finger /ˈfɪŋɡə(r)/
A *n* ▸ p. 698 **1** Anat doigt *m*; **to point one's ~ at sb/sth** montrer qn/qch du doigt; **to run one's ~s over sth** passer les doigts sur qch; **he didn't lift** *ou* **raise a ~ to help** il n'a pas levé le petit doigt pour aider; **I didn't lay a ~ on her** je ne l'ai pas touchée; **to put two ~s up at sb**○ GB, **to give sb the ~**○ US ≈ faire un bras d'honneur à qn; **2** (of glove) doigt *m*; **3** (narrow strip) (of land) bande *f*; (of mist, smoke) volute *f*; **4** (small amount) (of whisky etc) doigt *m*
B *vtr* toucher [*fruit, goods*]; tripoter○ [*necklace*]

Idioms **to get one's ~s burnt** se brûler les doigts; **to twist** *ou* **wrap sb around one's little ~** mener qn par le bout du nez; **to keep one's ~s crossed** croiser les doigts (**for sb** pour qn); **to point the ~ at sb** accuser qn; **to put the ~ on sb**○ moucharder qn○; **to pull one's ~ out**○ se grouiller○; **to slip through sb's ~s** [*opportunity*] passer sous le nez de qn; [*wanted man*] filer entre les doigts de qn

finger: **~ biscuit** *n* Culin ≈ boudoir *m*; **~board** *n* Mus touche *f*; **~ bowl** *n* rince-doigts *m inv*; **~ food** *n* Culin buffet *m* froid à consommer sans couverts; **~ hole** *n* Mus trou *m* (*sur flûte, clarinette etc*)

fingering /ˈfɪŋɡərɪŋ/ *n* Mus doigté *m*

finger: **~less glove** *n* mitaine *f*; **~-nail** *n* ongle *m*; **~-paint** *vi* peindre avec les doigts; **~print** *n* empreinte *f* digitale; **~printing** *n* prise *f* d'empreintes digitales

fingertip /ˈfɪŋɡətɪp/ *n* bout *m* du doigt

Idiom **to have sth at one's ~s** connaître qch sur le bout des doigts

fingertip control *n* contrôle *m* digital

finicky /ˈfɪnɪkɪ/ *adj* [*person*] difficile (**about** pour); [*job, task*] minutieux/-ieuse

finish /ˈfɪnɪʃ/
A *n* (*pl* **~es**) **1** (end) fin *f*; **from start to ~** du début (jusqu')à la fin; **it will be a fight to the ~** fig la partie va être serrée; **2** Sport arrivée *f*; **an athlete with a good ~** un athlète bon au sprint final; **3** (surface, aspect) (of clothing, wood, car) finition *f*; (of fabric, leather) apprêt *m*; **paint with a matt/silk ~** peinture mate/satinée
B *vtr* **1** (complete) finir, terminer [*chapter, sentence, task*]; terminer, achever [*building, novel, sculpture, opera*]; **to ~ doing** finir de faire; **2** (leave) finir [*work, studies*]; **3** (consume) finir [*cigarette, drink, meal*]; **4** (put an end to) briser [*career*]; **5** ○(exhaust, demoralize) achever○ [*person*]
C *vi* **1** (end) [*conference, programme*] finir, se terminer; [*holidays*] se terminer; **the film ~es on Thursday** le film ne passe plus à partir de jeudi; **I'll see you when the concert ~es** je te verrai à la fin du concert; **2** (reach end of race) arriver; **the horse/the athlete failed to ~** le cheval/l'athlète n'a pas fini la course; **3** (conclude) [*speaker*] finir de parler, conclure; **4** (leave employment) **I ~ed at the bank yesterday** j'ai quitté mon travail à la banque hier
D **finished** *pp adj* **1** **beautifully ~ed** [*furniture, interior etc*] avec des finitions soignées; **~ed in marble** avec des finitions en marbre; **the ~ed product** le produit fini; **2** (accomplished) [*performance*] accompli; **3** (ruined) [*person, career*] fini, fichu○

Phrasal verbs

■ **finish off**: ▸ **~ [sth] off**, **~ off [sth]** (complete) finir, terminer [*letter, meal, task*]; ▸ **~ [sb] off** **1** (exhaust, demoralize) achever○ [*person*]; **2** (kill) achever [*person, animal*]

■ **finish up**: ▸ **~ up** [*person*] (at end of journey) se retrouver; (in situation) finir; **to ~ up (by) doing** finir par faire; ▸ **~ [sth] up**, **~ up [sth]** finir [*milk, paint, cake*]

■ **finish with**: ▸ **~ with [sth]** finir avec [*book, tool, pen*]; **I'm ~ed with school/politics!** j'en ai assez de l'école/de la politique!; ▸ **~ with [sb]** **1** (split up) rompre avec [*girlfriend, boyfriend*]; **2** (stop punishing) **you'll be sorry when I've ~ed with you!** tu vas voir ce que tu vas voir○!

finish: **~ing line** GB, **~ line** US *n* Sport, fig ligne *f* d'arrivée; **~ing post** *n* Sport poteau *m* d'arrivée; **~ing school** *n* Sch pension pour jeunes filles de bonne famille

finishing touch /ˈfɪnɪʃɪŋ/ *n* touche *f* finale; **the ~es** la touche finale

finite /ˈfaɪnaɪt/ *adj* **1** gen [*resources*] limité; **2** Math, Philos, Ling fini

Finland /ˈfɪnlənd/ ▸ p. 774 *pr n* Finlande *f*

Finn /fɪn/ ▸ p. 1032 *n* **1** (citizen) Finlandais/-e *m/f*; **2** (speaker) Finnois/-e *m/f*

f

Finnish /'fınıʃ/ ▸ p. 1032, p. 969
A n (language) finnois m
B adj finlandais
fiord n = fjord
fir /fɜː(r)/ n (also ~ **tree**) sapin m
fir cone n pomme f de pin
fire /'faıə(r)/
A n [1] (element) feu m; **to set ~ to sth, to set sth on ~** mettre le feu à qch; **to be on ~** être en feu; **to catch ~** prendre feu; [2] (blaze) incendie m; **to start a ~** provoquer un incendie; [3] (for warmth) feu m; [4] **₵** (shots) coups mpl de feu; **to open ~ on sb** ouvrir le feu sur qn; **the police/passers-by came under ~** on a tiré sur la police/les passants; **to be under ~** fig être vivement critiqué (**from** par); **to return sb's ~** riposter; [5] (verve) fougue f
B excl [1] (raising alarm) au feu!; [2] (order to shoot) feu!
C vtr [1] Mil, gen décharger [gun, weapon]; tirer [shot]; lancer [arrow, missile]; **to ~ questions at sb** bombarder qn de questions; [2] (inspire) **to be ~d with enthusiasm** s'enthousiasmer; **to ~ sb's imagination** enflammer l'imagination de qn; [3] (dismiss) renvoyer, virer° [person]; [4] Tech cuire [ceramics]
D vi [1] Mil, gen tirer (**at, on** sur); [2] [engine] démarrer
(Idioms) ~ **away!** allez-y!; **to hang ~** faire long feu; fig [plans, project, person] traîner; **to play with ~** jouer avec le feu; **he'll never set the world on ~**° il ne fera jamais de miracles; ▸ **house**
(Phrasal verb)
■ **fire up:** ▸ ~ [sb] **up,** ~ **up** [sb] gonfler [qn] à bloc
fire: ~ **alarm** n alarme f incendie; ~**arm** n arme f à feu; ~**back** n plaque f de cheminée; ~**ball** n boule f de feu; ~ **bell** n sonnerie f d'alarme
firebomb /'faıəbɒm/
A n bombe f incendiaire
B vtr incendier [building]
fire: ~**brand** n fig semeur m de discordes; ~**break** n pare-feu m inv; ~ **brigade** n pompiers mpl; ~ **chief** n US chef m des pompiers; ~**cracker** n pétard m; ~**damaged** adj endommagé par le feu; ~ **department** n US pompiers mpl; ~ **door** n porte f coupe-feu; ~ **drill** n exercice m d'évacuation en cas d'incendie; ~**eater** n cracheur/-euse m/f de feu; ~ **engine** n voiture f de pompiers; ~ **escape** n escalier m de secours; ~ **exit** n sortie f de secours; ~ **extinguisher** n extincteur m; ▸ p. 1181 **fighter** n pompier m; ~**fighting** n lutte f contre l'incendie; ~**fly** n luciole f; ~**guard** n pare-étincelles m inv; ~ **hazard** n risque m d'incendie; ~ **house** n US caserne f de pompiers; ~ **hydrant** n bouche f d'incendie; ~ **insurance** n assurance-incendie f; ~**light** n lueur f du feu; ~**lighter** n allume-feu m inv; ▸ p. 1181 m pompier m; ~ **marshall** n US pompier m responsable de la prévention; ~**place** n cheminée f; ~ **plug** n US bouche f d'incendie; ~ **power** n puissance f de feu; ~ **practice** n = fire drill; ~**proof** adj [door, clothing] ignifugé; ~ **risk** n risque m d'incendie; ~ **screen** n écran m de cheminée; ~ **service** n (sapeurs-)pompiers mpl; ~**side** n coin m du feu; ~ **station** n caserne f de pompiers; ~**truck** n US voiture f de pompiers; ~**wall** n rampart pare-feu m, barrière f de sécurité; ~**warden** ▸ p. 1181 n responsable mf de la lutte contre l'incendie; ~**wood** n bois m à brûler; ~**work** n feu m d'artifice; ~**works display** n feu m d'artifice
firing /'faıərıŋ/ n [1] (of guns) tir m; [2] (of ceramics) cuisson f
firing line n **to be in the ~** lit être dans la ligne de tir; fig (under attack) faire l'objet de violentes critiques
firing squad n peloton m d'exécution; **to face the ~** être fusillé
firm /fɜːm/
A n (business) entreprise f, société f; ~ **of architects** cabinet m d'architecte
B adj [1] (hard) [mattress, fruit, handshake] ferme; **to give sth a ~ tap/tug** taper/tirer qch d'un coup sec; [2] (steady) [table, ladder] solide; [3] fig (strong) [foundation, basis, grasp] solide; **it's my ~ belief that** je crois fermement que; [4] (definite) [offer, intention, refusal] ferme; [date] définitif/-ive; [evidence] concret/-ète; [5] (resolute) [person, stand, leadership] ferme (**with sb** avec qn); **he needs a ~ hand** il a besoin qu'on soit ferme avec lui; [6] Fin [dollar, market] ferme

C adv **to stand ~** tenir bon (**against** contre); **to remain** ou **hold ~** [currency] rester ferme (**against** par rapport à)
firmly /'fɜːmlı/ adv [1] (with authority) [say, answer, state] d'un ton ferme; **tell him ~ but politely...** dis-lui fermement mais poliment...; **to deal ~ with sb/sth** traiter qn/qch avec fermeté; [2] (strongly) [believe, deny, be convinced] fermement; [3] (tightly) [hold, push, press] fermement; [attach, tie] solidement; **we have it ~ under control** nous l'avons bien en main
firmness /'fɜːmnıs/ n [1] gen fermeté f; [2] Fin stabilité f
first /fɜːst/ ▸ p. 1044, p. 788
A pron [1] (of series, group) premier/première m/f (**to do** à faire); [2] (of month) **the ~ (of May)** le premier (mai); [3] **First** (in titles) **Elizabeth the First** Elisabeth Première; [4] (initial moment) **the ~ I knew about his death was a letter from his wife** c'est par une lettre de sa femme que j'ai appris qu'il était mort; **that's the ~ I've heard of it!** première nouvelle!; [5] (beginning) début m; **at ~** au début; **from the (very) ~** dès le début; [6] (new experience) première f; **a ~ for sb/sth** une première pour qn/qch; [7] Aut (gear) première f; ▸ **gear**; [8] GB Univ (degree) ≈ mention f très bien (à la licence)
B adj [1] (of series, group) premier/-ière (before n); **the ~ three pages** or **the three ~ pages** les trois premières pages; [2] (in phrases) **at ~ glance** ou **sight** à première vue; **I'll ring ~ thing tomorrow** je vous appellerai demain à la première heure; **I'll do it ~ thing** je le ferai dès que possible; [3] (slightest) **he doesn't know the ~ thing about politics** il ne connaît absolument rien à la politique
C adv [1] (before others) [arrive, leave] le premier/la première; **you go ~!** après vous!; **women and children ~** les femmes et les enfants d'abord; **to come ~** Games, Sport terminer premier/première (**in** à); fig [career, family] passer avant tout; [2] (to begin with) d'abord; ~ **of all** tout d'abord; ~ **she tells me one thing, then something else** elle commence par me dire une chose puis elle me dit le contraire; **there are two reasons: ~...** il y a deux raisons: d'abord...; **when we were ~ married** tout au début de notre mariage; **when he ~ arrived** quand il est arrivé; [3] (for the first time) pour la première fois; **I ~ met him in Paris** je l'ai rencontré pour la première fois à Paris; [4] (rather) plutôt
(Idioms) ~ **come ~ served** les premiers arrivés sont les premiers servis; ~ **things ~** chaque chose en son temps
first aid n [1] **₵** gen premiers soins mpl; [2] (as skill) secourisme m
first aid: ~ **kit** n trousse f de secours; ~ **officer** n secouriste mf
first class
A n [1] Rail première f (classe f); [2] Post tarif m rapide
B first-class adj [1] Tourism, Rail [compartment, hotel, ticket] de première (classe); [2] Post [stamp] (au) tarif rapide; ~ **mail** courrier m (au tarif) rapide; [3] GB Univ [degree] avec mention très bien; [4] (excellent) excellent
C adv [1] Rail [travel] en première (classe); [2] Post [send] au tarif rapide
first: ~ **course** n (of meal) entrée f; ~ **cousin** n (male) cousin n germain; (female) cousine n germaine; ~ **degree murder** n US Jur meurtre m avec préméditation; ~ **edition** n édition f originale; ~**ever** adj tout premier/toute première; ~ **floor** n GB premier étage m; US rez-de-chaussée m; ~ **form** n GB Sch (classe f de) sixième f; ~**generation** adj de la première génération; ~ **grade** n US Sch cours m préparatoire; ~**hand** adj, adv de première main; **First Lady** n US Pol première dame f; ~ **light** n premières lueurs fpl
firstly /'fɜːstlı/ adv premièrement
first mate n Naut second m
first name n prénom m; **to be on ~ terms with sb** appeler qn par son prénom
first: ~ **night** n Theat première f; ~ **person** n Ling première personne f; ~ **principle** n principe m premier; ~**rate** adj excellent; ~ **school** n GB Sch école f préparatoire; ~**time buyer** n personne f qui achète sa première maison; ~ **violin** n premier violon m
first past the post n GB ~ **system** majorité simple des suffrages
first year n Sch, Univ (group) première année f; (pupil) élève mf en première année; (student) étudiant/-e m/f en première année
firth /fɜːθ/ n estuaire m

fiscal /ˈfɪskl/ *adj* fiscal
fiscal year *n* exercice *m* budgétaire *or* fiscal
fish /fɪʃ/
A *n* (*pl* ~, ~**es**) poisson *m*
B *noun modifier* [*course, bone, glue*] de poisson; [*knife, fork*] à poisson
C *vi* **1** lit pêcher; **to** ~ **for** trout/cod pêcher la truite/la morue; **2** fig (test for response) **to** ~ **for information** chercher à dénicher des renseignements; **to** ~ **for compliments** rechercher les compliments
(Idioms) **to be neither** ~ **nor fowl** n'être ni chair ni poisson; **to be like a** ~ **out of water** ne pas se sentir dans son élément; **to drink like a** ~○ boire comme un trou; **to have other** ~ **to fry** avoir d'autres chats à fouetter; **there are plenty more** ~ **in the sea** un de perdu, dix de retrouvés
(Phrasal verbs)
■ **fish around** farfouiller (**in** dans; **for** pour trouver)
■ **fish out**: ▸ ~ **out** [sth], ~ [sth] **out** **1** (from bag, pocket, box) sortir [*money, pen*] (**of** de); **2** (from water) repêcher [*body, object*] (**of** de)
fish: ~ **and chips** *n* poisson *m* frit avec des frites; ~ **and chip shop** ▸ p. 1181 *n* GB friterie *f*; ~**bowl** *n* bocal *m* (à poissons); ~ **cake** *n* croquette *f* de poisson
fisherman /ˈfɪʃəmən/ ▸ p. 1181 *n* pêcheur *m*
fishery /ˈfɪʃərɪ/ *n* (processing plant) pêcherie *f*
fish: ~ **farm** *n* centre *m* de pisciculture; ~ **farming** *n* pisciculture *f*; ~ **finger** *n* GB bâtonnet *m* de poisson; ~ **hook** *n* hameçon *m*
fishing /ˈfɪʃɪŋ/
A *n* pêche *f*; **to go** ~ aller à la pêche
B *noun modifier* [*boat, fleet, port, line, net*] de pêche
fishing: ~ **ground** *n* lieu *m* de pêche; ~ **rod** *n* canne *f* à pêche; ~ **village** *n* port *m* de pêche
fish market *n* halle *f* aux poissons
fishmonger /ˈfɪʃmʌŋɡə(r)/ ▸ p. 1181 *n* GB poissonnier/-ière *m/f*; ~**'s** (shop) poissonnerie *f*
fish: ~**net** *adj* [*stockings*] à résille; ~ **paste** *n* GB ≈ beurre *m* de poisson; ~**pond** *n* (ornamental) bassin *m*; (at fish farm) vivier *m*; ~ **shop** GB, ~ **store** US ▸ p. 1181 *n* poissonnerie *f*; ~ **slice** *n* (for frying) spatule *f*; (for serving at table) pelle *f* à poisson; ~ **tank** *n* aquarium *m*
fishy /ˈfɪʃɪ/ *adj* **1** lit [*smell, taste*] de poisson; **2** ○fig (suspect) louche○
fission /ˈfɪʃn/ *n* **1** (*also* **nuclear** ~) Phys fission *f*; **2** Biol fissiparité *f*
fissure /ˈfɪʃə(r)/ *n* **1** (in ground) crevasse *f*; (in wood, wall) fissure *f*; **2** Anat scissure *f*
fist /fɪst/ *n* poing *m*; **to shake one's** ~ **at sb** menacer qn du poing
(Idioms) **to make money hand over** ~ gagner des mille et des cents; **to make a good/poor** ~ **of doing sth** bien/mal faire qch
fistful /ˈfɪstfʊl/ *n* poignée *f* (**of** de)
fit /fɪt/
A *n* **1** Med crise *f*, attaque *f*; **to have a** ~ (unspecified) avoir une attaque *or* une crise; **2** gen (of rage, passion, panic) accès *m*; ~ **of coughing** quinte *f* de toux; **to have sb in** ~**s**○ donner le fou rire à qn; **to have** *ou* **throw a** ~ (be mad) piquer○ une crise; **3** (of garment) **to be a good/poor** ~ être/ne pas être à la bonne taille
B *adj* **1** [*person*] (in trim) en forme; (not ill) en bonne santé; **you're looking** ~ **and well!** tu as l'air en pleine forme!; **to get** ~ retrouver la forme; **2** (suitable, appropriate) **to be** ~ **for** (worthy of) être digne de [*person, hero, king*]; (capable of) être capable de faire [*job*]; **to be** ~ **for nothing** n'être plus bon/bonne à rien; ~/**not** ~ **for human consumption** propre/impropre à la consommation; **to be** ~ **to drive** être en état de conduire; ~ **to drink** potable; ~ **to live in** habitable; **I'm not** ~ **to be seen!** je ne suis pas présentable!; **to see** *ou* **think** ~ **to do** juger *ou* trouver bon de faire; **to be in no** ~ **state to do** ne pas être en état de faire; **3** ○(in emphatic phrases) **to laugh** ~ **to burst** se tordre de rire; **to cry** ~ **to burst** pleurer comme une madeleine
C *vtr* (*prét* **fitted, fit** US; *pp* **fitted**) **1** (be the right size) [*garment*] être à la taille de; [*shoe*] être à la pointure de; [*key*] aller dans [*lock*]; aller [*envelope, space*]; **to** ~ **size X to Y** correspondre aux tailles X à Y; **to** ~ **ages 3 to 5** convenir aux enfants de 3 à 5 ans; **2** (make or find room for) **to** ~ **sth in** *ou* **into** trouver de la place pour qch dans [*room, house, car*];

3 (install) mettre [qch] en place [*lock, door, kitchen, shower*]; **to** ~ **A to B, to** ~ **A and B together** assembler A avec B; **to** ~ **sth with** équiper qch de [*attachment, lock*]; **to** ~ **sb for** [*tailor*] prendre les mesures de qn pour [*garment, uniform*]; **to** ~ **sb with** [*doctor*] pourvoir qn de [*hearing aid, prosthesis*]; **4** (be compatible with) correspondre à [*description, requirements*]; aller avec [*decor*]; **the punishment should** ~ **the crime** la punition devrait être proportionnée à la faute; ▸ **bill**
D *vi* (*prét* **fitted, fit** US; *pp* **fitted**) **1** (be the right size) [*garment*] être à ma/ta/sa taille, aller; [*shoes*] être à ma/ta/sa pointure, aller; [*key, lid, sheet*] aller; **2** (have enough room) [*toys, books etc*] tenir (**into** dans); **will the table** ~ **in that corner?** y a-t-il de la place pour la table dans ce coin?; **3** (go into place) **to** ~ **inside one another** aller *or* se mettre les uns dans les autres; **to** ~ **into place** [*part, handle*] bien aller; [*cupboard, brick*] bien rentrer; **4** fig (tally, correspond) **something doesn't quite** ~ **here** il y a quelque chose qui ne va pas ici; **to** ~ **with** correspondre à [*story, facts*]; **to** ~ **into** aller avec [*ideology, colour scheme*]
(Idiom) **by** *ou* **in** ~**s and starts** par à-coups
(Phrasal verbs)
■ **fit in**: ▸ ~ **in** **1** lit [*key, object*] aller; **will you all** ~ **in?** (to car, room) est-ce qu'il y a de la place pour vous tous?; **2** fig (be in harmony) [*person*] s'intégrer (**with** à); **I'll** ~ **in with your plans** j'accorderai mes projets avec les vôtres; ▸ ~ [sth/sb] **in**, ~ **in** [sth/sb] **1** (find room for) caser [*books, objects*]; faire entrer [*key*]; **2** (find time for) caser [*game, meeting, break*]; trouver le temps pour voir [*patient, colleague*]
■ **fit out**: ▸ ~ [sth] **out**, ~ **out** [sth] équiper (**with** de); **to** ~ **sb out with** mettre [qch] à qn [*costume, garment, hearing aid*]
fitful /ˈfɪtfl/ *adj* [*sleep*] agité; [*wind*] changeant
fitfully /ˈfɪtfəlɪ/ *adv* [*sleep, rain, shine*] par intermittence
fitness /ˈfɪtnɪs/
A *n* **1** (physical condition) forme *f*; **2** (aptness) (of person) aptitude *f* (**for, to do** à faire)
B *noun modifier* [*club, centre, room*] de culture physique
fitness: ~ **test** *n* test *m* de condition physique; ~ **training** *n* ⓒ exercices *mpl* physiques, fitness *m*
fitted /ˈfɪtɪd/ *adj* [*wardrobe*] encastré; [*kitchen*] intégré
fitted: ~ **carpet** *n* moquette *f*; ~ **sheet** *n* drap-housse *m*
fitter /ˈfɪtə(r)/ ▸ p. 1181 *n* Tech monteur/-euse *m/f*
fitting /ˈfɪtɪŋ/
A *n* **1** (standardized part) (bathroom, electrical, gas) installation *f*; **2** (for clothes, hearing aid) essayage *m*; **3** (width of shoe) largeur *f*
B *adj* (apt, appropriate) [*description, language, site*] adéquat; [*memorial, testament*] qui convient; **a** ~ **tribute to her work** un hommage mérité à son œuvre
fittingly /ˈfɪtɪŋlɪ/ *adv* [*named*] de façon appropriée
fitting room *n* salon *m* d'essayage
five /faɪv/ ▸ p. 1044, p. 647, p. 745
A *n* (numeral) cinq *m inv*
B *adj* cinq *inv*
(Idiom) **to take** ~○ US faire une pause
five-a-side /ˌfaɪvəˈsaɪd/ *n* (*also* ~ **football**) GB football *m* à cinq (joueurs)
fiver○ /ˈfaɪvə(r)/ *n* GB billet *m* de cinq livres
five spot○ *n* US billet *m* de cinq dollars
fix /fɪks/
A *n* **1** ○(quandary) pétrin○ *m*; **to be in a** ~ être dans le pétrin○; **2** ○(dose) (of drugs) shoot○ *m*; **3** (means of identification) **to take a** ~ **on sth** Aviat, Naut déterminer la position de qch; **4** ○(rigged arrangement) **it was a** ~ c'était truqué
B *vtr* **1** (establish, set) fixer [*date, venue, price, limit*]; déterminer [*chronology, position*]; **to** ~ **tax at 20%** établir un impôt de 20%; **nothing is** ~**ed yet** il n'y a encore rien d'arrêté; **2** (organize) arranger [*meeting, visit*]; préparer [*drink, meal*]; **to** ~ **one's hair** se donner un coup de peigne; **how are we** ~**ed for time/money?** qu'est-ce qu'on a comme temps/argent?○; **3** (mend) réparer [*article, equipment*]; (sort out) régler [*problem*]; **4** (attach, insert) fixer [*curtain, handle, shelf, notice*] (**on** sur; **to** à); attacher [*rope*] (**to** à); fig faire peser [*suspicion*] (**on** sur); rejeter [*blame*] (**on** sur); **5** (concentrate) fixer [*attention*] (**on** sur); placer [*hopes*] (**on** dans); tourner [*thoughts*] (**on** vers); **to** ~ **one's eyes** *ou* **gaze on sb** regarder qn fixement; **6** ○(rig, corrupt) truquer [*contest, election*];

[7] Art, Biol, Chem, Phot, Tech fixer

C **fixed** pp adj [gaze, idea, income, order, price] fixe; [intervals] régulier/-ière; [method] immuable; [aim] arrêté; [desire] tenace; [intention] ferme; [proportion] constant; [expression] figé; [menu] à prix fixe

(Phrasal verbs)

■ **fix on**, **fix upon**: ▸ ~ **on** [sb/sth] choisir [person, place, food, object]; fixer [date, venue, amount]

■ **fix up**: ▸ ~ **up** [sth], ~ [sth] **up** **[1]** (organize) organiser [holiday, meeting]; décider de [date]; **[2]** (decorate) refaire [room, house]; ▸ ~ **sb up with sth** trouver qch à qn [accommodation, vehicle]; faire avoir qch à qn [ticket, meal]; ▸ ~ **sb up with sb**° monter une baraque à qn avec qn°

fixation /fɪk'seɪʃn/ n **[1]** gen, Psych fixation f; **[2]** Chem fixation f

fixative /'fɪksətɪv/ n gen, Tech produit m fixateur; (for hair) fixateur m; Art fixatif m; Phot fixateur m

fixed assets /fɪkst/ npl immobilisations fpl, actif m immobilisé

fixedly /'fɪksɪdlɪ/ adv [look, gaze] fixement

fixed-term contract n contrat m à durée déterminée

fixer /'fɪksə(r)/ n **[1]** °(schemer) magouilleur/-euse° m/f; **[2]** Phot fixateur m

fixture /'fɪkstʃə(r)/ n **[1]** Constr, Tech installation f; ~**s and fittings** équipements mpl; **[2]** Sport rencontre f

fizz /fɪz/
A n (of drink) pétillement m; (of match, firework) crépitement m
B vi [drink] pétiller; [match, firework] crépiter

(Phrasal verb)

■ **fizz up** mousser

fizzle /'fɪzl/ v:

■ **fizzle out** [interest, romance] s'éteindre; [strike, campaign, project] faire fiasco; [story] se terminer en queue de poisson; [firework] faire long feu

fizzy /'fɪzɪ/ adj gazeux/-euse

fjord /fɪ'ɔːd/ n fjord m

FL US Post abrév écrite = **Florida**

flab° /flæb/ n chair f flasque

flabbergast /'flæbəɡɑːst, US -ɡæst/ vtr sidérer

flabby /'flæbɪ/ adj [skin, muscle] flasque; [person] aux chairs flasques

flaccid /'flæsɪd/ adj flasque, mou/molle

flag /flæɡ/
A n **[1]** (national symbol) drapeau m; **to sail under the Panamanian** ~ Naut battre pavillon panaméen; **[2]** (as signal) Naut pavillon m; Rail drapeau m; **[3]** (on map) drapeau m; **[4]** (stone) dalle f; **[5]** Comput drapeau m
B vtr (p prés etc -gg-) **[1]** (mark with tab) baliser [text]; **[2]** (signal) signaler [problem]; **[3]** Comput signaler [qch] au moyen d'un drapeau
C vi (p prés etc -gg-) [interest] faiblir; [morale, strength] baisser; [conversation] languir; [athlete, campaigner] flancher°
D **flagging** pres p adj [strength] qui baisse; [energy, economy, industry etc] chancelant

(Idioms) **to fly the** ~ représenter son pays (à l'étranger); **to wave the** ~ faire des déclarations patriotiques

(Phrasal verb)

■ **flag down**: ▸ ~ [sth] **down**, ~ **down** [sth] faire signe de s'arrêter à [train]; héler [taxi]

flagellation /ˌflædʒə'leɪʃn/ n flagellation f

flageolet /ˌflædʒə'let, 'flædʒ-/ n flageolet m

flagon /'flæɡən/ n (bottle) grosse bouteille f; (jug) pichet m

flagpole /'flæɡpəʊl/ n mât m (de drapeau)

flagrant /'fleɪɡrənt/ adj flagrant

flagrantly /'fleɪɡrəntlɪ/ adv [behave, do sth] de façon flagrante; [artificial, dishonest etc] manifestement

flagship /'flæɡʃɪp/
A n Naut vaisseau m amiral
B noun modifier [company, product] vedette

flag: ~**stone** n dalle f; ~ **stop** n US arrêt m facultatif

flail /fleɪl/
A n fléau m
B vtr **[1]** Agric battre [qch] au fléau [corn]; **[2]** gen ▸ **flail about**
C vi ▸ **flail about**

■ **flail about**, **flail around**: ▸ ~ **around** [person] se débattre; [arms, legs] s'agiter; ▸ ~ [sth] **around**, ~ **around** [sth] agiter [arms, legs]

flair /'fleə(r)/ n **[1]** (talent) don; **[2]** (style) classe f

flak /flæk/ n **C** **[1]** Mil tirs mpl des batteries antiaériennes; **[2]** °fig (criticism) critiques fpl

flake /fleɪk/
A n (of snow, cereal) flocon m; (of soap) paillette f; (of chocolate, cheese) copeau m; (of paint, rust) écaille f; (of rock, flint) éclat m
B vi (also ~ **off**) [paint, varnish] s'écailler; [plaster, stone] s'effriter; [skin] peler; [fish] s'émietter

(Phrasal verb)

■ **flake out**° s'endormir comme une masse

flak jacket GB, **flack vest** US n gilet m pare-balles

flaky /'fleɪkɪ/ adj [paint] qui s'écaille; [skin] qui pèle; [plaster, rock, statue] qui s'effrite

flaky pastry n pâte f feuilletée

flamboyant /flæm'bɔɪənt/ adj [person] haut en couleur; [lifestyle, image] exubérant°; [colour, clothes] voyant; [gesture] extravagant

flame /fleɪm/
A n **[1]** lit flamme f; **in** ~**s** en flammes; **to go up in** ~**s** s'enflammer; **to burst into** ~**s** s'embraser; **to be shot down in** ~**s** lit, fig être descendu en flammes; **[2]** fig (also ~**s**) feu m (**of** de); **an old** ~° (person) un ancien flirt°; **[3]** (colour) rouge m feu
B vi [fire, torch] flamber

flamenco /flə'meŋkəʊ/ n (also ~ **dancing**) flamenco m

flame: ~**proof** adj qui va au feu; [substance, chemical] ignifuge; [furniture, fabric] ignifugé; ~**thrower** n lance-flammes m inv

flaming /'fleɪmɪŋ/
A n (on Internet) campagne f d'insultes
B adj **[1]** [vehicle, building] en flammes; [torch] allumé; **[2]** (épith) [row] violent

flamingo /flə'mɪŋɡəʊ/ n (pl ~**s** ou **-oes**) flamant m (rose)

flammable /'flæməbl/ adj inflammable

flan /flæn/ n (savoury) quiche f, tarte f; (sweet) tarte f

Flanders /'flɑːndəz/ pr n les Flandres fpl

flange /flændʒ/ n (on wheel) boudin m; (on pipe) bride f; (on tool) collet m; (on beam) aile f

flank /flæŋk/
A n **[1]** (of animal, mountain) flanc m; **[2]** Mil flanc m; **[3]** Pol, Sport aile f; **[4]** Culin flanchet m
B vtr flanquer [person, door]; border [path, area]

flannel /'flænl/ n **[1]** (wool) flanelle f; (cotton) pilou m; **[2]** GB (also **face** ~) ≈ gant m de toilette

flannels /'flænəlz/ npl pantalon m de flanelle

flap /flæp/
A n **[1]** (on pocket, envelope, tent) rabat m; (on table, bar) abattant m; (of trapdoor) trappe f; (for cat) chatière f; **[2]** (movement) (of wings) battement m (**of** de); (of sail) claquement m (**of** de); **[3]** Aviat volet m; **[4]** °(panic) **to get into a** ~ s'affoler; **[5]** Ling battement m
B vtr (p prés etc -pp-) [wind] claquer [sail, cloth]; faire voleter [paper, clothes]; [person] secouer [sheet]; agiter [paper, letter] (**at sb** en direction de qn); **the bird** ~**ped its wings** l'oiseau battait des ailes
C vi (p prés etc -pp-) **[1]** (move) [wing] battre; [sail, flag, door] claquer; [paper, clothes] voleter; **[2]** °(panic) s'affoler

flapjack /'flæpdʒæk/ n Culin **[1]** GB biscuit m au müesli; **[2]** US crêpe f

flare /fleə(r)/
A n **[1]** (light signal) Aviat (on runway) balise f lumineuse; Mil (on target) fusée f éclairante; Naut (distress signal) fusée f (de détresse); **[2]** (burst of light) (of match, lighter) lueur f; (of fireworks) flamboiement m; **[3]** (also **solar** ~) éruption f solaire
B flares npl (trousers) pantalon m à pattes d'éléphant
C vi **[1]** (burn briefly) [firework, match] jeter une brève lueur; **[2]** (erupt) [violence] éclater; **[3]** (also ~ **out**) (widen) [skirt] s'évaser; [nostrils] se dilater

(Phrasal verb)

■ **flare up [1]** (burn brightly) [fire] s'embraser; **[2]** fig (erupt) [anger, violence] éclater; [person] s'emporter; **[3]** (recur) [illness] réapparaître; [pain] se réveiller

flared /fleə(r)d/ *adj* [*skirt*] évasé; [*trousers*] à pattes d'éléphant

flash /flæʃ/

A *n* ① (sudden light) (of torch, headlights) lueur *f* soudaine; (of jewels, metal) éclat *m*; **a ～ of lightning** un éclair; ② fig **a ～ of inspiration/genius** un éclair d'inspiration/de génie; **it came to him in a ～ that** l'idée lui est soudain venue que; **in** *ou* **like a ～** en un clin d'œil; ③ Phot flash *m*; ④ (bulletin) flash *m* (d'information); ⑤ (stripe) (on clothing) parement *m*; (on car) bande *f*

B ○*adj* (posh) [*hotel*] luxueux/-euse; [*car, suit*] tape-à-l'œil *inv*

C *vtr* ① ○(display) [*person*] montrer [*qch*] rapidement [*card, money*]; ② (flaunt) = **～ about**; ③ (shine) **to ～ a signal/message to sb** envoyer un signal/message à qn avec une lampe; **to ～ one's headlights (at)** faire un appel de phares (à); ④ (send) fig lancer [*look, smile*] (**at** à); ⑤ (transmit) faire apparaître [*message*]

D *vi* ① (shine) [*light*] clignoter; [*jewels*] étinceler; [*eyes*] lancer des éclairs; **to ～ on and off** clignoter; ② (appear suddenly) **a thought ～ed through my mind** une pensée m'a traversé l'esprit; ③ ○(expose oneself) [*man*] faire l'exhibitionniste (**at** devant)

(Idioms) **to be a ～ in the pan** être un feu de paille; **quick as a ～** vif/vive comme l'éclair

(Phrasal verbs)
■ **flash about, flash around: ～ [sth] about** exhiber [*credit card*]; étaler [*money*]
■ **flash by, flash past** [*person, bird*] passer comme un éclair; [*landscape*] défiler
■ **flash up: ▸ ～ [sth] up, ～ up [sth]** afficher [*message*] (**on** sur)

flashback /'flæʃbæk/ *n* ① Cin flash-back *m* (**to** à); ② (memory) souvenir *m*

flash: ～bulb *n* ampoule *f* de flash; **～ card** *n* Sch carte *f* (de support visuel); **～ cube** *n* cube-flash *m*; **～ flood** *n* crue *f* soudaine; **～ gun** *n* Phot flash *m*

flashing /'flæʃɪŋ/
A *n* ① Constr solin *m*; ② ○(exhibitionism) exhibitionnisme *m*
B *adj* [*light, sign*] clignotant

flash: ～ light *n* lampe *f* de poche; **～ memory** *n* Comput mémoire *f* flash

flashpoint /'flæʃpɔɪnt/ *n* ① Chem point *m* d'éclair; ② fig (trouble spot) point *m* chaud; ③ fig (explosive situation) point *m* critique

flashy○ /'flæʃɪ/ *adj* péj [*driver, player*] frimeur/-euse; [*car, dress, tie, campaign, image*] tape-à-l'œil *inv*; [*jewellery*] clinquant

flask /flɑːsk, US flæsk/ *n* ① Chem (large) flacon *m*; (small) (round-bottomed) ballon *m*; (flat-bottomed) fiole *f*; ② gen (large) bonbonne *f*; (small) bouteille *f*; (vacuum) thermos® *f or m inv*; (hip) ～ flasque *f*

flat /flæt/
A *n* ① GB (apartment) appartement *m*; **one-bedroom ～** deux pièces *m inv*; ② (level part) **the ～ of** le plat de [*hand, sword*]; **on the ～** GB [*walk, park*] sur le plat; ③ ○(tyre) pneu *m* à plat; ④ Mus bémol *m*
B *flats npl* ① ○US (shoes) chaussures *fpl* plates; ② Geog (marshland) marécage *m*
C *adj* ① (level, not rounded) gen plat; (of flat appearance) [*nose, face*] aplati; **squashed ～** écrasé; ② (deflated) [*tyre, ball*] dégonflé; **to have a ～ tyre** avoir un pneu à plat; ③ (pressed close) **her feet ～ on the floor** les pieds bien à plat sur le sol; ④ (low) [*shoes, heels*] plat; ⑤ (absolute) [*refusal, denial*] catégorique; ⑥ (standard) [*fare, fee*] forfaitaire; [*charge*] fixe; ⑦ (monotonous) [*voice, tone*] plat, monocorde; (unexciting) [*performance, style*] plat; ⑧ (not fizzy) [*beer etc*] éventé; ⑨ (depressed) **to feel ～** [*person*] se sentir déprimé; ⑩ GB [*battery*] Elec usé; Aut à plat; ⑪ Comm, Fin (slow) [*market, trade*] languissant; [*profits*] stagnant; ⑫ Mus [*note*] bémol *inv*; (off key) [*voice, instrument*] faux/fausse
D *adv* ① (horizontally) [*lay, lie*] à plat; [*fall*] de tout son long; **to knock sb ～** terrasser qn; **to lie ～** [*person*] s'étendre; [*hair*] s'aplatir; [*pleat*] être aplati; **～ on one's back** sur le dos; **to fall ～ on one's face** fig se casser la figure○; ② (in close contact) **she pressed her nose ～ against the window** elle a collé son nez à la vitre; ③ (exactly) **in 10 minutes ～** en 10 minutes pile; ④ ○(absolutely) carrément; **to turn [sth] down ～** refuser [*qch*] tout net [*offer, proposal*]; ⑤ Mus [*sing, play*] faux

(Idiom) **to fall ～** [*performance*] faire un bide○; [*joke*] tomber à plat; [*party, evening*] tourner court; [*plan*] tomber à l'eau

flat: ～-bottomed *adj* [*boat*] à fond plat; **～ broke**○ *adj* fauché○, à sec○

flat-footed /ˌflæt'fʊtɪd/ *adj* ① Med [*person*] aux pieds plats; **to be ～** avoir les pieds plats; ② ○péj (tactless) [*attempt*] maladroit

flat-hunting /'flæthʌntɪŋ/ *n* GB **to go ～** chercher un appartement

flat: ～iron *n* Hist fer *m* à repasser (*qu'on chauffe sur un fourneau*); **～ jockey ▸ p. 1181** *n* jockey *m* spécialisé dans les courses de plat; **～lands** *npl* plaine *f*; **～mate** *n* GB colocataire *mf* (*personne avec qui on partage un appartement*)

flat out○ /ˌflæt'aʊt/
A *adj* GB (also **～ tired** US) KO○, épuisé
B *adv* [*drive*] à fond de train; [*work*] d'arrache-pied; **it only does 120 km per hour ～** elle ne monte qu'à 120 km à l'heure, pied au plancher

(Idiom) **to go ～ for sth** se mettre en quatre○ pour faire qch

flat: ～-pack *adj* en kit; **～ racing** *n* 𝄢 courses *fpl* de plat

flat rate /ˌflæt'reɪt/
A *n* taux *m* fixe
B **flat-rate** *noun modifier* [*fee, tax*] forfaitaire

flat screen *adj* [*TV, computer monitor*] à écran plat

flat-sharing /'flætʃeərɪŋ/ *n* colocation *f*

> ⓘ **Flat-sharing** Système de partage du logement très répandu aux États-Unis et en Grande-Bretagne. Des étudiants, des jeunes salariés ou des célibataires louent un appartement ou une maison (*house-sharing*) à plusieurs, et chacun paie sa part des charges et du loyer.

flat spin /ˌflæt'spɪn/ *n* Aviat vrille *f* à plat

(Idiom) **to be in a ～**○ être affolé

flatten /'flætn/
A *vtr* ① (level) [*rain*] coucher [*crops, grass*]; abattre [*tree, fence*]; [*bombing*] raser [*building*]; **he'll ～ you**○! il va te casser la figure○!; ② (smooth out) aplanir [*surface*]; aplatir [*metal*]; ③ (crush) écraser [*animal, fruit, object*]; ④ Mus baisser (le ton de) [*note*]
B *vi* = **flatten out**
C *v refl* **to ～ oneself** s'aplatir (**against** contre)

(Phrasal verb)
■ **flatten out: ▸ ～ out** [*slope, road, ground*] s'aplanir; [*graph, curve, flight path*] se redresser; [*growth, exports, decline*] se stabiliser; **▸ ～ out [sth], ～ [sth] out** aplanir [*ground, road*]

flatter /'flætə(r)/
A *vtr* ① (compliment) flatter (**on** sur); ② (enhance) [*light, dress, portrait*] flatter
B *v refl* **to ～ oneself** se flatter (**on being** d'être)

flatterer /'flætərə(r)/ *n* flatteur/-euse *m/f*

flattering /'flætərɪŋ/ *adj* [*remark, portrait etc*] gen flatteur/-euse

flattery /'flætərɪ/ *n* flatterie *f*

(Idiom) **～ will get you nowhere** la flatterie ne mène à rien

flatware /'flætweə(r)/ *n* US (cutlery) couverts *mpl*; (crockery) assiettes *fpl*

flaunt /flɔːnt/ *vtr* péj étaler [*wealth*]; faire étalage de [*charms*]; afficher [*ability, lover*]; exhiber [*possession*]

flautist /'flɔːtɪst/ **▸ p. 1181, p. 1028** *n* flûtiste *mf*

flavour GB, **flavor** US /'fleɪvə(r)/
A *n* ① Culin goût *m*; (subtler) saveur *f*; **coffee ～** au café; **full of ～** plein de saveurs; ② (atmosphere) (of period, place) atmosphère *f*; (hint) idée *f*
B *vtr* ① Culin (improve taste) donner du goût à; (add specific taste) parfumer (**with** à); ② fig assaisonner (**with** de)

(Idiom) **to be ～ of the month**○ [*thing*] être en vogue; [*person*] être la coqueluche du moment

flavour-enhancer GB, **flavor-enhancer** US *n* exhausteur *m* de goût

flavouring GB, **flavoring** US /'fleɪvərɪŋ/ *n* (for sweet taste) parfum *m*; (for meat, fish) assaisonnement *m*

flavourless GB, **flavorless** US /'fleɪvəlɪs/ *adj* insipide

flaw /flɔː/ *n* gen défaut *m*; (in theory) faille *f*

f

flawed /'flɔːd/ adj gen défectueux; [character, person] vicié

flea /fliː/
A n puce f
B noun modifier [collar] antipuce; [powder] antiparasitaire
(Idiom) **to send sb away with a ~ in their ear**○ envoyer promener○ qn

flea: **~-bitten** adj lit infesté de puces; fig miteux/-euse; **~ market** n marché m aux puces; **~pit**○ n GB péj cinéma m miteux

fleck /flek/
A n (of colour) moucheture f; (of light) tache f; (of foam) flocon m; (of blood, paint) petite tache f; (of dust) particule f
B vtr **~ed with** [fabric] moucheté de [colour]; [eye] piqueté de [colour]; tacheté de [paint, light]

fled /fled/ prét, pp ▶ **flee**

fledg(e)ling /'fledʒlɪŋ/
A n Zool oisillon m
B noun modifier fig [party, group] naissant; [democracy, enterprise] jeune

flee /fliː/ (prét, pp **fled**) vtr, vi fuir

fleece /fliːs/
A n (on animal) toison f; **2** Tex molleton m; (for sportswear) laine f polaire; **3** (garment) (vêtement m en laine) polaire f
B ○vtr (overcharge) estamper○; (swindle) plumer○

fleecy /'fliːsɪ/ adj [fabric] laineux/-euse; [clouds] floconneux/-euse

fleet /fliːt/ n **1** (of ships etc) flotte f; (of small vessels) flottille f; **2** (of vehicles) (in reserve) parc m; (on road) convoi m

fleeting /'fliːtɪŋ/ adj [memory, pleasure] fugace; [visit, moment] bref/brève; [glance] rapide

Fleet Street n la presse f (londonienne)

Flemish /'flemɪʃ/ ▶ p. 1032
A n **1** (language) flamand m; **2** **the ~** les Flamands mpl
B adj flamand

flesh /fleʃ/ n **1** (of human, animal) chair f; **2** (of fruit) chair f, pulpe f; **3** fig I'm only ~ **and blood** je ne suis qu'un être humain; **one's own ~ and blood** la chair de sa chair; **in the ~** en chair et en os; **it makes my ~ creep** ça me donne la chair de poule
(Idiom) **to demand one's pound of ~** exiger son dû impitoyablement
(Phrasal verb)
■ **flesh out**: ▶ **~ [sth] out**, **~ out [sth]** étayer [article]

flesh: **~-eating** adj carnivore; **~ wound** n blessure f superficielle

fleshy /'fleʃɪ/ adj [arm, fruit, leaf] charnu

flew /fluː/ prét ▶ **fly**

flex /fleks/
A n GB (for electrical appliance) fil m
B vtr **1** (contract) faire jouer [muscle]; **2** (bend and stretch) fléchir [limb]; plier [finger]

flexibility /,fleksə'bɪlɪtɪ/ n souplesse f, flexibilité f

flexible /'fleksəbl/ adj **1** [arrangement] flexible, souple; [plan, agenda] souple; [repayment plan] à échéances variables; **2** [person] souple (about en ce qui concerne); **3** [tube, wire, stem] flexible, souple

flexible response n Mil riposte f graduée

flexi disc /'fleksɪ dɪsk/ n Audio disque m souple

flexitime /'fleksɪtaɪm/ n horaire m flexible or souple

flick /flɪk/
A n **1** (with finger) chiquenaude f; (with whip, cloth) petit coup m; **2** (movement) gen, Sport petit coup m; **at the ~ of a switch** rien qu'en appuyant sur un bouton
B flicks○ npl cinéma m
C vtr **1** (strike) (with finger) donner une chiquenaude à; (with tail, cloth) donner un petit coup à; **to ~ sth at sb** (with finger) envoyer or lancer qch à qn d'une chiquenaude; **he ~ed his ash onto the floor** il a fait tomber sa cendre par terre; **2** (press) appuyer sur [switch]; **3** Sport donner un petit coup à [ball]
(Phrasal verbs)
■ **flick back**: ▶ **~ [sth] back** rejeter [qch] en arrière [hair]
■ **flick off**: ▶ **~ [sth] off**, **~ off [sth]** (with finger) enlever [qch] d'une chiquenaude; (with tail, cloth) enlever [qch] d'un petit geste

■ **flick over**: ▶ **~ [sth] over**, **~ over [sth]** feuilleter [pages]
■ **flick through**: ▶ **~ through [sth]** feuilleter [book, report]; **to ~ through the channels** TV zapper

flicker /'flɪkə(r)/
A n **1** (unsteady light) **the ~ of a candle** la flamme vacillante d'une bougie; **2** (slight sign) (of interest, anger) lueur f (of de); **3** (movement) (of eyelid) clignement m; (of indicator) oscillation f
B vi **1** (shine unsteadily) [fire, light, flame] vaciller, trembloter; [image] clignoter; **2** (move) [eye, eyelid] cligner
C flickering pres p adj [light, flame] vacillant; [image] tremblant

flick knife n GB couteau m à cran d'arrêt

flier /'flaɪə(r)/ n **1** **a powerful ~** (of bird) un oiseau au vol puissant; **2** (handbill) prospectus m

flight /flaɪt/
A n **1** Aerosp, Aviat (journey) vol m (to vers; from de); **a scheduled ~** un vol régulier; **the ~ from Dublin to London** le vol Dublin-Londres; **we hope you enjoyed your ~** nous espérons que vous avez fait un bon voyage; **we took the next ~ (out)** nous avons pris l'avion suivant; **2** (course) (of bird, insect) vol m; (of missile, bullet) trajectoire f; **3** (locomotion) vol m; **in full ~** lit en plein vol; fig en plein élan; **4** (group) **a ~ of** un vol de, une volée de [birds]; une troupe de [angels]; une volée de [arrows]; **5** (escape) fuite f (from devant); **to take ~** prendre la fuite; **6** (set) **a ~ of steps** une volée de marches; **six ~s (of stairs)** six étages; **four ~s up** au quatrième; **a ~ of** une série de [hurdles]; une série de [locks]; un étagement de [terraces]; **7** (display) **~s of imagination** élans mpl d'imagination; **~s of rhetoric** envolées fpl oratoires; **a ~ of fancy** une invention
B noun modifier [simulator, plan, recorder] de vol
(Idiom) **to be in the top ~** être parmi les meilleurs

flight: **~ attendant** ▶ p. 1181 n Aviat (male) steward m; (female) hôtesse f de l'air; **~ bag** n bagage m à main; **~ deck** n (compartment) Aviat poste m de pilotage; Naut pont m d'envol; **~ engineer** ▶ p. 1181 n mécanicien m navigant; **~ lieutenant** ▶ p. 1123 n Mil capitaine m (de l'armée de l'air); **~ path** n route f de vol; **~-test** vtr essayer [qch] en vol

flighty /'flaɪtɪ/ adj [imagination, mind] écervelé; [partner] volage

flimsy /'flɪmzɪ/ adj [fabric] léger/-ère; [structure] peu solide; [argument, excuse] futile; [evidence] mince, piètre (before n)

flinch /flɪntʃ/ vi (psychologically) hésiter (from doing à faire); (physically) tressaillir; **without ~ing** sans broncher; **to ~ at** tiquer sur [criticism, insult etc]

fling /flɪŋ/
A n **1** ○(spree) bon temps m; **to have a ~** se payer du bon temps; **2** ○(affair) (with person) aventure f; (intellectual) flirt○ m
B vtr (prét, pp **flung**) (throw) lancer [ball, grenade] (onto sur; into dans); lancer [insult] (at à); **to ~ a scarf around one's shoulders** jeter une écharpe sur ses épaules; **to ~ sb to the ground** [person] jeter qn à terre; [blast] projeter qn à terre; **I flung my arms around her neck** je me suis jeté à son cou
C v refl **to ~ oneself** se jeter (across en travers de; over par dessus); **to ~ oneself off sth** sauter de [bridge, cliff]
(Phrasal verbs)
■ **fling about**, **~ around**: ▶ **~ [sth] around** gaspiller [money]
■ **fling away**: ▶ **~ [sth] away** jeter qch
■ **fling back**: ▶ **~ [sth] back**, **~ back [sth]** renvoyer [ball, keys]; rejeter [qch] en arrière [head]; ouvrir [qch] brusquement [door]
■ **fling down**: ▶ **~ [sth] down**, **~ down [sth]** jeter [qch] par terre
■ **fling on**: ▶ **~ on [sth]** enfiler [qch] rapidement [dress, coat]
■ **fling open**: ▶ **~ [sth] open**, **~ open [sth]** ouvrir [qch] brusquement [door]; ouvrir [qch] tout grand [window]

flint /flɪnt/ n **1** (rock) silex m; **2** (primitive tool) éclat m de silex; **3** †(for kindling) pierre f à feu; **4** (in lighter) pierre f à briquet

flintlock n pistolet m à pierre

flip /flɪp/
A n **1** (of finger) chiquenaude f; **to decide sth by the ~ of a**

coin décider qch à pile ou face; **2)** Aviat, Sport (somersault) tour *m*

B *vtr* (*p prés etc* **-pp-**) **1)** (toss) lancer [*coin*]; faire sauter [*pancake*]; **let's ~ a coin to decide** décidons à pile ou face; **2)** (flick) basculer [*switch*]; **to ~ sth open** ouvrir qch rapidement

C *vi* (*p prés etc* **-pp-**) **1)** (get angry) se mettre en rogne○; **2)** (go mad) perdre la boule○; **3)** (get excited) devenir dingue○ (**over** de)

(Idiom) **to ~ one's lid** sortir de ses gonds○

(Phrasal verbs)

■ **flip over:** ▶ ~ **over** [*vehicle, plane*] se retourner (complètement); ▶ ~ **[sth] over**, ~ **over [sth]** retourner [*pancake, coin*]; feuilleter [*pages*]

■ **flip through:** ▶ ~ **through [sth]** feuilleter [*book*]

flipchart *n* tableau *m* de conférence, paperboard *m*

flip-flop /'flɪpflɒp/ *n* **1)** (sandal) tong *f*; **2)** Comput (device) bascule *f*; **3)** US (about-face) volte-face *f inv*

flippant /'flɪpənt/ *adj* (not serious) [*remark, person*] désinvolte; (lacking respect) [*tone, attitude*] cavalier/-ière

flipper /'flɪpə(r)/ *n* **1)** Zool nageoire *f*; **2)** (for swimmer) palme *f*

flipping○ /'flɪpɪŋ/ GB
A *adj* fichu○
B *adv* [*stupid, painful, cold*] drôlement○

flip: ~ **side** *n* Mus (on record) face *f* B; fig (other side) envers *m*; ~**-top** *n* capsule *f* à charnière

flirt /flɜːt/
A *n* (person) flirteur/-euse *m/f*; péj dragueur/-euse○ *m/f* pej
B *vi* flirter; **to ~ with** flirter avec [*person*]; jouer avec [*danger, image*]; caresser [*idea*]

flirtatious /ˌflɜː'teɪʃəs/ *adj* [*person, glance, wink*] charmeur/-euse, dragueur/-euse○ pej; [*laugh*] qui cherche à séduire

flit /flɪt/
A *n* (move) **to do a ~**○ (move house) déménager à la cloche de bois○; (leave) filer à l'anglaise
B *vi* (*p prés etc* **-tt-**) **1)** (also ~ **about**) [*bird, moth*] voleter; **2)** (move quickly) [*person*] aller d'un pas léger; **3)** (flash) **a look of panic ~ted across his face** une expression de panique lui traversa le visage

float /fləʊt/
A *n* **1)** (on net) flotteur *m*; (on line) bouchon *m*; **2)** Aviat flotteur *m*; **3)** (in plumbing) flotteur *m*; **4)** GB (swimmer's aid) planche *f*; US (life jacket) gilet *m* de sauvetage; **5)** (carnival vehicle) char *m*; **6)** (also **cash ~**) (in till) fonds *m* de caisse; **7)** US (drink) soda avec une boule de glace
B *vtr* **1)** [*person*] faire flotter [*boat, logs*]; [*tide*] mettre à flot [*ship*]; **2)** Fin émettre [*shares, securities, loan*]; lancer [qch] en Bourse [*company*]; laisser flotter [*currency*]; **3)** (propose) lancer [*idea, suggestion*]
C *vi* **1)** (on liquid, in air) flotter; **to ~ on one's back** [*swimmer*] faire la planche; **to ~ down the river** descendre la rivière; **the boat was ~ing out to sea** le bateau voguait vers le large; **to ~ up into the air** s'envoler; **2)** fig (waft) [*smoke, mist*] flotter; **to ~ across** [*cloud*] traverser lentement [*sky*]; **music ~ed out into the garden** la musique parvenait dans le jardin; **3)** Fin [*currency*] flotter

(Phrasal verbs)

■ **float about, float around 1)** (circulate) [*idea, rumour*] circuler; **2)** ○(be nearby) **are my keys ~ing around?** mes clés sont-elles par ici?; **3)** ○(aimlessly) [*person*] traîner

■ **float away** = **float off**

■ **float off** [*boat*] dériver; [*balloon*] s'envoler; [*person*] partir d'un pas léger

floating /'fləʊtɪŋ/ *adj* (on water) [*bridge*] flottant; fig (unstable) [*population*] instable

floating: ~ **assets** *npl* Fin actif *m* circulant; ~ **capital** *n* Fin capital *m* disponible, fonds *mpl* de roulement; ~ **rate interest** *n* Fin intérêt *m* à taux flottant *ou* variable; ~ **restaurant** *n* bateau-restaurant *m*; ~ **voter** *n* Pol électeur *m* indécis

flock /flɒk/
A *n* **1)** (of sheep, goats) troupeau *m*; (of birds) volée *f*; (of people) foule *f*; **in ~s** en masse; **2)** ₵ Relig ouailles *fpl*; **3)** (textile) bourre *f*; **4)** (tuft) flocon *m*
B *vi* [*animals, people*] affluer (**around** autour de; **into** dans); **to ~ together** [*people*] s'assembler; [*animals*] se rassembler

floe /fləʊ/ *n* banquise *f*

flog /flɒg/ *vtr* (*p prés etc* **-gg-**) **1)** (beat) flageller; **2)** ○GB (sell) fourguer○, vendre

(Idioms) **to ~ sth to death**○ GB bousiller○ qch; **to ~ a joke to death**○ rabâcher une plaisanterie

flogging /'flɒgɪŋ/ *n* (beating) flagellation *f*

flood /flʌd/
A *n* **1)** lit inondation *f*; '~!' (on roadsign) 'attention, route inondée!'; **in ~** en crue; **2)** fig **a ~ of** un flot de [*people, light, memories*]; un déluge de [*letters, complaints*]; **to be in ~s of tears** verser des torrents de larmes
B *vtr* **1)** lit inonder [*area*]; faire déborder [*river*]; **2)** fig [*light, mail*] inonder; **3)** Comm (over-supply) inonder [*shops*] (**with** de); **4)** Aut noyer [*engine*]
C *vi* **1)** [*meadow, street, cellar*] être inondé; [*river*] déborder; '**road liable to ~ing**' 'chaussée inondable'; **2)** fig **to ~ into sth** [*light*] inonder qch; [*people*] envahir qch; **to ~ over sb** [*emotion*] envahir qn

(Phrasal verbs)

■ **flood back** [*memories*] remonter à la surface.

■ **flood in** [*light etc*] entrer à flots; fig [*people, money*] affluer

■ **flood out:** ▶ ~ **out** [*liquid*] jaillir à flots; ▶ ~ **[sth/sb] out** inonder

flood: ~**bank** *n* berge *f* inondable; ~ **control** *n* prévention *f* des inondations; ~ **damage** *n* dégât *m* des eaux

floodgate /'flʌdgeɪt/ *n* lit vanne *f*; **to open the ~s** fig laisser entrer le flot (**to, for** de)

flood level *n* niveau *m* des eaux

floodlight /'flʌdlaɪt/
A *n* projecteur *m*; **under ~s** Sport en nocturne
B *vtr* (*prét, pp* **floodlit**) illuminer [*building*]; éclairer [*stage*]

flood: ~**mark** *n* indicateur *m* de niveau de crue; ~**plain** *n* plaine *f* inondable; ~ **tide** *n* marée *f* haute; ~**waters** *n* eaux *fpl* d'inondation

floor /flɔː(r)/
A *n* **1)** (of room) (wooden) plancher *m*, parquet *m*; (stone) sol *m*; (of car, lift) plancher *m*; **dance ~** piste *f* de danse; **on the ~** par terre; **to take the ~** [*dancer*] se lancer sur la piste de danse; **2)** (of sea, tunnel, valley) fond *m*; **the forest ~** le tapis forestier; **3)** (of Stock Exchange) parquet *m*; (of debating Chamber) auditoire *m*; (of factory) atelier *m*; **to hold the ~** garder la parole; **4)** (storey) étage *m*; **on the first ~** GB au premier étage; US au rez-de-chaussée; **ground ~, bottom ~** GB rez-de-chaussée *m*; **six ~s up** (on the sixth storey) au sixième étage; (six storeys above this storey) six étages plus haut; **5)** Fin (of prices) plancher *m* (**on** sur)
B *vtr* **1)** **an oak-~ed room** une pièce avec un parquet de chêne; **2)** (knock over) terrasser [*attacker, boxer*]; **3)** fig (silence) réduire [qn] au silence [*person, critic*]; (stump) [*question*] décontenancer [*candidate*]

(Idiom) **to wipe the ~ with sb** battre qn à plates coutures

floor: ~ **area** *n* superficie *f*; ~**board** *n* latte *f*, planche *f* (de plancher); ~ **cloth** *n* serpillière *f*; ~ **covering** *n* revêtement *m* de sol; ~ **exercises** *npl* exercices *mpl* au sol; ~ **lamp** *n* US lampadaire *m*

floor manager ▸ p. 1181 *n* **1)** TV régisseur *m* de plateau; **2)** Comm gérant/-e *m/f* de magasin

floor: ~ **polish** *n* encaustique *f*, cire *f*; ~ **show** *n* spectacle *m* (de cabaret); ~ **space** *n* espace *m* (au sol); ~**walker** *n* US chef *m* de rayon

flop /flɒp/
A *n* ○(failure) fiasco○ *m*
B *vi* (*p prés etc* **-pp-**) **1)** (move heavily) **to ~ down** s'effondrer; **to ~ down on** s'affaler sur [*bed, sofa*]; **2)** (hang loosely) [*hair, ear*] retomber; **3)** ○(fail) [*play, film*] faire un four○; [*project, venture*] être un fiasco○

(Phrasal verbs)

■ **flop out** US (rest) se reposer; (sleep) s'endormir

■ **flop over**○ US: ▶ ~ **over** changer d'avis; ▶ ~ **over to [sth]** adopter [*idea*]

floppy /'flɒpɪ/ *adj* [*ears, hair*] pendant; [*hat*] à bords tombants; [*clothes*] large; [*flesh, body*] mou/molle

floppy disk *n* Comput disquette *f*

flora /'flɔːrə/ *n* (+ *v sg*) flore *f*

floral /'flɔːrəl/ *adj* [*design, fabric*] à fleurs; [*arrangement, art, fragrance*] floral

Florentine /'flɒrəntaɪn/ *adj* florentin

florid /'florid, US 'flɔːr-/ adj **1** (ornate) [writing, style, language] fleuri; **2** (ruddy) [person, face] rougeaud

Florida /'florɪdə/ ▸ p. 1222 pr n Floride f

florist /'florɪst, US 'flɔːrɪst/ ▸ p. 1181 n (person) fleuriste mf; **to go to the ~'s** aller chez le fleuriste

floss /flɒs, US flɔːs/
A n **1** (for embroidery) soie f floche; **2** (for teeth) fil m dentaire
B vtr **to ~ one's teeth** utiliser du fil dentaire

flotation tank /fləʊ'teɪʃn/ n caisson m d'isolation sensorielle

flotsam /'flɒtsəm/ n ¢ épave f flottante

flounce /flaʊns/
A n **1** (movement) mouvement m vif; **2** (frill) volant m
B vi **1** **to ~ in/off** (indignantly) entrer/partir dans un mouvement d'indignation; **2** (also ~ **around**, ~ **about**) se démener

flounder /'flaʊndə(r)/
A n **1** GB flet m; **2** US poisson m plat
B vi **1** (also ~ **about**) [animal, person] se débattre (**in** dans); **2** fig (falter) [speaker] bredouiller; [economy] stagner; [career, company, leader] piétiner

flour /'flaʊə(r)/
A n farine f
B vtr saupoudrer [qch] de farine [cake tin, board]

flourish /'flʌrɪʃ/
A n **1** (gesture) geste m théâtral; **with a ~** [do] de façon théâtrale; **2** (detail, touch) **with a rhetorical ~** ou **an emphatic ~** avec emphase; (in piece of music) **the final ~** le bouquet final; **the opening ~** le brio des premiers accords; **3** (ornamental) (in style) fioriture f
B vtr brandir [ticket, document]
C vi [plant, bacteria] prospérer; [child] s'épanouir; [firm, democracy] prospérer

flourishing /'flʌrɪʃɪŋ/ adj [garden, industry] florissant; [business, town] prospère

floury /'flaʊəri/ adj [hands] couvert de farine; [potato] farineux/-euse

flout /flaʊt/ vtr se moquer de [convention, rules]

flow /fləʊ/
A n **1** (of liquid) écoulement m; (of blood, electricity) circulation f; (of refugees, words) flot m; (of information) circulation f; **in full ~** fig en plein discours; **traffic ~** circulation f; **2** Geog (of tide) flux m
B vi **1** (move) [liquid, gas] couler (**into** dans); **to ~ in/back** affluer/refluer; **to ~ downwards** tomber; **to ~ past sth** passer devant qch; **the river ~s into the sea** le fleuve se jette dans la mer; **2** (be continuous) [conversation, words] couler; [wine, beer] couler à flots; **3** (circulate) [blood, electricity etc] circuler (**through, round** dans); **4** (move gracefully) [hair, dress] flotter; [pen] courir (**across** sur); **5** [tide] monter

flowchart /'fləʊtʃɑːt/ n organigramme m

flower /'flaʊə(r)/
A n **1** (bloom, plant) fleur f; **to be in ~** être en fleur; **in full ~** en pleine floraison; **2** fig **the ~ of** la fine fleur de [age, era, group]; **in the ~ of her youth** dans la fleur de l'âge
B vi lit [flower, tree] fleurir; [love, person, talent] s'épanouir

flower: **~ arrangement** n composition f florale; **~ arranging** n décoration f florale; **~ garden** n jardin m d'agrément

flowering /'flaʊərɪŋ/
A n **1** Bot floraison f (**of** de); **2** fig (development) épanouissement m (**of** de)
B adj [shrub, tree] (producing blooms) à fleurs; (in bloom) en fleurs; **early-/late-~** à floraison précoce/tardive

flower: **~ shop** ▸ p. 1181 n fleuriste m; **~ show** n (large) floralies fpl; (amateur) exposition f florale

flowery /'flaʊəri/ adj [field] fleuri; [fabric] à fleurs; [wine] parfumé; [scent] floral; [speech, style] fleuri

flowing /'fləʊɪŋ/ adj [style, movement] coulant; [rhythm] berceur/-euse; [line] doux/douce; [hair, clothes] flottant

flown /fləʊn/ pp ▸ fly

fl oz abrév écrite = **fluid ounce(s)**

flu /fluː/ ▸ p. 933
A n grippe f; **to come down with ~** attraper une grippe
B noun modifier [victim, virus] de la grippe; [attack, epidemic] de grippe; [vaccine] contre la grippe

fluctuate /'flʌktjʊeɪt/ vi gen, Fin [rate, mood] fluctuer (**between** entre)

flue /fluː/ n (of chimney) conduit m; (of stove, boiler) tuyau m

fluency /'fluːənsɪ/ n (all contexts) aisance f; **sb's ~ in German** l'aisance de qn à s'exprimer en allemand

fluent /'fluːənt/ adj **1** (in language) **her French is ~** elle parle couramment le français; **a ~ Greek speaker** une personne qui parle grec couramment; **in ~ English** dans un anglais parfait; **2** (eloquent) [account, speech, speaker] éloquent; [writer] qui a la plume facile; **3** (graceful) [style] coulant; [movement] fluide

fluff /flʌf/
A n **1** (down) (on clothes) peluche f; (on carpet) poussière f; (under furniture) mouton m, flocon m de poussière; (on animal) duvet m; **2** ○(mistake) gaffe○ f; **3** ○US ¢ (trivia) frivolités fpl
B vtr **1** (also ~ **up**) hérisser [feathers]; faire bouffer [cushion, hair]; **2** ○(get wrong) rater [cue, exam, note]

fluffy /'flʌfɪ/ adj **1** [animal, down] duveteux/-euse; [fur] ébouriffé; [rug, sweater] moelleux/-euse; [hair] bouffant; [toy] en peluche; **2** (light) [mixture] léger/-ère; [egg white, rice] moelleux/-euse

fluid /'fluːɪd/
A n **1** gen, Biol liquide m; **2** Chem, Tech fluide m
B adj **1** gen liquide; Chem, Tech fluide; **2** (flexible) [arrangement, situation] vague; **3** (graceful) [movement, style, lines] fluide

fluid: **~ assets** npl US Fin disponibilités fpl; **~ capital** n US ¢ Fin fonds mpl de roulement; **~ ounce** n once f liquide

fluke /fluːk/ n **1** (lucky chance) coup m de veine○; **by a (sheer) ~** (tout à fait) par hasard; **2** Naut (of anchor) patte f (d'une ancre); (of harpoon, arrow) barbelure f; **3** Zool douve f; **blood ~** douve du sang

fluky, flukey /'fluːkɪ/ adj (lucky) [coincidence] heureux/-euse; [circumstances, goal, shot] dû au hasard; [winner] par hasard

flummox○ /'flʌməks/ vtr sidérer○

flung /flʌŋ/ prét, pp ▸ **fling**

flunk○ /flʌŋk/ vtr US Sch, Univ **1** [student] rater○ [exam]; sécher sur○ [subject]; **2** [teacher] coller○ [class, pupil]

flunkey GB, **flunky** US /'flʌŋkɪ/ n (pl **-eys** GB, **-ies** US) **1** (servant) laquais m; **2** fig, péj larbin m pej

fluorescent /flɔː'resənt, US flʊə'r-/ adj fluorescent

fluoride /'flɔːraɪd, US 'flʊəraɪd/ n fluorure m

fluorine /'flɔːriːn, US 'flʊər-/ n fluor m

flurry /'flʌrɪ/ n **1** (gust) (of rain etc) rafale f; (of leaves) tourbillon m; **2** (bustle) agitation f soudaine; **a ~ of activity** un tourbillon d'activité; **a ~ of interest** un mouvement d'intérêt; **3** (of complaints, enquiries) vague f

flush /flʌʃ/
A n **1** (blush) (on skin) rougeur f; **2** (surge) **a ~ of** un élan de [pleasure, pride]; un accès de [anger, shame]; **to be in the first ~ of youth** être de la première jeunesse; **3** (toilet device) chasse f d'eau; (sound) bruit m de la chasse d'eau; **4** Games (set) floche f
B adj **1** (level) **to be ~ with** être dans l'alignement de [wall]; **2** ○(rich) **to feel ~** se sentir en fonds
C vtr **1** (clean with water) **to ~ the toilet** tirer la chasse (d'eau); **to ~ (out)** nettoyer un tuyau à grande eau; **2** (colour) **to ~ sb's cheeks** empourprer les joues de qn
D vi **1** (redden) rougir (**with** de); **2** (operate) **the toilet doesn't ~** la chasse d'eau ne fonctionne pas

(Phrasal verbs)

■ **flush away**: ▸ ~ [sth] away, ~ away [sth] faire partir [waste]

■ **flush out**: ▸ ~ out [sb/sth] débusquer [sniper, spy]; **to ~ sb/sth out of** faire sortir qn/qch de [shelter]

flushed /flʌʃt/ adj **1** (reddened) [cheeks] rouge (**with** de); **to be ~** avoir les joues rouges; **2** (glowing) **~ with** [person] rayonnant de [pride etc]

fluster /'flʌstə(r)/
A n agitation f
B vtr énerver; **to look ~ed** avoir l'air énervé

flute /fluːt/ ▸ p. 1028 n **1** Mus flûte f; **2** Archit cannelure f; **3** (glass) flûte f

fluted /'fluːtɪd/ adj [collar] tuyauté; [glass, flan tin] à cannelures; [column] cannelé

flutist /'fluːtɪst/ ▸ p. 1181, p. 1028 n US flûtiste mf

flutter /ˈflʌtə(r)/

A n **1** (of wings, lashes) battement m; (of leaves, papers) voltigement m; (of bunting) flottement m; **heart ~** Med palpitations fpl cardiaques; **2** (stir) **a ~ of** un surcroît de [excitement]; **to be all of a ~** GB être tout en émoi; **3** ○GB (bet) **to have a ~ on the horses** faire un petit pari aux courses; **to have a ~ on the Stock Exchange** faire une spéculation à la Bourse; **4** Elec (in sound) pleurage m; **5** Aviat (fault) vibration f

B vtr **1** (beat) **the bird ~ed its wings** l'oiseau battait des ailes; **2** (move) agiter [fan, handkerchief]; **to ~ one's eyelashes** battre des cils

C vi **1** (beat) [bird] battre des ailes; **2** (fly rapidly) voleter; **3** (move rapidly) [flag] flotter; [clothes, curtains, fans] s'agiter; [eyelids, lashes] battre; **4** (also ~ **down**) [leaves] tomber en voltigeant; **5** (beat irregularly) [heart] palpiter (**with** de); [pulse] battre faiblement

flux /flʌks/ n **1** (uncertainty) **in (a state of) ~** dans un état de perpétuel changement; **2** Phys, Med flux m; **3** (for metals) fondant m

fly /flaɪ/

A n **1** Zool mouche f; **2** (of flag) (outer edge) bord m flottant; **3** GB Hist (carriage) fiacre m

B flies npl **1** (of trousers) braguette f; **2** Theat cintres mpl

C ○adj **1** US chic; **2** GB (clever) malin

D vtr (prét **flew**; pp **flown**) **1** (operate) piloter [aircraft, balloon]; faire voler [model aircraft, kite]; **the pilot flew the plane to...** le pilote a emmené l'avion jusqu'à...; **2** (transport by air) emmener [qn] par avion [person]; transporter [qch/qn] par avion [wounded, supplies]; **3** (cross by air) traverser [qch] en avion [Atlantic]; **4** (cover by air) [bird, aircraft] parcourir [distance]; **I ~ over 10,000 km a year** [passenger] je vole plus de 10 000 km par an; [pilot] je fais plus de 10 000 km par an; **5** (display) [ship] arborer [flag]; **the embassy was ~ing the German flag** le drapeau allemand flottait sur l'ambassade

E vi (prét **flew**; pp **flown**) **1** [bird, insect, aircraft, kite] voler (**from** de; **to** à); **to ~ over** ou **across sth** survoler qch; **to ~ over(head)** passer dans le ciel; **to ~ past the window** passer devant la fenêtre (en volant); **to ~ into Gatwick** atterrir à Gatwick; **there's a mosquito ~ing around** il y a un moustique; **2** [passenger] voyager en avion, prendre l'avion; [pilot] piloter, voler; **to ~ from Orly** partir d'Orly; **to ~ from Rome to Athens** aller de Rome à Athènes en avion; **to ~ in Concorde** prendre le Concorde; **we ~ to Boston twice a day** [airline] nous avons deux vols par jour pour Boston; **to ~ out to** s'envoler pour; **3** (be propelled) [bullet, glass, sparks, insults] voler; **a splinter flew into his eye** il a reçu une écharde dans l'œil; **to ~ off** s'envoler; **to ~ open** s'ouvrir brusquement; **to go ~ing**○ [person] faire un vol plané; [object] valdinguer○; **to send sb ~ing**○ jeter qn sur le carreau○; **to ~ into a rage** fig se mettre en colère; [go, hurry] **I must ~!** il faut que je file○! **to ~ past/in** passer/entrer en trombe○; **5** (also ~ **past**, ~ **by**) [time, holidays] passer vite, filer○; **6** (flutter, wave) [flag, scarf, hair] flotter; **to ~ in the wind** flotter au vent

(Idioms) **to drop like flies** tomber comme des mouches; **he wouldn't hurt a ~** il ne ferait pas de mal à une mouche; **there are no flies on her** elle n'est pas née de la dernière pluie; **to ~ in the face of** (defy) [authority, danger, tradition]; (contradict) être en contradiction flagrante avec [evidence]; **to let ~ (with)** lit tirer [arrow etc]; lancer [stream of abuse]; **to let ~ at sb** s'en prendre à qn

(Phrasal verbs)
■ **fly away** lit, fig s'envoler
■ **fly in:** ▸ **~ in** [person] accourir en avion; ▸ **~ [sth/sb] in**, **~ in [sth/sb]** acheminer [qch] par avion [supplies]

fly: **~away** adj [hair] indiscipliné; **~-by-night** adj [company] douteux/-euse; [person] irresponsable; **~catcher** n Zool gobe-mouches m inv; **~-drive** adj Tourism avec formule avion plus voiture

flyer /ˈflaɪə(r)/ n = **flier**

fly: **~-fishing** ▸ p. 881 n pêche f à la mouche; **~-half** n Sport demi m d'ouvertures

flying /ˈflaɪɪŋ/

A n **1** (in plane) **to be afraid of ~** avoir peur de l'avion; **to take up ~** apprendre à piloter; **2** (by bird, animal) vol m; **adapted for ~** adapté au vol

B noun modifier [lesson, instructor, school] de pilotage; [goggles, helmet, jacket] d'aviateur; [suit] de vol

C adj **1** (able to fly) [insect, machine, trapeze] volant; **2** (in pro-

cess of flying) [object, broken glass] qui vole; **3** (as if flying) **to take a ~ leap** sauter avec élan; **4** (fleeting) [visit] éclair inv

(Idiom) **with ~ colours** [pass] haut la main

flying: **~ buttress** n arc-boutant m; **~ doctor** n médecin m volant; **~ picket** n piquet m de grève volant; **~ squad** n brigade f volante

flying start n Sport départ m lancé; **to get off to a ~** fig prendre un très bon départ

fly: **~leaf** n garde f volante; **~-on-the-wall** adj [documentary, programme etc] pris sur le vif

flyover /ˈflaɪəʊvə(r)/ n **1** GB pont m routier; **2** US Aviat défilé m aérien

flypast n GB Aviat défilé m aérien

fly sheet n **1** (of tent) double-toit m; **2** (handbill) prospectus m

fly: **~ spray** n bombe f insecticide; **~ swatter** n tapette f à mouches; **~weight** n poids m mouche

FM n **1** Mil abrév ▸ **field marshal**; **2** Radio (abrév = **frequency modulation**) FM f

FO n GB abrév ▸ **Foreign Office**

foal /fəʊl/ n poulain m; **to be in ~** être pleine

foam /fəʊm/

A n **1** (on sea) écume f; (on drinks, bath) mousse f; **2** (on animal) sueur f; **3** (from mouth) écume f; **4** (chemical) mousse f; **5** (made of rubber, plastic) mousse f

B noun modifier **1** [bath] moussant; **2** [rubber, mattress] mousse

C vi **1** (also ~ **up**) [beer] mousser; [sea] se couvrir d'écume; **to ~ at the mouth** lit écumer; fig écumer de rage; **2** (sweat) [horse] suer

foam-filled adj en mousse

fob /fɒb/ n (pocket) gousset m; (chain) chaîne f

(Phrasal verb)
■ **fob off** (p prés etc **-bb-**): ▸ **~ [sb] off**, **~ off [sb]** se débarrasser de [enquirer, customer]; ▸ **~ off [sth]** rejeter [enquiry]; **to ~ sth off onto sb** refiler qch à qn

FOB adj, adv: abrév ▸ **free on board**

focal /ˈfəʊkl/ adj focal

focal point n **1** (in optics) foyer m; **2** (of village, building) point m de convergence (**of** de; **for** pour); **the room lacks a ~** cette pièce n'a pas de coin qui attire l'œil; **3** (main concern) point m central

focus /ˈfəʊkəs/

A n (pl **~es**, **foci**) **1** (focal point) foyer m; **in ~** au point; **to go out of ~** [device] se dérégler; [image] devenir flou; **to come into ~** se rapprocher de la mise au point; **2** (device on lens) mise f au point; **3** (centre of interest) centre m; **to become a ~ for the press** devenir le centre d'intérêt de la presse; **4** (emphasis) accent m

B vtr (p prés etc **-s-** ou **-ss-**) **1** (direct) concentrer [ray] (**on** sur); fixer [eyes] (**on** sur); **2** (adjust) mettre [qch] au point, régler [lens, camera]; **3** (concentrate) concentrer [mind] (**on** sur)

C vi (p prés etc **-s-** ou **-ss-**) **1** (home in) **to ~ on** [rays] converger sur; [camera] faire le point or la mise au point sur [eyes, attention] se fixer sur; **2** (concentrate) **to ~ on** [report] se concentrer sur

D **focused**, **focussed** pp adj [person] déterminé

fodder /ˈfɒdə(r)/ n (for animals) fourrage m

foe /fəʊ/ n littér ennemi/-e m/f also fig

FoE n: abrév ▸ **Friends of the Earth**

foetus, **fetus** US /ˈfiːtəs/ n fœtus m

fog /fɒg/

A n **1** Meteorol brouillard m; **a patch/blanket of ~** une nappe/un manteau de brouillard; **a ~ of** un nuage épais de [cigarette smoke]; **2** Phot voile m

B vtr (p prés etc **-gg-**) **1** lit (also ~ **up**) [steam] embuer [glass]; [light] voiler [film]; **2** fig (confuse) **to ~ the issue** (unwittingly) embrouiller les choses; (deliberately) noyer le poisson

fog bank n banc m de brume

fogey○ /ˈfəʊgɪ/ n péj vieille baderne f pej

foggy /ˈfɒgɪ/ adj **1** [day, weather] brumeux/-euse; **it will be ~ tomorrow** il y a aura du brouillard demain; **2** fig [idea, notion] confus; **I haven't the foggiest idea**○ je n'en ai pas la moindre idée

foghorn /ˈfɒghɔːn/ n Naut corne f de brume; **like a ~** [voice] de stentor

f

foglamp, foglight n Aut feu m de brouillard

foible /ˈfɔɪbl/ n petite manie f

foil /fɔɪl/
A n ①▸ (for wrapping) papier m d'aluminium; **silver/gold** ~ papier argenté/doré; ②▸ Sport fleuret m; ③▸ (deterrent) repoussoir m
B vtr contrecarrer [person]; déjouer [attempt]

foist /fɔɪst/ vtr (off-load) **to** ~ **sth on sb** repasser qch à qn

fold /fəʊld/
A n ①▸ (crease) (in fabric, paper, skin) pli m; **to hang in soft** ~**s** faire des plis souples; ②▸ Geog repli m; ③▸ (in rock formation) plissement m; ④▸ Agric parc m
B -**fold** combining form **to increase twofold/threefold** doubler/tripler; **the problems are threefold** il y a trois problèmes
C vtr ①▸ (crease) plier [paper, shirt, chair, umbrella]; replier [wings]; ~ **some newspaper around the vases** enveloppe les vases dans du papier journal; ②▸ (intertwine) croiser [arms]; joindre [hands]; **he** ~**ed his arms across his chest** il a croisé les bras; **with her legs** ~**ed under her** les jambes repliées sous elle; ③▸ Culin (add) incorporer (**into** à)
D vi ①▸ [chair] se plier; ②▸ (fail) [play] quitter l'affiche; [company] fermer; [project] échouer; [course] cesser

(Idiom) **to return to the** ~ rentrer au bercail
(Phrasal verbs)
■ **fold away**: ▸ ~ **away** [bed, table] se plier; ▸ ~ **away** [sth], ~ [sth] **away** plier et ranger [clothes, linen]; replier [chair]
■ **fold back**: ▸ ~ **back** [door, shutters] se rabattre (**against** contre); ▸ ~ **back** [sth], ~ [sth] **back** rabattre [shutters, sheet, sleeve]
■ **fold down**: ▸ ~ **down** [seat, pram hood] se rabattre; ▸ ~ [sth] **down**, ~ **down** [sth] replier [collar, flap, sheets]; rabattre [seat, pram hood]
■ **fold in**: ▸ ~ **in** [sth], ~ [sth] **in** incorporer [sugar, flour]
■ **fold out**: ▸ ~ **out** [sth], ~ [sth] **out** déplier [map]
■ **fold over**: ▸ ~ **over** se rabattre; ▸ ~ [sth] **over** rabattre [flap]
■ **fold up**: ▸ ~ **up** [chair, pram, umbrella] se plier; ▸ ~ [sth] **up**, ~ **up** [sth] plier [newspaper, chair, umbrella]

foldaway /ˈfəʊldəweɪ/ adj [bed] escamotable, pliant; [table] pliant

folder /ˈfəʊldə(r)/ n ①▸ (for papers) chemise f; ②▸ (for artwork) carton m; ③▸ (brochure) prospectus m; ④▸ Tech plieuse f, machine f à plier; ⑤▸ Comput dossier m

folding /ˈfəʊldɪŋ/ adj [bed, bicycle, table, umbrella] pliant; [camera] à soufflet; [door] en accordéon

folding: ~ **seat** n strapontin m; ~ **stool** n (siège m) pliant m; ~ **top** n Aut capote f

foldout n encart m

foliage /ˈfəʊlɪdʒ/ n feuillage m

folk /fəʊk/
A n ①▸ (people) (+ v pl) gens mpl; **old/young** ~ les vieux mpl/ jeunes mpl; ②▸ Mus (+ v sg) folk m
B **folks** npl ①▸ °(parents) parents mpl, vieux° mpl; ②▸ °(addressing people) **that's all,** ~**s**°! c'est tout, messieurs-dames°!
C noun modifier ①▸ (traditional) [dance etc] folklorique; ②▸ (modern) [music] folk inv; [club, group] de musique folk; ③▸ [hero] populaire

folk: ~**lore** n folklore m; ~ **medicine** n médecine f traditionnelle; ~ **memory** n mémoire f collective; ~ **wisdom** n (knowledge) savoir m populaire

follow /ˈfɒləʊ/
A vtr ①▸ (move after) suivre [person, car] (**into** dans); **to** ~ **sb in** entrer derrière qn; **she** ~**ed her father into politics** elle est entrée dans la politique comme son père; **they'll** ~ **us on a later flight** ils nous rejoindront par un autre vol; ②▸ (come after in time) suivre [event, item on list]; succéder à [leader]; ~**ed by** suivi de; ③▸ (be guided by) suivre [clue, path, fashion, instinct, instructions]; ④▸ (adhere to) suivre [teachings, example]; pratiquer [religion]; adhérer à [faith, ideas]; être le disciple de [person, leader]; ⑤▸ (watch closely) suivre [stock market, serial, trial]; ⑥▸ (understand) suivre [explanation, reasoning, plot]; **if you** ~ **my meaning** si tu vois ce que je veux dire; ⑦▸ (practise) exercer [trade, profession]; poursuivre [career]; continuer [way of life]
B vi ①▸ (move after) suivre; **she** ~**ed on her bike** elle a suivi en vélo; **to** ~ **in sb's footsteps** suivre les traces de qn;

②▸ (come after in time) suivre; **there** ~**ed a lengthy debate** il s'ensuivit un débat interminable; **there's ice cream to** ~ ensuite il y a de la glace; **the results were as** ~**s** les résultats ont été les suivants; ③▸ (be logical consequence) s'ensuivre; **it** ~**s that** il s'ensuit que; **it doesn't necessarily** ~ **that** ça ne veut pas forcément dire que; **that doesn't** ~ ce n'est pas évident; **that** ~**s** ça me paraît logique; **I don't** ~ (understand) suivre; **I don't** ~ je ne suis pas

(Phrasal verbs)
■ **follow about, follow around**: ▸ ~ [sb] **around** suivre [qn]
■ **follow out** US: ▸ ~ **out** [sth] suivre [orders, instructions, advice]
■ **follow through**: ▸ ~ **through** Sport faire un swing complet; ▸ ~ **through** [sth], ~ [sth] **through** mener [qch] à terme [project]; mettre [qch] à exécution [threat]; aller jusqu'au bout de [idea, theory]
■ **follow up**: ▸ ~ **up** [sth], ~ [sth] **up** ①▸ (reinforce) confirmer [victory, success] (**with** par); consolider [good start] (**with** par); donner suite à [letter, threat] (**with** par); **to** ~ **up with** [boxer] enchaîner avec; ②▸ (act upon, pursue) suivre [story, lead]; donner suite à [complaint, offer, call, article]; examiner [suggestion]; ▸ ~ **up** [sb], ~ [sb] **up** suivre [patient]

follower /ˈfɒləʊə(r)/ n ①▸ (of thinker, artist) disciple m; (of political leader) partisan/-e m/f; (of teachings, tradition) adepte mf; ②▸ (of soap opera, of TV series) fidèle mf; (of team) supporter m; ③▸ (not a leader) suiveur m

following /ˈfɒləʊwɪŋ/
A n ①▸ ₵ (of theorist, religion, cult) adeptes mfpl; (of party, political figure) partisans/-anes mpl/fpl; (of soap opera, show) public m; (of sports team) supporters mpl; ②▸ (before list or explanation) **you will need the** ~ vous aurez besoin des choses suivantes; **the** ~ **is a guide to...** ce qui suit est un guide sur...
B adj (tjrs épith) ①▸ (next) [year, article, remark] suivant (after n); ②▸ (from the rear) [wind] arrière
C prep suite à, à la suite de [incident, allegation]

follow-on /ˈfɒləʊˈɒn/ n suite f

follow-up /ˈfɒləʊʌp/
A n ①▸ (film, record, single, programme) suite f (**to** à); ②▸ (of patient, socialwork case) suivi m
B noun modifier ①▸ (supplementary) [survey, work] de suivi; [interview, check] de contrôle; [discussion, article, programme, meeting] complémentaire; [letter] de rappel; ②▸ (of patient, ex-inmate) [visit] de contrôle

folly /ˈfɒlɪ/ n ①▸ (madness) folie f; ②▸ Archit folie f

foment /fəʊˈment/ vtr Med, fig fomenter

fond /fɒnd/ adj ①▸ (loving) [gesture, person] affectueux/-euse; [eyes, heart] tendre; ~ **memories** de très bons souvenirs; **'with** ~**est love, Julie'** 'je t'embrasse affectueusement, Julie'; ②▸ (heartfelt) [wish, ambition] cher/chère; ③▸ (naive) **in the** ~ **hope that** bercé par la conviction que; ④▸ (partial) **to be** ~ **of sb** aimer beaucoup qn; **to be** ~ **of sth** aimer qch; **to be very** ~ **of sb/sth** adorer qn/qch; ⑤▸ (irritatingly prone) **to be** ~ **of doing** aimer bien faire

fondle /ˈfɒndl/ vtr caresser

fondness /ˈfɒndnɪs/ n ①▸ (love) (for person) tendresse f (**for** pour); (for thing, activity) passion f (**for** pour); ②▸ (irritating penchant) tendance f (**for doing** à faire)

font /fɒnt/ n ①▸ Relig fonts mpl baptismaux; ②▸ (in printing) fonte f; ③▸ Comput police f de caractères

food /fuːd/
A n ①▸ (sustenance) nourriture f, alimentation f; ②▸ ₵ (foodstuffs) aliments mpl; **frozen** ~ aliments surgelés; ③▸ ₵ (provisions) provisions fpl; ④▸ (cuisine, cooking) cuisine f; **is the** ~ **good in Japan?** on mange bien au Japon?; **to be a lover of good** ~ être gourmet; **to like one's** ~ avoir bon appétit; ⑤▸ (fuel) **that's** ~ **for thought** ça donne à réfléchir
B noun modifier [additive, industry, product] alimentaire; [production] d'aliments; [shop] d'alimentation

food: **Food and Drug Administration, FDA** n US organisme gouvernemental de contrôle pharmaceutique et alimentaire; ~ **parcel** n colis m de vivres; ~ **poisoning** n intoxication f alimentaire; ~ **processor** n robot m ménager; ~ **science** n diététique f; ~**stuff** n denrée f alimentaire

fool /fuːl/
A n ①▸ (silly person) idiot/-e m/f (**to do** de faire); **you stupid** ~°! espèce d'idiot/-e!; **to make sb look a** ~ faire passer qn pour un/-e idiot/-e; ~ **enough to agree** assez stupide pour

accepter; **she's no ∼** elle n'est pas si bête; **any ∼ could do that**[○] le premier imbécile venu pourrait faire ça[○]; **to act ou play the ∼** faire l'imbécile, faire le pitre; **2** Hist (jester) fou m; **3** GB Culin **fruit ∼** crème f aux fruits

B [○]*noun modifier* US [*politician*] idiot; **that's a ∼ thing to do** c'est vraiment stupide de faire ça

C *vtr* tromper, duper; **don't let that ∼ you!** ne t'y trompe pas!; **who are you trying to ∼?** à qui veux-tu faire croire ça?; **you don't ∼ me for a minute** je ne te crois pas un seul instant; **to ∼ sb into believing that...** faire croire à qn que...; **to be ∼ed** se laisser abuser (**by** par); **you really had me ∼ed!** tu m'as vraiment fait marcher[○]!

(Idioms) **a ∼ and his money are soon parted** Prov aux idiots l'argent file entre les doigts; **you could have ∼ed me**[○]! tu m'en diras tant[○]!

(Phrasal verb)

■ **fool about**[○] GB, **fool around**[○] GB (waste time) perdre son temps; (act stupidly) faire l'imbécile

foolhardy /ˈfuːlhɑːdɪ/ *adj* téméraire

foolish /ˈfuːlɪʃ/ *adj* **1** [*person*] bête (**to do** de faire); **2** [*grin, expression*] stupide; **to feel ∼** se sentir ridicule; **to make sb look ∼** ridiculiser qn; **3** (*misguided*) [*decision, question, remark*] idiot

foolproof /ˈfuːlpruːf/ *adj* **1** [*method, plan*] infaillible; **2** [*machine*] d'utilisation très simple

foolscap /ˈfuːlskæp/ *n* GB (paper) papier m ministre

foot /fʊt/ ▸ p. 698, p. 977

A *n* (*pl* **feet**) **1** gen, Anat (of person, horse) pied m; (of rabbit, cat, dog, cow) patte f; (of sock, chair) pied m; **on ∼** à pied; **soft under ∼** doux/douce sous le pied; **to set ∼ in** mettre les pieds dans; **from head to ∼** de la tête aux pieds; **to help sb to their feet** aider qn à se lever; **her speech brought the audience to its feet** toute l'audience s'est levée pour applaudir son discours; **to get sb/sth back on their/its feet** (after setback) remettre qn/qch sur pied; **bound hand and ∼** pieds et poings liés; **to wait on sb hand and ∼** faire tout pour qn; **to put one's ∼ down** (accelerate) appuyer sur l'accélérateur; (act firmly) mettre le holà; **2** (measurement) pied m (anglais) (= 0,3048 m); **3** (bottom) (of mountain) pied m (**of** de); **at the ∼ of** au pied de [*bed*]; à la fin de [*list, letter*]; en bas de [*page, stairs*]; en bout de [*table*]; **4** (in sewing) pied m

B *vtr* **to ∼ the bill** payer la facture (**for** pour)

(Idioms) **not to put a ∼ wrong** ne pas commettre la moindre erreur; **under sb's feet** fig dans les jambes de qn; **rushed off one's feet** débordé; **to catch sb on the wrong ∼** prendre qn au dépourvu; **to cut the ground from under sb's feet** couper l'herbe sous les pieds de qn; **to fall on one's feet** fig retomber sur ses pieds; **to keep one's feet on the ground** avoir les pieds sur terre; **to have two left feet** être maladroit; **to put one's best ∼ forward** (do one's best) faire de son mieux; (hurry) se dépêcher; **to put one's ∼ in it**[○] faire une gaffe; **to put one's feet up** se reposer, décompresser[○]; **to stand on one's own (two) feet** se débrouiller tout seul; **to get off on the wrong/right ∼** mal/bien commencer

footage /ˈfʊtɪdʒ/ *n* **Ȼ** Cin (piece of film) film m, pellicule f; **news ∼** des informations filmées

foot and mouth (disease) *n* fièvre f aphteuse

football /ˈfʊtbɔːl/ ▸ p. 881 *n* **1** (game) GB football m; US football m américain; **2** (ball) ballon m de football

football coupon *n* GB bulletin m de (participation au) loto sportif

footballer ▸ p. 1181 *n* GB joueur/-euse m/f de football

football pools *npl* GB ≈ loto m sportif (*limité aux matchs de football*)

foot: **∼bath** *n* (at home) bain m de pieds; (at pool) pédiluve m; **∼ brake** *n* Aut frein m (à pied); **∼bridge** *n* passerelle f; **∼fall** *n* (bruit m de) pas m; **∼hills** *npl* contreforts *mpl*

foothold /ˈfʊthəʊld/ *n* lit prise f (de pied); **to gain a ∼** fig [*company*] prendre pied; [*ideology*] s'imposer; [*plant, insect*] se propager

footing /ˈfʊtɪŋ/ *n* **1** (basis) **on a firm ∼** sur une base solide; **on a war ∼** sur le pied de guerre; **to put sth on a legal ∼** légaliser qch; **to be on an equal ou even ∼ with sb**

être sur un pied d'égalité avec qn; **2** (grip for feet) **to lose one's ∼** perdre pied

footlights /ˈfʊtlaɪts/ *npl* Theat rampe f

footloose /ˈfʊtluːs/ *adj* libre comme l'air

(Idiom) **∼ and fancy free** sans attache

foot: **∼mark** *n* trace f (de pas); **∼note** *n* lit note f de bas de page; fig (additional comment) post-scriptum m; **∼ passenger** *n* passager m sans véhicule; **∼path** *n* (in countryside) sentier m; (in town) trottoir m; **∼print** *n* empreinte f (de pied); **∼rest** *n* repose-pied m

footsore /ˈfʊtsɔː(r)/ *adj* **to be ∼** avoir mal aux pieds

footstep /ˈfʊtstep/ *n* pas m

(Idiom) **to follow in sb's ∼s** suivre les traces de qn

foot: **∼stool** *n* repose-pied m; **∼wear** *n* **Ȼ** chaussures *fpl*

for /fə(r), fɔː(r)/

A *prep* **1** (intended to be used or belong to) pour; **who are the flowers ∼?** pour qui sont les fleurs?; **to buy sth ∼ sb** acheter qch pour or à qn; **∼ young people** pour les jeunes; **keep some pancakes ∼ us!** garde-nous des crêpes!; **not ∼ me thanks** pas pour moi merci; **2** (intended to help or benefit) pour; **to do sth ∼ sb** faire qch pour qn; **he cooked dinner ∼ us** il nous a préparé à manger; **3** (indicating purpose) pour; **what's it ∼?** c'est pour quoi faire?, ça sert à quoi?; **it's ∼ removing stains** c'est pour enlever les taches; **it's not ∼ cleaning windows** ce n'est pas fait pour nettoyer les vitres; **'I need sth'—'what ∼'** 'j'en ai besoin'—'pourquoi?'; **what did you say that ∼?** pourquoi as-tu dit cela?; **to do sth ∼ a laugh** faire qch pour rigoler[○]; **to go ∼ a swim** aller nager; **I need something ∼ my cough** j'ai besoin de quelque chose contre la toux; **I sent it away ∼ cleaning** je l'ai renvoyé pour qu'il soit nettoyé; **the bell rang ∼ class to begin** la cloche a sonné pour indiquer le début du cours; **the idea was ∼ you to work it out yourself** le but était que tu trouves (*subj*) la réponse tout seul; **4** (as member, employee of) [*work, play*] pour; (as representative) [*MP, Minister*] de; **5** (indicating cause or reason) pour; **the reason ∼ doing** la raison pour laquelle on fait; **∼ this reason, I'd rather...** pour cette raison je préfère...; **grounds ∼ divorce** des motifs de divorce; **to jump ∼ joy** sauter de joie; **imprisoned ∼ murder** emprisonné pour meurtre; **she's been criticized ∼ her views** on lui a reproché ses opinions; **I was unable to sleep ∼ the noise** je ne pouvais pas dormir à cause du bruit; **if it weren't ∼ her...** sans elle...; **she is annoyed with me ∼ contradicting her** elle m'en veut parce que je l'ai contredite; **6** (indicating consequence) pour que (+ *subj*); **I haven't the patience ∼ sewing** je n'ai pas la patience qu'il faut pour coudre; **there's not enough time ∼ us to have a drink** nous n'avons pas le temps de prendre un verre; **7** (indicating person's attitude) pour; **to be easy ∼ sb to do** être facile pour qn de faire; **the film was too earnest ∼ me** le film était trop sérieux pour moi; **living in London is not ∼ me** je ne suis pas fait pour vivre à Londres; **8** (stressing particular feature) pour; **∼ further information write to...** pour plus de renseignements écrivez à...; **I buy it ∼ flavour** je l'achète pour le goût; **9** (considering) pour; **to be mature ∼ one's age** être mûr pour son âge; **10** (towards) pour; **to have respect ∼ sb** avoir du respect pour qn; **to feel sorry ∼ sb** avoir de la peine pour qn; **to feel contempt ∼ sb** mépriser qn; **11** (on behalf of) pour; **to be pleased ∼ sb** être content pour qn; **say hello to him ∼ me** dis-lui bonjour de ma part; **I can't do it ∼ you** je ne peux pas le faire à ta place; **let her answer ∼ herself** laisse-la répondre elle-même; **I speak ∼ everyone here** je parle au nom de toutes les personnes ici présentes; **12** (as regards) **she's a great one ∼ jokes** on peut toujours compter sur elle pour raconter des blagues; **to be all right ∼ money** avoir assez d'argent; **13** (taking account of past events) depuis; (stressing expected duration) pour; (stressing actual duration) pendant; **this is the best show I've seen ∼ years** c'est le meilleur spectacle que j'aie vu depuis des années; **we've been together ∼ 2 years** ça fait 2 ans que nous sommes ensemble; **she's off to Paris ∼ the weekend** elle va à Paris pour le week-end; **will he be away ∼ long?** est-ce qu'il sera absent longtemps?; **to stay ∼ a year** rester un an; **to be away ∼ a year** être absent pendant un an; **I was in Paris ∼ 2 weeks** j'étais à Paris pendant 2 semaines; **to last ∼ hours** durer des heures; **14** (indicating a deadline) pour; (in negative constructions) avant; **it will be ready ∼ Saturday** ça sera prêt pour samedi; **the car**

for

When *for* is used as a preposition, followed by a noun or pronoun, it is translated by *pour*:

for my sister
= pour ma sœur

for the garden
= pour le jardin

for me
= pour moi

For particular usages see the entry **for**.

When *for* is used as a preposition indicating purpose followed by a verb it is translated by *pour* + infinitive:

for cleaning windows
= pour nettoyer les vitres

When *for* is used in the construction

to be + adjective + *for* + pronoun + infinitive the translation in French is

être + indirect pronoun + adjective + *de* + infinitive:

it's impossible for me to stay
= il m'est impossible de rester

it was hard for him to understand that ...
= il lui était difficile de comprendre que ...

it will be difficult for her to accept the changes
= il lui sera difficile d'accepter les changements

For the construction *to be waiting for sb to do* see the entry **wait**.

For particular usages see the entry **for**.

··

In time expressions

for is used in English after a verb in the progressive present perfect tense to express the time period of something that started in the past and is still going on. To express this French uses a verb in the present tense + *depuis*:

I have been waiting for three hours (and I am still waiting)
= j'attends depuis trois heures

we've been together for two years (and we're still together)
= nous sommes ensemble depuis deux ans

When *for* is used in English after a verb in the past perfect tense, French uses the imperfect + *depuis*:

I had been waiting for two hours (and was still waiting)
= j'attendais depuis deux heures

for is used in English negative sentences with the present perfect tense to express the time that has elapsed since something has happened. To express this, French uses the same tense as English (the perfect) + *depuis*:

I haven't seen him for ten years (and I still haven't seen him)
= je ne l'ai pas vu depuis dix ans

In spoken French, there is another way of expressing this: *ça fait* or *il y a dix ans que je ne l'ai pas vu*.

When *for* is used in English in negative sentences after a verb in the past perfect tense, French uses the past perfect + *depuis*:

I hadn't seen him for ten years
= je ne l'avais pas vu depuis dix ans,
  or (in spoken French) ça faisait
  or il y avait dix ans que je ne l'avais pas vu

for is used in English after the preterite to express the time period of something that happened in the past and is no longer going on. Here French uses the present perfect + *pendant*:

last Sunday I gardened for two hours
= dimanche dernier, j'ai jardiné pendant deux heures

for is used in English after the present progressive tense or the future tense to express an anticipated time period in the future. Here French uses the present or the future tense + *pour*:

I'm going to Rome for six weeks
= je vais à Rome pour six semaines

I will go to Rome for six weeks
= j'irai à Rome pour six semaines

Note, however, that when the verb *to be* is used in the future with *for* to emphasize the period of time, French uses the future + *pendant*:

I will be in Rome for six weeks
= je serai à Rome pendant six semaines

he will be away for three days
= il sera absent pendant trois jours

For particular usages see **A 13, 14, 15** and **16** in the entry **for**.

for is often used in English to form a structure with nouns, adjectives and verbs (*weakness for, eager for, apply for, fend for* etc.). For translations, consult the appropriate noun, adjective or verb entry (**weakness, eager, apply, fend** etc.).

won't be ready ~ another 6 weeks la voiture ne sera pas prête avant 6 semaines; [15] (on the occasion of) pour; **invited ~ Easter** invité pour Pâques; [16] (indicating scheduled time) pour; **scheduled ~ next month** prévu pour le mois prochain; **I have an appointment ~ 4 pm** j'ai rendez-vous à 16h 00; **it's time ~ bed** c'est l'heure d'aller au lit; [17] (indicating distance) pendant; **to drive ~ miles** rouler pendant des kilomètres; **the last shop ~ 30 miles** le dernier magasin avant 50 kilomètres; [18] (indicating destination) pour; **a ticket ~ Dublin** un billet pour Dublin; **to leave ~ work** partir travailler; **to swim ~ the shore** nager vers la rive; [19] (indicating cost, value) pour; **it was sold ~ £100** ça s'est vendu (pour) 100 livres sterling; **I wouldn't do it ~ anything!** je ne le ferais pour rien au monde!; **I'll let you have it ~ £20** je vous le laisse à 20 livres sterling; **a cheque ~ £20** un chèque de 20 livres sterling; [20] (in favour of) **to be ~** être pour [*peace, divorce, reunification*]; **to be all ~ it** être tout à fait pour; **who's ~ a game of football?** qui veut jouer au football?; [21] (stressing appropriateness) **she's the person ~ the job** elle est la personne qu'il faut pour le travail; **that's ~ us to decide** c'est à nous de décider; [22] (in support

of) en faveur de; **the argument ~ recycling** l'argument en faveur du recyclage; **there's no evidence ~ that** ce n'est absolument pas prouvé; [23] (indicating availability) **~ sale** à vendre; [24] (as part of ratio) pour; **one teacher ~ five pupils** un professeur pour cinq élèves; [25] (equivalent to) **T ~ Tom** T comme Tom; **what's the French ~ 'boot'?** comment dit-on 'boot' en français?; **the technical term ~ it is 'chloasma'** 'chloasme' c'est le terme technique; [26] (in explanations) **~ one thing... and ~ another...** premièrement... et deuxièmement...; **I, ~ one, agree with her** en tout cas moi, je suis d'accord avec elle; [27] (when introducing clauses) **it would be unwise ~ us to generalize** il serait imprudent pour nous de généraliser; **the best thing would be ~ them to leave** le mieux serait qu'ils s'en aillent; **there's no need ~ people to get upset** il n'y a pas de quoi s'énerver

B *conj* sout car, parce que

(Idioms) **oh ~ a nice hot bath!** je rêve d'un bon bain chaud!; **I'll be (in) ~ it if...**° GB ça va être ma fête si...°; **that's adolescents ~ you!** que voulez-vous, c'est ça les adolescents!; **there's gratitude ~ you!** c'est comme ça qu'on me/vous etc remercie!

forage /ˈfɒrɪdʒ, US ˈfɔːr-/
A n ① (animal feed) fourrage m; ② (search) **to go on a ~ for** aller faire provision de [food, wood]
B vtr affourager [animals]
C vi **to ~ (about** ou **around) for** lit, fig fouiller pour trouver

foray /ˈfɒreɪ, US ˈfɔːreɪ/ n gen, Mil incursion f (**into** dans); **to make a ~ into** s'essayer à [politics, acting, sport]; Mil faire une incursion dans [territory]

forbad(e) /fɔːˈbæd, US fəˈbeɪd/ prét ▸ **forbid**

forbear /fɔːˈbeə(r)/ vi (prét **-bore**; pp **-borne**) sout s'abstenir (**from** de; **from doing, to do** de faire)

forbid /fəˈbɪd/ vtr (p prés **-dd-**; prét **-bad(e)**; pp **-bidden**) ① (disallow) défendre, interdire; **~ sb to do** défendre or interdire à qn de faire; **~ sb sth** défendre or interdire qch à qn; ② (prevent, preclude) interdire; **God ~!** Dieu m'en/l'en etc garde!; **God ~ she should do that!** pourvu qu'elle ne fasse pas cela!

forbidden /fəˈbɪdn/ adj [subject, fruit] défendu; [place] interdit; **smoking is ~** il est interdit de fumer

forbidding /fəˈbɪdɪŋ/ adj [edifice] intimidant; [landscape] inhospitalier/-ière; [expression] rébarbatif/-ive

forbore /fɔːˈbɔː(r)/ prét ▸ **forbear**

forborne /fɔːˈbɔːn/ pp ▸ **forbear**

force /fɔːs/
A n ① (of blow, explosion, collision) force f; (of fall) choc m; **by the ~ of the blast** sous la force de l'explosion; ② gen, Mil force f; **by ~** par la force; **by ~ of arms** à la force des armes; ③ fig force f; **from ~ of habit/of circumstance** par la force de l'habitude/des circonstances; ④ (influence) force f; **a ~ for good** une force agissant pour le bien; **a world ~** une puissance mondiale; ⑤ **⊄** (organized group) forces fpl; **expeditionary ~** forces expéditionnaires; ⑥ (also **Force**) (police) **the ~** la police; ⑦ Phys force f; **centrifugal ~** force centrifuge; **~ of gravity** pesanteur f; ⑧ Meteorol force f; **a ~ 10 gale** un vent de force 10
B forces npl Mil (also **armed ~s**) **the ~s** les forces fpl armées
C in force adv phr ① (in large numbers, strength) en force; ② gen, Jur [law, prices, ban] en vigueur
D vtr ① (compel, oblige) forcer (**to do** à faire); **to be ~d to do** ou **into doing** gen être forcé de faire; **the earthquake ~d the evacuation** le tremblement de terre a provoqué l'évacuation; ② (push) **to ~ one's way through** [sth] se frayer un chemin à travers or dans [crowd, jungle]; **to ~ sb up against sth** plaquer qn contre qch; **to ~d him to his knees** elle l'a forcé à se mettre à genoux; ③ (apply great pressure to) forcer [door, window, safe]; forcer sur [screw]; **to ~ an entry** Jur entrer par effraction; ④ Agric forcer [plant]; engraisser [animal]
E v refl ① (push oneself) **to ~ oneself** se forcer (**to do** à faire); ② (impose oneself) **I wouldn't want to ~ myself on you** je ne cherche pas à m'imposer

(Idiom) **to ~ sb's hand** forcer la main à qn

(Phrasal verbs)
■ **force back**: ▸ **~ [sth] back, ~ back [sth]** ① lit repousser [crowd, army]; ② fig réprimer [tears]
■ **force down**: ▸ **~ [sth] down, ~ down [sth]** ① (cause to land) forcer [qch] à se poser [aircraft]; ② (eat reluctantly) se forcer à avaler [food]; **to ~ sth down sb** forcer qn à manger qch; ③ (reduce) diminuer [qch] (de force) [prices, wages]; réduire [qch] (de force) [value, profits, inflation]; **to ~ down unemployment** faire baisser le taux de chômage; ④ (squash) tasser [contents, objects]
■ **force in**: ▸ **~ [sth] in, ~ in [sth]** gen faire entrer [qch] de force; (into small opening) enfoncer [qch] de force
■ **force on**: ▸ **~ [sth] on sb** imposer [qch] à qn, forcer qn à accepter [qch]; **the decision was ~d on him** il a été forcé de prendre cette décision
■ **force open**: ▸ **~ [sth] open, ~ open [sth]** forcer [door, window, box, safe]
■ **force out**: ▸ **~ [sth] out, ~ out [sth]** faire sortir [qch] par la force [enemy, object]; enlever [qch] de force [cork]; **~ one's way out (of sth)** s'échapper (de qch) par la force; **to ~ sth out of sb** arracher qch à qn [information, apology, smile, confession]
■ **force through**: ▸ **~ [sth] through, ~ through [sth]** faire adopter [legislation, measures]
■ **force up**: ▸ **~ [sth] up, ~ up [sth]** [situation] faire augmenter [prices, demand, unemployment]; [company] augmenter (de force) [output]; relever [exchange rate]

forced /fɔːst/ adj (all contexts) forcé

force-feed vtr (prét, pp **-fed**) gaver [animal, bird] (**on, with** de); alimenter [qn] de force

forceful /ˈfɔːsfl/ adj [person, behaviour] énergique; [attack, defence, speech] vigoureux/-euse

forcibly /ˈfɔːsəblɪ/ adv [restrain, repatriate] de force

forcing house n Bot forcerie f; fig pépinière f

ford /fɔːd/
A n gué m
B vtr **to ~ a river** passer une rivière à gué

fore /fɔː(r)/
A n **to the ~** en vue, en avant; fig **to come to the ~** [person] se faire connaître; [issue] attirer l'attention; [quality] ressortir; [team, party, competitor] commencer à dominer
B excl (in golf) gare!

forearm /ˈfɔːrɑːm/ n avant-bras m inv

forebears /ˈfɔːbeəz/ npl sout aïeux mpl

foreboding /fɔːˈbəʊdɪŋ/ n pressentiment m; **to have ~s about** avoir de sombres pressentiments quant à

forecast /ˈfɔːkɑːst, US -kæst/
A n ① (also **weather ~**) météo○ f; bulletin m météorologique; ② Comm, Econ, Fin prévisions fpl; ③ (in horseracing) **a (racing) ~** pronostics mpl des courses; ④ gen (outlook) pronostics mpl
B vtr (prét, pp **-cast**) (all contexts) prévoir (**that** que); **sunshine is forecast for tomorrow** on prévoit du soleil pour demain; **investment is forecast to fall** on prévoit une chute de l'investissement

forecaster /ˈfɔːkɑːstə(r), US -kæst-/ n ① (of weather) spécialiste mf de la météorologie; ② (economic) conjoncturiste mf; ③ gen, Sport pronostiqueur/-euse m/f

forecastle, fo'c'sle /ˈfəʊksl/ n poste m d'équipage

foreclose /fɔːˈkləʊz/ vtr sout ① Fin, Jur saisir [mortgage, loan]; ② (remove) exclure [possibility]

forecourt /ˈfɔːkɔːt/ n ① GB (of shop) parking m; (of garage) aire f de stationnement; ② Rail (of station) cour f de la gare; ③ (of church) ≈ parvis m; (of castle) avant-cour f

forefathers /ˈfɔːfɑːðəz/ npl ancêtres mpl

forefinger /ˈfɔːfɪŋgə(r)/ n index m

forefront /ˈfɔːfrʌnt/ n **at** ou **in the ~ of** à la pointe de [change, research, debate]; au premier plan de [campaign, struggle]; **it's in the ~ of my mind** c'est ma première préoccupation

forego vtr = **forgo**

foregone /ˈfɔːgɒn, US -gɔːn/ adj **it is/was a ~ conclusion** c'est/c'était couru d'avance

fore: **~ground** n premier plan m; **~hand** n Sport coup m droit; **~head** n front m

foreign /ˈfɒrən, US ˈfɔːr-/ adj ① [country, imports, company] étranger/-ère; [market] extérieur; [trade, travel] à l'étranger; ② (alien) [concept] étranger/-ère (**to** à)

foreign: **~ affairs** npl affaires fpl étrangères; **Foreign and Commonwealth Office, FCO** n GB = **Foreign Office**; **~ body** n corps m étranger; **~ correspondent** ▸ p. 1181 n correspondant/-e m/f à l'étranger

foreigner /ˈfɒrənə(r)/ n étranger/-ère m/f

foreign: **~ exchange dealer** ▸ p. 1181 n cambiste m, courtier/-ière m/f en devises; **~ exchange market** n marché m des changes; **~ legion** n légion f étrangère; **~ minister**, **~ secretary** GB n ministre m des Affaires étrangères; **Foreign Office, FO** n GB ministère m des Affaires étrangères

foreleg /ˈfɔːleg/ n patte f avant; (of horse) (membre m) antérieur m

foreman /ˈfɔːmən/ ▸ p. 1181 n ① (supervisor) contremaître m; ② Jur président m (d'un jury)

foremost /ˈfɔːməʊst/
A adj plus grand; **we have many problems, ~ among these are...** nous avons beaucoup de problèmes, les premiers d'entre eux sont...
B adv **first and ~** avant tout

forename /ˈfɔːneɪm/ n prénom m

forensic /fəˈrensɪk, US -zɪk/
A forensics npl US (public speaking) art m oratoire
B adj ① (in crime detection) **~ tests** expertises fpl médico-légales; **~ evidence** résultats mpl des expertises médico-légales; ② (in debate) sout [skill, eloquence] consommé; [attack] dévastateur/-trice

forensic: ∼ **medicine**, ∼ **science** n médecine f légale; ∼ **scientist** ▸ p. 1181 n médecin m légiste

forerunner /'fɔːrʌnə(r)/ n ① (predecessor) (person) précurseur m; (institution, invention, model) ancêtre m; ② (sign) signe m avant-coureur

foresee /fɔː'siː/ vtr (prét **-saw**; pp **-seen**) prévoir

foreseeable /fɔː'siːəbl/ adj prévisible (**that** que); **for the** ∼ **future** dans l'immédiat

foreshadow /fɔː'ʃædəʊ/ vtr annoncer

foreshore /'fɔːʃɔː(r)/ n laisse f de mer

foresight /'fɔːsaɪt/ n prévoyance f (**to do** de faire)

foreskin /'fɔːskɪn/ n Anat gen prépuce m; (of horse) fourreau m

forest /'fɒrɪst, US 'fɔːr-/ n forêt f

forestall /fɔː'stɔːl/ vtr empêcher [action, event, discussion]; prévenir [person]

forested /'fɒrɪstɪd, US 'fɔːr-/ adj boisé

forester /'fɒrɪstə(r), US 'fɔːr-/ n forestier/-ière m/f

forest: ∼ **fire** n incendie m de forêt; ∼ **ranger** n US forestier m

forestry /'fɒrɪstrɪ, US 'fɔːr-/ n (science) sylviculture f; (industry) exploitation f des forêts

Forestry Commission n GB l'office britannique des forêts

foretaste /'fɔːteɪst/ n avant-goût m (**of** de)

foretell /fɔː'tel/ vtr (prét, pp **-told**) prédire

forethought /'fɔːθɔːt/ n prévoyance f

forever /fə'revə(r)/ adv ① (also **for ever**) pour toujours; **it can't go on** ou **last** ∼ [situation, trend, success] ça ne peut pas toujours durer; ∼ **after(wards)** pour toujours; **the desert seemed to go on** ∼ le désert semblait ne pas avoir de limites; ② (persistently) **to be** ∼ **doing sth** faire qch sans arrêt; ③ °(also **for ever**) (ages) **to take** ∼ [task] prendre un temps fou°; [person] mettre un temps fou° (**to do** pour faire); **to go on** ∼ [pain, noise] durer une éternité; ④ (always) toujours; ∼ **on the brink of doing** toujours sur le point de faire

forevermore /fə,revə'mɔː(r)/ adv pour toujours

forewarn /fɔː'wɔːn/ vtr avertir (**of** de; **that** que)

(Idiom) ∼ed is forearmed Prov un homme averti en vaut deux Prov

foreword /'fɔːwɜːd/ n avant-propos m inv

forfeit /'fɔːfɪt/
A n ① (action, process) confiscation f (**of** de); ② (sum, token) gage m; ③ (in game) gage m; ④ Jur, Comm (fine) amende f; (for breach of contract) dédit m
B adj **to be** ∼ sout [property] être confiscable (**to** au profit de)
C vtr ① (under duress) perdre [right, liberty]; ② (voluntarily) renoncer à [right]; ③ Jur, Comm verser [sum]

forfeiture /'fɔːfɪtʃə(r)/ n (of property) confiscation f; (of right) déchéance f

forgave /fə'geɪv/ prét ▸ **forgive**

forge /fɔːdʒ/
A n forge f
B vtr ① forger [metal]; ② (fake) contrefaire [banknotes, signature]; **a** ∼**d passport** un faux passeport; ③ (alter) falsifier [date, will]; ④ (establish) forger [alliance]; établir [identity, link]
C vi **to** ∼ **ahead** accélérer; fig [industry] être en plein essor; **to** ∼ **ahead with** aller de l'avant dans

forger /'fɔːdʒə(r)/ n ① (of documents) faussaire m; ② (of artefacts) contrefacteur/-trice m/f; ③ (of money) faux-monnayeur m

forgery /'fɔːdʒərɪ/ n ① (of document) faux m; (of picture, banknotes) contrefaçon f; ② (signature, banknote) contrefaçon f; (picture, document) faux m

forget /fə'get/ (p prés **-tt-**; prét **-got**; pp **-gotten**)
A vtr ① (not remember) oublier (**that** que; **to do** de faire; **how** comment); ∼ **it!** (no way) n'y compte pas!; (drop the subject) laisse tomber!; (think nothing of it) ce n'est rien!; ② (put aside) oublier; **she'll never let me** ∼ **it** elle n'est pas près de me le faire oublier; ③ lit, fig (leave behind) oublier
B vi oublier

(Phrasal verb)

■ **forget about**: ▸ ∼ **about** [sth/sb] (overlook) oublier

forgetful /fə'getfl/ adj ① (absent-minded) distrait; **to become** ∼ perdre un peu la mémoire; ② (negligent) **to be** ∼ **of one's duties** négliger ses responsabilités

forgetfulness /fə'getflnɪs/ n ① (absent-mindedness) distraction f, perte f de mémoire; ② (carelessness) étourderie f

forget-me-not n myosotis m

forgettable /fə'getəbl/ adj [day, fact, film] peu mémorable; [actor, writer] sans grand intérêt

forgivable /fə'gɪvəbl/ adj pardonnable

forgive /fə'gɪv/ vtr (prét **-gave**; pp **-given**) pardonner à [person]; pardonner [act, remark]; annuler [debt]; **to** ∼ **sb sth** pardonner qch à qn; **to** ∼ **sb for doing** pardonner à qn d'avoir fait; **to** ∼ **oneself** se pardonner; **he could be forgiven for believing her** on ne peut pas lui reprocher de l'avoir crue

forgiveness /fə'gɪvnɪs/ n ① (for action, crime) pardon m; **to be full of** ∼ être très indulgent; ② (of debt) annulation f

forgiving /fə'gɪvɪŋ/ adj [person] indulgent; [climate] clément

forgo /fɔː'gəʊ/ vtr (prét **-went**; pp **-gone**) renoncer à

forgot /fə'gɒt/ prét ▸ **forget**

forgotten /fə'gɒtn/ pp ▸ **forget**

fork /fɔːk/
A n ① (for eating) fourchette f; ② (tool) fourche f; ③ (in tree, in river, on bicycle) fourche f; (in railway) embranchement m; (in road) bifurcation f; ④ (in chess) fourchette f
B vtr (all contexts) fourcher
C vi (also ∼ **off**) bifurquer

(Phrasal verbs)

■ **fork out**° casquer° (**for** pour)
■ **fork over**: ▸ ∼ [sth] **over**, ∼ **over** [sth] retourner à la fourche [hay, manure, garden]

forked /fɔːkt/ adj fourchu

forked lightning n éclair m en zigzag

fork: ∼**lift truck** n GB (also **forklift** US) chariot m élévateur à fourche; ∼ **spanner** n clé f plate

forlorn /fə'lɔːn/ adj ① (sad) [appearance] malheureux/-euse; [landscape] morne; [sight] triste; ② (desperate) [attempt] désespéré

form /fɔːm/
A n ① (kind, manifestation) (of exercise, transport, government, protest) forme f; (of entertainment, taxation, disease) sorte f; **some** ∼ **of control is needed** un système de contrôle est nécessaire; **in the** ∼ **of** sous forme de; **he won't touch alcohol in any** ∼ il évite l'alcool sous toutes ses formes; ② (document) formulaire m; **blank** ∼ formulaire vierge; ③ (shape) forme f; ④ (of athlete, horse, performer) forme f; **to be in good** ∼ être en bonne or pleine forme; **to return to** ∼ retrouver la forme; **to study the** ∼ étudier le tableau des performances; **true to** ∼, **she...** fidèle à elle-même, elle...; ⑤ Literat, Art (structure) forme f; (genre) genre m; ∼ **and content** la forme et le fond; ⑥ (etiquette) **it is bad** ∼ cela ne se fait pas (**to do** de faire); **purely as a matter of** ∼ purement par politesse or pour la forme; ⑦ GB Sch classe f; **in the first** ∼ ≈ en sixième; ⑧ (prescribed set of words) formule f; **I agree with the** ∼ **of words used** je suis d'accord avec la formulation; ⑨ Ling forme f; **in question** ∼ à la forme interrogative
B vtr ① (organize or create) gen former (**from** avec); nouer [friendship, relationship]; **how are stalactites** ∼**ed?** comment se forment les stalactites?; **to** ∼ **part of** faire partie de; **to** ∼ **the basis of** constituer la base de; ② (conceive) se faire [impression, opinion]; concevoir [admiration]; ③ (mould) former; **tastes** ∼**ed by television** des goûts formés par la télévision; ④ (constitute) former [jury, cabinet, panel]
C vi (all contexts) se former

(Phrasal verb)

■ **form into**: ▸ ∼ **into** [sth] [people] former [groups, teams]; **to** ∼ **sth into** mettre qch en [paragraphs, circle]; séparer [qch] en [groups, teams, classes]

formal /'fɔːml/ adj ① (official) [agreement, complaint, interview, invitation, reception] officiel/-ielle; ② (not casual) [language] soutenu; [occasion] solennel/-elle; [manner] cérémonieux/-ieuse; [clothing] habillé; (on invitation) '**dress:** ∼' 'tenue de soirée'; ③ (structured) [logic, linguistics] formel/-elle; ④ (in recognized institution) [training] professionnel/-elle; [qualification] reconnu; ⑤ Literat, Art formel/-elle

formal: ∼ **dress** n gen tenue f de soirée; Mil tenue f de cérémonie; ∼ **garden** n jardin m à la française

Forms of address

■ *Only those forms of address in frequent use are included here; titles of members of the nobility or of church dignitaries are not covered; for the use of military ranks as titles* ▸ p. 1123.

Speaking to someone

■ *Where English puts the surname after the title, French normally uses the title alone (note that when recording dialogue, French does not use a capital letter for* monsieur, madame *and* mademoiselle, *unlike English* Mr *etc., nor for titles such as* docteur).

good morning, Mr Johnson
= bonjour, monsieur

good evening, Mrs Jones
= bonsoir, madame

goodbye, Miss Smith
= au revoir, mademoiselle

■ *The French* monsieur *and* madame *tend to be used more often than the English* Mr X *or* Mrs Y. *Also, in English, people often say simply* Good morning *or* Excuse me; *in the equivalent situation in French, they might say* Bonjour, monsieur *or* Pardon, madame. *However, the French are slower than the British, and much slower than the Americans, to use someone's first name, so* hi there, Peter! *to a colleague may well be simply* bonjour!, *or* bonjour, monsieur; bonjour, cher ami; bonjour, mon vieux *etc., depending on the degree of familiarity that exists.*

■ *In both languages, other titles are also used, e.g.:*

hallo, Dr. Brown or hallo, Doctor
= bonjour, docteur

■ *In some cases where titles are not used in English, they are used in French, e.g.* bonjour, Monsieur le directeur *or* bonjour, Madame la directrice *to a head teacher, or* bonjour, maître *to a lawyer of either sex. Other titles, such as* professeur *(in the sense of* professor), *are used much less than their English equivalents in direct address. Where in English one might say* Good morning, Professor, *in French one would probably say* Bonjour, monsieur *or* Bonjour, madame.

■ *Titles of important positions are used in direct forms of address, preceded by* Monsieur le *or* Madame le *or* Madame la, *as in:*

yes, Chair
= oui, Monsieur le président
  or (to a woman) oui, Madame la présidente

yes, Minister
= oui, Monsieur le ministre
  or (to a woman) oui, Madame le ministre

■ *Note the use of* Madame le *when the noun in question, like* ministre *here, or* professeur *and other titles, has no feminine form, or no acceptable feminine. A woman Member of Parliament is addressed as* Madame le député, *a woman Senator* Madame le sénateur, *a woman judge* Madame le juge *and a woman mayor* Madame le maire. *Women often prefer the masculine word even when a feminine form does exist, as in* Madame l'ambassadeur *to a woman ambassador,* Madame l'ambassadrice *being reserved for the wife of an ambassador.*

Speaking about someone

Mr Smith is here
= monsieur Smith est là

Mrs Jones phoned
= madame Jones a téléphoné

Miss Black has arrived
= mademoiselle Black est arrivée

Ms Brown has left
= madame Brown *or (as appropriate)* mademoiselle Brown est partie

(French has no equivalent of Ms.)

■ *When the title accompanies someone's name, the definite article must be used in French:*

Dr Blake has arrived
= le docteur Blake est arrivé

Professor Jones spoke
= le professeur Jones a parlé

This is true of all titles:

Prince Charles
= le prince Charles

Princess Marie
= la princesse Marie

■ *Note that with royal etc. titles, only* 1er *is spoken as an ordinal number (*premier*) in French; unlike English, all the others are spoken as cardinal numbers (*deux, trois, *and so on).*

King Richard I
= le roi Richard 1er (*say* Richard premier)

Queen Elizabeth II
= la reine Elizabeth II (*say* Elizabeth deux)

Pope John XXIII
= le pape Jean XXIII (*say* Jean vingt-trois)

---

formalin /'fɔːməlɪn/ *n* formol *m*

formality /fɔː'mælətɪ/ *n* **1** (legal or social convention) formalité *f*; **2** (formal nature) (of occasion, manner) solennité *f*; (of dress) caractère *m* habillé; (of room) caractère *m* cérémonieux; (of language) caractère *m* soutenu

formalize /'fɔːməlaɪz/ *vtr* **1** *gen* officialiser; **2** Comput formaliser

formally /'fɔːməlɪ/ *adv* **1** (officially) officiellement; **2** (not casually) cérémonieusement

format /'fɔːmæt/
A *n* **1** (general formulation) (of product, publication, passport) format *m*, présentation *f*; (of musical group) formation *f*; **2** (size, style of book or magazine) format *m*; **folio** ∼ format folio; **3** TV, Radio formule *f* (**for** pour); **4** Comput format *m*; **in tabular** ∼ sous forme de tableau
B *vtr* (*p prés etc* **-tt-**) Comput formater

formation /fɔː'meɪʃn/ *n* **1** (creation) *gen* formation *f*; (of relationship) établissement *m*; **2** (shape, arrangement) gen, Mil,

Geog formation *f*; **a cloud** ∼ une masse nuageuse

formative /'fɔːmətɪv/ *adj* **1** *gen* formateur/-trice; **2** Ling [*element, affix*] de formation

formatting /'fɔːmætɪŋ/ *n* formatage *m*

former /'fɔːmə(r)/
A *n* **the** ∼ (the first of two) le premier/la première *m/f*, celui-là/celle-là *m/f*
B *adj* **1** (earlier) [*era, life*] antérieur; [*size, state*] initial, original; **of** ∼ **days** *ou* **times** d'autrefois; **he's a shadow of his** ∼ **self** il n'est plus que l'ombre de lui-même; **2** [*leader, husband, champion*] ancien/-ienne (*before n*); **3** (first of two) premier/-ière (*before n*)
C **-former** *combining form* GB Sch **fourth-**∼ ≈ élève *mf* de troisième

formerly /'fɔːməlɪ/ *adv* **1** (in earlier times) autrefois; **2** (no longer) anciennement; ∼ **Miss Martin** née Martin

formidable /'fɔːmɪdəbl, fɔː'mɪd-/ *adj* **1** (intimidating) redoutable; **2** (awe-inspiring) impressionnant

formless /ˈfɔːmlɪs/ adj [mass] informe; [novel] mal construit

form: ~ **of address** n formule f (de politesse); ~ **teacher** n GB Sch ≈ professeur m principal

formula /ˈfɔːmjʊlə/
A n (pl **-lae** ou **~s**) **1** formule f (**for** de; **for doing** pour faire); **2** US (for babies) (powder) lait m en poudre; (also ~ **milk**) lait m reconstitué
B Formula noun modifier Sport ~ **One/Two** de formule 1/2

formulate /ˈfɔːmjʊleɪt/ vtr élaborer [rules, principles]; formuler [idea, design, reply, bill, policy]

formulation /ˌfɔːmjʊˈleɪʃn/ n (of idea, reply, bill) formulation f; (of principles, strategy) élaboration f

fornication /ˌfɔːnɪˈkeɪʃn/ n fornication f

forsake /fəˈseɪk/ vtr (prét **-sook**; pp **-saken**) sout abandonner

forswear /fɔːˈsweə(r)/ vtr (prét **-swore**; pp **-sworn**) sout **1** (renounce) renoncer à; **2** Jur (deny) nier

fort /fɔːt/ n fort m

(Idiom) **to hold** ou US **hold down the** ~ s'occuper de tout

forte /ˈfɔːteɪ, US fɔːrt/ n **1** (strong point) **to be sb's** ~ être le fort de qn; **2** Mus forte m inv

forth /fɔːθ/

⚠ Forth often appears in English after a verb (bring forth, set forth, sally forth). For translations, consult the appropriate verb entry (bring, set, sally). For further uses of forth, see the entry below.

adv (onwards) **from this day** ~ à partir d'aujourd'hui; **from that day** ~ à dater de ce jour; ▸ **back, so**

forthcoming /ˌfɔːθˈkʌmɪŋ/ adj **1** (happening soon) prochain (before n); **2** (available) (jamais épith) disponible; **3** (communicative) affable, ouvert; **to be** ~ **about sth** être disposé à parler de qch

forthright /ˈfɔːθraɪt/ adj [person, manner] direct; [reply] sans détours; **in** ~ **terms** sans ambiguïté

forthwith /fɔːθˈwɪθ, US -ˈwɪð/ adv sout aussi Jur immédiatement

fortieth /ˈfɔːtɪəθ/ ▸ p. 1044

A n **1** (in order) quarantième mf; **2** (fraction) quarantième m
B adj, adv quarantième

fortification /ˌfɔːtɪfɪˈkeɪʃn/ n fortification f (**of** de)

fortify /ˈfɔːtɪfaɪ/ vtr **1** gen fortifier (**against** contre); **to** ~ **oneself** se donner du courage; **2** corser [wine]; **fortified wine** vin m doux, vin m de liqueur

fortitude /ˈfɔːtɪtjuːd, US -tuːd/ n détermination f

fortnight /ˈfɔːtnaɪt/ ▸ p. 1267 n GB quinze jours mpl; **the first** ~ **in August** la première quinzaine d'août

fortnightly /ˈfɔːtnaɪtlɪ/ GB adj [meeting, visit] qui a lieu toutes les deux semaines; [magazine] publié toutes les deux semaines

Fortran /ˈfɔːtræn/ Comput n fortran m

fortress /ˈfɔːtrɪs/ n forteresse f

fortuitous /fɔːˈtjuːɪtəs, US -ˈtuː-/ adj sout fortuit

fortunate /ˈfɔːtʃənət/ adj heureux/-euse; **it was** ~ **for him that** heureusement pour lui que; **to be** ~ (enough) **to do** avoir la chance or le bonheur de faire; **those less** ~ **than ourselves** ceux qui n'ont pas notre chance

fortunately /ˈfɔːtʃənətlɪ/ adv heureusement

fortune /ˈfɔːtʃuːn/
A n **1** (wealth) fortune f; **to make a** ~ faire fortune; **to seek fame and** ~ chercher fortune; **2** (luck) chance f; **to have the good** ~ **to do** avoir la chance or le bonheur de faire; **by good** ~ par chance; **to tell sb's** ~ dire la bonne aventure à qn
B fortunes npl (of team, country) destin m

(Idiom) ~ **favours the brave** la fortune sourit aux audacieux

fortune: ~ **cookie** n US petit gâteau m sec (renfermant une prédiction); **~-teller** n diseur/-euse m/f de bonne aventure

forty /ˈfɔːtɪ/ ▸ p. 1044, p. 647, p. 745 n, adj quarante (m) inv

(Idiom) **to have** ~ **winks** faire un petit somme

forum /ˈfɔːrəm/ n (pl ~**s** ou **fora**) forum m (**for** de); **in an open** ~ en débat ouvert

forward /ˈfɔːwəd/
A n Sport avant m
B adj **1** (bold) effronté; **2** (towards the front) [roll, gears] avant inv; ~ **pass** (in rugby) en-avant m; **to be too far** ~ [seat] être trop en avant; **3** (advanced) [season, plant] avancé; **how far** ~ **are you?** où en êtes-vous?; **4** Fin [market, price, rate] à terme
C adv **1** (ahead) **to step** ~ faire un pas en avant; **to fall** ~ tomber en avant; **to go** ou **walk** ~ avancer; **to rush** ~ se précipiter; **to move sth** ~ lit, fig avancer qch; **a seat facing** ~ une place dans le sens de la marche; **a way** ~ une solution; **2** (towards the future) **to go** ~ **in time** voyager dans le futur; **from this day** ~ à partir d'aujourd'hui; Audio, Video **to wind sth** ~ faire défiler qch en avance rapide
D vtr **1** (dispatch) expédier [goods]; envoyer [catalogue, parcel]; **2** (send on) faire suivre, réexpédier [mail]

forwarder /ˈfɔːwədə(r)/ n (of freight) transitaire m; (of mail) expéditeur m

forwarding /ˈfɔːwədɪŋ/ n Comm transport m; (of mail) expédition f

forwarding: ~ **address** n nouvelle adresse f (pour faire suivre le courrier); ~ **agent** n transitaire m; ~ **charges** npl frais mpl d'expédition

forward-looking adj [company, person] tourné vers l'avenir

forwardness /ˈfɔːwədnɪs/ n (of child, behaviour) impertinence f

forward planning n planification f à long terme

forwards /ˈfɔːwədz/ adv = forward C; ▸ **backwards**

forward slash n barre f oblique

fossil /ˈfɒsl/ n (remains) fossile m

fossil fuel n combustible m fossile

fossilized /ˈfɒsəlaɪzd/ adj **1** lit fossilisé; **2** fig sclérosé

foster /ˈfɒstə(r)/
A adj adoptif/-ive (dans une famille de placement)
B vtr **1** (encourage) encourager [attitude]; promouvoir [activity]; **2** (cherish) entretenir; **3** (act as parent to) prendre [qn] en placement; **4** (place in care of) **to** ~ **sb with a family** mettre qn dans une famille

foster: ~ **family** n famille f de placement; ~ **home** n foyer m de placement

fought /fɔːt/ prét, pp ▸ **fight**

foul /faʊl/
A n Sport faute f (**by** de; **on** sur)
B adj **1** (putrid) [conditions] répugnant; [smell, air] fétide; [water] putride; [taste] infect; **2** (grim) épouvantable; **to be in a** ~ **mood** être d'une humeur massacrante°; **to have a** ~ **temper** avoir un sale caractère; **3** (evil) odieux/-ieuse; **4** (offensive) ordurier/-ière; **to have a** ~ **mouth** être grossier/-ière; **5** (unsporting) déloyal
C adv **to taste** ~ avoir un goût infect
D vtr **1** (pollute) polluer [environment]; souiller [pavement]; **2** (become tangled) **the propeller was** ~**ed by nets** des filets de pêche étaient emmêlés dans l'hélice; **3** (clog) bloquer [mechanism]; obstruer [channel]; **4** Sport commettre une faute contre

(Idiom) **to fall** ~ **of sb** (fall out with) se brouiller avec qn; (lose favour) s'attirer le mécontentement de qn

(Phrasal verb)
▪ **foul up**°: ▸ ~ **up** faire des erreurs or des bourdes°; ▸ ~ **up** [sth], ~ [sth] **up 1** (bungle) ruiner [plan]; abîmer [system]; **2** (pollute) polluer

foully /ˈfaʊlɪ/ adv [treated] de façon scandaleuse

foul: **~-mouthed** adj péj grossier/-ière; ~ **play** n (malicious act) acte m criminel; Sport jeu m irrégulier; **~-smelling** adj puant; **~-tasting** adj infect; **~-up**° n cafouillage° m

found /faʊnd/
A prét, pp ▸ **find B, C**
B vtr **1** (establish) fonder; **2** (base) fonder (**on** sur); **to be** ~**ed on fact** s'appuyer sur les faits; **3** Tech fondre

foundation /faʊnˈdeɪʃn/ n **1** (base) (man-made) fondations fpl; (natural) base f; fig (of society, belief) fondements mpl; **to lay the** ~**s for** lit poser les fondations de; fig jeter les fondements de; **2** fig (truth) **without** ~ sans fondement; **3** (of school, town etc) fondation f (**of** de); **4** Fin (trust) fondation f

foundation course n GB Univ année f de préparation à des études supérieures

founder /'faʊndə(r)/
A n fondateur/-trice m/f
B vi [ship] sombrer (**on** sur); [car, person] s'embourber (**in** dans); [marriage] être en difficultés; [career, talks] être compromis (**on** par)

founder member n GB membre m fondateur

founding /'faʊndɪŋ/
A n fondation f
B adj fondateur/-trice

foundry /'faʊndrɪ/ n fonderie f

fount /faʊnt/ n **1** littér source f; **2** (in printing) fonte f

fountain /'faʊntɪn, US -tn/ n **1** (structure) fontaine f; **2** (spray) (of water) jet m; (of sparks, light) gerbe f

fountain: ∼**head** n lit, fig source f; ∼ **pen** n stylo m (à encre)

four /fɔː(r)/ n ▸ p. 1044 n, adj quatre (m) inv

(Idioms) **on all** ∼**s** à quatre pattes; **to the** ∼ **winds** aux quatre vents

four: ∼**-door** adj Aut [model] quatre portes; ∼**-by-**∼ n Aut quatre-quatre m inv; ∼**-engined** adj Aviat quadrimoteur

four-four time n Mus **in** ∼ à quatre-quatre

four: ∼**-leaf clover** n trèfle m à quatre feuilles; ∼**-letter word** n mot m grossier; ∼**-piece band** n (jazz) quartette m; (classical) quatuor m; ∼**-poster (bed)** n lit m à baldaquin; ∼**some**○ n quatuor○ m; ∼**square** adj [building] cubique; [attitude] loyal

four-star /'fɔːstɑː(r)/
A n GB (also ∼ **petrol**) super(carburant) m
B adj [hotel, restaurant] quatre étoiles

four-stroke /'fɔːstrəʊk/ adj Aut [engine] à quatre temps

fourteen /ˌfɔː'tiːn/ ▸ p. 1044 n, adj quatorze (m) inv

fourteenth /ˌfɔː'tiːnθ/ ▸ p. 1044, p. 788
A n **1** (in order) quatorzième mf; **2** (of month) quatorze m inv; **3** (fraction) quatorzième m
B adj, adv quatorzième

fourth /fɔːθ/ ▸ p. 1044, p. 788
A n **1** (in order) quatrième mf; **2** (of month) quatre m inv; **3** (fraction) quatrième m; **4** Mus quarte f; **5** (also ∼ **gear**) Aut quatrième f
B adj quatrième
C adv [come, finish] quatrième, en quatrième position

fourthly /'fɔːθlɪ/ adv quatrièmement

fourth-rate /ˌfɔːθ'reɪt/ adj péj [job, hotel, film] de seconde zone

four-wheel drive (vehicle) /'fɔːˌwiːl, US -'hwiːl/ n quatre-quatre m inv, 4 x 4 m inv

fowl /faʊl/ n gen, Culin (one bird) poulet m; (group) volaille f; ▸ **fish**

fox /fɒks/
A n renard m
B vtr dérouter

fox: ∼ **cub** n renardeau m; ∼ **fur** n (skin) (peau f de) renard m; (coat) (manteau m en) renard m; ∼**glove** n digitale f; ∼**hound** n fox-hound m; ∼ **hunt**, ∼**hunting** n chasse f au renard; ∼ **terrier** n fox-terrier m; ∼**trot** n fox-trot m

foxy /'fɒksɪ/ adj **1** (crafty) rusé; **2** ○(sexy) sexy

fr Fin abrév écrite = **franc**

Fr Relig abrév écrite = **Father**

fracas /'fræka:, US 'freɪkəs/ n altercation f, accrochage m

fraction /'frækʃn/ n **1** gen, Math (portion) fraction f (**of** de); **2** (tiny amount) part f infime; **a** ∼ **higher** un tout petit peu plus haut

fractional /'frækʃənl/ adj **1** gen infime; **2** Math fractionnaire

fractionally /'frækʃənəlɪ/ adv légèrement

fracture /'fræktʃə(r)/
A n gen, Med fracture f
B vtr fracturer [bone, rock]; fig fissurer [unity]
C vi [bone] se fracturer; [pipe, masonry] se fissurer

fragile /'frædʒaɪl, US -dʒl/ adj **1** (delicate) fragile; **to feel** ∼ (ill) se sentir patraque○; (emotionally) être fragile; **2** (tenuous) [link] ténu

fragility /frə'dʒɪlətɪ/ n fragilité f

fragment
A /'frægmənt/ n (of shell, manuscript) fragment m; (of glass) morceau m; (of food) miette f
B /fræg'ment/ vi [party, system] se fractionner

fragmentary /'frægməntrɪ, US -terɪ/ adj **1** [evidence, nature] fragmentaire; **2** Geog [material] détritique

fragmented /'frægmentɪd/ adj [account] décousu; [group] dispersé; [job] morcelé; [system] fragmenté

fragrance /'freɪgrəns/ n parfum m

fragrant /'freɪgrənt/ adj odorant

frail /freɪl/ adj [person] frêle; [health, hope] précaire

frailty /'freɪltɪ/ n (of person) fragilité f; (of health, state) précarité f

frame /freɪm/
A n **1** (of building, boat, roof) charpente f; (of car) châssis m; (of bicycle, racquet) cadre m; (of bed) sommier m; (of tent) armature f; **2** (of picture, window) cadre m; (of door) encadrement m; **3** (context) cadre m; **4** Anat (skeleton) ossature f; (body) corps m; **5** (picture) Cin photogramme m; TV, Phot image f; **6** (for weaving) métier m; **7** (in snooker) (triangle) triangle m; (single game) manche f; **8** Comput bloc m; (window) cadre m
B frames npl (of spectacles) monture f
C vtr **1** (enclose, surround) lit, fig encadrer [picture, face, view]; **2** (formulate in words) formuler; **3** (devise) élaborer [plan, policy]; rédiger [legislation]; **4** (mouth) articuler; **5** ○(set up) [police] monter une machination contre; [criminal] faire porter les soupçons sur
D **-framed** combining form timber-∼d à charpente de bois

frame of mind n état m d'esprit; **to be in the wrong** ∼ **for sth** ne pas être d'humeur pour qch

framer /'freɪmə(r)/ ▸ p. 1181 n encadreur m

framework /'freɪmwɜːk/ n **1** lit structure f; **2** fig (basis) (of society, system) cadre m; (of agreement, theory) base f; (of novel, play) structure f; **legal** ∼ cadre m juridique; **a** ∼ **for sth** un cadre pour qch

framing /'freɪmɪŋ/ n **1** gen encadrement m; **2** Cin cadrage m

franc /fræŋk/ n Hist franc m

France /frɑːns/ ▸ p. 774 pr n France f

franchise /'fræntʃaɪz/
A n **1** Pol droit m de vote; **universal** ∼ suffrage m universel; **2** Comm franchise f
B noun modifier [business, chain] franchisé; [holder] de franchise
C vtr US (subcontract) franchiser [product, service]

francophile /'fræŋkəʊfaɪl/ n, adj francophile (mf)

francophobe /'fræŋkəʊfəʊb/ n, adj francophobe (mf)

francophone /'fræŋkəfəʊn/ n, adj francophone (mf)

frank /fræŋk/
A adj franc/franche (**about** en ce qui concerne)
B vtr affranchir [letter, parcel]; oblitérer [stamp]

Frankfurt /'fræŋkfət/ ▸ p. 1276 pr n Francfort

frankfurter /'fræŋkfɜːtə(r)/ n saucisse f de Francfort

frankincense /'fræŋkɪnsens/ n encens m

franking machine /'fræŋkɪŋ/ n machine f à affranchir

frankly /'fræŋklɪ/ adv franchement

frankness /'fræŋknɪs/ n franchise f

frantic /'fræntɪk/ adj **1** (wild) [activity] frénétique; **2** (desperate) [effort, search] désespéré; [shout] éperdu; [person] surexcité; **to be** ∼ **with** être fou/folle de

frantically /'fræntɪklɪ/ adv **1** (wildly) frénétiquement; **2** (desperately) désespérément

fraternal /frə'tɜːnl/ adj fraternel/-elle

fraternity /frə'tɜːnətɪ/ n **1** (brotherhood) fraternité f also US Univ; **2** (sharing profession) aussi péj confrérie f also pej

fraternize /'frætənaɪz/ vi fraterniser; pej frayer

fraud /frɔːd/ n fraude f

Fraud Squad n GB Service m de répression des fraudes

fraudulence /'frɔːdjʊləns, US -dʒʊ-/ n **1** = **fraud**; **2** (of signature, figures) caractère m frauduleux

fraudulent /'frɔːdjʊlənt, US -dʒʊ-/ adj [system, practice, dealing, use] frauduleux/-euse; [signature, cheque] falsifié; [statement] faux/fausse; [application, claim] indu; [gain, earnings] illicite

fraught /frɔːt/ *adj* [*situation, atmosphere*] tendu; [*person*] accablé (**with** de); **to be ~ with** être lourd de [*danger, difficulty*]

fray /freɪ/
A *n* sout **the ~** la bataille
B *vi* [*material, rope*] s'effilocher; [*nerves*] craquer○

frayed /freɪd/ *adj* [*material*] effiloché; [*nerves*] à bout; **tempers were ~** les gens s'énervaient

frazzle○ /'fræzl/ *n* **to burn sth to a ~** calciner qch; **to be worn to a ~** être lessivé○

freak /friːk/
A *n* ❶ (deformed person) lit, fig injur monstre *m*; ❷ (strange person) original/-e *m/f*; ❸ (unusual occurrence) aberration *f*; **a ~ of nature** une bizarrerie de la nature; ❹ ○(enthusiast) mordu/-e○ *m/f*, fana○ *mf*
B *adj* [*accident, storm*] exceptionnel/-elle
(Phrasal verb)
■ **freak out**○: ▶ **~ out** (get angry) piquer une crise○; (get excited) se défouler; ▶ **~ [sb] out**, **~ out [sb]** (upset) faire paniquer [qn]

freakish /'friːkɪʃ/ *adj* ❶ (monstrous) grotesque; ❷ (surprising) exceptionnel/-elle; ❸ (unusual) bizarre

freckle /'frekl/
A *n* tache *f* de rousseur
B *vi* [*skin*] se couvrir de taches de rousseur

free /friː/
A *n* (also **~ period**) Sch ≈ heure *f* de libre
B *adj* ❶ (unhindered, unrestricted) [*person, country, election, press, translation*] libre (*after* n); [*access, choice*] libre (*before* n); **to be ~ to do** être libre de faire; **to leave sb ~ to do** laisser qn libre de faire; **to feel ~ to do** ne pas hésiter à faire; **to break ~ of** être libérer de; **to set sb ~ from** libérer qn de; **to be allowed ~ expression** pouvoir s'exprimer librement; **I oiled the hinges to allow ~ movement** j'ai graissé les gonds pour faciliter le mouvement; ❷ (not captive or tied) [*person, limb*] libre; [*animal, bird*] en liberté; **one more tug and my shoe was ~** un coup de plus et ma chaussure était dégagée; **to set [sb/sth] ~** libérer [*person*]; rendre la liberté à [*animal*]; **to pull sth ~** dégager qch; **they had to cut the driver ~ (from his car)** on a dû couper la tôle de la voiture pour dégager le chauffeur; **to break ~** se libérer (des ses liens); **the boat broke ~ from** *ou* **of its moorings** le bateau a rompu ses amarres; ❸ (devoid) **to be ~ from** *ou* **of sb** être libéré de qn; **~ from** *ou* **of pollution** dépourvu de pollution; **a day ~ from** *ou* **of interruptions** une journée sans interruptions; **she was ~ from** *ou* **of any hatred** elle n'éprouvait aucune haine; **this soup is ~ from** *ou* **of artificial colourings** cette soupe ne contient pas de colorants artificiels; ❹ (costing nothing) gratuit; **'admission ~'** 'entrée gratuite'; **~ gift** Comm cadeau *m*; **you can't expect a ~ ride** fig on n'a rien pour rien; ❺ (not occupied) libre; **are you ~ for lunch on Monday?** es-tu libre lundi pour déjeuner?; **is this seat ~?** cette place est-elle libre?; **I'm trying to keep Tuesday ~** j'essaie de garder mon mardi libre; ❻ (generous, lavish) **to be ~ with** être généreux/-euse avec [*food*]; être prodigue de [*advice*]; **to be very ~ with money** dépenser sans compter; ❼ (familiar) familier/-ière; ❽ Chem libre; ❾ Ling [*form*] non lié; [*vowel, stress*] libre
C *adv* ❶ (at liberty) librement, en toute liberté; **to go ~** [*hostage*] être libéré; [*criminal*] circuler en toute liberté; ❷ (without payment) gratuitement; **children are admitted ~** l'entrée est gratuite pour les enfants
D *vtr* ❶ (from captivity) libérer; (from wreckage) dégager; **to ~ sb from** débarrasser qn de [*prejudice*]; décharger qn de [*blame*]; délivrer qn de [*oppression, guilt*]; soulager qn de [*suffering*]; ❷ (make available) débloquer [*money, resources*]; libérer [*person, hands*]
E *v refl* **to ~ oneself from** se dégager de [*chains, wreckage*]; se libérer de [*influence*]; se débarrasser de [*burden*]; se décharger de [*blame*]; se délivrer de [*guilt*]
F **-free** *combining form* **smoke/sugar-~** sans fumée/sucre; **interest-~** Fin sans intérêt
G **for free** *adv phr* gratuitement
(Idioms) **to have a ~ hand** avoir carte blanche (**in** pour); **~ as a bird** *ou* **the air** libre comme l'air

free agent *n* **to be a ~** pouvoir agir à sa guise

free and easy *adj* gen décontracté; pej désinvolte

freebie○, **freebee**○ /'friːbiː/ *n* (free gift) cadeau *m*; (newspaper) journal *m* gratuit; (trip) voyage *m* gratuit

free: **~booter** *n* lit pilleur *m*; fig jouisseur/-euse *m/f*; **~ climbing** *n* escalade *f* libre

freedom /'friːdəm/ *n* ❶ (liberty) liberté *f* (**to do** de faire); **~ of information** libre accès *m* à l'information; **~ of movement** (of person) liberté de mouvement; (of part, screw etc) jeu *m*; **to give sb his/her ~** rendre sa liberté à qn; ❷ (entitlement to use) **they gave us the ~ of their house** ils nous ont laissé le plein usage de leur maison; **to give sb the ~ of a city** nommer qn citoyen d'honneur d'une ville; ❸ **~ from** (lack of) absence *f* de; (immunity from) immunité *f* contre

freedom fighter *n* combattant *m* de la liberté

free: **~ enterprise** *n* libre entreprise *f*; **~fall** *n* chute *f* libre; **Freefone®**, **Freephone®** ≈ numéro *m* vert®; **~-for-all** *n* mêlée *f* générale; **~hand** *adj*, *adv* à main levée; **~ hit** *n* coup *m* franc; **~hold** *n* pleine propriété *f*, propriété *f* foncière perpétuelle et libre; **~holder** *n* propriétaire *mf* foncier/-ière à perpétuité; **~ house** *n* GB pub *m* indépendant; **~ kick** *n* coup *m* franc

freelance /'friːlɑːns, US -læns/
A *n* (also **freelancer**) free-lance *mf*
B *adj* [*journalist*] free-lance
C *adv* [*work*] en free-lance

freeloader○ *n* parasite *m*

freely /'friːlɪ/ *adv* ❶ (without restriction) gen librement; [*breathe*] lit aisément; fig librement; (abundantly) [*spend, give*] sans compter; [*perspire*] abondamment; **to move ~** [*part of body*] bouger aisément; [*person*] (around building, country) se déplacer librement; **to be ~ available** (easy to find) se trouver facilement; (accessible) être ouvert à tous; ❷ (willingly) volontiers; ❸ [*translate, adapt*] librement

free: **~man of the city** *n* citoyen *m* d'honneur d'une ville; **~ market** *n* (also **~ economy**) économie *f* de marché; **~ marketeer** *n* libéral/-e *m/f*, partisan *m* de l'économie de marché; **Freemason** *n* franc-maçon/-onne *m/f*; **~ of charge** *adj* gratuit; **~ on board**, **FOB** *adj*, *adv* GB franco à bord, FAB; US franco à destination; **~ period** *n* ≈ heure *f* de libre; **Freephone®** *n*, *adj* = Freefone; **~ port** *n* port *m* franc; **~post** *n* GB (also on envelope) port *m* payé; **~-range** *adj* élevé en plein air; **~ school** *n* école *f* privée spécialisée; **~ speech** *n* liberté *f* d'expression

free spirit *n* **to be a ~** aimer sa liberté

free: **~-standing** *adj* [*lamp, statue, heater*] sur pied; [*cooker, bath*] nonencastré; **~style** *n* (in swimming) nage *f* libre; (in skiing) figures *fpl* libres; (in wrestling) lutte *f* libre; **~thinker** *n* libre penseur/-euse *m/f*; **~ throw** *n* (in basketball) lancer *m* franc; **~ trade** *n* libre-échange *m*; **~ trader** *n* partisan *m* du libre-échange; **~ verse** *n* vers *m* libre; **~ vote** *n* ≈ vote *m* de conscience; **~way** *n* US autoroute *f*; **~wheel** *vi* lit être *or* rouler en roue libre; **~wheeling** *adj* [*person*] insouciant; [*attitude*] libre

free will *n* libre arbitre *m*; **to do sth of one's (own) ~** faire qch de son plein gré *or* de son propre chef

freeze /friːz/
A *n* ❶ Meteorol gelées *fpl*; ❷ Econ, Fin (of credits, assets) gel *m* (**on** de); (of prices, wages) gel *m*, blocage *m*
B *vtr* (*prét* **froze**; *pp* **frozen**) ❶ congeler [*food*]; (*cold weather*) geler [*liquid, pipes*]; ❷ Econ, Fin bloquer, geler; ❸ Cin arrêter; ❹ (anaesthetize) insensibiliser; ❺ Comput figer
C *vi* (*prét* **froze**; *pp* **frozen**) ❶ (become solid) [*water, pipes*] geler; [*food*] se congeler; ❷ (feel cold) geler; **to be freezing to death** mourir de froid; ❸ (become motionless) se figer (**with** de); **~!** pas un geste!; ❹ (become haughty) devenir glacial
D *v impers* Meteorol geler
(Phrasal verbs)
■ **freeze out**: ▶ **~ [sb/sth] out**, **~ out [sb/sth]** gen tourner le dos à [*person*]; Comm supplanter [*competitor*]; éliminer [qch] du marché [*goods*]
■ **freeze over** [*lake*] geler; [*window*] se couvrir de givre

freeze: **~-dried** *adj* lyophilisé; **~ frame** *n* Video arrêt *m* sur image

French provinces and regions

■ Both traditional pre-Revolution regions and modern administrative regions usually take the definite article as in l'Alsace, la Champagne etc.:

I like Alsace
= j'aime l'Alsace

Champagne is beautiful
= la Champagne est belle

■ For names which have a compound form, such as Midi-Pyrénées or Rhône-Alpes, it is safer to include the words la région:

do you know Midi-Pyrénées?
= connaissez-vous la région Midi-Pyrénées?

In, to and from somewhere

■ There are certain general principles regarding names of French provinces and regions. However, usage is sometimes uncertain; doubtful items should be checked in the dictionary.

■ For in and to, with feminine names and with masculine ones beginning with a vowel, use en without the definite article:

to live in Burgundy
= vivre en Bourgogne

to go to Burgundy
= aller en Bourgogne

to live in Anjou
= vivre en Anjou

to go to Anjou
= aller en Anjou

■ For in and to with masculine names beginning with a consonant, use dans le:

to live in the Berry
= vivre dans le Berry

to go to the Berry
= aller dans le Berry

■ For from with feminine names and with masculine ones beginning with a vowel, use de without the definite article:

to come from Burgundy
= venir de Bourgogne

to come from Anjou
= venir d'Anjou

■ For from with masculine names beginning with a consonant, use du:

to come from the Berry
= venir du Berry

Regional adjectives

■ Related adjectives and nouns exist for most of the names of provinces and regions. Here is a list of the commonest:

Alsace	alsacien(ne)	Flandre	flamand(e)
Anjou	angevin(e)	Franche-Comté	franc-comtois(e)
Aquitaine	aquitain(e)	Jura	jurassien(ne)
Auvergne	auvergnat(e)	Languedoc	languedocien(ne)
Béarn	béarnais(e)	Limousin	limousin(e)
Berry	berrichon(ne)	Lorraine	lorrain(e)
Bourbonnais	bourbonnais(e)	Normandie	normand(e)
Bourgogne	bourguignon(ne)	Périgord	périgourdin(e)
Bresse	bressan(e)	Picardie	picard(e)
Bretagne	breton(ne)	Poitou	poitevin(e)
Cévennes	cévenol(e)	Provence	provençal(e)
Champagne	champenois(e)	Savoie	savoyard(e)
Charente	charentais(e)	Touraine	tourangeau(-elle)
Corse	corse	Vendée	vendéen(ne)
Dauphiné	dauphinois(e)	Vosges	vosgien(ne)

■ These adjectives mean of X, as in the following (where alsacien stands for any of them):

an Alsace accent
= un accent alsacien

Alsace costume
= le costume alsacien

the Alsace countryside
= les paysages alsaciens

Alsace traditions
= les traditions alsaciennes

Alsace villages
= les villages alsaciens

■ These words can also be used as nouns, meaning a person from X; in this case they are written with a capital letter:

a person from Alsace
= un Alsacien

an Alsace woman
= une Alsacienne

the people of Alsace
= les Alsaciens mpl

---

freezer /'friːzə(r)/ n congélateur m
freezer compartment n freezer m
freezing /'friːzɪŋ/
A n **1** Meteorol **below ~** en-dessous de zéro; **2** Fin, gen gel m; (of prices) gel m, blocage m
B adj [room, weather] glacial; **I'm ~** je suis gelé; **it's ~ in here** on gèle ici
freezing: ~ cold adj [room, wind] glacial; [water] glacé; **~ fog** n brouillard m givrant; **~ point** n point m de congélation
freight /freɪt/
A n **1** (goods) fret m, marchandises fpl; **2** (transport system) transport m; **3** (cost) (frais mpl de) port m
B noun modifier [company, route, service] de transport; [transport, car, wagon, train, yard] de marchandises
freight: ~ charges npl frais mpl de transport; **~ collect** adv US contre paiement à la livraison, port dû
freighter /'freɪtə(r)/ n **1** Naut cargo m; **2** Aviat avion-cargo m

freight: ~ forward adv GB contre paiement à la livraison, port dû; **~ note** n lettre f de voiture; **~ operator** ▸ p. 1181 n transporteur m; **~ terminal** n aérogare f de fret
French /frentʃ/ ▸ p. 1032, p. 969
A n **1** (language) français m; **2** (people) **the ~** les Français mpl
B adj français
(Idioms) **to take ~ leave** filer à l'anglaise; **pardon my ~** hum si vous me passez l'expression
French bean n haricot m vert
French Canadian ▸ p. 1032, p. 969
A n **1** (person) Canadien/-ienne m/f francophone; **2** (language) français m du Canada
B adj [person] canadien/-ienne m/f francophone; [accent] franco-canadien/-ienne; [town, custom] du Canada francophone
French: ~ chalk n craie f de tailleur; **~ doors** npl US porte-fenêtre f; **~ dressing** n GB vinaigrette f; US sauce f mayonnaise; **~ fried potatoes** npl pommes fpl

frites; ~ **fries** *npl* frites *fpl*; ~ **horn** ► p. 1028 *n* cor *m* (d'harmonie); ~ **horn player** ► p. 1181 *n* corniste *mf*

Frenchify /'frentʃɪfaɪ/ *vtr* péj *ou* hum franciser

French: ~ **kiss** *n* patin○ *m*; ~ **knickers** *npl* culotte *f* flottante; ~ **loaf** *n* baguette *f*; ~**man** *n* Français *m*; ~ **mustard** *n* moutarde *f* douce

French pleat *n* ❶ (in sewing) pli *m* plat; ❷ (hairstyle) (roll) chignon *m* banane; (pleat) natte *f* africaine

French: ~ **polish** *n* vernis *m* à l'alcool; ~ **Riviera** *n* Côte *f* d'Azur; ~ **seam** *n* couture *f* anglaise; ~**speaking** *adj* francophone; ~ **stick** *n* baguette *f*; ~ **toast** *n* pain *m* perdu; ~ **window** *n* porte-fenêtre *f*; ~**woman** *n* Française *f*

frenetic /frə'netɪk/ *adj* [activity] frénétique; [lifestyle] trépidant

frenzied /'frenzɪd/ *adj* [activity] frénétique; [passion] déchaîné; [attempt] désespéré; [mob] (happy) en délire; (angry) déchaîné

frenzy /'frenzɪ/ *n* frénésie *f*, délire *m*; **to be in a state of** ~ être exalté; **to drive [sb/sth] into a** ~ exciter [crowd]; rendre [qn] fou/folle [person]; **there was a** ~ **of activity** ça grouillait d'activité

frequency /'fri:kwənsɪ/ *n* fréquence *f* (**of** de); **to occur with increasing** ~ être de plus en plus fréquent

frequency: ~ **band** *n* bande *f* de fréquence; ~ **modulation** *n* modulation *f* de fréquence

frequent
A /'fri:kwənt/ *adj* ❶ (common, usual) [expression, use] courant; ❷ (happening often) fréquent; **to make** ~ **use of sth** se servir souvent *or* fréquemment de qch; **to be in** ~ **contact with sb** être en contact régulier avec qn
B /frɪ'kwent/ *vtr* fréquenter

frequently /'fri:kwəntlɪ/ *adv* souvent, fréquemment

fresco /'freskəʊ/ *n* (*pl* -**oes**) fresque *f*

fresh /freʃ/ *adj* ❶ (not old) [foodstuff] frais/fraîche; **to look** ~ avoir l'air frais; **to feel** ~ être frais au toucher; **to taste/smell** ~ avoir un goût frais/une odeur fraîche; **bread** ~ **from the oven** du pain frais sorti du four; ❷ Culin [herbs, pasta, coffee] frais/fraîche; ~ **orange juice** jus d'orange pressée; ❸ (renewed, other) gen nouveau/-elle (before *n*); [linen] propre; [ammunition] supplémentaire; **to take a** ~ **look at sth** regarder qch d'un œil neuf; **to make a** ~ **start** prendre un nouveau départ; ❹ (recent) [fingerprint, blood] frais/fraîche; **while it is still** ~ **in your mind** tant que tu l'as tout frais à l'esprit; ❺ (recently returned) **from** *ou* **out of school** à peine sorti de l'école; **to be** ~ **from a trip abroad** être tout frais débarqué d'un voyage à l'étranger; ❻ (refreshing, original) (tout) nouveau/(toute) nouvelle (before *n*); ❼ (energetic, alert) **to feel** ~ *ou* **be** ~ être plein d'entrain; ❽ (cool, refreshing) frais/fraîche; ❾ ○US (over-familiar) impertinent; **to be** ~ **with sb** être un peu familier/-ière avec qn; ❿ Meteorol **a** ~ **breeze** une brise moyenne

⟨Idiom⟩ **to be** ~ **out of** ○ être en panne de○ [supplies]

fresh air *n* air *m* frais; **to get some** ~ prendre l'air, s'oxygéner

freshen /'freʃn/ *v*:
■ **freshen up** faire un brin de toilette

fresh-faced /ˌfreʃ'feɪst/ *adj* au teint frais

freshly /'freʃlɪ/ *adv* fraîchement; ~ **ironed/washed** qui vient d'être repassé/lavé

freshman /'freʃmən/ *n* ❶ (also **fresher**○ GB) Univ étudiant/-e *m/f* de première année; ❷ US fig (in Congress, in firm) nouveau venu/nouvelle venue *m/f*

freshness /'freʃnɪs/ *n* (all contexts) fraîcheur *f*

fresh water *n* eau *f* douce

fret /fret/
A *n* Mus frette *f*, touche *f*
B *vtr* (*p* prés *etc* -**tt**-) chantourner [wood, screen]
C *vi* (*p* prés *etc* -**tt**-) ❶ (be anxious) s'inquiéter (**over, about** pour, au sujet de); ❷ [child] pleurer, pleurnicher

fretful /'fretfl/ *adj* [child] grognon; [adult] énervé, agité

fretfully /'fretfəlɪ/ *adv* [speak] avec énervement; **to cry** ~ pleurnicher

fret: ~**saw** *n* scie *f* à découper; ~**work** *n* découpure *f*

Freudian /'frɔɪdɪən/ *n, adj* freudien/-ienne (*m/f*)

Freudian slip *n* lapsus *m*

Fri abrév écrite = **Friday**

friar /'fraɪə(r)/ *n* frère *m*, moine *m*

friction /'frɪkʃn/ *n* ❶ Ling, Phys friction *f*; ❷ gen (rubbing) frottement *m*; ❸ **ⓒ** fig (conflict) conflits *mpl* (**between** entre); **to cause** ~ être cause de friction

Friday /'fraɪdɪ/ ► p. 1322 *n* vendredi *m*

fridge /frɪdʒ/ *n* GB frigo○ *m*, réfrigérateur *m*

fried /fraɪd/ *pp* ► **fry B, C**

friend /frend/ *n* ❶ (person one likes) ami/-e *m/f* (**of** de); **to make** ~**s** se faire des amis; **to be/make** ~**s with sb** être/devenir ami/-e *m/f* avec qn; **to be a good** ~ **to sb** gen être un véritable ami; (in crisis) être un soutien pour qn; **Maura is a** ~ **of mine** Maura est une amie; **that's what** ~**s are for** c'est à ça que servent les amis; ❷ fig (supporter, fellow-member, ally) ami/-e *m/f*; **to have** ~**s in high places** avoir des amis influents; ❸ fig (familiar object) ami *m*

⟨Idiom⟩ **a** ~ **in need is a** ~ **indeed** Prov c'est dans le besoin que l'on connaît ses vrais amis Prov

friendless /'frendlɪs/ *adj* sans amis

friendliness /'frendlɪnɪs/ *n* gentillesse *f* (**of** de)

friendly /'frendlɪ/
A *n* Sport match *m* amical
B *adj* [person] amical, sympathique; [animal] affectueux/-euse; [attitude, argument, match] amical; [smile] (polite) aimable; (warm) amical; [government, nation] ami *inv* (after *n*); [shop] accueillant; [agreement] à l'amiable; **to be** ~ **with sb** être ami/-e *m/f* avec qn; **to get** *ou* **become** ~ **with sb** se lier d'amitié avec qn; **to be on** ~ **terms with sb** être en bons termes avec qn; **to be** ~ **to** être réceptif/-ive à [new ideas]; être bien disposé envers [small firms, local groups]; **to have a** ~ **relationship with sb** avoir de bonnes relations avec qn; **the people round here are very** ~ les gens par ici sont très gentils; **he's very** ~ **with the boss** il est très copain○ avec le patron
C -**friendly** combining form **environment-**~ qui ne nuit pas à l'environnement; **user-**~ d'utilisation facile, convivial

friendly: ~ **fire** *n* Mil euph feu *m* allié; **Friendly Islands** ► p. 954 *n* Tonga *m*, îles *fpl* des Amis; ~ **society** *n* GB mutuelle *f*

friendship /'frendʃɪp/ *n* amitié *f*; **to form** ~**s** se faire des amis

Friends of the Earth, FoE *n* Amis *mpl* de la Terre

fries○ /fraɪz/ *npl* US frites *fpl*

frieze /fri:z/ *n* frise *f*

frigate /'frɪgɪt/ *n* frégate *f*

fright /fraɪt/ *n* ❶ (feeling of terror) peur *f*; (more sudden) frayeur *f*, effroi *m*; **to take** ~ prendre peur, s'effrayer; ❷ (shock) frayeur *f*, peur *f*; **to have** *ou* **get a** ~ avoir peur; **to give sb a** ~ faire peur à qn, effrayer qn; **I had the** ~ **of my life!** j'ai cru mourir de peur!; ❸ ○(person) épouvantail *m*, horreur *f*

frighten /'fraɪtn/ *vtr* faire peur à, effrayer; **to** ~ **sb into doing** faire tellement peur à qn qu'il/elle finit par faire

⟨Phrasal verb⟩
■ **frighten off**: ► ~ **off [sb]**, ~ **[sb] off** chasser [intruder]; effaroucher [rival, buyer, bidder]

frightened /'fraɪtnd/ *adj* apeuré; **to be** ~ avoir peur (**of** de; **to do** de faire); **to be** ~ **that** craindre que (+ *subj*), avoir peur que (+ *subj*); **to be too** ~ **even to look** avoir tellement peur qu'on n'ose même pas regarder

frightening /'fraɪtnɪŋ/ *adj* ❶ lit (scary) [story, experience] terrifiant; [statistics] effarant; ❷ fig (alarming, disturbing) effrayant

frighteningly /'fraɪtnɪŋlɪ/ *adv* terriblement

frightful /'fraɪtfl/ *adj* ❶ (inducing horror) abominable, épouvantable; ❷ ○(terrible, bad) [prospect, mistake] terrible; [possibility] horrible; [headache] affreux/-euse; ❸ ○(expressing disgust) [person] épouvantable; [decor] affreux/-euse

frightfully /'fraɪtfəlɪ/ *adv* GB terriblement; **I'm** ~ **sorry** je suis vraiment désolé

frigid /'frɪdʒɪd/ *adj* ❶ Med [woman] frigide; ❷ Geog [zone] glacial

frigidity /frɪ'dʒɪdətɪ/ *n* ❶ Med frigidité *f*; ❷ fig froideur *f*

frill /frɪl/
A *n* (on dress) volant *m*; (on shirt) jabot *m*; Culin papillotte *f*
B **frills** *npl* ❶ (on clothes, furniture) fanfreluches *fpl*; ❷ (on car, appliance) options *fpl*; ❸ (in writing, drawing) fioritures *fpl*

frilled /frɪld/ *adj* [garment, collar] à volants

frilly /'frɪlɪ/ adj [garment] à froufrous; [underwear] avec des dentelles

fringe /frɪndʒ/

A n **1** GB (of hair) frange f; **2** (decorative trim) frange f; **3** (edge) (of forest) lisière f, orée f; (of town) abords mpl, périphérie f; **to be on the ~ of the crowd** être au bord de la foule; **4** Pol (group) frange f, élément m; **5** Theat **the ~** théâtre m alternatif

B **fringes** npl **on the (outer) ~s of the town** à la périphérie or aux abords de la ville; **on the ~s of society** en marge de la société

fringe benefits npl **1** (pensions, life or medical cover) avantages mpl sociaux; **2** (of job) avantages mpl en nature

fringed /frɪndʒd/ adj **1** [garment] à franges; **2** (edged) bordé (**with, by** de)

frippery /'frɪpərɪ/ n **1** ¢ (trivia) frivolités fpl; **2** (item) frivolité f

Frisian /'frɪzɪən/ ▸ p. 1032, p. 969 n **1** (person) Frison/-onne m/f; **2** (language) frison m

frisk /frɪsk/

A vtr fouiller [person]

B vi [lamb, puppy] gambader

frisky /'frɪskɪ/ adj [puppy] joueur/-euse; [horse] nerveux/-euse, chaud

fritter /'frɪtə(r)/ n beignet m

(Phrasal verb)

■ **fritter away**: ▸ **~ away [sth]**, **~ [sth] away** gaspiller

fritz /frɪts/: **on the fritz** adj phr US en panne

frivolity /frɪ'vɒlətɪ/ n (all contexts) frivolité f

frivolous /'frɪvələs/ adj **1** [person, attitude] frivole; **2** péj [allegation, enquiry] pas sérieux/-ieuse

frizz /frɪz/ vtr friser [hair]

frizzle /'frɪzl/ vtr, vi grésiller

frizzy /'frɪzɪ/ adj [hair] crépu

frock /frɒk/ ▸ p. 1191 n **1** (dress) robe f; **2** (of monk) bure f

frog /frɒg, US frɔːg/ n Zool grenouille f

(Idiom) **to have a ~ in one's throat** avoir un chat dans la gorge

frog: **~man** n homme-grenouille m; **~-march** vtr GB conduire [qn] de force; **~s' legs** npl cuisses fpl de grenouille; **~-spawn** n ¢ œufs mpl de grenouille

frolic /'frɒlɪk/

A n **1** (fun) ébats mpl; **2** (film) comédie f; (play) farce f

B vi lit s'ébattre, gambader; fig faire la fête

from /frəm, frɒm/

When from is used as a straightforward preposition in English it is translated by de in French: from Rome = de Rome; from the sea = de la mer; from Lisa = de Lisa. Remember that de + le always becomes du: from the office = du bureau, and de + les always becomes des: from the United States = des États-Unis.

from is often used after verbs in English (suffer from, benefit from etc). For translations, consult the appropriate verb entry (**suffer, benefit** etc).

from is used after certain nouns and adjectives in English (shelter from, exemption from, free from, safe from etc). For translations, consult the appropriate noun or adjective entry (**shelter, exemption, free, safe** etc).

This dictionary contains usage notes on such topics as nationalities, countries and continents, provinces and regions. Many of these use the preposition from. For the index to these Notes ▸ p. 1354.

For examples of the above and particular usages of from, see the entry below.

prep **1** (indicating place of origin) **paper ~ Denmark** du papier provenant du Danemark; **a flight ~ Nice** un vol en provenance de Nice; **a friend ~ Chicago** un ami (qui vient) de Chicago; **a colleague ~ Japan** un collègue japonais; **people ~ Spain** les Espagnols; **where is he ~?** d'où est-il?, d'où vient-il?; **she comes ~ Oxford** elle vient d'Oxford; **a tunnel ~ X to Y** un tunnel qui relie X à Y; **the road ~ A to B** la route qui va de A à B; **noises ~ upstairs** du bruit venant d'en-haut; **to take sth ~ one's bag** sortir qch de son sac; **to take sth ~ the shelf** prendre qch sur l'étagère; **~ under the table** de dessous la table; **2** (expressing distance)

10 km ~ the sea à 10 km de la mer; **it's not far ~ here** ce n'est pas loin d'ici; **the journey ~ A to B** le voyage de A à B; **3** (expressing time span) **open ~ 2 pm until 5 pm** ouvert de 14 à 17 heures; **~ June to August** du mois de juin au mois d'août; **15 years ~ now** dans 15 ans; **one month ~ now** dans un mois, d'ici un mois; **~ today** à partir d'aujourd'hui; **deaf ~ birth** sourd de naissance; **~ the age of 8** depuis l'âge de 8 ans; **~ day to day** de jour en jour; **4** (using as a basis) **~ a short story by Maupassant** d'après un conte de Maupassant; **to speak ~ experience** parler d'expérience; **5** (working for) **a man ~ the council** un homme qui travaille pour le conseil municipal; **a representative ~ Grunard and Co** un représentant de chez Grunard et Cie; **6** (among) **to select** ou **choose** ou **pick ~** choisir parmi; **7** (indicating a source) **a card ~ Pauline** une carte de Pauline; **a letter ~ them** une lettre de leur part; **where did it come ~?** d'où est-ce que ça vient?; **a quote ~ sb** une citation de qn; **8** (expressing extent, range) **wine ~ £5 a bottle** du vin à partir de 5 livres la bouteille; **children ~ the ages of 12 to 15** les enfants de 12 à 15 ans; **to rise ~ 10 to 17%** passer de 10 à 17%; **everything ~ paperclips to wigs** tout, des trombones aux perruques; **~ start to finish** du début à la fin; **9** (in subtraction) **10 ~ 27 leaves 17** 27 moins 10 égale 17; **10** (because of, due to) **I know ~ speaking to her that** j'ai appris en lui parlant que; **he knows her ~ work** il la connaît car ils travaillent ensemble; **11** (judging by) d'après; **~ the way he talks you'd think he was an expert** à l'entendre, on dirait un spécialiste

frond /frɒnd/ n (of fern) fronde f; (of palm) feuille f

front /frʌnt/

A n **1** (of house) façade f; (of shop) devanture f; (of cupboard, box) devant m; (of sweater) devant m; (of book) couverture f; (of card, coin, banknote) recto m; (of car, boat) avant m; (of fabric) endroit m; **to button at the ~** se boutonner sur le devant; **on the ~ of the envelope** au recto de l'enveloppe; **2** (of train, queue) tête f; (of building) devant m; (of auditorium) premier rang m; **at the ~ of the line** en tête de la file; **at the ~ of the house** sur le devant de la maison; **to sit at the ~ of the class** s'asseoir au premier rang de la classe; **I'll sit in the ~** je vais m'asseoir devant; **at the ~ of the coach** à l'avant du car; **3** Mil, Pol front m; **4** (stomach) ventre m; **to spill sth down one's ~** se renverser qch sur le devant; **5** GB (promenade) front m de mer, bord m de mer; **on the sea ~** au bord de la mer; **6** Meteorol front m; **7** (area of activity) côté m; **changes on the domestic** ou **home ~** Pol des changements côté politique intérieure; **8** fig (outer appearance) façade f; **9** °(cover) couverture f

B adj (épith) **1** (facing street) [entrance] côté rue; [garden, window] de devant; [bedroom] qui donne sur la rue; **2** (furthest from rear) [wheel] avant (after n); [seat] (in cinema) au premier rang; (in vehicle) de devant; [leg, paw, tooth] de devant; [carriage] de tête (after n); **3** (first) [page] premier/-ière (before n); [racing car] de tête; **4** (head-on) [view] de face (after n)

C in front adv phr **who's in ~?** qui gagne?; **I'm 30 points in ~** j'ai 30 points d'avance

D in front of prep phr (all contexts) devant

E vtr **1** = F **1**; **2** °(lead) être à la tête de [band]; **3** TV présenter

F vi **1** (face) **to ~ onto** GB ou **on** US donner sur; **2** (serve as a cover) **to ~ for** servir de couverture à

frontage /'frʌntɪdʒ/ n **1** Archit (of house) façade f; (of shop) devanture f; **2** (access) **with ocean/river ~** avec accès direct sur la mer/rivière

frontal /'frʌntl/ adj **1** (head-on) [assault] de front (after n); **2** Anat frontal; **3** Meteorol frontal; **4** Cin, Phot [lighting] de face

front bench /ˌfrʌnt 'bentʃ/ n GB Pol ¢ **1** (seats) rangs mpl du gouvernement; **2** (also **frontbenchers**°) députés mpl membres du gouvernement

front: **~ cover** n couverture f; **~ door** n porte f d'entrée

frontier /'frʌntɪə(r), US frʌn'tɪər/

A n lit, fig frontière f; **the ~ between France and Spain** la frontière franco-espagnole

B noun modifier [town, zone] frontière inv (after n), frontalier/-ière

frontier: **~ post** n poste m frontière; **~sman** n homme m de la frontière

front line /ˈfrʌntlaɪn/
A n **1** Mil front m; **2** fig (exposed position) **to be in** GB *ou* **on** US **the ~** être en première ligne; **3** (in rugby) **the ~** les avants *mpl* première ligne
B **front-line** *noun modifier* **1** Mil [*troops*] de front; [*positions*] de première ligne; **2** Pol [*state*] frontalier/-ière avec un État en guerre

frontman /ˈfrʌntmən/ n **1** (figurehead) homme m de paille **(for** de); **2** (TV presenter) présentateur m; **3** (lead musician) leader m

front: **~ matter** n ¢ pages *fpl* liminaires; **~ of house** n GB Theat foyer m

front page
A n (of newspaper, book) première page f
B **front-page** *noun modifier* [*picture, story*] à la une○; **the ~ headlines** les gros titres, la manchette

front-runner /ˌfrʌntˈrʌnə(r)/ n **1** Pol, gen (favourite) favori/-ite *m/f* **(in** de); **2** Sport coureur qui aime se positionner en tête de course

front-wheel drive n traction f avant

frost /frɒst/ n **1** (weather condition) gel m; **10° of ~** moins 10°, 10° au-dessous de zéro; **there may be a touch of ~ tonight** il pourrait geler cette nuit; **2** (one instance) gelée f; **3** (icy coating) givre m **(on** sur)
(Phrasal verb)
■ **frost over, frost up** se couvrir de givre

frost: **~bite** n ¢ gelures *fpl*; **~bitten** adj gelé

frosted /ˈfrɒstɪd/ adj **1** [*nail varnish*] nacré; **2** [*cake*] recouvert de glaçage; **3** (opaque) [*glass*] dépoli, opaque; **4** (chilled) [*drinking glass*] givré

frosting /ˈfrɒstɪŋ/ n glaçage m

frost-resistant /ˈfrɒstrɪzɪstənt/ adj [*vegetable*] résistant au gel

frosty /ˈfrɒstɪ/ adj **1** [*morning*] glacial; [*windscreen*] couvert de givre; **it was a ~ night** il gelait cette nuit-là; **2** fig [*reception*] glacial

froth /frɒθ, US frɔːθ/
A n **1** (on beer, champagne) mousse f; (on water) écume f; (around mouth) écume f; **2** ¢ (trivia) futilités *fpl*
B vi écumer; **to ~ at the mouth** lit écumer; fig écumer de rage

frothy /ˈfrɒθɪ, US ˈfrɔːθɪ/ adj **1** (foamy) [*beer, coffee, liquid*] mousseux/-euse; [*surface of sea*] écumeux/-euse; **2** (lacy) [*lingerie*] vaporeux/-euse

frown /fraʊn/
A n froncement m de sourcils
B vi froncer les sourcils; **to ~ at sb** regarder qn en fronçant les sourcils
(Phrasal verb)
■ **frown on, frown upon**: ▶ **~ on** *ou* **upon [sth]** désapprouver, critiquer; **to be ~ed upon** être mal vu

froze /frəʊz/ *prét* ▶ **freeze** B, C

frozen /ˈfrəʊzn/
A pp ▶ **freeze** B, C
B adj **1** lit gelé; **I'm ~** je suis gelé; **to be ~ stiff** être transi de froid; **2** fig **to be ~ with fear** être paralysé par la peur; **to be ~ to the spot** être cloué sur place; **3** Culin (bought) surgelé; (home-prepared) congelé; **4** Fin, Econ [*prices, assets*] bloqué, gelé

fructify /ˈfrʌktɪfaɪ/ vi fructifier

frugal /ˈfruːgl/ adj [*person*] économe **(with** de); [*lifestyle, meal*] frugal

frugally /ˈfruːgəlɪ/ adv [*live*] frugalement; [*stock*] avec parcimonie

fruit /fruːt/
A n (pl inv for collective sense) **1** Bot (edible, inedible) fruit m; **a piece of ~** un fruit; **have some ~** prenez un fruit *or* des fruits; **to bear ~** donner des fruits; **2** fig fruit m; **to enjoy the ~(s) of one's labours** jouir des fruits de son travail
B vi donner des fruits

fruit: **~ bowl** n (large) coupe f à fruits; (individual) coupelle f à fruits; **~ cake** n Culin cake m; **~ cocktail** n macédoine f de fruits; **~ drop** n bonbon m (aromatisé) aux fruits; **~ farmer** ▶ p. 1181 n producteur/-trice *m/f* de fruits; **~ farming** n culture f fruitière; **~ fly** n mouche f du vinaigre

fruitful /ˈfruːtfl/ adj **1** [*discussion*] fructueux/-euse; [*source*] fertile; **2** littér fertile, fécond

fruitfully /ˈfruːtfəlɪ/ adv [*teach*] avec succès; [*spend time*] de façon fructueuse

fruitfulness /ˈfruːtflnɪs/ n **1** littér fécondité f; **2** (of approach) utilité f

fruit gum n ≈ pastille f, bonbon m aux fruits

fruition /fruːˈɪʃn/ n **to come to ~** se réaliser; **to bring sth to ~** (effect) réaliser qch; (conclude) concrétiser qch

fruitless /ˈfruːtlɪs/ adj [*attempt*] vain; [*discussion*] stérile

fruit: **~ machine** n machine f à sous; **~ salad** n salade f de fruits; **~s of the forest** npl fruits mpl de la forêt; **~ tree** n arbre m fruitier

fruity /ˈfruːtɪ/ adj **1** [*wine, fragrance*] fruité; **2** [*voice, tone*] timbré; **3** [*joke*] salé

frump /frʌmp/ n péj femme f mal fagotée

frustrate /frʌˈstreɪt, US ˈfrʌstreɪt/ vtr **1** (irk, annoy) énerver [*person*]; **2** (thwart) réduire [qch] à néant [*effort*]; contrarier [*plan*]; entraver [*attempt*]

frustrated /frʌˈstreɪtɪd, US ˈfrʌst-/ adj **1** (irritated) énervé; **he became ~ at people's ignorance** l'ignorance des gens l'énervait; **2** (in aspirations) [*person*] frustré; [*desire*] inassouvi; **3** (thwarted) [*plan*] contrarié; [*effort*] réduit à néant; [*attempt*] vain (before n); **4** (would-be) **a ~ diplomat** un diplomate manqué; **5** (sexually) frustré

frustrating /frʌˈstreɪtɪŋ, US ˈfrʌst-/ adj **1** (irritating) énervant; **there's nothing more ~!** il n'y a rien de plus énervant! **2** (unsatisfactory, thwarting) frustrant

frustratingly /frʌˈstreɪtɪŋlɪ, US ˈfrʌst-/ adv désespérément

frustration /frʌˈstreɪʃn/ n **1** (thwarted feeling) frustration f **(at, with** quant à); **to feel anger and ~** se sentir en colère et frustré; **in ~, he... frustré, il...; 2** (annoying aspect) **the ~s of house-buying are endless** acheter une maison est une entreprise longue et frustrante; **3** (ruination) anéantissement m; **4** (sexual) frustration f

fry /fraɪ/
A n **1** Zool fretin m; **2** fig **small ~** (children) petits mpl, mioches○ mpl; (unimportant people) menu fretin m
B vtr (prét, pp **fried**) Culin faire frire
C vi (prét, pp **fried**) Culin frire
D **fried** pp adj frit; **fried fish** poisson m frit; **fried food** friture f; **fried eggs** œufs mpl au plat; **fried potatoes** pommes fpl de terre sautées

frying pan GB n poêle f (à frire)
(Idiom) **to jump out of the ~ into the fire** tomber de Charybde en Scylla

ft abrév écrite = **foot, feet**

fuchsia /ˈfjuːʃə/ n fuchsia m

fuddled /ˈfʌdld/ adj **1** (confused) [*brain*] confus, embrouillé; [*state*] de confusion; [*person*] désorienté; **2** (slightly drunk) éméché

fuddy-duddy○ /ˈfʌdɪdʌdɪ/ n schnock○ mf

fudge /fʌdʒ/
A n **1** Culin (soft sweet) caramels mpl mous; **have a piece of ~** prends un caramel; **2** US Culin (also **~ sauce**) (hot sauce) sauce f au chocolat; **3** ○(compromise) **it's a ~** c'est flou
B ○vtr **1** (evade) esquiver [*issue*]; **2** (falsify) truquer [*figures*]

fuel /ˈfjuːəl/
A n **1** gen combustible m; (for car, plane) carburant m; **2** fig **to provide ~ for** rajouter du poids à [*claims*]; attiser [*hatred*]
B vtr (p prés etc **-ll-, -l-** US) **1** (make run) alimenter [*furnace, engine*]; **to be ~led by gas** marcher au gaz; **2** (put fuel into) ravitailler [*plane*]; **3** fig aggraver [*tension*]; attiser [*hatred*]; susciter [*speculation*]
(Idiom) **to add ~ to the flames** *ou* **fire** jeter de l'huile sur le feu

fuel: **~ consumption** n (of plane, car) consommation f de carburant; (in industry) consommation f de combustible; **~-efficient** adj économique; **~ injection** n injection f (de carburant); **~ injection engine** n moteur m à injection; **~ pump** n pompe f d'alimentation; **~ saving** n économie f d'énergie; **~ tank** n (of car) réservoir m; (of plane, ship) réservoir m de carburant

fuggy /ˈfʌgɪ/ adj GB (smoky) enfumé; (airless) confiné

fugitive /ˈfjuːdʒətɪv/
A n fugitif/-ive *m/f*; fuyard/-e *m/f*
B adj **1** littér [*happiness*] éphémère, fugace; [*impression, sensation*] fugitif/-ive; **2** (in flight) [*person*] fugitif/-ive, en fuite

fugue /fjuːɡ/ n ① Mus fugue f; ② Psych amnésie f d'identité

fulcrum /'fʊlkrəm/ n (pl ~s ou -cra) lit point m d'appui; fig pivot m

fulfil GB, **fulfill** US /fʊl'fɪl/ vtr (p prés etc -ll-) ① (realize, carry out) réaliser [ambition, prophecy]; tenir [promise]; répondre à [desire, need]; **to ~ one's potential** se réaliser; ② (satisfy) **to ~ oneself** s'épanouir; **to feel** ~led se sentir comblé; ③ (satisfy requirements of) remplir [duty, conditions, contract]

fulfilling /fʊl'fɪlɪŋ/ adj [job, marriage] épanouissant; [experience] enrichissant

fulfilment GB, **fulfillment** US /fʊl'fɪlmənt/ n ① (satisfaction) épanouissement m; **sexual ~** épanouissement sexuel; **personal ~** accomplissement m de soi; **to seek ~** rechercher la plénitude; ② (realization) **the ~ of** la réalisation de [ambition, need]; l'accomplissement m de [promise]; ③ (of role, duty, obligation) accomplissement m; ④ (meeting requirements) **the ~ of the contract will entail...** pour remplir le contrat, il faudra...

full /fʊl/

A adj ① (completely filled) [box, glass, room] plein; [hotel, flight, car park] complet/-ète; [theatre] comble; **a ~ bottle of whisky** une pleine bouteille de whisky; **~ to the brim** plein à ras bord; **~ to overflowing** [bucket] plein à déborder; [suitcase] plein à craquer○; **I've got my hands ~** lit j'ai les mains pleines; fig je suis débordé; **don't speak with your mouth ~** ne parle pas la bouche pleine; **~ of** plein de; **he's ~ of his holiday plans** il ne parle que de ses projets de vacances; **to be ~ of one's own importance** être plein de suffisance; ② (also **~ up**) [stomach] plein; **I'm ~**○ je n'en peux plus; ③ (busy) [day, week] chargé, bien rempli; **my diary is ~ for this week** mon agenda est complet pour cette semaine; **a very ~ life** une vie très remplie; ④ (complete) [name, breakfast, story] complet/-ète; [price, control, understanding] total; [responsibility] entier/-ière; [support] inconditionnel/-elle; [inquiry] approfondi; **the ~ extent of the damage** l'ampleur des dégâts; **the ~ implications of** toutes les implications de, toute la portée de; **he has a ~ head of hair** il a tous ses cheveux; **to be in ~ view** parfaitement visible; ⑤ (officially recognized) [member] à part entière; [right] plein (before n); ⑥ (maximum) [employment, bloom] plein (before n); **at ~ volume** à plein volume; **at ~ speed** à toute vitesse; **in ~ sunlight** en plein soleil; **to make ~ use of sth, to use sth to ~ advantage** profiter pleinement de qch; **to get ~ marks** GB obtenir la note maximale; ⑦ (for emphasis) [hour, kilo, month] bon/bonne (before n); ⑧ (rounded) [cheeks] rond; [lips] charnu; [figure] fort; [skirt, sleeve] ample; ⑨ **there's a ~ moon** c'est la pleine lune; ⑩ (rich) [flavour, tone] riche

B adv ① (directly) **to hit sb ~ in the face** frapper qn en plein visage; **to look sb ~ in the face** regarder qn droit dans les yeux; ② (very) **to know ~ well** that savoir fort bien que; ③ (to the maximum) **with the heating up ~** avec le chauffage à fond

C in full adv phr [describe, pay] intégralement

(Idiom) **to live life to the ~** profiter pleinement de l'existence

full: **~-back** n Sport arrière m; **~ beam** n Aut pleins phares mpl

full blast○ /ˌfʊl'blɑːst/ adv **the TV was on (at) ~** la télé marchait à pleins tubes○

full-blooded /ˌfʊl'blʌdɪd/ adj ① (vigorous) vigoureux/-euse; ② (committed) pur et dur inv; ③ (pure bred) [person] de race pure; [horse] pur sang

full-blown /ˌfʊl'bləʊn/ adj ① Med [disease] déclaré; [epidemic] extensif/-ive; **to have ~ Aids** être atteint d'un sida avéré; ② (qualified) [doctor] diplômé; ③ (large-scale) [crisis, war] à grande échelle; ④ [rose] épanoui

full: **~ board** n Tourism pension f complète; **~-bodied** adj [wine] corsé; **~-cream milk** n GB lait m entier; **~ dress** n gén tenue f de cérémonie; Mil grande tenue f; **~-face** adj, adv de face; **~-frontal** adj [photograph] nu de face; **~-grown** adj adulte

full house n ① Theat **to have a ~** faire salle comble; ② (in poker) full m

full-length /ˌfʊl'leŋθ/ adj ① Cin **a ~ film** un long métrage; ② (head to toe) [portrait] en pied; **a ~ window** baie f vitrée; ③ (long) [coat, curtain] long/longue; [opera] grand (before n)

full name n nom m et prénom m

fullness /'fʊlnɪs/ n ① (width) (of sleeve, dress) ampleur f; ② (roundness) (of breasts) rondeur f; (of lips) épaisseur f; ③ (of flavour) richesse f

(Idiom) **in the ~ of time** (with the passage of time) avec le temps; (eventually) en temps et lieu

full: **~-page** adj [advertisement] pleine page; **~ pay** n traitement m intégral; **~ price** adv au prix fort

full-scale /ˌfʊl'skeɪl/ adj ① (in proportion) [drawing] grandeur f nature; ② (extensive) [operation] de grande envergure; [investigation, study] approfondi; ③ (total) [alert] général; [crisis] généralisé; ④ (complete) [performance] grand (before n)

full-size(d) /ˌfʊl'saɪz(d)/ adj ① (large) grand format inv; ② [violin, bike] pour adulte

full stop n GB (in punctuation) point m; **I'm not leaving, ~!** je ne pars pas, point final!

full time **A** n Sport fin m du match **B** **full-time** noun modifier ① Sport [score] final; ② (permanent) [job, student] à plein temps **C** adv [study, teach, work] à plein temps

fully /'fʊlɪ/ adv ① (completely) [understand] très bien; [succeed, recover] tout à fait; [furnished, dressed] entièrement; [awake, developed] complètement; [aware] parfaitement; **to be ~ qualified** avoir obtenu tous ses diplômes; ② (to the maximum) [open] à fond; [stretched] complètement; **~ booked** complet/-ète; ③ (comprehensively) [study] à fond; [explain] de façon détaillée; ④ (at least) au moins

fully-fledged /ˌfʊlɪ'fledʒd/ adj ① Zool [bird] qui a toutes ses plumes; ② (established) [member] à part entière; [lawyer] diplômé

fulminate /'fʌlmɪneɪt, US 'fʊl-/ vi fulminer, pester

fulsome /'fʊlsəm/ adj sout [compliments] excessif/-ive; [manner] obséquieux/-ieuse

fumble /'fʌmbl/ **A** n US Sport échappé m **B** vtr ① Sport mal attraper [ball]; ② (bungle) rater [entrance, attempt] **C** vi **to ~ (about) in one's bag for a cigarette** fouiller dans son sac pour trouver une cigarette; **to ~ with** manier maladroitement

(Phrasal verb) **■ fumble about** (in dark) tâtonner (**to do** pour faire); **to ~ about in** fouiller dans

fume /fjuːm/ vi ① (in anger) **to be fuming** fulminer, être furibond○; **to be fuming with anger** bouillonner de colère; ② [mixture, chemical] fumer

fumes /fjuːmz/ npl émanations fpl; **petrol ~** GB, **gas ~** US vapeurs fpl d'essence; **traffic ~** fumée f des pots d'échappement

fumigate /'fjuːmɪɡeɪt/ vtr désinfecter [qch] par fumigation

fun /fʌn/ n plaisir m, amusement m; **to have ~** s'amuser (**doing** en faisant; **with** avec); **we had great ~** nous nous sommes beaucoup amusés; **doing this is ~** c'est amusant de faire qch; **to do sth for ~**, **to do sth for the ~ of it** faire qch pour s'amuser; **to do sth in ~** faire qch pour plaisanter; **half the ~ of doing is...** le plus beau de faire est...; **it's not much ~** ce n'est pas très amusant (**for** pour); **to spoil sb's ~** gâcher le plaisir de qn; **to have a sense of ~** avoir de l'humour; **he's (such) ~** il est (tellement) drôle; **she is great ~ to be with** on s'amuse beaucoup avec elle

(Idioms) **to become a figure of ~** devenir la risée (**for** de); **to have ~ and games** s'amuser comme des petits fous; **to make ~ of ou poke ~ at** se moquer de

function /'fʌŋkʃn/ **A** n ① (role, of body, organ, tool) fonction f; (of person) fonction f, charge f; **to fulfil a ~** [person] remplir une fonction; **in her ~ as...** en sa qualité de...; **the ~ of the heart is to do** le cœur a pour fonction de faire; ② (reception) réception f; (ceremony) cérémonie f (officielle); ③ Comput, Math fonction f **B** vi ① (work properly) fonctionner; ② (operate as) **to ~ as** [object] faire fonction de, servir de; [person] jouer le rôle de

functional /'fʌŋkʃənl/ adj [design] fonctionnel/-elle; (in working order) opérationnel/-elle

functionary /'fʌŋkʃənərɪ, US -nerɪ/ n gen fonctionnaire mf; péj bureaucrate mf, rond-de-cuir m

function : ~ **key** n touche f de fonction; ~ **room** n salle f de réception; ~ **word** n mot m grammatical, mot-outil m

fund /fʌnd/
A n [1] (cash reserve) fonds m; **emergency/relief** ~ caisse f de prévoyance/secours; **disaster** ~ collecte f en faveur des sinistrés; [2] fig (store) **she's a** ~ **of wisdom** c'est un puits de sagesse
B **funds** npl [1] (capital) fonds mpl, capitaux mpl; **to be in** ~**s** avoir de l'argent; [2] (credit balance) (of individual) argent m; (of company) capitaux mpl; [3] (on cheque) **'No** ~**s', 'insufficient** ~**s'** 'défaut de provision'
C vtr [1] Fin financer [company, project]; [2] (convert) consolider [debt]

fundamental /ˌfʌndə'mentl/
A **fundamentals** npl **the** ~**s** (of abstract ideas) les fondements mpl (**of** de); (of skill) les règles fpl de base
B adj [issue, meaning] fondamental (**to** pour); [error, importance] capital; [concern] principal; **to be** ~ **to** être essentiel à

fundamentalist /ˌfʌndə'mentəlɪst/ n, adj gen fondamentaliste (mf); (Islam) intégriste (mf)

fundamentally /ˌfʌndə'mentəlɪ/ adv [opposed, flawed] fondamentalement; [incompatible] foncièrement; [change] radicalement

funding /'fʌndɪŋ/ n [1] (financial aid) financement m; **to receive** ~ **from** être financé par; **self-**~ autofinancé; [2] (of debt) consolidation f

funding body, **funding agency** n organisme m de subvention

fund : ~ **manager** n Fin gestionnaire mf de fonds; ~**-raiser** n (person) collecteur/-trice m/f de fonds; (event) collecte f; ~**-raising** n collecte f de fonds

funeral /'fju:nərəl/
A n gen enterrement m, obsèques fpl fml
B noun modifier [march, oration, service] funèbre
(Idiom) **that's your/her** ~○! c'est ton/son problème○!

funeral : ~ **director** ▸ p. 1181 n entrepreneur m de pompes funèbres; ~ **parlour**, ~ **home** US, ~ **parlor** US n chambre f mortuaire (chez un entrepreneur de pompes funèbres)

funereal /'fju:'nɪərɪəl/ adj lugubre

fun : ~ **fair** n fête f foraine; ~ **fur** n fausse fourrure f

fungal /'fʌŋgl/ adj fongique

fungi /'fʌngaɪ, -dʒaɪ/ pl ▸ **fungus**

fungus /'fʌŋgəs/ n (pl **-gi**) [1] Bot, Med champignon m; [2] (mould) moisissure f

funicular /fju:'nɪkjʊlə(r)/ n, adj funiculaire (m)

fun-loving /'fʌnlʌvɪŋ/ adj [person] qui aime s'amuser

funnel /'fʌnl/
A n (for liquids) entonnoir m; (on ship) cheminée f
B vtr [1] lit **to** ~ **sth into/through** faire passer qch dans/par; **to** ~ **sth out** évacuer qch; [2] fig acheminer [funds, aid] (**to** vers)

funnily /'fʌnɪlɪ/ adv curieusement

funny /'fʌnɪ/
A adj (amusing) drôle; (odd) bizarre; **it's** ~ **that she hasn't phoned** c'est drôle or bizarre qu'elle n'ait pas appelé; **to feel** ~○ se sentir tout/-e chose○
B adv○ [walk, talk, act] bizarrement, drôlement
(Idiom) ~ **peculiar or** ~ **ha-ha?** drôle-bizarre ou drôle-amusant?

funny : ~ **business**○ n **C** magouilles○ fpl; ~ **money**○ n fausse monnaie f

fur /fɜ:(r)/
A n **C** [1] (on animal) poils mpl; (for garment) fourrure f; [2] GB (in kettle, pipes) tartre m
B noun modifier [collar, lining, coat] de fourrure
(Idiom) **that'll make the** ~ **fly!** ça va chauffer○!
(Phrasal verb)
  ■ **fur up** GB [kettle, pipes] s'entartrer

furious /'fjʊərɪəs/ adj [1] (angry) furieux/-ieuse (**with, at** contre); **he's** ~ **about it** cela l'a rendu furieux; **I was** ~ **with her for coming** j'étais furieux qu'elle soit venue; [2] (violent) gen acharné; [storm] déchaîné; **at a** ~ **rate** à un rythme effréné

(Idiom) **the pace was fast and** ~ le rythme était endiablé

furiously /'fjʊərɪəslɪ/ adv furieusement; [struggle] avec acharnement

furl /fɜ:l/ vtr ferler [sail]; rouler [flag]

furnace /'fɜ:nɪs/ n [1] (boiler) chaudière f; (in foundry) fourneau m; (for forging) four m; [2] fig fournaise f

furnish /'fɜ:nɪʃ/
A vtr [1] meubler [room, apartment] (**with** avec); [2] fournir [document, facts, excuse]; **to** ~ **sb with sth** fournir qch à qn
B **furnished** pp adj [apartment] meublé

furnishing /'fɜ:nɪʃɪŋ/
A n (action) ameublement m
B **furnishings** npl (complete décor) ameublement m
C noun modifier [fabric] d'ameublement; ~ **department** rayon m ameublement

furniture /'fɜ:nɪtʃə(r)/
A n **C** mobilier m, meubles mpl; **door** ~ plaques fpl et poignées fpl; **mental** ~ univers m intellectuel; **a piece of** ~ un meuble
B noun modifier [shop, business, factory, maker, restorer] de meubles; [industry] du meuble
(Idiom) **to be part of the** ~○ hum faire partie des meubles○

furniture : ~ **depot** n garde-meubles m inv; ~ **polish** n encaustique f; ~ **remover** ▸ p. 1181 n GB déménageur m; ~ **store** n magasin m de meubles; ~ **van** n camion m de déménagement

furore /fjʊ'rɔ:rɪ/, **furor** US /'fjʊ:rɔ:r/ n (acclaim) enthousiasme m; (criticism) scandale m; **to cause a** ~ (reaction, excitement) soulever les passions; (outrage) faire scandale; (acclaim) provoquer l'enthousiasme

furrow /'fʌrəʊ/
A n (in earth, snow) sillon m; (on brow) pli m
B vi **his brow** ~**ed** il a plissé le front

furry /'fɜ:rɪ/ adj [toy] en peluche; [kitten] au poil touffu

further /'fɜ:ðə(r)/
A adv (comparative of far) [1] (a greater distance) (also **farther**) lit, fig plus loin; **how much** ~ **is it?** c'est encore loin?; **how much** ~ **have they got to go?** est-ce qu'ils vont encore loin?; **to get** ~ **and** ~ **away** s'éloigner de plus en plus; ~ **back/forward** plus en arrière/en avant; ~ **away** ou **off** plus loin; ~ **on** encore plus loin; **I'll go so far but no** ~ j'irai jusque là mais pas plus loin; **she didn't get any** ~ **with him than I did** elle n'est arrivée à rien de plus avec lui que moi; **we're** ~ **forward than we thought** on est plus avancé qu'on ne le pensait; [2] (in time) (also **farther**) ~ **back than 1964** avant 1964; **a year** ~ **on** un an plus tard; **we must look** ~ **ahead** nous devons regarder plus vers l'avenir; **I haven't read** ~ **than page twenty** je n'ai pas lu au-delà de la page vingt; [3] (a greater extent) **prices fell (even)** ~ les prix ont baissé encore plus; **we will enquire** ~ **into the matter** nous nous renseignerons davantage sur la question; [4] (furthermore) de plus, en outre
B adj (comparative of **far**) [1] (additional) **a** ~ **500 people** 500 personnes de plus; ~ **changes** d'autres changements; **there have been** ~ **allegations that** il y a eu de nouvelles allégations selon lesquelles; ~ **research** des recherches plus approfondies; ~ **details can be obtained by writing to the manager** pour plus de renseignements, adressez-vous à la direction; **to have no** ~ **use for sth** ne plus avoir besoin de qch; **without** ~ **delay** sans plus attendre; **there's nothing** ~ **to discuss** il n'y a rien d'autre à discuter; [2] (more distant) (also **farther**) autre
C vtr augmenter [chances]; faire avancer [career, plan]; servir [cause]
D **further to** prep phr sout suite à

further education n GB Univ ≈ enseignement m professionnel

furthermore /ˌfɜ:ðə'mɔ:(r)/ adv de plus, en outre

furthest /'fɜ:ðɪst/
A adj (superl of **far**) le plus éloigné
B adv [1] (in space) (also **the** ~) le plus loin; **this plan goes** ~ **towards solving the problem** fig c'est ce projet qui s'approche le plus de la solution du problème; [2] (in time) **the** ~ **back I can remember is 1970** je ne me rappelle rien avant 1970; **the** ~ **ahead we can look is next week** nous ne pouvons rien prévoir au-delà de la semaine prochaine

furtive /'fɜ:tɪv/ adj [glance, movement] furtif/-ive; [person] agissant subrepticement; [behaviour] suspect; [deal, meeting] subreptice

furtively /'fɜːtɪvlɪ/ adv [glance] furtivement; [act] subrepticement; [eat, smoke] en cachette

fury /'fjʊərɪ/ n fureur f; (of storm, sea) violence f; **to be in a ∼** être en fureur; **he flew at her in a ∼** il se rua sur elle dans un accès de rage

(Idiom) **to do sth like ∼**○ faire qch comme un fou○/une folle○

fuse /fjuːz/

A n **1** Elec fusible m; **to blow a ∼** lit faire sauter un fusible; fig○ piquer une crise○; **2** (for bomb) mèche f; (detonator) détonateur m

B vtr **1** lit munir [qch] d'un fusible [plug]; amorcer [bomb]; souder [wires]; amalgamer [metals]; **2** fig faire fusionner [ideas, images]

C vi **1** lit [metals, chemicals] se fondre (ensemble); **the lights have ∼d** GB un fusible a sauté; **2** fig fusionner

D fused pp adj Elec [plug] avec fusible incorporé

(Idiom) **to be on a short ∼** être soupe au lait

fuse box n boîte f à fusibles

fuselage /'fjuːzəlɑːʒ, -lɪdʒ/ n fuselage m

fuse wire n fusible m

fusillade /ˌfjuːzə'leɪd, US -sə-/ n Mil fusillade f; fig avalanche f

fusion /'fjuːʒn/ n gen, Phys fusion f; (of styles) mélange m

fuss /fʌs/

A n **1** (agitation) remue-ménage m inv; (verbal) histoires fpl; **to make a ∼** faire des histoires; **to make a ∼ about sth** faire toute une histoire à propos de qch; **to make a big ∼ about nothing** faire un tas d'histoires pour rien; **I don't see what all the ∼ is about** je ne vois pas où est le problème; **2** (angry scene) tapage m; **to kick up a ∼ about sth**○ piquer une crise○ à propos de qch; **3** (attention) **to make a ∼ of** être aux petits soins avec or pour [person]; caresser [animal]; **she doesn't want any ∼** elle veut qu'on la reçoive simplement

B vi **1** (worry) se faire du souci (**about** pour); **he's always ∼ing over** ou **about his appearance** il est obsédé par son apparence; **2** (be agitated) s'agiter; **3** (show attention) **to ∼ over sb**○ être aux petits soins avec or pour qn

fussily /'fʌsɪlɪ/ adv **1** (anxiously) avec maniaquerie; **2** (ornately) de manière tarabiscotée

fussiness /'fʌsɪnɪs/ n (of decoration) tarabiscotage m; (choosiness) maniaquerie f

fussing /'fʌsɪŋ/ n maniaquerie f

fussy /'fʌsɪ/ adj **1** (difficult to please) **to be ∼ about one's food/about details** être difficile sur la nourriture/maniaque sur les détails; **2** [furniture, style, decoration] tarabiscoté; [pattern] trop chargé

futile /'fjuːtaɪl, US -tl/ adj **1** (vain) vain; **2** (inane) futile

futility /fjuː'tɪlətɪ/ n inutilité f

future /'fjuːtʃə(r)/

A n **1** (on time scale) avenir m; **in the ∼** dans l'avenir; **in the near** ou **not too distant ∼** dans un proche avenir; **in ∼** à l'avenir; **the train of the ∼** le train du futur; **to see into the ∼** lire l'avenir; **2** (prospects) avenir m; **3** Ling (also **∼ tense**) futur m; **in the ∼** au futur

B futures npl Fin contrats mpl à terme

C adj (épith) [generation, developments, investment, earnings] futur; [prospects] d'avenir; [queen, prince etc] futur (before n); **at some ∼ date** à une date ultérieure

future: **∼ perfect** n futur m antérieur; **∼s market** n Fin marché m de contrats à terme

fuze n US = **fuse**

fuzz /fʌz/

A n **1** (hair) tignasse f bouclée; (beard) barbiche f; (downy hair) duvet m; **2** ○(police) **the ∼** les flics○ mpl

B vtr brouiller [image, vision]

C vi (also **∼ over**) [image, vision] se brouiller

fuzziness /'fʌzɪnɪs/ n (of image) flou m; (of idea) caractère m confus

fuzzy /'fʌzɪ/ adj **1** [hair, beard] (curly) crépu; (downy) duveteux/-euse; **2** (blurry) [image] flou; [idea, mind] confus; [distinction] flou

Gg

g, **G** /dʒiː/ n ① (letter) g, G m; ② **G** Mus sol m; ③ **g** (abrév écrite = **gram(s)**) g; ④ **g** Phys g m

GA US Post abrév écrite = **Georgia**

gab○:

(Idiom) **to have the gift of the ~**○ avoir du bagou(t)○

gabble /'gæbl/
A n charabia○ m
B vi bredouiller
(Phrasal verb)
■ **gabble away**, **gabble on** baragouiner○

gable /'geɪbl/ n pignon m

Gabon /gə'bɒn/ ▸ p. 774 pr n Gabon m

gadget /'gædʒɪt/ n gadget m

gadgetry /'gædʒɪtrɪ/ n ¢ gadgets mpl

Gaelic /'geɪlɪk, 'gæ-/ ▸ p. 969 n, adj gaélique (m)

> ⓘ **Gaelic** Langue celtique parlée en Irlande et dans la région des Highlands et des Hébrides en Écosse. C'est, avec l'anglais, la langue officielle de la République d'Irlande où elle est enseignée à l'école. En Écosse, la diffusion de programmes en gaélique à la radio et à la télévision est obligatoire. Il existe des différences considérables entre le gaélique parlé en Irlande et celui qui est parlé en Écosse, mais les locuteurs de ces deux langues se comprennent.

gaff /gæf/:
(Idiom) **to blow the ~**○ GB vendre la mèche○; **to blow the ~ on sth**○ GB révéler la vérité sur [conspiracy]

gaffe /gæf/ n bévue f

gaffer /'gæfə(r)/ n ① GB (foreman) contremaître m; ② GB (boss) patron m; ③ Cin, TV éclairagiste mf

gag /gæg/
A n ① lit, fig bâillon m; **to put a ~ on the press** bâillonner la presse; ② ○(joke) blague○ f
B vtr (p prés etc **-gg-**) lit bâillonner [hostage]; fig bâillonner [media]; museler [journalist]
C vi (p prés etc **-gg-**) avoir un haut-le-cœur; **he ~ged on his soup** il s'est étouffé en mangeant sa soupe

gage /geɪdʒ/ n, vtr US = **gauge A**, **B**

gaiety /'geɪətɪ/ n gaieté f

gaily /'geɪlɪ/ adv ① [laugh] de bon cœur; [say] joyeusement; **~ coloured** GB, **~ colored** US aux couleurs gaies; ② (casually) [announce, reveal] avec désinvolture

gain /geɪn/
A n ① (increase) augmentation f (**in** de); ② (profit) profit m, gain m; **financial ~** gain financier; **to do sth for material ~** faire qch pour l'argent; ③ (advantage) gen gain m; (in status, knowledge) acquis m; **to make ~s** [political party] se renforcer
B gains npl Fin gains mpl; **losses and ~s** pertes fpl et profits mpl; **to make ~s** [currency, shares] être en hausse
C vtr ① (acquire) acquérir [experience] (**from** de); obtenir [advantage, information] (**from** grâce à); gagner [respect, support, time]; conquérir [freedom]; **to ~ popularity** gagner en popularité; **we have nothing to ~** nous n'avons rien à gagner; **to ~ control of sth** prendre le contrôle de qch; **to ~ possession of sth** s'assurer la possession de qch; **to ~ ground** gagner du terrain (**on** sur); ② (increase) **to**

~ speed prendre de la vitesse or de l'élan; **to ~ weight** prendre du poids; **to ~ 4 kilos** prendre 4 kilos; **to ~ 3 minutes** prendre 3 minutes d'avance; ③ (win, reach) gagner [point, place]; **they ~ed four seats from the Democrats** ils ont pris quatre sièges aux Démocrates; **to ~ the upper hand** prendre le dessus
D vi ① (improve) **to ~ in prestige/popularity** gagner en prestige/en popularité; **to ~ in confidence** prendre de l'assurance; ② (profit) **she hasn't ~ed by it** cela ne lui a rien rapporté; **do you think we'll ~ by adopting this strategy?** pensez-vous que nous y gagnerons en adoptant cette stratégie?
(Phrasal verb)
■ **gain on:** ▸ **~ on [sb/sth]** rattraper [person, vehicle]; **the opposition are ~ing on the government** l'opposition est en train de prendre l'avantage sur le gouvernement

gainful /'geɪnfl/ adj [employment] rémunéré

gainsay /ˌgeɪn'seɪ/ vtr (prét, pp **gainsaid**) sout réfuter [argument]; contredire [person]

gal /gæl/ n: abrév écrite = **gallon**

galaxy /'gæləksɪ/ n lit galaxie f; fig pléiade f

gale /geɪl/ n vent m violent; **a force 9 ~** un vent force 9; **~s of laughter** fig éclats mpl de rire

gale warning n avis m de coup de vent

Galicia /gə'lɪsɪə/ pr n (in Central Europe) Galicie f; (in Spain) Galice f

gall /gɔːl/
A n ① Med bile f; ② (cheek) impudence f
B vtr exaspérer

gallant /'gælənt/ adj ① (courageous) [soldier] vaillant, brave; [attempt] héroïque; ② †(courteous) galant

gallantry /'gæləntrɪ/ n ① (courage) bravoure f; ② †(courtesy) galanterie f

gall bladder ▸ p. 698 n vésicule f biliaire

gallery /'gælərɪ/ n ① (also **art ~**) (public) musée m; (private) galerie f; (part of museum) galerie f; ② Archit gen galerie f; (for press, public) tribune f; ③ Theat dernier balcon m
(Idiom) **to play to the ~** chercher à épater la galerie

galley /'gælɪ/ n (ship) galère f; (ship's kitchen) cuisine f; Aviat office m

Gallic /'gælɪk/ adj gen français; Hist gaulois

gallicism /'gælɪsɪzəm/ n gallicisme m

galling /'gɔːlɪŋ/ adj [remark, criticism] vexant

gallivant /'gælɪvænt/ v
■ **gallivant around**, **gallivant about** se balader

gallon /'gælən/ ▸ p. 723 n gallon m (GB = 4.546 litres; US = 3.785 litres)

gallop /'gæləp/
A n lit, fig galop m; **to go for a ~** aller faire un galop; **to break into a ~** prendre le galop; **at a ~** au galop also fig
B vtr, vi ① lit galoper; **to ~ away** partir au galop; ② fig **he came ~ing down the stairs** il a descendu l'escalier à toute allure; **Japan is ~ing ahead in this field** le Japon est largement en tête dans ce domaine

galloping /'gæləpɪŋ/ adj [horse] au galop; [inflation, consumption] galopant

gallows /'gæləʊz/ n gibet m

Games and sports

With or without the definite article?

■ *French normally uses the definite article with names of games and sports:*

football
= le football

bridge
= le bridge

chess
= les échecs *mpl*

marbles
= les billes *fpl*

cops and robbers
= les gendarmes et les voleurs

to play football
= jouer au football

to play bridge
= jouer au bridge

to play chess
= jouer aux échecs

to play marbles *or* **at marbles**
= jouer aux billes

to play cops and robbers *or* **at cops and robbers**
= jouer aux gendarmes et aux voleurs

to like football
= aimer le football

to like chess
= aimer les échecs

■ *But most compound nouns (e.g.* saute-mouton, colin-maillard, pigeon vole) *work like this:*

hide-and-seek
= cache-cache *m*

to play at hide-and-seek
= jouer à cache-cache

to like hide-and-seek
= aimer jouer à cache-cache

■ *Names of other 'official' games and sports follow the same pattern as* bridge *in the following phrases:*

to play bridge with X against Y
= jouer au bridge avec X contre Y

to beat sb at bridge
= battre qn au bridge

to win at bridge
= gagner au bridge

to lose at bridge
= perdre au bridge

she's good at bridge
= elle joue bien au bridge

a bridge club
= un club de bridge

Players and events

a bridge player
= un joueur de bridge

but

I'm not a bridge player
= je ne joue pas au bridge

he's a good bridge player
= il joue bien au bridge

a game of bridge
= une partie de bridge

a bridge champion
= un champion de bridge

the French bridge champion
= le champion de France de bridge

a bridge championship
= un championnat de bridge

to win the French championship
= gagner le championnat de France

the rules of bridge
= les règles du bridge

Playing cards

■ *The names of the four suits work like* club *here:*

clubs	**I've no clubs left**
= les trèfles *mpl*	= je n'ai plus de trèfle
to play a club	**have you any clubs?**
= jouer un trèfle	= as-tu du trèfle?
a high/low club	**clubs are trumps**
= un gros/petit trèfle	= l'atout est trèfle
the eight of clubs	**to call two clubs**
= le huit de trèfle	= demander deux trèfles
the ace of clubs	
= l'as de trèfle	

■ *Other games vocabulary can be found in the dictionary at* **match, game, set, trick** *etc.*

g

---

gallstone /'gɔːlstəʊn/ *n* calcul *m* biliaire

galore /gə'lɔː(r)/ *adv* [*prizes, bargains, nightclubs*] à profusion; [*drinks, sandwiches*] à volonté, à gogo○

galvanize /'gælvənaɪz/ *vtr* ① Ind galvaniser; ② *fig* galvaniser [*group, community*]; relancer [*campaign*]; **to ~ sb into doing** pousser qn à faire

Gambia /'gæmbɪə/ ▸ p. 774 *pr n* **the ~** la Gambie

gambit /'gæmbɪt/ *n* ① tactique *f*; **opening ~** tactique pour entrer en matière; ② (*in chess*) gambit *m*

gamble /'gæmbl/
A *n* pari *m*; **to have a ~ on sth** faire un pari sur qch; **to take a ~** faire un pari; **that's a bit of a ~** c'est un peu risqué; **his ~ paid off** il a réussi *or* gagné son pari
B *vtr* jouer [*money*]; *fig* miser (**on** sur)
C *vi* (*at cards, on shares*) jouer; (*on horses*) parier; *fig* miser; **to ~ for high stakes** *lit, fig* jouer gros
(*Phrasal verb*)
■ **gamble away**: ▸ **~ away** [sth], **~** [sth] **away** perdre [qch] au jeu

gambler /'gæmblə(r)/ *n* joueur/-euse *m/f*; **heavy ~** flambeur *m*

gambling /'gæmblɪŋ/
A *n* jeu *m* (d'argent)
B *noun modifier* [*syndicate, table, debt*] de jeu

gambol /'gæmbl/ *vi* (*p prés etc* **-ll-**, US **-l-**) *littér* gambader

game /geɪm/
A *n* ① (*activity*) jeu *m*; **to play a ~** jouer à un jeu; **to play the ~** *fig* jouer franc jeu; **don't play ~s with me!** (*tell me the truth*) ne me fais pas marcher! (*don't try to be smart*) n'essaie pas de jouer au plus fin avec moi!; ② (*match*) (*of indoor game*) partie *f* (**of** de); (*of football etc*) match *m* (**of** de); **let's have a ~ of cowboys** on joue aux cowboys?; ③ (*part of match*) (*in tennis*) jeu *m*; (*in bridge*) manche *f*; **we're two ~s all** nous sommes à deux jeux partout; **~ to Hadman** jeu Hadman; **~, set and match** jeu, set et match; **grass suits my ~** je joue bien sur gazon; **to put sb off his/her ~** distraire qn; ④ (*trick*) scheme) jeu *m*; **what's your ~?** à quoi joues-tu?; **so that's his ~!** c'est donc ça sa combine○!; ⑤ ○(*occupation*) péj *ou* hum **the insurance ~** le domaine de l'assurance; **I've been**

in this ~ **10 years** je suis dans la partie depuis 10 ans; **he's new to this** ~ il est nouveau dans la partie; **6** Culin gibier m

B **games** npl **1** GB Sch sport m; **2** (also **Games**) (sporting event) Jeux mpl

C noun modifier **1** [pâté, dish, stew] de gibier; **2** **games** GB [teacher, lesson] d'éducation physique

D adj **1** (willing to try) partant°; **he's** ~ **for anything** il est toujours partant°; **she's always** ~ **for a laugh** elle est toujours prête à rire; **OK, I'm** ~ d'accord, j'en suis; **2** (plucky) courageux/-euse

(Idioms) **that's the name of the** ~ c'est la règle du jeu; **the** ~**'s up** tout est fichu°; **to beat sb at their own** ~ battre qn à son propre jeu; **to be on the** ~° GB faire le trottoir°; **to give the** ~ **away** vendre la mèche; **two can play at that** ~ à bon chat, bon rat Prov

game: ~ **bird** n gibier m à plumes; ~**keeper** ▸ p. 1181 n garde-chasse m

gamely /'geɪmlɪ/ adv courageusement

game: ~ **park** n = game reserve; ~ **plan** n Sport, gen stratégie f; ~ **point** n (tennis) balle f de jeu; ~ **reserve** n (for hunting) réserve f de chasse; (for preservation) réserve f naturelle (de grands fauves); ~ **show** n jeu m télévisé

gamesmanship /'geɪmzmənʃɪp/ n ȼ péj stratagèmes mpl

game warden n garde-chasse m

gaming: ~ **laws** npl réglementation f des jeux; ~ **machine** n machine f à sous

gammon /'gæmən/ n jambon m

gamut /'gæmət/ n gamme f; **to run the** ~ **of sth** passer par tout l'éventail de qch

gander /'gændə(r)/ n Zool jars m

gang /gæŋ/ n **1** (of criminals) gang m; (of youths, friends) bande f; **2** (of workmen, prisoners) équipe f

(Phrasal verbs)
■ **gang together** se grouper (**to do** pour faire)
■ **gang up** se coaliser (**on, against** contre)

Ganges /'gændʒiːz/ ▸ p. 1146 pr n Gange m

gangland /'gæŋlænd/ n ≈ le Milieu

gang leader n chef m de bande

gangling /'gæŋglɪŋ/ adj dégingandé

gang: ~**plank** n passerelle f; ~**rape** n viol m collectif

gangrene /'gæŋgriːn/ ▸ p. 933 n gangrène f

gangrenous /'gæŋgrɪnəs/ adj gangreneux/-euse

gangster /'gæŋstə(r)/
A n gangster m
B noun modifier [film, story, tactics] de gangsters

gangway /'gæŋweɪ/ n **1** (passage) allée f; **'Gangway!'** 'Dégagez!'; **2** Naut passerelle f

gaol n, vtr GB = **jail**

gap /gæp/ n **1** (space) (between planks, curtains) interstice m (**in** entre); (in fence, wall, timetable, records, report, text, diagram) trou m (**in** dans); (between buildings, cars) espace m (**in** entre); (in hills, cloud) trouée f (**in** dans); **to fill a** ~ lit, fig combler un vide; **2** (break) (in conversation) silence m; (of time) intervalle m; (in event, performance) interruption f; **3** (discrepancy) (in age, scores) différence f; (between opinions) divergence f; (of status) écart m; **a 15-year age** ~ une différence d'âge de 15 ans; **to close the** ~ supprimer l'écart; **4** (in knowledge, education) lacune f (**in** dans); **there's a** ~ **in my memory** j'ai un trou de mémoire; **technology** ~ insuffisance f en matière de technologie; **5** Comm créneau m; **to look for a** ~ **in the market** chercher un créneau sur le marché; **to fill a** ~ **in the market** répondre à un besoin réel du marché; **6** Fin déficit m; **trade** ~ déficit commercial

gape /geɪp/ vi **1** (stare) rester bouche bée; **to** ~ **at sth/sb** regarder qn/qch bouche bée; **2** [chasm] s'ouvrir tout grand; [wound] être béant; [garment] bâiller

gaping /'geɪpɪŋ/ adj [person] bouche bée; [beak] grand ouvert; [wound, hole] béant

gap year n année f de coupure (avant d'entrer à l'université)

garage /'gæraːʒ, 'gærɪdʒ, US gə'raːʒ/
A n garage m
B noun modifier [wall, door] du garage
C vtr mettre [qch] au garage

garage: ~ **mechanic** ▸ p. 1181 n mécanicien m; ~ **owner** n garagiste m; ~ **sale** n brocante f à domicile

garb /gaːb/ n costume m

garbage /'gaːbɪdʒ/ n ȼ **1** US ordures fpl; **2** fig **to be** ~ être très mauvais

(Idiom) ~ **in** ~ **out** Comput à instructions incorrectes, résultats incorrects; fig on ne fait pas de bon pain avec du mauvais levain

garbage: ~ **can** n US poubelle f; ~ **chute** n US vide-ordures m inv; ~ **collector**, ~ **man** ▸ p. 1181 n US éboueur m; ~ **disposal unit** n US broyeur m d'ordures; ~ **truck** n US camion m des éboueurs

garbled /'gaːbld/ adj [account, instructions] confus

Garda /'gaːdə/ ▸ p. 968 pr n **1** Geog **Lake** ~ le lac de Garde; **2** (pl **-dai**) (in Ireland) membre de la police d'Irlande du Sud

garden /'gaːdn/
A n **1** GB jardin m; **front/back** ~ jardin situé devant/ derrière la maison; **2** US (flower) platebande f; (vegetable) potager m
B **gardens** npl jardin m public
C noun modifier [furniture] de jardin; [wall, fence, shed] du jardin
D vi jardiner, faire du jardinage

(Idiom) **to lead sb up** ou US **down the** ~ **path**° mener qn en bateau°

garden: ~ **apartment** n US appartement dans un immeuble bas entouré d'un jardin; ~ **centre** GB, ~ **center** US n jardinerie f; ~ **city** n GB cité-jardin f

gardener /'gaːdnə(r)/ ▸ p. 1181 n jardinier/-ière m/f; **to be a keen** ~ être un passionné de jardinage

garden flat n GB appartement m en rez-de-jardin

gardening /'gaːdnɪŋ/ n jardinage m

garden: ~ **produce** n ȼ produits mpl maraîchers; ~ **shears** npl cisailles fpl (de jardinier); ~ **suburb** n banlieue f verte; ~**variety** adj US [writer, book] insignifiant

gargle /'gaːgl/ vi se gargariser (**with** avec)

gargoyle /'gaːgɔɪl/ n gargouille f

garish /'geərɪʃ/ adj [colour, garment] tape-à-l'œil inv; [light] cru

garishly /'geərɪʃlɪ/ adj [dressed, decorated] de façon voyante; ~ **lit** à la lumière crue

garland /'gaːlənd/
A n guirlande f
B vtr enguirlander (**with** de)

garlic /'gaːlɪk/
A n ail m
B noun modifier [sausage, mushrooms] à l'ail; [crouton, sauce] aillé; [salt] d'ail; ~ **butter** beurre m d'ail; ~ **bread**: pain chaud tartiné de beurre d'ail

garlic press n presse-ail m inv

garment /'gaːmənt/ n vêtement m

garnet /'gaːnɪt/ n grenat m

garnish /'gaːnɪʃ/
A n Culin garniture f (**of** de)
B vtr Culin garnir (**with** de)

garret† /'gærət/ n mansarde f

garrison /'gærɪsn/
A n garnison f
B noun modifier [town, troops, life] de garnison
C vtr [officer] placer une garnison dans [town]

garrotte GB, **garrote** US /gə'rɒt/
A n garrot m
B vtr (officially) exécuter [qn] au garrot; (strangle) étrangler

garrulous /'gærʊləs/ adj loquace

garter /'gaːtə(r)/ n **1** (for stocking) jarretière f; (for sock) fixe-chaussette m; **2** US (suspender) jarretelle f

(Idiom) **I'll have your guts for** ~**s**°! j'aurai ta peau°!

garter belt n US porte-jarretelles m inv

gas /gæs/
A n **1** gen, Chem gaz m; **to cook with** ~ cuisiner au gaz; **to turn up/turn down the** ~ augmenter/baisser le gaz; **on a low/medium** ~ à feu doux/moyen; **2** (anaesthetic) anesthésie f; **3** Mil gaz m de combat; **4** US (petrol) essence f; **5** °US (also ~ **pedal**) accélérateur m

B *noun modifier* [*industry, company*] du gaz; [*explosion, pipe*] de gaz

C *vtr* (*p prés etc* -**ss**-) gen, Mil gazer

D ○*vi* GB (*chatter*) papoter

E *v refl* (*p prés etc* -**ss**-) **to ~ oneself** se suicider au gaz

(Idiom) **to step on the ~** appuyer sur le champignon○

(Phrasal verb)
■ **gas up** US prendre de l'essence

gas : **~ burner** *n* brûleur *m* à gaz; **~ chamber** *n* chambre *f* à gaz

Gascony /ˈgæskəni/ ▸ p. 873 *pr n* Gascogne *f*

gas cooker *n* cuisinière *f* à gaz

gaseous /ˈgæsɪəs, ˈgeɪsɪəs/ *adj* gazeux/-euse

gas : **~ fire** *n* GB (*appareil m de*) chauffage *m* à gaz; **~-fired** *adj* [*boiler, water heater*] à gaz; [*central heating*] au gaz; **~ fitter** ▸ p. 1181 *n* chauffagiste *m*

gash /gæʃ/
A *n* gen entaille *f* (**in, on** à)
B *vtr* entailler

gas : **~ heater** *n* (*for room*) (*appareil m de*) chauffage *m* à gaz; (*for water*) chauffe-eau *m inv*; **~holder** *n* gazomètre *m*; **~ jet** *n* (*burner*) brûleur *m*

gasket /ˈgæskɪt/ *n* Tech (*in pump*) garniture *f*; (*in joint*) joint *m* (*d'étanchéité*)

gas : **~ lamp** *n* (*domestic*) lampe *f* à gaz; (*in street*) bec *m* de gaz; **~light** *n* ⊄ (*illumination*) lueur *f* d'une lampe à gaz; (*of street lamp*) lueur *f* d'un réverbère; **~ lighter** *n* (*for cooker*) allume-gaz *m inv*; **~ main** *n* canalisation *f* de gaz; **~ man** ▸ p. 1181 *n* employé *m* du gaz; **~ mask** *n* masque *m* à gaz; **~ meter** *n* compteur *m* à gaz; **~ oil** *n* gazole *m*

gasoline /ˈgæsəliːn/ *n* US essence *f*

gas oven *n* four *m* à gaz

gasp /gɑːsp/
A *n* (*breathing*) halètement *m*; **to let out** *ou* **give a ~** avoir le souffle coupé; **to give a ~ of horror** avoir le souffle coupé par l'épouvante; **at the last ~** fig au dernier moment
B *vi* ①(*for air*) haleter; ②(*show surprise*) perdre le souffle; **to ~ in** *ou* **with amazement** avoir le souffle coupé par la surprise; ③○**to be ~ing for a drink** mourir d'envie de boire un verre

gas : **~ pedal** *n* US accélérateur *m*; **~ pipeline** *n* gazoduc *m*; **~ ring** *n* GB (*fixed*) brûleur *m* à gaz; (*portable*) réchaud *m* à gaz; **~ station** *n* US station-service *f*; **~ stove** *n* cuisinière *f* à gaz

gassy /ˈgæsi/ *adj* [*drink*] gazeux/-euse

gas : **~ tank** *n* US Aut réservoir *m*; **~ tap** *n* robinet *m* du gaz

gastric /ˈgæstrɪk/ *adj* gastrique; **~ flu** grippe *f* intestinale

gastritis /gæˈstraɪtɪs/ ▸ p. 933 *n* gastrite *f*

gastro-enteritis /ˌgæstrəʊˌentəˈraɪtɪs/ ▸ p. 933 *n* gastro-entérite *f*

gastronomic /ˌgæstrəˈnɒmɪk/ *adj* gastronomique

gasworks *n* usine *f* à gaz

gate /geɪt/ *n* ①(*of field, level crossing*) barrière *f*; (*in underground*) portillon *m* automatique; (*in town, prison, airport, garden*) porte *f*; (*of courtyard, palace*) portail *m*; **at the ~** à l'entrée; ②Sport **a ~ of 29,000** 29 000 spectateurs; ③Comput porte *f*

gatecrash ○ /ˈgeɪtkræʃ/
A *vtr* (*without paying*) resquiller○ à; (*without invitation*) se pointer○ sans invitation à
B *vi* (*at concert*) resquiller○; (*at party*) se pointer○ sans invitation

gatecrasher ○ /ˈgeɪtkræʃə(r)/ *n* (*at concert*) resquilleur/-euse *m/f*; (*at party*) intrus/-e *m/f*

gate : **~house** *n* maison *f* de gardien; **~keeper** *n* gardien/-ienne *m/f*; **~ money** *n* Sport recette *f*; **~post** *n* poteau *m* d'angle; **~way** *n* porte *f*

gather /ˈgæðə(r)/
A *n* (*in sewing*) fronce *f*
B *vtr* ①lit (*pick*) cueillir; (*pick up*) ramasser; ②fig recueillir [*information*]; rassembler [*followers, strength, courage*]; **the movement is ~ing strength** le mouvement devient plus puissant; **to ~ dust** lit prendre la poussière; fig tomber dans l'oubli; **to ~ speed** prendre de la vitesse; **we are ~ed here today** nous sommes réunis aujourd'hui; ③(*deduce, conclude*) **to**

~ that déduire que; **I ~ (that) he was there** d'après ce que j'ai compris il était là; **as you will have ~ed** comme vous avez dû le deviner; **as far as I can ~** autant que je sache; ④(*in sewing*) faire des fronces à; **~ed at the waist** froncé à la taille
C *vi* [*people, crowd*] se rassembler; [*family*] se réunir; [*clouds*] s'amonceler; [*darkness*] s'épaissir

(Phrasal verbs)
■ **gather around** = **gather round**
■ **gather in** : ▸ **~ [sth] in**, **~ in [sth]** ramasser [*papers, crop*]; recueillir [*money, contributions*]
■ **gather round** : ▸ **~ round** se rassembler; **~ round!** approchez-vous!; ▸ **~ round [sth]** se rassembler autour de; ▸ **~ [sth] round oneself** s'envelopper dans
■ **gather together** : ▸ **~ together** se réunir; ▸ **~ [sth] together**, **~ together [sth]** rassembler [*belongings, notes, followers*]; recueillir [*information*]
■ **gather up** : ▸ **~ [sth] up**, **~ up [sth]** ramasser

gathering /ˈgæðərɪŋ/
A *n* ①(*meeting*) réunion *f*; **social/family ~** réunion entre amis/de famille; ②(*in sewing*) fronces *fpl*
B *adj* croissant

gauche /gəʊʃ/ *adj* [*remark*] maladroit; [*person*] gauche

gaudy /ˈgɔːdi/ *adj* tape-à-l'œil *inv*

gauge /geɪdʒ/
A *n* ①(*for gun, screw*) calibre *m*; (*of metal*) épaisseur *f*; (*of needle*) diamètre *m*; ②Rail écartement *m* (*des voies*); **narrow ~ voie** *f* étroite; ③(*measuring instrument*) jauge *f*; **fuel ~** jauge d'essence; ④(*way of judging*) moyen *m* de jauger
B *vtr* ①(*accurately*) mesurer [*diameter*]; jauger [*distance, quantity*]; calibrer [*screw, gun*]; ②(*estimate*) évaluer [*reaction*]

Gaul /gɔːl/ *n* (*country*) Gaule *f*; (*inhabitant*) Gaulois/-e *m/f*

Gaullist /ˈgɔːlɪst/ *n, adj* gaulliste (*mf*)

gaunt /gɔːnt/ *adj* [*person*] décharné

gauntlet /ˈgɔːntlɪt/ *n* (*for protection*) gant *m* à crispin

(Idioms) **to throw down the ~** fig lancer un défi; **to pick up the ~** fig relever le défi

gauze /gɔːz/
A *n* (*fabric*) gaze *f*; (*wire*) grillage *m*
B *noun modifier* [*curtain, bandage*] de gaze

gauzy /ˈgɔːzi/ *adj* transparent

gave /geɪv/ *prét* ▸ **give**

gawky /ˈgɔːki/ *adj* dégingandé

gay /geɪ/
A ○*n* homosexuel/-elle *m/f*, gay *mf*
B *adj* ①(*homosexual*) homosexuel/-elle; [*club, magazine*] gay; ②(*lively*) gai; [*laughter*] joyeux/-euse; [*street*] animé; ③(*carefree*) joyeux/-euse

gay lib ○, **gay liberation** *n*: *mouvement pour la reconnaissance des droits des homosexuels*

Gaza strip /ˌgɑːzə ˈstrɪp/ *pr n* bande *f* de Gaza

gaze /geɪz/
A *n* regard *m*; **to hold sb's ~** soutenir le regard de qn
B *vi* **to ~ at** regarder qn/qch; (*in wonder*) contempler qn/qch

(Phrasal verb)
■ **gaze about**, **gaze around** regarder autour de soi

gazette /gəˈzet/ *n* (*newspaper title*) **Gazette** Gazette *f*; (*official journal*) journal *m* officiel

gazetteer /ˌgæzəˈtɪə(r)/ *n* index *m* géographique

gazump ○ /gəˈzʌmp/ *vtr* péj GB *en immobilier, revenir sur un accord pour vendre à plus offrant*

GB *n* (*abrév* = **Great Britain**) G.-B

GBH *n* (*abrév* ▸ **grievous bodily harm**

Gbyte *n* Comput (*abrév* = **gigabyte**) Go *m*, gigaoctet *m*

GCSE *n* (*pl* **~s**) GB (*abrév* = **General Certificate of Secondary Education**) certificat *m* d'études secondaires

> ⓘ GCSE Examen que les élèves d'Angleterre, du pays de Galles et d'Irlande du Nord passent à l'âge de 16 ans après cinq années d'études secondaires. Ils peuvent présenter autant de matières qu'ils désirent (ils en préparent en général entre 5 et 8). Pour obtenir un *GCSE* dans une discipline, ils doivent obtenir une note comprise entre A et G à l'examen. En Écosse, l'équivalent des *GCSEs* sont les *Standard Grades*.

GDP *n* (*abrév* = **gross domestic product**) PIB *m*

gear /gɪə(r)/
A *n* ①(*equipment*) matériel *m*; **climbing ~** matériel d'alpinis-

g

me; ☑ ○(possessions) affaires *fpl*; ☒ (clothes) fringues○ *fpl*;
football ~ tenue *f* de football; ☐ Aut vitesse *f*; **bottom** *ou*
first ~ première vitesse; **to be in third ~** être en troisième; **to put a car in ~** passer la vitesse; **you're not in ~**
tu es au point mort; **'keep in low ~'** 'utilisez votre frein
moteur'; **to get (oneself) into ~ for sth** fig se préparer pour
qch; ☑ Tech roue *f* dentée

B **gears** *npl* ☐ Aut changement *m* de vitesse; ☒ Tech engrenage *m*

C *noun modifier* [*box, change, lever, stick*] de vitesses; **~ wheel**
(on bicycle) pignon *m*

D *vtr* **to be ~ed to** *ou* **towards sb** s'adresser à qn

(Phrasal verb)

■ **gear up: ▸ ~ up** se préparer; **▸ ~ [sb] up** préparer; **to
be ~ed up** être prêt (**for** pour)

gearshift /ˈgɪəʃɪft/ *n* US (lever) levier *m* de vitesses

gee○ /dʒiː/ US *excl* (in surprise) ça alors!; (in disappointment, commiseration) mince alors!

geek● /giːk/ *n* (computer buff) passionné/-e *m/f* d'informatique

geese /giːs/ *pl* ▸ **goose**

gel /dʒel/
A *n* ☐ (for bath, hair) gel *m*; ☒ Chem colloïde *m*
B *vi* (*p prés etc* **-ll-**) Culin prendre; fig prendre forme

gelatin(e) /ˈdʒelətiːn, -tɪn/ *n* (all contexts) gélatine *f*

gelding /ˈgeldɪŋ/ *n* ☐ (horse) hongre *m*; ☒ (castration) castration *f*

gelignite /ˈdʒelɪgnaɪt/ *n* plastic *m*

gem /dʒem/ *n* ☐ lit pierre *f* précieuse; ☒ fig [*person*] perle
f; **this book is a real ~** ce livre est une vraie merveille

Gemini /ˈdʒemɪnaɪ, -niː/ ▸ **p. 1350** *n* Gémeaux *mpl*

gen○ /dʒen/ GB
A *n* tuyaux○ *mpl*; **what's the ~ on this?** qu'est-ce qu'il faut
savoir là-dessus?
B *adj, adv: abrév* = **general, generally**

(Phrasal verb)

■ **gen up**○ GB: **▸ ~ up** se renseigner (**on** sur); **▸ ~ [sb]
up** donner tous les tuyaux à (**on** sur); **to be ~ned up on** *ou*
about sth être au parfum○ de qch

Gen. *abrév écrite* = **General**

gender /ˈdʒendə(r)/ *n* Ling genre *m*; (of person, animal)
sexe *m*

gene /dʒiːn/ *n* Biol gène *m*; **it's in his ~s** gen, hum c'est
héréditaire

genealogist /ˌdʒiːnɪˈælədʒɪst/ ▸ **p. 1181** *n* généalo-
giste *mf*

genealogy /ˌdʒiːnɪˈælədʒɪ/ *n* généalogie *f*

gene pool *n* patrimoine *m* héréditaire

general /ˈdʒenrəl/ ▸ **p. 1123**
A *n* ☐ Mil général *m*; ☒ **the ~ and the particular** le général
et le particulier
B *adj* ☐ (widespread) gen général; **to be a ~ favourite** être
apprécié de tous; **in ~ use** [*word, term*] d'usage courant;
[*equipment*] d'utilisation courante; ☒ (overall) gen général;
do you get the ~ idea? tu vois en gros de quoi il s'agit?;
that's the ~ idea en gros, c'est ça l'idée; **as a ~ rule** normalement, en règle générale; ☒ (miscellaneous, not specific)
gen général; [*promise, assurance*] vague; **to talk in ~** terms
parler en termes généraux; **a ~ discussion** une discussion d' ensemble; **to give sb a ~ idea of** donner à qn une
idée d'ensemble de; **in the ~ direction of** en direction de;
☐ (not specialized) [*medicine, linguistics*] général; [*user, reader*]
moyen/-enne; **~ office duties** travail *m* de bureau;
~ assistant employé/-e *m/f* de bureau; ☑ (normal) général;
in the ~ way of things en règle générale
C **in general** *adv phr* (usually or non-specifically) en général; (overall, mostly) dans l'ensemble; **things in ~** tout

general: ~ degree *n* GB diplôme *m* sanctionnant des études
universitaires; **~ delivery** *n* US poste *f* restante;
~ election *n* élections *fpl* législatives; **~ headquarters** *n* (+ *v sg ou pl*) quartier *m* général

generality /ˌdʒenəˈrælətɪ/ *n* ☐ (remark) généralité *f*;
☒ (majority) **the ~ of people** la plupart des gens

generalization /ˌdʒenrəlaɪˈzeɪʃn/ US -lɪˈz-/ *n* généralisation *f* (**about** sur)

generalize /ˈdʒenrəlaɪz/ *vtr, vi* généraliser (**about** à
propos de)

general knowledge *n* culture *f* générale

generally /ˈdʒenrəlɪ/ *adv* ☐ (widely, usually) en général,
généralement; **a ~ accepted definition** une définition
couramment acceptée; **~ available** disponible pour le
grand public; **it's ~ best to wait** en général, il vaut mieux
attendre; **~ (speaking)...** en règle générale...; ☒ (overall)
the industry ~ will be affected l'ensemble de l'industrie
sera touché; **he's ~ unwell at the moment** en ce moment
il n'est vraiment pas en forme; **the quality is ~ good** dans
l'ensemble la qualité est bonne; ☒ (vaguely) d'une
manière générale

general: ~ manager ▸ **p. 1181** *n* directeur/-trice *m/f*
général/-e; **~ meeting** *n* assemblée *f* générale

general practice *n* ☐ (field of doctor's work) médecine *f*
générale; **to go into ~** devenir (médecin) généraliste;
☒ (health centre) cabinet *m* de médecine générale

general: ~ practitioner, GP ▸ **p. 1181** *n* (médecin *m*)
généraliste *m*; **~ public** *n* (grand) public *m*;
~-purpose *adj* à usages multiples; **~ science** *n* Sch
la physique, la chimie et les sciences naturelles; **~ secretary** *n* secrétaire *m* général; **~ staff** *n* état-major *m*;
~ store *n* bazar *m* (*qui fait aussi épicerie*)

generate /ˈdʒenəreɪt/ *vtr* ☐ gen produire; créer [*employment*]; susciter [*interest, debate, tension, ideas*]; entraîner [*loss,
profit, publicity*]; ☒ Elec produire

generating station *n* centrale *f* électrique

generation /ˌdʒenəˈreɪʃn/ *n* ☐ gen (time span) génération *f*;
the younger/older ~ la jeune/l'ancienne génération; **it's
been like this for ~s** cela fait des générations qu'il en est
ainsi; ☒ (in product development) génération *f*; **second
~ robots** des robots de la deuxième génération; ☒ (of
electricity, income, traffic, data) production *f*; (of employment) création *f*

generation gap *n* fossé *m* des générations

generative /ˈdʒenərətɪv/ *adj* générateur/-trice

generator /ˈdʒenəreɪtə(r)/ *n* ☐ Elec générateur *m*; (in hospital, on farm, etc) groupe *m* électrogène; ☒ (of ideas) créateur *m*

generic /dʒɪˈnerɪk/ *adj* générique

generically /dʒɪˈnerɪklɪ/ *adv* génériquement; **~ similar**
apparenté; **~ distinct** d'espèce(s) différente(s)

generosity /ˌdʒenəˈrɒsɪtɪ/ *n* générosité *f* (**to, towards**
envers); **~ of mind** *ou* **spirit** esprit *m* généreux

generous /ˈdʒenərəs/ *adj* ☐ (beneficent, lavish) généreux/
-euse; **to be ~ with** ne pas être avare de [*praise, time*];
☒ (magnanimous) [*person*] magnanime; **the most ~ interpretation** is that l'interprétation la plus charitable est
que; ☒ (large) [*quantity, supply, funding*] libéral; [*size*] grand;
[*hem*] bon/bonne

generously /ˈdʒenərəslɪ/ *adv* gen généreusement; [*sprinkle, grease*] abondamment; **~ cut** ample; **give ~!** soyez
généreux!

genesis /ˈdʒenəsɪs/
A *n* (*pl* **-ses**) fig genèse *f*
B **Genesis** *pr n* Bible la Genèse

genetic /dʒɪˈnetɪk/ *adj* génétique

genetically /dʒɪˈnetɪklɪ/ *adv* génétiquement; **~ engin-
eered, ~ manipulated** obtenu par manipulation génétique; **~ modified** transgénique, génétiquement modifié

genetic: ~ engineering *n* génie *m* génétique; **~ fingerprinting** *n* empreintes *fpl* génétiques

geneticist /dʒɪˈnetɪsɪst/ ▸ **p. 1181** *n* généticien/
-ienne *m/f*

genetic manipulation *n* ₵ manipulations *fpl* génétiques

genetics /dʒɪˈnetɪks/ *n* (+ *v sg*) génétique *f*

genetic testing *n* ₵ tests *mpl* de dépistage génétique

Geneva /dʒɪˈniːvə/ ▸ **p. 1276, p. 968** *pr n* Genève; **Lake ~** le
lac Léman *or* de Genève

genial /ˈdʒiːnɪəl/ *adj* (cheerful) cordial

geniality /dʒiːnɪˈælɪtɪ/ *n* cordialité *f*

genie /ˈdʒiːnɪ/ *n* (*pl* **-nii** *ou* **-nies**) djinn *m*, génie *m*

genital /ˈdʒenɪtl/ *adj* génital

genitalia /ˌdʒenɪˈteɪlɪə/ *npl* = **genitals**

genitals /ˈdʒenɪtlz/ ▸ **p. 698** *npl* organes *mpl* génitaux

genitive /ˈdʒenətɪv/
A *n* génitif *m*; **in the ~ (case)** au génitif
B *adj* génitif/-ive

genius /'dʒi:nɪəs/ n ⓵ (prodigy) génie m; **a mathematical** ∼ un mathématicien de génie; **a mechanical** ∼ un génie de la mécanique; ⓶ (skill) **to have a** ∼ **for doing** être très doué pour faire

Genoa /'dʒenəʊə/ ▸ p. 1276 pr n Gênes

genocide /'dʒenəsaɪd/ n génocide m

genotype /'dʒe:nəʊtaɪp/ n génotype m

genteel /dʒen'ti:l/ adj ⓵ (refined) distingué; ⓶ péj, iron (affected) [person] maniéré; [behaviour] affecté

gentility /dʒen'tɪləti/ n ⓵ †(refinement) distinction f; ⓶ iron ou péj (affectation) affectation f

gentle /'dʒentl/ adj ⓵ (not harsh) gen doux/douce; [dentist, nurse] qui a la main douce; [hint, reminder] discret/-ète; [teasing, parody] anodin/-e; **be** ∼ **with her, she's tired** ne la brusque pas, elle est fatiguée; **the** ∼ **sex** littér ou iron le sexe faible; ⓶ (gradual) [slope, curve] doux/douce; [stop] en douceur; [transition] sans heurts; ⓷ (light) [pressure, touch, breeze] léger/-ère; [exercise] modéré; [massage] en douceur; [stroll] petit

gentleman /'dʒentlmən/ n (pl **-men**) (man) monsieur m; (well-bred) gentleman m; (congressman) député m; **a** ∼ **of leisure** un rentier

gentlemanly /'dʒentlmənli/ adj courtois

gentlemen /'dʒentlmən/ npl ▸ gentleman

gentleness /'dʒentlnɪs/ n douceur f

gently /'dʒentli/ adv ⓵ (not harshly) [rock, blow, stir] doucement; [comb, treat, cleanse] avec douceur; [cook] à feu doux; ⓶ (kindly) gentiment; **treat her** ∼ soyez gentil avec elle; **to break the news** ∼ annoncer la nouvelle avec ménagement; ⓷ (lightly) [exercise] sans forcer; **he kissed her** ∼ **on the cheek** il lui posa un léger baiser sur la joue; **'squeeze** ∼**'** 'presser sans tordre'; ⓸ (gradually) **to slope** ∼ **up/down** monter/descendre en pente douce; ∼ **does it!** doucement!

gentrification /ˌdʒentrɪfɪ'keɪʃn/ n péj embourgeoisement m

gentry /'dʒentri/ n †ou hum haute bourgeoisie f

gents /dʒentz/ npl (toilets) toilettes fpl (pour hommes); (on sign) 'messieurs'

genuine /'dʒenjʊɪn/ adj ⓵ (real) [reason, motive] vrai; **in case of** ∼ **emergency** s'il y a vraiment urgence; ⓶ (authentic) [work of art] authentique; [jewel, substance] véritable; **it's the** ∼ **article**○ c'est du vrai○; ⓷ (sincere) [person, effort, interest] sincère; [simplicity] vrai; [inability] non feint (after n); [buyer] sérieux/-ieuse

genuinely /'dʒenjʊɪnli/ adv (really and truly) vraiment; (in reality) réellement

genuineness /'dʒenjʊɪnnɪs/ n (of person) sincérité f; (of work of art) authenticité f

genus /'dʒi:nəs/ n (pl **-nera** ou **-ses**) genre m

geo- /'dʒi:əʊ/ combining form géo-

geographer /dʒɪ'ɒɡrəfə(r)/ ▸ p. 1181 n géographe mf

geographic(al) /ˌdʒɪə'ɡræfɪkl/ adj géographique

geographically /ˌdʒɪə'ɡræfɪkli/ adv géographiquement; ∼ **speaking** du point de vue géographique

geographical mile n Naut mille m marin

geography /dʒɪ'ɒɡrəfi/
A n (study) géographie f; (lay-out) topographie f
B noun modifier [student, teacher, lesson, book] de géographie

geological /dʒɪə'lɒdʒɪkl/ adj géologique

geologist /dʒɪ'ɒlədʒɪst/ ▸ p. 1181 n géologue mf

geology /dʒɪ'ɒlədʒi/
A n géologie f
B noun modifier [course, department, degree] de géologie

geometric(al) /ˌdʒɪəʊ'metrɪk(l)/ adj géométrique

geometry /dʒɪ'ɒmətri/
A n géométrie f
B noun modifier [lesson, book] de géométrie; ∼ **set** nécessaire m de géométrie

geopolitical /ˌdʒi:əʊpə'lɪtɪkl/ adj géopolitique

Georgia /'dʒɔ:dʒə/ ▸ p. 1222, p. 774 pr n Géorgie f

Georgian /'dʒɔ:dʒən/ ▸ p. 1032, p. 969
A n ⓵ (person) Géorgien/-ienne m/f; ⓶ (language) géorgien m
B adj ⓵ Geog (all contexts) géorgien/-ienne; ⓶ GB Hist, Archit, Literat georgien/-ienne; **the** ∼ **period** la période allant de 1714 à 1830

geoscience /ˌdʒi:əʊ'saɪəns/ n ℃ sciences fpl de la Terre; **a** ∼ une des sciences de la Terre

gerbil /'dʒɜ:bɪl/ n gerbille f

geriatric /ˌdʒerɪ'ætrɪk/
A n Med ⓵ personne f âgée; ⓶ péj personne f sénile
B adj ⓵ Med [hospital, ward] gériatrique; ∼ **care** soins mpl aux vieillards; ∼ **medicine** gériatrie f; ⓶ ○péj, hum gâteux/-euse○

geriatrician /ˌdʒerɪə'trɪʃn/ ▸ p. 1181 n gériatre mf

geriatrics /ˌdʒerɪ'ætrɪks/ n (+ v sg) gériatrie f

germ /dʒɜ:m/ n ⓵ (microbe) microbe m; ⓶ (seed) lit, fig germe m

German /'dʒɜ:mən/ ▸ p. 1032, p. 969
A n ⓵ (person) Allemand/-e m/f; ⓶ (language) allemand m
B adj [custom, food etc] allemand; [ambassador, embassy] d'Allemagne; [teacher, course] d'allemand

germane /dʒɜ:'meɪn/ adj [point, remark] approprié; ∼ **to** se rapportant à [inquiry, topic]

Germanic /dʒɜ:'mænɪk/ adj gen, Ling germanique

German: ∼ **measles** ▸ p. 933 n rubéole f; ∼ **shepherd** n US berger m allemand; ∼-**speaking** adj germanophone

Germany /'dʒɜ:məni/ ▸ p. 774 pr n Allemagne f

germinate /'dʒɜ:mɪneɪt/
A vtr lit, fig faire germer
B vi lit, fig germer

germination /ˌdʒɜ:mɪ'neɪʃn/ n germination f

germ warfare n guerre f bactériologique

gerrymandering /ˌdʒerɪ'mændərɪŋ/ n charcutage m électoral

gerund /'dʒerənd/ n nom m verbal

gerundive /dʒe'rʌndɪv/
A n adjectif m verbal
B adj du gérondif

gestate /dʒe'steɪt/ vi ⓵ Biol être en gestation; ⓶ fig mûrir

gestation /dʒe'steɪʃn/ n ⓵ lit gestation f; ⓶ fig mûrissement m

gesticulate /dʒe'stɪkjʊleɪt/ vi gesticuler

gesture /'dʒestʃə(r)/
A n lit, fig geste m (of de); **a nice** ∼ un beau geste; **an empty** ∼ un geste qui ne signifie rien
B vi faire un geste; **to** ∼ **at** ou **towards sth** désigner qch d'un geste; **to** ∼ **to sb** faire signe à qn

get /get/

⚠ This much-used verb has no multi-purpose equivalent in French and therefore is very often translated by choosing a synonym: to get lunch = to prepare lunch = préparer le déjeuner.
     get is used in many idiomatic expressions (to get something off one's chest etc) and translations will be found in the appropriate entry (chest etc). This is also true of offensive comments (get lost etc) where the appropriate entry would be **lost**.
     Remember that when get is used to express the idea that a job is done not by you but by somebody else (to get a room painted etc) faire is used in French followed by an infinitive (faire repeindre une pièce etc).
     When get has the meaning of become and is followed by an adjective (to get rich/drunk etc) devenir is sometimes useful but check the appropriate entry (**rich, drunk** etc) as a single verb often suffices (s'enrichir, s'enivrer etc).
     For examples and further uses of get see the entry below.

A vtr (p prés **-tt-**; prét **got**; pp **got**, **gotten** US) ⓵ (receive) recevoir [letter, grant]; recevoir, percevoir [salary, pension]; TV, Radio capter [channel]; **did you** ∼ **much for it?** est-ce que tu en as tiré beaucoup d'argent?; **what did you** ∼ **for your car?** combien as-tu revendu ta voiture?; **we** ∼ **a lot of rain** il pleut beaucoup ici; **our garden** ∼**s a lot of sun** notre jardin est bien ensoleillé; **we** ∼ **a lot of tourists** nous avons beaucoup de touristes; **you** ∼ **what you pay for** si on veut de la qualité il faut y mettre le prix; **he's** ∼**ting help with his science** il se fait aider en sciences; ⓶ (inherit) **to** ∼ **sth from sb** lit hériter qch de qn [article, money]; fig tenir qch de qn [*trait, feature*]; **3▸** (obtain) (by applying) obtenir [*permission, divorce, licence*]; trouver [*job*]; (by contacting) trouver [*plumber*]; appeler [*taxi*]; (by buying) acheter [*item*] (from chez); avoir [*ticket*]; **to ~ something for nothing/at a discount** avoir qch gratuitement/avec une réduction; **to ~ sb sth, to ~ sth for sb** (by buying) acheter qch à qn; **I'll ~ sth to eat at the airport** je mangerai qch à l'aéroport; **4▸** (subscribe to) acheter [*newspaper*]; **5▸** (acquire) se faire [*reputation*]; **6▸** (achieve) obtenir [*grade, mark, answer*]; **he got it right** (of calculation) il a obtenu le bon résultat; (of answer) il a répondu juste; **7▸** (fetch) chercher [*object, person, help*]; **go and ~ a chair** va chercher une chaise; **to ~ sb sth, to ~ sth for sb** aller chercher qch pour qn; **can I ~ you your coat?** est-ce que je peux vous apporter votre manteau?; **8▸** (manoeuvre, move) **to ~ sb/sth upstairs/downstairs** faire monter/descendre qn/qch; **I'll ~ them there somehow** je les ferai parvenir d'une façon ou d'une autre; **can you ~ between the truck and the wall?** est-ce que tu peux te glisser entre le camion et le mur?; **9▸** (help progress) **is this discussion ~ting us anywhere?** est-ce que cette discussion est bien utile?; **I listened to him and where has it got me?** je l'ai écouté mais à quoi ça m'a avancé?; **10▸** (contact) **did you ~ Harry on the phone?** tu as réussi à avoir Harry au téléphone?; **11▸** (deal with) **I'll ~ it** (of phone) je réponds; (of doorbell) j'y vais; **12▸** (prepare) préparer [*breakfast, lunch etc*]; **13▸** (take hold of) attraper [*person*] (by par); **I've got you, don't worry** je te tiens, ne t'inquiète pas; **to ~ sth from ou off** prendre qch sur [*shelf, table*]; **to ~ sth from ou out of** prendre qch dans [*drawer, cupboard*]; **14▸** ○(oblige to give) **to ~ sth from ou out of sb** faire sortir qch à qn [*money*]; fig obtenir qch de qn [*truth*]; **15▸** ○(catch) gen arrêter [*escapee*]; **got you!** gen je t'ai eu!; (caught in act) vu!; **16▸** Med attraper [*disease*]; **he got measles from his sister** sa sœur lui a passé la rougeole; **17▸** (use as transport) prendre [*bus, train*]; **18▸** (have) **to have got** avoir [*object, money, friend etc*]; **I've got a headache** j'ai mal à la tête; **19▸** (start to have) **to ~ (hold of) the idea ou impression that** se mettre dans la tête que; **20▸** (suffer) **to ~ a surprise** être surpris; **to ~ a shock** avoir un choc; **to ~ a bang on the head** recevoir un coup sur la tête; **21▸** (be given as punishment) prendre [*five years etc*]; avoir [*fine*]; **22▸** (hit) **to ~ sb/sth with** toucher qn/qch avec [*stone, arrow*]; **got it!** (of target) touché!; **23▸** (understand, hear) comprendre; **now let me ~ this right…** alors si je comprends bien…; **'where did you hear that?'—'I got it from Paul'** 'où est-ce que tu as entendu ça?'—'c'est Paul qui me l'a dit'; **~ this! he was arrested this morning** tiens-toi bien! il a été arrêté ce matin; **24▸** ○(annoy, affect) **what ~s me is…** ce qui m'agace c'est que…; **25▸** (learn, learn of) **to ~ to do** finir par faire; **to ~ to like sb** finir par apprécier qn; **how did you ~ to know ou hear of our organization?** comment avez-vous entendu parler de notre organisation?; **we got to know them last year** on a fait leur connaissance l'année dernière; **26▸** (have opportunity) **to ~ to do** avoir l'occasion de faire, pouvoir faire; **27▸** (start) **to ~ (to be)** commencer à devenir; **to ~ to doing**○ commencer à faire; **then I got to thinking that…** puis je me suis dit que…; **we'll have to ~ going** il va falloir y aller; **28▸** (must) **to have got to do** devoir faire [*homework, chore*]; **it's got to be done** il faut le faire; **you've got to realize that…** il faut que tu te rendes compte que…; **there's got to be a reason** il doit y avoir une raison; **29▸** (persuade) **to ~ sb to do** demander à qn de faire; **I got her to talk** j'ai réussi à la faire parler; **did you ~ anything out of her?** est-ce que tu as réussi à la faire parler?; **30▸** (have somebody do) **to ~ sth done** faire faire qch; **to ~ the car repaired** faire réparer la voiture; **to ~ one's hair cut** se faire couper les cheveux; **how do you ever ~ anything done?** comment est-ce que tu arrives à travailler?; **31▸** (cause) **to ~ the car going** faire démarrer la voiture; **as hot as you can ~ it** aussi chaud que possible; **to ~ one's socks wet** mouiller ses chaussettes; **to ~ one's finger trapped** se coincer le doigt

B vi (p prés **-tt-**; prét **got**; pp **got, gotten** US) **1▸** (become) devenir [*suspicious, old*]; **how lucky/stupid can you ~!** il y en a qui ont de la chance/qui sont vraiment stupides!; **it's ~ting late** il se fait tard; **how did he ~ like that?** comment est-ce qu'il en est arrivé là?; **2▸** (forming passive) **to ~ (oneself) killed** se faire tuer; **to ~ hurt** être blessé; **3▸** (become involved in) **to ~ into**○ (as hobby) se mettre à; (as job) commencer dans; fig **to ~ into a fight** se battre; **4▸** (arrive) **to ~ there** arriver; **to ~ to the airport** arriver à l'aéroport; **how did your coat ~ here?** comment est-ce que ton manteau est arrivé là?; **how did you ~ here?** (by what miracle) comment

est-ce que tu es arrivé là?; (by what means) comment est-ce que tu es venu?; **where did you ~ to?** où est-ce que tu étais passé?; **we've got to page 5** nous en sommes à la page 5; **5▸** (progress) **it got to 7 o'clock** il était 7 heures; **I'd got as far as the title** j'en étais au titre; **I'm ~ting nowhere with this essay** je n'avance pas dans cette dissertation; **now we're ~ting somewhere** il y a du progrès; **6▸** ○(put on) **to ~ into** mettre, enfiler○ [*pyjamas, overalls*]

(Idioms) **~ along with you!**○ ne sois pas ridicule!; **~ away with you!**○ arrête de raconter n'importe quoi!○; **~ him in that hat!** regarde-le avec ce chapeau!; **I'll ~ you**○ **for that** je vais te le faire payer○; **I'm ~ting there** je progresse; **he's got it bad**○ il est vraiment mordu; **I've got it** j'ai compris; **to ~ above oneself** commencer à avoir la grosse tête○; **to ~ it together**○ se ressaisir; **to tell sb where to ~ off** envoyer promener qn; **to ~ with it**○ se mettre dans le coup○; **what's got into her?** qu'est-ce qui lui a pris?; **you've got me there!** alors là tu me poses une colle○!

(Phrasal verbs)

■ **get about 1▸** (manage to move) se déplacer; **2▸** (travel) voyager; **he ~s about a bit** (travels) il voyage pas mal; (knows people) il connaît du monde

■ **get across: 1▸** (pass to other side) traverser; **2▸** [*message*] passer; ▸ **~ across [sth]** traverser [*river, road etc*]; ▸ **~ [sth] across 1▸** (transport) **how will we ~ it across?** comment est-ce qu'on le/la fera passer de l'autre côté?; **2▸** (communicate) faire passer [*message*] (**to** à)

■ **get ahead 1▸** (make progress) progresser; **to ~ ahead of** prendre de l'avance sur [*competitor*]; **2▸** (go too fast) **let's not ~ ahead of ourselves** n'anticipons pas

■ **get along 1▸** (progress) **how's the project ~ting along?** comment est-ce que le projet se présente?; **how are you ~ting along?** (in job, school) comment ça se passe?; (to sick or old person) comment ça va?; **2▸** (be suited as friends) bien s'entendre (**with** avec); **3▸** (go) **I must be ~ting along** il faut que j'y aille

■ **get around:** ▸ **~ around 1▸** (move, spread) = **get about**; **2▸ to ~ around to doing: she'll ~ around to visiting us eventually** elle va bien finir par venir nous voir; **I must ~ around to reading his article** il faut vraiment que je lise son article; **I haven't got around to it yet** je n'ai pas encore eu le temps de m'en occuper; ▸ **~ around [sth]** (circumvent) contourner [*problem, law*]; **there's no ~ting around it** il n'y a rien à faire

■ **get at**○: ▸ **~ at [sb/sth] 1▸** (reach) atteindre [*object*]; arriver jusqu'à [*person*]; fig découvrir [*truth*]; **2▸** (spoil) **the ants have got at the sugar** les fourmis ont attaqué le sucre; **3▸** (criticize) être après [*person*]; **4▸** (insinuate) **what are you ~ting at?** où est-ce que tu veux en venir?

■ **get away:** ▸ **~ away 1▸** (leave) partir; **2▸** (escape) s'échapper; **3▸** fig (escape unpunished) **to ~ away with a crime** échapper à la justice; **you'll never ~ away with it!** tu ne vas pas t'en tirer comme ça!; **she can ~ away with bright colours** elle peut se permettre de porter des couleurs vives

■ **get away from:** ▸ **~ away from [sth] 1▸** (leave) quitter; **I must ~ away from here!** il faut que je parte d'ici!; **'~ away from it all'** 'évadez-vous de votre quotidien'; **2▸** fig (deny) nier; **there's no ~ting away from it** on ne peut pas le nier; **3▸** fig abandonner [*practice*]; ▸ **~ away from [sb]** lit, fig échapper à

■ **get back:** ▸ **~ back 1▸** (return) gen rentrer; (after short time) revenir; **when we ~ back** à notre retour; **2▸** (move backwards) reculer; **3▸** (take revenge) **to ~ back at** se venger de; ▸ **~ back to [sth] 1▸** (return to) rentrer à [*house, city*]; revenir à [*office, point*]; **when we ~ back to London** à notre retour à Londres; **2▸** (return to former condition) revenir à [*job*]; **to ~ back to sleep** se rendormir; **to ~ back to normal** redevenir normal; **3▸** (return to earlier stage) revenir à [*main topic, former point*]; ▸ **~ back to [sb]** (return to) revenir à; (on telephone) **I'll ~ right back to you** je vous rappelle tout de suite; ▸ **~ [sth] back 1▸** (return) (personally) ramener; (by post etc) renvoyer; **2▸** (regain) récupérer [*lost object, loaned item*]; fig reprendre [*strength*]; **she got her money back** elle a été remboursée; **she got her old job back** on lui a redonné son travail

■ **get behind:** ▸ **~ behind** (delayed) prendre du retard; ▸ **~ behind [sth]** se mettre derrière

■ **get by 1▸** (pass) passer; **2▸** (survive) s'en sortir (**on, with** avec)

■ **get down:** ▸ **~ down 1▸** (descend) descendre (**from, out** of de); [2] (leave table) quitter la table; [3] (lower oneself) (to floor) se coucher; (crouch) se baisser; **to ~ down to** arriver à [lower level etc]; atteindre [trapped person etc]; se mettre à [work]; **to ~ down to sb's level** fig se mettre à la portée de qn; **let's ~ down to business** parlons affaires; **when you ~ right down to it** quand on regarde d'un peu plus près; **to ~ down to doing** se mettre à faire; ▸ **~ down [sth]** descendre [slope]; ▸ **~ [sth] down, ~ down [sth]** [1] (from height) descendre; [2] (swallow) avaler; [3] (record) noter; ▸ **~ [sb] down** (from height) faire descendre; [2] ○(depress) déprimer

■ **get in**: ▸ **~ in** [1] lit (to building) entrer; (to vehicle) monter; [2] fig **to ~ in on** réussir à s'introduire dans [project, scheme]; **to ~ in on the deal**○ faire partie du coup; [3] (return home) rentrer; [4] (arrive at destination) arriver; [5] (penetrate) pénétrer; [6] Pol [party] passer; [candidate] être élu; [7] Sch, Univ [applicant] être admis; [8] (associate) **to ~ in with** se mettre bien avec [person]; ▸ **~ [sth] in, ~ in [sth]** [1] (buy) acheter; [2] (fit into space) **I can't ~ the drawer in** je n'arrive pas à faire rentrer le tiroir; [3] (harvest) rentrer; (plant) planter; [4] (hand in) rendre [essay]; [5] (include) placer; **I'll try to ~ a bit of tennis**○ j'essayerai de faire un peu de tennis; ▸ **~ [sb] in** faire entrer

■ **get into**: ▸ **~ into [sth]** [1] (enter) entrer dans [building]; monter dans [vehicle]; [2] (be admitted) (as member) devenir membre de; (as student) être admis à; **I didn't know what I was ~ting into** fig je ne savais pas dans quoi je m'embarquais; [3] (squeeze into) rentrer dans [garment, size]; ▸ **~ [sb/sth] into** faire entrer [qn/qch] dans

■ **get off**: ▸ **~ off** [1] (from bus etc) descendre (**at** à); [2] (start on journey) partir; [3] (leave work) finir; [4] ○(escape punishment) s'en tirer (**with** avec); [5] **to ~ off to** partir pour [destination]; (make headway) **to ~ off to a good start** prendre un bon départ; **to ~ off to sleep** s'endormir; ▸ **~ off [sth]** [1] descendre de [wall, bus etc]; [2] fig s'écarter de [subject]; ▸ **~ off**○ [sb] (leave hold) **~ off me!** lâche-moi!; ▸ **~ [sb/sth] off** [1] (lift down) descendre [object]; faire descendre [person]; [2] (dispatch) envoyer [letter, person]; [3] (remove) enlever [stain]; [4] ○endormir [baby]

■ **get on**: ▸ **~ on** [1] (climb aboard) monter; [2] (work) **~ on a bit faster! let's ~ on!** continuons!; **let's ~ on!** continuons!; [3] GB (like each other) bien s'entendre; [4] (fare) **how did you ~ on?** comment est-ce que ça s'est passé?; [5] (cope) **how are you ~ting on?** comment est-ce que tu t'en sors?; [6] GB (approach) **he's ~ting on for 40** il approche des quarante ans; **it's ~ting on for midnight** il est presque minuit; [7] (grow late) **time's ~ting on** le temps passe; [8] (grow old) **to be ~ting on a bit** se faire vieux/vieille; ▸ **~ on [sth]** (board) monter dans [vehicle]; ▸ **~ [sth] on, ~ on [sth]** gen mettre; monter [tyre]

■ **get onto**: ▸ **~ onto [sth]** [1] (board) monter dans [vehicle]; [2] (be appointed to) être nommé à [committee]; [3] (start to discuss) arriver à parler de [subject]; [4] GB (contact) contacter

■ **get on with**: ▸ **~ on with [sth]** (continue to do) **to ~ on with one's work** continuer à travailler; **let's ~ on with the job!** au travail!; ▸ **~ on with [sb]** GB s'entendre avec [person]

■ **get out**: ▸ **~ out** [1] (exit) sortir (**through, by** par); **~ out and don't come back!** va-t'en et ne reviens pas!; [2] (make social outing) sortir; [3] (resign) partir; [4] (alight) descendre; [5] (be let out) [prisoner] être libéré; [6] (leak) être révélé; ▸ **~ [sth] out, ~ out [sth]** [1] (bring out) sortir; **I couldn't ~ the words out** les mots ne voulaient pas sortir; [2] (extract) retirer [cork]; [3] enlever [stain]; [4] emprunter [library book]; ▸ **~ [sb] out** (release) faire libérer [prisoner]; **to ~ sth out of sth** (bring out) sortir qch de qch; (find and remove) récupérer qch dans qch [stuck object]; **I can't ~ it out of my mind** je ne peux pas l'effacer de mon esprit

■ **get out of**: ▸ **~ out of [sth]** [1] sortir de [building, bed, meeting]; descendre de [vehicle]; être libéré de [prison]; quitter [organization, profession]; échapper à [responsibilities]; [2] (avoid doing) s'arranger pour ne pas aller à [appointment, meeting]; perdre [habit]; **I'll try to ~ out of it** j'essaierai de me libérer; **to ~ out of doing** s'arranger pour ne pas faire; [3] (no longer do) perdre [habit]; [4] (gain from) **what do you ~ out of your job?** qu'est-ce que ton travail t'apporte?; **what will you ~ out of it?** qu'est-ce que vous en retirerez?

■ **get over**: ▸ **~ over** (cross) passer; ▸ **~ over [sth]** [1] (cross) traverser; [2] se remettre de [illness, shock]; **I can't ~ over it** (in amazement) je n'en reviens pas; **she never got**

over him elle ne l'a jamais oublié; [3] surmonter [problem]; **to ~ sth over with** en finir avec qch; ▸ **~ [sb/sth] over** faire passer [qn/qch] au-dessus de [bridge, wall etc]; **~ the plumber over here** faites venir le plombier

■ **get round** GB: ▸ **~ round = get around**; ▸ **~ round [sth] = get around [sth]**; ▸ **~ round**○ [sb] persuader [qn]

■ **get through**: ▸ **~ through** [1] (squeeze through) passer; [2] (on phone) **to ~ through to sb** avoir qn au téléphone; **I couldn't ~ through** je n'ai pas réussi à l'avoir; [3] (communicate with) **to ~ through to** communiquer avec [person]; [4] [news, supplies] arriver; [5] [examinee] réussir; ▸ **~ through [sth]** [1] traverser [checkpoint, mud]; terminer [book, revision]; finir [meal, task]; réussir à [exam, qualifying round]; **I thought I'd never ~ through the week** j'ai cru que je ne tiendrais pas la semaine; [2] (use) manger [food]; boire [drink]; dépenser [money]; **I ~ through two notebooks a week** il me faut deux carnets par semaine; ▸ **~ [sb/sth] through** [1] lit faire passer; fig (help to endure) aider qn à tenir le coup○; [2] Sch, Univ (help to pass) permettre à [qn] de réussir; [3] Pol faire passer [bill]

■ **get together**: ▸ **~ together** (assemble) se réunir (**about, over** pour discuter de); ▸ **~ [sb/sth] together, ~ together [sb/sth]** gen réunir; rassembler [food parcels]; former [company, action group]

■ **get under**: ▸ **~ under** passer en-dessous; ▸ **~ under [sth]** passer sous

■ **get up**: ▸ **~ up** [1] (from bed, chair etc) se lever (**from** de); [2] (on ledge etc) monter; [3] Meteorol [storm] se préparer; [wind] se lever; [4] **to ~ up to** (reach) arriver à; **what did you ~ up to?** fig (sth enjoyable) qu'est-ce que tu as fait de beau?; (sth mischievous) qu'est-ce que tu as fabriqué○?; ▸ **~ up [sth]** [1] arriver en haut de [hill, ladder]; [2] (increase) augmenter [speed]; [3] (muster) former [group]; faire [petition]; obtenir [support]; ▸ **~ [sth] up** organiser

getaway /ˈgetəweɪ/ n **to make a quick ~** décamper vite fait○; **the robbers had a ~ car** une voiture attendait les voleurs

get: **~-together** n réunion f (entre amis); **~up**○ n péj accoutrement m; **~-up-and-go** n dynamisme m; **~ well** adj [card, wishes] de prompt rétablissement

G-force n force f de gravité

Ghana /ˈgɑːnə/ ▸ **p. 774** pr n Ghana m

ghastly /ˈgɑːstlɪ, US ˈgæstlɪ/ adj horrible

gherkin /ˈgɜːkɪn/ n cornichon m

ghetto /ˈgetəʊ/ n (pl ~ ou ~es) ghetto m

ghetto blaster○ n (gros) radiocassette m portable

ghost /gəʊst/ n [1] (spectre) fantôme m; **you look as if you've seen a ~!** on dirait que tu as vu un revenant!; [2] fig **the ~ of a smile** l'ombre f d'un sourire; **they haven't the ~ of a chance!** ils n'ont pas la moindre chance!

(Idiom) **to give up the ~** rendre l'âme

ghostly /ˈgəʊstlɪ/ adj spectral

ghost: **~ site** n Comput site m fantôme; **~ story** n histoire f de fantômes; **~ town** n ville f fantôme; **~ train** n train m fantôme; **~ writer** n nègre m

ghoulish /ˈguːlɪʃ/ adj (all contexts) macabre

GHQ n (abrév = **General Headquarters**) GQG m

GI n (pl **GIs**) GI n inv, soldat m américain

giant /ˈdʒaɪənt/ n, adj (all contexts) géant (m)

giant-killer n vainqueur m surprise

gibber /ˈdʒɪbə(r)/ vi [person] bafouiller; [monkey] baragouiner

gibberish /ˈdʒɪbərɪʃ/ n charabia m

gibbet /ˈdʒɪbɪt/ n potence f, gibet m

gibe = **jibe**

giblets /ˈdʒɪblɪts/ npl abats mpl

giddiness /ˈgɪdɪnɪs/ n (dizziness) vertige m; (frivolity) légèreté f

giddy /ˈgɪdɪ/ adj [1] (dizzy) **to feel ~** avoir la tête qui tourne; [2] (exhilarating) [height, speed] vertigineux/-euse; [success] enivrant; [3] (frivolous) [person] écervelé; [behaviour] irréfléchi

giddy spell n vertige m, étourdissement m

gift /gɪft/ n [1] (present) cadeau m; **to give a ~ to sb, to give sb a ~** faire or offrir un cadeau à qn; **to give sb a ~ of money** offrir de l'argent à qn; **they gave it to us as a ~** ils nous en ont fait cadeau; **it's for a ~** c'est pour offrir; **the ~ of life/sight** le don de la vie/la vue; [2] (donation) don m;

to make a ~ of sth to sb faire don de qch à qn; **3)** (talent) don *m*; **to have a ~ for** *ou* **of doing** avoir le don de faire

(Idiom) **don't look a ~ horse in the mouth** Prov à cheval donné, on ne regarde pas les dents Prov

gifted /'gɪftɪd/ *adj* (talented) doué; (intellectually) surdoué

gift: ~ **shop** *n* magasin *m* de cadeaux; ~ **token**, ~ **voucher** *n* GB chèque-cadeau *m*

gift wrap

A /'gɪftræp/ *n* papier *m* cadeau

B gift-wrap /ˌgɪft'ræp/ *vtr* (*p prés etc* **-pp-**) would you like it ~ped? est-ce que je vous fais un paquet-cadeau?

gig /gɪg/ *n* **1)** ○Mus concert *m* de rock; **2)** (carriage) cabriolet *m*

gigantic /dʒaɪ'gæntɪk/ *adj* gigantesque

giggle /'gɪgl/

A *n* **1)** (silly) petit rire *m* bête; (nervous) petit rire *m* nerveux; **to get the ~s** attraper un fou rire; **2)** ○GB (joke) **to do sth for a ~**○ faire qch pour rigoler○

B *vi* (stupidly) rire bêtement; (nervously) rire nerveusement

giggly /'gɪglɪ/ *adj* péj [*person*] qui n'arrête pas de glousser; **to be in a ~ mood** se mettre à rire pour un rien

gild /gɪld/ *vtr* (*prét, pp* **gilded** *ou* **gilt**) dorer

gilding /'gɪldɪŋ/ *n* dorure *f*

gill¹ /gɪl/ *n* (of fish) branchie *f*

(Idiom) **green about the ~s**○ blanc/blanche comme un linge

gill² /dʒɪl/ ▸ p. 723 *n* (measure) quart *m* de pinte

gilt /gɪlt/

A *pp* ▸ gild

B *n* dorure *f*

C *adj* [*frame, paint*] doré

gilt-edged /ˌgɪlt'edʒd/ *adj* **1)** [*page*] doré sur tranche; **2)** [*investment*] en or

gilt-edged securities, **gilt-edged stock(s)** *n* obligations *fpl* et titres *mpl* d'État

gimlet /'gɪmlɪt/ *n* vrille *f*

(Idiom) **to have eyes like ~s** avoir un regard perçant

gimmick /'gɪmɪk/ *n* péj (scheme) truc○ *m*; (object) gadget *m*

gimmicky /'gɪmɪkɪ/ *adj* péj [*production*] plein d'effets gratuits; [*clothes*] fantaisiste; [*idea*] à la mode

gin /dʒɪn/ *n* gin *m*

gin: ~ **and it** *n* GB gin-vermouth *m*; ~ **and tonic** *n* gin tonic *m*

ginger /'dʒɪndʒə(r)/

A *n* **1)** Bot, Culin gingembre *m*; **root** *ou* **fresh ~** gingembre frais; **2)** (hair colour) roux *m*

B *noun modifier* **1)** [*cake, biscuit*] au gingembre; **2)** [*hair, beard*] roux/rousse; [*cat*] roux/rousse

(Phrasal verb)

■ **ginger up** stimuler [*metabolism*]

ginger: ~ **ale** *n*: boisson gazeuse au gingembre; ~ **beer** *n*: boisson légèrement alcoolisée à base de gingembre

gingerbread /'dʒɪndʒəbred/ *n* ≈ pain *m* d'épice

(Idiom) **that takes the gilt off the ~** ça change tout

ginger: ~ **group** *n* GB groupe *m* de pression; ~**-haired** *adj* roux/rousse

gingerly /'dʒɪndʒəlɪ/ *adv* avec précaution

gingernut, **ginger snap** *n* Culin biscuit *m* au gingembre

gingery /'dʒɪndʒərɪ/ *adj* [*hair, beard*] roux/rousse

gingham /'gɪŋəm/

A *n* vichy *m*

B *noun modifier* [*garment*] en vichy

gin rummy ▸ p. 881 *n* gin-rami *m*

gipsy *n* = gypsy

giraffe /dʒɪ'rɑːf, US dʒə'ræf/ *n* girafe *f*

gird /gɜːd/ littér *vtr* ceindre liter

(Idiom) **to ~ (up) one's loins** fig, hum revêtir son armure

girder /'gɜːdə(r)/ *n* poutre *f*

girdle /'gɜːdl/ *n* **1)** (corset) gaine *f*; **2)** (belt) ceinture *f*

girl /gɜːl/ *n* **1)** (child) fille *f*; (teenager) jeune fille *f*; (woman) femme *f*; **baby ~** petite fille *f*, bébé *m*; **little ~** petite fille *f*, fillette *f*; **teenage ~** adolescente *f*; **young ~** jeune fille; **when I was a ~** (referring to childhood) quand j'étais petite; (to adolescence) quand j'étais jeune; **the new ~** gen, Sch la nouvelle *f*; **2)** (daughter) fille *f*; **3)** (servant) bonne *f*; **factory ~**

ouvrière *f*; **office ~** employée *f* de bureau; **sales** *ou* **shop ~** vendeuse *f*; **4)** (sweetheart) (petite) amie *f*

girl: ~ **band** *n* girls band *m*; ~ **Friday** *n* aide *f* de bureau; ~**friend** *n* (sweetheart) (petite) amie *f*; gen amie *f*; ~ **guide** GB, ~ **scout** US *n* éclaireuse *f*

girlie mag(azine)○ *n* magazine *m* pour hommes

girlish /'gɜːlɪʃ/ *adj* de jeune fille

girl power *n* girl power *m* (*'le pouvoir aux femmes', revendication lancée par des groupes de pop britanniques dans les années 90*)

giro /'dʒaɪrəʊ/

A *n* GB Fin (system) système *m* de virement bancaire; (cheque) mandat *m*

B *noun modifier* ~ **payment**, ~ **transfer** (at bank) virement *m* bancaire; (at post office) virement *m* postal

girth /gɜːθ/ *n* (of person) tour *m* de taille; (of object) circonférence *f*

gist /dʒɪst/ *n* essentiel *m* (**of** de)

give /gɪv/

A *n* élasticité *f*

B *vtr* (*prét* **gave**; *pp* **given**) **1)** (hand over) gen donner (**to** à); offrir [*present, drink, sandwich*] (**to** à); **to ~ sb sth** gen donner qch à qn; (politely, as gift) offrir qch à qn; ~ **it me!**, ~ **me it!** donne-moi ça!; **how much will you ~ me for it?** combien m'en donnes-tu?; **what wouldn't I ~ for...!** je donnerais cher pour...!; **2)** (cause to have) **to ~ sb sth**, **to ~ sth to sb** donner qch à qn [*headache, nightmares, advice, information*]; transmettre *or* passer qch à qn [*disease*]; **to ~ sb pleasure** faire plaisir à qn; **3)** (provide, produce) donner [*milk, flavour, result, answer, sum*]; apporter [*heat, light, nutrient*]; faire [*total*]; **she gave him two sons** elle lui donna deux fils; **4)** (allow, accord) accorder [*custody, grant*]; laisser [qch] à qn [*seat*]; **to ~ sb sth** donner *or* accorder qch à qn [*time, time period*]; **to ~ sb enough room** laisser suffisamment de place à qn; **how long do you ~ their marriage?** combien de temps donnes-tu à leur mariage?; **she can sing, I'll ~ her that** elle sait chanter, je lui reconnais au moins ça; **it's original, I'll ~ you that** c'est original, je te l'accorde; **she could ~ her opponent five years** elle a au moins cinq ans de plus que son adversaire; **the polls ~ Labour a lead** les Travaillistes sont en tête dans les sondages; **I was given to understand that** on m'a laissé entendre que; **5)** Med **to ~ sb sth**, **to ~ sth to sb** donner qch à qn [*treatment, medicine*]; greffer qch à qn [*organ*]; poser qch à qn [*device*]; faire qch à qn [*injection, massage*]; **6)** Telecom **to ~ sb sth** passer qch à qn [*number, department*]; ~ **me the sales manager, please** passez-moi le directeur commercial, s'il vous plaît

C *vi* (*prét* **gave**; *pp* **given**) **1)** (contribute) donner, faire un don; **'please ~ generously'** 'merci (de vos dons)'; **2)** (bend) [*mattress, sofa*] s'affaisser; [*shelf, floorboard*] fléchir; [*branch*] ployer; [*leather, fabric*] s'assouplir; **3)** (yield, break) = **give way**; **4)** (yield) [*person, side*] céder; **something has to ~** ça va finir par craquer

(Idioms) **don't ~ me that**○! ne (me) raconte pas d'histoires!; ~ **or take an inch (or two)** à quelques centimètres près; **if this is the big city, ~ me a village every time**○ si c'est ça la ville, alors vive les petits villages; **'I ~ you the bride and groom!'** 'je bois à la santé des mariés!'; **I'll ~ you something to complain about**○! je vais t'apprendre à te plaindre!; **to ~ and take** faire des concessions; **to ~ as good as one gets** rendre coup pour coup; **to ~ it all one's got**○ (y) mettre le paquet; **to ~ sb what for**○ passer un savon à qn○; **what ~s?**○ qu'est-ce qui se passe?

(Phrasal verbs)

■ **give away**: ▸ ~ **away [sth]**, ~ **[sth] away 1)** donner [*item, sample*]; **we're practically giving them away!** à ce prix-là, c'est donné!; **2)** (reveal) révéler; **3)** (lose carelessly) laisser échapper [*match, goal, advantage*] (**to** au bénéfice de); ▸ ~ **[sb] away**, ~ **away [sb] 1)** (betray) [*expression, fingerprints*] trahir; [*person*] dénoncer (**to** à); **to ~ oneself away** se trahir; **2)** (in marriage) conduire [qn] à l'autel

■ **give back**: ▸ ~ **[sth] back**, ~ **back [sth] 1)** (return) rendre (**to** à); **...or we'll ~ you your money back** ...ou vous serez remboursé; **2)** renvoyer [*echo*]

■ **give in**: ▸ ~ **in 1)** (yield) céder (**to** à); **2)** (stop trying) abandonner; **I ~ in—tell me!** je donne ma langue au chat○—dis-le moi!; ▸ ~ **in [sth]**, ~ **[sth] in** rendre [*written work*]; remettre [*ticket, key*]

■ **give off**: ▸ ~ **off [sth]** émettre [*signal, scent, radiation, light*]; dégager [*heat, fumes, oxygen*]

■ **give onto**: ► ∼ **onto [sth]** donner sur

■ **give out**: ► ∼ **out** gen s'épuiser; [*engine, machine*] tomber en panne; ► ∼ **out [sth]**, ∼ **[sth] out** ① (distribute) distribuer (**to** à); ② (emit) = **give off**; ③ (announce) annoncer

■ **give over**: ► ∼ **over**○ arrêter; ► ∼ **over [sth]**, ∼ **[sth] over** ① affecter or réserver [*place, room*] (**to** à); ② consacrer [*time, life*] (**to** à); ③ (hand over) remettre [qch] à; ► ∼ **oneself over to** (devote oneself) se consacrer à; (let oneself go) s'abandonner à [*despair*]

■ **give up**: ► ∼ **up** abandonner; **don't** ∼ **up!** tiens bon!; **to** ∼ **up on** laisser tomber [*diet, crossword, pupil, patient*]; ne plus compter sur [*friend, partner*]; ► ∼ **up [sth]**, ∼ **[sth] up** ① (renounce or sacrifice) renoncer à [*vice, habit, title, claim*]; sacrifier [*free time*]; quitter [*job*]; **to** ∼ **up smoking/drinking** cesser de fumer/de boire; ② (abandon) abandonner [*search, hope, struggle, subject*]; renoncer à [*idea*]; **to** ∼ **up trying** abandonner; ③ (surrender) céder [*seat, territory*]; remettre [*passport, key*]; ► ∼ **up [sb]**, ∼ **[sb] up** ① (hand over) livrer (**to** à); **to** ∼ **oneself up** se livrer (**to** à); ② (drop) laisser tomber [*lover*]; délaisser [*friend*]

■ **give way** ① (collapse) gen s'effondrer; [*fence, cable*] céder; **his legs gave way** ses jambes se sont dérobées sous lui; ② GB (when driving) céder le passage (**to** à); ③ (yield) céder; **to** ∼ **way to** faire place à

give-and-take *n* ₵ concessions *fpl* mutuelles

giveaway /'gɪvəweɪ/ *n* **to be a** ∼ être révélateur/-trice

given /'gɪvn/
A *pp* ► **give**
B *adj* ① (specified) [*point, level, number*] donné; [*volume, length*] déterminé; **the** ∼ **date** la date convenue; **at any** ∼ **moment** à n'importe quel moment; ② (prone) **to be** ∼ **to sth/to doing** avoir tendance à qch/à faire; **I am not** ∼ **to doing** je n'ai pas l'habitude de faire
C *prep* ① (in view of) étant donné (**that** que); (assuming that) à supposer que; ② (with) avec [*training, proper care*]; ∼ **an opportunity I'll tell her this evening** si j'en ai l'occasion je le lui dirai ce soir; ∼ **the right conditions** dans de bonnes conditions

given name *n* prénom *m*

give way sign *n* GB panneau *m* 'cédez le passage'

gizzard /'gɪzəd/ *n* gésier *m*

glacier /'glæsɪə(r)/ *n* glacier *m*

glad /glæd/ *adj* ① (pleased) content, heureux/-euse (**about** de; **that** que; **to do** de faire); **I am** ∼ **(that) you are able to come** je suis content que vous puissiez venir; **he was only too** ∼ **to help me** il ne demandait qu'à m'aider; ② (cheering) **the** ∼ **tidings** la bonne nouvelle

(Idioms) **to give sb the** ∼ **eye** faire de l'œil à qn; **in one's** ∼ **rags**○ sur son trente-et-un○; **I'll be** ∼ **to see the back** *ou* **last of them**○ je serai content de les voir partir

gladden /'glædn/ *vtr* réjouir

glade /gleɪd/ *n* clairière *f*

gladiator /'glædɪeɪtə(r)/ *n* gladiateur *m*

gladiolus /ˌglædɪ'əʊləs/ *n* glaïeul *m*

gladly /'glædlɪ/ *adv* (willingly) volontiers; (with pleasure) avec plaisir

(Idiom) **she doesn't suffer fools** ∼ elle a du mal à supporter les imbéciles

glamorize /'glæməraɪz/ *vtr* (change) embellir [*person, room*]; (describe as attractive) valoriser [*place, attitude, idea*]; peindre [qch] sous de belles couleurs [*event*]

glamorous /'glæmərəs/ *adj* [*person, image, look*] séduisant; [*older person*] élégant; [*dress*] splendide; [*occasion*] brillant; [*job*] prestigieux/-ieuse

glamour, glamor US /'glæmə(r)/ *n* (of person) séduction *f*; (of job) prestige *m*; (of travel, cars) fascination *f*

glance /glɑːns, US glæns/
A *n* coup *m* d'œil; **to have a** ∼ **at** jeter un coup d'œil sur; **you can tell at a** ∼ **that** un coup d'œil suffit pour comprendre que; **without a backward** ∼ sans se retourner
B *vi* **to** ∼ **at** jeter un coup d'œil à; **to** ∼ **out of the window** jeter un coup d'œil par la fenêtre; **to** ∼ **around the room** parcourir la pièce du regard

(Phrasal verb)

■ **glance off**: ► ∼ **off [sth]** [*bullet, stone*] ricocher sur *or* contre; [*ball*] rebondir sur *or* contre; [*ray, beam*] se réfléchir sur

glancing /'glɑːnsɪŋ, US 'glænsɪŋ/ *adj* [*blow, kick*] oblique

gland /glænd/ *n* Anat glande *f*; **to have swollen** ∼**s** avoir des ganglions

glandular fever ► p. 933 *n* mononucléose *f* infectieuse

glare /gleə(r)/
A *n* ① (angry look) regard *m* furieux; ② (from light, headlights etc) lumière *f* éblouissante; **in the** ∼ **of publicity** fig sous le feu des médias
B *vi* [*person*] lancer un regard furieux (**at** à)

glaring /'gleərɪŋ/ *adj* ① (obvious) flagrant; ② (dazzling) éblouissant; ③ (angry) furieux/-ieuse

glaringly /'gleərɪŋlɪ/ *adv* **it's** ∼ **obvious** c'est l'évidence même

glass /glɑːs, US glæs/
A *n* ① (substance) verre *m*; **a piece of** ∼ un morceau de verre; (tiny) un éclat de verre; ② (drinking vessel) verre *m*; **wine** ∼ verre à vin; **a** ∼ **of wine** un verre de vin; ₵ (also ∼**ware**) verrerie *f*; ④ (mirror) miroir *m*; ⑤ (barometer) baromètre *m*
B *noun modifier* [*bottle, ornament, shelf*] en verre
C **glasses** *npl* ① (spectacles) lunettes *fpl*; **a pair of** ∼**es** une paire de lunettes; **he wears reading** ∼**es** il doit porter des lunettes quand il lit; ② (binoculars) jumelles *fpl*

glass: ∼ **blowing** *n* soufflage *m* du verre; ∼ **case** *n* (box) vitrine *f* en verre; (dome) globe *m*; ∼ **cloth** *n* essuie-verres *m inv*; ∼ **door** *n* porte *f* vitrée; ∼ **eye** *n* œil *m* de verre; ∼ **fibre** GB, ∼ **fiber** US *n* fibre *f* de verre; ∼**ful** *n* verre *m*

glasshouse /'glɑːshaʊs, US 'glæs-/ *n* GB serre *f*

(Idiom) **people in glass houses shouldn't throw stones** mieux vaut balayer devant sa porte avant de critiquer

glass: ∼**making** *n* fabrication *f* du verre; ∼ **paper** *n* papier *m* de verre; ∼**works** *n* verrerie *f*

glassy /'glɑːsɪ, US 'glæsɪ/ *adj* ① (resembling glass) [*substance*] vitreux/-euse; ② (slippery) [*road*] (from ice) verglacé; (from rain) glissant; ③ [*waters*] (calm) lisse (comme un miroir); (clear) transparent; ④ [*eyes*] (from drink, illness) vitreux/-euse; (hostile) glacé

glassy-eyed /ˌglɑːsɪ'aɪd, US ˌglæs-/ *adj* (from drink, illness) aux yeux vitreux; (hostile) au regard glacial

Glaswegian /glæz'wiːdʒən/
A *n* (inhabitant) habitant/-e *m/f* de Glasgow; (native) originaire *mf* de Glasgow
B *adj* [*accent, humour*] de Glasgow

glaucoma /glɔː'kəʊmə/ ► p. 933 *n* glaucome *m*

glaze /gleɪz/
A *n* ① gen vernis *m*; (on fabric) lustre *m*; ② (for ceramics) glaçure *f*; (in oil painting) glacis *m*; Culin (on pastry) dorure *f*; (of jelly) nappage *m*; (on meat) glaçage *m*; ③ US (ice) verglas *m*
B *vtr* ① vitrer [*window*]; mettre [qch] sous verre [*picture*]; ② (coat) vernisser [*ceramics*]; vernir [*leather*]; Phot glacer; Culin glacer [*meat*]; dorer [*pastry*]
C *vi* (also ∼ **over**) [*eyes*] devenir vitreux

glazed /gleɪzd/ *adj* [*door, window*] vitré; [*ceramics*] vernissé; [*fabric*] lustré; [*paper*] glacé; Culin [*meat, ham*] glacé; fig **to have a** ∼ **look in one's eyes** avoir les yeux vitreux

glazier /'gleɪzɪə(r), US -ʒər/ ► p. 1181, *n* vitrier *m*

gleam /gliːm/
A *n* (of light) lueur *f* also fig; (of sunshine) rayon *m*; (of gold, polished surface) reflet *m*; (of water) miroitement *m*
B *vi* [*light*] luire; [*knife, leather, surface*] reluire; [*jewel, water*] miroiter; [*eyes, teeth*] briller

gleaming /'gliːmɪŋ/ *adj* [*eyes, teeth, light*] brillant; [*leather, polished surface*] reluisant; [*water*] miroitant; [*jewel*] rutilant; [*kitchen etc*] étincelant (de propreté)

glean /gliːn/ *vtr, vi* lit, fig glaner

glee /gliː/ *n* allégresse *f*; (spiteful) jubilation *f*

gleeful /'gliːfl/ *adj* jubilant

glib /glɪb/ *adj* péj désinvolte

glide /glaɪd/
A *n* (in skating etc) pas *m* glissé; (in air) vol *m* plané
B *vi* gen glisser (**on, over** sur); (in air) planer

glider /'glaɪdə(r)/ *n* Aviat planeur *m*

gliding /'glaɪdɪŋ/ ► p. 881 *n* Sport vol *m* à voile

glimmer /'glɪmə(r)/
A *n* (light) faible lueur *f*; (trace) lueur *f*
B *vi* jeter une faible lueur

glimmering /'glɪmərɪŋ/
A n lit scintillement m; **the ~ of an idea** l'ébauche f d'une idée
B adj [sea, star] scintillant

glimpse /glɪmps/
A n **1** (sighting) vision f fugitive (**of** de); **to catch a ~ of sth** entrevoir qch; **2** fig (insight) aperçu m (**of, at** de)
B vtr lit, fig entrevoir

glint /glɪnt/
A n gen reflet m; (in eye) lueur f
B vi étinceler

glisten /'glɪsn/ vi [eyes, hair, surface] luire; [tears] briller; [water] scintiller; [silk] chatoyer

glitch○ /glɪtʃ/ n gen pépin○ m; Comput problème m technique

glitter /'glɪtə(r)/
A n (substance) paillettes fpl; (sparkle) éclat m; (of frost) scintillement m
B vi scintiller

(Idiom) **all that ~s is not gold** Prov tout ce qui brille n'est pas or Prov

glittering /'glɪtərɪŋ/ adj lit scintillant; fig brillant

gloat /gləʊt/ vi jubiler (**at, over** à l'idée de)

gloating /'gləʊtɪŋ/ adj triomphant

global /'gləʊbl/ adj (world wide) mondial; (comprehensive) global; (spherical) sphérique

globalize /'gləʊbəlaɪz/ vtr mondialiser

globally /'gləʊbəlɪ/ adv [compete, produce] à l'échelle mondiale; [famous, influential] dans le monde entier

global: **~ village** n village m planétaire; **~ warming** n réchauffement m de l'atmosphère

globe /gləʊb/ n **1** (world) **the ~** le globe; **2** (model) globe m terrestre

globe artichoke n artichaut m

globetrotting /'gləʊbtrɒtɪŋ/
A n voyages mpl à travers le monde
B adj voyageur/-euse

globule /'glɒbjuːl/ n gouttelette f (**of** de)

gloom /gluːm/ n **1** lit obscurité f; **2** fig morosité f (**about, over** à propos de); **to cast a ~ over sb** attrister qn; **to cast a ~ over sth** assombrir qch

gloomily /'gluːmɪlɪ/ adv [say, do] d'un air lugubre

gloomy /'gluːmɪ/ adj **1** (dark) sombre; **2** (sad) [expression, person, voice] lugubre; [weather] morose; [news, outlook] déprimant; **to be ~ about sth** être pessimiste à propos de qch

glorify /'glɔːrɪfaɪ/
A vtr (all contexts) glorifier
B glorified pp adj **the 'villa' was a glorified bungalow** la 'villa' n'était rien de plus qu'un simple pavillon

glorious /'glɔːrɪəs/ adj **1** (marvellous) gen magnifique; [holiday, outing] merveilleux/-euse; **2** (illustrious) glorieux/-ieuse

gloriously /'glɔːrɪəslɪ/ adv merveilleusement

glory /'glɔːrɪ/
A n **1** (honour) also Relig gloire f; **2** (splendour) splendeur f; **3** (source of pride) fierté f
B vi **to ~ in** être très fier/fière de

Glos n GB Post abrév écrite = **Gloucestershire**

gloss /glɒs/
A n **1** (lustre) (of wood, metal etc) lustre m; (of hair) éclat m; fig (glamour) clinquant m; **to lose its ~** lit, fig perdre (de) son éclat; **to take the ~ off** fig gâcher [occasion]; **2** fig (appearance) vernis m; **3** (in text) glose f; **4** (paint) laque f (brillante)
B vtr (explain) gloser [word, text]

(Phrasal verb)
■ **gloss over**: ▸ **~ over** [sth] (pass rapidly over) glisser sur; (hide) dissimuler

glossary /'glɒsərɪ/ n glossaire m

gloss: **~ finish** n brillant m; **~ paint** n laque f (brillante)

glossy /'glɒsɪ/ adj [hair, fur, material] luisant; [wood, metal] brillant; [leaves] vernissé; [photograph] brillant; [brochure] luxueux/-euse; fig [production, film, interior] qui a un éclat plutôt superficiel

glossy magazine n magazine m illustré (de luxe)

glottal stop n Ling coup m de glotte

glove /glʌv/ n gant m; **with the ~s off** fig sans prendre de gants; **her ~d hands** ses mains gantées

(Idioms) **it fits like a ~** cela me/lui etc va comme un gant; **to be hand in ~ with sb** être de mèche avec qn○

glove: **~ box**, **~ compartment** n boîte f à gants; **~ puppet** n marionnette f à gaine

glow /gləʊ/
A n **1** (of coal, furnace) rougeoiement m; (of room, candle) lueur f; **2** (colour) éclat m; **3** (feeling) douce sensation f; **it gives you a warm ~** ça fait chaud au cœur
B vi **1** (give off light) [coal, metal, furnace] rougeoyer; [lamp, paint, cigarette] luire; **2** (look vibrant) [colour] être éclatant; **her skin ~ed** elle avait un teint éblouissant; **to ~ with health** resplendir de santé; **to ~ with pride** rayonner de fierté

glower /'glaʊə(r)/ vi lancer des regards noirs (**at** à)

glowering /'glaʊərɪŋ/ adj [face] courroucé; [sky] menaçant

glowing /'gləʊɪŋ/ adj **1** (bright) [ember] rougeoyant; [lava] incandescent; [face, cheeks] (from exercise) rouge; (from pleasure) radieux/-ieuse; [colour] chaud; **2** (complimentary) élogieux/-ieuse

glowworm /'gləʊwɜːm/ n ver m luisant

glucose /'gluːkəʊs/
A n glucose m
B noun modifier [powder, syrup, tablets] de glucose; [drink] au glucose

glue /gluː/
A n lit colle f; **to sniff ~** inhaler de la colle
B vtr coller; **to ~ sth on** ou **down** coller qch
C glued○ pp adj **to have one's eyes ~d to sb/sth** avoir les yeux fixés sur qn/qch; **to be ~d to the TV** être collé○ devant la télé; **to be ~d to the spot** être cloué sur place

glue: **~ pen** n stylo m colle transparente; **~-sniffing** n inhalation f de colle

glum /glʌm/ adj morose

glut /glʌt/
A n gen surabondance f, excès m
B vtr (p prés etc **-tt-**) inonder
C glutted pp adj lit, fig rassasié (**with** de)

glutinous /'gluːtənəs/ adj gluant

glutton /'glʌtn/ n (greedy) glouton/-onne m/f; fig **a ~ for punishment** un masochiste

gluttony /'glʌtənɪ/ n gloutonnerie f

glycerin(e) /'glɪsəriːn, US -rɪn/ n glycérine f

gm n (abrév écrite = **gram**) g

GM adj (abrév = **genetically modified**) [crops, seed, ingredients] transgénique, génétiquement modifié

GMO n (abrév = **genetically modified organism**) OGM m, organisme m génétiquement modifié

GMT n (abrév = **Greenwich Mean Time**) TU

gnarled /nɑːld/ adj noueux/-euse

gnash /næʃ/ vtr **to ~ one's teeth** grincer des dents

gnat /næt/ n moucheron m

gnaw /nɔː/
A vtr lit ronger; fig (torment) [hunger, remorse] tenailler; [pain] lanciner
B vi **to ~ at** ou **on sth** ronger qch

gnawing /'nɔːɪŋ/ adj [hunger, guilt] tenaillant; [pain] lancinant

gnome /nəʊm/ n **1** (goblin) gnome m; **garden ~** petit nain m (en plâtre); **2** ○**~ of Zurich** banquier m international

GNP n (abrév = **gross national product**) PNB m

go /gəʊ/
A vi (3e pers sg prés **goes**; prét **went**; pp **gone**) **1** (move, travel) aller (**from** de; **to** à, en); **to ~ to Paris** aller à Paris; **to ~ to Wales/to California** aller au Pays de Galles/en Californie; **to ~ to town/to the country** aller en ville/à la campagne; **they went home** ils sont rentrés chez eux; **to ~ up/down/across** monter/descendre/traverser; **I went into the room** je suis entré dans la pièce; **to ~ by bus/train** voyager en bus/train; **to ~ by** ou **past** [person, vehicle] passer; **that car's**

go

As an intransitive verb

go as a simple intransitive verb is translated by *aller*:

we're going to Paris
= nous allons à Paris

where are you going?
= où vas-tu?

Sasha went to London last week
= Sasha est allée à Londres la semaine dernière

Note that *aller* conjugates with *être* in compound tenses. For the conjugation of *aller* see the French verb tables. For more examples and particular usages see the entry **go**. The verb *go* produces a great many phrasal verbs in English (*go up*, *go down*, *go out*, *go back* etc.). Many of these are translated by a single verb in French (*monter*, *descendre*, *sortir*, *retourner* etc.). The phrasal verbs are listed separately at the end of the entry **go**.

As an auxiliary verb

When *go* is used as an auxiliary to show intention, it is also translated by *aller*:

I'm going to buy a car tomorrow
= je vais acheter une voiture demain

I was going to talk to you about it
= j'allais t'en parler

he's not going to ask for a rise
= il ne va pas demander d'augmentation

For more examples and particular usages see **A23** in the entry **go**.

For all other uses see the entry **go**.

---

going very fast! cette voiture roule très vite!; **there he goes again!** (that's him again) le revoilà!; fig (he's starting again) le voilà qui recommence!; **where do we ~ from here?** fig et maintenant qu'est-ce qu'on fait?; ② (on specific errand, activity) aller; **to ~ shopping** aller faire des courses; **to ~ on a journey/on holiday** partir en voyage/en vacances; **to ~ for a drink** aller prendre un verre; ③ (attend) aller; **to ~ to school/work** aller à l'école/au travail; **to ~ to the doctor's** aller chez le médecin; ④ (used as auxiliary with present participle) **she went running up the stairs** elle a monté l'escalier en courant; ⑤ (depart) partir; ⑥ euph (die) mourir, disparaître; **when I am gone** quand je ne serai plus là; ⑦ (disappear) partir; **the money goes on school fees** l'argent part en frais de scolarité; **the money has all gone** il ne reste plus d'argent; **I left my bike outside and now it's gone** j'ai laissé mon vélo dehors et il n'est plus là; **there goes my chance of winning!** c'en est fait de mes chances de gagner!; ⑧ (be sent, transmitted) **it can't ~ by post** on ne peut pas l'envoyer par la poste; **these proposals will ~ before parliament** ces propositions seront soumises au parlement; ⑨ (become) **to ~ red** rougir; **to ~ white** blanchir; **to ~ mad** devenir fou/folle; ⑩ (change over to new system) **to ~ Labour** Pol [*country, constituency*] voter travailliste; **to ~ metric** adopter le système m étrique; ⑪ (be, remain) **the people went hungry** les gens n'avaient rien à manger; **we went for two days without food** nous avons passé deux jours sans rien manger; **to ~ unnoticed** passer inaperçu; **the question went unanswered** la question est restée sans réponse; **he was allowed to ~ free** il a été libéré; ⑫ (weaken, become impaired) **his memory is going** il perd la mémoire; **his hearing is going** il devient sourd; **my voice is going** je n'ai plus de voix; **the battery is going** la batterie est presque à plat; ⑬ (of time) **there are only three days to ~ before Christmas** il ne reste plus que trois jours avant Noël; **how's the time going?** quelle heure est-il?; **it's just gone seven o'clock** il est sept heures passées; ⑭ (be got rid of) **he'll have to ~!** il va falloir qu'on se débarrasse de

lui!; **the car will have to ~** il va falloir vendre la voiture; **either she goes or I do!** c'est elle ou moi!; **six down and four to ~!** six de faits, et encore quatre à faire!; ⑮ (operate, function) [*vehicle, machine, clock*] marcher, fonctionner; **to set [sth] going** mettre [qch] en marche; **to get going** [*engine, machine*] se mettre en marche; fig [*business*] démarrer; **to get the fire going** allumer le feu; **to keep going** [*person, business, machine*] se maintenir; **we have several projects going at the moment** nous avons plusieurs projets en route en ce moment; ⑯ (start) **let's get going!** allons-y!; **to get things going** mettre les choses en train; **here goes!, here we ~!** c'est parti!; **once he gets going, he never stops** une fois lancé, il n'arrête pas; ⑰ (lead) aller, conduire (**to** à); **the road goes down/goes up** la route descend/monte; ⑱ (extend in depth or scope) **the roots ~ very deep** les racines s'enfoncent très profondément; **these habits ~ very deep** ces habitudes sont profondément ancrées; **it's true as far as it goes** c'est vrai dans un sens; **a hundred pounds doesn't ~ far these days** on ne va pas loin avec cent livres sterling de nos jours; **this goes a long way towards explaining his attitude** ceci explique en grande partie son attitude; **you can make £5 ~ a long way** on peut faire beaucoup de choses avec 5 livres sterling; ⑲ (belong, be placed) aller; **the suitcases will have to ~ in the back** il va falloir mettre les valises derrière; ⑳ (fit) gen rentrer; **five into four won't ~** quatre n'est pas divisible par cinq; ㉑ (be expressed in particular way) **I can't remember how the poem goes** je n'arrive pas à me rappeler le poème; **how does the song ~?** quel est l'air de la chanson?; **as the saying goes** comme dit le proverbe; ㉒ (be accepted) **what he says goes** c'est lui qui fait la loi; **it goes without saying that** il va sans dire que; **anything goes** tout est permis; ㉓ (be about to) **to be going to do** aller faire; **it's going to snow** il va neiger; ㉔ (happen) **the party went very well** la soirée s'est très bien passée; **the way things are going** si ça continue comme ça; **how's it going○?, how are things going?** comment ça va○?; **how goes it?** hum comment ça va○?; ㉕ (be on average) **it's old, as Australian towns ~** c'est une ville assez vieille pour une ville australienne; **it wasn't a bad party, as parties ~** c'était une soirée plutôt réussie par rapport à la moyenne; ㉖ (be sold) **the house went for over £100,000** la maison a été vendue à plus de 100 000 livres; **'going, going, gone!'** 'une fois, deux fois, trois fois, adjugé!'; ㉗ (be on offer) **I'll have some coffee, if there's any going** je prendrai bien un café, s'il y en a; **it's the best machine going** c'est la meilleure machine sur le marché; **there's a job going** il y a un poste libre; ㉘ (contribute) **the money will ~ towards a new roof** l'argent servira à payer un nouveau toit; **everything that goes to make a good teacher** toutes les qualités d'un bon enseignant; ㉙ (be given) [*award, prize*] aller (**to** à); [*estate, inheritance, title*] passer (**to** à); **the job went to a local man** le poste a été donné à un homme de la région; ㉚ (emphatic use) **why did he ~ and spoil it?** pourquoi est-il allé tout gâcher?; **he went and won the competition!** il s'est débrouillé pour gagner le concours!; **you've really gone and done it now!** tu peux être fier de toi!; iron; **then he had to ~ and lose his wallet** comme s'il ne manquait plus que ça, il a perdu son portefeuille; ㉛ (of money) (be spent, used up) **all his money goes on drink** tout son argent passe dans l'alcool; **I don't know where all my money goes (to)!** je ne sais pas ce que je fais de mon argent!; ㉜ (make sound, perform action or movement) gen faire; [*bell, alarm*] sonner; **the cat went 'miaow'** le chat a fait 'miaou'; **wait until the bell goes** attends que la cloche sonne (*subj*); **she went like this with her fingers** elle a fait comme ça avec ses doigts; ㉝ (resort to, have recourse to) **to ~ to war** [*country*] entrer en guerre; [*soldier*] partir à la guerre; **to ~ to law** GB ou **to the law** US aller en justice; ㉞ (break, collapse etc) [*roof*] s'effondrer; [*cable, rope*] se rompre; [*light bulb*] griller; ㉟ (take one's turn) **you ~ next** c'est ton tour après, c'est à toi après; **you ~ first** après vous; ㊱ (be in harmony) **those two colours don't ~ together** ces deux couleurs ne vont pas ensemble; ㊲ (in takeaway) **to ~** à emporter.

B *vtr* (3ᵉ pers sg prés **goes**; *prét* **went**; *pp* **gone**) faire [*number of miles*]; **are you going my way?** tu vas dans la même direction que moi?

C *n* (*pl* **goes**) ① GB (turn) tour *m*; (try) essai *m*; **whose ~ is it?** gen à qui le tour?; (in game) à qui de jouer?; **I had to have several goes before passing** j'ai dû m'y reprendre à plusieurs fois avant de réussir; ② ○(energy) **to be full of ~, to be all ~** être très dynamique

(Idioms) **all systems are** ∼! Aerosp tout est paré pour le lancement; **to have a** ∼ **at sb** s'en prendre à qn; **to make a** ∼ **of sth** réussir qch; **she's always on the** ∼ elle n'arrête jamais; **he's all** ∼○! il n'arrête pas!; **we have several different projects on the** ∼ nous avons plusieurs projets différents en chantier; **(it's) no** ∼! pas question!; **from the word** ∼ dès le départ; **in one** ∼ d'un seul coup; **to** ∼ **one better than sb** renchérir sur qn; **that's how it goes!, that's the way it goes!** c'est la vie!; **there you** ∼○! voilà!

(Phrasal verbs)

■ **go about**: ▶ ∼ **about** ① = go around; ② Naut virer de bord; ▶ ∼ **about [sth]** ① (undertake) s'attaquer à [task]; **he knows how to** ∼ **about it** il sait s'y prendre; ② (be busy with) **to** ∼ **about one's business** vaquer à ses occupations

■ **go across**: ▶ ∼ **across** traverser; **he's gone across to the shop** il est allé au magasin en face; ▶ ∼ **across [sth]** traverser

■ **go after**: ▶ ∼ **after [sth/sb]** ① (chase) poursuivre; ② fig (try hard to get) **he really went after that job** il a fait tout son possible pour avoir ce travail

■ **go against**: ▶ ∼ **against [sb/sth]** ① (prove unfavourable to) **the vote/decision went against them** le vote/la décision leur a été défavorable; **the war is going against them** la guerre tourne à leur désavantage; ② (conflict with) être contraire à [rules, principles]; **to** ∼ **against the trend** aller à l'encontre de la tendance; ③ (resist, oppose) s'opposer à

■ **go ahead** ① (go in front) ∼ **ahead, I'll follow you on** partez devant, je vous suis; ② fig (proceed) [event] avoir lieu; ∼ **ahead and shoot!** vas-y, tire!; **they are going ahead with the project** ils ont décidé de mettre le projet en route; **we can** ∼ **ahead without them** nous pouvons continuer sans eux

■ **go along** ① (move along) [person, vehicle] aller, avancer; **to make sth up as one goes along** fig inventer qch au fur et à mesure; ② (attend) aller; **I went along** j'y suis allé

■ **go along with**: ▶ ∼ **along with [sb/sth]** être d'accord avec

■ **go around**: ▶ ∼ **around** ① (move, travel about) se promener, circuler; **she goes around on a bicycle** elle circule à bicyclette; **they** ∼ **around everywhere together** ils vont partout ensemble; ② (circulate) [rumour] courir; **there isn't enough money to** ∼ **around** il n'y a pas assez d'argent pour tout le monde; ▶ ∼ **around [sth]** faire le tour de [house, shops]

■ **go at**: ▶ ∼ **at [sb]** (attack) attaquer; ▶ ∼ **at [sth]** s'attaquer à

■ **go away** [person] partir; ∼ **away and leave me alone!** va-t'en et laisse-moi tranquille!; **don't** ∼ **away thinking that** ne va pas croire que; **this cold just won't** ∼ **away!** je n'arrive pas à me débarrasser de ce rhume!

■ **go back** ① (return) retourner; (turn back) rebrousser chemin; (resume work) reprendre le travail; (resume classes, studies) reprendre les cours; **let's** ∼ **back to France** retournons en France; **to** ∼ **back to the beginning** recommencer; **to** ∼ **back to sleep** se rendormir; **to** ∼ **back to work** se remettre au travail; **there's no going back** fig vous ne pouvez plus reculer; ② (in time) remonter; **this tradition goes back a century** cette tradition est vieille d'un siècle; **we** ∼ **back a long way** ça fait longtemps qu'on se connaît; ③ (revert) revenir (**to** à)

■ **go back on**: ▶ ∼ **back on [sth]** revenir sur [promise, decision]

■ **go before**: ▶ ∼ **before** (go in front) aller au devant; fig (in time) se passer avant; ▶ ∼ **before [sb/sth]** comparaître devant [court, judge]; **the bill went before parliament** le projet de loi a été soumis au parlement

■ **go below** gen, Naut descendre

■ **go by**: ▶ ∼ **by** passer; **as time goes by** avec le temps; ▶ ∼ **by [sth]** ① (judge by) juger d'après; **you mustn't** ∼ **by what you read in the papers** il ne faut pas croire tout ce que disent les journaux; ② (proceed by) **to** ∼ **by the rules** suivre or observer le règlement

■ **go down**: ▶ ∼ **down** ① (descend) descendre; [sun] se coucher; **to** ∼ **down to the pub** aller au pub; ② (fall) tomber; (sink) couler; **the plane went down in flames** l'avion s'est écrasé en flammes; ③ (be received) **to** ∼ **down well/badly** être bien/mal reçu; ④ (become lower) [water level, price, temperature, standard] baisser; [tide] descendre; (abate) [storm, wind] se calmer; (fall in price) devenir moins cher; ⑤ (be deflated) [swelling] désenfler; [tyre] se dégonfler; ⑥ GB Univ (for holiday) terminer les cours; (permanently) quitter l'université; ⑦ gen, Sport (be defeated) perdre; (be downgraded)

redescendre; ⑧ (be remembered) **he will** ∼ **down as a great statesman** on se souviendra de lui comme d'un grand homme d'État; ⑨ (be recorded) être noté; ⑩ (be stricken) **to** ∼ **down with flu/malaria** attraper la grippe/la malaria; ⑪ ○GB (go to prison) être envoyé en prison; ⑫ Comput tomber en panne; ▶ ∼ **down [sth]** descendre [hill]; descendre dans [mine]

■ **go for**: ▶ ∼ **for [sb/sth]** ① ○(favour, have liking for) craquer○ pour [person]; aimer [style of music, literature etc]; ② (apply to) être valable pour, s'appliquer à; ▶ ∼ **for [sb]** ① (attack) attaquer; ② **he has a lot going for him** il a beaucoup de choses pour lui; ▶ ∼ **for [sth]** ① (attempt to achieve) essayer d'obtenir [honour, victory]; **she's going for the world record** elle vise le record mondial; ∼ **for it**○! vas-y, fonce○!; ② (choose) choisir, prendre

■ **go forward(s)** avancer

■ **go in** ① (enter) entrer; (go back in) rentrer; ② Mil [troops] attaquer; ③ (disappear) [sun] se cacher

■ **go in for**: ▶ ∼ **in for [sth]** ① (be keen on) aimer; ② (take up) **to** ∼ **in for teaching** entrer dans l'enseignement; **to** ∼ **in for politics** se lancer dans la politique; ③ (take part in) s'inscrire à [exam, competition]

■ **go into**: ▶ ∼ **into [sth]** ① (enter) entrer dans; fig (take up) se lancer dans [business, profession]; ② (examine) étudier [question]; ③ (explain) **I won't** ∼ **into why I did it** je n'expliquerai pas pourquoi je l'ai fait; **let's not** ∼ **into that now** laissons cela de côté pour l'instant; ④ (be expended) **a lot of work went into this project** beaucoup de travail a été investi dans ce projet; ⑤ (hit) [car, driver] rentrer dans, heurter

■ **go off**: ▶ ∼ **off** ① (explode, fire) [bomb] exploser; **the gun didn't** ∼ **off** le coup n'est pas parti; ② [alarm clock] sonner; [fire alarm] se déclencher; ③ (depart) partir, s'en aller; **he went off to work** il est parti au travail; ④ GB (go bad) [milk, cream] tourner; [meat] s'avarier; [butter] rancir; (deteriorate) [performer, athlete etc] perdre sa forme; [work] se dégrader; ⑤ ○(fall asleep) s'endormir; ⑥ (cease to operate) [lights, heating] s'éteindre; ⑦ (happen, take place) [evening, organized event] se passer; ⑧ Theat quitter la scène; ▶ ∼ **off [sb/sth]** GB **I've gone off whisky** je n'aime plus tellement le whisky; **I think she's gone off the idea** je crois qu'elle a renoncé à l'idée

■ **go off with**: ▶ ∼ **off with [sb/sth]** partir avec

■ **go on**: ▶ ∼ **on** ① (happen, take place) se passer; **how long has this been going on?** depuis combien de temps est-ce que ça dure?; **a lot of stealing goes on** il y a beaucoup de vols; ② (continue on one's way) poursuivre son chemin; ③ (continue) continuer; **the meeting went on into the afternoon** la réunion s'est prolongée jusque dans l'après-midi; **the list goes on and on** la liste est infinie; **that's enough to be going on with** ça suffit pour le moment; **here's £20 to be going on with** voici 20 livres pour te dépanner; ∼ **on (with you)**○! allons donc!; ④ (of time) (elapse) **as time went on, they...** avec le temps, ils...; **as the evening went on** au fur et à mesure que la soirée avançait; ⑤ (keep talking) **to** ∼ **on about sth** ne pas arrêter de parler de qch; **the way she goes on, you'd think she was an expert!** à l'entendre, on croirait qu'elle est experte!; ⑥ (proceed) passer; **let's** ∼ **on to the next item** passons au point suivant; **he went on to say that** puis il a dit que; ⑦ (go into operation) [heating, lights] s'allumer; ⑧ Theat entrer en scène; ⑨ (approach) **it's going on three o'clock** il est presque trois heures; **she's four going on five** elle va sur ses cinq ans; ⑩ (fit) **these gloves won't** ∼ **on** ces gants ne m'iront pas; **the lid won't** ∼ **on properly** le couvercle ne ferme pas bien; ▶ ∼ **on [sth]** se fonder sur [piece of evidence, information]; **that's all we've got to** ∼ **on** tout ce que nous savons avec certitude; **we've got nothing else to** ∼ **on** nous n'avons pas d'autre point de départ

■ **go on at**: ▶ ∼ **on at [sb]** s'en prendre à

■ **go out** ① (leave, depart) sortir; **to** ∼ **out walking** aller se promener; **to** ∼ **out for a drink** aller prendre un verre; **she's gone out to Australia** elle est partie pour l'Australie; ② (have relationship) **to** ∼ **out with sb** sortir avec qn; ③ [tide] descendre; ④ (become unfashionable) passer de mode; (no longer be used) ne plus être utilisé; ⑤ (be extinguished) [fire, light] s'éteindre; ⑥ (invitation, summons) être envoyé; Radio, TV (be broadcast) être diffusé; ⑦ (be eliminated) gen, Sport être éliminé; ⑧ (expressing sympathy) **my heart goes out to them** je les plains de tout mon cœur; ⑨ (disappear) **all the spirit seemed to have gone out of her** elle semblait avoir perdu tout son entrain

■ **go over**: ▶ ~ **over** [1] (cross over) aller (**to** vers); **we are now going over to Washington** Radio, TV nous passons maintenant l'antenne à Washington; [2] (be received) être reçu; [3] (switch to other side or alternative) passer (**to** à); ▶ ~ **over** [sth] [1] (review, inspect) passer [qch] en revue [*details, facts*]; vérifier [*accounts, figures*]; relire [*article*]; **to ~ over a house** faire le tour d'une maison; [2] (clean) **he went over the room with a duster** il a donné un coup de chiffon dans la pièce; [3] (exceed) dépasser

■ **go round** GB: ▶ ~ **round** [1] (turn) tourner; [2] (call round) **to ~ round to see sb** aller voir qn; [3] (suffice) **there isn't enough food to ~ round** il n'y a pas assez de nourriture pour tout le monde; [4] (make detour) faire un détour; **we had to ~ the long way round** il a fallu qu'on prenne un chemin plus long; ▶ ~ **round** [sth] (visit) faire le tour de

■ **go through**: ▶ ~ **through** [1] (come in) entrer; [2] (be approved) [*law, agreement*] passer; [*divorce*] être prononcé; [*business deal*] être conclu; ▶ ~ **through** [sth] [1] endurer, subir [*experience, ordeal*]; passer par [*stage, phase*]; **she's gone through a lot** elle a beaucoup souffert; **the country has gone through two civil wars** le pays a connu deux guerres civiles; **to ~ through a crisis** traverser une crise; **as you ~ through life** au fur et à mesure que tu vieillis; **you have to ~ through the switchboard** il faut passer par le standard; **it went through my mind that** l'idée m'a traversé l'esprit que; [2] (check, inspect) examiner; (rapidly) parcourir [*documents, files, list*]; [3] (search) fouiller; [4] (perform, rehearse) répéter [*scene*]; expliquer [*procedure*]; remplir [*formalities*]; [5] (consume, use up) dépenser [*money*]; **we went through three bottles of wine** nous avons bu trois bouteilles de vin

■ **go through with**: ▶ ~ **through with** [sth] réaliser, mettre [qch] à exécution [*plan*]; **in the end they decided to ~ through with the wedding** finalement ils ont décidé que le mariage aurait lieu; **I can't ~ through with it** je ne peux pas le faire

■ **go together** [1] (harmonize) aller ensemble; [2] (entail each other) aller de pair

■ **go under** (sink) couler; fig [*person*] succomber; [*business, company*] faire faillite

■ **go up**: ▶ ~ **up** [1] (ascend, rise) monter; **to ~ up to bed** monter se coucher; [2] (rise) [*price, temperature*] monter; [*figures*] augmenter; Theat [*curtain*] se lever (**on** sur); **petrol has gone up (in price)** (le prix de) l'essence a augmenté; [3] (be erected) [*building*] être construit; [*poster*] être affiché; [4] (blown up) sauter, exploser; [5] GB Univ (start university) entrer à l'université; (start term) reprendre les cours; [6] (be upgraded) **the team has gone up to the first division** l'équipe est passée en première division; [7] (continue) **the book goes up to 1990** le livre va jusqu'en 1990; ▶ ~ **up** [sth] [1] (mount) monter, gravir [*hill, mountain*]; [2] **to ~ up a class** Sch passer dans une classe supérieure

■ **go with**: ▶ ~ **with** [sth] [1] (match, suit) aller avec; [2] (accompany) aller de pair avec

■ **go without**: ▶ ~ **without** s'en passer; ▶ ~ **without** [sth] se passer de

goad /gəʊd/
A n lit, fig aiguillon m
B vtr [1] (prod) aiguillonner; [2] fig (provoke) provoquer; **to ~ sb into doing sth** pousser qn à faire qch

go-ahead○ /'gəʊəhed/ n **to give sb the ~**○ donner le feu vert à qn; **to get the ~** recevoir le feu vert

goal /gəʊl/ n gen, Sport but m; **to keep ~** ou **to play in ~** être gardien de but; **to score** ou **kick a ~** marquer un but; **to score an own ~** lit, fig marquer un but pour le compte de l'adversaire

goal: ~ **area** n surface f de but; ~**keeper** ▸ p. 1181 n gardien m de but; ~ **kick** n (in soccer) dégagement m aux six

goalless /'gəʊllɪs/ adj ~ **match** ou **draw** match m nul

goalpost /'gəʊlpəʊst/ n poteau m de but

(Idiom) **to move the ~s** changer les règles du jeu

goat /gəʊt/
A n [1] Zool, Culin chèvre f; [2] ○GB (fool) andouille○ f; [3] ○(lecher) vieux cochon m○
B noun modifier [*cheese, meat, milk, stew*] de chèvre

(Idioms) **he really gets my ~**○ il me tape sur les nerfs○; **that will separate the sheep from the ~s** cela permettra de voir ce que vaut chacun

goatskin /'gəʊtskɪn/ n (leather) cuir m de chèvre; (pelt) peau f de chèvre

gobble /'gɒbl/
A n (cry of turkey) glouglou m
B vtr (also ~ **down**) engloutir [*food*]
C vi [1] [*turkey*] glouglouter; [2] [*person*] se goinfrer○

(Phrasal verb)

■ **gobble up** lit, fig: ▶ ~ [sth] **up**, ~ **up** [sth] engloutir

gobbledygook○ /'gɒblɪdɪguːk/ n charabia○ m

go-between /'gəʊbɪtwiːn/ n intermédiaire mf

goblet /'gɒblɪt/ n verre m à pied

goblin /'gɒblɪn/ n lutin m

gobsmacked○ /'gɒbsmækt/ adj GB estomaqué○

god /gɒd/
A n lit, fig dieu m
B **God** pr n [1] Relig Dieu m; **so help me God** je le jure devant Dieu; **a man of God** un prêtre; [2] (in exclamations) (exasperated) zut○!; (surprised) ça alors○!; **God forbid**○! grands dieux, non!
C **Gods**○ npl Theat paradis m, poulailler○ m

(Idioms) **God helps those who help themselves** aide-toi, le ciel t'aidera; **to put the fear of God into sb** faire une peur bleue à qn; **to think one is God's gift (to women)**○ se croire irrésistible auprès des femmes

God Almighty
A n Relig Dieu m Tout-Puissant
B excl mon Dieu!

(Idiom) **he thinks he's ~** il se prend pour Dieu le père

godchild n filleul/-e m/f

goddamn○ /'gɒdæm/ adj sacré○, fichu○

goddaughter /'gɒddɔːtə(r)/ n filleule f

goddess /'gɒdɪs/ n (divinity, woman) déesse f

god: ~**father** n parrain m; ~**fearing** adj pieux/pieuse; ~**forsaken** adj [*country, place*] perdu

godless /'gɒdlɪs/ adj impie

godlike /'gɒdlaɪk/ adj divin

godly /'gɒdlɪ/ adj pieux/pieuse

godmother /'gɒdmʌðə(r)/ n marraine f

godparent /'gɒdpeərənt/ n parrain/marraine m/f; **the ~s** le parrain et la marraine

God Save the Queen/King n GB hymne national britannique

> ⓘ **God Save the Queen/King** *God Save the King* est une chanson patriotique dont on ne connaît pas l'auteur, entendue pour la première fois en public à Londres en 1745. Elle devint l'hymne national britannique à partir du XIXᵉ siècle.

god: ~**send** n aubaine f; ~**son** n filleul m

goer /'gəʊə(r)/
A ○ n GB **to be a ~** être plein d'allant
B **-goer** combining form **theatre-~** personne f qui va au théâtre; (regular) amateur m de théâtre; **cinema-~** personne f qui va au cinéma; (regular) cinéphile mf

goes /gəʊz/ ▸ **go**

go: ~**faster stripes** n Aut bandes fpl horizontales; ~**getter**○ n fonceur/-euse○ m/f; ~**getting**○ adj fonceur/-euse○

goggle○ /'gɒgl/ vi [*person*] ouvrir des yeux ronds○

goggle: ~**box**○ n GB télé○ f; ~**eyed** adj avec des yeux ronds○

goggles /'gɒglz/ npl (cyclist's, worker's) lunettes fpl protectrices; (skier's) lunettes fpl de ski; (for swimming) lunettes fpl de plongée

go-go /'gəʊgəʊ/ adj [*dancing, girl*] de boîte○ (de nuit)

going /'gəʊɪŋ/
A n [1] (departure) départ m; [2] (progress) **that's not bad ~!**, **that's good ~!** c'est rapide!; **it was slow ~, the ~ was slow** (on journey) ça a été long; (at work) ça n'avançait pas vite; **the conversation was heavy ~** la conversation était laborieuse; [3] (condition of ground) état m du sol; **the ~ was hard** le terrain était lourd; [4] fig (conditions) **when the ~ gets tough** quand les choses vont mal; **she finds her new job hard ~** elle trouve que son nouveau travail est difficile; **they got out while the ~ was good** ils s'en sont tirés avant qu'il ne soit trop tard
B adj [1] (current) [*price*] actuel, en cours; **the ~ rate** le tarif en vigueur; [2] (operating) ~ **concern** Comm affaire f qui marche; **they bought the business as a ~ concern** quand

ils ont acheté l'entreprise elle était déjà montée; **3** (exist-ing) **it's the best model** ~ c'est le meilleur modèle sur le marché

C **-going** *combining form* **theatre-~** la fréquentation des théâtres; **the theatre-~ public** les amateurs *mpl* de théâtre

going-over○ /ˌɡəʊɪŋˈəʊvə(r)/ *n* (*pl* **goings-over**) **1** (examination) (of vehicle, machine) révision *f*; (of document) véri-fication *f*; (cleaning) (of room, house) nettoyage *m*; **the doctor gave me a thorough** ~ le médecin m'a soigneusement examiné; **2** **to give sb a** ~ (beat up) rouer qn de coups

goings-on○ /ˌɡəʊɪŋzˈɒn/ *npl* (events) événements *mpl*; péj (activities) activités *fpl*; (behaviour) conduite *f*

go-kart /ˈɡəʊkɑːt/ *n* kart *m*

go-karting /ˈɡəʊkɑːtɪŋ/ *n* karting *m*; **to go** ~ faire du karting

Golan /ˈɡəʊlæn/ *pr n* **the** ~ **Heights** le (plateau *m* du) Golan

gold /ɡəʊld/
A *n* **1** gen, Fin or *m*; **to strike** ~ découvrir un filon; **2** (colour) (couleur *f*) or *m*; **3** = **gold medal**
B *noun modifier* [*jewellery, cutlery, tooth*] en or; [*coin, medal, ingot, wire*] d'or; [*ore, deposit, alloy*] d'or
(Idioms) **as good as** ~ sage comme une image; **to be worth one's weight in** ~ valoir son pesant d'or

Gold Coast *n* **1** Hist (Ghana) Côte-de-l'Or *f*; **2** (in Australia) série de stations balnéaires dans l'est de l'Australie; **3** US ban-lieue *f* huppée

gold: ~ **digger** *n* chercheur *m* d'or; ~ **disc** *n* disque *m* d'or

gold dust *n* lit poudre *f* d'or; **to be like** ~ fig être une denrée rare

golden /ˈɡəʊldən/ *adj* **1** (made of gold) en or, d'or; **2** (gold coloured) doré, d'or; ~ **hair** cheveux *mpl* dorés; **3** fig [*summer*] idyllique; [*voice, age, days*] d'or; **a** ~ **opportunity** une occasion en or

golden: ~ **anniversary** *n* = **golden jubilee**; ~ **boy** *n* enfant *m* chéri; ~**brown** ▶ p. 752 *n*, *adj* mordoré (*m*); **Golden Delicious** *n* golden *f inv* (*pomme*); ~ **eagle** *n* aigle *m* royal; **Golden Fleece** *n* Toison *f* d'or; ~ **girl** *n* enfant *f* chérie

golden goose *n* **to kill the** ~ tuer la poule aux œufs d'or

golden: ~ **handshake** *n* GB prime *f* de départ; ~ **hello** *n* prime *f* d'embauche; ~ **jubilee** *n* (wedding anniversary) noces *fpl* d'or; (other) jubilé *m*

golden mean *n* (happy medium) **the** ~ le juste milieu

golden: ~ **oldie** *n* (song) vieux succès *m* (de la chanson); (film) vieux succès *m* (du cinéma); ~ **parachute** *n* US = **golden handshake**; ~ **rule** *n* règle *f* d'or; ~ **syrup** *n* GB ≈ sirop *m* de sucre roux; ~ **wedding** *n* noces *fpl* d'or; ~ **yellow** *n*, *adj* jaune (*m*) d'or *inv*

gold: ~ **fever** *n* fièvre *f* de l'or; ~**field** *n* terrain *m* aurifère; ~**fish** *n* (*pl* **-fish** *ou* **-fishes**) poisson *m* rouge

Goldilocks /ˈɡəʊldɪlɒks/ *pr n* Boucles d'Or

gold: ~ **leaf** *n* feuille *f* d'or; ~ **medal** *n* médaille *f* d'or; ~ **mine** *n* lit, fig mine *f* d'or; ~ **mining** *n* extraction *f* de l'or; ~ **plate** *n* (coating) fine couche *f* d'or; (dishes) vais-selle *f* d'or; ~**plated** *adj* plaqué or *inv*; ~ **rush** *n* ruée *f* vers l'or; ~**smith** ▶ p. 1181 *n* orfèvre *m*; ~ **stand-ard** *n* étalon or *m*

golf /ɡɒlf/ ▶ p. 881
A *n* golf *m*
B *noun modifier* [*ball, umbrella, bag, equipment*] de golf

golf club *n* **1** (place) club *m* de golf; **2** (stick) crosse *f* de golf

golf course *n* (terrain *m* de) golf *m*

golfer /ˈɡɒlfə(r)/ *n* joueur/-euse *m/f* de golf, golfeur/-euse *m/f*

golfing /ˈɡɒlfɪŋ/ *n* **to go** ~ faire du golf

golf links *n* = **golf course**

gondola /ˈɡɒndələ/ *n* **1** (boat) gondole *f*; **2** (under airship, balloon) nacelle *f*; (cable car) cabine *f* (de téléphérique); **3** US Rail (*also* ~ **car**) wagon *m* plat; **4** US (barge) barge *f*

gone /ɡɒn/
A *pp* ▶ **go**
B *adj* **1** [*person*] (departed) parti; (dead) disparu; **to be far** ~ (ill) être très malade; (with drink) être complètement bourré○;

(with drugs) planer○ complètement; **to be long** ~ [*person*] être mort depuis longtemps; [*era*] être révolu; ~ **with the wind** autant en emporte le vent; **2** ○GB (pregnant) enceinte; **3** GB (past) **it's** ~ **six o'clock** il est six heures passées; **she's** ~ **eighty** elle a plus de quatre-vingts ans

goner○ /ˈɡɒnə(r)/ *n* **to be a** ~○ être fichu○

gong /ɡɒŋ/ *n* gong *m*; **dinner** ~ cloche *f* du dîner

gonna○ /ˈɡɒnə/ = **going to**

gonorrh(o)ea /ˌɡɒnəˈrɪə/ ▶ p. 933 *n* blennorragie *f*

good /ɡʊd/
A *n* **1** (virtue) bien *m*; **to do** ~ faire le bien; **to be up to no** ~○ mijoter qch○; **to come to no** ~ mal tourner; **2** (bene-fit) bien *m*; **for all the** ~ **it did me** pour le peu de bien que ça m'a fait; **she's too generous for her own** ~ elle est trop généreuse et ça lui jouera des tours; **for the** ~ **of his health** lit pour sa santé; **it didn't do my migraine any** ~ ça n'a pas arrangé ma migraine; **no** ~ *ou* **will come of it** rien de bon n'en sortira; **no** ~ **will come of waiting** il vaut mieux agir tout de suite; **to be all to the** ~ être pour le mieux; **3** (use) **it's no** ~ **crying** ça ne sert à rien de pleu-rer; **what** ~ **would it do me?** à quoi cela me servirait-il?; **4** GB (profit) **to be £20 to the** ~ avoir 20 livres sterling à son crédit
B **goods** *npl* **1** (for sale) gen articles *mpl*, marchandise *f*; **stolen** ~ marchandise volée; **electrical** ~s appareils *mpl* électro-ménagers; ~**s and services** biens *mpl* de consom-mation et services; **2** GB Rail marchandises *fpl*; **3** (prop-erty) affaires *fpl*, biens *mpl*; ~ **and chattels** biens et effets personnels; **4** ○**to deliver** *ou* **come up with the** ~**s** répon-dre à l'attente de qn; **that's the** ~**s!** c'est parfait!
C **goods** *noun modifier* GB Rail [*depot, station, train, wagon*] de marchandises
D *adj* (*comparative* **better**; *superlative* **best**) **1** (enjoyable) gen bon/bonne; [*party*] réussi; **the** ~ **weather** le beau temps; **to have a** ~ **time** bien s'amuser; **have a** ~ **day!** bonne journée!; **the** ~ **things in life** les petits plaisirs de l'existen-ce; **the** ~ **life** la dolce vita; **it's** ~ **to see you again** je suis content de vous revoir; **2** (happy) **to feel** ~ **about/doing** être content de/de faire; **I didn't feel very** ~ **about lying to him** je n'étais pas très fier de lui avoir menti; **3** (healthy) [*eye, ear etc*] bon/bonne; **you don't look too** ~ tu as mau-vaise mine; **I don't feel too** ~ je ne me sens pas très bien; **4** (high quality) bon/bonne; (best) [*coat, china*] beau/belle; [*degree*] avec mention (*after n*); **I'm not** ~ **enough for her** je ne suis pas assez bien pour elle; **nothing is too** ~ **for her son** rien n'est trop beau pour son fils; **5** (prestigious) (*épith*) [*address, marriage*] bon/bonne; **6** (obedient) [*child, dog*] sage; [*manners*] bon/bonne; **there's a** ~ **boy** *ou* **girl!** c'est bien!; **7** (favourable) bon/bonne; **the** ~ **thing is that** ce qui est bien c'est que; **New York is** ~ **for shopping** New York est un bon endroit pour faire les magasins; **8** (attractive) beau/belle; **to look** ~ **with** [*garment, accessories*] aller bien avec; **she looks** ~ **in blue** le bleu lui va bien; **9** (tasty) [*meal*] bon/bonne; **to taste** ~ avoir bon goût; **to smell** ~ sentir bon *inv*; **to look** ~ avoir l'air bon; **10** (virtuous) (*épith*) [*man, life*] vertueux/-euse; [*Christian*] bon/bonne; **the** ~ **guys** les bons *mpl*; **11** [*person*] gentil/-ille; **a** ~ **deed** une bonne action; **to do sb a** ~ **turn** rendre ser-vice à qn; **would you be** ~ **enough to do**, **would you be so** ~ **as to do** auriez-vous la gentillesse de faire; **12** (pleasant) [*humour, mood*] bon/bonne; **to be in a** ~ **mood** être de bonne humeur; **to be very** ~ **about** se montrer très com-préhensif au sujet de [*mistake*]; **13** (competent) bon/bonne; **she's a** ~ **swimmer** elle nage bien; **to be** ~ **at** être bon en [*Latin, physics*]; être bon à [*badminton, chess*]; **she's** ~ **at dan-cing** elle danse bien; **to be no** ~ **at** être nul/nulle en [*tennis, chemistry*]; être nul/nulle à [*chess, cards*]; **I'm no** ~ **at knitting** je ne sais pas tricoter; **to be** ~ **with** savoir com-ment s'y prendre avec [*children, animals*]; aimer [*figures*]; **to be** ~ **with one's hands** être habile de ses mains; **to be** ~ **with words** savoir manier la langue; **14** (beneficial) **to be** ~ **for** faire du bien à [*person, plant*]; être bon pour [*health, business, morale*]; **exercise is** ~ **for you** l'exercice fait du bien; **he eats more than is** ~ **for him** il mange plus qu'il ne devrait; **say nothing if you know what's** ~ **for you** si je peux te donner un conseil, ne dis rien; **15** (effective, suitable, accurate, sensible) bon/bonne; **to look** ~ [*design*] faire de l'effet; **to keep** ~ **time** être très précis; **this will look** ~ **on your CV** *ou* **résumé** US cela fera bien sur votre CV; **that's a** ~ **point** tout à fait; **16** (fluent) **he speaks** ~ **Spanish** il parle bien espagnol; **17** (fortunate) **it's a** ~ **job** *ou* **thing (that)** heureusement que; **it's a** ~ **job** *ou* **thing too!** tant

mieux!; **we've never had it so** ∼○ les affaires n'ont jamais été aussi prospères; **it's too** ∼ **to be true** c'est trop beau pour être vrai; [18] (serviceable) **this season ticket is** ∼ **for two more months** cette carte d'abonnement est valable encore deux mois; **the car is** ∼ **for another 10,000 km** la voiture fera encore 10 000 km; **it's as** ∼ **a reason as any** c'est une raison comme une autre; **to be** ∼ **for a loan** avoir de l'argent à prêter; [19] (substantial) (épith) [salary, size, hour] bon/bonne; **it must be worth a** ∼ **2,000 dollars** ça doit valoir au moins 2 000 dollars; **a** ∼ **thick mattress** un matelas bien épais; ∼ **and early** de très bonne heure; **give it a** ∼ **clean** nettoie-le bien; **we had a** ∼ **laugh** on a bien ri; ▸ **better**, **best**

E **as good as** adv phr [1] (virtually) quasiment; **to be as** ∼ **as new** être comme neuf/neuve; [2] (tantamount to) **it's as** ∼ **as saying yes** c'est comme si tu disais oui; **he as** ∼ **as called me a liar** il m'a plus ou moins traité de menteur

F **for good** adv phr pour toujours

G excl (expressing pleasure, satisfaction) c'est bien!; (with relief) tant mieux!; (to encourage, approve) très bien!

(Idioms) ∼ **for you!** (approvingly) bravo!; (sarcastically) tant mieux pour toi!; **that's a** ∼ **one!** (of joke, excuse) elle est bonne celle-là!; ∼ **on you**○! GB bravo!; ∼ **thinking** bien vu!; **to be onto a** ∼ **thing**○, **to have a** ∼ **thing going**○ être sur un bon filon; **you can have too much of a** ∼ **thing** il ne faut pas abuser des bonnes choses

good: ∼ **afternoon** excl (in greeting) bonjour; (in farewell) au revoir; ∼**bye** n, excl au revoir; ∼ **evening** excl bonsoir; ∼**-for-nothing** n bon/bonne m/f à rien; **Good Friday** pr n Relig Vendredi m saint; ∼**-hearted** adj généreux/-euse

good-humoured GB, **good-humored** US /ˌɡʊdˈhjuː-məd/ adj [crowd, discussion] détendu; [rivalry] amical; [banter] innocent; [remark, smile] plaisant; **to be** ∼ être de bonne humeur

good-humouredly GB, **good-humoredly** US /ˌɡʊdˈhjuːmədlɪ/ adv [smile] plaisamment; [say] avec bonne humeur

goodish○ /ˈɡʊdɪʃ/ adj assez bon/bonne

good: ∼**-looking** adj beau/belle (before n); ∼ **looks** npl beauté f; ∼ **morning** excl (in greeting) bonjour; (in farewell) au revoir; ∼**-natured** adj [person] agréable; [animal] placide; [discussion] détendu; [remark] amical; [criticism] bien intentionné

goodness /ˈɡʊdnɪs/
A n [1] (virtue, kindness) bonté f; [2] (nutritive value) **to be full of** ∼ être plein de bonnes choses; **the carrots will lose all their** ∼ les carottes perdront toutes leurs vertus
B excl (also ∼ **gracious!**) mon Dieu!
(Idioms) **I hope to** ∼ **that** je prie le ciel que (+ subj); ∼ **only knows how/when** Dieu (seul) sait comment/quand; **for** ∼' **sake!** pour l'amour de Dieu!

good: ∼**night** n, excl bonne nuit; ∼**-sized** adj [kitchen, room] spacieux/-ieuse; ∼**-tempered** adj [person] facile; [animal] placide; ∼**-time girl** n péj (fun-loving) fêtarde○ f; euph (prostitute) fille f de joie

goodwill /ˌɡʊdˈwɪl/
A n [1] (helpful attitude) bonne volonté f; [2] (kindness) **to show** ∼ **to** ou **towards sb** faire preuve de bienveillance à l'égard de qn; **in a spirit of** ∼ en toute amitié; **the season of** ∼ le temps de Noël; [3] Comm (reputation) actif m incorporel (constitué par sa réputation); (customers) clientèle f
B noun modifier [gesture] de bonne volonté; [visite] d'amitié

goof○ /ɡuːf/
A n (idiot) dingue○ mf; (blunder) gaffe○ f
B vi faire une gaffe○ or une bévue○
(Phrasal verb)
■ **goof around**○ (fool around) faire l'imbécile○ mf; (laze about) glander○

goon○ /ɡuːn/ n (clown) cinglé/-e○ mf; (thug) homme m de main

goose /ɡuːs/
A n (pl **geese**) Zool, Culin oie f; **you silly** ∼○! idiot/-e!
B ○vtr pincer les fesses de
(Idiom) **to cook sb's** ∼○ couler qn

gooseberry /ˈɡʊzbərɪ, US ˈɡuːsberɪ/ n (fruit) groseille f à maquereau
(Idiom) **to be a** ou **play** ∼ tenir la chandelle

gooseberry: ∼ **bush** n groseillier m; ∼ **fool** n: purée de groseilles à maquereau à la crème

goose: ∼**bumps** npl = goose pimples; ∼**flesh** n = goose pimples; ∼ **pimples** npl chair f de poule

goose-step /ˈɡuːstep/
A n pas m de l'oie
B vi défiler au pas de l'oie

gore /ɡɔː(r)/
A n (blood) sang m
B vtr encorner; **to** ∼ **sb to death** tuer qn d'un coup de corne

gorge /ɡɔːdʒ/
A n Anat, Geog gorge f
B v refl **to** ∼ **oneself** se gaver (**on** de)
(Idiom) **to make sb's** ∼ **rise** dégoûter or écœurer qn

gorgeous /ˈɡɔːdʒəs/ adj [1] ○(lovely) [food, cake, scenery] formidable○; [kitten, baby] adorable; [weather, day, person] splendide; [2] (sumptuous) somptueux/-euse

gorilla /ɡəˈrɪlə/ n Zool, fig gorille m

gorse /ɡɔːs/ n **C** ajoncs mpl

gory /ˈɡɔːrɪ/ adj [film, battle] sanglant

gosh○ /ɡɒʃ/ excl ça alors○!

gosling /ˈɡɒzlɪŋ/ n oison m

go-slow /ˌɡəʊˈsləʊ/ GB n grève f perlée

gospel /ˈɡɒspl/
A n Évangile m; **to take sth as** ∼ ou ∼ **truth** prendre qch pour parole d'évangile
B noun modifier Mus ∼ **music** gospel m; ∼ **singer** chanteur/-euse m/f de gospel; ∼ **song** gospel m

gossamer /ˈɡɒsəmə(r)/ n (cobweb) fils mpl de la Vierge; (fabric) étoffe f très légère

gossip /ˈɡɒsɪp/
A n [1] (news) (malicious) commérages mpl (**about** sur); (not malicious) nouvelles fpl (**about** sur); **do come for coffee and a** ∼ viens chez moi prendre un café et papoter; [2] (person) bavard/-e m/f
B vi bavarder; péj faire des commérages (**about** sur)

gossip: ∼ **column** n échos mpl; ∼ **columnist** n échotier/-ière m/f

gossipy /ˈɡɒsɪpɪ/ adj [person] péj cancanier/-ière pej; [letter] plein de potins○; [style] vivant

got /ɡɒt/ [1] prét, pp ▸ **get**; [2] **to have** ∼ avoir; **we've** ∼ **three children** nous avons trois enfants; [3] **I've** ∼ **to go** il faut que j'y aille; **you've** ∼ **to meet Flora** il faut absolument que tu fasses la connaissance de Flora
(Idiom) **to feel** ∼ **at**○ se sentir persécuté

gothic, **Gothic** /ˈɡɒθɪk/
A n gothique m
B adj Archit, Literat (also in printing) gothique m; fig [gloom, horror] noir

gotta○ /ˈɡɒtə/ [1] = **got to**; [2] = **got a**

gotten /ˈɡɒtn/ pp US ▸ **get**

gouge /ɡaʊdʒ/ vtr (dig) creuser (**in** dans)
(Phrasal verb)
■ **gouge out**: ▸ ∼ **out** [sth], ∼ [sth] **out** creuser [pattern]; enlever [bad bit]; **to** ∼ **sb's eyes out** arracher les yeux de qn

gourd /ɡʊəd/ n (container) gourde f; (fruit) calebasse f

gout /ɡaʊt/ ▸ p. 933 n Med goutte f

govern /ˈɡʌvn/
A vtr [1] Admin, Pol gouverner [country, state, city]; administrer [colony, province]; [2] (control) gen régir [use, conduct, treatment]; [3] (determine) déterminer [decision, development]; [4] maîtriser [feelings, temper]; [5] Ling régir; [6] Elec, Tech régler
B vi [parliament, president] gouverner; [administrator, governor] administrer

governess /ˈɡʌvənɪs/ n (pl ∼**es**) gouvernante f

governing /ˈɡʌvənɪŋ/ adj [party] au pouvoir; [factor] décisif/-ive; [class] dirigeant; **the** ∼ **principle** l'idée directrice

governing body n [1] GB (of school) conseil m d'établissement; (of university) conseil m d'Université; (of hospital, prison) conseil m d'administration; [2] (of sport) organisation f dirigeante; [3] (of trade, professional organization) comité m directeur

government /ˈɡʌvənmənt/
A n [1] (system) (political) gouvernement m; (administrative) admi-

nistration *f*; **parliamentary** ∼ régime *m* parlementaire; ② (body) gouvernement *m*; (the State) l'État *m*; **in** ∼ au pouvoir

B *noun modifier* [*minister, official, plan, intervention*] du gouvernement; [*decree, department, majority, policy, publication*] gouvernemental; [*expenditure, borrowing*] de l'État; [*loan, funds*] public/-ique

governmental /ˌgʌvən'mentl/ *adj* gouvernemental

government: ∼ **bond** *n* Fin obligation *f* d'État; ∼ **corporation** *n* US régie *f* d'État; ∼ **employee** ▸ p. 1181 *n* agent *m* du secteur public; ∼**-funded** *adj* financé par l'État; ∼ **official** ▸ p. 1181 *n* fonctionnaire *mf*

governor /'gʌvənə(r)/ *n* (of state, colony) gouverneur *m*; GB (of bank) gouverneur *m*; (of prison) directeur *m*; (of school) membre *m* du conseil d'établissement

governorship /'gʌvənəʃɪp/ *n* (office of governor) fonctions *fpl* de gouverneur; (governing) direction *f*

govt *n*: *abrév écrite* = **government**

gown /gaʊn/ *n* (for evening wear) robe *f*; (of judge, academic) toge *f*; (of surgeon) blouse *f*; (of patient) chemise *f* (d'hôpital)

GP ▸ p. 1181 *n* (*abrév* = **general practitioner**) médecin *m* généraliste

GPO *n* ① GB (*abrév* = **General Post Office**) service *m* postal; ② US (*abrév* = **Government Printing Office**) ≈ Imprimerie *f* nationale

GPS *n* (*abrév* = **global positioning system**) GPS *m*

gr
A *n*: *abrév écrite* = **gram**
B *n, adj*: *abrév écrite* = **gross**

grab /græb/
A *n* ① (snatch) **to make a** ∼ **at** *ou* **for** essayer d'attraper; **to be up for** ∼**s**○ être bon à prendre; ② (on excavator) pelle *f* automatique
B *vtr* (*p prés etc* **-bb-**) ① (seize) empoigner [*money, toy*]; saisir [*arm, person, opportunity*]; **to** ∼ **sth from sb** arracher qch à qn; **to** ∼ **hold of** se saisir de; **to** ∼ **sb by the arm** saisir qn par le bras; ② (illegally) accaparer; ③ (snatch) **to** ∼ **some sleep** dormir un peu; **to** ∼ **a snack** manger en vitesse; ④ ○(impress) **how does that** ∼ **you?** qu'est-ce que tu en dis?

grace /greɪs/
A *n* ① (physical charm) grâce *f*; ② (dignity, graciousness) grâce *f*; **to do sth with (a) good/bad** ∼ faire qch de bonne/mauvaise grâce; **to have the** ∼ **to do** avoir la bonne grâce de faire; ③ (spiritual) grâce *f*; **to fall from** ∼ Relig perdre la grâce; (fig) tomber en disgrâce; ④ (time allowance) **to give sb two days'** ∼ accorder un délai de deux jours à qn; (to debtor) accorder un délai de deux jours à qn; ⑤ (prayer) (before meal) bénédicité *m*; (after meal) grâces *fpl*; ⑥ (quality) **sb's saving** ∼ ce qui sauve qn; ⑦ (mannerism) **to have all the social** ∼**s** avoir beaucoup de savoir-vivre
B *vtr* ① (decorate) orner, embellir; ② (honour) honorer; **to** ∼ **sb with one's presence** aussi iron honorer qn de sa présence also iron

(Idioms) **there but for the** ∼ **of God go I** ça aurait aussi bien pu m'arriver; **to put on airs and** ∼**s** péj prendre des airs

Grace /greɪs/ ▸ p. 869 *n* ① (title of archbishop) **his/your** ∼ Monseigneur; ② (title of duke) **his/your** ∼ Monsieur le duc; (of duchess) **her/your** ∼ Madame la duchesse

graceful /'greɪsfl/ *adj* ① [*dancer, movement*] gracieux/-ieuse; [*person, building*] élégant; ② [*apology*] élégant; **to make a** ∼ **exit** fig quitter discrètement les lieux

gracefully /'greɪsfəlɪ/ *adv* [*move*] avec grâce; [*concede*] gracieusement

gracefulness /'greɪsflnɪs/ *n* grâce *f*

graceless /'greɪslɪs/ *adj* [*manner*] inélégant; [*city, person*] dépourvu de charme

gracious /'greɪʃəs/ *adj* ① (generous, dignified) [*person*] affable; **to be** ∼ **(to sb)** **about** ne pas en vouloir à qn pour; **to be** ∼ **in defeat** accepter la défaite avec bonne grâce; ② (aristocratic) (pleasant) affable; (condescending) condescendant; ③ (in royal title) **by** ∼ **permission of** par la grâce de

graciously /'greɪʃəslɪ/ *adv* gracieusement; **he** ∼ **agreed to come** iron il a daigné venir iron

gradation /grə'deɪʃn/ *n* ① (on a continuum) gradation *f*; **colour** ∼**s** Art gradations *fpl* de couleurs; ∼**s of feeling** des degrés *mpl* d'émotion; ② (on scale) graduation *f*

grade /greɪd/
A *n* ① Comm qualité *f*; **high-/low-**∼ de qualité supérieure/

inférieure; ② Sch, Univ (mark) note *f* (**in** en); **to get good** ∼**s** avoir de bonnes notes; **to get** ∼ **A** *ou* **an A** ≈ avoir plus de 16 sur 20; ③ (rank) Admin échelon *m*; Mil rang *m*; **a top-**∼ **civil servant** un fonctionnaire de haut rang; **salary** ∼ échelon *m* de salaire; ④ US Sch (class) classe *f*; **she's in the eighth** ∼ ≈ elle est en (classe de) quatrième; ⑤ (*also* **Grade**) (level) niveau *m*; ∼ **IV piano** Mus niveau 4 de piano; ⑥ US (gradient) pente *f*
B *vtr* ① (categorize) (by quality) classer (**according to** selon); (by size) calibrer (**according to** selon); ② Sch (in level of difficulty) graduer [*tasks*] (**according to** selon); ③ US (mark) noter [*work*]; ④ Art (blend) dégrader; ⑤ Agric améliorer par sélection
C **graded** *pp adj* [*tests*] classé par ordre de difficulté; [*hotel*] classé NN

(Idiom) **to make the** ∼ se montrer à la hauteur

grade: ∼ **book** *n* US carnet *m* de notes; ∼ **crossing** *n* US Rail passage *m* à niveau

grader /'greɪdə(r)/
A *n* (of produce) (machine) calibreur *m*; (person) classeur/-euse *m/f*
B **-grader** *combining form* US **eighth/ninth-**∼ ≈ élève de quatrième/de troisième

grade school *n* US école *f* primaire

gradient /'greɪdɪənt/ *n* ① (slope) pente *f*; ② (degree of slope) inclinaison *f*; ③ Math, Phys gradient *m*

grading /'greɪdɪŋ/ *n* ① (classification) gen classification *f*; (of personnel) échelonnement *m*; ② Sch (marking) notation *f*

gradual /'grædʒʊəl/ *adj* ① (slow) [*change, increase*] progressif/-ive; ② (gentle) [*slope*] doux/douce

gradually /'grædʒʊlɪ/ *adv* progressivement; ∼**, he...** peu à peu, il...

graduate
A /'grædʒʊət/ *n* Univ diplômé/-e *m/f* (**in** en; **of, from** de); **arts** ∼ diplômé/-e *m/f* en lettres
B /'grædʒʊət/ *noun modifier* [*course, student*] ≈ de troisième cycle
C /'grædʒʊ‚eɪt/ *vtr* ① US (give degree to) conférer un diplôme à [*student*]; ② Tech graduer [*container, scale*]
D /'grædʒʊ‚eɪt/ *vi* ① Univ terminer ses études (**at** *ou* **from** à); US Sch ≈ finir le lycée; ② (progress) **to** ∼ **(from sth) to** passer (de qch) à

E **graduated** /'grædʒʊ‚eɪtɪd/ *pp adj* [*scale, system, tax*] proportionnel/-elle

graduate: ∼ **assistant** *n* US assistant/-e *m/f* (*chargé de TD*); ∼ **school** *n* US ≈ troisième cycle *m*; ∼ **teacher** *n* professeur *m* licencié; ∼ **training scheme** *n* GB programme *m* de formation professionnelle pour étudiants diplômés

graduation /‚grædʒʊ'eɪʃn/ *n* ① Univ (*also* ∼ **ceremony**) (cérémonie *f* de) remise *f* des diplômes; (end of course) obtention *f* d'un diplôme; ② (calibration) graduation *f*

graffiti /grə'fiːtɪ/ *n* (+ *v sg ou pl*) graffiti *mpl*

graffiti artist *n* tagger *m*

graft /grɑːft, US græft/
A *n* ① Bot, Med greffe *f*; **skin** ∼ greffe de la peau; ② (work) **hard** ∼ boulot○ *m* acharné
B *vtr* Bot, Med, fig greffer (**onto** sur)

grain /greɪn/ *n* ① (commodity) céréales *fpl*; ② (seed) (of rice, wheat) grain *m*; **long** ∼ **rice** riz *m* long; ③ (of sand, salt) grain *m*; ④ (fig, comfort) brin *m*; ⑤ (pattern) (in wood, stone) veines *fpl*; (in leather, paper, fabric) grain *m*; **to cut along/across the** ∼ couper dans le fil/contre le fil; ⑥ Phot grain *m*

(Idiom) **it goes against the** ∼ c'est contre nature

grainy /'greɪnɪ/ *adj* ① Phot [*photograph*] qui a du grain; ② (resembling wood/leather) veiné/grainé; ③ (granular) granuleux/-euse

gram(me) /græm/ ▸ p. 1323 *n* gramme *m*

grammar /'græmə(r)/
A *n* ① grammaire *f*; **that's bad** ∼ c'est grammaticalement incorrect; ② (*also* ∼ **book**) grammaire *f*
B *noun modifier* [*rule, lesson, exercise*] de grammaire

grammar checker *n* Comput correcteur *m* de grammaire

grammarian /grə'meərɪən/ *n* grammairien/-ienne *m/f*

grammar school *n* GB ≈ lycée *m* (*à recrutement sélectif*)

grammatical /grə'mætɪkl/ *adj* ① Ling [*error*] de grammaire; [*meaning, gender*] grammatical; ② (correct) grammaticalement correct

grammatically /grə'mætɪklɪ/ adv grammaticalement

Grammy /'græmɪ/ n (pl ~**s** ou -**mmies**) US Mus **to win a** ~ être primé aux Victoires de la musique

gramophone† /'græməfəʊn/ n phonographe m, gramophone® m

gran○ /græn/ n mémé○ f, mamie○ f

granary /'grænərɪ/
A n (grain store) grenier m
B noun modifier GB [bread] complet/-ète (avec des grains de céréales broyés)

grand /grænd/
A n GB mille livres fpl sterling; US mille dollars mpl
B adj **1** (impressive) [building, ceremony] grandiose; [park] magnifique; **in** ~ **style** en grande pompe; **on the** ~ **scale** (expensively) sur un grand pied; **the** ~ **old man** of theatre le grand monsieur du théâtre; **2** (self-important) **she's very** ~ elle joue à la grande dame pej; **3** ○(fine) **to have a** ~ **time** passer un moment formidable; **'is everything all right?'—'it's** ~ **thanks'** 'tout va bien?'—'très bien merci'

grandchild /'græntʃaɪld/ n (pl -**children**) (girl) petite-fille f; (boy) petit-fils m; **his grandchildren** ses petits-enfants mpl

granddad○ /'grændæd/ n pépé○ m, papy○ m, papi m

granddaddy○ /'grændædɪ/ n **1** (grandfather) pépé○ m, papy○ m, papi m; **2** fig **it's the** ~ **of them all** hum c'est l'ancêtre

grand: ~**daughter** n petite-fille f; ~ **duchess** n grande-duchesse f; ~ **duke** n grand-duc m

grandee /græn'diː/ n grand personnage m

grandeur /'grændʒə(r)/ n **1** (of scenery) majesté f; (of building) caractère m grandiose; **2** (of character) noblesse f; (power, status) éminence f

grand: ~**father** n grand-père m; ~**father clock** n horloge f comtoise; ~ **finale** n finale m

grandiose /'grændɪəʊs/ adj grandiose

grand: ~ **jury** n US jury qui décide s'il y a motif à inculpation; ~ **larceny** n US vol m qualifié

grandma /'grænmɑː/ n mémé○ f, mamy○ f, mamie○ f

grand master n (in chess) grand maître m

grandmother /'grænmʌðə(r)/ n grand-mère f

(Idiom) **to teach one's** ~ **to suck eggs** apprendre à un vieux singe à faire la grimace

Grand Old Party, **GOP** n US Pol parti m républicain

grandpa○ /'grænpɑː/ n pépé○ m, papy○ m, papi○ m

grandparent /'grænpeərənt/ n (male) grand-père m; (female) grand-mère f; **my** ~**s** mes grands-parents mpl

grand: ~ **piano** ▸ p. 1028 n piano m à queue; ~ **prix** n (pl inv) grand prix m; ~ **slam** n Games, Sport grand chelem m; ~**son** n petit-fils m

grandstand /'grænstænd/ n **1** (at stadium) tribune f; **to have a** ~ **view** ou **seat** lit, fig être aux premières loges; **2** (audience) public m

grand total n total m; **the** ~ **for the repairs came to £3,000** en tout, les travaux sont revenus à 3 000 livres sterling

grand tour n **1** **he took me on a** ~ **of the house** il m'a fait visiter toute la maison; **2** (also **the Grand Tour**) Hist le tour m d'Europe

grange /greɪndʒ/ n GB (house) manoir m

granite /'grænɪt/ n granit(e) m

granny○ /'grænɪ/ n **1** (grandmother) mémé○ f; **2** pej (fusspot, gossip) vieille mémère○

granny flat n GB petit appartement m indépendant (pour parent âgé)

granola /grə'nəʊlə/ n US muesli m

grant /grɑːnt, US grænt/
A n (from government, local authority) subvention f (**for** pour; **to do** pour faire); (for study) Sch, Univ bourse f; **research** ~ subvention f de recherche
B vtr **1** sout (allow) accorder [permission]; accéder à [request]; **permission** ~**ed!** permission accordée!; **2** (give) **to** ~ **sb sth, to** ~ **sth to sb** accorder qch à qn [interview, leave, visa]; concéder qch à qn [citizenship]; **3** (concede) **to** ~ **that** reconnaître que; **I** ~ **you that he's gifted** je vous accorde qu'il est doué; ~**ed that, ~ing that** en admettant que (+ subj)

(Idiom) **to take sth for** ~**ed** considérer qch comme allant de soi; **he takes his mother for** ~**ed** il croit que sa mère est à son service

grant aid /'grɑːnteɪd, US 'grænt-/ n **₡** (within a country) subventions fpl (**for** pour); (to Third World) aide f au développement (**for** pour)

grant-aided /,grɑːnt'eɪdɪd, US ,grænt-/ adj subventionné

granted /'grɑːntɪd, US 'grænt-/ adv ~, **it's magnificent, but very expensive** c'est magnifique, soit, mais cela coûte très cher

grant-maintained adj [school] subventionné par l'État

granular /'grænjʊlə(r)/ adj [texture] granuleux/-euse

granulated adj [paper] grenelé; [sugar] cristallisé

granule /'grænjuːl/ n (of sugar, salt) grain m; (of instant coffee) granulé m

grape /greɪp/ n grain m de raisin; **a bunch of** ~**s** une grappe de raisin; **I love** ~**s** j'adore le raisin; **to harvest the** ~**s** vendanger

(Idiom) **sour** ~**s!** les raisins sont trop verts!

grapefruit /'greɪpfruːt/ n pamplemousse m

grape: ~ **harvest** n vendange f; ~**seed oil** n huile f de pépins de raisin; ~**shot** n mitraille f

grapevine /'greɪpvaɪn/ n (in vineyard) pied m de vigne; (in greenhouse, garden) vigne f

(Idiom) **to hear sth on the** ~ apprendre qch par le téléphone arabe

graph /grɑːf, US græf/ n graphique m

graphic /'græfɪk/
A graphics npl **1** Comput visualisation f graphique; **computer** ~**s** infographie f; **2** (in film, TV) images fpl; (in book) illustrations fpl
B adj **1** Art, Comput graphique; **2** [account] (of sth pleasant) vivant; (of sth unpleasant) cru

graphical user interface, **GUI** n Comput interface m utilisateur graphique

graphic: ~ **artist** ▸ p. 1181 n graphiste mf; ~ **arts** npl arts mpl graphiques; ~ **design** n Art graphisme m; ~ **designer** ▸ p. 1181 n graphiste mf; ~ **display** n Comput visualisation f graphique; ~ **equalizer** n Audio égaliseur m graphique; ~**s tablet** n tablette f graphique

graphite /'græfaɪt/
A n graphite m
B noun modifier [fishing rod] en fibre de carbone

graphologist /grə'fɒlədʒɪst/ ▸ p. 1181 n graphologue mf

graphology /grə'fɒlədʒɪ/ n graphologie f

graph paper n papier m millimétré

grapple /'græpl/ vi **to** ~ **with** lit lutter avec [person]; fig se colleter avec [problem]

grasp /grɑːsp, US græsp/
A n **1** (hold, grip) prise f; (stronger) poigne f; **to hold sth in one's** ~ lit tenir qch fermement; fig tenir qch bien en main; **to take a firm** ~ **of sth** empoigner fermement qch; **the pen slipped from his** ~ le stylo lui a glissé des doigts; **success is within their** ~ fig le succès est à leur portée; **2** (understanding) maîtrise f; **to have a good** ~ **of a subject** avoir une bonne maîtrise d'un sujet
B vtr **1** lit empoigner [rope, hand]; fig saisir [opportunity]; **to** ~ **hold of** saisir; **2** (comprehend) saisir, comprendre [concept, subject]; suivre [argument]; se rendre compte de [situation, significance]
C vi **to** ~ **at** lit tenter de saisir; fig s'efforcer de comprendre [idea]; saisir [excuse]

grasping /'grɑːspɪŋ, US 'græspɪŋ/ adj cupide

grass /grɑːs, US græs/
A n **1** **₡** (wild) herbe f; **a blade of** ~ un brin d'herbe; **to put out to** ~ lit, fig hum mettre au vert; **2** **₡** (lawn) pelouse f; **keep off the** ~! défense de marcher sur les pelouses!; **3** **₡** (in tennis) gazon m; **4** Bot **C** graminée f; **5** ○**₡** (marijuana) herbe○ f; **6** ○GB (informer) mouchard○ m
B noun modifier [slope, verge] gazonné

(Idioms) **the** ~ **is greener (on the other side of the fence)** on croit toujours que c'est mieux ailleurs; **he doesn't let the** ~ **grow under his feet** il ne laisse pas traîner les choses

grass: ~ **court** n court m en gazon; ~ **cuttings** npl herbe f coupée **₡**

grasshopper /ˈɡrɑːʃɒpə(r), US ˈɡræs-/ *n* Zool sauterelle *f*

(Idiom) **kneehigh to a** ~ haut comme trois pommes

grassland /ˈɡrɑːslənd, US ˈɡræs-/ *n* prairie *f*

grassroots /ˌɡrɑːˈsruːts, US ˌɡræs-/
A *npl* the ~ le peuple
B *adj* [*movement*] populaire; [*support*] de base

grass snake *n* couleuvre *f*

grassy /ˈɡrɑːsɪ, US ˈɡræsɪ/ *adj* herbeux/-euse

grate /ɡreɪt/
A *n* (fire-basket) grille *f* de foyer; (hearth) âtre *m*
B *vtr* râper; **to** ~ **cheese over sth** parsemer qch de fromage râpé
C *vi* [1] [*metal object*] grincer (**on** sur); [2] (annoy) agacer; **her voice** ~**s** sa voix m'agace; **to** ~ **on sb's nerves** taper sur les nerfs de qn○

grateful /ˈɡreɪtfl/ *adj* [*person*] reconnaissant (**to** à; **for** de); [*letter, kiss*] de reconnaissance; **to be** ~ **that** être heureux/ -euse que (+ *subj*); **let's be** ~ **that** estimons-nous heureux que (+ *subj*); **I would be** ~ **if you could reply** je vous serais reconnaissant de bien vouloir répondre; **with** ~ **thanks** avec mes *or* nos plus sincères remerciements

gratefully /ˈɡreɪtfəlɪ/ *adv* [*speak*] avec reconnaissance

grater /ˈɡreɪtə(r)/ *n* râpe *f*

gratification /ˌɡrætɪfɪˈkeɪʃn/ *n* satisfaction *f*

gratify /ˈɡrætɪfaɪ/ *vtr* faire plaisir à [*person*]; satisfaire [*desire*]; **to be gratified that** être très heureux que (+ *subj*); **it is gratifying to know that** il est agréable d'apprendre que

grating /ˈɡreɪtɪŋ/
A *n* [1] (bars) grille *f*; [2] (noise) grincement *m*
B *adj* [*noise*] grinçant; [*voice*] désagréable

gratitude /ˈɡrætɪtjuːd, US -tuːd/ *n* reconnaissance *f* (**to, towards** envers; **for** de)

gratuitous /ɡrəˈtjuːɪtəs, US -ˈtuː-/ *adj* gratuit

gratuity /ɡrəˈtjuːətɪ, US -ˈtuː-/ *n* (tip) pourboire *m*; GB (bonus) prime *f*

grave /ɡreɪv/
A *n* tombe *f*; **beyond the** ~ après la mort; **to go to one's** ~ **believing that** rester convaincu jusque dans la tombe que; **to go to an early** ~ avoir une fin prématurée
B *adj* [1] (dangerous) [*illness*] grave; [*risk*] sérieux/-ieuse; [*danger*] grand (*before n*); [2] (solemn) sérieux/-ieuse

(Idioms) **to dig one's own** ~ creuser sa propre tombe; **to have one foot in the** ~ avoir un pied dans la tombe; **to turn in one's** ~ se retourner dans sa tombe

gravedigger /ˈɡreɪvdɪɡə(r)/ ▶ p. 1181 *n* fossoyeur *m*

gravel /ˈɡrævl/ *n* **C** [1] gen (coarse) graviers *mpl*; (fine) gravillons *mpl*; [2] Med calculs *mpl*

gravelly /ˈɡrævəlɪ/ *adj* [*path*] caillouteux/-euse; [*voice*] râpeux/-euse

gravel pit *n* gravière *f*

gravely /ˈɡreɪvlɪ/ *adv* [1] (extremely) [*concerned*] sérieusement; [*displeased*] extrêmement; [*ill*] gravement; [2] (solemnly) gravement

graven /ˈɡreɪvn/ *adj* † *ou* littér gravé also fig; ~ **image** Bible idole *f*

graverobber /ˈɡreɪvˌrɒbə(r)/ *n* déterreur *m* de cadavres

graveside /ˈɡreɪvsaɪd/ *n* **the mourners were gathered at the** ~ tout le monde était rassemblé autour de la tombe

gravestone /ˈɡreɪvstəʊn/ *n* pierre *f* tombale

graveyard /ˈɡreɪvjɑːd/ *n* cimetière *m*

graveyard shift○ *n* équipe *f* de nuit

gravitas /ˈɡrævɪtæs, -tɑːs/ *n* envergure *f*

gravitate /ˈɡrævɪteɪt/ *vi* **to** ~ **to(wards)** graviter vers

gravity /ˈɡrævətɪ/ *n* [1] Phys pesanteur *f*; **centre of** ~ centre *m* de gravité; **the pull of the earth's** ~ l'attraction *f* terrestre; [2] (of situation) gravité *f*; [3] (of demeanour) sérieux *m*

gravy /ˈɡreɪvɪ/ *n* Culin sauce *f* (au jus de rôti)

(Idiom) **he is on the** ~ **train**○ il a trouvé le filon○

gravy boat *n* saucière *f*

gray US = **grey**

graze /ɡreɪz/
A *n* écorchure *f*
B *vtr* [1] (scrape) **to** ~ **one's knee** s'écorcher le genou (**on**,

against sur); [2] [*bullet*] érafler; [3] Agric faire paître [*animal*]; utiliser comme pacage [*land*]
C *vi* Agric [*sheep*] brouter; [*cow*] paître

grazing /ˈɡreɪzɪŋ/ *n* Agric pacage *m*; ~ **land** pâturage *m*; ~ **rights** droit *m* de pacage

grease /ɡriːs/
A *n* [1] (lubricant) graisse *f*; (black) cambouis *m*; [2] (dirt) graisse *f*; [3] (from hair) sébum *m*
B *vtr* (all contexts) graisser

grease: ~**paint** *n* maquillage *m* de théâtre; ~**proof paper** *n* papier *m* sulfurisé

greaser○ /ˈɡriːsə(r)/ *n* (motorcyclist) motard○ *m*

greasiness /ˈɡriːsɪnɪs/ *n* (of hair, surface) aspect *m* graisseux; (of food) aspect *m* huileux

greasing /ˈɡriːsɪŋ/ *n* graissage *m*

greasy /ˈɡriːsɪ/ *adj* [*skin, food*] gras/grasse; [*overalls*] graisseux/-euse

great /ɡreɪt/
A *n* **the** ~ (+ *v pl*) les grands *mpl*
B *adj* [1] (large) [*height, speed, majority, object, danger, improvement*] grand (*before n*); [*number*] grand (*before n*), important; [*increase*] fort (*before n*), important; [2] (as intensifier) [*excitement, surprise, relief, success, tragedy*] grand (*before n*); [*heat*] fort (*before n*); **a** ~ **deal (of)** beaucoup (de); **a** ~ **many people** beaucoup de personnes, un grand nombre de personnes; **to have** ~ **difficulty doing** avoir beaucoup de mal à faire; **in** ~ **detail** dans les moindres détails; **the map was a** ~ **help** la carte a été très utile; **you're a** ~ **help!** iron tu m'aides vraiment beaucoup!; [3] (remarkable) [*person, name, painting, discovery*] grand (*before n*); [4] ○(excellent) [*book, party, weather*] génial○, formidable○; [*opportunity*] formidable○; **to feel** ~ se sentir en pleine forme; **you look** ~! (healthy) tu as l'air en pleine forme!; (attractive) tu es superbe!; **that dress looks** ~ **on you** cette robe est géniale○ sur toi; **to have a** ~ **time** bien s'amuser; **X is the** ~**est!** X est génial○!; [5] ○(talented) génial○, formidable○; **to be** ~ **at** être un as○ à [*tennis, football*]; **to be** ~ **with** être génial○ avec [*children, animals*]; **to be** ~ **on** être imbattable○ sur [*history, architecture*]; [6] ○(inveterate) [*worrier, organizer*] de première○; [*admirer, fan*] grand (*before n*)
C *adv* **I'm doing** ~ ça marche très bien pour moi○

(Idiom) **to cross the** ~ **divide** faire le grand saut

great: ~ **aunt** *n* grand-tante *f*; **Great Barrier Reef** *pr n* Grande Barrière *f* de Corail; ~ **big** *adj* (très) grand (*before n*), énorme

Great Britain ▶ p. 774 *pr n* Grande-Bretagne *f*

> ℹ️ **Great Britain** La Grande-Bretagne est la plus grande des îles britanniques. Elle comprend l'Angleterre, l'Écosse et le pays de Galles. Toutefois, le mot *Britain* est souvent utilisé abusivement pour désigner l'ensemble du Royaume-Uni. ▶ **United Kingdom**

great: **Great Dane** *n* danois *m*; **Greater London** *pr n* l'agglomération *f* londonienne; ~ **grandchild** *n* (girl) arrière-petite-fille *f*; (garçon) arrière-petit-fils *m*; ~ **granddaughter** *n* arrière-petite-fille *f*; ~ **grandfather** *n* arrière-grand-père *m*; ~ **grandmother** *n* arrière-grand-mère *f*; ~ **grandson** *n* arrière-petit-fils *m*; ~-**great grandchild** *n* (girl) arrière-arrière-petite-fille *f*; (boy) arrière-arrière-petit-fils *m*; **Great Lakes** ▶ p. 968 *npl* Grands Lacs *mpl*

greatly /ˈɡreɪtlɪ/ *adv* [*admire, regret, influence*] beaucoup, énormément; [*exceed*] de beaucoup; [*admired, surprised, distressed*] très, extrêmement; [*improved, changed*] considérablement; [*superior, inferior*] bien

great nephew *n* petit-neveu *m*

greatness /ˈɡreɪtnɪs/ *n* (of achievement) importance *f*; (of person) grandeur *f*

great: ~ **niece** *n* petite-nièce *f*; **Great Power** *n* Pol grande puissance *f*; ~ **uncle** *n* grand-oncle *m*; **Great War** *pr n* Hist Grande Guerre *f*

Grecian /ˈɡriːʃn/ *adj* grec/grecque

Greece /ɡriːs/ ▶ p. 774 *pr n* Grèce *f*

greed /ɡriːd/ *n* [1] (for money, power) avidité *f* (**for** de); [2] (also **greediness**) (for food) gourmandise *f*

greedy /ˈɡriːdɪ/ *adj* [1] [*person*] (for food) gourmand; (stronger) goulu; [*look*] avide; **a** ~ **pig**○ un goinfre○; [2] (for money, power) avide (**for** de)

Greek /griːk/ ▶ p. 1032, p. 969

A n **1** (person) Grec/Grecque m/f; **2** (language) grec m

B adj **1** [food, government, island, alphabet] grec/grecque; **2** [teacher, lesson, dictionary] de grec

(Idioms) **beware of ~s bearing gifts** ne faites jamais confiance à un ennemi; **it's all ~ to me** c'est du chinois pour moi

green /griːn/ ▶ p. 752

A n **1** (colour) vert m; **2** (grassy area) espace m vert; (vegetation) verdure f; **3** (in bowling) boulingrin m; (in golf) green m; **4** Ecol, Pol écologiste m/f; **the Greens** les Verts

B greens npl GB (vegetables) légumes mpl vert

C adj **1** (in colour) vert; **to go** ou **turn ~** [traffic lights] passer au vert; fig [person] verdir, devenir vert; **2** (with vegetation) verdoyant; **3** (not ready) [fruit] vert; **4** ○(naïve) naïf/naïve; **5** (inexperienced) novice; **6** Ecol, Pol [policies, candidate, issues] écologiste; [marketing, washing-powder] écologique; **7** Econ [currency] vert; **8** ○(off-colour) patraque○

(Idiom) **to have ~ fingers** GB ou **a ~ thumb** US avoir la main verte

green: **~back**○ n US dollar m; **~ bean** n haricot m vert; **~ belt** n Sport ceinture f verte

green card n **1** (driving insurance) carte f verte (internationale); **2** US carte f de séjour (permettant de travailler aux États-Unis)

greenery /ˈgriːnəri/ n verdure f

green-eyed monster n the **~** la jalousie

green: **~finch** n verdier m; **~fly** n puceron m (du rosier); **~gage** n reine-claude f; **~grocer** ▶ p. 1181 n marchand m de fruits et légumes

greenhorn○ /ˈgriːnhɔːn/ n péj **1** (gullible) benêt○ m; **2** (new) débutant/-e m/f; **he's a ~** il débarque○

green: **~house** n serre f; **~house effect** n effet m de serre

greenish /ˈgriːnɪʃ/ ▶ p. 752 adj tirant sur le vert, verdâtre péj

Greenland /ˈgriːnlənd/ ▶ p. 774 pr n Groenland m

greenness /ˈgriːnnɪs/ n **1** (of pigment) verdeur f; (of countryside) verdure f; **2** (of fruit, wood) verdeur f; **3** Ecol (awareness) conscience f écologique; **4** (inexperience) inexpérience f

green: **~ onion** n US ciboule f; **~ paper** n GB livre m blanc; **~ pepper** n poivron m vert; **~room** n Theat foyer m des artistes; **~ salad** n salade f verte; **~ tea** n thé m vert; **~-welly brigade** n GB grande bourgeoisie rurale

Greenwich Mean Time, GMT /ˌgrenɪtʃ ˈmiːntaɪm/ n temps m universel, TU

greet /griːt/ vtr **1** (welcome) accueillir [person, decision]; **2** (salute) saluer; **to ~ sb in the street** dire bonjour à qn dans la rue; **3** (receive) **to be ~ed with** ou **by** provoquer [dismay, amusement]; être salué par [jeers, applause]; **4** (confront) **an amazing sight ~ed me** une scène extraordinaire s'offrait à moi

greeter /ˈgriːtə(r)/ n personne f qui accueille les clients (dans un restaurant)

greeting /ˈgriːtɪŋ/

A n salutation f; **~s!** salutations!; **to exchange ~s** se saluer; (passing) se dire bonjour

B greetings npl **Christmas ~s** vœux mpl de Noël; **Season's ~s** meilleurs vœux

greetings card GB, **greeting card** US n carte f de vœux

gregarious /grɪˈgeərɪəs/ adj [person] sociable; [animal] grégaire

gremlin /ˈgremlɪn/ n hum diablotin m

Grenada /grəˈneɪdə/ ▶ p. 774, p. 1276 pr n (city, country) Grenade f

grenade /grəˈneɪd/ n grenade f

grenadier /ˌgrenəˈdɪə/ n Mil grenadier m

grew /gruː/ prét ▶ **grow**

grey GB, **gray** US /greɪ/ ▶ p. 752

A n **1** (colour) gris m; **2** (horse) cheval m gris

B adj **1** (colour) gris; **2** (grey-haired) aux cheveux gris, grisonnant; **to go** ou **turn ~** grisonner; **3** (dull, boring) [existence, day] morne; [person, town] terne

C vi grisonner; **to be ~ing at the temples** avoir les tempes grisonnantes

grey: **~ area** n zone f floue; **~ economy** n économie f parallèle; **~-haired** adj aux cheveux gris; **~hound** n lévrier m; **~hound racing** ▶ p. 881 n course f de lévriers; **~hound track** n piste f de course de lévriers

greyish GB, **grayish** US /ˈgreɪɪʃ/ ▶ p. 752 adj tirant sur le gris, grisâtre péj

grey: **~ matter** n (brain) matière f grise; **~ seal** n phoque m gris; **~ squirrel** n écureuil m gris

grid /grɪd/ n **1** (grating) grille f; **2** gen, Geog (pattern) quadrillage m; (of street layout) damier m; **3** GB (network) réseau m; **the national ~** le réseau électrique national; **4** (in motor racing) grille f de départ

griddle /ˈgrɪdl/ n (for meat) gril m en fonte; (for pancakes) plaque f en fonte

gridiron /ˈgrɪdaɪən/ n **1** Culin gril m; **2** US terrain m de football américain

gridlock /ˈgrɪdlɒk/ n **1** lit embouteillage m; **2** fig (deadlock) impasse f

grid reference n coordonnées fpl

grief /griːf/ n **1** (sorrow) chagrin m; **his ~ at** ou **over her death** le chagrin qu'il a ressenti à sa mort; **2** ○(trouble) **to give sb ~** ennuyer qn

(Idiom) **to come to ~** (have an accident) avoir un accident; (fail) échouer; [business] péricliter

grief-stricken /ˈgriːfstrɪkn/ adj accablé de douleur (after n)

grievance /ˈgriːvns/ n griefs mpl (against contre)

grievance: **~ committee** n commission f d'arbitrage; **~ procedure** n instance f prud'hommale

grieve /griːv/

A vi **to ~ for** ou **over** pleurer

B v impers littér **it ~s me that** cela me fait de la peine que (+ subj)

grievous /ˈgriːvəs/ adj sout [loss] cruel/-elle; [damage] grave; **to do sb a ~ wrong** faire cruellement tort à qn

grievous bodily harm, GBH n Jur coups mpl et blessures fpl

grievously /ˈgriːvəslɪ/ adv [hurt] grièvement; [offended] cruellement

grill /grɪl/

A n **1** GB (on cooker) gril m; **cook it in** ou **under the ~** faites-le griller; **2** US (barbecue) gril m; **3** (dish) grillade f; **4** (restaurant) grill m, restaurant m servant des grillades

B vtr **1** Culin faire griller; **2** ○(interrogate) mettre [qn] sur la sellette○ (about à propos de)

C vi [steak, fish] griller

grille /grɪl/ n gen grille f; (on car) calandre f

grill pan n GB plateau m à poignée (allant sous le gril)

grim /grɪm/ adj **1** (depressing) [news, town] sinistre; [sight, conditions] effroyable; [reality] dur; **her future looks ~** son avenir s'air sombre; **2** (unrelenting) [struggle] acharné; [resolve] terrible; **3** (unsmiling) grave; **to be ~-faced** avoir l'air grave; **4** ○(poor) [accommodation, food] très mauvais; **I'm feeling pretty ~** je ne me sens pas bien; **5** (black) [humour] macabre

grimace /grɪˈmeɪs, US ˈgrɪməs/

A n grimace f (of de)

B vi (involuntary) faire une grimace (with, in de); (pull a face) faire la grimace

grime /graɪm/ n (of city) saleté f; (on object, person) crasse f

grimly /ˈgrɪmlɪ/ adv **1** (sadly) [speak] d'un ton grave; **2** (relentlessly) [pursue, cling] avec acharnement

Grim Reaper /ˌgrɪm ˈriːpə(r)/ n the **~** la Faucheuse

grimy /ˈgraɪmɪ/ adj [city] noir; [hands, window] crasseux/-euse

grin /grɪn/

A n sourire m; **her face broke into a ~** elle a souri

B vi (p prés etc **-nn-**) sourire (at à; with de)

(Idiom) **to ~ and bear it** souffrir en silence

grind /graɪnd/

A n **1** ○(hard work) boulot○ m or travail m monotone; **the daily ~**○ le boulot○ or le train-train○ quotidien; **it'll be a long hard ~** ça va être très dur; **2** ○US péj (student) bûcheur/-euse○ m/f

B vtr (prét, pp **ground**) **1** (crush) moudre [corn, coffee beans]; écraser, broyer [grain]; hacher [meat]; **to ~ sth to dust**

réduire qch en poussière; **to ~ one's teeth** grincer des dents; ② (sharpen) affûter or aiguiser [qch] (à la meule) [*knife*]; ③ (polish) polir [*lenses*]; égriser [*gems*]; ④ (turn) tourner [*handle*]; jouer de [*barrel organ*]

C *vi* (*prét, pp* **ground**) ① (make harsh sound) [*machine*] grincer; **to ~ to a halt** *gen* s'arrêter; [*vehicle*] s'arrêter avec un grincement de freins; ② ○US (swot) bûcher○, potasser○

(Phrasal verbs)

■ **grind down**: ▸ **~ down** [sth], **~** [sth] **down** (crush) écraser; (pulverize) pulvériser; **to be ground down by poverty** *fig* être accablé par la misère

■ **grind on** se poursuivre inexorablement

■ **grind out**: ▸ **~ out** [sth], **~** [sth] **out** ① (extinguish) écraser [*cigarette*]; ② (play) **to ~ out a tune on a barrel organ** jouer un air sur un orgue de Barbarie

grinder /'graɪndə(r)/ *n* ① (crushing device) (industrial) broyeur *m*; (domestic) moulin *m*; ② Tech (for sharpening) meule *f* (à aiguiser); ③ (person) rémouleur/-euse *m/f*; ④ US (sandwich) gros sandwich *m* mixte

grinding /'graɪndɪŋ/
A *n* (sound) grincement *m*
B *adj* [*noise*] grinçant; **~ poverty** misère *f* noire

grindstone /'graɪndstəʊn/ *n* meule *f or* pierre *f* à aiguiser

(Idiom) **to keep** *ou* **have one's nose to the ~** travailler sans relâche

grip /grɪp/
A *n* ① (hold) prise *f* (**on** sur); **to tighten/relax one's ~ on** resserrer/relâcher sa prise sur; **she lost her ~ on the rope** elle a perdu prise et lâché la corde; ② (control) **to take a firm ~ on the party** prendre le parti bien en main; **to lose one's ~ on reality** perdre contact avec la réalité; **to come to ~s with sth** en venir aux prises avec qch; **to get to ~s with sth** attaquer qch de front; **get a ~ on yourself!** ressaisis-toi!; ③ (ability to hold) (of tyre) adhérence *f*; **these shoes have no ~** ces chaussures n'accrochent pas au sol; ④ (clutches) **to be in the ~ of an obsession** être en proie à une obsession; **in the ~ of winter** paralysé par l'hiver; ⑤ (bag) sac *m* de voyage; ⑥ Cin accessoiriste *mf*
B *vtr* (*p prés etc* **-pp-**) ① (grab) agripper; (hold) serrer; ② (adhere to) [*tyres*] adhérer à [*road*]; [*shoes*] accrocher à [*ground*]; ③ (captivate) captiver

gripe /graɪp/
A *n* ① (complaint) sujet *m* de plainte; ② Med **to have the ~s** avoir des coliques *fpl*
B *vi* (complain) râler○ (**about** à propos de; **that** que)

gripe water *n* GB calmant *m* (*pour coliques des nourrissons*)

griping /'graɪpɪŋ/
A *n*○ ✿ ronchonnements *mpl*
B *adj* Med **to have ~ pains** avoir des coliques *fpl*

gripping /'grɪpɪŋ/ *adj* captivant

grisly /'grɪzlɪ/ *adj* [*story, sight*] horrible; [*remains*] macabre

grist /grɪst/ *n* **it's all ~ to the mill** tout sert

gristle /'grɪsl/ *n* (in meat) cartilage *m*; **piece of ~** du cartilage

grit /grɪt/
A *n* ① ✿ (on lens) grains *mpl* de poussière; (sandy dirt) grains *mpl* de sable; (in wound) saletés *fpl*; ② GB (for roads) sable *m*; ③ (courage) cran○ *m*
B *vtr* (*p prés etc* **-tt-**) GB sabler [*road*]

(Idiom) **to ~ one's teeth** serrer les dents

grits /grɪts/ *npl* GB (oats) gruau *m* d'avoine; US (corn) gruau *m* de maïs

gritter /'grɪtə(r)/ *n* GB Aut sableuse *f*

gritty /'grɪtɪ/ *adj* ① (sandy) plein de sable; (gravelly) graveleux/-euse; ② (realistic, tough) [*personality*] solide et terre à terre; [*novel*] réaliste

grizzle /'grɪzl/ *vi* GB (cry) pleurnicher

grizzled /'grɪzld/ *adj* [*hair, beard, person*] grisonnant

grizzly /'grɪzlɪ/ *n* (also **~ bear**) grizzli *m*

groan /grəʊn/
A *n* (of pain, despair) gémissement *m*; (of disgust, protest) grognement *m*
B *vi* ① (in pain) gémir; (in disgust, protest) grogner; **to ~ in** *ou* **with pain** pousser un gémissement de douleur; ② (creak) [*timbers*] gémir

grocer /'grəʊsə(r)/ ▸ p. 1181 *n* (person) épicier/-ière *m/f*; **~'s (shop)** épicerie *f*

groceries /'grəʊsərɪz/ *npl* ① (shopping) provisions *fpl*; ② Comm épicerie *f* ✿

grocery /'grəʊsərɪ/ ▸ p. 1181 *n* (also **~ shop** GB, **~ store**) épicerie *f*

groggy /'grɒgɪ/ *adj* groggy; **to feel ~** avoir les jambes en coton○

groin /grɔɪn/ ▸ p. 698 *n* ① Anat aine *f*; **in the ~** *lit* à l'aine; *euph* dans les testicules; ② Archit arête *f*; ③ US = **groyne**

grommet /'grɒmɪt/ *n* ① (eyelet) œillet *m*; ② Med diabolo *m*

groom /gru:m/
A *n* ① (bridegroom) **the ~** le jeune marié; ② *gen* palefrenier/-ière *m/f*; (for racehorse) lad *m*
B *vtr* ① (see to toilette of [*dog, cat*]) (professionally) toiletter [*dog, cat*]; panser [*horse*]; **to ~ oneself carefully** s'habiller et se coiffer avec soin; ② (prepare) **to ~ sb for** préparer qn à [*exam, career*]

grooming /'gru:mɪŋ/ *n* (of horse) pansage *m*; (of dog) toilettage *m*; **personal ~** US présentation *f*, tenue *f*

groove /gru:v/ *n* ① *lit* (on record) sillon *m*; (for sliding door) coulisse *f*; (in joinery) rainure *f*; (on head of screw) fente *f*, creux *m*; ② (routine) **to be stuck in a ~** s'encroûter; ③ Mus rythme *m*

grope /grəʊp/
A *vtr* ① (feel) **he ~d his way past the furniture** il contourna les meubles à tâtons; ② ○(sexually) tripoter○
B *vi* **to ~ for sth** chercher qch à tâtons; **to ~ in the dark** *fig* tâtonner

gross /grəʊs/
A *n* (*pl* **~**) (twelve dozen) grosse *f*
B *adj* ① Comm, Fin [*income, profit*] brut; ② (serious) *gen*, Jur [*error, exaggeration*] grossier/-ière; [*ignorance*] crasse; [*abuse, inequality*] choquant; [*injustice*] flagrant; **~ negligence** Jur faute *f* lourde; ③ (coarse) [*behaviour*] vulgaire; [*language*] cru; ④ ○(revolting) dégoûtant; ⑤ ○(obese) obèse
C *vtr* faire un bénéfice brut de [*x million*]

(Phrasal verb)

■ **gross out**○ US: ▸ **~** [sb] **out** dégoûter [qn]

gross: **~ domestic product**, **GDP** *n* produit *m* intérieur brut, PIB *m*; **~ indecency** *n* Jur outrage *m* à la pudeur

grossly /'grəʊslɪ/ *adv* ① [*exaggerate*] grossièrement; [*misleading, irresponsible*] extrêmement; [*underpaid*] scandaleusement; **~ overweight** obèse; ② (crudely) de façon grossière

gross national product, **GNP** *n* produit *m* national brut, PNB *m*

gross: **~ ton** *n* tonne *f* britannique (1 016 *kilogrammes*); **~ tonnage** *n* Naut jauge *f* brute

grotesque /grəʊ'tesk/ *n*, *adj* grotesque (*m*)

grotto /'grɒtəʊ/ *n* (*pl* **~s** *ou* **~es**) grotte *f*

grotty○ /'grɒtɪ/ *adj* GB *gen* minable○; **to feel ~** se sentir tout chose○

grouch○ /'graʊtʃ/ *vi* rouspéter○ (**about sb** après qn; **about sth** contre qch)

grouchy○ /'graʊtʃɪ/ *adj* grognon

ground /graʊnd/
A *prét, pp* ▸ **grind B, C**
B *n* ① (surface underfoot) sol *m*, terre *f*; **to throw sth on the ~** jeter qch par terre; **to sit on the ~** s'asseoir par terre; **to fall to the ~** tomber (par terre); **get up off the ~** lève-toi; **to get off the ~** [*plane*] décoller; *fig* [*idea*] prendre *fig*; **to get sth off the ~** faire démarrer qch; **to burn to the ~** brûler complètement; **to prepare the ~** *fig* ouvrir la voie (**for** à); **to clear the ~** *lit, fig* déblayer le terrain; ② (area, territory) *lit, fig* terrain *m*; **to cover a lot of ~** *lit* faire beaucoup de chemin; *fig* avancer beaucoup; **to go over the same ~** se répéter; **to break fresh** *ou* **new ~** innover; **on neutral ~** en terrain neutre; **to be sure of one's ~** être sûr de ce qu'on avance; **on dangerous ~** (in discussion) sur un terrain miné; (in dealings) dans une position délicate; ③ *gen*, Sport (for specific activity) terrain *m*; ④ (reason) *gen*, Jur motifs *mpl*, raisons *fpl*; ⑤ *fig* (in contest, discussion) **to gain ~** gagner du terrain (**on**, **over** sur); **to lose ~** perdre du terrain (**to** au profit de); **to give ~** céder du terrain (**to** devant; **on**, **over** au niveau de); **to make up lost ~** regagner du terrain perdu; **to hold** *ou* **stand (one's) ~** tenir bon; **to shift one's ~** *fig* changer son fusil d'épaule (**on** au sujet de); ⑥ US Elec terre *f*; ⑦ Art fond *m*

G grounds npl **1** (of house, institution) parc m (**of** de); **private ~s** propriété f privée; **2** (reasons) **~s for** motifs de [divorce, criticism, hope]; **to have ~s for complaint** avoir des motifs de se plaindre; **~s for doing** motifs pour faire; **there are no ~s for supposing that** il n'y a aucun motif pour supposer que; **to give sb good ~s for doing** donner à qn de bonnes raisons de faire; **on (the) ~s of** en raison de [cost, public interest]; pour cause de [adultery, negligence]; **on (the) ~s of ill-health** pour raisons de santé; **on compassionate ~s** pour raisons personnelles; **on the ~s that** en raison du fait que

D ground pp adj [coffee, pepper] moulu

E vtr **1** Aviat immobiliser [aircraft]; **2** Naut **to be ~ed** s'échouer; **3** (base) **to ~ sth on** ou **in** fonder qch sur; **4** ○(keep in) priver [qn] de sortie; **5** US Elec relier [qch] à la terre

(Idioms) **to be thin on the ~** ne pas être légion inv; **to go to ~** se terrer; **to run sb/sth to ~** dénicher○ qn/qch; **to run** ou **drive oneself into the ~** s'user au travail; **that suits me down to the ~** ça me convient parfaitement

ground: ~ almonds npl poudre f d'amandes; **~ beef** n US bœuf m haché; **~ control** n contrôle m au sol; **~ crew** n personnel m au sol

ground floor surtout GB n rez-de-chaussée m; **on the ~** au rez-de-chaussée

ground: ~ forces npl forces fpl terrestres; **~ frost** n givre m; **Groundhog Day** n US le 2 février (dans la croyance populaire, jour décisif quant à la durée de l'hiver); **~ hostess** ▸ p. 1181 n hôtesse f au sol

grounding /'graʊndɪŋ/ n **1** ₵ (preparation) bases fpl (**in** en, de); **to have a good ~ in sth** avoir de bonnes bases en qch; **2** Aviat (of plane) immobilisation f

ground: ~less adj [fear, rumour] sans fondement; **~ level** n Constr rez-de-chaussée m; **~nut** n GB arachide f; **~nut oil** n GB huile f d'arachide; **~ rent** n rente f foncière; **~ rice** n semoule f de riz

ground rules npl grands principes mpl; **to change the ~** modifier les règles du jeu

ground: ~sheet n tapis m de sol; **~ speed** n vitesse f au sol

groundstaff /'graʊndstɑːf, US -stæf/ n **1** (for maintenance) personnel m d'entretien d'un terrain de sports; **2** Aviat personnel m au sol

groundswell /'graʊndswel/ n **1** fig (upsurge) **~ of support for** une vague de soutien pour; **2** lit, Naut raz-de-marée m

ground: ~-to-air missile n missile m sol-air; **~ troops** npl troupes fpl terrestres; **~ wire** n US fil m de terre; **~work** n travail m préparatoire (**for** à); **~ zero** n point m zéro

group /gruːp/
A n groupe m; **in ~s** en groupes
B noun modifier [dynamics, therapy] de groupe
C vtr (also **~ together**) grouper; **to ~ sth according to price** grouper qch en fonction du prix
D vi (also **~ together**) se grouper

group booking n réservation f de groupe

grouping /'gruːpɪŋ/ n (group, alliance) groupe m

group: ~ insurance n assurance f collective; **Group of Eight** n groupe m des Huit; **~ practice** n Med cabinet m médical collectif; **~ work** n travail m en groupes

grouse /graʊs/
A n (pl **~**) (bird, meat) tétras m
B ○vi (complain) râler○ (**about** après)

grove /graʊv/ n bosquet m; **lemon ~** verger m de citronniers

grovel /'grɒvl/ vi (p prés etc **-ll-**, US **-l-**) **1** fig (humbly) ramper (**to, before** devant); **2** (crawl) **to ~ around** être à quatre pattes

grovelling, groveling US /'grɒvlɪŋ/ adj obséquieux/-ieuse

grow /graʊ/ (prét **grew**; pp **grown**)
A vtr **1** (cultivate) cultiver; **2** (increase, allow to increase) laisser pousser [beard, nails]; **to ~ 5 cm** [person] grandir de 5 cm; [plant] pousser de 5 cm
B vi **1** (increase physically) [plant, hair] pousser (**by** de); [person] grandir (**by** de); [tumour] se développer; **to let one's nails ~** laisser pousser ses ongles; **to ~ to a height of 4 metres**

atteindre 4 mètres de hauteur; **2** (of something abstract) [spending, crime, population, tension] augmenter (**by** de); [company, economy] être en expansion; [movement, opposition, support, problem] devenir plus important; [poverty, crisis] s'aggraver; [pressure, influence] devenir plus fort; **fears are ~ing that** on craint de plus en plus que (**+** subj); **to ~** atteindre [level]; **to ~ in** acquérir plus de [authority, strength]; **to ~ in popularity** devenir plus populaire; **3** (become) devenir [hotter, stronger]; **to ~ old** vieillir; **to ~ more and more impatient** s'impatienter de plus en plus; **to ~ to do** finir par faire; **I soon grew to like him** j'ai vite fini par l'aimer

(Phrasal verbs)
■ **grow apart** s'éloigner l'un de l'autre
■ **grow into**: ▸ **~ into** [sth] **1** (become) devenir [adult]; **2** (fit into) s'accoutumer à [role]; **he'll ~ into it** (of garment) quand il aura un peu grandi il pourra le mettre
■ **grow on**: ▸ **~ on** [sb] [habit] s'imposer; **it ~s on you** on finit par l'aimer
■ **grow out of**: ▸ **~ out of** [sth] **1** (get too big for) **he's grown out of his suit** son costume est devenu trop petit pour lui; **she's grown out of discos** elle a passé l'âge des discothèques; **2** (develop from) naître de
■ **grow together** (become close) se rapprocher
■ **grow up 1** (grow, get bigger) [child] grandir; [movement] se développer; **to ~ up believing that** grandir dans l'idée que; **2** (become adult, mature) devenir adulte; **when I ~ up** quand je serai grand

grow bag n sac m de culture

grower /'graʊə(r)/ n (person) (of fruit) producteur/-trice m/f; (of cereal crops) cultivateur/-trice m/f; (of flowers) horticulteur/-trice m/f

growing /'graʊɪŋ/
A n Agric culture f
B adj **1** (physically) [child] en pleine croissance; [business] en expansion; **2** (increasing) [number, demand] croissant; [pressure, optimism, opposition] grandissant

growing pains npl fig (of firm, project) difficultés fpl dans le développement

growl /graʊl/
A n (of dog) grondement m; (of person) grognement m
B vi [dog] gronder; [person] **to ~ at sb** grogner après qn

grown /graʊn/
A pp ▸ **grow**
B adj a **~ man/woman** un/-e adulte

grown-up
A /'graʊnʌp/ n adulte mf, grande personne f
B /ˌgraʊn'ʌp/ adj adulte; **~ son** fils m adulte; **what do you want to be when you're ~?** qu'est-ce que tu veux faire quand tu seras grand?; **to be ~ for one's age** être mûr pour son âge

growth /graʊθ/ n **1** (physical) (of person, plant) croissance f; (of hair, nails) pousse f; **2** (increase) (of population, movement, idea) croissance f (**in, of** de); (of economy) expansion f (**in, of** de); (of numbers, productivity, earnings) augmentation f (**in** de); (of expenditure) hausse f (**in** de); **3** Med grosseur f, tumeur f; **4** Bot pousse f

growth: ~ area n secteur m en expansion; **~ industry** n industrie f en expansion; **~ rate** n Econ taux m de croissance; (of person) rythme m de croissance; **~ ring** n Bot (on tree) anneau m

groyne GB, **groin** US /grɔɪn/ n épi m (pour retenir le sable)

grub /grʌb/ n **1** Zool larve f; (in fruit) ver m; **2** ○(food) bouffe○ f

(Phrasal verb)
■ **grub around**: ▸ **~ around for** fouiner pour trouver

grubby /'grʌbɪ/ adj lit malpropre; fig infâme

Grub Street n: le monde des écrivaillons nécessiteux

grudge /grʌdʒ/
A n **to bear sb a ~** en vouloir à qn; **to harbour** ou **bear** ou **nurse a ~ against** garder de la rancune contre
B vtr **to ~ sb their success** en vouloir à qn de sa réussite; **to ~ doing** rechigner à faire

grudging /'grʌdʒɪŋ/ adj [acceptance, admiration] réticent; **to treat sb with ~ respect** respecter qn malgré soi; **to be ~ in one's praise** être avare de compliments

grudgingly /'grʌdʒɪŋlɪ/ adv [admit] avec réticence

gruel /'gruːəl/ n gruau m

gruelling, grueling US /'gru:əlɪŋ/ *adj* exténuant

gruesome /'gru:səm/ *adj* (gory) horrible; (horrifying) épouvantable

gruff /grʌf/ *adj* bourru

grumble /'grʌmbl/
A *n* ⓵ (complaint) ronchonnement *m*; **to have a ~ about** ronchonner après; ⓶ (of thunder) grondement *m*; (of stomach) gargouillement *m*
B *vi* ⓵ [*person*] ronchonner (**at sb** après qn; **to** auprès de); **to ~ about** se plaindre de; ⓶ [*stomach*] gargouiller

grumbling /'grʌmblɪŋ/
A *n* ⓵ **ℂ** (complaining) plaintes *fpl*; ⓶ (of thunder) grondement *m*; (of stomach) gargouillement *m*
B *adj* ⓵ (complaining) ronchon/-onne○; **~ appendix** appendicite *f* chronique

grumpily /'grʌmpɪlɪ/ *adv* [*speak*] en bougonnant; [*act*] d'un air maussade

grumpy /'grʌmpɪ/ *adj* grincheux/-euse, grognon

grunge○ /'grʌndʒ/ *n* (dirt) crasse *f*; (style) grunge *m*

grunt /grʌnt/
A *n* grognement *m*
B *vi* [*pig*] grogner; [*person*] grogner (**with, in** de)

GSM *n* (*abrév* = **Global System for Mobile**) GSM *m*

G-string *n* (garment) string *m*

Gt *abrév écrite* = **Great**

guarantee /,gærən'ti:/
A *n* ⓵ (warranty, document) garantie *f* (**against** contre); **there is a ~ on the vehicle** le véhicule est sous garantie; **this television carries a one-year ~** cette télévision est garantie un an; ⓶ (assurance) garantie *f* (**against** contre); **there is no ~ that** il n'est pas certain que; ⓷ Jur (of financial liability, sb's debts) garantie *f*; ⓸ (security) (cash) caution *f*; (object) gage *m*, garantie *f*; **to give [sth] as a ~** donner [qch] en caution [*money*]; donner [qch] en gage [*object*]
B *vtr* ⓵ Comm garantir (**against** contre); **it's ~d for five years** il est garanti cinq ans; **~d waterproof** garanti étanche; ⓶ (assure) garantir, assurer; **to ~ to do** s'engager à faire; **I can ~ that...** je peux vous garantir que...; **I can't ~ that it's true** je ne peux pas garantir que ce soit vrai; **it's a ~d bestseller** ce sera un bestseller à coup sûr; ⓷ Jur **to ~ a loan** se porter garant *or* caution d'un emprunt; **to ~ a cheque** garantir un chèque

guarantor /,gærən'tɔ:(r)/ *n* caution *f*, garant/-e *m/f*; **to stand ~ for sb** se porter garant de qn

guard /gɑ:d/
A *n* ⓵ (for person) surveillant/-e *m/f*; (for place, object) gardien/-ienne *m/f*; ⓶ (at prison) gardien/-ienne *m/f*; (soldier) garde *m*; ⓷ Mil (duty) garde *f*, surveillance *f*; **to be on ~** (duty) être de garde; **to go on/come off ~** prendre/finir son tour de garde; **to keep** *ou* **stand ~** monter la garde (**over** auprès de); **the changing of the ~** GB la relève de la garde; ⓸ (watchfulness) **to drop one's ~** baisser la garde; **to catch sb off ~** prendre qn au dépourvu; **to be on one's ~** se méfier (**against** de); ⓹ (group of soldiers, police etc) under **armed ~** sous escorte armée; ⓺ GB Rail chef *m* de train; ⓻ (for safety) (on printer) couvercle *m*; (on industrial machinery) carter *m* de protection; ⓼ (in Ireland) (policeman) policier *m* (irlandais)
B *vtr* ⓵ (protect) surveiller [*place, object*]; protéger [*person*]; **a dog ~s the house** un chien garde la maison; **the house is heavily ~ed** la maison est sous haute surveillance; **to ~ sth with one's life** protéger qch au péril de sa vie; ⓶ (prevent from escaping) surveiller; ⓷ (from discovery) garder [*secret*]

(Phrasal verb)

■ **guard against**: ▸ **~ against [sth]** se prémunir contre; **to ~ against doing** prendre garde à ne pas faire

guard dog *n* chien *m* de garde

guarded /'gɑ:dɪd/ *adj* circonspect (**about** à propos de)

guardian /'gɑ:dɪən/ *n* Jur tuteur/-trice *m/f*; gen gardien/-ienne *m/f* (**of** de)

guardian angel *n* lit, fig ange *m* gardien

guard: **~ of honour** *n* garde *f* d'honneur; **~ rail** *n* Aut glissière *f* de sécurité; (on bridge, window) garde-fou *m*; **~room** *n* salle *f* d'arrêt(s); **~'s van** *n* GB Rail fourgon *m* à bagages

Guatemala /,gwɑ:tə'mɑ:lə/ ▸ p. 774 *pr n* Guatemala *m*

Guatemalan /,gwɑ:tə'mɑ:lən/ ▸ p. 1032
A *n* Guatémaltèque *mf*

B *adj* guatémaltèque

guava /'gwɑ:və, US 'gwɔ:və/ *n* (tree) goyavier *m*; (fruit) goyave *f*

Guernsey /'gɜ:nzɪ/ ▸ p. 954 *pr n* Geog Guernesey *f*

guerrilla /gə'rɪlə/ *n* guérillero *m*; **urban ~s** guérilla *f* urbaine

guerrilla: **~ war** *n* guérilla *f*; **~ warfare** *n* guérilla *f*

guess /ges/
A *n* supposition *f*, conjecture *f*; **to have** *ou* **make a ~** essayer de deviner; **to have** *ou* **make a ~ at sth** essayer de deviner qch; **my ~ is that they will lose** à mon avis ils vont perdre; **at a (rough) ~ I would say that...** au hasard je dirais que...; **I'll give you three ~es!** devine un peu!; **that was a good ~!** tu as deviné juste!; **to make a wild ~** deviner au hasard; **your ~ is as good as mine** je n'en sais pas plus que toi; **it's anybody's ~!** les paris sont ouverts!
B *vtr* ⓵ (intuit) deviner; **to ~ that** supposer que; **to ~ sb's age** (correctly) deviner l'âge de qn; (make estimate) donner un âge à qn; **you'll never ~ what has happened!** tu ne devineras jamais ce qui vient d'arriver!; **I ~ed as much!** je m'en doutais!; **~ what! I've won a prize!** tu sais quoi○! j'ai gagné un prix!; **~ who!** devine qui c'est!; ⓶ US (suppose) supposer; (believe, think) penser, croire; **'he's right, you know'—'I ~ so'** 'il a raison, tu sais'—'oui, je suppose'
C *vi* ⓵ deviner; **to ~ at** faire des suppositions *or* des conjectures quant à [*plans, outcome*]; **to ~ right** deviner juste; **to ~ wrong** se tromper; **to keep sb ~ing** laisser qn dans le doute

guess: **~timate** *n* calcul *m* approximatif; **~work** *n* conjecture *f*

guest /gest/
A *n* ⓵ gen invité/-e *m/f*; (of hotel) client/-e *m/f*; (of boarding house) pensionnaire *mf*; **~ of honour** invité/-e *m/f* d'honneur; **house ~** invité/-e *m/f*; **be my ~!** je vous en prie!; ⓶ Biol hôte *m*
B *noun modifier* [*speaker*] invité; **~ book** livre *m* d'or; **~ list** liste *f* des invités; **~ star** gen invité/-e *m/f* d'honneur; (in film credits) avec la participation de

guest: **~house** *n* pension *f* de famille; **~ room** *n* chambre *f* d'amis; **~worker** *n* travailleur *m* immigré, travailleuse *f* immigrée

guff○ /gʌf/ *n* **ℂ** sottises *fpl*

guffaw /gə'fɔ:/ *n* gros éclat *m* de rire

GUI *n*: *abrév* ▸ **graphical user interface**

guidance /'gaɪdns/ *n* **ℂ** (advice) conseils *mpl* (**from** de); **~ on legal procedures** conseils en matière de procédures légales; **~ on how to do** conseils sur la façon de faire; **to give sb ~** donner des conseils à qn; **to seek ~ on a matter** demander conseil sur une (certaine) question; **this leaflet is for your ~** ce prospectus est pour vous, à titre d'information; **under the ~ of sb** sous la direction de qn

guide /gaɪd/
A *n* ⓵ (person) guide *m*; **tour ~** guide (touristique); **to act as a ~** servir de guide; ⓶ (estimate, idea) indication *f*; **as a rough ~** à titre d'indication; ⓷ gen Tourism (book) guide *m* (**to** de); TV **~** programme *m* de télé(vision); **user's ~** manuel *m* d'utilisation; ⓸ (*also* **Girl Guide**) guide *f*
B *vtr* ⓵ (steer) guider, conduire (**to** vers); ⓶ (influence) [*person*] guider; [*reason*] dicter; **to be ~d by sb's advice** suivre les conseils de qn; ⓷ Aerosp, Mil (télé)guider

guide: **~ book** *n* guide *m*; **~ dog** *n* chien *m* d'aveugle; **~d tour** *n* visite *f* guidée

guideline /'gaɪdlaɪn/ *n* ⓵ (rough guide) indication *f*; ⓶ Admin, Pol directive *f*; **pay ~s** base *f* des négociations salariales; ⓷ (advice) conseil *m*

guiding /'gaɪdɪŋ/ *adj* **~ force** fig moteur *m*; **~ principle** principe *m* directeur; **~ light** (person) flambeau *m*

guild /gɪld/ *n* (medieval) guilde *f*; (modern) association *f*

guilder /'gɪldə(r)/ ▸ p. 782 *n* florin *m*

guile /gaɪl/ *n* **full of ~** rusé; **without ~** candide

guileless /'gaɪllɪs/ *adj* candide

guillotine /'gɪlətiːn/ *n* ⓵ (for execution) guillotine *f*; ⓶ (for paper) massicot *m*; ⓷ GB Pol *système qui limite la durée des débats parlementaires*

guilt /gɪlt/ *n* ⓵ (blame) gen, Jur culpabilité *f*; ⓶ (feeling) sentiment *m* de culpabilité (**about sb** envers qn; **about** *ou* **over sth** pour qch)

guiltily /'gɪltɪlɪ/ *adv* [*say, look*] d'un air coupable

guiltless /'gɪltlɪs/ adj sout innocent

guilty /'gɪltɪ/ adj **1** Jur coupable; **to be found ~/not ~ of sth** être reconnu coupable/déclaré non coupable de qch; **the ~ party** le/la coupable; **2** (remorseful) [expression] de culpabilité; [appearance, look] coupable; **to feel ~ about** se sentir coupable vis-à-vis de

Guinea /'gɪnɪ/ ▸ p. 774 pr n Guinée f

guinea-fowl /'gɪnɪfaʊl/, **guinea-hen** /'gɪnɪhen/ n pintade f

guinea-pig /'gɪnɪpɪg/ n **1** Zool cochon m d'Inde; **2** fig cobaye m

guise /gaɪz/ n littér **in** ou **under the ~ of a joke** sous (le) couvert de la plaisanterie; **in various ~s** sous différentes formes

guitar /gɪ'tɑː(r)/ ▸ p. 1028

A n guitare f; **on the ~** à la guitare

B noun modifier [lesson, player, string, teacher] de guitare; **~ case** étui m à guitare

guitarist /gɪ'tɑːrɪst/ ▸ p. 1181, p. 1028 n guitariste mf

Gulag /'guːlæg/ n Goulag m

gulch /gʌltʃ/ n US ravin m

gulf /gʌlf/ n **1** fig fossé m (**between** qui sépare); **2** Geog golfe m

Gulf /gʌlf/ pr n **the ~** la région du Golfe

Gulf States pr npl **the ~** (in Middle East) les États mpl du Golfe; (on US/Mexican border) les États bordant le golfe du Mexique

Gulf War pr n guerre f du Golfe

Gulf War syndrome ▸ p. 933 n Med, Mil syndrome m de la guerre du Golfe

gull /gʌl/ n mouette f; (larger) goéland m

gullet /'gʌlɪt/ n (throat) gosier m; (oesophagus) œsophage m

gullibility /ˌgʌlə'bɪlətɪ/ n crédulité f

gullible /'gʌləbl/ adj crédule

gully /'gʌlɪ/ n Geog ravin m

gulp /gʌlp/

A n **1** (mouthful) (of liquid) gorgée f; (of air) bouffée f, goulée f; (of food) bouchée f; **she drained her glass in one ~** elle a vidé son verre d'un trait; **2** (nervous) serrement m de gorge; (tearful) hoquet m

B vtr engloutir [food, drink]; aspirer [air]

C vi avoir la gorge serrée

(Phrasal verb)

■ **gulp back**: ▸ **~ back [sth]**, **~ [sth] back** ravaler [tears]

gum /gʌm/

A n **1** Anat gencive f; **2** (also **chewing ~**) chewing-gum m; **a piece of ~** un chewing-gum; **3** (adhesive) colle f; **4** (resin) gomme f

B vtr (p prés etc **-mm-**) coller (**to** à; **on to** sur)

gum: **~boot** n GB botte f en caoutchouc; **~drop** n boule f de gomme

gumption○ /'gʌmpʃn/ n (common sense) jugeote○ f; (courage) cran○ m

gumshoe○ n (private investigator) détective m privé; (police detective) policier m en civil

gum tree n gommier m

(Idiom) **to be up a ~** être en position délicate

gun /gʌn/

A n **1** (weapon) gen arme f à feu; (revolver) revolver m; (rifle) fusil m; (cannon) canon m; **to fire a ~** tirer; **to draw a ~ on sb** braquer une arme sur qn; **he's got a ~!** il est armé!; **2** (tool) pistolet m; **paint ~** pistolet à peinture; **3** ○US **a hired ~** un tueur à gages

B vtr (p prés etc **-nn-**) **to ~ an engine** mettre les gaz○

(Idioms) **to go great ~s** [business] marcher très fort○; [person] avoir la frite○; **to hold a ~ to sb's head** mettre le couteau sous la gorge de qn; **to jump the ~** agir prématurément; **to stick to one's ~s**○ (in one's actions) s'accrocher○

(Phrasal verbs)

■ **gun down**: ▸ **~ [sb] down**, **~ down [sb]** abattre, descendre

■ **gun for**: **to be ~ning for [sb]** chercher des crosses à○

gun: **~ barrel** n canon m de fusil; **~boat** n canonnière f; **~dog** n chien m de chasse; **~fire** n **C** (from hand-held gun) coups mpl de feu; (from artillery) fusillade f

gunge○ /gʌndʒ/ GB n magma m répugnant

gung ho○ /ˌgʌŋ'həʊ/ adj hum ou péj (eager for war) va-t-en guerre inv; (overzealous) (trop) enthousiaste

gun: **~ laws** npl législation f sur les armes à feu; **~ licence** n permis m de port d'armes; **~man** n homme m armé

gunner /'gʌnə(r)/ n GB (in navy) canonnier m; (in army) artilleur m

gunpoint /'gʌnpɔɪnt/ n **to hold sb up at ~** tenir qn sous la menace d'une arme

gun: **~powder** n poudre f; **Gunpowder Plot** pr n Hist Conspiration f des Poudres; **~running** n trafic m d'armes; **~shot** n (report) coup m de feu; **~shot wound** n blessure f par balle; **~slinger**○ n US bandit m armé; **~smith** ▸ p. 1181 n armurier m

gunwale /'gʌnl/ n plat-bord m; **full to the ~s** plein à ras bords

gurgle /'gɜːgl/

A n (of water) gargouillement m; (of baby) gazouillis m

B vi [water] gargouiller; [baby] gazouiller

guru /'gʊruː, US gə'ruː/ n gourou m

gush /gʌʃ/

A n (of liquid) jaillissement m

B vi **1** [liquid] jaillir; **tears ~ed down her cheeks** ses joues ruisselaient de larmes; **2** fig **to ~ over** s'extasier devant

(Phrasal verb)

■ **gush in** [water, oil etc] pénétrer

gushing /'gʌʃɪŋ/, **gushy** /'gʌʃɪ/ adj [person] hyperexpansif/-ive○; [letter, style] dithyrambique○

gusset /'gʌsɪt/ n soufflet m

gust /gʌst/ n **1** (of wind, rain, snow) rafale f; **a ~ of hot air** une bouffée d'air chaud; **2** (of anger) bouffée f

gusto /'gʌstəʊ/ n **with ~** avec enthousiasme

gusty /'gʌstɪ/ adj [day, weather] de grand vent

gut /gʌt/

A n **1** ○(abdomen, belly) bide○ m; **beer ~** brioche f (de buveur de bière); **2** Anat (intestine) intestin m; **3** (for racket, bow) boyau m

B guts○ npl **1** (insides) (of human) tripes○ fpl; (of animal, building) entrailles fpl; **2** (courage) cran○ m

C noun modifier (basic) [feeling, reaction] viscéral, instinctif/-ive; [instinct] premier/-ière (before n)

D vtr (p prés etc **-tt-**) **1** Culin vider; **2** (destroy) [fire] ravager; [looters] saccager; **3** (strip) **to ~ a house** tout refaire dans une maison

E gutted○ pp adj GB abattu, découragé

gutless /'gʌtlɪs/ adj mou/molle

gutsy○ /'gʌtsɪ/ adj (spirited) fougueux/-euse; (brave) courageux/-euse

gutter /'gʌtə(r)/

A n **1** (on roof) gouttière f; (in street) caniveau m; **2** fig bas-fonds mpl

B vi [flame] crépiter et vaciller

guttering /'gʌtərɪŋ/ n **C** gouttières fpl

gutter: **~ press** n presse f à sensation; **~snipe** n péj gosse mf des rues

guttural /'gʌtərəl/ adj guttural

guv○ /gʌv/, **guvnor**○ /'gʌvnər/ n GB chef○ m

guy○ /gaɪ/ n **1** (man) type○ m; **a good/bad ~** (in films etc) un bon/méchant; **hey, you ~s!** (to men, mixed group) eh! vous, les gars○!; (to women) eh! les filles○!; **2** GB effigie de Guy Fawkes qu'on brûle le 5 novembre; **3** (also **~rope**) corde f d'attache

Guyana /gaɪ'ænə/ ▸ p. 774 pr n Guyana f

Guy Fawkes Day /'gaɪ fɔːks deɪ/ n GB le 5 novembre (anniversaire de la Conspiration des Poudres)

guzzle○ /'gʌzl/ vtr engloutir

guzzler○ /'gʌzlə(r)/ n goinfre○ mf

gym /dʒɪm/ ▸ p. 881 n **1** (abrév = **gymnasium**) salle f de gym, gymnase m; **2** (abrév = **gymnastics**) gym○ f

gymkhana /dʒɪm'kɑːnə/ n jeux mpl à poney

gymnasium /dʒɪm'neɪzɪəm/ n (pl **~s** ou **-ia**) gymnase m

gymnast /'dʒɪmnæst/ n gymnaste mf

gymnastic /dʒɪm'næstɪk/ adj de gymnastique

gymnastics /dʒɪm'næstɪks/ ▸ p. 881 npl (all contexts) gymnastique f

g

gym: ∼ **shoe** n (chaussure f de) tennis f; ∼**slip** n GB robe f chasuble (*faisant partie d'un uniforme scolaire*)

gynaecologist GB, **gynecologist** US /ˌgaɪnəˈkɒlə-dʒɪst/ ▸ p. 1181 n gynécologue mf

gynaecology GB, **gynecology** US /ˌgaɪnəˈkɒlədʒɪ/ n gynécologie f

gyp○ /dʒɪp/
A n ① GB (pain) **my back is giving me** ∼ j'ai mal au dos en ce moment; ② US (con) arnaque○ f
B vtr US (p prés etc **-pp-**) **to get** ∼**ped** se faire arnaquer○

gypsophila /dʒɪpˈsɒfɪlə/ n gypsophile f

gypsum /ˈdʒɪpsəm/ n gypse m

gypsy /ˈdʒɪpsɪ/
A n gen bohémien/-ienne m/f; (Central European) tzigane mf; (Spanish) gitan/-e m/f
B noun modifier [camp] de bohémiens; [music] tzigane

gypsy cab○ n US taxi m clandestin

gyrate /ˌdʒaɪˈreɪt, US ˈdʒaɪreɪt/ vi [dancer] se trémousser; [kite] décrire des cercles

h, H /eɪtʃ/ *n* h, H *m*

ha /hɑː/
A *n: abrév écrite* = **hectare**
B *excl* ah; '∼! ∼!' (laughter) 'ah, ah, ah!'; (ironic) très drôle! iron

haberdasher /ˈhæbədæʃə(r)/ ▸ p. 1181 *n* ① GB mercier/-ière *m/f*; ② US marchand/-e *m/f* de vêtements pour hommes

haberdashery /ˈhæbədæʃərɪ/ ▸ p. 1181 *n* ① GB (in department store) rayon *m* mercerie; ② (goods) GB mercerie *f*; ③ US magasin *m* de vêtements pour hommes

habit /ˈhæbɪt/ *n* ① (custom) gen habitude *f*; **to have a ∼ of doing, to be in the ∼ of doing** avoir l'habitude de faire; **I'm not in the ∼ of borrowing money** ce n'est pas dans mes habitudes d'emprunter de l'argent; **to get into/out of the ∼ of doing sth** prendre/perdre l'habitude de faire qch; **to be a creature of ∼** avoir ses petites habitudes; ② (addiction) accoutumance *f*; **to kick the ∼**○ (of addiction) décrocher○; (of smoking) arrêter; ③ Relig habit *m*; ④ (for horseriding) tenue *f* d'équitation

habitable /ˈhæbɪtəbl/ *adj* habitable

habitat /ˈhæbɪtæt/ *n* habitat *m*

habitation /ˌhæbɪˈteɪʃn/ *n* sout ① (house) habitation *f*; ② (being inhabited) **to show signs of ∼** paraître habité; **unfit for human ∼** insalubre

habit-forming /ˈhæbɪtfɔːmɪŋ/ *adj* **to be ∼** créer une accoutumance

habitual /həˈbɪtʃʊəl/ *adj* [behaviour, reaction] habituel/-elle; [drinker, smoker, liar] invétéré

habitually /həˈbɪtʃʊəlɪ/ *adv* habituellement

hack /hæk/
A *n* ① ○péj (writer) écrivaillon *m* pej; ② Comput = **hacker**; ③ ○Pol (also **party ∼**) militant/-e *m/f*
B *vtr* ① (strike, chop) taillader [branch, object] (**with** avec, à coups de); tailler dans [bushes] (**à coups de**); **to ∼ sb (to death) with sth** frapper qn (à mort) à coups de qch; **to ∼ sth/sb to pieces** tailler *or* mettre qch/qn en pièces; **to ∼ a path** *ou* **one's way through sth** se tailler un chemin à travers qch; ② Comput s'introduire dans [system, database]; ③ ○(cope with) **I can't ∼ it** je ne le supporte pas; **how long do you think he will ∼ it?** combien de temps tu penses qu'il va tenir?
C *vi* ① (chop) taillader (**with** à coups de); **to ∼ through sth** tailler dans qch; ② ○Comput pirater○; **to ∼ into** s'introduire dans [system]

⸨Phrasal verbs⸩
■ **hack down**: ▸ ∼ **down** [sth], ∼ [sth] **down** abattre [grass, bush, enemy]
■ **hack off**: ▸ ∼ **off** [sth], ∼ [sth] **off** tailler [piece, branch]; trancher [hand, head]

hacker /ˈhækə(r)/ *n* Comput pirate○ *m* informatique

hacking /ˈhækɪŋ/ *n* Comput piratage○ *m* informatique

hacking cough *n* toux *f* sèche et spasmodique

hackles /ˈhæklz/ *npl* (on animal) poils *mpl* du cou; **the dog's ∼ began to rise** le chien se hérissait; **to make sb's ∼ rise** fig hérisser qn

hackney cab /ˌhæknɪˈkæb/ *n* fiacre *m*

hackneyed /ˈhæknɪd/ *adj* [joke] éculé; [subject] rebattu; **∼ phrase, ∼ expression** cliché *m*

hack: **∼ reporter** *n* journaliste *mf* qui fait la rubrique des chiens écrasés; **∼saw** *n* scie *f* à métaux

had /hæd/ *prét, pp* ▸ **have**

haddock /ˈhædək/ *n* (*pl* **∼s** *ou* **∼**) églefin *m*

hadn't /ˈhædnt/ = **had not**

haematoma GB, **hematoma** US /ˌhiːməˈtəʊmə/ *n* (*pl* **∼s** *ou* **-mata**) hématome *m*

haemoglobin GB, **hemoglobin** US /ˌhiːməˈgləʊbɪn/ *n* hémoglobine *f*

haemophilia GB, **hemophilia** US /ˌhiːməˈfɪlɪə/ ▸ p. 933 *n* hémophilie *f*

haemophiliac GB, **hemophiliac** US /ˌhiːməˈfɪlɪæk/ *n*, *adj* hémophile (*mf*)

haemorrhage GB, **hemorrhage** US /ˈhemərɪdʒ/
A *n* lit, fig hémorragie *f*
B *vi* faire une hémorragie

haemorrhoids GB, **hemorrhoids** US /ˈhemərɔɪdz/ *npl* hémorroïdes *fpl*

hag /hæg/ *n* (witch) (vieille) sorcière *f*

haggard /ˈhægəd/ *adj* [appearance, person] exténué; [face, expression] défait

haggle /ˈhægl/ *vi* marchander; **to ∼ about** *ou* **over sth** discuter du prix de qch

Hague /heɪg/ ▸ p. 1276 *pr n* **The ∼** La Haye

haiku /ˈhaɪkuː/ *n* Literat haïku *m*

hail /heɪl/
A *n* lit grêle *f*; fig (of bullets, insults) grêle *f* (**of** de)
B *vtr* ① (call, signal to) héler [person, taxi, ship]; ② (praise) **to ∼ sb as** acclamer qn comme; **to ∼ sth as sth/as being** saluer qch comme/comme étant
C *v impers* grêler
D *excl* **Hail!** Salut!

⸨Phrasal verb⸩
■ **hail from** sout être de, venir de

hail: **Hail Mary** *n* 'Je vous salue Marie' *m inv*; **∼stone** *n* grêlon *m*; **∼storm** *n* averse *f* de grêle

hair /heə(r)/ *n* ① **C** (collectively) (on head) cheveux *mpl*; (on body) poils *mpl*; (of animal) poil *m*; **a fine head of ∼** une belle chevelure; **to have one's ∼ done** se faire coiffer; ② (individually) (on head) cheveu *m*; (on body) poil *m*; (animal) poil *m*; **long/short-∼ed** [person] aux cheveux longs/courts; [animal] à poil long/court

⸨Idioms⸩ **by a ∼, by a ∼'s breadth** d'un poil○; **he didn't turn a ∼** il n'a pas bronché; **he was perfect, not a ∼ out of place** il était impeccable, tiré à quatre épingles; **it made my ∼ stand on end** cela m'a fait dresser les cheveux sur la tête; **to get in sb's ∼**○ taper sur les nerfs de qn○; **to have sb by the short ∼s**○ US tenir le couteau sous la gorge de qn; **to let one's ∼ down**○ se défouler○; **to split ∼s** couper les cheveux en quatre; **to tear one's ∼ out** s'arracher les cheveux; **you need a ∼ of the dog (that bit you)** il te faut un petit verre pour faire passer la gueule de bois○

hair: **∼band** *n* bandeau *m*; **∼brush** *n* brosse *f* à cheveux; **∼clip** *n* GB barrette *f*; **∼ curler** *n* bigoudi *m*; **∼cut** *n* coupe *f* (de cheveux); **∼do**○ *n* coiffure *f*; **∼dresser** ▸ p. 1181, p. 000 *n* coiffeur/-euse *m/f*; **∼dressing** *n* coiffure *f*; **∼drier** *n* (hand-held) sèche-cheveux *m inv*; (hood) casque *m*; **∼ gel** *n* gel *m* coiffant; **∼grip** *n* GB pince *f* à cheveux; **∼less** *adj* [body, chin] glabre; [animal] sans poils; **∼line** *n* naissance *f* des cheveux; **∼line crack** *n* fêlure *f*; **∼line fracture** *n* Med fêlure *f*; **∼net** *n* filet *m* à cheveux; **∼piece** *n* postiche *m*; **∼pin** *n* épingle *f* à cheveux; **∼pin bend** *n* virage *m* en épingle à cheveux; ∼-**raising** *adj* à vous faire dresser les cheveux sur la tête; ∼ **remover** *n* crème *f* dépilatoire; ∼-**slide** *n* GB barrette *f*; ∼ **splitting** *n* ergotage *m*; ∼**spray** *n* laque *f*; ∼**style** *n* coiffure *f*; ∼ **stylist** ▸ p. 1181 *n* coiffeur/-euse *m/f*; ∼ **transplant** *n* greffe *f* de cheveux; ∼ **trigger** *n* détente *f* ultrasensible

hairy /'heərɪ/ *adj* **1** [*coat, dog, chest*] poilu; Bot [*stem*] villeux/-euse; **2** °[*adventure, moment*] atroce°

Haiti /'heɪtɪ/ ▸ p. 774, p. 954 *pr n* Haïti *m*

Haitian /'heɪʃn/ ▸ p. 1032, p. 969
A *pr n* **1** (person) Haïtien/-ienne *m/f*; **2** (language) (créole *m*) haïtien *m*
B *adj* haïtien/-ienne

hake /heɪk/ *n* **1** (*pl* ∼ *ou* ∼**s**) Zool merlu *m*; **2** ℂ Culin colin *m*

halcyon /'hælsɪən/ *adj* [*time, period*] paradisiaque; ∼ **days** jours heureux

hale /heɪl/ *adj* [*old person*] vigoureux/-euse; **to be** ∼ **and hearty** *gen* être en pleine forme

half /hɑːf, US hæf/ ▸ p. 745
A *n* (*pl* **halves**) **1** (one of two parts) moitié *f*; ∼ (**of**) **the page** la moitié de la page; **to cut sth in** ∼ couper qch en deux; **2** (fraction) demi *m*; **four and a** ∼ quatre et demi; **3** Sport (time period) mi-temps *f*; (pitch area) moitié *f* de terrain; **4** Sport = **halfback**; **5** °GB (half pint) demi-pinte *f*; **6** GB (half fare) demi-tarif *m*
B *adj* **a** ∼ **circle** un demi-cercle; **a** ∼-**litre**, **a litre** un demi-litre; **two and a** ∼ **cups** deux tasses et demie
C *pron* **1** (50%) moitié *f*; **only** ∼ (**of the students) passed** seule la moitié (des étudiants) a réussi; **to cut sth by** ∼ réduire qch de moitié; **that was a meal and a** ∼°! ça a été un sacré repas°!; **2** (in time) demi/-e *m/f*; **an hour and a** ∼ une heure et demie; ∼ **past two** GB, ∼ **two**° deux heures et demie; **it starts at** ∼ **past** ça commence à la demie; **the buses run at** ∼ **past the hour** les bus passent à la demie de chaque heure; **she is ten and a** ∼ elle a dix ans et demi
D *adv* **1** à moitié; **to** ∼ **close the window** fermer la fenêtre à moitié; **it's** ∼ **the price** c'est moitié moins cher; ∼ **as much money/as many people** moitié moins d'argent/de personnes; ∼ **as big** moitié moins grand; **he's** ∼ **Spanish** ∼ **Irish** il est mi-espagnol mi-irlandais; **he was only** ∼ **serious** il n'était qu'à moitié sérieux; ∼ **disappointed** ∼ **relieved** mi-déçu mi-soulagé; **if it was** ∼ **as easy as they say** si c'était vraiment aussi facile qu'on le dit; **I was** ∼ **hoping that...** j'espérais presque que...; **2** °(in phrases) **not** ∼ **old** pas jeune iron; **he wasn't** ∼ **surprised**° il était drôlement° surpris; **it doesn't** ∼ **stink**°! ça pue drôlement°!; **not** ∼°! et comment!; **not** ∼ **bad**° pas mauvais *or* mal du tout

(Idioms) ∼ **a minute** *ou* **second** *ou* **tick**° GB *ou* **mo**° une petite minute, un instant; **how the other** ∼ **lives** comment vivent les riches; **if given** ∼ **a chance** à la première occasion; **to have** ∼ **a mind to do** avoir bien envie de faire; **one's better** *ou* **other** ∼ sa (douce) moitié; **to go halves with sb** se mettre de moitié avec qn; **too clever by** ∼° un peu trop malin/-igne

half: ∼-**and-half** *adj, adv* moitié-moitié; ∼**back** *n* Sport demi *m*; ∼-**baked**° *adj* bancal°; ∼-**board** *n* demi-pension *f*; ∼-**breed** *n*, *adj* injur métis/-isse (*m/f*); ∼ **brother** *n* demi-frère *m*; ∼-**caste** *n*, *adj* injur métis/-isse (*m/f*); ∼ **century** *n* demi-siècle *m*

half cock *n* at ∼ lit au cran de sûreté

(Idioms) **to go off at** ∼, **to go off half-cocked** (flop) partir en eau de boudin; (be hasty) être impulsif/-ive

half: ∼-**conscious** *adj* à demi conscient; ∼ **crown**, ∼-**a-crown** *n* GB Hist demi-couronne *f*; ∼-**cut**° *adj* ivre; ∼ **day** *n* demi-journée *f*; ∼-**dead**° *adj* lit, fig à moitié mort; ∼-**dozen** *n, pron, adj* demi-douzaine (*f*); ∼ **fare** *n* demi-tarif *m*; ∼-**hearted** *adj* [*attempt, smile, participation*] peu enthousiaste; ∼-**heartedly** *adv* sans conviction

half hour /hɑːf'aʊə(r), US ,hæf-/ ▸ p. 1267 *n* demi-heure *f*; **on the** ∼ à la demie

half: ∼-**hourly** *adj, adv* toutes les demi-heures; ∼-**length** *adj* [*portrait*] en buste; ∼-**light** *n* littér demi-jour *m*

half-mast /,hɑːf'mɑːst, US ,hæf-/ *n* at ∼ en berne

half-moon /,hɑːf'muːn, US ,hæf-/
A *n* **1** demi-lune *f*; **2** (of fingernail) lunule *f*
B *noun modifier* [*spectacles, shape*] en demi-lune

half pay *n* **to be on** ∼ avoir un demi-salaire

halfpenny *n* GB Hist demi-penny *m*

half-pint /,hɑːf'paɪnt, US ,hæf-/ ▸ p. 723 *n* demi-pinte *f* (*GB* = *0.28 l*, *US* = *0.24 l*); **a** ∼ **of milk** ≈ un quart de litre de lait

half: ∼ **price** *adv, adj* à moitié prix; ∼ **sister** *n* demi-sœur *f*

half size
A *n* (of shoe) demi-pointure *f*
B *adj* [*copy*] réduit de moitié

half: ∼ **slip** *n* jupon *m*; ∼ **smile** *n* demi-sourire *m*; ∼-**staff** *n* US = **half-mast**; ∼-**starved** *adj* à demi mort de faim; ∼ **term** GB Sch *n* vacances *fpl* de demi-trimestre; ∼-**timbered** *adj* à colombages

half-time /,hɑːf'taɪm, US ,hæf-/ *n* Sport mi-temps *f*; **at** ∼ à la mi-temps

half-truth *n* demi-vérité *f*

halfway /,hɑːf'weɪ, US ,hæf-/
A *adj* **the** ∼ **stage** la mi-étape; **to reach the** ∼ **mark** *ou* **point** être à la moitié
B *adv* **1** (at the mid-point) à mi-chemin (**between** entre; **to** de); **I went** ∼ j'ai fait la moitié du chemin; ∼ **up** *ou* **down** à mi-hauteur de [*stairs, tree*]; ∼ **down the page** à mi-page; ∼ **across** au milieu de [*room, ocean*]; **to travel** ∼ **across** *ou* **round the world for sth** faire des kilomètres et des kilomètres pour qch; ∼ **through (sth)** au milieu (de qch); **to be** ∼ **through doing sth** avoir à moitié fini de faire qch; **2** fig **to go** ∼ *ou* **towards sth/doing** être à mi-chemin de qch/de faire; **I met him** ∼ j'ai fait un compromis avec lui; **3** °(in the least) [*decent, competent*] raisonnablement

halfway house *n* **1** (compromise) compromis *m*; **2** (rehabilitation centre) centre *m* de réadaptation

half: ∼**way line** *n* Sport ligne *f* médiane; ∼**wit**° *n* péj abruti/-e° *m/f*

half-year /,hɑːf'jɪə(r), US ,hæf-/ Fin, Comm
A *n* semestre *m*
B *noun modifier* [*profit, results*] semestriel/-ielle

half-yearly *adj* [*meeting, payment*] semestriel/-ielle

halibut /'hælɪbət/ *n* (*pl* ∼ *ou* ∼**s**) flétan *m*

halitosis /,hælɪ'təʊsɪs/ *n* mauvaise haleine *f*

hall /hɔːl/ *n* **1** (in house) entrée *m*; (corridor) couloir *m*; (in hotel, airport) hall *m*; (for public events) (grande) salle *f*; **2** Univ (residence) résidence *f* universitaire; **3** (country house) manoir *m*

hallelujah /,hælɪ'luːjə/ *excl* alléluia

hallmark /'hɔːlmɑːk/
A *n* **1** GB (on metal) poinçon *m*; **2** (typical feature) caractéristique *f*
B *vtr* poinçonner; **to be** ∼**ed** porter un poinçon

hallo /hə'ləʊ/ *excl* GB = **hello**

hall: **Hall of Fame** *n* (all contexts) panthéon *m*; ∼ **of residence** *n* résidence *f* universitaire

hallow /'hæləʊ/
A *vtr* littér sanctifier
B *pp adj* **hallowed** **1** (venerated) [*tradition*] vénéré; **2** (sanctified) [*ground*] saint

Halloween /,hæləʊ'iːn/ *n* Halloween *m*; **on** *ou* **at** ∼ le soir de Halloween

hallstand /'hɔːlstænd/ *n* portemanteau *m*

hallucinate /hə'luːsɪneɪt/ *vi* avoir des hallucinations

hallucination /hə,luːsɪ'neɪʃn/ *n* hallucination *f*

hallucinatory /hə'luːsɪnətrɪ, US -tɔːrɪ/ *adj* [*drug*] hallucinogène; [*image*] onirique; [*effect*] hallucinatoire

hallucinogenic /hə,luːsɪnə'dʒenɪk/ *adj* hallucinogène

hallway /'hɔːlweɪ/ *n* entrée *f*

halo /'heɪləʊ/ *n* (*pl* ∼**s** *ou* ∼**es**) **1** (around head) auréole *f*; **his** ∼ **has become a bit tarnished** fig son image s'est un peu ternie; **2** (in astronomy) halo *m*

halogen /'hælədʒn/ *n* halogène *m*

halt /hɔːlt/
A *n* **1** (stop) arrêt *m*; **to come to a** ∼ [*group, vehicle*] s'arrêter, cesser; [*negotiations*] être interrompu; **to call a** ∼ **to sth** mettre fin à qch; **shall we call a** ∼? on s'arrête?; **2** (temporary) (in activity) suspension *f* (**in** dans); (in proceedings) pause *f*

h

(**in** au cours de); ③ Mil (rest) halte *f*; ④ GB Rail halte *f*
B *excl* halte!
C *vtr* interrompre [*proceedings*]; mettre fin à [*arms sales, experiments*]; arrêter [*inflation, offensive*]
D *vi* [*vehicle*] s'arrêter; [*army*] faire halte

halter /'hɔːltə(r)/ *n* ① (for horse) licol *m*; ② (for hanging) corde *f* (de pendaison)

halterneck /'hɔːltənek/ *n, adj* dos (*m inv*) nu

halting /'hɔːltɪŋ/ *adj* [*steps, attempts*] hésitant

halve /hɑːv, US hæv/
A *vtr* réduire [qch] de moitié [*number, rate*]; couper [qch] en deux [*carrot, cake*]
B *vi* [*number, rate, time*] diminuer de moitié

halves /hɑːvz, US hævz/ *npl* ▸ **half**

ham /hæm/ *n* ① Culin jambon *m*; ② (of animal) cuisse *f*; ③ ○(poor actor) cabotin/-e *m/f*; ④ (*also* **radio** ~) radioamateur *m*
(Idiom) **to ~ it up**○ jouer de façon exagérée

ham and eggs *npl* US Culin œufs *mpl* au jambon

hamburger /'hæmbɜːgə(r)/ *n* ① (patty) hamburger *m*; ② US (ground beef) pâté *m* de viande

ham-fisted○ GB, **ham-handed**○ US /,hæm'fɪstɪd, ,hæm'hændɪd/ *adj péj* maladroit

hamlet /'hæmlɪt/ *n* hameau *m*

hammer /'hæmə(r)/
A *n* ① gen, Mus marteau *m*; **to come** *ou* **go under the ~** être vendu aux enchères; ② Sport (discipline) lancer *m* de marteau
B *vtr* ① lit (beat) marteler [*metal, table, keys*]; **to ~ sth into** enfoncer qch dans [*wall, fence*]; **to ~ sth into shape** façonner qch au marteau; **to ~ sth flat** aplatir qch à coups de marteau; ② fig (insist forcefully) **to ~ sth into sb** faire entrer qch dans la tête de qn; **they had Latin ~ed into them** on leur a bien inculqué le latin; **to ~ home a message** bien faire comprendre un message; ③ (attack) critiquer; ④ ○Sport (defeat) battre [qn] à plates coutures
C *vi* ① (use hammer) frapper à coups de marteau; ② (pound) tambouriner (**on, at** contre
(Phrasal verbs)
■ **hammer in**: ▸ ~ **in [sth]**, ~ **[sth] in** enfoncer [qch] à coups de marteau
■ **hammer out**: ▸ ~ **out [sth]**, ~ **[sth] out** (negotiate) parvenir à [qch] après maintes discussions [*agreement, policy, formula*]

hammer and sickle *n* **the ~** la faucille et le marteau

hammering /'hæmərɪŋ/ *n* ① (noise) (bruit *m* de) martèlement *m* (**at** sur); ② ○(defeat) **to take** *ou* **get a ~** prendre une dérouillée○

hammock /'hæmək/ *n* hamac *m*

hamper /'hæmpə(r)/
A *n* ① (for picnic) panier *m* à pique-nique; ② GB (from shop etc) panier vendu avec une sélection de produits alimentaires de luxe
B *vtr* entraver [*movement, career, progress*]; handicaper [*person*]

hamster /'hæmstə(r)/ *n* hamster *m*

hamstring /'hæmstrɪŋ/
A *n* (of human) tendon *m* du jarret; (of horse) corde *f* du jarret
B *vtr* fig (*prét, pp* **-strung**) fig paralyser

hand /hænd/ ▸ p. 698
A *n* ① main *f*; **he had a pencil/book in his ~** il avait un crayon/livre à la main; **she had a pistol/an umbrella in her ~** elle avait un pistolet/un parapluie à la main; **to get** *ou* **lay one's ~s on sth** mettre la main sur qch; **to keep one's ~s off sth** ne pas toucher à [*computer, money*]; **to keep one's ~s off sb** laisser qn tranquille; **they were holding ~s** ils se donnaient la main; **to hold sb's ~** lit tenir qn par la main; fig (give support) [*person*] tenir la main à qn; **to do** *ou* **make sth by ~** faire qch à la main; **the letter was delivered by ~** la lettre a été remise en mains propres; **'by ~'** (on envelope) 'par porteur'; **to have one's ~s full** lit avoir les mains pleines; fig avoir assez à faire; **to give sb a (helping) ~** donner un coup de main à qn; **~s up, or I shoot!** les mains en l'air, ou je tire!; **to be on one's ~s and knees** être à quatre pattes; **we can always use another pair of ~s** une autre paire de bras ne serait pas de trop; (round of applause) **to give sb a big ~** applaudir qn très fort; (consent to marriage) **to ask for/win sb's ~ (in marriage)** demander/obtenir la main de qn (en mariage); **to be in**

sb's ~s être entre les mains de qn; **to change ~s** changer de mains; **I got the information first/second ~** j'ai eu l'information de première main/par l'intermédiaire de quelqu'un; **to fall** *ou* **get into sb's ~s** tomber entre les mains de qn; **to fall** *ou* **get into the wrong ~s** tomber en mauvaises mains; **in the right ~s this information could be useful** en bonnes mains, cette information pourrait être utile; **to be in good** *ou* **safe ~s** [*child, money*] être en bonnes mains; **to place** *ou* **put sth in sb's ~s** confier qch à qn [*department, office*]; remettre qch entre les mains de qn [*matter, affair*]; **to play into sb's ~s** jouer le jeu de qn; **his treatment at the ~s of his captors** la façon dont il a été traité par ses ravisseurs; **the matter is out of my ~s** cette affaire n'est plus de mon ressort; **to have sth/sb on one's ~s** avoir qch/qn sur les bras; **to take sb/sth off sb's ~s** débarrasser qch de qn; **to have sth to ~** avoir qch sous la main; **to be on ~** [*person*] être disponible; **the fire extinguisher was close to ~** *ou* **near at ~** l'extincteur n'était pas loin; **to grab the first coat that comes to ~** attraper n'importe quel manteau; **~s off**○! pas touche○!; ② (control) **to get out of ~** [*inflation*] déraper; [*children, fans*] devenir incontrôlable; [*demonstration, party*] dégénérer; **things are getting out of ~** on est en train de perdre le contrôle de la situation; **to take sth/sb in ~** prendre qch/qn en main [*situation, person*]; ③ (writing) écriture *f*; ④ Games (cards dealt) jeu *m*; (game) partie *f*; **to show one's ~** lit, fig montrer son jeu; ⑤ (worker) gén ouvrier/-ière *m/f*; Naut membre *m* de l'équipage; ⑥ (skill) **to try one's ~ at sth** s'essayer à; **to set** *ou* **turn one's ~ to sth/doing** entreprendre qch/de faire; **to keep/get one's ~ in** garder/se faire la main; ⑦ (pointer) (on clock, dial) aiguille *f*; ⑧ (aspect, side) **on the one ~..., on the other ~...** d'une part... d'autre part...; **on the other ~** (conversely) par contre
B *vtr* **to ~ sb sth, to ~ sth to sb** donner qch à qn
C **in hand** *adj phr* ① (current) en cours; **the job/matter in ~** le travail/l'affaire en cours; **the preparations are well in ~** les préparatifs sont bien avancés; ② (to spare) **she finished the exam with 20 minutes in ~** elle a terminé l'examen avec 20 minutes d'avance; **I'll do it when I have some time in ~** je le ferai quand j'aurai du temps devant moi
D **out of hand** *adv phr* [*reject*] d'emblée
(Idioms) **to have a ~ in sth** prendre part à qch; **to know sth like the back of one's ~** connaître qch comme le dos de la main; **many ~s make light work** plus on est nombreux plus ça va vite; **I could do that with one ~ tied behind my back!** je pourrais le faire les doigts dans le nez○!; **you've got to ~ it to her/them...** il faut lui/leur faire cette justice...; **he never does a ~'s turn** il ne remue pas le petit doigt; **to stay** *ou* **hold one's ~** patienter; **to win ~s down** gagner haut la main
(Phrasal verbs)
■ **hand back**: ▸ ~ **[sth] back**, ~ **back [sth]** rendre
■ **hand down**: ▸ ~ **[sth] down**, ~ **down [sth]** lit passer [*object*]; fig transmettre [*property, skill*]
■ **hand in**: ▸ ~ **[sth] in**, ~ **in [sth]** remettre [*form, petition, ticket*] (**to** à); rendre [*homework, keys*]
■ **hand out**: ▸ ~ **[sth] out**, ~ **out [sth]** distribuer
■ **hand over**: ▸ ~ **over [sb]** TV, Radio passer l'antenne à [*reporter*]; passer la main à [*deputy, successor*]; (on telephone) **I'll just ~ you over to Rosie** je te passe Rosie; ▸ ~ **over [sth]**, ~ **[sth] over** rendre [*weapon*]; céder [*territory, title, business*]; transmettre [*power*]; remettre [*keys, money*]; ▸ ~ **[sb] over**, ~ **over [sb]** (transfer) livrer [*prisoner*]; confier [*child, patient*]
■ **hand round**: ▸ ~ **[sth] round**, ~ **round [sth]** faire circuler [*leaflets, drinks, sandwiches*]

hand: ~**bag** *n* sac *m* à main; ~ **baggage** *n* bagage *m* à main

handball /'hændbɔːl/ *n* Sport ① ▸ p. 881 Sport handball *m*; ② (fault in football) faute *f* de main

hand: ~**basin** *n* lavabo *m*; ~**bell** *n* clochette *f*; ~**bill** *n* prospectus *m*; ~**book** *n* (textbook) manuel *m*; (technical manual) livret *m* technique; (guide) guide *m*; ~**brake** *n* Aut frein *m* à main; ~**cart** *n* charrette *f* à bras; ~ **cream** *n* crème *f* pour les mains

handcuff /'hændkʌf/
A **handcuffs** *npl* menottes *fpl*
B *vtr* passer les menottes à [*person*]; **to ~ sb to sth** attacher qn à qch avec des menottes

hand-dryer, hand-drier /'hændraɪə(r)/ *n* sèche-mains *m inv*

handful /'hændfʊl/ n **1** (fistful) poignée f; **2** (small number) (of people) poignée f; (of buildings, objects, works) petit nombre m; **3** ○(person, animal) **to be a ~** être épuisant

hand: **~ grenade** n grenade f (à main); **~gun** n arme f de poing; **~-held** adj [camera] de reportage; [tool] à main; [device] portatif/-ive; [computer] de poche

handicap /'hændɪkæp/
A n gen, Sport handicap m
B vtr (p prés etc **-pp-**) gen, Sport handicaper

handicapped /'hændɪkæpt/ adj [person] handicapé; **mentally/physically ~ children** des enfants handicapés mentaux/physiques

handicraft /'hændɪkrɑːft, US 'hændkræft/ n **1** (object) objet m artisanal; **'~s'** (sign on shop) 'artisanat' m; **2** (skill) travail m artisanal

handily /'hændɪlɪ/ adv [located] bien (before adj)

hand in hand adv lit [run, walk] la main dans la main; **to go ~** fig aller de pair

handiwork /'hændɪwɜːk/ n gen ouvrage m; iron œuvre f

handkerchief /'hæŋkətʃɪf, -tʃiːf/ n mouchoir m

handle /'hændl/
A n **1** (on door, drawer, bag) poignée f; (on bucket, cup, basket) anse f; (on frying pan) queue f; (on saucepan, cutlery, hammer, spade) manche m; (on wheelbarrow, pump) bras m; **2** fig (hold) **to get a ~ on sb** comprendre qn
B vtr **1** (touch) manipuler [explosives, samples, food]; manier [gun, tool]; **to ~ sb gently/roughly** traiter qn gentiment/rudement; **to ~ sth gently/roughly** manier qch délicatement/brutalement; **to ~ stolen goods** faire du trafic de marchandises volées; **'~ with care'** 'fragile'; **to ~ the ball** (in football) faire une faute de main; **2** (manage) manier [horse]; manœuvrer [car]; **to know how to ~ children** savoir s'y prendre avec les enfants; **he's hard to ~** il n'a pas un caractère facile; **3** (deal with) traiter [case, negotiations]; faire face à [situation, crisis]; supporter [stress, pace]; **4** (process) [organization] traiter [money, clients, order]; [airport, port] accueillir [passengers, cargo]; [factory] traiter [waste]; [person] manier [information, money, accounts]; [computer] manipuler [graphics, information]; [department, official] s'occuper de [complaints, enquiries]; [agent] s'occuper de [sale]; [lawyer] s'occuper de [case]; traiter [theme]
C vi Aut **the car ~s well/badly** la voiture manœuvre bien/mal
(Idioms) **to fly off the ~**○ piquer une crise○; **to be too hot to ~** (of situation) être trop risqué

handle: **~bar moustache** n moustache f en crocs; **~bars** npl guidon m

handler /'hændlə(r)/ n **1** (of dog) maître-chien m; (of other animals) dresseur/-euse m/f; **2** (adviser) (of star) agent m; (of politician) conseiller/-ère m/f

handling /'hændlɪŋ/ n **1** (holding, touching) (of food, waste) manipulation f; (of tool, weapon) maniement m; **old books require careful ~** les livres anciens doivent être manipulés avec soin; **2** (way of dealing) **her ~ of the theme** sa façon de traiter le thème; **the bank's ~ of the affair** la façon dont la banque a traité l'affaire; **their ~ of the economy** leur gestion de l'économie; **3** Comm (storage, shipping) manutention f; **4** (processing) (of data, documents) traitement m; (of process, business) gestion f; **5** (training) **dog ~** entraînement m des chiens

handling charge n **1** Comm frais mpl de manutention; **2** Admin, Fin frais mpl administratifs

hand: **~ lotion** n lotion f pour les mains; **~ luggage** n bagage m à main; **~made** adj fait à la main; **~maid**, **~maiden‡** n servante f; **~-me-down**○ n vieux vêtement m

handout /'hændaʊt/ n **1** (payment) péj (welfare) allocation f; (subsidy) subvention f; (charitable) don m; **to live off/rely on ~s** vivre de/dépendre de la charité des autres; **2** (document) document m; (leaflet) prospectus m

hand: **~over** n (of property, power, territory) transfert m; (of prisoner, ransom) remise f; **~pick** vtr choisir [qch] soi-même [produce]; trier [qn] sur le volet [staff]; **~rail** n (on stairs) rampe f; (on balcony, pier) garde-fou m; **~-reared** adj [animal] élevé au biberon; **~set** n Telecom combiné m; **~s-free headset** n Telecom (for mobile phone) kit m mains libres piéton; **~s-free kit** n Aut, Telecom kit m mains libres conducteur; **~shake** n poignée f de main; **~ signal** n gen, Aut signe m de la main; **~s-off** adj

[manager] qui pratique la délégation du pouvoir; [policy] de non-intervention

handsome /'hænsəm/ adj **1** (fine) [person, town, building] beau/belle; **2** (appreciable) [dividend] [sum] beau/belle; [reward] généreux/-euse

handsomely /'hænsəmlɪ/ adv (amply) **to pay off ~** [investment] être d'un bon rapport; **to be ~ rewarded** recevoir une généreuse récompense

hand: **~s-on** adj [experience, manager] de terrain; [control] direct; [approach] pragmatique; **~spring** n saut m de mains, salto m; **~stand** n Sport équilibre m; **~-to-hand** adj, adv corps à corps; **~-to-mouth** adj précaire; **~ towel** n essuie-mains m inv; **~-woven** adj tissé à la main; **~writing** n écriture f; **~written** adj manuscrit

handy /'hændɪ/ adj **1** (useful) [book, skill] utile; [tool, pocket] pratique; **to come in ~ for sb/sth/doing** servir à qn/qch/faire; **that's ~ to know** c'est bon à savoir; **2** (convenient) [format, shape, size] pratique; [location] bon/bonne; [shop] bien situé; **to keep/have sth ~** garder/avoir qch sous la main [keys, passport]; **3** ○(skilful) [player] doué (**at doing** pour faire); **to be ~ with a paintbrush** savoir se servir d'un pinceau

handyman /'hændɪmæn/ n bricoleur m, homme m à tout faire

hang /hæŋ/
A n **1** (of garment) tombant m; **2** ○(knack) **to get the ~ of sth**○/**of doing**○ piger○ qch/comment faire; **you're getting the ~ of it** tu as pigé○
B vtr (prét, pp **hung**) **1** (suspend) (from projection, hook, coat-hanger) accrocher (**from** à; **by** par; **on** à); (from string, rope) suspendre (**from** à); (drape over) étendre, mettre (**over** sur); (peg up) étendre [washing] (**on** sur); **2** (also **~ down**) (let dangle) suspendre [rope, line etc] (**out of** par); laisser pendre [arm, leg]; **to ~ one's head in shame** baisser la tête de honte; **3** (decorate with) **to be hung with** être orné de [flags, tapestries]; être décoré de [garlands]; **4** (interior decorating) poser [wallpaper]; **5** Constr, Tech poser [door, gate]; **6** (prét, pp **hanged**) pendre [criminal, victim]
C vi (prét, pp **hung**) **1** (be suspended) (on hook) être accroché; (from height) être suspendu; (on washing line) être étendu; [arm, leg] pendre; **her arm hung over the arm of the chair** son bras pendait de l'accoudoir; **my feet ~ over the end** mes pieds dépassent; **the children were ~ing out of the window** les enfants se penchaient à la fenêtre; **2** (drape) [curtain, garment] tomber; **3** (float) [fog, cloud, smoke, smell] flotter; **4** (die) être pendu (**for** pour)
D v refl (prét, pp **hanged**) **to ~ oneself** se pendre (**from** à)
(Idioms) **~ the expense**○! au diable la dépense!; **~ed if I know**○! je n'en sais fichtre rien○!; **to let it all ~ out**○ être relax○; ▸ **sheep**

(Phrasal verbs)
■ **hang around**○: ▸ **~** (also **~ about**) (wait) attendre (aimlessly) traîner; **to ~ around with sb** passer son temps avec qn; ▸ **~ around [sb]** (inflict oneself on) être toujours à tourner autour○ de qn
■ **hang back** (in fear) rester derrière; (waiting) rester; (reluctant) lit rester à la traîne; fig être réticent
■ **hang down** pendre; [hem] être défait
■ **hang on**: ▸ **~ on 1** (wait) attendre; **2** ○(survive) tenir○; **~ on in there**○! tiens bon!; ▸ **~ on [sth] 1** (depend on) dépendre de; **2** (listen attentively) **to ~ on sb's every word** être pendu aux lèvres de qn
■ **hang on to**: ▸ **~ on to [sth/sb] 1** (hold) s'agripper à [object, rail]; agripper [person]; **~ on to your hat!** lit tiens bien ton chapeau!; fig accroche-toi!; **2** ○fig (retain) s'accrocher à○ [possession, power]
■ **hang out**: ▸ **~ out 1** (protrude) dépasser; **2** ○(live) crécher○; **3** ○(sit around) traîner○; ▸ **~ out [sth], ~ [sth] out** étendre [washing]; accrocher [sign]; sortir [flag]
■ **hang over**: ▸ **~ over [sb/sth]** [threat, suspicion] planer sur [person, project]
■ **hang together** (be consistent) se tenir
■ **hang up**: ▸ **~ up** (on phone) raccrocher; **to ~ up on sb** raccrocher au nez de qn; ▸ **~ up [sth], ~ [sth] up 1** (on hook) accrocher; (on hanger, string) suspendre; (on line) étendre; **2** fig, hum **to ~ up one's skis** mettre ses skis au rancart

hangar /'hæŋə(r)/ n hangar m

hangdog /'hæŋdɒg/ adj [expression, look] de chien battu

hanger /'hæŋə(r)/ n **1** (coat hanger) cintre m; **2** (loop) boucle f

hanger-on° /ˌhæŋərˈɒn/ n parasite m

hang: **∼-glider** n (craft) deltaplane m; (pilot) deltaplaniste mf; **∼-gliding** ► p. 881 n deltaplane m

hanging /ˈhæŋɪŋ/

A n **1** (strangulation) pendaison f; **2** (curtain) rideau m; (on wall) tenture f; **3** (suspending) (of picture) accrochage m; (wallpaper) pose f

B adj Jur [offence] passible de pendaison

hanging basket /ˈhæŋɪŋ/ n panier m suspendu

hangman /ˈhæŋmən/ n **1** (at gallows) bourreau m; **2** ► p. 881 (game) potence f

hangover /ˈhæŋəʊvə(r)/ n **1** (from drink) gueule f de bois°; **2** fig (legacy) héritage m (**from** de)

hang-up° /ˈhæŋʌp/ n complexe m, problème m

hank /hæŋk/ n (of wool etc) écheveau m

hanker /ˈhæŋkə(r)/ vi to ∼ after rêver de

hankering /ˈhæŋkərɪŋ/ n grande envie f (**for** de)

hanky, **hankie**° /ˈhæŋkɪ/ n mouchoir m

hanky-panky° /ˌhæŋkɪˈpæŋkɪ/ n hum (sexual) polissonneries fpl; (dishonest) friponneries fpl

Hants n GB Post abrév écrite = **Hampshire**

ha'penny /ˈheɪpnɪ/ n GB abrév ► **halfpenny**

haphazard /hæpˈhæzəd/ adj peu méthodique

haphazardly /hæpˈhæzədlɪ/ adv n'importe comment

hapless /ˈhæplɪs/ adj littér pauvre, infortuné

happen /ˈhæpən/ vi **1** (occur) arriver, se passer, se produire; **what's ∼ing?** qu'est-ce qui se passe?; **the accident ∼ed yesterday** l'accident est arrivé or s'est produit hier; **we must make sure this never ∼s again** nous devons faire en sorte que cela ne se reproduise jamais; **he reacted as if nothing had ∼ed** il a réagi comme si de rien n'était; **whatever ∼s, don't get out of the car** quoi qu'il arrive, ne sors pas de la voiture; **it had to ∼**, **it was bound to ∼** GB ça devait arriver; **anything might ∼!** il faut s'attendre à tout!; **she's the sort of person who makes things ∼** elle fait bouger les choses; **2** (befall) to ∼ **to sb** arriver à qn; **if anything ∼s to her**... si quoi que ce soit lui arrive...; **3** (occur by chance) **there ∼s to be a free parking space** il se trouve qu'il y a une place libre; **it so ∼s that**... il se trouve que...; **as it ∼ed**, **the weather that day was bad** il s'est trouvé qu'il faisait mauvais ce jour-là; **if you ∼ to see her say hello** si par hasard tu la vois, salue-la de ma part; **4** (become of) devenir; **what will ∼ to the children?** que deviendront les enfants?; **5** (used assertively) **he just ∼s to be the best actor in Britain!** il se trouve que c'est le meilleur acteur de Grande-Bretagne!; **I ∼ to think that**... je trouve que...

(Phrasal verb)

■ **happen on**: ► ∼ **on [sth]** tomber sur [qch] [object]

happening /ˈhæpənɪŋ/ n (occurrence) incident m

happily /ˈhæpɪlɪ/ adv **1** (cheerfully) [laugh, chat, play, say] joyeusement; **a ∼ married man** un mari heureux; **they all lived ∼ ever after** ils vécurent heureux jusqu'à la fin de leurs jours; **2** (luckily) heureusement; **3** (willingly) [admit, agree, leave] volontiers; **4** (successfully) avec bonheur

happiness /ˈhæpɪnɪs/ n bonheur m

happy /ˈhæpɪ/ adj **1** (cheerful) [life, memory, person] heureux/-euse (**about** de; **with sb** avec qn; **that** que + subj); **to be ∼ doing** bien aimer faire; **2** (pleased) content; **to be ∼ with sth** être satisfait de qch; **he's not ∼ about it** il n'est pas content; **to keep sb ∼** faire plaisir à qn; **3** (willing) **to be ∼ to do** être heureux/-euse de faire; **he's quite ∼ to leave on Monday** cela ne le dérange pas de partir lundi; **4** (in greetings) **Happy birthday!** Bon anniversaire!; **Happy Christmas!** Joyeux Noël!; **Happy New Year!** Bonne année!; **5** (fortunate) [choice, phrase] heureux/-euse; **he's in the ∼ position of having no debts** il a la chance de ne pas avoir de dettes

(Idiom) **to be as ∼ as Larry** ou **as a sandboy** GB être heureux comme un poisson dans l'eau

happy couple n **the ∼** les mariés mpl

happy ending n heureux dénouement m

happy: **∼-go-lucky** adj insouciant; **∼ hour** n: dans un bar, période durant laquelle les boissons sont vendues à prix réduit; **∼ hunting ground** n paradis m; **∼ medium** n juste milieu m

harangue /həˈræŋ/

A n (political) harangue f; (moral) sermon m

B vtr (p prés **haranguing**) (politically) haranguer; (morally) sermonner

harass /ˈhærəs, US həˈræs/

A vtr harceler

B **harassed** pp adj excédé

harassment /ˈhærəsmənt, US ˌhəˈræsmənt/ n harcèlement m; **racial ∼** persécution f raciste

harbinger /ˈhɑːbɪndʒə(r)/ n signe m annonciateur

harbour GB, **harbor** US /ˈhɑːbə(r)/

A n port m

B vtr **1** (nurse) nourrir [emotion, suspicion, illusion]; **2** (shelter illegally) receler [criminal]

hard /hɑːd/

A adj **1** (firm) dur; **to go** ou **grow** ou **become ∼** durcir; **a ∼ frost** une forte gelée; **frozen ∼** complètement gelé; ► **hard lens**; **2** (difficult) [problem, question, task] dur, difficile; [choice, decision] difficile; [bargaining, negotiations, fight] dur, serré; **I've had a ∼ day** j'ai eu une dure journée; **to be ∼ to open** être dur or difficile à ouvrir; **to be ∼ to please** être exigeant; **it's ∼ to do** c'est dur or difficile à faire; **it was ∼ for us to understand his decision** il nous était difficile de comprendre sa décision; **to find it ∼ to do sth** avoir du mal à faire qch, trouver dur or difficile de faire qch; **it's ∼ to accept/believe** on a du mal à accepter/croire (**that** que); **I'm not afraid of ∼ work** le travail ne me fait pas peur; **it was ∼ work** ou **going** ça a été dur or difficile; **∼ work never hurt** ou **killed anybody!** le travail n'a jamais fait de mal à personne!; **it's too much like ∼ work** c'est trop fatigant; **to be a ∼ worker** être travailleur/-euse; **to do things the ∼ way** se compliquer la tâche; **to find sth out** ou **learn sth the ∼ way** apprendre qch à ses dépens; **3** (harsh) [life, year] difficile; [blow] fig dur, terrible; [winter] rude; **to be ∼ on sb** être dur envers qn; **this tax is very ∼ on the unemployed** cet impôt frappe durement les chômeurs; **∼ luck** ou **lines**° GB! pas de chance!; **to take a ∼ line** adopter une attitude ferme (**on sth** à propos de qch; **with sb** envers qn); **it's a ∼ life** gen, hum, iron la vie est dure; **no ∼ feelings!** sans rancune!; **I bear her no ∼ feelings** je ne lui en veux pas; **to fall on ∼ times** connaître des temps difficiles; **he's having a ∼ time (of it)** il traverse une période difficile; **to give sb a ∼ time**° (make things difficult) rendre la vie impossible à qn; (tell off) passer un savon° à qn; **4** (stern, cold) [person, look, words] dur, sévère; **5** (concrete) [evidence, fact] solide; **6** (stark) [colour, light] dur; **7** (strong) [liquor] fort; [drug] dur; [pornography] hard° (inv); **to be a ∼ drinker** boire des alcools forts; **8** Pol **the ∼ left/right** la gauche/droite (pure et) dure; **9** Chem [water] dur, calcaire; **10** Ling [consonant] dur; **11** °(tough) [person] dur; **12** Fin [currency] fort

B adv **1** (strongly, energetically) [push, hit, cry] fort; [work] dur; [study, think] sérieusement; [rain] à verse; [snow] abondamment; [look, listen] attentivement; **to ∼ hit** fig être durement frappé (**by** par); **to try ∼** (intellectually) faire beaucoup d'efforts; (physically) essayer de toutes ses forces; **no matter how ∼ I try/work, I**... j'ai beau essayer/travailler, je...; **to be ∼ at it**° ou **at work** être en plein travail; **to take sth (very) ∼** prendre (très) mal qch; **2** (with directions) **turn ∼ left** at the traffic lights aux feux tournez tout de suite à gauche; **∼ behind** juste derrière; ► **heel**

(Idioms) **to play ∼ to get** se faire désirer; **to be ∼ put to do** avoir du mal à faire; **to be/feel ∼ done by** être/se sentir brimé

hard and fast adj [rule, distinction, category] absolu

hardback /ˈhɑːdbæk/

A n livre m relié; **in ∼** en édition reliée

B noun modifier [book] cartonné, relié

hardball /ˈhɑːdbɔːl/ ► p. 881 n US Sport baseball m

hard: **∼bitten** adj [person] endurci; **∼board** n aggloméré m

hard-boiled /ˌhɑːdˈbɔɪld/ adj **1** lit [egg] dur; **2** fig [person] endurci

hard: **∼ cash** n (argent m) liquide m; **∼ copy** n Comput tirage m

hard core

A n **1** (of group, demonstrators) noyau m dur; **2** Constr remblai m

B **hard-core** adj **1** (established) [supporter, opponent, protest] irréductible; **2** (extreme) [pornography, video] hard° (inv)

hard: **∼ court** n Sport court m en dur; **∼ disk** n Comput disque m dur; **∼-drinking** adj qui boit beaucoup;

~-earned *adj* [*cash*] durement gagné
harden /'hɑːdn/
A *vtr* **1** lit gen (faire) durcir; **2** fig endurcir [*person*] (**to** à); renforcer [*resolve*]; durcir [*attitude*]; **to ~ one's heart** s'endurcir (**to** à)
B *vi* **1** lit durcir; **2** fig [*voice, stance*] se durcir
hardened /'hɑːdnd/ *adj* **1** lit [*glue, clay*] durci; **2** fig [*criminal*] endurci; [*drinker, addict*] invétéré; **to become ~ to** s'accoutumer à
hard: **~-faced** *adj* lit [*person*] aux traits durs; fig froid; **~-fought** *adj* [*battle*] âprement mené; [*election, competition*] âprement disputé; **~ hat** *n* (helmet) gen casque *m*; (for riding) bombe *f*; **~-headed** *adj* réaliste; **~-hearted** *adj* insensible; **~-hitting** *adj* [*speech, criticism*] musclé; [*report*] très critique; **~ labour** GB, **~ labor** US *n* travaux *mpl* forcés; **~ lens** *n* lentille *f* de contact rigide
hardline *adj* [*policy*] (très) ferme; [*communist, conservative, regime*] intransigeant; **~ approach** jusqu'au-boutisme *m*
hardliner *n* jusqu'au-boutiste *mf*; Pol partisan/-e *m/f* de la ligne dure
hard-luck story *n* **to tell** *ou* **give sb a ~** raconter ses malheurs à qn pour essayer de l'attendrir
hardly /'hɑːdlɪ/ *adv* **1** (only just, barely) [*begin, know, see*] à peine; **~ had they set off than** à peine étaient-ils partis que; **2** (not really) [*expect, hope*] difficilement; **it's ~ a secret!** c'est loin d'être un secret!; **it's ~ likely** c'est peu probable; **it's ~ surprising** ce n'est guère étonnant; **~!** certainement pas!; **I need ~ remind you that** inutile de vous rappeler que; **I can ~ wait!** gen il me tarde d'y être; iron je meurs d'envie d'y être; **I can ~ believe it!** j'ai peine à le croire!; **3** (almost not) **~ any/ever/anybody** presque pas/jamais/personne
hardness /'hɑːdnɪs/ *n* dureté *f*
hard-nosed /ˌhɑːd'nəʊzd/ *adj* (unsentimental) [*person*] résolu; pej [*attitude, businessman, government*] dur
hard of hearing *adj* **to be ~** entendre mal
hard porn○ *n* hard○ *m*
hard-pressed /ˌhɑːd'prest/, **hard-pushed** /ˌhɑːd'pʊʃt/ *adj* gen en difficulté; (for time) pressé; **to be ~ to do** avoir du mal à faire
hard rock *n* Mus hard rock *m*, hard *m*
hard sell *n* vente *f* selon des méthodes agressives; **to give sb the ~** essayer de forcer qn à acheter
hardship /'hɑːdʃɪp/ *n* **1** **¢** (difficulty) détresse *f*; (poverty) privations *fpl*; **2** **C** (ordeal) épreuve *f*
hard: **~ shoulder** *n* GB bande *f* d'arrêt d'urgence; **~ standing** *n* place *f* de stationnement
hard up○ /ˌhɑːd'ʌp/ *adj* fauché○; **~ for** à court de
hardware /'hɑːdweə(r)/ *n* **1** Comput matériel *m* (informatique), hardware *m*; **2** Mil équipement *m*; **3** (household goods) articles *mpl* de quincaillerie
hard: **~ware shop**, **~ware store** ▸ p. 1181 *n* quincaillerie *f*; **~-wearing** *adj* résistant; **~-won** *adj* durement acquis; **~wood** *n* bois *m* dur, bois *m* de feuillu; **~-working** *adj* travailleur/-euse
hardy /'hɑːdɪ/ *adj* [*person*] robuste; [*plant*] résistant
hare /heə(r)/ *n* Zool, Culin lièvre *m*
(Idiom) **to be as mad as a March ~** être complètement toqué○
(Phrasal verb)
■ **hare off** GB partir en trombe○
hare: **~brained** *adj* [*person*] écervelé; [*scheme*] farfelu○; **~lip** *n* bec-de-lièvre *m*
haricot /'hærɪkəʊ/ *n* GB (also **~ bean**) (dried) haricot *m* blanc; (fresh) haricot *m* vert
hark /hɑːk/ *v*
■ **hark back to**: ▸ **~ back to [sth]** (recall) rappeler; (evoke) [*style, song*] évoquer
harm /hɑːm/
A *n* mal *m*; **to do ~ to sb, to do sb ~** faire du mal à qn; **to do ~ to sth** endommager qch; **I meant no ~ (by it)** je n'ai pas dit ça méchamment; **it would do no ~ to do** tu ne ferais *or* on ferait mieux de faire; **you'll come to no ~** il ne t'arrivera rien; **no ~ done!** il n'y a pas de mal!; **where's the ~ in it?** quel mal y a-t-il à ça?; **out of ~'s way** en sûreté
B *vtr* faire du mal à [*person, baby*]; endommager [*crops, lungs*]; nuire à [*population, economy*]

harmful /'hɑːmfl/ *adj* [*bacteria, chemical, ray*] nocif/-ive; [*behaviour, gossip, allegation*] nuisible (**to** pour)
harmless /'hɑːmlɪs/ *adj* **1** (not dangerous) [*chemical, virus*] inoffensif/-ive (**to** pour); [*growth, cyst*] bénin/bénigne; [*rash, bite*] sans danger; **2** (inoffensive) [*person*] inoffensif/-ive; [*fun, joke*] innocent
harmonica /hɑːˈmɒnɪkə/ ▸ p. 1028 *n* harmonica *m*
harmonious /hɑːˈməʊnɪəs/ *adj* harmonieux/-ieuse
harmonize /'hɑːmənaɪz/
A *vtr* harmoniser
B *vi* **1** [*law, practice, people*] s'accorder; [*colour*] se marier; **2** Mus jouer *or* chanter *or* être en harmonie
harmony /'hɑːmənɪ/ *n* harmonie *f*
harness /'hɑːnɪs/
A *n* (for horse, dog, person) harnais *m*; **I'm back in ~** j'ai repris le collier
B *vtr* **1** (put harness on) harnacher; **2** (attach) atteler [*animal*] (**to** à); **3** (use) exploiter [*power*]
harp /hɑːp/ ▸ p. 1028 *n* harpe *f*
(Phrasal verb)
■ **harp on** péj rabâcher○ toujours la même chose sur [*issue, event*]
harpist /'hɑːpɪst/ ▸ p. 1181 *n* harpiste *mf*
harpoon /hɑːˈpuːn/
A *n* harpon *m*
B *vtr* harponner
harpsichord /'hɑːpsɪkɔːd/ ▸ p. 1028 *n* clavecin *m*
harpy /'hɑːpɪ/ *n* Mythol harpie *f*; péj mégère *f* pej
harridan /'hærɪdən/ *n* péj mégère *f* pej
harrow /'hærəʊ/ *n* Agric herse *f*
harrowing /'hærəʊɪŋ/ *adj* [*experience, ordeal*] atroce; [*film, story, image*] déchirant
harry /'hærɪ/ *vtr* (pursue, harass) harceler
harsh /hɑːʃ/ *adj* **1** (severe, cruel) [*punishment, measures*] sévère; [*regime, person*] dur; [*conditions*] difficile; **to have ~ words for sb/sth** critiquer qn/qch; **2** (unpleasant) [*light, colour*] cru; [*voice, sound*] rude; **3** (strong) [*chemical, cleaner*] corrosif/-ive
harshly /'hɑːʃlɪ/ *adv* [*treat, judge, speak*] durement; [*punish, condemn*] sévèrement
harshness /'hɑːʃnɪs/ *n* (of punishment, law, regime) sévérité *f*; (of criticism) dureté *f*; (of climate) rigueur *f*; (of conditions) difficulté *f*; (of sound) rudesse *f*
harvest /'hɑːvɪst/
A *n* (of wheat, fruit) récolte *f*; (of grapes) vendange *f*; **to get in the ~** faire la récolte; **to reap a rich ~** fig récolter les fruits de ses efforts; **to reap a bitter ~** fig payer les pots cassés
B *vtr* **1** lit moissonner [*corn*]; récolter [*vegetables*]; cueillir [*fruit*]; **2** fig (collect) récolter [*information*]
C *vi* faire la récolte; (of grapes) faire la vendange
harvester /'hɑːvɪstə(r)/ *n* **1** (machine) moissonneuse *f*; **2** (person) moissonneur/-euse *m/f*
harvest festival /'hɑːvɪst/ *n* fête *f* de la moisson
has ▸ **have**
has-been○ /'hæzbiːn/ *n* péj homme fini/femme finie *m/f*
hash /hæʃ/ *n* **1** Culin hachis *m*; **2** ○(mess) **to make a ~ of sth** râter qch
hash browns *npl* US pommes *fpl* de terre sautées
hasn't = has not
hassle○ /'hæsl/
A *n* complications *fpl*; **to cause (sb) ~** créer des complications (à qn); **it was a real ~** c'était vraiment embêtant○; **to give sb ~** embêter qn○ (**about** à propos de)
B *vtr* talonner (**about** à propos de); **~d** stressé
haste /heɪst/ *n* hâte *f*; **to act in ~** agir à la hâte; **to make ~** se dépêcher (**to do** de faire); **with undue ~** avec une hâte excessive
(Idiom) **more ~ less speed** hâte-toi lentement
hasten /'heɪsn/
A *vtr* accélérer [*ageing, destruction*]; précipiter [*departure, death, decline*]
B *vi* se hâter; **to ~ to do** s'empresser de faire
hastily /'heɪstɪlɪ/ *adv* [*do*] à la hâte; [*say*] précipitamment; **too ~** avec trop de précipitation
hasty /'heɪstɪ/ *adj* **1** (hurried) [*talks, marriage, departure*] précipité; [*meal*] rapide; [*note, sketch*] fait à la hâte; **to beat a**

~ **retreat** hum se sauver; **2** (rash) [*decision*] inconsidéré; [*judgment, conclusion*] hâtif/-ive; **to be too ~ in doing** aller trop vite en besogne en faisant

hat /hæt/ n chapeau m; **to draw the winners out of a ~** déterminer les gagnants par un tirage au sort

(Idioms) **at the drop of a ~** pour un oui, pour un non; **old ~ dépassé; I'll eat my ~ (if he wins)!** je vous parie tout ce que vous voulez (qu'il ne gagnera pas)!; **to keep sth under one's ~** garder qch pour soi; **to pass the ~ around** faire la quête; **to put** ou **throw one's ~ into the ring** se porter candidat; **to take one's ~ off to sb** fig tirer son chapeau à qn; **to talk through one's ~** parler à tort et à travers

hat: **~band** n ruban m de chapeau; **~box** n carton m à chapeau

hatch /hætʃ/
A n **1** Aviat, Aerosp panneau m mobile; Naut écoutille f; Aut portière f; **2** (in dining room) passe-plats m inv
B vtr **1** (incubate) faire éclore [*eggs*]; **2** (plan secretly) tramer [*plot, scheme*]
C vi [*chicks, fish eggs*] éclore
(Idiom) **down the ~!** cul sec!; ▶ **chicken**

hatchback /'hætʃbæk/ n (car) voiture f avec hayon; (car door) hayon m

hatchet /'hætʃɪt/ n hachette f
(Idiom) **to bury the ~** faire la paix

hate /heɪt/
A n haine f; ▶ **pet hate**
B vtr **1** (feel antagonism towards) détester; (violently) haïr; **to ~ sb for sth/for doing** en vouloir à qn de qch/d'avoir fait; **he's someone you love to ~** c'est quelqu'un sur qui on aime bien taperᴼ; **2** (not enjoy) avoir horreur de [*sport, food, activity*]; **I ~ it when** je ne supporte pas quand; **3** (regret) (in apology) **to ~ to do, to ~ doing** être désolé de faire

hated /'heɪtɪd/ adj détesté

hateful /'heɪtfl/ adj odieux/-ieuse (**to** avec)

hate mail n lettres fpl d'injures

hatpin /'hætpɪn/ n épingle f à chapeau

hatred /'heɪtrɪd/ n (of person, group, system, war) haine f (**of** de; **for** pour); (less violent) aversion f (**of** pour)

hat: **~ stand** GB, **~ tree** US n portemanteau m (sur pied); **~ trick** n Sport triplé m

haughtily /'hɔːtɪlɪ/ adv avec hauteur

haughtiness /'hɔːtɪnɪs/ n hauteur f

haughty /'hɔːtɪ/ adj [*person*] hautain; [*manner*] altier/-ière

haul /hɔːl/
A n **1** (taken by criminals) butin m; **a £2m ~** un butin d'une valeur de 2 millions de livres; **2** (found by police, customs) saisie f; **arms/heroin ~** saisie d'armes/d'héroïne; **3** (journey) **it will be a long ~** lit, fig l'étape sera longue; **the long ~ from Dublin to London** le long voyage de Dublin à Londres; **4** (in transportation) courrier m; **long/medium/short ~** long/moyen/court courrier; **5** (of fish) pêche f
B vtr **1** (drag) tirer; **to ~ oneself up on the roof** se hisser sur le toit; **2** (by lorry) transporter
(Idiom) **to ~ sb over the coals** passer un savon à qnᴼ

haulage /'hɔːlɪdʒ/ n **1** (transport) transport m routier; **2** (cost) frais mpl de roulage or de transport

haulier /'hɔːlɪə(r)/ GB, **hauler** /'hɔːlə(r)/ US ▶ p. 1181 n (owner of firm) transporteur m; (firm) société f de transports routiers; (truck driver) routier m

haunch /hɔːntʃ/ n hanche f

haunt /hɔːnt/
A n lieu m de prédilection
B vtr lit, fig hanter; **he is ~ed by the fear of dying** il a la hantise de la mort

haunted /'hɔːntɪd/ adj [*house*] hanté; [*face, look*] tourmenté

haunting /'hɔːntɪŋ/ adj [*film, book, image, music, beauty, doubt*] lancinant; [*memory*] obsédant

Havana /hə'vænə/ ▶ p. 1276
A pr n La Havane f
B n (cigar) havane m

have /hæv, həv/ ▶ p. 912
A vtr (uses not covered in NOTE) **1** (possess) avoir; **she has (got) a dog** elle a un chien; **2** (consume) prendre; **to ~ a sandwich** manger un sandwich; **to ~ a whisky** boire un whisky; **to ~ a cigarette** fumer une cigarette; **to ~ breakfast** prendre le petit déjeuner; **to ~ dinner** dîner; **to**

~ **lunch** déjeuner; **I had some more cake** j'ai repris du gâteau; **3** (want) vouloir, prendre; **what will you ~?** qu'est-ce que vous prendrez or voulez?; **she won't ~ him back** elle ne veut plus de lui; **I wouldn't ~ it any other way** ça me convient comme ça; **I wouldn't ~ him/her any other way** c'est comme ça que je l'aime; **4** (receive, get) recevoir [*letter, information*]; **I've had no news from him** je n'ai pas eu de nouvelles de lui; **I must ~ the information soon** il me faut l'information bientôt; **to let sb ~ sth** donner qch à qn; **5** (hold) faire [*party, celebration*]; tenir [*meeting*]; organiser [*competition, ballot, exhibition*]; avoir [*conversation*]; mener [*enquiry*]; **6** (exert, exhibit) avoir [*effect, influence*]; avoir [*courage, courtesy*] (**to do** de faire); **7** (spend) passer; **to ~ a nice day/evening** passer une journée/soirée agréable; **to ~ a good time** bien s'amuser; **to ~ a hard** ou **bad time** traverser une période difficile; **to ~ a good vacation** passer de bonnes vacances; **8** (be provided with) (also ~ **got**) **to ~ sth to do** avoir qch à faire; **I ~** ou **I've got letters to write** j'ai du courrier à faire; **9** (undergo, suffer) avoir; **to ~ (the) flu/a heart attack** avoir la grippe/une crise cardiaque; **to ~ toothache** avoir mal aux dents; **to ~ a shock** subir un choc; **he had his car stolen** il s'est fait voler sa voiture; **she has had her windows broken** on lui a cassé ses vitres; **they like having stories read to them** ils aiment qu'on leur lise des histoires; **to ~ an interview** avoir or passer un entretien; **10** (cause to be done) **to ~ sth done** faire faire qch; **to ~ the house painted** faire peindre la maison; **to ~ one's hair cut** se faire couper les cheveux; **to ~ an injection** se faire faire une piqûre; **to ~ sb do sth** faire faire qch à qn; **she had him close the door** elle lui a fait fermer la porte; **they would ~ us believe that...** ils voudraient nous faire croire que...; **I would ~ you know that...** je voudrais que vous sachiez que...; **he had them laughing** il les a fait rire; **11** (cause to become) **he had his revolver ready** il avait son revolver prêt; **we'll soon ~ everything ready/clean** nous aurons bientôt fini de tout préparer/nettoyer; **if you're not careful you'll ~ that glass over** si tu ne fais pas attention tu vas renverser le verre; **she had them completely baffled** elle les a complètement déroutés; **I had it finished by 5 o'clock** je l'avais fini avant 5 heures; **12** (allow) tolérer; **I won't ~ this kind of behaviour!** je ne tolérerai pas ce comportement!; **I won't ~ it!** ça ne va pas se passer comme ça!; **I won't ~ them exploit him** je ne tolérerai pas qu'ils l'exploitent; **I won't ~ him hurt** je ne laisserai personne le blesser; **we can't ~ them staying in a hotel** on ne peut pas les laisser aller à l'hôtel; **13** (physically hold) tenir; **she had the glass in her hand** elle tenait le verre dans la main; **she had him by the throat/by the arm** elle le tenait à la gorge/par le bras; **he had his hands over his eyes** il avait les mains sur les yeux; **14** (give birth to) [*woman*] avoir [*child*]; [*animal*] mettre bas, avoir [*young*]; **has she had it yet?** est-ce qu'elle a accouché?; **she's having a baby (in May)** elle va avoir un enfant (en mai); **15** (as impersonal verb) **over here, we ~ a painting by Picasso** ici vous avez un tableau de Picasso; **what we ~ here is a small group of extremists** ce à quoi nous avons affaire ici, est un petit groupe d'extrémistes; **16** (puzzle) **you ~** ou **you've got me there!** là tu me poses une colleᴼ!; **17** (have at one's mercy) (also ~ **got**) **I've got you/him now!** maintenant je te/le tiens!; **I'll ~ you!** je vais te montrer!
B modal aux **1** (must) **I ~ (got) to leave now** je dois partir maintenant, il faut que je parte maintenant; **2** (need to) **you don't ~ to** ou **you haven't got to leave so early** tu n'as pas besoin de or tu n'es pas obligé de partir si tôt; **why did this ~ to happen?** pourquoi fallait-il que ça arrive?; **something has (got) to be done** il faut faire quelque chose; **3** (for emphasis) **this has (got) to be the most difficult decision I've ever made** c'est sans doute la décision la plus difficile que j'aie jamais eu à prendre
C v aux **1** gen avoir; (with movement and reflexive verbs) être; **she has lost her bag** elle a perdu son sac; **she has already left** elle est déjà partie; **she has hurt herself** elle s'est blessée; **2** (in tag questions etc) **you've seen the film, haven't you?** tu as vu le film, n'est-ce pas?; **you haven't seen the film, ~ you?** tu n'as pas vu le film?; **you haven't seen my bag, ~ you?** tu n'as pas vu mon sac, par hasard?; **'he's already left'—'has he indeed!'** 'il est déjà parti'—'vraiment!'; **'you've never met him'—'yes I ~!'** 'tu ne l'as jamais rencontré'—'mais si!'
D having v aux **1** (in time clauses) **having finished his breakfast, he went out** après avoir fini son petit déjeuner, il est

h

have

When used as an auxiliary in present perfect, future perfect and past perfect tenses, *have* is normally translated by *avoir*:

I have seen
= j'ai vu

I had seen
= j'avais vu

However, some verbs in French, especially verbs of movement and change of state (*e.g. aller, venir, descendre, mourir*), take *être* rather than *avoir* in these tenses:

he has left
= il est parti

In this case, remember the past participle agrees with the subject of the verb:

she has gone
= elle est allée

Reflexive verbs (*e.g. se lever, se coucher*) always conjugate with *être*:

she has fainted
= elle s'est évanouie

For translations of time expressions using *for* or *since* (*he has been in London for six months, he has been in London since June*), see the entries **for** and **since**.

For translations of time expressions using *just* (*I have just finished my essay, he has just gone*), see the entry **just**[1].

to have to meaning *must* is translated by either *devoir* or the impersonal construction *il faut que* + subjunctive:

I have to leave now
= il faut que je parte maintenant
or je dois partir maintenant

In negative sentences, *not to have to* is generally translated by *ne pas être obligé de* e.g.

you don't have to go
= tu n'es pas obligé d'y aller

For examples and particular usages see the entry **have**.

When *have* is used as a straightforward transitive verb meaning *possess, have* (or *have got*) can generally be translated by *avoir, e.g.*

I have (got) a car
= j'ai une voiture

she has a good memory
= elle a une bonne mémoire

they have (got) problems
= ils ont des problèmes

For examples and particular usages see entry; see also **got**.

have is also used with certain noun objects where the whole expression is equivalent to a verb:

to have dinner = to dine

to have a try = to try

to have a walk = to walk

In such cases the phrase is very often translated by the equivalent verb in French (*dîner, essayer, se promener*). For translations consult the appropriate noun entry (**dinner, try, walk**).

had is used in English at the beginning of a clause to replace an expression with *if*. Such expressions are generally translated by *si* + past perfect tense, *e.g.*

had I taken the train, this would never have happened
= si j'avais pris le train, ce ne serait jamais arrivé

had there been a fire, we would all have been killed
= s'il y avait eu un incendie, nous serions tous morts

For examples of the above and all other uses of *have* see the entry.

---

sorti; **2** (because, since) **having already won twice** comme il a déjà gagné deux fois

Idioms **to ~ done with sth** en finir avec qch; **this car/TV has had it**○ cette voiture/télé est foutue○; **when your father finds out, you've had it**○! (in trouble) quand ton père l'apprendra, ça va être ta fête○!; **I can't do any more, I've had it**○! (tired) je n'en peux plus, je suis crevé○!; **I've had it (up to here) with...**○ j'en ai marre de...○; **to ~ it in for sb**○ avoir qn dans le collimateur○; **she has/doesn't ~ it in her to do** elle est capable/incapable de faire; **to ~ it out with sb** s'expliquer avec qn; **he will ~ it that** il soutient que; **I've got it!** je sais!; **and the ayes/noes ~ it** les oui/non l'emportent; **the ~s and the ~-nots** les riches et les pauvres; **...and what ~ you** ...etc; **there is no milk/there are no houses to be had** on ne trouve pas de lait/de maisons

Phrasal verbs

■ **have around** US = **have over, have round**

■ **have back** : ▸ **~ [sth] back** (have returned) **when can I ~ my car back?** quand est-ce que tu me rends ma voiture?

■ **have in** : ▸ **~ [sb] in** faire venir [*doctor, priest*]

■ **have on** : ▸ **~ [sth] on, ~ on [sth]** (be wearing) porter [*coat, skirt etc*]; **to ~ (got) nothing on** être nu; ▸ **~ [sth] on** (be busy) avoir [qch] de prévu; ▸ **~ [sb] on**○ (tease) faire marcher○; ▸ **~ sth on sb** (have evidence about) avoir des preuves contre qn

■ **have over, have round** : ▸ **~ [sb] over** inviter [*person*]

■ **have up**○: ▸ **to be had up** être jugé (**for** pour)

haven /'heɪvn/ n **1** (safe place) refuge m (**for** pour); **2** fig havre m; **3** (harbour) port m

haven't = **have not**

haver /'heɪvə(r)/ vi (dither) vaciller

haversack /'hævəsæk/ n gen sac m à dos; Mil musette f

havoc /'hævək/ n dévastation f; **to wreak ~ on** dévaster [*building, landscape*]; **to play ~ with** chambouler [*plans etc*]; **to cause ~** lit provoquer des dégâts; fig tout mettre sens dessus dessous

haw /hɔː/ n Bot cenelle f

Idiom **to hum** GB ou **hem** US **and ~** balbutier

Hawaii /hə'waɪɪ/ ▸ p. 954 pr n Hawaï m

Hawaiian /hə'waɪən/ ▸ p. 1032, p. 969
A n **1** (person) Hawaïen/-ïenne m/f; **2** (language) hawaïen m
B adj [*culture, landscape*] hawaïen/-ïenne

hawk /hɔːk/
A n lit, fig, Pol faucon m
B vtr gen vendre; (door-to-door) colporter

Idioms **to have eyes like a ~** avoir des yeux de lynx

hawker /'hɔːkə(r)/ n colporteur m

hawkish /'hɔːkɪʃ/ adj Pol belliciste

hawthorn /'hɔːθɔːn/ n (tree, flower) aubépine f

hay /heɪ/ n foin m; **to make ~** faire les foins

Idiom **to make ~ while the sun shines** saisir l'occasion au vol

hay : **~cock** n meulon m; **~ fever** ▸ p. 933 n rhume m des foins; **~ fork** n fourche f à foin; **~ loft** n grenier m à foin; **~making** n fenaison f

haystack /'heɪstæk/ n meule f de foin

Idiom **it is/was like looking for a needle in a ~** autant chercher une aiguille dans une botte de foin

haywire○ /'heɪwaɪə(r)/ adj **1** (faulty) (*jamais épith*) **to go ~** [*plan*] dérailler; [*machinery, system*] se détraquer; **2** US (crazy) détraqué○

h

hazard /ˈhæzəd/
A n **1** (risk) risque m (**to** pour); **the ~s of doing** les risques qu'il y a à faire; **to be a health ~** constituer un risque pour la santé; **fire/occupational ~** risque d'incendie/du métier; **2** (chance) hasard m
B vtr (venture) hasarder [*opinion, explanation*]; **to ~ a guess** hasarder une idée

hazardous /ˈhæzədəs/ adj dangereux/-euse

haze /heɪz/ n (mist) brume f; (of smoke, dust) nuage m

hazel /ˈheɪzl/
A n (tree) noisetier m; (wood) bois m de noisetier
B ▸ p. 752 adj [*eyes*] (couleur de) noisette inv

hazelnut /ˈheɪzlnʌt/ n noisette f

hazy /ˈheɪzɪ/ adj [*weather, morning*] brumeux/-euse; [*sunshine*] voilé; [*image, outline*] flou; [*recollection, idea*] vague; **to be ~ about sth** être dans le vague en ce qui concerne qch

H bomb n bombe f H

HDTV n (abrév = **high-definition television**) TVHD f

he /hiː, hɪ/

> ⚠ *He* is almost always translated by *il*: *he closed the door* = il a fermé la porte. The emphatic form is *lui*.
> For exceptions and particular usages, see the entry below.

A pron il; **~'s seen us** il nous a vus; **here ~ is** le voici; **there ~ is** le voilà; HE **didn't take it** ce n'est pas lui qui l'a pris; **she lives in Oxford but ~ doesn't** elle habite Oxford mais lui non; **~'s a genius** c'est un génie; **~ who** celui qui; **~ and I** lui et moi
B n **it's a ~**○ (of baby) c'est un garçon; (of animal) c'est un mâle

head /hed/ ▸ p. 698
A n **1** tête f; **she put her ~ round the door** elle a mis la nez à la porte; **my ~ aches** j'ai mal à la tête; **a fine ~ of hair** une belle chevelure; **to keep one's ~ down** lit garder la tête baissée; fig (be inconspicuous) ne pas se faire remarquer; (work hard) avoir le nez sur son travail; **from ~ to foot** ou **toe** de la tête aux pieds; **the decision was made over their ~s** la décision a été prise sans les consulter; **to stand on one's ~** faire le poirier; **~s turned at the sight of...** tout le monde s'est retourné en voyant...; **to hold a gun to sb's ~** lit presser un pistolet contre la tête de qn; fig tenir le couteau sous la gorge de qn; **to have a bad ~**○ avoir mal à la tête; **to be a ~ taller than sb** dépasser qn d'une tête; **to win by a (short) ~** [*horse*] gagner d'une (courte) tête; **£10 a ~** ou **per ~** 10 livres sterling par personne; **50 ~ of cattle** Agric 50 têtes de bétail; **2** (mind) tête f; **I can't get it into her ~ that** je n'arrive pas à lui enfoncer dans la tête que; **he has got it into his ~ that** il s'est mis dans la tête que; **he has taken it into his ~ to resign** il s'est mis en tête de démissionner; **you can put that idea out of your ~!** tu peux oublier cette idée!; **the name has gone right out of my ~** le nom m'est complètement sorti de la tête; **I can't add them up in my ~** je ne peux pas les additionner de tête; **to be over sb's ~** (too difficult) passer par-dessus la tête de qn; **use your ~!** sers-toi de tes méninges○!; **her success has turned her ~** son succès lui a tourné la tête; **to have a (good) ~ for figures** être doué pour le calcul; **to have no ~ for heights** avoir le vertige; **3** (leader) (of family, church, agency) chef m; (of social service, organization) responsable mf, directeur/-trice m/f; **at the ~ of** à la tête de; **~ of government/State** chef de gouvernement/d'État; **~ of department** Admin chef de service; Sch professeur principal; **~ of personnel** Comm chef du personnel; **4** (of pin, nail, hammer, golf club) tête f; (of axe, spear, arrow) fer m; (of tennis racquet) tamis m; (of stick) pommeau m; (of cabbage, lettuce) pomme f; (of garlic) tête f; **5** (of tape recorder) also Comput tête f; **6** (top end) (of bed) tête f; (of table) (haut) bout m; (of procession) tête f; (of pier, river, valley) extrémité f; **at the ~ of the stairs/list** en haut de l'escalier/de la liste; **at the ~ of the queue** en tête de la file d'attente; **7** Med (on boil, spot) tête f; **to come to a ~** lit, Med mûrir; fig [*crisis*] arriver au point critique; **to bring sth to a ~** Med faire mûrir; fig précipiter [*crisis*]; amener [qch] au point critique [*situation*]; **8** (on beer) mousse f
B heads npl (tossing coin) face f; **'~s or tails?'** 'pile ou face?'; **~s I win/we go** face je gagne/on y va
C noun modifier **1** [*injury*] à la tête; **2** (chief) [*cashier, cook, gardener*] en chef

D vtr **1** être en tête de [*list, queue*]; être à la tête de [*firm, team*]; mener [*expedition, inquiry*]; **2** (entitle) intituler [*chapter*]; **~ed writing paper** papier m à lettres à en-tête; **3** (steer) diriger [*vehicle*]; naviguer [*boat*]; **he ~ed the sheep away from the cliff** il a éloigné les moutons de la falaise; **4** Sport **to ~ the ball** faire une tête; **he ~ed the ball into the net** il a marqué un but de la tête
E vi **where was the train ~ed** ou **~ing?** où allait le train?; **to ~ south/north** Naut mettre le cap au sud/au nord; **to ~ home** rentrer; **he's ~ing this way!** il se dirige par ici!; ▸ **head for**
F -**headed** combining form **black-~ed bird** oiseau à tête noire; **red-~ed boy** garçon (aux cheveux) roux; **two-~ed monster** monstre à deux têtes

(Idioms) **on your own ~ be it!** à tes risques et périls!; **to go to sb's ~** monter à la tête de qn; **to go off one's ~**○ perdre la boule○; **are you off your ~?** tu as perdu la boule○?; **to keep/lose one's ~** garder/perdre son sang-froid; **to be soft** ou **weak in the ~**○ être faible d'esprit; **he's not right in the ~**○ il a un grain○; **to laugh one's ~ off**○ rire aux éclats; **to shout one's ~ off**○ crier à tue-tête; **to talk one's ~ off**○ ne pas arrêter de parler; **off the top of one's ~** [*say, answer*] sans réfléchir; **to give a horse its/sb their ~** lâcher la bride à un cheval/à qn; **to be able to do sth standing on one's ~** faire qch les doigts dans le nez○; **I can't make ~ (n)or tail of it** je n'y comprends rien, ça n'a ni queue ni tête; **if we all put our ~s together** si nous nous y mettons tous; **the leaders put their ~s together** les dirigeants se sont consultés; **two ~s are better than one** Prov deux avis valent mieux qu'un

(Phrasal verbs)
■ **head for**: ▸ **~ for [sth]** se diriger vers; Naut mettre le cap sur; **to ~ for home** prendre le chemin du retour; **to be ~ing for a fall** courir à l'échec
■ **head off**: ▸ **~ off** partir (**for, towards** vers); ▸ **~ off [sb/sth]**, **~ [sb/sth] off** bloquer, barrer la route à [*person*]; fig éluder [*question*]; éviter [*quarrel*]

headache /ˈhedeɪk/ ▸ p. 933 n mal m de tête; **to have a ~** avoir mal à la tête; **to be a ~ (to sb)** fig causer des ennuis (à qn)

head: **~band** n bandeau m; **~board** n tête f de lit; **~ boy** n GB Sch élève qui représente l'école et qui a des responsabilités; **~butt** vtr donner un coup de tête à

head case○ n **to be a ~** avoir un grain○

head cold ▸ p. 933 n rhume m de cerveau

headcount /ˈhedkaʊnt/ n **to do a ~** compter (les personnes présentes)

headdress /ˈhedres/ n (of feathers) coiffure f; (of lace) coiffe f

header /ˈhedə(r)/ n **1** ○(dive) **to take a ~** piquer une tête○; **2** Sport tête f

head: **~first** adv lit [*fall, plunge*] la tête la première; fig [*rush into*] tête baissée; **~ gear** n ¢ couvre-chef m; **~ girl** n GB Sch élève qui représente l'école et qui a des responsabilités

head-hunt /ˈhedhʌnt/ vtr (seek to recruit) (chercher à) recruter; **she has been ~ed several times** elle a été contactée plusieurs fois par des chasseurs de tête

head: **~-hunter** n Comm chasseur m de têtes; **~-hunting** n Comm chasse f aux têtes

heading /ˈhedɪŋ/ n (of article, column) titre m; (of subject area, topic) rubrique f; (on notepaper, letter) en-tête m; **chapter ~** (quotation) tête f de chapitre; (title) titre m (de chapitre)

head: **~lamp** n (of car) phare m; (of train) fanal m; **~land** n (high) promontoire m; (flat) pointe f; **~light** n (of car) phare m; (of train) fanal m

headline /ˈhedlaɪn/ n gros titre m; Radio, TV titre m; **to hit the ~s** faire la une○; **the front-page ~** la manchette; **the news ~s** les grands titres (de l'actualité)

headlong /ˈhedlɒŋ/
A adj [*fall*] tête la première; **a ~ dash** une ruée
B adv [*fall*] la tête la première; [*run*] à toute vitesse; **to rush ~ into sth** fig se jeter tête baissée dans

head: **~louse** n (pl **~lice**) pou m; **~master** ▸ p. 1181, p. 869 n directeur m; **~mistress** ▸ p. 1181, p. 869 n directrice f; **~ office** n siège m social

head-on /ˌhedˈɒn/
A adj lit [*crash, collision*] de front; fig [*confrontation, approach*] direct

E adv [collide, crash, attack] de front

headphones /'hedfəʊnz/ npl casque m; **a pair of** ~ un casque

head:~**quarters** npl (+ v sg ou pl) gen, Comm, Admin siège m social; Mil quartier m général; ~ **rest** n gen appui-tête m; Aut repose-tête m inv

headroom /'hedrʊm/ n **I haven't got enough** ~ le plafond est trop bas pour moi; **'max** ~ **4 metres'** (on road sign) 'hauteur limitée à 4 mètres'

head:~**scarf** n (pl **-scarves**) foulard m; ~**set** n casque m; (with microphone) micro-casque m

headstand /'hedstænd/ n **to do a** ~ faire le poirier

head start n **to have a** ~ avoir une longueur d'avance (**over** sur)

head:~**stone** n (grave) pierre f tombale; ~**strong** adj [person] têtu; [attitude, behaviour] obstiné; ~ **teacher** ▸ p. 1181 n directeur/-trice m/f

head to head n, adj **to come together in a** ~ ou in a head-to-head battle s'affronter

head waiter ▸ p. 1181 n maître m d'hôtel

headway /'hedweɪ/ n **to make** ~ lit progresser; fig faire des progrès

headwind n gen vent m contraire; Naut vent m debout

heady /'hedɪ/ adj [wine, mixture] capiteux/-euse; [perfume] entêtant; fig [experience] grisant

heal /hiːl/
A vtr lit, fig guérir
B vi [wound, cut] se cicatriser; [fracture, scar] guérir

healer /'hiːlə(r)/ n guérisseur/-euse m/f; **time is a great** ~ le temps apporte l'oubli

healing /'hiːlɪŋ/
A n guérison f
B adj [power] curatif/-ive; [lotion] cicatrisant; [effect] salutaire; **the** ~ **process** lit, fig le rétablissement

health /helθ/ n **I** Med santé f; fig (of economy) santé f; **in good/bad** ~ en bonne/mauvaise santé; **to drink (to) sb's** ~ boire à la santé de qn; **here's (to your)** ~!, **good** ~! à votre santé!

health:**Health Authority** n GB administration f régionale de la santé publique; ~ **care** n gen soins mpl médicaux; Admin services mpl médicaux; ~ **centre** n GB centre m médico-social; ~ **check** n visite f médicale; ~ **club** n club m de remise en forme; ~ **education** n ≈ hygiène f publique; ~ **farm** n: établissement pour cures d'amaigrissement, de rajeunissement etc; ~ **food shop** ▸ p. 000 n magasin m de produits diététiques; ~ **hazard** n risque m pour la santé

healthily /'helθɪlɪ/ adv sainement

health:~ **inspector** ▸ p. 1181 n inspecteur/-trice m/f de l'hygiène; ~ **insurance** n assurance f maladie; ~ **officer** ▸ p. 1181 n inspecteur/-trice m/f de la santé; ~ **resort** n (by sea) station f balnéaire; (in mountains) station f climatique; (spa town) station f thermale; **Health Secretary** n GB ministre m de la Santé

Health Service n **I** GB services mpl de santé; **2** US Univ infirmerie f

health:~ **visitor** ▸ p. 1181 n GB infirmier/-ière m/f des services sociaux; ~ **warning** n mise f en garde du ministère de la Santé

healthy /'helθɪ/ adj [person, animal, plant, skin, lifestyle, diet] sain; [air] salutaire; [appetite] robuste; [crop] abondant; [economy] sain; [profit] excellent; [lead] confortable; **to have a** ~ **respect for** apprécier [qn] à sa juste valeur [opponent, sb's talents]; craindre [teacher]

heap /hiːp/
A n tas m; **to pile sth up in a** ~ ou in ~s mettre qch en tas; **to lie in a** ~ [person] être affalé; [objects, bodies] être entassés; ~s of ° plein de [money, food]; un tas° de [work, problems]; **we've got** ~s of time on a tout notre temps
B vtr **I** **to heap up** = **heap up**; **2** fig **to** ~ **sth on sb** couvrir qn de [praise]; accabler qn de [work, insults]

(Phrasal verb)
■ **heap up** : ▸ ~ [sth] up, ~ up [sth] entasser [leaves, bodies]; empiler [food]

heaped /hiːpt/ adj **a** ~ **spoonful** Culin une bonne cuillerée

hear /hɪə(r)/ (prét, pp **heard**)
A vtr **I** entendre; **she heard a man coming up the stairs**

elle a entendu un homme qui montait l'escalier; **I can** ~ **the train whistling** j'entends siffler le train; **to** ~ **her talk, you'd think (that)** à l'entendre, on croirait que; **we haven't heard the end** ou last of it on n'a pas fini d'en entendre parler; **to make oneself** ou **one's voice heard** lit se faire entendre; fig faire entendre sa voix; **2** (learn) apprendre [news, rumour]; **to** ~ **(tell) of sth** entendre parler de qch; **to** ~ **that** apprendre que; **to** ~ **it said that** entendre dire que; **I've heard so much about you** on m'a tant parlé de vous; **I've heard it all before!** je connais la chanson°!; **have you heard the one about...?** (joke) tu connais celle de...?; **have you heard?** tu es au courant?; **I** ~ **you want to be a doctor** il paraît que tu veux devenir médecin; **so I** ~, **so I've heard** c'est ce que j'ai entendu dire; **to** ~ **whether/why/how** savoir si/pourquoi/comment; **3** (listen to) écouter [lecture, broadcast]; [judge] entendre [case, evidence]; **to** ~ **what sb has to say** entendre ce que qn a à dire; **do you** ~ **(me)?** tu m'entends?; **to** ~ **Mass** sout assister à la messe
B vi entendre; **to** ~ **about** entendre parler de

(Idiom) ~! ~! bravo!

(Phrasal verbs)
■ **hear from** : ▸ ~ **from [sb]** **I** (get news) avoir des nouvelles de; **I'm waiting to** ~ **from the hospital** j'attends une réponse de l'hôpital; **you'll be** ~ing **from me!** (threat) tu auras de mes nouvelles!; **2** (on TV etc) entendre le point de vue de [expert]; écouter le récit de [witness]
■ **hear of** : ▸ ~ **of [sb/sth]** entendre parler de; **that's the first I've heard of it!** première nouvelle!; **I won't** ~ **of it!** il n'en est pas question!
■ **hear out** : ▸ ~ **out [sb]**, ~ **[sb] out** écouter [qn] jusqu'au bout

heard /hɜːd/ prét, pp ▸ **hear**

hearing /'hɪərɪŋ/
A n **I** (sense) ouïe f, audition f; **his** ~ **is not very good** il n'a pas l'oreille très fine; **2** (earshot) **in my** ~ en ma présence; **3** (before court) audience f; ~ **of an appeal** audition f d'un appel; **closed** ou **private** ~ audience à huis clos; **4** (chance to be heard) **to get a** ~ se faire entendre; **to give sb/sth a** ~ écouter qn/qch
B noun modifier [loss, test] d'audition

hearing:~ **aid** n prothèse f auditive; ~ **dog for the deaf** n chien m de malentendant; ~-**impaired** adj malentendant

hearsay /'hɪəseɪ/ n ¢ ouï-dire m inv, on-dit m inv; **based on** ~ fondé sur des ouï-dire or on-dit

hearse /hɜːs/ n corbillard m

heart /hɑːt/ ▸ p. 881
A n **I** cœur m; **my** ~ **missed a beat** mon cœur a fait un bond; **to win/steal sb's** ~ gagner/prendre le cœur de qn; **to break sb's** ~ briser le cœur de qn; **to break one's** ~ se briser le cœur (**over sb** pour qn); **it does my** ~ **good to see...** cela me réchauffe le cœur de voir...; **with a heavy/light** ~ le cœur lourd/léger; **to lose one's** ~ **to sb** tomber amoureux/-euse de qn; **to sob one's** ~ **out** pleurer toutes les larmes de son corps; **to know/learn sth off by** ~ savoir/apprendre qch par cœur; **my** ~ **goes out to you** je suis avec vous de tout cœur; **from the bottom of one's** ~, **from the** ~ du fond du cœur; **to open one's** ~ **to sb** ouvrir son cœur à qn; **to take sth to** ~ prendre qch à cœur; **to wish with all one's** ~ **that** souhaiter de tout cœur que (+ subj); **in my** ~ **(of** ~s) au fond de moi-même; **my** ~ **is not in sth/doing sth** je n'ai pas le cœur à qch/à faire qch; **it is close to my** ~ cela me tient à cœur; **I have your interests at** ~ tes intérêts me tiennent à cœur; **he's a child at** ~ au fond, c'est toujours un enfant; **to have no** ~ ne pas avoir de cœur; **to be all** ~ avoir très bon cœur; **I didn't have the** ~ **to refuse** je n'ai pas eu le cœur de refuser; **have a** ~! pitié!; **to have a change of** ~ changer de sentiment; **2** (courage) courage m; **to take/lose** ~ prendre/perdre courage; **she took** ~ **from the fact that** elle puisait son courage dans le fait que; **to be in good** ~ avoir le moral; **3** (centre) (of district) cœur m; **right in the** ~ **of London** en plein cœur de Londres; **in the** ~ **of the jungle** en pleine jungle; **the** ~ **of the matter** le fond du problème; **4** (in cards) cœur m; **5** (of vegetable) cœur m
B noun modifier [patient, specialist] du cœur; [muscle, valve] cardiaque; [surgery] du cœur, cardiaque; **to have a** ~ **condition** être cardiaque

(Idioms) **a man after my own ~** un homme comme je les aime; **cross my ~ (and hope to die)** croix de bois, croix de fer (si je mens je vais en enfer); **his/her ~ is in the right place** il/elle a bon cœur; **home is where the ~ is** Prov où le cœur aime, là est le foyer; **to have one's ~ set on sth** vouloir à tout prix qch; **don't set your ~ on it** n'y compte pas trop

heart: ~ache n chagrin m; **~ attack** n crise f cardiaque, infarctus m; **~beat** n battement m de cœur; **~break** n déchirement m, douleur f; **~breaking** adj [sight, story] navrant; [cry, appeal] déchirant

heartbroken /'hɑːtbrəʊkn/ adj **to be ~** avoir le cœur brisé

heart: ~burn n brûlures fpl d'estomac; **~ disease** n ₵ maladies fpl cardiaques

hearten /'hɑːtn/ vtr encourager

heartening /'hɑːtnɪŋ/ adj encourageant

heart: ~ failure n arrêt m du cœur; **~felt** adj sincère

hearth /hɑːθ/ n foyer m; **~ rug** petit tapis m

heartily /'hɑːtɪlɪ/ adv [greet] chaleureusement; [agree] tout à fait; [laugh, eat] de bon cœur; [glad] vraiment; **I'm ~ sick of it**○ j'en ai ras le bol○

heartiness /'hɑːtɪnɪs/ n (of person, manner) jovialité f

heartland /'hɑːtlənd/ n (also **~s** pl) (industrial, rural centre) cœur m; (of region, country) centre m; Pol fief m

heartless /'hɑːtlɪs/ adj [person] sans cœur; [attitude, behaviour] sans pitié; [treatment] cruel

heart: ~-lung machine n cœur-poumon m (artificiel); **~ monitor** n moniteur m cardiaque; **~ rate** n rythme m or fréquence f spec cardiaque

heartrending /'hɑːtrendɪŋ/ adj [cry, appeal] déchirant; [sight, story] navrant

heart-searching /'hɑːtsɜːtʃɪŋ/ n **after much ~** après un examen de conscience approfondi

heart: ~ surgeon ▸ p. 1181 n chirurgien m cardiaque, cardiochirurgien m; **~throb**○ n idole f

heart-to-heart /ˌhɑːtəˈhɑːt/

A n **to have a ~** parler à cœur ouvert (**with** avec)

B adj, adv à cœur ouvert

heart: ~ transplant n greffe f du cœur, transplantation f cardiaque spec; **~ transplant patient** n greffé/-e m/f du cœur

heart-warming adj qui réchauffe le cœur

hearty /'hɑːtɪ/ adj **1** (jolly) [welcome] cordial; [person] jovial; [laugh] franc/franche; [slap] vigoureux/-euse; **2** [appetite, meal] solide; [approval] chaleureux/-euse; **he's a ~ eater** c'est un gros mangeur; **to have a ~ dislike of sth** détester cordialement qch

heat /hiːt/

A n **1** gen, Phys, Meteorol chaleur f; **the plants wilted in the ~** les plantes se sont fanées à la chaleur; **in this ~** par cette chaleur; **in the ~ of** [afternoon, summer] au plus chaud de; fig [debate] dans le feu de; **in the ~ of the moment** dans le feu de l'action; **to take the ~ off sb** soulager qn; **2** Culin (of hotplate, gas ring) feu m; (of oven) température f; **cook at a low ~** faire cuire à feu doux; (in oven) faire cuire à basse température; **3** (heating) chauffage m; **4** Sport épreuve f éliminatoire; (in athletics) série f; **5** Zool **to be on** ou **in ~** être en chaleur

B vtr chauffer [house, pool]; faire chauffer [food, oven]; **~ the oven to 180°** faire chauffer le four à 180°

C vi chauffer

(Phrasal verb)

■ **heat up:** ▸ **~ up** [food, drink] chauffer; [air] se réchauffer; **wait until the radiator ~s up** attends que le radiateur soit chaud; ▸ **~ [sth] up, ~ up [sth]** faire chauffer [food]; (reheat) faire réchauffer

heated /'hiːtɪd/ adj lit [water, pool] chauffé; [windscreen, device] chauffant; fig [debate, argument] animé; [denial] véhément

heatedly /'hiːtɪdlɪ/ adv avec véhémence

heater /'hiːtə(r)/ n appareil m de chauffage

heath /hiːθ/ n (moor) lande f; (heather) bruyère f

heat haze n brume f de chaleur

heathen /'hiːðn/ n, adj (irreligious) païen/-ïenne (m/f); (uncivilized) barbare (mf)

heather /'heðə(r)/ n bruyère f

heating /'hiːtɪŋ/ n chauffage m

heating engineer ▸ p. 1181 n chauffagiste m

heat: ~ loss n déperdition f de chaleur; **~ rash** n éruption f cutanée due à la chaleur; **~-resistant** adj gen résistant à la chaleur; **~ stroke** n coup m de chaleur (avec collapsus); **~ treatment** n Med thermothérapie f; Agric thermisation f; **~wave** n vague f de chaleur

heave /hiːv/

A vtr (prét, pp **heaved**) (lift) hisser; (pull) traîner péniblement; (throw) lancer (**at** sur); **to ~ a sigh** pousser un soupir; **to ~ oneself up** se hisser (**onto** sur)

B vi (prét, pp **heaved**) **1** [sea, ground] se soulever et s'abaisser; **2** (pull) tirer de toutes ses forces; **3** (retch) avoir un haut-le-cœur; (vomit) vomir; **it made my stomach ~** ça m'a donné un haut-le-cœur

C heaving pres p adj [bosom, breast] haletant

heaven /'hevn/ n **1** (also **Heaven**) ciel m, paradis m; **~ and earth** ciel m et terre; **~ and hell** le paradis et l'enfer; **the kingdom of ~** le royaume des cieux; **the dinner was ~** le dîner était divin; **2** (in exclamations) **~s (above)!**, **good ~s!** grands dieux!; **~ forbid she should realize!** pourvu qu'elle ne s'en rende pas compte!; **~ help us!** que Dieu nous vienne en aide!; **thank ~(s)!** Dieu soit loué!; **3** (sky) ciel m; **the ~s** le ciel; **the ~s opened** des trombes d'eau se sont abattues

(Idioms) **to be in seventh ~** être au septième ciel; **to move ~ and earth** remuer ciel et terre (**to do** pour faire); **to stink** ou **smell to high ~** puer

heavenly /'hevnlɪ/ adj, n **1** [choir, body] céleste; [peace] divin; **Heavenly Father** père céleste; **2** ○(wonderful) divin

heaven-sent /'hevnsent/ adj providentiel/-ielle

heavily /'hevɪlɪ/ adv **1** [lean, fall, move, weigh] lourdement; [sleep, sigh] profondément; [breathe] (noisily) bruyamment; (with difficulty) péniblement; **~ built** solidement bâti; **~ underlined** souligné d'un gros trait; **2** (abundantly) [rain] très fort; [snow, invest, smoke, drink, rely] beaucoup; [bleed] abondamment; [taxed, armed, in debt] fortement; **to be ~ subsidized** bénéficier de beaucoup de subventions; **~ made-up** très maquillé; **to be ~ fined** avoir une forte amende; **to lose ~** (financially) perdre beaucoup; (in game) se faire écraser; **to be ~ into sth**○ s'adonner à qch

heavy /'hevɪ/ ▸ p. 1323

A ○n (person) grosse brute f

B adj **1** [person, load, bag] lourd; Mil, Ind [machinery] gros/grosse (before n), lourd; [artillery] lourd; **to make sth heavier** alourdir qch; **he's 5 kg heavier than me** il pèse 5 kilos de plus que moi; **2** [fabric, coat] lourd; [shoes, frame] gros/grosse (before n); [line, features] épais/épaisse; [movement, step] pesant, lourd; [blow] violent; [perfume, accent] fort; [irony, responsibility, sigh] lourd; **with a ~ heart** le cœur gros; **to be a ~ sleeper** avoir le sommeil lourd; **a ~ thud** un bruit sourd; **the interview was ~ going** l'interview a été laborieuse; **3** (abundant) [traffic] dense; [gunfire] nourri; [bleeding] abondant; **to be a ~ drinker/smoker** boire/fumer beaucoup; **4** (severe) [loss, debt] lourd; [attack] intense; [sentence, fine] sévère; [criticism] fort (before n); [cold] gros/grosse (before n); **~ fighting** de violents combats; **5** Meteorol [rain, frost] fort; [fog] épais/épaisse; [snow] abondant; [sky] chargé; **it's very ~ today** il fait très lourd aujourd'hui; **in ~ seas** par grosse mer; **6** Culin [meal, food] lourd; **7** (busy) [timetable] chargé; [book, film, lecture] ardu; **this book makes ~ reading** ce livre n'est pas d'une lecture facile

C adv **time hung ~ on her hands** le temps lui pesait

heavy: ~-duty adj [equipment] à usage industriel; **~ goods vehicle, HGV** n poids m lourd; **~-handed** adj maladroit; **~ industry** n industrie f lourde; **~ metal** n Mus hard rock m

heavyweight /'hevɪweɪt/

A n (boxer) poids m lourd; ○fig (in industry) grosse légume○ f; (intellectual) grosse tête○ f

B noun modifier [boxer, title] poids lourd; [fabric] lourd

Hebrew /'hiːbruː/ ▸ p. 969

A n **1** (language) hébreu m; **2** Hist Hébreu m

B adj [person] hébreu; [calendar, alphabet] hébraïque

heck○ /hek/

A n **what the ~ is going on?** que diable se passe-t-il?; **what the ~!** je m'en fiche○!; **a ~ of a lot of** énormément de

B excl zut!

heckle /'hekl/
A *vtr* (barrack) interpeller; (interrupt) interrompre grossièrement
B *vi* chahuter

heckler /'heklə(r)/ *n* chahuteur/-euse *m/f* (*qui interrompt un orateur*)

heckling /'heklɪŋ/ *n* **ℭ** interpellations *fpl*, chahut *m*

hectare /'hekteə(r)/ ▸ p. 1240 *n* hectare *m*

hectic /'hektɪk/ *adj* [*activity*] intense, fiévreux/-euse; [*period*] mouvementé, agité; [*day, week, schedule*] chargé, mouvementé; **at a ∼ pace** très rapidement; **to have a ∼ life(style)** avoir une vie trépidante

hector /'hektə(r)/
A *vtr* haranguer
B hectoring *pres p adj* dictatorial

hedge /hedʒ/
A *n* haie *f*; fig protection *f*
B *vi* (equivocate) se dérober
C hedged *pp adj* **∼d with** bordé de; **∼d about with** fig truffé de [*problems, restrictions*]
(Idiom) **to ∼ one's bets** se couvrir

hedge: **∼-clippers** *npl* cisailles *fpl* à haies; **∼hog** *n* hérisson *m*; **∼row** *n* haie *f*

hedonism /'hi:dənɪzəm/ *n* hédonisme *m*

hedonistic /ˌhi:də'nɪstɪk/ *adj* hédoniste, hédonistique; **a ∼ existence** une vie de sybarite

heebie-jeebies○ /ˌhi:bɪ'dʒi:bɪz/ *npl* **the ∼** la frousse○, le trac○

heed /hi:d/
A *n* **to pay ∼** *ou* **take ∼ of sb** tenir compte de ce que dit qn; **to pay ∼** *ou* **take ∼ of sth** tenir compte de qch
B *vtr* tenir compte de

heedless /'hi:dlɪs/ *adj* (thoughtless) irréfléchi

heedlessly /'hɪdlɪslɪ/ *adv* à la légère, imprudemment

heel /hi:l/
A *n* (of foot, shoe, sock) talon *m*; **to turn on one's ∼** tourner les talons; **at sb's ∼s** sur les talons de qn; **to bring a dog to ∼** rappeler un chien; **to bring [sb] to ∼** fig mettre [qn] au pas; **to come to ∼** [*dog*] venir au pied; [*person*] fig se soumettre; **to click one's ∼s** claquer des talons
B *npl* **heels** (*also* **high ∼s**) chaussures *fpl* à (hauts) talons
(Idioms) **to cool** *ou* **kick one's ∼s** attendre, faire le pied de grue○; **to dig one's ∼ in** se braquer○; **to go head over ∼s** culbuter; **to fall/be head over ∼ in love with sb** tomber/être éperdument amoureux/-euse de qn; **hard** *ou* **close on sb's ∼s** sur les talons de qn; **to be hot on sb's ∼s** talonner qn; **to follow hard on the ∼s of sth** suivre de près qch; **to take to one's ∼s** hum prendre ses jambes à son cou, s'enfuir

heel bar ▸ p. 1181 *n* talon-minute *m*

hefty /'heftɪ/ *adj* [*person*] costaud○; [*object*] pesant; [*blow*] puissant; [*portion*] imposant; [*profit, sum*] considérable

heifer /'hefə(r)/ *n* génisse *f*

height /haɪt/ ▸ p. 977 *n* **1** (of person) taille *f*; (of table, tower, tree) hauteur *f*; **what is your ∼?** combien mesurez-tu?; **to be 1 metre 60 cm in ∼** [*person*] mesurer 1 mètre 60; [*object*] faire 1 mètre 60 de haut; **to draw oneself up to one's full ∼** se redresser; **2** (distance from ground) (of mountain, plane) altitude *f*; **at a ∼ of 200 metres** à 200 mètres d'altitude; **to fall from a ∼ of 20 metres** tomber d'une hauteur de 20 mètres; **from a great ∼** de très haut; **to be scared of ∼s** avoir le vertige; **to rise to great ∼s** fig aller loin; **3** fig (peak) **at the ∼ of the season** en pleine saison; **at the ∼ of** au plus fort de [*storm, crisis*]; **to be at the ∼ of one's popularity/powers** être au sommet de sa popularité/son talent; **the violence was at its ∼** la violence était à son comble; **the ∼ of** le comble de [*luxury, stupidity, cheek*]; **to be the ∼ of fashion** être ce que l'on fait de plus à la mode

heighten /'haɪtn/
A *vtr* intensifier [*emotion*]; augmenter [*tension, suspense*]; accentuer [*effect*]; **to ∼ sb's awareness of** rendre qn plus conscient de; **a ∼ed awareness of** une conscience plus grande de
B *vi* [*tension*] monter

heinous /'heɪnəs/ *adj* sout abominable; **a ∼ crime** un crime odieux

heir /eə(r)/ *n* héritier/-ière *m/f* (**to** de); **his son and ∼** son héritier; **to be ∼ to** fig hériter de

heiress /'eərɪs/ *n* héritière *f*

heirloom /'eəlu:m/ *n* héritage *m*; **a family ∼** un objet de famille

heist○ /haɪst/ US *n* vol *m*; (armed) hold-up *m inv*

held /held/ *prét, pp* ▸ **hold**

helices /'helɪsi:z, 'hi:-/ *pl* ▸ **helix**

helicopter /'helɪkɒptə(r)/
A *n* hélicoptère *m*
B *vtr* héliporter

heliport /'helɪpɔ:t/ *n* héliport *m*

helium /'hi:lɪəm/ *n* hélium *m*

helix /'hi:lɪks/ *n* (*pl* **-lices** *ou* **-lixes**) hélice *f*

hell /hel/
A *n* **1** (*also* **Hell**) Relig enfer *m*; **in ∼** en enfer; **2** ○fig enfer *m*; **to make sb's life ∼** rendre la vie infernale à qn; **to go through ∼** en baver○; **a neighbour from ∼**○ un voisin infernal *or* insupportable; **3** ○(as intensifier) **a ∼ of a shock** un choc terrible; **a ∼ of a lot worse** nettement pire; **he's one ∼ of a smart guy** US c'est fou ce qu'il est intelligent○; **we had a ∼ of a time** (bad) on en a bavé○; (good) on s'est payé du bon temps○; **it sure as ∼ wasn't me** une chose est sûre, ce n'était pas moi; **to run like ∼** courir de toutes ses forces; **let's get the ∼ out of here!** barrons-nous○!; **get the ∼ out of here!** dégage○!; **like ∼ I will/you are!** pas question!; **'it's a good film'—'like ∼ it is!'** 'c'est un bon film'—'tu rigoles○!'; **why/who the ∼?** pourquoi/qui bon Dieu○?; **how the ∼ should I know?** comment je pourrais le savoir, bon Dieu○?; **oh, what the ∼!** (too bad) tant pis!; **to ∼ with it!** je laisse tomber○!
B ○*excl* bon Dieu○!; **go to ∼**○! va te faire voir○!
(Idioms) **all ∼ broke loose** le raffut a éclaté; **come ∼ or high water**○ coûte que coûte; **there was ∼ to pay** il/elle l'a payé cher; **to catch ∼**○ US prendre un savon○; **to do sth for the ∼ of it**○ faire qch pour le plaisir; **to give sb ∼**○ (cause to suffer) rendre la vie dure à qn; (scold) engueuler○ qn; **to raise (merry) ∼**○ faire une scène (**with sb** à qn)

hell-bent /ˌhel'bent/ *adj* **∼ on doing** décidé à faire

Hellenic /he'li:nɪk, US he'lenɪk/ *adj* [*civilization, language*] hellénique; [*people*] hellène

hellfire /ˌhel'faɪə(r)/ *n* tourments *mpl* de l'enfer

hell-for-leather○ *adj, adv* à toute allure

hellish /'helɪʃ/ *adj* lit d'enfer (after *n*); ○(awful) infernal○

hello /hə'ləʊ/ *excl* **1** (greeting) bonjour!; (on phone) (receiving a call) allô!; (making a call) allô bonjour!; **2** (in surprise) tiens!

Hell's angel *n* ≈ blouson *m* noir

helm /helm/ *n* lit, fig barre *f*; **at the ∼** à la barre

helmet /'helmɪt/ *n* gen casque *m*; Hist heaume *m*

help /help/
A *n* **1** aide *f*; (in emergency) secours *m*; **with the ∼ of** à l'aide de [*stick, knife*]; avec l'aide de [*person*]; **to be of ∼ to sb** [*person*] rendre service à qn; [*information, map*] être utile à qn; **you're a great ∼!** iron tu es vraiment d'un grand secours!; **to come to sb's ∼** venir au secours de qn, venir en aide à qn; **to cry for ∼** appeler au secours; **it's a ∼ if you can speak the language** ça aide de parler la langue; **she needs (professional) ∼** (from psychiatrist) elle devrait voir un psychiatre; **2** (*also* **daily ∼**) (cleaning woman) femme *f* de ménage
B *excl* au secours!
C *vtr* **1** aider (**to do** à faire); (more urgently) secourir; **to ∼ each other** s'entraider; **can you ∼ me with this sack?** est-ce que tu peux m'aider à porter ce sac?; **can I ∼ you?** (in shop) vous désirez?; (on phone) j'écoute; **to ∼ sb across/down/out** aider qn à traverser/descendre/sortir; **I ∼ed him to his feet** je l'ai aidé à se lever; **to ∼ sb on/off with** aider qn à mettre/enlever [*garment, boot*]; **he didn't ∼ matters by writing that letter** il n'a rien arrangé en écrivant cette lettre; **2** (serve) **to ∼ sb to** servir [qch] à qn [*food, wine*]; **3** (prevent) **it can't be ∼ed!** on n'y peut rien!, tant pis!; **he can't ∼ being stupid!** ce n'est pas de sa faute s'il est stupide!; **not if I can ∼ it!** sûrement pas!; **he won't win if I can ∼ it** je vais faire tout mon possible pour l'empêcher de gagner; **don't tell her any more than you can ∼** ne lui dis pas plus qu'il n'en faut; **I can't ∼ that** je n'y peux rien; **you can't ∼ but pity him** on ne peut pas s'empêcher d'avoir pitié de lui
D *vi* aider; **he never ∼s with the housework** il n'aide jamais à faire le ménage; **to ∼ with the expenses** participer aux frais; **this map doesn't ∼ much** cette carte n'est pas d'un

grand secours; **every little ~s** (donating money) tous les dons sont les bienvenus; (saving) les petits ruisseaux font les grandes rivières; **would it ~ if I turned the light off?** est-ce que ce serait mieux si j'éteignais?

E *v refl* **to ~ oneself** se servir; **~ yourselves to coffee** prenez du café; **to ~ oneself to the petty cash** piquer○ (de l'argent) dans la caisse

(Phrasal verb)

■ **help out**: ▸ **~ out** aider, donner un coup de main○; ▸ **~ [sb] out** gen aider, donner un coup de main○ à; (financially) dépanner○; (in crisis) tirer [qn] d'embarras [*person*]

helpdesk /'helpdesk/ *n* service *m* d'assistance

helper /'helpə(r)/ *n* gen aide *mf*, assistant/-e *m/f*; (for handicapped person) aide *f* sociale

helpful /'helpfl/ *adj* [*tool, machine*] utile; [*person*] serviable; [*advice, suggestion*] utile; **I was only trying to be ~!** j'essayais seulement de me rendre utile!

helpfully /'helpfəlɪ/ *adv* obligeamment, gentiment

helping /'helpɪŋ/ *n* portion *f*; **would you like another ~ of meat?** voulez-vous encore de la viande?; **he took a second ~ of strawberries** il a repris des fraises

helping hand *n* **to give** *ou* **lend sb a ~** donner un coup de main à qn

help key *n* Comput touche *f* d'aide

helpless /'helplɪs/ *adj* **1** (powerless) [*person*] impuissant; (because of infirmity, disability) impotent; **~ with laughter** mort de rire○; **2** (defenceless) [*person*] sans défense; [*victim*] malheureux/-euse (*before n*); (destitute) [*orphan, family*] démuni

helplessly /'helplɪslɪ/ *adv* [*watch*] sans pouvoir rien faire; [*struggle, try*] en vain, désespérément

helplessness /'helplɪsnɪs/ *n* impuissance *f*; (because of infirmity, disability) impotence *f*; (of baby) vulnérabilité *f*

helpline *n* service *m* d'assistance (téléphonique)

helter-skelter /ˌheltə'skeltə(r)/
A *n* GB toboggan *m* (en spirale)
B *adv* **to run ~** courir comme un dératé○ (*or* des dératés○)

hem /hem/
A *n* ourlet *m*; **to take up/let down the ~ on** raccourcir/rallonger [*garment*]
B *vtr* (*p prés etc* **-mm-**) faire un ourlet à [*garment*]

(Phrasal verb)

■ **hem in**: ▸ **~ [sb/sth] in**, **~ in [sb/sth]** cerner; **to feel ~med in** fig se sentir coincé

hemisphere /'hemɪsfɪə(r)/ *n* Med, Geog hémisphère *m*; **the western ~** journ le monde occidental

hemlock /'hemlɒk/ *n* ciguë *f*

hemp /hemp/ *n* chanvre *m*

hen /hen/
A *n* poule *f*
B *adj* femelle

hence /hens/ *adv* sout **1** (from now) d'ici; **three days ~** d'ici *or* dans trois jours; **2** (for this reason) (*before n*) d'où; (*before adj*) donc; **3** ‡(from this place) d'ici

henceforth /ˌhens'fɔːθ/, **henceforward** /hens'fɔːwəd/ *adv* littér (from now on) dorénavant; (from then on) dès lors

henchman /'hentʃmən/ *n* péj acolyte *m*

hen: **~ coop** *n* cage *f* à poules; **~house** *n* poulailler *m*

henna /'henə/ *n* henné *m*

hen party *n* soirée *f* passée entre femmes

hen-pecked /'henpekt/ *adj* **~ husband** mari *m* mené par le bout du nez

hepatitis /ˌhepə'taɪtɪs/ ▸ **p. 933** *n* hépatite *f*

her /hɜː(r), hə(r)/
A *pron* (direct object) la, l'; (indirect object) lui; **it's ~** c'est elle; **I did it for ~** je l'ai fait pour elle
B *det* son/sa/ses

herald /'herəld/
A *n* lit héraut *m*; fig signe *m* avant-coureur
B *vtr* (*also* **~ in**) annoncer

heraldic /he'rældɪk/ *adj* héraldique

heraldry /'herəldrɪ/ *n* (study, history) héraldique *f*

herb /hɜːb/ *n* herbe *f*; **mixed ~s** ≈ herbes de Provence

herbaceous border /hɜː'beɪʃəs 'bɔːdə(r)/ *n* bordure *f* de plantes herbacées

herbal /'hɜːbl/ *adj* [*remedy*] à base de plantes

herbalist /'hɜːbəlɪst/ ▸ **p. 1181** *n* herboriste *mf*

herb garden *n*: *jardin de plantes aromatiques utilisées en cuisine*

herb tea, **herbal tea** *n* tisane *f*, infusion *f*

herd /hɜːd/
A *n* gen troupeau *m*; (of reindeer) harde *f*; (of people) troupeau *m*; **~ instinct** instinct *m* grégaire
B *vtr* rassembler
C *vi* **to ~ into sth** s'assembler dans qch

(Idiom) **to follow the ~** fig être un mouton de Panurge

(Phrasal verb)

■ **herd together** se rassembler; (closely) se masser

here /hɪə(r)/

⚠️ When *here* is used to indicate the location of an object/point etc close to the speaker, it is generally translated by *ici*: **come and sit here** = viens t'asseoir ici.

  When the location is not so clearly defined, *là* is the usual translation: **he's not here at the moment** = il n'est pas là pour l'instant.

  Remember that *voici* is used to translate *here is* and *here are* when the speaker is drawing attention to an object/a place/a person etc physically close to him or her.

  For examples and particular usages, see entry below.

A *adv* **1** ici; **far from/near ~** loin/près d'ici; **two kilometres from ~** à deux kilomètres d'ici; **come over ~** venez par ici; **up to ~**, **down to ~** jusqu'ici; **I'm up ~** je suis là-haut; **~ lies** (on tombstone) ci-gît; **since you were last ~** depuis ta

---

her

When used as a direct object pronoun, *her* is translated by *la* (*l'* before a vowel). Note that the object pronoun normally comes before the verb in French and that, in compound tenses like perfect and past perfect, the past participle agrees with the pronoun:

I know her	*I've already seen her*
= je la connais	= je l'ai déjà vue

In imperatives, the direct object pronoun is translated by *la* and comes after the verb:

catch her!
= attrape-la!

(*note the hyphen*)

When used as an indirect object pronoun, *her* is translated by *lui*:

I've given her the book	*I've given it to her*
= je lui ai donné le livre	= je le lui ai donné

In imperatives, the indirect object pronoun is translated by *lui* and comes after the verb:

phone her	*give them to her*
= téléphone-lui	= donne-les-lui

(*note the hyphens*)

After prepositions and after the verb *to be* the translation is *elle*:

he did it for her	*it's her*
= il l'a fait pour elle	= c'est elle

When translating *her* as a determiner (*her house* etc.) remember that in French possessive adjectives, like most other adjectives, agree in gender and number with the noun they qualify; *her* is translated by *son* + masculine singular noun (*son chien*), *sa* + feminine singular noun (*sa maison*) BUT *son* + feminine noun beginning with a vowel or mute 'h' (*son assiette*), and *ses* + plural noun (*ses enfants*).

For *her* used with parts of the body ▸ **p. 698**.

h

dernière visite ici; ∼ **and there** par endroits; ∼ **they are/ she comes!** les/la voici!; ∼ **is my key/are my keys** voici ma clé/mes clés; ∼ **comes the bus** voilà le bus; ∼ **you are** (offering sth) tiens, tenez; **my colleague** ∼ mon/ma collègue; **which one? this one** ∼ **or that one?** lequel? celui-ci ou celui-là?; ∼'**s what you do** voilà ce qu'il faut faire; [2] (indicating presence, arrival) **she's not** ∼ **right now** elle n'est pas là pour le moment; '**John?**'—'∼ **sir**' (telling whereabouts) 'John?'—'ici Monsieur'; (during roll call) '**John?**'—'présent Monsieur'; ∼ **we are at last** nous voilà enfin; **the train will be** ∼ **any minute** le train va arriver d'un moment à l'autre; **we get off** ∼ c'est là qu'on descend; **now that summer's** ∼ maintenant que c'est l'été; ∼'**s our chance** voilà notre chance; [3] ᵒ(emphatic) **this** ∼ **contraption** ce truc°; **look** ou **see** ∼, **you!** écoute-moi bien toi!

B ᵒexcl hé!

(Idioms) ∼ **goes!** c'est parti!; ∼'**s hoping** j'espère; ∼'**s to our success/to you!** à notre succès/la tienne!; ∼ **there and everywhere** partout, par-ci par-là; **it's neither** ∼ **nor there** (unimportant) c'est sans importance; (irrelevant) ça n'a aucun rapport

hereabout US, **hereabouts** GB /'hɪərəbaʊt(s)/ adv par ici

hereafter /hɪər'ɑːftə(r)/
A n **the** ∼ l'au-delà m
B adv Jur ci-après

here and now
A n **the** ∼ (present) le présent
B adv immédiatement

hereby /hɪə'baɪ/ adv Admin, Jur **I** ∼ **declare that** (in document) je déclare par la présente que

hereditary /hɪ'redɪtrɪ, US -terɪ/ adj héréditaire

heredity /hɪ'redətɪ/ n hérédité f

heresy /'herəsɪ/ n (all contexts) hérésie f

heretic /'herətɪk/ n hérétique m

heretical /hɪ'retɪkl/ adj hérétique

herewith /hɪəwɪð/ adv sout ci-joint

heritage /'herɪtɪdʒ/ n patrimoine m

hermetic /hɜː'metɪk/ adj hermétique

hermetically /hɜː'metɪklɪ/ adv hermétiquement

hermit /'hɜːmɪt/ n ermite m

hernia /'hɜːnɪə/ n (pl ∼s ou ∼e) hernie f

hero /'hɪərəʊ/ n (pl ∼es) héros m; **a** ∼'**s welcome** un accueil triomphal

heroic /hɪ'rəʊɪk/ adj héroïque

heroically /hɪ'rəʊɪklɪ/ adv héroïquement

heroics /hɪ'rəʊɪks/ npl mélodrame m

heroin /'herəʊɪn/ n héroïne f

heroin addict n héroïnomane mf

heroine /'herəʊɪn/ n héroïne f

heroism /'herəʊɪzəm/ n héroïsme m

heron /'herən/ n héron m

hero-worship /'hɪərəʊwɜːʃɪp/
A n culte m du héros, adulation f
B vtr (p prés etc **-pp-**, US **-p-**) aduler

herpes /'hɜːpiːz/ ▸ p. 933 n herpès m

herring /'herɪŋ/ n hareng m

herringbone n (design) motif m à chevrons

hers /hɜːz/

⚠️ In French, possessive pronouns reflect the gender and number of the noun they are standing for; *hers* is translated by *le sien, la sienne, les siens, les siennes*, according to what is being referred to.
For examples and particular usages, see the entry below.

pron **my car is red but** ∼ **is blue** ma voiture est rouge mais la sienne est bleue; **the green pen is** ∼ le stylo vert est à elle; **which house is** ∼? sa maison c'est laquelle?; **I'm a friend of** ∼ c'est une amie à moi; **it's not** ∼ ce n'est pas à elle, ce n'est pas le sien or la sienne; **the money wasn't** ∼ **to give away** elle n'avait pas le droit de donner cet argent; ∼ **was not an easy task** sa tâche n'était pas facile

herself /hə'self/

⚠️ When used as a reflexive pronoun, direct and indirect, *herself* is translated by *se* (s' before a vowel): *she's enjoying herself* = elle s'amuse bien; *she's cut herself* = elle s'est coupée.
When used in emphasis, the translation is *elle-même*: *she herself didn't know* = elle ne le savait pas elle-même.
After a preposition the translation is *elle* or *elle-même*: *she can be proud of herself* = elle peut être fière d'elle or d'elle-même.

pron **she's hurt** ∼ elle s'est blessée; **for** ∼ pour elle, pour elle-même; **(all) by** ∼ toute seule; **she's not** ∼ **today** elle n'est pas dans son assiette aujourd'hui

Herts n GB Post abrév écrite = **Hertfordshire**

he's /hiːz/ = **he is**, **he has**

hesitancy /'hezɪtənsɪ/ n hésitation f

hesitant /'hezɪtənt/ adj hésitant; **to be** ∼ **about doing** hésiter à faire; **to be** ∼ **about** (reticent) être réticent quant à [plan, scheme]

hesitantly /'hezɪtəntlɪ/ adv [act] avec hésitation; [speak] d'un ton hésitant

hesitate /'hezɪteɪt/ vi hésiter (**over** sur; **to do** à faire)

(Idiom) **he who** ∼ **is lost** Prov à hésiter on n'obtient rien

hesitation /ˌhezɪ'teɪʃn/ n hésitation f; **to have no** ∼ **in doing** n'avoir aucune hésitation à faire

hessian /'hesɪən, US 'heʃn/ n toile f de jute

heterogeneous /ˌhetərə'dʒiːnɪəs/ adj hétérogène

heterosexual /ˌhetərə'sekʃʊəl/ n, adj hétérosexuel/-elle (m/f)

het upᵒ /ˌhet'ʌp/ adj énervé; **to get** ∼ **about sth** s'énerver à cause de qch

hew /hjuː/ (pp **hewn**) vtr abattre [wood, coal]; tailler [statue, canoe] (**out of** dans)

hexagon /'heksəgən, US -gɒn/ n hexagone m

heyᵒ /heɪ/ excl (call for attention) hé!, eh!; (in protest) dis donc!

heyday /'heɪdeɪ/ n (of movement etc) âge m d'or; (of person) beaux jours mpl; **in her** ∼ quand elle était au sommet de sa gloire

hey presto /ˌheɪ 'prestəʊ/ excl ô miracle!, et passez muscade!; (in narrative) comme par miracle

hiᵒ /haɪ/ excl salut°!

HI US Post abrév écrite = **Hawaii**

hiatus /haɪ'eɪtəs/ n (pl ∼es ou ∼) (pause) temps m d'arrêt; (gap) lacune f; Ling, Literat hiatus m

hibernate /'haɪbəneɪt/ vi hiberner

hibernation /ˌhaɪbə'neɪʃn/ n hibernation f

hiccup, hiccough /'hɪkʌp/
A n [1] lit hoquet m; **to have (the)** ∼s avoir le hoquet; [2] fig (setback) anicroche f
B vi (p prés etc **-p-** ou **-pp-**) hoqueter

hickᵒ /hɪk/ péj n plouc◆ mf; ∼ **town** trou° m

hid /hɪd/ prét ▸ **hide**

hidden /'hɪdn/
A pp ▸ **hide**
B adj caché; ∼ **from view** caché, invisible

hide /haɪd/
A n (skin) peau f; (leather) cuir m
B vtr (prét **hid**; pp **hidden**) cacher [object, person] (**from** à); ne pas montrer [feeling] (**from** à)
C vi (prét **hid**; pp **hidden**) se cacher

(Phrasal verbs)
■ **hide away**: ▸ ∼ [sth] **away**, ∼ **away** [sth] cacher
■ **hide out** GB, **hide up** US se cacher, se planquer°

hide: ∼ **and seek** GB, ∼**-and-go-seek** US ▸ p. 881 n cache-cache m inv; ∼**away** n retraite f

hidebound /'haɪdbaʊnd/ adj conventionnel/-elle

hideous /'hɪdɪəs/ adj [person, monster, object] hideux/-euse; [noise] affreux/-euse; [murder] odieux/-ieuse, atroce

hideously /'hɪdɪəslɪ/ adv atrocement

hideout n cachette f

hiding /'haɪdɪŋ/ n [1] **to go into** ∼ se cacher; **to come out of** ∼ sortir de sa cachette; ∼ **place** cachette f; [2] (beating) correction f; **to give sb a (good)** ∼ administrer une (bonne) correction à qn

(Idiom) **to be on a** ∼ **to nothing** ne pas avoir la moindre chance de réussir or de gagner

hierarchic(al) /ˌhaɪəˈrɑːkɪk(l)/ adj hiérarchique

hierarchy /ˈhaɪərɑːkɪ/ n hiérarchie f

hieroglyph, **hieroglyphic** /ˈhaɪərəglɪf, ˌhaɪərəˈglɪfɪk/ n lit, fig hiéroglyphe m

hi-fi /ˈhaɪfaɪ/ n **1** (set of equipment) chaîne f hi-fi inv, hi-fi f inv; **2** (abrév = **high fidelity**) hi-fi f inv, haute-fidélité f inv

higgledy-piggledy /ˌhɪɡldɪˈpɪɡldɪ/ adj, adv pêle-mêle (inv)

high /haɪ/ ▸ p. 977
A n **1** **an all-time** ~ un niveau record; **to reach a new** ~ atteindre son niveau le plus élevé; **2** ○**to give sb a** ~ [drug] défoncer○ qn; [success] monter à la tête de qn; **to be on a** ~ être en pleine euphorie; **3** ○US Sch = **high school**

B adj **1** [building, wall, cliff] haut; [table, forehead, collar] haut (after n); ~ **cheekbones** pommettes fpl saillantes; **how** ~ **is the cliff?** quelle est la hauteur de la falaise?; **it is 50 m** ~ ça fait 50 m de haut; **I've known him since he was so** ~ il n'était pas plus grand que ça quand je l'ai connu; **at** ~ **tide** à marée haute; **how** ~ **(up) are we?** (on top of building) on est à combien de mètres au-dessus du sol?; (on plane, mountain) quelle est notre altitude?; **2** [number, ratio, price, frequency, volume] élevé; [wind] violent; [hope, expectation] grand (before n); **at** ~ **speed** à grande vitesse; **to have a** ~ **temperature** avoir de la fièvre; ~ **in** riche en [fat, iron]; **on a** ~ **heat** à feu vif; **to have a** ~ **colour** avoir le teint rougeaud; **a moment of** ~ **drama** un moment de grande émotion; **in** ~ **summer** au cœur de l'été; **feelings are running** ~ les esprits s'échauffent; **3** (important) [quality, standard, rank] supérieur; **I have it on the** ~**est authority** je tiens cela des autorités les plus haut placées; **to have friends in** ~ **places** avoir des amis haut placés; **to be** ~ **up** être haut placé; **to go on to** ~**er things** faire son chemin dans le monde; **4** (noble) [ideal, principle] noble; **5** (acute) [pitch, sound, voice] aigu/-guë; [note] haut; **6** Culin [game] faisandé; **7** ○(euphoric) (on drug) défoncé○; (happy) ivre de joie; **to be** ~ **on** être défoncé à [drug]; **to get** ~ se défoncer○

C adv **1** (to a great height) haut; ~**er up** plus haut; **to climb** ~**er and** ~**er** [person, animal] grimper de plus en plus haut; fig [figures, unemployment] augmenter de plus en plus; **don't go any** ~**er than £5,000** ne dépasse pas 5 000 livres sterling; **from on** ~ gen de haut; Relig du Ciel; **2** (at a high level, pitch) [set, turn on] fort; [sing, play] haut; **to turn sth up** ~ monter qch

(Idioms) **it's** ~ **time that sb went** il est grand temps que qn y aille; **to hold one's head (up)** marcher la tête haute; **to search** ~ **and low for sth** remuer ciel et terre pour trouver qch

high and dry adj **to leave sb** ~ fig laisser qn en plan○

high: ~ **beam** n US pleins phares mpl; ~**born** adj de haute naissance; ~**brow** n, adj intellectuel/-elle (m/f); ~ **chair** n chaise f haute; **High Church** adj de la Haute Église; ~**class** adj [hotel, shop, car, prostitute] de luxe; [goods] de première qualité; [area] de grand standing; ~ **command** n haut commandement m; ~ **commission** n haut-commissariat m; ~ **commissioner** ▸ p. 1181 n haut-commissaire m; ~ **court** n cour f suprême; ~**definition** adj (à) haute définition inv; ~ **diving** ▸ p. 881 n plongeon m de haut vol; ~**er education** n enseignement m supérieur; ~**er mathematics** n (+ v sg) mathématiques fpl abstraites; ~**falutin(g)**○ adj [language] ampoulé; [ideas] prétentieux/-ieuse; ~ **fashion** n haute couture f; ~**fibre** adj riche en fibres; ~**fidelity** n, adj haute-fidélité (f) (inv); ~ **finance** n haute finance f; ~**flier** n jeune loup m, ambitieux/-ieuse m/f; ~**flown** adj ampoulé; ~**flying** adj [aircraft] capable de voler à haute altitude; fig [person] ambitieux/-ieuse; [career] de haut vol; ~**frequency** adj (à) haute fréquence; **High German** ▸ p. 969 n haut allemand m; ~**grade** adj de haute qualité

Higher /ˈhaɪə(r)/ n Scot Sch certificat m de fin d'études en Écosse (à 17 ans). ▸ **A level**

high ground n colline(s) f(pl); **on** ~ [built] sur une colline; [rain] en altitude; **to take the (moral)** ~ fig prendre une position moraliste

high: ~**handed** adj despotique; ~**handedly** adv despotiquement; ~**heeled** adj à talon haut; ~ **heels** npl hauts talons mpl

high jinks○ /ˌhaɪ ˈdʒɪŋks/ npl **to get up to** ~ se payer du bon temps○

high jump ▸ p. 881 n Sport saut m en hauteur

Highland: ~ **fling** n danse f écossaise; ~ **games** npl jeux mpl écossais

highlands /ˈhaɪləndz/ npl régions fpl montagneuses

Highlands /ˈhaɪləndz/ pr npl Highlands mpl, Hautes-Terres fpl (d'Écosse)

high: ~**level** adj [talks] à haut niveau; [official] de haut niveau; ~ **life** n grande vie f

highlight /ˈhaɪlaɪt/
A n **1** Art rehaut m; **2** (in hair) (natural) reflet m; (artificial) mèche f; **3** fig (of exhibition) clou m; (of match, show) point m culminant; (of week, year) point m fort

B highlights npl Sport, Radio, TV résumé m

C vtr (prét, pp -lighted) **1** Art rehausser; Phot mettre [qch] en valeur; **2** [sun, light] éclairer; **3** (with fluorescent pen) surligner; **4** fig (emphasize) mettre l'accent sur, souligner

highlighter /ˈhaɪlaɪtə(r)/ n (pen) surligneur m

highly /ˈhaɪlɪ/ adv [dangerous, developed, intelligent] extrêmement; ~ **unlikely** fort peu probable; **to speak/think** ~ **of sb** dire/penser beaucoup de bien de qn; **to praise sb** ~ chanter les louanges de qn

highly: ~**charged** adj [atmosphere] très tendu; ~**coloured** GB, ~**colored** US adj aux couleurs vives; fig enjolivé; ~**paid** adj très bien payé; ~**polished** adj d'un beau poli; ~**strung** adj très tendu

high: **High Mass** n grand-messe f; ~**minded** adj [person] à l'âme noble; ~**necked** adj à col montant

Highness /ˈhaɪnɪs/ ▸ p. 869 n **His** ou **Her (Royal)** ~ Son Altesse f

high noon n plein midi m; **at** ~ en plein midi

high: ~**performance** adj performant; ~**pitched** adj [voice, sound] aigu/-guë; ~ **point** n fig point m culminant; ~**powered** adj [car, engine] de grande puissance; [person] dynamique; [job] de haute responsabilité

high pressure
A n Meteorol hautes pressions f
B noun modifier Tech à haute pression; fig [job] à haute responsabilité

high: ~ **priest** n Relig grand prêtre m; fig pape m (**of** de); ~ **priestess** n Relig, fig grande prêtresse f (**of** de); ~**principled** adj [person] de haute moralité; ~**profile** adj [politician, group] bien en vue; [visit] qui fait beaucoup de bruit; ~**ranking** adj de haut rang; ~ **rise (building)** n tour f (d'habitation); ~**risk** adj à haut risque; ~ **road** n grand-route f

high school n US Sch ≈ lycée m; GB Sch établissement m secondaire

> ℹ️ **High school** Établissement d'enseignement secondaire aux États-Unis, souvent subdivisé en Junior high school (élèves de 12 à 14 ans) et Senior high school (élèves de 15 à 17 ans). À l'issue de ce cycle d'études, les élèves passent un examen (ACT, SAT) pour être admis dans un college. ▸ **College**

high sea n **on the** ~**s** en haute mer

high: ~ **season** n haute saison f; ~ **society** n haute société f; ~**sounding** adj ronflant; ~**speed** adj [train] à grande vitesse; [boat] rapide; [film] ultrarapide; ~**spirited** adj plein d'entrain

high spirits npl entrain m; **to be in** ~ être plein d'entrain

high spot n point m culminant

high street GB (also **High Street**) n (in town) rue f principale; (in village) grand-rue f; ~ **spending** dépenses fpl de consommation courante

high: ~**street shop** ▸ p. 1181 n boutique f appartenant à une chaîne; ~ **tea** n GB goûter m dînatoire

high tech /ˌhaɪ ˈtek/
A n (interior design) high-tech m
B ○**high-tech** adj [industry] de pointe; [equipment, car] ultramoderne; [furniture] high-tech inv

high: ~ **tide** n marée f haute; ~ **treason** n haute trahison f; ~ **voltage** n haute tension f

highway /ˈhaɪweɪ/ n GB route f nationale; US autoroute f; **public** ou **king's** ou **queen's** ~ GB voie f publique; **~s and byways** chemins et sentiers

highway: **Highway Code** n GB Code m de la Route; **~man** n bandit m de grand chemin; ~ **patrol** n US police f de la route; ~ **robbery** n lit banditisme m

high wire n corde f raide

hijack /ˈhaɪdʒæk/
A n détournement m d'avion
B vtr détourner [*plane*]; fig s'approprier [*theory*]; récupérer [*event, demonstration*]

hijacker /ˈhaɪdʒækə(r)/ n (of plane) pirate m (de l'air); (of bus, truck) pirate m (de la route)

hijacking /ˈhaɪdʒækɪŋ/ n détournement m

hike /haɪk/
A n randonnée f; **to go on** ou **for a** ~ faire une randonnée
B vi faire de la randonnée
C vtr (also ~ **up**) augmenter [*rate, price*]

hiker /ˈhaɪkə(r)/ n randonneur/-euse m/f

hiking /ˈhaɪkɪŋ/ ▸ p. 881 n randonnée f

hilarious /hɪˈleərɪəs/ adj désopilant, hilarant

hilarity /hɪˈlærətɪ/ n hilarité f

hill /hɪl/ n colline f; (hillside) coteau m; (incline) pente f, côte f; **over** ~ **and dale** littér par monts et par vaux

(Idioms) **as old as the** ~**s** vieux comme Hérode; **to be over the** ~ ne plus être de première jeunesse

hillbilly /ˈhɪlbɪlɪ/ n US péj péquenaud/-e° m/f péj

hillock /ˈhɪlək/ n petite colline f

hillside /ˈhɪlsaɪd/ n **on the** ~ à flanc de coteau

hilltop n sommet m de colline

hilly /ˈhɪlɪ/ adj vallonné

hilt /hɪlt/ n (of sword) poignée f; **(up) to the** ~ lit jusqu'à la garde; fig (in debt) jusqu'au cou; **to back sb (up) to the** ~ donner son appui inconditionnel à qn

him /hɪm/

⚠️ When used as a direct object pronoun, *him* is translated by *le* (*l'* before a vowel). Note that the object pronoun normally comes before the verb in French: *I know him* = je le connais; *I've already seen him* = je l'ai déjà vu.
In imperatives, the direct object pronoun is translated by *le* and comes after the verb: *catch him!* = attrape-le! (note the hyphen).
When used as an indirect object pronoun, *him* is translated by *lui*: *I've given him the book* = je lui ai donné le livre; *I've given it to him* = je le lui ai donné.
In imperatives, the indirect object pronoun is translated by *lui* and comes after the verb: *phone him!* = téléphone-lui!; *give it to him* = donne-le-lui (note the hyphens).
After prepositions and after the verb *to be* the translation is *lui*: *she did it for him* = elle l'a fait pour lui; *it's him* = c'est lui.

pron ① (direct object) le, l'; **I like** ~ je l'aime bien; **catch** ~! attrape-le!; ② (indirect object, after prep) lui

Himalayas /ˌhɪməˈleɪəz/ pr npl (montagnes fpl de) l'Himalaya m

himself /hɪmˈself/

⚠️ When used as a reflexive pronoun, direct and indirect, *himself* is translated by *se* (*s'* before a vowel): *he's enjoying himself* = il s'amuse bien; *he's cut himself* = il s'est coupé.
When used in emphasis the translation is *lui-même*: *he himself didn't know* = il ne le savait pas lui-même.
After a preposition, the translation is *lui* or *lui-même*: *he can be proud of himself* = il peut être fier de lui or de lui-même.
For particular usages see below.

pron **he's hurt** ~ il s'est blessé; **for** ~ pour lui, pour lui-même; **(all) by** ~ tout seul; **he's not** ~ **today** il n'est pas dans son assiette aujourd'hui

hind /haɪnd/
A n (pl ~**s** ou ~) Zool biche f
B adj de derrière; ~ **legs** pattes fpl de derrière

hinder /ˈhɪndə(r)/ vtr (hamper) entraver; (delay) freiner [*progress, efforts*]; retarder [*plan*]

hindquarters /ˌhaɪndˈkwɔːtəz/ npl arrière-train m

hindrance /ˈhɪndrəns/ n entrave f; **to be a** ~ **to sb/sth** gêner qn/qch

hindsight /ˈhaɪndsaɪt/ n **with (the benefit of)** ~ avec du recul, rétrospectivement

Hindu /ˌhɪnˈduː:, US ˈhɪnduː/ ▸ p. 1032
A n Hindou/-e m/f
B adj hindou

Hinduism /ˈhɪnduːɪzəm/ n hindouisme m

Hindustani /ˌhɪnduˈstɑːnɪ/ ▸ p. 969 n, adj hindoustani (m), hindi (m)

hinge /hɪndʒ/
A n gen charnière f; (lift-off) gond m; **to come off its** ~**s** [*door*] sortir de ses gonds
B vi (p prés hingeing) **to** ~ **on** dépendre de

hint /hɪnt/
A n allusion f (**about** à); fig (of spice, flavouring, accent) pointe f; (of colour) touche f; (of smile) ébauche f; (of irony, humour) soupçon m; **broad** ~ allusion transparente; **to give a** ~ faire allusion (**about** à); **to drop** ~**s** faire des allusions; **to drop** ~**s that** laisser entendre que; **to take a** ~ ou **the** ~ saisir l'allusion; **all right, I can take a** ~ c'est bon, j'ai compris; **to give sb some useful** ~**s** donner quelques conseils utiles à qn
B vtr **to** ~ **that** laisser entendre que (**to** à)

(Phrasal verb)
■ **hint at**: ▸ ~ **at [sth]** faire allusion à

hinterland /ˈhɪntəlænd/ n arrière-pays m inv

hip /hɪp/
A n ① ▸ p. 698 hanche f; **to break one's** ~ se casser le col du fémur; ② Bot gratte-cul m
B °adj [*person*] branché
C excl ~ ~ **hurrah!** hip hip hip hourra!

hip: ~**bone** n os m iliaque; ~ **flask** n flasque f

hip measurement, hip size n tour m de hanches

hippie, hippy /ˈhɪpɪ/ n, adj hippie (mf), hippy (mf)

hippo /ˈhɪpəʊ/ n hippopotame m

hip pocket n poche f revolver

Hippocratic /ˌhɪpəˈkrætɪk/ adj ~ **oath** serment m d'Hippocrate

hippopotamus /ˌhɪpəˈpɒtəməs/ n (pl **-muses** ou **-mi**) hippopotame m

hip replacement n prothèse f de la hanche

hire /ˈhaɪə(r)/
A n location f; **car** ~ location de voitures; **to let sth out on** ~ louer qch; **for** ~ [*boat, skis*] à louer; [*taxi*] libre
B noun modifier [*car, charge, firm*] de location
C vtr louer [*equipment*]; engager [*person*]

hire purchase, HP n achat m à crédit; **on** ~ à crédit

his /hɪz/

⚠️ In French determiners agree in gender and number with the noun they qualify. So *his* when used as a determiner is translated by *son* + masculine singular noun (son chien), by *sa* + feminine singular noun (sa maison) BUT by *son* + feminine noun beginning with a vowel or mute h (son assiette) and by *ses* + plural noun (ses enfants).
When *his* is stressed, *à lui* is added after the noun: *his house* = sa maison à lui.
For *his* used with parts of the body ▸ p. 698.
In French possessive pronouns reflect the gender and number of the noun they are standing for. When used as a possessive pronoun *his* is translated by *le sien, la sienne, les siens* or *les siennes* according to what is being referred to.
For examples and particular usages see the entry below.

A det son/sa/ses
B pron **all the drawings were good but** ~ **was the best** tous les dessins étaient bons mais le sien était le meilleur; **the blue car is** ~ la voiture bleue est la sienne, la voiture bleue est à lui; **it's not** ~ ce n'est pas à lui; **which house is** ~? sa maison c'est laquelle?; **I'm a colleague of** ~ je suis un/-e de ses collègues; **that dog of** ~ péj son sale chien°; **the money was not** ~ **to give away** il n'avait pas le droit de donner cet argent

Hispanic /hɪˈspænɪk/ adj (Spanish) hispanique, (Latin American) latino-américain

hiss /hɪs/
A n sifflement m; (of tape) grésillement m
B vtr siffler [person, performance, speech]
C vi [person, steam, snake] siffler; [cat] cracher; [fat, cassette] grésiller

historian /hɪˈstɔːrɪən/ ▸ p. 1181 n historien/-ienne m/f; **ancient ~** spécialiste mf d'histoire de l'Antiquité

historic /hɪˈstɒrɪk, US -ˈstɔːr-/ adj **1** gen historique; **2** Ling **past ~** passé m simple; **~ present** présent m de narration

historical /hɪˈstɒrɪkl, US -ˈstɔːr-/ adj historique

historically /hɪˈstɒrɪklɪ, US -ˈstɔːr-/ adv historiquement; **~ speaking** d'un point de vue historique

history /ˈhɪstrɪ/
A n **1** histoire f; **French ~** histoire de France; **18th century French ~** histoire de la France au XVIIIᵉ siècle; **~ of art** histoire de l'art; **a place in ~** une place dans l'histoire; **to make ~** entrer dans l'histoire; **to go down in ~ as** entrer dans l'histoire comme; **2** (past experience) antécédents mpl; **to have a ~ of heart trouble** avoir des antécédents cardiaques; **to have a ~ of violence** avoir un passé violent; **3** (account) histoire f; **4** (tradition) tradition f
B noun modifier [book, teacher] d'histoire
(Idiom) **the rest is ~** tout le monde connaît la suite

histrionic /ˌhɪstrɪˈɒnɪk/
A histrionics npl cinéma° m
B adj péj mélodramatique, théâtral

hit /hɪt/
A n **1** (blow, stroke in sport) coup m; (in fencing) touche f; **to score a ~** Sport, fig marquer un point; **2** (success) (play, film etc) succès m; (record) tube° m; **to be a big ou smash ~** avoir un succès fou; **to make a ~ with sb** faire grosse impression sur qn; **3** Comput (visit to website) visite f; (websearch match) page f trouvée
B vtr (p prés -tt-; prét, pp hit) **1** (strike) frapper [person, ball]; [head, arm] cogner contre [wall]; **to ~ one's head on sth** se cogner la tête contre qch; **his father used to ~ him** son père le battait; **to ~ a good shot** (in tennis, cricket) jouer une bonne balle; **2** (strike at target) atteindre [victim, target, enemy]; **3** (collide violently with) heurter [wall]; (more violently) percuter [wall]; [vehicle] renverser [person]; **4** (affect adversely) affecter, toucher; **5** (become apparent to) **it suddenly hit me that** je me suis soudain rendu compte que; **6** (reach) arriver à [motorway]; fig [figures, weight] atteindre [level]; **7** (come upon) rencontrer [traffic, bad weather]; **8** °(go to) **to ~ the town** sortir s'amuser; **9** °(attack) [robbers] attaquer [bank]
(Idioms) **a colour which ~s you between the eyes** une couleur criarde; **to ~ the roof**° sauter au plafond°; **to ~ it off with sb** bien s'entendre avec qn; **not to know what has hit one**° être sidéré
(Phrasal verbs)
■ **hit back**: ▸ **~ back** riposter; ▸ **~ [sb] back** rendre un coup à [qn]; ▸ **~ [sth] back** renvoyer [ball]
■ **hit out at**: ▸ **~ out at [sth]** (criticise) attaquer
■ **hit upon, hit on**: ▸ **~ (up)on [sth]** avoir [idea]; découvrir [evidence, solution]; tomber sur [problem]

hit-and-miss adj [method] approximatif/-ive; [affair, undertaking] hasardeux/-euse

hit-and-run adj [raid, attack] éclair inv; [accident] où le chauffeur a pris la fuite; **~ driver** chauffeur m en délit de fuite

hitch /hɪtʃ/
A n **1** (problem) problème m, pépin° m; **a slight ~** un petit pépin°; **2** (knot) nœud m
B vtr **1** (fasten) attacher [trailer]; atteler [horse]; accrocher [rail carriage]; **2** °(thumb) **to ~ a lift** faire du stop°
C °vi faire du stop°
(Idiom) **to get ~ed**° convoler en justes noces°
(Phrasal verb)
■ **hitch up**: ▸ **~ up [sth], ~ [sth] up 1** (pull up) retrousser [skirt]; remonter [trousers, covers]; **2** = **hitch B 1**

hitchhike /ˈhɪtʃhaɪk/ vi faire du stop° m; **to ~ to Paris** aller à Paris en stop°

hitch: **~hiker** n auto-stoppeur/-euse m/f; **~hiking** n auto-stop m

hi-tech = high tech

hither‡ /ˈhɪðə(r)/ adv ici; **~ and thither** de ci, de là

hitherto /ˌhɪðəˈtuː/ adv (until now) jusqu'à présent; (until then) jusqu'alors

hit: **~ list** n liste f noire; **~ man** n tueur m (à gages); **~ parade** n palmarès m, hit-parade m; **~ single** n tube° m

HIV n (abrév = **human immunodeficiency virus**) (virus m) VIH m

hive /haɪv/
A n **1** (beehive) ruche f; **a ~ of activity ou industry** fig une vraie ruche; **2** (swarm) essaim m
B hives npl ▸ p. 933 urticaire f
(Phrasal verb)
■ **hive off** (separate off) séparer; (sell off) céder

HIV: **~-infected** adj contaminé (par le virus du SIDA); **~-negative** adj séronégatif/-ive (au virus VIH); **~-positive** adj séropositif/-ive (au virus VIH)

HMI n (abrév = **His/Her Majesty's Inspector**) inspecteur m (qui se rend dans les écoles)

HMS n (abrév = **His/Her Majesty's Ship**) ≈ bâtiment m de Sa Majesté; **~ Victory** le (HMS) Victoire

HMSO n (Hist) (abrév = **His/Her Majesty's Stationery Office**) service gouvernemental de publication

HNC n GB (abrév = **Higher National Certificate**) ≈ BTS m

HND n GB (abrév = **Higher National Diploma**) diplôme supérieur d'aptitudes techniques

hoard /hɔːd/
A n (of treasure) trésor m; (of provisions) provisions fpl; (of miser) magot° m
B vtr [person] stocker [supplies] also pej; amasser [objects, money]; [animal] amasser [food]

hoarding /ˈhɔːdɪŋ/ n GB **1** (billboard) panneau m publicitaire; **2** (fence) palissade f; **3** (saving) accumulation f

hoarfrost /ˈhɔːfrɒst, US -frɔːst/ n gelée f blanche, givre m

hoarse /hɔːs/ adj [voice] rauque; **to be ~** être enroué; **to shout oneself ~** s'enrouer à force de crier

hoary /ˈhɔːrɪ/ adj **1** [person] chenu, aux cheveux blancs; **2** fig **a ~ old joke** une plaisanterie éculée

hoax /həʊks/
A n (practical joke) canular m; **it was a ~** (bomb) c'était une fausse alerte à la bombe
B noun modifier [call, warning] bidon° inv

hob /hɒb/ n (on stove) table f de cuisson; (on open fire) plaque f (sur laquelle on tient la bouilloire au chaud)

hobble /ˈhɒbl/ vi (limp) boitiller; **to ~ in/along** entrer/avancer clopin-clopant°

hobby /ˈhɒbɪ/ n passe-temps m inv; **hobbies and interests** (on CV) centres mpl d'intérêt

hobby horse n **1** (toy) bâton emmanché d'une tête de cheval en bois; **2** (obsession) dada m péj; cheval m de bataille

hobgoblin /ˈhɒbgɒblɪn/ n gnome m, lutin m

hobnob /ˈhɒbnɒb/ vi (p prés etc **-bb-**) **to ~ with sb** frayer° avec qn

hobo /ˈhəʊbəʊ/ n (pl **~s** ou **~es**) clochard/-e m/f, vagabond/-e m/f

hock /hɒk/ n **1** (of horse etc) jarret m; Culin jarret m (de porc); **2** (wine) vin m du Rhin; **3** °(pawn) **to be in ~** être au clou°, être engagé au mont-de-piété

hockey /ˈhɒkɪ/ n ▸ p. 881 n GB hockey m; US hockey m sur glace; **~ stick** crosse f de hockey

hocus-pocus /ˌhəʊkəsˈpəʊkəs/ n péj (trickery) supercherie f, tour m de passe-passe

hod /hɒd/ n (for coal) seau m à charbon; (for bricks) oiseau m, hotte f

hoe /həʊ/
A n houe f, binette f
B vtr biner [ground]; sarcler [plants, flowerbeds]

hoedown /ˈhəʊdaʊn/ n bal m (de village)

hog /hɒg/
A n **1** GB (castrated pig) porc m châtré; **2** US (pig) porc m, verrat m; **3** °(person) pourceau m
B °vtr (prét, pp **-gg-**) (monopolize) monopoliser
(Idiom) **to go the whole ~**° (be extravagant) voir les choses en grand; (go to extremes) aller jusqu'au bout

Hogmanay /ˈhɒgmənеɪ/ n GB dial Saint-Sylvestre f, réveillon m

h

hog-tie /'hɒgtaɪ/ *vtr* lier les pattes de [*pig, cow*]; US *fig* réduire [qn] à l'impuissance [*person*]

hogwash /'hɒgwɒʃ/ *n* foutaise○ *f*

hoi polloi /,hɔɪ pə'lɔɪ/ *npl* péj plèbe *f* pej, populace *f*

hoist /hɔɪst/
A *n* palan *m*; **to give sb a ~ (up)** faire la courte échelle à qn
B *vtr* hisser [*flag, sail, heavy object*]

hoity-toity○ /,hɔɪtɪ'tɔɪtɪ/ *adj* péj prétentieux/-ieuse

hokum○ /'həʊkəm/ *n* **Ȼ** US (nonsense) absurdités *fpl*, niaiseries *fpl*; (sentimentality) mièvrerie *f*

hold /həʊld/ ▸ p. 723
A *n* ⓵ (grasp) prise *f*; **to get ~ of** attraper; **to keep (a) ~ of** ou **on** tenir; ⓶ (possession) **to get ~ of** se procurer [*book, ticket*]; [*press*] avoir vent de [*story*]; découvrir [*information*]; ⓷ (contact) **to get ~ of** (by phone) joindre; (by other means) trouver; ⓸ (control) emprise *f* (**on, over** sur); **to have a ~ on** ou **over sb** avoir de l'emprise sur qn; **to get a ~ of oneself** se reprendre; ⓹ Telecom **on ~** en attente; **to put a call on ~** mettre un appel en attente; **to put a project on ~** gen laisser un projet en suspens; ⓺ (storage, area) Aviat soute *f*; Naut cale *f*; ⓻ (in wrestling) prise *f*; ⓼ (of spray, gel) fixation *f*
B *vtr* (*prét*, *pp* **held**) ⓵ (clasp) tenir; **to ~ sth in one's hand** tenir qch à la main [*brush, pencil*]; (enclosed) tenir qch dans la main [*coin, sweet*]; **to ~ sb by** tenir qn par [*sleeve, leg*]; **to ~ sb (in one's arms)** serrer qn dans ses bras; **to ~ each other** se serrer l'un contre l'autre; **to ~ one's head still** tenir sa tête immobile; **to ~ oneself well** se tenir bien; **to ~ sth in place** ou **position** maintenir qch en place; ⓷ (arrange) gen organiser; avoir [*conversation*]; célébrer [*church service*]; mener [*enquiry*]; faire passer [*interview*]; **to be held** avoir lieu; ⓸ (have capacity for) (pouvoir) contenir [*350 people*]; **the bus ~s ten (people)** le bus a dix places; ⓹ (contain) [*drawer, cupboard, box, case*] contenir [*objects, possessions*]; ⓺ (support) supporter [*weight, load, crate*]; ⓻ (restrain) tenir [*dog*]; **there'll be no ~ing him** fig on ne pourra plus l'arrêter; ⓼ (keep against will) détenir [*person*]; **to ~ sb hostage** garder qn en otage; ⓽ (possess) détenir, avoir [*shares, power, record*]; être titulaire de [*degree, sporting title*]; occuper [*job, position*]; avoir, être en possession de [*passport, licence*]; porter [*title*]; avoir [*mortgage*]; [*computer*] conserver [*information*]; ⓾ (keep back) garder [*place, ticket*]; faire attendre [*train, flight*]; mettre [qch] en attente [*letter, order*]; **~ it**○! minute○!; ⑪ (believe) avoir [*opinion, belief*]; **to ~ sb/sth to be** tenir qn/qch pour; **to ~ sb liable** ou **responsible** tenir qn pour responsable; **to ~ that** [*person*] soutenir que; [*law*] dire que; ⑫ (defend successfully) tenir [*territory, city*]; conserver [*title, seat, lead*]; **to ~ one's own** se défendre tout seul; ⑬ (captivate) captiver [*audience*]; capter, retenir [*attention*]; ⑭ Telecom **can you ~ the line please** ne quittez pas s'il vous plaît; ⑮ Mus tenir [*note*]; ⑯ Aut **to ~ the road** tenir la route
C *vi* (*prét*, *pp* **held**) ⓵ (remain intact) tenir; fig (*also* **~ good**) tenir; ⓶ (continue) [*weather*] rester beau, se maintenir; [*luck*] continuer, durer; ⓷ Telecom patienter; ⓸ (remain steady) **~ still!** tiens-toi tranquille!

Phrasal verbs

■ **hold against**: **to ~ sth against sb** reprocher qch à qn; **to ~ it against sb (that)** en vouloir à qn (parce que); **it could be held against you** [*age, sex*] ça pourrait jouer en ta défaveur

■ **hold back**: ▸ **~ back** se retenir (**from doing** de faire); ▸ **~ [sb/sth] back**, **~ back [sb/sth]** ⓵ (restrain) contenir [*water, crowd, anger*]; retenir [*hair, tears, person*]; refouler [*feelings*]; ⓶ (prevent progress of) entraver [*production, development*]; [*timidity, inexperience*] retenir [*person*]; ⓷ (withhold) différer [*payment*]; cacher [*information*]; (to protect privacy) tenir [qch] secret, ne pas divulguer

■ **hold down**: ▸ **~ [sb/sth] down**, **~ down [sb/sth]** ⓵ (prevent from moving) maintenir [qch] en place [*carpet*]; tenir, maîtriser [*person*]; ⓶ (keep at certain level) limiter [*expenditure, inflation*]; limiter l'augmentation de [*wages, prices*]; ⓷ (not lose) garder [*job*]

■ **hold forth** péj disserter, pérorer pej (**about, on** sur)

■ **hold in**: ▸ **~ [sth] in**, **~ in [sth]** (restrain) réprimer, contenir [*feeling*]; (pull in) rentrer [*stomach*]

■ **hold off**: ▸ **~ off** [*creditors*] accorder un délai; **I hope the rain ~s off** j'espère qu'il ne pleuvra pas; ▸ **~ [sb] off**, **~ off [sb]** tenir [qn] à distance; ▸ **~ [sth] off** repousser [*attack*]

■ **hold on**: ▸ **~ on** ⓵ (wait) gen attendre; '**~ on…**' (on

telephone) 'ne quittez pas…'; ⓶ (grip) tenir (**with** de, avec); '**~ on (tight)!**' 'tiens-toi (bien)!'; ⓷ (endure) tenir; ▸ **~ [sth] on** maintenir (**with** par)

■ **hold on to**: ▸ **~ on to [sb/sth]** ⓵ (grip) s'agripper à; (to prevent from falling) agripper, retenir [*person*]; serrer [*object, purse*]; ⓶ (retain) conserver [*power, lead*]; garder [*shares, car*]; **to ~ on to the belief that** persister à croire que; ⓷ (look after) garder (**for** pour)

■ **hold out**: ▸ **~ out** ⓵ (endure) tenir le coup, tenir bon; **to ~ out against** tenir bon devant; **to ~ out for** insister pour obtenir; **to ~ out on sb**○ cacher des choses à qn; ⓶ (remain available) durer; ▸ **~ [sth] out**, **~out [sth]** tendre [*hand*] (**to** à); **I don't ~ out much hope** je ne me fais guère d'illusions

■ **hold over** ⓵ (postpone) ajourner; ⓶ (continue to show) prolonger [*show, exhibition*]

■ **hold to**: ▸ **~ to [sth]** s'en tenir à [*belief, decision*]; ▸ **~ sb to [sth]** faire tenir [qch] à qn [*promise*]; faire honorer [qch] à qn [*contract, offer*]

■ **hold together**: ▸ **~ together** ⓵ (not break) tenir; ⓶ (remain united) rester uni; ▸ **~ [sth] together** ⓵ (keep intact) faire tenir [*machine, chair*]; maintenir ensemble [*pieces*]; ⓶ (unite) assurer la cohésion de

■ **hold up**: ▸ **~ up** ⓵ (remain intact) tenir, résister; ⓶ (remain valid) tenir; ▸ **~ [sb/sth] up**, **~ up [sb/sth]** ⓵ (support) soutenir [*shelf*]; tenir [*trousers*]; (raise) lever; **to ~ one's hand up** lever la main; ⓷ (display) **to ~ sb/sth up as an example** ou **model of** présenter qn/qch comme un exemple de; **to ~ sb up to ridicule** tourner qn en ridicule, ridiculiser qn; ⓸ (delay) retarder [*person, flight*]; ralentir [*production, traffic*]; ⓹ (rob) attaquer

■ **hold with**: **not to ~ with** être contre

holdall /'həʊldɔːl/ *n* fourre-tout *m*, sac *m*

holder /'həʊldə(r)/ *n* ⓵ (of passport, degree, post) titulaire *mf*; (of ticket, record) détenteur/-trice *m/f*; (of title) tenant/-e *m/f*; (of shares) porteur/-euse *m/f*; **account ~** titulaire d'un compte; ⓶ (stand) support *m*

hold-up /'həʊldʌp/ *n* ⓵ (delay) gen retard *m*; (on road) embouteillage *m*, bouchon *m*; ⓶ (robbery) hold-up *m*, attaque *f* à main armée

hole /həʊl/
A *n* ⓵ (in clothing, hedge etc) trou *m*; ⓶ (in wall) brèche *f*; ⓷ GB (in tooth) cavité *f*; ⓸ (in road) (pothole) nid *m* de poule; (man-made) trou *m*; ⓹ fig (flaw) faille *f*; **to pick ~s in an argument** repérer les failles d'un raisonnement; ⓺ (of mouse) trou *m*; (of fox, rabbit) terrier *m*; ⓻ Ecol (in ozone layer) trou *m*; ⓼ (financial) trou *m*; **that holiday made a ~ in my pocket** ces vacances ont fait un trou dans mon budget; ⓽ ○(place) péj trou○ *m* pej; ⑩ (golf) trou *m*; **a nine-~ course** un parcours de neuf trous
B *vtr* [*iceberg*] faire une brèche dans [*ship*]

⟨Idiom⟩ **to get sb out of a ~** tirer qn du pétrin○

⟨Phrasal verb⟩

■ **hole up** se terrer

hole-and-corner *adj* clandestin

hole-in-the-wall○ *n* distributeur *m* de billets (*de banque*)

holiday /'hɒlədeɪ/
A *n* ⓵ GB (vacation) vacances *fpl*; **on ~** en vacances; **the school ~s** les vacances scolaires; **the summer ~s** les vacances d'été, les grandes vacances; **family ~** vacances en famille; ⓶ GB (time off work) congé *m*; ⓷ (public, bank) jour *m* férié; ⓸ US **the ~s** les fêtes (de fin d'année)
B *vi* passer les vacances

holiday: **~ atmosphere** *n* air *m* de fête; **~ home** *n* résidence *f* secondaire; **~ job** *n* GB (in summer) job○ *m* d'été; **~maker** *n* GB gen vacancier/-ière *m/f*; (summer visitor) estivant/-e *m/f*; **~ resort** *n* lieu *m* de villégiature

holier-than-thou /,həʊlɪəðən'ðaʊ/ *adj* péj **to be ~** se prendre pour un petit saint

holiness /'həʊlɪnɪs/ *n* sainteté *f*

Holland /'hɒlənd/ ▸ p. 774 *pr n* Hollande *f*, Pays-Bas *mpl*; **in ~** en Hollande, aux Pays-Bas

holler○ /'hɒlə(r)/ *vi* brailler, gueuler❶ (**at sb** après qn)

hollow /'hɒləʊ/
A *n* ⓵ (in tree, of hand, back) creux *m*; ⓶ (small valley) cuvette *f*
B *adj* ⓵ (not solid) creux/creuse; **to sound ~** sonner creux; ⓶ (sunken) creux/creuse; ⓷ (booming) caverneux/-euse; ⓸ (insincere) [*words*] faux/fausse; [*promise*] vain; **a ~ laugh** un rire forcé; **to sound ~** sonner faux

(Idiom) **to beat sb ~**○ battre qn à plates coutures
(Phrasal verb)
∎ **hollow out: ▸ ~ [sth] out, ~ out [sth]** creuser

hollow: ~-cheeked adj aux joues creuses; **~-eyed** adj aux yeux caves

holly /'hɒlɪ/ n (tree, wood) houx m

holocaust /'hɒləkɔːst/ n holocauste m; **the Holocaust** l'Holocauste m

hologram /'hɒləgræm/ n hologramme m

holograph /'hɒləgrɑːf, US -græf/ n (also ~ **document**) document m olographe

hols○ /hɒlz/ n GB (abrév = **holidays**) vacances fpl

holster /'həʊlstə(r)/ n étui m de revolver

holy /'həʊlɪ/ adj [place, day, city, person] saint; [water] bénit; **~ picture** image f pieuse; **on ~ ground** en lieu saint

holy: Holy Bible n Sainte Bible f; **Holy Communion** n sainte communion f; **Holy Father** n Saint-Père m; **Holy Grail** n Saint-Graal m; **Holy Land** n Terre f Sainte; **Holy See** n Saint-Siège m; **Holy Spirit** n Saint-Esprit m; **Holy Trinity** n sainte Trinité f; **Holy Week** n semaine f sainte

holy writ n Saintes Écritures fpl; **it's ~** c'est sacré

homage /'hɒmɪdʒ/ n hommage m; **to pay ~ to** rendre hommage à

homburg /'hɒmbɜːg/ n chapeau m mou

home /həʊm/
A n **1** (dwelling) gen logement m; (house) maison f; **to be far from ~** être loin de chez soi; **a ~ of one's own** un chez-soi; **to work from ~** travailler à domicile; **to set up ~ in Madrid** s'installer à Madrid; **I've made my ~ in France** je suis installé or je vis en France; **it's ~ to me now** je m'y sens chez moi; **2** (for residential care) maison f; **to put sb in a ~** mettre qn dans un établissement spécialisé; **3** (family base) foyer m; **broken ~** foyer désuni; **'good ~ wanted'** 'cherche foyer accueillant'; **to leave ~** quitter la maison; **4** (country) pays m; **to consider France (as) ~** considérer la France comme son pays; **5** (source) **~ of** [country, area] pays m de [speciality]
B noun modifier **1** (family) [life] de famille; [background] familial; [comforts] du foyer; **2** (national) [market, affairs] intérieur; [news] national; **3** Sport [match, win] à domicile; [team] qui reçoit
C adv **1** [come, go, arrive] (to house) à la maison, chez soi; (to country) dans son pays; **on the way ~** en rentrant chez moi/nous etc; (by boat, plane) pendant le voyage de retour; **to take sb ~** raccompagner qn à la maison; **to be ~** (around) être à la maison; (from work) être rentré; **2** (to required effect) **to push one's point ~** enfoncer le clou fig; **to bring sth ~ to** fig faire voir qch à; **to strike ~** fig toucher juste
D **at home** adv phr **1** (in house) à la maison; **to live at ~** habiter chez ses parents; **2** Sport (on own ground) [play] à domicile; **3** fig (comfortable) à l'aise; **make yourself at ~** fais comme chez toi

(Idioms) **it's nothing to write ~ about** ça n'a rien d'extraordinaire; **it's ~ from ~** GB, **it's ~ away from ~** US c'est un second chez-soi; **to be a bit too close to ~** être blessant; **to be ~ and dry** être sauvé
(Phrasal verb)
∎ **home in on: ▸ ~ in on [sth]** se diriger sur [target]

home address n (on form) domicile m; (personal) adresse f personnelle

homebound /'həʊmbaʊnd/ adj surtout US **1** (housebound) confiné chez soi; **2** [traffic, car, traveller] rentrant chez soi; [train] du retour

home: ~ brew n bière f (brassée) maison; **~ centre** GB, **~ center** US n maisonnerie f

homecoming /'həʊmkʌmɪŋ/ n **1** (return home) retour m à la maison; **2** US Sport match de football annuel du lycée suivi d'un bal

home: ~ computer n ordinateur m, PC m; **~ cooking** n bonne cuisine f familiale; **Home Counties** npl GB comtés mpl limitrophes de Londres; **~ economics** n Sch cours m d'économie domestique

home front n (during war) **the ~** l'arrière m; **on the ~** (in politics) pour les affaires intérieures

home ground n fig terrain m familier; **on one's ~** Sport à domicile

home: ~grown adj lit du jardin; fig [idea] bien de chez soi; **~ help** n GB aide f familiale; **~land** n pays m

d'origine, patrie f; (in S. Africa) bantoustan m

homeless /'həʊmlɪs/
A n **the ~** (+ v pl) les sans-abri mpl inv
B adj gen sans abri, sans logement; (after flood etc) sinistré

home life n vie f de famille

home: ~ loan n prêt m immobilier; **~loving** adj casanier/-ière

homely /'həʊmlɪ/ adj **1** GB (cosy, welcoming) accueillant; **2** GB (unpretentious) [room, cooking] sans prétention; [person] simple; **3** US péj (plain) [person] sans attraits

home: ~made adj (fait) maison; **~maker** n femme f d'intérieur; **~ movie** n film m d'amateur; **Home Office** n Pol ministère m de l'Intérieur

homeopathic /ˌhəʊmɪə'pæθɪk/ adj [medicine, clinic] homéopathique; [doctor] homéopathe

homeopathy /ˌhəʊmɪ'ɒpəθɪ/ n homéopathie f

home: ~ owner n propriétaire mf; **~ ownership** n fait m d'être propriétaire de son logement; **~ plate** n Sport marbre m; **~ port** n port m d'attache; **~ rule** n Pol gouvernement m autonome; **~ run** n Sport point m marqué par le batteur (s'il réussit à toucher toutes les bases); **Home Secretary** n Pol Ministre m de l'Intérieur

homesick /'həʊmsɪk/ adj **to be ~** (for country) avoir le mal du pays; [child] s'ennuyer de ses parents

home: ~sickness n mal m du pays; **~ side** n = home team

homespun /'həʊmspʌn/ adj **1** [cloth] artisanal; **2** fig [wisdom, virtue] naturel-elle, sans artifices

homestead /'həʊmsted/ n **1** (house and land) domaine m; **2** (farm) ferme f; **3** US Admin terres fpl (acquises pour leur occupation et leur exploitation)

home: ~ team n équipe f qui reçoit; **~ town** n ville f natale; **~ video** n vidéo f d'amateur; **~ visit** n Med visite f à domicile

homeward /'həʊmwəd/ adv **to travel ~(s)** rentrer; **to be ~ bound** être sur le chemin de retour

home waters npl Naut, Pol eaux fpl territoriales

homework /'həʊmwɜːk/ n ¢ **1** Sch devoirs mpl; **2** (research) **to do some ~ on** faire quelques recherches au sujet de

home: ~worker n travailleur/-euse m/f à domicile; **~working** n travail m à domicile

homey /'həʊmɪ/ adj (cosy) accueillant; (simple) sans prétention

homicidal /ˌhɒmɪ'saɪdl/ adj homicide

homicide /'hɒmɪsaɪd/ n **1** (murder) homicide m; **justifiable ~** Jur homicide justifiable; **~ bureau** US brigade f criminelle; **2** (person) meurtrier/-ière m/f

homily /'hɒmɪlɪ/ n homélie f

homing /'həʊmɪŋ/ adj [missile] autoguidé; [system, device] d'autoguidage; **~ instinct** faculté f d'orientation; **~ pigeon** pigeon m voyageur

hominy grits /'hɒmɪnɪ grɪts/ n US (dish) bouillie f de maïs

homogeneity /ˌhɒmədʒɪ'niːɪtɪ/ n homogénéité f

homogeneous /ˌhɒmə'dʒiːnɪəs, ˌhɒməʊ-/ adj homogène

homogenize /hə'mɒdʒɪnaɪz/ vtr homogénéiser

homogenous /hə'mɒdʒɪnəs/ adj homogène

homograph /'hɒməgrɑːf, US -græf/ n homographe m

homonym /'hɒmənɪm/ n homonyme m

homophobia /ˌhɒmə'fəʊbɪə/ n intolérance f envers les homosexuels

homosexual /ˌhɒmə'sekʃʊəl/ n, adj homosexuel/-elle (m/f)

homosexuality /ˌhɒmə,sekʃʊ'ælətɪ/ n homosexualité f

Hon **1** (abrév écrite = **Honourable**) **the ~ Anne Grey** l'honorable Anne Grey; **2** (abrév écrite = **Honorary**) honoraire

honcho○ /'hɒntʃəʊ/ n (pl **~s**) US **he's the head ~** c'est le grand chef○

hone /həʊn/ vtr **1** (perfect) aiguiser [technique, skill]; affûter [argument, style]; **2** (sharpen) aiguiser

honest /'ɒnɪst/
A adj **1** (truthful) [person] intègre; [answer, account] sincère; **to be ~ about** être honnête au sujet de; **the ~ truth** la pure

vérité; **2** (trustworthy) honnête; **3** (sincere) franc/franche; **to be ~ with sb** être franc avec qn; **to be ~ with oneself** être honnête avec soi-même; **be ~!** sois franc!; **to be ~,...** à dire vrai...; **4** (legal) [*profit, money*] honnêtement acquis; [*price*] juste; **by ~ means** par des moyens légitimes; **to make an ~ living** gagner honnêtement sa vie

B *excl* ○ *ou* **~ to God!** parole d'honneur!

honestly /'ɒnɪstlɪ/ *adv* **1** (truthfully) honnêtement; **2** (legally) honnêtement; **3** (sincerely) [*believe*] franchement; [*say*] sincèrement; **quite ~,... ~, there's no problem** je vous assure, il n'y a aucun problème; **4** ○(in exasperation) franchement!

honest-to-goodness *adj* **1** (simple) simple; **2** US (authentic) véritable

honesty /'ɒnɪstɪ/ *n* honnêteté *f*

(Idiom) **~ is the best policy** l'honnêteté est toujours récompensée

honey /'hʌnɪ/ *n* **1** (food) miel *m*; **clear ~** miel liquide; **2** ○(endearment) chéri/-e *m/f*

honey: **~bee** *n* abeille *f*; **~bunch**○, **~bun** *n* US chéri/-e *m/f*; **~-coloured** GB, **~-colored** US ▸ p. 752 *adj* (couleur de) miel *inv*

honeycomb /'hʌnɪkəʊm/ *n* **1** (in hive) rayon *m* de miel; **2** (for sale) gâteau *m* de miel

honeycombed /'hʌnɪkəʊmd/ *adj* **~ with** percé de [*holes*]; creusé de [*passages, tunnels*]

honeydew melon *n* melon *m* d'Espagne

honeymoon /'hʌnɪmuːn/ *n* **1** (wedding trip) voyage *m* de noces; **2** fig (also **~ period**) (calm spell) lune *f* de miel

honeypot /'hʌnɪpɒt/ *n*

(Idiom) **like bees around a ~** comme des mouches sur un pot de miel

honeysuckle /'hʌnɪsʌkl/ *n* chèvrefeuille *m*

Hong Kong /,hɒŋ 'kɒŋ/ ▸ p. 1276 *pr n* Hongkong *m*

honk /hɒŋk/

A *n* (of horn) coup *m* de klaxon®; (of geese) cri *m* (de l'oie)

B *vtr* **to ~ one's horn (at sb)** klaxonner (qn)

C *vi* [*geese*] cacarder; [*car horn*] faire tut-tut; [*driver*] klaxonner

honky-tonk /'hɒŋkɪtɒŋk/ *adj* [*piano*] bastringue○

honor *n, vtr* US = **honour**

honorable *adj* US = **honourable**

honorably *adv* US = **honourably**

honorary /'ɒnərərɪ, US 'ɒnərerɪ/ *adj* [*doctorate*] honorifique, honoris causa *inv*; [*member*] honoraire

honorific /,ɒnə'rɪfɪk/ *adj* honorifique

honor roll *n* US **1** Sch, Sport tableau *m* d'honneur; **2** Mil liste *f* des soldats tombés au champ d'honneur

honor: **~ society** *n* US Sch club *m* des meilleurs élèves; **~ system** *n* US Sch système *m* de l'autodiscipline

honour GB, **honor** US /'ɒnə(r)/

A *n* **1** (privilege) honneur *m*; **place of ~** place d'honneur; **to give sb ~** do sb the **~ of doing** faire à qn l'honneur de faire; **in ~ of** en l'honneur de; **to what do I owe this ~?** sout *ou* iron que me vaut cet honneur? sout *ou* iron; **2** (high principles) honneur *m*; **to impugn sb's ~** sout mettre en doute l'honneur de qn; **to give one's word of ~** donner sa parole d'honneur; **3** (in titles) **Your Honour** Votre Honneur

B **honours** *npl* Univ **first/second class ~s** ≈ licence avec mention très bien/bien

C *vtr* **1** (show respect for) honorer; **to feel/be ~ed** se sentir/être honoré (**by** par); **to ~ sb by doing** sout faire l'honneur à qn de faire; **our ~ed guests** nos honorables invités; **2** (fulfil, be bound by) honorer [*cheque, contract, obligation*]; tenir [*promise, commitment*]; remplir [*agreement*]

(Idiom) **to do the ~s** (serve food, drinks) faire les honneurs; (introduce guests) faire les présentations

honourable GB, **honorable** US /'ɒnərəbl/ *adj* **1** (principled) honnête; **to do the ~ thing** faire la seule chose convenable; **2** (worthy) honorable; **3** ▸ p. 869 (in titles) **the Honourable Mr Justice Jones** Monsieur le Juge Jones; **the Honourable Gentleman** Pol Monsieur le député

honourable: **~ discharge** *n* libération *f* honorable; **~ mention** *n* mention *f* honorable

honourably GB, **honorably** US /'ɒnərəblɪ/ *adv* [*acquit oneself, fight, withdraw*] honorablement; [*behave*] honnêtement

honour: **~-bound** *adj* tenu par l'honneur (**to do** de faire); **~s course** *n*: cours universitaire réservé aux meilleurs étudiants; **~s degree** *n*: licence réservée aux meilleurs étudiants; **Honours List** *n* GB liste de distinctions honorifiques

hood /hʊd/ *n* **1** (head gear) (attached) capuchon *m*; (detached) capuche *f*; (balaclava) cagoule *f*; (for falcon) chaperon *m*; **2** (cover) (on cooker) hotte *f*; (on printer) capot *m* (antibruit); **3** GB (on car, pram) capote *f*; **4** US Aut (bonnet) capot *m*; **5** Univ (part of robes) épitoge *f*

hooded /'hʊdɪd/ *adj* **1** [*garment*] à capuchon; **2** [*attacker*] en cagoule; **3** **to have ~ eyes** avoir les paupières tombantes

hoodlum /'huːdləm/ *n* **1** (hooligan) vandale *m*; **2** US (crook) truand *m*

hoodwink /'hʊdwɪŋk/ *vtr* tromper

hoof /huːf/ *n* (*pl* **~s** *ou* **hooves**) sabot *m* (d'animal); **bought on the ~** acheté sur pied

(Idiom) **to ~ it**○ aller à pinces○ *or* à pied

hoo-ha○ /'huːhɑː/ *n* pagaille *f*

hook /hʊk/

A *n* **1** (for clothing, picture) crochet *m*; **2** (on fishing line) hameçon *m*; **3** (fastener) agrafe *f*; **~s and eyes** agrafes *fpl*; **4** (on pole) crosse *f*; **5** Telecom **to take the phone off the ~** décrocher le téléphone; **6** (boxing) crochet *m*; **left ~** crochet du gauche; **7** (golf) coup *m* hooké; **8** US (bend) coude *m*, courbe *f*

B *vtr* **1** (hang) accrocher (**on, onto** à); **2** (pull through) faire passer [*string*] (**through** dans); passer [*finger, stick*] (**through** dans); **3** (catch) prendre [*fish*]; fig, hum○ mettre le grappin sur○ [*spouse*]

(Idiom) **to get sb off the ~** tirer qn d'affaire

(Phrasal verbs)

■ **hook on** s'accrocher (**to** à)

■ **hook up**: ▸ **~ up** [*garment*] s'agrafer; ▸ **~ up** [*sth*], **~ [sth] up** **1** (attach) agrafer [*garment*]; accrocher [*trailer, picture*]; **2** Radio, TV faire un duplex entre [*stations*]; **3** Elec, Tech connecter [*appliance*]

hookah /'hʊkə/ *n* narguilé *m*

hooked /hʊkt/ *adj* **1** [*nose, beak*] crochu; [*stick*] avec une crosse; **2** (addicted) **to be ~ on** se camer○ à [*drugs*]; être mordu○ de [*computer games*]

hook nose *n* nez *m* crochu

hook-up /'hʊkʌp/ *n* **1** Radio, TV relais *m*; **2** US (in trailer park) borne *f* de raccordement

hooky○, **hookey** /'hʊkɪ/ *n* US **to play ~** faire l'école buissonnière†

hooligan /'huːlɪgən/ *n* vandale *m*, voyou *m*; **soccer ~** hooligan *m*

hooliganism /'huːlɪgənɪzəm/ *n* vandalisme *m*

hoop /huːp/ *n* (ring) cerceau *m*; (in croquet) arceau *m*

(Idioms) **to go through the ~s, to jump through ~s** faire des pieds et des mains

hoopla /'huːplɑː/ ▸ p. 881 *n* **1** GB (at fair) jeu *m* d'anneaux; **2** ○US (fuss) pagaille *f*

hooray /hʊ'reɪ/ *excl* hourra

Hooray Henry *n* GB péj fils *m* à papa pej

hoot /huːt/

A *n* **1** (noise) (of owl) (h)ululement *m*; (of train) sifflement *m*; (of ship or factory siren) mugissement *m*; (of car) coup *m* de klaxon®; (shout) rire *m* moqueur; **2** ○(funny) **to be a ~** être très marrant○

B *vtr* huer [*speaker, actor*]; **to ~ one's horn** donner un coup de klaxon○ (**at sb** pour avertir qn)

C *vi* [*owl*] (h)ululer; [*train*] siffler; [*siren*] mugir; [*car*] klaxonner; [*person, crowd*] (derisively) huer; **to ~ with laughter** éclater de rire

(Idiom) **I don't give two ~s**○! je m'en fiche○ comme de l'an quarante!

hooter /'huːtə(r)/ *n* **1** (siren) sirène *f*; **2** ○GB (nose) pif○ *m*, nez *m*

hoover /'huːvə(r)/ *vtr* GB **to ~ a room** passer l'aspirateur dans une pièce

Hoover® /'huːvə(r)/ *n* GB aspirateur *m*

hooves /huːvz/ *pl* ▸ **hoof**

hop /hɒp/

A *n* **1** (movement) (of frog, rabbit, child) bond *m*; (of bird) sautillement *m*; ⓶ ○(journey) **a short** ∼ un saut (de puce); ⓷ ○(dance) bal *m* (populaire)

B **hops** *npl* (crop) houblon *m* **₵**

C *vtr* (*p prés etc* **-pp-**) ⓵ (jump over) franchir [qch] d'un bond [*fence*]; ⓶ ○US (board) sauter dans [*flight, train, bus*]

D *vi* (*p prés etc* **-pp-**) ⓵ (jump) [*person*] sauter; **to** ∼ **off a wall** sauter d'un mur; **to** ∼ **up and down with rage** trépigner de rage; ⓶ (on one leg) sauter à cloche-pied; **to** ∼ **up the path** monter le sentier à cloche-pied; ⓷ [*animal*] sauter; [*bird*] sautiller; **a rabbit** ∼**ped across the road** un lapin traversa la route en quelques bonds; ⓸ (move speedily) **to** ∼ **into bed/off a bus** sauter dans son lit/d'un bus; ∼ **in!** (into car) vas-y, monte!

(Idioms) **to be** ∼**ping mad**○ être fou furieux/folle furieuse; **to catch sb on the** ∼○ GB prendre qn au dépourvu; **to** ∼ **it**○ GB déguerpir○; **to keep sb on the** ∼○ GB maintenir qn sous pression

hope /həʊp/

A *n* ⓵ (desire, expectation) espoir *m* (**of** de); (cause for optimism) espoir *m*; **in the** ∼ **of sth** dans l'espoir de qch; **to have high** ∼**s of sb/sth** fonder de grands espoirs sur qn/qch; **to have** ∼**s of doing** avoir l'espoir de faire; **there is no** ∼ **left for them** il n'y a plus d'espoir pour eux; **to set one's** ∼**s on doing** espérer de tout cœur faire; **to be beyond (all)** ∼, **to be without** ∼ être sans espoir; **to keep one's** ∼**s high** garder espoir; **to raise sb's** ∼**s** faire naître l'espoir chez qn; **to dash sb's** ∼**s** anéantir l'espoir de qn; ⓶ (chance) chance *f*, espoir *m*; **to have no** ∼ **of sth** n'avoir aucune chance de qch; **there is little** ∼ **that he will come** il y a peu de chances qu'il vienne; **there is no** ∼ **of an improvement** on ne peut pas s'attendre à une amélioration; **my last** ∼ mon dernier espoir; **what a** ∼○!, **some** ∼○! il ne faut pas rêver!; **he hasn't got a** ∼ **in hell**○ il n'a pas la moindre chance; ⓷ (promising person) espoir *m*

B *vtr* espérer (**that** que); **to** ∼ **to do** espérer faire; **it is to be** ∼**d that** il faut espérer que (+ *indic*); **we cannot** ∼ **to compete** nous n'avons aucune chance de rivaliser; **I only** ∼ **just** ∼ **he remembers** j'espère seulement qu'il s'en souviendra; **I (do)** ∼ **so/not** j'espère (bien) que oui/que non; **hoping to hear from you** dans l'espoir d' avoir de vos nouvelles

C *vi* espérer; **to** ∼ **for sth** espérer avoir qch; **all we can do is** ∼ nous ne pouvons qu'espérer; **to** ∼ **for the best** être optimiste

(Idiom) **to** ∼ **against** ∼ espérer en dépit de tout

hope chest *n* US (chest) coffre *m* à trousseau; (trousseau) trousseau *m*

hopeful /ˈhəʊpfl/

A *n* **young** ∼ jeune espoir *m*; (ambitious) ambitieux/-ieuse *m/f*

B *adj* ⓵ (filled with hope) [*person, expression*] plein d'espoir; [*attitude, mood*] optimiste; **to be** ∼ **about** être optimiste quant à; **to be** ∼ **of doing** avoir bon espoir de faire; ⓶ (encouraging) [*news, sign, situation*] encourageant; [*development*] prometteur/-euse

hopefully /ˈhəʊpfəlɪ/ *adv* ⓵ (with luck) avec un peu de chance; **'will he pay?'—'**∼**'** 'c'est lui qui paiera?'—'je l'espère'; ⓶ (with hope) [*say*] avec optimisme

hopeless /ˈhəʊplɪs/ *adj* ⓵ (desperate) [*attempt, case, grief, struggle*] désespéré; [*muddle*] inextricable; **it was** ∼ **trying to convince her** il était impossible de la convaincre; **it's** ∼**!** inutile!; ⓶ ○(incompetent) nul/nulle○; **to be** ∼ **at sth** être nul/nulle○ en qch; **to be** ∼ **at doing** être incapable de faire

hopelessly /ˈhəʊplɪslɪ/ *adv* ⓵ (irretrievably) [*drunk, inadequate*] complètement; [*in love*] éperdument; ⓶ (despairingly) désespérément

hopelessness /ˈhəʊplɪsnɪs/ *n* ⓵ (despair) désespoir *m*; ⓶ (futility) futilité *f* (**of doing** de faire)

hop: ∼ **field** *n* houblonnière *f*; ∼**sack** *n* US sac *m* en jute; ∼**scotch** ▸ p. 881 *n* marelle *f*

horde /hɔːd/ *n* (of people) foule *f*; (of insects) nuée *f*; (of animals) horde *f*; **the** ∼**(s)** la horde

horizon /həˈraɪzn/ *n* ⓵ (skyline) horizon *m*; **on the** ∼ (visible) à l'horizon; (imminent) en vue; ⓶ (of ideas, interests) horizon *m*; **to broaden one's** ∼**s** élargir ses horizons

horizontal /ˌhɒrɪˈzɒntl, US ˌhɔːr-/

A *n* horizontale *f*

B *adj* horizontal; ∼ **bar** barre *f* fixe

hormonal /hɔːˈməʊnl/ *adj* hormonal

hormone replacement therapy, **HRT** *n* hormonothérapie *f* substitutive

horn /hɔːn/ *n* ⓵ Zool (of animal, snail) corne *f*; (of owl) aigrette *f*; fig (on moon, anvil) corne *f*; ⓶ Mus ▸ p. 1028 cor *m*; **to play the** ∼ jouer du cor; **for** ∼ pour cor; ⓷ (of car) klaxon® *m*, avertisseur *m* (sonore); (of ship) sirène *f*; ⓸ **₵** (substance) corne *f*

(Idioms) **to draw in one's** ∼**s** (feeling hurt) rentrer dans sa coquille; (financially) réduire son train de vie; **to lock** ∼**s with sb** croiser le fer avec qn

hornet /ˈhɔːnɪt/ *n* frelon *m*

(Idiom) **to stir up a** ∼**'s nest** donner un coup de pied dans la fourmilière

horn: ∼ **of plenty** *n* corne *f* d'abondance; ∼**-rimmed** *adj* [*spectacles*] à monture d'écaille; [*frames*] d'écaille

horny /ˈhɔːnɪ/ *adj* ⓵ (hornlike) [*claws, carapace*] corné; [*protuberance*] cornu; ⓶ (calloused) calleux/-euse

horoscope /ˈhɒrəskəʊp, US ˈhɔːr-/ *n* horoscope *m*

horrendous /hɒˈrendəs/ *adj* [*crime, conditions, accident*] épouvantable; [*problem, mistake, cost, noise*] effroyable

horrible /ˈhɒrɪbl, US ˈhɔːr-/ *adj* ⓵ (unpleasant) [*place, clothes, smell, thought*] affreux/-euse; [*weather, food, person*] épouvantable; **to be** ∼ **to sb** être méchant avec qn; ⓶ (shocking) horrible

horribly /ˈhɒrɪblɪ, US ˈhɔːr-/ *adv* ⓵ [*embarrassed, rude*] terriblement; ⓶ [*disfigured*] horriblement

horrid /ˈhɒrɪd, US ˈhɔːrɪd/ *adj* (awful) affreux/-euse

horrific /həˈrɪfɪk/ *adj* atroce

horrified /ˈhɒrɪfaɪd, US ˈhɔːr-/ *adj* horrifié (**at, by** par; **to do** de faire; **that** que + *subj*)

horrifying /ˈhɒrɪfaɪɪŋ, US ˈhɔːr-/ *adj* [*experience, idea, sight*] horrifiant; [*behaviour*] effroyable

horror /ˈhɒrə(r), US ˈhɔːr-/ *n* ⓵ (feeling) horreur *f* (**at** devant); **to have a** ∼ **of sth/of doing** avoir horreur de qch/ de faire; ∼ **of** ∼**s!** ô horreur!; ⓶ (person) **a little** ∼○ un petit monstre○

horror: ∼ **film** *n* film *m* d'épouvante; ∼ **story** *n* histoire *f* d'épouvante; ∼**-stricken**, ∼**-struck** *adj* frappé d'horreur

horse /hɔːs/ *n* ⓵ cheval *m*; **the** ∼**s** fig (horseracing) les courses *fpl* (de chevaux); ⓶ (in gym) cheval *m* de saut; (pommel) cheval *m* d'arçons; ⓷ Mil **₵** cavalerie *f*

(Idioms) **I could eat a** ∼ j'ai une faim de loup; **to eat like a** ∼ manger comme quatre; **to flog** GB *ou* **beat** US **a dead** ∼○ perdre sa peine et son temps; **from the** ∼**'s mouth** de source sûre; **hold your** ∼**s**○! arrêtez!, une minute!; **it's** ∼**s for courses** ce qui convient à l'un ne convient pas nécessairement à l'autre; **that's a** ∼ **of a different colour** ça c'est une autre paire de manches; **wild** ∼**s wouldn't drag it out of me** pour rien au monde je ne le révélerais

(Phrasal verb)

■ **horse about**, **horse around** chahuter

horseback /ˈhɔːsbæk/ *n* **on** ∼ à cheval

horseback riding ▸ p. 881 *n* US équitation *f*

horse: ∼**box** *n* van *m*; ∼ **chestnut** *n* (tree) marronnier *m* (d'Inde); (fruit) marron *m* (d'Inde); ∼ **dealer** *n* maquignon/-onne *m/f*; ∼**-drawn** *adj* tiré par des chevaux; ∼**flesh** *n* (horses collectively) chevaux *mpl*; (meat) viande *f* de cheval; ∼**fly** *n* taon *m*; ∼**hair** *n* crin *m* (de cheval); ∼**man** *n* cavalier *m*; ∼ **manure** *n* crottin *m* de cheval; ∼**meat** *n* viande *f* de cheval; ∼**play** *n* chahut *m*

horsepower /ˈhɔːspaʊə(r)/ *n* puissance *f* (en chevaux); **a 90** ∼ **engine** un moteur de 90 chevaux

horse: ∼ **race** *n* course *f* de chevaux; ∼**racing** *n* courses *fpl* de chevaux, courses *fpl* hippiques; ∼**radish sauce** *n* sauce *f* au raifort; ∼**riding** ▸ p. 881 *n* équitation *f*; ∼**shoe** *n* fer *m* à cheval; ∼**show** *n* concours *m* hippique; ∼**trader** ▸ p. 1181 *n* lit, fig maquignon/-onne *m/f*; ∼ **trials** *npl* concours *m* complet d'équitation; ∼**whip** *n* cravache *f*; ∼**woman** *n* cavalière *f*, écuyère *f*

hors(e)y /ˈhɔːsɪ/ *adj* [*face*] chevalin; [*person*] passionné de chevaux

horticultural /ˌhɔːtɪˈkʌltʃərəl/ *adj* horticole

horticulture /ˈhɔːtɪkʌltʃə(r)/ *n* horticulture *f*

horticulturist /ˌhɔːtɪˈkʌltʃərɪst/ ▸ p. 1181 *n* horticulteur/-trice *m/f*

h

hose /həʊz/ n 1 (for garden) tuyau m d'arrosage; (for cleaning) jet m d'eau; 2 (also **fire** ∼) lance f à incendie; 3 Aut (in engine) tuyau m; 4 (tubing) tuyau m; 5 Hist (garment) haut-de-chausses m

hosepipe /'həʊzpaɪp/ GB n 1 (for garden) tuyau m d'arrosage; 2 (fire hose) lance f à incendie

hosiery† /'həʊzɪərɪ, US 'həʊʒərɪ/ n bonneterie f

hospice /'hɒspɪs/ n (for the dying) établissement m de soins palliatifs

hospitable /hɒ'spɪtəbl/ adj [person, country] hospitalier/-ière (**to** envers); [conditions] favorable

hospital /'hɒspɪtl/
A n hôpital m; **to/from** ∼ GB ou **the** ∼ US à/de l'hôpital; **to be taken to** ∼ **with...** être hospitalisé pour...
B noun modifier [facilities, staff, treatment, ward] hospitalier/-ière; ∼ **beds** lits mpl d'hôpital; ∼ **patient** patient/-e m/f

hospital: ∼ **administrator** ▸ p. 1181 n directeur/-trice m/f d'hôpital; ∼ **doctor** ▸ p. 1181 n médecin m d'hôpital

hospitality /ˌhɒspɪ'tælətɪ/ n hospitalité f

hospitalize /'hɒspɪtəlaɪz/ vtr hospitaliser

hospital: ∼ **nurse** ▸ p. 1181 n infirmier/-ière m/f d'hôpital; ∼ **porter** ▸ p. 1181 n GB brancardier m; ∼ **ship** n navire-hôpital m

host /həʊst/
A n 1 (to guests, visitors) hôte m; **to play** ∼ **to sb** recevoir or accueillir qn; 2 Bot, Zool hôte m; 3 Radio, TV animateur/-trice m/f; 4 (multitude) foule f (**of** de); 5 Relig hostie f; 6 Comput hôte m, serveur m
B vtr 1 organiser [function]; Radio, TV animer; 2 Comput héberger [website]

hostage /'hɒstɪdʒ/ n otage m; **to hold sb** ∼ garder qn en otage

host country n pays m hôte or d'accueil

hostel /'hɒstl/ n (for workers, refugees etc) foyer m; (**youth**) ∼ auberge f de jeunesse

hostess /'həʊstɪs/ n 1 (to guests etc) hôtesse f, maîtresse f de maison; (on plane etc) hôtesse f; 2 TV animatrice f

hostile /'hɒstaɪl, US -tl/ adj hostile (**to** à)

hostility /hɒ'stɪlətɪ/ n hostilité f (**towards sb/sth** à l'égard de qn/à qch)

hot /hɒt/ adj 1 (very warm) [season, country, bath, plate, hands] chaud; [sun] chaud; [food, drink] (bien) chaud; **it's** ∼ **here** il fait chaud ici; **the weather is** ∼ **in July** il fait un temps chaud au mois de juillet; **it was a** ∼ **day** il faisait chaud ce jour-là; **to be** ou **feel** ∼ [person] avoir chaud; **to get** ∼ [person] commencer à avoir trop chaud; [parked car] devenir chaud; [engine, oven] chauffer; [weather] se réchauffer; **the room feels** ∼ il fait chaud dans cette pièce; **your forehead feels** ∼ tu as le front chaud; **digging is** ∼ **work** ça donne chaud de bêcher; **when the sun is at its** ∼**test** quand le soleil chauffe le plus; **how** ∼ **should I have the oven?** à quelle température dois-je régler le four? **to be** ∼ **from the oven** sortir du four; **to go** ∼ **and cold** (with fever) être fiévreux/-euse; (with fear) avoir des sueurs froides; 2 Culin [mustard, spice] fort; [sauce, dish] épicé; 3 (new, fresh) [trail, news] tout chaud; ∼ **off the press** tout chaud sorti de la presse; 4 (fierce, keen) [competition] acharné; 5 (short) **to have a** ∼ **temper** s'énerver facilement; 6 ᵒUS (in demand) **to be** ∼ avoir un succès fou; 7 ᵒ(good) **a** ∼ **tip** un bon tuyauᵒ; **the** ∼ **favourite** le grand favori; **to be** ∼ **on sth** (knowledgeable) être calé en qch; (keen) être très à cheval sur qch; 8 ᵒ(stolen) volé; 9 (bright) [colour] chaud; ∼ **pink** rose bonbon; 10 (radioactive) radioactif/-ive; 11 (close) **to be** ∼ **on the trail of sth** être sur la piste de qch; **to set off in** ∼ **pursuit of sb** se lancer à la poursuite de qn; **you're getting** ∼ (in games) tu chauffes

[Idioms] **to be in** ∼ **water** être dans le pétrinᵒ; **to blow** ∼ **and cold** être d'humeur changeante; **to get all** ∼ **and bothered** se mettre dans tous ses états

[Phrasal verb]
■ **hot up** [match] s'animer; [election campaign] s'intensifier; **things are** ∼**ting up** ça commence à chaufferᵒ; **the pace is** ∼**ting up** l'allure s'accélère

hot: ∼ **air**ᵒ n paroles fpl en l'air; ∼ **air balloon** n montgolfière f; ∼**bed** n foyer m (**of** de); ∼**-blooded** adj [reaction] passionné

hot cake n US ≈ crêpe f
[Idiom] **to sell like** ∼**s** se vendre comme des petits pains

hotchpotch /'hɒtʃpɒtʃ/ n GB mélange m, mixture f

hot cross bun n ≈ brioche f du vendredi saint

hot desking n pratique f du bureau partagé, bureau m tournant

hot dog n hot dog m

hot dogging ▸ p. 881 n ski m acrobatique

hotel /həʊ'tel/
A n hôtel m
B noun modifier [room, manager] d'hôtel; [industry] hôtelier/-ière; [work] dans l'hôtellerie

hotelier /həʊ'telɪə(r)/, **hotelkeeper** /ˌhəʊtel'kiːpə(r)/ ▸ p. 1181 n hôtelier/-ière m/f

hot: ∼**foot** adv hum, iron [go] à toute vitesse or allure; ∼**head** n péj tête f brûlée, exalté/-e m/f; ∼**-headed** adj [person] impétueux/-euse; [decision] précipité

hothouse /'hɒthaʊs/ n lit serre f (chaude); fig milieu m protégé

hothousing /'hɒthaʊzɪŋ/ n Sch enseignement intensif destiné aux enfants surdoués

hot key n Comput raccourci m clavier

hotline /'hɒtlaɪn/ n 1 ligne f ouverte, permanence f téléphonique; 2 Mil, Pol téléphone m rouge; 3 (for customer support) service m d'assistance (téléphonique), hotline f

hotlink /'hɒtlɪŋk/ n Comput hyperlien m

hotly /'hɒtlɪ/ adv [say, exclaim] passionnément; [disputed, denied] violemment

hot: ∼**plate** n plaque f de cuisson; ∼**pot** n GB ragoût m

hot potatoᵒ n sujet m brûlant

[Idiom] **to drop sb like a** ∼ laisser tomber qn du jour au lendemain

hot rod n voiture f au moteur gonflé

hot seatᵒ n:
[Idiom] **to be in the** ∼ être sur la sellette

hot: ∼ **shoe** n griffe f porte-flash; ∼**shot**ᵒ n gen crackᵒ m; péj gros bonnetᵒ m

hot spotᵒ n 1 Pol point m chaud; 2 Tourism pays m du soleil, destination f au soleil; 3 (nightclub) boîte f de nuit; 4 Comput zone f cliquable, zone f sensible

hot spring n source f chaude

hot stuffᵒ n **to be** ∼ [person] être un crackᵒ; **he thinks he's** ∼ il ne se prend pas pour rien

hot: ∼ **swap** n Comput changement m de pièce sous tension; ∼**-tempered** adj colérique; ∼ **tub** n US ≈ jacuzzi m de jardin; ∼ **water bottle** n bouillotte f

hound /haʊnd/
A n 1 (in hunting) chien m de chasse; 2 hum (dog) chien m; 3 ᵒ(enthusiast) **autograph** ∼ chasseur/-euse m/f d'autographes
B vtr (harass) harceler, traquer [person]
[Phrasal verb]

■ **hound out**: ▸ ∼ **[sb] out** chasser (**of** de)

hound-dogᵒ /'haʊnddɒg/ n US chien m (de meute)

houndstooth (check) /'haʊndztuːθ/ n pied-de-poule m

hour /aʊə(r)/ ▸ p. 1267, p. 745
A n 1 (60 minutes) heure f; **an** ∼ **ago** il y a une heure; **it's an** ∼ (**away**) **from London** c'est à une heure de Londres; **twice an** ∼ deux fois par heure; **£10 per** ∼ 10 livres sterling (de) l'heure; **to be paid by the** ∼ être payé à l'heure; 2 (time of day) heure f; **the bus leaves on the** ∼ le bus part à l'heure juste; **in the early** ∼**s** au petit matin; **to stay out until all** ∼**s** rentrer très tard dans la nuit; **at this** ∼? à l'heure qu'il est?; 3 (point in time) heure f; **her finest** ∼ son heure de gloire; **in my** ∼ **of need** dans un moment difficile
B **hours** npl 1 (times) heures fpl; **business** ou **opening** ∼**s** heures fpl d'ouverture; **office** ∼**s** heures fpl de permanence; **to keep late** ∼**s** se coucher tard; 2 Relig heures fpl

hour: ∼**glass** n sablier m; ∼ **hand** n aiguille f des heures

hourly /'aʊəlɪ/
A adj 1 (every hour) horaire; **the buses are** ∼ les bus partent toutes les heures; 2 (per hour) [rate] horaire; **on an** ∼ **basis** à l'heure
B adv 1 (every hour) [arrive, phone] toutes les heures; 2 (per hour) **to pay sb** ∼ payer qn à l'heure

house

A /haʊs, pl haʊzɪz/ n **1** (home) maison f; **at my/his** ∼ chez moi/lui; **to go to sb's** ∼ aller chez qn; **to be good around the** ∼ aider à la maison; **to keep** ∼ tenir la maison (**for** de); **2** Pol (also **House**) Chambre f; **the bill before the** ∼ le projet de loi soumis à la Chambre; **3** Comm maison f; **on the** ∼ aux frais de la maison; **4** Theat (audience) assistance f; (auditorium) salle f; (performance) séance f; '∼ **full**' 'complet'; **to bring the** ∼ **down** faire crouler la salle sous les applaudissements; **5** (also **House**) (family line) maison f; **the** ∼ **of Windsor** la Maison des Windsor; **6** Relig maison f; **7** GB Sch (team) maison f; **8** (music) house music f (musique de discothèque)

B /haʊz/ vtr **1** (give lodging to) (permanently) loger; (temporarily) héberger; **badly** ou **poorly** ∼d mal logé; **2** (contain) [building] abriter [books, exhibition]

⟨Idioms⟩ **to put one's** ∼ **in order** mettre de l'ordre dans ses affaires; **to get on like a** ∼ **on fire**○ s'entendre à merveille

house arrest n résidence f surveillée

houseboat /'haʊsbəʊt/ n **1** (house-shaped) habitation f flottante; **2** (barge) péniche f aménagée

house: ∼**bound** adj confiné chez soi; ∼**breaking** n Jur cambriolage m par effraction; ∼**broken** adj US [pet] propre; ∼ **call** n visite f à domicile; ∼**cleaning** n US ménage m; ∼ **clearance sale** n vente f de mobilier à la suite d'un décès; ∼**coat** n déshabillé m, peignoir m; ∼**fly** n mouche f domestique

houseguest /'haʊsgest/ n invité/-e m/f (pour quelques jours)

household /'haʊshəʊld/

A n maison f; (in census etc) ménage m; **head of the** ∼ chef m de famille

B noun modifier [accounts, bill] du ménage; [chore, item] ménager/-ère

household: ∼ **appliance** n appareil m électroménager; **Household Cavalry** n GB cavalerie f de la Garde royale

householder /'haʊshəʊldə(r)/ n gen occupant/-e m/f; (owner) propriétaire mf; (tenant) locataire mf

household: ∼ **insurance** n assurance f de l'habitation; ∼ **linen** n linge m de maison

household name n **he's a** ∼ il est célèbre

house-hunting /'haʊshʌntɪŋ/ n **to go** ∼ se lancer à la recherche d'une maison (à acheter)

house husband n homme m au foyer

house: ∼**keeper** ▸ p. 1181 n (in house) gouvernante f; (in institution) responsable mf du personnel d'entretien; ∼**keeping** n (money) argent m du ménage; (managing of money) gestion f de l'argent du ménage; ∼ **lights** npl Theat éclairage m; ∼**maid** ▸ p. 1181 n femme f de chambre; ∼**martin** n hirondelle f de fenêtre; ∼**master** n GB Sch enseignant m responsable d'un groupe d'enfants (dans un internat britannique); **House of Commons** n Chambre f des communes; ∼ **officer** ▸ p. 1181 n GB Med interne mf; **House of Lords** n GB Chambre f des lords, Chambre f haute; **House of Representatives** n US Chambre f des représentants; ∼ **painter** ▸ p. 1181 n peintre m en bâtiment; ∼**parent** n responsable mf des enfants (dans une institution); ∼ **party** n réception f; ∼**plant** n plante f d'intérieur; ∼ **prices** npl prix mpl du marché immobilier; ∼**proud** adj toujours en train d'astiquer; ∼ **sales** npl ventes fpl immobilières; ∼**-sit** vi garder une maison; **Houses of Congress** npl US le Sénat et la Chambre des représentants; **Houses of Parliament** n GB Parlement m Britannique; ∼**-to-house** adj [search] de maison en maison; ∼**-trained** adj GB propre; ∼**-warming (party)** n pendaison f de crémaillère; ∼**wife** n (not employed outside home) femme f au foyer; (with emphasis on domestic labour) ménagère f; ∼ **wine** n cuvée f maison or du patron; ∼**wives** npl ▸ **housewife**

housework /'haʊswɜːk/ n travaux mpl ménagers; **to do the** ∼ gen s'occuper de la maison; (clean) faire le ménage

housing /'haʊzɪŋ/

A n (houses, flats) logements mpl

B noun modifier [crisis, problem] du logement; [conditions] de logement; [shortage] de logements

housing: ∼ **benefit** n GB ≈ allocation f logement; ∼ **development** n (large) cité f; (small) lotissement m; ∼ **estate** n GB (large) cité f; (small) lotissement m; (council-

run) ≈ cité f or lotissement m HLM; ∼ **project** US n ≈ cité f or lotissement m HLM

HOV n US (abrév = **high occupancy vehicle**) ∼ **lane** voie prioritaire sur autoroute

hove /həʊv/ pp, prét Naut ▸ **heave**

hovel /'hɒvl/ n taudis m

hover /'hɒvə(r)/ vi **1** [bird] voleter, planer; [helicopter] faire du surplace; **to** ∼ **around sb/sth** tourner autour de qn/qch; **2** (vacillate) vaciller; **country** ∼**ing on the brink of war** pays au bord de la guerre

hovercraft n (pl ∼) aéroglisseur m

how /haʊ/

⚠ When *how* is used as a question word meaning *in what way?* or *by what means?* (*how did you get here?*, *how will you do it?*) it is almost always translated by *comment*: comment es-tu arrivé ici?; comment le feras-tu?

When *how* is used as a conjunction meaning *the way in which* it is often translated by *comment*: *I don't know how they did it* = je ne sais pas comment ils l'ont fait; *tell me how you make a curry* = dis-moi comment on fait un curry.

When *how* is used as a conjunction meaning *that* it is almost always translated by *que*: *he told me how he had stolen the money* = il m'a dit qu'il avait volé l'argent; *it's amazing how they survived* = c'est étonnant qu'ils aient survécu.

For more examples and particular usages see below.

A adv, conj **1** (in what way, by what means) comment; **to know** ∼ **to do** savoir faire; **I learned** ∼ **to do it** j'ai appris à le faire; ∼ **do you feel about it?** qu'en penses-tu?; **2** (when enquiring) ∼ **are you?** comment allez-vous?; ∼**'s your foot?** comment va ton pied?; ∼'s **your brother?** comment va ton frère?; ∼ **did you like the party?** la fête t'a plu?; ∼ **are things?** comment ça va?; ∼ **do you do!** (greeting) enchanté!; **3** (in number, quantity etc questions) ∼ **much does this cost?**, ∼ **much is this?** combien ça coûte?; ∼ **much do you weigh?** combien pèses-tu?; ∼ **many times have you been to France?** combien de fois es-tu allé en France?; ∼ **many people?** combien de personnes?; ∼ **long will it take?** combien de temps cela va-t-il prendre?; ∼ **long is the rope?** de quelle longueur est cette corde?; ∼ **tall is the tree?** combien mesure l'arbre?; ∼ **big is the garden?** de quelle taille est le jardin?; ∼ **far is it?** c'est à quelle distance?; ∼ **old is she?** quel âge a-t-elle?; **4** (in exclamations) ∼ **wonderful!** c'est fantastique!; ∼ **nice you look!** que tu es beau/belle!; ∼ **clever of you!** comme c'est intelligent de ta part!; ∼ **wrong I was!** comme j'ai eu tort!; ∼ **it rained!** qu'est-ce qu'il a plu○!; **5** ○(in whichever way) comme; **you can decorate it** ∼ **you like** tu peux le décorer comme tu veux; **6** (why) ∼ **could you?** comment as-tu pu faire ça?; **7** (that) que; **you know** ∼ **he always arrives late** tu sais qu'il arrive toujours en retard

B ○**how come** adv phr '∼ **come?'** 'pourquoi?'; ∼ **come you always win?** comment ça se fait que tu gagnes toujours?

C how's that adv phr **I'll take you home,** ∼**'s that?** je te ramènerai chez toi, ça te va?; ∼**'s that for an honest answer** ça c'est une réponse honnête

howdy○ /'haʊdɪ/ excl US salut○!

however /haʊ'evə(r)/

A conj toutefois, cependant; ∼**, the recession is not over yet** toutefois, la récession n'est pas encore terminée; **they can,** ∼**, explain why** ils peuvent, cependant, expliquer pourquoi; **if,** ∼**, you prefer to do** si, toutefois, vous préférez faire

B adv **1** (no matter how) ∼ **hard I try, I can't** j'ai beau essayer de toutes mes forces, je n'y arrive pas; ∼ **difficult the task is** ou **may be, we can't give up** si difficile que soit la tâche, nous ne pouvons pas abandonner; ∼ **small she is** ou **may be** si petite soit-elle; ∼ **everyone,** ∼ **poor** chacun, si pauvre soit-il; ∼ **much it costs** quel que soit le prix; ∼ **long it takes** quel que soit le temps que ça prendra; **2** (in whatever way) ∼ **you like** comme tu veux; ∼ **they travel, they will find it difficult** quelle que soit la façon dont ils voyagent, ça va être difficile; **3** (how) ∼ **did you guess?** comment as-tu deviné?

howl /haʊl/

A n hurlement m; **a** ∼ **of pain** un hurlement de douleur; **a**

~ **of laughter** un éclat de rire; ~**s of protest** des protestations *fpl* bruyantes

B *vtr* hurler (**at** à)

C *vi* [*child*] hurler, pousser des hurlements; [*dog, wind*] hurler; **to** ~ **with rage** hurler de rage

howling /ˈhaʊlɪŋ/

A *n* **1** (of animal, wind) hurlement *m*; **2** **C** (of baby, crowd) hurlements *mpl*

B *adj* **1** [*child, animal*] qui hurle, hurlant; **the** ~ **wind** les hurlements du vent; **2** °fig [*success*] retentissant

hp *n* (*abrév* = **horse power**) CV *m*

HP *n* GB *abrév* ▸ **hire purchase**

HQ *n* Mil (*abrév* = **headquarters**) QG *m*

hr *n* (*abrév écrite* = **hour**) h

HR *npl*: *abrév* ▸ **human resources**

HRH *n* (*abrév* = **Her** *ou* **His Royal Highness**) Son Altesse Royale

HRT *n*: *abrév* ▸ **hormone replacement therapy**

HT *n, adj* (*abrév* = **high tension**) HT

HTML *n* (*abrév* = **HyperText Mark-up Language**) HTML *m*

hub /hʌb/ *n* Tech moyeu *m*; fig centre *m*

hubbub /ˈhʌbʌb/ *n* (noise) brouhaha *m*; (turmoil) tohubohu *m*

hubcap /ˈhʌbkæp/ *n* Aut enjoliveur *m*

huckleberry /ˈhʌklbərɪ, US -berɪ/ *n* US myrtille *f*

huckster /ˈhʌkstə(r)/ *n* US **1** (pedlar) camelot *m*; **2** péj (salesman) bonimenteur *m*; péj (swindler) escroc *m*

huddle /ˈhʌdl/

A *n* **1** (of people) petit groupe *m*; (of buildings) entassement *m*; **2** (of footballers) regroupement *m* (*pour mettre au point la stratégie à adopter*)

B *vi* **he was huddling in a corner** il était blotti dans un coin; **she** ~**d under the bushes** elle se blottit sous les buissons; **to** ~ **around** se presser autour de

hue /hjuː/ *n* **1** littér (shade) nuance *f*; (colour) couleur *f*, teinte *f*; **rose** ~**d** teinté de rose; **2** fig (political) tendance *f*

hue and cry *n* tollé *m*

huff° /hʌf/

A *n* **in a** ~ vexé; **to go into a** ~ prendre la mouche

B *vi* **to** ~ **and puff** lit haleter; fig faire toute une histoire

huffiness /ˈhʌfnɪs/ *n* mauvaise humeur *f*

hug /hʌɡ/

A *n* étreinte *f*; **to give sb a** ~ serrer qn dans ses bras

B *vtr* (*p prés etc* **-gg-**) **1** (embrace) serrer [qn] dans ses bras; **2** (keep close to) [*boat, vehicle*] raser; [*road*] longer; **to** ~ **the coast** serrer la côte

huge /hjuːdʒ/ *adj* [*country, room*] immense; [*building, person, animal*] gigantesque; [*appetite, success*] énorme; [*debts, sum*] gros/grosse (*before n*)

hugely /ˈhjuːdʒlɪ/ *adv* **1** (emphatic) extrêmement; **2** [*increase, vary*] considérablement; [*enjoy*] énormément

hugeness /ˈhjuːdʒnɪs/ *n* (of area, object) immensité *f*

huh° /hə/ *excl* (in surprise, inquiry) hein!; (in derision, disgust) pff!

hulk /hʌlk/ *n* **1** (of ship) épave *f*; (of machine, tank) carcasse *f*; **2** fig (bulk) masse *f* gigantesque

hulking /ˈhʌlkɪŋ/ *adj* énorme

hull /hʌl/

A *n* (of ship, plane) coque *f*; (of tank) carcasse *f*

B *vtr* décortiquer [*rice, grain*]; équeuter [*strawberries*]

hullabaloo° /ˌhʌləbəˈluː/ *n* (outcry) esclandre *m*; (noise) raffut° *m*

hullo /hʌˈləʊ/ *excl* = **hallo**

hum /hʌm/

A *n* (of insect, engine, traffic, voices) bourdonnement *m*; (of machinery) ronronnement *m*

B *vtr* (*p prés etc* **-mm-**) fredonner [*tune*]

C *vi* (*p prés etc* **-mm-**) lit [*person*] fredonner; [*insect, aircraft*] bourdonner; [*machine*] ronronner; fig [*office*] bourdonner

human /ˈhjuːmən/

A *n* humain *m*; **fellow** ~ semblable *mf*

B *adj* **1** (not animal) [*race, behaviour, body, population*] humain; [*characteristic, rights*] de l'homme; **he's only** ~ il a ses faiblesses comme tout le monde; ~ **being** être *m* humain; **2** (sympathetic) humain; **to lack the** ~ **touch** manquer de chaleur humaine

humane /hjuːˈmeɪn/ *adj* **1** [*person, régime*] humain; [*act*] d'humanité; **2** [*slaughter, culling*] sans cruauté

humanely /hjuːˈmeɪnlɪ/ *adv* sans cruauté

human engineering *n* (in industry) gestion *f* des ressources humaines

humane society *n* US société *f* américaine pour la protection des animaux, *cf* SPA *f*

human interest story *n* histoire *f* vécue

humanism /ˈhjuːmənɪzəm/ *n* humanisme *m*

humanist /ˈhjuːmənɪst/ *n, adj* humaniste (*mf*)

humanitarian /hjuːˌmænɪˈteərɪən/

A *n* humaniste *mf*

B *adj* humanitaire

humanity /hjuːˈmænətɪ/ *n* **1** (the human race) humanité *f*; **2** (kindness) humanité *f*; **3** **humanities** Univ humanités *fpl*

humanize /ˈhjuːmənaɪz/

A *vtr* **1** gen humaniser; **2** Art, Cin donner un visage humain à

B **humanizing** *pres p adj* [*influence*] humanisant

humanly /ˈhjuːmənlɪ/ *adv* humainement

human nature *n* nature *f* humaine; **it's** ~ **to...** c'est humain de...

human: ~ **resources, HR** *npl* ressources *fpl* humaines, RH *fpl*; ~ **resources manager** ▸ p. 1181 *n* responsable *mf* de la gestion des ressources humaines; ~ **rights** *npl* droits *mpl* de l'homme; ~ **rights activist** *n* militant/-e *m/f* pour les droits de l'homme; ~ **rights campaign** *n* mouvement *m* pour les droits de l'homme; ~ **shield** *n* bouclier *m* humain

humble /ˈhʌmbl/

A *adj* **1** (lowly) [*origin, position*] modeste; **2** (unpretentious) aussi hum [*dwelling, gift*] modeste; **3** (deferential) humble; **please accept my** ~ **apologies** sout je vous prie d'accepter mes humbles excuses fml; **4** (showing humility) humble

B *vtr* humilier; **to** ~ **oneself** s'humilier

Idiom **to eat** ~ **pie** aller à Canossa

humbling /ˈhʌmblɪŋ/ *adj* humiliant, salutaire

humbly /ˈhʌmblɪ/ *adv* humblement; ~ **born** d'origine modeste

humbug /ˈhʌmbʌɡ/ *n* **1** °(dishonesty) tromperie *f*; **2** °(nonsense) fumisterie° *f*; **3** GB bonbon à la menthe

humdrum /ˈhʌmdrʌm/ *adj* monotone

humid /ˈhjuːmɪd/ *adj* [*climate*] humide; [*weather*] lourd

humidifier /hjuːˈmɪdɪfaɪə(r)/ *n* humidificateur *m*

humidity /hjuːˈmɪdətɪ/ *n* humidité *f*

humiliate /hjuːˈmɪlɪeɪt/ *vtr* humilier

humiliating /hjuːˈmɪlɪeɪtɪŋ/ *adj* humiliant

humiliation /hjuːˌmɪlɪˈeɪʃn/ *n* humiliation *f*

humility /hjuːˈmɪlətɪ/ *n* humilité *f*

humming /ˈhʌmɪŋ/ *n* (of insect, aircraft) bourdonnement *m*; (of machine) ronronnement *m*; (of person) fredonnement *m*

humming bird *n* oiseau-mouche *m*, colibri *m*

hummock /ˈhʌmək/ *n* (of earth) monticule *m*

hummus /ˈhʊməs/ *n* hoummos *m*

humor *n* US = **humour**

humorist /ˈhjuːmərɪst/ *n* humoriste *mf*

humorless *adj* US = **humourless**

humorous /ˈhjuːmərəs/ *adj* **1** (amusing) humoristique; **2** (amused) plein d'humour

humorously /ˈhjuːmərəslɪ/ *adv* avec humour

humour GB, **humor** US /ˈhjuːmə(r)/

A *n* **1** (wit) humour *m*; **a good sense of** ~ le sens de l'humour; **2** (mood) humeur *f*; **to be in good** ~ être de bonne humeur; **to be in no** ~ **for arguing** ne pas être d'humeur à discuter; **when the** ~ **takes me** quand l'envie m'en prend

B *vtr* amadouer [*person*]; se plier à [*request*]; ▸ **good-humoured**

humourless GB, **humorless** US /ˈhjuːmələs/ *adj* [*person*] qui manque d'humour; [*description, tone*] dépourvu d'humour

hump /hʌmp/

A *n* lit (all contexts) bosse *f*; **road** ~ ralentisseur *m*, dos-d'âne *m inv*

B ᵒvtr GB (lift, carry) porter, traîner

humpback(ed) bridge n pont m en dos d'âne

humpy /'hʌmpɪ/ adj [land, field] bosselé

humus /'hjuːməs/ n humus m

hunch /hʌntʃ/
A n intuition f; **to have a ~ that** avoir l'intuition que
B vtr **to ~ one's shoulders** rentrer les épaules
C vi **to ~ over one's desk** se tenir penché à son bureau

hunch: **~back** n injur bossu/-e m/f; **~backed** adj bossu

hunched /hʌntʃt/ adj [back] voûté; [shoulders] rentré

hundred /'hʌndrəd/ ▸ p. 1044
A n cent m; **two ~** deux cents; **two ~ and one** deux cent un; **a ~ to one** cent contre un; **it was a ~ to one chance** il y avait une chance sur cent; **sold in ~s** ou **by the ~** vendu par centaines; **in nineteen ~** en mille neuf cents; **in nineteen ~ and three** en mil neuf cent trois; **~s of times** des centaines de fois
B adj cent; **two ~ francs** deux cents francs; **two ~ and five francs** deux cent cinq francs; **about a ~ people** une centaine de personnes

hundred-and-one ▸ p. 1044
A n cent un
B adj lit cent un/une; **I've a ~ things to do** fig j'ai mille choses à faire

hundredfold /'hʌndrədfəʊld/ adv **a ~** par cent; **to increase ~** centupler

hundreds and thousands npl Culin nonpareilles fpl

hundredth /'hʌndrətθ/ ▸ p. 1044
A n [1] (fraction) centième m; [2] (in order) centième mf
B adj, adv centième

hundredweight ▸ p. 1323 n GB = 50,80 kg; US = 45,36 kg

hung /hʌŋ/
A prét, pp ▸ hang
B adj Pol [jury, parliament] en suspens

Hungarian /hʌŋˈɡeərɪən/ ▸ p. 1032, p. 969
A n (person) Hongrois/-e m/f; (language) hongrois m
B adj hongrois

Hungary /'hʌŋɡərɪ/ ▸ p. 774 pr n Hongrie f

hunger /'hʌŋɡə(r)/
A n faim f; fig désir m ardent (**for** de)
B vi **to ~ for** fig avoir faim de

hunger strike n grève f de la faim

hung-overᵒ /ˌhʌŋˈəʊvə(r)/ adj **to be ~** avoir la gueule de boisᵒ

hungrily /'hʌŋɡrɪlɪ/ adv lit avec voracité; fig avec avidité

hungry /'hʌŋɡrɪ/ adj [1] lit **to be** ou **feel ~** avoir faim; **to make sb ~** donner faim à qn; **to go ~** (from necessity) souffrir de la faim; **I'd rather go ~!** je préfère me passer de manger!; [2] fig avide; **~ for** assoiffé de [success]; **power-~** assoiffé de pouvoir

hung-upᵒ /hʌŋˈʌp/ adj [1] (tense) complexé; [2] (obsessed with) **to be ~ on sb/sth** être dingueᵒ de qn/qch

hunk /hʌŋk/ n (of bread) gros morceau m; (man)ᵒ beau mecᵒ m

hunkerᵒ /'hʌŋkə(r)/
A hunkers npl **to sit on one's ~s** s'accroupir; **to be on one's ~s** être accroupi
B vi (also **~ down**) s'accroupir

hunky-doryᵒ /ˌhʌŋkɪˈdɔːrɪ/ adj superᵒ, au poilᵒ

hunt /hʌnt/
A n [1] (search) recherche f (**for** de); **the ~ is on for the terrorists** on recherche les terroristes; [2] (activity) chasse f; **lion ~** chasse au lion; [3] (fox-hunting group, area) chasse f à courre
B vtr [1] (seek, pursue) rechercher; **to ~ sb out of** ou **off** faire sortir qn de; [2] (pursue) chasser [game, fox]
C vi [1] (for prey) chasser; [2] (search) **to ~ for sth** chercher [qch] partout [object, person, address]; être à la recherche de [truth, cure]

(Phrasal verbs)
▪ **hunt down** [1] forcer [animal]; [2] (find) traquer [criminal]; persécuter [victim, minority]
▪ **hunt up** s'enquérir de [old friend, person]

hunted /'hʌntɪd/ adj traqué

hunter /'hʌntə(r)/ n [1] (person who hunts) chasseur/-euse m/f; (in fox-hunting) chasseur/-euse m/f à courre; (animal that hunts) prédateur m (**of** de); [2] (horse) cheval m de chasse;

[3] (dog) chien m de chasse; [4] (collector) collectionneur/-euse m/f

hunter-killer n Mil Naut navire m d'un groupe de recherche et d'attaque

hunting /'hʌntɪŋ/
A n chasse f (**of** à); **to go ~** aller à la chasse
B noun modifier [boot, knife, season] de chasse

hunting: **~ crop** n cravache f; **~ lodge** n pavillon m de chasse; **~ pink** n veste f de veneur

hunt saboteur n GB opposant/-e m/f à la chasse au renard

huntsman /'hʌntsmən/ n [1] (hunter) gen chasseur m; (fox-hunter) chasseur m à courre; [2] (trainer of hounds) veneur m

hunt the thimble ▸ p. 881 n cache-tampon m inv

hurdle /'hɜːdl/
A n ▸ p. 881 Sport haie f; **the 100m ~s** le 100 m haies; fig obstacle m; **to clear a ~** lit franchir une haie; fig surmonter un obstacle
B vi Sport faire de la course de haies

hurdler /'hɜːdlə(r)/ n coureur m de haies

hurdling /'hɜːdlɪŋ/ ▸ p. 881 n course f de haies

hurdy-gurdy /'hɜːdɪɡɜːdɪ/ ▸ p. 1028 n orgue m de Barbarie

hurl /hɜːl/
A vtr [1] lancer (**at** sur); **to be ~ed to the ground** être projeté au sol; [2] fig **to ~ insults at sb** accabler qn d'injures
B v refl **to ~ oneself** lit se précipiter; fig se jeter

hurly-burly /'hɜːlɪbɜːlɪ/ n tohu-bohu m

hurrah, **hurray** /hʊˈrɑː/ n, excl hourra (m); **~ for X!** vive X!

hurricane /'hʌrɪkən, US -keɪn/ n ouragan m; **~ force wind** vent soufflant en ouragan

hurried /'hʌrɪd/ adj [note, visit, meal] rapide; [job, work] fait à la va-vite; [departure] précipité

hurriedly /'hʌrɪdlɪ/ adv [dress, pack, write] en toute hâte; [leave] précipitamment

hurry /'hʌrɪ/
A n hâte f, empressement m; **to be in a ~** être pressé (**to do** de faire); **there's no ~** il n'y a pas le presse pas; **what's the ~?** qu'est-ce qui presse?; **to do sth in a ~** faire qch à la hâte; **I won't forget that in a ~!** je ne suis pas près d'oublier ça!
B vtr [1] (do hastily) terminer [qch] à la hâte [meal, task]; [2] (rush, bustle) bousculer [person]; **to ~ sb in/out** faire entrer/sortir qn en toute hâte
C vi se dépêcher (**over doing of** faire); **to ~ out** sortir précipitamment; **to ~ home** se dépêcher de rentrer

(Phrasal verbs)
▪ **hurry along**: ▸ **~ along** se presser, se dépêcher; ▸ **~ along [sth]**, **~ [sth] along** faire accélérer, activer [process]
▪ **hurry back** (to any place) se dépêcher de retourner (**to** à); (to one's home) se dépêcher de rentrer (chez soi)
▪ **hurry off** se sauver
▪ **hurry up**: ▸ **~ up** se dépêcher; **~ up!** dépêche-toi!; ▸ **~ [sth] up** faire accélérer, activer [process]

hurt /hɜːt/
A n blessure f; **his sense of ~** son sentiment d'avoir été blessé
B adj peiné, blessé; **I am more angry than ~** je suis plus fâché que blessé; **she was ~ not to have been invited** elle a été peinée de ne pas avoir été invitée; **to sound** ou **look/feel ~** avoir l'air/être peiné
C vtr (prét, pp **hurt**) [1] (injure) **to ~ oneself** se blesser, se faire mal; **to ~ one's back** se blesser or se faire mal au dos; **was anybody hurt?** y a-t-il eu des blessés?; **somebody's going to get hurt** quelqu'un va se faire mal; **it wouldn't ~ her to apologize** ça ne lui ferait pas de mal de s'excuser; [2] (cause pain to) faire mal à; **you're ~ing my arm** vous me faites mal au bras; **it ~s him to walk** il a mal quand il marche; [3] (emotionally) blesser; (offend) froisser; **to ~ sb's feelings** blesser quelqu'un; **to ~ sb's pride** blesser quelqu'un dans son amour-propre; **she's afraid of getting hurt** elle a peur de souffrir; [4] [prices, inflation] nuire à
D vi (prét, pp **hurt**) [1] (be painful) faire mal; **my throat ~s** j'ai mal à la gorge; **where does it ~?** où est-ce que vous avez mal?; **my shoes ~** mes chaussures me font mal; **it ~s when I laugh** j'ai mal quand je ris; [2] (take effect) [sanctions, taxes] se faire sentir; [3] (emotionally) blesser; **the truth often ~s** la vérité est souvent cruelle

h

hurtful /'hɜːtfl/ *adj* blessant

hurtle /'hɜːtl/ *vi* **to ~ down sth** dévaler qch; **to ~ along a road** foncer sur une route; **to ~ through the air** fendre l'air; **a stone ~d through the window** une pierre vola à travers la vitre

husband /'hʌzbənd/
A *n* mari *m*; Admin époux *m*; **to live as ~ and wife** vivre maritalement
B *vtr* (manage prudently) bien gérer [*resources*]

husbandry /'hʌzbəndrɪ/ *n* **animal ~** élevage *m*

hush /hʌʃ/
A *n* silence *m*
B *excl* (all contexts) chut!
C *vtr* faire taire [*person*]; faire cesser [*bruit*]; calmer [*baby*]
⌜Phrasal verb⌝
■ **hush up:** ► **~ up** se taire; ► **~ up [sth], ~ [sth] up** étouffer [*affair*]; ► **~ up [sb], ~ [sb] up** faire taire [*person*]

hushed /hʌʃt/ *adj* [*conversation*] étouffé; [*room, crowd*] silencieux/-ieuse; **in ~ tones** à voix basse

hush-hush○ /ˌhʌʃ'hʌʃ/ *adj* très confidentiel/-ielle

hush money○ *n* **to pay sb ~** acheter le silence de qn

husk /hʌsk/
A *n* (of grains) enveloppe *f* also fig
B *vtr* décortiquer

husky /'hʌskɪ/
A *n* (dog) husky *m*
B *adj* [*voice*] enroué

hussar /hʊ'zɑː(r)/ *n* hussard *m*

hustings /'hʌstɪŋz/ *n* **at/on the ~** pendant la campagne électorale

hustle /'hʌsl/
A *n* **~ (and bustle)** (lively) effervescence *f*; (tiring) agitation *f*
B *vtr* **1** (push) pousser, bousculer [*person*]; **to ~ sb into a building** pousser qn dans un bâtiment; **2** (urge) **to ~ sb (into doing)** pousser qn (à faire); **3** ○US (sell illegally) vendre illégalement; **4** ○US (obtain by dubious means) soutirer [*money*]; dégoter○ [*job*]; **5** (hurry) précipiter [*negotiations*]; bousculer [*person*]
C *vi* **1** (hurry) se dépêcher; **2** ○US (struggle, work) se démener; **3** ○US (get money dishonestly) pratiquer l'arnaque○

hustler○ /'hʌslə(r)/ *n* US **1** (swindler) arnaqueur/-euse○ *m/f*; **2** (prostitute) prostitué/-e *m/f*

hut /hʌt/ *n* (in garden) cabane *f*; (in shanty town) bicoque○ *f*; (on building site) baraque *f* (de chantier); (for climbers, shepherds) refuge *m*; (native type) hutte *f*, case *f*; (grass) paillote *f*; (on beach) cabine *f* (de plage)

hutch /hʌtʃ/ *n* **1** (for animals) gen cage *f*; (for rabbits) clapier *m*; **2** fig pej (house) clapier *m*; **3** US (furniture) dressoir *m*

hyacinth /'haɪəsɪnθ/ *n* (flower) jacinthe *f*

hybrid /'haɪbrɪd/ *n, adj* (all contexts) hybride (*m*)

hydra /'haɪdrə/ *n* (*pl* **~e** *ou* **~s**) hydre *f* also fig

hydrangea /haɪ'dreɪndʒə/ *n* hortensia *m*

hydrant /'haɪdrənt/ *n* **1** gen prise *f* d'eau; **2** (also fire **~**) bouche *f* d'incendie

hydrate /'haɪdreɪt/
A *n* hydrate *m*
B *vtr* hydrater

hydraulic /haɪ'drɔːlɪk/ *adj* (all contexts) hydraulique

hydraulic ramp *n* Aut pont-élévateur *m*

hydraulics /haɪ'drɔːlɪks/ *n* (+ *v sg*) hydraulique *f*

hydro /'haɪdrəʊ/ *n* GB établissement *m* thermal

hydroelectric /ˌhaɪdrəʊɪ'lektrɪk/ *adj* hydroélectrique

hydroelectricity /ˌhaɪdrəʊɪlek'trɪsətɪ/ *n* hydroélectricité *f*

hydrofoil /'haɪdrəfɔɪl/ *n* **1** (craft) hydroptère *m*; **2** (foil) aile *f* portante

hydrogen /'haɪdrədʒən/ *n* hydrogène *m*

hydrogen: ~ bomb *n* bombe *f* à hydrogène; **~ perox-ide** *n* eau *f* oxygénée

hydrolysis /haɪ'drɒləsɪs/ *n* hydrolyse *f*

hydrophobia /ˌhaɪdrə'fəʊbɪə/ *n* hydrophobie *f*

hydroplane /'haɪdrəpleɪn/ *n* (boat) hydroglisseur *m*; US (seaplane) hydravion *m*

hydroplaning /ˌhaɪdrə'pleɪnɪŋ/ *n* aquaplanage *m*

hydrotherapy /ˌhaɪdrəʊ'θerəpɪ/ *n* hydrothérapie *f*

hyena /haɪ'iːnə/ *n* Zool hyène *f*; fig requin *m*

hygiene /'haɪdʒiːn/ *n* hygiène *f*; **food ~** hygiène alimen-taire

hygienic /haɪ'dʒiːnɪk/ *adj* hygiénique

hygienist /'haɪdʒiːnɪst/ ► p. 1181 *n* hygiéniste *mf*

hymn /hɪm/ *n* (song) cantique *m*; fig hymne *m* (**to** à)

hymnbook /'hɪmbʊk/ *n* livre *m* de cantiques

hype○ /haɪp/ *n* battage *m* publicitaire; **media ~** battage *m* médiatique, médiatisation *f* à outrance
⌜Phrasal verb⌝
■ **hype up:** ► **~ up [sth], ~ [sth] up** doper○ [*sales, econ-omy*]; faire du battage pour [*film, star, book*]; gonfler [*issue, story*]

hyped up○ /ˌhaɪpt'ʌp/ *adj* [*person*] surexcité

hyper○ /'haɪpə(r)/ *adj* surexcité

hyperactive /ˌhaɪpər'æktɪv/ *adj* gen, Med, Psych hyperactif/-ive

hyperactivity /ˌhaɪpəræk'tɪvətɪ/ *n* hyperactivité *f*

hyperbole /haɪ'pɜːbəlɪ/ *n* hyperbole *f*

hypercritical /ˌhaɪpə'krɪtɪkl/ *adj* excessivement cri-tique

hyperdocument /'haɪpədɒkjʊmənt/ *n* Comput hyperdo-cument *m*

hyperlink /'haɪpəlɪŋk/ *n* Comput hyperlien *m*

hypermarket /'haɪpəmɑːkɪt/ *n* GB hypermarché *m*

hypersensitive /ˌhaɪpə'sensətɪv/ *adj* hypersensible

hypertension /ˌhaɪpə'tenʃn/ *n* hypertension *f*

hyperventilate /ˌhaɪpə'ventɪleɪt/ *vi* être en hyperventi-lation

hyphen /'haɪfn/ *n* trait *m* d'union

hyphenate /'haɪfəneɪt/ *vtr* **to be ~d** s'écrire avec un trait d'union

hypnosis /hɪp'nəʊsɪs/ *n* hypnose *f*

hypnotherapy /ˌhɪpnə'θerəpɪ/ *n* hypnothérapie *f*

hypnotic /hɪp'nɒtɪk/ *n, adj* hypnotique (*m*)

hypnotism /'hɪpnətɪzəm/ *n* hypnotisme *m*

hypnotist /'hɪpnətɪst/ *n* hypnotiseur *m*

hypnotize /'hɪpnətaɪz/ *vtr* hypnotiser

hypoallergenic /ˌhaɪpəʊælə'dʒenɪk/ *adj* hypoaller-gique

hypochondria /ˌhaɪpə'kɒndrɪə/ *n* hypocondrie *f*

hypochondriac /ˌhaɪpə'kɒndrɪæk/ *n, adj* hypocondria-que (*mf*)

hypocrisy /hɪ'pɒkrəsɪ/ *n* hypocrisie *f*

hypocrite /'hɪpəkrɪt/ *n* hypocrite *mf*

hypocritical /ˌhɪpə'krɪtɪkl/ *adj* hypocrite

hypocritically /ˌhɪpə'krɪtɪklɪ/ *adv* hypocritement

hypodermic /ˌhaɪpə'dɜːmɪk/ *adj* hypodermique

hypotenuse /haɪ'pɒtənjuːz, US -tnuːs/ *n* hypoténuse *f*

hypothermia /ˌhaɪpəʊ'θɜːmɪə/ *n* hypothermie *f*

hypothesis /haɪ'pɒθəsɪs/ *n* (*pl* **-theses**) hypothèse *f*

hypothesize /haɪ'pɒθəsaɪz/ *vi* émettre une hypothèse

hypothetic(al) /ˌhaɪpə'θetɪk(l)/ *adj* hypothétique

hysterectomy /ˌhɪstə'rektəmɪ/ *n* hystérectomie *f*

hysteria /hɪ'stɪərɪə/ *n* hystérie *f*

hysterical /hɪ'sterɪkl/ *adj* [*person, behaviour*] hystérique; [*sob*] convulsif/-ive; [*demand, speech*] délirant; **~ laughter** fou rire *m*

hysterically /hɪ'sterɪklɪ/ *adv* **1** [*funny*] follement; **2** **to sob ~** avoir une violente crise de larmes; **to laugh ~** avoir le fou rire; **to shout ~** hurler comme un/-e hysté-rique

hysterics /hɪ'sterɪks/ *n* **1** gen (fit) crise *f* de nerfs; **to go into** *ou* **have ~** avoir une crise de nerfs; **2** (laughter) **to be in ~** rire aux larmes

Ii

i, I /aɪ/ n i, I m

(Idiom) **to dot the i's and cross the t's** mettre les points sur les i

I /aɪ/

⚠ *I* is almost always translated by *je* which becomes *j'* before a vowel or mute h: *I closed the door* = j'ai fermé la porte. The emphatic form is *moi*. For exceptions and particular uses see below.

pron je, j'; **he's a student but I'm not** il est étudiant mais moi pas; **he and I went to the cinema** lui et moi sommes allés au cinéma

IA US Post *abrév écrite* = **Iowa**

ibex /'aɪbeks/ n bouquetin m

ice /aɪs/

A n ① gen glace f; (on roads) verglas m; (in drinks) glaçons mpl; **to put sth on ~** lit mettre qch à rafraîchir; fig mettre qch en attente; ② GB (ice cream) glace f; ③ ○**₵** (diamonds) diamants mpl

B vtr Culin glacer

C iced pp adj [water] avec des glaçons; [tea] glacé; [coffee] frappé

(Idioms) **to break the ~** rompre la glace; **to cut no ~ (with sb)** ne faire aucun effet (à qn); **to be treading** ou **skating on thin ~** s'aventurer sur un terrain glissant

(Phrasal verb)
■ **ice over** [windscreen, river] se couvrir de glace

ice: **~ age** n période f glaciaire; **~ axe** n piolet m

iceberg /'aɪsbɜːɡ/ n iceberg m

(Idiom) **the tip of the ~** la partie visible de l'iceberg

iceberg lettuce n laitue f croquante

icebox /'aɪsbɒks/ n ① GB (freezer compartment) freezer m; ② US (fridge) réfrigérateur m

ice: **~breaker** n Naut brise-glace m inv; **~ bucket** n seau m à glace; **~cap** n calotte f glaciaire; **~-cold** adj glacé; **~ cream** n Culin glace f; **~-cream parlour** GB, **~-cream parlor** US n Comm glacier m; **~-cream soda** n US boule de glace servie dans un soda; **~-cream sundae** n coupe f glacée; **~-cube** n glaçon m; **~ dancer** n ▸ p. 881 n danseur/-euse m/f sur glace; **~ floe** n glace f flottante; **~ hockey** n ▸ p. 881 n hockey m sur glace

Iceland /'aɪslənd/ ▸ p. 774 pr n Islande f

ice: **~ pack** n poche f de glace; **~ pick** n Culin pic m à glace; **~ rink** n patinoire f

iceskate /'aɪsskeɪt/ ▸ p. 881

A n patin m à glace

B vi gen patiner; (as a hobby) faire du patinage

ice: **~-skating** ▸ p. 881 n patinage m sur glace; **~-tray** n bac m à glaçons

icicle /'aɪsɪkl/ n stalactite f (de glace)

icily /'aɪsɪlɪ/ adv [stare] de façon glaciale; [say] d'un ton glacial

icing /'aɪsɪŋ/ n glaçage m

(Idiom) **to be the ~ on the cake** être la cerise sur le gâteau

icing sugar n GB sucre m glace

icon /'aɪkɒn/ n icône f; fig (person) idole f; (object) symbole m

iconoclast /aɪ'kɒnəklæst/ n iconoclaste mf

iconography /ˌaɪkə'nɒɡrəfɪ/ n lit iconographie f

icy /'aɪsɪ/ adj ① [road] verglacé; **~ patches** plaques fpl de verglas; ② (cold) [wind] glacial; [hands] glacé; ③ fig [look, reception] glacial

id /ɪd/ n the ~ le ça

I'd /aɪd/ = **I had, I should, I would**

ID n ① (abrév = **identification, identity**) pièce f d'identité; **~ card** carte f d'identité; ② US Post abrév écrite = **Idaho**

idea /aɪ'dɪə/ n ① (thought) idée f (about, on sur); **he came up with** ou **hit on the ~ of buying a farm** l'idée lui est venue d'acheter une ferme; **to be full of ~s** avoir plein d'idées; **don't start getting ~s!** ne commence pas à te faire des idées!; **you can get** ou **put that ~ out of your head!** il n'en est pas question!; ② (notion) conception f (about, of de); **if that's your ~ of a joke...** si c'est ça que tu appelles une plaisanterie...; ③ (impression) impression f; **whatever gave you that ~!** qu'est-ce qui t'a fait croire une chose pareille!; ④ (knowledge) idée f; **to have no ~ why/how etc** ne pas savoir pourquoi/comment etc; **to have no ~ of** ou **about** n'avoir aucune idée de [price, time]; **you've no ~ how pleased I was!** tu ne peux pas savoir combien j'étais content!; ⑤ (theory) idée f; **I've an ~ that he might be lying** j'ai dans l'idée qu'il ment; ⑥ (aim) but m (behind, of de); ⑦ (gist) **do you get the ~?** tu vois?; **that's the ~!** c'est ça!

(Idiom) **the very ~!** quelle idée!

ideal /aɪ'diːəl/

A n idéal m (of de)

B adj idéal (**for** pour; **to do** pour faire)

idealism /aɪ'dɪəlɪzəm/ n idéalisme m

idealist /aɪ'dɪəlɪst/ n idéaliste mf

idealistic /ˌaɪdɪə'lɪstɪk/ adj idéaliste

idealize /aɪ'dɪəlaɪz/ vtr idéaliser

ideally /aɪ'dɪəlɪ/ adv ① (preferably) **~, the tests should be free** l'idéal serait que les examens soient gratuits; **~, we'd like to stay** l'idéal pour nous, ce serait de rester; ② (perfectly) **~ situated** idéalement situé; **to be ~ suited** [couple] être parfaitement assortis; **to be ~ suited for** être parfait pour [job]

identical /aɪ'dentɪkl/ adj identique (**to, with** à); [twin] vrai

identically /aɪ'dentɪklɪ/ adv de façon identique

identifiable /aɪˌdentɪ'faɪəbl/ adj identifiable (**as** comme étant); **~ by sth** reconnaissable à qch

identification /aɪˌdentɪfɪ'keɪʃn/ n ① (of species, person) identification f (**from** à partir de); ② (empathy) identification f (**with** à); ③ (proof of identity) pièce f d'identité

identifier /aɪ'dentɪfaɪə(r)/ n (unique code) identifiant m

identify /aɪ'dentɪfaɪ/

A vtr (establish identity of) identifier (**as** comme étant; **to** à); (pick out) distinguer; (consider as equivalent) **to ~ sb/sth with sb/sth** identifier qn/qch à qn/qch

B vi (empathize) **to ~ with** s'identifier à

C v refl **to ~ oneself** donner son identité

identikit /aɪ'dentɪkɪt/ n (also **Identikit®, identikit picture**) portrait-robot m

identity /aɪ'dentətɪ/ n identité f; **have you any proof of ~?** avez-vous une pièce d'identité?; **mistaken ~** erreur f d'identité

identity: **~ bracelet** n gourmette f; **~ card** n carte f d'identité; **~ parade** n GB séance f d'identification

ideogram /'ɪdɪəɡræm/, **ideograph** /'ɪdɪəɡrɑːf, US -ɡræf/ n idéogramme m

ideological /ˌaɪdɪəˈlɒdʒɪkl/ *adj* idéologique

ideologically /ˌaɪdɪəˈlɒdʒɪklɪ/ *adv* d'un point de vue idéologique

ideology /ˌaɪdɪˈɒlədʒɪ/ *n* idéologie *f*

idiocy /ˈɪdɪəsɪ/ *n* (stupidity) idiotie *f*; (stupid remark) bêtise *f*

idiom /ˈɪdɪəm/ *n* ① (phrase) idiome *m*; ② (language) (of speakers) parler *m*; (of theatre, sport) langue *f*; (of music) style *m*

idiomatic /ˌɪdɪəˈmætɪk/ *adj* idiomatique

idiosyncrasy /ˌɪdɪəˈsɪŋkrəsɪ/ *n* particularité *f*

idiosyncratic /ˌɪdɪəsɪŋˈkrætɪk/ *adj* particulier/-ière

idiot /ˈɪdɪət/ *n* idiot/-e *m/f*

idiotic /ˌɪdɪˈɒtɪk/ *adj* bête

idiotically /ˌɪdɪˈɒtɪklɪ/ *adv* bêtement

idle /ˈaɪdl/

A *adj* ① (lazy) [*person*] paresseux/-euse, fainéant; ② (vain) [*boast, threat*] vain; [*curiosity*] oiseux/-euse; [*chatter*] inutile; ③ (without occupation) [*person*] oisif/-ive; [*day, hour, moment*] de loisir; ④ (not functioning) [*port, dock, mine*] à l'arrêt; [*machine*] arrêté; **to lie** *ou* **stand ~** [*machine, factory*] être à l'arrêt; [*land*] rester inexploité

B *vi* [*engine*] tourner au ralenti

(Idiom) **the devil makes work for ~ hands** Prov l'oisiveté est mère de tous les vices Prov

(Phrasal verb)

■ **idle away:** ▸ **~ away [sth]**, **~ [sth] away** passer [qch] à ne rien faire [*day*]; **to ~ away one's life/time** passer sa vie/son temps à ne rien faire

idleness /ˈaɪdlnɪs/ *n* (inaction) inactivité *f*; (laziness) paresse *f*

idler /ˈaɪdlə(r)/ *n* paresseux/-euse *m/f*

idly /ˈaɪdlɪ/ *adv* (not doing anything) paresseusement; (aimlessly) [*chat*] pour passer le temps

idol /ˈaɪdl/ *n* idole *f*

idolatry /aɪˈdɒlətrɪ/ *n* idolâtrie *f*

idolize /ˈaɪdəlaɪz/ *vtr* adorer [*friend*]; idolâtrer [*star*]

idyll /ˈɪdɪl, US ˈaɪdl/ *n* idylle *f*

idyllic /ɪˈdɪlɪk, US aɪˈd-/ *adj* idyllique

ie (*abrév* = **that is**) c-à-d

if /ɪf/

⚠ *If* is almost always translated by *si*, except in the case of a very few usages which are shown below

A *conj* ① (in the event that, supposing that) si; **I'll help you ~ you pay me** je t'aiderai si tu me paies; **~ he dies** *ou* **~ he should die** s'il meurt; **~ she is to be believed** si on l'en croit; **~ asked, I would say that** si on me posait la question, je dirais que; **~ you like** si tu veux; **~ I were you, I…** (moi) à ta place, je…; **~ it were to snow** s'il neigeait; **~ it were not for the baby** s'il n'y avait pas le bébé; **~ so** si c'est le cas; **~ not** sinon; **tomorrow, ~ not sooner** demain au plus tard, demain ou même avant; **~ I'm not mistaken** si je ne me trompe; ② (whenever) si; **~ you mention his name, she cries** il suffit de prononcer son nom pour qu'elle pleure; ③ (whether) si; **I wonder ~ they will come** je me demande s'ils vont venir; ④ (functioning as *that*) **I'm sorry ~ she doesn't like it but…** je suis désolé que cela ne lui plaise pas mais…; **do you mind ~ I smoke?** cela vous dérange si je fume?; **I don't care ~ he is married!** cela m'est égal qu'il soit marié!; ⑤ (although) si; **we'll go even ~ it's dangerous** nous irons même si c'est dangereux; **it's a good shop, ~ a little expensive** c'est un bon magasin, bien qu'un peu cher; **it was interesting, ~ nothing else** au moins c'était intéressant; ⑥ (as polite formula) **~ you would follow me please** si vous voulez bien me suivre; ⑦ (expressing surprise, dismay etc) **~ it isn't our old friend Mr Pivachon!** tiens, mais voilà notre vieil ami M. Pivachon!; **well, ~ she didn't try and hit him!** je vous jure, elle a essayé de le battre!; ⑧ (used with *what*) **what ~ he died?** et s'il mourait?; **what ~ I say no?** et si je dis non?; **(so) what ~ he** (*ou* **I etc**) **did?** et alors?

B **if only** *conj phr* **~ only because (of)** ne serait-ce qu'à cause de; **~ only for a moment** ne serait-ce que pour un instant; **~ only I had known!** si (seulement) j'avais su!

(Idiom) **it's a very big ~** c'est loin d'être sûr

iffy° /ˈɪfɪ/ *adj* (dubious) suspect; (undecided) incertain

igloo /ˈɪgluː/ *n* igloo *m*, iglou *m*

ignite /ɪgˈnaɪt/

A *vtr* faire exploser [*fuel*]; enflammer [*material*]

B *vi* [*petrol, gas*] s'enflammer; [*rubbish, timber*] prendre feu

ignition /ɪgˈnɪʃn/ *n* Aut (system) allumage *m*; (starting mechanism) contact *m*

ignition: **~ key** *n* clé *f* de contact; **~ switch** *n* contact *m*

ignominious /ˌɪgnəˈmɪnɪəs/ *adj* sout ignominieux/-ieuse

ignoramus /ˌɪgnəˈreɪməs/ *n* (*pl* **-muses**) ignare *mf*

ignorance /ˈɪgnərəns/ *n* (of person) ignorance *f*; **to be in ~ of sth** ignorer qch

(Idiom) **~ is bliss** l'ignorance est salvatrice

ignorant /ˈɪgnərənt/ *adj* [*person*] (of a subject) ignorant; (uneducated) inculte; [*remark*] d'ignorant; **to be ~ about** tout ignorer de [*subject*]; **to be ~ of** [*possibilities*]

ignorantly /ˈɪgnərəntlɪ/ *adv* par ignorance

ignore /ɪgˈnɔː(r)/ *vtr* ignorer [*person*]; ne pas relever [*criticism, mistake, remark*]; ne pas tenir compte de [*feeling, fact*]; ne pas respecter [*rule*]; ne pas suivre [*advice*]; se désintéresser complètement de [*problem*]; **to ~ sb's very existence** faire comme si qn n'existait pas

IL US Post *abrév écrite* = **Illinois**

ilk /ɪlk/ *n* (*sans pl*) espèce *f*

ill /ɪl/

A *n* mal *m*; **to wish sb ~** souhaiter du mal à qn; **economic ~s** les maux de l'économie

B *adj* malade; **to be ~ with sth** (serious illness) être atteint de qch; (less serious) souffrir de qch; **to be taken ~**, **to fall ~** tomber malade

C *adv* sout ① (badly) **he is ~ suited to the post** il n'est guère fait pour ce poste; **to speak ~ of sb** dire du mal de qn; **to bode** *ou* **augur ~ for sth** littér être de mauvais augure pour qch; ② (scarcely) **it ~ becomes you to criticize** il ne vous sied guère de critiquer

(Idiom) **it's an ~ wind (that blows nobody any good)** Prov à quelque chose malheur est bon Prov

I'll /aɪl/ = **I shall, I will**

ill: **~-advised** *adj* malavisé; **~-assorted** *adj* mal assorti; **~ at ease** *adj* gêné, mal à l'aise; **~-bred** *adj* mal élevé; **~-considered** *adj* [*remark*] irréfléchi; [*measure*] hâtif/-ive; **~-disposed** *adj* mal disposé; **~ effect** *n* conséquence *f* néfaste

illegal /ɪˈliːgl/

A *n* US immigrant/-e *m/f* clandestin/-e

B *adj* (unlawful) gen illégal; [*parking*] illicite; [*immigrant*] clandestin; Sport irrégulier/-ière

illegality /ˌɪliːˈgælətɪ/ *n* illégalité *f*

illegally /ɪˈliːgəlɪ/ *adv* [*import, work*] illégalement; [*park*] en infraction

illegible /ɪˈledʒəbl/ *adj* illisible

illegibly /ɪˈledʒəblɪ/ *adv* de façon illisible

illegitimacy /ˌɪlɪˈdʒɪtɪməsɪ/ *n* illégitimité *f*

illegitimate /ˌɪlɪˈdʒɪtɪmət/ *adj* illégitime

ill: **~-equipped** *adj* mal équipé; **~-fated** *adj* malheureux/-euse; **~ feeling** *n* ressentiment *m*; **~-fitting** *adj* [*garment, shoe*] qui va mal; **~-founded** *adj* sans fondement; **~-gotten** *adj* mal acquis; **~ health** *n* mauvaise santé *f*

illicit /ɪˈlɪsɪt/ *adj* illicite

illicitly /ɪˈlɪsɪtlɪ/ *adv* (illegally) de manière illicite; (secretly) clandestinement

ill-informed *adj* mal informé

illiteracy /ɪˈlɪtərəsɪ/ *n* analphabétisme *m*

illiterate /ɪˈlɪtərət/ *n, adj* analphabète (*mf*)

ill: **~-judged** *adj* peu judicieux/-ieuse; **~ luck** *n* malchance *f*; **~-mannered** *adj* grossier/-ière

illness /ˈɪlnɪs/ *n* maladie *f*

illogical /ɪˈlɒdʒɪkl/ *adj* illogique

illogicality /ɪˌlɒdʒɪˈkælətɪ/ *n* illogisme *m*

illogically /ɪˈlɒdʒɪklɪ/ *adv* illogiquement

ill: **~-prepared** *adj* mal préparé; **~-starred** *adj* littér infortuné fml; **~-tempered** *adj* désagréable, déplaisant; **~-timed** *adj* [*arrival*] inopportun; [*campaign*] malencontreux/-euse; **~-treat** *vtr* maltraiter; **~ treatment** *n* mauvais traitements *mpl*

illuminate /ɪˈluːmɪneɪt/ *vtr* gen éclairer; (light for effect) illuminer; Art enluminer; **~d** [*sign*] lumineux/-euse

Illnesses, aches and pains

Where does it hurt?

where does it hurt?
= où est-ce que ça vous fait mal?
  or (more formally) où avez-vous mal?

his leg hurts
= sa jambe lui fait mal

(*Do not confuse* faire mal à qn *with the phrase* faire du mal à qn, *which means* to harm sb.)

he has a pain in his leg
= il a mal à la jambe

■ *Note that with* avoir mal à *French uses the definite article* (la) *with the part of the body, where English has a possessive* (his)*, hence:*

his head was aching
= il avait mal à la tête

■ *English has other ways of expressing this idea, but* avoir mal à *fits them too:*

he had toothache
= il avait mal aux dents

his ears hurt
= il avait mal aux oreilles

. . . .

Accidents

she broke her leg
= elle s'est cassé la jambe

■ Elle s'est cassé la jambe *means literally* she broke to herself the leg; *because the* se *is an indirect object, the past participle* cassé *does not agree. This is true of all such constructions:*

she sprained her ankle
= elle s'est foulé la cheville

they burned their hands
= ils se sont brûlé les mains

. . . .

Chronic conditions

■ *Note that the French often use* fragile (*weak*) *to express a chronic condition:*

he has a weak heart
= il a le cœur fragile

he has kidney trouble
= il a les reins fragiles

he has a bad back
= il a le dos fragile

. . . .

Being ill

■ *Mostly French uses the definite article with the name of an illness:*

to have flu
= avoir la grippe

to have measles
= avoir la rougeole

to have malaria
= avoir la malaria

■ *This applies to most infectious diseases, including childhood illnesses. However, note the exceptions ending in* -ite (*e.g.* une hépatite, une méningite) *below.*

■ *When the illness affects a specific part of the body, French uses the indefinite article:*

to have cancer
= avoir un cancer

to have cancer of the liver
= avoir un cancer du foie

to have pneumonia
= avoir une pneumonie

to have cirrhosis
= avoir une cirrhose

to have a stomach ulcer
= avoir un ulcère à l'estomac

■ *Most words in* -ite (*English* -itis) *work like this:*

to have bronchitis
= avoir une bronchite

to have hepatitis
= avoir une hépatite

■ *When the illness is a generalized condition, French tends to use* du, de l', de la *or* des:

to have rheumatism
= avoir des rhumatismes

to have emphysema
= avoir de l'emphysème

to have asthma
= avoir de l'asthme

to have arthritis
= avoir de l'arthrite

One exception here is:

to have hay fever
= avoir le rhume des foins

■ *When there is an adjective for such conditions, this is often preferred in French:*

to have asthma
= être asthmatique

to have epilepsy
= être épileptique

■ *Such adjectives can be used as nouns to denote the person with the illness, e.g.* un/une asthmatique *and* un/une épileptique *etc.*

■ *French has other specific words for people with certain illnesses:*

someone with cancer
= un cancéreux/une cancéreuse

■ *If in doubt check in the dictionary.*

■ *English* with *is translated by* qui a *or* qui ont, *and this is always safe:*

someone with malaria
= quelqu'un qui a la malaria

people with Aids
= les gens qui ont le Sida

. . . .

Falling ill

■ *The above guidelines about the use of the definite and indefinite articles in French hold good for talking about the onset of illnesses.*

■ *French has no general equivalent of* to get. *However, where English can use* catch, *French can use* attraper:

to catch mumps
= attraper les oreillons

☛ See next page

i

Illnesses, aches and pains *continued*

to catch malaria
= attraper la malaria

to catch bronchitis
= attraper une bronchite

to catch a cold
= attraper un rhume

■ *Similarly where English uses* contract, *French uses* contracter:

to contract Aids
= contracter le Sida

to contract pneumonia
= contracter une pneumonie

to contract hepatitis
= contracter une hépatite

■ *For attacks of chronic illnesses, French uses* faire une crise de:

to have a bout of malaria
= faire une crise de malaria

to have an asthma attack
= faire une crise d'asthme

to have an epileptic fit
= faire une crise d'épilepsie

Treatment

to be treated for polio
= se faire soigner contre la polio

to take something for hay fever
= prendre quelque chose contre le rhume des foins

he's taking something for his cough
= il prend quelque chose contre la toux

to prescribe something for a cough
= prescrire un médicament contre la toux

malaria tablets
= des cachets contre la malaria

to have a cholera vaccination
= se faire vacciner contre le choléra

to be vaccinated against smallpox
= se faire vacciner contre la variole

to be immunized against smallpox
= se faire immuniser contre la variole

to have a tetanus injection
= se faire vacciner contre le tétanos

to give sb a tetanus injection
= vacciner qn contre le tétanos

to be operated on for cancer
= être opéré d'un cancer

to operate on sb for appendicitis
= opérer qn de l'appendicite

---

illuminating /ɪˈluːmɪneɪtɪŋ/ *adj* fig éclairant

illumination /ɪˌluːmɪˈneɪʃn/ *n* (lighting) (of building, sign) éclairage *m*; (for effect) illumination *f*; (enlightenment) illumination *f*; Art (of manuscript) enluminure *f*

illusion /ɪˈluːʒn/ *n* illusion *f*; **to be** *ou* **to labour under the** ∼ **that** avoir l'illusion que

illusive /ɪˈluːsɪv/, **illusory** /ɪˈluːsərɪ/ *adj* (misleading) trompeur/-euse; (apparent) illusoire

illustrate /ˈɪləstreɪt/ *vtr* illustrer; ∼**d** [*book, poem*] illustré; [*lecture*] support visuel

illustration /ˌɪləˈstreɪʃn/ *n* illustration *f*

illustrative /ˈɪləstrətɪv, US ɪˈlʌs-/ *adj* ∼ **material** illustrations *fpl*; **it is** ∼ **of...** cela illustre bien...

illustrator /ˈɪləstreɪtə(r)/ ▸ p. 1181 *n* illustrateur/-trice *m/f*

illustrious /ɪˈlʌstrɪəs/ *adj* [*person*] illustre; [*career*] glorieux/-ieuse

ill will *n* rancune *f*

I'm /aɪm/ = **I am**

image /ˈɪmɪdʒ/ *n* gen, also Comput image *f*; (of company, personality) image *f* de marque; **the popular** ∼ **of life in the north** l'idée que les gens se font de la vie dans le nord; **he is the (spitting)** ∼ **of you** c'est toi tout craché

image: ∼ **builder**, ∼ **maker** *n* professionnel/-elle *m/f* de l'image de marque; ∼**-conscious** *adj* conscient de son image de marque

imagery /ˈɪmɪdʒərɪ/ *n* ₵ images *fpl*

imaginable /ɪˈmædʒɪnəbl/ *adj* imaginable; **the funniest thing** ∼ la chose la plus amusante qu'on puisse imaginer

imaginary /ɪˈmædʒɪnərɪ, US -əneɪ/ *adj* imaginaire

imagination /ɪˌmædʒɪˈneɪʃn/ *n* imagination *f*; **to show** ∼ faire preuve d'imagination; **is it my** ∼, **or...?** je rêve, ou...?; **not by any stretch of the** ∼ **could you say...** même en faisant un grand effort d'imagination on ne pourrait pas dire...

imaginative /ɪˈmædʒɪnətɪv, US -əneɪtɪv/ *adj* [*person, performance*] plein d'imagination; [*mind*] imaginatif/-ive; [*solution, device*] ingénieux/-ieuse

imaginatively /ɪˈmædʒɪnətɪvlɪ, US -əneɪtɪvlɪ/ *adv* avec imagination

imagine /ɪˈmædʒɪn/ *vtr* ① (visualize) (s')imaginer [*object, scene*]; **to** ∼ **being rich/king** s'imaginer riche/roi; **just** ∼**!**, **just** ∼ **that!** tu t'imagines!; **just** ∼ **my surprise** imagine un peu ma surprise; **I can't** ∼ **him travelling alone** je ne le vois pas en train de voyager seul; **I can't** ∼ **her liking that, I can't** ∼ **(that) she liked that** je ne crois pas qu'elle ait aimé ça; **you must have** ∼**d it** ce doit être un effet de ton imagination; ② (suppose) (s')imaginer (**that** que); **you would** ∼ **he'd be more careful** on aurait pu croire qu'il serait plus prudent

imaging /ˈɪmɪdʒɪŋ/ *n* imagerie *f*

imaginings /ɪˈmædʒɪnɪŋz/ *npl* fantaisies *fpl*; **never in my worst** ∼ jamais dans mes rêves les plus horribles

imbalance /ˌɪmˈbæləns/ *n* déséquilibre *m*; **trade** ∼ Econ déséquilibre des échanges commerciaux

imbecile /ˈɪmbəsiːl, US -sl/ *n, adj* imbécile (*mf*)

imbecility /ˌɪmbəˈsɪlətɪ/ *n* (stupidity) stupidité *f*

imbibe /ɪmˈbaɪb/
A *vtr* sout ① (drink) boire; ② (take in) absorber [*knowledge*]
B *vi* hum boire

imbue /ɪmˈbjuː/ *vtr* imprégner (**with** de)

IMF *n* (*abrév* = **International Monetary Fund**) FMI *m*

imitate /ˈɪmɪteɪt/ *vtr* ① imiter; **to** ∼ **a cock crowing** imiter le chant du coq; ② (copy) copier [*handwriting*]

imitation /ˌɪmɪˈteɪʃn/
A *n* imitation *f*; **in** ∼ **of** à l'imitation de; (fake) contrefaçon *f*
B *adj* [*snow*] artificiel/-ielle; ∼ **fur** imitation *f* de fourrure; ∼ **gold** similor *m*; ∼ **jewel** faux bijou *m*; ∼ **leather** similicuir *m*; ∼ **mink** imitation *f* vison

(Idiom) ∼ **is the sincerest form of flattery** l'imitation est la plus sincère des flatteries

imitative /ˈɪmɪtətɪv, US -teɪtɪv/ *adj* imitatif/-ive

imitator /ˈɪmɪteɪtə(r)/ *n* imitateur/-trice *m/f*

immaculate /ɪˈmækjʊlət/ *adj* [*dress, manners*] impeccable; [*performance*] parfait; **the Immaculate Conception** Relig l'Immaculée Conception *f*

immaculately /ɪˈmækjʊlətlɪ/ *adv* de façon impeccable

immaterial /ˌɪməˈtɪərɪəl/ adj ① (unimportant) sans importance; **it's ~ (to me) whether you like it or not** peu m'importe que vous l'aimiez ou non; ② (intangible) immatériel/-ielle

immature /ˌɪməˈtjʊə(r), US -tʊər/ adj ① (not fully grown) [animal] qui n'a pas atteint la maturité; [plant] qui n'est pas arrivé à maturité; ② (childish) immature; **don't be so ~!** ne te conduis pas comme un enfant!

immaturity /ˌɪməˈtjʊərətɪ, US -tʊər-/ n ① (of plant, animal) immaturité f; ② pej (childishness) manque m de maturité

immeasurable /ɪˈmeʒərəbl/ adj incommensurable

immediacy /ɪˈmiːdɪəsɪ/ n immédiateté f

immediate /ɪˈmiːdɪət/ adj ① (instant) [effect, reaction] immédiat; [thought] premier/-ière; ② (urgent, current) [concern, goal] premier/-ière; [problem, crisis] urgent; **the patient is not in ~ danger** les jours du patient ne sont pas en danger; ③ (near) [prospects] immédiat; **his ~ family** ses proches; **in the ~ future** dans l'avenir proche; **on my ~ left** juste à ma gauche

immediately /ɪˈmiːdɪətlɪ/
A adv ① (at once) immédiatement, tout de suite; **~ at** ou **to hand** sous la main; ② (directly) [threatened, affected] immédiatement; **~ after/before** juste avant/après
B conj GB dès que

immemorial /ˌɪməˈmɔːrɪəl/ adj immémorial

immense /ɪˈmens/ adj immense

immensely /ɪˈmenslɪ/ adv [enjoy, help] énormément; [complicated, popular] extrêmement, infiniment

immensity /ɪˈmensətɪ/ n immensité f

immerse /ɪˈmɜːs/
A vtr plonger (**in** dans)
B v refl **to ~ oneself** se plonger (**in** dans)

immersed /ɪˈmɜːst/ adj ① (in liquid) immergé (**in** dans); ② (in book, task etc) absorbé (**in** dans)

immersion /ɪˈmɜːʃn, US -ʒn/ n immersion f (**in** dans)

immersion: **~ course** n GB cours m avec immersion linguistique; **~ heater** n chauffe-eau m électrique

immigrant /ˈɪmɪgrənt/ n, adj (recent) immigrant/-e (m/f); (established) immigré/-e (m/f)

immigrate /ˈɪmɪgreɪt/ vi immigrer (**to** à, **en**)

immigration /ˌɪmɪˈgreɪʃn/ n immigration f

immigration: **~ authorities** npl services mpl de l'immigration; **~ control** n (system) contrôle m de l'immigration; (office) services mpl de l'immigration; **Immigration Service** n GB services mpl de l'immigration

imminence /ˈɪmɪnəns/ n imminence f

imminent /ˈɪmɪnənt/ adj imminent; **rain is ~** la pluie menace

immobile /ɪˈməʊbaɪl, US -bl/ adj immobile

immobility /ˌɪməˈbɪlətɪ/ n immobilité f

immobilize /ɪˈməʊbɪlaɪz/ vtr paralyser [traffic, organization]; immobiliser [engine, patient, limb]

immobilizer /ɪˈməʊbɪlaɪzə(r)/ n Aut système m antidémarrage

immoderate /ɪˈmɒdərət/ adj sout immodéré

immodest /ɪˈmɒdɪst/ adj (boastful) présomptueux/-euse; (improper) indécent

immodesty /ɪˈmɒdɪstɪ/ n présomption f

immoral /ɪˈmɒrəl, US ɪˈmɔːrəl/ adj immoral

immorality /ˌɪməˈrælətɪ/ n immoralité f

immortal /ɪˈmɔːtl/ n, adj immortel/-elle (m/f)

immortality /ˌɪmɔːˈtælətɪ/ n immortalité f

immortalize /ɪˈmɔːtəlaɪz/ vtr immortaliser

immovable /ɪˈmuːvəbl/
A immovables npl Jur biens mpl immeubles
B adj (immobile) fixe; (unchanging) [opinion] inébranlable; [person] immuable; Jur [goods] immeuble

immune /ɪˈmjuːn/ adj ① Med [person] immunisé (**to** contre); [reaction, system] immunitaire; **~ deficiency** déficience f immunitaire, immunodéficience f; ② (oblivious) **~ to** insensible à; ③ (exempt) **to be ~ from** être à l'abri de [attack, arrest]; être exempté de [tax]

immunity /ɪˈmjuːnətɪ/ n ① Med, Admin immunité f (**to**, **against** contre); **tax/legal ~** exemption f fiscale/légale; ② (to criticism) impassibilité f (**to** devant)

immunization /ˌɪmjʊnaɪˈzeɪʃn, US -nɪˈz-/ n immunisation f (**against** contre)

immunize /ˈɪmjuːnaɪz/ vtr immuniser

immunology /ˌɪmjʊˈnɒlədʒɪ/ n immunologie f

immutable /ɪˈmjuːtəbl/ adj immuable

imp /ɪmp/ n lutin m

impact
A /ˈɪmpækt/ n ① (effect) impact m (**on** sur); ② (violent contact) (of hammer, vehicle) choc m; (of bomb, bullet) impact m; **on ~** au moment de l'impact
B /ɪmˈpækt/ vtr (affect) avoir un impact sur; (hit) percuter
C /ɪmˈpækt/ vi avoir un impact (**on** sur)

impacted /ɪmˈpæktɪd/ adj ① Med [tooth] inclus; [fracture] engrené; ② Aut **two ~ cars** deux voitures encastrées

impair /ɪmˈpeə(r)/ vtr affecter [performance]; diminuer [ability]; affaiblir [hearing, vision]; détériorer [health]

impaired /ɪmˈpeəd/ adj [hearing, vision] affaibli; [mobility] réduit; **his speech is ~** il a des problèmes d'élocution; ▸ **visually impaired, hearing-impaired**

impairment /ɪmˈpeəmənt/ n **mental/physical ~** troubles mpl mentaux/moteurs

impale /ɪmˈpeɪl/ vtr empaler (**on** sur)

impalpable /ɪmˈpælpəbl/ adj (intangible) impalpable; (hard to describe) indéfinissable

impart /ɪmˈpɑːt/ vtr ① (communicate) transmettre [knowledge, enthusiasm] (**to** à); communiquer [information] (**to** à); ② (add) donner [atmosphere]

impartial /ɪmˈpɑːʃl/ adj [advice, judge] impartial; [account] objectif/-ive

impartiality /ˌɪmˌpɑːʃɪˈælətɪ/ n impartialité f

impassable /ɪmˈpɑːsəbl, US -ˈpæs-/ adj [obstacle] infranchissable; [road] impraticable

impassioned /ɪmˈpæʃnd/ adj [debate] passionné; [plea] véhément

impassive /ɪmˈpæsɪv/ adj (expressionless) impassible; (unruffled) imperturbable

impatience /ɪmˈpeɪʃns/ n ① (irritation) agacement m (**with** à l'égard de; **at** devant); **my worst fault is ~** mon plus grand défaut est mon manque de patience; ② (eagerness) impatience f (**to do** de faire)

impatient /ɪmˈpeɪʃnt/ adj ① (irritable) agacé (**at** par); **to be/get ~ with sb** s'impatienter contre qn; ② (eager) [person] impatient; [gesture, tone] d'impatience; **to be ~ to do** être impatient or avoir hâte de faire

impatiently /ɪmˈpeɪʃntlɪ/ adv [wait] impatiemment; [fidget] avec impatience; [say] d'un ton agacé

impeach /ɪmˈpiːtʃ/ vtr mettre [qn] en accusation

impeccable /ɪmˈpekəbl/ adj [behaviour] irréprochable; [appearance] impeccable

impeccably /ɪmˈpekəblɪ/ adv [dressed] impeccablement; [behave] de façon irréprochable

impede /ɪmˈpiːd/ vtr entraver

impediment /ɪmˈpedɪmənt/ n ① (hindrance) entrave f (**to** à); ② (also **speech ~**) défaut m d'élocution

impel /ɪmˈpel/ vtr (p prés etc **-ll-**) ① (drive) [emotion, idea] pousser [person] (**to do** à faire); ② (urge) [person, speech] inciter [person] (**to** à; **to do** à faire); **to feel ~led to do** se sentir obligé de faire

impending /ɪmˈpendɪŋ/ adj (avant n) imminent

impenetrable /ɪmˈpenɪtrəbl/ adj impénétrable

imperative /ɪmˈperətɪv/
A n gen, Ling impératif m
B adj [need] urgent; [tone] impérieux/-ieuse; **it is ~ that she write** il est impératif qu'elle écrive

imperceptible /ˌɪmpəˈseptəbl/ adj imperceptible

imperfect /ɪmˈpɜːfɪkt/
A n Ling imparfait m
B adj (incomplete) incomplet/-ète; (defective) [goods] défectueux/-euse; [logic] imparfait; Ling **the ~ tense** l'imparfait m

imperfection /ˌɪmpəˈfekʃn/ n (in object) défectuosité f; (in person) défaut m; (state) imperfection f

imperial /ɪmˈpɪərɪəl/ adj ① (of empire, emperor) impérial; ② GB Hist de l'Empire; ③ GB [measure] conforme aux normes britanniques

imperialism /ɪmˈpɪərɪəlɪzəm/ n impérialisme m

imperialist /ɪmˈpɪərɪəlɪst/ n, adj impérialiste (mf)

imperil /ɪmˈperəl/ vtr (p prés etc **-ll-** GB, **-l-** US) menacer [existence]; compromettre [security, plan, scheme]

imperious /ɪmˈpɪərɪəs/ adj impérieux/-ieuse

impermeable /ɪmˈpɜːmɪəbl/ adj imperméable

impersonal /ɪmˈpɜːsənl/ adj gen, Ling impersonnel/-elle

impersonality /ɪmˌpɜːsəˈnælətɪ/ n (of person) froideur f; (of style, organization) impersonnalité f

impersonate /ɪmˈpɜːsəneɪt/ vtr (imitate) imiter; (pretend to be) se faire passer pour [police officer etc]

impersonation /ɪmˌpɜːsəˈneɪʃn/ n imitation f

impersonator /ɪmˈpɜːsəneɪtə(r)/ n imitateur/-trice m/f

impertinence /ɪmˈpɜːtɪnəns/ n impertinence f

impertinent /ɪmˈpɜːtɪnənt/ adj impertinent (**to** envers)

impertinently /ɪmˈpɜːtɪnəntlɪ/ adv [act, say, reply] avec impertinence

imperturbable /ˌɪmpəˈtɜːbəbl/ adj imperturbable

impervious /ɪmˈpɜːvɪəs/ adj (to water, gas) imperméable (**to** à); fig (to charm, suffering) indifférent (**to** à); (to demands) imperméable (**to** à)

impetuosity /ɪmˌpetʃʊˈɒsətɪ/ n (of person) impétuosité f; (of action) impulsivité f

impetuous /ɪmˈpetʃʊəs/ adj [person] impétueux/-euse; [action] impulsif/-ive

impetus /ˈɪmpɪtəs/ n (trigger) impulsion f; (momentum) élan m; Phys impulsion f

impiety /ɪmˈpaɪətɪ/ n gen manque m de respect; Relig impiété f

impinge /ɪmˈpɪndʒ/ vi **to** ~ **on** (restrict) empiéter sur; (affect) affecter

impious /ˈɪmpɪəs/ adj gen irrespectueux/-euse; Relig impie

impish /ˈɪmpɪʃ/ adj espiègle

implacable /ɪmˈplækəbl/ adj implacable

implacably /ɪmˈplækəblɪ/ adv implacablement

implant
A /ˈɪmplɑːnt, US -plænt/ n implant m
B /ɪmˈplɑːnt, US -ˈplænt/ vtr Med, fig implanter

implausible /ɪmˈplɔːzəbl/ adj peu plausible

implement
A /ˈɪmplɪmənt/ n gen instrument m; (tool) outil m; **farm** ~**s** outillage m agricole
B /ˈɪmplɪment/ vtr 1 gen, Jur exécuter [contract, idea]; mettre [qch] en application [law]; 2 Comput implanter [software]; implémenter [system]

implementation /ˌɪmplɪmenˈteɪʃn/ n (of contract, idea) exécution f; (of law, policy) mise f en application; Comput implémentation f

implicate /ˈɪmplɪkeɪt/ vtr impliquer (**in** dans)

implication /ˌɪmplɪˈkeɪʃn/ n (possible consequence) implication f; (suggestion) insinuation f

implicit /ɪmˈplɪsɪt/ adj (implied) implicite (**in** dans); (absolute) [faith, trust] absolu

implicitly /ɪmˈplɪsɪtlɪ/ adv (tacitly) [assume, admit, recognize] implicitement; (absolutely) [trust, believe] sans réserve

implied /ɪmˈplaɪd/ adj implicite

implore /ɪmˈplɔː(r)/ vtr conjurer (**to do** de faire)

imploring /ɪmˈplɔːrɪŋ/ adj implorant

implosion /ɪmˈpləʊʒn/ n implosion f

imply /ɪmˈplaɪ/ vtr 1 [person] (insinuate) insinuer (**that** que); (make known) laisser entendre (**that** que); 2 [argument] (mean) impliquer; 3 [term, word] (mean) laisser supposer (**that** que)

impolite /ˌɪmpəˈlaɪt/ adj impoli (**to** envers)

impolitely /ˌɪmpəˈlaɪtlɪ/ adv [behave] de manière impolie; [say] avec impolitesse

impoliteness /ˌɪmpəˈlaɪtnɪs/ n impolitesse f

import
A /ˈɪmpɔːt/ n 1 Comm, Econ importation f; 2 (cultural borrowing) apport m (**from** à); 3 sout (meaning) signification f (**in** à); 4 sout (importance) importance f; **of no (great)** ~ de peu d'importance
B /ɪmˈpɔːt/ vtr importer (**from** de; **to** en)

importance /ɪmˈpɔːtns/ n importance f; **her career is of great** ~ **to her** sa carrière est très importante ou compte beaucoup pour elle; **it is of great** ~ **that** il est essentiel que (+ subj); **an event of great political** ~ un événement d'une grande portée politique; **it is a matter of the utmost** ~ c'est une question de la plus haute importance

important /ɪmˈpɔːtnt/ adj important; **it is** ~ **that** il est important que (+ subj); **his children are very** ~ **to him** ses enfants comptent beaucoup pour lui; **he's an** ~ **social figure** c'est une personne en vue

importantly /ɪmˈpɔːtntlɪ/ adv 1 (significantly) d'une manière importante; **and, more** ~,... et, plus important encore,...; **most** ~, **it means** mais surtout, cela signifie; 2 (pompously) [announce] d'un air important

importation /ˌɪmpɔːˈteɪʃn/ n Comm importation f

import duty n taxe f à l'importation

importer /ɪmˈpɔːtə(r)/ n importateur/-trice m/f

import-export /ˌɪmpɔːˈtekspɔːt/ n import-export m

importing /ɪmˈpɔːtɪŋ/
A n importation f (**of** de)
B adj [country, business] importateur/-trice; **oil-**~ **country** pays m importateur de pétrole

import licence GB, **import license** US n licence f d'importation

importunate /ɪmˈpɔːtʃʊnət/ adj importun

importune /ˌɪmpɔːˈtjuːn/ vtr importuner [person]

impose /ɪmˈpəʊz/
A vtr imposer [embargo, rule] (**on sb** à qn; **on sth** sur qch); infliger [sanction] (**on** à); **to** ~ **a fine on sb** frapper qn d'une amende; **to** ~ **a tax on tobacco** imposer le tabac
B vi s'imposer; **to** ~ **on sb's kindness** abuser de la bienveillance de qn
C v refl **to** ~ **oneself on sb** s'imposer à qn

imposing /ɪmˈpəʊzɪŋ/ adj [person] imposant; [sight] impressionnant

imposition /ˌɪmpəˈzɪʃn/ n 1 (exploitation) **I hope it's not too much of an** ~ j'espère que je n'abuse pas de votre bienveillance; 2 (of tax) imposition f

impossibility /ɪmˌpɒsəˈbɪlətɪ/ n impossibilité f; **a physical** ~ une impossibilité matérielle

impossible /ɪmˈpɒsəbl/
A n **the** ~ l'impossible m
B adj impossible; **to make it** ~ **for sb to do sth** mettre qn dans l'impossibilité de faire qch

impossibly /ɪmˈpɒsəblɪ/ adv (appallingly) affreusement; (amazingly) incroyablement

impostor /ɪmˈpɒstə(r)/ n imposteur m

imposture /ɪmˈpɒstʃə(r)/ n imposture f

impotence /ˈɪmpətəns/ n impuissance f

impotent /ˈɪmpətənt/ adj impuissant

impound /ɪmˈpaʊnd/ vtr emmener [qch] à la fourrière [vehicle]; confisquer [goods]

impoverish /ɪmˈpɒvərɪʃ/ vtr appauvrir

impoverishment /ɪmˈpɒvərɪʃmənt/ n appauvrissement m

impracticable /ɪmˈpræktɪkəbl/ adj impraticable

impractical /ɪmˈpræktɪkl/ adj (unworkable) irréalisable; (unrealistic) peu réaliste; [person] **to be** ~ manquer d'esprit pratique

impracticality /ɪmˌpræktɪˈkælətɪ/ n gen caractère m irréalisable; (of person) manque m d'esprit pratique

imprecise /ˌɪmprɪˈsaɪs/ adj imprécis

imprecision /ˌɪmprɪˈsɪʒn/ n imprécision f

impregnable /ɪmˈpregnəbl/ adj imprenable

impregnate /ˈɪmpregneɪt/ US ɪmˈpreg-/ vtr (pervade) imprégner (**with** de); (fertilize) féconder

impresario /ˌɪmprɪˈsɑːrɪəʊ/ n impresario m

impress
A /ˈɪmpres/ n sout empreinte f
B /ɪmˈpres/ vtr 1 (arouse respect) impressionner (**with** par; **by doing** en faisant); **to be easily** ~**ed** se laisser facilement impressionner; **they were (favourably)** ~**ed** ça leur a fait bonne impression; 2 (emphasize) **to** ~ **sth (up)on sb** faire bien comprendre qch à qn; 3 (imprint) **to** ~ **sth on/in** marquer qch sur/faire une empreinte de qch dans
C /ɪmˈpres/ vi faire bonne impression

impression /ɪmˈpreʃn/ n 1 (idea) impression f; **to be under** ou **have the** ~ **that** avoir l'impression que; 2 (impact) impression f; **to make a good/bad** ~ faire bonne/mauvaise impression (**on** sur); **to make (quite) an** ~ faire impression or de l'effet; 3 (perception) impression f; **to give**

ou **create an ～ of sth** faire l'effet de qch; **an artist's ～ of the building** le bâtiment vu par un artiste; **first ～s count** les premières impressions sont souvent les meilleures; ④▸ (imitation) imitation *f*; ⑤▸ (imprint) (of weight, hand) impression *f*; (from teeth) marque *f*; (of hoof) empreinte *f*

impressionable /ɪmˈpreʃənəbl/ *adj* [*child*, *mind*] influençable

impressionist /ɪmˈpreʃənɪst/ *n* ①▸ (*also* **Impressionist**) Art, Mus impressionniste *mf*; ②▸ (mimic) imitateur/-trice *m/f*

impressionistic /ɪmˌpreʃəˈnɪstɪk/ *adj* impressionniste

impressive /ɪmˈpresɪv/ *adj* [*achievement*, *display*, *result*] impressionnant; [*building*, *sight*] imposant; **she is very ～** elle en impose

impressively /ɪmˈpresɪvlɪ/ *adv* de manière impressionnante

imprint

Ⓐ /ˈɪmprɪnt/ *n* empreinte *f*

Ⓑ /ɪmˈprɪnt/ *vtr* ①▸ (fix) graver (**on** dans); ②▸ (print) imprimer (**on** sur)

imprison /ɪmˈprɪzn/ *vtr* emprisonner

imprisonment /ɪmˈprɪznmənt/ *n* emprisonnement *m*

improbability /ɪmˌprɒbəˈbɪlətɪ/ *n* ①▸ (of something happening) improbabilité *f*; (of something being true) invraisemblance *f*; ②▸ (unlikely event) improbabilité *f*

improbable /ɪmˈprɒbəbl/ *adj* ①▸ (unlikely to happen) improbable; ②▸ (unlikely to be true) invraisemblable

improbably /ɪmˈprɒbəblɪ/ *adv* invraisemblablement

improper /ɪmˈprɒpə(r)/ *adj* (unseemly) malséant; (dishonest) irrégulier/-ière; (indecent) indécent; (incorrect) impropre, abusif/-ive

improperly /ɪmˈprɒpəlɪ/ *adv* (unsuitably) de manière malséante; (dishonestly) de manière irrégulière; (indecently) indécemment; (incorrectly) improprement, abusivement; **to be ～ dressed** ne pas être habillé comme il convient

impropriety /ˌɪmprəˈpraɪətɪ/ *n* (irregularity) irrégularité *f*; (unseemliness) inconvenance *f*; (indecency) indécence *f*

improve /ɪmˈpruːv/

Ⓐ *vtr* ①▸ (in quality) améliorer; **to ～ one's German** se perfectionner en allemand; **the new arrangements did not ～ matters** les nouveaux ～ n'ont pas arrangé les choses; **to ～ one's mind** se cultiver (l'esprit); ②▸ (in quantity) augmenter [*wages*, *chances*]; accroître [*productivity*]; ③▸ Constr aménager

Ⓑ *vi* ①▸ s'améliorer; ②▸ **to ～ on** (better) améliorer [*score*]; renchérir sur [*offer*]; **she has ～d on last year's result** elle a obtenu de meilleurs résultats que l'année dernière; ③▸ (increase) [*productivity*] augmenter

improvement /ɪmˈpruːvmənt/ *n* ①▸ (change for the better) amélioration *f* (**in**, **of**, **to** de); **an ～ on last year's performance** une amélioration par rapport aux résultats de l'an dernier; **the new edition is an ～ on the old one** la nouvelle édition est bien meilleure que l'ancienne; ②▸ (progress) progrès *mpl*; **there is room for ～** on pourrait encore faire mieux; ③▸ (alteration) aménagement *m*; **home ～s** aménagements *mpl* du domicile

improvident /ɪmˈprɒvɪdənt/ *adj* (heedless of the future) imprévoyant; (extravagant) prodigue

improvisation /ˌɪmprəvaɪˈzeɪʃn, US *also* ɪmˌprɒvəˈzeɪʃn/ *n* improvisation *f*

improvise /ˈɪmprəvaɪz/

Ⓐ *vtr* improviser; **an ～d table/screen** une table/un écran de fortune

Ⓑ *vi* improviser

imprudent /ɪmˈpruːdnt/ *adj* imprudent

impudence /ˈɪmpjʊdəns/ *n* effronterie *f*

impudent /ˈɪmpjʊdənt/ *adj* insolent, impudent

impulse /ˈɪmpʌls/ *n* impulsion *f*; **to have a sudden ～ to do** avoir une envie soudaine de faire; **on (an) ～** sur un coup de tête; **a generous ～** un élan de générosité

impulse: **～ buy**, **～ purchase** *n* achat *m* d'impulsion; **～ buying** *n* ₵ achat *m* d'impulsion

impulsion /ɪmˈpʌlʃn/ *n* envie *f* irrésistible

impulsive /ɪmˈpʌlsɪv/ *adj* (spontaneous) spontané; (rash) [*person*] impulsif/-ive; [*remark*] irréfléchi

impulsively /ɪmˈpʌlsɪvlɪ/ *adv* (on impulse) impulsivement; (rashly) sur un coup de tête

impulsiveness /ɪmˈpʌlsɪvnɪs/ *n* impulsivité *f*

impunity /ɪmˈpjuːnətɪ/ *n* impunité *f*

impure /ɪmˈpjʊə(r)/ *adj* [*water*, *thoughts*] impur

impurity /ɪmˈpjʊərətɪ/ *n* impureté *f*; **tested for impurities** pureté testée

imputation /ˌɪmpjuːˈteɪʃn/ *n* imputation *f* (**of** de; **to** à)

impute /ɪmˈpjuːt/ *vtr* imputer, attribuer (**to** à)

in /m/

⚠ *In* is often used after verbs in English (*join in*, *tuck in*, *result in*, *write in* etc). For translations, consult the appropriate verb entry (**join**, **tuck**, **result**, **write** etc).

If you have doubts about how to translate a phrase or expression beginning with *in* (*in a huff*, *in business*, *in trouble* etc) you should consult the appropriate noun entry (**huff**, **business**, **trouble** etc).

This dictionary contains usage notes on such topics as age, countries, dates, islands, months, towns and cities etc. Many of these use the preposition *in*. For the index to these notes ▸ p. 1354.

For examples of the above and particular functions and uses of *in*, see the entry below.

Ⓐ *prep* ①▸ (expressing location or position) **～ Paris** à Paris; **～ Spain** en Espagne; **～ school** à l'école; **～ prison/town** en prison/ville; **～ the film/newspaper** dans le film/journal; **I'm ～ here!** je suis là!; ▸ **bath**, **bed**; ②▸ (inside, within) dans; **～ the box** dans la boîte; **there's something ～ it** il y a quelque chose dedans *or* à l'intérieur; ③▸ (expressing a subject or field) dans; **～ insurance** dans les assurances; ▸ **course**, **expert**; ④▸ (included, involved) **to be ～ politics** faire de la politique; **to be ～ the team** faire partie de l'équipe; **to be ～ on the secret**○ être dans le secret; **I wasn't ～ on it**○ je n'étais pas dans le coup○; ⑤▸ (in expressions of time) **～ May** en mai; **～ 1987** en 1987; **～ the night** pendant la nuit; **～ the twenties** dans les années 20; **at four ～ the morning** à quatre heures du matin; **day ～ day out** tous les jours (sans exception); ⑥▸ (within the space of) en; **to do sth ～ 10 minutes** faire qch en 10 minutes; ⑦▸ (expressing the future) dans; **I'll be back ～ half an hour** je serai de retour dans une demi-heure; ⑧▸ (for) depuis; **it hasn't rained ～ weeks** il n'a pas plu depuis des semaines, ça fait des semaines qu'il n'a pas plu; ⑨▸ (during, because of) dans; **～ his hurry he forgot his keys** dans sa précipitation il a oublié ses clés; ⑩▸ (with reflexive pronouns) **it's no bad thing ～ itself** ce n'est pas une mauvaise chose en soi; **how do you feel ～ yourself?** est-ce que tu as le moral?; ▸ **itself**; ⑪▸ (present in, inherent in) **you see it ～ children** on le rencontre chez les enfants; **it's rare ～ cats** c'est rare chez les chats; **he hasn't got it ～ him to succeed** il n'est pas fait pour réussir; **there's something ～ what he says** il y a du vrai dans ce qu'il dit; ⑫▸ (expressing colour, composition) en; **available ～ several colours** disponible en plusieurs couleurs; ⑬▸ (dressed in) en; **～ a skirt** en jupe; **dressed ～ black** habillé en noir; ⑭▸ (expressing manner or medium) **～ German** en allemand; **～ B flat** en si bémol; **'no,' he said ～ a whisper** 'non,' a-t-il chuchoté; **chicken ～ a white wine sauce** du poulet à la sauce au vin blanc; **～ pencil/～ ink** au crayon/à l'encre; ⑮▸ (as regards) **rich/poor ～ minerals** riche/pauvre en minéraux; **deaf ～ one ear** sourd d'une oreille; **10 cm ～ length** 10 cm de long; ⑯▸ (by) **～ accepting** en acceptant; **～ doing so** en faisant cela; ⑰▸ (in superlatives) **the tallest tower ～ the world** la plus grande tour du monde; ⑱▸ (in measurements) **there are 100 centimetres ～ a metre** il y a 100 centimètres dans un mètre; **～ centimetres** en centimètres; **～ a smaller size** dans une taille plus petite; ⑲▸ (in ratios) **a gradient of 1 ～ 4** une pente de 25%; **a tax of 20 pence ～ the pound** une taxe de 20 pence par livre sterling; **to have a one ～ five chance** avoir une chance sur cinq; ⑳▸ (in approximate amounts) **～ their hundreds** *ou* **thousands** par centaines *or* milliers; **to cut sth ～ three** couper qch en trois; ㉑▸ (expressing age) **she's ～ her twenties** elle a entre vingt et trente ans; **people ～ their forties** les gens qui ont entre quarante et cinquante ans; **～ old age** avec l'âge, en vieillissant

Ⓑ **in and out** *prep phr* **to come ～ and out** entrer et sortir; **to weave ～ and out of** se faufiler entre [*traffic*, *tables*]; **to be ～ and out of prison all one's life** passer la plus grande partie de sa vie en prison

Ⓒ **in that** *conj phr* dans la mesure où

Ⓓ *adv* ①▸ (indoors) **to come ～** entrer; **to run ～** entrer en courant; **to ask** *ou* **invite sb ～** faire entrer qn; ②▸ (at home, at work) **to be ～** être là; **I'm usually ～ by 9 am** j'arrive généralement à 9 heures; **to come ～ two days a week** venir deux jours par semaine; **to be ~ by midnight** être rentré avant minuit; ▸ **keep, stay**; ③ (in prison, in hospital) **he's ~ for murder** il a été emprisonné pour meurtre; **she's ~ for a biopsy** elle est entrée à l'hôpital pour une biopsie; ④ (arrived) **the train is ~** le train est en gare; **the ferry is ~** le ferry est à quai; **the sea** *ou* **tide is ~** c'est marée haute; ▸ **come, get**; ⑤ Sport **the ball is ~** la balle est bonne; ⑥ (gathered) **the harvest is ~** la moisson est rentrée; ⑦ (in supply) **we don't have any ~** nous n'en avons pas en stock; **we've got some new titles ~** on a reçu quelques nouveaux titres; **to get some beer ~** aller chercher de la bière; ⑧ (submitted) **applications must be ~ by the 23rd** les candidatures doivent être déposées avant le 23; **the homework has to be ~ tomorrow** le devoir doit être rendu demain; ▸ **get, power, vote**

E °*adj* **to be ~, to be the ~ thing** être à la mode

Idioms **to know the ~s and outs of an affair** connaître une affaire dans les moindres détails; **to have an ~ with sb** US avoir ses entrées chez qn; **to have it ~ for sb**° avoir qn dans le collimateur°; **you're ~ for it**° tu vas avoir des ennuis; **he's ~ for a shock/surprise** il va avoir un choc/être surpris

in. *abrév écrite* = **inch**

IN US Post *abrév écrite* = **Indiana**

inability /ˌɪnəˈbɪlətɪ/ *n* (to drive, pay) incapacité *f* (**to do** de faire); (to help) impuissance *f* (**to do** à faire)

in absentia /ˌɪn æbˈsentɪə/ *adv* en son/leur etc absence

inaccessible /ˌɪnækˈsesəbl/ *adj* (out of reach) inaccessible; (hard to understand) peu accessible (**to** à)

inaccuracy /ɪnˈækjərəsɪ/ *n* ① ℂ (of report, estimate) inexactitude *f*; (of person) manque *m* d'exactitude *or* de précision; ② (error) inexactitude *f*

inaccurate /ɪnˈækjʊrət/ *adj* inexact

inaccurately /ɪnˈækjʊərətlɪ/ *adv* inexactement

inaction /ɪnˈækʃn/ *n* (failure to act) inaction *f*; (not being active) inactivité *f*

inactive /ɪnˈæktɪv/ *adj* inactif/-ive

inactivity /ˌɪnækˈtɪvətɪ/ *n* inactivité *f*

inadequacy /ɪnˈædɪkwəsɪ/ *n* (insufficiency) insuffisance *f*; (defect) défaut *m*

inadequate /ɪnˈædɪkwət/ *adj* [*funding, measures, knowledge*] insuffisant (**for** pour); [*system, facilities*] inadéquat; **to feel ~** être complexé

inadequately /ɪnˈædɪkwətlɪ/ *adv* insuffisamment

inadmissible /ˌɪnədˈmɪsəbl/ *adj* inadmissible; Jur [*evidence*] irrecevable

inadvertent /ˌɪnədˈvɜːtənt/ *adj* (accidental) involontaire; (inattentive) inattentif/-ive

inadvertently /ˌɪnədˈvɜːtəntlɪ/ *adv* (unintentionally) involontairement; (unthinkingly) par mégarde

inadvisable /ˌɪnədˈvaɪzəbl/ *adj* inopportun, à déconseiller

inalienable /ɪnˈeɪlɪənəbl/ *adj* inaliénable

inane /ɪˈneɪn/ *adj* [*person, conversation*] idiot; [*programme*] débile°

inanely /ɪˈneɪnlɪ/ *adv* de façon idiote

inanimate /ɪnˈænɪmət/ *adj* inanimé

inanity /ɪˈnænətɪ/ *n* ineptie *f*

inapplicable /ɪnˈæplɪkəbl/, /ˌɪnəˈplɪk-/ *adj* inapplicable

inappropriate /ˌɪnəˈprəʊprɪət/ *adj* ① (unsuitable) [*behaviour*] inconvenant, peu convenable; [*remark*] inopportun; ② (incorrect) [*advice, word*] qui n'est pas approprié

inappropriately /ˌɪnəˈprəʊprɪətlɪ/ *adv* inopportunément, mal à propos

inapt /ɪnˈæpt/ *adj* ① (inappropriate) inconvenant; ② (inept) incompétent

inarticulate /ˌɪnɑːˈtɪkjʊlət/ *adj* ① (unable to express oneself) **to be ~** ne pas savoir s'exprimer; ② (indistinct) [*mumble*] inarticulé; [*speech*] inintelligible; ③ (defying expression) [*rage*] inexprimable; ④ Zool inarticulé

inasmuch /ˌɪnəzˈmʌtʃ/: **inasmuch as** *conj phr* (insofar as) dans la mesure où; (seeing as) vu que

inattention /ˌɪnəˈtenʃn/ *n* inattention *f*

inattentive /ˌɪnəˈtentɪv/ *adj* [*pupil*] inattentif/-ive; [*audience, lover*] peu attentif/-ive

inattentively /ˌɪnəˈtentɪvlɪ/ *adv* distraitement

inaudible /ɪnˈɔːdəbl/ *adj* [*sound*] inaudible; **he was almost ~** on l'entendait à peine

inaugural /ɪˈnɔːɡjʊrəl/ *adj* inaugural

inaugurate /ɪˈnɔːɡjʊreɪt/ *vtr* inaugurer [*exhibition*]; investir [qn] de ses fonctions [*president, official*]

inauguration /ɪˌnɔːɡjʊˈreɪʃn/ *n* (of exhibition) inauguration *f*; (of president) investiture *f*

inauspicious /ˌɪnɔːˈspɪʃəs/ *adj* (unpromising) peu propice, de mauvais augure; (unfortunate) malencontreux/-euse

inauspiciously /ˌɪnɔːˈspɪʃəslɪ/ *adv* [*begin, start*] mal

in-between *adj* intermédiaire

inborn /ɪnˈbɔːn/ *adj* (innate) inné; (inherited) congénital

in-box /ˈɪnbɒks/ *n* (for email) boîte *f* de réception

inbred /ˌɪnˈbred/ *adj* (innate) inné; (produced by inbreeding) [*animal*] résultant de croisements entre animaux de même souche; [*characteristic*] résultant de croisement consanguin

inbreeding /ɪnˈbriːdɪŋ/ *n* (in animals) croisement *m* d'animaux de même souche; (in humans) croisement *m* consanguin, consanguinité *f*

inbuilt /ˌɪnˈbɪlt/ *adj* intrinsèque

Inc US (*abrév écrite* = **incorporated**) SA

incalculable /ɪnˈkælkjʊləbl/ *adj* incalculable

incandescence /ˌɪnkænˈdesns/ *n* incandescence *f*

incandescent /ˌɪnkænˈdesnt/ *adj* incandescent

incapability /ɪnˌkeɪpəˈbɪlɪtɪ/ *n* gen, Jur incapacité *f* (**to do** de faire)

incapable /ɪnˈkeɪpəbl/ *adj* incapable (**of doing** de faire); **drunk and ~** Jur en état d'ivresse publique

incapacitate /ˌɪnkəˈpæsɪteɪt/ *vtr* [*accident, illness*] immobiliser; **severely ~d** infirme, invalide

incapacity /ˌɪnkəˈpæsətɪ/ *n* gen, Jur incapacité *f* (**to do** de faire)

incapacity benefit *n* GB Soc Admin allocation *f* d'invalidité

incarcerate /ɪnˈkɑːsəreɪt/ *vtr* incarcérer

incarnate
A /ɪnˈkɑːnet/ *adj* incarné
B /ˈɪnkɑːneɪt/ *vtr* incarner; **to be ~d in** *ou* **as** s'incarner en

incarnation /ˌɪnkɑːˈneɪʃn/ *n* incarnation *f*

incautious /ɪnˈkɔːʃəs/ *adj* imprudent, irréfléchi

incendiary /ɪnˈsendɪərɪ, US -dɪerɪ/
A *n* (bomb) engin *m* incendiaire
B *adj* incendiaire

incendiary: **~ attack** *n* attaque *f* à la bombe incendiaire; **~ device** *n* engin *m* incendiaire

incense
A /ˈɪnsens/ *n* encens *m*
B /ɪnˈsens/ *vtr* mettre [qn] en fureur [*person*]

incensed /ɪnˈsenst/ *adj* outré (**at** de; **by** par)

incentive /ɪnˈsentɪv/ *n* ① (motivation) **to give sb the ~ to do sth** donner envie à qn de faire; **there is no ~ for people to save** rien n'incite les gens à faire des économies; **there are strong ~s to join a union** on a tout intérêt à adhérer à un syndicat; ② Fin, Comm prime *f*; **export ~** prime à l'exportation

incentive bonus, incentive payment *n* prime *f* d'encouragement

inception /ɪnˈsepʃn/ *n* commencement *m*; **from** *ou* **since its ~ in 1962** depuis ses débuts en 1962

incessant /ɪnˈsesnt/ *adj* incessant

incessantly /ɪnˈsesntlɪ/ *adv* sans cesse

incest /ˈɪnsest/ *n* inceste *m*

incestuous /ɪnˈsestjʊəs, US -tʃʊəs/ *adj* incestueux/-euse

inch /ɪntʃ/ ▸ p. 977
A *n* (*pl* **~es**) ① (measurement) pouce *m* (= 2,54 cm); ② fig (small amount) **~ by ~** petit à petit; **to come within an ~ of winning** passer à deux doigts de la victoire; **she won't give** *ou* **budge an ~** elle ne veut pas bouger d'un pouce
B *vtr* **to ~ sth forward** faire avancer qch petit à petit
C *vi* **to ~ towards sth** lit se diriger petit à petit vers qch; fig parvenir petit à petit à qch [*solution*]

Idioms **give her an ~ and she'll take a mile** *ou* **yard** plus on lui en donne, plus elle en veut; **there is no ~ for people to** °n'ai pas la moindre confiance en lui; **to fight every ~ of the way** lutter pied à pied

incidence /'ɪnsɪdəns/ n (occurrence) **the ~ of** la fréquence de [*thefts, deaths*]; **high/low ~ of sth** taux élevé/faible taux de qch

incident /'ɪnsɪdənt/ n incident m

incidental /ˌɪnsɪ'dentl/

A n détail m

B **incidentals** npl Comm faux-frais mpl

C adj (minor) [*detail, remark*] secondaire; [*error*] mineur; **to be ~ to** accompagner [*activity, job*]

incidental: **~ damages** npl Jur dommages-intérêts mpl indirects; **~ expenses** npl faux-frais mpl

incidentally /ˌɪnsɪ'dentlɪ/ adv (by the way) à propos; (by chance) par la même occasion

incidental music n Cin musique f de film; Theat musique f de scène

incident room n GB bureau m des enquêteurs

incinerate /ɪn'sɪnəreɪt/ vtr incinérer

incineration /ɪnˌsɪnə'reɪʃn/ n incinération f

incinerator /ɪn'sɪnəreɪtə(r)/ n (industrial, domestic) incinérateur m; (in crematorium) four m crématoire

incipient /ɪn'sɪpɪənt/ adj [*disease, crisis*] à ses débuts; [*baldness*] naissant

incise /ɪn'saɪz/ vtr (cut) inciser; (engrave) graver

incision /ɪn'sɪʒn/ n incision f

incisive /ɪn'saɪsɪv/ adj [*remark, mind*] pénétrant; [*style, criticism*] incisif/-ive

incisively /ɪn'saɪsɪvlɪ/ adv d'une manière précise

incisor /ɪn'saɪzə(r)/ n incisive f

incite /ɪn'saɪt/ vtr **to ~ violence** inciter à la violence; **to ~ sb to do** pousser ou inciter qn à faire

incitement /ɪn'saɪtmənt/ n incitation f **(to** à)

incl ① (abrév écrite = **including**) compris; **£20,000 ~ bonuses** 20 000 livres, primes comprises; ② (abrév = **inclusive**) TTC; **£110 ~** 110 livres sterling TTC

inclement /ɪn'klemənt/ adj (all contexts) inclément

inclination /ˌɪnklɪ'neɪʃn/ n ① (tendency) tendance f, inclination f; (to, towards à); **by ~** par nature; **to follow one's own ~s** suivre ses penchants naturels; ② (desire) envie f, désir m (**for** de); (liking) goût m; **to have an ~ to do** avoir envie de faire

incline

A /'ɪnklaɪn/ n (slope) pente f

B /ɪn'klaɪn/ vtr ① (tilt) incliner; ② **to be ~d to do** (have tendency) avoir tendance à faire; (have desire) avoir envie de faire; **if you feel so ~d** si l'envie vous en prend; **he was not ~d to listen** il n'était pas disposé à écouter; **to be artistically ~d** avoir un goût pour l'art; ③ sout (persuade) **to ~ sb to do** porter qn à faire

C /ɪn'klaɪn/ vi ① (tend) **to ~ to** ou **towards** [*ideas, politics*] tendre vers; **to ~ towards the opinion that** avoir tendance à penser que; ② (lean) s'incliner

include /ɪn'kluːd/ vtr inclure, comprendre; **all the ministers, Blanc ~d** tous les ministres, Blanc inclu; **breakfast is ~d in the price** le petit déjeuner est compris; **your duties ~ answering the phone** répondre au téléphone fait partie de vos fonctions; **does that ~ me?** est-ce que cela s'adresse aussi à moi?

including /ɪn'kluːdɪŋ/ prep (y) compris; **~ July** y compris juillet; **not ~ July** sans compter juillet; **up to and ~ Monday** jusqu'à lundi inclus; **~ service** service compris

inclusion /ɪn'kluːʒn/ n inclusion f (**of** de; **in** dans)

inclusive /ɪn'kluːsɪv/ adj [*charge*] inclus; [*price*] forfaitaire; [*terms*] tout compris; **those aged 17–24 ~** les personnes âgées de 17 à 24 ans inclus; **the price ~ of delivery** le prix, livraison comprise

incognito /ˌɪnkɒg'niːtəʊ, US ɪŋ'kɒgnətəʊ/

A adj **to be ~** rester dans l'incognito; **to remain ~** garder l'incognito

B adv [*travel*] incognito

incoherence /ˌɪŋkəʊ'hɪərəns/ n incohérence f

incoherent /ˌɪŋkəʊ'hɪərənt/ adj incohérent

income /'ɪŋkʌm/ n revenus mpl; **an ~ of £1,000 per month** 1 000 livres sterling par mois de revenus; **to be on an ~ of £20,000 per year** gagner 20 000 livres par an; **to live within/beyond one's ~** vivre dans la limite de/au-delà de ses moyens

income: **~ bracket**, **~ group** n tranche f de revenu; **~s policy** n politique f des revenus; **~ tax** n impôt m sur le revenu; **~ tax inspector** n inspecteur/-trice m/f des impôts

incoming /'ɪnkʌmɪŋ/ adj [*call, mail*] qui vient de l'extérieur; [*aircraft*] qui arrive; [*president, government*] nouveau/-elle; [*tide*] montant; **this phone only takes ~ calls** ce téléphone ne peut que recevoir des appels

incommunicado /ˌɪnkəˌmjuːnɪ'kɑːdəʊ/ adj (by choice) injoignable; (involuntarily) sans contact avec l'extérieur

incomparable /ɪn'kɒmprəbl/ adj sans pareil/-eille

incomparably /ɪn'kɒmprəblɪ/ adv [*better*] infiniment; **~ beautiful** d'une beauté sans pareille

incompatible /ˌɪnkəm'pætɪbl/ adj [*person, computer, drug*] incompatible; [*idea, activity*] inconciliable

incompetence /ɪn'kɒmpɪtəns/, **incompetency** /ɪn'kɒmpɪtənsɪ/ n (of professional) incompétence f; (of person, child) inaptitude f; Jur incompétence f

incompetent /ɪn'kɒmpɪtənt/

A n incapable mf

B adj ① [*doctor, government*] incompétent; [*work, performance*] mauvais; ② Jur [*person, child*] incompétent; [*witness*] récusé; [*evidence*] irrecevable

incomplete /ˌɪnkəm'pliːt/ adj ① (unfinished) [*work, building*] inachevé; ② (lacking parts) [*set*] incomplet/-ète; ③ (imperfect) [*success*] incomplet/-ète

incompletely /ˌɪnkɒm'pliːtlɪ/ adv incomplètement

incomprehensible /ɪnˌkɒmprɪ'hensəbl/ adj [*reason*] incompréhensible; [*speech*] inintelligible

incomprehension /ɪnˌkɒmprɪ'henʃn/ n incompréhension f

inconceivable /ˌɪnkən'siːvəbl/ adj inconcevable

inconceivably /ˌɪnkən'siːvəblɪ/ adv [*tall, difficult*] incroyablement

inconclusive /ˌɪnkən'kluːsɪv/ adj [*meeting*] sans conclusion véritable; [*election*] sans résultat clair; [*evidence*] peu concluant

inconclusively /ˌɪnkən'kluːsɪvlɪ/ adv [*end*] sans conclusion véritable; [*argue*] de manière peu concluante

incongruity /ˌɪnkɒŋ'gruːətɪ/ n (of appearance) incongruité f; (of situation) absurdité f

incongruous /ɪn'kɒŋgrʊəs/ adj [*sight*] déconcertant; [*appearance*] surprenant

incongruously /ɪn'kɒŋgrʊəslɪ/ adv bizarrement

inconsequential /ˌɪnkɒnsɪ'kwenʃl/ adj (unimportant) sans importance; (illogical) illogique

inconsiderate /ˌɪnkən'sɪdərət/ adj [*person*] peu attentif/-ive à autrui; [*remark*] maladroit; **to be ~ towards sb** manquer d'égards envers qn

inconsiderately /ˌɪnkən'sɪdərətlɪ/ adv sans aucune considération

inconsistency /ˌɪnkən'sɪstənsɪ/ n incohérence f

inconsistent /ˌɪnkən'sɪstənt/ adj [*work*] inégal; [*behaviour*] changeant; [*argument*] incohérent; [*attitude*] inconsistant; **~ with** en contradiction avec

inconsolable /ˌɪnkən'səʊləbl/ adj inconsolable

inconspicuous /ˌɪnkən'spɪkjʊəs/ adj [*person*] qui passe inaperçu, qui ne se fait pas remarquer; [*place, clothing*] discret/-ète

inconspicuously /ˌɪnkən'spɪkjʊəslɪ/ adv discrètement

inconstancy /ɪn'kɒnstənsɪ/ n inconstance f

inconstant /ɪn'kɒnstənt/ adj [*lover*] inconstant; [*conditions*] instable

incontestable /ˌɪnkən'testəbl/ adj incontestable

incontinence /ɪn'kɒntɪnəns/ n incontinence f

incontinent /ɪn'kɒntɪnənt/ adj incontinent

incontrovertible /ˌɪnkɒntrə'vɜːtəbl/ adj [*evidence, sign*] indéniable; [*argument, statement*] irréfutable

incontrovertibly /ˌɪnkɒntrə'vɜːtəblɪ/ adv [*true, wrong*] incontestablement; [*demonstrate, prove*] de façon incontestable

inconvenience /ˌɪnkən'viːnɪəns/

A n ① (trouble) dérangement m; **to put sb to great ~** causer beaucoup de dérangement à qn; ② (disadvantage) inconvénient m

B vtr déranger

inconvenient /ˌɪnkən'viːnɪənt/ adj ① [location, arrangement, device] incommode; [time] inopportun; **if it's not ~** si cela ne vous/les etc dérange pas; ② (embarrassing) gênant

inconveniently /ˌɪnkən'viːnɪəntlɪ/ adv de façon peu pratique

incorporate /ɪn'kɔːpəreɪt/ vtr ① (make part of sth) incorporer (**into** dans); ② (contain) comporter; ③ (unite) regrouper; ④ Comm, Jur **Smith and Brown Incorporated** Smith et Brown SA

incorporation /ɪnˌkɔːpə'reɪʃn/ n ① gen incorporation f (**into** dans); ② Jur constitution f en société

incorrect /ˌɪnkə'rekt/ adj incorrect (**to do** de faire); **to be ~ in doing** faire erreur en faisant

incorrectly /ˌɪnkə'rektlɪ/ adv incorrectement

incorrigible /ɪn'kɒrɪdʒəbl, US -'kɔːr-/ adj incorrigible

incorruptible /ˌɪnkə'rʌptəbl/ adj incorruptible

increase

Ⓐ /'ɪnkriːs/ n ① (in amount) augmentation f (**in, of** de); **price ~** augmentation de prix; **a 5% ~** une augmentation de 5%; ② (in degree) accroissement m; **to be on the ~** être en progression

Ⓑ /ɪn'kriːs/ vtr ① gen augmenter [sales, grant, offer, temperature] (**by** de; **to** jusqu'à); prolonger [life expectancy]; **I ~d my offer to $100** je suis monté à 100 dollars; ② (in knitting) augmenter de [stitch]

Ⓒ /ɪn'kriːs/ vi ① [output, sales, volume] augmenter (**by** de); [appetite] grandir; [workload] s'accroître; [wind] redoubler; **to ~ in number/value** augmenter en nombre/valeur; **to ~ in volume** augmenter de volume; **to ~ in size** s'agrandir; **to ~ from... to** passer de... à; ② (in knitting) augmenter

Ⓓ increasing pres p adj [prices, number] croissant

Ⓔ increased pp adj [demand, probability] plus grand; [risk] accru; [attacks] plus fréquent

increasingly /ɪn'kriːsɪŋlɪ/ adv de plus en plus

incredible /ɪn'kredəbl/ adj ① (unbelievable) incroyable; ② ○(wonderful) fantastique

incredibly /ɪn'kredəblɪ/ adv (astonishingly) incroyablement; (extremely) extrêmement

incredulity /ˌɪnkrɪ'djuːlətɪ, US -duː-/ n incrédulité f

incredulous /ɪn'kredjʊləs, US -dʒə-/ adj incrédule

incredulously /ɪn'kredjʊləslɪ, US -dʒə-/ adv [say] d'un ton incrédule; [look] d'un air incrédule; [listen] d'une oreille incrédule

increment /'ɪnkrəmənt/

Ⓐ n ① (on salary) augmentation f (automatique); ② Comput, Math incrément m

Ⓑ vtr ① Fin augmenter (automatiquement); ② Comput, Math incrémenter

incremental /ˌɪnkrə'mentl/ adj ① Comput, Math incrémentiel/-ielle; ② (increasing) [effect] cumulatif/-ive; [measures] progressif/-ive

incriminate /ɪn'krɪmɪneɪt/ vtr incriminer; **to ~ sb in** impliquer qn dans [crime, activity]

incriminating /ɪn'krɪmɪneɪtɪŋ/ adj [statement, document] compromettant; [evidence] incriminant

in-crowd○ /'ɪnkraʊd/ n **to be in with the ~** fréquenter les gens à la mode

incrust vtr = encrust

incrustation /ˌɪnkrʌ'steɪʃn/ n (of gems) incrustation f; (of salt) dépôt m

incubate /'ɪnkjʊbeɪt/

Ⓐ vtr [hen] couver; faire incuber [bacteria, culture]

Ⓑ vi [eggs, bacteria] être en incubation

incubation /ˌɪnkjʊ'beɪʃn/ n incubation f

incubator /'ɪnkjʊbeɪtə(r)/ n (for child) couveuse f; (for eggs, bacteria) incubateur m

inculcate /'ɪnkʌlkeɪt, US ɪn'kʌl-/ vtr **to ~ sth in sb, ~ sb with sth** inculquer qch à qn

incumbent /ɪn'kʌmbənt/

Ⓐ n sout ① Admin, Pol personne f exerçant une charge; (minister) ministre m; ② Relig pasteur m (chargé d'une paroisse)

Ⓑ adj ① (morally) **to be ~ on** ou **upon sb to do** incomber à qn de faire; ② (in office) en exercice

incur /ɪn'kɜː(r)/ vtr (p prés etc **-rr-**) contracter [debts]; subir [loss]; encourir [expense, penalty, risk, wrath]

incurable /ɪn'kjʊərəbl/

Ⓐ n incurable mf

Ⓑ adj [disease] incurable; [optimism] incorrigible

incurably /ɪn'kjʊərəblɪ/ adv **to be ~ ill** souffrir d'une maladie incurable; fig **to be ~ romantic** être d'un romantisme incorrigible

incurious /ɪn'kjʊərɪəs/ adj indifférent

incursion /ɪn'kɜːʃn, US -ʒn/ n gen intrusion f; Mil incursion f

indebted /ɪn'detɪd/ adj ① (grateful) **to be ~ to sb** (under an obligation) redevable à qn; (grateful) être reconnaissant à qn; ② Fin endetté

indecency /ɪn'diːsnsɪ/ n indécence f; (offence) attentat m à la pudeur; **gross ~** outrage m à la pudeur

indecent /ɪn'diːsnt/ adj (sexually) indécent; (unseemly) malséant

indecent: **~ assault** n attentat m à la pudeur (**on** contre); **~ exposure** n outrage m public à la pudeur

indecently /ɪn'diːsntlɪ/ adv [behave, dress] d'une manière indécente; **~ soon** avec une rapidité malséante; **~ early** plus tôt que nécessaire

indecipherable /ˌɪndɪ'saɪfrəbl/ adj indéchiffrable

indecision /ˌɪndɪ'sɪʒn/ n indécision f (**about** quant à)

indecisive /ˌɪndɪ'saɪsɪv/ adj [person, reply, result] indécis (**about** quant à); [battle, election] peu concluant

indecisively /ˌɪndɪ'saɪsɪvlɪ/ adv [speak, reply] d'un ton indécis; [behave] d'une manière indécise

indecorous /ɪn'dekərəs/ adj inconvenant

indeed /ɪn'diːd/ adv ① (certainly) en effet, effectivement; **'it's unfair'—'~!'** 'c'est injuste'—'en effet!'; **'~ I am!'** 'bien sûr que oui!'; **'~ you can'** ou **'you can ~'** 'bien sûr que oui'; **'he's not coming, is he?'—'~ he is!'** 'lui, il ne vient pas?'—'bien sûr que si!'; ② (in fact) en fait; **she is polite, ~ charming** elle est polie et même charmante; **if ~ that is what consumers want** si c'est vraiment ce que veulent les consommateurs; ③ (for emphasis) vraiment; **that was praise ~** c'était vraiment un compliment; **thank you very much ~** merci mille fois; ④ iron (expressing surprise) **'does he ~?'** 'ah bon?', 'vraiment?'; **a bargain ~!** tu parles d'une affaire!; **'why did she do it?'—'why ~?'** 'pourquoi est-ce qu'elle l'a fait?'—'ça c'est une bonne question'

indefatigable /ˌɪndɪ'fætɪgəbl/ adj inlassable

indefensible /ˌɪndɪ'fensəbl/ adj ① (morally) inexcusable; (logically) indéfendable; ② Mil indéfendable

indefinable /ˌɪndɪ'faɪnəbl/ adj indéfinissable

indefinably /ˌɪndɪ'faɪnəblɪ/ adv vaguement

indefinite /ɪn'defmət/ adj ① (vague) vague; ② (without limits) [period, delay] illimité; [number] indéterminé; [ban] pour une durée indéterminée; ③ Ling **the ~ article** l'article m indéfini

indefinitely /ɪn'defɪnətlɪ/ adv [continue, stay] indéfiniment; [postpone, ban] pour une durée indéterminée

indelible /ɪn'deləbl/ adj [ink, mark] indélébile; [impression] ineffaçable; [part] indélébile

indelibly /ɪn'deləblɪ/ adv ① lit [marked, printed] de manière indélébile; ② fig [impressed, imprinted] de manière ineffaçable

indelicacy /ɪn'delɪkəsɪ/ n (tactlessness) indélicatesse f; (coarseness) grossièreté f

indelicate /ɪn'delɪkət/ adj (tactless) indélicat; (coarse) grossier/-ière

indemnification /ɪnˌdemnɪfɪ'keɪʃn/ n ① (protection) assurance f; ② (compensation) indemnisation f (**for** de)

indemnify /ɪn'demnɪfaɪ/ vtr ① (protect) assurer (**against** contre); ② (compensate) indemniser (**for** de)

indemnity /ɪn'demnətɪ/ n ① (protection) assurance f; ② (payment) indemnité f; ③ (exemption) décharge f

indent

Ⓐ /'ɪndent/ n ① GB Comm commande f (**for** de); ② (of first line) alinéa m; ③ (incision) entaille f

Ⓑ /ɪn'dent/ vtr renfoncer [line, text, word]; faire un alinéa pour [new paragraph]; denteler [edge]

Ⓒ /ɪn'dent/ vi GB Comm passer une commande

Ⓓ indented pp adj ① [paragraph] en alinéa; ② [coastline] découpé; [edge] dentelé

indentation /ˌɪnden'teɪʃn/ n ① (dent) marque f; (in metal) bosse f; ② (in coastline) échancrure f

independence /ˌɪndɪ'pendəns/ n indépendance f

Independence Day n US fête f de l'Indépendance

ℹ Independence Day (4th July) Jour de fête nationale aux États-Unis pour commémorer la ratification de la Déclaration d'Indépendance par le Congrès
le 4 juillet 1776. ▸ Declaration of Independence

independent /ˌɪndɪ'pendənt/
A n **1)** Pol candidat/-e m/f indépendant/-e; **2)** (company) indépendant m, compagnie f indépendante
B adj **1)** (self-reliant) [person] indépendant; **~ means, an
~ income** des revenus personnels; **2)** Pol indépendant;
3) (impartial) [observer, inquiry] indépendant; [evidence,
account] objectif/-ive; **4)** (unconnected) [complaint] indépendant; **5)** (not part of an organization) indépendant; **6)** (not state
run) privé

independently /ˌɪndɪ'pendəntlɪ/ adv **1)** (without help) de
façon indépendante; **2)** (separately) individuellement, de
façon indépendante; **~ of** indépendamment de; **3)** (impar-
tially) [monitored] par une autorité extérieure

in-depth /ˌɪn'depθ/
A adj [analysis, study, knowledge] approfondi, détaillé; [guide]
détaillé; [interview] en profondeur
B in depth adv phr [examine, study] en détail

indescribable /ˌɪndɪ'skraɪbəbl/ adj [chaos, noise, smell]
indescriptible; [pleasure, beauty] inexprimable

indescribably /ˌɪndɪ'skraɪbəblɪ/ adv **~ beautiful/sad**
d'une beauté/tristesse inexprimable; **~ boring** incroyablement ennuyeux

indestructible /ˌɪndɪ'strʌktɪbl/ adj indestructible

indeterminate /ˌɪndɪ'tɜːmɪnət/ adj indéterminé

index /'ɪndeks/
A n (pl **~es** ou **-ices**) **1)** (of book) index m inv; **thumb ~**
index à onglets; **2)** (catalogue) catalogue m; **card ~** fichier
m; **3)** Math (of power) exposant m; (of radical) indice m; **4)** Econ
indice m; **cost-of-living ~** GB, **consumer price ~** US indice
des prix à la consommation; **share ~, stock ~** indice
boursier; **5)** Phys indice m; **6)** (indication) indice m (**of** de);
7) Comput index m inv
B vtr **1)** munir [qch] d'un index [book]; indexer [word];
2) (catalogue) classer, cataloguer (**under** sous, à); **3)** Econ
indexer (**to** sur); **4)** Comput indexer

indexation /ˌɪndek'seɪʃn/ n indexation f (**to** sur)

index: **~ card** n fiche f; **~ finger** n index m inv;
~-linked adj indexé

India /'ɪndɪə/ ▸ p. 774 pr n Inde f

India ink n US encre f de Chine

Indian /'ɪndɪən/ ▸ p. 1032
A n **1)** (from India) Indien/-ienne m/f; **2)** (American) Indien/
-ienne m/f d'Amérique
B adj (of India) [people, culture] indien/-ienne; [ambassador,
embassy] de l'Inde; [Empire] des Indes; (American) indien/
-ienne, amérindien/-ienne

Indian: **~ corn** n US maïs m; **~ elephant** n éléphant
m d'Asie

Indian file n **in ~** en file indienne, à la queue leu leu

Indian ink n GB encre f de Chine

Indian Ocean ▸ p. 1049 pr n **the ~** l'océan m Indien

Indian: **~ summer** n été m de la Saint Martin;
~ wrestling n US bras m de fer

indicate /'ɪndɪkeɪt/
A vtr **1)** (show) indiquer (**that** que; **with** de); **2)** (recommend) **to
be ~d** être indiqué; **3)** (make known) faire savoir [intentions,
feelings] (**to** à)
B vi [driver] mettre son clignotant; [cyclist] faire signe

indication /ˌɪndɪ'keɪʃn/ n indication f, indice m; **to be an
~ of** indiquer; **it is an ~** that c'est signe que; **to give no
~ that** [person] ne pas laisser entrevoir que; **to give no
~ of who/how** [person] ne rien dire qui permette de savoir
qui/comment; [letter, speech] ne pas permettre de savoir
qui/comment; **to give sb an ~ of sth** donner une idée de
qch à qn; **all the ~s are that** tout porte à croire que

indicative /ɪn'dɪkətɪv/
A n Ling indicatif m; **in the ~** à l'indicatif
B adj **1) to be ~ of** montrer; **2)** Ling indicatif/-ive

indicator /'ɪndɪkeɪtə(r)/ n **1)** (pointer) aiguille f; **2)** Rail
tableau m; **3)** Aut clignotant m; **4)** Chem, Ling, Tech indicateur m

indices /'ɪndɪsiːz/ npl ▸ **index**

indict /ɪn'daɪt/ vtr Jur inculper

indictable /ɪn'daɪtəbl/ adj passible de poursuites;
~ offence délit m

indictment /ɪn'daɪtmənt/ n **1)** Jur acte m d'accusation;
under ~ for murder inculpé/-e de meurtre; **2)** (criticism)
mise f en accusation

indie○ /'ɪndɪ/ n, adj Cin, Mus indépendant (m)

indifference /ɪn'dɪfrəns/ n indifférence f (**to, towards**
envers); **it is a matter of ~ to him** cela lui est indifférent

indifferent /ɪn'dɪfrənt/ adj **1)** (uninterested) indifférent (**to,
as to** à); (to charms) insensible (**to** à); **2)** (mediocre)
médiocre

indifferently /ɪn'dɪfrəntlɪ/ adv **1)** (without caring) avec
indifférence; **2)** (equally) indifféremment; **3)** (not well)
médiocrement

indigenous /ɪn'dɪdʒɪnəs/ adj indigène (**to** à)

indigestible /ˌɪndɪ'dʒestəbl/ adj indigeste

indigestion /ˌɪndɪ'dʒestʃn/ n indigestion f

indignant /ɪn'dɪgnənt/ adj indigné (**at** de; **about, over**
par); **to become** ou **get ~** s'indigner (**at, about** de)

indignantly /ɪn'dɪgnəntlɪ/ adv [say] avec indignation;
[leave, look] d'un air indigné

indignation /ˌɪndɪg'neɪʃn/ n indignation f (**at** devant;
over au sujet de)

indignity /ɪn'dɪgnətɪ/ n indignité f

indigo /'ɪndɪgəʊ/ ▸ p. 752
A n indigo m
B adj indigo inv

indirect /ˌɪndɪ'rekt, -daɪ'r-/ adj indirect

indirectly /ˌɪndɪ'rektlɪ, -daɪ'r-/ adv indirectement

indirect speech n discours m indirect

indiscernible /ˌɪndɪ'sɜːnəbl/ adj imperceptible

indiscreet /ˌɪndɪ'skriːt/ adj indiscret/-ète

indiscretion /ˌɪndɪ'skreʃn/ n **1)** (lack of discretion) manque
m de discrétion; **2)** (act) indiscrétion f

indiscriminate /ˌɪndɪ'skrɪmɪnət/ adj (general) sans distinction; (not fussy) sans discernement; **to be ~ in** manquer
de discernement dans

indiscriminately /ˌɪndɪ'skrɪmɪnətlɪ/ adv (without distinction)
sans distinction; (uncritically) sans discernement

indispensable /ˌɪndɪ'spensəbl/ adj indispensable

indisposed /ˌɪndɪ'spəʊzd/ adj **1)** (ill) souffrant; **2)** (unwilling) peu disposé (**to do** à faire)

indisputable /ˌɪndɪ'spjuːtəbl/ adj [champion] indiscuté;
[fact] indiscutable; [logic] irrécusable

indisputably /ˌɪndɪ'spjuːtəblɪ/ adv indiscutablement

indissoluble /ˌɪndɪ'sɒljʊbl/ adj indissoluble

indistinct /ˌɪndɪ'stɪŋkt/ adj [sound, markings] indistinct;
[memory] confus; [photograph] flou

indistinctly /ˌɪndɪ'stɪŋktlɪ/ adv indistinctement

indistinguishable /ˌɪndɪ'stɪŋgwɪʃəbl/ adj **1)** (identical)
impossible à distinguer (**from** de); **2)** (indiscernible) indis-
cernable

individual /ˌɪndɪ'vɪdʒʊəl/
A n (person) individu m
B adj **1)** (for or from one person) [effort, freedom, portion]
individuel/-elle; [comfort, attitude] personnel/-elle; [tuition]
particulier/-ière; **2)** (separately) **each ~ article** chaque article (individuellement); **3)** (idiosyncratic) particulier/-ière

individualism /ˌɪndɪ'vɪdʒʊəlɪzəm/ n individualisme m

individualist /ˌɪndɪ'vɪdʒʊəlɪst/ n **1)** (idiosyncratic) individualiste mf; **2)** (supporter of individualism) partisan/-e m/f de
l'individualisme

individualistic /ˌɪndɪˌvɪdʒʊə'lɪstɪk/ adj individualiste

individuality /ˌɪndɪˌvɪdʒʊ'ælətɪ/ n individualité f

individually /ˌɪndɪ'vɪdʒʊəlɪ/ adv (personally, in person) individuellement; (one at a time) séparément

indivisible /ˌɪndɪ'vɪzəbl/ adj indivisible; **~ from** inséparable de

Indochina /ˌɪndəʊ'tʃaɪnə/ pr n Indochine f

indoctrinate /ɪn'dɒktrɪneɪt/ vtr endoctriner

indoctrination /ɪnˌdɒktrɪ'neɪʃn/ n endoctrinement m

Indo-European /ˌɪndəʊˌjʊərə'pɪən/ adj indo-européen/-
-éenne

indolence /'ɪndələns/ n indolence f

indolent /'ɪndələnt/ adj indolent

indomitable /ɪnˈdɒmɪtəbl/ adj invincible

Indonesia /ˌɪndəʊˈniːzjə/ ▸ p. 774 pr n Indonésie f

Indonesian /ˌɪndəʊˈniːzjən/
A n ▸ p. 1032, p. 969 **1** (person) Indonésien/-ienne m/f; **2** (language) indonésien m
B adj indonésien/-ienne

indoor /ˈɪndɔː(r)/ adj [pool, court] couvert; [lavatory] à l'intérieur; [photography, shoes] d'intérieur

indoors /ˌɪnˈdɔːz/ adv (in the main house) à l'intérieur; (at home) à la maison; ~ **and outdoors** dedans et dehors; **to go ~** rentrer

indubitable /ɪnˈdjuːbɪtəbl, US -ˈduː-/ adj indubitable

induce /ɪnˈdjuːs, US -ˈduːs/ vtr **1** (persuade) persuader (**to do** de faire); (stronger) inciter (**to à**; **to do** à faire); **2** (bring about) provoquer [emotion, response]; **drug-/stress-~d** provoqué par la drogue/le stress; **to ~ labour** Med provoquer l'accouchement

inducement /ɪnˈdjuːsmənt, US -ˈduː-/ n **1** (reward) récompense f; (bribe) pot-de-vin m; **financial ~** avantage m pécuniaire; **2** ₵ (incentive) motivation f (**to do** pour faire); **to be an ~ to sth** encourager qch

induction /ɪnˈdʌkʃn/ n **1** Elec induction f; **2** (of labour) déclenchement m; **3** (inauguration) installation f; **4** US Mil incorporation f

induction: ~ **ceremony** n cérémonie f de prise de fonctions; ~ **course** n GB stage m d'introduction

indulge /ɪnˈdʌldʒ/
A vtr **1** (satisfy) céder à [passion, whim, desire]; **she can ~ her love of music** elle peut donner libre cours à sa passion pour la musique; **2** (humour) gâter [child]; céder à [adult]
B vi gen se laisser tenter; euph (drink) boire de l'alcool; **to ~ in** se livrer à [speculation]; se complaire dans [nostalgia]; se laisser tenter par [food]
C v refl **to ~ oneself** se faire plaisir

indulgence /ɪnˈdʌldʒəns/ n **1** (tolerance) indulgence f (**towards** envers; **for** pour); **2** (act of indulging) ~ **in food** gourmandise f; ~ **in nostalgia** abandon m à la nostalgie; **it's my one ~** c'est mon péché mignon; **3** (enjoyment) plaisir m

indulgent /ɪnˈdʌldʒənt/ adj indulgent (**to, towards** pour, envers)

indulgently /ɪnˈdʌldʒəntlɪ/ adv avec indulgence

industrial /ɪnˈdʌstrɪəl/ adj [city, area, sector, park, machinery] industriel/-ielle; [accident] du travail; [tool] à usage industriel; [worker] de l'industrie

industrial: ~ **action** n GB (strike) grève f; ~ **arts** npl US Sch cours mpl de technologie; ~ **design** n esthétique f or conception f industrielle; ~ **designer** n concepteur/-trice m/f industriel/-ielle; ~ **disease** n maladie f professionnelle; ~ **dispute** n conflit m social; ~ **engineering** n génie m industriel; ~ **estate** n GB zone f industrielle

industrialist /ɪnˈdʌstrɪəlɪst/ n industriel m

industrialize /ɪnˈdʌstrɪəlaɪz/ vtr industrialiser

industrial: ~ **relations** npl relations fpl entre les patrons et les ouvriers; ~ **tribunal** n ≈ conseil m des prud'hommes; ~ **unrest** n agitation f ouvrière; ~ **vehicle** n véhicule m utilitaire; ~ **waste** n déchets mpl industriels

industrious /ɪnˈdʌstrɪəs/ adj diligent

industriously /ɪnˈdʌstrɪəslɪ/ adv avec diligence

industriousness /ɪnˈdʌstrɪəsnɪs/ n zèle m au travail

industry /ˈɪndəstrɪ/ n **1** industrie f; **the oil ~** l'industrie du pétrole; **the Shakespeare ~** fig péj le filon Shakespeare; **2** (diligence) sout zèle m (au travail)

inebriate /ɪˈniːbrɪeɪt/ vtr enivrer

inedible /ɪnˈedɪbl/ adj [meal] immangeable; [plants] non comestible

ineffective /ˌɪnɪˈfektɪv/ adj inefficace

ineffectively /ˌɪnɪˈfektɪvlɪ/ adv sans succès

ineffectiveness /ˌɪnɪˈfektɪvnɪs/ n inefficacité f

ineffectual /ˌɪnɪˈfektʃʊəl/ adj [person] incapable; [policy] inefficace; [attempt] infructueux/-euse; [gesture] sans effet

ineffectually /ˌɪnɪˈfektʃʊəlɪ/ adv en vain

inefficiency /ˌɪnɪˈfɪʃnsɪ/ n (lack of organization) manque m d'organisation; (incompetence) incompétence f; (of machine, method) inefficacité f

inefficient /ˌɪnɪˈfɪʃnt/ adj (disorganized) mal organisé; (incompetent) incompétent; (not effective) inefficace

inefficiently /ˌɪnɪˈfɪʃntlɪ/ adv d'une manière inefficace

ineligible /ɪnˈelɪdʒəbl/ adj **to be ~** (for job) ne pas remplir les conditions pour poser sa candidature (**for** à); (for election) être inéligible; (for pension, benefit) ne pas avoir droit (**for** à); **to be ~ to vote** ne pas avoir le droit de vote

inept /ɪˈnept/ adj **1** (incompetent) incompétent; **2** (tactless) maladroit

ineptitude /ɪˈneptɪtjuːd, US -tuːd/, **ineptness** /ɪˈneptnɪs/ n **1** (inefficiency) incompétence f; **2** (tactlessness) maladresse f

ineptly /ɪˈneptlɪ/ adv **1** (inefficiently) de façon incompétente; **2** (tactlessly) maladroitement

inequality /ˌɪnɪˈkwɒlətɪ/ n inégalité f

ineradicable /ˌɪnɪˈrædɪkəbl/ adj indéracinable

inert /ɪˈnɜːt/ adj gen, Chem inerte; [gas] rare

inertia /ɪˈnɜːʃə/ n inertie f

inescapable /ˌɪnɪˈskeɪpəbl/ adj indéniable

inevitable /ɪnˈevɪtəbl/
A n **the ~** l'inévitable m
B adj inévitable (**that** que + subj)

inevitably /ɪnˈevɪtəblɪ/ adv inévitablement

inexact /ˌɪnɪgˈzækt/ adj inexact

inexactly /ˌɪnɪgˈzæktlɪ/ adv inexactement

inexcusable /ˌɪnɪkˈskjuːzəbl/ adj inexcusable (**that** que + subj)

inexcusably /ˌɪnɪkˈskjuːzəblɪ/ adv de façon inexcusable

inexhaustible /ˌɪnɪgˈzɔːstəbl/ adj inépuisable

inexorable /ɪnˈeksərəbl/ adj inexorable

inexorably /ɪnˈeksərəblɪ/ adv inexorablement

inexpensive /ˌɪnɪkˈspensɪv/ adj pas cher/chère

inexpensively /ˌɪnɪkˈspensɪvlɪ/ adv à peu de frais

inexperience /ˌɪnɪkˈspɪərɪəns/ n inexpérience f

inexperienced /ˌɪnɪkˈspɪərɪənst/ adj inexpérimenté

inexpert /ɪnˈekspɜːt/ adj [sailor] amateur inv; [repair] maladroit; [eye] de néophyte

inexpertly /ɪnˈekspɜːtlɪ/ adv de façon maladroite

inexplicable /ˌɪnɪkˈsplɪkəbl/ adj inexplicable

inexplicably /ˌɪnɪkˈsplɪkəblɪ/ adv inexplicablement

inexpressible /ˌɪnɪkˈspresəbl/ adj inexprimable

inexpressibly /ˌɪnɪkˈspresəblɪ/ adv au-delà de toute expression

inexpressive /ˌɪnɪkˈspresɪv/ adj inexpressif/-ive

inextricable /ɪnˈekstrɪkəbl, ˌɪnɪkˈstrɪk-/ adj inextricable

inextricably /ɪnˈekstrɪkəblɪ, ˌɪnɪkˈstrɪk-/ adv inextricablement

infallibility /ɪnˌfæləˈbɪlətɪ/ n infaillibilité f

infallible /ɪnˈfæləbl/ adj infaillible

infallibly /ɪnˈfæləblɪ/ adv infailliblement

infamous /ˈɪnfəməs/ adj (notorious) [person] tristement célèbre; (evil) [conduct, crime] infâme

infancy /ˈɪnfənsɪ/ n **1** (childhood) petite enfance f; **in early ~** dans la toute petite enfance; **in (one's) ~** en bas âge; **2** fig débuts mpl; **in its ~** à ses débuts

infant /ˈɪnfənt/ n **1** (baby) bébé m; (child) petit enfant m; **2** GB Sch enfant mf (entre 4 et 7 ans); **the ~s** les petites classes fpl

infanticide /ɪnˈfæntɪsaɪd/ n infanticide m

infantile /ˈɪnfəntaɪl/ adj **1** péj infantile, puéril; **2** Med infantile

infantry /ˈɪnfəntrɪ/ n infanterie f, fantassins mpl

infantryman /ˈɪnfəntrɪmən/ n (pl **-men**) fantassin m

infant school n ≈ école f maternelle

infatuate /ɪnˈfætʃʊeɪt/ vtr ~**d with** entiché de; **to become ~d with** s'éprendre de [person]; s'engouer de or pour [idea, object]

infatuation /ɪnˌfætʃʊˈeɪʃn/ n engouement m (**with** pour); **a passing ~** une amourette

infect /ɪnˈfekt/ vtr **1** gen, Med contaminer [person, blood, food]; infecter [wound]; **to ~ sb/sth with sth** transmettre qch à qn/qch; **to become ~ed** [wound] s'infecter; [person, blood] être contaminé; **2** fig (influence negatively) corrompre [person, society]

infection /ɪnˈfekʃn/ n **1** (of wound, organ) infection f; (of person, blood) contamination f; **to be exposed to** ~ [person] être exposé à la contagion; **2** (disease) infection f; fig contamination f

infectious /ɪnˈfekʃəs/ adj [disease] infectieux/-ieuse; [person] contagieux/-ieuse; [laughter] communicatif/-ive

infelicity /ˌɪnfɪˈlɪsətɪ/ n sout maladresse f

infer /ɪnˈfɜː(r)/ vtr (p prés etc **-rr-**) **1** (deduce) inférer fml, déduire; **2** usage critiqué (imply) suggérer

inference /ˈɪnfərəns/ n **1** (act, process) déduction f, inférence f; **by** ~ par déduction, par voie de conséquence; **2** (conclusion) conclusion f, déduction f; **the** ~ **is that** on en conclut or déduit que; **to draw an** ~ **from** tirer une conclusion de; **3** usage critiqué (implication) suggestion f

inferior /ɪnˈfɪərɪə(r)/
A n inférieur/-e m/f; Mil subalterne mf
B adj **1** (poor quality) de qualité inférieure; **2** [position] inférieur; **to make sb feel** ~ donner un sentiment d'infériorité à qn; **3** [letter, number] en indice

inferiority /ɪnˌfɪərɪˈɒrətɪ, US -ˈɔːr-/ n infériorité f (**to** vis-à-vis de); ~ **complex** complexe m d'infériorité

infernal /ɪnˈfɜːnl/ adj **1** ○(damned) [phone] maudit○ (before n); (appalling) [noise] infernal○; **2** (of hell) infernal

infernally /ɪnˈfɜːnəlɪ/ adv abominablement

inferno /ɪnˈfɜːnəʊ/ n **1** (conflagration) brasier m; **2** (hell) enfer m also fig

infertile /ɪnˈfɜːtaɪl, US -tl/ adj [land] infertile, stérile; [person] stérile

infertility /ˌɪnfəˈtɪlətɪ/ n (of land) stérilité f, infertilité f; (of person) stérilité f

infest /ɪnˈfest/ vtr infester (**with** de)

infestation /ˌɪnfesˈteɪʃn/ n infestation f

infidelity /ˌɪnfɪˈdelətɪ/ n infidélité f

infighting /ˈɪnfaɪtɪŋ/ n conflits mpl internes

infiltrate /ˈɪnfɪltreɪt/ vtr infiltrer [organization, group]

infiltration /ˌɪnfɪlˈtreɪʃn/ n infiltration f

infinite /ˈɪnfɪnət/
A n **the** ~ l'infini m
B adj **1** (boundless) [patience, variety] infini; [wealth] illimité; **2** Math infini

infinitely /ˈɪnfɪnətlɪ/ adv infiniment

infinitive /ɪnˈfɪnətɪv/ n Ling infinitif m; **in the** ~ à l'infinitif

infinity /ɪnˈfɪnətɪ/ n gen, Math, Phot infini m; **to** ~ à l'infini; fig **an** ~ **of...** une infinité de...

infirm /ɪnˈfɜːm/ adj (weak) infirme, invalide

infirmary /ɪnˈfɜːmərɪ/ n gen hôpital m; (in school, prison) infirmerie f

infirmity /ɪnˈfɜːmətɪ/ n infirmité f

in flagrante delicto /ɪn flæɡrænteɪ ˌdeɪˈlɪktəʊ/ adv phr en flagrant délit

inflame /ɪnˈfleɪm/ vtr enflammer [imagination, crowd]; exacerber [passion]; aggraver [situation]; Med enflammer

inflammable /ɪnˈflæməbl/ adj inflammable

inflammation /ˌɪnfləˈmeɪʃn/ n inflammation f

inflammatory /ɪnˈflæmətrɪ, US -tɔːrɪ/ adj **1** [speech, remarks] incendiaire; **2** Med inflammatoire

inflatable /ɪnˈfleɪtəbl/
A n gen objet m gonflable; (dinghy) canot m pneumatique; (toy) jouet m gonflable
B adj [mattress, dinghy] pneumatique; [toy] gonflable

inflate /ɪnˈfleɪt/
A vtr lit, fig gonfler
B vi [tyre, toy] se gonfler

inflated /ɪnˈfleɪtɪd/ adj **1** (excessive) [price] gonflé; [fee, salary] excessif/-ive; [claim] exagéré; [style] boursouflé; **an** ~ **ego** une très haute opinion de soi-même; **2** [tyre] gonflé

inflation /ɪnˈfleɪʃn/ n **1** Econ inflation f; **2** (of dinghy, tyre) gonflement m, gonflage m

inflationary /ɪnˈfleɪʃnrɪ, US -nerɪ/ adj Econ inflationniste

inflect /ɪnˈflekt/
A vtr **1** Ling conjuguer [verb]; décliner [noun, adjective]; **2** (modulate) moduler [voice]
B vi [verb] se conjuguer; [noun, adjective] se décliner

inflected /ɪnˈflektɪd/ adj [language] flexionnel/-elle; [form] fléchi

inflection /ɪnˈflekʃn/ n **1** Ling (of radical) flexion f; (of vowel) inflexion f; **2** (modulation) (of voice) inflexion f

inflexibility /ɪnˌfleksəˈbɪlətɪ/ n **1** (of attitude, will, rule) inflexibilité f; (of system, method) rigidité f; **2** (of material, structure) rigidité f

inflexible /ɪnˈfleksəbl/ adj **1** fig [person, attitude, will] inflexible; [system] rigide; **2** [material] rigide

inflexion n GB = **inflection**

inflict /ɪnˈflɪkt/ vtr infliger [pain, presence, defeat] (**on** à); causer [damage] (**on** à); **to** ~ **a wound on sb** blesser qn

in-flight /ˌɪnˈflaɪt/ adj en vol

inflow /ˈɪnfləʊ/ n (of cash, goods, people) afflux m; (into tank) arrivée f; ~ **pipe** tuyau m d'arrivée

influence /ˈɪnfluəns/
A n **1** (force, factor affecting sth) influence f (**on** sur); **to be** ou **have an** ~ avoir une influence; **to be under sb's** ~ subir l'influence de qn; **under the** ~ **of** sous l'influence de; **to be under the** ~ euph, hum être éméché○; **to drive while under the** ~ **of alcohol** Jur conduire en état d'ébriété; **2** (power to affect sth) influence f (**with sb** auprès de qn; **over** sur)
B vtr influencer [person] (**in** dans); influer sur [decision, choice, result]; **don't let him** ~ **you!** ne le laisse pas t'influencer!; **to be** ~**d by sb/sth** se laisser influencer par qn/qch

influential /ˌɪnfluˈenʃl/ adj **1** (respected) [theory, artist] très suivi; [newspaper, commentator] très écouté; [work] très remarqué; **2** (key) déterminant; **3** (powerful) [person] influent, qui compte; ~ **friends** des amis importants or en place

influenza /ˌɪnfluˈenzə/ ▸ p. 933 n grippe f

influx /ˈɪnflʌks/ n **1** (of people, money) afflux m; **2** (of liquid) arrivée f

info○ /ˈɪnfəʊ/ n renseignements mpl, tuyaux○ mpl

infomercial /ˌɪnfəʊˈmɜːʃl/ n TV documentaire m publicitaire

inform /ɪnˈfɔːm/
A vtr **1** (notify, tell) informer, avertir (**of, about** de; **that** du fait que); **to keep sb** ~**ed** tenir qn informé or au courant (**of, as to** de); **I** ~**ed him of my views** je lui ai fait part de mes vues; **I am pleased to** ~ **you that** j'ai le plaisir de vous informer que; **2** (pervade) guider [work, law]
B vi **1** (denounce) **to** ~ **on** ou **against** dénoncer; **2** (give information) informer

informal /ɪnˈfɔːml/ adj **1** (unaffected) [person] sans façons; [manner, style] simple; **2** (casual) [language] familier/-ière; ~ **clothes** vêtements mpl de tous les jours; **'dress** ~**'** (on invitation) 'tenue f de ville'; **3** (relaxed) [mood] décontracté; [group] informel/-elle; **4** (unofficial) [announcement] officieux/-ieuse; [visit] privé; [invitation] verbal; [discussion, interview] informel/-elle; **on an** ~ **basis** de façon informelle

informality /ˌɪnfɔːˈmælətɪ/ n (of person, event) simplicité f; (of arrangement, meeting) caractère m informel; (of workplace) ambiance f décontractée; (of language) style m familier

informally /ɪnˈfɔːmlɪ/ adv **1** (without ceremony) [dress] en tenue décontractée; [speak, meet] en toute simplicité; **2** (unofficially) [act, discuss] officieusement

informant /ɪnˈfɔːmənt/ n (source of information) informateur/-trice m/f; (informer) indicateur/-trice m/f

information /ˌɪnfəˈmeɪʃn/ n **1** ¢ (facts, details) renseignements mpl, informations fpl (**on, about** sur); **a piece** ou **item of** ~ un renseignement, une information; **my** ~ **is that** selon mes renseignements or informations; **'for** ~**'** 'pour information', 'à titre de renseignement'; **for your** ~**, I've never even met him!** au cas où tu ne le saurais pas, je ne l'ai jamais rencontré!; **2** US Telecom (service m des) renseignements mpl; **3** Comput informations fpl

information desk, **information office** n bureau m des renseignements

information officer n (PR person, press officer) préposé/-e m/f à l'information

information: ~ **pack** n documentation f; ~ **processing** n traitement m de l'information; ~ **retrieval** n recherche f documentaire; ~ **scientist** n informaticien/-ienne m/f; ~ **service** n service m de renseignements; ~ **system** n système m informatique; ~ **technology**, **IT** n informatique f

informative /ɪnˈfɔːmətɪv/ adj [lecture, book] riche en renseignements; [trip, day] instructif/-ive; [guide] savant

informed /ɪnˈfɔːmd/ adj [decision, opinion] fondé; [person] averti; [source] informé; **well-/ill-~** bien/mal informé or renseigné

informer /ɪnˈfɔːmə(r)/ n indicateur/-trice m/f; **to turn ~** dénoncer or vendre ses complices

infotainment /ˌɪnfəʊˈteɪnmənt/ n information-spectacle f

infrared /ˌɪnfrəˈred/ adj infrarouge

infrastructure /ˈɪnfrəstrʌktʃə(r)/ n infrastructure f

infrequent /ɪnˈfriːkwənt/ adj rare

infrequently /ɪnˈfriːkwəntlɪ/ adv rarement

infringe /ɪnˈfrɪndʒ/
A vtr enfreindre [rule]; ne pas respecter [rights]; commettre une contrefaçon de [patent]
B vi **to ~ on** ou **upon** empiéter sur [rights]

infringement /ɪnˈfrɪndʒmənt/ n (of rule) infraction f (**of** à); (of rights) violation f; (of patent) contrefaçon f

infuriate /ɪnˈfjʊərɪeɪt/ vtr exaspérer, faire rager

infuriating /ɪnˈfjʊərɪeɪtɪŋ/ adj exaspérant

infuriatingly /ɪnˈfjʊərɪeɪtɪŋlɪ/ adv [laugh, reply] de façon exaspérante; **~ slow** d'une lenteur exaspérante

infuse /ɪnˈfjuːz/
A vtr **1** (imbue) **to ~ sth with sth** insuffler qch à qch; **2** Culin faire infuser
B vi infuser

infusion /ɪnˈfjuːʒn/ n (of cash, aid) injection f; Culin infusion f

ingenious /ɪnˈdʒiːnɪəs/ adj ingénieux/-ieuse, astucieux/-ieuse

ingeniously /ɪnˈdʒiːnɪəslɪ/ adv ingénieusement, astucieusement

ingenuity /ˌɪndʒɪˈnjuːɪtɪ, US -ˈnuː-/ n ingéniosité f

ingenuous /ɪnˈdʒenjʊəs/ adj ingénu, candide

ingenuously /ɪnˈdʒenjʊəslɪ/ adv ingénument, candidement

ingest /ɪnˈdʒest/ vtr ingérer [food]; assimiler [fact]

inglorious /ɪnˈglɔːrɪəs/ adj déshonorant, infamant

ingot /ˈɪŋgət/ n lingot m

ingrained /ɪnˈgreɪnd/ adj [dirt] bien incrusté; [habit, hatred] enraciné; **~ in** ancré dans [society]

ingratiate /ɪnˈgreɪʃɪeɪt/ v refl **to ~ oneself** se faire bien voir (**with** de)

ingratiating /ɪnˈgreɪʃɪeɪtɪŋ/ adj péj doucereux/-euse

ingratitude /ɪnˈgrætɪtjuːd, US -tuːd/ n ingratitude f

ingredient /ɪnˈgriːdɪənt/ n Culin ingrédient m; fig élément m (**of** de)

ingrowing toenail /ˌɪnˌgrəʊɪŋ ˈtəʊˌneɪl/, **ingrown toenail** /ˈɪnˌgrəʊn ˈtəʊˌneɪl/ n ongle m de pied incarné

inhabit /ɪnˈhæbɪt/ vtr **1** lit habiter [house, region, planet]; **2** fig vivre dans [fantasy world, milieu]

inhabitable /ɪnˈhæbɪtəbl/ adj habitable

inhabitant /ɪnˈhæbɪtənt/ n habitant/-e m/f

inhalation /ˌɪnhəˈleɪʃn/ n inhalation f, aspiration f

inhale /ɪnˈheɪl/
A vtr aspirer, inhaler [vapour, fumes]; avaler [smoke, vomit]; humer, respirer [scent]
B vi (breathe in) inspirer; (smoke) avaler la fumée

inhaler /ɪnˈheɪlə(r)/ n inhalateur m

inherent /ɪnˈhɪərənt, ɪnˈherənt/ adj **~ in** inhérent or propre à

inherently /ɪnˈhɪərəntlɪ, ɪnˈher-/ adv [evil] naturellement; [difficult] en soi; [involve] par sa nature

inherit /ɪnˈherɪt/ vtr hériter de [money, property]; hériter de, succéder à [title]; fig hériter de [problem, tradition]; **to ~ sth from sb** hériter qch de qn

inheritance /ɪnˈherɪtəns/ n **1** (thing inherited) héritage m also fig; **to come into an ~** faire un héritage; **2** (succession) succession f; **by** ou **through ~** par voie de succession; **3** Biol patrimoine m héréditaire

inherited /ɪnˈherɪtɪd/ adj Biol héréditaire; [wealth] hérité

inheritor /ɪnˈherɪtə(r)/ n (all contexts) héritier/-ière m/f

inhibit /ɪnˈhɪbɪt/ vtr **1** (restrain) inhiber [person, reaction]; entraver [activity, progress]; **to ~ sb from doing** (prevent) empêcher qn de faire; (discourage) dissuader qn de faire; **2** Jur (prohibit) interdire

inhibited /ɪnˈhɪbɪtɪd/ adj [person] inhibé, refoulé; [development] entravé; **~ by** [person] handicapé par

inhibiting /ɪnˈhɪbɪtɪŋ/ adj inhibiteur/-trice

inhibition /ˌɪnhɪˈbɪʃn, ˌɪnɪˈb-/ n inhibition f; **to get rid of one's ~s** se libérer de ses inhibitions

inhospitable /ˌɪnhɒˈspɪtəbl/ adj inhospitalier/-ière

in-house /ˈɪnhaʊs, -ˈhaʊs/ adj interne

inhuman /ɪnˈhjuːmən/ adj inhumain

inhumanity /ˌɪnhjuːˈmænətɪ/ n inhumanité f (**to** envers)

inhumation /ˌɪnhjuːˈmeɪʃn/ n sout inhumation f

inimical /ɪˈnɪmɪkl/ adj inamical, hostile; **to be ~ to** aller à l'encontre de [aim]; être nuisible à [unity]

inimitable /ɪˈnɪmɪtəbl/ adj inimitable

iniquitous /ɪˈnɪkwɪtəs/ adj inique, injuste

iniquity /ɪˈnɪkwətɪ/ n iniquité f

initial /ɪˈnɪʃl/
A n initiale f
B adj [shock, reaction] initial, premier/-ière; [shyness] initial; **~ letter** initiale f; **in the ~ stages** au début
C vtr (p prés etc GB **-ll-**, US **-l-**) parapher or parafer

initialize /ɪˈnɪʃəlaɪz/ vtr Comput initialiser

initially /ɪˈnɪʃəlɪ/ adv au départ

initiate
A /ɪˈnɪʃɪət/ n initié/-e m/f
B /ɪˈnɪʃɪeɪt/ vtr **1** (start up) mettre en œuvre [project, reform]; amorcer [talks]; Jur entamer, engager [proceedings]; **2** (admit) **to ~ sb into** admettre qn au sein de [secret society]; initier qn à [astrology]; **3** Comput lancer [programme]; établir [communication]

initiation /ɪˌnɪʃɪˈeɪʃn/ n **1** (of negotiations) amorce f; (of scheme, process) lancement m; **2** (into sect) admission f (**into** au sein de); (into knowledge) initiation f (**into** à); **3** (ceremony) cérémonie f d'initiation

initiative /ɪˈnɪʃətɪv/ n **1** (quality) initiative f; **to have** ou **show ~** faire preuve d'initiative; **on one's own ~** de son propre chef; **2** (lead) initiative f; **to take/lose the ~** prendre/perdre l'initiative

initiator /ɪˈnɪʃɪeɪtə(r)/ n instigateur/-trice m/f

inject /ɪnˈdʒekt/
A vtr injecter [vaccine, fuel] (**into** dans); fig apporter [new ideas] (**into** à); insuffler [enthusiasm] (**into** à); injecter [cash] (**into** dans); **to ~ sb with sth** faire une injection or une piqûre de qch à qn
B v refl **to ~ oneself** se faire des piqûres (**with** de)

injection /ɪnˈdʒekʃn/ n Med piqûre f; Tech injection f

in-joke /ˈɪndʒəʊk/ n **it's an ~** c'est une plaisanterie entre nous

injudicious /ˌɪndʒuːˈdɪʃəs/ adj peu judicieux/-ieuse

injunction /ɪnˈdʒʌŋkʃn/ n injonction f

injure /ˈɪndʒə(r)/
A vtr **1** Med blesser [person]; **to ~ one's hand** se blesser la main; **2** (damage) nuire à, compromettre [health, reputation]; blesser [self-esteem]; **to ~ sb's feelings** faire de la peine à qn
B v refl **to ~ oneself** se blesser

injured /ˈɪndʒəd/
A n **the ~** (+ v pl) les blessés mpl
B adj **1** Med [person, limb, back] blessé; **2** fig [pride] blessé; [tone] offensé, blessé; **3** (wronged) [wife, husband] trompé; **the ~ party** Jur la partie lésée

injurious /ɪnˈdʒʊərɪəs/ adj sout **1** (harmful) **~ to** nuisible or préjudiciable à; **2** (abusive) [remark] blessant, offensant

injury /ˈɪndʒərɪ/ n **1** Med blessure f; **head injuries** blessures à la tête; **to do sb an ~** blesser qn; **to do oneself an ~** hum se faire mal; **2** (to reputation) atteinte f (**to** à); **3** Jur préjudice m, dommage m

injury time n Sport arrêts mpl de jeu

injustice /ɪnˈdʒʌstɪs/ n injustice f; **to do sb an ~** être or se montrer injuste envers qn

ink /ɪŋk/
A n encre f; **in ~** à l'encre
B vtr encrer

(Phrasal verb)

■ **ink in:** ▸ **~ in** [sth], **~** [sth] **in** repasser [qch] à l'encre

ink: ~**blot** n tache f d'encre, pâté m; ~**blot test** n test m de Rorschach; ~**jet printer** n imprimante f à jet d'encre

inkling /'ɪŋklɪŋ/ n petite idée f; **to have an** ~ **that** avoir l'idée que; **to have no** ~ **that** ne pas avoir la moindre idée que; **that was the first** ~ **I had that…** c'est alors que j'ai commencé à me douter que…

inky /'ɪŋkɪ/ adj lit taché d'encre; fig [sky] noir comme de l'encre

inlaid /ˌɪn'leɪd/
A prét, pp ▸ **inlay**
B adj [jewellery] incrusté (**with** de); [box, furniture] marqueté; [sword] damasquiné

inland
A /'ɪnlənd/ adj **1** (not coastal) intérieur; ~ **waterways** canaux mpl et rivières fpl; **2** GB (domestic) [mail, trade] intérieur
B /ˌɪn'lænd/ adv [travel, lie] à l'intérieur des terres

Inland Revenue n GB service m des impôts britannique

in-laws /'ɪnlɔːz/ npl (parents) beaux-parents mpl; (other relatives) belle-famille f, parents mpl par alliance

inlay
A /'ɪnleɪ/ n (on brooch) incrustation f; (on wood) marqueterie f
B /ˌɪn'leɪ/ vtr incruster [brooch] (**with** de); marqueter [wood]

inlet /'ɪnlet/ n **1** (of sea) bras m de mer, crique f; (of river) bras m de rivière; **2** (for fuel, air) arrivée f

in-line skate n patin m en ligne

inmate /'ɪnmeɪt/ n (of hospital) malade mf; (of mental hospital) interné/-e m/f; (of prison) détenu/-e m/f

inn /ɪn/ n **1** (hotel) (small) auberge f; (larger) hôtellerie f; **2** (pub) pub m

innards /'ɪnədz/ npl lit, fig entrailles fpl

innate /ɪ'neɪt/ adj inné, naturel/-elle

inner /'ɪnə(r)/ adj (épith) intérieur; **the** ~ **circle** le petit groupe

inner city
A n **the** ~ les quartiers mpl déshérités
B **inner-city** noun modifier [problems] des quartiers déshérités; [area] déshérité

inner ear n oreille f interne

innermost /'ɪnəməʊst/ adj (épith) **sb's** ~ **thoughts** les pensées les plus intimes de qn; **his** ~ **self** ou **being** le tréfonds de son âme

inner: ~ **sanctum** n hum antre m, saint m des saints; ~ **tube** n chambre f à air

inning /'ɪnɪŋ/ n US (in baseball) tour m de batte

innings /'ɪnɪŋz/ n GB **1** (in cricket) (+ v sg) tour m de batte; **2** fig **to have had a good** ~ (when dead) avoir bien profité de l'existence; (when leaving) avoir fait son temps

innkeeper /'ɪnkiːpə(r)/ n aubergiste mf

innocence /'ɪnəsns/ n innocence f

innocent /'ɪnəsnt/
A n innocent/-e m/f
B adj **1** (not guilty) innocent (**of** de); **2** (innocuous) [fun] innocent, inoffensif/-ive; [remark] innocent, sans malice; [error] bénin/-igne; [explanation] anodin; **3** (unaware) innocent; ~ **of** inconscient de [effect]

innocently /'ɪnəsntlɪ/ adv [ask, reply, say] innocemment; [act, become involved] en toute innocence

innocuous /ɪ'nɒkjʊəs/ adj inoffensif/-ive

innovate /'ɪnəveɪt/ vi innover

innovation /ˌɪnə'veɪʃn/ n innovation f

innovative /'ɪnəvətɪv/ adj innovateur/-trice

innovator /'ɪnəveɪtə(r)/ n innovateur/-trice m/f

innuendo /ˌɪnju:'endəʊ/ n (pl ~**s** ou ~**es**) (veiled slights) insinuations fpl; (sexual references) allusions fpl grivoises

innumerable /ɪ'nju:mərəbl, US 'nu:-/ adj innombrable, sans nombre

inoculate /ɪ'nɒkjʊleɪt/ vtr vacciner (**against** contre); **to** ~ **sb with sth** inoculer qch à qn

inoculation /ɪˌnɒkjʊ'leɪʃn/ n vaccination f, inoculation f

inoffensive /ˌɪnə'fensɪv/ adj inoffensif/-ive

inoperative /ɪn'ɒpərətɪv/ adj inopérant

inopportune /ɪn'ɒpətjuːn, US -tu:n/ adj inopportun

inopportunely /ɪn'ɒpətjuːnlɪ, US -tu:n-/ adv inopportunément

inordinate /ɪn'ɔːdɪnət/ adj [appetite, size, cost] démesuré; [desire] immodéré; [amount] excessif/-ive

inordinately /ɪn'ɔːdɪnətlɪ/ adv extrêmement

in-patient /'ɪnpeɪʃnt/ n malade mf hospitalisé/-e

input /'ɪnpʊt/
A n **1** (of money) apport m; (of energy) alimentation f (**of** en); **2** (contribution) contribution f; **her** ~ **was minimal** elle a fourni un minimum d'effort; **3** Comput (action) saisie f des données; (data) données fpl d'entrée or à traiter
B vtr (p prés -**tt**-; prét, pp -**put** ou -**putted**) Comput saisir [data]; **to** ~ **data into a computer** entrer des données dans un ordinateur

input: ~ **data** n Comput données fpl d'entrée or à traiter; ~-**output** n entrée-sortie f

inquest /'ɪŋkwest/ n gen, Jur enquête f (**on, into** sur); **to hold an** ~ mener or conduire une enquête

inquire /ɪn'kwaɪə(r)/
A vtr demander
B vi se renseigner (**about** sur); **to** ~ **after sb** demander des nouvelles de qn; **to** ~ **into** (ask for information about) se renseigner sur; (research) faire des recherches sur; Admin, Jur enquêter sur; '~ **within**' 's'adresser ici'

inquiring /ɪn'kwaɪərɪŋ/ adj [look, voice] interrogateur/-trice; [mind] curieux/-ieuse

inquiringly /ɪn'kwaɪərɪŋlɪ/ adv d'un air interrogateur

inquiry /ɪn'kwaɪərɪ, US 'ɪŋkwərɪ/
A n **1** (request for information) demande f de renseignements; **to make an** ~ **about** ou **into** se renseigner sur; **to make inquiries** demander des renseignements (**about** sur); **'all inquiries to…'** 'pour tous renseignements, s'adresser à…'; **with reference to your** ~ (by letter) en réponse à votre courrier; (by phone) suite à votre appel téléphonique; **2** Admin, Jur enquête f, investigation f (**into** sur); **murder** ~ enquête criminelle; **to conduct an** ~ mener une enquête (**into** sur); **to set up** ou **launch an** ~ ouvrir une enquête; **line of** ~ piste f
B **inquiries** npl bureau m or service m de renseignements

inquisition /ˌɪnkwɪ'zɪʃn/
A n enquête f
B **Inquisition** pr n Hist Inquisition f

inquisitive /ɪn'kwɪzətɪv/ adj curieux/-ieuse

inquisitively /ɪn'kwɪzətɪvlɪ/ adv avec curiosité

inquorate /ɪn'kwɔːreɪt/ adj **the meeting is** ~ le quorum n'a pas été atteint pour cette réunion

inroad /'ɪnrəʊd/ n **to make** ~**s into** ou **on** faire une avancée sur [market]; entamer [savings]; réduire [lead]

inrush /'ɪnrʌʃ/ n irruption f

insalubrious /ˌɪnsə'lu:brɪəs/ adj (dirty) insalubre; (sleazy) sordide

insane /ɪn'seɪn/ adj gen [person] fou/folle; Jur aliéné; [idea, desire] fou/folle, insensé; **to go** ~ perdre la raison; **to drive sb** ~ rendre qn fou

insanely /ɪn'seɪnlɪ/ adv [act] de façon insensée; ~ **jealous** fou/folle de jalousie

insanitary /ɪn'sænɪtərɪ, US -terɪ/ adj insalubre, malsain

insanity /ɪn'sænətɪ/ n gen folie f; Jur aliénation f mentale

insatiable /ɪn'seɪʃəbl/ adj insatiable

insatiably /ɪn'seɪʃəblɪ/ adv ~ **curious** d'une curiosité insatiable

inscribe /ɪn'skraɪb/ vtr **1** (write) inscrire (**in** dans); (engrave) graver (**on** sur); ~**d with his name** gravé à son nom; **the book was** ~**d 'To Bruno'** le livre portait l'inscription 'À Bruno'; **2** (sign) dédicacer; ~**d copy** exemplaire avec envoi

inscription /ɪn'skrɪpʃn/ n gen inscription f; (in book) envoi m

inscrutable /ɪn'skru:təbl/ adj énigmatique

insect /'ɪnsekt/ n insecte m; ~ **bite** piqûre f d'insecte

insecticide /ɪn'sektɪsaɪd/ n, adj insecticide (m)

insect: ~ **repellent** n insectifuge m, produit m anti-insecte; ~ **spray** n bombe f insecticide

insecure /ˌɪnsɪ'kjʊə(r)/ adj **1** (lacking confidence) qui manque d'assurance; **to be** ~ manquer d'assurance; **2** Psych insécurisé; **3** (not reliable) [job] précaire; [investment] risqué; **4** (unsafe, loose) [screw] qui tient mal; [lock] peu sûr; [rope] mal attaché; [door] qui ferme mal; [foothold] mal assuré; **5** (inadequately protected) peu sûr

i

insecurity /ˌɪnsɪˈkjʊərəti/ n ① (psychological) manque m d'assurance; **his feelings of** ~ son sentiment d'insécurité; ② (of position, situation) insécurité f; (of income) précarité f

insemination /ɪnˌsemɪˈneɪʃn/ n insémination f

insensibility /ɪnˌsensəˈbɪləti/ n ① (indifference) insensibilité f (**to** à); ② (to stimuli) insensibilité f; ③ (unconsciousness) inconscience f

insensible /ɪnˈsensəbl/ adj ① (to plea, stimuli, criticism) insensible (**to** à); ② (unconscious) sans connaissance; ③ (unaware) inconscient (**of, to** de)

insensitive /ɪnˈsensətɪv/ adj [person] (tactless) sans tact; (unfeeling) insensible (**to** à); [remark] indélicat; [attitude, policy] peu compréhensif/-ive

insensitivity /ɪnˌsensəˈtɪvəti/ n insensibilité f (**to** à)

inseparable /ɪnˈseprəbl/ adj inséparable (**from** de)

insert
A /ˈɪnsɜːt/ n = insertion 2
B /ɪnˈsɜːt/ vtr insérer [word, clause] (**in** dans); introduire, insérer [knife, finger] (**in** dans); insérer [advertisement, page] (**in** dans)

insertion /ɪnˈsɜːʃn/ n ① (action) insertion f, introduction f; ② Journ (enclosed page, leaflet) encart m; (advertisement, amendment) insertion f

in-service training n formation f continue

inset /ˈɪnset/
A n ① (map) insert m; (photo) photographie f en médaillon; ② (in sewing) entre-deux m inv
B vtr (p prés -tt-; prét, pp inset) insérer

inshore /ˌɪnˈʃɔː(r)/
A adj côtier/-ière
B adv [swim] vers la côte; [fish] près de la côte

inside
A /ˈɪnsaɪd/ n ① (inner area or surface) intérieur m; **to be on the** ~ [runner] être dans le couloir intérieur or à la corde; [horse] tenir la corde; [car] gen être sur or dans la voie de droite; (in GB, Australia) être sur or dans la voie de gauche; **to overtake on the** ~ (in Europe, US etc) doubler à droite; (in GB, Australia etc) doubler à gauche; ② (position of trust) **sb on the** ~ qn dans la place; ③ ○(prison) **on the** ~ en taule○
B **insides**○ /ɪnˈsaɪdz/ npl (intestines) (of animal) entrailles fpl; (of human) intestin m, estomac m, boyaux○ mpl
C /ɪnˈsaɪd/ prep (also US ~ **of**) ① (in the interior of) à l'intérieur; ~ **the box** à l'intérieur de or dans la boîte; **to be** ~ **(the house)** être à l'intérieur (de la maison); **you'll feel better with some food** ~ **you** tu te sentiras mieux après avoir mangé quelque chose; ② (within an area, organization) à l'intérieur de; ③ (under) ~ **(of) an hour** en moins d'une heure; **to be** ~ **the world record** battre le record mondial; ~ **the permitted time** dans les limites du temps imparti
D /ˈɪnsaɪd/ adj ① (interior) [cover, pocket, surface] intérieur; [toilet] à l'intérieur; ② (first-hand) [information] de première main; **the** ~ **story** la vérité; ③ (within an organization) **an** ~ **source** un informateur dans la place; **an** ~ **job** un coup monté de l'intérieur or par quelqu'un de la maison; ④ **the** ~ **lane** (of road) (in Europe, US etc) la voie de droite; (in GB, Australia etc) la voie de gauche; (of athletics track) le couloir intérieur
E /ɪnˈsaɪd/ adv ① (indoors) à l'intérieur; (in a container) à l'intérieur, dedans; **she's** ~ elle est à l'intérieur; **to look** ~ regarder à l'intérieur or dedans; **to go** ou **come** ou **step** ~ entrer; **to bring sth** ~ rentrer [chairs]; ② ○GB (in prison) en taule○
F **inside out** /ˌɪnsaɪdˈaʊt/ adv phr à l'envers; **to turn sth** ~ **out** retourner [bag]; **to know sth** ~ **out** connaître qch à fond

inside: ~ **forward** n intérieur m, inter m; ~ **leg** n entrejambes m inv; ~ **leg measurement** n hauteur f de l'entrejambes

insider /ɪnˈsaɪdə(r)/ n initié/-e m/f

insider: ~ **dealer**, ~ **trader** n initié m; ~ **dealing**, ~ **trading** n Fin délit m d'initié

insidious /ɪnˈsɪdɪəs/ adj insidieux/-ieuse

insight /ˈɪnsaɪt/ n ① (revealing glimpse) aperçu m, idée f; **a fascinating** ~ **into** un aperçu fascinant sur; **to give an** ~ **into** donner une idée de; **the book provides no new** ~s le livre n'apporte rien de nouveau (**into** sur); **to gain an** ~ **into sth** arriver à mieux connaître qch; ② (intuition) perspicacité f, intuition f; ③ (understanding) compréhension f (**into** de)

insightful /ˈɪnsaɪtfʊl/ adj [person] perspicace; [analysis] pénétrant

insignia /ɪnˈsɪgnɪə/ npl ① (symbols) insigne m; ② (medals) insigne m

insignificance /ˌɪnsɪgˈnɪfɪkəns/ n insignifiance f; **to pale** ou **fade into** ~ devenir dérisoire

insignificant /ˌɪnsɪgˈnɪfɪkənt/ adj [cost, difference] négligeable; [person, detail] insignifiant

insincere /ˌɪnsɪnˈsɪə(r)/ adj [person, compliment] peu sincère; **to be** ~ manquer de sincérité

insincerity /ˌɪnsɪnˈserəti/ n (of person) manque m de sincérité; (of smile, remark, compliment) hypocrisie f

insinuate /ɪnˈsɪnjʊeɪt/ vtr insinuer (**that** que)

insinuating /ɪnˈsɪnjʊeɪtɪŋ/ adj plein de sous-entendus

insinuation /ɪnˌsɪnjʊˈeɪʃn/ n insinuation f; **he made all sorts of** ~**s about me** il a insinué toutes sortes de choses à mon propos

insipid /ɪnˈsɪpɪd/ adj (all contexts) fade

insist /ɪnˈsɪst/
A vtr ① (demand) insister (**that** pour que); (authoritatively) exiger (**that** que + subj); ② (maintain forcefully) affirmer (**that** que)
B vi insister; **if you** ~ puisque tu insistes; **to** ~ **on** exiger; **to** ~ **on doing** vouloir à tout prix faire, tenir à faire; **to** ~ **on sb doing** insister pour que qn fasse

insistence /ɪnˈsɪstəns/ n insistance f; **to do sth at** ou **on sb's** ~ faire qch devant l'insistance de qn; **her** ~ **on doing** son obstination à faire

insistent /ɪnˈsɪstənt/ adj [person, noise] insistant; [demand] pressant; **to be** ~ insister (**about** sur; **that** pour que + subj)

insistently /ɪnˈsɪstəntli/ adv avec insistance

insofar /ˌɪnsəˈfɑː(r)/: **insofar as** conj phr ~ **as** dans la mesure où; ~ **as possible** dans la mesure du possible; ~ **as I can** dans la mesure de mes moyens; ~ **as X is concerned** en ce qui concerne X

insole /ˈɪnsəʊl/ n semelle f (intérieure)

insolence /ˈɪnsələns/ n insolence f

insolent /ˈɪnsələnt/ adj insolent

insolently /ˈɪnsələntli/ adv avec insolence

insoluble /ɪnˈsɒljʊbl/ adj insoluble

insolvency /ɪnˈsɒlvənsi/ n insolvabilité f

insolvent /ɪnˈsɒlvənt/ adj insolvable

insomnia /ɪnˈsɒmnɪə/ n insomnie f

insomniac /ɪnˈsɒmnɪæk/ n insomniaque mf

insomuch /ˌɪnsəʊˈmʌtʃ/ adv ~ **as** (to the extent that) dans la mesure où; (seeing that) vu que

inspect /ɪnˈspekt/ vtr ① examiner [qch] de près [document, product]; contrôler, vérifier [accounts]; inspecter [school, factory, pitch, wiring]; contrôler [passport, ticket, luggage]; ② Mil passer [qch] en revue [soldiers]

inspection /ɪnˈspekʃn/ n ① (of document, picture) examen m, inspection f; (of school, machinery, wiring) inspection f; (of ticket, passport) contrôle m; **to make** ou **carry out an** ~ procéder à une inspection; **on closer** ~ en y regardant de plus près; ② Mil (routine) inspection f; (at ceremony) revue f

inspection: ~ **copy** n spécimen m; ~ **pit** n fosse f de visite

inspector /ɪnˈspektə(r)/ n ① gen inspecteur/-trice m/f; ② GB (in police) inspecteur m de police; ③ GB Sch inspecteur/-trice m/f; ④ GB (on bus) contrôleur/-euse m/f

inspiration /ˌɪnspəˈreɪʃn/ n ① inspiration f (**for** pour); **to draw one's** ~ **from sth** s'inspirer de qch; **she is an** ~ **to us all!** elle est un exemple pour nous tous!; ② (sudden idea) inspiration f

inspirational /ˌɪnspəˈreɪʃənl/ adj ① (inspiring) inspirateur/-trice; ② (inspired) inspiré

inspire /ɪnˈspaɪə(r)/ vtr ① (give rise to) inspirer [person, work, idea]; motiver [decision]; **to be** ~**d by sth** s'inspirer de qch; **French-**~**d** d'inspiration française; **to** ~ **love in sb** inspirer de l'amour à qn; **he doesn't** ~ **much confidence** il n'inspire guère confiance; ② (incite) inciter, encourager (**to do** à faire)

inspired /ɪnˈspaɪəd/ adj [person, performance] inspiré; [idea] lumineux/-euse; **an** ~ **guess** une heureuse inspiration

inspiring /ɪnˈspaɪərɪŋ/ adj [person, speech] enthousiasmant; [thought, music] exaltant

instability /ˌɪnstəˈbɪləti/ n instabilité f

instal(l) /ɪnˈstɔːl/
A vtr lit installer [equipment]; poser [windows]; fig **to** ∼ **sb in office** installer qn
B v refl **to** ∼ **oneself** s'installer
installation /ˌɪnstəˈleɪʃn/ n installation f
installment plan n US contrat m de vente à crédit; **on the** ∼ à crédit
instalment GB, **installment** US /ɪnˈstɔːlmənt/ n
1 (payment) versement m partiel; **monthly** ∼ mensualité f, versement m mensuel; **to pay an** ∼ faire un versement partiel; **in** ∼**s** en plusieurs versements; **2** (of story, serial) épisode m; (of novel) feuilleton m
instance /ˈɪnstəns/
A n **1** (case) cas m; **in the first** ∼ en premier lieu; **2** (example) exemple m; **for** ∼ par exemple
B vtr (cite) citer [qch] en exemple
instant /ˈɪnstənt/
A n instant m; **at that (very)** ∼ à l'instant même; **come here this** ∼! viens ici tout de suite!; **the** ∼ **we saw him** dès que nous l'avons vu
B adj **1** (immediate) [access, effect, rapport, success] immédiat; [solution] instantané; ∼ **camera** polaroïd® m; **2** Culin [coffee, soup] instantané; [potato] déshydraté; [meal] à préparation rapide
instantaneous /ˌɪnstənˈteɪnɪəs/ adj instantané
instantly /ˈɪnstəntlɪ/ adv gen immédiatement; [die] sur le coup
instant replay n US Sport répétition f d'une séquence
instead /ɪnˈsted/
A adv **we didn't go home, we went to the park** ∼ au lieu de rentrer nous sommes allés au parc; **try camping** ∼ essaie plutôt le camping; **let's take a taxi** ∼ prenons plutôt un taxi; **she didn't go to London,** ∼ **she decided to go to Oxford** au lieu d'aller à Londres elle a décidé d'aller à Oxford; **I was going to phone but wrote** ∼ j'allais téléphoner mais finalement j'ai écrit; **her son went** ∼ son fils y est allé à sa place
B **instead of** prep phr ∼ **of doing** au lieu de faire; ∼ **of sth** au lieu de qch; **use oil** ∼ **of butter** utilisez de l'huile à la place du beurre; ∼ **of sb** à la place de qn
instep /ˈɪnstep/ n cou-de-pied m; **to have a high** ∼ avoir le pied cambré
instigate /ˈɪnstɪɡeɪt/ vtr lancer [attack]; engager [proceedings]
instigation /ˌɪnstɪˈɡeɪʃn/ n **at the** ∼ **of sb** à l'instigation de qn; **he stole the car at her** ∼ c'est elle qui l'a incité à voler la voiture
instil GB, **instill** US /ɪnˈstɪl/ vtr (p prés etc **-ll-**) inculquer [attitude, belief] (**in** à); donner [confidence] (**in** à); insuffler [fear] (**in** à)
instinct /ˈɪnstɪŋkt/ n instinct m (**for** de); **the** ∼ **to do** l'instinct qui pousse à faire; **her** ∼ **is to fight back** lit, fig elle se défend d'instinct; **follow your** ∼**(s)** laisse-toi guider par ton intuition
instinctive /ɪnˈstɪŋktɪv/ adj instinctif/-ive
instinctively /ɪnˈstɪŋktɪvlɪ/ adv d'instinct, instinctivement
institute /ˈɪnstɪtjuːt, US -tuːt/
A n **1** (organization) institut m; **2** US (course) stage m
B vtr **1** (initiate) instituer, instaurer [custom, prize]; engager [proceedings]; **2** (found) fonder, constituer
institution /ˌɪnstɪˈtjuːʃn, US -tuːʃn/ n **1** Admin, Pol institution f also fig; **financial** ∼ organisme m financier; **2** (home, hospital) établissement m spécialisé; (old people's home) asile m de vieillards; (mental hospital) hôpital m psychiatrique; **3** (establishment) (of rule, body, prize) institution f; ∼ **of legal proceedings** Jur introduction f d'instance; **4** US = **institute A 1**
institutional /ˌɪnstɪˈtjuːʃənl, US -tuː-/ adj **1** [structure, reform] institutionnel/-elle; [food] de collectivité; **to be put in** ∼ **care** [child] être placé dans un établissement spécialisé; **2** Comm institutionnel/-elle
institutionalize /ˌɪnstɪˈtjuːʃənəlaɪz, US -tuː-/ vtr **1** (place in care) placer [qn] dans un établissement spécialisé; (in mental hospital) interner; **to become** ∼**d** [patient] être marqué par la vie réglementée d'un établissement spécialisé; **2** (establish officially) institutionnaliser, donner un caractère officiel à; ∼**d** [racism, violence] institutionnalisé; **to become** ∼**d** s'institutionnaliser

instruct /ɪnˈstrʌkt/ vtr **1** (direct) **to** ∼ **sb to do** donner l'ordre à qn de faire; **to be** ∼**ed to do** recevoir l'ordre de faire; **to** ∼ **sb how to do** indiquer à qn comment faire; **2** (teach) instruire; **to** ∼ **sb in** enseigner [qch] à qn [subject]; **to** ∼ **sb how to do** enseigner à qn comment faire; **3** GB Jur **to** ∼ **a solicitor** confier son/une affaire à un avocat
instruction /ɪnˈstrʌkʃn/
A n **1** (order) instruction f (**to** à); **to give** ∼**s to sb to do** donner l'ordre à qn de faire; **I have** ∼**s to do** j'ai reçu l'ordre de faire; **to be under** ∼**s to do** être chargé de faire; **2** ¢ (teaching) instruction f; **the language of** ∼ la langue d'enseignement; **to give sb an** ∼ **in sth** enseigner qch à qn
B instructions npl instructions fpl; ∼**s for use** mode m d'emploi
instruction: ∼ **book** n livret m de l'utilisateur; ∼ **manual** n manuel m d'utilisation
instructive /ɪnˈstrʌktɪv/ adj instructif/-ive
instructor /ɪnˈstrʌktə(r)/ ▸ p. 1181 n **1** (in sports, driving, flying) moniteur/-trice m/f (**in** de); (military) instructeur m; **2** US (in university) ≈ assistant/-e m/f; (any teacher) professeur m
instructress /ɪnˈstrʌktrɪs/ n monitrice f
instrument /ˈɪnstrəmənt/ ▸ p. 1028 n **1** Mus instrument m; **to play an** ∼ jouer d'un instrument; **2** Aut, Aviat, Tech instrument m
instrumental /ˌɪnstrʊˈmentl/
A n instrumental m
B instrumentals npl partie f instrumentale
C adj **1** **to be** ∼ **in sth/in doing** contribuer à qch/à faire; **2** Mus instrumental
instrumentalist /ˌɪnstrʊˈmentəlɪst/ n instrumentiste mf
instrument panel n tableau m de bord
insubordination /ˌɪnsəˌbɔːdɪˈneɪʃn/ n insubordination f
insubstantial /ˌɪnsəbˈstænʃl/ adj **1** (small) [meal] peu nourrissant; [helping] mesquin; **2** (flimsy) [building] peu solide; [evidence] insuffisant; **3** (unreal) insaisissable
insufferable /ɪnˈsʌfrəbl/ adj [heat, conditions] insupportable; [rudeness] intolérable; **he's an** ∼ **bore** il est assommant
insufferably /ɪnˈsʌfrəblɪ/ adv ∼ **rude** d'une impolitesse insupportable
insufficient /ˌɪnsəˈfɪʃnt/ adj **there are** ∼ **copies** il n'y a pas assez d'exemplaires (**to do** pour faire); **to be** ∼ **for** être insuffisant pour
insufficiently /ˌɪnsəˈfɪʃntlɪ/ adv (not enough) pas assez; (badly) mal
insular /ˈɪnsjʊlə(r), US -sələr/ adj **1** péj (narrow-minded) [outlook] étriqué; **to be** ∼ [person] avoir des vues étroites; **2** Geog insulaire
insularity /ˌɪnsjʊˈlærətɪ, US -səˈl-/ n étroitesse f d'esprit
insulate /ˈɪnsjʊleɪt, US -səˈl-/ vtr **1** (against cold, heat) isoler [roof, room]; calorifuger [water tank]; (against noise) insonoriser [room]; **2** Elec isoler; **3** fig (protect) protéger (**from** de; **against** contre); ∼**d** [wire] isolé; [handle] isolant; [tank] calorifugé; [room] (against cold, heat) isolé; (against noise) insonorisé
insulating /ˈɪnsjʊˌleɪtɪŋ, US -səˈl-/ adj isolant; ∼ **tape** ruban m isolant
insulation /ˌɪnsjʊˈleɪʃn, US -səˈl-/ n **1** (thermal) gen isolation f; (of tank) calorifugeage m; **loft** ∼ isolation du comble; **2** (acoustic) isolation f (acoustique), insonorisation f; **3** (material) isolant m; **4** Elec isolation f
insulator /ˈɪnsjʊleɪtə(r), US -səl-/ n **1** (substance) isolant m; **2** Elec isolateur m
insulin /ˈɪnsjʊlɪn, US -səl-/ n insuline f
insult
A /ˈɪnsʌlt/ n (remark) insulte f, injure f; (action) insulte f, affront m; **and to add** ∼ **to injury...** et pour comble d'insulte...
B /ɪnˈsʌlt/ vtr (verbally) insulter, injurier; (by one's behaviour) insulter
insulting /ɪnˈsʌltɪŋ/ adj insultant
insultingly /ɪnˈsʌltɪŋlɪ/ adv de façon injurieuse
insuperable /ɪnˈsuːpərəbl, ɪnˈsjuː-/ adj insurmontable

insurance /ɪn'ʃɔːrəns, US -'ʃʊər-/ n ① ₵ (contract) assurance f (**against** contre; **for** pour); (policy) police f d'assurance; **to take out ~ against sth** s'assurer contre qch; **to pay the ~ on sth** payer l'assurance de qch; **accident/fire ~** assurance contre les accidents/l'incendie; **travel ~** assurance voyage; ② (amount paid) assurance f; **I pay £500 in ~ on the car** je paie 500 livres sterling d'assurance pour la voiture; ③ (profession) **he works in ~** il travaille dans les assurances; ④ fig (precaution) protection f (**against** contre)

insurance: ~ **agent** n agent m d'assurances; ~ **broker** n courtier m en assurances; ~ **claim** n demande f d'indemnité; ~ **company** n compagnie f d'assurances; ~ **plan** n US régime m d'assurances; ~ **policy** n (police f d')assurance f; ~ **premium** n prime f d'assurance; ~ **scheme** n GB régime m d'assurances

insure /ɪn'ʃɔː(r), US -'ʃʊər/ vtr ① assurer (**against** contre); **to ~ oneself** ou **one's life** prendre une assurance-vie; ~**d for £50** assuré pour une valeur déclarée de 50 livres; ② (take precautions) **to ~ against delay** se garantir contre les retards; ③ US = **ensure**

insured party n assuré/-e m/f

insurer /ɪn'ʃɔːrə(r), US -'ʃʊər-/ n assureur m

insurgent /ɪn'sɜːdʒənt/ n, adj insurgé/-e (m/f)

insurmountable /ˌɪnsə'maʊntəbl/ adj insurmontable

insurrection /ˌɪnsə'rekʃn/ n insurrection f

intact /ɪn'tækt/ adj intact; **to survive ~** rester intact

intake /'ɪnteɪk/ n ① (consumption) consommation f; ② Sch, Univ (admissions) (+ v sg ou pl) admissions fpl; **the new ~** (at school) les nouveaux élèves mpl; (into training, job) les nouvelles recrues fpl; ③ (inhalation) **an ~ of breath** une inspiration f; ④ (inlet) arrivée f

intangible /ɪn'tændʒəbl/ adj ① (undefinable) insaisissable; ② Jur incorporel/-elle

integral /'ɪntɪgrəl/
A n intégrale f
B adj ① (intrinsic) [part, feature] intégrant; ~ **to** intrinsèque à; ② (built-in) [lighting, component] incorporé; [garage] intégré; ③ (whole) intégral

integrate /'ɪntɪgreɪt/
A vtr ① (incorporate) intégrer [region, company, system] (**into** dans; **with** à); [minority] (**into** dans); **to be ~d with** s'intégrer à; ② (combine) combiner [systems]; ③ Pol (desegregate) rendre [qch] accessible à tous [school, activity]
B vi (mix) [person] s'intégrer (**with** à; **into** dans)

integrated /'ɪntɪgreɪtɪd/ adj [system, service, circuit] intégré; [sect, ethnic group] mixte

integration /ˌɪntɪ'greɪʃn/ n (all contexts) intégration f (**with** à)

integrity /ɪn'tegrətɪ/ n intégrité f; **a man of ~** un homme intègre

intellect /'ɪntəlekt/ n ① (intelligence) intelligence f; ② (person) esprit m

intellectual /ˌɪntə'lektʃʊəl/ n, adj intellectuel/-elle (m/f)

intellectualize /ˌɪntə'lektʃʊəlaɪz/
A vtr intellectualiser [problem]
B vi philosopher, pérorer pej (**about** sur)

intellectually /ˌɪntə'lektʃʊəlɪ/ adv intellectuellement

intelligence /ɪn'telɪdʒəns/ n ① intelligence f (**to do** de faire); **to be of low ~** être peu intelligent; **use your ~!** réfléchis!; **that's an insult to his ~!** c'est le prendre pour un imbécile!; ② gen, Mil (information) renseignements mpl; **latest ~** informations fpl de dernière minute; ③ Mil (secret service) services mpl de renseignements; **military ~** service de renseignements de l'armée de terre

intelligence: ~ **agent** n agent m de renseignements; **Intelligence Corps** n GB ≈ service m de renseignements de l'armée; ~ **quotient, IQ** n quotient m intellectuel; **Intelligence Service** n service m de renseignements; ~ **test** n test m d'aptitude intellectuelle

intelligent /ɪn'telɪdʒənt/ adj intelligent

intelligent card n carte f à puce

intelligently /ɪn'telɪdʒəntlɪ/ adv intelligemment, avec intelligence

intelligible /ɪn'telɪdʒəbl/ adj intelligible (**to** à)

intemperate /ɪn'tempərət/ adj ① [remark] immodéré; [attack] sans retenue; [person] intempérant; ② [weather] rigoureux/-euse

intend /ɪn'tend/
A vtr ① (have in mind) vouloir [outcome]; **as I ~ed** comme je le voulais; **sooner than I had ~ed** plus tôt que je ne voulais; **to ~ to do, to ~ doing** avoir l'intention de faire; ② (mean) **to ~ sth as a joke** dire qch pour plaisanter; **no insult ~ed** (to one person) sans vouloir t'offenser; (to group) sans vouloir offenser personne; **it was clearly ~ed as a reference to...** c'était manifestement une allusion à...; **to be ~ed for** être destiné à [person]; être prévu pour [purpose]; **I ~ed it as a compliment** je voulais faire un compliment; **the law is ~ed to prevent...** la loi vise à empêcher...
B intending pres p adj [applicant, traveller] éventuel/-elle

intended /ɪn'tendɪd/
A † n her/his ~ son/sa futur/-e m/f
B adj ① (desired) [result] voulu; ② (planned) [visit, purchase] projeté; **the ~ victim** la personne visée

intense /ɪn'tens/ adj ① [activity, feeling, colour, pressure] intense; [interest, satisfaction] vif/vive (before n); ② [person] sérieux/-ieuse

intensely /ɪn'tenslɪ/ adv [curious, problematic] extrêmement; [dislike, hate] profondément

intensifier /ɪn'tensɪfaɪə(r)/ n Ling intensif m

intensify /ɪn'tensɪfaɪ/
A vtr intensifier
B vi s'intensifier

intensity /ɪn'tensətɪ/ n intensité f (**of** de)

intensive /ɪn'tensɪv/
A adj (all contexts) intensif/-ive
B -**intensive** combining form energy-~ à forte consommation en énergie; **technology-~** à fort niveau technologique

intensive care n in ~ en réanimation

intensive care unit n service m de soins intensifs

intent /ɪn'tent/
A n ① (intention) intention f; **with ~** [act, say] à dessein, intentionnellement; ② Jur **with (criminal) ~** avec une intention criminelle
B adj ① (determined) ~ **on doing** résolu à faire; ② (absorbed) absorbé (**on** par; **on doing** à faire)
⟨Idiom⟩ **to all ~s and purposes** quasiment, en fait

intention /ɪn'tenʃn/ n intention f (**to do, of doing** de faire); **our ~ is to do** nous avons l'intention de faire; **the ~ is to do** l'objectif est de faire; **she hasn't the slightest ~ of doing** elle n'a nullement l'intention de faire; **with the best of ~s** avec les meilleures intentions du monde

intentional /ɪn'tenʃənl/ adj [action, insult] intentionnel/-elle; [effect] voulu

intentionally /ɪn'tenʃənəlɪ/ adv [act] intentionnellement, exprès; [ambiguous] délibérément

intently /ɪn'tentlɪ/ adv attentivement

interact /ˌɪntər'ækt/ vi [two factors, phenomena] agir l'un sur l'autre, s'influencer mutuellement; [people] communiquer; Comput dialoguer

interactive: ~ **computing** n informatique f conversationnelle; ~ **mode** n mode m conversationnel or interactif; ~ **terminal** n terminal m interactif; ~ **video** n vidéo f interactive

interbreed /ˌɪntə'briːd/
A vtr (prét, pp -bred) croiser
B vi (prét, pp -bred) se croiser

interbreeding /ˌɪntə'briːdɪŋ/ n croisement m

intercede /ˌɪntə'siːd/ vi (plead) intercéder (**with** auprès de; **on sb's behalf** en faveur de qn); (mediate) intervenir comme médiateur/-trice m/f

intercept /ˌɪntə'sept/
A n ① Telecom, US Sport interception f; ② Math intersection f
B vtr intercepter

intercession /ˌɪntə'seʃn/ n ① (intervention) intercession f (**with** auprès de); ② (mediation) médiation f

interchange
A /'ɪntətʃeɪndʒ/ n ① (road junction) échangeur m; ② (exchange) échange m
B /ˌɪntə'tʃeɪndʒ/ vtr (exchange) échanger

interchangeably /ˌɪntə'tʃeɪndʒəblɪ/ adv de façon interchangeable

inter-city /ˌɪntəˈsɪtɪ/
A n GB (train) rapide m
B adj interurbain

intercom /ˈɪntəkɒm/ n interphone® m; **over** ou **on the ∼** par l'interphone®

interconnect /ˌɪntəkəˈnekt/
A vtr raccorder [parts]
B vi [components] se connecter; [rooms] communiquer; Comput être raccordé

interconnecting /ˌɪntəkəˈnektɪŋ/ adj [rooms] communicant; [cable] de connexion

intercourse /ˈɪntəkɔːs/ n (social) rapports mpl avec autrui; (sexual) rapports mpl (sexuels)

interdepartmental /ˌɪntəˌdiːpɑːˈtmentl/ adj Univ entre départements; Admin, Comm entre services; Pol interministériel/-ielle

interdependence /ˌɪntədɪˈpendəns/ n interdépendance f

interdisciplinary /ˌɪntəˌdɪsɪˈplɪnərɪ, US -nerɪ/ adj interdisciplinaire

interest /ˈɪntrəst/
A n ① **Ȼ** (enthusiasm) intérêt m (**in** pour); **to add to the ∼ of sth** ajouter un certain intérêt à qch; **of no ∼ to sb** sans intérêt pour qn; **we've had a lot of ∼ from Europe** beaucoup de gens en Europe nous ont manifesté leur intérêt; **to hold sb's ∼** retenir l'attention de qn; **just for ∼** pour le plaisir; **as a matter of ∼...** juste pour savoir...; ② (hobby) centre m d'intérêt; **he has wide ∼s** il s'intéresse à énormément de choses; ③ (benefit) intérêt m; **in the ∼(s) of** (to help, to promote) dans l'intérêt de [peace, freedom, person]; (out of concern for) par souci de [hygiene, justice]; **it's in your (own) ∼(s) to do it** il est dans ton intérêt de faire; **I have an ∼ in doing** il est de mon intérêt de faire; **to have a vested ∼ in doing** avoir d'excellentes raisons de faire; **to have sb's best ∼s at heart** vouloir le bien de qn; ④ (concern) gen intérêt m; Fin participation f; **to declare one's ∼s** faire état de ses participations personnelles; ⑤ (accrued monies) intérêts mpl (**on** de); **overdraft ∼ charges** intérêts sur un découvert; **account paying ∼** compte rémunéré; ⑥ Comm (share) intérêts mpl; **business ∼s** intérêts commerciaux
B vtr ① (provoke curiosity) intéresser (**in** à); **can I ∼ you in buying some insurance?** est-ce qu'une assurance vous intéresserait?; **can I ∼ you in our new range?** permettez-moi d'attirer votre attention sur notre nouvelle gamme; ② (concern) [problem, policy] concerner

interested /ˈɪntrəstɪd/ adj [expression, onlooker] intéressé; **to be ∼ in** s'intéresser à [subject, activity]; **I am ∼ in doing** ça m'intéresse de faire; **we're just not ∼** ça ne nous intéresse pas; **to get sb ∼ in** intéresser qn à [subject]; **the ∼ parties** les intéressés

interest group n groupement m d'intérêt

interesting /ˈɪntrəstɪŋ/ adj intéressant

interestingly /ˈɪntrəstɪŋlɪ/ adv ① **∼, he...** (worthy of note) chose intéressante, il...; (strangely) iron chose curieuse, il...; **∼ enough...** ce qui est très intéressant...; ② (speak, write) d'une façon intéressante

interest rate n Fin taux m d'intérêt

interface /ˈɪntəfeɪs/
A n Comput, fig interface f
B vtr ① Tech connecter, relier; ② (in sewing) entoiler

interfacing /ˈɪntəfeɪsɪŋ/ n (in sewing) entoilage m

interfere /ˌɪntəˈfɪə(r)/ vi ① péj (involve oneself) **to ∼ in** se mêler de [affairs]; **she never ∼s** elle ne se mêle jamais de ce qui ne la regarde pas; ② (intervene) intervenir; **to ∼ in** s'ingérer dans [private life]; ③ (touch, mess with) **to ∼ with** toucher, traficoter◯ [machine]; ④ (hinder) [activity] **to ∼ with** empiéter sur [family life, freedom]; déranger [sleep]; ⑤ Phys interférer

interference /ˌɪntəˈfɪərəns/ n ① (by government, boss) ingérence f (**in** dans); (by family) immixtion f (**in** dans); ② (of sound waves, light waves) brouillage m, interférence f; (on radio) parasites mpl

interfering /ˌɪntəˈfɪərɪŋ/ adj péj [person] envahissant

interim /ˈɪntərɪm/
A n **in the ∼** entre-temps
B adj [arrangement, bond, government] provisoire; [interest, payment] intermédiaire; [post, employee] intérimaire; **∼ profits** résultats mpl semestriels; **∼ report** comptes mpl semestriels

interior /ɪnˈtɪərɪə(r)/
A n ① (inside) intérieur m; **a Vermeer ∼** Art une scène d'intérieur de Vermeer; ② (of country, continent) intérieur m; **Secretary/Department of the Interior** US Pol ministre m/ministère m de l'Intérieur
B adj ① [wall, paintwork] intérieur; ② Cin, TV [shot] en intérieur; [scene] d'intérieur; ③ (inner) [motive, impulse] intérieur

interior: **∼ decorator** ▸ p. 1181 n décorateur/-trice m/f; **∼ designer** ▸ p. 1181 n (of colours, fabrics etc) designer m; (of walls, space) architecte mf d'intérieur

interject /ˌɪntəˈdʒekt/ vtr placer [word, comment]; **..., he ∼ed ...,** lança-t-il

interjection /ˌɪntəˈdʒekʃn/ n Ling interjection f; (interruption) interruption f

interleave /ˌɪntəˈliːv/ vtr intercaler

interlink /ˌɪntəˈlɪŋk/
A vtr **to be ∼ed** être lié (**with** à)
B vi [aspects, problems] être liés

interlock
A /ˈɪntəlɒk/ n ① Comput verrouillage m; ② (knitted fabric) interlock m
B /ˌɪntəˈlɒk/ vi [pipes] s'emboîter; [mechanisms] s'enclencher; [fingers] s'entrelacer; [systems] être intimement liés

interloper /ˈɪntələʊpə(r)/ n intrus/-e m/f

interlude /ˈɪntəluːd/ n ① (interval) gen intervalle m; Cin, Mus, Theat entracte m; ② (brief entertainment) Theat intermède m; Mus interlude m

intermarriage /ˌɪntəˈmærɪdʒ/ n (within a family) intermariage m; (between racial groups) mariage m mixte; (between families, tribes) mariage m entre membres de familles/tribus différentes

intermediary /ˌɪntəˈmiːdɪərɪ, US -dɪerɪ/ n, adj intermédiaire (mf)

intermediate /ˌɪntəˈmiːdɪət/
A n ① (mediator) intermédiaire mf; ② US Aut automobile f de taille moyenne
B adj ① [stage] intermédiaire; ② Sch [exam] de difficulté moyenne; [course] de niveau moyen; [level] moyen/-enne; ③ Fin [credit] à moyen terme

interment /ɪnˈtɜːmənt/ n sout inhumation f

interminably /ɪnˈtɜːmɪnəblɪ/ adv [talk] interminablement, pendant des heures; **∼ long** interminable

intermingle /ˌɪntəˈmɪŋgl/ vi [patterns, themes] s'entremêler; [colours] se mélanger (**with** à)

intermission /ˌɪntəˈmɪʃn/ n Cin, Theat entracte m

intermittent /ˌɪntəˈmɪtənt/ adj [noise, activity] intermittent; [use] occasionnel/-elle

intermittently /ˌɪntəˈmɪtəntlɪ/ adv par intermittence

intern
A /ˈɪntɜːn/ n US ① Med interne mf; ② gen stagiaire mf
B /ɪnˈtɜːn/ vtr Mil, Pol interner

internal /ɪnˈtɜːnl/ adj ① (inner) [mechanism] interne; [pipe] intérieur; ② Med [organ, bleeding] interne; **∼ injuries** lésions fpl internes; **∼ examination** toucher m vaginal; ③ (within organization) [problem, mail, phone call] interne; [candidate] interne à l'entreprise; ④ (within country) [security, flight, trade] intérieur; **∼ revenue** revenus mpl fiscaux; **∼ affairs** Pol affaires fpl internes; **∼ fighting** luttes fpl intestines

internalize /ɪnˈtɜːnəlaɪz/ vtr intérioriser

internally /ɪnˈtɜːnəlɪ/ adv ① (inside) à l'intérieur; **'not to be taken ∼'** 'médicament à usage externe'; **to bleed ∼** faire une hémorragie interne; ② (within organization) [recruit] au sein de l'entreprise

Internal Revenue Service n US ≈ fisc m

international /ˌɪntəˈnæʃnəl/
A n Sport (fixture) match m international; (player) international/-e m/f
B adj international

internationally /ˌɪntəˈnæʃnəlɪ/ adv [known, respected] dans le monde entier; **∼, the situation is even worse** sur le plan international, la situation est encore pire

international: **International Monetary Fund**, **IMF** n Fonds m monétaire international, FMI m; **∼ money order** n mandat-poste m international; **International Phonetic Alphabet**, **IPA** n alphabet m phonétique international, API m; **∼ reply**

i

coupon n coupon-réponse m international
internee /ˌɪntɜː'niː/ n Mil, Pol interné/-e m/f
Internet /'ɪntənet/
A n Internet m; **to be on the** ~ avoir Internet; **to find sth on the** ~ trouver qch sur Internet
B modif [access] à Internet; [auction, banking, search] sur Internet; [account, address, connection] Internet; [use, user] d'Internet

Internet service provider, ISP n fournisseur m d'accès Internet

internist /ɪn'tɜːnɪst/ n US Med interniste mf

internship /ɪn'tɜːnʃɪp/ n US 1 gen stage m; 2 Med internat m

interpersonal /ˌɪntə'pɜːsənl/ adj [skills] de communication; [relations] humain; ~ **communications** communication f

interpret /ɪn'tɜːprɪt/
A vtr interpréter (**as** comme)
B vi faire l'interprète

interpretation /ɪnˌtɜːprɪ'teɪʃn/ n interprétation f (**by** par; **of** de); **open to** ~ sujet à interprétation

interpreter /ɪn'tɜːprɪtə(r)/ n 1 interprète mf; 2 (machine) traductrice f; (program) interpréteur m

interpreting /ɪn'tɜːprɪtɪŋ/ n (job) interprétariat m

interrelate /ˌɪntərɪ'leɪt/
A vtr mettre [qch] en corrélation; ~**d parts** parties interdépendantes
B vi [events, ideas] être étroitement liés

interrogate /ɪn'terəgeɪt/ vtr interroger

interrogation /ɪnˌterə'geɪʃn/
A n interrogatoire m; **under** ~ pendant mon/son etc interrogatoire
B noun modifier [procedure, room] d'interrogatoire

interrogative /ˌɪntə'rɒgətɪv/
A n Ling interrogatif m; **in the** ~ à la forme interrogative
B adj gen [look] interrogateur/-trice; Ling interrogatif/-ive

interrogator /ɪn'terəgeɪtə(r)/ n interrogateur/-trice m/f

interrupt /ˌɪntə'rʌpt/
A n Comput interruption f
B vtr 1 (cut in) interrompre, couper la parole à [person]; 2 (disturb) déranger [person]; interrompre [meeting, lecture]; 3 (block) gêner [view]; 4 (stop) couper [supply]
C vi interrompre

interruption /ˌɪntə'rʌpʃn/ n interruption f; **there are constant** ~**s** on est constamment interrompu

intersect /ˌɪntə'sekt/
A vtr gen, Math croiser
B vi 1 [roads, wires, ideas] se croiser; **to** ~ **with** croiser; 2 Math se couper

intersection /ˌɪntə'sekʃn/ n intersection f

intersperse /ˌɪntə'spɜːs/ vtr gen parsemer (**with** de); (with music, breaks) entrecouper (**with** de)

interstate /ˌɪntə'steɪt/
A n (also ~ **highway**) autoroute f (inter-États)
B adj US [commerce, links] entre États

intertwine /ˌɪntə'twaɪn/
A vtr entrelacer
B vi [fingers, threads] s'entrelacer; [lives, destinies] se croiser

interval /'ɪntəvl/ n 1 (in time, space) intervalle m; **at regular** ~**s** à intervalles réguliers; **at four-hourly** ~**s** toutes les quatre heures; **at 100 metre** ~**s** à 100 mètres d'intervalle; **bright** ~**s** Meteorol belles éclaircies fpl; 2 GB Theat entracte m; Sport (during match) pause f, mi-temps f inv

intervene /ˌɪntə'viːn/ vi 1 (take action) intervenir (**on behalf of** en faveur de); 2 (happen) arriver; **if nothing** ~**s** si rien n'arrive entre-temps; 3 (mediate) s'interposer

intervening /ˌɪntə'viːnɪŋ/ adj **in the** ~ **period** ou **hours** entre-temps; **in the** ~ **years** dans les années qui ont suivi

intervention /ˌɪntə'venʃn/ n gen, Econ intervention f (**on behalf of** en faveur de)

interventionist /ˌɪntə'venʃənɪst/ n, adj interventionniste (mf)

interview /'ɪntəvjuː/
A n 1 (also **job** ~) entretien m; 2 Journ interview f; **in an** ~ **with the Gazette** dans une interview accordée au journal la Gazette
B vtr 1 (for job, place) faire passer un entretien à [candidate]; 2 (call to interview) convoquer [qn] pour un entretien; 3 Journ interviewer [celebrity]; [police] interroger [suspect]
C vi [candidate] passer un entretien; [employer] faire passer des entretiens

interviewee /ˌɪntəvjuː'iː/ n 1 (for job, place) candidat/-e m/f; 2 (on TV, radio) personne f interviewée; 3 (in survey) personne f interrogée

interviewer /'ɪntəvjuːə(r)/ n 1 (for job, course) personne f faisant passer l'entretien; 2 (on Radio, TV, in newspaper) intervieweur/-euse m/f; 3 (for survey) enquêteur/-trice m/f

interwar /ˌɪntə'wɔː(r)/ adj **the** ~ **period** ou **years** l'entre-deux-guerres

interweave /ˌɪntə'wiːv/ (prét **-wove** /-'wəʊv/; pp **-woven** /-'wəʊvn/) vtr entrelacer [fingers, threads]; mêler [themes, rhythms] (**with** à)

intestate /ɪn'testeɪt/ adj Jur intestat inv

intestinal /ɪn'testɪnl, ˌɪntes'taɪnl/ adj intestinal; **to have** ~ **fortitude** US avoir quelque chose dans le ventre○

intestine /ɪn'testɪn/ n intestin m

intimacy /'ɪntɪməsɪ/ n 1 (closeness) intimité f; 2 euph (sexual relations) relations fpl (sexuelles)

intimate
A /'ɪntɪmət/ n intime mf
B /'ɪntɪmət/ adj 1 (personal) gen intime; [belief, friendship] profond; [life] privé; **to be on** ~ **terms with sb** être intime avec qn; 2 [relationship] intime; **to be** ~ **with** euph avoir des relations sexuelles avec; 3 (cosy) intime; 4 (close) [bond, connection] intime; **an** ~ **knowledge of** une connaissance approfondie de
C /'ɪntɪmeɪt/ vtr 1 (hint) laisser entendre [wishes]; 2 (announce) annoncer; **to** ~ **that** faire savoir que

intimately /'ɪntɪmətlɪ/ adv 1 [know] intimement; [speak] de façon intime; 2 (deeply) ~ **aware of** profondément conscient de; 3 [connected, related] intimement; ~ **involved in** ou **with sth** mêlé de près à qch

intimation /ˌɪntɪ'meɪʃn/ n 1 (hint) indication f; **she gave me no** ~ **that she was leaving** rien ne m'a laissé présager qu'elle allait partir; **he gave her an** ~ **that** il lui a laissé entendre que; 2 (announcement) gen, Relig annonce f

intimidate /ɪn'tɪmɪdeɪt/ vtr intimider; **to** ~ **sb into doing** forcer qn à faire qch par des mesures d'intimidation

intimidating /ɪn'tɪmɪdeɪtɪŋ/ adj [behaviour, experience, person] intimidant; [obstacle, sight, size] impressionnant; [prospect] redoutable

intimidation /ɪnˌtɪmɪ'deɪʃn/ n intimidation f (**by** de la part de)

into /'ɪntə, 'ɪntuː/

⚠️ Into is used after certain nouns and verbs in English (change into, wander into etc). For translations, consult the appropriate noun or verb entry (change, wander etc).
into is used in the structure verb + sb + into + doing (to bully sb into doing, to fool sb into doing). For translations of these structures see the appropriate verb entry (bully, fool etc).
For translations of expressions like get into trouble, go into detail, get into debt etc you should consult the appropriate noun entry (trouble, detail, debt etc).

prep 1 (indicating change of location) [put, go, disappear] dans [place]; **pour the mixture** ~ **it** versez-y le mélange; **to move sth** ~ **the shade** mettre qch à l'ombre; **to go** ~ **town**/ ~ **the office** aller en ville/au bureau; **to get** ~ **bed** se mettre au lit; **to help sb** ~ **bed** aider qn à se mettre au lit; 2 (indicating change of form) en [new shape, foreign currency, different language]; 3 (indicating duration) ~ **the 18th century** jusqu'au XVIIIe siècle; **well** ~ **the afternoon** jusque tard dans l'après-midi; 4 (indicating a point in a process) **we were well** ~ **1988 when...** l'année 1988 était bien entamée quand...; **well** ~ **the second half** bien après le début de la deuxième mi-temps; **to be (well)** ~ **one's thirties** avoir une bonne trentaine d'années; 5 (indicating direction) dans; **to speak** ~ **the microphone** parler dans le microphone; 6 ○(keen on) **to be** ~ être fana○ de [jazz etc]; **to be** ~ **drugs** se droguer; 7 (indicating impact) dans; **to run** ~ **sth** rentrer dans qch; **to bang** ~ **sb/sth** heurter qn/qch; 8 Math **8** ~ **24 goes 3 times** ou **is 3** 24 divisé par 8 égale 3

(Idiom) **to be** ~ **everything** [child] toucher à tout

intolerable /ɪn'tɒlərəbl/ adj intolérable, insupportable

intolerably /ɪnˈtɒlərəblɪ/ adv [behave] d'une façon insupportable; [painful, possessive, long] horriblement

intolerance /ɪnˈtɒlərəns/ n gen, Med intolérance f (**of**, **towards** vis-à-vis de; **to** à)

intolerant /ɪnˈtɒlərənt/ adj intolérant (**of**, **towards** vis-à-vis de; **with** envers)

intone /ɪnˈtəʊn/ vtr psalmodier [prayer]; débiter [speech]

intoxicate /ɪnˈtɒksɪkeɪt/ vtr ① (inebriate) enivrer; ② (poison) intoxiquer; ③ fig griser

intoxicated /ɪnˈtɒksɪkeɪtɪd/ adj lit ivre; fig grisé (**by**, **with** par)

intoxicating /ɪnˈtɒksɪkeɪtɪŋ/ adj ① lit [drink] alcoolisé; [effect, substance] toxique; ② fig [perfume] enivrant; [sensation] grisant

intoxication /ɪnˌtɒksɪˈkeɪʃn/ n lit, fig ivresse f

intractable /ɪnˈtræktəbl/ adj [person] intraitable; [opinion] inflexible; [illness, problem] rebelle

intramural /ˌɪntrəˈmjʊərl/ adj [studies] dispensé dans l'établissement; US Sport interclasse (inv)

intranet /ˈɪntrənet/ n Comput intranet m

intransigence /ɪnˈtrænsɪdʒəns/ n intransigeance f (**about**, **over** sur; **towards** envers)

intransitive /ɪnˈtrænsətɪv/ adj intransitif/-ive

intrauterine device, **IUD** n Med stérilet m

intravenous /ˌɪntrəˈviːnəs/ adj intraveineux/-euse

intravenous: ~ **drip** n perfusion f intraveineuse; ~ **drug user** n usager m de drogues par voie intraveineuse; ~ **injection** n (piqûre f) intraveineuse f

in-tray /ˈɪntreɪ/ n corbeille f arrivée

intrepid /ɪnˈtrepɪd/ adj intrépide

intricacy
Ⓐ /ˈɪntrɪkəsɪ/ n complexité f
Ⓑ **intricacies** npl (of story) subtilités fpl; (of law) méandres mpl

intricate /ˈɪntrɪkət/ adj [mechanism, pattern, plot, task] compliqué; [problem, relationship] complexe

intrigue
Ⓐ /ˈɪntriːɡ, ɪnˈtriːɡ/ n Ȼ (plotting) intrigue f; **political** ~ les intrigues politiques
Ⓑ /ɪnˈtriːɡ/ vtr (fascinate) intriguer [person]; **he's** ~**d to know...** il est curieux de savoir...

intriguing /ɪnˈtriːɡɪŋ/ adj [person, smile] fascinant; [story] curieux/-ieuse, intéressant

intrinsic /ɪnˈtrɪnzɪk, -sɪk/ adj intrinsèque (**to** à)

introduce /ˌɪntrəˈdjuːs, US -duːs/ vtr ① (make known) présenter [person, idea] (**as** comme); **to** ~ **sb to** fig initier qn à [painting, drugs]; **she** ~**d me to Mozart** elle m'a fait connaître Mozart; **introducing Abigail Bond** Cin pour la première fois à l'écran, Abigail Bond; ② (cause to enter) introduire [liquid, object, theme]; **she tried to** ~ **the subject into the conversation** elle a essayé d'amener le sujet dans la conversation; ③ (establish) introduire [law, reform]; introduire [word, product, change] (**in**, **into** dans); ④ (preface) introduire [talk, article] (**with** par); TV, Radio présenter [programme]; ⑤ (present for debate) présenter [bill, proposal]

introduction /ˌɪntrəˈdʌkʃn/ n ① (making known) présentation f; **'our guest needs no** ~' 'il est inutile de présenter notre invité'; **letter of** ~ lettre de recommandation; ② (insertion) introduction f (**into** dans); ③ (establishing of system, reform) introduction f (**into** dans); **this system is a recent** ~ ce système a été introduit récemment; ④ (initiation) (to art, drugs) premier contact m (**to** avec); ⑤ (preface) (to speech, article) introduction f (**to** de); ⑥ (beginner's guide) initiation f; **'An Introduction to French'** 'Initiation au français'; ⑦ Pol, Admin (of bill, proposal) présentation f

introduction agency n club m de rencontres

introductory /ˌɪntrəˈdʌktərɪ/ adj ① [speech, paragraph] préliminaire; [course] d'initiation; ② Comm [offer] de lancement

introspective /ˌɪntrəˈspektɪv/ adj [person] introspectif/-ive; [tendency] à l'introspection

introvert /ˈɪntrəvɜːt/ n introverti/-e m/f

introverted /ˈɪntrəvɜːtɪd/ adj introverti

intrude /ɪnˈtruːd/
Ⓐ vtr imposer [opinions]
Ⓑ vi ① (interfere) **to** ~ **in(to)** s'immiscer dans [affairs]; ② (encroach) **to** ~ **(up)on sb's privacy** être importun; **I**

don't want to ~ **on a family gathering** je ne veux pas m'imposer dans une réunion de famille; **I don't wish to** ~ je ne veux pas vous déranger

intruder /ɪnˈtruːdə(r)/ n (all contexts) intrus/-e m/f

intruder alarm n sonnerie f d'alarme

intrusion /ɪnˈtruːʒn/ n ① (interruption, unwelcome arrival) intrusion f (**into** dans); ② (interference) ingérence f, immixtion f (**into** dans); **it's an** ~ **into my affairs** on se mêle de mes affaires

intrusive /ɪnˈtruːsɪv/ adj [question, cameras] indiscret/-ète; [phone call, presence] importun

intuition /ˌɪntjuːˈɪʃn, US -tuː-/ n intuition f (**about** concernant); **to have an** ~ **that** avoir l'intuition que

intuitive /ɪnˈtjuːɪtɪv, US -tuː-/ adj intuitif/-ive

inundate /ˈɪnʌndeɪt/ vtr gen inonder; fig submerger

inure /ɪˈnjʊə(r)/ vtr endurcir (**to** à)

invade /ɪnˈveɪd/ vtr lit, fig envahir; **to** ~ **sb's privacy** s'immiscer dans la vie privée de qn

invading /ɪnˈveɪdɪŋ/ adj [troops, army] d'invasion; [fans, bacteria] envahisseur/-euse

invalid
Ⓐ /ˈɪnvəliːd, ˈɪnvəlɪd/ n (sick person) malade mf; (disabled person) infirme mf
Ⓑ /ˈɪnvəliːd, ˈɪnvəlɪd/ noun modifier [parent, relative] (sick) malade; (disabled) infirme
Ⓒ /ɪnˈvælɪd/ adj ① (without foundation) [argument, claim] sans fondement; ② (not acceptable) [claim, passport] pas valable; [contract, marriage] nul/nulle
Ⓓ /ˈɪnvəliːd, ˈɪnvəlɪd/ vtr ~**ed out of the army** GB réformé (pour raisons de santé)

invalidate /ɪnˈvælɪdeɪt/ vtr infirmer [judgment, argument]; annuler [claim]; vicier [contract]; rendre [qch] nul et sans effet [will]

invaluable /ɪnˈvæljʊəbl/ adj ① (useful) [assistance, advice, experience] inestimable; [person, machine, service] précieux/-ieuse; ② (priceless) inestimable

invariable /ɪnˈveərɪəbl/ adj invariable

invasion /ɪnˈveɪʒn/ n invasion f; ~ **of (sb's) privacy** atteinte f à la vie privée (de qn)

invasive /ɪnˈveɪsɪv/ adj [plant] envahissant; [cancer] invasif/-ive; [treatment] chirurgical

inveigle /ɪnˈveɪɡl/ vtr péj **to** ~ **sb into doing** convaincre qn de faire (par la ruse)

invent /ɪnˈvent/ vtr inventer

invention /ɪnˈvenʃn/ n invention f

inventive /ɪnˈventɪv/ adj inventif/-ive

inventiveness /ɪnˈventɪvnɪs/ n créativité f, esprit m d'invention

inventor /ɪnˈventə(r)/ n inventeur/-trice m/f

inventory /ˈɪnvəntrɪ, US -tɔːrɪ/ n ① (list) inventaire m; ② US (stock) stock m; ~ **of fixtures** état m des lieux

inverse /ˌɪnˈvɜːs/ n, adj Math, gen inverse (m)

inversion /ɪnˈvɜːʃn, US ɪnˈvɜːrʒn/ n inversion f

invert /ɪnˈvɜːt/ vtr ① (reverse) gen, Mus, Phot renverser [image, values]; inverser [word order]; **it's** ~**ed snobbery** c'est du snobisme à rebours; ② (upend) retourner [object]; **it's** ~**ed** c'est à l'envers

invertebrate /ɪnˈvɜːtɪbreɪt/ n, adj invertébré (m)

inverted commas /ˌɪnvɜːtɪd ˈkɒməz/ npl GB guillemets mpl; **in** ~ entre guillemets

invest /ɪnˈvest/
Ⓐ vtr ① (commit) investir, placer [money]; consacrer [time, energy] (**in** à); ② (bestow) **to** ~ **sb with** investir qn de [right, authority, power]; ③ Pol investir [president]
Ⓑ vi Fin investir; **to** ~ **in shares** placer son argent en valeurs; ② (buy) **to** ~ **in** investir dans [equipment]; **I** ~**ed in a carpet** je me suis acheté un tapis

investigate /ɪnˈvestɪɡeɪt/ vtr ① (inquire into) enquêter sur [crime, case]; faire une enquête sur [person]; vérifier [allegation, story]; ② (study) examiner [question, possibility, report]; étudier [subject, culture]; Comm sonder [market, sector]; ③ (try out) essayer [restaurant, club]; ④ (think) **it's worth investigating whether** il faudrait se renseigner pour savoir si

investigation /ɪnˌvestɪˈɡeɪʃn/ n ① (inquiry) enquête f (**of**, **into** sur); **the crime is still under** ~ on enquête encore sur le crime; **he is under** ~ il fait l'objet d'une enquête; ② Comm, Med (study) étude f (**of** de); **the matter under** ~ la question (actuellement) à l'étude; ③ Jur (of accounts, reports) vérification f

investigative /ɪn'vestɪgətɪv, US -geɪtɪv/ adj [committee, mission, journalist, reporting] d'investigation

investigator /ɪn'vestɪgeɪtə(r)/ n (in police) enquêteur/-trice m/f

investiture /ɪn'vestɪtʃə(r), US -tʃʊər/ n cérémonie f d'investiture

investment /ɪn'vestmənt/ n ① Fin investissement m, placement m; ② (commitment) **a huge emotional** ~ un énorme engagement personnel; ③ Mil investissement m

investment: ~ **analyst** ▸ p. 1181 n analyste mf financier/-ière; ~ **income** n revenu m de portefeuille de titres; ~ **management** n gestion f de portefeuille; ~ **manager** ▸ p. 1181 n gérant/-e m/f de portefeuille; ~ **trust** n société f d'investissement

investor /ɪn'vestə(r)/ n investisseur/-euse m/f (**in** dans); (in shares) actionnaire mf; **big** ~**s** gros actionnaires; **private** ~ petit porteur m

inveterate /ɪn'vetərət/ adj invétéré

invidious /ɪn'vɪdɪəs/ adj [position] délicat; [choice] difficile

invigilate /ɪn'vɪdʒɪleɪt/
Ⓐ vtr surveiller [examination]
Ⓑ vi être de surveillance

invigorate /ɪn'vɪgəreɪt/ vtr revigorer

invincible /ɪn'vɪnsəbl/ adj [person, power] invincible; [will] irréductible

inviolate /ɪn'vaɪələt/ adj (inviolable) [law] inviolable; [group, institution] intouchable; [treaty] inviolé

invisible /ɪn'vɪzəbl/ adj (all contexts) invisible

invisible: ~ **ink** n encre f sympathique; ~ **mending** n stoppage m

invisibly /ɪn'vɪzəblɪ/ adv invisiblement

invitation /ˌɪnvɪ'teɪʃn/ n ① (request, card) invitation f; **an** ~ **to dinner** une invitation à dîner; **thank you for your kind** ~ je vous remercie de votre aimable invitation; **to receive an** ~ **to do** être invité à faire; ② ₵ (act of inviting) invitation f; **'by** ~ **only'** 'entrée sur invitation uniquement'; **at sb's** ~ à or sur l'invitation de qn; ③ Ind (summons) offre f; **an urgent** ~ **to talks** une offre pressante de négociations; ④ Fin **an** ~ **to bid** ou **tender** un appel d'offres; ⑤ fig (encouragement) incitation f; **an open** ~ **to burglars** une incitation manifeste pour les cambrioleurs

invite
Ⓐ ○/'ɪnvaɪt/ n invitation f (**to do** à faire)
Ⓑ /ɪn'vaɪt/ vtr ① inviter [person]; **to** ~ **sb for a drink** inviter qn à prendre un verre; **why don't we** ~ **Tara along?** pourquoi ne pas inviter Tara à venir avec nous?; **to be** ~**d back** (repaying hospitality) être invité en retour; (a second time) être invité de nouveau; **to** ~ **sb out/in** inviter qn à sortir avec soi/à entrer; **to** ~ **sb over** ou **round** (to one's house) inviter qn chez soi; **to** ~ **sb for (an) interview** convoquer qn pour un entretien; ② (ask for) solliciter [comments]; **he** ~**d questions from the audience** il invita l'auditoire à poser des questions; ③ (court) chercher [trouble]; ④ Fin **to** ~ **bids** ou **tenders** faire un appel d'offres

inviting /ɪn'vaɪtɪŋ/ adj [room] accueillant; [smile] engageant; [meal] appétissant; [prospect] alléchant, tentant

invitingly /ɪn'vaɪtɪŋlɪ/ adv [smile] d'un air engageant

in vitro fertilization, IVF n fécondation f in vitro

invoice /'ɪnvɔɪs/
Ⓐ n facture f
Ⓑ vtr envoyer une facture à; **to** ~ **sb for sth** facturer qch à qn; **to be** ~**d** recevoir une facture

invoicing /'ɪnvɔɪsɪŋ/ n facturation f

invoke /ɪn'vəʊk/ vtr invoquer

involuntary /ɪn'vɒləntrɪ, US -terɪ/ adj involontaire; ~ **repatriation** rapatriement m forcé

involve /ɪn'vɒlv/
Ⓐ vtr ① (entail) impliquer, nécessiter [effort, travel]; entraîner [problems]; **there is a lot of work/effort** ~**d** cela implique beaucoup de travail/d'efforts; ② (cause to participate) gen faire participer [person] (**in** à); **to be** ~**d in** (positive) participer à, être engagé dans [business, project]; (negative) être mêlé à [scandal, robbery]; **to be** ~**d in doing** s'occuper de faire; **not to get** ~**d in** ou **with sth** rester à l'écart de qch; **it will** ~ **them in heavy expenditure** ça va les entraîner à de grosses dépenses; ③ (affect) concerner, impliquer [person,

animal, vehicle]; **their safety is** ~**d** leur sécurité est en jeu; ④ (engross) [film, book] faire participer, prendre [person]; **to get** ~**d in** se laisser prendre par, se plonger dans [film, book, work]; ⑤ (get emotionally attached) **to get** ~**d with sb** devenir proche de qn; **you're too** ~**d to make a judgment** tu es trop concerné pour porter un jugement; ⑥ (make commitment) **to get** ~**d** s'engager
Ⓑ v refl **to** ~ **oneself in** ou **with** prendre part à

involved /ɪn'vɒlvd/ adj ① (complicated) [explanation, problem] compliqué; ② (après n) [person, group] (implicated) impliqué; (affected) concerné; ③ (necessary) (après n) [expense, effort, problems] inhérent

involvement /ɪn'vɒlvmənt/ n ① (participation) (in activity) participation f (**in** à); (commitment) (in enterprise, politics) engagement m (**in** dans); ② (connections) (with group) liens mpl; (with person) relations fpl; ③ (relationship) relation f; ④ (engrossment) (in film, book) (vif) intérêt m (**in** pour)

inward /'ɪnwəd/
Ⓐ adj (inner) [satisfaction] personnel/-elle; [relief, calm] intérieur
Ⓑ adv = inwards

inward: ~**-bound** adj [journey, flight, cargo] de retour; [ship] en retour; ~ **investment** n Fin investissements mpl étrangers; ~**-looking** adj [society, person] replié sur soi-même; [policy] nombriliste○

inwardly /'ɪnwədlɪ/ adv gen intérieurement; [know, feel] en son for intérieur

inwards /'ɪnwədz/ adv [fold, open, move, grow] vers l'intérieur; [freight, invoice] à l'arrivée

iodine /'aɪədiːn, US -daɪn/ n (element) iode m; (antiseptic) teinture f d'iode

iota /aɪ'əʊtə/ n ① lit iota m; ② fig **not an** ou **one** ~ **of** pas un grain de [truth etc]; **it hasn't changed one** ~ ça n'a pas changé d'un iota

IOU n (abrév = **I owe you**) reconnaissance f de dette; **an** ~ **for £500** un reçu pour 500 livres sterling

IPA n (abrév = **International Phonetic Alphabet**) API m

IQ n (abrév = **intelligence quotient**) QI m

IRA n (abrév = **Irish Republican Army**) IRA f

Iran /ɪ'rɑːn/ ▸ p. 774 pr n Iran m

Iranian /ɪ'reɪnɪən/ ▸ p. 1032, p. 969
Ⓐ n ① (person) Iranien/-ienne m/f; ② (language) iranien m
Ⓑ adj iranien/-ienne

Iraq /ɪ'rɑːk/ ▸ p. 774 pr n Iraq m

Iraqi /ɪ'rɑːkɪ/ ▸ p. 1032
Ⓐ n (person) Iraquien/-ienne m/f
Ⓑ adj iraquien/-ienne

irate /aɪ'reɪt/ adj furieux/-ieuse (**about** au sujet de)

Ireland /'aɪələnd/ ▸ p. 774 pr n Irlande f; **the Republic of** ~ la République d'Irlande

Irish /'aɪərɪʃ/ ▸ p. 969, p. 1032
Ⓐ n ① (language) irlandais m; ② (people) **the** ~ les Irlandais mpl
Ⓑ adj irlandais

Irish: ~ **Free State** n État m libre d'Irlande; ~**man** n Irlandais m; ~ **Republic** ▸ p. 774 n République f d'Irlande; ~ **sea** ▸ p. 1049 n mer f d'Irlande; ~**woman** n Irlandaise f

irksome /'ɜːksəm/ adj agaçant

iron /'aɪən, US 'aɪərn/
Ⓐ n ① (metal) fer m; **old** ou **scrap** ~ ferraille f; ~ **and steel works** usine f sidérurgique; **a will of** ~ fig une volonté de fer; ② (for clothes) fer m (à repasser); **with a cool** ~ à fer doux; **to run the** ~ **over sth** donner un coup de fer à qch; ③ (golf) fer m; **a six-**~ un fer six; ④ (splint) attelle f
Ⓑ **irons** npl fers mpl; **in** ~**s** aux fers
Ⓒ noun modifier lit [bar, gate] en fer; ~ **sheet** tôle f
Ⓓ adj fig [constitution, grip, will] de fer; [rule] draconien/-ienne
Ⓔ vtr repasser [clothes]
(Idioms) **to have a lot of** ~**s in the fire** avoir beaucoup d'affaires en train; **to strike while the** ~ **is hot** battre le fer pendant qu'il est chaud
(Phrasal verb)
■ **iron out**: ▸ ~ **out [sth]** lit faire partir [qch] au fer [creases]; fig aplanir [problem, difficulty]

Iron Curtain n Pol Hist rideau m de fer; **behind the** ~ au-delà du rideau de fer

iron: ～ **filings** *npl* limaille *f* de fer; ～ **fist**, ～ **hand** *n* fig poigne *f* de fer

ironic(al) /aɪ'rɒnɪk(l)/ *adj* ironique

ironically /aɪ'rɒnɪklɪ/ *adv* ironiquement; ～, **she...** l'ironie, c'est qu'elle...

ironing /'aɪənɪŋ, US 'aɪərn-/ *n* repassage *m*

ironing board *n* planche *f* à repasser

iron lung *n* poumon *m* d'acier

iron: ～**monger** /'aɪənmʌŋɡə(r), US 'aɪərn-/ ▸ p. 1181 *n* quincaillier/-ière *m/f*; ～**monger's (shop)** quincaillerie *f*; ～**-on** *adj* [*label, patch*] à poser au fer à repasser

iron: ～ **ore** *n* minerai *m* de fer; ～ **oxide** *n* oxyde *m* de fer; ～ **rations** *npl* vivres *mpl* or rations *fpl*

irony /'aɪərənɪ/ *n* ironie *f*; **one of life's little ironies** une des ironies du sort

irradiate /ɪ'reɪdɪeɪt/ *vtr* (all contexts) irradier

irradiation /ɪ,reɪdɪ'eɪʃn/ *n* (all contexts) irradiation *f*

irrational /ɪ'ræʃənl/ *adj* [*behaviour*] irrationnel/-elle; [*fear, hostility*] sans fondement; **he's rather** ～ il n'est pas très raisonnable; **she's becoming quite** ～ elle déraisonne

irrationally /ɪ'ræʃənəlɪ/ *adv* [*act*] d'une façon déraisonnable or irrationnelle; [*angry, happy*] sans raison

irreconcilable /ɪ'rekənsaɪləbl, ɪ,rekən'saɪləbl/ *adj* [*opponents*] irréconciliable (**with** avec); [*ideas*] incompatible (**with** avec); [*conflict*] inconciliable

irrecoverable /,ɪrɪ'kʌvərəbl/ *adj* [*object*] irrécupérable; [*loss*] irréparable; Fin [*debt*] irrécouvrable

irredeemable /,ɪrɪ'di:məbl/ *adj* [1] Relig [*sinner*] incorrigible; [2] [*loss*] irrémédiable; [3] Fin [*shares*] irremboursable; [*loan*] non amortissable

irregular /ɪ'reɡjʊlə(r)/
A *n* Mil irrégulier/-ière *m/f*
B *adj* [1] gen, Ling irrégulier/-ière; [2] US Comm [*merchandise*] de second choix

irregularity /ɪ,reɡjʊ'lærətɪ/ *n* irrégularité *f*

irregularly /ɪ'reɡjʊləlɪ/ *adv* irrégulièrement

irrelevance /ɪ'reləvəns/, **irrelevancy** /ɪ'reləvənsɪ/
[1] (of fact, remark, question) manque *m* d'à-propos; ～ **to sth** manque *m* de rapport avec qch; [2] (unimportant thing) **to be an** ～ ne pas avoir d'importance

irrelevant /ɪ'reləvnt/ *adj* [1] (unconnected) [*remark*] hors de propos; [*facts*] hors du sujet; [*question*] sans rapport avec le sujet; **to be** ～ **to sth** n'avoir aucun rapport avec qch; [2] (unimportant) **the money's** ～ ce n'est pas l'argent qui compte

irreparable /ɪ'repərəbl/ *adj* irréparable

irreplaceable /,ɪrɪ'pleɪsəbl/ *adj* irremplaçable

irrepressible /,ɪrɪ'presəbl/ *adj* [*high spirits*] irrépressible; [*sense of humour, enthusiasm*] inextinguible; [*person*] infatigable

irreproachable /,ɪrɪ'prəʊtʃəbl/ *adj* irréprochable

irresistible /,ɪrɪ'zɪstəbl/ *adj* irrésistible

irresolute /ɪ'rezəlu:t/ *adj* irrésolu, indécis

irrespective /,ɪrɪ'spektɪv/: **irrespective of** *prep phr* sans tenir compte de [*age, class*]; sans distinction de [*race*]; **everyone,** ～ **of who they are** tous, sans exception; ～ **of whether it rains** qu'il pleuve ou non

irresponsible /,ɪrɪ'spɒnsəbl/ *adj* irresponsable

irresponsibly /,ɪrɪ'spɒnsəblɪ/ *adv* de façon irresponsable

irretrievable /,ɪrɪ'tri:vəbl/ *adj* [*loss, harm*] irrémédiable, irréparable

irretrievably /,ɪrɪ'tri:vəblɪ/ *adv* irrémédiablement

irreverent /ɪ'revərənt/ *adj* irrévérencieux/-ieuse

irreversible /,ɪrɪ'vɜːsəbl/ *adj* [*process, decision*] irréversible; [*disease*] incurable

irreversibly /,ɪrɪ'vɜːsəblɪ/ *adv* irréversiblement

irrevocable /ɪ'revəkəbl/ *adj* irrévocable

irrigation /,ɪrɪ'ɡeɪʃn/ *n* Agric, Med irrigation *f*

irritability /,ɪrɪtə'bɪlətɪ/ *n* irritabilité *f*

irritable /'ɪrɪtəbl/ *adj* irritable

irritant /'ɪrɪtənt/ *n, adj* irritant (*m*)

irritate /'ɪrɪteɪt/ *vtr* gen, Med irriter

irritating /'ɪrɪteɪtɪŋ/ *adj* gen, Med irritant

is /ɪz/ *3ᵉ pers. du prés de* **be**

ISA /'aɪsə/ *n* GB Fin (*abrév* ▸ **Individual Savings Account**) compte *m* épargne individuel (dont les revenus ne sont pas imposables)

-ish /ɪʃ/ *suffix* [1] ▸ p. 752 **greenish** tirant sur le vert, verdâtre pej; **darkish** plutôt sombre; **earlyish** assez tôt; [2] **he's thirtyish** il a dans les trente ans, il a la trentaine; **at four-ish** vers quatre heures

Islam /'ɪzlɑːm, -læm, -'lɑːm/ *n* (faith) islam *m*; (Muslims) Islam *m*

Islamic /ɪz'læmɪk/ *adj* islamique

island /'aɪlənd/
A *n* [1] île *f*; (small) îlot *m*; ～ **of peace** fig îlot de paix; [2] ▸ **traffic island**
B *noun modifier* (of particular island) de l'île; (of islands generally) des îles

islander /'aɪləndə(r)/ *n* insulaire *mf*, habitant/-e *m/f* d'une île (or de l'île)

island hopping *n* **to go** ～ aller d'île en île

isle /aɪl/ ▸ p. 954 *n* littér île *f*; **Isle of Man** île *f* de Man

ism /'ɪzəm/ *n* péj idéologie *f*

isn't /'ɪznt/ = **is not**

isobar /'aɪsəbɑː(r)/ *n* isobare *f*

isolate /'aɪsəleɪt/ *vtr* (all contexts) isoler (**from** de)

isolation /,aɪsə'leɪʃn/ *n* isolement *m*; **in** ～ dans l'isolement; **splendid** ～ splendide isolement

Isolde /ɪ'zɒldə/ *pr n* Iseult, Iseut

isometrics /,aɪsəʊ'metrɪks/ *npl* exercices *mpl* musculaires isométriques

isosceles /aɪ'sɒsəli:z/ *adj* isocèle

ISP *n*: *abrév* ▸ **Internet service provider**

Israel /'ɪzreɪl/ ▸ p. 774 *pr n* Israël (*never with article*); **in** ～ en Israël

Israeli /ɪz'reɪlɪ/ ▸ p. 1032
A *n* Israélien/-ienne *m/f*
B *adj* israélien/-ienne

issue /'ɪʃuː, 'ɪsjuː/
A *n* [1] (topic) problème *m*, question *f*; **to force the** ～ précipiter la solution d'une question; **to make an** ～ **(out) of** faire une histoire de; **the point at** ～ ce qui est en cause; **her beliefs are not at** ～ ses croyances ne sont pas en question; **I must take** ～ **with you on that** je dois vous signifier mon désaccord sur ce point; [2] (allocation) (of supplies) distribution *f*; [3] (official release) (of stamps, shares) émission *f*; (of book) publication *f*; [4] (journal etc) numéro *m*; **back** ～ vieux numéro *m*; [5] (flowing out) écoulement *m*; [6] (outcome) résultat *m*; [7] (offspring) descendance *f*; **without** ～ sans laisser de descendance
B *vtr* [1] (allocate) distribuer; **to** ～ **sb with sth** fournir qch à qn; **to be** ～**d with** recevoir; [2] (make public) délivrer [*declaration, ultimatum*]; émettre [*order, warning*]; [3] (release officially) émettre [*stamps, shares*]; [4] (publish) publier
C *vi* **to** ～ **from** [*liquid*] s'écouler de; [*gas*] émaner de; [*shouts, laughter*] provenir de

issuer /'ɪʃʊə(r)/ *n* Fin émetteur *m*

it /ɪt/ *pron* ▸ p. 955 [1] (in questions) **who is** ～? qui est-ce?, qui c'est○?; ～**'s me** c'est moi; **where is** ～? (of object) où est-il/elle?; (of place) où est-ce?, où est-ce que c'est?, c'est où○?; **what is** ～? (of object, noise etc) qu'est-ce que c'est?, c'est quoi○?; (what's happening?) qu'est-ce qui se passe?; (what is the matter?) qu'est-ce qu'il y a?; **how was** ～? comment cela s'est-il passé?, ça s'est passé comment○?; [2] Games **you're** ～! c'est toi le chat!

(Idioms) **I didn't have** ～ **in me to refuse** je n'ai pas eu le cœur de refuser; **the worst of** ～ **is that** ce qu'il y a de pire là-dedans c'est que; **that's** ～! (in triumph) voilà!, ça y est!; (in anger) ça suffit!

Islands

■ *In French, some names of islands always have the definite article and some never do.*

Island names with definite article

■ *These behave like the names of countries ▸ p. 774, with different constructions depending on gender and number:*

Corsica	**to Corsica**
= la Corse	= en Corse
in Corsica	**from Corsica**
= en Corse	= de Corse

■ *Note that where the English has the definite article, French normally has as well:*

the Balearics	**to the Balearics**
= les Baléares *fpl*	= aux Baléares
in the Balearics	**from the Balearics**
= aux Baléares	= des Baléares

Islands without definite article

■ *As in English, most island names have no definite article; these work like names of towns ▸ p. 1276:*

Cyprus	**to Cyprus**
= Chypre	= à Chypre
in Cyprus	**from Cyprus**
= à Chypre	= de Chypre

Cyprus sherry
= le sherry de Chypre

■ *English uses* on *with the names of small islands; there is no such distinction in French:*

on St. Helena	**on Naxos**
= à Sainte-Hélène	= à Naxos

■ *As with names of cities and towns, it is safest to avoid explicit genders; use* l'île d... *instead:*

Cuba is beautiful
= l'île de Cuba est belle

Names with or without *île* in them

■ *English and French tend to work the same way in this respect:*

Guernsey	**the island of Guernsey**
= Guernesey	= l'île de Guernesey
the Balearics	**the Balearic Islands**
= les Baléares	= les îles Baléares
the Orkney Isles	
= les îles Orcades	

Exceptions

■ *There are some exceptions to these rules, e.g. Fiji, Samoa, Jamaica. If in doubt, look up island name in the dictionary.*

IT *n: abrév* ▸ **information technology**

Italian /ɪˈtæljən/ ▸ p. 1032, p. 969
A *n* ① (person) Italien/-ienne *m/f*; ② (language) italien *m*
B *adj* italien/-ienne

italic /ɪˈtælɪk/
A **italics** *npl* italique *m*; **in ~s** en italique
B *adj* italique

italicize /ɪˈtælɪsaɪz/ *vtr* mettre [qch] en italique

Italy /ˈɪtəlɪ/ ▸ p. 774 *pr n* Italie *f*

itch /ɪtʃ/
A *n* ① (physical) démangeaison *f*; **to relieve an ~** soulager des démangeaisons; ② ○(hankering) **I had an ~ to travel** l'envie de voyager me démangeait○
B *vtr* US (scratch) gratter
C *vi* ① (physically) avoir des démangeaisons; **my back is ~ing** j'ai le dos qui me démange; **these socks make me** *ou* **my feet ~** ces chaussettes me démangent; ② **to be ~ing for sth/to do sth** mourir○ d'envie de qch/de faire qch

itching powder *n* poil *m* à gratter

itchy○ /ˈɪtʃɪ/ *adj* **I feel ~ all over** ça me gratte partout
(Idiom) **to have ~ feet**○ avoir la bougeotte○

it'd /ˈɪtəd/ = **it had**, **it would**

item /ˈaɪtəm/ *n* ① gen, Comput article *m*; **luxury ~** produit *m* de luxe; **an ~ of furniture** un meuble; **~s of clothing** vêtements *mpl*; ② Admin Pol (on agenda) point *m*; ③ (in newspaper, on news bulletin) article *m* (**about** sur); **news ~** article *m*; **the main ~** Radio, TV le titre principal; ④ Mus morceau *m*; (in show) numéro *m*; ⑤ ○(couple) **to be an ~** être ensemble, sortir ensemble

itemize /ˈaɪtəˌmaɪz/ *vtr* détailler

itinerant /aɪˈtɪnərənt, ɪ-/ *adj* [*life, preacher*] itinérant; [*tribe*] nomade

itinerary /aɪˈtɪnərərɪ, ɪ-, US -rerɪ/ *n* itinéraire *m*

it'll /ˈɪtl/ = **it will**

its /ɪts/

> ⚠ In French determiners agree in number and gender with the noun they qualify. *its* is translated by *son + masculine noun*: *its nose* = son nez; by *sa + feminine noun*: *its tail* = sa queue; BUT by *son + feminine noun beginning with a vowel or mute h*: *its ear* = son oreille; and by *ses + plural noun*: *its ears* = ses oreilles

det son/sa/ses

it's /ɪts/ = **it is**, **it has**

itself /ɪtˈself/

> ⚠ When used as a reflexive pronoun, direct and indirect, *itself* is translated by *se* (*s'* before a vowel or mute h): *the cat hurt itself* = le chat s'est fait mal; *a problem presented itself* = un problème s'est présenté.
> When used for emphasis *itself* is translated by *lui-même* when standing for a masculine noun and *elle-même* when standing for a feminine noun: *the car itself was not damaged* = la voiture elle-même n'était pas endommagée.
> For examples and particular usages see the entry below.
> For uses with prepositions (*by itself etc*) see **3** below.

pron ① (refl) se, s'; ② (emphatic) lui-même/elle-même; **the house ~ was pretty** la maison elle-même était jolie; **in the university ~** dans l'université même *or* dans l'université elle-même; **he was kindness ~** c'était la bonté même *or* personnifiée; ③ (after prepositions) **the heating comes on by ~** le chauffage se met en marche tout seul; **the house stands by ~** la maison est toute seule; **the library is a fine building in ~** la bibliothèque par elle-même est un beau bâtiment; **learning French is not difficult in ~** l'apprentissage du français n'est pas difficile en soi

IUD *n: abrév* ▸ **intrauterine device**

IV *n: abrév* ▸ **intravenous drip**

I've /aɪv/ = **I have**

it

When *it* is used as a subject pronoun to refer to a specific object (or animal) *il* or *elle* is used in French according to the gender of the object referred to:

'where is the book/chair?' 'it's in the kitchen'
= 'où est le livre/la chaise?' 'il/elle est dans la cuisine'

'do you like my skirt?' 'it's lovely'
= 'est-ce que tu aimes ma jupe?' 'elle est très jolie'

However, if the object referred to is named in the same sentence, *it* is translated by *ce* (*c'* before a vowel):

it's a good film
= c'est un bon film

When *it* is used as an object pronoun it is translated by *le* or *la* (*l'* before a vowel) according to the gender of the object referred to:

it's my book/my chair and I want it
= c'est mon livre/ma chaise et je le/la veux

Note that the object pronoun normally comes before the verb in French and that in compound tenses like the perfect and the past perfect, the past participle agrees with it:

I liked his shirt – did you notice it?
= j'ai aimé sa chemise – est-ce que tu l'as remarquée? or l'as-tu remarquée?

In imperatives only, the pronoun comes after the verb:

it's my book – give it to me
= c'est mon livre – donne-le-moi (note the hyphens)

When *it* is used vaguely or impersonally followed by an adjective the translation is *ce* (*c'* before a vowel):

it's difficult	**it's sad**
= c'est difficile	= c'est triste

But when *it* is used impersonally followed by an adjective + verb the translation is *il*:

it's difficult to understand how ...
= il est difficile de comprendre comment ...

If in doubt consult the entry for the adjective in question.

For translations for impersonal verb uses (*it's raining*, *it's snowing*) consult the entry for the verb in question.

it is used in expressions of days of the week (*it's Friday*) and clock time (*it's 5 o'clock*). This dictionary contains usage notes on these and many other topics. For the index to these notes ▸ **p. 1354**. For other impersonal and idiomatic uses see the entry **it**.

When *it* is used after a preposition in English the two words (prep + *it*) are often translated by one word in French. If the preposition would normally be translated by *de* in French (*e.g. of*, *about*, *from* etc.) the prep + *it* = *en*:

I've heard about it
= j'en ai entendu parler

If the preposition would normally be translated by *à* in French (*e.g. to*, *in*, *at* etc.) the prep + *it* = *y*:

they went to it
= ils y sont allés

For translations of *it* following prepositions not normally translated by *de* or *à* (*e.g. above*, *under*, *over* etc.) consult the entry for the preposition.

IVF *n* (*abrév* =**in vitro fertilization**) FIV *f*, fécondation *f* in vitro; **to have ~ (treatment)** recourir à la FIVETE

ivory /'aɪvərɪ/ *n*, *adj* (all contexts) ivoire (*m*)

ivory: **Ivory Coast** ▸ **p. 774** *pr n* Côte *f* d'Ivoire; **~ tower** *n* fig tour *f* d'ivoire

ivy /'aɪvɪ/ *n* lierre *m*

Ivy League *adj* US ≈ bon chic bon genre; **the ~ colleges** *les huit universités prestigieuses de la côte est américaine*

> ⓘ The **Ivy League** Ce sont les huit universités les plus anciennes et les plus renommées de la côte est des États-Unis (*Harvard*, *Yale*, *Columbia*, *Cornell*, *Dartmouth*, *Brown*, *Princeton*, *Pennsylvania*). Elles doivent ce nom collectif au lierre qui pousse (ou est censé pousser) sur les murs des bâtiments anciens. Le coût des études y est très élevé, mais il est possible d'obtenir une bourse.

Jj

j, J /dʒeɪ/ n j, J m

jab /dʒæb/
A n **1** GB Med (vaccination) vaccin m; (injection) piqûre f; **2** (poke) petit coup m; (in boxing) direct m
B vtr **to ~ sth into sth** planter qch dans qch
C vi **to ~ at** taper sur; (in boxing) envoyer des directs à

jabber /'dʒæbə(r)/
A vtr baragouiner
B vi (chatter) jacasser; (in foreign language) baragouiner

jack /dʒæk/ n **1** (for car etc) cric m; **2** (in cards) valet m (**of** de); **3** (in bowls) cochonnet m; **4** Elec jack m
⚬ (Idioms) **every man ~ of them** jusqu'au dernier; **to be (a) ~ of all trades** être un/-e touche-à-tout inv; **to have an I'm all right Jack attitude** ne s'occuper que de sa petite personne

(Phrasal verbs)
■ **jack in**° GB: ▶ ~ **in [sth]**, ~ **[sth] in** plaquer°, laisser tomber [job]
■ **jack up**: ▶ ~ **up [sth]**, ~ **[sth] up** **1** soulever [qch] avec un cric [vehicle]; **2** °fig faire grimper [price]; **3** °US chauffer° [crowd]

jackal /'dʒækɔːl, US -kl/ n chacal m

jack: ~**ass** n lit, fig âne m; ~**boot** n botte f militaire; ~**daw** n choucas m

jacket /'dʒækɪt/ ▶ p. 1191
A n **1** (garment) veste f; (man's) veste f, veston m; **2** (also **dust ~**) jaquette f; **3** US (of record) pochette f; **4** Tech enveloppe f isolante
B noun modifier **1** [pocket] de veste; ~ **potato** Culin pomme f de terre en robe des champs (au four); **2** [design] de couverture

jack: ~**hammer** n marteau-piqueur m; ~**-in-the-box** n diable m à ressort

jackknife /'dʒæknaɪf/
A n (knife) couteau m pliant
B vi [lorry] se mettre en portefeuille

jackpot /'dʒækpɒt/ n gros lot m
⚬ (Idiom) **to hit the ~** (win prize) gagner le gros lot; (have great success) faire un tabac

jackrabbit n lièvre m (du nord-ouest américain)

jade /dʒeɪd/ n **1** (stone) jade m; **2** ▶ p. 752 (also ~ **green**) vert m jade

jaded /'dʒeɪdɪd/ adj **1** (exhausted) fatigué; **2** (bored) [person, palate] blasé

jagged /'dʒægɪd/ adj [rock, cliff] déchiqueté; [knife, saw] dentelé

jail /dʒeɪl/
A n prison f; **to be in/go to ~** être/aller en prison; **to go to ~ for 10 years** faire 10 ans de prison; **sentenced to 14 days in ~** condamné à 14 jours de réclusion criminelle
B vtr emprisonner; Admin, Jur incarcérer

jail: ~**bird**° n taulard/-e° m/f; (habitual) récidiviste mf; ~**break** n évasion f; ~ **sentence** n peine f de prison

jam /dʒæm/
A n **1** Culin confiture f; **2** (congestion) (of people) foule f; (of traffic) embouteillage m; **3** (of machine, system, department) blocage m; **4** °(difficult situation) pétrin° m; **to help sb out of a ~** tirer qn du pétrin°; **5** (also ~ **session**) Mus bœuf° m, jam-session f
B vtr (p prés etc **-mm-**) **1** (stuff, pile) **to ~ things into** entasser des choses dans [small space, suitcase, box]; **to ~ one's foot**

on the brake freiner à bloc; **2** (fix firmly, wedge) coincer; **the key's ~med in the lock** la clé s'est coincée dans la serrure; **3** (also ~ **up**) (crowd) gen encombrer; **cars ~med (up) the roads** les routes étaient embouteillées; **4** (also ~ **up**) (block) [dirt, malfunction, person] enrayer [mechanism]; coincer [lock, door, window, system]; **5** Radio, Telecom brouiller [frequency, transmission]
C vi (p prés etc **-mm-**) **1** (become stuck) [mechanism, switch] s'enrayer; [lock, door, window] se coincer, se bloquer; **2** Mus improviser

(Phrasal verb)
■ **jam in**: ▶ ~ **in** [people] s'entasser; ▶ ~ **[sth/sb] in** **1** (trap, wedge) coincer; **2** (pack in) entasser

Jamaica /dʒə'meɪkə/ ▶ p. 774 pr n la Jamaïque

jamb /dʒæm/ n chambranle m

James /dʒeɪmz/ pr n Jacques

jam-full /ˌdʒæm'fʊl/ adj bondé; **to be ~ of** être bourré de

jamjar, jampot n pot m à confitures

jammy /'dʒæmɪ/ adj **1** °GB [person] veinard°; [job] de planqué; **2** lit [fingers, face] plein de confiture

jam-packed /ˌdʒæm'pækt/ adj bondé; **to be ~ with sth** être bourré de qch

Jan abrév écrite = **January**

jangle /'dʒæŋgl/
A n (of bells, pots) tintement m; (of keys) cliquetis m; (of alarm) bruit m strident
B vtr faire tinter [bells]; faire cliqueter [keys]
C vi (make noise) [bells] tinter; [bangles] cliqueter

jangling /'dʒæŋglɪŋ/
A n = **jangle A**
B adj [noise] métallique; [alarm] strident

janitor /'dʒænɪtə(r)/ n US, Scot gardien m

January /'dʒænjʊərɪ, US -jʊerɪ/ ▶ p. 1020 n janvier m

Japan /dʒə'pæn/ ▶ p. 774 pr n Japon m

Japanese /ˌdʒæpə'niːz/ ▶ p. 1032, p. 969
A n **1** (person) Japonais/-e m/f; **2** (language) japonais m
B adj japonais

jar /dʒɑː(r)/
A n **1** gen pot m; (large) bocal m; (earthenware) jarre f; **2** (jolt) lit, fig secousse f, choc m
B vtr (p prés etc **-rr-**) **1** lit, fig ébranler, secouer; **to ~ one's shoulder** se cogner l'épaule; **2** US **to ~ sb into action** pousser qn à agir
C vi (p prés etc **-rr-**) **1** rendre un son discordant; **to ~ on sb ou sb's nerves** agacer qn; **2** (rattle) [windows] trembler; **3** (clash) [colours] jurer; [note] sonner faux; [opinions] ne pas s'accorder

jargon /'dʒɑːgən/ n jargon m

jasmine /'dʒæsmɪn, US 'dʒæzmən/ n jasmin m

jaundice /'dʒɔːndɪs/ ▶ p. 933 n jaunisse f

jaundiced /'dʒɔːndɪst/ adj (cynical) négatif/-ive

jaunt /dʒɔːnt/ n balade° f

jaunty /'dʒɔːntɪ/ adj [appearance] guilleret/-ette

javelin /'dʒævlɪn/ ▶ p. 881 n javelot m

jaw /dʒɔː/ ▶ p. 698 n mâchoire f
⚬ (Idiom) **his ~ dropped** les bras lui en sont tombés

jaw: ~**bone** n mâchoire f; ~**line** n menton m

jay /dʒeɪ/ n geai m

jaywalk /'dʒeɪwɔːk/ vi traverser en dehors des passages pour piétons

jazz /dʒæz/ n Mus jazz m

(Idiom) **and all that** ~○ et tout le bataclan○

(Phrasal verb)
■ **jazz up**○: ▶ ~ **up [sth]**, ~ **[sth] up** ① rajeunir [dress]; égayer [room]; ranimer [party]; ② faire une version jazz de [tune]

jazz: ~ **band** n jazz-band m; ~ **dance** n modern-jazz m; ~**man** n musicien m de jazz

jazzy /'dʒæzɪ/ adj ① (bright) [colour] voyant; [pattern, dress, wallpaper] bariolé; ② [music] jazzy inv

jealous /'dʒeləs/ adj jaloux/-ouse (**of** de); **to feel** ~ être jaloux

jealousy /'dʒeləsɪ/ n jalousie f

jean /dʒiːn/
A noun modifier (made of denim) en jean
B jeans npl jean m; **a pair of** ~s un jean

jeer /dʒɪə(r)/
A n (from crowd) huée f; (from person) raillerie f
B vtr huer
C vi se moquer; **to** ~ **at** se moquer de [idea]; [crowd] huer [person]; [individual] railler [person]

jeering /'dʒɪərɪŋ/
A n ₵ huées fpl
B adj railleur/-euse

jell /dʒel/ vi =**gel B**

jellied /'dʒelɪd/ adj en aspic; ~ **eels** anguilles fpl en gelée

Jell-o ® /'dʒeləʊ/ n US gelée f de fruits

jelly /'dʒelɪ/ n ① Culin (savoury) gelée f; (sweet) gelée f de fruits; ② (preserve) gelée f; ③ US (jam) confiture f

(Idiom) **to shake like a** ~ trembler comme une feuille

jelly: ~ **baby** n bonbon m; ~ **bean** n bonbon m fourré à la gelée; ~**fish** n (pl ~ ou ~es) méduse f; ~ **shoe** n sandale f en plastique, méduse® f

jeopardize /'dʒepədaɪz/ vtr compromettre [career, chance, plans]; mettre [qch] en péril [lives, troops]

jeopardy /'dʒepədɪ/ n **in** ~ en péril, menacé

jerk /dʒɜːk/
A n ① (jolt) gen secousse f; (twitch) (of muscle, limb) tressaillement m, (petit) mouvement m brusque; **with a** ~ **of his head** d'un brusque mouvement de la tête; **to start off with a** ~ [vehicle] démarrer avec un soubresaut; ② ○péj (obnoxious man) salaud❶ m; (stupid) crétin○ m
B vtr tirer brusquement [object]
C vi ① (jolt) **to** ~ **to a halt** [vehicle] s'arrêter avec un soubresaut; ② (twitch) [person, muscle] tressaillir

jerkily /'dʒɜːkɪlɪ/ adv [move] par saccades; [speak] d'une voix saccadée

jerkin /'dʒɜːkɪn/ n gilet m

jerky /'dʒɜːkɪ/
A n US Culin bœuf m séché
B adj [movement] saccadé; [style, phrase] haché

jerry-built /'dʒerɪbɪlt/ adj péj construit à la va-vite

jersey /'dʒɜːzɪ/
A n ① (sweater) pull-over m; **football** ~ maillot m de football; ② (fabric) jersey m
B noun modifier [garment] en jersey

Jerusalem /dʒə'ruːsələm/ ▸ p. 1276 pr n Jérusalem

jest /dʒest/
A n plaisanterie f; **in** ~ pour plaisanter
B vi plaisanter

(Idiom) **many a true word is spoken in** ~ Prov plus d'une vérité est dite en plaisantant

jester /'dʒestə(r)/ n bouffon m

Jesuit /'dʒezjʊɪt, US 'dʒeʒəwət/ n, adj jésuite (m)

Jesus /'dʒiːzəs/ pr n Jésus; ~ **Christ** Jésus-Christ

jet /dʒet/
A n ① (also ~ **plane**) jet m, avion m à réaction; ② (of water, flame) jet m; ③ (on hob) brûleur m; (of engine) gicleur m; ④ (stone) jais m
B vi (p prés etc -**tt-**) **to** ~ **off to** s'envoler pour

jet: ~**black** adj de jais inv; ~ **engine** n moteur m à réaction, réacteur m; ~ **fighter** n chasseur m à réaction; ~**foil** n hydroglisseur m; ~**lag** n décalage m horaire; ~**-powered**, **jet-propelled** adj à réaction; ~ **propulsion** n propulsion f par réaction

jet setter n **to be a** ~ faire partie du jet-set

jet-skiing ▸ p. 881 n jet-ski m

jettison /'dʒetɪsn/ vtr ① (from ship) jeter [qch] par-dessus bord; (from plane) larguer; ② fig rejeter [idea]

jetty /'dʒetɪ/ n (of stone) jetée f; (of wood) appontement m

Jew /dʒuː/ n juif/juive m/f

jewel /'dʒuːəl/ n ① (gem) pierre f précieuse; (piece of jewellery) bijou m; (in watch) rubis m; ② fig (person) perle f; (town, object) joyau m

jewelled GB, **jeweled** US /'dʒuːəld/ adj orné de pierres précieuses

jeweller GB, **jeweler** US /'dʒuːələ(r)/ ▸ p. 1181 n (person) bijoutier/-ière m/f; ~**'s** (**shop**) bijouterie f

jewellery GB, **jewelry** US /'dʒuːəlrɪ/ n gen bijoux mpl; (in shop, workshop) bijouterie f; **a piece of** ~ un bijou

Jewess /'dʒuːes/ n juive f

Jewish /'dʒuːɪʃ/ adj juif/juive

Jewry /'dʒʊərɪ/ n communauté f juive

Jew's harp n Mus guimbarde f

jib /dʒɪb/
A n ① Naut foc m; ② (of crane) flèche f
B vi (p prés etc -**bb-**) [person] rechigner (**at** à); **to** ~ **at** [horse] refuser [fence]

jibe /dʒaɪb/
A n moquerie f
B vi ① (mock) **to** ~ **at sb/sth** se moquer de qn/qch; ② ○US (match) coller○ (**with** avec)

jiff(y)○ /'dʒɪfɪ/ n seconde f, instant m; **in a** ~ en moins de deux○

Jiffy bag ® n enveloppe f matelassée

jig /dʒɪg/
A n Mus gigue f
B vtr, vi =**jiggle**

(Idiom) **the** ~ **is up** US c'est cuit○

jiggle /'dʒɪgl/
A vtr agiter
B vi (also ~ **about**, ~ **around**) gigoter; (impatiently) se trémousser

jigsaw /'dʒɪgsɔː/ n ① (also ~ **puzzle**) puzzle m; ② Tech scie f sauteuse

jihad /dʒɪ'hɑːd/ n Relig djihad m

jilt /dʒɪlt/ vtr abandonner, plaquer○

Jim Crow○ /ˌdʒɪm 'krəʊ/ n US ~ **policies** politique f ségrégationniste

jingle /'dʒɪŋgl/
A n ① (of bells) tintement m; (of keys) cliquetis m; ② (verse) ritournelle f; (for advert) refrain m publicitaire, sonal m
B vtr faire tinter
C vi [bells] tintinnabuler; [keys, coins] cliqueter

jingoist /'dʒɪŋgəʊɪst/ n, adj chauvin/-e (m/f) Pol

jinx /dʒɪŋks/
A n ① (curse) sort m; **to put a** ~ **on** jeter un sort à; **there's a** ~ **on me** j'ai la poisse○; ② (unlucky person, object) porte-malheur m inv
B vtr porter la poisse○ à [person]

jitters /'dʒɪtəz/ npl **to have the** ~ [person, stock market] être nerveux/-euse; [actor] avoir le trac

jittery /'dʒɪtərɪ/ adj nerveux/-euse

jive /dʒaɪv/
A n ① Mus swing m; ② ○US (talk) salades○ fpl
B vi (dance) danser le swing

Jnr adj: abrév écrite =**junior**

job /dʒɒb/
A n ① (employment) emploi m; (post) poste m; **to get a** ~ trouver un emploi; **a teaching** ~ un poste d'enseignant; **what's her** ~? qu'est-ce qu'elle fait (comme travail)?; **to have a** ~ **as a secretary** être employé comme secrétaire; **out of a** ~ sans emploi; ② (rôle) fonction f; **it's my** ~ **to do** c'est à moi de faire; ③ (duty) travail m; **she's only doing her** ~ elle fait son travail; ④ (task) travail m; **to find a** ~ **for sb to do** trouver du travail pour qn; ⑤ (assignment) tâche f; **the** ~ **of building the theatre went to X** la construction du théâtre a été confiée à X; ⑥ (result of work) **a poor** ~ du mauvais travail; **to make a good** ~ **of sth** faire du bon travail avec qch; ⑦ (difficult activity) **a real** ~, **quite a** ~ toute une affaire○ (**to do, doing** de faire); ⑧ (crime, theft) coup○ m; ⑨ Comput job○ m
B noun modifier [advert, offer] d'emploi; [analysis] de poste;

[*pages*] des emplois; [*creation*] d'emplois

(Idioms) **(and a) good ~ too!** GB et c'est une bonne chose!; **it's a good ~ that** GB heureusement que; **~s for the boys** des planques○ pour les copains; **just the ~** tout à fait ce qu'il faut; **on the ~** (working) au travail; **to learn on the ~** apprendre sur le tas○; **to fall asleep on the ~** s'endormir à la tâche; **to do the ~** fig faire l'affaire; **to give sth up as a bad ~** GB laisser tomber qch; **to make the best of a bad ~** GB faire contre mauvaise fortune bon cœur

Job /dʒəʊb/ *pr n* Bible Job

(Idioms) **to be a ~'s comforter** être totalement décourageant; **to have the patience of ~** avoir une patience d'ange

job action *n* US mouvement *m* de revendication

jobber /'dʒɒbə(r)/ *n* US grossiste *mf*

jobbing /'dʒɒbɪŋ/ *adj* [*gardener*] à la tâche

job: **Job Centre** *n* GB bureau *m* des services nationaux de l'emploi; **~ description** *n* description *f* de poste; **~-hunting** *n* chasse *f* à l'emploi

jobless /'dʒɒblɪs/
A *n* the **~** les sans-emploi *mpl*
B *noun modifier* [*total*] des sans-emploi; [*rate, figures*] du chômage

job: **~ lot** *n* (at auction) lot *m*; fig ramassis *m*; **~ satisfaction** *n* satisfaction *f* dans le travail; **~ security** *n* sécurité *f* de l'emploi; **~-share** *adj* [*scheme*] de partage de poste; [*position*] partagé; **~ sharing** *n* partage *m* de poste

jockey /'dʒɒkɪ/
A *n* jockey *m*
B *vi* **to ~ for position** lit lutter pour la première place; fig jouer des coudes

jockey shorts *n* US slip *m* (d'homme)

jockstrap○ /'dʒɒkstræp/ *n* suspensoir *m*

jocular /'dʒɒkjʊlə(r)/ *adj* [*remark, mood*] badin; [*person*] enjoué

jodhpurs /'dʒɒdpəz/ *npl* Sport jodhpurs *mpl*

Joe Bloggs GB, **Joe Blow** US *n* Monsieur Tout-le-Monde

Joe Public○ /dʒəʊ'pʌblɪk/ *n* GB le grand public *m*, Monsieur Tout-le-Monde

jog /dʒɒg/
A *n* **1** (with elbow) coup *m* de coude; **2** **at a ~** au petit trot○; **3** Sport **to go for a ~** aller faire un jogging; **4** US (in road) coude *m*
B *vtr* (*p prés etc* **-gg-**) heurter; (with elbow) donner un coup de coude à; **to ~ sb's memory** rafraîchir la mémoire de qn
C *vi* (*p prés etc* **-gg-**) Sport faire du jogging *or* footing

(Phrasal verb) ■ **jog along** fig [*person, business*] se maintenir

jogger /'dʒɒgə(r)/ *n* joggeur/-euse *m/f*

jogging /'dʒɒgɪŋ/ ▸ p. 881 jogging *m*, footing *m*

John /dʒɒn/ *pr n* Jean

John: **~ Bull** *n* (Englishman) l'Anglais *m* moyen; **~ Doe** *n* US l'homme *m* de la rue; **~ Q Public**○ *n* US l'homme *m* de la rue

join /dʒɔɪn/
A *n* raccord *m*
B *vtr* **1** (meet up with) rejoindre [*person*]; **may I ~ you?** (sit down) puis-je me joindre à vous?; (accompany) puis-je venir avec vous?; **2** (go to the end of) se mettre dans [*queue*]; se mettre au bout de [*row*]; ajouter son nom à [*list*]; **3** (become member of) devenir membre de [*organization, team, church*]; adhérer à [*club*]; s'inscrire à [*library*]; s'engager dans [*army*]; **to ~ a union** se syndiquer; **~ the club!** fig tu n'es pas le seul/la seule!; **4** (become part of) se joindre à [*crowd, rush*]; **5** (become employee) entrer dans [*firm*]; **to ~ Ford** entrer chez Ford; **6** (participate in) ▸ **join in**; **7** (associate with) gen se joindre à [*person*] (**to do, in doing** pour faire); (professionally) s'associer à [*colleague*] (**to do, in doing** pour faire); **to ~ forces with** (merge) s'allier à; (co-operate) collaborer avec; **8** (board) monter dans [*train*]; monter à bord de [*ship*]; **9** (attach) réunir, joindre [*ends, pieces*]; assembler [*parts*]; **10** (link) relier [*points, towns*] (**to** à); **to ~ hands** lit se prendre par la main; fig collaborer; **11** (merge with) [*road*] rejoindre [*motorway*]; [*river*] se jeter dans [*sea*]
C *vi* **1** (become member) (of party, club) adhérer; (of group, class) s'inscrire; **2** (meet) [*pieces*] se joindre; [*wires*] se raccorder; [*roads*] se rejoindre

(Phrasal verbs) ■ **join in**: ▸ **~ in** participer; ▸ **~ in [sth]** participer à [*talks, game*]; prendre part à [*strike, demonstration, bidding*]; **to ~ in the fun** se joindre à la fête

■ **join on**: ▸ **~ [sth] on**, **~ on [sth]** (fasten) fixer; (add) ajouter

■ **join up**: ▸ **~ up 1** Mil (enlist) s'engager; **2** (meet up) [*people*] se retrouver; [*roads, tracks*] se rejoindre; ▸ **~ up [sth]**, **~ [sth] up** relier [*characters, dots*]; assembler [*pieces*]; **~ed-up writing** écriture *f* liée

joined-up government *n* GB Pol initiative *f* de coordination gouvernementale (*pour simplifier la vie des personnes et des entreprises*)

joiner /'dʒɔɪnə(r)/ ▸ p. 1181 *n* Constr menuisier/-ière *m/f*

joint /dʒɔɪnt/
A *n* **1** Anat articulation *f*; **to be out of ~** [*shoulder, knee*] être déboîté; **to have stiff** *ou* **aching ~s** avoir des douleurs articulaires; **2** Tech (in carpentry) assemblage *m*; (in metalwork) joint *m*; (of pipes, tubes) raccord *m*; **3** Culin rôti *m*; **4** ○pej (place) gen endroit *m*; (nightclub, office, workplace) boîte○ *f*; (café) boui-boui○ *m*; **5** ○(cannabis cigarette) joint○ *m*
B *adj* [*action*] collectif/-ive; [*programme, session*] mixte; [*measures, procedure*] commun; [*winner*] ex aequo *inv*; [*talks*] multilatéral

(Idiom) **to have one's nose put out of ~** être dépité

joint: **~ account** *n* compte *m* joint; **~ agreement** *n* convention *f* collective; **~ committee** *n* comité *m* mixte

jointed /'dʒɔɪntɪd/ *adj* **1** Culin [*chicken*] découpé; **2** (doll, puppet) articulé; **3** (rod, pole) démontable

joint: **~ effort** *n* collaboration *f*; **~ honours** *npl* GB Univ licence *f* combinée

jointly /'dʒɔɪntlɪ/ *adv* [*manage, publish, own*] conjointement; **to be ~ owned by X et Y** être la copropriété de X et Y

joint: **~ management** *n* cogestion *f*; **~ owner** *n* copropriétaire *mf*; **~-stock company** *n* société *f* par actions

joint venture *n* **1** Econ, Fin coentreprise *f*; **2** gen projet *m* en commun

joist /dʒɔɪst/ *n* solive *f*

jojoba /həʊ'həʊbə/ *n* jojoba *m*

joke /dʒəʊk/
A *n* **1** (amusing story) plaisanterie *f*, blague○ *f* (**about** sur); **to have a ~ about sth** plaisanter sur qch; **2** (laughing matter) plaisanterie *f*; **the ~ is on you** la plaisanterie se retourne contre toi; **this is getting beyond a ~** la plaisanterie a assez duré; **can't you take a ~?** tu ne supportes pas la plaisanterie?; **it's no ~ doing** ce n'est pas facile de faire; **3** (prank) farce *f*; **to play a ~ on sb** faire une farce à qn; **4** (object of ridicule) (person) guignol *m* pej; (event, situation) farce *f*
B *vi* plaisanter, blaguer○; **you must be joking!** tu veux rire!; **it's no joking matter** ça n'a rien de drôle

joker /'dʒəʊkə(r)/ *n* **1** (who tells jokes) blagueur/-euse○ *m/f*; (who plays tricks) farceur/-euse *m/f*; **2** ○pej (person) type○ *m*; **3** (in cards) joker *m*

(Idiom) **the ~ in the pack** l'exception à la règle

joking /'dʒəʊkɪŋ/ *n* ₵ plaisanterie *f*, blague○ *f*

jokingly /'dʒəʊkɪŋlɪ/ *adv* [*say*] en plaisantant

jollity /'dʒɒlətɪ/ *n* gaieté *f*; (of person) bonne humeur *f*

jolly /'dʒɒlɪ/
A *adj* (cheerful) [*person*] enjoué; [*tune*] joyeux/-euse; **what a ~ time we had!** qu'est-ce qu'on s'est bien amusé!
B *adv* GB (emphatic) drôlement
C *vtr* **to ~ sb along** amadouer qn

Jolly Roger *n* pavillon *m* noir

jolt /dʒəʊlt/
A *n* **1** (jerk) secousse *f*; **2** (shock) choc *m*
B *vtr* lit, fig secouer
C *vi* [*vehicle*] cahoter

Jordan /'dʒɔːdn/ ▸ p. 774, p. 1146 *pr n* **1** (country) Jordanie *f*; **2** (river) Jourdain *m*

joss stick /'dʒɒstɪk/ *n* bâtonnet *m* d'encens

jostle /'dʒɒsl/
A *vtr* bousculer [*person*]
B *vi* se bousculer (**for** pour; **to do** pour faire)

jot /dʒɒt/
A *n* **he doesn't care a ~** il s'en fiche○ complètement; **it**

doesn't matter a ～ cela n'a pas la moindre importance
B *vtr* (*p prés etc* **-tt-**) = **jot down**
(Phrasal verb)
■ **jot down**: ▸ ～ **[sth] down**, ～ **down [sth]** noter [*ideas, names*]

jotter /'dʒɒtə(r)/ *n* GB (pad) bloc-notes *m inv*
jottings /'dʒɒtɪŋz/ *npl* notes *fpl*
journal /'dʒɜːnl/ *n* ① (diary) journal *m*; ② (periodical) revue *f*; (newspaper) journal *m*
journalism /'dʒɜːnəlɪzəm/ *n* journalisme *m*
journalist /'dʒɜːnəlɪst/ *n* journaliste *mf*
journey /'dʒɜːnɪ/
A *n* ① (trip) (long) voyage *m*; (short or habitual) trajet *m*; **bus** ～ trajet en bus; **to go on a** ～ partir en voyage; **to break a** ～ faire étape; ② (distance covered) trajet *m*
B *vi* voyager; **to** ～ **on** continuer son voyage
jovial /'dʒəʊvɪəl/ *adj* [*person, mood*] jovial; [*remark*] enjoué; [*company*] joyeux/-euse
jowl /dʒaʊl/ *n* (jaw) mâchoire *f*; (fleshy fold) bajoue *f*
(Idiom) **cheek by** ～ **with sb** coude à coude avec qn
joy /dʒɔɪ/ *n* ① (delight) joie *f* (**at** devant); ② (pleasure) plaisir *m*; **the** ～ **of doing** le plaisir de faire; ③ ᴼGB (success) **I got no** ～ **out of the bank manager** mon entretien avec le directeur de banque n'a rien donné
(Idiom) **to be full of the** ～**s of spring** être en pleine forme
joyful /'dʒɔɪfl/ *adj* joyeux/-euse
joyless /'dʒɔɪlɪs/ *adj* [*marriage*] malheureux/-euse; [*occasion*] triste; [*production*] terne; [*existence*] morne
joyrider /'dʒɔɪraɪdə(r)/ *n* jeune chauffard *m* en voiture volée
joyriding /'dʒɔɪraɪdɪŋ/ *n* rodéo *m* à la voiture volée
joystick /'dʒɔɪstɪk/ *n* Aviat manche *m* à balai; (video games) manette *f*

JP *n* GB *abrév* ▸ **Justice of the Peace**
Jr *adj*: *abrév écrite* = **junior**
jubilant /'dʒuːbɪlənt/ *adj* [*person*] exultant; [*crowd*] en liesse; [*expression, mood*] réjoui
jubilation /ˌdʒuːbɪ'leɪʃn/ *n* jubilation *f* (**about, at, over** devant)
jubilee /'dʒuːbɪlɪ/ *n* jubilé *m*
Judaic /dʒuː'deɪɪk/ *adj* judaïque
Judaism /'dʒuːdeɪɪzəm, US -dɪɪzəm/ *n* judaïsme *m*
judder /'dʒʌdə(r)/ GB
A *n* secousse *f*
B *vi* être agité de violentes secousses
judge /dʒʌdʒ/
A *n* ① ▸ p. 869 Jur juge *m*; ② (adjudicator) (at competition) membre *m* du jury; Sport juge *m*; ③ fig **to be a good** ～ **of character** savoir juger les gens; **to be no** ～ **of** ne pas s'y connaître en [*art, wine*]
B *vtr* ① gen, Jur juger [*person*]; ② (adjudicate) faire partie du jury de [*show, competition*]; ③ (estimate) (currently) estimer [*distance, age*]; (in the future) prévoir [*outcome, reaction*]; ④ (consider) juger, estimer
C *vi* juger; **judging by** *ou* **from...** à en juger par, d'après...
(Idiom) **to be as sober as a** ～ (not drunk) ne pas être ivre du tout; (solemn) être sérieux comme un pape
judgment, **judgement** /'dʒʌdʒmənt/ *n* ① gen, Jur jugement *m*; **to sit in** ～ **on** *ou* **over** juger [*person, situation*]; ② (opinion) avis *m*, opinion *f*; **to do sth against one's better** ～ faire qch en sachant que l'on fait une erreur; ③ (discernment) jugement *m*; **use your own** ～ (in assessing) c'est à vous de juger; (in acting) faites comme bon vous semblera; ④ (punishment) punition *f*
judgmental, **judgemental** /ˌdʒʌdʒ'mentl/ *adj* **don't be so** ～! ne juge pas tant les autres!
judicial /dʒuː'dɪʃl/ *adj* ① [*inquiry, process*] judiciaire; [*decision*] jurisprudentiel/-ielle; ② (wise) [*mind*] pondéré; ③ (impartial) [*silence*] réfléchi
judiciary /dʒuː'dɪʃɪərɪ, US -ʃɪerɪ/
A *n* Jur ① (system of courts) système *m* judiciaire; ② (judges) magistrature *f*; ③ (authority) pouvoir *m* judiciaire
B *noun modifier* [*system, reforms*] judiciaire
judicious /dʒuː'dɪʃəs/ *adj* judicieux/-ieuse
judo /'dʒuːdəʊ/ ▸ p. 881 *n* judo *m*
jug /dʒʌɡ/
A *n* ① GB (glass) carafe *f*; (earthenware) pichet *m*; (pot-bellied)

cruche *f*; (for cream, milk, water) pot *m*; ② US (earthenware) cruche *f*
B *vtr* (*p prés etc* **-gg-**) Culin cuire [qch] à l'étuvée
jugful /'dʒʌɡfʊl/ *n* ① GB carafe *f*; ② US cruche *f*
juggernaut /'dʒʌɡənɔːt/ *n* ① GB (truck) poids *m* lourd; ② (irresistible force) poids *m* écrasant
juggle /'dʒʌɡl/
A *vtr* jongler avec
B *vi* jongler (**with** avec)
juggler /'dʒʌɡlə(r)/ *n* jongleur/-euse *m/f*
jugular /'dʒʌɡjʊlə(r)/ *n, adj* jugulaire (*f*)
(Idiom) **to go (straight) for the** ～ frapper au point sensible
juice /dʒuːs/ *n* ① Culin jus *m*; ② Bot suc *m*
juicy /'dʒuːsɪ/ *adj* ① Culin juteux/-euse; ② ᴼ(racy) [*story*] croustillant
jukebox /'dʒuːkbɒks/ *n* juke-box *m*
Jul *abrév écrite* = **July**
julep /'dʒuːlɪp/ *n* (*also* **mint** ～) boisson *f* à la menthe
July /dʒuː'laɪ/ ▸ p. 1020 *n* juillet *m*
jumble /'dʒʌmbl/
A *n* ① (of papers, objects) tas *m*; (of ideas) fouillis *m*; (of words) fatras *m*; ② GB (items for sale) bric-à-brac *m*, vieux objets *mpl*
B *vtr* brouiller [*ideas*]; mélanger [*words, letters*]
(Phrasal verb)
■ **jumble up**: ▸ ～ **[sth] up**, ～ **up [sth]** mélanger [*letters, shapes*]
jumble sale *n* GB vente *f* de charité
jumbo /'dʒʌmbəʊ/
A *n* ① (elephant) lang enfantin éléphant *m*; ② = **jumbo jet**
B *noun modifier* (*also* ～**-sized**) [*packet, size*] géant
jumbo jet *n* gros-porteur *m*
jump /dʒʌmp/
A *n* ① (leap) saut *m*, bond *m*; **to be one** ～ **ahead** fig avoir une longueur d'avance (**of sb** sur qn); ② (for horse) obstacle *m*; ③ (sudden increase) (in price, wages etc) bond *m* (**in** dans); **she's made the** ～ **from deputy to director** elle est passée d'un bond du poste d'adjointe à celle de directrice
B *vtr* ① (leap over) sauter [*obstacle, ditch*]; ② (anticipate) **to** ～ **the lights** [*motorist*] passer au feu rouge; **to** ～ **the queue** passer devant tout le monde; ③ (escape) **to** ～ **ship** [*crewman*] ne pas rejoindre son bâtiment; ④ (miss) [*stylus*] sauter [*groove*]; [*disease*] sauter [*generation*]; ⑤ ᴼ(attack) sauter sur [*person*]
C *vi* ① (leap) sauter; **to** ～ **across** *ou* **over sth** franchir qch d'un bond; **to** ～ **up and down** [*gymnast*] sautiller; [*child*] sauter en l'air; fig (in anger) trépigner de colère; ② (start in surprise) [*person*] sursauter; ③ (rise) [*prices, rate*] monter en flèche; ④ (move) **the film** ～**s from 1800 to 1920** le film passe d'un seul coup de 1800 à 1920; ⑤ (welcome) **to** ～ **at** sauter sur [*opportunity*]; accepter [qch] avec enthousiasme [*offer*]
(Idiom) ～ **to it!** et que ça saute ᴼ!
(Phrasal verbs)
■ **jump about**, **jump around** sauter
■ **jump back** [*person*] faire un bond en arrière; [*lever, spring*] reprendre sa place initiale
■ **jump down** [*person*] sauter (**from** de)
■ **jump on**: ▸ ～ **on [sth]** (mount) sauter dans [*bus, train*]; sauter sur [*bicycle, horse*]; ～ **on!** montel; ▸ ～ **on [sb]** lit, fig sauter sur qn
■ **jump out** [*person*] sauter; **to** ～ **out in front of sb** surgir devant qn
■ **jump up** [*person*] se lever d'un bond
jumped-up /'dʒʌmptʌp/ *adj* péj [*clerk, waiter*] prétentieux/-ieuse
jumper /'dʒʌmpə(r)/ ▸ p. 1191 *n* ① GB (sweater) pull *m*, pull-over *m*; ② US (pinafore) robe *f* chasuble; ③ Tech barre *f* à mine
jumper cables *npl* US Aut câbles *mpl* de démarrage
jump: ～**-jet** *n* avion *m* à décollage vertical; ～ **leads** *npl* câbles *mpl* de démarrage; ～ **rope** *n* US corde *f* à sauter; ～**-start** *vtr* démarrer [qch] avec des câbles [*car*]; ～ **suit** *n* combinaison *f*
jumpy ᴼ /'dʒʌmpɪ/ *adj* [*person*] nerveux/-euse; [*market*] instable
Jun *abrév écrite* = **June**

junction /'dʒʌŋkʃn/ n **1** (of two roads) carrefour m; (on motorway) échangeur m; **2** Rail (of railway lines) nœud m ferroviaire; (station) gare f de jonction; **3** Tech (point m de) raccordement m; **4** fig sout fusion f

June /dʒuːn/ ▸ p. 1020 n juin m

Jungian /'jʊŋɪən/ n, adj jungien/-ienne (m/f)

jungle /'dʒʌŋgl/ n lit, fig jungle f

junior /'dʒuːnɪə(r)/
A n **1** (younger person) cadet/-ette m/f; **2** (low-ranking worker) subalterne mf; **3** GB Sch élève mf du primaire; **4** US Univ ≈ étudiant/-e mf de premier cycle; (in high school) ≈ élève mf de première
B adj **1** (low-ranking) [colleague, worker] (inferior) subalterne; (trainee) débutant; [post, rank, position] subalterne; **he's very ~** il a très peu d'expérience; **2** (young) [person] jeune; [fashion, activity] pour les jeunes; **3** Sport [race, team] des cadets; [player, high-jumper] jeune; **4** (the younger) (also **Junior**) **Bob Mortimer ~** Bob Mortimer fils or junior

junior: **~ college** n US premier cycle m universitaire; **Junior Common Room** n GB Univ (room) salle f des étudiants; (student body) (+ v sg ou pl) étudiants mpl; **~ doctor** n médecin m des hôpitaux; **~ high school** n US ≈ collège m; **~ manager** n jeune cadre m; **~ minister** n secrétaire m d'État; **~ miss** n US (size) fillettes fpl; **~ school** n GB école f (primaire)

juniper /'dʒuːnɪpə(r)/ n genièvre m

junk /dʒʌŋk/ n **1** ᵒpéj (poor quality) (furniture, merchandise) camelote f; **clear your ~ off the table!** dégage ton bazarᵒ de la table!; **how can you read that ~?** comment peux-tu lire ces bêtises?; **2** (second-hand) bric-à-brac m; **3** (boat) jonque f

junk bond n obligation f à haut rendement et à risque élevé

junk food n **he only eats ~** il se nourrit mal; **obesity is largely due to ~** l'obésité est un grande partie le résultat de la malbouffe

junkieᵒ /'dʒʌŋkɪ/ n drogué/-e m/f

junk: **~ mail** n ₵ prospectus mpl; **~ shop** n boutique f de bric-à-brac; **~ yard** n (for scrap) dépotoir m; (for old cars) cimetière f de voitures

junta /'dʒʌntə/ n junte f

jurisdiction /ˌdʒʊərɪs'dɪkʃn/ n **1** gen, Admin compétence f (over sur); **2** Jur juridiction f (over sur); **3** US (court) juridiction f

jurisprudence /ˌdʒʊərɪs'pruːdns/ n **1** (philosophy) philosophie f du droit; **2** (precedents) jurisprudence f

jurist /'dʒʊərɪst/ ▸ p. 1181 n juriste mf

juror /'dʒʊərə(r)/ n juré m

jury /'dʒʊərɪ/ n gen, Jur jury m; **'members of the ~'** Jur 'mesdames et messieurs les jurés'

jury: **~ box** n banc m des jurés; **~ duty** n US = **jury service**

jury service n GB **to do ~** faire partie d'un jury

just¹ /dʒʌst/
A adv **1** (very recently) **to have ~ done** venir (juste) de faire; **2** (immediately) juste; **~ before** juste avant; **it's ~ after 10 am** il est 10 heures passées de quelques minutes; **3** (slightly) (with quantities) un peu; (indicating location or position) juste; **~ over/under 20 kg** un peu plus/moins de 20 kg; **~ after the station** juste après la gare; **4** (only, merely) juste; **~ a cup of tea** juste une tasse de thé; **~ for fun** juste pour rire; **~ two days ago** il y a juste deux jours; **~ last week** pas plus tard que la semaine dernière; **he's ~ a child** ce n'est qu'un enfant; **not ~ men** pas seulement les hommes; **5** (purposely) exprès; **he did it ~ to annoy us** il l'a fait exprès pour nous embêter; **6** (barely) tout juste; **~ on time** tout juste à l'heure; **he's ~ 20** il a tout juste 20 ans; **I ~ caught the train** j'ai eu le train de justesse; **7** (simply) tout simplement; **~ tell the truth** dis la vérité, tout simplement; **she ~ won't listen** elle ne veut tout simplement pas écouter; **'~ a moment'** 'un instant'; **8** (exactly, precisely) exactement; **that's ~ what I suggested** c'est exactement ce que j'ai suggéré; **it's ~ what you were expecting** c'est bien à ce à quoi tu t'attendais; **~ how do you hope to persuade him?** comment espères-tu le persuader au juste?; **it's ~ right** c'est parfait; **he likes everything to be ~ so** il aime que les choses soient parfaitement en ordre; **she looks ~ like her father** elle ressemble énormément à son père; **it's ~ like him/you to forget** c'est bien de lui/toi d'oublier; **9** (possibly, conceivably) **it might ou could ~ be true** il se peut que ce soit vrai; **10** (at this or that very moment) **to be ~ doing** être en train de faire; **to be ~ about to do** être sur le point de faire; **he was ~ leaving** il partait; **11** (positively, totally) vraiment; **that was ~ ridiculous** c'était vraiment ridicule; **12** (easily) **I can ~ imagine her as president** je n'ai aucun mal à l'imaginer présidente; **I can ~ smell the pineforests** je sens déjà l'odeur des pins; **13** (with imperatives) donc; **~ keep quiet!** tais-toi donc!; **~ look at the time!** regarde donc l'heure qu'il est!; **~ think, you could have been hurt!** mais tu te rends compte? tu aurais pu être blessé!; **14** (in requests) **if I could ~ interrupt you** si je peux me permettre de vous interrompre; **15** (for emphasis in responses) **'that film was dreadful'—'wasn't it ~!'** 'ce film était absolument nul!'—'ah, ça oui!'; **16** (equally) **~ as big/well as...** aussi grand/bien que...
B just about adv phr presque; **~ about cooked/finished** presque cuit/fini; **~ about everything** à peu près tout; **I can ~ about see it** je peux tout juste le voir; **I've had ~ about enough!** j'en ai marreᵒ!; **it's ~ about the most boring film I've seen** c'est sans doute le film le plus ennuyeux que j'aie vu
C just now adv phr (at the moment) en ce moment; (a short time ago) **I saw him ~ now** je viens juste de le voir
D just as conj phr juste au moment où

(Idioms) **~ as well!** tant mieux!; **I'd ~ as soon you didn't mention it** j'aimerais autant que tu le gardes pour toi; **take your raincoat ~ in case it rains** prends ton imperméable au cas où il pleuvrait

just² /dʒʌst/ adj **1** (fair) [person, society, decision, cause, comment, war] juste; [action, complaint, demand] justifié; [anger, claim, criticism, suspicion] légitime; **it's his ~ reward** il l'a bien mérité; **as is only ~** à juste titre; **without ~ cause** sans raison valable; **2** (exact) [account, calculation] juste, exact; **3** Jur [claim] fondé; [title, request] valable

justice /'dʒʌstɪs/ n **1** (fairness) justice f; **to do sb ~, to do ~ to sb** rendre justice à qn; **the portrait doesn't do her ~** le portrait ne l'avantage pas; **I couldn't do ~ to it** (refusing food) je ne pourrais pas y faire honneur; **2** (the law) justice f; **to bring sb to ~** traduire qn en justice; **3** (judge) GB juge m; US juge m de la Cour Suprême

justice: **Justice Department** n US ministère m de la justice; **Justice of the Peace**, **JP** n juge m de paix

justifiable /'dʒʌstɪfaɪəbl/ adj (that is justified) légitime; (that can be justified) justifiable

justifiably /'dʒʌstɪfaɪəblɪ/ adv à juste titre

justification /ˌdʒʌstɪfɪ'keɪʃn/ n **1** (reason) raison f; **to have some ~ for doing** avoir des raisons de faire; **in ~ of sth** en justification à qch; **with some ~** non sans raison; **2** (of text) justification f; Comput (moving of data) cadrage m

justified /'dʒʌstɪfaɪd/ adj **1** gen justifié; **to be ~ in doing** avoir raison de faire; **to feel ~ in doing** se sentir en droit de faire; **2** [margin] justifié; **3** Comput [text, data] cadré

justify /'dʒʌstɪfaɪ/ vtr **1** gen justifier; **2** justifier [margins]; **3** Comput cadrer [text, data]

justly /'dʒʌstlɪ/ adv **1** (equitably) avec justice; **2** (justifiably) à juste titre

justness /'dʒʌstnɪs/ n **1** (aptness) justesse f; **2** (reasonableness) (of claim, request) caractère m justifié

jut /dʒʌt/ vi (p prés etc **-tt-**) (also **~ out**) [cape, promontory] s'avancer en saillie (**into** dans); [balcony] faire saillie (**over** sur)

jute /dʒuːt/ n jute m

juvenile /'dʒuːvənaɪl/
A n **1** sout (young person) jeune mf; Jur mineur/-e m/f; **2** Bot, Zool jeune mf
B adj **1** pej (childish) puéril; **2** Bot, Zool juvénile

juvenile: **~ crime** n criminalité f juvénile; **~ delinquency** n délinquance f juvénile; **~ delinquent** n jeune délinquant/-e m/f; **~ offender** n Jur délinquant/-e m/f mineur/-e

juxtaposition /ˌdʒʌkstəpə'zɪʃn/ n juxtaposition f

k, K /keɪ/ n [1] (letter) k, K *m*; [2] **K** *abrév* = **kilo** ; [3] **K** Comput (*abrév* = **kilobyte**) K *m*; [4] **K** (*abrév* = **thousand**) mille; **he earns £50 K** il gagne 50 000 livres sterling

Kabul /'kɑːbl/ ▸ p. 1276 *pr n* Kaboul

kaftan /'kæftæn/ *n* caftan *m*

kale /keɪl/ *n* (*also* **curly** ∼) chou *m* frisé

kaleidoscope /kə'laɪdəskəʊp/ *n* lit, fig kaléidoscope *m*

kangaroo /ˌkæŋgə'ruː/ *n* kangourou *m*

kangaroo court *n* péj tribunal *m* irrégulier

kaolin /'keɪəlɪn/ *n* kaolin *m*

kapok /'keɪpɒk/ *n* kapok *m*

kaput○ /kæ'pʊt/ *adj* kaput○ *inv*

karaoke /ˌkærɪ'əʊkeɪ, -kɪ/ *n* karaoké *m*

karat /'kærət/ *n* US ▸ **carat**

karate /kə'rɑːtɪ/ ▸ p. 881 *n* karaté *m*; ∼ **chop** coup de karaté

kart /kɑːt/ *n* kart *m*

Kashmir /kæʃ'mɪə/ *pr n* Cachemire *m*

Kashmiri /kæʃ'mɪərɪ/ ▸ p. 1032, p. 969 *n* [1] (person) Cachemirien/-ienne *m/f*; [2] (language) cachemirien *m*

kayak /'kaɪæk/ *n* kayak *m*

kazoo /kə'zuː/ *n* mirliton *m*

KB *n* Comput (*abrév* = **kilobyte**) Ko *m*

kebab /kɪ'bæb/ *n* (*also* **shish** ∼) chiche-kebab *m*

kedgeree /'kedʒərɪː, ˌkedʒə'riː/ *n* GB pilaf *m* de poisson

keel /kiːl/ *n* quille *f*; **my finances are back on an even** ∼ fig mes finances sont revenues à la normale

(Phrasal verb)
■ **keel over** [*boat*] chavirer; [*person*] s'écrouler; [*tree*] s'abattre

keen /kiːn/ *adj* [1] (eager) [*admirer*] fervent; [*candidate*] motivé; **to be** ∼ **on** tenir à [*plan, project*]; être chaud○ pour [*idea*]; **to be** ∼ **on doing** *ou* **to do** tenir à faire; **to be** ∼ **for sb to do** *ou* **that sb should do** tenir à ce que qn fasse; **to look** ∼ avoir l'air tenté *or* partant○; [2] (enthusiastic) [*artist, sportsplayer, supporter*] enthousiaste; [*student*] assidu; **to be** ∼ **on** être passionné de [*activity*]; avoir une passion pour [*animals*]; **he's** ∼ **on my sister**○ il en pince○ pour ma sœur; **mad** ∼○ GB fana○; [3] (intense) [*appetite, desire, interest*] vif/vive; [*admiration, sense of loss*] intense; [4] (acute) [*eye, intelligence*] vif/vive; [*sight*] perçant; [*hearing, sense of smell*] fin; **to have a** ∼ **eye for sth** avoir l'œil pour qch; [5] (sharp) [*blade*] acéré; [*wit*] vif/vive; [*wind*] pénétrant; [*air*] vif/vive; [6] (competitive) [*price*] défiant toute concurrence; [*competition*] intense; [*demand*] fort; [*debate*] animé

keenly /'kiːnlɪ/ *adv* [*interested*] vivement; [*awaited*] ardemment; [*aware*] parfaitement; [*feel, contest, debate*] vivement

keenness /'kiːnnɪs/ *n* (enthusiasm) enthousiasme *m*; (of senses) acuité *f*

keep /kiːp/
A *n* [1] (maintenance) pension *f*; **to pay for one's** ∼ payer une pension; **to earn one's** ∼ gagner de quoi vivre; [2] Archit donjon *m*

B *vtr* (*prét, pp* **kept**) [1] (cause to remain) **to** ∼ **sb indoors** [*person*] garder qn à l'intérieur; [*illness*] retenir qn à l'intérieur; **to** ∼ **sth/sb clean** garder qch/qn propre; **to** ∼ **sth warm** garder qch au chaud; **to** ∼ **sb warm** protéger qn du froid; **to be kept clean/locked** rester propre/fermé (à clé); **to** ∼ **sb talking/waiting** retenir/faire attendre qn; **I won't** ∼ **you to your promise** tu n'es pas obligé de tenir ta promesse; **to** ∼ **an engine running** laisser un moteur en marche; [2] (detain) retenir; **I won't** ∼ **you a minute** je n'en ai pas pour longtemps; [3] (retain) garder; [4] (have and look after) tenir [*shop*]; avoir [*dog*]; élever [*chickens*]; [5] (sustain) **to** ∼ **sth going** entretenir qch [*conversation, fire, tradition*]; **I'll make you a sandwich to** ∼ **you going** je te ferai un sandwich pour que tu tiennes le coup; **have you got enough work to** ∼ **you going?** avez-vous assez de travail pour vous occuper?; [6] (store) mettre, ranger; **I** ∼ **a spare key** j'ai un double de la clé; [7] (have in stock) vendre, avoir; [8] (support financially) faire vivre, entretenir [*family*]; avoir [*servant*]; [9] (maintain by writing in) tenir [*accounts, diary*]; [10] (conceal) **to** ∼ **sth from sb** taire *or* cacher qch à qn; [11] (prevent) **to** ∼ **sb from doing** empêcher qn de faire; [12] (observe) tenir [*promise*]; garder [*secret*]; se rendre à [*appointment*]; célébrer [*occasion*]; observer [*commandments*]; [13] Mus **to** ∼ **time** *ou* **the beat** battre la mesure; [14] (maintain) entretenir [*car, house*]

C *vi* (*prét, pp* **kept**) [1] (continue) **to** ∼ **doing** continuer à *or* de faire, ne pas arrêter de faire; **to** ∼ **going** continuer; ∼ **at it!** persévérez!; ∼ **straight on** continuez tout droit; '∼ **left**' 'tenez votre gauche'; [2] (remain) **to** ∼ **indoors** rester à l'intérieur; **to** ∼ **out of the rain** se protéger de la pluie; **to** ∼ **warm** se protéger du froid; **to** ∼ **calm** rester calme; **to** ∼ **silent** garder le silence; [3] (stay in good condition) [*food*] se conserver, se garder; [4] (wait) [*news, business*] attendre; [5] (in health) **'how are you** ∼**ing?'** 'comment allez-vous?'; **she's** ∼**ing well** elle va bien

D *v refl* **to** ∼ **oneself** subvenir à ses propres besoins; **to** ∼ **oneself warm** se protéger du froid; **to** ∼ **oneself healthy** rester en forme; **to** ∼ **oneself to oneself** ne pas être sociable

E **for keeps** *adv phr* pour de bon, pour toujours

(Idiom) **to** ∼ **in with sb** rester en bons termes avec qn

(Phrasal verbs)
■ **keep at**: ▸ ∼ **at [sb]** harceler [*person*]; ▸ ∼ **at it** persévérer

■ **keep away**: ▸ ∼ **away** ne pas s'approcher (**from** de); ▸ ∼ **[sth/sb] away** empêcher [qch/qn] de s'approcher; **to** ∼ **sb away from** empêcher qn de s'approcher de [*person, fire*]; tenir qn éloigné de [*family*]

■ **keep back**: ▸ ∼ **back** ne pas s'approcher (**from** de); ▸ ∼ **[sth/sb] back**, ∼ **back [sth]** [1] (prevent from advancing) empêcher [qn] de s'approcher [*crowd*] (**from** de); faire redoubler [*student*]; [*dam*] retenir [*water*]; [2] (retain) garder; [3] (conceal) cacher (**from** à)

■ **keep down**: ▸ ∼ **down** rester allongé; ∼ **down!** bougez pas!; ▸ ∼ **[sth] down**, ∼ **down [sth]** [1] (cause to remain at a low level) limiter [*number, speed, inflation*]; limiter l'augmentation de [*prices, unemployment*]; maîtriser [*inflation*]; ∼ **your voice down!** baisse la voix!; ∼ **the noise down!** faites moins de bruit!; [2] (retain in stomach) **he can't** ∼ **anything down** il vomit tout ce qu'il avale; ▸ ∼ **[sb] down** opprimer [*people*]

■ **keep in**: ▸ ∼ **in** [*car, cyclist*] GB tenir sa gauche; (elsewhere) tenir sa droite; ▸ ∼ **[sb/sth] in** [1] (cause to remain inside) empêcher [qn/qch] de sortir [*person, animal*]; garder [*contact lenses*]; **they're** ∼**ing her in** (in hospital) ils la gardent; [2] (restrain) rentrer [*stomach*]; réprimer [*emotions*]; [3] Sch garder [qn] en retenue [*pupil*]

■ **keep off**: ∼ **off!** n'avancez pas!; ▸ ∼ **off [sth]** [1] (stay away from) ne pas marcher sur; **'Please** ∼ **off the grass'** 'Défense de marcher sur la pelouse'; [2] (refrain from) éviter [*alcohol*]; s'abstenir de parler de [*subject*]; ▸ ∼ **[sth] off**, ∼ **off [sth]** (prevent from touching) éloigner [*insects*]; **to** ∼ **the rain off** protéger contre la pluie

■ **keep on**: ▸ ∼ **on doing** continuer à faire; **to** ∼ **on** about sth ne pas arrêter de parler de qch; **to ~ on at sb** harceler qn (**to do** pour qu'il fasse); ▸ **~ [sb/sth] on** garder

■ **keep out**: ▸ **~ out of [sth]** ⓵ (not enter) ne pas entrer dans [*house*]; '**~ out!**' 'défense d'entrer'; ⓶ (avoid being exposed to) rester à l'abri de [*sun, rain, danger*]; ⓷ (avoid getting involved in) ne pas se mêler de [*argument*]; **to ~ out of sb's way, to ~ out of the way of sb** (not hinder) ne pas encombrer qn; (avoid seeing) éviter qn; **try to ~ out of trouble!** essaie de bien te conduire!; ▸ **~ [sb/sth] out, ~ out [sb/sth]** ne pas laisser entrer [*person, animal*]; **to ~ the rain out** empêcher la pluie d'entrer; **to ~ sb out of sth** (not involve in) ne pas vouloir mêler qn à qch; (not allow to enter) ne pas laisser entrer qn dans qch

■ **keep to**: ▸ **~ to [sth]** (stick to) lit ne pas s'écarter de [*road, path*]; respecter, s'en tenir à [*timetable, facts*]; respecter [*law, rules*]; '**~ to the left**' 'tenez votre gauche'; ▸ **~ [sth] to** (restrict) limiter [qch] à [*number*]; **to ~ sth to oneself** garder qch pour soi

■ **keep under**: ▸ **~ [sb] under** ⓵ (dominate) assujettir, soumettre; ⓶ (cause to remain unconscious) maintenir [qn] inconscient

■ **keep up**: ▸ **~ up** ⓵ (progress at same speed) [*car, runner, person*] suivre; [*competitors*] rester à la hauteur; ⓶ (continue) [*price*] se maintenir; **if the rain ~s up I'm not going** s'il continue à pleuvoir je n'y vais pas; ▸ **~ [sth] up, ~ up [sth]** ⓵ (cause to remain in position) tenir [*trousers*]; ⓶ (continue) continuer [*attack, studies*]; entretenir [*correspondence, friendship*]; maintenir [*membership, tradition*]; garder [*pace*]; **to ~ up the pressure** continuer à faire pression (**for** pour obtenir; **on** sur); **to ~ up one's strength/spirits** garder ses forces/le moral; ▸ **~ [sb] up** [*noise, illness*] empêcher [qn] de dormir

■ **keep up with**: ▸ **~ up with [sb/sth]** ⓵ (progress at same speed as) aller aussi vite que [*person*]; suivre [*class*]; se maintenir à la hauteur de [*competitors*]; [*wages*] suivre [*inflation*]; faire face à [*demand*]; ⓶ (be informed about) suivre [*fashion, developments*]; ⓷ (remain in contact with) garder le contact avec [*friends*]

keeper /'ki:pə(r)/ *n* ⓵ (in zoo) gardien/-ienne *m/f*; ⓶ (in football) gardien/-ienne *m/f* (de but); ⓷ (curator) conservateur/-trice *m/f*; ⓸ (guard) gardien/-ienne *m/f*

keep fit /ˌki:p 'fɪt/ *n* gymnastique *f* d'entretien

keeping /'ki:pɪŋ/ *n* ⓵ (custody) **in sb's ~, in the ~ of sb** à la garde de qn; **to put sb/sth in sb's ~** confier qn/qch à qn; ⓶ (conformity) **in ~ with** conforme à [*law, tradition*]; **to be in ~ with** correspondre à [*image, character*] s'harmoniser avec [*surroundings*]; **to be out of ~ with** ne pas correspondre à [*character, image*]; ne pas convenir à [*occasion*]

keepsake /'ki:pseɪk/ *n* souvenir *m*

keg /keg/ *n* (for liquid) fût *m*; (for gunpowder) baril *m*

kelp /kelp/ *n* laminaire *f*

kelvin /'kelvɪn/ *n* degré *m* Kelvin

kennel /'kenl/ *n* ⓵ GB (for dog) niche *f*; (for several dogs) chenil *m*; ⓶ (GB **kennels** + *v sg*) (establishment) chenil *m*

Kenya /'kenjə/ ▸ p. 774 *pr n* Kenya *m*; **in ~** au Kenya

kept /kept/
A *prét, pp* ▸ **keep**
B *adj* [*man, woman*] entretenu

kerb /kɜ:b/ *n* GB bord *m* du trottoir; **to draw up at the ~** se ranger le long du trottoir; **to pull away from the ~** s'éloigner du trottoir

kernel /'kɜ:nl/ *n* ⓵ (of nut, fruitstone) amande *f*; (whole seed) grain *m*; fig **a ~ of truth** un fond de vérité

kerosene, kerosine /'kerəsi:n/ *n* ⓵ US, Austral (paraffin) pétrole *m* (lampant); ⓶ (aircraft fuel) kérosène *m*

kestrel /'kestrəl/ *n* (faucon *m*) crécerelle *f*

ketchup /'ketʃəp/ GB *n* ketchup *m*

kettle /'ketl/ *n* bouilloire *f*; **to put the ~ on** mettre l'eau à chauffer; **the ~'s boiling** l'eau bout

(Idiom) **a different ~ of fish** une tout autre affaire

kettledrum /'ketldrʌm/ ▸ p. 1028 *n* timbale *f*

key /ki:/
A *n* ⓵ (locking device) clé *f*; **a front-door ~** une clé de maison; **a set** *ou* **bunch of ~s** un jeu de clés; **under lock and ~** sous clé; ⓶ (for clock) clé *f* (de pendule), remontoir *m*; ⓷ Tech clé *f*; **radiator ~** clavette *f* à radiateur; ⓸ (on computer, piano, phone) touche *f*; (on oboe, flute) clé *f*; ⓹ fig (vital clue)

clé *f*, secret *m* (**to** de); **to hold the ~ to the mystery** renfermer la clé du mystère; **exercise is the ~ to health** l'exercice est le secret de la santé; ⓺ (explanatory list) (on map) légende *f*; (to abbreviations, symbols) liste *f*; (for code) clé *f*; ⓻ (answers) (to test, riddle) solutions *fpl*; Sch corrigé *m*; ⓼ Mus ton *m*, tonalité *f*; **in a major ~** en majeur; **to sing in/off ~** chanter juste/faux; ⓽ Geog caye *n*
B *noun modifier* [*industry, job, document, figure, role*] clé *inv* (*after n*); [*difference, point*] capital
C *vtr* ⓵ (type) saisir; ⓶ (adapt) adapter (**to** à)
(Phrasal verb)

■ **key in**: ▸ **~ [sth] in, ~ in [sth]** saisir [*data*]

keyboard /'ki:bɔ:d/ ▸ p. 1028
A *n* clavier *m*
B **keyboards** *npl* Mus synthétiseur *m*
C *vtr* saisir

keyboarder /'ki:bɔ:də(r)/ *n* opérateur/-trice *m/f* de saisie

keyboarding /'ki:bɔ:dɪŋ/ *n* saisie *f*

keyboard: **~ operator** *n* = keyboarder; **~s player** *n* joueur/-euse *m/f* de synthétiseur; **~ shortcut** *n* raccourci *m* clavier

key: **~ card** *n* carte *f* magnétique; **~ combination** *n* Comput combinaison *f* de touches

keyed-up /ˌki:d'ʌp/ *adj* (excited) excité; (tense) tendu

keyhole /'ki:həʊl/ *n* trou *m* de serrure

keyhole journalism *n* reportages *mpl* à sensation

keying /'ki:ɪŋ/ *n* saisie *f*

key money *n* (for business) pas-de-porte *m inv*; (for apartment) reprise *f*

keynote /'ki:nəʊt/ *n* ⓵ Mus tonique *f*; ⓶ (main theme) thème *m* principal

keynote: **~ speaker** *n* intervenant/-e *m/f* principal/-e; **~ speech** *n* discours *m* programme

key: **~-pad** *n* Comput pavé *m* numérique; Telecom clavier *m* numérique; **~-ring** *n* porte-clés *m inv*; **~ signature** *n* armature *f*; **~stroke** *n* Comput frappe *f*; **~word** *n* mot *m* clé

kg *n* (*abrév* = **kilogram**) kg *m*

khaki /'kɑ:kɪ/
A *n* kaki *m*; **in ~** en kaki
B *adj* kaki *inv*

kibbutz /kɪ'bʊts/ *n* (*pl* **~es** *ou* **~im**) kibboutz *m*

kibosh○ /'kaɪbɒʃ/ *n*:
(Idiom) **to put the ~ on sth** mettre fin à qch

kick /kɪk/
A *n* ⓵ (of person, horse) coup *m* de pied; (of donkey, cow, goat) coup *m* de sabot; (of swimmer) battement *m* de pieds; (of footballer) tir *m*; **to give sb/the door a ~** donner un coup de pied à qn/dans la porte; **to aim** *ou* **take a ~ at sb/sth** [*person*] lancer un coup de pied à qn/dans qch; ⓶ (thrill) **to get a ~ from doing** prendre plaisir à faire; ⓷ (of firearm) recul *m*; ⓸ ○(strength, zest) dynamisme *m*; **this punch has quite a ~ (to it)** ce punch est assez costaud○
B *vtr* gen (once) [*person*] donner un coup de pied à [*person*]; donner un coup de pied dans [*table, door, ball, tin can*]; [*horse*] botter; [*donkey, cow, goat*] donner un coup de sabot à [*person*]; (repeatedly) donner des coups de pied à [*person*]; donner des coups de pieds dans [*object*]; **to ~ sb on the leg** [*person, horse*] donner à qn un coup *ou* des coups de pied à la jambe; [*donkey, cow*] donner à qn un coup de sabot dans la jambe; **to ~ sth over a wall** envoyer qch par-dessus un mur d'un coup de pied; **to ~ sth away** éloigner qch d'un coup de pied; **to ~ a hole in sth** défoncer qch d'un coup de pied; **to ~ one's legs (in the air)** [*baby*] pédaler; **to ~ a goal** marquer un but
C *vi* ⓵ gen [*person*] (once) donner un coup de pied; (repeatedly) donner des coups de pied; [*swimmer*] faire des battements de pieds; [*dancer*] lancer la jambe; [*cow*] ruer; [*horse*] botter; ⓶ (recoil) [*gun*] reculer
(Idioms) **to ~ sb when they're down** frapper un homme à terre; **to ~ the habit** gen décrocher○, arrêter; (of smoking) arrêter de fumer; **I could have ~ed myself** je me serais donné des claques○; **to be alive and ~ing** être bien vivant; **to ~ over the traces** ruer dans les brancards○
(Phrasal verbs)

■ **kick around, kick about**: ▸ **~ around**○ [*objects, clothes*] traîner○; **he's been ~ing around Europe for a year**○ il se balade○ en Europe depuis un an; ▸ **~ [sth]**

around *ou* **about** ⬚1⬚ lit donner des coups de pied dans, s'amuser avec [*ball*, *object*]; ⬚2⬚ ᴼdiscuter de, explorer [*idea*]

■ **kick against**: ▸ **~ against [sth]** résister à [*idea*]; lutter contre [*system*]

■ **kick down**: ▸ **~ [sth] down**, **~ down [sth]** enfoncer [qch] d'un coup de pied *or* à coups de pied [*door*]; [*horse*] renverser [*fence*]

■ **kick in**: **~ [sth] in**, **~ in [sth]** enfoncer [qch] d'un coup de pied *or* à coups de pied [*door*]

■ **kick off**: ▸ **~ off** ⬚1⬚ Sport donner le coup d'envoi; ⬚2⬚ ᴼ(start) commencer; ▸ **~ off [sth]**, **~ [sth] off** ⬚1⬚ enlever [*shoes*]; ⬚2⬚ ᴼ(start) commencer; ▸ **~ [sb] off** ᴼ exclure [qn] de [*committee*]

■ **kick out**: ▸ **~ out** [*animal*] ruer; [*person*] lancer des coups de pied; **to ~ out at sb** [*person*] lancer des coups de pied à qn; ▸ **~ [sb] out**, **~ out [sb]** ᴼ virer [*troublemaker*, *employee*]

■ **kick over**: ▸ **~ [sth] over**, **~ over [sth]** renverser [qch] (d'un coup de pied *or* à coups de pied)

■ **kick up**: ▸ **~ [sth] up**, **~ up [sth]** soulever [*dust*]; **to ~ up a fuss** *ou* **stink**ᴼ faire des histoires ᴼ (about à propos de)

kick: **~back** *n* pot-de-vin *m*; **~boxing** *n* kick-boxing *m*; **~-off** *n* Sport coup *m* d'envoi

kick-start /ˈkɪkstɑːt/

A *n* (also **~-starter**) (on motorbike) kick *m*

B *vtr* lit démarrer [qch] au pied [*motorbike*]; fig relancer

kid /kɪd/

A *n* ⬚1⬚ ᴼ(child) enfant *mf*, gosse ᴼ *mf*; (youth) gamin/-e ᴼ *m/f*; ⬚2⬚ (young goat) chevreau/-ette *m/f*; ⬚3⬚ (goatskin) chevreau *m*

B *vtr* (*p prés etc* **-dd-**) ⬚1⬚ (tease) charrier ᴼ (**about** à propos de); ⬚2⬚ (fool) faire marcher ᴼ; **to ~ sb into believing that** faire croire à qn que

C *vi* (*p prés etc* **-dd-**) (tease) rigoler ᴼ; **no ~ding!** sans blague ᴼ!

D *v refl* (*p prés etc* **-dd-**) **to ~ oneself** se faire des illusions

kid glove *n* gant *m* en chevreau

(Idiom) **to treat sb with ~s** prendre des gants avec qn

kidnap /ˈkɪdnæp/

A *n* enlèvement *m*

B *vtr* (*p prés etc* **-pp-**) enlever

kidnapper /ˈkɪdnæpə(r)/ *n* ravisseur/-euse *m/f*

kidnapping /ˈkɪdnæpɪŋ/ *n* enlèvement *m*

kidney /ˈkɪdnɪ/ *n* Anat rein *m*; Culin rognon *m*; **to have ~ trouble** souffrir de troubles rénaux

kidney: **~ bean** *n* haricot *m* rouge; **~ dialysis** *n* dialyse *f*; **~ donor** *n* donneur/-euse *m/f* de rein; **~ failure** *n* défaillance *f* rénale

kidney machine *n* rein *m* artificiel; **to be on a ~** être en dialyse

kidney: **~ shaped** *adj* en forme de haricot; **~ stone** *n* calcul *m* rénal

kill /kɪl/

A *n* ⬚1⬚ (in hunting) mise *f* à mort; **to be in at the ~** lit assister à la mise à mort; fig assister au dénouement; ⬚2⬚ (prey) proie *f*

B *vtr* ⬚1⬚ (cause to die) tuer; **they ~ed one another** *ou* **each other** ils se sont entre-tués; **~ed in action** *ou* **battle** tombé au champ d'honneur; **I'll do it, even if it ~s me**ᴼ! je le ferai, même si je dois y laisser ma peau ᴼ!; ⬚2⬚ ᴼ(make effort) **it wouldn't ~ you to turn up on time** tu pourrais faire l'effort d'arriver à l'heure; ⬚3⬚ ᴼ(hurt) **my feet are ~ing me** j'ai mal aux pieds; ⬚4⬚ (end, stop) arrêter [*rumour*]; supprimer [*story*]; faire échouer [*idea*]; **that remark ~ed the conversation dead** cette remarque a jeté un froid dans la conversation; ⬚5⬚ (deaden) tuer [*smell*, *flavour*]; faire disparaître [*pain*]; ôter [*appetite*]; ⬚6⬚ ᴼ(turn off) couper [*engine*]; éteindre [*television*, *light*]; ⬚7⬚ (spend) **to ~ time** tuer le temps (**by doing** en faisant); **I have two hours to ~** j'ai deux heures à attendre

C *vi* tuer

D *v refl* **to ~ oneself** se suicider; **to ~ oneself doing** fig se tuer à faire; **to ~ oneself laughing** être mort de rire

(Phrasal verb)

■ **kill off**: ▸ **~ off [sth]**, **~ [sth] off** éliminer

killer /ˈkɪlə(r)/

A *n* ⬚1⬚ (illness, poison) **heroin/cancer is a ~** l'héroïne/le cancer

tue; **cancer is a major ~** le cancer est l'une des principales causes de mortalité; ⬚2⬚ (person) meurtrier *m*; (animal) tueur/-euse *m/f*

B *noun modifier* [*disease*] mortel/-elle; [*drug*] qui tue

killer: **~ application** *n* Comput application *f* à grand succès; **~ instinct** *n* lit instinct *m* de tuer; fig agressivité *f*; **~ whale** *n* épaulard *m*

killing /ˈkɪlɪŋ/ *n* (of individual) meurtre *m* (**of** de); (of animal) mise *f* à mort (**of** de)

(Idiom) **to make a ~** ᴼ ramasser un joli paquet ᴼ

killjoy *n* rabat-joie *mf inv*

kiln /kɪln/ *n* four *m*

kilo /ˈkiːləʊ/ ▸ p. 1323 *n* kilo *m*

kilobyte /ˈkɪləbaɪt/ *n* kilo-octet *m*

kilogram(me) /ˈkɪləɡræm/ ▸ p. 1323 *n* kilogramme *m*

kilometre /kɪˈlɒmɪtə(r)/ GB, **kilometer** /kɪˈlɒmɪtə(r)/ US ▸ p. 977 *n* kilomètre *m*

kilowatt /ˈkɪləwɒt/ *n* kilowatt *m*

kilt /kɪlt/ *n* kilt *m*

kin /kɪn/ *n* ¢ parents *mpl*, famille *f*

kind /kaɪnd/

A *n* ⬚1⬚ (sort, type) sorte *f*, genre *m*, type *m*; **this ~ of book/person** ce genre *or* type de livre/personne; **all ~s of people, people of all ~s** toutes sortes de personnes; **what ~ of dog is it?** qu'est-ce que c'est comme chien?; **what ~ of person is she?** comment est-elle?, quel genre de personne est-ce?; **what ~ of person does he think I am?** pour qui me prend-il?; **what ~ of (a) person would do a thing like that?** qui pourrait faire une chose pareille?; **what ~ of an answer is that?** qu'est-ce que c'est que cette réponse?; **what ~ of talk is that?** en voilà des façons de parler!; **I don't believe anything of the ~** je n'en crois rien; **a criminal of the worst ~** un criminel de la pire espèce; **they could find no food of any ~** ils n'ont pas trouvé la moindre nourriture; **this is the only one of its ~, this is one of a ~** c'est unique en son genre; **he must be some ~ of idiot** ça doit être un imbécile; **they found a fossil of some ~** ils ont trouvé une sorte de fossile; **it's some ~ of cleaning device** ce doit être un système de nettoyage; **books, toys, that ~ of thing** des livres, des jouets, ce genre de choses; **what ~ of thing(s) does he like?** qu'est-ce qu'il aime?; **that's the ~ of person she is** elle est comme ça; **I'm not that ~ of person** ce n'est pas mon genre; **they found a solution of a ~** ils ont trouvé une sorte de solution; ⬚2⬚ (expressing vague classification) **a ~ of** une sorte de; **a ~ of handbag/soup** une sorte de sac à main/de soupe; **a ~ of intuition** une sorte d'intuition; **I heard a ~ of rattling noise** j'ai entendu comme un cliquetis; **I felt a ~ of apprehension** j'ai ressenti une certaine appréhension; ⬚3⬚ (classified type) espèce *f*, genre *m*; **I know his ~** je connais les gens de son espèce

B in kind *adv phr* ⬚1⬚ (in goods) en nature; **to pay in ~** payer en nature; ⬚2⬚ (in same way) **to repay sb in ~** rendre la pareille à qn

C ᴼ**kind of** *adv phr* **he's ~ of cute/forgetful** il est plutôt mignon/distrait; **they were ~ of frightened** en fait, ils avaient un peu peur; **I ~ of like him** en fait, je l'aime bien; **we ~ of thought that...** nous pensions que...; **'is it interesting?'—'~ of'** 'est-ce que c'est intéressant?'—'plutôt, oui'

D *adj* ⬚1⬚ (caring) [*person*] gentil/-ille; [*act*] bon/bonne; [*gesture*, *words*] gentil/-ille; **to be ~ to sb** être gentil avec qn; '**Sudso is ~ to your skin**' 'Sudso respecte votre peau'; **to be ~ to animals** bien traiter les animaux; **life has not been ~ to him** la vie ne l'a pas épargné; **that's very ~ of you** c'est très gentil *or* aimable de votre part; **would you be ~ enough to pass me the salt?** auriez-vous l'amabilité de me passer le sel?; **she was ~ enough to give me a lift home** elle a eu la gentillesse de me ramener chez moi

kindergarten /ˈkɪndəɡɑːtn/ *n* jardin *m* d'enfants

kind: **~-hearted** *adj* [*person*] de cœur; **~-heartedly** *adv* très gentiment; **~-heartedness** *n* bonté *f*

kindle /ˈkɪndl/

A *vtr* allumer [*fire*]; mettre le feu à [*wood*]; fig attiser [*desire*]; susciter [*interest*]

B *vi* [*wood*] s'enflammer, prendre feu

kindling /ˈkɪndlɪŋ/ *n* petit bois *m*, bois *m* d'allumage

kindly /ˈkaɪndlɪ/

A *adj* [*person*, *nature*] gentil/-ille; [*smile*, *interest*] bienveillant; [*face*] sympathique

B *adv* ⬚1⬚ (in a kind way) avec gentillesse; **to speak ~ of sb** avoir

k

un mot gentil pour qn; **2** (obligingly) gentiment; **would you ~ do/refrain from doing** auriez-vous l'amabilité de faire/de ne pas faire; **3** (favourably) **to look ~ on** approuver [*activity*]; **to think ~ of** avoir une bonne opinion de; **to take ~ to** apprécier

kindness /'kaɪndnɪs/ n **1** ₵ (quality) gentillesse *f*; **to show ~ to** *ou* **towards sb** témoigner de la gentillesse à l'égard de *or* envers qn; **an act of ~** un acte de bonté; **out of ~** par gentillesse; **2** C (instance) gentillesse *f*; **to do sb a ~** rendre service à qn

(Idioms) **out of the ~ of one's heart** par pure gentillesse; **to be full of the milk of human ~** être pétri d'humanité

kindred /'kɪndrɪd/
A n (+ v pl ou sg) famille *f*, parents *mpl*
B adj [*language*] apparenté; [*activity*] semblable

kindred spirit n âme *f* sœur

kinetic /kɪ'netɪk/ adj cinétique

kinetics /kɪ'netɪks/ n (+ v sg) cinétique *f*

king /kɪŋ/ ▸ p. 869 n **1** (monarch) roi *m*; **King Charles** le roi Charles; **to live like a ~** fig vivre comme un coq en pâte; **2** fig (of comedy, wines etc) roi *m* (**of** de); **3** (in chess, cards) roi *m*; (in draughts, checkers) dame *f*

kingdom /'kɪŋdəm/ n **1** (monarchy) lit, fig royaume *m*; **2** Bot, Zool règne *m*

(Idiom) **to send** *ou* **knock sb to ~ come** envoyer qn ad patres° *or* dans l'autre monde

kingfisher n martin-pêcheur *m*

kingly /'kɪŋlɪ/ adj lit, fig royal, de roi

kingpin n Tech, fig cheville *f* ouvrière

king-size(d) /'kɪŋsaɪzd/ adj [*cigarette*] extra-longue; [*packet*] géant; [*portion, garden*] énorme; **~ bed** grand lit *m* (qui fait 1,95 m de large)

kink /kɪŋk/
A n **1** (in rope, tube) nœud *m*; **the hosepipe has a ~ in it** le tuyau d'arrosage est tordu; **2** fig (in personality) aberration *f*
B vi [*rope, cable*] s'entortiller

kinky /'kɪŋkɪ/ adj **1** °(perverse) pervers, bizarre; **2** (wavy) ondulé

kinship /'kɪnʃɪp/ n **1** (blood relationship) parenté *f*; **2** fig (empathy) affinité *f* (**with** avec)

kiosk /'kiːɒsk/ n **1** (stand) kiosque *m*; **2** GB Telecom cabine *f*

kip° /kɪp/ GB
A n roupillon° *m*; **to get some ~** piquer un roupillon°
B vi (p prés etc **-pp-**) (also **~ down**) se pieuter°, roupiller°

kipper /'kɪpə(r)/ n GB hareng *m* fumé et salé, kipper *m*

Kirghizstan /'kɜːgɪstæn/ ▸ p. 774 pr n Kirghizistan *m*, Kirghizie *f*

kirk /kɜːk/ n Scot église *f*

kiss /kɪs/
A n baiser *m*; **to give sb a ~** embrasser qn, donner un baiser à qn
B vtr embrasser, donner un baiser à [*person*]; baiser [*hand, ring*]; **to ~ sb on** embrasser qn sur [*cheek, lips*]; **we ~ed each other** nous nous sommes embrassés; **to ~ sb goodnight** souhaiter bonne nuit à qn en l'embrassant; **let me ~ it better!** un petit bisou et ça ira mieux après!; **you can ~ your money goodbye!** fig tu peux dire adieu à ton argent!
C vi s'embrasser; **to ~ and make up** se réconcilier; **to ~ and tell** avoir une liaison et le faire savoir publiquement

kiss of death n coup *m* fatal; **to be the ~** porter le coup fatal

kiss of life n GB bouche-à-bouche *m* inv; **to give sb the ~** faire le bouche à bouche à qn

kissogram /'kɪsəgræm/ n: service par lequel une personne en tenue légère est employée pour aller embrasser et présenter des vœux à quelqu'un

kit /kɪt/ n **1** (implements) trousse *f*; **2** ₵ (gear, clothes) affaires *fpl*; **football/tennis ~** affaires de football/de tennis; **3** (parts for assembly) kit *m*; **to come in ~ form** être vendu en kit; **4** Mil paquetage *m*

(Phrasal verb)
■ **kit out** GB: ▸ **~ out** [sb/sth], **~** [sb/sth] **out** équiper (**with** de)

kit: **~bag** n (for sport) sac *m* de sport; (for travel) sac *m* de voyage; Mil (soldier's) sac *m* de soldat; **~car** n voiture *f* en kit

kitchen /'kɪtʃɪn/ n cuisine *f*

(Idiom) **if you can't stand the heat get out of the ~** si tu trouves la situation insupportable, tu n'es pas obligé de rester

kitchenette /ˌkɪtʃɪ'net/ n kitchenette *f*

kitchen: **~ foil** n papier *m* d'aluminium; **~ garden** n jardin *m* potager; **~ paper** n essuie-tout *m* inv, sopalin® *m*; **~ roll** n essuie-tout *m* inv; **~ scales** npl balance *f* de cuisine

kitchen sink n évier *m*

(Idiom) **to take everything but the ~** tout emporter sauf les meubles

kitchen: **~ sink drama** n GB théâtre *m* naturaliste; **~ unit** n élément *m* de cuisine; **~ware** n ₵ (implements) ustensiles *mpl* de cuisine; (crockery) vaisselle *f*; **~ waste** n ₵ déchets *mpl* domestiques

kite /kaɪt/ n **1** (toy) cerf-volant *m*; **to fly a ~** lit faire voler un cerf-volant; fig lancer un ballon d'essai; **2** (bird) milan *m*

kitemark /'kaɪtmɑːk/ n GB label *m* de qualité

kitsch /kɪtʃ/ n, adj kitsch (*m*)

kitten /'kɪtn/ n chaton *m*; fig **to have ~s** piquer une crise°

kitty /'kɪtɪ/ n **1** °(cat) minet *m*, minou° *m*; **2** (of money) cagnotte *f*

kiwi /'kiːwiː/ n Zool kiwi *m*

kiwi fruit n kiwi *m*

kleptomania /ˌkleptə'meɪnɪə/ n kleptomanie *f*

kleptomaniac /ˌkleptə'meɪnɪæk/ n, adj kleptomane (*mf*)

km (abrév écrite = **kilometre**) km

kmh (abrév écrite = **kilometres per hour**) km/h

knack /næk/ n **1** (dexterity) tour *m* de main (**of doing** pour faire); **to get the ~** attraper le tour de main; **to lose the ~** perdre la main; **2** (talent) don *m* (**of** ou **for doing** de faire)

knapsack /'næpsæk/ n sac *m* à dos

knave /neɪv/ n **1** (in cards) valet *m*; **2** ‡(rogue) coquin‡ *m*

knead /niːd/ vtr pétrir [*dough*]; masser [*flesh*]

knee /niː/
A ▸ p. 698 n Anat genou *m*; **to be on/fall to one's ~s** être/tomber à genoux; **on (one's) hands and ~s** à quatre pattes; **to go down on bended ~ to sb** se mettre à genoux devant qn
B vtr donner un coup de genou à [*person*]

(Idioms) **to bring** *ou* **force sb/sth to his/its ~s** mettre qn/qch à genoux; **to go weak at the ~s** avoir les jambes qui flageolent

knee-breeches n knickers *mpl*

kneecap /'niːkæp/
A n rotule *f*
B vtr briser les rotules à [*person*]

knee-deep /ˌniː'diːp/ adj **the water was ~** l'eau arrivait aux genoux; **to be ~ in paperwork** fig être dans les papiers jusqu'au cou

knee: **~-high** adj à hauteur des genoux; **~-jerk** adj [*reaction, response*] automatique

kneel /niːl/ vi (also **~ down**) (prét, pp **kneeled, knelt**) gen se mettre à genoux; (in prayer) s'agenouiller; **~ing** à genoux; (in prayer) agenouillé

knee: **~-length** adj [*skirt*] qui s'arrête au genou; [*boots*] haut; [*socks*] long/longue; **~-pad** n genouillère *f*

knell /nel/ n glas *m*; **to sound the death ~ for sth** sonner le glas de qch

knelt /nelt/ prét, pp ▸ **kneel**

knew /njuː, US nuː/ prét ▸ **know**

knickerbocker glory n coupe *f* glacée

knickerbockers /'nɪkəbɒkəz/ npl knickers *mpl*

knickers /'nɪkəz/ ▸ p. 1191 npl GB petite culotte *f*

knick-knack /'nɪknæk/ n bibelot *m*

knife /naɪf/
A n (pl **knives**) couteau *m*
B vtr donner un coup de couteau à [*person*] (**in** dans); **to be**

~d recevoir un coup de couteau

(Idioms) **to have one's ~ into sb**○ en avoir après qn○; **to put the ~ in** critiquer; **to twist the ~ in the wound** remuer le couteau dans la plaie

knife-edge *n* fig **to be on a ~** [negotiations] ne tenir qu'à un fil; **to be (living) on a ~** [person] être au bord de l'abîme

knife-point *n* **at ~** sous la menace d'un couteau

knife sharpener *n* aiguisoir *m*

knifing /'naɪfɪŋ/ *n* attaque *f* au couteau

knight /naɪt/
A *n* **1** gen, Hist chevalier *m*; **2** (in chess) cavalier *m*
B *vtr* GB anoblir [person] (**for** pour)

knighthood /'naɪthʊd/ *n* (title) titre *m* de chevalier; (chivalry) chevalerie *f*

knit /nɪt/
A *n* (garment) tricot *m*; **cotton ~** tricot en coton
B *vtr* (*prét*, *pp* **knitted**, **knit**) tricoter; **to ~ sb sth** tricoter qch pour qn
C *vi* (*prét*, *pp* **knitted**, **knit**) **1** (with wool) tricoter; **~ted** en tricot; **2** (join together) [broken bones] se souder

(Idiom) **to ~ one's brows** froncer les sourcils

(Phrasal verb)
■ **knit together**: ▸ **~ together** [bones] se souder; ▸ **~ [sth] together**, **~ together [sth]** lit tricoter [qch] ensemble [strands]; fig entrelacer [themes]; unir [community]

knitter /'nɪtə(r)/ *n* tricoteur/-euse *m/f*

knitting /'nɪtɪŋ/
A *n* tricot *m*
B *noun modifier* [bag] à tricot; [machine, needle, wool] à tricoter

knitwear /'nɪtweə(r)/ *n* ₵ tricots *mpl*

knives /naɪvz/ *pl* ▸ **knife**

knob /nɒb/ *n* **1** (of door, drawer) bouton *m*; (of cane) pommeau *m*; (on bannister, furniture) boule *f*; **2** (control button) bouton *m*; **3** (of butter etc) noix *f*

knobbly /'nɒblɪ/ GB, **knobby** /'nɒbɪ/ US *adj* [fingers] noueux/-euse; [knees] saillant

knock /nɒk/
A *n* **1** (blow) coup *m* (**on** sur; **with** de); **a ~ at the door** un coup à la porte; **I'll give you a ~ at 7.30** je frapperai à ta porte à 7 h 30; **2** onomat **~! ~!** toc! toc!; **3** fig (setback) coup *m*; **to take a ~** en prendre un coup; **to take the ~s** encaisser○ (les coups)
B *vtr* **1** (strike) cogner [object]; **to ~ one's head on sth** se cogner la tête contre qch; **to ~ sb on the arm** donner un coup sur le bras de qn; **to ~ sb against** projeter qch contre; **to ~ sb unconscious** ou **silly**○ assommer qn; **to ~ a hole in sth** faire un trou dans qch; **2** (cause to move) **to ~ sth off** ou **out of sth** faire tomber qch de qch; **to ~ sth over sth** envoyer qn/qch par-dessus qch; **to ~ a nail into sth** enfoncer un clou dans qch; **to ~ sb off his feet** [blast, wave] soulever qn; **to ~ sb flat** étendre qn par terre; **3** ○(criticize) critiquer [method, achievement]; dénigrer [person]
C *vi* **1** (make sound) [branch, engine, object] cogner (**on, against** contre); [person] frapper (**at, on** à); **2** (collide) **to ~ into** ou **against sth** heurter qch; **to ~ into each other** se heurter

(Idioms) **his knees were ~ing** ses genoux s'entrechoquaient de peur; **to ~ sth on the head**○ mettre fin à qch; **to be ~ing on a bit**○ commencer à se faire vieux

(Phrasal verbs)
■ **knock about**○, **knock around**○: ▸ **~ about** traîner; **to ~ about with sb**○ fréquenter qn; ▸ **~ about [sth]** [object] traîner dans [house]
■ **knock back**: ▸ **~ back [sth]**, **~ [sth] back 1** (return) [player] renvoyer [ball]; **2** (swallow) descendre○ [drink]; **3** ○(reject) rejeter [offer]; refuser [invitation]; ▸ **~ [sb] back** (surprise) [news] secouer [person]
■ **knock down**: ▸ **~ [sb/sth] down**, **~ down [sb/sth] 1** (cause to fall) (deliberately) [aggressor] jeter [qn] à terre [victim, opponent]; défoncer [door]; démolir [building]; (accidentally) renverser [person, object]; abattre [fence]; **2** (reduce) [buyer] faire baisser [price]; [seller] baisser [price]; **3** (allocate) [auctioneer] adjuger [lot]
■ **knock in**: ▸ **~ [sth] in**, **~ in [sth]** planter [nail, peg]
■ **knock off**: ▸ **~ off**○ [worker] arrêter de travailler; ▸ **~ [sb/sth] off**, **~ off [sb/sth] 1** (cause to fall) [person, blow, force] faire tomber [person, object]; **2** ○(reduce) **I'll**

~ £10 off for you je vous ferai une réduction de 10 livres; **3** ○(steal) subtiliser [car, object]; **4** ○(stop) **~ it off!** ça suffit!

■ **knock out**: ▸ **~ [sb/sth] out**, **~ out [sb/sth] 1** (dislodge) casser [tooth]; arracher [nail, support]; [person, blow] vider [contents]; **2** (make unconscious) [person, blow] assommer; [drug] endormir; [boxer] mettre [qn] au tapis [opponent]; **3** (destroy) faire sauter [tank]; mettre [qch] hors service [factory]; **4** Sport (eliminate) éliminer [opponent, team]; **5** (straighten) redresser [dent, metal]; **6** ○(overwhelm) émerveiller [person]; ▸ **~ oneself out** s'assommer
■ **knock over**: ▸ **~ [sb/sth] over**, **~ over [sb/sth]** renverser
■ **knock together**: ▸ **~ together** [knees, objects] s'entrechoquer; ▸ **~ [sth] together**, **~ together [sth]**○ **1** (create) bricoler [furniture]; confectionner [meal]; **2** (bang together) cogner l'un contre l'autre
■ **knock up**: ▸ **~ up** (in tennis) faire des balles (**with** avec); ▸ **~ [sth] up**, **~ up [sth] 1** ○(make) bricoler [furniture]; confectionner [meal, outfit]; **2** ○Sport [competitor] totaliser [points]; réaliser [score]; ▸ **~ [sb] up**, **~ up [sb]** (awaken) réveiller [person]

knockabout /'nɒkəbaʊt/
A *n* **1** Sport échange *m* de balles; **2** US Naut dériveur *m*
B *adj* [comedy, comedian] loufoque

knockdown /'nɒkdaʊn/ *adj* [price] sacrifié

knocker /'nɒkə(r)/ *n* heurtoir *m*

knocking /'nɒkɪŋ/ *n* gen coups *mpl*; (in engine) cognement *m*

knocking-off time○ /ˌnɒkɪŋɒftaɪm/ *n* heure *f* de la sortie

knock: **~-kneed** *adj* cagneux/-euse; **~-on effect** *n* implications *fpl*

knock-out /'nɒkaʊt/
A *n* **1** (in boxing) knock-out *m*; **2** ○(show etc) réussite *f*
B *adj* **1** Sport [competition] avec tours éliminatoires; **2** ○(incapacitating) [pills, injection] sédatif/-ive

knoll /nəʊl/ *n* butte *f*

knot /nɒt/
A *n* **1** (tied part) nœud *m*; **to tie sth in a ~** nouer qch; **2** (tangle) nœud *m*; **to comb the ~s out of one's hair** se démêler les cheveux avec un peigne; **3** (in wood) nœud *m*; **4** (group) petit groupe *m* (**of** de); **5** (tense feeling) **to have a ~ in one's stomach** avoir l'estomac noué; **6** Naut nœud *m*
B *vtr* (*p prés etc* **-tt-**) nouer (**together** ensemble); **to ~ one's tie** faire un nœud à sa cravate

(Idioms) **at a rate of ~s** à toute allure; **to get tied up in ~s** s'embrouiller; **to tie the ~** se marier

knotty /'nɒtɪ/ *adj* [wood] noueux/-euse; [problem] épineux/-euse

know /nəʊ/
A *vtr* (*prét* **knew** /njuː/; *pp* **known** /nəʊn/) **1** (have knowledge of) connaître [person, place, name, opinion, result, value, rules, situation, system, way]; savoir, connaître [answer, language, reason, truth, words]; **he ~s everything** il sait tout; **to ~ sb by name/sight** connaître qn de nom/vue; **to ~ sth by heart** savoir or connaître qch par cœur; **to ~ how to do** savoir faire; (stressing method) savoir comment faire; **to ~ that...** savoir que...; **to ~ for certain** ou **for sure that** savoir avec certitude que; **I wasn't to ~ that...** je ne pouvais pas deviner que...; **you ~ what children are** tu sais comment sont les enfants; **to ~ sb/sth as** connaître qn/qch sous le nom de; **Virginia known as Ginny to her friends** Virginia ou Ginny pour ses amis; **to let it be known** ou **to make it known that** faire savoir que; **to have known sb/sth to do** avoir déjà vu qn/qch faire; **it has been known to snow here** il est arrivé qu'il neige ici; **if I ~ him** tel que je le connais; **he is known to the police** il est connu de la police; **I ~ all about redundancy!** je sais ce que c'est que le chômage!; **as you well ~** comme tu le sais bien; **(do) you ~ something?**, **do you ~ what?** tu sais quoi?; **there's no ~ing whether** on ne peut pas savoir si; **to ~ one's way home** connaître le chemin pour rentrer chez soi; **to ~ one's way around a town** bien connaître une ville; **to ~ one's way around an engine** savoir se débrouiller avec les moteurs; **to ~ what for a fact** j'en suis absolument sûr; **I ~ what!** j'ai une idée!; **he ~s all about it** il est au courant; **2** (feel certain) être sûr; **I knew it!** j'en étais sûr!; **I don't ~ that I want to go really** je ne suis pas vraiment sûr

d'avoir envie d'y aller; ③ (realize) se rendre compte; **you don't ~ how pleased I am** tu ne peux pas savoir comme je suis content; **don't I ~ it!** ne m'en parle pas!; ④ (recognize) reconnaître (**by** à; **from** de); **only their parents ~ one from the other** il n'y a que leurs parents qui sachent les distinguer; **she ~s a bargain when she sees one** elle sait repérer les bonnes affaires; ⑤ (acknowledge) **to be known for sth/for doing** être connu pour qch/pour faire; ⑥ (experience) connaître

B vi (prét **knew**; pp **known**) ① (have knowledge) savoir; **as you ~** comme vous le savez; **I wouldn't ~** je ne saurais dire; **to ~ about** (have information) être au courant de [event]; (have skill) s'y connaître en [computing, engines]; **to ~ of** (from experience) connaître; (from information) avoir entendu parler de; **not that I ~ of** pas que je le sache; **to let sb ~ of** ou **about** tenir qn au courant de; **we'll let you ~** nous vous tiendrons au courant; **how should I ~!** comment veux-tu que je sache!; **if you must ~** si tu veux tout savoir; **you ~ better than to argue with him** tu as mieux à faire que de te disputer avec lui; **you ought to have known better** tu n'aurais pas dû; **he says he came home early but I ~ better** il dit qu'il est rentré tôt mais je n'en crois rien; **they don't ~ any better** ils n'en savent pas plus; ② (feel certain) **'he won't win'—'oh I don't ~'** 'il ne va pas gagner'—'oh je n'en suis pas si sûr'; **'I'll take the morning off'—'I don't ~ about that!'** 'je vais prendre ma matinée'—'c'est ce que vous croyez○!'; **I don't ~ about you but...** je ne sais pas ce que tu en penses, mais...

(Idioms) **it takes one to ~ one** qui se ressemble s'assemble; **not to ~ what to do with oneself** ne pas savoir quoi faire de son temps; **not to ~ where** ou **which way to turn** fig ne pas savoir à quel saint se vouer; **not to ~ where to put oneself** ne pas savoir où se mettre; **not to ~ whether one is coming or going** ne plus savoir ce qu'on fait; **to be in the ~**○ être bien informé; **to be in the ~ about sth**○ être au courant de qch

know: **~-all**○ n GB je-sais-tout mf inv; **~-how**○ n savoir-faire m inv

knowing /'nəʊɪŋ/ adj [look, smile] entendu

knowingly /'nəʊɪŋlɪ/ adv (intentionally) délibérément; (with understanding) d'un air entendu

know-it-all○ n US = **know-all**

knowledge /'nɒlɪdʒ/ n ① (awareness) connaissance f; **to bring sth to sb's ~** porter qch à la connaissance de qn; **to my ~** à ma connaissance; **with the full ~ of sb** au vu et au su de qn; **to have ~ of** avoir connaissance de; **he has no ~ of what happened** il ne sait pas ce qui s'est passé; **to my certain ~ he...** je sais de façon certaine qu'il...; **without sb's ~** à l'insu de qn; ② (factual wisdom) gen connaissances fpl; (of specific field) connaissance f; **technical ~** connaissances techniques; **~ of Monet's work** la connaissance des œuvres de Monet

knowledgeable /'nɒlɪdʒəbl/ adj [person] savant; [article] bien documenté; **to be ~ about** s'y connaître en [subject]

knowledgeably /'nɒlɪdʒəblɪ/ adv en connaissance de cause

knowledge-based system n système m expert

known /nəʊn/
A pp ▸ **know**
B adj [authority, danger] reconnu; [celebrity, cure] connu; [quantity] défini

knuckle /'nʌkl/ n ① (of person) jointure f, articulation f; **to crack one's ~s** faire craquer ses doigts; **to rap sb on** ou **over the ~s** lit, fig taper sur les doigts de qn; ② (on animal) jarret m; ③ Culin (of lamb, mutton) manche m de gigot; (of pork, veal) jarret m

(Phrasal verbs)
■ **knuckle down**○ s'y mettre (sérieusement)
■ **knuckle under**○ se soumettre, céder

knuckle: **~bone** n articulation f, jointure f; **~-duster** n coup-de-poing m américain

koala (bear) /kəʊ'ɑːlə/ n koala m

kohl /kəʊl/ n khôl m

kookie○, **kooky**○ /'kuːkɪ/ adj US dingue○

Koran /kə'rɑːn/ n Coran m

Korea /kə'rɪə/ ▸ p. 774 pr n Corée f

Korean /kə'rɪən/ ▸ p. 1032, p. 969
A n ① (person) Coréen/-éenne m/f; ② (language) coréen m
B adj coréen/-éenne; **the ~ War** la guerre de Corée

korma /'kɔːmə/ n: sorte de curry à la crème et à la noix de coco

kosher /'kəʊʃə(r)/ adj ① Relig casher; ② ○fig (legitimate) **it's ~** c'est réglo○; **there's something not quite ~ about it** il y a quelque chose de pas très catholique○ là-dedans

Kosovan /'kɒsəvn/ ▸ p. 1032 adj kosovar/-e

Kosovar /'kɒsəvɑː(r)/ ▸ p. 1032 n Kosovar/-e m/f

kowtow /ˌkaʊ'taʊ/ vi (lit) courber l'échine; **to ~ to sb** faire des courbettes à qn pej

kph (abrév écrite = **kilometres per hour**) km/h

KS US Post abrév écrite = **Kansas**

Kt n: abrév = **knight**

kudos○ /'kjuːdɒs/ n prestige m

kumquat /'kʌmkwɒt/ n kumquat m

Kurdish /'kɜːdɪʃ/ ▸ p. 969
A n (language) kurde m
B adj kurde

Kurdistan /ˌkɜːdɪ'stæn/ pr n Kurdistan m

Kuwaiti /kʊ'weɪtɪ/ ▸ p. 1032
A n Kuweitien/-ienne m/f
B adj kuweitien/-ienne

kW (abrév écrite = **kilowatt**) kW

kWh n (abrév = **kilowatt-hour**) kWh

KY US Post abrév écrite = **Kentucky**

l, L /el/ n ① (letter) l, L m; ② **L** (abrév écrite = **litre(s)** GB, **liter(s)** US) l; ③ **L** GB Aut (abrév écrite = **Learner**) élève m conducteur accompagné; ④ **L** US Rail **the L** le métro aérien; ⑤ **L** abrév écrite = **Lake**; ⑥ **L** abrév écrite = **left**; ⑦ **l** (abrév écrite = **line**) (in poetry) V; (in prose) l; ⑧ **L** (abrév écrite = **large**) L

LA ① US (abrév = **Los Angeles**) LA; ② US Post abrév écrite = **Louisiana**

lab /læb/ n labo⁰ m

Lab. GB Pol abrév écrite = **Labour (Party)**

lab coat n blouse f blanche

label /'leɪbl/
A n ① lit (on clothing, jar) étiquette f; (on diagram) légende f; ② fig étiquette f; ③ Mus (also **record** ∼) label m; ④ Comput label m; ⑤ Ling (in grammar) étiquette f; (in dictionary) marqueur m
B vtr (p prés etc **-ll-**, US **-l-**) ① lit (stick label on) étiqueter [clothing, jar]; mettre des légendes sur [diagram]; ② fig (pigeonhole) classer, étiqueter péj [person, work] (**as** comme); ③ Ling étiqueter

labelling /'leɪblɪŋ/ n étiquetage m

labor n US = **labour**

laboratory /lə'bɒrətrɪ, US 'læbrətɔːrɪ/ n laboratoire m

laboratory: ∼ **assistant** n laborantin/-e m/f; ∼ **technician** n technicien-ienne m/f de laboratoire

labor: **Labor Day** n US fête f du travail; **Labor Department** n US ministère m du travail

laborious /lə'bɔːrɪəs/ adj laborieux/-ieuse

labor union n US syndicat m

labour GB, **labor** US /'leɪbə(r)/
A n ① gen (work) travail m, labeur m liter; **to withdraw one's** ∼ se mettre en grève; ② Ind (workforce) gen main-d'œuvre f; ③ Med accouchement m; **to go into** ou **begin** ∼ commencer à avoir des contractions
B noun modifier Ind [costs] de la main-d'œuvre; [dispute, relations] ouvriers-patronat inv; [market] du travail; [shortage] de main-d'œuvre; [leader] syndical
C vi ① (work, try hard) travailler (dur) (**at** à; **on** sur; **to do** pour faire); ② (have difficulties) peiner (**to do** à faire); **to** ∼ **up** monter avec peine or péniblement; **to be** ∼**ing under the illusion** ou **misapprehension that** s'imaginer que
(Idioms) **a** ∼ **of love** une tâche demandant beaucoup de passion; **to** ∼ **the point** insister lourdement

Labour /'leɪbə(r)/
A pr n GB (+ v pl) le parti travailliste
B adj GB [supporter, view, manifesto] du parti travailliste; [MP, vote] travailliste

labour camp n camp m de travaux forcés, bagne m

laboured GB, **labored** US /'leɪbəd/ adj ① (difficult) [movement] pénible; [breathing] difficile; ② (showing effort) [joke, humour, speech] lourd

labourer GB, **laborer** US /'leɪbərə(r)/ ▸ p. 1181 n ouvrier-ière m/f du bâtiment

labour: ∼ **exchange**† n GB Bourse f du Travail; ∼ **force** n main-d'œuvre f

labour-intensive adj Ind **to be** ∼ nécessiter une main-d'œuvre importante

labour: ∼ **law** n législation f or droit m du travail; **Labour Party** n GB parti m travailliste

labour-saving adj [equipment, feature, system] qui facilite le travail; ∼ **device** appareil m ménager

labour ward n (ward) salles fpl d'accouchement

labrador /'læbrədɔː(r)/ n Zool labrador m

laburnum /lə'bɜːnəm/ n cytise m, faux ébénier m

labyrinth /'læbərɪnθ/ n Mythol, fig labyrinthe m, dédale m

lace /leɪs/
A n ① ₵ (fabric) dentelle f; ② **C** (on shoe, boot, dress) lacet m; (on tent) cordon m
B noun modifier [curtain, dress] en dentelle
C vtr ① (tie) lacer [shoes, corset]; attacher [tent flap]; ② (add substance to) **to** ∼ **a drink with sth** mettre qch dans une boisson

(Phrasal verb)
■ **lace up**: ▸ ∼ **[sth] up**, ∼ **up [sth]** lacer [shoes, corset]; attacher [tent flap]

lacerate /'læsəreɪt/ vtr lacérer

laceration /ˌlæsə'reɪʃn/ n gen, Med lacération f

lace-up (shoe) n chaussure f à lacet

lack /læk/
A n manque m (**of** de); **for** ou **through** ∼ **of** par manque de
B vtr manquer de [confidence, humour, funds]
C vi **to be** ∼**ing** manquer (**in** de)

lackadaisical /ˌlækə'deɪzɪkl/ adj [person, attitude] nonchalant

lackey /'lækɪ/ n laquais m also fig, pej

lacklustre GB, **lackluster** US /'læklʌstə(r)/ adj [person, performance, style] terne

laconic /lə'kɒnɪk/ adj laconique

lacquer /'lækə(r)/
A n ① (for hair) laque f; ② (varnish) laque f; ③ Art (ware) laques mpl
B vtr ① laquer [surface]; ② GB mettre de la laque sur [hair]

lactate
A /'lækteɪt/ n lactate m
B /læk'teɪt/ vi produire du lait

lactation /læk'teɪʃn/ n lactation f

lactic /'læktɪk/ adj lactique; ∼ **acid** acide m lactique

lactose /'læktəʊs/ n lactose m

lacy /'leɪsɪ/ adj en or de dentelle

lad⁰ /læd/ n ① (boy) garçon m; ② (in racing stables) lad m; (in riding stables) palefrenier m

ladder /'lædə(r)/
A n ① (for climbing) échelle f also fig; **to work one's way up the** ∼ fig gravir les échelons; ② GB (in stockings) échelle f, maille f filée
B vtr filer [stocking]
C vi [stocking] filer

ladderproof adj GB [stockings] indémaillable

laddish⁰ /'lædɪʃ/ adj péj macho⁰ inv

laden /'leɪdn/ adj [lorry, cart] en pleine charge; ∼ **with** lit chargé de [supplies, fruit]; fig littér accablé de [remorse, guilt]

ladette⁰ /læ'det/ n GB jeune femme qui se comporte comme un homme machiste

ladle /'leɪdl/
A n ① Culin louche f; ② Ind cuillère f de coulée
B vtr servir [qch] à la louche [soup, sauce]

(Phrasal verb)
■ **ladle out**: ▸ ∼ **[sth] out**, ∼ **out [sth]** ① lit = **ladle B**; ② fig se répandre en [compliments]; prodiguer [money, advice]

lady /'leɪdɪ/ (pl **ladies**)
A n ① (woman) dame f; **ladies and gentlemen** mesdames et

Lakes

■ *Normally, English* Lake X *becomes* le lac X *in French (note the* small l *at* lac):

Lake Michigan   **Lake Victoria**
= le lac Michigan   = le lac Victoria

■ *But when a lake shares its name with a town, English* Lake X *becomes* le lac de X *in French:*

Lake Annecy   **Lake Constance**
= le lac d'Annecy   = le lac de Constance

Lake Como
= le lac de Côme

■ *Sometimes English can drop the word* Lake *but it is always safe to keep the word* lac *in French:*

Trasimeno   **Balaton**
= le lac Trasimène   = le lac Balaton

■ Loch *and* Lough *in names are normally not translated (note the use of the definite article and the small* l *in French):*

Loch Ness   **Lough Erne**
= le loch Ness   = le lough Erne

---

messieurs; **behave yourself, young ∼!** (to child) sois sage, ma petite!; **a little old ∼** une petite vieille; **she's a real ∼** fig elle est très distinguée; **the ∼ of the house** la maîtresse de maison; ② (aristocrat) aristocrate f; ③ ▸ p. 869 (in titles) **Lady Churchill** Lady Churchill
B **Ladies** npl (on toilets) 'Dames'; **where's the Ladies?** où sont les toilettes?

lady: **∼bird** n coccinelle f; **∼-in-waiting** n dame f d'honneur; **∼-killer**○ n tombeur○ m; **∼like** adj [behaviour] distingué; **∼ mayoress** ▸ p. 869 n GB titre officiel de la femme du lord-maire

Ladyship /ˈleɪdɪʃɪp/ ▸ p. 869 n **her/your ∼** Madame (la baronne or la comtesse etc)

lady's maid n femme f de chambre

lag /læg/
A n ① (time period) (lapse) décalage m; (delay) retard m; ② ○(criminal) **old ∼** repris m de justice
B vtr (p prés etc -**gg**-) calorifuger [pipe, tank]; isoler [roof]
(Phrasal verb)
■ **lag behind**: ▶ **∼ behind** [person, prices] être à la traîne; ▶ **∼ behind [sb/sth]** traîner derrière [person]; fig être en retard sur [rival, product]

lager /ˈlɑːgə(r)/ n bière f blonde

lager lout n GB péj voyou○ m (qui se soûle à la bière)

lagging /ˈlægɪŋ/ n (material) isolant m

lagoon /ləˈguːn/ n lagune f

lah, la /lɑː/ n Mus la m

laid /leɪd/ prét, pp ▸ **lay**

laidback○ /ˌleɪdˈbæk/ adj décontracté

lain /leɪn/ pp ▸ **lie C 2, 3, 4, 5**

lair /leə(r)/ n repaire m also fig

laird /ˈleəd/ n Scot propriétaire m foncier, laird m

lake /leɪk/ n lac m
(Idiom) **go and jump in the ∼**○! va te faire voir ailleurs○!

lakeside /ˈleɪksaɪd/
A n **by the ∼** au bord du lac
B noun modifier [café, scenery] de bord de lac

La-la land○ /ˈlɑːlɑː lænd/ n ① (unreal world) **to be living in ∼** vivre sur un nuage, planer; ② (US film industry) monde m du cinéma américain

lama /ˈlɑːmə/ n lama m

lamb /læm/
A n ① (animal) agneau m; **leg of ∼** gigot m d'agneau; ② (term of endearment) ange m
B noun modifier Culin [chops, stew] d'agneau
C vi [ewe] mettre bas; [farmer] aider les brebis à mettre bas

lambast(e) /læmˈbeɪst/ vtr sout ① (beat) rosser; ② (censure) vilipender [person, organization]

lambskin /ˈlæmskɪn/
A n peau f d'agneau
B noun modifier [garment, rug] en agneau

lamb: **∼'s tails** npl Bot chatons mpl; **∼'s wool** n laine f d'agneau, lambswool m

lame /leɪm/ adj lit, fig [person, animal, excuse] boiteux/-euse; **to be ∼** lit [person, animal] boiter

lame duck
A n canard m boiteux
B noun modifier US Pol **∼ president/government** président/ gouvernement vaincu aux élections

lamely /ˈleɪmlɪ/ adv [say] sans conviction

lament /ləˈment/
A n ① (expression of grief) lamentation f, pleurs mpl (**for** pour); ② Literat (song) complainte f (**for** pour); (poem) élégie f (**for** à)
B vtr ① (grieve over) pleurer [wife, loss, death]; se lamenter sur [fate, misfortune]; ② (complain about) déplorer [lack, weakness]; **to ∼ that** déplorer que (+ subj)

lamentable /ˈlæməntəbl/ adj déplorable

lamentably /ˈlæməntəblɪ/ adv lamentablement

lamentation /ˌlæmənˈteɪʃn/ n (expression of grief) lamentation f

laminate
A /ˈlæmɪnət/ n (plastic) stratifié m; (metal) laminé m
B /ˈlæmɪneɪt/ vtr laminer [metal]

laminated /ˈlæmɪneɪtɪd/ adj [plastic, surface] stratifié; [metal] laminé; [wood] contreplaqué; [glass] feuilleté; [card, cover] plastifié

lamp /læmp/ n lampe f

lamp bracket n applique f

lampoon /læmˈpuːn/
A n satire f
B vtr railler [person, institution]

lamppost /ˈlæmppəʊst/ n réverbère m
(Idiom) **between you, me and the ∼** entre nous

lampshade /ˈlæmpʃeɪd/ n abat-jour m

lance /lɑːns, US læns/
A n ① (weapon) lance f; ② Med lancette f
B vtr Med percer [boil, abscess]

lance corporal ▸ p. 1123 n GB soldat m de première classe

lancet /ˈlɑːnsɪt, US ˈlæn-/ n Med lancette f

land /lænd/
A n ① (terrain, property) terrain m; (very large) terres fpl; **the lie** GB ou **lay** US **of the ∼** lit le relief du terrain; **to get the lie** GB ou **lay** US **of the ∼** fig savoir de quoi il retourne; **private/public ∼** propriété f privée/publique; ② Agric (farmland) terre f; **to work the ∼** travailler la terre; ③ (countryside) campagne f; ④ (country) pays m; ⑤ (not sea) terre f; **to reach ∼** toucher terre; **by ∼** par voie de terre
B noun modifier [clearance, drainage, prices] du terrain; [purchase, sale] de terrain; [deal, tax] foncier/-ière; [law] agraire; [battle, forces, animal] terrestre
C vtr ① Aviat [pilot] poser [aircraft]; faire atterrir [space capsule]; ② (in fishing) prendre [fish]; ③ ○fig (secure) décrocher○ [job, contract, prize]; ④ ○(leave with problem) **he ∼ed me with washing the car** il m'a refilé○ la voiture à laver; **to be ∼ed with sb/sth** se retrouver avec qn/qch sur les bras; **now you've really ∼ed her in it!** tu l'as vraiment fichue○ dans de beaux draps!; ⑤ ○(deliver) flanquer○ [blow, punch]
D vi ① Aviat [aircraft, passenger] atterrir; **as the plane came in to ∼** alors que l'avion se préparait à atterrir; ② Naut [passenger] débarquer; [ship] accoster; ③ Sport, gen [person, animal, object] atterrir; [ball] toucher le sol; **most of the paint ∼ed on me** presque toute la peinture m'est tombée dessus; **the punch ∼ed on his chin** le coup de poing l'a touché au menton
E v refl **to ∼ oneself in** se mettre dans [situation]; **to ∼ oneself with**○ se retrouver avec [task, problem]
(Idiom) **to find out how the ∼ lies** savoir de quoi il retourne
(Phrasal verb)
■ **land up**○: ▶ **∼ up** (end up) **to ∼ up in the river** finir dans la rivière; **to ∼ up with the bill** se retrouver avec la facture; ▶ **∼ up doing** finir par faire

land: **∼ agent** ▸ p. 1181 n (on estate) régisseur m; (broker) expert m foncier; **∼ army** n GB Hist corps de femmes

Languages

■ *Note that names of languages in French are always written with a small letter, not a capital as in English; also, French almost always uses the definite article with languages, while English does not. In the examples below the name of any language may be substituted for* French *and* français:

French is easy
= le français est facile

I like French
= j'aime le français

to learn French
= apprendre le français

■ *However, the article is never used after* en:

say it in French
= dis-le en français

a book in French
= un livre en français

to translate sth into French
= traduire qch en français

and it may be omitted with parler:

to speak French
= parler français *or* parler le français

■ *When* French *means* in French *or* of the French, *it is translated by* français:

a French expression
= une expression française

the French language
= la langue française

a French proverb
= un proverbe français

a French word
= un mot français

■ *and when you want to make it clear you mean* in French *and not* from France, *use* en français:

a French book
= un livre en français

a French broadcast
= une émission en français

■ *When* French *means* relating to French *or* about French, *it is translated by* de français:

a French class
= une classe de français

a French course
= un cours de français

a French dictionary
= un dictionnaire de français

a French teacher
= un professeur de français

but

a French-English dictionary
= un dictionnaire français-anglais

■ *See the dictionary entry for* -speaking *and* speaker *for expressions like* Japanese-speaking *or* German speaker. *French has special words for some of these expressions:*

English-speaking
= anglophone

a French speaker
= un/une francophone

■ *Note also that language adjectives like* French *can also refer to nationality e.g.* a French tourist ▸ **p. 1032**, *or to the country e.g.* a French town ▸ **p. 774**.

---

employées aux travaux agricoles pendant la guerre

landed /ˈlændɪd/ *adj* [*class*] de propriétaires terriens; [*property, estates*] foncier/-ière

landfall /ˈlændfɔːl/ *n* Naut (land reached or sighted) escale *f*; **to make** ~ [*boat, person*] accoster; [*hurricane*] atteindre la terre

land: ~**fill site** *n* site *m* d'enfouissement des déchets; ~**form** *n* relief *m* (du sol)

landing /ˈlændɪŋ/ *n* ①ⓘ (at turn of stairs) palier *m*; (storey) étage *m*; ② (from boat) (of people) débarquement *m*; (of cargo) déchargement *m*; (from plane) (by parachute) parachutage *m*; (on runway) largage *m*; ③ Aviat atterrissage *m* (**on** sur); ④ Sport, gen (of animal, athlete) réception *f*; (of parachutist, bird) atterrissage *m*

landing: ~ **beacon** *n* balise *f* d'atterrissage; ~ **card** *n* Aviat, Naut carte *f* de débarquement; ~ **craft** *n* péniche *f* de débarquement; ~ **gear** *n* train *m* d'atterrissage; ~ **lights** *npl* (on plane) phares *mpl* d'atterrissage; (on airfield) balises *fpl* d'atterrissage; ~ **party** *n* Mil commando *m* de débarquement; ~ **stage** *n* embarcadère *m*

land: ~**lady** *n* (owner of property) propriétaire *f*; (living-in) logeuse *f*; (of pub) patronne *f*; ~**locked** *adj* sans débouché sur la mer; ~**lord** *n* (owner of property) propriétaire *m*; (living in) logeur *m*; (of pub) patron *m*; ~**lubber** *n* hum *ou* péj marin *m* d'eau douce

landmark /ˈlændmɑːk/
Ⓐ *n* point *m* de repère; fig étape *f* importante
Ⓑ *noun modifier* [*reform, speech, victory*] décisif/-ive

land: ~**mass** *n* masse *f* terrestre; ~ **mine** *n* Mil mine *f* terrestre; ~**owner** *n* propriétaire *mf* foncier/-ière; ~ **reform** *n* réforme *f* agraire; ~ **registry** *n* cadastre *m*

landscape /ˈlændskeɪp/
Ⓐ *n* paysage *m*

Ⓑ *noun modifier* [*gardening*] paysagiste; [*architecture, art, design*] paysager/-ère
Ⓒ *vtr* aménager [*grounds*]

landscape: ~ **architect** ▸ **p. 1181** *n* architecte *mf* paysagiste; ~ **format** *n* gen, Comput format *m* horizontal, présentation *f* à l'italienne; ~ **gardener** ▸ **p. 1181** *n* jardinier/-ière *m/f* paysagiste

landscaping /ˈlændskeɪpɪŋ/ *n* aménagement *m*

landslide /ˈlændslaɪd/
Ⓐ *n* ①ⓘ lit glissement *m* de terrain; ② fig Pol victoire *f* écrasante
Ⓑ *noun modifier* Pol [*victory, majority*] écrasant

land: ~**slip** *n* glissement *m* de terrain; ~ **surveyor** ▸ **p. 1181** *n* géomètre *m*; ~ **yacht** *n* char *m* à voile

lane /leɪn/ *n* ①ⓘ (narrow road) (in country) chemin *m*, petite route *f*; (in town) ruelle *f*; ② (of road) voie *f*, file *f*; Aviat, Naut, Sport couloir *m*; **'get in** ~' GB 'mettez-vous sur la bonne file'

lane: ~ **closure** *n* fermeture *f* de voie; ~ **discipline** *n* respect *m* du marquage au sol; ~ **markings** *n* marquage *m* au sol

language /ˈlæŋgwɪdʒ/ *n* (system) langage *m*; (of a particular nation) langue *f*; gen, Comput langage *m*; **formal/legal** ~ langage formel/juridique; **spoken** ~ langue parlée; **bad** *ou* **strong** *ou* **foul** ~ langage grossier; **mind your** ~! sois poli!; **don't use that** ~ **with me!** ne me parle pas de cette façon!

language: ~ **barrier** *n* obstacle *m* or barrière *f* de la langue; ~ **laboratory**, ~ **lab** *n* laboratoire *m* de langues

languid /ˈlæŋgwɪd/ *adj* languissant

languidly /ˈlæŋgwɪdlɪ/ *adv* avec langueur

languish /ˈlæŋgwɪʃ/ *vi* ①ⓘ (remain neglected) [*person*] languir; [*object*] traîner; ② (lose strength) dépérir

languor /'læŋɡə(r)/ *n* langueur *f*

lank /læŋk/ *adj* [hair] plat

lanky /'læŋkɪ/ *adj* (grand et) maigre

lanolin /'lænəlɪn/ *n* lanoline *f*

lantern /'læntən/ *n* lanterne *f*

lantern jawed *adj* aux joues creuses

lanyard /'lænjəd/ *n* Naut (rope) ride *f* de hauban

Laos /'laːɒs, laʊs/ ▸ p. 774 *pr n* Laos *m*

lap /læp/
A *n* **1** (area of body) genoux *mpl*; **in one's ~** sur les genoux; **2** Sport (of track) tour *m* de piste; (of racecourse) tour *m* de circuit; **a ten-~ race** une course en dix tours; **to be on the last ~** lit faire le dernier tour; fig en être à la dernière étape; **3** (part of journey) étape *f*
B *vtr* (*p prés etc* **-pp-**) **1** Sport avoir un tour d'avance sur [*person*]; **2** (drink) laper [*water*]
C *vi* (*p prés etc* **-pp-**) (splash) [*water*] clapoter

(Idioms) **in the ~ of the gods** entre les mains des dieux; **in the ~ of luxury** dans le plus grand luxe; **to drop a problem in sb's ~** se décharger d'un problème sur qn; **to fall into sb's ~** tomber tout cuit dans le bec de qn○

(Phrasal verb)
■ **lap up**: ▸ **~ [sth] up**, **~ up [sth]** **1** lit laper [*milk, water*]; **2** fig boire [qch] comme du petit lait [*compliment, flattery*]

lap: **~ and shoulder belt** *n* Aut, Aviat ceinture *f* trois points; **~ belt** *n* Aut, Aviat ceinture *f* ventrale; **~ dancer** *n* strip-teaseuse *f* en salle

lapdog *n* **1** lit chien *m* de salon; **2** (person) péj **he's her ~** elle le mène par le bout du nez

lapel /lə'pel/ *n* revers *m*

Lapland /'læplænd/ ▸ p. 774 *pr n* Laponie *f*

lapping /'læpɪŋ/ *n* (sound) clapotis *m*

lapse /læps/
A *n* **1** (slip) défaillance *f*; **a ~ of memory** un trou de mémoire; **a ~ in concentration** un relâchement de l'attention; **2** (moral error) écart *m* de conduite; **3** (interval) intervalle *m*, laps *m* de temps
B *vi* **1** (drift) **to ~ into** se mettre à parler [*slang, jargon, German*]; tomber dans [*coma*]; **to ~ into bad habits** prendre de mauvaises habitudes; **2** (expire) [*right, patent, law*] tomber en désuétude; [*contract, policy, membership*] expirer; **3** (slip, slide) [*standard*] baisser; **to ~ from** manquer à [*virtue, principle*]
C **lapsed** *pp adj* [*patent, policy*] caduc/caduque; [*contract*] périmé; [*Catholic*] qui n'est plus pratiquant

laptop /'læptɒp/ *n* (also **~ computer**) Comput portable *m*

lapwing /'læpwɪŋ/ *n* vanneau *m*

larceny /'laːsənɪ/ *n* vol *m*

larch /laːtʃ/ *n* mélèze *m*

lard /laːd/
A *n* saindoux *m*
B *vtr* **1** Culin larder [*meat*]; **2** fig (embellish) **to ~ sth with** truffer qch de [*quotations, allusions*]

larder /'laːdə(r)/ *n* garde-manger *m inv*

large /laːdʒ/ ▸ p. 1191
A *adj* **1** (big) [*area, car, feet, house*] grand (*before n*); [*appetite, piece, nose*] gros/grosse (*before n*); **2** (substantial) [*amount*] important, gros/grosse (*before n*); [*part*] gros/grosse (*before n*); [*number, quantity*] grand (*before n*); [*population*] fort (*before n*), important; [*crowd, family*] nombreux/-euse (*after n*); **3** (fat) [*person*] gros/grosse (*before n*)
B **at large** *adj phr* **1** (free) [*prisoner*] en liberté; **2** (in general) [*society, population*] en général, dans son ensemble

(Idioms) **by and ~** en général; **~r than life** exubérant; **as ~ as life** bien vivant

large intestine *n* gros intestin *m*

largely /'laːdʒlɪ/ *adv* [*ignored, obsolete, responsible*] en grande partie; **they are ~ children** pour la plupart ce sont des enfants

largeness /'laːdʒnɪs/ *n* (of body, object) grandeur *f*; (of quantity, sum) importance *f*

large-scale *adj* à grande échelle

largish /'laːdʒɪʃ/ *adj* [*amount, sum*] assez important; [*crowd, house, town*] assez grand (*before n*)

lark /laːk/ *n* **1** Zool alouette *f*; **2** ○(fun) rigolade○ *f*

(Idiom) **to be up with the ~** se lever au chant du coq

(Phrasal verb)
■ **lark about**○ GB faire l'idiot

larkspur /'laːkspɜː(r)/ *n* pied *m* d'alouette, delphinium *m*

larva /'laːvə/ *n* (*pl* **-vae**) larve *f*

laryngitis /ˌlærɪn'dʒaɪtɪs/ ▸ p. 933 *n* laryngite *f*

larynx /'lærɪŋks/ *n* larynx *m*

lasagne /lə'zænjə/ *n* lasagnes *fpl*

lascivious /lə'sɪvɪəs/ *adj* lascif/-ive

laser /'leɪzə(r)/
A *n* laser *m*
B *noun modifier* [*beam, disc*] laser *inv*; [*guided*] par laser; [*printer*] à laser; [*surgery, treatment*] au laser

lash /læʃ/
A *n* **1** Anat (eyelash) cil *m*; **2** (whipstroke) coup *m* de fouet; **3** (whip) lanière *f*
B *vtr* **1** lit (whip) fouetter; [*rain*] cingler [*windows*]; [*storm*] balayer [*region*]; [*waves*] fouetter [*shore*]; **2** (criticize) **to ~ sb with one's tongue** faire des remarques cinglantes à qn; **3** (secure) attacher (**to** à)

(Phrasal verb)
■ **lash out** **1** (hit out) [*person*] devenir violent, se démener; [*cat*] donner un coup de patte; **to ~ out at** [*person*] frapper; [*tiger*] donner un coup de patte à; **2** (verbally) **to ~ out at** *ou* **against sb/sth** invectiver qn/qch; **3** (spend freely) **to ~ out on sth** faire une folie et acheter qch

lass /læs/ *n* GB dial jeune fille *f*

lasso /læ'suː/
A *n* (*pl* **-oes**) lasso *m*
B *vtr* attraper [qch] au lasso

last /laːst, US læst/ ▸ p. 1267
A *n* **1** (for shoes) forme *f*; **2** (end of life) **to the ~** jusqu'au bout
B *pron* (final) **the ~** le dernier/la dernière *m/f* (**to do** à faire); **he poured out the ~ of the whisky** il a versé ce qui restait de whisky; **the ~ of the guests** les derniers invités; **that was the ~ I saw of her** c'est la dernière fois que je l'ai vue; **I thought we'd seen the ~ of him!** je croyais qu'on en avait fini avec lui!; **you haven't heard the ~ of this!** l'affaire n'en restera pas là!; **the ~ I heard...** aux dernières nouvelles...; **the ~ but one** l'avant-dernier/-ière; **the night before ~** (evening) avant-hier soir; (night) la nuit d'avant-hier; **the week before ~** il y a deux semaines
C *adj* **1** (final) [*hope, novel, time*] dernier/-ière (*before n*); **the ~ person to do** la dernière personne à faire; **for the ~ time, will you be quiet!** c'est la dernière fois que je vous le dis, taisez-vous!; **your ~ name please?** votre nom de famille s'il vous plaît?; **in my ~ job** là où je travaillais avant; **every ~ one of them** tous jusqu'au dernier; **the ~ building but one** l'avant-dernier bâtiment; **his name is ~ but two on the list** son nom est le troisième à partir de la fin de la liste; **the ~ few children** les deux ou trois derniers enfants; **2** (describing past time) dernier/-ière; **~ week/year** la semaine/l'année dernière; **~ Christmas** à Noël l'an dernier; **in** *ou* **over the ~ ten years** durant ces dix dernières années; **Anne has been in Cambridge for the ~ eight months** Anne est à Cambridge depuis huit mois; **~ night** (evening) hier soir; (night-time) la nuit dernière; **3** (most unlikely) dernier/-ière; **he's the ~ person I'd ask!** c'est la dernière personne à qui je m'adresserais!; **the ~ thing they want is publicity!** la publicité, c'est vraiment ce qu'ils souhaitent le moins!; **the ~ thing I need is guests for the weekend** il ne me manquait plus que des invités pour le week-end *iron*
D *adv* **1** (in final position) **to come in ~** [*runner, racing car*] arriver en dernier; **to be placed ~** être classé dernier/-ière; **the girls left ~** les filles sont parties les dernières; **to leave sth till ~** s'occuper de qch en dernier (lieu); **~ of all** en dernier lieu; **2** (most recently) **she was ~ in Canada in 1976** la dernière fois qu'elle est allée au Canada, c'était en 1976
E *vtr* **a loaf ~s me two days** un pain me fait deux jours; **we have enough food to ~ (us) three days** nous avons assez de provisions pour trois jours
F *vi* **1** (extend in time) durer; **it won't ~!** ça ne durera pas longtemps!; **it's too good to ~!** c'est trop beau pour que ça dure!; **he won't ~ long in this place** il ne tiendra pas longtemps ici; **that beer didn't ~ long** cette bière n'a pas fait long feu○; **2** (maintain condition) [*fabric*] faire de l'usage; [*perishables*] se conserver

(Phrasal verb)
■ **last out:** ▸ ~ **out** ①① (not run out) [*money*] suffire; [*supplies*] durer; ②② (persist) [*person*] tenir; ▸ ~ **out [sth]** tenir jusqu'à la fin de [*siege*]

last-ditch *adj* [*attempt, stand*] désespéré, ultime

lasting /'lɑːstɪŋ, US 'læstɪŋ/ *adj* [*effect, impression, contribution*] durable; [*relationship*] sérieux/-ieuse; [*damage*] irréparable

lastly /'lɑːstlɪ, US 'læstlɪ/ *adv* enfin, finalement

last: ~**-minute** *adj* de dernière minute; ~ **number redial** *n* Telecom fonction *f* bis; ~ **post** *n* (each evening) retraite *f* au clairon; ~ **rites** *npl* Relig derniers sacrements *mpl*; **Last Supper** *n* Cène *f*

latch /lætʃ/ *n* (fastening) loquet *m*; (spring lock) serrure *f* (de sûreté); **to put the door on the** ~ bloquer le verrou en position ouverte

(Phrasal verb)
■ **latch on**◯: ▸ ~ **on** (understand) saisir◯; ▸ ~ **on to [sth/sb]** ①① (seize on) lit s'accrocher à [*object, person*]; (exploit) exploiter [*idea*]; reprendre [*weakness*]; ②② (realize) se rendre compte de [*truth, fact*]

latch: ~**key** *n* clé *f* plate; ~**key child**, ~**key kid**◯ *n* GB enfant *mf* laissé/-e à lui-/elle-même

late /leɪt/
A *adj* ①① (after expected time) [*arrival, rains, publication, implementation*] tardif/-ive; **in case of** ~ **delivery** en cas de retard de livraison; **to be** ~ **(for sth)** être en retard (pour qch); **to be** ~ **for lunch** déjeuner plus tard que d'habitude; **to be** ~ **with the rent** payer son loyer avec du retard; **dinner will be a bit** ~ le dîner sera retardé; **to be more than three days** ~ avoir plus de trois jours de retard; ②② (towards end of day, season etc) [*hour, supper, date, pregnancy*] tardif/-ive; **to take a** ~ **holiday** GB *ou* **vacation** US prendre ses vacances en fin de saison; **to have a** ~ **night** (aller) se coucher tard; **in** ~ **life** plus tard dans la vie; **to be in one's** ~ **fifties** approcher de la soixantaine; **to be a** ~ **starter** commencer tard; **at this** ~ **stage** à ce stade avancé; **in** ~ **January** (à la) fin janvier; **in the** ~ **50's** à la fin des années 50; ~ **Victorian** de la fin de l'époque victorienne; **it will be** ~ **afternoon when I arrive** j'arriverai en fin d'après-midi; **the** ~**st appointment is at 4 pm** le dernier rendez-vous est à 16 h; **in one of her** ~**r films** dans un de ses derniers films; **in a** ~**r novel** dans un roman postérieur; **her** ~**r experiments** ses expériences ultérieures; ③③ (deceased) **the** ~ **President** feu le Président *fml*; **my** ~ **husband** mon pauvre mari
B *adv* ①① (after expected time) [*arrive, start, finish*] en retard; **to be running** ~ [*person*] être en retard; [*train, bus*] avoir du retard; **to start three months** ~ commencer avec trois mois de retard; ②② (towards end of time period) [*get up, open, close*] tard; ~ **last night/in the evening** tard hier soir/dans la soirée; ~ **last week** à la fin de la semaine dernière; ~**r on** plus tard; **it's a bit** ~ **(in the day) to do** fig c'est un peu tard pour faire; **too** ~! trop tard!; **don't leave it too** ~! n'attendez pas trop (longtemps)!; **to leave no** ~**r than 6 am** partir au plus tard à 6 h; **to marry** ~ se marier sur le tard; **he left for Italy six months** ~**r** il est parti pour l'Italie six mois après; **see you** ~**r!** à tout à l'heure!; ③③ Admin (formerly) **Miss Stewart,** ~ **of 48 Temple Rd** Mlle Stewart, autrefois domiciliée au 48 Temple Rd
C **of late** *adv phr* dernièrement, ces jours-ci

latecomer /'leɪtkʌmə(r)/ *n* (to event) retardataire *mf*

late developer *n* **to be a** ~ [*child*] être lent; [*adult*] hum être un peu en retard

lately /'leɪtlɪ/ *adv* ces derniers temps

lateness /'leɪtnɪs/ *n* (of person, train etc) retard *m*

late-night *adj* [*film*] dernier/-ière (before n); [*session*] en nocturne; **it's** ~ **shopping on Thursdays** les magasins restent ouverts tard le jeudi

latent /'leɪtnt/ *adj* latent

lateral /'lætərəl/ *adj* latéral

late riser *n* lève-tard *mf inv*

latest /'leɪtɪst/
A *superlative adj* ▸ **late**
B *adj* (most recent) dernier/-ière
C *pron* ①① (news etc) **have you heard the** ~? est-ce que tu connais la dernière◯?; **what's the** ~ **on her condition?** quoi de neuf sur son état de santé?; ②② (most recent) **the** ~ **in modern technology** la technologie moderne
D **at the latest** *adv phr* au plus tard

latex /'leɪteks/ *n* latex *m*

lath /lɑːθ, US læθ/ *n* latte *f*

lathe /leɪð/ *n* tour *m*

lather /'lɑːðə(r), 'læðə(r)/ *n* ①① (of soap) mousse *f*; ②② (frothy sweat) écume *f*; **he was in a real** ~◯ fig il était dans tous ses états◯

Latin /'lætɪn, US 'lætn/ ▸ p. 969
A *n* ①① (language) latin *m*; ②② (hispanic) Latin/-e *m/f*
B *adj* latin

Latin America *pr n* Geog Amérique *f* latine
Latin American
A *n* Latino-Américain/-e *m/f*
B *adj* latino-américain

Latino /læˈtiːnəʊ/ *n* US Latino-Américain/-e *m/f*

latitude /'lætɪtjuːd, US -tuːd/ *n* Geog, gen latitude *f*

latrine /ləˈtriːn/ *n* latrines *fpl*

latter /'lætə(r)/
A *n* **the** ~ ce dernier/cette dernière *m/f*
B *adj* (of several) dernier/-ière; (of two) deuxième; **the former or the** ~ **explanation** la première ou la deuxième explication; **in the** ~ **part of the evening** vers la fin de la soirée

latterday /ˌlætəˈdeɪ/ *adj* [*crusader, pilgrim*] des temps modernes; [*invention, technique*] d'aujourd'hui

latterly /'lætəlɪ/ *adv* ①① (recently) dernièrement; ②② (in later times) (pendant) les dernières années

lattice /'lætɪs/ *n* (screen) treillis *m*; (fence, plant support) treillage *m*

lattice: ~ **window** *n* fenêtre *f* à croisillons de plomb; ~ **work** *n* treillis *m*

Latvia /'lætvɪə/ ▸ p. 774 *pr n* Lettonie *f*

laudable /'lɔːdəbl/ *adj* louable

laudatory /'lɔːdətərɪ, US -tɔːrɪ/ *adj* élogieux/-ieuse

laugh /lɑːf, US læf/
A *n* ①① (amused noise) rire *m*; **she gave a loud** ~ elle a ri bruyamment; **with a** ~ en riant; **to like a good** ~ aimer bien rire; **to get** *ou* **raise a** ~ faire rire; ②② ◯(source of amusement) **to do sth for a** ~ faire qch pour rigoler◯; **their brother is a real** ~ leur frère est très drôle *or* marrant◯; **let's go to the party, it will be a** ~◯ allons à la fête, on va bien s'amuser; **the script isn't exactly full of** ~**s** le scénario n'est pas ce qu'on peut appeler hilarant
B *vi* rire (about, over de); **to make sb** ~ faire rire qn; **to** ~ **out loud** rire aux éclats, rire tout haut; **to** ~ **to oneself** rire en soi-même, rire tout bas; **to** ~ **at sb/sth** rire de qn/qch; **the children** ~**ed at the clown** les enfants ont ri du clown; **we're** ~**ing with you not at you** on ne rit pas méchamment; **he** ~**ed nervously** il a eu un rire nerveux; **I don't know whether to** ~ **or cry!** je ne sais pas si je dois rire ou bien pleurer!; **he's afraid of being** ~**ed at** il a peur qu'on se moque de lui; **he doesn't have much to** ~ **at** *ou* **about these days** ce n'est pas drôle pour lui en ce moment

(Idioms) **we're** ~**ing**◯ (in good position) on n'a plus à s'en faire; **he who** ~**s last** ~**s longest** Prov rira bien qui rira le dernier Prov; ~ **and the world** ~**s with you** celui qui rit s'entoure d'amis; **you'll be** ~**ing on the other side of your face** tu riras jaune, ça va t'ôter l'envie de rire; **to be** ~**ing all the way to the bank** remplir ses poches; **to have the last** ~ **over sb** l'emporter finalement sur qn; **she had the last** ~ finalement c'est elle qui a bien ri; **to** ~ **in sb's face** rire au nez de qn; **to** ~ **oneself sick** *ou* **silly** se tordre de rire

(Phrasal verb)
■ **laugh off:** ▸ ~ **[sth] off,** ~ **off [sth]** écarter [qch] par une plaisanterie [*rumour, accusation*]; choisir de rire de [*criticism, insult*]; **she** ~**ed the matter off** elle a tourné la chose en plaisanterie

laughable /'lɑːfəbl, US 'læf-/ *adj* ridicule

laughing /'lɑːfɪŋ, US 'læfɪŋ/ *adj* [*person*] qui rit; [*eyes, face, expression*] rieur/rieuse; **it's no** ~ **matter** il n'y a pas de quoi rire

laughing gas *n* gaz *m* hilarant

laughingly /'lɑːfɪŋlɪ, US 'læf-/ *adv* [*say, explain*] en riant; **it is** ~ **called a hotel** cela porte pompeusement le nom d'hôtel

laughing stock *n* risée *f*

laughter /'lɑːftə(r), US 'læf-/ *n* ¢ rires *mpl*; **to roar** *ou* **howl with** ~ hurler de rire; **a fit of** ~ un fou rire

laughter line GB, **laugh line** US *n* ≈ ride *f* d'expression

launch /lɔːntʃ/
A *n* **1** Naut (*also* **motor** ~) (for patrolling) vedette *f*; (for pleasure) bateau *m* de plaisance; **2** (setting in motion) (of new boat, rocket) lancement *m*; (of lifeboat) mise *f* à l'eau; (of campaign, product) lancement *m*
B *vtr* **1** Naut mettre [qch] à l'eau [*dinghy, lifeboat*]; **2** (fire) lancer [*new ship, missile, rocket*] (**against, at** sur); **air-**/**sea-**~**ed** lancé du ciel/depuis la mer; **3** (start) lancer [*attack, campaign, career, company, product, computer program*]; ouvrir [*investigation*]; mettre [qch] en action [*plan*]
C *vi* **to** ~ **(forth) into** se lancer dans [*description, story*]; attaquer [*chorus, song*]; **to** ~ **oneself at sb/sth** se lancer sur qn/qch

launcher /ˈlɔːntʃə(r)/ *n* lanceur *m*

launch : ~ **pad**, ~**ing pad** *n* (for rocket) aire *f* de lancement; fig tremplin *m* (**for** pour); ~ **party** *n* réception *f* (*pour le lancement d'un produit*); ~ **vehicle** *n* lanceur *m*

launder /ˈlɔːndə(r)/ *vtr* lit laver [*clothes, linen*]; fig blanchir [*money, profits*]

launderette /lɔːnˈdret, ˌlɔːndəˈret/ GB, **laundromat** /ˈlɔːndrəmæt/ US *n* laverie *f* automatique

laundering /ˈlɔːndərɪŋ/ *n* lit, fig blanchissage *m*

laundrette *n* GB = **launderette**

laundromat *n* US = **launderette**

laundry /ˈlɔːndrɪ/ *n* **1** (place) (commercial) blanchisserie *f*; (in hotel, house) laverie *f*; **2** (linen) linge *m*; **to do the** ~ faire la lessive; ~ **basket** panier *m* à linge

laureate /ˈlɒrɪət, US ˈlɔː-/ *n, adj* lauréat/-e (*m*/*f*)

laurel /ˈlɒrəl, US ˈlɔːrəl/ *n* lit, fig laurier *m*

(Idioms) **to look to one's** ~**s** veiller à la concurrence; **to rest on one's** ~**s** se reposer *or* s'endormir sur ses lauriers

lav○ /læv/ *n* GB (*abrév* = **lavatory**) toilettes *fpl*

lava /ˈlɑːvə/ *n* lave *f*

lavatorial /ˌlævəˈtɔːrɪəl/ *adj* [*humour*] scatologique

lavatory /ˈlævətrɪ, US -tɔːrɪ/ *n* toilettes *fpl*

lavatory : ~ **attendant** ▸ p. 1181 *n* employé/-e *m*/*f* à l'entretien des toilettes; ~ **paper** *n* papier *m* hygiénique

lavender /ˈlævəndə(r)/ ▸ p. 752 *n, adj* lavande (*f*)

lavender blue ▸ p. 752 *n, adj* bleu (*m*) lavande *inv*

lavish /ˈlævɪʃ/
A *adj* [*party, home, lifestyle*] somptueux/-euse; **to be** ~ **with sth** être généreux avec qch
B *vtr* prodiguer [*money, affection*] (**on** à); **to** ~ **praise on sth/sb** se répandre en louanges sur qch/qn

lavishly /ˈlævɪʃlɪ/ *adv* [*decorated, furnished*] luxueusement; [*spend*] sans compter; [*entertain*] généreusement

law /lɔː/ *n* **1** ℂ (body of rules) loi *f*; **to be against the** ~ être contraire à la loi fml, être interdit; **it's required by** ~ c'est obligatoire légalement; **the bill became** ~ **yesterday** le projet de loi a été adopté hier; **court of** ~ cour *f* de justice; **to take the** ~ **into one's own hands** faire justice soi-même; **2** Jur (rule) loi *f*; **a** ~ **against sth** une loi interdisant qch; **the** ~**s on sth** les lois sur qch; **there ought to be a** ~ **against it** ça devrait être interdit; **3** (scientific principle) loi *f*; **4** ○ (police) police *f*; **5** (academic subject) droit *m*; **to study** ~ faire son droit

(Idioms) **to be a** ~ **unto oneself** être un peu original; **to lay down the** ~ dicter *or* imposer sa loi

law : ~**-abiding** *adj* respectueux/-euse des lois; ~ **and order** *n* ordre *m* public; ~**breaker** *n* personne *f* qui enfreint la loi; ~**breaking** *n* violation(s) *f*(*pl*) de la loi; ~ **court** *n* tribunal *m*; ~ **enforcement agency** *n* US organisme *m* responsable du maintien de l'ordre; ~ **enforcement officer** *n* US personne *f* responsable du maintien de l'ordre; ~ **faculty** *n* faculté *f* de droit

lawful /ˈlɔːfl/ *adj* [*custody, owner, strike, excuse*] légal; [*conduct*] licite; [*wife, husband*] légitime

lawfully /ˈlɔːfəlɪ/ *adv* légalement

lawfulness /ˈlɔːflnɪs/ *n* légalité *f*

lawgiver /ˈlɔːɡɪvə(r)/ *n* législateur/-trice *m*/*f*

lawless /ˈlɔːlɪs/ *adj* [*period, society*] anarchique; [*area, town*] tombé dans l'anarchie

lawlessness /ˈlɔːlɪsnɪs/ *n* anarchie *f*

law : **Law Lord** *n* GB juge *m* (*siégeant à la Chambre des Lords*); ~**man** *n* US policier *m*

lawn /lɔːn/ *n* pelouse *f*

lawn : ~**mower** *n* tondeuse *f* (à gazon); ~ **tennis** ▸ p. 881 *n* gen tennis *m*; (on grass) tennis *m* sur gazon

law : ~ **school** *n* faculté *f* de droit; ~**suit** *n* procès *m*

lawyer /ˈlɔːjə(r)/ ▸ p. 1181 *n* (who practises law) avocat/-e *m*/*f*; (expert in law) juriste *mf*

lax /læks/ *adj* [*government*] laxiste; [*security*] relâché

laxative /ˈlæksətɪv/
A *n* laxatif *m*
B *adj* laxatif/-ive

laxity /ˈlæksətɪ/, **laxness** /ˈlæksnɪs/ *n* laxisme *m*

lay /leɪ/
A *prét* ▸ **lie** C 2, 3, 4, 5
B *adj* **1** gen [*helper, worker*] non initié; **2** Relig [*preacher, member, reader*] laïque; [*brother, sister*] lai
C *vtr* (*prét, pp* **laid**) **1** lit (place) poser [*object, card*] (**in** dans; **on** sur); (spread out) étaler [*rug, covering, newspaper*] (**on** sur); (arrange) disposer (**on** sur); déposer [*wreath*]; **he laid his hand on my forehead** il a posé sa main sur mon front; **she laid the baby in the cot** elle a couché le bébé dans le berceau; **to** ~ **hands on sth** fig (find) mettre la main sur qch; **to** ~ **hands on sb** Relig imposer les mains à qn; **2** (set for meal) **to** ~ **the table (for)** mettre la table (pour); **to** ~ **an extra place** ajouter un couvert; **3** (prepare) préparer [*plan, trail*]; poser [*basis, foundation*]; tendre [*trap*]; **4** (fix in place) poser [*carpet, tiles, paving, turf, cable, mine*]; construire [*railway, road, sewer*]; **5** Zool pondre [*egg*]; **6** fig (attribute) porter [*charge, accusation*]; déposer [*complaint*]; jeter [*curse, spell*] (**on** à); **to** ~ **stress** *ou* **emphasis on sth** mettre l'accent sur qch; **7** (bet) **to** ~ **a bet** *ou* **money on sth** parier sur qch
D *vi* (*prét, pp* **laid**) [*bird*] pondre

(Idioms) **to** ~ **it on the line** ne pas mâcher ses mots; **to** ~ **a finger** *ou* **hand on sb** (beat) lever la main sur qn; **to** ~ **it on a bit thick** forcer un peu la dose○

(Phrasal verbs)
■ **lay about** : ▸ ~ **about [sb]** rouer [qn] de coups
■ **lay aside** : ▸ ~ **aside [sth]**, ~ **[sth] aside** (for another activity) poser [*book, sewing, toy*]; (after one stage in process) mettre [qch] de côté [*part-finished dish, model*]; abandonner [*studies, cares*]; renoncer à [*responsibility, principle, doubt*]
■ **lay before** : ▸ ~ **[sth] before sb** soumettre [qch] à qn [*law, bill*]; exposer [qch] à qn [*case, facts*]
■ **lay by** : ▸ ~ **by [sth]**, ~ **[sth] by** mettre [qch] de côté
■ **lay down** : ▸ ~ **down [sth]**, ~ **[sth] down** **1** lit coucher [*object, baby, patient*]; étaler [*rug, garment, cards*]; poser [*book, implement, suitcase*]; déposer [*weapon, arms*]; **to** ~ **down one's life for sb/sth** sacrifier sa vie pour qn/qch; **3** (establish) établir [*rule, procedure, plan*]; poser [*condition*]; **it is laid down that...** il est stipulé que...
■ **lay in** : ▸ ~ **in [sth]** faire provision de
■ **lay into** : ▸ ~ **into [sb]** **1** lit bourrer [qn] de coups; **2** ○ fig (abuse) **she laid into me** elle m'est tombée dessus○
■ **lay off** (stop) ○ arrêter; ▸ ~ **off [sb]**, **lay [sb] off** (sack) (temporarily) mettre [qn] en chômage technique; (permanently) licencier; ▸ ~ **off [sb]** (leave alone) ○ laisser [qn] tranquille
■ **lay on** : ▸ ~ **on [sth]**, ~ **[sth] on** **1** (apply) appliquer [*paint, plaster*]; **2** GB (install) installer [*gas, electricity*]; **3** (supply) prévoir [*meal, transport*]; organiser [*entertainment, excursion*]
■ **lay open** : ▸ ~ **[sth] open** exposer (**to** à); **to** ~ **oneself open to sth** s'exposer à qch
■ **lay out** : ▸ ~ **[sth] out**, ~ **out [sth]** **1** lit (spread out) disposer [*goods, food*]; (unfold) étaler [*map, garment, fabric*]; **2** (design) concevoir [*building, book, advertisement*]; mettre [qch] en page [*letter, illustrations*]; monter [*page*]; dessiner [*town, garden*]; **3** (explain) exposer [*reasons, demands, facts*]; **4** ○ (spend) débourser [*sum*]; ▸ ~ **out [sb]**, ~ **[sb] out** **1** (prepare for burial) faire la toilette mortuaire de [*person*]; **2** ○ (knock unconscious) mettre [qn] KO○
■ **lay up** : ▸ ~ **up [sth]**, ~ **[sth] up** (store away) lit faire provision de [*food, supplies*]; fig s'attirer [*trouble*]; ▸ ~ **[sb] up** (confine to bed) **to be laid up** être alité

lay : ~**about**○ *n* péj fainéant/-e○ *m*/*f*; ~**-by** *n* GB aire *f* de repos

layer /ˈleɪə(r)/
A *n* couche *f*; ~ **of clothing** épaisseur *f* de vêtements

B *vtr* **1** (in hairdressing) couper [qch] en dégradé; **2** (arrange in layers) disposer [qch] en couches

laying /'leɪɪŋ/ n (of floor, stone, cable, mines) pose f; (of railway) construction f; (of egg) ponte f

layman /'leɪmən/ n gen profane m; Relig laïc m

lay-off /'leɪɒf/ n (permanent) licenciement m; (temporary) mise f en chômage technique

layout /'leɪaʊt/ n (of page, book, computer screen) mise f en page; (of advertisement, article) présentation f; (of building) agencement m; (of rooms, cards) disposition f; (of town, estate, engine) plan m; (of garden, park) dessin m

lay: **~out artist** ► p. 1181 n maquettiste mf; **~person** n profane mf

laze /leɪz/ vi (also **about**, **~ around**) paresser; **to ~ in bed** traîner° au lit

lazily /'leɪzɪlɪ/ adv [move, wonder etc] nonchalamment; (relaxedly) [lie, float] mollement; [flow, bob] doucement

laziness /'leɪzɪnɪs/ n paresse f

lazy /'leɪzɪ/ adj [person] paresseux/-euse; [smile] nonchalant; [yawn] indolent; [day, holiday] paisible; [movement, pace] lent

lazy: **~bones** n paresseux/-euse m/f; **~ eye** n amblyopie f; **~ Susan** n plateau m tournant

lb abrév écrite = **pound**

LCD n (abrév = **liquid crystal display**) affichage m à cristaux liquides, LCD spec

LDS n (abrév = **Licentiate of Dental Surgery**) diplômé en chirurgie dentaire

LEA n (abrév = **Local Education Authority**) GB administration locale qui gère les affaires scolaires

lead¹ /liːd/

A n **1** (winning position) **to be in the ~**, **to have the ~** être en tête; **to go into the ~**, **to take the ~** passer en tête; **2** (amount by which one is winning) avance f (**over** sur); **to have a ~ of three points** avoir trois points d'avance; **to increase one's ~** creuser l'écart (**by** de); **3** (initiative) **to take the ~** prendre l'initiative; **to take the ~ in doing** être le premier/la première à faire; **to follow sb's ~** suivre l'exemple de qn; **4** (clue) piste f; **5** Theat, Cin (rôle) rôle m principal; **6** (in newspaper) **to be the ~** être à la une°; **7** Elec (wire) fil m; **8** GB (for dog) laisse f

B noun modifier [guitarist, guitar] premier/-ière (before n); [role, singer] principal

C vtr (prét, pp **led**) **1** (guide, escort) mener, conduire [person] (**to sth** à qch; **to sb** auprès de qn; **out of** hors de; **through** à travers); **to ~ sb away** éloigner qn (**from** de); **to ~ sb across the road** faire traverser la rue à qn; **2** (bring) [path, sign, smell] mener [person] (**to** à); **to ~ sb to do** amener qn à faire; **he led me to expect that...** d'après ce qu'il m'avait dit je m'attendais à ce que (+ subj); **everything ~s me to conclude** tout me porte à conclure que; **to be easily led** être très influençable; **this ~s me to my main point** ceci m'amène à mon sujet principal; **3** (be leader of) mener [army, team, attack, strike, procession]; diriger [orchestra, research]; **to ~ a congregation in prayer** entonner les prières; **4** Sport, Comm (be ahead of) avoir une avance sur [rival, team]; **to ~ the world** être au premier rang mondial; **to ~ the field** (in commerce, research) être le plus avancé; (in race) mener, être en tête; **to ~ the market** être le leader du marché; **5** (conduct, have) mener [active life]; **to ~ a life of luxury** vivre dans le luxe

D vi (prét, pp **led**) **1** (go, be directed) **to ~ to** [path] mener à; [door] s'ouvrir sur; [exit, trapdoor] donner accès à; **2** (result in) **to ~ to** entraîner [complication, discovery, accident, response]; **it was bound to ~ to trouble** ça devait mal finir; **one thing led to another, and we...** de fil en aiguille, nous...; **3** (be ahead) [runner, car, company] être en tête; [team, side] mener; **to ~ by 15 seconds** avoir 15 secondes d'avance; **4** (go first) (in walk, procession) aller devant; (in action, discussion) prendre l'initiative; **5** (in dancing) conduire; **6** (in newspaper) **to ~ with** mettre [qch] à la une° [story, headline]; **7** (in boxing) **to ~ with one's left/right** attaquer de gauche/de droite

(Idioms) **to ~ the way** (go first) passer devant; (guide others) montrer le chemin; (be ahead, winning) être en tête; **to ~ the way in space research** être le numéro un dans le domaine de la recherche spatiale

(Phrasal verbs)
■ **lead on:** ► **~ [sb] on 1** (give false hope) mener [qn] en bateau° [client, investor]; **2** (sexually) provoquer

■ **lead up to:** ► **~ up to [sth] 1** (precede) précéder; **2** (culminate in) se terminer par [argument, outburst]; **3** (introduce) amener [topic]

lead² /led/ n **1** (metal) plomb m; **red ~** minium m; **2** °fig (bullets) pruneaux° mpl; **3** (also **black ~**) (graphite) mine f de plomb; (in pencil) mine f; **4** (of window) (baguette f de) plomb m; **~s** (of windows) plomburc f **⊄**; **5** GB (for roofing) couverture f de plomb **⊄**

(Idioms) **to fill** ou **pump sb full of ~**° cribler qn de balles°; **to get the ~ out**° US (stop loafing) se bouger; (speed up) se grouiller°; **to go over** US ou **down** GB **like a ~ balloon**° tomber à plat°

lead led: **~ed petrol** GB, **~ed gasoline** US n essence f au plomb; **~ed window** n fenêtre f à petits carreaux

leaden /'ledn/ adj **1** (made of lead) de plomb, en plomb; **2** (lead coloured) [sky, clouds] de plomb; [complexion] grisâtre; **3** fig [silence] de mort; [atmosphere] écrasant; [footsteps, pace] lourd; [performance] raide

leader /'liːdə(r)/ n **1** (chief) (of nation) chef m d'État, dirigeant/-e m/f; (of gang, group, team) chef m; (of council, club, association) président/-e m/f; (of party, opposition) leader m; (of trade union) secrétaire mf; (of army, troops) commandant/-e m/f; (of expedition) responsable mf; (of strike, movement) meneur/-euse m/f; (of project, operation) directeur/-trice m/f; **2** (one in front) (in race or competition) premier/-ière m/f; (of procession, line of walkers) chef m de file; (horse) cheval m de tête; (in market, field) leader m; **3** (in newspaper) éditorial m

leadership /'liːdəʃɪp/ n **1** (of party, union etc) dirigeants mpl, direction f; **during her ~** pendant son mandat; **under the ~ of** sous la direction de; **2** (quality) qualités fpl de leader

leadership contest, **leadership election** n Pol élection f à la direction du parti

lead-free adj sans plomb

lead-in n préambule m

leading /'liːdɪŋ/ adj **1** (top) [lawyer, politician etc] éminent, important; [company, bank] important; [brand] dominant; [position] de premier plan; **2** (main) [role] Theat principal; gen majeur; **3** Sport (in race) [driver, car] en tête de course; (in league) [club, team] en tête du classement; **4** (at the front) [aircraft, car] de tête

leading article n éditorial m

leading edge
A n **1** Aviat bord m d'attaque; **2** fig **at the ~ of** à la pointe de [technology]
B **leading-edge** noun modifier [technology] de pointe

leading: **~ lady** n Theat, Cin actrice f principale; **~ light** n membre m très actif (**in** de); **~ man** n acteur m principal; **~ question** n question f qui suggère la réponse

lead led: **~ pencil** n crayon m à papier; **~ shot** n grenaille f de plomb

lead story /liːd/ n histoire f à la une°

leaf /liːf/ n (pl **leaves**) **1** (of plant) feuille f; **to come into ~** se couvrir de feuilles; **2** (of paper) feuille f; (of book) page f; **3** (of gold, silver) feuille f; **4** (of table) (sliding, removable) rallonge f; (hinged) abattant m

(Idioms) **to shake like a ~** trembler comme une feuille; **to take a ~ out of sb's book** s'inspirer de qn; **to turn over a new ~** tourner la page.

(Phrasal verb)
■ **leaf through:** ► **~ through [sth]** feuilleter [pages, papers, book]

leaflet /'liːflɪt/
A n gen dépliant m; (advertising) prospectus m; (polemic) tract m; **information ~** notice f explicative
B vtr **to ~ a town/an area** couvrir une ville/un quartier de prospectus ou de tracts

leaf vegetable n légume m dont on consomme la feuille

leafy /'liːfɪ/ adj [tree, wood] touffu; [suburb, area] vert

league /liːg/ n **1** (alliance) gen, Pol ligue f; **to be in ~ with** être allié avec; **2** GB Sport (competition) championnat m; (association of clubs) ligue f; **3** fig (class) niveau m; **they're not in the same ~** ils ne sont pas comparables; **to be in the big ~** être dans le peloton de tête

(Idiom) **to be ~s ahead of sth/sb** être bien meilleur que qch/qn

league table n GB classement m

leak /liːk/

A n [1] (crack) (in container, roof) fuite f; (in ship) voie f d'eau; **to spring a ~** [pipe, tank] se mettre à fuir; [2] (escape) fuite f; [3] Journ (disclosure) fuite f (**about** au sujet de)

B vtr (disclose) divulguer [information, document]; [2] (expel) répandre [oil, effluent]; dégager [fumes]

C vi [1] (have crack) [container, pipe, roof] fuir; [boat] faire eau; [2] (seep) [liquid, gas] s'échapper (**from, out of** de); **to ~ into** se répandre dans [sea, soil]

(Idiom) **to take a ~**⁰ aller se soulager○

(Phrasal verb)

■ **leak out** [information, news, secret] être divulgué; [water, gas] se répandre

leakage /ˈliːkɪdʒ/ n [1] (leaking) fuite f; [2] (of information, secrets) fuite f; [3] Comm (natural loss) perte f

leaky /ˈliːkɪ/ adj [container, pipe] qui fuit; [boat] qui prend l'eau

lean /liːn/

A adj [person, body, face] mince; [meat] maigre; fig (difficult) [year, times] difficile; [company] dégraissé

B vtr (prét, pp **leaned** ou **leant**) appuyer (**against** contre); **to ~ one's head out of the window** se pencher par la fenêtre; **to ~ one's elbows on sth** s'accouder à qch

C vi (prét, pp **leaned** ou **leant**) [wall, building] pencher; [bicycle, ladder] être appuyé contre qch; **to ~ against sth** [person] s'appuyer contre qch

(Idiom) **to have a ~ time of it** manger de la vache enragée○

(Phrasal verbs)

■ **lean across**: ▸ **~ across** [person] se pencher; ▸ **~ across [sth]** se pencher par-dessus [desk, table]

■ **lean back** se pencher en arrière

■ **lean forward** se pencher en avant

■ **lean on**: ▸ **~ on [sth/sb]** lit s'appuyer sur [stick, person]; s'accouder à [windowsill]; ▸ **~ on [sb]** [1] lit s'appuyer sur [person]; [2] fig (depend on) compter sur [person]; [3] fig (pressurize) faire pression sur [person]

■ **lean out**: ▸ **~ out** se pencher au dehors; **to ~ out of [sth]** se pencher par [window]

■ **lean over**: ▸ **~ over** [person] gen se pencher; ▸ **~ over [sth]** se pencher par-dessus [qch]

leaning /ˈliːnɪŋ/ adj [tree, tower, post] penché

leanings /ˈliːnɪŋz/ npl (gift, predisposition) dispositions fpl; (tendencies) tendances fpl

leant /lent/ prét, pp ▸ **lean**

lean-to /ˈliːntuː/ n appentis m

leap /liːp/

A n [1] lit, gen saut m, bond m; Sport saut m; **in** ou **at one ~** d'un bond; [2] fig (big step) bond m (en avant); **a ~ of the imagination** un grand effort de l'imagination; [3] (in price, demand) bond m (**in** dans)

B vtr (prét, pp **leapt, leaped**) franchir [qch] d'un bond [hedge, chasm]; **to ~ three metres** sauter trois mètres

C vi (prét, pp **leapt, leaped**) [1] [person, animal] bondir, sauter; **to ~ to one's feet** se lever d'un bond; **to ~ across** ou **over sth** franchir qch d'un bond; **to ~ out of bed** sauter du lit; [2] fig [heart] bondir (**with** de); **to ~ to sb's defence** fig bondir au secours de qn; [3] (increase) [price, profit, stock market] grimper (**by** de)

(Idioms) **look before you ~** Prov il faut réfléchir avant d'agir; **to come on in ~s and bounds** faire des progrès à pas de géant

(Phrasal verbs)

■ **leap about, leap around** sautiller

■ **leap at**: ▸ **~ at [sth]** sauter sur [chance, offer]

■ **leap in** (with answer, retort) se lancer

■ **leap out** lit surgir (**from behind** de derrière); ▸ **~ out at [sb]** lit surgir devant [passer-by]; fig sauter aux yeux de

■ **leap up** [1] (jump to one's feet) bondir sur ses pieds; **to ~ up at sb** bondir sur qn; [2] [price, rate] grimper

leapfrog /ˈliːpfrɒg/

A n saute-mouton m

B vtr (p prés etc **-gg-**) sauter par-dessus [obstacle]

leapt /lept/ pp, prét ▸ **leap**

leap year n année f bissextile

learn /lɜːn/

A vtr (prét, pp **learned** ou **learnt**) [1] (through study, practice) apprendre [language, facts, trade]; acquérir [skills] (**from** de);

to ~ (how) to do apprendre à faire; **to ~ to live with sth** finir par se faire à qch; [2] (discover) **to ~ that** apprendre que

B vi (prét, pp **learned** ou **learnt**) apprendre (**that** que); **to ~ about sth** apprendre qch; **to ~ from one's mistakes** tirer la leçon de ses erreurs; **it's been a ~ing experience** ça a été une expérience pleine d'enseignements; **you'll ~!** un jour tu comprendras!

(Idiom) **(you) live and ~** c'est une bonne leçon

learned adj [1] /ˈlɜːnɪd/ (erudite) [person, book] érudit; [remark, speech] savant; [journal] spécialisé; [society] savant; **my ~ friend** Jur mon distingué confrère; [2] /lɜːnd/ (acquired) [behaviour, response] acquis

learner /ˈlɜːnə(r)/ n apprenant/-e m/f; **he's only a ~** ce n'est qu'un débutant; **to be a quick/slow ~** apprendre/ne pas apprendre vite

learner driver n GB personne f qui apprend à conduire

learning /ˈlɜːnɪŋ/ n [1] (erudition) érudition f; [2] (process) apprentissage m

(Idiom) **a little ~ is a dangerous thing** Prov il est dangereux de jouer aux experts

learning: ~ difficulties npl (of schoolchildren) difficultés fpl scolaires; (of adults) difficultés fpl d'apprentissage; **~ disability** n US Sch difficultés fpl scolaires

learnt /lɜːnt/ prét, pp ▸ **learn**

lease /liːs/

A n bail m

B vtr louer [qch] à bail [house]; louer [car]

(Idioms) **to give sb a new ~ of** GB ou **on life** [operation, drug] redonner vie à qn; [news, experience] redonner des forces à qn; **to give a new ~ of life to** donner un second souffle à [party, company, movement]

leasehold /ˈliːshəʊld/

A n (tenure) bail m

B adj [property] loué à bail

leaseholder n locataire mf à bail

leash /liːʃ/ n (for dog) laisse f; **to keep sb on a tight ~** fig tenir la bride haute à qn; **to be straining at the ~** fig [person] brûler d'impatience

leasing /ˈliːsɪŋ/

A n (by company) crédit-bail m; (by individual) location f avec option d'achat

B noun modifier [company, scheme] de leasing

least /liːst/ (superlative of **little**)

> ⚠️ When the least is used as a quantifier followed by a noun to mean the smallest quantity of it is translated by le moins de: to have the least food = avoir le moins de nourriture.
> But when the least is used as a quantifier to mean the slightest it is translated by le ou la moindre: I haven't the least idea = je n'en ai pas la moindre idée.
> For examples of these and particular usages see A below.
> For translations of least as a pronoun or adverb see B and C below.
> The phrase at least is usually translated by au moins.
> For examples and exceptions see D below.
> For the phrase in the least see E below.

A quantif (**the**) **~** (le) moins de; (in negative constructions) (le or la) moindre; **they have the ~ food** ce sont eux qui ont le moins de nourriture or le moins à manger; **they haven't the ~ chance of winning** ils n'ont pas la moindre chance de gagner; **I haven't the ~ idea** je n'en ai pas la moindre idée; **the ~ thing annoys him** la moindre chose l'agace; **he wasn't the ~ bit jealous** il n'était pas jaloux du tout

B pron le moins; **we have the ~** c'est nous qui en avons le moins; **it was the ~ I could do!** c'est la moindre des choses!; **the ~ he could have done was phone the police** il aurait au moins pu appeler la police; **that's the ~ of our problems!** c'est le cadet de nos soucis!; **that's the ~ of it** ce n'est pas tout; **she was surprised, to say the ~ (of it)** le moins qu'on puisse dire, c'est qu'elle était surprise

C adv [1] (with adjective or noun) **the ~** le/la moins; (with plural noun) les moins; **the ~ wealthy families** les familles les moins riches; [2] (with verbs) le moins inv; **I like that one (the) ~** c'est celui-là que j'aime le moins; **those ~ able to cope** ceux qui ont le plus de mal à se débrouiller; **nobody liked it, John ~ of all** ou **~ of all John** personne ne l'aimait,

John encore moins que les autres

D **at least** adv phr (at the minimum) au moins; (qualifying statement) du moins; **at ~ 50 people** au moins 50 personnes; **she's at ~ 40** elle a au moins 40 ans; **he's at ~ as qualified as she is** il est au moins aussi qualifié qu'elle; **they could at ~ have phoned!** ils auraient au moins pu téléphoner!; **he's gone to bed—at ~ I think so** il est allé se coucher—du moins, je pense; **such people are at the very ~ guilty of negligence** de telles personnes sont au moins coupables de négligence

E **in the least** adv phr **I'm not worried in the ~**, **I'm not in the ~ (bit) worried** je ne suis pas inquiet le moins du monde; **I'm not hungry in the ~**, **I'm not in the ~ (bit) hungry** je n'ai absolument pas faim; **it doesn't matter in the ~** ça n'a pas la moindre importance

(Idioms) **last but not ~**, **last but by no means ~** enfin et surtout

leather /'leðə(r)/
A n ① (material) cuir m; ② (also **wash ~**) peau f de chamois
B **leathers** npl vêtements mpl en cuir
C noun modifier [garment, object] de cuir, en cuir
(Idiom) **to go hell for ~**○ aller à un train d'enfer○

leatherette /ˌleðə'ret/ n similicuir m

leathery /'leðərɪ/ adj [skin] tanné; [meat] coriace

leave /liːv/
A n ① (also **~ of absence**) (time off) gen congé m; Mil permission f; **to take three days' ~** prendre trois jours de congé; ② (permission) autorisation f; **to give sb ~ to do** donner à qn l'autorisation de faire; **by** ou **with your ~** avec votre permission; ③ (departure) **to ~ of sb** prendre congé de qn; **he took his ~** il a pris congé
B vtr (prét, pp **left**) ① (depart from) gen partir de [house, station etc]; (more permanently) quitter [country, city etc]; (by going out) sortir de [room, building]; **he left home early** il est parti tôt de chez lui; **to ~ school** (permanently) quitter l'école; **to ~ the road/table** quitter la route/table; **to ~ the track** [train] dérailler; **to ~ the ground** [plane] décoller; **to ~ one's seat** se lever; **I left him cleaning his car** quand je suis parti, il nettoyait sa voiture; **the smile left her face** fig son sourire s'est effacé; ② (leave behind) (forgetfully) laisser [person]; oublier [object]; (deliberately) quitter [partner]; laisser [key, instructions, name, tip] (**for** pour; **with** à); (permanently) abandonner [animal, family]; **to ~ sth in sb's care** confier qn/qch à qn; ③ (let remain) laisser [food, drink, gap]; **you ~ me no choice** ou **alternative but to...** vous ne me laissez pas d'autre choix que de...; **he left us in no doubt as to** ou **about his feelings** il ne nous a laissé aucun doute quant à ses sentiments; **to ~ sth lying around** laisser traîner qch; **to ~ sth tidy** laisser qch en ordre; **there are/we have five minutes left** il reste/il nous reste cinq minutes; **he was left short of money** il ne lui restait plus beaucoup d'argent; **the accident left him an orphan/a cripple** l'accident a fait de lui un orphelin/un invalide; **the attack left her with a scar** elle garde une cicatrice de l'agression; **where does that ~ me?** qu'est-ce que je vais devenir?; ④ (allow to do) **to ~ sth to sb** laisser [qch] à qn [job, task]; **to ~ it (up) to sb to do** laisser à qn le soin de faire; **to ~ the decision (up) to sb** laisser à qn le soin de décider; **~ him to sleep** laisse-le dormir; **to ~ sb to it** (to do something) laisser qn se débrouiller; (to be alone) laisser qn tranquille; **to ~ sb to himself**, **to ~ sb be**○ laisser qn tranquille; **~ it to** ou **with me** je m'en occupe; ⑤ (result in) [oil, wine] faire [stain]; [cup, plate etc] laisser [stain, mark]; faire [hole, dent]; ⑥ (postpone) laisser [task, homework]; **~ it till tomorrow/the end** laisse ça pour demain/la fin; ⑦ (stop and agree) **to ~ it that** convenir que; **to ~ it at that** en rester là; ⑧ Jur (bequeath) léguer (**to sb** à qn); ⑨ (pass) **to ~ sth on one's left/right** passer qch à gauche/à droite
C vi (prét, pp **left**) partir (**for** pour)
D v refl (prét, pp **left**) **to ~ oneself (with)** se réserver [time, money]

(Phrasal verbs)
■ **leave about**, **leave around**: ▸ **~ [sth] around** (carelessly) laisser traîner [books, toys]; (deliberately) disposer [cushions, books]
■ **leave aside**: ▸ **~ [sth] aside**, **~ aside [sth]** laisser [qch] de côté; **leaving aside the question of...** (not mentioning) sans parler du problème de...
■ **leave behind**: ▸ **~ [sb/sth] behind** ① (go faster than)

distancer [person, competitor]; **to be** ou **get left behind** (physically) [person] se faire distancer; (intellectually) ne pas suivre, être largué○; (in business) [country, company] se laisser distancer; ② (move away from) [vehicle, plane] s'éloigner de [coast, country, ground]; [traveller] laisser [qch] derrière soi [town, country]; [person] quitter [family, husband]; fig en finir avec [past, problems]; ③ (fail to bring) oublier, laisser [object, child, animal]; ④ (cause to remain) [person] laisser [chaos, problems, bitterness]; [earthquake, storm, flood] faire [damage]
■ **leave go**, **leave hold** usage critiqué lâcher; **to ~ go** ou **hold of sb/sth** lâcher qn/qch
■ **leave off**: ▸ **~ off** [rain] cesser; [person] s'interrompre; **to carry on** ou **continue where one left off** reprendre là où on en était; ▸ **~ off doing** (stop) arrêter de faire; ▸ **~ [sth] off** ① (not put on) ne pas mettre [coat, lid, blanket]; (not put back on) ne pas remettre [coat, lid, blanket]; ② (not switch on) ne pas allumer [light, TV]; ne pas brancher [iron, kettle]; (from switched off) laisser [qch] éteint [light, central heating, TV]; laisser [qch] débranché [iron, kettle]; ③ (omit) omettre, oublier [name, item, letter]
■ **leave on**: ▸ **~ [sth] on** ① (not remove) garder [coat, hat]; laisser [lid, blanket, bandage]; ② (not switch off) laisser [qch] allumé [light, TV, central heating]; laisser [qch] branché [iron]; laisser [qch] ouvert [gas, tap]
■ **leave out**: ▸ **~ [sth/sb] out**, **~ out [sb/sth]** ① (fail to include) (accidentally) oublier [word, fact, ingredient, person]; (deliberately) omettre [name, fact, reference]; ne pas mettre [ingredient, object]; (from social group, activity) tenir [qn] à l'écart; **to feel left out** se sentir tenu à l'écart; **to ~ sth out of** omettre qch de [text]; **to ~ sb out of** exclure qn de [group]; ② (let remain outdoors) laisser [qch] dehors
■ **leave over**: ▸ **~ [sth] over** ① (cause to remain) laisser [food, drink]; **there is/we have some money left over** il reste/il nous reste de l'argent; ② (postpone) remettre [qch] à plus tard

leaven /'levn/ vtr Culin faire lever; fig relever (**with** de)

leaves /liːvz/ npl ▸ **leaf**

leaving /'liːvɪŋ/
A n départ m
B noun modifier [party, present] d'adieu

Lebanon /'lebənən/ ▸ p. 774 pr n (also **the ~**) (le) Liban m

lecher /'letʃə(r)/ n péj coureur m de jupons

lecherous /'letʃərəs/ adj lubrique

lectern /'lektɜːn/ n (in church) lutrin m; (for lecture notes) pupitre m

lecture /'lektʃə(r)/
A n ① (public talk) conférence f (**on** sur); GB Univ cours m magistral (**on** sur); **to give a ~** (public talk) donner une conférence (**to** à); GB Univ faire un cours (**to** à); ② (scolding) **he gave me a ~** il m'a fait la leçon
B vtr ① GB Univ donner un cours à; ② (scold) faire la leçon à
C vi ① GB Univ (on specific subject) faire un cours (**to** à; **on** sur); **she ~s in mathematics** elle enseigne les mathématiques (à l'université); ② (give public talk) donner une conférence (**on** sur)

lecture: **~ hall** n US amphithéâtre m; **~ notes** npl GB Univ notes fpl de cours

lecturer /'lektʃərə(r)/ ▸ p. 1181 n ① (speaker) conférencier/-ière m/f; ② GB Univ enseignant/-e m/f (du supérieur); **junior ~** ≈ assistant/-e m/f; **senior ~** ≈ maître m de conférences; **she's a maths ~** elle enseigne les maths (à l'université); ③ US Univ ≈ chargé m de cours

lecture: **~ room** n GB Univ salle f de conférences; **~ship** n GB Univ poste m d'enseignant à l'université; **~ theatre** n GB Univ amphithéâtre m

led /led/ prét, pp ▸ **lead¹**

LED n (abrév = **light-emitting diode**) DEL f, diode f électroluminescente

ledge /ledʒ/ n ① (shelf) rebord m; ② (on mountain) saillie f (rocheuse); (tiny) aspérité f; (in climbing) vire f

ledger /'ledʒə(r)/ n (in book-keeping) registre m (de comptabilité), grand livre m

lee /liː/
A n côté m sous le vent; **in the ~ of** à l'abri de
B adj sous le vent

leech /liːtʃ/ n sangsue f; **to cling to sb like a ~** coller○ qn comme une sangsue

leek /liːk/ n poireau m

leer /lɪə(r)/ péj

A n (cunning) regard m sournois; (lustful) regard m libidineux

B vi **to ~ at sb/sth** lorgner○ qn/qch

lees /liːz/ npl (wine sediment) lie f

leeway /'liːweɪ/ n Naut, Aviat dérive f; fig liberté f de manœuvre

left /left/

A prét, pp ▸ **leave**

B ▸ p. 803 n **1** (side or direction) gauche f; **on the ~** sur la gauche; **on your ~** sur votre gauche; **to the ~** vers la gauche; **keep (to the) ~** Aut tenez votre or restez à gauche; **2** Pol **the ~** la gauche; **on the ~** à gauche; **3** Sport (poing m) gauche m

C adj gauche

D adv à gauche

(Idiom) **~, right and centre** (everywhere) partout

left: **~-click** vi cliquer en appuyant sur le bouton gauche (de la souris) (**on** sur); **~-hand** adj de gauche; **~-hand drive, lhd** adj [car] avec la conduite à gauche; **~-handed** adj [person] gaucher/-ère

leftie○ /'leftɪ/ n aussi péj gauchiste mf

leftist /'leftɪst/ Pol

A n homme/femme m/f de gauche

B adj de gauche

left: **~-luggage (office)** n GB consigne f; **~-over** adj restant; **~-overs** npl restes mpl

left wing Pol

A n **the ~** la gauche

B **left-wing** adj de gauche

left-winger n Pol homme/femme m/f de gauche

leg /leg/

A n **1** ▸ p. 698 (of person) jambe f; (of animal) gen patte f; (of horse) jambe f; **to stand on one ~** se tenir debout sur une jambe; **2** (of furniture) pied m; **3** Culin (of lamb) gigot m; (of veal) cuisseau m; (of poultry, pork, frog) cuisse f; (of venison) cuissot m; **4** (of trousers) jambe f; **to be too long in the ~** [trousers] avoir les jambes trop longues; **5** (of journey, race) étape f

B ○vtr (p prés etc **-gg-**) **to ~ it** (walk) marcher, aller à pied; (walk fast) galoper○; (run away) cavaler○

C **-legged** combining form **three-~ged** [furniture] à trois pieds; **four-~ged** [animal] à quatre pattes; **long-~ged** [person] à jambes longues

(Idioms) **she doesn't have a ~ to stand on** elle n'a rien sur quoi s'appuyer; **to be on its last ~s** [machine, car] avoir fait son temps; [regime] n'en avoir plus pour longtemps; [company] être au bord de la faillite; **he is on his last ~s** il n'en a plus pour longtemps; **to cost an arm and a ~** coûter les yeux de la tête; **to give sb a ~ up** faire la courte échelle à qn; fig dépanner qn○; **to pull sb's ~** faire marcher qn

legacy /'legəsɪ/ n **1** Jur legs m; **2** fig **the ~ of** l'héritage m de [era, artist]; les séquelles fpl de [war]

legal /'liːgl/ adj **1** (relating to the law) [document, matter, system, profession] juridique; [process, status] légal; [costs] de justice; **to take ~ advice** consulter un avocat; **2** (lawful) [act, age, heir, right, separation] légal; [owner, claim] légitime

legal action n poursuite f judiciaire; **to bring a** ou **take ~ against sb** intenter un procès à qn

legal: **~ aid** n Jur aide f juridique; **~ eagle** n as m du barreau○; **~ holiday** n US jour m férié

legality /liːˈgælətɪ/ n légalité f

legalization /ˌliːgəlarˈzeɪʃn, US -lɪˈz-/ n légalisation f

legalize /'liːgəlaɪz/ vtr légaliser

legally /'liːgəlɪ/ adv **1** [liable, valid, void] juridiquement; **~ represented** représenté par un avocat; **to be ~ entitled to do** avoir le droit de faire; **this contract is ~ binding** ce contrat vous engage; **2** (lawfully) [act] légalement

legal: **~ practitioner** n juriste mf; **~ proceedings** npl poursuites fpl judiciaires; **~ tender** n monnaie f légale

legate /'legɪt/ n légat m

legend /'ledʒənd/ n légende f (**of** de); **~ has it that** selon la légende; **to become a ~ in one's own lifetime** passer dans la légende de son vivant

legendary /'ledʒəndrɪ, US -derɪ/ adj légendaire

leggings /'legɪŋz/ npl gen cuissardes fpl; (for baby) collant m; (for woman) caleçon m

leggy /'legɪ/ adj [person] aux longues jambes

legibility /ˌledʒəˈbɪlətɪ/ n lisibilité f

legible /'ledʒəbl/ adj lisible

legion /'liːdʒən/

A n Mil légion f; fig multitude f

B adj (jamais épith) légion (inv)

legionnaire /ˌliːdʒəˈneə(r)/ n Mil légionnaire m

legionnaire's disease ▸ p. 933 n maladie f du légionnaire

legislate /'ledʒɪsleɪt/ vi légiférer (**on** sur); **to ~ against** faire des lois contre

legislation /ˌledʒɪsˈleɪʃn/ n législation f; **a piece of ~** une loi; **to introduce ~** faire adopter des lois

legislative /'ledʒɪslətɪv, US -leɪtɪv/ adj législatif/-ive

legislator /'ledʒɪsleɪtə(r)/ n Jur, Pol législateur/-trice m/f

legislature /'ledʒɪsleɪtʃə(r)/ n Jur, Pol législature f

legitimacy /lɪˈdʒɪtɪməsɪ/ n légitimité f

legitimate /lɪˈdʒɪtɪmət/ adj **1** (justifiable) [action, question, request, target] légitime; [excuse] valable; **2** (lawful) [business, organization] régulier/-ière; [act, child, claim, heir, owner] légitime

legitimately /lɪˈdʒɪtɪmətlɪ/ adv **1** (justifiably) légitimement; **2** (legally) légalement

legitimize /lɪˈdʒɪtɪmaɪz/ vtr **1** (legalize) légaliser; **2** (justify) justifier

legless /'leglɪs/ adj lit sans jambes; ○GB (drunk) hum soûl comme un cochon○

leg: **~-pulling** n mise f en boîte○; **~-room** n place f pour les jambes; **~ warmer** n jambière f

legwork /'legwɜːk/ n déplacements mpl; **to do the ~** déblayer le terrain○ fig

Leics GB Post abrév écrite = **Leicestershire**

leisure /'leʒə(r), US 'liːʒə(r)/

A n **C** (spare time) loisir(s) m(pl); (activities) loisirs mpl; **to do sth at (one's) ~** prendre son temps pour faire qch

B noun modifier [centre, facilities] de loisirs; **~ industry** industrie f des loisirs

leisured /'leʒəd, US 'liːʒəd/ adj **1** privilégié; **the ~ classes** les classes fpl privilégiées, les nantis mpl; **2** (tjrs épith) = **leisurely**

leisurely /'leʒəlɪ, US 'liː-/ adj [person] calme; [walk, breakfast] tranquille; **at a ~ pace** sans se presser

leisure: **~ time** n loisirs mpl, temps m libre; **~ wear** **C** vêtements mpl de sport

lemming /'lemɪŋ/ n lemming m

lemon /'lemən/ ▸ p. 752

A n **1** (fruit) citron m; (colour) jaune m citron; **2** ○hum **to look a ~** avoir l'air tout bête; **3** ○US pej (film, book etc) navet○ m

B adj (colour) jaune citron inv

lemonade /ˌleməˈneɪd/ n (fizzy) limonade f; (still) citronnade f; US (fresh) citron m pressé

lemon: **~ cheese, ~ curd** n GB crème f de citron; **~ juice** n jus m de citron; GB (drink) citron m pressé; **~ sole** n GB limande-sole f; **~ squash** n GB ≈ sirop m de citron; **~ tea** n thé m au citron; **~ tree** n citronnier m; **~ yellow** ▸ p. 752 n, adj jaune (m) citron inv

lend /lend/

A vtr (prét, pp **lent**) prêter [object, money]; conférer [quality, credibility] (**to** à); prêter [support]; **to ~ sb sth** prêter qch à qn; **to ~ a hand** prêter une main; **to ~ one's name to** prêter son nom à; **to ~ weight to sth** donner du poids à qch; **it doesn't ~ itself to...** il ne se prête pas à...

B vi (prét, pp **lent**) Comm prêter (**to** à); **to ~ at 15%** prêter à 15%

lender /'lendə(r)/ n prêteur/-euse m/f

lending /'lendɪŋ/

A n prêt m

B noun modifier [bank, library, scheme] de prêt; [agreement, rate] d'emprunt

length /leŋθ/ ▸ p. 977

A n **1** longueur f; **to be 15 cm/50 km in ~** faire 15 cm/50 km de long; **X is twice the ~ of Y** X est deux fois plus long que Y; **along the whole ~ of** sur toute la longueur de; **to cycle the (whole) ~ of Italy** faire l'Italie d'un bout à l'autre à bicyclette; **there was a ladder running the (whole) ~ of her stocking** son bas était filé sur toute sa hauteur;

Length measurement

■ *Note that French has a comma where English has a decimal point.*

1 in
= 2,54 cm* (*centimètres*)

1 ft
= 30,48 cm

1 yd
= 91,44 cm

1 furlong
= 201,17 m (*mètres*)

1 ml
= 1,61 km (*kilomètres*)

* *There are three ways of saying* 2,54 cm, *and other measurements like it:* deux virgule cinquante-quatre centimètres, *or* (*less formally*) deux centimètres virgule cinquante-quatre, *or* deux centimètres cinquante-quatre. *For more details on how to say numbers* ▸ **p. 1044.**

Length

how long is the rope?
= de quelle longueur est la corde?

it's ten metres long
= elle fait dix mètres

a rope about six metres long
= une corde d'environ six mètres de* long

A is longer than B
= A est plus long que B

B is shorter than A
= B est plus court que A

A is as long as B
= A est aussi long que B

A is the same length as B
= A a la même longueur que B

A and B are the same length
= A et B ont la même longueur
   or A et B sont de* la même longueur

it's three metres too short
= il est trop court de trois mètres

it's three metres too long
= il est trop long de trois mètres

ten metres of rope
= dix mètres de corde

sold by the metre
= vendu au mètre

■ *Note the French construction with* de, *coming after the noun it describes:*

a six-foot-long python
= un python de six pieds de* long

an avenue four kilometres long
= une avenue de quatre kilomètres de* long

* *The* de *is obligatory in these constructions.*

Height

People

how tall is he?
= quelle est sa taille?
   or combien est-ce qu'il mesure?

he's six feet tall
= il fait un mètre quatre-vingts
   or il mesure un mètre quatre-vingts

he's 1m 50
= il fait 1,50 m (*say* un mètre cinquante)

he's about five feet
= il fait à peu près un mètre cinquante

A is taller than B
= A est plus grand que B

B is smaller than A
= B est plus petit que A

A is as tall as B
= A est aussi grand que B

A is the same height as B
= A a la même taille que B

A and B are the same height
= A et B ont la même taille
   or A et B sont de* la même taille

■ *Note the French construction with* de, *coming after the noun it describes:*

a six-foot-tall athlete
= un athlète d'un mètre quatre-vingts

a footballer over six feet in height
= un footballeur de plus d'un mètre quatre-vingts

Things

how high is the tower?
= quelle est la hauteur de la tour?

it's 50 metres
= elle fait 50 mètres
   or elle mesure 50 mètres

about 25 metres high
= environ 25 mètres de* haut

it's 100 metres high
= elle fait cent mètres de* haut
   or elle fait cent mètres de hauteur

at a height of two metres
= à une hauteur de deux mètres
   or à deux mètres de hauteur

A is higher than B
= A est plus haut que B

B is lower than A
= B est moins haut que A

A is as high as B
= A est aussi haut que B

A is the same height as B
= A a la même hauteur que B

A and B are the same height
= A et B ont la même hauteur
   or A et B sont de* la même hauteur

■ *Note the French construction with* de, *coming after the noun it describes:*

a 100-metre-high tower
= une tour de 100 mètres de* haut

a mountain over 4,000 metres in height
= une montagne de plus de quatre mille mètres

how high is the plane?
= à quelle hauteur *or* à quelle altitude est l'avion?

what height is the plane flying at?
= à quelle altitude l'avion vole-t-il?

the plane is flying at 5,000 metres
= l'avion vole à une altitude de cinq mille mètres
   or à cinq mille mètres d'altitude*

* *The* de *is obligatory in these constructions.*

☛ See next page

L

Length measurement *continued*

Distance

what's the distance from A to B?
= quelle distance y a-t-il entre A et B?

how far is it from Paris to Nice?
= combien y a-t-il de kilomètres de Paris à Nice?

how far away is the school from the church?
= à quelle distance l'école est-elle de l'église?

it's two kilometres
= il y a deux kilomètres

at a distance of five kilometres
= à une distance de cinq kilomètres
　　or à cinq kilomètres de distance

C is nearer B than A is
= C est plus près de B que A

A is nearer to B than to C
= A est plus près de B que de C

A is as far away as B
= A est aussi loin que B

A and B are the same distance away
= A et B sont à la même distance

■ *Note the French construction with* de, *coming after the noun it describes:*

a ten-kilometre walk
= une promenade de dix kilomètres

Width/breadth

■ *In the following examples,* broad *may replace* wide *and* breadth *may replace* width, *but the French remains* large *and* largeur.

what width is the river?
= de* quelle largeur est la rivière?

how wide is it?
= combien fait-elle de* large?

about seven metres wide
= environ sept mètres de* large

it's seven metres wide
= elle fait sept mètres de* large *or* de* largeur

A is wider than B
= A est plus large que B

B is narrower than A
= B est plus étroit que A

A is as wide as B
= A est aussi large que B

A is the same width as B
= A a la même largeur que B

■ *Note the French construction with* de, *coming after the noun it describes:*

a ditch two metres wide
= un fossé de deux mètres de* large

a piece of cloth two metres in width
= une pièce de tissu de deux mètres de* largeur

a river 50 metres wide
= une rivière de 50 mètres de* largeur

* *The* de *is obligatory in these constructions.*

Depth

what depth is the river?
= de* quelle profondeur est la rivière?

how deep is it?
= combien fait-elle de* profondeur?

it's four metres deep
= elle fait quatre mètres de* profondeur

at a depth of ten metres
= à dix mètres de* profondeur
　　or à une profondeur de* dix mètres

A is deeper than B
= A est plus profond que B

B is shallower than A
= B est moins profond que A

■ *Note that French has no word for* shallow

A is as deep as B
= A est aussi profond que B

A is the same depth as B
= A a la même profondeur que B

■ *Note the French construction with* de, *coming after the noun it describes:*

a well 20 metres deep
= un puits de vingt mètres de* profondeur

* *The* de *is obligatory in these constructions.*

2▸ (duration) (of book, list, syllable) longueur *f*; (of event, activity, prison sentence) durée *f*; **a film three hours in** ∼ un film de trois heures *or* qui dure trois heures; **a considerable** ∼ **of time** un temps considérable; **he can't concentrate for any** ∼ **of time** il n'arrive pas à se concentrer pendant (très) longtemps; **3**▸ (piece) (of string, carpet, wood) morceau *m*; (of fabric) ≈ métrage *m*; (of piping, track) tronçon *m*; **dress/skirt** ∼ hauteur *f* de robe/de jupe; **4**▸ Sport longueur *f*
B lengths *npl* **to go to great** ∼**s to do sth** se donner beaucoup de mal pour faire qch; **to be willing to go to any** ∼**s** être prêt à faire n'importe quoi; **to go to the** ∼**s of doing** aller jusqu'à faire
C at length *adv phr* (for a long time) longuement; (at last) finalement
D -length *combining form* **shoulder-**∼ **hair** des cheveux qui arrivent aux épaules; **floor-**∼ **curtains** des rideaux qui descendent jusqu'au sol; ▸ **full-length**
lengthen /ˈleŋθən/
A *vtr* rallonger [*garment*] (**by** de, par); prolonger [*wall, shelf*] (**by** de, par); prolonger [*stay, visit*]; Ling allonger [*vowel, syllable*]
B *vi* [*queue, list, shadow*] s'allonger; [*skirts, trousers*] devenir plus long; [*days, nights*] rallonger
lengthily /ˈleŋθɪlɪ/ *adv* longuement

lengthwise /ˈleŋθwaɪz/, **lengthways** /ˈleŋθweɪz/ GB *adv* [*cut, fold, place*] dans le sens de la longueur; [*place, lay*] en long

lengthy /ˈleŋθɪ/ *adj* long/longue

lenience /ˈliːnɪəns/, **leniency** /ˈliːnɪənsɪ/ *n* (of person) indulgence *f* (**with** pour; **towards** envers); (of punishment) légèreté *f*

lenient /ˈliːnɪənt/ *adj* [*person, treatment*] indulgent (**with** pour; **towards** envers); [*punishment*] léger/-ère

lens /lenz/ *n* **1**▸ (in optical instruments) lentille *f*; (in spectacles) verre *m*; (in camera) objectif *m*; (contact) lentille *f*; **2**▸ Anat cristallin *m*

lens: ∼ **cap** *n* bouchon *m* d'objectif; ∼ **hood** *n* parasoleil *m*

lent /lent/ *prét, pp* ▸ **lend**

Lent /lent/ *n* carême *m*

lentil /ˈlentl/
A *n* Bot, Culin lentille *f*
B *noun modifier* [*soup*] aux lentilles

Leo /ˈliːəʊ/ ▸ p. 1350 *pr n* **1**▸ (star) Lion *m*; **2**▸ (name) Léon *m*

less

When *less* is used as a quantifier (*less money*) it is translated by *moins de*: *moins d'argent*. For examples and particular usages, see **A** in the entry **less**.

When *less* is used as a pronoun (*you should have taken less*), it is translated by *moins*: *tu aurais dû en prendre moins*.

less than is usually translated by *moins que* and *even less* by *encore moins*. For examples and particular usages of these see **B** in the entry **less**.

When *less* is used as an adverb followed by a verb, an adjective, or another adverb (*to eat less, less interesting, less often*) it is translated by *moins: manger moins, moins intéressant, moins souvent*. For examples and particular usages see **C** in the entry **less**.

For *less* used as a preposition (*less 10%*) see **D** in the entry **less**.

For the phrase *less and less* see **E** in the entry **less**.

let¹

When *let* is used in English with another verb in order to make a suggestion (*let's do it at once*), the first person plural *-ons* of the appropriate verb can generally be used to express this in French: *faisons-le tout de suite*. (Note that the verb alone translates *let us do* and no pronoun appears in French.)

In the spoken language, however, which is the usual context for such suggestions, French speakers will use the much more colloquial *on* + present tense or *si on* + imperfect tense:

let's do it at once
= on le fait tout de suite?
  or si on le faisait tout de suite?

let's go to the cinema tonight
= si on allait au cinéma ce soir?

let's go!
= allons-y! *or* on y va!

These translations can also be used for negative suggestions:

let's not take or *don't let's take the bus – let's walk*
= on ne prend pas le bus, on y va à pied
  or ne prenons pas le bus, allons-y à pied

For more examples and particular usages see **A1** in the entry **let¹**.

When *let* is used in English with another verb to express defiance or a command (*just let him try!*) the French uses the structure *que* + present subjunctive:

just let him try!
= qu'il essaie!

don't let me see you here again!
= que je ne te revoie plus ici!

For more examples and particular usages see **A 1** in the entry **let¹**.

When *let* is used to mean *allow*, it is generally translated by the verb *laisser*. For examples and particular usages see **A 2** in the entry **let¹**.

For translations of expressions such as *let fly, let loose, let slip* etc., consult the entry for the second word (**fly, loose, slip** etc.).

---

leopard /'lepəd/ *n* léopard *m*

[Idiom] **a ~ cannot change his spots** Prov chassez le naturel, il revient au galop Prov

leopardskin /'lepədskɪn/
A *n* peau *f* de léopard
B *noun modifier* [*garment, rug*] en peau de léopard

leotard /'liːətɑːd/ *n* justaucorps *m inv*

leper /'lepə(r)/ *n* Med, fig lépreux/-euse *m/f*

leprosy /'leprəsɪ/ *n* lèpre *f*

leprous /'leprəs/ *adj* [*person*] lépreux/-euse

lesbian /'lezbɪən/
A *n* lesbienne *f*
B *adj* lesbien/-ienne

lesion /'liːʒn/ *n* lésion *f*

less /les/ (*comparative of* **little**)
A *quantif* moins de; **~ beer** moins de bière; **I have ~ money than him** j'ai moins d'argent que lui; **of ~ importance** de moindre importance; **to grow ~** diminuer
B *pron* moins; **I have ~ than you** j'en ai moins que toi; **even ~ than half** moins de la moitié; **in ~ than three hours** en moins de trois heures; **13 is ~ than 18** 13 est plus petit que 18; **a sum of not ~ than £1,000** une somme qui s'élève au moins à 1 000 livres sterling; **he was ~ than helpful** il était loin d'être serviable; **it's an improvement, but ~ of one than I had hoped** c'est un progrès, mais pas au point que j'aurais espéré; **she's nothing ~ than a liar** elle n'est rien de moins qu'une menteuse; **it's nothing ~ than a scandal!** c'est un véritable scandale!; **they let me have it for ~** ils me l'ont laissé pour moins; **he's ~ of a fool than you think** il est moins bête que tu ne le penses; **they will think all the ~ of her for it** ça va la faire descendre dans leur estime; **£100 and not a penny ~!** cent livres et pas un centime de moins!; **the ~ said about it the better** moins on en parle, mieux ça vaut; **people have been shot for ~!** il y en a qui ont été tués pour moins que ça!
C *adv* moins; **I liked it ~ than you did** je l'ai moins aimé que toi; **I dislike him no ~ than you** je ne l'aime pas plus que toi; **it matters ~ than it did before** cela a moins d'importance qu'avant; **she is no ~ qualified than you** elle n'est pas moins qualifiée que toi; **it's ~ a village than a town** c'est plutôt une ville qu'un village; **the more I see him, the ~ I like him** plus je le vois, moins je l'aime; **no ~ than 85%** au moins 85%; **they live in Kensington, no ~!** ils habitent à Kensington, rien que ça!; **no ~ a person than the emperor** l'empereur en personne; **he was ~ offended than shocked** il était plus choqué qu'offensé
D *prep* moins; **~ 15% discount** moins 15% de remise; **~ tax** avant impôts
E **less and less** *adv phr* de moins en moins

lessee /le'siː/ *n* Jur preneur/-euse *m/f* à bail

lessen /'lesn/
A *vtr* gen diminuer, réduire [*cost, production*]; atténuer [*impact, pain*]

B *vi* diminuer

lessening /'lesnɪŋ/ *n* diminution *f*

lesser /'lesə(r)/
A *adj* gen moindre; [*life form*] peu évolué; **to a ~ degree** *ou* **extent** à un moindre degré; **~ being** *ou* **mortal** être inférieur; **the ~ works of an artist** les œuvres mineures d'un artiste
B *adv* moins

lesson /'lesn/ *n* [1] cours *m*, leçon *f*; **Spanish ~** cours d'espagnol; **driving ~** leçon de conduite; **to give ~s** donner des cours (**in** de); **to take/have ~s** prendre/suivre des cours (**in** de); **we have ~s from 9 to 12** nous avons cours de 9 heures à midi; [2] Relig leçon *f*; **to read the ~** lire la leçon; [3] fig leçon *f*; **let that be a ~ to you!** que cela te serve de leçon!; **I'm going to teach him a ~!** je vais lui donner une bonne leçon!; **that'll teach you a ~!** cela t'apprendra!

lessor /le'sɔː(r)/ *n* Jur bailleur/-eresse *m/f*

lest /lest/ *conj* sout (*for fear that*) de peur de (+ *infinitive*), de crainte de (+ *infinitive*), de crainte que (+ *ne* + *subj*); (*in case that*) au cas où; **'~ we forget'** ≈ 'In memoriam'

let¹ /let/
A *vtr* (*p prés* **-tt-**; *prét, pp* **let**) [1] (*when making suggestion, expressing command*) **~'s go** allons-y; **~'s go for a swim** allons nager; **~'s begin by doing** commençons par faire; **~'s get out of here!** sortons d'ici!; **~'s not** *ou* **don't ~'s** GB **talk about that!** n'en parlons pas!; **~'s see if...** voyons si...; **~'s**

pretend that... faisons comme si...; ∼'s face it soyons honnêtes; ∼ me see, ∼'s see... voyons...; ∼ me think about it laisse-moi réfléchir; **it's more complex than,** ∼'s say, a computer c'est plus compliqué que, disons, un ordinateur; ∼ there be no doubt about it! qu'il n'y ait aucun doute là-dessus!; ∼ the festivities begin! que la fête commence!; never ∼ it be said that qu'il ne soit pas dit que; just ∼ him try it! qu'il essaie!; if he wants tea, ∼ him make it himself! s'il veut du thé, qu'il le fasse lui-même!; ∼ me tell you... crois-moi, croyez-moi...; [2] (allow) to ∼ sb do sth laisser qn faire qch; ∼ me explain laisse-moi t'expliquer; she let herself be intimidated elle s'est laissée intimider; don't ∼ it get you down ne te laisse pas abattre; she wanted to go but they wouldn't ∼ her elle voulait y aller mais ils ne l'ont pas laissée faire; I won't ∼ them talk to me like that! je ne permets pas qu'on me parle sur ce ton!; don't ∼ me forget to do rappelle-moi de faire; ∼ me see, ∼ me have a look fais voir, fais-moi voir; ∼ me introduce you to... laissez-moi vous présenter à...; to ∼ sth fall laisser tomber qch; to ∼ one's hair grow se laisser pousser les cheveux; to ∼ sb through laisser passer qn; to ∼ sb on/off the bus laisser qn monter dans/descendre de l'autobus; can you ∼ me off here? pouvez-vous me déposer ici?; to ∼ the air out of dégonfler [*tyre, balloon*]

B let alone *conj phr* à plus forte raison

(Phrasal verbs)

■ **let down**: ▸ ∼ [sb] down [1] (disappoint) laisser tomber [qn]; **it has never let me down** [*technique, machine*] ça a toujours marché; to feel let down être déçu; [2] (embarrass) faire honte à [qn]; ▸ ∼ [sth] down, ∼ down [sth] [1] GB (deflate) dégonfler [*tyre*]; [2] (lower) faire descendre [*bucket*]; baisser [*window*]; [3] (lengthen) rallonger [*garment*]; [4] détacher [*hair*]

■ **let go** lit lâcher prise; to ∼ go of sb/sth lit lâcher qn/qch; fig se détacher de qn/qch; ▸ ∼ [sb] go, ∼ go [sb] [1] (free) relâcher [*prisoner*]; [2] lâcher [*person, arm*]; [3] euph licencier [*employee*]; [4] to ∼ oneself go se laisser aller; ▸ ∼ [sth] go, ∼ go [sth] [1] lâcher [*rope, bar*]; [2] fig to ∼ it go (not to react) laisser passer; (stop fretting about) ne plus y penser

■ **let in**: ▸ ∼ in [sth], ∼ [sth] in [*roof, window*] laisser passer [*rain*]; [*shoes*] prendre [*water*]; [*curtains*] laisser passer [*light*]; ▸ ∼ [sb] in, ∼ in [sb] [1] (show in) faire entrer; (admit) laisser entrer; I let myself in je suis entré avec ma clé; [2] to ∼ oneself in for aller au devant de [*trouble, disappointment*]; I had no idea what I was ∼ting myself in for je n'avais aucune idée de là où je mettais les pieds○; [3] to ∼ sb in on, to ∼ sb into mettre qn au courant de [*secret, joke*]

■ **let off**: ▸ ∼ off [sth] tirer [*fireworks*]; faire exploser [*bomb*]; faire partir [*gun*]; ▸ ∼ [sb] off [1] GB Sch laisser sortir [*pupils*]; [2] (excuse) to ∼ sb off dispenser qn de [*homework*]; [3] (leave unpunished) ne pas punir [*culprit*]; to be ∼ off with s'en tirer avec [*fine, caution*]; to ∼ sb off lightly laisser qn s'en tirer à bon compte

■ **let on** [1] (reveal) dire (to sb à qn); don't ∼ on that you speak German ne dis pas que tu parles allemand; [2] GB (pretend) to ∼ on that faire croire que

■ **let out**: ▸ ∼ out US [*movie, school*] finir (at à); ▸ ∼ out [sth] [1] laisser échapper [*cry, sigh*]; to ∼ out a roar beugler; [2] (reveal) révéler (that que); ▸ ∼ [sb] out, ∼ out [sth] [1] (release) faire sortir [*animal*]; fig donner libre cours à [*grief, anger*]; [2] élargir [*skirt, jacket*]; rallonger [*waistband*]; ▸ ∼ [sb] out [1] (release) laisser sortir [*prisoner*] (of de); faire sortir [*pupils, employees*] (of de); (show out) reconduire [qn] à la porte; I'll ∼ myself out ne vous dérangez pas, je peux sortir tout seul

■ **let through**: ▸ ∼ [sb] through, ∼ through [sb] [1] (in crowd) laisser passer; [2] Sch, Univ accorder un examen à; ▸ ∼ [sth] through, ∼ through [sth] laisser passer [*error, faulty product*]

■ **let up** [*rain, wind*] se calmer; [*pressure*] s'arrêter; [*heat*] diminuer; the rain never once let up il a plu sans arrêt; he never ∼s up (works hard) il travaille sans relâche; (talks) il n'arrête pas de parler

let² /let/

A *n* [1] GB (lease) bail *m*; [2] Sport let *m*, balle *f* let; to serve a ∼ jouer un let

B *vtr* (*p prés* -**tt**-; *prét, pp* **let**) (*also* GB ∼ **out**) (lease) louer (to à); 'to ∼' 'à louer'

letdown /'letdaʊn/ *n* déception *f*

---

lethal /'liːθl/ *adj* [*substance, gas, dose*] mortel-elle; [*disease, blow*] fatal; [*weapon*] meurtrier/-ière; [*machine, stretch of road*] très dangereux/-euse; a ∼ mixture (drink) fig, hum un mélange redoutable

lethargic /lɪ'θɑːdʒɪk/ *adj* lit léthargique; fig (lazy) apathique; to feel ∼ se sentir engourdi

lethargy /'leθədʒɪ/ *n* léthargie *f*

let's /lets/ = **let us**

letter /'letə(r)/

A *n* [1] lettre *f* (to pour; from de); to inform sb by ∼ informer qn par lettre; he receives a lot of ∼s il reçoit beaucoup de courrier; ∼s to the editor (in newspaper) courrier des lecteurs; the ∼s of Henry James la correspondance de Henry James; [2] (of alphabet) lettre *f*; (character) caractère *m*

B letters *npl* (literature) belles-lettres *fpl*; a man/woman of ∼s un homme/une femme de lettres

(Idioms) the ∼ of the law la lettre de la loi; to follow instructions to the ∼ suivre des instructions à la lettre

letter: ∼ **bomb** *n* lettre *f* piégée; ∼ **box** *n* boîte *f* à lettres; ∼**head** *n* en-tête *m*

lettering /'letərɪŋ/ *n* caractères *mpl*

letter: ∼ **post** *n* tarif *m* lettre; ∼ **rack** *n* porte-lettres *m inv*; ∼**s page** *n* (in newspaper) courrier *m* des lecteurs

letting /'letɪŋ/ *n* GB location *f*

lettuce /'letɪs/ *n* salade *f*, laitue *f*

letup /'letʌp/ *n gen* accalmie *f*; (respite) pause *f*

leuk(a)emia /luːˈkiːmɪə/ ▸ p. 933 *n* leucémie *f*; to have ∼ être atteint de leucémie

level /'levl/

A *n* [1] gen, Sch niveau *m*; an intermediate ∼ textbook un manuel pour le niveau intermédiaire; to be on the same ∼ as sb être du même niveau que qn; to talk to sb on their ∼ parler à qn d'égal à égal; on a ∼ with the first floor à la hauteur du premier étage; on the same ∼ au même niveau *or* à la même hauteur; at waist-/knee-∼ à la hauteur de la taille/des genoux; at street ∼ au niveau de la rue; that is on a ∼ with blackmail fig ça revient à faire du chantage; on a purely practical ∼ sur un plan strictement pratique; to be reduced to the same ∼ as être mis sur le même plan que; the ∼ of training la qualité de la formation; [2] (degree) (of pollution, noise) niveau *m*; (of unemployment) taux *m*; (of spending) montant *m*; (of satisfaction, anxiety) degré *m*; glucose ∼s taux de glucose; [3] (position in hierarchy) échelon *m*; at local ∼ à l'échelon local; at a lower ∼ à un échelon inférieur

B *adj* [1] (not at an angle) [*shelf, floor*] droit; [*surface*] plan; [*table*] horizontal; [2] (not bumpy) [*ground, surface, land*] plat; [3] Culin [*teaspoonful*] ras; [4] (equally high) to be ∼ [*shoulders, windows*] être à la même hauteur; [*floor, building*] être au même niveau; ∼ with the ground au ras du sol; [5] fig (in achievement, rank) to be ∼ [*competitors*] être à égalité; [6] fig (even) [*tone*] égal; to remain ∼ [*figures*] rester stable

C *adv* to draw ∼ arriver à la même hauteur (with que)

D *vtr* (*p prés* -**ll**- GB, -**l**- US) [1] raser [*village, area*]; [2] braquer [*gun, weapon*] (at sur); lancer [*accusation*] (at contre); adresser [*criticism*] (at à)

(Idioms) to ∼-pegging être à égalité; to be on the ∼ (trustworthy) être réglo○; to ∼ with sb○ être honnête avec qn; to keep a ∼ head garder son sang-froid; to try one's best to do faire tout son possible pour faire

(Phrasal verbs)

■ **level off**: ▸ ∼ off [1] [*path*] continuer sur terrain plat; fig [*prices, curve*] se stabiliser; [2] [*plane, pilot*] amorcer le vol en palier

■ **level out** [*terrain*] s'aplanir; fig se stabiliser

level: ∼ **crossing** *n* passage *m* à niveau; ∼-**headed** *adj* sensé

levelling /'levlɪŋ/

A *n* [1] (making smooth) nivellement *m*; [2] (demolition) démolition *f*

B *noun modifier* [*effect*] de nivellement

lever /'liːvə(r), US 'levər/

A *n* Aut, Tech levier *m*; (small) manette *f*

B *vtr* lit to ∼ sth up/off soulever/enlever qch à l'aide d'un levier; to ∼ sth open utiliser un levier pour ouvrir qch

leverage /'liːvərɪdʒ, US 'lev-/ *n* [1] Econ, Pol force *f* d'appui (on, over sur); [2] Phys puissance *f* de levier

leveret /'levərɪt/ *n* levraut *m*

levitate /ˈlevɪteɪt/
A vtr faire léviter
B vi léviter

levity /ˈlevətɪ/ n désinvolture f

levy /ˈlevɪ/
A n (tax) taxe f, impôt m; (act of collecting) perception f; **import** ~ taxe à l'importation
B vtr prélever [tax, duty]; imposer [fine]

lewd /ljuːd, US ˈluːd/ adj [joke, gesture, remark] obscène; [person, expression] lubrique

lewdness /ˈljuːdnɪs, US ˈluːd-/ n (of joke, remark) obscénité f; (of person, behaviour) lubricité f

lexical /ˈleksɪkl/ adj lexical

lexicographer /ˌleksɪˈkɒɡrəfə(r)/ ▸ p. 1181 n lexicographe mf

lexicography /ˌleksɪˈkɒɡrəfɪ/ n lexicographie f

lexicon /ˈleksɪkən, US -kɒn/ n gen, Ling lexique m

liability /ˌlaɪəˈbɪlətɪ/
A n 1 Jur responsabilité f; ~ **for tax** assujettissement m à l'impôt; 2 fig (drawback) handicap m
B liabilities npl passif m, dettes fpl

liable /ˈlaɪəbl/ adj 1 (likely) **to be** ~ **to do** risquer de faire; **it's** ~ **to rain** il risque de pleuvoir, il se peut qu'il pleuve; 2 (prone) **to be** ~ **to** être susceptible à; **she is** ~ **to colds** elle est sujette aux rhumes; **the contract is** ~ **to changes** le contrat peut faire l'objet de modifications; 3 (legally subject) **to be** ~ **to** être passible de [fine, prosecution]; **to be** ~ **for** ou **to tax** [person, company] être imposable; [goods] être soumis à l'impôt; ~ **for military service** astreint au service militaire; **to be** ~ **for sb's debts** répondre des dettes de qn; ~ **for damages** tenu de payer des dommages et intérêts

liaise /lɪˈeɪz/ vi travailler en liaison (**with** avec)

liaison /lɪˈeɪzn, US ˈlɪəzɒn/ n liaison f

liaison officer n Mil officier m de liaison; Admin responsable mf de la communication

liar /ˈlaɪə(r)/ n menteur/-euse m/f

Lib Dem○ n, adj GB Pol abrév = **Liberal Democrat**

libel /ˈlaɪbl/
A n 1 (crime) diffamation f; **to sue sb for** ~ intenter un procès en diffamation à qn; 2 (article, statement) écrit m diffamatoire; 3 (slander) calomnie f
B noun modifier [action, case, suit] en diffamation; [damages] pour diffamation; [laws] sur la diffamation
C vtr (p prés etc **-ll-**, US **-l-**) diffamer

libellous GB, **libelous** US /ˈlaɪbələs/ adj diffamatoire

liberal /ˈlɪbərəl/
A n gen, Pol libéral/-e m/f; gauchisant/-e m/f pej
B adj 1 [person, institution] gen, Pol, Relig libéral; péj bien intentionné; 2 (generous) [amount, offer] généreux/-euse; [person] prodigue (**with** de); **to make** ~ **use of sth** faire amplement usage de qch; 3 [interpretation] libre

Liberal /ˈlɪbərəl/ n, adj Pol libéral/-e (m/f)

Liberal Democrat n GB Pol libéral-démocrate mf; **the** ~**s** les libéraux-démocrates

liberalism /ˈlɪbərəlɪzəm/ n gen, Pol, Econ libéralisme m

liberality /ˌlɪbəˈrælətɪ/ n 1 (generosity) libéralité f; 2 (open-mindedness) libéralisme m

liberalize /ˈlɪbərəlaɪz/ vtr libéraliser

liberally /ˈlɪbərəlɪ/ adv 1 (generously) libéralement; 2 (tolerantly) de façon libérale; 3 [interpret] librement

liberal-minded adj large d'esprit

liberate /ˈlɪbəreɪt/
A vtr libérer (**from** de)
B liberated pp adj [lifestyle, woman] libéré
C liberating pres p adj libérateur/-trice

liberation /ˌlɪbəˈreɪʃn/ n gen, Pol libération f (**from** de); **women's** ~ libération de la femme

liberator /ˈlɪbəreɪtə(r)/ n libérateur/-trice m/f

Liberia /laɪˈbɪərɪə/ ▸ p. 774 pr n Liberia m

liberty /ˈlɪbətɪ/ n gen, Pol liberté f; **civil liberties** droits mpl civils; **to be at** ~ être en liberté; **to be at** ~ **to do** être libre de faire; **I am not at** ~ **to say** sout je n'ai pas le droit de vous le dire; **to take the** ~ **of doing** prendre la liberté de faire

(Idiom) **it's** ~ **hall here!** chacun fait comme il veut ici!

libido /lɪˈbiːdəʊ, ˈlɪbɪdəʊ/ n (pl **-os**) libido f

Libra /ˈliːbrə/ ▸ p. 1350 n Balance f

librarian /laɪˈbreərɪən/ ▸ p. 1181 n bibliothécaire mf

library /ˈlaɪbrərɪ, US -brerɪ/
A n bibliothèque f; **public** ~ bibliothèque municipale; **photo(graphic)** ~ photothèque f
B noun modifier [book, card, ticket] de bibliothèque

libretto /lɪˈbretəʊ/ n (pl **-tti** ou **-ttos**) livret m, libretto m

Libya /ˈlɪbɪə/ ▸ p. 774 pr n Libye f

lice /laɪs/ pl ▸ **louse**

licence GB, **license** US /ˈlaɪsns/ n 1 (for trading) licence f (**to do** de faire); **sold under** ~ (**from**) vendu sous licence (de); 2 (to drive, carry gun, fish) permis m (**to do** pour faire); (for TV) redevance f; **to lose one's (driving)** ~ se faire retirer son permis (de conduire); **to be married by special** ~ se marier avec dispense; **artistic** ~ liberté f de l'artiste; **this law is a** ~ **to harass the innocent** fig cette loi laisse le champ libre pour harceler les innocents; **a** ~ **to print money** un pactole

licence: ~ **agreement** GB, **license agreement** US n contrat m de licence; ~ **fee** n GB redevance f; ~ **number** n (of car) numéro m minéralogique or d'immatriculation; ~ **plate** GB, **license tag** US n plaque f minéralogique or d'immatriculation

license /ˈlaɪsns/
A n US = **licence**
B vtr 1 (authorize) autoriser (**to do** à faire); 2 obtenir un permis pour [gun]; faire immatriculer [vehicle]

licensed /ˈlaɪsnst/ adj 1 [restaurant, café, club] qui a une licence de débit de boissons; 2 [dealer, firm, taxi] agréé; [pilot] breveté; [vehicle] en règle; **to be** ~ **to carry a gun** avoir un permis de port d'armes

licensee /ˌlaɪsnˈsiː/ n (of pub etc) titulaire mf d'une licence de débit de boissons

licensing: ~ **hours** npl GB heures fpl d'ouverture des débits de boissons; ~ **laws** npl GB lois fpl réglementant la vente des boissons alcoolisées

licentious /laɪˈsenʃəs/ adj sout licencieux/-ieuse

lichen /ˈlaɪkən/ n lichen m

lick /lɪk/
A n 1 coup m de langue; **to give sth a** ~ lécher qch; 2 fig **a** ~ **of paint** un petit coup de peinture; 3 ○Mus (in jazz) chorus m
B vtr 1 lécher; **the cat was** ~**ing its paws** le chat se léchait les pattes; **to** ~ **sth clean** [animal] nettoyer qch à coups de langue; **to** ~ **one's chops**○ ou **lips** lit se lécher les babines; fig (at prospect) se délecter (**at** à); **to** ~ **sb's boots** lécher les bottes○ de or à qn; 2 ○(beat in game) écraser [team, opponent]; (beat physically) battre [person]; **to get** ~**ed** (in game) se faire écraser; **I think we've got the problem** ~**ed**○! je crois que nous avons réussi à venir à bout de ce problème

(Idioms) **at a fair** ou **good** ~○ à toute allure; **to** ~ **one's wounds** panser ses blessures

licorice n US = **liquorice**

lid /lɪd/ n 1 (cover) couvercle m; 2 (eyelid) paupière f

(Idioms) **to blow the** ~ **off sth**○ lever le voile sur qch; **to flip one's** ~○ éclater; **to keep the** ~ **on sth**○ contrôler qch; **that really puts the (tin)** ~ **on it**○! ça, c'est vraiment le pompon○!

lido /ˈliːdəʊ/ n (pl **-os**) (beach) plage f (aménagée); GB (pool) piscine f (en plein air)

lie /laɪ/
A n mensonge m; **to tell a** ~ mentir; **to give the** ~ **to sth/sb** démentir qch/qn
B vtr (p prés **lying**; prét, pp **lied**) mentir; **he** ~**d his way into the job** il a obtenu le poste grâce à des mensonges
C vi 1 (p prés **lying**; prét, pp **lied**) (tell falsehood) mentir (**to sb** à qn; **about** à propos de); **he** ~**d about her** il a menti à son propos; 2 (p prés **lying**; prét **lay**, pp **lain** also for 3, 4, 5) (in horizontal position) [person, animal] (action) s'allonger; (state) être allongé; [objects] être couché; **to** ~ **on one's back/on one's front** ou **face down** être allongé or s'allonger sur le dos/ventre; **to** ~ **in bed all morning** rester au lit toute la matinée; **don't** ~ **in the sun too long** ne reste pas allongé trop longtemps au soleil; ~ **still** ne bougez pas; **he lay dead** il gisait mort; **here** ~**s John Brown** ci-gît John Brown; 3 (be situated) être; (remain) rester; **their unhappy past lay behind them** leur passé malheureux était derrière eux; **that's where our future** ~**s** c'est là qu'est notre avenir; **to**

~ before sb [*life, career*] s'ouvrir devant qn; **what ~s ahead?** qu'est-ce qui nous attend?; **the toys lay all over the floor** le sol était couvert de jouets; **his clothes lay where he'd left them** ses vêtements étaient restés là où il les avait laissés; **4** (can be found) résider; **their interests ~ else-where** leurs intérêts résident ailleurs; **to ~ in** [*cause, secret, talent*] résider dans; [*popularity, strength, fault*] venir de; **to ~ in doing** [*solution, cure*] consister à faire; **to ~ behind** (be hidden) se cacher derrière; (instigate) être à l'origine de; **the responsibility ~s with them** c'est eux qui sont responsables; **5** lit, fig (as covering) [*snow*] tenir; **the snow lay thick** il y avait une épaisse couche de neige; **to ~ over** [*atmosphere*] recouvrir [*place, gathering*]

(Idioms) **to ~ low** garder un profil bas; **to live a ~** vivre dans le mensonge; **to take it lying down**○ se laisser faire

(Phrasal verbs)
■ **lie about = lie around**
■ **lie around:** ▸ **~ around** [*person, object*] traîner; **to leave sth lying around** laisser traîner qch; ▸ **~ around [sth]** traîner dans [*house*]
■ **lie back** (horizontally) s'allonger (**on** sur); **she lay back on the pillow** elle s'est adossée à l'oreiller
■ **lie down** (briefly) s'allonger; (for longer period) se coucher
■ **lie in** (in bed) faire la grasse matinée
■ **lie up** **1** (stay in bed) garder le lit; **2** (hide) se cacher

Liechtenstein /'lɪktənstaɪn/ ▸ p. 774 *pr n* Liechtenstein *m*

lie detector *n* détecteur *m* de mensonge

lie-down /'laɪdaʊn/ *n* **to have a ~** aller s'allonger

lie-in /'laɪɪn/ *n* **to have a ~** faire la grasse matinée

lieu /ljuː/
A **in lieu** *adv phr*: **one week's holiday in ~** une semaine de vacances pour compenser
B **in lieu of** *prep phr* à la place de

lieutenant, Lt /lef'tenənt, US luː't-/ ▸ p. 1123 *n* (GB army, US police) lieutenant *m*; (GB, US navy) lieutenant *m* de vaisseau

lieutenant: **~ colonel** *n* lieutenant-colonel *m*; **~ Governor** *n* gouverneur *m* adjoint

life /laɪf/ (*pl* **lives**)
A *n* **1** (as opposed to death) vie *f*; **a matter of ~ and death** une question de vie ou de mort; **to have a love of ~** aimer la vie; **to bring sb back to ~** gen rendre la vie à qn; Med ranimer qn; **plant ~** la vie végétale; **to take one's own ~** se donner la mort; **to take ~ as it comes** prendre la vie comme elle vient; **~ must go on** la vie continue; **that's ~!** c'est la vie!; **run for your ~!** sauve qui peut!; **2** (period from birth to death) vie *f*; **throughout one's ~** pendant toute sa vie; **the first time in my ~** la première fois de ma vie; **a day in the ~ of** une journée de la vie de; **a job for ~** un emploi à vie; **a friend for ~** un ami pour la vie; **in later ~** plus tard dans sa vie; **early in ~** très tôt; **in adult ~** à l'âge adulte; **at my time of ~** à mon âge; **for the rest of one's ~** pour le restant de ses jours; **the ~ and times of X** la vie et l'époque de X; **to write a ~ of sb** écrire une biographie de qn; **3** (animation) vie *f*, vitalité *f*; **full of ~** plein de vie; **there's not much ~ in this town** cette ville n'est pas très vivante; **to come to ~** [*person*] reprendre conscience; fig sortir de sa réserve; [*fictional character*] prendre vie; [*party*] s'animer; **to bring a subject to ~** traiter un sujet de manière très vivante; **put a bit of ~ into it**○ mettez-y un peu de tonus○; **4** (social activity, lifestyle) vie *f*; **private ~** vie privée; **his way of ~** son mode de vie; **a ~ of crime** une vie de criminel; **to live the good** *ou* **high ~** mener la grande vie; **it's no ~ for a child** ce n'est pas une vie pour un enfant; **5** (human being(s)) **without loss of ~** sans perte de vies humaines; **the ship sank with the loss of 500 lives** le naufrage du navire a fait 500 morts; **6** (useful duration) (of machine, vehicle, product) durée *f*; **7** Jur **to do**○ *ou* **serve ~** être emprisonné à vie; **to sentence sb to ~** condamner qn à perpétuité; **to get ~**○ se faire condamner à perpette○; **8** Art **from ~** [*draw, paint*] d'après nature
B *noun modifier* [*member, peer, membership*] à vie

(Idioms) **anything for a quiet ~** tout ce que tu voudras mais laisse-moi tranquille; **for dear ~** de toutes mes/ses etc forces; **he couldn't for the ~ of him see why** il n'arrivait absolument pas à comprendre pourquoi; **get a ~**○! lâche-moi les baskets○!; **not on your ~**! certainement pas!; **this is the ~**! c'est la belle vie!; **to frighten the ~ out of sb** faire mourir qn de peur; **to have the time of one's ~** s'amuser

comme un fou/une folle; **to take one's ~ in one's hands** risquer sa vie

life: **~-and-death** *adj* [*decision, issue*] crucial; **~belt** *n* bouée *f* de sauvetage; **~ blood** *n* fig force *f* vitale; **~boat** *n* canot *m* de sauvetage; **~buoy** *n* bouée *f* de sauvetage; **~ drawing** *n* Art dessin *m* d'après modèle; **~ expectancy** *n* Biol espérance *f* de vie; (of product) durée *f* probable; **~ force** *n* littér force *f* vitale; **~ form** *n* être *m* vivant; **~guard** ▸ p. 1181 *n* surveillant-e *m/f* de baignade; **~ imprisonment** *n* réclusion *f* à perpétuité; **~ insurance** *n* assurance-vie *f*; **~jacket** *n* gilet *m* de sauvetage

lifeless /'laɪflɪs/ *adj* inanimé; fig [*performance*] peu vivant; [*voice*] éteint

lifelike /'laɪflaɪk/ *adj* très ressemblant

lifeline /'laɪflaɪn/ *n* (on boat) bouée *f* de sauvetage; (safety line) corde *f* de sécurité; (in climbing) assurance *f*

lifelong /'laɪflɒŋ/ *adj* [*friendship, fear*] de toute une vie; **to have had a ~ ambition to do** avoir toujours rêvé de faire

life: **~ mask** *n* Art masque *m*, empreinte *f* du visage; **~ preserver** *n* = lifejacket, lifebuoy

lifesaver /'laɪfseɪvə(r)/ *n* (lifeguard) sauveteur *m*

lifesaving /'laɪfseɪvɪŋ/
A *n* gen sauvetage *m*; Med secourisme *m*
B *noun modifier* [*course*] (swimming) de sauvetage; Med de secourisme

life: **~ sentence** *n* Jur condamnation *f* à perpétuité; **~-size** *adj* grandeur nature *inv*; **~ span** *n* durée *f* de vie; **~ story** *n* vie *f*

lifestyle /'laɪfstaɪl/
A *n* mode *m* de vie
B *modif* [*product*] ciblé pour un mode de vie; [*comedy, magazine*] destiné à un public ayant un mode de vie spécifique

life-support machine *n* appareil *m* de respiration artificielle; **to be on a ~** être sous assistance respiratoire

lifetime /'laɪftaɪm/ *n* vie *f*; **the work of a ~** l'œuvre d'une vie; **in her ~** de son vivant; **the chance of a ~** la chance de ma/ta etc vie; **to seem like a ~** sembler une éternité

life vest *n* US = lifejacket

lift /lɪft/
A *n* **1** GB (elevator) (for people) ascenseur *m*; (for goods) monte-charge *m* *inv*; **2** (ride) **she asked me for a ~** elle m'a demandé de la conduire; **can I give you a ~?** je peux te déposer quelque part?; **to give ~s to hitchhikers** prendre des auto-stoppeurs; **don't accept ~s from strangers** ne monte jamais dans la voiture d'un inconnu; **3** ○(boost) **to give sb a ~** remonter le moral à qn; **4** Sport (in weightlifting) essai *m*
B *vtr* **1** soulever [*object, person*]; lever [*one's arm, head*] (**from** de); fig lever [*siege, ban, sanctions*]; **to ~ sth off a ledge** soulever qch d'un rebord; **to ~ sth out of the box** sortir qch de la boîte; **to ~ sth over the wall** faire passer qch par-dessus le mur; **she ~ed the spoon to her lips** elle a porté la cuillère à sa bouche; **I feel as if a great weight has been ~ed from my mind** je me sens soulagé d'un grand poids; **2** (boost) **to ~ sb's spirits** remonter le moral à qn; **3** ○(steal) piquer○, voler [*file, keys, ideas*] (**from** dans); copier [*article, passage*] (**from** sur); **4** Sport lifter [*ball*]; **to ~ weights** faire des haltères; **5** **to have one's face ~ed** se faire faire un lifting
C *vi* [*lid*] se soulever; [*bad mood, headache*] disparaître; [*fog*] se dissiper

(Idiom) **not to ~ a finger** ne pas lever le petit doigt

(Phrasal verbs)
■ **lift down:** ▸ **~ [sb/sth] down, ~ down [sb/sth]** descendre [*object*]
■ **lift off:** ▸ **~ off** [*rocket*] décoller; [*top, cover*] s'enlever; ▸ **~ [sth] off, ~ off [sth]** enlever [*cover, lid*]
■ **lift up:** ▸ **~ up** [*lid, curtain*] se soulever; ▸ **~ [sb/sth] up, ~ up [sb/sth]** soulever [*book, suitcase, lid*]; lever [*head, veil, eyes*]; relever [*jumper, coat*]

liftboy *n* GB liftier *m*

lifting /'lɪftɪŋ/ *n* (of ban, siege) levée *f*

lift-off /'lɪftɒf/ *n* (of rocket) lancement *m*

ligament /'lɪgəmənt/ *n* ligament *m*

light /laɪt/ ▸ p. 1323
A *n* **1** (brightness) lumière *f*; **by the ~ of** à la lumière de [*fire*]; à la clarté de [*moon*]; **in the ~ of day** lit, fig au grand jour;

to cast ou **throw** ou **shed ~ on** lit projeter de la lumière sur; fig éclaircir; **to hold sth up to the ~** tenir qch à la lumière; **against the ~** à contre-jour; **with the ~ behind her** le dos tourné à la lumière; ②ⓘ (in building, machine, oven) lumière f; (in street) réverbère m; (on ship) feu m; **to put** ou **turn a ~ on/off** allumer/éteindre une lumière; ③ⓘ (part of gauge, indicator, dashboard) voyant m (lumineux); ④ⓘ Aut (headlight) phare m; (rearlight) feu m arrière; (inside car) veilleuse f; ⑤ⓘ (flame) **to put a ~ to** allumer [fire, gas]; **to set ~ to** mettre le feu à; **have you got a ~?** (for cigarette) tu as du feu?; ⑥ⓘ fig (aspect) jour m; **to see sth in a different ~** voir qch sous un jour différent; **looking at it in that ~...** vu sous cet angle...; **to appear in a bad ~** apparaître sous un jour défavorable; **in the ~ of** compte tenu de; **to review sth in the ~ of** réexaminer qch à la lumière de [evidence, experience]; ⑦ⓘ fig (exposure) **to bring to ~** découvrir [fact, evidence, truth]; **to come to** ou **be brought to ~** être découvert

Ⓑ lights npl ①ⓘ (traffic) **~s** feu m, feux mpl; **the ~s are red** le feu est au rouge; **to stop at the ~s** s'arrêter au feu; **to shoot○** ou **jump○ the ~s** griller○ un feu rouge; ②ⓘ (decorative display) illuminations fpl

Ⓒ adj ①ⓘ (bright) [evening, room] clair; **to get** ou **grow ~er** [sky] s'éclaircir; **while it's still ~** pendant qu'il fait encore jour; ②ⓘ [colour, fabric, wood, skin] clair; [hair] blond; **~ blue** bleu clair inv; ③ⓘ (not heavy) [material, substance, snow, wind, clothing, meal] léger/-ère; [rain] fin; [drinker] modéré; [damage, sentence] léger/-ère; **to be a ~ sleeper** avoir le sommeil léger; **she is 2 kg ~er** elle pèse 2 kg de moins; ④ⓘ (delicate) [knock, footsteps] léger/-ère; [movement] délicat; **to be ~ on one's feet** avoir la démarche légère; ⑤ⓘ (not tiring) [work] ne pas fatiguer; [exercise] léger/-ère; **~ duties** petits travaux mpl; **to make ~ work of sth** faire qch sans peine; ⑥ⓘ [music, verse] léger/-ère; **a bit of ~ relief** un peu de divertissement; **some ~ reading** quelque chose de facile à lire; **it is no ~ matter** c'est une chose sérieuse; **to make ~ of** traiter [qch] à la légère [rumour, problem]; ne pas attacher d'importance à [injury]

Ⓓ vtr (prét, pp **lit** ou **lighted**) ①ⓘ allumer [candle, oven, cigarette]; enflammer [wood, paper]; tirer [firework]; craquer [match]; **to ~ a fire** faire un ou du feu; **to ~ the fire** allumer le feu; ②ⓘ (illuminate) éclairer

Ⓔ vi (prét, pp **lit**) [fire] prendre; [gas, match] s'allumer

(Idioms) **the ~ of sb's life** le rayon de soleil de qn; **many hands make ~ work** Prov à plusieurs la besogne va vite; **to go out like a ~** s'endormir tout de suite; **to see the ~** comprendre

(Phrasal verbs)
■ **light on**: ► **~ on [sth]** [eyes, person] tomber sur
■ **light up**: ► **~ up** ①ⓘ (light cigarette) allumer une cigarette (or une pipe etc); ②ⓘ [lamp] s'allumer; fig [face] s'éclairer; [eyes] briller de joie; ► **~ up [sth]**, **~ [sth] up** ①ⓘ allumer [cigarette, pipe]; ②ⓘ (illuminate) illuminer

light bulb n ampoule f

lighten /ˈlaɪtn/
Ⓐ vtr ①ⓘ éclairer [room, surroundings]; éclaircir [colour, hair, wood, skin]; fig détendre [atmosphere]; ②ⓘ alléger [burden, pressure]
Ⓑ vi ①ⓘ [sky, colour, hair] s'éclaircir; fig [atmosphere] se détendre; ②ⓘ [burden, pressure, workload] s'alléger

light entertainment n variétés fpl

lighter /ˈlaɪtə(r)/ n ①ⓘ (for smokers) gen briquet m; (for gas cooker) allume-gaz m inv; ②ⓘ Naut allège f

lighter fuel n (gas) gaz m à briquet; (liquid) essence f à briquet

light: **~-fingered** adj (thieving) chapardeur/-euse; (skilful) [thief] adroit; **~-footed** adj agile, au pied léger liter; **~-headed** adj [person] étourdi; **~-hearted** adj (happy) enjoué; (not serious) humoristique; **~house** n phare m; **~ industry** n industrie f légère

lighting /ˈlaɪtɪŋ/ n gen, Theat éclairage m

lightly /ˈlaɪtlɪ/ adv ①ⓘ (delicately) gen légèrement; [move, run] avec légèreté; (frivolously) [take decision] à la légère; **to sleep ~** avoir le sommeil léger; ②ⓘ (with little punishment) **to get off ~** s'en tirer à bon compte

lightness /ˈlaɪtnɪs/ n ①ⓘ (brightness) clarté f; ②ⓘ (in weight) légèreté f

lightning /ˈlaɪtnɪŋ/
Ⓐ n ¢ éclairs mpl; **a flash of ~** un éclair; **struck by ~** frappé par la foudre
Ⓑ adj [raid, visit] éclair (inv)

---

like¹

When like is used as a preposition (like a child, do it like this) it can generally be translated by comme.

Note however that be like and look like meaning resemble are translated by ressembler à:

she's like her father or **she looks like her father**
= elle ressemble à son père

like is used after certain other verbs in English to express particular kinds of resemblance (taste like, feel like, smell like etc.). For translations, consult the appropriate verb entry.

When like is used as a conjunction it is translated by comme:

songs like my mother sings
= des chansons comme celles que chante ma mère

When like is used to introduce an illustrative example (big cities like London) it can be translated by either comme or tel/telle/tels/telles que: les grandes villes comme Londres or les grandes villes telles que Londres.

For particular usages of like as a preposition or conjunction and for noun and adverb uses, see the entry **like¹**.

(Idioms) **as quick as ~** en un rien de temps; **like greased ~**, **like a streak of ~** en quatrième vitesse

lightning: **~ conductor** GB, **~ rod** n paratonnerre m; **~ strike** n grève f surprise

light: **~ opera** n opérette f; **~ pen** n (for computer screen) photostyle m, crayon m optique; **~ railway** n transport m urbain sur rail; **~-sensitive** adj photosensible; **~ switch** n interrupteur m

lightweight /ˈlaɪtweɪt/
Ⓐ n Sport poids m léger; fig péj personne f médiocre
Ⓑ adj gen léger/-ère; Sport [champion, title] des poids légers; fig péj médiocre

light year n année-lumière f; **it was ~s ago** ça fait des siècles

like¹ /laɪk/
Ⓐ prep ①ⓘ (in the same manner as) comme; **to act ~ a professional** agir comme un professionnel or en professionnel; **~ the liar that she is, she...** en bonne menteuse, elle...; **stop behaving ~ an idiot!** arrête de faire l'idiot!; **it happened ~ this** voilà comment cela s'est passé; **when I see things ~ that** quand je vois des choses pareilles; **I'm sorry to disturb you ~ this** je suis désolé de vous déranger comme ça; ②ⓘ (similar to, resembling) comme; **to be ~ sb/sth** être comme qn/qch; **you know what she's ~!** tu sais comment elle est!; **it was just ~ a fairytale!** on aurait dit un conte de fée!; **what's it ~?** c'est comment?; **so this is what it feels ~ to be poor** maintenant je sais (or on sait etc) ce que c'est d'être pauvre!; **there's nothing ~ a nice warm bath!** rien ne vaut un bon bain chaud!; **I've never seen anything ~ it!** je n'ai jamais rien vu de pareil!; **that's more ~ it!** voilà qui est mieux!; **I don't earn anything ~ as much as she does** je suis loin de gagner autant qu'elle; **what was the weather ~?** quel temps faisait-il?; ③ⓘ (typical of) **it's not ~ her to be late** ça ne lui ressemble pas or ce n'est pas son genre d'être en retard; **it's just ~ him to be so spiteful!** c'est bien lui d'être si méchant!; **just ~ a man!** c'est typiquement masculin!; ④ⓘ (expressing probability) **it looks ~ rain** on dirait qu'il va pleuvoir; **it looks ~ the war will be a long one** il y a des chances pour que la guerre dure; **you seem ~ an intelligent man** tu as l'air intelligent; ⑤ⓘ (close to) **it cost something ~ £20** cela a coûté dans les 20 livres or environ 20 livres; **with something ~ enthusiasm** avec un semblant d'enthousiasme
Ⓑ adj sout pareil/-eille, semblable, du même genre
Ⓒ conj ①ⓘ (in the same way as) comme; **~ I said, I wasn't there○** comme je vous l'ai déjà dit, je n'étais pas là; **~ they used to** comme ils le faisaient autrefois; ②ⓘ (as if) comme si; **he acts ~ he owns the place** il se conduit comme s'il était chez lui
Ⓓ adv (akin to, near) **it's nothing ~ as nice as...** c'est loin d'être

aussi beau que...; **'the figures are 10% more than last year'—'20%, more ~**⚬**!'** 'les chiffres sont de 10% supérieurs à l'année dernière'—'20%, plutôt!'

E *n* **fires, floods and the ~** des incendies, des inondations et autres catastrophes de ce genre; **I've never seen the ~ (of it)** je n'ai jamais vu une chose pareille; **the ~(s) of Al Capone** des gens comme Al Capone; **she won't even speak to the ~s of us**⚬! elle refuse même de parler à des gens comme nous!

F **-like** *combining form* **bird-~** qui fait penser à un oiseau; **child-~** enfantin; **king-~** royal

(Idioms) **~ enough, (as) ~ as not** probablement; **~ father ~ son** Prov tel père tel fils Prov

like² /laɪk/ *vtr* **1** aimer bien [*person*]; aimer (bien) [*artist, food, music, style*]; **to ~ A better than B** préférer A à B, aimer mieux A que B; **to ~ A best** préférer A; **to be well ~d** être apprécié; **to want to be ~d** vouloir plaire; **2** **how do you ~ your tea?** comment aimes-tu boire ton thé?; **what I ~ about him/this car is...** ce que j'aime (bien) chez lui/ dans cette voiture, c'est...; **she didn't ~ the look of the hotel** l'hôtel ne lui disait rien; **I don't ~ the look of that man** cet homme a une tête que ne me revient pas; **I don't ~ the look of her, call the doctor** elle a une drôle de mine, appelle le médecin; **I don't ~ the sound of that** ça ne me dit rien qui vaille; **if you ~ that sort of thing** à condition d'aimer ce genre de choses; **I ~ cheese but it doesn't ~ me**⚬ j'aime le fromage mais ça ne me réussit pas; **this plant ~s sunlight** cette plante se plaît au soleil; **I ~ doing, I ~ to do** j'aime (bien) faire; **I ~ to see people doing** j'aime (bien) que les gens fassent; **how do you ~ living in London?** ça te plaît de vivre à Londres?; **the boss won't ~ it if you're late** le patron ne sera pas content si tu arrives en retard; **she doesn't ~ to be kept waiting** elle n'aime pas qu'on la fasse attendre; **I ~ it!** ça me plaît!; **~ it or not we all pay tax** que ça nous plaise ou non nous payons tous des impôts; **3** (wish) vouloir, aimer; **I would** *ou* **should ~ a ticket** je voudrais un billet; **I would** *ou* **should ~ to do** je voudrais *or* j'aimerais faire; **would you ~ to come to dinner?** voudriez-vous venir dîner?; **I wouldn't ~ to think I'd upset her** j'espère bien que je ne lui ai pas fait de peine; **we'd ~ her to do** nous voudrions *or* aimerions qu'elle fasse; **would you ~ me to come?** voulez-vous que je vienne?; **if you ~** si tu veux; **you can do what you ~** tu peux faire ce que tu veux; **say what you ~, I think it's a good idea** tu peux dire ce que tu veux, je pense que c'est une bonne idée; **sit (any)where you ~** asseyez-vous où vous voulez; **4** (think important) **to ~ to do** tenir à faire

likeable /'laɪkəbl/ *adj* [*person*] sympathique; [*novel, music*] agréable

likelihood /'laɪklɪhʊd/ *n* probabilité *f*, chances *fpl*; **in all ~** selon toute probabilité; **the ~ is that she got lost** il est probable qu'elle se soit perdue; **there is no ~ of peace** il n'y a aucune chance de paix

likely /'laɪklɪ/
A *adj* **1** (probable) probable; [*explanation*] plausible; **to be ~ to fail** risquer d'échouer; **to be ~ to become president** avoir de fortes chances de devenir président; **the man most ~ to win** l'homme qui a le plus de chances de gagner; **it is** *ou* **seems ~ that** il est probable que; **it is not** *ou* **hardly ~ that** il y a peu de chances que (+ *subj*); **he looks ~ to fail** il échouera probablement; **a ~ story!** iron à d'autres⚬!; **2** (promising) [*person, candidate*] prometteur/ -euse; **3** (potential) [*client, candidate*] potentiel/-ielle
B *adv* (probably) probablement; **as ~ as not** probablement; **not ~!**⚬! GB que tu crois⚬!

like-minded /laɪk'maɪndɪd/ *adj* du même avis

liken /'laɪkən/ *vtr* comparer **(to** à)

likeness /'laɪknɪs/ *n* **1** (similarity) ressemblance *f* **(between** entre); **family ~** air *m* de famille; **to be a good ~** [*picture*] être ressemblant; **2** (form) **to assume** *ou* **take on the ~ of** se métamorphoser en

likewise /'laɪkwaɪz/ *adv* (similarly) également, de même; (also) aussi, de même; **to do ~** faire de même

liking /'laɪkɪŋ/ *n* **to have a ~ for** aimer; **to take a ~ to sb** se prendre d'affection pour qn; **you should find this more to your ~** ceci devrait vous plaire davantage; **he's too smart for my ~** il est trop malin à mon goût

lilac /'laɪlək/
A *n* lilas *m*
B ▸ p. 752 *adj* (colour) lilas *inv*

Lilo ® /'laɪləʊ/ *n* matelas *m* pneumatique

lilt /lɪlt/ *n* (of tune) cadence *f*; (of accent) intonation *f*

lilting /'lɪltɪŋ/ *adj* mélodieux/-ieuse

lily /'lɪlɪ/ *n* lys *m* *inv*

lily: **~-livered** *adj* poltron/-onne; **~ of the valley** *n* muguet *m*; **~ pond** *n* bassin *m* aux nénuphars

limb /lɪm/ *n* **1** Anat membre *m*; **2** (of tree) branche *f* (maîtresse)

(Idioms) **to be out on a ~** se retrouver isolé; **to go out on a ~** se mouiller⚬; **to risk life and ~** risquer sa vie; **to tear sb ~ from ~** mettre qn en pièces

limber /'lɪmbə(r)/ *adj* littér souple

(Phrasal verb)

■ **limber up** s'échauffer

limbo /'lɪmbəʊ/ *n* **1** ⦰ Relig, fig les limbes *mpl*; **2** (dance) limbo *m*

lime /laɪm/ *n* **1** (calcium) chaux *f*; **2** (fruit) citron *m* vert; (tree) tilleul *m*

lime: **~ green** ▸ p. 752 *n*, *adj* citron (*m*) vert *inv*; **~ juice** *n* jus *m* de citron vert

limelight /'laɪmlaɪt/ *n* vedette *f*; **to be in the ~** tenir la vedette

limerick /'lɪmərɪk/ *n* limerick *m*

limestone *n* calcaire *m*

limit /'lɪmɪt/
A *n* **1** (boundary) lit, fig limite *f*; **there will be no ~ to the violence** la violence ne connaîtra pas de limites; **within the ~s of what we can do** dans la limite de ce que l'on peut faire; **to be off ~s** Mil être interdit d'accès; **the garden is off ~s** l'accès au jardin est interdit; **to push sb to the ~** pousser qn à bout; **2** (legal restriction) limitation *f* (**on** sur); **speed ~** limitation de vitesse; **to be over the ~** (of alcohol) avoir trop d'alcool dans le sang
B *vtr* limiter; **places are ~ed to 60** le nombre de places est limité à 60; **to ~ oneself to** se limiter à

limitation /ˌlɪmɪ'teɪʃn/ *n* **1** (restriction) restriction *f* (**on** à); **2** (shortcoming) limite *f*; **to know one's (own) ~s** connaître ses propres limites

limited /'lɪmɪtɪd/ *adj* **1** [*resources, vocabulary, intelligence, space*] limité; **2** Comm **Nolan Computers Limited** Nolan Computers SA

limited: **~ company** *n* GB société *f* anonyme; **~ edition** *n* (book, lithograph) tirage *m* limité; (recording) production *f* limitée

limitless /'lɪmɪtlɪs/ *adj* illimité

limousine /'lɪməziːn, ˌlɪmə'ziːn/ *n* limousine *f*

limp /lɪmp/
A *n* **to have a ~** boiter
B *adj* [*material, gesture, handshake, style*] mou/molle; **I felt his body go ~** j'ai senti tous les muscles de son corps se relâcher
C *vi* **to ~ along** boiter; **to ~ in/away** entrer/s'éloigner en boitant

limpid /'lɪmpɪd/ *adj* limpide

limply /'lɪmplɪ/ *adv* mollement

limpness /'lɪmpnɪs/ *n* (of body) mollesse *f*

limp-wristed /ˌlɪmp'rɪstɪd/ *adj* péj efféminé

linchpin /'lɪntʃpɪn/ *n* (essential element) **the ~ of** [*person*] le pilier de; [*principle*] la base de

Lincs GB Post *abrév écrite* = **Lincolnshire**

linctus /'lɪŋktəs/ *n* sirop *m* (contre la toux)

linden (tree) /'lɪndən/ *n* littér tilleul *m*

line /laɪn/
A *n* **1** gen, Sport ligne *f*; (shorter, thicker) trait *m*; Art trait *m*; **a straight/curved ~** une ligne droite/courbe; **to put a ~ through sth** barrer qch; **the ~ AB** (in geometry) la droite AB; **2** (of people, cars) file *f*; (of trees) rangée *f*; **in straight ~s** [*plant, arrange*] en lignes droites; **to be in ~** [*buildings*] être dans l'alignement; **put the desks in ~** alignez les bureaux; **3** fig **to be in ~ for promotion** avoir des chances d'être promu; **you're next in ~** ça va être ton tour; **in ~ for** bien placé pour obtenir; **4** (queue) file *f*; **to stand in** *ou* **wait in ~** faire la queue; **to form a ~** [*people*] faire la queue; **please form a ~** mettez-vous en file s'il vous plaît; **5** (on face) ride *f*; **6** Archit (outline shape) ligne *f* (**of** de); **7** (boundary) frontière *f*; **there's a fine ~ between knowledge and pedantry** de la culture à la pédanterie il n'y a

qu'un pas; [8] (rope) corde *f*; (for fishing) ligne *f*; **to put the washing on the** ~ étendre le linge; [9] (cable) Elec ligne *f* (électrique); [10] Telecom (connection) ligne *f*; **to be on the** ~ **to sb** être en ligne avec qn; **to get off the** ~○ raccrocher; **at the other end of the** ~ au bout du fil; **the** ~ **is dead** il n'y a pas de tonalité; **the** ~ **went dead** la ligne a été coupée; [11] (rail route) ligne *f* (**between** entre); (rails) voie *f*; (shipping company, airline) compagnie *f*; [12] (in genealogy) lignée *f*; **the male** ~ la ligne par les hommes; **the Tudor** ~ la maison des Tudor; **to trace one's** ~ **back to sb** retracer son ascendance jusqu'à qn; **she is second in** ~ **to the throne** elle est la deuxième dans l'ordre de succession au trône; [13] (in prose) ligne *f*; (in poetry) vers *m*; (of music) ligne *f*; **100** ~**s** 100 lignes; **to start a new** ~ aller à la ligne; **a** ~ **from** une citation de [*poem etc*]; **he has all the best** ~**s** il a les meilleures répliques; **to learn one's** ~**s** Theat apprendre son texte; [14] (conformity) **to fall into** ~ **with** s'aligner sur; **to bring sb into** ~ ramener qn dans le rang; **to bring regional laws into** ~ **with federal laws** harmoniser les lois régionales et les lois fédérales; **to keep sb in** ~ tenir qn en main; **our prices are out of** ~ **with those of our competitors** nos prix ne s'accordent pas avec ceux de nos concurrents; **you're way out of** ~○! franchement, tu exagères!; [15] ○(piece of information) **to have a** ~ **on sth** avoir des informations sur qch; **don't give me that** ~! ne me raconte pas ces histoires!; [16] (stance) **the official** ~ la position officielle; **something along these** ~**s** quelque chose dans le même genre; **to be on the right** ~**s** être sur la bonne voie; **to take a firm** ~ **with sb** se montrer ferme avec qn; **I don't know what** ~ **to take** je ne sais pas quelle ligne de conduite adopter; [18] Mil **enemy** ~**s** lignes *fpl* ennemies; [19] (equator) **the** ~ la ligne; [20] ○(of cocaine) ligne○ *f* (**of** de)

B **in line with** *prep phr* en accord avec [*policy, trend*]; **to increase in** ~ **with** augmenter proportionnellement à; **to vary in** ~ **with** varier parallèlement à

C *vtr* doubler [*garment*] (**with** avec); tapisser [*box, shelf*] (**with** de); [*spectators*] border [*route*]

(Idioms) **all along the** ~, **right down the** ~ sur toute la ligne; **somewhere along the** ~ (at point in time) à un certain moment; (at stage) quelque part

(Phrasal verb)
■ **line up:** ▶ ~ **up** [1] (side by side) se mettre en rang; (one behind the other) se mettre en file; [2] (take sides) **to** ~ **up against sb** se regrouper contre qn; ▶ ~ **up** [sb], ~ [sb] **up** (in row) faire s'aligner; ▶ ~ [sth] **up**, ~ **up** [sth] [1] (align) aligner (**with** sur); [2] (organize) sélectionner [*team*]; **to have sb/sth** ~**d up** avoir qn/qch en vue [*work, candidate*]; **what have you got** ~**d up for us tonight?** qu'est-ce que tu nous as prévu pour ce soir○?

lineage /ˈlɪnɪɪdʒ/ *n* lignage *m*

linear /ˈlɪnɪə(r)/ *adj* linéaire

lined /laɪnd/ *adj* [*face*] ridé; [*paper*] ligné; [*curtains*] doublé

line: ~ **dancer** *n* danseur/-euse *m/f* en ligne; ~ **dancing** *n* danse *f* en ligne; ~ **drawing** *n* dessin *m* au trait; ~**man** *n* US Sport au football américain, joueur qui se place sur la ligne; ~ **management** *n* (system) direction *f* hiérarchique; ~ **manager** *n* responsable opérationnel/-elle *m/f*

linen /ˈlɪnɪn/
A *n* [1] (fabric) lin *m*; [2] (household) linge de maison; (underwear) linge *m* de corps
B *noun modifier* [*jacket, sheet*] en lin, de lin

(Idiom) **to wash one's dirty** ~ **in public** laver son linge sale en public

linen: ~ **basket** *n* panier *m* à linge sale; ~ **cupboard** GB, ~ **closet** US *n* armoire *f* à linge

line: ~ **of argument** *n* raisonnement *m*; ~ **of attack** *n* fig plan *m* d'action

line of duty *n* **killed in the** ~ [*policeman*] mort en service (commandé); [*soldier*] mort au combat

line: ~ **of enquiry** *n* (in investigation) piste *f*; (in research) ligne *f* de recherche; ~ **of fire** *n* ligne *f* de tir; ~ **of work** *n* métier *m*; ~**-out** *n* (rugby) remise *f* en touche

liner /ˈlaɪnə(r)/ *n* paquebot *m* de grande ligne

linesman /ˈlaɪnzmən/ *n* GB (in tennis) juge *m* de ligne; (in football, hockey) juge *m* de touche

line-spacing *n* interlignage *m*

line-up /ˈlaɪnʌp/ *n* [1] Sport équipe *f*; (personnel, pop group) groupe *m*; [2] (identification) séance *f* d'identification (*de suspects*)

linger /ˈlɪŋɡə(r)/ *vi* [1] [*person*] s'attarder; [*gaze*] s'attarder (**on** sur); **to** ~ **for a few weeks (before dying)** vivre encore quelques semaines; [2] [*memory, smell*] persister; [3] [*doubt, suspicion*] subsister

(Phrasal verbs)
■ **linger on** [*memory*] persister
■ **linger over**: ▶ ~ **over** [sth] savourer [*meal*]

lingerie /ˈlænʒəriː, US ˌlɑːndʒəˈreɪ/ *n* ***C*** lingerie *f*

lingering /ˈlɪŋɡərɪŋ/ *adj* [*look*] prolongé; [*death*] lent; **some** ~ **doubts remain** il subsiste encore quelques doutes

lingo○ /ˈlɪŋɡəʊ/ *n* baragouin○ *m*

linguist /ˈlɪŋɡwɪst/ *n* linguiste *mf*

linguistic /lɪŋˈɡwɪstɪk/ *adj* linguistique

linguistics /lɪŋˈɡwɪstɪks/
A *n* (+ *v sg*) linguistique *f*
B *noun modifier* [*course, lecturer*] de linguistique

liniment /ˈlɪnɪmənt/ *n* (ointment) pommade *f*

lining /ˈlaɪnɪŋ/ *n* doublure *f*

(Idiom) **every cloud has a silver** ~ à quelque chose malheur est bon

link /lɪŋk/
A *n* [1] (in chain) maillon *m*; fig **the weak** ~ le point faible; [2] (connection by rail, road) liaison *f*; [3] (connection between facts, events) rapport *m* (**between** entre); (between people) lien *m* (**with** avec); [4] (economic or trading tie) relation *f* (**with** avec; **between** entre); (historical or friendly tie) lien *m* (**with** avec; **between** entre); [5] Telecom, Radio, Comput liaison *f*; [6] (on a web page) lien *m*

B *vtr* [1] (connect physically) [*road, cable*] relier [*places, objects*]; **to** ~ **A to B** ou **A and B** relier A à B; **to** ~ **arms** [*people*] se donner le bras; **to** ~ **arms with sb** prendre qn par le bras; [2] (relate, establish connection between) **to** ~ **sth to** ou **with** lier qch à [*inflation*]; établir un lien entre qch et [*fact, crime, illness*]; **his name has been** ~**ed with** son nom a été associé à [*deed, name*]; [3] Comput connecter [*terminals*]; **to** ~ **sth to** ou **with** connecter qch à [*mainframe, terminal*]; [4] TV, Radio établir une liaison entre [*places*] (**by** par)

C **linked** *pp adj* [1] [*circles, symbols*] entrelacé; [2] fig [*issues, problems*] lié; **they are romantically** ~**ed** il y a quelque chose entre eux

(Phrasal verb)
■ **link up:** ▶ ~ **up** [*firms*] s'associer; **to** ~ **up with** s'associer avec [*college, firm*]

linkage /ˈlɪŋkɪdʒ/ *n* [1] (connection) lien *m* (**between** entre); [2] (of issues in international relations) association *f* (**between** entre); [3] (in genetics) linkage *m*

link: ~**man** *n* présentateur *m*; ~ **road** *n* GB route *f* de raccordement

links /lɪŋks/ *n* golf *m*, terrain *m* de golf

link-up /ˈlɪŋkʌp/ *n* [1] TV, Radio liaison *f*; [2] Comm association *f* (**between** entre; **with** avec)

lino /ˈlaɪnəʊ/ *n* lino *m*

lino cut, **lino print** *n* gravure *f* sur linoléum

linseed oil /ˈlɪnsiːd ɔɪl/ *n* huile *f* de lin

lint /lɪnt/ *n* [1] (bandage) tissu *m* ouaté; [2] (fluff) peluches *fpl*

lintel /ˈlɪntl/ *n* linteau *m*

lion /ˈlaɪən/ *n* lion *m*; **the** ~**'s den** lit, fig l'antre du lion; **literary** ~ célébrité *f* littéraire

(Idiom) **to take the** ~**'s share** se tailler la part du lion

lion cub *n* lionceau *m*

lioness /ˈlaɪənes/ *n* lionne *f*

lionize /ˈlaɪənaɪz/ *vtr* aduler

lip /lɪp/
A *n* [1] Anat lèvre *f*; **to read sb's** ~**s** lire sur les lèvres de qn; **my** ~**s are sealed!** bouche cousue○!; [2] (of bowl, crater) bord *m*; (of jug) bec *m*; [3] ○(cheek) insolence *f*
B *noun modifier* [*pencil*] à lèvres
C **-lipped** *combining form* **thin-/thick-**~**ped** aux lèvres minces/charnues

(Idiom) **to keep a stiff upper** ~ rester flegmatique

lip gloss *n* Cosmet brillant *m* à lèvres

liposuction /ˈlaɪpəʊsʌkʃn, ˈlɪpəʊ-/ *n* liposuccion *f*

lip : **∼-read** *vi* (*prét*, *pp* -**read** /-red/) lire sur les lèvres de quelqu'un; **∼reading** *n* lecture *f* sur les lèvres; **∼salve** *n* baume *m* pour les lèvres

lip service *n* péj **to pay ∼ to feminism** se dire féministe pour la forme

lipstick *n* rouge *m* à lèvres

liquefy /'lɪkwɪfaɪ/
A *vtr* liquéfier
B *vi* se liquéfier

liqueur /lɪ'kjʊə(r), US -'kɜːr/ *n* liqueur *f*

liqueur glass *n* verre *m* à liqueur

liquid /'lɪkwɪd/
A *n* (substance) liquide *m*; **drink plenty of ∼s** buvez beaucoup
B *adj* [*substance, nitrogen*] liquide; [*gaze*] clair

liquid assets *npl* liquidités *fpl*

liquidate /'lɪkwɪdeɪt/ *vtr* (all contexts) liquider

liquidation /ˌlɪkwɪ'deɪʃn/ *n* liquidation *f*

liquidator /'lɪkwɪdeɪtə(r)/ *n* liquidateur/-trice *m/f*

liquidity /lɪ'kwɪdətɪ/ *n* liquidité *f*

liquidize /'lɪkwɪdaɪz/ *vtr* GB Culin passer [qch] au mixeur

liquidizer /'lɪkwɪdaɪzə(r)/ *n* GB Culin mixeur *m*

liquid : **∼ lunch** *n* hum alcool *m* en fait de déjeuner; **∼ measure** *n* mesure *f* de capacité des liquides

liquor /'lɪkə(r)/ *n* (alcohol) alcool *m*

liquorice , licorice US /'lɪkərɪs/
A *n* ① (plant) réglisse *f*; ② (substance) réglisse *m*
B *noun modifier* [*root, stick*] de réglisse

liquor store *n* US magasin *m* de vins et spiritueux

lira /'lɪərə/ ▸ p. 782 *n* (*pl* **lire**) lire *f*

Lisbon /'lɪzbən/ ▸ p. 1276 *pr n* Lisbonne

lisle /laɪl/
A *n* fil *m* d'Écosse
B *noun modifier* ∼ **stockings** bas *mpl* de fil

lisp /lɪsp/
A *n* zézaiement *m*; **to have a ∼** zézayer
B *vi* zézayer, zozoter○

lissom /'lɪsəm/ *adj* svelte

list /lɪst/
A *n* ① (catalogue) liste *f* (**of** de); **to be at the top of the ∼** lit arriver en tête de liste; fig être en tête des priorités; **to be low on one's ∼ of priorities** ne pas figurer en tête de ses priorités; ② Naut (leaning) bande *f*
B *vtr* ① gen faire la liste de [*objets, people*]; **to be ∼ed under** être classé à; **to be ∼ed among** figurer parmi; **to be ∼ed in a directory** être repris dans un répertoire; ② Comput lister; ③ **to be ∼ed on the Stock Exchange** être coté en Bourse
C *vi* Naut donner de la bande
D listed *pp adj* GB [*building*] classé

listen /'lɪsn/
A *n* **have a ∼ to this**○! écoute un peu ça!
B *vi* ① (to words, music, sounds) écouter; **to ∼ at the door** écouter aux portes; **to ∼ to sb/sth** écouter qn/qch; ② (pay heed) écouter; **sorry, I wasn't ∼ing** excusez-moi, je n'écoutais pas; **∼, can you come tomorrow?** écoute, est-ce que tu peux venir demain?; **to ∼ to reason** écouter la voix de la raison; ③ (wait) **to ∼ (out) for** guetter [*sound*]

(Phrasal verb)

■ **listen in** écouter (indiscrètement); **to ∼ in on** *ou* **to sth** écouter qch indiscrètement

listener /'lɪsnə(r)/ *n* ① (personal) **to be a good ∼** savoir écouter; **a ready ∼** une oreille attentive; ② Radio auditeur/-trice *m/f*

listening /'lɪsnɪŋ/ *n* **it makes interesting ∼** c'est intéressant à écouter; **'easy ∼'** Mus 'variétés' *fpl*

listeria /lɪ'stɪərɪə/ *n* (bacteria) listéria *f*; (illness) listériose *f*

listeriosis /lɪˌstɪərɪ'əʊsɪs/ *n* Med listériose *f*

listing /'lɪstɪŋ/
A *n* ① gen inscription *f* (**in** dans); **Stock Exchange ∼** liste *f* des sociétés cotées en Bourse; ② Comput listing *m*
B listings *npl* pages *fpl* d'informations

listless /'lɪstlɪs/ *adj* [*person*] apathique

listlessly /'lɪstlɪslɪ/ *adv* [*speak*] sans enthousiasme; [*move*] mollement

list price *n* prix *m* au catalogue

lit /lɪt/
A *prét*, *pp* ▸ **light D , E**
B ○(*abrév* = **literature**) littérature *f*

litany /'lɪtənɪ/ *n* ① Relig litanies *fpl*; ② fig (of complaints etc) litanie *f*

literacy /'lɪtərəsɪ/
A *n* (in a population) taux *m* d'alphabétisation; **our goal is 100% adult ∼** notre but est que 100% des adultes soient alphabétisés
B *noun modifier* [*campaign, level*] d'alphabétisation

literal /'lɪtərəl/ *adj* ① [*meaning*] littéral; ② [*translation*] mot à mot; ③ [*rendering*] gen fidèle; péj sans imagination péj

literally /'lɪtərəlɪ/ *adv* ① [*mean*] littéralement; [*translate*] mot à mot; **to take sth ∼** prendre qch au pied de la lettre; ② (without exaggeration) bel et bien

literary /'lɪtərərɪ, US 'lɪtərerɪ/ *adj* littéraire

literary : ∼ **critic** *n* critique *m* littéraire; ∼ **criticism** *n* critique *f* littéraire; ∼ **theory** *n* théorie *f* littéraire

literate /'lɪtərət/ *adj* ① (able to read and write) **to be ∼** savoir lire et écrire; ② (cultured) [*person*] cultivé; [*work, film*] érudit

literati /ˌlɪtə'rɑːtɪ/ *npl* gens *mpl* de lettres

literature /'lɪtrətʃə/, US -tʃʊər/
A *n* ① (literary writings) littérature *f*; **a work of ∼** une œuvre littéraire; ② (pamphlets, brochures etc) documentation *f*
B *noun modifier* [*course*] de littérature

lithe /laɪð/ *adj* leste

lithograph /'lɪθəgrɑːf, US -græf/
A *n* lithographie *f*
B *vtr* lithographier

lithographer /lɪ'θɒgrəfə(r)/ ▸ p. 1181 *n* lithographe *mf*

lithography /lɪ'θɒgrəfɪ/ *n* lithographie *f*

Lithuania /ˌlɪθjuː'eɪnɪə/ ▸ p. 774 *pr n* Lituanie *f*

litigation /ˌlɪtɪ'geɪʃn/ *n* ∉ litiges *mpl*; **to come to ∼** être porté devant les tribunaux

litigious /lɪ'tɪdʒəs/ *adj* [*person*] procédurier/-ière

litmus : ∼ **paper** *n* papier *m* de tournesol; ∼ **test** *n* Chem réaction *f* au (papier de) tournesol; fig test *m* décisif

litre , liter US /'liːtə(r)/ ▸ p. 723
A *n* litre *m*
B *noun modifier* [*jug, measure*] d'un litre

litter /'lɪtə(r)/
A *n* ① (rubbish) détritus *mpl*; (more substantial) ordures *fpl*; (paper) papiers *mpl*; **'no ∼'** 'défense de déposer des ordures'; ② (random collection) fouillis *m* (**of** de); ③ (of animal) (young) portée *f*; **to make a ∼** mettre bas; ④ (for casualty) brancard *m*; (for dignitary) litière *f*; ⑤ (for pet tray) litière *f*
B *vtr* [*leaves, books*] joncher [*ground*]; **to ∼ the house with sth** [*person*] semer qch dans toute la maison; **to be ∼ed with corpses** [*ground*] être jonché de cadavres

litter : ∼ **bin** *n* poubelle *f*; ∼ **bug** *n* péj personne qui jette des détritus par terre; ∼ **lout** *n* GB = **litterbug**; ∼ **tray** *n* bac *m* à litière

little¹ /'lɪtl/ (comparative **less** ; superlative **least**)

⚠ When *little* is used as a quantifier (*little hope, little damage*) it is translated by *peu de*: peu d'espoir, peu de dégâts.
  For examples and particular usages see **A** below.
  When *a little* is used as a pronoun (*give me a little*) it is translated by *un peu*: donne-m'en un peu.
  When *little* is used alone as a pronoun (*there's little I can do*) it is very often translated by *pas grand-chose*: je ne peux pas faire grand-chose.
  For examples of these and other uses of *little* as a pronoun (*to do as little as possible* etc) see **B** below. For uses of *little* and *a little* as adverbs see the entry above.
  Note that **less** and **least** are treated as separate entries in the dictionary.

A *quantif* ∼ **chance** peu de chances; **there's so ∼ time** il y a si peu de temps; **too ∼ money** trop peu *ou* pas assez d'argent; ∼ **or no influence** presque pas d'influence; **I have ∼ time for cheats** je ne supporte pas les tricheurs; **I see ∼ of Paul these days** je ne vois pas beaucoup Paul en ce moment

B *pron* **save a ∼ for me** gardes-en un peu pour moi; **I only ate a ∼** je n'en ai mangé qu'un peu; **I did what ∼ I could**

j'ai fait le peu que j'ai pu; **he remembers very ~** il ne se souvient pas bien; **there's ~ I can do** je ne peux pas faire grand-chose; **age has ~ to do with it** l'âge n'a pas grand-chose à voir là-dedans; **to do as ~ as possible** faire le moins possible; **~ of note** rien de bien particulier; **~ or nothing** quasiment rien

C *adv* **1** (not much) peu; **I go there very ~** j'y vais très peu; **the next results were ~ better** les résultats suivants étaient à peine meilleurs; **~ more than an hour ago** il y a à peine plus d'une heure; **it's ~ short of madness** cela frise la folie; **a ~-known novel** un roman peu connu; **2** (not at all) **~ did she realize** elle ne s'est pas du tout rendu compte; **~ did they know that** ils étaient bien loin de se douter que

D a little (bit) *adv phr* (slightly) un peu; **a ~ (bit) anxious** un peu inquiet; **a ~ less/more** un peu moins/plus; **stay a ~ longer** reste encore un peu

E as little as *adv phr* **for as ~ as 10 dollars a day** pour seulement 10 dollars par jour; **as ~ as £60** juste 60 livres sterling

little² /ˈlɪtl/ *adj* **1** (small) [*house, smile, voice*] petit (*before n*); **poor ~ thing** pauvre petit/-e *m/f*; **she's a nice ~ thing** elle est adorable; **2** (young) [*sister, boy*] petit (*before n*); **when I was ~** quand j'étais petit; **3** (in a small way) [*farmer, businessman*] petit (*before n*); **4** (expressing scorn) **a poky ~ flat** un petit appartement minable; **a nasty ~ boy** un méchant petit garçon; **5** (short) [*snooze*] petit (*before n*); **a ~ holiday** quelques jours de vacances; **a ~ break** une petite pause

Idioms **~ by ~** petit à petit; **to make ~ of** (not understand) ne pas comprendre grand-chose à [*speech*].

⚠ Pour le comparatif et le superlatif on préférera les formes *smaller* et *smallest* à *littler* and *littlest*

Little Englander *n* péj partisan/-e *m/f* de l'anglocentrisme (opposé/-e à l'ouverture internationale)
little finger *n* petit doigt *m*, auriculaire *m*
Idiom **to wrap** *ou* **twist sb around one's ~** mener qn par le bout du nez
liturgy /ˈlɪtədʒɪ/ *n* liturgie *f*
live¹ /lɪv/

A *vtr* (conduct) vivre [*life*]; **to ~ a normal/peaceful life** vivre normalement/paisiblement; **to ~ a life of luxury** vivre dans le luxe; **to ~ the life of a recluse** vivre en reclus

B *vi* **1** (dwell) [*animal*] vivre; [*person*] gen vivre, habiter (**with** avec); (have one's address) habiter; **they ~ at number 7** ils habitent au numéro 7; **to ~ together** vivre *ou* habiter ensemble; **to ~ in** vivre dans, habiter [*house, apartment*]; **not fit to ~ in** insalubre; **easy to ~ with** facile à vivre; **it's a nice place to ~** il fait bon y vivre; **have you found anywhere to ~ yet?** avez-vous trouvé à vous loger?; **he ~s in jeans** il est toujours en jean; **2** (lead one's life) vivre; **to ~ in poverty** vivre dans la pauvreté; **we ~ in the computer age** nous vivons à l'ère de l'informatique; **to ~ for** ne vivre que pour [*sport, work*]; **to ~ through sth** vivre [*experience*]; **3** (remain alive) gen, fig vivre; (survive) survivre; **to ~ to be eighty** vivre jusqu'à l'âge de quatre-vingts ans; **to be still living** être encore en vie; **as long as I ~...** tant que je vivrai...; **I don't think he'll ~** je ne pense pas qu'il survive; **to ~ through the night** passer la nuit; **I'll ~!** hum je n'en mourrai pas!; **nothing left to ~ for** plus de raison de vivre; **to ~ to regret sth** en venir à regretter qch; **long ~ democracy!** vive la démocratie!; **4** (subsist) vivre; **to ~ by one's wits** vivre d'expédients; **to ~ on** *ou* **off** vivre de [*fruit, charity*]; vivre sur [*wage, capital*]; **that's not enough to ~ on** ça ne suffit pas pour vivre; **to ~ on junk food** ne manger que des cochonneries°; **5** (put up with) **to ~ with** accepter [*situation*]; supporter [*décor*]; **to ~ with the fact that** admettre que; **6** (experience life) vivre; **come on! ~ a little!** allez viens! laisse-toi vivre!; **you haven't ~d until you've been to...** tu n'as rien vu tant que tu n'es pas allé à...

Idioms **~ and let ~** il faut être tolérant; **to ~ it up**° faire la fête°; **we ~ and learn** on en apprend tous les jours; **to ~ sth down** faire oublier qch

Phrasal verbs
▪ **live in** [*caretaker*] avoir un logement de fonction; [*nanny, maid*] être logé et nourri
▪ **live on** [*reputation, tradition*] se perpétuer
▪ **live out**: ▶ **~ out** [*nanny*] ne pas être logé; [*teacher*] vivre en ville; ▶ **~ out [sth]** **1** (survive) passer [*winter*]; **2** (spend) **to ~ out one's days somewhere** finir ses jours quelque part; **3** (enact) vivre [*fantasies*]

▪ **live up to** [*person*] répondre à [*expectations*]; être à la hauteur de [*reputation*]; [*product*] ne pas démentir [*advertising*]
live² /laɪv/

A *adj* **1** (not dead) [*animal*] vivant; [*birth*] d'un enfant viable; **real ~** en chair et en os; **2** Radio, TV [*broadcast*] en direct; [*performance*] sur scène; [*theatre*] vivant; [*album*] enregistré sur scène; **before a ~ audience** devant un public; **3** (burning) [*coal*] ardent; **4** (capable of exploding) [*ammunition*] réel, réelle; (unexploded) [*shell*] nonexplosé; **5** Elec sous tension

B *adv* Radio, TV [*appear, broadcast*] en direct

lived-in° /ˈlɪvdɪn/ *adj* **to have that ~ look** donner une impression de confort
live-in /ˈlɪvɪn/ *adj* [*maid, nanny*] qui est logé et nourri; **to have a ~ lover** vivre en concubinage
livelihood /ˈlaɪvlɪhʊd/ *n* gagne-pain *m*; **to lose one's ~** perdre ses moyens d'existence
liveliness /ˈlaɪvlɪnɪs/ *n* (of place, person) gaieté *f*; (of style) vivacité *f*
lively /ˈlaɪvlɪ/ *adj* **1** (vivacious) [*person*] plein d'entrain; [*place, atmosphere, conversation*] animé; [*account*] vivant; [*interest, mind*] vif/vive; [*campaign*] percutant; **2** (fast) [*pace*] vif/vive; [*music, dance*] entraînant

Idiom **look ~!** réveillez-vous!
liven /ˈlaɪvn/ *v*
▪ **liven up**: ▶ **~ up** s'animer; ▶ **~ up [sth]**, **~ [sth] up** égayer [*person*]; animer [*event*]
liver /ˈlɪvə(r)/ *n* Culin, Med foie *m*
live rail /laɪv/ *n* rail *m* conducteur
liver paste, **liver pâté** *n* pâté *m* de foie
Liverpudlian /ˌlɪvəˈpʌdlɪən/ *n* (living there) habitant/-e *m/f* de Liverpool; (born there) natif/-ive *m/f* de Liverpool
liver:~ salts *npl* sels *mpl* pour le foie; **~ spot** *n* tache *f* de vieillesse; **~wurst** *n* US ≈ pâté *m* de foie
livery /ˈlɪvərɪ/ *n* **1** (uniform) livrée *f*; **2** (boarding horses) **at ~** en pension
lives /laɪvz/ *npl* ▸ **life**
live laɪv:**~stock** *n* bétail *m*; **~ wire** *n* fig boute-en-train *m inv*
livid /ˈlɪvɪd/ *adj* **1** °(furious) furieux/-ieuse; **2** [*face, scar*] livide; **~ with rage** blême de rage
living /ˈlɪvɪŋ/

A *n* **1** (livelihood) vie *f*; **to work for a ~** travailler pour gagner sa vie; **what do you do for a ~?** qu'est-ce que vous faites dans la vie?; **2** (lifestyle) vie *f*; **loose ~** une vie de débauche; **3** Relig (incumbency) cure *f*; **4** **the ~** (+ v pl) les vivants *mpl*

B *adj* vivant; **to be ~ proof of** être la preuve vivante de; **a ~ hell** un véritable enfer; **within ~ memory** de mémoire d'homme; **there wasn't a ~ soul** il n'y avait pas âme qui vive

Idiom **to be still in the land of the ~** être encore de ce monde

living: **~ conditions** *npl* conditions *fpl* de vie; **~ dead** *npl* morts-vivants *mpl*; **~ death** *n* fig enfer *m*, calvaire *m*; **~ expenses** *npl* frais *mpl* de subsistance; **~ quarters** *npl* quartiers *mpl*; **~ room** *n* salle *f* de séjour, salon *m*; **~ standards** *npl* niveau *m* de vie; **~ wage** *n* salaire *m* adéquat; **~ will** *n* Jur, Med testament *m* de vie
lizard /ˈlɪzəd/ *n* lézard *m*
llama /ˈlɑːmə/ *n* lama *m*
LLB *n* (abrév écrite = **Bachelor of Laws**) ≈ licence *f* en droit
LLD *n* (abrév écrite = **Doctor of Laws**) ≈ doctorat *m* en droit
load /ləʊd/

A *n* **1** (sth carried) charge *f*; (on vehicle, animal) chargement *m*; (on ship, plane) cargaison *f*; fig fardeau *m*; **to take a ~ off sb's mind** soulager qn (d'un grand poids); **a bus-~ of children** un autobus plein d'enfants; **2** Tech (weight) charge *f* (on sur); **3** (shipment, batch) (of sand, gravel) cargaison *f*; **four ~s of washing** quatre machines de linge; **4** Elec charge *f*; **5** fig (amount of work) travail *m*; **to lighten/spread the ~** alléger/répartir le travail; **6** °(a lot) **a ~** *ou* **a whole ~ of people** des tas° de gens; **that's a ~ of nonsense**° c'est de la blague°

B °**loads** *npl* **~s of** (plus plural nouns) des tas° de; **~s of times**

I

plein de or des tas⁰ de fois; **we've got ~s of time** nous avons tout notre temps; **we had ~s to drink** on n'a pas arrêté de boire; **~s of energy** de l'énergie à revendre; **~s of champagne** du champagne en quantité; **~s of work** un travail fou⁰; **~s of money** énormément d'argent

C vtr ① gen charger [vehicle, gun, washing machine] (**with** de); mettre un film dans [camera]; ② Comput charger [program]; ③ fig (inundate) **to ~ sb with** combler or couvrir qn de [presents, honours]

D vi charger

(Idioms) **get a ~ of this**⁰! (listen) écoute un peu ça⁰!; **get a ~ of that**⁰! (look) vise un peu ça⁰!; **the dice are ~ed against him** tout est contre lui

(Phrasal verb)

■ **load down**: ▸ ~ **[sb] down** charger qn (**with** de); **to be ~ed down with sth** plier sous le poids de qch

load-bearing adj [wall] porteur/-euse

loaded /'ləʊdɪd/ adj ① (full, laden) [tray, lorry, gun] chargé (**with** de); fig ~ **with meaning** plein de sens; ② (weighed down) [person] chargé (**with** de); fig **to be ~ with honours** être couvert d'honneurs; ③ ⁰fig (rich) plein aux as⁰, bourré de fric⁰; ④ (leading) [question] tendancieux/-ieuse; ⑤ ⁰US (drunk) bourré⁰

loading /'ləʊdɪŋ/ n (of vehicle) chargement m

loading bay n aire f or zone f de chargement

loaf /ləʊf/ n (pl **loaves**) pain m; **a ~ of bread** un pain

(Idioms) **half a ~ is better than none** Prov faute de grives on mange des merles; **use your ~⁰!** fais marcher tes méninges⁰!

(Phrasal verb)

■ **loaf about, loaf around** traînasser

loafer /'ləʊfə(r)/ n ① (shoe) mocassin m; ② (idler) flemmard/-e⁰ m/f

loam /ləʊm/ n terreau m

loan /ləʊn/

A n gen (when borrowing) emprunt m; (when lending) prêt m; **to have the ~ of sth** emprunter qch; **to be on ~** [museum object] être prêté (**to** à); **the book is already on ~** le livre a déjà été emprunté

B vtr prêter (also ~ **out**) prêter [object, money]

loan: ~ **account** n Comm compte m de prêt; ~ **agreement** n contrat m de prêt; ~ **facility** n facilité f de crédit; ~ **shark**⁰ n péj usurier/-ière m/f

loath /ləʊθ/ adj **to be ~ to do** répugner à faire

loathe /ləʊð/ vtr détester (**doing** faire)

loathing /'ləʊðɪŋ/ n répugnance f (**for** pour)

loathsome /'ləʊðsəm/ adj répugnant

loaves /ləʊvz/ npl ▸ **loaf**

lob /lɒb/

A n Sport lob m

B vtr (p prés etc **-bb-**) ① gen lancer; ② Sport lober

lobby /'lɒbɪ/

A n ① (of hotel) hall m; (of theatre) lobby m; ② GB Pol (also **division** ~) (where MPs vote) vestibule où les députés se répartissent pour voter; ③ (also ~ **group**) lobby m

B vtr [group] faire pression sur [group] (**about** à propos de); Pol appuyer [bill]

C vi faire pression (**for** pour obtenir)

lobbying /'lɒbɪɪŋ/ n lobbying m

lobbyist /'lɒbɪɪst/ n membre m d'un groupe de pression, lobbyiste mf

lobe /ləʊb/ n Anat, Bot lobe m

lobelia /lə'biːlɪə/ n lobélie f

lobster /'lɒbstə(r)/

A n Culin, Zool homard m

B noun modifier [salad, soup] au homard

lobster pot n casier m à homards

local /'ləʊkl/

A n ① (person) **is he a ~?** il est du coin?; **the ~s** les gens mpl du coin; ② (pub) pub m du coin

B adj ① (neighbourhood) [library, shop] du quartier; ② (of the town) [newspaper] local; ③ (regional) [radio, news] régional; [speciality] du pays; [tradition] local; [business] de la région; ④ (of a country) [currency, time] local

local: ~ **anaesthetic** n anesthésique m local; ~ **area network**, **LAN** n Comput réseau m local; ~ **authority** n GB Admin (+ v sg ou pl) autorités fpl locales; ~ **call** n Telecom communication f téléphonique

locale; ~ **colour** GB, ~ **color** US n couleur f locale; ~ **derby** n Sport derby m local

locale /ləʊ'kɑːl, US -'kæl/ n endroit m

Local Education Authority, **LEA** n GB administration locale qui gère les affaires scolaires

local: ~ **election** n élection f locale; ~ **government** n administration f locale

locality /ləʊ'kælətɪ/ n ① (neighbourhood) voisinage m; ② (place) endroit m

localize /'ləʊkəlaɪz/

A vtr localiser [problem]; restreindre [damage]

B localized pp adj localisé

locate /ləʊ'keɪt, US 'ləʊkeɪt/ vtr ① (find) retrouver [object]; localiser [fault]; ② (position) situer [site]; **to be ~d in London** se trouver à Londres

location /ləʊ'keɪʃn/ n gen endroit m; (in house particulars) **a central ~** un emplacement central; **to know the ~ of sth** savoir où se trouve qch; Cin **on ~** en extérieur

loch /lɒk, lɒx/ n loch m, lac m

lock /lɒk/

A n ① (with key) serrure f; (with bolt) verrou m; **under ~ and key** sous clé; ② (of hair) mèche f; **curly ~s** cheveux mpl bouclés; ③ Naut écluse f; ④ (in wrestling) clé f; ⑤ Aut **to have a good ~** [car] bien braquer; **to turn the wheel full ~** braquer le volant à fond; ⑥ Comput verrouillage m

B vtr ① (close securely) (with key) fermer [qch] à clé; (with bolt) verrouiller; **to ~ sth into a drawer** enfermer qch dans un tiroir; ② Comput verrouiller [file]; ③ **~ed in combat** aux prises; **to ~ horns** fig se disputer violemment

C vi ① (close securely) [door, drawer] fermer à clé; ② (seize up) [steering wheel] se bloquer

(Phrasal verbs)

■ **lock away**: ▸ ~ **[sth] away** mettre [qch] sous clé

■ **lock in**: ▸ ~ **[sb] in** enfermer [person]; **to ~ oneself in** s'enfermer

■ **lock out**: ▸ ~ **[sb] out** (on purpose) fermer la porte à clé pour empêcher qn d'entrer; (by mistake) laisser qn dehors sans clé; **to get ~ed out** se retrouver sans clé à la porte

■ **lock together** [components, pieces] s'emboîter

■ **lock up**: ▸ ~ **up** fermer; ▸ ~ **[sth] up**, ~ **up [sth]** fermer [qch] à clé [house]; immobiliser [capital]; ▸ ~ **[sb] up**, ~ **up [sb]** enfermer [hostage]; mettre [qn] sous les verrous [killer]

locker /'lɒkə(r)/ n casier m, vestiaire m

locker room n vestiaire m

locket /'lɒkɪt/ n médaillon m

lock gate n porte f d'écluse

locking /'lɒkɪŋ/

A n gen, Comput verrouillage m

B adj [petrol cap] antivol

lock: ~ **jaw** n tétanos m; ~ **keeper** n éclusier/-ière m/f; ~**-out** n lock-out m inv, grève f patronale; ~**smith** n serrurier m; ~**-up garage** n GB box m

loco /'ləʊkəʊ/

A ⁰n GB Rail loco⁰ f

B ⁰adj fou/folle

locomotive /ˌləʊkə'məʊtɪv/ n locomotive f

locum /'ləʊkəm/ n GB remplaçant/-e m/f

locust /'ləʊkəst/ n locuste f, sauterelle f

lodge /lɒdʒ/

A n ① (small house) pavillon m; (for gatekeeper) loge f (du gardien); (in castle) conciergerie f; **porter's ~** Univ loge du concierge; ② (Masonic) loge f

B vtr ① (accommodate) loger [person]; ② Jur **to ~ an appeal** faire appel; **to ~ a complaint** porter plainte; **to ~ a protest** protester

C vi ① (reside) loger (**with** chez); ② (stick) [bullet] se loger; [small object] se coincer; ③ (in memory) s'incruster

lodger /'lɒdʒə(r)/ n (room only) locataire mf; (with meals) pensionnaire mf

lodging /'lɒdʒɪŋ/

A n logement m; **board and ~** le gîte et le couvert

B lodgings npl logement m; **to take ~s** prendre une chambre (**with** chez)

loft /lɒft, US lɔːft/ n ① (attic) grenier m; ② US (apartment) loft m; ③ Archit **organ ~** tribune d'orgue

loft conversion n aménagement m de grenier

loftily /'lɒftɪlɪ, US 'lɔːftɪlɪ/ adv avec hauteur

lofty /'lɒftɪ, US 'lɔːftɪ/ adj **1** [building, peak] haut; **2** [manner] hautain; [ideals] noble

log /lɒg, US lɔːg/
A n **1** (of wood) rondin m; (for burning) bûche f; **2** (written record) registre m; **3** (of ship) journal m de bord; (of plane) carnet m de vol; **4** Comput carnet m d'exploitation; **5** Math logarithme m
B vtr (p prés etc -**gg**-) **1** (record) noter; **2** (clock up) (also ~ **up**) avoir à son actif [miles]; **3** [car, train] rouler à [speed]; [plane] voler à [speed]; [ship] filer [knots]
(Idiom) **to sleep like a ~** dormir comme une souche
(Phrasal verbs)
▪ **log in, log on** Comput ouvrir une session, se connecter
▪ **log off, log out** Comput clore une session, se déconnecter

logarithm /'lɒgərɪðəm, US 'lɔːg-/ n logarithme m

log book n **1** (of car) ≈ carte f grise; **2** (of ship) journal m de bord; (of plane) carnet m de vol; **3** (written record) registre m

log: ~ **cabin** n cabane f en rondins; ~ **fire** n feu m de bois

logger /'lɒgə(r)/ n bûcheron m

loggerheads /'lɒgəhedz/ npl **to be at** ~ être en désaccord (**with** avec)

logging /'lɒgɪŋ/ n abattage m (des arbres)

logic /'lɒdʒɪk/ n gen, Philos, Comput logique f

logical /'lɒdʒɪkl/ adj logique

logically /'lɒdʒɪklɪ/ adv logiquement

login /'lɒgɪn/ n Comput ouverture f de session

logistic /lə'dʒɪstɪk/ adj logistique

logistically /lə'dʒɪstɪklɪ/ adv d'un point de vue logistique

logistics /lə'dʒɪstɪks/ n (+ v sg ou pl) logistique f

log jam n lit embouteillage m (de bois de flottage); fig blocage m

logo /'ləʊgəʊ/ n logo m

logon /'lɒgɒn/ n Comput ouverture f de session

log: ~**rolling** n US Pol trafic m de faveurs; ~ **tables** npl tables fpl de logarithmes

loin /lɔɪn/
A n Culin GB ≈ côtes fpl premières; US ≈ filet m
B loins† npl Anat reins mpl; **to gird up one's ~s** lit ceindre les reins; fig s'armer de courage

loin: ~ **chop** n côte f première; ~**cloth** n pagne m

loiter /'lɔɪtə(r)/ vi (idly) traîner; (pleasurably) flâner; (suspiciously) rôder

loll /lɒl/ vi [person] se prélasser; [part of body] tomber; [tongue] pendre
(Phrasal verb)
▪ **loll about** traîner sans rien faire

lollipop /'lɒlɪpɒp/ n sucette f

lollop /'lɒləp/ vi galoper (maladroitement)

lolly /'lɒlɪ/ n GB **1** ○(money) fric m; **2** (sweet) sucette f; **ice** ~ glace f à l'eau (sur un bâton)

London /'lʌndən/ ▸ p. 1276
A pr n Londres; **in/to** ~ à Londres; **inner** ~ Londres intramuros; **outer** ~ la banlieue de Londres
B noun modifier [accent, train] de Londres

Londoner /'lʌndənə(r)/ n Londonien/-ienne m/f

lone /ləʊn/ adj littér (only one) seul

loneliness /'ləʊnlɪnɪs/ n (of person) solitude f; (of position) isolement m

lonely /'ləʊnlɪ/ adj [person] solitaire; [place] isolé; [decision] que l'on prend seul

lonely: ~ **hearts' club** club m de rencontres; ~ **hearts' column** n petites annonces fpl (de rencontre)

lone parent n parent m isolé

loner /'ləʊnə(r)/ n solitaire mf

lonesome /'ləʊnsəm/ adj US solitaire

long /lɒŋ, US lɔːŋ/ ▸ p. 977
A adj **1** (lengthy, protracted) [process, wait, journey, vowel] long/ longue; [delay] important; [bath, sigh] grand (before n); **to be 20 minutes** ~ durer 20 minutes; **how** ~ **is the interval?** combien de temps dure l'entracte?; **is an hour** ~ **enough?**

est-ce qu'une heure suffira?; **it's been a** ~ **day** la journée a été longue; **to get** ~**er** [days] s'allonger; **to take a** ~ **hard look at sth** réfléchir sérieusement à qch; **to work** ~ **hours** faire de longues journées; **a friend of** ~ **standing** un ami de longue date; **2** (in expressions of time) **she's been away a** ~ **time** elle est restée longtemps absente; **it's been a** ~ **time since I saw you** ça fait longtemps que je ne t'ai pas vu; **you've been a** ~ **time getting here** tu as mis longtemps pour arriver; **they've taken a** ~ **time to decide** il leur a fallu du temps pour se décider; **that's a** ~ **time** c'est long; **I've been a teacher for a** ~ **time** je suis professeur depuis longtemps; **she hasn't been well for a** ~ **time** ça fait longtemps qu'elle est malade; **for a** ~ **time I didn't believe her** pendant longtemps je ne l'ai pas crue; **a** ~ **time ago** il y a longtemps; **to take a** ~ **time** [person] être lent; [task] prendre longtemps; **3** (in measuring) [dress, hair, queue] long/ longue; [grass] haut; [detour] grand; **20 m** ~ de 20 m de long; **to be 20 m** ~ avoir 20 m de long; **to get** ~ [grass, hair] pousser; [list, queue] s'allonger; **she's growing her hair** ~ elle se laisse pousser les cheveux; **to make sth** ~**er** allonger [sleeve]; augmenter la longueur de [shelf]; **4** (in expressions of distance) **a** ~ **way** loin; **January is a** ~ **way off** janvier est loin; **don't fall, it's a** ~ **way down** ne tombe pas, c'est haut; **a** ~ **way down the list** loin sur la liste; **a** ~ **way out** (at sea) loin au large; (in calculations) loin du compte; **we've come a** ~ **way** nous avons fait beaucoup de chemin; **to go a** ~ **way** [person] (be successful) aller loin; **to make sth go a** ~ **way** faire durer qch; **to go a** ~ **way towards doing** contribuer largement à faire; **to have a** ~ **way to go** fig [worker, planner] avoir encore beaucoup d'efforts à faire; **by a** ~ **way** de loin; **to take the** ~ **way round** faire un long détour
B adv **1** (a long time) longtemps; **to be** ~ (doing sth) en avoir pour longtemps; **how** ~ **will you be in the meeting?** cette réunion va te prendre combien de temps?; **not very** ~ pas très longtemps; **don't be** ~ dépêche-toi; **how** ~ **will it be before we know?** dans combien de temps le saura-t-on?; **it won't be** ~ **before...** dans peu de temps...; **I've been here** ~**er than anyone else** je suis ici depuis plus longtemps que personne; **I can't stand it a day** ~**er** je ne le supporterai pas un jour de plus; **I can't stand it any** ~**er** j'en ai assez; **the** ~**er we stayed the hotter it grew** plus le temps passait et plus il faisait chaud; **it's not that** ~ **since...** il ne s'est pas passé tellement de temps depuis...; **it wasn't** ~ **before...** il n'a pas fallu longtemps pour que...; **has he been gone** ~? est-ce qu'il y a longtemps qu'il est parti?; **I haven't got** ~ je n'ai pas beaucoup de temps; ~ **enough** assez longtemps; **just** ~ **enough to...** juste le temps de...; **that doesn't give us** ~ ça ne nous laisse pas beaucoup de temps; **this won't take** ~ ça ne prendra pas longtemps; ~**er than expected** plus longtemps que prévu; **how** ~ **did it take him?** il lui a fallu combien de temps?; ~**er than he thought** plus de temps qu'il ne pensait; **three days at the** ~**est** trois jours tout au plus; **before** ~ (in past) peu après; (in future) dans peu de temps; **before much** ~**er** sous peu; **not for** ~ pas longtemps; **will you be gone for** ~? seras-tu longtemps absent?; ~ **after** longtemps après; **not** ~ **after** peu après; **it's** ~ **past your bedtime** tu devrais être couché depuis longtemps; ~ **ago** il y a longtemps; ~ **before** bien avant; **not** ~ **before lunch** peu de temps avant le déjeuner; ~ **since** depuis longtemps; **he's no** ~**er head** il n'est plus chef; **5 minutes, no** ~**er!** 5 minutes, pas plus!; **2** (for a long time) (avant pp) depuis longtemps; **those days are** ~ **gone** ce temps-là n'est plus; **3** (throughout) (après n) **all day** ~ toute la journée
C as long as, so long as conj phr **1** (in time) aussi longtemps que; **(for) as** ~ **as you like** aussi longtemps que tu veux; **as** ~ **as I live** toute ma vie; **2** (provided that) du moment que (+ indic), pourvu que (+ subj)
D vi **to** ~ **for sth/sb** avoir très envie de qch/de voir qn; **to** ~ **to do** (be impatient) être très impatient de faire; (desire sth elusive) rêver de faire
(Idioms) ~ **time no see**○! hum ça fait une paye○ qu'on ne s'est pas vus!; **she's not** ~ **for this world** elle ne fera pas de vieux os; **so** ~○! salut!; **why all the** ~ **faces?** vous en faites une tête○!; **to pull a** ~ **face** faire triste mine; **to have a** ~ **memory** être rancunier/-ière

long: ~**-awaited** adj longtemps attendu; ~**boat** n chaloupe f; ~**-delayed** adj longuement différé

long-distance
A adj [runner] de fond; [telephone call] (within the country) interurbain; (abroad) international; ~ **lorry driver** GB routier m

B *adv* de loin; (from abroad) de l'étranger

long: ~**-drawn-out** *adj* interminable; ~**ed-for** *adj* tant attendu; ~**-established** *adj* fondé il y a long-temps

longevity /lɒn'dʒevətɪ/ *n* (of person) longévité *f*

long-haired *adj* [*person*] aux cheveux longs; [*animal*] à poil long

longhand /'lɒŋhænd/ *n* **in** ~ écrit à la main

long-haul *adj* Aviat long-courrier *inv*

longing /'lɒŋɪŋ, US 'lɔːŋɪŋ/
A *n* grand désir *m* (**for** de; **to do** de faire); (stronger) convoitise *f* (**for** envers); (nostalgic) nostalgie *f* (**for** de)
B *adj* [*look*] (greedy) plein de convoitise

longingly /'lɒŋɪŋlɪ, US 'lɔːŋ-/ *adv* (greedily) avec convoitise; (nostalgically) avec nostalgie

longish /'lɒŋɪʃ, US 'lɔːŋɪʃ/ *adj* assez long/longue; **a** ~ **time** pas mal de temps

longitude /'lɒndʒɪtjuːd, US -tuːd/ *n* longitude *f*; **at a** ~ **of 52°** par 52° de longitude

long: ~ **johns**○ *npl* caleçon *m* long; ~ **jump** ▸ p. 881 *n* GB saut *m* en longueur; ~**-lasting** *adj* qui dure long-temps; ~**-life** *adj* [*milk*] longue conservation *inv*; [*battery*] longue durée *inv*; ~**-limbed** *adj* aux membres longs; ~**-line** *adj* long/longue; ~**-lived** *adj* [*tradition*] persist-ant; ~**-lost** *adj* [*relative*] perdu de vue depuis long-temps; ~**-range** *adj* [*missile*] (à) longue portée; [*forecast*] à long terme; ~**-running** *adj* [*play, dispute*] qui dure depuis longtemps; ~**-shoreman** *n* US docker *m*

long shot *n* (risky attempt) **it's a** ~ c'est risqué; (guess) **this is a** ~ je dis ça à tout hasard

long: ~**-sighted** *adj* Med presbyte; ~**-sleeved** *adj* à manches longues; ~**-standing** *adj* de longue date; ~**-suffering** *adj* qui supporte tout sans se plaindre; ~**-tailed** *adj* à longue queue

long term
A *n* **in the** ~ à long terme
B long-term *adj, adv* à long terme

long: ~**-time** *adj* de longue date; ~**-wave** *n* grandes ondes *fpl*; ~**ways** *adv* dans le sens de la longueur; ~**-winded** *adj* verbeux/-euse

loo○ /luː/ *n* GB vécés○ *mpl*, toilettes *fpl*

loofah /'luːfə/ *n* loufa *m*

look /lʊk/
A *n* **1** (glance) coup *m* d'œil; **to have** *ou* **take a** ~ **at sth** jeter un coup d'œil à *ou* sur qch; **to have** *ou* **take a good** ~ **at** fig examiner [qch] soigneusement; lit regarder [qch] de près; **I didn't get a good** ~ je n'ai pas bien vu; **to have a** ~ **inside/behind sth** regarder à l'intérieur de/derrière qch; **to have a** ~ **round** faire un tour de [*house, town*]; **to have a** ~ **round the shops** faire le tour des magasins; **to have a** ~ **through** (scan) chercher dans [*archives, files*]; parcourir [*essay, report*]; **I took one** ~ **at him and knew that he was ill** j'ai tout de suite vu qu'il était malade; **let's have a** ~ **at that grazed knee** voyons ce genou écorché; **to take a long hard** ~ **at sth** fig étudier sérieusement qch; **2** (search) **to have a (good)** ~ (bien) chercher; **3** (expression) regard *m*; **a** ~ **of sadness/anger** un regard triste/rempli de colère; **to give sb a pitying** ~ regarder qn avec pitié; **he got some odd** *ou* **funny** ~**s** on l'a regardé d'un drôle d'air; **I don't like the** ~ **on his face** je n'aime pas son air; **from the** ~ **on his face...** à son expression...; **4** (appearance) (of person) air *m*; (of building, scenery) aspect *m*; **to have a** ~ **of** ne pas faire très moderne; **she has a** ~ **of her father** elle a quelque chose de son père; **to have the** ~ **of a military man** avoir l'allure d'un militaire; **I like the** ~ **of it** ça a l'air bien; **I like the** ~ **of him** il a l'air sympa○; **I don't like the** ~ **of him** il ne m'inspire pas confiance; **I don't like the** ~ **of the weather** le ciel n'annonce rien de bon; **I don't like the** ~ **of that rash** ces rougeurs m'inquiètent; **by the** ~ **of him...** à le voir...; **5** (style) look○ *m*
B **looks** *npl* **he's got the** ~**s** il a le physique; ~**s aren't everything** il n'y a pas que la beauté qui compte; **to keep one's** ~**s** rester beau/belle; **he's losing his** ~**s** il n'est pas aussi beau qu'autrefois; **you can't go by** ~**s alone** il ne faut pas se fier aux apparences
C *vtr* **1** (gaze, stare) regarder; **to** ~ **sb in the eye/in the face** regarder qn dans les yeux/en face; **to** ~ **sb up and down** (appraisingly) regarder qn de haut en bas; ~ **who it is!** regarde qui voilà!; **2** (appear) **to** ~ **one's age** faire son âge; **she's 40 but she doesn't** ~ **it** elle a 40 ans mais elle ne les

fait pas; **he** ~**s about 50** il doit avoir la cinquantaine; **to** ~ **one's best** être à son avantage; **she still** ~**s the same** elle n'a pas changé; **to** ~ **a fool** avoir l'air ridicule; **it won't** ~ **good** ça sera mal vu; **he doesn't** ~ **himself** il n'a pas l'air dans son assiette
D *vi* **1** regarder (**into** dans; **over** par-dessus); **to** ~ **and see who's at the door** regarder qui est à la porte; **to** ~ **away** détourner le regard *or* les yeux; **to** ~ **out of the window** regarder par la fenêtre; **to** ~ **the other way** lit regarder ailleurs; fig fermer les yeux; **to** ~ **up and down the street** regarder partout dans la rue; **I didn't know where to** ~ fig je ne savais plus où me mettre; (in shop) **I'm just** ~**ing** je ne fais que regarder; **2** (search) chercher, regarder; **to** ~ **down** parcourir [*list*]; **3** (appear, seem) avoir l'air, paraî-tre; **you** ~ **cold** tu as l'air d'avoir froid; **he** ~**s young for his age** il fait jeune pour son âge; **that makes you** ~ **younger** ça te rajeunit; **how do I** ~? comment me trouves-tu?; **you** ~ **well** tu as bonne mine; **you** ~ **good in that hat** ce chapeau te va bien; **you** ~ **good enough to eat!** tu es mignon/-onne à croquer○; **the picture will** ~ **good in the study** le tableau ira bien dans le bureau; **it doesn't** ~ **right** ça ne va pas; **how does it** ~ **to you?** qu'est-ce que tu en penses?; **it** ~**s OK to me** ça m'a l'air d'aller; **things are** ~**ing good** les choses se présentent bien; **it** ~**s to me as if** *ou* **though**...; j'ai l'impression que...; **it** ~**s as if it will snow** on dirait qu'il va neiger; **it** ~**s likely that** il semble probable que (+ *subj*); **it** ~**s certain that** il semble certain que (+ *indic*); **to** ~ **like sb/sth** ressembler à qn/qch; **that photograph doesn't** ~ **like you** on ne te reconnaît pas du tout sur cette photo; **what does the house** ~ **like?** com-ment est la maison?; **it** ~**s like being fun** cela promet d'être amusant; **you** ~ **like being the only man there** il y a de fortes chances pour que tu sois le seul homme pré-sent; **it** ~**s like rain** on dirait qu'il va pleuvoir; **it certainly** ~**s like it** ça en a tout l'air; **it** ~**s like cancer to me** je pense que c'est un cancer; **4** (listen) écoute; ~ **here** écoute-moi bien; **5** (be oriented) **to** ~ **north** [*house, room*] être orienté au nord
E **-looking** *combining form* **distinguished-~ing** [*person*] à l'air distingué; **sinister-~ing** [*place*] à l'aspect sinistre; **he's not bad-~ing** il n'est pas mal

(Idiom) **if** ~**s could kill**... il/elle etc m'a fusillé du regard

(Phrasal verbs)
■ **look after**: ▸ ~ **after** [sb/sth] **1** (care for) soigner [*patient*]; garder [*child*]; s'occuper de [*customer, plant*]; entre-tenir [*car*]; prendre soin de [*belongings*]; **2** (be responsible for) s'occuper de [*finances, shop*]; surveiller [*class, luggage*]; **to** ~ **after sb's interests** veiller aux intérêts de qn; ▸ ~ **after oneself 1** (cope) se débrouiller tout seul; **2** (be careful) **safe journey, and** ~ **after yourself** bon voyage, fais bien attention à toi!
■ **look ahead** lit regarder devant soi; fig regarder vers l'avenir
■ **look around**: ▸ ~ **around 1** (glance around) regarder autour de soi; **2** (search) chercher; **to** ~ **around for sb/sth** chercher qn/qch; **3** (visit, examine) (in town) faire un tour; ▸ ~ **around** [sth] visiter [*church, town*]; **to** ~ **around the shops** faire les magasins
■ **look at**: ▸ ~ **at** [sth] **1** gen regarder; (briefly) jeter un coup d'œil sur; ~ **at the state of you!** regarde un peu de quoi tu as l'air!; **you'd never guess, to** ~ **at her** à la voir on ne devinerait jamais; **he's not much to** ~ **at** il ne paie pas de mine; **2** (examine) vérifier [*equipment*]; examiner [*patient*]; jeter un coup d'œil à [*car, plumbing*]; étudier [*problem, options*]; **3** (see, view) voir [*life, situation*]; envisager [*problem*]; **try and** ~ **at it my way** essaie de voir les choses de mon point de vue; **that's how I** ~ **at it** c'est comme ça que je vois les choses; **you can't be too careful,** ~ **at Tom!** il faut être très prudent, regarde ce qui est arrivé à Tom!; **4** (talk about) ~ **ing at about 3,000 dollars** ça va vous coûter aux alentours de 3 000 dollars
■ **look back**: ▸ ~ **back 1** (turn around) se retourner (**at** pour regarder); **2** (reminisce) **let's** ~ **back to 1964** revenons à l'année 1964; **if we** ~ **back to the 19th century** si l'on considère le dix-neuvième siècle; **she's never** ~**ed back** tout s'est bien passé pour elle; **to** ~ **back on** se tour-ner sur [*past*]; repenser à [*experience*]; ~**ing back on it** rétrospectivement
■ **look down**: ▸ ~ **down** (with modesty, shame) baisser les yeux; (from a height) regarder en bas; ▸ ~ **down on** [sb/sth] **1** lit regarder [qch] d'en haut; **2** fig mépriser; **3** (loom above) dominer

■ **look for**: ► ~ **for [sb/sth]** (search for) chercher qn/qch; ► ~ **for [sth]** (expect) attendre [*commitment, co-operation, result, reward*] (**from** de)

■ **look forward**: **to** ~ **forward to [sth]** attendre [qch] avec impatience; **she's** ~**ing forward to going on holiday** elle a hâte de partir en vacances; **I'm not** ~**ing forward to the interview** la perspective de l'entretien ne me réjouit pas; **I** ~ **forward to hearing from you** (to a friend) j'espère avoir bientôt de tes nouvelles; (formal) dans l'attente de votre réponse

■ **look in** (pay a visit) passer

■ **look into**: ► ~ **into [sth]** examiner, étudier [*matter, possibility, problem*]; examiner [*accounts*]; enquêter sur [*death, disappearance*]

■ **look on**: ► ~ **on** (watch) regarder; (be present) assister; ► ~ **on [sb/sth]** considérer [*person, event*] (**as** comme; **with** avec)

■ **look onto**: ► ~ **onto [sth]** [*house*] donner sur [*street*]

■ **look out**: ► ~ **out** (take care) faire attention (**for** à); (be wary) se méfier (**for** de); ~ **out!** attention!; ► ~ **out for [sb/sth]** guetter [*person*]; être à l'affût de [*bargain, new talent*]; être à la recherche de [*apartment*]; guetter l'apparition de [*symptoms*]; repérer [*examples*]; ► ~ **out for [oneself]** se débrouiller tout seul; ► ~ **out over [sth]** [*window*] donner sur [*sea*]

■ **look over**: ► ~ **[sb] over** passer [qn] en revue; ► ~ **[sth] over** examiner [*car, animal*]; ► ~ **over** ① (read) (in detail) examiner; (rapidly) parcourir; ② (visit) visiter [*factory, gardens*]

■ **look round** ① (look behind one) se retourner; ② (look about) regarder autour de soi; ③ (try to find) **we're** ~**ing round for a new house** nous cherchons une nouvelle maison; ► ~ **round [sth]** visiter [*town*]

■ **look through**: ► ~ **through [sth]** ① (read) consulter [*archive, files*]; parcourir [*essay, report, notes*]; (scan idly) feuilleter [*magazine*]; ② (search) fouiller dans [*belongings, briefcase*]; ► ~ **through [sb]** faire semblant de ne pas voir [*person*]

■ **look to**: ► ~ **to [sb/sth]** ① (rely on) compter sur qn/qch; ② (turn to) se tourner vers [*future, friends*]; ► ~ **to [sth]** (pay attention) veiller à [*interests*]; ► ~ **to do** (expect) espérer faire

■ **look up**: ► ~ **up** ① (raise one's eyes) lever les yeux (**from** de); ② (raise one's head) lever la tête; **to** ~ **up at the clouds** regarder les nuages; ③ (improve) [*business*] aller mieux; [*situation*] s'améliorer; [*property market*] reprendre; **things are** ~**ing up for us** les choses s'arrangent pour nous; ► ~ **[sb/sth] up**, ~ **up [sb/sth]** ① (check in book) chercher [*phone number, price*] (**in** dans); ② (visit) passer voir [*acquaintance*]; ► ~ **up to [sb]** admirer [*person*]

look: ~**-alike** n sosie m; ~**ed-for** adj (tjrs épith) [*result*] attendu; [*benefit*] escompté

look-in /'lʊkɪn/ n GB **to get a** ~ avoir sa chance; **to give sb a** ~ donner sa chance à qn

looking-glass n littér miroir m

look-out /'lʊkaʊt/
A n ① **to be on the** ~ **for** rechercher [*stolen vehicle*]; être à l'affût de [*bargain, new talent*]; guetter [*visitor*]; ② (sentry) (on ship) vigie f; (in army) guetteur m; ③ (place) poste m d'observation; ④ ○GB (private concern) **that's his** ~ c'est son affaire
B noun modifier [*tower*] d'observation; **to be on** ~ **duty** (on ship) être de quart; (in army) faire le guet

loom /luːm/
A n métier m à tisser
B vi ① (also ~ **up**) surgir (**out of** de; **over** au-dessus de); ② [*war, crisis*] menacer; [*exam, interview*] être imminent; **to** ~ **large** [*exam, issue*] peser lourd
C **looming** prés p adj ① fig [*crisis*] qui menace; [*deadline*] qui approche dangereusement; ② lit [*spire, cliff*] menaçant

loony○ /'luːnɪ/
A n (pl **-ies**) ① (eccentric) farfelu/-e m/f; ② (crazy) dingue○ mf; injur (mentally ill) taré/-e○ m/f offensive
B adj farfelu○

loony-bin○ n asile m de fous

loop /luːp/
A n ① boucle f; ② Aviat **to** ~ **the** ~ faire un looping; ③ Comput boucle f
B vtr nouer
C vi [*road, path*] faire une boucle
(Idiom) **to throw sb for a** ~ US sidérer qn

loophole /'luːphəʊl/ n fig lacune f

loopy○ /'luːpɪ/ adj loufoque○

loose /luːs/
A n **on the** ~ qui s'est échappé; **a gang of hooligans on the** ~ **in the town** une bande de voyous qui rôdent dans les rues de la ville; **he is still on the** ~ il est toujours en liberté
B adj ① lit (not firm or tight) [*knot, screw*] desserré; [*handle*] branlant; [*component*] mal fixé; [*button*] qui se découd; [*thread*] décousu; [*tooth*] qui se déchausse; **to come** ~ [*knot, screw*] se desserrer; [*handle*] être branlant; [*tooth*] se déchausser; **to hang** ~ [*hair*] être dénoué; [*rope*] pendre; ~ **connection** Elec faux contact; ② (free) **to break** ~ [*animal*] s'échapper (**from** de); **to cut sb** ~ détacher qn; **to let** ou **set** ou **turn** ~ libérer [*animal, prisoner*]; ③ Comm (not packed) [*tea, sweets*] en vrac; (as individual item) au détail; **just put the apples in the bag** ~ mettez donc les pommes à même le sac; ~ **change** petite monnaie; ④ (that has come apart) [*page*] volant; [*fragment*] détaché; **to come** ~ [*pages*] se détacher; '~ **chippings'** GB, '~ **gravel'** US (roadsign) 'attention gravillons'; ⑤ (not tight) [*jacket, trousers*] ample; [*collar*] lâche; [*skin*] flasque; ⑥ (not compacted) [*soil*] meuble; [*film, weave*] lâche; **to have** ~ **bowels** avoir la diarrhée; ⑦ (not strict or exact) [*translation, interpretation*] assez libre; [*wording*] imprécis; [*connection, guideline*] vague; [*style*] relâché; ⑧ (dissolute) [*morals*] dissolu; ~ **living** (vie f de) débauche f

(Idioms) **to be at a** ~ **end** GB, **to be at** ~ **ends** US ne pas trop savoir quoi faire

loose: ~**-box** n GB box m; ~ **cover** n GB housse f (de fauteuil); ~**-fitting** adj ample; ~**-leaf** adj à feuilles mobiles

loose-limbed adj souple

loosely /'luːslɪ/ adv ① lit (not tightly) [*fasten, wrap*] sans serrer; (not firmly) [*fix*] pas solidement; **his clothes hung** ~ **on him** il flottait dans ses vêtements; ② fig [*connected*] de façon souple; [*structured*] assez librement; ③ fig (imprecisely) [*translate*] assez librement; **the film is** ~ **based on the novel** le film est une adaptation assez libre du roman; ~ **termed Marxist** qualifié grossièrement de marxiste

loosely knit adj [*group, structure*] peu uni

loosen /'luːsn/
A vtr ① (make less tight) desserrer [*belt, strap, collar*]; dégager [*nail, post*]; relâcher [*rope, control*]; dénouer [*hair*]; **to** ~ **one's grip** ou **hold on sth** lit relâcher sa prise sur qch; fig relâcher son emprise sur qch; ② **to** ~ **the bowels** Med avoir une action laxative
B vi (become less tight) [*fastening, grip*] se desserrer
(Phrasal verb)
■ **loosen up**○: ► ~ **up** fig [*person*] se détendre, se dégeler○

looseness /'luːsnɪs/ n (of clothing) ampleur f; fig (of translation, argument) manque m de rigueur

loot /luːt/
A n ① (stolen goods) butin m; ② ○(money) fric○ m
B vtr piller
C vi se livrer au pillage

looter /'luːtə(r)/ n pillard/-e m/f

looting /'luːtɪŋ/ n pillage m

lop /lɒp/ (p prés etc **-pp-**) vtr élaguer [*branch*]; **she** ~**ped 10 seconds off the record** elle a retranché 10 secondes du record

lope /ləʊp/ vi **to** ~ **off** partir à grandes enjambées

lop-eared /'lɒpɪəd/ adj aux oreilles pendantes

lopsided /ˌlɒp'saɪdɪd/ adj ① [*object, smile*] de travers; ② fig [*argument, view*] irrationnel/-elle

lord /lɔːd/ ► p. 869 n ① Relig seigneur m (**of** de); ② (peer) lord m; **the (House of) Lords** la Chambre des Lords; **my Lord** (to noble) Monsieur le comte/duc etc
(Idiom) **to** ~ **it over sb**○ regarder qn de haut

Lord /lɔːd/ n ① Relig Seigneur m; **the year of our** ~ l'an de grâce; ② ○(in exclamations) **good** ~! grand Dieu!; ~ **knows where/why** Dieu sait où/pourquoi

Lord: ~ **Chancellor** n Lord m Chancelier; cf ministre m de la Justice; ~ **Chief Justice** n: le plus haut magistrat de la Haute Cour de Justice en Grande-Bretagne

lordly /'lɔːdlɪ/ adj ① (proud) [*manner*] hautain; ② (like a lord) [*bearing*] princier/-ière

Lord Mayor ► p. 869 n lord-maire m (titre des maires des grandes villes de Grande-Bretagne)

lordship /'lɔːdʃɪp/ ► p. 869 n (also **Lordship**) (title) **your/his** ~ (of noble) Monsieur; (of judge) Monsieur le Juge

Lord's Prayer n Notre Père m

lore /lɔː(r)/ n (of a people) traditions fpl

lorry /'lɒrɪ, US 'lɔːrɪ/ n (pl **-ies**) GB camion m; **heavy ~** poids m lourd; **army ~** camion militaire

(Idiom) **it fell off the back of a ~**○ euph c'est de la marchandise récupérée

lorry: **~ driver** ▸ p. 1181 n GB gen routier m, chauffeur m de poids lourd; **~ load** n GB chargement m, camion m

lose /luːz/

A vtr (prét, pp **lost**) **1** (mislay) perdre [object, person]; **to ~ one's way** lit se perdre; fig s'égarer; **2** (not have any longer) perdre; **to ~ interest in sth** se désintéresser de qch; **to ~ touch** (with person, reality) perdre contact; **to ~ the use of** perdre l'usage de [limb, muscle]; **to ~ one's life** mourir; **many lives were lost** il y a eu de nombreuses victimes; **200 jobs will be lost** 200 emplois vont être supprimés; **to ~ one's figure** s'épaissir; **he's losing his looks** il n'est plus aussi beau qu'autrefois; **nothing to ~**○ rien à perdre; **I've got too much to ~** c'est trop risqué; **3** (miss, waste) manquer [chance]; perdre [time]; **there's no time to ~** il n'y a pas de temps à perdre; **this allusion was not lost on him** cette allusion ne lui a pas échappé; **4** (be defeated in) gen, Jur, Pol, Sport perdre [war, race, bet, election]; avoir le dessous dans [argument]; perdre in [appeal]; **5** (lose sight of) perdre [qch] de vue [moving object]; fig **you've lost me there**○! je ne vous suis plus!; **6** (shake off, get rid of) se débarrasser de [habit]; semer○ [pursuer]; **7** (go slow) [clock] retarder de [minutes, seconds]; **8** (cause to forfeit) **to ~ sb sth** faire perdre qch à qn

B vi (prét, pp **lost**) **1** (be defeated) se faire battre (**to** par); **2** (be worse off, deteriorate) perdre; **they lost on the house** ils ont vendu la maison à perte; **3** [clock, watch] retarder

C v refl (prét, pp **lost**) **to ~ oneself in** se plonger dans [book]; se perdre dans [contemplation]

(Idiom) **to ~ it (totally)**○ péter les plombs○

(Phrasal verb) ■ **lose out** être perdant; **to ~ out on** perdre dans [deal]

loser /'luːzə(r)/ n gen, Sport perdant/-e m/f; **to be a good/bad ~** être bon/mauvais perdant

losing /'luːzɪŋ/ adj **1** gen, Sport [team] perdant; **2** Comm [concern] déficitaire

(Idioms) **it's a ~ battle** c'est une bataille perdue d'avance; **to be on a ~ streak** ne pas être en veine○

loss /lɒs, US lɔːs/ n **1** gen, Comm, Pol perte f (**of** de); **there was heavy ~ of life** il y a eu de nombreuses victimes; **~ of income** ou **earnings** manque m à gagner; **~ of sound/vision** TV interruption f du son/de l'image; **the ~ of 300 jobs** la suppression de 300 emplois; **a sense of ~** un sentiment de vide; **to make a ~** Comm enregistrer une perte; **2** **to be at a ~** (puzzled) être perplexe; (helpless) être perdu; **to be at a ~ as to what to do** ne pas savoir du tout quoi faire; **I'm at a ~ to explain it** je suis dans l'impossibilité de l'expliquer; **he was at a ~ for words** les mots lui manquaient; **she's never at a ~ for words** elle a toujours quelque chose à dire

(Idioms) **to cut one's ~es** arrêter les dégâts○; **it's his/their ~** tant pis pour lui/eux; **their ~ is our gain** autant de gagné pour nous

loss: **~ adjuster** n Comm expert m en assurances; **~ leader** n article m promotionnel (vendu à perte); **~-making** adj [product] vendu à perte; [company] travaillant à perte

lost /lɒst, US lɔːst/

A prét, pp ▸ **lose**

B adj **1** [person, animal] perdu; **we're ~** nous sommes perdus; **to get ~** [person, animal] se perdre; [object] s'égarer; **get ~**○! fiche le camp○!; **2** (wasted, vanished) [opportunity] manqué; [innocence] perdu; [civilisation] disparu; **to give sb/sth up for ~** considérer qn/qch comme perdu; **to be ~ on sb** passer au-dessus de la tête de qn; **3** (mystified) [person, look] perdu; **to be ~ for words** être interloqué; **4** **to be ~ in** être plongé dans [book, thought]; **5** (doomed) littér ou hum perdu; **a ~ cause** une cause perdue

lost: **~ and found** n objets mpl trouvés; **~ property** GB n objets mpl trouvés

lot¹ /lɒt/

A pron **1** (great deal) **a ~** beaucoup; **we bought a ~** nous avons acheté beaucoup de choses; **he spent a ~** il a beaucoup dépensé, il a dépensé beaucoup d'argent; **to get a**

---

lot¹

When a lot is used as a pronoun (they buy a lot, he spends a lot), it is translated by beaucoup: ils achètent beaucoup, il dépense beaucoup. For particular usages, see **A 1** in the entry **lot¹**.

When a lot is used to mean much in negative expressions (they didn't have a lot) it is translated by pas grand-chose: ils n'avaient pas grand-chose. For particular usages, see **A 1** in the entry **lot¹**.

When the lot is used as a pronoun (they took the lot), it is usually translated by tout: ils ont tout pris. For particular usages, see **A 2** in the entry **lot¹**.

When a lot of is used as a quantifier (a lot of money) it is translated by beaucoup de. For particular usages, see **B 1** in the entry **lot¹**. For translations of lots of, see **C** in the entry **lot¹**.

When a lot is used as an adverb (a lot stronger, he's changed a lot) it is translated by beaucoup: beaucoup plus fort, il a beaucoup changé. For particular usages, see **E** in the entry **lot¹**.

~ out of tirer beaucoup de [book]; **there's not a ~ to tell** il n'y a pas grand-chose à raconter; **he knows a ~ about sport** il s'y connaît beaucoup en sport; **you've taken (rather) a ~ on** tu en fais (un peu) trop; **I'd give a ~ to...** je donnerais cher pour...; **it says a ~ about her** ça en dit long sur elle; **that has a ~ to do with it** c'est très lié; **an awful ~** énormément; **quite a ~** beaucoup, pas mal○; **to mean quite a ~ to sb** avoir beaucoup d'importance pour qn; **such a ~** tellement; **2** ○(entire amount or selection) **the ~** (le) tout; **I'll write you a cheque for the ~** je vous ferai un chèque pour le tout; **the nicest dress of the ~** la plus belle robe de toutes; **heartburn, cramps, the ~!** des brûlures d'estomac, des crampes, bref tout!; **3** ○(specific group of people) **she's the nicest of the ~** c'est la plus gentille (de tous/toutes); **that ~** péj ces gens-là pej; **you ~** vous, vous autres; **my ~ can't even spell properly** les miens ne savent même pas écrire correctement; **they're not a bad ~** ils ne sont pas méchants; **the best of a bad ~**○ le moins pire○

B quantif **1** (great deal) **a ~ of** beaucoup de; **a ~ of money/time** beaucoup d'argent/de temps; **not a ~ of people know that** il n'y a pas beaucoup de personnes or gens qui savent ça; **I see a ~ of him** je le vois beaucoup; **an awful○ ~ of** énormément de; **quite a ~ of** beaucoup or pas mal○ de; **quite a ~ of our support...** une bonne part de notre soutien...; **what a ~ of people!** que de monde!; **2** ○(entire group) tous; **I'd sack the ~ of them!** je les mettrais tous à la porte!

C lots○ quantif, pron ~s (and ~s) of des tas○ de (+ pl nouns only); beaucoup de (+ any nouns); ~s of things des tas○ de choses; ...and ~s more ...et beaucoup d'autres choses

D lots○ adv ~s better beaucoup or vachement○ mieux

E a lot phr beaucoup; **a ~ better** beaucoup mieux; **a ~ worse** bien pire; **they talk a ~ about justice** ils parlent beaucoup de justice; **you find this a ~ on** on rencontre beaucoup ce problème; **the situation has improved a ~** la situation s'est beaucoup améliorée; **this happens quite a ~** cela arrive très souvent; **an awful ~ cheaper** beaucoup moins cher; **it would help an awful○ ~** ça aiderait beaucoup; **he travels abroad such a ~** il voyage beaucoup à l'étranger

lot² /lɒt/ n **1** (destiny) sort m; (quality of life) condition f; **to be the ~ of many** être le lot de beaucoup de gens; **to throw in one's ~ with sb** allier son destin à celui de qn; **2** US parcelle f (de terrain); **vacant ~** terrain m vague; **used car ~** garage m vendant des voitures d'occasion; **3** (at auction) lot m; **4** (decision-making process) tirage m au sort; **to draw** ou **cast ~s** tirer au sort; **5** Cin studio m; **6** (batch) (of students, tourists) fournée f

lotion /'ləʊʃn/ n lotion f

lottery /'lɒtərɪ/

A n lit loterie f, loto m; fig loterie f

B modif [winner] du loto; [win] au loto; [number, ticket] de loto

lotto /'lɒtəʊ/ ▸ p. 881 n loto m

loud /laʊd/
A adj ⟦1⟧ (noisy) [bang, music, voice] fort; [crash, scream] grand; [comment, laugh] bruyant; [applause] vif/vive; [whisper] audible; ⟦2⟧ (emphatic) [objection] vif/vive; ⟦3⟧ (vulgar) péj [colour, pattern] criard; [person, behaviour] exubérant
B adv fort; **out** ∼ à voix haute; ∼ **and clear** clairement
(Idiom) **for crying out** ∼○! pour l'amour de Dieu!

loudhailer /ˌlaʊd'heɪlə(r)/ n GB mégaphone m

loudly /'laʊdlɪ/ adv [knock, talk, sing] bruyamment; [play music, scream] fort; [protest] vivement

loud: ∼**mouth**○ n grande gueule⟨⟩ f; ∼**mouthed**○ adj fort en gueule⟨⟩

loudness /'laʊdnɪs/ n intensité f

loudspeaker n (for announcements) haut-parleur m; (for hi-fi) enceinte f

lounge /laʊndʒ/
A n ⟦1⟧ (in house, hotel) salon m; ⟦2⟧ (in airport) **departure** ∼ salle f d'embarquement; ⟦3⟧ US (also **cocktail** ∼) bar m
B vi (sprawl) s'avachir (**on** sur)
(Phrasal verb)
■ **lounge about**, **lounge around** paresser pej

lounge: ∼ **bar** n GB grande salle f de pub; ∼ **lizard**○ n salonnard○ m; ∼ **suit** n GB costume m

louse /laʊs/ n ⟦1⟧ (pl **lice**) (insect) pou m; ⟦2⟧ ⟨⟩(pl ∼**s**) pej salaud⟨⟩ m
(Phrasal verb)
■ **louse up**⟨⟩: ▸ ∼ [sth] up, ∼ up [sth] bousiller

lousy /'laʊzɪ/
A adj ○[book, holiday] mauvais; [meal, working conditions] infect○; [salary] minable○; **to feel** ∼ être mal fichu○; **a** ∼ **trick** un sale tour
B ⟨⟩adv US **to do** ∼ se débrouiller comme un manche○

lout /laʊt/ n (rude-mannered) malotru○ m

loutish /'laʊtɪʃ/ adj [person] grossier/-ière; [behaviour] de voyou

louvred GB, **louvered** US /'luːvəd/ adj à lamelles

lovable /'lʌvəbl/ adj [person] sympathique; [child] adorable

love /lʌv/
A n ⟦1⟧ (affection, devotion) amour m; **to do sth for the** ∼ **of it** faire qch par goût; **for the** ∼ **of God!** pour l'amour de Dieu!; **to be/fall in** ∼ être/tomber amoureux/-euse (**with** de); **he's in** ∼ **with the sound of his own voice** il s'écoute parler; **to make** ∼ (have sex) faire l'amour; ⟦2⟧ (in polite formulas) **give my** ∼ **to Jo** transmets mes amitiés à Jo; ∼ **to Don** baisers à Don; **Andy sends his** ∼ Andy t'embrasse; **with** ∼ **from Bob**, ∼ **Bob** affectueusement, Bob; ⟦3⟧ (object of affection) amour m; **be a** ∼○ GB sois gentil; ⟦4⟧ GB (term of address) (to adult) mon amour m, mon chéri/ma chérie m/f; (to child) mon chéri/ma chérie m/f; ⟦5⟧ (in tennis) zéro m
B noun modifier [letter, song, story] d'amour
C vtr ⟦1⟧ (feel affection for) aimer; **to** ∼ **sb very much** adorer qn; **to** ∼ **each other** s'aimer; ⟦2⟧ (appreciate) aimer beaucoup (**to do** faire); (accepting invitation) **'I'd** ∼ **to!'** 'avec plaisir!'; ⟦3⟧ ○(in exaggerated speech) adorer; **she'll** ∼ **that!** iron elle sera vraiment ravie! iron
(Idioms) ∼ **at first sight** le coup de foudre; **there's no** ∼ **lost between them** ils/elles se détestent cordialement

love affair n liaison f (**with** avec; **between** entre)

love: ∼ **child** n euph enfant mf de l'amour; ∼**-hate relationship** n relation f oscillant entre l'amour et la haine

loveless /'lʌvlɪs/ adj [marriage] sans amour

love-life n vie f amoureuse

loveliness /'lʌvlɪnɪs/ n beauté f

lovely /'lʌvlɪ/ adj ⟦1⟧ (beautiful) [colour, garden, woman] beau/belle, joli (before n); **you look** ∼ tu es ravissante; **the hat will look** ∼ **with it** le chapeau ira très bien avec; ⟦2⟧ (pleasant) [letter, person] charmant; [meal, smell] délicieux/-ieuse; [idea, surprise] bon/bonne (before n); [weekend outing] excellent; [present, weather] magnifique; **it's** ∼ **to do** c'est tellement agréable de faire; **to smell** ∼ sentir bon; **to taste** ∼ être délicieux/-ieuse; ⟦3⟧ (emphatic) ∼ **and hot/fresh** bien chaud/frais

love: ∼**making** n rapports mpl (sexuels); ∼ **match** n union f parfaite

lover /'lʌvə(r)/ n ⟦1⟧ amant m; **to take a** ∼ prendre un amant; ⟦2⟧ (person in love) amoureux/-euse m/f; ⟦3⟧ (enthusiast) amateur m (**of** de); **jazz** ∼ amateur de jazz

love: ∼ **seat** n confident m; ∼**sick** adj languissant d'amour

lovey-dovey○ /ˌlʌvɪ'dʌvɪ/ adj GB **to get all** ∼ se mettre à roucouler○

loving /'lʌvɪŋ/
A adj [mother, husband, look, smile] tendre; [kiss] amoureux/-euse; [care] affectueux/-euse; (in letter-writing) **your** ∼ **son** ton fils qui t'aime
B **-loving** combining form **football-/music-**∼ amateur de football/de musique

lovingly /'lʌvɪŋlɪ/ adv (all contexts) avec amour

low /ləʊ/
A n ⟦1⟧ Meteorol dépression f; ⟦2⟧ fig (low point) **to be at** ou **have hit an all-time** ∼ être au plus bas
B adj ⟦1⟧ (close to the ground) [branch, building, chair, cloud] bas/basse; **on** ∼ **ground** [flood] dans les basses terres; [built] dans une dépression; ⟦2⟧ (nearly depleted) [reservoir, stocks, level] bas/basse; [battery] faible; **the fire was getting** ∼ le feu baissait; **to be** ∼ **on staff** manquer de personnel; **I'm getting** ∼ **on petrol** je n'ai plus beaucoup d'essence; **to be** ∼ **in sugar** contenir peu de sucre; ⟦3⟧ (minimal) [price, wage] bas/basse; [capacity, speed] réduit; [number, rate] faible; [pressure, temperature] bas/basse; **on a** ∼ **heat** à feu doux; **the temperature was in the** ∼ **twenties** il faisait dans les vingt degrés; ⟦4⟧ (inferior) [mark, standard] mauvais; ⟦5⟧ (depressed) déprimé; ⟦6⟧ (deep) [tone, voice] bas/basse; **in a** ∼ **voice** tout bas; ⟦7⟧ (vulgar) [humour] peu relevé; (base) [behaviour] ignoble; ⟦8⟧ Naut ∼ **tide** marée f basse
C adv ⟦1⟧ (near the ground) [aim] bas; [bend] très bas; **to fly** ∼ voler à basse altitude; **I wouldn't sink** ou **stoop so** ∼ fig je ne m'abaisserais pas à ce point-là; ⟦2⟧ (near the bottom) **very** ∼ **(down) on the list** fig tout à fait secondaire; ⟦3⟧ (at a reduced level) [speak] bas; **to turn sth down** ∼ baisser [heating, light]; **stocks are running** ∼ les stocks sont en baisse; **to rate sb pretty** ∼ ne pas tenir qn en grande estime; ⟦4⟧ [sing] bas
D vi [cow] meugler
(Idioms) **to be the** ∼**est of the** ∼ être le dernier des derniers; **to be laid** ∼ **by** être cloué au lit par

low-alcohol adj peu alcoolisé

lowbrow /'ləʊbraʊ/ péj
A n personne f peu intellectuelle
B adj [person] peu intellectuel/-elle

low: ∼**-budget** adj à petit budget; ∼**-calorie** adj [diet] hypocalorique; [food] à faible teneur en calories; ∼**-cost** adj économique, bon marché; **Low Countries** pr npl Pays-Bas mpl; ∼**-cut** adj décolleté; ∼**-down** n tuyau○ m

lower¹ /'ləʊə(r)/
A vi littér (frown) prendre un air comminatoire (**at** avec)
B **lowering** pres p adj [sky] menaçant

lower² /'ləʊə(r)/
A adj (comparative of **low**) inférieur; **in the** ∼ **back** au bas du dos
B vtr ⟦1⟧ (bring down) baisser [barrier, curtain, flag]; abaisser [ceiling]; **to** ∼ **sb/sth** (let down) descendre qn/qch (**into** dans; **onto** sur); ⟦2⟧ (reduce) baisser [light, prices, standards]; réduire [pressure, temperature]; diminuer [resistance]; abaisser [age limit]; **to** ∼ **one's voice** baisser la voix; **to** ∼ **one's guard** relâcher sa vigilance; ⟦3⟧ (abolish) abolir [trade barrier]; ⟦4⟧ Naut affaler [sail]; mettre [qch] à la mer [lifeboat]
C v refl **to** ∼ **oneself** ⟦1⟧ (demean oneself) s'abaisser; ⟦2⟧ (sit carefully) **to** ∼ **oneself into** entrer lentement dans [bath]; s'asseoir précautionneusement dans [chair]

lower case /'ləʊə(r)/ n bas m de casse, minuscules fpl

lower class /'ləʊə(r)/
A n (pl ∼**es**) **the** ∼**(es)** la classe ouvrière
B **lower-class** adj gen de la classe ouvrière; [accent, district] populaire

lowering /'ləʊərɪŋ/ n gen baisse f; (of age limit) abaissement m; (of resistance) diminution f; (of flag, sail) abaissement m; (of trade barriers) abolition f

lower middle class /'ləʊə(r)/
A n (pl ∼**es**) **the** ∼**(es)** la petite bourgeoisie
B adj petit-bourgeois/petite-bourgeoise

lower sixth /'ləʊə(r)/ n GB Sch ≈ classe f de première; **to be in the** ∼ ≈ être en première

lowest common denominator n Math, fig plus petit dénominateur m commun

low: **~-fat** adj [diet] sans matières grasses; [cheese] allégé; [milk] écrémé; **~-flying** adj volant à faible altitude; **~-frequency** adj [sonar, sound] (à) basse fréquence (after n); **~-grade** adj [product] de qualité inférieure; [official] de grade inférieur; **~-heeled** adj plat, à talons plats; **~-income** adj [family] à faible revenu; [bracket] des bas salaires; **~-key** adj [approach] discret/-ète; [meeting, talks] informel/-elle

lowland /'ləʊlənd/
A n (also **~s**) basses-terres fpl
B noun modifier [area] à faible altitude

low-level adj [bombing] à basse altitude; [talks] informel/-elle; [radiation] faible

low-life
A n ᴼ(person) (pl **~s**) crapule f
B noun modifier [character, scene] des bas-fonds; [friend, contact] du milieu

low: **~-lying** adj à basse altitude; **~-necked** adj décolleté

lowness /'ləʊnɪs/ n **1** (of bridge, ceiling) faible hauteur f; **2** Meteorol, Phys the ~ of the temperature/pressure la basse température/pression

low-paid
A n the ~ (+ v pl) les petits salaires mpl
B adj [job] faiblement rémunéré; [worker] peu rémunéré

low: **~-priced** adj Comm à bas prix; **~-profile** adj (discreet) discret/-ète; **~-quality** adj de qualité inférieure; **~-rise** adj [building] bas/basse (after n); **~-risk** adj [investment] à risque limité; [borrower] fiable; **~-scoring** adj Sport [match] avec peu de points de marqués; **~ season** n Tourism basse saison f; **~-slung** adj [chassis] surbaissé; **~-tar** adj à faible teneur en goudrons; **~-tech** adj (de type) traditionnel; **~ tide** n marée f basse

low voltage
A n basse tension f
B low-voltage adj de basse tension

loyal /'lɔɪəl/ adj [friend] loyal (**to** envers); [customer] fidèle (**to** à)

loyalist /'lɔɪəlɪst/ n, adj loyaliste (mf)

loyally /'lɔɪəlɪ/ adv [serve] fidèlement; [speak] avec dévouement

loyalty /'lɔɪəltɪ/ n loyauté f (**to, towards** envers); **to have divided loyalties** se sentir écartelé

loyalty card n Comm carte f de fidélité

lozenge /'lɒzɪndʒ/ n pastille f

LP n (abrév = **long-playing record**) (disque m) 33 tours m

L-plate /'el pleɪt/ n GB Aut plaque f d'élève conducteur débutant accompagné

LSE n GB (abrév = **London School of Economics**) faculté des Sciences économiques de l'Université de Londres

L-shaped adj en (forme de) L

Lt abrév écrite ▸ **lieutenant**

Ltd GB (abrév écrite = **limited (liability)**) cf SARL

lubricant /'lu:brɪkənt/ n lubrifiant m

lubricate /'lu:brɪkeɪt/ vtr gen lubrifier

lucid /'lu:sɪd/ adj **1** (clear) clair; **2** (sane) [person] lucide; [moment] de lucidité

lucidity /lu:'sɪdətɪ/ n **1** (clarity) clarté f; **2** (sanity) lucidité f

luck /lʌk/ n **1** (good or bad) **good ~** chance f; **bad ~** malchance f; **to bring sb good/bad ~** porter bonheur/malheur à qn; **it's good ~** ça porte chance; **it is bad ~ that** ce n'est pas de chance que (+ subj); **to try one's ~** tenter sa chance; **as ~ would have it...** le hasard a voulu que... (+ subj); **bad** ou **hard ~!** pas de chance!; **just my ~!** c'est bien ma chance!; **good ~!** bonne chance!; **better ~ next time!** tu auras plus de chance la prochaine fois!; **to be down on one's ~** être dans une mauvaise passe; **2** (good luck) chance f; **with a bit of ~...** avec un peu de chance...; **our ~ ran out** notre chance a tourné; **to wear sth for ~** porter qch comme porte-bonheur; **by a stroke of ~** par un coup de chance; **any ~?** ça donne quelque chose?; **to be in/out of ~** avoir de la/ne pas avoir de chance

(Idioms) **it's the ~ of the draw** c'est une question de chance; **one for ~** un/une de plus tant qu'on y est; **my ~'s in!** c'est mon jour de chance!; **no such ~!** hélas non!; **once more for ~** encore une fois à tout hasard; **you'll have to take pot ~** (at meal) ce sera à la fortune du pot

(Phrasal verb)
■ **luck out**ᴼ US avoir de la veine ᴼ

luckily /'lʌkɪlɪ/ adv heureusement (**for** pour)

luckless /'lʌklɪs/ adj littér [person] infortuné

lucky /'lʌkɪ/ adj **1** (fortunate) **to be ~ to do/to be** avoir la chance de faire/d'être; **to be ~ to get out alive** avoir eu de la chance de s'en tirer vivant; **you'll be ~ to get a taxi** tu auras bien de la chance si tu trouves un taxi; **it was ~ for me** j'ai eu de la chance; **to be ~ enough to do** avoir la chance de faire; **I'm not ~** je n'ai jamais de chance; **~ you**ᴼ! veinard/-e ᴼ m/f!; **I/you etc should be so ~**ᴼ! GB iron ça serait trop beau!; **you should think** ou **count yourself ~** tu peux te considérer heureux/-euse; **to have a ~ escape** l'échapper belle; **2** (bringing good luck) [charm, colour, number] porte-bonheur inv; **it's my ~ day!** c'est mon jour de chance!

(Idioms) **to strike it ~** décrocher le gros lot ᴼ; **to thank one's ~ stars** remercier le ciel

lucrative /'lu:krətɪv/ adj lucratif/-ive

lucreᴼ† /'lu:kə(r)/ n fric ᴼ m

ludicrous /'lu:dɪkrəs/ adj grotesque

ludo /'lu:dəʊ/ ▸ p. 881 n GB jeu m des petits chevaux

lug /lʌg/
A n **1** Tech patte f; **2** ᴼGB = **lughole**
B vtr (p prés etc **-gg-**) traîner

luggage /'lʌgɪdʒ/ n ⊄ bagages mpl

luggage: **~ handler** ▸ p. 1181 n bagagiste mf; **~ rack** n compartiment m à bagages; **~ van** n GB fourgon m à bagages

lugholeᴼ /'lʌgəʊl/ n GB esgourde ᴼ f

lukewarm /ˌlu:k'wɔ:m/ adj tiède

lull /lʌl/
A n (in storm, fighting) accalmie f; (in conversation) pause f; (in trading) ralentissement m
B vtr apaiser [person]; **he ~ed them into thinking that...** il leur a fait croire que...; **to be ~ed into a false sense of security** se laisser aller à un sentiment de sécurité trompeur

lullaby /'lʌləbaɪ/ n berceuse f

lumbar /'lʌmbə(r)/ adj lombaire

lumber /'lʌmbə(r)/
A n US (wood) bois m de construction
B vtr ᴼGB **to get** ou **be ~ed with sb/sth** se retrouver avec qn/qch sur les bras; **to be ~ed with a chore** se taper une corvée
C vi **1** (also **~ along**) avancer d'un pas lourd; [vehicle] avancer péniblement; **to ~ away** ou **off** [person] s'éloigner d'un pas lourd; **2** US (cut timber) débiter le bois

lumbering /'lʌmbərɪŋ/ adj [animal, person] au pas lourd (after n); fig [bureaucracy] pesant

lumber: **~jack** ▸ p. 1181 n bûcheron/-onne m/f; **~jack shirt** n chemise f épaisse à carreaux; **~ mill** n scierie f

luminary /'lu:mɪnərɪ, US -nerɪ/ n fig (person) sommité f

luminous /'lu:mɪnəs/ adj lumineux/-euse

lump /lʌmp/
A n **1** morceau m; (of soil, clay) motte f; (in sauce) grumeau m; **in one ~** en bloc; **2** (on body) (from knock) bosse f (**on** sur); (tumour) grosseur f (**in, on** à); **3** ᴼ(idle person) (man) balourd ᴼ m; (woman) dondon ᴼ f
B vtr **to ~ X together with Y** regrouper X et Y; péj mettre X et Y dans le même panier ᴼ

(Idioms) **to have a ~ in one's throat** avoir la gorge serrée; **I'll/he'll have to ~ it**ᴼ il va falloir faire avec/qu'il fasse avec ᴼ; **like it or ~ it**ᴼ que ça te/lui etc chante ou pas ᴼ

lump: **~ sugar** n sucre m en morceaux; **~ sum** n Comm (complete payment) versement m unique

lumpy /'lʌmpɪ/ adj [sauce] grumeleux/-euse; [mattress, pillow, soil] défoncé

lunacy /'lu:nəsɪ/ n fig folie f

lunar /'lu:nə(r)/ adj [landscape, module, orbit] lunaire; [eclipse] de lune; [landing] sur la lune

lunatic /ˈluːnətɪk/
A n fig fou/folle m/f
B adj fig [person] fou/folle; [plan, idea] démentiel/-ielle
lunatic: ~ **asylum** n asile m d'aliénés†; ~ **fringe** n péj les jusqu'au-boutistes mfpl
lunch /lʌntʃ/
A n déjeuner m; **to have** ~ déjeuner; **to take sb out for** ~ emmener qn déjeuner au restaurant; **she's gone to** ~ elle est partie déjeuner; ~**!, time for** ~**!** à table!; **to close for** ~ fermer le midi; **to do good** ~**es** servir de bons repas le midi
B vi déjeuner (**on, off** de)
(Idioms) **out to** ~° dingue°; **there's no such thing as a free** ~ on ne fait jamais rien pour rien
lunch: ~**box** n boîte f à sandwichs; ~**break** n pause-déjeuner f
luncheon /ˈlʌntʃən/ n sout déjeuner m
luncheon: ~ **meat** n ≈ viande f en conserve; ~ **voucher, LV** n ticket-repas m, ticket-restaurant® m
lunch: ~ **hour** n heure f du déjeuner; ~**time** n heure f du déjeuner
lung /lʌŋ/
A n poumon m
B noun modifier [disease] pulmonaire; [transplant, cancer] du poumon
lunge /lʌndʒ/
A n brusque mouvement m vers l'avant; **a desperate** ~ **for the ball** un bond désespéré vers la balle
B vtr faire tourner [qch] à la longe [horse]
C vi gen bondir
lurch /lɜːtʃ/
A n **to give a** ~ [vehicle] faire une embardée
B vi lit [person, vehicle] tanguer; **to** ~ **forward** tressauter; **to** ~ **to a halt** faire une embardée et s'arrêter
(Idiom) **to leave sb in the** ~ abandonner qn
lurcher /ˈlɜːtʃə(r)/ n GB chien m de chasse (croisé entre un collie et un lévrier)
lure /lʊə(r)/
A n **1** (attraction) attrait m (**of** de); **2** (in hunting) leurre m
B vtr attirer (**into** dans; **with** avec); **they** ~**d him out of his house** ils ont réussi à le faire sortir de chez lui par la ruse; **to** ~ **sb away from her studies** détourner qn de ses études
lurid /ˈlʊərɪd/ adj [colour] criard; [detail] épouvantable
lurk /lɜːk/
A vi **1** **he was** ~**ing in the bushes** il était tapi dans les

buissons; **2** fig [danger] menacer; **3** (in a chatroom) observer passivement
B lurking pres p adj [doubt] persistant
luscious /ˈlʌʃəs/ adj [food] succulent; [woman]° pulpeux/-euse
lush /lʌʃ/
A °n poivrot/-ote° m/f
B adj [vegetation] luxuriant; [surroundings] luxueux/-euse
lust /lʌst/
A n gen désir m (**for** de); (deadly sin) luxure f; **the** ~ **for power** la soif du pouvoir
B vi **to** ~ **for** ou **after sb/sth** convoiter qn/qch
lustre GB, **luster** US /ˈlʌstə(r)/ n éclat m
lustreware GB, **lusterware** US /ˈlʌstəweə(r)/ n poterie f à reflet métallique
lusty /ˈlʌstɪ/ adj vigoureux/-euse
lute /luːt/ ▸ p. 1028 n luth m
Luxembourg /ˈlʌksəmbɜːg/ ▸ p. 774 pr n Luxembourg m
luxuriate /lʌgˈzjʊərɪeɪt/ vi **to** ~ **in** s'abandonner avec délices à [warmth, bath]; savourer [attention]
luxurious /lʌgˈzjʊərɪəs/ adj [apartment, lifestyle] de luxe (never after v); **his apartment is** ~ son appartement est luxueux
luxuriously /lʌgˈzjʊərɪəslɪ/ adv [decorate] luxueusement; [yawn, stretch] voluptueusement
luxury /ˈlʌkʃərɪ/
A n (all contexts) luxe m
B noun modifier [product, holiday] de luxe
LV n (abrév = **luncheon voucher**) ticket-repas m
LW n Radio (abrév = **long wave**) GO fpl
lychee /ˈlaɪtʃiː, ˌlaɪˈtʃiː/ n litchi m
lychgate /ˈlɪtʃgeɪt/ n porche m d'entrée du cimetière
lying /ˈlaɪɪŋ/ n ¢ mensonges mpl
lymph /lɪmf/ n lymphe f
lynch /lɪntʃ/ vtr lyncher
lynch mob n lyncheurs mpl
Lyons /ˈliːɔːŋ/ ▸ p. 1276 pr n Lyon m
lyric /ˈlɪrɪk/
A n Literat poème m lyrique
B lyrics npl (of song) paroles fpl (d'une chanson)
C adj lyrique
lyrical /ˈlɪrɪkl/ adj (all contexts) lyrique; **to wax** ~ (**about** ou **over sth**) disserter avec lyrisme (sur qch)
lyricism /ˈlɪrɪsɪzəm/ n (all contexts) lyrisme m
lyric-writer ▸ p. 1181 n parolier/-ière m/f

Mm

m, **M** /em/ n ① (letter) m, M m; ② **m** (abrév écrite = **metre(s)** GB, **meter(s)** US) m; ③ **M** (abrév = **motorway**) autoroute f; **the M3** l'autoroute M3; ④ **m** abrév écrite = **mile(s)**; ⑤ **m** abrév écrite = **million**

MA n ① (abrév = **Master of Arts**) diplôme m supérieur de lettres; ② US Post abrév écrite = **Massachusetts**

ma'am /mæm, mɑːm/ n (abrév = **madam**) gen madame f, mademoiselle f; (to Queen) madame f

mac○ /mæk/ n GB (abrév = **mackintosh**) imper○ m

macaroni /ˌmækəˈrəʊnɪ/ n ¢ macaronis mpl

macaroni cheese n gratin m de macaronis

macaroon /ˌmækəˈruːn/ n macaron m

mace /meɪs/ n ① (spice) macis m; ② (ceremonial staff) masse f

Macedonia /ˌmæsɪˈdəʊnɪə/ pr n Macédoine f

macerate /ˈmæsəreɪt/ vi macérer

machete /məˈtʃetɪ, US məˈʃetɪ/ n machette f

machination /ˌmækɪˈneɪʃn/ n machination f

machine /məˈʃiːn/
A n ① (piece of equipment) machine f (**for doing** à faire); **sewing** ∼ machine à coudre; **to operate a** ∼ faire fonctionner une machine; **by** ∼ à la machine; ② fig (apparatus) machine f; **publicity** ∼ machine publicitaire
B vtr Ind usiner

machine: ∼-**assisted translation**, **MAT** n traduction f assistée par ordinateur, TAO f; ∼ **gun** n mitrailleuse f; ∼ **intelligence** n intelligence f artificielle; ∼ **operator** n Ind opérateur/-trice m/f; ∼-**readable** adj Comput [data, text] directement exploitable; [passport] vérifiable par ordinateur

machinery /məˈʃiːnərɪ/ n ¢ ① (equipment) machines fpl; (working parts) mécanisme m, rouages mpl; **a piece of** ∼ une machine; **heavy** ∼ machines fpl lourdes; ② fig (apparatus) dispositifs mpl; **the** ∼ **to settle industrial disputes** le système mis en place pour régler les conflits sociaux; **the** ∼ **of justice** les rouages de la justice

machine: ∼-**stitch** vtr piquer à la machine; ∼ **translation**, **MT** n traduction f automatique; ∼-**washable** adj lavable en machine

machinist /məˈʃiːnɪst/ n ▸ p. 1181 opérateur/-trice m/f

machismo /məˈtʃɪzməʊ, -ˈkɪzməʊ/ n machisme m

macho /ˈmætʃəʊ/ adj péj macho; (manly) viril

mackerel /ˈmækrəl/ n maquereau m

mackintosh, **macintosh** /ˈmækɪntɒʃ/ n imperméable m

macro /ˈmækrəʊ/
A n Comput macro f
B **macro+** combining form macro-

macrocosm /ˈmækrəʊkɒzəm/ n macrocosme m

mad /mæd/ adj ① [person] fou/folle (**with** de); [dog, bull] enragé; **to go** ∼ devenir fou/folle; ② (foolish) [idea, scheme] insensé; **it is** ∼ **to do** ou **doing** c'est fou○ or de la folie de faire; **they are** ∼ **to do** c'est de la folie de leur part de faire; **to go** ∼○ (spend money) faire des folies; ③ ○(angry) (jamais épith) très en colère, furieux/-ieuse; **to be** ∼ **at** ou **with sb** être très en colère contre qn; **to get** ∼ **at** ou **with sb** se mettre en colère contre qn; **to be** ∼ **about sth** être en colère à cause de qch; **to go** ∼ être fou de rage; **to make sb** ∼ exaspérer qn; **to drive sb** ∼ rendre qn fou; ④ ○(enthusiastic) ∼ **about** ou **on** fou de○ [person, hobby]; **to be movie-**∼ être un passionné or un mordu○ de cinéma;

⑤ (frantic) [panic] infernal; **to be** ∼ **for blood** être assoiffé de sang or de vengeance; ∼ **for food** affamé; **the audience went** ∼ le public s'est déchaîné; **to be in a** ∼ **rush** être très pressé; **it was a** ∼ **scramble to do** ça a été la panique○ pour faire; **we made a** ∼ **dash for the bus** on a couru comme des fous pour attraper le bus
(Idiom) **to work like** ∼ travailler comme un fou/une folle

Madagascar /ˌmædəˈɡæskə/ ▸ p. 774 pr n Madagascar m

madam /ˈmædəm/ n ① (also **Madam**) (form of address) madame f; **Madam Chairman** Madame la Présidente; **Dear Madam** Madame; ② ○GB (young woman) (stuck up) pimbêche○ f; (cheeky) insolente f

mad: ∼**cap** adj (épith) [person, idea] insensé; ∼ **cow disease** n maladie f de la vache folle

madden /ˈmædn/ vtr [attitude] exaspérer; [pain, heat, insects] rendre [qn] fou; **it** ∼**s me to do/that** ça m'exaspère de faire/que (+ subj)

maddening /ˈmædnɪŋ/ adj [person] énervant; [delay, situation] exaspérant; **it's** ∼ **to** c'est exaspérant de

made /meɪd/
A prét, pp ▸ **make**
B adj **to be** ∼ avoir réussi; **a** ∼ **man** un homme qui a réussi
C -**made** combining form Italian-∼ fabriqué en Italie
(Idiom) **he's got it** ∼○ (sure to succeed) sa réussite est assurée; (has succeeded) il n'a plus à s'en faire

Madeira /məˈdɪərə/ ▸ p. 954 pr n ① (island) Madère; ② (wine) madère m

made-to-measure adj [garment] fait sur mesure

made-up /ˌmeɪdˈʌp/ adj ① (wearing make-up) maquillé; ② [story] fabriqué; ③ [road] goudronné; ④ [garment] de prêt-à-porter

madhouse○ /ˈmædhaʊs/ n (bedlam) maison f de fous

madly /ˈmædlɪ/ adv ① (frantically) frénétiquement; ② (extremely) follement; ∼ **in love (with sb)** follement or éperdument amoureux (de qn)

madman○ /ˈmædmən/ n fou○ m, malade○ m

madness /ˈmædnɪs/ n folie f; **it is** ∼ **to do** c'est de la folie de faire

madwoman○ /ˈmædwʊmən/ n folle○ f, malade○ f

MAFF n GB Hist (abrév = **Ministry of Agriculture, Fisheries and Food**) ministère m de l'Agriculture, de la pêche et de l'alimentation

mafia /ˈmæfɪə, US ˈmɑː-/ n **the Mafia** la Mafia; fig **the** ∼ la mafia

mag○ /mæg/ n: abrév ▸ **magazine 1**

magazine /ˌmæɡəˈziːn/ n ① (periodical) revue f; (mainly photos) magazine m; **computer** ∼ revue d'informatique; **monthly** ∼ revue mensuelle; **fashion** ∼ magazine de mode; **women's** ∼ journal m féminin; ② (on radio, TV) magazine m; ③ (of gun, camera) magasin m

maggot /ˈmæɡət/ n (in fruit) ver m; (for fishing) asticot m

magic /ˈmædʒɪk/
A n ① (supernatural power) magie f; **to do sth by** ∼ faire qch par magie; **as if by** ∼ comme par enchantement; **it works like** ∼! c'est miraculeux!; ② (enchantment) magie f (**of** de)
B adj magique; **the Magic Flute** la Flûte enchantée

magical /ˈmædʒɪkl/ adj ① (supernatural) magique; ② (enchanting) [moment] magique; [week, stay] merveilleux/-euse

magic carpet n tapis m volant

magician /mə'dʒɪʃn/ n (wizard) magicien m; (entertainer) illusionniste m

magisterial /ˌmædʒɪ'stɪərɪəl/ adj ① (authoritative) magistral; ② Jur [office, duties] de magistrat

magistrate /'mædʒɪstreɪt/ ▸ p. 1181 n magistrat m (non professionnel); **to appear before (the)** ∼s comparaître devant les magistrats

magistrates' court, Magistrates' Court n ≈ tribunal m de police

magna cum laude /ˌmægnə kʊm 'laʊdeɪ/ adv US Univ **to graduate** ∼ obtenir son diplôme avec mention très bien

magnanimity /ˌmægnə'nɪmətɪ/ n magnanimité f

magnanimous /mæg'nænɪməs/ adj magnanime

magnate /'mægneɪt/ n magnat m; **oil** ∼ magnat du pétrole

magnesia /mæg'niːʃə/ n magnésie f

magnesium /mæg'niːzɪəm/ n magnésium m

magnet /'mægnɪt/ n lit aimant m; fig pôle m d'attraction **(for** pour)

magnetic /mæg'netɪk/ adj ① [block, rod] aimanté; [force, properties] magnétique; ② [appeal, smile] irrésistible

magnetically /mæg'netɪklɪ/ adv ① lit par magnétisme; ② fig irrésistiblement

magnetic: ∼ **compass** n boussole f; ∼ **tape** n bande f magnétique

magnetism /'mægnɪtɪzəm/ n lit, fig magnétisme m

magnetize /'mægnɪtaɪz/ vtr ① lit aimanter; ② fig magnétiser

magnification /ˌmægnɪfɪ'keɪʃn/ n grossissement m

magnificence /mæg'nɪfɪsns/ n splendeur f

magnificent /mæg'nɪfɪsnt/ adj magnifique

magnificently /mæg'nɪfɪsntlɪ/ adv [play, perform] magnifiquement; [dressed, decorated] superbement

magnify /'mægnɪfaɪ/ vtr ① lit grossir; ② (exaggerate) exagérer

magnifying glass n loupe f

magnitude /'mægnɪtjuːd, US -tuːd/ n ① (of problem, disaster) ampleur f; **of the first** ∼ de la première importance; ② (in astronomy) magnitude f

magnolia /mæg'nəʊlɪə/ ▸ p. 752 n ① Bot (also ∼ **tree**) magnolia m; ② (colour) crème m

magnum opus /ˌmægnəm 'əʊpəs/ n œuvre f maîtresse

magpie /'mægpaɪ/ n Zool pie f

mahogany /mə'hɒgənɪ/ ▸ p. 752
A n (wood, tree, colour) acajou m
B noun modifier [table, chest] d'acajou, en acajou

maid /meɪd/ n (in house) bonne f; (in hotel) femme f de chambre; ∼ **of honour** demoiselle f d'honneur

maiden /'meɪdn/
A n littér jeune fille f
B adj [flight, voyage, speech] inaugural

maiden name n nom m de jeune fille

maidservant /'meɪdsɜːvənt/ n servante f

mail /meɪl/
A n ① (postal service) poste f; **by** ∼ par la poste; ② (correspondence) courrier m; ③ Mil Hist **a coat of** ∼ une cotte de mailles; ④ (emails) **to check one's** ∼ vérifier sa boîte à lettres électronique; **did you get any** ∼? as-tu reçu du courrier électronique or des messages électroniques?
B vtr envoyer, expédier [letter, parcel] **(to** à)

mail: ∼**bag** n (for transport) sac m postal; (of postman) sacoche f (du facteur); (correspondence) courrier m; ∼ **bomb** n colis m piégé

mailbox n ① surtout US (for posting) boîte f aux lettres; (for delivery) boîte f à lettres; ② (for email) boîte f à lettres électronique

∼ **car** n US wagon-poste m; ∼ **carrier** n US préposé/-e m/f; ∼ **coach** n Rail wagon-poste m; ∼ **delivery** n distribution f du courrier

mailing /'meɪlɪŋ/ n ① (dispatch) envoi m (par la poste); ② (for advertising) publipostage m, mailing m

mailing: ∼ **address** n adresse f postale; ∼ **house** n (company) société f de routage; (department) service m du courrier; ∼ **list** n Comm fichier-clientèle m; Theat liste f d'abonnés

mailman /'meɪlmən/ ▸ p. 1181 n US (pl **-men**) facteur m

mail order /'meɪl ɔːdə(r)/
A n **to buy (by)** ∼ acheter par correspondance; **available by** ∼ disponible sur commande
B noun modifier [business, goods] de vente f par correspondance

mail: ∼ **room** n (service m du) courrier m; ∼ **shot** n publipostage m; ∼ **slot** n boîte f à lettres; ∼ **train** n train m postal; ∼ **van** n (in train) wagon-poste m; (delivery vehicle) camionnette f de la poste

maim /meɪm/ vtr estropier

main /meɪn/
A n ① (pipe, conduit) (for water, gas, electricity) canalisation f; (for sewage) égout m (collecteur); ② (network) **the** ∼s (of water, gas, electricity) le réseau de distribution; (of sewage) le réseau d'évacuation; **to turn sth on/off at the** ∼s mettre/couper qch (au compteur); **to work** ou **run off the** ∼s fonctionner sur secteur
B **mains** noun modifier [gas] de ville; [electricity] du secteur; [water] courant; [radio, appliance] sur secteur; [plug, lead, voltage] de secteur
C adj principal; **the** ∼ **thing is to...** le principal, c'est de...; **that's the** ∼ **thing!** c'est le principal!

(Idiom) **in the** ∼ dans l'ensemble

main chance n:

(Idiom) **to have an eye for** ou **to the** ∼ ne jamais perdre de vue ses intérêts

main: ∼ **course** n plat m principal; ∼ **deck** n pont m supérieur

mainframe /'meɪnfreɪm/
A n (also ∼ **computer**, ∼ **processor**) ordinateur m central
B noun modifier [system, network] informatiquement centralisé

mainland /'meɪnlənd/ n territoire m continental; **on the** ∼ sur le continent; **the Chinese** ∼ la Chine continentale

main line
A /ˌmeɪn 'laɪn/ n Rail grande ligne f
B /'meɪnˌlaɪn/ noun modifier [station, terminus, train] de grande ligne
C ◦**mainline** /'meɪnlaɪn/ vi argot des drogués se piquer

mainly /'meɪnlɪ/ adv surtout, essentiellement

main: ∼ **man**◦ n US copain m, pote◦ m; ∼**mast** n grand mât m; ∼ **memory** n Comput mémoire f centrale; ∼ **office** n (of company, organization, newspaper) siège m (social); ∼ **road** n (country) route f principale; (in town) grande rue f; ∼**sail** n grand-voile f

mainspring /'meɪnsprɪŋ/ n ① fig (of action, plot) ressort m **(of** de); (of life) raison f d'être **(of** de); ② (of watch) ressort m principal

mainstream /'meɪnstriːm/
A n courant m dominant
B adj ① (conventional) traditionnel/-elle; ② Mus ∼ **jazz** jazz mainstream

maintain /meɪn'teɪn/ vtr ① (keep steady) maintenir [temperature, standards]; ② (support) subvenir aux besoins de [family]; entretenir [army]; garder [lifestyle]; ③ (look after) entretenir; ④ (assert) continuer à affirmer [innocence]; **to** ∼ **that** soutenir que

maintenance /'meɪntənəns/
A n ① (upkeep) entretien m **(of** de); ② (of standards etc) maintien m **(of** de); ③ GB Jur (alimony) pension f alimentaire
B noun modifier [contract, crew, fees] d'entretien; ∼ **man** ouvrier m chargé de l'entretien

maintenance: ∼ **grant** n (for student) bourse f (d'études); ∼ **order** n GB ordonnance f de versement de pension alimentaire

maisonette /ˌmeɪzə'net/ n duplex m

maize /meɪz/ n maïs m

Maj n: abrév écrite = **Major**

majestic /mə'dʒestɪk/ adj majestueux/-euse

majesty /'mædʒəstɪ/
A n ① (of building, ceremony) majesté f; ② (royal authority) majesté f
B n **Majesty** (in titles) **Her/His** ∼ sa Majesté; **Her/His** ∼**'s government** le gouvernement britannique

m

major /'meɪdʒə(r)/
A *n* **1▸** Mil commandant *m*; **2▸** US Univ (subject) matière *f* principale; (student) **I'm a physics ~** ma matière principale est la physique; **3▸** Jur majeur/-e *m/f*; **4▸** Mus ton *m* majeur
B *adj* **1▸** (important) [*championship, event*] important; [*difference, role*] majeur; [*influence, significance*] capital; **a ~ operation**, **~ surgery** Med une grosse opération; **2▸** (main) principal; **3▸** Mus majeur
C *vi* US Univ **to ~ in** se spécialiser en

Majorca /mə'jɔːkə, mə'dʒɔːkə/ ▸ p. 954 *pr n* Majorque *f*; **in ~** à Majorque

major-general /ˌmeɪdʒə'dʒenrəl/ *n* général *m* de division

majority /mə'dʒɒrəti, US -'dʒɔːr-/
A *n* **1▸** (greater part) (+ *v sg ou pl* GB) majorité *f* (**of** de); **the vast ~** la grande majorité; **to be in a** *ou* **the ~** être en majorité; **2▸** Pol majorité *f*; **by a ~ of 50** à une majorité de 50; **a three to one ~** une majorité de trois contre un; **a working ~** une majorité suffisante; **3▸** Jur majorité *f*
B *noun modifier* [*government, rule*] majoritaire; [*support, view*] de la majorité; [*verdict*] rendu à la majorité; [*decision*] pris à la majorité

make /meɪk/
A *n* (brand) marque *f*; **what ~ is your car?** de quelle marque est ta voiture?
B *vtr* (*prét*, *pp* **made**) **1▸** (create) faire [*cake, film, noise*]; **to ~ a rule** établir une règle; **to ~ sth from** faire qch avec; **wine is made from grapes** le vin se fait avec du raisin; **to ~ sth for sb**, **to ~ sb sth** faire qch pour qn; **to be made for sb** être fait pour qn; **to ~ room/the time for sth** trouver de la place/du temps pour qch; **to ~ sth out of** faire qch en; **it's made (out) of gold** c'est en or; **let's see what he's made of** voyons de quoi il est fait; **to ~ a house into apartments** transformer une maison en appartements; **made in France/by Macron** fabriqué en France/par Macron; **God made man** Dieu a créé l'homme; **to ~ the bed** faire le lit; **2▸** (cause to be or become, render) se faire [*friends, enemies*]; **to ~ sb happy** rendre qn heureux; **to ~ sb hungry** donner faim à qn; **to ~ oneself available** se rendre disponible; **to ~ oneself understood** se faire comprendre; **to ~ sth bigger/better/worse** agrandir/améliorer/aggraver qch; **to ~ passing exams easier**, **to ~ it easier to pass exams** faciliter les examens; **to ~ it possible to do** [*person*] faire en sorte qu'il soit possible de faire; **3▸** (cause to do) **to ~ sb cry** faire pleurer qn; **I made her smile** je l'ai fait sourire; **to ~ sb do sth** faire faire qch à qn; **I made her lose patience** je lui ai fait perdre patience; **it ~s me look fat** ça me grossit; **to ~ sth happen** faire que qch se produise; **to ~ the story end happily** faire en sorte que l'histoire se termine bien; **to ~ sth work** [*person*] réussir à faire marcher qch [*machine*]; **to ~ sth grow** [*person*] réussir à faire pousser qch; [*chemical, product*] faire pousser qch; **it ~s her voice sound funny** cela lui donne une drôle de voix; **4▸** (force, compel) **to ~ sb do** obliger *or* forcer qn à faire; **to ~ sb wait/talk** faire attendre/parler qn; **5▸** (turn into) **to ~ sb sth**, **to ~ sth of sb** faire de qn qch; **we made him treasurer** on l'a fait trésorier; **we made Tom treasurer** on a choisi Tom comme trésorier; **to ~ sb one's assistant** faire de qn son adjoint; **it'll ~ a man of you** ça fera de toi un homme; **he'll never ~ a teacher** il ne fera jamais un bon professeur; **to ~ sb a good husband** être un bon mari pour qn; **to ~ sth sth**, **to ~ sth of sth** faire de qch qch; **to ~ a habit/an issue of sth** faire de qch une habitude/une affaire; **it's been made into a film** on en a fait *or* tiré un film; **to ~ too much of sth** faire tout un plat de qch○; **that will ~ a good shelter** cela fera un bon abri; **6▸** (add up to, amount to) faire; **three and three ~ six** trois et trois font six; **that ~s ten altogether** ça fait dix en tout; **7▸** (earn) gagner [*salary, amount*]; **to ~ a living** gagner sa vie; **to ~ a profit** réaliser des bénéfices; **to ~ a loss** subir des pertes; **8▸** (reach, achieve) arriver jusqu'à [*place, position*]; atteindre [*ranking, level*]; faire [*speed, distance*]; **we'll never ~ it** nous n'y arriverons jamais; **to ~ the first team/the charts** entrer dans la première équipe/au hit-parade; **to ~ the front page** faire la une; **to ~ six spades** (in bridge) faire six piques; **9▸** (estimate, say) **I ~ it five o'clock** il est cinq heures à ma montre; **what time do you ~ it?** quelle heure as-tu?; **let's ~ it five dollars** disons cinq dollars; **can we ~ it a bit later?** peut-on dire un peu plus tard?; **what do you ~ of it?** qu'en dis-tu?; **I can't ~ anything of it** je n'y comprends rien; **10▸** (cause success of) assurer la réussite de [*holiday, meal, day*]; **it really ~s the room** [*feature, colour*] ça rend

bien; **it really made my day** ça m'a rendu heureux pour la journée; **to ~ or break** décider de l'avenir de; **11▸** Elec fermer [*circuit*]; **12▸** Games (shuffle) battre [*cards*]; **to ~ a trick** (win) faire une levée

Idioms **to be as clever as they ~ them** être malin comme pas un○; **to be on the ~**○ (for profit) avoir les dents longues; (for sex) être en chasse○; **to ~ it**○ (in career, life) y arriver; (to party, meeting) réussir à venir; (be on time for train etc) y être; **I can't ~ it** je ne peux pas y aller

Phrasal verbs
■ **make after**: ▸ **~ after [sb]** poursuivre
■ **make do** faire avec; **to ~ do with** se contenter de qch
■ **make for**: ▸ **~ for [sth]** **1▸** (head for) se diriger vers; **2▸** (help create) permettre, assurer; ▸ **~ for [sb]** **1▸** (attack) se jeter sur; **2▸** (approach) se diriger vers
■ **make good**: ▸ **~ good** réussir; ▸ **~ good [sth]** **1▸** réparer [*damage, omission*]; rattraper [*lost time*]; combler [*deficit*]; **2▸** tenir [*promise*]
■ **make off** filer○; **to ~ off with** se tirer○ avec
■ **make out**: ▸ **~ out** **1▸** (manage) s'en tirer○; **2▸** ○US (grope) se peloter○; **3▸** (claim) affirmer (**that** que); ▸ **~ out [sth]**, **~ [sth] out** **1▸** (see, distinguish) distinguer; **2▸** (claim) **to ~ sth out to be** prétendre que qch est; **3▸** (understand, work out) comprendre (**if** si); **I can't ~ him out** je n'arrive pas à le comprendre; **4▸** (write out) faire, rédiger; **to ~ out a cheque to sb** faire un chèque à qn; **it is made out to X** il est à l'ordre de X; **5▸** (expound) **to ~ out a case for** argumenter en faveur de; ▸ **~ oneself out to be** prétendre être [*rich, brilliant*]; faire semblant d'être [*stupid, incompetent*]
■ **make over**: ▸ **~ over [sth]**, **~ [sth] over** **1▸** (transform) transformer (**into** en); **2▸** (transfer) céder (**to** à)
■ **make towards**: ▸ **~ towards [sth/sb]** se diriger vers
■ **make up**: ▸ **~ up** **1▸** (put make-up on) se maquiller; **2▸** (after quarrel) se réconcilier (**with** avec); **3▸** (compensate for) **to ~ up for** rattraper [*lost time, lost sleep*]; combler [*deficit*]; compenser [*personal loss*]; **4▸** (seek favour) faire de la lèche à○; ▸ **~ up [sth]**, **~ [sth] up** **1▸** (invent) inventer; **2▸** (prepare) faire [*parcel, garment, bed*]; préparer [*prescription*]; **3▸** (constitute) faire; **to be made up of** être fait *or* composé de; **to ~ up 10% of** constituer 10% de; **4▸** (compensate for) rattraper [*loss, time*]; combler [*deficit*]; **5▸** (put make-up on) maquiller; **to ~ oneself up** se maquiller; **6▸** **to ~ it up** (make friends) se réconcilier (**with** avec); **to ~ it up to sb** (when at fault) se faire pardonner; (when not at fault) trouver quelque chose pour compenser

make-believe
A /'meɪkbɪliːv/ *n* fantaisie *f*; **it's only ~** ce n'est qu'une histoire imaginaire; **the land of ~** le pays des contes de fées
B **make believe** /ˌmeɪk bɪ'liːv/ *vtr* **to ~ that** imaginer que

make: **~-do-and-mend** *vi* faire avec; **~fast** *n* point *m* d'amarrage; **~over** *n* transformation *f*

maker /'meɪkə(r)/ *n* (of clothes, food, appliance) fabricant *m*; (of cars, aircraft) constructeur *m*; **the ~'s label** la marque du fabricant; ▸ **coffee maker**

Idiom **to (go to) meet one's Maker** rendre l'âme

makeshift /'meɪkʃɪft/ *adj* improvisé

make-up /'meɪkʌp/ *n* **1▸** gen, Theat maquillage *m*; **to wear ~** se maquiller; **to put on one's ~** se maquiller; **2▸** (character) caractère *m*; **to be part of sb's ~** faire partie du caractère de qn; **3▸** (of whole, committee) composition *f*; **4▸** (in printing) mise *f* en page

make-up: **~ artist** ▸ p. 1181 *n* maquilleur/-euse *m/f*; **~ bag** *n* trousse *f* de maquillage; **~ remover** *n* démaquillant *m*

making /'meɪkɪŋ/ *n* **1▸** (of film, programme) réalisation *f*; (of industrial product) fabrication *f*; (of clothes) confection *f*; **problems of sb's own ~** des problèmes du propre fait de qn; **a disaster is in the ~** une catastrophe est en train de se produire; **2▸** (of person, personality) **to be the ~ of sb** (past events) être ce qui a fait de qn ce qu'il/elle est; **this contract will be the ~ of her** ce contrat sera le point de départ de sa carrière

Idiom **to have all the ~s of** avoir tout pour faire

maladjusted /ˌmælə'dʒʌstɪd/ *adj* Psych inadapté

maladministration /ˌmælədˌmɪnɪ'streɪʃn/ *n* ₵ **1▸** Admin mauvaise gestion *f*; **2▸** Jur malversations *fpl*

Malagasy /ˌmælə'gæsɪ/ ▸ p. 1032, p. 969
A *n* (*pl* **-ies**) **1▸** (native of Madagascar) Malgache *mf*; **2▸** (language) malgache *m*

m

B *adj* malgache

malaria /məˈleərɪə/ ▸ p. 933 *n* paludisme *m*; **a ~ attack** une crise de paludisme; **anti-~ tablet** cachet *m* antipaludique

Malawi /məˈlɑːwɪ/ ▸ p. 774 *pr n* Malawi *m*

Malaya /məˈleɪə/ ▸ p. 774 *pr n* Malaisie *f*

Malaysia /məˈleɪzɪə/ ▸ p. 774 *pr n* Malaisie *f*

Malaysian /məˈleɪzɪən/ ▸ p. 1032
A *n* (inhabitant) Malaisien/-ienne *m/f*
B *adj* malaisien/-ienne

male /meɪl/
A *n* ① Biol, Zool mâle *m*; **in the ~** chez le mâle; ② (man) homme *m*; hum mâle *m*
B *adj* ① Biol, Zool mâle; ② (of men) [*population, role, trait*] masculin; [*company*] des hommes; **a ~ voice** une voix d'homme; **the ~ body** le corps de l'homme; **~ singer** chanteur *m*; **~ student** étudiant *m*; ③ Elec mâle

male: ~ chauvinism *n* machisme *m*; **~ chauvinist** *n* phallocrate *m*

male-dominated /ˌmeɪldɒmɪneɪtɪd/ *adj* ① (run by men) dominé par les hommes; ② (mainly masculine) où les hommes dominent

male: ~ menopause *n* retour *m* d'âge masculin; **~ model** *n* mannequin *m* homme *or* masculin; **~ voice choir** *n* chœur *m* d'hommes

malevolence /məˈlevələns/ *n* malveillance *f*

malevolent /məˈlevələnt/ *adj* malveillant

malformation /ˌmælfɔːˈmeɪʃn/ *n* malformation *f*

malformed /ˌmælˈfɔːmd/ *adj* [*limb, nose*] difforme; [*heart, kidney, leaf, shoot*] malformé

malfunction /ˌmælˈfʌŋkʃn/
A *n* ① (poor operation) mauvais fonctionnement *m*; ② (breakdown) défaillance *f*; **a computer ~** une défaillance de l'ordinateur
B *vi* mal fonctionner

Mali /ˈmɑːlɪ/ ▸ p. 774 *pr n* Mali *m*

malice /ˈmælɪs/ *n* (spite) méchanceté *f* (**towards** à); **there's no ~ in him** il n'est pas méchant; **with ~ aforethought** Jur avec préméditation

malicious /məˈlɪʃəs/ *adj* [*comment, person*] malveillant; [*act*] méchant; [*allegation*] calomnieux/-ieuse; **with ~ intent** Jur avec l'intention de nuire

malign /məˈlaɪn/
A *adj* nuisible
B *vtr* calomnier; **much-~ed** tant décrié

malignancy /məˈlɪgnənsɪ/ *n* ① Med malignité *f*; ② gen malveillance *f*

malignant /məˈlɪgnənt/ *adj* ① [*criticism, look*] malveillant; [*person*] malfaisant; [*nature*] cruel/-elle; ② Med malin/-igne

mall /mæl, mɔːl/ *n* ① (shopping arcade) (in town) galerie *f* marchande; (in suburbs) US centre *m* commercial; ② US (street) rue *f* piétonne

mallard /ˈmælɑːd, US ˈmælərd/ *n* (*pl* ~ *ou* ~s) colvert *m*

malleable /ˈmælɪəbl/ *adj* malléable

mallet /ˈmælɪt/ *n* Sport, Tech maillet *m*

malnutrition /ˌmælnjuːˈtrɪʃn, US -nuː-/ *n* gen sous-alimentation *f*; Med spéc malnutrition *f*

malpractice /ˌmælˈpræktɪs/ *n* **Ȼ** ① Admin, Jur malversations *fpl*; **electoral ~** fraude *f* électorale; **professional ~** faute *f* professionnelle; ② US Med erreur *f* médicale

malt /mɔːlt/ *n* ① (grain) malt *m*; ② (whisky) whisky *m* pur malt; ③ US (drink) lait *m* malté, milk-shake *m*

Malta /ˈmɔːltə/ ▸ p. 954 *pr n* Malte *f*

Maltese /ˌmɔːlˈtiːz/ ▸ p. 1032, p. 969
A *n* ① (person) Maltais/-e *m/f*; ② (language) maltais *m*
B *adj* maltais

maltreat /ˌmælˈtriːt/ *vtr* maltraiter

maltreatment /ˌmælˈtriːtmənt/ *n* mauvais traitement *m*

malt: ~ vinegar *n* vinaigre *m* de malt; **~ whisky** *n* whisky *m* pur malt

mammal /ˈmæml/ *n* mammifère *m*

mammary /ˈmæmərɪ/ *adj* mammaire

mammograph /ˈmæməgrɑːf, US -græf/ *n* mammographie *f*

mammoth /ˈmæməθ/
A *n* Zool mammouth *m*
B *adj* [*project, task*] gigantesque; [*organization, structure*] géant

man /mæn/
A *n* (*pl* **men**) ① (adult male) homme *m*; **middle-aged ~** homme d'âge mûr; **as one ~ to another** entre hommes; **he's not a ~ to do** ce n'est pas le genre d'homme à faire; **a blind ~** un aveugle; **an old ~** un vieillard; **a single ~** un célibataire; **a ladies' ~** un homme à femmes; **a beer ~** un buveur de bière; **a ~ of God** un homme de Dieu; **they've arrested the right ~** on a arrêté le vrai coupable; **he's your ~** c'est l'homme qu'il te faut; **~ of the match** héros *m* du match; **good ~!** (well done) bravo mon gars!; ② (husband, partner) homme *m*; **he is the right ~ for her** c'est l'homme qu'il lui fallait; **~ and wife** mari et femme; **to live as ~ and wife** vivre maritalement; ③ (person) homme *m*; **no ~ could have done more** personne n'aurait pu faire davantage; **as good as the next ~** aussi bien que n'importe qui; **the common ~** l'homme du commun; ④ (person of courage) homme *m*; **be a ~** sois un homme; **to make a ~ of sb** faire un homme de qn; ⑤ (mankind) (*also* **Man**) l'humanité *f*; ⑥ Sport (team member) joueur *m*; ⑦ (piece) (in chess) pièce *f*; (in draughts) pion *m*
B **men** *npl* Mil (subordinates) hommes *mpl*
C *vtr* (*p prés etc* **-nn-**) ① gen tenir [*switchboard, desk*]; **will the telephone be ~ned?** est-ce qu'il y aura quelqu'un pour répondre au téléphone?; ② Mil armer [*qch*] en hommes [*ship*]; assigner des hommes à [*barricade, gun*]
D **manned** *pp adj* [*flight, spacecraft, base*] habité; **fully ~ned** (of ship) avec un équipage complet

(Idioms) **every ~ for himself** chacun pour soi; **to a ~** sans exception; **as one ~** comme un seul homme; **to sort out the men from the boys** séparer les hommes des mauvietes○; **he took it like a ~** il a pris ça en homme; **to be a ~'s ~** aimer être entre hommes; **to be one's own ~** être son propre maître

manage /ˈmænɪdʒ/
A *vtr* ① (succeed) **to ~ to do** réussir à faire, se débrouiller○ pour faire; **he ~d to offend everybody** iron il a réussi à froisser tout le monde; ② (find possible) **she ~d a smile** elle a réussi à sourire; **I can ~ a few words in Italian** j'arrive à dire quelques mots en italien; **can you ~ lunch on Friday?** est-ce que tu seras libre pour déjeuner vendredi?; ③ (administer) administrer [*project, finances*]; diriger [*organization*]; gérer [*business, shop, hotel, estate*]; ④ (organize) gérer [*money, time*]; ⑤ (handle) savoir s'y prendre avec [*person, animal*]; manier [*tool, boat*]; **they ~d the situation very badly** ils s'y sont très mal pris
B *vi* se débrouiller○; **can you ~?** tu y arrives?

manageable /ˈmænɪdʒəbl/ *adj* [*size, car*] maniable; [*problem*] maîtrisable; [*boat*] facile à manœuvrer; [*person, animal*] docile; [*level*] raisonnable

management /ˈmænɪdʒmənt/
A *n* ① (control) gestion *f*; **her skilful ~ of the situation** sa façon adroite de gérer la situation; ② (managers collectively) direction *f*; **top ~** la haute direction, les cadres *mpl* dirigeants; **~ and unions** les partenaires *mpl* sociaux, les partenaires *mpl* sociaux; **'under new ~'** 'changement de direction'
B *noun modifier* [*committee, studies*] de gestion; [*career*] dans le management; [*job*] de cadre; [*staff*] d'encadrement; **the ~ team** l'équipe dirigeante

management: ~ accounting *n* comptabilité *f* analytique; **~ buyout, MBO** *n* rachat *m* d'une entreprise par ses cadres; **~ consultancy** *n* cabinet *m* de conseil; **~ consultant** ▸ p. 1181 *n* conseiller *m* en gestion *or* en management

manager /ˈmænɪdʒə(r)/ *n* (of firm, bank) directeur/-trice *m/f*; (of shop) gérant/-e *m/f*; (of farm) exploitant/-e *m/f*; (of project) chef *m*, directeur/-trice *m/f*; (of household) directeur/-trice *m/f* artistique; Sport manager *m*; **to be a good ~** gen être un bon gestionnaire; (of household) savoir bien gérer le budget domestique

manageress /ˌmænɪdʒəˈres/ *n* (of firm, bank) directrice *f*; (of shop) gérante *f*

managerial /ˌmænɪˈdʒɪərɪəl/ *adj* [*experience*] en gestion; [*decision*] de la direction; **~ staff** les cadres *mpl*; **at ~ level** au niveau des cadres

managing: ~ director *n* directeur/-trice *m/f* général/-e; **~ editor** *n* directeur/-trice *m/f* de la rédaction

m

Manchu /ˌmænˈtʃuː/ ▸ p. 1032, p. 969 n **1** (person) Mandchou/-e m/f; **2** (language) mandchou m

Manchuria /ˌmænˈtʃʊərɪə/ pr n Mandchourie f

mandarin /ˈmændərɪn/ n **1** (fruit) mandarine f; (tree) mandarinier m; **2** (person) mandarin m also pej

mandate /ˈmændeɪt/ n **1** (authority) gen autorité f; Pol mandat m; **to have a ~ to do** Pol avoir reçu mandat de faire; **this gives us a clear ~ to proceed** ceci nous donne toute latitude pour poursuivre; **2** Hist territoire m sous mandat; **3** Fin, Jur (document) procuration f, mandat m

mandatory /ˈmændətərɪ, US -tɔːrɪ/ adj obligatoire

mandible /ˈmændɪbl/ n (of vertebrate) mâchoire f inférieure; (of bird, insect) mandibule f

mandolin /ˌmændəˈlɪn/ ▸ p. 1028 n mandoline f

mandrake /ˈmændreɪk/ n mandragore f

mane /meɪn/ n lit, fig crinière f

maneuver US n, vtr, vi = **manoeuvre**

man Friday /ˌmæn ˈfraɪdeɪ/ n (helper) factotum m

mange /meɪndʒ/ n gale f

manger /ˈmeɪndʒə(r)/ n mangeoire f

mangle /ˈmæŋgl/
A n essoreuse f à rouleaux
B vtr mutiler [body]; broyer [vehicle]; fig massacrer [work, music]

mango /ˈmæŋgəʊ/ n (fruit) mangue f; (tree) manguier m

mangrove /ˈmæŋgrəʊv/ n palétuvier m, manglier m

mangy /ˈmeɪndʒɪ/ adj lit galeux/-euse; fig [rug] élimé; [hotel] miteux/-euse

manhandle /ˈmænhændl/ vtr **1** (treat roughly) malmener, maltraiter; **2** (move by manpower) manutentionner

man: **~hole** n (in road) regard m, bouche f d'égout; (of boiler, tank) regard m; **~hood** n (state) âge m d'homme; (masculinity) masculinité f; **~hour** n Ind heure f de main-d'œuvre; **~hunt** n chasse f à l'homme

mania /ˈmeɪnɪə/ n Psych manie f; **to have a ~ for doing** avoir la manie de faire

maniac /ˈmeɪnɪæk/ n **1** Psych maniaque mf; **2** ○fig fou/folle m/f

maniacal /məˈnaɪəkl/ adj Psych maniaque; fig dément

manic /ˈmænɪk/ adj **1** (manic-depressive) maniaco-dépressif/-ive; (obsessive) obsessionnel/-elle; **2** fig frénétique

manic depression n psychose f maniaco-dépressive

manicure /ˈmænɪkjʊə(r)/
A n manicure f
B vtr manucurer [person]; **to ~ one's nails** se faire les ongles

manicure set n trousse f de manucure

manicurist /ˈmænɪkjʊərɪst/ ▸ p. 1181 n manucure mf

manifest /ˈmænɪfest/
A n Naut, Aviat manifeste m
B adj manifeste, évident
C vtr manifester; **to ~ itself** se manifester

manifestation /ˌmænɪfeˈsteɪʃn/ n manifestation f

manifesto /ˌmænɪˈfestəʊ/ n manifeste m, programme m

manipulate /məˈnɪpjʊleɪt/ vtr **1** (handle, control) manipuler, manœuvrer [machine]; **2** péj manipuler [person, situation]; jouer sur [emotions]; **she ~d him into accepting the offer** elle l'a manipulé pour qu'il accepte la proposition; **to ~ sb's emotions** jouer sur les émotions de qn; **3** (falsify) péj falsifier [data]; **4** Med (in physiotherapy) manipuler

manipulation /məˌnɪpjʊˈleɪʃn/ n **1** (of machine) manipulation f, manœuvre f; **2** (of person, situation) péj manipulation f; **3** (of data) péj falsification f; **4** Med manipulation f

manipulative /məˈnɪpjʊlətɪv/ adj manipulateur/-trice

mankind /ˌmænˈkaɪnd/ n humanité f

manly /ˈmænlɪ/ adj viril

man-made /ˌmænˈmeɪd/ adj [fibre, fabric] synthétique; [pond] artificiel/-ielle; [environment] façonné par l'homme; [catastrophe] d'origine humaine

manna /ˈmænə/ n Bible, fig manne f

manner /ˈmænə(r)/
A n **1** (way, method) manière f, façon f; **in this ~** de cette manière or façon; **the ~ in which they were treated** la manière or la façon dont on les a traités; **to do sth in such a ~ that** faire qch de telle sorte que (+ subj); **in a ~ of**

speaking pour ainsi dire; **in** ou **after the ~ of** à la manière de; **2** (way of behaving) attitude f; **she has a bad ~** elle a une attitude déplaisante; **something in his ~ disturbed her** quelque chose dans son comportement la troublait; **to have a good telephone ~** savoir parler au téléphone; **3** littér (sort, kind) sorte f, genre m; **what ~ of man is he?** quel genre d'homme est-ce?; **by no ~ of means** pas du tout

B **manners** npl **1** (social behaviour) manières fpl; **to have good/bad ~s** avoir de bonnes/mauvaises manières; **it's bad ~s to do** il est mal élevé de faire; **he has no ~s** il n'a aucun savoir-vivre; (child) il ne sait pas se tenir; **to have the ~s to do** avoir la politesse de faire; **road ~s** politesse f au volant; **2** (social habits) mœurs fpl; **comedy of ~s** comédie f de mœurs

C **-mannered** combining form **ill/well-~ed** mal/bien élevé; **mild-~ed** doux/douce, aux manières douces

mannerism /ˈmænərɪzəm/ n (habit) particularité f; péj (quirk) manie f pej

manning /ˈmænɪŋ/ n **1** Mil armement m; **2** Ind effectifs mpl

mannish /ˈmænɪʃ/ adj masculin, péj hommasse○

manoeuvrable GB, **maneuverable** US /məˈnuːvrəbl/ adj maniable

manoeuvre GB, **maneuver** US /məˈnuːvə(r)/
A n lit, fig manœuvre f; **on ~s** Mil en manœuvres; **some room for ~** fig une marge de manœuvre
B vtr **1** lit manœuvrer [vehicle, object]; **to ~ sth in/out** faire entrer/sortir qch en manœuvrant; **to ~ sth into position** manœuvrer qch pour le mettre en position; **2** fig manœuvrer [person]; faire dévier [discussion] (**to** vers); **to ~ sb into doing** manœuvrer qn pour qu'il fasse
C vi manœuvrer

manoeuvring GB, **maneuvering** US /məˈnuːvərɪŋ/ n **C** manigances fpl

man-of-war /ˌmænəvˈwɔː(r)/ n (ship) navire m de guerre

manor /ˈmænə(r)/ n (also ~ **house**) manoir m; Hist (estate) domaine m seigneurial; **Lord/Lady of the ~** châtelain/châtelaine m/f

manpower /ˈmænpaʊə(r)/ n **1** gen main-d'œuvre f; Mil hommes mpl; **2** (physical force) force f; **by sheer ~** à la force des poignets

manse /mæns/ n presbytère m (de pasteur)

manservant /ˈmænsɜːvənt/ n valet m

mansion /ˈmænʃn/ n (in countryside) demeure f; (in town) hôtel m particulier

man: **~-sized** adj [tissues] grand modèle inv; **~slaughter** n Jur homicide m involontaire

mantelpiece /ˈmæntlpiːs/ n (manteau m de) cheminée f

mantis /ˈmæntɪs/ n (also **praying ~**) mante f (religieuse)

man-to-man /ˌmæntəˈmæn/ adj d'homme à homme

manual /ˈmænjʊəl/
A n **1** (book) manuel m; **2** Mus clavier m
B adj [labour, worker] manuel/-elle; [gearbox, typewriter] mécanique

manufacture /ˌmænjʊˈfæktʃə(r)/
A n (of materials, tools) fabrication f; (of food products, arms) production f; **car ~** construction f automobile
B vtr lit fabriquer; fig péj fabriquer (de toutes pièces) [excuse]
C **manufactured** pp adj **~d goods** biens manufacturés

manufacturer /ˌmænjʊˈfæktʃərə(r)/ n gen fabricant m (**of** de); **car ~** constructeur m automobile

manufacturing /ˌmænjʊˈfæktʃərɪŋ/
A n **1** Econ (sector) industrie f de transformation; **the importance of ~** l'importance de la production industrielle; **2** (making) gen fabrication f; (of cars, heavy machinery) construction f
B noun modifier [output, workforce] industriel/-ielle; [capacity, costs, engineer] de production; [process] de fabrication; **~ plant** usine f

manufacturing base n tissu m industriel, base f industrielle

manure /məˈnjʊə(r)/ n fumier m; **liquid ~** purin m; **horse ~** crottin m de cheval

manuscript /ˈmænjʊskrɪpt/ n manuscrit m; **in ~** (not yet printed) sous forme de manuscrit

Manx /mæŋks/ ▸ p. 969 n **1** (language) mannois m; **2** (people) **the ~** les habitants mpl de l'île de Man

many /ˈmenɪ/ (*comparative* **more**; *superlative* **most**)

A *quantif* beaucoup de, un grand nombre de; ~ **times** de nombreuses fois, bien des fois; **for** ~ **years** pendant de nombreuses années; **in** ~ **ways** à bien des égards; **his** ~ **friends** ses nombreux amis; **the** ~ **advantages of city life** les nombreux avantages de la vie citadine; **how** ~ **people/times?** combien de personnes/fois?; **there are too** ~ **people** il y a trop de monde; **for a great** ~ **years** pendant de nombreuses années; **a good** ~ **people attend-ed** de nombreuses personnes sont venues; **like so** ~ **other women** comme tant d'autres femmes; **I have as** ~ **books as you (do)** j'ai autant de livres que toi; **five exams in as** ~ **days** cinq examens en autant de jours; ~ **a man would be glad of such an opportunity** plus d'un homme se réjouirait d'une telle occasion; ~**'s the time I've been there** j'y suis allé maintes fois

B *pron* beaucoup; **not** ~ pas beaucoup; **too** ~ trop; **how** ~? combien?; **as** ~ **as you like** autant que tu veux; **I didn't know there were so** ~ je ne savais pas qu'il y en avait autant; **we don't need** ~ **more** il ne nous en faut pas beaucoup plus; ~ **of them were killed** beaucoup d'entre eux ont été tués; **there were too** ~ **of them** ils étaient trop nombreux; **a good** ~ **of the houses were damaged** bon nombre de maisons ont été endommagées; **one too** ~ un de trop; **you've set one place too** ~ tu as mis un couvert de trop; **to have had one too** ~° avoir bu un coup de trop°

many: ~**-coloured** littér *adj* multicolore; ~**-sided** *adj* [*personality, phenomenon*] à multiples facettes

map /mæp/

A *n* (of region) carte *f* (**of** de); (of town, underground) plan *m* (**of** de); **weather** ~ carte météo(rologique); **street** ~ plan des rues; **the political** ~ **of Europe** fig le paysage politique de l'Europe

B *vtr* 1 faire la carte de [*region, planet*]; faire le plan de [*town*]; 2 Comput faire une projection de

(Idiom) **to put sb/sth on the** ~ mettre qn/qch en vedette

(Phrasal verb)

■ **map out**: ▸ ~ **out** [*sth*], ~ [*sth*] **out** élaborer, mettre [qch] au point [*plans, strategy*]; planifier [*schedule*]; tracer [*sb's future*]

maple /ˈmeɪpl/ *n* 1 (tree) érable *m*; 2 (wood) bois *m* d'érable

mapping /ˈmæpɪŋ/ *n* 1 Geog, Biol cartographie *f*; 2 Comput projection *f* topographique

mar /mɑː(r)/ *vtr* (*p prés etc* **-rr-**) (*souvent au passif*) gâcher

Mar *abrév écrite* = **March**

marathon /ˈmærəθən, US -θɒn/

A *n* (all contexts) marathon *m*

B *noun modifier* 1 Sport ~ **runner** marathonien/-ienne *m/f*; 2 (massive) -marathon *inv*; **a** ~ **session** une séance-marathon

marauding /məˈrɔːdɪŋ/ *adj* en maraude

marble /ˈmɑːbl/ *n* 1 (stone, sculpture) marbre *m*; 2 Games bille *f*; **to play the** ~ US ~**s** jouer aux billes

(Idioms) **to lose one's** ~**s**° perdre la boule°; **she still has all her** ~**s**° elle garde toute sa tête

march /mɑːtʃ/

A *n* 1 Mil marche *f*; **a 40 km** ~ une marche de 40 km; **to be on the** ~ lit être en marche; fig [*prices*] être en hausse; **quick/slow** ~ marche au pas accéléré/au pas de parade; 2 (demonstration) marche *f* (**against** contre; **for** pour); **peace** ~ marche *f* pacifiste; 3 Mus marche *f*; 4 fig **the** ~ **of time** la marche du temps

B *vtr* **he** ~**ed him into the office** elle l'a emmené d'autorité dans le bureau

C *vi* 1 Mil marcher au pas; **to** ~ **on Rome** marcher sur Rome; **to** ~ **(for) 40 km** faire une marche de 40 km; **forward** ~! en avant, marche!; 2 (in protest) manifester (**against** contre; **for** pour); 3 (walk briskly) marcher d'un pas vif; (angrily) marcher l'air furieux; **he** ~**ed out of the room** il est sorti l'air furieux; **she** ~**ed up to his desk** elle s'est dirigée droit sur son bureau

(Idiom) **to give sb their** ~**ing orders** renvoyer qn avec perte et fracas

March /mɑːtʃ/ ▸ p. 1020 *n* mars *m*

(Idiom) **to be as mad as a** ~ **hare** être complètement fou

marcher /ˈmɑːtʃə(r)/ *n* (in demonstration) manifestant/-e *m/f*; (in procession, band) marcheur/-euse *m/f*

---

marchioness /ˌmɑːʃəˈnes/ *n* marquise *f*

march-past /ˈmɑːtʃpɑːst/ *n* défilé *m*

mare /meə(r)/ *n* (horse) jument *f*; (donkey) ânesse *f*

margarine /ˌmɑːdʒəˈriːn/ *n* margarine *f*

marge° /mɑːdʒ/ *n* GB *abrév* = **margarine**

margin /ˈmɑːdʒɪn/ *n* 1 (on paper) marge *f*; **in the** ~ dans la marge; **left** ~ marge à gauche; 2 (of wood, field) lisière *f*; (of river) bord *m*; 3 marge *f* (**of** de); **by a narrow** ~ de peu, de justesse; **to lose by a small** ~ perdre de peu; 4 fig (fringe) (*souvent pl*) marge *f*; **at** *ou* **on the** ~**(s) of** en marge de; 5 (allowance) marge *f*; ~ *ou* **for error** marge d'erreur; **safety** ~ marge de sécurité; 6 (*also* **profit** ~) marge *f* bénéficiaire

marginal /ˈmɑːdʒɪnl/ *adj* 1 (minor or peripheral) marginal; 2 GB disputé; 3 [*note*] marginal

marginalize /ˈmɑːdʒɪnəlaɪz/ *vtr* marginaliser

marginally /ˈmɑːdʒɪnəlɪ/ *adv* très légèrement

marigold /ˈmærɪɡəʊld/ *n* Bot souci *m*

marijuana /ˌmærjuˈɑːnə/ *n* marijuana *f*

marinade /ˌmærɪˈneɪd/

A *n* marinade *f*

B *vtr* (*also* **marinate**) faire mariner (**in** dans)

marine /məˈriːn/

A *n* 1 (soldier) fusilier *m* marin; **the Marines** les marines *mpl*; 2 (navy) **the merchant** ~ la marine marchande

B *adj* [*mammal, biology*] marin; [*explorer, life*] sous-marin; [*insurance, law, transport*] maritime

(Idiom) **tell it to the** ~**s!** raconte ça à d'autres!

marine: **Marine Corps** *n* corps *m* des marines améri-cains; ~ **engineer** ▸ p. 1181 *n* ingénieur *m* du génie maritime

marital /ˈmærɪtl/ *adj* conjugal; ~ **status** Admin situation *f* de famille

maritime /ˈmærɪtaɪm/ *adj* (all contexts) maritime

marjoram /ˈmɑːdʒərəm/ *n* Bot, Culin marjolaine *f*

mark /mɑːk/

A *n* 1 (stain, animal marking) tache *f*; (from injury) marque *f*; **to make one's** ~ lit signer d'une croix; fig faire ses preuves; 2 (lasting impression) **to leave one's** ~ **on sth** [*person*] marquer qch de son influence [*company*]; [*recession*] marquer qch [*country*]; 3 (symbol) **as a** ~ **of** en signe de [*esteem*]; 4 Sch, Univ note *f*; **he gets no** ~**s for effort** fig pour l'effort, il mérite zéro; 5 (number on scale) **the 3-mile** ~ la borne de trois miles; **unemployment has reached the two million** ~ le chômage a atteint la barre des deux millions; **the high-tide** ~ le maximum de la marée haute; **at gas** ~ 7 à thermostat 7; 6 Sport (starting line) marque *f*; **on your** ~**s!** à vos marques!; **to get off the** ~ prendre le départ; **he's very quick/a bit slow off the** ~ fig il a l'esprit vif/un peu lent; **you were quick off the** ~! fig tu n'as pas perdu de temps!; 7 (target) (in archery etc) but *m*; **to find its** ~ [*arrow*] atteindre son but; fig [*remark*] mettre dans le mille; **to be (way) off the** ~, **to be wide of the** ~ fig être à côté de la plaque°; 8 Sport (in rugby) arrêt *m* de volée; 9 (*also* **Mark**) (model in series) Mark; **Jaguar Mark II** Jaguar Mark II; 10 ▸ p. 782 (*also* **Deutschmark**) deutschmark *m*

B *vtr* 1 (make visible impression on) (stain) tacher [*clothes*]; [*bruise, scar*] marquer [*skin*]; (with pen) marquer [*map, belongings*]; **to** ~ **sb for life** (physically) défigurer qn à vie; (mentally) marquer qn à vie; 2 (indicate, label) [*person*] marquer [*name, price*] (**on** sur); [*arrow, sign, label*] indiquer [*position, road*]; fig [*event*] marquer [*end, change*]; **to** ~ **the occasion with** marquer l'occasion par [*firework display, party*]; **X** ~**s the spot** l'en-droit est indiqué par une croix; **to** ~ **one's place** (in book) marquer la page; 3 (characterize) caractériser; 4 Sch, Univ corriger; **to** ~ **sb absent** noter qn absent; 5 (pay attention to) noter (bien); **he'll not live long,** ~ **my words!** tu verras, il ne vivra pas longtemps!; 6 Sport marquer

C *vi* 1 Sch, Univ faire des corrections; 2 (stain) se tacher; 3 Sport marquer

D mark you *conj phr* n'empêche que (+ *indic*)

(Idioms) **to be an easy** ~ être une poire°; **to** ~ **time** Mil marquer le pas; **I'm** ~**ing time working as a waitress until I go to France** fig je travaille comme serveuse en attendant d'aller en France

(Phrasal verbs)

■ **mark down**: ▸ ~ [*sth*] **down**, ~ **down** [*sth*] démarquer [*product*]; ▸ ~ [*sb*] **down** baisser les notes de [*person*]

■ **mark out**: ▸ ∼ **[sb] out**, ∼ **out [sb]** ⟦1⟧ (distinguish) distinguer (**from** de); ⟦2⟧ (select) désigner (**for** pour)

■ **mark up**: ▸ ∼ **[sth] up**, ∼ **up [sth]** [company] majorer le prix de [item] (**by** de); [shopkeeper] augmenter le prix de [item] (**by** de); ▸ ∼ **[sb] up** Sch, Univ remonter les notes de [person]

marked /mɑːkt/ adj ⟦1⟧ (noticeable) gen marqué, net/nette (before n); [accent] prononcé; ⟦2⟧ (in danger) **he's a ∼ man** on en veut à sa vie

marker /'mɑːkə(r)/ n ⟦1⟧ (pen) marqueur m; ⟦2⟧ (tag) repère m; ⟦3⟧ (scorekeeper) marqueur/-euse m/f; ⟦4⟧ Sch, Univ examinateur/-trice m/f; ⟦5⟧ Sport marqueur/-euse m/f

market /'mɑːkɪt/
A n ⟦1⟧ Econ marché m; **the job ∼** le marché du travail; **cars at the upper** ou **top end of the ∼** les voitures haut de gamme; **to come onto the ∼** arriver sur le marché; **to be in the ∼ for** chercher (à acquérir); ⟦2⟧ Comm (potential customers) marché m (**for** pour); **domestic/French ∼** marché intérieur/français; **a poor/steady ∼ for** une demande faible/stable de; **the teenage ∼** les adolescents; **a gap in the ∼** un créneau, un besoin du marché; ⟦3⟧ (place) marché m; **fish ∼** halle f aux poissons; **to go to ∼** aller au marché; ⟦4⟧ (stock market) Bourse f; **to play the ∼** spéculer
B noun modifier [share] de marché; [conditions, rates] du marché
C vtr ⟦1⟧ (sell) commercialiser, vendre; ⟦2⟧ (promote) lancer or mettre [qch] sur le marché

market: ∼ **analyst** n analyste mf de marché; ∼ **capitalization** n capitalisation f boursière; ∼ **day** n jour m du marché; ∼ **economy** n économie f de marché; ∼ **forces** npl forces fpl du marché; ∼ **gardener** ▸ p. 1181 n maraîcher/-ère m/f; ∼ **gardening** n culture f maraîchère

marketing /'mɑːkɪtɪŋ/ n ⟦1⟧ (process, theory) marketing m, mercatique f; ⟦2⟧ (department) service m de marketing

marketing: ∼ **agreement** n accord m de commercialisation; ∼ **campaign** n campagne f de vente; ∼ **man** n commercial m; ∼ **process** n processus m de commercialisation; ∼ **strategy** n stratégie f commerciale

market: ∼ **leader** n (product) produit m vedette; (company) leader m du marché; ∼**-led** adj gen déterminé par le marché; [economy] de marché; ∼ **opportunity** n créneau m; ∼**place** n (square) place f du marché; Econ, Fin marché m; ∼ **price** n prix m du marché; ∼ **research** n étude f de marché; ∼ **researcher** ▸ p. 1181 n chargé/-e m/f d'études de marketing; ∼ **square** n place f du marché; ∼ **stall** n étal m; ∼ **town** n bourg m; ∼ **trader** n vendeur/-euse m/f sur un marché; ∼ **value** n valeur f marchande or d'échange

marking /'mɑːkɪŋ/ n ⟦1⟧ (on animal) tache f; (on aircraft) marque f; **road ∼s** signalisation f horizontale; ⟦2⟧ GB Sch, Univ (process) **C** corrections fpl; (marks given) notation f; ⟦3⟧ Sport marquage m

mark: ∼**sman** n Mil, Sport tireur m d'élite; ∼**smanship** n Mil, Sport adresse f au tir; ∼**-up** n (retailer's margin) marge f; (increase) augmentation f

marmalade /'mɑːməleɪd/ n confiture f or marmelade f d'oranges

marmalade cat n chat/chatte m/f roux/rousse

marmoset /'mɑːməzet/ n ouistiti m

marmot /'mɑːmət/ n marmotte f

maroon /mə'ruːn/ ▸ p. 752
A n ⟦1⟧ (colour) bordeaux m; ⟦2⟧ GB (rocket) fusée f de détresse
B vtr **to be ∼ed on an island** être bloqué sur une île; **the ∼ed sailors** les naufragés

marquee /mɑː'kiː/ n ⟦1⟧ GB (tent) grande tente f; (of circus) chapiteau m; ⟦2⟧ US (canopy) (grand) auvent m

marquess /'mɑːkwɪs/ n marquis m

marquetry /'mɑːkɪtrɪ/ n marqueterie f

marquis /'mɑːkwɪs/ n marquis m

marriage /'mærɪdʒ/
A n ⟦1⟧ (ceremony, contract) mariage m (**to** avec); **broken ∼** mariage brisé; **proposal of ∼** proposition f de mariage; **by ∼** par alliance; ⟦2⟧ fig (alliance) mariage m; ⟦3⟧ (in cards) mariage m
B noun modifier [guidance] conjugal; [contract, vows] de mariage

marriage: ∼ **bureau** n agence f matrimoniale; ∼ **ceremony** n cérémonie f nuptiale; ∼ **certificate** n extrait m d'acte de mariage; ∼ **guidance counsellor** n conseiller/-ère m/f conjugal/-e; ∼ **of convenience** n mariage m de convenance

married /'mærɪd/ adj [person] marié (**to** à); [life] conjugal; ∼ **couple** couple m

marrow /'mærəʊ/ n ⟦1⟧ Anat moelle f; **frozen to the ∼** gelé jusqu'à la moelle; ⟦2⟧ GB Bot courge f; **baby ∼** GB courgette f

marrowbone /'mærəʊbəʊn/ n os m à moelle

marry /'mærɪ/
A vtr ⟦1⟧ lit [priest] marier [couple]; se marier avec, épouser [fiancé(e)]; **to get married** se marier (**to** avec); **will you ∼ me?** veux-tu m'épouser?; ⟦2⟧ fig marier [ideas, colours]; **to be married to one's job** hum ne vivre que pour son travail
B vi se marier; **to ∼ into a family** entrer dans une famille par le mariage; **to ∼ for love** faire un mariage d'amour; **to ∼ into money** épouser un homme ou une femme riche; **to ∼ beneath oneself** se mésallier

(Phrasal verb)

■ **marry off**: ▸ ∼ **off [sb]**, ∼ **[sb] off** marier (**to** à, avec)

marsh /mɑːʃ/ n (also **marshland**) (terrain) marécage m; (region) marais m

marshal /'mɑːʃl/
A n ⟦1⟧ Mil maréchal m; ⟦2⟧ GB Jur avocat accompagnant un juge itinérant; ⟦3⟧ (at rally, ceremony) membre m du service d'ordre; ⟦4⟧ US Jur ≈ huissier m de justice; ⟦5⟧ US Hist (sheriff) marshal m; ⟦6⟧ US (in fire service) capitaine m des pompiers
B (p prés **-ll-** GB, **-l-** US) vtr ⟦1⟧ gen, Mil rassembler [troops]; diriger [crowd]; Rail trier [wagons]; fig rassembler [facts]; ⟦2⟧ (guide) conduire [person]

marshalling yard n GB Rail gare f de triage

marsh: ∼ **fever** ▸ p. 933 n paludisme m; ∼ **harrier** n busard m des roseaux; ∼**mallow** n Culin pâte f de guimauve

marten /'mɑːtɪn, US -tn/ n martre f

martial /'mɑːʃl/ adj [music, art, law] martial; [spirit] guerrier/-ière

martinet /ˌmɑːtɪ'net, US -tn'et/ n **to be a ∼** être stricte en matière de discipline

martyr /'mɑːtə(r)/
A n Relig, fig martyr/-e m/f; **a ∼ to the cause** un martyr de la cause; **to play the ∼** jouer les martyrs
B vtr lit, fig martyriser

martyrdom /'mɑːtədəm/ n martyre m

marvel /'mɑːvl/
A n merveille f; **it was a ∼ to behold** c'était merveilleux à voir; **to work ∼s** faire des merveilles; **he's a ∼ of patience** il est merveilleusement patient
B vtr (p prés etc GB **-ll-**, US **-l-**) **to ∼ that** s'étonner de ce que (+ subj)
C vi s'étonner (**at** de), être émerveillé (**at** par)

marvellous GB, **marvelous** US /'mɑːvələs/ adj [weather, holiday] merveilleux/-euse; **but that's ∼!** mais c'est formidable!

marvellously GB, **marvelously** US /'mɑːvələslɪ/ adv [sing, get on] à merveille; [clever, painted] merveilleusement

marzipan /'mɑːzɪpæn, ˌmɑːzɪ'pæn/ n pâte f d'amandes

mascot /'mæskət, -skɒt/ n mascotte f; **lucky ∼** porte-bonheur m inv

masculine /'mæskjʊlɪn/ n, adj masculin (m)

masculinity /ˌmæskjʊ'lɪnətɪ/ n masculinité f

mash /mæʃ/
A n ⟦1⟧ Agric pâtée f; ⟦2⟧ (in brewing) trempe f; ⟦3⟧ ○GB Culin purée f (de pommes de terre)
B vtr ⟦1⟧ (also ∼ **up**) écraser [fruit]; **to ∼ potatoes** faire de la purée; ⟦2⟧ (in brewing) brasser

MASH /mæʃ/ n US (abrév = **mobile army surgical hospital**) unité f médicale de campagne

mask /mɑːsk, US mæsk/
A n gen masque m; (for eyes only) loup m
B vtr masquer [face]; dissimuler [truth, emotions]; masquer [taste, drug]

mask: ∼**ed ball** n bal m masqué; ∼**ing tape** n ruban m adhésif

masochist /'mæsəkɪst/ *n, adj* masochiste (*mf*)

mason /'meɪsn/ ▸ p. 1181 [1] Constr maçon *m*; [2] **Mason** (*also* **Free~**) franc-maçon *m*

masonic /mə'sɒnɪk/ *adj* maçonnique

masonry /'meɪsənrɪ/ *n* maçonnerie *f*

masquerade /ˌmɑːskə'reɪd, US ˌmæsk-/
A *n* [1] (ball) bal *m* masqué; [2] *fig* (pretence) mascarade *f*
B *vi* **to ~ as sb** se faire passer pour qn

mass /mæs/
A *n* [1] (vast body) masse *f* (**of** de); (cluster) amas *m* (**of** de); [2] (amount) (of people) foule *f* (**of** de); (of details) quantité *f* (**of** de); [3] Relig messe *f*; [4] Phys, Art masse *f*
B **masses** *npl* [1] (the people) **the ~es** *gen* la foule; (working class) les masses *fpl*; [2] ○GB (lots) **~es of work** beaucoup *or* plein○ de travail; **~es of people** une foule de gens; **to have ~es of time** avoir largement le temps
C *noun modifier* [1] (large scale) [*audience*] de masse; [*destruction, exodus, protest, unemployment*] massif/-ive; [*sackings*] en masse; **~ meeting** rassemblement *m* de masse; [2] (of the people) [*movement, tourism*] de masse; **to have ~ appeal** avoir un succès de masse
D *vi* [*troops*] se regrouper; [*bees*] se masser; [*clouds*] s'amonceler

massacre /'mæsəkə(r)/
A *n* lit, fig massacre *m*
B *vtr* [1] lit massacrer; [2] fig massacrer [*tune*]; démolir○ [*team*]

massage /'mæsɑːʒ, US mə'sɑːʒ/
A *n* massage *m*
B *vtr* masser [*person*]; fig tricher sur [*figures*]; flatter [*ego*]

mass: **~ cult**○ *n* US culture *f* de masse; **~-energy** *n* masse-énergie *f*; **~ grave** *n* charnier *m*, fosse *f* commune; **~ hysteria** *n* hystérie *f* collective

massive /'mæsɪv/ *adj* [*object, amount, error*] énorme; [*explosion*] retentissant; [*majority*] écrasant; [*campaign, task*] de grande envergure; [*increase, cut*] massif/-ive; [*haemorrhage*] grave

massively /'mæsɪvlɪ/ *adv* [*reduce, increase*] énormément; [*overrated*] considérablement

mass: **~ market** *n* marché *m* grand public; **~-marketing** *n* commercialisation *f* massive; **~ media** *n* (+ *v sg ou pl*) (mass) médias *mpl*; **~ murder** *n* massacre *m*; **~ murderer** *n* auteur *m* d'un massacre; **~-produce** *vtr* fabriquer [qch] en série; **~ production** *n* fabrication *f* en série; **~ screening** *n* Med dépistage *m* systématique

mast /mɑːst, US mæst/ *n* [1] (on ship, for flags) mât *m*; Radio, TV pylône *m*; **the ~s of a ship** la mâture d'un navire; [2] ¢ Agric glands *mpl* et faînes *fpl*

(Idiom) **to nail one's colours to the ~** afficher ses opinions (une fois pour toutes)

master /'mɑːstə(r), US 'mæs-/
A *n* [1] (man in charge) maître *m*; **the ~ of the house** le maître de maison; **to be ~ in one's own house** être maître chez soi; [2] (person in control) maître/-esse *m/f*; **to be one's own ~** être son propre maître; [3] (person who excels) maître *m*; **a ~ of** un maître de [*violin, narrative*]; un/-e expert/-e en [*tactics, public relations*]; **to be a ~ at doing** être maître dans l'art de faire; [4] (*also* **Master**) Art maître *m*; [5] Sch (primary) maître *m*, instituteur *m*; (secondary) professeur *m*; (headmaster) proviseur *m*; [6] GB Univ (of college) principal *m*; [7] (*also* **~ copy**) original *m*; [8] Univ (graduate) ≈ titulaire *mf* d'une maîtrise; **~'s (degree)** maîtrise *f* (**in** en, de); [9] Naut capitaine *m*; [10] (title of young man) monsieur *m*; **Master Ian Todd** (on envelope) Monsieur Ian Todd
B *noun modifier* [*architect, chef*] maître (*before n*); [*smuggler, spy*] professionnel/-elle
C *vtr* [1] (learn) maîtriser [*subject*]; posséder [*skill*]; [2] (control) dominer [*feelings*]; surmonter [*phobia*]

master: **~ bedroom** *n* chambre *f* principale; **~ builder** ▸ p. 1181 *n* maître *m* d'œuvre; **~ copy** *n* original *m*; **~ disk** *n* Comput disque *m* d'exploitation

master key *n* passe-partout *m inv*

masterly /'mɑːstəlɪ, US 'mæs-/ *adj* [*technique, writing*] magistral

mastermind /'mɑːstəmaɪnd/
A *n* cerveau *m* (**of, behind** de)
B *vtr* échafauder [*crime*]; organiser [*event*]

master: **Master of Arts** *n* ≈ maîtrise *f* de lettres; **~ of ceremonies** *n* (presenting entertainment) animateur/-trice *m/f*; (at formal occasion) maître *m* des cérémonies; **Master of Science** *n* ≈ maîtrise *f* de sciences; **~piece** *n* chef-d'œuvre *m* also fig; **~ plan** *n* plan *m* d'ensemble; **~ race** *n* race *f* supérieure; **~stroke** *n* (piece of skill) coup *m* de maître; (idea) idée *f* de génie; **~ tape** *n* bande *f* mère

mastery /'mæstərɪ, US 'mæs-/ *n* [1] (competence) maîtrise *f* (**of** de); [2] (control) domination *f*, maîtrise *f*; **to have ~ over sb/sth** dominer qn/qch

masticate /'mæstɪkeɪt/ *vi* mastiquer, mâcher

mat /mæt/
A *n* [1] (on floor) (petit) tapis *m*; (for wiping feet) paillasson *m*; **exercise ~** tapis; [2] (on table) (heatproof) dessous-de-plat *m inv*; (ornamental) napperon *m*; **place ~** set *m* de table
B *adj* = **matt**
C *vi* (*p prés etc* **-tt-**) [*hair*] s'emmêler; [*wool*] se feutrer; [*fibres*] s'enchevêtrer

MAT *n* (*abrév* = **machine-assisted translation**) TAO *f*

match /mætʃ/
A *n* [1] Sport match *m*; [2] (for lighting fire) allumette *f*; **to put a ~ to sth** mettre le feu à qch; [3] (equal) **to be a ~ for sb** être un adversaire à la mesure de qn; **to be no ~ for sb** être trop faible pour qn; **to meet one's ~** trouver quelqu'un à sa hauteur; **to be more than a ~ for sb** surpasser qn; [4] (thing that harmonizes) **to be a good ~ for sth** [*shoes, curtains, colour*] aller très bien avec qch; **to be an exact ~ with** correspondre parfaitement à; [5] (marriage) union *f*, mariage *m*; **to make a good ~** épouser un bon parti
B *vtr* [1] (correspond to) [*colour, bag*] être assorti à; [*blood type*] correspondre à; [*product, supply*] répondre à [*demand*]; [*word*] correspondre à [*definition*]; [2] (equal) égaler [*record, achievements*]; **the government will ~ your donation** le gouvernement donnera la même somme que vous; **his wit cannot be ~ed** il a une intelligence hors pair; **she more than ~ed him in aggression** elle le valait bien sur le plan de l'agressivité; **he is to be ~ed against the champion** on a organisé une rencontre entre lui et le champion; **there's nobody to ~ him** (disparagingly) il n'y en a pas deux comme lui; [3] (find a match for) **to ~ trainees with companies** mettre en rapport des stagiaires avec des sociétés
C *vi* [*colours, clothes, curtains*] être assortis/-ies; [*components*] aller ensemble; **that button doesn't ~** ce bouton n'est pas identique aux autres; **with gloves to ~** avec des gants assortis

(Phrasal verb)
■ **match up**: ▸ **~ up** [*pieces, bits*] aller ensemble; ▸ **~ up** [sth], **~** [sth] **up** ajuster [*pieces*]; **to ~ up to** être à la hauteur de [*expectation*]

matchbox /'mætʃbɒks/ *n* boîte *f* d'allumettes

matchmaker /'mætʃmeɪkə(r)/ *n* (for couples) marieur/-euse *m/f*; (for business) intermédiaire *mf*

match point *n* balle *f* de match; **at ~** à la balle de match

matchstick /'mætʃstɪk/
A *n* (bois *m* d') allumette *f*
B *noun modifier* [*man, figure*] stylisé, filiforme

mate /meɪt/
A *n* [1] ○GB (friend) copain○ *m*; (at work, school) camarade *mf*; [2] Zool (male) mâle *m*; (female) femelle *f*; [3] (assistant) aide *mf*; **builder's ~** aide-maçon *m*; [4] (in chess) mat *m*
B *vtr* [1] accoupler [*animal*] (**with** à *or* avec); [2] (in chess) faire mat
C *vi* [*animal*] s'accoupler (**with** à, avec)

material /mə'tɪərɪəl/
A *n* [1] (data) documentation *f*, documents *mpl*; **teaching ~** matériel *m* pédagogique; **reference ~** ouvrages *mpl* de référence; [2] (subject matter) contenu *m*; [3] Theat, TV (script) texte *m*; (show) spectacle *m*; **she writes all her own ~** elle écrit ses textes elle-même; Mus elle est auteur-compositeur; [4] (substance) *gen* matière *f*, substance *f*; Constr, Tech matériau *m*; **packing ~** matériaux *mpl* d'emballage; **waste ~** déchets *mpl*; [5] (fabric) tissu *m*, étoffe *f*; [6] (personal potential) étoffe *f*; **she is star ~** elle a l'étoffe d'une vedette; **to be university ~** être capable d'entreprendre des études universitaires
B **materials** *npl* (equipment) matériel *m*; **art ~s, artist's ~s** fournitures *fpl* de dessin; **cleaning ~s** produits *mpl* d'entretien

m

C adj **1** (significant, relevant) [assistance, benefit, change, damage, evidence] matériel/-ielle; [question] important; [fact] pertinent; **to be ~ to sth** se rapporter à qch; **2** (concrete) [comfort, gains, possessions, success] matériel/-ielle; **in ~ terms** sur le plan matériel; **to do sth for ~ gain** faire qch par intérêt

materialist /məˈtɪərɪəlɪst/ n, adj matérialiste (mf)

materialistic /məˌtɪərɪəˈlɪstɪk/ adj matérialiste

materialize /məˈtɪərɪəlaɪz/ vi **1** (happen) [hope, offer, plan, threat] se concrétiser; [event, situation] se réaliser; [idea] prendre forme; **the strike failed to ~** la grève n'a pas eu lieu; **2** (appear) [person, object] surgir; [spirit] se matérialiser; **I waited, but he failed to ~** hum j'ai attendu, mais il ne s'est pas montré

materially /məˈtɪərɪəlɪ/ adv **1** (considerably) sensiblement; **2** (physically) matériellement

maternal /məˈtɜːnl/ adj maternel/-elle (**towards** avec)

maternity /məˈtɜːnətɪ/
A n maternité f
B noun modifier [clothes] de grossesse; [leave, benefit] de maternité

maternity: ~ department n (in store) rayon m future maman; **~ hospital** n maternité f; **~ unit** n service m d'obstétrique; **~ ward** n maternité f

matey /ˈmeɪtɪ/ adj GB copain○ (**with** avec)

math○ /mæθ/ n US = **maths**○

mathematical /ˌmæθəˈmætɪkl/ adj mathématique; **it's a ~ impossibility** c'est mathématiquement impossible

mathematician /ˌmæθəməˈtɪʃn/ ▸ p. 1181 n mathématicien/-ienne m/f

mathematics /ˌmæθəˈmætɪks/ n (subject) (+ v sg) mathématiques fpl; (operations) (+ v sg ou v pl) calculs mpl

maths○ /mæθs/ GB
A n (+ v sg) maths○ fpl
B noun modifier [class, teacher] de maths

matinée /ˈmætɪneɪ, ˈmætneɪ, US ˌmætnˈeɪ/
A n Cin, Theat matinée f
B noun modifier [performance] en matinée

mating /ˈmeɪtɪŋ/ n accouplement m

mating: ~ call n chant m nuptial; **~ season** n saison f des amours

matriarchal /ˌmeɪtrɪˈɑːkl/ adj matriarcal

matrices /ˈmeɪtrɪsiːz/ pl ▸ **matrix**

matriculate /məˈtrɪkjʊleɪt/
A vtr inscrire [student]
B vi (enrol) (student) s'inscrire

matrimony /ˈmætrɪmənɪ, US -məʊnɪ/ n mariage m; **united in holy ~** unis dans le sacrement du mariage

matrix /ˈmeɪtrɪks/ n (pl **-trices**) matrice f

matron /ˈmeɪtrən/ n **1** GB (nurse) (in hospital) infirmière f en chef; (in school) infirmière f (chargée également de l'intendance); **2** (of nursing home) directrice f; **3** US (warder) gardienne f; **4** (woman) péj matrone f péj

matronly /ˈmeɪtrənlɪ/ adj [duties, manner] de mère de famille, de matrone; [figure] fort, corpulent

matron-of-honour GB, **matron-of-honor** US n dame f d'honneur

matt GB, **matte** US /mæt/ adj [paint] mat; [photograph] sur papier mat

matter /ˈmætə(r)/
A n **1** (affair) (of specified nature) affaire f; (requiring solution) problème m; (on agenda) point m; **business ~s** affaires fpl; **the ~ in hand** l'affaire en question; **it will be no easy ~** cela ne sera pas (une affaire) facile; **important ~s to discuss** des choses importantes à discuter; **~s arising** (in meeting) points non inscrits à l'ordre du jour; **private ~** affaire privée; **a ~ for the police** un problème qui relève de la police; **that's another ~** c'est une autre histoire; **it's no small ~** ce n'est pas une broutille; **to let the ~ drop** en rester là; **to take the ~ further** aller plus loin; **the fact of the ~ is that** la vérité est que; **I know nothing of the ~** je ne suis au courant de rien; **2** (question) question f; **it's a ~ of urgency** c'est urgent; **a ~ of life and death** une question de vie ou de mort; **it will just be a ~ of months** ce ne sera qu'une question de mois; **a ~ of a few days** l'affaire de quelques jours; **it's only a ~ of time before they separate** ils vont se séparer, ce n'est plus qu'une question de

temps; **3** (trouble) **is anything the ~?** y a-t-il un problème?; **what's the ~?** qu'est-ce qu'il y a?; **there's nothing the ~ with me** je n'ai rien; **what's the ~ with Louise?** qu'est-ce qu'elle a Louise?; **4** (substance) matière f; **vegetable ~** matière végétale; **colouring ~** colorant m; **5** (on paper) printed ~ imprimés mpl; **advertising ~** publicité f; **reading ~** lecture f; **6** (content of book, speech etc) contenu m; **subject ~** contenu m; **~ and style** le fond et la forme; **7** Med (pus) pus m
B vi être important; **to ~ to sb** [behaviour, action] avoir de l'importance pour qn; [person] compter pour qn; **it ~s little to me where you go** peu m'importe où tu vas; **it doesn't ~ whether** peu importe que (+ subj); **it doesn't ~** ça n'a aucune importance, ça ne fait rien; **does it really ~?** qu'est-ce que ça peut faire?

(idioms) **as a ~ of course** automatiquement; **as a ~ of fact** en fait; **for that ~** d'ailleurs; **no ~!** peu importe!; **no ~ how late it is** peu importe l'heure; **that's the end of the ~** c'est mon/son etc dernier mot; **to make ~s worse** pour ne rien arranger; **to take ~s into one's own hands** prendre les choses en main

Matterhorn /ˈmætəhɔːn/ pr n **the ~** le (mont) Cervin

matter-of-fact adj [voice, tone] détaché; [person] terre à terre

Matthew /ˈmæθjuː/ pr n Mathieu; Bible Matthieu

mattress /ˈmætrɪs/ n matelas m

maturation /ˌmætjʊˈreɪʃn/ n (of tree, body) maturation f; (of whisky, wine) vieillissement m; (of cheese) affinage m

mature /məˈtjʊə(r), US -ˈtʊər/
A adj **1** [plant, animal] adulte; **~ garden** beau jardin (planté depuis quelques années); **2** (psychologically) [person] mûr; [attitude, reader] adulte; **her most ~ novel** son roman le plus achevé; **after ~ consideration** après mûre réflexion; **3** [hard cheese] fort; [soft cheese] affiné; [whisky] vieux; **4** Fin [policy] arrivé à échéance
B vi **1** (physically) [person, animal] devenir adulte; [plant] atteindre la taille adulte; **2** (psychologically) [person] mûrir; **3** [idea] mûrir; **4** [wine] vieillir; [cheese] s'affiner; **5** Fin [policy] arriver à échéance

mature student n GB personne f qui reprend des études (après un temps au foyer ou dans la vie active)

maturity /məˈtjʊərətɪ, US -ˈtʊə-/ n gen maturité f; Fin échéance f; **to reach ~** [person] atteindre l'âge adulte; [tree] arriver à maturité

maudlin /ˈmɔːdlɪn/ adj [song] larmoyant; [person] mélancolique

maul /mɔːl/
A n **1** (hammer) masse f; **2** (in rugby) maul m
B vtr **1** (attack) [animal] mutiler; (fatally) déchiqueter; **2** (manhandle) malmener; **3** (sexually) tripoter○ [woman]; **4** fig [critics] démolir

Maundy Thursday n jeudi m saint

Mauritius /məˈrɪʃəs/ ▸ p. 774, p. 954 pr n l'île f Maurice

mausoleum /ˌmɔːsəˈliːəm/ n **1** (tomb) mausolée m; **2** (big house) grande baraque○ f

mauve /məʊv/ ▸ p. 752 n, adj mauve (m)

maverick /ˈmævərɪk/ n, adj nonconformiste (mf)

mawkish /ˈmɔːkɪʃ/ adj péj **1** (sentimental) mièvre; **2** (insipid) fade

maxi /ˈmæksɪ/ n **1** (also **~ dress**) robe f maxi; **2** (also **~ skirt**) jupe f maxi

maxim /ˈmæksɪm/ n maxime f

maxima /ˈmæksɪmə/ pl ▸ **maximum**

maximization /ˌmæksɪmaɪˈzeɪʃn/ n maximalisation f

maximize /ˈmæksɪmaɪz/ vtr gen maximiser [profit, sales]; Comput agrandir

maximum /ˈmæksɪməm/
A n (pl **-imums, -ima**) maximum m; **to hold a ~ of 300** contenir 300 personnes au maximum
B adj [price] maximum; [temperature] maximal; [speed] maximum, maximal; [load] limite
C adv au maximum

maximum security prison n prison f de haute surveillance

may¹ /meɪ/ modal aux **1** (possibility) **he ~ come** il se peut qu'il vienne, il viendra peut-être; **'are you going to**

may¹

When *may* (or *may have*) is used with another verb in English to convey possibility, French will generally use the adverb *peut-être* (perhaps) with the equivalent verb:

it may rain
= il pleuvra peut-être

we may never know what happened
= nous ne saurons peut-être jamais ce qui s'est passé

he may have got lost
= il s'est peut-être perdu

Alternatively, and more formally, the construction *il se peut que* + subjunctive may be used: *il se peut qu'il pleuve*; *il se peut que nous ne sachions jamais*. For particular usages, see **1** in the entry **may¹**.

peut-être is also used in French to convey concession:

he may be slow but he's not stupid
= il est peut-être lent mais il n'est pas bête

you may think I'm crazy but ...
= tu penses peut-être que je suis fou mais...

When *may* is used to convey permission, the French equivalent is *pouvoir*:

you may close the door
= vous pouvez fermer la porte

Note that the polite question *may I ... ?* is translated by *puis-je ... ?*:

may I make a suggestion?
= puis-je faire une suggestion?

For particular usages, see **2** in the entry **may¹**.

When *may* is used in rather formal English to convey purpose in the construction *in order that + may*, the French equivalent is *pour que* + subjunctive:

in order that he may know
= pour qu'il sache

When *may* is used with another verb to express a wish, the French uses *que* + subjunctive:

may they be happy!
= qu'ils soient heureux!

long may it last!
= que ça dure!

When *may well* + verb is used to convey likelihood, the French uses *il est fort possible que* + subjunctive:

he may well have gone elsewhere
= il est fort possible qu'il soit allé ailleurs

But note:

that may well be but ...
= c'est possible mais ...

In the phrase *may as well*, *may* is used interchangeably with *might*, which is more frequently used. For translations see the entry **might¹**.

---

accept?'—'I ∼' 'tu vas accepter?'—'peut-être'; **this medicine ∼ cause drowsiness** ce médicament peut provoquer des réactions de somnolence; **they're afraid she ∼ die** ils ont peur qu'elle (ne) meure; **even if I invite him he ∼ not come** même si je l'invite il risque de ne pas venir; **that's as ∼ be, but...** peut-être bien, mais...; **come what ∼** advienne que pourra; **be that as it ∼** quoi qu'il en soit; ② (permission) **∼ I come in?** puis-je entrer?; **I'll sit down, if I ∼** je vais m'asseoir si vous le permettez; **if I ∼ say so** si je puis me permettre; **and who are you, ∼ I ask?** iron qui êtes-vous au juste?; ▸ **well¹ B 2**

may² /meɪ/ n (hawthorn) aubépine *f*

May /meɪ/ ▸ p. 1020 n (month) mai *m*

maybe /'meɪbi:/
A adv peut-être; **∼ they'll arrive early** peut-être arriveront-ils tôt; **∼ three weeks ago** il y a peut-être trois semaines
B n **'is that a yes?'—'it's a ∼'** 'c'est oui?'—'c'est peut-être'

May: ∼ beetle, ∼ bug n hanneton *m*; **∼day** n Radio mayday *m*; **∼ Day** n premier mai *m*, fête *f* du travail

mayhem /'meɪhem/ n ① (chaos) désordre *m*; (violence) grabuge° *m*; **to create ∼** semer la pagaille°; ② US Jur (crime *m* de) mutilation *f*

mayn't /'meɪənt/ = **may not**

mayor /meə(r), US 'meɪər/ ▸ p. 869 n maire *m*

mayoress /'meərɪs, US 'meɪə-/ ▸ p. 869 n ① (wife of mayor) femme *f* du maire; (lady mayor) US mairesse *f*

May: maypole n mât *m* (de fête) (à l'occasion du premier mai); **∼ queen** n reine *f* du premier mai

maze /meɪz/ n (puzzle) labyrinthe *m*; fig (of streets, corridors) dédale *m*; (of pipes) enchevêtrement *m*

Mb n Comput (abrév = **megabyte**) Mo

MBA n Univ (abrév = **Master of Business Administration**) ≈ maîtrise *f* de gestion

MBE n GB (abrév = **Member of the Order of the British Empire**) membre de l'ordre de l'empire britannique

MBO n: abrév ▸ **management buyout**

Mbyte n (abrév = **megabyte**) mégaoctet *m*

MC n ① (abrév = **Master of Ceremonies**) (in cabaret) animateur *m*; (at banquet) maître *m* de cérémonie; ② Mus (rapper) MC *m*; ③ US Pol abrév écrite = **Member of Congress**

McCoy /mə'kɔɪ/ n:
(Idioms) **it's the real ∼** c'est de l'authentique

MD n ① Med, Univ (abrév = **Doctor of Medicine**) docteur *m* en médecine; ② US Post abrév écrite = **Maryland**; ③ (abrév = **Managing Director**) directeur *m* général

MDF n (abrév = **medium-density fibreboard**) lamifié *m*

me¹ /mi:, mɪ/

⚠ When used as a direct or indirect object pronoun *me* is translated by *me* (or *m'* before a vowel): *she knows me* = elle me connaît; *he loves me* = il m'aime.
Note that the object pronoun normally comes before the verb in French and that in compound tenses like the present perfect and past perfect, the past participle of the verb agrees with the direct object pronoun: *he's seen me* (female speaker) = il m'a vue.
In imperatives the translation for both the direct and the indirect object pronoun is *moi* and comes after the verb: *kiss me!* = embrasse-moi!; *give it to me!* = donne-le-moi! (note the hyphens).
After prepositions and the verb *to be* the translation is *moi*: *she did it for me* = elle l'a fait pour moi; *it's me* = c'est moi.
For particular expressions see below.

pron me; (before vowel) m'; **it's for ∼** c'est pour moi; **poor little ∼°** pauvre de moi; **if you were ∼** à ma place

me² /mi:/ n Mus mi *m*

ME n ① Med abrév ▸ **myalgic encephalomyelitis**; ② US Post abrév écrite = **Maine**; ③ Ling abrév ▸ **Middle English**; ④ US Med abrév ▸ **medical examiner**

mead /mi:d/ n hydromel *m*

meadow /'medəʊ/ n ① (field) pré *m*; ② **₡** (also **∼land**) prés *mpl*, prairies *fpl*; ③ (also **water ∼**) prairie *f* inondable

meadowsweet n reine-des-prés *f*

meagre GB, **meager** US /'mi:gə(r)/ adj [income, sum, meal] maigre (before n); [living] chiche; [response, returns] piètre (before n)

meal /mi:l/ n ① (food) repas *m*; **to enjoy one's ∼** bien manger; **to go out for a ∼** aller (manger) au restaurant; ② (from grain) farine *f*
(Idiom) **don't make a ∼ of it**! n'en fais pas tout un plat°!

meal ticket n ① (voucher) ticket-repas *m*; ② °fig (quality, qualification) gagne-pain *m* inv; (person) **I'm just a ∼ for you!** pour toi je ne suis qu'un portefeuille!

mean /miːn/

A n **1** gen, Math moyenne f; **above the** ∼ au-dessus de la moyenne; **2** fig (middle point) milieu m

B adj **1** (average) [weight, age] moyen/-enne; **2** (ungenerous) [person] avare, radin○; [attitude, nature] mesquin; [examiner] sévère; **he's** ∼ **with his time** il est avare de son temps; **he's** ∼ **with money** il est près de ses sous; **3** (unkind) [person] méchant (**to** avec); **a** ∼ **trick** un sale tour; **4** (vicious) [animal, person, expression] méchant; **that dog has got a** ∼ **streak** ce chien a la méchanceté en lui; **5** (tough) [city] implacable; [street] hostile; **6** ○(skilful) [artist, cook, cocktail] formidable, du tonnerre○ (after n); **7** (small) **that's no** ∼ **feat!** ce n'est pas un mince exploit!; **8** (lowly) littér [dwelling] misérable; [birth] bas/basse; [origin] modeste; **9** ○US (off colour) **to feel** ∼ ne pas être dans son assiette○

C vtr (prét, pp **meant**) **1** (signify) [word, phrase, symbol] signifier, vouloir dire; [sign] vouloir dire; **the term** ∼**s nothing to him** le terme ne lui dit rien; **2** (intend) **to** ∼ **to do** avoir l'intention de faire; **to** ∼ **sb to do** GB, **to** ∼ **for sb to do** US vouloir que qn fasse; **to be meant for sb** [question, bomb] être destiné à qn; **I meant it as a joke** c'était une blague de ma part; **she meant no offence** elle n'y entendait pas malice; **he doesn't** ∼ **you any harm** il ne te veut aucun mal; **what do you** ∼ **by opening my letters?** qu'est-ce qui te prend d'ouvrir mon courrier?; **to** ∼ **well** avoir de bonnes intentions; **she** ∼**s business** elle ne plaisante pas; **he** ∼**s what he says** il est sérieux; (he is menacing) il ne plaisante pas; **I didn't** ∼ **to do it** je ne l'ai pas fait exprès; **without** ∼**ing to** par inadvertance; **3** (entail) [strike, law] entraîner [shortages, changes]; **4** (intend to say) vouloir dire; **what do you** ∼ **by that remark?** qu'est-ce que tu veux dire par là?; **do you** ∼ **me?** c'est de moi que tu parles?; **I** ∼ **to say**○, who wants a car that won't start? non mais, qui voudrait d'une voiture qui ne démarre pas?; **I know what you** ∼ je comprends; **5** (be of value) **a promise** ∼**s nothing** une promesse ne veut pas dire grand-chose; **money** ∼**s a lot to him** l'argent compte beaucoup pour lui; **your friendship** ∼**s a lot to me** ton amitié est très importante pour moi; **6** (be destined) **to be meant to do** être destiné à faire; **it was meant to be** ou happen cela devait arriver; **they were meant for each other** ils étaient faits l'un pour l'autre; **7** (be supposed to be) **he's meant to be** il est censé être

meander /mɪˈændə(r)/ vi **1** (wind) [river, road] serpenter; ∼**ing path** sentier sinueux; **2** (wander) [person] flâner; [thoughts] vagabonder

meaning /ˈmiːnɪŋ/ n **1** (sense) (of word, remark) sens m; (of symbol, film, dream) signification f; **a word with two** ∼**s** un mot à double sens; **what is the** ∼ **of this?** qu'est-ce que cela signifie?; **yes, I get your** ∼○ oui, je vois ce que tu veux dire; **2** (purpose) sens m; **my life no longer has any** ∼ ma vie n'a plus aucun sens; **to give new** ∼ **to** donner un sens nouveau à [life, work]; **full of** ∼ lourd de sens

meaningful /ˈmiːnɪŋfl/ adj **1** (significant) [word, statement, result] significatif/-ive; **2** (profound) [relationship, comment, lyric] sérieux/-ieuse; [experience] riche; [insight] poussé; **3** (eloquent) [look, smile] entendu; [gesture] significatif/-ive; **4** (constructive) [talk] constructif/-ive; [work] utile; [process, input] positif/-ive

meaningless /ˈmiːnɪŋlɪs/ adj **1** (having no sense) [claim, phrase] dépourvu de sens; [code, figure] incompréhensible; **2** (worthless) [chatter, role, title] insignifiant; [action, remark] sans importance; [effort] inutile; **a** ∼ **exercise** une opération inutile; **3** (pointless) [act, sacrifice, violence] insensé; **my life is** ∼ ma vie n'a pas de sens

meanness /ˈmiːnnɪs/ n **1** (stinginess) (of person) avarice f; (of portion) maigreur f; **2** (nastiness) méchanceté f (**to** envers; **towards** à l'égard de); **3** (humbleness) littér pauvreté f

means /miːnz/

A n (pl ∼) (way) moyen m (**of doing** de faire); **whatever** ∼ **possible** tous les moyens; **a** ∼ **of** un moyen de [communication, transport]; **by** ∼ **of** au moyen de; **yes, by all** ∼ oui, certainement; **if you wish to leave, then by all** ∼ **do** si vous voulez partir, cela ne tient qu'à vous; **it is by no** ∼ **certain** c'est loin d'être sûr

B npl (resources) moyens mpl, revenus mpl; **of moderate** ∼ [person, family] aux revenus modestes; **to live within one's** ∼ vivre selon ses moyens; **a man of** ∼ un homme riche or fortuné

(Idioms) **by fair** ∼ **or foul** par tous les moyens; **a** ∼ **to an end** un moyen d'arriver à ses fins

mean-spirited adj petit, mesquin

means test

A n enquête f sur les ressources

B **means-test** vtr soumettre [qn] à un examen de ressources

meant /ment/ prét, pp ▸ **mean C**

meantime /ˈmiːntaɪm/ adv **for the** ∼ pour le moment; **(in the)** ∼ pendant ce temps

meanwhile /ˈmiːnwaɪl/

A adv **1** (during this time) pendant ce temps; **2** (until then) en attendant; **3** (since then) entre-temps; **4** (by way of contrast) au même moment

B **in the meanwhile** adv phr = **meanwhile A**

measles /ˈmiːzlz/ ▸ p. 933 n (+ v sg) rougeole f

measly○ /ˈmiːzlɪ/ adj [amount] misérable; [gift, result] minable○

measurable /ˈmeʒərəbl/ adj **1** (perceptible) [difference] notable; **2** (quantifiable) [change] mesurable; [phenomena] quantifiable

measure /ˈmeʒə(r)/ ▸ p. 977, p. 1240, p. 723, p. 1311, p. 1323, p. 1191

A n **1** (unit) unité f de mesure; **weights and** ∼**s** les poids mpl et mesures fpl; **liquid** ∼ mesure f de capacité pour les liquides; **it's made to** ∼ (garment) c'est fait sur mesure, c'est du sur mesure; **2** (of alcohol) mesure f; **he gave me short** ∼ il a triché sur la quantité; **3** (device for measuring) instrument m de mesure; **4** (qualified amount, extent) **a** ∼ **of success** un certain succès; **a small** ∼ **of support** un soutien limité; **a good** ou **wide** ∼ **of autonomy** une grande autonomie; **in large** ∼ dans une large mesure; **in full** ∼ [feel, possess, contribute] pleinement; **5** (way of estimating) (of price rises) mesure f; (of success, anger) mesure f, indication f; (of efficiency, performance) critère m; **to be the** ∼ **of** donner la mesure de; **to give some** ∼ **of** donner une idée de [delight, talent]; **to use sth as a** ∼ **of** utiliser qch pour mesurer [effects, impact]; **this is a** ∼ **of how dangerous it is** ceci montre à quel point c'est dangereux; **beyond** ∼ [change] énormément; [beautiful] extrêmement; **it has improved beyond** ∼ il y a eu d'énormes progrès; **to take the** ∼ **of sb** jauger qn; **I have the** ∼ **of them** je sais ce qu'ils valent; **6** (action, step) mesure f; **to take** ∼**s** prendre des mesures; **safety** ∼ mesure de sécurité; **as a precautionary** ∼ par mesure de précaution; **as a preventive** ∼ à titre préventif; **as a temporary** ∼ provisoirement

B vtr **1** (assess size) mesurer [length, rate, person]; **to** ∼ **sth in** mesurer qch en [metres]; **to get oneself** ∼**d for** faire prendre ses mesures pour; **2** (have measurement of) mesurer; **to** ∼ **four by five metres** mesurer quatre mètres sur cinq; **a tremor measuring 5.2 on the Richter scale** une secousse de 5,2 sur l'échelle de Richter; **3** (assess) mesurer [performance, ability] (**against** à); **4** (compare) **to** ∼ **sth against** comparer qch à [achievement]

(Idioms) **for good** ∼ pour faire bonne mesure; **to do things by half-**∼**s** se contenter de demi-mesures

(Phrasal verbs)

■ **measure off:** ▸ ∼ **off [sth]** mesurer [fabric]

■ **measure out:** ▸ ∼ **out [sth]** mesurer [land, flour, liquid]; doser [medicine]; compter [drops]

■ **measure up:** ▸ ∼ **up** [person] avoir les qualités requises; **to** ∼ **up to** être à la hauteur de [expectations]; soutenir la comparaison avec [achievement]; ▸ ∼ **up [sth]** mesurer [room etc]

measured /ˈmeʒəd/ adj [tone] mesuré; [comment] circonspect

measurement /ˈmeʒəmənt/ ▸ p. 1240, p. 1191 n **1** (of room, object) dimension f; **2** (of person) **to take sb's** ∼**s** prendre les mensurations de qn; **chest** ∼ tour m de poitrine; **leg** ∼ longueur f de jambe

measuring: ∼ **jug** n verre m gradué; ∼ **spoon** n cuillère-mesure f

meat /miːt/ n (flesh) viande f; **red** ∼ viande rouge; **crab** ∼ chair f de crabe; ∼ **and two veg**○ viande garnie de deux légumes

(Idioms) **political scandals are** ∼ **and drink to them** ils se repaissent de scandales politiques; **to be strong** ∼ être choquant; **one man's** ∼ **is another man's poison** Prov le malheur des uns fait le bonheur des autres Prov

meatball /ˈmiːtbɔːl/ n **1** Culin (gén pl) boulette f de viande; **2** ○US (person) andouille○ f

meat-eater /ˈmiːtiːtə(r)/ n [1] (animal) carnivore m; [2] (person) **they're not great ~s** ils ne mangent pas beaucoup de viande

meat: ~ **hook** n croc m de boucherie; ~ **loaf** n pain m de viande; ~ **pie** n ≈ pâté m en croûte

meaty /ˈmiːtɪ/ adj [1] (with meat) [stew, sauce] riche en viande; [chop] beau/belle; [flavour, smell] de viande; [2] fig [role, story] riche

Mecca /ˈmekə/ ▸ p. 1276 pr n La Mecque; **a ~ for** fig la Mecque des [tourists, scholars]

mechanic /mɪˈkænɪk/ ▸ p. 1181 n mécanicien/-ienne m/f

mechanical /mɪˈkænɪkl/ adj mécanique

mechanical: ~ **drawing** n US Tech dessin m industriel; ~ **engineering** n construction f mécanique

mechanics /mɪˈkænɪks/ npl [1] (subject) (+ v sg) mécanique f; [2] (workings) (+ v pl) lit, fig mécanisme m; **the ~ of** le mécanisme de [engine, pump]; les mécanismes de [management, law]; **the ~ of doing** la méthode pour faire

mechanism /ˈmekənɪzəm/ n [1] Tech, Biol, Psych, Philos mécanisme m; [2] (procedure) mécanisme m (**of** de); **legal ~s** procédures fpl légales

mechanization /ˌmekənaɪˈzeɪʃn, US -nɪˈz-/ n mécanisation f

medal /ˈmedl/ n médaille f; **gold/silver ~** médaille d'or/d'argent

medallion /mɪˈdælɪən/ n (all contexts) médaillon m

medallist GB, **medalist** US /ˈmedəlɪst/ n médaillé/-e m/f; **gold/silver ~** médaillé/-e m/f d'or/d'argent

Medal of Honor n US Mil Médaille f d'honneur (la plus haute décoration militaire des États-Unis)

meddle /ˈmedl/ vi péj **stop meddling!** mêle-toi de tes affaires!; **to ~ in** s'immiscer dans [affairs]; **to ~ with** toucher à [property]

media /ˈmiːdɪə/
A n (+ v pl ou sg) **the ~** les médias pl; **news ~** presse f d'information; **in the ~** dans les médias
B noun modifier [advertising] dans les médias; [analyst, interest] des médias; [coverage, image] médiatique; [consultant] de médias; [sales] par les médias; [person] qui travaille dans les médias

median /ˈmiːdɪən/
A n [1] (in maths, statistics) médiane f; [2] (also ~ **strip**) US Aut terre-plein m central
B adj [1] (in statistics) [price, income, sum] moyen/-enne; [2] (in maths) [point, line] médian; [value] moyen/-enne

media studies npl communication f et journalisme m

mediate /ˈmiːdɪeɪt/
A vtr négocier [settlement, peace]
B vi arbitrer; **to ~ in/between** servir de médiateur dans/entre

mediator /ˈmiːdɪeɪtə(r)/ n médiateur/-trice m/f

medic○ /ˈmedɪk/ n [1] (doctor) toubib○ m, médecin m; [2] (student) étudiant/-e m/f en médecine; [3] Mil infirmier/-ière m/f militaire

Medicaid /ˈmedɪkeɪd/ n US assistance f médicale aux économiquement faibles

medical /ˈmedɪkl/
A n (in school, army, for job) visite f médicale; (private) examen m médical
B adj médical; **on ~ grounds** pour raisons de santé

medical advice n conseils mpl d'un médecin; **to seek ~** consulter un médecin; **against ~** contre l'avis du médecin

medical: ~ **board** n Mil commission f médicale; ~ **care** n ¢ gen soins mpl médicaux; Admin assistance f médicale; ~ **check-up** n bilan m de santé; ~ **doctor** ▸ p. 1181 n docteur m en médecine; ~ **emergency** n urgence f; ~ **examination** n = medical A; ~ **examiner** n US Jur médecin m légiste; ~ **history** n (background) antécédents mpl médicaux; (notes) dossier m médical; ~ **insurance** n assurance-maladie f

medically /ˈmedɪklɪ/ adv ~ **fit/unfit** en bonne/mauvaise santé; **a ~ qualified person** une personne ayant une formation médicale

medical officer, **MO** n Mil médecin m militaire; Ind médecin m du travail

medical profession n **the ~** (doctors collectively) le corps médical; (occupation) la médecine

medical: **Medical Research Council** n GB institut national britannique de la recherche médicale; ~ **school** n faculté f de médecine; ~ **student** n étudiant/-e m/f en médecine

Medicare /ˈmedɪkeə(r)/ n US assistance f médicale aux personnes âgées

medicated /ˈmedɪkeɪtɪd/ adj [bandage] médical; [shampoo] traitant

medication /ˌmedɪˈkeɪʃn/ n [1] ¢ (drug treatment) médicaments mpl; **to be on ~** prendre des médicaments; **to put sb on/take sb off ~** prescrire/supprimer des médicaments à qn; [2] C (medicine) médicament m

medicinal /mɪˈdɪsɪnl/ adj [property, use] thérapeutique; [herb] médicinal; ~ **drugs** médicaments mpl; **I drink brandy for ~ purposes** hum je bois du cognac à des fins thérapeutiques

medicine /ˈmedsn, US ˈmedɪsn/ n [1] ¢ médecine f; **to study ~** étudier la médecine; **doctor of ~** docteur m en médecine; [2] C (drug) médicament m (**for** pour); **the best ~** lit, fig le meilleur remède

(Idioms) **to give sb a taste of their own ~** rendre à qn la monnaie de sa pièce; **to take one's ~ like a man** avaler la pilule○

medicine: ~ **ball** n médecine-ball m; ~ **bottle** n fiole f; ~ **cabinet**, ~ **cupboard** n armoire f à pharmacie; ~ **man** n sorcier m guérisseur

medico○ /ˈmedɪkəʊ/
A n = **medic**
B medico+ combining form médico-

medieval /ˌmedɪˈiːvl, US ˌmiːd-, also mɪˈdiːvl/ adj médiéval; fig (primitive) moyenâgeux/-euse péj

mediocre /ˌmiːdɪˈəʊkə(r)/ adj médiocre

mediocrity /ˌmiːdɪˈɒkrətɪ/ n [1] (state) médiocrité f; [2] (person) médiocre mf

meditate /ˈmedɪteɪt/ vtr, vi méditer

meditative /ˈmedɪtətɪv, US -teɪt-/ adj [person, expression] méditatif/-ive; [music, experience] contemplatif/-ive; [calm] recueilli

Mediterranean /ˌmedɪtəˈreɪnɪən/ ▸ p. 1049
A pr n [1] (also ~ **sea**) **the ~** la (mer) Méditerranée; [2] (region) **the ~** les pays méditerranéens; [3] (native) méditerranéen/-éenne m/f
B adj méditerranéen/-éenne

medium /ˈmiːdɪəm/ ▸ p. 1191
A n [1] (pl -iums ou -ia) Cin, Radio, Theat, TV moyen m d'expression; **advertising ~** support m publicitaire; **through the ~ of** par l'intermédiaire de; [2] (pl -ia) Art (technique) technique f; (material) matériel m; [3] (mid-point) milieu m; **to find ou strike a happy ~** trouver le juste milieu; [4] (pl -iums) Biol, Bot milieu m; [5] (pl -iums) (spiritualist) médium m
B adj [1] [size, temperature] moyen/-enne; **in the ~ term** à moyen terme; [2] Radio [wave] moyen/-enne; **on ~ wave** sur les ondes moyennes

medium: ~-**dry** adj [drink] demi-sec; ~-**fine** adj [pen] à pointe moyenne; [tip, point] moyen/-enne; ~-**length** adj [book, film, article] de longueur moyenne; [hair, skirt] mi-long/mi-longue; ~-**range** adj [missile] à moyenne portée; ~-**rare** adj [meat] à point; ~-**sized** adj de taille moyenne

medlar /ˈmedlə(r)/ n [1] (fruit) nèfle f; [2] (tree) néflier m

medley /ˈmedlɪ/ n [1] Mus pot-pourri m (**of** de); [2] (in swimming) ~ **relay** relais m quatre nages; [3] (mixture) (of people, groups) mélange m

meek /miːk/ adj docile

meet /miːt/
A n [1] Sport rencontre f (sportive); **track ~** US rencontre f d'athlétisme; [2] GB (in hunting) rendez-vous m de chasseurs
B vtr (prét, pp **met**) [1] (encounter) rencontrer [person, team, enemy]; **to ~ one's death** trouver la mort; [2] (make acquaintance of) faire la connaissance de [person]; **Paul, ~ Frances** (as introduction) Paul, je vous présente Frances; [3] (await) attendre; (fetch) chercher; **she went to ~ them** elle est allée les attendre or chercher; **to ~ sb off** GB ou at US **the plane** attendre qn à l'aéroport; [4] (come into contact with) rencontrer; **his eyes met hers** son regard a rencontré le sien; **an incredible sight met her eyes** un spectacle incroyable s'est

offert à ses yeux; **5** (fulfil) satisfaire [*order*]; répondre à, satisfaire à [*criteria, standards, needs*]; payer [*bills, costs*]; couvrir [*debts, overheads*]; compenser [*loss*]; faire face à [*obligations, commitments*]; remplir [*conditions*]; **6** (rise to) se montrer à la hauteur de [*challenge*]; **7** (respond to) répondre à [*criticism*]

C vi (*prét, pp* met) **1** (come together) [*people, teams*] se rencontrer; [*committee, parliament*] se réunir; [*cars*] se croiser; **the two trains met head-on** les deux trains se sont heurtés de front; **to ~ again** [*people*] se revoir; **goodbye, till we ~ again!** au revoir! à la prochaine fois!; **2** (make acquaintance) [*people*] faire connaissance; **3** (come into contact) [*lips, roads*] se rencontrer; **their eyes met** leurs regards se croisèrent

(Idioms) **there's more to this than ~s the eye** ce n'est pas aussi clair que cela n'en a l'air; **to make ends ~** joindre les deux bouts

(Phrasal verbs)
▪ **meet up**° se retrouver; **to ~ up with**° retrouver [*friend*]
▪ **meet with**: ▸ **~ with [sb]** rencontrer [*person, delegation*]; ▸ **~ with [sth]** rencontrer [*opposition, success, suspicion*]; être accueilli avec [*approval*]; subir [*failure*]; **he met with an accident** il lui est arrivé un accident; **to ~ with no response** ne susciter aucune réaction; **to be met with** être accueilli par [*silence, shouts*]; se heurter à [*disapproval*]; susciter [*anger*]

meeting /ˈmiːtɪŋ/ n **1** (official assembly) réunion f; **to call a ~** convoquer une réunion; **in a ~** en réunion; **2** (coming together) rencontre f; **a ~ of minds** fig une profonde entente; **3** GB Sport rencontre f (sportive)

meeting: **~-place** n (lieu m de) rendez-vous m; **~ point** n point m de rencontre

mega /megə/ **mega+** combining form méga-

megabyte /ˈmegəbaɪt/ n Comput mégaoctet m

megalith /ˈmegəlɪθ/ n mégalithe m

megalomaniac /ˌmegələˈmeɪnɪæk/ n, adj mégalomane (mf)

megaphone /ˈmegəfəʊn/ n porte-voix m inv

megaton /ˈmegətʌn/ n mégatonne f

melancholy /ˈmelənkəlɪ/
A n mélancolie f
B adj [*person*] mélancolique; [*music, occasion*] triste

Melanesia /ˌmeləˈniːzɪə/ ▸ p. 774 pr n Mélanésie f

Melba: **~ sauce** n coulis m de framboises; **~ toast** n ≈ toast m très mince

mellow /ˈmeləʊ/
A adj **1** [*wine*] moelleux/-euse; [*flavour*] suave; [*tone*] mélodieux/-ieuse; [*colour, light, sound*] doux/douce; [*fruit*] fondant; **2** (weathered) [*stone*] patiné par l'âge; **3** (calm) **to get** ou **grow ~ with age** s'assagir avec l'âge; **4** (relaxed) [*person*] détendu; [*atmosphere*] serein
B vtr **1** (calm) [*experience*] assagir [*person*]; [*music, wine*] détendre [*person*]; **2** (ripen) faire mûrir [*fruit*]; donner du moelleux à [*wine*]
C vi **1** (calm down) [*person, behaviour*] s'assagir; **2** (tone down) [*attitude*] s'adoucir; **3** (ripen) [*fruit*] mûrir; [*taste*] prendre du moelleux

melodic /mɪˈlɒdɪk/ adj gen mélodieux/-ieuse; Mus mélodique

melodrama /ˈmelədrɑːmə/ n mélodrame m also fig

melodramatic /ˌmelədrəˈmætɪk/ adj mélodramatique; **you're being ~!** tu dramatises les choses!

melody /ˈmelədɪ/ n mélodie f

melon /ˈmelən/ n (fruit) melon m

melt /melt/
A n **1** (thaw) dégel m, fonte f des neiges; **2** US Culin sandwich m recouvert de fromage fondu
B vtr lit [*heat, sun, person*] faire fondre [*snow, plastic, butter*]; fig attendrir [*heart*]
C vi **1** lit fondre; **to ~ in your mouth** fondre dans la bouche; **2** fig (soften) [*heart, person*] fondre (**with** de); **3** (merge) **to ~ into** se fondre dans [*crowd*]

(Phrasal verbs)
▪ **melt away** **1** lit [*snow, ice*] fondre complètement; **2** fig [*fear, confidence*] se dissiper; [*crowd, people*] se disperser; [*money*] fondre
▪ **melt down**: ▸ **~ down [sth]**, **~ [sth] down** fondre [*metal*]

meltdown /ˈmeltdaʊn/ n **1** (of reactor) fusion f du cœur d'un réacteur; **in ~** en fusion; **2** °Fin (crash) chute f des actions, krach m boursier

melting point n point m de fusion

melting pot n (of people, nationalities) melting-pot m

(Idiom) **to be in the ~** être remis en question

member /ˈmembə(r)/
A n **1** (of group, commission) membre m; **to be a ~ of** faire partie de [*group*]; être membre de [*club, committee*]; **~ of staff** gen employé/-e m/f; (in school) professeur m; **~ of the opposite sex** personne f de l'autre sexe; '**~s only**' 'réservé aux membres'; **~ of the public** (in street) passant/-e m/f; (in theatre, cinema) spectateur/-trice m/f; **an ordinary ~ of the public** un simple citoyen; **like any other ~ of the public** comme tout le monde; **2** (also **Member**) Pol (of parliament) député m; **3** Constr pièce f; **cross ~** traverse f; **4** Math (of set) élément m; **5** (limb) membre m
B noun modifier [*nation, state*] membre

Member of Congress, **MC** n US Pol membre m du Congrès

Member of Parliament, **MP** ▸ p. 869 n GB Pol député m (**for** de)

member: **Member of the European Parliament**, **MEP** n député m au Parlement européen; **Member of the Northern Ireland Assembly** n membre m de l'Assemblée d'Irlande du Nord; **Member of the Scottish Parliament**, **MSP** n député m du Parlement écossais; **Member of the Welsh Assembly** n membre m de l'Assemblée galloise

membership /ˈmembəʃɪp/ n **1** adhésion f (**of** à); **EC ~** adhésion à la CE; **full/group ~** adhésion à part entière/en groupe; **to resign one's ~** rendre sa carte de membre; **~ of** GB ou in US **the club is open to all** le club est ouvert à tous; **to take out joint ~ of** GB ou in US **the club** adhérer en couple au club; **2** (fee) cotisation f; **3** (people belonging) (+ v sg ou pl) membres mpl; **it has a ~ of 200** il y a 200 membres; **~ is declining** le nombre des membres décroît

membrane /ˈmembreɪn/ n (all contexts) membrane f

memento /mɪˈmentəʊ/ n (pl **~s** ou **~es**) souvenir m (**of** de); **as a ~** en souvenir

memo /ˈmeməʊ/ n (abrév = **memorandum**) Admin note f de service

memo board n tableau m d'affichage

memoirs /ˈmemwɑː(r)z/ npl mémoires mpl

memo pad n bloc-notes m

memorabilia /ˌmemərəˈbɪlɪə/ npl souvenirs mpl

memorable /ˈmemərəbl/ adj [*event*] mémorable; [*person, quality*] inoubliable

memorandum /ˌmeməˈrændəm/ n (pl **memoranda**) **1** Admin note f de service (**to** à l'attention de; **from** de la part de); **2** Pol mémorandum m

memorial /məˈmɔːrɪəl/
A n **1** (monument) mémorial m (**to** à); **2** (reminder) **as a ~ to** à la mémoire de; **3** (document) mémoire m
B adj commémoratif/-ive; **~ service** messe f commémorative

Memorial Day n US jour de commémoration des soldats américains morts à la guerre

memorize /ˈmeməraɪz/ vtr apprendre [qch] par cœur

memory /ˈmemərɪ/ n **1** (faculty) mémoire f; **to have a good ~** avoir bonne mémoire; **to have a bad ~** ne pas avoir de mémoire; **from ~** de mémoire; **to have a good ~ for faces** avoir la mémoire des physionomies; **if my ~ serves me right** si je me souviens bien; **to have a long ~** être rancunier/-ière f; **2** (recollection) (souvent pl) souvenir m; **3** (period of time) **in living** ou **recent ~** de mémoire d'homme; **4** (posthumous fame) souvenir m; **their ~ lives on** leur souvenir est toujours vivant; **to keep sb's ~ alive** maintenir le souvenir de qn en vie; **5** (commemoration) **in (loving) ~ of** à la mémoire de; **6** Comput mémoire f

(Idiom) **to take a trip down ~ lane** se pencher sur ses souvenirs

memory bank n bloc m mémoire

men /men/ pl ▸ **man**

menace /ˈmenəs/
A n **1** (threat) menace f; **with ~s** Jur par des menaces; **2** (danger) **a ~ to other motorists** un danger public;

③ ○(nuisance) **he's a real** ∼ c'est une vraie plaie

B *vtr* menacer (**with** de, avec)

mend /mend/

A *n* ① (in fabric) (stitched) raccommodage *m*; (darned) reprise *f*; (patched) rapiéçage *m*; ② fig **to be on the** ∼ [*person*] être en voie de guérison; [*economy*] reprendre; [*weather, situation*] s'améliorer

B *vtr* ① (repair) réparer [*object, road*]; ② (in sewing) (stitch) raccommoder; (darn) repriser; (add patch) rapiécer; ③ (improve) **to** ∼ **relations with** améliorer les relations avec; **that won't** ∼ **matters** ça n'arrangera pas les choses

C *vi* [*injury*] guérir; [*person*] se rétablir

(Idiom) **to** ∼ **one's ways** s'amender

mending /ˈmendɪŋ/ *n* raccommodage *m*

menfolk /ˈmenfəʊk/ *npl* hommes *mpl*

menial /ˈmiːnɪəl/ *adj* [*job*] subalterne; [*attitude*] servile; ∼ **tasks** basses besognes

meningitis /ˌmenɪnˈdʒaɪtɪs/ ▸ p. 933 *n* méningite *f*

menopause /ˈmenəpɔːz/ *n* ménopause *f*

Menorca /mɪˈnɔːkə/ ▸ p. 954 *pr n* Minorque *f*

men's room /ˈmenzruːm, -rʊm/ *n* US toilettes *fpl* pour hommes

menstruate /ˈmenstrʊeɪt/ *vi* avoir ses règles

menswear /ˈmenzweə(r)/ *n* prêt-à-porter *m* pour hommes

mental /ˈmentl/ *adj* ① Med [*handicap, illness, patient*] mental; [*hospital, institution*] psychiatrique; [*ward*] de psychiatrie; ② (of the mind) [*ability, effort, energy*] intellectuel/-elle; [*process, age*] mental; ③ (in one's head) [*arithmetic, picture*] mental; **to make a** ∼ **note to do** se dire qu'il faut faire; ④ ○(mad) fou/folle, malade○

mental: ∼ **block** *n* blocage *m* psychologique; ∼ **health** *n* (of person) santé *f* mentale; Admin psychiatrie *f*; ∼ **home** *n* clinique *f* psychiatrique

mentality /menˈtælətɪ/ *n* mentalité *f*

mentally /ˈmentəlɪ/ *adv* ① Med ∼ **handicapped** handicapé mental; ∼ **retarded** retardé; **the** ∼ **ill** les malades mentaux; **to be** ∼ **deranged** avoir l'esprit dérangé; ② (regarding the mind) ∼ **exhausted** surmené intellectuellement; **to be** ∼ **alert** avoir l'esprit alerte; ∼ **slow** lent d'esprit; ③ (inwardly) [*resolve*] dans son for intérieur; [*calculate*] mentalement

mentholated /ˈmenθəleɪtɪd/ *adj* au menthol

mention /ˈmenʃn/

A *n* ① (reference) mention *f* (**of** de); **the mere** ∼ **of my name** la seule évocation de mon nom; **to make no** ∼ **of** [*report, person*] ne pas faire mention de; **it got a** ∼ **on the radio** on en a parlé à la radio; ② (acknowledgement) mention *f*; **honourable** ∼ gen mention honorable; Mil citation *f*

B *vtr* ① (allude to) faire mention de [*person, topic, fact*]; **please don't** ∼ **my name** ne mentionnez pas mon nom; **she never** ∼**s her work** elle ne parle jamais de son travail; **to** ∼ **sb/sth to sb** parler de qn/qch à qn; **to** ∼ **that...** dire (en passant) que...; **I hardly need to** ∼ **that...** inutile de signaler que...; **not to** ∼ sans parler de; **without** ∼**ing any names** sans nommer personne; **too numerous to** ∼ trop nombreux pour être cités; **to be** ∼**ed in a will** figurer sur un testament; **just** ∼ **my name** dis-leur que tu viens de ma part; **don't** ∼ **it!** je vous en *or* je t'en prie!; ② (acknowledge) citer [*name*]; mentionner [*service*]

menu /ˈmenjuː/ *n* (all contexts) menu *m*

MEP *n* (*abrév* = **Member of the European Parliament**) député *m* au Parlement européen

mercantile /ˈmɜːkəntaɪl, US -tiːl, -tɪl/ *adj* [*ship, nation*] marchand; [*law*] commercial; [*system, theory*] mercantile

mercenary /ˈmɜːsɪnərɪ, US -nerɪ/

A *n* mercenaire *mf*

B *adj* [*action, person*] intéressé; [*business interest*] mercantile

merchandise /ˈmɜːtʃəndaɪz/

A *n* marchandise(s) *f(pl)*

B *vtr* (also **merchandize**) ① (buy and sell) faire le commerce de; ② (promote) assurer la promotion de

merchant /ˈmɜːtʃənt/

A *n* gen négociant *m*; (selling small quantities) marchand *m*; (retailer) détaillant *m*; **speed** ∼○ fou/folle *m/f* du volant

B *noun modifier* [*ship*] marchand; [*sailor*] de la marine marchande

merchant: ∼ **bank** *n* GB banque *f* d'affaires; ∼ **banker** ▸ p. 1181 *n* GB (executive) cadre *m* d'une banque

d'affaires; (owner) banquier *m* d'affaires; ∼**man** *n* Naut navire *m* marchand; ∼ **navy** GB, ∼ **marine** US *n* marine *f* marchande

merciful /ˈmɜːsɪfl/ *adj* ① (kind) [*person, sentence*] clément (**to, towards** envers); [*act*] charitable; [*God*] miséricordieux/-ieuse; ② (fortunate) [*occurrence*] heureux/-euse; **a** ∼ **release** une délivrance

mercifully /ˈmɜːsɪfəlɪ/ *adv* ① (compassionately) avec clémence; ② (fortunately) par bonheur, par chance

merciless /ˈmɜːsɪlɪs/ *adj* [*ruler, criticism*] impitoyable (**to, towards** envers); [*heat*] implacable

mercurial /mɜːˈkjʊərɪəl/ *adj* ① Chem [*compound, poisoning*] au mercure; ② (quick-witted) [*person*] vif/vive; (changeable) [*temperament, person*] lunatique

mercury /ˈmɜːkjʊrɪ/

A *n* mercure *m*

B **Mercury** *pr n* ① (planet) Mercure *f*; ② Mythol Mercure *m*

mercy /ˈmɜːsɪ/ *n* ① (clemency) clémence *f*; **to show** ∼ **to sb** se montrer clément à l'égard de qn; **to have** ∼ **on sb** avoir pitié de qn; **to beg for** ∼ demander grâce; **an act of** ∼ un acte de compassion; **a mission of** ∼ une mission humanitaire; ② (power) merci *f*; **at the** ∼ **of** à la merci de; **to throw oneself on sb's** ∼ s'en remettre au bon vouloir de qn; ③ (fortunate event) **it's a** ∼ **that** c'est une chance que (+ *subj*)

(Idiom) **let's be grateful for small mercies** sachons apprécier notre chance

mercy killing *n* ① ¢ euthanasie *f*; ② (act) **C** acte *m* d'euthanasie

mere /mɪə(r)/ *adj* ① (simple) [*coincidence, nonsense*] pur (*before n*); [*fiction, formality*] simple (*before n*); **he's a** ∼ **child** ce n'est qu'un enfant; **a** ∼ **nothing** trois fois rien; **he's a** ∼ **nobody** c'est quelqu'un d'insignifiant; ② (least) [*sight, idea*] simple, seul; **the** ∼ **mention of her name** la simple évocation de son nom; **the** ∼ **sight of her** sa seule vue; **the** ∼ **presence of asbestos...** le seul fait qu'il y ait de l'amiante...; ③ (bare) seulement; **the beach is a** ∼ **2 km from here** la plage n'est qu'à 2 km d'ici; **to last a** ∼ **20 minutes** durer tout juste 20 minutes

merely /ˈmɪəlɪ/ *adv* simplement, seulement; **his accusations** ∼ **damaged his reputation** ses accusations n'ont fait que nuire à sa réputation; **it is not enough** ∼ **to do** il ne suffit pas de faire

merge /mɜːdʒ/

A *vtr* ① (join) **to** ∼ **sth with sth** fusionner qch avec qch [*company, group*]; ② (blend) mélanger [*colour, design*]

B *vi* ① (also ∼ **together**) [*companies, departments*] fusionner; [*roads, rivers*] se rejoindre; **to** ∼ **with** fusionner avec [*company, department*]; rejoindre [*river, road*]; ② (blend) [*colours, sounds*] se confondre; **to** ∼ **into** se fondre avec [*colour, sky, trees*]

merger /ˈmɜːdʒə(r)/ *n* ① (of companies) fusion *f*; ② (process of merging) fusionnement *m*

meridian /məˈrɪdɪən/

A *n* lit méridien *m*; fig (peak) apogée *m*

B *noun modifier* [*time*] méridien/-ienne

merit /ˈmerɪt/

A *n* (of idea) valeur *f*; (of person) mérite *m*; **to judge sb on their own** ∼**s/sth on its own** ∼**s** juger qn selon son mérite/qch selon ses qualités propres; **there's little** ∼ **in his work** son œuvre a peu de valeur; **certificate of** ∼ accessit *m*

B *vtr* mériter

merit: ∼ **award** *n* récompense *f* honorifique; ∼ **list** *n* tableau *m* d'honneur; ∼ **mark,** ∼ **point** *n* Sch bon point *m*

meritorious /ˌmerɪˈtɔːrɪəs/ *adj* méritoire

mermaid /ˈmɜːmeɪd/ *n* sirène *f*

merman /ˈmɜːmæn/ *n* (*pl* **-men**) triton *m*

merrily /ˈmerɪlɪ/ *adv* ① (happily) joyeusement; ② (unconcernedly) avec insouciance

merriment /ˈmerɪmənt/ *n* (fun) joie *f*; (laughter) hilarité *f*

merry /ˈmerɪ/ *adj* ① (happy) joyeux/-euse, gai; ∼ **Christmas!** joyeux Noël!; ② ○(tipsy) éméché; ③ ‡ *ou* hum (also **merrie**) ∼ **England** l'Angleterre du bon vieux temps; **the** ∼ **month of May** le joli mois de mai

(Idioms) **the more the merrier!** Prov plus on est de fous, plus on rit Prov; **to give sb** ∼ **hell**○ passer un bon savon à qn○; **to make** ∼ faire la noce

merry: ~**-go-round** n lit manège m; fig tourbillon m; ~**maker** n noceur/-euse° m/f

mesh /meʃ/
A n ① (of string) filet m; (of metal) grillage m; ② (net) mailles fpl; ③ Tech engrenure f; **in** ~ engrené
B vi ① (also ~ **together**) [branches] s'enchevêtrer; ② (also ~ **together**) [ideas] concorder; ③ **with** être en accord avec; ③ Tech [cogs] s'engrener; **to** ~ **with** s'emboîter dans

mesmerize /ˈmezməraɪz/
A vtr hypnotiser
B **mesmerized** pp adj fasciné, médusé

mess /mes/
A n ① (untidy or dirty state) désordre m; **what a** ~! quel désordre!, quelle pagaille°!; **to make a** ~ [person] mettre du désordre; **in a** ~ en désordre; **to tidy** ou **clear up the** ~ mettre de l'ordre; **this report is a** ~! ce rapport est fait n'importe comment!; **my hair is a** ~ je suis complètement décoiffée; **you look a** ~! GB, **you look like a** ~! US tu es dans un bel état!; **to make a** ~ **on the carpet** salir la moquette; ② fig (muddled state) **my life is a** ~ ma vie est un désastre; **to be in a terrible** ~ [economy] être dans une situation catastrophique; **to make a** ~ **of the job** massacrer° le travail; **how did we get into this** ~? comment a-t-on fait pour en arriver là?; **this is a fine** ~ **we're in** nous voilà dans de beaux draps!; ③ °(pitiful state) **his face was a** ~ il avait le visage amoché; **he's a** ~° (psychologically) il est dans un sale état; ④ (excrement) saletés fpl; **to make a** ~ [dog] faire ses saletés; **dog** ~° crotte° f de chien; ⑤ Mil cantine f; **officers'** ~ (in the army) mess m; (in the navy) carré m des officiers; ⑥ °US portion f
B °vi (meddle) **to** ~ **with** toucher à [drugs]; **don't** ~ **with him** évite-le

(Phrasal verbs)

■ **mess about**°, **mess around**°: ▸ ~ **around** ① (act the fool) faire l'imbécile; **to** ~ **around with** jouer avec [chemicals, matches]; toucher à [drugs]; ② (potter) **to** ~ **around in the garden** s'amuser dans le jardin; ③ (sexually) **he** ~**es around** c'est un coureur; ▸ ~ **[sb] around**° faire tourner qn en bourrique°

■ **mess up**°: ▸ ~ **up** US faire l'imbécile; ▸ ~ **[sth] up**, ~ **up [sth]** ① (muddle up) semer la pagaille dans [papers]; mettre du désordre dans [kitchen]; salir [napkin, sheets]; ② (ruin) bricoler [exam, work]; gâcher [chances]; ▸ ~ **[sb] up** [drugs, alcohol] détruire [person]; [experience] faire perdre les pédales° à qn

message /ˈmesɪdʒ/ n ① (communication) message m also Comput (**about** au sujet de); **a telephone** ~ un message téléphonique; **to send sb a** ~ **that** envoyer un message à qn pour lui dire que; **to receive a** ~ **that** recevoir un message selon lequel; ② (meaning) gen, Relig, Pol message m; **to get one's** ~ **across** (be understood) se faire comprendre; (convince people) faire passer son message; **to get the** ~° comprendre; **his** ~ **isn't getting through** son message ne passe pas

message box n Comput boîte f de dialogue

messaging /ˈmesɪdʒɪŋ/ n Comput messagerie f électronique

mess dress n Mil grand uniforme m

messenger /ˈmesɪndʒə(r)/ n gen messager/-ère m/f; (for hotel, company) garçon m de courses, coursier/-ière m/f

messenger boy ▸ p. 1181 n garçon m de courses, coursier m

messiah /mɪˈsaɪə/ n messie m; **the Messiah** le Messie

Messrs /ˈmesəz/ n (abrév écrite = **messieurs**) MM

messy /ˈmesɪ/ adj ① (untidy) [house] en désordre; [appearance] négligé; [handwriting] peu soigné; ② (dirty) [activity] salissant; **he's a** ~ **eater** il mange salement; ③ (confused) [lawsuit, business] sale [business]; pénible [business]

mestizo /meˈstiːzəʊ/ n (pl **-zoes** ou **-zos**) métis/métisse m/f (d'ascendants européen et amérindien)

met /met/ prét, pp ▸ **meet**

metabolic /ˌmetəˈbɒlɪk/ adj [disease, needs, stress] du métabolisme

metabolism /mɪˈtæbəlɪzəm/ n métabolisme m

metal /ˈmetl/
A n métal m
B noun modifier [coin, container] en métal

metal: ~ **detector** n détecteur m de métaux; ~ **fatigue** n fatigue f du métal

metallic /mɪˈtælɪk/ adj ① [substance] métallique; ② [paint, finish] métallisé; ③ (resembling metal) [sound, appearance] métallique; [taste] de métal

metallurgist /mɪˈtælədʒɪst, US ˈmetəlɜːrdʒɪst/ ▸ p. 1181 n métallurgiste m

metallurgy /mɪˈtælədʒɪ, US ˈmetəlɜːrdʒɪ/ n métallurgie f

metal: ~ **polish** n produit m à astiquer les métaux; ~ **work** n ferronnerie f

metamorphose /ˌmetəˈmɔːfəʊz/
A vtr métamorphoser (**into** en)
B vi se métamorphoser (**into** en)

metamorphosis /ˌmetəˈmɔːfəsɪs/ n (pl **-phoses**) métamorphose f (**into** en)

metaphor /ˈmetəfɔː(r)/ n métaphore f; **to mix one's** ~**s** faire des métaphores incohérentes

metaphoric(al) /ˌmetəˈfɒrɪk(l)/ adj métaphorique

metaphorically /ˌmetəˈfɒrɪklɪ/ adv métaphoriquement; ~ **speaking** pour employer une métaphore

metaphysical /ˌmetəˈfɪzɪkl/ adj ① Philos métaphysique; ② (abstract) abstrait

mete /miːt/ v
■ **mete out**: ▸ ~ **[sth] out**, ~ **out [sth]** infliger [punishment]; rendre [justice]

meteor /ˈmiːtɪə(r)/ n météore m

meteoric /ˌmiːtɪˈɒrɪk, US -ˈɔːr-/ adj lit météorique; fig [rise] fulgurant

meteorite /ˈmiːtɪəraɪt/ n météorite f

meteorological /ˌmiːtɪərəˈlɒdʒɪkl/ adj météorologique

Meteorological Office n: météorologie nationale britannique

meteorologist /ˌmiːtɪəˈrɒlədʒɪst/ ▸ p. 1181 n météorologue mf

meteorology /ˌmiːtɪəˈrɒlədʒɪ/ n météorologie f

meter /ˈmiːtə(r)/
A n ① (measuring device) compteur m; **gas** ~ compteur de gaz; **to read the** ~ relever le compteur; ② (also **parking** ~) parcmètre m; ③ US = **metre**
B vtr ① mesurer [electricity, gas, pressure]; ② affranchir [qch] à la machine [letter]

meter reader n releveur m de compteur

methane /ˈmiːθeɪn/ n méthane m

method /ˈmeθəd/ n ① (of teaching, contraception, training) méthode f (**for doing** pour faire); (of payment, treatment) mode m (**of** de); ~ **of transport** moyen m de transport; **production** ~**s** modes de production; ② (orderliness) méthode f; **a man of** ~ un homme méthodique

method: ~ **acting** n méthode f Stanislavski, jeu m 'Actor's Studio'; ~ **actor** n adepte mf de 'l'Actor's Studio'

methodical /mɪˈθɒdɪkl/ adj méthodique

Methodist /ˈmeθədɪst/ n, adj méthodiste (mf)

methodology /ˌmeθəˈdɒlədʒɪ/ n méthodologie f

methyl /ˈmeθɪl/ n méthyle m

methylated /ˈmeθəleɪtɪd/ adj méthylique

methylated spirit(s) n (+ v sg) alcool m à brûler

meticulous /mɪˈtɪkjʊləs/ adj méticuleux/-euse; ~ **about** méticuleux/-euse dans [work]; **to be** ~ **about doing** faire très attention à faire

métier /ˈmetɪeɪ/ n vocation f

Met Office n GB abrév ▸ **Meteorological Office**

metre /ˈmiːtə(r)/ ▸ p. 977 n ① GB (measurement) mètre m; ② Literat mètre m; ③ Mus mesure f

metric /ˈmetrɪk/ adj métrique; **to go** ~° adopter le système métrique

metricate /ˈmetrɪkeɪt/ vtr faire passer [qch] au système métrique

metrics /ˈmetrɪks/ n (+ v sg) métrique f

metronome /ˈmetrənəʊm/ n métronome m

metropolis /məˈtrɒpəlɪs/ n métropole f

metropolitan /ˌmetrəˈpɒlɪtən/ adj ① (of city) [area, population] urbain; [buildings, traffic, values] des grandes villes; ~ **New York** l'agglomération de New York; ② (home territory) ~ **France** la France métropolitaine; ③ Relig métropolitain

metropolitan: ~ **district** n GB Admin circonscription f administrative (d'une conurbation); **Metropolitan**

police *n* GB police *f* de Londres

mettle /'metl/ *n* courage *m*; **to be on one's** ∼ être sur la sellette; **to put sb on his** ∼ amener qn à montrer de quoi il est capable

mew /mju:/
A *n* ① (of cat) miaulement *m*; ② (seagull) mouette *f*
B *vi* miauler

mews /mju:z/ *n* GB ① (+ *v sg*) (street) ruelle *f*; (yard) cour *f*; ② (+ *v pl*) (stables) écuries *fpl*

Mexican /'meksɪkən/ ▸ p. 1032
A *n* (person) Mexicain/-e *m/f*
B *adj* mexicain

Mexican: ∼ **jumping bean** *n* pois *m* sauteur; ∼ **stand off** *n* US impasse *f*; ∼ **wave** *n* ola *f* (*mouvement de vague engendré par les spectateurs qui se lèvent successivement autour du terrain*)

Mexico /'meksɪkəʊ/ ▸ p. 774 *pr n* Mexique *m*

Mexico City ▸ p. 1276 *pr n* Mexico

mezzanine /'mezəni:n/ *n* ① gen mezzanine *f*; ② Theat US corbeille *f*; GB premier dessous *m*

MF *n* (*abrév* = **medium frequency**) FM *f*

Mgr (*abrév écrite* = **Monseigneur, Monsignor**) Mgr

mi /mi:/ *n* mi *m*

MI US Post *abrév écrite* = **Michigan**

MI5 *n* (*abrév* = **Military Intelligence Section Five**) service *m* britannique de contre-espionnage

MI6 *n* (*abrév* = **Military Intelligence Section Six**) service *m* britannique de surveillance du territoire; *cf* DST

miaow /mi:'aʊ/
A *n* miaou *m*
B *vi* miauler

miasma /mɪ'æzmə/ *n* miasmes *mpl*

mice /maɪs/ *pl* ▸ **mouse**

Michaelmas /'mɪklməs/ *pr n* la Saint-Michel

Michaelmas: ∼ **daisy** *n* GB aster *m*; ∼ **Term** *n* GB Univ premier trimestre *m*

Michelangelo /ˌmaɪkəl'ændʒələʊ/ *pr n* Michel-Ange

mickey /'mɪkɪ/ *n* GB

(Idioms) **are you taking the** ∼ **out of me?** tu te paies ma tête?

micro /'maɪkrəʊ/
A *n* Comput micro *m*
B **micro +** *combining form* micro-

microbe /'maɪkrəʊb/ *n* microbe *m*

microchip /'maɪkrəʊtʃɪp/
A *n* puce *f*, circuit *m* intégré
B *noun modifier* [*industry, technology*] du circuit intégré; [*factory*] de circuits intégrés

microcomputing /ˌmaɪkrəʊkəm'pju:tɪŋ/ *n* micro-informatique *f*

microcosm /'maɪkrəkɒzəm/ *n* microcosme *m*

microfibre GB, **microfiber** US /'maɪkrəʊˌfaɪbə(r)/ *n* Tex microfibre *f*

microfilm /'maɪkrəʊfɪlm/
A *n* microfilm *m*
B *vtr* microfilmer

microlighting /'maɪkrəˌlaɪtɪŋ/ ▸ p. 881 *n* ULM *m*, ultra léger *m* motorisé

micromesh /'maɪkrəʊmeʃ/ *adj* ∼ **tights** GB, ∼ **pantyhose** US collant *m* mousse

microphone /'maɪkrəfəʊn/ *n* microphone *m*

microphysics /'maɪkrəʊfɪzɪks/ *n* (+ *v sg*) microphysique *f*

microprocessing /ˌmaɪkrəʊ'prəʊsesɪŋ/ *n* micro-informatique *f*

microscope /'maɪkrəskəʊp/ *n* microscope *m*; **under the** ∼ lit, fig au microscope

microscopic /ˌmaɪkrə'skɒpɪk/ *adj* ① (minute) microscopique; ② (using a microscope) au microscope

microsurgery /ˌmaɪkrəʊ'sɜ:dʒərɪ/ *n* microchirurgie *f*

microsurgical /ˌmaɪkrəʊ'sɜ:dʒɪkl/ *adj* [*technique, procedure*] de microchirurgie; [*specialist, knowledge*] en microchirurgie

microwave /'maɪkrəweɪv/
A *n* ① (wave) micro-onde *f*; ② (oven) four *m* à micro-ondes

B *noun modifier* [*transmitter*] à micro-ondes; [*cookery*] au four à micro-ondes
C *vtr* passer [qch] au four à micro-ondes

microwaveable /'maɪkrəweɪvəbl/ *adj* [*food*] micro-ondable, qui peut être cuit au four à micro-ondes; [*container*] pour four à micro-ondes

mid+ /mɪd/ *combining form* **in the** ∼**-20th century** au milieu du vingtième siècle; ∼**-afternoon** milieu *m* de l'après-midi; **(in)** ∼**-May** (à la) mi-mai; **he's in his** ∼**-forties** il a environ quarante-cinq ans

midair /ˌmɪd'eə(r)/
A *adj* [*collision*] en plein vol
B **in midair** *adv phr* (in mid-flight) en plein vol; (in the air) en l'air; **to leave sth in** ∼ fig laisser qch en suspens

midday /ˌmɪd'deɪ/ ▸ p. 745
A *n* midi *m*
B *noun modifier* [*sun, meal*] de midi

middle /'mɪdl/
A *n* ① milieu *m*; **in the** ∼ **of** au milieu de; **to be caught in the** ∼ être pris entre deux feux; **I was in the** ∼ **of a book when...** j'étais plongé dans un livre quand...; **in the** ∼ **of May** à la mi-mai; **right in the** ∼ **of** en plein milieu de; **to be in the** ∼ **of doing** être en train de faire; **to split [sth] down the** ∼ partager [qch] en deux [*bill, work*]; diviser [qch] en deux [*group, opinion*]; ② °(waist) taille *f*
B *adj* [*door, shelf*] du milieu; [*price*] modéré; [*size, difficulty*] moyen/-enne; **in** ∼ **life** au milieu de ma/ta etc vie; **to be in one's** ∼ **thirties** GB avoir environ 35 ans; **there must be a** ∼ **course** *ou* **way** il doit y avoir un juste milieu; **to steer** *ou* **take** *ou* **follow a** ∼ **course** adopter une position intermédiaire

(Idiom) **in the** ∼ **of nowhere** dans un trou perdu

middle: ∼ **age** *n* âge *m* mûr; ∼**-aged** *adj* [*person*] d'âge mûr; fig [*outlook, view*] vieux jeu *inv*

Middle Ages *n* **the** ∼ le Moyen Âge; **the early/late** ∼ le bas/haut Moyen Âge

middle: ∼**-age spread** *n* embonpoint *m* dû à l'âge; **Middle America** *n* (social group) *Américains aisés et aux idées conservatrices*; ∼**brow** *adj* [*book, person*] sans prétentions intellectuelles

middle class
A *n* classe *f* moyenne
B **middle-class** *adj* [*person*] de la classe moyenne; [*attitude, view*] bourgeois

middle distance
A *n* ① Art, Phot, Cin second plan *m*; ② gen **in the** ∼ au loin; **to gaze into the** ∼ regarder dans le vague
B **middle-distance** *adj* Sport [*event, athlete*] de demi-fond

Middle East
A *pr n* Moyen-Orient *m*
B *noun modifier* [*affairs*] du Moyen-Orient; [*talks*] sur le Moyen-Orient

middle-eastern: *adj* [*nation, politics*] du Moyen-Orient

Middle England *n* classes *fpl* moyennes de province

> ⓘ **Middle England** Par cette expression, on désigne au Royaume-Uni les classes moyennes qui forment la plus grande partie de l'électorat et dont tous les partis cherchent à gagner les voix. On parle aussi de *middle-income Britain*.

middle: **Middle English** *n* moyen anglais *m*; ∼ **finger** ▸ p. 698 *n* majeur *m*

middle ground *n* gen juste milieu *m*; (in argument) terrain *m* d'entente; Pol **the** ∼ les modérés *mpl*

middle: ∼**-income** *adj* [*person, family, country*] aux revenus moyens; ∼**man** *n* gen, Comm intermédiaire *m*; ∼ **manager** *n* cadre *m* moyen; ∼**-of-the-road** *adj* (banal) très ordinaire; (with wide appeal) populaire; [*policy*] gen modéré; péj tiède; ∼**-ranking** *adj* d'un rang intermédiaire; ∼ **school** *n* GB école pour élèves entre 9 et 13 ans; US école pour élèves entre 12 et 14 ans; ∼**-size(d)** *adj* de taille moyenne; ∼**weight** *n* poids *m* moyen

middling /'mɪdlɪŋ/ *adj* [*ability*] moyen/-enne

(Idiom) **fair to** ∼ pas trop mal

Middx GB Post *abrév écrite* = **Middlesex**

midfield /ˌmɪd'fi:ld/ *n* milieu *m* du terrain

mid-flight /ˌmɪd'flaɪt/
A *adj* en plein vol
B **in mid-flight** *adv phr* en plein vol

m

might¹

Although usage shows that *may* and *might* are interchangeable in many contexts, *might* indicates a more remote possibility than *may*. French generally translates this element of possibility using *peut-être* with the appropriate verb tense:

it might snow
= il va peut-être neiger

(It is also possible to translate this more formally using *il se peut* + subjunctive: *il se peut qu'il neige*). For particular examples see **might¹ 1**.

It is possible to translate *might* differently depending on the nature of the context and the speaker's point of view:

he might not come
= il risque de ne pas venir

implies that this is not a desirable outcome for the speaker;

he might not come
= il pourrait ne pas venir *or* il se peut qu'il ne vienne pas

however, is neutral in tone. Where there is the idea of a possibility in the past which has not in fact occurred (see **might¹ 2**), French uses the past conditional of the verb (which is often *pouvoir*):

it might have been serious (but wasn't in fact)
= ça aurait pu être grave

This is also the case where something which could have taken place did not, thus causing annoyance:

you might have said thanks!
= tu aurais pu dire merci! (see **might¹ 7**).

Might, as the past tense of *may*, will automatically occur in instances of reported speech:

he said you might be hurt
= il a dit que tu serais peut-être blessé

For more examples see the entry **might¹** and bear in mind the rules for the agreement of tenses.

Where there is a choice between *may* and *might* in making requests, *might* is more formal and even rather dated. French uses inversion (*je peux* = *puis-je?*) in this context and *puis-je me permettre de ... ?* (= *might I ... ?*) is extremely formal.

Might can be used to polite effect – to soften direct statements: *you might imagine that ...* or to offer advice tactfully: *it might be wise to ...* In both cases, French uses the conditional tense of the verb: *on pourrait penser que ...* ; *ce serait peut-être une bonne idée de ...* The use of *well* in phrases such as *he might well be right* etc. implies a greater degree of likelihood.

For translations of *might well*, *may well*, see **B 2** in the entry **well¹**.

For translations of the phrase *might as well* (*we might as well go home*), see **well¹ B 2**.

---

midge /mɪdʒ/ *n* moucheron *m*
midget /'mɪdʒɪt/
A *n* nain/-e *m/f*
B *adj* miniature; **∼ submarine** Mil sous-marin *m* de poche
Midlands /'mɪdləndz/ *pr n* (+ *v sg*) **the ∼s** la région *f* des Midlands (*au centre de l'Angleterre*)
midlife /'mɪdlaɪf/
A *n* âge *m* mûr
B *noun modifier* [*crisis, problems*] de la cinquantaine
midnight /'mɪdnaɪt/ ▸ p. 745 *n* minuit *m*
⟨Idiom⟩ **to burn the ∼ oil** travailler jusqu'à l'aube
mid-range /,mɪd'reɪndʒ/
A *n* **to be in the ∼** [*product, hotel*] être en milieu de gamme
B *noun modifier* [*car, hotel*] de milieu de gamme
midriff /'mɪdrɪf/ *n* ventre *m*
mid-season /,mɪd'siːzn/ *adj* de milieu de saison
midshipman /'mɪdʃɪpmən/ *n* (*pl* **-men**) **1** GB (officer) aspirant *m* (*de la Marine*); **2** US (trainee) élève *m* de l'École navale
midst /mɪdst/ *n* **in the ∼ of** au beau milieu de; **in the ∼ of change/war** en plein changement/pleine guerre; **in our ∼** parmi nous
midstream /,mɪd'striːm/: **in midstream** *adv phr* (in river) au milieu du courant; fig (in speech) en plein milieu d'une phrase
midsummer /,mɪd'sʌmə(r)/
A *n* (high summer) milieu *m* de l'été; (solstice) solstice *m* d'été
B *noun modifier* [*heat, days*] de plein été
Midsummer('s) Day *n* la Saint-Jean
midterm /,mɪd'tɜːm/
A *n* **in ∼** Pol au milieu de son/leur etc mandat; Sch au milieu du trimestre; (of pregnancy) au milieu de ma/sa etc grossesse
B *noun modifier* Pol [*crisis, reshuffle*] de milieu de mandat; Sch [*report, test*] de milieu de trimestre
midtown /'mɪdtaʊn/ *n* US centre-ville *m*
midway /,mɪd'weɪ/
A *n* US attractions *fpl* foraines
B *adj* [*post, position*] de mi-course; [*stage, point*] de mi-parcours
C *adv* **∼ between/along** à mi-chemin entre/le long de; **∼ through** au milieu de

midweek /,mɪd'wiːk/
A *adj* de milieu de semaine
B *adv* en milieu de semaine
midwife /'mɪdwaɪf/ ▸ p. 1181 *n* (*pl* **-wives**) sage-femme *f*; **male ∼** homme *m* sage-femme
midwifery /'mɪdwɪfərɪ, US -waɪf-/ *n* profession *f* de sage-femme
midwinter /,mɪd'wɪntə(r)/
A *n* **1** (season) milieu *m* de l'hiver; **2** (solstice) solstice *m* d'hiver
B *noun modifier* [*day, weather*] de plein hiver
miffed○ /mɪft/ *adj* **to be** *ou* **feel ∼** être vexé
might¹ /maɪt/ *modal aux* (*nég* **might not, mightn't**) **1** (indicating possibility) **she ∼ be right** elle a peut-être raison; **they ∼ not go** peut-être qu'ils n'iront pas; **'will you come?'—'I ∼'** 'tu viendras?'—'peut-être'; **you ∼ finish the painting before tonight** il se peut que tu finisses de peindre avant ce soir; **they ∼ have got lost** ils se sont peut-être perdus; **you ∼ have guessed that...** vous aurez peut-être deviné que...; **the plane ∼ have landed by now** il se peut que l'avion ait déjà atterri; **I ∼ (well) lose my job** je risque de perdre mon travail; **it ∼ well improve the standard** ça pourrait bien améliorer le niveau; **try as I ∼, I can't do it** j'ai beau essayer, je n'y arrive pas; **however unlikely that ∼ be** si improbable que cela puisse paraître; **2** (indicating unrealized possibility) **I ∼ have been killed!** j'aurais pu être tué!; **he was thinking about what ∼ have been** il pensait à ce qui se serait passé si les choses avaient été différentes; **if they had acted quickly he ∼ well be alive** s'ils avaient agi plus vite il serait peut-être encore en vie; **3** (*prét de* **may**) (in sequence of tenses, in reported speech) **I said I ∼ go into town** j'ai dit que j'irais en ville; **I thought it ∼ rain** j'ai pensé qu'il risquait de pleuvoir; **she asked if she ∼ leave** elle demanda si elle pouvait partir; **4** sout (when making requests) **∼ I make a suggestion?** puis-je me permettre de faire une suggestion?; **∼ I ask who's calling?** c'est de la part de qui s'il vous plaît?; **and who, ∼ I ask, are you?** et qui, sout; **and who ∼ you be?** (aggressive) on peut savoir qui vous êtes?; **5** (when making suggestions) **it ∼ be a good idea to do** ce serait peut-être une bonne idée de faire; **you ∼ try making some enquiries** tu devrais essayer de te renseigner; **we ∼ go out for a meal later** nous pourrions aller manger au restaurant plus tard; **you ∼ like to drop in later** tu veux peut-être passer plus tard; **6** (when

making statement, argument) one ∼ argue *ou* it ∼ be argued that on pourrait dire *or* faire valoir que; **as you** *ou* **one** ∼ **expect** comme de bien entendu; **as you** ∼ **imagine** comme vous pouvez le deviner; **7** (expressing reproach, irritation) **I** ∼ **have known** *ou* **guessed!** j'aurais dû m'en douter!; **he** ∼ **at least apologize!** il pourrait au moins s'excuser!; **you** ∼ **have warned me!** tu aurais pu me prévenir!; **8** (in concessives) **they** ∼ **not be fast but they're reliable** ils ne sont peut-être pas rapides mais on peut au moins compter sur eux; ▸ **well¹** B 2

might² /maɪt/ n **1** (power) puissance *f*; **2** (physical strength) force *f*; **with all his** ∼ de toutes ses forces

mightn't /ˈmaɪtnt/ = might not

mighty /ˈmaɪtɪ/

A *n* **the** ∼ les puissants

B *adj* **1** (powerful) puissant; **2** (large) imposant; **3** ○(huge, terrific) énorme

C ○*adv* (emphatic) vachement○, très

(Idioms) **how are the** ∼ **fallen!** comme tombent les puissants!; **high and** ∼ hautain

migrant /ˈmaɪgrənt/

A *n* (person) migrant/-e *m/f*; (bird) oiseau *m* migrateur; (animal) animal *m* migrateur

B *adj* [*labour*] saisonnier/-ière; [*bird, animal*] migrateur/-trice

migrate /maɪˈgreɪt, US ˈmaɪgreɪt/ *vi* **1** [*person*] émigrer; **2** [*bird, animal*] migrer

migration /maɪˈgreɪʃn/ *n* migration *f*

migratory /ˈmaɪgrətrɪ, maɪˈgreɪtərɪ, US ˈmaɪgrətɔːrɪ/ *adj* [*animal*] migrateur/-trice; [*journey, behaviour*] migratoire

mike○ /maɪk/ *n* (microphone) micro○ *m*

mild /maɪld/

A *n* GB (*also* ∼ **ale**) bière *f* anglaise brune (légère)

B *adj* **1** (moderate) [*amusement, surprise*] léger/-ère; [*interest, irritation*] modéré; **2** (not cold) [*weather, winter*] doux/douce; [*climate*] tempéré; **a** ∼ **spell** une période de beau temps; **3** (in flavour) [*beer, taste, tobacco*] léger/-ère; [*cheese*] doux/douce; [*curry*] peu épicé; **4** [*soap, detergent, cream*] doux/douce; **5** [*case, infection*] bénin/-igne; [*attack, sedative*] léger/-ère; **a** ∼ **heart attack** une petite crise cardiaque; **6** (gentle) [*person, voice*] doux/douce

mildew /ˈmɪldjuː, US -duː/ *n* **1** (on plant) mildiou *m*; **2** (mould) moisissure *f*

mildly /ˈmaɪldlɪ/ *adv* **1** (moderately) légèrement; **to put it** ∼ pour dire les choses avec modération; **that's putting it** ∼ c'est un euphémisme; **2** (gently) [*speak*] avec douceur; [*rebuke*] légèrement

mildness /ˈmaɪldnɪs/ *n* (of weather, product) douceur *f*; (of taste) légèreté *f*; (of protest) modération *f*

mile /maɪl/ ▸ p. 977, p. 1116

A *n* **1** lit mile *m* (= 1609 mètres); **it's 50** ∼**s away** ≈ c'est à 80 kilomètres d'ici; **2** fig **to walk for** ∼**s** marcher pendant des kilomètres; **it's** ∼**s away!** c'est au bout du monde; **to be** ∼**s away** (daydreaming) être complètement ailleurs; ∼**s from anywhere** loin de tout; **not a million** ∼**s from here** pas très loin d'ici; **you could smell it a** ∼ **off** on pouvait le sentir à cent lieues à la ronde; **to stand out a** ∼ sauter aux yeux; **I'd run a** ∼ je prendrais mes jambes à mon cou

B ○**miles** *npl* (as intensifier) beaucoup; ∼**s better** bien meilleur; **to be** ∼**s out** [*estimate, figure*] être complètement faux; [*person*] être très loin du compte

(Idiom) **a miss is as good as a** ∼ Prov rater, même de peu, c'est rater

mileage /ˈmaɪlɪdʒ/ *n* **1** nombre *m* de miles; **what's the** ∼ **for the trip?** ≈ combien de kilomètres fait l'ensemble du voyage?; **2** (done by car) kilométrage *m*; **3** (miles per gallon) consommation *f*; **4** fig (use) **he's had plenty of** ∼ **out of that coat** ce manteau lui a beaucoup servi; **the press got maximum** ∼ **out of the story** la presse a exploité l'histoire au maximum; **5** = **mileage allowance**

mileage: ∼ **allowance** *n* ≈ indemnité *f* kilométrique; ∼ **indicator** *n* ≈ compteur *m* kilométrique; ∼ **post** *n* borne *f* (milliaire)

milestone /ˈmaɪlstəʊn/ *n* **1** lit borne *f* (milliaire); **2** fig étape *f* importante

militant /ˈmɪlɪtənt/

A *n* (activist) agitateur/-trice *m/f*; (armed) partisan/-e *m/f* de la lutte armée

B *adj* militant

militarism /ˈmɪlɪtərɪzəm/ *n* péj militarisme *m*

militarize /ˈmɪlɪtəraɪz/ *vtr* militariser; ∼**d zone** zone *f* militarisée

military /ˈmɪlɪtrɪ, US -terɪ/

A *n* **the** ∼ (army) l'armée *f*; (soldiers) les militaires *mpl*

B *adj* militaire

military: ∼ **academy** *n* école *f* militaire; ∼ **policeman**, **MP** *n* membre *m* de la police militaire

military service *n* service *m* militaire; **to be called up for** ∼ être appelé sous les drapeaux

militate /ˈmɪlɪteɪt/ *vi* **to** ∼ **against sth** compromettre qch; **to** ∼ **for** militer en faveur de

militia /mɪˈlɪʃə/ *n* **1** (citizen army) milice *f*; **2** US (liable for draft) **the** ∼ la réserve

milk /mɪlk/

A *n* lait *m*; **baby** ∼ lait *m* pour bébé; **condensed** ∼ lait concentré sucré; **powdered/evaporated** ∼ lait en poudre/concentré; **full cream** ∼ lait entier; **long-life** ∼ lait longue conservation; **skimmed** ∼ lait écrémé; **breast** ∼ lait maternel; **cleansing** ∼ lait démaquillant

B *vtr* **1** (milk) traire; **2** fig (exploit) (for money) pomper (**for** de); **to** ∼ **sb dry** saigner qn à blanc

C *vi* [*cow, goat*] donner du lait; [*farmer*] faire la traite

(Idiom) **it's no good crying over spilt** ∼ Prov il est trop tard pour pleurer

milk: ∼**-and-water** *adj* insipide; ∼ **chocolate** *n* chocolat *m* au lait; ∼ **diet** *n* régime *m* lacté; ∼ **float** *n* GB camionnette *f* de laitier; ∼ **jug** *n* pot *m* à lait; ∼**man** ▸ p. 1181 *n* laitier *m*; ∼ **products** *npl* produits *mpl* laitiers; ∼ **pudding** *n* dessert *m* à base de lait; ∼ **run** *n* Aviat vol *m* de routine; ∼ **tooth** *n* dent *f* de lait; ∼ **train** *n* premier train *m* du matin; ∼ **truck** *n* US camionnette *f* de laitier

milky /ˈmɪlkɪ/ *adj* **1** (containing milk) [*drink*] au lait; [*diet*] lacté; **2** [*skin, liquid, colour*] laiteux/-euse

Milky Way *pr n* Voie *f* lactée

mill /mɪl/

A *n* **1** (building) (for flour) moulin *m*; **water** ∼ moulin à eau; **2** (factory) fabrique *f*; **steel** ∼ aciérie *f*; **3** (for pepper) moulin *m*; **4** fig (routine) routine *f* ardue; **5** US fig usine *f*; **diploma** ∼ usine à diplômes

B *vtr* moudre [*flour, pepper*]; fabriquer [*steel*]; broyer [*paper*]; filer [*cotton*]; tisser [*textiles*]; moleter [*screw*]; fraiser [*nut, bolt*]; denteler [*coin*]

(Idioms) **there'll be trouble at t'mill**○ hum on va avoir des ennuis; **to go through the** ∼ en voir de toutes les couleurs○; **to put sb through the** ∼ mettre qn à rude épreuve

(Phrasal verb)

■ **mill around**, **mill about** grouiller

millennium /mɪˈlenɪəm/ *n* (*pl* **-niums** *ou* **-nia**) **1** millénaire *m*; **2** Relig, fig millénium *m*

miller /ˈmɪlə(r)/ ▸ p. 1181 *n* **1** (person) Agric meunier/-ière *m/f*; Ind fraiseur/-euse *m/f*; **2** (machine) fraiseuse *f*

millet /ˈmɪlɪt/ *n* **1** (grass) (European) millet *m* des roseaux; (Indian) millet *m* commun; **2** (seed) millet *m*

milligram(me) /ˈmɪlɪgræm/ ▸ p. 1323 *n* milligramme *m*

millimetre GB, **millimeter** US /ˈmɪlɪmiːtə(r)/ ▸ p. 977 *n* millimètre *m*

milliner /ˈmɪlɪnə(r)/ ▸ p. 1181 *n* modiste *f*

milling /ˈmɪlɪŋ/

A *n* (of corn) mouture *f*; (of paper) broyage *m*; (of cloth) tissage *m*; (of metal) fraisage *m*; (on coin) dentelage *m*

B *adj* [*crowd*] grouillant

million /ˈmɪljən/ ▸ p. 1044

A *n* million *m*; **thanks a** ∼○! merci mille fois!; iron merci quand même○!; **to have** ∼**s** être riche à millions

B **millions** *npl* des millions (**of** de); **the starving** ∼**s** les masses *fpl* affamées

C *adj* **a** ∼ **people/pounds** un million de personnes/de livres

(Idioms) **to feel like a** ∼ **dollars**○ se sentir des ailes; **to look like a** ∼ **dollars**○ être superbe; **to be one in a** ∼○ être un oiseau rare○; **a chance in a** ∼○ (slim) une chance sur un million; (exceptional) une chance unique

millipede /ˈmɪlɪpiːd/ *n* mille-pattes *m inv*

m

mill pond n bassin m de retenue (d'un moulin)

millstone /'mɪlstəʊn/ n meule f

(Idiom) **to be a ~ round one's neck** être un boulet au pied

mill: **~stream** n bief m de moulin; **~wheel** n roue f de moulin

milometer /maɪ'lɒmɪtə(r)/ n GB ≈ compteur m kilométrique; **to turn back the ~** trafiquer le compteur

mime /maɪm/

A n ⒈ (art) mime m; ⒉ (performance) pantomime f; ⒊ (performer) mime mf

B vtr, vi mimer

mime artist ▸ p. 1181 n mime mf

mimic /'mɪmɪk/

A n imitateur/-trice m/f

B vtr (p prés etc -ck-) ⒈ gen imiter; (to ridicule) parodier; ⒉ (simulate) simuler; Zool imiter [colouring]; ⒊ péj (copy) singer péj

mimicry /'mɪmɪkrɪ/ n gen imitation f; Zool mimétisme m

mince /mɪns/

A n GB Culin viande f hachée; **beef ~** bœuf m haché

B vtr hacher [meat]

C vi péj (walk) marcher en se trémoussant

(Idiom) **not to ~ matters** ou **one's words** ne pas mâcher ses mots

mincemeat /'mɪnsmiːt/ n GB Culin garniture composée de fruits secs et d'épices

(Idiom) **to make ~ of sb** ne faire qu'une bouchée de qn

mince pie n: tartelette garnie d'une pâte de fruits secs

mincer /'mɪnsə(r)/ n hachoir m; **to put sth through the ~** passer qch au hachoir

mincing /'mɪnsɪŋ/ adj affecté

mind /maɪnd/

A n ⒈ (centre of thought, feelings) esprit m; **peace of ~** tranquillité d'esprit; **it's all in the ~** c'est tout dans la tête○; **to cross sb's ~** venir à l'esprit de qn; **at the back of my ~ I had my doubts** au fond de moi j'avais des doutes; **that's a load ou weight off my ~** ça me soulage beaucoup; **to feel easy in one's ~ about sth** se sentir rassuré quant à qch; **to have something on one's ~** être préoccupé; **to set sb's ~ at rest** rassurer qn; **nothing could be further from my ~** loin de moi cette pensée; ⒉ (brain) intelligence f; **with the ~ of a two-year-old** avec l'intelligence d'un enfant de deux ans; **to have a very good ~** être très intelligent; **he has a fine legal ~** c'est un brillant juriste; **it's a case of ~ over matter** c'est la victoire de l'esprit sur la matière; ⒊ (way of thinking) esprit m; **to have a logical ~** avoir l'esprit logique; **the criminal ~** l'esprit criminel; ⒋ (opinion) avis m; **to be of one ~** être du même avis; **to my ~** à mon avis; **to make up one's ~ about/to do** se décider à propos de/à faire; **my ~'s made up** je suis décidé; **to change one's ~ about sth** changer d'avis sur qch; **to keep an open ~ about sth** ne pas avoir de préjugés sur qch; **to know one's own ~** avoir des idées bien à soi; **to speak one's ~** dire ce qu'on a à dire; ⒌ (attention) esprit m; **to concentrate ou keep one's ~ on sth** se concentrer sur; **to give ou put one's ~ to sth** accorder son attention à qch; **to take sb's ~ off sth** distraire qn de qch; ⒍ (memory) esprit m; **I can't get him out of my ~** je n'arrive pas à l'oublier; **try to put it out of your ~** essaie de ne plus y penser; **my ~'s a blank** j'ai un trou de mémoire; **it went right ou clean ou completely out of my ~** cela m'est complètement sorti de la tête; **to bring sth to ~** rappeler qch; ⒎ (sanity) raison f; **his ~ is going** il n'a plus toute sa raison; **are you out of your ~**○? tu es fou/folle○?; ⒏ (person as intellectual) esprit m

B in mind adv phr **I bought it with you in ~** je l'ai acheté en pensant à toi; **I have something in ~ for this evening** j'ai une idée pour ce soir; **with the future in ~** en prévision de l'avenir; **with this in ~,...** avec cette idée en tête,...; **to have it in ~ to do sth** avoir l'intention de faire qch; **to put sb in ~ of sb/sth** rappeler qn/qch à qn

C vtr ⒈ (pay attention to) faire attention à [hazard]; surveiller [manners, language]; **don't ~ me** gen ne faites pas attention à moi; iron ne vous gênez pas!; **~ how you go** GB faites bien attention à vous; **it's a secret, ~**○ c'est un secret, n'oublie pas; **~ you**○, it won't be easy remarque, ce ne sera pas facile; ⒉ (object to) **I don't ~ the cold** le froid ne me dérange pas; **I don't ~ cats, but I prefer dogs** je n'ai rien contre les chats, mais je préfère les chiens; **'today or tomorrow?'—'I don't ~'** 'aujourd'hui ou demain?'—'ça m'est égal'; **will they ~ us being late?** est-ce qu'ils seront

fâchés si nous sommes en retard?; **would you ~ keeping my seat for me?** est-ce que ça vous ennuierait de garder ma place?; **if you don't ~ my asking...** si ce n'est pas une question indiscrète...; **'like a cigarette?'—'don't ~ if I do'**○ 'une cigarette?'—'c'est pas de refus'○; **I wouldn't ~ a glass of wine** je prendrais volontiers un verre de vin; **if you don't ~** si cela ne vous fait rien also iron; ⒊ (care) se soucier de; **do you ~!** iron non mais!; **never ~** (don't worry) ne t'en fais pas; (it doesn't matter) peu importe; **he can't afford an apartment, never ~ a big house** il ne peut pas se permettre un appartement encore moins une grande maison; ⒋ (look after) s'occuper de [animal, children]; tenir [shop]

(Idioms) **great ~s think alike** les grands esprits se rencontrent; **to read sb's ~** lire dans les pensées de qn; **if you've a ~ to** si le cœur vous en dit; **to see sth in one's ~'s eye** imaginer qch; **to have a good ~ ou half a ~ to do** GB avoir bien envie de faire; **to have a ~ of one's own** savoir ce qu'on veut

(Phrasal verb)

■ **mind out** faire attention; **~ out of the way**○! dégage○!

mind: **~-bending** adj [drug] psychotrope; [problem] très complexe; **~-blowing**○ adj époustouflant○; **~-boggling**○ adj stupéfiant

minded /'maɪndɪd/

A adj sout **if you're so ~** si ça vous dit

B -minded combining form ⒈ (with certain talent) **to be mechanically-/business-~** avoir le sens de la mécanique/ des affaires; ⒉ (with certain attitude) **to be small-/open-~** avoir l'esprit étroit/ouvert; ⒊ (with certain trait) **to be feeble-~** être simplet/-ette

minder /'maɪndə(r)/ n GB ⒈ ○(bodyguard) garde m du corps; ⒉ (also **child ~**) nourrice f

mindful /'maɪndfl/ adj **~ of** soucieux/-ieuse de

mindless /'maɪndlɪs/ adj péj (stupid) [person, programme] bête; [work] abrutissant; [vandalism] gratuit; [task] machinal

mindreader /'maɪndriːdə(r)/ n télépathe mf; **you must be a ~** hum mais tu lis dans mes pensées

mine¹ /maɪn/

> ⚠ In French, pronouns reflect the gender and number of the noun they are standing for. So mine is translated by le mien, la mienne, les miens, les miennes, according to what is being referred to: the blue car is mine = la voiture bleue est la mienne; his children are older than mine = ses enfants sont plus âgés que les miens.
> For examples and particular usages, see the entry below.

pron **his car is red but ~ is blue** sa voiture est rouge mais la mienne est bleue; **which (glass) is ~?** lequel (de ces verres) est le mien?; **~'s a whisky**○ un whisky pour moi; **she's a friend of ~** c'est une amie à moi; **it's not ~** ce n'est pas à moi; **that brother of ~** gen mon frère; péj mon imbécile de frère○

mine² /maɪn/

A n ⒈ lit, fig mine f; **to work in ou down the ~s** travailler dans les mines; **to have a ~ of experience to draw on** pouvoir s'appuyer sur son expérience; **a ~ of information** une mine de renseignements; ⒉ (explosive) mine f; **to lay a ~** (on land) poser une mine; (in sea) mouiller une mine

B vtr ⒈ extraire [gems, mineral]; exploiter [area]; ⒉ Mil miner [area]

C vi exploiter un gisement; **to ~ for** extraire [gems, mineral]

minefield /'maɪnfiːld/ n lit champ m de mines; fig terrain m miné; **a political ~** une poudrière politique

miner /'maɪnə(r)/ ▸ p. 1181 n mineur m

mineral /'mɪnərəl/

A n ⒈ (substance, class) minéral m; (for extraction) minerai m; ⒉ GB (drink) eau f minérale

B adj gen minéral; **~ ore** minerai m

mineralogy /ˌmɪnəˈrælədʒɪ/ n minéralogie f

mineral: **~ oil** n pétrole m; US (paraffin) huile f minérale; **~ rights** npl concession f d'exploitation minière; **~ water** n eau f minérale

mine maɪn: **~sweeper** n dragueur m de mines; **~worker** ▸ p. 1181 n mineur m

mingle /ˈmɪŋgl/
A vtr mêler [quality, feeling] (**with** à); mélanger [sand, colour, taste] (**with** avec)
B vi **1** to ~ **with** se mêler à [crowd, guests]; fréquenter [social group]; **2** [sounds] se confondre (**with** à); [smells, feelings] se mêler (**with** à)

mini /ˈmɪnɪ/
A n mini-jupe f
B mini+ combining form mini-

miniature /ˈmɪnətʃə(r), US ˈmɪnɪətʃʊər/
A n (all contexts) miniature f
B adj gen miniature; [breed, dog, horse] nain

miniature: ~ **golf** ▸ p. 881 n mini-golf m; ~ **railway** n petit train m

minibudget /ˌmɪnɪˈbʌdʒɪt/ n GB Pol budget m provisoire

minicab /ˈmɪnɪkæb/ n GB taxi m (non agréé)

minicourse /ˈmɪnɪkɔːs/ n US Univ stage m

minidisc /ˈmɪnɪdɪsk/ n minidisque m

minim /ˈmɪnɪm/ n **1** Mus GB blanche f; **2** (liquid measure) goutte f

minima /ˈmɪnɪmə/ pl ▸ **minimum**

minimal /ˈmɪnɪml/ adj **1** (very small) minime; **2** (minimum) minimal

minimalist /ˈmɪnɪməlɪst/ n, adj minimaliste (mf)

minimally /ˈmɪnɪməlɪ/ adv très légèrement

minimarket /ˈmɪnɪmɑːkɪt/, **minimart** /ˈmɪnɪmɑːt/ n supérette f

minimize /ˈmɪnɪmaɪz/ vtr **1** (reduce) réduire [qch] au maximum [cost, risk]; **2** (play down) minimiser [incident]; **3** Comput réduire

minimum /ˈmɪnɪməm/
A n minimum m (**of** de); **to keep to a/the** ~ maintenir à un/au minimum; **to reduce to a** ou **to the** ~ réduire au maximum; **the bare** ou **absolute** ~ le strict minimum
B adj minimum, minimal

mining /ˈmaɪnɪŋ/
A n **1** exploitation f minière; **2** Mil (on land) pose f de mines; (at sea) mouillage m de mines
B noun modifier [area, industry, town] minier/-ière; [family, union] de mineurs; [accident] de mine

mining: ~ **engineer** ▸ p. 1181 n ingénieur m des mines; ~ **engineering** n génie m minier

minister /ˈmɪnɪstə(r)/ ▸ p. 869
A n **1** GB Pol ministre m; ~ **of** ou **for Defence, Defence** ~ ministre de la Défense; **2** Relig ministre m (du culte)
B vi (care for) sout **to** ~ **to** donner des soins à [person]; **to** ~ **to sb's needs** pourvoir aux besoins de qn

ministering angel n ange m de dévouement

minister of state n GB Pol ministre m délégué; **Minister of State for Education** ministre délégué auprès du ministre de l'Éducation

ministry /ˈmɪnɪstrɪ/ n **1** GB Pol (department, building) ministère m; **Ministry of Transport** ministère des Transports; **2** Relig **the** ~ le ministère

mink /mɪŋk/
A n (animal, fur, coat) vison m
B noun modifier [coat] de vison

minnow /ˈmɪnəʊ/ n **1** (fish) vairon m; **2** fig menu fretin m

minor /ˈmaɪnə(r)/
A n Jur mineur/-e m/f
B adj **1** [change, repair, role] mineur; ~ **road** route secondaire; **2** (not serious) [injury, burn, fracture] léger/-ère; [operation, surgery] mineur; **3** Mus mineur; **C** ~ **Do** mineur; **in a** ~ **key** en mineur
C vi US Univ **to** ~ **in sth** prendre qch en matière secondaire

Minorca /mɪˈnɔːkə/ ▸ p. 954 pr n Minorque f

minority /maɪˈnɒrətɪ, US -ˈnɔːr-/
A n gen minorité f (**of** de); **to be in the** ~ être en minorité; **vocal** ~ minorité agissante; **to be in a** ~ **of one** être le seul/la seule à penser cela; **2** US Pol opposition f
B noun modifier minoritaire

minority: ~ **leader** n US Pol chef m de l'opposition; ~ **president** n US Pol président dont le parti n'a pas la majorité au Congrès; ~ **rule** n gouvernement m par la minorité

minor: ~ **league** US Sport n division f secondaire; ~ **offence** GB, ~ **offense** US n délit m mineur

minster /ˈmɪnstə(r)/ n (cathedral) cathédrale f; (large church) église f abbatiale

minstrel /ˈmɪnstrəl/ n ménestrel m

mint /mɪnt/
A n **1** Bot, Culin menthe f; **2** (sweet) bonbon m à la menthe; **after-dinner** ~ chocolat m à la menthe; **3** (for coins) hôtel m des Monnaies; **the Royal Mint** GB l'hôtel de la Monnaie (à Londres); **4** ○ (vast sum) fortune f
B noun modifier [sauce, tea] à la menthe; [essence, flower, leaf] de menthe
C adj (new) **in** ~ **condition** à l'état neuf
D vtr **1** frapper [coin]; **2** forger [word, expression]

mint: ~ **-flavoured** adj parfumé à la menthe; ~ **green** n, adj couleur (f) menthe à l'eau inv

minuet /ˌmɪnjʊˈet/ n menuet m

minus /ˈmaɪnəs/
A n **1** Math moins m; **two** ~**es make a plus** moins par moins égale plus; **2** (drawback) inconvénient m
B adj **1** [sign, symbol, button] moins; [number, quantity, value] négatif/-ive; **2** [factor, point] négatif/-ive; **on the** ~ **side...** pour ce qui est des inconvénients...
C prep **1** Math moins; **what is 20** ~ **8?** combien font 20 moins 8? **it is** ~ **15 (degrees)** il fait moins 15 (degrés); **2** hum (without) sans; **he woke up** ~ **his passport** quand il s'est réveillé il n'avait plus son passeport

minuscule /ˈmɪnəskjuːl/ n, adj (letter) minuscule (f)

minute¹ /ˈmɪnɪt/ ▸ p. 1267, p. 745
A n **1** (unit of time, short moment) minute f; **five** ~**s past ten** dix heures cinq; **it's five** ~**s' walk away** c'est à cinq minutes à pied; **we arrived at eight o'clock to the** ~ nous sommes arrivés à huit heures pile; **without a** ~ **to spare** au tout dernier moment; **just a** ~ **please** une minute, s'il vous plaît; **she won't be a** ~ elle sera là dans un instant; **it won't take a** ~ ce ne sera pas long; **2** (exact instant) **the** ~ **I heard the news** dès que j'ai entendu la nouvelle; **at that very** ~ à cet instant précis; **any** ~ **now** d'une minute à l'autre; **stop it this** ~**!** arrêtez immédiatement! **I was just this** ~ **going to phone you** j'allais t'appeler à l'instant; **he's at this** ~ **starting his speech** il est en train de commencer son discours; **to put sth off to the last** ~ repousser qch au dernier moment; **he's always up to the** ~ **with the news** il est toujours au courant des dernières nouvelles
B minutes npl Admin compte-rendu m; **to take the** ~**s** rédiger le compte-rendu
C vtr inscrire [qch] au procès-verbal

minute² /maɪˈnjuːt, US -ˈnuːt/ adj [particle] minuscule; [quantity] infime; [risk, variation] minime

minute hand /ˈmɪnɪt hænd/ n aiguille f des minutes

minutely /maɪˈnjuːtlɪ, US -ˈnuːtlɪ/ adv [describe, examine] minutieusement; [vary, differ] de manière infime

minutiae /maɪˈnjuːʃɪiː, US mɪˈnuːʃɪiː/ npl menus détails mpl

miracle /ˈmɪrəkl/
A n miracle m; **to work** ou **perform** ~**s** faire des miracles; **a** ~ **of** un prodige de [efficiency etc]
B noun modifier [cure, drug] miracle; [recovery] miraculeux

miraculous /mɪˈrækjʊləs/ adj **1** [cure, escape, recovery] miraculeux/-euse; **2** [speed, efficiency] prodigieux/-ieuse

mirror /ˈmɪrə(r)/
A n gen miroir m, glace f; Aut rétroviseur m; fig reflet m
B vtr lit, fig refléter; **to be** ~**ed in** se refléter dans

mirror image n fig image f inversée

mirth /mɜːθ/ n (laughter) hilarité f; (joy) joie f

mirthless /ˈmɜːθlɪs/ adj [laugh] forcé; [account] dépourvu d'humour; [occasion] triste

misadventure /ˌmɪsədˈventʃə(r)/ n sout mésaventure f; **verdict of death by** ~ GB Jur verdict de mort accidentelle

misapprehension /ˌmɪsæprɪˈhenʃn/ n malentendu m, erreur f; **to be (labouring) under a** ~ se tromper

misappropriate /ˌmɪsəˈprəʊprɪeɪt/ vtr détourner [funds]

misbehave /ˌmɪsbɪˈheɪv/
A vi [child] se tenir mal; [adult] se conduire mal
B v refl **to** ~ **oneself** = **misbehave**

misbehaviour, **misbehavior** US /ˌmɪsbɪˈheɪvɪə(r)/ n gen mauvais comportement m; Sch mauvaise conduite f

miscalculation /ˌmɪskælkjʊˈleɪʃn/ n lit erreur f de calcul; fig mauvais calcul m

miscarriage /'mɪskærɪdʒ, ˌmɪs'kærɪdʒ/ n ①► Med fausse couche f; ②► Jur **a ~ of justice** une grave erreur judiciaire

miscarry /ˌmɪs'kæri/ vi ① Med [woman] faire une fausse couche; [animal] avorter; ② [plan, attack, strategy] échouer

miscellaneous /ˌmɪsə'leɪnɪəs/ adj divers

miscellany /mɪ'seləni, US 'mɪsəleɪni/ n (of people, things) collection f disparate (**of** de); Literat (anthology) morceaux mpl choisis; TV, Radio choix m

mischief /'mɪstʃɪf/ n (playfulness) espièglerie f; (witty) malice f; (done by children) bêtises fpl; **to get into ~** faire des bêtises; **he's up to ~** il prépare quelque chose; **it keeps them out of ~** ça les occupe

mischievous /'mɪstʃɪvəs/ adj [child, comedy, humour] espiègle; [smile, eyes] malicieux/-ieuse

misconceived /ˌmɪskən'siːvd/ adj [idea, argument] mal fondé; [agreement, project] mal conçu

misconception /ˌmɪskən'sepʃn/ n idée f fausse; **it is a popular ~ that** on croit souvent à tort que

misconduct /ˌmɪs'kɒndʌkt/ n (moral) inconduite f; **professional ~** faute professionnelle

misconstrue /ˌmɪskən'struː/ vtr sout mal interpréter

miscount /ˌmɪs'kaʊnt/
Ⓐ n Pol **to make a ~** faire une erreur dans le compte des suffrages exprimés
Ⓑ vtr, vi gen, Pol mal compter

misdeed /ˌmɪs'diːd/ n méfait m

misdemeanour, misdemeanor US /ˌmɪsdɪ'miːnə(r)/ n Jur délit m

misdirect /ˌmɪsdaɪ'rekt, -dɪ'rekt/ vtr ① mal orienter; **to ~ sb to** diriger qn par erreur vers; ② (address wrongly) mal libeller l'adresse de [letter, parcel]; **the letter was ~ed to our old address** la lettre a été envoyée par erreur à notre ancienne adresse

miser /'maɪzə(r)/ n avare mf

miserable /'mɪzrəbl/ adj ① (gloomy) [person, event, expression] malheureux/-euse; [thoughts] noir; [weather] sale (before n); **to feel ~** avoir le cafard; ② (pathetic) [quantity] misérable; [wage] de misère; [attempt, failure, performance, result] lamentable; ③ (depressing) [life] de misère; [dwelling] misérable

miserably /'mɪzrəblɪ/ adv ① (unhappily) [speak] d'un ton malheureux; [stare] d'un air malheureux; **he was ~ cold** il avait horriblement froid; ② (pathetically) [fail, perform] lamentablement; **a ~ low wage** un salaire de misère

miserly /'maɪzəlɪ/ adj [person] avare; [habits] mesquin; [allowance, amount] maigre

misery /'mɪzərɪ/ n ① (unhappiness) souffrance f; (gloom) abattement m; **to make sb's life a ~** faire de la vie de qn un enfer; **to put sb out of their ~** euph (kill) abréger les souffrances de qn euph; **to put an animal out of its ~** euph achever un animal; ② (misfortune) **the miseries of unemployment** le chômage et son cortège de misères; ③ ○GB (child) pleurnicheur/-euse m/f; (adult) rabat-joie mf inv

misfire /ˌmɪs'faɪə(r)/ vi lit [gun, rocket] faire long feu; [engine] avoir des ratés; fig [plan, joke] tomber à plat

misfit /'mɪsfɪt/ n (at work, in a group) marginal/-e m/f; **social ~** inadapté/-e m/f social/-e

misfortune /ˌmɪs'fɔːtʃuːn/ n (unfortunate event) malheur m; (bad luck) malchance f; **to have the ~ to do** avoir la malchance de faire

misgiving /ˌmɪs'ɡɪvɪŋ/ n crainte f; **to have ~s about sth** avoir des craintes quant à qch; **to have ~s about sb** avoir des doutes au sujet de qn; **not without ~(s)** non sans appréhension

misguided /ˌmɪs'ɡaɪdɪd/ adj [strategy, attempt] peu judicieux/-ieuse; [politicians, teacher] malavisé

mishandle /ˌmɪs'hændl/ vtr ① (inefficiently) mal conduire [operation, meeting]; ne pas savoir comment s'y prendre avec [person]; ② (roughly) manier [qch] sans précaution [object]; malmener [person, animal]

mishap /'mɪshæp/ n incident m; **a slight ~** un incident sans importance; **without ~** sans incident

mishear /ˌmɪs'hɪə(r)/ vtr (prét, pp **-heard**) mal entendre

mishmash○ /'mɪʃmæʃ/ n méli-mélo○ m; **a ~ of** un ramassis de

misinform /ˌmɪsɪn'fɔːm/ vtr mal renseigner

misinformation /ˌmɪsɪnfə'meɪʃn/ n (intentional) désinformation f; (unintentional) renseignements mpl inexacts (**about** sur)

misinterpret /ˌmɪsɪn'tɜːprɪt/ vtr mal interpréter

misinterpretation /ˌmɪsɪntɜːprɪ'teɪʃn/ n interprétation f erronée

misjudge /ˌmɪs'dʒʌdʒ/ vtr mal évaluer [speed, distance, public feeling]; mal calculer [shot]; mal juger [person, character]

miskick GB /ˌmɪs'kɪk/
Ⓐ vtr mal envoyer [ball]; rater [penalty]
Ⓑ vi rater son tir

mislay /ˌmɪs'leɪ/ vtr (prét, pp **-laid**) égarer

mislead /ˌmɪs'liːd/ vtr (prét, pp **-led**) (deliberately) tromper; (unintentionally) induire [qn] en erreur

misleading /ˌmɪs'liːdɪŋ/ adj [impression, title, information] trompeur/-euse; [claim, statement, advertising] mensonger/-ère

mismanage /ˌmɪs'mænɪdʒ/ vtr (administratively) mal diriger; (financially) mal gérer

mismanagement /ˌmɪs'mænɪdʒmənt/ n (of economy, funds) mauvaise gestion f; (of company, project) mauvaise direction f

mismatch /'mɪsmætʃ/ n (of styles, colours) discordance f (**between** de); (of concepts, perceptions) disparité f (**between** de)

misname /ˌmɪs'neɪm/ vtr (incorrectly) appeler à tort; (unsuitably) mal nommer

misnomer /ˌmɪs'nəʊmə(r)/ n appellation f impropre

misogynist /mɪ'sɒdʒɪnɪst/ n misogyne mf

misplace /ˌmɪs'pleɪs/
Ⓐ vtr ① (mislay) égarer; ② (put in wrong place) mal ranger
Ⓑ **misplaced** pp adj [fears, criticisms] déplacé; [money, passport] égaré

misprint /'mɪsprɪnt/ n coquille f, faute f typographique

mispronounce /ˌmɪsprə'naʊns/ vtr mal prononcer

mispronunciation /ˌmɪsprəˌnʌnsɪ'eɪʃn/ n (act) prononciation f incorrecte (**of** de); (instance) erreur f de prononciation

misquote /ˌmɪs'kwəʊt/ vtr déformer les propos de [person]; déformer [text]; citer incorrectement [price]

misread /ˌmɪs'riːd/ vtr (prét, pp **-read** /-'red/) ① (read wrongly) mal lire [sentence, map]; mal relever [meter]; ② (misinterpret) mal interpréter [actions]

misrepresent /ˌmɪsˌreprɪ'zent/ vtr présenter [qn] sous un faux jour [person]; déformer [views, intentions, facts]; **to ~ sb as sth** présenter qn à tort comme qch

misrepresentation /ˌmɪsˌreprɪzen'teɪʃn/ n (of facts, opinions) déformation f

miss /mɪs/
Ⓐ n ① (failure to score) (in game) coup m manqué or raté; **the first shot was a ~** le premier coup a manqué; ② **to give [sth] a ~**○ ne pas aller à [film, lecture]; se passer de [dish, drink, meal]; ③ (failure) échec m
Ⓑ **Miss** ▸ p. 869 (woman's title) Mademoiselle f; (written abbreviation) Mlle; (mode of address) mademoiselle f
Ⓒ vtr ① (fail to hit or reach) manquer [target]; passer à côté de [record]; **the stone just ~ed my head** la pierre m'a frôlé la tête; **he just ~ed the other car/a pedestrian** il a failli emboutir l'autre voiture/renverser un piéton; ② (fail to catch or take) rater [bus, plane, event, meeting]; laisser passer [chance, opportunity]; **I ~ed the train by five minutes** j'ai raté le train de cinq minutes; **it's wonderful, don't ~ it!** c'est génial, à ne pas rater!; ③ (fail to see) rater; **the shop's easy to ~** la boutique peut facilement se rater; ④ (fail to hear or understand) ne pas saisir [joke, remark]; **he doesn't ~ a thing** rien ne lui échappe; **you've ~ed the whole point!** tu n'as rien compris!; ⑤ (omit) sauter [line, class]; ⑥ (fail to attend) manquer [school]; ⑦ (avoid) échapper à [death, injury]; éviter [traffic, bad weather, rush hour]; **he just ~ed being caught** il a failli être pris; **how she ~ed being run over I'll never know!** comment elle n'a pas été renversée je ne le saurai jamais!; ⑧ (notice absence of) remarquer la disparition de; **oh, is it mine? I hadn't ~ed it** c'est le mien? je n'avais pas remarqué qu'il avait disparu; **keep it, I won't**

~ **it** garde-le, je n'en aurai pas besoin; **9** (regret absence of) **I ~ you** tu me manques; **he ~ed Paris** Paris lui manquait; **I'll ~ coming to the office** le bureau va me manquer; **she'll be greatly** *ou* **sadly ~ed** son absence sera très regrettée; **he won't be ~ed**○! bon débarras!

D vi **1** Games, Mil, Sport rater son coup; **2** Aut [*engine*] avoir des ratés

(Idiom) **to ~ the boat** *ou* **bus**○ rater le coche

(Phrasal verb)

■ **miss out**: ▸ **~ out** être lésé; ▸ **~ out on [sth]** laisser passer; ▸ **~ out [sb/sth]**, **~ [sth] out** sauter [*line, verse*]; omettre [*fact, point, person*]

misshapen /ˌmɪsˈʃeɪpən/ *adj* [*leg*] difforme; [*object*] déformé

missile /ˈmɪsaɪl, US ˈmɪsl/
A *n* Mil missile *m*; gen (rock, bottle) projectile *m*
B *noun modifier* [*attack, base, site*] de missiles; **~ launcher** lance-missiles *m inv*

missing /ˈmɪsɪŋ/ *adj* **the ~ jewels/child** les bijoux disparus/l'enfant disparu; **there are two books ~** il manque deux livres; **the ~ link** le chaînon manquant; **to be ~** manquer; **the book was ~ from its usual place** le livre n'était pas à sa place habituelle; **to go ~** [*person, object*] disparaître; **to report sb ~** signaler la disparition de qn; **~ presumed dead** porté disparu, présumé mort

missing in action, MIA *adj* Mil porté disparu

mission /ˈmɪʃn/
A *n* (all contexts) mission *f*; **our ~ was to do** nous avions pour mission de faire; **to be on a ~** être en mission
B *noun modifier* [*hospital, school*] géré par une mission

missionary /ˈmɪʃənrɪ, US -nerɪ/ ▸ p. 1181 *n* Relig missionnaire *mf*

mission statement *n* déclaration *f* de mission

misspelling /ˌmɪsˈspelɪŋ/ *n* faute *f* d'orthographe

misspent /ˌmɪsˈspent/ *adj* **a ~ youth** une folle jeunesse

mist /mɪst/
A *n* gen brume *f*; (from breath, on window) buée *f*; (of tears) voile *m*
B *vtr* vaporiser [*plant*]

(Idiom) **in the ~s of time** dans la nuit des temps

(Phrasal verbs)

■ **mist over** [*lens, mirror*] s'embuer; [*landscape*] s'embrumer
■ **mist up** [*lens, window*] s'embuer

mistake /mɪˈsteɪk/
A *n* (error) gen erreur *f*; (in text, spelling, typing) faute *f*; **to make a stupid ~** faire une bêtise; **to make a ~ about sb/sth** se tromper sur le compte de qn/sur qch; **it was a ~ to leave my umbrella at home** j'ai eu tort de laisser mon parapluie à la maison; **by ~** par erreur; **she took my keys in ~ for hers** elle a pris mes clés au lieu des siennes; **we all make ~s** des erreurs, on en fait tous; **there is no ~** il n'y a pas d'erreur possible; **you'll be punished, make no ~ about it** *ou* that! tu seras puni, fais-moi confiance!; **there must be some ~** il doit y avoir erreur; **my ~!** mea culpa!; **...and no ~** ...il n'y a pas de doute; **to learn by one's ~s** tirer la leçon de ses erreurs
B *vtr* (*prét* **-took**, *pp* **-taken**) **1** (confuse) **to ~ sth for sth else** prendre qch pour qch d'autre; **to ~ sb for sb else** confondre qn avec qn d'autre; **there's no mistaking that voice** il est impossible de ne pas reconnaître cette voix; **2** (misinterpret) mal interpréter [*meaning*]

mistaken /mɪˈsteɪkən/
A *pp* ▸ **mistake**
B *adj* **1** **to be ~** avoir tort; **he was ~ in thinking it was over** il avait tort de croire que c'était fini; **unless I'm very much ~** si je ne me trompe; **to do sth in the ~ belief that** faire qch croyant à tort que; **it's a case of ~ identity** Jur il y a erreur sur la personne; **2** [*enthusiasm, generosity*] mal placé

mistakenly /mɪˈsteɪkənlɪ/ *adv* à tort

mister /ˈmɪstə(r)/ *n: forme complète de* **Mr**, *assez rare*

mistletoe /ˈmɪsltəʊ/ *n* gui *m*

mistook /mɪˈstʊk/ *prét* ▸ **mistake**

mistranslate /ˌmɪstrænsˈleɪt/ *vtr* mal traduire

mistranslation /ˌmɪstrænsˈleɪʃn/ *n* erreur *f* de traduction

mistreat /ˌmɪsˈtriːt/ *vtr* maltraiter

mistreatment /ˌmɪsˈtriːtmənt/ *n* mauvais traitement *m*

mistress /ˈmɪstrɪs/ *n* **1** maîtresse *f*; **2** †GB (teacher) professeur *m*

mistrust /ˌmɪsˈtrʌst/
A *n* méfiance *f* (**of, towards** à l'égard de)
B *vtr* se méfier de

misty /ˈmɪstɪ/ *adj* [*conditions, morning*] brumeux/-euse; [*hills, view*] embrumé; [*lens, window*] embué; [*photo*] flou

misty-eyed /ˈmɪstɪˌaɪd/ *adj* [*look*] tendre; **he goes all ~ about it** il est tout ému quand il en parle

misunderstand /ˌmɪsˌʌndəˈstænd/
A *vtr* (*prét, pp* **-stood**) mal comprendre; (completely) ne pas comprendre; **don't ~ me** (to clarify oneself) comprends-moi bien
B *vtr* **misunderstood** *pp adj* **to feel misunderstood** se sentir incompris; **much misunderstood** souvent mal compris

misunderstanding /ˌmɪsˌʌndəˈstændɪŋ/ *n* malentendu *m*

misuse
A /ˌmɪsˈjuːs/ *n* (of equipment) mauvais usage *m*; (of word) usage *m* impropre; (of talents) mauvais emploi *m*; **~ of funds** détournement *m* de fonds
B /ˌmɪsˈjuːz/ *vtr* faire mauvais usage de [*equipment*]; mal employer [*word, resources*]; abuser de [*authority*]

mite /maɪt/ *n* **1** (child) **poor little ~!** pauvre petit!; **2** (animal) acarien *m*

miter *n* US = **mitre**

mitigate /ˈmɪtɪɡeɪt/ *vtr* atténuer [*effects, distress, sentence*]; réduire [*risks*]; minimiser [*loss*]; **mitigating circumstances** *ou* **factors** Jur circonstances *fpl* atténuantes

mitre GB, **miter** US /ˈmaɪtə(r)/ *n* (of bishop) mitre *f*

mitt /mɪt/ *n* **1** (mitten) moufle *f*; **2** ○(hand) main *f*; **3** Sport gant *m* de baseball

mitten /ˈmɪtn/ *n* moufle *f*

mix /mɪks/
A *n* **1** gen, Culin mélange *m*; **a cake ~** une préparation pour gâteau; **2** Mus mixage *m*, mix *m*
B *vtr* **1** (combine) mélanger [*colours, ingredients*] (**with** avec; **and** à); combiner [*styles, methods, systems*] (**with** avec; **and** à); **to ~ sth into** (add to) incorporer qch à; **to ~ and match** assortir; **2** (make) préparer [*drink*]; malaxer [*cement, paste*]; **3** Mus mixer
C *vi* **1** (combine) (*also* **~ together**) se mélanger (**with** avec; à); **2** (socialize) être sociable; **to ~ with** fréquenter

(Phrasal verbs)

■ **mix in**: ▸ **~ [sth] in**, **~ in [sth]** incorporer [*ingredient, substance*] (**with** à)
■ **mix up**: ▸ **~ [sth] up, ~up [sth]** **1** (confuse) confondre; **to get two things ~ed up** confondre deux choses; **2** (jumble up) mélanger, mêler [*papers, photos*]; **3** (involve) **to ~ sb up in** impliquer qn dans; **to get ~ed up in** se trouver mêlé à

mixed /mɪkst/ *adj* **1** (varied) [*collection, programme, diet*] varié; [*nuts, sweets*] assorti; [*salad*] composé; [*group, community*] (socially, in age) mélangé; (racially) d'origines diverses; **of ~ blood** de sang mêlé; **2** (for both sexes) [*school, team, sauna*] mixte; **in ~ company** en présence d'hommes et de femmes; **3** (contrasting) [*reaction, feelings, reception*] mitigé

mixed: ~ ability *adj* Sch [*class, teaching*] sans groupes de niveau; **~ bag** *n* fig mélange *m*

mixed blessing *n* **to be a ~** avoir ses avantages et ses inconvénients

mixed: ~ doubles *n* double *m* mixte; **~ economy** *n* économie *f* mixte; **~ grill** *n* assortiment *m* de grillades; **~ marriage** *n* mariage *m* mixte; **~ media** *adj* multimédia; **~ metaphor** *n* métaphore *f* incohérente

mixed race *n* race *f* mêlée; **of ~** métis/-isse

mixed: ~-up○ *adj* [*person*] perturbé; [*emotions*] confus; **~ vegetables** *npl* macédoine *f* de légumes

mixer /ˈmɪksə(r)/ *n* **1** Culin (electric) batteur *m* électrique; **2** (drink) boisson *f* nonalcoolisée (*à ajouter à une boisson alcoolisée*); **3** (for cement) bétonnière *f*; **4** Mus (engineer) ingénieur *m* du son; (device) mélangeur *m* de son; **5** (sociable person) **to be a good/bad ~** être très/peu sociable

mixing /ˈmɪksɪŋ/ *n* **1** (combining) (of people, objects, ingredients) mélange *m*; (of cement) malaxage *m*; **2** Mus mixage *m*

mixing: ~ bowl *n* bol *m* à mixer, saladier *m*; **~ desk** *n* Mus console *f* de mixage

mixture /'mɪkstʃə(r)/ n mélange m (**of** de)

mix-up /'mɪksʌp/ n confusion f (**over** sur)

MLA n (abrév = Member of the Legislative Assembly) GB Pol membre m de l'Assemblée d'Irlande du Nord

mm (abrév écrite = **millimetre(s)**) mm

MN US Post abrév écrite = **Minnesota**

MO [1] Mil abrév ▸ **Medical Officer**; [2] US Post abrév écrite = **Missouri**; [3] abrév ▸ **money order**

moan /məʊn/
[A] n [1] (of person, wind) gémissement m; [2] ○(complaint) plainte f (**about** au sujet de)
[B] vi [1] (wail) gémir (**with** de); [2] ○(complain) râler○ (**about** contre)

moat /məʊt/ n douve f

mob /mɒb/
[A] n [1] (crowd) foule f (**of** de); (gang) gang m; **the Mob** la Mafia; [2] ○(group) clique○ f also pej; **and all that** ~ et toute la clique○; [3] (masses) péj **the** ~ la populace f
[B] noun modifier [1] (Mafia) [boss, leader] de la Mafia; [2] [violence, hysteria] de la foule
[C] vtr (p prés etc **-bb-**) assaillir [person]; envahir [place]

mobile /'məʊbaɪl, US -bl, also -biːl/
[A] n gen, Art mobile m; [2] (also ~ **phone**) portable m, téléphone m portable or mobile
[B] adj [1] (moveable) gen mobile; [canteen, classroom] ambulant; [2] (expressive) [features] mobile; [3] **to be** ~ (able to walk) pouvoir marcher; (able to travel) pouvoir se déplacer

mobile: ~ **communications** npl téléphonie f mobile; ~ **library** n GB bibliobus m; ~ **phone** n téléphone m portable or mobile; ~ **shop** n commerce m ambulant

mobility /məʊ'bɪlətɪ/ n (ability to move) mobilité f; (agility) agilité f; **social** ~ mobilité f

mobility allowance n GB allocation de transport pour personnes à mobilité réduite

mobilization /ˌməʊbɪlaɪ'zeɪʃn, US -lɪ'z-/ n gen, Mil mobilisation f

mobilize /'məʊbɪlaɪz/ vtr, vi gen, Mil mobiliser (**against** contre); **to** ~ **the support of sb** essayer de trouver du soutien auprès de qn

mocha /'mɒkə, US 'məʊkə/ n [1] (coffee) moka m; [2] (flavour) arôme m de café et de chocolat

mock /mɒk/
[A] n GB Sch examen m blanc
[B] adj (before n) [1] (imitation) [suede, ivory] faux/fausse; ~ **leather** similicuir m; [2] (feigned) simulé; **in** ~ **terror** en feignant la terreur
[C] vtr se moquer de
[D] vi se moquer

mockery /'mɒkərɪ/ n [1] (ridicule) moquerie f; **to make a** ~ **of** tourner [qn/qch] en dérision [person, process, report, work]; bafouer [law, rule]; [2] (travesty) parodie f

mock-heroic /ˌmɒkhɪ'rəʊɪk/ adj héroï-comique

mocking /'mɒkɪŋ/
[A] n ₵ moqueries fpl
[B] adj moqueur/-euse

mock ~ **orange** n Bot seringa m; ~-**up** n maquette f

MoD n GB (abrév = Ministry of Defence) ministère m de la Défense

mod con /ˌmɒd 'kɒn/ n GB (abrév = **modern convenience**) confort m (moderne); **'all** ~**s'** (in advert) 'tout confort'

mode /məʊd/ n [1] (style) mode m; ~ **of dress** tenue f; ~ **of expression** façon f de s'exprimer; ~ **of leadership** façon f de diriger; [2] (method) ~ **of funding** type m de financement; ~ **of production** méthode f de production; ~ **of transport** moyen m de transport; [3] (state) (of equipment) mode m; (of person) humeur f

model /'mɒdl/
[A] n [1] (scale representation) maquette f (**of** de); [2] (version of car, appliance, garment) modèle m; **computer** ~ modèle informatique; [3] (person) (for artist) modèle m; (showing clothes) mannequin m; [4] (example, thing to be copied) modèle m (**of** de)
[B] adj [1] (railway, soldier, village) miniature; [aeroplane, boat, car] modèle réduit; [2] (pilot) [hospital, prison] modèle; [3] (perfect) [husband, student] modèle
[C] vtr (p prés etc **-ll-**, -**l**- US) [1] **to** ~ **sth on sth** modeler qch sur qch; [2] présenter [garment, design]; [3] modeler [clay, figure] (**in** en)

[D] vi (p prés etc **-ll-**, **-l-** US) [1] [artist's model] poser; [2] [fashion model] travailler comme mannequin; [3] [sculptor, artist] **to** ~ **in** modeler en [clay, wax]
[E] **modelled, modeled** US pp adj [1] [clothes] présenté (**by** par); [2] ~**led on sth** modelé sur qch
[F] v refl **to** ~ **oneself on sb** se modeler sur qn

modelling, modeling US /'mɒdəlɪŋ/ n [1] (of clothes) **to take up** ~ devenir mannequin; **have you done any** ~? as-tu déjà travaillé comme mannequin? [2] (for artist) **to do some** ~ poser comme modèle; [3] (with clay etc) modelage m; [4] Comput modélisation f

modelling clay n pâte f à modeler

moderate
[A] /'mɒdərət/ adj [1] (not extreme) also Pol modéré (**in** dans); [2] (of average extent) moyen/-enne
[B] /'mɒdərət/ vtr gen, Pol modérer
[C] /'mɒdəreɪt/ vi se modérer; [wind, storm] s'apaiser; [rain] se calmer

moderate: ~ **breeze** n jolie brise f; ~ **gale** n grand frais m

moderately /'mɒdərətlɪ/ adv [1] (averagely) moyennement, assez; ~ **priced** de milieu de gamme; ~ **sized** de taille moyenne; [2] (restrainedly) avec modération

moderating /'mɒdəreɪtɪŋ/ adj [influence, role] modérateur/-trice

moderation /ˌmɒdə'reɪʃn/ n modération f (**in** dans); **in** ~ avec modération

modern /'mɒdn/
[A] n moderne mf
[B] adj gen moderne; **all** ~ **conveniences** tout confort (moderne); [world] contemporain; ~ **China** la Chine d'aujourd'hui

modern-day adj des temps modernes

modernism /'mɒdənɪzəm/ n (also **Modernism**) modernisme m

modernity /mɒ'dɜːnətɪ/ n modernité f

modernization /ˌmɒdɜːnaɪ'zeɪʃn, US -nɪ'z-/ n modernisation f

modernize /'mɒdənaɪz/
[A] vtr moderniser
[B] vi se moderniser

modern language
[A] **modern languages** npl langues fpl vivantes
[B] noun modifier (also ~**s**) [student] en langues vivantes; [lecturer, teacher] de langues vivantes

modest /'mɒdɪst/ adj [1] (unassuming) modeste (**about** au sujet de); **he's just being** ~! il fait le modeste!; [2] (moderate) [gift, aim] modeste; [sum, salary] modique; [3] (demure) [dress] décent; [person] pudique

modestly /'mɒdɪstlɪ/ adv (unassumingly) avec modestie; (demurely) décemment; (moderately) **he has been** ~ **successful** il a remporté un succès modeste

modesty /'mɒdɪstɪ/ n [1] (humility) modestie f; [2] (demureness) (of person) pudeur f; (of dress) décence f; [3] (smallness) modicité f

modicum /'mɒdɪkəm/ n minimum m (**of** de)

modification /ˌmɒdɪfɪ'keɪʃn/ n modification f; **we accept it without further** ~**s** nous l'acceptons tel quel

modifier /'mɒdɪfaɪə(r)/ n Ling modificateur m

modify /'mɒdɪfaɪ/ vtr [1] (alter) gen, Ling modifier; [2] (moderate) modérer [demand, statement, policy]; atténuer [punishment] (**to** en)

modular /'mɒdjʊlə(r), US -dʒʊ-/ adj (all contexts) modulaire

modulation /ˌmɒdjʊ'leɪʃn, US -dʒʊ-/ n (all contexts) modulation f

module /'mɒdjuːl, US -dʒʊ-/ n (all contexts) module m

modus operandi /ˌməʊdəs ˌɒpə'rændɪ/ n manière f de procéder

mogul /'məʊgl/ n [1] (magnate) magnat m; [2] (in skiing) bosse f

Mohammed /məʊ'hæmed/ pr n Mahomet

Mohammedan /məʊ'hæmɪdən/
[A] n ‡ Mahométan/-e m/f
[B] adj ‡ mahométan

Mohammedanism /məʊ'hæmɪdənɪzəm/ n ‡ mahométisme m

mohican /məʊ'hiːkən/ n [1] (hairstyle) iroquois m; [2] ▸ p. 1032 **Mohican** (person) Mohican m

moist /mɔɪst/ *adj* [*soil*] humide; [*cake*] moelleux/-euse; [*hands*] (with sweat) moite; [*skin*] bien hydraté

moisten /'mɔɪsn/ *vtr* gen humecter; Culin mouiller légèrement

moisture /'mɔɪstʃə(r)/ *n* (of soil, in walls) humidité *f*; (on glass) buée *f*; (in skin) hydratation *f*; (sweat) moiteur *f*

moisturize /'mɔɪstʃəraɪz/
A *vtr* hydrater [*skin*]
B **moisturizing** *pres p adj* hydratant

moisturizer /'mɔɪstʃəraɪzə(r)/ *n* (lotion) lait *m* hydratant; (cream) crème *f* hydratante

molar /'məʊlə(r)/ *n, adj* molaire (*f*)

molasses /mə'læsɪz/ *n* (+ *v sg*) mélasse *f*

mold *n, vtr* US ▸ **mould**

mole /məʊl/ *n* ⒈ Zool taupe *f*; ⒉ (spy) taupe *f*; ⒊ (on skin) grain *m* de beauté; ⒋ (breakwater) môle *m*

molecular /mə'lekjʊlə(r)/ *adj* moléculaire

molecule /'mɒlɪkjuːl/ *n* molécule *f*

molehill /'məʊlhɪl/ *n* taupinière *f*

(Idiom) **to make a mountain out of a** ~ faire une montagne d'une taupinière

moleskin /'məʊlskɪn/ *n* (fur) (peau *f* de) taupe *f*; (cotton) moleskine *f*

molest /mə'lest/ *vtr* (sexually assault) agresser [qn] sexuellement

molester *n* ▸ **child molester**

mollify /'mɒlɪfaɪ/ *vtr* apaiser, calmer

mollusc, mollusk US /'mɒləsk/ *n* mollusque *m*

mollycoddle /'mɒlɪkɒdl/ *vtr* dorloter

molt *n, vi* US ▸ **moult**

molten /'məʊltən/ *adj* (*épith*) en fusion

moment /'məʊmənt/ *n* ⒈ (instant) instant *m*; **it will only take you a** ~ tu en as pour un instant; **just for a** ~ **I thought you were Paul** l'espace d'un instant j'ai cru que tu étais Paul; **at any** ~ à tout instant; **I don't believe that for one** ~ je ne le crois pas du tout; **and not a** ~ **too soon!** il était temps!; **the car hasn't given me a** ~**'s trouble** la voiture ne m'a pas créé le moindre ennui; ⒉ (point in time) moment *m*; **at the right** ~ au bon moment; **to choose one's** ~ choisir le bon moment; **phone me the** ~ (**that**) **he arrives** appelle-moi dès qu'il arrivera; **I've only this** ~ **arrived** je viens tout juste d'arriver; **at this** ~ **in time** à l'heure actuelle; ⒊ (good patch) **the film had its** ~**s** le film avait ses bons moments; **he has his** ~**s** il a ses bons côtés; ⒋ (importance) littér importance *f*

momentarily /'məʊməntrəlɪ, US ˌməʊmən'terəlɪ/ *adv* ⒈ (for an instant) momentanément; ⒉ US (very soon) dans un instant; (at any moment) d'un moment à l'autre

momentary /'məʊməntrɪ, US -terɪ/ *adj* ⒈ (temporary) momentané; **a** ~ **silence** un moment de silence; ⒉ (fleeting) gen passager/-ère; [*glimpse*] rapide

momentous /mə'mentəs, məʊ'm-/ *adj* capital

momentum /mə'mentəm, məʊ'm-/ *n* lit, fig élan *m*; Phys vitesse *f*

Mon *abrév écrite* = **Monday**

Mona Lisa /ˌməʊnə 'liːzə/ *pr n* **the** ~ la Joconde

monarch /'mɒnək/ *n* monarque *m*

monarchy /'mɒnəkɪ/ *n* monarchie *f*

monastery /'mɒnəstrɪ, US -terɪ/ *n* monastère *m*

monastic /mə'næstɪk/ *adj* ⒈ Relig monastique; ⒉ (ascetic) monacal

Monday /'mʌndeɪ, -dɪ/ ▸ **p. 1322** *n* lundi *m*

monetarism /'mʌnɪtərɪzəm/ *n* monétarisme *m*

monetary /'mʌnɪtrɪ, US -terɪ/ *adj* monétaire

money /'mʌnɪ/
A *n* argent *m*; **to make** ~ (person) gagner de l'argent; (business, project) rapporter de l'argent; **to get one's** ~ **back** (in shop) être remboursé; (after loan, resale) rentrer dans ses frais; (after risky venture, with difficulty) récupérer son argent; **there's no** ~ **in it** ça ne rapporte pas; **to raise** ~ se trouver des capitaux; (for charity) collecter des fonds; **to pay good** ~ payer en bel et bon argent; **to earn good** ~ bien gagner sa vie; **to make one's** ~ **in business** faire (sa) fortune dans les affaires; **there's a lot of** ~ (**to be made**) **in** computing l'informatique, ça peut rapporter
B **monies, moneys** *npl* (funds) fonds *mpl*; (sums) sommes *fpl*

C *noun modifier* [*matters, problems, worries*] d'argent

(Idioms) **not for love nor** ~ pour rien au monde; **for my** ~… à mon avis…; **it's** ~ **for jam, it's** ~ **for old rope** c'est de l'argent facile; ~ **talks** avec l'argent on obtient ce qu'on veut; **to be in the** ~ être en fonds; **to be made of** ~ être cousu d'or; **to get one's** ~**'s worth** en avoir pour son argent; **to have** ~ **to burn** avoir de l'argent à ne savoir qu'en faire; **to put one's** ~ **where one's mouth is** sortir son portefeuille; **to throw good** ~ **after bad** investir en pure perte; **your** ~ **or your life!** la bourse ou la vie!

money: ~ **belt** *n* ceinture *f* porte-monnaie; ~**box** *n* tirelire *f*; ~**grubbing** *adj* péj rapace fig; ~**lender** ▸ p. 1181 *n* prêteur/-euse *m/f*; ~**maker** *n* (product) article *m* qui rapporte beaucoup; (activity) activité *f* lucrative; ~**making** *adj* [*scheme*] pour faire fortune; ~**man** *n* financier *m*; ~ **market** *n* marché *m* monétaire; ~ **order, MO** *n* mandat *m* postal; ~ **rate** *n* taux *m* du loyer de l'argent; ~ **spinner** *n* GB mine *f* d'or fig; ~ **supply** *n* masse *f* monétaire

mongrel /'mʌŋgrl/ *n* (chien *m*) bâtard *m*

monitor /'mɒnɪtə(r)/
A *n* ⒈ Tech dispositif *m* de surveillance; (security TV) écran *m* de contrôle; ⒉ Med, Audio, Comput moniteur *m*; ~ **program** moniteur *m*; ⒊ Radio permanencier *m*
B *vtr* gen, Tech, Med surveiller; Sch suivre [*student, progress*]; Radio être à l'écoute de

monitoring /'mɒnɪtərɪŋ/
A *n* ⒈ Tech, Med (by person) surveillance *f*; (by device) monitoring *m*; **careful** ~ **for problems** contrôle *m* systématique des problèmes éventuels; ⒉ GB Sch suivi *m*; ⒊ Radio service *m* d'écoute
B *noun modifier* [*device, equipment*] de surveillance

monk /mʌŋk/ *n* moine *m*

monkey /'mʌŋkɪ/ *n* ⒈ Zool singe *m*; ⒉ ○(rascal) galopin○ *m*

(Idioms) **I don't give a** ~**'s about it**○ je m'en fous complètement○; **to make a** ~ **out of sb**○ se payer la tête de qn○

monkey: ~ **business** *n* 𝒞 (fooling) bêtises *fpl*; (cheating) grenouillage○ *m*; ~ **nut**○ *n* GB cacahuète *f*; ~ **tricks**○ *npl* = **monkey business**; ~ **wrench** *n* clé *f* à molette

monkfish /'mʌŋkfɪʃ/ *n* (*pl* ~) lotte *f*

mono /'mɒnəʊ/
A *n* Audio monophonie *f*; **in** ~ en mono
B *adj* Audio mono *inv*
C **mono+** *combining form* mono-

monochrome /'mɒnəkrəʊm/
A *n* ⒈ (technique) **in** ~ Art, Phot en monochrome; Cin, TV en noir et blanc; ⒉ (print) monochrome *m*
B *adj* ⒈ Cin, TV [*film*] en noir et blanc; Art, Comput, Phot monochrome; ⒉ fig (dull) monotone

monogamy /mə'nɒgəmɪ/ *n* monogamie *f*

monogram /'mɒnəgræm/ *n* monogramme *m*

monograph /'mɒnəgrɑːf, US -græf/ *n* monographie *f*

monolith /'mɒnəlɪθ/ *n* monolithe *m*

monologue, monolog US /'mɒnəlɒg/ *n* monologue *m*

monomania /ˌmɒnə'meɪnɪə/ *n* monomanie *f*

monoplane /'mɒnəpleɪn/ *n* monoplan *m*

monopolize /mə'nɒpəlaɪz/ *vtr* Econ détenir le monopole de; fig monopoliser

monopoly /mə'nɒpəlɪ/ *n* Econ, fig monopole *m*

monoski /'mɒnəskiː/
A *n* monoski *m*
B *vi* faire du monoski

monosodium glutamate /ˌmɒnəʊˌsəʊdɪəm 'gluːtəmeɪt/ *n* glutamate *m* (de sodium)

monosyllable /'mɒnəsɪləbl/ *n* monosyllabe *m*

monotonous /mə'nɒtənəs/ *adj* monotone

monotony /mə'nɒtənɪ/ *n* monotonie *f*

monsoon /mɒn'suːn/ *n* mousson *f*

monster /'mɒnstə(r)/
A *n* lit, fig monstre *m*; **sea** ~ monstre marin
B *noun modifier* géant

monstrosity /mɒn'strɒsɪtɪ/ *n* (eyesore) horreur *f*; (of act) monstruosité *f*

monstrous /'mɒnstrəs/ *adj* ⒈ (odious) gen monstrueux/-euse; [*building*] hideux/-euse; **it is** ~ **that** il est scandaleux

The months of the year

■ *Don't use capitals for the names of the months in French, and note that there are no common abbreviations in French as there are in English (Jan, Feb and so on). The French only abbreviate in printed calendars etc.*

January	= janvier	**July**	= juillet
February	= février	**August**	= août
March	= mars	**September**	= septembre
April	= avril	**October**	= octobre
May	= mai	**November**	= novembre
June	= juin	**December**	= décembre

Which month?

■ (May *in this note stands for any month; they all work the same way; for more information on dates in French* ▸ p. 788.)

what month is it?
= quel mois sommes-nous?
or (*very informally*) on est quel mois?

it was May
= nous étions en mai

what month was he born?
= de quel mois est-il?

When?

in May
= en mai *or* au mois de mai

they're getting married this May
= ils se marient en mai

that May
= cette année-là en mai

next May
= en mai prochain

in May next year
= l'an prochain en mai

last May
= l'année dernière en mai

the May after next
= dans deux ans en mai

the May before last
= il y a deux ans en mai

Which part of the month?

at the beginning of May
= au début de mai

in early May
= début mai

at the end of May
= à la fin de mai

in late May
= fin mai

in mid-May
= à la mi-mai

for the whole of May
= pendant tout le mois de mai

throughout May
= tout au long du mois de mai

Regular events

every May
= tous les ans en mai

every other May
= tous les deux ans en mai

most Mays
= presque tous les ans en mai

Uses with other nouns

one May morning
= par un matin de mai

one May night
= par une nuit de mai *or* (*if evening*) par un soir de mai

■ *For other uses, it is always safe to use* du mois de:

May classes
= les cours du mois de mai

May flights
= les vols du mois de mai

the May sales
= les soldes du mois de mai

Uses with adjectives

the warmest May
= le mois de mai le plus chaud

a rainy May
= un mois de mai pluvieux

a lovely May
= un beau mois de mai

---

que (+ *subj*); **2** (huge) énorme

montage /mɒnˈtɑːʒ/ *n* Art, Cin montage *m*; Phot photomontage *m*

month /mʌnθ/ ▸ p. 1267 *n* mois *m*; **in two ∼s, in two ∼s' time** dans deux mois; **the ∼ before last** pas le mois dernier, celui d'avant; **the ∼ after next** pas le mois prochain, celui d'après; **every other ∼** tous les deux mois; **in the ∼ of June** au mois de juin; **at the end of the ∼** à la fin du mois; Admin, Comm fin courant; **what day of the ∼ is today?** nous sommes le combien aujourd'hui?; **a ∼'s rent** un mois de loyer; **six ∼s' pay** six mois de salaire; **your salary for the ∼ beginning May 15** votre salaire du 15 mai au 15 juin

(Idiom) **it's her time of the ∼** euph elle est indisposée

monthly /ˈmʌnθlɪ/
A *n* (journal) mensuel *m*
B *adj* mensuel/-elle; **∼ instalment** mensualité *f*
C *adv* [*pay, earn*] au mois; [*happen, visit, publish*] tous les mois

monty /ˈmɒntɪ/ *n* GB
(Idiom) **the full ∼** la totale

monument /ˈmɒnjʊmənt/ *n* lit, fig monument *m*; **the building is a ∼ to his art** le bâtiment témoigne de son art

monumental /ˌmɒnjʊˈmentl/ *adj* (all contexts) monumental

monumentally /ˌmɒnjʊˈmentəlɪ/ *adv* [*boring*] mortellement; **∼ ignorant** d'une ignorance monumentale

moo /muː/ *vi* meugler

mooch /muːtʃ/
A *n* US tapeur/-euse *m/f*
B *vtr* US (cadge) **to ∼ sth from** *ou* **off sb** taper qch à qn
C *vi* GB **to ∼ along** *ou* **about** traîner

mood /muːd/ *n* **1** (frame of mind) humeur *f*; **in a good/bad ∼** de bonne/mauvaise humeur; **to be in the ∼ for doing** *ou* **to do** avoir envie de faire; **to be in a relaxed ∼** être détendu; **when he's in the ∼** quand l'envie l'en prend; **when** *ou* **as the ∼ takes him** selon son humeur; **I'm not in the ∼ for**

joking *ou* jokes je ne suis pas d'humeur à plaisanter; **'are you coming to the beach?'**—'no, I'm not in the ~' 'tu viens à la plage?'—'non, ça ne me dit rien'; ②⟩ (bad temper) saute *f* d'humeur; **to be in a ~** être de mauvaise humeur; ③⟩ (atmosphere) (in room, meeting) ambiance *f*; (of place, era, artwork) atmosphère *f*; (of group, party) état *m* d'esprit; **the general ~ was one of despair** le sentiment général était au désespoir; ④⟩ Ling mode *m*; **in the subjunctive ~** au subjonctif

moodily /'muːdɪlɪ/ *adv* [*say*] d'un ton maussade; [*look, sit, stare*] d'un air morose

moody /'muːdɪ/ *adj* ①⟩ (unpredictable) d'humeur changeante, lunatique; ②⟩ (sulky) de mauvaise humeur

moon /muːn/
A⟩ *n* gen lune *f*; **the ~** (of the earth) la Lune; **there will be a ~ tonight** il y aura clair de lune cette nuit
B⟩ *vi* (daydream) rêvasser (**over sth/sb** à qch/qn)

(Idioms) **to be over the ~** être aux anges; **once in a blue ~** tous les trente-six du mois○; **the man in the ~** le visage de la Lune

(Phrasal verb)
■ **moon about**○, **moon around**○ musarder

moon: **~beam** *n* rayon *m* de lune; **~ buggy** *n* jeep *f* lunaire; **~-faced** *adj* aux joues rondes

moonlight /'muːnlaɪt/
A⟩ *n* clair *m* de lune
B⟩ *vi* travailler au noir

(Idiom) **to do a ~ flit**○ GB filer de nuit sans payer

moonlit /'muːnlɪt/ *adj* [*sky, evening*] éclairé par la lune; **a ~ night** une nuit de lune

moonshine /'muːnʃaɪn/ *n* ①⟩ (nonsense) fadaises○ *fpl*; ②⟩ US (liquor) alcool *m* de contrebande

moor /mɔː(r), US mʊər/
A⟩ *n* lande *f*; **on the ~s** sur la lande
B⟩ *vtr* Naut amarrer
C⟩ *vi* Naut mouiller

moorhen /'mɔːhen, US 'mʊər-/ *n* GB poule *f* d'eau

mooring /'mɔːrɪŋ, US 'mʊər-/
A⟩ *n* mouillage *m*; **a boat at its ~s** un bateau amarré
B⟩ **moorings** *npl* amarres *fpl*

Moorish /'mʊərɪʃ/ *adj* mauresque

moorland /'mɔːlənd, US 'mʊər-/ *n* lande *f*

moose /muːs/ *n* (*pl* ~) (Canadian) orignal *m*; (European) élan *m*

moot point *n* **that is a ~** c'est difficile à dire

mop /mɒp/
A⟩ *n* ①⟩ (for floors) (of cotton) balai *m* à franges; (of sponge) balai *m* éponge; (for dishes) lavette *f*; ②⟩ (hair) crinière○ *f*
B⟩ *vtr* (*p prés etc* **-pp-**) ①⟩ (wash) laver [qch] à grande eau; ②⟩ (wipe) **to ~ one's face/brow** s'éponger le visage/le front

(Phrasal verbs)
■ **mop down**: ▶ **~ [sth] down**, **~ down [sth]** laver [qch] à grande eau [*floor, deck*]
■ **mop up**: ▶ **~ up** éponger; ▶ **~ up [sth]**, **~ [sth] up** ①⟩ lit éponger; ②⟩ fig balayer [*resistance, rebels*]; engloutir [*savings, profits, surplus*]

mope /məʊp/ *vi* (brood) se morfondre

(Phrasal verb)
■ **mope about**, **mope around** traîner (comme une âme en peine)

moped /'məʊped/ *n* vélomoteur *m*

moral /'mɒrəl, US 'mɔːrəl/
A⟩ *n* morale *f*; **to draw a ~ from sth** tirer une leçon de qch
B⟩ **morals** *npl* ①⟩ (habits) mœurs *fpl*; ②⟩ (morality) moralité *f*; **to have no ~s** être sans moralité
C⟩ *adj* (all contexts) moral; **to take the ~ high ground** prendre une position moraliste

morale /məˈrɑːl, US -ˈræl/ *n* moral *m*

morale-booster *n* **his comment was a ~** sa remarque m'a/leur a *etc* remonté le moral

moral fibre GB, **moral fiber** US /ˌmɒrəl ˈfaɪbə(r), US ˌmɔːr-/ *n* force *f* morale

moralist /'mɒrəlɪst, US 'mɔːrəlɪst/ *n* moraliste *mf*

moralistic /ˌmɒrəˈlɪstɪk, US ˌmɔːr-/ *adj* moralisateur/-trice

morality /məˈrælətɪ/ *n* moralité *f*

moralize /'mɒrəlaɪz, US 'mɔːr-/ *vi* moraliser

morally /'mɒrəlɪ, US 'mɔːr-/ *adv* moralement; **~ wrong** contraire à la morale

moral: **~ majority** *n* majorité *f* bien-pensante; **~ philosopher** *n* Philos moraliste *mf*; **~ philosophy** *n* morale *f*

morass /məˈræs/ *n* lit, fig bourbier *m*

moratorium /ˌmɒrəˈtɔːrɪəm/ *n* (*pl* **-toria**) moratoire *m* (**on** sur)

morbid /'mɔːbɪd/ *adj* (all contexts) morbide

morbidly /'mɔːbɪdlɪ/ *adv* de façon malsaine

more /mɔː(r)/

⚠ When used to modify an adjective or an adverb to form the comparative *more* is very often translated by *plus*: *more expensive* = plus cher/chère; *more beautiful* = plus beau/belle; *more easily* = plus facilement; *more regularly* = plus régulièrement. For examples and further uses see **A 1** below.
When used as a quantifier to indicate a greater amount or quantity of something *more* is very often translated by *plus de*: *more money/cars/people* = plus d'argent/de voitures/de gens. For examples and further uses see below.

A⟩ *adv* ①⟩ (comparative) **it's ~ serious than we thought** c'est plus grave que nous ne pensions; **the ~ intelligent (child) of the two** (l'enfant) le plus intelligent des deux; **he's no ~ honest than his sister** il n'est pas plus honnête que sa sœur; ②⟩ (to a greater extent) plus, davantage; **you must work/rest ~** il faut que tu travailles/te reposes davantage; **he sleeps ~ than I do** il dort plus que moi; **the ~ you think about it, the harder it will seem** plus tu y penseras, plus ça te paraîtra dur; **he is (all) the ~ angry because** il est d'autant plus en colère que; ③⟩ (longer) **I don't work there any ~** je n'y travaille plus; ④⟩ (again) **once ~** une fois de plus; ⑤⟩ (rather) **~ surprised than angry** plus étonné que fâché

B⟩ *quantif* **~ cars than people** plus de voitures que de gens; **~ cars than expected** plus de voitures que prévu; **some ~ books** quelques livres de plus; **a little/lot ~ wine** un peu/beaucoup plus de vin; **~ bread** encore un peu de pain; **there's no ~ bread** il n'y a plus de pain; **have some ~ beer!** reprenez de la bière; **have you any ~ questions?** avez-vous d'autres questions?; **nothing ~** rien de plus; **something ~** autre chose

C⟩ *pron* ①⟩ (larger amount or number) plus; **it costs ~ than the other one** il/elle coûte plus cher que l'autre; **he eats ~ than you** il mange plus que toi; **the children take up ~ of my time** les enfants prennent une plus grande partie de mon temps; **many were disappointed, ~ were angry** beaucoup de gens ont été déçus, un plus grand nombre étaient fâchés; **we'd like to see ~ of you** nous voudrions te voir plus souvent; ②⟩ (additional amount) davantage; (additional number) plus; **I need ~ of them** il m'en faut plus; **I need ~ of it** il m'en faut davantage; **several/a few ~ (of them)** plusieurs/quelques autres; **I can't tell you any ~** je ne peux pas t'en dire plus; **I have nothing ~ to say** je n'ai rien à ajouter; **in Mexico, of which ~ later...** au Mexique, dont nous reparlerons plus tard...; **let's** *ou* **we'll say no ~ about it** n'en parlons plus

D⟩ **more and more** *det phr, adv phr* de plus en plus; **~ and ~ work** de plus en plus de travail; **to sleep ~ and ~** dormir de plus en plus; **~ and ~ regularly** de plus en plus régulièrement

E⟩ **more or less** *adv phr* plus ou moins

F⟩ **more so** *adv phr* encore plus; **in York, and even ~ so in Oxford** à York et encore plus à Oxford; **he is just as active as her, if not ~ so** *ou* **or even ~ so** il est aussi actif qu'elle, si ce n'est plus; **they are all disappointed, none ~ so than Mr Lowe** ils sont tous déçus, en particulier M. Lowe; **no ~ so than usual** pas plus que d'habitude

G⟩ **more than** *adv phr, prep phr* ①⟩ (greater amount or number) plus de; **~ than 20 people** plus de 20 personnes; **~ than half** plus de la moitié; **~ than enough** plus qu'assez; ②⟩ (extremely) **~ than generous** plus que généreux; **the cheque ~ than covered the cost** le chèque a amplement couvert les frais

(Idioms) **she's nothing ~ (nor less) than a thief**, **she's a thief, neither ~ nor less** c'est une voleuse, ni plus ni moins; **he's nothing** *ou* **no** *ou* **not much ~ than a servant** ce n'est qu'un serviteur; **and what is ~...** et qui plus est...;

m

there's ∼ where that came from ce n'est qu'un début

moreish○ /'mɔːrɪʃ/ adj GB **to be** ∼ avoir un petit goût de revenez-y

moreover /mɔː'rəʊvə(r)/ adv de plus, qui plus est

morgue /mɔːg/ n morgue f

MORI /'mɒrɪ/ n (abrév = **Market and Opinion Research Institute**) institut de sondage britannique

morning /'mɔːnɪŋ/ ▸ p. 745

A n matin m; (with emphasis on duration) matinée f; **at 3 o'clock in the** ∼ à 3 heures du matin; **on Monday** ∼**s** le lundi matin; **(on) Monday** ∼ lundi matin; **later this** ∼ plus tard dans la matinée; **the previous** ∼ la veille au matin; **the following** ∼, **the** ∼ **after, the next** ∼ le lendemain matin; **early** ou **first thing in the** ∼ (dawn) tôt le matin; **I'll do it first thing in the** ∼ je le ferai dès demain matin; **to be on** ∼**s** être du matin

B noun modifier du matin; **that early** ∼ **feeling** la torpeur matinale

C excl (also **good** ∼) bonjour!

(Idiom) **the** ∼ **after the night before** un lendemain de cuite○

morning: ∼**-after pill** n pilule f du lendemain; ∼ **coffee** n pause-café f; ∼ **dress** n habit m; ∼ **sickness** n nausées fpl du matin

Moroccan /mə'rɒkən/ ▸ p. 1032

A n Marocain/-e m/f

B adj marocain

morocco (leather) /mə'rɒkəʊ/

A n maroquin m

B noun modifier [binding, shoes] en maroquin

Morocco /mə'rɒkəʊ/ ▸ p. 774 pr n Maroc m

moronic /mə'rɒnɪk/ adj débile

morph /mɔːf/

A n morphe m

B vi se morpher (**into** en)

morris dance n: danse folklorique anglaise

Morse (code) /mɔːs/

A n morse m; **in** ∼ en morse

B noun modifier [signal] en morse

morsel /'mɔːsl/ n (of food) morceau m; (of sense, self-respect) once f

mortal /'mɔːtl/

A n mortel/-elle m/f

B adj [enemy, danger, sin] mortel/-elle; [injury, blow] fatal

mortal combat n lutte f à mort

mortality /mɔː'tælətɪ/ n mortalité f

mortally /'mɔːtəlɪ/ adv (all contexts) mortellement

mortar /'mɔːtə(r)/ n mortier m

mortgage /'mɔːgɪdʒ/

A n emprunt-logement m (**on** pour); **to raise/take out a** ∼ obtenir/faire un emprunt-logement

B noun modifier [agreement, deed] hypothécaire

C vtr hypothéquer (**for** pour)

mortgage: ∼ **broker** ▸ p. 1181 n courtier m en prêts hypothécaires; ∼ **rate** n taux m de l'emprunt-logement; ∼ **relief** n: dégrèvement fiscal pour emprunt-logement; ∼ **repayment** n mensualité f de remboursement

mortician /mɔː'tɪʃn/ ▸ p. 1181 n US entrepreneur m de pompes funèbres

mortification /ˌmɔːtɪfɪ'keɪʃn/ n (all contexts) mortification f

mortify /'mɔːtɪfaɪ/

A vtr mortifier

B mortifying pres p adj mortifiant

mortuary /'mɔːtʃərɪ, US 'mɔːtʃʊerɪ/

A n morgue f

B adj mortuaire

mosaic /məʊ'zeɪɪk/

A n lit, fig mosaïque f

B noun modifier [floor, pattern] en mosaïque

Moscow /'mɒskəʊ/ ▸ p. 1276 pr n Moscou

Moses /'məʊzɪz/ pr n Moïse; **Holy** ∼○! grand Dieu!

Moslem /'mɒzləm/

A n Musulman/-e m/f

B adj musulman

mosque /mɒsk/ n mosquée f

mosquito /məs'kiːtəʊ, mɒs-/ n moustique m

mosquito: ∼ **bite** n piqûre f de moustique; ∼ **net** n moustiquaire f; ∼ **repellent** n antimoustique m

moss /mɒs, US mɔːs/ n Bot mousse f

(Idiom) **a rolling stone gathers no** ∼ Prov pierre qui roule n'amasse pas mousse Prov

mossy /'mɒsɪ, US 'mɔːsɪ/ adj moussu

most /məʊst/

⚠ When used to form the superlative of adjectives **most** is translated by **le plus** or **la plus** depending on the gender of the noun and by **les plus** with plural noun: **the most beautiful woman in the room** = la plus belle femme de la pièce; **the most expensive hotel in Paris** = l'hôtel le plus cher de Paris; **the most difficult problems** = les problèmes les plus difficiles. For examples and further uses see the entry below

A det **1** (the majority of, nearly all) la plupart de; ∼ **people** la plupart des gens; **2** (superlative: more than all the others) le plus de; **she got the** ∼ **votes/money** c'est elle qui a obtenu le plus de voix/d'argent

B pron **1** (the greatest number) la plupart (**of** de); (the largest part) la plus grande partie (**of** de); ∼ **of the time** la plupart du temps; ∼ **of us** la plupart d'entre nous; ∼ **of the money** la plus grande partie de l'argent; **for** ∼ **of the day** pendant la plus grande partie de la journée; ∼ **of the bread** presque tout le pain; ∼ **agreed** la plupart étaient d'accord; **the** ∼ **you can expect is...** tout ce que tu peux espérer c'est...; **the** ∼ **I can do is...** tout ce que je peux faire, c'est..., le mieux que je puisse faire, c'est...; **2** (the maximum) le plus; **John has got the** ∼ c'est John qui en a le plus

C adv **1** (used to form superlative) **the** ∼ **beautiful château in France** le plus beau château de France; ∼ **easily** le plus facilement; **2** (very) très, extrêmement; ∼ **encouraging** très or extrêmement encourageant; ∼ **probably** très vraisemblablement; **3** (more than all the rest) le plus; **what** ∼ **annoyed him** ou **what annoyed him** ∼ **(of all) was** ce qui l'ennuyait le plus c'était que; **those who will suffer** ∼ ceux qui souffriront le plus; **4** ○US (almost) presque; ∼ **everyone** presque tout le monde

D at (the) most adv phr au maximum, au plus

E for the most part adv phr (most of them) pour la plupart; (most of the time) la plupart du temps; (basically) essentiellement, surtout; **for the** ∼ **part, they...** pour la plupart, ils...; **for the** ∼ **part he works in his office** la plupart du temps, il travaille dans son bureau; **his experience is, for the** ∼ **part, in publishing** son expérience est surtout or essentiellement dans l'édition

F most of all adv phr par-dessus tout

(Idiom) **to make the** ∼ **of** tirer le meilleur parti de [situation, resources, looks, rest, abilities, space]; profiter de [holiday, opportunity, good weather]

mostly /'məʊstlɪ/ adv **1** (chiefly) surtout, essentiellement; (most of them) pour la plupart; **he composes** ∼ **for the piano** il compose surtout pour le piano; **200 people,** ∼ **Belgians** 200 personnes, des Belges pour la plupart; **2** (most of the time) la plupart du temps; ∼ **we travelled by train** la plupart du temps, nous avons pris le train

MOT /ˌeməʊ'tiː/ GB Aut (abrév = **Ministry of Transport**)

A n (also ∼ **test**, ∼ **inspection**) contrôle m technique des véhicules; **to pass the** ∼ obtenir le certificat de contrôle; '∼ **until June**' 'certificat de contrôle valable jusqu'à juin'

B noun modifier [certificate, centre] de contrôle technique

C vtr effectuer le contrôle technique de [car]

moth /mɒθ, US mɔːθ/ n gen papillon m de nuit; (in clothes) mite f

mothball /'mɒθbɔːl, US 'mɔːθ-/

A n boule f de naphtaline; **to put sth in/take sth out of** ∼**s** fig mettre qch au/sortir qch du placard fig

B vtr mettre [qch] en sommeil

moth-eaten /'mɒθiːtn, US 'mɔːθ-/ adj (shabby) miteux/-euse; (damaged by moths) mité

mother /'mʌðə(r)/

A n **1** (parent) mère f; **2** (form of address) mère f fml, maman f

B Mother pr n Relig Mère f; **Reverend Mother** révérende Mère

C vtr lit materner; fig dorloter also pej

(Idioms) **every ∼'s son (of them)** tous sans exception; **to learn sth at one's ∼'s knee** apprendre qch dans sa plus tendre enfance

motherhood /'mʌðəhʊd/ n maternité f; **the responsibilities of ∼** les responsabilités incombant à une mère de famille; **to combine ∼ with a career** combiner les enfants et le travail

mothering /'mʌðərɪŋ/ n ¢ (motherly care) soins mpl maternels; (being a mother) fait m d'être mère

Mothering Sunday n GB fête f des Mères

mother: **∼-in-law** n (pl **mothers-in-law**) belle-mère f; **∼land** n patrie f

motherless /'mʌðəlɪs/ adj [child] orphelin de mère; [animal] sans mère

motherly /'mʌðəlɪ/ adj maternel/-elle

mother-of-pearl /ˌmʌðərəv'pɜ:l/
A n nacre f
B noun modifier [necklace, box] de or en nacre

mother: **∼'s boy** n fils m à maman○; **Mother's Day** n fête f des Mères; **∼'s help** GB, **∼'s helper** US n aide f maternelle; **∼-to-be** n future mère f, future maman f; **∼ tongue** n langue f maternelle

motif /məʊ'ti:f/ n (in art, music) motif m; (in literature) thème m

motion /'məʊʃn/
A n [1] (movement) mouvement m; **to set sth in ∼** lit mettre qch en marche; fig mettre qch en route [plan]; déclencher [chain of events]; **to set the wheels in ∼** fig mettre les choses en route; [2] (gesture) (of hands) geste m; (of head, body) mouvement m; [3] Admin, Pol motion f; **to table/second the ∼** déposer/appuyer la motion; **to carry/defeat the ∼** adopter/rejeter la motion; [4] Med selles fpl
B vtr **to ∼ sb to approach** faire signe à qn de s'approcher
C vi faire signe (**to** à)
(Idioms) **to go through the ∼s** agir machinalement; **to go through the ∼s of doing** faire mine de faire

motionless /'məʊʃnlɪs/ adj [cloud] immobile; [sit, stand] sans bouger

motion picture
A n film m
B noun modifier [industry] du cinéma; [director] de cinéma

motion sickness n mal m des transports

motivate /'məʊtɪveɪt/
A vtr motiver [person, décision]; **to ∼ sb to do** inciter or pousser qn à faire
B **motivating** pres p adj [force, factor] motivant

motivated /'məʊtɪveɪtɪd/ adj [1] [person, pupil] motivé; [2] **politically/racially ∼** [act] politique/raciste

motivation /ˌməʊtɪ'veɪʃn/ n (all contexts) motivation f (**for** de; **for doing, to do** pour faire)

motive /'məʊtɪv/
A n [1] gen motif m (**for, behind** de); **sb's ∼ in** ou **for doing** le motif qui pousse qn à faire; [2] Jur mobile m (**for** de)
B adj [force, power] moteur/-trice

motley /'mɒtlɪ/ adj [crowd, gathering] bigarré; [collection] hétéroclite

motor /'məʊtə(r)/
A n (engine) moteur m
B noun modifier [1] Aut [industry, insurance, racing, vehicle] automobile; [show] de l'automobile; [2] Med [activity, area of brain, disorder, function, nerve] moteur/-trice; [3] [mower] à moteur
C vi [1] †(travel by car) voyager en voiture; [2] ○(go fast) tracer○

motorail /'məʊtəreɪl/ n GB train m auto-couchettes

motor: **∼bike** n moto f; **∼boat** n canot m automobile; **∼cade** n cortège m (de véhicules); **∼ car**† n automobile† f; **∼ court**, **∼ inn** n US = **motor lodge**; **∼cycle** n motocyclette f; **∼cycle escort** n escorte f de motards; **∼cycle messenger** n coursier/-ière m/f à moto; **∼cycling** ▸ p. 881 n motocyclisme m; **∼cyclist** n motocycliste mf; **∼ home** n auto-caravane f

motoring /'məʊtərɪŋ/
A †n promenade f en voiture
B noun modifier [organization, correspondent, magazine] automobile; [accident] de voiture; [holiday] en voiture; [offence] de conduite

motorist /'məʊtərɪst/ n automobiliste mf

motorize /'məʊtəraɪz/
A vtr motoriser [vehicle, troops, police]; équiper [qch] d'un moteur [system, device]
B **motorized** pp adj [transport, vehicle, regiment] motorisé; [camera, device] équipé d'un moteur

motor: **∼ launch** n vedette f; **∼ lodge** n US motel m; **∼man** ▸ p. 1181 n US machiniste m; **∼ mechanic** ▸ p. 1181 n mécanicien/-ienne m/f auto(mobile); **∼mouth**○ n moulin m à paroles○; **∼ oil** n huile f de graissage; **∼ scooter** n scooter m

motorway /'məʊtəweɪ/ GB
A n autoroute f
B noun modifier [markings, police, service station] de l'autoroute; [traffic, system, junction] autoroutier/-ière; [crash] sur l'autoroute; [driving] sur autoroute

mottled /'mɒtld/ adj [skin, paper] marbré; [hands] tacheté

motto /'mɒtəʊ/ n devise f

mould GB, **mold** US /məʊld/
A n [1] (cast, container) moule m; fig moule m; [2] (fungi) moisissure f; [3] (soil) terreau m
B vtr lit modeler [plastic, clay] (**into sth** pour en faire qch); modeler [sculpture, shape] (**out of, from, in** en); fig façonner (**into** pour en faire)
C vi to ∼ to sth, to ∼ round sth mouler qch; **to be ∼ed to sb's body** [dress] mouler (le corps de) qn

moulder GB, **molder** US /'məʊldə(r)/ vi (also **∼ away**) lit [ruins] tomber en poussière; [corpse, refuse] se décomposer; fig pourrir

moulding GB, **molding** US /'məʊldɪŋ/ n [1] (of clay, model) moulage m; [2] (of opinion, character) modelage m; [3] (trim) moulure f

mouldy GB, **moldy** US /'məʊldɪ/ adj moisi; **to go ∼** moisir

moult GB, **molt** US /məʊlt/
A n mue f
B vi [cat, dog] perdre ses poils; [bird] muer

mound /maʊnd/ n (hillock) tertre m; (heap) monceau m (**of** de)

mount /maʊnt/
A n [1] (mountain) mont m; [2] (horse) monture f; [3] (surround) (for jewel, lens) monture f; (for picture) carton m de montage
B vtr [1] (ascend) gravir [stairs]; monter sur [platform, scaffold, horse, bicycle]; [2] (fix into place) monter [jewel, picture] (**on** sur); coller [stamp]; monter [exhibit, specimen]; installer [engine]; [3] (set up, hold) monter [campaign]; organiser [demonstration]; [4] Zool monter
C vi monter (**to** jusqu'à); [number, toll] augmenter; [concern] grandir; (on horse) se mettre en selle
D **mounting** pres p adj croissant

mountain /'maʊntɪn, US -ntn/
A n lit, fig montagne f; **in the ∼s** à la montagne; **meat/butter ∼** Econ excédents mpl de viande/de beurre
B noun modifier [road, stream, scenery] de montagne; [air] de la montagne; [tribe] des montagnes

mountain: **∼ bike** n vélo m tout-terrain, VTT m; **∼ climbing** ▸ p. 881 n alpinisme m

mountaineer /ˌmaʊntɪ'nɪə(r), US -ntn'ɪər/ ▸ p. 1181 n (climber) alpiniste mf; US montagnard/-e m/f

mountaineering /ˌmaʊntɪ'nɪərɪŋ, US -ntn'ɪərɪŋ/ ▸ p. 881 n alpinisme m

mountainous /'maʊntɪnəs, US -ntənəs/ adj lit montagneux/-euse; fig gigantesque

mountain: **∼ range** n chaîne f de montagnes; **∼ top** n cime f

mounted police n (+ v pl) police f montée

mourn /mɔ:n/
A vtr pleurer
B vi porter le deuil; **to ∼ for sth/sb** pleurer qch/qn

mournful /'mɔ:nfl/ adj mélancolique

mourning /'mɔ:nɪŋ/ n [1] (state, clothes) deuil m; **to be in deep ∼** être en grand deuil; **to go into/come out of ∼** prendre/quitter le deuil; [2] (wailing) lamentations fpl

mouse /maʊs/ n (pl **mice**) lit, fig, Comput souris f

mouse: **∼hole** n trou m de souris; **∼trap** n souricière f

mousey /'maʊsɪ/ adj [1] (colour) châtain terne inv; [2] (timid) péj effacé; [3] [odour] de souris

moustache /mə'stɑ:ʃ/, **mustache** US /'mʌstæʃ/ n moustache f

mousy *adj* = **mousey**

mouth /maʊθ/

A *n* **1** (of human, horse) bouche *f*; (of other animal) gueule *f*; **with my/his etc ~ open** gen la bouche ouverte; (in surprise, admiration) bouche bée *inv*; **2** (of cave, tunnel) entrée *f*; (of river) embouchure *f*; (of geyser, volcano) bouche *f*; (of valley) débouché *m*; (of jar, bottle, decanter) goulot *m*; (of bag, sack) ouverture *f*

B *vtr* **1** articuler silencieusement; **2** débiter [*platitudes, rhetoric*]

Idioms **by word of ~** de bouche à oreille; **don't put words in my ~** ne me fais pas dire ce que je n'ai pas dit; **his heart was in his ~** son cœur battait la chamade; **to be down in the ~** être tout triste; **to leave a bad** *ou* **nasty taste in one's** *ou* **the ~** fig laisser un arrière-goût amer; **to take the words right out of sb's ~** ôter les mots de la bouche de qn; **wash your ~ out!** ne dis pas de gros mots!

mouthful /'maʊθfʊl/ *n* **1** (of food) bouchée *f*; (of liquid) gorgée *f*; **2** ○(word) mot *m* long d'un kilomètre○; (name) nom *m* à coucher dehors○; **3** ○**to give sb a ~** passer une engueulade○ à qn

mouth organ ▸ p. 1028 *n* harmonica *m*

mouthpiece /'maʊθpiːs/ *n* **1** (of musical instrument) embouchure *f*; (of telephone) microphone *m*; (of pipe, snorkel) embout *m*; **2** (person) porte-parole *m* (**of, for** de); (newspaper) organe *m* (**of** de)

mouth: **~-to-mouth** *adj* [*technique, method*] du bouche-à-bouche *inv*; **~-to-mouth resuscitation** *n* bouche-à-bouche *m inv*; **~wash** *n* eau *f* dentifrice; **~-watering** *adj* appétissant

movable /'muːvəbl/ *adj* gen mobile; Jur mobilier/-ière

move /muːv/

A *n* **1** (movement) gen mouvement *m*; (gesture) geste *m*; **to watch sb's every ~** surveiller chacun des gestes de qn; **2** (transfer) (of residence) déménagement *m*; (of company) transfert *m*; **to make the ~ to London** [*family*] s'installer à Londres; [*firm*] être transféré à Londres; [*employee*] être muté à Londres; **she made the ~ from sales to management** elle est passée des ventes à la direction; **3** Games coup *m*; **white has the first ~** les blancs jouent en premier; **it's your ~** c'est ton tour; **4** (step, act) manœuvre *f*; **a good/bad ~** une bonne/mauvaise idée; **to make the first ~** faire le premier pas; **they have made no ~(s) to allay public anxiety** ils n'ont rien fait pour rassurer l'opinion publique; **in a ~ to counter opposition attacks…** pour tenter de parer aux attaques de l'opposition…

B **on the move** *adj phr* **to be on the ~** être en mouvement; [*train*] être en marche; **to be always on the ~** [*diplomat, family*] être tout le temps en train de déménager; [*nomad, traveller*] être toujours sur les routes

C *vtr* **1** (change position of) gen déplacer; transporter [*patient, army*]; (to clear a space) enlever [*object*]; **~ your head, I can't see!** pousse ta tête, je ne vois rien!; **to ~ sth into** transporter qch dans [*room, garden*]; **to ~ sth upstairs/downstairs** monter/descendre qch; **to ~ sth further away/closer** éloigner/rapprocher qch; (set in motion) [*person*] bouger [*limb, head*]; [*wind, mechanism*] faire bouger [*leaf, wheel*]; **3** (to new location or job) muter [*staff*]; transférer [*office*]; **4** (to new house, site) déménager; **to ~ house** déménager; **5** (affect) émouvoir; **6** (motivate) **to ~ sb to do** amener qn à faire; **7** (propose) proposer; **to ~ that the matter be put to the vote** proposer que la question soit soumise au vote; **8** (sell) vendre

D *vi* **1** (stir) gen bouger; [*lips*] remuer; **will you please ~!** veux-tu te pousser?; **2** (travel) [*vehicle*] rouler; [*person*] avancer; [*procession, army*] être en marche; **we must get things moving** fig nous devons faire avancer les choses; **things are starting to ~ on the job front** les choses commencent à avancer côté travail; **go on, get moving!** allez, avance!; **to ~ back** reculer; **to ~ forward** s'avancer; **to ~ away** s'éloigner; **3** ○(proceed quickly) **that car's really moving!** t'as vu comme elle va vite cette voiture○!; **4** (change home, location) déménager; **to ~ to the countryside/to Japan** s'installer à la campagne/au Japon; **5** (change job) être muté; **6** (act) agir; **to ~ to do** intervenir pour faire; **7** Games [*player*] jouer; [*piece*] se déplacer; **8** Comm (sell) se vendre

Idioms **let's make a ~**○ si on bougeait○?; **it's time I made a ~**○ il est temps de partir; **to get a ~ on**○ se dépêcher; **to ~ with the times** vivre avec son temps

Phrasal verbs

■ **move about**, **move around**: ▸ **~ about** **1** (to different position) [*person*] remuer; [*object*] bouger; **2** (to different home) déménager; ▸ **~ [sb/sth] about** déplacer; **they ~ him around a lot between branches** on le fait souvent changer de succursale

■ **move along**: ▸ **~ along** **1** (stop loitering) circuler; (proceed) avancer; (squeeze up) se pousser; **2** fig (progress) **things are moving along nicely** les choses se mettent en place; ▸ **~ [sb/sth] along** faire circuler [*loiterers, crowd*]; faire avancer [*herd, group*]

■ **move away** **1** (by moving house) déménager; (by leaving scene) partir; **to ~ away from** quitter; ▸ **~ [sb/sth] away**, **~ away [sb/sth]** faire reculer [*crowd*]; déplacer [*obstruction*]

■ **move down**: ▸ **~ down** descendre; ▸ **~ [sb] down**, **~ down [sb]** GB Sch faire repasser [qn] au niveau inférieur; gen faire redescendre; ▸ **~ [sth] down**, **~ down [sth]** (to lower shelf etc) mettre [qch] plus bas

■ **move in**: ▸ **~ in** **1** (to house) emménager; **to ~ in with** s'installer avec [*friend, relative*]; aller vivre avec [*friend, relative*]; **2** (advance, attack) s'avancer; **to ~ in on** [*police, attackers, demolition men*] s'avancer sur; [*corporate raider, racketeer*] lancer une opération sur; **3** (intervene) [*company, government*] intervenir; ▸ **~ [sb] in**, **~ in [sb]** **1** (place in housing) installer; **2** (change residence) **a friend helped to ~ me in** un ami m'a aidé à emménager

■ **move off** [*procession*] partir; [*vehicle*] se mettre en route; [*troops*] se mettre en marche

■ **move on** **1** [*person, traveller*] se mettre en route; [*vehicle*] repartir; [*time*] passer; **to ~ on to** passer à [*next item*]; **let's ~ on** passons au point suivant; **2** (keep moving) circuler; **3** (develop) **things have ~d on since** depuis, les choses ont changé; ▸ **~ [sth] on**, **~ on [sth]** GB faire avancer; ▸ **~ [sb] on**, **~ on [sb]** GB faire circuler

■ **move out** **1** (of house) déménager; [*soldiers, tanks*] quitter les lieux; **to ~ out of** quitter; ▸ **~ [sb/sth] out**, **~ out [sb/sth]** évacuer [*residents*]; enlever [*object*]

■ **move over**: ▸ **~ over** **1** se pousser; **2** fig céder la place (**for sb** à qn); ▸ **~ [sb/sth] over** déplacer [*person, object*]

■ **move up**: ▸ **~ up** **1** (make room) se pousser; **2** (be promoted) être promu; **to ~ up to the first division** passer en première division; ▸ **~ [sb] up**, **~ up [sb]** **1** GB Sch faire passer [qn] au niveau supérieur; **2** Sport faire monter; ▸ **~ [sth] up** mettre [qch] plus haut

moveable *adj* = **movable**

movement /'muːvmənt/ *n* **1** gen, Econ, Mus mouvement *m*; (of hand, arm) geste *m*; **to watch sb's ~s** surveiller les faits et gestes de qn; **an upward/downward ~ in prices** une augmentation/diminution des prix; **a ~ towards liberalization** une évolution vers la libéralisation; **a ~ away from marriage** une tendance à rejeter le mariage; **2** (transporting) acheminement *m*; **3** (circulation) circulation *f*

movie /'muːvi/

A *n* surtout US film *m*

B **movies** *npl* **the ~s** le cinéma

movie: **~ camera** *n* caméra *f*; **~ director** ▸ p. 1181 *n* réalisateur/-trice *m/f* de cinéma; **~ film** *n* pellicule *f* cinématographique; **~goer** *n* spectateur/-trice *m/f* de cinéma; **~ star** *n* vedette *f* de cinéma; **~ theater** *n* US cinéma *m*

moving /'muːvɪŋ/ *adj* **1** [*vehicle*] en marche; [*parts, target*] mobile; [*staircase, walkway*] roulant; **2** (emotional) [*scene, speech*] émouvant; **3** fig **to be the ~ force** *ou* **spirit behind sth** être l'âme de qch

mow /məʊ/ *vtr* (*pp* **~ed**, **mown**) tondre [*grass, lawn*]; couper [*hay*]

Phrasal verb

■ **mow down**: ▸ **~ down [sb]**, **~ [sb] down** faucher

mower /'məʊə(r)/ *n* (machine) tondeuse *f* à gazon; (person) faucheur/-euse *m/f*

mown /məʊn/ *pp* ▸ **mow**

MP *n* **1** GB (*abrév* = **Member of Parliament**) député *m*; **2** (*abrév* = **military policeman**)

mpg *n* (*abrév* = **miles per gallon**) miles *mpl* au gallon

mph *n* (*abrév* = **miles per hour**) miles *mpl* à l'heure

MPhil *n* Univ (*abrév* = **Master of Philosophy**) diplôme *m* supérieur de lettres et sciences humaines

MPV n (abrév = **multipurpose vehicle**) véhicule m polyvalent

Mr /'mɪstə(r)/ ► p. 869 n (pl **Messrs**) M., Monsieur; ∼ **Right** le Prince Charmant; ∼ **President** Monsieur le Président

Mrs /'mɪsɪz/ ► p. 869 n Mme, Madame

Ms /mɪz, məz/ ► p. 869 n ≈ Mme.

> ⚠ Ms est l'équivalent féminin de Mr (M.) et permet de s'adresser à une femme dont on connaît le nom sans préciser sa situation de famille: Ms Brown

MS n ① abrév écrite = **manuscript**; ② abrév ► **multiple sclerosis**; ③ US Post abrév écrite = **Mississippi**

MSc n Univ (abrév = **Master of Science**) diplôme m supérieur en sciences

MSP n: abrév ► **Member of the Scottish Parliament**

MT n ① abrév ► **machine translation**; ② US Post abrév écrite = **Montana**

much /mʌtʃ/

> ⚠ When much is used as an adverb, it is translated by beaucoup: it's much longer = c'est beaucoup plus long; she doesn't talk much = elle ne parle pas beaucoup.
> For particular usages, see **A** below.
> When much is used as a pronoun, it is usually translated by beaucoup: there is much to learn = il y a beaucoup à apprendre. However, in negative sentences grand-chose is also used: I didn't learn much = je n'ai pas beaucoup appris or je n'ai pas appris grand-chose.
> When much is used as a quantifier, it is translated by beaucoup de: they don't have much money = ils n'ont pas beaucoup d'argent.
> For particular usages see **C** below.

A adv ① (to a considerable degree) beaucoup; ∼ **smaller** beaucoup plus petit; **the film is** ∼ **better** le film est bien meilleur; **it's** ∼ **better organized** c'est beaucoup mieux organisé; **she doesn't worry** ∼ **about it** ça ne l'inquiète pas beaucoup; **we'd** ∼ **rather stay here** nous préférerions de beaucoup rester ici; **they are** ∼ **to be pitied** ils sont bien à plaindre; ∼ **loved by her friends** très aimée de ses amis; **your comments would be** ∼ **appreciated** tous vos commentaires seront les bienvenus; **he's not** ∼ **good at doing** il n'est pas très doué pour faire; **does it hurt** ∼? est-ce que ça fait très mal?; **she's** ∼ **the best teacher here** elle est de loin le meilleur professeur ici; ∼ **to my surprise** à ma grande surprise; ② (often) beaucoup, souvent; **we don't go out** ∼ nous ne sortons pas beaucoup; **do you go to concerts** ∼? est-ce que tu vas souvent au concert?; ③ (nearly) plus ou moins, à peu près; **it's** ∼ **the same** c'est à peu près pareil (**as** que); **it's pretty** ∼ **like driving a car** c'est plus ou moins la même chose que de conduire une voiture; **in** ∼ **the same way** à peu près de la même façon (**as** que); ∼ **the same is true of China** la situation est à peu près la même en Chine; ④ (specifying degree to which something is true) **too** ∼ trop; **very** ∼ (a lot) beaucoup; (absolutely) tout à fait; **he misses you very** ∼ tu lui manques beaucoup; **it's very** ∼ **the norm** c'est tout à fait la norme; **I feel very** ∼ **the foreigner** je me sens tout à fait étranger; **so** ∼ tellement; **as** ∼ autant (**as** que); **I like them as** ∼ **as you (do)** je les aime autant que toi; **they hated each other as** ∼ **as ever** ils se détestaient toujours autant; **I thought as** ∼ ça ne m'étonne pas, je m'en doutais; **however** ∼ même si; **you'll have to accept the decision however** ∼ **you disagree** il va falloir que tu acceptes la décision même si tu n'es pas d'accord; ⑤ (emphatic: setting up a contrast) **the discovery wasn't so** ∼ **shocking as depressing** la découverte était moins choquante que déprimante

B pron ① (a great deal) beaucoup; (in negative sentences) grand-chose; **do you have** ∼ **left?** est-ce qu'il vous en reste beaucoup?; **we didn't eat** ∼ nous n'avons pas mangé grand-chose; **there isn't** ∼ **to do** il n'y a pas grand-chose à faire; **he doesn't have** ∼ **to complain about** il n'a pas à se plaindre; **it leaves** ∼ **to be desired** ça laisse (vraiment) à désirer; **there's** ∼ **to be said for it** ça présente des avantages; ∼ **of** une grande partie de; ∼ **of the difficulty lies in...** une grande partie de la difficulté réside dans...; **I don't see** ∼ **of them now** je ne les vois plus beaucoup maintenant; **to make** ∼ **of sth** (focus on) insister sur qch; (understand) comprendre qch; ② (expressing a relative amount, degree) **so** ∼

tellement, tant; **we'd eaten so** ∼ **that** nous avions tellement mangé que; **so** ∼ **of her work is gloomy** une si grande partie de son œuvre est sombre; **so** ∼ **of the time,** it's a question of patience la plupart du temps c'est une question de patience; **too** ∼ trop; **it costs too** ∼ c'est trop cher; **it's too** ∼! lit c'est trop!; (in protest) c'en est trop!; **she was too** ∼ **of an egotist to do** elle était trop égoïste pour faire; **the heat was too** ∼ **for them** ils n'ont pas pu supporter la chaleur; **he was too** ∼ **for his opponent** il était trop fort pour lui, il est honnête; **this** ∼ **is certain, we'll have no choice** une chose est certaine, nous n'aurons pas le choix; **twice as** ∼ deux fois plus; **if we had half as** ∼ **as you** si nous avions la moitié de ce que tu as; **as** ∼ **as possible** autant que possible; **it can cost as** ∼ **as £50** ça peut coûter jusqu'à 50 livres sterling; **it was as** ∼ **as I could do not to laugh** il a fallu que je me retienne pour ne pas rire; **as** ∼ **as to say...** d'un air de dire...; **how** ∼? combien?; **tell them how** ∼ **you won** dis-leur combien tu as gagné; **do you know how** ∼ **this means to me?** est-ce que tu sais à quel point or combien c'est important pour moi?; ③ (focusing on limitations, inadequacy) **it's not** ou **nothing** ∼ ce n'est pas grand-chose; **it's not up to** ∼ GB ça ne vaut pas grand-chose; **he's not** ∼ **to look at** il n'est pas très beau; **she doesn't think** ∼ **of him** elle n'a pas très bonne opinion de lui; **I'm not** ∼ **of a reader** je n'aime pas beaucoup lire; **it wasn't** ∼ **of a life** ce n'était pas une vie; **I'm not** ∼ **of a one for cooking**○ la cuisine ce n'est pas mon fort○

C quantif beaucoup de; **I haven't got (very)** ∼ **time** je n'ai pas beaucoup de temps; **she didn't speak** ∼ **English** elle ne connaissait que quelques mots d'anglais; **to spend too** ∼ **money** dépenser trop d'argent; **we don't have too** ∼ **time** nous n'avons pas beaucoup de temps; **don't use so** ∼ **salt** ne mets pas tant de sel; **we paid twice as** ∼ **money** nous avons payé deux fois plus d'argent; **how** ∼ **time have we got left?** combien de temps nous reste-t-il?

D much+ combining form ∼-**loved**/-**respected** très apprécié/respecté; ∼-**maligned** tant décrié; ∼-**needed** indispensable

E much as conj phr bien que (+ subj); ∼ **as we regret our decision we have no choice** bien que nous regrettions or nous avons beau regretter notre décision, nous n'avons pas le choix

F much less conj phr encore moins; **I've never seen him** ∼ **less spoken to him** je n'ai jamais eu l'occasion de le voir encore moins de lui parler

G so much as adv phr without so ∼ **as saying goodbye/as an apology** sans même dire au revoir/s'excuser; **if you so** ∼ **as move** si tu fais le moindre mouvement

(Idioms) **there isn't** ∼ **in** GB ou **to** US **it** (in contest, competition) ils se suivent de près; **there isn't** ∼ **in it for us** (to our advantage) ça ne va pas nous apporter grand-chose; **she's late again?** **that's a bit** ∼! elle est encore en retard? elle exagère!; **they're** ∼ **of a muchness** il n'y a pas beaucoup de différence entre eux

muck /mʌk/ n ① lit saletés fpl; (mud) boue f; (manure) fumier m; **dog** ∼ crotte f de chien; ② ○fig (book, film, dish) saleté f; **it's** ∼ c'est dégoûtant

(Phrasal verbs)

■ **muck about**○, **muck around**○: ► ∼ **about** (fool about) faire l'imbécile; (do nothing) traîner; **to** ∼ **about with** trafico-ter○ [appliance]; toucher à [object]; ► ∼ [sb] **about** se ficher de○

■ **muck in** (share task) mettre la main à la pâte○; (share accommodation) partager le gîte et le couvert

■ **muck out**: ► ∼ **out [sth]** nettoyer [cowshed, stable]

■ **muck up**: ► ∼ **up [sth]** ① (spoil) chambouler○ [plans]; cochonner○ [task]; louper○ [exam, interview, opportunity]; ② salir [clothes, carpet]

muckraking /'mʌkreɪkɪŋ/

A n course f au scandale

B adj [story] infâme; [campaign] de diffamation

mucus /'mjuːkəs/ n mucus m, mucosités fpl

mud /mʌd/ n boue f

(Idioms) **his name is** ∼ on l'exècre, il est très mal vu; **it's as clear as** ∼○! c'est d'un clair○!; **to drag sb's name in** ou **through the** ∼ traîner qn dans la boue

muddle /'mʌdl/

A n ① (mess) 𝒞 (of papers) pagaille○ f; (of string) embrouillami-

m

ni *m*; fig (in administration) confusion *f*; **2** (mix-up) malentendu *m* (**over** à propos de); **3** (mental confusion) **to be in a ~** avoir les idées embrouillées; **to get into a ~** s'embrouiller

B *vtr* = **muddle up**

(Phrasal verbs)

■ **muddle along** vivoter○

■ **muddle through** se débrouiller

■ **muddle up**: ▸ **~ [sth] up**, **~ up [sth]** (disorder) semer la pagaille○ dans; ▸ **~ [sb] up** embrouiller les idées de; **to get sth ~d up** s'embrouiller dans qch [*dates, names*]; **I got you ~d up with Martin** je t'ai confondu avec Martin

muddled /'mʌdld/ *adj* confus

muddle-headed /,mʌdl'hedɪd/ *adj* [*plan*] confus; [*person*] aux idées confuses

muddy /'mʌdɪ/
A *adj* [*hand*] couvert de boue; [*shoe, garment*] crotté; [*road, water, coffee*] boueux/-euse; [*pink*] sale; [*green, yellow*] terne; [*complexion*] terreux/-euse
B *vtr* couvrir [qch] de boue [*hands*]; crotter [*shoes, clothes*]; troubler [*water*]

(Idiom) **to ~ the waters** brouiller les pistes

mud; **~ flat** *n* laisse *f*; **~guard** *n* garde-boue *m inv*; **~ hut** *n* hutte *f* de terre; **~pack** *n* masque *m* de beauté à l'argile; **~ pie** *n* pâté *m* de boue; **~slide** *n* éboulement *m* de terrain; **~-slinging** *n* dénigrement *m*

muff /mʌf/
A *n* (mitten) manchon *m*
B ○*vtr* louper○ [*shot*]; rater○ [*chance*]; se tromper dans [*lines*]

muffle /'mʌfl/ *vtr* **1** (wrap up) emmitoufler (**in** dans); **2** assourdir [*bell, drum*]; étouffer [*voice, laughter*]

muffler /'mʌflə(r)/ *n* **1** cache-nez *m inv*; **2** US Aut silencieux *m*

mug /mʌg/
A *n* **1** (for tea, coffee) grande tasse *f*; (for beer) chope *f*; **2** (contents) (*also* **~ful**) grande tasse *f* (**of** de); **3** ○(face) gueule○ *f*; **4** GB (fool) poire○ *f*; **it's a ~'s game** c'est un attrape-nigaud
B *vtr* (*p prés etc* **-gg-**) agresser; **to be ~ged** se faire agresser

(Phrasal verb)

■ **mug up**○ GB: ▸ **~ up [sth]** potasser○ [*subject*]

mugger /'mʌgə(r)/ *n* agresseur *m*

mugging /'mʌgɪŋ/ *n* **1** (attack) agression *f*; **2** ¢ (crime) agressions *fpl*

muggy /'mʌgɪ/ *adj* [*room, day*] étouffant; [*weather*] lourd

Muhammad /mə'hæmɪd/ *pr n* Mahomet

mujaheddin, **mujahedeen** /,mu:dʒə'di:n/ *npl* **the ~** les Moudjahidin *mpl*

mulatto /mju:'lætəʊ, US mə'l-/
A *n* mulâtre/-esse *m/f*
B *adj* mulâtre

mulberry /'mʌlbrɪ, US -berɪ/ *n* (tree) mûrier *m*; (fruit) mûre *f*

mule /mju:l/ *n* (animal) mulet *m*; (stubborn person)○ tête *f* de mule; (slipper) mule *f*

mulish /'mju:lɪʃ/ *adj* entêté

mull /mʌl/ *vtr* Culin chauffer et épicer [*wine*]

(Phrasal verb)

■ **mull over**: ▸ **~ over [sth]**, **~ [sth] over** retourner [qch] dans sa tête

mullet /'mʌlɪt/ *n* (red) rouget *m*; (grey) mulet *m*

mullioned /'mʌlɪənd/ *adj* [*windows*] à meneaux

multi+ /'mʌltɪ/ combining form multi-

multi-access /,mʌltɪ'ækses/ *n* Comput accès *m* multiple

multicellular /,mʌltɪ'seljʊlə(r)/ *adj* pluricellulaire

multichannel /,mʌltɪ'tʃænl/ *adj* [*television*] à canaux multiples; [*reception*] de plusieurs chaînes

multicultural /,mʌltɪ'kʌltʃərəl/ *adj* multiculturel/-elle

multidisciplinary /,mʌltɪdɪsɪ'plɪnərɪ, US -nerɪ/ *adj* Sch, Univ pluridisciplinaire

multi-faceted /,mʌltɪ'fæsɪtɪd/ *adj* **1** [*career, personality*] à multiples facettes; **2** [*gemstone*] facetté

multi-function /,mʌltɪ'fʌŋkʃn/ *adj* [*watch, calculator, computer*] multifonctions *inv*

multigym /'mʌltɪdʒɪm/ *n* appareil *m* de musculation

multilateral /,mʌltɪ'lætərəl/ *adj* Pol multilatéral; Math à plusieurs côtés

multilevel /,mʌltɪ'levl/ *adj* **1** [*parking, access, analysis*] à plusieurs niveaux; [*building, complex*] de plusieurs étages; **2** Comput multiniveaux *inv*

multilingual /,mʌltɪ'lɪŋgwəl/ *adj* plurilingue

multimedia /,mʌltɪ'mi:dɪə/ *adj* (all contexts) multimédia *inv*

multi-million /,mʌltɪ'mɪljən/ *adj* de plusieurs millions

multinational /,mʌltɪ'næʃnl/
A *n* (*also* **~ company**) multinationale *f*
B *adj* [*company, force, agreement*] multinational

multi-party /,mʌltɪ'pɑ:tɪ/ *adj* Pol [*government, system*] pluripartite

multiple /'mʌltɪpl/
A *n* **1** Math multiple *m* (**of** de); **sold in ~s of six** vendus par six; **2** GB (chain of shops) magasin *m* à succursales multiples; **3** Fin action *f* multiple
B *adj* (all contexts) multiple

multiple: **~ choice** *adj* [*test, question*] à choix multiple; **~ entry visa** *n* visa *m* valable pour plusieurs entrées; **~ occupancy** *n*: occupation d'une maison par plusieurs personnes; **~ ownership** *n* multipropriété *f*; **~ pile-up** *n* carambolage *m*; **~ sclerosis**, **MS** *n* sclérose *f* en plaques; **~ store** *n* GB magasin *m* à succursales multiples

multiplex /'mʌltɪpleks/
A *n* **1** Telecom multiplex *m*; **2** US Cin complexe *m* multisalles
B *adj* Telecom multiplex *inv*
C *vtr* Telecom multiplexer

multiplication /,mʌltɪplɪ'keɪʃn/ *n* gen, Math multiplication *f*; **to do ~** faire des multiplications

multiplier /'mʌltɪplaɪə(r)/ *n* (all contexts) multiplicateur *m*

multiply /'mʌltɪplaɪ/
A *vtr* (all contexts) multiplier (**by** par)
B *vi* **1** Math multiplier; **2** gen, Biol (increase) se multiplier

multiply handicapped /,mʌltɪplɪ 'hændɪkæpt/ *adj* polyhandicapé

multiprocessing /,mʌltɪ'prəʊsesɪŋ/ *n* Comput multitraitement *m*

multipurpose /,mʌltɪ'pɜ:pəs/ *adj* [*tool, gadget*] à usages multiples; [*area, organization*] polyvalent

multi-screen /,mʌltɪskri:n/ *adj* [*cinema*] multisalles

multistorey /,mʌltɪ'stɔ:rɪ/ *adj* GB [*carpark*] à niveaux multiples; [*building*] à étages

multitrack /'mʌltɪtræk/ *adj* Audio multipiste *inv*

multitude /'mʌltɪtju:d, US -tu:d/ *n* multitude *f*

(Idiom) **to hide** *ou* **cover a ~ of sins** hum (servir à) camoufler pas mal de choses

multiuser /,mʌltɪ'ju:zə(r)/ *adj* Comput [*computer*] à utilisateurs multiples; [*system, installation*] multiposte *inv*

mum○ /mʌm/ *n* GB maman *f*

(Idioms) **~'s the word** motus et bouche cousue; **to keep ~** ne pas piper mot

mumble /'mʌmbl/
A *n* marmonnement *m*
B *vtr, vi* marmonner

mumbo jumbo /,mʌmbəʊ 'dʒʌmbəʊ/ *n* péj (speech, writing) charabia○ *m*; (ritual) cérémonial *m*

mummify /'mʌmɪfaɪ/ *vtr* momifier

mummy /'mʌmɪ/ *n* **1** ○GB maman *f*; **2** (embalmed body) momie *f*

mummy's boy *n* GB péj fils *m* à maman

mumps /mʌmps/ ▸ p. 933 *n* (+ *v sg*) oreillons *mpl*

munch /mʌntʃ/ *vtr* [*person*] mâcher; [*animal*] mâchonner; **to ~ one's way through** dévorer

mundane /mʌn'deɪn/ *adj* terre-à-terre, quelconque

municipal /mju:'nɪsɪpl/ *adj* municipal

municipal court *n* US Jur tribunal *m* d'instance

municipality /mju:,nɪsɪ'pælətɪ/ *n* municipalité *f*

munitions /mju:'nɪʃnz/
A *npl* Mil munitions *fpl*
B noun modifier [*factory, industry*] de munitions

mural /'mjʊərəl/
A *n* peinture *f* murale; (in cave) peinture *f* rupestre
B *adj* [*art, decoration*] mural

murder /'mɜ:də(r)/
A *n* **1** meurtre *m*; **attempted ~** tentative *f* de meurtre *or*

d'assassinat; **2** ○**it's ~ in town today!** c'est infernal en ville aujourd'hui○!

B *noun modifier* [*inquiry, investigation*] sur un meurtre; [*scene, weapon*] du crime; [*squad, trial*] criminel/-elle; [*story, mystery*] policier/-ière; **~ hunt** chasse *f* à l'assassin; **~ suspect** meurtrier/-ière *m/f* présumé/-e; **~ victim** victime *f* (d'un meurtre)

C *vtr* **1** (kill) assassiner (**with** avec); **2** ○**I could ~ her**○! je l'étranglerais volontiers!; **3** ○massacrer○ [*language, piece of music*]; **4** ○(defeat) écraser○

D murdered *pp adj* **the ~ed man/woman** la victime

(Idioms) **to get away with ~** [*dishonest person*] exercer ses talents en toute impunité; **that child gets away with ~!** on lui passe tout à cet enfant!; **to yell blue ~** GB [*child*] crier comme un putois

murder: **~ case** *n* (for police) affaire *f* d'homicide; (for court) procès *m* en homicide; **~ charge** *n* inculpation *f* de meurtre

murderer /'mɜːdərə(r)/ *n* assassin *m*, meurtrier *m*

murderess /'mɜːdərɪs/ *n* meurtrière *f*

murderous /'mɜːdərəs/ *adj* **1** (deadly) [*regime, expression, look*] assassin; [*deeds, tendencies, thoughts*] meurtrier/-ière; [*intent*] de meurtre; **2** ○[*heat, conditions, pressure*] infernal; [*route, conditions*] meurtrier/-ière

murky /'mɜːkɪ/ *adj* **1** [*water, colour*] glauque; [*weather*] maussade; [*distance*] opaque; **2** [*past*] trouble

murmur /'mɜːmə(r)/

A *n* gen murmure *m* (**of** de); (of traffic) bourdonnement *m* (**of** de)

B *vtr, vi* (all contexts) murmurer

murmuring /'mɜːmərɪŋ/

A *n* murmure *m*

B murmurings *npl* (complaints) murmures *mpl* (**about** contre); (rumours) rumeurs *fpl*

C *adj* [*stream*] murmurant

muscle /'mʌsl/

A *n* **1** (in arm, leg etc) muscle *m*; (tissue) muscles *mpl*; **without moving a ~** sans bouger; **don't move a ~!** ne bouge pas!; **2** fig puissance *f*; **we have the ~ to compete with them** nous sommes assez forts pour leur faire concurrence; **to give ~** to donner du poids à

B *noun modifier* [*exercise, relaxant*] pour les muscles; [*fatigue, injury, tissue*] musculaire

C *vtr* **to ~ one's way into sth** essayer de s'imposer dans [*discussion*].

(Phrasal verb)

■ **muscle in**○ s'imposer (**on** dans)

muscle strain *n* élongation *f*

muscular /'mʌskjʊlə(r)/ *adj* [*disease, tissue*] musculaire; [*body, limbs*] musclé; [*attitude, pose*] musclé; **to have a ~ build** être tout en muscles

muscular dystrophy ▸ p. 933 *n* dystrophie *f* musculaire

museum /mjuːˈzɪəm/

A *n* musée *m*

B *noun modifier* [*curator, collection*] de musée

mushroom /'mʌʃrʊm, -ruːm/ ▸ p. 752

A *n* Bot, Culin champignon *m*; (colour) beige *m* rosé

B *noun modifier* Culin [*soup*] aux champignons

C *vi* [*towns, groups*] proliférer; [*demand, profits*] s'accroître rapidement

mushroom: **~ cloud** *n* champignon *m* atomique; **~ growth** *n* croissance *f* rapide

mushrooming /'mʌʃruːmɪŋ, -rʊmɪŋ/

A *n* **1** (activity) **to go ~** aller aux champignons; **2** (spread) prolifération *f*

B *adj* [*demand*] croissant; [*trade*] florissant

mushy○ /'mʌʃɪ/ *adj* **1** (pulpy) [*texture*] pâteux/-euse; [*vegetables*] en bouillie; **2** (sentimental) [*film, story*] à l'eau de rose

music /'mjuːzɪk/

A *n* **1** (art, composition) musique *f*; **to set sth to ~** mettre qch en musique; **2** (printed) partition *f*

B *noun modifier* [*exam, lesson, teacher, festival*] de musique; [*critic, practice*] musical

(Idioms) **to face the ~** affronter l'orage; **to be ~ to sb's ears** être doux à l'oreille de qn

musical /'mjuːzɪkl/

A *n* (also **~ comedy**) comédie *f* musicale

B *adj* **1** [*person*] (gifted) musicien/-ienne; (interested) mélomane; **2** [*voice, laughter*] mélodieux/-ieuse; [*accompaniment, director, score*] musical

musical: **~ box** *n* GB boîte *f* à musique; **~ instrument** *n* instrument *m* de musique

music: **~ box** *n* boîte *f* à musique; **~ case** *n* porte-musique *m inv*; **~ centre** *n* GB chaîne *f* compacte stéréo

musician /mjuːˈzɪʃn/ ▸ p. 1181 *n* musicien/-ienne *m/f*

music lover *n* mélomane *mf*

musicology /ˌmjuːzɪˈkɒlədʒɪ/ *n* musicologie *f*

music: **~ stand** *n* pupitre *m* à musique; **~ stool** *n* tabouret *m* de piano; **~ video** *n* clip *m* (vidéo)

musing /'mjuːzɪŋ/

A musings *npl* songeries *fpl*

B *adj* [*stare, way*] songeur/-euse

musk /mʌsk/ *n* musc *m*

musket /'mʌskɪt/ *n* mousquet *m*

musketeer /ˌmʌskɪˈtɪə(r)/ *n* mousquetaire *m*

musky /'mʌskɪ/ *adj* musqué

Muslim /'mʊzlɪm, US 'mʌzləm/ = **Moslem**

muslin /'mʌzlɪn/

A *n* (cloth) mousseline *f*; Culin étamine *f*

B *noun modifier* [*apron, curtain*] en mousseline

mussel /'mʌsl/ *n* moule *f*

mussel bed *n* parc *m* à moules

must /mʌst, məst/

⚠ When *must* indicates obligation or necessity, French tends to use either the verb *devoir* or the impersonal construction *il faut que + subjunctive*: *I must go* = je dois partir, il faut que je parte. For examples and particular usages see **A 1** and **A 3** below. See also **have B 1** and the related usage note.

When *must* expresses assumption or probability, the verb *devoir* is always used: *it must strike you as odd that* = ça doit te sembler bizarre que (+ *subj*). See **A 7** below for further examples.

For the conjugation of *devoir*, see the French verb tables.

A *modal aux* (*nég* **must not, mustn't**) **1** (indicating obligation, prohibition) **you ~ check your rearview mirror** il faut regarder dans le rétroviseur; **the feeding bottles ~ be sterilized** les biberons doivent être stérilisés; **they said she ~ be consulted first** ils ont dit qu'il fallait d'abord la consulter; **you mustn't mention this to anyone** il ne faut en parler à personne, tu ne dois en parler à personne; **all visitors ~ leave the premises** tous les visiteurs doivent quitter les lieux; **the loan ~ be repaid in one year** le prêt est remboursable en un an; **withdrawals ~ not exceed £200** les retraits ne doivent pas dépasser 200 livres sterling; **it ~ eventually have an effect** ça doit finir par avoir un effet; **2** (indicating requirement, condition) **candidates ~ be EC nationals** les candidats doivent être ressortissants d'un des pays de la CE; **to gain a licence you ~ spend 40 hours in the air** pour obtenir son brevet il faut avoir 40 heures de vol; **3** (stressing importance, necessity) **you ~ be patient** il faut que tu sois patient, tu dois être patient; **tell her she mustn't worry** dis-lui de ne pas s'inquiéter; **we ~ never forget** il ne faut jamais oublier; **I ~ ask you not to smoke** je dois vous demander de ne pas fumer; **I feel I ~ tell you that…** je pense devoir te dire que…; **it ~ be said that** il faut dire que; **I ~ apologize for being late** je vous demande d'excuser mon retard; **I ~ say I was impressed** je dois avouer que j'ai été impressionné; **that was pretty rude I ~ say!** je dois dire que c'était assez impoli!; **very nice, I ~ say!** iron très gentil vraiment! iron; **4** (expressing intention) **I ~ check the reference** je dois vérifier la référence, il faut que je vérifie la référence; **5** (indicating irritation) **well, come in if you ~** bon, entre si tu y tiens; **why ~ she always be so cynical?** pourquoi faut-il toujours qu'elle soit si cynique?; **he's ill, if you ~ know** il est malade si tu veux vraiment le savoir; **~ you make such a mess?** est-ce que tu as vraiment besoin de mettre le désordre?; **6** (in invitations, suggestions) **we really ~ get together soon** il faudrait vraiment qu'on se voie bientôt; **you**

Musical instruments

Playing an instrument

■ *Note the use of* de *with* jouer*:*

to play the piano
= jouer du piano

to play the clarinet
= jouer de la clarinette

but

to learn the piano
= apprendre le piano

Players

■ *English* -ist *is often French* -iste*; the gender reflects the sex of the player.*

a violinist
= un *or* une violoniste

a pianist
= un *or* une pianiste

■ *A phrase with* joueur/joueuse de X *is usually safe.*

a piccolo player
= un joueur *or* une joueuse de piccolo

a horn player
= un joueur *or* une joueuse de cor

■ *But note the French when these words are used with* good *and* bad *like this:*

he's a good pianist
= il joue bien du piano

he's not a good pianist
= il ne joue pas bien du piano

he's a bad pianist
= il joue mal du piano

■ *As in English, the name of the instrument is often used to refer to its player:*

she's a first violin
= elle est premier violon

Music

a piano piece
= un morceau pour piano

a piano arrangement
= un arrangement pour piano

a piano sonata
= une sonate pour piano

a concerto for piano and orchestra
= un concerto pour piano et orchestre

the piano part
= la partie pour piano

Use with another noun

■ De *is usually correct:*

to take piano lessons
= prendre des leçons de piano

a violin maker
= un fabricant de violons

a violin solo
= un solo de violon

a piano teacher
= un professeur de piano

■ *but note the* à *here:*

a violin case
= un étui à violon

~ **meet Flora Brown** il faut absolument que tu fasses la connaissance de Flora Brown; **7** (expressing assumption, probability) **it ~ be difficult living there** ça doit être difficile de vivre là-bas; **there ~ be some mistake!** il doit y avoir une erreur!; **what ~ people think?** qu'est-ce que les gens doivent penser?; **viewers ~ have been surprised** les téléspectateurs ont dû être surpris; **we thought he ~ be shy** nous pensions qu'il devait être timide; **they ~ really detest each other** ils doivent vraiment se détester; **anyone who believes her ~ be naïve** il faut vraiment être naïf pour la croire; **you ~ be out of your mind!** tu es fou!; **8** (expressing strong interest, desire) **this I ~ see!** il faut que je voie ça!; **we simply ~ get away from this town!** il faut à tout prix que nous quittions cette ville!
B *n* **it's a ~** c'est indispensable; **this film is a ~** ce film est à voir *or* à ne pas rater; **a visit to the Louvre is a ~** une visite au Louvre s'impose

mustache *n* US = moustache

mustard /'mʌstəd/ ▸ p. 752
A *n* **1** (plant, condiment) moutarde *f*; **2** (colour) (jaune *m*) moutarde *m*
B *noun modifier* [*powder, seed*] de moutarde; [*pot, spoon*] à moutarde
(Idiom) **to be as keen as ~** déborder d'enthousiasme

muster /'mʌstə(r)/
A *n* Mil rassemblement *m*
B *vtr* (*also* ~ **up**) (summon) rassembler [*energy, troops*]; rallier [*support*]; préparer [*argument*]
C *vi* gen, Mil se rassembler
(Idiom) **to pass ~** être acceptable

must-have○ /'mʌsthæv/
A *n* must○ *m*
B *adj* [*accessory, gadget*] indispensable, must○ *inv*; **a mobile is**
a ~ item for teenagers le portable est must pour les ados○

mustn't /'mʌsnt/ *abrév* = must not

musty /'mʌstɪ/ *adj* **1** [*room*] qui sent le renfermé; [*book, clothing*] qui a une odeur de moisi; **to smell ~** sentir le moisi *or* le renfermé; **2** *fig* [*ideas*] vieux jeu

mutant /'mju:tənt/ *n, adj* mutant/-e (*m/f*)

mutate /mju:'teɪt, US 'mju:teɪt/
A *vtr* faire subir une mutation à
B *vi* [*cell, organism*] subir une mutation; [*alien, monster*] se métamorphoser (**into** en)

mutation /mju:'teɪʃn/ *n* **1** gen, Biol mutation *f*; **2** Ling altération *f*

mute /mju:t/
A *n* Mus sourdine *f*
B *adj* muet/-ette

muted /'mju:tɪd/ *adj* **1** (subdued) [*response*] tiède; [*celebration, pleasure*] mitigé; [*criticism*] voilé; [*colour*] sourd; [*sound*] assourdi; **2** Mus [*trumpet*] bouché

mutilate /'mju:tɪleɪt/ *vtr* mutiler

mutilation /ˌmju:tɪ'leɪʃn/ *n* **1** (of body, property) mutilation *f*; **2** (injury) blessure *f*

mutinous /'mju:tɪnəs/ *adj* gen rebelle; [*soldier, sailor*] mutiné

mutiny /'mju:tɪnɪ/ *n* mutinerie *f*

mutter /'mʌtə(r)/
A *n* marmonnement *m*
B *vtr, vi* marmonner

mutton /'mʌtn/
A *n* Culin mouton *m*
B *noun modifier* [*stew, pie*] de mouton

(Idioms) **as dead as** ~ mort et bien mort; ~ **dressed as lamb** habillé trop jeune pour son âge

mutton chops *npl* (whiskers) (favoris *mpl* en) côtelettes *fpl*

mutual /'mjuːtʃʊəl/ *adj* (reciprocal) réciproque; (common) commun; [*society, consent*] mutuel/-elle; **by** ~ **agreement** d'un commun accord; **it is to their** ~ **advantage** c'est dans leur intérêt à tous deux

mutual aid, **mutual assistance** *n* entraide *f*

mutually /'mjuːtʊəlɪ/ *adv* mutuellement; ~ **acceptable** acceptable pour les deux parties; ~ **agreed** fixé d'un commun accord

Muzak ® /'mjuːzæk/ *n* péj musique *f* d'ambiance (enregistrée)

muzzle /'mʌzl/
A *n* (snout) museau *m*; (worn by animal) muselière *f*; (of gun) canon *m*; (of canon) bouche *f*
B *vtr* museler

MW *n* Radio (*abrév* = **medium wave**) ondes *fpl* moyennes

my /maɪ/

⚠ In French, determiners agree in gender and number with the noun that follows. So *my* is translated by *mon* + masculine singular noun (mon chien), *ma* + feminine singular noun (ma maison) BUT by *mon* + feminine noun beginning with a vowel or mute h (mon assiette) and by *mes* + plural noun (mes enfants).
When *my* is stressed, *à moi* is added after the noun: MY *house* = ma maison à moi.
For *my* used with parts of the body see the usage note ▸ p. 698.

A *det* ① gen mon/ma/mes; ② (used emphatically) MY **house** ma maison à moi
B *excl* ~ ~! ça alors!

myalgic encephalomyelitis, **ME** /maɪˌældʒɪk enˌsefələʊˌmaɪəˈlaɪtɪs/ ▸ p. 933 *n* encéphalomyélite *f* myalgique

myopia /maɪˈəʊpɪə/ *n* Med myopie *f* also fig

myopic /maɪˈɒpɪk/ *adj* ① [*vision*] myope; ② fig [*policy*] myope; [*view*] étroit

myself /maɪˈself, məˈself/

⚠ When used as a reflexive pronoun, direct and indirect, *myself* is translated by *me* which is always placed before the verb: *I've hurt myself* = je me suis fait mal.
When used as an emphatic the translation is *moi-même*: *I did it myself* = je l'ai fait moi-même.
When used after a preposition *myself* is translated by *moi* or *moi-même*: *I did it for myself* = je l'ai fait pour moi *or* moi-même.
For particular usages see below.

pron ① (refl) me, (before vowel) m'; ② (emphatic) moi-même; **I saw it** ~ je l'ai vu moi-même; **for** ~ pour moi, pour moi-même; **(all) by** ~ tout seul; ③ (expressions) **I'm not much of a dog-lover** ~ personnellement je n'aime pas trop les chiens; **I'm not** ~ **today** je ne suis pas dans mon assiette aujourd'hui

mysterious /mɪˈstɪərɪəs/ *adj* mystérieux/-ieuse; **to be** ~ **about** faire grand mystère de

mysteriously /mɪˈstɪərɪəslɪ/ *adv* [*die, disappear, appear*] mystérieusement; [*say, smile, signal*] d'un air mystérieux

mystery /'mɪstərɪ/
A *n* ① mystère *m*; **it's a** ~ **to me how** je n'arrive pas à comprendre comment; **it's a** ~ **how** on ne sait pas comment; **there is no** ~ **about her success** son succès n'a rien de mystérieux; ② (book) roman *m* policier; ③ Relig mystère *m*
B *noun modifier* [*death, illness, voice*] mystérieux/-ieuse; [*guest, visitor*] mystère; [*prize, tour*] surprise; **the** ~ **man/woman** l'inconnu/-e

mystery: ~ **play** *n* mystère *m*; ~ **tour** *n* voyage *m* surprise

mystic(al) /'mɪstɪk(l)/ *adj* gen mystique

mysticism /'mɪstɪsɪzəm/ *n* mysticisme *m*

mystification /ˌmɪstɪfɪˈkeɪʃn/ *n* ① (of issue, process) mystification *f*; ② (of person) perplexité *f*; **in some** ~, **he...** quelque peu perplexe, il...

mystify /'mɪstɪfaɪ/ *vtr* laisser [qn] perplexe; **I am completely mystified** je suis tout à fait perplexe

mystifying /'mɪstɪfaɪɪŋ/ *adj* intrigant

myth /mɪθ/ *n* (fallacy) mythe *m*; (mythology) mythologie *f*

mythic(al) /'mɪθɪk(l)/ *adj* mythique

mythological /ˌmɪθəˈlɒdʒɪkl/ *adj* mythologique

mythology /mɪˈθɒlədʒɪ/ *n* mythologie *f*

m

n, N /en/ n **[1]** (letter) n, N m; **for the nth time** pour la énième fois; **[2]** N Geog (abrév écrite = **north**) N

n/a, N/A (abrév = **not applicable**) s/o

NA n: abrév ▸ **North America**

nab /næb/ vtr (p prés etc **-bb-**) (catch) pincer○ [wrongdoer]; coincer○ [passer-by]; (steal) piquer○

nadir /'neɪdɪə(r)/ n lit nadir m; fig point m le plus bas

naff○ /næf/ adj GB ringard○

nag /næg/
A vtr (p prés etc **-gg-**) **[1]** (pester) enquiquiner○ (**about** au sujet de); **[2]** (niggle) lanciner
B vi (p prés etc **-gg-**) **[1]** (moan) faire des remarques continuelles; **to ~ at sb** enquiquiner○ qn; **[2]** (niggle) **to ~ (away) at sb** travailler qn
C nagging pres p adj **[1]** (complaining) péj **his ~ging wife** sa mégère de femme péj; **[2]** (niggling) [pain, doubt, suspicion] tenace; [problem] obsédant

nail /neɪl/
A n **[1]** Anat ongle m; **to bite one's ~s** se ronger les ongles; **[2]** Tech clou m
B vtr **[1]** (attach with nails) clouer; **[2]** ○(pin down) coincer○ [wrongdoer]; démasquer [liar]; **[3]** ○(expose) démentir [rumour]; démolir [myth]

(Idioms) **to hit the ~ on the head** mettre le doigt dessus; **cash on the ~** argent m comptant; **to be as hard ou as tough as ~s** être sans cœur; **to fight tooth and ~** se battre avec acharnement

(Phrasal verbs)
■ **nail down: ▸ ~ down [sth], ~ [sth] down [1]** clouer; **[2]** fig (define) définir; **▸ ~ [sb] down** coincer○ [person]; **to ~ sb down to a time** obtenir de qn qu'il fixe (subj) une heure
■ **nail up: ▸ ~ up [sth], ~ [sth] up** gen clouer; (board up) condamner (avec des planches)

nail-biting /'neɪlbaɪtɪŋ/
A n habitude f de se ronger les ongles
B adj [match, finish] palpitant; [wait] angoissant

nail: **~brush** n brosse f à ongles; **~ clippers** npl coupe-ongles m inv; **~ file** n lime f à ongles; **~ polish** n vernis m à ongles; **~ polish remover** n dissolvant m; **~ scissors** npl ciseaux mpl à ongles; **~ varnish** n vernis m à ongles

naïve /naɪ'iːv/ adj gen, Art naïf/-ïve

naïvely /naɪ'iːvlɪ/ adv [believe, say, behave] naïvement; [draw, write] dans un style naïf

naked /'neɪkɪd/ adj **[1]** lit nu; **~ to the waist** torse nu; **[2]** [flame, light bulb, sword] nu; **[3]** [truth] tout nu; [facts] brut; [emotion] non déguisé

name /neɪm/
A n **[1]** (title) gen nom m; (of book, film) titre m; **first ~** prénom m; **my ~ is Louis** je m'appelle Louis; **what ~ shall I say?** (on phone) c'est de la part de qui?; (in person) qui dois-je annoncer?; **he goes by the ~ of Max** il s'appelle Max; **I know it by another ~** je le connais sous un autre nom; **I only know the company by ~** je ne connais la société que de nom; **he's president in ~ only** il n'a de président que le nom; **to be party leader in all ou everything but ~** être chef du parti en pratique, sinon en titre; **to take ou get one's ~ from** porter le nom de; **to put one's ~ down for** s'inscrire à; **[2]** (reputation) réputation f; **[3]** (insult) **to call sb ~s** injurier qn; **he called me all sorts of ~s** il m'a traité de tous les noms
B vtr **[1]** (call) appeler [person, area]; baptiser [boat, planet];

they **~d her after** GB ou for US **her mother** ils l'ont appelée comme sa mère; **we'll ~ him Martin after Martin Luther King** on l'appellera Martin en souvenir de Martin Luther King; **a boy ~d Joe** un garçon nommé Joe; **the product is ~d after its inventor** le produit porte le nom de son inventeur; **[2]** (cite) citer; **~ three American States** citez trois États américains; **illnesses? you ~ it, I've had it!** des maladies? je les ai toutes eues!; **[3]** (reveal identity of) citer [names]; révéler [sources]; révéler l'identité de [suspect]; **to ~ ~s** donner des noms; **naming no ~s** sans vouloir dénoncer personne; **to be ~d as a suspect** être désigné comme suspect; **[4]** (appoint) nommer [captain]; donner la composition de [team]; désigner [heir]; nommer [successor]; **[5]** (state) indiquer [place, time]; fixer [price, terms]

(Idioms) **that's the ~ of the game** c'est la règle du jeu; **to see one's ~ in lights** devenir célèbre

name: ~ day n Relig fête f; **~-drop** vi péj citer des gens célèbres (qu'on prétend connaître)

nameless /'neɪmlɪs/ adj [person] anonyme; [fear, dread] inexprimable

namely /'neɪmlɪ/ adv à savoir

name: ~ plate n plaque f; **~sake** n homonyme m; **~ tag** n étiquette f (sur laquelle est marqué le nom du propriétaire); **~ tape** n nom m tissé

Namibia /nə'mɪbɪə/ ▸ p. 774 pr n Namibie f

nanny /'nænɪ/ n GB (nurse) bonne f d'enfants; (grandmother)○ mamie f

nanny goat n chèvre f

nano+ /'nænəʊ/ (dans composés) nano

nap /næp/
A n **[1]** (snooze) petit somme m; **afternoon ~** sieste f; **[2]** (pile) poil m; (direction of cut) sens m; **against the ~** à rebrousse-poil
B vi (p prés etc **-pp-**) sommeiller

(Idiom) **to catch sb ~ping**○ prendre qn au dépourvu

napalm /'neɪpɑːm/ n napalm m

nape /neɪp/ n nuque f; **the ~ of the neck** la nuque

napkin /'næpkɪn/ n (serviette) serviette f (de table); **~ ring** rond m de serviette

nappy /'næpɪ/ n GB couche f (de bébé)

nappy: ~ liner n lange m fin; **~ rash** n GB érythème m fessier

narcotic /nɑː'kɒtɪk/
A n (soporific) lit, fig narcotique m; (illegal drug) stupéfiant m
B adj lit, fig narcotique

narcotics agent n US agent m de la brigade des stupéfiants

narked○ /nɑːkt/ adj en rogne○, en boule

narration /nə'reɪʃn/ n récit m, narration f

narrative /'nærətɪv/
A n (account) récit m; (storytelling) narration f
B noun modifier [prose, poem] narratif/-ive; [skill, talent] de conteur

narrator /nə'reɪtə(r)/ n Literat narrateur/-trice m/f; Mus récitant/-e m/f

narrow /'nærəʊ/ ▸ p. 977
A narrows npl goulet m
B adj **[1]** (in breadth, size, shape) étroit; **to grow ou become ~** [road, river] se rétrécir; [valley] se resserrer; **[2]** (in scope) [range, choice] restreint; [issue, field, boundaries, group, sense, definition] étroit; [vision, life, interests, understanding] limité;

[*views, version*] étriqué pej; **3** (in degree) [*majority, margin*] faible; **to have a ~ lead** avoir une légère avance; **to win a ~ victory** gagner de justesse; **to have a ~ escape** *ou* **a ~ squeak**○ GB l'échapper belle

C *vtr* **1** (limit) gen limiter (**to** à); restreindre [*sense, definition*] (**to** à); **2** (reduce) réduire (**from** de; **to** à); **Elliott has ~ed the gap** (in race, poll) Elliott a réduit l'écart; **3** (reduce breadth of) rétrécir [*road, path, arteries*]; **to ~ one's eyes** plisser les yeux

D *vi* **1** lit gen se rétrécir; [*valley, arteries*] se resserrer; **2** fig [*gap, deficit, margin, lead*] se réduire (**to** à); [*choice*] se limiter (**to** à)

(Idiom) **the straight and ~** le droit chemin

(Phrasal verb)

■ **narrow down** [*investigation, search*] se limiter (**to** à); [*field of contestants, suspects*] se réduire (**to** à); ► **~ [sth] down**, **~ down [sth]** réduire [*numbers, list, choice*] (**to** à); limiter [*investigation, research*] (**to** à)

narrow boat *n* GB péniche *f*

narrowly /ˈnærəʊlɪ/ *adv* (barely) de justesse; (strictly) strictement

narrow-minded /ˌnærəʊˈmaɪndɪd/ *adj* péj borné

nasal /ˈneɪzl/
A *n* Ling nasale *f*
B *adj* Ling nasal; gen nasillard

nasal spray *n* nébuliseur *m* (*pour le nez*)

nastily /ˈnɑːstɪlɪ/ *adv* [*behave, speak, laugh*] d'une façon désagréable; **to say sth ~** dire qch d'un ton sarcastique

nastiness /ˈnɑːstɪnɪs/ *n* gen méchanceté *f*; (of food, medicine) mauvais goût *m*

nasturtium /nəˈstɜːʃəm/ *n* capucine *f*

nasty /ˈnɑːstɪ/
A ○*n* (in food, water, air) saleté *f*; **video ~** film *m* d'épouvante en vidéo
B *adj* **1** (unpleasant) [*crime, experience, sight, taste, surprise, suspicion*] horrible; [*feeling, task*] désagréable; [*habit, weather, smell, taste*] mauvais; [*expression, look*] méchant; [*rumour*] inquiétant; [*stain*] gros/grosse; [*affair, business*] sale (*before n*); **I got a ~ fright** j'ai vraiment eu un choc; **things could get ~** les choses pourraient mal tourner; **to turn ~** [*person, dog*] devenir méchant; [*weather*] se gâter; **to be a ~ piece of work**○ GB être un sale type○/une sale bonne femme○; **2** (unkind) [*person*] désagréable; [*trick*] sale (*before n*), vilain; [*gossip, remark, letter*] méchant; **you've got a ~ mind** tu vois toujours le mal partout; **to be ~** être dur envers; **3** (serious) [*cut, bruise*] vilain (*before n*); [*bump, crack, fall, accident*] grave; [*cold*] mauvais (*before n*); **4** (ugly) affreux/-euse; **5** (tricky) [*problem, question*] difficile; [*bend*] dangereux/-euse

nation /ˈneɪʃn/ *n* Pol (entity) nation *f*; (people) peuple *m*

national /ˈnæʃənl/
A *n* **1** (citizen) ressortissant/-e *m/f*; **2** ○GB (newspaper) **the ~s** les grands quotidiens *mpl*
B *adj* national; **the ~ press** *ou* **newspapers** GB les grands quotidiens *mpl*; **~ affairs** les affaires du pays

national: **~ anthem** *n* hymne *m* national; **National Curriculum** *n* GB programme *m* scolaire national; **~ debt** *n* dette *f* publique; **National Front**, **NF** *n* GB parti britannique d'extrême droite; **~ grid** *n* Elec réseau *m* national haute-tension

National Health *n* GB **to get sth on the ~** ≈ se faire rembourser qch par la Sécurité Sociale

national: **National Health Service**, **NHS** *n* GB services *mpl* de santé britanniques, ≈ Sécurité *f* Sociale; **National Insurance**, **NI** *n* GB sécurité *f* sociale britannique; **National Insurance number** *n* numéro *m* de sécurité sociale

nationalism /ˈnæʃnəlɪzəm/ *n* nationalisme *m*

nationality /ˌnæʃəˈnælɪtɪ/ *n* nationalité *f*

nationalization /ˌnæʃnəlaɪˈzeɪʃn/, US -lɪ'z-/ *n* nationalisation *f*

nationalize /ˈnæʃnəlaɪz/ *vtr* nationaliser [*industry*]

nationally /ˈnæʃnəlɪ/ *adv* **1** (at national level) à l'échelon national; **2** (nationwide) [*broadcast, enforce, employ, distribute*] sur l'ensemble du pays; [*known, respected, available*] dans tout le pays

national: **National Minimum Wage** *n* GB Soc Admin ≈ SMIC *m*; **~ monument** *n* monument *m* historique; **National Savings Bank** *n* GB ≈ Caisse *f* d'Épargne;

~ service *n* GB Hist service *m* militaire

National Trust, **NT** *n* GB commission *f* nationale des sites et monuments historiques

nation-state *n* État-nation *m*

nationwide /ˌneɪʃnˈwaɪd/
A *adj* [*appeal, coverage, scheme, strike*] sur l'ensemble du territoire; [*campaign*] national; [*survey, poll*] à l'échelle nationale
B *adv* [*broadcast, travel, compete*] dans tout le pays

native /ˈneɪtɪv/
A *n* (person) autochtone *mf*; Bot, Zool espèce *f* indigène; **to be a ~ of** [*person, plant*] être originaire de; **to speak a language like a ~** parler une langue comme si c'était sa langue maternelle
B *adj* **1** (original) [*land*] natal; [*tongue*] maternel/-elle; **~ German speaker** personne *f* de langue maternelle allemande; **~ English speaker** anglophone *mf*; **2** Bot, Zool indigène; **to go ~** hum adopter les coutumes locales; **3** [*cunning*] inné; [*wit*] naturel/-elle

Native American *n, adj* amérindien/-ienne (*m/f*)

> **Native American** Longtemps appelés *Indians*, les Amérindiens veulent que soit reconnu le fait qu'ils occupaient le territoire américain des centaines d'années avant l'arrivée des Européens. À peu près un million d'entre eux vivent dans des réserves qui ont chacune leur propre gouvernement et leur propre force de police.

native speaker *n* locuteur natif/locutrice native *m/f*; **'we require a ~ of English'** 'recherchons personne de langue maternelle anglaise'

Nativity /nəˈtɪvətɪ/ *n* Relig, Art nativité *f*

Nato, **NATO** *n* (abrév = **North Atlantic Treaty Organization**) OTAN *f*

natter○ /ˈnætə(r)/ GB
A *n* causette○ *f* (**about** sur)
B *vi* (*also* **~ on**) papoter

natty○ /ˈnætɪ/ *adj* (smart) chic *inv*; (clever) astucieux/-ieuse

natural /ˈnætʃrəl/
A *n* **1** ○(person) **as an actress, she's a ~** c'est une actrice née; **2** Mus (sign) bécarre *m*; (note) note *f* naturelle
B *adj* **1** naturel/-elle, normal; **it's only ~** c'est tout à fait naturel; **to die of ~ causes** mourir de mort naturelle; **2** (innate) [*gift, emotion, trait*] inné; [*artist, professional*] né; [*affinity*] naturel/-elle; **a ~ advantage** un atout; **3** (unaffected) simple, naturel/-elle; **4** Mus naturel/-elle

natural childbirth *n* accouchement *m* sans douleur

naturalist /ˈnætʃrəlɪst/ *n, adj* naturaliste (*mf*)

naturalization /ˌnætʃrəlaɪˈzeɪʃn, US -lɪ'z-/ *n* **1** Admin naturalisation *f*; **2** Bot, Zool acclimatation *f*

naturalize /ˈnætʃrəlaɪz/
A *vtr* **1** Admin naturaliser [*person*]; **to be ~d** se faire naturaliser; **2** Bot, Zool acclimater
B *vi* Bot, Zool s'acclimater

natural justice *n*: principes d'égalité s'appliquant au règlement de disputes

naturally /ˈnætʃrəlɪ/ *adv* **1** (obviously, of course) naturellement, bien entendu; **~ enough**, **she refused** naturellement, elle a refusé; **2** (by nature) de nature; **her hair is ~ blonde** elle a des cheveux blond naturel; **I was doing what comes ~** j'ai fait ce qui me semblait naturel; **politeness comes ~ to him** il est d'un naturel poli; **3** (unaffectedly) avec naturel; **4** (in natural world) à l'état naturel

nature /ˈneɪtʃə(r)/
A *n* **1** (the natural world) nature *f*; **let ~ take its course** laissez faire la nature; **~ versus nurture** l'inné et l'acquis; **to obey a call of ~** euph aller se soulager○; **2** (character, temperament) nature *f*, naturel *m*; **it's not in her ~ to be aggressive** elle n'est pas agressive de nature; **3** (kind, sort) nature *f*, sorte *f*; **matters of a medical ~** des choses d'ordre médical; **her letter was something in the ~ of a confession** sa lettre tenait de la confession; **'~ of contents'** 'désignation du contenu'; **4** (essential character) nature *f*, essence *f*; **it is in the ~ of things** il est dans l'ordre des choses
B **-natured** combining form **sweet-/pleasant-~d** d'un naturel doux/agréable

nature: **~ conservancy** *n* protection *f* de la nature; **~ reserve** *n* réserve *f* naturelle; **~ trail** *n* sentier *m* écologique

Nationalities

■ Words like French can also refer to the language (e.g. a French textbook ▸ **p. 969**) and to the country (e.g. French history ▸ **p. 774**).

■ *Note the different use of capital letters in English and French; adjectives never have capitals in French:*

a French student
= un étudiant français/une étudiante française

a French nurse
= une infirmière française/un infirmier français

a French tourist
= un touriste français/une touriste française

■ *Nouns have capitals in French when they mean a person of a specific nationality:*

a Frenchman
= un Français

a Frenchwoman
= une Française

French people or *the French*
= les Français *mpl*

a Chinese man
= un Chinois

a Chinese woman
= une Chinoise

Chinese people or *the Chinese*
= les Chinois *mpl*

■ *English sometimes has a special word for a person of a specific nationality; in French, the same word can almost always be either an adjective (no capitals) or a noun (with capitals):*

Danish
= danois

a Dane
= un Danois, une Danoise

the Danes
= les Danois *mpl*

■ *Note the alternatives using either adjective (il/elle est ... etc.) or noun (c'est ...) in French:*

he is French
= il est français or c'est un Français

she is French
= elle est française or c'est une Française

they are French
= (men or mixed) ils sont français or ce sont des Français (women) elles sont françaises or ce sont des Françaises

■ *When the subject is a noun, like* the teacher *or* Paul *below, the adjective construction is normally used in French:*

the teacher is French
= le professeur est français

Paul is French
= Paul est français

Anne is French
= Anne est française

Paul and Anne are French
= Paul et Anne sont français

■ *Other ways of expressing someone's nationality or origins are:*

he's of French extraction
= il est d'origine française

she was born in Germany
= elle est née en Allemagne

he is a Spanish citizen
= il est espagnol

a Belgian national
= un ressortissant belge

she comes from Nepal
= elle vient du Népal

---

naturist /'neɪtʃərɪst/ *n, adj* naturiste (*mf*)

naughtily /'nɔːtɪlɪ/ *adv* (disobediently) **to behave** ∼ être vilain; (suggestively) **she winked at him** ∼ hum elle lui a fait un clin d'œil coquin

naughtiness /'nɔːtɪnɪs/ *n* ① (of child, pet) mauvaise conduite *f*; ② (of joke, suggestion) grivoiserie *f*

naughty /'nɔːtɪ/ *adj* ① (disobedient) [*child*] vilain; **a** ∼ **word** un gros mot; ② (suggestive) coquin; **the** ∼ **nineties** ≈ la Belle Époque

nausea /'nɔːsɪə, US 'nɔːʒə/ *n* nausée *f*

nauseate /'nɔːzɪeɪt, US 'nɔːz-/ *vtr* lit, fig écœurer

nauseating /'nɔːzɪeɪtɪŋ, US 'nɔːz-/ *adj* écœurant

nauseatingly /'nɔːzɪeɪtɪŋlɪ, US 'nɔːz-/ *adv* ∼ **sweet/rich** d'une douceur/richesse écœurante

nauseous /'nɔːsɪəs, US 'nɔːʃəs/ *adj* [*taste, smell*] écœurant; **to feel** ∼ avoir la nausée

nautical /'nɔːtɪkl/ *adj* [*instrument, almanac, term, mile*] nautique; [*rules*] de navigation; [*theme*] marin

naval /'neɪvl/ *adj* naval; [*officer, recruit, uniform, affairs*] de la marine; [*traditions, strength, building*] maritime

naval: ∼ **base**, ∼ **station** base *f* navale; ∼ **dockyard** *n* chantier *m* naval; ∼ **stores** *npl* (depot) entrepôt *m* maritime; (supplies) fournitures *fpl* maritimes

nave /neɪv/ *n* Archit nef *f*

navel /'neɪvl/ *n* nombril *m*

navigable /'nævɪgəbl/ *adj* [*river*] navigable

navigate /'nævɪgeɪt/
Ⓐ *vtr* ① (sail) parcourir [*seas*]; ② (guide) piloter [*plane, ship*]; ③ (steer) piloter [*plane*]; gouverner [*ship*]; **to** ∼ **one's way through** retrouver son chemin dans [*streets*]; ④ (on the Internet) **to** ∼ **the Web** naviguer sur le web

Ⓑ *vi* Naut, Aviat naviguer; Aut (in a rally) faire le copilote; (on a journey) tenir la carte; (without a map) retrouver son chemin

navigation /ˌnævɪ'geɪʃn/ *n* navigation *f*

navigational /ˌnævɪ'geɪʃənl/ *adj* [*instruments*] de navigation; [*science*] de la navigation

navigation laws *npl* code *m* maritime

navigator /'nævɪgeɪtə(r)/ *n* Aviat, Naut navigateur/-trice *m/f*; Aut copilote *mf*

navy /'neɪvɪ/
Ⓐ *n* ① (fleet) flotte *f*; (fighting force) marine *f*; ② (also ∼ **blue**) bleu *m* marine

Ⓑ *adj* ▸ **p. 752** ① (also ∼ **blue**) bleu marine *inv*; ② Mil, Naut [*life, uniform, wife*] de marin

nay /neɪ/ ‡ *ou* littér
Ⓐ *n* (negative vote) non *m*

Ⓑ *adv* et même

Nazi /'nɑːtsɪ/ *n, adj* nazi/-e (*m/f*)

NBC *n* US TV (abrév = **National Broadcasting Company**) chaîne nationale de la télévision américaine

NC ① Comm (abrév = **no charge**) gratuit; ② US Post *abrév écrite* = **North Carolina**

NCO *n* Mil (abrév = **noncommissioned officer**) sous-officier *m*

ND US Post *abrév écrite* = **North Dakota**

NE ① ▸ **p. 1089** (abrév = **northeast**) NE *m*; ② *abrév écrite* = **Nebraska**

near /nɪə(r)/
Ⓐ *adv* ① (nearby) **to live quite** ∼ habiter tout près; **to move** *ou* **draw** ∼**er** s'approcher davantage (**to** de); **to bring sth** ∼**er** approcher qch; ② (close in time) **the time is** ∼ **when...** dans peu de temps,...; **how** ∼ **are they in age?** combien ont-ils de différence d'âge?; ③ (nearly) **as** ∼ **perfect as it could be**

aussi proche de la perfection que possible; **nowhere ~ finished** loin d'être fini

B near enough *adv phr* **1** (approximately) à peu près; **2** (sufficiently close) **that's ~ enough** (not any closer) tu es assez près; (acceptable as quantity) ça ira

C *prep* **1** (in space) près de; **2** (in time) **~er the time** quand la date approchera; **it's getting ~ Christmas** Noël approche; **on or ~ the 12th** autour du 12; **3** (in degree) proche de; **~ the beginning of the article** presque au début de l'article; **he's no ~er (making) a decision** il n'est pas plus décidé; **she's nowhere ~ finishing** elle est loin d'avoir fini; **£400? it cost ~er £600** 400 livres sterling? je dirais plutôt 600; **nobody comes anywhere ~ her** *fig* personne ne lui arrive à la cheville

D near to *prep phr* **1** (in space) près de; **~ to where** près de l'endroit où; **how ~ are we to Dijon?** à quelle distance sommes-nous de Dijon?; **2** (on point of) au bord de [*tears, hysteria, collapse*]; **to be ~ to doing** être sur le point de faire; **how ~ are you to completing…?** est-ce que vous êtes sur le point de finir…?; **3** (in degree) **to come ~est to** s'approcher le plus de; **to come ~ to doing** faillir faire

E *adj* **1** (close in distance, time) proche; **2** (in degree) **he's the ~est thing to an accountant we've got** c'est lui qui a le plus de connaissances en comptabilité parmi nos employés; **it's the ~est thing** (to article, colour required) c'est ça le plus approchant; **3** (short) **the ~est route** le chemin le plus court

F near + *combining form* presque; **a ~-catastrophic blunder** une gaffe presque catastrophique

G *vtr* lit, fig (draw close to) approcher de; **to ~ completion** toucher à sa fin; **to ~ retirement** partir bientôt à la retraite

nearby /nɪəˈbaɪ/

A *adj* [*person*] qui se trouve/trouvait etc à proximité; [*town, village*] d'à côté; **they drove to a ~ garage** ils ont conduit jusqu'au garage le plus proche

B *adv* à proximité; **~, there's a village** tout près il y a un village

Near East *pr n* Proche-Orient *m*

nearly /ˈnɪəlɪ/ *adv* **1** (almost) presque; **have you ~ finished?** as-tu bientôt fini?; **he ~ laughed** il a réprimé un rire; **I very ~ gave up** j'ai bien failli abandonner; **2** (used with negatives) **not ~ long enough** loin d'être; **not ~ as talented as** loin d'être aussi doué que

nearly new *adj* [*clothes*] d'occasion

near miss *n* risque *m* de collision; **to have a ~** [*planes*] frôler la collision; [*cars*] faillir se percuter

nearness /ˈnɪənɪs/ *n* gen proximité *f*; (of event) approche *f*

nearside /ˈnɪəsaɪd/

A *n* GB côté *m* gauche; (elsewhere) côté *m* droit

B *noun modifier* GB [*lane*] gauche; (elsewhere) [*lane*] droit

near: ~-sighted *adj* myope; **~-sightedness** *n* myopie *f*

neat /niːt/

A *adj* **1** (tidy) [*person*] (in habits) ordonné; (in appearance) soigné; [*room, house, desk*] bien rangé; [*garden, handwriting*] soigné; **in ~ piles** en piles régulières; **2** (adroit) [*explanation, solution*] habile; [*formula, slogan*] bien trouvé; [*summary*] concis; **that's a ~ way of doing it!** c'est astucieux!; **3** (trim) [*figure*] bien fait; [*features*] régulier/-ière; **4** US (very good) [*plan, party, car*] super; [*sum of money*] joli; **5** [*alcohol, spirits*] sans eau

B *adv* sec, sans eau

Idiom **to be as ~ as a new pin** être propre comme un sou neuf

neaten /ˈniːtn/ *vtr* arranger [*tie, skirt*]; ranger [*pile of paper*]

neatly /ˈniːtlɪ/ *adv* **1** (tidily) gen avec soin; [*write*] proprement; **his hair was ~ combed** ses cheveux étaient impeccablement peignés; **2** (perfectly) gen parfaitement; [*link*] habilement; **~ put!** bien *or* joliment dit!; **the case is designed to fit ~ into your pocket** l'étui est conçu pour rentrer facilement dans la poche

neatness /ˈniːtnɪs/ *n* **1** (tidiness, orderliness) (of person, garden) aspect *m* soigné; (in habits) méticulosité *f*; (of room, house) propreté *f*; (of handwriting) netteté *f*; **extra marks are given for ~** on tiendra compte de la présentation dans la notation; **2** (of figure, features) finesse *f*; (of explanation, solution) habileté *f*

necessarily /ˌnesəˈserɪlɪ, ˈnesəsərɪlɪ/ *adv* (definitely) forcément; (of necessity) nécessairement

necessary /ˈnesəsərɪ, US -serɪ/

A *n* **1** ○(money) fric○ *m*; **2** (needed thing) **to do the ~** faire le nécessaire

B *adj* (required, essential, inevitable) gen nécessaire; [*qualification*] requis; **if ~, as ~** si besoin est; **'no experience ~'** 'aucune expérience requise'; **to become ~** devenir urgent; **to find it ~ to do** éprouver le besoin de faire; **it is ~ for him to do** il faut qu'il fasse; **it is ~ that she should do** il faut vraiment qu'elle fasse

necessitate /nɪˈsesɪteɪt/ *vtr* nécessiter; **the job would ~ your moving** le travail t'obligerait à déménager

necessity /nɪˈsesətɪ/ *n* **1** (need) nécessité *f*; **from** *ou* **out of ~** par nécessité; **the ~ for** le besoin de; **of ~** nécessairement; **2** (essential item) **the necessities of life** les produits *mpl* de première nécessité; **to be a ~** être indispensable; **3** (essential measure) impératif *m*; **to be an absolute ~** être indispensable; **4** †(poverty) besoin *m*

neck /nek/

A *n* ▸ p. 698 **1** (of person) cou *m*; (of horse, donkey) encolure *f*; **to fling one's arms around sb's ~** sauter au cou de qn; **the back of the ~** la nuque; **2** (collar) col *m*; (neckline) encolure *f*; **with a high ~** à *or* avec un col montant; **with a low ~** décolleté; **3** Culin (also **best end of ~**) collet *m*; **4** (of bottle, vase, womb) col *m*

B ○*vi* se bécoter○

Idioms **to be a pain in the ~** ○ être casse-pieds○; **to be ~ and ~** lit, fig être à égalité; **to get** *ou* **catch it in the ~** ○ en prendre pour son grade○; **to risk one's ~** ○ risquer sa peau○; **to stick one's ~ out** ○ prendre des risques; **in this ~ of the woods** ○ par ici; **to be dead from the ~ up** ○ être abruti

necking ○ /ˈnekɪŋ/ *n* **¢** papouilles○ *fpl*

neck: ~lace *n* collier *m*; (longer) sautoir *m*; **~line** *n* encolure *f*; **~tie** *n* US cravate *f*

nectar /ˈnektə(r)/ *n* (all contexts) nectar *m*

nectarine /ˈnektərɪn/ *n* (fruit) nectarine *f*, brugnon *m*; (tree) brugnonier *m*

need /niːd/

> ⚠ When *need* is used as a verb meaning *to require* or *to want* it is generally translated by *avoir besoin de* in French: *I need help* = j'ai besoin d'aide.
> When *need* is used as a verb to mean *must* or *have to* it can generally be translated by *devoir* + *infinitive* or by *il faut que* + subjunctive: *I need to leave* = je dois partir, il faut que je parte.
> When *need* is used as a modal auxiliary in the negative to say that there is no obligation it is generally translated by *ne pas être obligé de* + *infinitive*: *you needn't finish it today* = tu n'es pas obligé de le finir aujourd'hui.
> When *needn't* is used as a modal auxiliary to say that something is not worthwhile or necessary it is generally translated by *ce n'est pas la peine de* + *infinitive* or *ce n'est pas la peine que* + subjunctive: *I needn't have hurried* = ce n'était pas la peine de me dépêcher *or* ce n'était pas la peine que je me dépêche.
> For examples of the above and further uses of *need*, see the entry below.

A *modal aux* **1** (must, have to) **'I waited'—'you needn't have'** 'j'ai attendu'—'ce n'était pas la peine'; **~ he reply?** est-ce qu'il faut qu'il réponde?, est-ce qu'il doit répondre?; **~ I say more?** tu vois ce que je veux dire?; **I hardly ~ say that…** inutile de dire que…; **did you ~ to be so unpleasant to him?** est-ce que tu avais besoin d'être si désagréable avec lui?; **'previous applicants ~ not apply'** 'les candidats ayant déjà répondu à l'annonce sont priés de ne pas se représenter'; **2** (be logically inevitable) **~ that be true?** est-ce que c'est forcément vrai?; **they needn't have died** leur mort aurait pu être évitée

B *vtr* **1** (require) **to ~ sth** avoir besoin de qch; **my shoes ~ to be polished, my shoes ~ polishing** mes chaussures ont besoin d'être cirées; **I ~ you to hold the ladder** j'ai besoin de toi pour tenir l'échelle; **more money is ~ed** nous avons besoin de plus d'argent; **everything you ~** tout ce qu'il vous faut; **I gave it a much-~ed clean** je l'ai nettoyé, il en avait grand besoin; **this job ~s a lot of concentration** ce travail demande beaucoup de concentration; **to raise the money ~ed for the deposit** réunir l'argent nécessaire pour la caution; **they ~ to have things explained to them**

n

il faut tout leur expliquer; **you don't ~ me to tell you that...** vous n'êtes pas sans savoir que...; **everything you ~ to know about computers** tout ce que vous devez savoir sur les ordinateurs; **that's all I ~!** il ne me manquait plus que ça; ② (have to) **you'll ~ to work hard** il va falloir que tu travailles dur; **something ~ed to be done** il fallait faire quelque chose; **it ~ only be said that** il suffit de dire que; **nobody ~ know** que cela reste entre nous; **nobody ~ know that I did it** personne ne doit savoir que c'est moi qui l'ai fait

C n ① (necessity) nécessité f (**for** de); **I can't see the ~ for it** je n'en vois pas la nécessité; **without the ~ for an inquiry** sans qu'une enquête soit nécessaire; **to feel the ~ to do** éprouver le besoin de faire; **there's no ~ to wait** inutile d'attendre; **there's no ~ to worry** ce n'est pas la peine de s'affoler; **there's no ~ for panic** ça ne sert à rien de s'affoler; **if ~ be** s'il le faut; **if the ~ arises** si le besoin s'en fait sentir; **there's no ~, I've done it** inutile, c'est fait; ② (want, requirement) besoin m (**for** de); **to satisfy a ~** répondre à un besoin; **to meet sb's ~s** répondre aux besoins de qn; **a list of your ~s** une liste de ce dont vous avez besoin; **my ~s are few** j'ai peu de besoins; **energy ~s** besoins mpl en énergie; ③ (adversity, distress) **to help sb in times of ~** aider qn à faire face à l'adversité; **she was there in my hour of ~** elle était là quand j'ai eu besoin d'elle; **your ~ is greater than mine** tu en as plus besoin que moi; ④ (poverty) besoin m; **to be in ~** être dans le besoin

needful /ˈniːdfl/
A n **to do the ~** faire le nécessaire
B adj sout nécessaire

needle /ˈniːdl/
A n lit (all contexts) aiguille f
B vtr (annoy) harceler

(Idioms) **as sharp as a ~** rusé comme un singe; **to have pins and ~s** avoir des fourmis

needless /ˈniːdlɪs/ adj [anxiety, delay, suffering] inutile; [intrusion, intervention] inopportun

needlessly /ˈniːdlɪslɪ/ adv pour rien

needlework n couture f

needs /niːdz/ adv **~ must** † il faut bien

need-to-know adj **we operate on a ~ basis, we have a ~ policy** nous avons pour principe de ne divulguer les informations qu'aux personnes strictement concernées

needy /ˈniːdɪ/
A n **the ~** (+ v pl) les indigents mpl
B adj [person] nécessiteux/-euse; [sector, area] sans ressources

negate /nɪˈɡeɪt/ vtr (cancel out) réduire [qch] à néant; (deny) nier; (contradict) contredire; Ling mettre [qch] à la forme négative

negation /nɪˈɡeɪʃn/ n gen, Ling négation f; (denial) réfutation f

negative /ˈneɡətɪv/
A n ① (refusal) réponse f négative; **to answer** ou **reply in the ~** répondre par la négative; ② Phot, Elec négatif m; ③ Ling négation f; **in the ~** à la forme négative
B adj ① gen (negating, unpleasant, pessimistic) négatif/-ive; [effect, influence] néfaste; ② Phot en négatif

negatively /ˈneɡətɪvlɪ/ adv [react, respond] négativement; [affect, influence] de façon néfaste

neglect /nɪˈɡlekt/
A n ① (lack of care) (of person) négligence f; (of building, garden equipment) manque m d'entretien; (of health, appearance) manque m de soin; **to fall into ~** être laissé à l'abandon; ② (lack of interest) indifférence f (**of** à l'égard de)
B vtr ① (fail to care for) ne pas s'occuper de [person, dog, plant]; ne pas entretenir [garden, house]; négliger [health, appearance]; ② (ignore) négliger [problem, friend, artist, subject, work]; se désintéresser de [industry, economy, sector]; ne pas tenir compte de [needs, wishes]; ignorer [offer, opportunity]; ③ (fail) **to ~ to do** négliger de faire; **to ~ to mention** omettre de mentionner
C v refl **to ~ oneself** se laisser aller

neglected /nɪˈɡlektɪd/ adj gen négligé; [garden, building] mal entretenu; **to feel ~** se sentir délaissé

neglectful /nɪˈɡlektfl/ adj négligent

negligence /ˈneɡlɪdʒəns/ n gen négligence f

negligent /ˈneɡlɪdʒənt/ adj [person, procedure] négligent; [air, manner] nonchalant

negligible /ˈneɡlɪdʒəbl/ adj négligeable

negotiable /nɪˈɡəʊʃəbl/ adj ① Fin, Comm négociable; 'not ~' [cheque] 'non à ordre'; ② [road, pass] praticable; [obstacle] franchissable

negotiate /nɪˈɡəʊʃɪeɪt/
A vtr ① (discuss) gen, Fin négocier (**with** avec); **'to be ~d'** 'à négocier'; ② (manoeuvre around) négocier [bend, turn]; franchir [obstacle]; ③ résoudre [problem]; surmonter [difficulty]
B vi négocier (**with** avec; **for** pour obtenir)
C **negotiated** pp adj [settlement, peace, solution] négocié

negotiating /nɪˈɡəʊʃɪeɪtɪŋ/ adj ① [ploy, position] de négociation; [rights] à la négociation; **the ~ table** la table des négociations; ② [team, committee] qui conduit les négociations

negotiation /nɪˌɡəʊʃɪˈeɪʃn/ n négociation f; **to be under ~** être en cours de négociations; **to be open for ~** être négociable; **to be up for ~** être à négocier

negotiator /nɪˈɡəʊʃɪeɪtə(r)/ n négociateur/-trice m/f

Negro /ˈniːɡrəʊ/
A n (pl **-es**) injur nègre m
B adj [descent, race] noir, nègre

neigh /neɪ/ vi hennir

neighbour, neighbor US /ˈneɪbə(r)/
A n ① voisin/-e m/f; **next-door-~** voisin/-e m/f d'à côté; **England's nearest ~ is France** le pays le plus proche de l'Angleterre est la France; ② Relig, littér prochain m
B vi **to ~ on sth** [building] avoisiner qch; [country] border qch

neighbourhood GB, **neighborhood** US /ˈneɪbəhʊd/
A n ① (district) quartier m; ② (vicinity) **in the ~** dans le voisinage
B noun modifier [facility, shop, office] du quartier

neighbourhood: ~ television n télévision f locale; **~ watch (scheme)** n surveillance f par les gens du quartier

neighbouring GB, **neighboring** US /ˈneɪbərɪŋ/ adj voisin

neighbourly GB, **neighborly** US /ˈneɪbəlɪ/ adj [person, act] gentil/-ille; [relations] de bon voisinage

neither /ˈnaɪðə(r), ˈniːð-/

> ⚠ When used as co-ordinating conjunctions neither...nor are translated by ni...ni: she speaks neither English nor French = elle ne parle ni anglais ni français; he is neither intelligent nor kind = il n'est ni intelligent ni gentil; neither tea, nor milk = ni (le) thé, ni (le) lait. Note that the preceding verb is negated by ne.
>
> For examples and particular usages see the entry **neither A 1**.
>
> When used as a conjunction to show agreement or similarity with a negative statement, neither is translated by non plus: 'I don't like him'—'neither do I' = 'je ne l'aime pas'—'moi non plus'; 'he's not Spanish' —'neither is John' = 'il n'est pas espagnol'—'John non plus'; 'I can't sleep'—'neither can I' = 'je n'arrive pas à dormir'—'moi non plus'.
>
> When used to give additional information to a negative statement neither can often be translated by non plus preceded by a negative verb: she hasn't written, neither has she telephoned = elle n'a pas écrit, et elle n'a pas téléphoné non plus; I don't wish to insult you, but neither do I wish to lose money = je ne veux pas vous offenser, mais je ne souhaite pas non plus perdre de l'argent.
>
> For examples and particular usages see the entry **neither A 2**.

A conj ① (not either) ni...ni; **I have ~ the time nor the money** je n'ai ni le temps ni l'argent; **I've seen ~ him nor her** je ne les ai vus ni l'un ni l'autre; ② (nor) **he doesn't have the time, ~ does he have the money** il n'a pas le temps, et il n'a pas l'argent non plus; **you don't have to tell him, ~ should you** tu n'es pas obligé de le lui dire, tu ferais même mieux d'éviter
B det (neither of the two): **~ book is suitable** aucun des deux livres ne convient; **~ girl replied** aucune des deux filles n'a répondu
C pron ni l'un/-e, ni l'autre m/f; **~ of them came** ni l'un ni l'autre n'est venu; **'which one is responsible?'—'~'** 'lequel des deux est responsable?'—'ni l'un ni l'autre'

nem con /ˌnemˈkɒn/ *adv* (*abrév* = **nemine contradi-cente**) à l'unanimité

neo+ /niːəʊ/ *combining form* néo-

neologism /niːˈɒlədʒɪzəm/ *n* néologisme *m*

neon /ˈniːɒn/
A *n* néon *m*
B *noun modifier* [*light, lighting, sign*] au néon; [*atom*] de néon

nephew /ˈnevjuː, ˈnef-/ *n* neveu *m*

nephritis /nɪˈfraɪtɪs/ ▸ p. 933 *n* néphrite *f*

nerve /nɜːv/
A *n* **1** Anat nerf *m*; Bot nervure *f*; **2** (*courage*) courage *m*; (*confidence*) assurance *f*; **to keep one's ~** conserver son sang-froid; **to recover one's ~** retrouver son assurance; **3** ○(*cheek*) culot○ *m*
B **nerves** *npl* (*nervousness*) nerfs *mpl*; (*stage fright*) trac○ *m*; **to have an attack of ~s** faire une crise de nerfs; **it's only ~s!** c'est nerveux!; **his ~s were on edge** il était sur les nerfs; **to calm sb's ~s** calmer qn
C *vtr* **to ~ oneself to do** s'armer de courage pour faire
(Idioms) **to touch** *ou* **hit a raw ~** toucher un point sensible; **to strain every ~ to do** s'évertuer à faire

nerve racking, **nerve wracking** *adj* angoissant

nerviness /ˈnɜːvɪnɪs/ *n* GB nervosité *f*; US aplomb *m*

nervous /ˈnɜːvəs/ *adj* **1** [*person*] (*fearful*) timide; (*anxious*) angoissé; (*highly strung*) nerveux/-euse; [*smile, laugh, habit*] nerveux/-euse; **to be ~ of** GB *ou* **around** US avoir peur de [*strangers, animals*]; **to be ~ of** GB *ou* **about** US redouter [*change, disagreement*]; **to be ~ about doing** avoir peur de faire; **to feel ~** (*apprehensive*) gen être angoissé; (*before performance*) avoir le trac○; (*afraid*) avoir peur; (*ill at ease*) se sentir mal à l'aise; **she makes me feel ~** (*intimidates me*) elle me met mal à l'aise; (*puts my nerves on edge*) elle me rend nerveux; **2** Anat, Med nerveux/-euse; **3** Fin instable

nervous: **~ breakdown** *n* dépression *f* nerveuse; **~ energy** *n* énergie *f*

nervously /ˈnɜːvəslɪ/ *adv* nerveusement

nervousness /ˈnɜːvəsnɪs/ *n* **1** (*of person*) (*shyness*) timidité *f*; (*fear*) peur *f*; (*anxiety*) inquiétude *f*; (*stage fright*) trac○ *m*; (*physical embarrassment*) agitation *f*; (*tenseness*) nervosité *f*; **2** Fin instabilité *f*

nervous: **~ system** *n* système *m* nerveux; **~ wreck**○ *n* boule *f* de nerfs○

nervy○ /ˈnɜːvɪ/ *adj* GB (*anxious*) nerveux/-euse; US (*cheeky*) gonflé○

nest /nest/
A *n* **1** (*of animal*) nid *m*; (*group of baby birds, mice*) nichée *f* (**of** de); **2** (*of criminals, traitors*) nid *m*; (*of boxes, bowls*) série *f*; **~ of tables** tables *fpl* gigognes
B *vi* [*bird*] faire son nid; [*pans*] s'emboîter
(Idiom) **to feather one's (own) ~** se remplir les poches

nested /ˈnestɪd/ *adj* Comput imbriqué

nest egg *n* magot○ *m*

nesting /ˈnestɪŋ/
A *n* Zool construction *f* de nid; Comput imbrication *f*
B *noun modifier* [*place*] propice à la construction des nids; [*habit, season*] de construction des nids

nestle /ˈnesl/
A *vtr* **to ~ one's head** appuyer sa tête (**on** sur; **against** contre); **to ~ a baby in one's arms** tenir un bébé dans ses bras
B *vi* **1** [*person, animal*] se blottir (**against** contre; **under** sous); **2** [*village, house, object*] être niché
(Phrasal verbs)
■ **nestle down** s'installer confortablement
■ **nestle up** se blottir (**against, to** contre)

nestling /ˈneslɪŋ/ *n* oisillon *m*

net /net/
A *n* **1** lit filet *m*; **2** Sport (*in tennis*) filet *m*; **to come (up) to the ~** monter au filet; (*in football*) filets *mpl*; **3** fig piège *m*; **to slip through the ~** passer à travers les mailles du filet; **4** Telecom réseau *m*; **5** (*fabric*) voile *m*, tulle *m*
B *adj* (*also* **nett**) **1** gen, Fin, Comm net/nette; [*loss*] sec/sèche; **~ of tax** net après impôt; **terms strictly ~** prix nets; **2** gen [*result, effect, increase*] net/nette
C *vtr* (*p prés etc* **-tt-**) **1** (*catch*) prendre [*sale*] (au filet; **2** Comm, Fin [*person*] faire un bénéfice de; [*sale, export, deal*] rapporter; **3** (*in football*) marquer [*goal*]; gagner [*trophy*]
(Idiom) **to cast one's ~ wide** ratisser large

Net /net/ *n* (*also* **net**) Comput Net *m*, Internet *m*

net: **~ball** *n*: *sport d'équipe proche du basket joué par les femmes*; **~ cord** *n* Sport (*in tennis*) (*shot*) net *m*; (*cord*) corde *f* (du filet); **~ curtain** *n* voilage *m*

Netherlands /ˈneðələndz/ ▸ p. 774
A *pr n* **the ~** les Pays-Bas *mpl*, la Hollande
B *adj* [*tradition, climate*] hollandais, des Pays-Bas

netiquette /ˈnetɪket/ *n* nétiquette *f*

netting /ˈnetɪŋ/ *n* (*of rope*) filet *m*; (*of metal, plastic*) grillage *m*; (*fabric*) voile *m*, tulle *m*

nettle /ˈnetl/
A *n* (*also* **stinging ~**) ortie *f*
B *vtr* agacer
(Idiom) **to grasp** *ou* **seize the ~** prendre le taureau par les cornes

net ton ▸ p. 1323 *n* US tonne *f* courte

network /ˈnetwɜːk/
A *n* (*all contexts*) réseau *m* (**of** de)
B *vtr* TV, Radio diffuser; Comput interconnecter
C *vi* tisser un réseau de relations
D **networked** *pp adj* [*computer, workstation*] interconnecté

networking /ˈnetwɜːkɪŋ/ *n* **1** Comm constitution *f* de réseaux; **2** Comput interconnexion *f*; **3** (*establishing contacts*) **~ is important** c'est important d'avoir des contacts

network television *n* US chaîne *f* nationale

neuralgia /ˌnjʊəˈrældʒə, US ˌnʊ-/ ▸ p. 933 *n* névralgie *f*

neuritis /ˌnjʊəˈraɪtɪs, US ˌnʊ-/ ▸ p. 933 *n* névrite *f*

neurologist /ˌnjʊˈrɒlədʒɪst, US ˌnʊ-/ ▸ p. 1181 *n* neurologue *mf*

neurosis /njʊəˈrəʊsɪs, US nʊ-/ *n* (*pl* **-oses**) névrose *f*; fig **to have a ~ about sth** avoir une idée fixe à propos de qch

neurosurgeon /ˌnjʊərəʊˈsɜːdʒn, US ˌnʊ-/ ▸ p. 1181 *n* neurochirurgien *m*

neurotic /njʊəˈrɒtɪk, US nʊ-/
A *n* névrosé/-e *m/f*
B *adj* névrosé; **to be ~ about sth/about doing** être complètement maniaque en ce qui concerne qch/quand il s'agit de faire

neurotically /njʊəˈrɒtɪklɪ, US nʊ-/ *adv* de façon obsessionnelle

neuter /ˈnjuːtə(r), US ˈnuː-/
A *n* Ling neutre *m*
B *adj* neutre
C *vtr* châtrer

neutral /ˈnjuːtrəl, US ˈnuː-/
A *n* **1** Mil, Pol neutre *mf*; **2** Aut point *m* mort; **in/into ~** au point mort
B *adj* (*all contexts*) neutre (**about** en ce qui concerne); **to have a ~ policy** pratiquer une politique de neutralité; **to have a ~ effect on sth** ne pas avoir d'effet sur qch

neutrality /njuːˈtrælətɪ, US nuː-/ *n* **1** Chem, Pol (*status*) neutralité *f*; **2** Pol, gen (*attitude*) attitude *f* de neutralité (**towards** vis-à-vis)

neutralize /ˈnjuːtrəlaɪz, US ˈnuː-/ *vtr* aussi euph neutraliser *also euph*

neutron /ˈnjuːtrɒn, US ˈnuː-/
A *n* neutron *m*
B *noun modifier* [*bomb, star*] à neutrons

never /ˈnevə(r)/

⚠️ When *never* is used to modify a verb (*she never wears a hat, I've never seen him*) it is translated *ne...jamais* in French; *ne* comes before the verb, and before the auxiliary in compound tenses, and *jamais* comes after the verb or auxiliary: *elle ne porte jamais de chapeau, je ne l'ai jamais vu*.
When *never* is used without a verb, it is translated by *jamais* alone: *'admit it!'—'never!'* = *'avoue-le!'—'jamais'*.
For examples and particular usages, see the entry below.

adv **1** (*not ever*) **I ~ go to London** je ne vais jamais à Londres; **she ~ says anything** elle ne dit jamais rien; **I've ~ known him to be late** ce n'est pas le genre à être en retard; **~ have I seen such poverty** je n'ai jamais vu une telle pauvreté; **it's now or ~** c'est le moment ou jamais; **~ again** plus jamais; **he ~ ever drinks alcohol** il ne boit absolument jamais d'alcool; **~ one to refuse a free meal,** he agreed il a accepté parce qu'il ne dit jamais non à un repas gratuit; ∼ **a day passes but he phones me** pas un jour ne passe sans qu'il me téléphone; **2** (as an emphatic negative) **he** ∼ **said a word** il n'a rien dit; **I** ∼ **knew that** je ne le savais pas; **he** ∼ **so much as apologized** il ne s'est même pas excusé; **she mustn't catch you crying! that would** ∼ **do** il ne faut surtout pas qu'elle te voie pleurer; **3** (expressing surprise, shock) **you're** ∼ **40!** GB ce n'est pas possible, tu n'as pas 40 ans!; **you've** ∼ **gone and broken it have you** ○! GB ne me dis pas que tu l'as cassé!; ∼**!** pas possible!; **well I** ∼ **(did)!** ça par exemple!

never-ending /ˌnevərˈendɪŋ/ adj interminable

nevermore /ˌnevəˈmɔː(r)/ adv plus jamais

never-never ○ /ˌnevəˈnevə(r)/ n GB **to buy sth on the** ∼ acheter qch à crédit

never-never land n pays m imaginaire

nevertheless /ˌnevəðəˈles/ adv **1** (all the same) quand même; **thanks** ∼ merci quand même; **2** (nonetheless) pourtant, néanmoins; **so strong yet** ∼ **so gentle** si fort et pourtant si doux; **3** (however) pourtant, néanmoins; **he did** ∼ **say that...** il a pourtant or néanmoins dit que...

new /njuː, US nuː/ adj (recent, different, not known, seen, owned etc before) nouveau/-elle; (brand new) neuf/neuve; **I bought a** ∼ **computer** (to replace old one) j'ai acheté un nouvel ordinateur; (a brand new model) j'ai acheté un ordinateur neuf; **the area is** ∼ **to me** la région m'est inconnue; **the subject is** ∼ **to me** je ne connais rien au sujet; **as good as** ∼ lit, fig comme neuf; **'as** ∼**'** (in advertisement) 'état neuf'; **I feel like a** ∼ **man** je suis transformé; **someone/something** ∼ quelqu'un/quelque chose d'autre; **could I have a** ∼ **plate? this one is dirty** est-ce que je pourrais avoir une autre assiette? celle-ci est sale; **to be** ∼ **to** ne pas être habitué à [job, way of life]; **we're** ∼ **to the area** nous sommes nouveaux venus dans la région

New Age
A n New Age m
B noun modifier [music, ideas, sect] New Age inv

new blood n sang m frais

newborn /ˈnjuːbɔːn, US ˈnuː-/ adj nouveau-né/-née; ∼ **baby** nouveau-né/-née m/f

new: **New Caledonia** ▸ p. 954 pr n Nouvelle-Calédonie f; ∼**comer** n (in place, job, club) nouveau venu/nouvelle venue m/f; (in sport, theatre, cinema) nouveau/-elle m/f; ∼**fangled** adj péj moderne; ∼**found** adj tout nouveau/toute nouvelle

Newfoundland /njuːˈfaʊndlənd, US nuː-/ pr n Geog Terre-Neuve f; **to/in** ∼ à Terre-Neuve

New Guinea ▸ p. 774 pr n Nouvelle-Guinée f

newish /ˈnjuːɪʃ, US ˈnuː-/ adj assez neuf/neuve

New Labour n GB Pol nouveau parti m travailliste

new look
A n nouveau style m
B new-look adj [product] nouvelle version inv; [car, team] nouveau/-elle (before n); [edition, show] remanié

newly /ˈnjuːlɪ, US ˈnuː-/ adv (recently) gen nouvellement; [washed] fraîchement; (differently) différemment

newlyweds /ˈnjuːlɪwedz, US ˈnuː-/ npl jeunes mariés mpl

news /njuːz, US nuːz/ n **1** (political, public, personal) nouvelle(s) f(pl); **an item** ou **piece of** ∼ gen une nouvelle; (in newspaper) une information; **a sad bit of** ∼ une triste nouvelle; **have you heard the** ∼? tu connais la nouvelle?; **the latest** ∼ **is that all is quiet** aux dernières nouvelles tout était calme; **the** ∼ **that she had resigned** la nouvelle selon laquelle elle aurait démissionné; ∼ **is just coming in of an explosion** on vient d'apprendre qu'une explosion s'est produite; **here now with** ∼ **of today's sport is X** et voici maintenant, pour nous parler du sport aujourd'hui, X; **these events are not** ∼ ces événements n'ont rien de nouveau; **to be in the** ∼, **to make (the)** ∼ défrayer la chronique; **she's always in the** ∼ on parle beaucoup d'elle dans les médias; **have I got** ∼ **for you** ○! j'ai une nouvelle à t'apprendre!; **tell me all your** ∼! raconte-moi ce que tu deviens!; **that's** ∼ **to me** ○! ça, c'est du nouveau ○!; **2** Radio, TV (programme) **the** ∼ les informations fpl, le journal m; **to see sth/sb on the** ∼ voir qch/qn aux informations; **3** (in newspaper) **'financial** ∼**'** 'chronique f financière'; **'Home News'** 'les informations fpl nationales'

Idiom no ∼ **is good** ∼ pas de nouvelles, bonnes nouvelles

news: ∼ **agency** n agence f de presse; ∼**agent** ▸ p. 1181 n GB marchand m de journaux; ∼**agent's** n GB magasin m de journaux; ∼ **bulletin** GB, ∼**cast** US n Radio, TV bulletin m d'information; ∼**caster** ▸ p. 1181 n présentateur/-trice m/f des informations; ∼ **conference** n conférence f de presse; ∼**dealer** ▸ p. 1181 n US marchand m de journaux; ∼ **desk** n (at newspaper) (salle f de) rédaction f; ∼ **editor** ▸ p. 1181 n rédacteur/-trice m/f; ∼ **headlines** npl TV titres mpl de l'actualité; ∼ **item** n sujet m d'actualité; ∼**letter** n bulletin m; ∼**man** ▸ p. 1181 n journaliste m

newspaper /ˈnjuːspeɪpə(r), US ˈnuːz-/
A n (item) journal m; (substance) papier m journal
B noun modifier [article, cutting, photograph] de presse; [archives] du journal, de la rédaction

newspaper: ∼**man** ▸ p. 1181 n journaliste m; ∼ **office** n bureau m de rédaction; ∼**woman** ▸ p. 1181 n journaliste f

newspeak /ˈnjuːspiːk, US ˈnuː-/ n péj jargon m administratif pej

news: ∼**print** n (paper) papier m journal; (ink) encre f d'imprimerie; ∼**reader** ▸ p. 1181 n GB présentateur/-trice m/f des informations; ∼**reel** n Cin Hist actualités fpl; ∼**room** n (salle f de) rédaction f; ∼ **service** n (agency) agence f de presse; (service provided by media) service m d'information; ∼ **sheet** n bulletin m; ∼**stand** n kiosque m à journaux; ∼ **value** n valeur f médiatique; ∼**worthy** adj médiatique

newsy /ˈnjuːzɪ, US ˈnuː-/ adj [letter] plein de nouvelles

New Testament, NT pr n Nouveau Testament m

new wave n, adj nouvelle vague (f)

New Year n **1** (January 1st) le nouvel an m; **closed for** ∼ ou US ∼**'s** Comm fermé pour les fêtes du nouvel an; **to see in the** ∼ fêter la Saint-Sylvestre; **Happy** ∼**!** bonne année!; **2** (next year) (whole) l'année f prochaine; (the beginning) la nouvelle année

New Year: ∼ **Honours list** n GB liste f des décorés du 1ᵉʳ janvier; ∼ **resolution** n résolution f pour la nouvelle année; ∼**'s day** GB, ∼**'s** US n le jour m de l'an; ∼**'s Eve** n la Saint-Sylvestre

New Zealand /ˌnjuːˈziːlənd, US ˌnuː-/
A ▸ p. 774 pr n Nouvelle-Zélande f
B adj néo-zélandais

next /nekst/

⚠ When next is used as an adjective it is generally translated by prochain when referring to something which is still to come or happen and by suivant when referring to something which has passed or happened: I'll be 40 next year = j'aurai 40 ans l'année prochaine; the next year, he went to Spain = l'année suivante il est allé en Espagne.
For examples and further usages see the entry below.
See also the usage note on time units ▸ p. 1267.

A pron after this train the ∼ is at noon le train suivant est à midi; **he's happy one minute, sad the** ∼ il passe facilement du rire aux larmes; **I hope my** ∼ **will be a boy** j'espère que mon prochain enfant sera un garçon; **from one minute to the** ∼ d'un instant à l'autre; **to survive from one day to the** ∼ survivre au jour le jour; **the** ∼ **to speak was Emily** ensuite, c'est Emily qui a parlé; **the week/month after** ∼ dans deux semaines/mois

B adj **1** (in list, order or series) (following) suivant; (still to come) prochain; **get the** ∼ **train** prenez le prochain train; **he got on the** ∼ **train** il a pris le train suivant; **what's** ∼ **on the list?** qu'est-ce qu'on doit faire maintenant?; **the** ∼ **thing to do is** ce qu'il faut faire maintenant c'est; **'∼!'** 'au suivant!'; **'who's** ∼?' 'c'est à qui le tour?'; **'you're** ∼' 'c'est à vous'; **you're** ∼ **in line** la prochaine fois c'est ton tour; **you're** ∼ **but one** plus qu'une personne et c'est à toi; ∼ **to last** avant-dernier/-ière; **the** ∼ **size (up)** la taille au-dessus; **2** (in expressions of time) (in the future) prochain; (in the past) suivant; ∼ **Thursday, Thursday** ∼ jeudi prochain; **I'll phone in the** ∼ **few days** je téléphonerai d'ici quelques jours; **he's due to arrive in the** ∼ **10 minutes** il devrait arriver d'ici 10 minutes; **this time** ∼ **week** dans une semaine; **the** ∼ **week she was late** la semaine suivante elle était en retard; **the** ∼ **day** le lendemain; **the** ∼ **day**

but one le surlendemain; **the ~ moment** l'instant d'après; **(the) ~ thing I knew, the police were at the door** la police était à la porte avant que j'aie eu le temps de comprendre ce qui se passait; ③ (adjacent) [*room, street*] voisin; [*building, house*] voisin, d'à côté

C adv ① (afterwards) ensuite, après; **what happened ~?** que s'est-il passé ensuite?; **what word comes ~?** quel mot vient après?; **whatever ~!** et quoi encore!; ② (now) **~, I'd like to say...** je voudrais dire maintenant...; **what shall we do ~?** qu'est-ce qu'on fait maintenant?; ③ (on a future occasion) **when I ~ go there** la prochaine fois que j'irai; **they ~ met in 1981** ils se sont ensuite revus en 1981; ④ (nearest in order) **the ~ tallest is Patrick** ensuite c'est Patrick qui est le plus grand; **after 65, 50 is the ~ best score** c'est 65 le meilleur score, ensuite c'est 50; **the ~ best thing would be to...** à défaut, le mieux serait de...

D next to adv phr presque; **~ to impossible** presque impossible; **to get sth for ~ to nothing** avoir qch pour quasiment rien; **in ~ to no time it was over** en un rien de temps c'était fini

E next to prep phr à côté de; **two seats ~ to each other** deux sièges l'un à côté de l'autre; **to wear silk ~ to the skin** porter de la soie à même la peau; **~ to Picasso, my favourite painter is Chagall** après Picasso c'est Chagall mon peintre préféré

(Idiom) **he's as honest as the ~ man** ou **person** il est aussi honnête que n'importe qui

next door

A n (people) les voisins mpl; **~'s cat** le chat des voisins; **~'s garden** le jardin d'à côté

B adj (also **next-door**) d'à côté; **the girl ~** lit la fille d'à côté; fig une fille très simple

C adv [*live, move in*] à côté

next-door neighbour n voisin/-e m/f (d'à côté); **we're ~s** nous habitons à côté l'un de l'autre

next of kin n to be sb's **~** être le parent le plus proche de qn

nexus /ˈneksəs/ n (pl **~** ou **-uses**) (link) connexion f; (network) réseau m

NF n ① GB Pol abrév ▸ **National Front**; ② Fin (also **N/F**) (abrév = **no funds**) défaut m de provision

NH US Post abrév écrite = **New Hampshire**

NHS

A n GB (abrév = **National Health Service**) services mpl de santé britanniques; **on the ~** ≈ remboursé par la sécurité sociale

B noun modifier [*hospital, bed*] conventionné; [*treatment*] remboursé par la sécurité sociale

NI n ① GB abrév ▸ **National Insurance**; ② Geog (abrév écrite = **Northern Ireland**) Irlande f du Nord

nib /nɪb/ n plume f

nibble /ˈnɪbl/

A n ① (snack food) (gén pl) amuse-gueule m inv; ② (action) mordillement m; **to have** ou **take a ~ at** grignoter; ③ (small meal) collation f

B vtr (eat) ① [*rodent, person*] grignoter; [*sheep, goat*] brouter; ② (playfully) mordiller [*ear, neck*]

C vi ① lit [*animal*] mordiller; [*person*] grignoter; **to ~ at** [*mouse, rabbit*] grignoter; [*sheep, goat*] brouter; [*fish*] mordre à [*bait*]; [*person*] manger [qch] du bout des dents; ② fig **to ~ at** considérer [*idea, proposal*]

Nicaragua /ˌnɪkəˈrægjuːə/ ▸ p. 774 pr n Nicaragua m

nice /naɪs/ adj ① (enjoyable) agréable; **it would be ~ to do** ce serait bien de faire; **did you have a ~ time?** tu t'es bien amusé?; **weather isn't it?** beau temps, n'est-ce pas?; **a ~ cool drink** une boisson bien fraîche; **it's ~ and sunny** il fait beau; **to have a ~ long chat** bien bavarder; **~ work if you can get it!** hum il y en a qui ont de la veine○!; **~ to have met you** ravi d'avoir fait votre connaissance; **have a ~ day!** bonne journée!; ② (attractive) gen beau/belle; [*place*] agréable; **you look very ~** tu es très chic; ③ (tasty) bon/bonne; **to taste ~** avoir bon goût; ④ (kind) sympathique; **to be ~ to** être gentil avec; **he says really ~ things about you** il dit beaucoup de bien de toi; [*behaviour, neighbourhood, school*] comme il faut inv; **it is not ~ to do** ce n'est pas bien de faire; **that's not very ~!** ça ne se fait pas!; ⑥ (used ironically) **~ friends you've got!** ils sont bien tes amis!; **a ~ mess you've got us into!** tu nous as fichus dans un beau pétrin○!; **that's a ~ way to talk to your father!** en voilà une façon de parler à ton père!; **this is a ~ state of**

affairs! c'est du propre!; ⑦ sout (subtle) subtil

(Idiom) **~ one!** (in admiration) bravo!; iron il ne manquait plus que ça!

nice-looking /ˌnaɪsˈlʊkɪŋ/ adj beau/belle

nicely /ˈnaɪslɪ/ adv ① (kindly) gentiment; ② (attractively) agréablement; **she sings very ~** elle chante très bien; ③ (satisfactorily) bien; **to be ~ chilled** être juste frais/fraîche comme il faut; **that will do ~** cela fera l'affaire; ④ (politely) [*eat, speak*] convenablement; [*ask, explain*] poliment

niceness /ˈnaɪsnɪs/ n (kindness) gentillesse f; (subtlety) subtilité f

nicety /ˈnaɪsətɪ/ n subtilité f; **the social niceties** les raffinements mpl mondains

niche /niːtʃ, niːʃ/ n (role) place f; (recess) niche f; Comm créneau m; Ecol niche f écologique

niche market n marché m spécialisé

nick /nɪk/

A n ① (notch) encoche f (**in** dans); ② ○GB **to be in good/bad ~** [*object*] être en bon/mauvais état; [*person*] être/ne pas être en forme; ③ ○GB (jail) taule○ f; (police station) poste m

B vtr ① (cut) faire une entaille dans; ② ○GB (steal) piquer○; (arrest) pincer○; ③ ○US (strike) donner un coup léger à

C v refl **to ~ oneself** s'écorcher

(Idiom) **just in the ~ of time** juste à temps

nickel /ˈnɪkl/ n ① US (coin) pièce f de cinq cents; ② (metal) nickel m

nickel-and-dime○ adj US qui ne vaut pas un clou○

nickelodeon /ˌnɪkəˈləʊdɪən/ n US (juke box) juke-box m

nickname /ˈnɪkneɪm/

A n surnom m

B vtr surnommer

nicotine /ˈnɪkətiːn/

A n nicotine f

B noun modifier [*addiction, poisoning, chewing gum, patch*] à la nicotine; [*stain*] de nicotine

niece /niːs/ n nièce f

nifty○ /ˈnɪftɪ/ adj (skilful) habile; (attractive) chouette○

Nigeria /naɪˈdʒɪərɪə/ ▸ p. 774 pr n Nigeria m

niggardly /ˈnɪgədlɪ/ adj ① [*person*] avare; ② [*portion, amount*] mesquin

niggle○ /ˈnɪgl/

A n (complaint) remarque f; **I've a ~ at the back of my mind** il y a quelque chose qui me travaille

B vtr (irritate) tracasser

C vi (complain) se plaindre sans arrêt (**about, over** de; **that** que)

niggling /ˈnɪglɪŋ/

A n chicanerie f

B adj [*person*] tatillon/-onne; [*doubt, worry*] insidieux/-ieuse

night /naɪt/ ▸ p. 1267 n ① (period of darkness) nuit f; (before going to bed) soir m; **at ~** la nuit; **all ~ long** toute la nuit; **Moscow by ~** Moscou la nuit; **eight o'clock at ~** huit heures du soir; **late at ~** tard le soir; **he arrived last ~** il est arrivé hier soir; **I slept badly last ~** j'ai mal dormi la nuit dernière; **he arrived the ~ before** last il est arrivé avant-hier soir; **she had arrived the ~ before** elle était arrivée la veille au soir; **on Tuesday ~s** le mardi soir; **to sit up all ~ reading** passer toute la nuit à lire; **to have a good/bad ~** bien/mal dormir; **to have a late ~** se coucher tard; **to get an early ~** se coucher tôt; **to stay out all ~** ne pas rentrer de la nuit; ② (evening) soir m; (evening as a whole) soirée f; **it's his ~ out** c'est son soir de sortie; **to take a ~ off** se libérer une soirée; **it's my ~ off** ce soir je suis libre; **a ~ to remember** une soirée mémorable; **to make a ~ of it** faire la fête○; ③ (darkness) nuit f

nightcap /ˈnaɪtkæp/ n ① (hat) bonnet m de nuit; ② (drink) **to have a ~** boire quelque chose (avant d'aller se coucher)

nightclub n boîte f de nuit

nightclubbing n **to go ~** aller en boîte○

nightdress n chemise f de nuit

nightie○ /ˈnaɪtɪ/ n chemise f de nuit

nightingale /ˈnaɪtɪŋgeɪl, US -tŋg-/ n rossignol m

night: **~life** /ˈnaɪtlaɪf/ n vie f nocturne; **~-light** n veilleuse f

nightly /ˈnaɪtlɪ/ adj gen de tous les soirs; [*revels, visitor, disturbance*] littér nocturne

n

nightmare /ˈnaɪtmeə(r)/ n cauchemar m; **to have a ~** faire un cauchemar

night: **~marish** adj cauchemardesque; **~ owl** n couche-tard mf inv; **~ porter** n portier m de nuit; **~ school** n cours mpl du soir; **~ shelter** n asile m de nuit

night shift n ① (period) **to be/work on the ~** être/travailler de nuit; ② (workers) équipe f de nuit

nightshirt n chemise f de nuit (d'homme)

night: **~ spot** n boîte f de nuit○; **~stand** n US table f de nuit; **~stick** n US matraque f

night-time /ˈnaɪttaɪm/
A n nuit f; **at ~** la nuit
B noun modifier nocturne

night: **~ vision** n vision f nocturne; **~ watchman** ▸ p. 1181 n veilleur m de nuit; **~wear** n vêtements mpl de nuit

nil /nɪl/ n ① **to be ~** [courage, enthusiasm] être à zéro; [progress] être zéro; ② Sport zéro m; ③ (on forms) néant m

Nile /naɪl/ ▸ p. 1146 pr n Nil m

nimble /ˈnɪmbl/ adj [person] agile (**at doing** pour faire; **with** de); [fingers] habile; [mind] vif/vive

nincompoop○ /ˈnɪŋkəmpuːp/ n nigaud/-e m/f

nine /naɪn/ ▸ p. 1044 n, adj neuf (m) inv

Idioms **a ~ day(s') wonder** la merveille d'un jour; **to be dressed up to the ~s**○ être sur son trente et un○

ninepin /ˈnaɪnpɪn/ n quille f

Idiom **to go down** ou **fall like ~s** tomber comme des mouches

nineteen /ˌnaɪnˈtiːn/ ▸ p. 1044 n, adj dix-neuf (m) inv

Idiom **to talk ~ to the dozen** parler à n'en plus finir

nineteenth /ˌnaɪnˈtiːnθ/ ▸ p. 1044, p. 788
A n ① (in order) dix-neuvième mf; ② (of month) dix-neuf m inv; ③ (fraction) dix-neuvième m
B adj, adv dix-neuvième

ninetieth /ˈnaɪntɪəθ/ ▸ p. 1044
A n ① (in order) quatre-vingt-dixième mf; ② (fraction) quatre-vingt-dixième m
B adj, adv quatre-vingt-dixième

nine-to-five /ˌnaɪntəˈfaɪv/
A adj [job, routine] de bureau
B nine to five adv [work] de neuf à cinq

ninety /ˈnaɪntɪ/ ▸ p. 1044 n, adj quatre-vingt-dix (m) inv

nip /nɪp/
A n (pinch) pincement m; (bite) morsure f; fig **there's a ~ in the air** il fait frisquet○
B vtr (p prés etc **-pp-**) (pinch) pincer; (bite) donner un petit coup de dent à; (playfully) mordiller
C vi ① (bite) [animal] mordre; (playfully) mordiller; [bird] donner un petit coup de bec à; ② ○GB (go) **to ~ into a shop** entrer rapidement dans un magasin; **to ~ in front of sb** passer devant qn; **to ~ over to France** faire un saut en France

Idioms **to ~ sth in the bud** étouffer qch dans l'œuf; **~ and tuck**○ (cosmetic surgery) chirurgie f esthétique; (neck and neck) US au coude à coude

Phrasal verbs
■ **nip along** aller à bonne allure
■ **nip off**: ▸ **~ off**○ [person] se sauver; ▸ **~ off [sth]**, **~ [sth] off** couper [flower]; pincer [bud]

nipple /ˈnɪpl/ n ① Anat mamelon m; ② Tech graisseur m

nippy○ /ˈnɪpɪ/ adj ① (cold) [air] piquant; **it's a bit ~** il fait frisquet○; ② GB (quick) [person] vif/vive; [car] rapide; **be ~ about it!** fais vite!

nit /nɪt/ n (egg) lente f; (larva) larve f de pou

nit-pick vi chercher la petite bête○

nitrate /ˈnaɪtreɪt/ n ① Chem nitrate m; ② (fertilizer) engrais m azoté

nitric /ˈnaɪtrɪk/ adj nitrique

nitrogen /ˈnaɪtrədʒən/ n azote m

nitty-gritty○ /ˌnɪtɪˈgrɪtɪ/ n **the ~** la réalité pure et dure; **to get down to the ~** passer aux choses sérieuses

nitwit○ /ˈnɪtwɪt/ n imbécile mf

NJ abrév écrite US Post = **New Jersey**

NM abrév écrite US Post = **New Mexico**

no /nəʊ/
A particle non
B det ① (none, not any) **to have ~ money/shoes** ne pas avoir d'argent/de chaussures; **~ intelligent man would have done that** aucun homme intelligent n'aurait fait cela; **~ two people would agree on this** il n'y a pas deux personnes qui seraient d'accord là-dessus; **of ~ interest** sans intérêt; **there's ~ chocolate like Belgian chocolate** il n'y a pas de meilleur chocolat que le chocolat belge; ② (with gerund) **there's ~ knowing what will happen** (il est) impossible de savoir ce qui va arriver; **there's ~ denying that...** (il est) inutile de nier que...; ③ (prohibiting) **~ smoking** défense de fumer; **~ parking** stationnement interdit; **~ talking!** silence!; **~ job losses!** non aux licenciements!; ④ (for emphasis) **he's ~ expert** ce n'est certes pas un expert; **this is ~ time to cry** ce n'est pas le moment de pleurer; **at ~ time did I say that...** je n'ai jamais dit que...; ⑤ (hardly any) **in ~ time** en un rien de temps; **it was ~ distance** ce n'était pas loin
C n gen non m inv; (vote against) non m inv
D adv **it's ~ further/easier than** ce n'est pas plus loin/facile que; **I ~ longer work there** je n'y travaille plus; **~ later than Wednesday** pas plus tard que mercredi; **it's ~ different from driving a car** c'est exactement comme conduire une voiture; **~ fewer than 50 people** pas moins de 50 personnes; **they need ~ less than three weeks** ils ont besoin d'au moins trois semaines

no., No. (abrév écrite = **number**) n○

Noah /ˈnəʊə/ pr n Noé; **~'s Ark** l'arche f de Noé

nobility /nəʊˈbɪlətɪ/ n noblesse f

noble /ˈnəʊbl/
A n noble m
B adj noble

noble: **~man** n noble m; **~-minded** adj au grand cœur; **~ savage** n bon sauvage m

nobly /ˈnəʊblɪ/ adv gen noblement; (selflessly) généreusement; **~ born** de haute naissance

nobody /ˈnəʊbədɪ/

⚠ When nobody is used as a pronoun it is almost always translated by personne.
When the pronoun nobody is the subject or object of a verb, the French requires ne before the verb (or auxiliary): nobody likes him = personne ne l'aime; I heard nobody = je n'ai entendu personne.
For examples and particular usages, see the entry below.

A pron (also **no-one**) personne; **~ saw her** personne ne l'a vue; **there was ~ in the car** il n'y avait personne dans la voiture; **~ but me** personne sauf moi
B n to be a **~** être insignifiant; **I knew her when she was still a ~** je la connaissais alors qu'elle n'était encore qu'une inconnue

Idioms **to work like ~'s business**○ GB travailler comme un fou/une folie; **he's ~'s fool** on ne la lui fait pas○

nocturnal /nɒkˈtɜːnl/ adj (all contexts) nocturne

nod /nɒd/
A n signe m de (la) tête; **she gave him a ~** gen elle lui a fait un signe de (la) tête; (as greeting) elle l'a salué d'un signe de tête; (indicating assent) elle a fait oui de la tête
B vtr (p prés etc **-dd-**) **to ~ one's head** gen faire un signe de tête; (to indicate assent) hocher la tête; **he ~ded his assent/approval** il a hoché la tête en signe d'assentiment/d'approbation
C vi (p prés etc **-dd-**) ① gen faire un signe de tête (**to** à); (in assent) faire oui de la tête; ② (sway) [flowers, treetops] onduler; ③ (be drowsy) sommeiller

Idioms **to give sb/sth the ~**○ GB donner le feu vert à qn/qch; **on the ~**○ GB sans discussion; **a ~ is as good as a wink (to a blind man)** ne t'en fais pas○, on a compris

Phrasal verb
■ **nod off** s'endormir

no-fly zone n Mil Aviat zone f d'exclusion aérienne

no-go○ /ˈnəʊgəʊ/ adj **it's (a) ~** ça ne sert à rien

no: **~-go area** n quartier m chaud (où la police etc ne s'aventure plus); **~-hoper**○ n raté/-e m/f

noise /nɔɪz/ n gen bruit m; (shouting) tapage m; **background ~** bruit de fond; **a rattling ~** un cliquetis

Idioms **to be a big** ~ **(in sth)**○ être une grosse légume (de qch)○; **to make a** ~ **about sth** se plaindre de qch; **she made** ~**s about leaving** elle a laissé entendre qu'elle voulait partir; **to make polite** ~**s** dire des choses polies; **to make the right** ~**s** dire ce qui convient

noise: ~**less** adj silencieux/-ieuse; ~ **level** n niveau m sonore; ~ **nuisance,** ~ **pollution** n nuisances fpl sonores

noisily /ˈnɔɪzɪlɪ/ adv bruyamment

noisy /ˈnɔɪzɪ/ adj [person, place] bruyant; [meeting, protest] tumultueux/-euse

nomad /ˈnəʊmæd/ n nomade mf

nominal /ˈnɒmɪnl/ adj gen nominal; [fee, sum] minimal; [fine, penalty] symbolique

nominally /ˈnɒmɪnəlɪ/ adv (in name) nominalement; (in theory) théoriquement

nominate /ˈnɒmɪneɪt/ vtr ⓵ (propose) proposer; **to** ~ **sb for a prize** sélectionner qn pour un prix; ⓶ (appoint) nommer; **to** ~ **sb (as) chairman** nommer qn président; **to** ~ **sb to do** désigner qn pour faire

nomination /ˌnɒmɪˈneɪʃn/ n (as candidate) proposition f de candidat; (for award) sélection f; (appointment) nomination f **(to** à)

nominative /ˈnɒmɪnətɪv/ n, adj nominatif (m)

nominee /ˌnɒmɪˈniː/ n candidat/-e m/f désigné/-e

non+ /nɒn-/ combining form (+ noun) non-; (+ adj) non

nonacademic /ˌnɒnækəˈdemɪk/ adj [course] pré-professionnel/-elle; [staff] non enseignant

nonaddictive /ˌnɒnəˈdɪktɪv/ adj qui ne crée pas de dépendance

nonalcoholic /ˌnɒnælkəˈhɒlɪk/ adj non alcoolisé

nonattendance /ˌnɒnəˈtendəns/ n absence f

nonbeliever /ˌnɒnbɪˈliːvə(r)/ n non-croyant/-e m/f

non-budgetary /ˌnɒnˈbʌdʒɪtrɪ/ adj extrabudgétaire

nonchalant /ˈnɒnʃələnt/ adj nonchalant

nonclassified /ˌnɒnˈklæsɪfaɪd/ adj [information] non confidentiel/-ielle

noncombustible /ˌnɒnkəmˈbʌstəbl/ adj incombustible

non-commercial /ˌnɒnkəˈmɜːʃəl/ adj [event, activity] à but non lucratif

noncommissioned officer n Mil sous-officier m

noncommittal /ˌnɒnkəˈmɪtl/ adj [person, reply] évasif/-ive **(about** au sujet de)

noncompliance /ˌnɒnkəmˈplaɪəns/ n (with standards) (of substance, machine) non-conformité f **(with** à); (with orders) (of person) non-obéissance f **(with** à)

non compos mentis /ˌnɒn ˌkɒmpəs ˈmentɪs/ adj phr **to be** — Jur être en état de démence (au moment des faits); gen ne pas avoir toutes ses facultés

nonconformist /ˌnɒnkənˈfɔːmɪst/
Ⓐ n non-conformiste mf
Ⓑ adj non conformiste

noncooperation /ˌnɒnkəʊˌɒpəˈreɪʃn/ n refus m de coopération

nondenominational /ˌnɒndɪˌnɒmɪˈneɪʃənl/ adj [church] œcuménique; [school] laïque

nondescript /ˈnɒndɪskrɪpt/ adj [person, clothes] insignifiant; [building] quelconque; [colour] indéfinissable; [performance, book] sans intérêt

none /nʌn/
Ⓐ pron ⓵ (not any) aucun/-e m/f; ~ **of them** aucun d'entre eux; **'have you any pens?'—'**~ **at all'** 'as-tu des stylos?'—'pas un seul'; **he saw three dogs,** ~ **of which had a tail** il a vu trois chiens, dont aucun n'avait de queue; ~ **of the wine/milk** pas une goutte de vin/lait; ~ **of the bread** pas une miette de pain; ~ **of the cheese** pas un morceau de fromage; **'is there any money left?'—'**~ **at all'** 'est-ce qu'il reste de l'argent?'—'pas du tout'; **'did you have any difficulty?'—'**~ **whatsoever** ou **at all'** 'as-tu eu des difficultés?'—'aucune'; **we have** ~ nous n'en avons pas; **there's** ~ **left** il n'y en a plus; ~ **of it was true** il n'y avait rien de vrai; **he was having** ~ **of it** il ne voulait rien entendre; ⓶ (nobody, not one person) personne; ~ **can sing so well as her** personne ne chante aussi bien qu'elle; **there's** ~ **better than** il n'y en a pas de meilleur que; ~ **but him** personne sauf lui; **it was** ~ **other than** ce n'était autre que; ⓷ (on form, questionnaire) néant m

Ⓑ adv (not, not at all) **it was** ~ **too easy** c'était loin d'être facile; **I was** ~ **too sure** je n'étais pas trop sûr; **he was** ~ **the worse for the experience** il ne se portait pas plus mal après cette expérience; **the play is long, but** ~ **the worse for that** la pièce est longue mais ce n'est pas un défaut

non-EC adj Hist [country] hors CEE; [national] non ressortissant de la CEE

nonentity /nɒˈnentɪtɪ/ n péj (person) personne f insignifiante

nonessentials /ˌnɒnɪˈsenʃlz/ npl (objects) accessoires mpl; (details) accessoire m sg; **forget the** ~ oublie l'accessoire

nonetheless /ˌnʌnðəˈles/ adv ▸ **nevertheless**

nonexistent /ˌnɒnɪgˈzɪstənt/ adj inexistant

non-family /ˌnɒnˈfæməlɪ/ adj en dehors de la famille

nonfat /ˌnɒnˈfæt/ adj sans matières grasses

nonfiction /ˌnɒnˈfɪkʃn/ n œuvres fpl non fictionnelles

nonflammable /ˌnɒnˈflæməbl/ adj ininflammable

non-fulfilment /ˌnɒnfʊlˈfɪlmənt/ n (of contract, obligation) inexécution f; (of desire) inaccomplissement m

non-infectious /ˌnɒnɪnˈfekʃəs/ adj intransmissible

noniron /ˌnɒnˈaɪən, US -ˈaɪərn/ adj infroissable

nonjudgmental /ˌnɒndʒʌdʒˈmentl/ adj neutre

non-league /ˌnɒnˈliːg/ adj Sport hors division

no-no○ /ˈnəʊnəʊ/ n **that's a** ~ ça ne se fait pas

no-nonsense /ˌnəʊˈnɒnsəns/ adj [manner, look, tone, attitude, policy] direct; [person] franc/franche

nonpartisan /ˌnɒnpɑːtɪˈzæn/ adj impartial

nonparty /ˌnɒnˈpɑːtɪ/ adj [issue, decision] non partisan; [person] non affilié au parti

nonperson /ˈnɒnˈpɜːsn/ n ⓵ péj (insignificant person) être m falot; ⓶ Pol **officially, he's a** ~ officiellement, il n'a jamais existé

nonplussed /ˌnɒnˈplʌst/ adj perplexe

nonprofessional /ˌnɒnprəˈfeʃənl/ n, adj amateur (m)

non-profitmaking /ˌnɒnˈprɒfɪtmeɪkɪŋ/ adj [organization] à but non lucratif

non-redeemable /ˌnɒnrɪˈdiːməbl/ adj Fin perpétuel/-elle

nonrefillable /ˌnɒnriːˈfɪləbl/ adj [lighter, pen] non rechargeable; [can, bottle] non réutilisable

nonreligious /ˌnɒnrɪˈlɪdʒəs/ adj laïque

nonresident /ˌnɒnˈrezɪdənt/
Ⓐ n non-résident/-e m/f
Ⓑ adj ⓵ [guest] de passage; [student, visitor] non résident; [caretaker] de jour; ⓶ (also **non-residential**) [job, course] sans hébergement; ⓷ Comput [routine] qui ne réside pas en permanence en mémoire centrale

nonreturnable /ˌnɒnrɪˈtɜːnəbl/ adj [bottle] non consigné

nonsegregated /ˌnɒnˈsegrɪgeɪtɪd/ adj [area] sans ségrégation; [society] non ségrégationniste

nonsense /ˈnɒnsns, US -sens/ n (foolishness) absurdités fpl; **it's a** ~ **that** c'est absurde que; **to make (a)** ~ **of** être en totale contradiction avec; **what's all this** ~ **about leaving work?** qu'est-ce que c'est que ces histoires de quitter le travail?; **there's no** ~ **about him** il ne permet pas de fantaisie

nonsensical /nɒnˈsensɪkl/ adj (stupid) absurde

non sequitur /ˌnɒn ˈsekwɪtə(r)/ n ⓵ gen **to be a** ~ être illogique; ⓶ (in philosophy) illogisme m

nonskid /ˌnɒnˈskɪd/, **nonslip** /ˌnɒnˈslɪp/ n antidérapant m

non-specialized /ˌnɒnˈspeʃəlaɪzd/ adj généraliste

nonstarter /ˌnɒnˈstɑːtə(r)/ n fig **to be a** ~ [person] être hors-course; [plan, idea] être voué à l'échec

nonstick /ˌnɒnˈstɪk/ adj antiadhésif/-ive

nonstop /ˌnɒnˈstɒp/
Ⓐ adj [flight] sans escale; [journey] sans arrêt; [train] direct; [talk, work, pressure, noise] incessant; [service, show] permanent; [coverage] non-stop inv
Ⓑ adv [fly] sans arrêt; [fly] sans escale

non-taxable /ˌnɒnˈtaksabl/ adj non imposable

non-union /ˌnɒnˈjuːnɪən/ adj non syndiqué

non-white, non-White /ˌnɒnˈwaɪt/ n personne f de couleur

n

noodles /'nuːdlz/ npl Culin nouilles fpl

nook /nʊk/ n coin m

(Idiom) **every ~ and cranny** tous les coins et recoins

noon /nuːn/ n midi m; **at 12 ~** à midi; **at high ~** en plein midi

(Idiom) **morning, ~ and night** du matin au soir

no-one /'nəʊwʌn/ pron = **nobody A**

noose /nuːs/ n (loop) nœud m coulant; (for hanging) corde f; **the hangman's ~** la corde de la potence

(Idiom) **to put one's head in a ~** se jeter dans la gueule du loup

nor /nɔː(r), nə(r)/

⚠ If you want to know how to translate *nor* when used in combination with *neither* look at the entry **neither**.
When used as a conjunction to show agreement or similarity with a negative statement, *nor* is very often translated by *non plus*: 'I don't like him'—'nor do I' = 'je ne l'aime pas'—'moi non plus'; 'he's not Spanish'—'nor is John' = 'il n'est pas espagnol'—'John non plus'; 'I can't sleep'—'nor can I' = 'je n'arrive pas à dormir'—'moi non plus'.
When used to give additional information to a negative statement *nor* can very often be translated by *non plus* preceded by a negative verb: *she hasn't written, nor has she telephoned* = elle n'a pas écrit, et elle n'a pas téléphoné non plus; *I do not wish to insult you, (but) nor do I wish to lose money* = je ne veux pas vous offenser, mais je ne souhaite pas non plus perdre de l'argent.
For examples and further uses of *nor* see the entry below.

conj **you don't have to tell him, ~ should you** tu n'es pas obligé de le lui dire, et même tu ne devrais pas; **he was not a cruel man, ~ a mean one** il n'était ni cruel, ni méchant

norm /nɔːm/ n norme f (**for** pour; **to do** de faire)

normal /'nɔːml/

Ⓐ n gen, Math normale f; **above/below ~** au-dessus/en dessous de la norme

Ⓑ adj gen, Math, Psych normal; [*place, time*] habituel/-elle; **as ~** comme d'habitude; **in the ~ course of events** si tout va bien; **in ~ circumstances** en temps normal

normality /nɔː'mælətɪ/ n normalité f

normally /'nɔːməlɪ/ adv normalement

Norman /'nɔːmən/

Ⓐ n ① gen, Hist Normand/-e m/f; ② (also **~ French**) Ling normand m

Ⓑ adj ① gen, Hist [*landscape, village*] normand; [*produce*] de Normandie; ② Archit roman

Norse /nɔːs/ adj [*mythology, saga*] nordique

north /nɔːθ/ ► p. 1089

Ⓐ n (compass direction) nord m; **true ~** le nord géographique

Ⓑ n pr n Pol, Geog (part of world, country) **the North** le Nord; **the far North** le Grand Nord

Ⓒ adj gen nord inv; [*wind*] du nord; **in/from ~ London** dans le/du nord de Londres

Ⓓ adv [*move*] vers le nord; [*lie, live*] au nord (**of** de); **to go ~ of sth** passer au nord de qch

north: North Africa ► p. 774 n Afrique f du Nord; **North America** ► p. 774 n Amérique f du Nord

Northants n GB Post abrév écrite = **Northamptonshire**

northbound adj en direction du nord

Northd n GB Post abrév écrite ► **Northumberland**

northeast /,nɔː'θiːst/ ► p. 1089

Ⓐ n nord-est m

Ⓑ adj [*coast, side*] nord-est inv; [*wind*] de nord-est

Ⓒ adv [*move*] vers le nord-est; [*lie, live*] au nord-est

northeasterly /,nɔː'θiːstəlɪ/

Ⓐ n vent m de nord-est

Ⓑ adj [*wind*] de nord-est; [*point*] au nord-est

northeastern /,nɔː'θiːstən/ ► p. 1089 adj [*coast*] nord-est inv; [*town, accent*] du nord-est

northerly /'nɔːðəlɪ/

Ⓐ n vent m du nord

Ⓑ adj [*wind, area*] du nord; [*point*] au nord

northern /'nɔːðən/ ► p. 1089 adj [*coast*] nord inv; [*town, accent*] du nord; [*latitude*] boréal; [*hemisphere*] Nord inv;

~ England le nord de l'Angleterre

northerner /'nɔːðənə(r)/ n **~s** les gens mpl du Nord

northern: Northern Ireland ► p. 774 n Irlande f du Nord; **Northern Lights** npl aurore f boréale

North Pole n pôle m Nord

North Sea ► p. 1049 n **the ~** la mer du Nord

North Star n étoile f polaire

northward /'nɔːθwəd/ ► p. 1089

Ⓐ adj [*side*] nord inv; [*wall, slope*] du côté nord; [*journey*] vers le nord

Ⓑ adv (also **~s**) vers le nord

northwest /,nɔː'θ'west/ ► p. 1089

Ⓐ n nord-ouest m

Ⓑ adj [*coast*] nord-ouest inv; [*wind*] de nord-ouest

Ⓒ adv [*move*] vers le nord-ouest; [*lie, live*] au nord-ouest

northwesterly /,nɔː'θ'westəlɪ/

Ⓐ n vent m de nord-ouest, noroît m

Ⓑ adj [*wind*] de nord-ouest; [*point*] au nord-ouest

northwestern /,nɔː'θ'westən/ adj [*coast*] nord-ouest inv; [*town, accent*] du nord-ouest

Norway /'nɔːweɪ/ ► p. 774 pr n Norvège f

Norwegian /nɔː'wiːdʒən/ ► p. 1032, p. 969

Ⓐ n ① (person) Norvégien/-ienne m/f; ② (language) norvégien m

Ⓑ adj norvégien/-ienne

nose /nəʊz/

Ⓐ ► p. 698 n ① Anat nez m; **to speak through one's ~** parler du nez; ② (of plane, boat) nez m; (of car) avant m; **to travel ~ to tail** rouler à touche-touche; ③ (sense of smell) gen odorat m; (of wine or perfume expert) nez m; (of dog) flair m; ④ (smell of wine) bouquet m; ⑤ fig (instinct) **to have a ~ for sth** avoir du flair pour qch; **to follow one's ~** se fier à son instinct

Ⓑ vtr (manœuvre) **to ~ sth in/out** faire entrer/sortir qch avec précaution [*boat, vehicle*]

Ⓒ vi **to ~ into/out of sth** entrer dans/sortir de qch avec prudence; **the car ~d into the traffic** la voiture s'est faufilée dans la circulation

(Idioms) **to hit sth on the ~** US taper qch dans le mille; **to lead sb by the ~** mener qn par le bout du nez; **to look down one's ~ at sb/sth** prendre qn/qch de haut; **to pay through the ~ for sth** payer le prix fort pour qch; **to poke ou stick one's ~ into sth°** fourrer° son nez dans qch; **to turn one's ~ up at sth** faire le dégoûté/la dégoûtée devant qch; **(right) under sb's ~** sous le nez de qn; **with one's ~ in the air** d'un air supérieur

(Phrasal verbs)

■ **nose about, nose around** fouiner (**in** dans)

■ **nose out:** ► ■ **~ out** [*vehicle*] déboîter prudemment; [*boat*] sortir avec prudence; ► **~ out** [sth], **~** [sth] **out** lit dépister [*animal*]; fig dénicher [*facts, secret*]

nosebleed n saignement m de nez

nose-dive /'nəʊzdaɪv/

Ⓐ n Aviat piqué m; fig **to go into ou take a ~** [*currency, rate*] chuter

Ⓑ vi [*plane*] descendre en piqué; [*demand, prices, sales*] chuter

nosey° adj = **nosy**

no-show n: personne ayant fait une réservation qui ne se présente pas à l'hôtel, l'aéroport etc

nosily /'nəʊzɪlɪ/ adv indiscrètement

nostalgia /nʊ'stældʒə/ n nostalgie f

nostalgic /nʊ'stældʒɪk/ adj nostalgique; **to feel ~ for** avoir la nostalgie de

nostril /'nɒstrɪl/ n (of person) narine f; (of horse) naseau m

nosy° /'nəʊzɪ/ adj fouineur/-euse°

not /nɒt/

Ⓐ adv ne...pas; **she isn't at home** (voir note ci-dessous) elle n'est pas chez elle; **we won't need a car** nous n'aurons pas besoin d'une voiture; **has he ~ seen it?** il ne l'a pas vu alors?; **I hope ~** j'espère que non; **certainly ~** sûrement pas; **~ only ou just** non seulement; **whether it rains or ~** qu'il pleuve ou non; **why ~?** pourquoi pas?; **they live in caves, ~ in houses** ils habitent non pas dans des maisons, mais dans des grottes; **he's ~ so much aggressive as assertive** il est plutôt sûr de lui qu'agressif; **a ~ ou ~ an (entirely) unexpected response** une réponse prévisible; **~ three hours from here** à moins de trois heures

not

When *not* is used without a verb before an adjective, an adverb, a verb or a noun, it is translated by *pas*:

it's a cat not a dog
= c'est un chat pas un chien

not at all
= pas du tout

not bad
= pas mal

For examples and particular usages see the entry **not**.

When *not* is used to make the verb *be* negative (*it's not a cat*) it is translated by *ne ... pas* in French; *ne* comes before the verb or the auxiliary in compound tenses and *pas* comes after the verb or auxiliary: *ce n'est pas un chat*;

she hasn't been ill
= elle n'a pas été malade.

When *not* is used with the auxiliary *do* to make a verb negative (*he doesn't like oranges*) *do* + *not* is translated by *ne ... pas* in French: *il n'aime pas les oranges*.

When *not* is used in the present perfect tense (*I haven't seen him*, *she hasn't arrived yet*),

ne ... pas is again used in French on either side of the appropriate auxiliary (*avoir* or *être*): *je ne l'ai pas vu*, *elle n'est pas encore arrivée*.

When *not* is used with *will* to make a verb negative (*will not*, *won't*), *ne ... pas* is used with the future tense in French:

she won't come by car
= elle ne viendra pas en voiture

When used with a verb in the infinitive, *ne ... pas* are placed together before the verb:

he decided not to go
= il a décidé de ne pas y aller

you were wrong not to tell her
= tu as eu tort de ne pas le lui dire

When *not* is used in question tags, the whole tag can usually be translated by the French *n'est-ce pas*, e.g.

she bought it, didn't she?
= elle l'a acheté, n'est-ce pas?

For usages not covered in this note see the entry **not**.

---

d'ici; **hadn't we better leave?** est-ce qu'on ne ferait pas mieux de partir?; ~ **everyone likes it** tout le monde ne l'aime pas; **it's ~ every day that** ce n'est pas tous les jours que; ~ **a sound was heard** on n'entendait pas un bruit
B **not at all** *adv phr* gen pas du tout; (responding to thanks) de rien
C **not that** *conj phr* ~ **that I know of** pas (autant) que je sache; **if she refuses,** ~ **that she will...** si elle refuse, je ne dis pas qu'elle le fera...

⚠️ Dans la langue parlée ou familière, *not* utilisé avec un auxiliaire ou un modal prend parfois la forme *n't* qui est alors accolée au verbe (eg *you can't go*, *he hasn't finished*)

notable /ˈnəʊtəbl/ *adj* [*person*] remarquable; [*event, success, difference*] notable

notably /ˈnəʊtəblɪ/ *adv* (in particular) notamment; (markedly) remarquablement; **most** ~ plus *or* tout particulièrement

notary /ˈnəʊtərɪ/ ▸ p. 1181 *n* notaire *m*

notation /nəʊˈteɪʃn/ *n* notation *f*

notch /nɒtʃ/
A *n* (in plank) entaille *f*; (in fabric, belt) cran *m*; (in lid, as record) encoche *f*; **to go up a** ~ [*opinion*] monter d'un cran
B *vtr* (mark) encocher [*stick*]; cranter [*fabric*]
(Phrasal verb)
■ **notch up**°: ▸ ~ **up** [sth] remporter [*point, prize*]

note /nəʊt/
A *n* **1** gen note *f*; (short letter) mot *m*; **to make a** ~ **of** noter [*date, address*]; **to take** ~ **of** lit, fig prendre note de; **2** fig **to hit the right** ~ trouver le ton juste; **to strike** *ou* **hit a wrong** ~ commettre un impair; **on a less serious** ~ en passant à un registre moins sérieux; **3** Mus (sound, symbol) note *f*; (piano key) touche *f*; **4** (banknote) billet *m*
B **of note** *adj phr* [*person*] éminent, réputé; [*development, contribution*] digne d'intérêt
C *vtr* gen noter; (pay attention to) prendre bonne note de
D **noted** *pp adj* [*intellectual, criminal*] célèbre; **to be** ~**d for** être réputé pour [*tact, wit*]
(Idiom) **to compare** ~**s** échanger ses impressions (**with** avec)
(Phrasal verb)
■ **note down**: ▸ ~ **down** [sth], ~ [sth] **down** noter

note: ~**book** *n* gen carnet *m*; Comput agenda *m* électronique; ~**pad** *n* bloc-notes *m*; ~**paper** *n* papier *m* à lettres; ~**worthy** *adj* remarquable

not guilty *adj* Jur [*person*] non coupable; [*verdict*] d'acquittement

nothing

When *nothing* is used alone as a reply to a question in English, it is translated by *rien*:

'what are you doing?' 'nothing'
= 'que fais-tu?' 'rien'

nothing as a pronoun when it is the subject of a verb is translated by *rien ne* in French:

nothing changes   **nothing has changed**
= rien ne change   = rien n'a changé

nothing as a pronoun when it is the object of a verb is translated by *ne rien*; *ne* comes before the verb, and before the auxiliary in compound tenses, and *rien* comes after the verb or auxiliary:

I see nothing   **I saw nothing**
= je ne vois rien   = je n'ai rien vu

When *ne rien* is used with an infinitive the two words are not separated:

I prefer to say nothing
= je préfère ne rien dire

For examples and particular usages, see **A** in the entry **nothing**.

For translations of *nothing* as an adverb (*it's nothing like as difficult*) and for the phrases *nothing but*, *nothing less than*, *nothing more than*, see **B, E, F** and **G** respectively in the entry **nothing**.

nothing /ˈnʌθɪŋ/
A *pron* rien; (as object of verb) ne...rien; (as subject of verb) rien...ne; **I knew** ~ **about it** je n'en savais rien; **we can do** ~ **(about it)** nous n'y pouvons rien; **next to** ~ presque rien; ~ **much** pas grand-chose; ~ **more** rien de plus; **is there** ~ **more you can do?** vous ne pouvez rien faire de plus?; **she's just a friend,** ~ **more or less** c'est une amie, c'est tout; ~ **else** rien d'autre; **if** ~ **else it will be a change for us** au moins ça nous changera les idées; **I had** ~ **to do with it!** je n'y étais pour rien!; **it's** ~ **to do with us** ça ne nous regarde pas; **to come to** ~ n'aboutir à rien; **to stop at** ~ ne reculer devant rien (**to do** pour faire); **to have** ~ **on** (no clothes) être nu; (no engagements, plans) n'avoir rien de prévu; **you've got** ~ **on me**°! (to incriminate) vous n'avez rien contre moi!; **he's got** ~ **on you**°! (to rival) il ne t'arrive

n

pas à la cheville◦|; **we were talking about** ∼ much nous parlions de tout et de rien; **he means** ou **is** ∼ **to me** il n'est rien pour moi; **it meant** ∼ **to me** ça lui était complètement égal (**that, whether** que + *subj*); **the names meant** ∼ **to him** les noms ne lui disaient rien; **he cares** ∼ **for convention** il se moque des conventions; **to think** ∼ **of doing** (consider normal) trouver tout à fait normal de faire; (not baulk at) ne pas hésiter à faire; **think** ∼ **of it!** ce n'est rien!; **there's really** ∼ **to it** c'est tout ce qu'il y a de plus facile; **it costs next to** ∼ ça ne coûte presque rien; **for** ∼ (for free) gratuitement; (pointlessly) pour rien; **it's money for** ∼ c'est de l'argent vite gagné; **it seems easy but it's** ∼ **of the kind** cela paraît facile mais il n'en est rien; **you'll do** ∼ **of the sort!** tu n'en feras rien!; **there's** ∼ **like it!** il n'y a rien de tel or de mieux!; **I can think of** ∼ **worse than** je ne peux rien imaginer de pire que; **to say** ∼ **of** sans parler de; **you get** ∼ **out of it** ça ne rapporte rien; **there's** ∼ **in it for me** ça n'a aucun intérêt pour moi; **there's** ∼ **in it** (in gossip, rumour) il n'y a rien de vrai là-dedans; (in magazine, booklet) c'est sans intérêt

B *adv* **it is** ∼ **like as difficult as** c'est loin d'être aussi difficile que; **she is** or **looks** ∼ **like her sister** elle ne ressemble pas du tout à sa sœur; **it's** ∼ **short of brilliant** c'est tout à fait génial; ∼ **short of a miracle can save them** il n'y a qu'un miracle qui puisse les sauver; **I'm** ∼ **if not stubborn!** le moins qu'on puisse dire c'est que je suis têtu!

C *adj* **to be** ∼ **without sb/sth** ne rien être sans qn/qch

D *n* néant *m*; **it's a mere** ∼ **compared to** ce n'est pratiquement rien par rapport à; ▸ **sweet**

E **nothing but** *adv phr* **he's** ∼ **but a coward** ce n'est qu'un lâche; **they've done** ∼ **but moan**◦ ils n'ont fait que râler◦; **it's caused me** ∼ **but trouble** ça ne m'a valu que des ennuis; **she has** ∼ **but praise for them** elle ne tarit pas d'éloges sur eux

F **nothing less than** *adv phr* **it's** ∼ **less than a betrayal** c'est une véritable trahison; ∼ **less than real saffron will do** il n'y a que du vrai safran qui fera l'affaire

G **nothing more than** *adv phr* **it's** ∼ **more than a strategy to do** ce n'est qu'une stratégie pour faire; **the stories are** ∼ **more than gossip** ces histoires ne sont rien d'autre que des ragots; **they'd like** ∼ **more than to do** ils ne demandent pas mieux que de faire

notice /'nəʊtɪs/

A *n* **1** (written sign) pancarte *f*; (advertisement) annonce *f*; (announcing birth, marriage, death) avis *m*; (review of a play) compte-rendu *m*; **2** (attention) attention *f*; **to take** ∼ faire attention (**of** à); **it was beneath her** ∼ ça ne méritait pas son attention; **it has come to my** ∼ **that** il m'a été signalé que; **3** (notification) préavis *m*; **one month's** ∼ un mois de préavis; **to do sth at short** ∼ faire qch au pied levé; **to give sb** ∼ **of sth** avertir or prévenir qn de qch; **until further** ∼ jusqu'à nouvel ordre; **I'm sorry it's such short** ∼ je suis désolé de vous prévenir si tard; **to give in** ou **hand in one's** ∼ donner sa démission; [domestic servant] donner ses huit jours; **to give sb (their)** ∼ congédier qn; **to get one's** ∼ recevoir son congé

B *vtr* remarquer [absence, mark]; **I** ∼ **that** je vois que; **to get oneself** ∼d se faire remarquer; **I can't say I** ∼d je n'ai pas fait attention

noticeable /'nəʊtɪsəbl/ *adj* visible

noticeably /'nəʊtɪsəblɪ/ *adv* [increase, improve] sensiblement; [better, colder] nettement

notice: ∼**board** *n* panneau *m* d'affichage; ∼ **to pay** *n* avis *m* de paiement

notification /ˌnəʊtɪfɪ'keɪʃn/ *n* gen notification *f*; (in newspaper) avis *m*; **to receive** ∼ **that** être avisé que

notify /'nəʊtɪfaɪ/ *vtr* **1** GB (give notice of) notifier; **to** ∼ **sb of** ou **about** aviser qn de [result, incident]; avertir qn de [intention]; **2** (announce formally) **to** ∼ **sb of** informer qn de [birth, death]

notion /'nəʊʃn/ *n* **1** (idea) idée *f*; **I never had any** ∼ **of asking her** il ne m'est jamais venu à l'idée de lui demander; **2** (vague understanding) notion *f*; **some** ∼ **of** quelques notions de; **3** (whim, desire) idée *f*; **he had** ou **took a sudden** ∼ **to go for a swim** il a eu l'envie soudaine d'aller nager

notorious /nəʊ'tɔːrɪəs/ *adj* [criminal, organization] notoire; [district, venue] mal famé; [example, case] tristement célèbre; ∼ **for/as sth** [person, place] connu pour/comme qch

notoriously /nəʊ'tɔːrɪəslɪ/ *adv* notoirement; **they're** ∼ **unreliable** il est bien connu qu'on ne peut pas compter sur eux

Notts *n* GB Post abrév écrite = **Nottinghamshire**

notwithstanding /ˌnɒtwɪθ'stændɪŋ/

A *adv* sout néanmoins

B *prep* (in spite of) en dépit de; (excepted) exception faite de; Jur nonobstant

nought /nɔːt/ *n* zéro *m*

noughts and crosses ▸ p. 881 *n* (+ *v sg*) (jeu *m* de) morpion *m*

noun /naʊn/ *n* nom *m*, substantif *m*

nourish /'nʌrɪʃ/ *vtr* nourrir (**with** avec; **on** de)

nourishment /'nʌrɪʃmənt/ *n* (food) nourriture *f*

Nov abrév écrite = **November**

novel /'nɒvl/

A *n* roman *m*

B *adj* original

novelette /ˌnɒvə'let/ *n* péj (over-sentimental) roman *m* à l'eau de rose

novelist /'nɒvəlɪst/ ▸ p. 1181 *n* romancier/-ière *m/f*

novelty /'nɒvltɪ/

A *n* **1** nouveauté *f* (**of doing** de faire); **to be a** ∼ **to sb** avoir l'attrait de la nouveauté pour qn; **2** (trinket) babiole *f*

B *noun modifier* [key ring, mug] fantaisie

November /nə'vembə(r)/ ▸ p. 1020 *n* novembre *m*

novice /'nɒvɪs/ *n* débutant/-e *m/f*; Relig novice *mf*

now /naʊ/

A *conj* ∼ **(that)** maintenant que

B *adv* **1** (at the present moment) maintenant; **I'm doing it** ∼ je suis en train de le faire; ∼ **is the best time to do** c'est le meilleur moment pour faire; **right** ∼ tout de suite; **it's a week** ∼ **since she left** cela fait une semaine (maintenant) qu'elle est partie; **any time** ou **moment** ∼ d'un moment à l'autre; **I'll be more careful** ∼ je serai plus prudent dorénavant; ∼ **fast,** ∼ **slowly** tantôt vite, tantôt lentement; **(every)** ∼ **and then** ou **again** de temps en temps; ∼ **for the next question** passons à la question suivante; **2** (with preposition) **you should have phoned him before** ∼ tu aurais dû lui téléphoner avant; **before** ou **until** ∼ jusqu'à présent; **he should be finished by** ∼ il devrait avoir déjà fini; **between** ∼ **and next Friday** d'ici vendredi prochain; **between** ∼ **and then** d'ici là; **from** ∼ **on(wards)** dorénavant; **that's enough for** ∼ ça suffit pour le moment; **good-bye for** ∼ à bientôt; **3** (in the past) **it was** ∼ **4 pm** il était alors 16 heures; **by** ∼ **it was too late** à ce moment-là, il était trop tard; **4** (without temporal force) ∼ **there's a man I can trust!** ah! voilà un homme en qui on peut avoir confiance!; ∼ **Paul would never do a thing like that** Paul, lui, ne ferait jamais une chose pareille; **careful** ∼! attention!; ∼ **let's see** voyons donc; ∼! ∼!, **come** ∼! allons!; **there** ∼, **what did I tell you?** eh bien, qu'est-ce que je t'avais dit?; ∼ **then, let's get down to work** bon, reprenons le travail

nowadays /'naʊədeɪz/ *adv* (these days) de nos jours, aujourd'hui; (at present, now) actuellement, maintenant

nowhere /'nəʊweə(r)/

A *adv* nulle part; **I've got** ∼ **else to go** je n'ai nulle part où aller; ∼ **else will you find a better bargain** vous ne trouverez pas de meilleure affaire ailleurs; **there's** ∼ **to sit down** il n'y a pas d'endroit pour s'asseoir; ∼ **is this custom more widespread than in China** c'est en Chine que cette coutume est la plus répandue; **this company/this team is going** ∼ l'entreprise/l'équipe stagne; **£10 goes** ∼ **these days** avec 10 livres sterling on ne va pas loin de nos jours; **all this talk is getting us** ∼ tout ce bavardage ne nous avance à rien; **flattery will get you** ∼! tu n'arriveras à rien en me flattant

B **nowhere near** *adv phr*, *prep phr* loin de; ∼ **near sufficient** loin d'être suffisant

noxious /'nɒkʃəs/ *adj* nocif/-ive

nozzle /'nɒzl/ *n* (of hose, pipe) ajutage *m*; (of bellows) bec *m*; (of hoover) suceur *m*; (for icing) douille *f*

nr abrév écrite = **near**

NSPCC *n* GB (*abrév* = **National Society for the Prevention of Cruelty to Children**) société pour la protection de l'enfance

NT *abrév* ▸ **New Testament**

nth /enθ/ *adj* Math, fig énième; **to the ~ power** *ou* **degree** à la puissance n

nub /nʌb/ *n* (of problem) fond *m*; **the ~ of the matter** le cœur du sujet

nubile /'njuːbaɪl, US 'nuːbl/ *adj* (attractive) désirable

nuclear /'njuːklɪə(r), US 'nuː-/ *adj* nucléaire

nuclear: **~ bomb** *n* bombe *f* atomique; **~ deterrent** *n* force *f* de dissuasion nucléaire; **~ energy** *n* énergie *f* nucléaire *or* atomique; **~-free zone** *n* GB zone *f* où les expériences nucléaires sont interdites; **~ physics** *n* (+ *v sg*) physique *f* nucléaire

nuclear power *n* ①‌ (energy) = **nuclear energy**; ②‌ (country) puissance *f* nucléaire

nuclear: **~ power station** *n* centrale *f* nucléaire; **~ shelter** *n* abri *m* antiatomique

nucleus /'njuːklɪəs, US 'nuː-/ *n* (*pl* **-clei**) noyau *m*

nude /njuːd, US nuːd/
🅐 *n* Art nu/-e *m/f*; **in the ~** nu
🅑 *adj* [*person*] nu

nudge /nʌdʒ/
🅐 *n* coup *m* de coude, poussée *f*
🅑 *vtr* (push) pousser du coude; (accidentally) heurter; (brush against) frôler

nudist /'njuːdɪst, US 'nuː-/ *n* nudiste *mf*

nudity /'njuːdətɪ, US 'nuː-/ *n* nudité *f*

nugget /'nʌgɪt/ *n* pépite *f*

nuisance /'njuːsns, US 'nuː-/ *n* gen embêtement *m*; Jur nuisance *f*; **to be a ~** [*thing*] être gênant; [*person*] être pénible; **to make a ~ of oneself** embêter tout le monde; **the ~ is that...** l'ennui c'est que...; **what a ~!** que c'est agaçant!; **I'm sorry to be such a ~** excusez-moi de vous déranger tout le temps

nuisance call *n* Telecom appel *m* anonyme

null /nʌl/ *adj* Jur **~ and void** nul et non avenu

nullify /'nʌlɪfaɪ/ *vtr* invalider, annuler

numb /nʌm/
🅐 *adj* ①‌ [*limb, face*] (due to cold, pressure) engourdi (**with** par); (due to anaesthetic) insensible; **to go ~** s'engourdir; ②‌ fig [*person*] hébété (**with** par)
🅑 *vtr* [*cold*] engourdir; [*anaesthetic*] insensibiliser; **to ~ the pain** endormir la douleur

number /'nʌmbə(r)/ ▸ p. 1044
🅐 *n* ①‌ gen, Ling nombre *m*; (written figure) chiffre *m*; **a three-figure ~** un nombre à trois chiffres; ②‌ (of bus, house, page, telephone) numéro *m*; **a wrong ~** un faux numéro; **there's no reply at that ~** ce numéro ne répond pas; **to be ~ three on the list** être troisième sur la liste; ③‌ (amount, quantity) nombre *m*; **a ~ of people/times** un certain nombre de personnes/fois; **for a ~ of reasons** pour plusieurs raisons; **large ~s of people** beaucoup de gens; **on a ~ of occasions** plusieurs fois; **they were sixteen in ~** ils étaient (au nombre de) seize; **one of our ~** un des nôtres; **in equal ~s** en nombre égal; **any ~ of times** maintes fois; ④‌ (issue) (of magazine, periodical) numéro *m*; **the May ~** le numéro de mai; ⑤‌ Mus, Theat (act) numéro *m*; (song) chanson *f*; ⑥‌ ○(object of admiration) **a little black ~** (dress) une petite robe noire; **that car is a neat little ~** elle est chouette○, cette voiture
🅑 **numbers** *npl* (in company, school) effectifs *mpl*; (of crowd, army) nombre *m*; **to win by force** *ou* **weight of ~s** gagner parce que l'on est plus nombreux; **to make up the ~s** pour compléter le nombre
🅒 *vtr* ①‌ (allocate number to) numéroter; ②‌ (amount to) compter; **the regiment ~ed 1,000 men** le régiment comptait 1 000 hommes; ③‌ (include) compter (**among** parmi)
🅓 *vi* (comprise in number) **a crowd ~ing in the thousands** une foule de plusieurs milliers de personnes; **to ~ among the great musicians** compter parmi les plus grands musiciens

⌈Idioms⌉ **your ~'s up**○! ton compte est bon!; **to do sth by the ~s** US *ou* **by ~s** faire qch mécaniquement; **his days are ~ed** ses jours sont comptés

numbering /'nʌmbərɪŋ/ *n* (action) numérotage *m*; (sequence of numbers) numérotation *f*

number one *n* ①‌ (most important) numéro un *m* (**in** de); ②‌ ○(oneself) **to look after** *ou* **take care of ~** penser avant tout à son propre intérêt

numberplate *n* GB plaque *f* minéralogique *or* d'immatriculation

numeracy /'njuːmərəsɪ, US 'nuː-/ *n* aptitude *f* au calcul; **to improve pupils' standards of ~** améliorer le niveau des élèves en calcul

numeral /'njuːmərəl, US 'nuː-/ *n* chiffre *m*, nombre *m*

numerate /'njuːmərət, US 'nuː-/ *adj* **to be ~** savoir compter

numerical /njuː'merɪkl, US 'nuː-/ *adj* numérique

numerous /'njuːmərəs, US 'nuː-/ *adj* nombreux/-euse

nun /nʌn/ *n* religieuse *f*, bonne sœur *f*; **to become a ~** entrer au couvent

nurse /nɜːs/ ▸ p. 1181
🅐 *n* ①‌ Med infirmier/-ière *m/f*; **male ~** infirmier *m*; ②‌ = **nursemaid**
🅑 *vtr* ①‌ Med soigner [*person, cold*]; ②‌ (clasp) serrer [*object*]; **to ~ a baby in one's arms** bercer un bébé dans ses bras; **~ one's drink** faire durer sa boisson; ③‌ (suckle) allaiter [*baby*]; ④‌ (foster) nourrir [*grievance, hope*]
🅒 *vi* ①‌ (be a nurse) être infirmier/-ière; ②‌ (feed) [*baby*] têter

nursemaid *n* nurse *f*, bonne *f* d'enfants

nursery /'nɜːsərɪ/ *n* ①‌ (also **day ~**) gen crèche *f*; (in hotel, shop) garderie *f*; ②‌ (room) chambre *f* d'enfants; ③‌ (for plants) pépinière *f*

nursery: **~ rhyme** *n* comptine *f*; **~ school** *n* école *f* maternelle; **~ slope** *n* GB piste *f* pour débutants

nurse's aide ▸ p. 1181 *n* US aide-soignant/-e *m/f*

nursing /'nɜːsɪŋ/ ▸ p. 1181
🅐 *n* (profession) profession *f* d'infirmier/-ière; (care) soins *mpl*
🅑 *adj* ①‌ [*mother*] qui allaite; ②‌ Med [*staff*] infirmier/-ière; [*methods, practice*] de soins

nursing auxiliary *n* GB aide-soignant/-e *m/f*

nursing home *n* ①‌ (old people's) maison *f* de retraite; (convalescent) maison *f* de repos; ②‌ GB (small private hospital) clinique *f*; (maternity) clinique *f* obstétrique

nurture /'nɜːtʃə(r)/ *sout*
🅐 *n* 🅒 soins *mpl*
🅑 *vtr* ①‌ lit élever [*child*]; soigner [*plant*]; ②‌ fig nourrir [*hope, feeling, talent*]

⌈Idiom⌉ **the nature ~ debate** la question de l'inné et de l'acquis

nut /nʌt/ *n* ①‌ Culin (walnut) noix *f*; (hazel) noisette *f*; (almond) amande *f*; (peanut) cacahuète *f*; ②‌ Tech écrou *m*

⌈Idioms⌉ **he's a hard** *ou* **tough ~ to crack** il est dur à convaincre; **to be ~s about sb/sth**○ être fou/folle de qn/qch; **the ~s and bolts** les détails pratiques (**of** de)

nut: **~cracker(s)** *n(pl)* casse-noisettes *m inv*; **~ cutlet** *n* côtelette *f* végétarienne (à base de noisettes); **~meg** *n* (spice) noix *f* de muscade

nutrient /'njuːtrɪənt, US 'nuː-/ *n* substance *f* nutritive

nutrition /njuː'trɪʃn, US 'nuː-/ *n* (process) nutrition *f*, alimentation *f*; (science) diététique *f*

nutritional /njuː'trɪʃənl, US nuː-/ *adj* [*value*] nutritif/-ive; [*composition, information*] nutritionnel/-elle

nutritious /njuː'trɪʃəs, US nuː-/ *adj* nourrissant

nutshell /'nʌtʃel/ *n* ①‌ lit coquille *f* de noix *or* noisette; ②‌ fig **in a ~** en un mot; **to put sth in a ~** résumer qch en un mot

nuzzle /'nʌzl/
🅐 *vtr* frotter son nez contre
🅑 *vi* = **nuzzle up**
⌈Phrasal verb⌉

▪ **nuzzle up**: **to ~ up against** *ou* **to sb** se blottir contre qn

NV US Post *abrév écrite* = **Nevada**

NY US Post *abrév écrite* = **New York**

NYC US *abrév écrite* = **New York City**

n

Numbers

Cardinal numbers in French

0	zéro*
1	un†
2	deux
3	trois
4	quatre
5	cinq
6	six
7	sept
8	huit
9	neuf
10	dix
11	onze
12	douze
13	treize
14	quatorze
15	quinze
16	seize
17	dix-sept
18	dix-huit
19	dix-neuf
20	vingt
21	vingt et un
22	vingt-deux
30	trente
31	trente et un
32	trente-deux
40	quarante
50	cinquante
60	soixante
70	soixante-dix
	septante
	(in Belgium, Canada, Switzerland etc.)
71	soixante et onze
	septante et un *(etc)*
72	soixante-douze
73	soixante-treize
74	soixante-quatorze
75	soixante-quinze
76	soixante-seize
77	soixante-dix-sept
78	soixante-dix-huit
79	soixante-dix-neuf
80	quatre-vingts‡
81	quatre-vingt-un§
82	quatre-vingt-deux
90	quatre-vingt-dix
	nonante
	(in Belgium, Canada, Switzerland, etc)
91	quatre-vingt-onze
	nonante et un
92	quatre-vingt-douze
	nonante-deux *(etc.)*
99	quatre-vingt-dix-neuf
100	cent
101	cent un†
102	cent deux
110	cent dix
111	cent onze
112	cent douze
187	cent quatre-vingt-sept
200	deux cents
250	deux cent¶ cinquante
300	trois cents
1 000‖	mille
1 001	mille un†
1 002	mille deux
1 020	mille vingt
1 200	mille** deux cents
2 000	deux mille††
10 000	dix mille
10 200	dix mille deux cents
100 000	cent mille
102 000	cent deux mille
1 000 000	un million‡‡
1 264 932	un million deux cent soixante-quatre mille neuf cent trente-deux
1 000 000 000	un milliard‡‡
1 000 000 000 000	un billion‡‡

* *In English 0 may be called* nought, zero *or even* nothing; *French is always* zéro; *a nought =* un zéro.

† *Note that* one *is* une *in French when it agrees with a feminine noun, so* un crayon *but* une table, une des tables, vingt et une tables, combien de tables? – il y en a une seule *etc.*

‡ *Also* huitante *in Switzerland. Note that when 80 is used as a page number it has no* s, *e.g.* page eighty = page quatre-vingt.

§ *Note that* vingt *has no* s *when it is in the middle of a number. The only exception to this rule is when* quatre-vingts *is followed by* millions, milliards *or* billions, *e.g.* quatre-vingts millions, quatre-vingts billions *etc.*

¶ *Note that* cent *does not take an* s *when it is in the middle of a number. The only exception to this rule is when it is followed by* millions, milliards *or* billions, *e.g.* trois cents millions, six cents billions *etc. It has a normal plural when it modifies other nouns, e.g.* 200 inhabitants = deux cents habitants.

‖ *Note that figures in French are set out differently; where English would have a comma, French has simply a space. It is also possible in French to use a full stop (period) here, e.g.* 1.000. *French, like English, writes dates without any separation between thousands and hundreds, e.g. in* 1995 = en 1995.

** *When such a figure refers to a date, the spelling* mil *is preferred to* mille, *i.e.* en 1200 = en mil deux cents. *Note however the exceptions: when the year is a round number of thousands, the spelling is always* mille, *so* en l'an mille, en l'an deux mille *etc.*

†† Mille *is invariable; it never takes an* s.

‡‡ *Note that the French words* million, milliard *and* billion *are nouns, and when written out in full they take* de *before another noun, e.g.* a million inhabitants *is* un million d'habitants, a billion francs *is* un billion de francs. *However, when written in figures,* 1,000,000 inhabitants *is* 1 000 000 habitants, *but is still spoken as* un million d'habitants. *When* million *etc. is part of a complex number,* de *is not used before the nouns, e.g.* 6,000,210 people = six millions deux cent dix personnes.

Use of *en*

■ *Note the use of* en *in the following examples:*

there are six	**I've got a hundred**
= il y en a six	= j'en ai cent

■ En *must be used when the thing you are talking about is not expressed (the French says literally* there of them are six, I of them have a hundred *etc.). However,* en *is not needed when the object is specified:*

there are six apples
= il y a six pommes

Approximate numbers

■ *When you want to say* about…, *remember the French ending* -aine:

about ten	**about fifteen people**
= une dizaine	= une quinzaine de personnes
about ten books	**about twenty**
= une dizaine de livres	= une vingtaine
about fifteen	**about twenty hours**
= une quinzaine	= une vingtaine d'heures

■ *Similarly* une trentaine, une quarantaine, une cinquantaine, une soixantaine *and* une centaine (*and* une douzaine *means* a dozen). *For other numbers, use* environ (*about*):

about thirty-five	**about thirty-five francs**
= environ trente-cinq	= environ trente-cinq francs
about four thousand	**about four thousand pages**
= environ quatre mille	= environ quatre mille pages

■ Environ *can be used with any number:* environ dix, environ quinze *etc. are as good as* une dizaine, une quinzaine *etc.*

■ *Note the use of* centaines *and* milliers *to express approximate quantities:*

hundreds of books
= des centaines de livres

I've got hundreds
= j'en ai des centaines

hundreds and hundreds of fish
= des centaines et des centaines de poissons

I've got thousands
= j'en ai des milliers

thousands of books
= des milliers de livres

thousands and thousands
= des milliers et des milliers

millions and millions
= des millions et des millions

☛ See next page

Numbers *continued*

Phrases

numbers up to ten
= les nombres jusqu'à dix

to count up to ten
= compter jusqu'à dix

almost ten
= presque dix

less than ten
= moins de dix

■ *Note the French word order:*

my last ten pounds
= mes dix dernières livres

the next twelve weeks
= les douze prochaines semaines

more than ten
= plus de dix

all ten of them
= tous les dix

all ten boys
= les dix garçons

the other two
= les deux autres

the last four
= les quatre derniers

Calculations in French

say

10 + 3= 13	dix et trois font *or* égalent treize
10 − 3= 7	trois ôté de dix il reste sept
	or dix moins trois égale sept
10 × 3= 30	dix fois trois égale trente
30 : 3= 10	(30 ÷ 3 = 10) trente divisé par trois égale dix

■ *Note how the French division sign differs from the English.*

5^2	cinq au carré
5^3	cinq puissance trois
5^4	cinq puissance quatre
5^{100}	cinq puissance cent
5^n	cinq puissance n
$\sqrt{12}$	racine carrée de douze
$\sqrt{25} = 5$	racine carrée de vingt-cinq égale cinq
B > A	B est plus grand que A
A < B	A est plus petit que B

Decimals in French

■ *Note that French uses a comma where English has a decimal point.*

say

0,25	zéro virgule vingt-cinq
0,05	zéro virgule zéro cinq
0,75	zéro virgule soixante-quinze
3,45	trois virgule quarante-cinq
8,195	huit virgule cent quatre-vingt-quinze
9,1567	neuf virgule quinze cent soixante-sept
	or neuf virgule mille cinq cent soixante-sept
9,3456	neuf virgule trois mille quatre cent cinquante-six

Percentages in French

say

25%	vingt-cinq pour cent
50%	cinquante pour cent
100%	cent pour cent
200%	deux cents pour cent
365%	troix cent soixante-cinq pour cent
4,25%	quatre virgule vingt-cinq pour cent

Fractions in French

say

1/2	un demi*
1/3	un tiers
1/4	un quart
1/5	un cinquième
1/6	un sixième
1/7	un septième
1/8	un huitième
1/9	un neuvième
1/10	un dixième
1/11	un onzième
1/12	un douzième (*etc.*)
2/3	deux tiers†
2/5	deux cinquièmes
2/10	deux dixièmes (*etc.*)
3/4	trois quarts
3/5	trois cinquièmes
3/10	trois dixièmes (*etc.*)
1¹/2	un et demi
1¹/3	un (et) un tiers
1¹/4	un et quart
1¹/5	un (et) un cinquième
1¹/6	un (et) un sixième
1¹/7	un (et) un septième (*etc.*)
5²/3	cinq (et) deux tiers
5³/4	cinq (et) trois quarts
5⁴/5	cinq (et) quatre cinquièmes

45/100ths of a second
= quarante-cinq centièmes de seconde

Ordinal numbers in French§

1st	1er‡	premier
		(*feminine* première)
2nd	2e	second *or* deuxième
3rd	3e	troisième
4th	4e	quatrième
5th	5e	cinquième
6th	6e	sixième
7th	7e	septième
8th	8e	huitième
9th	9e	neuvième
10th	10e	dixième
11th	11e	onzième
12th	12e	douzième
13th	13e	treizième
14th	14e	quatorzième
15th	15e	quinzième
16th	16e	seizième
17th	17e	dix-septième
18th	18e	dix-huitième
19th	19e	dix-neuvième
20th	20e	vingtième
21st	21e	vingt et unième
22nd	22e	vingt-deuxième
23rd	23e	vingt-troisième
24th	24e	vingt-quatrième
25th	25e	vingt-cinquième
30th	30e	trentième
31st	31e	trente et unième
40th	40e	quarantième
50th	50e	cinquantième
60th	60e	soixantième
70th	70e	soixante-dixième
		septantième (*in Belgium, Canada, Switzerland etc.*)
71st	71e	soixante et onzième
		septante et unième (*etc.*)
72nd	72e	soixante-douzième

☛ See next page

n

Numbers *continued*

73rd	73e	soixante-treizième
74th	74e	soixante-quatorzième
75th	75e	soixante-quinzième
76th	76e	soixante-seizième
77th	77e	soixante-dix-septième
78th	78e	soixante-dix-huitième
79th	79e	soixante-dix-neuvième
80th	80e	quatre-vingtième¶
81st	81e	quatre-vingt-unième
90th	90e	quatre-vingt-dixième
		nonantième (*in Belgium, Canada, Switzerland etc.*)
91st	91e	quatre-vingt-onzième
		nonante et unième (*etc.*)
99th	99e	quatre-vingt-dix-neuvième
100th	100e	centième
101st	101e	cent et unième
102nd	102e	cent-deuxième
196th	196e	cent quatre-vingt-seizième
200th	200e	deux centième
300th	300e	trois centième
400th	400e	quatre centième
1,000th	1000e	millième
2,000th	2000e	deux millième
1,000,000th	1000000e	millionième

■ *Like English, French makes nouns by adding the definite article:*

the first
= le premier (*or* la première, *or* les premiers *mpl or* les premières *fpl*)

the second
= le second (*or* la seconde *etc.*)

the first three
= les trois premiers *or* les trois premières

■ *Note the French word order in:*

the third richest country in the world
= le troisième pays le plus riche du monde
* *Note that* half, *when not a fraction, is translated by the noun* moitié *or the adjective* demi; *see the dictionary entry.*
† *Note the use of* les *and* d'entre *when these fractions are used about a group of people or things:* two-thirds of them = les deux tiers d'entre eux.
‡ *This is the masculine form; the feminine is* 1re *and the plural* 1ers (*m*) *or* 1res (*f*).
§ *All the ordinal numbers in French behave like ordinary adjectives and take normal plural endings where appropriate.*
¶ *Also* huitantième *in Switzerland.*

nylon /ˈnaɪlɒn/ *n* nylon® *m*
nylons /ˈnaɪlɒnz/ *npl* bas *mpl* nylon
nymph /nɪmf/ *n* nymphe *f*

nymphomaniac /ˌnɪmfəˈmeɪnɪæk/ *n, adj* nymphomane (*f*)

NZ *abrév écrite* = **New Zealand**

n

Oo

o, O /əʊ/ n **1** (letter) o, O m; **2** **O** (spoken number) zéro

o' /ə/ prep (abrév = **of**) de

oaf /əʊf/ n (clumsy) balourd/-e m/f; (loutish) mufle m

oak /əʊk/
A n chêne m
B noun modifier [table] de ou en chêne
(Idiom) **great ~s from little acorns grow** Prov les petits ruisseaux font les grandes rivières Prov

OAP n GB **1** (abrév = **old age pensioner**) retraité/-e m/f; **2** (abrév = **old age pension**) retraite f de la sécurité sociale

oar /ɔː(r)/ n rame f; (person) rameur/-euse m/f

OAS n US (abrév = **Organization of American States**) Organisation f des États américains

oasis /əʊˈeɪsɪs/ n (pl **oases**) (in desert) oasis f; fig (of peace) havre m

oatcake /ˈəʊtkeɪk/ n galette f d'avoine

oath /əʊθ/ n **1** Jur serment m; **under ~, on ~** GB sous serment; **to take the ~** prêter serment; **to swear** ou **take an ~** prêter serment (**to do** de faire; **that** que); **to administer the ~ to sb, to put sb under ~** faire prêter serment à qn; **2** (swearword) juron m

oatmeal /ˈəʊtmiːl/
A n C **1** (cereal) farine f d'avoine; **2** US (porridge) bouillie f d'avoine; **3** (colour) grège m
B ▶ p. 752 adj grège

oats /əʊts/ n avoine f
(Idiom) **to sow one's wild ~s** jeter sa gourme

obdurate /ˈɒbdjʊrət, US -dər-/ adj **1** (stubborn) obstiné, entêté; **2** (hardhearted) endurci

OBE n GB (abrév = **Officer of the (Order of the) British Empire**) officier m de l'ordre de l'empire britannique

obedience /əˈbiːdɪəns/ n gen obéissance f (**to** à); Relig obédience f; **in ~ to** conformément à

obedient /əˈbiːdɪənt/ adj obéissant

obediently /əˈbiːdɪəntlɪ/ adv docilement

obelisk /ˈɒbəlɪsk/ n Archit obélisque m

obese /əʊˈbiːs/ adj obèse

obesity /əʊˈbiːsətɪ/ n obésité f

obey /əˈbeɪ/
A vtr obéir à; se conformer à [instructions]; Jur obtempérer à [summons, order]
B vi obéir

obituary /əˈbɪtʃʊərɪ, US -tʃʊerɪ/
A n (also ~ **notice**) nécrologie f
B noun modifier [column, page] nécrologique

object
A /ˈɒbdʒɪkt/ n **1** (item) objet m; **2** (goal) but m (**of** de); **with the ~ of doing** dans le but de faire; **3** (focus) **to be the ~ of** être l'objet de; **4** Ling complément m d'objet
B /ˈɒbdʒekt/ vtr objecter (**that** que)
C /əbˈdʒekt/ vi soulever des objections; **'I ~!'** 'je proteste!'; **to ~ to** s'opposer à [plan, law]; se plaindre de [noise]; récuser [witness, juror]; **to ~ strongly to** s'opposer catégoriquement à; **to ~ to sb on grounds of sex/age** objecter à qn son sexe/âge; **to ~ to sb('s) doing** s'opposer à ce que qn fasse; **do you ~ to my** ou **me smoking?** est-ce que cela vous ennuie que je fume?
(Idiom) **money is no ~** l'argent n'est pas un problème

objection /əbˈdʒekʃn/ n objection f (**to** à; **from** de la part de); **I've no ~(s)** je n'y vois pas d'inconvénient; **I've no**

~ to them coming cela ne me dérange pas qu'ils viennent; **to make ~ to** Jur marquer son opposition à [argument, statement]

objectionable /əbˈdʒekʃənəbl/ adj [remark] désobligeant; [behaviour] choquant; [person] insupportable

objective /əbˈdʒektɪv/
A n gen objectif m; Ling accusatif m
B adj (unbiased) objectif/-ive, impartial (**about** en ce qui concerne); Ling accusatif/-ive

objectively /əbˈdʒektɪvlɪ/ adv objectivement

objectivity /ˌɒbdʒekˈtɪvətɪ/ n objectivité f

object lesson n démonstration f (**in** de)

objector /əbˈdʒektə(r)/ n opposant/-e m/f

obligation /ˌɒblɪˈɡeɪʃn/ n **1** (duty) devoir m (**towards, to** envers); **to be under (an) ~ to do** être obligé de faire; **2** (commitment) (contractual) obligation f (**to** envers; **to do** de faire); (personal) engagement m (**to** envers); **3** (debt) (financial) dette f; (of gratitude) dette f de reconnaissance; **to be under ~ to sb for sth** être redevable à qn de qch

obligatory /əˈblɪɡətrɪ, US -tɔːrɪ/ adj (compulsory) obligatoire (**to do** de faire); (customary) de rigueur

oblige /əˈblaɪdʒ/ vtr **1** (compel) obliger (**to do** à faire); **2** (be helpful) rendre service à; **could you ~ me with a lift?** auriez-vous l'amabilité de me déposer?; **anything to ~!** à votre service!; **3** (be grateful) **to be ~d to sb** être reconnaissant à qn (**for** de; **for doing** d'avoir fait); **I would be ~d if you'd stop smoking** je vous saurais gré de ne pas fumer; **much ~d!** merci beaucoup!

obliging /əˈblaɪdʒɪŋ/ adj serviable; **it is ~ of them** c'est aimable de leur part (**to do** de faire)

oblique /əˈbliːk/
A n (in printing) oblique f
B adj gen oblique; [reference, compliment] indirect

obliquely /əˈbliːklɪ/ adv [drawn] obliquement, de biais; [answer, refer] indirectement

obliterate /əˈblɪtəreɪt/ vtr **1** (destroy) anéantir [landmark, city]; (remove) effacer [trace, word]; **2** (cover) masquer [sun, view]; **3** (erase from mind) effacer [memory]

obliteration /əˌblɪtəˈreɪʃn/ n (of mark, memory) effacement m; (of city) anéantissement m

oblivion /əˈblɪvɪən/ n **1** (obscurity) oubli m; **2** (unconsciousness) néant m

oblivious /əˈblɪvɪəs/ adj **1** (unaware) inconscient; **to be ~ of** ou **to** ne pas être conscient de; **2** (forgetful) oublieux/-ieuse (**of** de)

oblong /ˈɒblɒŋ, US -lɔːŋ/
A n rectangle m
B adj [table, building] oblong/-ongue, rectangulaire

obnoxious /əbˈnɒkʃəs/ adj [person, behaviour] odieux/-ieuse, exécrable; [smell] nauséabond

oboe /ˈəʊbəʊ/ ▶ p. 1028 n hautbois m

obscene /əbˈsiːn/ adj **1** [film, publication, remark] obscène; **2** [wealth] indécent; [war] monstrueux/-euse

obscenely /əbˈsiːnlɪ/ adv [leer, suggest] de manière obscène; **to be ~ rich** être tellement riche que c'en est indécent

obscenity /əbˈsenətɪ/ n obscénité f

obscure /əbˈskjʊə(r)/
A adj gen obscur; (indistinct) vague
B vtr gen obscurcir; cacher [view]; **to ~ the issue** embrouiller la question

obscurity /əb'skjʊərətɪ/ n obscurité f

obsequious /əb'si:kwɪəs/ adj obséquieux/-ieuse

observable /əb'zɜ:vəbl/ adj (discernible) observable; (noteworthy) notable

observance /əb'zɜ:vəns/ n ⓵ (of law, right) respect m (of de); (of sabbath) observance f (of de); ⓶ (ceremony) observance f

observant /əb'zɜ:vənt/ adj observateur/-trice

observation /ˌɒbzə'veɪʃn/ n ⓵ gen, Med observation f (of de); **to be under ~** (in hospital) être en observation; **to keep sb/sth under ~** gen surveiller qn/qch; ⓶ (remark) remarque f; (critical) observation f; **to make the ~ that** faire observer que

observation: **~ car** n wagon m panoramique; **~ tower** n mirador m

observatory /əb'zɜ:vətrɪ, US -tɔ:rɪ/ n observatoire m

observe /əb'zɜ:v/ vtr ⓵ (see, notice) observer (**that** que); ⓶ (watch) [doctor, police] surveiller; [scientist, researcher] observer; ⓷ (remark) faire observer (**that** que); ⓸ (adhere to) observer [law, custom, festival]

observer /əb'zɜ:və(r)/ n gen observateur/-trice m/f (of de); (commentator) spécialiste mf

obsess /əb'ses/ vtr obséder

obsession /əb'seʃn/ n obsession f; **she has an ~ with tidiness** elle a la manie de l'ordre; **sailing is an ~ with him** sa passion pour la voile tient de l'obsession

obsessive /əb'sesɪv/ adj [person] maniaque; [neurosis] obsessionnel/-elle; [thought, memory] obsédant; **his ~ fear of illness** sa hantise de la maladie

obsessively /əb'sesɪvlɪ/ adv **~ clean** d'une propreté maniaque; **to be ~ interested in sth** s'intéresser à qch au point d'en être obsédé

obsolescence /ˌɒbsə'lesns/ n gen désuétude f; Econ obsolescence f; **built-in ~, planned ~** obsolescence planifiée

obsolete /'ɒbsəli:t/ adj [technology] dépassé; [custom, idea] démodé; [word] désuet

obstacle /'ɒbstəkl/ n lit, fig obstacle m; **to be an ~ to sth, to put an ~ in the way of sth** faire obstacle à qch; **to put an ~ in sb's way** faire obstacle à qn

obstacle: **~ course** n Mil parcours m du combattant; fig course f d'obstacles; **~ race** n course f d'obstacles

obstetric /əb'stetrɪk/
Ⓐ obstetrics n (+ v sg) obstétrique f
Ⓑ adj [service, technique] obstétrical

obstetrician /ˌɒbstə'trɪʃn/ ▸ p. 1181 n obstétricien/-ienne m/f

obstinacy /'ɒbstənəsɪ/ n (of person) entêtement m (**in doing** à faire); (of cough, illness) persistance f

obstinate /'ɒbstənət/ adj [person] têtu (**about** en ce qui concerne); [behaviour, silence, effort] obstiné; [resistance] acharné; [illness, cough] persistant; [fever, stain] rebelle

obstreperous /əb'strepərəs/ adj [drunk, child] tapageur/-euse; [crowd] tumultueux/-euse

obstruct /əb'strʌkt/ vtr ⓵ (block) cacher [view]; bloquer [road]; Med obstruer (**with** de); ⓶ (impede) gêner [traffic, person, progress]; faire obstacle à [plan]; faire obstruction à [player]; entraver le cours de [justice]; **to ~ the police** gêner la police dans l'exercice de ses fonctions

obstruction /əb'strʌkʃn/ n ⓵ ℭ (act, state) (of road) encombrement m; (of pipe, artery) engorgement m; Pol obstruction f; ⓶ (blockage) (to traffic, progress) obstacle m; (in pipe) bouchon m; Med obstruction f; ⓷ Sport obstruction f

obstructive /əb'strʌktɪv/ adj ⓵ [policy, tactics] obstructionniste; [person] peu coopératif/-ive; [behaviour] récalcitrant; ⓶ Med qui obstrue, obstruant

obtain /əb'teɪn/
Ⓐ vtr obtenir [information, permission, degree, visa, prize]; (for oneself) se procurer [money, goods]; acquérir [experience]; **to ~ sth for sb** procurer qch à qn; **our products may be ~ed from any supermarket** vous trouverez nos produits dans tous les supermarchés
Ⓑ vi sout [situation] avoir cours; [rule] être de rigueur

obtainable /əb'teɪnəbl/ adj **~ in all good bookstores** disponible dans toutes les bonnes librairies; **petrol is easily ~** on peut se procurer de l'essence facilement

obtrude /əb'tru:d/ vi ⓵ sout (impinge) **to ~ on** empiéter sur; ⓶ sout (become apparent) transparaître; ⓷ (stick out) sortir

obtrusive /əb'tru:sɪv/ adj ⓵ (conspicuous) [decor] choquant; [stain] visible; [noise] gênant; ⓶ (indiscreet) [person, behaviour] importun

obtuse /əb'tju:s, US -'tu:s/ adj ⓵ [person] obtus; [remark] stupide; **he's being deliberately ~** il joue les abrutis○; ⓶ Math obtus

obverse /'ɒbvɜ:s/ adj ⓵ (contrary) [argument] contraire; ⓶ (of coin) **the ~ side** ou **face** l'avers m

obviate /'ɒbvɪeɪt/ vtr sout obvier à [difficulty]; éviter [delay, requirement]; écarter [danger]

obvious /'ɒbvɪəs/
Ⓐ n **to state the ~** enfoncer les portes ouvertes
Ⓑ adj ⓵ (evident) évident (**to** pour); **it's ~ that** il est évident que; **her anxiety was ~** il était évident qu'elle était inquiète; **she is the ~ choice for the job** c'est la personne qu'il nous faut pour ce poste; **it was the ~ solution to choose** la solution s'imposait d'elle-même; **the ~ thing to do** la chose à faire; **for ~ reasons** pour des raisons évidentes; ⓶ (unsubtle) [lie] flagrant; [joke] lourd; **she was too ~ about it** elle a un peu trop manqué de finesse

obviously /'ɒbvɪəslɪ/
Ⓐ adv manifestement; **she ~ needs help** il est évident qu'elle a besoin d'aide; **he's ~ lying** il est clair qu'il ment; **he was ~ in pain** il souffrait visiblement; **'hasn't he heard of them?'—'~ not'** iron 'n'en a-t-il pas entendu parler?'—'on dirait que non'
Ⓑ excl (indicating assent) bien sûr!, évidemment!

occasion /ə'keɪʒn/
Ⓐ n ⓵ (particular time) occasion f; **on that ~** à cette occasion, cette fois-là; **on one ~** une fois; **on a previous ~** précédemment; **on ~** à l'occasion; **on the ~ of** à l'occasion de; **when the ~ demands it** lorsque les circonstances l'exigent; **to rise to the ~** se montrer à la hauteur des circonstances; ⓶ sout (opportunity) occasion f; **to have ~ to do** avoir l'occasion de faire; **it's no ~ for laughter** ce n'est pas le moment de rire; **should the ~ arise** si l'occasion se présente; ⓷ (event, function) occasion f, événement m; **on special ~s** dans les grandes occasions; **for the ~** pour l'occasion; **the wedding was quite an ~** le mariage a été un événement; **state ~** cérémonie f officielle; ⓸ sout (cause) raison f; **there is no ~ for alarm** il n'y a pas lieu de s'inquiéter
Ⓑ vtr sout occasionner, provoquer

occasional /ə'keɪʒənl/ adj ⓵ [event] qui a lieu de temps en temps; **the ~ letter** une lettre de temps en temps; **~ showers** Meteorol averses fpl intermittentes; ⓶ sout [poem, music] de circonstance

occasionally /ə'keɪʒənəlɪ/ adv de temps à autre; **very ~** très rarement, presque jamais

occlude /ə'klu:d/ vtr occlure

occult /'ɒkʌlt/
Ⓐ /ɒ'kʌlt, US ə'kʌlt/ n **the ~** (+ v sg) les sciences fpl occultes
Ⓑ /ɒ'kʌlt/ adj [powers, arts, literature] occulte

occupancy /'ɒkjʊpənsɪ/ n occupation f; **sole ~ of a house** occupation d'une maison par une seule personne; **a change of ~** un changement d'occupant/-e m/f; **available for immediate ~** libre immédiatement

occupant /'ɒkjʊpənt/ n ⓵ (of building, bed) occupant/-e m/f; ⓶ (of vehicle) passager/-ère m/f; ⓷ (of post) titulaire mf

occupation /ˌɒkjʊ'peɪʃn/ n ⓵ (of house) **to be in ~** être installé; **ready for ~** prêt à être habité; **to take up ~** s'installer (**of** dans); ⓶ Mil, Pol occupation f (**de** of); **to come under ~** être envahi; ⓷ (job) (trade) métier m; (profession) profession f; ⓸ (leisure activity) occupation f

occupational /ˌɒkjʊ'peɪʃənl/ adj [accident] du travail; [activity] professionnel/-elle; [risk] du métier; [safety] au travail

occupational: **~ hazard** n risque m professionnel; **~ health** n médecine f du travail; **~ pension** n GB retraite f professionnelle; **~ psychologist** ▸ p. 1181 n psychologue mf du travail; **~ therapist** ▸ p. 1181 n ergothérapeute mf; **~ therapy** n ergothérapie f

occupier /'ɒkjʊpaɪə(r)/ n occupant/-e m/f

occupy /'ɒkjʊpaɪ/ vtr ⓵ (inhabit) occuper [premises]; ⓶ (fill) occuper [bed, seat, room]; ⓷ (take over) occuper [country, building]; ⓸ (take up) prendre [time]; [activity] durer [afternoon]; occuper [area, surface]; ⓹ (keep busy) occuper [person, mind]; capter [attention]; **I'm fully occupied with the garden** le jardin prend tout mon temps; **to keep oneself occupied**

Oceans and seas

■ *Note that the words* océan *and* mer *do not have capitals in French.*

the Atlantic Ocean
= l'océan Atlantique

the Pacific Ocean
= l'océan Pacifique

the Indian Ocean
= l'océan Indien

the Caspian Sea
= la mer Caspienne

the Baltic Sea
= la mer Baltique

■ *As in English, French often drops the words* océan *or* mer. *When this happens, oceans have masculine gender (from the masculine word* océan) *and seas have feminine gender (from the feminine* mer):

the Pacific
= le Pacifique

the Baltic
= la Baltique

but

the Aegean
= la mer Égée

■ *If in doubt, look up the name in the dictionary.*

Use with other nouns

■ *Here are some useful patterns, using* Pacifique *as a typical name:*

the Pacific coast
= la côte du Pacifique

a Pacific crossing
= une traversée du Pacifique

a Pacific cruise
= une croisière dans le Pacifique

Pacific currents
= les courants du Pacifique

Pacific fish
= les poissons du Pacifique

the Pacific islands
= les îles du Pacifique

s'occuper (**by doing** en faisant); **6** (hold) remplir [*post*]

occur /ə'kɜː(r)/ vi (*p prés etc* **-rr-**) **1** (happen) [*change, delay, fault*] se produire; [*epidemic*] se déclarer; [*symptom*] apparaître; [*opportunity*] se présenter; [*sale, visit*] s'effectuer; **2** (be present) [*disease, infection*] se produire; [*species, toxin, misprint*] se trouver; [*phrase*] se rencontrer; **3** (suggest itself) **the idea ∼red to me that** l'idée m'est venue à l'esprit que; **it ∼s to me that she's wrong** il me semble qu'elle a tort; **it didn't ∼ to me to do** il ne m'est pas venu à l'idée de faire

occurrence /ə'kʌrəns/ n **1** (event) fait *m*; **to be a rare ∼** se produire rarement; **2** (instance) occurrence *f*; **3** (of disease, phenomenon) cas *m*

ocean /'əʊʃn/
A *n* lit océan *m*
B **oceans**° *npl* **∼s of** plein de° [*food, space, time, work etc*]
C *noun modifier* [*voyage, wave*] océanique; **∼ bed** fond *m* de l'océan

ocean-going /'əʊʃngəʊɪŋ/ *adj* [*vessel, ship*] de haute mer

ochre GB, **ocher** US /'əʊkə(r)/ ▸ p. 752 *n, adj* (colour) ocre (*mf*) *inv*

o'clock /ə'klɒk/ ▸ p. 745 *adv* **at one ∼** à une heure; **it's two ∼/12 ∼ midday** il est deux heures/midi; **the 10 ∼ screening** la séance de 10 heures

Oct *abrév écrite* = **October**
octagon /'ɒktəgən, US -gɒn/ *n* octogone *m*
octane /'ɒkteɪn/ *n* octane *m*
octave /'ɒktɪv/ *n* Mus octave *f*; Literat huitain *m*
octavo /ɒk'teɪvəʊ/ *n, noun modifier* in-octavo (*m*)
octet /ɒk'tet/ *n* Mus octuor *m*; Comput octet *m*; Literat huitain *m*
October /ɒk'təʊbə(r)/ ▸ p. 1020 *n* octobre *m*
octogenarian /ˌɒktədʒɪ'neərɪən/ *n, adj* octogénaire (*mf*)
octopus /'ɒktəpəs/ *n* **1** Zool pieuvre *f*; Culin poulpe *m*; **2** GB (elastic straps) fixe-bagages *m inv*
oculist /'ɒkjʊlɪst/ ▸ p. 1181 *n* ophtalmologiste *mf*
OD° /əʊdiː/
A *n* = **overdose** A
B *vi* (*3e pers sg prés* **OD's**; *p prés* **OD'ing**; *prét, pp* **OD'd, OD'ed**) **to ∼ on** lit prendre une dose mortelle de [*tablets*]; prendre une overdose de [*drugs*]; fig se gaver de [*chocolate*]; s'abrutir de [*television*]

odd /ɒd/
A *adj* **1** (strange, unusual) [*person, object, occurrence*] bizarre; **there is something ∼ about** il y a quelque chose de bizarre dans [*appearance, statement*]; **it is ∼ how...** c'est bizarre de voir comme...; **to be an ∼ couple** former un drôle de couple; **that's ∼** (c'est) bizarre; **he's a bit ∼** il est un peu loufoque°; **to ∼ on** lit prendre une ∼ drink il m'arrive de boire un verre; **to write the ∼ article** écrire un article de temps en temps; **except for the ∼ tree** à part un arbre ou deux; **3** [*socks, gloves*] dépareillés; **4** (miscellaneous) **there were some ∼ bits of cloth left** il restait encore quelques bouts de tissu; **a few ∼ coins** un reste de monnaie; **5** Math [*number*] impair; **6** (different) **spot the ∼ man ou one out** trouvez l'intrus; **to feel the ∼ one out** ne pas se sentir à sa place
B **-odd** *combining form* (approximately) **there were sixty-∼ people** il y avait soixante et quelques personnes; **twenty-∼ years later** une vingtaine d'années plus tard

odd: **∼ball**° *n* farfelu/-e° *m/f*; **∼ bod**° *n* GB drôle de mec°/nana° *m/f*

oddity /'ɒdɪtɪ/ *n* (odd thing) bizarrerie *f*; (person) excentrique *mf*

odd job *n* (for money) petit boulot *m*; **to do ∼s around the house** bricoler dans la maison

odd-jobman *n* homme *m* à tout faire

odds /ɒdz/ *npl* **1** (in betting) cote *f* (**on** sur); **what are the ∼?** quelle est la cote?; **the ∼ are 20 to 1** la cote est 20 contre 1; **the ∼ on X are short/long** X est bien/mal coté; **2** (chance, likelihood) chances *fpl*; **the ∼ are against/in favour of sth** qch est improbable/probable; **the ∼ are against it** il y a peu de chances; **the ∼ against/in favour of sth happening** les chances que qch n'arrive pas/arrive; **the ∼ are in our favour** (in venture) nous avons toutes les chances de réussir; **to win against the ∼** gagner contre toute attente; **to shorten/lengthen the ∼ on sth** rendre qch plus/moins probable

Idioms **it makes no ∼** GB ça n'a pas d'importance; **to pay over the ∼ for sth** payer le prix fort pour qch; **at ∼** (in dispute) être en conflit; (inconsistent) en contradiction

odds and ends, **odds and sods**° GB *npl* bricoles° *fpl*

odds-on /ˌɒdz'ɒn/ *adj* **1** °(likely) **it is ∼ that** il y a de fortes chances que (+ *subj*); **he has an ∼ chance of doing** il a de fortes chances de faire; **2** (in betting) **to be the ∼ favourite** être le grand favori

odious /'əʊdɪəs/ *adj* odieux/-ieuse

odium /'əʊdɪəm/ *n* réprobation *f* générale

odometer /ɒ'dɒmɪtə(r)/ *n* Aut US odomètre *m*

odour GB, **odor** US /'əʊdə(r)/ *n* odeur *f*

odourless GB, **odorless** US /'əʊdəlɪs/ *adj* [*gas*] inodore; [*cosmetic*] non parfumé

odyssey /'ɒdɪsɪ/ *n* odyssée *f*; **the Odyssey** l'Odyssée *f*

OECD *n* (*abrév* = **Organization for Economic Cooperation and Development**) OCDE *f*

oedema GB, **edema** US /ɪ'diːmə/ *n* œdème *m*

o'er /ɔː(r)/ *littér* = **over**[1]

oesophagus GB, **esophagus** US /ɪ'sɒfəgəs/ *n* œsophage *m*

of

In almost all its uses the preposition *of* is translated by *de*. Exceptions to this are substances (*made of gold*), uses with a personal pronoun (*that's kind of you*), proportions (*some of us, of the 12 of us* ...) and time expressions (*of an evening*). For translations of these, see the entry **of**. Remember that *de* + *le* always becomes *du* and that *de* + *les* always becomes *des*.

To find translations for phrases beginning with *of* (*of course, of all, of interest, of late, of old*) you should consult the appropriate noun etc. entry (**course, all, interest, late, old** etc.).

of also often appears as the second element of a verb (*consist of, deprive of, die of, think of*). For translations, consult the appropriate verb entry.

of is used after certain nouns, pronouns and adjectives in English (*a member of, a game of, some of, most of, afraid of, capable of, ashamed of*). For translations, consult the appropriate noun, pronoun or adjective entry.

When *of it* or *of them* are used for something already referred to, they are translated by *en*:

there's a lot of it   *there are several of them*
= il y en a beaucoup   = il y en a plusieurs

Note, however, the following expressions used when referring to people:

there are six of them   *there were several of them*
= ils sont six   = ils étaient plusieurs

For particular usages see the entry of.

This dictionary contains usage notes on such topics as **age, capacity measurement, dates, illnesses, length measurement, quantities, towns and cities,** and **weight measurement,** many of which use *of*.

For the index to these notes ▶ **p. 1354.**

oestrogen GB, **estrogen** US /ˈiːstrədʒən/ *n* œstrogène *m*

of /ɒv, əv/ *prep* ① (in most uses) de; **the leg ~ the table** le pied de la table; ② (made of) **a ring (made) ~ gold** une bague en or; **a will ~ iron** fig une volonté de fer; ③ (indicating an agent) **that's kind ~ you** c'est très gentil de votre part *or* à vous; ④ (indicating a proportion) **some ~ us** quelques-uns d'entre nous; **of the twelve ~ us...** sur les douze (que nous sommes/étions)...; ⑤ GB (in expressions of time) **I like to play golf ~ an afternoon** j'aime jouer au golf l'après-midi

off /ɒf, US ɔːf/

⚠️ *Off* is often found as the second element in verb combinations (*fall off, run off* etc) and in offensive interjections (*clear off* etc). For translations consult the appropriate verb entry (**fall, run, clear** etc). *off* is used in certain expressions such as *off limits, off colour* etc and translations for these will be found under the noun entry (**limit, colour** etc). For other uses of *off* see the entry below.

A ○*n* (from) **the ~** (dès) le départ; **just before the ~** (of race) juste avant le départ

B *adv* ① (leaving) **to be ~** partir, s'en aller; **it's time you were ~** il est temps que tu partes; **I'm ~** gen je m'en vais; (to avoid sb) je ne suis pas là; **to be ~ to a good start** avoir pris un bon départ; **he's ~ again talking about his exploits!** fig et voilà c'est reparti, il raconte encore ses exploits!; ② (at a distance) **to be 30 metres ~** être à 30 mètres; **some way ~** assez loin; ③ (ahead in time) **Easter is a month ~** Pâques est dans un mois; **the exam is still several months ~** l'examen n'aura pas lieu avant plusieurs mois; ④ Theat **trumpet sound ~** on entend une trompette dans les coulisses

C *adj* ① (free) **Tuesday's my day ~** je ne travaille pas le mardi; **to have the morning ~** avoir la matinée libre; ② (turned off) **to be ~** [*water, gas*] (at mains) être coupé; [*tap*] être fermé; [*light, TV*] être éteint; ③ (cancelled) **to be ~** [*match, party*] être annulé; **our engagement's ~** nous avons rompu nos fiançailles; **the 'coq au vin' is ~** (from menu) il n'y a plus de 'coq au vin'; ④ (removed) **the lid is ~** il n'y a pas de couvercle; **with her make-up ~** sans maquillage; **to have one's leg ~**○ se faire couper la jambe; **25% ~** Comm 25% de remise; ⑤ ○(bad) **to be ~** [*food*] être avarié; [*milk*] avoir tourné

D **off and on** *adv phr* par périodes

E *prep* ① (away from in distance) **~ the west coast** au large de la côte ouest; **three metres ~ the ground** à trois mètres (au-dessus) du sol; ② (away from in time) **to be a long way ~ doing** être encore loin de faire; ③ (also **just ~**) **just ~** côté de [*kitchen etc*]; **just ~ the path** à quelques mètres du sentier; ④ (astray from) **it is ~ the point** là n'est pas la question; **to be ~ centre** être mal centré; ⑤ (detached from) **to be ~ its hinges** être sorti de ses gonds; **there's a button ~** [*cuff etc*] il manque un bouton à; ⑥ ○(no longer interested in) **to be ~ one's food** ne pas avoir d'appétit; **I'm ~ her at the moment!** il ne faut pas me parler d'elle en ce moment!; ⑦ ○(also **~ of**) **to borrow sth ~ a neighbour** emprunter qch à un voisin; **to eat ~ a tray** manger sur un plateau

Idioms **how are we ~**○ **for...?** qu'est-ce qu'il nous reste comme...? [*flour etc*]; **~ with her head!** qu'on lui coupe la tête!; **that's a bit ~**○ GB ça c'est un peu fort○; **to feel a bit ~**○(**-colour**) GB ne pas être dans son assiette○; **to have an ~ day** ne pas être dans un de ses bons jours

offal /ˈɒfl, US ˈɔːfl/ *n* abats *mpl*

off: **~beat** *adj* Mus [*rhythm*] à temps faible; fig [*humour*] cocasse; **~-centre** GB, **~-center** US *adj* décentré

off-chance /ˈɒftʃɑːns, US -tʃæns/ *n* chance *f*; **there's just an ~ that** il y a une chance pour que (+ *subj*); **just on the ~ that** au cas où

off: **~-color** *adj* US [*story, joke*] indécent; **~-colour**○ *adj* GB (unwell) patraque○

offence GB, **offense** US /əˈfens/ *n* ① Jur infraction *f*; **it is an ~ to do** il est illégal de faire; ② (insult) offense *f*; **to cause** *ou* **give ~ to sb** offenser qn; **to take ~ (at)** s'offenser (de); **no ~ intended, but...** je ne voudrais pas te vexer, mais...; **no ~ taken** il n'y a pas de mal; ③ (attack) atteinte *f* (**against** à); ④ Mil offensive *f*; ⑤ US Sport **the ~** les attaquants *mpl*

offend /əˈfend/

A *vtr* ① (hurt) blesser, offenser [*person*]; [*behaviour, remark*]; **to get ~ed** se vexer; ② (displease) outrager [*sense of justice*]; **to ~ the eye** [*building etc*] choquer la vue

B *vi* Jur commettre une infraction (**against** à); **to ~ again** récidiver

C **offending** *pres p adj* (responsible) [*object*] en cause; [*person*] responsable.

Phrasal verb

■ **offend against**: ▶ **~ against [sth]** ① enfreindre [*law*]; ② (violate) offenser [*good taste*]; être un outrage à [*common sense*]

offender /əˈfendə(r)/ *n* ① Jur (against the law) délinquant/-e *m/f*; (against regulations) contrevenant/-e *m/f* (**against** à); ② (culprit) coupable *mf*; **the worst ~** le/la plus à blâmer

offense *n* US ▶ **offence**

offensive /əˈfensɪv/

A *n* ① Mil, Pol, Sport offensive *f* (**against** contre); **to go on the ~** passer à l'offensive; **to be on the ~** être passé à l'attaque; ② Comm (campaign) campagne *f*

B *adj* ① (insulting) [*remark*] injurieux/-ieuse (**to** pour); [*behaviour*] insultant; ② (vulgar) [*language*] grossier/-ière; [*behaviour, gesture*] choquant; ③ (revolting) [*smell*] repoussant; [*behaviour, idea*] répugnant; ④ Mil, Sport, [*action, play*] offensif/-ive

offer /ˈɒfə(r), US ˈɔːf-/

A *n* ① (proposition) gen, Fin offre *f* (**to do** de faire); **job ~** offre d'emploi; **an ~ of marriage** une proposition de mariage; **that's my final** *ou* **best ~** c'est mon dernier mot; **to be open to ~s** être ouvert à toute proposition; **the house is under ~** il y a une promesse d'achat sur cette maison; **or near(est) ~** (in property ad) à débattre; **~s in the region of £80,000** prix 80 000 livres, à débattre; ② Comm (promotion) promotion *f*; **to be on special ~** être en promotion; ③ (available) **the goods/cases on ~ were dear** les marchandises/valises en vente étaient chères; **there's a lot/nothing on ~** il y a beaucoup/peu de choix; **what's on**

∼ **in the catalogue?** qu'est-ce qu'on propose dans le catalogue?

B *vtr* **1** (proffer) donner [*advice, explanation, information, friendship*]; offrir [*cigarette, help, job, reward, suggestion, support*]; émettre [*opinion*]; faire [*reduction*]; proposer [*service*]; accorder [*discount*]; **to ∼ sb sth, to ∼ sth to sb** offrir qch à qn; **to ∼ to do** se proposer pour faire; **she has a lot to ∼ the company** elle peut beaucoup apporter à la société; **he had little to ∼ in the way of news** il n'avait pas beaucoup de nouvelles à apporter; **2** (provide) offrir [*facilities, advantages, guarantee, resistance*]; donner [*insight*]; **3** (possess) posséder [*language*]; avoir [*experience*]; **4** (sell) offrir [*goods*]; **the radios were being ∼ed at bargain prices** les radios étaient vendues à prix réduit; **to ∼ sth for sale** mettre qch en vente; **5** (present) présenter

C *vi* (volunteer) se proposer

D *v refl* **to ∼ oneself** se proposer (**for** pour); **to ∼ itself** [*opportunity*] se présenter

(Phrasal verb)

■ **offer up:** ▸ ∼ **[sth] up,** ∼ **up [sth]** offrir [*prayer*]; faire l'offrande de [*animal, sacrifice*]

offering /'ɒfərɪŋ, US 'ɔːf-/ *n* **1** (act of giving) offre *f*; **2** (gift) cadeau *m*; **the band's latest ∼** *iron, péj* le dernier album du groupe; **3** Relig collecte; **4** (sacrifice) offrande *f*

offer price *n* Comm prix *m* de vente

offertory /'ɒfətrɪ, US 'ɔːfətɔːrɪ/ *n* Relig offertoire *m*

offhand /ˌɒf'hænd, US ˌɔːf-/

A *adj* (impolite) désinvolte

B *adv* ∼, **I don't know** comme ça au pied levé je ne sais pas

office /'ɒfɪs, US 'ɔːf-/

A *n* **1** (place) bureau *m*; **the accounts ∼** le service comptable; **lawyer's ∼** cabinet *m* de notaire; **2** (position) fonction *f*, charge *f*; **public ∼** fonctions *fpl* officielles; **to perform the ∼ of** remplir les fonctions de; **to hold ∼** [*president, mayor*] être en fonction; [*minister*] avoir un portefeuille; [*political party*] être au pouvoir; **to take ∼** [*president, mayor*] entrer en fonction; [*political party*] arriver au pouvoir; **to go out of ∼** [*president, mayor*] quitter ses fonctions; [*minister*] perdre son portefeuille; [*political party*] perdre le pouvoir; **to stand** GB *ou* **run** US **for ∼** être candidat aux élections; **to rise to high ∼** être promu à un poste élevé; **3** Relig office *m* (**for** de)

B offices *npl* **1** *sout* (services) offices *mpl*, aide *f*; **2** GB (of property) **'the usual ∼s'** 'cuisine *f* et dépendances *fpl*'; (in smaller house) 'cuisine *f* et salle *f* de bains'

office automation *n* bureautique *f*

office: ∼ **block,** ∼ **building** *n* GB immeuble *m* de bureaux; ∼ **junior** *n* employé/-e *m/f* de bureau; ∼ **politics** *n* intrigues *fpl* de bureau

officer /'ɒfɪsə(r), US 'ɔːf-/ *n* **1** Mil, Naut officier *m*; **2** (official) (in a company) responsable *mf*; (in government) fonctionnaire *mf*; (in committee, union, club) membre *m* du comité directeur; **3** (*also* **police ∼**) policier *m*

office worker ▸ p. 1181 *n* employé/-e *m/f* de bureau

official /ə'fɪʃl/

A *n* Pol, Admin fonctionnaire *mf*; (of party, trade union) officiel/-ielle *m/f*; (of police, customs) agent *m*; (at town hall) employé/-e *m/f*

B *adj* *gen* officiel/-ielle; [*biography*] autorisé

officialdom /ə'fɪʃldəm/ *n* bureaucratie *f*

Official Secrets Act *n* GB loi *f* relative aux secrets d'État; **to have signed the ∼** être astreint au secret

officiate /ə'fɪʃɪeɪt/ *vi* [*official*] présider; [*priest*] officier; [*referee, umpire*] arbitrer

officious /ə'fɪʃəs/ *adj* *péj* trop empressé, zélé

offing /'ɒfɪŋ/: **in the offing** *adv phr* [*storm, war*] imminent; [*deal, wedding*] en perspective

off: ∼**-key** *adj* Mus faux/fausse; ∼**-licence** *n* GB magasin *m* de vins et de spiritueux; ∼**-limits** *adj* interdit; ∼**-line** *adj* Comput [*equipment, system*] autonome; [*processing*] en différé; [*storage*] non connecté

offline, off-line /ɒf'laɪn/

A *adj* **1** (not connected to the Internet) [*access, service*] hors connexion; **to be ∼** ne pas être en ligne, ne pas être connecté; **2** Comput [*equipment, system*] autonome; [*processing*] en différé; [*storage*] non connecté

B *adv* [*write, work, read*] hors connexion

off-load /ˌɒf'ləʊd, US ˌɔːf-/ *vtr* **1** *fig* (get rid of) écouler [*goods, stock*]; se dégager de [*investments*]; **to ∼ the blame onto sb** rejeter la responsabilité sur qn; **2** Comput décharger

off-peak /ˌɒf'piːk, US ˌɔːf-/

A *adj* [*electricity*] au tarif de nuit; [*travel*] en période creuse; ∼ **call** Telecom appel *m* au tarif réduit

B *adv* Telecom [*call, cost*] aux heures de tarif réduit

offprint /'ɒfprɪnt, US 'ɔːf-/ *n* tiré *m* or tirage *m* à part

off-putting /ˌɒf'pʊtɪŋ, US ˌɔːf-/ *adj* [*manner*] peu engageant; **it was very ∼** c'était déroutant

off-screen /ˌɒf'skriːn, US ˌɔːf-/

A *adj* Cin [*action*] hors-champ; [*voice*] off *inv*; [*relationship*] dans la vie

B *adv* en privé

off-season /ˌɒf'siːzn, US ˌɔːf-/ *adj* [*cruise*] hors saison; [*losses, deficit*] de basse saison

offset /'ɒfset, US 'ɔːf-/ *vtr* (*p prés* **-tt-**; *prét, pp* **offset**) compenser (**by** par); **to ∼ sth against sth** mettre qch et qch en balance

offset printing *n* offset *m*

offshoot /'ɒfʃuːt, US 'ɔːf-/ *n* (of tree, organization) ramification *f*; (of plant) rejeton *m*; (of idea, decision) conséquence *f*

offshore /ˌɒf'ʃɔː(r), US ˌɔːf-/

A *adj* **1** Naut [*waters*] du large; [*fishing*] au large; ∼ **wind** brise *f* de terre; **2** Fin [*funds*] hors-lieu *inv*; **3** [*oil rig*] offshore

B *adv* **1** **to invest ∼** faire des investissements hors-lieu; **2** (in oil industry) [*work*] en mer, offshore

offside /ˌɒf'saɪd, US ˌɔːf-/

A *n* GB Aut côté *m* conducteur

B *adj* GB Aut [*lane*] *gen* de gauche; GB de droite; **the ∼ rear wheel** la roue arrière côté conducteur; **2** Sport [*position*] hors jeu

off: ∼**-spring** *n* (*pl* ∼) progéniture *f* *also hum*; ∼**-stage** *adj, adv* Theat dans les coulisses; ∼**-the-cuff** *adj* [*remark, speech*] impromptu; ∼**-the-peg** *adj* [*garment*] de prêt-à-porter

off-the-shelf *adj* **1** Comm [*goods*] disponible en magasin; **2** Comput [*software*] fixe

off-the-shoulder *adj* **an ∼ dress** une robe qui dégage les épaules

off: ∼**-the-wall**○ *adj* loufoque○; ∼**-white** *adj* blanc cassé *inv*

often /'ɒfn, 'ɒftən, US 'ɔːfn/ *adv* souvent; **as ∼ as not, more ∼ than not** le plus souvent; **how ∼ do you meet?** vous vous voyez tous les combien?; **how ∼ do the planes depart?** les avions partent tous les combien?; **it cannot be said too ∼ that** on ne répétera jamais assez que; **once too ∼** une fois de trop; **every so ∼** (in time) de temps en temps; (in distance, space) ça et là

ogle○ /'əʊgl/ *vtr* reluquer○

ogre /'əʊgə(r)/ *n* **1** (giant) ogre *m*; **2** *fig* (man) monstre *m*; (woman) dragon○ *m*; **3** (grim vision) spectre *m*

oh /əʊ/ *excl* oh!; ∼ **dear!** (sympathetic) oh là là!; (dismayed, cross) mon Dieu!; ∼ **(really)?** (interested) ah bon?; (sceptical) tiens donc!; ∼ **really!** (cross) ah c'est pas possible○!; ∼ **by the way** ah au fait; ∼ **no it isn't!** mais non!; ∼ **yes?** (pleased) ah bon?; (sceptical) tiens donc!; ∼ **for some sun!** oh si seulement il faisait beau!

OH US Post *abrév écrite* = **Ohio**

OHMS GB (*abrév écrite* = **On Her/His Majesty's Service**) au service de sa majesté (*formule apparaissant sur le courrier officiel de l'administration*)

oil /ɔɪl/

A *n* **1** (for fuel) pétrole *m*; (for lubrication) huile *f*; **crude ∼** pétrole brut; **engine ∼** huile de moteur; **heating ∼** fioul *m*, mazout *m*; **to check the ∼** Aut vérifier le niveau d'huile; **to change the ∼** Aut faire la vidange; **to strike ∼** *lit* découvrir du pétrole; *fig* découvrir une mine d'or; **2** (for cooking) huile *f*; **corn/sunflower ∼** huile de maïs/tournesol; **an ∼ and vinegar dressing** une vinaigrette; **3** Art (medium, picture) huile *f* ₵; **to work in ∼s** peindre à l'huile; **4** Art (picture) huile *f*; **5** (medicinal, beauty) huile *f*; ∼ **of cloves** essence *f* de girofle

B *noun modifier* [*deposit, exporter, producer*] de pétrole; [*prices*] du pétrole; [*company, crisis, industry, reserves*] pétrolier/-ière

C *vtr* huiler

Idioms to ~ **the wheels** mettre de l'huile dans les rouages; **to pour ~ on troubled waters** apaiser les esprits

oil: ~**-burning** adj [stove, boiler] à mazout; ~**can** n (applicator) burette f (d'huile); (container) bidon m (d'huile); ~ **change** n vidange f; ~**cloth** n toile f cirée

oiler /'ɔɪlə(r)/ n 1 (ship) pétrolier m; 2 (worker) pétrolier m; 3 ᴼ(oilcan) burette f

oil: ~ **field** n champ m pétrolifère; ~ **filter** n filtre m à huile; ~**-fired** adj [furnace, heating] au fuel or fioul; ~ **gauge** n jauge f de niveau d'huile; ~ **heater** n poêle m à mazout; ~ **lamp** n lampe f à pétrole; ~ **man** n pétrolier m; ~ **paint** n couleur f à l'huile; ~ **painting** n peinture f à l'huile; ~ **pan** n US carter m; ~ **pipeline** n oléoduc m; ~ **pollution** n pollution f aux hydrocarbures; ~ **pressure** n pression f d'huile; ~**-producing** adj [country] producteur/-trice de pétrole; ~ **refinery** n raffinerie f de pétrole; ~ **rig** n (offshore) plate-forme f pétrolière; (on land) tour f de forage; ~**seed rape** n colza m

oilskin /'ɔɪlskɪn/ GB
A n (fabric) toile f huilée
B **oilskins** npl ciré m

oil: ~ **slick** n marée f noire; ~ **spill** n déversement m accidentel d'hydrocarbures; ~ **stove** n poêle m à mazout; ~ **tank** n (domestic) cuve f à mazout; (industrial) réserve f de stockage de pétrole; ~ **tanker** n pétrolier m; ~ **well** n puits m de pétrole

oily /'ɔɪlɪ/ adj 1 (saturated) [cloth, food, hair] gras/grasse; [hand] plein de graisse; 2 (in consistency) [dressing] huileux/-euse; [lotion] gras/grasse; 3 péj [person, manner] onctueux/-euse

ointment /'ɔɪntmənt/ n pommade f

Idiom **the fly in the ~** (thing) le hicᴼ

o.i.r.o. GB (abrév écrite = **offers in the region of**) ~ **£75,000** 75 000 livres à débattre

OK 1 = **okay**; 2 US Post abrév écrite = **Oklahoma**

okay, OKᴼ /ˌəʊ'keɪ/
A n accord m; **to give sth the ~** donner le feu vert à qch
B 1 **it's ~ by me/him** ça ne me/le dérange pas; **is it ~ if ...?** est-ce que ça va si ...?; **to be ~ for** avoir assez de [time, money]; **he's ~** il est sympaᴼ; **to feel ~** aller bien; '**how was the meeting?**'—'**~**' 'comment ça s'est passé la réunion?'—'ça s'est bien passé'; 2 (acceptable) **that's ~ for men, but...** les hommes peuvent se le permettre, mais...; **it's ~ to call him by his nickname** tu peux l'appeler par son petit nom; 3 (in agreement, confirmation) [reply, signal] d'accord
C adv [cope, work out] (assez) bien
D particle 1 (giving agreement) d'accord; 2 (seeking consensus) d'accord?; 3 (seeking information) bon d'accord; **~, whose idea was this?** bon d'accord, qui a eu cette idée?; 4 (introducing topic) bien; **~, let's move on to...** bien, passons à...
E vtr approuver [change, plan]

old /əʊld/ ▸ p. 647
A n 1 (old people) **the ~** (+ v pl) les personnes fpl âgées; 2 (in days) of **~** (au temps) jadis; **I know him of ~** je le connais depuis longtemps
B adj 1 (not young) vieux/vieille, âgé; **an ~ man** un vieil homme, un vieillard; ~ **people** les vieux; **to get ~** vieillir; ~ **before one's time** vieux avant l'âge; ~ **Mr Salter or young Mr Salter?** M Salter père ou fils?; 2 (of a particular age) **how ~ are you?** quel âge as-tu?; **to know how ~ sth is** connaître l'âge de qch; **a six-year-~ boy** un garçon (âgé) de six ans; **a week ~** [bread etc] vieux d'une semaine; **to be as ~ as sb** avoir le même âge que qn; **she is 10 years ~er than him** elle a 10 ans de plus que lui; **my ~er brother** mon frère aîné; **the ~er children play here** les grands jouent ici; **I'll tell you when you're ~er** je te le dirai quand tu seras plus grand; **I'm the ~est** c'est moi l'aîné/-e; **to be ~ enough to do** être en âge de faire; **you're ~ enough to know better** à ton âge tu devrais avoir plus de bon sens; **that dress is too ~ for you** cette robe fait trop vieux pour toi; **to be ~ for one's age** être mûr pour son âge; 3 (not new) [object, song, tradition, family] vieux/vieille; [excuse] classique; [joke] rebattu; **an ~ firm** une maison établie depuis longtemps; 4 (former, previous) [address, school, job, admirer, system] ancien/-ienne (before n); **in the ~ days** autrefois; **just like ~ times** comme au bon vieux temps; 5 ᴼ(as term of affection) vieux/vieille; **good ~ British weather!** iron ce sacréᴼ climat anglais!; 6 ᴼ(as intensifier) **a right ~ mess** une sacrée pagaille; **any ~ how** n'importe comment; **any ~ doctor** n'importe quel docteur.

⚠ The irregular form vieil of the adjective vieux/vieille is used before masculine nouns beginning with a vowel or a mute 'h'

old age n vieillesse f

old: ~**-age pension** n GB retraite f de la sécurité sociale; ~**-age pensioner, OAP** n GB retraité/-e m/f

old boy n 1 (ex-pupil) ancien élève m; 2 ᴼ(old man) vieux m; 3 ᴼ†(dear chap) (mon) vieux m

old country n mère f patrie

olden /'əʊldən/ adj **the ~ days** l'ancien temps

old-established adj établi depuis longtemps

olde-worlde /ˌəʊld'wɜːld/ adj hum ou péj pseudo-ancien/-ienne

old-fashioned /ˌəʊld'fæʃnd/ adj 1 [person, ways, manners] vieux jeu inv; [idea, attitude, garment, machine] à l'ancienne, démodé pej; 2 ~ **look** (reproving) regard m réprobateur; (quizzical) regard m perplexe

old: ~ **favourite** n (song, film) succès m de toujours; (book, play) classique m; ~ **flame** n ancien flirt m

old girl n 1 (ex-pupil) ancienne élève f; 2 ᴼ(old lady) (petite) vieille f

Old Glory n drapeau m des États-Unis

old hand n vieux routier m; **to be an ~ at sth/at doing** s'y connaître en qch/à faire

old hatᴼ adj **to be ~** être dépassé

oldieᴼ /'əʊldɪ/ n 1 (film, song) vieux succès m; 2 (person) ancien/-ienne m/f

old lady n 1 (elderly woman) vieille dame f; 2 ᴼ**my ~** (wife) la bourgeoiseᴼ; (mother) ma maternelleᴼ

old maid n péj vieille fille f pej

old man n 1 (elderly man) vieil homme m, vieillard m; 2 ᴼ**my ~** (husband) mon hommeᴼ; (father) mon paternelᴼ; 3 ᴼ†(dear chap) (mon) vieuxᴼ; 4 ᴼ(boss) **the ~** le patronᴼ, le singe

old: ~ **master** n (work) tableau m de maître ancien; ~ **people's home** n maison f de retraite; ~ **soldier** n (former soldier) ancien combattant m; ~ **stager** n GB ancien/-ienne m/f; ~ **style** adj à l'ancienne (after n); **Old Testament** n Ancien Testament m; ~**-time** adj du temps jadis; ~**-time dancing** n danses fpl de salon; ~ **timer** n ancien/-ienne m/f; ~ **wives' tale** n conte m de bonne femme

old woman n 1 (elderly lady) vieille femme f, vieille f; 2 péj (man) **to be an ~** avoir des manies de petite vieille; 3 ᴼ**my ~** (wife) la bourgeoiseᴼ; (mother) ma maternelleᴼ

old-world adj [cottage, charm, courtesy] d'autrefois

oleander /ˌəʊlɪ'rændə(r)/ n laurier-rose m

olive /'ɒlɪv/
A n 1 (fruit) olive f; **green/black ~** olive verte/noire; 2 (also ~ **tree**) olivier m; 3 (colour) vert m olive
B adj [dress, eyes] vert olive inv; [complexion] olivâtre

Idiom **to hold out** ou **extend an ~ branch to** fig tendre la main à

olive: ~ **green** ▸ p. 752 n, adj vert (m) olive inv; ~ **grove** n oliveraie f; ~ **oil** n huile f d'olive; ~**-skinned** adj au teint olivâtre

Olympic /ə'lɪmpɪk/ adj olympique; **the ~ Games** les jeux Olympiques

ombudsman /'ɒmbʊdzmən/ n Admin médiateur m

omelette /'ɒmlɪt/ n omelette f

omen /'əʊmən/ n présage m

ominous /'ɒmɪnəs/ adj [presence, cloud] menaçant; [development, news] inquiétant; [sign] de mauvais augure

omission /ə'mɪʃn/ n 1 gen, Jur omission f; 2 (from list, team) absence f

omit /ə'mɪt/ vtr (p prés etc **-tt-**) omettre (**from** de; **to do** de faire)

omnibus /'ɒmnɪbəs/
A n 1 (also ~ **edition**) GB TV rediffusion des épisodes de la semaine; 2 (also ~ **volume**) recueil m; 3 †(bus) omnibus† m
B adj US de portée générale

omnipotent /ɒm'nɪpətənt/ adj omnipotent

on /ɒn/

⚠️ When *on* is used as a straightforward preposition expressing position (*on the beach*, *on the table*) it is generally translated by *sur*: sur la plage, sur la table; *on it* is translated by dessus: *there's a table over there, put the key on it* = il y a une table là-bas, mets la clé dessus.

on is often used in verb combinations in English (*depend on*, *rely on* etc). For translations, consult the appropriate verb entry (**depend**, **rely** etc).

If you have doubts about how to translate a phrase or expression beginning with *on* (*on demand*, *on impulse*, *on top* etc) consult the appropriate noun or other entry (**demand, impulse, top** etc).

This dictionary contains usage notes on such topics as dates, islands, rivers etc. Many of these use the preposition *on*.
▸ p. 1354.

For the index to these notes
For examples of the above and further uses of *on*, see the entry below.

A *prep* **1** (position) sur [*table, coast, motorway etc*]; ~ **top of the piano** sur le piano; ~ **the floor** par terre; **there's a stain** ~ **it** il y a une tache dessus; **to live** ~ **Park Avenue** habiter Park Avenue; **a studio** ~ **Avenue Montaigne** un studio Avenue Montaigne; **the paintings** ~ **the wall** les tableaux qui sont au mur; **2** (indicating attachment, contact) **to hang sth** ~ **a nail** accrocher qch à un clou; ~ **a string** au bout d'une ficelle; **3** (on or about one's person) **I've got no small change** ~ **me** je n'ai pas de monnaie sur moi; **a girl with sandals** ~ **her feet** une fille avec des sandales aux pieds; **to have a smile** ~ **one's face** sourire; **4** (about, on the subject of) sur; **a programme** ~ **Africa** une émission sur l'Afrique; **have you heard him** ~ **electoral reform?** est-ce qu tu l'as entendu parler de la réforme électorale?; **we're** ~ **fractions** nous en sommes aux fractions; **5** (employed, active) **to be** ~ faire partie de [*team*]; être membre de [*board, committee*]; **to be** ~ **the Gazette** travailler pour la Gazette; **a job** ~ **the railways** un travail dans les chemins de fer; **there's a bouncer** ~ **the door** il y a un videur à la porte; **6** (in expressions of time) ~ **22 February** le 22 février; ~ **or about the 23rd** vers le 23; ~ **sunny days** quand il fait beau; **7** (immediately after) ~ **his arrival** à son arrivée; ~ **hearing the truth she...** quand elle a appris la vérité, elle...; **8** (taking, using) **to be** ~ **steroids** prendre des stéroïdes; **to be** ~ **drugs** se droguer; **to be** ~ **40 (cigarettes) a day** fumer 40 cigarettes par jour; **9** (powered by) **to run** ~ **batteries** fonctionner sur piles; **to run** ~ **electricity** marcher à l'électricité; **10** (indicating support) sur; **to stand** ~ **one leg** se tenir sur un pied; **11** (indicating a medium) ~ **TV** à la télé; **I heard it** ~ **the news** j'ai entendu ça aux informations; ~ **video** en vidéo; **with Lou Luciano** ~ **drums** avec Lou Luciano à la batterie; **12** (income, amount of money) **to be** ~ **£20,000 a year** gagner 20 000 livres sterling par an; **to be** ~ **a low income** avoir un bas salaire; **13** (paid for by, at the expense of) **this round is** ~ **me** c'est ma tournée; **have a beer** ~ **me** je te paye une bière; **14** (in scoring) **to be** ~ **25 points** avoir 25 points; **15** (indicating means of transport) **to travel** ~ **the bus** voyager en bus; ~ **the plane** dans l'avion; **to be** ~ **one's bike** être à vélo; **to leave** ~ **the first train** prendre le premier train

B *adj* **1** (taking place, happening) **is the match still** ~**?** est-ce que le match aura lieu quand même?; **the engagement is back** ~ **again** ils sont à nouveau fiancés; **while the meeting is** ~ pendant la réunion; **there's a war** ~ il y a une guerre; **I've got nothing** ~ **tonight** je n'ai rien de prévu pour ce soir; **I've got a lot** ~ je suis très occupé; **2** (being performed) **the news is** ~ **in 10 minutes** les informations sont dans 10 minutes; **what's** ~**?** (on TV) qu'est-ce qu'il y a à la télé?; (at the cinema, at the theatre) qu'est-ce qu'on joue?; **there's nothing** ~ il n'y a rien de bien; **3** (functional, live) **to be** ~ [*TV, oven, light*] être allumé; [*handbrake*] être serré; [*dishwasher, radio*] marcher; [*tap*] être ouvert; **the power is** ~ il y a du courant; **the power is back** ~ le courant est rétabli; **in the '~' position** en position 'allumé'; **4** GB (permissible) **it's just** *ou* **simply not** ~ (out of the question) c'est hors de question; (not the done thing) ça ne se fait pas; (unacceptable) c'est inadmissible; **5** (attached, in place) **to be** ~ [*lid*] être mis; **not properly** ~ mal mis; **once the roof is** ~ une fois le toit construit

C *adv* **1** (on or about one's person) **to have a hat** ~ porter un chapeau; **to have nothing** ~ être nu; ~ **with your coats!** allez, mettez vos manteaux!; **to have make-up** ~ être maquillé; **with slippers** ~ en pantoufles; **2** (ahead in time)

---

20 years ~ **he was still the same** 20 ans plus tard, il n'avait pas changé; **a few years** ~ **from now** dans quelques années; **from that day** ~ à partir de ce jour-là; **to be well** ~ **in years** ne plus être tout jeune; **3** (further) **to walk** ~ continuer à marcher; **to go to Paris then** ~ **to Marseilles** aller à Paris et de là à Marseille; **a little further** ~ un peu plus loin; **4** (on stage) **I'm** ~ **after the juggler** je passe juste après le jongleur; **to come** ~ entrer en scène

D **on and off** *adv phr* (also **off and on**) **to see sb** ~ **and off** voir qn de temps en temps; **she's been working at the novel** ~ **and off for years** ça fait des années que son roman est en chantier; **to flash** ~ **and off** clignoter

E **on and on** *adv phr* **to go** ~ **and** ~ [*speaker*] parler pendant des heures; [*speech*] durer des heures; **to go** ~ **and** ~ **about** ne pas arrêter de parler de; **the list goes** ~ **and** ~ la liste n'en finit pas

(Idioms) **you're** ~ d'accord; **to be always** ~ **at sb** être toujours sur le dos de qn; **what's he** ~ **about?** GB qu'est-ce qu'il raconte?; **he's been** ~ **to me about the lost files** GB il m'a contacté à propos des dossiers perdus

on-board /'ɒnbɔːd/ *adj* Aut embarqué

once /wʌns/
A *n* **I've only been there the** ~ je n'y suis allé qu'une seule fois; **just this** ~ pour cette fois; **for** ~ pour une fois
B *adv* **1** (one time) une fois; ~ **before** une fois déjà; **I will tell you** ~ **only** je ne te le dirai qu'une seule fois; **if I've told you** ~ **I've told you a hundred times** je te l'ai dit mille fois; ~ **and for all** une bonne fois pour toutes; **never** ~ **did he offer to help** il ne s'est pas une seule fois proposé pour aider; ~ **too often** une fois de trop; ~ **a day** une fois par jour; **(every)** ~ **in a while** de temps en temps; **it was a** ~**-in-a-lifetime experience** c'était une expérience unique; **if** ~ **you forget the code** si jamais vous oubliez le code; ~ **a thief, always a thief** qui a volé, volera; **2** (formerly) autrefois; **she was** ~ **very famous** (autrefois) elle était très célèbre; **I'm not as young as I** ~ **was** je ne suis plus très jeune; ~ **upon a time there was** il était une fois
C **at once** *adv phr* **1** (immediately) tout de suite; **all at** ~ tout d'un coup; **2** (simultaneously) à la fois
D *conj* une fois que; ~ **you've signed, it's too late to...** une fois qu'on a signé, il est trop tard pour...; ~ **he had eaten he...** après avoir mangé il...

once-over○ /'wʌnsəʊvə(r)/ *n* **1** (quick look) **to give sth the** ~ jeter un rapide coup d'œil à qch; **to give sb the** ~ gen évaluer qn au premier coup d'œil; [*doctor*] faire un rapide bilan de santé à qn; **2** (quick clean) **to give sth a quick** ~ (with duster) donner un coup de chiffon à qch

oncoming /'ɒnkʌmɪŋ/ *adj* [*car, vehicle*] venant en sens inverse; **'beware of** ~ **traffic'** 'circulation dans les deux sens'

one /wʌn/ ▸ p. 1044, p. 647, p. 745

⚠️ When *one* is used as a personal pronoun it is translated by *on* when it is the subject of the verb: *one never knows* = on ne sait jamais. When *one* is the object of the verb or comes after a preposition it is usually translated by *vous*: *it can make one ill* = cela peut vous rendre malade.
For more examples and all other uses, see the entry below.

A *det* **1** (single) un/une; **to raise** ~ **hand** lever la main; **no** ~ **person can do it alone** personne ne peut faire cela tout seul; **2** (unique, sole) seul; **she's the** ~ **person who can help** c'est la seule personne qui puisse nous aider; **the** ~ **and only Edith Piaf** l'incomparable Edith Piaf; **she's** ~ **fine artist** US c'est une très grande artiste; **3** (same) même; **at** ~ **and the same time** en même temps; ~ **and the same thing** exactement la même chose; **to be of** ~ **mind** être d'accord; **it's all** ~ **to me** ça m'est égal; **4** (for emphasis) ~ **Simon Richard** un certain Simon Richard
B *pron* **1** (indefinite) un/une *m*/*f*; **can you lend me** ~**?** tu peux m'en prêter un/une?; **every** ~ **of them** tous/toutes sans exception (+ *v pl*); **she's** ~ **of us** elle est des nôtres; **2** (impersonal) (as subject) on; (as object) vous; ~ **would like to think that...** on aimerait penser que...; **it can make** ~ **ill** cela peut vous rendre malade; **3** (referring to specific person) **the advice of** ~ **who knows** les conseils de quelqu'un qui s'y connaît; **I'm not** ~ **for doing** ce n'est pas mon genre de faire; **she's a clever** ~ elle est intelligente; **you're a** ~○**!** toi alors!; **I for** ~ **think that...** pour ma part je crois que...;

0

4⟩ (demonstrative) **the grey ~** le gris/la grise; **this ~** celui-ci/celle-ci; **which ~?** lequel/laquelle?; **that's the ~** c'est celui-là/celle-là; **he's the ~ who** c'est lui qui; **5⟩** (in knitting) **knit ~, purl ~** une maille à l'endroit, une maille à l'envers; **6⟩** (in currency) **~-fifty** (in sterling) une livre cinquante; (in dollars) un dollar cinquante; **7⟩** ○(drink) **he's had ~ too many** il a bu un coup○ de trop; **8⟩** ○(joke) **have you heard the ~ about...?** est-ce que tu connais l'histoire de...?; **9⟩** ○(blow) **to land** ou **sock sb ~** en coller une à qn○; **10⟩** ○(question, problem) **that's a tricky ~** c'est une question difficile

C n **1⟩** (number) un m; (referring to feminine) une f; **to throw a ~** (on dice) faire un un; **~ o'clock** arriver en ~s and twos arriver par petits groupes; **2⟩** (person) **her loved ~s** ceux qui lui sont/étaient chers; **the little ~s** les petits

D as one adv phr [rise] comme un seul homme; [shout, reply] tous ensemble

E one by one adv phr [pick up, wash] un par un/une par une

(Idioms) **to down a drink in ~** boire un verre cul sec○; **you've got it in ~** tu as trouvé tout de suite; **to be ~ up on sb**○ avoir un avantage sur qn; **to go ~ better than sb** faire mieux que qn; **to have a thousand** ou **million and ~ things to do** avoir un tas de choses à faire

one another

⚠ *One another* is very often translated by using a reflexive pronoun (*nous, vous, se, s'*).
For examples and particular usages see the entry below.

pron **they love ~** ils s'aiment; **to help ~** s'aider mutuellement; **we often use ~'s cars** souvent nous échangeons nos voitures; **to worry about ~** s'inquiéter l'un pour l'autre

one: **~-armed** adj manchot; **~-armed bandit** n machine f à sous

one-dimensional /ˌwʌndɪ'menʃənl/ adj **1⟩** gen, Math unidimensionnel/-elle; **2⟩** fig **to be ~** [character] Literat manquer d'épaisseur

one: **~-eyed** adj borgne; **~-for-one** adj = one-to-one A 2; **~-handed** adv [catch, hold] d'une seule main; **~-horse town** n péj bled○ m; **~-legged** adj unijambiste; **~-liner** n bon mot m

one-man /'wʌnmæn/ adj **1⟩** (for one person) **it's a ~ outfit** ou **operation** il est tout seul; **she's a ~ woman** elle est fidèle en amour; **2⟩** Sport [bobsled] monoplace

one-man band n lit homme-orchestre m; fig **to be a ~** faire tout soi-même

one: **~-off** adj GB [experiment, order, deal, design] unique; [event, decision, offer, payment] exceptionnel/-elle; [example] peu courant; [issue, magazine] spécial; **~-parent family** n famille f monoparentale

one-piece /'wʌnpiːs/ adj gen, Tech d'une seule pièce; **~ swimsuit** maillot m de bain une pièce

one-room flat, one-room apartment n studio m

onerous /'ɒnərəs/ adj [task] lourd; Jur [terms] dur

one's /wʌnz/

⚠ In French determiners agree in gender and number with the noun they qualify. So when *one's* is used as a determiner it is translated by *son* + masculine singular noun (*son argent*), by *sa* + feminine noun (*sa voiture*) BUT by *son* + feminine noun beginning with a vowel or mute h (*son assiette*) and by *ses* + plural noun (*ses enfants*).
When *one's* is stressed, *à soi* is added after the noun.
When *one's* is used as a reflexive pronoun it is translated by *se* (or *s'* before a vowel or mute h): *to brush one's teeth* = se brosser les dents; ▸ p. 698.
For examples and particular usages see the entry below.

A = one is, one has

B det son/sa/ses; **~ books/friends** ses livres/amis; **to wash ~ hands** se laver les mains; **to do ~ best** faire de son mieux; **it upsets ~ concentration** ça perturbe la concentration; **a house of ~ own** une maison à soi

oneself /wʌn'self/

⚠ When used as a reflexive pronoun, direct and indirect, *oneself* is translated by *se* (or *s'* before a vowel): *to hurt oneself* = se blesser; *to enjoy oneself* = s'amuser.
When used in emphasis the translation is *soi-même*: *to do something oneself* = faire quelque chose soi-même.
After a preposition, the translation is *soi*.
For particular usages see the entry below.

pron **1⟩** (refl) se, s'; **to wash/cut ~** se laver/couper; **2⟩** (for emphasis) soi-même; **3⟩** (after prep) **sure of ~** sûr de soi; **to have the house all to ~** avoir la maison pour soi tout seul/toute seule; **to talk to ~** parler tout seul/toute seule; **(all) by ~** tout seul/toute seule

one-shot adj US = one-off

one-sided /ˌwʌn'saɪdɪd/ adj **1⟩** (biased) [account] partial; **2⟩** (unequal) [decision] unilatéral; [contest] inégal; [deal] inéquitable

one: **~-size** adj [garment] taille unique; **~-time** adj ancien/-ienne (before n)

one-to-one /ˌwʌntə'wʌn/
A adj **1⟩** (private) **~ meeting** tête-à-tête m inv; **~ session** gen, Psych face m à face; **~ tuition** cours mpl particuliers; **2⟩** Math biunivoque; **3⟩** Sport [contest] à deux (after n); [marking] individuel/-elle
B adv [discuss] en tête à tête

one-upmanship /ˌwʌn'ʌpmənʃɪp/ n art m de paraître supérieur aux autres

one-way /ˌwʌn'weɪ/
A adj **1⟩** [traffic] à sens unique; **~ street** ou **system** sens m unique; **2⟩** (single) **~ ticket** aller m simple; **3⟩** [process, conversation] à sens unique; [friendship] non partagé; [transaction] unilatéral; **4⟩** Elec, Telecom [circuit] unidirectionnel/-elle
B adv **it costs £10 ~** l'aller simple coûte 10 livres sterling

one-woman /ˌwʌn'wʊmən/ adj **it's a ~ outfit**○ elle est toute seule; **he's a ~ man** il est fidèle en amour

ongoing /'ɒngəʊɪŋ/ adj [process] continu; [battle, saga] continuel/-elle

onion /'ʌnɪən/ n oignon m

(Idiom) **to know one's ~s**○ GB connaître son affaire

onionskin n (paper) papier m pelure

on-line /ˌɒn'laɪn/
A adj **1⟩** (on the Internet) [help, service, ordering, shopping, bank, retailer, bookshop] en ligne; **to be ~** être en ligne, être connecté; **2⟩** Comput [access] direct; [mode] connecté; [data processing] en direct; [storage] en ligne
B adv [bank, search, shop] en ligne

onlooker /'ɒnlʊkə(r)/ n spectateur/-trice m/f

only /'əʊnlɪ/
A conj (but) mais; **I'd come ~ I'm working tonight** je viendrais bien mais ce soir je travaille; **it's like a mouse ~ bigger** c'est comme une souris mais en plus gros
B adj **1⟩** (sole) seul; **~ child** enfant unique; **the ~ one left** le seul/la seule m/f qui reste; **one and ~** seul; **the ~ thing is, I'm broke**○ le seul problème, c'est que je suis fauché○; **2⟩** (best, preferred) **skiing is the ~ sport for me** pour moi, aucun sport ne vaut le ski
C adv **1⟩** (exclusively) **~ in Italy can one...** il n'y a qu'en Italie que l'on peut...; **I'll go but ~ if you'll go too** je n'irai que si tu y vas aussi; **~ Annie saw her** Annie est la seule à l'avoir vue; **~ time will tell** seul l'avenir nous le dira; **'men ~'** 'réservé aux hommes'; **'for external use ~'** 'usage externe'; **2⟩** (nothing more than) **it's ~ fair to let him explain** ce n'est que justice de le laisser s'expliquer; **it's ~ polite** c'est la moindre des politesses; **3⟩** (in expressions of time) **~ yesterday** pas plus tard qu'hier; **it seems like ~ yesterday** j'ai l'impression que c'était hier; **I saw him ~ recently** je l'ai vu très récemment; **4⟩** (merely) **you ~ had to ask** tu n'avais qu'à demander; **he ~ grazed his knees** il s'est juste égratigné les genoux; **~ half the money** juste la moitié de l'argent; **~ twenty people turned up** seules vingt personnes sont venues; **you've ~ got to look around** you il suffit de regarder autour de soi; **I was ~ joking!** je plaisantais!; **5⟩** (just) **I ~ hope she'll realize** j'espère simplement qu'elle s'en rendra compte; **I can ~ think that Claire did it** la seule explication qui me vienne à l'esprit c'est que c'est Claire qui l'a fait; **open up, it's ~ me** ouvre, c'est moi; **I got home ~ to find (that) I'd been burgled**

quand je suis rentré à la maison j'ai découvert que j'avais été cambriolé

D only just *adv phr* ⓵ (very recently) **to have ∼ just done** venir juste de faire; ⓶ (barely) **it's ∼ just tolerable** c'est à peine tolérable; **∼ just wide enough** juste assez large; **I caught the bus, but ∼ just** j'ai eu le bus mais de justesse

E only too *adv phr* **I remember it ∼ too well** je m'en souviens trop bien; **they were ∼ too pleased to help** ils étaient trop contents de se rendre utiles

(Idiom) **goodness** *ou* **God** *ou* **Heaven ∼ knows!** Dieu seul le sait!

o.n.o. GB (*abrév écrite* = **or nearest offer**) à débattre

on-off *adj* [*button, control*] marche-arrêt

onrush /ˈɒnrʌʃ/ *n* (of water) torrent *m*; (of people) ruée *f*; (of pain) accès *m*

on-screen /ˌɒnˈskriːn/ *adj* Cin, Comput sur l'écran

onset /ˈɒnset/ *n* début *m* (**of** de)

onshore /ˈɒnʃɔː(r)/ *adj* [*work*] à terre; [*wind*] du large

onside /ˌɒnˈsaɪd/ *adj, adv* Sport en jeu

on-site /ˌɒnˈsaɪt/ *adj* sur place

onslaught /ˈɒnslɔːt/ *n* attaque *f* (**on** contre)

onstage /ˌɒnˈsteɪdʒ/ *adj, adv* sur scène

on-the-job *adj* [*training*] sur le lieu de travail

on-the-spot

A *adj* [*team, reporting*] sur place; [*investigation*] sur les lieux; [*advice, quotation*] immédiat

B on the spot *adv phr* [*decide etc*] *gen* sur place

onto /ˈɒntuː/ *prep* (*also* **on to**) sur

(Idioms) **to be ∼ something**○ être sur une piste; **I think I'm ∼ something big**○ je suis sur un gros coup○; **the police are ∼ him**○ la police est après lui

onus /ˈəʊnəs/ *n* obligation *f*; **the ∼ is on sb to do sth** il incombe à qn de faire qch; **to put the ∼ on sb to do sth** obliger qn à faire qch

onward /ˈɒnwəd/

A *adj* **∼ flight** correspondance *f* (**to** à destination de); **the ∼ march of progress** la marche inéluctable du progrès

B *adv* = **onwards**

onwards /ˈɒnwədz/ *adv* ⓵ (forwards) **the journey ∼ to Tokyo** le voyage jusqu'à Tokyo; **to go ∼ and upwards** gravir les échelons de la hiérarchie; ⓶ (in time phrases) **from tomorrow ∼** à partir de demain; **from now ∼** à partir d'aujourd'hui; **from that day ∼** à dater de ce jour

oodles○ /ˈuːdlz/ *n des* masses○ *fpl*

ooh /uː/ *excl* oh!; **∼s and ahs** des oh et des ah

oomph○ /ʊmf/ *n* punch○ *m*, dynamisme *m*

oops○ /uːps, ʊps/ *excl* oh là là!

ooze /uːz/

A *n* (silt) vase *f*

B *vtr* ⓵ **the wound ∼d blood** du sang suintait de la blessure; **to ∼ butter** déborder de beurre; ⓶ *fig* [*person*] rayonner de [*charm*]

C *vi* **to ∼ with** déborder de [*butter, cream*]; rayonner de [*charm*]

(Phrasal verb)

■ **ooze out** s'écouler

op○ /ɒp/ *n* Med, Comput *abrév* = **operation 2, 6**

opal /ˈəʊpl/ *n* opale *f*

opaque /əʊˈpeɪk/ *adj* lit, fig opaque

Opec, OPEC /ˈəʊpek/ *n* (*abrév* = **Organization of Petroleum Exporting Countries**) OPEP *f*

open /ˈəʊpən/

A *n* ⓵ (outside) **in the ∼** dehors, en plein air; ⓶ (exposed position) **in/into the ∼** en terrain découvert; *fig* **out in the ∼** étalé en plein jour; **to bring sth out into the ∼** mettre qch au grand jour; ⓷ (*also* **Open**) Sport (tournoi *m*) open *m*

B *adj* ⓵ (not closed) [*door, box, book, eyes, shirt, wound, flower*] ouvert; [*arms, legs*] écarté; (to the public) [*bank, bridge, meeting*] ouvert; **to get sth ∼** ouvrir qch; **to burst** *ou* **fly ∼** s'ouvrir brusquement; **the book lay ∼** le livre était ouvert; **the door was partly** *ou* **half ∼** la porte était entrouverte; **∼ for business** ouvert au public; **in ∼ court** en audience publique; ⓶ (not obstructed) **to be ∼** [*road*] être ouvert (à la circulation); [*canal, harbour*] être ouvert (à la navigation); [*telephone line, frequency*] être libre; **the ∼ air** le plein air; **∼ country** la rase campagne; **∼ ground** un terrain vague; **the ∼ road** la grand-route; **the ∼ sea** la haute mer; **the**

(wide) ∼ spaces les (grands) espaces libres; **an ∼ view** une vue dégagée (**of** de); ⓷ (not covered) [*car, carriage*] découvert, décapoté; [*mine, sewer*] à ciel ouvert; **an ∼ fire** un feu (de cheminée); ⓸ (susceptible) **∼ to** exposé à [*air, wind, elements*]; **∼ to attack** exposé à l'attaque; **to be ∼ to** prêter le flanc à [*criticism*]; **I'm ∼ to offers** je suis ouvert à toute proposition; **to be ∼ to persuasion** être prêt à se laisser convaincre; **to lay oneself ∼ to criticism** s'exposer (ouvertement) à la critique; **it is ∼ to question whether** on peut douter que (+ *subj*); ⓹ (accessible) (*jamais épith*) [*job, position*] libre, vacant; [*access, competition*] ouvert à tous; [*meeting, session*] public/-ique; **there are several courses of action ∼ to us** nous avons le choix entre plusieurs lignes de conduite; ⓺ (candid) [*person, discussion, declaration, statement*] franc/franche (**about** à propos de); ⓻ (blatant) [*hostility, contempt*] non dissimulé; [*disagreement, disrespect*] manifeste; ⓼ (undecided) **to leave the date ∼** laisser la date en suspens; **the election is (wide) ∼** l'issue de l'élection est indécise; **to keep an ∼ mind about sth** réserver son jugement sur qch; **∼ ticket** (for traveller) billet *m* ouvert; **she kept my job ∼** elle m'a gardé mon travail; **I have an ∼ invitation to visit him** je suis invité chez lui quand je veux; ⓽ (with spaces) [*weave*] ajouré; ⓾ Sport [*contest*] open; ⑪ Mus [*string*] à vide; ⑫ Ling ouvert

C *vtr* ⓵ (cause not to be closed) *gen* ouvrir; **to ∼ a door slightly** *ou* **a little** entrouvrir une porte; **to ∼ one's mind (to sth)** s'ouvrir (à qch); ⓶ (begin) entamer [*discussions, meeting*]; ouvrir [*account, enquiry, show, shop*]; **to ∼ fire** ouvrir le feu; ⓷ (inaugurate) inaugurer [*shop, bridge*]; ouvrir [*exhibition*]; ⓸ (make wider) ▸ **open up**

D *vi* ⓵ (become open) [*door, flower, curtain*] s'ouvrir; **his eyes ∼ed** il a ouvert les yeux; **to ∼ into** *ou* **onto sth** [*door, window*] donner sur qch; **∼ wide!** (at dentist's) ouvrez grand!; **to ∼ slightly** *ou* **a little** [*window, door*] s'entrouvrir; ⓶ Comm (operate) [*shop, bar*] ouvrir; ⓷ (begin) [*meeting, discussion, play*] commencer (**with** par); **to ∼ by doing** [*person*] commencer par faire; ⓸ (have first performance) [*film*] sortir (sur les écrans); [*exhibition*] ouvrir; **the play ∼s on the 25th** la première de la pièce aura lieu le 25; ⓹ (be first speaker) [*person*] ouvrir le débat; ⓺ (become wider) ▸ **open up**; ⓻ Fin [*shares*] débuter

(Phrasal verbs)

■ **open out**: ▸ **∼ out** [*river, path, view*] s'élargir; [*countryside*] s'étendre; **to ∼ out into** [*passage*] déboucher sur [*room*]; [*stream*] se jeter dans [*pool*]; ▸ **∼ [sth] out, ∼ out [sth]** déplier [*map*]

■ **open up**: ▸ **∼ up** ⓵ (unlock a building) ouvrir; **I'll ∼ up for you** je t'ouvre; ⓶ (appear) [*gap*] se creuser; [*crack*] lit, fig se former; ⓷ (speak freely) se confier; **to ∼ up to sb about sth** s'ouvrir à qn de qch; ⓸ (develop) [*opportunities, market*] s'ouvrir; ⓹ Comm (start up) [*shop, branch*] ouvrir; ▸ **∼ [sth] up, ∼ up [sth]** ⓵ (make open) ouvrir [*parcel, suitcase, wound*]; ⓶ (make wider) creuser [*gap*]; **to ∼ up a lead** [*athlete*] creuser l'écart; ⓷ (unlock) ouvrir [*building*]; ⓸ (start up) ouvrir [*shop*]; ⓹ (make accessible) ouvrir [*area, road*]; exploiter [*forest, desert*]; *fig* ouvrir [*possibilities, career*]

open: ∼-air *adj* [*pool, market, stage*] en plein air; **∼cast mining** *n* GB exploitation *f* minière à ciel ouvert; **∼ competition** *n* concours *m*; **∼ day** *n* journée *f* portes ouvertes; **∼-door** *adj* Econ, Pol [*policy*] de la porte ouverte; **∼-ended** *adj* [*strategy*] flexible; [*contract*] modifiable; [*debate, question*] ouvert; [*relationship, situation*] flou; [*stay*] de durée indéterminée; [*period*] indéterminé

opener /ˈəʊpnə(r)/

A *n* ⓵ TV, Theat (first act) premier numéro *m*; (first episode) premier épisode *m*; ⓶ Games (in bridge) (bid) ouverture *f*; (player) ouvreur/-euse *m/f*; ⓷ (for bottles) décapsuleur *m*; (for cans) ouvre-boîte *m*

B for openers○ *adv phr* pour commencer

open: ∼-face(d) sandwich *n* US canapé *m*; **∼ government** *n* Pol politique *f* de transparence; **∼-handed** *adj* généreux/-euse; **∼-hearted** *adj* chaleureux/-euse; **∼-heart surgery** *n* Med (operation) opération *f* à cœur ouvert

open house *n* ⓵ **it's always ∼ at the Batemans'** les Bateman sont très hospitaliers; ⓶ US (open day) journée *f* portes ouvertes

opening /ˈəʊpnɪŋ/

A *n* ⓵ (start) (of book, film, piece of music) début *m*; ⓶ (official act of opening) (of exhibition, shop) ouverture *f*; (of play, film) première *f*; ⓷ (gap) (in wall, garment, forest) trouée *f*; ⓸ (opportunity) *gen* occasion f (**to do** de faire); Comm (in market etc) débouché m; marché m (**for** pour); (for employment) (in company) poste m (disponible); (in field) possibilité f de travail; **5** Games ouverture f

B adj [scene, move] premier/-ière (before n); [remarks, speech, statement] préliminaire; Fin [price, offer, bid] de départ; [share price] d'ouverture

opening: ~ **balance** n Fin (of individual) solde m initial; (of company) solde m en début d'exercice; ~ **ceremony** n (cérémonie f d')inauguration f; ~ **hours** n Comm heures fpl d'ouverture

open market n Econ marché m libre

open-minded /ˌəʊpən'maɪndɪd/ adj **to be** ~ avoir l'esprit ouvert; **to be** ~ **about** n'avoir aucun préjugé sur

open: ~**-mouthed** adj bouche bée inv; ~**-necked** n [shirt] à col ouvert

openness /'əʊpənnɪs/ n **1** (candour) (of person) franchise f; (of manner) caractère m franc; (of government, atmosphere) transparence f; **2** (receptiveness) ouverture f d'esprit (**to** en ce qui concerne)

open: ~**-plan** adj [office] paysagé; ~ **scholarship** n Univ bourse f décernée par un concours ouvert à tous; ~ **season** n (in hunting) saison f de la chasse; ~ **secret** n secret m de Polichinelle

Open University, OU n GB Univ: enseignement universitaire par correspondance

> **ⓘ** **Open University** Organisme britannique d'enseignement universitaire par correspondance. Les cours sont également diffusés à la télévision et à la radio. Les étudiants de tous âges travaillent chez eux et envoient leurs travaux écrits à leur directeur d'études (tutor). Les diplômes obtenus ont la même valeur que ceux délivrés par les universités traditionnelles.

open verdict n Jur verdict m constatant l'impossibilité de déterminer les causes d'un décès

opera /'ɒprə/ n opéra m

operable /'ɒprəbl/ adj **1** [plan] réalisable; [machine] en état de marche; [system] capable de fonctionner; **2** Med [tumour] opérable

opera: ~ **glasses** n jumelles fpl de théâtre; ~ **house** n opéra m

operate /'ɒpəreɪt/
A vtr **1** (run) faire marcher [appliance, vehicle]; **2** (enforce) pratiquer [policy, system]; mettre [qch] en vigueur [ban]; **3** (manage) gérer [service, radio station]; exploiter [mine, racket]; [bank] avoir [pension plan]
B vi **1** (do business) opérer; **they** ~ **out of London** ils ont Londres comme base d'opérations; **2** (function) marcher; **3** (take effect) agir; **4** fig jouer (**in favour of** en faveur de; **against** contre); **5** (run) [service] fonctionner; **6** Med opérer; **to** ~ **on** opérer [person]; **to** ~ **on sb's leg/on sb for appendicitis** opérer qn à la jambe/qn de l'appendicite

operatic /ˌɒpə'rætɪk/ adj [voice] de chanteur/-euse d'opéra; [composer] d'opéras

operating /'ɒpəreɪtɪŋ/ adj [costs] d'exploitation

operating: ~ **instructions** npl mode m d'emploi; ~ **room** n US salle f d'opération; ~ **system** n système m d'exploitation; ~ **table** n table f d'opération; ~ **theatre** n GB salle f d'opération

operation /ˌɒpə'reɪʃn/ n **1** (working) fonctionnement m; **2** Med opération f; **to have an** ~ subir une opération; **to have a major/minor** ~ subir une grosse/petite opération; **to have a heart** ~ se faire opérer du cœur; **3** (use) (of machinery) utilisation f; (of plant, mine) exploitation f; (of law, scheme) mise f en vigueur; **to be in** ~ [plan] être en vigueur; [oil rig, mine] être en exploitation; [machine] fonctionner; **out of** ~ hors service; **4** (undertaking) opération f; **a big** ~ une grosse opération; **5** (business) **their European** ~ **is expanding** ils étendent leurs activités en Europe; **6** Comput, Fin opération f

operational /ˌɒpə'reɪʃənl/ adj **1** gen, Mil (ready to operate) opérationnel/-elle; **2** [budget, costs, manager] d'exploitation

operations: ~ **research** n US recherche f opérationnelle; ~ **room** n Mil salle f d'opérations; (police) centre m d'opérations

operative /'ɒpərətɪv, US -reɪt-/
A n (worker) employé/-e m/f; (secret agent) agent m
B adj **1** (effective) [rule, law, system] en vigueur; **2** (important) **X being the** ~ **word** X étant le mot qui compte

operator /'ɒpəreɪtə(r)/ ▸ p. 1181 n **1** Telecom standardiste mf; **2** Comput, Radio, Tech opérateur m; **3** Tourism compagnie f de voyages organisés; **4** Comm (of business) entrepreneur m; **he's a smooth** ou **shrewd** ~ pej il sait s'y prendre

operetta /ˌɒpə'retə/ n opérette f

ophthalmic /ɒf'θælmɪk/ adj GB [nerve] ophtalmique; [surgeon, clinic, research] ophtalmologique

opiate /'əʊpɪət/ n (from opium) opiacé m; (narcotic) narcotique m

opinion /ə'pɪnɪən/ n **1** (belief, view) opinion f (**about** de), avis m (**about**, **on** sur); **conflicting** ~**s** avis contradictoires; **informed** ~ les gens bien informés; **to be of the** ~ **that** estimer que; **if you want my honest** ~ si vous voulez savoir ce que je pense honnêtement; **that's a matter of** ~ chacun ses opinions; **in the experts'** ~ d'après les experts; **2** (evaluation) opinion f (**of** de); **high/low** ~ **of sb/sth** bonne/mauvaise opinion de qn/qch; **to get a second** ~ gen demander un autre avis; Med consulter un autre médecin; **3** 𝓒 (range of views) opinions fpl; **a difference of** ~ une divergence d'opinions; ~ **is divided** les opinions sont partagées

opinionated /ə'pɪnɪəneɪtɪd/ adj [person] qui a des avis sur tout; [tone] dogmatique

opinion poll n sondage m d'opinion

opium /'əʊpɪəm/ n lit, fig opium m

opponent /ə'pəʊnənt/ n gen adversaire mf; (of regime) opposant/-e m/f (**of** à)

opportune /'ɒpətjuːn, US -tuːn/ adj [moment] opportun

opportunist /ˌɒpə'tjuːnɪst, US -'tuːn-/ n, adj opportuniste (mf)

opportunity /ˌɒpə'tjuːnəti, US -'tuːn-/ n **1** (occasion) occasion f (**for** de); **an** ~ **for discussion** une occasion de or pour discuter; **to give sb every** ~ donner à qn toutes les chances (**to do** de faire); **I should like to take this** ~ **to say** j'aimerais profiter de cette occasion pour dire; **at the earliest** ~ à la première occasion; **2** (possibility) possibilité f; **training opportunities** possibilités de formation

‿Idiom‿ ~ **knocks!** la chance frappe à la porte!

oppose /ə'pəʊz/
A vtr gen, Pol s'opposer à [plan, bill]; faire opposition à [bail]; **to be** ~**d to/to doing** être contre/contre l'idée de
B as opposed to prep phr par opposition à
C opposing pres p adj [party, team] adverse; [army] ennemi; [view, style] opposé

opposite /'ɒpəzɪt/
A n contraire m (**to**, **of** de); **the exact** ~ tout le contraire; **it does the** ~ **of what one expects** cela fait l'inverse de ce à quoi on pourrait s'attendre
B adj **1** (facing) [direction, side, pole] opposé also Math; [building] d'en face; [page] ci-contre; **at** ~ **ends** aux deux bouts de [table, street]; **2** (different) [viewpoint, camp] opposé; [effect, approach] inverse; [sex] autre
C adv [live, stand] en face; **directly** ~ juste en face
D prep gen en face de [building, park, person]; Naut devant [port]

opposite number n gen, Pol homologue m; Sport adversaire mf

opposition /ˌɒpə'zɪʃn/
A n **1** gen opposition f (**to** à); **to put up** ~ **against** faire opposition à; **2** (also **Opposition**) Pol opposition f; **3** Sport the ~ l'adversaire m
B noun modifier Pol [politician, debate, party etc] de l'opposition

oppress /ə'pres/ vtr **1** (subjugate) opprimer; **2** [anxiety, responsibility] accabler

oppression /ə'preʃn/ n oppression f

oppressive /ə'presɪv/ adj **1** [law] oppressif/-ive; **2** [heat] oppressant

oppressively /ə'presɪvlɪ/ adv [govern, rule] de façon oppressive; **it's** ~ **hot** il fait une chaleur accablante

oppressor /ə'presə(r)/ n oppresseur m

opt /ɒpt/ vi **to** ~ **for sth** opter pour qch; **to** ~ **to do/not to do** choisir de faire/de ne pas faire

(Phrasal verb)

■ **opt out** [*person, country*] décider de ne pas participer (**of** à); [*school, hospital*] choisir d'assurer sa propre gestion

optic /'ɒptɪk/ *adj* [*nerve, disc, fibre*] optique

optical /'ɒptɪkl/ *adj* (all contexts) optique

optical: ~ **illusion** *n* illusion *f* d'optique; ~ **wand** *n* crayon-lecteur *m* optique

optician /ɒp'tɪʃn/ ▸ p. 1181 *n* (selling glasses) opticien/-ienne *m/f*; (eye specialist) GB optométriste *mf*

optics /'ɒptɪks/ *n* (+ *v sg*) optique *f*

optimism /'ɒptɪmɪzəm/ *n* optimisme *m*

optimist /'ɒptɪmɪst/ *n* optimiste *mf*

optimistic /ˌɒptɪ'mɪstɪk/ *adj* optimiste (**about** quant à); **wildly/cautiously** ~ exagérément/raisonnablement optimiste; **to be** ~ **that sth will happen** avoir bon espoir que qch arrivera

optimize /'ɒptɪmaɪz/ *vtr* optimiser

optimum /'ɒptɪməm/ *n, adj* optimum (*m*)

option /'ɒpʃn/ *n* **1** gen, Comput option *f* (**to do** de faire); *soft/safe* ~ solution *f* facile/la plus sûre; *zero* ~ option zéro; **it's the only** ~ **for us** nous n'avons pas d'autre possibilité; **the only** ~ **open to me** la seule possibilité que j'aie; **to keep one's** ~**s open** ne pas s'engager; **2** (possibility of choosing) choix *m*; **to have the** ~ **of doing sth** pouvoir choisir de faire qch; **I had little** ~ je n'avais guère le choix; **3** Comm, Fin option *f* (**on** sur; **to do** pour faire); **to take up an** ~ lever une option; **to have first** ~ avoir priorité d'option

optional /'ɒpʃənl/ *adj* [*activity, subject*] facultatif/-ive; [*colour, size*] au choix; ~ **extras** accessoires *mpl* en option

opulent /'ɒpjʊlənt/ *adj* [*lifestyle*] opulent; [*hotel, furnishings*] somptueux/-euse

opus /'əʊpəs/ *n* (*pl* ~**es** *ou* **opera**) opus *m*

or /ɔː(r)/

⚠ In most uses *or* is translated by *ou*. There are two exceptions to this:
When used to link alternatives after a negative verb (*I can't come today or tomorrow*). For translations see 2 below.
When used to indicate consequence (*be careful or you'll cut yourself*) or explanation (*it can't be serious or she'd have called us*) the translation is *sinon*: fais attention sinon tu vas te couper; ça ne nous pas être grave sinon elle nous aurait appelés. See 5 below.

conj **1** (linking two or more alternatives) ou; **with** ~ **without sugar?** avec ou sans sucre?; **any brothers** ~ **sisters?** tu as des frères et sœurs?; **either here** ~ **at Dave's** soit ici soit chez Dave; **whether he likes it** ~ **not** que cela lui plaise ou non; **rain** ~ **no rain** qu'il pleuve ou non; **car** ~ **no car, you've got to get to work** voiture ou pas, il faut que tu ailles travailler; **2** (linking alternatives in the negative) **not today** ~ **tomorrow** ni aujourd'hui ni demain; **I couldn't eat** ~ **sleep** je ne pouvais ni manger ni dormir; **she doesn't drink** ~ **smoke** elle ne boit pas et ne fume pas non plus; **3** (indicating approximation, vagueness) ou; **once** ~ **twice a week** une ou deux fois par semaine; **someone** ~ **other** quelqu'un; **in a week** ~ **so** dans huit jours environ; **4** (introducing qualification, correction, explanation) ou; ~ **rather** ou plutôt; ~ **should I say** ou bien devrais-je dire; **5** (indicating consequence: otherwise) sinon, autrement; **be careful** ~ **you'll cut yourself** fais attention sinon tu vas te couper; **do as you're told**—~ **else**[○]! fais ce qu'on te dit—sinon (gare[○] à toi)!

OR US Post *abrév écrite* = **Oregon**

oracle /'ɒrəkl/, US 'ɔːr-/ *n* **1** gen, Hist, Relig oracle *m*; **2** Oracle® GB TV *cf* Antiope *f*

oral /'ɔːrəl/
🇦 *n* oral *m*
🇧 *adj* gen oral; [*contraceptive, medicine*] par voie orale; [*hygiene*] buccal; [*history*] transmis oralement; [*evidence*] verbal

orally /'ɔːrəlɪ/ *adv* (verbally) oralement; (by mouth) par voie orale

orange /'ɒrɪndʒ/, US 'ɔːr-/ ▸ p. 752
🇦 *n* **1** (fruit) orange *f*; **2** (colour) orange *m*
🇧 *noun modifier* [*drink, pudding, sauce*] à l'orange; [*jam*] d'orange
🇨 *adj* (colour) orange *inv*

orange: ~ **blossom** *n* fleur *f* d'oranger; ~ **grove** *n* orangeraie *f*; ~ **juice** *n* jus *m* d'orange; ~ **peel** *n* gen écorce *f* d'orange; Culin zeste *m* d'orange; ~ **squash** *n* GB ≈ sirop *m* d'orange; ~ **tree** *n* oranger *m*

oration /ɔː'reɪʃn/ *n* sout harangue *f*

oratory /'ɒrətrɪ, US 'ɔːrətɔːrɪ/ *n* (art) art *m* oratoire; (talent) éloquence *f*

orb /ɔːb/ *n* littér (all contexts) globe *m*

orbit /'ɔːbɪt/
🇦 *n* orbite *f*
🇧 *vtr* décrire une orbite autour de
🇨 *vi* [*spacecraft*] orbiter

orbital road /'ɔːbɪtl rəʊd/ *n* rocade *f*

orchard /'ɔːtʃəd/ *n* verger *m*

orchestra /'ɔːkɪstrə/ *n* orchestre *m*; **chamber** ~ orchestre de chambre

orchestral /ɔː'kestrəl/ *adj* [*concert, music*] orchestral; [*instrument*] d'orchestre

orchestra: ~ **pit** *n* fosse *f* d'orchestre; ~ **seats** US, ~ **stalls** GB *n* fauteuils *mpl* d'orchestre

orchestrate /'ɔːkɪstreɪt/ *vtr* lit, fig orchestrer

orchid /'ɔːkɪd/ *n* orchidée *f*

ordain /ɔː'deɪn/ *vtr* **1** (decree) décréter (**that** que); **2** Relig ordonner

ordeal /ɔː'diːl, 'ɔːdiːl/ *n* gen épreuve *f*

order /'ɔːdə(r)/
🇦 *n* **1** (logical arrangement) ordre *m*; **to set** *ou* **put one's life in** ~ remettre de l'ordre dans sa vie; **2** (sequence) ordre *m*; **in alphabetical** ~ dans l'ordre alphabétique; **to do things in** ~ procéder par ordre; **in the right/wrong** ~ dans le bon/ mauvais ordre; **to be out of** ~ [*files, records*] être déclassé; **3** (discipline, control) ordre *m*; **to restore** ~ rétablir l'ordre; **to keep** ~ [*teacher*] maintenir la discipline; **4** (established state) ordre *m*; **the existing** ~ l'ordre actuel; **5** (command) ordre *m* (**to do** de faire) also Jur; **to have** *ou* **to be under** ~**s to do** avoir reçu (l')ordre de faire; **I'm not taking** ~**s from you** je ne suis pas à vos ordres; **until further** ~**s** jusqu'à nouvel ordre; **6** (in shop, restaurant) commande *f*; **a rush/repeat** ~ une commande urgente/renouvelée; **the books are on** ~ les livres ont été commandés; **made to** ~ fait sur commande; **7** (operational state) **in good** ~ en bon état; **in working** ~ en état de marche; **to be out of** ~ [*phone line*] être en dérangement; [*lift, machine*] être en panne; **8** (in public debate) ~! ~! un peu de silence, s'il vous plaît!; **to call sb to** ~ rappeler qn à l'ordre; **out of** ~ contraire à la procédure; **9** (all right) **in** ~ [*documents*] en règle; **that is perfectly in** ~ aucune objection; **that remark was way out of** ~ cette remarque était tout à fait déplacée; **I hear that congratulations are in** ~! il paraît que les félicitations sont à l'ordre du jour!; **economy is the** ~ **of the day** l'austérité est de mise; **10** Relig ordre *m*; **11** (rank, scale) **craftsmen of the highest** ~ des artisans de premier ordre; **talent of this** ~ un tel talent; **the lower** ~**s** les classes inférieures; **of the** ~ **of 15%** GB, **in the** ~ **of 15%** US de l'ordre de 15%; **12** Fin **pay to the** ~ **of** (on cheque, draft) payer à l'ordre de; **13** GB (honorary association, title) ordre *m*
🇧 **orders** *npl* Relig ordres *mpl*; **to take Holy** ~**s** entrer dans les ordres
🇨 **in order that** *conj phr* (with the same subject) afin de (+ *infinitive*), pour (+ *infinitive*); (with different subjects) afin que (+ *subj*), pour que (+ *subj*); **I've come in** ~ **that I might help you** je suis venu pour t'aider; **he brought the proofs in** ~ **that I might check them** il a apporté les épreuves pour que je puisse les vérifier
🇩 **in order to** *prep phr* pour (+ *infinitive*), afin de (+ *infinitive*); **in** ~ **to talk to him** pour lui parler
🇪 *vtr* **1** (command) ordonner [*inquiry, retrial*]; **to** ~ **sb to do** ordonner à qn de faire; **to** ~ **the building to be demolished** ordonner la démolition du bâtiment; **the soldiers were** ~**ed to disembark** les soldats ont reçu l'ordre de débarquer; **2** commander [*goods, meal*]; réserver [*taxi*] (**for** pour); **3** (put in order) classer [*files, cards*]; mettre [qch] dans l'ordre [*names, dates*]; **to** ~ **one's affairs** s'organiser
🇫 *vi* [*diner, customer*] commander
🇬 **ordered** *pp adj* [*series*] ordonné

(Phrasal verbs)

■ **order about**, **order around**: ▸ ~ [**sb**] **around** donner des ordres à
■ **order off** Sport: ▸ ~ [**sb**] **off** expulser [*player*]

order book *n* carnet *m* de commandes

o

ordered /ˈɔːdəd/ adj ▸1▸ [list] méthodique; [structure] régulier/-ière; **an ∼ whole** un ensemble ordonné; **in ∼ ranks** en rangs réguliers; ▸2▸ Math [set] ordonné

order form n bon m or bulletin m de commande

orderly /ˈɔːdəlɪ/
▸**A**▸ n ▸1▸ Mil planton m; ▸2▸ Med aide-soignant/-e m/f
▸**B**▸ adj ▸1▸ (well-regulated) [clothes] ordonné; [queue, line] ordonné; [arrangement, pattern] régulier/-ière; [file, row, rank] régulier/-ière; [mind, system] méthodique; [lifestyle, society] bien réglé; ▸2▸ (calm) [crowd, demonstration, debate] calme; **in an ∼ fashion** ou **manner** [leave etc] dans le calme

orderly officer n Mil officier m de service

ordinal /ˈɔːdɪnl, US -dənl/ n, adj ordinal (m)

ordinarily /ˈɔːdənrəlɪ, US ˌɔːrdn'erəlɪ/ adv (normally) d'ordinaire

ordinary /ˈɔːdənrɪ, US ˈɔːrdənerɪ/
▸**A**▸ n (normal) **to be out of the ∼** sortir de l'ordinaire
▸**B**▸ adj ▸1▸ (normal) [clothes] de tous les jours (after n); [citizen, life, family] ordinaire; **to be just ∼ people** n'être que des gens bien ordinaires; **this is no ∼ case** c'est un cas inhabituel; **in the ∼ way** normalement; ▸2▸ (average) [consumer, family] moyen/-enne; ▸3▸ péj (uninspiring) **very ∼** très quelconque

ordination /ˌɔːdɪ'neɪʃn, US -dn'eɪʃn/ n ordination f

ordnance /ˈɔːdnəns/ n ¢ (supplies) matériel m (militaire)

ordnance: **Ordnance Survey, OS** n GB institut géographique national de Grande-Bretagne; **Ordnance Survey map** n ≈ carte f d'état-major

ore /ɔː(r)/ n minerai m; **iron ∼** minerai de fer

oregano /ˌɒrɪ'gɑːnəʊ/ n origan m

organ /ˈɔːgən/ ▸ p. 1028
▸**A**▸ n ▸1▸ Bot, Anat organe m; **donor ∼, transplant ∼** (sought) don m d'organe; (transplanted) transplant m; **male ∼** membre m viril; ▸2▸ Mus (also **pipe ∼**) orgue m; **on the ∼** à l'orgue; **to play the ∼** jouer de l'orgue; (as job) tenir l'orgue; ▸3▸ fig (publication, organization) organe m (**of** de)

organ donor n Med donneur/-euse m/f d'organes

organic /ɔːˈgænɪk/ adj ▸1▸ gen, Biol organique; [produce, farming] biologique; [fertilizer] naturel/-elle; ▸2▸ (integrated) [society, whole] intégré

organic chemistry n chimie f organique

organism /ˈɔːgənɪzəm/ n (all contexts) organisme m

organist /ˈɔːgənɪst/ ▸ p. 1181 n organiste mf

organization /ˌɔːgənaɪ'zeɪʃn, US -nɪ'z-/ n ▸1▸ (group) gen organisation f; (bureaucratic) organisme m; (voluntary) association f; **human rights ∼** association de défense des droits de l'homme; ▸2▸ (arrangement) organisation f (**of** de)

organizational /ˌɔːgənaɪ'zeɪʃənl, US -nɪ'z-/ adj [ability, role] d'organisateur/-trice; [problem] d'organisation

organize /ˈɔːgənaɪz/
▸**A**▸ vtr organiser [event, day, time]; ranger [books, papers]; **to ∼ sth into chapters** répartir qch en chapitres; **I'll ∼ the drinks** je m'occuperai des boissons; **to ∼ a babysitter** trouver une babysitter; **to get (oneself) ∼d** s'organiser
▸**B**▸ vi (unionize) se syndiquer

organized: **∼ crime** n grand banditisme m; **∼ labour** n main-d'œuvre f syndiquée

organizer /ˈɔːgənaɪzə(r)/ n ▸1▸ (person) organisateur/-trice m/f (**of** de); **union ∼, labour ∼** militant/-e m/f syndicaliste; ▸2▸ (also **personal ∼**) (agenda m) organisateur m; **electronic ∼** agenda électronique; ▸3▸ (container) **desk ∼** (pot m) range-tout m inv

organizing /ˈɔːgənaɪzɪŋ/
▸**A**▸ n organisation f; **she did all the ∼** c'est elle qui a tout organisé
▸**B**▸ adj [group, committee] organisateur/-trice

organ: **∼ loft** n tribune f d'orgue; **∼ stop** n Mus (register) jeu m d'orgues; (knob) registre m d'orgues; **∼ transplant** n Med transplantation f d'organe

orgasm /ˈɔːgæzəm/ n orgasme m

orgy /ˈɔːdʒɪ/ n (all contexts) orgie f

orient /ˈɔːrɪənt/
▸**A**▸ n the Orient l'Orient m
▸**B**▸ vtr fig orienter [person, society] (**towards** en faveur de)
▸**C**▸ v refl **to ∼ oneself** fig s'adapter (**to, in** à); lit s'orienter

oriental /ˌɔːrɪ'entl/
▸**A**▸ Oriental n Oriental/-e m/f

▸**B**▸ adj gen oriental; [appearance, eyes] d'Oriental; [carpet] d'Orient

orientate /ˈɔːrɪənteɪt/ vtr, v refl = **orient B, C**

-orientated /-ˈɔːrɪənteɪtɪd/ combining form = **-oriented**

orientation /ˌɔːrɪən'teɪʃn/
▸**A**▸ n ▸1▸ (beginning of studies) cours m d'introduction; ▸2▸ (inclination) (political, intellectual) orientation f; (sexual) tendance f
▸**B**▸ noun modifier [week] d'introduction

-oriented /-ˈɔːrɪəntɪd/ combining form **family-∼** orienté vers la famille

orienteering /ˌɔːrɪən'tɪərɪŋ/ n course f d'orientation

origin /ˈɒrɪdʒɪn/ n ▸1▸ (of person, custom, idea etc) origine f; **the problem has its ∼(s) in...** le problème provient de...; ▸2▸ (of goods) provenance f; **country of ∼** pays d'origine

original /əˈrɪdʒənl/
▸**A**▸ n (genuine article) original m; **to read sth in the ∼** lire qch dans le texte original
▸**B**▸ adj ▸1▸ (initial) [inhabitant, owner] premier/-ière; [version] original; [question, site, strategy] originel/-elle; [member] originaire; ▸2▸ (not copied) [manuscript, painting] original; [invoice, receipt] d'origine; ▸3▸ (creative) [design, suggestion] original; **he's ∼** il est créatif; **an ∼ thinker** un esprit novateur; ▸4▸ (eccentric) original

original cost n Comm, Econ prix m d'achat

originality /əˌrɪdʒə'næləti/ n originalité f

originally /əˈrɪdʒənəlɪ/ adv ▸1▸ (initially) au départ; ▸2▸ (in the first place) à l'origine; **I am** ou **come from France ∼** je suis originaire de France

originate /əˈrɪdʒɪneɪt/ vi [custom, style, tradition] voir le jour; [fire] se déclarer; **to ∼ from** [goods] provenir de; [proposal] émaner de

originator /əˈrɪdʒɪneɪtə(r)/ n ▸1▸ (of idea, rumour) auteur m; ▸2▸ (of invention, system) créateur/-trice m/f

Orkney /ˈɔːknɪ/ ▸ p. 954 pr npl (also **∼ Islands**) (îles fpl) Orcades f; **in/on ∼** dans les Orcades

ornament /ˈɔːnəmənt/ n ▸1▸ ¢ (trinket) bibelot m; ▸2▸ ¢ (ornamentation) ornement m

ornamental /ˌɔːnə'mentl/ adj [plant] ornemental; [garden, lake] d'agrément; [motif, artwork] décoratif/-ive

ornate /ɔː'neɪt/ adj gen richement orné; [style] très fleuri

ornithologist /ˌɔːnɪ'θɒlədʒɪst/ ▸ p. 1181 n ornithologue mf

ornithology /ˌɔːnɪ'θɒlədʒɪ/ n ornithologie f

orphan /ˈɔːfn/
▸**A**▸ n orphelin/-e m/f
▸**B**▸ adj orphelin

orphanage /ˈɔːfənɪdʒ/ n orphelinat m

orthodontist /ˌɔːθə'dɒntɪst/ ▸ p. 1181 n orthodontiste mf

orthodox /ˈɔːθədɒks/ adj gen, Relig orthodoxe; **Greek Orthodox church** église orthodoxe grecque

orthopaedic, orthopedic US /ˌɔːθə'piːdɪk/ adj orthopédique; **∼ surgeon** chirurgien m orthopédiste

orthopaedics, orthopedics US /ˌɔːθə'piːdɪks/ n (+ v sg) orthopédie f

OS ▸1▸ abrév ▸ **outsize**; ▸2▸ GB Geog abrév ▸ **Ordnance Survey**

Oscar /ˈɒskə(r)/ n Oscar m

ⓘ Oscars Cérémonie annuelle à Los Angeles où the Academy of Motion Picture Arts récompense les talents cinématographiques par des Academy Awards. La statuette en or qui matérialise cette récompense s'appelle un Oscar. Ce nom viendrait d'une remarque de l'un des premiers membres du jury qui aurait dit en voyant une statuette : He reminds me of my uncle Oscar.

oscillate /ˈɒsɪleɪt/ vi gen, Phys, Tech osciller

osmosis /ɒz'məʊsɪs/ n osmose f; **by ∼** par osmose

ossify /ˈɒsɪfaɪ/ vi fig se scléroser

ostensible /ɒ'stensəbl/ adj apparent

ostensibly /ɒ'stensəblɪ/ adv (supposedly) soi-disant

ostentatious /ˌɒsten'teɪʃəs/ adj [house, surroundings] tape-à-l'œil

ostentatiously /ˌɒsten'teɪʃəslɪ/ adv avec ostentation

osteopath /ˈɒstɪəpæθ/ ▸ p. 1181 n ostéopathe mf

osteopathy /ˌɒstɪˈɒpəθɪ/ n ostéopathie f

osteoporosis /ˌɒstɪəʊpəˈrəʊsɪs/ ▸ p. 933 n ostéoporose f

ostracism /ˈɒstrəsɪzəm/ n ostracisme m

ostracize /ˈɒstrəsaɪz/ vtr ostraciser

ostrich /ˈɒstrɪtʃ/

A n Zool, fig autruche f

B noun modifier [feather, egg] d'autruche

other /ˈʌðə(r)/

A adj **1** (what is left, the rest) autre; **the ~ one** l'autre; **the ~ 25** les 25 autres; **2** (alternative, additional) autre; **I only have one ~ shirt** je n'ai qu'une seule autre chemise; **3** (alternate) **every ~ year** tous les deux ans; **every ~ Saturday** un samedi sur deux; **4** (different, not the same) autre; **~ people** les autres; **I wouldn't have him any ~ way** je ne voudrais pas qu'il change; **some ~ time perhaps** une autre fois peut-être; **at all ~ times** en dehors de ces heures-là; **the '~ woman'** (mistress) la maîtresse; **5** (opposite) autre; **he was going the ~ way** il allait dans la direction opposée; **6** (recent) **the ~ day** l'autre jour; **7** (in lists) **she will visit Japan, among ~ places** entre autres, elle ira au Japon

B **other than** prep phr **1** (except) **~ than that** à part ça; **there's nobody here ~ than Carole** il n'y a personne ici à part Carole; **we can't get home ~ than by car** nous ne pouvons pas rentrer autrement qu'en voiture; **I have no choice ~ than to fire her** je n'ai pas d'autre solution que de la renvoyer; **2** (anything but) **he could scarcely be ~ than relieved** il aurait difficilement pu être autre chose que soulagé

C pron **the ~s** les autres; **~s** (as subject) d'autres; (as object) les autres; **one after the ~** l'un après l'autre; **one or ~ of them** un d'entre eux; **somebody** ou **someone or ~** quelqu'un; **some book or ~** un livre, je ne sais plus lequel; **somehow or ~** d'une manière ou d'une autre; **Bob something or ~** Bob quelque chose

(Idiom) **my ~ half**° ma moitié° f

otherwise /ˈʌðəwaɪz/

A adv **1** (differently, in other ways) **to do ~** faire autrement; **improve or ~ change sth** améliorer ou modifier qch d'une manière ou d'une autre; **no woman, married or ~** aucune femme, mariée ou non; **unless we are told ~** à moins qu'on ne nous dise le contraire; **I know ~** je sais que ce n'est pas le cas; **William ~ known as Bill** William, qu'on connaît aussi sous le nom de Bill; **2** (in other respects) à part cela, par ailleurs; **less damage than might ~ have been the case** moins de dégâts qu'on aurait pu s'y attendre

B conj (or else, in other circumstances) sinon; **it's quite safe, ~ I wouldn't do it** ce n'est pas dangereux du tout, sinon je ne le ferais pas

otherworldly /ˌʌðəˈwɜːldlɪ/ adj **to be ~** ne pas avoir les pieds sur terre

OTT adj: abrév ▸ **over-the-top**

otter /ˈɒtə(r)/ n loutre f; **sea ~** loutre marine

OU n GB Univ abrév ▸ **Open University**

ouch /aʊtʃ/ excl aïe

ought /ɔːt/

> ⚠ In virtually all cases, ought is translated by the conditional tense of devoir: you ought to go now = tu devrais partir maintenant; they ought to arrive tomorrow ils devraient arriver demain.
> The past ought to have done/seen etc is translated by the past conditional of devoir: he ought to have been more polite = il aurait dû être plus poli. For further examples, including negative sentences, see the entry below.
> The French verb devoir is irregular. For its conjugation see the French verb tables.

modal aux **1** (expressing probability, expectation) **that ~ to fix it** ça devrait arranger les choses; **2** (making polite but firm suggestion) **oughtn't we to ask?** ne croyez-vous pas que nous devrions demander?; **3** (indicating moral obligation) **someone ~ to have accompanied her** quelqu'un aurait dû l'accompagner; **4** (when prefacing important point) **you ~ to know that** il vaudrait mieux que tu saches que

ounce /aʊns/ ▸ p. 1323, p. 723 n **1** (weight) once f (= 28,35 g); **2** GB (fluid) = 0,028 l; US = 0,035 l; **3** fig once f

our /ˈaʊə(r), ɑː(r)/

> ⚠ In French, determiners agree in gender and number with the noun they qualify. So our is translated by notre + masculine or feminine singular noun (notre chien, notre maison) and nos + plural noun (nos enfants).
> When our is stressed, à nous is added after the noun: OUR house = notre maison à nous.
> For our used with parts of the body ▸ p. 698.

det notre/nos

ours /ˈaʊəz/

> ⚠ In French, pronouns reflect the number and gender of the noun they are standing for. Thus ours is translated by le nôtre, la nôtre or les nôtres according to what is being referred to: the blue car is ours = la voiture bleue est la nôtre; their children are older than ours = leurs enfants sont plus âgés que les nôtres

pron le nôtre/la nôtre/les nôtres; **which tickets are ~?** lesquels de ces billets sont les nôtres?; **a friend of ~** un ami à nous; **~ is not an easy task** sout notre tâche n'est pas facile

ourselves /aʊəˈselvz, ɑː-/

> ⚠ When used as a reflexive pronoun, direct and indirect, ourselves is translated by nous in standard French: we've hurt ourselves = nous nous sommes fait mal. However, if the more informal on is used to translate we, the translation of ourselves will be se (or s' before a vowel): on s'est fait mal.
> When used as an emphatic the translation is nous-mêmes: we did it ourselves = nous l'avons fait nous-mêmes.
> When used after a preposition ourselves is translated by nous or nous-mêmes.

pron **1** (refl) nous; **2** (emphatic) nous-mêmes; **3** (after prep) **for ~** pour nous, pour nous-mêmes; **(all) by ~** tout seuls/toutes seules

oust /aʊst/ vtr évincer [person] **(from** de; **as** comme); forcer [qn] à démissionner [government]

out /aʊt/

> ⚠ Out is used after many verbs in English to alter or reinforce the meaning of the verb (hold out, wipe out, filter out etc). Very often in French, a verb alone will be used to translate these combinations. For translations you should consult the appropriate verb entry (**hold, wipe, filter** etc).
> When out is used as an adverb meaning outside, it often adds little to the sense of the phrase: they're out in the garden = they're in the garden. In such cases out will not usually be translated: ils sont dans le jardin.
> out is used as an adverb to mean absent or not at home. In this case she's out really means she's gone out and the French translation is elle est sortie.
> For the phrase out of see **C** in the entry below.
> For examples of the above and other uses, see the entry below.

A vtr révéler l'homosexualité de [person]

B adv **1** (outside) dehors; **to stand ~ in the rain** rester (dehors) sous la pluie; **to be ~ in the garden** être dans le jardin; **~ there** dehors; **~ here** ici; **to tear a page ~** arracher une page; **2** (from within) **to be ~** sortir; **to pull/take sth ~** retirer/sortir qch; **I couldn't find my way ~** je ne trouvais pas la sortie; **3** (at a distance) **~ in China** en Chine; **two days ~ from port** à deux jours du port; **when the tide is ~** à marée basse; **further ~** plus loin; **4** (in the world at large) **there are a lot of people ~ there looking for work** il y a beaucoup de gens qui cherchent du travail en ce moment; **5** (absent) **to be ~** gen être sorti; [strikers] être en grève; **6** (for social activity) **to invite sb ~ to dinner** inviter qn au restaurant; **a day ~** une sortie pour la journée; **7** (published, now public) **to be ~** [book, exam results] être publié; **my secret is ~** mon secret est révélé; **8** (in bloom) **to be ~** [tree, shrub] être en fleurs; **to be fully ~** [flower] être épanoui; **9** (shining) **to be ~** [sun, moon, stars] briller; **10** (extinguished) **to be ~** [fire, light] être éteint; **lights ~** extinction des feux; **11** Sport, Games **to be ~** [player] être éliminé; **'~!'** (of ball) 'out!'; **12** (unconscious) **to be ~ (cold)** gen être dans les pommes°; [boxer] être K.O.; **13** (over, finished) **before the week is ~** avant la fin de la

o

semaine; **14** GB (incorrect) **to be ~ in one's calculations** s'être trompé dans ses calculs; **my watch is two minutes ~** (slow) ma montre retarde de deux minutes; (fast) ma montre avance de deux minutes; **15** ○(not possible) exclu; **no, that option is ~** non, cette solution est exclue; **16** ○(actively in search of) **to be ~ to do sth** être bien décidé à faire qch; **he's just ~ for what he can get** péj c'est l'intérêt qui le guide; **he's ~ to get you** il t'en veut à mort; (killer) il veut ta peau○; **17** ○(not in fashion) passé de mode

C out of *prep phr* **1** (from) **to go** *ou* **walk** *ou* **come ~** sortir; **get ~ of here!** sors d'ici!; **to jump ~ of the window** sauter par la fenêtre; **to take sth ~ of a box** retirer qch d'une boîte; **to take sth ~ of one's bag** prendre qch dans son sac; **2** (expressing ratio) sur; **two ~ of every three** deux sur trois; **3** (part of whole) **~ of a book** tiré d'un livre; **4** Jur **to be ~** [*jury*] être en délibération; **5** (beyond defined limits) hors de [*reach, sight*]; en dehors de [*city*]; **6** (free from confinement) **~ of hospital** sorti de l'hôpital; [*sheltered*] à l'abri de [*sun*]; **8** (lacking) **to be (right) ~ of** ne plus avoir de [*item*]; **9** (made from) en [*wood, metal*]; **10** (due to) par [*respect*]

(Idioms) **I want ~○!** je ne marche plus avec vous/eux etc○; **come on, ~ with it○!** allez, dis ce que tu as à dire!; **to be ~ and about** (after illness) être à nouveau sur pied; **to be ~ of it○** être dans les vapes○; **to feel ~ of it** se sentir exclu; **you're well ~ of it** c'est mieux comme ça

out-and-out /ˌaʊtənˈaʊt/ *adj* [*villain, liar*] fieffé; [*supporter*] pur et dur; [*success, failure*] total

outback /ˈaʊtbæk/ *n* **the ~** la brousse (australienne)

outbid /ˌaʊtˈbɪd/ *vtr* (*p prés* **-dd-**; *prét, pp* **outbid**) surenchérir sur

outboard motor /ˈaʊtbɔːdˈməʊtə(r)/ *n* moteur *m* horsbord

out-box /ˈaʊtbɒks/ *n* (in email) boîte *f* d'envoi

outbreak /ˈaʊtbreɪk/ *n* (of war, unrest) déclenchement *m*; (of violence, spots) éruption *f*; (of disease) déclaration *f*; **at the ~ of war** quand la guerre a éclaté

outbuilding /ˈaʊtbɪldɪŋ/ *n* dépendance *f*

outburst /ˈaʊtbɜːst/ *n* (of laughter) éclat *m*; (of anger) accès *m*; fig (of trouble) éruption *f*

outcast /ˈaʊtkɑːst, US -kæst/ *n* exclu/-e *m/f*

outclass /ˌaʊtˈklɑːs, US -ˈklæs/ *vtr* dominer

outcome /ˈaʊtkʌm/ *n* résultat *m*

outcrop /ˈaʊtkrɒp/ *n* affleurement *m*

outcry /ˈaʊtkraɪ/ *n* tollé *m* (**about, against** contre)

outdated /ˌaʊtˈdeɪtɪd/ *adj* gen dépassé; [*clothing*] démodé

outdistance /ˌaʊtˈdɪstəns/ *vtr* lit, fig distancer

outdo /ˌaʊtˈduː/ *vtr* (*prét* **outdid**; *pp* **outdone**) surpasser

outdoor /ˈaʊtdɔː(r)/ *adj* [*life, activity, sport*] de plein air; [*restaurant, cinema*] en plein air; [*shoes*] de marche; **to be an ~ type** être sportif

outdoors /ˌaʊtˈdɔːz/
A *n* **the great ~** (+ *v sg*) la pleine nature
B *adv* gen dehors; [*live*] en plein air

outer /ˈaʊtə(r)/ *adj* **1** (furthest) [*limit*] extrême; **2** (outside) gen extérieur; [*clothing*] de dessus

outer: **~ space** *n* espace *m* extra-atmosphérique *or* extérieur; **~ suburbs** *npl* grande banlieue *f*

outfit /ˈaʊtfɪt/ *n* **1** (set of clothes) tenue *f*; **2** ○(company) boîte○ *f*

outfitter /ˈaʊtfɪtə(r)/ *n* **ladies'/men's ~** spécialiste *mf* de confection pour femmes/hommes

outflank /ˌaʊtˈflæŋk/ *vtr* Mil, fig déborder

outflow /ˈaʊtfləʊ/ *n* (of money) sortie *f*

outgoing /ˈaʊtɡəʊɪŋ/ *adj* **1** (sociable) ouvert et sociable; **2** (departing) [*government*] sortant; [*mail*] en partance; [*tide*] descendant; Telecom **~ call** appel téléphonique

outgoings /ˈaʊtɡəʊɪŋz/ *npl* GB sorties *fpl* (de fonds)

outgrow /aʊtˈɡrəʊ/ *vtr* (*prét* **outgrew**; *pp* **outgrown**) **1** (grow too big for) devenir trop grand pour; **2** (grow too old for) se lasser de [*qch*] avec le temps; **he'll ~ it** ça lui passera; **3** (grow taller than) devenir plus grand que

outhouse /ˈaʊthaʊs/ *n* (separate) dépendance *f*; (adjoining) appentis *m*

outlandish /aʊtˈlændɪʃ/ *adj* bizarre

outlast /ˌaʊtˈlɑːst, US -læst/ *vtr* durer plus longtemps que

outlaw /ˈaʊtlɔː/
A *n* hors-la-loi *m inv*
B *vtr* déclarer illégal [*practice, organization*]

outlay /ˈaʊtleɪ/ *n* dépenses *fpl* (**on** en); **capital ~** frais *mpl* d'établissement; **initial ~** mise *f* de fonds initiale

outlet /ˈaʊtlet/ *n* **1** lit (for gas, air, water) tuyau *m* de sortie; **2** Comm (market) débouché *m*; **retail ~**, **sales ~** point *m* de vente; **3** fig (for emotion, talent) exutoire *m*; **4** US Elec prise *f* de courant

outline /ˈaʊtlaɪn/
A *n* **1** (of object) contour *m*; **2** (of plan, policy) grandes lignes *fpl*; (of essay) plan *m*
B *vtr* **1** (give summary of) exposer brièvement [*aims, plan, reasons*]; **2** (draw round) dessiner le contour de [*eye, picture*] (**in, with** en); **to be ~ed against the sky** se découper sur le ciel

outline agreement *n* accord-cadre *m*

outlive /ˌaʊtˈlɪv/ *vtr* survivre à [*person*]; **it has ~d its usefulness** il/elle a fait son temps

outlook /ˈaʊtlʊk/ *n* **1** (attitude) conception *f*, vue *f*; **to be conservative in ~** avoir une vue conservatrice des choses; **2** (prospects) perspectives *fpl*; **3** **the ~ for tomorrow is rain** demain on prévoit un temps pluvieux; **4** (from window) vue *f* (**over, onto** sur)

outlying /ˈaʊtlaɪɪŋ/ *adj* (away from city centre) excentré; (remote) isolé

outmanoeuvre GB, **outmaneuver** US /ˌaʊtməˈnuːvə(r)/ *vtr* déjouer les plans de

outmoded /ˌaʊtˈməʊdɪd/ *adj* dépassé

outnumber /ˌaʊtˈnʌmbə(r)/ *vtr* être plus nombreux que; **~ed two to one** deux fois moins nombreux

out of bounds *adj, adv* **1** **to be ~** [*area*] être interdit (**to** à); **2** Sport **to be ~** être hors jeu

out-of-date *adj* [*ticket, passport*] périmé; [*clothing*] démodé; [*theory, concept*] dépassé

out-of-pocket *adj* **1** **~ expenses** frais *mpl* complémentaires; **2** **to be out of pocket** être perdant

out-of-the-way
A *adj* [*places*] à l'écart
B **out of the way** *adv phr* **get out of the way!** pousse-toi!

outpatient /ˈaʊtpeɪʃnt/ *n* malade *mf* externe; **~s' department** service *m* de consultation

outpost /ˈaʊtpəʊst/ *n* Mil, gen avant-poste *m*; **the last ~** le dernier bastion

output /ˈaʊtpʊt/
A *n* **1** gen (yield) rendement *m*; (of factory) production *f*; **2** Comput (données *fpl* de) sortie *f*; **computer ~** sortie *f* d'ordinateur
B *noun modifier* Comput [*data, equipment*] de sortie
C *vtr* (*p prés* **-tt-**; *prét, pp* **-put** *ou* **-putted**) [*computer*] sortir [*data*]

outrage /ˈaʊtreɪdʒ/
A *n* **1** (anger) indignation *f* (**at** devant); **2** (horrifying act) attentat *m*; **3** (scandal) (against decency) outrage *m*; **it's an ~ that** c'est un scandale que (+ *subj*)
B *vtr* scandaliser [*public*]
C **outraged** *pp adj* outragé (**by** par)

outrageous /aʊtˈreɪdʒəs/ *adj* **1** (disgraceful) scandaleux/-euse; **2** (unconventional) [*person, outfit*] incroyable; [*remark*] outrancier/-ière

outré /ˈuːtreɪ, US uːˈtreɪ/ *adj* outrancier/-ière

outrider /ˈaʊtraɪdə(r)/ *n* (also **motorcycle ~**) motard *m* (d'une escorte)

outright /ˈaʊtraɪt/
A *adj* **1** (absolute) [*control, defiance, majority*] absolu; [*ban, rejection*] catégorique; **2** (obvious) [*favourite, victory, winner*] incontesté; **3** (unreserved) [*disbelief, hostility*] pur et simple
B *adv* **1** (completely) gen catégorique; [*killed*] sur le coup; **to own one's house ~** être pleinement propriétaire; **2** (openly) franchement

outrun /ˌaʊtˈrʌn/ *vtr* (*p prés* **-nn-**; *prét, pp* **-ran**) **1** lit distancer; **2** fig (exceed) dépasser

outsell /ˌaʊtˈsel/ *vtr* [*product*] se vendre mieux que

outset /ˈaʊtset/ *n* **at the** ∼ au début; **from the** ∼ dès le début

outside /aʊtˈsaɪd, ˈaʊtsaɪd/

A *n* **1** extérieur *m*; **on the** ∼ à l'extérieur; **on the** ∼ **of** (on surface itself) sur l'extérieur de [*box, file*]; **2** (maximum) **at the** ∼ au maximum

B *adj* **1** (outdoor) [*temperature*] extérieur; [*broadcast*] enregistré hors studio; **2** (outer) [*edge, world, wall*] extérieur; **3** Telecom [*line*] extérieur; [*call*] de l'extérieur; **4** (leisure) ∼ **interests** centres *mpl* d'intérêt personnels; **5** (from elsewhere) [*help*] de l'extérieur; [*opinion, influence*] extérieur; **6** ∼ **lane** (in GB) voie *f* de droite; (in US, Europe) voie *f* de gauche; (on athletics track) couloir *m* extérieur; **7** (faint) **an** ∼ **chance** une faible chance

C *adv* dehors

D *prep* (*also* ∼ **of**) **1** (not within) en dehors de [*city*]; de l'autre côté de [*boundary*]; à l'extérieur de [*prison*]; **2** (in front of) devant [*house*]; **3** (over) **to wear a shirt** ∼ **one's trousers** porter une chemise sur son pantalon; **4** fig (beyond) ∼ **office hours** en dehors des heures de bureau

outsider /ˌaʊtˈsaɪdə(r)/ *n* **1** (in community) étranger/-ère *m/f*; (to organization, company) personne *f* de l'extérieur; **2** (unlikely to win) outsider *m*

outsize /ˈaʊtsaɪz/

A *n* (large garment) grandes tailles *fpl*

B *adj* gen (*also* ∼**d**) énorme

outskirts /ˈaʊtskɜːts/ *npl* (of town) périphérie *f*

outsmart /ˌaʊtˈsmɑːt/ *vtr* se montrer plus futé que

outspoken /ˌaʊtˈspəʊkən/ *adj* **to be** ∼ parler sans détour

outspread /ˌaʊtˈspred/ *adj* [*arms*] grand ouvert; [*wings*] déployé; [*fingers*] écarté

outstanding /ˌaʊtˈstændɪŋ/ *adj* **1** (praiseworthy) remarquable; **2** (striking) frappant; **3** (unresolved) [*issue*] en suspens; [*work*] inachevé; [*account*] impayé; [*interest*] échu; ∼ **debts** créances *fpl* à recouvrer

outstandingly /ˌaʊtˈstændɪŋlɪ/ *adv* remarquablement; ∼ **good** remarquable

outstay /ˌaʊtˈsteɪ/ *vtr* **to** ∼ **one's welcome** s'éterniser

outstretched /ˌaʊtˈstretʃt/ *adj* [*hand, arm, fingers*] tendu; [*wings*] déployé; [*legs*] allongé

outstrip /ˌaʊtˈstrɪp/ *vtr* (*p prés etc* **-pp-**) dépasser [*person*]; excéder [*production, demand*]

out-tray /ˈaʊtreɪ/ *n* corbeille *f* départ

outvote /ˌaʊtˈvəʊt/ *vtr* **to be** ∼**d** être battu aux voix

outward /ˈaʊtwəd/

A *adj* [*appearance, sign*] extérieur; [*calm*] apparent; ∼ **journey** aller *m*

B *adv* = **outwards**

outwardly /ˈaʊtwədlɪ/ *adv* (apparently) en apparence

outwards /ˈaʊtwədz/ *adv* (*also* **outward**) [*open, turn*] vers l'extérieur

outweigh /ˌaʊtˈweɪ/ *vtr* l'emporter sur

outwit /ˌaʊtˈwɪt/ *vtr* (*p prés etc* **-tt-**) gen être plus futé que; déjouer la surveillance de [*guard*]; déjouer les manœuvres de [*opponent*]

outworker /ˈaʊtwɜːkə(r)/ *n* GB travailleur/-euse *m/f* à domicile

outworn /ˌaʊtˈwɔːn/ *adj* (outmoded) désuet/-ète

oval /ˈəʊvl/

A *n* ovale *m*

B *adj* (*also* ∼**-shaped**) ovale

ovary /ˈəʊvərɪ/ *n* Anat, Bot ovaire *m*

ovation /əʊˈveɪʃn/ *n* ovation *f*; **to give sb a standing** ∼ se lever pour ovationner qn

oven /ˈʌvn/ *n* four *m*; **cook in a slow** ∼ faites cuire à four doux

oven: ∼ **chip** *n* frite *f* à four; ∼ **cleaner** *n* nettoyant *m* pour four; ∼ **glove** *n* manique *f*; ∼**proof** *adj* qui va au four; ∼**-ready** *adj* prêt à cuire

over /ˈəʊvə(r)/

⚠️ *Over* is used after many verbs in English (*change over, fall over, lean over etc*). For translations, consult the appropriate verb entry (**change, fall, lean** etc).

over is often used with another preposition in English (*to, in, on*) without altering the meaning. In this case *over* is usually not translated in French: *to be over in France* = être en France; *to swim over to sb* = nager vers qn.

over is often used with nouns in English when talking about superiority (*control over etc*) or when giving the cause of something (*concern over, worries over etc*). For translations, consult the appropriate noun entry (**control, concern, worry** etc).

over is often used as a prefix in verb combinations (*overeat*), adjective combinations (*overconfident*) and noun combinations (*overcoat*). These combinations are treated as headwords in the dictionary.
For particular usages see the entry below.

A *prep* **1** (across the top of) par-dessus; **he jumped** ∼ **it** il a sauté par-dessus; **a bridge** ∼ **the Thames** un pont sur la Tamise; **2** (from or on the other side of) **the house** ∼ **the road** la maison d'en face; **it's just** ∼ **the road** c'est juste de l'autre côté de la rue; ∼ **here/there** par ici/là; **come** ∼ **here!** viens (par) ici!; **3** (above) au-dessus de; **they live** ∼ **the shop** ils habitent au-dessus de la boutique; **4** (covering, surrounding) gen sur; **to wear a sweater** ∼ **one's shirt** porter un pull par-dessus sa chemise; **shutters** ∼ **the windows** des volets aux fenêtres; **5** (physically higher than) **the water came** ∼ **my ankles** j'avais de l'eau jusqu'aux chevilles; **6** (more than) plus de; **children** ∼ **six** les enfants de plus de six ans; **temperatures** ∼ **40°** des températures supérieures à 40°; **7** (in the course of) **to stay with sb** ∼ **the weekend** pendant le week-end; ∼ **a period of** sur une période de; ∼ **the last few days** au cours de ces derniers jours; ∼ **the years** avec le temps; ∼ **Christmas** à Noël; **to stay with sb** ∼ **Easter** passer les vacances de Pâques chez qn; **8** (recovered from) **to be** ∼ s'être remis de [*illness, operation*]; **to be** ∼ **the worst** avoir passé le pire; **9** (by means of) ∼ **the phone** par téléphone; ∼ **the radio** à la radio; **10** (everywhere) **all** ∼ **the house** partout dans la maison; **to show sb** ∼ **a house** faire visiter une maison à qn

B **over and above** *prep phr* ∼ **and above that** en plus de cela; ∼ **and above the minimum requirement** au-delà du minimum requis

C *adj, adv* **1** (use with verbs not covered in NOTE) ∼ **you go!** allez hop!; **2** (finished) **to be** ∼ [*term, meeting*] être terminé; [*war*] être fini; **to get sth** ∼ **with** en finir avec qch; **3** (more) **children of six and** ∼ les enfants de plus de six ans; **4** (remaining) **there's one** ∼ il en reste un; **there's nothing** ∼ il ne reste rien; **5** (to one's house, country) **to invite** *ou* **ask sb** ∼ inviter qn; **we had them** ∼ **on Sunday** ils sont venus dimanche; **when you're next** ∼ **this way** la prochaine fois que tu passes dans le coin; **6** Radio, TV ∼ **to you** à vous; **now** ∼ **to Tim for the weather** laissons la place à Tim pour la météo; **now** ∼ **to our Paris studios** nous passons l'antenne à nos studios de Paris; **7** (showing repetition) **five times** ∼ cinq fois de suite; **to start all** ∼ **again** recommencer à zéro; **I had to do it** ∼ US j'ai dû recommencer; **I've told you** ∼ **and** ∼ **(again)...** je t'ai dit je ne sais combien de fois...; **8** GB (excessively) **I'm not** ∼ **keen** je ne suis pas très enthousiaste

overact /ˌəʊvərˈækt/ *vi* en faire trop

overactive /ˌəʊvərˈæktɪv/ *adj* [*imagination*] débordant

overall /ˈəʊvərɔːl/

A *n* GB (coat-type) blouse *f*; (child's) tablier *m*

B **overalls** *npl* GB combinaison *f*; US salopette *f*

C /ˌəʊvərˈɔːl/ *adj* [*cost*] global; [*improvement, increase, trend*] général; [*control, impression, effect*] d'ensemble; [*majority*] absolu; [*winner*] au classement général

D *adv* **1** (in total) en tout; **2** (in general) dans l'ensemble

overarm /ˈəʊvərɑːm/ *adj, adv* Sport par le haut

overate /ˌəʊvərˈeɪt/ *prét* ▸ **overeat**

overawe /ˌəʊvərˈɔː/ *vtr* intimider

overbalance /ˌəʊvəˈbæləns/ *vi* [*person*] perdre l'équilibre; [*pile of objects*] s'écrouler

overbearing /ˌəʊvəˈbeərɪŋ/ *adj* dominateur/-trice

overblown /ˌəʊvəˈbləʊn/ *adj* [*style*] ampoulé

overboard /ˈəʊvəbɔːd/ *adv* à l'eau; **man** ∼**!** un homme à la mer!; **to go** ∼° fig aller trop loin

overbook /ˌəʊvəˈbʊk/ *vtr*, *vi* surréserver

overburden /ˌəʊvəˈbɜːdn/ *vtr* (with work) surcharger (**with** de); (with responsibility, debt, guilt) accabler

overcapacity /ˌəʊvəkəˈpæsəti/ *n* surcapacité *f*

overcast /ˌəʊvəˈkɑːst, US -ˈkæst/ *adj* Meteorol couvert

overcharge /ˌəʊvəˈtʃɑːdʒ/
A *vtr* faire payer trop cher à; **they ~d him by £10** ils lui ont fait payer 10 livres de trop
B *vi* pratiquer des prix trop élevés

overcoat /ˈəʊvəkəʊt/ *n* pardessus *m*

overcome /ˌəʊvəˈkʌm/
A *vtr* (*prét* **-came**; *pp* **-come**) **1** (defeat) battre [*opponent*]; vaincre [*enemy*]; maîtriser [*nerves*]; surmonter [*dislike, fear*]; **2** (overwhelm) **to be overcome by smoke** être suffoqué par la fumée; **to be overcome with despair** succomber au désespoir; **to be quite overcome** être bouleversé
B *vi* (*prét* **-came**, *pp* **-come**) triompher

overcompensate /ˌəʊvəˈkɒmpenseɪt/ *vi* **to ~ for sth** trop compenser qch (**by doing** en faisant)

overconfident /ˌəʊvəˈkɒnfɪdənt/ *adj* trop sûr de soi

overcook /ˌəʊvəˈkʊk/ *vtr* trop cuire

overcrowded /ˌəʊvəˈkraʊdɪd/ *adj* [*train, room*] (with people) bondé (**with** de); [*road*] surencombré; [*institution, city*] surpeuplé (**with** de); [*class*] surchargé

overcrowding /ˌəʊvəˈkraʊdɪŋ/ *n* (in city, institution) surpeuplement *m*; (in transport) surencombrement *m*; **~ in classrooms** les classes surchargées

overdo /ˌəʊvəˈduː/ *vtr* (*prét* **overdid**; *pp* **overdone**) **1** (exaggerate) **to ~ it** (when describing) exagérer; (when performing) forcer la note○; (when working) en faire trop○; **2** (use too much of) avoir la main lourde○ sur [*salt, makeup*]; **3** (overcook) faire trop cuire [*meat*]

overdone /ˌəʊvəˈdʌn/ *adj* (exaggerated) exagéré; (overcooked) trop cuit

overdose /ˈəʊvədəʊs/
A *n* **1** (large dose) surdose *f*, dose *f* excessive; **2** (lethal dose) (of medicine) dose *f* mortelle; (of drugs) overdose *f*; **to take an ~** absorber une dose excessive de médicaments
B *vi* (on medicine) prendre une dose mortelle de médicaments; (on drugs) faire une overdose

overdraft /ˈəʊvədrɑːft, US -dræft/ *n* découvert *m*; **to have an ~** être à découvert

overdraw /ˌəʊvəˈdrɔː/
A *vtr* (*prét* **overdrew**, *pp* **overdrawn**) faire un découvert sur [*account*]
B *vi* être à découvert

overdressed /ˌəʊvəˈdrest/ *adj* trop habillé

overdrive /ˈəʊvədraɪv/ *n* **1** Aut vitesse *f* surmultipliée; **2** fig **to go into ~** s'activer intensivement

overdue /ˌəʊvəˈdjuː, US -ˈduː/ *adj* [*baby, work*] en retard (**by** de); [*bill*] impayé; [*cheque*] présenté tardivement; **this measure is long ~** cette mesure aurait dû être prise il y a longtemps; **the book is ~** ce livre aurait déjà dû être rendu

over easy *adj* US [*egg*] cuit des deux côtés

overeat /ˌəʊvərˈiːt/ *vi* (*prét* **overate**, *pp* **overeaten**) manger à l'excès

overemphasize /ˌəʊvəˈremfəsaɪz/ *vtr* accorder trop d'importance à [*aspect, fact*]; exagérer [*importance*]

overenthusiastic /ˌəʊvərɪnˌθjuːzɪˈæstɪk, US -ˌθuː-/ *adj* trop enthousiaste

overestimate /ˌəʊvərˈestɪmeɪt/ *vtr* surestimer

overexcited /ˌəʊvərɪkˈsaɪtɪd/ *adj* surexcité

overexert /ˌəʊvərɪɡˈzɜːt/ *v refl* **to ~ oneself** se surmener

overexposure /ˌəʊvərɪkˈspəʊʒə(r)/ *n* **1** Phot surexposition *f*; **2** Cin, TV médiatisation *f* excessive

overfeed /ˌəʊvəˈfiːd/ *vtr* (*prét*, *pp* **-fed**) suralimenter [*child, pet*]; donner trop d'engrais à [*plant*]

overflow
A /ˈəʊvəfləʊ/ *n* **1** (surplus) **the ~ of students** les étudiants en surnombre; **2** (from bath, sink) trop-plein *m*; (from dam) déversoir *m*; **3** Comput dépassement *m* de capacité
B /ˌəʊvəˈfləʊ/ *vtr* [*river*] inonder [*banks*]
C /ˌəʊvəˈfləʊ/ *vi* déborder (**into** dans; **with** de); **to be full to ~ing** [*room*] être plein à craquer
D **overflowing** /ˌəʊvəˈfləʊɪŋ/ *pres p adj* [*school*] saturé; [*prison*] surpeuplé

overgenerous /ˌəʊvəˈdʒenərəs/ *adj* trop généreux/-euse (**with** avec); [*amount*] excessif/-ive

overgrown /ˌəʊvəˈɡrəʊn/ *adj* [*garden*] envahi par la végétation; **to behave like an ~ schoolboy** se conduire comme un collégien

overhang
A /ˈəʊvəhæŋ/ *n* (of cliff) surplomb *m*; (of roof) avancée *f*
B /ˌəʊvəˈhæŋ/ *vtr* surplomber

overhanging /ˌəʊvəˈhæŋɪŋ/ *adj* [*ledge, cliff*] en surplomb; [*tree, branch*] qui surplombe

overhaul
A /ˈəʊvəhɔːl/ *n* (of machine) révision *f*; fig (of system) restructuration *f*
B /ˌəʊvəˈhɔːl/ *vtr* réviser [*car, machine*]; restructurer [*system*]

overhead /ˈəʊvəhed/
A **overheads** *npl* Comm frais *mpl* généraux
B *adj* [*cable, railway*] aérien/-ienne
C /ˌəʊvəˈhed/ *adv* **1** (in the sky) dans le ciel; **2** (above sb's head) au-dessus de ma/sa etc tête

overhead: **~ light** *n* plafonnier *m*; **~ locker** *n* Aviat compartiment *m* à bagages; **~ projector** *n* rétroprojecteur *m*

overhear /ˌəʊvəˈhɪə(r)/ *vtr* (*p prés*, *pp* **-heard**) entendre par hasard; **I overheard a conversation between...** j'ai surpris une conversation entre...

overheat /ˌəʊvəˈhiːt/
A *vtr* Culin faire trop chauffer
B *vi* [*car, equipment*] chauffer; [*oven*] chauffer trop; [*economy*] être en surchauffe

overindulge /ˌəʊvərɪnˈdʌldʒ/
A *vtr* gâter [*child*]
B *vi* faire des excès

overindulgence /ˌəʊvərɪnˈdʌldʒəns/ *n* **1** (excess) abus *m* (**in** de); **2** (laxity) trop grande indulgence *f* (**of, towards** envers)

overjoyed /ˌəʊvəˈdʒɔɪd/ *adj* [*person*] fou/folle de joie (**at** devant)

overkill /ˈəʊvəkɪl/ *n* (excess publicity) matraquage *m*

overland /ˈəʊvəlænd/
A *adj* [*route*] terrestre; [*journey*] par route
B *adv* par route

overlap
A /ˈəʊvəlæp/ *n* chevauchement *m* (**between** de); (undesirable) empiétement *m*
B /ˌəʊvəˈlæp/ *vi* (*p prés etc* **-pp-**) **1** fig [*theories*] se chevaucher; [*duties*] se recouvrir partiellement; [*visits, holidays*] coïncider en partie; **2** lit [*materials, edges*] se recouvrir partiellement; [*one edge*] dépasser; [*roof tiles*] s'imbriquer

overlay /ˌəʊvəˈleɪ/ *vtr* (*prét*, *pp* **-laid**) recouvrir (**with** de)

overleaf /ˌəʊvəˈliːf/ *adv* au verso

overload
A /ˈəʊvələʊd/ *n* fig surcharge *f*
B /ˌəʊvəˈləʊd/ *vtr* surcharger (**with** de)

overlook /ˌəʊvəˈlʊk/ *vtr* **1** (have a view of) [*building, window*] donner sur; **2** (miss) ne pas voir [*detail, error*]; **to ~ the fact that** négliger le fait que; **3** (ignore) laisser passer [*behaviour*]; ignorer [*effect, fact, need, problem*]

overly /ˈəʊvəli/ *adv* trop, excessivement

overmanned /ˌəʊvəˈmænd/ *adj* en sureffectif

overmanning /ˌəʊvəˈmænɪŋ/ *n* sureffectif *m*, effectif *m* pléthorique

overmuch /ˌəʊvəˈmʌtʃ/ *adv* trop

overnight /ˈəʊvənaɪt/
A *adj* **1** (night-time) [*journey, train*] de nuit; [*stay*] d'une nuit; [*guest*] pour la nuit; [*stop*] pour une nuit; **2** fig (rapid) [*success*] immédiat
B /ˌəʊvəˈnaɪt/ *adv* **1** (during the night) dans la nuit; (for the night) pour la nuit; **to stay ~** passer la nuit; **2** fig (rapidly) du jour au lendemain

overnight bag *n* petit sac *m* de voyage

overpass /ˈəʊvəpɑːs, US -pæs/ *n* (for cars) toboggan *m*

overpay /ˌəʊvəˈpeɪ/ *vtr* (*prét*, *pp* **-paid**) **I was overpaid by £500** on m'a versé 500 livres de trop; **they are overpaid** ils sont trop bien payés

overplay /ˌəʊvəˈpleɪ/ *vtr* (exaggerate) exagérer

(Idiom) **to ~ one's hand** aller trop loin

overpopulated /ˌəʊvəˈpɒpjʊleɪtɪd/ *adj* surpeuplé

overpower /ˌəʊvəˈpaʊə(r)/ vtr 1 lit maîtriser [thief]; vaincre [army]; 2 fig [smell, smoke] accabler

overpowering /ˌəʊvəˈpaʊərɪŋ/ adj [person] intimidant; [personality] écrasant; [desire, urge] irrésistible; [heat] accablant; [smell] irrespirable

overpriced /ˌəʊvəˈpraɪst/ adj it's ∼ c'est trop cher pour ce que c'est

overproduction /ˌəʊvəprəˈdʌkʃn/ n surproduction f

overqualified /ˌəʊvəˈkwɒlɪfaɪd/ adj surqualifié

overrate /ˌəʊvəˈreɪt/ vtr surestimer

overrated /ˌəʊvəˈreɪtɪd/ adj [person, work] surfait; his films are ∼ ses films sont loin d'être aussi bien qu'on le dit

overreach /ˌəʊvəˈriːtʃ/ v refl to ∼ oneself se fixer des objectifs trop ambitieux

overreact /ˌəʊvərɪˈækt/ vi réagir de façon excessive

override /ˌəʊvəˈraɪd/ vtr (prét -rode; pp -ridden) 1 (take precedence over) l'emporter sur [consideration]; 2 (quash) passer outre à [decision]

overriding /ˌəʊvəˈraɪdɪŋ/ adj [importance] primordial; [priority] numéro un

overripe /ˌəʊvəˈraɪp/ adj [fruit] trop mûr, blet/blette; [cheese] trop fait

overrule /ˌəʊvəˈruːl/ vtr to be ∼d [decision] être annulé; I was ∼d mon avis n'a pas prévalu

overrun /ˈəʊvərʌn/
A n Fin dépassement m (of de); cost ∼ dépassement m du budget, surcoût m
B /ˌəʊvəˈrʌn/ vtr (p prés -nn-; prét overran; pp overrun) 1 (invade) envahir [country, site]; 2 (exceed) dépasser [time, budget]
C vi the lecture overran by an hour la conférence a duré une heure de plus que prévu

overseas /ˌəʊvəˈsiːz/
A adj 1 (from abroad) [student, investor] étranger/-ère; 2 (in or to other countries) [travel, investment] à l'étranger; [trade, market] extérieur
B adv (abroad) [work, retire] à l'étranger; (across the sea) outre-mer

oversee /ˌəʊvəˈsiː/ vtr (prét -saw; pp -seen) superviser

oversell /ˌəʊvəˈsel/ vtr (prét, pp -sold) trop vanter [idea, plan]

oversensitive /ˌəʊvəˈsensɪtɪv/ adj [personne] trop susceptible

oversexed○ /ˌəʊvəˈsekst/ adj to be ∼ être un/une obsédé/-e sexuel/-elle

overshadow /ˌəʊvəˈʃædəʊ/ vtr éclipser [achievement]

overshoe /ˈəʊvəʃuː/ n (rubber) caoutchouc m

overshoot /ˌəʊvəˈʃuːt/ vtr (prét, pp -shot) dépasser
(Idiom) to ∼ the mark se planter○

oversight /ˈəʊvəsaɪt/ n erreur f; (viewed critically) négligence f; due to an ∼ par inadvertance

oversimplification /ˌəʊvəˌsɪmplɪfɪˈkeɪʃn/ n simplification f excessive

oversimplify /ˌəʊvəˈsɪmplɪfaɪ/
A vtr simplifier [qch] à l'excès
B oversimplified pp adj simpliste, trop simple

oversize(d) /ˈəʊvəsaɪzd/ adj gen énorme

oversleep /ˌəʊvəˈsliːp/ vi (prét, pp -slept) se réveiller trop tard; I overslept je ne me suis pas réveillé

overspend /ˌəʊvəˈspend/ vi (prét, pp -spent) trop dépenser

overspending /ˌəʊvəˈspendɪŋ/ n ⊄ gen dépense f excessive; Fin, Admin dépassement m budgétaire

overspill /ˈəʊvəspɪl/
A n excédent m de population
B noun modifier an ∼ (housing) development une cité de relogement; ∼ population population f excédentaire

overstaffed /ˌəʊvəˈstɑːft, US -ˈstæft/ adj to be ∼ avoir du personnel en surnombre

overstaffing /ˌəʊvəˈstɑːfɪŋ, US -ˈstæfɪŋ/ n ∼ is a problem les sureffectifs sont un problème

overstate /ˌəʊvəˈsteɪt/ vtr gen exagérer; to ∼ the case exagérer; its importance cannot be ∼d son importance ne saurait être trop soulignée

overstatement /ˌəʊvəˈsteɪtmənt/ n exagération f

overstay /ˌəʊvəˈsteɪ/ vtr to ∼ one's visa dépasser la limite de validité de son visa; to ∼ one's time ne pas rentrer à temps

overstep /ˌəʊvəˈstep/ vtr (p prés etc -pp-) dépasser [bounds]; to ∼ the mark aller trop loin

overstretched /ˌəʊvəˈstretʃt/ adj [budget] excessivement serré; [resources] surexploité; she is ∼ elle a beaucoup trop à faire

oversubscribed /ˌəʊvəsəbˈskraɪbd/ adj [offer, tickets] en excès de demandes; [share issue] sursouscrit

overt /ˈəʊvɜːt, US əʊˈvɜːrt/ adj déclaré

overtake /ˌəʊvəˈteɪk/ (prét -took; pp -taken)
A vtr 1 (pass) [vehicle, person] dépasser; 2 fig [disaster] frapper [project, country]; [storm] surprendre [person]; to be overtaken by events être pris de vitesse
B vi GB dépasser; 'no overtaking' 'dépassement interdit'

overtax /ˌəʊvəˈtæks/
A vtr 1 to ∼ one's brain se surmener; to ∼ one's heart fatiguer son cœur; 2 Fin surimposer [taxpayer]
B v refl to ∼ oneself se surmener

over-the-counter /ˌəʊvəðəˈkaʊntə(r)/
A adj (épith) [medicines] vendu sans ordonnance
B adv to sell sth over the counter vendre qch sans ordonnance

over-the-top○ /ˌəʊvəðəˈtɒp/, **OTT** adj 1 (épith) outrancier/-ière; 2 (après v) to go over the top aller trop loin

overthrow /ˈəʊvəθrəʊ/
A n renversement m
B /ˌəʊvəˈθrəʊ/ vtr (prét -threw; pp -thrown) renverser [government, system]

overtime /ˈəʊvətaɪm/
A n (time, money) heures fpl supplémentaires
B adv to work ∼ [person] faire des heures supplémentaires

overtired /ˌəʊvəˈtaɪəd/ adj gen épuisé; (baby, child) énervé

overtly /ˈəʊvɜːtlɪ, US əʊˈvɜːrtlɪ/ adv ouvertement

overtone /ˈəʊvətəʊn/ n (nuance) sous-entendu m, connotation f

overture /ˈəʊvətjʊə(r)/ n 1 Mus ouverture f (to de); 2 (approach) (gén pl) (social) ouverture f (to à); (business) proposition f

overturn /ˌəʊvəˈtɜːn/
A vtr 1 (roll over) renverser [car, chair]; faire chavirer [boat]; 2 (reverse) faire annuler [decision, sentence]; casser [judgment, ruling]; faire basculer [majority]
B vi [car, chair] se renverser; [boat] chavirer

overvalue /ˌəʊvəˈvæljuː/ vtr Fin surévaluer [currency, property]

overview /ˈəʊvəvjuː/ n vue f d'ensemble (of de)

overweening /ˌəʊvəˈwiːnɪŋ/ adj démesuré

overweight /ˌəʊvəˈweɪt/ adj 1 [person] trop gros/grosse; to be ∼ avoir des kilos en trop; 2 [suitcase]; to be ∼ être trop lourd; my case is 10 kilos ∼ j'ai un excédent de bagages de 10 kilos

overwhelm /ˌəʊvəˈwelm, US -ˈhwelm/
A vtr 1 lit [wave, avalanche] submerger; [enemy] écraser; 2 fig [shame] accabler; [grandeur] impressionner
B overwhelmed pp adj (with letters, offers, phone calls, kindness) submergé (with, by de); (with shame, unhappiness, work) accablé (with, by de); (by sight, experience) ébloui (by par); to be quite ∼ed (with emotion) être très ému

overwhelming /ˌəʊvəˈwelmɪŋ, US -ˈhwelm-/ adj [defeat, victory, majority, argument, evidence] écrasant; [desire] irrésistible; [heat, sorrow] accablant; [concern, impression] dominant; [support] massif/-ive; [conviction] absolu

overwhelmingly /ˌəʊvəˈwelmɪŋlɪ, US -ˈhwelm-/ adv [generous] extraordinairement; [vote, accept, reject] à une écrasante majorité; ∼ Protestant presque exclusivement protestant

overwork /ˈəʊvəwɜːk/
A n surmenage m
B /ˌəʊvəˈwɜːk/ vtr surmener [employee, heart]
C vi se surmener

overworked /ˌəʊvəˈwɜːkt/ adj [employee] surmené; [excuse, word] éculé

overwrite /ˌəʊvəˈraɪt/ vtr (prét -wrote; pp -written) Comput remplacer [data, memory]

overwrought /ˌəʊvəˈrɔːt/ *adj* à bout de nerfs

ow /aʊ/ *excl* aïe!

owe /əʊ/ *vtr* ① (be indebted for) devoir [*money, invention, life, success*]; **to ~ sth to sb** devoir qch à qn [*failure, artistic style, money*]; **can I ~ it to you?** (borrowing money) est-ce que je peux te le rendre plus tard?; **my mother, to whom I ~ so much** ma mère, à qui je dois tant; **I ~ you one**○ *ou* **a favour** je te revaudrai ça; **he ~s me one**○ il me doit bien ça; ② (be morally bound to give) devoir [*duty, loyalty, explanation*]; **I ~ you an apology** je te dois des excuses; **you ~ it to yourself to try everything** tu te dois de tout essayer; **he thinks the world ~s him a living** il s'imagine que tout lui est dû

owing /ˈəʊɪŋ/
A *adj* (*après n, après v*) à payer, dû (**for** pour); **£20 is still ~** il y a encore 20 livres à payer
B **owing to** *prep phr* en raison de

owl /aʊl/ *n* hibou *m*; (with tufted ears) chouette *f*

own /əʊn/
A *adj* propre; **her ~ car/house/business** sa propre voiture/maison/affaire; **he has his ~ ideas about it** il a son idée là-dessus; **he has his ~ problems** il a assez de problèmes comme ça; **he's very nice in his ~ way** il est très gentil à sa manière; **the house has its ~ garage/garden** c'est une maison avec garage/jardin (privatif); **she does her ~ cooking** c'est elle qui se fait à manger; **he makes his ~ decisions** il prend ses décisions tout seul
B *pron* **my ~** le mien, la mienne; **his/her ~** le sien, la sienne; **they have problems of their ~** ils ont assez de problèmes comme ça; **when you have children of your ~** quand tu auras des enfants; **he has a room of his ~** il a sa propre chambre; **a house of our (very) ~** une maison (bien) à nous; **my time's not my ~** je n'ai pas une minute à moi
C *vtr* ① (possess) avoir [*car, house, dog*]; **she ~s three shops** elle est propriétaire de trois magasins; **who ~s that house?** à qui est cette maison?; **he walks around as if he ~s the place** il se conduit comme s'il était chez lui; ② (admit) reconnaître, avouer
D *vi* **to ~ to misgivings** avouer son appréhension
(Idioms) **to come into one's ~** s'épanouir fig; **to do one's ~ thing** être indépendant; **each to his ~** chacun son goût○; **to get one's ~ back** se venger (**on sb** de qn); **to hold one's ~** bien se défendre; **on one's ~** tout seul; **to get sb on their ~** voir qn en privé
(Phrasal verb)
■ **own up** avouer; **to ~ up to the murder** avouer avoir commis le meurtre

owner /ˈəʊnə(r)/ *n* propriétaire *mf*; **car ~** automobiliste *mf*; **home ~** propriétaire *mf*; **previous ~** ancien/-ienne propriétaire; **proud ~** heureux/-euse propriétaire; **rightful ~** possesseur *m* légitime

owner: **~-driver** *n* conducteur/-trice *m/f* propriétaire; **~-occupied** *adj* occupé par le propriétaire; **~-occupier** *n* propriétaire *mf* occupant/-e

ownership /ˈəʊnəʃɪp/ *n* propriété *f*; (of land) possession *f*; **joint ~** copropriété *f*; **to be in private ~** appartenir à une personne privée; **share ~** participation *f* dans le capital d'une société; **to take into public ~** nationaliser; **'under new ~'** 'changement de propriétaire'; **home ~ is increasing** le nombre de personnes propriétaires de leur logement augmente; **to provide proof of ~** prouver qu'on est propriétaire

ox /ɒks/ *n* (*pl* **~en**) bœuf *m*
(Idiom) **as strong as an ~** fort comme un bœuf

oxblood *adj* [*shoes, polish*] rouge foncé *m inv*

Oxbridge /ˈɒksbrɪdʒ/ *n* universités *fpl* d'Oxford et de Cambridge

> ❶ **Oxbridge** Formé de la combinaison de Oxford et Cambridge, ce mot-valise est fréquemment employé pour désigner les universités de ces deux villes, en particulier quand on veut les distinguer des autres universités britanniques, car ce sont les plus prestigieuses.

ox cart *n* char *m* à bœufs

oxen /ˈɒksn/ *pl* ▸ **ox**

oxfords /ˈɒksfədz/ *npl* chaussures *fpl* d'homme (*basses, à lacets et bouts renforcés*)

oxidize /ˈɒksɪdaɪz/
A *vtr* oxyder
B *vi* s'oxyder

Oxon /ˈɒksən/ ① GB Post *abrév écrite* = **Oxfordshire**; ② GB Univ (*abrév écrite* = **Oxoniensis**) d'Oxford

oxygen /ˈɒksɪdʒən/
A *n* oxygène *m*
B *noun modifier* [*bottle, supply, tank*] d'oxygène; [*mask, tent*] à oxygène

oyster /ˈɔɪstə(r)/
A *n* (fish) huître *f*
B *noun modifier* [*knife*] à huîtres; [*sauce*] aux huîtres; [*shell*] d'huître
(Idiom) **the world's your ~** le monde est à toi

oyster: **~ bed** *n* banc *m* d'huîtres; **~ cracker** *n* US petit biscuit *m* salé; **~ farm** *n* parc *m* à huîtres

oz *abrév écrite* = **ounce(s)**

ozone /ˈəʊzəʊn/ *n* ① Chem ozone *m*; ② ○(sea air) air *m* pur marin

ozone: **~ depletion** *n* destruction *f* de la couche d'ozone; **~ layer** *n* couche *f* d'ozone

Pp

p, P /piː/ n **1** (letter) p, P m; **2** p GB (*abrév* = **penny, pence**) (nouveau) penny m, (nouveaux) pence mpl

Idiom **to mind one's p's and q's** veiller aux convenances

p.a. (*abrév écrite* = **per annum**) par an

PA 1 (*abrév* = **personal assistant**) secrétaire mf de direction; **2** US Post *abrév écrite* = **Pennsylvania**

pace /peɪs/
A n (short stride, unit of measurement) pas m; (rate of movement) (of person walking, of life) rythme m; **at a fast/slow ∼** vite/ lentement; **to quicken one's ∼** presser le pas; **to keep ∼ with developments** rester à la page; **I can't stand the ∼** lit, fig je n'arrive pas à suivre; **to step up/slow the ∼** accélérer/ralentir le rythme; **to set the ∼** fig donner le ton
B vtr arpenter [*cage, room*]
C vi **to ∼ up and down** (impatiently) faire les cent pas; **to ∼ up and down sth** arpenter qch

Idiom **to put sb through their ∼s** mettre qn à l'épreuve

pacemaker /ˈpeɪsmeɪkə(r)/ n **1** Med stimulateur m cardiaque; **2** (athlete) lièvre m

pacesetter /ˈpeɪssetə(r)/ n (athlete) lièvre m; (leader, inspiration) locomotive f

pacific /pəˈsɪfɪk/ adj pacifique

Pacific /pəˈsɪfɪk/ ▸ p. 1049 pr n **the ∼** le Pacifique

Pacific: ∼ Ocean n océan m Pacifique; **∼ Standard Time, PST** n heure f du Pacifique

pacifier /ˈpæsɪfaɪə(r)/ n US (for baby) tétine f, sucette f

pacifist /ˈpæsɪfɪst/ n, adj pacifiste (mf)

pacify /ˈpæsɪfaɪ/ vtr apaiser [*person*]

pack /pæk/
A n **1** US (container) (box) paquet m; (large box) boîte f; (bag) sachet m; **2** (group) bande f; (of hounds) meute f; (of scouts) section f; **3** (in rugby) pack m; **4** (of cards) jeu m de cartes; **5** (backpack) sac m à dos; (carried by animal) ballot m
B -pack combining form **a four-∼** (of cassettes) un lot de quatre; (of beer) un pack de quatre
C vtr **1** (stow) (in suitcase) mettre [qch] dans une valise [*clothes*]; (in box, crate) emballer [*ornaments, books*]; **2** (put things into) emballer [*box, crate*]; **to ∼ one's suitcase** faire sa valise; **to ∼ one's bags** lit, fig faire ses valises; **3** (package commercially) conditionner [*fruit, meat, goods*]; **4** (cram into) [*crowd*] remplir complètement [*church, theatre*]; **to be ∼ed with** être bondé de [*people*]; être plein de [*ideas*]; **5** (press firmly) tasser [*snow, earth*]
D vi **1** (get ready for departure) [*person*] faire ses valises; **2** (crowd) **to ∼ into** s'entasser dans [*place*]

Idioms **a ∼ of lies** un tissu de mensonges; **to send sb ∼ing** envoyer promener qn

Phrasal verbs
■ **pack in:** ▸ **∼ [sth] in, ∼ in [sth] 1** (cram in) entasser [*people*]; **2** °(give up) plaquer° [*job, boyfriend*]; **∼ it in!** arrête!, ça suffit!
■ **pack off:** ▸ **∼ [sb] off, ∼ off [sb]** expédier
■ **pack up:** ▸ **∼ up 1** (prepare to go) [*person*] faire ses valises°; **2** °(break down) [*TV, machine*] se détraquer°; [*car*] tomber en panne; [*heart, liver*] lâcher°; ▸ **∼ [sth] up, ∼ up [sth]** (put away) ranger [*books*]; (in boxes, crates) emballer [*books, objects*]

package /ˈpækɪdʒ/
A n **1** (parcel) paquet m, colis m; **2** (collection) (of reforms, measures, proposals) ensemble m (**of** de); **part of the ∼** compris dans le prix; **3** Comput progiciel m

B vtr **1** (put into packaging) emballer [*goods, object*]; **2** (design image for) concevoir un conditionnement pour [*product*]; présenter [*policy, proposal*]

package: ∼ deal n offre f globale; **∼ holiday** GB, **∼ tour** n voyage m organisé

packaging /ˈpækɪdʒɪŋ/ n **1** Comm (materials) emballage m; **2** (promotion) (of product) conditionnement m; (of policy, film, singer) image f publique

packed /pækt/ adj (crowded) comble; **∼ with** plein de; **I'm ∼** j'ai fait mes valises

packed lunch n panier-repas m

packer /ˈpækə(r)/ n Ind (person) emballeur/-euse m/f; (machine) emballeuse f

packet /ˈpækɪt/
A n (box) paquet m; (bag) sachet m; (parcel) paquet m; (for drinks) brique f
B noun modifier [*soup*] en sachet; [*drink*] en brique

Idiom **to cost a ∼°** coûter un argent fou°

pack ice n pack m, banquise f

packing /ˈpækɪŋ/ n **1** Comm emballage m; **2** **to do one's ∼** faire ses valises; **3** Tech garniture f d'étanchéité; ▸ **postage**

packing: ∼ case n caisse f d'emballage; **∼ density** n Comput densité f d'enregistrement

pact /pækt/ n gen, Pol pacte m; **to make a ∼ to do** se mettre d'accord pour faire

pad /pæd/
A n **1** (of paper) bloc m; **2** (to prevent chafing) protection f; (to absorb liquid) tampon m; (to give shape) rembourrage m; **3** (sticky part on object, plant) ventouse f; **4** (of paw) coussinet m; (of finger) pulpe f; **5** (sanitary towel) serviette f hygiénique; **6** Sport (in general) protection f; (for leg) jambière f; **7** (also **launch ∼**) rampe f de lancement
B vtr (p prés etc **-dd-**) **1** (put padding in, on) rembourrer [*chair, shoulders, jacket*] (**with** avec); capitonner [*walls, floor, large surface*]; **to ∼ a wound with cotton wool** mettre un tampon de coton sur une plaie; **2** (make longer) = **pad out**
C vi (p prés etc **-dd-**) **to ∼ along/around** avancer/aller à venir à pas feutrés

Phrasal verb
■ **pad out:** ▸ **∼ out [sth], ∼ [sth] out 1** fig étoffer, délayer pej [*essay, speech*] (**with** à l'aide de); allonger [*meal, dish*] (**with** avec); **2** lit rembourrer [*garment*]

padded: ∼ cell n cellule f capitonnée; **∼ envelope** n enveloppe f matelassée

padding /ˈpædɪŋ/ n **1** (stuffing) rembourrage m; (on large surface) capitonnage m; **2** (in speech, essay) remplissage m

paddle /ˈpædl/
A n **1** (oar) pagaie f; **2** US Sport raquette f de ping-pong®; **3** **to go for a ∼** faire trempette f
B vtr **1** (row) **to ∼ a canoe** pagayer; **2** (dip) agiter [*feet, fingers*] (**in** dans); **3** US donner une fessée à
C vi **1** (row) pagayer; **2** (wade) patauger; **3** [*duck, swan*] barboter

paddling pool n (public) pataugeoire f; (inflatable) piscine f gonflable

paddock /ˈpædək/ n (field) paddock m

paddy: ∼field n rizière f; **∼ wagon°** n US panier m à salade°

padlock /ˈpædlɒk/
A n gen cadenas m; (for bicycle) antivol m
B vtr cadenasser [*door, gate*]; mettre un antivol à [*bicycle*]

p

paediatric *adj* = pediatric

pagan /'peɪɡən/ *n, adj* païen/païenne (*m/f*)

page /peɪdʒ/
A *n* **1** (in book) page *f*; **on ~ two** à la page deux; **2** Comput page-écran *f*; **3** (attendant) groom *m*; US coursier *m*; Hist page *m*
B *vtr* (on pager) rechercher; (over loudspeaker) faire appeler; **'paging Mr Jones'** 'on demande M. Jones'

pageant /'pædʒənt/ *n* (play) reconstitution *f* historique; (carnival) fête *f* à thème historique

pageantry /'pædʒəntrɪ/ *n* pompe *f*

page: **~boy** *n* (bride's attendant) garçon *m* d'honneur; **~ break** *n* Comput fin *f* de page; **~ number** *n* numéro *m* de page; **~ proof** *n* tierce *f*

pager /'peɪdʒə(r)/ *n* Telecom récepteur *m* d'appel

page: **~ reference** *n* page *f*; **~ set-up** *n* Comput mise *f* en page; **~ three** *n* GB page *f* des pin-up

paging /'peɪdʒɪŋ/ *n* Comput pagination *f*

paid /peɪd/
A *prét, pp* ▸ **pay**
B *adj* [*job*] rémunéré; [*holiday*] payé; **~ assassin** tueur *m* à gages
(Idiom) **to put a ~ to sth** GB mettre un terme à qch

paid: **~-up** *adj* rémunéré [*payment, instalment*] à jour; [*share, capital*] remboursé; **~-up member** *n* GB adhérent/-e *m/f*

pail /peɪl/ *n* seau *m* (**of** de)

pain /peɪn/
A *n* **1** gen, Med douleur *f*; **to feel ~, to be in ~** souffrir; **he's caused me a lot of ~** il m'a fait beaucoup souffrir; **period ~s** règles *fpl* douloureuses; **where is the ~?** où avez-vous mal?; **2** °(annoying person, thing) **she can be a real ~** elle peut être très enquiquinante°; **it's a real ~** c'est très enquiquinant°; **he's a ~ in the neck**° il est casse-pieds°; **3** **on ~ of death** sous peine de mort
B *n pl* **to be at ~s to do sth** prendre grand soin de faire qch; **to take great ~s over** *ou* **with sth** se donner beaucoup de mal pour faire qch
C *vtr* **1** (hurt) **my leg ~s me a little** ma jambe me fait un peu mal; **2** sout (grieve) chagriner
D **pained** *pp adj* **with a ~ed expression** d'un air affligé

painful /'peɪnfl/ *adj* **1** (injury, swelling etc) douloureux/-euse; fig [*lesson, progress, memory, reminder, task*] pénible; [*blow*] dur; **2** °(bad) lamentable

painfully /'peɪnfəlɪ/ *adv* **1** (excruciatingly) **his arm is ~ swollen** son bras est enflé et lui fait mal; **to be ~ shy** être d'une timidité maladive; **I am ~ aware of that** je n'en ai que trop conscience; **2** fig **progress has been ~ slow** les progrès ont été terriblement lents

painkiller *n* analgésique *m*

painless /'peɪnlɪs/ *adj* **1** [*operation, injection*] indolore; [*death*] sans souffrance; **2** (trouble-free) sans peine

painlessly /'peɪnlɪslɪ/ *adv* lit sans douleur; (easily) sans trop de mal

painstaking /'peɪnzteɪkɪŋ/ *adj* minutieux/-ieuse

paint /peɪnt/
A *n* gen, Art peinture *f*; **'wet ~'** 'peinture fraîche'
B *n pl* Art couleurs *fpl*
C *vtr* **1** lit peindre [*wall, subject*]; peindre le portrait de [*person*]; **to ~ sth on** appliquer [*varnish, undercoat*]; **to ~ sth out** peindre par-dessus qch; **to ~ one's nails** se vernir les ongles; **2** fig (depict) dépeindre; **3** Med badigeonner [*cut, wound*] (**with** de)
D *vi* peindre
(Idiom) **to ~ the town red** faire la noce

paint: **~box** *n* boîte *f* de couleurs; **~brush** *n* pinceau *m*

painter /'peɪntə(r)/ ▸ p. 1181 *n* **1** (artist, workman) peintre *m*; **2** Naut amarre *f*

painting /'peɪntɪŋ/ *n* **1** ¢ (activity, art form) peinture *f*; **2** (work of art) tableau *m*; (unframed) toile *f*; (of person) portrait *m*; **3** ¢ (decorating) peintures *fpl*

paint: **~pot** *n* pot *m* de peinture; **~ remover** *n* (for removing stains) solvant *m*; **~ roller** *n* rouleau *m* à peinture; **~ spray** *n* bombe *f* de peinture; **~ stripper** *n* (chemical) décapant *m*; (tool) racloir *m*; **~ tray** *n* bac *m* à peinture; **~work** *n* ¢ gen peintures *fpl*; (on car) peinture *f*

pair /peə(r)/
A *n* **1** (two matching items) paire *f*; **to be one of a ~** faire partie d'une paire; **to work in ~s** travailler en groupes de deux; **these gloves are not a ~** ces gants sont dépareillés; **2** (two people, animals etc) (sexually involved) couple *m*; (grouped together) paire *f*; **a coach and ~** une voiture à deux chevaux
B **pairs** *noun modifier* Sport [*competition, final*] pour équipes de deux
C *vtr* ranger par deux [*gloves, socks*]; **to ~ Paul with Julie** mettre Paul avec Julie; **to ~ each name with a photograph** associer chaque nom à une photo
(Phrasal verbs)
■ **pair off** (as a couple) se mettre ensemble; (for temporary purposes) se mettre par deux
■ **pair up** [*dancers, lovers*] former un couple; [*competitors*] faire équipe

paisley /'peɪzlɪ/ *n* tissu *m* à motifs cachemire

pajamas *npl* US = pyjamas

Pakistani /ˌpɑːkɪ'stɑːnɪ, ˌpækɪ-/ ▸ p. 1032
A *n* Pakistanais/-e *m/f*
B *adj* pakistanais

pal° /pæl/ *n* copain°/copine° *m/f*

PAL /pæl/ *n* TV (*abrév* = **phase alternative line**) PAL *m*

palace /'pælɪs/ *n* (of monarch) palais *m*; (of bishop) évêché *m*

palatable /'pælətəbl/ *n* [*food*] savoureux; [*solution, law*] acceptable

palate /'pælət/ *n* palais *m*; **too sweet for my ~** trop sucré à mon goût

palatial /pə'leɪʃl/ *adj* immense

palaver° /pə'lɑːvə(r), US '-læv-/ *n* **1** (bother) bazar° *m*; **2** (talks) discussion *f*

pale /peɪl/
A *adj* [*colour, complexion*] pâle; [*light, dawn*] blafard; **to turn** *ou* **go ~** pâlir
B *vi* lit pâlir; fig **to ~ into insignificance** devenir dérisoire
(Idiom) **to be beyond the ~** [*remark, behaviour*] être inadmissible; [*person*] être infréquentable

Palestine Liberation Organization, **PLO** *n* Organisation *f* de Libération de la Palestine

palette /'pælɪt/ *n* (object, colours) palette *f*

palette knife *n* **1** Art couteau *m* à palette; **2** Culin palette *f*

paling /'peɪlɪŋ/
A *n* (stake) palis *m*
B **palings** *npl* (fence) palissade *f*

palisade /ˌpælɪ'seɪd/
A *n* (fence) palissade *f*
B **palisades** *npl* US muraille *f* de falaises à pic

pall /pɔːl/
A *n* **1** (coffin-cloth) drap *m* mortuaire; (coffin) cercueil *m*; **2** fig (of smoke, dust) nuage *m*; (of gloom, mystery, silence) manteau *m*
B *vi* **it never ~s** on ne s'en lasse jamais

pallet /'pælɪt/ *n* (for loading) palette *f*

palliative /'pælɪətɪv/ *adj*
A *n* gen, Med palliatif *m*
B *adj* gen, Med palliatif/-ive *m/f*

pallid /'pælɪd/ *adj* [*skin, light*] blafard

pallor /'pælə(r)/ *n* pâleur *f*

palm /pɑːm/
A *n* **1** (of hand) paume *f*; **in the ~ of one's hand** dans le creux de la main; **he read my ~** il m'a lu les lignes de la main; **2** Bot (plant) (*also* **~ tree**) palmier *m*; (branch) branche *f* de palmier; (leaf) palme *f*; **3** Relig rameau *m*
B *vtr* escamoter [*card, coin*]; subtiliser [*money*]
(Idiom) **you have him in the ~ of your hand!** tu pourrais lui faire faire tout ce que tu veux!
(Phrasal verb)
■ **palm off**°: ▸ **~ [sth] off, ~ off [sth]** faire passer qch (as pour); **to ~ sth off on sb, to ~ sb off with sth** refiler° qch à qn

palmistry /'pɑːmɪstrɪ/ *n* chiromancie *f*

Palm Sunday *n* dimanche *m* des Rameaux

palmy /'pɑːmɪ/ *adj* **in the ~ days of sth** aux beaux jours de qch

palpable /'pælpəbl/ *adj* [*fear, tension*] palpable; [*lie, error, nonsense*] manifeste

palpitate /ˈpælpɪteɪt/ vi (all contexts) palpiter (**with** de)

paltry /ˈpɔːltrɪ/ adj [sum] dérisoire; [excuse] piètre

pampas /ˈpæmpəs, US -əz/ n (+ v sg) pampa f

pamper /ˈpæmpə(r)/
A vtr choyer [person, pet]
B v refl **to ~ oneself** se bichonner○

pamphlet /ˈpæmflɪt/ n gen brochure f; (political) tract m; Hist (satirical) pamphlet m

pan /pæn/
A n **1** Culin (saucepan) casserole f; **heat up a ~ of water** faites bouillir de l'eau dans une casserole; **2** (on scales) plateau m; **3** (in lavatory) cuvette f
B vtr (p prés etc **-nn-**) **1** ○(criticize) éreinter; **2** Cin, Phot, TV faire un panoramique de
C vi **1** Phot (p prés etc **-nn-**) [camera] faire un panoramique; **2** (prospect) **to ~ for** chercher [gold]
D Pan+ combining form **Pan-American** panaméricain/-aine; **Pan-African** panafricain/-aine
(Phrasal verb)
■ **pan out** (turn out) marcher; (turn out well) s'arranger

pancake /ˈpæŋkeɪk/ n **1** Culin crêpe f; **2** Theat (make-up) fond m de teint
(Idiom) **as flat as a ~**○ plat comme une galette

pancake: **~ day** n mardi m gras; **~ filling** n garniture f pour crêpes

panda car○ n GB voiture f pie

pandemonium /ˌpændɪˈməʊnɪəm/ n tohu-bohu m

pander /ˈpændə(r)/ vi **to ~ to** céder aux exigences de [person]; flatter [whim]

pane /peɪn/ n vitre f, carreau m; **a ~ of glass** une vitre, un carreau

panel /ˈpænl/
A n **1** (of experts, judges) commission f; TV, Radio (on discussion programme) invités mpl; (on quiz show) jury m; **to be on a ~** (of experts) être membre d'un comité; TV, Radio faire partie d'un jury; **2** Archit, Constr (section of wall) panneau m; **3** Aut, Tech (section) panneau m; (of instruments, switches) tableau m
B vtr (p prés etc **-ll-**, **-l-** US) recouvrir [qch] de panneaux
C panelled, paneled US pp adj [fencing] en panneaux; [wall, ceiling] lambrissé; [bath] cloisonné

panel: **~ beater** ▸ p. 1181 n tôlier m; **~ discussion** n Radio, TV débat m; **~ game** n Radio jeu m radiophonique; TV jeu m télévisé

panelling, paneling US /ˈpænlɪŋ/ n lambris m

panellist, panelist US /ˈpænlɪst/ n Radio, TV invité/-e m/f

panel truck n US camionnette f

pan-fry /ˈpænfraɪ/ vtr faire sauter

pang /pæŋ/ n **1** (emotional) serrement m de cœur; **a ~ of jealousy** une pointe de jalousie; **~s of conscience** ou **guilt** remords mpl de conscience; **2** (physical) **~s of hunger** crampes fpl d'estomac; **birth ~s** fig difficultés fpl initiales

panhandler○ /ˈpænhændlə(r)/ n US mendiant/-e m/f

panic /ˈpænɪk/
A n affolement m; **to get into a ~** s'affoler (**about** à cause de); **to throw sb into a ~** affoler qn
B noun modifier [decision] pris dans un moment de panique; [reaction] de panique
C vtr (p prés etc **-ck-**) affoler [person, animal]; semer la panique dans [crowd]; **to be ~ked into doing** se laisser affoler et faire
D vi (p prés etc **-ck-**) s'affoler; **don't ~!** pas de panique!

panic: **~ button** n signal m d'alarme; **~ buying** n ¢ achats mpl par crainte de la pénurie

panicky /ˈpænɪkɪ/ adj affolé

panic: **~ measure** n Pol, Econ disposition f précipitée; **~ selling** n ¢ Fin mouvements mpl de panique chez les petits porteurs

pannier /ˈpænɪə(r)/ n (on bike) sacoche f; (on mule) panier m de bât

pan scourer, pan scrubber n tampon m à récurer

pansy /ˈpænzɪ/ n Bot pensée f

pant /pænt/
A n halètement m
B vtr = **pant out**
C vi haleter; **to be ~ing for breath** être tout essoufflé

(Phrasal verb)
■ **pant out**: ▸ **~ out [sth]**, **~ [sth] out** dire [qch] d'une voix haletante

panther /ˈpænθə(r)/ n **1** (leopard) panthère f; **2** US (puma) puma m

panties /ˈpæntɪz/ ▸ p. 1191 npl slip m (de femme)

pantomime /ˈpæntəmaɪm/ n **1** GB Theat spectacle m pour enfants (à Noël); **2** (mime) mime m

pantry /ˈpæntrɪ/ n **1** (larder) garde-manger m inv; **2** (butler's etc) office m

pants /pænts/ ▸ p. 1191 npl US (trousers) pantalon m; GB (underwear) slip m

(Idioms) **to bore the ~ off sb**○ faire mourir d'ennui qn; **to scare the ~ off sb**○ flanquer la trouille à qn○; **to catch sb with his/her ~ down**○ prendre qn au dépourvu; **to fly by the seat of one's ~** [pilot] naviguer à l'instinct; **that's ~**○ c'est nul○

pantsuit /ˈpæntsuːt, -sjuːt/ n US tailleur-pantalon m

panty: **~ girdle** n gaine-culotte f; **~ hose** n ¢ US collant m; **~-liner** n protège-slip m

papacy /ˈpeɪpəsɪ/ n papauté f

papal /ˈpeɪpl/ adj papal, pontifical

paper /ˈpeɪpə(r)/
A n **1** (substance) (for writing etc) papier m; **to get** ou **put sth down on ~** mettre qch par écrit; **it's a good idea on ~** c'est une bonne idée en théorie; **this contract isn't worth the ~ it's written on** ce contrat ne vaut absolument rien; **2** (also **wall~**) papier m peint; **3** (newspaper) journal m; **4** (scholarly article) article m (**on** sur); (lecture) communication f (**on** sur); (report) exposé m (**on** sur); **5** (examination) épreuve f (**on** de); **6** Fin effet f de commerce; **7** (government publication) livre m
B papers npl Admin papiers mpl
C noun modifier **1** lit [bag, hat, handkerchief, napkin] en papier; [plate, cup] en carton; [industry] du papier; [manufacture] de papier; **2** fig [loss, profit] théorique; [promise, agreement] sans valeur
D vtr (also **wall~**) tapisser [room, wall]
E vi **to ~ over the existing wallpaper** recouvrir le papier actuel; **to ~ over one's differences** passer sur ses différences
(Idiom) **to ~ over the cracks** passer sur les problèmes

paperback /ˈpeɪpəbæk/
A n livre m de poche
B noun modifier [edition, version] de poche

paper: **~ bank** n conteneur m de récupération de vieux papiers; **~ boy** n livreur m de journaux; **~ chain** n guirlande f de papier; **~ chase** n jeu m de piste; **~clip** n trombone m; **~ currency** n monnaie f de papier; **~ fastener** n attache f parisienne; **~ feed tray** n Comput bac m d'alimentation en papier; **~ knife** n coupe-papier m inv

paperless /ˈpeɪpəlɪs/ adj Comput [office] électronique; [system] informatisé

paper: **~ mill** n papeterie f; **~ qualifications** npl diplômes mpl

paper round n he has ou does a **~** il livre des journaux

paper: **~ shop** n marchand m de journaux; **~ shredder** n déchiqueteuse f à papier; **~ tape** n Comput bande f perforée; **~ thin** adj mince comme du papier à cigarette; **~ towel** n essuie-tout m inv; **~weight** n presse-papier m inv; **~work** n (administration) travail m administratif; (documentation) documents mpl

papery /ˈpeɪpərɪ/ adj [texture, leaves] mince comme du papier; [skin] parcheminé

Papua New Guinea /ˌpɑːpʊə njuː ˈgɪniː, US nuː-/ ▸ p. 774 pr n Papouasie-Nouvelle-Guinée f

par /pɑː(r)/ n **1** gen **to be on a ~ with** [performance] être comparable à; [person] être l'égal de; **to be up to ~** être à la hauteur; **to be below** ou **under ~** [performance] être en dessous de la moyenne; [person] ne pas se sentir en forme; **2** (in golf) par m; **3** Econ, Fin pair m
(Idiom) **to be ~ for the course** être typique

para /ˈpærə/ n **1** abrév écrite = **paragraph**; **2** ○GB Mil (abrév = **paratrooper**) para○ m

parable /ˈpærəbl/ n parabole f

parachute /ˈpærəʃuːt/
A n parachute m
B vtr parachuter
C vi descendre en parachute
parachute: ~ **drop** n parachutage m; ~ **jump** n saut m en parachute
parachuting /ˈpærəʃuːtɪŋ/ ► p. 881 n **to go** ~ faire du parachutisme
parade /pəˈreɪd/
A n ① (procession) parade f; ② Mil (march) défilé m; (review) prise f d'armes; (in barracks) appel m; **to be on** ~ être à l'exercice; ③ (display) (of designs) défilé m; (of ideas) souvent péj étalage m; ④ GB (row) **a** ~ **of shops** une rangée de magasins
B vtr ① (display) faire étalage de; ② (claim) **to** ~ **sth as sth** présenter qch comme qch
C vi ① (march) défiler (**through** dans); **to** ~ **up and down** [soldier, model] défiler; [child, person] parader
parade ground n champ m de manœuvres
paradise /ˈpærədaɪs/ n paradis m; **in** ~ au paradis
paradox /ˈpærədɒks/ n paradoxe m
paradoxical /ˌpærəˈdɒksɪkl/ adj paradoxal
paraffin /ˈpærəfɪn/
A n ① GB (fuel) pétrole m; ② (also ~ **wax**) paraffine f
B noun modifier GB [lamp, heater] à pétrole
paragliding /ˈpærəˌɡlaɪdɪŋ/ ► p. 881 n parapente m
paragon /ˈpærəɡən, US -ɡɒn/ n modèle m (**of** de)
paragraph /ˈpærəɡrɑːf, US -ɡræf/
A n ① (section) paragraphe m; **new** ~ (in dictation) à la ligne; ② (article) entrefilet m
parallel /ˈpærəlel/
A n ① Math parallèle f; ② (comparison) parallèle m; **to be on a** ~ **with sth** être comparable à qch; **without** ~ sans pareil; ③ Geog parallèle m
B adj ① Comput, Math parallèle; ② (similar) analogue (**to, with** à); ③ (simultaneous) parallèle
C adv ~ **to**, ~ **with** parallèlement à
D vtr (p prés GB -**ll**-, US -**l**-) (equal) égaler; (find a comparison) trouver un équivalent à
parallel: ~ **processing** n Comput traitement m en parallèle; ~ **turn** n Sport virage m parallèle
paralyse GB, **paralyze** US /ˈpærəlaɪz/ vtr Med, fig paralyser
paralysis /pəˈræləsɪs/ n Med, fig paralysie f
paralytic /ˌpærəˈlɪtɪk/ adj ① Med [person] paralytique; [arm, leg] paralysé; ② ◦GB (drunk) complètement bourré◦
paramedic /ˌpærəˈmedɪk/ ► p. 1181 n auxiliaire mf médical/-e
parameter /pəˈræmɪtə(r)/ n paramètre m; **within the** ~**s of** fig dans les limites de
paramilitary /ˌpærəˈmɪlɪtrɪ, US -terɪ/
A n membre m d'une organisation paramilitaire
B adj paramilitaire
paramount /ˈpærəmaʊnt/ adj [consideration, goal] suprême; **to be** ~, **to be of** ~ **importance** être d'une importance capitale
paranoid /ˈpærənɔɪd/
A n paranoïaque mf
B adj ① Psych paranoïde; ② (suspicious) paranoïaque (**about** au sujet de); **to be** ~ **about being burgled** avoir une peur maladive d'être cambriolé
parapet /ˈpærəpɪt/ n Archit, Mil parapet m
paraphernalia /ˌpærəfəˈneɪlɪə/ n (+ v sg) ① (articles, accessories) attirail m; ② GB (rigmarole) comédie◦ f
paraphrase /ˈpærəfreɪz/
A n paraphrase f
B vtr paraphraser
paraplegic /ˌpærəˈpliːdʒɪk/
A n paraplégique mf
B adj [person] paraplégique; [games] pour les paraplégiques
parascending /ˈpærəsendɪŋ/ n GB parachutisme m ascensionnel
parasite /ˈpærəsaɪt/ n lit, fig parasite m
paratrooper /ˈpærətruːpə(r)/ n parachutiste m
parboil /ˈpɑːbɔɪl/ vtr faire cuire [qch] à demi
parcel /ˈpɑːsl/ n ① gen, Fin paquet m; ② ◦(of people, problems) tas◦ m

Idiom **to be part and** ~ **of** faire partie intégrante de
Phrasal verbs
■ **parcel out**: ► ~ **out** [sth], ~ [sth] **out** répartir
■ **parcel up**: ► ~ **up** [sth], ~ [sth] **up** emballer
parcel: ~ **bomb** n colis m piégé; ~ **office** n (bureau m des) messageries fpl; ~ **post** n service m de colis postaux; ~**s service** n société f d'expédition des colis postaux
parched /pɑːtʃt/ adj ① [earth] desséché; ② **to be** ~◦ mourir de soif
parchment /ˈpɑːtʃmənt/ n (document) parchemin m; (paper) papier-parchemin m
pardon /ˈpɑːdn/
A n ① gen pardon m; **to beg sb's** ~ demander pardon à qn; ② Jur (also **free** ~) grâce f
B excl (what?) pardon?; (sorry!) pardon!
C vtr gen pardonner; Jur gracier [criminal]
pare /peə(r)/ vtr peler [apple]; rogner [nails]

Idiom **to** ~ **sth to the bone** réduire qch au minimum vital
Phrasal verb
■ **pare off**: ► ~ [sth] **off**, ~ **off** [sth] peler [rind, peel]; réduire [amount, percentage]
pared-down /ˌpeəd ˈdaʊn/ adj [budget] réduit; [version] abrégé; [prose, plot] dépouillé
parent /ˈpeərənt/ n ① (of child) parent m; **as a** ~ en ma/votre etc qualité de parent; ② Comm (company) maison f mère; (organization) organisation f mère
parentage /ˈpeərəntɪdʒ/ n ascendance f
parental /pəˈrentl/ adj parental fml, des parents
parent: ~ **company** n maison f mère; ~**-governor** n GB Sch membre du conseil d'établissement et représentant des parents d'élèves
parenthesis /pəˈrenθəsɪs/ n (pl -**eses**) parenthèse f
parenthood /ˈpeərənthʊd/ n (fatherhood) paternité f; (motherhood) maternité f
parenting /ˈpeərəntɪŋ/ n éducation f des enfants
parent: ~ **organization** n organisation f mère; ~ **power** n Sch pouvoir m décisionnel des parents d'élèves; ~**s' evening** n Sch réunion f pour les parents d'élèves; ~**-teacher association** n ► PTA
parer /ˈpeərə(r)/ n épluche-légumes m inv
parings /ˈpeərɪŋz/ npl ① (of fruit) épluchures fpl; ② (of nails) rognures fpl
Paris /ˈpærɪs/ ► p. 1276
A pr n Paris
B noun modifier [fashion, metro, restaurant] parisien/-ienne
parish /ˈpærɪʃ/
A n ① Relig paroisse f; ② GB (administrative) commune f
B noun modifier [church, hall, meeting, register] paroissial
parishioner /pəˈrɪʃənə(r)/ n paroissien/-ienne m/f
parish priest n (Protestant) pasteur m; (Catholic) curé m
Parisian /pəˈrɪzɪən/
A n Parisien/-ienne m/f
B adj parisien/-ienne
parity /ˈpærətɪ/ n (equality) parité f (**with** avec)
park /pɑːk/
A n ① (public garden) jardin m public; ② (estate) parc m also Comm, Ind; ③ GB (pitch) terrain m; US (stadium) stade m; ④ (in automatic gearbox) position f parking
B vtr ① Aut garer; ② ◦(deposit) laisser
C vi [driver] se garer
D **parked** pp adj en stationnement
E ◦v refl **to** ~ **oneself** s'installer
park-and-ride n GB parking m de dissuasion
parking /ˈpɑːkɪŋ/
A n ① (action) stationnement m; '**No** ~' 'stationnement interdit'; ② (space for cars) place f de stationnement
B noun modifier [area, bay, charge, permit, problem, regulations, restrictions] de stationnement; [facilities] pour le stationnement
parking: ~ **attendant** ► p. 1181 n gardien/-ienne m/f de parking; ~ **light** n Aut feu m de position; ~ **lot** n US parking m; ~ **meter** n parcmètre m; ~ **offence** GB, ~ **offense** US n infraction f aux règles de stationnement; ~ **place**, ~ **space** n place f; ~ **ticket** n (from machine) ticket m de stationnement; (fine) contravention f, PV◦

park: ∼**land** n parc m boisé; ∼ **ranger**, ∼ **warden**
▶ p. 1181 n (on estate) garde m forestier; (in game reserve) garde-chasse m

parliament /'pɑːləmənt/
A n Pol parlement m
B **Parliament** pr n GB **1** (institution) Parlement m; **to get into Parliament** se faire élire député; **2** (parliamentary session) session f parlementaire

> ℹ **Parliament** Corps législatif britannique composé de la Chambre des communes et de la Chambre des lords qui siègent au Palais de Westminster. Le souverain convoque et dissout le Parlement, ouvre chaque session parlementaire et signe les textes de lois. Des élections législatives ont lieu au minimum tous les cinq ans et renouvellent la totalité de la Chambre des communes.

parliamentarian /ˌpɑːləmənˈteəriən/ n **1** (member) parlementaire m; **2** (expert in procedure) expert m des procédures parlementaires

parliamentary /ˌpɑːləˈmentrɪ, US -terɪ/ adj parlementaire

parliamentary: ∼ **election** n élections fpl législatives; ∼ **privilege** n immunité f parlementaire; ∼ **secretary** n GB député m attaché ministériel

parlour GB, **parlor** US /'pɑːlə(r)/ n **1** †(in house) petit salon m; **2** (in convent) parloir m

parochial /pəˈrəʊkɪəl/ adj **1** péj [interest, view] de clocher; **2** US (of parish) paroissial

parody /'pærədɪ/
A n (all contexts) parodie f
B vtr parodier [person, style]

parole /pəˈrəʊl/
A n **1** Jur liberté f conditionnelle; **2** Mil parole f (d'honneur)
B vtr Jur mettre [qn] en liberté conditionnelle

paroxysm /'pærəksɪzəm/ n crise f (of de)

parquet /'pɑːkeɪ, US pɑːrˈkeɪ/
A n (floor) parquet m; US Theat parterre m
B vtr parqueter

parrot /'pærət/
A n Zool, péj (person) perroquet m
B vtr péj répéter comme un perroquet
(Idiom) **as sick as a** ∼○ en rage

parry /'pærɪ/
A n **1** Sport parade f; **2** (verbal) riposte f
B vtr **1** Sport parer; **2** éluder [question]
C vi (in fencing, boxing) parer

parse /pɑːz/ vtr Ling, Comput faire l'analyse grammaticale de

parsimonious /ˌpɑːsɪˈməʊnɪəs/ adj sout parcimonieux/-ieuse fml

parsley /'pɑːslɪ/ n persil m

parsnip /'pɑːsnɪp/ n panais m

parson /'pɑːsn/ n pasteur m

part /pɑːt/
A n **1** (of whole) gen partie f; (of country) région f; **in** ou **around these** ∼ dans la région; ∼ **of the reason is...** c'est en partie parce que...; **to be (a)** ∼ **of** faire partie de; **the early** ∼ **of my life** ma jeunesse; **it's all** ∼ **of being young** il faut bien que jeunesse se passe; **that's the best/hardest** ∼ c'est ça le meilleur/le plus dur; **that's the** ∼ **I don't understand** voilà ce que je ne comprends pas; **to be good in** ∼**s** GB avoir de bons passages; **for the most** ∼ dans l'ensemble; **my** ∼ **of the world** mon pays; **what are you doing in this** ∼ **of the world?** qu'est-ce que tu fais par ici?; **2** Tech (component) pièce f; **spare** ∼**s** pièces détachées; **3** TV (of serial, programme) partie f; **a two-**∼ **series** une série en deux épisodes; **4** (share, role) rôle m (**in** dans); **to do one's** ∼ jouer son rôle; **I want no** ∼ **in it, I don't want any** ∼ **of it** je ne veux pas m'en mêler; **to take** ∼ participer (**in** à); **they took no further** ∼ **in it** ils n'ont rien fait de plus; **5** Theat, TV, Cin rôle m (**of** de); **6** (equal measure) mesure f; **mix X and Y in equal** ∼**s** mélangez une quantité égale de X et Y; **in a concentration of 30,000** ∼**s per million** dans une concentration de 3%; **7** Mus (for instrument, voice) partie f; (score) partition f; **8** (behalf) **on the** ∼ **of** de la part de; **for my** ∼ pour ma part; **to take sb's** ∼ prendre le parti de qn; **9** US (in hair) raie f

B adv (partly) en partie; **it was** ∼ **fear**, ∼ **greed** c'était à la fois de la crainte et de la cupidité
C vtr **1** (separate) séparer [two people]; écarter [legs]; entrouvrir [lips, curtains]; fendre [crowd, ocean, waves]; **2** (make parting in) **to** ∼ **one's hair** se faire une raie
D vi **1** (split up) se séparer; **we** ∼**ed friends** nous nous sommes quittés bons amis; **to** ∼ **from sb** quitter qn; **2** [crowd, clouds] (divide) s'ouvrir; [rope, cable] se rompre
(Idioms) **a man of (many)** ∼**s** un homme qui a plusieurs cordes à son arc; **to look the** ∼ avoir la tête de l'emploi; **to take sth in good** ∼ prendre qch en bonne part
(Phrasal verb)
∎ **part with**: ▶ ∼ **with [sth]** se défaire de [money]; se séparer de [object]

partake /pɑːˈteɪk/ vi sout **1** **to** ∼ **of** prendre [food, drink]; tenir de [quality]; **2** **to** ∼ **in** participer à

part exchange n GB reprise f; **to take sth in** ∼ reprendre qch

partial /'pɑːʃl/ adj **1** (not complete) partiel/-ielle; **2** (biased) partial; **3** (fond) **to be** ∼ **to** avoir un faible pour

partiality /ˌpɑːʃɪˈælətɪ/ n **1** (bias) partialité f; **2** (liking) ∼ **to** ou **for** penchant m pour

partially /'pɑːʃəlɪ/ adv **1** (incompletely) partiellement; **2** (with bias) avec partialité

partially sighted
A n **the** ∼ (+ v pl) les malvoyants mpl
B adj malvoyant

participant /pɑːˈtɪsɪpənt/ n participant/-e m/f (**in** à)

participate /pɑːˈtɪsɪpeɪt/ vi participer (**in** à)

participation /pɑːˌtɪsɪˈpeɪʃn/ n participation f (**in** à)

participle /'pɑːtɪsɪpl/ n participe m

particle /'pɑːtɪkl/ n (all contexts) particule f

particular /pəˈtɪkjʊlə(r)/
A n **1** detail m; **in every** ∼ dans tous les détails; **in one** ∼ sur un point précis; **in several** ∼**s** à plus d'un titre; **2** **in** ∼ en particulier; **are you looking for anything in** ∼? vous cherchez quelque chose de précis?
B **particulars** npl (information) détails mpl; (from person) (name, address etc) coordonnées fpl; (for missing person, suspect) signalement m; Admin (for vehicle, stolen goods etc) description f; **for further** ∼**s please phone...** pour plus amples renseignements veuillez téléphoner à...
C adj **1** (specific) particulier/-ière; **this** ∼ **colour doesn't really suit me** cette couleur-là ne me va pas très bien; **is there any** ∼ **colour you would prefer?** est-ce que vous désirez une couleur en particulier?; **no** ∼ **time has been arranged** on n'a pas fixé d'heure précise; **2** (special, exceptional) particulier/-ière; **to take** ∼ **care over sth** faire qch avec un soin tout particulier; **he is a** ∼ **friend of mine** c'est un de mes meilleurs amis; **3** (fussy) méticuleux/-euse; **to be** ∼ **about** être exigeant sur [cleanliness, punctuality]; faire attention à [appearance]; être difficile pour [food]; **'any special time?'—'no, I'm not** ∼ '**y** a-t-il une heure spéciale qui vous convient?'—'non, je n'ai pas de préférence'

particularize /pəˈtɪkjʊləraɪz/ vtr, vi préciser

particularly /pəˈtɪkjʊləlɪ/ adv **1** (in particular) en particulier; **2** (especially) spécialement

parting /'pɑːtɪŋ/
A n **1** (division) séparation f; **the** ∼ **of the ways** la croisée des chemins; **2** GB (in hair) raie f
B adj [gift, words] d'adieu also iron; ∼ **shot** flèche f du Parthe

partisan /'pɑːtɪzæn, ˌpɑːtɪˈzæn, US 'pɑːrtɪzn/
A n Mil, gen partisan m
B adj **1** (biased) partisan; **2** Mil de partisans

partition /pɑːˈtɪʃn/
A n **1** (in room, house) cloison f; **2** Pol (of country) partition f; **3** Jur (of property) morcellement m
B vtr **1** = **partition off**; **2** Pol diviser; **3** Jur morceler
(Phrasal verb)
∎ **partition off**: ▶ ∼ **off [sth]**, ∼ **[sth] off** cloisonner [area, room]

partitive /'pɑːtɪtɪv/ adj partitif/-ive

partly /'pɑːtlɪ/ adv en partie

partner /'pɑːtnə(r)/
A n **1** Comm, Jur associé/-e m/f (**in** dans); **active** ∼ associé-

gérant *m*; **business** ~ associé/-e *m/f*; **general** ~ commandité *m*; **limited** ~ commanditaire *m*; [2] Econ, Pol, Sport partenaire *m*; [3] (married) époux/-se *m/f*; (unmarried) partenaire *mf*; [4] (workmate) collègue *mf*

B *vtr* être le collègue de [*workmate*]; être le partenaire de [*dancer*]; faire équipe avec [*player*]

(Idiom) **to be** ~**s in crime** être complices

partnership /'pɑːtnəʃɪp/ *n* [1] Jur association *f*; **to go into** ~ **with** s'associer à; **to take sb into** ~ prendre qn pour associé/-e *m/f*; ~ **society** *f* en nom collectif; **professional** ~, **non-trading** ~ association professionnelle; [2] (alliance) partenariat *m*; [3] (pairing) association *f*; **a working** ~ une équipe

part: ~ **of speech** *n* partie *f* du discours; ~ **owner** *n* copropriétaire *mf*; ~ **payment** *n* règlement *m* partiel

partridge /'pɑːtrɪdʒ/ *n* perdrix *f*

part song *n* chant *m* polyphonique

part-time /,pɑːt'taɪm/
A *n* temps *m* partiel
B *adj, adv* [*work, worker*] à temps partiel

partway /,pɑːt'weɪ/ *adv* ~ **through the evening** à un moment de la soirée; ~ **down the page** vers le bas de la page; **to be** ~ **through doing** être en train de faire

party /'pɑːtɪ/
A *n* [1] (social event) fête *f*; (in evening) soirée *f*; (formal) réception *f*; **birthday** ~ (fête d')anniversaire *m*; **children's** ~ goûter *m* d'enfants; **leaving** ~ pot *m* de départ; [2] (group) groupe *m*; Mil détachement *m*; **rescue** ~ équipe *f* de secouristes; [3] Pol parti *m*; [4] Jur (individual, group) partie *f*; [5] sout **to be a** ~ **to** être complice de
B *noun modifier* [*spirit*] de fête; [*game*] de société; [2] Pol [*member, policy*] du parti
C ᵒ*vi* faire la fête

party: ~ **dress** *n* (formal) robe *f* de soirée; ~**goer** *n* fêtard/-eᵒ *m/f*; ~ **hat** *n* chapeau *m* en papier

party line *n* [1] Pol, fig **the** ~ la ligne du parti; [2] Telecom ligne *f* commune

party piece *n* **to do one's** ~ᵒ faire son numéroᵒ

party: ~ **political broadcast** *n* émission *f* dans laquelle un parti expose sa politique; ~ **politics** *n* péj politique *f* politicienne; ~ **wall** *n* mur *m* mitoyen

pass /pɑːs, US pæs/
A *n* [1] (to enter, leave) laisser-passer *m inv*; (for journalists) coupe-file *m*; (to be absent) permission *f* also Mil; (of safe conduct) sauf-conduit *m*; [2] (travel document) carte *f*; [3] Sch, Univ (success) moyenne *f* (**in** en); **to get a** ~ être reçu; [4] Sport (in ball games) passe *f*; (in fencing) botte *f*; [5] Geog (in mountains) col *m*; [6] Aviat **to make a** ~ **over sth** survoler qch
B *vtr* [1] (go past) (to far side) passer [*checkpoint, customs*]; franchir [*lips*]; (alongside and beyond) passer devant [*building, area*]; dépasser [*level, understanding, expectation, vehicle*]; **to** ~ **sb in the street** croiser qn dans la rue; [2] (hand over) (directly) passer; (indirectly) faire passer; [3] (move) passer also Sport; [4] (spend) passer [*time*] (**doing** à faire); [5] (succeed in) [*person*] réussir [*car, machine etc*] passer [qch] (avec succès); [6] (declare satisfactory) admettre [*candidate*]; approuver [*invoice*]; **to** ~ **sth** (**as being**) **safe** juger qch sans danger; [7] adopter [*bill, motion*]; [8] (pronounce) prononcer; **to** ~ **a remark about sb/sth** faire une remarque sur qn/qch; [9] Med **to** ~ **water** uriner; **to** ~ **blood** avoir du sang dans les urines
C *vi* [1] (go past, be transferred, accepted) passer also Sport, Games; [*letter, knowing look*] être échangé; **to** ~ **through sth** traverser qch; ~ **down the bus please** avancez dans le fond s'il vous plaît; **let the remark** ~ laissez couler; **I'm afraid I must** ~ **on that** fig (in discussion) je cède mon tour de parole; **she** ~**es for 40** on lui donnerait 40 ans; [2] littér (happen) se passer; [3] (in exam) réussir

(Idioms) **to come to such a** ~ **that** arriver à un tel point que; **to make a** ~ **at sb** faire du platᵒ à qn; **to** ~ **the word** passer la consigne

(Phrasal verbs)

■ **pass along**: ▸ ~ [sth] **along**, ~ **along** [sth] faire passer

■ **pass around, pass round**: ▸ ~ [sth] **around**, ~ **around** [sth] faire circuler [*document, photos*]; faire passer [*food, plates etc*]

■ **pass away** euph décéder

■ **pass by** [*procession*] défiler; [*person*] passer; **life seems**

to have ~**ed me by** j'ai le sentiment d'être passé à côté de la vie

■ **pass down**: ▸ ~ [sth] **down**, ~ **down** [sth] transmettre (**from** de; **to** à)

■ **pass off**: ▸ ~ **off** [1] (take place) [*demonstration*] se dérouler; [*fête*] se passer; [2] (disappear) se dissiper; ▸ ~ [sb/sth] **off**, ~ **off** [sb/sth] faire passer (**as** pour)

■ **pass on**: ▸ ~ **on** poursuivre; **to** ~ **on to sth** passer à qch; ▸ ~ [sth] **on**, ~ **on** [sth] transmettre [*good wishes, condolences, message, title*]; passer [*book, clothes, cold*] (**to** à); répercuter [*costs*]

■ **pass out**: ▸ ~ **out** [1] (faint) perdre connaissance; (fall drunk) tomber ivre mort; [2] Mil (complete training) sortir avec ses diplômes (**of, from** de); ▸ ~ [sth] **out**, ~ **out** [sth] distribuer [*leaflets*]

■ **pass over**: ▸ ~ **over**† = **pass away**; ▸ ~ [sb] **over** délaisser; **he was** ~**ed over in favour of another candidate** on lui a préféré un autre candidat; ▸ ~ **over** [sth] ne pas tenir compte de

■ **pass through**: ▸ ~ **through** [sth] traverser; **I'm just** ~**ing through** je suis de passage

■ **pass up**ᵒ: ▸ ~ **up** [sth] laisser passer

passable /'pɑːsəbl, US 'pæs-/ *adj* [1] (acceptable) gen passable; [*knowledge, performance*] assez bon/bonne; **only** ~ moyen/-enne sans plus; [2] (traversable) [*road*] praticable; [*river*] franchissable

passage /'pæsɪdʒ/ *n* [1] (also ~**way**) (indoors) corridor *m*; (outdoors) passage *m*; [2] Anat conduit *m*; **nasal** ~**s** fosses *fpl* nasales; [3] Mus, Literat passage *m*; **selected** ~**s** Literat morceaux *mpl* choisis; [4] (movement) passage *m*; ~ **of arms** passe *f* d'armes; [5] (journey) traversée *f*; **the bill had a stormy** ~ **through parliament** fig la discussion de ce projet de loi au parlement a été mouvementée

pass: ~**book** *n* Fin livret *m* (bancaire); ~ **degree** *n* Univ diplôme *m* avec mention passable

passé /'pæseɪ, US pæ'seɪ/ *adj* péj démodé

passenger /'pæsɪndʒə(r)/ *n* [1] (in car, plane, ship) passager/-ère *m/f*; (in train, bus, tube) voyageur/-euse *m/f*; [2] GB péj parasite *m*

passenger: ~ **compartment** *n* GB Aut habitacle *m*; ~ **ferry** *n* ferry *m*; ~ **plane** *n* avion *m* de ligne; ~ **service** *n* ligne *f*; ~ **train** *n* train *m* de voyageurs

passe-partout /,pæspɑː'tuː, ,pɑːs-/ *n* (key) passe-partout *m inv*; (frame) sous-verre *m inv*

passerby /'pɑːsə'baɪ/ *n* passant/-e *m/f*

passing /'pɑːsɪŋ, US 'pæs-/
A *n* [1] (movement) passage *m*; **with the** ~ **of time** avec le temps; [2] (end) fin *f*; [3] euph (death) disparition *f* euph
B *adj* [1] (going by) [*motorist, policeman*] qui passe; **with each** ~ **day** de jour en jour; [2] [*whim*] passager/-ère; [3] (cursory) [*reference*] en passant *inv*; [4] (vague) [*resemblance*] vague (*before n*)

passing: ~ **place** *n* aire *f* de croisement; ~ **shot** *n* (in tennis) tir *m* passant

passion /'pæʃn/ *n* [1] (love, feeling) passion *f*; [2] (anger) colère *f*; [3] Relig Passion *f*

passionate /'pæʃənət/ *adj* [*kiss, person, nature, speech*] passionné; [*advocate, belief, plea*] fervent; [*relationship*] passionnel/-elle

passionately /'pæʃənətlɪ/ *adv* [1] [*love, kiss*] passionnément; [*write, defend*] avec passion; [*believe, want*] ardemment; [*oppose*] farouchement; **to be** ~ **fond of sb/sth** adorer qn/qch

Passion Sunday *n* dimanche *m* d'avant les Rameaux

passive /'pæsɪv/
A *n* Ling **the** ~ le passif, la voix passive
B *adj* (all contexts) passif/-ive

passively /'pæsɪvlɪ/ *adv* [1] [*gaze, stare*] d'un air passif; [*wait, react*] passivement; [2] Ling au passif

pass: ~**key** *n* passe *m*; ~ **mark** *n* Sch, Univ moyenne *f*

Passover /'pɑːsəʊvə(r), US 'pæs-/ *n* Pâque *f* juive

passport /'pɑːspɔːt, US 'pæs-/ *n* passeport *m* also fig; **visitor's** ~ GB Hist passeport temporaire

passport holder *n* détenteur/-trice *m/f* d'un passeport

pass: ~**-through** *n* US passe-plat *m*; ~**word** *n* (all contexts) mot *m* de passe

past /pɑːst, US pæst/

⚠️ For a full set of translations for *past* used in clocktime consult the Usage Note ▸ p. 745

A *n* **1** gen passé *m*; **in the ~** dans le passé; **she has a ~** elle a un passé chargé; **2** Ling (*also* **~ tense**) passé *m*; **in the ~** au passé

B *adj* **1** (preceding) dernier/-ière; **2** (former) [*times, achievements, problems, experience*] passé; [*president, incumbent*] ancien/-ienne; [*government*] précédent; **in times ~** autrefois, jadis; **3** (finished) **summer is ~** l'été est fini; **that's all ~** c'est du passé

C *prep* **1** (moving) **to walk** *ou* **go ~ sb/sth** passer devant qn/qch; **to drive ~ sth** passer devant qch (en voiture); **2** (in time) **it's ~ 6** il est 6 heures passées; **twenty ~ two** deux heures vingt; **half ~ two** deux heures et demie; **he is ~ 70** il a 70 ans passés; **3** (beyond in position) après; **~ the church** après l'église; **4** (beyond a certain level) **the temperature soared ~ 40°C** la température est montée brutalement à plus de 40°C; **he didn't get ~ the first chapter** il n'est pas allé plus loin que le premier chapitre; **he didn't get ~ the first interview** il n'a pas passé la barrière du premier entretien; **5** (beyond scope of) **to be ~ understanding** dépasser l'entendement; **to be ~ caring** ne plus s'en faire; **he is ~ playing football** ce n'est plus de son âge de jouer au foot

D *adv* **1** (onwards) **to go** *ou* **walk ~** passer; **2** (ago) **two years ~** il y a deux ans

(Idioms) **to be ~ it**○ avoir passé l'âge; **to be ~ its best** [*food*] être un peu avancé; [*wine*] être un peu éventé; **I wouldn't put it ~ him to do** je ne pense pas que ça le gênerait de faire

pasta /ˈpæstə/ *n* ⦰ pâtes *fpl* (alimentaires)

paste /peɪst/
A *n* **1** (glue) colle *f*; **2** (mixture) pâte *f*; **3** Culin (fish, meat) pâté *m*; (vegetable) purée *f*; **4** (in jewellery) strass *m*
B *vtr* **1** (stick) coller *also* Comput; **2** (coat in glue) encoller; **3** ○(defeat) battre [qn] à plates coutures○
(Phrasal verb)
■ **paste up**: ▸ **~ [sth] up, ~ up [sth]** afficher [*notice, poster*]; faire une maquette de [*article, page*]

pasteboard /ˈpeɪstbɔːd/ *n* carton *m*

pastel /ˈpæstl, US pæˈstel/
A *n* (medium, stick) pastel *m*; (drawing) dessin *m* au pastel
B *noun modifier* [*colour, green, pink, shade*] pastel; [*drawing*] au pastel

pasteurize /ˈpɑːstʃəraɪz, US ˈpæst-/ *vtr* pasteuriser

past historic *n* Ling passé *m* simple

pastime /ˈpɑːstaɪm, US ˈpæs-/ *n* passe-temps *m inv*

pasting○ /ˈpeɪstɪŋ/ *n* (defeat) gamelle○ *f*; (criticism) **to take a ~** se faire descendre en flammes

past master *n* **to be a ~ at doing** avoir l'art de faire

pastor /ˈpɑːstə(r), US ˈpæs-/ ▸ p. 1181 *n* pasteur *m*

pastoral /ˈpɑːstərəl, US ˈpæs-/
A *n* pastorale *f*
B *adj* **1** Art, Literat, Relig pastoral; **2** GB Sch, Univ [*role, work*] de conseiller/-ère; **he looks after students' ~ needs** il s'occupe du bien-être des étudiants

past perfect *n* Ling plus-que-parfait *m*

pastrami /pæˈstrɑːmɪ/ *n* bœuf *m* fumé

pastry /ˈpeɪstrɪ/ *n* **1** (mixture) pâte *f*; **to roll out ~** étaler une pâte; **2** (cake) pâtisserie *f*

pastry: **~ case** *n* fond *m* de tarte; **~ cook** *n* pâtissier/-ière *m/f*; **~ shell** *n* = pastry case

past tense *n* Ling passé *m*

pasture /ˈpɑːstʃə(r), US ˈpæs-/ *n* (land) pré *m*, pâturage *m*; (grass) herbe *f*

(Idioms) **to leave for ~s new** partir vers de nouveaux horizons; **to put sb out to ~** mettre qn au vert

pasty
A /ˈpæstɪ/ *n* GB Culin petit pâté en croûte
B /ˈpeɪstɪ/ *adj* **1** [*skin*] terreux/-euse; **2** [*mixture*] pâteux/-euse

pat /pæt/
A *n* **1** (gentle tap) petite tape *f*; **2** (of butter) noix *f*; (larger) morceau *m*
B *adj* **1** (glib) tout prêt; **2** (apt) pertinent
C *vtr* (*p prés etc* **-tt-**) tapoter [*ball, hand*]; caresser [*dog*]; **to ~ one's hair into place** arranger ses cheveux

---

(Idioms) **to have sth off** GB *ou* **down** US **~** connaître qch par cœur; **to get a ~ on the back** se faire féliciter; **to stand ~** US demeurer inflexible

patch /pætʃ/
A *n* (*pl* **~es**) **1** (in clothes) pièce *f*; (on tyre, airbed) rustine® *f*; (on eye) bandeau *m*; **2** (small area) (of snow, ice) plaque *f*; (of colour, damp, rust, sunlight) tache *f*; (of fog) nappe *f*; (of oil) flaque *f*; (of blue sky) coin *m*; **in ~es** par endroits; **3** (area of ground) gen zone *f*; (for planting) carré *m*; **a ~ of grass** coin d'herbe; **4** GB○ (territory) (of gangster, salesman) territoire *m*; (of policeman, official) secteur *m*; **5** ○(period) période *f*
B *vtr* **1** rapiécer [*hole, trousers*]; réparer [*tyre*]; **2** Comput corriger

(Idiom) **the film isn't a ~ on the book** le film est loin de valoir le livre

(Phrasal verbs)
■ **patch together**: ▸ **~ [sth] together** rafistoler○ [*fragments*]; concocter [*deal, report*]
■ **patch up**: ▸ **~ up [sth], ~ [sth] up** soigner [*person*]; rapiécer [*hole, trousers*]; réparer [*ceiling, tyre*]; fig rafistoler○ [*marriage*]; ▸ **~ up [sth]** résoudre [*differences, quarrel*]

patch: **~ pocket** *n* poche *f* plaquée; **~ test** *n* Med test *m* cutané; **~ work** *n* lit, fig patchwork *m*

patchy /ˈpætʃɪ/ *adj* [*colour, essay, quality*] inégal; [*knowledge*] incomplet/-ète; **~ cloud** nuages *mpl* épars; **~ fog** nappes *fpl* de brouillard

patent /ˈpætnt, ˈpeɪtnt, US ˈpætnt/
A *n* (document) brevet *m* (**for, on** pour); **to hold/take out a ~** détenir/obtenir un brevet; **to come out of ~** *ou* **off ~** tomber dans le domaine public; **~ pending** en cours de brevetage *m*
B *adj* **1** (obvious) manifeste; **2** Jur (licensed) breveté
C *vtr* Jur faire breveter

patent leather *n* cuir *m* verni

patently /ˈpeɪtntlɪ, US ˈpæt-/ *adv* manifestement

patent: **~ medicine** *n*: médicament de marque déposée; **Patent Office** GB, **Patent and Trademark Office** US *n* ≈ Institut *m* national de la propriété industrielle

paternal /pəˈtɜːnl/ *adj* (all contexts) paternel/-elle

paternity /pəˈtɜːnətɪ/ *n* paternité *f*

paternity: **~ leave** *n* congé *m* de paternité; **~ suit** *n* action *f* en recherche de paternité

path /pɑːθ, US pæθ/ *n* **1** (track) (*also* **~way**) chemin *m*; (narrower) sentier *m*; (in garden) allée *f*; **2** (course) (of projectile, vehicle) trajectoire *f*; (of planet, river, sun) cours *m*; (of hurricane) passage *m*; **to stand in sb's ~** lit, fig barrer le chemin à qn; **3** (option) voie *f*; **4** (means) (difficult) chemin *m* (**to** de); (easy) route *f* (**to** de); **5** (*abrév* = **pathology**) pathologie *f*

pathetic /pəˈθetɪk/ *adj* **1** (full of pathos) pathétique; **2** péj (inadequate) misérable; **3** ○péj (contemptible) lamentable

pathetically /pəˈθetɪklɪ/ *adv* **1** [*vulnerable*] pathétiquement; [*grateful*] éperdument; **2** ○péj de façon lamentable

pathetic fallacy *n* ≈ sophisme *m* sentimental

pathological /ˌpæθəˈlɒdʒɪkl/ *adj* **1** [*fear, hatred*] pathologique; **he's a ~ liar**○ c'est pathologique chez lui, il ment sans arrêt○; **2** [*journal*] médical; [*research*] des causes pathologiques

pathologically /ˌpæθəˈlɒdʒɪklɪ/ *adv* **he's ~ jealous** sa jalousie est pathologique

pathologist /pəˈθɒlədʒɪst/ ▸ p. 1181 *n* (doing post-mortems) médecin *m* légiste; (specialist in pathology) pathologiste *mf*

pathology /pəˈθɒlədʒɪ/ *n* pathologie *f*

patience /ˈpeɪʃns/ *n* **1** patience *f* (**with** avec); **2** ▸ p. 881 (game) réussite *f*

patient /ˈpeɪʃnt/
A *n* patient/-e *m/f*; **heart ~** patient souffrant d'une maladie cardiaque
B *adj* patient (**with** avec)

patiently /ˈpeɪʃntlɪ/ *adv* avec patience, patiemment

patio /ˈpætɪəʊ/ *n* **1** (terrace) terrasse *f*; **2** (courtyard) patio *m*

patio: **~ doors** *npl* porte-fenêtre *f*; **~ furniture** *n* meubles *mpl* de jardin; **~ garden** *n* patio *m*

patriarch /ˈpeɪtrɪɑːk, US ˈpæt-/ *n* patriarche *m*

patriot /ˈpætrɪət, US ˈpeɪt-/ *n* patriote *mf*

p

patriotic /ˌpætrɪˈɒtɪk, US ˈpeɪt-/ adj [mood, song] patriotique; [person] patriote

patriotism /ˈpætrɪətɪzəm, US ˈpeɪt-/ n patriotisme m

patrol /pəˈtrəʊl/
A n (all contexts) patrouille f; **to carry out a ~** faire une ronde
B noun modifier [helicopter, vehicle] de patrouille
C vtr, vi (p prés etc **-ll-**) patrouiller

patrol: ~ boat, ~ vessel n patrouilleur m; **~ car** n voiture f de police

patrolman /pəˈtrəʊlmən/ ▸ p. 1181 n **1** US (policeman) agent m de police; **2** GB Aut agent d'un service d'assistance routière privé

patrol wagon n US fourgon m cellulaire

patron /ˈpeɪtrən/ n **1** (supporter) (of artist) mécène m; (of person) protecteur/-trice m/f; (of charity) bienfaiteur/-trice m/f; **to be ~ of an organization** parrainer une organisation; **2** (client) client/-e m/f (**of de**)

patronage /ˈpætrənɪdʒ/ n **1** (support) patronage m; **~ of the arts** mécénat m; **2** Pol (right to appoint) droit m de présentation; **political ~** péj copinage m péj

patronize /ˈpætrənaɪz/ vtr **1** péj traiter [qn] avec condescendance; **don't ~ me!** ne prends pas cet air supérieur avec moi!; **2** Comm fréquenter [restaurant, cinema]; se fournir chez [shop]; **3** (support) protéger [charity, the arts]

patronizing /ˈpætrənaɪzɪŋ/ adj péj condescendant

patron saint n saint/-e m/f patron/-onne (**of de**)

patter /ˈpætə(r)/
A n **1** (of rain) crépitement m; **~ of footsteps** bruit m de pas rapides et légers; **we'll soon be hearing the ~ of tiny feet** hum la maison retentira bientôt de rires enfantins; **2** ○(of salesman etc) baratin○ m
B vi [child, mouse] trottiner; [rain, hailstones] crépiter

pattern /ˈpætn/
A n **1** (design) dessin m, motif m; **2** (regular way of happening) **~ of behaviour, behaviour ~** mode m de comportement; **working ~s in industry** l'organisation f du travail dans l'industrie; **the current ~ of events** la situation actuelle; **a clear ~ emerges from these statistics** une tendance nette ressort de ces statistiques; **he could detect a ~ in the plot** il arrivait à discerner une logique dans l'intrigue; **to follow a set ~** se dérouler toujours de la même façon; **traffic ~** distribution f de la circulation; **weather ~s** tendances fpl climatiques; **3** (model) modèle m also Ling; **4** (in dressmaking) patron m; (in knitting) modèle m; **5** (style of manufacture) style m; **6** (sample) échantillon m
B vtr (model) modeler (**on, after** sur)

patterned /ˈpætnd/ adj [fabric etc] à motifs

patty /ˈpætɪ/ n **1** US (in hamburger etc) steak m haché; **2** (pie) petit feuilleté m

paunch /pɔːntʃ/ n (of person) ventre m

pauper /ˈpɔːpə(r)/ n indigent/-e m/f

pause /pɔːz/
A n **1** (brief silence) silence m; **2** (break) pause f (**in** dans; **for** pour); **3** (stoppage) interruption f; **4** Mus point m d'orgue
B vi **1** (stop speaking) marquer une pause; **2** (stop) s'arrêter; **to ~ in** interrompre [activity]; **to ~ for thought** faire une pause pour réfléchir; **3** (hesitate) hésiter

(Phrasal verb)
■ **pause over:** ▸ **~ over [sth]** s'arrêter sur

pave /peɪv/ vtr paver (**with** de)

(Idiom) **to ~ the way for sth** ouvrir la voie à qch

pavement /ˈpeɪvmənt/ n **1** GB (footpath) trottoir m; **2** US (roadway) chaussée f; (road surface) revêtement m (de la chaussée); **3** (paved area) surface f pavée; **4** US (material) dallage m

pavement café n GB ≈ café m avec terrasse

pavilion /pəˈvɪlɪən/ n (all contexts) pavillon m

paving /ˈpeɪvɪŋ/ n **C** dalles fpl

paving slab, paving stone n dalle f

pavlova /pævˈləʊvə, ˌpævˈləʊvə/ n GB gâteau meringué aux fruits

paw /pɔː/
A n (of animal) patte f; péj (hand) patte○ f
B vtr **1** [animal] donner des coups de patte à; **to ~ the ground** [horse] piaffer; [bull] frapper le sol du sabot; **2** péj [person] peloter○

pawn /pɔːn/
A n **1** (in chess) pion m also fig; **2** Comm gage m; **to be in ~** être au mont-de-piété
B vtr mettre [qch] au mont-de-piété

pawn: ~broker ▸ p. 1181 n prêteur/-euse m/f sur gages; **~shop** n mont-de-piété m

pay /peɪ/
A n gen salaire m; (to soldier) solde f; Admin traitement m; **back ~** rappel m de salaire; **extra ~** prime f de salaire; **to be in the ~ of sb** péj être à la solde de qn; **~ and allowances** rémunération principale et indemnités; **the ~ is good** c'est bien payé
B noun modifier [agreement, claim, negotiations, deal] salarial; [rise, cut] de salaire; [freeze, structure, policy] des salaires
C vtr (prét, pp **paid**) **1** (for goods, services) gen payer; verser [down payment]; **to ~ cash** payer comptant; **to ~ £100 on account** verser un acompte de 100 livres; **to ~ sth into** verser qch sur [account]; **to ~ high/low wages** payer bien/mal; **all expenses paid** tous frais payés; **2** Fin (accrue) rapporter [interest]; **to ~ dividends** fig finir par rapporter; **3** (give) **to ~ attention/heed to** faire/prêter attention à; **to ~ a tribute to sb** rendre hommage à qn; **to ~ sb a compliment** faire des compliments à qn; **to ~ sb a visit** rendre visite à qn; **4** (benefit) **it would ~ him/her etc to do** fig il/elle etc y gagnerait à faire; **it doesn't ~ to do** cela ne sert à rien de faire
D vi (prét, pp **paid**) **1** gen payer; **to ~ for sth** payer qch also fig; **I'll make you ~ for this!** fig tu me le paieras!; **they're paying for him to go to college** ils lui paient ses études; **'~ on entry'** 'paiement à l'entrée'; **you have to ~ to get in** l'entrée est payante; **'~ and display'** (in carpark) 'payez et laissez le ticket en évidence'; **~ on demand** (on cheque) payer à vue; **to ~ one's own way** payer sa part; **the work doesn't ~ very well** le travail est mal payé; **2** (bring gain) [business] rapporter; [activity, quality] payer; **to ~ handsomely** rapporter gros; **to ~ for itself** [business, purchase] s'amortir; **to make sth ~** rentabiliser qch

(Idioms) **there'll be hell○ ou the devil to ~** ça va barder○; **to ~ a visit○** euph aller au petit coin○

(Phrasal verbs)
■ **pay back:** ▸ **~ [sb] back** rembourser; **I'll ~ him back for the trick he played on me** je lui revaudrai le tour qu'il m'a joué; ▸ **~ [sth] back, ~ back [sth]** rembourser
■ **pay down:** ▸ **~ [sth] down** verser un acompte de
■ **pay in:** GB ▸ **~ [sth] in, ~ in [sth]** déposer
■ **pay off:** ▸ **~ off** fig être payant; ▸ **~ [sb] off, ~ off [sb] 1** (dismiss) congédier [worker]; **2** ○(buy silence) acheter le silence de; ▸ **~ off [sth], ~ [sth] off** rembourser
■ **pay out:** ▸ **~ out [sth] 1** (hand over) débourser (**in** pour); **he paid out £300 for his new washing machine** il a payé 300 livres sa nouvelle machine à laver; **2** (release) laisser filer [rope]
■ **pay up○:** ▸ **~ up** payer

payable /ˈpeɪəbl/ adj **1** (which will be paid) à payer; **to make a cheque ~ to** faire un chèque à l'ordre de; **2** (requiring payment) **to be ~** être payable; **~ on demand** payable à vue; **3** (may be paid) payable; **4** (profitable) rentable

pay: ~-as-you-earn, PAYE n GB (tax) prélèvement m de l'impôt à la source; **~back** (of debt) remboursement m; **~ channel** n TV chaîne f payante or à péage; **~ cheque** GB, **~ check** US n chèque m de paie; **~day** n (for wages) jour m de paie; (in Stock Exchange) séance f de liquidation; **~desk** n caisse f

PAYE n GB abrév ▸ **pay-as-you-earn**

payee /peɪˈiː/ n bénéficiaire mf

payer /ˈpeɪə(r)/ n gen payeur/-euse m/f

pay gate n tourniquet m

paying /ˈpeɪɪŋ/ adj [proposition] rentable

paying: ~ guest n hôte m payant; **~-in slip** GB, **~-in deposit slip** US n bordereau m de versement

payload /ˈpeɪləʊd/ n **1** (of aircraft, ship) passagers et fret mpl; **2** (of bomb) charge f explosive

paymaster /ˈpeɪmɑːstə(r), US -mæstər/ n **1** gen caissier m; Naut commissaire m; Mil trésorier m; **2** péj (employer) commanditaire m

payment /ˈpeɪmənt/ n gen paiement m; (in settlement) règlement m; (into account, of instalments) versement m; (to creditor) remboursement m; fig (for help) récompense f also iron; **cash ~** (not credit) paiement comptant; (not cheque) paiement en liquide; **~ in full is now requested** un règlement complet est désormais exigé; **in monthly ~s of £30** en mensualités de 30 livres sterling; **~ on** (instalment) traite de [*television, washing machine etc*]; **on ~ of £30** moyennant 30 livres sterling; **Social Security ~s** prestations *fpl* de la Sécurité sociale

pay: **~off** *n* (reward) récompense *f*; fig bouquet *m*; **~-packet** *n* enveloppe *f* de paie; fig paie *f*; **~ phone** *n* téléphone *m* public

payroll /ˈpeɪrəʊl/ *n* (list) fichier *m* des salaires; (sum of money) paie *f* (de tous les employés); (employees collectively) ensemble *m* du personnel; **to be on a company's ~** être employé par une entreprise; **to take sb off the ~** licencier qn; **a ~ of 500 workers** un effectif de 500 ouvriers

payslip *n* bulletin *m* de salaire

pc *n* ① (also **PC**) abrév ▸ **personal computer**; ② abrév ▸ **per cent**; ③ abrév ▸ **postcard**; ④ (also **PC**) abrév ▸ **politically correct**

PC *n* GB abrév ▸ **Police Constable**

pd (abrév = **paid**) payé

PD *n* US abrév ▸ **Police Department**

PDA *n*: abrév ▸ **personal digital assistant**

PDO *n* (abrév = **protected designation of origin**) appellation *f* d'origine protégée, AOP *f*

PDQ machine *n* TPV *m*, terminal *m* point de vente

PE *n*: abrév ▸ **physical education**

pea /piː/ *n* ① Bot pois *m*; ② Culin (also **green ~**) petit pois *m*

peace /piːs/
Ⓐ *n* (all contexts) paix *f*; **to be at ~** (free from war) être en paix; (dead) avoir trouvé la paix; **to keep the ~** (between countries, individuals) maintenir la paix; (in town) [*police*] maintenir l'ordre public; [*citizen*] ne pas troubler l'ordre public; **I need a bit of ~ and quiet** j'ai besoin d'un peu de calme; **to find ~ of mind** trouver la paix
Ⓑ *noun modifier* [*plan, talks*] de paix; [*campaign, march, moves*] pour la paix

(Idioms) **to hold one's ~** rester muet; **to make one's ~ with sb** faire la paix avec qn

peaceable /ˈpiːsəbl/ *adj* [*person*] pacifique

peace: **~ campaigner** *n* militant/-e *m/f* pacifiste; **Peace Corps** *n* US Admin organisation composée de volontaires pour l'aide aux pays en voie de développement; **~ envoy** *n* négociateur/-trice *m/f* de paix

peaceful /ˈpiːsfl/ *adj* ① (tranquil) paisible; ② (without conflict) pacifique

peacefully /ˈpiːsfəlɪ/ *adv* ① (without disturbance) [*sleep*] paisiblement; [*situated*] à un endroit paisible; ② (without violence) pacifiquement

peacekeeping /ˈpiːskiːpɪŋ/
Ⓐ *n* Mil, Pol maintien *m* de la paix
Ⓑ *noun modifier* [*force, troops*] de maintien de la paix

peace: **~-loving** *adj* pacifique; **~maker** *n* Pol artisan *m* de la paix; (in family) conciliateur *m*; **~ offering** *n* gage *m* de réconciliation; **~ pipe** *n* calumet *m* de la paix; **~ process** *n* Pol processus *m* de paix

peacetime /ˈpiːstaɪm/
Ⓐ *n* temps *m* de paix
Ⓑ *noun modifier* [*army, alliance, training*] en temps de paix; [*planning, government*] de temps de paix

peach /piːtʃ/
Ⓐ *n* ① (fruit, colour) pêche *f*; (tree) pêcher *m*; ② ○**a ~ of a game**○ un match formidable
Ⓑ *noun modifier* [*jam, yoghurt*] aux pêches; [*stone*] de pêche

peacock /ˈpiːkɒk/ *n* paon *m*

peacock: **~ blue** ▸ p. 752 *n*, adj bleu (*m*) canard *inv*; **~ butterfly** *n* paon *m* de jour

peak /piːk/
Ⓐ *n* ① (of mountain) pic *m* (of de); ② (of cap) visière *f*; ③ (of inflation, demand, price) maximum *m* (**in** dans; **of** de); (on a graph) sommet *m*; ④ (high point) (of career, empire, creativity) apogée *m* (**of** de); (of fitness, form) meilleur *m* (**of** de); **in the ~ of condition** en excellente santé; **to be past its** ou **one's ~** avoir fait son temps; ⑤ (busiest time) gen heure *f* de pointe; Telecom heures *fpl* rouges
Ⓑ *noun modifier* [*figure, level, price, risk*] maximum; [*fitness, form, performance*] meilleur
Ⓒ *vi* lit, fig culminer (**at** à); **to ~ too early** [*runner*] se lancer

trop tôt; [*prodigy*] s'épanouir trop tôt; (in career) réussir trop tôt

(Phrasal verb)
■ **peak out**○ [*athlete, prowess, skill, luck*] commencer à décliner; [*inflation, rate*] commencer à décroître

peak demand *n* gen demande *f* record; Elec période *f* de consommation de pointe

peaked /piːkt/ *adj* ① [*cap, hat*] à visière; [*roof*] pointu; ② US = **peaky**

peak: **~ period** *n* période *f* de pointe; **~ rate** *n* Telecom tarif *m* rouge; **~ season** *n* haute saison *f*; **~ time** *n* (on TV) heures *fpl* de grande écoute; (for switchboard, traffic) heures *fpl* de pointe

peaky○ /ˈpiːkɪ/ *adj* pâlot/-otte

peal /piːl/ *n* (of bells) carillonnement *m*; (of doorbell) sonnerie *f*; (of thunder) grondement *m*; (of organ) retentissement *m*; **~s of laughter** éclats *mpl* de rire

(Phrasal verb)
■ **peal out** [*bells*] carillonner; [*thunder*] gronder; [*organ*] retentir; [*laughter*] éclater

peanut /ˈpiːnʌt/
Ⓐ *n* (nut) cacahuète *f*; (plant) arachide *f*
Ⓑ **peanuts**○ *npl* clopinettes○ *fpl*

peanut: **~ butter** *n* beurre *m* de cacahuètes; **~ oil** *n* huile *f* d'arachide

pear /peə(r)/ *n* (fruit) poire *f*; (tree) poirier *m*

(Idiom) **to go ~-shaped**○ foirer●

pearl /pɜːl/ ▸ p. 752
Ⓐ *n* ① lit, fig perle *f* (**of** de); (city, building) joyau *m*; **~s of wisdom** trésors *mpl* de sagesse; ② (colour) (couleur *f*) perle *f*
Ⓑ *noun modifier* [*necklace, brooch etc*] de perles; [*button*] en nacre

pearl: **~ barley** *n* orge *m* perlé; **~ diver** *n* pêcheur/-euse *m/f* de perles; **~ grey** ▸ p. 752 *n*, adj gris (*m*) perle *inv*

pearly /ˈpɜːlɪ/ *adj* nacré

Pearly Gates *npl* the **~** hum les portes *fpl* du Paradis

peasant /ˈpeznt/
Ⓐ *n* aussi péj paysan/-anne *m/f*
Ⓑ *noun modifier* [*class, custom, cuisine, craft, life*] paysan/-anne; [*costume*] de paysan/-anne

peat /piːt/ *n* (substance) tourbe *f*

pebble /ˈpebl/ *n* caillou *m*; (on beach) galet *m*

pebbledash /ˈpebldæʃ/ *n* crépi *m*, mouchetis *m*

pecan /ˈpiːkən, pɪˈkæn, US pɪˈkɑːn/ *n* ① (nut) noix *f* de pécan; ② (tree) pacanier *m*

peck /pek/
Ⓐ *n* ① (from bird) coup *m* de bec; ② ○(kiss) bise *f*
Ⓑ *vtr* [*bird*] picorer [*food*]; donner un coup de bec à [*person, animal*]; **to ~ a hole in sth** faire un trou dans qch à (force de) coups de bec
Ⓒ *vi* ① (with beak) **to ~ at** picorer [*food*]; donner des coups de bec contre [*window, tree*]; ② ○fig **to ~ at one's food** chipoter

(Phrasal verb)
■ **peck out**: ▸ **~ [sth] out**, **~ out [sth]** arracher [qch] à coups de bec [*kernel, seeds*]

pecking order *n* lit, fig ordre *m* hiérarchique

peckish○ /ˈpekɪʃ/ *adj* GB **to be** ou **feel ~** avoir un petit creux○

pectoral /ˈpektərəl/
Ⓐ **pectorals** *npl* (also **pecs**○) pectoraux *mpl*
Ⓑ *adj* pectoral

peculiar /pɪˈkjuːlɪə(r)/ *adj* ① (odd) bizarre; **to feel ~** se sentir bizarre; **funny ~**○ hum bizarre; ② (exceptional) situation, circumstances] particulier/-ière; ③ (exclusive to) particulier/-ière; **to be ~ to** [*feature, trait*] être particulier/-ière à ou propre à

peculiarity /pɪˌkjuːlɪˈærətɪ/ *n* ① (feature) particularité *f*; ② (strangeness) bizarrerie *f*

peculiarly /pɪˈkjuːlɪəlɪ/ *adv* ① (strangely) de façon étrange; ② (particularly) particulièrement

pecuniary /pɪˈkjuːnɪərɪ, US -erɪ/ *adj* pécuniaire

pedagogic(al) /ˌpedəˈgɒdʒɪkl/ *adj* pédagogique

pedal /ˈpedl/
Ⓐ *n* (all contexts) pédale *f*

p

B vtr (p prés etc -ll- GB, -l- US) to ~ a bicycle pédaler
C vi (p prés etc -ll- GB, -l- US) 1 (use pedal) pédaler; to ~ hard pédaler dur; 2 (cycle) to ~ down/through descendre/traverser à vélo

pedal: ~ bin n GB poubelle f à pédale; ~ boat n pédalo® m; ~ cycle n bicyclette f; ~ pushers npl (pantalon m) corsaire m

pedantic /pɪ'dæntɪk/ adj pédant

pedantry /'pedntrɪ/ n pédantisme m

peddle /'pedl/ vtr colporter [wares, ideas]; to ~ drugs faire du trafic de drogue (à petite échelle)

peddler /'pedlə(r)/ n 1 (street vendor) colporteur m; 2 drug ~ trafiquant m

pedestal /'pedɪstl/ n (of statue, ornament) socle m, piédestal m; (of washbasin) colonne f
(Idioms) to put sb on a ~ mettre qn sur un piédestal; to knock sb off their ~ détrôner qn

pedestrian /pɪ'destrɪən/ n
A n piéton m
B noun modifier [street, area] piétonnier/-ière, piéton/-onne
C adj (humdrum) terre à terre inv

pedestrian: ~ crossing n passage m pour piétons; ~ precinct n GB zone f piétonne

pediatric /ˌpiːdɪ'ætrɪk/ adj [ward] de pédiatrie; [illness] infantile; ~ nursing puériculture f

pediatrician /ˌpiːdɪə'trɪʃn/ ▸ p. 1181 n pédiatre mf

pediatrics /ˌpiːdɪ'ætrɪks/ n (+ v sg) pédiatrie f

pedicure /'pedɪkjʊə(r)/ n to have a ~ se faire soigner les pieds

pedigree /'pedɪgriː/
A n 1 (ancestry) (of animal) pedigree m; (of person, family) (line) ascendance f; (tree, chart) arbre m généalogique; (background) origines fpl; 2 (purebred animal) animal m avec pedigree; 3 fig (of sportsman, artist) antécédents mpl
B noun modifier [animal] de pure race

pediment /'pedɪmənt/ n fronton m

pedlar n = peddler 1

pee○ /piː/ n pipi○ m; to have ou do a ~ faire pipi○

peek /piːk/
A n to have a ~ at jeter un coup d'œil furtif à
B vi jeter un coup d'œil furtif (at à, sur)

peekaboo /ˌpiːkə'buː/ excl coucou!

peel /piːl/
A n (before peeling) peau f; (after peeling) épluchures fpl
B vtr éplucher [carrot etc]; décortiquer [prawn]; écorcer [stick]
C vi [skin] peler; [fruit, vegetable] s'éplucher
(Phrasal verb)
■ peel off: ▸ ~ off [label] se détacher (from de); [paint] s'écailler; [paper] se décoller; ▸ ~ off [sth], ~ [sth] off enlever [clothing, label, leaves]

peeler /'piːlə(r)/ n (manual) économe m; (electric) éplucheur m électrique; potato ~ épluche-légumes m inv

peeling /'piːlɪŋ/
A peelings npl épluchures fpl
B adj [walls, paint] qui s'écaille; [skin] qui pèle

peep /piːp/
A n 1 (look) (quick) coup m d'œil; to have a ~ at sth jeter un coup d'œil à qch; (furtively) regarder qch à la dérobée; 2 (noise) (of chick) pépiement m; there wasn't a ~ out of him il n'a pas pipé mot
B vi 1 (look) jeter un coup d'œil (over par-dessus; through par); to ~ at sth/sb gen jeter un coup d'œil à qch/qn; (furtively) regarder qch/qn furtivement; 2 (make noise) [chick] pépier
(Phrasal verb)
■ peep out [person, animal] se montrer, apparaître; [gun, hanky] dépasser (of de)

peep: ~hole /'piːphəʊl/ n gen trou m; (in door) judas m; Peeping Tom○ n voyeur m

peer /pɪə(r)/
A n 1 (equal) (in status) pair m also GB Pol; (in profession) collègue m/f; 2 (contemporary) (adult) personne f de la même génération; (teenager) adolescent/-e m/f du même âge; (child) enfant mf du même âge; 3 (person of equal merit) égal/-e m/f
B vi to ~ at regarder (fixement); to ~ shortsightedly at sth regarder qch avec des yeux de myope

peerage /'pɪərɪdʒ/ n 1 GB Pol pairie f; to be given a ~ être anobli; 2 (book) nobiliaire m

peer group n 1 (of same status) pairs mpl; 2 (contemporary) (adults) personnes fpl de la même génération; (children) enfants mpl du même âge

peer group pressure n pression f du groupe

peerless /'pɪəlɪs/ adj hors pair inv

peeved○ /piːvd/ adj [person, expression] irrité

peevish /'piːvɪʃ/ adj grognon/-onne

peg /peg/
A n 1 (to hang garment) patère f; 2 GB (also clothes ~) pince f à linge; 3 (to mark place) piquet m; 4 (in carpentry, music) cheville f; 5 Econ indice m; 6 (barrel stop) fausset m
B vtr (p prés etc -gg-) 1 (fasten cloth) to ~ sth on ou onto a line accrocher qch sur une corde avec des pinces; to ~ sth down ou in place fixer qch avec des piquets; 2 (fasten wood) cheviller (to à; together ensemble); 3 Econ indexer (to sur); to ~ sth at 10% indexer qch à 10%; 4 US (characterize) cataloguer
(Idioms) to be a square ~ (in a round hole) ne pas être dans son élément; to take ou bring sb down a ~ (or two)○ remettre qn à sa place
(Phrasal verb)
■ peg away○ travailler ferme, bosser○ (at sur)

pegboard /'pegbɔːd/ n panneau m alvéolé

pejorative /pɪ'dʒɒrətɪv, US -'dʒɔːr-/ adj péjoratif/-ive

Pekin(g)ese /ˌpiːkɪ'niːz/ ▸ p. 969 n pékinois m

Peking /ˌpiː'kɪŋ/ ▸ p. 1276 pr n Pékin f

pelican /'pelɪkən/ n pélican m

pelican crossing n GB passage m pour piétons

pellet /'pelɪt/ n 1 (of paper, wax, mud) boulette f; 2 (of shot) plomb m; 3 Agric granulé m

pell-mell /ˌpel'mel/ adv pêle-mêle

pelmet /'pelmɪt/ n cantonnière f

pelt /pelt/
A n (fur) fourrure f; (hide) peau f
B at full pelt adv phr à toute vitesse
C vtr bombarder; to ~ sb with sth lancer une volée de qch à qn
D vi 1 (also ~ down) tomber à verse; the ~ing rain la pluie battante; 2 ○(run) courir à toutes jambes; to ~ down the road descendre la rue à toutes jambes

pelvis /'pelvɪs/ ▸ p. 698 n bassin m, pelvis m spec

pen /pen/
A n 1 (for writing) stylo m; to run one's ~ through sth barrer qch; to put ~ to paper (write) écrire, prendre la plume; (give signature) signer; 2 (for animals) parc m, enclos m; 3 Zool cygne m femelle; 4 ○US (prison) taule○ f, prison f
B vtr (p prés etc -nn-) 1 (write) écrire; 2 (also ~ in) enfermer, parquer

penal /'piːnl/ adj [reform, law, code, system] pénal; [colony, institution] pénitentiaire; ~ servitude Hist travaux mpl forcés

penalize /'piːnəlaɪz/ vtr pénaliser

penalty /'penltɪ/ n 1 Jur, gen (punishment) peine f, pénalité f; (fine) amende f; on ~ of sous peine de; 2 fig (unpleasant result) prix m (for de); 3 Sport (in soccer) penalty m; (in rugby) pénalité f; to take a ~ tirer un penalty; 4 Games amende f

penalty: ~ area n Sport surface f de réparation; ~ clause n Comm, Jur clause f pénale; ~ goal n (in rugby) but m sur pénalité; ~ kick n (in rugby) coup m de pied de pénalité; (in soccer) penalty m

penance /'penəns/ n gen, Relig pénitence f

pence /pens/ npl GB ▸ penny

penchant /'pɑːnʃɑːn, US 'pentʃənt/ n penchant m; to have a ~ for doing avoir tendance f à faire

pencil /'pensl/
A n crayon m; in ~ au crayon
B vtr (p prés etc -ll- GB, -l- US) écrire [qch] au crayon
(Phrasal verb)
■ pencil in: ▸ ~ [sth] in, ~ in [sth] lit écrire [qch] au crayon; let's ~ in the second of May disons le deux mai pour l'instant

pencil: ~ case n trousse f (à crayons); ~ pusher○ n US péj gratte-papier m inv péj; ~ sharpener n taille-crayon m

pendant /'pendənt/ n ☐1 (necklace) pendentif m; ☐2 (bauble) pendeloque f

pending /'pendɪŋ/
A adj ☐1 Jur [case, charge] en instance; gen [matter] en souffrance; **patent** ∼ modèle m déposé; ☐2 (imminent) imminent
B prep en attendant

pending tray n corbeille f des affaires en souffrance

pendulum /'pendjʊləm, US -dʒʊləm/ n pendule m, balancier m

penetrate /'penɪtreɪt/
A vtr ☐1 (enter into or through) pénétrer [protective layer, territory, surface]; percer [cloud, silence, defences]; traverser [wall]; ☐2 fig (permeate) pénétrer [market, mind, ideas]; [spy] infiltrer [organization]; ☐3 (understand) percer [disguise, mystery]
B vi ☐1 (enter) pénétrer (**into** dans; **as far as** jusqu'à); ☐2 [sound] parvenir (**to** à); **nothing I say seems to** ∼ j'ai l'impression de parler à un mur

penetrating /'penɪtreɪtɪŋ/ adj ☐1 (invasive) [cold, eyes, wind] pénétrant; [sound, voice] perçant; ☐2 (perceptive) [analysis, question] pénétrant

penetratingly /'penɪtreɪtɪŋlɪ/ adv ☐1 (loudly) d'une voix pénétrante; ☐2 (perceptively) avec pénétration

penetration /,penɪ'treɪʃn/ n ☐1 (entering) pénétration f; (by spies) infiltration f; ☐2 (insight) perspicacité f

pen friend n correspondant/-e m/f

penguin /'peŋgwɪn/ n pingouin m, manchot m

penicillin /,penɪ'sɪlɪn/ n pénicilline f

peninsula /pə'nɪnsjʊlə, US -nsələ/ n péninsule f

penis /'piːnɪs/ n pénis m

penitence /'penɪtəns/ n gen, Relig pénitence f

penitent /'penɪtənt/ n, adj pénitent/-e (m/f)

penitentiary /,penɪ'tenʃərɪ/ n US prison f

pen: ∼**knife** n canif m; ∼**manship** n calligraphie f; ∼ **name** n pseudonyme m, nom m de plume

pennant /'penənt/ n ☐1 (flag) (on boat) flamme f; (in competition, procession, on car) fanion m; ☐2 US Sport championnat m

penniless /'penɪlɪs/ adj sans le sou, sans ressources

penny /'penɪ/ n ☐1 (pl **pennies**) (small amount of money) ≈ centime m; **when he died she didn't get a** ∼ quand il est mort elle n'a pas eu un sou; **not to have a** ∼ **to one's name** être sans le sou; ☐2 GB (pl **pence** ou **pennies**) (unit of currency) penny m; **a five pence** ou **five p piece** une pièce de cinq pence; **a 25 pence** ou **25p stamp** un timbre-poste à 25 pence; ☐3 US (pl **pennies**) cent m

Idioms **a** ∼ **for your thoughts** ou **for them**○ à quoi penses-tu?; **a pretty** ∼○ une jolie somme; **in for a** ∼ **in for a pound** lorsque le vin est tiré, il faut le boire; **take care of the pennies and the pounds will take care of themselves** Prov il n'y a pas de petites économies; **the** ∼ **dropped**○ ça a fait tilt○; **they are ten a** ∼ on les ramasse à la pelle○; **to spend a** ∼○ GB euph aller au petit coin euph; **to turn up like a bad** ∼ revenir continuellement.

⚠ Le pluriel de penny est pence pour une somme spécifique: 10 pence, 24 pence. À l'oral et à l'écrit on utilise souvent l'abréviation p: 47p, 1p. Le pluriel de penny est pennies pour les pièces en tant qu'objets comptables: a bag of pennies

penny: ∼**-farthing** n grand bi m; ∼**-pinching** adj grippe-sou inv; ∼ **whistle** n flûteau m

pen: ∼ **pal**○ n correspondant/-e m/f; ∼ **pusher**○ n péj gratte-papier○ m inv péj

pension /'penʃn/ n ☐1 (from state) pension f; **to be** ou **live on a** ∼ être pensionné; **old age** ∼ pension f de retraite; ☐2 (from employer) retraite f; **company** ∼ retraite f de société; ☐3 (hotel) pension f

pensionable /'penʃənəbl/ adj [post, service] donnant droit à la retraite; [employee] ayant droit à la retraite

pensioner /'penʃənə(r)/ n retraité/-e m/f

pension: ∼ **fund** n fonds m d'assurance-vieillesse; ∼ **plan**, ∼ **scheme** n plan m de retraite; ∼ **rights** npl droit m à une retraite complémentaire

pensive /'pensɪv/ adj songeur/-euse, pensif/-ive

pentagon /'pentəgən, US -gɒn/ n ☐1 Math pentagone m; ☐2 **Pentagon** US Pol **the** ∼ le Pentagone m

ℹ **Pentagon** Grand bâtiment pentagonal situé à Arlington (Virginie), qui abrite le ministère de la défense américain. Par extension ce mot est employé dans les médias pour désigner tout l'état-major américain.

pentathlon /pen'tæθlən, -lɒn/ n pentathlon m

Pentecost /'pentɪkɒst, US -kɔːst/ n Pentecôte f

penthouse /'penthaʊs/
A n ☐1 (flat) appartement m de grand standing (construit au dernier étage d'un immeuble); ☐2 (roof) auvent m
B noun modifier [accommodation, suite] de grand standing

pent-up /pent'ʌp/ adj [energy, frustration] contenu; [feelings] réprimé

penultimate /pen'ʌltɪmət/ adj avant-dernier/-ière

penury /'penjʊrɪ/ n indigence f

peony /'piːənɪ/ n pivoine f

people /'piːpl/
A n (nation) peuple m, peuplade f; **the English-speaking** ∼s les anglophones mpl
B npl ☐1 (in general) gens mpl; (specified or counted) personnes fpl; **old** ∼ les personnes âgées; **they're nice** ∼ ce sont des gens sympathiques; **there were a lot of** ∼ il y avait beaucoup de monde; **other** ∼ **say that...** d'autres disent que...; **other** ∼**'s property** la propriété des autres; **he likes helping** ∼ il aime aider les autres; **you shouldn't do that in front of** ∼ tu ne devrais pas faire ça en public; ∼ **in general** le grand public; **what do you** ∼ **want?** que voulez-vous?; **you of all** ∼**!** je n'aurais jamais pensé ça de toi!; **you of all** ∼ **should know that...** tu devrais savoir encore mieux que les autres que...; ☐2 (inhabitants) (of town) habitants mpl; (of a country) peuple m; ☐3 (citizens, subjects) **the** ∼ le peuple; **a man of the** ∼ un homme du peuple; ☐4 ○(experts) gens○ mpl; **the tax** ∼ les gens○ des impôts; ☐5 ○(relations) famille f; (parents) parents mpl.

⚠ gens is masculine plural and never countable (you CANNOT say 'trois gens'). When used with gens, some adjectives such as vieux, bon, mauvais, petit, vilain placed before gens take the feminine form: les vieilles gens

people: ∼ **mover** n US tapis m roulant; ∼**'s democracy** n démocratie f populaire; **People's Republic of China** ▸ p. 774 pr n République f populaire de Chine

pep /pep/ v
■ **pep up**: ▸ ∼ **up** [person] retrouver des forces; [business] reprendre; ▸ ∼ **[sb/sth] up**, ∼ **up [sb/sth]** remettre [qn] d'aplomb [person]; animer [party, team]

pepper /'pepə(r)/
A n ☐1 (spice) poivre m; **black/white** ∼ poivre noir/blanc; ☐2 (vegetable) poivron m
B vtr ☐1 lit poivrer [food]; ☐2 fig **to be** ∼**ed with** être parsemé de [swearwords, criticisms]; ☐3 (fire at) cribler (**with** de)

pepper: ∼**-and-salt** adj [hair] poivre et sel; [material] chiné noir et blanc; ∼**corn** n grain m de poivre; ∼ **mill** n moulin m à poivre

peppermint /'pepəmɪnt/
A n ☐1 (sweet) pastille f de menthe; ☐2 (plant) menthe f poivrée
B noun modifier (also ∼**-flavoured**) à la menthe

pepper pot, **pepper shaker** n poivrier m

peppery /'pepərɪ/ adj ☐1 (spicy) poivré; ☐2 (irritable) irascible

pep: ∼ **pill**○ n excitant m; ∼ **talk**○ n laïus○ m d'encouragement

peptic /'peptɪk/ adj gen digestif/-ive; ∼ **ulcer** ulcère m de l'estomac

per /pɜː(r)/ prep ☐1 (for each) par; ∼ **head** par tête or personne; ∼ **annum** par an; **80 km** ∼ **hour** 80 km à l'heure; **£5** ∼ **hour** 5 livres (de) l'heure; **revolutions** ∼ **minute** tours-minute; **as** ∼ **usual**○ comme d'habitude; ☐2 (by means of) ∼ **post** par la poste; ☐3 Comm **as** ∼ **invoice** suivant facture; **as** ∼ **your instructions** conformément à vos instructions

per capita adj, adv par habitant

perceive /pə'siːv/
A vtr percevoir; **to** ∼ **oneself as (being) sth** se percevoir comme qch
B **perceived** pp adj [need, success] perçu/-e comme tel/telle

per cent, pc /pə'sent/
A *n* pour-cent *m*
B *adv* pour cent

percentage /pə'sentɪdʒ/
A *n* pourcentage *m*; **to get a ∼ on** toucher un pourcentage sur [*sale*]
B *noun modifier* [*increase, decrease, change*] en pourcentage

perceptible /pə'septəbl/ *adj* perceptible (**to** à)

perceptibly /pə'septəblɪ/ *adv* sensiblement

perception /pə'sepʃn/ *n* [1] Philos, Psych perception *f*; [2] (view) **my ∼ of him** l'idée que je me fais de lui; **the popular ∼ of** l'idée que les gens se font de; [3] (also **perceptiveness**) (of person) perspicacité *f*; (of essay, novel) finesse *f*; [4] Comm, Fin perception *f*

perceptive /pə'septɪv/ *adj* [1] [*person*] perspicace; [*study*] pertinent; [*comedy*] spirituel/-elle; [2] Psych perceptif/-ive

perceptively /pə'septɪvlɪ/ *adv* avec perspicacité

perch /pɜːtʃ/
A *n* [1] (for bird) perchoir *m*; [2] fig (vantage point) position *f* élevée; [3] (fish) perche *f*
B *vtr* percher
C *vi* se percher (**on** sur)
(Idiom) **to knock sb off their ∼**○ détrôner qn

percolate /'pɜːkəleɪt/
A *vtr* **∼d coffee** café fait dans une cafetière à pression
B *vi* (also **∼ through**) [*coffee*] passer; [*water*] passer, filtrer; [*information*] filtrer (**into, to** jusqu'à)

percolator /'pɜːkəleɪtə(r)/ *n* cafetière *f* à pression

percussion /pə'kʌʃn/ *n* ₵ Mus percussions *fpl*

percussionist /pə'kʌʃənɪst/ *n* percussionniste *mf*

peremptory /pə'remptərɪ, US 'perəmptɔːrɪ/ *adj* péremptoire

perennial /pə'renɪəl/
A *n* plante *f* vivace; **hardy ∼** plante *f* vivace
B *adj* [1] (recurring) perpétuel/-elle; [2] Bot [*plant*] vivace

perfect
A /'pɜːfɪkt/ *n* Ling parfait *m*; **in the ∼** au parfait
B /'pɜːfɪkt/ *adj* [1] (flawless) gen parfait (**for** pour); [*choice, holiday, moment, name, opportunity, place, partner, solution*] idéal (**for** pour); [*hostess*] exemplaire; **that screw will be ∼ for the job** cette vis fera parfaitement l'affaire; **that jacket is a ∼ fit** cette veste va parfaitement; **to do sth with ∼ timing** faire qch au bon moment; [2] (total) [*stranger, fool*] parfait (*before n*); [*pest*] véritable (*before n*); [3] Ling **the ∼ tense** le parfait
C /pə'fekt/ *vtr* perfectionner

perfection /pə'fekʃn/ *n* perfection *f* (**of** de); **to ∼** à la perfection

perfectionist /pə'fekʃənɪst/ *n, adj* perfectionniste (*mf*)

perfective /pə'fektɪv/ *n* Ling (verb) verbe *m* perfectif

perfectly /'pɜːfɪktlɪ/ *adv* [1] (totally) gen tout à fait; **to be ∼ entitled to do** avoir parfaitement le droit de faire; [2] (very well) [*fit, illustrate*] parfaitement

perfidious /pə'fɪdɪəs/ *adj* perfide

perforate /'pɜːfəreɪt/ *vtr* perforer

perform /pə'fɔːm/
A *vtr* [1] (carry out) exécuter [*task*]; accomplir [*duties*]; procéder à [*operation*]; [2] (for entertainment) jouer [*play*]; chanter [*song*]; exécuter [*dance, trick*]; [3] (enact) célébrer [*ceremony*]
B *vi* [1] [*actor, musician*] jouer; [2] (conduct oneself) **to ∼ well/badly** [*team*] bien/mal jouer; [*interviewee*] faire bonne/mauvaise impression; [*exam candidate*] avoir de bons/de mauvais résultats; [3] Comm, Fin [*company, department*] avoir de bons résultats; **sterling ∼ed badly** la livre sterling a baissé

performance /pə'fɔːməns/ *n* [1] (rendition) interprétation *f* (**of** de); [2] (concert, show, play) représentation *f* (**of** de); **to put on a ∼** monter un spectacle; [3] (of team, sportsman) performance *f* (**in** à); [4] ₵ (economic, political record) performances *fpl*; [5] (of duties) exercice *m* (**of** de); (of rite) célébration *f* (**of** de); (of task) exécution *f* (**of** de); [6] ₵ Aut (of car, engine) performances *fpl*; [7] ○ (outburst) scène *f*; (elaborate procedure) affaire *f*; [8] Art art *m* vivant

performance: **∼ artist** ▸ p. 1181 *n* artiste *mf* de performances; **∼-enhancing drug** *n* Med, Sport substance *f* dopante; **∼ indicators** *npl* tableau *m* de bord

performer /pə'fɔːmə(r)/ *n* [1] (artist) artiste *mf*; [2] (achiever) **the car is a good ∼ on hilly terrain** la voiture se comporte bien en terrain vallonné

performing /pə'fɔːmɪŋ/ *adj* [*seal, elephant*] savant

performing arts *npl* arts *mpl* scéniques

perfume /'pɜːfjuːm, US pər'fjuːm/
A *n* parfum *m*
B *vtr* parfumer

perfunctory /pə'fʌŋktərɪ, US -tɔːrɪ/ *adj* [*search, greeting*] pour la forme; [*kiss, nod*] sans conviction; [*investigation*] sommaire

perhaps /pə'hæps/ *adv* peut-être; **∼ she's forgotten** elle a peut-être oublié

peril /'perəl/ *n* péril *m*, danger *m*

perilous /'perələs/ *adj* périlleux/-euse

perilously /'perələslɪ/ *adv* dangereusement; **he came ∼ close to doing** il a failli faire

perimeter /pə'rɪmɪtə(r)/ *n* périmètre *m*; **on the ∼ of** aux abords de [*park, site*]

perimeter fence *n* clôture *f* grillagée

perineum /ˌperɪ'niːəm/ *n* (*pl* **-nea**) périnée *m*

period /'pɪərɪəd/
A *n* [1] gen, Art, Geog, Hist période *f*; (longer) époque *f*; **trial ∼** période d'essai; **bright ∼s** Meteorol éclaircies *fpl*; **rainy ∼s** Meteorol averses *fpl*; **over a two-year ∼** en deux ans; **for a long ∼** pendant longtemps; [2] US (full stop) lit, fig point *m*; [3] (menstruation) règles *fpl*; [4] Sch (lesson) cours *m*, leçon *f*; **a double ∼ of French** deux cours de français à la suite; **to have a free ∼** ≈ avoir une heure de libre; [5] Sport période *f* de jeu
B *noun modifier* (of a certain era) [*costume, furniture, instrument*] d'époque; (reproduction) [*costume, instrument*] caractéristique de l'époque; [*furniture*] de style (ancien)

periodic /ˌpɪərɪ'ɒdɪk/ *adj* périodique

periodical /ˌpɪərɪ'ɒdɪkl/ *n, adj* périodique (*m*)

periodically /ˌpɪərɪ'ɒdɪklɪ/ *adv* périodiquement

periodic: **∼ law** *n* principe *m* de classification périodique des éléments chimiques; **∼ table** *n* tableau *m* de classification périodique des éléments

period: **∼ of office** *n* Pol, Admin mandat *m*; **∼ pains** *npl* règles *fpl* douloureuses; **∼ piece** *n* curiosité *f* d'époque

peripheral /pə'rɪfərəl/ *adj* [*equipment, vision, suburb*] périphérique; [*issue, investment*] annexe; **to be ∼ to** être secondaire par rapport à

periphery /pə'rɪfərɪ/ *n* [1] (edge) périphérie *f*; [2] fig (fringes) **to be on the ∼ of** être dans la mouvance de [*party*]; **to remain on the ∼ of** rester à l'écart de [*event, movement*]

periscope /'perɪskəʊp/ *n* périscope *m*

perish /'perɪʃ/ *vi* [1] littér (die) périr (**from** de); **to do sth or ∼ in the attempt** hum faire qch coûte que coûte; **∼ the thought!** le Ciel nous en préserve!; [2] (rot) [*food*] se gâter; [*rubber*] se détériorer

perishable /'perɪʃəbl/ *adj* périssable

perished○ /'perɪʃt/ *adj* **to be ∼** [*person*] être gelé○

peritonitis /ˌperɪtə'naɪtɪs/ ▸ p. 933 *n* péritonite *f*

periwinkle /'perɪwɪŋkl/ *n* [1] Bot pervenche *f*; [2] Zool bigorneau *m*; [3] ▸ p. 752 (also **∼ blue**) bleu *m* pervenche

perjure /'pɜːdʒə(r)/ *v refl* **to ∼ oneself** Jur faire un faux témoignage; (morally) se parjurer

perjury /'pɜːdʒərɪ/ *n* Jur faux témoignage *m*

perk○ /pɜːk/ *n* gen avantage *m*; (benefit in kind) avantage *m* en nature
(Phrasal verb)
■ **perk up:** ▸ **∼ up** [*person*] se ragaillardir; [*business, life, plant*] reprendre; [*weather*] s'adoucir; ▸ **∼ [sth] up, ∼ up [sth]** revigorer [*person, plant, business*]; égayer [*dress*]

perky /'pɜːkɪ/ *adj* guilleret/-ette

perm /pɜːm/
A *n* permanente *f*; **to have a ∼** se faire faire une permanente
B *vtr* **to ∼ sb's hair** faire une permanente à qn

permanence /'pɜːmənəns/ *n* permanence *f*

permanent /'pɜːmənənt/
A *n* US permanente *f*

B *adj* [*job, disability, exhibition, address*] permanent; [*premises, closure*] définitif/-ive; [*contract*] à durée indéterminée; [*staff*] ayant un contrat à durée indéterminée

permanently /'pɜ:mənəntlɪ/ *adv* (constantly) [*happy, tired*] en permanence; (definitively) [*employed, disabled*] de façon permanente; [*appointed*] à titre définitif; [*close, emigrate, settle*] définitivement

permanent secretary (of state) *n* GB Pol Admin directeur/-trice *m/f* de cabinet

permeate /'pɜ:mɪeɪt/
A *vtr* **1)** [*liquid, gas*] s'infiltrer dans; [*odour*] pénétrer dans; **2)** fig [*ideas*] imprégner
B permeated *pp adj* **to be** ∼**d with** être imprégné de also fig

permissible /pə'mɪsɪbl/ *adj* [*level, conduct*] admissible; [*error*] acceptable; **to tell sb what is** ∼ dire à qn ce qui est permis

permission /pə'mɪʃn/ *n* gen permission *f*; (official) autorisation *f*; **to have** ∼ **to do** avoir la permission *or* l'autorisation de faire; **to get** ∼ **to do** obtenir la permission *or* l'autorisation de faire; **written** ∼ **to do** l'autorisation écrite de faire; **by kind** ∼ **of** avec l'aimable autorisation de

permissive /pə'mɪsɪv/ *adj* **1)** (morally lax) permissif/-ive; **2)** (liberal) [*view, law*] libéral

permit
A /'pɜ:mɪt/ *n* **1)** (document) permis *m*; (official permission) autorisation *f*; **to apply for a** ∼ faire une demande de permis; **work** ∼ permis *m* de travail: **2)** US Aut permis *m* (de conduire)
B /pə'mɪt/ *vtr* (*p prés etc* **-tt-**) **1)** (allow) permettre [*action, measure*]; **smoking is not** ∼**ted** il est interdit de fumer; **to** ∼ **sb to do** permettre à qn de faire; **to** ∼ **oneself** se permettre [*smile, drink*]; **2)** (allow formally, officially) autoriser
C /pə'mɪt/ *vi* (*p prés etc* **-tt-**) permettre; **weather** ∼**ting** si le temps le permet; **time** ∼**ting** à condition d'en avoir le temps

permutation /ˌpɜ:mjʊ'teɪʃn/ *n* permutation *f*

pernicious /pə'nɪʃəs/ *adj* pernicieux/-ieuse

pernickety○ GB /pə'nɪkətɪ/ *adj* **1)** (detail-conscious) pointilleux/-euse (**about** sur); **2)** (choosy) péj tatillon/-onne (**about** quant à)

peroxide /pə'rɒksaɪd/ *n* **1)** Chem peroxyde *m*; **2)** (also hydrogen ∼) eau *f* oxygénée

peroxide blonde *n* péj blonde *f* décolorée

perpendicular /ˌpɜ:pən'dɪkjʊlə(r)/
A *n* gen, Math verticale *f* (**to** à)
B *adj* [*line*] perpendiculaire; **a** ∼ **cliff face** un à-pic

perpetrate /'pɜ:pɪtreɪt/ *vtr* perpétrer [*deed, fraud*]; monter [*hoax*]

perpetrator /'pɜ:pɪtreɪtə(r)/ *n* auteur *m* (**of** de)

perpetual /pə'petʃʊəl/ *adj* [*meetings, longing, turmoil*] perpétuel/-elle; [*darkness, stench*] permanent; [*banter*] éternel/-elle

perpetually /pə'petʃʊəlɪ/ *adv* perpétuellement

perpetuate /pə'petjʊeɪt/ *vtr* perpétuer

perpetuity /ˌpɜ:pɪ'tju:ətɪ, US -'tu:-/ *n* perpétuité *f*

perplexed /pə'plekst/ *adj* perplexe; **to be** ∼ **as to why/how** se demander pourquoi/comment

perplexing /pə'pleksɪŋ/ *adj* [*behaviour*] curieux/-ieuse; [*situation*] confus; [*question*] difficile

perquisite /'pɜ:kwɪzɪt/ *n* avantage *m*

per se /ˌpɜ: 'seɪ/ *adv* en soi

persecute /'pɜ:sɪkju:t/ *vtr* persécuter (**for** pour; **for doing** pour avoir fait)

persecution /ˌpɜ:sɪ'kju:ʃn/ *n* persécution *f*

persecution complex *n* délire *m* de persécution

perseverance /ˌpɜ:sɪ'vɪərəns/ *n* persévérance *f*

persevere /ˌpɜ:sɪ'vɪə(r)/ *vi* persévérer (**with, at** dans)

Persian /'pɜ:ʃn/ ▸ p. 1032, p. 969
A *n* **1)** (person) (ancient) Perse *mf*; (from 7th century on) Persan/-e *m/f*; **2)** (language) persan *m*
B *adj* (ancient) perse; (from 7th century on) persan

Persian: ∼ **cat** *n* chat *m* persan; ∼ **Gulf** ▸ p. 1049 *pr n* Golfe *m* persique; ∼ **lamb** *n* astrakan *m*

persimmon /pɜ:'sɪmən/ *n* (tree) plaqueminier *m*; (fruit) kaki *m*

---

persist /pə'sɪst/ *vi* persister (**in** dans; **in doing** à faire)

persistence /pə'sɪstəns/ *n* gen persévérance *f*; pej persistance *f* (**in** dans; **in doing** à faire)

persistent /pə'sɪstənt/ *adj* **1)** (persevering) persévérant; (obstinate) obstiné pej (**in** dans); **2)** (continual) [*rain, denial*] persistant; [*inquiries, noise, pressure*] continuel/-elle; [*illness, fears, idea*] tenace

persistently /pə'sɪstəntlɪ/ *adv* continuellement

persistent offender *n* Jur récidiviste *mf*

persistent vegetative state, PVS *n* Med état *m* végétatif chronique

person /'pɜ:sn/ *n* **1)** (human being) (*pl* **people, persons** sout) personne *f*; **the average** ∼ **cannot afford** une personne ordinaire ne peut se permettre; **to do sth in** ∼ faire qch en personne; **he's not the kind of** ∼ **who would do such a thing** ce n'est pas le genre à faire ça; **single** ∼ célibataire *mf*; **the** ∼ **concerned** l'interessé/-e *m/f*; **there's no such** ∼ cette personne n'a jamais existé; **the very** ∼ **I was looking for!** c'est justement toi que je cherchais!; **2)** (type) **I didn't know he was a horsey** ∼○! je ne savais pas que c'était un passionné de cheval!; **what's she like as a** ∼? en tant que femme, elle est comment?; **he's a very discreet** ∼ il est très discret; **3)** (body) **with drugs concealed about his** ∼ avec de la drogue cachée sur lui; **offences against the** ∼ Jur atteintes à la personne; **4)** Ling personne *f*; **the first** ∼ **singular** la première personne du singulier

persona /pɜ:'səʊnə/ *n* Theat, Psych personnage *m*

personable /'pɜ:sənəbl/ *adj* qui présente bien

personage /'pɜ:sənɪdʒ/ *n* personnalité *f*

personal /'pɜ:sənl/
A *n* US petite annonce *f* personnelle
B *adj* [*opinion, life, problem, attack, call, matter*] personnel/-elle; [*safety, freedom, choice, income, profit, insurance*] individuel/-elle; [*service*] personnalisé; **don't be so** ∼! ne fais pas d'allusions personnelles!; **the discussion became rather** ∼ la discussion a pris un ton personnel; **on** *ou* **at a** ∼ **level** sur le plan personnel; **to take care of one's** ∼ **appearance** prendre soin de son apparence; **to make a** ∼ **appearance** venir en personne (**at** à); **he paid them a** ∼ **visit** il leur a rendu visite en personne; ∼ **belongings** *ou* **effects** *ou* **possessions** effets *mpl* personnels; ∼ **hygiene** hygiène *f* intime; **my** ∼ **best is 10 seconds** mon meilleur temps est de 10 secondes; **as a** ∼ **favour to you** pour te faire plaisir

personal: ∼ **ad** *n* petite annonce *f* personnelle; ∼ **assistant** ▸ p. 1181 *n* (secretary) (also **PA**) secrétaire *mf* de direction; (assistant) assistant/-e *m/f*; ∼ **column** *n* petites annonces *fpl* personnelles; ∼ **computer, PC** *n* ordinateur *m* (personnel); ∼ **details** *npl* gen renseignements *mpl* d'ordre personnel; (more intimate) détails *mpl* intimes; (on application form) état civil *m* et coordonnées *fpl*; ∼ **digital assistant, PDA** *n* Comput assistant *m* personnel; ∼ **injury** *n* Jur préjudices *m* individuels

personality /ˌpɜ:sə'nælətɪ/ *n* **1)** (character) personnalité *f*; **2)** (person) personnalité *f*; **a TV** ∼ une vedette de la télévision

personalize /'pɜ:sənəlaɪz/ *vtr* **1)** personnaliser [*stationery, clothing*]; **2)** ramener [qch] à un plan personnel [*issue, dispute*]

personal loan *n* Fin (borrowed) emprunt *m* (à titre personnel); (given by bank etc) prêt *m* personnel

personally /'pɜ:sənəlɪ/ *adv* personnellement; **to take sth** ∼ se sentir visé personnellement par qch

personal: ∼ **organizer** *n* ≈ agenda *m*; ∼ **pension plan,** ∼ **pension scheme** *n* plan *m* de retraite; ∼ **pronoun** *n* Ling pronom *m* personnel; ∼ **property** *n* ¢ Jur biens *mpl* personnels; ∼ **shopper** *n* conseiller personnel/conseillère personnelle *m/f* en shopping; ∼ **stereo** *n* Audio baladeur *m*

personification /pəˌsɒnɪfɪ'keɪʃn/ *n* **1)** (embodiment) incarnation *f* (**of** de); **2)** Literat personnification *f*

personify /pə'sɒnɪfaɪ/ *vtr* **1)** incarner [*ideal*]; **2)** Literat personnifier

personnel /ˌpɜ:sə'nel/ *n* **1)** gen, Mil (staff, troops) personnel *m*; **2)** Admin (also **Personnel**) service *m* du personnel

personnel: ∼ **carrier** *n* véhicule *m* de transport de troupes; ∼ **department** *n* service *m* du personnel;

~ **manager** ▸ p. 1181 *n* directeur/-trice *m/f* du personnel; ~ **officer** ▸ p. 1181 *n* responsable *m/f* du personnel

person-to-person *adj* Telecom avec préavis

perspective /pə'spektɪv/ *n* gen, Art perspective *f*; **from one's (own)** ~ de son (propre) point de vue; **to keep things in** ~ garder un sens de la mesure; **to put things into** ~ relativiser les choses

perspex® /'pɜːspeks/ *n* plexiglas® *m*

perspiration /ˌpɜːspɪ'reɪʃn/ *n* **1**▸ (sweat) sueur *f*; **2**▸ (sweating) transpiration *f*

perspire /pə'spaɪə(r)/ *vi* transpirer

persuade /pə'sweɪd/ *vtr* **1**▸ (influence) persuader [*person*]; **to** ~ **sb to do** persuader qn de faire; **2**▸ (convince intellectually) convaincre (**of** de); **to** ~ **oneself** réussir à se convaincre (**that** que)

persuasion /pə'sweɪʒn/ *n* **1**▸ **₵** (persuading, persuasiveness) persuasion *f*; **no amount of** ~ **will make her change her mind** on aura beau essayer de la persuader, rien ne la fera changer d'avis; **to be open to** ~ être prêt à se laisser convaincre; **2**▸ Relig confession *f*; **3**▸ (political view) conviction *f*; **4**▸ (kind, sort) sorte *f*

persuasive /pə'sweɪsɪv/ *adj* [*person*] persuasif/-ive; [*argument, evidence*] convaincant

persuasively /pə'sweɪsɪvlɪ/ *adv* [*speak*] d'un ton persuasif; [*demonstrate*] d'une manière convaincante

pert /pɜːt/ *adj* [*person, manner*] espiègle; [*hat, nose*] coquin

pertain /pə'teɪn/ *vi* **to** ~ **to** Jur dépendre de; gen se rapporter à

pertinent /'pɜːtɪnənt, US -tənənt/ *adj* [*question, point*] pertinent; **to be** ~ **to** avoir rapport à; **to be** ~ **to do** être approprié de faire

perturb /pə'tɜːb/ *vtr* perturber; **to be** ~**ed by** [*person*] être troublé par; (more deeply) être alarmé par

perturbing /pə'tɜːbɪŋ/ *adj* troublant; (more deeply) alarmant

Peru /pə'ruː/ ▸ p. 774 *pr n* Pérou *m*

peruse /pə'ruːz/ *vtr* sout parcourir [*paper*]

pervade /pə'veɪd/ *vtr* imprégner

pervasive /pə'veɪsɪv/ *adj* [*smell*] pénétrant; [*feeling*] envahissant

perverse /pə'vɜːs/ *adj* **1**▸ (twisted) [*person*] retors; [*desire*] pervers; **2**▸ (contrary) [*refusal, attempt, attitude*] illogique; [*effect*] contraire; **to take a** ~ **pleasure in doing** prendre un malin plaisir à faire

perversely /pə'vɜːslɪ/ *adv* avec un malin plaisir

perversion /pə'vɜːʃn, US -ʒn/ *n* **1**▸ (deviation) perversion *f* (**of** de); **2**▸ (wrong interpretation) (of facts, justice) travestissement *m* (**of** de)

perversity /pə'vɜːsətɪ/ *n* (corruptness) (of person) mauvais esprit *m*; (of action) malignité *f*

pervert
A /'pɜːvɜːt/ *n* pervers/-e *m/f*
B /pə'vɜːt/ *vtr* **1**▸ (corrupt) corrompre; **2**▸ (misrepresent) travestir [*truth*]; dénaturer [*meaning*]; fausser [*values*]; **to** ~ **the course of justice** Jur entraver l'action de la justice

perverted /pə'vɜːtɪd/ *adj* **1**▸ (sexually deviant) pervers; **2**▸ (distorted) [*idea*] tordu; [*act*] vicieux/-ieuse

pessimism /'pesɪmɪzəm/ *n* pessimisme *m*

pessimist /'pesɪmɪst/ *n* pessimiste *mf*

pessimistic /ˌpesɪ'mɪstɪk/ *adj* pessimiste

pest /pest/ *n* **1**▸ Agric (animal) animal *m* nuisible; (insect) insecte *m* nuisible; **2**▸ ○(person) gen enquiquineur/-euse○ *m/f*; (little boy) garnement *m*; (little girl) chipie○ *f*

pest control *n* (of insects) désinsectisation *f*; (of rats) dératisation *f*

pester /'pestə(r)/ *vtr* **1**▸ (annoy) harceler; **stop** ~**ing me!** fiche-moi la paix○!; **2**▸ (harass sexually) harceler, poursuivre [qn] de ses assiduités

pesticide /'pestɪsaɪd/ *n* pesticide *m*

pestilential /ˌpestɪ'lenʃl/ *adj* **1**▸ hum (annoying) satané○ (*before n*); **2**▸ (unhealthy) sout pestilentiel/-ielle

pestle /'pesl/ *n* pilon *m*

pet /pet/
A *n* **1**▸ (animal) animal *m* de compagnie; **'no** ~**s'** 'les animaux domestiques ne sont pas acceptés'; **2**▸ (favourite)

chouchou/chouchoute○ *m/f*; **3**▸ (sweet person) chou○ *m*
B *adj* (favourite) [*charity, theory*] favori/-ite; ~ **dog** chien
C *vtr* (*p prés etc* -**tt**-) **1**▸ (spoil) chouchouter○; **2**▸ (caress) caresser

petal /'petl/ *n* pétale *m*

peter /'piːtə(r)/ *v*
■ **peter out** [*conversation*] tarir; [*meeting*] tourner court; [*plan*] tomber à l'eau; [*supplies*] s'épuiser

Peter /'piːtə(r)/ *pr n* Pierre

Ⓘⓓⓘⓞⓜ **to rob** ~ **to pay Paul** déshabiller Pierre pour habiller Paul

pet: ~ **food** *n* aliments *mpl* pour chiens et chats; ~ **hate** GB *n* bête *f* noire

petite /pə'tiːt/ *adj* [*woman*] menue; [*size*] petite

petition /pə'tɪʃn/
A *n* **1**▸ (document) pétition *f* (**to** à); **a** ~ **calling for** une pétition réclamant; **2**▸ (formal request) pétition *f*; **3**▸ Jur demande *f*; **a** ~ **for divorce** une demande de divorce
B *vtr* adresser une pétition à [*person, body*]
C *vi* **1**▸ gen faire une pétition; **2**▸ Jur **to** ~ **for divorce** demander le divorce

petitioner /pə'tɪʃnə(r)/ *n* **1**▸ (signatory) pétitionnaire *mf*; **2**▸ Jur gen requérant/-ante *m/f*; (in divorce) demandeur/-deresse *m/f*

pet: ~ **name** *n* petit nom *m*; ~ **project** *n* enfant *m* chéri *m*

petrified /'petrɪfaɪd/ *adj* (all contexts) pétrifié

petrify /'petrɪfaɪ/ *vi* [*substance*] se pétrifier; [*civilisation, system*] se fossiliser

petrifying /'petrɪfaɪɪŋ/ *adj* (terrifying) terrifiant

petrochemical /ˌpetrəʊ'kemɪkl/ *n* produit *m* pétrochimique

petrodollar /'petrəʊdɒlə(r)/ *n* pétrodollar *m*

petrol /'petrəl/ GB
A *n* essence *f*; **to fill up with** ~ faire le plein (d'essence); **to run on** ~ fonctionner à l'essence; **to run out of** ~ [*car*] tomber en panne d'essence; [*garage*] ne plus avoir d'essence
B *noun modifier* [*prices, rationing*] d'essence; [*tax*] sur l'essence

petrol: ~ **bomb** *n* GB cocktail *m* Molotov; ~ **can** *n* GB bidon *m* à essence; ~ **cap** *n* GB bouchon *m* de réservoir (d'essence); ~ **engine** *n* GB moteur *m* à essence

petroleum /pə'trəʊlɪəm/
A *n* pétrole *m*
B *noun modifier* [*product, industry, engineer*] pétrolier/-ière

petroleum jelly *n* vaseline® *f*

petrol: ~ **gauge** *n* GB jauge *f* d'essence; ~ **pump** *n* GB (at garage, in engine) pompe *f* à essence; ~ **station** *n* GB station *f* d'essence; ~ **tank** *n* GB réservoir *m* d'essence; ~ **tanker** *n* GB (ship) pétrolier *m*; (lorry) camion-citerne *m*

pet: ~ **shop** GB, ~ **store** US *n* animalerie *f*; ~ **subject** *n* sujet *m* favori, dada *m*

petticoat /'petɪkəʊt/ *n* (full slip) combinaison *m*; (half slip) jupon *m*

pettifogging /'petɪfɒgɪŋ/ *adj* péj pointilleux/-euse

pettiness /'petɪnɪs/ *n* mesquinerie *f*

petting /'petɪŋ/ *n* caresses *fpl*, pelotage○ *m*

pettish /'petɪʃ/ *adj* grincheux/-euse

petty /'petɪ/ *adj* [*person, squabble*] mesquin; [*detail*] insignifiant; [*regulation*] tracassier/-ière; [*snobbery*] étroit

petty: ~ **cash, p/c** *n* petite caisse *f*; ~ **crime** *n* petite délinquance *f*; ~ **expenses** *npl* menues dépenses *fpl*; ~**-minded** *adj* mesquin; ~ **officer** *n* Naut ≈ maître *m*; ~ **official** *n* péj petit fonctionnaire *m*; ~ **theft** *n* Jur larcin *m*

petulant /'petjʊlənt, US -tʃʊ-/ *adj* irascible

petulantly /'petʊləntlɪ, US -tʃʊ-/ *adv* avec humeur

pew /pjuː/ *n* banc *m* (d'église)

pewter /'pjuːtə(r)/ *n* **1**▸ (metal) étain *m*; **2**▸ (colour) (gris *m*) anthracite *m inv*

PG *n* Cin (*abrév* = **Parental Guidance**) *tous publics avec accord parental suggéré*

PGCE *n* (*abrév* = **postgraduate certificate in education**) diplôme *m* de spécialisation dans l'enseignement

phallus /'fæləs/ n (pl **-luses** ou **-li**) phallus m

phantom /'fæntəm/ n 1 (ghost) fantôme m; 2 Aviat Phantom m

pharaoh /'feərəʊ/ n (also **Pharaoh**) pharaon m; (title) Pharaon m

pharmaceutical /ˌfɑːmə'sjuːtɪkl, US -'suː-/ adj pharmaceutique

pharmaceuticals /ˌfɑːmə'sjuːtɪklz, US -'suː-/
A npl produits mpl pharmaceutiques
B noun modifier [industry, factory] pharmaceutique

pharmacist /'fɑːməsɪst/ ▸ p. 1181 n (person) pharmacien/-ienne m/f

pharmacology /ˌfɑːmə'kɒlədʒɪ/ n pharmacologie f

pharmacy /'fɑːməsɪ/ ▸ p. 1181 n 1 (shop) pharmacie f; 2 (also **pharmaceutics**) pharmaceutique f

phase /feɪz/
A n (all contexts) phase f; **it's just a ~ (she's going through)** ça lui passera; **to be out of ~** Elec être déphasé; fig ne pas être en harmonie
B vtr échelonner [changes] (**over** sur)
(Phrasal verb)
  ■ **phase out**: ▸ ~ **out** [sth] supprimer [qch] peu à peu

PhD n (abrév = **Doctor of Philosophy**) doctorat m

pheasant /'feznt/ n faisan/-e m/f

phenix n US = **phoenix**

phenomena /fə'nɒmɪnə/ pl ▸ **phenomenon**

phenomenal /fə'nɒmɪnl/ adj phénoménal

phenomenally /fə'nɒmɪnəlɪ/ adv [grow, increase] de manière phénoménale; [stupid, successful] extraordinairement

phenomenon /fə'nɒmɪnən/ n (pl **-na**) phénomène m

phew /fjuː/ excl (in relief) ouf; (when too hot) pff; (in surprise) oh

phial /'faɪəl/ n fiole f

Phi Beta Kappa /ˌfaɪ biːtə 'kæpə/ n US Univ (group) association d'anciens étudiants d'élite

Philadelphia lawyer /ˌfɪlə'dɛlfɪə/ n US péj avocat m retors

philanderer /fɪ'lændərə(r)/ n coureur m de juponsᵒ

philanthropist /fɪ'lænθrəpɪst/ n philanthrope mf

philatelist /fɪ'lætəlɪst/ n philatéliste mf

philharmonic /ˌfɪlɑː'mɒnɪk/ adj philharmonique

philistine /'fɪlɪstaɪn/
A n béotien/-ienne m/f
B adj [attitude, article] béotien/-ienne; [public] de béotiens

Phillips screwdriver /'fɪlɪps/ n tournevis m cruciforme

philology /fɪ'lɒlədʒɪ/ n philologie f

philosopher /fɪ'lɒsəfə(r)/ ▸ p. 1181 n lit, fig philosophe mf

philosophic(al) /ˌfɪlə'sɒfɪk(l)/ adj 1 [knowledge, question, treatise] philosophique; 2 fig (calm, stoical) philosophe (**about** à propos de)

philosophically /ˌfɪlə'sɒfɪklɪ/ adv philosophiquement; **he took it all very ~** fig il a pris tout ça avec philosophie

philosophize /fɪ'lɒsəfaɪz/ vi philosopher (**about** sur)

philosophy /fɪ'lɒsəfɪ/ n philosophie f

phlebitis /flɪ'baɪtɪs/ ▸ p. 933 n phlébite f

phlegm /flem/ n 1 Med mucosité f; 2 (calm) flegme m

phlegmatic /fleg'mætɪk/ adj flegmatique (**about** au sujet de)

phobia /'fəʊbɪə/ n phobie f

phobic /'fəʊbɪk/ adj phobique

phoenix /'fiːnɪks/ n phénix m

phone /fəʊn/
A n téléphone m; **to be on the ~** (be talking) être au téléphone (**to sb** avec qn); (be subscriber) avoir le téléphone
B vtr passer un coup de fil àᵒ, téléphoner à [person, company]; **to ~ France** téléphoner en France
C vi téléphoner; **to ~ for a taxi** appeler un taxi
(Phrasal verbs)
  ■ **phone in** téléphoner; **she ~d in sick** elle a téléphoné au bureau pour dire qu'elle était malade
  ■ **phone up**: ▸ ~ **up** [sb], ~ [sb] **up** téléphoner à, appeler [person, organization]

phone: ~ **book** n annuaire m (du téléphone); ~ **booth**, ~ **box** GB n cabine f téléphonique; ~ **call**

n gen coup m de filᵒ; Admin communication f (téléphonique); ~ **card** n GB télécarte f; ~**-in** n émission f à ligne ouverte; ~ **link** n liaison f téléphonique

phoneme /'fəʊniːm/ n phonème m

phone: ~ **number** n numéro m de téléphone; ~ **tapping** n ₡ écoutes fpl téléphoniques

phonetic /fə'netɪk/ adj phonétique

phonetics /fə'netɪks/ n phonétique f

phoneyᵒ /'fəʊnɪ/ péj
A n (affected person) poseur/-euse m/f; (impostor) charlatan m; (forgery, fake) faux m
B adj [address, accent, jewel] faux/fausse (before n); [company, excuse] bidonᵒ; [emotion] simulé

phoney war n Hist the ~ la drôle de guerre

phonology /fə'nɒlədʒɪ/ n phonologie f

phooey /'fuːɪ/ excl peuh!, pfft!

phosphate /'fɒsfeɪt/
A n Chem phosphate m
B **phosphates** npl Agric phosphates mpl, engrais mpl phosphatés

phosphorescent /ˌfɒsfə'resnt/ adj phosphorescent

phosphorus /'fɒsfərəs/ n phosphore m

photo /'fəʊtəʊ/
A n photo f; ▸ **photograph**
B **photo+** combining form photo-

photo: ~ **album** n album m de photos; ~ **booth** n photomaton® m; ~**call** n GB séance f de photos

photocell /'fəʊtəʊsel/ n cellule f photoélectrique

photocopier /'fəʊtəʊkɒpɪə(r)/ n photocopieuse f

photocopy /'fəʊtəʊkɒpɪ/
A n photocopie f
B vtr photocopier

photoengraving /ˌfəʊtəʊɪn'greɪvɪŋ/ n photogravure f

photo finish n (in picture) photo-finish f; (result) arrivée f départagée au photo-finish

Photofit® /'fəʊtəʊfɪt/ n GB portrait-robot m

photoflash n ampoule f de flash

photogenic /ˌfəʊtəʊ'dʒenɪk/ adj photogénique

photograph /'fəʊtəɡrɑːf, US -ɡræf/
A n photo f; **in the ~** sur la photo; **to take a ~ of sb/sth** prendre qn/qch en photo
B vtr photographier, prendre [qn/qch] en photo
C vi **to ~ well** [person] être photogénique

photograph album n album m de photos

photographer /fə'tɒɡrəfə(r)/ ▸ p. 1181 n photographe mf

photographic /ˌfəʊtə'ɡræfɪk/ adj [image, reproduction, equipment] photographique; [studio] de photo; [shop, agency, exhibition] de photos; **to have a ~ memory** avoir une mémoire visuelle exceptionnelle

photographically /ˌfəʊtə'ɡræfɪklɪ/ adv en termes de photographie

photographic library n photothèque f

photography /fə'tɒɡrəfɪ/ n photographie f

photojournalist /ˌfəʊtəʊ'dʒɜːnəlɪst/ ▸ p. 1181 n photojournaliste mf

photo-offset /ˌfəʊtəʊ'ɒfset/ n offset m

photo opportunity n séance f de photos

photorealism /ˌfəʊtəʊ'rɪəlɪzəm/ n hyperréalisme m

photosensitive /ˌfəʊtəʊ'sensətɪv/ adj photosensible

photo session n séance f de photos

photoset /'fəʊtəʊset/ vtr (p prés **-tt-**; prét, pp **-set**) photocomposer

Photostat® /'fəʊtəʊstæt/ n photocopie f

photosynthesis /ˌfəʊtəʊ'sɪnθəsɪs/ n photosynthèse f

phrasal verb n verbe m à particule

phrase /freɪz/
A n 1 (expression) gen expression f, Ling locution f; 2 Ling (part of clause) syntagme m; **noun ~** syntagme nominal; 3 Mus phrase f
B vtr 1 (formulate) exprimer [idea]; formuler [question, speech]; 2 Mus phraser

phrase: ~**book** n manuel m de conversation; ~ **marker** n marqueur m syntagmatique

phrasing /'freɪzɪŋ/ n 1 gen formulation f; 2 Mus phrasé m

p

phut○ /fʌt/ adv **to go ~** [car] rendre l'âme; [plan] tomber à l'eau○

phylogenesis /ˌfaɪləʊˈdʒenəsɪs/, **phylogeny** /faɪˈlɒdʒɪnɪ/ n phylogénie f

physical /ˈfɪzɪkl/
A ○n bilan m de santé; **to have a ~** se faire faire un bilan de santé
B adj **1** (of the body) [strength, pain etc] physique; **~ abuse** sévices mpl; **it's a ~ impossibility** c'est physiquement impossible; **she's very ~** (demonstrative) elle est très démonstrative; **did he get ~?** (become violent) est-ce qu'il en est venu aux mains?; **2** [chemistry, science, property] physique

physical: **~ education**, **PE** n éducation f physique; **~ examination** n examen m médical; **~ fitness** n forme f physique; **~ geography** n géographie f physique

physically /ˈfɪzɪklɪ/ adv physiquement

physically handicapped adj **to be ~** être handicapé/-e m/f physique

physical: **~ sciences** npl sciences fpl physiques; **~ therapist** ▸ p. 1181 n US Med kinésithérapeute mf; **~ therapy** n US Med kinésithérapie f; **~ training**, **PT** n éducation f physique

physician /fɪˈzɪʃn/ ▸ p. 1181 n GB†, US médecin m; GB spécialiste mf

physicist /ˈfɪzɪsɪst/ ▸ p. 1181 n physicien/-ienne m/f

physics /ˈfɪzɪks/ n (+ v sg) physique f

physio○ /ˈfɪzɪəʊ/ ▸ p. 1181 n GB **1** (abrév = **physiotherapist**) kinési○ mf, kinésithérapeute mf; **2** (abrév = **physiotherapy**) kinési○ f, kinésithérapie f

physiological /ˌfɪzɪəˈlɒdʒɪkl/ adj physiologique

physiologist /ˌfɪzɪˈɒlədʒɪst/ ▸ p. 1181 n physiologiste mf

physiology /ˌfɪzɪˈɒlədʒɪ/ n physiologie f

physiotherapist /ˌfɪzɪəʊˈθerəpɪst/ ▸ p. 1181 n kinésithérapeute mf

physiotherapy /ˌfɪzɪəʊˈθerəpɪ/ n kinésithérapie f

physique /fɪˈziːk/ n physique m

pianist /ˈpɪənɪst/ ▸ p. 1181, p. 1028 n pianiste mf

piano /pɪˈænəʊ/ ▸ p. 1028
A n piano m
B noun modifier [lesson, teacher] de piano; [concerto, music] pour piano

piano: **~ accordion** ▸ p. 1028 n accordéon m à clavier; **~ bar** n piano-bar m

pianola® /pɪəˈnəʊlə/ ▸ p. 1028 n (also **piano organ**) piano m mécanique

piano stool n tabouret m (de piano)

piazza /pɪˈætsə/ n **1** (public square) place f; **2** US (veranda) véranda f

piccalilli /ˌpɪkəˈlɪlɪ/ n ₵ pickles mpl à la moutarde

pick /pɪk/
A n **1** (tool) gen pioche f, pic m; (of climber) piolet m; (of mason) smille f; **to dig with a ~** creuser à la pioche; **2** (choice) choix m; **to have one's ~** of avoir le choix parmi; **take your ~** choisis; **3** (best) meilleur/-e m/f; **the ~ of the crop** (fruit) les meilleurs fruits; **the ~ of the bunch** le/la etc meilleur/-e etc du lot
B vtr **1** (choose, select) gen choisir (**from** parmi); Sport sélectionner [player] (**from** parmi); former [team]; **you ~ed the wrong person** tu as choisi la mauvaise personne; **to ~ a fight** (physically) chercher à se bagarrer○ (**with** avec); **to ~ a fight** ou **a quarrel** chercher querelle (**with** à); **2** (navigate) **to ~ one's way through** avancer avec précaution parmi [rubble, litter]; **3** (pluck, gather) cueillir [fruit, flowers]; **4** (poke at) gratter [spot, scab]; **to ~ sth from** ou **off** enlever qch de; **to ~ one's nose** mettre les doigts dans son nez; **to ~ one's teeth** se curer les dents; **to ~ a lock** crocheter une serrure; **to ~ sb's pocket** faire les poches de qn
C vi choisir; **to ~ and choose** faire le/la difficile (**among**, **between** pour choisir parmi)

(Phrasal verbs)
■ **pick at**: ▸ **~ at [sth]** **1** [person] manger [qch] du bout des dents [food]; gratter [spot, scab]; **2** [bird] picorer [crumbs]
■ **pick off**: ▸ **~ [sb] off**, **~ off [sb]** (kill) abattre; ▸ **~ [sth] off**, **~ off [sth]** enlever [qch]; ▸ **~ [sth] off sth** cueillir

[qch] sur qch [apple, cherry]; **to ~ sth off the floor** ramasser qch qui était par terre
■ **pick on**: ▸ **~ on [sb]** harceler
■ **pick out**: ▸ **~ [sb/sth] out**, **~ out [sb/sth]** **1** (select) gen choisir; (single out) repérer; **to ~ out three winners** sélectionner trois gagnants (**from** parmi); **2** (make out) distinguer [landmark]; saisir [words]; reconnaître [person in photo]; repérer [person in crowd]; **3** (highlight) [torch etc] révéler; **to be ~ed out in red** [pattern] être mis en valeur par le rouge
■ **pick over**: ▸ **~ [sth] over**, **~ over [sth]** lit trier; fig analyser
■ **pick up**: ▸ **~ up** **1** (improve) [trade, market] reprendre; [weather, performance, health] s'améliorer; [ill person] se rétablir; **2** (resume) reprendre; **to pick up (from) where one left off** reprendre là où on s'est arrêté; ▸ **~ [sb/sth] up**, **~ up [sb/sth]** **1** (lift, take hold of) (to tidy) ramasser; (to examine) prendre; (after fall) relever; (for cuddle) prendre [qn] dans ses bras; **to ~ sth up in** ou **with one's left hand** prendre qch de sa main gauche; **to ~ up the telephone** décrocher le téléphone; **to ~ up the bill** régler l'addition; **2** (collect) prendre [passenger, cargo]; (passer) prendre [ticket, keys]; **could you ~ me up?** est-ce que tu peux venir me chercher?; ▸ **~ [sth] up**, **~ up [sth]** **1** (buy) prendre, acheter; dénicher [bargain]; **2** (learn, acquire) apprendre [language]; prendre [habit, accent]; développer [skill]; **you'll soon ~ it up** tu t'y mettras vite; **3** (catch) attraper [illness]; **4** (notice, register) [person] repérer [error]; [person, machine] détecter [defect]; **5** (detect) trouver [trail, scent]; [radar] détecter la présence de [aircraft, person, object]; Radio, Telecom capter [signal]; **6** (gain, earn) gagner [point, size]; acquérir [reputation]; **to ~ up speed** prendre de la vitesse; **7** (resume) reprendre [conversation, career]; **you'll soon ~ up your French again** ton français te reviendra vite; ▸ **~ [sb] up**, **~ up [sb]** **1** (rescue) recueillir [person]; **2** (arrest) arrêter [suspect]; **3** (meet) péj ramasser [partner, prostitute]; **4** (find fault with) faire des remarques à [person] (**on** sur); ▸ **~ oneself up** (get up) se relever; (recover) se reprendre

pickaxe GB, **pickax** US /ˈpɪkæks/ n pioche f

picker /ˈpɪkə(r)/ n cueilleur/-euse m/f

picket /ˈpɪkɪt/
A n **1** (in strike) (group of people) piquet m (de grève); (one person) gréviste mf (qui fait partie d'un piquet); **to be on a ~** faire partie d'un piquet de grève; **2** Mil (detachment) détachement m; (one soldier) factionnaire m; **3** (stake) piquet m, pieu m
B vtr **1** (to stop work) installer un piquet de grève aux portes de [factory]; (to protest) former un cordon de protestation devant [meeting place, embassy]; **2** (fence in) clôturer, palissader

picket duty n **to be on ~** Ind faire partie d'un piquet de grève; Mil être (de service) de guet

picket: **~ fence** n palissade f; **~ line** n (in strike) (cordon m de) piquet m de grève; (in protest) cordon m de protestation

picking /ˈpɪkɪŋ/
A n (of crop) cueillette f
B **pickings** npl (rewards) gains mpl

pickle /ˈpɪkl/
A n **1** ₵ (preserved food) conserves fpl au vinaigre; **2** C (gherkin) cornichon m; **~s** pickles mpl; **3** ₵ (brine) saumure f; (vinegar) vinaigre m
B vtr conserver [qch] dans du vinaigre or dans de la saumure

(Idiom) **to be in a ~** hum être dans le pétrin○

pickled /ˈpɪkld/ adj **1** Culin au vinaigre; **2** ○GB (drunk) bourré○

pick: **~-me-up** n remontant m; **~pocket** n voleur m à la tire

pickup /ˈpɪkʌp/ n **1** (also **~ arm**) lecteur m; **2** (on electric guitar) capteur m; **3** Radio, TV (reception) réception f; **4** (collection) (of goods) ramassage m; (passenger) passager/-ère m/f ramassé/-e en route; **5** ₵ Aut (acceleration) reprises fpl; **6** (in business, economy) reprise f (**in** de); **7** = **pickup truck**

pickup: **~ point** n (for passengers) point m de ramassage; (for goods) point m de chargement; **~ truck**, **~ van** GB n pick-up m inv

picky○ /ˈpɪkɪ/ adj difficile (**about** pour ce qui est de)

picnic /ˈpɪknɪk/
A n pique-nique m

B *noun modifier* [*basket, hamper*] à pique-nique

(Idiom) **it's no ~!** ce n'est pas une partie de plaisir!

picnic lunch *n* pique-nique *m*

pictogram /'pɪktəgræm/ *n* **1** (symbol) pictogramme *m*; **2** (chart) carte *f* thématique

pictorial /pɪk'tɔːrɪəl/ *adj* **1** (in pictures) [*magazine*] illustré; [*record, information*] graphique; [*technique*] artistique; **2** (resembling pictures) [*language, description*] imagé

picture /'pɪktʃə(r)/

A *n* **1** (visual depiction) (painting) peinture *f*, tableau *m*; (drawing) dessin *m*; (in book) gen illustration *f*; (in child's book) image *f*; (in mind) image *f*; **to paint a ~ of sb/sth** peindre qn/qch; **to paint sb's ~** faire le portrait de qn; **2** fig (description) description *f*; **to paint a ~ of sb/sth** dépeindre qn/qch; **to give** *ou* **present a clear ~ of sth** présenter qch avec clarté; **3** Phot photo *f*, photographie *f*; **to take a ~ (of)** prendre une photo (de); **4** fig (overview) situation *f*; **to get the ~** comprendre la situation; **to be in the ~** être au courant; **5** Cin (film) film *m*; **to make a ~** faire un film; **6** TV image *f*

B **pictures** *npl* the **~s** le cinéma

C *vtr* **1** (form mental image of) s'imaginer; **2** (show in picture form) **to be ~d** être représenté; **the vase (~d above) is...** le vase (voir photo ci-dessus) est...

(Idioms) **to be the ~ of health** respirer la santé; **to look a ~** être ravissant; **her face was a ~!** son expression en disait long!

picture: **~ book** *n* livre *m* d'images; **~ card** *n* Games figure *f* (*carte*); **~ desk** *n* (of newspaper) service *m* photo; **~ editor** ▸ p. 1181 *n* (of newspaper) directeur/-trice *m/f* du service photo; **~ frame** *n* cadre *m*; **~ framing** *n* encadrement *m*; **~ gallery** *n* galerie *f* de peinture; **~ hook** *n* crochet *m* (à tableaux); **~ postcard** *n* carte *f* postale; **~ rail** *n* cimaise *f*

picturesque /ˌpɪktʃə'resk/ *adj* pittoresque

piddle○ /'pɪdl/ *vi* (urinate) faire pipi○

piddling○ /'pɪdlɪŋ/ *adj* insignifiant

pidgin /'pɪdʒɪn/ *n* **1** (also **~ English**) pidgin *m*; **2** (also **~ French**) gen petit nègre *m*; (French with Arab) sabir *m*; **3** péj charabia *m*

pie /paɪ/ *n* **1** (savoury) gen tourte *f*; **meat ~** tourte à la viande; **pork ~** pâté *m* de porc en croûte; **2** (sweet) tarte *f* (*recouverte de pâte*)

(Idioms) **it's all ~ in the sky** c'est de l'utopie; **as easy as ~** simple comme bonjour; **to have a finger in every ~** être mêlé à tout; **as nice as ~** gen gentil/-ille comme tout, péj tout sucre tout miel

piebald /'paɪbɔːld/ *n* cheval *m* pie

piece /piːs/ *n* **1** gen morceau *m*; (of string, ribbon) bout *m*; **2** (unit) **a ~ of furniture** un meuble; **a ~ of luggage** une valise; **a ~ of advice** un conseil; **a ~ of information** un renseignement; **a ~ of legislation** une loi; **a ~ of work** gen un travail; (referring to book etc) une œuvre; **a ~ of luck** un coup dde chance; **to be paid by the ~** être payé à la pièce; **3** (of jigsaw, machine, model) pièce *f*; **in ~s** en pièces (détachées); **to come in ~s** [*furniture*] être livré en kit; **to take sth to ~s** démonter qch; **4** (broken fragment) morceau *m*; **to fall to ~s** [*object*] tomber en morceaux; fig [*argument*] s'effondrer; **to go to ~s** fig (from shock) s'effondrer; (emotionally) craquer○; (in interview) paniquer complètement; **5** (artistic work) (of music) morceau *m*; (sculpture) sculpture *f*; (painting) peinture *f*; (article) article *m* (**on** sur); (play) pièce *f*; (in book) passage *m*; **6** (instance) **a ~ of** un exemple de [*propaganda*]; **a wonderful ~ of running/acting** une très belle course/ interprétation; **7** (coin) pièce *f*; **a 50p ~** une pièce de 50 pence; **8** Games (in chess) pièce *f*; (in draughts) pion *m*; **9** Mil (gun) fusil *m*; (cannon) pièce *f* (d'artillerie); **10** ○(gun) flingue○ *m*, pistolet *m*

(Idioms) **to be (all) of a ~ with** s'accorder avec; **to be still in one ~** lit être intact; fig être sain et sauf; **to give sb a ~ of one's mind** dire ses quatre vérités à qn

(Phrasal verb)
  ■ **piece together:** ▸ **~ [sth] together**, **~ together [sth]** reconstituer [*vase, garment, letter*]; assembler [*puzzle*]; fig reconstituer [*facts, evidence*]

piecemeal /'piːsmiːl/

A *adj* [*approach, reforms*] fragmentaire; [*description*] décousu; [*research, construction, development*] (random) fragmentaire; (at different times) irrégulier/-ière

B *adv* petit à petit

piecework /'piːswɜːk/ *n* **to be on ~** être payé à la pièce

pie: **~ chart** *n* diagramme *m* circulaire sectorisé, camembert○ *m*; **~ crust** *n* croûte *f*; **~ dish** *n* tourtière *f*; **~-eyed**○ *adj* rond○, soûl○

pier /pɪə(r)/ *n* **1** (at seaside) jetée *f* (sur pilotis) (*où les gens viennent se promener*); **2** (part of harbour) (built of stone) digue *f*; (landing stage) embarcadère *f*; **3** Constr (of bridge, dam, foundations) pile *f*; (pillar in church, of gateway) pilier *m*; (wall between openings) trumeau *m*

pierce /pɪəs/ *vtr* **1** (make hole in) percer; (penetrate) transpercer [*armour, skin*]; **2** fig (penetrate) [*cry, light*] percer; [*wind*] transpercer; **3** Mil pénétrer [*enemy lines*]

piercing /pɪəsɪŋ/ *adj* [*noise*] perçant; [*light*] intense; [*wind*] glacial, pénétrant

piety /'paɪətɪ/ *n* (religiousness) piété *f*

piffling○ /'pɪflɪŋ/ *adj* GB insignifiant

pig /pɪg/ *n* **1** (animal) porc *m*, cochon *m*; **2** ○(greedy) goinfre○ *m*; (dirty) cochon/-onne○ *m/f*; (nasty) sale type○ *m*; **to make a ~ of oneself** manger comme un goinfre○; **3** ○péj **the ~s** les flics○ *mpl*

(Idioms) **to buy a ~ in a poke** acheter chat en poche; **~s might fly!** le jour où les poules auront des dents!; **in a ~'s eye**○!, US mon œil○!; **to make a ~'s ear of sth** bousiller○ qch

(Phrasal verb)
  ■ **pig out**○ se goinfrer○, s'empiffrer○ (**on** de)

pigeon /'pɪdʒɪn/ *n* pigeon *m*

(Idiom) **to put** *ou* **set the cat among the ~s** jeter *or* lancer un pavé dans la mare

pigeon: **~-breasted**, **~-chested** *adj* à la poitrine bombée; **~ fancier** *n* colombophile *mf*

pigeonhole /'pɪdʒɪnhəʊl/ GB

A *n* casier *m*

B *vtr* étiqueter, cataloguer

pigeon: **~ house**, **~ loft** *n* pigeonnier *m*; **~ racing** *n* **¢** courses *fpl* de pigeons voyageurs

pigeon-toed *adj* **to be ~** marcher les pieds en dedans

pig farming *n* élevage *m* de porcs

piggery /'pɪgərɪ/ *n* (pigsty) porcherie *f*

piggy /'pɪgɪ/ *n* lang enfantin cochon *m*

(Idiom) **to be ~ in the middle** se trouver entre deux chaises

piggyback /'pɪgɪbæk/

A *n* (also **~ ride**) **to give sb a ~** porter qn sur son dos *or* sur ses épaules

B *adv* [*ride, carry*] sur le dos

piggy bank *n* tirelire *f* (*en forme de cochon*)

pigheaded /ˌpɪg'hedɪd/ *adj* péj entêté, obstiné

pig iron *n* métal *m* en gueuse

piglet /'pɪglɪt/ *n* porcelet *m*, petit cochon *m*

pigment /'pɪgmənt/ *n* Biol, Art pigment *m*

pigmentation /ˌpɪgmən'teɪʃn/ *n* pigmentation *f*

pig: **~pen** *n* US = pigsty; **~skin** *n* peau *f* de porc; **~sty** *n* (*pl* **-sties**) lit, fig porcherie *f*; **~tail** *n* (hair) natte *f*

pike /paɪk/ *n* **1** Hist (spear) pique *f*; **2** (fish) brochet *m*

pikestaff /'paɪkstɑːf, US -stæf/ *n*:

(Idiom) **it's as plain as a ~** ça se voit comme le nez au milieu de la figure

pilchard /'pɪltʃəd/ *n* pilchard *m*

pile /paɪl/

A *n* **1** (untidy heap) tas *m* (**of** de); (stack) pile *f* (**of** de); **in a ~** en tas *or* en pile; **2** (of fabric, carpet) poil *m*; **3** ○(large amount) **a ~** *ou* **~s of** un tas○ *or* des tas○ de; **to have ~s of money** avoir plein d'argent○; **4** Constr pilier *m*; **5** Elec pile *f*; **6** littér *ou* hum (building) édifice *m*

B **piles** *npl* Med hémorroïdes *fpl*

C *vtr* (en heap) entasser (**on** sur; **into** dans); **a plate ~d high with cakes** une assiette avec une montagne de gâteaux

D *vi* **to ~ into** (board) s'engouffrer dans [*vehicle*]; (crash) rentrer dans [*vehicle*]

(Idiom) **to make one's ~**○ faire fortune

(Phrasal verbs)
  ■ **pile in**○: **the bus came and we all ~d in** le bus est arrivé et nous y sommes montés en nous serrant

■ **pile on**°: **to ~ on the charm** jouer à fond sur la séduction; **to ~ it on** mettre le paquet°
■ **pile up**: ▸ **~ up** [*leaves, snow, rubbish*] s'entasser; [*money*] s'amasser; [*debts, problems, work*] s'accumuler; ▸ **~ [sth] up**, **~ up [sth]** (in a heap) entasser; (in a stack) empiler

pile: **~ driver** n sonnette f de battage; **~ fabric** n (velvet) velours m; (other) fourrure f synthétique; **~up** n Aut carambolage m

pilfer /'pɪlfə(r)/
A vtr dérober (**from** dans)
B vi commettre des larcins

pilgrim /'pɪlgrɪm/ n pèlerin m (**to** de)

pilgrimage /'pɪlgrɪmɪdʒ/ n Relig, fig pèlerinage m; **to go on** ou **make a ~** faire un pèlerinage (**to** à)

pill /pɪl/ n Med (for general use) comprimé m, cachet m; **to be on the ~** (contraceptive) prendre la pilule

(Idioms) **it was a bitter ~ to swallow** la pilule était amère; **to sugar** ou **sweeten the ~** dorer la pilule°

pillage /'pɪlɪdʒ/
A n pillage m
B vtr, vi piller

pillar /'pɪlə(r)/ n **1** Archit pilier m; fig (of smoke, fire etc) colonne f; **a ~ of salt** Bible une statue de sel; **2** fig (of institution, society) pilier m (**of** de); **to be a ~ of strength to sb** être d'un grand soutien à qn

(Idiom) **to be sent from ~ to post**° (for information, papers) se faire renvoyer de service en service°

pillar box n GB boîte f aux lettres

pillbox /'pɪlbɒks/ n **1** (for pills) boîte f à pilules; **2** (also **~ hat**) toque f

pillion /'pɪlɪən/
A n (also **~ seat**) siège m de passager
B noun modifier [*passenger*] arrière inv
C adv **to ride ~** monter en croupe

pillory /'pɪlərɪ/
A n Hist pilori m
B vtr lit, fig mettre [qn] au pilori (**for** pour)

pillow /'pɪləʊ/ n oreiller m

pillow: **~case** n taie f d'oreiller; **~ talk**° n 𝒞 confidences fpl sur l'oreiller

pilot /'paɪlət/ ▸ p. 1181
A n **1** Aviat, Aerosp, Naut pilote m; **2** Radio, TV (programme) émission f pilote (**for** pour); **3** (also **~ light**) (gas) veilleuse f; (electric) voyant m lumineux
B noun modifier **1** Comm, Ind [*course, project, study*] pilote; Radio, TV [*programme, series*] expérimental; **2** Aviat [*instruction, training*] des pilotes; [*error*] de pilotage
C vtr **1** Aviat, Naut (navigate) piloter; **to ~ sb through** fig guider qn à travers [*crowd, streets*]; **to ~ a bill through parliament** assurer le passage d'un projet de loi au parlement; **2** (test) mettre [qch] au banc d'essai [*course, system*]

pilot: **~ boat** n bateau-pilote m; **~ burner** n (gas) veilleuse f; (electric) voyant m lumineux; **~ scheme** n projet-pilote m; **~'s licence** n brevet m de pilote

pimp /pɪmp/
A n proxénète m
B vi faire du proxénétisme

pimple /'pɪmpl/ n bouton m

pimply /'pɪmplɪ/ adj boutonneux/-euse also pej

pin /pɪn/
A n **1** (for sewing, fastening cloth or paper) épingle f; **2** Elec (of plug) fiche f; **two-/three-~ plug** prise f à deux/trois fiches; **3** Tech (to attach wood or metal) goujon m; (machine part) goupille f; **4** Med (in surgery) broche f; **5** (brooch) barrette f; **6** (in bowling) quille f; **7** (in golf) drapeau m (de trou)
B pins n (legs) npl quilles f, jambes fpl
C vtr (p prés etc **-nn-**) **1** (attach with pins) épingler [*dress, hem, curtain*]; **to ~ sth on(to)** (with drawing pin) fixer qch avec une punaise sur [*board, wall*]; **to ~ sth with** attacher qch avec [*brooch, grip, pin*]; **2** (trap, press) coincer [*person, part of body*]; **to ~ sb against** ou **to** coincer qn contre [*wall, sofa, floor*]; **her arms were ~ned to her sides** elle avait les bras plaqués au corps; **3** °(attribute, attach) **to ~ sth on sb** imputer qch à qn [*blame, crime*]; **4** Mil, Sport coincer, bloquer

(Idioms) **for two ~s I would do** pour un peu je le ferais; **to ~ one's ears back**° ouvrir grand les oreilles°; **you could have heard a ~ drop** on aurait entendu voler une mouche

■ **pin down**: ▸ **~ down [sb]**, **~ [sb] down 1** (physically) immobiliser (**to** à); **2** fig coincer; **to ~ sb down to a definite date** arriver à soutirer une date fixe à qn; **to ~ sb down to doing** obliger qn à s'engager à faire; ▸ **~ down [sth]**, **~ [sth] down 1** lit accrocher [*piece of paper, cloth*]; épingler [*sheet*]; **2** fig (define) identifier [*concept, feeling*]; **I can't ~ it down** je n'arrive pas à mettre le doigt dessus
■ **pin up**: ▸ **~ up [sth]**, **~ [sth] up** accrocher [*poster, notice*] (**on** à); remonter [*hair*]

PIN /pɪn/ n (also **~ number**) (abrév = **personal identification number**) code m confidentiel (*pour carte bancaire*)

pinafore /'pɪnəfɔː(r)/ n (apron) tablier m; (overall) blouse f

pinball ▸ p. 881 n flipper m

pincer /'pɪnsə(r)/
A n Zool pince f
B pincers npl (tool) tenailles fpl

pinch /pɪntʃ/
A n **1** pincement m; **to give sb a ~ on the cheek** pincer la joue de qn; **2** (of salt, spice) pincée f; (of snuff) prise f
B vtr **1** pincer; **2** [*shoe*] serrer; **3** °(steal) faucher° (**from** à); **4** (remove) **to ~ out** ou **off** enlever [*bud, tip*]
C vi [*shoe*] serrer

(Idioms) **at** GB ou **on** US **a ~** à la rigueur; **to feel the ~** avoir de la peine à joindre les deux bouts; **to ~ and scrape** rogner sur tout

pinched /pɪntʃt/ adj **to look ~** avoir les traits tirés

pincushion /'pɪnkʊʃn/ n pelote f à épingles

pine /paɪn/
A n pin m; **stripped ~** pin décapé
B noun modifier [*furniture*] en pin
C vi languir (**for** après; **to do** de faire)

■ **pine away** se laisser dépérir

pineapple /'paɪnæpl/ n (fruit, plant) ananas m

pine: **~cone** n pomme f de pin; **~ kernel** n pignon m de pin; **~-needle** n aiguille f de pin

ping /pɪŋ/
A n (of bell) tintement m; (of bullet) claquement m
B vi [*bell*] tinter; [*bullet*] claquer

ping-pong® /'pɪŋpɒŋ/ ▸ p. 881 n ping-pong® m

pinhead /'pɪnhed/ n **1** lit tête f d'épingle; **2** °péj abruti/-e° m/f

pinion /'pɪnɪən/
A n Tech pignon m
B vtr **to ~ sb against** plaquer qn contre [*wall, door*]; **to ~ sb's arms** tenir les bras de qn

pink /pɪŋk/ ▸ p. 752
A n **1** (colour) rose m; **2** Bot œillet m mignardise
B adj **1** (rosy) rose; **to go** ou **turn ~** rosir; (blush) rougir (**with** de); **2** (leftwing) gauchisant

(Idiom) **to be in the ~** être en pleine forme

pinking shears, **pinking scissors** npl ciseaux mpl cranteurs

pin money n argent m de poche

pinnacle /'pɪnəkl/ n Archit pinacle m; (of rock) cime f (**of** de); fig apogée m (**of** de)

pinpoint /'pɪnpɔɪnt/
A n tête f d'épingle; **a ~ of light** un point lumineux
B vtr **1** (identify, pick out) indiquer [*problem, risk, causes*]; **2** (place exactly) indiquer [*location, position, site*]; déterminer [*time, exact moment*]

pinprick /'pɪnprɪk/ n **1** lit coup m d'épingle; (feeling caused) sensation f de piqûre; **2** fig (of jealousy, remorse) pointe f

pinstripe /'pɪnstraɪp/
A pinstripes npl (suit) costume m à fines rayures
B noun modifier (also **pinstriped**) [*fabric, suit*] à fines rayures

pint /paɪnt/ ▸ p. 723 n **1** pinte f (GB = 0.57 l, US = 0.47 l); **a ~ of milk** ≈ un demi-litre de lait; **2** °GB **to go for a ~** aller boire une bière

pint: **~ glass**, **~ pot** n ≈ chope f (d'un demi-litre); **~-size(d)** adj petit

pinup /'pɪnʌp/ n **1** (woman) pin-up° f; (man) photo f d'homme à moitié nu; **2** (poster of star) affiche f de vedette; (star) idole f

pioneer /ˌpaɪə'nɪə(r)/
A n pionnier m (**of, in** de)

B *noun modifier* [*research*] novateur/-trice; **a ~ astronaut** un des premiers astronautes
C *vtr* **to ~ the use of** être le premier à utiliser
D **pioneering** *pres p adj* [*scientist, scheme*] innovateur/-trice

pious /'paɪəs/ *adj* pieux/pieuse; *pej* plein de componction

pip /pɪp/
A *n* **1** (seed) pépin *m*; **2** GB Telecom **the ~s** tonalité *f* (*indiquant qu'il faut introduire à nouveau de l'argent*); **3** Radio top *m* (*signal pour indiquer l'heure*); **4** (on card, dice, domino) point *m*
(Idioms) **to be ~ped at** *ou* **to the post** se faire souffler la victoire; **to give sb the ~**† énerver qn

pipe /paɪp/ ▸ p. 1028
A *n* **1** (for gas, water etc) (in building) tuyau *m*; (underground) conduite *f*; **2** (smoker's) pipe *f*; **3** Mus (on organ) tuyau *m* (d'orgue); (flute) chalumeau *m*
B **pipes** *npl* Mus cornemuse *f*
C *vtr* **1** (carry) **to ~ water into a house** alimenter un foyer en eau; **oil is ~d across/to le** pétrole est transporté par canalisation à travers/jusqu'à; **2** (transmit) diffuser [*music*] (**to** dans); **3** (in sewing) passepoiler [*cushion, collar*]; Culin **to ~ icing onto a cake** décorer un gâteau; **5** Naut siffler [*order*]; **to ~ sb aboard** accueillir qn à bord au son du sifflet
D *vi* siffler

(Phrasal verbs)
■ **pipe down**○ (quieten down) faire moins de bruit
■ **pipe up** [*voice*] se faire entendre; **'it's me!' she ~d up** 'c'est moi!' dit-elle d'une petite voix

pipe: **~clay** *n* terre *f* de pipe; **~-cleaner** *n* cure-pipe *m*; **~d music** *n* musique *f* d'ambiance; **~-dream** *n* chimère *f*

pipeline /'paɪplaɪn/ *n* Tech oléoduc *m*; **to be in the ~** *fig* être en cours

pipe: **~ of peace** *n* calumet *m* de la paix; **~ organ** *n* Mus orgue *m*

piper /'paɪpə(r)/ ▸ p. 1181, p. 1028 *n* (bag-pipe player) joueur/ -euse *m/f* de cornemuse; (flute-player) joueur/-euse *m/f* de chalumeau
(Idiom) **he who pays the ~ calls the tune** *Prov* l'argent c'est le pouvoir

pipe: **~-smoker** *n* fumeur/-euse *m/f* de pipe; **~ tobacco** *n* tabac *m* à pipe

piping /'paɪpɪŋ/
A *n* **1** *C* (pipes) tuyauterie *f*; **2** (in sewing) passepoil *m*; **3** Culin décoration *f* (en sucre)
B *adj* [*voice, tone*] flûté

piping hot *adj* fumant

piquant /'piːkənt/ *adj* piquant

pique /piːk/
A *n* dépit *m*; **in a fit of ~** dans un accès de dépit
B *vtr* **1** (hurt) froisser; **2** (arouse) piquer [*interest*]

piqued /piːkt/ *adj* vexé (**at, by** par; **to do** de faire)

piracy /'paɪərəsɪ/ *n* **1** Naut piraterie *f*; **2** (of tapes, software) duplication *f* pirate (**of** de)

pirate /'paɪərət/
A *n* **1** Naut pirate *m*; **2** (copy of tape etc) contrefaçon *f*; **3** (*also* **~ station**) station *f* pirate; **4** (entrepreneur) pirate *m*; **5** (copier) contrefacteur *m*
B *noun modifier* [*video, tape*] pirate; [*ship*] de pirates
C *vtr* pirater [*tape, video, software*]

pirate radio *n* radio *f* pirate

Pisces /'paɪsiːz/ ▸ p. 1350 *n* Poissons *mpl*

pistachio /pɪ'stɑːʃɪəʊ, US -æʃɪəʊ/ *n* (*pl* **~s**) **1** (nut, flavour) pistache *f*; **2** (tree) pistachier *m*

pistol /'pɪstl/ *n* pistolet *m*

piston /'pɪstən/ *n* piston *m*

piston: **~ engine** *n* moteur *m* à pistons; **~ pin** *n* axe *m* de piston; **~ rod** *n* tige *f* de piston

pit /pɪt/
A *n* **1** (for storage, weapons, bodies) *also* Aut fosse *f*; (trap) trappe *f*; (at racetrack) stand *m*; **gravel ~** carrière *f* de gravier; **the ~ of the stomach** le creux du ventre; **2** (mine) mine *f*; **to go down the ~** aller travailler à la mine; **3** Theat parterre *m*; **orchestra ~** fosse *f* d'orchestre; **4** US (in peach, olive) noyau *m*
B *vtr* (*p prés etc* **-tt-**) **1** (in struggle) **to ~ sb against** opposer qn

à [*opponent*]; **2** (mark) marquer [*surface, stone*]; **3** US dénoyauter [*peach, olive*]
C *v refl* **to ~ oneself against sb** se mesurer à qn
(Idiom) **it's the ~s**○! c'est l'enfer!

pitapat /ˌpɪtə'pæt/ *n* **to go ~** faire toc-toc

pit bull terrier *n* pit bull *m*

pitch /pɪtʃ/
A *n* **1** Sport terrain *m*; **football ~** terrain de foot(ball); **2** (sound level) gen (of note, voice) hauteur *f*; Mus ton *m*; **absolute ~**, **perfect ~** oreille *f* absolue; **3** (degree) degré *m*; (highest point) comble *m*; **excitement was at full ~** l'excitation était à son comble; **4** (sales talk) gen, Comm boniment *m*; **5** Constr, Naut (tar) brai *m*; **6** (for street trader) emplacement *m*
B *vtr* **1** (throw) jeter [*object*] (**into** dans); Sport lancer; **to be ~ed forward** [*person*] être projeté vers l'avant; **2** (aim) adapter [*campaign, speech*] (**at** à); (set) fixer [*price*]; **programme ~ed at young people** émission qui vise un public jeune; **the exam was ~ed at a high level** l'examen a été ajusté à un haut niveau; **3** Mus [*singer*] trouver [*note*]; [*player*] donner [*note*]; **to ~ one's voice higher/lower** hausser/baisser le ton de la voix; **4** (erect) planter [*tent*]; **to ~ camp** établir un camp
C *vi* **1** (be thrown) [*rider, passenger*] être projeté; **to ~ and roll** *ou* **toss** Naut tanguer; **2** US (in baseball) lancer (la balle)

(Phrasal verbs)
■ **pitch in**○ (set to work) s'atteler à la tâche; (start to eat) attaquer○; (join in) y mettre du sien○; (help) donner un coup de main○
■ **pitch into**: ▸ **~ into [sth]** (attack) attaquer [*opponent, speaker*]; attaquer [*work, meal*]; ▸ **~ [sb] into** propulser [qn] dans [*situation*]
■ **pitch out**○: ▸ **~ out [sb/sth]**, **~ [sb/sth] out** éjecter [*person*] (**from** de)

pitch: **~-and-putt** *n* mini-golf *m*; **~-black**, **~ dark** *adj* tout noir; **~ed battle** *n* *lit, fig* bataille *f* rangée

pitcher /'pɪtʃə(r)/ *n* **1** (jug) cruche *f*; **2** US Sport lanceur *m*

pitchfork /'pɪtʃfɔːk/
A *n* fourche *f*
B *vtr* **1** Agric ramasser à la fourche; **2** *fig* **to ~ sb into** parachuter qn dans [*situation*]

piteous /'pɪtɪəs/ *adj* [*sight, story*] pitoyable; [*state*] piteux/ -euse

pitfall /'pɪtfɔːl/ *n* *fig* écueil *m* (**of** de)

pith /pɪθ/ *n* (of fruit) peau *f* blanche; (of stem) moelle *f*; *fig* essence *f* (**of** de)

pit head *n* carreau *m* de mine

pithy /'pɪθɪ/ *adj* [*remark, style, writing*] (concise) concis; (incisive) piquant

pitiable /'pɪtɪəbl/ *adj* [*existence, sight*] pitoyable; [*salary*] misérable; [*attempt, excuse*] lamentable

pitiful /'pɪtɪfl/ *adj* [*cry, sight*] pitoyable; [*income*] misérable; [*attempt, excuse, state*] lamentable; [*amount*] ridicule

pitifully /'pɪtɪfəlɪ/ *adv* [*thin*] à faire peur; [*cry, suffer*] pitoyablement; [*poor, small*] lamentablement

pitiless /'pɪtɪlɪs/ *adj* impitoyable

pittance /'pɪtns/ *n* **to live on/earn a ~** vivre avec/gagner trois fois rien

pitted /'pɪtɪd/ *adj* **1** [*surface*] rongé; [*face, skin*] grêlé (**with** de); **2** [*olive*] dénoyauté

pitter-patter /'pɪtəpætə(r)/ *n* = pitapat

pituitary /pɪ'tjuːɪtərɪ, US -tuːəterɪ/ *adj* pituitaire; **~ gland** hypophyse *f*

pit worker ▸ p. 1181 *n* mineur *m* de fond

pity /'pɪtɪ/
A *n* **1** (compassion) pitié *f* (**for** pour); **out of ~** par pitié; **to feel ~** avoir de la pitié; **2** (shame) dommage *m*; **what a ~!** quel dommage!; **I'm not rich, more's the ~** je ne suis pas riche, c'est bien dommage
B *vtr* avoir pitié de; **he's to be pitied** il faut avoir pitié de lui; **it's the police I ~, not the criminals** c'est la police que je plains, pas les criminels

pityingly /'pɪtɪɪŋlɪ/ *adv* **1** (compassionately) avec pitié; **2** (scornfully) avec mépris

pivot /'pɪvət/
A *n* Mil, Tech, *fig* pivot *m*
B *vtr* faire pivoter [*lever*]; orienter [*lamp*]

C vi [*lamp, device*] pivoter (**on** sur); fig [*outcome, success*] reposer (**on** sur)

pivotal /'pɪvətl/ *adj* [*role, decision*] essentiel/-ielle; [*moment*] crucial

pixie /'pɪksɪ/ *n* lutin *m*

pizza /'pi:tsə/
A *n* pizza *f*
B *noun modifier* [*base, oven, pan*] à pizza

pizza parlour GB, **pizza parlor** US *n* pizzeria *f*

pizzazz○ /pɪ'zæz/ *n* panache *m*

placard /'plækɑ:d/ *n* (at protest march) pancarte *f*; (on wall) affiche *f*

placate /plə'keɪt, US 'pleɪkeɪt/ *vtr* apaiser, calmer

placatory /plə'keɪtərɪ, US 'pleɪkətɔːrɪ/ *adj* apaisant

place /pleɪs/
A *n* ①（location, position) endroit *m*; **from ~ to ~** d'un endroit à l'autre; **same time, same ~** même heure, même endroit; **in ~s** [*hilly, damaged, worn*] par endroits; **in several ~s** (in region) dans plusieurs endroits; (on body) à plusieurs endroits; **~ of birth/work** lieu *m* de naissance/travail; **~ of residence** domicile *m*; **this is the ~ for me!** c'est le rêve ici!; **to be in the right ~ at the right time** être là où il faut quand il le faut; **I can't be in two ~s at once!** je ne peux pas être partout à la fois!; **in Oxford, of all ~s!** à Oxford, figure-toi!; **to lose/find one's ~** (in book) perdre/retrouver sa page; (in paragraph, speech) perdre/retrouver le fil; **he had no ~ to go**○ surtout US il n'avait nulle part où aller; **some ~**○ surtout US quelque part; ②（town, hotel etc) endroit *m*; **a good ~ to eat** une bonne adresse (pour manger); **a little ~ called...** un petit village du nom de...; **in a ~ like Kent** dans une région comme le Kent; **to be seen in all the right ~s** se montrer dans les lieux qui comptent; **all over the ~** (everywhere) partout; fig○ [*speech, lecture*] complètement décousu; [*hair*] en bataille; ③（home) **David's ~** chez David; **a ~ by the sea** une maison au bord de la mer; **a ~ of one's own** un endroit à soi; **your ~ or mine?** chez toi ou chez moi?; ④（seat, space) (on bus, at table, in queue) place *f*; (setting) couvert *m*; **to keep a ~** garder une place (**for** pour); **please take your ~s** veuillez prendre place; **to lay** *ou* **set a ~ for sb** mettre un couvert pour qn; ⑤（on team, with firm) place *f* (**on** dans); (on committee, board) siège *m* (**on** au sein de); **a ~ as** une place comme [*au pair, cook, cleaner*]; ⑥ GB Univ place *f* (**at** à); **to get a ~ on** obtenir une place dans [*course*]; **she has a ~ on a carpentry course** elle a été acceptée pour suivre des cours de menuiserie; ⑦（in competition, race) place *f*; **to finish in first ~** terminer premier/-ière *ou* à la première place; **to take second ~** fig (in importance) passer au deuxième plan; **in the first ~** fig (firstly) en premier lieu; (at the outset) pour commencer; ⑧（in order, correct position) **everything is in its ~** tout est bien à sa place; **to hold sth in ~** maintenir qch en place; **in ~** [*law, system, scheme*] en place; **to put sb in his/her ~** remettre qn à sa place; **to know qn's ~** rester à sa place; ⑨（role) **it's not my ~ to do** ce n'est pas à moi de faire; **to take sb's ~** prendre la place de qn; **to have no ~ in** n'avoir aucune place dans [*organization, philosophy*]; ⑩（situation) **in my/his ~** à ma/sa place; **to change ~s with sb** changer de place avec qn; ⑪（moment) moment *m*; **in ~s** [*funny, boring, silly*] par moments

B out of place *adj phr* déplacé; **to look out of ~** [*building, person*] détonner; **to feel out of ~** ne pas se sentir à l'aise

C in place of *prep phr* à la place de [*person, object*]

D *vtr* ①（put) placer, mettre [*object*]; mettre [*advertisement*]; **to ~ sth back on** remettre qch sur [*shelf, table*]; **to ~ an order for sth** passer une commande pour qch; **to ~ emphasis on sth** mettre l'accent sur qch; **to ~ one's trust in** placer sa confiance en; **to ~ sb at risk** faire courir des risques à qn; ②（locate) placer; **to be awkwardly ~d** être mal placé; **he is not well ~d to judge** il est mal placé pour juger; ③（rank) (in competition) classer; (in exam) GB classer; **to be ~d third** [*horse, athlete*] arriver troisième; ④（identify) situer [*person*]; reconnaître [*accent*]; **I can't ~ his face** je ne le reconnais pas; ⑤ Admin (send, appoint) placer [*student, trainee*] (**in** dans); (find home for) placer [*child*]; **to ~ sb in charge of a project** confier la direction d'un projet à qn

(Idioms) **that young man is really going ~s**○ voilà un jeune homme qui ira loin; **to have friends in high ~s** avoir des amis haut placés; **to fall** *ou* **fit into ~** devenir clair; ▸ **take place**

placebo /plə'si:bəʊ/ *n* ① Med placebo *m*; ② fig os *m* à ronger

place mat *n* set *m* de table

placement /'pleɪsmənt/ *n* ① GB (also **work ~**) (trainee post) stage *m*; **to get a ~** trouver un stage; ②（in accommodation, employment) (of child, unemployed person) placement *m* (**in** dans); ③ Fin placement *m*

place-name /'pleɪsneɪm/ *n* nom *m* de lieu

placid /'plæsɪd/ *adj* [*person, animal, nature, smile*] placide

placing /'pleɪsɪŋ/ *n* ①（position) (in race, contest, league) classement *m*, place *f*; ②（of ball, players) (positioning) positionnement *m*; (location) position *f*; ③ Fin placement *m*

plagiarism /'pleɪdʒərɪzəm/ *n* plagiat *m*

plagiarize /'pleɪdʒəraɪz/ *vtr, vi* plagier

plague /pleɪg/
A *n* Med (bubonic) peste *f*; (epidemic) épidémie *f*; fig (of ants, rats, locusts etc) invasion *f*; **what a ~ that boy is!** quelle plaie ce garçon!
B *vtr* ①（beset) **to be ~d by** *ou* **with** être en proie à [*doubts, remorse, difficulties*]; **he's ~d by ill health** il a sans arrêt des ennuis de santé; ②（harass) harceler

(Idiom) **to avoid sb/sth like the ~** fuir qn/qch comme la peste

plaice /pleɪs/ *n* (*pl* **~**) plie *f*, carrelet *m*

plaid /plæd/
A *n* (fabric) tissu *m* écossais; (pattern) motif *m* écossais
B *noun modifier* [*scarf, shirt, design*] écossais

plain /pleɪn/
A *n* plaine *f*
B *adj* ①（simple) [*dress, food, language*] simple; [*building, furniture*] sobre; **a ~ man** un homme simple; ②（background, fabric) uni; [*envelope*] sans inscription; [*paper*] (unlined) non réglé; (unheaded) libre; **under ~ cover** Post sous pli discret; ③ euph (unattractive) [*woman*] quelconque; **she's rather ~** elle n'a rien d'une beauté; ④（obvious) évident, clair; **it's ~ to see** ça saute aux yeux; **to make it ~ to sb that** faire comprendre clairement à qn que; ⑤（direct) [*answer, language*] franc/franche; **~ speaking** franchise *f*; **in ~ English, this means that...** en clair, ceci veut dire que...; ⑥（tjrs épith) (downright) [*common sense*] simple (before *n*); [*ignorance, laziness*] pur et simple (after *n*); ⑦ [*yoghurt, crisps, rice*] nature inv; ⑧（in knitting) [*stitch, row*] à l'endroit
C *adv* [*stupid, wrong*] tout bonnement

(Idioms) **to be as ~ as day** être clair comme l'eau de roche; **to be ~ sailing** [*project, task etc*] marcher comme sur des roulettes

plain chocolate *n* chocolat *m* à croquer

plain clothes
A *npl* **to wear ~, to be in ~** être en civil
B **plain-clothes** *adj* [*policeman etc*] en civil

plain flour *n* Culin farine *f* (*sans levure*)

plainly /'pleɪnlɪ/ *adv* ①（obviously) manifestement; ②（distinctly) [*hear*] distinctement; [*see, remember, state*] clairement; ③（frankly) [*speak*] franchement; ④ [*dress, eat*] simplement; [*furnished*] sobrement

plainness /'pleɪnnɪs/ *n* ①（of decor, dress) sobriété *f*; (of food, language) simplicité *f*; ②（unattractiveness) manque *m* de beauté

plain: ~song *n* plain-chant *m*; **~-spoken** *adj* direct

plaintiff /'pleɪntɪf/ *n* Jur plaignant/-e *m/f*

plaintive /'pleɪntɪv/ *adj* plaintif/-ive

plait /plæt/
A *n* natte *f*; **to wear ~s** avoir des nattes
B *vtr* tresser [*hair, rope*]; **to ~ one's hair** se faire des nattes

plan /plæn/
A *n* ①（scheme, course of action) plan *m*; **the ~ is to leave very early** nous avons prévu de partir très tôt; **to go according to ~** se passer comme prévu; ②（definite aim) projet *m* (**for** de; **to do** pour faire); **to have a ~ to do** projeter de faire; ③（outline, map) also Archit, Constr, Tech plan *m*
B **plans** *npl* ①（arrangements) projets *mpl*; **what are your ~s for the future?** quels sont vos projets d'avenir?; **to make ~s for sth** (organize arrangements) organiser qch; (envisage) projeter qch; **I have no particular ~s** (for tonight) je n'ai rien de prévu; (for the future) je n'ai pas de projets bien déterminés; **but Paul had other ~s** mais Paul avait prévu autre chose; ② Archit, Constr **the ~s** les plans *mpl*
C *vtr* (*p prés etc* **-nn-**) ①（prepare, organize) planifier [*future, economy*]; organiser, préparer [*timetable, meeting, expedition*]; préparer [*retirement*]; organiser [*day*]; faire un plan de [*career*]; faire le plan de [*essay, book*]; préméditer [*crime*]; **he**

~ned it so he could leave early il s'est organisé pour pouvoir partir tôt; **to ~ a family** planifier les naissances; **2** (intend, propose) projeter [*visit, trip*]; prévoir [*new development, factory*]; **to ~ to do** projeter de faire; **3** Archit, Constr (design) concevoir [*kitchen, garden, city centre*]

D *vi* (*p prés* **-nn-**) prévoir; **to ~ on doing/on sth** (expect) s'attendre à faire/à qch; (intend) compter faire/sur qch

(Phrasal verb)

■ **plan ahead** (vaguely) faire des projets; (look, think ahead) prévoir

plane /pleɪn/

A *n* **1** Aviat avion *m*; **2** (in geometry) plan *m*; (face of cube, pyramid) face *f*; **3** Tech (tool) rabot *m*; **4** Bot (*also* ~ **tree**) platane *m*

B *adj* (flat) plan, uni

C *vtr* raboter [*wood, edge*]; **to ~ sth smooth** lisser qch au rabot

D *vi* [*bird, aircraft, glider*] planer

planet /'plænɪt/ *n* planète *f*

plank /plæŋk/

n planche *f*; fig (of policy, argument) point *m*; **to walk the ~** Naut Hist être exécuté par noyade

(Idiom) **to be as thick as two (short) ~s**⊘ en tenir une couche⊘

planner /'plænə(r)/ *n* gen planificateur/-trice *m/f*; (in town planning) urbaniste *mf*

planning /'plænɪŋ/

A *n* **1** (of industry, economy, work) planification *f*; (of holiday, party) organisation *f*; **2** Archit (in town) urbanisme *m*; (out of town) aménagement *m* du territoire

B *noun modifier* gen, Admin [*decision*] prévisionnel/-elle; Archit [*department, authorities*] de l'urbanisme; **at the ~ stage** à l'état de projet

planning application *n* demande *f* de permis de construire

planning board *n* **1** (in town-planning) commission *f* d'urbanisme; **2** Econ commission *f* de planification

planning: ~ committee *n* = **planning board 1**; **~ permission** *n* permis *m* de construire

plant /plɑːnt, US plænt/

A *n* **1** Bot plante *f*; **2** Ind (factory) usine *f*; (power station) centrale *f*; **3** *C* Ind (buildings and machinery) installations *fpl* industrielles et commerciales; (fixed machinery) installations *fpl*; (movable machinery) matériel *m*

B *vtr* **1** planter [*seed, bulb, tree*]; **to ~ a field with wheat** semer un champ de blé; **2** (illicitly) placer [*bomb, spy*]; **to ~ a weapon on sb** placer une arme sur qn pour l'incriminer; **3** (place) **to ~ a kiss on sth** planter un baiser sur qch; **to ~ an idea in sb's mind** mettre une idée dans la tête de qn

C *v refl* **to ~ oneself between/in front of** se planter entre/devant

(Phrasal verb)

■ **plant out**: ▸ ~ [sth] out, ~ out [sth] repiquer [*seedlings*]

plantation /plæn'teɪʃn/ *n* (all contexts) plantation *f*

planter /'plɑːntə(r), US 'plænt-/ *n* (person) planteur/-euse *m/f*; (machine) planteuse *f*

plant: ~ food *n* engrais *m*; **~ hire** *n* GB location *f* de machines

planting /'plɑːntɪŋ, US 'plænt-/ *n* plantation *f*

plant: ~ kingdom *n* règne *m* végétal; **~ life** *n* flore *f*

plaque /plɑːk, US plæk/ *n* **1** (on wall, monument) plaque *f*; **2** (dental) ~ plaque *f* dentaire

plasma /'plæzmə/ *n* Med, Phys plasma *m*

plasma screen *n* écran *m* à plasma

plaster /'plɑːstə(r), US 'plæs-/

A *n* **1** Constr, Med, Art plâtre *m*; **2** GB (bandage) sparadrap *m*; **a (piece of)** ~ un pansement

B *vtr* **1** Constr **to ~ the walls of a house** faire les plâtres d'une maison; **2** (cover) (with posters, pictures) couvrir (**with** de)

(Phrasal verbs)

■ **plaster down**: ▸ ~ down [sth], ~ [sth] down plaquer [*hair*]

■ **plaster over**: ▸ ~ over [sth] Constr boucher [*crack, hole*]

plaster: ~board *n* placoplâtre® *m*; **~ cast** *n* Med plâtre *m*; Art (mould) moulage *m*; (sculpture) plâtre *m*

plastered⊘ /'plɑːstəd, US 'plæst-/ *adj* (drunk) beurré⊘

plasterer /'plɑːstərə(r), US 'plæst-/ ▸ p. 1181 *n* plâtrier *m*

plastic /'plæstɪk/

A *n* plastique *m*

B **plastics** *npl* (matières *fpl*) plastiques *mpl*

C *adj* **1** [*bag*] en plastique; **2** Art plastique

plastic: ~ bomb *n* bombe *f* au plastic; **~ bullet** *n* balle *f* (de) plastique; **~ foam** *n* polystyrène *m* expansé

Plasticine® /'plæstɪsiːn/ *n* pâte *f* à modeler

plastic: ~ money⊘ *n* cartes *fpl* de crédit; **~ surgeon** ▸ p. 1181 *n* chirurgien *m* esthétique; **~ surgery** *n* (cosmetic) chirurgie *f* esthétique; Med chirurgie *f* plastique

plate /pleɪt/

A *n* **1** (dish) (for eating) assiette *f*; (for serving) plat *m*; **to hand ou present sth to sb on a ~** lit, GB fig apporter or présenter qch à qn sur un plateau; **2** (dishful) assiette *f*; **3** (sheet of metal) plaque *f*, tôle *f*; **4** (name plaque) plaque *f*; **5** (registration plaque) plaque *f* minéralogique; **6** *C* (silverware) gen argenterie *f*; Relig trésor *m*; **7** (metal coating) plaqué *m*; **8** (illustration) planche *f*; **9** Phot plaque *f*; **10** (in dentistry) dentier *m*; **11** Geog, Zool plaque *f*; **12** Sport (trophy) plaque *f*; (competition) coupe *f*; **13** Med plaque *f*

B *vtr* plaquer [*bracelet, candlestick*] (**with** avec, de)

C **-plated** *combining form* **gold/silver-~d** plaqué or/argent

(Idiom) **to have a lot on one's ~** avoir beaucoup à faire

plateau /'plætəʊ, US plæ'təʊ/ *n* (*pl* ~**s** *or* ~**x**) **1** Geog plateau *m*; **2** fig palier *m*

plate glass

A *n* verre *m* à vitre

B *noun modifier* [*window, door*] en verre à vitre

platelet /'pleɪtlɪt/ *n* plaquette *f*

plate: ~-rack *n* (for draining) égouttoir *m*; **~ warmer** *n* chauffe-assiettes *m inv*

platform /'plætfɔːm/ *n* **1** (stage) (for performance) estrade *f*; (at public meeting) tribune *f*; **to provide a ~ for sb/sth** offrir une tribune à qn/qch; **2** (in oil industry, in scaffolding, on vehicle, for guns) plate-forme *f*; (on weighing machine) plateau *m*; **3** Pol plate-forme *f* électorale; **4** Rail quai *m*

platform: ~ scales *n* bascule *f*; **~ shoes** *npl* chaussures *fpl* à plateforme; **~ ticket** *n* GB Rail ticket *m* de quai

platinum /'plætɪnəm/

A *n* platine *m*

B *noun modifier* [*ring, jewellery*] de *or* en platine

platinum blonde *n* blonde *f* platine *or* platinée

platitude /'plætɪtjuːd, US -tuːd/ *n* platitude *f*

Platonic /plə'tɒnɪk/ *adj* **1** (*also* **platonic**) [*love, relationship*] platonique; **2** Philos platonicien/-ienne

platoon /plə'tuːn/ *n* (+ *v sg ou pl*) Mil (of soldiers, police, firemen) section *f*; (in cavalry, armoured corps) peloton *m*; fig régiment *m*

platter /'plætə(r)/ *n* **1** (dish) plat *m*; **2** Culin **seafood ~** assiette *f* de fruits de mer

platypus /'plætɪpəs/ *n* ornithorynque *m*

plausible /'plɔːzəbl/ *adj* [*story, plot, alibi*] plausible, vraisemblable; [*person*] convaincant

plausibly /'plɔːzəblɪ/ *adv* [*speak*] avec vraisemblance

play /pleɪ/ ▸ p. 881, p. 1028

A *n* **1** Theat pièce *f* (**about** sur); **a radio ~** une pièce radiophonique; **2** (amusement, recreation) **the sound of children at ~** le bruit d'enfants en train de jouer; **to learn through ~** apprendre par le jeu; **3** Sport, Games **~ starts at 11** la partie commence à 11 heures; **the ball is out of ~/in ~** la balle est hors jeu/en jeu; **there was some fine ~ from the Danish team** l'équipe danoise a bien joué; **4** fig (movement, interaction) jeu *m*; **to come into ~** entrer en jeu; **it has brought new factors into ~** cela a introduit de nouveaux éléments; **a ~ on words** un jeu de mots

B *vtr* **1** jouer à [*game, match, cards*]; jouer [*card*]; **to ~ a club** jouer du trèfle; **to ~ goal** (in football) être gardien de but; **to ~ the ball to sb** (in basketball) passer la balle à qn; **to ~ hide and seek** jouer à cache-cache; **to ~ a joke on sb** jouer un tour à qn; **2** Mus jouer de [*instrument*]; jouer [*tune, symphony, chord*]; **they're ~ing the jazz club on Saturday** ils jouent au club de jazz samedi; ③ (act out) Theat interpréter, jouer [*role*]; ④ Audio mettre [*tape, video, CD*]; ~ **me the record** mets-moi le disque; **to** ~ **music** écouter de la musique; **let me** ~ **the tape for you** je vais vous faire entendre la cassette; ⑤ Fin **to** ~ **the stock market** boursicoter○

C *vi* ① [*children*] jouer (**with** avec); ② fig **to** ~ **at being an artist** jouer à l'artiste; **what does he think he's** ~**ing at?** GB○ qu'est-ce qu'il fabrique○?; ③ Sport, Games jouer; **do you** ~? est-ce que tu sais jouer?; **to** ~ **fair** jouer franc-jeu; **to** ~ **into the net** envoyer la balle dans le filet; ④ Mus [*musician, band, orchestra*] jouer (**for** pour); **to** ~ **to large audiences** jouer devant un grand public; ⑤ Cin, Theat [*play*] se jouer; [*film*] passer; [*actor*] jouer; **she's** ~**ing opposite him in 'Macbeth'** elle lui donne la réplique dans 'Macbeth'; ⑥ [*fountain, water*] couler; Mus [*record*] jouer; **I could hear music** ~**ing** j'entendais de la musique

(Idioms) **to** ~ **for time** essayer de gagner du temps; **all work and no** ~ (**makes Jack a dull boy**) Prov il n'y a pas que le travail dans la vie; **to make great** ~ **of sth** accorder beaucoup d'importance à qch

(Phrasal verbs)
■ **play along: to** ~ **along with sb** Mus accompagner qn; fig entrer dans le jeu de qn
■ **play around** (act the fool) faire l'imbécile; **to** ~ **around with** trafiquer [*figures*]; **how much money do we have to** ~ **around with?** combien d'argent avons-nous à notre disposition?
■ **play back:** ▸ ~ [**sth**] **back,** ~ **back** [**sth**] repasser [*song, film, video*]
■ **play down:** ▸ ~ **down** [**sth**] minimiser
■ **play off: to** ~ **sb off against sb** monter qn contre qn (pour en tirer avantage)
■ **play on:** ▸ ~ **on** [*musicians, footballers*] continuer à jouer; ▸ ~ **on** [**sth**] exploiter [*fears, prejudices*]
■ **play out:** ▸ ~ **out** [**sth**] vivre [*fantasy*]; **the drama which is being** ~**ed out in India** le drame qui se déroule en Inde
■ **play up:** ▸ ~ **up**○ [*computer, person*] commencer à faire des siennes○; ▸ ~ **up** [**sth**] mettre l'accent sur [*dangers, advantages*]
■ **play upon = play on**

play: ~**-acting** *n* comédie *f*, simagrées *fpl*; ~ **area** *n* (outside) aire *f* de jeu; (inside) coin-jeu *m*; ~**bill** *n* Theat affiche *f*; ~**boy** *n* playboy *m*; ~**-by-play** *n* US Sport commentaire *m* suivi

player /'pleɪə(r)/ *n* Sport, Mus joueur/-euse *m/f*; Theat comédien/-ienne *m/f*; fig (in negotiations, crisis) protagoniste *mf*; **tennis** ~ joueur/-euse *m/f* de tennis

playful /'pleɪfl/ *adj* [*remark*] taquin; [*child, kitten*] joueur/ -euse

playfully /'pleɪfəlɪ/ *adv* avec espièglerie

play: ~**ground** *n* (in school) cour *f* de récréation; fig (for the rich) lieu *m* de divertissement; ~**group** *n* ≈ halte-garderie *f*; ~**house** *n* théâtre *m*

playing /'pleɪɪŋ/ *n* Mus, Theat interprétation *f*; Sport jeu *m*

playing: ~ **card** *n* carte *f* à jouer; ~ **field** *n* terrain *m* de sport

play: ~**mate** *n* camarade *mf* de jeu; ~**-off** *n* GB (at end of match) prolongation *f*; US match *m* crucial; ~**pen** *n* parc *m* (*pour bébé*); ~**room** *n* salle *f* de jeux; ~**school** *n* ≈ halte-garderie *f*; ~**thing** *n* lit, fig jouet *m*; ~**wright** *n* auteur *m* dramatique

plaza /'plɑːzə, US 'plæzə/ *n* ① (public square) place *f*; **shopping** ~ centre *m* commercial; ② US (services point) aire *f* de service; (toll point) péage *m*

plc, PLC (abrév = **public limited company**) GB SA

plea /pliː/ *n* ① (for tolerance, mercy etc) appel *m* (**for** à); (for money, food) demande *f* (**for** de); **to make a** ~ **for aid** lancer un appel à l'aide; ② Jur **to make** *ou* **enter a** ~ **of guilty/not guilty** plaider coupable/non coupable; ③ (excuse) excuse *f*; **on the** ~ **that** sous prétexte que

plead /pliːd/
A *vtr* (*prét, pp* **pleaded**, US **pled**) ① (beg) supplier; ② (argue) plaider; **to** ~ **sb's case** Jur, fig plaider la cause de qn; ③ (give as excuse) **to** ~ **ignorance** plaider l'ignorance
B *vi* (*prét, pp* **pleaded**, US **pled**) ① (beg) supplier; (more fervently) implorer; ② Jur plaider

pleading /'pliːdɪŋ/
A *n* ① **C** (requests) supplications *fpl*; ② Jur (presentation of a case) plaidoirie *f*
B *adj* [*voice, look*] suppliant

pleasant /'pleznt/ *adj* [*taste, voice, place etc*] agréable; [*person*] agréable, aimable (**to** avec); **it makes a** ~ **change from work!** ça change du travail!

pleasantly /'plezntlɪ/ *adv* [*say, smile, behave*] aimablement; ~ **surprised** agréablement surpris; **it was** ~ **warm** il faisait bon

pleasantry /'plezntrɪ/
A *n* sout (joke) plaisanterie *f*
B **pleasantries** *npl* (polite remarks) civilités *fpl*; **to exchange pleasantries** bavarder aimablement

please /pliːz/
A *adv* gen s'il vous plaît; (to close friend) s'il te plaît; ~ **be seated** sout veuillez vous asseoir fml; '~ **do not smoke**' 'prière de ne pas fumer'; ~, **come in** entrez, je vous en prie; '**may I?**'—'~ **do**' 'je peux?'—'oui, je vous en prie'; ~ **tell me if you need anything** n'hésitez pas à me dire si vous avez besoin de quelque chose; ~ **don't!** pas ça, s'il vous plaît!; **he married a countess, if you** ~! il a épousé une comtesse, rien que ça!
B *vtr* faire plaisir à [*person*]; **she is hard to** ~ elle est difficile à contenter; **you're easily** ~**d!** ce n'est pas dur de te faire plaisir!; **there's no pleasing him** il n'est jamais satisfait
C *vi* plaire; **we aim to** ~ vous satisfaire est notre priorité; **do as you** ~ fais comme tu veux
D *v refl* **to** ~ **oneself** faire comme on veut

pleased /pliːzd/ *adj* content (**that** que + *subj*; **about, at** de; **with** de; **for sb** pour qn); **to look** ~ **with oneself** avoir l'air content de soi; **I am** ~ **to announce that...** j'ai le plaisir d'annoncer que...; **I'm** ~ **to hear it!** quelle bonne nouvelle!; ~ **to meet you** enchanté

pleasing /'pliːzɪŋ/ *adj* [*appearance, shape, colour, voice*] agréable; [*manner, smile, personality*] avenant; [*effect, result*] heureux/-euse

pleasingly /'pliːzɪŋlɪ/ *adv* agréablement

pleasurable /'pleʒərəbl/ *adj* agréable

pleasure /'pleʒə(r)/ *n* ① **C** (enjoyment) plaisir *m* (**of** de; **of doing** de faire); **to take all the** ~ **out of** enlever tout le plaisir de; **to do sth for** ~ faire qch par plaisir; **it gives me no** ~ **to do** il ne m'est pas agréable de faire; ② **C** (enjoyable activity, experience) plaisir *m* (**of** de); **it is/was a** ~ **to do** c'est/ c'était agréable de faire; **to mix business and** ~ joindre l'utile à l'agréable; **are you in Paris for business or** ~? êtes-vous à Paris pour affaires ou pour le plaisir?; ③ (in polite formulae) **it gives me great** ~ **to do** c'est avec plaisir que je fais; **I look forward to the** ~ **of meeting you** (some day) j'espère avoir un jour le plaisir de vous rencontrer; **my** ~ (replying to request for help) avec plaisir; (replying to thanks) je vous en prie; **what an unexpected** ~! gen quelle excellente surprise!; iron ça! par exemple!; '**Mr and Mrs Moor request the** ~ **of your company at their daughter's wedding**' 'M. et Mme Moor vous prient d'assister à la cérémonie de mariage de leur fille'; **at one's** ~ à son gré

pleasure: ~ **boat** *n* bateau *m* de plaisance; ~ **craft** *n* **C** bateaux *mpl* de plaisance; ~ **cruise** *n* croisière *f*

pleat /pliːt/
A *n* pli *m*
B *vtr* plisser
C **pleated** *pp adj* [*skirt*] plissé; [*trousers*] à plis

plebeian /plɪ'biːən/ *n, adj* péj plébéien/-ienne (*m/f*)

pled /pled/ US *pp* ▸ **plead**

pledge /pledʒ/
A *n* ① (promise) promesse *f*; **to give** *ou* **make a** ~ **to do** prendre l'engagement de faire; ② (deposited as security) (to creditor, pawnbroker) gage *m*; **as a** ~ **of her friendship** fig en gage or en témoignage de son amitié; ③ (money promised to charity) promesse *f* de don
B *vtr* ① (promise) promettre [*allegiance, aid, support*] (**to** à); **to** ~ (**oneself**) **to do, to** ~ **that one will do** s'engager à faire; **the treaty** ~**s the signatories to do** le traité engage les signataires à faire; **to be** ~**d to secrecy** être tenu au secret; **to** ~ **one's word** donner sa parole; ② (to creditor, pawnbroker) mettre [qch] en gage

Pledge of Allegiance *n* US Serment *m* au drapeau

ℹ️ **Pledge of Allegiance** Dans les écoles américaines, les élèves se rassemblent tous les jours dans la *Homeroom* avant le début des cours pour l'appel et pour prêter serment au drapeau. Debout, la main droite sur le cœur, ils jurent fidélité et loyauté aux États-Unis d'Amérique en prononçant ces paroles : *I pledge allegiance to the flag of the United States of America and to the republic for which it stands, one nation under God, indivisible, with liberty and justice for all.* Les immigrants qui prennent la nationalité américaine prêtent ce même serment.

plenary /'pliːnərɪ, US -erɪ/ *adj* (*before n*) [*session*] plénier/-ière; [*powers*] plein (*épith*); [*authority*] absolu

plenipotentiary /ˌplenɪpə'tenʃərɪ, US -erɪ/ *adj* [*powers*] plein; [*authority, ambassador*] plénipotentiaire

plentiful /'plentɪfl/ *adj* [*diet, food, harvest*] abondant; **a ~ supply of** une abondance de

plenty /'plentɪ/
A *quantif* **1** (a lot, quite enough) **to have ~ of** avoir beaucoup de [*time, money, friends*]; **there is ~ of time/money** on a tout le temps/l'argent qu'il faut; **there's ~ more where that came from**○**!** (of food, joke etc) profites-en, j'en ai toute une réserve!; **that's ~** c'est bien assez; **£10 will be ~** 10 livres sterling suffiront largement; **2** ¢ (abundance) **a time of ~** une époque prospère; **in ~** en abondance
B ○*adv* **that's ~ big enough!** c'est bien assez grand!; **he cried ~** US il a beaucoup pleuré

pleurisy /'plʊərəsɪ/ ▸ p. 933 *n* pleurésie *f*

pliable /'plaɪəbl/ *adj* [*twig, plastic*] flexible; [*person*] malléable

pliers /'plaɪəz/ *npl* pinces *fpl*; **a pair of ~** des pinces

plight /plaɪt/ *n* **1** (dilemma) situation *f* désespérée; **2** (suffering) détresse *f*; **the ~ of the homeless** la détresse des sans-abri

plimsoll /'plɪmsəl/ *n* GB chaussure *f* de tennis

plinth /plɪnθ/ *n* Archit plinthe *f*; (of statue) socle *m*

PLO *n* (*abrév* = **Palestine Liberation Organization**) OLP *f*

plod /plɒd/ *vi* (*p prés etc* **-dd-**) (walk) marcher péniblement
(Phrasal verbs)
■ **plod along** lit, fig avancer d'un pas lent
■ **plod away** travailler ferme, bosser○
■ **plod on** lit continuer à marcher; fig persévérer
■ **plod through**: ▸ **~ through [sth]** fig faire [qch] laborieusement

plodder /'plɒdə(r)/ *n* bûcheur/-euse○ *m/f*

plodding /'plɒdɪŋ/ *adj* [*step*] lourd; fig laborieux/-ieuse

plonk /plɒŋk/
A *n* **1** (sound) plouf○ *m*, son *m* creux; **2** ○(wine) vin *m* ordinaire, pinard● *m*
B ○*vtr* planter [*plate, bottle*] (on sur)
(Phrasal verb)
■ **plonk down**○: ▸ **~ [sth] down** poser [*box, sack*] (on sur); **to ~ oneself down on** s'installer sur [*sofa*]; ▸ **~ down [sth]** US (pay) allonger○, payer [*sum*]

plop /plɒp/
A *n* floc *m*
B *vi* (*p prés etc* **-pp-**) faire floc

plot /plɒt/
A *n* **1** (conspiracy) complot *m*; **2** Cin, Literat (of novel, film, play) intrigue *f*; **the ~ thickens** l'histoire se corse; **3** Agric (allotment) **~ of land** parcelle *f* de terre; **a vegetable ~** un carré de légumes; **4** Constr (site) terrain *m* à bâtir
B *vtr* (*p prés etc* **-tt-**) **1** (plan) comploter [*murder, attack, return*]; fomenter [*revolution*]; **2** (chart) relever [qch] sur une carte [*course*]; tracer [qch] sur une carte [*progress*]; **we ~ted our position on the map** nous avons pointé notre position sur la carte; **3** Math (on graph) tracer [qch] point par point [*curve, graph*]; reporter [*figures, points*]; **to ~ the progress of sth** tracer la courbe de progression de qch; **4** Literat (invent) inventer [*episode, story, destiny*]
C *vi* (conspire) conspirer (**against** contre)

plotter /'plɒtə(r)/ *n* **1** (schemer) conspirateur/-trice *m/f*; **2** Comput traceur *m* (de courbes)

plotting /'plɒtɪŋ/ *n* ¢ (scheming) complots *mpl*; **to be accused of ~** être accusé d'avoir tramé un complot

plough GB, **plow** US /plaʊ/
A *n* Agric charrue *f*

B *Plough* *pr n* **the Plough** le Grand Chariot *m*
C *vtr* **1** Agric labourer [*land, field*]; creuser [*furrow*]; **2** (invest) **to ~ money into** investir beaucoup d'argent dans [*project, company*]
D *vi* Agric labourer
(Phrasal verbs)
■ **plough back**: ▸ **~ [sth] back**, **~ back [sth]** réinvestir [*profits, money*] (**into** dans)
■ **plough into**: ▸ **~ into [sth]** **1** [*vehicle*] percuter [*tree, wall*]; **the car ~ed into the crowd** la voiture a foncé dans la foule; **2** US se lancer à corps perdu dans [*work*]
■ **plough through**: ▸ **~ through [sth]** fig [*person*] ramer○ sur [*book, task*]; [*walker, vehicle*] avancer péniblement dans [*mud, snow*]
■ **plough up**: ▸ **~ [sth] up**, **~ up [sth]** Agric mettre [qch] en labour [*field*]; fig [*car, person*] défoncer [*ground*]

ploughing GB, **plowing** US /'plaʊɪŋ/ *n* labourage *m*

plough: **~man** GB, **plow-man** US ▸ p. 1181 *n* laboureur *m*; **~man's lunch** *n* GB plat servi dans les pubs composé de fromage, de pain et de salade

plow *n, vtr, vi* US = **plough**

ploy /plɔɪ/ *n* stratagème *m* (**to do** pour faire)

pluck /plʌk/
A *n* (courage) courage *m*, cran○ *m*
B *vtr* **1** cueillir [*flower, fruit*]; **to ~ sth from sb's grasp** arracher qch à qn; **2** Culin plumer [*chicken*]; **3** Mus pincer [*strings*]; pincer les cordes de [*guitar*]; **4** **to ~ one's eyebrows** s'épiler les sourcils
(Idiom)
to ~ up one's courage prendre son courage à deux mains
(Phrasal verbs)
■ **pluck at**: **to ~ at sb's sleeve/arm** tirer qn par la manche/le bras
■ **pluck off**: ▸ **~ off [sth]**, **~ [sth] off** arracher
■ **pluck out**: ▸ **~ out [sth]**, **~ [sth] out** arracher

pluckily /'plʌkɪlɪ/ *adv* vaillamment

plucky /'plʌkɪ/ *adj* courageux/-euse

plug /plʌg/
A *n* **1** Elec (on appliance) prise *f* (de courant); (connecting device) (on computer, for phone) fiche *f*; **to pull out the ~** débrancher la prise; **to pull the ~ on**○ retirer son soutien à [*scheme, project*]; **a mains ~** une prise secteur; **2** (in bath, sink, barrel) bonde *f*; **to pull out the ~** retirer la bonde; **3** Constr (for screw) cheville *f*; **4** (stopper) bonde *f*; (for leak) bouchon *m*; (for medical purpose) tampon *m*; **5** Aut (also **spark ~**) bougie *f*; **6** (in advertising) **to give sth a ~** faire de la publicité pour qch
B *vtr* (*p prés etc* **-gg-**) **1** (block) colmater [*leak*] (**with** avec); boucher [*hole*] (**with** avec); **2** ○(promote) faire de la publicité pour [*book, show, product*]; **3** Elec **to ~ sth into** brancher qch à
C *vi* (*p prés etc* **-gg-**) **to ~ into** se brancher à [*TV, computer*]; fig se mettre au courant de [*public opinion, mood*]
(Phrasal verbs)
■ **plug away**○ s'acharner (**at** sur)
■ **plug in**: ▸ **~ in** se brancher; ▸ **~ [sth] in**, **~ in [sth]** brancher [*appliance*]
■ **plug up**: ▸ **~ up [sth]**, **~ [sth] up** boucher [*hole, gap*] (**with** avec)

plug-and-play *n* Comput plug and play, équipement *m* prêt à l'emploi

plughole /'plʌghəʊl/ *n* GB bonde *f*; **to go down the ~** [*ring etc*] tomber dans le trou de l'évier; fig○ s'en aller à vau-l'eau

plug-in
A *n* Comput module *m* complémentaire, plug-in *m inv*
B *adj* [*appliance*] enfichable

plum /plʌm/ ▸ p. 752
A *n* Bot (fruit) prune *f*; (tree) prunier *m*
B *noun modifier* Culin [*tart*] aux prunes; [*jam*] de prunes
C *adj* **1** (also **~-coloured**) prune *inv*; **2** ○(good) **to get a ~ job/part** décrocher un boulot/rôle en or○

plumage /'pluːmɪdʒ/ *n* plumage *m*

plumb /plʌm/
A *n* **1** (weight) **~ line** Constr fil *m* à plomb; Naut sonde *f*; **2** **to be out of ~** *ou* **off ~** ne pas être d'aplomb
B *adv* **1** ○US [*crazy, wrong*] complètement; **2** ○(precisely) **~ in the middle** en plein milieu

P

G vtr sonder [sea, depths]; **to ~ the depths of** fig toucher le fond de [despair, misery]

plumber /'plʌmə(r)/ n plombier m

plumbing /'plʌmɪŋ/ n plomberie f

plume /pluːm/ n (feather) plume f; (of several feathers) panache m; fig (of steam, smoke etc) panache m (**of** de)

plumed /pluːmd/ adj [horse, helmet] empanaché; [hat] à plumes

plummet /'plʌmɪt/ vi [bird, aircraft] tomber à pic; fig [prices, profits, sales] s'effondrer; [temperature, popularity] baisser brusquement

plummy○ /'plʌmɪ/ adj GB [voice] maniéré; [accent] affecté

plump /plʌmp/ adj [person, arm, leg] potelé; [cheek, face] rond, plein

(Phrasal verbs)
- **plump down**○ [person] s'asseoir (lourdement) (**into** dans; **onto** sur)
- **plump for**○: ▸ **~ for [sth]** opter pour
- **plump up**: ▸ **~ up [sth]** redonner du volume à [cushion]

plumpness /'plʌmpnɪs/ n (of person) embonpoint m; (of arms, legs etc) rondeur f

plunder /'plʌndə(r)/
A n **1** (act) pillage m; **2** (booty) butin m
B vtr piller
G vi se livrer au pillage

plunge /plʌndʒ/
A n **1** (from height) plongeon m; **to take a ~** (dive) piquer une tête; **2** Fin (of share prices etc) chute f libre
B vtr plonger (**into** dans); **to be ~d into** être plongé dans [darkness, crisis, strike]; être submergé de [debt]
G vi [road, cliff, waterfall] plonger; [bird, plane] piquer; [person] (dive) plonger; (fall) tomber (**from** de); fig [rate, value] chuter; **to ~ into** fig se lancer dans [activity, career]; sombrer dans [chaos]

(Idiom) **to take the ~** se jeter à l'eau
(Phrasal verb)
- **plunge in** [swimmer] plonger; fig (impetuously) se lancer

plunger /'plʌndʒə(r)/ n (for sink) ventouse f

plunging /'plʌndʒɪŋ/ adj **~ neckline** décolleté m plongeant

pluperfect /ˌpluː'pɜːfɪkt/ Ling
A n plus-que-parfait m
B noun modifier [tense] au plus-que-parfait; [form] du plus-que-parfait

plural /'plʊərəl/
A n Ling pluriel m; **in the ~** au pluriel
B adj Ling [noun, adjective] au pluriel; [form, ending] du pluriel

pluralism /'plʊərəlɪzəm/ n pluralisme m

plus /plʌs/
A n Math plus m; fig (advantage) avantage m
B adj Math, Elec positif/-ive; **~ factor**, **~ point** fig atout m; **the ~ side** le côté positif; **the 65-~ age group** les personnes qui ont 65 ans et plus
G prep Math plus; **15 ~ 12** 15 plus 12
D conj et; **bedroom ~ bathroom** chambre et salle de bains

plus-fours /ˌplʌs'fɔːz/ npl culotte f de golf

plush /plʌʃ/
A n (textile) peluche f
B ○adj [room, hotel] somptueux/-euse; [area] riche

plus sign n Math signe m plus

Pluto /'pluːtəʊ/ pr n **1** Mythol Pluton m; **2** (planet) Pluton f

plutonium /pluː'təʊnɪəm/ n plutonium m

ply /plaɪ/
A n épaisseur f; **two ~ wool** laine deux fils; **three ~ wood** contreplaqué trois plis
B vtr **1** vendre [wares]; **to ~ one's trade** exercer son métier; **2** † manier [pen, oars]; **3** **to ~ sb with** assaillir qn de [questions]; **to ~ sb with food/drink** ne cesser de remplir l'assiette/le verre de qn
G vi [boat, bus] faire la navette (**between** entre)

plywood /'plaɪwʊd/ n contreplaqué m

pm ▸ p. 745 adv (abrév = **post meridiem**) **two pm** deux heures de l'après-midi; **nine pm** neuf heures du soir

PM n GB abrév ▸ **Prime Minister**

PMS n (abrév = **premenstrual syndrome**) SPM m

PMT n (abrév = **premenstrual tension**) SPM m

pneumatic /njuː'mætɪk, US nuː-/ adj pneumatique

pneumatic drill n marteau m piqueur

pneumonia /njuː'məʊnɪə, US nuː-/ ▸ p. 933 n pneumonie f

PO **1** abrév ▸ **post office**; **2** abrév ▸ **postal order**

poach /pəʊtʃ/
A vtr **1** chasser [qch] illégalement [game]; fig (steal) débaucher [staff, players] (**from** de); s'approprier [idea] (**from** de); **2** Culin faire pocher
B vi (hunt) lit braconner; **to ~ on sb's territory** fig empiéter sur le territoire de qn
G poached pp adj Culin [egg, fish] poché

poacher /'pəʊtʃə(r)/ n **1** (hunter) braconnier m; **2** (for eggs) pocheuse f

poaching /'pəʊtʃɪŋ/ n (of game) braconnage m

PO Box (abrév écrite = **Post Office Box**) **~ 20** BP 20

pocket /'pɒkɪt/
A n **1** poche f; **to go through sb's ~s** faire les poches de qn; **he paid for it out of his own ~** il l'a payé de sa poche; **prices to suit every ~** fig des prix à la portée de tout le monde; **2** (in billiards) bourse f
B noun modifier [flask, diary, dictionary, edition] de poche
G vtr lit, vtr empocher

(Idioms) **to be in ~** GB être en fonds; **to be out of ~** GB en être de sa poche; **to have sb in one's ~** avoir qn dans sa poche; **to live in each other's ~s** être tout le temps l'un sur l'autre; **to ~ one's pride** ravaler sa fierté

pocketbook /'pɒkɪtbʊk/ n **1** (wallet) portefeuille m; **2** US (also **pocket book**) livre m de poche; **3** US (handbag) sac m à main

pocketful /'pɒkɪtfʊl/ n poche f pleine (**of** de)

pocket: **~-handkerchief** n pochette f; **~knife** n couteau m de poche; **~ money** n argent m de poche; **~-size(d)** adj [book, map, edition etc] de poche; fig (tiny) tout petit

pockmarked adj [skin, face] grêlé

pod /pɒd/ n (of peas, beans) (intact) gousse f; (empty) cosse f; (of vanilla) gousse f

podgy○ /'pɒdʒɪ/ adj grassouillet/-ette

podium /'pəʊdɪəm/ n (pl **-iums**, **-ia**) (for speaker, conductor) estrade f; (for winner) podium m

poem /'pəʊɪm/ n poème m

poet /'pəʊɪt/ n poète m

poetic /pəʊ'etɪk/ adj poétique

poetically /pəʊ'etɪklɪ/ adv avec poésie

poetic: **~ justice** n justice f immanente; **~ licence** GB, **~ license** US n licence f poétique

poetry /'pəʊɪtrɪ/ n poésie f; **to write/read ~** écrire/lire des poèmes; **a collection of ~** un recueil de poèmes

po-faced○ /'pəʊfeɪst/ adj GB **to look/be ~** avoir l'air pincé

pogo-stick /'pəʊɡəʊstɪk/ n Games échasse f à ressort

poignant /'pɔɪnjənt/ adj poignant

point /pɔɪnt/
A n **1** (of knife, needle, pencil etc) pointe f; **2** (location, position on scale) point m; (less specific) endroit m; **embarkation ~** lieu m d'embarquement; **~ of entry** (into country) point d'arrivée; (of bullet into body) point d'impact; (into atmosphere) point d'entrée; **~ of no return** point de non-retour; **3** (extent, degree) point m; **I've got to the ~ where I can't take any more** j'en suis arrivé au point où je n'en peux plus; **up to a ~** jusqu'à un certain point; **4** (moment) (precise) moment m; (stage) stade m; **to be on the ~ of doing** être sur le point de faire; **at this ~ he broke down** à ce moment-là il a fondu en larmes; **at some ~ in the future** plus tard; **at one ~** à un moment donné; **when it came to the ~ of deciding** quand il a fallu décider; **at this ~ in time** dans l'état actuel des choses; **5** (question, idea) point m; **to take up ou return to sb's ~** revenir sur un point soulevé par qn; **this proves my ~** cela confirme ce que je viens de dire; **to make a ~** faire une remarque (**about** sur); **to make the ~ that** faire remarquer que; **you've made your ~, please let me speak** vous vous êtes exprimé, laissez-moi parler; **to make a ~ of doing sth** (as matter of pride) mettre un point d'honneur à faire qch; (do deliberately) faire qch exprès; **to raise a ~ about sth** soulever la question de qch; **my**

Points of the compass

- *abbreviated as*

north	= nord	N
south	= sud	S
east	= est	E
west	= ouest	O

- *nord, sud, est, ouest is the normal order in French as well as English.*

northeast	= nord-est	NE
northwest	= nord-ouest	NO
north-northeast	= nord-nord-est	NNE
east-northeast	= est-nord-est	ENE

Where?

- *Compass points in French are not normally written with a capital letter. However, when they refer to a specific region in phrases such as* I love the North *or* he lives in the North, *and it is clear where this* North *is, without any further specification such as* of France *or* of Europe, *then they are written with a capital letter, as they often are in English, too. In the following examples,* north *and* nord *stand for any compass point word.*

I love the North
= j'aime le Nord

to live in the North
= vivre dans le Nord

- *Normally, however, these words do not take a capital letter:*

in the north of Scotland
= dans le nord de l'Écosse

Take care to distinguish this from

to the north of Scotland
(i.e. further north than Scotland)
= au nord de l'Écosse

in the south of Spain
= dans le sud de l'Espagne*

it is north of the hill
= c'est au nord de la colline

a few kilometres north
= à quelques kilomètres au nord

due north of here
= droit au nord

* *Note that the south of France is more usually referred to as* le Midi.

- *There is another set of words in French for* north, south *etc., some of which are more common than others:*

(north)	septentrion *(rarely used)*	septentrional(e)
(south)	midi	méridional(e)
(east)	orient	oriental(e)
(west)	occident	occidental(e)

Translating *northern* etc.

a northern town
= une ville du Nord

a northern accent
= un accent du Nord

the most northerly outpost
= l'avant-poste le plus au nord

- *Regions of countries and continents work like this:*

northern Europe
= l'Europe du Nord

eastern France
= l'est de la France

the northern parts of Japan
= le nord du Japon

- *For names of countries and continents which include these compass point words, such as* North America *or* South Korea, *see the dictionary entry.*

Where to?

- *French has fewer ways of expressing this than English has;* vers le *is usually safe:*

to go north
= aller vers le nord

to head towards the north
= se diriger vers le nord

to go northwards
= aller vers le nord

to go in a northerly direction
= aller vers le nord

a northbound ship
= un bateau qui se dirige vers le nord

- *With some verbs, such as* to face, *the French expression changes:*

the windows face north
= les fenêtres donnent au nord

a north-facing slope
= une pente orientée au nord

- *If in doubt, check in the dictionary.*

Where from?

- *The usual way of expressing* from the *is* du:

it comes from the north
= cela vient du nord

from the north of Germany
= du nord de l'Allemagne

- *Note also these expressions relating to the direction of the wind:*

the north wind
= le vent du nord

a northerly wind
= un vent du nord

prevailing north winds
= des vents dominants du nord

the wind is in the north
= le vent est au nord

the wind is coming from the north
= le vent vient du nord

Compass point words used as adjectives

- *The French words* nord, sud, est *and* ouest *are really nouns, so when they are used as adjectives they are invariable.*

the north coast
= la côte nord

the north side
= le côté nord

the north door
= la porte nord

the north wall
= le mur nord

the north face (of a mountain)
= la face nord

Nautical bearings

- *The preposition* by *is translated by* quart *in expressions like the following:*

north by northwest
= nord quart nord-ouest

southeast by south
= sud-est quart sud

p

p

~ **was that** ce que je voulais dire, c'était que; **that's a good** ~ c'est une remarque judicieuse; **I take your** ~ (agreeing) je suis d'accord avec vous; **I take your** ~, **but** je vois bien où vous voulez en venir, mais; **all right,** ~ **taken!** très bien, j'en prends note; **good** ~**!** très juste!; **you've got a** ~ **there** vous n'avez pas tort; **in** ~ **of fact** en fait; **6** (central idea) point *m* essentiel; **to come straight to the** ~ aller droit au fait; **to keep** *ou* **stick to the** ~ rester dans le sujet; **to miss the** ~ ne pas comprendre; **what she said was short and to the** ~ ce qu'elle a dit était bref et pertinent; **that's beside the** ~ là n'est pas la question; **to get the** ~ comprendre; **that's not the** ~ il ne s'agit pas de cela; **7** (purpose) objet *m*; **what's the** ~ **of doing…?** à quoi bon faire…?; **there's no** ~ **in doing** ça ne sert à rien de faire; **I don't see the** ~ **of doing** je ne vois pas l'intérêt de faire; **8** (feature, characteristic) point *m*, côté *m*; **her strong** ~ son point fort; **9** Sport, Fin (in scoring) point *m*; **to win by 4** ~**s** gagner à 4 points près; **to win on** ~**s** (in boxing) remporter une victoire aux points; **match** ~ (in tennis) balle *f* de match; **10** (dot) point *m*; (decimal point) virgule *f*; (diacritic) signe *m* diacritique; Math point *m*; **11** Geog (headland) pointe *f*

B points *npl* **1** GB Rail aiguillages *mpl*, aiguilles *fpl*; **2** Aut électrodes *fpl*; **3** (in ballet) **to dance on** ~**(s)** faire des pointes *fpl*

C *vtr* **1** (aim, direct) **to** ~ **sth at sb** braquer qch sur qn [*camera, gun*]; **to** ~ **one's finger at sb** montrer qn du doigt; **to** ~ **the finger at sb** (accuse) accuser qn; **to** ~ **sth towards** (of car, boat) diriger qch vers; **to** ~ **sb in the right direction** lit, fig mettre qn dans la bonne direction; **2** (show) **to** ~ **the way** to lit (person, signpost) indiquer la direction de; **to** ~ **the way to a fairer system** ouvrir la voie à un système plus équitable; **3** (in ballet, gym) **to** ~ **one's toes** faire des pointes; **4** Constr jointoyer [*wall*]

D *vi* **1** (indicate) indiquer *or* montrer (du doigt); **to** ~ **at sb/sth** montrer qn/qch du doigt; **2** [*signpost, arrow*] indiquer; **to** ~ **at sb** *ou* **in sb's direction** [*gun, camera*] être braqué sur qn; **everything** ~**s in that direction** tout semble indiquer que c'est ainsi; **to** ~ **to sth as evidence of success** citer qch comme preuve d'une réussite

(Phrasal verbs)
■ **point out:** ▸ ~ **out [sth/sb],** ~ **[sth/sb] out** (show) montrer (**to** à); ▸ ~ **out [sth]** faire remarquer [*fact, discrepancy*]; **as he** ~**ed out** comme il l'a fait remarquer
■ **point up:** ▸ ~ **up [sth]** souligner [*contrast, need*]

point-blank /ˌpɔɪntˈblæŋk/ *adv* **1** lit [*shoot*] à bout portant; **2** fig [*refuse, deny*] catégoriquement; [*ask, reply*] de but en blanc

point duty *n* GB **to be on** ~ être affecté à la circulation

pointed /ˈpɔɪntɪd/ *adj* **1** (sharp) [*hat, stick, chin*] pointu; [*window*] en pointe; [*arch*] en ogive; **2** fig [*remark*] qui vise quelqu'un

pointedly /ˈpɔɪntɪdlɪ/ *adv* [*ignore, look*] ostensiblement

pointer /ˈpɔɪntə(r)/ *n* **1** (piece of information) indication *f*; **2** (dog breed) pointer *m*; **3** (for teaching) baguette *f*; **4** (on projector screen) flèche *f*; **5** Comput pointeur *m*

pointillism /ˈpɔɪntɪlɪzəm, ˈpwæntiːlɪzəm/ *n* pointillisme *m*

pointing /ˈpɔɪntɪŋ/ *n* Constr jointoiement *m*

pointless /ˈpɔɪntlɪs/ *adj* [*request, activity*] absurde; [*gesture*] inutile; [*attempt*] vain; **it's** ~ **to do/for me to do** ça ne sert à rien de faire/que je fasse

pointlessly /ˈpɔɪntlɪslɪ/ *adv* pour rien

pointlessness /ˈpɔɪntlɪsnɪs/ *n* absurdité *f*

point: ~ **of contact** *n* contact *m*; ~ **of departure** *n* point *m* de départ; ~ **of order** *n* question *f* relative à la procédure; ~ **of reference** *n* point *m* de référence; ~ **of sale** *n* point *m* de vente; ~**-of-sale advertising** *n* publicité *f* sur les lieux de vente, PLV *f*; ~ **of view** *n* point *m* de vue; ~**(s) system** *n* système *m* de points

poise /pɔɪz/
A *n* **1** (confidence) assurance *f*; **2** (physical elegance) aisance *f*
B *vtr* tenir [*javelin, spade*]

poised /pɔɪzd/ *adj* **1** (self-possessed) [*person*] plein d'assurance; [*manner*] posé; **2** (elegant) plein d'aisance; **3** (suspended) [*pen, knife, hand*] en suspens; **4** (balanced) **to be** ~ **on** se tenir sur [*rock, platform, cliff*]; **5** (on the point of) **to be** ~ **to do** être sur le point de faire

poison /ˈpɔɪzn/
A *n* lit, fig poison *m*
B *vtr* **1** (give poison to) [*person*] empoisonner [*person, animal*] (**with** avec); [*lead, fumes*] intoxiquer; **2** (make poisonous) mettre du poison dans [*foodstuffs, water*]; Ecol (contaminate) empoisonner [*environment, air, rivers*] (**with** avec); fig (damage) empoisonner [*relationship, life*]; corrompre [*mind*]

poisoner /ˈpɔɪzənər/ *n* empoisonneur/-euse *m/f*

poison gas *n* gaz *m* asphyxiant *or* toxique

poisoning /ˈpɔɪzənɪŋ/ *n* empoisonnement *m*

poisonous /ˈpɔɪzənəs/ *adj* **1** (noxious) [*chemicals, gas*] toxique; [*plant, mushroom, berry*] vénéneux/-euse; Zool [*snake, insect, bite*] venimeux/-euse; **2** fig (vicious) [*rumour, propaganda*] pernicieux/-ieuse; [*person*] malveillant

poison-pen letter *n* lettre *f* anonyme pleine de venin

poke /pəʊk/
A *n* (prod) coup *m*
B *vtr* **1** (jab, prod) pousser [qn] du bout du doigt [*person*]; donner un coup dans [*pile, substance*]; tisonner [*fire*] **he** ~**d his food with his fork** il inspecta le contenu de son assiette avec sa fourchette; **2** (push, put) **to** ~ **sth into** enfoncer qch dans [*hole, pot*]; **to** ~ **one's finger into a hole/pot** mettre le doigt dans un trou/pot; **to** ~ **one's head round the door/out of the window** passer la tête par la porte/par la fenêtre; **3** (pierce) **to** ~ **a hole in sth** faire un trou dans qch (**with** avec)

(Idiom) **it's better than a** ~ **in the eye** (with a sharp stick) c'est mieux que rien

(Phrasal verbs)
■ **poke around, poke about** GB fouiner, farfouiller (**in** dans)
■ **poke at:** ▸ ~ **at [sb/sth]** (with finger) pousser [qn] du bout du doigt [*person*]; enfoncer son doigt dans [*pile of objects, cake*]; tâter du bout du doigt [*vegetables, fruit*]; (with stick) piquer dans [*pile of objects*]; chipoter dans [*food*]
■ **poke out:** ▸ ~ **out** [*elbow, toe, blade, spring*] dépasser; [*flower*] poindre; ▸ **to** ~ **out [sth], to** ~ **[sth] out** sortir [*head, nose, tongue*]; **to** ~ **sb's eye out** crever l'œil de qn

poker /ˈpəʊkə(r)/ ▸ p. 881 *n* **1** (for fire) tisonnier *m*; **2** (cardgame) poker *m*

(Idiom) **(as) stiff as a** ~ raide comme la justice

poker-faced /ˈpəʊkəfeɪst/ *adj* [*person*] au visage impénétrable

poky /ˈpəʊkɪ/ *adj* (small) [*room*] minuscule

Poland /ˈpəʊlənd/ ▸ p. 774 *pr n* Pologne *f*

polar /ˈpəʊlə(r)/ *adj* Geog, Elec [*icecap, lights, bear, region*] polaire; [*attraction*] (one) du pôle; (both) des pôles

polarity /pəˈlærətɪ/ *n* **1** Elec, Phys polarité *f*; **2** fig opposition *f*

polarize /ˈpəʊləraɪz/
A *vtr* **1** Elec, Phys polariser; **2** (divide) diviser [*opinion*]
B *vi* (divide) [*opinions*] diverger

pole /pəʊl/ *n* **1** (stick) gen perche *f*; (for tent, flag) mât *m*; (in show jumping) barre *f*; (for skiing) bâton *m*; (piste marker) piquet *m*; **2** Geog, Phys pôle *m*; **to be at the opposite** ~ **from** fig être aux antipodes de; **3** (in fishing) canne *f* à pêche

(Idiom) **to be** ~**s apart** [*people*] être complètement différents; [*theories, methods, opinions*] être diamétralement opposés

Pole /pəʊl/ ▸ p. 1032 *n* Polonais/-e *m/f*

polecat /ˈpəʊlkæt/ *n* **1** (ferret) putois *m*; **2** US (skunk) mouf(f)ette *f*

polemic /pəˈlemɪk/ *n* polémique *f* (**about** sur)

polemical /pəˈlemɪkl/ *adj* polémique

pole: ~ **position** *n* pole position *f*; ~ **star** *n* étoile *f* polaire; ~ **vault** *n* saut *m* à la perche

police /pəˈliːs/
A *n* **1** (+ v pl) (official body) **the** ~ la police; **2** ₵ (individuals) policiers *mpl*
B *vtr* **1** (keep order) maintenir l'ordre dans [*area*]; **2** (patrol) surveiller [*area, frontier*]; organiser le service d'ordre pour [*demonstration, match*]; **3** (monitor) contrôler l'application de [*measures*]

police: ~ **chief** *n* commissaire *m* divisionnaire; ~ **college** *n* centre *m* de formation de la police; ~ **constable, PC** *n* agent *m* de police; ~ **court** *n* tribunal de police et correctionnel; ~ **custody** *n* garde *f* à vue; **Police Department, PD** *n* US services *mpl* de police (d'une ville); **~ escort** n escorte f policière; **~ force** n police f; **~ headquarters** npl administration f centrale de la police; **~man** n agent m de police; **~ officer** n policier m; **~ record** n casier m judiciaire; **~ state** n péj État m policier; **~ station** n poste m de police; (larger) commissariat m; **~ van** n fourgon m cellulaire; **~woman** n femme f policier

police work n ① *C* (detection) investigations fpl policières; ② (profession) métier m de policier

policing /pə'li:sɪŋ/ n ① (maintaining law and order) maintien m de l'ordre; ② (patrolling) surveillance f; ③ (of demonstration, match) organisation f du service d'ordre; ④ (of measures, regulations) contrôle m de l'application

policy /'pɒləsɪ/
A n ① (plan, rule) politique f (on sur); **it is our ~ to do** nous avons pour politique de faire; **to have** ou **follow a ~ of doing** avoir pour politique de faire; **it is our ~ that** notre politique est de; **our company has a no-smoking ~** notre société a mis en place des mesures de restriction du tabagisme; ② (in insurance) (type of cover) contrat m; (document) police f
B noun modifier [decision, statement] de principe; [discussion, matter, meeting, paper] de politique générale

policy: ~holder n assuré/-e m/f; **~-making** n *C* décisions fpl; **~ unit** n comité m de conseillers politiques

polio /'pəʊlɪəʊ/, **poliomyelitis** /ˌpəʊlɪəʊˌmaɪə'laɪtɪs/ ▸ p. 933 n poliomyélite f

polish /'pɒlɪʃ/
A n ① (substance) (for wood, floor) cire f; (for shoes) cirage m; (for brass, silver) pâte f à polir; (for car) lustre m; ② (shiny surface) éclat m; ③ fig (elegance) (of manner, performance) brio m; (of person) chic m
B vtr ① lit cirer [shoes, furniture]; astiquer [leather, car, glass, brass]; polir [stone]; ② fig (refine) soigner [performance, image]; affiner [style]
C vi cirer

(Phrasal verbs)
■ **polish off**○: ▸ **~ off [sth]**, **~ [sth] off** (eat, finish) expédier○ [food, job]
■ **polish up**: ▸ **~ up [sth]**, **~ [sth] up** ① lit astiquer [glass, car, silver]; cirer [wood, floor]; ② ○(perfect) parfaire [Spanish, piano playing]; perfectionner [sporting skill]; **to ~ up one's act** fignoler○ son numéro

Polish /'pəʊlɪʃ/ ▸ p. 1032, p. 969
A n (language) polonais m
B adj polonais

polished /'pɒlɪʃt/ adj ① lit [surface, wood] poli; [floor, shoes] ciré; [silver, brass] astiqué; ② fig (refined) [manner] raffiné; ③ (accomplished) [man] rodé

polite /pə'laɪt/ adj poli (to avec, envers fml); **to be ~ about sth** faire des commentaires polis sur qch; **to make ~ conversation** échanger des politesses; **in ~ company** ou **society** en bonne société; **to keep a ~ distance** rester à une distance respectueuse; **to use the ~ form** Ling utiliser le vouvoiement

politely /pə'laɪtlɪ/ adv poliment

politeness /pə'laɪtnɪs/ n politesse f

politic /'pɒlətɪk/ adj sout (wise) avisé; ▸ **body politic**

political /pə'lɪtɪkl/ adj politique

political: ~ analyst, **~ commentator** ▸ p. 1181 n commentateur/-trice m/f politique; **~ football** n enjeu m politique

politically /pə'lɪtɪklɪ/ adv [motivated, biased] politiquement; **~ (speaking)...** du point de vue politique...

politically correct, PC adj politiquement correct

ⓘ **Politically correct, PC** Apparue dans les années 1980, la notion de 'politiquement correct' désigne les comportements et formes d'expression qui ne trahissent aucun préjugé sexuel, raciste ou xénophobe afin de ne choquer personne. Si certains changements de formulation rétablissent une vérité historique (*African American* plutôt que *Black*, ou *Native American* plutôt que *Indian*), certains euphémismes semblent excessifs, par exemple *involuntarily leisured* pour exprimer *unemployed*.
---

political: ~ prisoner n prisonnier/-ière m/f politique; **~ science** n sciences fpl politiques

politician /ˌpɒlɪ'tɪʃn/ ▸ p. 1181 n homme/femme m/f politique

politicize /pə'lɪtɪsaɪz/ vtr politiser

politics /'pɒlətɪks/ n ① (+ v sg) (political life, affairs) politique f; ② (+ v sg) Sch, Univ sciences fpl politiques; ③ (+ v pl) (political views) opinions fpl politiques

polka dot n pois m

poll /pəʊl/
A n ① (vote casting) scrutin m, vote m; (election) élections fpl; (number of votes cast) voix fpl; **the result of the ~** les résultats du scrutin; **to go to the ~s** se rendre aux urnes; **a heavy defeat at the ~s** une lourde défaite aux élections; ② (list of voters) liste f électorale; (list of taxpayers) liste f de contribuables; ③ (survey) sondage m (on sur); **a ~ of teachers** un sondage effectué auprès des enseignants
B vtr ① (obtain in election) obtenir [votes]; ② (canvass) interroger [group]; ③ Comput interroger
C vi (obtain votes) **to ~ badly/well** recueillir peu de/beaucoup de voix

pollen /'pɒlən/ n pollen m

pollen: ~ count n taux m de pollen dans l'atmosphère; **~ sac** n sac m pollinique

polling /'pəʊlɪŋ/ n ① (voting) vote m; (election) élections fpl; (turnout) participation f électorale; ② Comput interrogation f

polling: ~ booth n isoloir m; **~ day** n jour m des élections; **~ place** n US = polling station; **~ station** n bureau m de vote

pollster /'pəʊlstə(r)/ n (person) sondeur m; (organization) institut m de sondage

poll tax n GB ≈ impôts mpl locaux.

⚠ Le terme officiel était **community charge**. Il a été remplacé par **council tax** en avril 1993
---

pollutant /pə'lu:tənt/ n polluant m

pollute /pə'lu:t/ vtr ① Ecol polluer (with avec); ② fig (morally) corrompre; (physically) souiller

polluter /pə'lu:tə(r)/ n pollueur/-euse m/f

pollution /pə'lu:ʃn/ n ① Ecol pollution f (of de); ② fig (moral) corruption f

polo /'pəʊləʊ/ n ① ▸ p. 881 Sport polo m; ② GB (sweater) col m roulé

polo neck n GB (collar, sweater) col m roulé

poltergeist /'pɒltəgaɪst/ n esprit m frappeur

poly /'pɒlɪ/
A ○n GB abrév ▸ **polytechnic**
B poly+ combining form poly-

polyanthus /ˌpɒlɪ'ænθəs/ n (pl ~ ou -thuses) primevère f

polychrome /'pɒlɪkrəʊm/ adj polychrome

polycotton /ˌpɒlɪ'kɒtn/ n polyester m et coton m

polyester /ˌpɒlɪ'estə(r)/ n polyester m

polygamy /pə'lɪgəmɪ/ n polygamie f

polyglot /'pɒlɪglɒt/ n, adj polyglotte (mf)

polymath /'pɒlɪmæθ/ n esprit m universel

polymer /'pɒlɪmə(r)/ n polymère m

polyp /'pɒlɪp/ n Med, Zool polype m

polystyrene /ˌpɒlɪ'staɪri:n/ n polystyrène m

polystyrene cement n colle f polystyrène

polytechnic /ˌpɒlɪ'teknɪk/ n GB établissement m d'enseignement supérieur

polythene /'pɒlɪθi:n/ n GB polyéthylène m

polyunsaturates /ˌpɒlɪʌn'sætʃərɪts/ npl acides mpl gras polyinsaturés; **high in ~** riche en acides gras polyinsaturés

polyurethane /ˌpɒlɪ'jʊərəθeɪn/ n, noun modifier polyuréthane (m)

pomade /pə'mɑːd/ n brillantine f

pomander /pə'mændə(r)/ n diffuseur m de parfum

pomegranate /'pɒmɪgrænɪt/ n (fruit) grenade f; (tree) grenadier m

pomp /pɒmp/ n pompe f; **with great ~** en grande pompe; **~ and circumstance** grand apparat

pompom, pompon /'pɒmpɒm/ n pompon m

pomposity /pɒm'pɒsətɪ/ n air m or ton m pompeux

P

pompous /'pɒmpəs/ adj [person] plein de suffisance; [air, speech, style] pompeux/-euse

pompously /'pɒmpəslɪ/ adv de manière pompeuse

pond /pɒnd/ n (large) étang m; (smaller) mare f; (in garden) bassin m

ponder /'pɒndə(r)/
A vtr considérer [options]; réfléchir à [past events]
B vi réfléchir (**on** à); (more deeply) méditer (**on** sur)

ponderous /'pɒndərəs/ adj [movement] lourd; [tone] pesant

pong○ /pɒŋ/ GB
A n puanteur f; **what a ~!** ça pue○!
B vi puer○

pontiff /'pɒntɪf/ n pontife m

pontifical /pɒn'tɪfɪkl/ adj **1** Relig pontifical; **2** péj [manner, tone] pontifiant

pontificate
A /pɒn'tɪfɪkət/ n pontificat m
B /pɒn'tɪfɪkeɪt/ vi pontifier (**about, on** sur)

pontoon /pɒn'tuːn/ n **1** (pier) ponton m; **2** Aviat (float) flotteur m; **3** ▸ p. 881 GB Games vingt-et-un m

pony /'pəʊnɪ/ n poney m

ponytail /'pəʊnɪteɪl/ n queue f de cheval

pooch○ /puːtʃ/ n clebs○ m, chien m

poodle /'puːdl/ n caniche m

poof○ /pʊf/, **poofter**○ /'pʊftə(r)/ n GB injur (homosexual) homosexuel m

pooh /puː/
A n GB lang enfantin caca○ m baby talk
B excl (expressing disgust) berk○!; (expressing scorn) peuh!

pooh-pooh○ /,puː'puː/ vtr faire peu de cas de [idea]

pool /puːl/
A n **1** (pond) étang m; (artificial) bassin m; (still spot in river) plan m d'eau; (underground: of oil, gas) nappe f; **2** (also **swimming ~**) piscine f; **3** (puddle) flaque f; **a ~ of blood** une mare de sang; **a ~ of light** une flaque de lumière; **4** (kitty, in cards) mises fpl; gen cagnotte f; **5** (common supply) (of money, resources) pool m; (of ideas, experience) réservoir m; (of labour) réserve f; (of teachers, players, candidates) liste f; Sport (billiards) billard m américain; ▸ **gene pool**
B pools npl GB (also **football ~s**) ≈ loto m sportif
C vtr mettre [qch] en commun [money, resources, information]

pool: **~ attendant** ▸ p. 1181 n surveillant/-e m/f de baignade; **~ liner** n revêtement m de piscine; **~ party** n réception f au bord de la piscine; **~ room** n salle f de billard américain; **~side** adj au bord de la piscine; **~ table** n table f de billard américain

pooped○ /puːpt/ adj **to be ~ (out)** être crevé○

poor /pɔː(r), US pʊər/ adj **1** (not wealthy) [person, country] pauvre (never before n) (**in** en); **to become** ou **get ~er** s'appauvrir; **2** (inferior) gen mauvais; [school, work] faible; [soil] pauvre; [appetite] petit; [chance, attendance] faible; **to be ~ at** [person] être faible en [maths, French]; **I'm a ~ traveller** je supporte mal les voyages; **3** (deserving pity) pauvre; **~ you!** pauvre de toi!; **4** (sorry, pathetic) [attempt, creature] pauvre; [excuse] piètre (before n)

Idiom **as ~ as a church mouse** pauvre comme Job

poorly /'pɔːlɪ, US 'pʊərlɪ/
A adj malade, souffrant
B adv **1** (not richly) [live, dress, dressed] pauvrement; **2** (badly) [written, managed, lit, paid, argued] mal

poorness /'pɔːnɪs, US 'pʊərnɪs/ n (of land, diet) pauvreté f; (of education, pay) médiocrité f; (of eyesight, hearing) défaillance f

poor relation n lit, fig parent m pauvre

pop /pɒp/
A n **1** (sound) (aussi onomat) pan m; **to go ~** faire pan; **2** (drink) soda m; **3** (popular music) musique f pop; **4** ○US (dad) (also **~s**) papa m
B noun modifier [concert, group, music, song, video] pop; [record, singer, star] de pop
C vtr (p prés etc **-pp-**) **1** ○(burst) faire éclater [balloon, bubble]; **2** (remove) faire sauter [cork]; **3** ○(put) **to ~ sth in(to)** mettre qch dans [oven, cupboard, mouth]; **to ~ one's head through the window** passer la tête par la fenêtre; **4** ○(take) prendre [pills]
D vi (p prés etc **-pp-**) **1** (go bang) [balloon] éclater; [cork, buttons] sauter; **2** [ears] se déboucher brusquement; **her eyes were ~ping out of her head** les yeux lui sortaient de la

tête; **3** ○GB (go) **to ~ into town/the bank** faire un saut○ en ville/à la banque

Idiom **to ~ the question** faire sa demande en mariage

Phrasal verbs
■ **pop back**○ GB repasser
■ **pop in**○ GB passer
■ **pop off** GB **1** (leave) filer○; **2** (die) crever○
■ **pop out** GB sortir
■ **pop round, pop over** GB passer
■ **pop up**○ [head] surgir; [missing person] refaire surface○

pope /pəʊp/ n pape m; **Pope Paul VI** le Pape Paul VI

poplar /'pɒplə(r)/ n peuplier m

poplin /'pɒplɪn/ n popeline f

popover /'pɒpəʊvə(r)/ n US Culin chausson m

poppet○ /'pɒpɪt/ n GB **my (little) ~** ma puce; **she's a real ~** c'est un amour

poppy /'pɒpɪ/ n Bot pavot m; **wild ~** coquelicot m

Poppy Day○ n GB anniversaire m de l'armistice (de 1918)

> ⓘ **Poppy Day** C'est ainsi que les Britanniques ont surnommé la commémoration de l'Armistice de 1918 (aussi appelée *Remembrance Sunday* ou *Armistice Day*). Ce dimanche-là, de nombreuses personnes portent à la boutonnière des coquelicots en papier ou en plastique, vendus par les associations caritatives au profit des mutilés de guerre. Ils évoquent ainsi les fleurs des champs de France ou de Belgique où reposent les morts de la première guerre mondiale.

Popsicle® /'pɒpsɪkl/ n US glace f à l'eau (en bâtonnet)

pop sock n mi-bas m

populace /'pɒpjʊləs/ n population f

popular /'pɒpjʊlə(r)/ adj **1** (generally liked) [actor, politician] populaire (**with, among** parmi); [profession, hobby, sport] répandu (**with, among** chez); [food, dish] prisé (**with, among** par); [product, resort, colour, design] en vogue (**with, among** chez); **John is very ~** John a beaucoup d'amis; **Smith was a ~ choice as chairman** comme de Smith comme président a été très apprécié; **she's ~ with the boys** elle a du succès auprès des garçons; **I'm not very ~ with my husband at the moment** je n'ai pas tellement la cote○ auprès de mon mari en ce moment; **2** (of or for the people) [music, song] populaire; [entertainment, TV programme] grand public inv; [science, history etc] de vulgarisation; [enthusiasm, interest, support] du public; [discontent, uprising] du peuple; [movement, press] populaire; **contrary to ~ belief** contrairement à ce qu'on pense généralement; **the ~ view** ou **perception of sth** l'opinion générale sur qch; **by ~ demand** ou **request** à la demande générale

popularity /,pɒpjʊ'lærətɪ/ n popularité f (**of** de; **with** auprès de)

popularization /,pɒpjʊləraɪ'zeɪʃn, US -rɪ'z-/ n popularisation f; (of ideas, science) vulgarisation f

popularize /'pɒpjʊləraɪz/ vtr **1** (make fashionable) généraliser; **2** (make accessible) vulgariser

popularly /'pɒpjʊləlɪ/ adv généralement

populate /'pɒpjʊleɪt/ vtr peupler (**with** de)

population /,pɒpjʊ'leɪʃn/
A n population f
B noun modifier [increase, decrease, explosion, figure] démographique; **~ control** contrôle m des naissances

populist /'pɒpjʊlɪst/ n, adj populiste (mf)

populous /'pɒpjʊləs/ adj populeux/-euse

pop: **~-up book** n livre m avec découpes en relief, livre m animé; **~-up menu** n Comput menu m déroulant mobile; **~-up toaster** grille-pain m vertical

porcelain /'pɔːsəlɪn/ n porcelaine f

porch /pɔːtʃ/ n **1** (of house, church) porche m; **2** US (veranda) véranda f

porcupine /'pɔːkjʊpaɪn/ n porc-épic m

pore /pɔː(r)/ n pore m

Phrasal verb
■ **pore over**: ▸ **over [sth]** être plongé dans [book]; étudier soigneusement [map, details]

pork /pɔːk/ n (viande f de) porc m; **a leg of ~** un jambon

pork scratchings n: **~ butcher** n charcutier/-ière m/f; **~ chop** n côte f de porc; **~ sausage** n saucisse f; **~ scratchings** npl GB grattons mpl

porn○ /pɔːn/ n (abrév = **pornography**) porno○ m

pornographic /ˌpɔːnəˈgræfɪk/ adj pornographique

pornography /pɔːˈnɒgrəfɪ/ n pornographie f

porous /ˈpɔːrəs/ adj [rock, wood, substance] poreux/-euse

porpoise /ˈpɔːpəs/ n Zool marsouin m

porridge /ˈpɒrɪdʒ, US ˈpɔːr-/ n porridge m (bouillie de flocons d'avoine)

port /pɔːt/
A n ① (harbour) port m; **in ~** au port; **the ship left ~** le bateau a appareillé; **~ of call** Naut escale f; fig (stop) arrêt m; ② (drink) porto m; ③ Aviat, Naut (window) = **porthole**; ④ Mil Naut (gunport) sabord m; ⑤ Aviat, Naut (left) bâbord m; ⑥ Tech (in engine) orifice m; ⑦ Comput port m
B noun modifier (harbour) [area, authorities, facilities, security] portuaire
C vtr Comput transporter [qch] (d'un système à l'autre)
⊙ (Idiom) **any ~ in a storm** nécessité fait loi

portable /ˈpɔːtəbl/
A n portable m
B adj gen, Comput portable

Portakabin® /ˈpɔːtəkæbɪn/ n gen bâtiment m préfabriqué; (on building site) baraque f (de chantier)

portal /ˈpɔːtl/ n gen, Comput portail m

portcullis /ˌpɔːtˈkʌlɪs/ n herse f (de forteresse)

portentous /pɔːˈtentəs/ adj littér ① (ominous) sinistre; ② (significant) très important, capital; ③ (solemn) grave; ④ (pompous) pompeux/-euse

portentously /pɔːˈtentəslɪ/ adv littér ① (ominously) [say, announce] d'un ton solennel; ② (pompously) [say, announce] d'un ton pompeux

porter /ˈpɔːtə(r)/ ▸ p. 1181 n ① (in station, airport, hotel) porteur m; (in hospital) brancardier m; (in market) débardeur m; ② GB (at entrance) (of hotel) portier m; (of apartment block) gardien/-ienne m/f; (of school) concierge mf; ③ US Rail (steward) employé m des wagons-lits

portfolio /pɔːtˈfəʊlɪəʊ/ n ① (case) porte-documents m inv; (for drawings) carton m (à dessins); ② Art, Phot (sample) portfolio m; ③ Pol (post) portefeuille m (ministériel); ④ Fin (of investments) portefeuille m

porthole /ˈpɔːthəʊl/ n hublot m

portico /ˈpɔːtɪkəʊ/ n portique m

portion /ˈpɔːʃn/ n ① (part, segment) (of house, machine, document, country) partie f (**of** de); ② (share) (of money, food) part f (**of** de); (of responsibility, blame) part f (**of** de); ③ (at meal) portion f; ④ littér (fate) destin m

portly /ˈpɔːtlɪ/ adj corpulent

portrait /ˈpɔːtreɪt, -trɪt/ n portrait m

portray /pɔːˈtreɪ/ vtr ① (depict) décrire [place, era, event]; présenter [person, group, situation]; ② Cin, Theat [actor] interpréter [character]; ③ Art [artist] peindre [person]; [picture, artist] représenter [scene]

portrayal /pɔːˈtreɪəl/ n ① (by actor) interprétation f (**of** de); ② (by author, filmmaker) portrait m

Portugal /ˈpɔːtʃʊgl/ ▸ p. 774 pr n Portugal m

Portuguese /ˌpɔːtjʊˈgiːz/ ▸ p. 1032, p. 969
A n ① (person) Portugais/-e m/f; **the ~** les Portugais mpl; ② (language) portugais m
B adj [course] portugais

pose /pəʊz/
A n ① (for portrait, photo) pose f; ② péj (posture) pose f; **to strike a ~** prendre une pose; **to strike an aggressive ~** prendre un air agressif
B vtr (present) poser [problem] (**for** pour); présenter [challenge] (**to** à); représenter [threat, risk] (**to** pour); soulever [question] (**about** de)
C vi [artist's model] poser; [performer] prendre des poses; ② (masquerade) **to ~ as** se faire passer pour; ③ péj (posture) frimer

poser○ /ˈpəʊzə(r)/ n ① (person) frimeur/-euse○ m/f; ② (puzzle) colle○ f

poseur /pəʊˈzɜː(r)/ n frimeur/-euse○ m/f

posh○ /pɒʃ/ adj ① (high-class) [person] huppé○; [house, resort, area, clothes, car] chic inv; [voice] distingué; [party] mondain; ② péj [school, district] de rupins○; **to talk ~**○ parler comme les gens de la haute○

position /pəˈzɪʃn/
A n ① (situation, state) situation f; **in a strong ~** en position de

force; **to be in a ~ to do** être en mesure de faire; **to be in a good/in no ~ to do** être bien/mal placé pour faire; **to be ou find oneself in the happy/unhappy ~ of doing** avoir la chance/malchance de faire; **if I were in your ~** si j'étais à ta place; ② (attitude, stance) position f; **the official ~** la position officielle; ③ (place, location) position f; **to be in ~** (in place) être en place; (ready) être prêt; **to get into ~** se mettre en place; **the house is in a good ~** la maison est bien située; ④ (posture) position f; **to be in a sitting ~** être assis; ⑤ (of lever, switch) position f; ⑥ (ranking) place f, rang m; (in sport, competition) position f; ⑦ Sport poste m; **what ~ does he play?** quel est son poste?; ⑧ (job) poste m; **to hold ou occupy a senior ~** occuper un poste responsable; ⑨ (place in society, army) position f; ⑩ (counter) guichet m; **'~ closed'** 'guichet fermé'
B vtr ① (station) poster [policemen, soldiers]; ② (situate) disposer [object]; ③ (get correct angle) orienter [telescope, lamp, aerial]
C v refl **to ~ oneself** prendre position

positive /ˈpɒzətɪv/
A n ① Ling (degré m) affirmatif m; ② Phot positif m; ③ Math nombre m positif; ④ Elec (pôle m) positif m
B adj ① (affirmative) [answer] positif/-ive; ② (optimistic) [message, person, response, tone] positif/-ive; **to be ~ about** être enthousiaste à propos de [idea, proposal]; **to think ~** voir les choses de façon positive; ③ (constructive) [contribution, effect, progress] positif/-ive; [advantage, good] réel/réelle; ④ (pleasant) [experience, feeling] positif/-ive; ⑤ (sure) [identification, proof] formel/-elle; [fact] indéniable; **to be ~** être sûr (**about** de; **that** que); **'~!'** 'certain!'; ⑥ (forceful) [action, measure] catégorique; ⑦ Med [reaction, result, test] positif/-ive; ⑧ Chem, Elec, Math, Phot, Phys positif/-ive; ⑨ (épith) (extreme) [pleasure] pur (before n); [disgrace, outrage, genius] véritable (before n)

positive discrimination n discrimination f positive

positively /ˈpɒzətɪvlɪ/ adv ① (constructively) [contribute, criticize] de façon constructive; ② (favourably) [react, refer, speak] favorablement; ③ (actively) [participate, prepare, promote] activement; ④ (definitely) [identify, prove] formellement; ⑤ (absolutely) [disgraceful, beautiful, dangerous, idiotic] vraiment; [refuse, forbid] catégoriquement

positive vetting n enquête f administrative

posse /ˈpɒsɪ/ n détachement m

possess /pəˈzes/
A vtr ① (have) posséder [property, weapon, proof, charm]; avoir [power, advantage]; (illegally) détenir [arms, drugs]; **to be ~ed of** sout avoir [charm, feature]; ② (take control of) [anger, fury] s'emparer de [person]; [devil] posséder [person]; **to be ~ed by** être obsédé par [idea, illusion]; **what ~ed you to do that?** qu'est-ce qui t'a pris de faire ça?
B **possessed** pp adj (by demon) possédé

possession /pəˈzeʃn/
A n ① (state of having) possession f (**of** de); **to be in ~ of** être en possession de; **to have ~ of sth** posséder qch; ② Jur (illegal) détention f (**of** de); ③ Jur (of property) jouissance f (**of** de); **to take ~ of** prendre possession de [premises, property]; **to be in ~** occuper les lieux; ④ Sport **to be in ~** have ~ contrôler le ballon; ⑤ (by demon) possession f (**by** par); ⑥ (colonial) possession f
B **possessions** npl (belongings) biens mpl
⊙ (Idiom) **~ is nine-tenths of the law** Prov possession vaut titre Prov

possessive /pəˈzesɪv/
A n Ling possessif m
B adj gen, Ling [person, behaviour] possessif/-ive (**towards** à l'égard de; **with** avec)

possessor /pəˈzesə(r)/ n possesseur m

possibility /ˌpɒsəˈbɪlətɪ/
A n ① (chance, prospect) possibilité f; **there is a definite ~ that he'll come** il y a de très grandes chances qu'il vienne; **there is no ~ of changing the text** il est impossible de changer le texte; **within the bounds of ~** dans la limite du possible; ② (eventuality) éventualité f; **the ~ of a refusal/of failure** l'éventualité d'un refus/d'un échec; **the collapse of the company is now a ~** l'effondrement de la société est à présent de l'ordre du possible
B **possibilities** npl (potential) **the idea has possibilities** l'idée a un fort potentiel

possible /ˈpɒsəbl/
A n Ⓒ ① (possibility) possible m; ② (potential candidate) (for job)

candidat *m* possible; (for team) joueur/-euse *m/f* possible

B *adj* possible; **he did as much as** ∼ il a fait tout son possible; **as far as** ∼ dans la mesure du possible; **as quickly as** ∼ le plus vite possible; **of what** ∼ **interest/benefit can it be to you?** quel intérêt/avantage cela peut-il bien avoir pour toi?

possibly /'pɒsəblɪ/ *adv* **1** (maybe) peut-être; **2** (for emphasis) **how could they** ∼ **understand?** comment donc pourraient-ils comprendre?; **what can he** ∼ **do to you?** qu'est-ce que tu veux qu'il te fasse?; **we can't** ∼ **afford it** nous n'en avons absolument pas les moyens; **I'll do everything I** ∼ **can** je ferai (absolument) tout mon possible

possum○ /'pɒsəm/ *n* opossum *m*; **to play** ∼ faire le mort

post /pəʊst/

A *n* **1** Admin (job) poste *m* (**as** comme; **of** de); **to hold a** ∼ occuper un poste; **2** GB Post (system) poste *f*; (letters) courrier *m*; (delivery) distribution *f*; **by return of** ∼ par retour du courrier; **it was lost in the** ∼ cela s'est égaré dans le courrier; **to catch the** ∼ ne pas manquer la levée; **3** (duty, station) gen, Mil poste *m*; **at one's** ∼ à son poste; **4** (pole) gen, Sport poteau *m*; **to be the first past the** ∼ Sport être le premier à l'arrivée; *fig* Pol obtenir la majorité

B **post-** *combining form* post-; **in** ∼**-1992 Europe** dans l'Europe d'après 1992

C *vtr* **1** (send by post) poster *or* expédier (par la poste); (put in letterbox) mettre [qch] à la poste; **2** (stick up) afficher [*notice, poster*]; annoncer [*details, results*]; **3** gen, Mil (send abroad) affecter (**to** à); **4** (station) gen, Mil poster [*guard, sentry*]

(Idiom) **to keep sb** ∼**ed (about sth)** tenir qn au courant (de qch)

(Phrasal verb)

■ **post on** GB: ▸ ∼ **on [sth]**, ∼ **[sth] on** faire suivre

postage /'pəʊstɪdʒ/ *n* affranchissement *m*; **including** ∼ **and packing** frais *mpl* d'expédition inclus; ∼ **extra** affranchissement en supplément; ∼ **free** franc de port

postage: ∼ **meter** *n* US machine *f* à affranchir; ∼ **stamp** *n* timbre-poste *m*

postal /'pəʊstl/ *adj* [*charges, district*] postal; [*application*] par la poste

postal order, PO *n* GB mandat *m* (**for** de)

postal service *n* **1** (institution) Service *m* des Postes; **2** (service) Post distribution *f* du courrier; (of company) service *m* de ventes par correspondance

postal vote *n* GB vote *m* par correspondance

postbag /'pəʊstbæg/ *n* GB **1** lit sac *m* postal; **2** (mail) courrier *m*

post: ∼**box** *n* GB boîte *f* aux lettres; ∼**card**, **pc** *n* carte *f* postale; ∼ **code** *n* GB code *m* postal

postdate /ˌpəʊst'deɪt/ *vtr* postdater

poster /'pəʊstə(r)/ *n* (for information) affiche *f*; (decorative) poster *m*

posterior /pɒ'stɪərɪə(r)/

A *n* hum (buttocks) derrière *m*

B *adj* sout postérieur (**to** à)

posterity /pɒ'sterətɪ/ *n* postérité *f*

poster paint *n* gouache *f*

postgraduate /ˌpəʊst'grædʒʊət/

A *n* ≈ étudiant/-e *m/f* de troisième cycle

B *adj* ≈ de troisième cycle

posthumous /'pɒstjʊməs, US 'pɒstʃəməs/ *adj* posthume

posthumously /'pɒstjʊməslɪ, US 'pɒstʃəməslɪ/ *adv* [*publish*] après la mort de l'auteur; [*award*] à titre posthume

posting /'pəʊstɪŋ/ *n* **1** (job) affectation *f* (**to** à); **2** GB Post envoi *m*; **proof of** ∼ justificatif *m* d'expédition

postman /'pəʊstmən/ ▸ p. 1181 *n* facteur *m*

postmark /'pəʊstmɑːk/

A *n* cachet *m* de la poste

B *vtr* timbrer

post: ∼**master** ▸ p. 1181 *n* receveur *m* des Postes; **Postmaster General** *n* Hist ministre *m* des Postes et Télécommunications; ∼**mistress** ▸ p. 1181 *n* receveuse *f* des Postes

postmodernist /ˌpəʊst'mɒdənɪst/ *n*, *adj* postmoderniste (*mf*)

post-mortem /ˌpəʊst'mɔːtəm/ *n* Med autopsie *f*; *fig* analyse *f* rétrospective

post-natal /ˌpəʊst'neɪtl/ *adj* post-natal

post: ∼ **office, PO** *n* poste *f*; **Post Office Box, PO Box** *n* boîte *f* postale

post-operative /ˌpəʊst'ɒpərətɪv, US -reɪt-/ *adj* Med post-opératoire

postpone /pə'spəʊn/ *vtr* reporter, remettre (**until** à; **for** de)

postponement /pə'spəʊnmənt/ *n* report *m*, renvoi *m* (**until** à)

postscript /'pəʊsskrɪpt/ *n* (at end of letter) post-scriptum *m inv* (**to** à); (to book, document) postface *f* (**to** à); *fig* suite *f* (**to** à)

post-tax /ˌpəʊst'tæks/ *adj, adv* après paiement des impôts

post-traumatic /ˌpəʊsttrɔː'mætɪk, US -traʊ-/ *adj* ∼ **stress disorder** syndrome *m* de stress post-traumatique

postulate /'pɒstjʊleɪt, US -tʃʊ-/ *vtr* poser comme postulat; **to** ∼ **that** postuler que

posture /'pɒstʃə(r)/

A *n* **1** (pose) posture *f*; *fig* (stance) position *f*; **2** (bearing) maintien *m*; **to have good/bad** ∼ se tenir bien/mal

B *vi* péj poser, prendre des poses

posturing /'pɒstʃərɪŋ/ *n* péj affectation *f*

post-viral (fatigue) syndrome ▸ p. 933 *n* encéphalomyélite *f* myalgique

postwar /ˌpəʊst'wɔː(r)/ *adj* d'après-guerre

posy /'pəʊzɪ/ *n* petit bouquet *m* (de fleurs)

pot /pɒt/

A *n* **1** (container) pot *m*; **a** ∼ **of tea for two** deux thés; **to make a** ∼ **of tea/coffee** faire du thé/du café; ∼**s and pans** casseroles; **2** (piece of pottery) poterie *f*; **3** ○(hashish) hasch○ *m*; **4** (for infant) pot *m*

B *vtr* (-tt-) **1** mettre [qch] en pot [*jam*]; **2** (in billiards) blouser [*ball*]; **3** (*also* ∼ **up**) mettre [qch] en pot [*plant*]

C potted *pp adj* **1** Culin ∼**ted meat** GB terrine *f* de viande; ∼**ted shrimps** crevettes *fpl* conservées (*dans du beurre*); **2** [*palm, plant*] en pot; **3** (condensed) [*biography, history*] bref/brève

(Idioms) **to go to** ∼○ (person) se laisser aller; (thing) aller à vau-l'eau; **to have** ∼**s of money**○ GB avoir un tas○ d'argent; **a watched** ∼ **never boils** Prov quand on est impatient chaque seconde semble durer une éternité; **to take** ∼ **luck** (for meal) GB manger à la fortune du pot; (for hotel room etc) prendre ce que l'on trouve

potash /'pɒtæʃ/ *n* potasse *f*

potassium /pə'tæsɪəm/ *n* potassium *m*

potato /pə'teɪtəʊ/ *n* (*pl* **-es**) Bot Culin pomme *f* de terre

potato: ∼ **crisps** GB, ∼ **chips** US *npl* chips *fpl*; ∼ **masher** *n* presse-purée *m inv*; ∼ **peeler** *n* épluche-légumes *m inv*

pot: ∼ **bellied** *adj* [*person*] bedonnant○; [*stove*] renflé; ∼ **belly** *n* bedaine *f*; ∼**boiler** *n* péj œuvre *f* alimentaire

potency /'pəʊtnsɪ/ *n* **1** (of drug, remedy, image, voice) puissance *f*; (of drink) force *f*; **2** (sexual) virilité *f*

potent /'pəʊtnt/ *adj* **1** [*argument, force, symbol, drug*] puissant; [*drink, mixture*] fort; **2** (sexually) viril

potentate /'pəʊtnteɪt/ *n* potentat *m*

potential /pə'tenʃl/

A *n* potentiel *m* (**as** en tant que; **for** de); **the** ∼ **to do** les qualités *fpl* nécessaires pour faire; **to fulfil one's** ∼ montrer de quoi on est capable

B *adj* [*buyer, danger, energy, market, value, victim*] potentiel/-ielle; [*champion, rival*] en puissance; [*investor*] éventuel/-elle; **to be a** ∼ **success** avoir toutes les qualités pour réussir

potentially /pə'tenʃəlɪ/ *adv* potentiellement

pot: ∼**hole** *n* (in road) fondrière *f*, nid *m* de poule; ∼**holer** *n* GB spéléologue *mf*; ∼**holing** ▸ p. 881 *n* GB spéléologie *f*; ∼**hook** *n* crémaillère *f*

potion /'pəʊʃn/ *n* potion *f*

pot: ∼**pie** *n* US tourte *f* à la viande; ∼ **plant** *n* plante *f* d'appartement; ∼ **roast** *n* rôti *m* (*cuit dans une cocotte*)

potshot /'pɒtʃɒt/ *n* **to take a** ∼ **at sth** tirer à vue sur qch

potter /ˈpɒtə(r)/ ▸ p. 1181 n potier m

(Phrasal verb)
■ **potter about**, **potter around** GB (do odd jobs) bricoler○; (go about daily chores) suivre son petit train-train○; (pass time idly) traîner

potter's wheel n tour m de potier

pottery /ˈpɒtəri/ n ① (craft, subject) poterie f; ② ₵ (ware) poteries fpl; ③ (factory, workshop) poterie f

pot: ~**ting compost** n terreau m; ~**ting shed** n abri m de jardin

potty○ /ˈpɒti/
Ⓐ n lang enfantin pot m (d'enfant)
Ⓑ adj GB ① (crazy) dingue○; [idea] farfelu○; ② (enthusiastic) to be ~ about sb/sth être toqué○ de qn/qch

potty-train /ˈpɒtitreɪn/ vtr to ~ a child apprendre à un enfant à aller sur le pot

pouch /paʊtʃ/ n ① (bag) petit sac m; (for tobacco) blague f (à tabac); (for ammunition) étui m (à munitions); (for cartridges) giberne f; (for mail) sac m postal; (for money) bourse f; (of clothes, skin) poche f; ② Zool (of marsupials) poche f ventrale; (of rodents) abajoue f

pouf(fe) /puːf/ n (cushion) pouf m

poultice /ˈpəʊltɪs/ n cataplasme m

poultry /ˈpəʊltri/ n ₵ (birds) volailles fpl; (meat) volaille f

poultry: ~ **farm** n (ferme f d')élevage m de volailles; ~ **farming** n élevage m de volailles; ~**man** ▸ p. 1181 n US volailleur m

pounce /paʊns/
Ⓐ n bond m
Ⓑ vi bondir; to ~ on [animal] bondir sur [prey, object]; [person] se jeter sur [victim]

pound /paʊnd/
Ⓐ n ① ▸ p. 1323 (weight measurement) livre f (de 453,6g); **two** ~**s of apples** ≈ un kilo de pommes; **pears are 80 pence a** ou **per** ~ ≈ les poires sont à 80 pence la livre; ~ **for** ~ **chicken is better value than pork** tout compté le poulet revient moins cher que le porc; ② (unit of currency) ▸ p. 782 livre f; **I'll match your donation** ~ **for** ~ je donnerai exactement la même somme que toi; ③ (compound) (for dogs, cars) fourrière f
Ⓑ vtr ① Culin (crush) piler [spices, grain, salt]; aplatir [meat]; to ~ **sth to** réduire qch en [powder, paste, pieces]; ② (beat) [waves] battre [shore]; to ~ **sth with one's fists** frapper sur qch avec ses poings [door, table]; ③ (bombard) [artillery] pilonner [city]; ④ (tread heavily) to ~ **the streets** battre le pavé
Ⓒ vi ① (knock loudly) to ~ **on** marteler [door, wall]; ② (beat) [heart] battre; to ~ **on** [waves] battre contre [beach, rocks]; ③ (run noisily) to ~ **up/down the stairs** monter/descendre l'escalier d'un pas lourd; ④ (throb) **my head is** ~**ing** j'ai des élancements dans la tête

(Phrasal verb)
■ **pound away**: ▸ ~ **away at [sth]** ① (strike hard) taper à tour de bras sur [piano, typewriter]; ② (work doggedly) travailler d'arrache-pied sur

pounding /ˈpaʊndɪŋ/ n (sound) (of waves, drums, heart) battement m; (of fists, hooves) martèlement m; (of guns) pilonnage m

pour /pɔː(r)/
Ⓐ vtr ① verser [liquid]; couler [cement, metal, wax]; ② (also ~ **out**) (serve) servir [drink]; **can I** ~ **you some more coffee?** puis-je vous resservir du café? to ~ **oneself a drink** se servir un verre; ③ (supply freely) to ~ **money into sth** investir des sommes énormes dans qch; to ~ **one's energies into one's work** mettre toute son énergie dans son travail
Ⓑ vi ① (flow) [liquid] couler (à flots); to ~ **into** [water, liquid] couler dans; [smoke, fumes] se répandre dans; [light] inonder [room]; to ~ **out of** ou **from** [smoke, fumes] s'échapper de; [water] ruisseler de; **tears** ~**ed down her face** les larmes ruisselaient sur son visage; **water** ~**ed down the walls** l'eau coulait le long des murs; **light** ~**ed through the window** la lumière entrait à flots par la fenêtre; **relief** ~**ed over me** j'ai été envahi par une sensation de soulagement; ② fig (come in) to ~ **into** [people] affluer dans; to ~ **from** ou **out of** [people, cars] sortir en grand nombre de; [supplies, money] sortir en masse de; to ~ **across** ou **over** [people] traverser [qch] en grand nombre [border, bridge]; ③ (serve tea, coffee) **shall I** ~? je vous sers?; ④ [jug, teapot] verser
Ⓒ **pouring** pres p adj [rain] battant

Ⓓ v impers **it's** ~**ing (with rain)** il pleut à verse
(Idiom) **to** ~ **cold water on** se montrer peu enthousiaste pour

(Phrasal verbs)
■ **pour away**: ▸ ~ **away [sth]**, ~ **[sth] away** vider
■ **pour down** pleuvoir à verse
■ **pour in**: ▸ ~ **in** [people] affluer; [letters, money, requests] pleuvoir; [water] entrer à flots
■ **pour off**: ▸ ~ **off [sth]**, ~ **[sth] off** vider
■ **pour out**: ▸ ~ **out** [liquid, smoke] se déverser; [people] sortir en grand nombre. ▸ ~ **out [sth]**, ~ **[sth] out** ① verser, servir [coffee, wine etc]; ② fig donner libre cours à [ideas, feelings, troubles] (**to sb** devant qn); rejeter [fumes, sewage]; to ~ **out one's troubles** ou **heart to sb** s'épancher auprès de qn

pout /paʊt/
Ⓐ n moue f
Ⓑ vi faire la moue

poverty /ˈpɒvəti/ n ① (lack of money) pauvreté f; (more severe) misère f; ② (of imagination, resources) pauvreté f

poverty: ~ **line**, ~ **level** n seuil m de pauvreté; ~**-stricken** adj misérable

POW n (abrév = **prisoner of war**) prisonnier/-ière m/f de guerre

powder /ˈpaʊdə(r)/
Ⓐ n gen poudre f; (snow) poudreuse f; **in** ~ **form** en poudre
Ⓑ vtr to ~ **one's face** se poudrer le visage
Ⓒ **powdered** pp adj [egg, milk, coffee] en poudre
(Idioms) **to keep one's** ~ **dry** être paré; **to** ~ **one's nose** euph hum se refaire une beauté euph hum

powder: ~ **blue** ▸ p. 752 n, adj bleu (m) pastel inv; ~ **compact** n poudrier m; ~ **keg** n fig poudrière f fig; ~ **puff** n houppette f; ~ **room** n euph toilettes fpl pour dames

powdery /ˈpaʊdəri/ adj ① (in consistency) [snow] poudreux/-euse; [stone] friable; ② (covered with powder) couvert de poudre

power /ˈpaʊə(r)/
Ⓐ n ① gen, Pol (control) pouvoir m; **to be in/come to** ~ être/accéder au pouvoir; **to be in sb's** ~ être à la merci de qn; ② (strength) puissance f; ③ (influence) influence f (**over** sur); ④ (capability) pouvoir m; **to do everything in one's** ~ faire tout ce qui est en son pouvoir (**to do** pour faire); **to lose the** ~ **of speech** perdre l'usage de la parole; **to be at the height of one's** ~**s** gen avoir atteint la plénitude de ses moyens; [artist] être au sommet de son art; ⑤ ₵ (also ~**s**) (authority) attributions fpl; **police** ~**s** les attributions de la police; ⑥ (physical force) (of person, explosion) force f; (of storm) violence f; ⑦ Phys, Tech, gen énergie f; (current) courant m; **to switch on the** ~ mettre le courant; ⑧ (of vehicle, plane) puissance f; **to be running at full/half** ~ fonctionner à plein/mi-régime; ⑨ (magnification) puissance f; ⑩ Math **8 to the** ~ **of 3** 8 puissance 3; ⑪ (country) puissance f
Ⓑ noun modifier Tech, Elec [drill, circuit, cable] électrique; [steering, brakes] assisté; [mower] à moteur; [shovel] mécanique; [breakfast, lunch] de travail
Ⓒ vtr faire marcher [engine]; propulser [plane, boat]; ~**ed by** propulsé par [engine]; alimenté par [electricity, gas, generator]
(Idioms) **to do sb a** ~ **of good** faire à qn un bien fou; **the** ~**s of darkness** les puissances des ténèbres; **the** ~**s that be** les autorités

power: ~**-assisted** adj [steering] assisté; ~ **base** n base f politique; ~**boat** n hors-bord m inv; ~ **broker** n: celui/celle qui détient les clés du pouvoir; ~ **cut** n coupure f de courant; ~ **dressing** n tenue f vestimentaire qui en impose (portée par les femmes cadres au travail)

powerful /ˈpaʊəfl/ adj [person, arms, engine, computer, description] puissant; [bomb] de forte puissance; [smell, emotion, impression, light, voice, government] fort; [blow] bon/bonne; [argument, evidence] solide; [portrayal] saisissant; [performance] magistral

powerfully /ˈpaʊəfəli/ adv [influenced, affected] fortement; [portrayed] d'une manière saisissante; [argue] avec force; [smell] fortement (**of** de); **to be** ~ **built** avoir une forte carrure

powerhouse /ˈpaʊəhaʊs/ n ① lit centrale f électrique; ② ○fig (of ideas etc) laboratoire m; ③ fig (person) locomotive f

powerless /'paʊəlɪs/ adj impuissant (**against** face à); **to be ~ to do** ne pas pouvoir faire

power: **~ line** n ligne f à haute tension; **~ of attorney** n procuration f; **~ plant** US = **power station**; **~ play** n US fig coup m de force; **~ point** n prise f (de courant); **~ politics** npl (using military force) politique f de la force armée; (using coercion) politique f d'intimidation; **~ sharing** n partage m du pouvoir; **~ station** n centrale f (électrique)

powwow /'paʊwaʊ/ n [1] (meeting) assemblée f (d'Indiens d'Amérique); [2] ᵒfig discussion f importante

pp [1] (on document) (abrév = per procurationem) po; [2] (abrév = pages) pp.

p & p n (abrév = postage and packing) frais mpl d'expédition

PR n [1] abrév ▸ public relations; [2] abrév ▸ proportional representation

practicability /ˌpræktɪkə'bɪlətɪ/ n faisabilité f

practicable /'præktɪkəbl/ adj [proposal, plan] réalisable

practical /'præktɪkl/
A n (exam) épreuve f pratique; (lesson) travaux mpl pratiques
B adj [1] (concrete, not theoretical) pratique; **in ~ terms** en pratique; [2] [person] (sensible) pratique; (with hands) adroit; [3] (functional) [clothes, furniture, equipment] pratique; [4] (viable) [plan etc] réalisable

practicality /ˌpræktɪ'kælətɪ/
A n [1] (of person) esprit m pratique; (of clothes, equipment) facilité f d'utilisation; [2] (of scheme, idea, project) aspect m pratique
B practicalities npl détails mpl pratiques

practical joke n farce f

practically /'præktɪklɪ/ adv [1] (almost, virtually) pratiquement; [2] (in a practical way) d'une manière pratique

practice /'præktɪs/
A n [1] ₵ (exercises) exercices mpl; (experience) entraînement m; **to have had ~ in** ou **at sth/in** ou **at doing** avoir l'expérience en qch/pour ce qui est de faire; **to be in ~** (for sport) être bien entraîné; (for music) être bien exercé; **to be out of ~** être rouilléᵒ; [2] (meeting) (for sport) entraînement m; (for music, drama) répétition f; [3] (procedure) pratique f, usage m; **it's standard ~ to do** il est d'usage de faire; **business ~** usage m en affaires; [4] ₵ (habit) habitude f; **as is my usual ~** comme je le fais d'habitude; [5] (custom) coutume f; [6] (business of doctor, lawyer) cabinet m; **to be in ~** exercer; **to set up in** ou **go into ~** s'établir en tant que médecin or juriste; [7] ₵ (as opposed to theory) pratique f; **in ~** en pratique
B noun modifier [game, match] d'essai; [flight] d'entraînement
C vtr, vi US = **practise**

(Idiom) **~ makes perfect** Prov c'est en forgeant qu'on devient forgeron Prov

practise GB, **practice** US /'præktɪs/
A vtr [1] (work at) travailler [song, speech, French]; s'exercer à [movement, shot]; réviser [technique]; répéter [play]; **to ~ the piano** travailler le piano; **to ~ doing** ou **how to do** s'entraîner à faire; [2] (use) pratiquer [restraint, kindness]; utiliser [method]; [3] (follow a profession) exercer [method]; [4] (observe) pratiquer [custom, religion]
B vi [1] (train) (at piano, violin) s'exercer; (for sports) s'entraîner; (for play, concert) répéter; [2] (follow a profession) exercer; **to ~ as** exercer la profession de [doctor, lawyer]

(Idiom) **to ~ what one preaches** prêcher d'exemple

practised GB, **practiced** US /'præktɪst/ adj [player, lawyer, cheat] expérimenté; [eye, ear, movement] expert; **to be ~ in/in doing** être fort dans/pour faire

practising GB, **practicing** US /'præktɪsɪŋ/ adj [Christian, Muslim] pratiquant; [doctor, lawyer] en exercice; [homosexual] actif/-ive

practitioner /præk'tɪʃənə(r)/ n praticien/-ienne m/f; **dental ~** dentiste mf

pragmatic /præg'mætɪk/ adj pragmatique

pragmatics /præg'mætɪks/ n (+ v sg) [1] Ling pragmatique f; [2] (of scheme, situation) détails mpl pratiques

pragmatism /'prægmətɪzəm/ n pragmatisme m

pragmatist /'prægmətɪst/ n gen, Ling pragmatiste mf

prairie /'preərɪ/ n plaine f (herbeuse), prairie f

prairie wolf n US coyote m

praise /preɪz/
A n gen éloges mpl, louanges fpl; **in ~ of sb** à la louange de qn; **in ~ of sth** louant qch; **to be highly ~d** être couvert d'éloges; **that's ~ indeed coming from her** venant d'elle c'est un compliment
B vtr [1] gen faire l'éloge de [person, book, achievement] (**as** en tant que); **to ~ sb for sth/for doing** féliciter qn pour qch/d'avoir fait; **to ~ sb/sth to the skies** porter qn/qch aux nues; [2] Relig louer [God]

praiseworthy /'preɪzwɜːðɪ/ adj digne d'éloges

pram /præm/ n GB landau m

prance /prɑːns, US præns/ vi [horse] caracoler; [person] sautiller; **to ~ in/out** [person] entrer/sortir allègrement

prank /præŋk/ n farce f

prattle /'prætl/
A n bavardage m; (of children) babillage m
B vi bavarder; [children] babiller; **to ~ on about sth** parler de qch à n'en plus finir

prawn /prɔːn/
A n crevette f rose, bouquet m
B noun modifier [salad, sandwich] aux crevettes; **~ cocktail** salade f de crevettes

pray /preɪ/
A ‡ ou iron adv je vous prie
B vtr prier (**that** pour que + subj)
C vi gen, Relig prier (**for** pour)

prayer /'preə(r)/
A n Relig prière f; fig (hope) souhait m; **to say one's ~s** faire sa prière; **his ~s were answered** lit, fig sa prière a été exaucée
B prayers npl (informal) prière f; (formal) office m

(Idiom) **on a wing and a ~**ᵒ Dieu sait comment

prayer: **~ beads** npl chapelet m; **~ book** n livre m de prières; **~ shawl** n taled m; **~ wheel** n moulin m à prière

preach /priːtʃ/
A vi Relig prêcher (**to** à); fig pej sermonner
B vtr Relig prêcher (**to** à); fig prêcher, prôner [tolerance, virtue, pacifism]

(Idioms) **to practise what one ~es** conformer ses actes à ses paroles; **to ~ to the converted** prêcher les convertis

preacher /'priːtʃə(r)/ n pasteur m

preamble /priː'æmbl/ n préambule m (**to** à)

prearrange /ˌpriːə'reɪndʒ/ vtr fixer [qch] à l'avance

precarious /prɪ'keərɪəs/ adj précaire

precast /ˌpriː'kɑːst, US -'kæst/ adj [concrete] précoulé

precaution /prɪ'kɔːʃn/ n précaution f (**against** contre)

precautionary /prɪ'kɔːʃənərɪ, US -nerɪ/ adj préventif/-ive

precede /prɪ'siːd/ vtr précéder

precedence /'presɪdəns/ n [1] (in importance) priorité f (**over** sur); [2] (in rank) préséance f (**over** sur)

precedent /'presɪdənt/ n précédent m

preceding /prɪ'siːdɪŋ/ adj précédent

precept /'priːsept/ n précepte m

preceptor /prɪ'septə(r)/ n US Univ ≈ moniteur/-trice m/f

precinct /'priːsɪŋkt/ n [1] GB (also **shopping ~**) quartier m commerçant; [2] GB (also **pedestrian ~**) zone f piétonne; [3] US Admin circonscription f

precious /'preʃəs/
A n (as endearment) mon trésor
B adj [1] (valuable) précieux/-ieuse; [2] (held dear) [person] cher/chère (**to** à) also iron; [3] pej (affected) [person, style] précieux/-ieuse, affecté
C adv (very) **~ little time** fort peu de temps; **~ few cars** fort peu de voitures

precipice /'presɪpɪs/ n lit, fig précipice m

precipitate
A /prɪ'sɪpɪteɪt/ n Chem précipité m
B /prɪ'sɪpɪtət/ adj (hasty) [action] précipité

precipitately /prɪ'sɪpɪtətlɪ/ adv sout précipitamment

precipitation /prɪˌsɪpɪ'teɪʃn/ n [1] Chem précipitation f; [2] ₵ Meteorol précipitations fpl

precipitous /prɪ'sɪpɪtəs/ adj [1] sout (steep) [cliff] à pic inv; [road] escarpé; [steps] raide; [2] (hasty) = **precipitate B**

précis /'preɪsiː, US preɪ'siː/
A n résumé m

B *vtr* faire un résumé de [*text, speech*]

precise /prɪˈsaɪs/ *adj* **1** (exact) [*sum, measurement*] précis; **2** (meticulous) [*person, mind*] méticuleux/-euse

precisely /prɪˈsaɪslɪ/ *adv* **1** (exactly) exactement, précisément; **at ten o'clock** ~ à dix heures précises; **2** (accurately) [*describe, record*] avec précision

precision /prɪˈsɪʒn/ *n* précision *f*

preclude /prɪˈkluːd/ *vtr* exclure [*possibility*]; empêcher [*action*]

precocious /prɪˈkəʊʃəs/ *adj* gen précoce

precociousness /prɪˈkəʊʃəsnɪs/, **precocity** /prɪˈkɒsətɪ/ *n* précocité *f*

preconceived /ˌpriːkənˈsiːvd/ *adj* préconçu

preconception /ˌpriːkənˈsepʃn/ *n* opinion *f* préconçue

precondition /ˌpriːkənˈdɪʃn/
A *n* condition *f* requise
B *vtr* Psych conditionner

precook /ˌpriːˈkʊk/ *vtr* précuire

precursor /ˌpriːˈkɜːsə(r)/ *n* (person) précurseur *m*; (sign) signe *m* avant-coureur; (prelude) prélude *m* (**to, of** à); (earlier form) ancêtre *m*

predate /ˌpriːˈdeɪt/ *vtr* **1** (put earlier date) antidater [*cheque, document*]; **2** (exist before) [*discovery, building*] être antérieur à

predator /ˈpredətə(r)/ *n* lit, fig prédateur *m*

predatory /ˈpredətrɪ, US -tɔːrɪ/ *adj* prédateur/-trice

predecessor /ˈpriːdɪsesə(r), US ˈpredə-/ *n* prédécesseur *m*

predestination /ˌpriːdestɪˈneɪʃn/ *n* prédestination *f*

predestine /ˌpriːˈdestɪn/ *vtr* prédestiner

predetermine /ˌpriːdɪˈtɜːmɪn/ *vtr* **1** (fix beforehand) déterminer d'avance; **2** Relig, Philos prédéterminer

predicament /prɪˈdɪkəmənt/ *n* situation *f* difficile

predicate
A /ˈpredɪkət/ *n* Ling, Philos prédicat *m*
B /ˈpredɪkət/ *adj* Ling, Philos prédicatif/-ive
C /ˈpredɪkeɪt/ *vtr* **1** gen (assert) avancer [*theory*]; **to** ~ **that** poser que; **2** Philos (affirm) affirmer (**of** de); **3** (base) fonder (**on** sur)

predicative /prɪˈdɪkətɪv, US ˈpredɪkeɪtɪv/ *adj* Ling prédicatif/-ive

predict /prɪˈdɪkt/ *vtr* prédire

predictable /prɪˈdɪktəbl/ *adj* prévisible

predictably /prɪˈdɪktəblɪ/ *adv* [*boring, late*] comme prévu; ~**, he came** comme on pouvait s'y attendre, il est venu

prediction /prɪˈdɪkʃn/ *n* prédiction *f* (**that** selon laquelle)

predigested /ˌpriːdaɪˈdʒestɪd/ *adj* prédigéré

predilection /ˌpriːdɪˈlekʃn, US ˌpredlˈek-/ *n* prédilection *f*

predispose /ˌpriːdɪˈspəʊz/ *vtr* prédisposer

predisposition /ˌpriːdɪspəˈzɪʃn/ *n* prédisposition *f*

predominance /prɪˈdɒmɪnəns/ *n* prédominance *f* (**of** de; **over** sur)

predominant /prɪˈdɒmɪnənt/ *adj* prédominant

predominantly /prɪˈdɒmɪnəntlɪ/ *adv* [*represent, feature*] principalement; [*Muslim, female*] essentiellement; **the flowers were** ~ **pink** la plupart des fleurs étaient roses

predominate /prɪˈdɒmɪneɪt/ *vi* prédominer

pre-eminence /ˌpriːˈemɪnəns/ *n* gen suprématie *f*; Sport supériorité *f*

pre-eminent /ˌpriːˈemɪnənt/ *adj* **1** (distinguished) [*celebrity, scientist*] éminent; **2** (leading) [*nation, cult, company*] dominant

pre-eminently /ˌpriːˈemɪnəntlɪ/ *adv* **1** (highly) [*successful, distinguished*] particulièrement; **2** (above all) [*religious, political*] avant tout

pre-empt /ˌpriːˈempt/ *vtr* **1** (anticipate) anticiper [*question, decision, move*]; devancer [*person*]; **2** (thwart) contrecarrer [*action, plan*]

pre-emptive /ˌpriːˈemptɪv/ *adj* [*strike, move, attack*] préventif/-ive

preen /priːn/
A *vi* [*bird*] se lisser les plumes
B *v refl* **to** ~ **oneself** [*bird*] se lisser les plumes; [*person*] péj se pomponner

pre-exist /ˌpriːɪgˈzɪst/
A *vtr* préexister à
B *vi* [*situation*] préexister; [*person, soul*] avoir une vie antérieure
C **pre-existing** *pres p adj* préexistant

prefab /ˈpriːfæb, US ˌpriːˈfæb/ *n* (bâtiment *m*) préfabriqué *m*

prefabricate /ˌpriːˈfæbrɪkeɪt/ *vtr* préfabriquer

preface /ˈprefɪs/
A *n* (to book) préface *f*; (to speech) préambule *m*
B *vtr* préfacer [*livre*]; **to** ~ **sth with sth** faire précéder qch de qch

prefatory /ˈprefətrɪ, US -tɔːrɪ/ *adj* [*comments*] préliminaire; [*pages, notes*] liminaire

prefect /ˈpriːfekt/ *n* **1** GB Sch élève chargé de la surveillance; **2** Pol préfet *m*

prefecture /ˈpriːfektjʊə(r), US -tʃər/ *n* préfecture *f*

prefer /prɪˈfɜː(r)/
A *vtr* **1** (like better) préférer, aimer mieux; **I** ~ **painting to drawing** je préfère la peinture au dessin; **to** ~ **it if** aimer mieux que (+ *subj*); **2** Jur **to** ~ **charges** porter plainte; **3** (appoint) élever [*clergyman*]
B **preferred** *pp adj* (*tjrs épith*) [*method, option, solution*] préféré; [*creditor, candidate*] prioritaire

preferable /ˈprefrəbl/ *adj* préférable (**to** à)

preferably /ˈprefrəblɪ/ *adv* de préférence

preference /ˈprefrəns/ *n* préférence *f* (**for** pour); **in** ~ **to** de préférence à; **in** ~ **to doing** plutôt que de faire

preference share *n* GB Fin action *f* privilégiée

preferential /ˌprefəˈrenʃl/ *adj* (all contexts) préférentiel/-ielle

preferment /prɪˈfɜːmənt/ *n* Admin élévation *f*

prefigure /ˌpriːˈfɪgə(r), US -gjər/ *vtr* **1** (be an early sign of) [*event*] préfigurer; [*person*] être le précurseur de; **2** (imagine beforehand) imaginer d'avance

prefix /ˈpriːfɪks/
A *n* (*pl* **-es**) Ling préfixe *m*
B *vtr* préfixer [*word*]; **to** ~ **X to Y** faire précéder Y de X

pregnancy /ˈpregnənsɪ/ *n* (of woman) grossesse *f*; (of animal) gestation *f*

pregnant /ˈpregnənt/ *adj* **1** Med [*woman*] enceinte; [*animal*] pleine; **to get sb** ~° faire un enfant à qn°; **2** fig [*pause*] éloquent; ~ **with meaning/danger** lourd de sens/danger

preheat /ˌpriːˈhiːt/ *vtr* préchauffer [*oven*]

prehistoric /ˌpriːhɪˈstɒrɪk, US -tɔːrɪk/ *adj* préhistorique also fig

prehistory /ˌpriːˈhɪstrɪ/ *n* **1** Hist préhistoire *f*; **2** **¢** fig (beginnings) débuts *mpl*

pre-ignition /ˌpriːɪgˈnɪʃn/ *n* autoallumage *m*

prejudge /ˌpriːˈdʒʌdʒ/ *vtr* juger [qn] d'avance [*person*]; préjuger [*issue*]

prejudice /ˈpredʒʊdɪs/
A *n* **1 C** préjugé *m*; **2 ¢** préjugés *mpl*; **racial/political** ~ préjugés raciaux/en matière de politique; **3** (harm) gen, Jur préjudice *m*
B *vtr* **1** (bias) influencer; **to** ~ **sb against/in favour of** prévenir qn contre/en faveur de; **2** (harm, jeopardize) porter préjudice à [*claim, case*]; léser [*person*]; compromettre [*chances*]

prejudiced /ˈpredʒʊdɪst/ *adj* [*person*] plein de préjugés; [*judgment, account*] partial; [*opinion*] préconçu

prejudicial /ˌpredʒʊˈdɪʃl/ *adj* sout préjudiciable

prelate /ˈprelət/ *n* prélat *m*

prelim /priːˈlɪm/ *n* (*gén pl*) **1** GB Univ examen *m* de passage en deuxième année; **2** GB Sch ≈ bac *m* blanc

preliminary /prɪˈlɪmɪnərɪ, US -nerɪ/
A *n* **1 as a** ~ **to** en prélude à; **2** Sport épreuve *f* éliminatoire
B **preliminaries** *npl* préliminaires *mpl* (**to** à)
C *adj* [*comment, data, test*] préliminaire; [*heat, round*] éliminatoire; Jur [*hearing, inquiry, ruling*] préliminaire; ~ **to** préalable à

prelude /ˈpreljuːd/ *n* gen, Mus prélude *m* (**to** à)

premarital /ˌpriːˈmærɪtl/ *adj* avant le mariage

premature /ˈpremətjʊə(r), US ˌpriːməˈtʊər/ *adj* gen, Med prématuré; [*ejaculation, menopause*] précoce; **to be born two weeks** ~ naître deux semaines avant terme

p

prematurely /'prematjʊəlɪ, US ˌpriːmə'tʊərlɪ/ adv prématurément

premedication /ˌpriːmedɪ'keɪʃn/ n (also **premed**) Med prémédication f

premeditate /ˌpriː'medɪteɪt/ vtr préméditer

premenstrual: ∼ **syndrome**, **PMS** n spéc syndrome m prémenstruel; ∼ **tension**, **PMT** n syndrome m prémenstruel

premier /'premɪə(r), US 'priːmɪər/
A n **1** (prime minister) premier ministre m; **2** (head of government) chef m du gouvernement
B adj premier/-ière

première /'premɪeə(r), US 'priːmɪər/
A n première f
B vtr donner [qch] en première [film, play]
C vi [film] passer en première

premiership /'premɪeəʃɪp, US prɪ'mɪərʃɪp/ n Pol fonction f de premier ministre or de chef du gouvernement; (period of office) ministère m

premise /'premɪs/
A n GB (also **premiss** GB) prémisse f; **on the** ∼ **that** en supposant que (+ subj)
B **premises** npl locaux mpl; **on the** ∼**s** sur place; **off the** ∼**s** à l'extérieur; **to leave the** ∼**s** quitter les lieux

premium /'priːmɪəm/ n **1** gen (extra payment) supplément m; **2** (Stock Exchange) prime f d'émission; **3** (in insurance) prime f (d'assurance); **4** Comm (payment for lease) reprise f; **5** fig **to be at a** ∼ valoir de l'or; **to put** ou **place** ou **set a (high)** ∼ **on sth** mettre qch au (tout) premier plan

premium: ∼ **bond** GB n obligation f à lots; ∼ **rate** n [call, number] ≈ à tarification normale

prenatal /ˌpriː'neɪtl/ adj surtout US prénatal

preoccupation /ˌpriːɒkjʊ'peɪʃn/ n préoccupation f; **to have a** ∼ **with** se préoccuper de; **his** ∼ **with** son obsession pour

preoccupied /ˌpriː'ɒkjʊpaɪd/ adj préoccupé

preoccupy /ˌpriː'ɒkjʊpaɪ/ vtr (prét, pp **-pied**) préoccuper

preoperative /ˌpriː'ɒpərətɪv, US -reɪt-/ adj préopératoire

preordained /ˌpriːɔː'deɪnd/ adj **1** gen [decree, order] prescrit d'avance; **2** Relig, Philos [outcome] prédestiné; [pattern] préétabli

prep° /prep/ n **1** GB Sch **¢** (homework) devoirs mpl; (study period) étude f; **2** US Sch élève mf d'un lycée privé

prepack /ˌpriː'pæk/, **prepackage** /ˌpriː'pækɪdʒ/ vtr pré-emballer

prepaid /ˌpriː'peɪd/ adj gen payé d'avance; **carriage** ∼ port payé; ∼ **envelope** enveloppe f affranchie pour la réponse

preparation /ˌprepə'reɪʃn/ n **1** (of meal, report, lecture, event) préparation f; ∼**s** préparatifs mpl; **in** ∼ **for sth** en vue de qch; **2** (physical, psychological) préparation f (for pour); (sporting) entraînement (for pour); **3** (substance) préparation f; **4** **¢** GB (homework) devoirs mpl

preparatory /prɪ'pærətrɪ, US -tɔːrɪ/ adj [training, course, drawing] préparatoire; [meeting, report, investigations] préliminaire; ∼ **to sth/to doing** en vue de qch/de faire

preparatory school n **1** GB école f primaire privée; **2** US lycée m privé

prepare /prɪ'peə(r)/
A vtr (plan) préparer [food, room, class, speech, report]; préparer [surprise]; **to** ∼ **to do** se préparer à faire; **to** ∼ **sb for** préparer qn à [exam, situation, shock]
B vi **to** ∼ **for** se préparer à [trip, talks, exam, election, storm, war]; se préparer pour [party, ceremony, game]
C v refl **to** ∼ **oneself** se préparer

prepared /prɪ'peəd/ adj **1** (willing) **to be** ∼ **to do** être prêt à faire; **2** (ready) **to be** ∼ **for** [event, conflict, change] être prêt à; **to be well-/ill-**∼ (with materials) être bien/mal équipé; **to come** ∼ venir bien préparé; **to be** ∼ **for the worst** s'attendre au pire; **I really wasn't** ∼ **for this!** je ne m'attendais pas du tout à ça!; **3** (ready-made) [speech, response] préparé d'avance; [meal] tout prêt

preparedness /prɪ'peərɪdnɪs/ n **1** ∼ **for** préparation f en cas de; **a state of** ∼ Mil un état d'alerte; **2** (willingness) **her** ∼ **to address major issues** son empressement à aborder des problèmes importants

prepay /ˌpriː'peɪ/ vtr payer [qch] d'avance

prepayment /ˌpriː'peɪmənt/ n paiement m d'avance

preponderantly /prɪ'pɒndərəntlɪ/ adv principalement

preponderate /prɪ'pɒndəreɪt/ vi prédominer

preposition /ˌprepə'zɪʃn/ n préposition f

prepositional /ˌprepə'zɪʃənəl/ adj prépositionnel/-elle; ∼ **phrase** (used as preposition) locution f prépositive; (introduced by preposition) syntagme m prépositionnel

prepossessing /ˌpriːpə'zesɪŋ/ adj avenant

preposterous /prɪ'pɒstərəs/ adj grotesque

preposterously /prɪ'pɒstərəslɪ/ adv ridiculement

preppy°, **preppie**° /'prepɪ/ US
A n Sch (student) élève mf d'une école privée; (alumnus) ancien élève/ancienne élève m/f d'une école privée
B adj ≈ BCBG° inv

preprogrammed /ˌpriː'prəʊgræmd, US -grəmd/ adj gen programmé; Comput préprogrammé

prep school /'prepskuːl/ n GB école f primaire privée; US lycée m privé

> **ⓘ Prep school** Au Royaume-Uni, école privée qui accueille des élèves âgés de 7 à 13 ans et les prépare à l'entrée dans une bonne école, le plus souvent une *public school*. Aux États-Unis, école secondaire privée très sélective qui prépare les élèves à l'entrée dans les meilleures universités. ▸ The **Ivy League**, **Public schools**

prequel /'priːkwəl/ n Literat, Cin épisode m précédent

prerecord /ˌpriːrɪ'kɔːd/
A vtr TV, Radio enregistrer [qch] à l'avance
B **prerecorded** pp adj [broadcast] préenregistré, en différé inv

prerequisite /ˌpriː'rekwɪzɪt/
A n **1** gen préalable m (of de; for à); **2** US Univ unité f de valeur
B adj [condition] préalable

prerogative /prɪ'rɒgətɪv/ n (official) prérogative f; (personal) droit m

presage /'presɪdʒ/ sout
A n présage m (of de)
B vtr laisser présager [disaster]

preschool /ˌpriː'skuːl/
A n US (kindergarten) école f maternelle; **in** ∼ à l'école maternelle
B adj [child] d'âge préscolaire inv; [years] préscolaire

prescribe /prɪ'skraɪb/
A vtr **1** Med fig prescrire (**for sb** à qn; **for sth** pour qch); **2** (lay down) imposer [rule]
B **prescribed** pp adj **1** Med, fig prescrit; **2** (set) [rule] imposé; Sch, Univ [book] inscrit au programme

prescription /prɪ'skrɪpʃn/
A n **1** Med ordonnance f; **repeat** ∼ ordonnance renouvelable; **2** fig (formula) recette f; (set of rules) prescription f
B noun modifier Med [glasses, lenses] correcteur/-trice; ∼ **drug** préparation médicinale

prescription charges npl GB Med frais mpl d'ordonnance

prescriptive /prɪ'skrɪptɪv/ adj gen, Ling normatif/-ive; Jur prescriptible

presence /'prezns/ n (all contexts) présence f; **signed in the** ∼ **of X** Jur signé par-devant X; **your** ∼ **is requested at** vous êtes prié d'assister à; **a heavy police** ∼ (in streets) une forte présence policière; (at match, demonstration) un important service d'ordre

(Idiom) **to make one's** ∼ **felt** ne pas passer inaperçu

presence of mind n présence f d'esprit

present
A /'preznt/ n **1** (gift) cadeau m; **to give sb sth as a** ∼ offrir qch à qn; **2** **the** ∼ (now) le présent; **for the** ∼ pour le moment, pour l'instant; **3** Ling (also ∼ **tense**) présent m; **in the** ∼ au présent
B /'preznt/ adj **1** (attending) présent; **to be** ∼ **at** assister à; ∼ **company excepted** à l'exception des personnes ici présentes; **all** ∼ **and correct!** tous présents à l'appel!; **2** (current) actuel/-elle; **up to the** ∼ **day** jusqu'à ce jour; **at the** ∼ **time** ou **moment** actuellement; **the** ∼ **writer feels that** l'auteur (de cet article) pense que; **3** Ling présent

C **at present** adv phr (at this moment) en ce moment; (nowadays) actuellement, à présent

D /prɪ'zent/ vtr **1** (raise) présenter [problem, challenge, risk]; offrir [chance, opportunity]; **2** (proffer, show) présenter; to be ~ed with a choice se trouver face à un choix; to be ~ed with a huge bill se retrouver avec une énorme facture; **3** (submit for consideration) présenter [plan, figures, petition]; fournir [evidence]; **4** (formally give) remettre [prize, certificate]; présenter [apologies, respects, compliments]; may I ~ my son Piers? permettez-moi de vous présenter mon fils Piers; **5** (portray) présenter [person, situation] (as comme étant); to ~ sth in a different light présenter qch sous un jour différent; **6** TV, Radio, Theat présenter [programme, show]; donner [production, play, concert]; **7** Mil présenter [arms]

E vi Med [patient, baby] se présenter; [symptom, condition] apparaître

F v refl **1** to ~ oneself se présenter; to learn how to ~ oneself apprendre à mettre en avant ses qualités; **2** to ~ itself [opportunity, thought] se présenter

(Idiom) there is no time like the ~ il ne faut jamais remettre au lendemain ce que l'on peut faire le jour même

presentable /prɪ'zentəbl/ adj présentable

presentation /ˌprezən'teɪʃn/ n **1** (of plan, report, bill, idea, person etc) présentation f; **2** (by salesman, colleague, executive etc) exposé m; **3** (of gift, award) remise f (**of** de); the chairman will make the ~ le président remettra le prix; there will be a ~ at 5.30 il y aura une cérémonie à 17 h 30; **4** (portrayal) gen, Theat représentation f; **5** Med (of baby) présentation f

presentation : ~ **box** n coffret-cadeau m; ~ **copy** n hommage m (de l'auteur ou de l'éditeur); ~ **pack** n présentoir m

presentation skills npl to have good ~ avoir le sens de la communication

present-day /ˌprezənt'deɪ/ adj actuel/-elle

presenter /prɪ'zentə(r)/ ▸ p. 1181 n TV, Radio présentateur/-trice m/f

presently /'prezntlɪ/ adv (currently) à présent; (soon afterwards, in past) peu de temps après; (soon, in future) bientôt

present perfect n passé m composé

preservation /ˌprezə'veɪʃn/ n (of building, wildlife, tradition, peace, dignity) préservation f (**of** de); (of food) conservation f (**of** de); (of life) protection f (**of** de)

preservation order n to put a ~ on sth classer qch

preservative /prɪ'zɜːvətɪv/

A n (for food) agent m de conservation; (for wood) revêtement m (protecteur)

B adj [mixture, product, effect] de conservation

preserve /prɪ'zɜːv/

A n **1** Culin (also ~s) confiture f; (pickle) conserve f; **2** (territory) lit, fig chasse f gardée (**of** de)

B vtr **1** (rescue, save from destruction) préserver [land, building, tradition] (**for** pour); entretenir [wood, leather, painting]; **2** (maintain) préserver [peace, standards, rights]; maintenir [order]; **3** (keep, hold onto) garder [humour, dignity, health]; **4** Culin (stop rotting) conserver; (make into jam) faire de la confiture de

C preserved pp adj [food] en conserve; [site, castle] protégé; ~d on film conservé sur la pellicule

preserving pan n bassine f à confiture

preset /ˌpriː'set/ vtr (prét, pp -**set**) régler (à l'avance) [timer, cooker]; programmer [magnétoscope]

preshrunk /ˌpriː'ʃrʌŋk/ adj [fabric] irrétrécissable

preside /prɪ'zaɪd/ vi présider; to ~ at sth présider qch; to ~ over présider [conference, committee]; présider à [activity, change]

presidency /'prezɪdənsɪ/ n présidence f

president /'prezɪdənt/ ▸ p. 869 n **1** gen, Pol président/-e m/f; to run for ~ être candidat/-e à la présidence; **2** US Comm président-directeur m général

presidential /ˌprezɪ'denʃl/ adj [election, government, term] présidentiel/-ielle; [race, candidate] à la présidence; [adviser, office, policy] du président

pre-soak /ˌpriː'səʊk/ vtr faire tremper [washing]

press /pres/

A n **1** the ~, the Press la presse f; to get a good/bad ~ lit, fig avoir bonne/mauvaise presse; **2** (also **printing** ~) presse f; to go to ~ être mis sous presse; at ou in (the) ~ sous presse; **3** (publishing house) maison f d'éditon; (print

works) imprimerie f; the Starlight Press les Éditions Starlight; **4** (device for flattening) presse f; **5** (act of pushing) pression f; to give sth a ~ appuyer sur qch; **6** (with iron) repassage m; to give sth a ~ repasser qch; **7** (crowd) foule f (**of** de)

B noun modifier [acclaim, freedom, criticism] de la presse; [campaign, photo, photographer] de presse; [announcement, advertising] par voie de presse; ~ **story**, ~ **report** reportage m

C vtr **1** (push) appuyer sur; to ~ sth in enfoncer qch; ~ the pedal right down appuie à fond sur la pédale; ~ the switch down pousse l'interrupteur vers le bas; to ~ sth into enfoncer qch dans [clay, mud, ground, pillow]; to ~ sth into sb's hand glisser qch dans la main de qn; **2** (apply) to ~ one's nose against sth coller son nez contre qch; to ~ one's hands to one's ears se plaquer les mains contre les oreilles; to ~ one's knees together serrer les genoux; **3** (squeeze) presser [fruit, flower]; serrer [arm, hand, person]; to ~ sb to one presser qn contre soi; **4** (iron) repasser [clothes]; **5** (urge) faire pression à fond sur [person]; insister sur [point]; mettre [qch] en avant [matter, issue]; défendre [qch] avec insistance [case]; to ~ sb to do presser qn de faire; to ~ sb into doing forcer qn à faire; I must ~ you for an answer je dois avoir une réponse; when ~ed, he admitted that… quand on a insisté, il a reconnu que…; to ~ a point insister; **6** Tech former [shape, object]; presser [record, CD]; emboutir [steel, metal, car body]

D vi **1** (push with hand, foot, object) to ~ down appuyer; **2** [crowd, person] se presser (**against** contre; **around** autour de; **forward** vers l'avant)

E v refl to ~ oneself against se plaquer contre [wall]; se presser contre [person]

(Phrasal verbs)

■ **press ahead** aller de l'avant; to ~ ahead with [sth] faire avancer [reform, plan, negotiations]

■ **press for**: ▸ ~ for [sth] faire pression pour obtenir [change, support, release]; to be ~ed for sth ne pas avoir beaucoup de qch

■ **press on**: ▸ ~ on **1** (on journey) continuer; to ~ on regardless continuer malgré tout; **2** (move on) fig passer à la suite; to ~ on with faire avancer [reform, plan]; passer à [next item]; ▸ ~ [sth] on sb forcer qn à prendre

press : ~ **agency** n agence f de presse; ~ **agent** ▸ p. 1181 n attaché /-e m/f de presse; **Press Association** n GB agence f de presse britannique; ~ **attaché** n = press agent; ~ **baron** n magnat m de la presse; ~ **card** n carte f de presse; ~ **conference** n conférence f de presse; ~ **corps** n ₵ journalistes mpl; ~ **cutting** n coupure f de presse; ~ **gallery** n tribune f de la presse

press-gang /'presgæŋ/ vtr Hist racoler; to ~ sb into doing fig forcer qn à faire

pressing /'presɪŋ/

A n **1** (of olives) pression f; **2** (of records) pressage m

B adj **1** (urgent) urgent; **2** (insistent) [invitation] pressant; [anxiety] oppressant

press lord n magnat m de la presse

pressman /'presmən/ ▸ p. 1181 n **1** (printer) imprimeur/-euse m/f; **2** GB (journalist) journaliste m

press : ~ **officer** n = press agent; ~ **pass** n coupe-file m; ~ **release** n communiqué m de presse; ~**room** n (for printing) salle f des presses; (for press conferences) salle f de presse; ~ **run** n tirage m; ~ **secretary** n = press agent; ~**stud** n GB (bouton-)pression m; ~**up** n pompe° f

pressure /'preʃə(r)/

A n **1** gen, fig, Tech, Meteorol pression f; to put ~ on sb faire pression sur qn; to do sth under ~ faire qch sous la contrainte; she has come under a lot of ~ to do on exerce de fortes pressions sur elle pour l'amener à faire; due to ~ of work pour cause d'emploi du temps chargé; financial ~s contraintes financières; the ~s of modern life le stress de la vie moderne; **2** (volume) (of traffic, tourists, visitors) flux m

B vtr = pressurize

pressure : ~-**cook** vtr cuire [qch] à la cocotte-minute®; ~ **cooker** n cocotte-minute f®; ~ **gauge** n manomètre m; ~ **group** n groupe m de pression; ~ **point** n point m de compression

pressurize /'preʃəraɪz/ vtr **1** lit pressuriser; **2** fig faire pression sur [person]; to be ~d into doing être contraint de faire

presswoman /ˈpreswʌmən/ ▸ p. 1181 n journaliste f

prestige /preˈstiːʒ/
A n prestige m
B noun modifier [car, site] de prestige; [housing, hotel] de grand standing

prestigious /preˈstɪdʒəs/ adj prestigieux/-ieuse

presumably /prɪˈzjuːməblɪ, US -ˈzuːm-/ adv sans doute

presume /prɪˈzjuːm, US -ˈzuːm/
A vtr **1** (suppose) supposer, présumer; **I ~d him to be honest** je le croyais honnête; **'does he know?'—'I ~ so'** 'le sait-il?'—'probablement'; **2** (presuppose) présupposer; **3** (dare) **to ~ to do** se permettre de faire
B vi **to ~ upon** abuser de [person, kindness]; **I hope I'm not presuming** j'espère que je ne m'avance pas trop

presumption /prɪˈzʌmpʃn/ n **1** (supposition) supposition f (**that** que); **on the ~ that** en supposant que; **to make a ~** supposer; **2** (basis) arguments mpl; **3** (impudence) audace f

presumptive /prɪˈzʌmptɪv/ adj gen par présomption

presumptuous /prɪˈzʌmptʃʊəs/ adj audacieux/-ieuse

presuppose /ˌpriːsəˈpəʊz/ vtr présupposer (**that** que)

pre-tax /ˌpriːˈtæks/ adj avant impôts inv

pretence GB, **pretense** US /prɪˈtens/ n **1** (false show) faux-semblant m; **to make a ~ of sth** feindre qch; **to make a ~ of doing** faire semblant de faire; **to make no ~ of sth** ne pas se donner la peine de feindre qch; **to keep up the ~ of doing** entretenir l'illusion de faire; **2** (sham) simulacre m (**of** de); (of illness) simulation f (**of** de)

pretend /prɪˈtend/
A °adj lang enfantin [gun, car] imaginaire; [jewels] faux/fausse (before n); **it's only ~!** c'est pour rire!
B vtr **1** (feign) simuler; **to ~ that** faire comme si; **to ~ to do** faire semblant de faire; **a thief ~ing to be a policeman** un voleur se faisant passer pour un policier; **2** (claim) **to ~ to understand** avoir la prétention de comprendre; **to ~ to be** prétendre être
C vi **1** (feign) faire semblant; **2** (maintain deception) jouer la comédie; **I was only ~ing** c'était pour rire
D **pretended** pp adj [emotion, ignorance] simulé

pretender /prɪˈtendə(r)/ n prétendant/-e m/f (**to** à)

pretense n US = **pretence**

pretension /prɪˈtenʃn/ n prétention f; **to have ~s to sth** prétendre à qch

pretentious /prɪˈtenʃəs/ adj prétentieux/-ieuse

preterite /ˈpretərət/ n prétérit f

pretext /ˈpriːtekst/ n prétexte m

prettily /ˈprɪtɪlɪ/ adv [arrange, dress, decorate, perform, talk] joliment; [blush, smile] de façon charmante; [apologize, thank] gentiment

pretty /ˈprɪtɪ/
A adj **1** (attractive) joli; **it was not a ~ sight** ce n'était pas beau à voir; **2** péj (trite) joli
B °adv **1** (very) vraiment; (fairly) assez; (almost) pratiquement; **~ good** pas mal du tout; **~ well all** pratiquement tout; **'how are you?'—'~ well'** 'comment ça va?'—'très bien'
(Idioms) **~ as a picture** ravissant; **I'm not just a ~ face**° hum j'ai aussi quelque chose dans la tête; **this is a ~ mess** ou **a ~ state of affairs** iron voilà du beau travail iron; **that must have cost you a ~ penny**° ça a dû te coûter cher; **to be sitting ~**° se la couler douce°; **things have come to a ~ pass when...** ça commence à ne plus aller du tout quand...
(Phrasal verb)
■ **pretty up**: ▸ ~ [sth] up, ~ up [sth] enjoliver

pretty: **~ boy**° n péj minet° m pej; **~-pretty** adj péj trop coquet/-ette

prevail /prɪˈveɪl/ vi **1** (win) prévaloir (**against** contre); **2** (be usual) prédominer
(Phrasal verb)
■ **prevail upon**: ▸ ~ **upon [sb]** persuader

prevailing /prɪˈveɪlɪŋ/ adj gen [attitude, style] qui prévaut; [rate] en vigueur; [wind] dominant

prevalence /ˈprevələns/ n **1** (widespread nature) fréquence f; **2** (superior position) prédominance f

prevalent /ˈprevələnt/ adj **1** (widespread) répandu; **2** (ruling) qui prévaut

prevaricate /prɪˈværɪkeɪt/ vi sout se dérober

prevent /prɪˈvent/ vtr prévenir [fire, illness, violence]; éviter [conflict, disaster, damage]; faire obstacle à [marriage]; **to ~ the outbreak of war** empêcher le déclenchement d'une guerre

preventable /prɪˈventəbl/ adj évitable

preventative /prɪˈventətɪv/ adj = **preventive**

prevention /prɪˈvenʃn/ n prévention f; **accident ~** gen prévention f des accidents; (on road) prévention f routière; **crime ~** lutte f contre la délinquance
(Idiom) **~ is better than cure** Prov mieux vaut prévenir que guérir Prov

preventive /prɪˈventɪv/ adj préventif/-ive

preview /ˈpriːvjuː/
A n (of film, play) avant-première f; (of exhibition) vernissage m; (of match, programme) présentation f (**of** de)
B vtr présenter [match, programme]

previous /ˈpriːvɪəs/
A adj **1** (before) [day, meeting, manager] gen précédent; (further back in time) antérieur; **on a ~ occasion** (une fois) déjà; **on ~ occasions** à plusieurs reprises; **he has no ~ convictions** Jur il a un casier judiciaire vierge; **to have a ~ engagement** être déjà pris; **'~ experience essential'** 'expérience préalable indispensable'; **2** °(hasty) [decision] hâtif/-ive; [action] prématuré
B **previous to** prep phr avant

previously /ˈpriːvɪəslɪ/ adv (before) auparavant, avant; (already) déjà

prewar /ˌpriːˈwɔː(r)/ adj d'avant-guerre inv

prewash /ˌpriːˈwɒʃ/ n prélavage m

prey /preɪ/ n lit, fig proie f
(Phrasal verb)
■ **prey on**: ▸ ~ **on [sth]** **1** (hunt) chasser; **2** fig (worry) **to ~ on sb's mind** préoccuper qn; **3** (exploit) exploiter [fears, worries]; ▸ ~ **on [sb]** [conman] choisir ses victimes parmi; [mugger, rapist] s'attaquer à

price /praɪs/
A n **1** gen, Comm, lit, fig (cost) prix m; **the ~ per kilo** le prix du kilo; **'we pay top ~s for...'** 'nous payons le prix fort pour...'; **cars have gone up in ~** les voitures ont augmenté; **what sort of ~ did you have to pay?** à peu près combien est-ce que tu as eu à payer?; **to pay a high ~ for sth** lit, fig payer qch cher; **that's a small ~ to pay for sth** fig ce n'est pas un gros sacrifice pour obtenir qch; **2** gen, Comm, lit, fig (value) valeur f; **beyond** ou **above ~** (d'une valeur) inestimable; **to put a ~ on** lit évaluer [object, antique]; **to put** ou **set a high ~ on** attacher beaucoup de prix à [loyalty, hard work]; **what ~ all his good intentions now!** qu'en est-il maintenant de ses bonnes intentions!
B vtr **1** (fix, determine the price of) fixer le prix de (**at** à); **a dress ~d at £30** une robe à 30 livres; **a moderately-~d hotel** un hôtel aux tarifs raisonnables; **2** (evaluate the worth of) estimer la valeur de; **3** (mark the price of) marquer le prix de
(Idiom) **to put a ~ on sb's head** mettre à prix la tête de qn
(Phrasal verb)
■ **price out**: **~ oneself** ou **one's goods out of the market** perdre un marché en pratiquant des prix trop élevés

price: **~ bracket** n = **price range**; **~ control** n contrôle m des prix; **~ cut**, **~ cutting** n baisse f du prix; **~ fixing** n détermination f illégale des prix; **~ freeze** n blocage m des prix; **~ index** n indice m des prix; **~ label** n étiquette f

priceless /ˈpraɪslɪs/ adj **1** (extremely valuable) inestimable; **2** °(amusing) impayable

price list n (in shop, catalogue) liste f des prix; (in bar, restaurant) tarif m

price range n fourchette f; **that's out of my ~** cela n'est pas dans mes prix

price: **~ restrictions** n contrôle m des prix; **~ ring** n cartel m de vendeurs; **~ rise** n hausse f des prix; **~ tag** n (label) étiquette f; fig (cost) coût m; **~ ticket** n étiquette f; **~ war** n guerre f des prix

prick /prɪk/
A n (of needle etc) (feeling) piqûre f; (hole) trou m (d'épingle); **to give sth a ~** piquer qch
B vtr **1** (cause pain) piquer; **to ~ one's finger** se piquer le doigt; **his conscience ~ed him** fig il avait mauvaise conscience; **2** (pierce) percer [paper, plastic, hole]; crever [bubble, balloon]; Culin piquer [potato etc]; **3** = **prick up**

C *vi* **1** [*eyes*] piquer; [*skin*] picoter; **2** [*thorn*] piquer

(Idiom) **to kick against the ~s** s'obstiner pour rien

(Phrasal verbs)

■ **prick out** : ▶ **~ out** [sth], **~** [sth] **out** repiquer [*seedlings*]; Art piquer [*design, outline*]

■ **prick up** : ▶ **~ up** [*dog's ears*] se dresser; **to ~ up its** *ou* **one's ears** [*dog*] dresser les oreilles; [*person*] dresser l'oreille

prickle /'prɪkl/

A *n* (of hedgehog, plant) piquant *m*

B *vtr* [*clothes, jumper*] gratter

C *vi* [*hairs*] se hérisser (**with** de)

prickly /'prɪklɪ/ *adj* **1** [*bush, leaf*] épineux/-euse; [*animal*] armé de piquants; [*thorn*] piquant; **2** (itchy) qui gratte; **3** ○(touchy) irritable (**about** à propos de)

pride /praɪd/

A *n* **1** (source of satisfaction) fierté *f* (**in** sb/sth éprouvée pour qn/qch); **to take ~ in** être fier/fière de [*ability, achievement*]; soigner [*appearance, work*]; **to be sb's ~ and joy** être la (grande) fierté de qn; **2** (self-respect) amour-propre *m*; *péj* orgueil *m*; **family ~** honneur *m* familial; **national ~** sentiment *m* de fierté nationale; **3** (of lions) troupe *f*

B *v refl* **to ~ oneself on sth/on doing** être fier/fière de qch/de faire

(Idioms) **to have ~ of place** être mis en vedette; **~ comes before a fall** *Prov* péché d'orgueil ne va pas sans danger

priest /priːst/ *n* prêtre *m*; **parish ~** curé *m*

priesthood /'priːsthʊd/ *n* (calling) prêtrise *f*; (clergy) clergé *m*; **to enter the ~** entrer dans les ordres

prig /prɪg/ *n* bégueule *mf*

prim /prɪm/ *adj* (*also* **~ and proper**) [*person, manner, appearance*] guindé; [*expression*] pincé; [*voice*] affecté; [*clothing*] très convenable

prima ballerina /ˌpriːmə ˌbælə'riːnə/ *n* danseuse *f* étoile

primacy /'praɪməsɪ/ *n* gen primauté *f*; (of party, power) suprématie *f*; *Relig* primatie *f*

primaeval *adj* = **primeval**

prima facie /ˌpraɪmə 'feɪʃɪ/

A *adj* *Jur*, gen légitime (à première vue)

B *adv* *Jur*, gen de prime abord

primal /'praɪml/ *adj* [*quality, myth, feeling*] primitif/-ive; [*stage, cause, origins*] premier/-ière

primarily /'praɪmərəlɪ, US praɪ'merəlɪ/ *adv* (chiefly) essentiellement; (originally) à l'origine

primary /'praɪmərɪ, US -merɪ/

A *n* **1** US *Pol* (*also* **~ election**) primaire *f*; **2** *Sch* ▶ **primary school**

B *adj* **1** (main) gen principal; [*sense, meaning, stage*] premier/-ière; **of ~ importance** de première importance; **2** *Sch* [*teaching, education*] primaire; [*post*] dans l'enseignement primaire; **3** *Econ* [*industry, products*] de base

> **ℹ** **Primaries** Aux États-Unis, les partis politiques choisissent leurs délégués au cours des élections primaires. Les délégués se réunissent ensuite dans une convention nationale pour désigner le candidat du parti à la présidence et le candidat à la vice-présidence : c'est le *presidential ticket*.

primary : **~ colour** *n* couleur *f* primaire; **~ health care** *n* soins *mpl* de premier recours; **~ school** *n* école *f* primaire; **~ sector** *n* *Econ* secteur *m* primaire; **~ (school) teacher** ▶ p. 1181 *n* surtout GB instituteur/-trice *m/f*

primate /'praɪmeɪt/ *n* **1** *Zool* (mammal) primate *m*; **2** *Relig* (*also* **Primate**) primat *m* (**of** de)

prime /praɪm/

A *n* **1** (peak period) **in one's ~** (professionally) à son apogée; (physically) dans la fleur de l'âge; **in its ~** à son apogée; **to be past its ~** avoir connu des jours meilleurs; **2** *Math* (*also* **~ number**) nombre *m* premier

B *adj* **1** (chief) gen principal; [*importance*] primordial; **2** *Comm* (good quality) [*site*] de premier ordre; [*meat, cuts*] de premier choix; [*foodstuffs*] d'une parfaite fraîcheur; **in ~ condition** [*machine*] en parfait état; [*livestock*] en parfaite condition; **of ~ quality** de première qualité; **3** (épith) (classic) [*example, instance*] excellent; **4** *Math* premier/-ière

C *vtr* **1** (brief) préparer; **to ~ sb about** mettre qn au courant de; **to ~ sb to say** souffler à qn de dire; **2** (apply primer to)

appliquer un apprêt sur; **3** *Mil*, *Tech* amorcer

prime : **~ cost** *n* prix *m* de revient; **~ minister**, **PM** ▶ p. 869 *n* Premier ministre *m*; **~-ministerial** *adj* de Premier ministre

prime mover *n* **1** (person) promoteur/-trice *m/f*; (instinct) moteur *m* principal; **2** *Phys*, *Tech* force *f* motrice

primer /'praɪmə(r)/ *n* **1** (paint) apprêt *m*; **2** (for detonating) amorce *f*

prime time

A *n* heures *fpl* de grande écoute

B **prime-time** *noun modifier* [*advertising, programme*] passant aux heures de grande écoute

primeval /praɪ'miːvl/ *adj* primitif/-ive

primitive /'prɪmɪtɪv/

A *n* *Art* primitif *m*

B *adj* (all contexts) primitif/-ive

primly /'prɪmlɪ/ *adv* **1** (starchily) [*behave, smile*] d'une manière guindée; [*say, reply*] d'un ton guindé; **2** (demurely) [*behave, sit*] très sagement

primordial /praɪ'mɔːdɪəl/ *adj* primitif/-ive

primrose /'prɪmrəʊz/ *n* primevère *f* (jaune)

(Idiom) **the ~ path** le chemin de la facilité

prince /prɪns/ ▶ p. 869 *n* prince *m* *also fig*

princely /'prɪnslɪ/ *adj* [*amount, style*] princier/-ière; [*life, rôle*] de prince

princess /prɪn'ses/ ▶ p. 869 *n* princesse *f*

principal /'prɪnsəpl/

A *n* **1** ▶ p. 869 (of senior school) proviseur *m*; (of junior school, college) directeur/-trice *m/f*; **2** *Theat* acteur/-trice *m/f* principal/-e; **3** *Mus* chef *m* de pupitre; **4** (client) mandant *m*; **5** *Fin* capital *m*; (debt before interest) principal *m*

B *adj* **1** (main) principal; **2** [*violin, clarinet*] premier/-ière (*before n*); [*dancer*] étoile; **3** *Ling* [*clause*] principal; **the ~ parts of a verb** les temps primitifs d'un verbe

principality /ˌprɪnsə'pælətɪ/ *n* principauté *f*

principally /'prɪnsəplɪ/ *adv* principalement

principle /'prɪnsəpl/ *n* (all contexts) principe *m*; **to have high ~s** avoir beaucoup de principes; **in ~** en principe; **on ~** par principe; **to make it a ~** se faire un devoir ou principe de faire; **to get back to first ~s** repartir sur des bases concrètes

principled /'prɪnsəpld/ *adj* [*decision*] de principe; [*person*] de principes; **to be ~** avoir des principes

print /prɪnt/

A *n* **1** **C** (typeface) caractères *mpl*; **the ~ is very small** c'est écrit très petit; **the small** *ou* **fine ~** fig les détails; **don't forget to read the small ~** n'oubliez pas de lire tous les détails; **2** (published form) **in ~** disponible en librairie; **out of ~** épuisé; **to go into ~** être publié; **to put** *ou* **get sth into ~** publier qch; **to see sth in ~** voir qch noir sur blanc; **to see oneself in ~** se voir publié; **'at the time of going to ~'** 'à l'heure où nous mettons sous presse'; **3** *Art* (etching) estampe *f*; (engraving) gravure *f*; **4** *Phot* épreuve *f*; **5** *Cin* copie *f*; **6** (of finger, hand, foot) empreinte *f*; (of tyre) trace *f*; **7** (fabric) tissu *m* imprimé; **8** (handwriting) script *m*

B *noun modifier* [*curtains, dress*] en tissu imprimé

C *vtr* **1** (on press) imprimer *also Art*; **2** (publish) publier; **3** *Phot* [*copy*] tirer; faire développer [*photos*]; **4** (write) écrire [qch] en script

D *vi* **1** (write) écrire en script; **2** (on press) imprimer

E **printed** *pp adj* imprimé; **'~ed matter'** *Post* 'imprimés' *mpl*; **~ed notepaper** papier *m* à lettres à en-tête

(Phrasal verbs)

■ **print off** : ▶ **~ off** [sth], **~** [sth] **off** tirer [*copies*]

■ **print out** : ▶ **~ out** [sth], **~** [sth] **out** gen, *Comput* imprimer

printer /'prɪntə(r)/ *n* (person, firm) imprimeur *m*; (machine) imprimante *f*

printing /'prɪntɪŋ/ *n* (technique) imprimerie *f*; (result) impression *f*; (print run) tirage *m*

printing : **~ business**, **~ house**, **~industry** *n* imprimerie *f*; **~ press** *n* presse *f* (typographique); **~ works** *n* imprimerie *f*

print : **~ journalism** *n* (journalisme *m* de) presse *f* écrite; **~out** *n* sortie *f* sur imprimante; (perforated) listing *m*; **~-preview** *n* *Comput* aperçu *m* avant impression; **~ run** *n* tirage *m*; **~ shop** *n* (workshop) imprimerie *f*; (art shop) boutique *f* d'art

prior /'praɪə(r)/
A n Relig prieur m
B adj **1** (previous) préalable; **~ notice** préavis m; **2** (more important) prioritaire
C prior to prep phr avant

priority /praɪ'ɒrətɪ, US -'ɔːr-/
A n (all contexts) priorité f; **the main** ou **highest ~** la priorité absolue; **to get one's priorities right/wrong** définir correctement/mal définir l'ordre de ses priorités
B noun modifier [case, debt, expense, mail] prioritaire; [call] de priorité; [appointment] en priorité

priory /'praɪərɪ/ n prieuré m

prise /praɪz/ v
■ **prise apart:** ▶ **~ [sth] apart** séparer [layers, people]; ouvrir [qch] de force [lips, teeth]
(Phrasal verbs)
■ **prise away: to ~ sb away from** fig arracher qn à [TV, work]
■ **prise off:** ▶ **~ [sth] off** enlever [qch] en forçant
■ **prise open:** ▶ **~ [sth] open, ~ open [sth]** ouvrir [qch] en forçant
■ **prise out:** ▶ **~ [sth] out** lit retirer (**of, from** de); **to ~ sth out of sb** fig arracher qch à qn; **to ~ sb out of** lit arracher qn de
■ **prise up:** ▶ **~ [sth] up** soulever [qch] en forçant

prism /'prɪzəm/ n prisme m

prison /'prɪzn/
A n **1** **to put sb in ~** emprisonner qn; **to have been in ~** avoir fait de la prison
B noun modifier [administration, authorities, regulation] pénitentiaire; [population, reform] pénal; [cell, governor, visitor, guard, yard] de prison; [chapel, kitchen] de la prison; [conditions] de détention

prison camp n camp m de prisonniers

prisoner /'prɪznə(r)/ n gen, fig prisonnier/-ière m/f; (in jail) détenu/-e m/f; **they took me ~** ils m'ont fait prisonnier; **~ of conscience** prisonnier/-ière m/f d'opinion

prison: ~ issue adj fourni par la prison; **~ officer** ▸ p. 1181 n GB (officially) surveillant/-e m/f de prison; gen gardien/-ienne m/f de prison; **~ sentence, ~ term** n peine f de prison; **~ service** n administration f pénitentiaire; **~ van** n fourgon m cellulaire

prissy /'prɪsɪ/ adj [person] collet monté inv; [style] surchargé

pristine /'prɪstiːn, 'prɪstaɪn/ adj immaculé

privacy /'prɪvəsɪ, 'praɪ-/ n **1** (private life) vie f privée; **to invade sb's ~** s'immiscer dans la vie privée de qn; **2** (solitude) intimité f

private /'praɪvɪt/
A ▸ p. 1123 n simple soldat m
B adj **1** (not for general public) privé; **room with ~ bath** chambre avec salle de bains particulière; **the funeral will be ~** l'enterrement aura lieu dans la plus stricte intimité; **2** (personal, not associated with company) [letter, phone call, capacity] personnel/-elle; [sale] de particulier à particulier; **~ life** vie privée; **the ~ citizen** le (simple) particulier; **3** (not public, not state-run) gen privé; [housing, accommodation, landlord, lesson] particulier/-ière; **~ industry** le (secteur) privé; **4** [talk, meeting, matter] privé; [reason, opinion, thought] personnel/-elle; **to come to a ~ understanding** s'arranger à l'amiable; **to keep sth ~** préserver l'intimité de qch; **a ~ joke** une plaisanterie pour initiés; **5** [place] tranquille; **6** (secretive) renfermé (sur soi-même)
C in private adv phr en privé
(Idiom) **to go ~** GB Med se faire soigner dans le (secteur) privé

private: ~ company n société f privée; **~ enterprise** n entreprise f privée; **~ eye**○ n détective m privé; **~ hotel** n ≈ pension f de famille; **~ investor** n petit porteur m

privately /'praɪvɪtlɪ/ adv **1** (in private) en privé; (out of public sector) dans le privé; **~ managed** à gestion privée; **~ funded, ~ financed** à financement privé; **2** (in one's heart) [believe, doubt] en mon/son etc for intérieur

private parts npl euph parties fpl génitales

private practice n GB Med cabinet m privé; **to work** ou **be in ~** travailler hors des services de santé de l'État

private secretary n gen secrétaire mf particulier/-ière; Pol conseiller/-ère mf particulier/-ière

private treaty n **by ~** de gré à gré

private view n Art vernissage m

privatization /praɪvətaɪ'zeɪʃn, US -tɪ'z-/ n privatisation f

privatize /'praɪvətaɪz/ vtr privatiser

privilege /'prɪvəlɪdʒ/ n **1** (honour, advantage) privilège m; **tax ~s** avantages mpl fiscaux; **2** (prerogative) apanage m; **3** US Fin option f

privileged /'prɪvəlɪdʒd/ adj [minority, life, position] privilégié; [information] confidentiel/-ielle

prize /praɪz/
A n **1** (award) prix m; (in lottery) lot m; **first ~** premier prix; (in lottery) gros lot; **2** littér (valued object) trésor m; (reward for effort) récompense f
B noun modifier **1** [vegetable, bull etc] (for competitions) de concours; (prize-winning) primé; [pupil] hors-pair inv; **a ~ example of** un parfait exemple de; **2** [possession] précieux/-ieuse
C vtr **1** priser [independence, possession]; **2** = prise
D prized pp adj [possession, asset] précieux/-ieuse; **to be ~d for sth** être prisé pour qch
(Idiom) **no ~s for guessing who was there!** il n'est pas difficile de deviner qui était là!

prize: ~ day n jour m de la distribution des prix; **~ draw** n (for charity) tombola f; (for advertising) tirage m au sort; **~ fighter** n boxeur m professionnel; **~-giving** n remise f des prix; **~ money** n (for one prize) argent m du prix; (total amount given out) montant m total des prix; **~winner** n (in lottery etc) gagnant/-e m/f; (of literary award) lauréat/-e m/f; **~-winning** adj primé

pro /prəʊ/
A n **1** ○(professional) pro○ mf; **2** (advantage) **the ~s and cons** le pour et le contre; **the ~s and cons of sth** les avantages et les inconvénients de qch
B ○prep (in favour of) pour
C pro- combining form **to be ~-democracy** être pour la démocratie; **to be a ~-abortionist** être partisan/-e de l'avortement

PRO n **1** abrév ▸ public relations officer; **2** abrév ▸ Public Records Office

probability /prɒbə'bɪlətɪ/ n **1** (likelihood) (of desirable event) chances fpl; (of unwelcome event) risques mpl; **in all ~** selon toute probabilité; **2** (likely result) probabilité f also Math

probable /'prɒbəbl/ adj probable

probably /'prɒbəblɪ/ adv probablement

probate /'prəʊbeɪt/ n Jur (process) homologation f; **to grant ~ (of a will)** homologuer un testament

probation /prə'beɪʃn, US prəʊ-/ n **1** Jur (for adult) sursis m avec mise à l'épreuve; (for juvenile) mise f en liberté surveillée; **2** (trial period) période f d'essai

probationary /prə'beɪʃnrɪ, US prəʊ'beɪʃənerɪ/ adj **1** (trial) [period, year] d'essai; **2** (training) [month, period] probatoire

probationary teacher n GB Sch ≈ professeur m en stage pratique

probationer /prə'beɪʃənə(r)/ n (trainee) stagiaire mf; (employee on trial) employé/-e m/f engagé/-e à l'essai

probation: ~ officer ▸ p. 1181 n Jur (for juveniles) délégué/-e m/f à la liberté surveillée; (for adults) agent m de probation; **~ order** n Jur ordonnance f de probation; **~ service** n Jur comité m de probation

probe /prəʊb/
A n **1** (investigation) enquête f; **2** (instrument) sonde f; (operation) sondage m; **3** (in space) sonde f
B vtr **1** (investigate) enquêter sur [affair, mystery]; **2** [dentist] examiner [qch] avec une sonde [tooth]; **3** Med, Tech sonder [ground, wound] (**with** avec); **4** Aerosp explorer [space]; **5** (explore) explorer [qch] avec soin [hole, surface]
C vi faire des recherches
(Phrasal verb)
■ **probe into:** ▶ **~ into [sth]** enquêter sur [suspicious activity]; regarder [qch] de plus près, fouiller dans pej [private affairs]; sonder [mind]; scruter [thoughts]

probing /'prəʊbɪŋ/
A n lit exploration f; (questions) questions fpl
B adj [look] inquisiteur/-trice; [question] pénétrant; [study, examination] très poussé

problem /'prɒbləm/
A n gen, Math problème m; **to have a drink ~** avoir un pro-

blème d'alcoolisme; **to cause** ou **present a** ∼ poser un problème; **to be a** ∼ **to sb** poser des problèmes à qn
B *noun modifier* Psych, Sociol [*child*] difficile; [*family*] à problèmes; [*group*] qui pose des problèmes

problematic(al) /ˌprɒblə'mætɪk(l)/ *adj* problématique

problem: ∼ **case** *n* Sociol cas *m* social; ∼ **page** *n* courrier *m* du cœur

procedural /prə'siːdʒərəl/ *adj* [*detail, error*] de procédure

procedure /prə'siːdʒə(r)/ *n* (all contexts) procédure *f*

proceed /prə'siːd, prəʊ-/
A *vtr* **to** ∼ **to do** entreprendre de faire; '**so…,' he** ∼**ed** 'alors…,' a-t-il continué
B *vi* **1** (act) (set about) procéder; (continue) poursuivre; **to** ∼ **with** poursuivre [*idea, plan, sale*]; procéder à [*election*]; **to** ∼ **to** passer à [*item, problem*]; **let us** ∼ (begin) commençons; (continue) poursuivons; **2** (be in progress) [*project, work*] avancer; [*interview, talks, trial*] se poursuivre; (take place) [*work, interview, talks*] se dérouler; **everything is** ∼**ing according to plan** tout se passe comme prévu; **3** (move along) [*person, road*] continuer; [*vehicle*] avancer; **4** sout (issue) **to** ∼ **from** provenir de

proceeding /prə'siːdɪŋ/
A *n* (procedure) procédure *f*
B **proceedings** *npl* **1** gen (meeting) réunion *f*; (ceremony) cérémonie *f*; (discussion) débats *mpl*; **to direct** ∼**s** diriger les opérations; **2** Jur poursuites *fpl*; **extradition** ∼**s** procédure *f* d'extradition; **to take** ou **institute** ∼**s** engager des poursuites; **to start divorce** ∼**s** intenter un procès en divorce; **3** (report) gen rapport *m*; (of conference, society) actes *mpl*

proceeds /'prəʊsiːdz/ *npl* (of deal) produit *m*; (of event) recette *f*

process
A /'prəʊses, US 'prɒses/ *n* **1** gen, Comput processus *m* (**of** de); **the** ∼ **of doing** le processus consistant à faire; **to begin the** ∼ **of doing** entreprendre de faire; **to be in the** ∼ **of doing** être en train de faire; **in the** ∼ **of doing this, he…** pendant qu'il faisait cela, il…; **it's a long** ou **slow** ∼ cela prend du temps; **2** (method) procédé *m*
B /'prəʊses, US 'prɒses/ *vtr* **1** gen, Admin, Comput traiter; **2** Ind transformer [*raw materials, food product*]; traiter [*chemical, waste*]; **3** Phot développer [*film*]; **4** Culin (mix) mixer; (chop) hacher
C /prə'ses/ *vi* **1** Relig, Hist faire des processions; **2** sout (move) **to** ∼ **down/along** défiler dans/le long de [*road*]
D **processed** /'prəʊsest/ *pp adj* [*food*] qui a subi un traitement; [*meat, peas*] en conserve; [*steel*] traité

processing /'prəʊsesɪŋ, US 'prɒ-/ *n* **1** gen traitement *m*; **2** Ind (of raw material, food product) transformation *f*; (of chemical waste) traitement *m*; **the food** ∼ **industry** l'industrie alimentaire; **3** Phot développement *m*

procession /prə'seʃn/ *n* (of demonstration, carnival) défilé *m*; (formal) cortège *m*; Relig procession *f*

processor /'prəʊsesə(r), US 'prɒ-/ *n* **1** Comput unité *f* centrale; **2** = **food processor**

pro-choice /prəʊ'tʃɔɪs/ *adj* favorable à l'avortement

proclaim /prə'kleɪm/ *vtr* (all contexts) proclamer

proclamation /ˌprɒklə'meɪʃn/ *n* proclamation *f*

proclivity /prə'klɪvətɪ/ *n* propension *f*; **sexual proclivities** tendances *fpl* sexuelles

procrastinate /prəʊ'kræstɪneɪt/ *vi* atermoyer

procrastination /prəʊˌkræstɪ'neɪʃn/ *n* **C** atermoiements *mpl*

(Idiom) ∼ **is the thief of time** ≈ ne remettez pas à demain ce que vous pouvez faire aujourd'hui

procreate /'prəʊkrɪeɪt/
A *vtr* procréer [*children, young*]
B *vi* se reproduire

procreation /ˌprəʊkrɪ'eɪʃn/ *n* (human) procréation *f*; (animal) reproduction *f*

procure /prə'kjʊə(r)/
A *vtr* (obtain) procurer also Jur; **to** ∼ **sth for sb** (directly) procurer qch à qn; (indirectly) faire obtenir qch à qn
B *vi* Jur (in prostitution) faire du proxénétisme

procurement /prə'kjʊəmənt/ *n* gen obtention *f*; Mil, Comm acquisition *f*

procurer /prə'kjʊərə(r)/ *n* Comm acheteur/-euse *m/f*; Jur proxénète *m*

prod /prɒd/
A *n* **1** lit (poke) petit coup *m*; **to give sth/sb a** ∼ (with implement)

donner un petit coup à qch/qn; (with finger) toucher qch/qn; **2** ○fig (reminder) **to give sb a** ∼ secouer○ qn; **he/she needs a** ∼ **to do** il faut le/la pousser pour qu'il/elle fasse
B *vtr* (*p prés etc* **-dd-**) (also ∼ **at**) **1** (poke) (with foot, instrument, stick) donner des petits coups à; (with finger) toucher; (with fork) piquer; **stop** ∼**ding me!** arrête de me bousculer!; **2** ○(remind) pousser; **to** ∼ **sb into doing** pousser qn à faire; **3** (interrogate) interroger

prodding /'prɒdɪŋ/ *n* **1** (reminding) **after a bit of** ∼ **he agreed** il a fallu insister pour qu'il donne son accord; **she needs a bit of** ∼ elle a besoin d'être poussée; **2** **C** (interrogation) questions *fpl*

prodigal /'prɒdɪgl/ *adj* littér [*expenditure, generosity*] extravagant; [*government, body, son*] prodigue; **to be** ∼ **with** ou **of** être prodigue de

prodigiously /prə'dɪdʒəslɪ/ *adv* gen prodigieusement; [*eat, drink*] énormément

prodigy /'prɒdɪdʒɪ/ *n* (all contexts) prodige *m*

produce
A /'prɒdjuːs, US -duːs/ *n* **C** produits *mpl*
B /prə'djuːs, US -'duːs/ *vtr* **1** (cause) gen, Biol produire [*result, effect, plant*]; provoquer [*reaction, change*]; **2** Agric, Ind [*region, farmer, company*] produire (**from** à partir de); [*worker, machine*] fabriquer; **3** (generate, create) produire [*heat, sound, energy*]; rapporter [*gains, profits, returns*]; **4** (present) produire [*passport, report*]; fournir [*evidence, argument, example*]; **to** ∼ **sth from** sortir qch de [*pocket, bag*]; **5** Cin, Mus, Radio, TV produire [*show, film*]; GB Theat mettre [qch] en scène [*play*]; **well-**∼**d** bien réalisé; **6** (put together) préparer [*meal*]; mettre au point [*argument, timetable, package, solution*]; éditer [*brochure, guide*]; **a well-**∼**d brochure** une brochure bien faite

producer /prə'djuːsə(r), US -'duːs-/ ▸ p. 1181 *n* **1** (of produce, food) producteur *m*; (of machinery, goods) fabricant *m*; **2** Cin, Radio, TV producteur/-trice *m/f*; GB Theat metteur *m* en scène

producer goods *npl* biens *mpl* d'équipement

producing /prə'djuːsɪŋ, US -'duːs-/
A *adj* producteur/-trice
B **-producing** *combining form* producteur/-trice de; **oil-**∼ **countries** pays producteurs de pétrole

product /'prɒdʌkt/
A *n* Comm, Math produit *m*; **consumer** ∼**s** produits de consommation; **the end** ∼ le résultat final
B *noun modifier* [*design, launch, development, testing*] d'un produit; ∼ **range** gamme *f* de produits; ∼ **designer** créateur/-trice *m/f* de produit

production /prə'dʌkʃn/
A *n* **1** Agric, Ind (of crop, foodstuffs, metal) production *f* (**of** de); (of machinery, furniture, cars) fabrication (**of** de); **to go into** ou **be in** ∼ être fabriqué; **to be in full** ∼ tourner à plein rendement; **to take land out of** ∼ cesser l'exploitation d'une terre; **2** (output) production *f* also Biol, Phys; **3** (presentation) (of document, ticket, report) présentation *f* (**of** de); (of evidence) production *f*; **4** Cin, Mus production *f* (**of** de); Theat mise *f* en scène (**of** de); **X's** ou **of 'Le Cid'** 'Le Cid', mis en scène par X; **to work in TV** ∼ être producteur/-trice à la télévision; **to put on a** ∼ **of** Theat mettre en scène [*play*]
B *noun modifier* [*costs, difficulties, levels, methods, company, quota, unit*] de production; [*control, department, manager*] de la production

production line *n* chaîne *f* de fabrication

productive /prə'dʌktɪv/ *adj* **1** (efficient) [*factory, land*] productif/-ive; [*system, method, use*] efficace; **2** (constructive) [*discussion*] fructueux/-euse; [*day, phase, period*] productif/-ive; **3** Econ productif/-ive; **4** (resulting in) **to be** ∼ **of** être générateur/-trice de

productively /prə'dʌktɪvlɪ/ *adv* [*work*] de façon profitable; [*cultivate*] de façon rentable; [*spend time*] utilement

productivity /ˌprɒdʌk'tɪvətɪ/
A *n* productivité *f*
B *noun modifier* [*agreement, bonus, drive, gains, growth*] de productivité

product: ∼ **liability** *n* responsabilité *f* de produits; ∼ **licence** *n* autorisation *f* de mise sur le marché; ∼ **manager** ▸ p. 1181 *n* chef *m* de produit

profane /prə'feɪn, US prəʊ'feɪn/
A *adj* **1** (blasphemous) impie; **2** (secular) profane
B *vtr* profaner [*shrine, tradition, honour*]

p

profanity /prəˈfænətɪ, US prəʊ-/ n sout **①** (behaviour) impiété f; **②** (oath) blasphème m

profess /prəˈfes/ vtr **①** (claim) prétendre (**to do** de faire; **that** que); **②** (declare openly) faire profession de [opinion, religion]

professed /prəˈfest/ adj gen (genuine) déclaré; (pretended) soi-disant; Relig profès/-esse

professedly /prəˈfesɪdlɪ/ adv sout (avowedly) de son/leur etc propre aveu; (with notion of insincerity) soi-disant

profession /prəˈfeʃn/ n **①** (occupation, group) profession f; **by** ~ de profession; **the** ~**s** les professions libérales; **to enter a** ~ embrasser une profession; **the legal** ~ le corps judiciaire; **②** (statement) déclaration f

professional /prəˈfeʃənl/
A n **①** (not amateur) professionnel/-elle m/f; **②** (in small ad) salarié/-e m/f
B adj (all contexts) gen professionnel/-elle; [diplomat, soldier] de carrière; ~ **career** carrière f; **he needs** ~ **help** il devrait consulter un spécialiste; **they are** ~ **people** ils exercent une profession libérale; **to turn** ~ [actor, singer] devenir professionnel/-elle; [footballer, athlete] passer professionnel/-elle

professional: ~ **fee** n honoraire m; ~ **foul** n Sport faute f délibérée

professionalism /prəˈfeʃənəlɪzəm/ n (of person, organization) professionnalisme m also Sport; (of performance, piece of work) (haute) qualité f

professionally /prəˈfeʃənəlɪ/ adv **①** (expertly) [designed] par un professionnel; ~ **qualified** diplômé; **he is** ~ **trained** il a reçu une formation professionnelle; **②** (from an expert standpoint) d'un point de vue professionnel; **③** (in work situation) dans un cadre professionnel; **he is known** ~ **as Tim Jones** dans le métier, il est connu sous le nom de Tim Jones; **④** [play sport] en professionnel/-elle; **he sings/dances** ~ il est chanteur/danseur professionnel; **⑤** (to a high standard) de manière professionnelle

professional school n US Univ (business school) école f de commerce; (law school) faculté f de droit; (medical school) faculté f de médecine

professor /prəˈfesə(r)/ ▸ p. 869 n Univ (chair holder) professeur m d'Université; US Univ (teacher) professeur m

professorial /ˌprɒfɪˈsɔːrɪəl/ adj **①** Univ [duties, post, salary] de professeur (d'Université); US professoral; **②** (imposing) imposant

professorship /prəˈfesəʃɪp/ n (chair) chaire f; US poste m de professeur

proffer /ˈprɒfə(r)/ vtr sout (hold out) tendre; fig (offer) offrir

proficiency /prəˈfɪʃnsɪ/ n (practical) compétence f (**in, at** en; **in doing** à faire); (academic) niveau m (**in** en)

proficient /prəˈfɪʃnt/ adj compétent; **she is a highly** ~ **musician** c'est une très bonne musicienne

profile /ˈprəʊfaɪl/
A n **①** (of face) profil m also fig; **in** ~ de profil; **to have/maintain a high** ~ fig occuper/rester sur le devant de la scène; **he enjoys a high** ~ **in the literary world** il est très en vue dans le monde littéraire; **to raise one's** ~ se rendre plus connu; **②** (of body, mountain) silhouette f; **③** (by journalist) portrait m (**of** de); **④** (graph, table, list) profil m
B vtr dresser le portrait de [person]
C profiled pp adj (silhouetted) **to be** ~**d** se profiler

profit /ˈprɒfɪt/
A n **①** Comm bénéfice m, profit m; **gross/net** ~ bénéfice brut/net; **to operate at a** ~ être rentable; **there isn't much** ~ **in that line of business** ce genre de métier ne rapporte pas gros; **②** fig (benefit) profit m
B vtr littér profiter à
C vi **to** ~ **by** ou **from sth** tirer profit de qch

profitability /ˌprɒfɪtəˈbɪlətɪ/ n rentabilité f

profitable /ˈprɒfɪtəbl/ adj Comm rentable; fig fructueux/-euse; **to make** ~ **use of sth** mettre qch à profit

profitably /ˈprɒfɪtəblɪ/ adv **①** Fin [sell, trade] à profit; [invest] avec profit; **②** (usefully) utilement

profiteer /ˌprɒfɪˈtɪə(r)/ péj
A n profiteur/-euse m/f
B vi faire des bénéfices excessifs

profiteering /ˌprɒfɪˈtɪərɪŋ/ péj
A n réalisation f de bénéfices excessifs
B adj profiteur/-euse

profit: ~-**making organization** n organisation f à but lucratif; ~ **margin** n marge f bénéficiaire; ~ **sharing** n intéressement m des salariés aux bénéfices; ~ **squeeze** n Fin contraction f des marges bénéficiaires; ~ **taking** n prise f de bénéfices

profligate /ˈprɒflɪgət/ adj sout **①** (extravagant) [government, body] extrêmement prodigue; [spending] excessif/-ive; **②** (dissolute) débauché

profound /prəˈfaʊnd/ adj profond

profoundly /prəˈfaʊndlɪ/ adv **①** (very) profondément; **②** (wisely) avec profondeur

profuse /prəˈfjuːs/ adj [praise, thanks] profus; [growth, bleeding] abondant

profusely /prəˈfjuːslɪ/ adv [sweat, bleed] abondamment; [bloom] à profusion; [thank] avec effusion; **to apologize** ~ se confondre en excuses

prognosis /prɒgˈnəʊsɪs/ n **①** Med pronostic m (**on, about** sur); **②** (prediction) pronostics mpl (**for** sur)

prognosticate /prɒgˈnɒstɪkeɪt/ vtr pronostiquer

program /ˈprəʊɡræm, US -ɡrəm/
A n **①** Comput programme m; **to run a** ~ lancer un programme; **②** US Radio, TV émission f
B vtr, vi (p prés etc -mm- GB, -m- US) gen, Comput programmer (**to do** pour faire)

programer n US = **programmer**

programing n US = **programming**

programme GB, **program** US /ˈprəʊɡræm, US -ɡrəm/
A n **①** TV, Radio (single broadcast) émission f (**about** sur); (schedule of broadcasting) programme m; **②** (schedule) programme m; **③** Mus, Theat programme m
B vtr (set) programmer [machine] (**to do** pour faire)

programme: ~ **music** n Mus musique f à programme; ~ **note** n commentaire m de programme

programmer GB, **programer** US /ˈprəʊɡræmə(r)/, US -ɡrəm-/ ▸ p. 1181 n programmeur/-euse m/f

programming GB, **programing** US /ˈprəʊɡræmɪŋ, US -ɡrəm-/ n (all contexts) programmation f

progress
A /ˈprəʊɡres, US ˈprɒɡres/ n **①** (advances) progrès m; **to make slow/steady** ~ progresser lentement/régulièrement; **the patient is making** ~ l'état de santé du malade s'améliore; **②** (course, evolution) (of person, vehicle, inquiry, event) progression f; (of talks, dispute, disease, career) évolution f; **to make (slow/steady)** ~ progresser (lentement/régulièrement); **to be in** ~ [discussions, meeting, exam, work] être en cours
B /prəˈɡres/ vi **①** (develop, improve) [person, work, studies] progresser; **to** ~ **towards democracy** s'acheminer vers la démocratie; **②** (follow course) [person, vehicle, discussion] progresser

progression /prəˈɡreʃn/ n **①** (development) (evolution) évolution f; (improvement) progression f; **②** (series) suite f also Math; **③** Mus progression f

progressive /prəˈɡresɪv/
A n progressiste mf
B adj **①** (gradual) [increase, change] progressif/-ive; [illness] évolutif/-ive; **to show a** ~ **improvement** s'améliorer progressivement; **②** (radical) [person, art, idea, policy] progressiste; [school] parallèle; [age, period] progressif/-ive; **③** Ling progressif/-ive

progressively /prəˈɡresɪvlɪ/ adv progressivement

progress report n (on construction work) rapport m sur l'état des travaux; (on project) rapport m sur l'état du projet; (on patient) bulletin m de santé; (on pupil) bulletin m scolaire

prohibit /prəˈhɪbɪt, US prəʊ-/ vtr (forbid) interdire; **to** ~ **sb from doing** interdire à qn de faire; **'smoking** ~**ed'** 'défense de fumer'

prohibition /ˌprəʊhɪˈbɪʃn, US ˌprəʊəˈbɪʃn/
A n interdiction f (**on, against** de)
B **Prohibition** pr n **the Prohibition** US Hist la prohibition

prohibitive /prəˈhɪbɪtɪv, US prəʊ-/ adj [cost, price] prohibitif/-ive

prohibitively /prəˈhɪbɪtɪvlɪ, US prəʊ-/ adv **prices are** ~ **high** les prix sont prohibitifs

project
A /ˈprɒdʒekt/ n **①** (scheme) projet m (**to do** pour faire); **②** Sch dossier m (**on** sur); Univ mémoire m (**on** sur); **research** ~ programme m de recherches; **③** US (state housing) (large) ≈ cité f HLM; (small) ≈ lotissement m HLM

B /ˈprɒdʒekt/ *noun modifier* [*budget, funds*] d'un projet; ~ **manager** gen directeur/-trice *m/f* de projet; Constr maître *m* d'œuvre; ~ **outline** avant-projet *m*

C /prəˈdʒekt/ *vtr* **1** (throw, send) projeter [*object*]; envoyer [*missile*]; faire porter [*voice*]; donner [*image*]; **2** (transfer) projeter [*guilt, doubts, anxiety*]; **3** (estimate) prévoir; **4** Cin, Phys, Math projeter; **5** Geog faire la projection de

D /prəˈdʒekt/ *vi* **1** gen (stick out) faire saillie (**from** sur); **to** ~ **over** surplomber; **2** Theat [*actor*] passer la rampe

E **projected** *pp adj* [*figure, deficit*] prévu

F /prəˈdʒekt/ *v refl* **to** ~ **oneself** **1** (make an impression) faire impression; **to** ~ **oneself as being** donner l'impression d'être; **2** **to** ~ **oneself into the future** se projeter dans l'avenir

projectile /prəˈdʒektaɪl, US -tl/ *n* projectile *m*

projecting /prəˈdʒektɪŋ/ *adj* saillant

projection /prəˈdʒekʃn/ *n* **1** (of object, thoughts, emotions) projection *f* also Cin, Math, Geog; **2** (estimate) prévision *f*

projection room *n* cabine *f* de projection

projector /prəˈdʒektə(r)/ *n* projecteur *m*

proletarian /ˌprəʊlɪˈteərɪən/

A *n* prolétaire *mf*

B *adj* Pol, Econ prolétarien/-ienne; gen ouvrier/-ière

pro-life /ˌprəʊˈlaɪf/ *adj* contre l'avortement

proliferate /prəˈlɪfəreɪt, US prəʊ-/ *vi* proliférer

prolific /prəˈlɪfɪk/ *adj* (productive) [*writer, plant, parent*] prolifique; [*decade*] fécond; [*growth*] rapide

prologue /ˈprəʊlɒg/ *n* Literat prologue *m* (**to** de); fig prélude *m* (**to** à)

prolong /prəˈlɒŋ, US -ˈlɔːŋ/ *vtr* prolonger

prom○ /prɒm/ *n* **1** GB concert *m*; **2** US (at high school) bal *m* de lycéens; (college) bal *m* d'étudiants; **3** GB (at seaside) front *m* de mer

> **ⓘ** Proms Festival annuel de musique classique qui se déroule au Royal Albert Hall à Londres. La dernière soirée (*Last Night of the Proms*) est toujours un événement ; on y joue des airs célèbres (*Land of Hope and Glory, Rule, Britannia!*) que l'auditoire reprend avec l'orchestre. *Proms* est l'abréviation de *promenade concerts*, car une partie des auditeurs reste debout.
> ▸ Britannia

promenade /ˌprɒməˈnɑːd, US -ˈneɪd/

A *n* **1** (path) promenade *f*; (by sea) front *m* de mer; **2** (dance) promenade *f*

B *vtr* sout promener [*virtues etc*]

C *vi* sout se promener

promenade concerts *npl* GB série *f* annuelle de concerts

prominence /ˈprɒmɪnəns/ *n* (of person, issue) importance *f*; (of object, feature) proéminence *f*; **to rise to** ~ devenir connu

prominent /ˈprɒmɪnənt/ *adj* **1** [*figure, campaigner*] très en vue; [*artist, intellectual, industrialist*] éminent; **to play a** ~ **part** *ou* **role in sth** jouer un rôle de premier plan dans qch; **2** [*position, place, feature*] proéminent; [*peak, ridge, cheekbone*] saillant; [*marking*] bien visible; [*eye*] exorbité

prominently /ˈprɒmɪnəntlɪ/ *adv* [*displayed*] en évidence; **to feature** *ou* **figure** ~ **in sth** jouer un rôle important dans qch

promiscuity /ˌprɒmɪˈskjuːətɪ/ *n* (sexual) vagabondage *m* sexuel

promiscuous /prəˈmɪskjʊəs/ *adj* péj [*person*] aux mœurs légères; ~ **behaviour** mœurs légères

promise /ˈprɒmɪs/

A *n* **1** (undertaking) promesse *f*; **to break one's** ~ manquer à sa promesse; **they held him to his** ~ ils lui ont fait tenir sa promesse; **2** ◬ (hope) espoir *m*; **3** ◬ (likelihood of success) **she shows great** ~ elle promet beaucoup

B *vtr* **1** (pledge) **to** ~ **sb sth** promettre qch à qn; **as** ~**d** comme promis; **2** (give prospect of) annoncer; **it** ~**s to be a fine day** la journée s'annonce belle; **3** (assure) assurer; **it won't be easy, I** ~ **you** cela ne sera pas facile, je te l'assure

C *vi* **1** (give pledge) promettre; **do you** ~**?** c'est promis?; **2** fig **to** ~ **well** [*young talent, candidate*] être très prometteur; [*result, situation, event*] s'annoncer bien; **this doesn't** ~ **well for the future** cela ne présage rien de bon pour le futur

promising /ˈprɒmɪsɪŋ/ *adj* [*situation, result, future*] prometteur/-euse; [*artist, candidate*] qui promet; **the future looks more** ~ l'avenir s'annonce meilleur; **'I've been shortlisted for the job'—'that's** ~**'** 'je suis sur la liste des candidats retenus'—'c'est bon signe'

promisingly /ˈprɒmɪsɪŋlɪ/ *adv* d'une façon prometteuse

promo○ *n* (d'un produit) vidéo *f* publicitaire; (d'un artiste) vidéo *f* de présentation

promontory /ˈprɒməntrɪ, US -tɔːrɪ/ *n* promontoire *m*

promote /prəˈməʊt/

A *vtr* **1** (in rank) promouvoir (**to** à); **2** (advertise) faire de la publicité pour; (market) promouvoir; **to** ~ **a candidate** mettre un candidat en avant; **3** (encourage) promouvoir; **4** GB (in football) **to be** ~**d from the fourth to the third division** passer de quatrième en troisième division; **5** US Sch **to be** ~**d** être admis dans la classe supérieure

B *vtr* **to** ~ **oneself** se mettre en avant

promoter /prəˈməʊtə(r)/ *n* (all contexts) promoteur/-trice *m/f*

promotion /prəˈməʊʃn/ *n* **1** (of employee) promotion *f*; **to gain** ~ être promu; **to apply for** ~ demander une promotion; **to be in line for** ~ avoir des chances d'être promu; **2** Comm promotion *f* (**of** de); **3** (encouragement) promotion *f* (**of** de); **4** US Sch admission *f* dans la classe supérieure

promotional /prəˈməʊʃənl/ *adj* Comm promotionnel/-elle; **the** ~ **ladder** les échelons *mpl*

promotional video *n* (d'un produit) vidéo *f* publicitaire; (d'un artiste) vidéo *f* de présentation

promotion: ~ **prospects** *npl* (long-term) perspectives *fpl* d'avenir; (immediate) possibilités *fpl* d'avenir; ~**s manager** ▸ p. 1181 *n* directeur/-trice *m/f* de la publicité

prompt /prɒmpt/

A *n* **1** Comput message *m* guide-opérateur; **2** Comm délai *m* de paiement

B *adj* rapide; **to be** ~ **to do** être prompt à faire

C *adv* pile; **at six o'clock** ~ à six heures pile

D *vtr* **1** (cause) provoquer [*reaction, decision*]; susciter [*concern, accusation, comment, warning*]; **to** ~ **sb to do sth** inciter qn à faire qch; **2** (encourage to talk) **'and then what?' she** ~**ed** 'et puis quoi?' demanda-t-elle; **3** gen, Theat (remind) souffler à [*person*]

E *vi* gen, Theat souffler

prompt box *n* Theat trou *m* du souffleur

prompter /ˈprɒmptə(r)/ *n* **1** Theat souffleur/-euse *m/f*; **2** US TV téléprompteur *m*

prompting /ˈprɒmptɪŋ/ *n* encouragement *m*; **without any** ~ de mon/son etc plein gré

promptly /ˈprɒmptlɪ/ *adv* **1** (immediately) immédiatement; **2** (without delay) rapidement; **3** (punctually) à l'heure; ~ **at six o'clock** à six heures précises

promptness /ˈprɒmptnɪs/ *n* (speed) rapidité *f* (**in doing** à faire); (punctuality) ponctualité *f*

prompt note *n* Comm rappel *m* de paiement

promulgate /ˈprɒmlgeɪt/ *vtr* (promote) répandre; (proclaim) promulguer

prone /prəʊn/

A *adj* **1** (liable) **to be** ~ être sujet/-ette à [*migraines, colds*]; être enclin à [*depression, violence*]; **2** (prostrate) **to lie** ~ (sleeping, sunbathing) être allongé sur le ventre; (injured) être allongé face contre terre

B **-prone** *combining form* **accident-**~ sujet/-ette aux accidents

prong /prɒŋ, US prɔːŋ/ *n* (on fork) dent *f*

-pronged /prɒŋd, US prɔːŋd/ *combining form* **1** **two/three** ~ **attack** attaque *f* sur deux/trois fronts; **2** [*fork, spear*] **two/three** ~ à deux/trois dents

pronoun /ˈprəʊnaʊn/ *n* pronom *m*

pronounce /prəˈnaʊns/

A *vtr* **1** Ling prononcer [*letter, word*]; **2** gen prononcer [*judgment, sentence*]; rendre [*verdict*]; émettre [*opinion*]; **to** ~ **sb dead** déclarer qn mort

B *vi* Jur prononcer; **to** ~ **for/against sb** rendre un jugement favorable/défavorable à qn

C *v refl* **to** ~ **oneself satisfied/bored** se déclarer satisfait/ennuyé.

(Phrasal verb)

■ **pronounce on:** ▸ ~ **on** [sth] se prononcer sur [*case, matter*]; affirmer [*existence, truth*]

pronounceable /prəˈnaʊnsəbl/ *adj* prononçable

pronounced /prəˈnaʊnst/ *adj* ① (noticeable) [*accent, limp, tendency*] prononcé; [*change, difference, increase*] marqué; ② (strongly felt) [*idea, opinion*] arrêté

pronouncement /prəˈnaʊnsmənt/ *n* (statement) déclaration *f*; (verdict) verdict *m*

pronunciation /prəˌnʌnsɪˈeɪʃn/ *n* prononciation *f*

proof /pruːf/
A *n* ① (evidence) preuve *f* also Math; **to have ~ that** pouvoir prouver que; **there is no ~ that** rien ne prouve que; **to produce sth as ~** produire qch à titre de preuve; **to be ~ of sb's worth** prouver la valeur de qn; **~ of identity** pièce *f* d'identité; ② (in printing) épreuve *f*; **to read sth in ~** lire qch sur épreuves; ③ Phot épreuve *f*; ④ (of alcohol) niveau *m* étalon; **to be 70° ou 70% ~** ≈ titrer 40° d'alcool
B *adj* **to be ~ against** être à l'épreuve de [*heat, infection*]; être à l'abri de [*temptation, charms*]
C **-proof** *combining form* (resistant to) **vandal-~** protégé contre les vandales; **earthquake-~** antisismique
D *vtr* ① imperméabiliser [*fabric*]; insonoriser [*room, house*]; ② = **proofread**

proof: **~ of delivery** *n* reçu *m* de livraison; **~ of ownership** *n* titre *m* de propriété; **~ of postage** *n* certificat *m* d'expédition; **~ of purchase** *n* justificatif *m* d'achat

proofread /ˈpruːfriːd/
A *vtr* (*prét, pp* **-read** /red/) ① (check copy) corriger; ② (check proofs) corriger les épreuves de
B *vi* (*prét, pp* **-read** /red/) ① (check copy) corriger; ② (check proofs) corriger des épreuves

proof: **~reader** ▸ p. 1181 *n* correcteur/-trice *m/f*; **~reading** *n* correction *f* d'épreuves; **~ spirit** *n* GB alcool *m* à 57,1°; US alcool *m* à 50°

prop /prɒp/
A *n* ① Constr, Tech étai *m*; ② (supportive person) soutien *m* (**for** pour); ③ Theat (*abrév* = **property**) accessoire *m*; ④ (in rugby) pilier *m*
B *vtr* (*p prés etc* **-pp-**) ① (support) étayer; **I ~ed his head on a pillow** je lui ai soutenu la tête avec un oreiller; ② (lean) **to ~ sb/sth against sth** appuyer qn/qch contre qch
C *v refl* (*p prés etc* **-pp-**) **to ~ oneself against sth** s'appuyer à qch

<u>Phrasal verb</u>
■ **prop up**: ▸ **~ [sth] up, ~ up [sth]** *lit* étayer; *fig* soutenir

propaganda /ˌprɒpəˈɡændə/
A *n* propagande *f*
B *noun modifier* [*campaign, exercise, film, war*] de propagande

propagate /ˈprɒpəɡeɪt/
A *vtr lit, fig* propager
B *vi* se propager

propagator /ˈprɒpəɡeɪtə(r)/ *n* (tray) germoir *m*

propel /prəˈpel/ *vtr* (*p prés etc* **-ll-**) ① (power) propulser [*vehicle, ship*]; ② (push) pousser [*person*]; (more violently) propulser [*person*]

propellant /prəˈpelənt/ *n* ① (in aerosol) gaz *m* propulseur; ② (in rocket) poudre *f* propulsive; ③ (in gun) charge *f* propulsive

propeller /prəˈpelə(r)/ *n* Aviat, Naut hélice *f*

propeller shaft *n* Aut arbre *m* de transmission; Naut arbre *m* porte-hélice; Aviat arbre *m* de propulsion

propelling pencil *n* GB portemine *m*

propensity /prəˈpensətɪ/ *n* propension *f* (**to, for** à)

proper /ˈprɒpə(r)/ *adj* ① (right) [*term, spelling*] correct; [*order, manner, tool, choice, response*] bon/bonne; [*sense*] propre; [*precautions*] nécessaire; [*clothing*] qu'il faut; **it's only ~ for her to keep the money** il est tout naturel qu'elle garde l'argent; **everything is in the ~ place** tout est à sa place; **to go through the ~ channels** passer par la filière officielle; **in the ~ way** correctement; ② (adequate) [*funding, recognition*] convenable; [*education, training*] bon/bonne; [*care, control*] requis; **we have no ~ tennis courts** nous n'avons pas de courts de tennis convenables; **it has ~ facilities** c'est bien équipé; ③ (fitting) **~ to** *sout* convenant à [*position, status*]; **I did as I thought ~** j'ai agi comme je l'ai jugé bon; ④ (respectably correct) [*person*] correct; [*upbringing*] convenable; ⑤ (real, full) [*doctor, holiday, job*] vrai (*before n*); **he did a ~ job of repairing the car** il a bien réparé la voiture; ⑥ ᴼ(complete) **I felt a ~ fool!** je me suis senti complètement stupide!; ⑦ (actual) (*après n*) **in the**

village ~ dans le village même; **the competition ~** le concours proprement dit

<u>Idiom</u> **to beat sb good and ~** *fig* battre qn haut la main

properly /ˈprɒpəlɪ/ *adv* ① (correctly) correctement; **~ speaking** à proprement parler; **behave ~!** tiens-toi comme il faut!; ② (fully) complètement; **read the letter ~** lis la lettre correctement; **~ prepared for the interview** bien préparé pour l'entretien; **I didn't have time to thank you ~** je n'ai pas eu le temps de vous remercier; ③ (adequately) convenablement; ④ (suitably) [*dressed*] correctement

proper name, **proper noun** *n* Ling nom *m* propre

property /ˈprɒpətɪ/
A *n* ① (belongings) propriété *f*, bien(s) *m(pl)*; **government ~** propriété *f* de l'État; **that is not your ~** cela ne vous appartient pas; ② Ȼ (real estate) biens *mpl* immobiliers; **to invest in ~** investir dans l'immobilier; **~ was damaged** il y a eu des dégâts matériels; ③ (house) propriété *f*; **the ~ is detached** c'est une maison indépendante; ④ Chem, Phys, Jur propriété *f*
B **properties** *npl* ① Fin immobilier *m*; ② Theat accessoires *mpl*
C *noun modifier* (real estate) [*company, development, group, law, speculator, value*] immobilier/-ière; [*market, prices*] de l'immobilier

<u>Idiom</u> **to be hot ~** être demandé

property: **~ dealer** *n* marchand *m* de biens; **~ developer** *n* promoteur *m* immobilier; **~ insurance** *n* assurance *f* des biens; **~ owner** *n* propriétaire *mf*; **~ sales** *npl* vente *f* immobilière; **~ speculation** *n* spéculation *f* foncière; **~ tax** *n* impôt *m* foncier

prophecy /ˈprɒfəsɪ/ *n* prophétie *f*

prophesy /ˈprɒfəsaɪ/
A *vtr* prophétiser (**that** que)
B *vi* faire des prophéties (**about** sur)

prophet /ˈprɒfɪt/ *n* prophète *m*

prophetic /prəˈfetɪk/ *adj* prophétique

prophylactic /ˌprɒfɪˈlæktɪk/
A *n* ① Med (treatment) traitement *m* prophylactique; (measure) mesure *f* prophylactique; ② (condom) préservatif *m*
B *adj* prophylactique

propitiate /prəˈpɪʃɪeɪt/ *vtr* se concilier [*person, gods*]

propitious /prəˈpɪʃəs/ *adj sout* propice (**for** à)

propitiously /prəˈpɪʃəslɪ/ *adv sout* [*start*] sous de bons auspices; [*arrive*] fort à propos; [*disposed*] favorablement

proponent /prəˈpəʊnənt/ *n* partisan/-e *m/f* (**of** de)

proportion /prəˈpɔːʃn/
A *n* ① (part, quantity) (of group, population etc) proportion *f* (**of** de); (of income, profit, work etc) part *f* (**of** de); ② (ratio) also Math proportion *f*; **productivity increases in ~ to the incentives offered** l'augmentation de la productivité est directement proportionnelle aux primes de rendement; **tax should be in ~ to income** les contributions devraient être en fonction des revenus; ③ (harmony, symmetry) **out of/in ~** hors de/en proportion; ④ *fig* (perspective) **to get sth out of all ~** faire tout un drame de qch; **to be out of all ~** être tout à fait disproportionné (**to** par rapport à); **you've got to have a sense of ~** il faut avoir le sens de la mesure
B **proportions** *npl lit, fig* dimensions *fpl*
C **-proportioned** *combining form* **well-/badly-~ed** bien/mal proportionné

proportional /prəˈpɔːʃənl/ *adj* proportionnel/-elle

proportionally /prəˈpɔːʃənəlɪ/ *adv* proportionnellement

proportional representation, **PR** *n* représentation *f* proportionnelle

proportionate /prəˈpɔːʃənət/ *adj* proportionnel/-elle

proportionately /prəˈpɔːʃənətlɪ/ *adv* [*larger, higher*] proportionnellement; [*distribute*] en proportion

proposal /prəˈpəʊzl/ *n* ① (suggestion) proposition *f* (**for sth** de qch); ② (offer of marriage) demande *f* en mariage; ③ (insurance) (*also* **~ form**) proposition *f* d'assurance

propose /prəˈpəʊz/
A *vtr* (nominate, intend, suggest) proposer; présenter [*motion*]
B *vi* faire sa demande en mariage (**to** à)
C **proposed** *pp adj* [*action, reform*] envisagé

proposer /prəˈpəʊzə(r)/ *n* ① (of motion) auteur *m*; ② (of candidate) personne proposant un candidat à un poste; ③ (of member) parrain/marraine *m/f*

proposition /ˌprɒpəˈzɪʃn/
A *n* **1** (suggestion) proposition *f* also Math; **2** (assertion) assertion *f*; **3** (enterprise) affaire *f*
B *vtr* faire une proposition à [*person*]

propound /prəˈpaʊnd/ *vtr* avancer

proprietary /prəˈpraɪətrɪ, US -terɪ/ *adj* **1** [*rights, duties*] du propriétaire; [*manner, attitude*] de propriétaire; **2** Comm [*information*] qui est la propriété de la compagnie; [*system*] breveté

proprietary: ~ **brand** *n* marque *f* déposée; ~ **medicine** *n* spécialité *f* pharmaceutique

proprietor /prəˈpraɪətə(r)/ *n* propriétaire *mf* (**of** de)

propriety /prəˈpraɪətɪ/ *n* **1** (politeness) correction *f*; **2** (morality) décence *f*

propulsion /prəˈpʌlʃn/ *n* propulsion *f*

pro rata /ˌprəʊ ˈrɑːtə/
A *adj* **on a** ~ **basis** en rapport, au prorata
B *adv* [*increase*] dans la même proportion; **salary £15,000** ~ salaire 15 000 livres sterling au prorata des heures travaillées

prosaic /prəˈzeɪɪk/ *adj* prosaïque

proscenium /prəˈsiːnɪəm/ *n* Theat avant-scène *f*

proscribe /prəˈskraɪb, US prəʊ-/ *vtr* proscrire

prose /prəʊz/ *n* **1** (not verse) prose *f*; **2** GB (translation) thème *m*

prosecute /ˈprɒsɪkjuːt/
A *vtr* **1** Jur poursuivre [qn] en justice; **to** ~ **sb for doing** poursuivre qn pour avoir fait; **2** (pursue) poursuivre
B *vi* engager des poursuites

prosecuting: ~ **attorney** *n* US (lawyer) avocat/-e *m/f* de la partie civile; (public official) procureur *m*; ~ **lawyer** *n* avocat/-e *m/f* de l'accusation

prosecution /ˌprɒsɪˈkjuːʃn/ *n* **1** Jur (accusation) poursuites *fpl* (judiciaires); **the** ~ **process** la procédure d'inculpation; **2** Jur (party) **the** ~ (private individual) le/les plaignant/-s; (state, Crown) le ministère public; **3** (of war, research) poursuite *f* (**of** de)

prosecutor /ˈprɒsɪkjuːtə(r)/ *n* Jur **1** (instituting prosecution) **to be the** ~ être chargé des poursuites; **2** (in court) procureur *m*; **3** US (prosecuting attorney) avocat/-e *m/f* de la partie civile; (public official) procureur *m*

prospect
A /ˈprɒspekt/ *n* **1** (hope) (of change, improvement) espoir *m*; (of success) chance *f*; **a bleak/gloomy** ~ une perspective triste/sombre; **2** (outlook) perspective *f*; **to be in** ~ être à prévoir; **3** (good option) (for job) recrue *f* potentielle; (for sports team) espoir *m*; **4** Comm (likely client) client/-e *m/f* potentiel/-ielle; **5** (view) littér vue *f*
B prospects *npl* perspectives *fpl*; **she has good career** ~**s** elle a de bonnes perspectives de carrière; **to have no** ~**s** [*person*] ne pas avoir d'avenir; [*job*] être sans avenir
C /prəˈspekt, US ˈprɒspekt/ *vtr* prospecter [*land, region*]
D /prəˈspekt, US ˈprɒspekt/ *vi* prospecter; **to** ~ **for** chercher

prospecting /prəˈspektɪŋ/
A *n* prospection *f*
B *noun modifier* [*rights, licence*] de prospection

prospective /prəˈspektɪv/ *adj* [*buyer, candidate*] potentiel/-ielle; [*son-in-law, mother-in-law*] futur

prospector /prəˈspektə(r), US ˈprɒspektər/ *n* prospecteur/-trice *m/f*; **gold** ~ chercheur/-euse *m/f* d'or

prospectus /prəˈspektəs/ *n* gen brochure *f*; (for shares, flotation) prospectus *m* d'émission; **university** ~, **college** ~ ≈ livret *m* de l'étudiant

prosper /ˈprɒspə(r)/ *vi* prospérer

prosperity /prɒˈsperətɪ/ *n* prospérité *f*

prosperous /ˈprɒspərəs/ *adj* [*person, farm, country*] prospère; [*appearance*] de prospérité

prostate /ˈprɒsteɪt/ *n* (also ~ **gland**) prostate *f*

prostitute /ˈprɒstɪtjuːt, US -tuːt/
A *n* (woman) prostituée *f*; **male** ~ prostitué *m*
B *vtr* prostituer [*person, talent*]

prostitution /ˌprɒstɪˈtjuːʃn, US -tuːt-/ *n* prostitution *f*

prostrate
A /ˈprɒstreɪt/ *adj* **1** (on stomach) allongé à plat ventre; **2** fig (incapacitated) prostré; ~ **with grief** accablé de chagrin
B /prɒˈstreɪt, US ˈprɒstreɪt/ *vtr* **to be** ~**d by** être abattu par

C /prɒˈstreɪt, US ˈprɒstreɪt/ *v refl* **to** ~ **oneself** se prosterner (**before** devant)

prostration /prɒˈstreɪʃn/ *n* (from illness, overwork) prostration *f*

protagonist /prəˈtægənɪst/ *n* **1** Literat, Cin protagoniste *mf*; **2** (advocate) partisan/-e *m/f* (**of** de); (participant) participant/-e *m/f*

protect /prəˈtekt/
A *vtr* **1** (keep safe) protéger; **2** (defend) défendre [*consumer, interests, privilege*] (**against** contre); préserver [*privacy*]; protéger [*investment, standards, economy*]
B *v refl* **to** ~ **oneself** (against threat) se protéger; (against attack) se défendre

protection /prəˈtekʃn/ *n* **1** (safeguard) lit, fig protection *f*; **to give** *ou* **offer sb** ~ **against sth** protéger qn contre qch; **for his own** ~ (moral) pour son bien; (physical) pour le protéger; **2** Econ (also **trade** ~) protectionnisme *m*; **3** (extortion) **to pay sb** ~ payer un impôt à qn (*pour être protégé*) iron; **to buy** ~ acheter sa tranquillité (*à un racketteur*); **4** Comput protection *f*; **data** ~ protection *f* de données; **5** (protective clothing) **head** ~ casque *m*; **eye** ~ lunettes *fpl*

protection factor *n* (of sun cream) indice *m* de protection

protectionist /prəˈtekʃənɪst/ *n, adj* protectionniste (*mf*)

protection: ~ **money** *n* euph argent versé à un racketteur; ~ **racket** *n* racket *m*

protective /prəˈtektɪv/
A *n* US (condom) préservatif *m*
B *adj* **1** (providing security) [*clothing, layer*] protecteur/-trice; [*measure*] de protection; **2** (caring) protecteur/-trice; **to be** ~ **of** veiller jalousement sur [*possessions*]; protéger [*discovery, research*]; **3** Econ [*tarif, system*] protectionniste

protective custody *n* Jur **to place sb in** ~ détenir qn pour sa (propre) protection

protector /prəˈtektə(r)/ *n* **1** (defender) gen protecteur/-trice *m/f*; (of rights) défenseur *m*; **2** (pads etc) **ear** ~**s** casque *m* antibruit; **elbow** ~ protège-coude *m*

protein /ˈprəʊtiːn/ *n* protéine *f*; **high-**~ riche en protéines

protest
A /ˈprəʊtest/ *n* **1** *C* (disapproval) protestation *f*; **in** ~ en signe de protestation; **without** ~ sans protester; **I followed him under** ~ je l'ai suivi contre mon gré; **2** *C* (complaint) réclamation *f*; **as a** ~ **against** *ou* **at sth** pour protester contre qch; **to lodge a** ~ faire une réclamation; **3** (demonstration) manifestation *f*
B /ˈprəʊtest/ *noun modifier* [*march, movement, song*] de protestation
C /prəˈtest/ *vtr* **1** (declare) affirmer [*truth*]; **to** ~ **one's innocence** protester de son innocence; **2** (complain) **'that's unfair!' they** ~**ed** 'c'est injuste!' s'écrièrent-ils; **to** ~ **that** protester que; **3** US (complain about) protester contre (**to** auprès de)
D /prəˈtest/ *vi* **1** (complain) protester; **2** (demonstrate) manifester

Protestant /ˈprɒtɪstənt/
A *n* protestant/-e *m/f*
B *adj* protestant; **the** ~ **Church** gen l'Église protestante; (in official names) l'Église Réformée

protestation /ˌprɒtɪˈsteɪʃn/ *n* protestation *f*; **in** ~ pour protester

protester /prəˈtestə(r)/ *n* manifestant/-e *m/f*

protocol /ˌprəʊtəˈkɒl, US -kɔːl/ *n* gen, Pol, Comput protocole *m*

prototype /ˈprəʊtətaɪp/
A *n* prototype *m* (**of** de)
B *noun modifier* [*vehicle, aircraft*] prototype

protrude /prəˈtruːd, US prəʊ-/ *vi* gen dépasser

protruding /prəˈtruːdɪŋ, US prəʊ-/ *adj* [*rock*] en saillie; [*nail*] qui dépasse; [*eyes*] globuleux/-euse; [*ears*] décollé; [*ribs*] saillant; [*chin*] en avant; **to have** ~ **teeth** avoir les dents qui avancent

protrusion /prəˈtruːʒn, US prəʊ-/ *n* sout (on rocks) saillie *f*; (part of building) avancée *f*; (on skin) protubérance *f*

proud /praʊd/ *adj* **1** (satisfied, self-respecting) gen fier/fière; [*owner*] heureux/-euse; **2** (great) [*day, moment*] grand; **3** GB **fill the hole** ~ bouchez le trou en laissant une protubérance

(Idioms) **to do sb** ~ (entertain) traiter qn royalement; (praise) faire honneur à qn; **to do oneself** ~ ne rien se refuser

proudly /'praʊdlɪ/ adv [display, show] avec fierté; [move, speak] fièrement; **Disney Studios** ~ **present** Cin les studios Disney ont le plaisir de présenter

provable /'pruːvəbl/ adj démontrable

prove /pruːv/
A vtr ① (show) gen prouver; (by demonstration) démontrer; **to** ~ **a point** montrer qu'on a raison; ② Jur authentifier [will]; ③ Culin faire lever [dough]
B vi ① (turn out) s'avérer; **it** ~**d otherwise** il en est allé autrement; **if I** ~ **to be mistaken** s'il arrive que j'ai tort; ② Culin [dough] lever
C v refl **to** ~ **oneself** faire ses preuves; **to** ~ **oneself (to be)** se révéler

proven /'pruːvn/ adj éprouvé

proverb /'prɒvɜːb/ n proverbe m

proverbial /prə'vɜːbɪəl/ adj ① [wisdom, saying] proverbial; ② (widely known) légendaire

proverbially /prə'vɜːbɪəlɪ/ adv **he is** ~ **stupid/mean** il est d'une stupidité/avarice légendaire

provide /prə'vaɪd/
A vtr ① (supply) fournir [opportunity, evidence, jobs, meals] (**for** à); apporter [answer, support, understanding] (**for** à); donner [satisfaction] (**for** à); assurer [service, food, access, training, shelter] (**for** à); **to** ~ **an incentive to do** être un encouragement à faire; **please use the bin** ~**d** veuillez utiliser la poubelle mise à votre disposition; ② Jur, Admin (stipulate) prévoir; **except as** ~**d** sauf indication contraire
B vi pourvoir aux besoins

(Phrasal verbs)
■ **provide against:** ▶ ~ **against [sth]** parer à
■ **provide for:** ▶ ~ **for [sth]** ① (account for) envisager; ② Jur prévoir; ▶ ~ **for [sb]** subvenir aux besoins de; **to be well** ~**d for** être à l'abri du besoin

provided /prə'vaɪdɪd/, **providing** /prə'vaɪdɪŋ/ conj (also ~ **that**) à condition que (+ subj); ~ **always that** Jur, Admin sous réserve que

providence /'prɒvɪdəns/ n (fate) providence f

provident /'prɒvɪdənt/ adj prévoyant

providential /ˌprɒvɪ'denʃl/ adj sout providentiel/-ielle

provider /prə'vaɪdə(r)/ n ① (in family) **to be a good** ~ bien subvenir aux besoins de sa famille; ② Comm pourvoyeur/-euse m/f

providing /prə'vaɪdɪŋ/ conj = provided

province /'prɒvɪns/ n ① (region) province f; **in the** ~**s** en province; ② fig (field, area) domaine m

provincial /prə'vɪnʃl/
A n (from provinces) provincial/-e m/f also pej
B adj ① [doctor, newspaper, capital] de province; [life] provincial; [tour] en province; ② péj (narrow) provincial

proving ground n terrain m d'essai

provision /prə'vɪʒn/
A n ① (of housing, information, facility, equipment) mise f à disposition; (of food) approvisionnement m; (of service) prestation f; **health care** ~ services mpl pour la santé; **to be responsible for the** ~ **of transport** être responsable d'assurer le transport; ② (for future) dispositions fpl; ③ Jur, Admin (of agreement) clause f; (of bill, act) disposition f; ~ **to the contrary** stipulation f du contraire; **to make** ~ **for** prévoir; **under the** ~**s of** aux termes de; **with the** ~ **that** à la condition que; **within the** ~**s of the treaty** dans le cadre du traité
B provisions npl (food) provisions fpl

provisional /prə'vɪʒənl/ adj provisoire

provisional driving licence n GB ≈ permis m de conduire d'élève conducteur

Provisional IRA n faction f dure de l'IRA

provisionally /prə'vɪʒnəlɪ/ adv provisoirement

proviso /prə'vaɪzəʊ/ n gen condition f

provisory /prə'vaɪzərɪ/ adj conditionnel/-elle

provocation /ˌprɒvə'keɪʃn/ n provocation f

provocative /prə'vɒkətɪv/ adj ① (causing controversy) provocant; **to be** ~ faire de la provocation; ② (sexually) provocant; ③ (challenging) [book, film] qui fait réfléchir

provoke /prə'vəʊk/ vtr ① (annoy) provoquer; **to** ~ **sb to do** ou **into doing sth** pousser qn à faire qch; ② (cause) susciter [anger, complaints]; provoquer [laughter, reaction, crisis]

provost /'prɒvəst/ n ① GB Univ, Sch principal m; ② US Univ doyen m; ③ (in Scotland) maire m; ④ Relig prévôt m

prow /praʊ/ n proue f

prowess /'praʊɪs/ n ① ¢ (skill) prouesses fpl; ② (bravery) vaillance f

prowl /praʊl/
A n **to be on the** ~ rôder (**for** en quête de); **to go on the** ~ [animal] partir en quête d'une proie; fig faire une virée
B vtr **to** ~ **the streets at night** rôder dans les rues la nuit
C vi (also ~ **around**, ~ **about** GB) [animal, person] gen rôder; (restlessly) [person] faire les cent pas; [animal] (in cage) tourner

proximity /prɒk'sɪmətɪ/ n proximité f

proxy /'prɒksɪ/ n ① (person) mandataire mf; **to be sb's** ~ avoir procuration pour qn; ② (authority) gen, Pol, Fin procuration f; **by** ~ par procuration

prude /pruːd/ n bégueule mf

prudent /'pruːdnt/ adj prudent

prudently /'pruːdntlɪ/ adv (with caution) avec circonspection; (wisely) prudemment

prudish /'pruːdɪʃ/ adj pudibond

prune /pruːn/
A n Culin pruneau m
B vtr lit (also ~ **back**) (cut back) tailler; (thin out) élaguer; fig élaguer [essay, article]; réduire [budget, expenditure]

pruning /'pruːnɪŋ/ n (of bush, tree) taille f

prurient /'prʊərɪənt/ adj sout lubrique

pry /praɪ/
A n US levier m
B vtr US ① lit **to** ~ **sth open** ouvrir qch en faisant levier; **to** ~ **the lid off a jar** forcer le couvercle d'un pot; ② fig **to** ~ **sth out of sb** soutirer qch à qn
C vi **to** ~ **into** mettre son nez dans [business]

prying /'praɪɪŋ/ adj curieux/-ieuse, indiscret/-ète

PS (abrév = postscriptum) PS m

psalm /sɑːm/ n psaume m

pseud° /sjuːd, US 'suːd/ n, adj prétentieux/-ieuse (m/f)

pseudo+ /'sjuːdəʊ, US 'suːdəʊ/ combining form pseudo-

pseudonym /'sjuːdənɪm, US 'suːd-/ n pseudonyme m

PST abrév ▸ **Pacific Standard Time**

PSV GB abrév ▸ **public service vehicle**

psych /saɪk/ v
■ **psych out**°: ▶ ~ **[sb/sth] out**, ~ **out [sb/sth]**° ① (unnerve) déstabiliser; ② US (outguess) deviner
(Phrasal verb)
■ **psych up**°: **to** ~ **oneself up** se préparer (psychologiquement) (**for** pour)

psychiatric /ˌsaɪkɪ'ætrɪk/ adj [hospital, care, nurse, treatment, help] psychiatrique; [illness, disorder] mental; [patient] d'un hôpital psychiatrique

psychiatrist /saɪ'kaɪətrɪst, US sɪ-/ ▸ p. 1181 n psychiatre mf

psychiatry /saɪ'kaɪətrɪ, US sɪ-/ n psychiatrie f

psychic /'saɪkɪk/
A n médium m, voyant/-e m/f
B adj ① (paranormal) parapsychologique; (telepathic) télépathe; **to have** ~ **powers** avoir des dons de voyance; ② (psychological) psychologique

psychical /'saɪkɪkl/ adj = psychic B

psychic: ~ **research** n parapsychologie f; ~ **surgery** n opération f à main nue

psycho+ /'saɪkəʊ/ combining form psycho

psychoanalyse GB, **psychoanalyze** US /ˌsaɪkəʊ'ænəlaɪz/ vtr psychanalyser

psychoanalysis /ˌsaɪkəʊə'næləsɪs/ n psychanalyse f; **to undergo** ~ se faire psychanalyser

psychoanalyst /ˌsaɪkəʊ'ænəlɪst/ ▸ p. 1181 n psychanalyste mf

psychological /ˌsaɪkə'lɒdʒɪkl/ adj (all contexts) psychologique; ~ **abuse** harcèlement m psychologique

psychologist /saɪ'kɒlədʒɪst/ ▸ p. 1181 n psychologue mf

psychology /saɪ'kɒlədʒɪ/ n (all contexts) psychologie f

psychopath /'saɪkəʊpæθ/ n psychopathe mf

psychopathic /ˌsaɪkəʊ'pæθɪk/ adj [personality] psychopathique

psychosis /saɪˈkəʊsɪs/ n psychose f

psychotherapist /ˌsaɪkəʊˈθerəpɪst/ ▸ p. 1181 n psychothérapeute mf

psychotic /saɪˈkɒtɪk/ n, adj psychotique (mf)

pt n: abrév écrite = pint

PT n: abrév ▸ physical training

PTA n (abrév = Parent-Teacher Association) association f des parents d'élèves et des professeurs

PTO (abrév = please turn over) TSVP

puberty /ˈpjuːbətɪ/ n puberté f

public /ˈpʌblɪk/

A n the ~ le public; the theatre-going ~ les amateurs mpl de théâtre

B adj [health, property, park, inquiry] public/-ique; [disquiet, enthusiasm, indifference, support] général; [library, amenity] municipal; [duty, spirit] civique; **to be in the ~ eye** être exposé à l'opinion publique; **she has decided to go ~ (with her story)** elle a décidé de rendre son histoire publique; **the company is going ~** la société va être cotée en Bourse; **it is ~ knowledge that** il est de notoriété publique que; **let's go somewhere less ~** allons dans un endroit plus discret; **at ~ expense** aux frais du contribuable

C in public adv phr en public

public address (system) n (système m de) sonorisation f

publican /ˈpʌblɪkən/ ▸ p. 1181 n GB patron/-onne m/f de pub

public assistance n US aide f sociale

publication /ˌpʌblɪˈkeɪʃn/ n publication f; **to accept sth for ~** accepter de publier qch; **on the day of ~** le jour de la sortie; **'not for ~'** 'confidentiel'

publications list n liste f de titres

public: ~ **company** n société f anonyme par actions; ~ **convenience** n GB toilettes fpl; ~ **corporation** n GB organisme m public; ~ **examination** n examen m ouvert à tous; ~ **gallery** n tribune f réservée au public; ~ **holiday** n GB jour m férié

public house n **1** GB pub m; **2** US auberge f

publicist /ˈpʌblɪsɪst/ n (advertiser) agent m de publicité; (press agent) attaché/-e m/f de presse

publicity /pʌbˈlɪsətɪ/

A n **1** (media attention) **to attract ~** attirer l'attention des médias; **to take place in a blaze of ~** avoir lieu sous les feux des médias; **to receive bad ou adverse ~** faire l'objet de critiques dans les médias; **2** (advertising) publicité f; **advance ~** promotion f; **3** **¢** (advertising material) (brochures) brochures fpl publicitaires; (posters) affiches fpl publicitaires; (films) films mpl publicitaires

B noun modifier [bureau, launch] de publicité

publicity: ~ **agency** n agence f de publicité; ~ **agent** ▸ p. 1181 n attaché/-e m/f de presse; ~ **campaign**, ~ **drive** n (to sell product) campagne f publicitaire; (to raise social issue) campagne f de sensibilisation; ~ **stunt** n coup m publicitaire

publicize /ˈpʌblɪsaɪz/ vtr **1** (raise awareness of) attirer l'attention du public sur; **well-~d**, **much-~d** [event] dont on parle beaucoup dans les médias; [scandal, controversy] qui fait ou qui a fait la une de tous les journaux; **2** (make public) rendre [qch] public; **3** (advertise) faire de la publicité pour; **well-~d**, **much-~d** annoncé à grand renfort de publicité

publicly /ˈpʌblɪklɪ/ adv publiquement; ~ **owned** (state-owned) public; (floated on market) à actionnaires multiples; **~-funded** réalisé à l'aide de fonds publics

public ownership n to be in ~, to be taken into ~ être nationalisé; **to bring [sth] under ou into ~** nationaliser [industry]

public: ~ **prosecutor** n procureur m général; ~ **purse** n Trésor m public; **Public Records Office**, **PRO** npl Archives fpl nationales

public relations, **PR**

A n relations fpl publiques

B noun modifier [manager, department] des relations publiques; [consultant, expert] en relations publiques; [firm] de relations publiques

public: ~ **relations officer**, **PRO** n responsable mf des relations publiques; ~ **restroom** n US toilettes fpl

public school n GB école f privée; US école f publique

> ⓘ **Public schools** Contrairement à ce que leur nom indique, les public schools anglaises sont des écoles privées. Elles sont en général réservées aux enfants de l'Establishment ou de milieux aisés, car le coût de la scolarité y est très élevé, notamment dans les plus prestigieuses d'entre elles (Eton, Harrow, Winchester, Rugby). Cependant, ces écoles accordent également la gratuité de la scolarité ou des bourses d'études à des élèves brillants mais peu fortunés.
> ▸ Secondary schools

public: ~ **sector** n secteur m public; ~ **servant** n fonctionnaire mf

public service n **1** C (transport, education etc) service m public; **2** **¢** (public administration, civil service) fonction f publique

public: ~ **service broadcasting** n **¢** chaînes fpl de télévision et radios fpl publiques; ~ **service corporation** n US service m public non étatisé; ~ **service vehicle**, **PSV** n véhicule m de transport en commun

public speaking n the art of ~ l'art de parler en public

public-spirited adj à l'esprit civique; **it was ~ of you to do** tu as fait preuve de civisme en faisant

public: ~ **transport** n transports mpl en commun; ~ **utilities** npl équipements mpl collectifs; ~ **utility** n service m public

publish /ˈpʌblɪʃ/

A vtr **1** (print commercially) publier [book, letter, guide]; éditer [newspaper, magazine]; **who ~es Amis?** qui est-ce qui édite Amis?; **to be ~ed weekly** paraître toutes les semaines; **2** (make public) publier; **3** [scholar, academic] publier

B vi [scholar, academic] faire une publication or des publications

publisher /ˈpʌblɪʃə(r)/ ▸ p. 1181 n (person) éditeur/-trice m/f; (company) maison f d'édition; **newspaper ~** (person) patron m de presse; (company) maison f de presse

publishing /ˈpʌblɪʃɪŋ/

A n édition f

B noun modifier [group, empire] de presse

publishing house n maison f d'édition

puce /pjuːs/ ▸ p. 752 adj rouge-brun inv; [curtains, silk] cramoisi

puck /pʌk/ n **1** (in ice-hockey) palet m; **2** (sprite) lutin m

pucker /ˈpʌkə(r)/ vi [fabric, face, mouth] se plisser; [skirt] goder; [seam, cloth] froncer

pudding /ˈpʊdɪŋ/ n **1** (cooked dish) pudding m; **steak-and-kidney ~** pain m de viande au bœuf et aux rognons; **2** GB (dessert) dessert m; **3** GB (sausage) **black/white ~** boudin m noir/blanc; **4** péj (fat person) patapouf○ mf; (slow person) empoté○/-e m/f

⟨Idiom⟩ **the proof of the ~ is in the eating** Prov la qualité se révèle à l'usage

pudding: ~ **basin**, ~ **bowl** n jatte f; ~ **rice** n riz m à grains ronds

puddle /ˈpʌdl/ n flaque f

Puerto Rico /ˌpwɜːtəʊ ˈriːkə/ ▸ p. 774 pr n Porto Rico f

puff /pʌf/

A n **1** (of air, smoke, steam) bouffée f; (of breath) souffle m; **to disappear in a ~ of smoke** lit disparaître dans un nuage de fumée; fig partir en fumée; **~s of cloud** quelques petits nuages; **2** ○GB (breath) souffle m; **3** Culin feuilleté m; **4** ○(favourable review) article m élogieux; (favourable publicity) battage○ m

B vtr **1** tirer sur [pipe]; **to ~ smoke** lancer des bouffées de fumée; **2** ○(praise) faire du battage○ autour de

C vi **1** souffler; **smoke ~ed from the chimney** des bouffées de fumée s'échappaient de la cheminée; **to ~ (away) at** tirer des bouffées de [cigarette]; **to ~ along** [train] avancer en lançant des bouffées de fumée; **2** (pant) souffler; **she came ~ing and blowing up the hill** elle s'essoufflait en montant la côte

⟨Phrasal verbs⟩

■ **puff out**: ▸ ~ **out** [sails] se gonfler; [sleeve, skirt] bouffer; ▸ ~ **out [sth]**, ~ **[sth] out 1** (swell) gonfler [sails]; **to ~ out one's cheeks** gonfler ses joues; **to ~ out one's chest** bomber le torse; **the bird ~ed out its feathers** l'oiseau a

p

hérissé ses plumes; **2** (give out) **to ~ out smoke** lancer des bouffées de fumée
■ **puff up**: ▸ **~ up** [*feathers*] se hérisser; [*eyes*] bouffir; [*rice*] gonfler; ▸ **~ up [sth]**, **~ [sth] up** hérisser [*feathers, fur*]; **to be ~ed up with pride** être rempli d'orgueil

puffed /pʌft/ *adj* **1** ○(breathless) essoufflé; **2** [*sleeve*] bouffant

puffiness /'pʌfɪnɪs/ *n* (of face, eyes) boursouflure *f*

puff pastry *n* pâte *f* feuilletée

puffy /'pʌfɪ/ *adj* bouffi

pug /pʌg/ *n* (also **~dog**) carlin *m*

pugnacious /pʌg'neɪʃəs/ *adj* combatif/-ive

pull /pʊl/
A *n* **1** (tug) coup *m*; **to give sth a ~** tirer sur qch; **2** (attraction) n force *f*; fig attrait m (**of** de); **3** ○(influence) influence *f* (**over, with** sur); **4** ○(swig) lampée° *f*; **5** ○(on cigarette etc) bouffée *f*; **6** Sport (in rowing) coup *m* d'aviron; (in golf) coup *m* hooké; **it was a hard ~ to the summit** cela a été très dur d'arriver jusqu'au sommet; **7** (snag) (in sweater) maille *f* tirée
B *vtr* **1** (tug) tirer [*chain, curtain, hair, tail*]; tirer sur [*cord, rope*]; **to ~ the sheets over one's head** se cacher la tête sous les draps; **to ~ a sweater over one's head** (put on) enfiler un pull-over; (take off) retirer un pull-over; **2** (tug, move) (towards oneself) tirer (**towards** vers); (by dragging) traîner (**along** le long de); (to show sth) entraîner [qn] par le bras [*person*]; **to ~ sb/sth through** faire passer qn/qch par [*hole, window*]; **3** (draw) gen tirer; [*vehicle*] tracter; **4** (remove) **to ~ sth off** [*child, cat*] faire tomber qch de; **he ~ed her attacker off her** il a fait lâcher prise à son assaillant; **to ~ sth out of** tirer qch de [*pocket, drawer*]; **to ~ sb out of** retirer qn de [*wreckage*]; sortir qn de [*river*]; **5** ○sortir [*gun, knife*]; **to ~ a gun on sb** menacer qn avec un pistolet; **6** (operate) appuyer sur [*trigger*]; tirer [*lever*]; **7** Med se faire une élongation à [*muscle*]; **8** (steer, guide) **to ~ a boat into the bank** amener une barque jusqu'à la berge; **to ~ a plane out of a dive** redresser un avion; **9** Sport [*golfer, batsman*] hooker; **to ~ one's punches** lit retenir ses coups; fig **he didn't ~ his punches** il n'a pas mâché ses mots; **10** ○GB tirer [*pint of beer*]; **11** ○(attract) attirer; **12** (make) **to ~ a face** faire la grimace
C *vi* **1** (tug) tirer (**at, on** sur); **to ~ at sb's sleeve** tirer qn par la manche; **2** (move, resist restraint) tirer (**at, on** sur); **to ~ ahead of sb** [*athlete, rally driver*] prendre l'avance sur qn; [*company*] avoir de l'avance sur; **3** Sport [*golfer, batsman*] hooker; (row) ramer

(Idiom) **~ the other one, (it's got bells on)**○! à d'autres (mais pas à moi)○!

(Phrasal verbs)
■ **pull along**: ▸ **~ [sth] along**, **~ along [sth]** tirer; ▸ **~ [sb] along** tirer qn par le bras
■ **pull apart**: ▸ **~ apart** se séparer; ▸ **~ [sb/sth] apart** **1** (dismantle) démonter; **2** (destroy) [*child*] mettre en pièces; [*animal*] déchiqueter; **3** fig (disparage) descendre [qch] en flammes; **4** (separate) séparer
■ **pull away**: ▸ **~ away 1** (move away, leave) [*car*] démarrer; [*person*] s'écarter; **2** (become detached, increase lead) se détacher; ▸ **~ away from [sb/sth]** s'éloigner de [*person, kerb*]; ▸ **~ [sb/sth] away** éloigner [*person*]; retirer [*hand*]; **to ~ sth away from sb** arracher qch à qn; **to ~ sb/sth away from** éloigner qn/qch de [*danger*]; écarter qn/qch de [*window, wall etc*]
■ **pull back**: ▸ **~ back 1** [*troops*] se retirer (**from** de); **2** [*car, person*] reculer; **3** (close the gap) rattraper mon/son etc retard; ▸ **~ [sb/sth] back**, **~ back [sb/sth]** (restrain) retenir; (tug back) **~ the rope back hard** tire fort sur la corde
■ **pull down**: ▸ **~ [sth] down**, **~ down [sth]** (demolish) démolir; (lower) baisser [*blind, trousers*]; réduire [*inflation*]; baisser [*prices*]; ▸ **~ [sb/sth] down**, **~ down [sb/sth]** lit tirer (**onto** sur); fig entraîner
■ **pull in**: ▸ **~ in** [*car, bus, driver*] s'arrêter; **to ~ in to the kerb** s'arrêter le long du trottoir; ▸ **~ [sb] in**, **~ in [sb] 1** [*police*] appréhender [*person*]; **2** [*exhibition, show*] attirer [*crowds, tourists*]; ▸ **~ [sth] in**, **~ in [sth] 1** (retract) rentrer; **2** ○(earn) réunir [*money*]; **3** arrêter [*car*]
■ **pull off**: ▸ **~ off** [*lid*] s'enlever; [*handle*] être amovible; ▸ **~ [sb/sth] off** (leave) quitter [*road*]; ▸ **~ off [sth]**, **~ [sth] off 1** (remove) ôter [*coat, sweater*]; enlever [*shoes, socks, tie, wrapping, sticker*]; **2** ○(clinch) réussir [*raid, robbery*]; conclure [*deal*]; réaliser [*coup, feat*]; décrocher [*win, victory*]

■ **pull out**: ▸ **~ out 1** (emerge) [*car, truck*] déboîter; **just as the train was ~ing out** au moment où le train partait; **to ~ out of sth** quitter qch; **2** (withdraw) se retirer (**of** de); **3** (come away) [*drawer*] s'enlever; [*component, section*] se détacher; ▸ **~ [sth] out**, **~ out [sth] 1** extraire [*tooth*]; enlever [*splinter*]; arracher [*weeds*]; **2** (from pocket) sortir; **3** (withdraw) retirer [*troops*]
■ **pull over**: ▸ **~ over** [*motorist, car*] s'arrêter (sur le côté); ▸ **~ [sb/sth] over** [*police*] forcer [qn/qch] à se ranger sur le côté
■ **pull through**: ▸ **~ through** [*accident victim*] s'en tirer; ▸ **~ [sb/sth] through** faire passer
■ **pull together**: ▸ **~ together** faire un effort; ▸ **~ [sth] together**: **~ the two pieces together** mettez les deux morceaux l'un contre l'autre; **to ~ oneself together** se ressaisir
■ **pull up**: ▸ **~ up 1** (stop) s'arrêter; **2** (regain lost ground) rattraper son retard; ▸ **~ up [sth]**, **~ [sth] up 1** (uproot) arracher; **2** (lift) lever; **to ~ up one's trousers/socks** remonter son pantalon/ses chaussettes; **3** (stop) arrêter [*horse*]; ▸ **~ [sb] up 1** (lift) hisser; **2** (reprimand) réprimander [*driver*]; disqualifier [*athlete*]

pull-down menu *n* Comput menu *m* déroulant

pulley /'pʊlɪ/ *n* poulie *f*

pull-in /'pʊlɪn/ *n* GB **1** ○(café) routier *m*; **2** (lay-by) aire *f* de stationnement (en bordure de la chaussée)

pulling power *n* pouvoir *m* d'attraction

Pullman /'pʊlmən/ *n* **1** (train) pullman *m*; (carriage) voiture *f* pullman; **2** US (suitcase) valise *f*

pull-off /'pʊlɒf/ *adj* détachable

pull-out /'pʊlaʊt/
A *n* **1** (in book etc) encart *m*; **2** (withdrawal) retrait *m*
B *adj* [*supplement*] détachable; [*map, diagram*] hors-texte *inv*

pullover /'pʊləʊvə(r)/ *n* pull-over *m*

pulmonary /'pʌlmənərɪ, US -nerɪ/ *adj* pulmonaire

pulp /pʌlp/
A *n* **1** (soft centre) pulpe *f*; (crushed mass) pâte *f*; **to beat sb to a ~**○ réduire qn en bouillie○; **2** ○pej (trashy books) littérature *f* de gare pej
B *noun modifier* [*novel, literature*] de gare; [*magazine*] à sensation
C *vtr* **1** (crush) écraser [*fruit, vegetable*]; réduire [qch] en pâte [*wood, cloth*]; mettre [qch] au pilon [*newspapers, books*]; **2** ○fig (kill) écrabouiller○

pulpit /'pʊlpɪt/ *n* (in church) chaire *f*

pulsate /pʌl'seɪt, US 'pʌlseɪt/
A *vi* [*vein, heart*] palpiter; [*blood*] circuler
B **pulsating** *pres p adj* **1** (beating) [*heart, vein*] qui palpite; [*beat, rhythm*] entraînant; **2** fig (exciting) palpitant

pulse /pʌls/
A *n* **1** Anat, Med pouls *m*; **his ~ raced** son cœur battait très vite; **to take/feel sb's ~** prendre/tâter le pouls de qn; **to have one's finger on the ~ of sth** fig être à l'écoute de qch; **2** (beat, vibration) (of music) rythme *m*; (of drums) battement *m* rythmique; **3** Audio, Elec, Phys impulsion *f*; **4** Bot, Culin graine *f* de légumineuse
B *vi* [*blood*] circuler; [*heart*] battre fort

pulse rate *n* pouls *m*

pulverize /'pʌlvəraɪz/ *vtr* lit, fig pulvériser

pumice /'pʌmɪs/ *n* (also **~ stone**) pierre *f* ponce

pummel /'pʌml/ *vtr* (*p prés etc* **-ll-** GB, **-l-** US) marteler

pump /pʌmp/
A *n* **1** Tech pompe *f*; **bicycle ~** pompe à bicyclette; **to prime the ~** lit amorcer la pompe; fig réamorcer la pompe; **2** (plimsoll) chaussure *f* de sport; (flat shoe) GB ballerine *f*; (shoe with heel) US chaussure *f* à talon
B *vtr* **1** (push) pomper (**out of** de); **to ~ air into a tyre** injecter de l'air dans un pneu; **to ~ sewage into the sea** déverser les eaux usées dans la mer; **the boiler ~s water to the radiators** la chaudière distribue l'eau dans les radiateurs; **to ~ bullets** cracher des balles; **to ~ sb full of drugs**○ gaver qn de médicaments; **to ~ iron**○ faire de la gonflette○; **2** actionner [*handle, lever*]; (shake) **to ~ sb's hand** donner une poignée de main vigoureuse à qn; **4** ○(question) cuisiner○ [*person*] (**about** à propos de); **5** Med **to ~ sb's stomach** faire un lavage d'estomac à qn
C *vi* **1** (function) [*machine, piston*] fonctionner; **2** (flow) gicler (**from, out of** de); **3** (beat) battre violemment

(Phrasal verbs)
■ **pump out**: ▶ ~ **out [sth]**, ~ **[sth] out** **1** (pour out) débiter [*music, propaganda*]; cracher [*fumes*]; déverser [*sewage*]; **2** (empty) pomper [qch] à sec; **to ~ sb's stomach out** faire un lavage d'estomac à qn
■ **pump up**: ▶ ~ **up [sth]**, ~ **[sth] up** **1** (inflate) gonfler; **2** ○monter [*volume*]

pump attendant ▸ p. 1181 *n* pompiste *mf*

pumpkin /'pʌmpkɪn/ *n* citrouille *f*

pun /pʌn/
A *n* jeu *m* de mots, calembour *m* (**on** sur)
B *vi* (*p prés etc* **-nn-**) faire des jeux de mots, faire des calembours

punch /pʌntʃ/
A *n* **1** (blow) coup *m* de poing; **2** fig (forcefulness) (of person) punch○ *m*; (of style, performance) énergie *f*; **it lacks ~** ça manque de nerf; **3** (tool) (for leather) alène *f*; (for metal) perçoir *m*; Comput perforateur *m*; **ticket ~** pince *f* à composter; **4** (drink) punch *m*
B *vtr* **1** (hit) **to ~ sb in the face** donner un coup de poing dans la figure de qn; **to ~ sb on the nose** donner un coup de poing dans le nez de qn; **2** Comput, Telecom perforer [*cards, tape*]; appuyer sur [*key*]; (make hole in) (manually) poinçonner; (in machine) composter [*ticket*]
C *vi* cogner, donner des coups de poing
(Idioms) **to pack a ~**○ [*boxer*] avoir du punch; [*cocktail*] être corsé; [*book, film*] avoir un fort impact; **to pull no ~es** lit, fig ne pas y aller de main morte
(Phrasal verbs)
■ **punch in**: ▶ ~ **in [sth]**, ~ **[sth] in** Comput introduire [*data*]
■ **punch out**: ▶ ~ **out [sth]**, ~ **[sth] out** (shape) découper qch à l'emporte-pièce; **to ~ out a number on the phone** composer un numéro au téléphone

Punch /pʌntʃ/ *pr n* Polichinelle
(Idiom) **to be as pleased as ~** être ravi

Punch-and-Judy show *n* ≈ (spectacle *m* de) guignol *m*

punch: **~bag** *n* GB Sport sac *m* de sable; **~ ball** *n* punching-ball *m*; **~ card** *n* carte *f* perforée; **~-drunk** *adj* (in boxing) abruti par les coups; fig (from tiredness) abruti de fatigue; **~ line** *n* chute *f* (*d'une histoire drôle*); **~-up**○ *n* GB bagarre○ *f*

punchy○ /'pʌntʃɪ/ *adj* [*person, style*] énergique; [*article*] percutant

punctilious /pʌŋk'tɪlɪəs/ *adj* sout scrupuleux/-euse

punctual /'pʌŋktʃʊəl/ *adj* [*person, delivery*] ponctuel/-elle; **to be ~ for sth** être à l'heure pour qch

punctuality /ˌpʌŋktʃʊ'ælətɪ/ *n* ponctualité *f*

punctually /'pʌŋktʃʊəlɪ/ *adv* [*start, arrive, leave*] à l'heure; **to arrive ~ at 10** arriver ponctuellement à 10 heures

punctuate /'pʌŋktʃʊeɪt/ *vtr, vi* ponctuer

punctuation /ˌpʌŋktʃʊ'eɪʃn/ *n* ponctuation *f*

punctuation mark *n* signe *m* de ponctuation

puncture /'pʌŋktʃə(r)/
A *n* (in tyre, balloon, airbed) crevaison *f*; (in skin) piqûre *f*; **we had a ~ on the way** on a crevé en chemin
B *vtr* **1** (perforate) crever [*tyre, balloon, airbed*]; ponctionner [*organ*]; **to ~ a lung** Med se perforer un poumon; **2** fig démolir [*myth*]; **to ~ sb's pride** *ou* **ego** décontenancer qn
C *vi* [*tyre, balloon*] crever

puncture: **~ (repair) kit** *n* boîte *f* de rustines®; **~-proof** *adj* increvable

pundit /'pʌndɪt/ *n* (expert) expert/-e *m/f*

pungency /'pʌndʒənsɪ/ *n* (of sauce, dish) goût *m* piquant; (of smoke, smell) âcreté *f*; (of speech, satire) mordant *m*

pungent /'pʌndʒənt/ *adj* [*flavour*] relevé; [*smell*] fort; [*gas, smoke*] âcre; [*speech, satire*] mordant, virulent

punish /'pʌnɪʃ/ *vtr* **1** punir; **2** ○(treat roughly) malmener [*opponent*]; fatiguer [*car, horse*]

punishable /'pʌnɪʃəbl/ *adj* [*offence*] punissable

punishing /'pʌnɪʃɪŋ/
A *n* punition *f*; **to take a ~**○ prendre une raclée○
B *adj* [*schedule, pace*] éprouvant; [*defeat*] cuisant

punishment /'pʌnɪʃmənt/ *n* **1** punition *f*; (stronger) châtiment *m*; **as ~ for** en punition de; **2** ○(rough treatment) **to take a lot of ~** être mis à rude épreuve

punitive /'pju:nətɪv/ *n* [*measure, action*] punitif/-ive; [*taxation*] très sévère; **~ damages** Jur dommages et intérêts à valeur répressive

punnet /'pʌnɪt/ *n* GB barquette *f*

punt /pʌnt/
A *n* **1** (boat) barque *f* (*à fond plat*); **2** (Irish pound) livre *f* irlandaise
B *vi* **1** (travel by punt) **to go ~ing** faire une promenade en barque; **2** (bet) miser

punter○ /'pʌntə(r)/ *n* GB **1** (at races) parieur *m*; (at casino) joueur/-euse *m/f*; **2** (average client) client/-e *m/f*

puny /'pju:nɪ/ *adj* [*person, body*] chétif/-ive; [*effort*] piteux/-euse

pup /pʌp/
A *n* (dog) chiot *m*; (seal, otter etc) petit *m*
B *vi* (*p prés etc* **-pp-**) [*bitch, seal*] mettre bas
(Idiom) **to be sold a ~**○ se faire avoir➐

pupil /'pju:pɪl/ *n* **1** Sch élève *mf*; **2** Anat pupille *f*

puppet /'pʌpɪt/
A *n* lit, fig marionnette *f*
B *noun modifier* [*government, state*] fantoche

puppy /'pʌpɪ/ *n* chiot *m*

puppy: **~ fat** *n* ℂ rondeurs *fpl* de l'enfance; **~ love** *n* amour *m* d'adolescent/-e

purchase /'pɜ:tʃəs/
A *n* **1** Comm achat *m*; **2** (grip) prise *f*; **to get** *ou* **gain (a) ~ on** [*climber*] trouver une prise sur; [*vehicle*] adhérer à
B *vtr* **1** Comm acheter; **2** fig acquérir [*liberty*]

purchaser /'pɜ:tʃəsə(r)/ *n* acheteur/-euse *m/f*

purchasing /'pɜ:tʃəsɪŋ/ *n* achat *m*

purchasing power *n* pouvoir *m* d'achat

purdah /'pɜ:də/ *n*: isolement des femmes conformément à certaines religions; **to go into ~** fig s'isoler

pure /pjʊə(r)/ *adj* (all contexts) pur; **~ new wool** laine *f* vierge; **by ~ accident** de façon purement accidentelle; **~ research** recherche *f* fondamentale

purebred /'pjʊəbred/
A *n* (horse) pur-sang *m inv*
B *adj* de race, pur-sang *inv*

puree /'pjʊəreɪ, US pjʊə'reɪ/
A *n* purée *f*
B *vtr* écraser; **~d vegetables** purée de légumes

purely /'pjʊəlɪ/ *adv* purement; **~ to be polite** uniquement pour être poli

purgatorial /ˌpɜ:gə'tɔ:rɪəl/ *adj* du purgatoire; fig infernal

purgatory /'pɜ:gətrɪ, US -tɔ:rɪ/ *n* purgatoire *m*

purge /pɜ:dʒ/
A *n* (all contexts) purge *f*
B *vtr* **1** gen, Med purger; **2** Pol purger [*country, party*]; éliminer [*extremists, dissidents etc*]; **3** Relig expier [*sin*]; purger liter [*mind, heart*]

purification /ˌpjʊərɪfɪ'keɪʃn/ *n* **1** (of water, air, chemicals) épuration *f*; **2** Relig purification *f*

purifier /'pjʊərɪfaɪə(r)/ *n* (for water) épurateur *m*; (for air) purificateur *m*

purify /'pjʊərɪfaɪ/ *vtr* gen, Tech épurer; Relig purifier

purist /'pjʊərɪst/ *n, adj* puriste (*mf*)

puritan /'pjʊərɪtən/ *n, adj* fig puritain/-e (*m/f*)

purity /'pjʊərətɪ/ *n* pureté *f*

purl /pɜ:l/
A *n* maille *f* à l'envers
B *vtr* tricoter [qch] à l'envers [*row, stitch*]

purple /'pɜ:pl/ ▸ p. 752
A *n* **1** (colour) violet *m*; **2** Relig **the ~** (rank) la pourpre; (bishops) GB évêques *mpl* anglicans
B *adj* (bluish) violet/-ette; (reddish) pourpre; **to turn ~** (in anger) devenir rouge de colère

purple passage, **purple patch** *n* Literat péj passage *m* ampoulé

purplish /'pɜ:plɪʃ/ ▸ p. 752 *adj* violacé

purport sout
A /'pɜ:pət/ *n* sens *m*
B /pə'pɔ:t/ *vtr* **to ~ to do** prétendre faire

purpose /'pɜ:pəs/
A *n* **1** (aim) but *m*; **for the ~ of doing** dans le but de faire;

for cooking ∼s pour la cuisine; for our ∼s, we can assume that... dans l'optique qui nous intéresse, nous pouvons considérer que...; for the ∼s of this book pour (les besoins de) ce livre; for all practical ∼s en pratique; ∼ unknown usage *m* inconnu; put it in the bin provided for the ∼ mets-le dans la poubelle prévue à cet effet; for some *ou* good ∼ utilement; to no ∼ inutilement; to the ∼ sout à propos; [2] (determination) (*also* strength of ∼) résolution *f*; to have a sense of ∼ savoir ce que l'on veut
B on ∼ *adv phr* exprès

purpose-built /ˌpɜːpəsˈbɪlt/ *adj* GB conçu pour un usage déterminé; a ∼ apartment ≈ un appartement indépendant

purposeful /ˈpɜːpəsfl/ *adj* résolu

purposely /ˈpɜːpəsli/ *adv* exprès, intentionnellement

purpose-made /ˌpɜːpəsˈmeɪd/ *adj* GB fait spécialement (for pour)

purr /pɜː(r)/
A *n* (of cat, engine) ronronnement *m*
B *vi* [*cat, engine*] ronronner

purse /pɜːs/ *n* [1] (for money) porte-monnaie *m inv*; US (handbag) sac *m* à main; [2] fig (resources) moyens *mpl*; [3] (prize) prix *m*
(idioms) to hold the ∼-strings tenir les cordons de la bourse; to ∼ one's lips faire une moue désapprobatrice

purser /ˈpɜːsə(r)/ ▸ p. 1181 *n* commissaire *m* de bord

purse snatcher *n* US voleur/-euse *m/f* de sacs à main

pursue /pəˈsjuː, US -ˈsuː/ *vtr* poursuivre [*person, aim, ambition, studies*]; mener [*policy*]; se livrer à [*occupation, interest*]; to ∼ a career faire carrière (in dans); to ∼ a line of inquiry suivre une piste

pursuer /pəˈsjuːə(r), US -ˈsuː-/ *n* poursuivant/-e *m/f*

pursuit /pəˈsjuːt, US -ˈsuː-/ *n* [1] 𝒞 (following) poursuite *f*; in ∼ of à la poursuite de; the ∼ of happiness la recherche du bonheur; in close *ou* hot ∼ à vos/ses etc trousses; [2] (hobby) passe-temps *m*; artistic ∼s activités *fpl* artistiques

push /pʊʃ/
A *n* [1] lit (shove, press) poussée *f*; to give sb/sth a ∼ pousser qn/qch; the car won't start—we need a ∼ la voiture ne veut pas démarrer—il faut la pousser; at the ∼ of a button en appuyant sur un bouton; [2] (campaign, drive) campagne *f*; [3] fig (stimulus) impulsion *f*; to give sth/sb a ∼ encourager qch/qn; this gave me the ∼ I needed c'est ça qui m'a décidé à faire quelque chose; to give sth a ∼ in the right direction faire avancer qch dans la bonne direction; [4] Mil poussée *f*; the big ∼ la grande offensive; [5] (spirit, drive) esprit *m* battant
B *vtr* [1] (move, shove, press) gen pousser; appuyer sur [*button, switch, bell*]; to ∼ sb/sth away repousser qn/qch; she ∼ed him down the stairs elle l'a poussé dans l'escalier; to ∼ one's finger into sth enfoncer son doigt dans; to ∼ sth into sb's hand mettre qch de force dans la main de qn; to ∼ sb/sth out of the way écarter qn/qch; to ∼ sb aside écarter qn; to ∼ one's way through sth se frayer un chemin à travers qch; to ∼ sth off the road enlever qch de la chaussée; to ∼ the door open, to ∼ the door shut pousser la porte; to ∼ sb too far fig pousser qn à bout; to be ∼ed° (under pressure) être à la bourre°; to be ∼ed for sth° (short of) être à court de qch; [2] °(promote) faire la promotion de [*product*]; promouvoir [*policy, theory*]; [3] °(sell) vendre [*drugs*]
C *vi* pousser; to ∼ against s'appuyer contre; to ∼ at sth repousser qch; to ∼ past sb bousculer qn; to ∼ through se frayer un chemin à travers
D *v refl* to ∼ oneself upright se redresser; to ∼ oneself through a gap passer par un trou; (drive oneself) se pousser (to do à faire)
(idioms) at a ∼° GB s'il le faut; if it comes to the ∼ si on en vient à cette extrémité; to be ∼ing 50 friser la cinquantaine; to give sb the ∼° GB (fire) virer qn°; (break up with) larguer qn°; to ∼ one's luck, to ∼ it° forcer sa chance; that's ∼ing it a bit°! (cutting it fine) c'est un peu juste *or* risqué!
(Phrasal verbs)
▪ **push ahead** (with plans) persévérer (with dans); (on journey) continuer
▪ **push around**°: ▶ ∼ [sb] around fig bousculer
▪ **push back**: ▶ ∼ [sth] back, ∼ back [sth] repousser [*forest, frontier, date, enemy*]; pousser [*object, furniture*]

▪ **push down**: ▶ ∼ [sth] down, ∼ down [sth] faire chuter; ▶ ∼ down [sb], ∼ [sb] down faire tomber
▪ **push for** [sth] faire pression en faveur de
▪ **push forward**: ▶ ∼ forward (with plans) persévérer (with dans); (on journey) continuer; ▶ ∼ [sth] forward, ∼ forward [sth] faire valoir; to ∼ oneself forward se mettre en avant
▪ **push in**: ▶ ∼ in s'introduire dans la file; ▶ ∼ [sth] in, ∼ in [sth] enfoncer [*button, stick, window*]
▪ **push off** [1] °GB filer°; [2] Naut pousser
▪ **push on** = push ahead
▪ **push over**: ▶ ∼ over° (move over) se pousser; ▶ ∼ over [sth/sb], ∼ [sth/sb] over renverser [*person, table, car*]
▪ **push through**: ▶ ∼ [sth] through, ∼ through [sth] faire voter [*bill, legislation*]; faire passer [*deal*]; to ∼ through a passport application accélérer l'obtention d'un passeport
▪ **push up**: ▶ ∼ up [sth], ∼ [sth] up faire monter

push-button /ˈpʊʃbʌtn/
A push button *n* bouton-poussoir *m*
B *adj* [*control, tuning, selection*] par bouton-poussoir; [*telephone*] à touches; [*radio*] à boutons-poussoirs; [*dialling*] au clavier

push: ∼cart *n* charrette *f* à bras; ∼chair *n* GB poussette *f*

pusher° /ˈpʊʃə(r)/ *n* (*also* drug ∼) revendeur/-euse *m/f* de drogue

pushiness /ˈpʊʃɪnɪs/ *n* (ambition) arrivisme *m*; (tenacity) obstination *f*

pushing /ˈpʊʃɪŋ/ *n* bousculade *f*

Pushkin /ˈpʊʃkɪn/ *pr n* Pouchkine

push: ∼over° *n* (easy to do, beat) jeu *m* d'enfant; ∼pin *n* US punaise *f*; ∼rod *n* poussoir *m*

push-start
A /ˈpʊʃstaːt/ *n* to give sth a ∼ pousser qch pour le/la faire démarrer
B /ˌpʊʃˈstaːt/ *vtr* pousser [qch] pour le/la faire démarrer [*vehicle*]

push-up /ˈpʊʃʌp/ *n* Sport pompe° *f*

pushy° /ˈpʊʃi/ *adj* (ambitious) arriviste; she's very ∼ (assertive) elle s'impose

puss° /pʊs/ *n* [1] (cat) minet° *m*; [2] US (mouth) gueule° *f*

pussy cat *n* [1] lang enfantin minou *m* baby talk; [2] °fig he's a real ∼ il est très conciliant

pussyfoot /ˈpʊsɪfʊt/ *vi* (*also* ∼ around) tourner autour du pot°

pussyfooting° /ˈpʊsɪfʊtɪŋ/
A *n* 𝒞 tergiversations *fpl*
B *adj* [*attitude, behaviour*] timoré

put /pʊt/
A *vtr* (*p prés* -tt-; *prét, pp* put) [1] (place) mettre [*object, person*]; to ∼ more sugar in one's tea ajouter du sucre dans son thé; to ∼ more soap in the bathroom remettre du savon dans la salle de bains; [2] (cause to go or undergo) to ∼ sth through glisser qch dans [*letterbox*]; passer qch par [*window*]; to ∼ one's head through the window passer la tête par la fenêtre; to ∼ one's fist through the window casser la fenêtre d'un coup de poing; to ∼ sth through a test faire passer un test à qch; to ∼ sth through a process faire suivre un processus à qch; to ∼ sb through envoyer qn à [*university, college*]; faire passer qn par [*suffering, ordeal*]; faire passer [qch] à qn [*test*]; faire suivre [qch] à qn [*course*]; after all you've put me through après tout ce que tu m'as fait subir; to ∼ one's hand to porter la main à [*mouth*]; to ∼ sb to washing sth faire laver qch à qn; [3] (devote, invest) to ∼ money/energy into sth investir de l'argent/son énergie dans qch; to ∼ a lot into s'engager à fond pour [*work, project*]; sacrifier beaucoup à [*marriage*]; [4] (add) to ∼ sth towards mettre qch pour; ∼ it towards some new clothes dépense-le en nouveaux vêtements; to ∼ tax/duty on sth taxer/imposer qch; to ∼ a penny on income tax GB augmenter l'impôt sur le revenu d'un pourcent; [5] (express) how would you ∼ that in French? comment dirait-on ça en français?; to ∼ it bluntly pour parler franchement; let me ∼ it another way laissez-moi m'exprimer différemment; that was very well put c'était très bien tourné; to ∼ one's feelings into words trouver les mots pour exprimer ses sentiments; [6] (offer for consideration) présenter [*point of view, proposal*]; to ∼ sth to soumettre qch à [*meeting, conference, board*]; to ∼ sth to the vote mettre qch au vote; [7] (rate, rank) placer; I ∼ a sense of

humour **first** pour moi le plus important c'est le sens de l'humour; **to ~ safety first** faire passer la sécurité avant tout; 8) (estimate) **to ~** sth at évaluer qch à [*sum*]; **I'd ~ him at about 40** je lui donnerais à peu près 40 ans; 9) Sport lancer [*shot*]

B *v refl* (*p prés* **-tt-**; *prét, pp* **put**) **to ~ oneself in a strong position/in sb's place** se mettre dans une position de force/à la place de qn

(Idioms) **I wouldn't ~ it past him!** je ne pense pas que ça le gênerait!; **to ~ one over** *ou* **across** GB **on sb**○ faire marcher qn○

(Phrasal verbs)

■ **put about**: ► **~ about** Naut virer de bord; ► **~ [sth] about**, **~ about [sth]** 1) (spread) faire circuler; **it is being put about that** le bruit court que; 2) Naut faire virer de bord

■ **put across**: ► **~ across [sth]**, **~ [sth] across** communiquer [*idea, message, case*]; mettre [qch] en valeur [*personality*]; **to ~ oneself across** se mettre en valeur

■ **put aside**: ► **~ aside [sth]**, **~ [sth] aside** mettre [qch] de côté

■ **put away**: ► **~ away [sth]**, **~ [sth] away** 1) (tidy away) ranger; 2) (save) mettre [qch] de côté; 3) ○avaler [*food*]; descendre○ [*drink*]; ► **~ away [sb]**○, **~ [sb] away**○ (in mental hospital) enfermer; (in prison) boucler○

■ **put back**: ► **~ back [sth]**, **~ [sth] back** 1) (return, restore) remettre; **to ~ sth back where it belongs** remettre qch à sa place; 2) (postpone) remettre [*meeting, departure*] (**to** à; **until** jusqu'à); repousser [*date*]; 3) retarder [*clock, watch*]; 4) (delay) retarder (**by** de); 5) ○(knock back) descendre○

■ **put by** GB: ► **~ [sth] by**, **~ by [sth]** mettre [qch] de côté

■ **put down**: ► **~ down** [*aircraft*] atterrir; ► **~ [sth] down**, **~ down [sth]** 1) poser [*object, plane*]; mettre [*rat poison etc*]; 2) (suppress) réprimer; 3) (write down) mettre (par écrit); 4) (ascribe) **to ~ sth down to** mettre qch sur le compte de; **to ~ sth down to the fact that** imputer qch au fait que; 5) (charge) **to ~ sth down to** mettre qch sur; 6) (destroy) (by injection) piquer; (by other method) abattre [*animal*]; 7) (deposit) **to ~ down a deposit** verser des arrhes; **to ~ £50 down on sth** verser 50 livres d'arrhes sur qch; 8) (store) mettre [qch] en cave [*wine*]; affiner [*cheese*]; 9) (put on agenda) inscrire [qch] à l'ordre du jour; ► **~ [sb] down**, **~ down [sb]** 1) déposer [*passenger*]; 2) ○(humiliate) rabaisser; 3) Sch (into lower group) faire descendre (**from** de; **to, into** à); 4) (classify, count in) **to ~ sb down as** considérer qn comme [*possibility, candidate, fool*]; **to ~ sb down for** (note as wanting or offering) compter [qch] pour qn [*contribution*]; (put on waiting list) inscrire qn sur la liste d'attente pour; **to ~ sb down for £10** compter 10 livres pour qn; **to ~ sb down for three tickets** réserver trois billets pour qn

■ **put forward**: ► **~ forward [sth]**, **~ [sth] forward** 1) (propose) avancer [*idea, theory, name*]; soumettre [*plan, suggestion*]; émettre [*opinion*]; 2) (in time) avancer [*meeting, date, clock*] (**by** de; **to** à); ► **~ [sb] forward**, **~ forward [sb]** présenter la candidature de (**for** pour); ► **~ sb forward as** présenter qn comme

■ **put in**: ► **~ in** 1) [*ship*] faire escale (**at** à; **to** dans; **for** pour); 2) (apply) **to ~ in for** postuler pour [*job, promotion, rise*]; demander [*transfer, overtime*]; ► **~ in [sth]**, **~ [sth] in** 1) (fit, install) installer; 2) (make) faire [*request, claim, offer*]; **to ~ in an application for** déposer une demande de [*visa etc*]; poser sa candidature pour [*job*]; **to ~ in a protest** protester; **to ~ in an appearance** faire une apparition; 3) passer [*time, hours, days*]; contribuer pour [*sum, amount*]; **to ~ in a lot of time doing** consacrer beaucoup de temps à faire; **to ~ in a good day's work** avoir une bonne journée de travail; **to ~ in a lot of work** se donner beaucoup de mal; 4) (insert) mettre [*paragraph, reference*]; 5) (elect) élire; ► **~ [sb] in for** présenter [qn] pour [*exam*]; poser la candidature de [qn] pour [*promotion, job*]; recommander [qn] pour [*prize, award*]

■ **put off**: ► **~ off** Naut partir; **to ~ off from** s'éloigner de [*quay, jetty*]; ► **~ off [sth]**, **~ [sth] off** 1) (delay, defer) remettre [qch] (**à** plus tard); 2) (turn off) éteindre [*light, radio*]; couper [*heating*]; ► **~ off [sb]**, **~ [sb] off** 1) (fob off, postpone seeing) décommander [*guest*]; dissuader [*person*]; **to be easily put off** se décourager facilement; 2) (repel) [*appearance, smell*] dégoûter; [*manner, person*] déconcerter; 3) GB (distract) distraire; 4) (drop off) déposer [*passenger*]

■ **put on**: ► **~ on [sth]**, **~ [sth] on** 1) mettre [*garment,*

make-up*]; 2) (switch on) allumer [*light, heating*]; mettre [*record, tape, music*]; **to ~ the kettle on mettre de l'eau à chauffer; **to ~ the brakes on** freiner; 3) prendre [*weight, kilo*]; rajouter [*extra duty, tax*]; 4) (produce) monter [*play, exhibition*]; 5) (adopt) prendre [*accent, expression*]; **he's ~ting it on** il fait semblant; 6) (offer) ajouter [*train, bus service*]; proposer [*meal*]; 7) avancer [*clock*]; 8) (bet) parier; ► **~ [sb] on** 1) Telecom passer; **I'll ~ him on** je vous le passe; 2) ○US faire marcher○; 3) (recommend) **to ~ sb on to sth** indiquer qch à qn; **who put you on to me?** qui vous a envoyé à moi?; 4) (put on track of) **to ~ sb on to** mettre qn sur la piste de

■ **put out**: ► **~ out** Naut partir; ► **~ out [sth]**, **~ [sth] out** 1) (extend) tendre [*hand*]; **to ~ out one's tongue** tirer la langue; 2) (extinguish) éteindre; 3) sortir [*bin, garbage*]; faire sortir [*cat*]; 4) (issue) diffuser [*report, warning, statement*]; 5) (arrange) mettre [*food, dishes, towels etc*]; 6) (sprout) [*plant*] déployer [*buds, shoots*]; 7) (distort) fausser [*figure, estimate, result*]; 8) (dislocate) se démettre [*shoulder*]; 9) (subcontract) confier [qch] en sous-traitance (**to** à); ► **~ [sb] out** 1) (inconvenience) déranger; **to ~ oneself out for sb** se donner beaucoup de mal pour qn; 2) (annoy) contrarier; 3) (evict) expulser

■ **put over = put across**

■ **put through**: ► **~ [sth/sb] through**, **~ through [sth/sb]** 1) (implement) faire passer; 2) Telecom passer

■ **put together**: ► **~ [sb/sth] together**, **~ together [sb/sth]** 1) (assemble) assembler; **to ~ sth together again**, **to ~ sth back together** reconstituer qch; **smarter than all the rest put together** plus intelligent que tous les autres réunis; 2) (place together) mettre ensemble; 3) (form) former; 4) (edit) constituer [*file, portfolio, anthology*]; rédiger [*newsletter, leaflet*]; établir [*list*]; faire [*film, programme, video*]; 5) (improvise) improviser [*meal*]; 6) (present) constituer [*case*]; construire [*argument, essay*]

■ **put up**: ► **~ up** 1) (stay) **to ~ up at sb's** se faire héberger par qn; **to ~ up in a hotel** descendre à l'hôtel; 2) **to ~ up with** (tolerate) supporter; ► **~ up [sth]** opposer [*resistance*]; **to ~ up a fight** *ou* **struggle** combattre; **to ~ up a good performance** Sport bien se défendre; **to ~ [sth] up**, **~ up [sth]** 1) hisser [*flag, sail*]; relever [*hair*]; **to ~ up one's hand** lever la main; **~ your hands up!** (in class) levez le doigt!; 2) (post up) mettre [*sign, plaque*]; afficher [*list*]; 3) (erect) dresser [*fence, barrier, tent*]; construire [*building*]; 4) (increase) augmenter [*rent, prices, tax*]; faire monter [*temperature, pressure*]; 5) (provide) fournir [*money*]; 6) (present) soumettre [*proposal, argument*]; 7) Aerosp placer [qch] en orbite [*satellite, probe*]; ► **~ [sb] up**, **~ up [sb]** 1) (lodge) héberger; 2) (propose) présenter [*candidate*]; **to ~ sb up for** proposer qn comme [*leader, chairman*]; proposer qn pour [*promotion, position*]; 3) (promote) faire passer [qn] au niveau supérieur; 4) (incite) **to ~ sb up to sth/to doing** pousser qn à qch/à faire

■ **put upon**: ► **~ upon [sb]** abuser de [*person*]; **to be put upon** se faire marcher sur les pieds

put: **~-down** *n* remarque *f* humiliante; **~-out**○ *adj* vexé

putt /pʌt/
A *n* putt *m*
B *vtr, vi* putter

putty /'pʌtɪ/
A *n* mastic *m*
B *vtr* mastiquer

put: **~-up job**○ *n* coup *m* monté; **~-you-up**○ *n* GB canapé-lit *m*

puzzle /'pʌzl/
A *n* (mystery) mystère *m*; Games casse-tête *m inv*
B *vtr* [*question, attitude*] déconcerter [*person*]
C *vi* **to ~ over sth** réfléchir à qch

(Phrasal verb)

■ **puzzle out**: ► **~ out [sth]**, **~ [sth] out** deviner

puzzle book *n* livre *m* de jeux

puzzled /'pʌzld/ *adj* [*person, smile*] perplexe; **to be ~ as to why** se demander pourquoi

puzzling /'pʌzlɪŋ/ *adj* curieux/-ieuse

pygmy /'pɪgmɪ/ *n* pygmée *mf*

pyjama GB, **pajama** US /pə'dʒɑːmə/
A *noun modifier* [*cord, jacket, trousers*] de pyjama
B **pyjamas** *npl* pyjama *m*; **a pair of ~s** un pyjama

pylon /'paɪlən, -lɒn/ *n* Elec, Aviat pylône *m*

pyramid /'pɪrəmɪd/ n pyramide f
pyramid selling n vente f en cascade
pyre /'paɪə(r)/ n bûcher m

pyromaniac /ˌpaɪrəʊ'meɪnɪæk/ n pyromane mf
pyrotechnics /ˌpaɪrə'tekniks/ n ① (science) pyrotechnie f; ② (display) feu m d'artifice also fig

Qq

q, Q /kju:/ *n* q, Q *m*

Q and A *n* (*abrév* = **question and answer**) questions-réponses *fpl*

Qatar /kæˈtɑː/ ▸ p. 774 *pr n* Qatar *m*

QC *n* GB Jur (*abrév* = **Queen's Counsel**) *titre conféré à un avocat éminent*

QED (*abrév* = **quod erat demonstrandum**) CQFD

qty *n*: *abrév écrite* = **quantity**

quack /kwæk/
A *n* ① (impostor) charlatan *m*; ② ○GB (doctor) toubib○ *m*; ③ onomat coin-coin *m inv*
B *vi* onomat cancaner

quad /kwɒd/ *n* ① *abrév* ▸ **quadrangle**; ② *abrév* ▸ **quadruplet**

quad bike *n* quad *m*

quadrangle /ˈkwɒdræŋgl/ *n* ① Math quadrilatère *m*; ② Archit cour *f* carrée

quadraphonics /ˌkwɒdrəˈfɒnɪks/ *n* (+ *v sg*) quadriphonie *f*

quadratic equation *n* équation *f* du second degré

quadrilateral /ˌkwɒdrɪˈlætərəl/
A *n* quadrilatère *m*
B *adj* quadrilatéral

quadriplegic /ˌkwɒdrɪˈpliːdʒɪk/ *adj* tétraplégique

quadruple
A /ˈkwɒdrʊpl, US kwɒˈdruːpl/ *n, adj* quadruple (*m*)
B /kwɒˈdruːpl/ *vtr, vi* quadrupler

quadruplet /ˈkwɒdrʊplət, US kwɒˈdruːp-/ *n* quadruplé-e *m/f*; **a set of ~s** des quadruplés

quadruplicate /kwɒˈdruːplɪkət/ *n* **in ~** en quatre exemplaires

quagmire /ˈkwɒgmaɪə(r), ˈkwæg-/ *n* bourbier *m*

quail /kweɪl/
A *n* (*pl* ~**s** *ou collective* ~) (bird) caille *f*
B *vi* trembler

quaint /kweɪnt/ *adj* ① (pretty) pittoresque; ② (old-world) d'un charme suranné; (slightly ridiculous) au charme vieillot; ③ (odd) bizarre; (unusual) original

quake /kweɪk/
A *n* (earthquake) tremblement *m* de terre
B *vi* [*earth, person*] trembler

qualification /ˌkwɒlɪfɪˈkeɪʃn/ *n* ① (diploma, degree etc) diplôme *m* (**in** en); (experience, skills) qualification *f*; **to have the (necessary ou right) ~s for sth** (on paper) avoir les titres requis pour qch; (in experience, skills) avoir les qualifications pour qch; ② GB (graduation) **my first job after ~** mon premier travail après avoir reçu mon diplôme; ③ (restriction) restriction *f*; **my only ~ is (that)** ma seule réserve est que; ④ Admin (eligibility) droit *m*; ⑤ Ling qualification *f*

qualified /ˈkwɒlɪfaɪd/ *adj* ① (for job) (having diploma) diplômé; (having experience, skills) qualifié; **to be ~ for sth** (on paper) avoir les titres requis pour qch; (by experience, skills) être qualifié pour qch; ② (competent) (having authority) qualifié; (having knowledge) compétent; ③ (modified) nuancé, mitigé

qualifier /ˈkwɒlɪfaɪə(r)/ *n* ① Sport (contestant) qualifié-e *m/f*; (match) éliminatoire *m*; ② Ling qualificatif *m*

qualify /ˈkwɒlɪfaɪ/
A *vtr* ① (make competent) **to ~ sb for a job** [*degree, diploma*] habiliter qn à exercer un emploi; [*experience, skills*] rendre qn apte à exercer un emploi; ② Admin **to ~ sb for sth**

donner droit à qch à qn; **to ~ sb to do** donner à qn le droit de faire; ③ gen (give authority to) **to ~ sb to do** autoriser qn à faire; ④ (modify) nuancer [*acceptance, approval, opinion*]; préciser [*statement, remark*]; ⑤ Ling qualifier
B *vi* ① (obtain diploma, degree etc) obtenir son diplôme (**as** de, en); (have experience, skill) avoir les connaissances requises (**for** pour); **to ~ to do** avoir les connaissances requises pour faire; **while she was ~ing as an engineer** pendant qu'elle faisait ses études d'ingénieur; ② Admin remplir les conditions (requises); **to ~ for** avoir droit à; **to ~ to do** avoir le droit de faire; ③ (meet standard) **he hardly qualifies as a poet** ce n'est pas vraiment ce que l'on peut appeler un poète; ④ Sport se qualifier

qualifying /ˈkwɒlɪfaɪɪŋ/ *adj* ① gen, Sport de qualification; **~ period** (until trained) (periode *f* de) stage *m*; (until eligible) période *f* d'attente; ② Ling qualificatif/-ive

qualitative /ˈkwɒlɪtətɪv, US -teɪt-/ *adj* qualitatif/-ive

quality /ˈkwɒlətɪ/
A *n* (all contexts) qualité *f*
B *noun modifier* [*car, workmanship, press*] de qualité

quality control
A *n* contrôle *m* de qualité
B *noun modifier* [*procedure*] de contrôle de qualité

quality controller ▸ p. 1181 *n* contrôleur/-euse *m/f* chargé/-e du contrôle de la qualité

quality time *n* (with loved one) temps *m* en tête à tête, temps *m* de qualité

qualm /kwɑːm/ *n* scrupule *m*

quandary /ˈkwɒndərɪ/ *n* embarras *m*; (serious) dilemme *m*

quango /ˈkwæŋgəʊ/ *n* (*pl* ~**s**) GB organisme *m* autonome d'État

quantifiable /ˌkwɒntɪˈfaɪəbl/ *adj* facile à évaluer

quantify /ˈkwɒntɪfaɪ/ *vtr* gen évaluer avec précision; Math, Phys quantifier

quantitative /ˈkwɒntɪtətɪv, US -teɪt-/ *adj* gen quantitatif/-ive

quantity /ˈkwɒntətɪ/ ▸ p. 1116
A *n* gen, Literat quantité *f*; **in ~** en grande quantité; **unknown ~** Math, fig inconnue *f*
B *noun modifier* [*purchase, sale*] en grande quantité; [*production*] en série

quantity: ~ surveying *n* métrage *m*; **~ surveyor** ▸ p. 1181 *n* métreur *m*

quantum /ˈkwɒntəm/
A *n* (*pl* **-ta**) quantum *m*
B *noun modifier* [*mechanics, theory*] quantique

quantum leap *n* Phys saut *m* quantique; fig bond *m* prodigieux

quarantine /ˈkwɒrəntiːn, US ˈkwɔːr-/
A *n* quarantaine *f*
B *noun modifier* [*hospital, period*] de quarantaine
C *vtr* mettre [qn/qch] en quarantaine

quarrel /ˈkwɒrəl, US ˈkwɔːrəl/
A *n* ① (argument) dispute *f* (**between** entre; **over** au sujet de); **to have a ~** se disputer; ② (feud) brouille *f* (**about, over** au sujet de); **to have a ~ with sb** être brouillé avec qn; ③ (difference of opinion) différend *m*; **to have no ~ with sb/sth** ne rien avoir contre qn/à redire à qch
B *vi* (*p prés etc* -**ll-**, US -**l-**) ① (argue) se disputer; ② (sever relations) se brouiller; ③ (dispute) **to ~ with** contester [*claim, idea*]; se plaindre de [*price, verdict*]

Quantities

■ *Note the use of* en *(of it or of them) in the following examples. This word must be included when the thing you are talking about is not expressed (the French says literally* there is of it a lot, there is of it two kilos, I have of them a lot *etc.). However,* en *is not needed when the commodity is specified e.g.* there is a lot of butter = il y a beaucoup de beurre.

how much is there?
= combien y en a-t-il?

there's a lot
= il y en a beaucoup*

there's not much
= il n'y en a pas beaucoup

there's two kilos
= il y en a deux kilos

how much sugar have you got?
= combien de sucre as-tu?

I've got a lot
= j'en ai beaucoup

I've not got much
= je n'en ai pas beaucoup

I've got two kilos
= j'en ai deux kilos

how many are there?
= combien y en a-t-il?

there are a lot
= il y en a beaucoup

there aren't many
= il n'y en a pas beaucoup

there are twenty
= il y en a vingt

how many apples have you?
= combien de pommes as-tu?
  or tu as combien de pommes?

I've got a lot
= j'en ai beaucoup

I haven't many
= je n'en ai pas beaucoup

I've got twenty
= j'en ai vingt

A has got more than B
= A en a plus que B

A has got more money than B
= A a plus d'argent que B

much more than
= beaucoup plus que

a little more than
= un peu plus que

A has got more apples than B
= A a plus de pommes que B

many more apples than B
= beaucoup plus de pommes que B

a few more apples than B
= quelques pommes de plus que B

a few more people than yesterday
= quelques personnes de plus qu'hier

B has got less money than A
= B a moins d'argent que A

B has got less than A
= B en a moins que A

much less than
= beaucoup moins que

a little less than
= un peu moins que

B has got fewer than A
= B en a moins que A

B has got fewer apples than A
= B a moins de pommes que A

many fewer than
= beaucoup moins que

Relative quantities

how many are there to the kilo?
= combien y en a-t-il au kilo?

there are ten to the kilo
= il y en a dix au kilo

you can count six to the kilo
= il faut en compter six au kilo

how many do you get for ten francs?
= combien peut-on en avoir pour dix francs?

you get five for ten francs
= il y en a cinq pour dix francs

how much does it cost a litre?
= combien coûte le litre?

it costs £5 a litre
= ça coûte cinq livres le litre

how much do apples cost a kilo?
= combien coûte le kilo de pommes?

apples cost ten francs a kilo
= les pommes coûtent dix francs le kilo

how much does it cost a metre?
= combien coûte le mètre?

how much does your car do to the gallon?
= combien consomme votre voiture?

it does 28 miles to the gallon
= elle fait dix litres aux cent

■ (*Note that the French calculate petrol consumption in litres per 100 km. To convert mpg to litres per 100 km and vice versa, simply divide 280 by the known figure.*)

how many glasses do you get to the bottle?
= combien y a-t-il de verres par bouteille?

you get six glasses to the bottle
= il y a six verres par bouteille

* *Never use* très *with* beaucoup.

---

quarrelling, quarreling US /'kwɒrəlɪn, US 'kwɔː-/ *n* ₵ disputes *fpl*

quarrelsome /'kwɒrəlsəm, US 'kwɔː-/ *adj* [*person, nature*] querelleur/-euse; [*remark*] agressif/-ive

quarry /'kwɒrɪ, US 'kwɔːrɪ/
A *n* ① (in ground) carrière *f*; ② (prey) proie *f*; (in hunting) gibier *m* also fig
B *vtr* (*also* ~ **out**) extraire [*stone*]
C *vi* **to** ~ **for** extraire [*stone, gravel*]

quarry tile *n* carreau *m* de terre cuite

quart /kwɔːt/ ▸ p. 723 *n* ≈ litre *m* (GB = *1.136 litres*, US = *0.946 litres*)

quarter /'kwɔːtə(r)/ ▸ p. 745, p. 782, p. 1323
A *n* ① (one fourth) quart *m*; ~ **of an hour** quart *m* d'heure; ② gen, Fin (three months) trimestre *m*; ③ (district) quartier *m*; ④ (group) milieu *m*; **don't expect help from that** ~ n'attends aucune aide de ce côté-là; ⑤ (mercy) littér **to get no** ~ **from sb** ne recevoir aucune pitié de la part de qn; **to**

give no ∼ ne pas faire de quartier; ⑥ US (25 cents) vingt-cinq cents *mpl*; ⑦ US (measurement) = 12,7 kg

B **quarters** *npl* Mil quartiers *mpl*, gen logement *m*; **to take up ∼s** se loger (**in** dans)

C *pron* ① (25%) quart *m*; **only a ∼ passed** seul le quart a réussi; ② (in time phrases) **at (a) ∼ to 11** GB, **at a ∼ of 11** US à onze heures moins le quart; **an hour and a ∼** une heure et quart; ③ (in age) **she's ten and a ∼** elle a dix ans et trois mois

D *adj* **a ∼ share in the company** un quart des actions de l'entreprise; **a ∼ century** un quart de siècle

E *adv* **a ∼ full** au quart plein; **a ∼ as big** quatre fois moins grand; **∼ the price** quatre fois moins cher

F **at close quarters** *adv phr* de près; **to fight at close ∼s** lutter au corps à corps

G *vtr* ① (divide into four) couper [qch] en quatre [*cake, apple*]; ② (accommodate) cantonner [*troops*]; loger [*people*]; abriter [*livestock*]

quarter: **∼back** *n* US quarterback *m* (*joueur qui dirige l'attaque*); **∼deck** *n* Naut (on ship) plage *f* arrière; **∼final** *n* quart *m* de finale

quarterly /ˈkwɔːtəlɪ/
A *adj* trimestriel/-ielle
B *adv* tous les trois mois

quarter: **∼master** ▸ p. 1123 *n* (in army) intendant *m*; (in navy) maître *m* de timonerie; **∼note** *n* US Mus noire *f*; **∼staff** *n* Mil Hist bâton *m*

quartet /kwɔːˈtet/ *n* gen, Mus quatuor *m*; **jazz ∼** quartette *m*

quarto /ˈkwɔːtəʊ/ *n*, *noun modifier* (*pl* **-tos**) in-quarto (*m*)

quartz /kwɔːts/
A *n* quartz *m*
B *noun modifier* [*crystal*] de quartz; [*clock*] à quartz

quash /kwɒʃ/ *vtr* rejeter [*proposal*]; réprimer [*rebellion*]

quasi+ /ˈkweɪzaɪ, ˈkwɑːzɪ/ *combining form* quasi (+ *adj*), quasi- (+ *noun*)

quatercentenary /ˌkwætəsenˈtiːnərɪ, US -ˈsentənerɪ/ *n* quatrième centenaire *m*

quaternary /kwəˈtɜːnərɪ/
A *n* ① Math quatre *m*; (set) ensemble *m* de quatre; ② **the Quaternary** (in geology) le quaternaire
B *adj* quaternaire

quaver /ˈkweɪvə(r)/
A *n* ① Mus GB croche *f*; ② (trembling) tremblement *m* (**in** dans)
B *vi* trembloter

quay /kiː/ *n* quai *m*; **on the ∼** sur le quai

queasiness /ˈkwiːzɪnɪs/ *n* nausée *f*

queasy /ˈkwiːzɪ/ *adj* ① lit **to be** *ou* **feel ∼** avoir mal au cœur; ② fig [*conscience*] mauvais; **to feel ∼ about** se sentir mal à l'aise en ce qui concerne

Quebec /kwɪˈbek/ ▸ p. 1276
A *pr n* ① (town) Québec *m*; **in ∼** à Québec; ② (province) Québec *m*; **in ∼** au Québec
B *noun modifier* [*people, culture*] québécois

queen /kwiːn/
A *n* ▸ p. 869 ① lit, fig reine *f*; ② Zool reine *f*; ③ (in chess) reine *f*; (in cards) dame *f*
B *vtr* (in chess) damer [*pawn*]

Idiom **to ∼ it over sb** prendre de grands airs avec qn

queen bee *n* ① Zool reine *f* des abeilles; ② fig **she thinks she's (the) ∼** elle se prend pour la reine

queenly /ˈkwiːnlɪ/ *adj* de reine

queen: **∼ mother** *n* Reine mère *f*; **Queen's Counsel**, **QC** *n* GB Jur avocat *m* éminent (*qui tient son titre de la Reine*)

Queen's English *n* **to speak the ∼** parler un anglais correct

Queen's evidence *n* **to turn ∼** GB Jur dénoncer ses complices contre promesse de pardon

Queensland /ˈkwiːnzlənd/ *pr n* Queensland *m*

Queen's Regulations *npl* GB Mil code *m* militaire

queer /kwɪə(r)/ *adj* ① (strange) étrange, bizarre; ② (suspicious) louche, suspect; ③ †GB (ill) patraque○; ④ ○injur (homosexual) pédé● offensive, homosexuel/-elle

Idiom **to ∼ sb's pitch** contrecarrer les plans de qn

queerly /ˈkwɪəlɪ/ *adv* singulièrement

quell /kwel/ *vtr* étouffer [*anger, anxiety, revolt*]; **to ∼ sb with a look** faire taire qn du regard

quench /kwentʃ/ *vtr* ① étancher [*thirst*]; étouffer [*desire*]; ② littér éteindre [*flame*]; ③ Tech tremper [*metal*]

querulous /ˈkwerʊləs/ *adj* grincheux/-euse

query /ˈkwɪərɪ/
A *n* ① (request for information) question *f* (**about** au sujet de); **a ∼ from sb** une question venant de qn; **queries from customers** demandes *fpl* de renseignement venant des clients; ② (expression of doubt) question *f* (**about** à propos de); ③ Comput interrogation *f*; ④ (question mark) point *m* d'interrogation
B *vtr* mettre en doute; **to ∼ whether** demander si; **nobody dares to ∼ that…** personne n'ose douter du fait que…; **to ∼ sb's ability** mettre en doute les capacités de qn; **some may ∼ my interpretation of the data** il se peut que certains doutent de mon interprétation des données

query window *n* Comput ① (dialogue box) boîte *f* de dialogue; ② (for web search) fenêtre *f* de requête

quest /kwest/ *n* quête *f*; **the ∼ for sb/sth** la recherche de qn/qch; **his ∼ to do** son désir de faire

question /ˈkwestʃən/
A *n* ① (request for information) question *f* (**about** sur); (in exam) question *f*; **to ask sb a ∼** poser une question à qn; **in reply to a ∼ from Mr John Molloy** en réponse à une question posée par M. John Molloy; **to do sth without ∼** faire qch sans poser de question; **what a ∼!** en voilà une question!; **a ∼ from the floor** (in parliament) une question provenant de l'assemblée; ② (practical issue) problème *m*; (ethical issue) question *f*; **the Palestinian ∼** la question palestinienne; **the ∼ of pollution** le problème de la pollution; **it's a ∼ of doing** il s'agit de faire; **the ∼ of where to live** le problème de savoir où habiter; **the ∼ arises as to who is going to pay the bill** la question se pose, à savoir qui va payer la note; **that's another ∼** c'est une autre affaire; **the ∼ is whether** il s'agit ici de savoir si; **there was never any ∼ of you paying** il n'a jamais été question que tu paies; **the person in ∼** la personne en question; **it's out of the ∼ for him to leave** il est hors de question qu'il parte; ③ (uncertainty) doute *m*; **to call sth into ∼** mettre qch en doute; **to prove beyond ∼ that** prouver sans l'ombre d'un doute que; **it's open to ∼** cela se discute; **his honesty was never in ∼** on n'a jamais douté de son honnêteté
B *vtr* ① (interrogate) questionner [*suspect, politician*]; ② (cast doubt upon) (on one occasion) mettre en doute [*tactics, methods*]; (over longer period) douter de [*tactics, methods*]; **to ∼ whether** douter que (+ *subj*)

questionable /ˈkwestʃənəbl/ *adj* (debatable) [*motive, decision*] discutable; (dubious) [*evidence, taste*] douteux/-euse; **it is ∼ whether** il est douteux que (+ *subj*)

questioner /ˈkwestʃənə(r)/ *n* interrogateur/-trice *m/f*

questioning /ˈkwestʃənɪŋ/
A *n* ① (of person) interrogation *f*; (relentless) interrogatoire *m*; **to bring sb in for ∼** amener qn pour interrogatoire; **he is wanted for ∼ in connection with the explosion** la police le recherche suite à l'explosion; **under ∼** [*admit*] pendant un interrogatoire; **a line of ∼** une série de questions; ② (of criteria) remise *f* en question (**of** de)
B *adj* ① [*look, tone*] interrogateur/-trice; ② [*techniques*] d'interrogation; (by official) d'interrogatoire

question mark *n* ① (in punctuation) point *m* d'interrogation; ② (doubt) **there is a ∼ about his honesty** on s'interroge quant à son honnêteté; **there is a ∼ about his suitability for the job** on se demande s'il est apte à occuper ce poste; **there is a ∼ hanging over his future** l'incertitude plane sur son avenir

question master *n* animateur/-trice *m/f* de jeu

questionnaire /ˌkwestʃəˈneə(r)/ *n* questionnaire *m* (**on** sur; **to do** pour faire)

question tag *n* Ling queue *f* de phrase interrogative, tag○ *m*

queue /kjuː/
A *n* GB (of people) queue *f*, file *f* (d'attente); (of vehicles) file *f*; **to stand in a ∼** faire la queue; **to join the ∼** [*person*] se mettre à la queue; [*car*] se mettre dans la file; **go to the back of the ∼!** à la queue!; **to jump the ∼**○ passer avant son tour
B *vi* GB (*also* **∼ up**) [*people*] faire la queue (**for** pour); [*taxis*] attendre en ligne; **to ∼ up to do sth** fig se précipiter pour faire qch

q

queue-jump vi GB resquiller, passer avant son tour

quibble /'kwɪbl/
A n chicane f (**about, over** sur)
B vi chicaner (**about, over** sur)

quick /kwɪk/
A n Anat, Med chair f vive; **to the ~** [bite nails] jusqu'au sang
B adj **1** (speedy) [pace, reply, profit, meal] rapide; [storm, shower] bref/brève; **to make a ~ phone call** passer un coup de téléphone rapide; **to have a ~ coffee** prendre un café en vitesse; **to have a ~ wash** faire une toilette rapide; **she's a ~ worker** elle travaille vite; **the ~est way to...** le meilleur moyen de...; **we're hoping for a ~ sale** nous espérons que cela se vendra rapidement; **we had a ~ chat about our plans** nous avons rapidement discuté de nos projets; **to make a ~ recovery** se rétablir vite; **to pay a ~ visit to sb** faire une petite visite à qn; **be ~ (about it)!** dépêche-toi!; **2** (clever) [child, student] vif/vive d'esprit; **to be ~ at** être bon/bonne en [arithmetic]; **3** (prompt) **to be a ~ learner** apprendre vite; **to be (too) ~ to condemn** condamner (trop) facilement; **she was ~ to see the advantages** elle a tout de suite vu les avantages; **4** (lively) **a ~ temper** un tempérament vif; **to have a ~ temper** s'emporter facilement
C adv ~! vite!; **~ as a flash** avec la rapidité de l'éclair
(Idioms) **a ~ one = quickie 1, 2**; **the ~ and the dead** les vivants et les morts; **to cut ou sting sb to the ~** piquer qn au vif; **to make a ~ buck**○ gagner de l'argent facile; **to make a ~ killing**○ faire fortune rapidement

quick-assembly adj facile à monter

quicken /'kwɪkən/
A vtr accélérer [pace]; fig stimuler [interest]
B vi **1** [pace] s'accélérer; fig [anger] s'intensifier; **2** [fœtus] bouger

quick fire /'kwɪkfaɪə/
A n lit tir m rapide
B **quick-fire** noun modifier [question, sketch] rapide

quick-freeze vtr (prét **-froze**; pp **-frozen**) surgeler

quickie○ /'kwɪkɪ/ n **1** (drink) pot○ m en vitesse; **2** (question) question f rapide; **3** US Cin film fait rapidement

quicklime n chaux f vive

quickly /'kwɪklɪ/ adv [arrive, resolve] (rapidly) vite, rapidement; (without delay) sans tarder; (come) ~! (viens) vite!; **I acted ~ on his advice** je me suis dépêché de suivre ses conseils; **I ~ changed the subject** je me suis empressé de changer de sujet

quick march n Mil ≈ pas m cadencé; ~! (as order) ≈ pas cadencé marche!

quickness /'kwɪknɪs/ n **1** (speed) (of person, movement) rapidité f; **~ to respond/react** promptitude f à répondre/réagir; **2** (nimbleness) (of person, movements) vivacité f; **3** (liveliness of mind) vivacité f d'esprit

quick:~**sand** n ¢ lit sables mpl mouvants; fig bourbier m; ~**setting** adj à prise rapide; ~**silver** n Chem mercure m; ~**tempered** adj coléreux/-euse; ~ **time** n US marche f rapide; ~ **trick** n (in bridge) levée f assurée; ~**witted** adj [person] à l'esprit vif; [reaction] vif/vive

quid○ /kwɪd/ n GB (pl ~) livre f (sterling)

quid pro quo /ˌkwɪd prəʊ 'kwəʊ/ n contrepartie f

quiescent /kwaɪˈesnt, kwɪˈesnt/ adj sout [person] passif/-ive; [mood, state] tranquille; [soul, spirit] en repos

quiet /'kwaɪət/
A n **1** (silence) silence m; **~ please!** silence, s'il vous plaît!; **2** (peace) tranquillité f; **3** ○(secret) **to do sth on the ~** faire qch discrètement
B adj **1** (silent) [church, person, room] silencieux/-ieuse; **to keep ~** garder le silence; **to go ~** [person, assembly] se taire; **to keep sb ~** faire taire [dog, child]; **be ~** (stop talking) tais-toi; (make no noise) ne fais pas de bruit; **2** (not noisy) [voice] bas/basse; [engine] silencieux/-ieuse; [music] doux/douce; [cough, laugh] discret/-ète; **in a ~ voice** à voix basse; **to keep the children ~** [activity] tenir les enfants tranquilles; **3** (discreet) [diplomacy] discret/-ète; [deal] en privé; [confidence] serein; [despair] voilé; [colour] sobre; **to have a ~ word with sb** prendre qn à part pour lui parler; **4** (calm) [village, holiday, night, life] tranquille; **the stock market is ~** la Bourse est calme; **5** (for few people) [meal] intime; [wedding] célébré dans l'intimité; **6** (docile) [pony] paisible; **7** (secret) **to keep [sth] ~** ne pas divulguer [plans]; garder [qch] secret/-ète [engagement]
C vtr US = **quieten**

quieten /'kwaɪətn/ vtr **1** (calm) calmer [person, animal]; **2** (allay) dissiper [doubts]; **3** (silence) faire taire [critics, children]
(Phrasal verb)
■ **quieten down**: ► **~ down 1** (become calm) [person, activity] se calmer; **2** (fall silent) se taire; ► **~ down [sb/sth]**, **~ [sb/sth] down 1** (calm) calmer; **2** (silence) faire taire

quietly /'kwaɪətlɪ/ adv **1** (not noisily) [move] sans bruit; [cough, speak, play] doucement; **2** (silently) [play, read, sit] en silence; **3** (discreetly) [pleased etc] modérément; **to be ~ confident that** avoir la conviction intime que; **4** (simply) [live] simplement; [get married] dans l'intimité; **5** (calmly) calmement; **6** (soberly) [dress] de façon discrète

quietness /'kwaɪətnɪs/ n **1** (silence) silence m; **2** (lowness) (of voice) faiblesse f; **3** (of place) tranquillité f

quiff /kwɪf/ n GB (on forehead) toupet m; (on top of head) houppe f

quill /kwɪl/ n **1** (feather) penne f; (stem of feather) tuyau m de plume; **2** (on porcupine) piquant m; **3** (also ~ **pen**) (for writing) plume f d'oie

quilt /kwɪlt/
A n **1** GB (duvet) couette f; **2** (bed cover) dessus m de lit
B vtr matelasser

quilting /'kwɪltɪŋ/ n (technique) matelassage m; (fabric) matelassure f

quince /kwɪns/ n (fruit) coing m; (tree) cognassier m

quincentenary /ˌkwɪnsenˈtiːnərɪ, US -ˈsentənerɪ/ n cinq centième anniversaire m

quinine /kwɪˈniːn, US ˈkwaɪnaɪn/ n quinine f

quintessential /ˌkwɪntɪˈsenʃl/ adj [quality] fondamental; **the ~ Renaissance man** l'homme de la Renaissance par excellence

quintet /kwɪnˈtet/ n Mus quintette m

quintuple
A /ˈkwɪntjʊpl, US kwɪnˈtuːpl/ adj quintuple
B /kwɪnˈtjʊpl/ vtr quintupler

quintuplet /ˈkwɪntjuːplet, US kwɪnˈtuːplɪt/ n quintuplé/-e m/f

quip /kwɪp/ n trait m d'esprit

quire /ˈkwaɪə(r)/ n (in printing) (4 sheets) cahier m; (24 or 25 sheets) main f

quirk /kwɜːk/ n (of person) excentricité f; (of fate, nature) caprice m

quisling /ˈkwɪzlɪŋ/ n péj collaborateur/-trice m/f pej

quit /kwɪt/
A vtr **1** (p prés **-tt-**; prét, pp **quit** ou **quitted**) (leave) démissionner de, laisser tomber○ [job]; quitter [place, person, profession]; **2** Comput quitter [application, program]
B vi (p prés **-tt-**; prét, pp **quit** ou **quitted**) **1** (give up) arrêter; **to ~ whilst one is ahead** pen s'arrêter avant que les choses se gâtent; (in career) partir au summum de la gloire; **2** (resign) [person] démissionner; **3** Comput quitter, sortir d'une application

quite /kwaɪt/ adv **1** (completely) [new, ready, understand] tout à fait; [alone, empty, exhausted, ridiculous] complètement; [impossible] totalement; [justified] entièrement; [extraordinary] vraiment; **I ~ agree** je suis tout à fait d'accord; **you're ~ right** vous avez entièrement raison; **it's ~ all right** (in reply to apology) c'est sans importance; **it's ~ out of the question** il n'en est pas du tout question; **I can ~ believe it** je veux bien le croire; **are you ~ sure?** en êtes-vous certain?; **to be ~ aware that** être tout à fait conscient du fait que; **~ clearly** [see] très clairement; **it's ~ clear** c'est parfaitement clair; **and ~ right too!** à juste titre!; **that's ~ enough!** ça suffit!; **2** (exactly) **not ~** pas exactement; **not ~ so much** un petit peu moins; **not ~ as many** pas tout à fait autant; **I don't ~ know** je ne sais pas du tout; **nobody knew ~ what he meant** personne ne savait exactement ce qu'il voulait dire; **that's not ~ all** (giving account of sth) et ce n'est pas tout; **3** (definitely) **it was ~ the best answer** c'était de loin la meilleure réponse; **he's ~ the stupidest man!** il est vraiment stupide!; **~ simply** tout simplement; **4** (rather) [big, easily, often] assez; **it's ~ small** ce n'est pas très grand; **it's ~ warm today** il fait bon aujourd'hui; **it's ~ likely that** il est très probable que; **I ~ like Chinese food** j'aime assez la cuisine chinoise; **~ a few** un bon nombre de [people, examples]; **~ a lot of money** pas mal d'argent; **~ a lot of opposition** une opposition assez forte; **I've thought about it** ～ **a bit** j'y ai pas mal réfléchi; **5** (as intensifier) ～ **a difference** une différence considérable; **that will be** ～ **a change for you** ça va te faire un grand changement; **she's** ～ **a woman!** quelle femme!; **to be** ～ **something** [*house, car*] valoir le coup d'œil○; **6** (expressing agreement) ～ **(so)** c'est sûr

quits○ /kwɪts/ *adj* **to be** ～ être quitte (**with sb** envers qn); **to call it** ～ en rester là

quiver /'kwɪvə(r)/
A *n* **1** (trembling) (of voice, part of body) tremblement *m*; (of leaves) frémissement *m*; (of excitement) frémissement *m*; **2** (for arrows) carquois *m*
B *vi* [*voice, lip, animal*] trembler (**with** de); [*leaves*] frémir; [*wings*] battre; [*flame*] vaciller

quixotic /kwɪk'sɒtɪk/ *adj* (unrealistic) chimérique

quiz /kwɪz/
A *n* (*pl* ～**zes**) **1** (game) jeu *m* de questions-réponses, quiz *m*; (written, in magazine) questionnaire *m* (**about** sur); **2** US Sch interrogation *f*
B *vtr* (*p prés etc* **-zz-**) questionner (**about** au sujet de)

quiz game, **quiz show** *n* jeu *m* de questions-réponses

quizzical /'kwɪzɪkl/ *adj* interrogateur/-trice

quoit /kɔɪt, US kwɔɪt/ *n* palet *m*

quorum /'kwɔːrəm/ *n* quorum *m*; **the** ～ **is ten** le quorum est fixé à dix; **to have a** ～ avoir atteint le quorum

quota /'kwəʊtə/ *n* **1** gen, Comm (prescribed number) quota *m* (**of, for** de); **this year's** ～ le quota fixé pour cette année; **2** (share) part *f* (**of** de); (officially allocated) quote-part *f*

quotation /kwəʊ'teɪʃn/ *n* **1** (phrase, passage cited) citation *f*; **2** (estimate) devis *m*; **3** Fin cours *m*, cote *f*

quotation marks *npl* guillemets *mpl*; **in** ～ entre guillemets

quote /kwəʊt/
A *n* **1** (quotation) citation *f* (**from** de); **2** (statement to journalist) déclaration *f*; **3** (estimate) devis *m*; **4** Fin cote *f*
B **quotes** *npl* = **quotation marks**
C *vtr* **1** (repeat, recall) citer [*person, passage, proverb*]; rapporter [*words*]; rappeler [*reference number*]; **don't** ～ **me on this, but...** ne répète pas ce que je dis, mais...; **she was** ～**d as saying that...** elle aurait dit que...; **2** Comm (state) indiquer [*price, figure*]; **they** ～**d us £200** dans leur devis, ils ont demandé £200; **3** (on stock exchange) coter [*share, price*] (**at** à); ～**d company** société *f* cotée en Bourse; **4** (in betting) **to** ～ **odds of** proposer une cote de; **to be** ～**d 6 to 1** être coté entre 6 et 1
D *vi* (from text, author) faire des citations; **to** ～ **from Keats** citer Keats; ～ **... unquote** (in dictation) ouvrez les guillemets ... fermez les guillemets; (in lecture, speech) je cite ... fin de citation; **on** ～ **'business' unquote** soi-disant pour affaires

quotient /'kwəʊʃnt/ *n* **1** Math quotient *m*; **2** gen niveau *m*

q

Rr

r, R /ɑ:(r)/ n **1** (letter) r, R m; **the three R's** l'écriture, la lecture et le calcul; **2** R abrév écrite = **right**; **3** R GB abrév = **Regina**

rabbi /'ræbaɪ/ n rabbin m

rabbit /'ræbɪt/ n (male) lapin m; (female) lapine f; (fur, meat) lapin m; **wild ~** lapin de garenne

(Idiom) **to pull a ~ out of a hat** fig faire un coup de théâtre

(Phrasal verb)
■ **rabbit on**○ GB parler sans cesse (**about** de)

Rabbit® /'ræbɪt/ pr n Telecom ≈ Bibop® m

rabbit: **~ burrow**, **~ hole** n terrier m de lapin; **~ hutch** n clapier m; **~ warren** n lit garenne f; fig (maze) labyrinthe m

rabble /'ræbl/ n péj (crowd) foule f; (populace) **the ~** la populace péj; **~-rousing** incitation f à la violence

rabid /'ræbɪd, US 'reɪbɪd/ adj **1** (with rabies) enragé; **2** (fanatical) fanatique

rabies /'reɪbi:z/ ▸ p. 933
A n rage f
B noun modifier [injection, legislation] antirabique; [virus] de la rage

RAC n GB (abrév = **Royal Automobile Club**) organisme m d'assistance pour les automobilistes

raccoon /rə'ku:n, US ræ-/ n (pl ~**s** ou ~) raton m laveur

race /reɪs/
A n **1** Sport course f; **to have a ~** faire la course; **to run a ~** courir (**with** contre); **boat ~** course nautique; **a ~ against the clock** ou **against time** lit, fig une course contre la montre; **2** fig (contest) course f (**for** à; **to do** pour faire); **the ~ to reach the moon** la course à la lune; **presidential ~** course à la présidence; **3** Sociol race f; **4** Bot, Zool espèce f
B noun modifier [attack, equality, law] racial
C vtr **1** (compete with) faire la course avec [person, car, horse] (**to** jusqu'à); **2** (enter for race) faire courir [horse, dog]; courir en [car, boat]; courir sur [Formula One]; faire voler [qch] en compétition [pigeon]; **3** (rev) faire ronfler [engine]
D vi **1** (compete in race) courir (**at** à; **to** vers; **for** pour atteindre); **to ~ around the track** faire le tour de la piste; **2** (rush) **to ~ in/away** entrer/partir en courant; **to ~ after sb/sth** courir après qn/qch; **to ~ through** faire [qch] rapidement [task]; **3** [pulse] battre précipitamment; [engine] s'emballer; **my mind started to ~** je me suis mis à imaginer toutes sortes de choses; **4** (hurry) se dépêcher (**to do** de faire)

(Phrasal verb)
■ **race by** [time, person] passer à toute allure

race: **~ card** n programme m des courses; **~goer** n turfiste mf; **~horse** n cheval m de course; **~ meeting** n GB réunion f de courses

racer /'reɪsə(r)/ n (bike) vélo m de course; (motorbike) moto f de course; (car) voiture f de course; (runner, cyclist etc) coureur/-euse m/f

race: **~ relations** npl relations fpl inter-raciales; **~track** n (for horses) champ m de courses; (for cars) circuit m; (for dogs, cycles) piste f; **~way** n US (for cars) circuit m; (for dogs, harness racing) piste f

racial /'reɪʃl/ adj (all contexts) racial

racialist /'reɪʃəlɪst/ n, adj raciste (mf)

racing /'reɪsɪŋ/
A n **1** (for horses) hippisme m; **did you see the ~?** as-tu vu les courses (de chevaux)?; **2** (with vehicle, dogs) course f
B noun modifier [car, yacht] de course; [fan, commentator] des courses; [stable] de courses

racing: **~ cyclist** n coureur/-euse m/f cycliste; **~ driver** n coureur/-euse m/f automobile; **~ pigeon** n pigeon m de compétition

racist /'reɪsɪst/ n, adj raciste (mf)

rack /ræk/
A n **1** (for plates) égouttoir m; (in dishwasher) panier m; (on train) compartiment m à bagages; (for clothes) portant m; (for cakes) grille f (à gâteau); (for bottles) casier m; (for newspapers) porte-revues m inv; (shelving) étagère f; ▸ **roof rack**; **2** (torture) chevalet m; **3** Culin **~ of lamb** carré m d'agneau
B vtr fig (torment) [pain, guilt, fear] torturer

(Idiom) **to ~ one's brains** se creuser la cervelle○; ▸ **ruin**

racket /'rækɪt/ n **1** Sport raquette f; **2** ○(noise) vacarme m, raffut○ m; **to make a ~** faire du vacarme, faire du raffut○; **3** (swindle) escroquerie f; **4** (illegal activity) trafic m; **in on the ~**○ dans le coup○

racketeering /,rækə'tɪərɪŋ/ n racket m

racking /'rækɪŋ/ adj [pain] atroce; [sobs] déchirant

racoon n = raccoon

racquet n = racket 1

racquetball /'rækɪtbɔ:l/ ▸ p. 881 n US ≈ squash m

racy /'reɪsɪ/ adj [account, style] plein de verve; (risqué) osé

radar /'reɪdɑ:(r)/ n, noun modifier radar (m)

radar trap n contrôle-radar m inv; **to get caught in a ~** se faire piéger par un radar

raddled /'rædld/ adj [features] marqué par la vie

radial /'reɪdɪəl/
A n (also **~ tyre**) pneu m radial
B adj [lines, roads] rayonnant

radiance /'reɪdɪəns/, **radiancy** /'reɪdɪənsɪ/ n lit, fig éclat m

radiant /'reɪdɪənt/
A n **1** (on electric fire) résistance f chauffante; **2** (of meteors) point m radiant
B adj **1** fig [person, beauty, smile] radieux/-ieuse; **~ with** rayonnant de [joy, health]; **2** (shining) éclatant; **3** Phys radiant

radiantly /'reɪdɪəntlɪ/ adv [shine] d'un vif éclat; [smile] d'un air radieux

radiate /'reɪdɪeɪt/
A vtr **1** rayonner de [health, happiness]; déborder de [confidence]; **2** Phys émettre [heat]
B vi **1** **to ~ from** [confidence, happiness] émaner de; [roads] rayonner (à partir) de; **2** Phys [heat] rayonner; [light] irradier

radiation /,reɪdɪ'eɪʃn/
A n **1** (medical, nuclear) radiation f; (rays) radiations fpl; **a low level of ~** un faible niveau de radiations; **2** Phys rayonnement m
B noun modifier [levels] de radiation; [effects] des radiations; [leak] de radiations

radiation: **~ exposure** n irradiation f; **~ sickness** n maladie f des rayons; **~ therapy** n radiothérapie f

radiator /'reɪdɪeɪtə(r)/ n gen, Aut radiateur m; **to turn up/down a ~** monter/baisser le chauffage

radical /'rædɪkl/ n, adj (all contexts) radical/-e (m/f)

radii /'reɪdɪaɪ/ pl ▸ **radius**

radio /'reɪdɪəʊ/
A n (pl ~**s**) **1** Audio radio f; **she was on the ~ this morning**

elle est passée à la radio ce matin; **2** Telecom radio *f*

B *noun modifier* [*contact, equipment, link, operator, signal*] radio *inv*; [*mast, programme*] de radio

C *vtr* (3ᵉ *pers sg prés* ~**s**; *prét, pp* ~**ed**) **to ~ sb for sth** appeler qn par radio pour demander qch; **to ~ sth (to sb)** communiquer qch par radio (à qn)

D *vi* (3ᵉ *pers sg prés* ~**s**; *prét, pp* ~**ed**) **to ~ for help** appeler au secours par radio

radio: ~**active** *adj* radioactif/-ive; ~ **alarm (clock)** *n* radio-réveil *m*; ~ **announcer** *n* speaker/-erine *m/f*; ~ **broadcast** *n* émission *f* de radio, émission *f* radiophonique; ~ **cab** *n* radio-taxi *m*; ~ **car** *n* voiture-radio *f*; ~**carbon dating** *n* datation *f* au carbone quatorze; ~ **cassette (recorder)** *n* radiocassette *f*; ~ **communication** *n* contact *m* radio *inv*; ~**controlled** *adj* [*toy, boat*] télécommandé; [*taxi*] radioguidé; ~ **frequency** *n* radiofréquence *f*

radiographer /ˌreɪdɪˈɒɡrəfə(r)/ ▸ p. 1181 *n* manipulateur/-trice *m/f* radiographe

radiography /ˌreɪdɪˈɒɡrəfɪ/ *n* radiographie *f*

radio: ~ **ham**○ *n* radio-amateur *m*; ~ **interview** *n* entretien *m* radiophonique

radiologist /ˌreɪdɪˈɒlədʒɪst/ ▸ p. 1181 *n* radiologue *mf*

radio: ~ **microphone**, ~ **mike**○ *n* micro *m* sans fil; ~ **station** *n* (channel) station *f* de radio; (installation) station *f* émettrice; ~**telephone** *n* radiotéléphone *m*; ~**therapy** *n* radiothérapie *f*

radish /ˈrædɪʃ/ *n* radis *m*

radius /ˈreɪdɪəs/ *n* (*pl* -**dii** *ou* -**diuses**) **1** gen, Math rayon *m*; **within a 10 km ~ of here** dans un rayon de 10 km; **2** Anat radius *m*

RAF *n* GB Mil *abrév* ▸ **Royal Air Force**

raffish /ˈræfɪʃ/ *adj* libertin

raffle /ˈræfl/
A *n* tombola *f*; **in a ~** à une tombola
B *vtr* (*also* ~ **off**) mettre [qch] en tombola

raft /rɑːft, US ræft/ *n* radeau *m*

rafter /ˈrɑːftə(r), US ˈræftə(r)/ *n* Constr chevron *m*

rag /ræg/
A *n* **1** (cloth) chiffon *m*; **a bit of ~** un chiffon; **2** ○(local newspaper) canard○ *m*
B **rags** *npl* (old clothes) loques *fpl*
C ○*vtr* (*p prés etc* -**gg**-) taquiner

◯(Idioms) **it's like a red ~ to a bull** ça a le don de l'exciter; **to go from ~s to riches** connaître une ascension spectaculaire; **to lose one's ~**○ GB sortir de ses gonds○

ragamuffin† /ˈræɡəmʌfɪn/ *n* va-nu-pieds *mf inv*

rag: ~**-and-bone man†** *n* GB chiffonnier *m*; ~**bag** *n* fig ramassis *m*

rage /reɪdʒ/
A *n* **1** (anger) rage *f*, colère *f*; **to fly into a ~** entrer dans une colère noire; **2** ○(fashion) **to be (all) the ~** faire fureur
B *vi* **1** [*storm, battle*] faire rage; [*controversy*] se déchaîner (**over, about** à propos de); **2** [*person*] tempêter (**at, against** contre); **3** ○(party) faire la fête

ragged /ˈræɡɪd/ *adj* **1** [*garment*] en loques; [*cuff, collar*] effiloché; [*person*] dépenaillé; **2** (uneven) irrégulier/-ière *m*; **3** (motley) [*group*] disparate; **4** (in quality) [*performance*] inégal

◯(Idiom) **to run sb ~**○ épuiser qn

raging /ˈreɪdʒɪŋ/ *adj* **1** [*passion, argument*] violent; [*thirst, pain*] atroce; **a ~ toothache** une rage de dents; **2** [*blizzard, sea*] déchaîné; **there was a ~ storm** la tempête faisait rage

ragtag○ /ˈræɡtæɡ/ *adj péj* [*group*] désordonné

◯(Idiom) **the ~ and bobtail**○ la canaille

rag trade○ *n* **the ~** la confection

rag week *n* GB Univ semaine *f* du carnaval étudiant (*au profit d'institutions caritatives*)

raid /reɪd/
A *n* Mil, Fin raid *m* (**on** sur); (on bank) hold-up *m* (**on** de); (on home) cambriolage *m* (**on** de, dans); (by police, customs) rafle *f* (**on** dans)
B *vtr* **1** (attack) [*military*] faire un raid sur; attaquer [*bank*]; cambrioler [*house*]; [*police*] faire une rafle dans; **2** fig casser [*piggybank*]; faire une razzia○ sur [*fridge*]; **3** Fin [*company*] entamer [*reserves*]

---

raider /ˈreɪdə(r)/ *n* (thief) pillard *m*; (corporate) raider *m*; (soldier) (membre *m* d'un) commando *m*

rail /reɪl/
A *n* **1** (in fence) barreau *m*; (on balcony) balustrade *f*; (on tower) garde-fou *m*; (handrail) rampe *f*; (on ship) bastingage *m*; **2** (for display) (in shop) présentoir *m*; **3** (for curtains) tringle *f*; **4** (for vehicle) rail *m*; fig **to go off the ~s** dérailler○
B **rails** *npl* (on racetrack) corde *f*; **to come up on the ~s** tenir la corde
C *noun modifier* [*network, traffic, transport*] ferroviaire; [*journey, travel*] en train; ~ **strike** grève *f* des cheminots

rail: ~**car** *n* autorail *m*; ~**card** *n* GB carte *f* d'abonnement; ~**head** *n* tête *f* de ligne

railing /ˈreɪlɪŋ/ *n* **1** (*also* ~**s**) (in park, stadium) grille *f*; **2** (on wall) main courante *f*; (on tower) garde-fou *m*; (on balcony) balustrade *f*

railroad /ˈreɪlrəʊd/
A *n* US Rail **1** (network) chemin *m* de fer; **2** (*also* ~ **track**) voie *f* ferrée; **3** (company) compagnie *f* des chemins de fer
B ○*vtr* (push) **to ~ sb into doing** forcer qn à faire; **to ~ the bill through** tout faire pour faire adopter le projet de loi

railroad car *n* US wagon *m*

railway /ˈreɪlweɪ/ GB Rail
A *n* **1** (network) chemin *m* de fer; **to use the ~s** voyager en train; **2** (*also* ~ **line**) ligne *f*; **light ~** ligne locale; **3** (line) voie *f* ferrée; **4** (company) compagnie *f* des chemins de fer
B *noun modifier* [*bridge*] de chemin de fer; [*museum*] des chemins de fer; [*link, tunnel, accident*] ferroviaire

railway: ~ **carriage** *n* GB wagon *m*; ~ **embankment** *n* remblai *m*; ~ **engine** *n* GB locomotive *f*; ~ **junction** *n* gare *f* de raccordement; ~ **line** *n* GB (route) ligne *f* de chemin de fer; (tracks) voie *f* ferrée; ~**man** ▸ p. 1181 GB *n* cheminot *m*; ~ **station** *n* GB gare *f*

rain /reɪn/
A *n* Meteorol pluie *f*; **the ~ stopped** il s'est arrêté de pleuvoir; **steady/driving/pouring ~** pluie régulière/battante/diluvienne; **in the ~** sous la pluie; **it looks like ~** le temps est à la pluie
B **rains** *npl* saison *f* des pluies
C *vtr* **to ~ blows on sb** rouer qn de coups
D *v impers* **1** Meteorol pleuvoir; **it's ~ing (hard)** il pleut (à verse); **2** fig = **rain down**

◯(Idioms) **come ~ or shine** qu'il pleuve ou qu'il vente; **it never ~s but it pours** un malheur n'arrive jamais seul; **to be (as) right as ~** GB [*person*] se porter comme un charme

◯(Phrasal verbs)

■ **rain down** [*blows, ash, insults*] pleuvoir

■ **rain off** GB, **rain out** US: **to be ~ed off** (cancelled) être annulé pour cause de pluie; (stopped) être interrompu par la pluie

rainbow /ˈreɪnbəʊ/ *n* lit, fig arc-en-ciel *m*

◯(Idiom) **at the ~'s end** du domaine du rêve

rainbow coalition *n* Pol coalition *f* arc-en-ciel

rain check *n* US Sport *billet pour un autre match si le premier est annulé pour cause de pluie*

◯(Idiom) **to take a ~ on sth** reporter qch

rain: ~**coat** *n* imperméable *m*; ~**drop** *n* goutte *f* de pluie

rainfall /ˈreɪnfɔːl/ *n* niveau *m* de précipitations; **heavy/low ~** fortes/faibles précipitations

rain: ~ **forest** *n* forêt *f* tropicale; ~**storm** *n* trombe *f* d'eau

rainy /ˈreɪnɪ/ *adj* [*afternoon, climate*] pluvieux/-ieuse; ~ **season** saison *f* des pluies

◯(Idiom) **to keep** *ou* **save something for a ~ day** mettre de l'argent de côté

raise /reɪz/
A *n* **1** US (pay rise) augmentation *f*; **2** Games (in poker) mise *f* supérieure
B *vtr* **1** (lift) lever [*baton, barrier, curtain*]; hisser [*flag*]; soulever [*box, lid*]; élever [*standard*]; renflouer [*sunken ship*]; **to ~ one's hand/head** lever la main/tête; **he ~d the glass to his lips** il a porté le verre à ses lèvres; **to ~ a glass to sb** lever son verre à l'honneur de qn; **I've never ~d a hand to my children** je n'ai jamais levé la main sur mes enfants;

nobody ∼d an eyebrow at my suggestion fig ma sugges-tion n'a fait sourciller personne; **2** (place upright) dresser [*mast*]; redresser [*patient*]; **3** (increase) augmenter [*price, offer, salary, volume*] (**from** de; **to** à); élever [*standard*]; reculer [*age limit*]; **to raise sb's awareness of** sensibiliser qn à; **to ∼ one's voice** (to be heard) parler plus fort; (in anger) élever la voix; **to ∼ the temperature** lit, fig faire monter la tempéra-ture; **4** (cause) faire naître [*doubts, fears*]; soulever [*dust*]; provoquer [*protests*]; **to ∼ a cheer** [*speech*] déclencher des hourras; **to ∼ a smile** [*joke*] faire sourire; **5** (mention) sou-lever; **6** (bring up) élever [*child, family*]; **to be ∼d (as) a Catholic** être élevé dans la religion catholique; **7** (breed) élever [*livestock*]; **8** (find) trouver [*capital*]; **9** (form) lever [*army*]; former [*team*]; **10** (collect) lever [*tax*]; obtenir [*sup-port*]; [*person*] collecter [*money*]; **the money ∼d from the concert** la recette du concert; **11** (erect) élever [*monument*] (**to sb** en l'honneur de qn); **12** (end) lever [*ban*]; **13** (con-tact) contacter [*person*]; **14** (give) **to ∼ the alarm** fig donner l'alarme; **15** (improve) **to ∼ the tone** hausser le ton; **to ∼ sb's spirits** remonter le moral à qn; **16** (increase the stake) **I'll ∼ you 200 dollars!** 200 dollars de mieux!; **to ∼ the bidding** (in gambling) monter la mise; (at auction) monter l'enchère; **17** Math élever [*number*]

C *v refl* **to ∼ oneself** se redresser

raised /reɪzd/ *adj* [*platform, jetty*] surélevé; **I heard ∼ voices** j'ai entendu des éclats de voix

raisin /'reɪzn/ *n* raisin *m* sec

Raj /rɑːdʒ/ *n* GB Hist empire *m* britannique aux Indes

rake /reɪk/

A *n* **1** (tool) râteau *m*; (in casino) râteau *m* de croupier; **2** †(liber-tine) débauché *m*

B *vtr* **1** (in gardening) ratisser; **2** (scan) balayer

C *vi* **to ∼ among** *ou* **through** fouiller dans

(Phrasal verbs)

■ **rake in**○: ▸ **∼ in [sth]** amasser [*money*]; **he's raking it in**○! il brasse l'argent à la pelle○!

■ **rake over**: ▸ **∼ over [sth]** ratisser [*soil*]

■ **rake up**: ▸ **∼ up [sth], ∼ [sth] up 1** lit ramasser [qch] avec un râteau [*leaves*]; **2** fig ressusciter [*grievance*]; remuer [*past*]

rake-off○ /'reɪkɒf/ *n* (legal) commission *f*; (illicit) ristourne *f* illicite

rakish /'reɪkɪʃ/ *adj* **1** †(dissolute) débauché; **2** (jaunty) désinvolte

rally /'rælɪ/

A *n* **1** (meeting) rassemblement *m*; **2** (race) rallye *m*; **3** (in tennis) échange *m*; **4** (recovery) gen amélioration *f* (**in** dans); Fin reprise *f*

B *vtr* rassembler [*support, troops*]; rallier [*opinion*]

C *vi* **1** (come together) [*people*] se rallier (**to** à); **to ∼ to the defence of sb** se porter au secours de qn; **2** (recover) [*dollar*] remonter; [*patient*] se rétablir; [*sportsperson*] se res-saisir

(Phrasal verb)

■ **rally round, rally around**: ▸ **∼ round** [*supporters*] se rallier; ▸ **∼ round [sb]** soutenir [*person*]

rallying: **∼ call, ∼ cry** *n* lit, fig cri *m* de ralliement; **∼ point** *n* lit, fig point *m* de ralliement

ram /ræm/

A *n* bélier *m*

B *vtr* (*p prés etc* **-mm-**) **1** (crash into) rentrer dans, heurter; **2** (push) enfoncer; **∼med home** enfoncé

C *vi* (*p prés etc* **-mm-**) **to ∼ into sth** [*vehicle*] rentrer dans qch, heurter qch

(Phrasal verb)

■ **ram home**: ▸ **∼ [sth] home, ∼ home [sth]** lit placer [*ball, fist*]; fig faire clairement comprendre [*message, point*]

RAM /ræm/ *n* (*abrév* = **random access memory**) RAM *f*

ramble /'ræmbl/

A *n* randonnée *f*, balade *f*

B *vi* (walk) faire une randonnée, faire une balade

(Phrasal verb)

■ **ramble on** discourir (**about** sur)

rambler /'ræmblə(r)/ *n* randonneur/-euse *m/f*

rambling /'ræmblɪŋ/

A *n* randonnée *f*

B *adj* **1** [*house*] plein de coins et de recoins; **2** [*talk, article*] décousu; **3** [*plant*] grimpant

ramification /ˌræmɪfɪ'keɪʃn/ *n* ramification *f*

ramify /'ræmɪfaɪ/ *vi* se ramifier

ramp /ræmp/ *n* gen rampe *f*; GB (in roadworks) dénivellation *f*; Aut, Tech pont *m* de graissage; Aviat passerelle *f*; US Aut (on, off highway) bretelle *f*; **hydraulic ∼** pont *m* élévateur

rampage

A /'ræmpeɪdʒ/ *n* **to be** *ou* **go on the ∼** tout saccager

B /ræm'peɪdʒ/ *vi* se déchaîner (**through** dans)

rampant /'ræmpənt/ *adj* [*crime, disease*] endémique

rampart /'ræmpɑːt/ *n* lit, fig rempart *m*

ramshackle /'ræmʃækl/ *adj* lit, fig délabré

ran /ræn/ *prét* ▸ **run**

ranch /rɑːntʃ, US ræntʃ/ *n* ranch *m*

rancher /'rɑːntʃə(r), US 'ræntʃə(r)/ *n* propriétaire *mf* de ranch

rancid /'rænsɪd/ *adj* rance; **to go ∼** rancir

rancorous /'ræŋkərəs/ *adj* rancunier/-ière

rancour GB, **rancor** US /'ræŋkə(r)/ *n* rancœur *f*

rand /rænd/ ▸ p. 782 *n* rand *m*

random /'rændəm/ *adj* (fait) au hasard

rang /ræŋ/ *prét* ▸ **ring**

range /reɪndʒ/

A *n* **1** (choice) (of prices, products) gamme *f*; (of activities, options) éventail *m*, choix *m*; (of people, abilities, beliefs, emotions) variété *f*; (of benefits, salaries) éventail *m*; (of issues, assumptions) série *f*; **a top of the ∼ computer** un ordinateur haut de gamme; **age ∼** tranche *f* d'âge; **price/salary ∼** éventail de prix/des salaires; **in the £50–£100 ∼** entre 50 et 100 livres sterling; **to have a wide ∼ of interests** s'intéresser à beaucoup de choses; **a wide ∼ of views** des vues très diverses; **2** (scope) (of influence, knowledge) étendue *f*; (of investigation, research) domaine *m*; **3** (of radar, weapon, transmitter) portée *f* (**of** de); **to be out of ∼** être hors de portée; **4** Aerosp, Aut, Aviat autono-mie *f*; **5** US (prairie) prairie *f*; **on the ∼** dans les pâturages; **6** (of mountains) chaîne *f*; **7** (stove) (wood etc) fourneau *m*; (gas, electric) cuisinière *f*; **8** (firing area) (for weapons) champ *m* de tir; (for missiles) zone *f* de tir; **9** (of actor) répertoire *m*; **10** Mus tessiture *f*

B *vtr* **1** (set) opposer (**against** à); **2** (draw up) aligner, ranger [*forces*]

C *vi* **1** (extend) aller (**from** de; **to** à); (vary) varier; **to ∼ over sth** couvrir qch; **2** (roam, wander) vagabonder

ranger /'reɪndʒə(r)/ *n* **1** (in forest) garde-forestier *m*; **2** US, Mil ranger *m*

rangy /'reɪndʒɪ/ *adj* élancé

rank /ræŋk/

A *n* **1** (in military, police) grade *m*; (in company, politics) rang *m*; (social status) rang *m*; **to pull ∼** abuser de son rang; **2** (line) (of people) rang *m*; (of objects) rangée *f*; **to break ∼s** lit [*soldiers*] rompre les rangs; fig [*politician*] se rebeller; **to close ∼s** lit, fig serrer les rangs; **3** (for taxis) station *f*; **taxi ∼** station de taxis

B ranks *npl* Mil, Pol, Ind rangs *mpl*; **to rise through the ∼s** sortir du rang

C *adj* **1** (absolute) [*outsider, beginner*] complet/-ète; [*favouritism, stupidity*] flagrant; **2** (foul) [*odour*] fétide; **3** (exuberant) [*ivy, weeds*] envahissant

D *vtr* **1** (classify) [*person*] classer [*player, novel, restaurant*] (**among** parmi; **above** au-dessus de; **below** au-dessous de); **2** US (be senior to) commander [*person*]

E *vi* **1** (rate) se classer (**among** parmi); **to ∼ as a great com-poser** être considéré comme un grand compositeur; **to ∼ above/alongside sb** occuper un rang supérieur/égal à qn; **this has to ∼ as one of the worst films I've ever seen** c'est un des films les pires que j'aie jamais vus; **that doesn't ∼ very high on my list** cela ne figure pas très haut dans ma liste; **2** US Mil (be most senior) commander

rank and file /ˌræŋk ən 'faɪl/

A *n* base *f*

B rank-and-file *noun modifier* [*opinion*] de la base; [*member*] de base

ranking /'ræŋkɪŋ/

A *n* Sport classement *m*

B -ranking *combining form* **high/low-∼** de haut/bas rang

rankle /'ræŋkl/ *vi* **to ∼ with sb** rester en travers de la gorge de qn○; **but it still ∼s** mais ça laisse toujours un goût saumâtre

ransack /'rænsæk, US ræn'sæk/ *vtr* fouiller [*drawer*] (**for** pour trouver); mettre [qch] à sac [*house*]

Military ranks and titles

■ *The following list gives the principal ranks in the French services. For translations, see the individual dictionary entries.*

The Navy = La marine nationale

amiral
vice-amiral d'escadre
vice-amiral
contre-amiral
capitaine de vaisseau
capitaine de frégate
capitaine de corvette
lieutenant de vaisseau
enseigne de vaisseau (1re et 2e classe)
aspirant
major
maître principal
premier maître
maître
second maître
quartier-maître (1re et 2e classe)
matelot

The Army = L'armée de terre

général d'armée
général de corps d'armée
général de division
général de brigade
colonel
lieutenant-colonel
commandant
capitaine
lieutenant
sous-lieutenant
aspirant
major
adjudant-chef
adjudant
sergent-chef *or* maréchal des logis-chef (*cavalry*)
sergent *or* maréchal des logis (*cavalry*)
caporal-chef *or* brigadier-chef (*cavalry*)
caporal *or* brigadier (*cavalry*)
soldat *or* cavalier (*cavalry*)

The Air Force = L'armée de l'air

général d'armée aérienne
général de corps aérien
général de division aérienne
général de brigade aérienne
colonel

lieutenant-colonel
commandant
capitaine
lieutenant
sous-lieutenant
aspirant
major
adjudant-chef
adjudant
sergent-chef
sergent
caporal-chef
caporal
aviateur

Speaking about someone

he's a colonel
= il est colonel

to be promoted to colonel
= être promu colonel

he has the rank of colonel
= il a le rang de colonel

she's a lieutenant in the Army
= elle est lieutenant dans l'armée de terre

he's just a private
= il est simple soldat

Colonel Smith has arrived
= le colonel Smith est arrivé

Speaking to someone

■ *In the* armée de terre, *the* mon *is used to superior officers from* lieutenant *upwards, except for* major. Mon *is never prefixed to ranks in the* marine nationale *or the* armée de l'air *and never used to personnel of inferior rank in any of the three services.*

Service personnel to superior officers

yes, sir
= oui, mon colonel
   (*or* mon capitaine, mon lieutenant *etc.*)

yes, ma'am
= oui, colonel (*or* capitaine, lieutenant *etc.*)

Service personnel to someone of lower rank

yes, sergeant
= oui, sergent

---

ransom /ˈrænsəm/ *n* rançon *f*; **to hold sb to** GB *ou* for US ∼ lit garder qn en otage; fig tenir qn en otage
⟨Idiom⟩ **a king's** ∼ une somme fabuleuse

rant /rænt/ *vi* déclamer; **to** ∼ **and rave** tempêter (**at** contre); **to** ∼ **on** divaguer (**about** sur)

ranting /ˈræntɪŋ/ *n* (*also* ∼**s**) rodomontades *fpl*

rap /ræp/
A *n* ⓵ (tap) coup *m* sec; ⓶ Mus rap *m*; ⓷ ᴼUS (conversation) conversation *f*; ⓸ ᴼ(accusation) accusation *f*; **to beat the** ∼ s'en tirer à bon compte
B *vtr* (*p prés etc* **-pp-**) (tap) frapper sur
C *vi* (*p prés etc* **-pp-**) ⓵ (tap) donner des coups secs (**on** sur); ⓶ Mus faire du rap; ⓷ ᴼUS (talk) parler

rapacious /rəˈpeɪʃəs/ *adj* rapace

rape /reɪp/
A *n* ⓵ (attack) viol *m*; ⓶ Agric colza *m*

B *vtr* violer

rape(seed) oil *n* huile *f* de colza

rapid /ˈræpɪd/ *adj gen* rapide; **in** ∼ **succession** coup sur coup

rapid: ∼ **deployment force** *n* Mil force *f* d'intervention rapide; ∼ **eye movement, REM** *n* mouvements *mpl* oculaires rapides

rapidity /rəˈpɪdətɪ/ *n* rapidité *f*

rapidly /ˈræpɪdlɪ/ *adv* rapidement

rapids /ˈræpɪdz/ *npl* rapides *mpl*

rapid transit *n* US transport *m* public

rapist /ˈreɪpɪst/ *n* violeur *m*

rapper /ˈræpə(r)/ *n* ⓵ Mus rappeur/-euse *m/f*; ⓶ US (door-knocker) heurtoir *m*

rapport /ræ'pɔː(r), US -'pɔːrt/ n bons rapports mpl; **in ~ with** en harmonie avec

rapt /ræpt/ adj gen absorbé; [smile] extasié

rapture /'ræptʃə(r)/ n ravissement m; **to go into ~s over** ou **about sth** s'extasier sur qch

rapturous /'ræptʃərəs/ adj [delight] extasié; [welcome] enthousiaste; [applause] frénétique

rare /reə(r)/ adj **1** (uncommon) rare; **2** [steak] saignant; **3** [atmosphere, air] raréfié

rarebit /'reəbɪt/ n ▸ **Welsh rarebit**

rarefied /'reərɪfaɪd/ adj lit raréfié; fig étouffant

rarely /'reəlɪ/ adv rarement

raring /'reərɪŋ/ adj **to be ~ to do** être très impatient de faire; **to be ~ to go** piaffer d'impatience

rarity /'reərətɪ/ n **1** (collector's item) pièce f rare; **2** (rare occurrence) phénomène m rare; **to be a ~** être rare; **3** (rareness) rareté f

rascal /'rɑːskl, US 'ræskl/ n **1** (used affectionately) coquin/-e m/f; **2** †(villain) voyou m

rash /ræʃ/
A n **1** (skin) rougeurs fpl; **2** fig vague f
B adj [person, decision] irréfléchi; **it was ~ to do** il n'était pas raisonnable de faire

rasher /'ræʃə(r)/ n tranche f

rashly /'ræʃlɪ/ adv sans réfléchir

rashness /'ræʃnɪs/ n inconséquence f

rasp /rɑːsp, US ræsp/
A n **1** (of saw, voice) grincement m; **2** (file) râpe f
B vtr (rub) râper
C vi [saw] grincer
D **rasping** pres p adj [voice, sound] râpeux/-euse

raspberry /'rɑːzbrɪ, US 'ræzberɪ/
A n **1** (fruit) framboise f; **2** (noise) **to blow a ~** faire un bruit de dérision
B noun modifier [ice cream, tart] à la framboise; [jam] de framboise

Rastafarian /ˌræstə'feərɪən/ n rasta mf, rastafari mf

rat /ræt/
A n **1** Zool rat m; **2** ○(person) **you ~!** canaille○!; **3** US (informer) mouchard/-e○ m/f
B ○vi (p prés etc **-tt-**) **~ on** moucharder○, dénoncer [person]; se dédire de [deal]
C **rats** excl mince alors○!

(Idioms) **to look like a drowned ~** être trempé comme une soupe○; **to smell a ~** flairer quelque chose de louche

ratcatcher /'rætkætʃə(r)/ n Hist chasseur m de rats

ratchet /'rætʃɪt/ n (toothed rack) crémaillère f

rate /reɪt/
A n **1** (speed) rythme m; **at this ~** ou **at the ~ we're going we'll never be able to afford a car** fig à ce train-là nous n'aurons jamais les moyens d'acheter une voiture; **at a terrific ~** à toute vitesse; **2** (level) taux m; **the interest ~** le taux d'intérêt; **3** (charge) tarif m; **at a reduced ~** à tarif réduit; **hourly ~** salaire m horaire; **4** (in foreign exchange) cours m
B **rates** npl GB (taxation) impôts mpl locaux; **business ~s** ≈ taxe f professionnelle
C vtr **1** (classify) **I ~ his new novel very highly** j'admire beaucoup son nouveau roman; **how do you ~ this restaurant?** que pensez-vous de ce restaurant?; **to ~ sb as a great composer** considérer qn comme un grand compositeur; **to ~ sb among** classer qn parmi; **highly ~d** très coté; **2** (deserve) mériter [medal, round of applause]; **3** (value) estimer [honesty, friendship, person]
D vi (rank) **she ~s among the best sopranos in Europe** elle compte parmi les meilleures sopranos européennes
E v refl **how do you ~ yourself as a driver?** comment vous jugez-vous en tant que conducteur?; **she doesn't ~ herself very highly** elle n'a pas une très haute opinion d'elle-même

(Idiom) **at any ~** en tout cas

rateable GB, **ratable** US /'reɪtəbl/ adj [property] imposable; **~ value** valeur f locative imposable

rate-cap /'reɪtkæp/ vtr (p prés etc **-pp-**) GB Pol, Econ imposer un plafond aux impôts locaux

rate: **~-capping** n GB plafonnement m des impôts locaux; **~payer** n GB contribuable mf

rather /'rɑːðə(r)/ adv **1** (somewhat) plutôt; **I ~ like him** je le trouve plutôt sympathique; **it's ~ like an apple** ça ressemble un peu à une pomme; **it's ~ a pity** c'est assez dommage; **it's ~ too/more difficult** c'est un peu trop/plus difficile; **2** (preferably) **~ than sth/do** plutôt que qch/de faire; **I would (much) ~ do** je préférerais (de loin) faire **(than do** que faire); **I'd ~ die!** plutôt mourir!; **I'd ~ not** j'aimerais mieux pas; **3** (more exactly) plutôt; **a tree, or ~ a bush** un arbre, ou plutôt un buisson; **practical ~ than decorative** pratique plutôt que décoratif

ratification /ˌrætɪfɪ'keɪʃn/ n ratification f

ratify /'rætɪfaɪ/ vtr ratifier

rating /'reɪtɪŋ/
A n **1** (score) cote f; **2** Fin (status) cote f; **share ~** cote f en Bourse; **3** GB (in taxation) (valuation) valeur f imposable; **4** Mil Naut ≈ matelot m
B **ratings** npl TV Radio indice m d'écoute, audimat® m

rating system n GB répartition f des impôts locaux

ratio /'reɪʃɪəʊ/ n gen proportion f, rapport m; Math raison f; **the pupil to teacher ~** le nombre d'élèves par enseignant; **the ~ of men to women is two to five** la proportion d'hommes est de deux pour cinq femmes; **in** ou **by a ~ of 60:40** dans une proportion de 60 à 40

ration /'ræʃn/
A n lit ration f; fig (of problems) compte m
B noun modifier [book, card] de rationnement
C vtr rationner [food etc] (**to** à); limiter la ration de [person] (**to** à)

rational /'ræʃənl/ adj [approach, argument] rationnel/-elle; [person] sensé; **it is ~ to do** il est logique de faire; **~ being** être m doué de raison

rationale /ˌræʃə'nɑːl, US -'næl/ n (sans pl) **1** (reasons) raisons fpl (**for** pour; **for doing** de faire); **2** (logic) logique f **(behind** de)

rationalist /'ræʃnəlɪst/ n, adj rationaliste (mf)

rationalization /ˌræʃnəlaɪ'zeɪʃn/ n **1** (justification) justification f (**for** de); **2** GB, Econ rationalisation f

rationalize /'ræʃnəlaɪz/ vtr **1** (justify) justifier; **2** GB Econ rationaliser

rationally /'ræʃnəlɪ/ adv rationnellement

rationing /'ræʃnɪŋ/ n rationnement m

rat: **~ pack**○ n paparazzis mpl; **~ poison** n mort-aux-rats f inv; **~ race** n péj foire f d'empoigne; **~-run** n GB Aut petite rue servant de raccourci

rattan /ræ'tæn/ n (tree, material) rotin m

rat-tat-tat /ˌrættæt'tæt/ n toc-toc m

rattle /'rætl/
A n **1** (noise) (of bottles, cutlery, chains) cliquetis m; (of window, engine) vibration f; (of car bodywork) bruit m de ferraille; (of rattlesnake) bruit m de crécelle; (of gun) crépitement m; **2** (of baby) hochet m; (of sports fan) crécelle f; **3** (snake's tail) cascabelle f
B vtr **1** (shake) [person] faire s'entrechoquer [bottles, cutlery, chains]; [wind] faire vibrer [window]; [person] s'acharner sur [handle]; **2** ○(annoy) énerver [person]
C vi [bottles, cutlery, chains] s'entrechoquer; [window] vibrer; **the car ~d along** la voiture avançait dans un bruit de ferraille

(Idiom) **to shake sb until his/her etc teeth ~** secouer qn comme un prunier

rattlesnake /'rætlsneɪk/ n serpent m à sonnette, crotale m

rattling /'rætlɪŋ/
A n = **rattle A 1**
B adj (vibrating) [chain, window] bruyant

rat trap n piège m à rats, ratière f

ratty○ /'rætɪ/ adj **1** GB (grumpy) grincheux/-euse; **2** US (shabby) miteux/-euse; **3** US (tangled) [hair] emmêlé

raucous /'rɔːkəs/ adj [laugh] éraillé; [person] bruyant

raucously /'rɔːkəslɪ/ adv [call] d'une voix éraillée

raunchy○ /'rɔːntʃɪ/ adj **1** (earthy) [performer, voice, song] torride; **2** US (bawdy) paillard

ravage /'rævɪdʒ/
A **ravages** npl ravages mpl (**of** de)
B vtr ravager

rave /reɪv/
A ○n GB (party) bringue○ f (branchée○)
B ○adj **a ~ review** une critique dithyrambique

C vi (enthusiastically) s'emballer (**about** au sujet de); (angrily) tempêter; (when fevered) délirer

raven /'reɪvn/ n grand corbeau m

raven-haired /ˌreɪvn'heəd/ adj aux cheveux de jais

ravenous /'rævənəs/ adj [animal] vorace; [appetite] féroce; **to be ~** avoir une faim de loup

ravenously /'rævənəslɪ/ adv avec voracité

rave-up○ /'reɪvʌp/ n GB fête f

ravine /rə'viːn/ n ravin m

raving /'reɪvɪŋ/
A ravings npl divagations fpl
B adj **1** (fanatical) enragé; **a ~ lunatic** un fou furieux/une folle furieuse; **2** (tremendous) [success] éclatant
(Idiom) **(stark) ~ mad**○ complètement fou

ravioli /ˌrævɪ'əʊlɪ/ n ravioli mpl

ravish /'rævɪʃ/ vtr littér (delight) ravir

ravishing /'rævɪʃɪŋ/ adj ravissant

raw /rɔː/ adj **1** [food] cru; [rubber, sugar] brut; [data] brut; [sewage] non traité; **2** (without skin) [patch] à vif; **3** (cold) [weather] froid et humide; [air] cru; [wind] pénétrant; **4** (inexperienced) inexpérimenté; **5** (realistic) [description] cru; **6** (undisguised) [emotion] à l'état brut; [energy] sauvage; **7** US (vulgar) obscène
(Idioms) **in the ~**○ GB (naked) nu; **life in the ~** la vie dans le vif; **to give sb a ~ deal**○ traiter qn de façon injuste; **to touch a ~ nerve** toucher un point sensible

raw: ~hide n (leather) cuir m brut; **~ material** n lit, fig matière f première

ray /reɪ/ n **1** (beam) rayon m; **~ gun** pistolet m à rayons; **a ~ of** fig une lueur de [hope etc]; **2** (fish) raie f

rayon /'reɪɒn/ n rayonne f

raze /reɪz/ vtr raser

razor /'reɪzə(r)/ n rasoir m
(Idiom) **to live on a ~('s) edge** être au bord de l'abîme

razor: ~ blade n lame f de rasoir; **~ burn** n feu m du rasoir; **~-sharp** adj lit tranchant comme un rasoir; fig acéré; **~ wire** n feuillard m

razzle○ /'ræzl/ n GB **to go on the ~**○ faire la fête○

razzledazzle /ˌræzl'dæzl/ n éclat m (trompeur)

razzmatazz○ /ˌræzmə'tæz/ n folklore○ m, cirque○ m

R & B n (abrév = **rhythm and blues**) rhythm and blues m

RC n, adj: abrév ▸ **Roman Catholic**

Rd n: abrév écrite = **road**

R&D n: abrév ▸ **research and development**

RDA n (abrév = **recommended daily amount**) AQR mpl

re¹ /reɪ/ n ré m

re² /riː/ prep (abrév = **with reference to**) (in letter head) 'objet:'; (about) au sujet de; **~ your letter...** suite à votre lettre...

RE n GB Sch (abrév = **Religious Education**) éducation f religieuse

reach /riːtʃ/
A n portée f; **beyond** ou **out of ~** hors de portée; **within (arm's) ~** à portée de (la) main; **within easy ~ of** à proximité de [shops, facility]; **within ~ for sb** à la portée de qn
B reaches npl **the upper/lower ~es** (of society) les échelons mpl les plus hauts/les plus bas; (of river) la partie supérieure/inférieure
C vtr **1** (arrive at) [person, train, river] atteindre [place, person]; [sound, news, letter] parvenir à [person, place]; **to ~ land** toucher terre; **the message took three days to ~ Paris** le message a mis trois jours pour arriver jusqu'à Paris; **easily ~ed by bus** facilement accessible par le bus; **2** (attain) atteindre [age, level]; **matters ~ed a point where...** les choses en sont arrivées à un point où...; **to ~ the finals** parvenir en finale; **3** (come to) arriver à [decision, understanding, conclusion]; **to ~ a verdict** Jur rendre un verdict; **4** (by stretching) atteindre [object, shelf, switch]; **5** (contact) joindre; **6** (make impact on) toucher [audience, market]; **7** (in height, length) arriver à [floor, ceiling]
D vi **1** (stretch) **to ~ up/down** lever/baisser le bras; **to ~ across** étendre le bras; **to ~ for one's gun** étendre le bras pour saisir son arme; **~ for the sky!** les mains en l'air!; **2** (extend) **to ~ (up/down) to** arriver jusqu'à

(Phrasal verb)
■ **reach out** lit étendre le bras; **to ~ out for** chercher [affection, success]; **to ~ out to** (help) aider; (make contact) établir un contact avec

react /rɪ'ækt/ vi gen, Chem réagir (**to** à; **against** contre; **with** avec; **on** sur)

reaction /rɪ'ækʃn/ n gen, Chem réaction f

reactionary /rɪ'ækʃənrɪ, US -ənerɪ/ n, adj réactionnaire (mf)

reactivate /rɪ'æktɪveɪt/ vtr remettre [qch] en fonction

reactor /rɪ'æktə(r)/ n Chem réacteur m

read
A /riːd/ n **to have a ~ of**○ lire [article, magazine]; **to be an easy ~** être facile à lire
B /riːd/ vtr (prét, pp **read** /red/) **1** (in text etc) lire [book, map, music, sign]; **to ~ sth to oneself** lire qch; **I can ~ German** je lis l'allemand; **2** (say) **the card ~s 'Happy Birthday Dad'** sur la carte il est écrit 'bon anniversaire Papa'; **3** (decipher) lire [braille, handwriting]; **4** (interpret) reconnaître [signs]; interpréter [intentions, reactions]; voir [situation]; **to ~ sb's thoughts** ou **mind** lire dans les pensées de qn; **to ~ sb's mood** connaître les humeurs de qn; **to ~ a remark as** considérer une remarque comme; **the book can be read as a satire** le livre peut se lire comme une satire; **don't ~ too much into his reply** ne va pas imaginer des choses qu'il n'a pas dites; **5** Univ faire des études de [history etc]; **6** (take a recording) relever [meter]; lire [dial]; **7** Radio, Telecom recevoir [person]; **I can ~ you loud and clear** je vous reçois cinq sur cinq
C /riːd/ vi (prét, pp **read** /red/) **1** (look at or articulate text) lire (**to** sb à qn); **to ~ about sth** lire quelque chose sur qch; **to ~ to sb from sth** lire qch à qn; **2** GB Univ **to ~ for a degree** ≈ préparer une licence (**in** de); **3** (create an impression) **the document ~s well/badly** le document se lit bien/mal; **the translation ~s like the original** la traduction est aussi bonne que l'original
(Idioms) **to take sth as read** considérer qch comme lu; **to ~ between the lines** lire entre les lignes
(Phrasal verbs)
■ **read back:** ▸ **~ [sth] back** relire [message, sentence]
■ **read on** continuer à lire
■ **read out:** ▸ **~ [sth] out, ~ out [sth]** lire [qch] à haute voix
■ **read over, read through:** ▸ **~ over** ou **through [sth], ~ [sth] over** ou **through** lire; (reread) relire
■ **read up: to ~ up on sth/sb** étudier qch/qn à fond

readable /'riːdəbl/ adj **1** (legible) lisible; **2** (enjoyable) agréable à lire

reader /'riːdə(r)/ n **1** gen lecteur/-trice m/f; **he's a slow ~** il lit lentement; **2** (anthology) recueil m de textes; **3** GB Univ chargé/-e m/f de cours; US Univ directeur/-trice m/f d'études

readership /'riːdəʃɪp/ n lecteurs mpl

read head n Comput tête f de lecture

readily /'redɪlɪ/ adv **1** (willingly) [accept, reply, give] sans hésiter; **2** (easily) facilement

readiness /'redɪnɪs/ n **1** (preparedness) niveau m de préparation; **in ~ for sth** en prévision de qch; **to be in a state of ~** être (fin) prêt; **2** (willingness) empressement m (**to do** à)

reading /'riːdɪŋ/ n **1** (skill, pastime) lecture f; **~ and writing** la lecture et l'écriture; **his ~ is poor** il lit mal; **her novels make light/heavy ~** ses romans sont faciles/difficiles à lire; **2** (measurement) (on meter) relevé m (**on** de); (on instrument) indication f (**on** de); **3** (interpretation) interprétation f (**of** de); **4** (spoken extract) lecture f (**from** de); **5** GB Pol (of bill) lecture f (**of** de)

reading: ~ age n Sch niveau m de lecture; **~ glass** n loupe f; **~ glasses** npl lunettes fpl (pour lire); **~ lamp** n (by bed) lampe f de chevet; (on desk) lampe f de bureau; **~ list** n Sch, Univ liste f d'ouvrages recommandés; **~ matter** n lecture ⊄ f; **~ room** n salle f de lecture

readjust /ˌriːə'dʒʌst/
A vtr rajuster [hat]; régler [qch] de nouveau [TV, lens]; remettre [qch] à l'heure [watch]; réajuster [salary]
B vi se réadapter (**to** à)

read: ~-only memory, ROM n Comput mémoire f morte; **~-out** n Comput extraction f

r

readvertise /ˌriːˈædvətaɪz/ vtr refaire paraître une annonce pour [post, sale, item]

ready /ˈredɪ/

A n **(to have) a gun/pen at the ~** (être) prêt à tirer/écrire

B ᵒ**readies** npl argent m

C adj **1** (prepared) prêt (**for** pour); **~ to do** prêt à faire; **to get ~ se préparer; to get sth ~ préparer qch; ~ when you are** quand tu veux; **~, steady, go** Sport à vos marques, prêts, partez!; **I'm ~, willing and able** je suis à votre service; **~ and waiting** fin prêt; **2** (willing) prêt (**to do** à faire); **more than ~ to do** plus que disposé à faire; **to be ~ for** avoir besoin de [meal, vacation]; **3** (quick) [answer] tout prêt; [wit] vif/vive; [smile] facile; **to be ~ with one's criticism** être prompt à critiquer; **4** (available) [market, supply] à portée (de main); [access] direct; **~ cash**ᵒ, **~ money**ᵒ (argent m) liquide m

D vtr préparer [ship, car] (**for sth** à qch)

ready-made /ˌredɪˈmeɪd/ adj [suit] de prêt-à-porter; [curtains] prêt à poser; [furniture] déjà monté; [excuse, phrase] tout fait

ready: **~ meal** n plat m cuisiné; **~-to-serve** adj [food] cuisiné; **~-to-wear** adj [garment] prêt-à-porter

reaffirm /ˌriːəˈfɜːm/ vtr réaffirmer

reafforestation GB, **reforestation** US /ˌriːəˌfɒrɪˈsteɪʃn, US ˌriːˌfɔːrəˈsteɪʃn/ n reboisement m

real /rɪəl/

A n réel m

B adj **1** (not imaginary) véritable, réel/réelle; **in ~ life** dans la réalité; **the ~ world** le monde réel, la réalité; **in ~ terms** en réalité; **2** (not artificial) [diamond, flower, leather] vrai (before n), authentique; **the ~ McCoy**ᵒ de l'authentique, du vrai de vraiᵒ; **this time it's the ~ thing** cette fois c'est pour de vraiᵒ; **3** (true, proper) [holiday, rest] véritable, vrai (before n); **he knows the ~ you** il connaît ta vraie personnalité; **the ~ Africa** l'Afrique profonde; **4** (for emphasis) [charmer, pleasure] vrai (before n); **it's a ~ shame** c'est vraiment dommage; **5** Fin, Comm [cost, value] réel/réelle; **6** Math réel/réelle

(Idiom) **for ~**ᵒ pour de vraiᵒ

real estate n **1** Jur, Comm (property) biens mpl immobiliers; **2** US (profession) immobilier m

real estate: **~ agent** n US agent m immobilier; **~ developer** n US promoteur m; **~ office** n US agence f immobilière

realign /ˌriːəˈlaɪn/

A vtr remettre [qch] dans l'alignement [objects]; fig redéfinir [views]

B vi Pol former de nouvelles alliances

realignment /ˌriːəˈlaɪnmənt/ n (of view) redéfinition f; Pol, Fin réalignement m

realism /ˈriːəlɪzəm/ n réalisme m

realist /ˈriːəlɪst/ n, adj réaliste (mf)

realistic /ˌrɪəˈlɪstɪk/ adj réaliste

realistically /ˌrɪəˈlɪstɪklɪ/ adv [look at, think, describe] de façon réaliste; **~,...** en réalité,...

reality /rɪˈælɪtɪ/ n réalité f (**of** de); **to be out of touch with ~** vivre hors des réalités

realization /ˌrɪəlaɪˈzeɪʃn, US -lɪˈz-/ n **1** (awareness) prise f de conscience (**of** de; **that** du fait que); **to come to the ~ that** se rendre compte que; **2** (achievement) réalisation f (**of** de)

realize /ˈrɪəlaɪz/ vtr **1** (know) se rendre compte de [error, significance, fact]; **to ~ that** se rendre compte que; **to ~ how/what** comprendre comment/ce que; **more/less than people ~** plus/moins que les gens n'en ont conscience; **to come to ~ sth** prendre conscience de qch; **to make sb ~ sth** faire comprendre qch à qn; **I didn't ~** je ne le savais pas!; **I ~ that!** oui, je sais bien!; **2** (make real) réaliser [idea, dream, goal, design]; **my worst fears were ~d** ce que je craignais le plus est arrivé; **to ~ one's potential** développer ses capacités; **3** Fin (liquidate) réaliser [assets]; **4** Comm [sale] rapporter [sum]; [person, vendor] faire [sum] (**on** en vendant)

reallocate /riːˈæləˌkeɪt/ vtr réattribuer

really /ˈrɪəlɪ/

A adv **1** (for emphasis) vraiment, réellement; **they ~ enjoyed the film** le film leur a vraiment plu; **you ~ must taste it** il faut absolument que tu y goûtes; **2** (very) [cheap, hot] très, vraiment; **3** (in actual fact) en fait, réellement; **what I**

~ mean is that... en fait, ce que je veux dire c'est que...; **he's a good teacher ~** en fait, c'est un bon professeur; **ghosts don't ~ exist** les fantômes n'existent pas; **I'll tell you what ~ happened** je vais te dire ce qui s'est réellement passé; **4** (seriously) vraiment; **I ~ don't know** je ne sais vraiment pas; **do you ~ think he'll apologize?** tu penses vraiment qu'il s'excusera?; **~?** (expressing disbelief) c'est vrai?; **does she ~?** c'est vrai?

B excl (also **well ~**) (annoyed) franchement!

realm /relm/ n (kingdom) royaume m; fig domaine m

real tennis ▸ p. 881 n jeu m de paume

realty /ˈriːəltɪ/ n US biens mpl immobiliers

ream /riːm/ n (of paper) rame f (de papier); **she wrote ~s about it** fig elle en a écrit toute une tartineᵒ

reanimate /ˌriːˈænɪˌmeɪt/ vtr ranimer

reap /riːp/

A vtr **1** Agric recueillir [crop]; **2** fig récolter [benefits]; **to ~ the rewards of one's efforts** recueillir le fruit de ses efforts

B vi moissonner

reaper /ˈriːpə(r)/ n (machine) moissonneuse f; (person) moissonneur/-euse m/f

reappear /ˌriːəˈpɪə(r)/ vi reparaître

reappearance /ˌriːəˈpɪərəns/ n réapparition f

reapply /ˌriːəˈplaɪ/ vi reposer sa candidature (**for** à)

reappoint /ˌriːəˈpɔɪnt/ vtr renommer (**to** à)

reappraise /ˌriːəˈpreɪz/ vtr réexaminer [question, policy]; réévaluer [writer, work]

rear /rɪə(r)/

A n **1** (of building, car, room etc) arrière m; **at the ~ of the house** derrière la maison; (of procession, train) queue f; Mil (of unit, convoy) arrière-garde f, arrières mpl; (of column) queue f; **to bring up the ~** fermer la marche; **2** euph (of person) derrièreᵒ m

B adj **1** [entrance, garden] de derrière; **2** Aut [light, seat, suspension] arrière inv

C vtr élever [child, animals]; cultiver [plants]

D vi (also **~ up**) [horse] se cabrer; [snake] se dresser

rear: **~ admiral** n contre-amiral m; **~-drive** adj à traction f arrière

rear end /ˌrɪər ˈend/

A n **1** (of vehicle) arrière m; **2** euph (of person) derrière m

B ᵒ**rear-end** vtr US emboutirᵒ l'arrière de [car]

rearguard /ˈrɪəɡɑːd/ n Mil, fig arrière-garde f

rearguard action n combat m d'arrière-garde

rearm /ˌriːˈɑːm/ vtr, vi réarmer

rearmament /ˌriːˈɑːməmənt/ n réarmement m

rearmost /ˈrɪəməʊst/ adj gen tout/-e dernier/-ière; [carriage] de queue

rearrange /ˌriːəˈreɪndʒ/ vtr réarranger [hair]; redisposer [furniture]; réaménager [room]; modifier [plans]

rear: **~-view mirror** n rétroviseur m; **~ wheel** n Aut roue f arrière inv; **~-wheel drive** n Aut traction f arrière; **~ window** n Aut vitre f arrière inv

reason /ˈriːzn/

A n **1** (cause) raison f (**for, behind** de); **for no (good) ~, without good ~** sans raison valable; **if you are late for any ~** si tu es en retard, pour une raison ou pour une autre; **I have ~ to believe that...** j'ai des raisons de croire que...; **by ~ of** sout en raison de; **for that ~ I can't do it** c'est pour cette raison que je ne peux pas le faire; **the ~ why...** la raison pour laquelle...; **I'll tell you the ~ why...** je vais te dire pourquoi...; **give me one ~ why I should!** et pourquoi donc devrais-je le faire?; **what was his ~ for resigning?** pour quelle raison a-t-il démissionné?; **the ~ is that...** la raison en est que...; **the ~ given is that...** la raison invoquée est que...; **to have every ou good ~ for doing ou to do** avoir toute ou de bonnes raisons de faire; **there was no ~ for you to worry** tu n'avais aucune raison de t'inquiéter; **all the more ~ to insist on it** raison de plus pour insister; **she was angry, and with good ~** elle était fâchée, et à juste titre; **2** (common sense) raison f; **to lose one's ~** perdre la raison; **to listen to ou see ~** entendre raison; **it stands to ~ that** il va sans dire que; **within ~** dans la limite du raisonnable

B vtr **1** (argue) soutenir; **2** (conclude) déduire

C vi **to ~ with sb** raisonner qn

D ᵒ**reasoned** pp adj raisonné

reasonable /ˈriːznəbl/ adj **1** (sensible) raisonnable; **2** (understanding) compréhensif/-ive (**about** au sujet de);

3) (justified) légitime; **it is ~ for sb to do** il est légitime que qn fasse; **beyond ~ doubt** Jur sans aucun doute possible; **4)** (moderately good) convenable; **there is a ~ chance that** il est fort possible que

reasonableness /'ri:znəblnɪs/ n (of remark, argument) bien-fondé m

reasonably /'ri:znəblɪ/ adv **1)** (legitimately) légitimement; (sensibly) raisonnablement; **2)** (rather) assez

reasoning /'ri:znɪŋ/ n raisonnement m

reassemble /ˌri:ə'sembl/
A vtr **1)** rassembler [troops, pupils]; **2)** Tech remonter [unit, engine etc]
B vi [people] se rassembler

reassert /ˌri:ə'sɜ:t/ vtr réaffirmer [authority, claim]

reassess /ˌri:ə'ses/ vtr gen réexaminer, reconsidérer [problem, situation]; recalculer [tax liability]

reassessment /ˌri:ə'sesmənt/ n (of situation) réexamen m; (of tax) nouveau calcul m

reassurance /ˌri:ə'ʃɔ:rəns, US -'ʃʊər-/ n **1)** (comfort) réconfort m; **2)** (official guarantee) garantie f

reassure /ˌri:ə'ʃɔ:(r), US -'ʃʊər-/ vtr rassurer [person] (**about** sur)

reassuring /ˌri:ə'ʃɔ:rɪŋ, US -'ʃʊər-/ adj rassurant

reassuringly /ˌri:ə'ʃɔ:rɪŋlɪ, US -'ʃʊər-/ adv d'une manière rassurante

reawaken /ˌri:ə'weɪkən/
A vtr **1)** sout réveiller à nouveau [person]; **2)** fig faire renaître [interest]
B vi sout [person] se réveiller de nouveau

reawakening /ˌri:ə'weɪkənɪŋ/ n sout réveil m

rebate /'ri:beɪt/ n (refund) remboursement m; (discount) remise f

rebel
A /'rebl/ n, noun modifier rebelle (mf)
B /rɪ'bel/ vi (p prés etc **-ll-**) lit, fig se rebeller

rebellion /rɪ'beliən/ n rébellion f, révolte f

rebellious /rɪ'beliəs/ adj [nation, child] rebelle, insoumis; [school, class] indiscipliné

rebirth /ˌri:'bɜ:θ/ n lit, fig renaissance f

reboot /ˌri:'bu:t/ vtr Comput réinitialiser, réamorcer

reborn /ˌri:'bɔ:n/ adj Relig **to be ~** renaître; fig **to be ~ as sth** réapparaître sous la forme de qch

rebound
A /'ri:baʊnd/ n (of ball) rebond m; (in basketball) panier m; **to marry sb on the ~** épouser qn sous le coup d'une déception amoureuse
B /rɪ'baʊnd/ vi lit (bounce) rebondir; **to ~ on** fig se retourner contre

rebuff /rɪ'bʌf/
A n rebuffade f
B vtr rabrouer [person]; repousser [suggestion, advances]

rebuild /ˌri:'bɪld/ vtr (prét, pp **rebuilt** /ˌri:'bɪlt/) reconstruire

rebuilding /ˌri:'bɪldɪŋ/ n reconstruction f

rebuke /rɪ'bju:k/
A n réprimande f
B vtr réprimander (**for** pour)

rebut /rɪ'bʌt/ vtr (p prés etc **-tt-**) réfuter

rebuttal /rɪ'bʌtl/ n réfutation f

recalcitrant /rɪ'kælsɪtrənt/ adj sout récalcitrant

recalculate /ˌri:'kælkjʊˌleɪt/ vtr recalculer

recall
A /'ri:kɔ:l/ n **1)** (memory) mémoire f; **to have total ~ of sth** se souvenir de qch dans les moindres détails; **2)** gen, Mil, Comput (summons) rappel m
B /rɪ'kɔ:l/ vtr **1)** (remember) se souvenir de; **I ~ seeing/what happened** je me souviens d'avoir vu/de ce qui est arrivé; **as I ~** si je m'en souviens bien; **2)** (remind of) rappeler; **3)** (summon back) gen rappeler; convoquer [parliament]

recant /rɪ'kænt/
A vtr abjurer [heresy]; désavouer [opinion]; rétracter [statement]
B vi gen se rétracter; Relig abjurer

recap
A °n /'ri:kæp/ abrév ▸ **recapitulation**
B °vtr /'ri:kæp/ (p prés etc **-pp-**) abrév ▸ **recapitulate**

recapitulate /ˌri:kə'pɪtʃʊleɪt/ vtr, vi récapituler

recapitulation /ˌri:kəpɪtʃʊ'leɪʃn/ n récapitulation f

recapture /ˌri:'kæptʃə(r)/
A n (of prisoner, animal) capture f; (of town, position) reprise f
B vtr lit recapturer [prisoner, animal]; Mil reprendre [town, position]; Pol reconquérir [seat]; fig retrouver [feeling]; recréer [period, atmosphere]

recast /ˌri:'kɑ:st, US -'kæst/ vtr (prét, pp **recast**) reformuler [sentence]; remanier [text, plan]

recede
A /rɪ'si:d/ vi **1)** lit, gen s'éloigner; [tide] descendre; fig [hope, memory, prospect] s'estomper; [threat] s'éloigner; [prices] baisser; **2)** (go bald) [person] se dégarnir
B /rɪ'si:dɪŋ/ pres p adj [chin, forehead] fuyant; **he has a receding hairline** son front se dégarnit

receipt /rɪ'si:t/
A n **1)** Comm (in writing) reçu m, récépissé m (**for** pour); (from till) ticket m de caisse; (for rent) quittance f; Post (on sending) reçu m; (on delivery) accusé m de réception (**for** pour); **2)** (of goods, letters) réception f; **to be in ~ of** recevoir [income, benefits]
B receipts npl Comm (takings) recette f (**from** de)

receive /rɪ'si:v/
A vtr **1)** (get) recevoir [letter, money, treatment, education]; receler [stolen goods]; **he ~d a 30-year sentence** il a été condamné à 30 ans de prison; **'~d with thanks'** Comm 'pour acquit'; **2)** (meet) accueillir, recevoir [visitor, proposal, play] (**with** avec); **to be well ou positively ~d** être bien reçu; **to be ~d into** être reçu or admis dans [church, order]; **3)** Radio, TV capter, recevoir
B received pp adj [ideas, opinions] reçu

Received Pronunciation, RP n GB prononciation f standard (de l'anglais)

> ℹ️ **Received Pronunciation, RP** Il s'agit d'une prononciation normalisée de l'anglais britannique, sans trace d'accent régional, généralement associée aux couches élevées de la société et employée à la radio et à la télévision. Les expressions *BBC English* et *Queen's English* y font également référence.

received: **Received Standard** n US = **Received Pronunciation**; **~ wisdom** n opinion f générale

receiver /rɪ'si:və(r)/ n **1)** (telephone) combiné m; **2)** Radio, TV (equipment) (poste m) récepteur m; **3)** GB Fin Jur (also **Official Receiver**) administrateur m judiciaire

receivership /rɪ'si:vəʃɪp/ n GB Fin Jur **to go into ~** être placé sous administration judiciaire

receiving /rɪ'si:vɪŋ/ n GB Jur recel m

(Idiom) **to be on the ~ end of** faire les frais de [criticism, hostility]; recevoir [blow, punch]

recent /'ri:snt/ adj [event, change, arrival, film] récent; [acquaintance, development] nouveau/-elle; **in ~ times** récemment; **in ~ years/weeks** au cours des dernières années/semaines

recently /'ri:sntlɪ/ adv récemment, dernièrement; **as ~ as Monday** pas plus tard que lundi; **until ~** jusqu'à ces derniers temps

receptacle /rɪ'septəkl/ n récipient m

reception /rɪ'sepʃn/ n **1)** (also **~ desk**) réception f; **2)** (gathering) réception f (**for sb** en l'honneur de qn; **for sth** à l'occasion de qch); **3)** (public response) accueil m (**for** de); **they gave us a great ~** [fans, audience] ils nous ont fait un accueil formidable; **4)** Radio, TV réception f (**on** sur)

reception: **~ area** n réception f; **~ camp, ~ centre** n centre m d'accueil (**for** pour); **~ class** n GB Sch ≈ cours m préparatoire; **~ committee** n comité m d'accueil also fig

receptionist /rɪ'sepʃənɪst/ ▸ p. 1181 n réceptionniste mf

reception room n **1)** (in house) (grande) pièce f, pièce f de réception; **2)** (in hotel) salle f de réception, salon m

receptive /rɪ'septɪv/ adj réceptif/-ive (**to** à)

recess /rɪ'ses, US 'ri:ses/
A n **1)** Jur, Pol vacances fpl; **2)** US (break) (in school) récréation f; (during meeting) pause f; **3)** Constr (for door, window) embrasure f; (alcove) alcôve f, niche f, recoin m
B recesses npl lit, fig recoins mpl (**of** de)
C vtr US (interrupt) suspendre [meeting, hearing]
D vi US Jur, Pol suspendre les séances

recession /rɪ'seʃn/ n Econ récession f

recessive /rɪ'sesɪv/ adj Biol récessif/-ive

r

recharge /ˌriːˈtʃɑːdʒ/ *vtr* recharger

rechargeable /ˌriːˈtʃɑːdʒəbl/ *adj* rechargeable

recidivism /rɪˈsɪdɪvɪzəm/ *n* récidive *f*

recidivist /rɪˈsɪdɪvɪst/ *n* récidiviste *mf*

recipe /ˈresəpɪ/ *n* Culin recette *f* (**for** de); ∼ **book** livre *m* de recettes; fig **a** ∼ **for business success** une recette pour réussir dans les affaires; **it's a** ∼ **for disaster** ça mène tout droit à la catastrophe

recipient /rɪˈsɪpɪənt/ *n* (receiver) (of mail) destinataire *mf*; (of benefits, aid, cheque) bénéficiaire *mf*; (of prize, award) lauréat/ -e *m/f*

reciprocal /rɪˈsɪprəkl/ *adj* réciproque

reciprocally /rɪˈsɪprəklɪ/ *adv* réciproquement

reciprocate /rɪˈsɪprəkeɪt/
A *vtr* retourner [*compliment*]; payer [qch] de retour [*love, kindness*]; rendre [*affection, invitation*]
B *vi* rendre la pareille

reciprocity /ˌresɪˈprɒsətɪ/ *n* réciprocité *f*

recital /rɪˈsaɪtl/ *n* (of music, poetry) récital *m*; (narration) récit *m*

recitation /ˌresɪˈteɪʃn/ *n* récitation *f*

recite /rɪˈsaɪt/ *vtr, vi* réciter

reckless /ˈreklɪs/ *adj* [*person, driving*] imprudent

recklessly /ˈreklɪslɪ/ *adv* [*act*] avec imprudence; [*promise, spend*] de manière inconsciente

recklessness /ˈreklɪsnɪs/ *n* imprudence *f*

reckon /ˈrekən/
A *vtr* **1** (judge) considérer (**that** que); **she is** ∼**ed (to be) the cleverest** elle est considérée comme la plus intelligente; **2** ᴼ(think) **to** ∼ (**that**) croire que; **I** ∼ **he's about 50** à mon avis il a à peu près 50 ans; **to** ∼ **to do** compter faire; **3** (calculate accurately) calculer [*amount*]; **4** ᴼ(believe to be good) **I don't** ∼ **your chances of success** je doute de vos chances de succès; **5** ᴼ(like) estimer [*person*]
B *vi* calculer
(Phrasal verbs)
■ **reckon on**ᴼ: ▶ ∼ **on [sb/sth]** compter sur; ▶ ∼ **on doing** compter faire
■ **reckon up** calculer
■ **reckon with**: ▶ ∼ **with [sb/sth]** compter avec

reckoning /ˈrekənɪŋ/ *n* gen (estimation) estimation *f*; (accurate calculation) calculs *mpl*

(Idiom) **day of** ∼ Relig jour *m* du Jugement (dernier)

reclaim /rɪˈkleɪm/ *vtr* **1** Ecol reconquérir [*coastal land*]; mettre en valeur [*site*]; assécher [*marsh*]; défricher [*forest*]; assainir [*polluted land*]; irriguer [*desert*]; (recycle) récupérer [*glass, metal*]; **2** (get back) récupérer [*deposit, money*]

reclaimable /rɪˈkleɪməbl/ *adj* [*waste product*] récupérable; [*expenses*] remboursable

reclamation /ˌrekləˈmeɪʃn/ *n* **1** (recycling) récupération *f*; **2** (of land) mise *f* en valeur; (of marsh) assèchement *m*; (of polluted land) assainissement *m*; (of forest) défrichement *m*

recline /rɪˈklaɪn/ *vi* [*person*] s'allonger; [*seat*] s'incliner

reclining /rɪˈklaɪnɪŋ/ *adj* **1** Art [*figure*] allongé; **2** [*seat*] inclinable

recluse /rɪˈkluːs/ *n* reclus/-e *m/f*

reclusive /rɪˈkluːsɪv/ *adj* solitaire

recognition /ˌrekəɡˈnɪʃn/ *n* **1** (identification) reconnaissance *f*; **they've changed the town beyond** ∼ ils ont rendu la ville méconnaissable; **2** (realization) reconnaissance *f* (**of** de); **3** gen, Pol (acknowledgement) reconnaissance *f*; **to receive** *ou* **win** ∼ **for** être reconnu pour [*talent, work*]; **in** ∼ **of** en reconnaissance de; **4** Comput (of data) reconnaissance *f*; **5** Aviat (identification) identification *f*

recognizable /ˌrekəɡˈnaɪzəbl, ˈrekəɡnaɪzəbl/ *adj* reconnaissable

recognizably /ˌrekəɡˈnaɪzəblɪ, ˈrekəɡnaɪzəblɪ/ *adv* manifestement

recognize /ˈrekəɡnaɪz/
A *vtr* **1** (identify) reconnaître [*person, voice, sound, place*] (**by** à; **as** comme étant); identifier [*sign, symptom*] (**as** comme étant); **2** (acknowledge) reconnaître [*problem, fact, government, claim*]; **3** US (in debate) donner la parole à [*speaker*]
B **recognized** *pp adj* **1** (acknowledged) [*expert, organization*] reconnu; Comm (accredited) [*firm, supplier*] accrédité; ∼**d dealer** concessionnaire *m* attitré

recoil
A /ˈriːkɔɪl/ *n* (of gun) recul *m*; (of spring) détente *f*
B /rɪˈkɔɪl/ *vi* **1** [*person*] (physically) avoir un mouvement de recul (**from, at** devant); (mentally) reculer (**from** devant); **to** ∼ **in horror** reculer d'horreur; **2** [*gun*] reculer en tirant; [*spring*] se détendre

recollect /ˌrekəˈlekt/
A *vtr* se souvenir de, se rappeler
B *vi* se souvenir; **as far as I** ∼ autant que je m'en souvienne

recollection /ˌrekəˈlekʃn/ *n* souvenir *m*; **to have some** ∼ **of** se souvenir vaguement de; **to the best of my** ∼ autant que je m'en souvienne

recommence /ˌriːkəˈmens/ *vtr, vi* recommencer (**doing à** faire)

recommend /ˌrekəˈmend/ *vtr* **1** (commend) recommander [*person, company, film*] (**as** comme étant); **2** (advise) conseiller, recommander; **3** (favour) **the strategy has much to** ∼ **it** la stratégie présente de nombreux avantages; **the hotel has little to** ∼ **it** on ne peut pas dire grand-chose en faveur de cet hôtel

recommendation /ˌrekəmenˈdeɪʃn/ *n* recommandation *f* (**to** à; **on** sur); **on the** ∼ **of** sur la recommandation de; **to give sb a** ∼ recommander qn; **to write sb a** ∼ donner une lettre de recommandation à qn

recommend: ∼**ed daily amount**, **RDA** *n* apports *mpl* quotidiens recommandés, AQR; ∼**ed reading** *n* livres *mpl* conseillés *or* recommandés; ∼**ed retail price** *n* prix *m* de vente conseillé

recompense /ˈrekəmpens/
A *n* **1** (reward) récompense *f* (**for** de); **2** Jur dédommagement *m* (**for** pour)
B *vtr* **1** sout (reward) récompenser (**for** de); **2** Jur dédommager (**for** de)

reconcilable /ˈrekənsaɪləbl/ *adj* [*differences*] conciliable; [*views*] compatible (**with** avec)

reconcile /ˈrekənsaɪl/ *vtr* **1** (after quarrel) réconcilier [*people*]; **to be** *ou* **become** ∼**d** se réconcilier (**with** avec); **2** (see as compatible) concilier [*attitudes, views*] (**with** avec); **3** (persuade to accept) **to** ∼ **sb to sth/to doing** réconcilier qn avec qch/avec l'idée de faire; **to become** ∼**d to sth** se résigner à qch

reconciliation /ˌrekənˌsɪlɪˈeɪʃn/ *n* réconciliation *f*

recondition /ˌriːkənˈdɪʃn/ *vtr* remettre [qch] à neuf

reconnaissance /rɪˈkɒnɪsns/ *n* reconnaissance *f*

reconnoitre GB, **reconnoiter** US /ˌrekəˈnɔɪtə(r)/ Mil
A *vtr* reconnaître
B *vi* faire une reconnaissance

reconsider /ˌriːkənˈsɪdə(r)/
A *vtr* réexaminer
B *vi* (think further) y repenser

reconstitute /ˌriːˈkɒnstɪtjuːt, US -tuːt/ *vtr* **1** Admin, Pol reconstituer; **2** Culin réhydrater

reconstruct /ˌriːkənˈstrʌkt/ *vtr* **1** (rebuild) reconstruire [*building*]; réédifier [*system*]; reconstituer [*text*]; Med reconstituer; **2** [*police*] faire une reconstitution de [*crime*]

reconstruction /ˌriːkənˈstrʌkʃn/ *n* **1** (of building) reconstruction *f*; (of system) réédification *f*; **2** (of object, event, crime) reconstitution *f*; **3** Med reconstitution *f*

reconvene /ˌriːkənˈviːn/ *vi* se réunir à nouveau

record
A /ˈrekɔːd, US ˈrekərd/ *n* **1** (written account) (of events) compte-rendu *m*; (of official proceedings) procès-verbal *m*; **to keep a** ∼ **of sth** noter qch; **I have no** ∼ **of your application** je n'ai aucune trace de votre demande; **the hottest summer on** ∼ l'été le plus chaud qu'on ait jamais enregistré; **to be on** ∼ **as saying that...** avoir déclaré officiellement que...; **to say sth off the** ∼ dire qch en privé; **I'd like to set the** ∼ **straight** je voudrais mettre les choses au clair; **2** (data) (*also* ∼**s**) (historical, public) archives *fpl*; (personal, administrative) dossier *m*; **3** (history) (of individual) passé *m*; (of organization, group) réputation *f*; **to have a good** ∼ **on sth** avoir une bonne réputation en ce qui concerne; **4** Audio disque *m* (**by, of** de); **5** (best performance) record *m* (**for, in** de); **6** Jur (*also* **criminal** ∼) casier *m* judiciaire
B /ˈrekɔːd, US ˈrekərd/ *noun modifier* **1** Audio [*company, label, shop*] de disques; [*industry*] du disque; **2** (best) [*result, sales, time*] record (inv, after n); **to be at a** ∼ **high/low** être à son niveau le plus haut/bas

C /rɪˈkɔːd/ *vtr* **1** (note) noter; **2** (on disc, tape) enregistrer; **3** (register) [*equipment*] enregistrer [*temperature*]; [*dial*] indiquer [*pressure, speed*]; **4** (provide an account of) rapporter [*event*]

D /rɪˈkɔːd/ *vi* [*video, tape recorder*] enregistrer

record book *n* livre *m* des records

record-breaker /ˈrekɔːdbreɪkə(r)/, US ˈrekərd-/ *n* **to be a** ∼ avoir battu un record

record: ∼**-breaking** *adj* record (*inv, after n*); ∼ **card** *n* fiche *f*; ∼ **deck** *n* Audio platine *f* disques

recorded /rɪˈkɔːdɪd/ *adj* **1** (on tape, record) enregistré; **2** (documented) [*case, sighting*] connu; [*fact*] reconnu; ∼ **delivery** GB Post recommandé *m*

recorder /rɪˈkɔːdə(r)/ *n* Mus flûte *f* à bec

record-holder /ˈrekɔːdhəʊldə(r), US ˈrekərd-/ *n* recordman/recordwoman *m/f*

recording /rɪˈkɔːdɪŋ/ *n* enregistrement *m*; **to make a** ∼ **of sth** enregistrer qch

record: ∼ **library** *n* discothèque *f* de prêt; ∼ **player** *n* tourne-disque *m*; ∼**s office** *n* (of births, deaths) bureau *m* des archives; Jur (of court records) greffe *m*; ∼ **token** *n* chèque-cadeau *m* pour disques

recount /rɪˈkaʊnt/ *vtr* raconter, conter

re-count

A /ˈriːkaʊnt/ *n* Pol deuxième compte *m* des suffrages

B /ˌriːˈkaʊnt/ *vtr* recompter

recoup /rɪˈkuːp/ *vtr* compenser [*losses*]; **to** ∼ **one's costs** rentrer dans ses frais

recourse /rɪˈkɔːs/ *n* recours *m* (**to** à)

recover /rɪˈkʌvə(r)/

A *vtr* **1** (get back) retrouver, récupérer [*money, vehicle*]; récupérer [*territory*]; (from water) repêcher, retrouver [*body, wreck*]; **to** ∼ **one's sight/health** recouvrer la vue/santé; **to** ∼ **one's confidence/one's strength** reprendre confiance/des forces; **2** (recoup) recouvrer [*loan, taxes, costs*] (**from** auprès de); réparer, compenser [*losses*]

B *vi* (from illness) se remettre, se rétablir (**from** de); (from defeat, mistake) se ressaisir (**from** après); [*economy*] se redresser; [*shares, currency*] remonter

recoverable /rɪˈkʌvərəbl/ *adj* **1** Fin recouvrable; **2** Ecol, Ind récupérable

recovered memory syndrome *n* Psych syndrome *m* des souvenirs retrouvés

recovery /rɪˈkʌvərɪ/ *n* **1** (getting better) rétablissement *m*, guérison *f*; fig (of team, player) ressaisissement *m*; **to be on the road to** ∼ être sur la voie de la guérison; **to make a** ∼ (from illness) se rétablir, guérir; (from mistake, defeat) se ressaisir; **2** Econ, Fin (of economy, country, company, market) relance *f*, reprise *f*; (of shares, prices) remontée *f*; **3** (getting back) (of vehicle) rapatriement *m*; (of money) récupération *f*; (of costs, debts) recouvrement *m*; (of losses) réparation *f*

recovery: ∼ **room** *n* Med salle *f* de réveil; ∼ **vehicle** *n* Aut (car) voiture *f* de dépannage; (truck) camion *m* de dépannage

recreate /ˈrekrɪeɪt, ˌriːkrɪˈeɪt/ *vtr* recréer

recreation /ˌrekrɪˈeɪʃn/

A *n* **1** (leisure) loisirs *mpl*; **what do you do for** ∼? que faites-vous pour vous détendre?; **2** (pastime) récréation *f*; **3** Sch (break) récréation *f*

B *noun modifier* [*facilities, centre*] de loisirs; ∼ **area** (indoor) salle *f* de récréation; (outdoor) terrain *m* de jeux; ∼ **ground** terrain *m* de jeux; ∼ **room** US salle *f* de jeux

recreational /ˌrekrɪˈeɪʃənl/ *adj* [*facilities*] de loisirs

recreational: ∼ **drug** *n*: drogue que l'on prend de façon occasionnelle; ∼ **vehicle**, **RV** *n* US camping-car *m*

recrimination /rɪˌkrɪmɪˈneɪʃn/ *n* récrimination *f*

rec room° /ˈrek ruːm/ *n* US salle *f* de jeux

recruit /rɪˈkruːt/

A *n* recrue *f*

B *vtr* Mil, Pol recruter [*soldier, member, agent*] (**from** dans); gen recruter, embaucher [*staff*]

C *vi* recruter

recruiting officer *n* officier *m* recruteur

recruitment /rɪˈkruːtmənt/ *n* recrutement *m*

rectangle /ˈrektæŋgl/ *n* rectangle *m*

rectangular /rekˈtæŋgjʊlə(r)/ *adj* rectangulaire

rectify /ˈrektɪfaɪ/ *vtr* gen, Math, Chem rectifier

rectitude /ˈrektɪtjuːd, US -tuːd/ *n* droiture *f*

rector /ˈrektə(r)/ *n* Relig pasteur *m*

rectory /ˈrektərɪ/ *n* presbytère *m* (anglican)

rectum /ˈrektəm/ *n* rectum *m*

recumbent /rɪˈkʌmbənt/ *adj* littér allongé

recuperate /rɪˈkuːpəreɪt/

A *vtr* réparer [*loss*]

B *vi* Med se rétablir (**from** de), récupérer

recuperation /rɪˌkuːpəˈreɪʃn/ *n* **1** (of losses) réparation *f*; **2** Med rétablissement *m* (**from** de), récupération *f*

recur /rɪˈkɜː(r)/ *vi* (*p prés etc* -**rr**-) [*event, error, dream*] se reproduire; [*problem, illness*] réapparaître; [*theme, phrase*] revenir; Math [*number*] se répéter à l'infini

recurrence /rɪˈkʌrəns/ *n* (of illness) récurrence *f*; (of symptom) réapparition *f*

recurrent /rɪˈkʌrənt/ *adj* récurrent

recurring /rɪˈkɜːrɪŋ/ *adj* [*thought, pain*] récurrent; Math ∼ **decimal** suite *f* décimale illimitée

recyclable /ˌriːˈsaɪkləbl/ *adj* recyclable

recycle /ˌriːˈsaɪkl/ *vtr* Ecol recycler [*paper, waste*]

recycling /ˌriːˈsaɪklɪŋ/ *n* Ecol recyclage *m*

red /red/ ▸ p. 752

A *n* **1** (colour) rouge *m*; **in** ∼ en rouge; **2** °pej (*also* **Red**) (communist) rouge *mf*; **3** (deficit) **to be in the** ∼ [*person, account*] être à découvert; [*company*] être en déficit; **4** (wine) rouge *m*; **5** (red ball) bille *f* rouge (*de billard/ snooker*)

B *adj* (in colour) gen rouge (**with** de); [*hair*] roux/rousse; **to go** *ou* **turn** ∼ rougir; ∼ **in the face** tout rouge; **there'll be** ∼ **faces when...** certains vont être bien gênés quand...

(Idioms) **to be caught** ∼**-handed** être pris/-e la main dans le sac°; **to see** ∼ voir rouge; **not to have a** ∼ **cent** US ne pas avoir un sou°

red: ∼ **admiral** *n* Zool vulcain *m*; ∼ **blood cell** *n* globule *m* rouge; ∼**-blooded** *adj* [*male*] ardent; ∼ **cabbage** *n* chou *m* rouge; ∼ **card** *n* Sport carton *m* rouge; ∼ **carpet** *n* tapis *m* rouge

redcoat /ˈredkəʊt/ *n* **1** GB (at camp) animateur/-trice *m/f*; **2** Mil soldat *m* anglais (*du XVIIIᵉ siècle*)

red: **Red Cross** *n* Croix-Rouge *f*; ∼**currant** *n* groseille *f*; ∼ **deer** *n* cerf *m* commun

redden /ˈredn/ *vtr, vi* rougir

reddish /ˈredɪʃ/ *adj* rougeâtre; ∼ **hair** cheveux tirant sur le roux

redecorate /ˌriːˈdekəreɪt/ *vtr* repeindre et retapisser, refaire

redeem /rɪˈdiːm/

A *vtr* **1** (exchange) échanger [*voucher*] (**for** contre); (for cash) convertir [qch] en espèces [*bond, security*]; **2** (pay off) racheter [*pawned goods*]; **her one** ∼**ing feature is... quality is...** ce qui la rachète, c'est...; **3** (salvage) rattraper [*occasion*]; sauver [*situation*]; racheter [*fault*]; **4** (satisfy) s'acquitter de [*obligation*]; tenir [*pledge*]; **5** Relig racheter

B *v refl* **to** ∼ **oneself** se racheter

redeemable /rɪˈdiːməbl/ *adj* **1** Fin [*bond, security*] convertible; [*loan, mortgage*] remboursable; **2** Comm [*voucher*] échangeable; [*pawned goods*] rachetable

Redeemer /rɪˈdiːmə(r)/ *n* Relig Rédempteur *m*

redefine /ˌriːdɪˈfaɪn/ *vtr* redéfinir

redemption /rɪˈdempʃn/ *n* **1** Fin (of loan, debt, bill) remboursement *m*; **2** Relig rédemption *f*; **beyond** *ou* **past** ∼ [*situation*] irrémédiable; [*machine*] irréparable; [*person*] hum irrécupérable

redesign /ˌriːdɪˈzaɪn/ *vtr* transformer [*area, building*]; **to** ∼ **a logo** créer un nouveau logo

redevelop /ˌriːdɪˈveləp/ *vtr* réaménager [*site, town*]

redevelopment /ˌriːdɪˈveləpmənt/ *n* réaménagement *m*

red: ∼**-eyed** *adj* aux yeux rouges; ∼**-faced** *adj* (temporarily) rouge; fig (embarrassed) penaud; (permanently) rougeaud; ∼ **grouse** *n* grouse *f*; ∼**-haired** *adj* roux/rousse; ∼**head** *n* roux/rousse *m/f*; ∼**headed** *adj* roux/rousse; ∼ **herring** *n* (distraction) faux problème *m*

red-hot /ˌredˈhɒt/

A °*n* US hot-dog *m*

B *adj* lit [*metal, coal*] chauffé au rouge; fig [*passion, lover*] ardent; [*news*] tout frais/toute fraîche

redial /ˌriːˈdaɪəl/ Telecom
A vtr refaire [number]
B vi recomposer le numéro
redial:~ **button** n touche f bis; ~ **facility** n rappel m du dernier numéro composé

redid /ˌriːˈdɪd/ prét ▸ redo

Red Indian n injur Peau-Rouge mf

redirect /ˌriːdɪˈrekt/ vtr canaliser [resources]; dévier [traffic]; faire suivre, réexpédier [mail]

rediscover /ˌriːdɪˈskʌvə(r)/ vtr redécouvrir

red: ~**-letter day** n jour m mémorable; ~ **light** n feu m rouge; ~ **light area** n quartier m chaud; ~ **meat** n viande f rouge; ~ **mullet** n rouget m

redneck /ˈrednek/
A n injur péquenaud/-e° m/f offensive
B adj ultraréactionnaire

redness /ˈrednɪs/ n rougeur f

redo /ˌriːˈduː/ vtr (3ᵉ pers sg prés **redoes**; prét **redid**; pp **redone**) refaire

redolent /ˈredələnt/ adj littér to be ~ of sth lit sentir qch; fig évoquer qch

redone /ˌriːˈdʌn/ pp ▸ redo

redouble /ˌriːˈdʌbl/ vtr, vi redoubler; to ~ one's efforts redoubler d'efforts

redoubtable /rɪˈdaʊtəbl/ adj redoutable

red pepper n poivron m rouge

redraft /ˌriːˈdrɑːft/ vtr rédiger [qch] à nouveau

redress /rɪˈdres/
A n gen, Jur réparation f; they have no (means of) ~ ils n'ont aucun recours
B vtr réparer [error, wrong]; redresser [situation]; to ~ the balance rétablir l'équilibre

red: **Red Sea** pr n mer f Rouge; ~**skin** n injur Peau-Rouge mf; ~ **snapper** n vivaneau m; **Red Square** pr n place f Rouge; ~ **squirrel** n écureuil m roux; ~ **tape** n paperasserie f

reduce /rɪˈdjuːs, US ˈduːs/
A vtr **1** (make smaller) réduire [inflation, number, pressure, impact] (by de); baisser [prices, temperature]; Med résorber [swelling]; faire baisser [fever]; the jackets have been ~d by 50% Comm le prix des vestes a été réduit de 50%; '~ speed now' Aut 'ralentir'; **2** (in scale) réduire [map, article]; **3** (alter the state of) to ~ sth to shreds réduire qch en pièces; to ~ sb to tears faire pleurer qn; to be ~d to begging en être réduit à la mendicité; **4** (simplify) réduire [argument, equation, existence]; **5** Jur réduire [sentence]; **6** Culin faire réduire [sauce, stock]
B vi Culin [sauce] réduire
C reduced pp adj réduit; ~d goods marchandises en solde; in ~d circumstances sout dans la gêne

reductio ad absurdum /rɪˌdʌktɪəʊ æd əbˈsɜːdəm/ n raisonnement m par l'absurde

reduction /rɪˈdʌkʃn/ n **1** (decrease) (of volume, speed) réduction f (in de); (of weight, size, cost) diminution f (in de); **2** Comm réduction f, rabais m; **3** (simplification) réduction f; **4** Chem réduction f

reductive /rɪˈdʌktɪv/ adj réducteur/-trice

redundancy /rɪˈdʌndənsɪ/ n Ind licenciement m

redundant /rɪˈdʌndənt/ adj **1** GB Ind [worker] licencié; to be made ~ être licencié; **2** (not needed) [information, device] superflu; [land, machinery] inutilisé; to feel ~ se sentir de trop; **3** GB (outdated) [technique, practice] inutile; [craft] dépassé; **4** Comput, Ling redondant

red: ~ **wine** n vin m rouge; ~ **wine vinegar** n vinaigre m de vin rouge; ~**wood** n séquoia m

reed /riːd/
A n **1** Bot roseau m; **2** Mus anche f
B noun modifier **1** [basket, hut] en roseau; **2** Mus [instrument] à anche
(Idiom) to be a broken ~ être quelqu'un sur qui on ne peut plus compter

re-educate /ˌriːˈedʒʊkeɪt/ vtr rééduquer

reedy /ˈriːdɪ/ adj [voice, tone] aigu/-uë

reef /riːf/ n (in sea) récif m, écueil m

reefer /ˈriːfə(r)/ n **1** (also ~ jacket) caban m; **2** ᴼ(to smoke) joint m, cigarette f de marijuana

reef knot n nœud m plat

reek /riːk/
A n lit, fig relent m
B vi (stink) to ~ of sth lit puer qch; fig avoir des relents de qch

reel /riːl/
A n **1** gen bobine f; (for fishing) moulinet m; ~**-to-~** [tape recorder] à bobines; **2** (dance) quadrille m écossais
B vi (sway) [person] tituber; he ~ed across the room il a traversé la pièce en titubant; the blow sent him ~ing le coup l'a projeté en arrière; the government is still ~ing after its defeat le gouvernement ne s'est pas encore remis de sa défaite
(Idiom) off the ~ US sans hésiter
(Phrasal verbs)
■ reel in ramener [fish]
■ reel off: ▸ ~ off [sth] débiter [list, names]

re-elect /ˌriːɪˈlekt/ vtr réélire

re-election /ˌriːɪˈlekʃn/ n réélection f; to stand for GB ou run for ~ se représenter (aux élections)

re-emerge /ˌriːɪˈmɜːdʒ/ vi [person, sun] réapparaître; [problem] resurgir

re-enact /ˌriːɪˈnækt/ vtr **1** reconstituer [crime]; rejouer [role]; **2** Jur remettre en vigueur

re-enlist /ˌriːɪnˈlɪst/ vi se rengager

re-enter /ˌriːˈentə(r)/
A vtr entrer à nouveau dans
B vi (come back in) [person, vehicle etc] revenir

re-entry /ˌriːˈentrɪ/ n gen, Aerosp rentrée f; fig (into politics etc) retour m (into dans)

re-entry visa n visa m aller-retour

re-examine /ˌriːɪɡˈzæmɪn/ vtr réexaminer [issue, problem]; interroger à nouveau [witness]

ref /ref/ n **1** Comm abrév écrite = **reference A 3**; **2** ᴼSport (abrév = **referee**) arbitre m

refectory /rɪˈfektrɪ, ˈrefɪktrɪ/ n réfectoire m

refer /rɪˈfɜː(r)/ (p prés etc **-rr-**)
A vtr **1** (pass on) renvoyer [task, problem, enquiry] (to à); to ~ sb to [person] envoyer qn à [department]; [critic, text] renvoyer qn à [article, footnote]; **2** Jur déférer [case] (to à); **3** Med to be ~red to a specialist être envoyé en consultation chez un spécialiste
B vi **1** (allude to, talk about) to ~ to parler de, faire allusion à [person, topic, event]; **2** (as name, label) she ~s to him as Bob elle l'appelle Bob; **3** (signify) to ~ to [number, date, term] se rapporter à; **4** (consult) to ~ to consulter [notes, article]

referee /ˌrefəˈriː/
A n **1** Sport arbitre m; **2** GB (giving job reference) personne f pouvant fournir des références
B vtr, vi arbitrer

reference /ˈrefərəns/
A n **1** (allusion) référence f (to à), allusion f (to à); to make ~ to sb/sth faire allusion à qn/qch; there are three ~s to his son in the article son fils est mentionné trois fois dans l'article; **2** (consultation) to do sth without ~ to sb/sth faire qch sans consulter qn/qch; 'for ~ only' (on library book) 'consultation sur place'; for future ~ pour information; without ~ to se tenir compte de [statistics, needs]; **3** (in book, letter, memo) référence f; please quote this ~ prière de rappeler cette référence; **4** (also~ **mark**) renvoi m; **5** (testimonial) références fpl; **6** (referee) personne f pouvant fournir des références; **7** Ling référence f; **8** Geog map ~s coordonnées fpl
B with reference to prep phr en ce qui concerne, quant à; with ~ to your letter/request suite à votre lettre/demande
C vtr fournir les sources de [book, article]

reference: ~ **book** n ouvrage m de référence; ~ **library** n bibliothèque f d'ouvrages de référence; ~ **number** n numéro m de référence; ~ **point** n fig point m de repère

referendum /ˌrefəˈrendəm/ n (pl **-da**) référendum m

referral /rɪˈfɜːrəl/ n **1** Med Admin (person) patient/-e m/f envoyé/-e à un confrère; (system) fait d'envoyer un malade chez un spécialiste; **2** gen (of matter, problem) renvoi m (to à)

refill
A /ˈriːfɪl/ n (for fountain pen) cartouche f; (for ball-point, lighter, perfume) recharge f
B /ˌriːˈfɪl/ vtr recharger [pen, lighter]; remplir [qch] à nouveau [glass, bottle]

refine /rɪ'faɪn/ vtr **1** Ind raffiner [oil, sugar etc]; **2** (improve) peaufiner [theory]; raffiner [manners]; affiner [method, taste, language]

refined /rɪ'faɪnd/ adj **1** Ind [oil, sugar etc] raffiné; [metal] affiné; **2** (cultured) raffiné; **3** (improved) [method, model] très au point; [theory, concept] peaufiné

refinement /rɪ'faɪnmənt/ n (elegance) raffinement m

refinery /rɪ'faɪnərɪ/ n raffinerie f

refit
A /'riːfɪt/ n (of shop, factory etc) rééquipement m; Naut réarmement m
B /ˌriː'fɪt/ vtr (p prés etc **-tt-**) réarmer [ship]; rééquiper [shop, factory]

reflate /ˌriː'fleɪt/ vtr Econ relancer

reflation /ˌriː'fleɪʃn/ n Econ relance f

reflect /rɪ'flekt/
A vtr **1** lit, fig refléter; **to be ~ed in sth** lit, fig se refléter dans qch; **he saw himself/her face ~ed in the mirror** il a vu son reflet/le reflet de son visage dans le miroir; **2** (throw back) renvoyer, réfléchir [light, heat]; **3** (think) se dire, penser
B vi **1** (think) réfléchir (on, upon à); **2** **to ~ well/badly on sb** faire honneur/du tort à qn; **how is this going to ~ on the school?** quelles vont être les conséquences pour l'école?

reflection /rɪ'flekʃn/ n **1** (image) lit, fig reflet m (of de), image f (of de); **2** (thought) réflexion f; **on ~** à la réflexion; **3** (idea) réflexion f, pensée f; (remark) remarque f; **4** (criticism) **it is a sad ~ on our society that** ce n'est pas à la gloire de notre société que

reflective /rɪ'flektɪv/ adj **1** [mood] pensif/-ive; [person] réfléchi; **2** [material, surface] réfléchissant

reflector /rɪ'flektə(r)/ n **1** (on vehicle) catadioptre m; **2** (of light, heat) réflecteur m

reflex /'riːfleks/
A n réflexe m
B adj gen, Anat réflexe; **a ~ action** un réflexe

reflexive /rɪ'fleksɪv/ Ling
A n (also **~ verb**) verbe m pronominal réfléchi
B adj réfléchi

refloat /ˌriː'fləʊt/ vtr Naut, Econ renflouer

reforestation /ˌriːfɒrə'steɪʃn/ n reboisement m

reform /rɪ'fɔːm/
A n réforme f
B vtr réformer
C vi se réformer
D **reformed** pp adj [state, system] réformé; [criminal] repenti; Relig [church] réformé; **he's a ~ed character** il s'est assagi

reformat /ˌriː'fɔːmæt/ vtr Comput reformater

reformation /ˌrefə'meɪʃn/ n gen réforme f; **the Reformation** Relig la Réforme

reformer /rɪ'fɔːmə(r)/ n réformateur/-trice m/f

refrain /rɪ'freɪn/
A n Mus, Literat, fig refrain m
B vi se retenir; **to ~ from doing** s'abstenir de faire; **he could not ~ from saying** il n'a pas pu s'empêcher de dire; **please ~ from smoking** sout ayez l'obligeance de ne pas fumer fml

refresh /rɪ'freʃ/ vtr [bath, drink] rafraîchir; [rest] reposer; **to ~ oneself** se rafraîchir; **to ~ sb's memory** rafraîchir la mémoire à qn

refresher course /rɪ'freʃə kɔːs/ n cours m de recyclage

refreshing /rɪ'freʃɪŋ/ adj [drink, shower] rafraîchissant; [rest] réparateur/-trice; [insight] original

refreshment /rɪ'freʃmənt/ n (rest) repos m; (food, drink) restauration f; **~s** (drinks) rafraîchissements mpl; **light ~s** repas m léger

refreshment bar, refreshment stall n buvette f

refrigerate /rɪ'frɪdʒəreɪt/
A vtr frigorifier; **'keep ~d'** 'conserver au réfrigérateur'
B **refrigerated** pp adj [product] frigorifié; [transport] frigorifique

refrigeration /rɪˌfrɪdʒə'reɪʃn/ n réfrigération f

refrigerator /rɪ'frɪdʒəreɪtə(r)/
A n (appliance) réfrigérateur m, frigidaire® m; (room) chambre f frigorifique
B noun modifier [truck, wagon] frigorifique

refuel /ˌriː'fjʊəl/ (p prés etc **-ll-** GB, **-l-** US)
A vtr lit ravitailler [qch] en carburant; fig ranimer
B vi se ravitailler en carburant

refuge /'refjuːdʒ/ n **1** refuge m (**from** contre); **to take ~ from** se mettre à l'abri de [danger, people]; s'abriter de [weather]; **to take ~ in** se réfugier dans [place, drink, drugs]; **2** (hostel) foyer m

refugee /ˌrefjʊ'dʒiː, US 'refjʊdʒiː/
A n réfugié/-e m/f
B noun modifier [camp] de réfugiés; [status] de réfugié

refund
A /'riːfʌnd/ n remboursement m
B /rɪ'fʌnd/ vtr rembourser

refurbish /ˌriː'fɜːbɪʃ/ vtr rénover

refurbishment /ˌriː'fɜːbɪʃmənt/ n rénovation f

refusal /rɪ'fjuːzl/ n **1** gen refus m (**to do** de faire); (to application, invitation) réponse f négative; **2** **to give sb first ~** Comm donner la priorité à qn

refuse¹ /rɪ'fjuːz/
A vtr refuser (**to do** de faire)
B vi refuser

refuse² /'refjuːs/ n GB (household) ordures fpl; (industrial) déchets mpl; (garden) déchets mpl de jardinage

refuse bin n GB poubelle f

refuse chute n GB vide-ordures m inv

refuse refjuːs: **~ collector** ▸ p. 1181 n GB éboueur m; **~ disposal** GB n traitement m des ordures; **~ disposal unit** n broyeur m d'ordures; **~ dump** n GB décharge f publique; **~ lorry** n GB camion m des éboueurs

refute /rɪ'fjuːt/ vtr réfuter

regain /rɪ'geɪn/ vtr retrouver [health, sight, freedom]; reconquérir [power, seat]; retrouver [balance, composure]; reprendre [lead, control]; rattraper [time]; **to ~ possession of** rentrer en possession de; **to ~ consciousness** reprendre connaissance

regal /'riːgl/ adj royal

regale /rɪ'geɪl/ vtr régaler (**with** de)

regalia /rɪ'geɪlɪə/ npl insignes mpl; **in full ~** lit, hum en grande tenue

regally /'riːgəlɪ/ adv majestueusement

regard /rɪ'gɑːd/
A n **1** (consideration) égard m fml; **out of ~ for** par égard pour; **2** (esteem) estime f (**for** pour); **to hold sb/sth in high ~** avoir beaucoup d'estime pour qn/qch; **to have little ~ for money** faire peu de cas de l'argent; **3** (connection) **with ~ to** ou **in ~ to** en ce qui concerne; **in this ~** à cet égard
B **regards** npl (good wishes) amitiés fpl; **kindest ~s** avec toutes mes (or nos) amitiés; **give them my ~s** transmettez-leur mes amitiés
C vtr **1** (consider) considérer; **to ~ sb with suspicion** se montrer soupçonneux à l'égard de qn; **highly ~ed** très apprécié; **2** (concern) sout concerner

regarding /rɪ'gɑːdɪŋ/ prep concernant

regardless /rɪ'gɑːdlɪs/
A prep **~ of cost/age** sans tenir compte du prix/de l'âge; **~ of the weather** quel que soit le temps
B adv malgré tout

regatta /rɪ'gætə/ n régate f

regency /'riːdʒənsɪ/ n régence f

regenerate /rɪ'dʒenəreɪt/
A vtr régénérer
B vi se régénérer

regeneration /rɪˌdʒenə'reɪʃn/ n gen régénération f; (urban) restauration f

regent /'riːdʒənt/ n Pol Hist régent/-e m/f

reggae /'regeɪ/ n reggae m

regime, régime /reɪ'ʒiːm, 'reɪʒiːm/ n Pol régime m

regiment /'redʒɪmənt/ n Mil, fig régiment m

regimental /ˌredʒɪ'mentl/ adj du régiment

regimented /'redʒɪmentɪd/ adj soumis à une discipline toute militaire

Regina /rə'dʒaɪnə/ n GB Jur **~ v Jones** la Couronne contre Jones

region /'riːdʒən/ n région f; **(somewhere) in the ~ of £300** environ 300 livres sterling

r

British regions and counties

■ *The names of British regions and counties usually have the definite article in French, except when used with the preposition* en.

. . . .

In, to and from somewhere

■ *Most counties and regions are masculine; with these,* in *and* to *are translated by* dans le, *and* from *by* du:

to live on Sussex
= vivre dans le Sussex

to go to Sussex
= aller dans le Sussex

to come from Sussex
= venir du Sussex

■ *Note however:*

Cornwall
= la Cornouailles

to live in Cornwall
= vivre en Cornouailles

to go to Cornwall
= aller en Cornouailles

to come from Cornwall
= venir de la Cornouailles

Uses with nouns

■ *There are rarely French equivalents for English forms like* Cornishmen, *and it is always safe to use* de *with the definite article:*

Cornishmen
= les habitants *mpl* de la Cornouailles

Lancastrians
= les habitants du Lancashire

■ *In other cases,* du *is often possible:*

a Somerset accent
= un accent du Somerset

the Yorkshire countryside
= les paysages du Yorkshire

■ *but it is usually safe to use* du comté de:

the towns of Fife
= les villes du comté de Fife

the rivers of Merioneth
= les rivières du comté de Merioneth

■ *or* de la région de:

Grampian cattle
= le bétail de la région des Grampians

---

regional /'riːdʒənl/ *adj* régional; ~ **development** Ind aménagement *m* du territoire

regionalism /'riːdʒənlɪzəm/ *n* régionalisme *m*

register /'redʒɪstə(r)/
A *n* **1** gen, Admin, Comm registre *m*; Sch cahier *m* des absences; ~ **of births, marriages and deaths** registre public de l'état civil; **2** Mus, Ling, Comput registre *m*; **3** US (till) caisse *f* enregistreuse
B *vtr* **1** [*member of the public*] déclarer [*birth, death, marriage*]; faire immatriculer [*vehicle*]; faire enregistrer [*luggage, company*]; déposer [*trademark, patent, complaint*]; [*official*] inscrire [*student*]; enregistrer [*name, birth, death, company*]; immatriculer [*vehicle*]; **to be ~ed (as) disabled** être officiellement reconnu handicapé; **2** [*instrument*] indiquer [*speed, temperature*]; [*person*] exprimer [*anger, disapproval*]; **to ~ six on the Richter scale** [*earthquake*] atteindre la magnitude six sur l'échelle de Richter; **3** (mentally) (notice) remarquer; (realize) se rendre compte; **4** (record) enregistrer [*loss, gain*]; **5** Post envoyer [qch] en recommandé [*letter*]; enregistrer [*luggage*]
C *vi* **1** [*person*] (to vote, for course, school) s'inscrire; (at hotel) se présenter; (with police, for taxes) se faire recenser (**for** pour); (for shares) souscrire (**for** à); **to ~ for a course** s'inscrire à un cours; **to ~ with a doctor** s'inscrire sur la liste des patients d'un médecin; **2** [*speed, temperature, earthquake*] être enregistré; **his name didn't ~ with me** fig son nom ne me disait rien

registered /'redʒɪstəd/ *adj* **1** [*voter*] inscrit; [*vehicle, student*] immatriculé; [*charity*] ≈ agréé; [*firearm*] déclaré; [*company*] inscrit au registre du commerce; [*nurse*] diplômé d'État; Comm [*shares*] nominatif/-ive; **2** Post [*letter*] recommandé; ~ **post** envoi *m* recommandé; **by ~ post** en recommandé

registered trademark *n* nom *m* déposé

registrar /ˌredʒɪs'trɑː(r), 'redʒ-/ ▶ p. 1181 *n* GB Admin officier *m* d'état civil; Univ responsable *mf* du bureau de la scolarité; GB Med adjoint *m*; GB Jur greffier/-ière *m/f* en chef

registration /ˌredʒɪ'streɪʃn/ *n* (of person) (for course) inscription *f*; (for taxes) ≈ déclaration *f*; (for national service) recensement *m* militaire; (of trademark, patent) dépôt *m*; (of birth, death, marriage) déclaration *f*; (of company, luggage) enregistrement *m*; Aut année *f* de première immatriculation

registration: ~ **number** *n* numéro *m* d'immatriculation *or* minéralogique; ~ **plate** *n* plaque *f* d'immatriculation *or* minéralogique

registry /'redʒɪstrɪ/ *n* GB salle *f* des registres

registry office *n* GB bureau *m* de l'état civil; **to get married in a ~** se marier civilement

regress /rɪ'gres/ *vi* Biol, Psych régresser (**to** au stade de); fig régresser; **to ~ to childhood** retomber en enfance

regression /rɪ'greʃn/ *n* régression *f*

regressive /rɪ'gresɪv/ *adj* Biol, Psych régressif/-ive

regret /rɪ'gret/
A *n* regret *m* (**about** à propos de; **that** que + *subj*); **to have no ~s about doing** ne pas regretter d'avoir fait; **to my great ~** à mon grand regret
B *vtr* (*p prés etc* **-tt-**) regretter (**that** que + *subj*); **to ~ doing** regretter d'avoir fait; **I ~ to say that...** je suis au regret de dire que...; **I ~ to inform you that** j'ai le regret de vous informer que; **it is to be ~ted that** il est regrettable que (+ *subj*)

regretful /rɪ'gretfl/ *adj* plein de regrets

regretfully /rɪ'gretflɪ/ *adv* (reluctantly) à regret

regrettable /rɪ'gretəbl/ *adj* regrettable (**that** que + *subj*)

regrettably /rɪ'gretəblɪ/ *adv* **1** (sadly) malheureusement; **2** (very) [*slow, weak*] fâcheusement

regroup /ˌriː'gruːp/ *vi* se regrouper

regular /'regjʊlə(r)/
A *n* **1** (habitual client, visitor) habitué/-e *m/f*; **2** GB Mil soldat *m* de métier; **3** US (petrol) ordinaire *m*
B *adj* **1** [*habit, job, income, interval etc*] also Med, Ling régulier/-ière; **on a ~ basis** de façon régulière; ~ **features** traits réguliers; **to take ~ exercise** prendre de l'exercice régulièrement; **to be in ~ employment** avoir un emploi permanent; **he's a ~ guy**○ US c'est un chic type○; **2** (usual) [*activity, customer, visitor*] habituel/-elle; Comm [*price, size*] normal; Radio, TV [*listener*] fidèle; **3** GB Admin, Mil [*army, soldier*] de métier; [*officer, policeman*] de carrière; [*staff*] permanent; **4** (honest) régulier/-ière; **5** ○(thorough) véritable (*before n*); **a ~ crook** un véritable escroc

regularity /ˌregjʊ'lærətɪ/ *n* régularité *f*

regularize /'regjʊləraɪz/ *vtr* régulariser

regularly /'regjʊləlɪ/ *adv* régulièrement

regulate /'regjʊleɪt/ *vtr* **1** réguler [*behaviour, activity*]; réglementer [*use*]; **well-~d** bien réglé; **state-~d** sous le contrôle de l'état; **2** (adjust) régler [*mechanism*]

regulation /ˌregjʊ'leɪʃn/
A *n* **1** (rule) (for safety, fire) consigne *f*; (for discipline) règlement *m*; (legal) disposition *f* réglementaire; **EC ~s** réglementation *f* communautaire; **fire ~s** (laws) normes *fpl* anti-incendie;

under the (new) ∼s selon la (nouvelle) réglementation; **against the ∼s** contraire au règlement *or* aux normes; **②** (process) réglementation *f*

B *noun modifier* [*width, length etc*] réglementaire; hum [*garment*] de rigueur

regulator /ˈregjʊleɪtə(r)/ *n* **①** (device) régulateur *m*; **②** (person) régulateur/-trice *m/f*; **③** Econ organisme *m* de contrôle

regulatory /ˈregjʊleɪtrɪ, US -tɔːrɪ/ *adj* de contrôle

rehabilitate /ˌriːəˈbɪlɪteɪt/ *vtr* **①** (medically) rééduquer; (to society) réinsérer [*handicapped person, ex-prisoner*]; réhabiliter [*addict*]; **②** gen, Pol réhabiliter

rehabilitation /ˌriːəbɪlɪˈteɪʃn/ *n* **①** (of person) (medical) rééducation *f*; (social) réinsertion *f*; **②** gen, Pol réhabilitation *f*

rehabilitation centre GB, **rehabilitation center** US *n* (for the handicapped) centre *m* de rééducation; (for addicts etc) centre *m* de réinsertion

rehash péj
A /ˈriːhæʃ/ *n* resucée○ *f*
B /ˌriːˈhæʃ/ *vtr* remanier, piller péj

rehearsal /rɪˈhɜːsl/ *n* Theat répétition *f* (**of** de); fig préparation *f* (**of** de); **in ∼** en répétition

rehearse /rɪˈhɜːs/
A *vtr* Theat répéter [*scene*]; faire répéter [*performer*]; fig préparer [*speech, excuse*]
B *vi* répéter (**for** pour)

reheat /ˌriːˈhiːt/ *vtr* réchauffer

rehouse /ˌriːˈhaʊz/ *vtr* reloger

reign /reɪn/
A *n* lit, fig règne *m*; **in the ∼ of** sous le règne de; **∼ of terror** fig règne de la terreur; **the Reign of Terror** Hist la Terreur
B *vi* lit, fig régner (**over** sur)

reigning /ˈreɪnɪŋ/ *adj* [*monarch*] régnant; [*champion*] en titre

reimburse /ˌriːɪmˈbɜːs/ *vtr* rembourser

reimbursement /ˌriːɪmˈbɜːsmənt/ *n* remboursement *m* (**of** de; **for** pour)

rein /reɪn/ *n* rêne *f*; **to hold the ∼s** lit, fig tenir les rênes; **to keep sb on a tight ∼** fig tenir qn de près; **to give full** *ou* **free ∼ to** donner libre cours à

⌐Phrasal verb⌐

■ **rein in: ▸ ∼ in [sth]** freiner [qch] (avec les rênes) [*horse*]; fig contenir

reincarnate /ˌriːɪnˈkɑːneɪt/ *vtr* **to be ∼d** se réincarner (**as** en)

reincarnation /ˌriːɪnkɑːˈneɪʃn/ *n* réincarnation *f*

reindeer /ˈreɪndɪə(r)/ *n* (*pl* ∼) renne *m*

reinforce /ˌriːɪnˈfɔːs/ *vtr* gen, Mil renforcer; fig renforcer [*feeling, trend*]; **∼d concrete** béton *m* armé

reinforcement /ˌriːɪnˈfɔːsmənt/ *n* **①** (action) renforcement *m* (**of** de); **②** (support) renfort *m*; **∼s** Mil, fig renforts

reinstate /ˌriːɪnˈsteɪt/ *vtr* réintégrer [*employee*]; rétablir [*legislation*]

reintegrate /ˌriːˈɪntɪgreɪt/ *vtr* réintégrer (**into** dans)

reinvigorate /ˌriːɪnˈvɪgəreɪt/ *vtr* revigorer

reissue /ˌriːˈɪʃuː/
A *n* (book, record) réédition *f*; Cin reprise *f*
B *vtr* rééditer [*book, record*]; ressortir [*film*]; Comm émettre [qch] à nouveau [*shares*]

reiterate /riːˈɪtəreɪt/ *vtr* réitérer

reiteration /riːˌɪtəˈreɪʃn/ *n* réitération *f*

reject
A /ˈriːdʒekt/ *n* Comm marchandise *f* de deuxième choix
B /rɪˈdʒekt/ *vtr* gen, Med, Psych rejeter; refuser [*candidate, manuscript*]; démentir [*claim, suggestion*]; repousser [*suitor*]

rejection /rɪˈdʒekʃn/ *n* gen, Med, Psych rejet *m*; (of candidate, manuscript) refus *m*; **to meet with ∼** se heurter à un refus

rejection: ∼ letter *n* lettre *f* de refus; **∼ slip** *n* avis *m* de refus

rejig /ˌriːˈdʒɪg/ GB, **rejigger** /ˌriːˈdʒɪgə(r)/ US *vtr* réviser

rejoice /rɪˈdʒɔɪs/
A *vtr* réjouir; **to ∼ that** se réjouir du fait que
B *vi* se réjouir (**at, over** de); **to ∼ in** se réjouir de

rejoicing /rɪˈdʒɔɪsɪŋ/ *n* (jubilation) allégresse *f*; **∼s** (celebrations) réjouissances *fpl*

rejoin /riːˈdʒɔɪn/ *vtr* gén rejoindre; réintégrer [*team, organization*]; [*road*] rejoindre [*coast, route*]; **to ∼ ship** Naut rallier le bord

rejoinder /rɪˈdʒɔɪndə(r)/ *n* gen, Jur réplique *f*

rejuvenate /rɪˈdʒuːvɪneɪt/ *vtr* lit, fig rajeunir

rejuvenation /rɪˌdʒuːvɪˈneɪʃn/ *n* lit, fig rajeunissement *m*

rekindle /ˌriːˈkɪndl/ *vtr* lit, fig ranimer

relapse
A /ˈriːlæps/ *n* Med, fig rechute *f*
B /rɪˈlæps/ *vi* gen retomber; Med rechuter

relate /rɪˈleɪt/
A *vtr* **①** (connect) **to ∼ sth and sth** établir un rapport entre qch et qch; **to ∼ sth to sth** associer qch à qch; **②** raconter [*story*] (**to** à)
B *vi* **①** (have connection) **to ∼ to** se rapporter à; **everything relating to him** tout ce qui a un rapport avec lui; **②** (communicate) **to ∼ to** s'entendre avec; **I can't ∼ to the character** le personnage ne me touche pas; **I can ∼ to that!** ça, je comprends!

related /rɪˈleɪtɪd/ *adj* **①** [*person, language*] apparenté (**by, through** par; **to** à); **to be ∼ by marriage** être parents par alliance; **②** (connected) [*subject*] connexe (**to** à); [*area, idea, incident*] lié (**to** à); [*species*] similaire (**to** à); **the murders are ∼** les crimes sont liés; **drug/work-∼** lié à la drogue/au travail

relation /rɪˈleɪʃn/
A *n* **①** (relative) parent/-e *m/f*; **my ∼s** ma famille; **②** (connection) rapport *m*; **to bear no ∼ to** n'avoir aucun rapport avec; **in ∼ to** par rapport à; **with ∼ to** en ce qui concerne
B **relations** *npl* gen (dealings) relations *fpl*; euph (intercourse) relations *fpl* sexuelles

relationship /rɪˈleɪʃnʃɪp/ *n* **①** (between people) relations *fpl*; **to form ∼s** se lier; **to have a good ∼** avoir de bonnes relations avec; **a working ∼** des relations professionnelles; **sexual ∼** relation sexuelle; **we have a good ∼** nous nous entendons bien; **②** (connection) rapport *m* (**to, with** avec); **③** (family bond) lien *m* de parenté (**to** avec)

relative /ˈrelətɪv/
A *n* **①** (relation) parent/-e *m/f*; **my ∼s** ma famille; **②** Ling relatif *m*
B *adj* relatif/-ive; **the ∼ merits of X and Y** les mérites respectifs de X et Y; **∼ to** (compared to) par rapport à; **supply is ∼ to demand** l'offre varie en fonction de la demande

relatively /ˈrelətɪvlɪ/ *adv* relativement; **∼ speaking** toutes proportions gardées

relativism /ˈrelətɪvɪzəm/ *n* relativisme *m*

relativity /ˌreləˈtɪvətɪ/ *n* relativité *f* (**of** de)

relax /rɪˈlæks/
A *vtr* relâcher [*grip, concentration*]; décontracter [*jaw, muscle*]; assouplir [*restrictions, discipline*]; détendre [*body*]
B *vi* **①** [*person*] se détendre; **∼!** ne t'en fais pas!; **②** [*grip*] se relâcher; [*jaw, muscle*] se décontracter; [*discipline, restrictions*] s'assouplir

relaxation /ˌriːlækˈseɪʃn/ *n* **①** (recreation) détente *f*; **what do you do for ∼?** qu'est-ce que vous faites pour vous détendre?; **②** (of grip, concentration) relâchement *m*; (of restrictions, discipline) assouplissement *m* (**in** de); (of body) détente *f*

relaxed /rɪˈlækst/ *adj* gen détendu, décontracté; [*muscle*] décontracté

relaxing /rɪˈlæksɪŋ/ *adj* [*atmosphere, activity*] délassant; [*period, vacation*] reposant

relay
A /ˈriːleɪ/ *n* **①** (of workers) équipe *f* (*de relais*); (of horses) attelage *m*; **②** Radio, TV émission *f* retransmise; **③** (*also* **∼ race**) course *f* de relais
B /ˈriːleɪ, rɪˈleɪ/ *vtr* (*prét, pp* **relayed**) Radio, TV relayer (**to** à); fig transmettre [*message*] (**to** à)

relay station *n* Radio, TV relais *m*

release /rɪˈliːs/
A *n* **①** (liberation) libération *f*; **on his ∼ from prison** à sa sortie de prison; **②** fig soulagement *m*; **death came as a merciful ∼** la mort est venue comme une délivrance; **③** Mil (of missile) lancement *m*; (of bomb) largage *m*; **④** (for press) communiqué *m*; **⑤** Cin sortie *f*; **the film is now on general ∼** le film passe maintenant dans toutes les grandes salles de cinéma; **⑥** (film, video, record) nouveauté *f*; **⑦** (discharge form) décharge *f*
B *vtr* **①** libérer [*prisoner*]; dégager [*accident victim*]; relâcher

[*animal*]; **to ~ sb from** fig dégager qn de [*promise, obligation*]; **2** faire jouer [*catch, clasp*]; Phot déclencher [*shutter*]; Aut desserrer [*handbrake*]; **3** décocher [*arrow*]; larguer [*bomb*]; lancer [*missile*]; **4** lâcher [*object, arm, hand*]; **to ~ one's grip** lâcher prise; **to ~ one's grip of sth** lâcher qch; **5** (to public) communiquer [*statement*]; publier [*photo*]; faire sortir [*film, video, record*]

relegate /ˈrelɪɡeɪt/ vtr **1** reléguer [*person, object, issue*] (**to** à); **2** GB Sport reléguer (**to** en); **to be ~d** descendre dans la division inférieure

relegation /ˌrelɪˈɡeɪʃn/ n gen relégation f (**to** à); GB Sport relégation f (**to** en)

relent /rɪˈlent/ vi [*person, government*] céder

relentless /rɪˈlentlɪs/ adj [*ambition*] implacable; [*noise, activity*] incessant; [*attack*] acharné

relentlessly /rɪˈlentlɪslɪ/ adv (incessantly) sans arrêt; (mercilessly) inexorablement

relevance /ˈreləvəns/ n pertinence f (**to** pour), intérêt m (**to** pour); **the ~ of politics to daily life** le rapport entre la politique et la vie quotidienne; **to be of ~ to** être lié à

relevant /ˈreləvənt/ adj **1** [*issue, facts, remark, point*] pertinent; [*information, resource*] utile; **to be ~ to** avoir rapport à; **2** (appropriate) [*chapter*] correspondant; [*period*] en question; **~ document** Jur pièce f justificative; **the ~ authorities** les autorités compétentes

reliability /rɪˌlaɪəˈbɪlətɪ/ n (of friend, witness) honnêteté f; (of employee, firm) sérieux m; (of car, machine) fiabilité f; (of information, memory) exactitude f

reliable /rɪˈlaɪəbl/ adj [*friend, witness*] digne de confiance, fiable; [*employee, firm*] sérieux/-ieuse; [*car, memory, account*] fiable; [*information, source*] sûr

reliably /rɪˈlaɪəblɪ/ adv [*work*] correctement; **to be ~ informed that** tenir de source sûre que

reliance /rɪˈlaɪəns/ n dépendance f (**on** vis-à-vis de)

reliant /rɪˈlaɪənt/ adj **to be ~ on** être dépendant de

relic /ˈrelɪk/ n **1** fig (custom, building) vestige m (**of** de); (object) relique f (**of** de); **2** Relig relique f

relief /rɪˈliːf/
A n **1** (from pain, distress) soulagement m; **to my ~** à mon grand soulagement; **it was a ~ to them that** ils ont été soulagés que (+ subj); **2** (help) aide f, secours m; **famine ~** aide aux victimes de la famine; **to come to the ~ of sb** venir à l'aide or au secours de qn; **tax ~** allégement fiscal; **to be on ~** US bénéficier des aides sociales; **3** (diversion) divertissement m; **to provide light ~** apporter un peu de divertissement; **4** (of garrison, troops) délivrance f; **5** Art, Archit, Geog relief m; **in ~** en relief; **to throw sth into ~** mettre qch en relief
B noun modifier [*operation*] de secours; [*programme, project, effort*] d'aide; [*guard, shift*] de relève; [*bus, train*] supplémentaire

relief: ~ agency n organisation f humanitaire; **~ fund** n gen fonds m d'aide; (in emergency) fonds m de secours; **~ map** n carte f en relief; **~ road** n route f de délestage; **~ supplies** npl secours mpl; **~ work** n travail m humanitaire; **~ worker** n secouriste mf

relieve /rɪˈliːv/
A vtr **1** soulager [*pain, suffering, tension*]; dissiper [*boredom*]; remédier à [*poverty, famine*]; alléger [*debt*]; rompre [*monotony*]; **to be ~d that** être soulagé que (+ subj); **to be ~d at** être soulagé par [*news, results*]; **to ~ congestion** Med, Aut décongestionner; **2** **to ~ sb of** débarrasser qn de [*plate, coat*]; soulager qn de [*burden*]; **to ~ sb of a post** relever qn de son poste; **3** (help) venir en aide à, secourir [*troops, population*]; **4** relever [*worker, sentry*]; **to ~ the guard** relever la garde; **5** Mil délivrer [*town*]
B v refl **to ~ oneself** euph se soulager euph

religion /rɪˈlɪdʒən/ n religion f; **what ~ is he?** de quelle religion est-il?; **it's against my ~ to...** c'est contraire à ma religion de... also hum; **to get ~**° péj devenir bigot; **to lose one's ~** perdre la foi

religious /rɪˈlɪdʒəs/
A n religieux/-ieuse m/f
B adj gen religieux/-ieuse; [*war*] de religion; [*person*] croyant; **Religious Education** ou **Instruction** instruction f religieuse

religiously /rɪˈlɪdʒəslɪ/ adv lit religieusement; fig rituellement

relinquish /rɪˈlɪŋkwɪʃ/ vtr sout renoncer à [*claim, right, privilege*] (**to** en faveur de); céder [*task, power*] (**to** à); abandonner [*responsibility*]; **to ~ one's hold** ou **grip on sth** lâcher qch

relish /ˈrelɪʃ/
A n **1** **with ~** [*eat, drink, perform*] avec un plaisir évident; [*say*] avec délectation or (gloatingly) en jubilant; **2** (flavour) saveur f; fig (appeal) attrait m; **3** Culin condiment m
B vtr savourer [*food*]; fig se réjouir de [*prospect*]; **I don't ~ the thought of telling her the news** je me passerais bien de lui annoncer la nouvelle

relocate /ˌriːləʊˈkeɪt, US riːˈləʊkeɪt/
A vtr muter
B vi [*company*] déménager; [*employee*] être muté

relocation /ˌriːləʊˈkeɪʃn/ n (of company) relocalisation f, déménagement m; (of employee) mutation f (**to** à, en); (of refugees) transfert m (**to** vers)

relocation: ~ allowance n prime f de relogement; **~ package** n indemnités fpl de déménagement

reluctance /rɪˈlʌktəns/ n gen réticence f (**to do** à faire); **to do sth with ~** faire qch à contrecœur

reluctant /rɪˈlʌktənt/ adj [*person*] peu enthousiaste; [*consent, promise*] accordé à contrecœur; **to be ~ to do** être peu disposé à faire; **she is a rather ~ celebrity** elle est devenue une célébrité malgré elle

reluctantly /rɪˈlʌktəntlɪ/ adv à contrecœur

rely /rɪˈlaɪ/ vi **1** (be dependent) **to ~ on** gen dépendre de; reposer sur [*method, technology, exports*]; **he relies on her for everything** il s'en remet à elle pour tout; **2** (count) **to ~ on sb/sth** compter sur qn/qch (**to do** pour faire); **she cannot be relied (up)on to help** on ne peut pas compter sur elle pour aider

remain /rɪˈmeɪn/
A vi **1** (be left) rester; **the fact ~s that** il reste que, toujours est-il que; **it ~s to be seen whether** il reste à voir si; **2** (stay) [*person, memory*] rester, demeurer; [*problem, doubt*] subsister; **to ~ standing** rester debout; **to ~ silent** garder le silence; **to ~ hopeful** continuer à espérer; **if the weather ~s fine** si le temps se maintient au beau
B remaining pres p adj restant; **for the ~ months of my life** pendant les mois qu'il me reste à vivre

remainder /rɪˈmeɪndə(r)/
A n (remaining things, money) also Math reste m; (people) autres mfpl; (time) reste m, restant m
B remainders npl Comm invendus mpl soldés

remains /rɪˈmeɪnz/ npl **1** (of meal, fortune) restes mpl; (of building) vestiges mpl, restes; **2** (corpse) restes mpl

remake
A /ˈriːmeɪk/ n nouvelle version f, remake m
B /ˌriːˈmeɪk/ vtr (prét, pp **remade**) refaire

remand /rɪˈmɑːnd, US rɪˈmænd/ Jur
A n **to be on ~** (in custody) être en détention provisoire; (on bail) être en liberté sous caution
B vtr renvoyer [*case, accused*]; **to be ~ed in custody** être placé en détention provisoire; **to be ~ed on bail** être mis en liberté sous caution

remand: ~ centre n GB centre m de détention (provisoire); **~ home** n GB centre m de détention (pour mineurs); **~ prisoner** n GB prisonnier/-ière m/f en détention provisoire

remark /rɪˈmɑːk/
A n remarque f (**about** à propos de, sur), réflexion f (**about** à propos de, sur)
B vtr **1** (comment) faire remarquer (**that** que; **to** à); **2** (notice) sout remarquer (**that** que)

(Phrasal verb)

■ **remark on, remark upon:** ▸ **~ on** ou **upon [sth]** faire des remarques sur or à propos de (**to** à)

remarkable /rɪˈmɑːkəbl/ adj remarquable (**that** que + subj)

remarkably /rɪˈmɑːkəblɪ/ adv remarquablement

remarry /ˌriːˈmærɪ/ vi se remarier

remaster /riːˈmɑːstə(r)/ vtr Audio remastériser

rematch /ˈriːmætʃ/ n Sport gen match m de retour; (in boxing) deuxième combat m

remedial /rɪˈmiːdɪəl/ adj gen [*measures*] de redressement; Med curatif/-ive; Sch [*class*] de rattrapage

remedy /ˈremədɪ/
A n Med, fig remède m (**for** à, contre)

B *vtr* remédier à; **the situation cannot be remedied** la situation est sans remède

remember /rɪˈmembə(r)/

A *vtr* **1** (recall) se souvenir de, se rappeler [*fact, name, place, event*]; se souvenir de [*person*]; **to ~ that** se rappeler que, se souvenir que; **to ~ doing** se rappeler avoir fait, se souvenir d'avoir fait; **I don't ~ anything about it** je n'en ai aucun souvenir; **that's worth ~ing** c'est bon à savoir; **a night to ~** une soirée mémorable; **2** (not forget) **to ~ to do** penser à faire, ne pas oublier de faire; **did you ~ to feed the cat?** tu as pensé à donner à manger au chat?; **~ that it's fragile** n'oublie pas que c'est fragile; **~ where you are!** un peu de tenue!; **she ~ed me in her will** euph elle ne m'a pas oublié dans son testament; **3** (commemorate) commémorer [*battle, war dead*]; **4** (convey greetings) **she asks to be ~ed to you** elle m'a prié de vous transmettre son bon souvenir

B *vi* se souvenir; **if I ~ rightly** si je me souviens bien; **not as far as I ~** pas que je sache; **as far as I can ~** pour autant que je me souvienne

remembrance /rɪˈmembrəns/ *n* souvenir *m*

Remembrance Day, **Remembrance Sunday** GB *n*: *jour consacré à la mémoire des soldats tués au cours des deux guerres mondiales et des conflits postérieurs*

remind /rɪˈmaɪnd/

A *vtr* rappeler; **to ~ sb of sth/sb** rappeler qch/qn à qn; **to ~ sb to do/that** rappeler à qn de faire/que; **you are ~ed that** nous vous rappelons que; **I forgot to ~ her about the meeting** j'ai oublié de lui reparler de la réunion; **that ~s me** à propos

B *v refl* **to ~ oneself** se dire (**that** que)

reminder /rɪˈmaɪndə(r)/ *n* rappel *m* (**of** de; **that** du fait que); **a ~ to sb to do** un rappel à qn lui demandant de faire; (**letter of**) ~ Admin (lettre *f* de) rappel *m*; **to be a ~ of sth** rappeler qch; **~s of the past** souvenirs *mpl* du passé

reminisce /ˌremɪˈnɪs/ *vi* évoquer ses souvenirs (**about** de)

reminiscence /ˌremɪˈnɪsns/ *n* (recalling) réminiscence *f*; (memory) souvenir *m*

reminiscent /ˌremɪˈnɪsnt/ *adj* **to be ~ of sb/sth** faire penser à qn/qch

remiss /rɪˈmɪs/ *adj* négligent; **it was ~ of him not to reply** c'était négligent de sa part de ne pas répondre

remission /rɪˈmɪʃn/ *n* (of sentence, debt) remise *f*; Med, Relig rémission *f*

remit /ˈriːmɪt/ *n* attributions *fpl* (**to do** pour faire; **for** pour); **it's outside my ~** ce n'est pas dans mes attributions

remittance /rɪˈmɪtns/ *n* (payment) versement *m*; (allowance) rente *f*

remix Mus

A /ˈriːmɪks/ *n* (version *f*) remix *m*

B /ˌriːˈmɪks/ *vtr* remixer

remnant /ˈremnənt/ *n* gen reste *m*; (of building, past) vestige *m*; Comm (of fabric) coupon *m*

remonstrate /ˈremənstreɪt/ *vi* protester; **to ~ with sb** faire des remontrances à qn

remorse /rɪˈmɔːs/ *n* remords *m* (**for** de); **a feeling of ~** un remords; **she felt no ~ for her crime** elle n'éprouvait aucun remords d'avoir commis ce crime

remorseful /rɪˈmɔːsfl/ *adj* plein de remords

remorseless /rɪˈmɔːslɪs/ *adj* **1** (brutal) impitoyable; **2** [*ambition*] implacable; [*optimism*] perpétuel/-elle

remorselessly /rɪˈmɔːslɪslɪ/ *adv* implacablement

remote /rɪˈməʊt/ *adj* **1** (distant) [*era*] lointain; [*antiquity*] haut; [*ancestor, country, planet*] éloigné; **in the ~ future/past** dans un avenir/passé lointain; **in the ~st corner of Asia** au fin fond de l'Asie; **2** [*area, village*] isolé; **~ from society** à l'écart de la société; **3** fig (aloof) [*person*] distant; **4** (slight) [*chance, connection*] vague, infime; **I haven't (got) the ~st idea** je n'en ai pas la moindre idée; **there is only a ~ possibility that** il est très peu probable que (+ *subj*)

remote access *n* Comput téléconsultation *f*, accès *m* à distance

remote control *n* télécommande *f*; **to operate sth by ~** télécommander qch

remote-controlled *adj* télécommandé

remotely /rɪˈməʊtlɪ/ *adv* **1** [*situated*] à l'écart de tout; **2** (slightly) [*resemble*] vaguement; **he's not ~ interested** ça ne l'intéresse pas du tout

remoteness /rɪˈməʊtnɪs/ *n* isolement *m* (**from** par rapport à); (in time) éloignement *m* (dans le temps) (**from** par rapport à); fig (of person) attitude *f* distante (**from** envers)

remould GB, **remold** US /ˈriːməʊld/ *n* GB pneu *m* rechapé

remount /ˌriːˈmaʊnt/ *vtr* enfourcher [qch] de nouveau [*bicycle*]; **to ~ a horse** se remettre en selle

removable /rɪˈmuːvəbl/ *adj* amovible

removal /rɪˈmuːvl/

A *n* **1** (of tax, barrier, threat) suppression *f*; (of doubt, worry) disparition *f*; (of demonstrators) expulsion *f*; (of troops) retrait *m*; Med ablation *f*; **stain ~** détachage *m*; **2** (change of home, location) déménagement *m* (**from** de; **to** à); **3** (of employee, official) renvoi *m*; (of leader) déposition *f*, révocation *f*

B *noun modifier* [*costs, firm, van*] de déménagement; **~ man** déménageur *m*

remove /rɪˈmuːv/

A *n* sout **to be at one ~ from/at many ~s from** être tout proche de/très loin de

B *vtr* **1** gen, Med enlever (**from** de); enlever, ôter [*clothes, shoes*]; enlever, faire partir [*stain*]; enlever, supprimer [*paragraph, word*]; supprimer [*tax, subsidy*]; **to ~ goods from the market** retirer des marchandises de la vente; **to ~ sb's name from a list** rayer qn d'une liste; **to be ~d to hospital** GB être emmené à l'hôpital; **to ~ one's make-up** se démaquiller; **to be far ~d from** être très éloigné de [*reality, truth*]; **cousin once/twice ~d** cousin au deuxième/troisième degré; **2** (oust) renvoyer [*employee*]; **to ~ sb from office** démettre qn de ses fonctions; **3** dissiper [*suspicion, fears*]; chasser [*doubt*]; écarter [*obstacle*]; supprimer [*threat*]; **4** euph (kill) supprimer; **5** Comput effacer

remover /rɪˈmuːvə(r)/ *n* (person) déménageur *m*; ▸ **stain remover etc**

remunerate /rɪˈmjuːnəreɪt/ *vtr* rémunérer (**for** pour)

remuneration /rɪ,mjuːnəˈreɪʃn/ *n* sout rémunération *f*

renal /ˈriːnl/ *adj* rénal

rename /ˌriːˈneɪm/ *vtr* rebaptiser

rend /rend/ *vtr* (*prét, pp* **rent**) lit, fig déchirer

render /ˈrendə(r)/ *vtr* **1** (make) **to ~ sth impossible** rendre qch impossible; **2** (give) rendre [*allegiance*] (**to** à); apporter [*assistance*] (**to** à); **'for services ~ed'** 'pour services rendus'; **3** Literat, Mus rendre [*style, nuance*]; traduire [*text*] (**into** en); **4** enduire [*wall*]

rendering /ˈrendərɪŋ/ *n* **1** Art, Literat, Mus interprétation *f* (**of** de); (translation) traduction *f* (**of** de); **2** (in building) enduit *m*

rendezvous /ˈrɒndɪvuː/

A *n* (*pl* ~) rendez-vous *m inv*; **to have a ~ with sb** avoir rendez-vous avec qn

B *vi* **to ~ with sb** rejoindre qn

rendition /renˈdɪʃn/ *n* interprétation *f*

renegade /ˈrenɪgeɪd/

A *n* (abandoning beliefs) renégat/-e *m/f*; (rebel) rebelle *mf*

B *adj* (abandoning beliefs) renégat; (rebel) rebelle

renege /rɪˈniːg, -ˈneɪg/ *vi* se rétracter; **to ~ on an agreement** revenir sur sa parole

renew /rɪˈnjuː, US -ˈnuː/

A *vtr* gen renouveler; renouer [*acquaintance*]; reprendre [*negotiations*]

B **renewed** *pp adj* [*interest, optimism*] accru; [*attack, call*] renouvelé

renewable /rɪˈnjuːəbl, US -ˈnuːəbl/ *adj* renouvelable

renewal /rɪˈnjuːəl, US -ˈnuːəl/ *n* gen renouvellement *m*; (of hostilities) reprise *f*; (of interest) regain *m*; **to come up for ~** arriver à expiration

renounce /rɪˈnaʊns/ *vtr* gen renoncer à; renier [*faith, friend*]; dénoncer [*agreement, treaty*]

renovate /ˈrenəveɪt/ *vtr* rénover [*building*]

renovation /ˌrenəˈveɪʃn/ *n* rénovation *f*; **~s** travaux *mpl* de rénovation; **property in need of ~** maison à rénover

renown /rɪˈnaʊn/ *n* renommée *f*

renowned /rɪˈnaʊnd/ *adj* célèbre (**for** pour)

rent /rent/

A *prét, pp* ▸ **rend**

r

B *n* ① (for accommodation) loyer *m*; **for** ∼ à louer; ② (rip) lit, fig déchirure *f*
C *vtr* ① (hire) louer [*car, house*]; ② (let) = **rent out**
D *vi* [*tenant*] être locataire; **he** ∼**s to students** [*landlord*] il loue des logements à des étudiants

⸨Phrasal verb⸩

■ **rent out:** ▸ ∼ [sth] out, ∼ out [sth] louer (**to** à)

rental *n* (of car, premises, equipment) location *f*; (of phone line) abonnement *m*; **car** ∼ location de voitures

rent-free /ˌrent'friː/
A *adj* [*house*] prêté
B *adv* [*live, use*] sans payer de loyer

renunciation /rɪˌnʌnsɪ'eɪʃn/ *n* gen renonciation *f* (**of** à); (of faith, friend) reniement *m* (**of** de)

reopen /ˌriː'əʊpən/ *vtr, vi* rouvrir

reopening /ˌriː'əʊpənɪŋ/ *n* réouverture *f*

reorganization /ˌriːˌɔːɡənaɪ'zeɪʃn/ *n* réorganisation *f*

reorganize /ˌriː'ɔːɡənaɪz/
A *vtr* réorganiser
B *vi* se réorganiser

rep /rep/ ▸ p. 1181 *n* ① Comm, Ind (*abrév* = **representative**) représentant *m* (de commerce); ② Theat *abrév* ▸ **repertory**; ③ (fabric) reps *m*

repackage /ˌriː'pækɪdʒ/ *vtr* ① Comm reconditionner [*product*]; ② fig reconditionner [*pay offer*]; modifier l'image publique de [*politician, media personality*]

repaid /ˌriː'peɪd/ *prét, pp* ▸ **repay**

repaint /ˌriː'peɪnt/ *vtr* repeindre

repair /rɪ'peə(r)/
A *n* ① gen réparation *f*; Naut (of hull) radoub *m*; **under** ∼ [*building*] en réparation; [*ship*] au radoub; **the** ∼**s to the roof** la réparation du toit; **to be (damaged) beyond** ∼ ne pas être réparable; **'road under** ∼' 'travaux'; ② sout (condition) **to be in good/bad** ∼ être en bon/mauvais état; **to keep sth in good** ∼ (bien) entretenir qch
B *vtr* ① réparer; Naut radouber [*hull*]
C *vi* (go) sout se retirer

repair: ∼ **kit** *n* trousse *f* de réparation; ∼**man** *n* réparateur *m*

reparation /ˌrepə'reɪʃn/ *n* sout réparation *f*; ∼**s** Pol indemnités *fpl* de guerre

repartee /ˌrepɑː'tiː/ *n* (conversation) échange *m* de bons mots; (wit) repartie *f*; (reply) réplique *f*, repartie *f*

repatriate /ˌriː'pætrɪeɪt, US -'peɪt-/ *vtr* rapatrier

repatriation /ˌriːpætrɪ'eɪʃn, US -peɪt-/ *n* rapatriement *m*

repay /rɪ'peɪ/ *vtr* (*prét, pp* **repaid**) rembourser [*person, sum*]; rendre [*hospitality, favour*]; **how can I ever** ∼ **you (for your kindness)?** comment pourrai-je jamais vous remercier (de votre gentillesse)?

repayment /rɪ'peɪmənt/ *n* remboursement *m* (**on** de); **to fall behind with one's** ∼**s** accumuler des arriérés de remboursement; ∼ **mortgage** emprunt *m* hypothécaire à remboursements

repeal /rɪ'piːl/
A *n* Jur abrogation *f* (**of** de)
B *vtr* abroger

repeat /rɪ'piːt/
A *n* gen répétition *f*; Radio, TV rediffusion *f*; Mus reprise *f*
B *vtr* gen répéter; Sch redoubler [*year*]; recommencer [*course*]; Radio, TV rediffuser [*programme*]; Mus reprendre; **to be** ∼**ed** gen se répéter; Radio, TV être rediffusé; Comm [*offer*] être renouvelé; **to** ∼ **oneself** se répéter

repeated /rɪ'piːtɪd/ *adj* [*warnings, requests, attempts*] répété; [*defeats, setbacks*] successif/-ive; Mus repris

repeatedly /rɪ'piːtɪdlɪ/ *adv* plusieurs fois, à plusieurs reprises

repel /rɪ'pel/ *vtr* (*p prés etc* **-ll-**) gen, Phys repousser; fig (disgust) dégoûter; **to be** ∼**led by sb** trouver qn repoussant

repellent /rɪ'pelənt/ *adj* repoussant; ▸ **insect repellent**

repent /rɪ'pent/
A *vtr* se repentir de
B *vi* se repentir

repentance /rɪ'pentəns/ *n* repentir *m*

repentant /rɪ'pentənt/ *adj* repentant fml

repercussion /ˌriːpə'kʌʃn/ *n* répercussion *f*

repertoire /'repətwɑː(r)/ *n* répertoire *m*

repertory /'repətrɪ, US -tɔːrɪ/ *n* ① **to work in** ∼ Theat jouer avec une troupe de province; ② = **repertoire**

repetition /ˌrepɪ'tɪʃn/ *n* répétition *f*

repetitious /ˌrepɪ'tɪʃəs/ *adj* répétitif/-ive

repetitive /rɪ'petɪtɪv/ *adj* répétitif/-ive

repetitiveness /rɪ'petɪtɪvnɪs/ *n* répétitivité *f*

repetitive strain injury, RSI *n* Med microtraumatismes *mpl* répétés, trouble *m* musculo-squelettique, TMS *m*

replace /rɪ'pleɪs/ *vtr* ① (put back) remettre [*lid, cork*]; remettre [qch] à sa place [*book, ornament*]; **to** ∼ **the receiver** raccrocher; ② remplacer [*goods*] (**with** par); (in job) remplacer [*person*]; ③ Comput remplacer

replacement /rɪ'pleɪsmənt/
A *n* ① (person) remplaçant/-e *m/f* (**for** de); **we will give you a** ∼ Comm (article) on vous le/la remplacera; ② (act) remplacement *m*; ③ (spare part) pièce *f* de rechange
B *noun modifier* [*staff*] intérimaire; [*engine, part*] de rechange

replay
A /'riːpleɪ/ *n* Sport match *m* rejoué; fig répétition *f*
B /ˌriː'pleɪ/ *vtr* Mus rejouer [*piece*]; Audio écouter [qch] à nouveau [*record*]; Sport rejouer

replenish /rɪ'plenɪʃ/ *vtr* gen remplir de nouveau (**with** de); reconstituer [*stocks*]

replete /rɪ'pliːt/ *adj* (after eating) rassasié (**with** de)

replica /'replɪkə/ *n* réplique *f*, copie *f* (**of** de)

replicate /'replɪkeɪt/
A *vtr* reproduire
B *vi* Med se reproduire (par réplication)

reply /rɪ'plaɪ/
A *n* gen, Jur réponse *f*
B *vtr, vi* répondre

report /rɪ'pɔːt/
A *n* ① (written account) gen, Admin rapport *m* (**on** sur); (of commission, enquiry) rapport *m* d'enquête; (verbal account, minutes) compte-rendu *m*; GB Sch bulletin *m* scolaire; US Sch (review) critique *f*; **have you had any** ∼**s of lost dogs?** est-ce qu'on a signalé des chiens perdus?; ② (in media) communiqué *m*; (longer) reportage *m*; ③ (noise) détonation *f*
B **reports** *npl* (unsubstantiated news) **we are getting** ∼**s of heavy fighting** des combats intensifs auraient lieu; **according to** ∼**s** selon certaines sources; **I've heard** ∼**s that** j'ai entendu dire que
C *vtr* ① gen, Admin signaler [*fact, event*]; (in media) faire le compte rendu de [*debate*]; **to** ∼ **sth to sb** transmettre qch à qn [*result, decision, news*]; **five people are** ∼**ed dead** on signale cinq morts; **he is** ∼**ed to have said that...** il aurait dit que...; **did she have anything of interest to** ∼? avait-elle quelque chose d'intéressant à raconter?; **he** ∼**ed that my parents are well** il m'a dit que mes parents vont bien; ② (make complaint about) signaler; péj dénoncer [*person*]
D *vi* ① (give account) **to** ∼ **on** faire un compte-rendu sur [*talks, progress*]; Journ faire un reportage sur [*events*]; **he will** ∼ **to Parliament on the negotiations** il fera un compte-rendu des négociations au parlement; ② (present findings) [*committee, group*] faire son rapport (**on** sur); ③ (present oneself) se présenter; ∼ **to reception** présentez-vous à la réception; **to** ∼ **for duty** prendre son service; **to** ∼ **sick** se faire porter malade; **to** ∼ **to one's unit** Mil rejoindre son unité; ④ Admin **to** ∼ **to** être sous les ordres (directs) de [*manager, superior*]

⸨Phrasal verb⸩

■ **report back** ① [*employee*] se présenter; ② (present findings) présenter un rapport

report card *n* US bulletin *m* scolaire

reportedly /rɪ'pɔːtɪdlɪ/ *adv* **he is** ∼ **unharmed** il serait indemne

reporter /rɪ'pɔːtə(r)/ ▸ p. 1181 *n* journaliste *mf*, reporter *mf*

reporting /rɪ'pɔːtɪŋ/ *n* Journ reportages *mpl*

repose /rɪ'pəʊz/ sout
A *n* repos *m*; **in** ∼ au repos
B *vi* (lie buried) reposer

repository /rɪ'pɒzɪtrɪ, US -tɔːrɪ/ *n* ① (of secret, authority) dépositaire *mf*; ② (place) dépôt *m* (**of, for** de)

repossess /ˌriːpə'zes/ *vtr* [*bank*] saisir [*house*]; [*creditor*] reprendre possession de [*property, goods*]

repossession /ˌriːpə'zeʃn/ *n* saisie *f* immobilière

reprehensible /ˌreprɪ'hensɪbl/ *adj* répréhensible

represent /ˌreprɪ'zent/ *vtr* **1)** (act on behalf of) gen, Jur, Pol représenter [*person*]; **under-~ed** insuffisamment représenté; **well ~ed** (numerous) bien représenté; **2)** (present) présenter [*person, event*] (**as** comme); **3)** (convey) exposer [*facts, reasons*]; **4)** [*painting etc*] représenter; (be symbol of) (on map etc) représenter; **5)** (constitute) représenter

representation /ˌreprɪzen'teɪʃn/ *n* **1)** gen, Pol représentation *f* (**of** de; **by** par); **2)** (requests) **to make ~s to sb** faire des démarches *fpl* auprès de qn; (complain) se plaindre officiellement auprès de qn

representational /ˌreprɪzen'teɪʃənl/ *adj* Art figuratif/-ive

representative /ˌreprɪ'zentətɪv/
A ▸ p. 1181 *n* gen représentant/-e *m/f*; Comm représentant/-e *m/f*, agent *m* (commercial); US Pol député *m*
B *adj* représentatif/-ive (**of** de), typique (**of** de)

repress /rɪ'pres/ *vtr* gen réprimer; Psych refouler

repression /rɪ'preʃn/ *n* gen répression *f*; Psych refoulement *m*

repressive /rɪ'presɪv/ *adj* répressif/-ive

reprieve /rɪ'priːv/
A *n* **1)** Jur remise *f* de peine; **2)** (delay) sursis *m*; **3)** (respite) répit *m*
B *vtr* **1)** Jur accorder une remise de peine à [*prisoner*]; **2)** **the school was ~d** (temporarily) l'école a bénéficié d'un sursis

reprimand /'reprɪmɑːnd, US -mænd/
A *n* Admin, gen réprimande *f*
B *vtr* Admin, gen réprimander

reprint
A /'riːprɪnt/ *n* réimpression *f*
B /ˌriː'prɪnt/ *vtr* réimprimer; **the book is being ~ed** le livre est en réimpression

reprisal /rɪ'praɪzl/ *n* représailles *fpl*; **in ~ for** *ou* **against** en représailles contre; **to take ~s** exercer des représailles

reproach /rɪ'prəʊtʃ/
A *n* reproche *m*; **above** *ou* **beyond ~** irréprochable
B *vtr* reprocher à [*person*]; **to ~ sb with** *ou* **for sth** reprocher qch à qn; **to ~ oneself for** *ou* **with sth** se reprocher qch

reproachful /rɪ'prəʊtʃfl/ *adj* [*person, remark, look*] réprobateur/-trice; [*letter, word*] de reproche

reproachfully /rɪ'prəʊtʃfəlɪ/ *adv* [*look at*] d'un air réprobateur; [*say*] d'un ton réprobateur

reprocess /ˌriː'prəʊses/ *vtr* retraiter

reprocessing plant /ˌriː'prəʊsesɪŋ/ *n* (*also* **nuclear ~**) usine *f* de retraitement (des déchets nucléaires)

reproduce /ˌriːprə'djuːs, US -'duːs/
A *vtr* reproduire
B *vi* Biol (*also* **~ oneself**) se reproduire

reproduction /ˌriːprə'dʌkʃn/ *n* reproduction *f*

reproduction furniture *n* meubles *mpl* de style

reproductive /ˌriːprə'dʌktɪv/ *adj* reproducteur/-trice

reproof /rɪ'pruːf/ *n* réprimande *f*

reprove /rɪ'pruːv/ *vtr* réprimander (**for doing** de faire)

reproving /rɪ'pruːvɪŋ/ *adj* réprobateur/-trice

reptile /'reptaɪl, US -tl/ *n* Zool reptile *m* also fig

republic /rɪ'pʌblɪk/ *n* république *f*

republican /rɪ'pʌblɪkən/
A *n* républicain/-e *m/f*
B *adj* républicain

Republican /rɪ'pʌblɪkən/
A *n* Pol Républicain/-e *m/f*
B *adj* républicain

republicanism /rɪ'pʌblɪkənɪzəm/ *n* gen républicanisme *m*; **Republicanism** Pol US tendance *f* républicaine; (in Northern Ireland) Républicanisme *m*

republish /ˌriː'pʌblɪʃ/ *vtr* rééditer

repudiate /rɪ'pjuːdɪeɪt/ *vtr* gen rejeter; abandonner [*violence, aim*]; Jur refuser d'honorer [*contract*]

repudiation /rɪˌpjuːdɪ'eɪʃn/ *n* (of charge, claim, violence) rejet *m*; (of treaty) refus *m* d'honorer

repugnance /rɪ'pʌgnəns/ *n* aversion *f* (**for sth** pour qch; **for sb** contre qn)

repugnant /rɪ'pʌgnənt/ *adj* répugnant; **to be ~ to sb** répugner à qn

repulse /rɪ'pʌls/ *vtr* gen, Mil repousser

repulsion /rɪ'pʌlʃn/ *n* répulsion *f*

repulsive /rɪ'pʌlsɪv/ *adj* repoussant

reputable /'repjʊtəbl/ *adj* de bonne réputation

reputation /ˌrepjʊ'teɪʃn/ *n* réputation *f* (**as** de); **to have a good/bad ~** avoir bonne/mauvaise réputation; **he has a ~ for honesty** il a la réputation d'être honnête

repute /rɪ'pjuːt/ *n* **of ~** réputé; **a house of ill ~** euph une maison close

reputed /rɪ'pjuːtɪd/ *adj* réputé; Jur putatif/-ive; **he is ~ to be very rich** à ce que l'on dit il serait très riche

reputedly /rɪ'pjuːtɪdlɪ/ *adv* à ce que l'on dit

request /rɪ'kwest/
A *n* **1)** demande *f* (**for** de; **to** à), requête *f* (**for** de; **to** à); **on ~** sur demande; **at the ~ of** sur la demande de; **by popular ~** à la demande générale; **2)** Radio dédicace *f*; **to play a ~ for sb** passer un disque à la demande de qn
B *vtr* demander (**from** à); **to ~ sth** demander à qn de faire; **to ~ sb's help** demander de l'aide à qn; **to ~ that** demander que (+ *subj*); **you are ~ed not to smoke** prière de ne pas fumer; **as ~ed** (in correspondance) conformément à votre demande

request stop *n* GB arrêt *m* facultatif

requiem /'rekwɪem/ *n* requiem *m*; **~ mass** messe *f* de requiem

require /rɪ'kwaɪə(r)/
A *vtr* **1)** (need) avoir besoin de [*help, money, staff*]; **as ~d** en cas de besoin; **2)** (necessitate) [*job, situation*] exiger [*funds, qualifications*]; **to ~ that** exiger que (+ *subj*); **to ~ sth of** *ou* **from** exiger qch de; **to be ~d to do** être tenu de faire
B **required** *pp adj* [*amount, size, qualification*] exigé; **by the ~d date** en temps voulu

requirement /rɪ'kwaɪəmənt/ *n* **1)** (need) besoin *m*; **to meet sb's ~s** satisfaire les besoins de qn; **2)** (condition) condition *f*; **university entrance ~s** conditions d'entrée à l'université; **to fulfil** *ou* **meet the ~s** remplir les conditions; **3)** (obligation) obligation *f* (**to do** de faire); **4)** US Univ matière *f* obligatoire

requisite /'rekwɪzɪt/
A *n* condition *f* (**for** pour)
B **requisites** *npl* (for artist, office) fournitures *fpl*; **toilet ~s** articles *mpl* de toilette
C *adj* exigé, requis

requisition /ˌrekwɪ'zɪʃn/
A *n* Mil réquisition *f*
B *vtr* Mil réquisitionner

reroof /ˌriː'ruːf/ *vtr* refaire la toiture de [*building*]

reroute /ˌriː'ruːt/ *vtr* changer l'itinéraire de [*flight*]; dévier [*traffic*]

rerun /'riːrʌn/ *n* (*also* **re-run**) Cin, Theat reprise *f*; TV rediffusion *f*; fig répétition *f*

resat /ˌriː'sæt/ *prét, pp* ▸ **resit** *vtr*

reschedule /ˌriː'ʃedjuːl, US -'skedʒʊl/ *vtr* gen (change time) changer l'heure de; (change date) changer la date de [*performance*]; Comm rééchelonner [*debt*]

rescind /rɪ'sɪnd/ *vtr* abroger [*law*]; annuler [*decision, treaty*]; résilier [*contract*]; casser [*judgment*]

rescue /'reskjuː/
A *n* **1)** (aid) secours *m*; **to come/go to sb's ~** venir/aller au secours de qn; **to come/go to the ~** venir/aller à la rescousse; **2)** (operation) sauvetage *m* (**of** de); **air-sea ~** service aéro-naval de sauvetage
B *noun modifier* [*bid, mission, operation*] de sauvetage
C *vtr* (save) sauver [*person*]; (salvage) récupérer [*object*]; (aid) porter secours à [*person, company*]; venir à l'aide de [*industry*]; (release) libérer

rescue party *n* équipe *f* de secours

rescuer /'reskjuːə(r)/ *n* sauveteur *m*

rescue worker *n* secouriste *mf*

research /rɪ'sɜːtʃ, 'riːsɜːtʃ/
A *n* gen, Univ, Med recherche *f* (**into, on** sur); (for media) documentation *f* (**into** sur); **animal ~** expériences *fpl* sur les animaux; **a piece of ~** une recherche
B *noun modifier* [*grant, project*] de recherche; [*student*] qui fait de la recherche; [*funding*] pour la recherche; **~ work** recherche *f*; **~ scientist** chercheur/-euse *m/f*
C *vtr* gen, Univ faire des recherches sur [*topic*]; préparer [*book, article*]; (in media) se documenter sur [*issue*]; **well ~ed** bien documenté; **to ~ the market** Comm faire une étude de marché

research: ∼ **and development**, **R&D** n recherche-développement f, recherche f et développement m; ∼ **assistant** ▸ p. 1181 n GB Univ assistant/-e m/f d'un chercheur

researcher /rɪ'sɜ:tʃə(r), 'rɪ:sɜ:tʃə(r)/ ▸ p. 1181 n gen chercheur/-euse m/f; TV documentaliste mf

research: ∼ **establishment** n centre m de recherches; ∼ **fellow** n GB Univ chercheur/-euse m/f universitaire

resell /ri:'sel/ vtr (prét, pp **resold**) revendre

resemblance /rɪ'zembləns/ n ressemblance f (**between** entre; **to** avec); **to bear a close** ∼ **to** ressembler fort à; **family** ∼ air m de famille

resemble /rɪ'zembl/ vtr ressembler à; **to** ∼ **each other** se ressembler

resent /rɪ'zent/ vtr en vouloir à [person] (**for doing** d'avoir fait); mal supporter [change, system]; ne pas aimer [tone, term]; **to** ∼ **having to do** ne pas supporter de faire; **I** ∼ **that remark** cette réflexion ne me plaît pas du tout; **to** ∼ **the fact that** ne pas supporter le fait que (+ subj)

resentful /rɪ'zentfl/ adj plein de ressentiment (**at** à; **of** à l'égard de)

resentment /rɪ'zentmənt/ n ressentiment m (**about** au sujet de; **against** envers; **at** à l'égard de)

reservation /ˌrezə'veɪʃn/ n 1 (doubt) réserve f; **without** ∼ sans réserve; **with some** ∼**s** avec certaines réserves; **to have** ∼**s about sth** avoir des doutes sur qch; 2 (booking) réservation f; **do you have a** ∼**?** avez-vous réservé?; 3 US (Indian land) réserve f

reservation desk n bureau m des réservations

reserve /rɪ'zɜ:v/
A n 1 (resource, stock) réserve f; **oil** ∼**s** réserves de pétrole; **to keep sth in** ∼ tenir qch en réserve; 2 (reticence) réserve f; **to lose one's** ∼ sortir de sa réserve; 3 (doubt) réserve f; 4 Mil **the** ∼, **the** ∼**s** la réserve; 5 Sport remplaçant/-e m/f; 6 (area of land) réserve f; **wildlife** ∼ réserve naturelle
B noun modifier [fund, supplies, steam, forces] de réserve; [player] remplaçant
C vtr 1 (set aside) réserver; **she** ∼**s her fiercest criticism for...** elle réserve ses critiques les plus féroces pour...; **to** ∼ **one's strength** ménager ses forces; **to** ∼ **the right to do sth** se réserver le droit de faire qch; **to** ∼ **judgment** réserver son jugement; 2 (book) réserver [room, seat]

reserved /rɪ'zɜ:vd/ adj 1 [person] réservé; **to be** ∼ **about sth** rester réservé sur qch; 2 [table, room] réservé; 3 Comm **all rights** ∼ tous droits réservés

reserve price n GB prix m minimum

reservist /rɪ'zɜ:vɪst/ n réserviste m

reservoir /'rezəvwɑ:(r)/ n réservoir m

reset /ˌri:'set/ vtr (p prés **-tt-**; prét, pp **reset**) gen régler [machine]; remettre [qch] à l'heure [clock]

resettle /ˌri:'setl/
A vtr réinstaller [person]; repeupler [area]
B vi se réinstaller

reshuffle /ˌri:'ʃʌfl/
A n Pol remaniement m; **cabinet** ∼ remaniement ministériel
B vtr 1 Pol remanier; 2 rebattre [cards]

reside /rɪ'zaɪd/ vi sout (live) résider, habiter (**with** avec); fig résider (**in** dans)

residence /'rezɪdəns/ n 1 sout (dwelling) maison f, demeure f; (in property ad) maison f; 2 Admin, Jur (in area, country) résidence f; **place of** ∼ lieu de résidence; **to take up** ∼ élire domicile; ∼ **permit** permis m de séjour; **to be in** ∼ sout [monarch] être au château; ▸ **hall of residence**; 3 US Univ (also ∼ **hall**) résidence f universitaire

resident /'rezɪdənt/
A n 1 (of city, region) résident/-e m/f; (of street) riverain/-e m/f; (of hostel) résident/-e m/f; (of guest house) pensionnaire mf; **the local** ∼**s** les habitants du quartier; ∼**s association** association f de quartier
B adj [population] local; [staff, tutor] à demeure; [band] permanent; **to be** ∼ **in** résider dans

residential /ˌrezɪ'denʃl/ adj [area] résidentiel/-ielle; [staff] à demeure; [course] en internat; ∼ **home** GB (for elderly) maison f de retraite; (for disabled) institution f pour handicapés; (for youth) foyer m d'accueil; **to be in** ∼ **care** être pris en charge par une institution

residual /rɪ'zɪdjʊəl, US -dʒʊ-/ adj 1 [prejudice, need] persistant; [income] résiduel/-elle; 2 Chem résiduel/-elle

residue /'rezɪdju:, US -du:/ n gen, Chem résidu m (**of** de); fig reste m (**of** de)

resign /rɪ'zaɪn/
A vtr démissionner de [post, job]
B vi démissionner (**as** du poste de; **from** de; **over** à cause de)
C v refl **to** ∼ **oneself** se résigner (**to** à)

resignation /ˌrezɪg'neɪʃn/ n 1 (from post) démission f (**from** de; **as** du poste de); **to hand in one's** ∼ donner sa démission; 2 (patience) résignation f

resigned /rɪ'zaɪnd/ adj résigné (**to** à)

resilience /rɪ'zɪlɪəns/ n (of person) (mental) détermination f; (physical) résistance f physique; (of industry, economy) faculté f de reprise; (of material) élasticité f

resilient /rɪ'zɪlɪənt/ adj 1 (morally) déterminé; (physically) résistant; 2 [material] élastique

resin /'rezɪn, US 'rezn/ n résine f

resist /rɪ'zɪst/
A vtr 1 s'opposer à [attempt, reform]; résister à [attack]; 2 résister à [temptation, suggestion]; **to** ∼ **doing** s'empêcher de faire; 3 résister à [rust, heat]
B vi résister

resistance /rɪ'zɪstəns/ n résistance f (**to** à); **to meet with** ∼ se heurter à une résistance; **to put up** ∼ résister; **his** ∼ **is low** sa résistance est amoindrie; **to build up a** ∼ **to sth** devenir plus résistant à qch
(Idiom) **to take the line** ou **path of least** ∼ choisir la voie de la facilité

Resistance /rɪ'zɪstəns/ n Pol Hist **the** ∼ la Résistance

resistance: ∼ **fighter** n résistant/-e m/f; ∼ **movement** n mouvement m de résistance

resistant /rɪ'zɪstənt/ adj 1 [virus] rebelle (**to** à); **heat-/rust-**∼ résistant à la chaleur/à la rouille; **water-**∼ imperméable; 2 (opposed) ∼ **to** réfractaire à

resit GB
A /'ri:sɪt/ n session f de rattrapage
B /ˌri:'sɪt/ vtr (prét, pp **resat**) repasser [exam, test]

resolute /'rezəlu:t/ adj [person] résolu

resolutely /'rezəlu:tlɪ/ adv résolument

resolution /ˌrezə'lu:ʃn/ n 1 (determination) résolution f; 2 (decree) résolution f (**against** contre; **that** selon laquelle); **to pass a** ∼ voter une résolution; 3 (promise) résolution f (**to do** de faire); **to make a** ∼ **to do** prendre la résolution de faire; 4 (solving of problem) résolution f (**of** de); 5 Comput résolution f

resolve /rɪ'zɒlv/
A n 1 (determination) détermination f; **to strengthen/weaken sb's** ∼ rendre qn plus/moins décidé; 2 (decision) résolution f
B vtr 1 (solve) résoudre [dispute]; dissiper [doubts]; 2 (decide) **to** ∼ **that** décider que; **to** ∼ **to do** résoudre de faire
C vi (decide) [person, government] résoudre; **to** ∼ **on doing** résoudre de faire
D v refl **to** ∼ **itself** se résoudre

resonant /'rezənənt/ adj [voice] sonore

resonate /'rezəneɪt/ vi résonner (**with** de)

resort /rɪ'zɔ:t/
A n 1 (resource) recours m; **as a last** ∼ en dernier recours; 2 (holiday centre) lieu m de villégiature; **seaside** ∼ station f balnéaire; **ski** ∼ station f de ski
B vi **to** ∼ **to** recourir à

resound /rɪ'zaʊnd/ vi 1 [noise] retentir (**through** partout dans); 2 [place] retentir (**with** de)

resounding /rɪ'zaʊndɪŋ/ adj [cheers] retentissant; [success] éclatant; **a** ∼ **'no'** un 'non' retentissant

resource /rɪ'sɔ:s, -'zɔ:s, US 'ri:sɔ:rs/
A n gen, Comput, Econ, Ind, Admin ressource f; **natural/energy** ∼**s** ressources naturelles/énergétiques; **the world's** ∼**s of coal** les ressources mondiales en charbon
B vtr accorder les ressources nécessaires à [institution]; **to be under-**∼**d** ne pas disposer de ressources suffisantes

resource centre GB, **resource center** US n centre m de documentation

resourceful /rɪ'sɔ:sfl, -'zɔ:sfl, US 'ri:sɔ:rsfl/ adj [person] plein de ressources, débrouillard○

resource(s) room n salle f de documentation

respect /rɪ'spekt/

A n **1** (admiration) respect m, estime f; **to win the ~ of sb** gagner l'estime de qn; **to command ~** imposer le respect; **2** (politeness) respect m; **out of ~** par respect (**for** pour); **you've got no ~!** tu ne respectes rien!; **with (all due) ~** sauf votre respect; **in ~ of** (as regards) pour ce qui est de; **with ~ to** par rapport à; **3** (regard) (for human rights, privacy) respect m (**for** de); **4** (aspect) égard m; **in this ~** à cet égard; **in many ~s** à bien des égards; **in what ~?** à quel égard?

B respects npl respects mpl; **to offer** ou **pay one's ~s to sb** présenter ses respects à qn; **to pay one's last ~s to sb** rendre un dernier hommage à qn

C vtr (honour) respecter; **as ~s sth** quant à qch

respectability /rɪ,spektə'bɪləti/ n respectabilité f

respectable /rɪ'spektəbl/ adj **1** (reputable) [person] respectable; [upbringing] bon/bonne; **in ~ society** entre gens convenables; **2** (adequate) [crowd] respectable; [performance] honorable; **to finish a ~ fourth** terminer honorablement quatrième

respectably /rɪ'spektəblɪ/ adv (reputably) convenablement, correctement; (creditably) honorablement

respectful /rɪ'spektfl/ adj respectueux/-euse (**to, towards** envers)

respectfully /rɪ'spektfəlɪ/ adv respectueusement

respecting /rɪ'spektɪŋ/ prep concernant

respective /rɪ'spektɪv/ adj respectif/-ive

respiration /,respɪ'reɪʃn/ n respiration f

respirator /'respɪreɪtə(r)/ n (apparatus) respirateur m; **to be on a ~** être sous respirateur

respiratory /rɪ'spɪrətrɪ, US -tɔːrɪ/ adj respiratoire

respite /'respaɪt, 'respɪt/ n **1** sout (relief) répit m (**from** dans); **a brief ~** un court répit; **2** Comm, Jur (delay) sursis m

resplendent /rɪ'splendənt/ adj sout resplendissant; **to look ~** être resplendissant

respond /rɪ'spɒnd/ vi **1** (answer) répondre (**to** à; **with** par); **2** (react) réagir (**to** à); [car] répondre; **to ~ to pressure** Pol, Admin céder aux pressions; **3** (listen, adapt) s'adapter; **4** Relig (by speaking) répondre

respondent /rɪ'spɒndənt/ n **1** (to questionnaire) personne f interrogée; **2** Jur défendeur/-eresse m/f

response /rɪ'spɒns/ n **1** (answer) réponse f (**to** à); **in ~ to** en réponse à; **2** (reaction) réaction f (**to** à; **from** de); **to meet with a favourable ~** être bien reçu; **3** Relig the **~s** les répons mpl

responsibility /rɪ,spɒnsə'bɪlətɪ/ n responsabilité f (**for** de); **to take ~ for sth** prendre la responsabilité de qch; **a sense of ~** le sens des responsabilités; **to take no ~** décliner toute responsabilité; **it's not my ~ to do sth** ce n'est pas à moi de faire; **it's your ~** c'est à vous de vous en occuper; **to claim ~ for an attack** revendiquer une attaque

responsible /rɪ'spɒnsəbl/ adj **1** (to blame) **~ for killing ten people** responsable de la mort de dix personnes; **2** (in charge) **~ for producing the leaflets** chargé de produire les brochures; **3** (accountable) **to be ~ to sb** être responsable devant qn; **I won't be ~ for my actions** je ne réponds plus de moi; **4** (trustworthy) responsable; **5** [job] à responsabilités

responsive /rɪ'spɒnsɪv/ adj **1** (alert) [audience, class, pupil] réceptif/-ive; **2** Aut [car] nerveux/-euse

respray

A /'riːspreɪ/ n **the car had been given a ~** on avait repeint la voiture

B /,riː'spreɪ/ vtr repeindre [vehicle]

rest /rest/

A n **1** (what remains) **the ~** (of food, day, story) le reste (**of** de); **the ~ of my life** pour le restant de mes jours; **for the ~...** pour ce qui est du reste...; **and all the ~ of it**○ et tout et tout○; **2** (other people) **he is no different from the ~ (of them)** il n'est pas différent des autres; **why can't you behave like the ~ of us?** pourquoi ne peux-tu pas faire comme nous?; **3** (repose, inactivity) repos m; **to have a ~** se reposer; **4** (break) pause f; **let's have a little ~** et si on faisait une petite pause?; **5** (lie-down) sieste f; **to have a ~** faire la sieste; **6** (support) support m; **7** Mus pause f; **8** (immobility) **to come to ~** s'arrêter

B vtr **1** (lean) **to ~ sth on** appuyer qch sur [surface]; **2** (allow to rest) reposer [legs]; ne pas utiliser [injured limb]; laisser

[qch] au repos [horse]; **3** Agric laisser [qch] en jachère [land]; **4** Jur **to ~ one's case** conclure; **I ~ my case** fig il n'y a rien à ajouter

C vi **1** se reposer; **I won't ~ until I know** je n'aurai de cesse de savoir; **to ~ easy** être tranquille; **2** (be supported) **to ~ on** reposer sur; **3** [actor] **to be ~ing** être sans engagement; **4** **to ~ in peace** reposer en paix; **God ~ his soul** Dieu ait son âme; **5** fig **to let the matter ~** en rester là; **you can't just let it ~ there!** tu ne peux pas laisser les choses en l'état!

(Idioms) **a change is as good as a ~** Prov le changement a les mêmes vertus que le repos; **and there the matter ~s** voilà la situation actuelle

(Phrasal verbs)

■ **rest on**: ▸ **~ on [sb/sth] 1** [eyes] s'arrêter sur; **2** [decision] reposer sur [assumption]

■ **rest up** se reposer

■ **rest with**: ▸ **~ with [sb/sth]** être entre les mains de

restart /,riː'stɑːt/ vtr **1** reprendre [talks]; **2** remettre [qch] en marche [engine]

restate /,riː'steɪt/ vtr réaffirmer

restaurant /'restrɒnt, US -tərənt/ n restaurant m

restaurant car n GB wagon-restaurant m

rest cure n lit cure f de repos; hum sinécure f

restful /'restfl/ adj [holiday] reposant; [place] paisible

rest home n maison f de retraite

resting place /'restɪŋ/ n **his last ~** sa dernière demeure

restitution /,restɪ'tjuːʃn, US -'tuː-/ n gen, Jur restitution f

restive /'restɪv/ adj [crowd] énervé; [animal] rétif/-ive

restless /'restlɪs/ adj [person] agité; **to get** ou **grow ~** [audience] commencer à donner des signes d'impatience; [populace] commencer à s'agiter; **to feel ~** (in job) avoir envie de changer

restlessly /'restlɪslɪ/ adv nerveusement

restlessness /'restlɪsnɪs/ n **1** (physical) agitation f; **2** (of character) instabilité f

restock /,riː'stɒk/

A vtr regarnir [shelf] (**with** en); réapprovisionner [shop] (**with** en); repeupler [river] (**with** de)

B vi se réapprovisionner

restoration /,restə'reɪʃn/ n **1** (of territory) restitution f (**to** à); **2** (of monarchy, painting) restauration f; (of democracy) rétablissement m

restore /rɪ'stɔː(r)/ vtr **1** (return) restituer, rendre [property] (**to** à); **2** (bring back) rétablir [health]; rendre [faculty]; redonner [good humour] (**to** à); rétablir [peace, monarchy, rights]; **to be ~d to health** être rétabli; **to ~ sb to power** ramener qn au pouvoir; **you ~ my faith in humanity** tu me redonnes confiance dans le genre humain; **3** (repair) restaurer; **4** Comput redimensionner [window]

restorer /rɪ'stɔːrə(r)/ n (person) restaurateur/-trice m/f

restrain /rɪ'streɪn/

A vtr **1** (hold back) retenir [person]; contenir [crowd]; maîtriser [animal]; **to ~ sb from doing sth** empêcher qn de faire qch; **2** (curb) limiter [spending]; maîtriser [inflation]

B v refl **to ~ oneself** se retenir

restrained /rɪ'streɪnd/ adj [style] sobre; [manner] calme; [reaction] modéré; [person] posé

restraining order /rɪ'streɪnɪŋ/ n injonction f

restraint /rɪ'streɪnt/ n **1** (moderation) modération f; **2** (restriction) restriction f; **wage ~** contrôle m des salaires; **3** (constraint) contrainte f

restrict /rɪ'strɪkt/

A vtr limiter [activity, growth] (**to** à); restreindre [freedom]; réserver [access, membership] (**to** à); **visibility was ~ed** la visibilité était limitée

B v refl **to ~ oneself to sth** se limiter à qch

restricted /rɪ'strɪktɪd/ adj [growth, movement] limité; [document] confidentiel/-ielle; [film] US interdit aux moins de 17 ans; [parking] réglementé

restriction /rɪ'strɪkʃn/ n **1** (rule) règlement m; **~s on** règlements mpl contrôlant [advertising, activities]; **~s on arms sales** limitations fpl de ventes d'armes; **credit ~s** encadrement m (sg) du crédit; **currency ~s** contrôle m (sg) des devises; **parking ~s** règles fpl de stationnement; **price ~s** contrôle m (sg) des prix; **speed ~s** limitations fpl de vitesse; **travel ~s** restrictions fpl à la libre circulation (des citoyens); **weight** ~**s** (for vehicles) limitations *fpl* de poids; **2)** (limiting) (of amount) limitation *f* (**on** de); (of freedom) restrictions *fpl* (**of** à)

restrictive /rɪˈstrɪktɪv/ *adj* restrictif/-ive

re-string /ˌriːˈstrɪŋ/ *vtr* (*prét, pp* **re-strung**) changer les cordes de [*instrument*]; recorder [*racket*]; renfiler [*necklace, beads*]

rest room *n* US toilettes *fpl*

restyle
A /ˈriːstaɪl/ *n* nouvelle coiffure *f*
B /ˌriːˈstaɪl/ *vtr* changer la ligne de [*car*]; transformer [*shop*]; **to ~ sb's hair** faire une nouvelle coupe (de cheveux) à qn

result /rɪˈzʌlt/
A *n* **1)** (consequence) résultat *m* (**of** de), conséquence *f* (**of** de); **as a ~ of** à la *or* par suite de; **as a ~** en conséquence; **2)** (outcome) résultat *m*; **exam(ination)** ~**s** résultats aux examens
B **results** *npl* Comm, Fin résultats *mpl*
C *vi* résulter; **to ~ in** avoir pour résultat

resume /rɪˈzjuːm, US -ˈzuːm/
A *vtr* reprendre [*talks*]; regagner [*seat*]; renouer [*relations*]
B *vi* reprendre

résumé /ˈrezjuːmeɪ, US ˌrezuˈmeɪ/ *n* **1)** (summary) résumé *m*; **2)** US (cv) curriculum vitae *m inv*

resumption /rɪˈzʌmpʃn/ *n* reprise *f* (**of** de)

resurface /ˌriːˈsɜːfɪs/
A *vtr* refaire (la surface de)
B *vi* [*submarine*] faire surface; [*rumour*] réapparaître; [*person*] refaire surface

resurgence /rɪˈsɜːdʒəns/ *n* gen résurgence *f*; (of interest) regain *m*; (of economy) reprise *f*

resurrect /ˌrezəˈrekt/ *vtr* ressusciter

resurrection /ˌrezəˈrekʃn/ *n* résurrection *f*; Relig **the Resurrection** la Résurrection

resuscitate /rɪˈsʌsɪteɪt/ *vtr* Med réanimer

resuscitation /rɪˌsʌsɪˈteɪʃn/ *n* réanimation *f*

retail /ˈriːteɪl/
A *n* vente *f* au détail
B *noun modifier* [*business, sector*] de détail
C *adv* au détail
D *vtr* vendre [qch] au détail
E *vi* **to ~ at** se vendre au détail à

retailer /ˈriːteɪlə(r)/ *n* détaillant *m*

retailing /ˈriːteɪlɪŋ/
A *n* distribution *f*
B *noun modifier* [*giant, sector*] de la distribution; [*group, operations*] de distribution

retail: ~ **price** *n* prix *m* de détail; ~ **price index**, **RPI** *n* indice *m* des prix à la consommation; ~ **sales** *npl* ventes *fpl* au détail; ~ **trade** *n* (companies) détaillants *mpl*; (industry) commerce *m* de détail

retain /rɪˈteɪn/ *vtr* garder [*control, identity*]; conserver [*heat, title*]; retenir [*water, fact*]; engager [*lawyer*]

retainer /rɪˈteɪnə(r)/ *n* **1)** (fee) somme *f* versée à l'avance (*pour s'assurer des services de quelqu'un*); **2)** ‡(servant) domestique *mf*

retaining wall *n* mur *m* de soutènement

retake
A /ˈriːteɪk/ *n* Cin nouvelle prise *f*
B /ˌriːˈteɪk/ *vtr* (*prét* **retook**; *pp* **retaken**) **1)** Cin faire une nouvelle prise de [*scene*]; **2)** Sch, Univ repasser [*exam*]; **3)** Mil reprendre [*town*]

retaliate /rɪˈtælɪeɪt/ *vi* réagir

retaliation /rɪˌtælɪˈeɪʃn/ *n* **in ~ for** en représailles de

retarded /rɪˈtɑːdɪd/ *adj* **1)** Psych retardé; **2)** ᵒUS (stupid) débile○

retch /retʃ/ *vi* avoir des haut-le-cœur

retd *abrév écrite* = **retired**

retention /rɪˈtenʃn/ *n* Med rétention *f*

retentive /rɪˈtentɪv/ *adj* [*memory*] fidèle, bon

rethink
A /ˈriːθɪŋk/ *n* **to have a ~** y repenser
B /ˌriːˈθɪŋk/ *vtr* (*prét, pp* **rethought**) repenser

reticence /ˈretɪsns/ *n* réticence *f* (**on, about** à propos de)

reticent /ˈretɪsnt/ *adj* réticent; **to be ~ about sth** être discret sur qch

retina /ˈretɪnə, US ˈretənə/ *n* rétine *f*

retinue /ˈretɪnjuː, US ˈretənuː/ *n* escorte *f*

retire /rɪˈtaɪə(r)/
A *vi* **1)** (from work) prendre sa retraite; **2)** (withdraw) se retirer (**from** de); **3)** †**to ~** (**to bed**) aller se coucher; **4)** Sport abandonner; **to ~ from sth** se retirer de qch
B **retired** *pp adj* retraité
C **retiring** *pres p adj* (leaving job) qui prend sa retraite; (shy) réservé

retirement /rɪˈtaɪəmənt/ *n* retraite *f*; **to take early ~** partir en retraite anticipée; **to come out of ~** reprendre ses activités (après avoir pris sa retraite)

retirement: ~ **age** *n* âge *m* de la retraite; ~ **bonus** *n* prime *f* de départ à la retraite

retirement home *n* **1)** (individual) maison *f* pour la retraite; **2)** (communal) maison *f* de retraite

retirement pension *n* (pension *f* de) retraite *f*

retort /rɪˈtɔːt/
A *n* (reply) riposte *f*
B *vtr* rétorquer (**that** que)

retrace /riːˈtreɪs/ *vtr* **to ~ one's steps** revenir sur ses pas

retract /rɪˈtrækt/
A *vtr* rétracter [*statement, claws*]; escamoter [*landing gear*]
B *vi* [*landing gear*] s'escamoter

retractable /rɪˈtræktəbl/ *adj* [*landing gear*] escamotable; [*pen*] à pointe rétractable

retrain /ˌriːˈtreɪn/
A *vtr* recycler
B *vi* se recycler

retraining /ˌriːˈtreɪnɪŋ/ *n* recyclage *m*

retread /ˈriːtred/ *n* pneu *m* rechapé

retreat /rɪˈtriːt/
A *n* **1)** (withdrawal) retraite *f*; **to beat a hasty ~** battre en retraite précipitamment; **to sound the ~** Mil sonner la retraite; **2)** (house) retraite *f*; **3)** Relig retraite *f*; **to go on a ~** faire une retraite
B *vi* **1)** gen [*person*] se retirer (**into** dans; **from** de); **2)** Mil [*army*] se replier (**to** sur); **3)** fig **to ~ into a dream world** se réfugier dans un monde imaginaire; **4)** [*flood water*] reculer

retrench /rɪˈtrentʃ/ *vi* sout se restreindre dans ses dépenses

retrenchment /rɪˈtrentʃmənt/ *n* sout (economizing) restriction *f* (des dépenses)

retrial /ˌriːˈtraɪəl/ *n* Jur nouveau procès *m*

retribution /ˌretrɪˈbjuːʃn/ *n* sout châtiment *m*

retrievable /rɪˈtriːvəbl/ *adj* **1)** gen recouvrable; **2)** Comput accessible

retrieval /rɪˈtriːvl/ *n* Comput extraction *f*

retrieve /rɪˈtriːv/ *vtr* récupérer [*object*]; redresser [*situation*]; rapporter [*pheasant*]; extraire [*data*]

retro /ˈretrəʊ/ *n, adj* rétro (*m*)

retrograde /ˈretrəgreɪd/ *adj* rétrograde

retrospect /ˈretrəʊspekt/: **in retrospect** *adv phr* rétrospectivement

retrospective /ˌretrəˈspektɪv/
A *n* (also ~ **exhibition** *ou* ~ **show**) Art, Cin rétrospective *f*
B *adj* **1)** gen rétrospectif/-ive; **2)** Jur, Admin rétroactif/-ive

retrospectively /ˌretrəˈspektɪvlɪ/ *adv* **1)** Jur, Admin rétroactivement; **2)** gen rétrospectivement

retrovirus /ˈretrəʊvaɪərəs/ *n* rétrovirus *m*

retry /ˌriːˈtraɪ/ *vtr* **1)** Jur juger à nouveau [*case*]; **2)** Comput essayer de relancer [*operation*]

retune /ˌriːˈtjuːn, US -ˈtuːn/ *vtr* Mus accorder; Radio, Telecom, Aut régler

return /rɪˈtɜːn/
A *n* **1)** lit, fig (getting back, going back) retour *m* (**to** à; **from** de); **on your ~ to work** dès que vous aurez repris votre travail; **2)** (recurrence) retour *m* (**of** de); **3)** (restitution, bringing back) (of law, practice) retour *m* (**of** de); (of object) restitution *f* (**of** de); **4)** (sending back) renvoi *m* (**of** de); **5)** Fin (yield on investment) rendement *m* (**on** de); (on capital) rémunération *f*; **the law of diminishing ~s** la loi des rendements décroissants; **6)** (travel ticket) aller-retour *m inv*; **7)** Theat billet *m* rendu à

la dernière minute; **8** (unsold book) invendu m

B **returns** npl Pol résultats mpl

C **in return** adv phr en échange (**for** de)

D vtr **1** (give back) rendre; (pay back) rembourser; **2** (bring back, take back) rapporter (**to** à); **3** (put back) remettre; **4** (send back) renvoyer; '**~ to sender**' 'retour à l'expéditeur'; **5** (give, issue in return) rendre [greeting]; **to ~ the favour** en faire autant; **6** (reciprocate) répondre à [love]; **7** Mil riposter à [fire]; **8** Sport renvoyer [ball]; **9** (rejoin) répliquer; **10** Jur prononcer [verdict]; **11** Fin rapporter [profit]; **12** Pol élire [candidate]; **13** Telecom **to ~ sb's call** rappeler qn

E vi **1** (come back) revenir (**from** de); **2** (go back) retourner (**to** à); **3** (get back from abroad) rentrer (**from** de); **4** (get back home) rentrer chez soi; **5** (resume) **to ~ to** reprendre [activity]; **to ~ to power** revenir au pouvoir; **6** (recur) [symptom, doubt] réapparaître; [days, times] revenir

(Idioms) **by ~ of post** par retour du courrier; **many happy ~s!** bon anniversaire!

returner /rɪˈtɜːnə(r)/ n femme f qui reprend le travail

return: **~ fare** n prix m d'un billet aller-retour; **~ing officer** n GB président/-e m/f d'un bureau d'élections; **~ ticket** n billet m aller-retour; **~ trip** n retour m; **~ visit** n retour m

reunification /ˌriːjuːnɪfɪˈkeɪʃn/ n réunification f

reunion /ˌriːˈjuːnɪən/ n réunion f

reunite /ˌriːjuːˈnaɪt/ vtr (gén au passif) réunir [family]; réunifier [party]; **he was ~d with his family** il a retrouvé sa famille

reusable /ˌriːˈjuːzəbl/ adj réutilisable

reuse /ˌriːˈjuːz/ vtr réutiliser

rev○ /rev/

A n Aut (abrév = **revolution** (**per minute**)) tour m (par minute)

B vtr (p prés etc **-vv-**) (also **~ up**) monter le régime de [engine]

Rev(d) n: abrév écrite = **Reverend**

revaluation /ˌriːvæljuːˈeɪʃn/ n réévaluation f

revalue /ˌriːˈvæljuː/ vtr Comm, Fin réévaluer

revamp /ˌriːˈvæmp/ vtr rajeunir [image]; réorganiser [company]; retaper○ [building, clothing]

rev counter○ n GB compte-tours m inv

reveal /rɪˈviːl/

A vtr **1** (make public) dévoiler [truth]; révéler [secret]; **to ~ that** révéler que; **to ~ sth to sb** révéler qch à qn; **to ~ all** (divulge) tout dire; **2** (make visible) découvrir [view, picture]; **~ed religion** religion f révélée

B v refl **to ~ oneself** [person] se montrer; [God] se révéler

revealing /rɪˈviːlɪŋ/ adj **1** [remark] révélateur/-trice; **2** [blouse] décolleté

revel /ˈrevl/

A npl **~s** festivités fpl

B vi (p prés etc **-ll-**, **-l-** US) **to ~ in sth** se délecter de qch

revelation /ˌrevəˈleɪʃn/ n révélation f

revelatory /ˈrevəleɪtrɪ, US -tɔːrɪ/ adj révélateur/-trice

reveller, US **reveler** /ˈrevələ(r)/ n fêtard/-e○ m/f

revelry /ˈrevəlrɪ/ n (also **revelries**) réjouissances fpl

revenge /rɪˈvendʒ/ n **1** (punitive act) vengeance f; **to take** ou **get one's ~** se venger (**for** de; **on** sur); **2** (getting even) revanche f

(Idiom) **~ is sweet** la vengeance est un plat qui se mange froid

revenue /ˈrevənjuː, US -ənuː/

A n revenus mpl

B **revenues** npl **oil ~s** revenus mpl pétroliers

reverberate /rɪˈvɜːbəreɪt/ vi [hills, sound] résonner (**with** de; **through** dans, par); [shock] se propager

revere /rɪˈvɪə(r)/ vtr révérer

reverence /ˈrevərəns/ n profond respect m

Reverend /ˈrevərənd/ ▸ p. 869 n **1** (Protestant) pasteur m; **2** (as title) **the ~ Jones** (Anglican) le révérend Jones; **~ Mother** Révérende Mère; **~ Father** Révérend Père

reverent /ˈrevərənt/ adj [hush] religieux/-ieuse; [expression] de respect

reverently /ˈrevərəntlɪ/ adv avec vénération

revers: /rɪˈvɪə(r)/ npl (lapels) revers mpl

reversal /rɪˈvɜːsl/ n gen (of policy, roles) renversement m; (of order, trend) inversion f; (of fortune) revers m

reverse /rɪˈvɜːs/

A n **1** (opposite) **the ~** le contraire; **2** (back) **the ~** (of coin) le revers; (of banknote) le verso; (of fabric) l'envers m; **3** (setback) revers m; **4** Aut (also **~ gear**) marche f arrière

B adj **1** (opposite) [effect] contraire; **2** (other) **the ~ side** (of coin) le revers; (of fabric) l'envers m; **3** [somersault] en arrière; **to answer the questions in ~ order** répondre aux questions en commençant par la dernière; **4** Aut **~ gear** marche f arrière

C **in reverse** adv phr [do, function] en sens inverse

D vtr inverser [trend, process]; renverser [roles]; faire rouler [qch] en marche arrière [car]; **to ~ a car out of a garage** sortir une voiture d'un garage en marche arrière; **to ~ the charges** appeler en PCV

E vi [driver] faire marche arrière; **to ~ down the lane/into a parking space** descendre l'allée/se garer en marche arrière

reverse charge call n appel m en PCV

reversible /rɪˈvɜːsəbl/ adj (all contexts) réversible

reversing light /rɪˈvɜːsɪŋ/ n feu m de recul

reversion /rɪˈvɜːʃn, US -ʒn/ n retour m (**to** à)

revert /rɪˈvɜːt/ vi **to ~ to** reprendre [habit, name]; redevenir [wilderness]; **to ~ to normal** redevenir normal; **to ~ to type** lit retourner au type primitif; **he ~ed to type** fig le naturel a repris le dessus

review /rɪˈvjuː/

A n **1** gen, Admin, Jur, Pol (reconsideration) révision f (**of** de); (report) rapport m (**of** sur); **under ~** [policy] en train d'être réexaminé; [salaries] en train d'être révisé; **to come under ~** être réexaminé; **to be subject to ~** pouvoir être reconsidéré; **2** (critical assessment) critique f (**of** de); **rave ~**○ revue f excellente; **to write a ~** faire une critique; **3** Journ (magazine) revue f; **4** Mil revue f; **5** US Sch, Univ (of lesson) révision f

B vtr **1** (re-examine) reconsidérer [situation]; réviser [attitude, policy]; passer [qch] en revue [troops]; **2** Literat faire la critique de [book, film etc]; **to be well/badly ~ed** se faire bien/mal accueillir par la critique; **3** US Sch, Univ réviser [subject, lesson]

review: **~ board** n Admin comité m de révision; **~ copy** n exemplaire m de service de presse

reviewer /rɪˈvjuːə(r)/ n critique m

revise /rɪˈvaɪz/

A n (in printing) seconde f (épreuve f)

B vtr **1** (alter) réviser [estimate, figures]; changer [attitude]; **to ~ one's position** revenir sur sa position; **to ~ one's opinion of sb/sth** réviser son jugement sur qn/qch; **~d upwards/downwards** [figures, profits etc] révisé à la hausse/à la baisse; **2** GB (for exam) réviser [subject]; **3** (correct) réviser [text]

C vi GB réviser

revision /rɪˈvɪʒn/ n révision f

revisit /ˌriːˈvɪzɪt/ vtr revisiter [museum etc]; retourner voir [person, childhood home]; fig revoir

revitalization /ˌriːvaɪtəlaɪˈzeɪʃn, US -lɪˈz-/ n **1** (of economy) relance f; **2** (of depressed area) renaissance f

revitalize /ˌriːˈvaɪtəlaɪz/ vtr **1** relancer [economy]; faire démarrer [company]; **2** revitaliser [complexion]

revival /rɪˈvaɪvl/ n **1** (of economy) reprise f; (of interest) regain m; (of custom, language) renouveau m; (of law) remise f en vigueur; Theat reprise f

revivalist /rɪˈvaɪvəlɪst/ adj **1** Relig revivaliste; **2** Archit, Mus etc **Greek/Gothic ~** néo-grec/-gothique

revive /rɪˈvaɪv/

A vtr **1** gen remonter; (from coma, faint etc) faire reprendre connaissance à [person]; **2** fig raviver [custom]; ranimer [interest, hopes]; remettre en vigueur [law]; relancer [debate, career, movement]; remettre [qch] à la mode [style, fashion]; revigorer [economy]; **to ~ sb's (flagging) spirits** remonter le moral à qn; **3** Theat reprendre [play]

B vi **1** [person] (from coma, faint) reprendre connaissance; [interest] renaître; [economy] reprendre

revocation /ˌrevəˈkeɪʃn/ n (of will, edict) révocation f; (of decision, order) annulation f

revoke /rɪˈvəʊk/ vtr révoquer [will, edict]; annuler [decision, order]

revolt /rɪˈvəʊlt/

A n (physical) révolte f (**against** contre); (verbal) rébellion f (**over**

contre); **to be in** ~ être en révolte *or* en rébellion; **to rise in** ~ se soulever

B *vtr* dégoûter, révolter

C *vi* (physically) se révolter (**against** contre); (verbally) se rebeller (**against, over** contre)

revolting /rɪ'vəʊltɪŋ/ *adj* **1)** (physically) répugnant; (morally) révoltant; **2)** ○[*food*] infect; [*person*] affreux/-euse

revolution /,revə'lu:ʃn/ *n* **1)** Pol, fig révolution *f* (**in** dans); **2)** Aut, Tech tour *m*; **3)** (of planet) révolution *f*

revolutionary /,revə'lu:ʃənərɪ, US -nerɪ/ *n, adj* révolutionnaire (*mf*)

revolutionize /,revə'lu:ʃənaɪz/ *vtr* révolutionner

revolve /rɪ'vɒlv/ *vi* **1)** lit tourner; **2)** fig **to** ~ **around** (be focused on) être axé sur

revolving /rɪ'vɒlvɪŋ/ *adj* [*chair*] pivotant; [*stage*] tournant; ~ **door** porte *f* à tambour

revue /rɪ'vju:/ *n* Theat revue *f*

revulsion /rɪ'vʌlʃn/ *n* dégoût *m* (**against** pour); **to feel** ~ **at sth** être dégoûté par qch

reward /rɪ'wɔ:d/

A *n* (recompense) récompense *f*; **a £50** ~ 50 livres sterling de récompense

B *vtr* récompenser (**for** de, pour)

(Idiom) **virtue is its own** ~ Prov la vertu est sa propre récompense

rewarding /rɪ'wɔ:dɪŋ/ *adj* [*experience*] enrichissant; [*job*] gratifiant; **financially** ~ rémunérateur/-trice

rewind /,ri:'waɪnd/ *vtr* (*prét, pp* **rewound**) rembobiner [*tape, film*]

rewind button *n* bouton *m* de retour en arrière

rewire /,ri:'waɪə(r)/ *vtr* refaire l'installation électrique de

reword /,ri:'wɜ:d/ *vtr* reformuler

rework /,ri:'wɜ:k/ *vtr* retravailler [*theme, metal*]

reworking /,ri:'wɜ:kɪŋ/ *n* nouvelle version *f*

rewrite /,ri:'raɪt/ *vtr* (*prét* **rewrote**; *pp* **rewritten**) ré(é)crire [*story, history*]

RFC *n* Sport (*abrév* = **rugby football club**) club *m* de rugby

rhapsodize /'ræpsədaɪz/ *vi* **to** ~ **about** *ou* **over sth** s'extasier sur qch

rhapsody /'ræpsədɪ/ *n* Mus rhapsodie *f*

rhd *n*: *abrév* ▸ **right-hand drive**

rhesus /'ri:səs/ *n* rhésus *m*

rhesus: ~ **baby** *n* enfant *m* rhésus; ~ **factor** *n* facteur *m* rhésus; ~ **negative** *adj* rhésus négatif *inv*; ~ **positive** *adj* rhésus positif *inv*

rhetoric /'retərɪk/ *n* Literat rhétorique *f*; **the** ~ **of terrorism** le discours terroriste; **empty** ~ mots *mpl* creux

rhetorical /rɪ'tɒrɪkl, US -'tɔ:r-/ *adj* rhétorique

rhetorically /rɪ'tɒrɪklɪ, US -'tɔ:r-/ *adv* [*ask*] sans s'attendre à une réponse; ~ **(speaking)** d'un point de vue tout à fait théorique

rheumatic /ru:'mætɪk/ *adj* [*joint*] rhumatisant; [*pain*] rhumatismal

rheumatic fever ▸ p. 933 *n* rhumatisme *m* articulaire aigu

rheumatism /'ru:mətɪzəm/ ▸ p. 933 *n* rhumatisme *m*

rheumatoid arthritis ▸ p. 933 *n* polyarthrite *f* rhumatoïde

rheumatologist /,ru:mə'tɒlədʒɪst/ ▸ p. 1181 *n* rhumatologue *mf*

rheumatology /,ru:mə'tɒlədʒɪ/ *n* rhumatologie *f*

rheumy /'ru:mɪ/ *adj* littér [*eyes*] chassieux/-ieuse

Rhine /raɪn/ ▸ p. 1146 *pr n* Rhin *m*

rhinestone /'raɪnstəʊn/

A *n* diamant *m* fantaisie

B *adj* en strass

rhino /'raɪnəʊ/ *n* (*pl* ~**s** *ou* ~) rhinocéros *m*

rhinoceros /raɪ'nɒsərəs/ *n* (*pl* -**eroses, -eri** *ou* ~) rhinocéros *m*

rhombus /'rɒmbəs/ *n* (*pl* -**buses** *ou* -**bi**) losange *m*

Rhone /rəʊn/ ▸ p. 1146 *pr n* Rhône *m*

rhubarb /'ru:bɑ:b/

A *n* **1)** Culin rhubarbe *f*; **2)** GB '~, ~' simulation du bruit d'une foule

B *noun modifier* [*pie*] à la rhubarbe; [*jam*] de rhubarbe; [*leaf*] de rhubarbe

rhyme /raɪm/

A *n* **1)** (poem) vers *mpl*; (children's) comptine *f*; **2)** (fact of rhyming) rime *f*; **to find a** ~ **for sth** trouver un mot qui rime avec qch

B *vi* rimer (**with** avec)

(Idiom) **without** ~ **or reason** sans rime ni raison

rhyming couplet *n* distique *m* rimé

rhyming slang *n* argot *m* rimé

> **ℹ** **Rhyming slang** L'argot rimé des Cockneys est impossible à comprendre par un non-initié. Le principe consiste à remplacer un mot par une expression qui rime avec ce mot. Par exemple, *Adam and Eve* pour *believe* ou *loaf of bread* pour *head*. Pour corser le tout, les Cockneys tronquent parfois la fin de ces expressions dans la conversation : *Use your loaf (of bread)!* pour *Use your head!.* ▸ **Cockney**

rhythm /'rɪðəm/ *n* gen Mus, Literat rythme *m*

rhythm and blues *n* rhythm and blues *m*

rhythmic(al) /'rɪðmɪk(l)/ *adj* [*beat*] rythmé; [*movement*] rythmique; [*breathing*] régulier/-ière

rhythm section *n* Mus section *f* rythmique

RI *n* **1)** Sch (*abrév* = **religious instruction**) ≈ catéchisme *m*; **2)** US Post *abrév écrite* = **Rhode Island**

rib /rɪb/

A *n* **1)** Anat, Culin côte *f*; **2)** (in umbrella) baleine *f*; (in plane, building) nervure *f*; **3)** (stitch) côte *f*

B *vtr*○ (*p prés etc* -**bb**-) (tease) taquiner

ribald /'rɪbld/ *adj* paillard

ribbed /rɪbd/ *adj* [*garment*] à côtes; [*ceiling, vault*] à nervures; [*seashell*] strié

ribbing /'rɪbɪŋ/ *n* **1)** (in knitting) côtes *fpl*; **2)** (teasing) **to give sb a** ~ taquiner qn

ribbon /'rɪbən/ *n* **1)** ruban *m*; **2)** fig **a** ~ **of smoke** un filet de fumée; **in** ~**s** en lambeaux *mpl*

ribbon development *n*: concentration d'habitations le long d'un axe routier

rib: ~ **cage** *n* cage *f* thoracique; ~ **roast** *n* côte *f* de bœuf; ~ **tickler**○ *n* histoire *f* drôle *or* tordante○

rice /raɪs/ *n* riz *m*

rice: ~**field** *n* rizière *f*; ~ **paper** *n* Culin galette *f* de pain azyme; Art papier *m* de riz; ~ **pudding** *n* riz *m* au lait

rich /rɪtʃ/

A *n* (+ *v* plural) **the** ~ les riches *mpl*

B **riches** *npl* richesses *fpl*

C *adj* [*person, soil, furnishings*] riche; **to grow** *ou* **get** ~ s'enrichir; **to make sb** ~ enrichir qn; ~ **in** riche en [*vitamins*]

D -**rich** *combining form* **oil-/protein-**~ riche en pétrole/protéines

(Idioms) **that's a bit** ~○! GB ça, c'est un peu fort○! iron; **to strike it** ~ faire fortune

richly /'rɪtʃlɪ/ *adv* [*ornamented, coloured*] richement; ~ **deserved** amplement mérité

richness /'rɪtʃnɪs/ *n* richesse *f*

Richter scale /'rɪktə/ *n* échelle *f* de Richter; **on the** ~ sur l'échelle de Richter

rick /rɪk/

A *n* (of hay) meule *f*

B *vtr* **to** ~ **one's ankle** GB se faire une entorse à la cheville

rickets /'rɪkɪts/ ▸ p. 933 *n* (+ *v sg*) rachitisme *m*

rickety /'rɪkətɪ/ *adj* **1)** (shaky) [*chair, coalition*] branlant; [*house*] délabré; **2)** Med rachitique

rickshaw /'rɪkʃɔ:/ *n* pousse-pousse *m inv*

rid /rɪd/

A *vtr* (*p prés* -**dd**-; *prét, pp* **rid**) **to** ~ **the house of mice** débarrasser la maison des souris; **to** ~ **the world of famine** venir à bout de la famine

B *pp adj* **to get** ~ **of** se débarrasser de [*old car, guests*]; faire cesser [*poverty*]; se défaire de [*prejudice*]

riddance /'rɪdns/ *n*:

(Idiom) **good** ~ **(to bad rubbish)!** bon débarras○!

ridden /'rɪdn/

A *pp* ▸ **ride**

B -**ridden** *combining form* **guilt-**~ rongé par un sentiment de culpabilité; **flea-~** infesté de puces; **cliché-~** bourré d'idées reçues

riddle /ˈrɪdl/
A n **1** (puzzle) devinette f; **2** (mystery) énigme f; **he's a ~** c'est une énigme
B vtr **1** (perforate) **to ~ sth with** cribler qch de [*bullets*]; **2** (undermine) **to be ~d with** être rongé par [*disease, guilt*]; fourmiller de [*errors, ambiguities*]; **it's ~d with corruption** la corruption règne

ride /raɪd/
A n **1** (from A to B) trajet m (**in, on** en, à); (for pleasure) tour m, promenade f, balade○ f; **it's a five-minute ~ by taxi** c'est à cinq minutes en taxi; **to go for a ~** aller faire un tour; **to give sb a ~** US emmener qn (en voiture); **2** (in horse race) course f; (for pleasure) promenade f à cheval; **3** fig (path) parcours m; **an easy ~** un parcours facile; **4** Aut smooth **~** confort m; **5** (bridlepath) allée f cavalière
B vtr (*prét* **rode**; *pp* **ridden**) **1** (as rider) monter [*animal*]; rouler à [*bike*]; **can you ~ a bike?** sais-tu faire du vélo?; **to ~ a good race** [*jockey*] courir une belle course; **do you want to ~ my bike/horse?** est-ce que tu veux prendre mon vélo/monter mon cheval?; **to ~ one's bike up/down the road** monter/descendre la rue à vélo; **2** US (travel on) prendre [*subway*]; parcourir [*range*]; **3** (float on) chevaucher [*wave*]
C vi (*prét* **rode**; *pp* **ridden**) **1** (sitting) **to ~ astride** être à califourchon; **to ~ behind** être en croupe; (journeying) **she rode to London on her bike** elle est allée à Londres à vélo; **to ~ across** traverser; **to ~ along sth** longer qch; (being carried) **to ~ in** *ou* **on** prendre [*bus*]; **riding on a wave of popularity** fig porté par une vague de popularité; **2** (horse-riding) faire du cheval; (as jockey) courir; **he ~s well** [*person*] c'est un bon cavalier; fig (of tricky situation) **there's a lot riding on this project** beaucoup de choses sont en jeu dans ce projet

Idioms **to be in for a rough** *or* **bumpy ~** avoir à affronter des temps difficiles; **to be riding for a fall** courir à sa perte; **to give sb a rough ~** donner du fil à retordre à qn; **to go along for the ~** y aller pour le plaisir; **to let sth** *ou* **things ~** laisser courir; **to take sb for a ~**○ (swindle) rouler qn○

Phrasal verbs
■ **ride about, ride around** se déplacer
■ **ride off** partir; **to ~ off to** se diriger vers
■ **ride out**: ▸ **~ out** aller (**to** jusqu'à); ▸ **~ [sth] out, ~ out [sth]** surmonter [*crisis*]; survivre à [*recession*]; **to ~ out the storm** fig surmonter la crise
■ **ride up 1** (approach) [*rider*] s'approcher (**to** de); **2** (rise) [*skirt*] remonter

rider /ˈraɪdə(r)/ n **1** (person) (on horse) cavalier/-ière m/f; (on motorbike) motocycliste mf; (on bike) cycliste mf; (in bike race) coureur/-euse m/f; (in horse race) jockey m; **2** (as proviso) correctif m; (to document) annexe f

ridge /rɪdʒ/ n **1** Geog (along mountain top) arête f, crête f; (on hillside) corniche f; **2** (raised strip) (on rock, metal surface) strie f; (in ploughed land) crête f, billon m; **3** (on roof) faîte m, faîtage m; **4** Meteorol **~ of high pressure** ligne f de hautes pressions

ridge tent n (tente f) canadienne f

ridicule /ˈrɪdɪkjuːl/
A n ridicule m; **to hold sb up to ~** tourner qn en ridicule
B vtr tourner [qch] en ridicule

ridiculous /rɪˈdɪkjʊləs/ adj ridicule

ridiculously /rɪˈdɪkjʊləslɪ/ adv ridiculement

riding /ˈraɪdɪŋ/ ▸ p. 881
A n équitation f; **to go ~** faire de l'équitation
B noun modifier [*clothes, boots, lesson*] d'équitation

riding: **~ breeches** npl culotte f d'équitation; **~ crop** n cravache f; **~ habit** n tenue f d'amazone; **~ school** n centre m équestre; **~ stables** n manège m

rife /raɪf/ adj (*après v*) **to be ~** [*crime*] régner; **speculation was ~** les conjectures allaient bon train

riff /rɪf/ n riff m; **guitar ~** un riff à la guitare

riffle /ˈrɪfl/ vtr (*also* **~ through**) feuilleter [*pages*]

riffraff /ˈrɪfræf/ n péj populace f pej

rifle /ˈraɪfl/
A n Mil fusil m; (at fairground) carabine f
B vtr vider [*wallet, safe*]

Phrasal verb
■ **rifle through**: ▸ **~ through [sth]** fouiller dans

rifle range n Mil champ m de tir; (at fairground) stand m de tir

rift /rɪft/ n **1** (disagreement) désaccord m; (permanent) rupture f; **2** (split) (in rock) fissure f; (in clouds) trouée f

rift valley n rift m

rig /rɪg/
A n (for drilling oil) (on land) tour f de forage; (offshore) plate-forme f pétrolière; (piece of equipment) appareil m; **lighting ~** système m d'éclairage
B vtr (*p prés etc* **-gg-**) (control fraudulently) truquer [*election, result*]

Phrasal verbs
■ **rig out** (dress) **he was ~ged out in his best clothes** il portait ses plus beaux habits
■ **rig up**: ▸ **~ up [sth]** installer [*equipment*]; improviser [*clothesline, shelter*]

rigging /ˈrɪgɪŋ/ n **1** Naut gréement m; **2** (fraudulent control) (of election, competition, result) truquage m

right /raɪt/ ▸ p. 803
A n **1** (side, direction) droite f; **keep to the ~** Aut tenez votre droite; **on** *ou* **to your ~** à votre droite; **take the second ~** prenez la deuxième à droite; **2** Pol (*also* **Right**) **the ~** la droite; **3** (morally) bien m; **to be in the ~** avoir raison; **4** (just claim) droit m; **to have a ~ to sth** avoir droit à qch; **the ~ to work/to strike** le droit au travail/de grève; **she has no ~ to do it** elle n'a pas le droit de le faire; **what ~ have you to criticize me?** de quel droit est-ce que vous me critiquez?; **I've got every ~ to be annoyed** j'ai toutes les raisons d'être agacé; **human ~s** droits de l'homme; **civil ~s** droits civils; **to be within one's ~s** être dans son droit; **her husband is a celebrity in his own ~** son mari est une célébrité à part entière; **the gardens are worth a visit in their own ~** à eux seuls, les jardins méritent la visite; **5** (in boxing) droite f
B rights npl **1** Comm, Jur droits mpl; **film ~s** droits d'adaptation cinématographique; **sole ~** l'exclusivité f des droits; **2** (moral) **the ~s and wrongs of a matter** les aspects mpl moraux d'une question
C adj **1** (as opposed to left) droit, de droite; **on my ~ hand** (position) sur ma droite; **2** (morally correct) bien; (fair) juste; **it's not ~ to steal** ce n'est pas bien de voler; **it's only ~** c'est normal; **I thought it ~ to tell him** j'ai jugé bon de le lui dire; **it is only ~ and proper** ce n'est que justice; **to do the ~ thing** faire ce qu'il faut; **I hope we're doing the ~ thing** j'espère que nous ne faisons pas une erreur; **to do the ~ thing by sb** faire son devoir envers qn; **3** (correct, true) [*choice, direction, size*] bon/bonne; [*word*] juste; (accurate) [*time*] exact; **to be ~** [*person*] avoir raison; [*answer*] être juste; **you're quite ~!** tu as tout à fait raison!; **that's the ~ answer** c'est la bonne réponse; **that's ~** c'est ça; **that can't be ~** ça ne peut pas être ça; **what's the ~ time?** quelle est l'heure exacte?; **it's not the ~ time** ce n'est pas le bon moment; **is that ~?** (asking) est-ce que c'est vrai?; (double-checking) c'est ça?; **am I ~ in thinking that...?** ai-je raison de penser que...?; **is this the ~ train for Dublin?** c'est bien le train pour Dublin?; **is this the ~ way to the station?** est-ce que c'est la bonne direction pour aller à la gare?; **the ~ side of a piece of material** l'endroit m d'un tissu; **to get one's facts ~** être sûr de ce qu'on avance; **you've got the spelling ~** l'orthographe est bonne; **let's hope he gets it ~ this time** espérons qu'il y arrivera cette fois-ci; **it wouldn't look ~ if we didn't attend** ça serait mal vu si on n'y assistait pas; **how ~ you are!** comme vous avez raison!; **time proved him ~** le temps lui a donné raison; **4** (most suitable) qui convient; **the ~ clothes for gardening** des vêtements qui conviennent au jardinage; **the model that's ~ for you** le modèle qui vous convient; **the ~ person for the job** la personne qu'il faut pour le poste; **you need to have the ~ equipment** il te faut le matériel approprié; **when the time is ~** quand le moment sera venu; **to be in the ~ place at the ~ time** être là où il faut au bon moment; **to know the ~ people** connaître des gens bien placés; **he was careful to say all the ~ things** il a pris grand soin de dire tout ce qu'il faut dire dans ce genre de situation; **5** (in good order) [*machine, vehicle*] en bon état, qui fonctionne bien; (healthy) [*person*] bien portant; **I don't feel quite ~ these days** je ne me sens pas très bien ces jours-ci; **the engine isn't quite ~** le moteur ne fonctionne pas très bien; **there's something not quite ~ about**

him il a quelque chose de bizarre; **I sensed that things were not quite ~** j'ai senti qu'il y avait quelque chose qui n'allait pas; ⑥ (in order) **to put** ou **set ~** corriger [*mistake*]; réparer [*injustice*]; arranger [*situation*]; réparer [*machine*]; **to put** ou **set one's watch ~** remettre sa montre à l'heure; **they gave him a month to put** ou **set things ~** ils lui ont donné un mois pour tout arranger; **to put** ou **set sb ~** détromper qn; ⑦ Math [*angle*] droit; **at ~ angles to** à angle droit avec, perpendiculaire à; ⑧ ○GB (emphatic) **he's a ~ idiot!** c'est un idiot fini!; **it's a ~ mess** c'est un vrai gâchis; ⑨ ○GB (ready) prêt

D *adv* ① (of direction) à droite; **to turn/look ~** tourner/ regarder à droite; **they looked for him ~, left and centre**○ ils l'ont cherché partout; **they are arresting people ~, left and centre**○ ils arrêtent les gens en masse; ② (directly) droit, directement; **it's ~ in front of you** c'est droit ou juste devant toi; **I'll be ~ back** je reviens tout de suite; **the path goes ~ down to the river** le chemin conduit tout droit à la rivière; **~ before/after** juste avant/après; **to walk ~ up to sb** marcher droit vers qn; ③ (exactly) **~ in the middle of the room** en plein milieu ou au beau milieu de la pièce; **~ now** (immediately) tout de suite; US (at this point in time) en ce moment; **I'm staying ~ here** je ne bougerai pas d'ici; **~ there** juste là; **~ on the river** juste au bord de la rivière; ④ (correctly) juste, comme il faut; **you're not doing it ~** tu ne fais pas ça comme il faut; **to guess ~** deviner juste; **if I remember ~** si je me souviens bien; ⑤ (completely) tout; **~ around the garden** tout autour du jardin; **go ~ back to the beginning** revenez tout au début; **~ at the bottom** tout au fond; **~ at the top of the house** tout en haut de la maison; **to read a book ~ through** lire un livre jusqu'au bout; **she looked ~ through me** *fig* elle a fait semblant de ne pas me voir; **to turn the central heating ~ up** mettre le chauffage central à fond; **~ up until the 1950s** jusque dans les années 50; **we're ~ behind you!** nous vous soutenons totalement!; ⑥ ▸ p. 869 GB (in titles) **the Right Honourable** le très honorable; **the Right Honourable Gentleman** (form of address in parliament) ≈ notre distingué collègue; ⑦ (very well) bon; **~, let's have a look** bon, voyons ça

E *vtr* ① (restore to upright position) redresser; ② (correct) réparer; **to ~ a wrong** redresser un tort

F *v refl* **to ~ oneself** [*person*] se redresser; **to ~ itself** [*ship, situation*] se rétablir

(Idioms) **to see sb's ~** (financially) dépanner○ qn; (in other ways) sortir qn d'affaire; **~ you are**○!, **~-oh**○! GB d'accord!; **~ enough**○ effectivement; **by ~s** normalement, en principe; **to put sth to ~s** arranger qch

right: **~ angle** *n* angle *m* droit; **~-angled triangle** *n* triangle *m* rectangle; **~ away** *adv* tout de suite; **~-click** *vi* Comput cliquer en appuyant sur le bouton droit (de la souris) (on sur)

righteous /ˈraɪtʃəs/ *adj* vertueux/-euse

righteously /ˈraɪtʃəslɪ/ *adv* de façon vertueuse

rightful /ˈraɪtfl/ *adj* légitime

rightfully /ˈraɪtfəlɪ/ *adv* [*mine*] légitimement; [*belong*] en droit

right-hand /ˈraɪthænd/ *adj* du côté droit; **on the ~ side** sur la droite

right: **~-hand drive, rhd** *n* conduite *f* à droite; **~-handed** *adv* [*person*] droitier/-ière; [*blow*] du droit; **~-hand man** *n* bras *m* droit

rightly /ˈraɪtlɪ/ *adv* ① (accurately) correctement; ② (justifiably) à juste titre; **and ~ so** et pour cause; **~ or wrongly** à tort ou à raison; ③ (with certainty) au juste; **I can't ~ say** je ne peux pas dire; **I don't ~ know** je ne sais pas au juste

right: **~-minded** *adj* bien-pensant; **~-of-centre** *adj* Pol centre-droite *inv*; **~ off** *adv* tout de suite

right of way *n* ① Aut priorité *f*; ② (over land) droit *m* de passage; **'no ~'** 'entrée *f* interdite'

right-on○ /ˈraɪtɒn/
A *adj péj* **they're very ~**○ ils s'appliquent à être idéologiquement corrects sur tout
B *excl* GB **right on** *excl* ça marche!

right: **~s issue** *n* émission *f* de droits de souscription; **~-thinking** *adj* bien-pensant; **~-to-die** *adj* [*movement, protester*] pro-euthanasie, pour le droit de mourir; **~-to-life** *adj* [*movement, protester*] pour le droit de vivre

right wing
A *n* Pol **the ~** la droite

B **right-wing** *adj* Pol [*attitude*] de droite; **they are very ~** ils sont très à droite

rigid /ˈrɪdʒɪd/ *adj* [*rules, person, material*] rigide; [*controls, timetable*] strict; **to stand ~** se tenir très raide
(Idiom) **to bore sb ~**○ ennuyer qn à mourir

rigidity /rɪˈdʒɪdətɪ/ *n* rigidité *f*

rigidly /ˈrɪdʒɪdlɪ/ *adv* [*oppose*] fermement; [*obey, control*] rigoureusement; [*stick to, apply*] strictement

rigmarole /ˈrɪgmərəʊl/ *n* (fuss) cirque○ *m*

rigorous /ˈrɪgərəs/ *adj* ① (strict) [*discipline*] rigoureux/ -euse; [*regime*] sévère; [*adherence*] strict; ② (scrupulous) rigoureux/-euse

rigorously /ˈrɪgərəslɪ/ *adv* rigoureusement

rigour GB, **rigor** US /ˈrɪgə(r)/ *n* rigueur *f*

rig-out○ /ˈrɪgaʊt/ *n* tenue *f*

rile /raɪl/ *vtr* énerver

rim /rɪm/
A *n* bord *m*; (in basketball) anneau *m*; **with a gold ~** cerclé d'or
B **-rimmed** *combining form* **gold-~med spectacles** lunettes *fpl* à monture d'or

rimless glasses /ˈrɪmlɪs/ *n* lunettes *fpl* non cerclées

rind /raɪnd/ *n* ① (on cheese) croûte *f*; (on bacon) couenne *f*; ② (on fruit) peau *f*; **lemon ~** Culin zeste *m* de citron

ring /rɪŋ/
A *n* ① (hoop) (for gymnast, attaching rope) anneau *m*; **a diamond/wedding ~** une bague de diamants/une alliance; ② (circle) (of people, on page) cercle *m*; **to put a ~ round** entourer [qch] d'un cercle [*ad*]; **to have ~s under one's eyes** avoir les yeux cernés; ③ (sound) (at door) coup *m* de sonnette; (of phone) sonnerie *f*; **to have a nice ~ to it** sonner bien; **that has a familiar ~ (to it)** j'ai déjà entendu ça quelque part; ④ GB (phone call) coup *m* de téléphone or fil○; ⑤ Sport (for horses, circus) piste *f*; (for boxing) ring *m*; ⑥ (of smugglers) réseau *m*; (of dealers, speculators) syndicat *m*; ⑦ (to mark bird) bague *f*; ⑧ (round planet) anneau *m*; ⑨ (on cooker) (electric) plaque *f*; (gas) brûleur *m*
B *vtr* ① (cause to sound) (*prét* **rang**; *pp* **rung**) faire sonner [*bell*]; **to ~ the doorbell** ou **bell** sonner; ② GB Telecom (*prét* **rang**; *pp* **rung**) appeler; ③ (encircle) (*prét, pp* **ringed**) [*trees*] entourer; [*police*] encercler; ④ Zool, Ecol (*prét, pp* **ringed**) baguer
C *vi* (*prét* **rang**; *pp* **rung**) ① (sound) [*bell, telephone*] sonner; **the doorbell rang** on a sonné à la porte; ② (sound bell) [*person*] sonner; **to ~ at the door** sonner à la porte; **'please ~ for service'** 'prière de sonner'; ③ (resonate) [*footsteps, laughter, words*] résonner; **that noise makes my ears ~** ce bruit fait bourdonner mes oreilles; **to ~ true/false** sonner vrai/creux; ④ GB Telecom téléphoner; **to ~ for** appeler [*taxi*]
(Idioms) **to ~ down/up the curtain** baisser/lever le rideau; *fig* **to ~ down the curtain on an era** marquer la fin d'une ère; **to ~ in the New Year** fêter le Nouvel An; **to run ~s round** éclipser

(Phrasal verbs)
■ **ring back** GB rappeler
■ **ring in** GB (to work) téléphoner au bureau
■ **ring off** GB raccrocher
■ **ring out**: ▸ **~ out** [*voice, cry*] retentir; [*bells*] sonner
■ **ring up** GB: ▸ **~ up** téléphoner; ▸ **~ up** [sth] ① (phone) téléphoner à [*station*]; ② (on till) enregistrer; ▸ **~ up [sb]**, **~ [sb] up** téléphoner à [*friend*]

ring: **~-a-ring-a-roses** ▸ p. 881 *n*: ronde et jeu enfantins; **~ binder** *n* classeur *m* à anneaux; **~-fence** *vtr* GB réserver; **~ finger** *n* annulaire *m*

ringing /ˈrɪŋɪŋ/ *n* ① (noise of bell, alarm) sonnerie *f*; ② (in ears) bourdonnement *m*

ring: **~leader** *n* meneur/-euse *m/f*; **~let** *n* anglaise *f*; **~master** *n* Monsieur Loyal; **~pull** *n* anneau *m*

ringroad /ˈrɪŋrəʊd/ *n* GB périphérique *m*; **inner ~** ceinture *f*

ringside /ˈrɪŋsaɪd/ *n* **at the ~** près du ring
(Idiom) **to have a ~ seat** *fig* être aux premières loges

rink /rɪŋk/ *n* patinoire *f*

rinse /rɪns/
A *n* rinçage *m*; **to give sth a ~** rincer qch
B *vtr* (to remove soap) rincer; (wash) laver

■ **rinse out**: ▸ ~ **out** [colour] partir au lavage; ▸ ~ [sth] **out**, ~ **out** [sth] rincer [glass]

rinse cycle n cycle m de rinçage

riot /'raɪət/
A n **1** gen (disturbance) émeute f, révolte f; **football** ~ affrontement m de supporters; **prison** ~ mutinerie f; **2** **a** ~ **of** une profusion de [colours]; **3** ○**to be a** ~ (hilarious) être tordant○

B vi gen se soulever; [prisoner] se mutiner

(Idiom) **to run** ~ (behave wildly) lit se déchaîner; fig [imagination] se débrider; [plant] proliférer

Riot Act n Jur, Hist loi f britannique antiémeutes

(Idiom) **to read sb the riot act** chapitrer qn

rioter /'raɪətə(r)/ n gen émeutier/-ière m/f; (in prison) mutin m

riot gear n tenue f antiémeutes

rioting /'raɪətɪŋ/ n ¢ émeutes fpl, bagarres fpl

riotous /'raɪətəs/ adj [laughter] exubérant; [welcome] délirant; [living, evening] débridé

riotously /'raɪətəslɪ/ adv ~ **funny** à se tordre or mourir de rire

riot: ~ **police** n forces fpl d'ordre; ~ **shield** n bouclier m antiémeutes; ~ **squad** n brigade f antiémeutes

rip /rɪp/
A n (tear) accroc m (**in** dans)

B vtr (p prés etc **-pp-**) **1** (tear) déchirer; **to** ~ **a hole in sth** faire un trou dans qch; **to** ~ **sth to pieces** ou **shreds** réduire qch en pièces; **2** (snatch, pull) **to** ~ **sth down** ou **out** arracher qch

C vi (p prés etc **-pp-**) [fabric] se déchirer

(Idiom) **to let** ~○ tempêter○; **to let** ~ **at sb** engueuler➌ qn

(Phrasal verbs)
■ **rip apart**: ▸ ~ [sth] **apart** **1** lit [bomb blast] déchiqueter; **2** ○fig défoncer [team, team's defences]
■ **rip off**: ▸ ~ **off** [sth], ~ [sth] **off** **1** lit arracher [garment, roof]; **2** ○(steal) rafler○ [idea, design]; ▸ ~ [sb] **off** arnaquer➌
■ **rip open**: ▸ ~ ~ **open** [sth], ~ [sth] **open** déchirer
■ **rip through**: ▸ ~ **through** [sth] [bomb blast] défoncer [building]
■ **rip up**: ▸ ~ ~ **up** [sth], ~ [sth] **up** déchirer [paper, contract]; arracher [floorboards]

RIP (abrév = requiescat ou requiescant in pace) qu'il/elle repose en paix or qu'ils/elles reposent en paix

ripcord /'rɪpkɔːd/ n poignée f d'ouverture

ripe /raɪp/ adj **1** [fruit] mûr; [cheese] fait; **2** **the time is** ~ c'est le moment; ~ **for development** (site) bon pour la construction; **3** [language] grossier/-ière m/f; **to smell** ~ sentir mauvais

(Idiom) **to live to a** ~ **old age** vivre jusqu'à un âge très avancé

ripen /'raɪpən/
A vtr mûrir [fruit]; affiner [cheese]
B vi [fruit] mûrir; [cheese] se faire

ripeness /'raɪpnɪs/ n lit, fig maturité f

rip: ~-**off**○ n arnaque➌ f; ~-**off artist**○, ~-**off merchant**○ n arnaqueur/-euse➌ m/f

ripping○ /'rɪpɪŋ/ adj GB épatant, sensationnel/-elle

ripple /'rɪpl/
A n **1** (in water, corn, hair) ondulation f; **2** (sound) **a** ~ **of applause** une cascade d'applaudissements; **3** (repercussion) répercussion f; **4** (ice cream) glace f panaché
B vtr faire des vaguelettes à la surface de [water]; **to** ~ **one's muscles** faire saillir ses muscles
C vi **1** [water] se rider; (making noise) clapoter; **2** [corn] ondoyer; [hair] onduler; [muscles] saillir

ripple effect n effet m secondaire

rip-roaring○ /'rɪprɔːrɪŋ/ adj [success] dingue○

rise /raɪz/
A n **1** (increase) (in amount, number, inflation, rates) augmentation f (**in** de); (in prices, pressure) hausse f (**in** de); (in temperature) élévation f (**in** de); (in standards) amélioration f (**in** de); **2** GB (also **pay** ~, **wage** ~) augmentation f (de salaire); **3** (progress) (of person) ascension f; (of empire) essor m; (of ideology) montée f; **her** ~ **to fame** son accession à la gloire; **4** (slope) montée f; **5** (hill) butte f; **6** **to give** ~ **to** fig donner lieu à [rumours, speculation]; susciter [resentment, frustration];

causer [problem, unemployment]

B vi (prét **rose**; pp **risen**) **1** (become higher) [water] monter; [price, temperature] augmenter; [voice] devenir plus fort; **to** ~ **above** [temperature, amount] dépasser; **2** fig (intensify) [pressure] augmenter; [tension] monter; [frustration, hopes] grandir; **3** (get up) [person] se lever; (after falling) se relever; **to** ~ **from the dead** ressusciter; '~ **and shine!**' 'debout!'; **4** (meet successfully) **to** ~ **to** se montrer à la hauteur de [occasion, challenge]; **5** (progress) [person] réussir; **to** ~ **to** devenir [director, manager]; s'élever à [rank]; **to** ~ **to fame** atteindre la célébrité; **to** ~ **through the ranks** gravir tous les échelons; **6** (slope upwards) [road] monter; [cliff] s'élever; **7** (appear over horizon) [sun, moon] se lever; **8** Geog (have source) **to** ~ **in** [river] prendre sa source dans [area]; **9** Culin [cake] lever; **10** [committee, parliament] lever la séance

(Idiom) **to get a** ~ **out of sb**○ faire enrager qn

(Phrasal verbs)
■ **rise above**: ▸ ~ **above** [sth] (overcome) surmonter
■ **rise up** (ascend) [bird, plane] s'élever; [smoke] monter; [building] se dresser; (rebel) se soulever

risen /'rɪzn/
A pp ▸ **rise**
B adj Relig ressuscité

riser /'raɪzə(r)/ n (person) **to be an early** ~ être un/une lève-tôt

rising /'raɪzɪŋ/
A n (rebellion) soulèvement m
B adj [costs, unemployment, temperature] en hausse; [demand] en augmentation; [tension] grandissant; [sun, moon] levant; [politician, singer] en pleine ascension; [talent] prometteur/-euse
C adv **to be** ~ **twelve** aller sur ses douze ans

risk /rɪsk/
A n **1** gen risque m; **is there any** ~ **of him catching the illness?** est-ce qu'il risque d'attraper la maladie?; **there is no** ~ **to consumers** il n'y a aucun danger pour le consommateur; **to run a** ~ courir un risque; **to take** ~**s** prendre des risques; **it's not worth the** ~ le risque est trop grand; **at** ~ menacé; **to put one's health at** ~ compromettre sa santé; **at one's own** ~ à ses risques et périls; **at the** ~ **of seeming ungrateful** au risque de paraître ingrat; **'at owner's** ~' 'aux risques et périls du propriétaire'; **2** (in banking, insurance) **to be a good/bad** ~ être un bon/mauvais risque
B vtr **1** (endanger) **to** ~ **one's life/neck** risquer sa vie/peau; **2** (venture) **to** ~ **doing** courir le risque de faire; **to** ~ **death** risquer la mort; **to** ~ **one's all** risquer le tout pour le tout; **we decided to** ~ **it** nous avons décidé de prendre le risque; **let's** ~ **it anyway** c'est un risque à prendre

risk-taker /'rɪskteɪkə(r)/ n fonceur/-euse○ m/f; **to be a** ~ aimer prendre des risques

risky /'rɪskɪ/ adj [decision, undertaking] risqué; [share, investment] à risques

risotto /rɪ'zɒtəʊ/ n (pl ~**s**) risotto m

risqué /'riːskeɪ, US rɪ'skeɪ/ adj osé

rite /raɪt/ n rite m; **to perform a** ~ accomplir un rite; ~ **of passage** rite de passage

ritual /'rɪtʃʊəl/
A n rituel m, rites mpl; **the courtship** ~ Zool le cérémonial d'approche
B adj [dance, murder] rituel/-elle; [visit] traditionnel/-elle

ritualistic /ˌrɪtʃʊə'lɪstɪk/ adj [activity] rituel/-elle; (religious) ritualiste

ritually /'rɪtʃʊəlɪ/ adv (ceremonially) selon le rituel; fig (routinely) rituellement

ritzy○ /'rɪtsɪ/ adj chic inv

rival /'raɪvl/
A n (person) rival/-e m/f; (company) concurrent/-e m/f
B adj [team, business] rival; [claim] opposé
C vtr (p prés etc **-ll-**, **-l-** US) (equal) égaler (**in** en); (compete favourably) rivaliser avec (**in** de); **to** ~ **sb/sth in popularity** rivaliser de popularité avec qn/qch

rivalry /'raɪvlrɪ/ n rivalité f (**between** entre)

river /'rɪvə(r)/ n **1** (flowing into sea) fleuve m; (tributary) rivière f; **up** ~/**down** ~ en amont/en aval; **2** fig (of lava, blood) fleuve m

(Idiom) **to sell sb down the** ~ trahir qn

riverbank /'rɪvəbæŋk/ n berge f; **along the** ~ le long de la rivière

r

Rivers

■ *The English word* river *can be either* fleuve *or* rivière *in French. Major rivers, all of which flow into the sea, are* fleuves: *the rest are* rivières. *Here are some examples of* fleuves *in France:* la Garonne, la Loire, la Seine, le Rhin, le Rhône *and* la Somme: *other* fleuves *include:* le Nil, le Danube, le Gange, le Tage, l'Indus, l'Amazone, le Congo, le Mississippi, le Niger *and* le Saint-Laurent.

■ *The following French rivers are* rivières: la Marne, l'Oise, l'Allier, la Dordogne, la Saône.

■ *As in English, French uses the definite article with names of rivers:*

the Thames
= la Tamise

to go down the Rhine
= descendre le Rhin

to live near the Seine
= habiter près de la Seine

the course of the Danube
= le cours du Danube

In English you can say the X, the X river *or* the river X. *In French it is always* le X (*or* la X):

the river Thames
= la Tamise

the Potomac river
= le Potomac

■ *When the name of the river is used as an adjective, French has* de + definite article:

Seine barges
= les péniches de la Seine

a Rhine castle
= un château des bords du Rhin

the Rhine estuary
= l'estuaire du Rhin

river: ~ **basin** n bassin m fluvial; ~**boat** n navire m à aubes; ~ **police** n police f fluviale

riverside /'rɪvəsaɪd/
A n berges fpl
B adj [pub] au bord de la rivière

river traffic n navigation f fluviale

rivet /'rɪvɪt/
A n rivet m
B vtr ① (captivate) **to be ~ed** être captivé; ② (fix) **to be ~ed to the spot** [person] être cloué sur place

riveting /'rɪvɪtɪŋ/ adj fascinant

Riviera /ˌrɪvɪ'eərə/ n **the Italian ~** la Riviera; **the French ~** la Côte d'Azur

rivulet /'rɪvjʊlɪt/ n (stream) ruisselet m

RN n GB abrév ▸ Royal Navy

roach /rəʊtʃ/ n ① (fish) (pl ~) gardon m; ② ○US (insect) cafard m

road /rəʊd/
A n ① (between places) route f; **the ~ to Leeds** la route de Leeds; **the ~ north** la route du nord; **the ~ home** la route qui mène à la maison; **the ~ back** to the route du retour à; **are we on the right ~ for Oxford?** c'est bien la route pour Oxford?; **follow the ~ ahead** allez tout droit; **three hours on the ~** trois heures de route; **across the ~** de l'autre côté de la route, en face; **it's just along the ~** c'est juste un peu plus loin; **down the ~** plus bas, plus loin; **by ~** par la route; **transported by ~** transporté par or sur route; **to take (to) the ~** prendre la route, se mettre en route; **to be on the ~** [car] être en état de rouler; [driver] être sur la route; [band, performers] être en tournée; **I've been on the ~ all night** j'ai roulé toute la nuit; **to be off the ~** [vehicle] être hors d'usage; ② (in built-up area) rue f; **he lives just along ou down the ~** il habite un peu plus loin dans la

rue; ③ fig (way) voie f (**to** de); **to be on the ~ to success** être sur la voie du succès; **to be on the right ~** être sur la bonne voie; **we don't want to go down that ~** nous ne voulons pas suivre cette voie; **somewhere along the ~ she learned** en cours de route elle a appris; **to reach the end of the ~** déboucher sur une impasse
B noun modifier [condition, network, map, safety] routier/-ière; [repair] des routes; [accident] de la route
(Idiom) **let's get this show on the ~!** c'est parti!

roadblock /'rəʊdblɒk/ n barrage m routier; **police ~** barrage de police

road: ~ **haulage** n transports mpl routiers; ~ **hog**○ n chauffard○ m; ~**holding** n tenue f de route; ~**house** n (inn) relais m (routier); ~ **hump** n ralentisseur m; ~ **manager** ▸ p. 1181 n organisateur/-trice m/f de tournée

road map n ① (for orientation) carte f routière; ② Pol **the ~ map to peace** la feuille de route pour la paix

road: ~**-mender** ▸ p. 1181 n cantonnier m; ~ **movie** n road-movie m; ~ **racing** ▸ p. 881 n compétition f sur route; ~ **rage** n violence f au volant; ~**roller** n rouleau m compresseur; ~ **sense** n conscience f des dangers de la route

roadshow /'rəʊdʃəʊ/ n ① (play, show) spectacle m de tournée; ② (publicity tour) tour m promotionnel

roadside /'rəʊdsaɪd/
A n bord m de la route; **at ou by ou on the ~** au bord de la route
B noun modifier au bord de la route; ~ **repairs** réparations fpl de fortune

road: ~**sign** n panneau m de signalisation; ~**sweeper** ▸ p. 1181 n (person) balayeur/-euse m/f; (machine) balayeuse f; ~ **tax** n taxe f routière; ~ **tax disc** n vignette f; ~ **test** n essai m sur route; ~ **transport** n transports mpl routiers; ~ **user** n usager m de la route; ~**works** npl travaux mpl (routiers); ~**worthy** adj en état de rouler

roam /rəʊm/
A vtr parcourir [countryside]; faire le tour de [shops]; **to ~ the streets** traîner dans les rues
B vi **to ~ through** parcourir [countryside]; faire le tour de [building]
(Phrasal verb)

■ **roam around** [person] vadrouiller○

roar /rɔː(r)/
A n (of lion) rugissement m; (of person) hurlement m; (of crowd) clameur f; (of engine) vrombissement m; (of traffic, waterfall) grondement m; (of sea) mugissement m; **to give a ~** [lion] rugir; [person] hurler; **a ~ of laughter** un éclat de rire; **a ~ of applause** un tonnerre d'applaudissements
B vi [lion] rugir; [person] vociférer (**at sb** devant qn); [sea, wind] mugir; [fire] ronfler; [crowd] hurler; [engine] vrombir; **to ~ with pain** rugir de douleur

roaring /'rɔːrɪŋ/
A n (of lion, person) rugissement m; (of crowd) clameur f; (of storm, wind, sea) mugissement m; (of thunder, waterfall) grondement m; (of engine) vrombissement m
B adj ① (loud) [engine, traffic] grondant; **a ~ fire** une belle flambée; ② [success] fou/folle; **to do a ~ trade** faire des affaires en or (**in** dans la vente de)

roast /rəʊst/
A n Culin rôti m; US barbecue m
B adj [meat, potatoes] rôti; ~ **beef** rôti m de bœuf, rosbif m; ~ **chestnuts** châtaignes fpl grillées
C vtr rôtir [meat, potatoes]; (faire) griller [chestnuts]; torréfier [coffee beans]; **to be ~ed alive** faire être grillé vif
D vi [meat] rôtir; **I'm ~ing**○! je crève de chaud○!

roaster /'rəʊstə(r)/ n Culin (chicken) poulet m à rôtir; (oven pan) plat m à rôtir

roasting /'rəʊstɪŋ/
A ○n **to give sb a ~** passer un bon savon à qn○
B adj Culin [chicken, pan] à rôtir

rob /rɒb/ vtr (p prés etc **-bb-**) ① [thief] voler [person]; dévaliser [bank, train]; **to be ~bed of sth** se faire voler qch; ② (deprive) **to ~ sb of** priver qn de
(Idiom) **to ~ sb blind** escroquer qn

robber /'rɒbə(r)/ n voleur/-euse m/f; **train ~** bandit m

robbery /'rɒbərɪ/ n vol m; **it's sheer ~!** fig c'est du vol!

robe /rəʊb/
A n robe f; **christening** ~ robe de baptême; **ceremonial** ~s vêtements mpl de cérémonie
B vtr vêtir; ~**d in white** vêtu de blanc

robin /'rɒbɪn/ n **1** rouge-gorge m; **2** US merle m migrateur

Robin Hood pr n Hist Robin des bois

robot /'rəʊbɒt/ n (in sci-fi, industry) robot m also pej

robotic /rəʊ'bɒtɪk/ adj [movement, voice] de robot; [tool, device, machine] robotisé

robotics /rəʊ'bɒtɪks/ n (+ v sg) robotique f

robotization /ˌrəʊbətaɪ'zeɪʃn, US -tɪ'z-/ n robotisation f

robust /rəʊ'bʌst/ adj [health, person, toy] robuste; [economy] solide; [humour] fruste; [reply, attitude, tackle] énergique; [wine, flavour] corsé

robustly /rəʊ'bʌstlɪ/ adv **1** [made] solidement; **2** fig [answer, defend] avec force; [confident] foncièrement

robustness /rəʊ'bʌstnɪs/ n **1** (of object) robustesse f; (of answer, defence) fermeté f; (of economy) solidité f

rock /rɒk/
A n **1** ⊄ (substance) roche f; **solid** ~ roche dure; **hewn out of solid** ~ taillé dans le roc; **2** C (boulder) rocher m; **on the** ~**s** [ship] sur les récifs; [drink] avec des glaçons; **to be on the** ~**s** [marriage] aller à vau-l'eau; **3** (stone) pierre f; **'falling** ~**s'** 'chute de pierres'; **4** (also ~ **music**) rock m; **5** GB (sweet) sucre m d'orge
B noun modifier [band, concert, musician] rock; [industry] du rock
C vtr **1** (move gently) balancer [cradle]; bercer [baby, boat]; **2** (shake) [tremor] secouer; [scandal] ébranler
D vi **1** (sway) se balancer; **to** ~ **back and forth** se balancer d'avant en arrière; **to** ~ **with laughter** être secoué de rire; **2** (shake) trembler; **3** (dance) danser le rock

(Idiom) **rock solid/hard as a** ~ solide/dur comme le roc

rock and roll /ˌrɒk ən 'rəʊl/ n (also **rock'n'roll**) rock and roll m

rock bottom /ˌrɒk 'bɒtəm/ n **to be at** ~ être au plus bas; **to hit** ~ toucher le fond

rock: ~ **bun** n GB petit gâteau aux raisins secs; ~ **candy** n US friandise à base de sucre candi; ~ **climber** n varappeur/-euse m/f

rock climbing ▸ p. 881 n varappe f; **to go** ~ faire de la varappe

rock crystal n cristal m de roche

rocker /'rɒkə(r)/ n **1** US (chair) fauteuil m à bascule; **2** (on cradle, chair) bascule f; **3** (also ~ **switch**) interrupteur m à bascule

(Idiom) **to be/go off one's** ~○ débloquer○

rockery /'rɒkərɪ/ n GB rocaille f

rocket /'rɒkɪt/
A n **1** gen, Mil fusée f; **2** Bot, Culin roquette f
B noun modifier [base] de lancement de fusées; [research] spatiale
C vi **1** [price, profit] monter en flèche; **to** ~ **from 10 to 100** grimper de 10 à 100; **2** [person, car] **to** ~ **past sb** passer en trombe devant qn

rocket: ~ **engine** n moteur-fusée m; ~ **launcher** n lance-fusées m inv; ~**-propelled** adj autopropulsé; ~ **ship** n vaisseau m spatial

rock: ~ **face** n paroi f rocheuse; ~**fall** n chute f de pierres; ~ **formation** n formation f rocheuse

Rockies /'rɒkiːz/ pr npl (montagnes fpl) Rocheuses fpl

rocking /'rɒkɪŋ/ n (gentle) balancement m; (vigorous) ballottement m

rocking: ~ **chair** n fauteuil m à bascule; ~ **horse** n cheval m à bascule

rock: ~ **lobster** n langouste f; ~ **painting** n peinture f rupestre; ~ **salmon** n GB Culin roussette f; ~ **salt** n sel m gemme; ~ **star** n rock-star f; ~**-steady** adj extrêmement stable

rocky /'rɒkɪ/ adj **1** [beach, path, road] rocailleux/-euse; [coast] rocheux/-euse; **a** ~ **road** fig un chemin difficile; **2** [relationship, period] difficile; [business] précaire

Rocky Mountains pr npl montagnes fpl Rocheuses

rod /rɒd/ n **1** gen, Tech (stick) tige f; **curtain/stair** ~ tringle à rideaux/de marche; **2** (for punishment) baguette f; **3** (for fishing) canne f à pêche; **4** (staff of office) bâton m de commandement

(Idioms) **to make a** ~ **for one's own back** s'attirer des ennuis; **spare the** ~ **and spoil the child** Prov qui aime bien châtie bien Prov

rode /rəʊd/ prét ▸ **ride**

rodent /'rəʊdnt/ n rongeur m

rodeo /'rəʊdɪəʊ/ n (pl ~**s**) rodéo m

roe /rəʊ/ n **1** ⊄ (eggs) œufs mpl (de poisson); **2** (milt) laitance f

roe: ~**buck** n (pl ~) chevreuil m; ~ **deer** n (pl ~) gen chevreuil m; (female) chevrette f

roger /'rɒdʒə(r)/ excl **1** Telecom reçu; **2** ○(OK) d'accord!

rogue /rəʊg/
A n **1** hum coquin m; **2** péj fripouille f; ~**s' gallery** (file) fichier de police
B noun modifier **1** (maverick) solitaire; **2** péj (dishonest) véreux/-euse; ~ **state** état m voyou

roguish /'rəʊgɪʃ/ adj espiègle, coquin

role /rəʊl/ n Theat, fig rôle m (**of** de); **to take a** ~ interpréter un rôle; ~ **title** ~ rôle-titre m

role: ~ **model** n gen, Psych modèle m; ~**-play** n Psych psychodrame m; Sch jeu m de rôle; ~ **reversal**, ~ **swapping** n permutation f de rôles

roll /rəʊl/
A n **1** (of paper, cloth) rouleau m; (of banknotes) liasse f; (of flesh) bourrelet m; **a** ~ **of film** une pellicule; **2** (bread) petit pain m; **cheese** ~ sandwich m au fromage; **3** (of ship, train) roulis m; **4** (in gymnastics) roulade f; **5** Aviat tonneau m; **6** Games (of dice) lancer m; **7** (of drums) roulement m; **8** (register) liste f; **electoral** ~ listes électorales; **to call the** ~ faire l'appel
B vtr **1** (push) rouler [ball, log]; **to** ~ **sth away** rouler qch pour l'éloigner (**from** de); **2** (make) **to** ~ **sth into a ball** faire une boulette de [paper]; faire une boule de [clay, dough]; faire une pelote de [wool]; **3** (flatten) étendre [dough]; rouler [lawn]; laminer [metal]; **4** (turn) **to** ~ **one's eyes** rouler des yeux; **5** faire tourner [camera, presses]; **6** Games faire rouler [dice]; **7** Ling **to** ~ **one's 'r's** rouler les 'r's
C vi **1** (move) rouler (**onto** sur); **to** ~ **backwards** reculer; **to** ~ **down** [car, rock] dévaler [hill]; **to** ~ **into** entrer en [station]; entrer dans [city]; **to** ~ **off** tomber de; **2** (rotate) [car, plane] faire un tonneau; [eyes] rouler dans leurs orbites; **3** (sway) [ship] tanguer; **4** (reverberate) [thunder] gronder; [drum] rouler; **5** (function) [camera, press] tourner

(Idioms) **heads will** ~**!** des têtes vont tomber!; ~ **on the holidays!** vivement les vacances!; **to be** ~**ing in it**○ rouler sur l'or; **to be X and Y** ~**ed into one** être à la fois X et Y

(Phrasal verbs)
■ **roll about** GB, **roll around** [animal, person] se rouler; [marbles, tins] rouler
■ **roll back**: ▸ ~ **[sth] back**, ~ **back [sth]** **1** (push back) rouler [carpet]; **2** fig faire reculer [years]; repousser [frontiers]
■ **roll down**: ▸ ~ **[sth] down**, ~ **down [sth]** baisser [blind, sleeve]
■ **roll in** [tourists, money] affluer; [clouds] se rassembler; [tanks, trucks] avancer; **2** (stroll in) s'amener○
■ **roll off**: ▸ ~ **off [sth]** sortir de [production line]
■ **roll on** [time] passer
■ **roll out**: ▸ ~ **[sth] out**, ~ **out [sth]** étirer [pastry]; dérouler [rug]
■ **roll over**: ▸ ~ **over** se retourner; **to** ~ **over on one's stomach** rouler sur le ventre; ▸ ~ **[sb] over** tourner [patient] (**onto** sur)
■ **roll up**: ▸ ~ **up** ○(arrive) s'amener○, arriver; ~ **up!** approchez!; ▸ ~ **up [sth]**, ~ **[sth] up** enrouler [rug, poster]; **to** ~ **up one's sleeves** retrousser ses manches; **to** ~ **sth/sb up in** enrouler qch/qn dans

roll-call n Mil appel m

rolled gold n or m plaqué; ~ **watch** montre f plaquée or

roll: ~**ed oats** npl flocons mpl d'avoine; ~**ed-up** adj roulé

roller /'rəʊlə(r)/ n **1** Ind, Tech rouleau m; **paint** ~ rouleau de peintre; **2** (curler) bigoudi m; **3** (wave) rouleau m

roller: ~**ball** n stylo m à bille; ~ **blind** n store m; ~**blade** n patin m en ligne; ~ **blader** n patineur/-euse m/f en ligne ~ **coaster** n montagnes fpl russes; ~**drome** n piste f de patin à roulettes

roller-skate /ˈrəʊləskeɪt/
A n patin m à roulettes
B vi faire du patin à roulettes
roller-skating /ˈrəʊləskeɪtɪŋ/ ▸ p. 881 n patinage m à roulettes; **to go ~** faire du patin à roulettes
roller: **~-skating rink** n patinoire f; **~ towel** n essuie-main m à enrouleur
rollicking /ˈrɒlɪkɪŋ/ adj [comedy] bouffon/-onne
rolling: **~ pin** n rouleau m à pâtisserie; **~ stock** n Rail matériel m roulant; **~ stone** n fig vagabond/-e m/f; **~ strike** n Ind grève f tournante
roll: **~mop** n Culin rollmops m; **~neck** n col m roulé; **~ of honour** GB, **~ of honor** US n Sch, Sport tableau m d'honneur; Mil liste f des soldats tombés au champ d'honneur; **~-on** n déodorant m à bille
roll-on roll-off
A n roulage m
B adj **~ ferry** navire m roulier
roll: **~over jackpot** n super-cagnotte f (en raison de l'absence d'un gagnant la fois précédente); **~-top desk** n bureau m cylindre
ROM /rɒm/ n: abrév ▸ **read-only memory**
roman /ˈrəʊmən/ n, adj (print) romain (m)
Roman /ˈrəʊmən/
A n Romain/-e m/f
B adj [empire, calendar, alphabet, law, road] romain
Roman: **~ candle** n chandelle f romaine; **~ Catholic**, **RC** n, adj catholique (mf); **~ Catholicism** n catholicisme m
romance /rəʊˈmæns/ n ① (of era, place) charme m; (of travel) côté m romantique; ② (love affair) histoire f d'amour; (love) amour m; (passing affair) aventure f; ③ (novel) roman m d'amour; (film) film m d'amour; ④ Literat (medieval) roman m du moyen âge
Romance /rəʊˈmæns/ n, adj Ling roman (m)
Romanesque /ˌrəʊməˈnesk/ adj roman
Romania /rəʊˈmeɪnɪə/ ▸ p. 774 pr n Roumanie f
Romanian /rəʊˈmeɪnɪən/ ▸ p. 1032, p. 969
A n ① (person) Roumain/-e m/f; ② (language) roumain m
B adj roumain
Roman: **~ nose** n nez m aquilin; **~ numerals** npl chiffres mpl romains
romantic /rəʊˈmæntɪk/
A n romantique mf
B adj [setting, story, person] romantique; ② (involving affair) sentimental; ③ [novel, film] d'amour
Romantic /rəʊˈmæntɪk/ n, adj romantique (mf)
romantically /rəʊˈmæntɪklɪ/ adv [behave, sing, play] de façon romantique
romantic: **~ comedy** n comédie f sentimentale; **~ fiction** n (genre) romans mpl d'amour; (in bookshop) 'sentiment' m
romanticism /rəʊˈmæntɪsɪzəm/ n romantisme m
romanticize /rəʊˈmæntɪsaɪz/ vtr idéaliser [person]; présenter [qch] sous un jour romantique [period]
Romany /ˈrɒmənɪ/ n Tzigane mf, Romani mf
Rome /rəʊm/ ▸ p. 1276 pr n Rome
(Idioms) **~ wasn't built in a day** Prov Rome ne s'est pas faite en un jour Prov; **when in ~ do as the Romans do** Prov il faut faire comme les gens du pays
Romeo /ˈrəʊmɪəʊ/ pr n ① (character) Roméo m; ② fig don Juan m
romp /rɒmp/
A n ① (frolic) ébats mpl; ② (easy victory) victoire f facile
B vi s'ébattre; **to ~ home** l'emporter facilement
rompers /ˈrɒmpəz/ npl (also **romper suit**) barboteuse f
roof /ruːf/
A n ① (of building, car etc) toit m; **under one ~** sous le même toit; **a room under the ~** une chambre sous les toits or combles; **to have a ~ over one's head** avoir un toit sur la tête; ② Anat **the ~ of the mouth** la voûte du palais
B vtr faire la couverture de [building]
(Idioms) **to go through** ou **hit the ~**○ [person] sauter au plafond○; [prices] battre tous les records○; **to raise the ~** (be angry) sauter au plafond○; (make noise) faire un boucan de tous les diables○

(Phrasal verb)
■ **roof in**, **roof over**: ▸ **~ in** [sth], **~ over** [sth], **~** [sth] **over** couvrir

roofer /ˈruːfə(r)/ ▸ p. 1181 n couvreur m
roofing /ˈruːfɪŋ/ n ① (material) toiture f, couverture f; ② (process) pose f de la toiture
roofing felt n carton m bitumé
roof: **~ light** n Archit, Constr fenêtre f de toit; **~ rack** n galerie f
rooftop /ˈruːftɒp/ n toit m; **to shout sth from the ~s** crier qch sur tous les toits
rook /rʊk/ n ① Zool (corbeau m) freux m; ② Games tour f
rookery /ˈrʊkərɪ/ n colonie f de freux
rookie○ /ˈrʊkɪ/ n US bleu○ m
room /ruːm, rʊm/
A n ① (for living) pièce f; (for sleeping) chambre f; (for working) bureau m; (for meetings, teaching, operating) salle f; **in the next ~** dans la pièce d'à côté; '**~s to let**' 'chambres à louer'; **~ 159** la chambre 159; **~ and board** chambre avec repas; **to get ~ and board** être logé (et) nourri; ② ¢ (space) place f; **to make ~** faire de la place; ③ (opportunity) **~ for improvement** possibilité f d'amélioration; **~ for manoeuvre** marge f de manœuvre
B vi US loger (**with** chez)
C **-roomed** combining form **4-~ed** de 4 pièces
rooming house /ˈruːmɪŋ/ n immeuble m locatif
roommate /ˈruːmmeɪt/ n ① (in same room) camarade mf de chambre; ② US (flatmate) compagnon/compagne m/f d'appartement
room service n service m de chambre
room temperature n température f ambiante; **at ~** [wine] chambré
roomy /ˈruːmɪ/ adj [car, house] spacieux/-ieuse; [garment] large; [bag, cupboard] grand
roost /ruːst/
A n (perch, tree) perchoir m
B vi (in trees) percher (pour la nuit); (in attic) se nicher
(Idiom) **to rule the ~** faire la loi
rooster /ˈruːstə(r)/ n coq m
root /ruːt/
A n ① Bot, Ling, Math, fig racine f; **to take ~** [plant] prendre racine; [idea, value] s'établir; [industry] s'implanter; **to pull sth up by the ~s** déraciner qch; **she has no ~s** elle n'a aucune racine; **to destroy sth ~ and branch** détruire complètement qch; ② (of problem) fond m; (of evil) origine f; **at the ~ of** à l'origine de; **to get to the ~ of the problem** prendre le problème à la racine
B noun modifier ① fig [cause, issue] fondamental; ② Bot [growth] des racines; [system] radiculaire
C vtr **to be ~ed in** être ancré dans; **deeply-~ed** lit, fig bien enraciné; **~ed to the spot** figé sur place
D vi ① Bot prendre racine; ② (search) fouiller

(Phrasal verbs)
■ **root around**, **root about** fouiller (**in** dans)
■ **root for**: ▸ **~ for** [sb] encourager
■ **root out**: ▸ **~ out** [sth], **~** [sth] **out** traquer [corruption]; ▸ **~ out** [sb], **~** [sb] **out** déloger [person]

root: **~ beer** n US boisson pétillante nonalcoolisée aux extraits de plantes; **~ canal work** n Med dévitalisation f; **~ ginger** n gingembre m frais; **~less** adj sans racines; **~ sign** n Math radical m; **~ word** n mot m racine
rope /rəʊp/
A n gen, Sport corde f; fig (of pearls) rang m; **the ~** (hanging) la corde; **to be on the ~s** (in boxing) être dans les cordes; fig avoir le dos au mur
B vtr ① attacher [victim, animal] (**to** à); encorder [climber]; ② US (lasso) prendre au lasso
(Idioms) **to give sb plenty of ~** laisser à qn toute la liberté qu'il/elle veut; **to know the ~s** connaître les ficelles○

(Phrasal verbs)
■ **rope in**: **~** [sb] **in**, **~ in** [sb] ① GB (to help with task) embaucher○; ② US (trick) **to get ~d in** se faire embringuer○

■ **rope off**: ▸ ~ **off** [sth], ~ [sth] **off** barrer [qch] avec une corde

rope ladder n échelle f de corde

rop(e)y○ /'rəʊpɪ/ adj GB **to feel** ~ se sentir patraque○

rosary /'rəʊzərɪ/ n (prayer) rosaire m; (beads) chapelet m

rose /rəʊz/
A prét ▸ **rise**
B n **1** Bot (flower) rose f; (shrub) rosier m; **an English** ~ une Anglaise au teint de porcelaine; **the Wars of the Roses** GB Hist la guerre des Deux-Roses; **2** (colour) rose m; **3** (nozzle) (on watering can) pomme f d'arrosoir; (on shower) pomme f de douche

(Idioms) **life is not a bed of** ~**s** ce n'est pas tous les jours la fête; **everything is coming up** ~**s** tout se passe merveilleusement bien; **to come up smelling of** ~**s** s'en tirer sans tache

rose: ~**bed** n parterre m de roses; ~**bowl** n vase n (spécialement conçu pour les roses); ~**bud** n bouton m de rose; ~ **bush** n rosier m

rose-coloured GB, **rose-colored** US /'rəʊzkʌləd/ ▸ p. 752 adj **1** (red) vermeil/-eille; **2** (optimistic) à l'eau de rose

(Idiom) **to see the world through** ~ **spectacles** voir la vie en rose

rose: ~**garden** n roseraie f; ~**hip** n gratte-cul m, cynorhodon m; ~**hip syrup** n sirop m d'églantine

rosemary /'rəʊzmərɪ, US -merɪ/ n romarin m

rose: ~ **petal** n pétale m de rose; ~ **pink** ▸ p. 752 adj rose; ~**red** ▸ p. 752 adj vermeil/-eille; ~**tinted** ▸ p. 752 adj = **rose-coloured**

rosette /rəʊ'zet/ n **1** (for winner) cocarde f; (on horse) flot m; (on gift) nœud m; **2** Bot rosette f

rose: ~**water** n eau f de rose; ~ **window** n rosace f; ~**wood** n bois m de rose

rosin /'rɒzɪn, US 'rɒzn/ n colophane f

roster /'rɒstə(r)/ n (also **duty** ~) tableau m de service

rostrum /'rɒstrəm/ n (pl **-trums** ou **-tra**) estrade f

rosy /'rəʊzɪ/ adj (pink) rose; [dawn] rosé; **things are looking** ~ fig les choses s'annoncent bien; **to paint a** ~ **picture** fig peindre un tableau favorable

(Idiom) **everything in the garden is** ~ tout va très bien

rot /rɒt/
A n lit pourriture f; fig mal m; **the** ~ **set in when...** les choses ont commencé à se gâter quand...
B vtr (p prés etc **-tt-**) pourrir
C vi (p prés etc **-tt-**) (also ~ **away**) lit pourrir; fig [person] moisir○

rota /'rəʊtə/ n GB tableau m de service; **on a** ~ **basis** à tour de rôle

rotary /'rəʊtərɪ/
A n US Aut rond-point m
B adj rotatif/-ive

rotary clothes line n séchoir m parapluie

rotate /rəʊ'teɪt, US 'rəʊteɪt/
A vtr **1** faire tourner [blade]; faire pivoter [mirror]; **2** (alternate) faire [qch] à tour de rôle [job]; alterner [roles]
B vi [blade, handle, wings] tourner

rotating /rəʊ'teɪtɪŋ, US 'rəʊteɪtɪŋ/ adj **1** [blade, globe] tournant; **2** [post, presidency] tournant

rotation /rəʊ'teɪʃn/ n **1** (of blade etc) rotation f; **2** (taking turns) **to work in** ~ travailler par roulement or à tour de rôle

rote /rəʊt/ n **by** ~ par cœur

rote learning n par cœur

rotisserie /rəʊ'tiːsərɪ/ n rôtissoire f

rotor: ~ **arm** n Aut toucheau m; ~ **blade** n pale f de rotor

rotproof /'rɒtpruːf/ adj imputrescible

rotten /'rɒtn/
A adj **1** [produce] pourri; [teeth] gâté; [smell] de pourriture; **2** (corrupt) pourri○; **3** ○(bad) [weather] pourri; [food] infect; [cook, driver] exécrable; **I feel** ~ **about it** j'en suis malade; **that was a** ~ **thing to do!** c'était vraiment un sale coup○!
B adv **to spoil sb** ~○ pourrir qn○

rotten apple n fig brebis f galeuse

rotund /rəʊ'tʌnd/ adj [person] grassouillet/-ette; [stomach] rebondi; [object, building] aux formes arrondies

rotunda /rəʊ'tʌndə/ n rotonde f

rouble /'ruːbl/ ▸ p. 782 n rouble m

rouge† /ruːʒ/ n rouge m à joues

rough /rʌf/
A n **1** (in golf) rough m; **2** (draft) brouillon m; (sketch) ébauche f; **in** ~ au brouillon
B adj **1** [hand, skin, material] rêche; [surface, rock] rugueux/-euse; [terrain] cahoteux/-euse; [landscape] sauvage; **to smooth (off) the** ~ **edges** (of stone, glass) polir; **2** (brutal) [person, behaviour, sport] brutal, violent; [area] dur; **to be** ~ **with** être brutal avec; **to get** ~ devenir violent; **3** (approximate) [description, map] sommaire; [figure, idea, estimate] approximatif/-ive; ~ **justice** justice f sommaire or expéditive; **4** (difficult) dur; **to be** ~ **on sb** [person] être dur avec qn; **it's** ~ **on you** c'est dur pour toi; **a** ~ **time** une période difficile; **to give sb a** ~ **ride** rendre la vie dure à qn; **5** (crude) grossier/-ière; **6** (harsh) [voice, taste, wine] âpre; **7** (stormy) [sea, crossing] agité; [weather] gros/ grosse; [landing] mouvementé; **8** ○**to feel** ~ se sentir patraque○
C adv (outdoors) **to sleep** ~ dormir à la dure

(Idiom) **to** ~ **it** vivre à la dure

(Phrasal verbs)
■ **rough out**: ▸ ~ **out** [sth] esquisser, ébaucher
■ **rough up**○: ▸ ~ [sb] **up**, ~ **up** [sb] (manhandle) malmener; (beat up) tabasser○

roughage /'rʌfɪdʒ/ n ¢ fibres fpl

rough: ~**-and-ready** adj [person, manner] fruste; [conditions] rudimentaire; [method, system] sommaire; ~**-and-tumble** n lit chahut m; fig mêlée f (**of** de); ~**cast** n Constr crépi m; ~ **diamond** n (gem) diamant m brut; GB (man) brave homme m

roughen /'rʌfn/ vtr rendre [qch] rêche or rugueux

rough-hewn /'rʌfhjuːn/ adj [wood] équarri

roughly /'rʌflɪ/ adv **1** [calculate, describe, indicate] grossièrement, rapidement; ~ **speaking** en gros, approximativement; ~ **10%** à peu près 10%; **2** [treat, hit] brutalement; **3** [make, grate] grossièrement

roughness /'rʌfnɪs/ n **1** (of skin, surface, material) rugosité f; (of terrain) inégalité f; **2** (violence) brutalité f; **3** (lack of sophistication) (of person) rudesse f

rough paper n feuille f de brouillon

roughrider n dresseur/-euse m/f de chevaux

roughshod /'rʌfʃɒd/ adj:

(Idiom) **to ride** ~ **over** se moquer (totalement) de

rough work n Sch brouillon m

roulette /ruː'let/ n roulette f

Roumania pr n = **Romania**

round /raʊnd/

⚠️ *Round* often appears after verbs in English (*change round, gather round, pass round*). For translations, consult the appropriate verb entry (**change, gather, pass**).
For *go round*, *get round* see the entries **go, get.**

A adv **1** GB (on all sides) **all** ~ tout autour; **whisky all** ~! du whisky pour tout le monde!; **to go all the way** ~ faire tout le tour; **2** GB (in circles) **to go** ~ and ~ [carousel] tourner (en rond); [person] fig tourner en rond; lit aller et venir; **3** GB (to specific place, home) **to go** ~ **to** passer à; **to ask sb** ~ dire qn de passer à la maison; **to invite sb** ~ **for lunch** inviter qn à déjeuner (chez soi); **I'll be** ~ **in a minute** j'arrive (dans un instant); **4** GB **three metres** ~ de trois mètres de circonférence; **5** GB (as part of cycle) **all year** ~ toute l'année; **this time** ~ cette fois-ci
B prep GB **1** (expressing location) autour de [table etc]; **to sit** ~ **the fire** s'asseoir au coin du feu; **the wall goes right** ~ **the house** le mur fait le tour de la maison; **what do you measure** ~ **the waist?** combien fais-tu de tour de taille?; **2** (expressing direction) **to go** ~ **the corner** tourner au coin de la rue; **just** ~ **the corner** tout près; **to go** ~ **a bend** (in road) prendre un virage; **to go** ~ **an obstacle** contourner un obstacle; **3** (on visit) **her sister took us** ~ **Oxford** sa sœur nous a fait visiter Oxford; **to go** ~ **the shops** faire les magasins
C **round about** adv phr **1** (approximately) à peu près, environ; **it happened** ~ **about here** ça s'est passé par ici; **2** (vicinity)

the people ~ about les gens des environs

D n **1** (set, series) série f (of de); **the daily ~ of activities** le train-train quotidien; **2** (in competition) rencontre f; **qualifying ~ match** m de qualification; **3** (in golf, cards) partie f; (in boxing, wrestling) round m; **4** (in showjumping) parcours m; **5** (in election) tour m; **6** (of drinks) tournée f; **7** Mil (unit of ammunition) balle f; **~ of ammunition** cartouche f; **8** Mil (shot fired) salve f; **9** (burst) **~ of applause** salve f d'applaudissements; **to get a ~ of applause** être applaudi; **10** (of bread) **a ~ of toast** un toast; **11** (route) tournée f; **to do one's ~s** [doctor] visiter ses malades; [postman] faire sa tournée; [guard] faire sa ronde; **to do** ou **go the ~s** [rumour, flu] circuler; **to go** ou **do the ~s of** faire le tour de; **12** (circular shape) rondelle f (of de); **13** Mus (canon) canon m

E adj **1** (circular, spherical, curved) rond; **~-faced** au visage rond; **her eyes grew ~** elle a ouvert des yeux ronds; **to have ~ shoulders** avoir le dos voûté; **2** (complete) [figure] rond; **in ~ figures, that's £100** ça fait 100 livres sterling en arrondissant; **a ~ dozen** une douzaine exactement; **a nice ~ sum** une somme rondelette°

F vtr contourner [headland]; **to ~ the corner** tourner au coin; **to ~ a bend** prendre un virage

(Phrasal verbs)
- **round down**: ▸ **~ [sth] down, ~ down [sth]** arrondir [qch] au chiffre inférieur
- **round off**: ▸ **~ off [sth], ~ [sth] off** **1** (finish off) finir [meal, evening] (**with** par); conclure [speech]; parfaire [education]; **2** (alter) arrondir [corner, edge, figure]
- **round on** GB: ▸ **~ on [sb]** attaquer violemment; **she ~ed on me** elle m'est tombée dessus°
- **round up**: ▸ **~ up [sb/sth], ~ [sb/sth] up** **1** regrouper [people]; rassembler [livestock]; **to be ~ed up** être pris dans une rafle; **2** arrondir [qch] au chiffre supérieur [figure]

roundabout /'raʊndəbaʊt/
A n GB (in fairground etc) manège m; GB (in playpark) tourniquet m; (for traffic) rond-point m
B adj **to come by a ~ way** faire un détour; **by ~ means** par des moyens détournés; **a ~ way of saying** une façon détournée or alambiquée° de dire

(Idiom) **it's swings and ~s** ce que tu gagnes d'un côté, tu le perds de l'autre

round brackets npl GB parenthèses fpl

rounded /'raʊndɪd/ adj **1** [shape, edge] arrondi; **2** [phrase] travaillé; [account] détaillé

rounders /'raʊndəz/ n GB Sport (+ v sg) ≈ baseball m

roundly /'raʊndlɪ/ adv [condemn] sans ambages; [defeat] joliment

round-neck(ed) sweater n pull-over m ras-de-cou inv

roundness /'raʊndnɪs/ n rondeur f

round robin n Sport tournoi m

round-shouldered /ˌraʊnd'ʃəʊldəd/ adj **to be ~** avoir le dos voûté

round-the-clock adj GB [care, surveillance] 24 heures sur 24; **~ shifts** les trois-huit m inv

round: **~-the-world** adj autour du monde; **~ trip** n aller-retour m

roundup /'raʊndʌp/ n **1** (swoop) rafle f; **2** (herding) rassemblement m (of de); **3** (summary) résumé m

roundworm n ascaris m

rouse /raʊz/ vtr **1** sout **to ~ sb from a deep sleep** tirer qn d'un sommeil profond; **2** (stir) réveiller [person]; susciter [anger, interest]; soulever [public opinion]; **to ~ sb to action** pousser qn à l'action

rousing /'raʊzɪŋ/ adj [reception] enthousiaste; [speech] galvanisant; [music] exaltant

rout /raʊt/
A n déroute f, défaite f
B vtr Mil mettre en déroute; fig battre à plates coutures

(Phrasal verb)
- **rout out** **1** (find) dénicher; **2** (force out) déloger

route /ruːt/
A n **1** gen (way) chemin m; (to work) trajet m (**to** pour aller à); **on the ~ to Oxford** sur le chemin d'Oxford; **to plan a ~** décider d'un itinéraire; **2** (for transport) route f; **shipping ~** route maritime; **domestic ~s** les lignes intérieures; **bus ~** ligne d'autobus; **Route 86** US l'autoroute f 86; **3** (official itinerary) parcours m; **4** fig (to power etc) voie f (**to** de);

5 US /raʊt/ (newspaper) ~ tournée f de livraison
B vtr expédier, acheminer [goods]; **this flight is ~d to Athens via Rome** ce vol va à Athènes via Rome

route march n marche f d'entraînement

routine /ruː'tiːn/
A n **1** (procedure) routine f; **office ~** travail m de routine; **to establish a ~** (at work) s'organiser; (for spare time) se faire un emploi du temps; **2** (drudgery) routine f (**of** de); **3** Mus, Theat (act) numéro m; **4** °péj (obvious act) numéro° m; **5** Comput sous-programme m; **6** Sport enchaînement m
B adj **1** (normal) [enquiry, matter] de routine; **it's fairly ~** c'est la routine; **~ maintenance** entretien m courant; **2** (uninspiring) routinier/-ière

routinely /ruː'tiːnlɪ/ adv **1** [check, review] systématiquement; **2** [tortured, abused] régulièrement

roving /'rəʊvɪŋ/ adj [ambassador] itinérant; **to have a ~ eye** être toujours à l'affût d'une aventure

row¹ /rəʊ/ ▸ p. 881
A n **1** (line) (of people, plants, stitches) rang m (**of** de); (of houses, seats, books) rangée f (**of** de); **seated in a ~** assis en rang; **a ~ of cars** une file de voitures; **~ after ~ of** rang après rang de; **in the front ~** au premier rang; **2** (succession) **six times in a ~** six fois de suite; **the third week in a ~** la troisième semaine d'affilée; **3** (in boat) **to go for a ~** faire de la barque
B vtr **to ~ a boat up the river** remonter la rivière à la rame; **to ~ a race** faire une course d'aviron
C vi ramer; **to ~ across** traverser [qch] à la rame [river, lake]

row² /raʊ/
A n **1** (dispute) (public) querelle f; (private) dispute f (**about, over** à propos de); **a family ~** une dispute (familiale); **to have a ~ with** se disputer avec; **2** (noise) tapage m; **to make a ~** faire du tapage
B vi se disputer (**with** avec; **about, over** à propos de)

rowan /'rəʊən, 'raʊ-/ n **1** (tree) sorbier m; **2** (berry) sorbe f

rowboat /'rəʊbəʊt/ n US bateau m à rames

rowdiness /'raʊdɪnɪs/ n (noise) tapage m; (violence) bagarre° f; (in class) chahut m

rowdy /'raʊdɪ/ adj (noisy) tapageur/-euse; (violent) bagarreur/-euse; (in class) chahuteur/-euse

rower /'rəʊə(r)/ n rameur/-euse m/f, nageur/-euse m/f

rowing /'rəʊɪŋ/ ▸ p. 881 n aviron m; **~ boat** GB bateau m à rames; **~ machine** rameur m

rowlock /'rəʊlɒk/ n GB dame f de nage, tolet m

royal /'rɔɪəl/
A °n (person) membre m de la famille royale
B adj royal; **the ~ 'we'** le pluriel de majesté; **to give sb a ~ welcome** faire un accueil royal à qn

royal: **Royal Air Force, RAF** n GB armée f de l'air britannique; **~ blue** ▸ p. 752 n, adj bleu (m) roi inv; **~ flush** n quinte f royale

Royal Highness ▸ p. 869 n **His ~** Son Altesse f royale; **Your ~** Votre Altesse f

royal: **~ icing** n GB glaçage m aux blancs d'œufs; **~ jelly** n gelée f royale; **Royal Mail** n GB service m postal britannique; **Royal Marines** npl GB fusiliers-marins mpl britanniques; **Royal Navy** n GB marine f britannique; **Royal Society** n GB Académie f des Sciences

royalty /'rɔɪəltɪ/ n **1** ℂ (person) membre m d'une famille royale; (persons) membres mpl d'une famille royale; **2** (state of royal person) royauté f; **3** (money) (to author, musician) droits mpl d'auteur; (on patent, coal deposits) royalties fpl

Royal Ulster Constabulary, RUC n GB Hist police f d'Irlande du Nord

RP n GB (abrév = Received Pronunciation) RP f (prononciation de l'anglais considérée comme standard)

RPI abrév ▸ retail price index

rpm (abrév = revolutions per minute) tr/min

RRP GB (abrév écrite = recommended retail price) prix m de détail conseillé

RSPCA n GB (abrév = Royal Society for the Prevention of Cruelty to Animals) société f protectrice des animaux

Rt Hon GB abrév écrite = **Right Honourable**

rub /rʌb/
A n **1** (massage) friction f; **to give [sth] a** ~ frictionner [back]; bouchonner [horse]; **2** (polish) coup m de chiffon; **to give [sth] a** ~ donner un coup de chiffon à [table]; frotter [stain]
B vtr (p prés etc **-bb-**) **1** (touch) se frotter [chin, eyes]; **2** (polish) frotter [stain, surface]; **to** ~ **sth away** faire disparaître qch; **3** (massage) frictionner; **4** (apply) **to** ~ **sth on to the skin** appliquer qch sur la peau; **to** ~ **sth into the skin** faire pénétrer qch dans la peau; **5** (incorporate) ~ **the cream into your skin** faire pénétrer la pommade en massant; **6** (chafe) blesser [heel]; frotter contre [mudguard]
C vi (p prés etc **-bb-**) **1** (scrub) frotter; **2** (chafe) **these shoes** ~ ces chaussures me blessent

(Idioms) **to** ~ **salt into sb's wounds** remuer le couteau dans la plaie; **to** ~ **sb up the wrong way** prendre qn à rebrousse-poil○; **to** ~ **shoulders with sb** côtoyer or fréquenter qn

(Phrasal verbs)
■ **rub along**○: **to** ~ **along with** s'entendre assez bien avec [person]
■ **rub down**: ▸ ~ **[sb] down**, ~ **down [sb]** frictionner [athlete]; ▸ ~ **[sth] down**, ~ **down [sth]** **1** (massage) bouchonner [horse]; **2** (smooth) poncer [plaster, wood]
■ **rub in**: ~ **[sth] in**, ~ **in [sth]** faire pénétrer [lotion]; **there's no need to** ~ **it in**○! fig inutile d'en rajouter○!
■ **rub off**: ▸ ~ **off** [dye, ink] déteindre; **the chalk** ~s **off easily** la craie s'efface facilement; ▸ ~ **[sth] off**, ~ **off [sth]** faire disparaître [stain]
■ **rub out**: ▸ ~ **out** s'effacer; ▸ ~ **[sth] out**, ~ **out [sth]** effacer

rubber /'rʌbə(r)/
A n **1** (substance) caoutchouc m; **made of** ~ en caoutchouc; **2** GB (eraser) gomme f; **3** (for cleaning) chiffon m; **4** ○US (condom) préservatif m, capote○ f; **5** (in games) partie f
B noun modifier [ball, sole] de or en caoutchouc

rubber: ~ **band** n élastique m; ~ **bullet** n balle f de caoutchouc; ~ **check**○ US chèque m en bois○; ~ **dinghy** n canot m pneumatique; ~ **glove** n gant m en or de caoutchouc

rubberneck○ /'rʌbənek/ n **1** (onlooker) curieux/-ieuse m/f; **2** (tourist) touriste mf

rubber: ~ **plant** n caoutchouc m; ~ **plantation** n plantation f d'hévéas; ~ **sheet** n alaise f; ~-**soled** adj à semelles de caoutchouc

rubber stamp n **1** lit tampon m; **2** fig péj **to be a** ~ **for sb's decisions** [body, group] entériner sans discuter les décisions de qn

rubber: ~ **tapping** n récolte f du latex par saignée; ~ **tree** n hévéa m

rubbery /'rʌbərɪ/ adj caoutchouteux/-euse

rubbing /'rʌbɪŋ/ n **1** (friction) frottement m; **2** (picture) reproduction f par frottement

rubbish /'rʌbɪʃ/
A n **1** (refuse) déchets mpl; (domestic) ordures fpl; (from garden) détritus mpl; (on site) gravats mpl; **2** (inferior goods) camelote○ f; (discarded objects) saletés○ fpl; **3** (nonsense) **to talk** ~ raconter n'importe quoi; **this book is** ~○! ce livre est nul○!
B vtr GB descendre [qn/qch] en flammes

rubbish: ~ **bin** n GB poubelle f; ~ **chute** n GB videordures m inv; ~ **collection** n GB ramassage m des ordures; ~ **dump** GB décharge f (publique); ~ **heap** n tas m d'ordures

rubble /'rʌbl/ n ¢ (after explosion) décombres mpl; (on site) gravats mpl

rub-down /'rʌbdaʊn/ n **to give sb a** ~ frictionner qn; **to give [sth] a** ~ bouchonner [horse]; poncer [woodwork, plaster]

rubella /ru:'belə/ ▸ p. 933 n rubéole f

rubric /'ru:brɪk/ n sout rubrique f

ruby /'ru:bɪ/ ▸ p. 752
A n **1** (gem) rubis m; **2** (also ~ **red**) rouge m rubis
B noun modifier [bracelet, necklace] de rubis; **a** ~ **ring** une bague rubis
C adj [liquid, lips] vermeil/-eille; ~ **port** porto m (ruby); ~ **wedding** noces fpl de vermeil

RUC n: abrév ▸ **Royal Ulster Constabulary**

ruck /rʌk/ n **1** (in rugby) mêlée f ouverte; **2** (crease) faux pli m

rucksack /'rʌksæk/ n sac m à dos

rudder /'rʌdə(r)/ n (on boat) gouvernail m; (on plane) gouverne f

ruddy /'rʌdɪ/ adj [cheeks] coloré; [sky] rougeâtre

rude /ru:d/ adj **1** (impolite) [comment] impoli; [person] mal élevé; **to be** ~ **to sb** être impoli envers qn; **it is** ~ **to do** il est impoli or c'est mal élevé de faire; **I don't mean to be** ~ **but...** je ne veux pas vous vexer mais...; **2** (indecent) [joke] grossier/-ière; [book] osé; **a** ~ **word** un gros mot; **3** (abrupt) brutal

(Idiom) **to be in** ~ **health** littér avoir une santé de fer

rudely /'ru:dlɪ/ adv (impolitely) de façon impolie; (abruptly) brutalement

rudeness /'ru:dnɪs/ n manque m de correction

rudimentary /,ru:dɪ'mentrɪ/ adj rudimentaire

rudiments /'ru:dɪmənts/ npl rudiments mpl (**of** de)

rue /ru:/
A n Bot rue f
B vtr littér se repentir de [decision]

rueful /'ru:fl/ adj [smile] attristé; [thought] triste

ruefully /'ru:fəlɪ/ adv tristement

ruff /rʌf/ n (of lace) fraise f; (of fur, feathers) collier m

ruffian† /'rʌfɪən/ n voyou m

ruffle /'rʌfl/
A n (at sleeve) manchette f; (at neck) ruche f; (on shirt front) jabot m; (on curtain) volant m
B vtr **1** ébouriffer [hair, fur]; hérisser [feathers]; rider [water]; **2** (disconcert) énerver; (upset) froisser

ruffled /'rʌfld/ adj:
(Idiom) **to smooth** ~ **feathers** calmer le jeu

rug /rʌg/ n **1** (mat, carpet) tapis m; (by bed) descente f de lit; **2** GB (blanket) plaid m, couverture f

(Idiom) **to be as snug as a bug in a** ~○ être bien au chaud

rugby /'rʌgbɪ/ ▸ p. 881 n rugby m

rugby: ~ **league** n rugby m à 13; ~ **tackle** n plaquage m; ~ **union** n rugby m à 15

rugged /'rʌgɪd/ adj **1** [landscape] accidenté; [coastline] déchiqueté; **2** [man, features] rude; **3** (tough) [character] coriace; [defence] acharné; **4** (durable) solide

ruin /'ru:ɪn/
A n **1** ¢ (collapse) (physical, financial) ruine f; (moral) perte f; **in a state of** ~, **in** ~s en ruines; **to fall into** ~ tomber en ruines; **2** (building) ruine f; ~s lit, fig ruines fpl (**of** de)
B vtr **1** (destroy) ruiner [economy, career]; **to** ~ **one's health** se ruiner la santé; **to** ~ **one's eyesight** s'abîmer la vue; **2** (spoil) gâcher [holiday, meal]; abîmer [clothes]; gâter [child, pet]; **it's** ~ing **our lives** ça nous gâche la vie

(Idiom) **to go to rack and** ~ se délabrer

ruined /'ru:ɪnd/ adj **1** (derelict) en ruines; **2** (spoilt) [holiday, meal] gâché; [clothes, furniture] abîmé; [reputation] ruiné; (financially) ruiné

ruinous /'ru:ɪnəs/ adj [costs] ruineux/-euse; [prices] exorbitant; [course of action] désastreux/-euse

rule /ru:l/
A n **1** (regulation) (of game, language) règle f; (of school, organization) règlement m; **the** ~s **of the game** les règles or la règle du jeu; **to bend the** ~s contourner les règles or le règlement; **against the** ~s contraire aux règles or au règlement (**to do** de faire); **it is a** ~ **that** il est de règle que (+ subj); ~s **and regulations** réglementation f; **I make it a** ~ **always to do** j'ai pour règle de toujours faire; **2** (usual occurrence) règle f; **as a** ~ généralement; **3** ¢ (authority) domination f, gouvernement m; **under the** ~ **of a tyrant** sous la domination d'un tyran; **majority** ~ gouvernement majoritaire; **4** (for measuring) règle f
B vtr **1** Pol [ruler, law] gouverner; [monarch] régner sur; [party] diriger; [army] commander; **2** (control) [person, money, consideration] diriger [behaviour, life]; [factor] dicter [strategy]; **to be** ~d **by sb** se laisser diriger par qn; **to let one's heart** ~ **one's head** laisser son cœur dominer sa raison; **3** (draw) faire, tirer [line]; ~d **paper** papier réglé; **4** [court, umpire] **to** ~ **that** décréter que
C vi **1** [monarch, anarchy] régner; **2** [court, umpire] statuer

Phrasal verb

■ **rule out**: ▸ **~ out [sth]**, **~ [sth] out** [1] (eliminate) exclure [*possibility, candidate*] (**of** de); **to ~ out doing** exclure de faire; [2] (prevent) interdire [*activity*]

rule: **~book** *n* règlement *m*; **~ of law** *n* Pol séparation *f* constitutionnelle de la justice et du pouvoir; **~ of thumb** *n* principe *m* de base

ruler /'ruːlə(r)/ *n* [1] (leader) dirigeant/-e *m/f*; [2] (measure) règle *f*

ruling /'ruːlɪŋ/
A *n* décision *f* (**against** à l'encontre de; **by** de; **on** sur); **to give a ~** rendre une décision
B *adj* [1] (in power) dirigeant; [2] (dominant) dominant

rum /rʌm/ *n* rhum *m*; **white ~** rhum blanc

rumble /'rʌmbl/
A *n* (of thunder, artillery, trucks) grondement *m*; (of stomach) gargouillement *m*
B *vtr* ○GB **we've been ~d!** on nous a démasqués!
C *vi* [1] [*thunder, artillery*] gronder; [*stomach*] gargouiller; [2] (trundle) **to ~ by** passer bruyamment

rumble: **~ seat** *n* US Aut spider *m*; **~ strip** *n* bande *f* sonore (*sur l'autoroute*)

rumbling /'rʌmblɪŋ/ *n* (of thunder, vehicles) grondement *m*; (of stomach, pipes) gargouillement *m*; **~s** fig murmures *mpl*

rumbustious /rʌm'bʌstɪəs/ *adj* bruyant

ruminant /'ruːmɪnənt/ *n, adj* ruminant (*m*)

ruminate /'ruːmɪneɪt/ *vi* [1] fig **to ~ on** *ou* **about** ruminer sur; [2] Zool ruminer

rummage /'rʌmɪdʒ/
A *n* [1] (look) **to have a ~ in** fouiller dans; [2] US (jumble) vieilleries *fpl*
B *vi* fouiller (**through** dans; **for** à la recherche de)

rummy /'rʌmɪ/ ▸ p. 881 *n* rami *m*

rumour GB, **rumor** US /'ruːmə(r)/ *n* rumeur *f*, bruit *m* (**about** sur); **to start a ~** faire courir une rumeur *or* un bruit; **~s are circulating that, ~ has it that** le bruit court que; **there is no truth in any of the ~s** les rumeurs sont dénuées de tout fondement

rumoured GB, **rumored** US /'ruːməd/ *adj* **it is ~ that** il paraît que, on dit que

rumourmonger GB, **rumormonger** US /'ruːməmʌŋgə(r)/ *n* personne *f* qui fait courir une rumeur

rump /rʌmp/ *n* [1] (*also* **~ steak**) rumsteck *m*; [2] (of animal) croupe *f*; (of bird) croupion *m*; [3] hum (of person) postérieur *m*; [4] (of party) vestiges *mpl*

rumple /'rʌmpl/ *vtr* ébouriffer [*hair*]; froisser [*clothes, sheets, papers*]

rumpus ○ /'rʌmpəs/ *n* (noise) boucan ○ *m*; (protest) esclandre *m* (**over** au sujet de)

rumpus room *n* US salle *f* de jeux

rum toddy *n* grog *m*

run /rʌn/
A *n* [1] (act of running) course *f*; **a two-mile ~** une course de deux miles; **to go for a ~** aller courir; **to take the dog for a ~** aller faire courir le chien; **to break into a ~** se mettre à courir; **to take a ~ at** prendre son élan pour franchir [*hedge*]; **to give sb a clear ~** fig laisser le champ libre à qn (**at doing** pour faire); [2] (flight) **on the ~** en fuite; **to be on the ~ from** fuir; **to have sb on the ~** lit mettre qn en fuite; fig réussir à effrayer qn; **to make a ~ for it** fuir, s'enfuir; [3] (series) série *f*; **to have a ~ of luck** être en veine; **to have a ~ of bad luck** jouer de malchance; [4] Theat série *f* de représentations; **to have a six-month ~** tenir l'affiche pendant six mois; [5] (trend) (of events, market) tendance *f*; **the ~ of the cards/dice was against me** le jeu était contre moi; **in the normal ~ of things** dans l'ordre normal des choses; [6] (series of thing produced) (in printing) tirage *m*; (in industry) série *f*; [7] Fin (on Stock Exchange) ruée *f* (**on** sur); [8] (trip, route) trajet *m*; **the ~ up to York** le trajet jusqu'à York; [9] (in cricket, baseball) point *m*; [10] (for rabbit, chickens) enclos *m*; [11] (in tights, material) échelle *f*; [12] (for skiing etc) piste *f*; [13] (in cards) suite *f*
B *vtr* (*p prés* **-nn-**; *prét* **ran**; *pp* **run**) [1] (cover by running) courir [*distance, marathon*]; **to ~ a race** faire une course; **she ran a very fast time** elle a fait un très bon temps; [2] (drive) **to ~ sb to the station** conduire qn à la gare; **to ~ sb home** reconduire qn; **to ~ sth over to sb's house** apporter qch

chez qn en voiture; **to ~ the car into a tree** jeter la voiture contre un arbre; [3] (pass, move) **to ~ one's hand over** passer la main sur; **to ~ one's eye(s) over** parcourir rapidement; **to ~ a duster over** passer un coup de chiffon sur; **to ~ one's pen through** rayer; [4] (manage) diriger; **a well-/badly-run organization** une organisation bien/mal dirigée; **stop trying to ~ my life!** arrête de vouloir diriger ma vie!; **who is ~ning things here?** qui est-ce qui commande ici?; [5] (operate) faire fonctionner [*machine*]; faire tourner [*motor*]; exécuter [*program*]; entretenir [*car*]; **to ~ tests on** effectuer des tests sur; **to ~ a check on sb** prendre des renseignements sur qn; [6] (organize, offer) organiser [*competition, course*]; mettre [qch] en place [*bus service*]; [7] (pass) passer [*cable*]; [8] (cause to flow) faire couler [*bath*]; ouvrir [*tap*]; [9] (publish) publier [*article*]; [10] (pass through) franchir [*rapids*]; forcer [*blockade*]; brûler [*red light*]; [11] (smuggle) faire passer [qch] en fraude; [12] (enter) faire courir [*horse*]; présenter [*candidate*]
C *vi* (*p prés* **-nn-**; *prét* **ran**; *pp* **run**) [1] (move quickly) [*person, animal*] courir; **to ~ across/down sth** traverser/descendre qch en courant; **to ~ around the house** courir dans toute la maison; **to ~ for** *ou* **to catch the bus** courir pour attraper le bus; **to ~ for the exit** courir vers la sortie; **to ~ in the 100 metres** courir le 100 mètres; **to come ~ning** courir (**towards** vers); [2] (flee) fuir, s'enfuir; **to ~ for one's life** s'enfuir pour sauver sa peau ○; **~ for your life!**, **~ for it** ○! sauve qui peut!, déguerpissons ○!; **there's nowhere to ~ (to)** il n'y a nulle part où aller; **to go ~ning to one's parents** se réfugier chez ses parents; [3] ○ (rush off) filer ○; [4] (function) [*machine*] marcher; **to leave the engine ~ning** laisser tourner le moteur; **to ~ off** fonctionner sur [*mains, battery*]; **to ~ on** marcher à [*diesel, unleaded*]; **to ~ fast/slow** [*clock*] prendre de l'avance/du retard; **the organization ~s very smoothly** l'organisation fonctionne parfaitement; [5] (continue, last) [*contract, lease*] courir; **to ~ from... to...** [*school year, season*] aller de... à...; [6] Theat [*play, musical*] tenir l'affiche (**for** pendant); **this show will ~ and ~!** ce spectacle tiendra à l'affiche pendant des mois!; [7] (pass) **to ~ past/through** [*frontier, path*] passer/traverser; **to ~ (from) east to west** aller d'est en ouest; **the road ~s north for about ten kilometres** la route va vers le nord sur une dizaine de kilomètres; **to ~ parallel to** être parallèle à; **a scar ~s down her arm** une cicatrice court le long de son bras; [8] (move) [*sledge, vehicle*] glisser; [*curtain*] coulisser; **to ~ through sb's hands** [*rope*] filer entre les mains de qn; **a pain ran up my leg** une douleur m'est remontée le long de la jambe; **a wave of excitement ran through the crowd** un frisson d'excitation a parcouru la foule; **his eyes ran over the page** il a parcouru la page des yeux; [9] (operate regularly) circuler; **a ferry ~s between X and Y** il existe un ferry entre X et Y; [10] (flow) couler; **my nose is ~ning** j'ai le nez qui coule; **tears ran down his face** les larmes coulaient sur son visage; **the streets will be ~ning with blood** fig le sang coulera à flots dans les rues; [11] (flow when wet or melted) [*dye, garment*] déteindre; [*makeup, butter*] couler; [12] (as candidate) se présenter; **to ~ for** être candidat/-e au poste de [*mayor, governor*]; **to ~ for president** être candidat/-e à la présidence; [13] (be worded) **the telex ~s...** le télex se présente or est libellé comme suit...; **so the argument ~s** selon l'argument habituellement avancé; [14] (snag) filer

Idioms **to give sb the ~ of sth** mettre qch à la disposition de qn; **in the long ~** à long terme; **in the short ~** à brève échéance

Phrasal verbs

■ **run about**, **run around**: ▸ **~ around** courir; **to ~ around** ○ **with** voir ○

■ **run across** ○: ▸ **~ across [sth/sb]** tomber sur ○

■ **run along** **to ~** se sauver ○, filer ○

■ **run at**: ▸ **~ at [sth]** [1] (charge towards) se précipiter sur; [2] (be at) atteindre, être de l'ordre de

■ **run away**: ▸ **~ away** [1] (flee) s'enfuir (**from sb** devant qn; **to do** pour faire); **to ~ away from home** s'enfuir de chez soi; [2] (run off) [*liquid*] couler; ▸ **~ away with [sth/sb]** [1] (flee) partir avec; [2] (carry off easily) rafler ○; [3] (get into one's head) **to ~ away with the idea that** s'imaginer que

■ **run down**: ▸ **~ down** [*battery*] se décharger; [*watch*] retarder; [*machine, company*] s'essouffler; ▸ **~ down [sth/sb]**, **~ [sth/sb] down** [1] (in vehicle) renverser; [2] (allow to decline) réduire [*production, defences*]; user [*battery*]; [3] (disparage) dénigrer; [4] (track down) retrouver [*person*]; dénicher ○ [*thing*]

■ **run in:** ▶ ~ **in [sth]**, ~ **[sth] in** roder [*car*]; '~**ning in**' 'en rodage'

■ **run into:** ▶ ~ **into [sth/sb]** ①⟩ (collide with) heurter, rentrer dans○ [*car, wall*]; ②⟩ (encounter) rencontrer [*person, difficulty*]; **to ~ into debt** s'endetter; ③⟩ (amount to) se compter en [*hundreds, millions*]

■ **run off** ①⟩ (leave) partir en courant; **to ~ off with** partir avec; ②⟩ [*liquid*] couler

■ **run on:** ▶ ~ **on** [*meeting*] se prolonger; ▶ ~ **on [sth]** (be concerned with) [*mind*] être préoccupé par; [*conversation*] porter sur; ▶ ~ **on [sth]**, ~ **[sth] on** ①⟩ (in printing) faire suivre [qch] sans alinéa; ②⟩ Literat faire enjamber [*line*]

■ **run out** ①⟩ (become exhausted) [*supplies, oil*] s'épuiser; **time is ~ning out** le temps manque; **my patience is ~ning out** je suis en train de perdre patience; ②⟩ (have no more) [*pen, machine*] être vide; **sorry, I've run out** désolé, je n'en ai plus; ③⟩ (expire) expirer; ▶ ~ **out of** ne plus avoir de [*petrol, time, money, ideas*]; **to be ~ning out of** n'avoir presque plus de [*petrol etc*]

■ **run out on:** ▶ ~ **out on [sb]** abandonner

■ **run over:** ▶ ~ **over** ①⟩ [*meeting, programme*] se prolonger; **to ~ over by an hour** dépasser l'horaire prévu d'une heure; ②⟩ (overflow) déborder; ▶ ~ **over [sth]** (run through) passer [qch] en revue [*arrangements*]; ▶ ~ **over [sth/sb]**, ~ **[sth/sb] over** ①⟩ (injure) renverser; (kill) écraser; ②⟩ (drive over) passer sur [*bump*]

■ **run through:** ▶ ~ **through [sth]** ①⟩ (be present in) se retrouver dans [*work*]; ②⟩ (look through) parcourir [*list, article*]; (discuss) passer [qch] en revue; ▶ ~ **through [sth]**, ~ **[sth] through** répéter [*scene, speech*]; **to ~ sth through the computer** passer qch dans l'ordinateur

■ **run to** fig (extend to) **her tastes don't ~ to** jazz elle n'est pas très portée sur le jazz

■ **run up:** ▶ ~ **up [sth]** ①⟩ (accumulate) accumuler [*debt*]; ②⟩ (make) fabriquer [*dress*]; ③⟩ (raise) hisser [*flag*]

■ **run up against:** ▶ ~ **up against [sth]** se heurter à [*difficulty*]

runaround /'rʌnəraʊnd/ *n* **he's giving me/her the ~**○ il se défile○

runaway /'rʌnəweɪ/ *adj* ①⟩ (having left) [*teenager*] fugueur/-euse; [*slave*] fugitif/-ive; [*father*] en fuite; ②⟩ (out of control) [*vehicle*] incontrôlé; [*horse*] emballé; [*inflation*] galopant; ③⟩ (great) [*success, victory*] éclatant

rundown /'rʌndaʊn/ *n* ①⟩ (report) récapitulatif *m* (**on** de); ②⟩ (of industry, factory) réduction *f* de l'activité

run-down /ˌrʌn'daʊn/ *adj* ①⟩ (exhausted) fatigué, à plat○; ②⟩ (shabby) décrépit

rung /rʌŋ/
Ⓐ *pp* ▸ **ring**
Ⓑ *n* ①⟩ (of ladder) barreau *m*; ②⟩ (in hierarchy) échelon *m*

run-in○ /'rʌnɪn/ *n* prise *f* de bec○

runner /'rʌnə(r)/ *n* ①⟩ (person, animal) coureur *m*; ②⟩ (horse) partant/-e *m/f*; ③⟩ (messenger) estafette *f*; ④⟩ (for door, seat) glissière *f*; (for drawer) coulisseau *m*; (for curtain) chariot *m*; (on sled) patin *m*; ⑤⟩ (in hall/on stairs) chemin *m* de couloir/ d'escalier

Ⓘⓓⓘⓞⓜ **to do a ~**○ (not pay) s'esquiver sans payer; (from home) déménager à la cloche de bois

runner: ~ **bean** *n* GB haricot *m* d'Espagne; ~ **up** *n* (*pl* ~**s up**) second/-e *m/f* (**to** après)

running /'rʌnɪŋ/
Ⓐ *n* ①⟩ (sport, exercise) course *f* à pied; ②⟩ (management) direction *f* (**of** de)
Ⓑ *adj* ①⟩ (flowing) [*water*] courant; [*tap*] ouvert; [*knot*] coulant; ~ **sore** lit plaie *f* suppurante; fig abcès *m*; ②⟩ **five days ~** cinq jours de suite

Ⓘⓓⓘⓞⓜⓢ **to be in/out of the ~** être/ne plus être dans la course (**for** pour); **to make the ~** lit, fig mener la course

running: ~ **battle** *n* éternel conflit *m* (**with** avec, contre); ~ **board** *n* marchepied *m*; ~ **commentary** *n* commentaire *m* ininterrompu; ~ **costs** *n* (of scheme) dépenses *fpl* courantes; (of car) frais *mpl* d'entretien; ~ **mate** *n* gen co-candidat/-e *m/f*; (vice-presidential) candidat/-e *m/f* à la vice-présidence; ~ **time** *n* durée *f*; ~ **total** *n* total *m* cumulé; ~ **track** *n* piste *f*

runny /'rʌnɪ/ *adj* [*jam, sauce*] liquide; [*butter*] fondu; [*omelette*] baveux/-euse; [*boiled egg*] mollet; **to have a ~ nose** avoir le nez qui coule

run: ~**-of-the-mill** *adj* ordinaire, banal; ~**proof** *adj* [*fabric*] indémaillable; [*makeup*] résistant à l'eau

runt /rʌnt/ *n* ①⟩ (of litter) le *plus faible d'une portée*; ②⟩ péj (weakling) avorton *m* pej

run-through /'rʌnθruː/ *n* (practice) répétition *f*; (summary) aperçu *m*

run-up /'rʌnʌp/ *n* ①⟩ Sport course *f* d'élan; **to take a ~** prendre son élan pour sauter; ②⟩ (preceding period) **the ~ to** la dernière ligne droite avant

runway /'rʌnweɪ/ *n* Aviat piste *f* d'aviation

rupee /ruːˈpiː/ ▸ **p. 782** *n* roupie *f*

rupture /'rʌptʃə(r)/
Ⓐ *n* ①⟩ Med (hernia) hernie *f*; (of blood vessel, kidney) rupture *f*; ②⟩ Tech (in tank, container) rupture *f*; ③⟩ (in relations) rupture *f* (**between** entre)
Ⓑ *vtr* ①⟩ Med **to ~ oneself** se faire une hernie; ~**d** éclaté; ②⟩ rompre [*relations, unity*]
Ⓒ *vi* ①⟩ [*appendix*] se rompre; ②⟩ [*container*] éclater

rural /'rʊərəl/ *adj* (country) rural; (pastoral) champêtre

ruse /ruːz/ *n* stratagème *m*

rush /rʌʃ/
Ⓐ *n* ①⟩ (of crowd) ruée *f* (**to do** pour faire); **a ~ for the door** une ruée vers la porte; **to make a ~ for sth** [*crowd*] se ruer vers qch; [*individual*] se précipiter vers qch; ②⟩ (hurry) **to be in a ~** être pressé (**to do** de faire); **there's no ~** ce n'est pas pressant; **in a ~** en vitesse; **it all happened in such a ~** tout s'est passé si vite; **what's the ~?** pourquoi faire vite?; **is there any ~?** y a-t-il urgence?; ③⟩ (peak time) (during day) heure *f* de pointe; (during year) période *f* de pointe; **the morning ~** l'heure de pointe du matin; **beat the ~!** évitez la foule!; ④⟩ (surge) (of liquid, adrenalin) montée *f*; (of air) bouffée *f*; (of emotion) vague *f*; (of complaints) flot *m*; **a ~ of blood to the head** fig un coup de tête; ⑤⟩ (plant) jonc *m*
Ⓑ **rushes** *npl* Cin rushes *mpl*, épreuves *fpl* de tournage
Ⓒ *vtr* ①⟩ (transport urgently) **to ~ sth to** envoyer qch d'urgence à; **to be ~ed to the hospital** être emmené d'urgence à l'hôpital; ②⟩ (do hastily) expédier [*task, speech*]; **don't try to ~ things** ne va pas trop vite; ③⟩ (pressurize, hurry) presser, bousculer [*person*]; ④⟩ (charge at) sauter sur [*person*]; prendre d'assaut [*building*]; ⑤⟩ US Univ essayer de devenir membre de [*sorority, fraternity*]
Ⓓ *vi* ①⟩ [*person*] (make haste) se dépêcher (**to do** de faire); (rush forward) se précipiter (**to do** pour faire); **don't ~** ne te précipite pas; **to ~ out of the room** se précipiter hors de la pièce; **to ~ at** se précipiter sur; **to ~ down the stairs/past** descendre l'escalier/passer à toute vitesse; **to ~ along** marcher à toute vitesse; ②⟩ (travel) **to ~ past** passer à toute vitesse; **to ~ along at 120 km/h** filer à 120 km/h; **the sound of ~ing water** le bruit de l'eau jaillissante

Ⓟⓗⓡⓐⓢⓐⓛ ⓥⓔⓡⓑⓢ

■ **rush into:** ▶ ~ **into [sth]** se lancer dans [*commitment, purchase, sale*]; ~ **into marriage** se marier précipitamment; ▶ ~ **[sb] into doing** pousser [qn] à faire; **don't be ~ed into it** ne te laisse pas bousculer

■ **rush out:** ▶ ~ **out** sortir en vitesse; ▶ ~ **[sth] out**, ~ **[sth] out** sortir *or* publier [qch] en vitesse

■ **rush through:** ▶ ~ **through [sth]** expédier [*task*]; parcourir [qch] en vitesse [*book*]; ▶ ~ **[sth] through**, ~ **through [sth]** adopter en vitesse [*legislation*]; traiter en priorité [*order, application*]; ▶ ~ **[sth] through to** envoyer [qch] d'urgence à

rushed /rʌʃt/ *adj* [*attempt, letter*] expédié

rush: ~ **hour** *n* heures *fpl* de pointe; ~ **job**○ *n* travail *m* urgent, urgence *f*

rusk /rʌsk/ *n* biscuit *m* pour bébés

russet /'rʌsɪt/
Ⓐ *n* ①⟩ (colour) brun *m* roux; ②⟩ (apple) canada *f* inv
Ⓑ *adj* roussâtre

Russia /'rʌʃə/ ▸ **p. 774** *pr n* Russie *f*

Russian /'rʌʃn/ ▸ **p. 1032, p. 969**
Ⓐ *n* ①⟩ (person) Russe *mf*; ②⟩ (language) russe *m*
Ⓑ *adj* russe; ~ **class** cours *m* de russe

Russian: ~ **Federation** *n* Fédération *f* de Russie; ~ **roulette** *n* roulette *f* russe; ~**-speaking** *adj* russophone

rust /rʌst/
Ⓐ *n* Agric, Chem rouille *f*
Ⓑ *vtr* lit rouiller; ~**ed** rouillé; **to become ~ed** se rouiller
Ⓒ *vi* lit se rouiller; fig [*skill*] s'altérer

rustic /'rʌstɪk/
Ⓐ *n* campagnard/-e *m/f*; pej rustaud/-e *m/f*

B *adj* [*furniture*] rustique; [*charm*] champêtre; [*accent*] rustique

rustle /'rʌsl/

A *n* (of paper, dry leaves) froissement *m*; (of leaves, silk) bruissement *m*

B *vtr* froisser [*papers etc*]; **stop rustling your newspaper!** arrête de faire du bruit avec ton journal!

(Phrasal verb)

■ **rustle up**: ▸ ∼ **up** [**sth**] préparer [qch] en vitesse

rustler /'rʌslə(r)/ *n* US voleur/-euse *m/f* de bétail *ou* de chevaux

rustling /'rʌslɪŋ/ *n* ▸ **rustle A**

rust-proof /'rʌstpruːf/ *adj* [*material*] inoxydable; [*paint, coating*] antirouille

rusty /'rʌstɪ/ *adj* lit, fig rouillé

rut /rʌt/ *n* **1** (in ground) ornière *f*; **2** (routine) **to get into/be in a** ∼ s'enliser/être enlisé dans la routine; **3** Zool (mating) **the** ∼ le rut

ruthless /'ruːθlɪs/ *adj* impitoyable (**in** dans)

ruthlessly /'ruːθlɪslɪ/ *adv* impitoyablement

rutting /'rʌtɪŋ/ *n* rut *m*; ∼ **season** saison du rut

RV *n* US Aut (*abrév* = **recreational vehicle**) camping-car *m*, auto-caravane *f*

Rwanda /rʊ'ændə/ ▸ p. 774 *pr n* Rwanda *m*

Rx US *n* Med *symbole signifiant 'ordonnance'*

rye /raɪ/ *n* **1** (cereal) seigle *m*; **2** US (*also* ∼ **whiskey**) whisky *m* à base de seigle

rye: ∼ **bread** *n* pain *m* de seigle; ∼ **grass** *n* ivraie *f* vivace

Ss

s, S /es/ n ⒈ (letter) s, S m; ⒉ S abrév écrite = **South**; ⒊ S (abrév écrite = **Saint**) St/Ste; ⒋ abrév écrite = **small**

SA n ⒈ abrév écrite = **South Africa**; ⒉ abrév écrite = **South America**

sabbath /'sæbəθ/ n (also **Sabbath**) (Jewish) sabbat m; (Christian) jour m du seigneur

sabbatical /sə'bætɪkl/
A n congé m sabbatique; **on ~** en congé sabbatique
B adj [leave, year] sabbatique

saber n US = **sabre**

sable /'seɪbl/
A n (fur, animal) zibeline f
B noun modifier [hat, garment] en zibeline; **~ coat/stole** zibeline f

sabotage /'sæbətɑːʒ/
A n sabotage m
B vtr saboter [equipment, campaign, discussion]

saboteur /ˌsæbə'tɜː(r)/ n saboteur/-euse m/f

sabre, saber US /'seɪbə(r)/ n sabre m; **~ rattling** rodomontade f

sac /sæk/ n ⒈ Anat, Bot sac m; ⒉ Zool poche f

saccharin /'sækərɪn/ n saccharine f

saccharine /'sækəriːn/ adj péj ⒈ [sentimentality, novel] à l'eau de rose; [smile] mielleux/-euse; ⒉ [drink, food] trop sucré

sachet /'sæʃeɪ, US sæ'ʃeɪ/ n sachet m

sack /sæk/
A n ⒈ (bag) sac m; **potato ~** sac à pommes de terre; **mail ~** sac postal; ⒉ ᴼ(dismissal) **to get the ~** se faire mettre à la porteᴼ; **to give sb the ~** mettre qn à la porteᴼ; **to be threatened with the ~** être menacé de renvoi; ⒊ ᴼ(bed) **to hit the ~**ᴼ se coucher; ⒋ (pillage) sac m
B vtr ⒈ ᴼ(dismiss) mettre [qn] à la porteᴼ; ⒉ (pillage) mettre [qch] à sac

sackcloth /'sækklɒθ/ n toile f à sac

(Idiom) **to wear ~ and ashes** faire son mea culpa

sackful /'sækfʊl/, **sackload** /'sækləʊd/ n sac m

sacking /'sækɪŋ/ n ⒈ (canvas) toile f à sac; ⒉ ᴼ(dismissal) licenciement m

sacrament /'sækrəmənt/ n (religious ceremony) sacrement m

Sacrament /'sækrəmənt/ n (Communion bread) Saint sacrement m; **to receive the ~(s)** communier

sacred /'seɪkrɪd/
A n **the ~** le sacré
B adj ⒈ (holy) sacré; **to hold sth ~** tenir qch pour sacré; ⒉ (revered) [name] sacré; [tradition] sacro-saint; **is nothing ~?** hum il n'y a rien de sacré?; ⒊ (binding) [duty] sacré; [trust] inviolable

sacred cow n fig vache f sacrée

sacrifice /'sækrɪfaɪs/
A n sacrifice m (**to** à; **of** de)
B vtr ⒈ fig sacrifier (**to** à); **principles ~d on the altar of profit** les principes immolés sur l'autel du profit; ⒉ Relig offrir [qch] en sacrifice (**to** à)
C v refl **to ~ oneself** se sacrifier (**for** pour)

sacrificial /ˌsækrɪ'fɪʃl/ adj [victim] offert en sacrifice; fig **to be the ~ lamb** être sacrifié

sacrilege /'sækrɪlɪdʒ/ n Relig, fig, hum sacrilège m

sacrilegious /ˌsækrɪ'lɪdʒəs/ adj sacrilège

sacristy /'sækrɪstɪ/ n sacristie f

sacrosanct /'sækrəʊsæŋkt/ adj sacro-saint

sad /sæd/ adj ⒈ (unhappy) triste; **to be ~ to do** [person] être triste de faire; **it makes me ~** cela me rend triste; **to be ~ that** [person] être triste que (+ subj); **we are ~ about the accident** l'accident nous attriste; **it's ~ that** c'est triste que (+ subj); **it was a ~ sight** c'était triste à voir; ⒉ (unfortunate) [fact, duty, truth] triste (before n); **~ to say,...** c'est malheureux à dire, mais...; ⒊ (deplorable) [attitude, situation] navrant; **it's a ~ state of affairs when one can't/one has to...** c'est lamentable de ne pas pouvoir/d'avoir à...; **it's a ~ day for democracy** c'est un sombre jour pour la démocratie

(Idiom) **to be a ~der but wiser person** avoir reçu une leçon dure mais profitable

sadden /'sædn/
A vtr attrister; **it ~s me that** cela m'attriste que (+ subj)
B **saddened** pp adj attristé; (stronger) affligé

saddle /'sædl/
A n ⒈ (on horse, bike) selle f; **to climb into the ~** se mettre en selle; ⒉ GB Culin **~ of lamb/venison** selle f d'agneau/de chevreuil; **~ of hare** râble m de lièvre; ⒊ Geog (ridge) col m
B vtr ⒈ seller [horse]; ⒉ (impose) **to ~ sb with sth** mettre qch sur les bras de qn [responsibility, task]
C v refl **to ~ oneself with sth** se mettre qch sur les bras

(Phrasal verb)
■ **saddle up:** ► **~ up** seller son cheval

saddle bag n sacoche f

saddler /'sædlə(r)/ ► p. 1181 n sellier m, bourrelier m

saddlery /'sædlərɪ/ n sellerie f

sadism /'seɪdɪzəm/ n sadisme m

sadist /'seɪdɪst/ n sadique mf

sadistic /sə'dɪstɪk/ adj sadique

sadly /'sædlɪ/ adv ⒈ (with sadness) tristement; **he will be ~ missed** il nous manquera beaucoup; ⒉ (unfortunately) malheureusement; ⒊ (emphatic) **he is ~ lacking in sense** le bon sens lui fait cruellement défaut; **you are ~ mistaken** vous vous trompez fortement

sadness /'sædnɪs/ n tristesse f

sae n: abrév ► **stamped addressed envelope**

safari /sə'fɑːrɪ/ n safari m; **to go on ~** aller faire un safari

safari: ~ hat n casque m colonial; **~ jacket** n saharienne f; **~ park** n parc m (zoologique) (où les animaux vivent en semi-liberté)

safe /seɪf/
A n coffre-fort m
B adj ⒈ (after ordeal, risk) [person] sain et sauf; [object] intact; **we know they are ~** nous les savons hors de danger; **to hope for sb's ~ return** espérer que qn reviendra sans encombre; **~ and sound** sain et sauf; ⒉ (free from threat, harm) **to be ~** [person] être en sécurité; [document, valuables] être en lieu sûr; [company, job, reputation] ne pas être menacé; **to feel ~** se sentir en sécurité; **is the bike ~ here?** est-ce qu'on peut laisser le vélo ici sans risque?; **he's ~ in bed** il dort tranquillement dans son lit; **have a ~ journey!** bon voyage!; **to keep sb ~** protéger qn (**from** contre, de); **to keep sth ~** (protect) mettre qch à l'abri (**from** de); (store) garder qch en lieu sûr; **to be ~ from** être à l'abri de [attack, curiosity]; **to be ~ with sb** ne rien risquer avec qn; ⒊ (risk-free) [product, toy, level, method] sans danger; [place, environment, vehicle, route] sûr; [structure, building]

solide; [*animal*] inoffensif/-ive; [*speed*] raisonnable; **the ~st way to do** la façon la plus sûre de faire; **to watch from a ~ distance** observer à distance respectueuse; **let's go—it's ~ allons-y**—il n'y a plus de danger; **it's not ~** c'est dangereux; **to be ~ for sb** être sans danger pour qn; **the toy/ park is not ~ for children** le jouet/parc est dangereux pour les enfants; **it is ~ to swim there** on peut s'y baigner sans danger; **it is not ~ to do** il est dangereux de faire; **that car is not ~ to drive** cette voiture est dangereuse; **to make sth ~** rendre [qch] (plus) sûr [*premises, beach*]; rendre [qch] inoffensif/-ive [*bomb*]; [4] (prudent) [*investment*] sûr; [*estimate, choice*] prudent; [*topic*] anodin; **the ~st thing to do would be to leave** le plus sûr serait de partir; **it would be ~r not to do** il vaudrait mieux ne pas faire; **it is ~ to say that** on peut dire à coup sûr que; **it's ~ to assume that** on peut raisonnablement penser que; [5] (reliable) [*driver*] prudent; **to be in ~ hands** être en bonnes mains

(Idioms) **as ~ as houses** GB (secure) [*person*] en sécurité; [*place*] sûr; (risk-free) sans risque; **better ~ than sorry!** mieux vaut prévenir que guérir!; **just to be on the ~ side** simplement par précaution; **to play (it) ~** être prudent

safe bet *n* **it's a ~** c'est quelque chose de sûr; **it's a ~ that** il est certain que

safe-breaker *n* perceur *m* de coffres-forts

safe-conduct /ˌseɪf'kɒndʌkt/ *n* [1] (guarantee) laissez-passer *m inv* (**to** pour); [2] (document) sauf-conduit *m*

safe-deposit box *n* coffre *m* (à la banque)

safeguard /'seɪfgɑːd/
A *n* garantie *f*
B *vtr* protéger (**against, from** contre)

safe: **~ haven** *n* lieu *m* de refuge; **~ house** *n* refuge *m*

safekeeping /ˌseɪf'kiːpɪŋ/ *n* **to give sth to sb for ~** confier qch à la garde de qn

safely /'seɪflɪ/ *adv* [1] (unharmed) [*come back*] (of person) sans encombre; (of parcel, goods) sans dommage; (of plane) [*land, take off*] sans problème; **I arrived ~** je suis bien arrivé; **you can walk around quite ~** vous pouvez vous promener en toute sécurité; [2] (without worry or risk) [*leave, do, go*] en toute tranquillité; [*assume, say*] avec certitude; [3] (causing no concern) [*locked, hidden*] bien; **to be ~ tucked up in bed** être bien bordé dans son lit; **he's ~ behind bars** heureusement il est sous les verrous; [4] (carefully) prudemment

safeness /'seɪfnɪs/ *n* (of structure) solidité *f*; (of method, product) sécurité *f*; (of investment) sûreté *f*

safe: **~ passage** *n* laissez-passer *m inv* (**to** pour; **for sb** pour qn); **~ seat** *n* Pol siège *m* assuré; **~ sex** *n* rapports *mpl* sexuels sans risque

safety /'seɪftɪ/
A *n* sécurité *f*; **there are fears for her ~** on est inquiet sur son sort; **in ~** en (toute) sécurité; **to help sb to ~** aider qn à se mettre à l'abri; **to flee to ~** (in building, place) courir se mettre à l'abri; (abroad) se réfugier à l'étranger; **to reach ~** parvenir en lieu sûr; **in the ~ of one's home** chez soi en sécurité; **road ~** sécurité routière; **~ in the home** la sécurité domestique
B *noun modifier* [*check, code, level, limit, measure, regulations, test*] de sécurité; [*bolt, blade, strap*] de sûreté

(Idiom) **there's ~ in numbers** plus on est nombreux, moins on court de risques

safety: **~ belt** *n* ceinture *f* de sécurité; **~ catch** *n* cran *m* de sûreté; **~ curtain** *n* rideau *m* de fer; **~ glass** *n* verre *m* de sécurité; **~ helmet** *n* casque *m* de protection; **~ match** *n* allumette *f* de sûreté; **~ net** *n* lit filet *m* (de protection); fig filet *m* de sécurité; **~ pin** *n* épingle *f* de sûreté

saffron /'sæfrən/
A *n* safran *m*; **~ rice** riz au safran
B ▸ p. 752 *adj* (also **~ yellow**) safran *inv*

sag /sæg/ *vi* (*p pres etc* **-gg-**) [1] (beam, mattress) s'affaisser; [*tent, rope*] ne pas être bien tendu; [2] [*flesh*] être flasque; [3] (weaken) **her spirits ~ged** elle a perdu courage; [4] (fall) [*currency*] baisser

saga /'sɑːgə/ *n* [1] ᵒ(lengthy story) histoire *f*; [2] Literat saga *f*

sagacious /sə'geɪʃəs/ *adj sout* [*person*] sagace

sagacity /sə'gæsətɪ/, **sagaciousness** /sə'geɪʃəsnɪs/ *n* sagacité *f*

sage /seɪdʒ/
A *n* [1] Bot sauge *f*; [2] (wise person) sage *m*

B *adj* (wise) avisé; **to give ~ advice** donner de sages conseils

sage green ▸ p. 752 *n, adj* vert (*m*) cendré *inv*

sagely /'seɪdʒlɪ/ *adv* [*reply, nod*] avec sagesse

sagging /'sægɪŋ/ *adj* [1] [*beam*] affaissé; [*cable*] mal tendu; [*flesh*] flasque; [2] [*spirits*] défaillant

Sagittarius /ˌsædʒɪ'teərɪəs/ ▸ p. 1350 *n* Sagittaire *m*

sago /'seɪgəʊ/ *n* sagou *m*; **~ pudding** bouillie *f* de sagou au lait

Sahara /sə'hɑːrə/ *pr n* Sahara *m*; **the ~ desert** le désert du Sahara

said /sed/
A *prét, pp* ▸ **say**
B *pp adj* dit; **the ~ Mr X** le dit M. X; **on the ~ day** le jour dit

sail /seɪl/
A *n* [1] (on boat) voile *f*; [2] (navigation) **to set ~** prendre la mer; **to set ~ from/for** partir en bateau de/pour; **to be under ~** être en mer; **a ship in full ~** un navire toutes voiles dehors; [3] (on windmill) aile *f*; [4] (journey) **to go for a ~** faire un tour en bateau
B *vtr* [1] (be in charge of) piloter [*ship*]; (steer) manœuvrer [*ship*]; [2] (travel across) traverser [qch] en bateau [*ocean, channel*]; [3] (own) avoir [*yacht*]
C *vi* [1] (travel) voyager en bateau; **to ~ around the world** faire le tour du monde en bateau; [2] (move across water) [*ship*] **to ~ across** traverser [*ocean*]; **to ~ into** entrer dans [*port*]; [3] (set sail) prendre la mer; **the boat ~s at 10 am** le bateau part à 10 h; [4] (as hobby) faire de la voile; **to go ~ing** faire de la voile; [5] (move smoothly) **to ~ past sb** [*person*] passer près de qn sans même le/la remarquer; **the ball ~ed over the fence** la balle est passée par-dessus la barrière

(Idioms) **to ~ close to the wind** jouer avec le feu; **to take the wind out of sb's ~s** rabattre le caquet à qn

(Phrasal verb)

■ **sail through:** ▸ **~ through [sth]** gagner [qch] facilement [*match*]; **to ~ through an exam** réussir un examen les doigts dans le nezᵒ

sail: **~board** *n* planche *f* à voile; **~boarder** *n* véliplanchiste *mf*; **~boarding** *n* planche *f* à voile; **~boat** *n* voilier *m*

sailing /'seɪlɪŋ/ ▸ p. 881
A *n* [1] (sport) voile *f*; [2] (departure) **the next ~** le prochain bateau; **three ~s a day** trois bateaux par jour
B *noun modifier* [*club, holiday, instructor*] de voile; [*boat*] à voiles; [*time, date*] de départ du bateau

sailing ship /'seɪlɪŋ/ *n* voilier *m*

sailor /'seɪlə(r)/ *n* ▸ p. 1123 (seaman) marin *m*; **to be a good/ bad ~** avoir/ne pas avoir le pied marin

sailor suit *n* costume *m* marin

sailplane /'seɪlpleɪn/ *n* planeur *m*

saint /seɪnt, snt/ *n* Relig, fig saint/-e *m/f*

sainthood /'seɪnthʊd/ *n* sainteté *f*

saintly /'seɪntlɪ/ *adj* [*person*] plein de bonté

saint's day *n* fête *f*

sake /seɪk/ *n* [1] (purpose) **for the ~ of principle** pour le principe; **for the ~ of clarity, for clarity's ~** pour la clarté; **for the ~ of argument** à titre d'exemple; **to kill for the ~ of killing** tuer pour le plaisir de tuer; **to do sth for its own ~** faire qch pour le plaisir; **for old times' ~** en souvenir du bon vieux temps; [2] (benefit) **for the ~ of sb, for sb's ~** par égard pour qn; **for all our ~s** dans notre intérêt à tous; **I'm telling you this for your own ~** c'est pour ton bien que je te dis cela; [3] (in anger, in plea) **for God's/heaven's ~!** pour l'amour de Dieu/du ciel!

salacious /sə'leɪʃəs/ *adj* salace

salad /'sæləd/ *n* salade *f*; **bean/ham ~** salade de haricots/ au jambon; **mixed ~** salade composée

salad: **~ bar** *n* buffet *m* de crudités; **~ bowl** *n* saladier *m*; **~ cream** *n* GB ≈ sauce *f* mayonnaise; **~ days** *npl* littér années *fpl* de jeunesse; **~ dressing** *n* sauce *f* pour salade; **~ oil** *n* huile *f* de table; **~ servers** *npl* couverts *mpl* à salade; **~ spinner** *n* essoreuse *f* à salade

salami /sə'lɑːmɪ/ *n* saucisson *m* sec

salaried /'sælərɪd/ *adj* salarié

salary /'sælərɪ/ *n* salaire *m*

sale /seɪl/
A *n* [1] (selling) vente *f*; **for ~** à vendre; **to put sth up for ~**

mettre qch en vente; **on** ~ GB en vente; US en solde; **to go on** ~ GB être mis en vente; US être mis en solde; **I'll take them on a** ~ **or return basis** je les prends sous condition de reprise des invendus; **2▸** (event) (in shop) solde *f*; (auction) vente *f*; **book** ~ vente de livres; **in the** ~**(s)** GB, **on** ~ US en solde; **to have a** ~ solder; **3▸** (by salesman) vente *f*; **to make a** ~ réaliser une vente

B **sales** *npl* **1▸** (amount sold) ventes *fpl*; **2▸** (career) commerce *m*; **3▸** (department) service *m* des ventes; **4▸** (event) **the** ~**s** les soldes *fpl*; **the** ~**s are on** c'est la saison des soldes; **the summer** ~**s** les soldes estivales

saleable /ˈseɪləbl/ *adj* vendable, demandé

sale: ~ **item** *n* article *m* soldé; ~ **of work** *n* vente *f* de charité; ~ **price** *n* prix *m* soldé; ~**room** *n* hôtel *m* des ventes; ~**s assistant** ▸ p. 1181 *n* GB vendeur/-euse *m/f*; ~**sclerk** ▸ p. 1181 *n* US vendeur/-euse *m/f*; ~**s director** ▸ p. 1181 *n* directeur/-trice *m/f* commercial/-e; ~**s executive** ▸ p. 1181 *n* cadre *m* commercial; ~**s figures** *npl* chiffre *m* de ventes, chiffre *m* d'affaires; ~**s force** *n* force *f* de vente; ~**sgirl** ▸ p. 1181 *n* vendeuse *f*

salesman /ˈseɪlzmən/ ▸ p. 1181 *n* (*pl* **-men**) **1▸** (representative) représentant *m*; **insurance** ~ représentant d'assurances; **2▸** (in shop, showroom) vendeur *m*; **used car** ~ revendeur *m* de voitures d'occasion

sale: ~**s manager** *n* = sales director; ~**s office** *n* bureau *m* des ventes; ~**sperson** ▸ p. 1181 *n* vendeur/-euse *m/f*; ~**s pitch** *n* baratin° *m* publicitaire; ~**s rep**, **sales representative** ▸ p. 1181 *n* représentant/-e *m/f*; ~**s staff** *n* commerciaux *mpl*, équipe *f* commerciale; ~**s tax** *n* US taxe *f* à l'achat; ~**swoman** ▸ p. 1181 *n* (representative) représentante *f*; (in shop) vendeuse *f*

salient /ˈseɪlɪənt/ *adj* saillant; (principal) essentiel/-ielle

saline /ˈseɪlaɪn/
A *n* Med (*also* ~ **solution**) sérum *m* physiologique; ~ **drip** perfusion *f* de sérum physiologique
B *adj* [*liquid, spring*] salé; [*deposit*] salin

saliva /səˈlaɪvə/ *n* salive *f*

salivate /ˈsælɪveɪt/ *vi* saliver

sallow /ˈsæləʊ/ *adj* (pale) cireux/-euse

sally /ˈsælɪ/ *n* **1▸** †Mil sortie *f*; **2▸** (witty remark) trait *m* d'esprit, saillie *f*

(Phrasal verb)

■ **sally forth** se mettre en route avec entrain

salmon /ˈsæmən/
A *n* saumon *m*
B *noun modifier* [*fillet, pâté*] de saumon; [*fishing, sandwich*] au saumon

salmonella /ˌsælməˈnelə/ ▸ p. 933 *n* (*pl* **-æ** *ou* **-as**) Biol salmonelle *f*

salmon: ~ **pink** ▸ p. 752 *n, adj* rose (*m*) saumon *inv*; ~ **steak** *n* darne *f* de saumon; ~ **trout** *n* truite *f* saumonée

salon /ˈsælɒn, US səˈlɒn/ *n* salon *m*; **hairdressing/beauty** ~ salon de coiffure/de beauté

saloon /səˈluːn/
A *n* **1▸** (*also* ~ **car**) GB Aut berline *f*; **2▸** GB (*also* ~ **bar**) salle *f* confortable (*d'un pub*); US (in Wild West) saloon *m*, bar *m* (*du Far West américain*); **3▸** (on boat) salon *m*

salsify /ˈsælsɪfɪ/ *n* salsifis *m*

salt /sɔːlt/
A *n* **1▸** Chem, Culin sel *m*; **there's too much** ~ **in the rice** le riz est trop salé; **to put** ~ **on** saler; **2▸** °†(sailor) **an old** ~ un vieux loup de mer
B *noun modifier* [*crystal, solution*] de sel; [*industry, refining*] du sel; [*water, lake*] salé; [*beef, pork*] salé
C *vtr* saler [*meat, fish, road, path*]

(Idioms) **to be the** ~ **of the earth** être le sel de la terre; **you should take his remarks with a grain** *ou* **a pinch of** ~ il ne faut pas prendre ses remarques pour argent comptant; **any teacher worth his** ~ **knows that** tout enseignant digne de ce nom sait cela

(Phrasal verb)

■ **salt away**: ▸ ~ **away [sth]**, ~ **[sth] away** mettre [qch] de côté

salt: ~**cellar** *n* salière *f*; ~ **flat** *n* marais *m* salant

saltiness /ˈsɔːltɪnɪs/ *n* **1▸** (taste) (of food) goût *m* salé; **2▸** (salt content) (of solution, water) teneur *f* en sel

salt: ~ **marsh** *n* salin *m*; ~**mine** *n* mine *f* de sel; ~**pan** *n* puits *m* de sel; ~**shaker** *n* salière *f*; ~**water** *adj* [*fish*] de mer; [*mammal*] marin

salty /ˈsɔːltɪ/ *adj* [*water, food, flavour*] salé

salubrious /səˈluːbrɪəs/ *adj* lit salubre; fig [*neighbourhood*] tout à fait respectable

salutary /ˈsæljʊtrɪ, US -terɪ/ *adj* salutaire

salutation /ˌsæljuˈteɪʃn/ *n* (greeting) salutation *f*; (in letter) forme *f* d'adresse

salute /səˈluːt/
A *n* **1▸** Mil, gen (greeting) salut *m*; **to give a** ~ faire un salut; **to take the** ~ assister au défilé des troupes; **victory** ~ V *m* de la victoire; **2▸** (firing of guns) salve *f*; **a 21-gun** ~ une salve de 21 coups de canon; **3▸** (tribute) hommage *m* (**to** à)
B *vtr, vi* (all contexts) saluer

salvage /ˈsælvɪdʒ/
A *n* **1▸** (rescue) sauvetage *m* (**of** de); **2▸** (reward) prime *f* de sauvetage
B *noun modifier* [*operation, team*] de sauvetage
C *vtr* **1▸** (rescue) sauver [*cargo, belongings*] (**from** de); effectuer le sauvetage de [*ship*]; **2▸** fig sauver [*plan, marriage, reputation*]; sauver [*game*]; préserver [*pride*]; **3▸** (save for recycling) récupérer

salvation /sælˈveɪʃn/ *n* salut *m*

Salvation Army *n* Armée *f* du Salut

salve /sælv, US sæv/
A *n* lit, fig (balm) baume *m*
B *vtr* **to** ~ **one's conscience** soulager sa conscience

salver /ˈsælvə(r)/ *n* plateau *m* (à boissons)

salvo /ˈsælvəʊ/ *n* (*pl* **-os** *ou* **-oes**) Mil fig salve *f*

same /seɪm/
A *adj* **1▸** (identical) même; **to be the** ~ être le *or* la même; **the result was the** ~ le résultat était le même; **people are the** ~ **everywhere** les gens sont partout les mêmes; **it's the** ~ **everywhere** c'est partout la même chose; **it is the** ~ **with** il en est de même pour; **to look the** ~ être pareil; **to be the** ~ **as sth** être comme qch; **it's the** ~ **as riding a bike** c'est comme de faire du vélo; **one wine is the** ~ **as another to him** pour lui un vin en vaut un autre; **the** ~ **time last week** la semaine dernière à la même heure; **the** ~ **time last year** l'année dernière à la même époque; ~ **time** ~ **place** même heure même endroit; **in the** ~ **way** (in a similar manner) de la même manière (**as** que); (likewise) de même; **to feel the** ~ **way about** avoir les mêmes sentiments à l'égard de; **to think the** ~ **way on** *ou* **about sth** être du même avis sur qch; **to go the** ~ **way as** lit aller dans la même direction que; fig connaître le même sort que; **the** ~ **thing** la même chose; **it's the** ~ **thing** c'est pareil; **it amounts** *ou* **comes to the** ~ **thing** cela revient au même; **it's all the** ~ **to me** ça m'est complètement égal; **if it's all the** ~ **to you** si ça ne te fait rien; **2▸** (for emphasis) (very) même (**as** que); **the** ~ **one** le/la même; **'ready the** ~ **day'** 'prêt dans la journée'; **that** ~ **week** la même semaine; **later that** ~ **day** plus tard dans la journée; **at the** ~ **time** en même temps; **they are one and the** ~ **(person)** il s'agit d'une seule et même personne; **the very** ~ exactement le *or* la même; **the very** ~ **day that** le jour même où; **3▸** (unchanged) même; **she's not the** ~ **woman** ce n'est plus la même femme; **to be still the** ~ être toujours le/la même; **things are just the** ~ **as before** rien n'a changé; **it's/he's the** ~ **as ever** c'est/il est toujours pareil; **my views are the** ~ **as they always were** mes opinions n'ont pas changé; **she's much the** ~ elle n'a pas beaucoup changé; **to remain** *ou* **stay the** ~ ne pas changer; **things were never the** ~ **again** rien n'était plus comme avant; **it's not the** ~ **without you** ce n'est pas pareil sans toi; **the** ~ **old excuse** toujours la vieille excuse
B **the same** *adv phr* de la même façon; **to feel the** ~ **as sb** penser comme qn; **to feel the** ~ **about** avoir les mêmes sentiments à l'égard de; **life goes on just the** ~ la vie continue comme d'habitude
C **the same** *pron* **1▸** (the identical thing) la même chose (**as** que); **I'll have the** ~ je prendrai la même chose; **the** ~ **applies to** *ou* **goes for** il en va de même pour; **to say the** ~ **about** en dire autant de; **the** ~ **as sb** faire comme qn; **we're hoping to do the** ~ on espère en faire autant; **I would do the** ~ **for you** j'en ferais autant pour toi; **I 'd do the** ~ again je recommencerais; **the** ~ **to you!** à toi aussi, à toi de même!; (of insult) et toi-même°!; **(the)** ~ **again please!** la même chose s'il vous plaît!; **it'll be**

more of the ～! péj c'est reparti pour un tour!; **2** Jur celui-ci/celle-ci *m/f*

(Idioms) **all the ～...., just the ～,...** tout de même,...; **thanks all the ～** merci quand même

same-day /ˌseɪmˈdeɪ/ *adj* [*processing, service*] effectué dans la journée

sameness /ˈseɪmnɪs/ *n* péj monotonie *f*

Samoa /səˈməʊə/ ▸ p. 774 *pr n* Samoa *m*

sample /ˈsɑːmpl, US ˈsæmpl/

A *n* **1** (of product, fabric, rock etc) échantillon *m*; **to take a soil ～** prélever un échantillon de sol; **2** Med, Biol (of individual for analysis) prélèvement *m*; (one of many kept in lab) échantillon *m*; **to take a blood ～** faire une prise de sang; **3** Ecol, Biol (of water etc) prélèvement *m*, échantillon *m*; **4** (of public, population) panel *m*, échantillon *m*

B *noun modifier* **1** Comm [*cassette, video*] de promotion; **～ bottle/packet** échantillon *m*; **2** (representative) [*question*] type; **～ prices** prix *mpl* donnés à titre d'exemple

C *vtr* **1** goûter (à) [*food, wine*]; **to ～ the delights of Paris** goûter aux plaisirs de Paris; **2** (test) essayer [*products*]; sonder [*opinion, market*]

sampling /ˈsɑːmplɪŋ, US ˈsæmpl-/ *n* **1** (taking of specimens) prélèvement *m*, échantillonnage *m*; **2** (of population group) échantillonnage *m*

sanatorium /ˌsænəˈtɔːrɪəm/ *n* (*pl* **～s** *ou* **-ria**) GB (clinic) sanatorium *m*; (in school) infirmerie *f*

sanctify /ˈsæŋktɪfaɪ/ *vtr* sanctifier

sanctimonious /ˌsæŋktɪˈməʊnɪəs/ *adj* péj supérieur

sanction /ˈsæŋkʃn/

A *n* **1** (authorization) autorisation *f*; (approval) sanction *f*; **2** (deterrent) **legal ～**, **criminal ～** sanction *f* pénale; **3** Pol, Econ sanction *f*

B sanctions *npl* sanctions *fpl*; **trade ～s** sanctions économiques/commerciales; **to impose ～s** prendre des sanctions; **to break ～s against a country** violer l'embargo contre un pays

C *vtr* (permit) autoriser; (approve) sanctionner

sanctity /ˈsæŋktətɪ/ *n* **1** (of life, law) inviolabilité *f*; **2** Relig sainteté *f*

sanctuary /ˈsæŋktʃʊərɪ, US -tʃuərɪ/ *n* **1** (safe place) refuge *m*; **a place of ～** un refuge; **to seek ～** chercher asile; **2** (holy place) sanctuaire *m*; **3** (for wildlife) réserve *f*; (for mistreated pets) refuge *m*

sanctum /ˈsæŋktəm/ *n* (*pl* **-tums** *ou* **-ta**) **1** (private place) refuge *m*; **2** Relig **the (inner) ～** (in temple) le Saint des Saints; (holy place) le sanctuaire

sand /sænd/

A *n* sable *m*

B sands *npl* **1** (beach) plage *f*; **2** (desert) sables *mpl*

C *vtr* **1** (*also* **～ down**) (smooth) poncer [*floor*]; frotter *or* passer [qch] au papier de verre [*woodwork*]; **2** (put sand on) sabler [*icy road*]

(Idiom) **to stick** *ou* **bury one's head in the ～** pratiquer la politique de l'autruche

sandal /ˈsændl/ *n* sandale *f*

sandalwood /ˈsændlwʊd/ *n* santal *m*

sandbag /ˈsændbæɡ/

A *n* sac *m* de sable

B *vtr* (*p prés etc* **-gg-**) (against gunfire) renforcer [qch] avec des sacs de sable [*position*]

sand: **～bank** *n* banc *m* de sable; **～blast** *vtr* décaper [qch] à la sableuse

sandboy /ˈsændbɔɪ/ *n*:

(Idiom) **as happy as a ～** gai comme un pinson

sand: **～ castle** *n* château *m* de sable; **～ dune** *n* dune *f*

sander /ˈsændə(r)/ *n* ponceuse *f*

sand: **～ lot** *n* US terrain *m* vague (*où les enfants jouent*); **～man** *n* marchand *m* de sable

sandpaper /ˈsændpeɪpə(r)/

A *n* papier *m* de verre

B *vtr* poncer [*plaster, wood*]; polir [*glass, metal*]

sandpit /ˈsændpɪt/ *n* (for children) bac *m* à sable

sandstone /ˈsændstəʊn/ *n* grès *m*; **white/red ～** grès blanc/rose

sandstorm *n* tempête *f* de sable

sandwich /ˈsænwɪdʒ, US -wɪtʃ/

A *n* **1** sandwich *m*; **cucumber ～** sandwich au concombre;

2 GB (cake) génoise *f* (*fourrée*)

B *vtr* **to be ～ed between** [*car, building, person*] être pris en sandwich entre, être coincé entre

sandwich: **～ bar** *n* sandwich bar *m*; **～ course** *n* GB cours *m* avec stage pratique, formation *f* en alternance; **～ loaf** *n* pain *m* en tranches; **～ man** ▸ p. 1181 *n* homme-sandwich *m*

sandy /ˈsændɪ/ *adj* **1** [*beach*] de sable; [*path, soil*] sablonneux/-euse; [*sediment*] sableux/-euse; **2** (yellow) [*hair*] blond roux *inv*; [*colour*] sable *inv* (*after n*)

sane /seɪn/ *adj* **1** (not mad) [*person*] sain d'esprit; **it's the only thing that keeps me ～** c'est la seule chose qui m'empêche de devenir fou; **2** (reasonable) [*policy, judgment*] sensé

sang /sæŋ/ *prét* ▸ **sing**

sanguine /ˈsæŋɡwɪn/ *adj* optimiste; **to take a ～ view** voir les choses avec optimisme

sanitarium US = **sanatorium**

sanitary /ˈsænɪtrɪ, US -terɪ/ *adj* **1** [*engineer, facilities*] sanitaire; **2** (hygienic) hygiénique; (clean) propre

sanitary: **～ protection** *n* garniture *f* périodique; **～ towel** GB, **～ napkin** US *n* serviette *f* hygiénique *or* périodique

sanitation /ˌsænɪˈteɪʃn/ *n* ▸ p. 1181 (toilets) ¢ installations *fpl* sanitaires; **～ worker** US éboueur *m*

sanitize /ˈsænɪtaɪz/ *vtr* **1** (tone down) aseptiser [*art, politics*]; expurger [*document*]; rendre [qch] plus acceptable [*violence*]; **2** (sterilize) désinfecter

sanity /ˈsænətɪ/ *n* **1** (mental health) équilibre *m* mental; **to preserve one's ～** rester sain d'esprit; **2** (sense) bon sens *m*; **～ prevailed** le bon sens l'emporta

sank /sæŋk/ *prét* ▸ **sink C**

San Marino /ˌsæn məˈriːnəʊ/ ▸ p. 774 *pr n* Saint-Marin *m*

Sanskrit /ˈsænskrɪt/ ▸ p. 969 *n* sanscrit *m*

Santa (Claus) /ˈsæntə (klɔːz)/ *pr n* le père Noël

Santiago /ˌsæntɪˈɑːɡəʊ/ ▸ p. 1276 *pr n* **1** (*also* **～ de Compostela**) (in Spain) Saint Jacques de Compostelle; **2** (in Chile) Santiago

sap /sæp/

A *n* sève *f*; **the ～ rises** la sève monte

B *vtr* (weaken) saper [*strength, courage, confidence*]

sapling /ˈsæplɪŋ/ *n* jeune arbre *m*

sapper /ˈsæpə(r)/ ▸ p. 1123 *n* GB Mil soldat *m* du génie

sapphire /ˈsæfaɪə(r)/ ▸ p. 752

A *n* **1** (stone) saphir *m*; **2** (colour) bleu *m* saphir

B *adj* (colour) bleu saphir *inv*

Saracen /ˈsærəsn/ *n* Sarrasin/-e *m/f*

saranwrap® /səˈrænræp/ *n* US ≈ scellofrais® *m*

sarcasm /ˈsɑːkæzm/ *n* sarcasme *m*

sarcastic /sɑːˈkæstɪk/ *adj* sarcastique

sarcastically /sɑːˈkæstɪklɪ/ *adv* d'un ton sarcastique

sarcophagus /sɑːˈkɒfəɡəs/ *n* (*pl* **-gi** *ou* **-guses**) sarcophage *m*

sardine /sɑːˈdiːn/ *n* Zool, Culin sardine *f*

Sardinia /sɑːˈdɪnɪə/ ▸ p. 954 *pr n* Sardaigne *f*

Sardinian /sɑːˈdɪnɪən/ ▸ p. 1032, p. 969

A *n* **1** (person) Sarde *mf*; **2** (language) sarde *m*

B *adj* sarde

sardonic /sɑːˈdɒnɪk/ *adj* [*laugh, look*] sardonique; [*person, remark*] acerbe

sardonically /sɑːˈdɒnɪklɪ/ *adv* [*laugh*] sardoniquement; [*comment, say*] de façon acerbe

Sargasso Sea ▸ p. 1049 *pr n* mer *f* des Sargasses

SARS /sɑːz/ *n* SRAS *m*; pneumonie *f* atypique

sartorial /sɑːˈtɔːrɪəl/ *adj* vestimentaire

SAS *n* GB (*abrév* = **Special Air Service**) commandos *mpl* britanniques aéroportés

sash /sæʃ/ *n* **1** (round waist) large ceinture *f* (*en tissu*); (ceremonial) écharpe *f* (*servant d'insigne*); **2** (window frame) châssis *m* d'une fenêtre à guillotine

sashay○ /ˈsæʃeɪ/ *vi* **1** (casually) marcher d'un air dégagé; (seductively) marcher de manière aguichante

sash window *n* fenêtre *f* à guillotine

sassy○ /ˈsæsɪ/ *adj* US (cheeky) culotté○; (smart) chic

sat /sæt/ *prét, pp* ▸ **sit**

Sat ▸ p. 1322 *abrév écrite* = **Saturday**

SAT /sæt/ *n* ① GB Sch *abrév* = **Standard Assessment Task**; ② US Sch *abrév* ▸ **Scholastic Aptitude Test**

Satan /ˈseɪtn/ *pr n* Satan

satanic /səˈtænɪk/ *adj* [*rites*] satanique

satanist, Satanist /ˈseɪtənɪst/ *n*: personne qui voue un culte à Satan

satchel /ˈsætʃəl/ *n* cartable *m* (à bandoulière)

sated /ˈseɪtɪd/ *adj sout* (*jamais épith*) [*desire*] assouvi; [*person*] rassasié; [*appetite*] satisfait; **to be ~ with** être repu de

satellite /ˈsætəlaɪt/
A *n* satellite *m*
B *noun modifier* [*broadcasting, transmission*] par satellite; [*town, country, photograph*] satellite

satellite: **~ dish**, **~ receiver** *n* antenne *f* parabolique; **~ television**, **~ TV** *n* télévision *f* par satellite

satiate /ˈseɪʃɪeɪt/ *vtr* rassasier [*person*]; satisfaire [*appetite*]; assouvir [*desire*]; **~d with** fig repu de

satiety /səˈtaɪətɪ/ *n* satiété *f*

satin /ˈsætɪn, US ˈsætn/
A *n* satin *m*
B *noun modifier* [*garment, shoe*] de satin; **with a ~ finish** satiné

satinwood /ˈsætɪnwʊd, US ˈsætn-/ *n* ① (tree) chloroxylon *m*; ② (wood) bois *m* satiné de l'Inde

satire /ˈsætaɪə(r)/ *n* satire *f* (**on** sur)

satiric(al) /səˈtɪrɪkl/ *adj* satirique

satirically /səˈtɪrɪklɪ/ *adv* d'une manière satirique

satirist /ˈsætərɪst/ *n* satiriste *mf*

satirize /ˈsætəraɪz/ *vtr* faire la satire de; **~d by** qui a été l'objet de la satire de

satisfaction /ˌsætɪsˈfækʃn/ *n* ℂ ① (pleasure) satisfaction *f*; **to express ~ with sth** se déclarer satisfait de qch; **to get** *ou* **derive ~ from sth** retirer des satisfactions de qch; **to get** *ou* **derive ~ from doing sth** éprouver du plaisir à faire qch; **he felt he had done the work to his own ~** il était satisfait de son travail; **the conclusions were to everybody's ~** les conclusions ont satisfait tout le monde; ② (fulfilment) satisfaction *f*; ③ (compensation) dédommagement *m*; (apology) réparation *f*; **to obtain ~ (for sth)** obtenir satisfaction (pour qch)

satisfactorily /ˌsætɪsˈfæktərəlɪ/ *adv* de manière satisfaisante

satisfactory /ˌsætɪsˈfæktərɪ/ *adj* satisfaisant; **to be ~ to sb** convenir à qn; **the solution is less than ~** la solution est loin d'être satisfaisante; **his work is far from ~** son travail laisse fort à désirer; **her condition was said to be ~** son état a été déclaré satisfaisant; **to bring a matter to a ~ conclusion** mener une affaire à bien

satisfied /ˈsætɪsfaɪd/ *adj* ① (pleased) satisfait (**with, about** de); **not ~ with winning the match, they...** non contents de gagner le match, ils...; **now are you ~?** tu es content maintenant?; ② (convinced) convaincu (**by** par; **that** que)

satisfy /ˈsætɪsfaɪ/
A *vtr* ① (fulfil) satisfaire [*person, need, desires, curiosity*]; assouvir [*hunger, desire*]; ② (persuade, convince) convaincre; ③ (meet) satisfaire à [*criteria, demand, requirements, conditions*]
B *v refl* **to ~ oneself** s'assurer (**that** que)

satisfying /ˈsætɪsfaɪɪŋ/ *adj* ① (filling) [*meal*] substantiel/-ielle; ② (rewarding) [*job*] qui apporte de la satisfaction; [*life*] bien rempli; [*relationship*] heureux/-euse; ③ (pleasing) [*result, progress*] satisfaisant

saturate /ˈsætʃəreɪt/ *vtr* ① (soak) tremper [*clothes, ground*] (**with** de); fig saturer [*market*] (**with** de); ② Chem saturer

saturation /ˌsætʃəˈreɪʃn/
A *n* saturation *f*
B *noun modifier* [*campaign, coverage*] de saturation; [*bombing*] intensif/-ive

saturation point *n* point *m* de saturation; **to reach ~** arriver à saturation

Saturday /ˈsætədeɪ, -dɪ/ ▸ p. 1322 *n* samedi *m*; **he has a ~ job** GB il a un petit boulot○ le samedi

Saturn /ˈsætən/ *pr n* ① Mythol Saturne *m*; ② (planet) Saturne *f*

sauce /sɔːs/ *n* ① Culin sauce *f*; **orange ~** sauce à l'orange; **tomato ~** sauce tomate; ② ○†(impudence) toupet○ *m*

(Idiom) **what's ~ for the goose is ~ for the gander** ce qui vaut pour l'un vaut pour l'autre

sauce: **~boat** *n* saucière *f*; **~pan** *n* casserole *f*

saucer /ˈsɔːsə(r)/ *n* soucoupe *f*

saucily /ˈsɔːsɪlɪ/ *adv* avec impertinence

saucy† /ˈsɔːsɪ/ *adj* ① (*person*) impertinent; (suggestive) égrillard; ② [*hat, dress etc*] aguichant

Saudi /ˈsaʊdɪ/ ▸ p. 1032 (*also* **~ Arabian**)
A *n* Saoudien/-ienne *m/f*
B *adj* saoudien/-ienne

Saudi Arabia /ˌsaʊdɪ əˈreɪbɪə/ ▸ p. 774 *pr n* Arabie *f* saoudite

sauerkraut /ˈsaʊəkraʊt/ *n* choucroute *f*

sauna /ˈsɔːnə, ˈsaʊnə/ *n* sauna *m*

saunter /ˈsɔːntə(r)/
A *n* **to go for a ~** faire une petite balade○
B *vi* (*also* **~ along**) marcher d'un pas nonchalant; **to ~ off** s'éloigner d'un pas nonchalant

sausage /ˈsɒsɪdʒ, US ˈsɔːs-/ *n* (for cooking) saucisse *f*; (ready to eat) saucisson *m*

sausage: **~ dog**○ *n* teckel *m*; **~ meat** *n* chair *f* à saucisse; **~ roll** *n* feuilleté *m* à la chair à saucisse

sauté /ˈsaʊteɪ, US saʊˈteɪ/ Culin
A *adj* (*also* **sauté(e)d**) sauté
B *vtr* (*p prés* **-éing** *ou* **-éeing**; *prét, pp* **-éd** *ou* **-éed**) faire sauter

savage /ˈsævɪdʒ/
A *n* sauvage *mf* *also pej*
B *adj* ① *lit* [*blow, beating*] violent; [*attack*] sauvage; ② *fig* [*temper*] violent; [*mood, satire*] féroce; [*criticism*] virulent; [*price increases*] violent
C *vtr* ① (maul) [*dog*] attaquer [qn/qch] sauvagement; [*lion*] déchiqueter; ② *fig* descendre [qch/qn] en flammes

savagely /ˈsævɪdʒlɪ/ *adv* ① *lit* [*beat, attack*] sauvagement; ② *fig* [*criticize, satirize*] férocement

savagery /ˈsævɪdʒrɪ/ *n* (of war, primitive people) barbarie *f*; (of attack) (physical) sauvagerie *f*; (verbal) férocité *f*

save /seɪv/
A *n* ① Sport arrêt *m* de but; ② Comput sauvegarde *f*
B *vtr* ① (rescue) sauver; **she ~d him from falling** elle l'a empêché de tomber; **she ~d the country from civil war** elle a évité au pays de sombrer dans la guerre civile; **to ~ sb from himself** protéger qn contre lui-même; **to ~ sb's life** *lit, fig* sauver la vie à qn; **he can't speak German to ~ his life**○ il ne parle pas un mot d'allemand!; **to ~ the day** *ou* **the situation** sauver la situation; ② (put by, keep) mettre [qch] de côté [*money, food*]; garder [*goods, documents*]; **to have money ~d** avoir de l'argent de côté; **to ~ sth for sb**, **to ~ sb sth** garder qch pour qn; ③ (economize on) économiser [*money, energy*]; gagner [*time, space*]; **to ~ one's energy/voice** ménager ses forces/sa voix; **you'll ~ money/£20** vous ferez des économies/une économie de 20 livres; **to ~ sb sth** faire économiser qch à qn [*money*]; éviter qch à qn [*trouble, expense, journey*]; faire gagner qch à qn [*time*]; **to ~ sb/sth (from) having to do** éviter à qn/qch de faire; **to ~ doing** éviter de faire; ④ Sport arrêter [*penalty*]; ⑤ Relig sauver; ⑥ Comput sauvegarder, enregistrer (**on, to** sur); ⑦ (*also* **~ up**) (collect) collectionner
C *vi* ① (put by funds) = **save up**; ② (economize) économiser, faire des économies; **to ~ on** faire des économies de [*energy, paper*]
D *v refl* **to ~ oneself** ① (rescue oneself) *lit, fig* s'en tirer; **to ~ oneself (from) having to do** éviter de faire; ② (keep energy) se réserver (**for** pour); ③ (avoid waste) **to ~ oneself money** économiser; **to ~ oneself time** gagner du temps; **to ~ oneself a journey** s'éviter un déplacement

(Phrasal verb)
■ **save up** faire des économies; **to ~ up for** mettre de l'argent de côté pour s'acheter [*car, house*]; mettre de l'argent de côté pour s'offrir [*holiday*]

saver /ˈseɪvə(r)/ *n* épargnant/-e *m/f*

saving /ˈseɪvɪŋ/
A *n* ① (reduction) économie *f* (**in** de; **on** sur); ② ℂ Fin (activity) épargne *f*; ③ (conservation) économie *f*; **energy ~** économies *fpl* d'énergie
B **savings** *npl* économies *fpl*; **to live off one's ~s** vivre de ses économies

S

G -**saving** *combining form* **energy-/fuel-**∼ qui réduit la con-sommation d'énergie/de carburant

saving grace *n* bon côté *m*; **it's his** ∼ c'est ce qui le sauve

saving: ∼**s account** *n* GB compte *m* d'épargne; US compte *m* rémunéré; ∼**s and loan (association)**, **S & L** *n* US société *f* d'investissement et de crédit immo-bilier; ∼**s bank** *n* caisse *f* d'épargne; ∼**s certifi-cate** *n* bon *m* de caisse

saviour GB, **savior** US /ˈseɪvɪə(r)/ *n* sauveur *m*

savoir-faire /ˌsævwɑːˈfeə(r)/ *n* **1** (social) savoir-vivre *m* *inv*; **2** (practical) savoir-faire *m* *inv*

savor /ˈseɪvə(r)/ *n* US = **savour**

savory /ˈseɪvərɪ/ *n, adj* US = **savoury**

savour GB, **savor** US /ˈseɪvə(r)/
A *n* **1** lit saveur *f*; **2** fig goût *m*; **life has lost its** ∼ **for her** elle a perdu goût à la vie; **3** (trace, hint) pointe *f*
B *vtr* lit, fig savourer
C *vi* **to** ∼ **of** sentir

savoury GB /ˈseɪvərɪ/
A *n* (pie, flan, stew) plat *m* salé; (after dessert) GB canapé *m* (*servi après le dessert*)
B *adj* **1** Culin (not sweet) salé; (appetizing) appétissant; ∼ **bis-cuits** biscuits *mpl* apéritif; **2** fig **not a very** ∼ **individual/area** un individu/quartier peu recommandable; **the less** ∼ **aspects of the matter** le côté plutôt louche de l'affaire

Savoy /səˈvɔɪ/ ▸ p. 873
A *pr n* Savoie *f*
B *noun modifier* [*cuisine, wines*] de Savoie; **the** ∼ **Alps** les Alpes *fpl* savoyardes

savoy cabbage *n* chou *m* de Milan

saw /sɔː/
A *prét* ▸ **see**
B *n* scie *f*; **electric/power** ∼ scie électrique/mécanique
C *vtr* (*prét* **sawed**; *pp* **sawn** GB, **sawed** US) scier; ∼ **through/down/off** scier

(Phrasal verb)
▪ **saw up**: ▸ ∼ **up [sth]**, ∼ **[sth] up** débiter qch à la scie

sawdust *n* sciure *f* (de bois)

sawed /sɔːd/ *pp* US ▸ **saw C**

saw- ∼**fish** *n* poisson-scie *m*; ∼**mill** *n* scierie *f*

sawn /sɔːn/ *pp* GB ▸ **saw C**

sawn-off /ˈsɔːnɒf/ *adj* GB [*shotgun*] à canon scié

sax○ /sæks/ ▸ p. 1028 *n* (*pl* ∼**es**) (*abrév* = **saxophone**) saxo○ *m*

Saxon /ˈsæksn/
A *pr n* (person) Saxon/-onne *m/f*; (language) saxon *m*
B *adj* saxon/-onne

saxophone /ˈsæksəfəʊn/ ▸ p. 1028 *n* saxophone *m*

saxophonist /sæksˈɒfənɪst/ ▸ p. 1181, p. 1028 *n* saxopho-niste *mf*

say /seɪ/
A *n* **to have one's** ∼ dire ce qu'on a à dire (**on** sur); **to have a** ∼**/no** ∼ **in sth** avoir/ne pas avoir son mot à dire sur qch; **to have no** ∼ **in the matter** ne pas avoir voix au chapitre; **to have a** ∼ **in appointing sb** avoir son mot à dire sur la nomination de qn; **they want more** *ou* **a bigger** ∼ ils veu-lent avoir davantage leur mot à dire; **to have the most** *ou* **biggest** ∼ avoir le plus de poids
B *vtr* (*prét, pp* **said**) **1** [*person*] dire [*words, prayer, hello, no*] (**to** à); **'hello,' he said** 'bonjour,' dit-il; ∼ **after me...** répète après moi...; **to** ∼ **one's piece** dire ce qu'on a à dire; **to** ∼ **(that)** dire que; **she** ∼**s he's ill** elle dit qu'il est malade; **how nice of you to** ∼ **so** merci, c'est gentil; **didn't I** ∼ **so?** je l'avais bien dit!; **if** *ou* **though I do** ∼ **so myself!** je ne devrais pas le dire, mais...!; **so they** ∼ (agreeing) il paraît; **or so they** ∼ (doubtful) du moins c'est ce qu'on dit; **or so he** ∼**s** du moins c'est ce qu'il prétend; **so to** ∼ pour ainsi dire; **as you** ∼**...** comme tu le dis...; **as they** ∼ comme on dit; **I don't care what anyone** ∼**s** je me moque du qu'en-dira-t-on; **people** *ou* **they** ∼ **she's very rich, she is said to be very rich** on dit qu'elle est très riche; **to** ∼ **sth on a subject** parler d'un sujet; **she'll have something to** ∼ **about that!** elle aura certainement quelque chose à dire là-dessus!; **to** ∼ **sth to oneself** se dire qch; **what do you** ∼ **to that?** qu'est-ce que tu en dis? **what do you** ∼ **to the argument that...?** que répondez-vous à l'argument

selon lequel...?; **what would you** ∼ **to a little walk?** qu'est-ce que tu dirais d'une petite promenade?; **what (do you)** ∼ **we eat now**○? et si on mangeait maintenant?; **that's for the committee to** ∼ c'est au comité de décider; **it's not for me to** ∼ ce n'est pas à moi de le dire; **you said it**○! tu l'as dit!; **you can** ∼ **that again**○! ça, tu peux le dire○!; **I should** ∼ **it is/they were!** et comment○!; **well said!** bien dit!; ∼ **no more**○ ça va, j'ai compris!○; **let's** ∼ **no more about it** n'en parlons plus; **enough said**○ ça va, j'ai compris○; **there's no more to be said** il n'y a rien à ajouter; **it goes without** ∼**ing that** il va sans dire que; **don't** ∼ **I didn't warn you!** tu ne pourras pas dire que je ne t'avais pas prévenu!; **don't** ∼ **it's raining again!** ne me dis pas qu'il recommence à pleuvoir!; **you might just as well** ∼ **education is useless** autant dire que l'instruction est inutile; **that is to** ∼ c'est-à-dire; **that's not to** ∼ **that** cela ne veut pas dire que; **he was displeased, not to** ∼ **furious** il était mécontent, pour ne pas dire furieux; **I'll** ∼ **this for her...** je dois dire à sa décharge que...; **I must** ∼ **(that)** je dois dire que; **to have a lot to** ∼ **for oneself** être bavard; **what have you got to** ∼ **for yourself?** (reprimand) qu'est-ce que tu as comme excuse?; (jocular greeting) qu'est-ce que tu deviens?; **that's** ∼**ing a lot**○ ce n'est pas peu dire; **2** [*writer, book, letter, report, map*] dire; [*painting, music, gift*] exprimer; [*sign, clock, poster, dial, gauge*] indiquer; [*gesture, signal*] signifier; **it** ∼**s on the radio/in the rules that** la radio/le règlement dit que; **it** ∼**s here that** il est dit ici que; **3** (guess) dire; **how high would you** ∼ **it is?** à ton avis, quelle en est la hau-teur?; **I'd** ∼ **it was a bargain** à mon avis c'est une bonne affaire; **I'd** ∼ **she was about 25** je lui donnerais environ 25 ans; **4** (assume) **to** ∼ **(that)** supposer que (+ *subj*), mettre que (+ *indic or subj*); **let's** ∼ **there are 20** mettons *ou* supposons qu'il y en ait 20
C *vi* (*prét*, *pp* **said**) **1** **stop when I** ∼ arrête quand je te le dirai; **he wouldn't** ∼ il n'a pas voulu le dire; **you don't** ∼! iron sans blague!, pas possible!; ∼**s you**○! (taunting) que tu dis○!; ∼**s who**○?, **who** ∼**s**○? (sceptical) ah oui?; (on whose authority) et sur les ordres de qui?; **2** †GB **I** ∼! (listen) écoute, dis donc
D *adv* disons, mettons; ∼, **£50 for petrol** disons *or* mettons, 50 livres sterling pour l'essence
E *excl* US dis-donc!

(Idioms) **it doesn't** ∼ **much for their marriage** cela en dit long sur leur mariage; **it** ∼**s a lot for sb/sth** c'est tout à l'honneur de qn/qch; **that** ∼**s it all** c'est tout dire, cela se passe de commentaires; **there's a lot to be said for that method** cette méthode est très intéressante à bien des égards; **there's a lot to be said for keeping quiet** il y a intérêt à se taire; **when all is said and done** tout compte fait, en fin de compte

saying /ˈseɪɪŋ/ *n* dicton *m*; **as the** ∼ **goes** comme on dit

s/c *adj* (*abrév écrite* = **self-contained**) indépendant

SC *n* US Post *abrév écrite* = **South Carolina**

scab /skæb/ *n* **1** Med croûte *f*; **2** (on plant, animal) gale *f*; **3** ○péj (strikebreaker) jaune○ *m* péj, briseur *m* de grève

scabby /ˈskæbɪ/ *adj* **1** [*skin*] couvert de croûtes *fpl*; **2** [*animal, plant*] attaqué par la gale; **3** ○(nasty) moche○

scab labour○ *n* péj personnel qui remplace des travailleurs en grève

scaffold /ˈskæfəʊld/ *n* (gallows) échafaud *m*; Tech échafau-dage *m*

scaffolding /ˈskæfəldɪŋ/ *n* échafaudage *m*

scald /skɔːld/
A *n* brûlure *f* (*causée par un liquide bouillant*)
B *vtr* **1** (burn) ébouillanter [*person*]; **2** Culin ébouillanter; (nearly boil) faire chauffer [qch] sans bouillir
C *v refl* **to** ∼ **oneself** s'ébouillanter

(Idiom) **to run off like a** ∼**ed cat** prendre ses jambes à son cou

scalding /ˈskɔːldɪŋ/ *adj* brûlant; ∼ **hot** brûlant

scale /skeɪl/
A *n* **1** (extent) (of crisis, disaster, success, violence) étendue *f*; (of reform, development, defeat, recession, task) ampleur *f*; (of activity, operation) envergure *f*; (of support, change) degré *m*; **on a large/small** ∼ [*map*] à grande/petite échelle; **on a modest** ∼ [*building*] d'une ampleur modeste; **to do sth on a large** ∼ fig faire qch sur une grande échelle; **2** (grading system) échelle *f*; **pay** ∼, **salary** ∼ échelle des salaires; **on a** ∼ **of 1 to 10** sur une échelle allant de 1 à 10; **3** (for maps, models)

échelle *f*; **on a ~ of 2 km to 1 cm** à une échelle de 1 cm pour 2 km; **4** (on gauge etc) graduation *f*; **5** (for weighing) balance *f*; **6** Mus gamme *f*; **7** (on fish, insect) écaille *f*; **8** (deposit) (in kettle) dépôt *m* calcaire *m*; (on teeth) tartre *m*
B scales *npl* balance *f*
C *vtr* **1** (climb) escalader; **2** (take scales off) écailler
(Idiom) **the ~s fell from my eyes** tout d'un coup j'ai compris
(Phrasal verbs)
▪ **scale down**: ▸ **~ [sth] down, ~ down [sth]** réduire l'échelle de [*drawing, map*]; fig réduire
▪ **scale up**: ▸ **~ [sth] up, ~ up [sth]** **1** augmenter l'échelle de [*drawing, map*]; **2** fig augmenter [*activity, work*]

scale: **~d-down** *adj* réduit; **~ drawing** *n* dessin *m* à l'échelle; **~ pan** *n* plateau *m* de balance

scallop, scollop /'skɒləp/
A *n* **1** Zool pecten *m*; **2** Culin coquille *f* Saint-Jacques; **3** (in sewing) feston *m*
B *vtr* **1** (in sewing) festonner; **2** Culin **~ed potatoes** ≈ gratin *m* de pommes de terre

scalp /skælp/
A *n* **1** Anat cuir *m* chevelu; **2** fig (trophy) scalp *m*; **he's after my ~**° il veut ma peau°
B *vtr* **1** (remove scalp) scalper; **2** °US fig (defeat) écraser; **3** °US (sell illegally) revendre [qch] au marché noir

scaly /'skeɪlɪ/ *adj* [*wing, fish*] écailleux/-euse; [*skin, fruit, bark*] squameux/-euse; [*plaster, wall*] écaillé

scam° /skæm/ *n* escroquerie *f*

scamper /'skæmpə(r)/ *vi* (*also* **~ about, ~ around**) [*child, dog*] gambader; [*mouse*] trottiner; **to ~ away** *ou* **off** détaler

scampi /'skæmpɪ/ *npl* (fresh) langoustines *fpl*; (breaded) scampi *mpl*

scan /skæn/
A *n* **1** Med (CAT) scanner *m*; (ultrasound) échographie *f*; **2** (radar, TV) balayage *m*; (picture) analyse *f*
B *vtr* (*p prés etc* **-nn-**) **1** (cast eyes over) lire rapidement [*page, newspaper*]; **2** (examine) scruter [*faces, crowd, horizon*]; **3** [*light, radar*] balayer; **4** Med faire un scanner de [*organ*]; **5** Comput scanner, numériser [*document, image*]
C *vi* (*p prés etc* **-nn-**) Literat pouvoir se scander

scandal /'skændl/ *n* **1** (incident, outcry) scandale *m*; **the Grunard ~** l'affaire *f* Grunard; **2** (gossip) potins° *mpl*; (shocking stories) histoires *fpl* scandaleuses

scandalize /'skændəlaɪz/ *vtr* (shock) scandaliser

scandalmonger /'skændlmʌŋgə(r)/ *n* mauvaise langue *f*

scandalmongering /'skændlmʌŋgə(r)ɪŋ/ *n* commérage *m*

scandalous /'skændələs/ *adj* scandaleux/-euse

scandal sheet *n* journal *m* à scandales

Scandinavia /ˌskændɪ'neɪvɪə/ *pr n* Scandinavie *f*

scanner /'skænə(r)/ *n* **1** Med (CAT) scanner *m*; **2** (for bar codes etc) lecteur *m* optique; **3** (radar) scanner *m*; **4** Comput scanneur *m*, numériseur *m*, scanner *m*

scant /skænt/ *adj* [*concern, coverage*] maigre; **a ~ five metres** à peine cinq mètres; **to show ~ regard for sth** avoir peu de respect pour qch

scantily /'skæntɪlɪ/ *adv* insuffisamment; **~ clad, ~ dressed** très légèrement vêtu; **~ cut** très échancré

scanty /'skæntɪ/ *adj* [*meal, report, supply*] maigre; [*information*] sommaire; [*knowledge*] rudimentaire; [*swimsuit*] minuscule

scapegoat /'skeɪpgəʊt/ *n* bouc *m* émissaire (**for** de)

scar /skɑː(r)/
A *n* lit, fig cicatrice *f*; (from knife on face) balafre *f*; **acne ~s** traces *fpl* d'acné
B *vtr* (*p prés etc* **-rr-**) lit, fig marquer; (with knife on face) balafrer; fig défigurer [*landscape*]; **to ~ sb for life** lit laisser à qn une cicatrice permanente; fig marquer qn pour la vie
C *vi* (*p prés etc* **-rr-**) se cicatriser

scarce /skeəs/ *adj* (rare) rare; (insufficient) limité; **to become ~** se faire rare
(Idiom) **to make oneself ~**° s'éclipser°

scarcely /'skeəslɪ/ *adv* **1** (hardly) à peine; **it ~ matters** il n'importe guère; **~ a week passes without someone telephoning me** presque chaque semaine quelqu'un me téléphone; **~ anybody** presque personne; **we have ~ any money** nous n'avons pratiquement pas d'argent; **~ ever** presque jamais; **2** (not really) iron difficilement; **I can ~ accuse him** je peux difficilement l'accuser

scarcity /'skeəsətɪ/ *n* **1** (dearth) pénurie *f* (**of** de); **2** (rarity) rareté *f* (**of** de); **~ value** valeur *f* de rareté

scare /skeə(r)/
A *n* **1** (fright) peur *f*; **to give sb a ~** faire peur à qn; **2** (alert) alerte *f*; **bomb ~** alerte à la bombe; **3** (rumour) bruits *mpl* alarmistes; **food ~** alerte *f* à l'intoxication *f* alimentaire
B *vtr* faire peur à; **to ~ sb into doing sth** forcer qn à faire qch par intimidation; **to ~ sb stiff**° paralyser qn de peur
C *vi* **to ~ easily** s'effrayer facilement
(Phrasal verb)
▪ **scare away, scare off**: ▸ **~ away [sth/sb], ~ [sth/sb] away** lit faire fuir; fig dissuader

scarecrow /'skeəkrəʊ/ *n* épouvantail *m*

scared /skeəd/ *adj* [*animal, person*] effrayé; [*look*] apeuré; **to be** *ou* **feel ~** avoir peur; **to be ~ about sth** craindre qch; **to be ~ stiff** of/of doing avoir une peur bleue de/de faire°

scare: **~mongering** *n* alarmisme *m*; **~ tactic** *n* tactique *f* alarmiste

scarf /skɑːf/ *n* (*pl* **scarves**) (long) écharpe *f*; (square) foulard *m*

scarlet /'skɑːlət/ ▸ **p. 752** *n, adj* (colour) écarlate (*f*)

scarlet: **~ fever** ▸ **p. 933** *n* scarlatine *f*; **~ woman** *n* femme *f* de mauvaise vie

scarper° /'skɑːpə(r)/ *vi* GB déguerpir

scarves /skɑːvz/ *pl* ▸ **scarf**

scary° /'skeərɪ/ *adj* (inspiring fear) qui fait peur

scathing /'skeɪðɪŋ/ *adj* [*remark, report, tone, wit*] cinglant; [*criticism*] virulent; [*look*] noir

scatter /'skætə(r)/
A *n* **1** (of houses, stars, papers) éparpillement *m* (**of** de); **2** (statistics) dispersion *f*
B *vtr* (*also* **~ around, ~ about**) (throw around) répandre [*seeds, earth*]; éparpiller [*books, papers, clothes*]; disperser [*debris*]; **to be ~ed around** être éparpillé; **to be ~ed with sth** être jonché de qch
C *vi* [*people, animals, birds*] se disperser

scatter-brained *adj* [*person*] étourdi; [*idea*] farfelu°

scattered /'skætəd/ *adj* [*houses, population, clouds*] épars; [*books, litter*] éparpillé; [*support*] clairsemé; **~ showers** averses *fpl* intermittentes

scattering /'skætərɪŋ/ *n* (of leaves, papers, people) éparpillement *m*; (of shops etc) constellation *f*

scatty° /'skætɪ/ *adj* GB étourdi

scavenge /'skævɪndʒ/
A *vtr* lit récupérer (**from** dans)
B *vi* **to ~ for food** [*bird, animal*] chercher de la nourriture; **to ~ in** *ou* **through the dustbins for sth** [*person*] faire les poubelles à la recherche de qch; [*dog*] fouiller les poubelles à la recherche de qch

scavenger /'skævɪndʒə(r)/ *n* **1** (animal) charognard *m*; **2** (for food) faiseur *m* de poubelles; **3** (for objects) récupérateur *m*

scenario /sɪ'nɑːrɪəʊ, US -'nær-/ *n* (*pl* **~s**) Cin scénario *m*; fig (hypothetical situation) cas *m* de figure

scene /siːn/ *n* **1** (in play, film, novel) scène *f*; **first, let's set the ~: a villa in Mexico** situons le décor d'abord: une villa au Mexique; **the ~ was set for a major tragedy** fig tous les éléments étaient réunis pour qu'une grande tragédie se produise; **2** Theat décor *m*; **behind the ~s** lit, fig dans les coulisses *fpl*; **3** (location) lieu *m*; **these streets have been the ~ of violent fighting** ces rues ont été le théâtre de violents affrontements; **to come on the ~** [*police, ambulance*] arriver sur les lieux; fig arriver; **you need a change of ~** tu as besoin de changer de décor; **4** (sphere, field) scène *f*; **the jazz/fashion ~** le monde du jazz/de la mode; **it's not my ~**° ce n'est pas mon genre; **5** (emotional incident) scène *f*; **there were ~s of violence** il y a eu des incidents violents; **6** (image, sight) image *f*; **7** (view) vue *f*, tableau *m*; Art scène *f*

scene designer, **scene painter** ▸ p. 1181 *n* Theat décorateur/-trice *m/f*

scenery /'si:nərɪ/ *n* **⊄** **1** (landscape) paysage *m*; fig décor *m*; **2** Theat décors *mpl*; **a piece of** ~ un élément de décor

scene shifter ▸ p. 1181 *n* machiniste *mf*

scenic /'si:nɪk/ *adj* [*drive, route, walk*] panoramique; [*location, countryside*] pittoresque

scent /sent/
A *n* **1** (smell) odeur *f*; (perfume) parfum *m*; **2** (body smell) (of animal) fumet *m*; (in hunting) piste *f*; fig relents *mpl*; **to pick up the** ~ lit, fig trouver la piste; **to throw the dogs off the** ~ brouiller la piste aux chiens; **to be (hot) on the** ~ **of sth/ sb** suivre qch/qn à la trace
B *vtr* (smell) flairer; fig pressentir [*danger*]

(Phrasal verb)

■ **scent out**: ▸ ~ **[sth] out**, ~ **out [sth]** flairer

scented /'sentɪd/
A *adj* gen parfumé (**with** de); [*air*] odorant
B **-scented** *combining form* (with scent added) parfumé à; (natural) à l'odeur de

sceptic GB, **skeptic** US /'skeptɪk/ *n* sceptique *mf*

sceptical GB, **skeptical** US /'skeptɪkl/ *adj* sceptique (**about, of** en ce qui concerne)

sceptically GB, **skeptically** US /'skeptɪklɪ/ *adv* avec scepticisme *m*

scepticism GB, **skepticism** US /'skeptɪsɪzəm/ *n* scepticisme *m* (**about** à propos de)

schedule /'ʃedju:l, US 'skedʒʊl/
A *n* **1** Admin, Comm, Tech programme *m*; (projected plan) prévisions *fpl*; **to be ahead of/behind** ~ être en avance/en retard sur les prévisions; **to work to a tight** ~ travailler selon un programme serré; **to draw up** *ou* **make out a** ~ établir un programme; **to be on** ~ progresser comme prévu; **finished on** ~ fini à temps; **according to** ~ comme prévu; **a** ~ **of events** un calendrier; **2** (of appointments) programme *m* also TV; **to fit sb/sth into one's** ~ intégrer qn/qch dans son programme; **3** (timetable) horaire *m*; **to arrive on/ahead of/behind** ~ arriver à l'heure/en avance/ en retard; **4** Comm, Jur (list) (of charges) barème *m*; (of repayments) taux *m*; (of contents) inventaire *m*; (to a contract) annexe *f*
B *vtr* prévoir; (arrange) programmer; **the plane is** ~**d to arrive at 2.00** l'avion est attendu à 2 h; **the station is** ~**d for completion in 2007** la gare doit être terminée en 2007

schedule: ~**d building** *n* GB immeuble *m* classé; ~**d flight** *n* vol *m* régulier; ~**d territories** *npl* GB zone *f* sterling

scheduling /'ʃedju:lɪŋ, US 'skedʒʊl-/ *n* (of project, work) programmation *f*; (of monument) GB classification *f*

scheme /ski:m/
A *n* **1** (plan) projet *m*, plan *m*; **a** ~ **for sth/for doing** un plan pour qch/pour faire; **2** GB Admin (system) système *m*, projet *m*; **road** ~ projet de développement routier; **insurance/ pension** ~ régime *m* d'assurances/de retraite; **3** péj (impractical idea) plan *m*; **4** (plot) combine *f*; **5** (for house, garden etc) plan *m*
B *vi* péj comploter (**to do** pour faire)

(Idioms) **in the overall** *ou* **whole** ~ **of things** si on considère la situation dans son ensemble; **she was unsure how she fitted into the** ~ **of things** elle ne savait pas où elle se situait

scheming /'ski:mɪŋ/ péj
A *n* **⊄** machinations *fpl*
B *adj* [*person*] intrigant

schizophrenic /ˌskɪtsəʊ'frenɪk/
A *n* schizophrène *mf*
B *adj* gen schizophrénique; [*patient*] schizophrène

schmal(t)zy○ /'ʃmɔːltsɪ/ *adj* gen larmoyant; [*music*] sirupeux/-euse

scholar /'skɒlə(r)/ *n* **1** (learned person) érudit/-e *m/f*; **Hebrew** ~ spécialiste *mf* de l'hébreu; **2** (student with scholarship) lauréat/-e *m/f* détenteur/-trice d'une bourse

scholarly /'skɒləlɪ/ *adj* **1** (erudite) érudit; **2** [*journal, periodical, circles*] (academic) universitaire; (serious) intellectuel/-elle; **3** [*appearance*] d'intellectuel

scholarship /'skɒləʃɪp/ *n* **1** (award) bourse *f* (**to** pour); **2** (meticulous study) érudition *f*; **3** (body of learning) savoir *m*; (of individual, work) érudition *f*

scholastic /skə'læstɪk/ *adj* **1** (philosopher) scolastique; **2** (of school) scolaire

Scholastic Aptitude Test, **SAT** *n* US examen *m* d'admission à l'université

school /sku:l/
A *n* **1** Sch, Univ école *f*; **broadcasts for** ~**s** émissions *fpl* scolaires; ~ **starts/finishes** les cours commencent/finissent; **no** ~ **today** pas de classe aujourd'hui; **to go to medical** ~ faire des études de médecine; **2** US (university) université *f*; **3** (of painting, literature, thought) école *f*; **4** (of whales etc) banc *m*
B *noun modifier* gen [*holiday, outing, life, uniform, year*] scolaire; (of particular school) [*facilities*] de l'école
C *vtr* dresser [*horse*]; **to** ~ **sb in sth** enseigner qch à qn

schoolbag *n* sac *m* de classe; (traditional) cartable *m*

schoolboy /'sku:lbɔɪ/
A *n* gen élève *m*; (of primary age) écolier *m*; (secondary) collégien *m*; (sixth former) GB lycéen *m*
B *noun modifier* **1** [*attitude, behaviour*] de collégien; [*slang, word*] d'élève; **2** [*champion, player*] junior

school: ~ **bus** *n* car *m* scolaire; ~ **captain** *n* GB Sch élève *choisi pour représenter l'école*; ~**child** *n* écolier/-ière *m/f*; ~ **council** *n*: conseil *d'enseignants et de représentants des élèves*; ~**days** *npl* années *fpl* d'école; ~ **dinner** *n* = **school lunch**; ~ **fees** *n* frais *mpl* de scolarité; ~**friend** *n* camarade *mf* de classe; ~**girl** *n* gen élève *f*; (of primary age) écolière *f*; (secondary) collégienne *f*; (sixth former) GB lycéenne *f*; ~ **graduation age** *n* US Sch = **school leaving age**; ~**house** *n* école *f*

schooling /'sku:lɪŋ/ *n* (of child) scolarité *f*; (of horse) dressage *m*

school: ~ **inspector** ▸ p. 1181 *n* inspecteur/-trice *m/f*; ~**kid**○ *n* (primary) écolier/-ière *m/f*; (junior) collégien/-ienne *m/f*; (senior) lycéen/-éenne *m/f*; ~**leaver** *n* GB jeune *mf* ayant fini sa scolarité; ~ **leaving age** *n* âge *m* de fin de scolarité; ~ **lunch** *n* repas *m* de la cantine scolaire; ~**master** ▸ p. 1181 *n* enseignant *m*; ~**mate** *n* camarade *mf* d'école; ~**mistress** ▸ p. 1181 *n* enseignante *f*; ~ **prefect** *n* GB Sch élève *de terminale chargé de la discipline*; ~ **record** *n* ≈ dossier *m* scolaire; ~ **report** GB, ~ **report card** US *n* bulletin *m* scolaire; ~**room** *n* salle *f* de classe; ~**teacher** ▸ p. 1181 *n* gen enseignant/-e *m/f*; (secondary) professeur *m*; (primary) gen instituteur/-trice *m/f*; Admin professeur *m* des écoles; ~**work** *n* travail *m* de classe

schooner /'sku:nə(r)/ *n* (boat) goélette *f*; (glass) US grande chope *f* (à bière); GB grand verre *m* à Xérès

sciatica /saɪ'ætɪkə/ ▸ p. 933 *n* Med sciatique *f*

science /'saɪəns/
A *n* science *f*; **to teach** ~ enseigner les sciences
B *noun modifier* [*exam, subject*] scientifique; [*faculty*] des sciences; [*teacher, textbook*] de sciences

(Idiom) **to blind sb with** ~ épater qn avec sa science

scientific /ˌsaɪən'tɪfɪk/ *adj* scientifique; **it's a very** ~ **game** c'est un jeu qui exige de l'analyse intellectuelle

scientifically /ˌsaɪən'tɪfɪklɪ/ *adv* [*investigate, show*] scientifiquement

scientist /'saɪəntɪst/ ▸ p. 1181 *n* gen scientifique *mf*; (eminent) savant *m*

Scillies /'sɪlɪz/, **Scilly Isles** /ˌsɪlɪ 'aɪlz/ ▸ p. 954 *pr n* (îles *fpl*) Sorlingues *fpl*

scintillate /'sɪntɪleɪt, US -təleɪt/ *vi* lit scintiller; fig briller

scintillating /'sɪntɪleɪtɪŋ, US -təleɪtɪŋ/ *adj* lit scintillant; fig [*person, conversation*] brillant; [*wit*] vif/vive

scissors /'sɪzəz/ *npl* ciseaux *mpl*; **a** ~**-and-paste job** fig péj un tissu d'idées glanées à droite à gauche

scoff /skɒf, US skɔːf/
A *vtr* **1** (mock) **'love!'** she ~**ed** 'l'amour!' dit-elle avec dédain; **2** ○ GB (eat) engloutir○, bouffer○
B *vi* se moquer (**at** de)

scold /skəʊld/
A *vtr* gronder (**for doing** pour avoir fait)
B *vi* râler○

scolding /'skəʊldɪŋ/ *n* **⊄** gronderie *f*; **to give sb a** ~ gronder qn

scone /skɒn, skəʊn, US skəʊn/ *n* GB scone *m* (*petit pain rond*)

scoop /sku:p/
A *n* **1** (implement) (for shovelling) pelle *f*; (for measuring) mesure *f*;

(for ice cream) cuillère *f* à glace; ② (scoopful) (of coffee, flour) mesure *f*; (of earth) pelletée *f*; (of coal) boule *f*; ③ (in journalism) exclusivité *f*; **to get a** ~ obtenir un scoop○
B ○*vtr* décrocher○ [*prize, sum, story*]

(Phrasal verbs)

■ **scoop out**: ▸ ~ **out** [sth], ~ [sth] **out** creuser; **to** ~ **the flesh out of a tomato** évider une tomate

■ **scoop up**: ▸ ~ [sth] **up**, ~ **up** [sth] pelleter [*earth, snow*]; recueillir [*water*]; soulever [*child*]

scooter /'sku:tə(r)/ *n* ① (child's) trottinette *f*; ② (motorized) scooter *m*; ③ US (boat) yacht *m* à glace

scope /skəʊp/ *n* ① (opportunity) possibilité *f*; **there is** ~ **for sb to do** il y a des possibilités pour qn de faire; **to give sb** ~ **to do** laisser toute latitude à qn de faire; ② (range) (of plan) envergure *f*; (of inquiry, report, study, book) portée *f*; (of changes, disaster, knowledge, power) étendue *f*; **to be within/ outside the** ~ **of the study** faire partie du/sortir du champ de l'étude; ③ (capacity) compétences *fpl*; **to be within/beyond the** ~ **of sb** entrer dans/dépasser les compétences de qn

scorch /skɔ:tʃ/
A *n* (*also* ~ **mark**) légère brûlure *f*
B *vtr* [*fire*] brûler; [*sun*] dessécher [*grass, trees*]; griller [*lawn*]; [*iron etc*] roussir [*fabric*]; ~**ed earth policy** Mil tactique *f* de la terre brûlée

scorcher○ /'skɔ:tʃə(r)/ *n* journée *f* de canicule

scorching○ /'skɔ:tʃɪŋ/ *adj* (*also* ~ **hot**) [*heat, day*] torride; [*sun*] brûlant; [*weather, summer*] caniculaire

score /skɔ:(r)/
A *n* ① (points gained) Sport score *m*; (in cards) marque *f*; **there is still no** ~ le score est toujours zéro à zéro; **the final** ~ **was 3–1** le score final était de 3 à 1; **to keep (the)** ~ gen marquer les points; (in cards) tenir la marque; **what's the** ~? (in game, match) où en est le jeu *or* le match?; **to know the** ~ fig savoir où on est; ② (in exam, test) note *f*, résultat *m*; ③ Mus (written music) partition *f*; (for ballet) musique *f* (du ballet); (for film) musique *f* (du film); ④ (twenty) **a** ~ vingt *m*, une vingtaine *f*; **three** ~ **years and ten** soixante-dix ans; **by the** ~ à la pelle; ~**s of requests** des tas de demandes; ⑤ (account) sujet *m*; **on this** *ou* **that** ~ à ce sujet
B *vtr* ① Sport marquer [*goal, point*]; remporter [*victory, success*]; **to** ~ **9 out of 10** avoir 9 sur 10; **to** ~ **a hit** in swordsmanship) toucher; (in shooting) mettre dans le mille; fig remporter un grand succès; ② Mus (arrange) adapter; (orchestrate) orchestrer; Cin composer la musique de [*film*]; ③ (mark) (with chalk, ink) marquer; (cut) entailler; inciser [*meat, fish*]
C *vi* ① Sport (gain point) marquer un point (obtain goal) marquer un but; **to** ~ **well** *ou* **highly** obtenir un bon résultat; **to** ~ **over** *ou* **against sb** (in argument, debate) prendre le dessus sur qn; ② (keep score) marquer les points; ③ ○(be successful) avoir du succès

(Idiom) **to settle a** ~ régler ses comptes

(Phrasal verb)

■ **score off**: ▸ ~ **off** [sth], ~ [sth] **off** rayer; ▸ ~ **off** [sb] (in argument) marquer des points sur

score: ~**board** *n* gen tableau *m* d'affichage; ~**card** *n* gen, Sport carte *f* de score; (in cards) feuille *f* de marque; ~**line** *n* score *m*

scorer /'skɔ:rə(r)/ *n* marqueur/-euse *m/f*

scoresheet /'skɔ:ʃi:t/ *n* feuille *f* de match

scoring /'skɔ:rɪŋ/ *n* ① Sport **to open the** ~ ouvrir la marque; ② Mus arrangement *m*

scorn /skɔ:n/
A *n* mépris *m*; **to pour** *ou* **heap** ~ **on** accabler [qn] de mépris [*person*]; dénigrer [*attempt, argument, organization*]
B *vtr* ① (despise) mépriser [*person, action*]; dédaigner [*fashion, make-up*]; ② (reject) gen rejeter; accueillir avec mépris [*claim, suggestion*]; ③ sout **to** ~ **to do** ne pas daigner faire

scornful /'skɔ:nfl/ *adj* méprisant; **to be** ~ **of** manifester du mépris pour

scornfully /'skɔ:nfəlɪ/ *adv* avec mépris, dédaigneusement

Scorpio /'skɔ:pɪəʊ/ ▸ p. 1350 *n* Scorpion *m*

Scot /skɒt/ ▸ p. 1032 *n* Écossais/-e *m/f*

scotch /skɒtʃ/ *vtr* étouffer [*rumour, revolt*]; contrecarrer [*plans*]; anéantir [*hopes*]

Scotch /skɒtʃ/ *n* (*also* ~ **whisky**) whisky *m*, scotch *m*

Scotch: ~ **egg** *n* GB œuf dur enrobé de chair à saucisse; ~ **mist** *n* bruine *f*, crachin *m*; ~ **pine** *n* = Scots pine; ~ **tape**® *n* US scotch® *m*

scot-free /ˌskɒt'fri:/ *adj* **to get off** *ou* **go** ~ (unpunished) s'en tirer sans être inquiété; (unharmed) s'en sortir indemne

Scotland /'skɒtlənd/ ▸ p. 774 *pr n* Écosse *f*

Scotland Office *n* Pol ministère *m* des Affaires écossaises

Scotland Yard *n* Scotland Yard (*police judiciaire britannique*)

Scots: ~**man** *n* Écossais *m*; ~ **pine** *n* pin *m* sylvestre; ~**woman** *n* Écossaise *f*

Scottish /'skɒtɪʃ/ ▸ p. 1032 *adj* écossais

Scottish: ~ **National Party**, **SNP** *n* Parti *m* national écossais; **Scottish Parliament** *n* Parlement *m* écossais

scoundrel /'skaʊndrəl/ *n* péj gredin *m*; hum chenapan *m*

scour /'skaʊə(r)/ *vtr* ① (scrub) récurer; ② (search) parcourir (**for** à la recherche de); **to** ~ **the shops for sth** faire le tour des magasins à la recherche de qch

scourer /'skaʊərə(r)/ *n* (pad) tampon *m* à récurer

scourge /skɜ:dʒ/
A *n* lit, fig fléau *m*
B *vtr* ① lit fouetter; ② fig [*ruler*] opprimer; [*famine, disease, war*] frapper

scouring powder *n* poudre *f* à récurer

scout /skaʊt/
A *n* ① (boy) (Catholic) scout *m*; (non-Catholic) éclaireur *m*; ② Mil éclaireur *m*; **to have a** ~ **around** Mil aller en reconnaissance; fig explorer; ③ (*also* **talent** ~) découvreur/-euse *m/f* de nouveaux talents
B *noun modifier* [*camp, leader, movement*] scout; [*uniform*] de scout; [*troop*] de scouts

(Phrasal verb)

■ **scout around** Mil aller en reconnaissance; gen explorer; **to** ~ **around for sth** rechercher qch

scouting /'skaʊtɪŋ/ *n* scoutisme *m*

scowl /skaʊl/
A *n* air *m* renfrogné; **with a** ~ d'un air renfrogné
B *vi* prendre un air renfrogné

scrabble /'skræbl/ *vi* ① (*also* ~ **around**) (search) fouiller; ② (scrape) gratter; **he** ~**d desperately for a hold** il a cherché désespérément à s'accrocher quelque part

scrag *n* Culin (*also* ~ **end**) collet *m* de mouton

scraggy /'skrægɪ/ *adj* [*person*] maigrichon/-onne; [*part of body*] décharné; [*animal*] famélique

scram○ /skræm/ *vi* (*p prés etc* **-mm-**) filer○

scramble /'skræmbl/
A *n* ① (rush) course *f*; ② (climb) escalade *f*; ③ Aviat, Mil décollage *m* d'urgence
B *vtr* ① Culin **to** ~ **eggs** faire des œufs brouillés; ② Radio, Telecom brouiller; TV coder; ③ Mil faire décoller [qch] d'urgence
C *vi* ① (clamber) grimper; **to** ~ **up/down** escalader; **to** ~ **over** escalader; **to** ~ **through** se frayer un passage à travers; **to** ~ **to one's feet** se lever en sursaut; ② (compete) **to** ~ **for** se disputer; **to** ~ **to do** se dépêcher de faire; ③ (rush) **to** ~ **for** se précipiter sur; **to** ~ **to do** se démener pour faire

scrambler /'skræmblə(r)/ *n* ① Radio, Telecom brouilleur *m*; ② GB (motorcyclist) trialiste *mf*

scrambling /'skræmblɪŋ/ ▸ p. 881 *n* ① Sport motocross *m*; ② Radio, Telecom brouillage *m*; TV cryptage *m*

scrap /skræp/
A *n* ① (fragment) (of paper, cloth) petit morceau *m*; (of news, information, verse) fragment *m*; (of conversation) bribe *f*; (cutting) coupure *f*; (of land) parcelle *f*; **there wasn't a** ~ **of evidence** fig il n'y avait pas la moindre preuve; **she never does a** ~ **of work** elle ne fiche○ jamais rien; ② ○(fight) bagarre○ *f*; ③ (old iron) ferraille *f*; **to sell sth for** ~ mettre qch à la casse
B **scraps** *npl* (of food) restes *mpl*
C *noun modifier* [*price, value*] à la casse
D *vtr* (*p prés etc* **-pp-**) ① ○fig (do away with) abandonner; ② lit détruire [*aircraft etc*]
E ○*vi* (*p prés etc* **-pp-**) (fight) se bagarrer○ (**with** avec)

scrap: ~**book** *n* album *m* (de coupures de journaux etc); ~ **(metal) dealer** ▸ p. 1181 *n* marchand *m* de ferraille

scrape /skreɪp/
A n ⓵ °(awkward situation) **to get into a ~** s'attirer des ennuis; **to get sb into a ~** mettre qn dans le pétrin°; ⓶ (sound) raclement m
B vtr ⓵ gratter [vegetables, shoes]; ⓶ (damage) érafler; ⓷ (injure) écorcher; ⓸ (making noise) racler; ⓹ °**to ~ a living** s'en sortir à peine (**doing** en faisant); **she ~d a ten in biology** elle a laborieusement décroché un dix en biologie
C vi ⓵ **to ~ against sth** [car part] érafler qch; ⓶ (economize) économiser le moindre sou
(Idiom) **to ~ the bottom of the barrel** être à court d'idées (or d'imagination or de personnes qualifiées etc)
(Phrasal verbs)
■ **scrape by** (financially) s'en sortir à peine; (in situation) s'en tirer de justesse
■ **scrape home** Sport gagner de justesse
■ **scrape in** (to university, class) entrer de justesse
■ **scrape off:** ▸ **~ off [sth], ~ [sth] off** enlever [qch] en grattant
■ **scrape out:** ▸ **~ out [sth], ~ [sth] out** nettoyer [qch] en grattant [saucepan]
■ **scrape through:** ▸ **~ through** s'en tirer de justesse; ▸ **~ through [sth]** réussir [qch] de justesse [exam, test]
■ **scrape together:** ▸ **~ [sth] together, ~ together [sth]** arriver à amasser [sum of money]
■ **scrape up** = **scrape together**

scraper /'skreɪpə(r)/ n (for decorating) couteau m de peinture; (for shoes) grattoir m

scrap heap /'skræp hi:p/ n **to be thrown on** ou **consigned to the ~** être mis au rebut

scrap: **~ iron** n ferraille f; **~ merchant** ▸ p. 1181 n marchand m de ferraille; **~ metal** n ferraille f; **~ paper** n papier m brouillon

scrappy /'skræpɪ/ adj ⓵ (disorganized) [report] décousu; [game] désordonné; [meal] de bric et de broc; ⓶ °US péj (pugnacious) bagarreur/-euse°

scrap yard /'skræp jɑːd/ n chantier m de ferraille, casse f

scratch /skrætʃ/
A n ⓵ (wound) gen égratignure f; (from a claw, fingernail) griffure f; ⓶ (on metal, furniture) éraflure f; (on record, disc, glass) rayure f; ⓷ (to relieve an itch) **to have a ~** se gratter; ⓸ (sound) grattement m; ⓹ °**he/his work is not up to ~** il/son travail n'est pas à la hauteur; ⓺ (zero) **to start from ~** partir de zéro; ⓻ Sport **to play off ~** jouer scratch
B adj [team] de fortune; [meal] improvisé; **he's a ~ golfer** il joue scratch
C vtr ⓵ (cancel) supprimer; effacer [file]; ⓶ (trace) **to ~ one's initials on sth** graver ses initiales sur qch; ⓷ [cat, person] griffer; [thorns, rosebush] égratigner; **to ~ sb's eyes out** arracher les yeux à quelqu'un; ⓸ (react to itch) gratter; **to ~ an itch** se gratter; **to ~ one's head** lit se gratter la tête; fig être perplexe; ⓹ (damage) gen érafler; rayer [record]; [cat] se faire les griffes sur [furniture]; ⓺ Sport retirer, scratcher
D vi ⓵ (relieve itch) se gratter; ⓶ (inflict injury) griffer
E v refl **to ~ oneself** se gratter
(Idioms) **you ~ my back and I'll ~ yours** un service en vaut un autre; **~ a translator and you'll find a writer underneath!** dans tout traducteur il y a un écrivain qui sommeille!
(Phrasal verb)
■ **scratch around** gratter (**in** dans)

scratch: **~ mark** n éraflure f; **~ pad** n bloc-notes m; **~ tape** n bande f de travail; **~ test** n Med test m cutané; **~ video** n cassette f de montage

scratchy /'skrætʃɪ/ adj [fabric, wool] rêche

scrawl /skrɔːl/
A n griboullage m
B vtr, vi gribouiller

scrawny /'skrɔːnɪ/ adj décharné, maigre

scream /skriːm/
A n ⓵ (of person, animal) cri m (perçant); (stronger) hurlement m; (of brakes) grincement m; (of tyres) crissement m; **~s of laughter** éclats mpl de rire; ⓶ °**to be a ~** être tordant°
B vtr lit crier; fig [headline] annoncer [en titre]
C vi [person, animal, bird] crier; (stronger) hurler; [brakes] grincer; [tyres] crisser; fig [colour] crier; **to ~ at sb** crier après qn°; **to ~ with** hurler de [fear, pain, rage]; pousser des cris

de [excitement, pleasure]; **to ~ with laughter** rire aux éclats
(Idioms) **to ~ the place down** pousser des hurlements; **to drag sb kicking and ~ing to the dentist** traîner qn de force chez le dentiste

screaming /'skriːmɪŋ/ n cris mpl; (stronger) hurlements mpl

scree /skriː/ n éboulis m

screech /skriːtʃ/
A n gen cri m strident; (of tyres) crissement m
B vtr hurler
C vi [person, animal] pousser un cri strident; [tyres] crisser

screen /skriːn/
A n ⓵ Cin, Comput, TV écran m; **on ~** Comput sur l'écran; Cin, TV à l'écran; **he writes for the ~** Cin il écrit pour le cinéma; ⓶ (folding panel) paravent m; (partition) cloison f mobile; (to protect) écran m; **a ~ of trees** un rideau d'arbres; ⓷ fig couverture f; ⓸ Med visite f de dépistage
B noun modifier Cin [actor, star] de cinéma; [appearance, debut] cinématographique, au cinéma
C vtr ⓵ (show on screen) Cin projeter; TV diffuser; ⓶ (conceal) cacher; (protect) protéger; ⓷ (test) examiner le cas de [applicants]; contrôler le statut de [refugees]; contrôler [baggage]; Med faire passer des tests de dépistage à [patient]; **to be ~ed** [staff] faire l'objet d'une enquête de sécurité; **to ~ sb for cancer** faire passer à qn des tests de dépistage du cancer
(Phrasal verb)
■ **screen off:** ▸ **~ off [sth], ~ [sth] off** isoler

screen: **~ door** n porte f munie d'une moustiquaire; **~ dump** n Comput recopie f d'écran

screening /'skriːnɪŋ/ n ⓵ (showing) Cin projection f; TV diffusion f; ⓶ (testing) sélection f; Med (of patients) examens mpl de dépistage; **cancer ~** dépistage m du cancer; ⓷ (vetting) filtrage m

screening: **~ room** n Cin salle f de projection; **~ service** n Med service m de dépistage

screen: **~play** n Cin scénario m; **~ printing** n sérigraphie f; **~ rights** npl droits mpl d'adaptation à l'écran; **~saver** n Comput économiseur m d'écran; **~ test** n Cin bout m d'essai; **~ wash** n (device) lave-glace m; (liquid) liquide m lave-glace; **~writer** ▸ p. 1181 n Cin, TV scénariste mf

screw /skruː/
A n ⓵ Tech vis f; ⓶ Aviat, Naut hélice f; ⓷ °GB (prison guard) maton/-onne° m/f
B vtr ⓵ Tech visser (**into** dans); ⓶ °(extort) **to ~ sth out of sb** extorquer qch à qn
C vi Tech **to ~ onto/into** se visser sur/dans
(Idioms) **to have one's head ~ed on** avoir la tête sur les épaules; **to put the ~s on sb°** forcer la main à qn
(Phrasal verbs)
■ **screw down:** ▸ **~ down** se visser; ▸ **~ [sth] down, ~ down [sth]** visser (à fond)
■ **screw in:** ▸ **~ in** se visser; ▸ **~ [sth] in, ~ in [sth]** visser
■ **screw on:** ▸ **~ on** se visser; ▸ **~ [sth] on, ~ on [sth]** visser
■ **screw round: to ~ one's head round** tourner la tête
■ **screw together:** ▸ **~ together** se visser l'un à l'autre; ▸ **~ [sth] together, ~ together [sth]** assembler [qch] avec des vis
■ **screw up:** ▸ **~ up°** (mess up) cafouiller°; ▸ **~ [sth] up, ~ up [sth]** ⓵ (crumple) froisser; **to ~ up one's eyes** plisser les yeux; **to ~ up one's face** faire la grimace; ⓶ °(make a mess of) faire foirer° [plan, task]; ⓷ (summon) **to ~ up the courage to do** trouver le courage de faire; ▸ **~ [sb] up°** perturber [person]; **~ed up°** perturbé

screw-cap n bouchon m à vis

screwdriver /'skruːdraɪvə(r)/ n ⓵ (tool) tournevis m; ⓶ (cocktail) vodka-orange f

screw-in adj [lightbulb] à vis

screw top
A n bouchon m à vis
B **screw-top** noun modifier [jar] avec un couvercle à vis; [bottle] avec un bouchon à vis

screwy° /'skruːɪ/ adj cinglé°

scribble /'skrɪbl/
A n griboullage m
B vtr, vi lit, fig griffonner, gribouiller

(Phrasal verbs)
- **scribble down:** ▸ ~ **[sth] down**, ~ **down [sth]** griffonner
- **scribble out:** ▸ ~ **[sth] out**, ~ **out [sth]** raturer

scrimmage /'skrɪmɪdʒ/ n ①ⴲ US (in football) mêlée f; ② (struggle) bousculade f

scrimp /skrɪmp/ vi économiser; **to ~ on sth** lésiner sur qch péj; **to ~ and save** se priver de tout

script /skrɪpt/
A n ① (text) Cin, Radio, TV script m; Theat texte m; ② (handwriting) écriture f; ③ GB Sch, Univ copie f (d'examen)
B vtr écrire le scénario de [film etc]

scripture /'skrɪptʃə(r)/ n Relig (also **Holy Scripture**, **Holy Scriptures**) (Christian) Saintes Écritures fpl; (other) textes mpl sacrés

scriptwriter /'skrɪptraɪtə(r)/ ▸ p. 1181 n Cin, Radio, TV scénariste mf

scroll /skrəʊl/
A n ① (manuscript, painting) rouleau m; ② Archit, Art volute f
B vtr Comput **to ~ sth up/down** faire défiler qch vers le haut/vers le bas
C vi Comput défiler

scroll bar n barre f de défilement

Scrooge○ /skruːdʒ/ n grippe-sou m

scrounge○ /skraʊndʒ/
A n **to be on the ~** être toujours en train de mendier
B vtr quémander [favour]; **to ~ sth off sb** piquer○ qch à qn [cigarette]; taper○ qn de qch [money]
C vi ① **to ~ off sb** vivre sur le dos de qn; ② **to ~ (around) for sth** chercher qch

scrounger○ /'skraʊndʒə(r)/ n parasite m

scrub /skrʌb/
A n ① (clean) **to give sth a (good) ~** (bien) nettoyer qch; ② Bot broussailles fpl; ③ (beauty product) gommage m
B vtr (p prés etc **-bb-**) ① (clean) gen frotter; nettoyer [vegetable]; **to ~ one's nails** se brosser les ongles; ② ○(scrap) laisser tomber○
C vi (p prés etc **-bb-**) nettoyer, frotter
D v refl (p prés etc **-bb-**) **to ~ oneself** se frotter

(Phrasal verbs)
- **scrub down:** ▸ ~ **down [sth/sb]**, ~ **[sth/sb] down** nettoyer [qch/qn] à fond
- **scrub off:** ▸ ~ **off [sth]**, ~ **[sth] off** nettoyer, enlever [stain, graffiti]
- **scrub out:** ▸ ~ **out [sth]**, ~ **[sth] out** (clean inside) récurer; (rub out) effacer
- **scrub up** se stériliser les mains (avant une opération)

scrubbing brush, **scrub brush** US n brosse f de ménage

scruff /skrʌf/ n ① (nape) **by the ~ of the neck** par la peau du cou; ② ○GB (untidy person) **he's a bit of a ~**○ il est peu soigné

scruffy /'skrʌfɪ/ adj [clothes, person] dépenaillé; [flat, town] délabré

scrum /skrʌm/ n ① (rugby) mêlée f; ② ○GB bousculade f

scrum half n Sport demi m de mêlée

scrummage /'skrʌmɪdʒ/ n (in rugby) mêlée f

scrunch /skrʌntʃ/
A n crissement m
B vi [footsteps, tyres] crisser

(Phrasal verbs)
- **scrunch up:** ▸ ~ **up** US se tasser; ▸ ~ **[sth] up**, ~ **up [sth]** faire une boule de

scruple /'skruːpl/
A n scrupule m (**about** vis-à-vis de)
B vi **not to ~ to do** n'avoir aucun scrupule à faire

scrupulous /'skruːpjʊləs/ adj scrupuleux/-euse

scrutinize /'skruːtɪnaɪz, US -tənaɪz/ vtr scruter [face, motives]; examiner [qch] minutieusement [document]; vérifier [accounts, votes]; surveiller [election]

scrutiny /'skruːtɪnɪ, US 'skruːtənɪ/ n ① (investigation) examen m; **close ~** examen approfondi; **to come under ~** être examiné; **to avoid ~** échapper au contrôle; ② (surveillance) surveillance f; ③ (look) regard m scrutateur

scuba diving ▸ p. 881 n plongée f sous-marine

scud /skʌd/ vi (p prés etc **-dd-**) [ship] fuir; **to ~ across the sky** [cloud] filer dans le ciel

scuff /skʌf/
A n (also **mark**) gen rayure f; (on leather) éraflure f
B vtr érafler [shoes]; rayer [floor, furniture]; **to ~ one's feet** traîner les pieds

scuffle /'skʌfl/
A n bagarre f
B vi se bagarrer

scull /skʌl/
A n (boat) outrigger m; (single oar) godille f; (one of a pair) aviron m
B vi (with one oar) godiller; (with two oars) ramer en couple

scullery /'skʌlərɪ/ n GB arrière-cuisine f

sculpt /skʌlpt/ vtr, vi sculpter

sculptor /'skʌlptə(r)/ ▸ p. 1181 n sculpteur m

sculpture /'skʌlptʃə(r)/
A n sculpture f
B noun modifier [class, gallery] de sculpture

scum /skʌm/ n ① (on pond) couche f d'algues, de mousse etc; ② (on liquid) mousse f; ③ (on bath) crasse f; **they're the ~ of the earth** ce sont des moins que rien

scurf /skɜːf/ n (dandruff) pellicules fpl; (dead skin) peau f morte

scurrilous /'skʌrɪləs/ adj calomnieux/-ieuse

scurry /'skʌrɪ/
A n (tjrs sg) **the ~ of feet** le bruit de pas rapides
B vi (prét, pp **-ried**) se précipiter; **to ~ to and fro** courir dans tous les sens; **to ~ away**, **to ~ off** se sauver

scuttle /'skʌtl/
A n ① (hatch) écoutille f; ② ▸ **coal scuttle**
B vtr lit saborder [ship]; fig faire échouer
C vi **to ~ away** ou **off** filer; **to ~ across sth** traverser qch à toute vitesse

scythe /saɪð/
A n faux f inv
B vtr faucher [grass]

SD n US Post abrév ▸ **South Dakota**

SDLP n Pol (in Ireland) (abrév = **Social Democratic and Labour Party**) SDLP m

SE ▸ p. 1089 n (abrév = **southeast**) SE m

sea /siː/ ▸ p. 1049
A n ① gen mer f; **beside** ou **by the ~** au bord de la mer; **the open ~** le large; **to be at ~** être en mer; **once out to ~** une fois en pleine mer; **to put (out) to ~**, **to go to ~** prendre la mer; **a long way out to ~** très loin de la côte; **by ~** [travel] en bateau; [send] par bateau; **to bury sb at ~** immerger le corps de qn; ② (as career) **to go to ~** (join Navy) s'engager dans la marine; (join ship) se faire engager comme marin; ③ (sailor's life) **the ~** la vie de marin; ④ fig **a ~ of** une nuée de [faces]
B **seas** npl **the heavy ~s** la tempête; **to sink in heavy ~s** couler par gros temps
C noun modifier [air, breeze] marin; [bird, water] de mer; [crossing, voyage] par mer; [battle] naval; [creature] de la mer; [power] maritime

(Idioms) **to be all at ~** être complètement perdu; **to get one's ~ legs** s'habituer au roulis

sea: **~ anemone** n anémone f de mer; **~ bass** n loup m de mer; **~bed** n fonds mpl marins; **~board** n côte f; **~ bream** n dorade f; **~ captain** ▸ p. 1123 n capitaine m de la marine marchande; **~ change** n transformation f radicale; **~ defences** GB, **~ defenses** US npl digues fpl; **~ dog** n (vieux) loup m de mer; **~ dumping** n déversement m de déchets en mer

seafaring /'siːfeərɪŋ/ adj [nation] de marins; **my ~ days** ma vie de marin; **a ~ man** un marin

seafood /'siːfuːd/
A n fruits mpl de mer
B noun modifier [dish] de fruits de mer; [sauce] aux fruits de mer

sea: **~front** n front m de mer; **~-green** ▸ p. 752 n, adj vert (m) d'eau inv; **~gull** n mouette f; **~ horse** n hippocampe m; **~kale** n chou m marin

seal /siːl/
A n ① Zool phoque m; ② Jur, gen (insignia) sceau m; **to set one's ~ on** lit apposer son cachet sur; fig conclure; **to set the ~ on** sceller [friendship]; confirmer [trend, regime]; **to give sth one's ~ of approval** approuver qch; **look for our ~ of quality** exigez le label de qualité; ③ (to keep intact) (on

Seasons

■ *French never uses capital letters for names of seasons as English sometimes does.*

spring　　　　**in spring**
= le printemps　　= au printemps

summer　　　　**in summer**
= l'été *m*　　　　= en été

autumn *or* **fall**　　**in autumn** *or* **fall**
= l'automne *m*　　　= en automne

winter　　　　**in winter**
= l'hiver *m*　　　　= en hiver

■ *In the following examples,* summer *and* été *are used as models for all the season names. French normally uses the definite article, whether or not English does.*

I like summer *or* **I like the summer**
= j'aime l'été

during the summer
= pendant l'été *or* au cours de l'été

in early summer
= au début de l'été

in late summer
= à la fin de l'été

for the whole summer
= pendant tout l'été

throughout the summer
= tout au long de l'été

last summer
= l'été dernier

next summer
= l'été prochain

the summer before last
= il y a deux ans en été

the summer after next
= dans deux ans en été

■ *However, words like* chaque, ce *etc. may replace the definite article:*

every summer　　　**this summer**
= tous les ans en été　= cet été

■ *There is never any article when en is used:*

in summer　　　　**until summer**
= en été　　　　　　= jusqu'en été

....

Seasons used as adjectives with other nouns

■ *De alone, without article, is the usual form, e.g.*

summer clothes　　　**a summer evening**
= des vêtements d'été　= un soir d'été

the summer collection　**a summer landscape**
= la collection d'été　　= un paysage d'été

the summer sales　　　**summer weather**
= les soldes d'été　　　= un temps d'été

a summer day
= une journée d'été

---

container) plomb *m*; (on package, letter) cachet *m*; (on door) scellés *mpl*; ④ (closure) fermeture *f*
B *vtr* ① cacheter [*letter*]; ② (close) sceller [*oil well, pipe*]; boucher [*gap*]; ③ (make airtight, watertight) fermer [qch] hermétiquement [*jar, tin*]; ④ fig sceller [*alliance*] (**with** par); conclure [*deal*] (**with** par); **to ~ sb's fate** décider du sort de qn
C sealed *pp adj* [*envelope*] cacheté; [*door*] scellé; [*orders*] sous pli cacheté; [*jar*] fermé hermétiquement
(Phrasal verbs)
■ **seal in** conserver [*flavour*]
■ **seal off**: ▸ ~ **[sth] off**, ~ **off [sth]** ① (isolate) isoler; ② (cordon off) gen boucler; barrer [*street*]
■ **seal up**: ▸ ~ **[sth] up**, ~ **up [sth]** fermer [qch] hermétiquement [*jar*]; boucher [*gap*]

sea lane *n* couloir *m* de navigation

sealant /'si:lənt/ *n* (coating) enduit *m* d'étanchéité; (filler) mastic *m*

seal cull, **seal culling** *n* massacre *m* des phoques

sea level *n* niveau *m* de la mer

sealing wax *n* cire *f* à cacheter

sea lion *n* lion *m* de mer

sealskin /'si:lskɪn/
A *n* peau *f* de phoque
B *noun modifier* [*coat, gloves*] en peau de phoque

seam /si:m/
A *n* ① (in garment) couture *f*; **to be bursting at the ~s** [*building*] être bondé; [*suitcase*] être plein à craquer; **to come apart at the ~** lit craquer; fig s'écrouler; ② (of coal) veine *f*
B *vtr* (in sewing) coudre

seaman /'si:mən/ ▸ p. 1123 *n* (*pl* **-men**) Mil Naut matelot *m*; (amateur) marin *m*

seamed /si:md/ *adj* [*stockings, tights*] à coutures

sea: ~ **mile** *n* mille *m* marin; ~ **mist** *n* brume *f*

seamless /'si:mlɪs/ *adj* [*garment, cloth*] sans coutures; [*transition*] sans heurts; [*process, whole*] continu

seamy /'si:mɪ/ *adj* [*scandal*] sordide; [*area*] malfamé

seance /'seɪɑ:ns/ *n* séance *f* de spiritisme

seaplane *n* hydravion *m*

sear /sɪə(r)/ *vtr* (scorch) calciner; (seal) cautériser [*wound*]; saisir [*meat*]; (wither) flétrir

search /sɜ:tʃ/
A *n* ① (seeking) recherches *fpl* (**for sb/sth** pour retrouver qn/qch); **in ~ of** à la recherche de; ② (examination) fouille *f* (**of** de); **to carry out a ~ of sth** fouiller qch; ③ Comput recherche *f*
B *vtr* ① (examine) gen fouiller; fouiller dans [*cupboard, drawer, memory*]; ② (scrutinize) examiner (attentivement) [*page, map, records*]; ~ **me**⊙! aucune idée!, j'en sais rien⊙!; ③ Comput rechercher dans [*file*]
C *vi* ① (seek) chercher; **to ~ for** *ou* **after sb/sth** chercher qn/qch; ② (examine) **to ~ through** fouiller dans [*cupboard, bag*]; examiner [*records, file*]; ③ Comput **to ~ for** rechercher [*data, item, file*]
(Phrasal verbs)
■ **search about**, **search around** chercher
■ **search out**: ▸ ~ **[sb/sth] out**, ~ **out [sb/sth]** découvrir

search-and-replace *n* Comput chercher-remplacer *m*

search engine *n* Comput moteur *m* de recherche

searcher /'sɜ:tʃə(r)/ *n* sauveteur/-euse *m/f*

searching /'sɜ:tʃɪŋ/ *adj* [*look, question*] pénétrant

search: ~**light** *n* projecteur *m*; ~ **party** *n* équipe *f* de secours; ~ **warrant** *n* Jur mandat *m* de perquisition

searing /'sɪərɪŋ/ *adj* [*heat*] incandescent; [*pace, pain*] fulgurant; [*criticism, indictment*] virulent

sea: ~ **route** *n* voie *f* maritime; ~ **salt** *n* Culin sel *m* de mer; Ind sel *m* marin; ~**shell** *n* coquillage *m*; ~**shore** *n* (part of coast) littoral *m*; (beach) plage *f*

seasick /'si:sɪk/ *adj* **to be** *ou* **get** *ou* **feel ~** avoir le mal de mer

seasickness /'si:sɪknɪs/ *n* mal *m* de mer

seaside /'si:saɪd/
A *n* **the ~** le bord de la mer
B *noun modifier* [*holiday*] à la mer; [*hotel*] en bord de mer; [*town*] maritime; ~ **resort** station *f* balnéaire

season /'si:zn/
A *n* ① (time of year) saison *f*; **strawberries are in/out of ~** c'est/ce n'est pas la saison des fraises; **out of ~** hors

saison; **late in the** ~ dans l'arrière-saison; **the holiday** ~ la période des vacances; **a** ~ **of French films** un cycle du cinéma français; **2** (festive period) **the Christmas** ~ la période de Noël; **Season's greetings!** (on Christmas cards) Joyeuses fêtes!

B *vtr* **1** Culin (with spices) relever; (with condiments) assaisonner; ~ **with salt and pepper** salez et poivrez; **2** Tech sécher [*timber*]; abreuver [*cask*]

seasonal /'si:zənl/ *adj* gen saisonnier/-ière; [*fruit, produce*] de saison

seasonally /'si:zənəlɪ/ *adv* selon la saison; ~ **adjusted figures** Fin chiffres *mpl* corrigés en fonction des variations saisonnières

seasoned /'si:znd/ *adj* **1** [*timber*] bien séché; **2** fig [*soldier*] aguerri; [*traveller*] grand (*before n*); [*politician, leader*] chevronné; [*campaigner, performer*] expérimenté; **3** Culin [*dish*] assaisonné; **highly** ~ relevé, épicé; **4** [*wine*] vieilli en fût

seasoning /'si:znɪŋ/ *n* Culin assaisonnement *m*

season: ~ **ticket** *n* (for travel) carte *f* d'abonnement; Sport, Theat abonnement *m*; ~ **ticket holder** *n* (for travel) détenteur/-trice *m/f* de carte d'abonnement; Sport, Theat abonné/-e *m/f*

seat /si:t/
A *n* **1** (allocated place) place *f*; **has everybody got a** ~? est-ce que tout le monde est assis?; **take** *ou* **have a** ~ asseyez-vous; **2** Pol siège *m*; **safe/marginal** ~ siège sûr/menacé; **to have a** ~ **on the council** siéger au conseil; **3** (type, object) gen, Aut siège *m*; (bench-type) banquette *f*; **the back** ~ la banquette arrière; **sit in the front** ~ assieds-toi à l'avant; **4** (location, centre) siège *m*; ~ **of government/learning** siège du gouvernement/savoir; **5** (residence) résidence *f* familiale; **6** (on horse) **to have a good** ~ avoir une bonne assiette; **7** euph postérieur *m*; **8** (of trousers) fond *m*

B **-seat** *combining form* **a 150-**~ **plane/cinema** un avion/cinéma de 150 places

C *vtr* **1** (assign place to) placer [*person*]; **2** **the car** ~**s five** c'est une voiture à cinq places; **the table** ~**s six** c'est une table de six couverts; **the room** ~**s 30 people** la salle peut accueillir 30 personnes

D *v refl* **to** ~ **oneself** prendre place (**at** à)

E **seated** *pp adj* assis

(Idiom) **to take/occupy a back** ~ fig se mettre/se tenir en retrait

seatbelt *n* ceinture *f* (de sécurité)

-seater /'si:tə(r)/ *combining form* **a two-**~ (plane) un avion *m* à deux places; (car) un coupé; (sofa) un (canapé) deux places; **all-**~ **stadium** GB stade *m* sans places debout

seating /'si:tɪŋ/
A *n* (chairs) sièges *mpl*; (places) places *fpl* assises; **to introduce extra** ~ ajouter plus de sièges; **I'll organize the** ~ je placerai les gens

B *noun modifier* ~ **capacity** nombre *m* de places assises; ~ **plan** plan *m* de table

sea: ~ **trout** *n* truite *f* de mer; ~ **urchin** *n* oursin *m*; ~ **view** *n* vue *f* sur la mer; ~**wall** *n* digue *f*

seaward /'si:wəd/
A *adj* [*side of building*] qui donne sur la mer; [*side of cape*] qui fait face au large
B *adv* (*also* ~**s**) [*fly, move*] vers la mer; [*gaze*] vers le large

sea: ~**weed** *n* algue *f* marine; ~**worthy** *adj* [*ship, vessel*] en état de naviguer

sec /sek/ *n* **1** (*abrév écrite* = **second**) s; **2** °(short instant) instant *m*

secateurs /ˌsekə'tɜːz, 'sekətɜːz/ *npl* GB sécateur *m*

secede /sɪ'si:d/ *vi* faire sécession (**from** de)

secession /sɪ'seʃn/ *n* sécession *f* (**from** de)

secluded /sɪ'klu:dɪd/ *adj* retiré

seclusion /sɪ'klu:ʒn/ *n* isolement *m* (**from** à l'écart de)

second ▸ p. 745, p. 1044, p. 788

A /'sekənd/ *n* **1** (unit of time) also Mus, Math, Phys seconde *f*; (instant) instant *m*; **they should arrive any** ~ **now** ils devraient arriver d'un instant à l'autre; **at six o'clock to the** ~ à six heures pile; **2** (ordinal number) deuxième *mf*, second/-e *m/f*; **X was the most popular in the survey, but Y came a close** ~ dans le sondage X était le plus populaire mais Y suivait de près; **he came a poor** ~ il est arrivé deuxième, mais loin derrière le premier; **the problem of crime was seen as** ~ **only to unemployment** le problème

du crime venait juste derrière le chômage; **3** (date) **the** ~ **of May** le deux mai; **4** GB Univ **upper/lower** ~ ≈ licence *f* avec mention bien/assez bien; **5** (*also* ~ **gear**) Aut deuxième *f*, seconde *f*; **6** (defective article) article *m* qui a un défaut; **7** (in boxing) soigneur *m*; (in duel) témoin *m*

B °**seconds** /'sekəndz/ *npl* rab° *m*

C /'sekənd/ *adj* deuxième, second; **the** ~ **teeth** les dents définitives; **every** ~ **Monday** un lundi sur deux; **to have** *ou* **take a** ~ **helping (of sth)** reprendre (de qch); **to have a** ~ **chance to do sth** avoir une nouvelle chance de faire; **to ask for a** ~ **opinion** (from doctor) demander l'opinion d'un autre médecin

D /'sekənd/ *adv* **1** (in second place) deuxième; **to come** *ou* **finish** ~ (in race, competition) arriver deuxième; **I agreed to speak** ~ j'ai accepté de parler le deuxième; **the** ~ **biggest building** le deuxième bâtiment de par sa grandeur; **the fact that he's my father comes** ~ le fait qu'il soit mon père est secondaire; **2** (*also* **secondly**) deuxièmement

E *vtr* **1** /'sekənd/ appuyer [*motion, proposal*]; **2** /sɪ'kɒnd/ Mil, Comm détacher (**from** de; **to** à)

(Idioms) **to be** ~ **nature** être automatique; **to be** ~ **to none** être sans pareil; **to do sth without (giving it) a** ~ **thought** faire qch sans réfléchir; **on** ~ **thoughts** à la réflexion; **to have** ~ **thoughts** avoir quelques hésitations *ou* doutes; **to have** ~ **thoughts about doing** avoir moins envie de faire

secondary /'sekəndrɪ, US -derɪ/
A *n* Med métastase *f*
B *adj* gen, Ling, Psych, Sch secondaire; [*sense, meaning*] dérivé; ~ **to sth** moins important que qch

secondary: ~ **health care** *n* ≈ soins *mpl* hospitaliers; ~ **infection** *n* surinfection *f*; ~ **modern (school)** *n* GB ≈ collège *m* d'enseignement général

secondary school *n* ≈ école *f* secondaire

ⓘ **Secondary schools** Plusieurs types d'établissements dispensent un enseignement secondaire au Royaume-Uni:
Comprehensive schools : écoles publiques mixtes où la scolarité est gratuite. Elles représentent environ 85% des établissements secondaires.
Grammar schools : écoles publiques ou privées, rarement mixtes. Les élèves y sont généralement admis à l'issue d'un examen d'entrée.
Public schools (*private schools* en Écosse): écoles privées qui sont généralement des internats. Les frais de scolarité y sont très élevés, mais elles accordent parfois des bourses d'études.
Secondary modern schools (Hist): écoles publiques à orientation plus technique que les précédentes.
▸ **Public schools**

second ballot *n* second tour *m*, deuxième tour *m* (du scrutin)

second best
A *n* pis-aller *m*; **as a** ~, **I suppose it will do** je suppose que faute de mieux, cela fera l'affaire
B *adv* **he came off** GB *ou* **out** US ~ il a été largement battu

second chamber *n* chambre *f* haute

second class
A *n* **1** (for post) ≈ acheminement *m* lent; **2** Rail deuxième classe *f*
B **second-class** *adj* **1** (for post) au tarif lent; **2** Rail deuxième classe; **3** GB Univ ~ **degree** ≈ licence *f* obtenue avec mention assez bien; **4** (second rate) de qualité inférieure; ~ **citizen** citoyen/-enne *m/f* de seconde zone
C *adv* [*travel*] en deuxième classe; [*send*] au tarif lent

second: ~ **cousin** *n* cousin/-e *m/f* issu/-e de germains; ~ **degree** *n* Univ ≈ diplôme *m* de troisième cycle

seconder /'sekəndə(r)/ *n* personne *f* qui appuie une motion

second-guess° /ˌsekənd'ges/ *vtr* anticiper

second hand
A /'sekəndhænd/ *n* (on watch, clock) trotteuse *f*
B **second-hand** /ˌsekənd'hænd/ *adj* [*clothes, car, goods*] d'occasion; [*market*] de l'occasion; [*news, information, report*] de seconde main; [*opinion*] d'emprunt; ~ **dealer** vendeur/-euse *m/f* d'objets d'occasion; ~ **car dealer** *ou* **salesman** vendeur/-euse *m/f* de voitures d'occasion; ~ **value** valeur *f* à la revente
C *adv* [*buy*] d'occasion; [*hear*] indirectement

second in command ▸ p. 1123 *n* Mil commandant *m* en second; gen second *m*, adjoint *m*

secondly /'sekəndlɪ/ *adv* deuxièmement

secondment /sɪ'kɒndmənt/ *n* **on** ~ en détachement

second name *n* [1] (surname) nom *m* de famille; [2] (second forename) deuxième prénom *m*

second: ~**-rate** *adj* gen de second ordre; [*product*] de qualité inférieure; ~ **sight** *n* double vue *f*

secrecy /'si:krəsɪ/ *n* secret *m*; **why all the** ~**?** pourquoi tous ces secrets?; **she's been sworn to** ~ on lui a fait jurer le secret; **an air of** ~ un air de mystère

secret /'si:krɪt/

A *n* [1] (unknown thing) secret *m*; **to tell sb a** ~ confier un secret à qn; **to let sb in on a** ~ mettre qn dans le secret; **I make no** ~ **of my membership of the party** je ne fais pas mystère de mon appartenance au parti; **it's an open** ~ **that** tout le monde sait que; **there's no** ~ **about who** tout le monde sait qui; [2] (ideal method) secret *m* (**of** de)

B *adj* gen secret/-ète; [*contributor*] anonyme; **to keep sth** ~ **from sb** cacher qch à qn; **to be a** ~ **drinker** boire en cachette

C **in secret** *adv phr* gen en secret

secretarial /ˌsekrə'teərɪəl/ *adj* [*course, skills, work*] de secrétaire; [*college, staff*] de secrétariat

secretariat /ˌsekrə'teərɪət/ *n* secrétariat *m*

secretary /'sekrətrɪ, US -rəterɪ/ ▸ p. 1181 *n* [1] Admin secrétaire *mf* (**to sb** de qn); [2] GB Pol **Foreign/Home Secretary** ministre *m* des Affaires étrangères/de l'Intérieur; **Secretary of State for the Environment** ministre *m* de l'Environnement; [3] US Pol **Defense Secretary** ministre *m* de la Défense; **Secretary of State** ministre *m* des Affaires étrangères

secrete /sɪ'kri:t/ *vtr* [1] Biol, Med sécréter [*fluid*]; [2] (hide) cacher

secretion /sɪ'kri:ʃn/ *n* Biol, Med sécrétion *f*

secretive /'si:krətɪv/ *adj* gen secret/-ète; [*expression, conduct*] mystérieux/-ieuse; **to be** ~ **about sth** faire un mystère de qch

secretively /'si:krətɪvlɪ/ *adv* (mysteriously) énigmatiquement; (furtively) furtivement

secretly /'si:krɪtlɪ/ *adv* secrètement

secret: ~ **police** *n* police *f* secrète; ~ **service** *n* services *mpl* secrets; **Secret Service** *n* US services *mpl* chargés de la protection du président; ~ **society** *n* société *f* secrète; ~ **weapon** *n* lit, fig arme *f* secrète

sect /sekt/ *n* secte *f*

sectarian /sek'teərɪən/ *n, adj* sectaire (*mf*)

section /'sekʃn/

A *n* [1] (part) (of train, aircraft, town, forest, area) partie *f*; (of pipe, tunnel, road, river) tronçon *m*; (of object, kit) élément *m*; (of fruit) quartier *m*; (of population, group) tranche *f*; [2] (department) gen service *m*; (of library, shop) rayon *m*; [3] (of act, bill, report) article *m*; (of newspaper) rubrique *f*; **under** ~ **24** aux termes de l'article 24; [4] (of book) passage *m* (**on** sur); (larger) partie *f* (**on** qui traite de); [5] Mil groupe *m*; [6] Biol lamelle *f*; [7] Math section *f*; [8] US (sleeping car) compartiment-couchettes *m*

B *vtr* sectionner [*document, text*]; segmenter [*computer screen*]

(Phrasal verb)

■ **section off:** ▸ ~ **off [sth]**, ~ **[sth] off** séparer [*part, area*]

sector /'sektə(r)/ *n* (all contexts) secteur *m*

secular /'sekjʊlə(r)/ *adj* [*politics, law, society, education*] laïque; [*belief, music*] profane; [*priest, power*] séculier/-ière

secularize /'sekjʊləraɪz/ *vtr* séculariser, laïciser [*society, education*]; séculariser [*church property*]

secure /sɪ'kjʊə(r)/

A *adj* [1] (not threatened) [*job, marriage, income*] stable; [*base, foundation*] solide; [*investment*] sûr; [2] [*hiding place, route*] sûr; **to be** ~ **against sth** être à l'abri de qch; [3] [*padlock, knot*] solide; [*structure, ladder*] stable; [*foothold*] sûr; [*rope*] bien attaché; [*door*] bien fermé; [4] Psych [*feeling*] de sécurité; [*background*] sécurisant; **to feel** ~ se sentir en sécurité; **to be** ~ **in the knowledge that** avoir la certitude que; [5] (fraud-proof) [*line, transaction*] sécurisé

B *vtr* [1] (procure, obtain) gen obtenir; atteindre [*objective*]; [2] (make firm, safe) bien attacher [*rope*]; bien fermer [*door*]; fixer [*wheel*]; stabiliser [*ladder*]; [3] (make safe) protéger [*house, camp*]; assurer [*position, future, job*]; [4] Fin garantir [*loan*]

securely /sɪ'kjʊəlɪ/ *adv* [1] (carefully) [*fasten, fix, tie*] solidement; [*wrap, tuck, pin*] soigneusement; [2] (safely) en sûreté; [3] fig (well and truly) bel et bien

secure unit *n* (in children's home) *section surveillée dans une maison de rééducation*; (in psychiatric hospital) quartier *m* de haute sécurité

securities /sɪ'kjʊərətɪz/ Fin

A *npl* titres *mpl*

B *noun modifier* [*company, market*] des titres

security /sɪ'kjʊərətɪ/

A *n* [1] (of person, child, financial position, investment) sécurité *f*; ~ **of employment, job** ~ sécurité de l'emploi; [2] (for site, prison, nation, VIP) sécurité *f*; **state** *ou* **national** ~ sûreté *f* de l'État; [3] (department) service *m* de sécurité; [4] (guarantee) garantie *f* (**on** sur); **to stand** ~ **for sb** se porter garant de qn; [5] Fin titre *m*

B *noun modifier* [*badge, camera, check, forces, measures*] de sécurité; [*firm, staff*] de surveillance

security: ~ **guard** ▸ p. 1181 *n* garde *m* sécurité, vigile *m*; ~ **leak** *n* fuite *f* (*d'information*); ~ **officer** ▸ p. 1181 *n* responsable *mf* de la sécurité; ~ **risk** *n* (person) danger *m* pour la sécurité; ~ **van** *n* GB fourgon *m* blindé

sedate /sɪ'deɪt/

A *adj* [*person*] posé; [*lifestyle, pace*] tranquille

B *vtr* mettre [qn] sous calmants [*patient*]

sedative /'sedətɪv/

A *n* sédatif *m*, calmant *m*

B *adj* [*effect, drug*] sédatif/-ive

sedentary /'sedntrɪ, US -terɪ/ *adj* sédentaire

sediment /'sedɪmənt/ *n* gen dépôt *m*; (in wine) lie *f*

seduce /sɪ'dju:s, US -'du:s/ *vtr* [1] (sexually) [*person*] séduire; [2] fig [*idea, project etc*] tenter; **to be** ~**d into doing** se laisser convaincre de faire

seduction /sɪ'dʌkʃn/ *n* [1] (act of seducing) séduction *f*; [2] (attractive quality) attrait *m* (**of** de)

seductive /sɪ'dʌktɪv/ *adj* [*person*] séduisant; [*argument, proposal*] alléchant; [*smile*] aguicheur/-euse

see /si:/

A *n* (of bishop) évêché *m*; (of archbishop) archevêché *m*

B *vtr* (*prét* **saw**; *pp* **seen**) [1] (perceive, look at) voir; **there's nobody to be seen** il n'y a personne en vue; **there was going to be trouble: I could** ~ **it coming** *ou* **I could** ~ **it a mile off** il allait y avoir des problèmes: je le sentais venir; **I don't know what you** ~ **in him**° je ne sais pas ce que tu lui trouves°; **I must be** ~**ing things!** j'ai des visions!; **to** ~ **one's way (clear) to doing sth** trouver le moyen de faire qch; [2] (visit) voir [*expert, country, building*]; **I'm** ~**ing a psychiatrist** je vais chez un psychiatre; **to** ~ **the sights** faire du tourisme; **they** ~ **a lot of each other** ils se voient souvent; ~ **you**°! salut!°; ~ **you next week**°! à la semaine prochaine!; **he's** ~**ing a married woman** il fréquente une femme mariée; [3] (receive) recevoir; [4] (understand) voir [*advantage, problem*]; comprendre [*joke*]; **do you** ~ **what I mean?** tu vois ce que je veux dire?; [5] (consider) voir; **to** ~ **sb as** considérer qn comme [*leader, hero*]; **I** ~ **it as an opportunity** je pense que c'est une occasion à saisir; **I** ~ **it as an insult** je prends ça pour une insulte; **it can be seen from this example that** cet exemple nous montre que; **it remains to be seen whether** *ou* **if** reste à voir si; [6] (envisage) **I can't** ~ **sb/sth doing** je ne pense pas que qn/qch puisse faire; **I can** ~ **a time when this country will be independent** je peux imaginer qu'un jour ce pays sera indépendant; [7] (make sure) **to** ~ **(to it) that** veiller à ce que (+ *subj*); [8] (witness) voir; (experience) connaître [*poverty, war*]; **next year will** ~ **the completion of the road** la route sera terminée l'année prochaine; [9] (accompany) **to** ~ **sb to the station** accompagner qn à la gare; **to** ~ **sb home** raccompagner qn chez lui/elle

C *vi* (*prét* **saw**; *pp* **seen**) [1] (with eyes) voir; **I can't** ~ je ne vois rien; ~ **for yourself** voyez vous-même; **so I** ~ c'est ce que je vois; **you can** ~ **for miles** on y voit à des kilomètres; [2] (understand) voir; **now I** ~ maintenant, je comprends; **as far as I can** ~ autant que je puisse en juger; [3] (check, find out) **I'll go and** ~ je vais voir; **we'll just have to wait and** ~ il ne nous reste plus qu'à attendre; [4] (think, consider) **I'll have to** ~ il faut que je réfléchisse; **let's** ~, **let me** ~ voyons (un peu)

D *v refl* (*prét* **saw**; *pp* **seen**) **to** ~ **oneself** lit, fig se voir; **I can't** ~ **myself as** *ou* **being...** je ne pense pas que je vais être...

Ⓘdioms **I'll ~ you right**○ je ne te laisserai pas tomber○; **now I've seen it all!** j'aurai tout vu!

Ⓟhrasal verbs

■ **see about**: ▶ **~ about [sth]** s'occuper de; **we'll soon ~ about that**○! iron c'est ce qu'on va voir!; **to ~ about doing** penser à faire

■ **see off**: ▶ **~ [sb] off, ~ [off] sb** ①▸ (say goodbye to) dire au revoir à qn; ②▸ (throw out) **the drunk was seen off the premises** on a mis l'ivrogne à la porte

■ **see out**: ▶ **~ [sth] out, ~ out [sth] we have enough coal to ~ the winter out** nous avons assez de charbon pour passer l'hiver; ▶ **~ [sb] out** raccompagner [qn] à la porte; **I'll ~ myself out** gen je m'en vais mais ne vous dérangez pas; (in big building) je trouverai la sortie, ne vous dérangez pas

■ **see through**: ▶ **~ through [sth]** déceler [deception, lie]; **it was easy enough to ~ through the excuse** il était évident que c'était une fausse excuse; ▶ **~ through [sb]** percer [qn] à jour; ▶ **~ [sth] through** mener [qch] à bonne fin; ▶ **~ [sb] through**: **there's enough food to ~ us through the week** il y a assez à manger pour tenir toute la semaine; **this money will ~ you through** cet argent te dépannera

■ **see to**: ▶ **~ to [sth]** s'occuper de

seed /siːd/

Ⓐ n ①▸ Bot (of plant) graine f; (fruit pip) pépin m; ②▸ ₵ (for sowing) semences fpl; Culin graines fpl; **to go** ou **run to ~** lit [plant] monter en graine; fig [person] se ramollir; [organization, country] être en déclin; ③▸ fig (beginning) germes mpl; ④▸ Sport tête f de série; **the top ~** la tête de série numéro un

Ⓑ vtr ①▸ (sow) ensemencer [field, lawn] (with de); ②▸ Culin (also **deseed**) épépiner; ③▸ Sport classer [qn] tête de série; **to be ~ed sixth** ou **(number) six** être classé tête de série numéro six; **a ~ed player** une tête de série

seed: **~bed** n lit semis m; fig pépinière f; **~ box** n = **seed tray**; **~cake** n gâteau m au carvi

seedless /ˈsiːdlɪs/ adj sans pépins

seedling /ˈsiːdlɪŋ/ n plant m

seed: **~ merchant** ▸ p. 1181 n (person) grainetier/-ière m/f; **~ tray** n germoir m

seedy /ˈsiːdɪ/ adj ①▸ (shabby) [hotel, street] miteux/-euse; [person] minable; ②▸ (disreputable) [activity, person] louche; [area, club] mal famé; ③▸ ○(ill) patraque○

seeing /ˈsiːɪŋ/ conj **~ that, ~ as** étant donné que, vu que

seek /siːk/ (prét, pp **sought**)

Ⓐ vtr ①▸ (try to obtain) chercher [agreement, means, refuge, solution]; demander [advice, help, backing, redress]; **to ~ revenge** chercher à se venger; **to ~ one's fortune** chercher fortune; ②▸ (look for) [police, employer, person] rechercher

Ⓑ **-seeking** combining form en quête de; **pleasure-~ing** en quête de plaisir

Ⓒ vi **to ~ for** ou **after sth** rechercher qch

Ⓟhrasal verb

■ **seek out**: ▶ **~ out [sth/sb], ~ [sth/sb] out** aller chercher, dénicher

seeker /ˈsiːkə(r)/ n **~ after** ou **for sth** personne f en quête de qch

seem /siːm/ vi ①▸ (give impression) sembler; (less formal) avoir l'air; **he ~s to be looking for...** on dirait qu'il cherche...; **it would ~ so/not** on dirait que oui/non; **the whole house ~ed to shake** on aurait dit que toute la maison tremblait; **things are not always what they ~** les apparences sont souvent trompeuses; **how does she ~ today?** comment va-t-elle aujourd'hui?; ②▸ (have impression) **it ~s to me that** il me semble que (+ indic); **it ~s as if** ou **as though** il semble que (+ subj); **I ~ to have offended him** j'ai l'impression que je l'ai vexé; **I ~ to have forgotten my money** je crois que j'ai oublié mon argent; **it ~s hours since we left** on dirait qu'il y a des heures que nous sommes partis; **it ~ed like a good idea at the time** cela avait l'air d'une bonne idée; ③▸ (expressing criticism) **he ~s to think that...** il a l'air de croire que...; **they don't ~ to realize that...** ils n'ont pas l'air de se rendre compte que...; **what ~s to be the problem?** quel est le problème?; ④▸ (despite trying) **he can't ~ to do** on dirait qu'il n'arrive pas à faire; **I just can't ~ to do** je n'arrive pas à faire

seeming /ˈsiːmɪŋ/ adj [ease, lack] apparent

seemingly /ˈsiːmɪŋlɪ/ adv apparemment

seen /siːn/ pp ▸ see

seep /siːp/ vi suinter; **to ~ away** s'écouler; **to ~ through sth** [water, gas] s'infiltrer à travers qch; [light] filtrer à travers qch

seepage /ˈsiːpɪdʒ/ n (trickle) suintement m; (leak) (from container) fuite f; (into structure, soil) infiltration f

seesaw /ˈsiːsɔː/

Ⓐ n lit tapecul m; fig (motion) va-et-vient m inv

Ⓑ vi lit faire du tapecul; fig [price, rate] osciller

seethe /siːð/ vi ①▸ [water] bouillonner; ②▸ **to ~ with rage** bouillir de colère; ③▸ (teem) grouiller; **seething with unrest** en proie à l'agitation

see-through /ˈsiːθruː/ adj transparent

segment

Ⓐ /ˈsegmənt/ n ①▸ Anat, Comput, Ling, Zool segment m; (of orange) quartier m; ②▸ (of economy, market) secteur m; (of population, vote) part f

Ⓑ /segˈment/ vtr segmenter [market, surface]; couper [qch] en quartiers [orange]

segregate /ˈsegrɪgeɪt/ vtr ①▸ (separate) séparer (from de); ②▸ (isolate) isoler (from de)

segregated /ˈsegrəgeɪtɪd/ adj [education, parliament, society] ségrégationniste; [area, school] où la ségrégation raciale (or religieuse) est en vigueur; [facilities] séparé

segregation /ˌsegrɪˈgeɪʃn/ n (of races, religions, social groups) ségrégation f (from de); (of rivals) séparation f; (of prisoners) isolement m

seismic /ˈsaɪzmɪk/ adj sismique

seismograph /ˈsaɪzməgrɑːf, US -græf/ n sismographe m

seismology /saɪzˈmɒlədʒɪ/ n sismologie f

seize /siːz/

Ⓐ vtr ①▸ lit (take hold of) saisir; **to ~ hold of** se saisir de [person]; s'emparer de [object]; sauter sur [idea]; ②▸ fig (grasp) saisir [opportunity, moment]; prendre [initiative]; **to be ~d by** être pris de [emotion]; ③▸ Mil, Pol (capture) s'emparer de [territory, prisoner, power]; prendre [control]; ④▸ Jur saisir [arms, drugs]; appréhender [person]

Ⓑ vi [engine, mechanism] se gripper

Ⓟhrasal verbs

■ **seize on, seize upon**: ▶ **~ on [sth]** sauter sur

■ **seize up** [engine] se gripper; [limb etc] se bloquer

seizure /ˈsiːʒə(r)/ n ①▸ (taking) (of territory, installation, power) prise f; (of arms, drugs, property) saisie f; (of person) (legal) arrestation f; (illegal) capture f; (of hostage) prise f; ②▸ Med, fig attaque f

seldom /ˈseldəm/ adv rarement; **~ if ever** rarement, pour ne pas dire jamais

select /sɪˈlekt/

Ⓐ adj [group, audience] privilégié; [hotel, restaurant] chic inv, sélect; [area] chic inv, cossu; **a ~ few** seulement quelques privilégiés

Ⓑ vtr sélectionner (**from, from among** parmi)

Ⓒ **selected** pp adj [poems, letters] choisi; [candidate, country, question, materials] sélectionné; [ingredients] de premier choix; **in ~ed stores** dans certains magasins; **pilot programmes in ~ed areas** des programmes pilotes dans les zones-test

select committee n commission f d'enquête

selection /sɪˈlekʃn/

Ⓐ n gen, Sport sélection f; **to make a ~** (for purchase) faire un choix; **~s from Mozart** morceaux mpl choisis de Mozart

Ⓑ noun modifier [panel, process] de sélection

selective /sɪˈlektɪv/ adj ①▸ (positively biased) [memory, recruitment] sélectif/-ive; [admission, education] basé sur la sélection; **she should be more ~ about the friends she makes** elle devrait mieux choisir ses amis; ②▸ (negatively biased) [account, perspective] tendancieux/-ieuse; ③▸ Agric [weedkiller] sélectif/-ive; **~ breeding** sélection f artificielle (en élevage)

selector /sɪˈlektə(r)/ n ①▸ GB Sport (person) sélectionneur/-euse m/f; ②▸ Tech (device) sélecteur m

self /self/ n (pl **selves**) ①▸ gen, Psych moi m; **he's back to his old ~ again** il est redevenu lui-même; **one's better ~** le meilleur de soi/de lui/d'elle etc; ②▸ Fin (on cheque) moi-même

self: **~-acting** adj automatique; **~-addressed envelope, SAE** n enveloppe f à mon/votre etc adresse; **~-adhesive** adj autocollant; **~-analysis** n auto-analyse f; **~-apparent** adj évident; **~-appointed** adj autonommé; **~-appraisal** n auto-évaluation f;

S

∼**-assembly** adj en kit; ∼**-assessment** n auto-évaluation f (fiscale); ∼**-assurance** n assurance f

self-assured /ˌselfəˈʃɔːd, US -ˈʃʊərd/ adj plein d'assurance; **to be very** ∼ avoir beaucoup d'assurance

self: ∼**-awareness** n conscience f de soi/de lui-même etc; ∼**-belief** n confiance f en soi/en elle etc

self-catering /ˌselfˈkeɪtərɪŋ/ adj GB [flat, accommodation] meublé; ∼ **holiday** vacances fpl en location

self: ∼**-centred** GB, ∼**-centered** US adj égocentrique; ∼**-coloured** GB, ∼**-colored** US adj uni; ∼**-confessed** adj avoué; ∼**-confidence** n assurance f; ∼**-confident** adj sûr de soi/de lui etc

self-conscious /ˌselfˈkɒnʃəs/ adj ① (shy) timide; **to be** ∼ **about** sth/**about doing** être gêné par qch/de faire; ② [style, artistry] conscient; ③ (aware) conscient de ma/sa etc personne

self-consciously /ˌselfˈkɒnʃəslɪ/ adv ① (shyly) timide-ment; ② (deliberately) consciemment

self-contained /ˌselfkənˈteɪnd/ adj ① [flat] indépen-dant; [project, unit] autonome; ② [person] réservé

self: ∼**-control** n sang-froid m; ∼**-controlled** adj [person] maître/maîtresse de soi/de lui-même/d'elle-même etc; [behaviour, manner] contrôlé; ∼**-correcting** adj à système autocorrecteur; ∼**-critical** adj critique à l'égard de soi/de lui-même/d'elle-même etc; ∼**-deception** n aveuglement m à son/votre etc propre égard

self-defeating /ˌselfdɪˈfiːtɪŋ/ adj autodestructeur/-trice; **that would be** ∼ cela irait à l'encontre du but recherché

self-defence GB, **self-defense** US /ˌselfdɪˈfens/
A n gen autodéfense f; Jur légitime défense f
B noun modifier [class, instructor] d'autodéfense

self: ∼**-denial** n abnégation f; ∼**-deprecating** adj [person] qui se dénigre; [joke, manner, remark] d'autodéni-grement

self-destruct /ˌselfdɪˈstrʌkt/
A adj d'autodestruction
B vi s'autodétruire

self: ∼**-destructive** adj autodestructeur/-trice; ∼**-determination** n gen, Pol autodétermination f; ∼**-determining** adj [country] autonome; [action, move] d'autodétermination; ∼**-drive** adj GB [car, van] de loca-tion sans chauffeur; [holiday] en voiture; ∼**-educated** adj autodidacte; ∼**-effacing** adj effacé; ∼**-elected** adj lit [committee] autoélu; [leader] autoproclamé

self-employed /ˌselfɪmˈplɔɪd/
A n the ∼ (+ v pl) les travailleurs mpl indépendants
B adj indépendant; **to be** ∼ travailler à son compte

self: ∼**-employment** n travail m indépendant; ∼**-esteem** n amour-propre m; ∼**-evident** adj évi-dent; ∼**-evidently** adv de toute évidence

self-examination /ˌselfɪɡˌzæmɪˈneɪʃn/ n ① (of con-science, motives) examen m de conscience; ② Med auto-examen m

self-explanatory /ˌselfɪkˈsplænətrɪ, US -tɔːrɪ/ adj expli-cite

self-expression /ˌselfɪkˈspreʃn/ n expression f de soi/de lui-même etc; **a means of** ∼ un moyen de s'exprimer

self-financing /ˌselfˈfaɪnænsɪŋ/
A n autofinancement m
B adj autofinancé

self: ∼**-fulfilment** n accomplissement m de soi; ∼**-governing** adj autonome; ∼**-governing trust** n GB organisme médical qui gère son budget de manière auto-nome; ∼**-government** n autonomie f

self-help /ˌselfˈhelp/
A n to learn ∼ apprendre à se débrouiller seul
B noun modifier [group, scheme, meeting] d'entraide; ∼ **book** manuel m d'aide

self: ∼**-image** n image f de soi-même/de lui-même etc; ∼**-important** adj péj suffisant; ∼**-imposed** adj auto-imposé; ∼**-improvement** n ¢ progrès mpl person-nels; ∼**-induced** adj auto-infligé; ∼**-indulgence** n complaisance f; ∼**-indulgent** adj complaisant; ∼**-inflicted** adj auto-infligé; ∼**-interest** n intérêt m personnel; ∼**-interested** adj intéressé

selfish /ˈselfɪʃ/ adj égoïste (**to do** de faire)

selfishly /ˈselfɪʃlɪ/ adv égoïstement

selfishness /ˈselfɪʃnɪs/ n égoïsme m

self-knowledge n connaissance f de soi/de lui-même etc

selfless /ˈselflɪs/ adj [person] dévoué; [action, devotion] dés-intéressé

selflessly /ˈselflɪslɪ/ adv [give, donate] sans penser à soi/à lui etc

selflessness /ˈselflɪsnɪs/ n (of person) dévouement m; (of action, devotion) désintéressement m

self: ∼**-loading** adj [gun, rifle] automatique; ∼**-locking** adj à verrouillage automatique

self-made /ˌselfˈmeɪd/ adj [star, millionaire] qui s'est fait tout seul (after n); ∼ **man** self-made man m

self: ∼**-management** n Comm autogestion f; ∼**-motivated** adj très motivé; ∼**-obsessed** adj obsédé par sa/ma etc personne; ∼**-perpetuating** adj qui se perpétue (after n); ∼**-pitying** adj [person] qui s'apitoie sur son sort; ∼**-portrait** n autoportrait m; ∼**-possessed** adj [person] maître/maîtresse de soi; ∼**-possession** n maîtrise f de soi/de lui-même etc; ∼**-preservation** n autoconservation f; ∼**-proclaimed** adj autoproclamé; ∼**-raising flour** GB, ∼**-rising flour** US n farine f à gâteau; ∼**-regard** n (concern for oneself) égard m pour soi-même/lui-même etc; ∼**-regulating**, ∼**-regulatory** adj autorégulateur/-trice; ∼**-regulation** n autorégulation f; ∼**-reliant** adj autosuffisant; ∼**-representation** n (before tribunal) possibilité f de se représenter; ∼**-respect** n respect m de soi/de lui-même etc; ∼**-respecting** adj [teacher, jour-nalist, comedian] (worthy of that name) qui se respecte (after n); [person] respectueux/-euse de ma/sa etc personne; ∼**-restraint** n retenue f; ∼**-righteous** adj péj satis-fait de soi/de lui-même etc; ∼**-righteously** adv péj [say, behave] en se donnant raison; ∼**-rising flour** n US = self-raising flour; ∼**-rule** n autonomie f; ∼**-ruling** adj autonome; ∼**-sacrifice** n abnégation f; ∼**-satisfied** adj péj satisfait de soi/de lui-même etc; ∼**-sealing** adj autocollant

self-seeking /ˌselfˈsiːkɪŋ/
A n égoisme m
B adj égoïste

self-service /ˌselfˈsɜːvɪs/
A n libre-service m
B adj [cafeteria] en libre-service

self: ∼**-styled** adj autoproclamé; ∼**-sufficiency** n (all contexts) autosuffisance f; ∼**-sufficient** adj autosuffi-sant (**in** en matière de); ∼**-supporting** adj (all contexts) indépendant; ∼**-taught** adj autodidacte; ∼**-willed** adj entêté

sell /sel/
A n (deception, disappointment) déception f; **it was a real** ∼! qu'est-ce qu'on s'est fait avoir○!
B vtr (prét, pp **sold**) ① gen, Comm vendre; **to** ∼ **sth at** ou **for £5 each** vendre qch 5 livres sterling pièce; **'stamps sold here'** 'ici on vend des timbres'; **the novel has sold millions (of copies)** le roman s'est vendu à des millions d'exemplai-res; **to** ∼ **sth back** revendre qch; ② (promote sale of) faire vendre; **her name will help to** ∼ **the film** son nom aidera à promouvoir le film; ③ (put across) faire accepter, vendre péj [idea, image, policy, party]; ④ ○(cause to appear true) **to** ∼ **sb sth, to** ∼ **sth to sb** faire avaler○ qch à qn [lie, story, excuse]; ⑤ (betray) trahir
C vi (prét, pp **sold**) ① [person, shop, dealer] vendre; '∼ **by June 27'** 'date limite de vente: 27 juin'; ② [goods, product, house, book] se vendre; **the new model is/isn't** ∼**ing (well)** le nouveau modèle se vend bien/mal
D v refl (prét, pp **sold**) ① (prostitute oneself) **to** ∼ **oneself** lit, fig se vendre (**to** à; **for** pour); ② (put oneself across) **to** ∼ **oneself** se vendre○

(Idiom) **to be sold on** être emballé○ par [idea, person]

(Phrasal verbs)

■ **sell off**: ▸ ∼ ∼ [sth] off, ∼ off [sth] gen liquider; (in sale) solder

■ **sell out**: ▸ ∼ out ① gen, Comm [merchandise] se vendre; **we've sold out of tickets** tous les billets ont été vendus; **sorry, we've sold out** désolé, mais nous avons tout vendu; ② Theat **the play has sold out** la pièce affiche complet; ③ Fin vendre ses parts (**to** à); ④ ○(betray one's principles) retourner sa veste; ▸ ∼ [sth] out, ∼ out [sth] ① gen, Comm

the concert is sold out le concert affiche complet; **2**▸ Fin vendre

■ **sell up**: ▸ ~ **up** vendre (tout)

sell-by date *n* date *f* limite de vente

seller /'selə(r)/ *n* **1** (person) vendeur/-euse *m/f*; **2** **it's a good/poor** ~ cela se vend bien/mal

seller's market *n* Fin marché *m* à la hausse; Comm marché *m* où la demande est forte

selling /'selɪŋ/
A *n* **¢** vente *f*; **telephone** ~ vente par téléphone
B *noun modifier* [*cost, price, rate*] de vente

selling: ~**-off** *n* (of company, assets) liquidation *f*; (of stock) écoulement *m*; ~ **point** *n* (all contexts) argument *m* de vente

Sellotape® /'seləʊteɪp/
A *n* scotch® *m*
B **sellotape** *vtr* scotcher

sellout /'selaʊt/
A *n* **1** **the show was a** ~ le spectacle affichait complet; **the product has been a** ~ le produit s'est très bien vendu; **2** ᴼ(betrayal) revirement *m*
B *noun modifier* [*concert, performance, production*] à guichets fermés

selvage, selvedge /'selvɪdʒ/ *n* lisière *f*

selves /selvz/ *pl* ▸ **self**

semantic /sɪ'mæntɪk/ *adj* sémantique

semantics /sɪ'mæntɪks/
A *n* (subject) (+ *v sg*) sémantique *f*
B *npl* (meaning) (+ *v pl*) sémantique *f*

semblance /'sembləns/ *n* semblant *m*; **to maintain a** ~ **of composure** garder un air dégagé

semi /'semɪ/
A ᴼ*n* **1** GB (house) maison *f* jumelée; **2** US Aut semi-remorque *f*
B **semi+** *combining form* **1** (half) semi-, demi-; **2** (partly) plus ou moins

semi: ~**automatic** *n, adj* semi-automatique (*m*); ~**autonomous** *adj* semi-autonome; ~**basement** *n* GB ≈ rez-de-jardin *m inv*; ~**circle** *n* demi-cercle *m*; ~**circular** *adj* semi-circulaire; ~**colon** *n* point-virgule *m*; ~**conscious** *adj* à peine conscient; ~**darkness** *n* pénombre *f*, demi-jour *m*; ~**-detached (house)** *n* maison *f* jumelée; ~**final** *n* demi-finale *f*; ~**finalist** *n* demi-finaliste *mf*

seminal /'semɪnl/ *adj* (major) déterminant

seminar /'semɪnɑː(r)/ *n* séminaire *m* (**on** sur)

semiotics /ˌsemɪ'ɒtɪks/ *n* (+ *v sg*) sémiotique *f*

semi: ~**precious** *adj* semi-précieux/-ieuse; ~**skilled** *adj* [*work*] d'ouvrier spécialisé; [*worker*] spécialisé; ~**skimmed** *adj* demi-écrémé

Semitic /sɪ'mɪtɪk/ *adj* **1** gen sémite; **2** Ling sémitique

semitone *n* Mus demi-ton *m*

semolina /ˌsemə'liːnə/ *n* semoule *f*

Sen **1** *abrév écrite* = **senator**; **2** *abrév écrite* = **senior**

senate /'senɪt/ *n* **1** Pol, Hist sénat *m*; **2** Univ conseil *m* (d'université)

senator /'senətə(r)/ ▸ **p. 869** *n* sénateur *m* (**for** de)

send /send/ *vtr* (*prét, pp* **sent**) **1** (dispatch) envoyer; **to** ~ **sth to sb, to** ~ **sb sth** envoyer qch à qn; **they'll** ~ **a car for you** ils enverront une voiture vous chercher; **to** ~ **sb home** (from school, work) renvoyer qn chez lui/elle; **to** ~ **sb to prison** mettre qn en prison; ~ **her my love!** embrasse-la de ma part; ~ **them my regards** transmettez-leur mes amitiés; **to** ~ **word that** faire dire que; **2** (cause to move) **the noise sent people running** le bruit a fait courir les gens; **to** ~ **share prices soaring** faire monter le cours des actions; **to** ~ **shivers down sb's spine** donner froid dans le dos à qn; **3** (cause to become) **to** ~ **sb mad** rendre qn fou; **to** ~ **sb into a rage** mettre qn dans une rage folle; **to** ~ **sb to sleep** endormir qn

(Idioms) **to** ~ **sb packing**ᴼ, **to** ~ **sb about her/his business**ᴼ envoyer balader qnᴼ

(Phrasal verbs)

■ **send around** US = **send round**
■ **send away**: ▸ ~ **away for [sth]** commander [qch] par correspondance; ▸ ~ **[sb/sth] away** faire partir; ▸ **to** ~ **a child away to boarding school** envoyer un enfant en pension

■ **send down**: ▸ ~ **[sb/sth] down**, ~ **down [sb/sth]** envoyer; ~ **him down to the second floor** dites-lui de descendre au deuxième étage; ▸ ~ **[sb] down** **1** GB Univ renvoyer [qn] de l'université; **2** ᴼGB envoyer qn en prison

■ **send for**: ▸ ~ **for [sb/sth]** appeler [*doctor, taxi, plumber*]; demander [*reinforcements*]

■ **send in**: ▸ ~ **[sb/sth] in**, ~ **in [sb/sth]** envoyer [*letter, form, troops*]; faire entrer [*visitor*]; **to** ~ **in one's application** poser sa candidature

■ **send off**: ▸ ~ **off for [sth]** commander [qch] par correspondance; ▸ ~ **[sth] off**, ~ **off [sth]** (post) expédier; ▸ ~ **[sb] off**, ~ **off [sb]** Sport expulser; ▸ ~ **[sb] off to** envoyer [qn] à

■ **send on**: ▸ ~ **[sb] on (ahead)** (as scout) envoyer [qn] en éclaireur; ~ **him on ahead to open up the shop** dites-lui de partir devant ouvrir le magasin; ▸ ~ **[sth] on**, ~ **on [sth]** (send in advance) expédier [qch] à l'avance; (forward) faire suivre

■ **send out**: ▸ ~ **out for [sth]** envoyer quelqu'un chercher; ▸ ~ **[sth] out**, ~ **out [sth]** **1** (post) envoyer; **2** émettre [*light*]; ▸ ~ **[sb] out** faire sortir [*pupil*]; **to** ~ **sb out for** envoyer qn chercher

■ **send round** GB: ▸ ~ **[sb/sth] round**, ~ **round [sb/sth]** **1** (circulate) faire circuler; **2** (cause to go) envoyer

■ **send up**: ▸ ~ **[sth] up** (post) envoyer; ▸ ~ **[sb] up**ᴼ **1** GB (parody) parodier; **2** US (put in prison) mettre *or* envoyer [qn] en prison; ▸ ~ **[sb/sth] up**, ~ **up [sb/sth]** **1** (into space) envoyer; **2** (to upper floor) **you can** ~ **him up now** vous pouvez lui dire de monter maintenant

sender /'sendə(r)/ *n* expéditeur/-trice *m/f*

send: ~**-off** *n* adieux *mpl*; ~**-up**ᴼ *n* GB parodie *f*

senile /'siːnaɪl/ *adj* sénile also pej

senile dementia *n* démence *f* sénile

senior /'siːnɪə(r)/
A *n* **1** (older person) aîné/-e *m/f*; **to be sb's** ~ **by ten years** avoir dix ans de plus que qn; **to be sb's** ~ être plus âgé que qn; **2** (superior) supérieur/-e *m/f*; **3** GB Sch élève *mf* dans les grandes classes; **4** US Sch élève *mf* de terminale; **5** US Univ étudiant/-e *m/f* de licence; **6** Sport senior *m*
B *noun modifier* **1** Sport [*league, player*] senior; **2** US Univ [*year, prom*] de fin d'études
C *adj* **1** (older) [*person*] plus âgé; **Mr Becket** ~ M. Becket père; **2** (superior) [*person*] plus haut placé; [*civil servant, diplomat*] haut (before *n*); [*aide, employee, minister*] haut placé; [*colleague*] plus ancien/-ienne; [*figure*] prédominant; [*job, post*] supérieur; **to be** ~ **to sb** être le supérieur de qn

senior: ~ **citizen** *n* personne *f* du troisième âge; ~ **editor** ▸ **p. 1181** *n* rédacteur/-trice *m/f* en chef; ~ **executive** *n* cadre *m* supérieur; ~ **high school** *n* US Sch ≈ lycée *m*

seniority /ˌsiːnɪ'ɒrətɪ, US -'ɔːr-/ *n* **1** (in years) âge *m*; (in rank) statut *m* supérieur; **in order of** ~ par ordre hiérarchique; **2** (in years of service) ancienneté *f*

senior: ~ **management** *n* Admin direction *f*; ~ **manager** *n* cadre *m* supérieur; ~ **officer** *n* (police) officier *m* de police supérieur; Admin haut/-e fonctionnaire *m/f*; ~ **partner** *n* associé/-e *m/f* principal/-e; ~ **school** *n* GB (secondary school) lycée *m*; (for older pupils) grandes classes *fpl*; ~ **staff** *n* Admin cadres *mpl* supérieurs

sensation /sen'seɪʃn/ *n* **1** (feeling, impression, stir) sensation *f*; **to cause** *ou* **create a** ~ faire sensation. **2** ᴼ(person) **to be a** ~ être formidable

sensational /sen'seɪʃənl/ *adj* **1** gen, péj sensationnel/-elle; ~ **story/article** histoire *f*/article *m* à sensation pej; **2** ᴼ(emphatic) sensationnel/-elle

sensationalism /sen'seɪʃənəlɪzəm/ *n* gen péj recherche *f* du sensationnel

sensationalist /sen'seɪʃənəlɪst/ *adj* péj [*headline, story, writer*] à sensation pej

sensationalize /sen'seɪʃənəlaɪz/ *vtr* péj faire un reportage à sensation sur [*event, story*]

sensationally /sen'seɪʃənəlɪ/ *adv* (luridly) [*write, describe*] en dramatisant pej

sense /sens/
A *n* **1** (faculty, ability) sens *m*; ~ **of hearing** ouïe *f*; ~ **of sight** vue *f*; ~ **of smell** odorat *m*; ~ **of taste** goût *m*; ~ **of touch** toucher *m*; **to dull/sharpen the** ~**s** émousser/aiguiser les sens; **a** ~ **of direction** le sens de l'orientation; **to lose all** ~ **of time** perdre toute notion du temps; **2** (feeling) **a** ~ **of**

un sentiment de; **a ~ of purpose** le sentiment d'avoir un but; **the town has a great ~ of community** la ville a un grand sens de la communauté; [3] (practical quality) bon sens *m*; **to have more ~ than to do** avoir suffisamment de bon sens pour ne pas faire; [4] (reason) **there's no ~ in doing** cela ne sert à rien de faire; **what's the ~ in getting angry?** à quoi sert-il de se fâcher?; **to make ~ of sth** comprendre qch; **I can't make ~ of this article** je ne comprends rien à cet article; **it makes ~ to do** c'est une bonne idée de faire; **to make ~** [*sentence, film, theory*] avoir un sens; **what he said didn't make much ~ to me** ce qu'il a dit ne m'a pas semblé très logique; [5] (meaning) gen, Ling sens *m*; **in the ~ that** en ce sens que; **he is in a** *ou* **some ~ right to complain, but...** dans un certain sens il a raison de se plaindre, mais...

B senses *npl* (sanity) raison *f*; **to bring sb to his ~s** ramener qn à la raison; **to take leave of one's ~s** perdre la raison *or* l'esprit *m*

C *vtr* [1] (be aware of) deviner (**that** que); **to ~ danger** sentir un danger; [2] [*machine*] détecter

(Idioms) **to knock** *ou* **pound** US **some ~ into sb** ramener qn à la raison; **to see ~** entendre raison; **to talk ~** dire des choses sensées

senseless /'senslɪs/ *adj* [1] (pointless) [*violence*] gratuit; [*idea, discussion*] absurde; [*act, waste*] insensé; [2] (unconscious) sans connaissance; **to knock sb ~** faire perdre connaissance à qn

senselessly /'senslɪslɪ/ *adv* de manière insensée

sensible /'sensəbl/ *adj* [1] (showing common sense) [*person, attitude*] raisonnable; [*policy, solution, investment*] judicieux/-ieuse; [2] (practical) [*garment*] pratique; [*diet*] intelligent; [3] (perceptible) sensible

sensibly /'sensəblɪ/ *adv* [*eat, act, talk*] de façon raisonnable; [*dressed*] de façon pratique; [*chosen*] de façon judicieuse; **~ priced** à un prix raisonnable

sensitive /'sensətɪv/ *adj* [1] (easily affected, aware) sensible; [2] (delicate) [*situation*] délicat; [*discussions, issue, job*] difficile; [*information*] confidentiel/-ielle

sensitively /'sensətɪvlɪ/ *adv* [*speak, treat, react*] avec délicatesse; [*chosen, portrayed*] avec sensibilité

sensitivity /ˌsensə'tɪvətɪ/ *n* sensibilité *f* (**to** à)

sensitize /'sensɪtaɪz/ *vtr* (all contexts) sensibiliser

sensor /'sensə(r)/ *n* détecteur *m*

sensory /'sensərɪ/ *adj* sensoriel/-ielle; **~ deprivation** perte *f* sensorielle

sensual /'senʃʊəl/ *adj* sensuel/-elle

sensuality /ˌsenʃʊ'ælətɪ/ *n* sensualité *f*

sensuous /'senʃʊəs/ *adj* sensuel/-elle

sent /sent/ *prét, pp* ▸ **send**

sentence /'sentəns/
A *n* [1] Jur peine *f*; **to be under ~ of death** être condamné à mort; **to serve a ~** purger une peine; **to pass ~ on sb** prononcer une peine contre qn; [2] Ling phrase *f*
B *vtr* condamner (**to** à; **to do** à faire; **for** pour)

sentiment /'sentɪmənt/ *n* [1] (feeling) sentiment *m*; **public ~** le sentiment général; [2] (opinion) opinion *f*; [3] (sentimentality) gen sentimentalité *f*; pej sensiblerie *f*

sentimental /ˌsentɪ'mentl/ *adj* sentimental also pej; **to be ~ about** faire du sentiment pour [*children, animals*]; évoquer [qch] avec émotion [*past*]

sentimentality /ˌsentɪmen'tælətɪ/ *n* sentimentalité *f*; pej sensiblerie *f*

sentimentally /ˌsentɪ'mentəlɪ/ *adv* sentimentalement

sentinel /'sentɪnl/ *n* factionnaire *m*

sentry /'sentrɪ/ *n* sentinelle *f*

sentry: **~ box** *n* guérite *f*; **~ duty** *n* faction *f*

separable /'sepərəbl/ *adj* séparable (**from** de)

separate
A separates /'sepərəts/ *npl* (garments) coordonnés *mpl*
B /'sepərət/ *adj* [1] (with singular noun) [*piece, organization*] à part; [*discussion, issue, occasion*] autre; **the flat is ~ from the rest of the house** l'appartement est indépendant du reste de la maison; **a ~ appointment for each child** un rendez-vous pour chaque enfant; **under ~ cover** Post sous pli séparé; [2] (with plural noun) [*sections, discussions, problems*] différent; [*organizations, agreements, treaties*] distinct; **they have ~ rooms** ils ont chacun leur chambre; **they asked**

for ~ bills (in restaurant) ils ont demandé chacun leur addition
C /'sepərət/ *adv* keep the knives **~** rangez les couteaux séparément; **keep the knives ~ from the forks** séparez les couteaux des fourchettes
D /'sepəreɪt/ *vtr* [1] (divide) lit séparer; fig diviser; **the child became ~d from his mother** l'enfant s'est retrouvé séparé de sa mère; **to ~ the issue of pay from that of working hours** dissocier la question des salaires de celle des heures de travail; [2] (also **~ out**) (sort out) répartir [*people*]; trier [*objects*]
E /'sepəreɪt/ *vi* (all contexts) se séparer (**from** de)
F separated /'sepəreɪtɪd/ *pp adj* séparé

separately /'sepərətlɪ/ *adv* (all contexts) séparément

separation /ˌsepə'reɪʃn/ *n* gen séparation *f*

separatist /'sepərətɪst/ *n, adj* séparatiste (*mf*)

sepia /'siːpɪə/ *n* [1] ▸ p. 752 (colour) sépia *f*; [2] Zool seiche *f*

Sept abrév écrite = **September**

September /sep'tembə(r)/ ▸ p. 1020 *n* septembre *m*

septic /'septɪk/ *adj* infecté; **to go ~** s'infecter

septicaemia /ˌseptɪ'siːmɪə/ ▸ p. 933 *n* septicémie *f*

septic tank *n* fosse *f* septique

sequel /'siːkwəl/ *n* (all contexts) suite *f* (**to** à)

sequence /'siːkwəns/ *n* [1] (of problems) succession *f*; (of photos) série *f*; **the ~ of events** la suite des événements; [2] (order) ordre *m*; [3] (in film) séquence *f*; **the dream ~** la scène de rêve; [4] (dance) numéro *m* de danse; [5] Ling **~ of tenses** concordance *f* des temps; [6] Mus séquence *f*; [7] Comput, Math séquence *f*

sequential /sɪ'kwenʃl/ *adj* séquentiel/-ielle

sequin /'siːkwɪn/ *n* paillette *f*

Serbia /'sɜːbɪə/ ▸ p. 774 pr *n* Serbie *f*

Serbo-Croat(ian) /ˌsɜːbəʊ'krəʊæt, -krəʊ'eɪʃn/ ▸ p. 969 *n, adj* (language) serbo-croate (*m*)

serene /sɪ'riːn/ *adj* serein

serenity /sɪ'renətɪ/ *n* sérénité *f*

sergeant /'sɑːdʒənt/ ▸ p. 1123 *n* [1] GB Mil sergent *m*; [2] US Mil caporal-chef *m*; [3] (in police) ≈ brigadier *m*

serial /'sɪərɪəl/
A *n* [1] (story) feuilleton *m*; TV **~** feuilleton télévisé; [2] (publication) périodique *m*
B *adj* Comput [*input, printer, transfer*] série inv

serialization /ˌsɪərɪəlaɪ'zeɪʃn, US -lɪ'z-/ *n* adaptation *f* en feuilleton

serialize /'sɪərɪəlaɪz/ *vtr* adapter [qch] en feuilleton

serial killer *n* meurtrier *m* en série

serial number *n* (of machine, car etc) numéro *m* de série; US (of soldier) numéro *m* matricule

series /'sɪəriːz/ *n* (*pl* **~**) [1] gen série *f*; **a ~ of books** une collection de livres; [2] Radio, TV, Literat série *f*; **this is the last in the present ~** voici la dernière partie de ce programme; [3] Sport championnat *m* (à *plusieurs épreuves*); [4] Elec série *f*

serious /'sɪərɪəs/ *adj* [1] (not frivolous or light) [*person, expression, discussion, issue, offer, purpose*] sérieux/-ieuse; [*work, literature, actor, survey*] de qualité; [*attempt, concern*] réel/réelle; **to be ~ about sth** prendre qch au sérieux; **to be ~ about doing** avoir vraiment l'intention de faire; **is he ~ about her?** est-ce qu'il tient vraiment à elle?; **to give ~ thought to sth** penser sérieusement à qch; **you can't be ~** tu veux rire○; **being a parent is a ~ business** être parent est une grande responsabilité; **to make ~ money**○ gagner beaucoup d'argent; **if you want to do some ~ shopping**○ si tu veux vraiment faire des courses; [2] (grave) [*accident, crime, problem*] grave; [*doubt, misgiving*] sérieux/-ieuse; **this is a very ~ matter** l'affaire est très grave

seriously /'sɪərɪəslɪ/ *adv* [1] (not frivolously) sérieusement; **are you ~ suggesting that...?** tu veux vraiment dire que...?; **but ~,...** blague à part,...○; **to take sb/sth ~** prendre qn/qch au sérieux; **he takes himself too ~** il se prend trop au sérieux; [2] (gravely) [*ill, injured, at risk, flawed*] gravement; [*mislead, underestimate*] vraiment; [3] ○(extremely) vraiment

seriousness /'sɪərɪəsnɪs/ n [1] (of person, film, study, approach) sérieux m; (of tone, occasion, reply) gravité f; (of intention) sincérité f; **in all** ~ sérieusement; [2] (of illness, damage, allegation, problem, situation) gravité f

sermon /'sɜːmən/ n sermon m

seropositive /ˌsɪərəʊ'pɒzɪtɪv/ adj séropositif/-ive

serpent /'sɜːpənt/ n (all contexts) serpent m

serrated /sɪ'reɪtɪd, US 'sereɪtɪd/ adj dentelé; ~ **knife** couteau-scie m

serum /'sɪərəm/ n sérum m; **snake-bite** ~ sérum antivenimeux

servant /'sɜːvənt/ n [1] ‣ p. 1181 (in household) domestique mf; **to keep a** ~ avoir un domestique; ~ **girl** bonne f; ~**'s hall** office m; [2] fig serviteur m

serve /sɜːv/

A n Sport service m; **it's my** ~ à moi de servir; **to have a big** ~ avoir un très bon service

B vtr [1] (work for) servir [country, cause, public]; travailler au service de [employer, family]; **to** ~ **sb/sth well** rendre de grands services à qn/qch; [2] (attend to customers) servir; **are you being** ~**d?** on vous sert?; [3] Culin servir; **to** ~ **sb with sth** servir qch à qn; ~**s four** (in recipe) pour quatre personnes; [4] (provide facility) [public utility, power station, reservoir] alimenter; [public transport, library, hospital] desservir; [5] (satisfy) servir [interests]; satisfaire [needs]; [6] (function) être utile à; **this old pen has** ~**d me well** ce vieux stylo m'a été très utile; **if my memory** ~**s me well** si j'ai bonne mémoire; **to** ~ **sb as sth** servir de qch à qn; **to** ~ **a purpose** ou **function** être utile; **to** ~ **no useful purpose** ne servir à rien; **to** ~ **sth's purpose** faire l'affaire; [7] (spend time) **to** ~ **a term** Pol remplir un mandat; **to** ~ **one's time** (in prison) purger sa peine; **to** ~ **a sentence** purger une peine (de prison); **to** ~ **five years** faire cinq ans de prison; [8] Jur **to** ~ **a writ on sb** assigner qn en justice; **to** ~ **a summons on sb** citer qn à comparaître; **to** ~ **notice of sth on sb** Jur, fig signifier qch à qn; [9] Sport servir

C vi [1] (in shop, church) servir; (at table) faire le service; [2] (on committee, in government) exercer ses fonctions (**as** de); **to** ~ **on** être membre de [committee, jury]; [3] Mil servir; [4] (meet a need) faire l'affaire; **to** ~ **as sth** servir de qch; **this should** ~ **as a warning** cela devrait nous servir d'avertissement; **the photo** ~**d as a reminder to me of the holidays** la photo me rappelait les vacances; [5] Sport servir; **Bruno to** ~ au service, Bruno

(Idiom) **it** ~**s you right!** ça t'apprendra!

(Phrasal verbs)

■ **serve out: ▸** ~ **out** [sth], ~ [sth] **out** finir [term of duty]; purger [prison sentence]

■ **serve up: ▸** ~ **up** Culin servir; **▸** ~ **up** [sth], ~ [sth] **up** [1] Culin servir; **to** ~ **sth up again** resservir qch; [2] °fig, pej resservir [idea, policy]; donner [excuse]

serve-and-volley adj [player] service-volée inv

server /'sɜːvə(r)/ n [1] Sport, Comput serveur m; [2] Culin couvert m de service; [3] Relig servant m

server-managed adj Comput géré par serveur

service /'sɜːvɪs/

A n [1] (department, facility) service m; **(accident and) emergency** ~ service des urgences; **for** ~**s rendered** Comm pour services rendus; **it's all part of the** ~ (don't mention it) c'est tout naturel; (it's all included) tout est compris; **'normal** ~ **will be resumed as soon as possible'** 'dans quelques instants le suite de votre programme'; **my** ~**s don't come cheap!** je me fais payer cher!; [2] (work, period of work done) gen, Admin, Mil service m; **I'm at your** ~ je suis à votre service; **to put** ou **place sth at sb's** ~ mettre qch à la disposition de qn; **he gave his life in the** ~ **of his country** il a donné sa vie pour servir son pays; **to be in** ~ Hist travailler comme domestique; [3] Comm (customer care) service m (**to** à); **to get good/bad** ~ être bien/mal servi; **15% for** ~ 15% pour le service; [4] (from machine, vehicle, product) usage m; **to give good** ou **long** ~ [machine] fonctionner longtemps; [vehicle, product, garment] faire de l'usage; **it went out of** ~ **years ago** il n'est plus en service depuis des années; **'out of** ~**'** ou **'hors service';** (on machine) 'en panne'; [5] (transport facility) service m (**to** pour); **to run a regular** ~ assurer un service régulier; **an hourly bus/train** ~ un autobus/train toutes les heures; **the number 28 bus** ~ la ligne du 28; [6] Aut, Tech (overhaul) révision f; [7] Relig office m; **Sunday** ~ office du dimanche; **marriage** ~ cérémonie f nuptiale; [8] (crockery) service

m; [9] Sport service m; **your** ~**!** à toi de servir!; [10] (good turn) service m; **to do sb a** ~ rendre service à qn; **to be of** ~ **to sb** [person] aider qn; [thing] être utile à qn

B services npl [1] **the** ~**s** Mil, Naut les armées; [2] (on motorway) aire m de services

C noun modifier Mil [pay, pension] militaire; [personnel] de l'armée; [life] dans l'armée

D vtr [1] (overhaul) faire la révision de [vehicle]; entretenir [machine]; **to have one's car** ~**d** faire réviser sa voiture; [2] Fin payer les intérêts de [debt]

serviceable /'sɜːvɪsəbl/ adj (usable) utilisable

service area n aire f de services

service break n Sport **to have a** ~ avoir fait le break

service centre GB, **service center** US n centre m de service après-vente

service charge n [1] (in restaurant) service m; **there is a** ~ le service n'est pas compris; **what is the** ~**?** le service est de combien?; [2] (in banking) frais mpl de gestion de compte; [3] (for property maintenance) charges fpl locatives

service: ~ **company** n société f de service; ~ **contract** n Comm contrat m d'entretien; ~ **department** n (office) service m entretien; (workshop) atelier m d'entretien; ~ **elevator** n US = **service lift**; ~ **engineer** ‣ p. 1181 n technicien m de maintenance; ~ **entrance** n entrée f des fournisseurs; ~ **flat** n GB appartement m (dont le ménage est assuré par l'agence de location); ~ **game** n service m; ~ **hatch** n passe-plats m inv; ~ **industry** n (company) industrie f de services; (sector) secteur m tertiaire; ~ **lift** n GB (in hotel, building) ascenseur m de service; (for heavy goods) monte-charge m; ~**man** n militaire m; ~ **road** n GB, gen voie f d'accès; Constr voie f de service; ~ **sector** n secteur m tertiaire; ~ **station** n station-service f; ~**woman** n femme f soldat

servicing /'sɜːvɪsɪŋ/ n Aut, Tech révision f

serving /'sɜːvɪŋ/

A n (helping) portion f; **enough for four** ~**s** pour quatre personnes

B adj [officer] Mil en activité; Admin en exercice

serving: ~ **dish** n plat m (de service); ~ **hatch** n passe-plats m inv; ~ **spoon** n cuillère f de service

session /'seʃn/ n [1] Pol (term) session f; [2] Admin, Jur, Pol, gen (sitting) séance f; **emergency** ~ séance exceptionnelle; **the court is in** ~ Jur le tribunal tient séance; **to go into closed** ou **private** ~ siéger à huis clos; [3] (meeting) réunion f; (informal discussion) discussion f; **drinking** ~° beuverie f; [4] GB Sch (year) année f scolaire; US (term) trimestre m; (period of lessons) cours mpl; [5] Mus, Sport séance f; **training** ~ Sport séance d'entraînement; [6] Fin séance f; **trading** ~ séance de Bourse

set /set/

A n [1] (collection) (of keys, spanners, screwdrivers) jeu m; (of golf clubs, stamps, coins, chairs) série f; (of cutlery) service m; (of encyclopedias) collection f; fig (of data, rules, instructions, tests) série f; **a new** ~ **of clothes** des vêtements neufs; **they're sold in** ~**s of 10** ils sont vendus par lots mpl de 10; **a** ~ **of fingerprints** des empreintes fpl digitales; **a** ~ **of traffic lights** des feux mpl (de signalisation); [2] (kit, game) **a chess** ~ un jeu d'échecs; **a magic** ~ une mallette de magie; [3] (pair) **a** ~ **of sheets** une paire de draps; **a** ~ **of false teeth** un dentier; **my top/bottom** ~ (of false teeth) la partie supérieure/inférieure de mon dentier; **one** ~ **of grandparents lives in Canada** deux de mes grands-parents habitent au Canada; **both** ~**s of parents agreed with us** ses parents comme les miens étaient d'accord avec nous; [4] Sport (in tennis) set m; [5] (television) poste m; [6] (group) (social) monde m; (sporting) milieu m; **the smart** ou **fashionable** ~ les gens mpl à la mode; [7] (scenery) Theat décor m; Cin, TV plateau m; [8] Math ensemble m; [9] GB Sch (class, group) groupe m; [10] (hair-do) mise f en plis; **to have a shampoo and** ~ se faire faire un shampooing et une mise en plis

B adj [1] (fixed) (épith) [procedure, rule, task] bien déterminé; [time, price] fixe; [menu] à prix fixe; [formula] toute faite; [idea] arrêté; **I had no** ~ **purpose** je n'avais pas d'objectif précis; ~ **phrase** expression f consacrée; ~ **expression** locution f figée; **to be** ~ **in one's ideas** ou **opinions** avoir des idées bien arrêtées; **to be** ~ **in one's ways** avoir ses habitudes; **the weather is** ~ **fair** le temps est au beau fixe; [2] (stiff) [expression, smile] figé; [3] Sch, Univ (prescribed) **there are five** ~ **topics on the history syllabus** il y a cinq sujets au programme d'histoire; ④ (ready) prêt (**for** pour); **to be (all)** ～ **to leave** être prêt à partir; ⑤ (determined) **to be (dead)** ～ **against sth/doing** être tout à fait contre qch/ l'idée de faire; **he's really** ～ **against my resigning** il est tout à fait contre ma démission; **to be** ～ **on sth/on doing** tenir absolument à qch/à faire; ⑥ (firm) [*jam, honey*] épais/ épaisse; [*cement*] dur; [*yoghurt*] ferme

C vtr (*p prés* **-tt-**; *prét, pp* **set**) ① (place, position) placer [*object*]; monter [*gem*]; **to** ～ **sth before sb** lit placer qch devant qn; fig présenter qch à qn; **to** ～ **sth in the ground** enfoncer qch dans le sol; **to** ～ **sth into sth** encastrer qch dans qch; **to** ～ **sth straight** lit (align) remettre qch droit [*painting*]; fig (tidy) remettre de l'ordre dans qch; **to** ～ **sth upright** redresser qch; **a house set among the trees** une maison située au milieu des arbres; **to** ～ **matters** *ou* **the record straight** fig mettre les choses au point; **his eyes are set very close together** ses yeux sont très rapprochés; ② (prepare) mettre [*table*]; tendre [*trap*]; ～ **three places** mets trois couverts; **to** ～ **the stage** *ou* **scene for sth** fig préparer le lieu de qch; **the stage is set for the final** tout est prêt pour la finale; **to** ～ **one's mark** *ou* **stamp on sth** laisser sa marque sur qch; ③ (affix, establish) fixer [*date, deadline, place, price, target*]; lancer [*fashion, trend*]; donner [*tone*]; établir [*precedent, record*]; **to** ～ **a good/bad example to sb** montrer le bon/ mauvais exemple à qn; ～ **one's sights on** viser; ④ (adjust) mettre [qch] à l'heure [*clock*]; mettre [*alarm clock, burglar alarm, timer*]; programmer [*magnétoscope*]; **to** ～ **the oven to 180°** mettre le four sur 180°; **to** ～ **the video to record the film** programmer le magnétoscope pour enregistrer le film; ～ **your watch by mine** règle ta montre sur la mienne; **I set the heating to come on at 6 am** j'ai réglé le chauffage pour qu'il se mette en route à six heures; ⑤ (start) **to** ～ **sth going** mettre qch en marche [*machine*]; **to** ～ **sb laughing/thinking** faire rire/réfléchir qn; **to** ～ **sb to work doing** charger qn de faire; ⑥ (impose, prescribe) [*teacher*] donner [*homework, essay*]; poser [*problem*]; créer [*crossword puzzle*]; **to** ～ **an exam** préparer les sujets d'examen; **to** ～ **a book for study** mettre un texte au programme; **to** ～ **sb the task of doing** charger qn de faire; ⑦ Cin, Literat, Theat, TV situer; **to** ～ **a book in 1960/New York** situer un roman en 1960/à New York; **the film is set in Munich** le film se passe à Munich; ⑧ Mus **to** ～ **sth to music** mettre qch en musique; ⑨ (in printing) composer [*text, type*] (**in** en); ⑩ Med immobiliser [*broken bone*]; ⑪ (style) **to** ～ **sb's hair** faire une mise en plis à qn; **to have one's hair set** se faire faire une mise en plis; ⑫ (cause to harden) faire prendre [*jam, concrete*]

D vi (*p prés* **-tt-**; *prét, pp* **set**) ① [*sun*] se coucher; ② [*jam, concrete*] prendre; [*glue*] sécher; ③ Med [*fracture*] se ressouder

(Idioms) **to be well set-up** (financially) avoir les moyens○; **to make a (dead)** ～ **at sb**○ GB se lancer à la tête de qn○

(Phrasal verbs)

■ **set about**: ▶ ～ **about [sth]** se mettre à [*work, duties*]; ～ **about doing** commencer à faire; **to** ～ **about the job** *ou* **task** *ou* **business of doing** commencer à faire; **I don't know how to** ～ **about it** je ne sais pas comment m'y prendre; ▶ ～ **about [sb]**○ attaquer qn (**with** avec)

■ **set against**: ▶ ～ **[sb] against** monter qn contre; **to** ～ **oneself against sth** s'opposer à qch; ▶ ～ **sth against sth** confronter qch à qch; **the benefits seem small, set against the risks** par rapport aux risques les bénéfices semblent maigres

■ **set apart**: ▶ ～ **[sb/sth] apart** distinguer (**from** de)

■ **set aside**: ▶ ～ **[sth] aside**, ～ **aside [sth]** ① (put down) poser [qch] de côté; ② (reserve) réserver [*area, room, time*] (**for** pour); mettre [qch] de côté [*money, stock*]; ③ (disregard) mettre [qch] de côté [*differences*]; ④ Admin, Jur (reject) rejeter [*decision, verdict*]; casser [*judgment, ruling*]

■ **set back**: ▶ ～ **[sth] back** ① (position towards the rear) reculer; **the house is set back from the road** la maison est située un peu en retrait de la route; ② retarder [*clock, watch*]; ▶ ～ **back [sth]**, ～ **[sth] back** (delay) retarder; ▶ ～ **[sb] back**○ coûter les yeux de la tête à○

■ **set by**: ▶ ～ **[sth] by**, ～ **by [sth]** mettre [qch] de côté

■ **set down**: ▶ ～ **[sb/sth] down** déposer [*passenger*]; poser [*object*]; ▶ ～ **down [sth]**, ～ **[sth] down** ① (establish) fixer [*conditions*]; ② (record) enregistrer [*event, fact*]; **to** ～ **down one's thoughts** consigner ses pensées par écrit; ③ poser [*helicopter*]

■ **set forth**: ▶ ～ **forth** se mettre en route; ▶ ～ **forth [sth]** exposer [*facts*]; présenter [*argument*]

■ **set in**: ▶ ～ **in** [*infection*] se déclarer; [*complications*] survenir; [*winter*] arriver; [*depression*] s'installer; **the rain has set in for the afternoon** la pluie va durer toute l'après-midi; ▶ ～ **[sth] in** rapporter [*sleeve*]

■ **set off**: ▶ ～ **off** partir (**for** pour); **to** ～ **off on a journey** partir en voyage; **to** ～ **off to do** partir faire; **he set off on a long description** il s'est lancé dans une longue description; ▶ ～ **[off] sth**, ～ **[sth] off** ① (trigger) faire partir [*firework*]; faire exploser [*bomb*]; déclencher [*riot, row, panic, alarm*]; ② (enhance) mettre [qch] en valeur; ▶ ～ **[sb] off** faire pleurer [*baby*]; **she laughed and that set me off** elle a ri et ça m'a fait rire à mon tour; **don't mention politics, you know it always** ～**s him off** ne parle pas de politique, tu sais bien que quand il est parti on ne peut plus l'arrêter

■ **set on**: ▶ ～ **on [sb]** attaquer qn; ▶ ～ **[sth] on sb** lâcher [qch] contre qn [*dog*]; **to** ～ **sb onto sb** *ou* **sb's track** mettre qn sur la piste de qn

■ **set out**: ▶ ～ **out** (leave) se mettre en route (**for** pour); **we set out from Paris at 9 am** nous avons quitté Paris à 9 heures; **to** ～ **out on a journey** partir en voyage; **to** ～ **out to do** (intend) [*book, report, speech*] avoir pour but de faire; [*person*] chercher à faire; ▶ ～ **[sth] out**, ～ **out [sth]** ① (spread out) disposer [*goods, chairs, chessmen*]; disposer [*food*]; étaler [*books, papers*]; organiser [*information*]; ② (state, explain) présenter [*ideas*]; formuler [*objections, terms*]

■ **set to** s'y mettre

■ **set up**: ▶ ～ **up** (establish oneself) [*business person, trader*] s'établir; **to** ～ **up on one's own** s'établir à son compte; **to** ～ **up (shop) as a decorator** s'établir en tant que décorateur; **to** ～ **up in business** monter une affaire; ▶ ～ **[sth] up**, ～ **up [sth]** ① (erect) monter [*stand, stall*]; assembler [*equipment, easel*]; déplier [*deckchair*]; ériger [*roadblock*]; dresser [*statue*]; **to** ～ **up home** *ou* **house** s'installer; **to** ～ **up camp** installer un campement; ② (prepare) préparer [*experiment*]; ③ (found, establish) créer [*business, company*]; implanter [*factory*]; former [*group, charity*]; constituer [*committee*]; ouvrir [*fund*]; lancer [*scheme*]; ④ (start) provoquer [*vibration*]; susciter [*reaction*]; ⑤ (organize) organiser [*conference, meeting*]; mettre [qch] en place [*procedures*]; ⑥ (in printing) composer [*page*]; ▶ ～ **[sb] up** ① (establish in business) **she set her son up (in business) as a gardener** elle a aidé son fils à s'installer comme jardinier; ② (improve one's health, fortune) remettre [qn] sur pied; **that deal has set her up for life** grâce à ce contrat elle n'aura plus à se soucier de rien; ③ ○GB (trap) [*police*] tendre un piège à [*criminal*]; [*colleague, friend*] monter un coup contre [*person*]; ④ Comput installer, configurer; ▶ ～ **[oneself] up** ① Comm **she set herself up as a financial adviser** elle s'est mise à son compte comme conseiller financier; **to** ～ **oneself up in business** se mettre à son compte; ② (claim) **I don't** ～ **myself up to be an expert** je ne prétends pas être expert; **she** ～**s herself up as an authority on French art** elle prétend faire autorité en matière d'art français

■ **set upon**: ▶ ～ **upon [sb]** attaquer qn

setback /'setbæk/ n ① gen, Mil revers m (**for** pour); **to suffer a** ～ essuyer un revers; **this would be a** ～ **to our plans** cela compromettrait nos projets; **a temporary** ～ un recul passager; ② Fin recul m

set: ～ **designer** ▸ p. 1181 n Theat décorateur/-trice m/f; ～ **piece** n Sport coup m préparé; Mus morceau m célèbre; Theat ferme f; ～ **play** n Sport, gen coup m préparé; ～ **point** n balle f de set; ～ **square** n GB Tech équerre f

settee /se'tiː/ n canapé m

setter /'setə(r)/ n (dog) setter m

setting /'setɪŋ/ n ① (for building, event, film, novel) cadre m; **a house in a riverside** ～ une maison au bord d'une rivière; **Milan will be the** ～ **for the film** le film va se passer à Milan; **Dublin is the** ～ **for her latest novel** l'action de son dernier roman se passe à Dublin; ② (in jewellery) monture f; ③ (position on dial) position f (de réglage); **speed** ～ vitesse f; **put the iron on the highest** ～ mets le fer à repasser au maximum; ④ Mus arrangement m; ⑤ **the** ～ **of the sun** le coucher du soleil

setting lotion n fixateur m

setting-up /ˌsetɪŋ'ʌp/ n (of committee, programme, scheme, business) création f; (of inquiry) ouverture f; (of factory) implantation f

settle /'setl/
A n banquette f coffre
B vtr **1** (position comfortably) installer [person, animal]; **to get the children ~d for the night** mettre les enfants au lit; **2** (calm) calmer [stomach, nerves]; **3** (resolve) régler [matter, business, dispute]; mettre fin à [conflict]; régler, résoudre [problem]; **~ it among yourselves** réglez ça entre vous; **that's ~d** voilà qui est réglé; **that ~s it! I'm leaving tomorrow!** (making decision) c'est décidé! je pars demain!; (in exasperation) c'en est trop! je pars demain!; **to ~ an argument** (as referee) trancher; **4** (agree on) fixer; **nothing is ~d yet** rien n'est encore fixé; **5** (put in order) **to ~ one's affairs** mettre de l'ordre dans ses affaires; **6** Comm régler [bill, debt]; **7** (colonize) coloniser
C vi **1** (come to rest) [bird, insect, wreck] se poser; [dust, dregs] se déposer; **to let the dust ~** lit laisser retomber la poussière; fig attendre que les choses se calment; **to ~ over** [clouds] descendre sur; [silence, grief] s'étendre sur; **2** (become resident) gen s'installer; (more permanently) se fixer; **3** (become compacted) se tasser; **4** (calm down) gen se calmer; (go to sleep) s'endormir; [weather] se mettre au beau fixe; **5** (take hold) **to be settling** [snow] tenir; [mist] persister; **6** Jur régler; **to ~ out of court** parvenir à un règlement à l'amiable
D v refl **to ~ oneself in** s'installer dans [chair, bed]
(Idiom) **to ~ a score with sb** régler ses comptes avec qn
(Phrasal verbs)
■ **settle back** s'installer confortablement; **to ~ back in** se caler dans [chair]
■ **settle down** **1** (get comfortable) s'installer (**on** sur; **in** dans); **2** (calm down) [person] se calmer; [situation] s'arranger; **~ down!** du calme!; **to ~ down to work** se concentrer sur son travail; **to ~ down to doing** se résoudre à faire; **3** (marry) se ranger
■ **settle for**: ▸ **~ for** [sth] se contenter de; **why ~ for less?** pourquoi se contenter de moins?
■ **settle in** **1** (move in) s'installer; **2** (become acclimatized) s'adapter
■ **settle on**: ▸ **~ on** [sth] choisir [name, colour]
■ **settle up** **1** (pay) payer; **to ~ up with** régler [waiter, tradesman]; **2** (sort out who owes what) faire les comptes

settled /setld/ adj stable; **I feel ~ here** (in home) je me sens chez moi

settlement /'setlmənt/ n **1** (agreement) accord m; **2** (resolving) règlement m also Jur; **3** Fin constitution f (**on** en faveur de); **4** (social work centre) centre m social; **5** (dwellings) village m; **6** (colonization) implantation f

settler /'setlə(r)/ n colon m

set-to° /'settu:/ n prise f de bec°, dispute f

set-top box /ˌset₁tɒp bɒks/ n TV décodeur m

set-up° /'setʌp/
A n (system) organisation f; (trap) traquenard° m
B noun modifier [costs] initial; [time] de préparation

seven /'sevn/ ▸ p. 1044, p. 647 n, adj sept (m) inv

seventeen /ˌsevn'ti:n/ ▸ p. 1044, p. 647 n, adj dix-sept (m) inv

seventeenth /ˌsevn'ti:nθ/ ▸ p. 1044, p. 788
A n **1** (in order) dix-septième mf; **2** (of month) dix-sept m inv; **3** (fraction) dix-septième m
B adj, adv dix-septième

seventh /'sevnθ/ ▸ p. 1044, p. 788
A n **1** (in order) septième mf; **2** (of month) sept m inv; **3** (fraction) septième m; **4** Mus septième f
B adj, adv septième

seventies /'sevntɪz/ ▸ p. 788, p. 647 npl **1** **the ~** les années fpl soixante-dix; **2** **to be in one's ~** avoir plus de soixante-dix ans; **a man in his ~** un septuagénaire

seventieth /'sevntɪəθ/ ▸ p. 1044
A n **1** (in order) soixante-dixième mf; **2** (fraction) soixante-dixième m
B adj, adv soixante-dixième

seventy /'sevntɪ/ ▸ p. 1044, p. 647 n, adj soixante-dix (m) inv

seventy-eight /ˌsevntɪ'eɪt/ n Audio **a ~** (record ou disc) un soixante-dix-huit tours m inv

seven-year itch n démon m de l'infidélité (après sept ans de mariage)

sever /'sevə(r)/ vtr **1** lit sectionner [wire, limb, artery]; couper [rope, branch]; **to ~ sth from** séparer qch de; **2** fig rompre [relations]; couper [contact]

several /'sevrəl/
A pron **~ of you/us** plusieurs d'entre vous/d'entre nous; **~ of our group** plusieurs membres de notre groupe
B quantif **1** (a few) plusieurs; **~ books** plusieurs livres; **2** sout (respective) respectif/-ive

severally /'sevrəlɪ/ adv séparément

severance /'sevərəns/ n **1** (separation) rupture f; **2** (redundancy) licenciement m; **~ pay** indemnités fpl de licenciement

severe /sɪ'vɪə(r)/ adj **1** (extreme) [problem, damage, shortage, injury, depression, shock] grave; [weather, cold, winter] rigoureux/-euse; [headache] violent; [loss] lourd; **2** (harsh) sévère; **3** (austere) austère

severely /sɪ'vɪəlɪ/ adv **1** (seriously) [restrict, damage] sévèrement; [affect, shock] durement; [disabled] gravement; [injured] grièvement; **2** (harshly) [treat, speak] sévèrement; [beat] violemment; **3** (austerely) de façon austère

severity /sɪ'verətɪ/ n **1** (seriousness) (of problem, situation, illness) gravité f; (of shock, pain) violence f; **2** (harshness) (of sentence, treatment) sévérité f; (of climate) rigueur f

Seville orange /sə,vɪl'ɒrəndʒ/ n orange f amère

sew /səʊ/ (prét **sewed**; pp **sewn, sewed**)
A vtr coudre; **to ~ sth on to sth** coudre qch; **he ~ed the button back on** il a recousu le bouton
B vi coudre, faire de la couture
(Phrasal verb)
■ **sew up**: ▸ **~ [sth] up, ~ up [sth]** **1** recoudre [hole, tear]; faire [seam]; (re)coudre [wound]; **2** °(settle) conclure [deal]; conclure [qch] victorieusement [game]; (control) dominer [market]; **they've got the match sewn up** ils sont sûrs de gagner le match; **the deal is all sewn up!** l'affaire est dans le sac°!

sewage /'su:ɪdʒ, 'sju:-/ n ¢ eaux fpl usées

sewage: **~ disposal** n évacuation f des eaux usées; **~ farm** n = sewage works; **~ works** n champ m d'épandage

sewer /'su:ə(r), 'sju:-/ n égout m

sewing /'səʊɪŋ/
A n (activity) couture f; (piece of work) ouvrage m
B noun modifier [scissors, thread] à coudre

sewing: **~ basket** n corbeille f à ouvrage; **~ machine** n machine f à coudre

sewn /səʊn/ pp ▸ sew

sex /seks/
A n **1** (gender) sexe m; **2** (intercourse) (one act) rapport m sexuel; (repeated) rapports mpl sexuels
B noun modifier [organ] sexuel/-elle
C vtr déterminer le sexe de [animal]

sex: **~ abuse** n violence f sexuelle; **~ act** n acte m sexuel; **~ appeal** n sex-appeal m; **~ attack** n agression f sexuelle

sex change n **to have a ~** changer de sexe

sex: **~ discrimination** n discrimination f sexuelle; **~ drive** n libido f; **~ education** n éducation f sexuelle

sexism /'seksɪzəm/ n sexisme m

sexist /'seksɪst/ n, adj sexiste (mf)

sex: **~ life** n vie f sexuelle; **~ offender** n délinquant/-e m/f sexuel/-elle

sexual /'sekʃʊəl/ adj sexuel/-elle

sexual: **~ abuse** n violence f sexuelle; **~ harassment** n harcèlement m sexuel; **~ intercourse** n rapports mpl sexuels

sexuality /ˌsekʃʊ'ælətɪ/ n **1** (sexual orientation) sexualité f; **2** (eroticism) érotisme m

sexually /'sekʃəlɪ/ adv [dominant, explicit, mature] sexuellement; [transmit, infect] par voie sexuelle; **~ abused** victime de violence sexuelle

sexually transmitted disease, **STD** n maladie f sexuellement transmissible, MST

sexy° /'seksɪ/ adj **1** (erotic) [book, film, show] érotique; [person, clothing] sexy° inv; **2** [image, product] accrocheur°/-euse

S Glam n GB Post abrév écrite = **South Glamorgan**

sh /ʃ/ excl chut!

shabbily /'ʃæbɪlɪ/ adv [dressed] pauvrement, de façon miteuse; [behave, treat] de manière peu élégante

shabby /'ʃæbɪ/ adj [person] habillé de façon miteuse; [room, furnishings, clothing] miteux/-euse; [treatment] mesquin

shack /ʃæk/ n cabane f

(Phrasal verb)

■ **shack up**○: to ~ up with sb se maquer◑ avec qn

shackle /'ʃækl/
A n lit fer m; fig chaîne f
B vtr mettre [qn] aux fers

shade /ʃeɪd/
A n **1** (shadow) ombre f; **2** (of colour) ton m; fig (of opinion, meaning) nuance f; **an attractive ~ of blue** un beau bleu; **a solution that should appeal to all ~s of opinion** une solution qui devrait plaire à toutes les tendances; **3** (small amount, degree) **a ~ too loud** un tout petit peu trop fort; **a ~ of resentment** un soupçon de ressentiment; **4** (also **lamp ~**) abat-jour m inv; **5** US (also **window ~**) store m
B shades npl **1** ○(sunglasses) lunettes fpl de soleil; **2** (undertones) **~s of Mozart** ça fait penser à Mozart
C vtr **1** (screen) donner de l'ombre à; **the hat ~d her face** le chapeau projetait une ombre sur son visage; **the garden was ~d by trees** le jardin était ombragé par des arbres; **to ~ one's eyes (with one's hand)** s'abriter les yeux de la main; **2** = **shade in**
D vi (blend) [colour, tone] se fondre (**into** en)
E shaded pp adj **1** (shady) ombragé; **2** [lamp] avec un abat-jour; **3** Art (also **~-in**) gen sombre; (produced by hatching) hachuré
(Idioms) **to put sb in the ~** éclipser qn; **to put sth in the ~** surpasser or surclasser qch
(Phrasal verb)

■ **shade in**: ▸ **~ in [sth]**, **~ [sth] in** ombrer [drawing]; (by hatching) hachurer; [child] colorier

shading /'ʃeɪdɪŋ/ n ¢ (in painting) ombres fpl; (hatching) hachures fpl

shadow /'ʃædəʊ/
A n **1** (shade) lit, fig ombre f; **to live in the ~ of** (near) vivre à proximité de [mine, power station]; (in fear of) vivre dans la crainte de [Aids, unemployment, war]; **to stand in the ~s** se tenir dans l'ombre; **she's a ~ of her former self** elle n'est plus que l'ombre d'elle-même; **the war casts a long ~** les effets de la guerre se font toujours sentir; **to have ~s under one's eyes** avoir les yeux cernés; **2** (person who follows another) gen ombre f; (detective) détective m qui file qn; **to put a ~ on sb** faire filer or suivre qn; **3** (hint) **not a ~ of suspicion** pas le moindre soupçon; **without ou beyond the ~ of a doubt** sans l'ombre d'un doute
B shadows npl littér (darkness) ténèbres fpl
C vtr **1** lit projeter une ombre sur; **2** (follow) filer

shadow: **~ box** vtr boxer à vide; **~ boxing** n lit entraînement de boxe sans adversaire; fig attaque f purement formelle; **~ cabinet** n GB Pol cabinet m fantôme; **~ minister** n GB Pol = **shadow secretary**; **~ play** n théâtre m d'ombres

shadow secretary n GB Pol **the ~ for employment/foreign affairs** le porte-parole de l'opposition dans le domaine de l'emploi/des affaires étrangères

shadowy /'ʃædəʊɪ/ adj **1** (dark) sombre; **2** (indistinct) [image, outline] flou; [form] indistinct; **3** (mysterious) mystérieux/-ieuse

shady /'ʃeɪdɪ/ adj **1** [place] ombragé; **2** (dubious) véreux/-euse

shaft /ʃɑːft, US ʃæft/ n **1** (rod) (of tool) manche m; (of arrow) tige f; (of spear, sword) hampe f; (in machine) axe m; (on a cart) brancard m; **2** (passage, vent) puits m; **3** fig (of wit) trait m; **~ of light** rai m; **~ of lightning** éclair m

shaggy /'ʃægɪ/ adj [hair, beard, eyebrows] en broussailles; [animal] poilu; [carpet] à longues mèches

shaggy dog story n histoire f drôle sans queue ni tête

shake /ʃeɪk/
A n **1** **to give sb/sth a ~** gen secouer qn/qch; **with a ~ of the ou one's head** avec un hochement de tête; **2** (also **milk-~**) milk-shake m
B vtr (prét **shook**, pp **shaken**) **1** secouer; **'~ before use'** 'agiter avant emploi'; **he shook the seeds out of the packet** il a fait tomber les graines du paquet; **to ~ powder over the carpet** répandre de la poudre sur le tapis; **to ~ salt over the dish** saupoudrer le plat de sel; **to ~ one's**

fist at sb menacer qn du poing; **I shook him by the shoulders** je l'ai pris par les épaules et je l'ai secoué; **to ~ one's head** hocher la tête; **to ~ hands with sb**, **to ~ sb's hand** serrer la main de qn, donner une poignée de main à qn; **to ~ hands on the deal** se serrer la main pour conclure l'affaire; **to ~ hands on it** (after argument) se serrer la main en signe de réconciliation; **2** fig ébranler [belief, confidence, faith, person]; [event, disaster] secouer; **it really shook me to find out that...** cela m'a vraiment donné un choc de découvrir que...; **3** US (get rid of) = **shake off**
C vi (prét **shook**; pp **shaken**) **1** (tremble) trembler; **to ~ with** trembler de [fear, cold, emotion]; se tordre de [laughter]; **2** (shake hands) **they shook on it** (on deal, agreement) ils se sont serré la main en signe d'accord; (after argument) ils se sont serré la main en signe de réconciliation; **'~!'** 'serrons-nous la main!'
D v refl (prét **shook**; pp **shaken**) **to ~ oneself** [person, animal] se secouer
(Idioms) **in a ~**○ ou **two ~s**○ en un clin d'œil; **to be no great ~s**○ ne pas valoir grand-chose; **to have the ~s**○ (from fear, cold, infirmity) avoir la tremblote○; (from alcohol, fever) trembler
(Phrasal verbs)

■ **shake about** GB, **shake around**: ▸ **~ about** ou **around** être secoué; ▸ **~ [sth] about** ou **around** secouer [qch] dans tous les sens

■ **shake off**: ▸ **~ [sb/sth] off**, **~ off [sb/sth]** se débarrasser de [cold, depression, habit, person]; se défaire de [feeling]

■ **shake out**: ▸ **~ [sth] out**, **~ out [sth]** secouer; **to ~ some tablets out of a bottle** secouer un flacon pour en faire tomber quelques comprimés; ▸ **~ [sb] out of** secouer [qn] pour le faire sortir de [mood]

■ **shake up**: ▸ **~ up [sth]**, **~ [sth] up** agiter [bottle, mixture]; ▸ **~ [sb/sth] up**, **~ up [sb/sth] 1** lit, fig secouer; **2** (reorganize) Comm réorganiser (radicalement); Pol remanier [cabinet]

shaken /'ʃeɪkən/
A pp ▸ **shake**
B adj (shocked) choqué; (upset) bouleversé

shaken baby syndrome n syndrome présenté par un nourrisson suite à des lésions causées par des secousses violentes

shaker /'ʃeɪkə(r)/ n (for cocktails) shaker m; (for dice) gobelet m à dés; (for salt) salière f; (for pepper) poivrière f; (for salad) saladier m

shake-up /'ʃeɪkʌp/ n Comm réorganisation f (importante); Pol remaniement m

shakily /'ʃeɪkɪlɪ/ adv [say, speak] d'une voix tremblante; [walk] d'un pas chancelant; **he writes ~** il écrit en tremblant; **they started rather ~** leur début était chancelant or mal assuré

shaky /'ʃeɪkɪ/ adj **1** [chair, ladder] branlant; **my hands are rather ~** j'ai les mains qui tremblent; **I feel a bit ~** je me sens un peu flageolant; **2** fig [relationship, position] instable; [argument] peu solide; [knowledge, memory] peu sûr; [regime] chancelant; **3** fig (uncertain) [start] chancelant; **we got off to a rather ~ start** (in relationship, business) au début cela a été difficile pour nous; (in performance) nous étions très peu sûrs de nous au début; **my French is a bit ~** mon français est un peu hésitant

shall /ʃæl, ʃəl/

> ⚠ When shall is used to form the future tense in English, the same rules apply as for will. You will find a note on this and on question tags and short answers near the entry **will**[1]

modal aux **1** (in future tense) **I ~** ou **I'll see you tomorrow** je vous verrai demain; **we ~ not** ou **shan't have a reply before Friday** nous n'aurons pas de réponse avant vendredi; **2** (in suggestions) **~ I set the table?** est-ce que je mets la table?; **~ we go to the cinema tonight?** et si on allait au cinéma ce soir?; **let's buy some peaches, ~ we?** si on achetait des pêches?; **3** sout (in commands, contracts etc) **you ~ do as I say** tu dois faire ce que je te dis; **the sum ~ be paid on signature of the contract** le montant devra être versé à la signature du contrat; **thou shalt not steal** Bible tu ne voleras point

shallot /ʃə'lɒt/ n **1** GB échalote f; **2** US cive f

shallow /'ʃæləʊ/ ▸ p. 977
A shallows npl bas-fonds mpl
B adj [container, hollow, water, grave] peu profond; [stairs] aux marches basses; [breathing, character, response] superficiel/

-ielle; [*writing, conversation*] plat; [*wit*] creux/creuse; **the ~ end of the pool** l'extrémité la moins profonde de la piscine

shallowness /ˈʃæləʊnɪs/ *n* (of water) peu *m* de profondeur; (of person) manque *m* de profondeur; (of conversation) caractère *m* superficiel

sham /ʃæm/
A *n* (person) imposteur *m*; (organization) imposture *f*; (democracy, election) parodie *f*; (ideas, views) mystification *f*; (activity) supercherie *f*
B *adj* (*épith*) [*election, democracy*] prétendu (*before n*); [*object, building*] factice; [*organization*] fantoche
C *vtr* (*p prés etc* **-mm-**) **to ~ sleep/death** faire semblant de dormir/d'être mort
D *vi* (*p prés etc* **-mm-**) faire semblant

shamble /ˈʃæmbl/ *vi* aller d'un pas traînant

shambles○ /ˈʃæmblz/ *n* (of administration, room) pagaille○ *f*; (of meeting etc) désastre *m*

shame /ʃeɪm/
A *n* **1** (embarrassment, disgrace) honte *f*; **he has no (sense of) ~** il n'a honte de rien; **to feel ~** at être honteux/-euse de; **to my eternal ~** à ma très grande honte; **the ~ of it!** quelle honte!; **to bring ~ on** être *or* faire la honte de; **~ on you!** tu devrais avoir honte!; **there were cries of '~!'** les gens criaient au scandale; **2** (pity) **it is a ~ that** c'est dommage que (+ *subj*); **it was a great** *ou* **such a ~ (that) she lost** c'est tellement dommage qu'elle ait perdu; **it's a ~ about the factory closing** c'est dommage que l'usine ait fermé *or* ferme; **it's a ~ about your father** (if not very serious matter) c'est dommage pour ton père; (if serious) je suis désolé pour ton père; **nice costumes—~ about the play**○! les costumes étaient réussis—mais la pièce○! **isn't it a ~?** c'est vraiment dommage
B *vtr* **1** (embarrass) faire honte à; **I was ~d by her words** ses paroles m'ont fait honte; **to ~ sb into doing** obliger qn à faire en lui faisant honte; **2** (disgrace) déshonorer (**by doing** en faisant); **they ~d the nation** ils ont fait la honte de la nation
(Idiom) **to put sb to ~** faire honte à qn; **your garden puts the others to ~** tous les jardins semblent minables comparés au tien

shamefaced /ˌʃeɪmˈfeɪst/ *adj* [*person, look*] penaud
shameful /ˈʃeɪmfl/ *adj* [*conduct, waste*] honteux/-euse; **it is ~ that** c'est une honte que (+ *subj*)
shamefully /ˈʃeɪmfəlɪ/ *adv* [*behave*] honteusement; [*mistreated*] abominablement; **~ ignorant** d'une ignorance crasse
shameless /ˈʃeɪmlɪs/ *adj* [*person*] éhonté; [*attitude, negligence*] effronté; **a ~ display of** un étalage impudique de [*emotion, wealth*]; **to be quite ~ about** n'avoir pas du tout honte de
shamelessly /ˈʃeɪmlɪslɪ/ *adv* [*behave*] sans vergogne
shaming /ˈʃeɪmɪŋ/ *adj* [*defeat, behaviour*] humiliant
shampoo /ʃæmˈpuː/
A *n* (all contexts) shampooing *m*
B *vtr* (3ᵉ *pers sg prés* **-poos**, *prét, pp* **-pooed**) faire un shampooing à [*customer, pet*]; **to ~ one's hair** se faire un shampooing

shamrock /ˈʃæmrɒk/ *n* trèfle *m*
shandy /ˈʃændɪ/, **shandygaff** /ˈʃændɪgæf/ US *n* panaché *m*
Shangri-La /ˌʃæŋgrɪˈlɑː/ *n* paradis *m* terrestre
shank /ʃæŋk/ *n* **1** Zool jambe *f*; Culin jarret *m*; **2** (of knife) soie *f*; (of golf-club) manche *m*; (of drill-bit) queue *f*; (of screw) tige *f*; (of shoe) cambrure *f*
shan't /ʃɑːnt/ = **shall not**
shanty /ˈʃæntɪ/ *n* **1** (hut) baraque *f*; **2** (song) chanson *f* de marins
shantytown /ˈʃæntɪtaʊn/ *n* bidonville *m*
shape /ʃeɪp/
A *n* **1** (of object, building etc) forme *f*; (of person) silhouette *f*; **a square ~** une forme carrée; **what ~ is it?** de quelle forme est-ce?; **to be an odd ~** avoir une drôle de forme; **to be the right ~** [*object*] avoir la forme qu'il faut; [*person*] avoir la silhouette qu'il faut; **it's like a leaf in ~** de forme cela ressemble à une feuille; **in the ~ of** en forme de [*star, cat*]; **to mould sth into ~** donner forme à qch en le modelant; **to keep one's ~**

[*person*] garder sa ligne; **to take ~** [*sculpture, building*] prendre forme; **to lose its ~** [*garment*] se déformer; **to bend sth out of ~** gauchir qch; **in all ~s and sizes** de toutes les formes et de toutes les tailles; **2** (optimum condition) forme *f*; **to be out of ~** ne pas être en forme; **to get in ~** se mettre en forme; **to knock sth into ~** mettre qch au point *or* en état [*project, idea, essay*]; **3** fig (character, structure) gen forme *f*; (of organization) structure *f*; **to take ~** [*plan, project, idea*] prendre forme; [*events*] prendre tournure; **the likely ~ of currency union** la forme que prendra probablement l'union monétaire; **my contribution took the ~ of helping…** j'ai contribué en aidant…; **developments which have changed the ~ of our lives** des développements qui ont changé notre mode de vie; **the ~ of things to come** ce que sera l'avenir; **tips in any ~ or form are forbidden** les pourboires de toutes sortes sont interdits; **I don't condone violence in any ~ or form** je n'approuve pas la violence, sous quelque forme que ce soit; **4** (guise) **in the ~ of** sous (la) forme de [*money etc*]; en la personne de [*policeman etc*]; **5** (vague form) forme *f*, silhouette *f*; **6** Culin (mould) moule *m*
B *vtr* **1** (fashion, mould) [*person*] modeler [*clay*]; sculpter [*wood*]; [*wind*] façonner, sculpter [*rock*]; [*hairdresser*] couper [*hair*]; **~ the dough into balls** faites des boules avec la pâte; **to ~ the cardboard into a triangle** faites un triangle dans le carton; **2** fig [*person, event*] influencer; (stronger) déterminer [*future, idea*]; modeler [*character*]; [*person*] formuler [*policy, project*]; **to play a part in shaping the country's future** avoir un rôle dans la détermination de l'avenir du pays; **3** (in sewing) (fit closely) ajuster [*garment*]
(Phrasal verb)
■ **shape up 1** (develop) [*person*] s'en sortir; **how are things shaping up at (the) head office?** quelle tournure prennent les choses au siège?; **2** (meet expectations) être à la hauteur; **if he doesn't ~ up, fire him** s'il n'est pas à la hauteur, renvoie-le; **3** (improve one's figure) se mettre en forme

shaped /ʃeɪpt/
A *adj* **to be ~ like sth** avoir la forme de qch; **a teapot ~ like a house** une théière en forme de maison
B **-shaped** *combining form* **star-/V-~** en forme d'étoile/de V; **oddly-~** de forme étrange
shapeless /ˈʃeɪplɪs/ *adj* sans forme, informe
shapely /ˈʃeɪplɪ/ *adj* [*leg*] bien galbé; [*woman*] bien fait
shard /ʃɑːd/ *n* tesson *m*
share /ʃeə(r)/
A *n* **1** (of money, food, profits, blame) part *f* (of de); **to have a ~ in** être pour quelque chose dans, contribuer à [*success etc*]; **to have more than one's fair ~ of** avoir plus que sa part de [*bad luck*]; **to do one's ~ of sth** faire sa part de qch; **to pay one's (fair) ~** payer sa part; **to have a ~ in a company** avoir une participation dans une société; **to own a half-~** posséder la moitié; **2** Fin action *f*; **3** Agric soc *m* (de charrue)
B *noun modifier* Fin [*capital, issue*] d'actions; [*price*] des actions
C *vtr* partager [*money, house, opinion*] (**with** avec); se partager [*chore*]; **we ~ a birthday** nous avons notre anniversaire le même jour; **we ~ an interest in animals** nous aimons tous les deux les animaux
D *vi* **to ~ in** prendre part à [*success, happiness, benefits*]
(Idiom) **~ and ~ alike** il faut partager
(Phrasal verb)
■ **share out**: ▸ **~ [sth] out**, **~ out [sth]** (amongst selves) partager [*food etc*]; (amongst others) répartir [*food etc*]; **we ~d the cakes out between us** nous nous sommes partagé les gâteaux

shared /ʃeəd/ *adj* [*house, interest, grief*] partagé; [*space, facilities etc*] commun
shareholder /ˈʃeəhəʊldə(r)/ *n* actionnaire *mf*; **the ~s** l'actionnariat *m*
share: **~ option scheme** *n* plan *m* de participation par achat d'actions; **~-out** *n* partage *m*, répartition *f*
shark /ʃɑːk/ *n* requin *m* also fig
sharp /ʃɑːp/
A *n* Mus dièse *m*
B *adj* **1** [*razor*] tranchant; [*edge*] coupant; [*blade, scissors, knife*] bien aiguisé; [*saw*] bien affûté; **2** [*tooth, fingernail, end, needle*] pointu; [*pencil*] bien taillé; [*features*] anguleux/-euse; [*nose*] pointu; **3** (abrupt) [*angle*] aigu/-uë;

[bend, reflex] brusque; [drop, incline] fort; [fall, rise] brusque, brutal; **4** (acidic) [taste, smell] âcre; [fruit] acide; **5** (piercing) [pain, cold] vif/vive; [cry] aigu/-uë; [blow] sévère; [frost] fort, intense; **6** fig (aggressive) [tongue] acéré; [tone] acerbe; **7** (alert) [person, mind] vif/vive; [eyesight] perçant; [hearing] fin; **to have a ~ wit** avoir de la repartie; **to keep a ~ look-out** rester sur le qui-vive (**for** pour); **to have a ~ eye for sth** fig avoir l'œil pour qch; **8** péj (clever) [businessman, person] malin/-igne; **~ operator** filou m; **9** (clearly defined) [image, sound, distinction] net/nette; [contrast] prononcé; **to bring sth into ~ focus** lit cadrer qch avec netteté; fig faire passer qch au premier plan; **10** ᴳᴮ [suit] tape-à-l'œil inv pej; **11** ᵁˢ (stylish) chic inv; **12** Mus dièse; (too high) aigu/-uë

C adv **1** (abruptly) [stop] net; **to turn ~ left** tourner brusquement vers la gauche; **2** ᵒ(promptly) **at 9 o'clock** à neuf heures pileᵒ; **3** Mus [sing, play] trop haut

(Idioms) **to be at the ~ end** être en première ligne; **to look ~ᵒ** se dépêcher

sharpen /'ʃɑːpən/
A vtr **1** lit aiguiser, affûter [blade]; tailler [pencil]; **to ~ its claws** [cat] se faire les griffes; **2** (accentuate) rendre [qch] plus net [contrast]; affiner [focus]; régler [image]; **3** (make stronger) aviver [anger, desire]; aiguiser [appetite]; affiner [reflexes]; **to ~ sb's wits** dégourdir l'esprit de qn
B vi [tone, voice, look] se durcir; [pain] s'aviver

sharpener /'ʃɑːpənə(r)/ n (for pencil) taille-crayon m; (for knife) fusil m, aiguisoir m

sharp-eyed /ˌʃɑːpˈaɪd/ adj à la vue perçante; fig vigilant

sharpishᵒ /'ʃɑːpɪʃ/ adv GB illicoᵒ, vite

sharply /'ʃɑːplɪ/ adv **1** (abruptly) [turn, change, rise, fall] brusquement, brutalement; [stop] net; **2** (harshly) [speak] d'un ton brusque; [criticize] vivement, sévèrement; [look] durement; **3** (distinctly) [differ, define] nettement; **to bring sth ~ into focus** lit cadrer qch avec netteté; fig faire passer qch au premier plan; **4** (perceptively) [drawn] avec acuité; [aware] vivement

sharpness /'ʃɑːpnɪs/ n **1** (of blade, scissors) tranchant m (**of** de); **2** (of turn, bend) angle m brusque (**of** de); **3** (of image, sound) netteté f (**of** de); **4** (of voice, tone) brusquerie f (**of** de); **5** (acidity) (of taste) piquant m; (of smell) âcreté f; (of fruit, drink) acidité f

sharp: **~ practice** n filouterie f; **~shooter** n tireur/-euse m/f d'élite

shatter /'ʃætə(r)/
A vtr lit fracasser [glass]; fig rompre [silence]; briser [life, hope]; démolir [nerves]
B vi [window, glass] voler en éclats

shattered /'ʃætəd/ adj **1** [dream] brisé; [life, confidence] anéanti; **2** (devastated) effondré; ᵒ(tired) crevéᵒ

shattering /'ʃætərɪŋ/ adj [blow, effect] accablant; [news] bouleversant

shave /ʃeɪv/
A n to have a ~ se raser; **to give sb a ~** raser qn
B vtr (pp ~**d** ou **shaven**) **1** lit [barber] raser [person]; **to ~ sb's beard off** raser la barbe de qn; **to ~ one's legs** se raser les jambes; **2** (plane) raboter [wood]; **3** fig réduire [prices, profits]
C vi (pp ~**d** ou **shaven**) [person] se raser

(Idiom) **that was a close ~!** je l'ai/il l'a etc échappé belle!

shaver /'ʃeɪvə(r)/ n (also **electric ~**) rasoir m électrique

shaving /'ʃeɪvɪŋ/
A n **1** (process) rasage m; **2** (of wood, metal) copeau m
B noun modifier [cream, foam] à raser; [kit] de rasage

shaving: **~ brush** n blaireau m; **~ mirror** n petit miroir m; **~ soap** n savon m à barbe

shawl /ʃɔːl/ n châle m

she /ʃiː/

⚠ *She* is translated by elle: *she closed the door* = elle a fermé la porte. For particular usages, see the entry below

A pron elle; **~'s not at home** elle n'est pas chez elle; **here ~ is** la voici; **there ~ is** la voilà; **sʜᴇ didn't take it** ce n'est pas elle qui l'a pris; **he lives in Dublin but ~ doesn't** il habite Dublin mais elle non; **~'s a genius** c'est un génie; **~ who** celle qui; **~ who must be obeyed** hum la patronne hum; **~ and I** elle et moi; **~'s a lovely boat** c'est un beau bateau

B n **it's a ~ᵒ** (of baby) c'est une fille; (of animal) c'est une femelle

sheaf /ʃiːf/ n (pl **sheaves**) (of corn, flowers) gerbe f; (of papers) liasse f

shear /ʃɪə(r)/
A vtr (prét **sheared**; pp **shorn**) tondre
B shorn pp adj fig dépouillé (**of** de)
(Phrasal verb)
■ **shear off**: ▸ **~ off** [metal component] céder; ▸ **~ off** [sth], **~** [sth] **off** tondre [hair, fleece]; [accident, storm] emporter [branch]

shears /ʃɪəz/ npl **1** (for garden) cisaille f; **2** (for sheep) tondeuse f

sheath /ʃiːθ/ n **1** (case) (of sword) fourreau m; (of knife, cable) gaine f; **2** Bot gaine f

sheathe /ʃiːð/ vtr rengainer [sword, dagger]; rentrer [claws]; gainer [cable]; **~d in** gainé de [silk etc]

sheaves /ʃiːvz/ npl ▸ **sheaf**

shebangᵒ /ʃɪˈbæŋ/ n US **the whole ~ᵒ** tout le tremblementᵒ

shed /ʃed/
A n gen remise f, abri m; (lean-to) appentis m; (bigger) (at factory site, port etc) hangar m
B vtr (prét, pp **shed**) **1** verser [tears]; perdre [leaves, weight]; [lorry] déverser [load]; enlever [clothes]; se débarrasser de [inhibitions, image]; **to ~ skin** [snake] muer; **to ~ blood** (one's own) perdre du sang; **too much blood has been shed** trop de sang a coulé; **to ~ jobs** ou **staff** supprimer des emplois; **2** (transmit) répandre [light, happiness]

she'd /ʃiːd, ʃɪd/ = **she had**, **she would**

sheen /ʃiːn/ n (of hair) éclat m; (of silk) lustre m

sheep /ʃiːp/ n (pl ~) mouton m; (ewe) brebis f; **black ~** fig brebis f galeuse; **lost ~** fig brebis f égarée

(Idioms) **to count ~** fig compter les moutons; **to make ~'s eyes at sb** faire les yeux doux à qn; **may as well be hung for a ~ as for a lamb** tant qu'à être condamné pour un crime, autant qu'il en vaille la peine

sheep: **~ dog** n chien m de berger; **~ farm** n ferme f d'élevage de moutons; **~ farmer** ▸ p. 1181 n éleveur m de moutons

sheepish /'ʃiːpɪʃ/ adj penaud

sheepshearing n tonte f

sheepskin /'ʃiːpskɪn/ n **1** peau f de mouton; **2** ᵒUS Univ diplôme m

sheep station n élevage m de moutons (en Australie)

sheer /ʃɪə(r)/
A adj **1** (pure) [boredom, hypocrisy, stupidity] pur; **out of ~ malice/stupidity** par pure méchanceté/bêtise; **by ~ hard work** uniquement grâce à son acharnement au travail; **by ~ accident** tout à fait par accident; **2** (utter) **the ~ immensity of it** son immensité même; **3** (steep) [cliff] à pic; **4** (fine) [fabric] léger/-ère, fin; [stockings] extra-fin
B adv [rise, fall] à pic
(Phrasal verb)
■ **sheer away**, **sheer off** faire une embardée

sheet /ʃiːt/ n **1** (of paper, stamps) feuille f; **2** (for bed) drap m; (shroud) linceul m; **waterproof ~** alaise f; **3** (printed) (periodical) périodique m; (newspaper) journal m; **fact ou information ~** bulletin m d'informations; **4** (of plastic, rubber) feuille f; (of canvas, tarpaulin) bâche f; (of metal) plaque f; (thinner) feuille f; (of glass) plaque f; (thinner) vitre f; **5** (of ice etc) couche f; (thicker) plaque f; (of mist, fog) nappe f; (of flame) rideau m; **in ~s** [rain] à torrents; **6** Naut écoute f; **7** ᵒUS Jur casier m

(Idiom) **to be as white as a ~** être blanc comme un linge

sheeting /'ʃiːtɪŋ/ n (fabric) toile f à draps; (iron) tôle f; **plastic ~** bâche f en plastique

sheet: **~ iron** n tôle f; **~ lightning** n ₵ éclairs mpl de chaleur; **~ metal** n Aut tôle f; **~ music** n ₵ partitions fpl

sheik /ʃeɪk, US ʃiːk/ n cheik m

shekel /'ʃekl/
A ▸ p. 782 n (currency) shekel m
B shekels npl (money) fricᵒ m, argent m

shelf /ʃelf/ n (pl **shelves**) **1** (at home) gen étagère f; (in oven) plaque f; (in shop, fridge) rayon m; **a set of shelves** une étagère; **2** Geog (of rock, ice) corniche f

(Idiom) **to be left on the ~** (remain single) rester vieille fille

shelf-life /'ʃelflaɪf/ n **1** lit (of product) durée f de conservation; **2** fig (of technology, pop music) durée f de vie; (of politician, star) période f de gloire

shelf mark n cote f

shell /ʃel/
A n **1** Bot, Zool (of egg, nut, snail) coquille f; (of crab, tortoise, shrimp) carapace f; **sea ~** coquillage m; **to develop a hard ~** fig [person] se forger une carapace; **to come out of one's ~** fig sortir de sa coquille; **2** Mil (bomb) obus m; (cartridge) cartouche f; **3** Tech (of vehicle) carcasse f; (of building) cage f; (of machine) enveloppe f; (of nuclear plant) enceinte f de confinement; **4** (remains) (of building) carcasse f
B vtr **1** Mil pilonner [town, installation]; **2** Culin écosser [peas]; décortiquer [prawn, nut]; écailler [oyster]

(Phrasal verb)
  ■ **shell out**○: ▸ **~ out** casquer○ (**for** pour); ▸ **~ out [sth]** débourser [sum] (**for** pour)

she'll /ʃiːl/ = she will

shellac /ʃə'læk, 'ʃelæk/ US
A n gomme-laque f
B vtr (p prés etc **-ck-**) (varnish) lacquer

shellfish /'ʃelfɪʃ/ npl **1** Zool crustacés mpl; (mussels, oysters) coquillages mpl; **2** Culin fruits mpl de mer

shelling /'ʃelɪŋ/ n pilonnage m

shell: **~ pink** ▸ p. 752 adj nacré; **~-proof** adj blindé; **~-shocked** adj lit [soldier] traumatisé (par un bombardement); fig en état de choc

shell suit n survêtement m en nylon®

shelter /'ʃeltə(r)/
A n **1** ₵ (protection) abri m; **in the ~ of** à l'abri de; **to take ~ from** se mettre à l'abri de [danger]; s'abriter de [weather]; **to give sb ~** [person] donner un abri à qn; [hut, tree] offrir un abri à qn; [country] donner asile à qn; **2** (covered place) abri m (**from** contre); **3** (for homeless) refuge m; (for refugee) asile m
B vtr **1** (protect) (against weather) abriter (**from, against** de); (from truth) protéger (**from** de); **2** (give refuge, succour to) accueillir [refugee, criminal]; **to ~ sb from sb/sth** accueillir qn pour qu'il échappe à qn/qch
C vi **1** se mettre à l'abri; **to ~ from the storm** s'abriter de l'orage; **2** [refugee, fugitive] se réfugier

sheltered accommodation n GB foyer-résidence m

shelve /ʃelv/
A vtr **1** (postpone) mettre [qch] en suspens [plan]; **2** (store on shelf) mettre [qch] sur les rayons; **3** (provide with shelves) garnir [qch] d'étagères
B vi [beach, sea bottom etc] descendre en pente

shelves /ʃelvz/ pl ▸ shelf

shelving /'ʃelvɪŋ/ n ₵ (at home) étagères fpl; (in shop) rayons mpl

shepherd /'ʃepəd/ ▸ p. 1181
A n berger m
B vtr **1** [host] escorter [person] (**into** jusque dans); **2** [herdsman] guider [animals]

shepherdess /,ʃepə'des, US 'ʃepərdɪs/ ▸ p. 1181 n bergère f

shepherd: **~'s crook** n houlette f; **~'s pie** n hachis m Parmentier

sherbet /'ʃɜːbət/ n **1** GB (powder) confiserie f en poudre f acidulée; **2** US (sorbet) sorbet m

sheriff /'ʃerɪf/ ▸ p. 1181 n shérif m

sherry /'ʃerɪ/ n xérès m, sherry m

she's /ʃiːz/ = she is, she has

Shetland /'ʃetlənd/ ▸ p. 954
A pr n (also **~ Islands**) îles fpl Shetland; **in ~, in the ~s** dans les îles Shetland
B noun modifier [scarf, sweater] en shetland
C adj [crofter, family] shetlandais

shhh /ʃ/ excl chut!

Shia(h) /'ʃiːə/
A n chiisme m
B adj chiite

shied /ʃaɪd/ prét, pp ▸ shy B

shield /ʃiːld/
A n **1** Mil bouclier m; (in heraldry) écusson m; fig protection f (**against** contre); **2** Sport ≈ trophée m; **3** Tech (on machine) écran m de protection; **4** US (policeman's badge) insigne m

B vtr (from weather, danger) protéger; (from authorities) (by lying) couvrir; (by harbouring) donner asile à [suspect, criminal]; **to ~ one's eyes** se protéger les yeux

shift /ʃɪft/
A n **1** (alteration) changement m (**in** de), modification f (**in** de); **a sudden ~ in public opinion** un retournement de l'opinion publique; **a ~ to the left** Pol un glissement vers la gauche; **the ~ from agriculture to industry** le passage de l'agriculture à l'industrie; **2** Ind (period of time) période f de travail; (group of workers) équipe f; **to be on night ~s** être (d'équipe) de nuit; **to work an eight-hour ~** faire les trois-huit; **3** (dress) robe f droite; †(undergarment) chemise f; **4** Ling mutation f; **5** US Aut = **gearshift**; **6** (on keyboard) = **shift key**
B vtr **1** (move) déplacer [furniture, vehicle]; bouger, remuer [arm]; Theat changer [scenery]; **to ~ sth away from** éloigner qch de [wall, window]; **to ~ one's position** fig changer de position or d'avis; **2** (get rid of) faire partir, enlever [stain, dirt]; **I can't ~ this cold**○! GB je n'arrive pas à me débarrasser de mon rhume!; **3** (transfer) (to another department) affecter; (to another town, country) muter [employee]; fig rejeter [blame]; (**onto** sur); **to ~ attention away from a problem** détourner l'attention d'un problème; **4** US Aut **to ~ gear** changer de vitesse
C vi **1** (also **~ about**) [load] bouger; **to ~ uneasily in one's chair** remuer dans son fauteuil l'air mal à l'aise; **to ~ from one foot to the other** se dandiner d'un pied sur l'autre; **2** (move) [scene] **the ~s to Ireland** Cin, Theat la scène se situe maintenant en Irlande; **this stain won't ~!** cette tache ne veut pas partir!; **~**○! GB pousse-toi○!; **3** (change) [attitude] se modifier; [wind] tourner; **opinion has ~ed to the right** l'opinion a glissé vers la droite; **4** ○GB (go quickly) [person] se grouiller○; [vehicle] foncer○; **5** US Aut **to ~ into second gear** passer en seconde
D v refl **to ~ oneself** se pousser

shifting /'ʃɪftɪŋ/ adj [belief] changeant; [population] toujours renouvelé

shift key n touche f de majuscule

shiftless /'ʃɪftlɪs/ adj **1** (lazy) paresseux/-euse, apathique; **2** (lacking initiative) qui manque d'ambition

shift: **~ lock** n touche f de verrouillage des majuscules; **~ system** n Ind travail m par équipes

shift work n travail m posté; **to be on ~** faire un travail posté

shifty /'ʃɪftɪ/ adj [person, manner] louche

Shiite /'ʃiːaɪt/
A n Chiite mf
B adj chiite

shilling /'ʃɪlɪŋ/ ▸ p. 782 n shilling m

(Idiom) **to take the King's** ou **Queen's ~** GB partir sous les drapeaux

shillyshally○ /'ʃɪlɪʃælɪ/ vi tergiverser

shimmer /'ʃɪmə(r)/ vi **1** [jewels, water] scintiller; [silk] chatoyer; **2** (in heat) [landscape] vibrer

shin /ʃɪn/ n tibia m

(Phrasal verbs)
  ■ **shin up**: ▸ **~ up [sth]** grimper à [tree]
  ■ **shin down**: ▸ **~ down [sth]** descendre [qch] en s'agrippant [tree]

shinbone /'ʃɪnbəʊn/ n tibia m

shindig○ /'ʃɪndɪg/, **shindy**○ /'ʃɪndɪ/ n **1** (disturbance) ramdam○ m; **to kick up a ~** faire du ramdam○; **2** (party) nouba○ f

shine /ʃaɪn/
A n gen lustre m; (of parquet) brillant m
B vtr **1** (prét, pp **shone**) braquer [light, torch] (**on** sur); **2** (prét, pp **shined**) faire reluire [brass]; cirer [shoes]
C vi (prét, pp **shone**) **1** [hair, light, sun] briller; [brass, floor] reluire; **to ~ through** percer [mist, gloom]; **the light is shining in my eyes** j'ai la lumière dans les yeux; **2** fig (be radiant) [eyes] briller (**with** de); [face] rayonner (**with** de); **3** (excel) briller; **to ~ at** être brillant en [science, languages etc]

(Idioms) **to ~ up to sb**○ US passer de la pommade○ à qn; **to take a ~ to sb**○ s'enticher○ de qn; fig **to take the ~ off sth** gâcher qch

(Phrasal verbs)
  ■ **shine in** pénétrer (**through** par)
  ■ **shine through** [talent] éclater au grand jour

■ **shine out** [*light*] briller, apparaître

shingle /'ʃɪŋgl/ n **1** ¢ (pebbles) galets *mpl*; **2** Constr (tile) bardeau *m*; **3** US (nameplate) plaque *f*

shingles /'ʃɪŋglz/ ▸ p. 933 *npl* Med zona *m*

shinguard, **shinpad** /'ʃɪŋgɑːd, 'ʃɪnpæd/ *n* jambière *f*

shining /'ʃaɪnɪŋ/ *adj* **1** (shiny) [*car*] étincelant; [*hair*] brillant; [*bald spot, metal*] luisant; [*floor*] reluisant; **2** (glowing) [*eyes*] brillant; [*face*] radieux/-ieuse; **3** fig [*achievement*] brillant; [*example*] parfait

shinty /'ʃɪntɪ/ *n* GB Sport hockey *m* (simplifié)

shiny /'ʃaɪnɪ/ *adj* **1** [*metal, surface, hair*] brillant; **2** [*shoes, wood*] bien ciré; **3** [*seat of trousers*] lustré

ship /ʃɪp/
A *n* navire *m*; (smaller) bateau *m*; **passenger ~** paquebot *m*
B *vtr* (*p prés etc* **-pp-**) **1** (send) (by sea) transporter [*qch*] par mer; (by air) transporter [*qch*] par avion; (overland) acheminer; **2** (take on board) charger [*cargo*]; rentrer [*oars*]; **to ~ water** embarquer de l'eau

(Idioms) **we are like ~s that pass in the night** nous ne faisons que nous croiser; **the ~ of state** le char de l'État; **the ~ of the desert** (camel) le vaisseau du désert; **to run a tight ~** mener tout le monde à la baguette; **when my ~ comes in** quand j'aurai fait fortune

(Phrasal verb)
■ **ship off**: ▸ **~ [sth/sb] off**, **~ off [sth/sb]** expédier also hum

ship: **~building** *n* construction *f* navale; **~load** *n* cargaison *f*

shipment /'ʃɪpmənt/ *n* **1** (cargo) (by sea) cargaison *f*; (by air, land) chargement *m*; **2** (sending) expédition *f*

ship owner *n* armateur *m*

shipper /'ʃɪpə(r)/ *n* expéditeur/-trice *m/f*

shipping /'ʃɪpɪŋ/
A *n* **1** (boats) navigation *f*, trafic *m* maritime; **attention all ~!** avis à toutes les embarcations!; **2** (sending) acheminement *m*
B *noun modifier* [*agent, office*] maritime; [*charges*] de transport

shipping: **~ clerk** ▸ p. 1181 *n* expéditionnaire *mf*; **~ company** *n* (sea) compagnie *f* maritime; (road) entreprise *f* de transport routier; **~ forecast** *n* météo *f* marine; **~ lane** *n* couloir *m* de navigation; **~ line** *n* compagnie *f* de navigation

ship: **~'s company** *n* équipage *m*; **~'s doctor** ▸ p. 1181 *n* médecin *m* de bord; **~shape** *adj* GB bien en ordre; **~-to-shore radio** *n* liaison *f* radio avec la côte

shipwreck /'ʃɪprek/
A *n* (event) naufrage *m*; (ship) épave *f*
B *vtr* **to be ~ed** faire naufrage; **a ~ed sailor** un marin naufragé

shipyard *n* chantier *m* naval

shire /'ʃaɪə(r)/ *n* GB **1** †comté *m* (du centre de l'Angleterre); **2** Pol **the ~s** les provinces

shirk /ʃɜːk/
A *vtr* esquiver [*task, duty*]; fuir [*responsibility*]; éluder [*problem*]; **to ~ doing sth** éviter de faire qch
B *vi* se défiler

shirker /'ʃɜːkə(r)/ *n* tire-au-flanc° *m inv*

shirt /ʃɜːt/ ▸ p. 1191 *n* (man's) chemise *f*; (woman's) chemisier *m*; (for sport) maillot *m*

(Idioms) **keep your ~ on**°! du calme!; **to lose one's ~**° laisser jusqu'à sa dernière chemise°; **to sell the ~ off one's back** vendre père et mère°

shirtfront *n* plastron *m*

shirt-sleeve /'ʃɜːtsliːv/ *n* manche *f* de chemise; **in one's ~s** en manches de chemise; **to roll up one's ~s** remonter ses manches (de chemise) also fig

shirttail /'ʃɜːtteɪl/ *n* **1** (of shirt) pan *m* de chemise; **2** US (in newspaper) *commentaire en bas d'un article*

shirttail cousin *n* US cousin/-e *m/f* à la mode de Bretagne

shirty° /'ʃɜːtɪ/ *adj* GB [*person*] de mauvais poil°; **to get ~** prendre la mouche°

shish-kebab /'ʃiːʃkəbæb/ *n* chiche-kebab *m*

shit❶ /ʃɪt/
A *n* **1** (excrement) merde❶ *f*, crotte° *f*; **2** (also **bull~**) conneries❶ *fpl*
B *excl* merde❶!; **tough ~!** tant pis!

shiver /'ʃɪvə(r)/
A *n* lit, fig frisson *m*; **to give a ~** avoir un frisson; **to send a ~ down sb's spine** faire courir un frisson dans le dos à qn
B **shivers** *npl* frissons *mpl*; **an attack of the ~s** un accès de frissons; **to give sb the ~s** lit donner des frissons à qn; fig donner froid dans le dos à qn
C *vi* (with cold) grelotter (**with** de); (with fear) frémir (**with** de); (with disgust) frissonner (**with** de)

shivery /'ʃɪvərɪ/ *adj* (feverish) fébrile

shoal /ʃəʊl/ *n* **1** (of fish) banc *m*; **2** Geog (of sand) banc *m* de sable; (shallows) bas-fond *m*

shock /ʃɒk/
A *n* **1** (psychological) choc *m*; **to get** *ou* **have a ~** avoir un choc; **to give sb a ~** faire un choc à qn; **the ~ of seeing** le choc de voir; **it came as a bit of a ~** cela m'a fait comme un choc; **her death came as a ~ to us** sa mort a été un choc pour nous; **it's a ~ to the system when…** c'est un vrai choc quand…; **to recover from** *ou* **get over the ~** surmonter le choc; **he's in for a nasty**° **~** il va avoir un sacré° choc; **to express one's ~** (indignation) exprimer son indignation; (amazement) exprimer sa surprise; **~! horror!** journ *ou* hum scandale épouvantable!; **2** Med état *m* de choc; **to be in (a state of) ~** être en état de choc; **to treat sb for ~** soigner qn en état de choc; **in deep ~** en grave état de choc; **to be suffering from ~** souffrir d'un choc; **3** Elec décharge *f*; **to get a ~** prendre une décharge; **to give sb a ~** donner une décharge à qn; **4** (impact) (of collision) choc *m*; (of earthquake) secousse *f*; (of explosion) souffle *m*; **5** (of corn) gerbe *f*; fig (of hair) tignasse *f*; **6** °(also **~ absorber**) amortisseur *m*
B °*noun modifier* [*effect*] de choc; [*result*] sidérant
C *vtr* (distress) consterner; (scandalize) choquer; **she's not easily ~ed** on ne la choque pas facilement

shock absorber *n* amortisseur *m*

shocking /'ʃɒkɪŋ/ *adj* **1** (upsetting) [*sight*] consternant; (scandalous) [*news*] choquant; **2** °(appalling) désastreux/-euse°

shocking pink ▸ p. 752 *n*, *adj* rose (*m*) vif *inv*

shock: **~proof**, **~ resistant** *adj* antichoc *inv*; **~ troops** *npl* troupes *fpl* de choc

shock wave *n* **1** lit onde *f* de choc; **2** fig remous *mpl*; **to send ~s through the stock market** provoquer des remous à la Bourse

shod /ʃɒd/
A *prét, pp* ▸ **shoe B**
B *pp adj* chaussé; **well/poorly ~** bien/mal chaussé

shoddily /'ʃɒdɪlɪ/ *adv* **1** **to be ~ made/built** être de fabrication/de construction sommaire; **2** [*behave*] avec bassesse

shoddy /'ʃɒdɪ/ *adj* **1** [*product*] de mauvaise qualité; [*work*] mal fait; **2** [*behaviour*] mesquin; **a ~ trick** un sale tour

shoe /ʃuː/ ▸ p. 1191
A *n* **1** (footwear) chaussure *f*; **2** (for horse) fer *m*; **3** (also **brake ~**) Aut sabot *m* de frein
B *vtr* (*p prés* **shoeing**; *prét, pp* **shod**) ferrer [*horse*]

(Idioms) **it's a question of dead men's ~s** il s'agit d'attendre la mort de quelqu'un pour prendre sa place; **in my/your etc ~s** à ma/ta etc place; **to save ~ leather** ménager ses semelles; **to shake** *ou* **shiver in one's ~s** avoir peur; **to step into sb's ~s** prendre la place de qn

shoe: **~horn** *n* chausse-pied *m*; **~lace** *n* lacet *m* de chaussure; **~maker** ▸ p. 1181 *n* cordonnier/-ière *m/f*; **~ polish** *n* cirage *m*; **~ rack** *m* porte-chaussures *m inv*; **~ repairer** ▸ p. 1181 *n* cordonnier *m*; **~shine (boy)** *n* cireur *m* de chaussures; **~ shop** ▸ p. 1181 *n* magasin *m* de chaussures; **~ size** ▸ p. 1191 *n* pointure *f*

shoestring /'ʃuːstrɪŋ/ *n* US lacet *m* de chaussure

(Idiom) **on a ~**° avec peu de moyens

shoe tree *n* embauchoir *m*

shone /ʃɒn/ *prét, pp* ▸ **shine**

shoo /ʃuː/
A *excl* ouste!
B *vtr* (also **~ away**) chasser

Shops, trades and professions

Shops

■ *In English you can say* at the baker's *or* at the baker's shop; *in French the construction with* chez (*at the house or premises of…*) *is common but you can also use the name of the particular shop:*

at the baker's
= chez le boulanger *or* à la boulangerie

I'm going to the grocer's
= je vais chez l'épicier *or* à l'épicerie

I bought it at the fishmonger's
= je l'ai acheté chez le poissonnier *or* à la poissonnerie

go to the chemist's
= va à la pharmacie *or* chez le pharmacien

at or to the hairdresser's
= chez le coiffeur/la coiffeuse

to work in a butcher's
= travailler dans une boucherie

■ Chez *is also used with the names of professions:*

at or to the doctor's
= chez le médecin

at or to the lawyer's
= chez le notaire

at or to the dentist's
= chez le dentiste

■ *Note that there are specific names for the place of work of some professions:*

the lawyer's office
= l'étude *f* du notaire

the doctor's surgery (*GB*) or ***office*** (*US*)
= le cabinet du médecin

■ Cabinet *is also used for architects and dentists. If in doubt, check in the dictionary.*

People

■ *Talking of someone's profession, we could say* he is a dentist. *In French this would be either* il est dentiste *or* c'est un dentiste. *Only when the sentence begins with* c'est, *can the indefinite article* (un *or* une) *be used.*

Paul is a dentist
= Paul est dentiste

she is a dentist
= elle est dentiste *or* c'est une dentiste

she's a geography teacher
= elle est professeur de géographie
or c'est un professeur de géographie

■ *With adjectives, only the* c'est *construction is possible:*

she is a good dentist
= c'est une bonne dentiste

■ *In the plural, if the construction begins with* ce sont *then you need to use* des (*or* de *before an adjective*):

they are mechanics
= ils sont mécaniciens *or* ce sont des mécaniciens

they are good mechanics
= ce sont de bons mécaniciens

Trades and professions

what does he do?
= qu'est-ce qu'il fait?

what's your job?
= qu'est-ce que vous faites dans la vie?

I'm a teacher
= je suis professeur

to work as a dentist
= travailler comme dentiste

to work for an electrician
= travailler pour un électricien

to be paid as a mechanic
= être payé comme mécanicien

he wants to be a baker
= il veut devenir boulanger

---

shook /ʃʊk/ *prét* ▸ **shake**

shoot /ʃuːt/
A *n* ⓵ Bot (young growth) pousse *f*; (offshoot) rejeton *m*; ⓶ GB (hunt meeting) partie *f* de chasse; ⓷ Cin tournage *m*
B *vtr* (*prét, pp* **shot**) ⓵ (fire) tirer [*bullet, arrow*] (**at** sur); lancer [*missile*] (**at** sur); ⓶ (hit with gun) tirer sur [*person, animal*]; (kill) abattre [*person, animal*]; **she shot him in the leg** elle lui a tiré dans la jambe; **to be shot in the back** recevoir une balle dans le dos; **to ∼ sb for desertion** fusiller qn pour désertion; **shot to pieces**○ lit criblé de balles; fig réduit à néant; ⓷ (direct) **to ∼ questions at sb** bombarder qn de questions; ⓸ Cin, Phot (film) tourner [*film, scene*]; prendre [qch] (en photo) [*subject*]; ⓹ (push) mettre [*bolt*]; ⓺ (in canoeing) **to ∼ the rapids** franchir les rapides; ⓻ (in golf) **to ∼ 75** faire un score de 75; ⓼ US Games jouer à [*pool, craps*]; ⓽ (in hunting) chasser [*game*]; ⓾ ○(inject) ▸ **shoot up**○
C *vi* (*prét, pp* **shot**) ⓵ (fire a gun) tirer (**at** sur); ⓶ (move suddenly) **to ∼ forward** s'élancer à toute vitesse; **the car shot past** la voiture est passée en trombe; **to ∼ to fame** fig percer, devenir célèbre subitement; ⓷ Cin tourner; ⓸ Sport (in football etc) tirer, shooter; ⓹ (in hunting) [*person*] chasser
D *v refl* (*prét, pp* **shot**) **to ∼ oneself** se tirer une balle
(Idioms) ∼○! US vas-y, parle!; **to ∼ a line**○ frimer○; **to ∼ oneself in the foot**○ agir contre son propre intérêt
(Phrasal verbs)
■ **shoot down:** ▸ ∼ **down** [sb/sth], ∼ [sb/sth] **down** Aviat, Mil abattre, descendre○ [*plane, pilot*]; **to ∼ [sb/sth]**

down in flames lit, fig descendre [qn/qch] en flammes [*person, plane, argument*]
■ **shoot out:** ▸ ∼ **out** [*flame, water*] jaillir; [*car*] sortir en trombe
■ **shoot up:** ▸ ∼ **up** ⓵ [*flames, spray*] jaillir; fig [*prices, profits*] monter en flèche; ⓶ (grow rapidly) [*plant*] pousser vite; **that boy has really shot up!** fig qu'est-ce que ce garçon a poussé!; ▸ ∼ **up [sth]**, ∼ [sth] **up** (inject)○ se shooter à○ [*heroin*]

shooting /'ʃuːtɪŋ/
A *n* ⓵ (act) (killing) meurtre *m* (par arme à feu); ⓶ (firing) coups *mpl* de feu, fusillade *f*; ⓷ (by hunters) chasse *f*; ⓸ ▸ p. 881 Sport (at target etc) tir *m*; ⓹ Cin tournage *m*
B *adj* [*pain*] lancinant

shooting: ∼ **gallery** *n* stand *m* de tir; ∼ **range** *n* stand *m* de tir; ∼ **star** *n* étoile *f* filante; ∼ **stick** *n* canne-siège *f*

shoot-out○ /'ʃuːtaʊt/ *n* fusillade *f*

shop /ʃɒp/
A *n* ⓵ (store) magasin *m*; (small, fashionable) boutique *f*; **to go to the ∼s** aller faire les courses *fpl*; **to set up** ∼ lit, fig s'installer; **to shut up** ∼○ lit, fig fermer boutique; ⓶ US (in department store) rayon *m*; ⓷ (workshop) atelier *m*; ⓸ US Sch atelier *m*; ⓹ ○GB (shopping) **the weekly ∼** les courses pour la semaine; **to do a big ∼** faire le plein○
B ○*vtr* (*p prés etc* **-pp-**) GB donner○, vendre
C *vi* (*p prés etc* **-pp-**) faire ses courses; **to go ∼ping** gen aller faire des courses; (as browser) aller faire les magasins

S

(Idioms) **all over the** ~° GB fig partout; **to talk** ~ parler boutique

(Phrasal verb)
■ **shop around** (compare prices) faire le tour des magasins (**for** pour trouver); fig (compare courses, services etc) bien chercher

shopaholic° /ʃɒpə'hɒlɪk/ n accro° mf du shopping

shop: ~ **assistant** ▸ p. 1181 n GB vendeur/-euse m/f; ~ **fitter** ▸ p. 1181 n GB installateur/-trice m/f de magasins

shopfloor /ʃɒp'flɔ:(r)/ n **problems on the** ~ des problèmes parmi les ouvriers

shop: ~ **front** n devanture f; ~**keeper** ▸ p. 1182 n commerçant/-e m/f; ~**lifter** n voleur/-euse m/f à l'étalage

shopping /'ʃɒpɪŋ/ n (activity, purchases) courses fpl

shopping: ~ **bag** n sac m à provisions; ~ **basket** n panier m; ~ **centre** GB, ~ **center** US, ~ **mall** US n centre m commercial; ~ **precinct** n zone f commerçante

shopping trip n to go on a ~ aller faire les magasins

shopping trolley n caddie® m

shop: ~**-soiled** adj [garment] sali; ~ **steward** n représentant/-e m/f syndical/-e; ~ **window** n vitrine f also fig; ~**-worn** adj US ▸ **shop-soiled**

shore /ʃɔ:(r)/ n 1 (edge) (of sea) côte f, rivage m; (of lake) rive f; (of island) côte f; **off the** ~ **of** Naut au large de; 2 (dry land) terre f; **on** ~ à terre; **from ship to** ~ en liaison avec la côte; 3 (beach) grève f, plage f

(Phrasal verb)
■ **shore up**: ▸ ~ **up** [sth], ~ [sth] **up** lit étayer; fig soutenir

shore leave n permission f de descendre à terre

shorn /ʃɔ:n/ pp ▸ **shear**

short /ʃɔ:t/ ▸ p. 977
A n 1 (drink) alcool m fort; 2 Elec = **short circuit**; 3 Cin court métrage m; 4 Fin (deficit) manque m, déficit m
B **shorts** npl short m; (underwear) caleçon m
C adj 1 (not long-lasting) [stay, memory, period] court (before n); [course] de courte durée; [conversation, speech, chapter] bref/brève; [walk] petit (before n); **a** ~ **time ago** il y a peu de temps; **in four** ~ **years** en quatre brèves années; **to work** ~**er hours** travailler moins d'heures; **the days are getting** ~**er** les jours diminuent or raccourcissent; **the** ~ **answer is that** la réponse est tout simplement que; 2 (not of great length) court (before n); **the suit is too** ~ **in the sleeves** les manches du costume sont trop courtes; **to have one's hair cut** ~ se faire couper les cheveux court; 3 (not tall) [person] petit; 4 (scarce) **to be in** ~ **supply** être difficile à trouver; **time is getting** ~ le temps presse; 5 (inadequate) [rations] insuffisant; **he gave me a** ~ **measure** (in shop) il a triché sur le poids; 6 (lacking) **he is** ~ **of sth** il lui manque qch; **to be** ~ **on** [person] manquer de [talent, tact]; **to be** ~ **of**, **to run** ~ **of** manquer de [clothes, money, food]; **my wages are £30** ~ il me manque 30 livres sterling sur mon salaire; 7 (in abbreviation) **Tom is** ~ **for Thomas** Tom est le diminutif de Thomas; **this is Nicholas, Nick for** ~! je te présente Nicholas, mais on l'appelle Nick; 8 (abrupt) **to be** ~ **with sb** être brusque avec qn; 9 Ling [vowel] bref/brève; 10 Fin [loan, credit] à court terme; 11 Culin [pastry] brisé
D adv (abruptly) [stop] net; **to stop** ~ **of doing** se retenir pour ne pas faire
E **in short** adv phr bref
F **short of** prep phr 1 (just before) un peu avant; 2 (just less than) pas loin de; **that's nothing** ~ **of blackmail!** c'est du chantage, ni plus ni moins!; 3 (except) ~ **of doing** à moins de faire
G vtr, vi Elec = **short-circuit**

(Idioms) ~ **and sweet** bref/brève; **to bring** ou **pull sb up** ~ couper qn dans son élan; **to sell oneself** ~ se sous-estimer; **to make** ~ **work of sth/sb** expédier qch/qn; **to be caught** ~ être pris d'un besoin pressant; **the long and** ~ **of it is that they...** en un mot (comme en cent), ils...

shortage /'ʃɔ:tɪdʒ/ n pénurie f, manque m (**of** de); **housing** ~ crise f du logement; **there is no** ~ **of applicants** les candidats ne manquent pas

short ~ **back and sides** n coupe f de cheveux masculine (dégageant la nuque et les oreilles); ~**bread**, ~**cake** n sablé m; ~**-change** vtr lit ne pas rendre

toute sa monnaie à; fig rouler°

short circuit /ʃɔ:t'sɜ:kɪt/
A n court-circuit m
B **short-circuit** vtr lit, fig court-circuiter
C **short-circuit** vi faire court-circuit

short: ~**comings** npl points mpl faibles; ~**crust pastry** n pâte f brisée

shortcut n 1 lit raccourci m; 2 fig **to take** ~**s** bâcler°; **there are no** ~**s to becoming a musician** on ne s'improvise pas musicien

shorten /'ʃɔ:tn/
A vtr abréger [visit, life]; raccourcir [garment, talk]; réduire [time, list]; alléger [syllabus]; **to** ~ **sail** Naut réduire la voilure
B vi [days, odds] diminuer

shortening /'ʃɔ:tnɪŋ/ n 1 Culin matière f grasse; 2 (reduction) réduction f; 3 (abridging) abrégement m

shortfall /'ʃɔ:tfɔ:l/ n (in budget, accounts) déficit m; (in earnings, exports etc) manque m; **there is a** ~ **of £10,000 in our budget** il manque 10 000 livres sterling dans notre budget; **to make up the** ~ fig combler le déficit

shorthand /'ʃɔ:thænd/
A n 1 Comm sténographie f, sténo° f; **in** ~ en sténo°; 2 fig (verbal shortcut) formule f consacrée
B noun modifier [notebook, qualification] de sténo°

short-handed /ʃɔ:t'hændɪd/ adj (in company) à court de personnel; (on site) à court de main-d'œuvre

shorthand-typist ▸ p. 1181 n sténo-dactylo f

shortlist /'ʃɔ:tlɪst/
A n liste f des candidats sélectionnés
B vtr sélectionner [applicant] (**for** pour)

short-lived /ʃɔ:t'lɪvd, US -'laɪvd/ adj [triumph, happiness] de courte durée; [effect] passager/-ère; **to be** ~ ne pas durer longtemps

shortly /'ʃɔ:tlɪ/ adv 1 (very soon) [return] bientôt; [be published] prochainement; 2 (a short time) ~ **after(wards)**, ~ **before** peu (de temps) après/avant

short: ~**-range** adj [weather forecast] à court terme; ~ **sight** n myopie f

shortsighted /ʃɔ:t'saɪtɪd/ adj 1 lit myope; 2 fig (lacking foresight) [person] peu clairvoyant; [policy, decision] à courte vue

shortsightedness /ʃɔ:t'saɪtɪdnɪs/ n 1 lit myopie f; 2 fig manque m de perspicacité (**about** à propos de)

short-sleeved /ʃɔ:t'sli:vd/ adj à manches courtes

short-staffed /ʃɔ:t'stɑ:ft, US -stæft/ adj **to be** ~ manquer de personnel

short: ~**-stay** adj [car park] de courte durée; [hostel, housing] à court terme; ~ **story** n Literat nouvelle f; ~**-tempered** adj coléreux/-euse

short term
A n **in the** ~ (looking to future) dans l'immédiat; (looking to past) pendant un temps, pour commencer
B **short-term** adj gen, Fin à court terme

short: ~ **time** n (in industry) chômage m partiel; ~**wave** n ondes fpl courtes

shot /ʃɒt/
A prét, pp ▸ **shoot**
B n 1 (from gun etc) coup m (de feu); **to fire** ou **take a** ~ **at sb/sth** tirer sur qn/qch; **to fire the opening** ~ fig ouvrir le feu; 2 Sport (in tennis, golf, cricket) coup m; (in football) tir m; **to have** ou **take a** ~ **at goal** (in football) tirer au but; **'good** ~**!'** 'bien joué!'; 3 Phot photo f (**of** de); 4 Cin plan m (**of** de); **action** ~ scène f d'action; **out of** ~ Cin hors champ; 5 (injection) piqûre f; **to give sb a** ~ faire une piqûre à qn; 6 (attempt) **to have a** ~ **at doing** essayer de faire qch; **to give it one's best** ~ faire de son mieux; 7 (in shotputting) poids m; 8 (pellet) **C** balle f, plomb m; (pellets collectively) **C** plomb m; 9 (person who shoots) **a good** ~ un bon tireur; 10 °(dose) **a** ~ **of** une lampée° de [whisky]
C adj 1 (also ~ **through**) [silk] changeant; 2 (also ~ **away**) **he is** ~ **(away)** il n'a plus toute sa tête; **his nerves were** ~ il était à bout de nerfs

(Idioms) **to call the** ~**s** dicter la loi; **to be** ~ **of** être débarrassé de; **to give sth a** ~ **in the arm** revigorer qch; **he'd go like a** ~ il partirait sans hésiter; **it was a** ~ **in the dark** ça a été dit au hasard

should

Meaning *ought to*

When *should* is used to mean *ought to*, it is translated by the conditional tense of *devoir*:

we should leave at seven
= nous devrions partir à sept heures

The past *should have* meaning *ought to have* is translated by the past conditional of *devoir*:

she should have told him the truth
= elle aurait dû lui dire la vérité

The same verb is used in negative sentences:

you shouldn't do that
= vous ne devriez pas faire ça

he shouldn't have resigned
= il n'aurait pas dû démissionner

For the conjugation of *devoir*, see the French verb tables.

In conditional sentences

When *should* is used as an auxiliary verb to form the conditional, *should* + verb is translated by the conditional of the appropriate verb in French:

I should like to go to Paris
= j'aimerais aller à Paris

I should have liked to go to Paris
= j'aurais aimé aller à Paris

As a subjunctive in purpose clauses

When *should* is used as an auxiliary verb in *that* clauses, *should* + verb is translated by the subjunctive of the appropriate verb in French:

in order that they should understand
= pour qu'ils comprennent

For particular usages see the entry **should**.

shotgun /'ʃɒtɡʌn/ n fusil m

shot: **~gun wedding** n mariage m forcé; **~ put** n Sport lancer m de poids

should /ʃʊd, ʃəd/ modal aux (conditional of **shall**) ⓵ (ought to) **you ~ have told me before** tu aurais dû me le dire avant; **why shouldn't I do it?** pourquoi est-ce que je ne le ferais pas?; **that ~ be them arriving now!** ça doit être eux qui arrivent!; **how ~ I know?** comment veux-tu que je le sache?; **as it ~ be** (in order) en ordre; ...**which is only as it ~ be** ...ce qui est parfaitement normal; **flowers! you shouldn't have!** des fleurs! il ne fallait pas!; ⓶ (in conditional sentences) **had he asked me, I ~ have accepted** s'il me l'avait demandé, j'aurais accepté; **I don't think it will happen, but if it ~...** je ne pense pas que cela arrive, mais si toutefois cela arrivait...; **if you ~ change your mind,...** si vous changez d'avis,...; **~ the opportunity arise** si l'occasion se présente; ⓷ (expressing purpose) **in order that they ~ understand** pour qu'ils comprennent; **we are anxious that he ~ succeed** nous souhaitons vivement qu'il réussisse; ⓸ (in polite formulas) **I ~ like a drink** je prendrais volontiers un verre; **I ~ like to go there** j'aimerais bien y aller; ⓹ (expressing opinion, surprise) **I ~ think so!** je l'espère!; **I ~ think not!** j'espère bien que non!; **'how long?'—'an hour, I ~ think'** 'combien de temps?'—'une heure, je suppose'; **I ~ think she must be about 40** à mon avis, elle doit avoir 40 ans environ; **I ~ say so!** et comment!; **who ~ walk in but John!** devine qui est arrivé—John!; **and then what ~ happen, but it began to rain!** et devine quoi—il s'est mis à pleuvoir!

shoulder /'ʃəʊldə(r)/
Ⓐ n ▸ p. 698 ⓵ Anat épaule f; **on ou over one's ~** à l'épaule; **on ou over one's ~s** sur les épaules; **too tight across the ~s** trop étroit d'épaules; **to put one's ~s back** rejeter les épaules en arrière; **if you need a ~ to cry on** si tu as besoin d'une épaule pour pleurer; **to have round ~s** avoir le dos rond; **to look over one's ~** lit, fig regarder derrière soi; **the burden is** ou **falls on my ~s** la charge m'incombe; **~ to ~** [stand] côte à côte; [work] coude à coude ou côte à côte; ⓶ (on mountain) replat m; ⓷ (on road) bas-côté m; ⓸ Culin épaule f
Ⓑ vtr ⓵ lit mettre [qch] sur l'épaule [bag, implement]; **to ~ arms** Mil se mettre au port d'armes; **~ arms!** Mil arme sur l'épaule!; ⓶ fig se charger de [burden, expense, task]; endosser [responsibility]; ⓷ (push) **to ~ sb aside** écarter qn d'un coup d'épaule
(Idioms) **to stand head and ~s above sb** lit dépasser qn d'une bonne tête; fig laisser qn loin derrière; **to have a good head on one's ~s** avoir la tête sur les épaules; **to have an old head on young ~s** être mûr avant l'âge; **to put one's ~ to the wheel** s'atteler à la tâche; **to rub ~s with sb** côtoyer qn; **straight from the ~**○ [comment, criticism] franc/franche

shoulder: **~ bag** n sac m à bandoulière; **~ blade** n omoplate f; **~-length** adj [hair] mi-long; **~ pad** n épaulette f; **~ strap** n (of garment) bretelle f; (of bag) bandoulière f

shouldn't /'ʃʊdnt/ = **should not**

shout /ʃaʊt/
Ⓐ n ⓵ (cry) cri m (of de); ⓶ ○GB (round of drinks) tournée f
Ⓑ vtr ⓵ (cry out) crier; (stronger) hurler; ⓶ ○GB (buy) **to ~ a round (of drinks)** payer une tournée
Ⓒ vi crier; **to ~ at sb** crier après qn; **to ~ at** ou **to sb to do** crier à qn de faire; **to ~ for help** crier pour demander de l'aide
(Idioms) **I'll give you a ~** je te ferai signe; **it's nothing to ~ about** ça n'a rien d'extraordinaire
(Phrasal verbs)
■ **shout down**: ▸ **~ [sb] down** faire taire [qn] (en criant plus fort que lui)
■ **shout out**: ▸ **~ out** pousser un cri; ▸ **~ out [sth]** lancer [qch] à haute voix [names, answers]

shouting /'ʃaʊtɪŋ/ n ₵ cris mpl
(Idiom) **it's all over bar the ~** c'est pratiquement terminé

shove○ /ʃʌv/
Ⓐ n **to give sb/sth a ~** pousser qn/qch
Ⓑ vtr ⓵ (push) pousser; **to ~ sth through** pousser qch dans [letterbox]; pousser qch par [gap]; **to ~ sb/sth aside** écarter qn/qch en le poussant; **to ~ sth in sb's face** fourrer○ qch sous le nez de qn; **to ~ sth down sb's throat** fig imposer qch à qn; ⓶ (stuff hurriedly) fourrer; ⓷ (jostle) bousculer [person]; **he ~d his way to the front of the crowd** il s'est frayé un chemin à travers la foule
Ⓒ vi pousser; **people were pushing and shoving** les gens poussaient et se bousculaient
(Idioms) **if push comes to ~** au pire; **~ off**○! tire-toi○!
(Phrasal verbs)
■ **shove over**○: ▸ **~ over** se pousser
■ **shove up**○ se pousser

shove halfpenny /,ʃʌv 'heɪpnɪ/ ▸ p. 881 n GB ≈ jeu m de palet (sur table)

shovel /'ʃʌvl/
Ⓐ n (spade) pelle f; (digger) pelleteuse f
Ⓑ vtr enlever [qch] à la pelle [dirt, leaves, snow] (off de); **to ~ sth into sth** verser qch dans qch à l'aide d'une pelle; **to ~ food into one's mouth**○ s'enfourner○ la nourriture dans la bouche
(Phrasal verb)
■ **shovel up**: ▸ **~ up [sth]**, **~ [sth] up** ramasser [qch] à la pelle

shovelful /'ʃʌvlfʊl/ n pelletée f (of de)

show /ʃəʊ/
Ⓐ n ⓵ (as entertainment) Theat, gen spectacle m; (particular performance) représentation f; Cin séance f; Radio, TV émission f; (of slides) projection f; **family ~** spectacle pour tous; **on with the ~!** (introduction) place au spectacle!; ⓶ Comm (of cars, boats etc) salon m; (of fashion) défilé m; (of flowers, crafts) exposition f; **to be on ~** être exposé; ⓷ (of feelings) semblant m; (of strength) démonstration f; (of wealth) étalage m; **to make** ou

S

put on a (great) ∼ of doing s'évertuer pour la galerie à faire; **he made a** ∼ **of concern** il a affiché sa sollicitude; **to be all for** or **just for** ∼ être de l'esbroufe○; **4**○ (performance) **the team put up a good** ∼ l'équipe s'est bien défendue; **it was a poor** ∼ **not to thank them** ce n'était pas très adroit de ne pas les remercier; **good** ∼! bravo!; **5** ○(business, undertaking) affaire f; **she runs the whole** ∼ c'est elle qui fait marcher l'affaire

B vtr (prét **showed**; pp **shown**) **1** (present for viewing) montrer [person, object, photo] (**to** à); présenter [ticket, fashion collection] (**to** à); [TV channel, cinema] passer [film]; **to** ∼ **sb sth** montrer qch à qn; **2** (display competitively) présenter [animal]; exposer [flower, vegetables]; **3** (reveal) montrer [feeling, principle, fact]; [garment] laisser voir [underclothes, dirt]; [patient] présenter [symptoms]; **to** ∼ **interest in** montrer de l'intérêt pour; **it** ∼**s that** cela montre bien que; **4** (indicate) montrer [object, trend, loss, difficulty]; indiquer [time, direction, area]; **5** (demonstrate) [reply] témoigner de [wit, intelligence]; [gesture, gift] témoigner de [respect, gratitude]; **to** ∼ **favouritism towards sb, to** ∼ **sb favouritism** favoriser qn; **to** ∼ **one's age** accuser son âge; **as shown in diagram 12** comme on le voit figure 12; **6** (prove) démontrer [truth, guilt]; **to** ∼ **that** [document] prouver que; [findings] démontrer que; [expression] montrer que; **7** (conduct) **to** ∼ **sb to their seat** [host, usher] placer qn; **to** ∼ **sb to their room** accompagner qn à sa chambre; **to** ∼ **sb to the door** reconduire qn; **8** ○(teach a lesson to) **I'll** ∼ **him!** (as revenge) je vais lui apprendre○!; (when challenged) je lui ferai voir○!

C vi (prét **showed**; pp **shown**) **1** (be noticeable) [stain, label] se voir; [emotion] gen se voir; (in eyes) se lire; **2** (be exhibited) [artist] exposer; [film] passer

(Idioms) **it just goes to** ∼ c'est ça la vie; ∼ **a leg**○! debout!; **to have nothing to** ∼ **for sth** ne rien avoir tiré de qch; **to** ∼ **one's face**○ montrer son nez○; **to** ∼ **one's hand** abattre son jeu; **to steal the** ∼ **be the way forward** ouvrir la voie; **to steal the** ∼ être l'attraction

(Phrasal verbs)
■ **show in**: ▸ ∼ **[sb] in** faire entrer
■ **show off**: ▸ ∼ **off**○ faire le fier/la fière; ▸ ∼ **[sb/sth] off,** ∼ **off [sb/sth]** mettre [qch] en valeur [special feature]; faire admirer [skill]; exhiber [baby, car]
■ **show out**: ▸ ∼ **[sb] out** accompagner [qn] à la porte
■ **show round**: ▸ ∼ **[sb] round** faire visiter
■ **show up**: ▸ ∼ **up 1** (be visible) [mark] se voir; [details, colour] ressortir; **2** ○(arrive) se montrer○; ▸ ∼ **up [sth]** révéler [fault, mark]; ▸ ∼ **[sb] up 1** (let down) faire honte à [person]; **2** (reveal truth about) **to** ∼ **sb up for what he/she is** montrer la vraie nature de qn

show biz○, **show business** n industrie f du spectacle

showboat n US bateau-théâtre m

showcase /'ʃəʊkeɪs/
A n **1** lit vitrine f; **2** fig (for paintings, ideas) vitrine f; (for new artist etc) tremplin m
B noun modifier [village, prison] modèle

showdown /'ʃəʊdaʊn/ n confrontation f

shower /'ʃaʊə(r)/
A n **1** (for washing) douche f; **in the** ∼ sous la douche; **2** Meteorol averse f; **light/heavy** ∼ petite/grosse averse; **3** (of confetti, sparks) pluie f; (of praise, gifts) avalanche f; **4** US fête f; **5** ○GB péj bande f
B vtr **1** (wash) doucher [dog, child]; **2** **to** ∼ **sth on** or **over sb/sth, to** ∼ **sb/sth with sth** [fire, volcano] faire pleuvoir qch sur qn/qch; [person] asperger qn/qch de qch [water etc]; **3** fig **to** ∼ **sb with sth, to** ∼ **sth on sb** couvrir qn de [gifts, compliments]
C vi **1** [person] prendre une douche; **2** (rain) **ash** ∼**ed down** une pluie de cendres est retombée

shower: ∼ **attachment** n douchette f de lavabo; ∼ **cap** n bonnet m de douche; ∼**proof** adj imperméabilisé

showery /'ʃaʊərɪ/ adj [day, weather] pluvieux/-ieuse

show: ∼**girl** n girl f; ∼**ground** n gen champ m de foire; (for horses) terrain m de concours; ∼ **house** n maison-témoin f

showing /'ʃəʊɪŋ/ n **1** Cin (screening) séance f; **2** (performance) gen prestation f; Sport performance f

showjumper /'ʃəʊdʒʌmpə(r)/ n **1** (person) cavalier/-ière m/f de saut; **2** (horse) cheval m de saut

showman /'ʃəʊmən/ n **to be a** ∼ fig avoir le sens du spectacle

shown /ʃəʊn/ pp ▸ **show B, C**

show: ∼**-off**○ n m'as-tu-vu○ mf inv; ∼ **of hands** n vote m à mains levées

showpiece /'ʃəʊpiːs/ n (exhibit) œuvre f exposée; (in trade fair) objet m exposé; **this hospital is a** ∼ fig cet hôpital est un modèle du genre

showroom /'ʃəʊruːm, -rʊm/ n exposition f; **to look at cars in a** ∼ regarder les voitures exposées; **in** ∼ **condition** dans un état impeccable

show: ∼**stopper**○ n clou○ m d'un spectacle; ∼ **trial** n procès m pour l'exemple

shrank /ʃræŋk/ prét ▸ **shrink B, C**

shrapnel /'ʃræpnl/ n ∉ éclats mpl d'obus

shred /ʃred/
A n **1** fig (of evidence, emotion, sense, truth) parcelle f; **2** (of paper, fabric) lambeau m
B vtr (p prés etc **-dd-**) déchiqueter [paper]; râper [vegetables]; ∼**ded newspaper** déchirures fpl de journaux

shredder /'ʃredə(r)/ n (for paper) déchiqueteuse f

shrew /ʃruː/ n **1** Zool musaraigne f; **2** †(woman) péj mégère f

shrewd /ʃruːd/ adj [person] habile; [face] plein d'astuce; [move, assessment, investment] astucieux/-ieuse; **to have a** ∼ **idea that** être porté à croire que; **to make a** ∼ **guess** deviner juste

shrewdly /'ʃruːdlɪ/ adv [act] habilement; [assess] avec perspicacité

shriek /ʃriːk/
A n **1** (of pain, fear) cri m perçant, hurlement m; (of delight) cri m; ∼**s of laughter** éclats mpl de rire; **2** (of bird) cri m
B vi crier, hurler (**in, with** de)

shrift /ʃrɪft/ n **to give sb/sth short** ∼ expédier qn/qch sans ménagements

shrill /ʃrɪl/
A adj **1** [voice, cry, laugh] perçant; [whistle, tone] strident; **2** péj [criticism] vigoureux/-euse
B vi [bird] pousser un cri aigu; [telephone] retentir

shrimp /ʃrɪmp/ n Zool, Culin crevette f grise

shrimping /'ʃrɪmpɪŋ/ n pêche f à la crevette

shrine /ʃraɪn/ n **1** (place) lieu m de pèlerinage (**to** consacré à); **2** (alcove) autel m; (building) chapelle f

shrink /ʃrɪŋk/
A ○n hum psy○ mf, psychiatre mf
B vtr (prét **shrank**; pp **shrunk** ou **shrunken**) faire rétrécir [fabric]; [tribesman] réduire [head]
C vi (prét **shrank**; pp **shrunk** ou **shrunken**) **1** [fabric] rétrécir; [forest, area] reculer; [boundaries] se rapprocher; [economy, sales] être en recul; [resources, funds] s'amenuiser; [old person, body] se tasser; **to** ∼ **from 200 to 50** tomber de 200 à 50; **to have shrunk to nothing** [team, household] être quasiment réduit à néant; [person] n'avoir plus que la peau sur les os; **2** (recoil) **to** ∼ **from** se dérober devant [conflict, responsibility]; **to** ∼ **from doing** hésiter à faire

shrinkage /'ʃrɪŋkɪdʒ/ n (of fabric) rétrécissement m; (of economy) recul m; (of resources, area) diminution f

shrinking /'ʃrɪŋkɪŋ/ adj [population, market] en baisse; [asset] qui se raréfie; [audience] qui s'amenuise

shrinking violet n hum personne f timorée

shrink-wrap /'ʃrɪŋkræp/
A n film m plastique
B vtr (p prés etc **-pp-**) emballer [qch] sous film plastique

shrivel /'ʃrɪvl/
A vtr (p prés etc **-ll-, -l-** US) [sun, heat] flétrir [skin]; dessécher [plant, leaf]
B vi (p prés etc **-ll-, -l-** US) (also ∼ **up**) [fruit, vegetable] se ratatiner; [skin] se flétrir; [plant, leaf, meat] se dessécher

shroud /ʃraʊd/
A n **1** (cloth) linceul m, suaire m; **2** fig voile m (**of** de); **3** Naut hauban m
B vtr envelopper [body, person] (**in** dans)

Shrove Tuesday n Relig mardi m gras

shrub /ʃrʌb/ n arbuste m

shrubbery /'ʃrʌbərɪ/ n (in garden) massif m d'arbustes; (collectively) arbustes mpl

shrug /ʃrʌg/
A n (also ∼ **of the shoulders**) haussement m d'épaules

B *vtr* (*p prés etc* **-gg-**) hausser les épaules *fpl*
(Phrasal verb)
 ■ **shrug off:** ▸ ～ **off [sth]**, ～ **[sth] off** ignorer [*problem, rumour*]

shrunk /ʃrʌŋk/ *pp* ▸ **shrink B, C**

shrunken /'ʃrʌŋkən/ *adj* [*person, body*] rabougri; [*budget*] réduit; [*head*] tête *f* réduite

shucks○ /ʃʌks/ *excl* US (in irritation) zut○, mince○; (in embarrassment) allons donc

shudder /'ʃʌdə(r)/
A *n* ① (of person) frisson *m* (**of** de); **the news sent a ～ of terror through them** à l'annonce de la nouvelle, un frisson de terreur les parcourut; **with a ～** en frissonnant; ② (of vehicle) secousse *f*; **to give a ～** avoir une secousse
B *vi* ① [*person*] frissonner; **to ～ with** frissonner de [*fear etc*]; **I ～ to think!** j'en ai des frissons rien que d'y penser!; ② [*vehicle*] (once) avoir un soubresaut; **to ～ to a halt** avoir quelques soubresauts et s'arrêter

shuffle /'ʃʌfl/
A *n* ① (way of walking) pas *mpl* traînants; ② (sound of walk) bruit *m* de pas traînants
B *vtr* ① (*also* ～ **about**) déplacer [*objects, people*]; ② **to ～ one's feet (in embarrassment)** agiter ses pieds (par embarras); ③ (mix together) mélanger [*papers*]; ④ Games battre [*cards*]
C *vi* traîner les pieds; **to ～ along** marcher en traînant les pieds
(Phrasal verb)
 ■ **shuffle off:** ▸ ～ **off** partir en traînant les pieds; ▸ ～ **off [sth]** se décharger de [*responsibility, blame, guilt*] (**on(to) sb** sur qn)

shufty○ /'ʃʊftɪ/ *n* GB **to have a ～ at sth** jeter un coup d'œil sur qch

shun /ʃʌn/ *vtr* (*p prés etc* **-nn-**) ① (avoid) fuir [*people, publicity*]; dédaigner [*work*]; ② (reject) rejeter

shunt /ʃʌnt/
A *n* Med, Elec shunt *m*
B *vtr* ① ○(send) expédier○; **to be ～ed from place to place** être expédié d'un endroit à l'autre; **to ～ sb back and forth** ballotter qn d'un côté à l'autre; ② Rail (move) aiguiller [*wagon, engine*] (**into** sur)
C *vi* **to ～ back and forth** manœuvrer

shush /ʃʊʃ/
A *excl* chut!
B ○*vtr* faire taire [*person*]

shut /ʃʌt/
A *adj* (closed) [*door, book, box, mouth, shop*] fermé; **to slam the door ～** claquer la porte (pour bien la fermer); **to slam ～** se refermer en claquant; **to keep one's mouth**○ ～ se taire
B *vtr* (*p prés* **-tt-**; *prét, pp* **shut**) ① (close) fermer; ～ **your mouth** *ou* **trap**○ *ou* **face**○! ferme-la○!; ② (confine) = **shut up 2**
C *vi* (*p prés* **-tt-**; *prét, pp* **shut**) ① [*door, book, box, mouth*] se fermer; ② [*office, factory*] fermer
(Phrasal verbs)
 ■ **shut away:** ▸ ～ **[sb/sth] away**, ～ **away [sb/sth]** (lock up) enfermer [*person*]; mettre [qch] sous clé [*valuables, medicine*]
 ■ **shut down:** ▸ ～ **down** [*business*] fermer; [*machinery*] s'arrêter; ▸ ～ **[sth] down**, ～ **down [sth]** fermer [*business*]; arrêter [*machinery*]
 ■ **shut in:** ▸ ～ **[sb/sth] in** enfermer [*person, animal*]; **to feel shut in** fig se sentir étouffé
 ■ **shut off:** ▸ ～ **[sth] off**, ～ **off [sth]** couper [*supply, motor*]; arrêter [*oven, fan*]; fermer [*valve*]
 ■ **shut out:** ▸ ～ **out [sth/sb]**, ～ **[sth/sb] out** ① (keep out) laisser [qch] dehors [*animal, noise*]; éliminer [*noise*]; **to be shut out** être à la porte; ② (keep at bay) chasser [*thought*]; ③ (reject) repousser [*world*]; **to feel shut out** se sentir exclu; ④ (block) empêcher [qch] d'entrer [*light*]; bloquer [*view*]
 ■ **shut up:** ▸ ～ **up**○ se taire (**about** au sujet de); ▸ ～ **[sb] up**, ～ **up [sb]** ① ○(silence) faire taire; ② (confine) enfermer (**in** dans); ③ (close) fermer [*house*]; **to ～ up shop**○ lit, fig fermer boutique○

shutdown /'ʃʌtdaʊn/ *n* gen fermeture *f*; (of nuclear reactor) arrêt *m* (du réacteur)

shut-eye○ /'ʃʌtaɪ/ *n* **to get some ～** (short sleep) piquer un roupillon○

shutout *n* US victoire *f* écrasante (*l'équipe perdante ne marquant aucun point*)

shutter /'ʃʌtə(r)/ *n* ① (on window) (wooden, metal) volet *m*; (on shopfront) store *m*; **to put up the ～s** lit fermer le magasin; fig fermer boutique○; ② Phot obturateur *m*; ～ **speed** vitesse *f* d'obturation

shuttle /'ʃʌtl/
A *n* ① (transport service) navette *f* also Aerosp; ② Sport (*also* ～**cock**) volant *m*
B *vtr* transporter [*passengers*]
C *vi* **to ～ between** faire la navette entre

shuttle: ～ **bus** *n* navette *f*; ～ **diplomacy** *n* Pol démarches *fpl* diplomatiques; ～ **service** *n* service *m* de navette

shy /ʃaɪ/
A *adj* ① (timid) [*person*] timide (**with, of** avec); [*animal*] farouche (**with, of** avec); ② (afraid) **to be ～ of** avoir peur de; ③ (avoid) **to fight ～ of** fuir devant
B *vi* [*horse*] faire un écart (**at** devant)
(Phrasal verb)
 ■ **shy away** se tenir à l'écart (**from** de); **to ～ away from doing** répugner à faire

shyness /'ʃaɪnɪs/ *n* timidité *f*

Siamese /ˌsaɪə'miːz/ ▸ p. 1032, p. 969
A *n* ① (person) Siamois/-e *m/f*; ② (language) siamois *m*; ③ (cat) siamois/-e *m/f*
B *adj* siamois

Siberia /saɪ'bɪərɪə/ ▸ p. 774 *pr n* Sibérie *f*

sibling /'sɪblɪŋ/ *n* frère/sœur *m/f*

Sicily /'sɪsɪlɪ/ ▸ p. 954 *pr n* Sicile *f*

sick /sɪk/
A *n* ① **the ～** (+ *v pl*) les malades *mpl*; ② ○GB (vomit) vomi *m*
B *adj* ① (ill) malade; **to feel ～** ne pas se sentir bien; **to take ～** GB tomber malade; **off ～** GB absent pour cause de maladie; **to go ～**○ se faire porter malade; ② (nauseous) **to be ～** vomir; **to feel ～** avoir mal au cœur; **you'll make yourself ～** tu vas te rendre malade; **to have a ～ feeling in one's stomach** (from nerves) avoir l'estomac noué; **worried ～** malade d'inquiétude; ③ (tasteless) [*joke, story*] malsain, de mauvais goût; ④ (disturbed) [*mind, imagination*] malsain; ⑤ (disgusted) écœuré, dégoûté; **you make me ～!** tu m'écœures!; **it's enough to make you ～!** il y a de quoi vous rendre malade!; ⑥ ○(fed-up) **to be ～ of sth/sb**○ en avoir assez *or* marre○ de qn/qch; **to be ～ and tired of sth/sb**○ en avoir ras le bol○ de qch/qn; **to be ～ of the sight of sth/sb**○ ne plus supporter qch/qn
(Phrasal verb)
 ■ **sick up**○ GB: ▸ ～ **up [sth]**, ～ **[sth] up**○ vomir

sick: ～ **bay** *n* infirmerie *f*; ～**bed** *n* lit *m* de malade

sicken /'sɪkən/
A *vtr* rendre [qn] malade; fig écœurer
B *vi* ① [*person, animal*] littér tomber malade, dépérir; **to be ～ing for something** couver quelque chose; ② fig (grow weary) **to ～ of** se lasser de

sickening /'sɪkənɪŋ/ *adj* ① [*sight*] qui soulève le cœur; [*smell, cruelty*] écœurant; ② ○(annoying) [*person, behaviour*] insupportable

sickle /'sɪkl/ *n* faucille *f*

sick leave *n* congé *m* de maladie

sickly /'sɪklɪ/ *adj* ① [*person*] maladif/-ive; [*plant*] mal en point; [*complexion*] blafard; ② [*smell, taste*] écœurant; [*colour*] fadasse; ～ **sweet** douceâtre

sickness /'sɪknɪs/ *n* ① (illness) maladie *f*; **in ～ and in health** ≈ pour le meilleur et pour le pire; ② (nausea) **bouts of ～** vomissements *mpl*

sickness: ～ **benefit** *n* ₵ GB prestations *fpl* de l'assurance-maladie; ～ **insurance** *n* assurance *f* maladie

sick: ～ **note**○ *n* (for school) mot *m* d'excuse; (for work) certificat *m* médical; ～**pay** *n* indemnité *f* de maladie; ～**room** *n* (in school, institution) infirmerie *f*; (at home) chambre *f* de malade

side /saɪd/
A *n* ① (part) (of person's body, object, table) côté *m*; (of animal's body, hill, boat) flanc *m*; (of ravine, cave) paroi *f*; (of box) (outer) côté *m*; (inner) paroi *f*; **on my left/right ～** à ma gauche/droite; **on one's/its ～** sur le côté; ～ **by** côte à côte; **don't leave my ～** reste près de moi; **the north ～ of town** le nord de la

ville; **'this ~ up'** (on box) 'haut'; [2] (surface of flat object) (of paper, cloth) côté *m*; (of record) face *f*; **the right ~** (of cloth) l'endroit *m*; (of coin) l'avers *m*; (of paper) le recto; **the wrong ~** (of cloth) l'envers *m*; (of coin) le revers; (of paper) le verso; [3] (edge) (of lake, road) bord *m*; (of building) côté *m*; **at** *ou* **by the ~ of** au bord de [*lake, road*]; [4] (aspect) (of person, argument) côté *m*; (of problem, question) aspect *m*; (of story) version *f*; **she's on the arts ~** (academically) elle a opté pour les lettres; **he's on the marketing ~** (in company) il fait partie du service de marketing; [5] (opposing group) côté *m*, camp *m*; **to take ~s** prendre position; [6] (team) équipe *f*; **you've really let the ~ down** tu nous as laissé tomber; [7] (page) page *f*; [8] (line of descent) **on his mother's ~** du côté de sa mère; [9] ◦(TV channel) chaîne *f*

B *noun modifier* [*door, window, entrance, view*] latéral

C **-sided** *combining form* **six-~d figure** figure *f* à six côtés; **many-~d problem** problème *m* complexe

D **on the side** *adv phr* **with salad on the ~** avec de la salade; **to do sth on the ~** (in addition) faire qch à côté; (illegally) faire qch au noir

(Idioms) **like the ~ of a house** énorme; **time is on our ~** le temps travaille pour nous; **to be on the safe ~** (allowing enough time) pour calculer large; (to be certain) pour être sûr; **(a bit) on the big ~** plutôt grand; **to get on the wrong ~ of sb** prendre qn à rebrousse-poil; **to get on the right ~ of sb** se mettre bien avec qn; **to have right on one's ~** être dans son droit; **to put sth to one ~** mettre [qch] de côté [*object, task*]; **to take sb to one ~** prendre qn à part

(Phrasal verb)
■ **side with** se mettre du côté de [*person*]

side: **~ arm** *n* arme *f* de protection; **~board** *n* buffet *m*; **~boards** GB, **sideburns** *npl* (on face) pattes *fpl*; **~ dish** *n* Culin plat *m* d'accompagnement; **~ effect** *n* lit (of drug) effet *m* secondaire; fig (of action) répercussion *f*; **~ issue** *n* question *f* annexe; **~kick**◦ *n* acolyte *m*

sidelight /'saɪdlaɪt/ *n* [1] Aut feu *m* de position; [2] (window) (in house) lucarne *f*; (in car) déflecteur *m*

sideline /'saɪdlaɪn/ *n* [1] (extra) à-côté *m*; **as a ~** comme à-côté; [2] Sport ligne *f* de touche; **over the ~** en touche; **on the ~s** lit, fig sur la touche

side: **~long** *adj* [*look*] oblique; **~ order** *n* Culin portion *f*; **~ plate** *n* petite assiette *f*; **~ road** *n* petite route *f*; **~ saddle** *n* selle *f* d'amazone; **~ show** *n* (at fair) attraction *f*; **~splitting**◦ *adj* très drôle; **~step** *vtr* (*p prés etc* **-pp-**) lit éviter [*opponent*]; fig éluder [*issue*]; **~ street** *n* petite rue *f*; **~swipe** *vtr* emboutir [qch] sur le côté

sidetrack *vtr* fig fourvoyer [*person*]; **to get ~ed** se fourvoyer

sidewalk *n* US trottoir *m*

sideways /'saɪdweɪz/
A *adj* [*look, glance*] de travers; **a ~ move in his career** une bifurcation dans sa carrière
B *adv* [*move*] latéralement; [*carry*] sur le côté; [*park*] de biais; [*look at*] de travers; **~ on** [*person*] de profil

(Idiom) **to knock sb ~** fig sidérer qn

side-whiskers /saɪd/ *npl* favoris *mpl*

siding /'saɪdɪŋ/ *n* [1] Rail voie *f* de garage; [2] US (weatherproof coating) revêtement *m* extérieur

sidle /'saɪdl/ *vi* **to ~ into/out of** se faufiler dans/hors de; **to ~ up to** s'avancer furtivement vers qn

SIDS /sɪdz/ *n* Med *abrév* ▸ **sudden infant death syndrome**

siege /si:dʒ/ *n* siège *m*; **to lay ~ to sth** lit, fig assiéger qch

Sierra Leone /sɪ,erəlɪ'əʊn/ ▸ p. 774 *n* Sierra Leone *f*

siesta /sɪ'estə/ *n* sieste *f*; **to have a ~** faire la sieste

sieve /sɪv/
A *n* (for draining) passoire *f*; (for sifting) tamis *m*; (for coal, stones) crible *m*; (for wheat) van *m*
B *vtr* tamiser [*earth, flour*]; passer [qch] au crible [*coal*]; vanner [*wheat*]

sift /sɪft/
A *vtr* [1] (sieve) tamiser, passer [qch] au tamis [*flour, soil*]; passer [qch] au crible [*coal*]; vanner [*wheat*]; [2] fig (sort) passer [qch] au crible [*data, evidence, information*]

(Phrasal verbs)
■ **sift out**: ▸ ~ **out [sb]** (dispose of) éliminer [*troublemakers*]; ▸ ~ **out [sth]** extraire [*gold etc*]
■ **sift through**: ▸ ~ **through [sth]** trier

sifter /'sɪftə(r)/ *n* saupoudreuse *f*

sigh /saɪ/
A *n* soupir *m*; **to breathe** *ou* **heave a ~** pousser un soupir
B *vi* [1] (exhale) soupirer, pousser un soupir; **to ~ with relief** pousser un soupir de soulagement; [2] (complain) **to ~ over sth** se lamenter sur qch; [3] (whisper) [*wind*] gémir; [*trees*] bruisser

sight /saɪt/
A *n* [1] (faculty) vue *f*; **to have good/poor ~** avoir une bonne/ mauvaise vue; [2] (act of seeing) vue *f*; **at first ~** à première vue; **at the ~ of** à la vue de [*blood*]; **at the ~ of her** en la voyant; **this was my first ~ of** c'était la première fois que je voyais; **to catch ~ of sb/sth** apercevoir qn/qch; **to lose ~ of sb/sth** lit, fig perdre qn/qch de vue; **we mustn't lose ~ of the fact that** fig nous ne devons pas perdre de vue que; **to know sb by ~** connaître qn de vue; **I can't stand the ~ of him!** je ne peux pas le voir (en peinture)!; [3] (range of vision) **to be in ~** [*land, border*] être en vue; [*peace, freedom*] être proche; **the end is in ~!** on approche de la fin!; **there wasn't a soldier in ~** il n'y avait pas un soldat en vue; **to come into ~** apparaître; **to be out of ~** (hidden) être caché; (having moved) ne plus être visible; **to do sth out of ~ of sb** faire qch sans être vu par qn; **to stay out of ~** rester caché; **to keep sb/sth out of ~** cacher qn/qch; **don't let her out of your ~!** ne la quitte pas des yeux!; [4] (thing seen) spectacle *m*; **a ~ to behold** un spectacle à voir; **it was not a pretty ~!** iron ce n'était pas beau à voir!; [5] (a shock to see) (place) porcherie *f*; (person) **you're a ~!** tu n'es pas présentable!
B **sights** *npl* [1] (places worth seeing) attractions *fpl* touristiques (**of** de); **to see the ~s** visiter; **to show sb the ~s** (in town) faire visiter la ville à qn; [2] (on rifle, telescope) viseur *m*; [3] fig **to have sth in one's ~s** avoir qch dans sa ligne de mire; **to have sb in one's ~s** avoir qn dans le collimateur◦; **to set one's ~s on sth** viser qch; **to raise/lower one's ~s** viser plus haut/plus bas

(Idioms) **a damned** *ou* **jolly** GB **~ better** beaucoup mieux; **out of ~, out of mind** Prov loin des yeux, loin du cœur Prov; **out of ~◦!** fantastique◦!

sighted /'saɪtɪd/ *adj* [*person*] doué de la vue

sight: **~-read** *vtr, vi* déchiffrer; **~-reading** *n* déchiffrage *m*

sightseeing /'saɪtsi:ɪŋ/ *n* tourisme *m*; **to go ~** faire du tourisme

sight: **~seer** *n* gen touriste *mf*; péj badaud/-e *m/f*; **~ unseen** *adv* Comm [*buy*] sur description

sign /saɪn/
A *n* [1] (symbolic mark) signe *m*, symbole *m*; **the pound ~** le symbole de la livre sterling; [2] (object) (roadsign, billboard) panneau *m*; (smaller, indicating opening hours) pancarte *f*; (outside inn, shop) enseigne *f*; [3] (gesture) geste *m*; **the ~ of the cross** le signe de la croix; [4] (signal) signal *m*; **the ~ for us to leave** le signal du départ; [5] (visible evidence) signe *m*; **there was no ~ of life** il n'y avait aucun signe de vie; **there was no ~ of any troops** il n'y avait pas l'ombre d'un soldat; [6] (indication, pointer) signe *m*; **this is a ~ that** c'est signe que, ça indique que; **the ~s are that** tout indique que; **there is no ~** *ou* **there are no ~s of** il n'y a rien qui annonce [*change, violence*]; **to show ~s of** montrer des signes de [*stress, talent*]; **to show ~s of doing** sembler faire; [7] ▸ p. 1350 (of zodiac) signe *m*; **what ~ are you?** tu es de quel signe?
B *vtr* [1] (put signature to) signer; **~ed, sealed and delivered** lit dûment signé et remis à qui de droit; fig terminé; [2] (on contract) engager [*footballer, band*]
C *vi* [1] (put signature) **to ~ for** signer un reçu pour; [2] Sport signer son contrat; [3] (signal) **to ~ to sb to do** faire signe à qn de faire; [4] (communicate) communiquer en langage des sourds-muets

(Phrasal verbs)
■ **sign away**: ▸ ~ **away [sth]**, ~ **[sth] away** renoncer à [qch] par écrit [*rights, inheritance*]
■ **sign in**: ▸ ~ **in** signer le registre (à l'arrivée); ▸ ~ **in [sb]**, ~ **[sb] in** inscrire [*guest*]
■ **sign off** (all contexts) terminer
■ **sign on**: ▸ ~ **on** [1] GB (for benefit) pointer au chômage; [2] (to course of study) s'inscrire (**for** à, dans)
■ **sign out** signer le registre (au départ)
■ **sign up**: ▸ ~ **up** [1] (in forces, by contract) s'engager;

2 (for course) s'inscrire (**for** à, dans); ▸ **~ up [sb]** engager [*player, filmstar*]

signal /'sɪgnl/
A *n* **1** (cue) signal *m* (**for** de); **to give the ~ to attack** donner le signal de l'attaque; **this is a ~ to do** cela indique qu'il faut faire; **2** (sign, indication) signe *m* (**of** de); **to be a ~ that** être signe que, indiquer que; **to send a ~ to sb that** indiquer (clairement) à qn que; **3** Rail signal *m*; **4** Radio, TV, Elec signal *m*; **to read the ~s** fig comprendre
B *adj* [*honour*] véritable (*before n*); [*failure*] notoire
C *vtr* (*p prés etc* **-ll-** GB, **-l-** US) **1** (gesture) **to ~ (to sb) that** faire signe (à qn) que; **to ~ sb to do** faire signe à qn de faire; **2** (indicate) indiquer [*shift, determination, support*]; annoncer [*release*]; **to ~ one's intention to do** annoncer son intention de faire; **to ~ that** indiquer que; **3** (mark) marquer [*end, beginning, decline*]
D *vi* (*p prés etc* **-ll-** GB, **-l-** US) faire des signes

signal: **~ box** *n* Rail poste *m* d'aiguillage *m*; **~man** ▸ p. 1181 *n* Rail aiguilleur *m*

signatory /'sɪgnətrɪ, US -tɔːrɪ/ *n, adj* signataire (*mf*)

signature /'sɪgnətʃə(r)/ *n* signature *f*; **to put** *ou* **set one's ~ to** apposer sa signature à [*letter, document*]

signature tune *n* indicatif *m*

signboard /'saɪnbɔːd/ *n* panneau *m* d'affichage

signet ring /'sɪgnɪtrɪŋ/ *n* chevalière *f*

significance /sɪg'nɪfɪkəns/ *n* **1** (importance) importance *f*; **not of any ~, of no ~** sans aucune importance; **2** (meaning) signification *f*

significant /sɪg'nɪfɪkənt/ *adj* **1** (substantial) considérable; **2** (important) important; **3** (meaningful) [*gesture*] éloquent; [*name, figure*] significatif/-ive; [*phrase*] lourd de sens; **it is ~ that** il est significatif que (+ *subj*)

significantly /sɪg'nɪfɪkəntlɪ/ *adv* **1** (considerably) sensiblement; **2** (meaningfully) [*named*] de façon significative

signify /'sɪgnɪfaɪ/ *vtr* **1** (denote) [*symbol, gesture, statement*] indiquer; [*dream*] signifier; **2** (display) exprimer [*disapproval, joy*]; **to ~ that** indiquer que

signing /'saɪnɪŋ/ *n* **1** (of treaty) signature *f*; **2** (of footballer) signature *f*; **3** = **sign language**

sign language *n* code *m* or langage *m* gestuel

signpost /'saɪnpəʊst/
A *n* **1** gen panneau *m* indicateur; **2** (old free-standing type) poteau *m* indicateur; **3** fig (pointer) indice *m*, indication *f*
B *vtr* indiquer; **to be ~ed** être indiqué

signposting *n* signalisation *f* routière

Sikh /siːk/ *n, adj* sikh (*mf*)

silage /'saɪlɪdʒ/ *n* fourrage *m* ensilé, ensilage *m*

silence /'saɪləns/
A *n* **1** (quietness) silence *m*; **in ~** en silence; **~ fell** le silence se fit; **2** (pause) silence *m*; **3** (absence of communication) silence *m* (**about, on, over** sur); **to break one's ~** sortir de son silence; **right of ~** Jur droit pour un accusé de se taire avant ou pendant son procès; **4** (discretion) silence *m*
B *vtr* **1** (quieten) faire taire [*person, enemy guns*]; **2** (gag) faire taire [*critic, press*]

silencer /'saɪlənsə(r)/ *n* Mil, GB Aut silencieux *m*

silent /'saɪlənt/ *adj* **1** (quiet) silencieux/-ieuse; **to be ~** se taire; **to remain** *ou* **stay ~** rester silencieux; **to fall ~** se taire; **2** (taciturn) taciturne; **3** (unexpressed) [*disapproval, prayer*] muet/muette; **4** Cin muet/muette; **the ~ screen** le cinéma muet; **5** Ling muet/muette

(Idiom) **as ~ as the grave** muet comme une tombe

silently /'saɪləntlɪ/ *adv* [*appear, leave, move*] silencieusement; [*listen, pray, stare, work*] en silence

silent: **~ majority** *n* majorité *f* silencieuse; **~ partner** *n* Comm, Jur commanditaire *m*

Silesia /saɪ'liːzɪə/ ▸ p. 774 *pr n* Silésie *f*

silhouette /ˌsɪluː'et/
A *n* silhouette *f*
B *vtr* **to be ~d against sth** se détacher sur qch

silicon /'sɪlɪkən/ *n* silicium *m*

silicon chip *n* Comput puce *f* électronique

silicone /'sɪlɪkəʊn/ *n* Chem silicone *f*; (in pharmacy) silicone *m*; **~ rubber** silicone *m* élastomère

Silicon Valley *pr n* Silicon Valley *f*, zone *f* d'industries électroniques

silk /sɪlk/
A *n* **1** (fabric) soie *f*; **2** (thread) fil *m* de soie; **3** (clothing)

soierie *f*; **4** (of spider) soie *f*; **5** GB, Jur avocat *m* de la couronne
B *noun modifier* [*garment*] de soie

(Idiom) **as soft** *ou* **smooth as ~** doux comme de la soie

silken /'sɪlkən/ *adj* **1** (shiny) soyeux/-euse; **2** (made of silk) de soie; **3** (soft) [*voice*] doux/douce; *péj* doucereux/-euse *péj*

silk: **~ factory** *n* soierie *f*; **~ farming** *n* sériciculture *f*; **~ finish** *adj* [*fabric*] soyeux/-euse; [*paint*] satiné; **~ hat** *n* haut-de-forme *m*; **~ route** *n* route *f* de la soie; **~-screen printing** *n* sérigraphie *f*; **~ square** *n* carré *m* de soie; **~worm** *n* ver *m* à soie

silky /'sɪlkɪ/ *adj* **1** [*fabric, hair, skin*] soyeux/-euse; **2** (soft) [*voice*] doux/douce; *péj* doucereux/-euse *péj*

sill /sɪl/ *n* (of window) (interior) rebord *m*; (exterior) appui *m*

silliness /'sɪlɪnɪs/ *n* sottise *f*, stupidité *f*

silly /'sɪlɪ/
A *adj* [*person*] idiot; [*question, game*] stupide; [*behaviour, clothes*] ridicule; **don't be ~** ne dis pas de bêtises; **what a ~ thing to do!** quelle bêtise!; **to make sb look ~** faire passer qn pour un/-e idiot/-e
B *adv* **to drink oneself ~** s'abrutir d'alcool; **to bore sb ~** assommer qn

silly season /'sɪlɪ/ *n* GB période *f* creuse (*où la presse se contente de frivolités*)

silo /'saɪləʊ/ *n* (*pl* **~s**) Agric, Mil silo *m*

silt /sɪlt/
A *n* limon *m*, vase *f*
B *vi* (*also* **~ up**) [*river*] (with mud) s'envaser; (with sand) s'ensabler

silver /'sɪlvə(r)/ ▸ p. 752
A *n* **1** (metal, colour) argent *m*; **2** (silverware) argenterie *f*; (cutlery) couverts *mpl* en argent; (coins) monnaie *f*; **3** (medal) médaille *f* d'argent
B *adj* [*ring, coin*] en argent; [*hair, moon*] argenté; [*paint*] gris métallisé *inv*

silver: **~ birch** *n* bouleau *m* argenté; **~ foil** *n* GB papier *m* d'aluminium; **~-gilt** *n* vermeil *m*; **~-grey** ▸ p. 752 *adj* [*hair, silk*] gris-argent *inv*; [*paint*] gris métallisé *inv*; **~-haired** *adj* aux cheveux argentés; **~ jubilee** *n* (date) vingt-cinquième anniversaire *m*; **~ paper** *n* papier *m* d'argent; **~ plated** *adj* plaqué argent; **~ screen** *n* Cin écran *m*; **~ service** *n* service *m* stylé; **~side** *n* Culin gîte *m*; **~smith** ▸ p. 1181 *n* orfèvre *mf*; **~ surfer**° *n* internaute *mf* senior, papy/mamy *m/f* internaute°; **~ware** *n* (solid) argenterie *f* massive; (plate) métal *m* argenté; **~ wedding** *n* noces *fpl* d'argent

silvery /'sɪlvərɪ/ *adj* **1** [*hair*] argenté; **2** [*sound*] argentin

SIM card /'sɪm kɑːd/ *n* Telecom carte *f* SIM

similar /'sɪmɪlə(r)/ *adj* similaire, analogue; **something ~** quelque chose de similaire; **~ to** analogue à, comparable à; **it's ~ to riding a bike** c'est comme faire du vélo; **~ in price** comparable pour ce qui est du prix; **it is ~ in appearance to...** ça ressemble à...; **~ in colour** dans les mêmes tons

similarity /ˌsɪmɪ'lærətɪ/ *n* (fact of resembling) ressemblance *f*, similarité *f* (**to, with** avec; **in** dans)

similarly /'sɪmɪləlɪ/ *adv* [*behave, dressed*] de la même façon; [*elaborate, hostile*] aussi (*before adj*); **and ~,...** et de même,...

simile /'sɪmɪlɪ/ *n* comparaison *f*

simmer /'sɪmə(r)/
A *vtr* faire cuire [qch] à feu doux [*soup*]; laisser frémir [*water*]
B *vi* **1** [*soup*] cuire à feu doux, mijoter; [*water*] frémir; **2** fig [*person*] (with discontent) bouillonner (**with** de); (with passion, excitement) frémir (**with** de); [*revolt, violence*] couver

(Phrasal verb)
■ **simmer down**° [*person*] se calmer

simper /'sɪmpə(r)/ *vi* péj minauder

simpering /'sɪmpərɪŋ/ *adj* péj [*person*] minaudier/-ière; [*smile*] affecté

simple /'sɪmpl/ *adj* **1** (not complicated) simple; **it's a ~ matter to change a wheel** c'est très simple de changer une roue; **the ~ truth** la vérité pure et simple; **I can't make it any ~r** je ne peux pas simplifier davantage; **what**

since

As a preposition

In time expressions

since is used in English after a verb in the present perfect or progressive present perfect tense to indicate when something that is still going on started. To express this French uses a verb in the present tense + *depuis*:

I've been waiting since Saturday
= j'attends depuis samedi

I've lived in Rome since 1988
= j'habite à Rome depuis 1988

When *since* is used after a verb in the past perfect tense, French uses the imperfect + *depuis*:

I had been waiting since nine o'clock
= j'attendais depuis neuf heures

In negative time expressions

Again *since* is translated by *depuis*, but in negative sentences the tenses used in French are the same as those used in English:

I haven't seen him since Saturday
= je ne l'ai pas vu depuis samedi

I hadn't seen him since 1978
= je ne l'avais pas vu depuis 1978

As a conjunction

In time expressions

When *since* is used as a conjunction, it is translated by *depuis que* and the tenses used in French parallel exactly those used with the preposition *depuis* (see above):

since she's been living in Oxford
= depuis qu'elle habite à Oxford

since he'd been in Paris
= depuis qu'il était à Paris

Note that in time expressions with *since* French native speakers will generally prefer to use a noun where possible when English uses a verb:

I haven't seen him since he left
= je ne l'ai pas vu depuis son départ

she's been living in Nice since she got married
= elle habite à Nice depuis son mariage

For particular usages see the entry **since**.

Meaning 'because'

When *since* is used to mean *because,* it is translated by *comme* or *étant donné que*:

since she was ill, she couldn't go
= comme elle était malade *or* étant donné qu'elle était malade, elle ne pouvait pas y aller

As an adverb

When *since* is used as an adverb it is translated by *depuis*:

he hasn't been seen since
= on ne l'a pas vu depuis

---

could be ~r? rien de plus facile!; **computing made ~** l'informatique à la portée de tous; ② (not elaborate) [*dress, furniture, style*] sobre; [*food, tastes*] simple; ③ (unsophisticated) simple; ④ (dimwitted) simplet/-ette°, simple d'esprit; ⑤ (basic) [*structure*] simple; [*sentence, tense*] simple
simple: ~ **fraction** *n* fraction *f*; **~-minded** *adj* péj [*person*] simple d'esprit; [*attitude*] naïf/naïve
simpleton /'sɪmpltən/ *n* simple *mf* d'esprit
simplicity /sɪm'plɪsətɪ/ *n* (all contexts) simplicité *f*
simplification /ˌsɪmplɪfɪ'keɪʃn/ *n* simplification *f*
simplify /'sɪmplɪfaɪ/ *vtr* simplifier
simplistic /sɪm'plɪstɪk/ *adj* simpliste
simply /'sɪmplɪ/ *adv* ① [*write, dress, live*] simplement, avec simplicité; **to put it ~...** en deux mots...; ② (merely) simplement; **it's ~ a question of explaining** il suffit d'expliquer; ③ (absolutely) absolument
simulate /'sɪmjʊleɪt/ *vtr* ① (feign) simuler [*anger, illness, grief*]; affecter [*interest*]; ② (reproduce) simuler [*behaviour, conditions*]; imiter [*blood, sound*]
simulated /'sɪmjʊleɪtɪd/ *adj* ① (fake) [*fur, pearls*] artificiel/-ielle; ② (feigned) [*anger, grief*] simulé, feint
simulation /ˌsɪmjʊ'leɪʃn/ *n* simulation *f*
simulator /'sɪmjʊleɪtə(r)/ *n* simulateur *m*
simulcast /'sɪməlkɑːst, US -kæst/ *vtr* diffuser [qch] simultanément à la radio et à la télévision
simultaneity /ˌsɪmltə'niːətɪ, US ˌsaɪm-/ *n* simultanéité *f*
simultaneous /ˌsɪml'teɪnɪəs, US ˌsaɪm-/ *adj* simultané; **to be ~** avoir lieu en même temps (**with** que)
simultaneously /ˌsɪml'teɪnɪəslɪ, US ˌsaɪm-/ *adv* simultanément
sin /sɪn/
A *n* péché *m*, crime *m*; **to live in ~** vivre dans le péché; **it's a ~ to steal** voler est un péché
B *vi* (*p prés etc* **-nn-**) pécher (**against** contre)
(Idiom) **for my ~s** hum malheureusement pour moi

since /sɪns/
A *prep* depuis; **she'd been a teacher ~ 1965** elle était professeur depuis 1965; **she's been waiting ~ 10 am** elle attend depuis 10 heures; **I haven't seen him ~ then** je ne l'ai pas vu depuis; **~ arriving** *ou* **~ his arrival** he... depuis son arrivée *or* depuis qu'il est arrivé, il...
B *conj* ① (from the time when) depuis que; **~ he's been away** depuis qu'il est absent; **ever ~ I married him** depuis que nous nous sommes mariés, depuis notre mariage; **it's 10 years ~ we last met** cela fait 10 ans que nous ne nous sommes pas revus; ② (because) comme, étant donné que; **~ you're so clever, why don't you do it yourself?** puisque tu es tellement malin, pourquoi ne le fais-tu pas toi-même?
C *adv* depuis
sincere /sɪn'sɪə(r)/ *adj* [*person, apology, thanks, belief*] sincère; [*attempt*] réel/réelle
sincerely /sɪn'sɪəlɪ/ *adv* sincèrement; **Yours ~, Sincerely yours** US (end of letter) Veuillez agréer, Monsieur/Madame, l'expression de mes sentiments les meilleurs; (less formally) Cordialement (vôtre)
sincerity /sɪn'serətɪ/ *n* sincérité *f*; **with ~** sincèrement
sine /saɪn/ *n* Math sinus *m*
sinew /'sɪnjuː/ *n* Anat tendon *m*
sinewy /'sɪnjuːɪ/ *adj* ① [*person, animal*] (mince et) musclé; ② [*meat*] tendineux/-euse
sinful /'sɪnfl/ *adj* [*pleasure, thought, waste*] immoral; [*world*] impie; **a ~ man** un pécheur
sing /sɪŋ/
A *vtr* (*prét* **sang**; *pp* **sung**) chanter; **to ~ a role** chanter dans un rôle; **to ~ the part of** chanter dans le rôle de; **to ~ sth for sb** chanter qch pour qn; **to ~ sb to sleep** chanter pour endormir qn; **to ~ sb's praises** chanter les louanges de qn
B *vi* (*prét* **sang**; *pp* **sung**) ① [*person*] chanter; **to ~ in/out of tune** chanter juste/faux; **to ~ to an accompaniment** chanter avec un accompagnement; ② [*bird, cricket, kettle*] chanter; [*wind*] siffler; **to make sb's ears ~** faire siffler les

oreilles de qn; ③ ○(confess) se mettre à table○

(Idiom) **to ∼ a different** ou **another song** changer d'avis.

(Phrasal verbs)
■ **sing out:** ▸ ∼ **out** (sing loud) entonner; (call out) appeler; ▸ ∼ **out [sth]** (shout) crier
■ **sing up** chanter plus fort

sing. abrév écrite = **singular**

sing-along /'sɪŋəlɒŋ/ n US **to have a ∼** chanter ensemble

Singapore /ˌsɪŋə'pɔː(r)/ ▸ p. 1276, p. 954, p. 774 pr n Singapour f; **in/to ∼** à Singapour

singe /sɪndʒ/
A n (also ∼ **mark**) gen légère brûlure f; (from iron) roussissure f
B vtr (p prés **singeing**) brûler [qch] légèrement [hair, clothing]; (when ironing) roussir [clothes]

singer /'sɪŋə(r)/ n chanteur/-euse m/f; **he's a good ∼** il chante bien

singing /'sɪŋɪŋ/
A n ① Mus chant m; **to teach ∼** enseigner le chant; **opera ∼** chant d'opéra; **to hear ∼** entendre chanter; ② (of kettle, wind) sifflement m
B noun modifier [lesson] de chant; [career] dans la chanson; **∼ voice** voix f

single /'sɪŋgl/
A n ① (also ∼ **ticket**) aller m simple; ② Tourism (also ∼ **room**) chambre f à une personne; ③ Mus (record) 45 tours m
B adj ① (sole) seul; **a ∼ rose** une seule rose; **in a ∼ day** en une seule journée; ② (not double) [sink] à un bac; [unit] simple; [door] à un battant; [wardrobe] à une porte; [sheet, duvet] pour une personne; **inflation is in ∼ figures** Econ l'inflation est inférieure à 10%; ③ (for one) [bed, tariff, portion] pour une personne; ④ (unmarried) célibataire; ⑤ (used emphatically) **every ∼ day** tous les jours sans exception; **every ∼ one of those people** chacune de ces personnes; **there wasn't a ∼ person there** il n'y avait absolument personne; **not a ∼ thing was left** il ne restait pas la moindre chose; ⑥ (describing main cause, aspect) **the ∼ most important factor** le facteur principal

(Phrasal verb)
■ **single out:** ▸ ∼ **[sb/sth] out, ∼ out [sb/sth]** [person] choisir; **to be ∼d out for** faire l'objet de [special treatment, praise]; être l'objet de [attention]; être la proie de [criticism]

single: **∼-breasted** adj [jacket] droit; **∼ combat** n combat m singulier; **∼ cream** n ≈ crème f fraîche liquide; **∼ currency** n monnaie f unique; **∼ decker** n autobus m sans impériale; **∼ file** adv en file indienne; **∼-handedly** adv tout seul; **∼ market** n marché m unique

single-minded /ˌsɪŋgl'maɪndɪd/ adj [determination] farouche; [person] tenace, résolu; **to be ∼ about doing** être résolu à faire

single mother n mère f qui élève ses enfants seule

single parent n parent m isolé; **∼ family** famille monoparentale

single-party /ˌsɪŋgl'pɑːtɪ/ adj [government, rule] à parti unique

singles /'sɪŋglz/ n ① Sport (event) **the women's ∼** le simple dames; ② (people) célibataires mpl

singles: **∼ bar** n bar m de rencontres pour célibataires; **∼ charts** npl palmarès m des 45 tours

single: **∼ seater** n avion m monoplace; **∼-sex** adj non mixte; **∼-sided disk** n disquette f simple face; **∼-storey** adj [house] de plain-pied

singlet /'sɪŋglɪt/ n GB ① Sport maillot m; ② (vest) maillot m de corps

single-track adj [line, road] à une voie; fig [commitment] entier/-ière

singly /'sɪŋglɪ/ adv ① (one by one) un à un; ② (alone) individuellement

singsong /'sɪŋsɒŋ/ GB
A n **to have a ∼** chanter ensemble
B adj [voice, dialect] chantant

singular /'sɪŋgjʊlə(r)/
A n Ling singulier m; **in the ∼** au singulier
B adj ① Ling [noun, verb] au singulier; ② (strange) singulier/-ière

sinister /'sɪnɪstə(r)/ adj sinistre

sink /sɪŋk/
A n ① (basin) (in kitchen) évier m; (in bathroom) lavabo m; **double ∼** évier à deux bacs; ② (cesspit) lit fosse f d'aisance; fig cloaque m; ③ (also **∼hole**) doline f
B vtr (prét **sank**; pp **sunk**) ① Naut (by scuttling) couler; (by torpedo) torpiller; ② (bore) forer [oil well]; creuser [foundations]; ③ (embed) enfoncer [post, pillar]; **to ∼ one's teeth into** mordre à pleines dents dans [sandwich]; **the dog sank its teeth into my arm** le chien a planté ses crocs dans mon bras; ④ ○GB (drink) descendre○ [drink]; ⑤ Sport mettre [qch] dans le trou [billiard ball]; rentrer [putt]; ⑥ (destroy) [scandal] faire couler [party]; **without capital we're sunk** sans capital nous sommes perdus; ⑦ (invest) **to ∼ money into sth** engloutir de l'argent dans qch
C vi (prét **sank**; pp **sunk**) ① (fail to float) couler; **to ∼ without a trace** fig tomber dans les oubliettes; ② (drop to lower level) [sun, water level, pressure] baisser; [cake] redescendre; **the sun ∼s in the West** le soleil disparaît à l'ouest; **to ∼ to the floor** s'effondrer; **to ∼ to one's knees** tomber à genoux; **∼ into a chair** s'affaler dans un fauteuil; **to ∼ into a deep sleep** sombrer dans un profond sommeil; ③ fig (fall) baisser; **he has sunk in my estimation** il a baissé dans mon estime; ④ (subside) [building, wall] s'effondrer; **to ∼ into** s'enfoncer dans [mud]; sombrer dans [anarchy, obscurity]; **∼ under the weight of** [shelf] plier sous le poids de [boxes etc]; [person, company] crouler sous le poids de [debt]

(Phrasal verb)
■ **sink in** ① [lotion, water] pénétrer; ② fig [news, announcement] faire son chemin; **it took several minutes for the truth to ∼ in** il m'a fallu plusieurs minutes pour accepter la vérité

sinker /'sɪŋkə(r)/ n ① (in fishing) plomb m; ② US Culin ≈ beignet m

(Idiom) **he fell for the story hook, line and ∼** il a gobé○ toute cette histoire

sinking /'sɪŋkɪŋ/
A n ① Naut (accidental) naufrage m; (by torpedo) torpillage m; ② (of well, shaft) forage m
B adj [feeling] angoissant

sink unit n évier m encastré

sinner /'sɪnə(r)/ n pécheur/-eresse m/f

sinuous /'sɪnjʊəs/ adj sinueux/-euse

sinus /'saɪnəs/ n (pl **∼es**) sinus m inv

sinusitis /ˌsaɪnə'saɪtɪs/ ▸ p. 933 n sinusite f

sip /sɪp/
A n petite gorgée f
B vtr (p prés etc **-pp-**) boire [qch] à petites gorgées

siphon /'saɪfn/
A n siphon m
B vtr (also ∼ **off**) ① siphonner [petrol, water]; ② détourner [money] (out of, from de; into au profit de)

sir /sɜː(r)/ ▸ p. 869 n ① (form of address) Monsieur; **yes ∼** gen oui, Monsieur; (to president) oui, Monsieur le président; (to headmaster) oui, Monsieur le directeur; Mil oui, mon commandant or mon lieutenant etc; **Dear Sir** Monsieur; ② GB **Sir James** Sir James; ③ ○US (emphatic) **yes/no ∼** ça oui/non○!

sire /'saɪə(r)/ vtr engendrer

siren /'saɪərən/ n ① (alarm) sirène f; ② Mythol sirène f also fig

sirloin /'sɜːlɔɪn/ n aloyau m

sirloin steak n biftek m dans l'aloyau

sissy○ /'sɪsɪ/
A n péj (coward) poule f mouillée○; **he's a real ∼!** (effeminate) c'est une vraie fille!
B adj **that's a ∼ game!** c'est un jeu de fille!

sister /'sɪstə(r)/
A n ① (sibling) sœur f; ② GB Med infirmière f chef; ③ Relig (also **Sister**) sœur f; ④ (fellow woman) sœur f
B noun modifier [company] sœur; [publication] apparenté; **∼ country, ∼ state** pays frère; **∼ nation** nation sœur

sisterhood /'sɪstəhʊd/ n ① Relig communauté f religieuse; ② (in feminism) solidarité f féminine

sister-in-law n (pl **sisters-in-law**) belle-sœur f

sisterly /'sɪstəlɪ/ adj ① [feeling] fraternel/-elle; [rivalry] entre sœurs; ② [solidarity] féminin

sit /sɪt/
A vtr (p prés **-tt-**; prét, pp **sat**) ① (put) **to ∼ sb in/near** asseoir

S

qn dans/près de; **to ~ sth on/near** placer qch sur/près de; **2)** GB Sch, Univ se présenter à, passer [*exam*]

B *vi* (*p prés* **-tt-**; *prét, pp* **sat**) **1)** (take a seat) s'asseoir; **to ~ on the floor** s'asseoir par terre; **2)** (be seated) être assis; [*bird*] être perché (**on** sur); **to be ~ting reading** être assis à lire; **to ~ over** être penché sur; **to ~ for two hours** rester assis pendant deux heures; **to ~ quietly** être tranquillement assis; **to ~ still** se tenir tranquille; **to ~ at home** rester à la maison; **don't just ~ there!** ne reste pas là à ne rien faire!; **3)** [*committee, court*] siéger; **4)** (hold office) **to ~ as** être [*judge, magistrate*]; **to ~ on** faire partie de [*committee, jury*]; **5)** (fit) **to ~ well/badly (on sb)** [*suit, jacket*] bien/mal tomber (sur qn); **power ~s lightly on her** fig le pouvoir ne lui pèse guère; **6)** (remain untouched) **the books were still ~ting on the desk** les livres étaient toujours sur le bureau; **7)** Agric, Zool **to ~ on** couver [*eggs*]

(Idiom) **to make sb ~ up and take notice** faire réagir qn

(Phrasal verbs)

■ **sit about, sit around** rester assis à ne rien faire

■ **sit back 1)** (lean back) se caler dans son fauteuil; **2)** (relax) se détendre; **to ~ back on one's heels** s'asseoir sur les talons

■ **sit down: ▸ ~ down** s'asseoir (**at** à; **in** dans; **on** sur); **to ~ down to dinner** se mettre à table; **▸ ~ [sb] down** asseoir qn; **to ~ oneself down** s'asseoir

■ **sit in** [*observer*] assister (**on** à)

■ **sit on○: ▸ ~ on** [*sth/sb*] (not deal with) garder [qch] sous le coude○

■ **sit out: ▸ ~ out** s'asseoir dehors; **▸ ~ [sth] out** (stay to the end) rester jusqu'à la fin de; (not take part in) ne pas jouer [*game*]; attendre la fin de [*war*]

■ **sit through: ▸ ~ through [sth]** assister à

■ **sit up: ▸ ~ up 1)** (raise oneself upright) se redresser; **to be ~ing up** être assis; **~ up straight!** tiens-toi droit!; **2)** (stay up late) rester debout (**doing** pour faire); **to ~ up with sb** veiller qn; **▸ ~ [sb/sth] up** redresser

sitcom○ /'sɪtkɒm/ *n* (*abrév* = **situation comedy**) sitcom *m*

sit-down /'sɪtdaʊn/ *n* GB **to have a ~** s'asseoir

sit-down strike *n* grève *f* sur le tas

site /saɪt/

A *n* **1)** (also **building ~**) (before building) terrain *m*; (during building) chantier *m*; **2)** (land for specific activity) terrain *m*; **caravan ~** terrain de caravaning; **3)** (of building, town) emplacement *m*, site *m*; **4)** (of recent event, accident) lieux *mpl*; **5)** (on the Web) site *m*

B *vtr* construire [*building*]; **to be ~d** être situé

sit-in /'sɪtɪn/ *n* sit-in *m inv*, manifestation *f* avec occupation des locaux

sitter /'sɪtə(r)/ *n* **1)** Art, Phot modèle *m*; **2)** (babysitter) baby-sitter *mf*

sitting /'sɪtɪŋ/

A *n* **1)** (session) séance *f*; **I read it at one ~** je l'ai lu d'un seul trait; **2)** (period in which food is served) service *m*; **3)** (incubation period) couvaison *f*

B *adj* **1)** (seated) **in a ~ position** assis; **2)** Agric [*hen*] couveuse *f*

sitting: **~ duck○** *n* lit, fig cible *f or* victime *f* facile; **~ room** *n* salon *m*; **~ target** *n* lit, fig cible *f* facile; **~ tenant** *n* Jur locataire *mf* dans les lieux

situate /'sɪtjʊeɪt, US 'sɪtʃʊeɪt/ *vtr* **1)** lit situer; **to be ~d** être situé, se trouver; fig **to be well ~d to do** être bien placé pour faire; **2)** (put into context) situer

situation /ˌsɪtjʊ'eɪʃn, US ˌsɪtʃʊ-/ *n* **1)** (set of circumstances) situation *f*; **in the present economic ~** dans la conjoncture économique *or* la situation économique actuelle; **in an interview ~** lors d'un entretien; **the housing ~ is worsening** la crise du logement s'aggrave; **he doesn't know how to behave in social ~s** il ne sait pas comment se conduire en société; **2)** (of house, town etc) situation *f*; **3)** † *ou* sout (job) situation *f*, emploi *m*; **'~s vacant'** 'offres *fpl* d'emploi'

situation comedy *n* comédie *f* de situation

sit-ups /'sɪtʌps/ *npl* abdominaux *mpl*

six /sɪks/ ▸ p. 1044, p. 647

A *n* six *m inv*

B *adj* six *inv*

(Idioms) **to be (all) at ~es and sevens** [*person*] ne pas savoir où donner de la tête; [*affairs*] être sens dessus dessous; **it's ~ of one and half a dozen of the other** c'est bonnet blanc

et blanc bonnet, c'est du pareil au même; **to be ~ foot** *ou* **feet under** être enterré; **knock sb for ~○** GB laisser qn KO○

six: **Six Counties** *pr npl* six comtés *mpl* de l'Irlande du Nord; **~-pack** *n* pack *m* de six; **~pence** *n* GB (ancienne) pièce *f* de six pence

sixteen /ˌsɪk'stiːn/ *n, adj* ▸ p. 1044, p. 647 seize (*m*) *inv*

sixteenth /sɪk'stiːnθ/ ▸ p. 1044, p. 788

A *n* **1)** (in order) seizième *mf*; **2)** (of month) seize *m inv*; **3)** (fraction) seizième *m*

B *adj, adv* seizième

sixth /sɪksθ/ ▸ p. 1044, p. 788

A *n* **1)** (in order) sixième *mf*; **2)** (of month) six *m inv*; **3)** (fraction) sixième *m*; **4)** Mus sixième *f*; **5)** GB Sch ▸ **sixth form**

B *adj, adv* sixième

sixth form GB Sch *n* (lower) ≈ classes *fpl* de première; (upper) ≈ classes *fpl* de terminale; **in the ~** ≈ en première *or* en terminale

sixth: **~ form college** *n* GB Sch lycée *m* (*n'ayant que des classes de première et terminale*); **~ former** *n* ≈ élève *mf* de terminale; **~ sense** *n* sixième sens *m*

sixties /'sɪkstɪz/ ▸ p. 647, p. 788 *npl* **1)** (decade) **the ~** les années *fpl* soixante; **2)** (age) **to be in one's ~** avoir entre soixante et soixante-dix ans

sixtieth /'sɪkstɪəθ/ ▸ p. 1044

A *n* **1)** (in order) soixantième *mf*; **2)** (fraction) soixantième *m*

B *adj, adv* soixantième

sixty /'sɪkstɪ/ ▸ p. 1044, p. 647 *n, adj* soixante (*m*) *inv*

size /saɪz/ ▸ p. 1191

A *n* **1)** (dimensions) (of person, head, tree, envelope, picture) taille *f*; (of container, room, building, region) grandeur *f*; (of apple, egg, book, parcel) grosseur *f*; (of carpet, bed, machine) dimensions *fpl*; **it's about the ~ of an egg/of this room** c'est à peu près de la grosseur d'un œuf/de la grandeur de cette pièce; **he's about your ~** il est à peu près de ta taille; **to increase in ~** [*tree*] pousser; [*company, town*] s'agrandir; **to cut sth to ~** découper qch à la dimension voulue; **to be of a ~** [*people, boxes*] être de la même taille; **2)** (number) (of population, audience) importance *f*; (of class, school, company) effectif *m*; **3)** (of garment) taille *f*; (of collar) encolure *f*; (of shoes, gloves) pointure *f*; **what ~ do you take?** (in clothes) quelle taille faites-vous?; (in shoes) quelle pointure faites-vous?, vous chaussez du combien?; **to take ~ X** (in clothes) faire du X; (in shoes) chausser *or* faire du X; **'one ~'** 'taille unique'; **try this for ~** lit essayez ceci pour voir si c'est votre taille; fig essayez ceci pour voir si cela vous convient; **4)** (substance) (for paper, textiles) apprêt *m*; (for plaster) colle *f*

B *vtr* **1)** classer [qch] selon la grosseur [*eggs, fruit*]; **2)** Tech apprêter [*textile, paper*]; encoller [*plaster*]; **3)** Comput dimensionner [*window*]

(Idioms) **that's about the ~ of it!** c'est à peu près ça!; **to cut sb down to ~** remettre qn à sa place

(Phrasal verb)

■ **size up: ▸ ~ up [sb/sth], ~ [sb/sth] up** se faire une opinion de [*person*]; évaluer [qch] du regard [*surroundings*]; évaluer [*situation*]; mesurer [*problem*]

sizeable /'saɪzəbl/ *adj* [*proportion*] non négligeable; [*amount, fortune*] assez important; [*house, field, town*] assez grand; **to have a ~ majority** être largement majoritaire

sizzle /'sɪzl/ *vi* grésiller

sizzling /'sɪzlɪŋ/ *adj* [*fat, sausage*] qui grésille; **a ~ sound** un grésillement

skate /skeɪt/

A *n* **1)** (ice) patin *m* à glace; (roller) patin *m* à roulettes; **2)** (fish) raie *f*

B *vi* patiner (**on, along** sur); **to ~ across** *ou* **over** traverser [qch] en patins [*pond, lake*]

(Idioms) **get your ~s on○!** grouille-toi○!; **to be skating on thin ice** s'aventurer sur un terrain glissant

skate: **~board** *n* skateboard *m*, planche *f* à roulettes; **~boarder** *n* skateur/-euse *m/f*; **~boarding** ▸ p. 881 *n* skateboard *m*, planche *f* à roulettes

skater /'skeɪtə(r)/ *n* patineur/-euse *m/f*

skating /'skeɪtɪŋ/ ▸ p. 881 *n* patinage *m*; **to go ice ~** faire du patin à glace

skating: **~ boots** *npl* GB patins *mpl* à glace; **~ rink** *n* (ice) patinoire *f*; (roller-skating) piste *f* de patins à roulettes

skein /skeɪn/ *n* (of wool) écheveau *m*

skeletal /'skelɪtl/ *adj* Anat, fig squelettique

Sizes

■ *In the following tables of equivalent sizes, French sizes have been rounded up, where necessary. (It is always better to have clothes a little too big than a little too tight.)*

■ *Note that for shoe and sock sizes French uses* pointure, *so a size 37 is* une pointure 37. *For all other types of garment (even stockings and tights) the word* taille *is used, so a size 16 shirt is* une chemise taille 40, *etc.*

Men's shoe sizes		Women's shoe sizes		
in UK & US	in France	In UK	US	in France
6	40	3	6	35
7	41	3½	6½	36
8	42	4	7	37
9	43	5	7½	38
10	44	6	8	39
11	45	7	8½	40
12	46	8	9	41

Men's clothing sizes		Women's clothing sizes		
in UK & US	in France	in UK	in US	in France
28	38	8	4	34
30	40	10	6	36
32	42	12	8	38–40
34	44	14	10	42
36	46	16	12	44–46
38	48	18	14	48
40	50	20	16	50
42	52			
44	54			
46	56			

Men's shirt collar sizes			
in UK & US	in France	in UK & US	in France
14	36	16½	41
14½	37	17	42
15	38	17½	43
15½	39	18	44
16	40		

what size are you?
= quelle taille faites-vous? *or* quelle pointure faites-vous?

I take size 40 (in clothes)
= je prends du 40 *or* je fais du 40

I take a size 7 (in shoes)
= je chausse du 40 *or* je fais du 40

my collar size is 15
= je porte un 38 *or* je porte du 38

I'm looking for collar size 16
= je cherche un 40

his shoe size is 39
= il chausse du 39

a pair of shoes size 39
= une paire de chaussures pointure 39

have you got the same thing in a 16?
= avez-vous ce modèle en 40?

have you got this in a smaller size?
= avez-vous ce modèle dans une plus petite taille (*or* pointure)? *or* avez-vous ce modèle en plus petit?

have you got this in a larger size?
= avez-vous ce modèle dans une plus grande taille (*or* pointure)? *or* avez-vous ce modèle en plus grand?

they haven't got my size
= ils n'ont pas ma taille (*or* ma pointure)

---

skeletal code n Comput séquence f paramétrable

skeleton /'skelɪtn/
A n Anat, Constr squelette m; (of plan, novel) grandes lignes fpl
B noun modifier fig [staff] réduit au strict minimum
(Idiom) **to have a ~ in the cupboard** GB *ou* **closet** US avoir un cadavre dans le placard○

skeleton key n passe-partout m inv

skeptic n, adj US = **sceptic**

skeptical adj US = **sceptical**

skeptically adv US = **sceptically**

skepticism n US = **scepticism**

sketch /sketʃ/
A n ① (drawing, draft) esquisse f; (hasty outline) croquis m; **rough ~** ébauche f; ② (comic scene) sketch m; ③ (brief account) aperçu m; **a character ~ of sb** une ébauche du personnage de qn
B vtr ① (make drawing of) faire une esquisse de; (hastily) faire un croquis de; ② (describe briefly) ébaucher
C vi (as art, hobby) faire des esquisses
(Phrasal verb)
■ **sketch in:** ▸ **~ in [sth], ~ [sth] in** (by drawing) ajouter l'esquisse de; fig (by describing) donner un aperçu de

sketch: **~book** n (for sketching) carnet m à croquis; (book of sketches) carnet m de croquis; **~pad** n bloc m à dessin

sketchy /'sketʃɪ/ adj [information, details] insuffisant; [memory] vague; [work] rapide

skew /skju:/
A n **on the ~** de travers
B vtr ① (distort) fausser [result, survey]; (deliberately) déformer [result]; ② (angle) incliner [object]
C vi (also **~ round**) [vehicle, ship] obliquer

skewer /'skju:ə(r)/
A n (for kebab) brochette f; (for joint) broche f
B vtr embrocher [joint]; mettre [qch] en brochette [chicken pieces]

ski /ski:/
A n ① Sport (for snow) ski m; (for water) ski m (nautique); **cross-country ~s** skis mpl de fond; **downhill ~s** skis mpl alpins; **on ~s** à ski; ② Aviat patin m
B vi (prét, pp **ski'd** ou **skied**) (as hobby) faire du ski; (move on skis) skier; **to ~ down a slope** descendre une pente à skis

ski binding n fixation f (de ski)

ski boot /ski:/ n chaussure f de ski

skid /skɪd/
A n ① (of car etc) dérapage m; **to correct a ~** redresser *or* contrôler un dérapage; ② fig (of prices) dérapage m; ③ (to help move sth) traîneau m
B vi (p prés etc **-dd-**) déraper (**on** sur); **to ~ off the road** déraper et sortir de la route; **to ~ across the floor** glisser sur le sol; **to ~ to a halt** [vehicle] s'arrêter dans un dérapage
(Idiom) **to put the ~s under sb** (undermine) faire échouer qn; (pressurize) obliger qn à faire vite

skid mark /skɪd/ n trace f de pneus

skier /'ski:ə(r)/ n skieur/-euse m/f

skies /skaɪz/ pl ▸ **sky**

skiff /skɪf/ n gen petite embarcation f légère; (working boat) youyou m

skiing /'ski:ɪŋ/ ▸ p. 881 n ski m; **to go ~** faire du ski; **cross country ~** ski m de fond; **downhill ~** ski m alpin

skiing: **~ holiday** n vacances fpl de neige; **~ instructor** ▸ p. 1181 n moniteur/-trice m/f de ski

ski jump
A n ① (jump) saut m à skis; ② (ramp) tremplin m (de ski)
B vi faire du saut à skis

ski jumping ▸ p. 881 n saut m à skis

skilful GB, **skillful** US /'skɪlfl/ adj ① (clever) [person] habile, adroit; [portrayal] excellent; **~ at sth** habile en qch; **~ at doing** habile à faire; **~ with his hands** adroit de ses mains; ② (requiring talent) [operation] délicat

skilfully GB, **skillfully** US /'skɪlfəlɪ/ adv ① (with ability) [play, write] habilement; [written] de façon habile; ② (with agility) adroitement

skilfulness GB, **skillfulness** US /'skɪlflnɪs/ n (mental) habileté f (**at doing** à faire); (physical) adresse f

ski lift *n* remontée *f* mécanique

skill /skɪl/
A *n* **1** **C** (flair) (intellectual) habileté *f*, adresse *f*; (physical) dextérité *f*; ~ **at** habileté *or* adresse à; ~ **at doing** habileté à faire; **to have** ~ être doué; **with** ~ avec talent; **2** **C** (special ability) (acquired) compétence *f*, capacités *fpl*; (innate) aptitude *f*; (practical) technique *f*; (gift) talent *m*; **your** ~**(s) as** vos talents de [*linguist, politician, mechanic*]; ~ **at** *ou* **in doing** talent à faire; ~ **at** *ou* **in sth** compétence en qch
B **skills** *npl* (training) connaissances *fpl*

skilled /skɪld/ *adj* **1** (trained) [*labour, work*] qualifié; **semi-**~ spécialisé; **2** (talented) [*actor, negotiator*] consommé; **to be** ~ **as** avoir des talents de [*writer, diplomat*]; **to be** ~ **at doing** savoir faire

skillet /'skɪlɪt/ *n* poêle *f* (à frire)

skillful *adj* US ▸ **skilful**

skillfully *adv* US ▸ **skilfully**

skillfulness *n* US ▸ **skilfulness**

skim /skɪm/
A *vtr* (*p prés etc* **-mm-**) **1** (remove cream) écrémer; (remove scum) écumer; (remove fat) dégraisser; **2** (touch lightly) [*plane, bird*] raser, frôler [*surface, treetops*]; **it only** ~**s the surface of the problem** ça ne fait qu'effleurer le problème; **3** (read quickly) parcourir; **4** ○US Fin ne pas déclarer [*part of income*]
B *vi* (*p prés etc* **-mm-**) **1** [*plane, bird*] **to** ~ **over** *ou* **across** *ou* **along sth** raser qch; **2** [*reader*] **to** ~ **through** *ou* **over sth** parcourir qch; **to** ~ **over** passer rapidement sur [*event, facts*]

ski mask *n* cagoule *f* de ski

skim milk, **skimmed milk** *n* lait *m* écrémé

skimp /skɪmp/ *vi* **to** ~ **on** lésiner sur [*expense, food, materials*]; économiser [*effort*]

skimpily /'skɪmpɪli/ *adv* [*work, make*] à la va-vite; [*stocked*] maigrement; ~ **dressed** en tenue minimale

skimpy /'skɪmpi/ *adj* [*garment*] minuscule; [*portion, allowance, income*] maigre (*before n*); [*work*] maigre

skin /skɪn/
A *n* **1** (of person) peau *f*; **2** (of animal) peau *f*; **leopard** ~ peau de léopard; **3** Culin (of fruit, vegetable, sausage) peau *f*; (of onion) pelure *f*; **remove the** ~ éplucher; **4** (on hot milk, cocoa) peau *f*
B *vtr* (*p prés etc* **-nn-**) **1** Culin dépecer [*animal*]; **2** (graze) **to** ~ **one's knee** s'écorcher le genou
(Idioms) **I've got you under my** ~ je t'ai dans la peau○; **to have a thick** ~ être insensible; **to jump out of one's** ~ sauter au plafond○; **to be** *ou* **get soaked to the** ~ être trempé jusqu'aux os○; **it's no** ~ **off my nose** *ou* **back**○ je m'en balance○; **to keep one's eyes** ~**ned** rester attentif *or* vigilant; **by the** ~ **of one's teeth** de justesse

skin: ~ **cancer** ▸ p. 933 *n* cancer *m* de la peau; ~ **care** *n* **C** soins *mpl* pour la peau; ~ **cream** *n* crème *f* pour la peau; ~**deep** *adj* superficiel/-ielle; ~ **disease** *n* maladie *f* de peau; ~ **diver** *n* plongeur/-euse *m/f*; ~ **diving** ▸ p. 881 *n* plongée *f* sous-marine; ~**flint** *n* radin/-e○ *m/f*

skin graft *n* **1** (*also* ~ **grafting**) greffe *f* de la peau; **2** (grafted area) greffon *m* de peau

skinhead /'skɪnhed/ *n* GB (youth) skinhead *m*

skinny○ /'skɪni/ *adj* maigre

skinny-ribbed sweater *n* pull-chaussette *m*

skint○ /skɪnt/ *adj* GB fauché○

skin: ~ **test** *n* cuti-réaction *f*; ~**tight** *adj* moulant

skip /skɪp/
A *n* **1** (jump) petit bond *m*; **2** GB (rubbish container) benne *f*
B *vtr* (*p prés etc* **-pp-**) **1** (not attend) sauter [*meeting, lunch, school*]; **2** (leave out) sauter [*pages, chapter*]; **to** ~ **the formalities** sauter les formalités; ~ **it**○! laisse tomber!; **3** ○(leave) **to** ~ **town** filer○ de la ville
C *vi* (*p prés etc* **-pp-**) **1** (jump) (once) bondir; (several times) sautiller; **2** (with rope) sauter à la corde; **3** (travel, move) **she** ~**ped from Paris to Lyons** elle a fait un saut de Paris à Lyon; **to** ~ **from one chapter to another** sauter d'un chapitre à l'autre

ski: ~ **pants** *n* fuseau *m* (de ski); ~ **pass** *n* forfait-skieur *m*

skipjack /'skɪpdʒæk/ *n* (*also* ~ **tuna**) (canned) ≈ thon *m* blanc

ski: ~ **plane** *n* avion *m* à skis; ~ **pole** *n* = **ski stick**

skipper /'skɪpə(r)/ *n* **1** Naut (of merchant ship) capitaine *m*; (of fishing boat) patron *m*; (of yacht) skipper *m*; **2** gen (leader) chef *m*

skipping /'skɪpɪŋ/ ▸ p. 881 *n* saut *m* à la corde

skipping rope *n* corde *f* à sauter

ski: ~ **racer** *n* skieur/-euse *m/f* alpin/-e; ~ **racing** ▸ p. 881 *n* ski *m* alpin; ~ **rack** *n* porte-skis *m inv*; ~ **resort** *n* station *f* de ski

skirl /skɜːl/ *n* son *m* aigu (de la cornemuse)

skirmish /'skɜːmɪʃ/ *n* **1** (fight) gen accrochage *m*; Mil escarmouche *f*; **2** (argument) prise *f* de bec○

skirt /skɜːt/ ▸ p. 1191
A *n* **1** (garment, of dress) jupe *f*; (of frock coat) basques *fpl*; **2** (of vehicle, machine) jupe *f*; **3** (woman) minette○ *f*
B *vtr* contourner [*wood, city*]; esquiver [*problem*]
(Idiom) **to cling to one's mother's** ~**s** s'accrocher aux jupes de sa mère
(Phrasal verb)
■ **skirt round**, **skirt around**: ▸ ~ **round** [sth] contourner

skirting board *n* plinthe *f*

skirt length *n* (piece of fabric) hauteur *f* de jupe; ~**s vary** la longueur des jupes varie

ski: ~ **run** *n* piste *f* de ski; ~ **slope** *n* piste *f*; ~ **stick** *n* bâton *m* de ski; ~ **suit** *n* combinaison *f* de ski

skit /skɪt/ *n* (parody) parodie *f* (**on** de); (sketch) sketch *m* (satirique) (**on, about** sur)

ski: ~ **touring** ▸ p. 881 *n* randonnée *f* à skis; ~ **tow** *n* téléski *m*

skittish /'skɪtɪʃ/ *adj* **1** (difficult to handle) capricieux/-ieuse; **2** (playful) joueur/-euse

skittle /'skɪtl/ ▸ p. 881
A *n* quille *f*
B **skittles** *npl* (jeu *m* de) quilles *fpl*

skive○ /skaɪv/ *vtr* GB (*also* ~ **off**) **1** (shirk) tirer au flanc○; **2** (be absent) (from school) sécher l'école○; (from work) ne pas aller au boulot○; **3** (leave early) se tirer○

ski wax *n* fart *m*

skivvy /'skɪvi/ *n*○ GB lit, fig bonne *f* à tout faire

skulduggery○ /skʌl'dʌgəri/ *n* **C** magouille○ *f*

skulk /skʌlk/ *vi* rôder; **to** ~ **out/off** sortir/s'éloigner furtivement

skull /skʌl/ *n* **1** Anat crâne *m*; **2** ○(brain) crâne *m*

skull: ~ **and crossbones** *n* (emblem) tête *f* de mort; (flag) pavillon *m* à tête de mort; ~ **cap** *n* (Catholic) calotte *f*; (Jewish) kippa *f*

skunk /skʌŋk/
A *n* Zool moufette *f*; (fur) sconse *m*
B *vtr* US (defeat) battre [qn] à plates coutures○ [*team, opponent*]

sky /skaɪ/
A *n* ciel *m*; **clear** ~ ciel dégagé; **open** ~ ciel dégagé; **in(to) the** ~ dans le ciel; **the** ~ **over Paris** le ciel de Paris; **a patch of blue** ~ une trouée de ciel bleu; **there are blue skies ahead** fig il y a une éclaircie à l'horizon
B **skies** *npl* Meteorol ciel *m*, fig, littér cieux *mpl*; Art ciels *mpl*; **summer skies** ciel d'été; **a day of rain and cloudy skies** un jour pluvieux et couvert; **to take to the skies** [*plane*] décoller
(Idiom) **the** ~**'s the limit** tout est possible; **reach for the** ~○! haut les mains!

sky: ~**-blue** ▸ p. 752 *n*, *adj* bleu (*m*) ciel *inv*; ~**cap** *n* US porteur *m* (dans un aéroport); ~**diver** *n* parachutiste *mf* (en chute libre); ~**diving** ▸ p. 881 *n* parachutisme *m* (en chute libre)

sky-high /,skaɪ'haɪ/
A *adj* [*prices, rates*] exorbitant
B *adv* **to rise** ~ monter en flèche; **to blow sth** ~ faire voler qch en éclats

sky: ~**jacker**○ *n* pirate *m* de l'air; ~**lark** *n* alouette *f* des champs; ~**larking**○ *n* chahut *m*; ~**light** *n* fenêtre *f* à tabatière; ~**line** *n* (in countryside) ligne *f* d'horizon; (in city) ligne *f* des toits

skyrocket /'skaɪrɒkɪt/
A *n* fusée *f*
B *vi* [*price, inflation*] monter en flèche

skyscraper *n* gratte-ciel *m inv*

sky: ~ **train** n aérotrain m; ~**ways** npl US Aviat couloirs mpl aériens; ~**writing** n publicité f tracée dans le ciel (par un avion)

S & L n US abrév ▸ **savings and loan (association)**

slab /slæb/ n ⒈ (piece) (of stone, wood, concrete) dalle f; (of meat, cheese, cake) pavé m; (of ice) plaque f; (of chocolate) tablette f; **fishmonger's** ~ étal m de poissonnier; ⒉ ○(operating table) billard○ m, table f d'opération; (mortuary table) table f d'autopsie

slack /slæk/
A n ⒈ lit (in rope, cable) mou m; **to take up the** ~ **in a rope** tendre une corde; **to take up the** ~ fig (take over) prendre le relais; ⒉ fig (in schedule etc) marge f; ⒊ (coal) poussier m
B **slacks** npl pantalon m; **a pair of** ~**s** un pantalon
C adj ⒈ (careless) [worker] peu consciencieux/-ieuse; [management] négligent; [student] peu appliqué; [work] peu soigné; **to be** ~ **about doing** négliger de faire; **to get** ~ [worker, discipline, surveillance] se relâcher; ⒉ (not busy) [period] creux/creuse (after n); [demand, sales] faible; **business is** ~ les affaires tournent au ralenti; ⒊ (loose, limp) détendu; **to go** ~ se détendre
D vi [worker] se relâcher dans son travail
(Phrasal verb)
■ **slack off** [business, trade] diminuer; [rain] se calmer

slacken /'slækən/
A vtr ⒈ (release) donner du mou à [rope, cable]; lâcher [reins]; relâcher [grip, pressure]; desserrer [nut]; ⒉ (reduce) réduire [pace]; ⒊ (loosen) assouplir [control]
B vi ⒈ (loosen) [grip, pressure, rope] se relâcher; [nut, bolt] se desserrer; **his grip on the rope** ~**ed** il a relâché sa prise sur la corde; ⒉ (ease off) [activity, pace, speed, business] ralentir; [pressure, interest] diminuer; [rain, gale] se calmer
(Phrasal verb)
■ **slacken off** = **slack off**

slackening /'slækənɪŋ/ n (of grip, discipline, skin) relâchement m; (of pace, business, economy) ralentissement m; (of tension) diminution f

slacker /'slækə(r)/ n gen fainéant/-e m/f, tire-au-flanc○ m inv

slackness /'slæknɪs/ n (of worker) laisser-aller m inv; (in trade, economy) stagnation f; (in discipline, security) relâchement m

slag /slæg/ n ¢ (from coal) GB stériles mpl; (from metal) scories fpl; ~ **heap** terril m

slain /sleɪn/ pp ▸ **slay**

slake /sleɪk/ vtr lit étancher [thirst]; fig assouvir

slalom /'slɑːləm/ ▸ p. 881 n slalom m

slam /slæm/
A n ⒈ (of door) claquement m; ⒉ Games chelem m
B vtr (p prés etc **-mm-**) ⒈ (shut loudly) [person] claquer [door]; [wind] faire claquer [door]; **to** ~ **sth shut** fermer brutalement qch; **to** ~ **the door behind one** sortir en claquant la porte derrière soi; **to slam the door in sb's face** lit, fig claquer la porte au nez de qn; ⒉ (with violence) **to** ~ **one's fist on the table** taper du poing sur la table; **to** ~ **sb into a wall** jeter qn contre le mur; **to** ~ **on the brakes** freiner à mort○; ⒊ ○(criticize) critiquer [qn] violemment; ⒋ ○(defeat) écraser
C vi (p prés etc **-mm-**) ⒈ [door] claquer (**against** contre); **to** ~ **shut** se refermer en claquant; ⒉ **to** ~ **into sth** [vehicle] s'écraser contre qch; [boxer, body] heurter violemment qch
(Phrasal verb)
■ **slam down**: ▸ ~ **down** [heavy object] s'écraser (**onto** sur); ▸ ~ **down** [sth], ~ [sth] **down** raccrocher violemment [phone]; refermer violemment [lid, car bonnet]; jeter brutalement [object] (**on**, **onto** sur)

slammer○ /'slæmə(r)/ n **the** ~ la taule○

slander /'slɑːndə(r), US 'slæn-/
A n ⒈ (statement) calomnie f; ⒉ ¢ Jur diffamation f orale; **to sue sb for** ~ intenter un procès en diffamation contre qn
B vtr gen calomnier; Jur diffamer

slanderous /'slɑːndərəs, US 'slæn-/ adj gen calomnieux/-ieuse; Jur diffamatoire

slang /slæŋ/ n argot m; **army** ~ argot militaire

slanging match n GB prise f de bec

slangy○ /'slæŋɪ/ adj [style] argotique

slant /slɑːnt, US slænt/
A n ⒈ (perspective) point m de vue (**on** sur); **with a European** ~ d'un point de vue européen; **to give a new** ~ **on sth** offrir un angle nouveau sur qch; ⒉ péj (bias) tendance f; ⒊ (slope) pente f; ⒋ (in printing) barre f oblique
B vtr ⒈ (twist) présenter [qch] avec parti pris [story, facts]; ⒉ (lean) incliner [object]
C vi ⒈ [floor, ground] être en pente; [handwriting] pencher (**to** vers); [painting] être de travers
D **slanting** pres p adj [roof] en pente; ~**ing eyes** yeux mpl bridés

slanted /'slɑːntɪd, US 'slæn-/ adj ⒈ (biased) orienté (**to**, **towards** vers); ⒉ (sloping) en pente

slantwise /'slɑːntwaɪz, US 'slæn-/ adv (also **slantways**) en biais

slap /slæp/
A n ⒈ (blow) tape f (**on** sur); (stronger) claque f (**on** sur); **a** ~ **on the face** une gifle; **it was a real** ~ **in the face for him** fig il a reçu une claque; **to give sb a** ~ **on the back** fig (in congratulation) féliciter qn; ⒉ (sound of blow) (bruit m d'une) claque f
B adv = **slap bang**
C vtr (p prés etc **-pp-**) ⒈ (hit) donner une tape à [person, animal]; **to** ~ **sb for/for doing** gifler qn pour/pour avoir fait; **to** ~ **sb on the leg, to** ~ **sb's leg** donner une tape à qn sur la jambe; **to** ~ **sb on the back** (in friendly way) donner une (grande) claque or tape dans le dos de qn; fig (congratulate) féliciter qn; **to** ~ **sb in the face** lit gifler qn; **to** ~ **sb on the wrist** fig taper sur les doigts de qn; ⒉ (put) **he** ~**ped the money (down) on the table** il a flanqué○ l'argent sur la table; **she** ~**ped some make-up on her face** elle s'est maquillée en vitesse; **they** ~**ped**○ **50p on the price** ils ont gonflé○ le prix de 50 pence
(Phrasal verb)
■ **slap down**: ▸ **to** ~ **sth down on** flanquer○ qch sur [table, counter]; ▸ ~ [**sb**] **down** rembarrer

slap bang○ /ˌslæp'bæŋ/ adv **he ran** ~ **into the wall** il s'est cogné en plein dans le mur en courant; ~ **in the middle (of)** au beau milieu (de)

slapdash○ /'slæpdæʃ/ adj [person] brouillon/-onne○; [work] bâclé○, fait à la va-vite; **in a** ~ **way** à la va-vite

slapstick /'slæpstɪk/ n comique m tarte à la crème, slapstick m

slap-up○ /'slæpʌp/ adj GB **a** ~ **meal** un bon gueuleton○

slash /slæʃ/
A n ⒈ (wound) balafre f (**on** à); ⒉ (cut) (in fabric, seat, tyre) lacération f; (in painting, wood) entaille f; ⒊ (in printing) barre f oblique; ⒋ Comm, Fin réduction f; **a 10%** ~ **in prices** une réduction de 10% sur les prix; ⒌ (in skirt) fente f; (in sleeve) crevé m
B vtr ⒈ (wound) balafrer [cheek]; faire une balafre à [person]; couper [throat]; [knife] entailler [face]; **to** ~ **one's wrists** se tailler les veines; ⒉ (cut) taillader [painting, fabric, tyres]; trancher [cord]; **to** ~ **one's way through** se tailler un chemin à travers [undergrowth]; ⒊ (reduce) réduire [qch] (considérablement), sacrifier [price]; réduire [qch] (considérablement) [amount, spending, size]; **to** ~ **40% off the price** réduire le prix de 40%; ⒋ (in dressmaking) fendre [skirt]
C vi **to** ~ **at** cingler [grass]; frapper [qch] d'un grand coup [ball]; **to** ~ **through** trancher [cord]; taillader [fabric]

slasher film○, **slasher movie**○ US n film m d'horreur sanglant

slat /slæt/ n ⒈ (of shutter, blind) lamelle f; (of table, bench, bed) lame f; ⒉ Aviat bec m de sécurité

slate /sleɪt/
A n ⒈ (rock) ardoise f; **made of** ~ en ardoise; ⒉ (piece, tablet) ardoise f; **a roof** ~ une ardoise; ⒊ US Pol liste f de candidature
B vtr ⒈ lit couvrir [qch] d'ardoises [roof]; ⒉ ○GB (criticize) [press, critic] taper sur○ [film, politician, policy] (**for** pour); ⒊ US Pol mettre [qn] sur la liste [candidate]
(Idioms) **to put sth on the** ~○ mettre qch sur l'ardoise○; **to wipe the** ~ **clean** faire table rase

slate: ~ **blue** ▸ p. 752 n, adj bleu (m) ardoise inv; ~ **grey** GB, ~ **gray** US ▸ p. 752 n, adj gris (m) ardoise inv

slater /'sleɪtə(r)/ ▸ p. 1181 n ⒈ (roofer) couvreur-ardoisier m; ⒉ (quarrier) ardoisier m; ⒊ Zool cloporte m

slating /'sleɪtɪŋ/ n **1** (laying slates) pose f des ardoises; **2** ○GB (criticism) **to get a ~ from sb** se faire démolir par qn○

slatted /'slætɪd/ adj [table] en lames; [shutter] à lamelles

slaughter /'slɔːtə(r)/
A n **1** (in butchery) abattage m; **to go to ~** aller à l'abattoir; **2** (massacre) massacre m, boucherie f; (road deaths) carnage m
B vtr **1** (in butchery) abattre; **2** (massacre) massacrer; **3** ○fig (defeat) écraser
(Idiom) **like a lamb to the ~** comme un agneau à l'abattoir

slaughterhouse /'slɔːtəhaʊs/ n abattoir m

Slav /slɑːv, US slæv/
A n Slave mf
B adj slave

slave /sleɪv/
A n **1** (servant) esclave mf; **2** fig **to be a ~ to** ou **of** être l'esclave de [fashion]; **a ~ to convention** l'esclave des conventions
B noun modifier **1** [colony] d'esclaves; [market] aux esclaves; **2** Comput asservi
C vi (also **~ away**) travailler comme un forçat, trimer○; **to ~ (away) at housework** s'escrimer à faire le ménage

slave: **~ driver** n lit Hist surveillant m d'esclaves; fig négrier/-ière m/f fig; **~ labour** n (activity) travail m de forçat; (manpower) main-d'œuvre f esclave

slaver /'slævə(r)/
A n salive f
B vi (drool) baver; **to ~ over** [animal] saliver devant; péj ou hum [person] baver devant

slavery /'sleɪvərɪ/ n **1** (practice, condition) esclavage m; **to be sold into ~** être vendu comme esclave; **2** fig **~ to** asservissement à [fashion]

slave ship n (vaisseau m) négrier m

slave trade n commerce m des esclaves; **the African ~** la traite des Noirs

slave-trader n marchand m d'esclaves, pej négrier m

slavish /'sleɪvɪʃ/ adj (all contexts) servile

slavishly /'sleɪvɪʃlɪ/ adv servilement

slaw /slɔ:/ n US = coleslaw

slay /sleɪ/ vtr (prét **slew**) pp **slain**) littér (kill) faire périr [enemy]; pourfendre [dragon]

SLD GB Pol n (abrév = **Social and Liberal Democrat**) parti m Démocrate Socio-Libéral

sleaze○ /sliːz/ n péj (pornography) pornographie f; (corruption) corruption f

sleazy○ /'sliːzɪ/ adj péj [club, area, character] louche; [story, aspect] scabreux/-euse; [café, hotel] borgne

sled /sled/
A n luge f; (pulled) traîneau m
B vi (p prés etc **-dd-**) faire de la luge; **to go ~ding** faire de la luge

sledge /sledʒ/
A n **1** GB luge f; **2** (pulled) traîneau m
B vi GB faire de la luge; **to go sledging** faire de la luge

sledgehammer /'sledʒhæmə(r)/ n masse f

sleek /sliːk/ adj **1** (glossy) [hair] lisse et brillant; [animal] au poil lisse et brillant; **2** (smooth) [elegance] raffiné; [shape] élégant; [figure] mince et harmonieux/-ieuse; **3** (prosperous-looking) à l'air cossu

sleep /sliːp/
A n sommeil m; **to go** ou **get to ~** s'endormir; **to go back to ~** se rendormir; **to send** ou **put sb to ~** endormir qn; **to get some ~** ou **to have a ~** gen dormir; (have a nap) faire un petit somme; **my leg has gone to ~**○ j'ai la jambe engourdie; **I didn't get any ~** ou **a wink of ~ last night** j'ai passé une nuit blanche, je n'ai pas fermé l'œil de la nuit; **I need my ~** il me faut beaucoup de sommeil; **to have a good night's ~** passer une bonne nuit, bien dormir; **to rock a baby to ~** bercer un bébé jusqu'à ce qu'il s'endorme; **to walk in one's ~** marcher en dormant; **I could do it in my ~**! je pourrais le faire les yeux fermés!; **she's losing ~ over it** ça l'empêche de dormir; **don't lose any ~ over it!** ne t'en fais pas pour ça!; **to put an animal to ~** euph faire piquer un animal
B vtr (prét, pp **slept**) **the house ~s six (people)** on peut loger ou coucher six personnes dans la maison
C vi (prét, pp **slept**) **1** dormir; **to ~ soundly** (deeply) dormir

profondément, dormir à poings fermés; (without worry) dormir tranquille, dormir sur ses deux oreilles; **to ~ on one's feet** dormir debout; **~ tight!** dors bien!; **2** (stay night) **to ~ at a friend's house** coucher chez un ami; **to ~ with sb** euph (have sex) coucher avec qn
(Idioms) **the big ~** le sommeil des morts; **to cry oneself to ~** pleurer jusqu'à épuisement; **to ~ like a log** ou **top** dormir comme une souche or un loir; **to ~ it off**○ cuver son vin○
(Phrasal verbs)
 ■ **sleep around**○ coucher à droite et à gauche○
 ■ **sleep in** (stay in bed late) faire la grasse matinée; (oversleep) dormir trop tard
 ■ **sleep on** continuer à dormir; **to ~ on a decision** attendre le lendemain pour prendre une décision; **I'd like to ~ on it** je préférerais dormir dessus
 ■ **sleep out** dormir or coucher à la belle étoile
 ■ **sleep over: to ~ over at sb's house** passer la nuit or coucher chez qn

sleeper /'sliːpə(r)/
A n **1** dormeur/-euse m/f; **to be a sound ~** avoir le sommeil profond; **2** Rail (berth) couchette f; (sleeping car) wagon-lit m, voiture-lit f; (train) train-couchettes m; **3** GB (on railway track) traverse f; **4** GB (earring) dormeuse f; **5** ○US (successful book, film etc) succès m à retardement; **6** (spy) espion/-ionne m/f en sommeil
B sleepers npl US grenouillère f

sleepily /'sliːpɪlɪ/ adv d'un ton or d'un air endormi

sleeping /'sliːpɪŋ/ adj qui dort, endormi
(Idiom) **let ~ dogs lie** il ne faut pas réveiller le chat qui dort

sleeping: **~ bag** n sac m de couchage; **~ car** n voiture-lit f, wagon-lit m; **~ partner** n GB Comm commanditaire mf; **~ pill** n somnifère m; **~ policeman**○ n GB ralentisseur m; **~ quarters** npl (in barracks) chambrée f; (dormitory) dortoir m; **~ sickness** ▸ p. 933 n maladie f du sommeil; **~ tablet** n somnifère m

sleepless /'sliːplɪs/ adj [vigil, hours] sans sommeil; **to pass a ~ night** passer une nuit blanche

sleeplessness /'sliːplɪsnɪs/ n insomnie f

sleep: **~walk** vi marcher en dormant, être somnambule; **~walking** n somnambulisme m

sleepy /'sliːpɪ/ adj [voice, village] endormi, somnolent; **to feel** ou **be ~** avoir envie de dormir, avoir sommeil; **to make sb ~** [fresh air] donner envie de dormir à qn; [wine] endormir qn, assoupir qn

sleepyhead○ /'sliːpɪhed/ n endormi/-e m/f; **'get up, ~!'** 'debout, paresseux/-euse!'

sleet /sliːt/ n neige f fondue

sleeve /sliːv/ n **1** (of garment) manche f; **to pull** ou **tug at sb's ~** tirer qn par la manche; **to roll up one's ~s** lit, fig retrousser ses manches; **2** (of record) pochette f; (of CD) boîtier m; **3** Tech (inner) chemise f; (outer) gaine f; (short outer) manchon m
(Idioms) **to laugh up one's ~** rire sous cape; **to wear one's heart on one's ~** laisser voir ses sentiments; **to have something up one's ~** avoir quelque chose en réserve; **to have a few tricks up one's ~** fig avoir plus d'un tour dans son sac

sleeveless /'sliːvlɪs/ adj sans manches

sleigh /sleɪ/ n traîneau m

sleight of hand /ˌslaɪtəv'hænd/ n **1** (dexterity) dextérité f; **2** (trick) tour m de passe-passe

slender /'slendə(r)/ adj **1** (thin) [person] mince; [waist] fin; [finger] effilé; [neck] gracile; [stem, arch] élancé; **2** (slight) [majority] faible (before n); **to win by a ~ margin** gagner de justesse; **3** (meagre) [income, means] modeste, maigre (before n)

slenderness /'slendənɪs/ n **1** (of person) sveltesse f; (of part of body) minceur f; **2** (of margin) étroitesse f

slept /slept/ prét, pp ▸ **sleep**

sleuth /sluːθ/ n limier m, détective m

S-level n GB Sch (abrév = **Special Level**) épreuve optionnelle d'un niveau supérieur que l'on passe à l'âge de dix-huit ans

slew /sluː/ pp ▸ **slay**

slice /slaɪs/
A n **1** (portion) (of bread, meat, fish) tranche f; (of cheese) morceau m; (of pie, tart) part m; (of lemon, cucumber, sausage) rondelle f;

2 (proportion) (of income, profits) part *f*; (of territory, population) partie *f*; **3** Culin (utensil) spatule *f*; **4** Sport slice *m*
B *vtr* **1** (section) couper [qch] (en tranches) [*loaf, roast*]; couper [qch] en rondelles [*lemon, cucumber*]; **2** (cleave) fendre [*water, air*]; **to ~ sb's throat** trancher la gorge à qn; **3** Sport slicer, couper [*ball*]
C *vi* **to ~ through** fendre [*water, air*]; trancher [*timber, rope, meat*]

sliced bread *n* pain *m* en tranches

(Idiom) **it's the best** *ou* **greatest thing since ~**○! hum on n'a pas fait mieux depuis l'invention du fil à couper le beurre

slice: **~d loaf** *n* pain *m* en tranches; **~ of life** *n* Cin, Theat tranche *f* de vie

slick /slɪk/
A *n* **1** (on water) nappe *f* de pétrole; (on shore) marée *f* noire; **2** (tyre) slick *m*
B *adj* **1** (adept) [*production, campaign*] habile; [*operation, deal*] mené rondement; **2** péj (superficial) qui a un éclat plutôt superficiel; **3** péj (insincere) [*person*] roublard○; [*answer*] astucieux/-ieuse; [*excuse*] facile; **~ salesman** vendeur qui a du bagou○; **4** US (slippery) [*road*] glissant; [*hair*] lissé

slicker /'slɪkə(r)/ *n* US (raincoat) ciré *m*

slickly /'slɪklɪ/ *adv* **1** (cleverly) [*presented*] de manière habile; [*worded*] habilement; **2** (smoothly) [*carried out*] efficacement; **3** (stylishly) [*dressed*] de manière branchée○

slickness /'slɪknɪs/ *n* (of film, style) brillant *m*; (of answer, person) habileté *f*; (of salesman) bagou○ *m*; (of magician) dextérité *f*; (of operation) efficacité *f*

slide /slaɪd/
A *n* **1** (chute) (in playground, factory) toboggan *m*; (for logs) glissoir *m*; (on ice) glissoire *f*; **2** Phot diapositive *f*; **lecture with ~s** conférence avec projections; **3** (microscope plate) lame *f* porte-objet; **4** GB (hair clip) barrette *f*; **5** Mus (slur) coulé *m*; **6** Mus (on trombone) coulisse *f*; **7** fig (decline) baisse *f* (in de)
B *vtr* (*prét, pp* **slid**) (move) faire glisser [*bolt, component*]; **to ~ sth forward** faire glisser quelque chose vers l'avant
C *vi* (*prét, pp* **slid**) **1** (*also* **~ about** GB, **~ around**) (slip) [*car, person*] glisser, partir en glissade (**into** dans; **on** sur); **to ~ off** glisser de [*roof, table, deck*]; sortir de [*road*]; **2** (move) **to ~ down** dévaler [*slope*]; glisser le long de [*bannister*]; **to ~ in and out** [*drawer, component*] coulisser; **to ~ up and down** [*window*] coulisser de bas en haut; **to ~ out of** se glisser hors de [*seat, room*]; **3** (decline) [*prices, shares*] baisser; **the economy is sliding into recession** l'économie est sur la pente de la récession; **to let sth ~** laisser qch aller à la dérive
(Phrasal verb)
■ **slide back**: ▸ **~** [*sth*] **back, ~ back** [*sth*] reculer [*car seat*]; tirer [*bolt*]; refermer [*hatch, sunroof*]
slide: **~ projector** *n* projecteur *m* de diapositives; **~ rule** GB, **~ ruler** US *n* règle *f* à calcul; **~ show** *n* (at exhibition) diaporama *m*; (at lecture, at home) séance *f* de projection; **~ trombone** ▸ p. 1028 *n* trombone *m* à coulisse

sliding /'slaɪdɪŋ/ *adj* [*door*] coulissant; [*roof*] ouvrant

sliding: **~ scale** *n* échelle *f* mobile; **~ seat** *n* (in car) siège *m* réglable; (in boat) banc *m* à glissière

slight /slaɪt/
A *n* affront *m* (**on** à; **from** de la part de)
B *adj* **1** [*change, delay, movement, rise*] léger/-ère (*before n*); [*risk, danger*] faible (*before n*); [*pause, hesitation*] petit (*before n*); **the chances of it happening are ~** il y a de faibles chances pour que cela arrive; **not to have the ~est difficulty** ne pas avoir la moindre difficulté; **not in the ~est** pas le moins du monde; **2** (in build) mince; **to be ~ of build** être mince
C *vtr* **1** (offend) humilier [*person*]; **2** US (underestimate) sous-estimer

slighting /'slaɪtɪŋ/ *adj* [*remark, reference*] offensant

slightly /'slaɪtlɪ/ *adv* légèrement; [*embarrassed, uneasy, unfair*] un peu; **~ built** mince

slim /slɪm/
A *adj* **1** (shapely) [*person, figure*] mince; **of ~ build** mince; **to get ~** devenir mince, s'amincir; **2** (thin) [*book, volume*] mince; [*watch, calculator*] plat; **3** (slight) [*chance, margin*] mince
B *vtr* (*p prés etc* **-mm-**) = **slim down**
C *vi* (*p prés etc* **-mm-**) GB (lose weight) maigrir; **I'm ~ming** je fais un régime pour maigrir

(Phrasal verb)
■ **slim down**: ▸ **~ down** **1** [*person*] maigrir, perdre du poids; **2** [*organization*] réduire ses effectifs; ▸ **~** [*sth*] **down, ~ down** [*sth*] réduire les effectifs de, dégraisser○ [*industry*]; réduire [*workforce*]

slime /slaɪm/ *n* gen dépôt *m* gluant *ou* visqueux; (on river-bed) vase *f*; (on beach) algues *fpl*; (of slug, snail) bave *f*

slimline /'slɪmlaɪn/ *adj* [*garment*] amincissant; [*drink*] diététique

slimmer /'slɪmə(r)/ *n* GB personne *f* suivant un régime amaigrissant; **~s' disease**○ anorexie *f* mentale

slimy /'slaɪmɪ/ *adj* **1** [*weed, mould*] visqueux/-euse; [*plate*] gluant; [*wall*] suintant; **2** GB péj (obsequious) servile; **3** US péj (sleazy) louche

sling /slɪŋ/
A *n* **1** (weapon) fronde *f*; (smaller) lance-pierres *m inv*; **2** (for support) Med écharpe *f*; (for carrying baby) porte-bébé *m*; (for carrying load) élingue *f*; **3** Sport (in climbing) boucle *f* d'assurance
B *vtr* (*prét, pp* **slung**) **1** ○(throw) lit, fig lancer [*object, insult*] (**at** à); **to ~ a bag over one's shoulder** mettre son sac sur son épaule; **2** (carry *or* hang loosely) **to ~ sth** suspendre qch à [*beam, branch, hook*]; **to be slung over/across/round sth** être jeté par dessus/en travers de/autour de qch; **to ~ sth over one's shoulder** porter [qch] en bandoulière [*bag, rifle*]
(Phrasal verb)
■ **sling out**: ▸ **~** [*sth*] **out, ~ out** [*sth*] jeter; ▸ **~** [*sb*] **out** flanquer [qn] à la porte

sling: **~back** *n* escarpin *m* à bride; **~shot** *n* lance-pierres *m inv*

slink /slɪŋk/ *vi* (*prét, pp* **slunk**) **to ~ in** entrer furtivement; **to ~ off** [*person*] s'éloigner furtivement; [*dog*] s'en aller la queue basse

slinky○ /'slɪŋkɪ/ *adj* [*dress*] moulant, sexy

slip /slɪp/
A *n* **1** (error) gen erreur *f*; (by schoolchild) faute *f* d'étourderie; (faux pas) gaffe○ *f*; **to make a ~** faire une erreur *or* une faute d'étourderie; **a ~ of the tongue** un lapsus; **2** (piece of paper) bout *m* de papier; (receipt) reçu *m*; **a ~ of paper** un bout de papier; **3** (slipping) glissade *f* involontaire; (stumble) faux pas *m*; **4** ○†(slender person) **a ~ of a girl** une fille frêle; **5** (petticoat) (full) combinaison *f*; (half) jupon *m*
B *vtr* (*p prés etc* **-pp-**) **1** (slide) **to ~** [*sth*] **into** sth glisser [qch] dans qch [*note, coin, joke*]; **to ~ one's feet into one's shoes** enfiler ses chaussures; **to ~** [*sth*] **out of** sth sortir [qch] de qch [*object, foot, hand*]; **she ~ped the shirt over her head** (put on) elle a enfilé la chemise; (take off) elle a retiré la chemise; **to ~ sth into place** mettre qch en place; **to ~ a car into gear** embrayer; **2** ○(give surreptitiously) **to ~ sb sth, to ~ sth to sb** glisser qch à qn; **3** (escape from) [*dog*] se dégager de [*leash*]; [*boat*] filer [*moorings*]; **it ~ped my notice** *ou* **attention that** je ne me suis pas aperçu que; **it had ~ped my mind (that)** j'avais complètement oublié que; **to let ~ an opportunity** *ou* **a chance (to do)** laisser échapper une occasion (de faire); **to let ~ a remark** laisser échapper une remarque; **4** (in knitting) **to ~ a stitch** glisser une maille; **5** Med **to ~ a disc** avoir une hernie discale; **6** Aut **to ~ the clutch** faire patiner l'embrayage
C *vi* (*p prés etc* **-pp-**) **1** (slide) **~ into** passer [*dress*]; s'adapter à [*rôle*]; tomber dans [*coma*]; sombrer doucement dans [*madness*]; **to ~ out of** enlever [*dress, coat*]; **2** (slide quietly) **to ~ into/out of** se glisser dans/hors de [*room, building*]; **to ~ across the border** passer la frontière en cachette; **3** (slide accidentally) [*person, vehicle*] glisser (**on** sur; **off** de); [*knife, pen*] glisser, déraper; [*load*] tomber; **the glass ~ped out of his hand** le verre lui a échappé des mains; **to ~ through sb's fingers** fig filer entre les doigts de qn; **4** ○(lose one's grip) **I must be ~ping!** je baisse○!
(Idiom) **to give sb the ~** semer○ qn
(Phrasal verbs)
■ **slip away** (leave unnoticed) partir discrètement
■ **slip back**: ▸ **~ back** [*person*] revenir discrètement (**to** à); ▸ **~** [*sth*] **back** glisser, remettre
■ **slip by** [*life, weeks, months*] s'écouler; [*time*] passer
■ **slip in**: ▸ **~ in** (enter quietly) [*person*] entrer discrètement; [*animal*] entrer furtivement; **a few errors have ~ped in** il y a quelques erreurs; ▸ **~** [*sth*] **in, ~in** [*sth*] glisser [*remark*]

■ **slip off**: ▸ ~ **off** partir discrètement; ▸ ~ **[sth] off**, ~ **off [sth]** enlever
■ **slip on**: ▸ ~ **[sth] on**, ~ **on [sth]** passer, enfiler
■ **slip out** ①（leave quietly）[*person*] sortir discrètement; **to** ~ **out to** faire un saut° à [*shop*]; ②**it just ~ped out!** ça m'a échappé!
■ **slip up**° faire une gaffe° (**on** à propos de)

slip: ~**knot** *n* nœud *m* coulant; ~-**on (shoe)** *n* mocassin *m*

slippage /ˈslɪpɪdʒ/ *n* ①（delay）retard *m*; ②（discrepancy）décalage *m*

slipped disc *n* Med hernie *f* discale

slipper /ˈslɪpə(r)/ *n*（houseshoe）pantoufle *f*

slippery /ˈslɪpərɪ/ *adj* ①（difficult to grip）[*road, fish*] glissant; ②（difficult to deal with）[*subject*] délicat; **a** ~ **customer**° un personnage suspect
Idiom **to be on the** ~ **slope** être sur une pente savonneuse

slippy° /ˈslɪpɪ/ *adj*（slippery）[*path, surface*] glissant

slip: ~ **road** *n* bretelle *f* d'accès à l'autoroute; ~**shod** *adj* [*person*] négligent (**about, in** dans); [*appearance, work*] négligé, peu soigné; ~**stream** *n* sillage *m*; ~-**up**° *n* bourde° *f*

slit /slɪt/
A *n* fente *f* (**in** dans); **to make a** ~ **in** sth faire une fente dans qch; **his eyes narrowed to** ~**s** il plissa les yeux
B *adj* [*eyes*] bridé; [*skirt*] fendu
C *vtr* (*prét, pp* **slit**)（on purpose）faire une fente dans; （by accident）déchirer; **to** ~ **a letter open** ouvrir une lettre; **to** ~ **sb's throat** égorger qn; **to** ~ **one's wrists** s'ouvrir les veines

slither /ˈslɪðə(r)/ *vi* glisser; **to** ~ **about on sth** avoir du mal à garder son équilibre sur qch

sliver /ˈslɪvə(r)/ *n*（of glass）éclat *m*; （of soap）reste *m*; （of food）mince tranche *f*

Sloane /sləʊn/ *n* GB péj（*also* ~ **Ranger**）≈ BCBG *mf*

slob° /slɒb/ *n*（lazy）flemmard/-e° *m/f*; （messy）cochon/-onne° *m/f*; **fat** ~! gros lard°!

slobber° /ˈslɒbə(r)/ *vi* baver; **to** ~ **over [sb/sth]**° baver d'attendrissement devant

sloe /sləʊ/ *n* ①（fruit）prunelle *f*; ②（bush）prunellier *m*

slog° /slɒg/
A *n* ①（hard work）**a hard** ~ un travail dur; **it was a real** ~ c'était vraiment dur; ②（hard stroke）coup *m* violent
B *vtr* (*p prés etc* -**gg**-) ①（hit hard）frapper [qn] violemment [*opponent*]; taper de toutes ses forces dans [*ball*]; **to** ~ **it out** lit, fig se battre; ②（progress with difficulty）**to** ~ **one's way through** se frayer un chemin à travers
C *vi* (*p prés etc* -**gg**-) ①（work hard）travailler dur, bosser°; ②（progress with difficulty）**we** ~**ged up the hill** nous avons escaladé la colline avec effort
Phrasal verb
■ **slog away** travailler dur (**at** sur)

slop /slɒp/
A *n* ①Agric（pigswill）pâtée *f*; ②péj（food）bouillie *f*; ③°péj（sentimentality）sentimentalité *f*
B **slops** *npl*（food）aliment *m* liquide; （dirty water）eaux *fpl* sales
C *vtr* (*p prés etc* -**pp**-) renverser
D *vi* (*p prés etc* -**pp**-)（*also* ~ **over**）déborder
Phrasal verbs
■ **slop around, slop about** [*person*] traînasser
■ **slop out** vider sa tinette (*en prison*)

slope /sləʊp/
A *n*（incline）gen pente *f*; （of writing）inclinaison *f*; （hillside）flanc *m*; **north/south** ~ versant *m* nord/sud; **uphill** ~ montée *f*; **downhill** ~ descente *f*; **upper** ~**s** sommet *m* de la montagne
B *vi* gen être en pente; [*writing*] pencher (**to** vers)

sloping /ˈsləʊpɪŋ/ *adj* [*ground, roof*] en pente; [*ceiling*] incliné; [*shoulders*] tombant; [*writing*] penché

sloppily /ˈslɒpɪlɪ/ *adv* n'importe comment; ~ **run** mal administré

sloppiness /ˈslɒpɪnɪs/ *n*（of thinking, discipline）manque *m* de rigueur; （of work）manque *m* de soin; （of dress）débraillé *m*

sloppy /ˈslɒpɪ/ *adj* ①°（careless）[*personal appearance*] débraillé; [*language, workmanship*] peu soigné; [*management, administration*] laxiste; [*discipline, procedure*] relâché; [*method, thinking*] qui manque de rigueur; **to be a** ~ **eater**

manger salement; ②°（over-emotional）sentimental; ③GB（baggy）ample

slosh /slɒʃ/
A *vtr* ①°（spill）répandre (en éclaboussant) [*liquid*]; ②°GB（hit）flanquer un coup° à
B °*vi*（*also* ~ **about**）clapoter
C °**sloshed** *pp adj* bourré°; **to get** ~**ed** prendre une cuite°

slot /slɒt/
A *n* ①（for coin, ticket）fente *f*; （for letters）ouverture *f*; （groove）rainure *f*; ②（in schedule）créneau *m*; **a prime-time** ~ une tranche horaire de grande écoute; ③（job）place *f*
B *vtr* (*p prés etc* -**tt**-) **to** ~ **sth into a machine** insérer qch dans une machine; **to** ~ **a film into the timetable** trouver un créneau pour un film dans le programme
C *vi* (*p prés etc* -**tt**-) **to** ~ **into sth** [*coin, piece*] s'insérer dans; **to** ~ **into place** *ou* **position** s'encastrer
Phrasal verbs
■ **slot in**: ▸ ~ **in** se mettre en place; ▸ ~ **[sth] in**, ~ **in [sth]** insérer [*coin, piece*]; trouver un créneau pour [*film, programme*]; placer [*person*]
■ **slot together**: ▸ ~ **together** s'emboîter; ▸ ~ **[sth] together** emboîter

sloth /sləʊθ/ *n* ①Zool paresseux *m*; ②sout（idleness）paresse *f*

slot: ~ **machine** *n* Games machine *f* à sous; （for vending）distributeur *m* automatique; ~ **meter** *n* (for gas, electricity) compteur *m* à pièces; （parking meter）parcmètre *m*; ~**ted spoon** *n* ≈ écumoire *f*

slouch /slaʊtʃ/
A *n* ①（to walk with a） ~ marcher le dos voûté; ②°（lazy person）traîne-savates *m inv*
B *vi* ①（sit or stand badly）être avachi; ②（*also* ~ **around**）traînasser

Slovakia /sləˈvækɪə/ ▸ **p. 774** *pr n* Slovaquie *f*

Slovenia /sləˈviːnɪə/ ▸ **p. 774** *pr n* Slovénie *f*

slovenliness /ˈslʌvnlɪnɪs/ *n* laisser-aller *m inv*

slovenly /ˈslʌvnlɪ/ *adj* [*person, dress, appearance, speech, style*] négligé; [*habits*] malpropre; [*work*] bâclé

slow /sləʊ/
A *adj* ①（not quick, dull）lent; **to be** ~ **to do** tarder à faire; **to be** ~ **in doing** être lent à faire; ②（slack）gen stagnant; [*economic growth*] lent; ③（dim）lent (d'esprit); ④[*clock, watch*] **to be** ~ retarder; **to be 10 minutes** ~ retarder de 10 minutes; ⑤[*oven*] doux/douce; ⑥[*pitch, court*] lourd
B *adv* gen lentement; **to go** ~ [*workers*] freiner la production; ~-**acting** à action lente
C *vtr, vi* ▸ **slow down**
Phrasal verbs
■ **slow down**: ▸ ~ **down** ralentir; **to** ~ **(down) to a crawl** rouler au pas; **to** ~ **(down) to 2%** tomber à 2%; ▸ ~ **down [sth/sb]**, ~ **[sth/sb] down** ralentir
■ **slow up** = **slow down**

slow: ~**coach**° *n* GB traînard/-e° *m/f*; ~ **cooker** *n* mijoteuse *f* électrique; ~**down** *n* ralentissement *m*; ~ **handclapping** *n*: applaudissements exprimant l'impatience *ou* le mécontentement; ~ **lane** *n*（in UK）voie *f* de gauche; （elsewhere）voie *f* de droite

slowly /ˈsləʊlɪ/ *adv* lentement

slow motion *n* ralenti *m*; **in** ~ au ralenti

slow-moving /ˌsləʊˈmuːvɪŋ/ *adj* lent

slowness /ˈsləʊnɪs/ *n* lit lenteur *f*; （of pitch, court, mind, intelligence）lourdeur *f*

slow: ~**poke**° *n* US = **slowcoach**; ~ **train** *n* omnibus *m*; ~-**witted** *adj* à l'esprit lent

sludge /slʌdʒ/ *n*（mud）vase *f*

slug /slʌg/
A *n* ①Zool limace *f*; ②°（bullet）balle *f*; ③（of alcohol）lampée° *f*; ④°（blow）coup *m*
B °*vtr* (*p prés etc* -**gg**-) ①°（hit）cogner [*person*]; **to** ~ **sb one**° en envoyer une à qn°; ②°US Sport taper° dans [*ball*]
Idiom **to** ~ **it out**° se tabasser°

slug bait *n* granulés *mpl* antilimaces

sluggish /ˈslʌgɪʃ/ *adj* ①[*person, animal*] léthargique; [*circulation, reaction*] lent; [*traffic*] engorgé; [*river*] stagnant; ②Fin qui stagne; **after a** ~ **start** après un démarrage difficile

slug pellets *npl* = **slug bait**

sluice /slu:s/ n (also ~**way**) canal m

(Phrasal verb)

■ **sluice down**: ▸ ~ **down [sth]**, ~ **[sth] down** laver [qch] à grande eau

sluice gate n vanne f

slum /slʌm/

A n ⓵ (poor area) quartier m pauvre; **the ~s** les bas-quartiers mpl; ⓶ (dwelling) taudis m

B vi◯ (p prés etc **-mm-**) (also ~ **it**) s'encanailler

slumber /'slʌmbə(r)/ littér

A n sommeil m

B vi lit, fig sommeiller

slum clearance n démolition f de taudis

slump /slʌmp/

A n ⓵ Fin, Econ effondrement m (**in** de); **to experience a ~** s'effondrer; ⓶ (in popularity) chute f (**in** de); (in support) baisse f (**in** de)

B vi [demand, trade, value, price] chuter (**from** de; **to** à; **by** de); [economy, market] s'effondrer; [support, popularity] être en forte baisse; [person, body] s'affaler◯

slung /slʌŋ/ prét, pp ▸ **sling**

slunk /slʌŋk/ prét, pp ▸ **slink**

slur /slɜ:(r)/

A n ⓵ (aspersion) calomnie f; **to cast a ~ on sb/sth** répandre des calomnies sur qn/qch; **to be a ~ on sb/sth** porter atteinte à qn/qch; **a racial ~** une diffamation raciale; ⓶ Mus liaison f

B vtr (p prés etc **-rr-**) ⓵ **to ~ one's speech** ou **words** manger ses mots; ⓶ Mus lier

C slurred pp adj [voice, words, speech] inarticulé

slurp /slɜ:p/ vtr aspirer [qch] bruyamment

slurry /'slʌrɪ/ n ⓵ (of cement) gâchis m; ⓶ (waste) (from animals) purin m; (from factory) déchets mpl

slush /slʌʃ/ n ⓵ (melted snow) neige f fondue; ⓶◯ péj (sentimentality) sensiblerie f; ⓷ US Culin granité m

slush fund n caisse f noire

slushy /'slʌʃɪ/ n ⓵ lit [snow] fondu; [street] couvert de neige fondue; ⓶◯fig [novel, film] à l'eau de rose, sentimental

slut◯ /slʌt/ n injur traînée◉ f offensive

sly /slaɪ/ adj (cunning) rusé; (secretive) entendu

(Idiom) **on the ~** en douce◯, en cachette

slyly /'slaɪlɪ/ adv (with cunning) malicieusement; (secretively) [say] d'un ton entendu; [smile, look] d'un air entendu

smack /smæk/

A n ⓵ (blow) (with hand) claque f; (on face) gifle f; (with bat) coup m; ⓶ (sound) (of object) bruit m sec; (by hand or person) coup m; ⓷ (loud kiss) gros baiser m

B adv◯ (also ~ **bang**, ~ **dab** US) en plein◯; ~ **in the middle of** en plein milieu de

C vtr (on face) gifler [person]; taper [object] (**on** sur; **against** contre); **she ~ed him (on the bottom)** ou **she ~ed his bottom** elle lui a donné une claque sur les fesses

D vi ⓵ (hit) **to ~ into** ou **against sth** taper contre qch; ⓶ (have suggestion of) **to ~ of** sentir

(Idioms) **to ~ one's lips** se lécher les babines (**at sth** à l'idée de qch); **a ~ in the eye** une gifle

small /smɔ:l/ ▸ p. 1191

A n **the ~ of the back** le creux du dos

B ◯**smalls** npl GB euph petit linge m

C adj ⓵ (not big) gen petit; [increase, majority, proportion, quantity, amount, stake] faible; **his influence was ~** son influence était négligeable; **the ~ matter of the £1,000 you owe me** iron la bagatelle de 1 000 livres sterling que tu me dois iron; **it is written with a ~ letter** ça s'écrit avec une minuscule; **in his** ou **her own ~ way** gen à sa façon; **to cut sth up ~** couper qch en petits morceaux; **the ~est room**◯ euph le petit coin◯ euph; ⓶ (petty) [person, act] mesquin; ⓷ (not much) **to have ~ cause** ou **reason for worrying** ou **to worry** n'avoir guère de raisons de s'inquiéter; **it is ~ comfort** ou **consolation to sb** c'est une piètre consolation pour qn; **~ wonder he left!** pas étonnant qu'il soit parti!; ⓸ (quiet) [voice, noise] petit; [sound] faible; ⓹ (humiliated) **to feel** ou **look ~** être dans ses petits souliers◯; **to make sb feel** ou **look ~** humilier qn

D adv [write] petit

small: ~ **ad** n GB petite annonce f; ~ **change** n petite monnaie f; ~ **claims court** n GB, Jur ≈ tribunal m d'instance; ~**holding** n GB Agric petite exploitation f;

~ **hours** npl petit matin m; ~ **intestine** n intestin m grêle; ~**-minded** adj mesquin; ~**pox** ▸ p. 933 n variole f

small print n ⓵ lit petits caractères mpl; ⓶ fig **to read the** ~ lire tout jusque dans les moindres détails; **to read the** ~ **of a contract** éplucher un contrat

small-scale /,smɔ:l'skeɪl/ adj [model] réduit; [map, plan] à petite échelle; [industry] petit (before n)

small talk n banalités fpl; **to make ~** faire la conversation

small-town adj péj provincial

smart /smɑ:t/

A adj ⓵ (elegant) élégant; ⓶◯ (intelligent) [child, decision] malin; [politician, journalist] habile; **it was definitely the ~ choice** c'est certainement ce qu'il fallait choisir; ⓷ [restaurant, hotel, street] chic inv; **the ~ set** le beau monde; ⓸ (stinging) [blow] vif/vive; [rebuke] cinglant; ⓹ (brisk) **to walk at a ~ pace** marcher à vive allure; **that was ~ work!** ça a été vite fait!; ⓺ Comput intelligent

B vi ⓵ (sting) brûler; ⓶ fig (emotionally) être piqué au vif; **they are ~ing over** ou **from their defeat** ils sont sous le coup de leur défaite

smart: ~ **alec(k)**◯ n gros malin◯/grosse maligne◯ m/f; ~ **bomb** n bombe f intelligente; ~ **card** n Comput, Fin carte f à puce

smarten /'smɑ:tn/ v

■ **smarten up**: ▸ ~ **[sth/sb] up**, ~ **up [sth/sb]** embellir; **he's really ~ed himself up** il s'est beaucoup arrangé

smartly /'smɑ:tlɪ/ adv ⓵ [dressed] (neatly) soigneusement; (elegantly) élégamment; ⓶ (quickly) sèchement; ⓷ (briskly) vivement; ⓸ (cleverly) avec malice

smart money◯ n **the ~ was on Desert Orchid** Desert Orchid était une mise sûre; **the ~ is on our shares** nos actions sont un investissement

smash /smæʃ/

A n ⓵ (crash) (of glass, china) bruit m fracassant; (of vehicles) fracas m; ~! **there goes another plate!** crac! encore une assiette cassée; ⓶ ◯(also ~**-up**) (accident) collision f; ⓷◯(also ~ **hit**) Mus tube◯ m; Cin film m à grand succès; **to be a ~** faire un tabac◯; ⓸ Fin (collapse) débâcle f; (on stock exchange) krach m; ⓹ Sport (tennis) smash m

B vtr ⓵ briser (**with** avec); (more violently) fracasser; **thieves ~ed their way into the shop** les voleurs sont entrés dans la boutique en cassant tout; **she ~ed the car into a tree** elle est rentrée dans un arbre; ⓶ (destroy) écraser [demonstration, opponent]; démanteler [drugs ring]; ⓷ Sport pulvériser◯ [record]; **to ~ the ball** faire un smash

C vi ⓵ (disintegrate) se briser, se fracasser (**on** sur, **against** contre); ⓶ (crash) **to ~ into** [vehicle] aller s'écraser contre; **the raiders ~ed through the door** les cambrioleurs ont enfoncé la porte; ⓷ Fin faire faillite

(Phrasal verbs)

■ **smash down**: ▸ ~ **[sth] down**, ~ **down [sth]** enfoncer

■ **smash in**: ▸ ~ **[sth] in** défoncer [door, skull]

■ **smash open**: ▸ ~ **[sth] open**, ~**open [sth]** défoncer

■ **smash up**: ▸ ~ **[sth] up**, ~ **up [sth]** démolir; **they'll ~ the place up!** ils vont tout casser!

smash-and-grab◯ GB n (also ~ **raid**) cambriolage m (avec destruction de vitrine)

smashed /smæʃt/ adj ⓵ ◯(on alcohol) bourré◯; (on drugs) défoncé◯ (**on** à); ⓶ [limb, vehicle] écrasé; [window] fracassé

smashing◯ /'smæʃɪŋ/ adj GB épatant◯

smattering /'smætərɪŋ/ n notions fpl; **to have a ~ of Russian** avoir quelques connaissances en russe; **a ~ of culture** quelques bribes de culture

smear /smɪə(r)/

A n ⓵ (mark) (spot) tache f; (streak) traînée f; ⓶ (defamation) propos m diffamatoire; **a ~ on sb's character** une tache sur la réputation de qn; ⓷ Med = **smear test**

B vtr ⓵ (dirty) faire des taches sur; **her face was ~ed with jam** elle avait le visage barbouillé de confiture; ⓶ (slander) diffamer [person]; salir [reputation]; ⓷ (spread) étaler [butter, paint]; appliquer [lotion]

C vi [ink, paint] s'étaler; [lipstick, make-up] couler

smear: ~ **campaign** n campagne f de diffamation (**against** contre); ~ **tactics** npl manœuvres fpl diffamatoires; ~ **test** n Med frottis m

S

smell /smel/
A n **1** (odour) odeur f; **what a ∼!** comme ça sent mauvais!; **2** (sense) odorat m; **sense of ∼** odorat m; **3** (action) to have a ∼ of sentir un peu; **4** fig relents mpl
B vtr (prét, pp **smelled**, **smelt** GB) **1** lit sentir; **I can ∼ burning** ça sent le brûlé; **2** fig (detect) gen flairer; repérer [liar, cheat]
C vi (prét, pp **smelled**, **smelt** GB) **1** (have odour) sentir; **this flower doesn't ∼** cette fleur ne sent rien; **to ∼ of roses** sentir la rose; **that ∼s like curry** ça sent le curry; fig **to ∼ of** sentir [corruption]; **2** (have sense of smell) avoir de l'odorat
(Phrasal verb)
■ **smell out**: ▸ **∼ [sth] out**, **∼ out [sth]** **1** lit [dog] flairer; **2** fig gen découvrir; démasquer [spy, traitor]; **3** (cause to stink) empester
smelling salts npl Med sels mpl
smelly /'smelɪ/ adj lit gen qui sent mauvais
smelt /smelt/
A prét, pp ▸ **smell**
B vtr extraire [qch] par fusion [metal]; fondre [ore]
smile /smaɪl/
A n sourire m; **to give a ∼** sourire; **to give sb a ∼** adresser un sourire à qn; **with a ∼** en souriant
B vtr **'Of course,' he ∼d** 'bien sûr', dit-il en souriant; **to ∼ a sad smile** avoir un sourire triste
C vi sourire (**at sb** à qn; **with** de); **we ∼d at the idea** cette idée nous a fait sourire; **to ∼ to oneself** sourire intérieurement; **keep smiling!** garde le sourire!
(Phrasal verb)
■ **smile on**: ▸ **∼ on [sb/sth]** [luck, fortune, weather] sourire à; [person, police, authority] être favorable à
smiley /'smaɪlɪ/ n **1** (happy symbol) souriant m; **2** (emoticon) frimousse f, binette f Can
smiling /'smaɪlɪŋ/ adj souriant
smirk /smɜːk/
A n (self-satisfied) petit sourire m satisfait; (knowing) sourire m en coin
B vi (in a self-satisfied way) avoir un petit sourire satisfait; (knowingly) avoir un sourire en coin
smith /smɪθ/ ▸ p. 1181 n maréchal-ferrant m
smithereens /ˌsmɪðə'riːnz/ npl **in ∼** en mille morceaux
smithy /'smɪðɪ/ n forge f
smitten /'smɪtn/ adj **1** (afflicted) **∼ by** rongé par [guilt, regret]; terrassé par [illness]; **2** (in love) fou/folle d'amour
smock /smɒk/
A n blouse f, sarrau m
B vtr faire des smocks à
smog /smɒg/ n smog m
smog mask n masque m antipollution
smoke /sməʊk/
A n **1** (fumes) fumée f; **to go up in ∼**○ lit brûler, partir en fumée; fig tomber à l'eau○; **2** ○(cigarette) clope○ f; **to have a ∼** fumer
B vtr **1** fumer [cigarette etc]; **2** Culin fumer
C vi (all contexts) fumer
D **smoked** pp adj fumé
(Idiom) **to ∼ like a chimney**○ fumer comme un pompier○
(Phrasal verb)
■ **smoke out**: ▸ **∼ [sth] out**, **∼ out [sth]** enfumer [animal]; ▸ **∼ [sb] out**, **∼ out [sb]** lit déloger qn en l'enfumant; fig débusquer
smoke: **∼ alarm** n détecteur m de fumée; **∼ bomb** n grenade f fumigène; **∼-dried** adj fumé; **∼-filled** adj enfumé
smokeless /'sməʊklɪs/ adj [fuel] non polluant
smoker /'sməʊkə(r)/ n **1** (person) fumeur/-euse m/f; **a light ∼** une personne qui fume peu; **2** (on train) compartiment m fumeurs
smoke screen n **1** Mil écran m de fumée; **2** fig diversion f; **to create** ou **throw up a ∼** faire diversion
smokey = **smoky**
smoking /'sməʊkɪŋ/
A n **∼ and drinking** le tabac et l'alcool; **to give up ∼** arrêter de fumer; **'no ∼'** 'défense de fumer'
B adj **1** (emitting smoke) qui fume; [cigarette] allumé; **2** (for smokers) [compartment, section] fumeurs (after n)

smoking: **∼ ban** n interdiction f de fumer; **∼ compartment** GB, **∼ car** US n compartiment m fumeurs; **∼-related** adj [disease] associé au tabac; **∼ room** n fumoir m
smoky /'sməʊkɪ/
A ○n US motard○ m (de la police)
B adj [atmosphere, room] enfumé; [fire] qui fume; [cheese, ham, bacon, glass] fumé
smolder vi US = **smoulder**
smooth /smuːð/
A adj **1** lit (even, without bumps) [stone, sea, surface, skin, fabric] lisse; [road] plan; [curve, line, breathing] régulier/-ière; [sauce, paste] homogène; [crossing, flight] sans heurts; [movement] aisé; [music, playing] fluide; **the tyres are worn ∼** les pneus sont lisses; **the engine is very ∼** le moteur tourne parfaitement rond; **2** (problem-free) paisible; **the bill had a ∼ passage through Parliament** la loi a été adoptée sans difficultés par le Parlement; **3** [taste, wine, whisky] moelleux/-euse; **4** (suave) gen, pej [person] mielleux/-euse; [manners, appearance] onctueux/-euse; **to be a ∼ talker** être enjôleur/-euse
B vtr **1** lit (flatten out) lisser; (get creases out) défroisser; **to ∼ the creases from sth** défroisser qch; **∼ the cream into your skin** étalez la crème sur votre peau; **2** fig (ease) faciliter [process, path]
(Idioms) **to take the rough with the ∼** prendre les choses comme elles viennent; **the course of true love never did run ∼** l'amour vrai n'a jamais été facile à vivre
(Phrasal verbs)
■ **smooth away**: ▸ **∼ away [sth]**, **∼ [sth] away** lit, fig faire disparaître
■ **smooth down**: ▸ **∼ [sth] down**, **∼ down [sth]** gen lisser; polir [wood, rough surface]
■ **smooth out**: ▸ **∼ [sth] out**, **∼ out [sth]** **1** lit (lay out) étendre; (remove creases) défroisser; **2** fig aplanir [difficulties]; faire disparaître [imperfections]
■ **smooth over**: ▸ **∼ over [sth]** fig atténuer [differences, awkwardness]; aplanir [difficulties, problems]; **to ∼ things over** arranger les choses
smoothly /'smuːðlɪ/ adv **1** (easily) lit [move, flow, glide] doucement; [start, stop, brake, land] en douceur; [write, spread] de façon unie; fig (without difficulties) sans heurts; **the key turned ∼ in the lock** la clé a tourné facilement dans la serrure; **to run ∼** lit tourner rond; fig marcher bien; [holiday] se dérouler sans problèmes; **things are going very ∼ for me** tout va bien pour moi; **2** (suavely) gen en douceur; pej mielleusement
smoothness /'smuːðnɪs/ n **1** lit (of surface, skin) aspect m lisse; (of crossing, flight) tranquillité f; (of car, machine) régularité f; (of music) fluidité f; (of movement) aisance f; **2** fig (absence of problems) harmonie f; **3** (of wine, taste) douceur f; **4** (suaveness) onctuosité f
smooth running
A n (of machinery) bon fonctionnement m; (of organization, event) bonne marche f
B **smooth-running** adj [machinery] qui tourne bien; [organization, event] qui marche bien
smooth-tongued adj péj enjôleur/-euse
smorgasbord /'smɔːgəsbɔːd/ n Culin buffet m (à la scandinave)
smother /'smʌðə(r)/ vtr **1** (stifle) étouffer; **2** (cover) couvrir (**with** de); **to be ∼ed in blankets** être tout emmitouflé dans des couvertures
smoulder GB, **smolder** US /'sməʊldə(r)/ vi lit se consumer; fig couver; **to ∼ with** se consumer de [resentment, jealousy]
smouldering GB, **smoldering** US /'sməʊldərɪŋ/ adj **1** lit [fire, cigarette] qui se consume; [ashes, ruins] fumant; **2** fig (intense) sourd; (sexy) ardent
smudge /smʌdʒ/
A n (mark) trace f
B vtr étaler [make-up, print, ink, wet paint]; faire des traces sur [paper, paintwork]
C vi [paint, ink, print, make-up] s'étaler
D **smudged** pp adj [paint, make-up] qui a coulé (after n); [writing, letter] maculé; [paper, cloth] taché
smudgy /'smʌdʒɪ/ adj **1** (marked) [paper, face] taché; [writing, letter] à moitié effacé; **2** (indistinct) [photograph, image] voilé; [outline] estompé

S

smug /smʌg/ *adj* suffisant; **to be ~ about winning** être fier d'avoir gagné

smuggle /ˈsmʌgl/
A *vtr* gen faire passer [qch] clandestinement [*message, food*] (**into** dans); faire du trafic de [*arms, drugs*]; (to evade customs) faire passer [qch] en contrebande; **to ~ sth/sb in** faire entrer qch/qn clandestinement; **to ~ sth through** *ou* **past customs** faire passer qch en fraude
B *vi* faire de la contrebande
C smuggled *pp adj* de contrebande

smuggler /ˈsmʌglə(r)/ *n* contrebandier/-ière *m/f*; **drug/arms ~** passeur/-euse *m/f* de drogue/d'armes

smuggling /ˈsmʌglɪŋ/ *n* gen contrebande *f*; **drug/arms ~** trafic *m* de drogue/d'armes

smut /smʌt/ *n* (vulgarity) grivoiseries *fpl*; (stain) tache *f*

smutty /ˈsmʌtɪ/ *adj* (crude) grivois; (dirty) noir

snack /snæk/
A *n* ①① (small meal) repas *m* léger; (instead of meal) casse-croûte *m inv*; **to have** *ou* **eat a ~** manger quelque chose; ②② (crisps, peanuts etc) amuse-gueule *m inv*
B *vi* grignoter, manger légèrement

snag /snæg/
A *n* ①① (hitch) inconvénient *m* (**in** de); **there's just one ~** il y a un problème; ②② (tear) accroc *m* (**in** à); ③③ (projection) aspérité *f* (**in** sur)
B *vtr* (*p prés etc* **-gg-**) (tear) filer [*tights, stocking*] (**on** contre); accrocher [*sleeve, garment, fabric*] (**on** à); se casser [*fingernail*]; s'égratigner [*hand, finger*]
C *vi* (*p prés etc* **-gg-**) (catch) **to ~ on** [*rope, fabric*] s'accrocher à; [*propeller, part*] frotter contre

snail /sneɪl/ *n* escargot *m*

snake /sneɪk/
A *n* Zool serpent *m*; péj (person) traître/traîtresse *m/f*
B *vi* [*road*] serpenter (**through** à travers)
(Idiom) **a ~ in the grass** péj un traître/une traîtresse

snake: **~bite** *n* morsure *f* de serpent; **~ charmer** *n* charmeur/-euse *m/f* de serpent; **~s and ladders** ▸ p. 881 *n* GB Games ≈ jeu *m* de l'oie

snap /snæp/ ▸ p. 881
A *n* ①① (of branch) craquement *m*; (of fingers, lid, elastic) claquement *m*; ②② (lid) claquement *m*; ③③ ○Phot photo *f*; ④④ Games ≈ bataille *f*
B *adj* [*decision, judgment, vote*] rapide
C ○*excl* **~! we're wearing the same tie!** coïncidence! nous portons la même cravate!
D *vtr* (*p prés etc* **-pp-**) ①① (click) faire claquer [*fingers, jaws, elastic*]; **to ~ sth shut** fermer qch avec un bruit sec; ②② (break) (faire) casser net; ③③ (say crossly) dire [qch] hargneusement; ④④ ○Phot prendre une photo de
E *vi* (*p prés etc* **-pp-**) ①① lit (break) se casser; ②② fig (lose control) [*person*] craquer○; **my patience finally ~ped** ma patience était arrivée à bout; ③③ (click) **to ~ open/shut** s'ouvrir/se fermer d'un coup sec; ④④ (speak sharply) parler hargneusement
(Idioms) **~ out of it!**○ cesse de faire la tête!; **~ to it!**○ et plus vite que ça○!; **to ~ to attention** Mil se figer au garde-à-vous
(Phrasal verbs)
■ **snap at**: ▶ **~ at** [*sth/sb*] ①① (speak sharply) parler hargneusement à; ②② (bite) essayer de mordre
■ **snap off**: ▶ **~ off** casser net; ▶ **~ off** [sth], **~** [sth] **off** casser net
■ **snap up**: ▶ **~ up** [sth] sauter sur [*bargain, chance*]

snap: **~ fastener** *n* bouton-pression *m*; **~-on** *adj* [*lid, attachment*] à pression

snappy /ˈsnæpɪ/ *adj* ①① (bad-tempered) hargneux/-euse; ②② (lively) [*rhythm, reply*] rapide; (punchy) [*advertisement*] accrocheur/-euse; ③③ ○(smart) [*clothing*] chic *inv*
(Idiom) **make it ~**○! grouille-toi○!

snapshot /ˈsnæpʃɒt/ *n* photo *f*

snare /sneə(r)/
A *n* piège *m* also fig
B *vtr* prendre [qn/qch] au piège [*animal, person*]

snarl /snɑːl/
A *n* ①① (growl) grondement *m*; **'you'd better watch out!' he said with a ~** 'tu ferais mieux de faire attention!' dit-il d'un ton hargneux; ②② (grimace) mine *f* hargneuse; ③③ (tangle) (in single rope, flex) nœud *m*; (of several ropes, flexes) enchevêtrement *m*

B *vtr* rugir; **'don't be so stupid,' he ~ed** 'ne sois pas si stupide,' dit-il d'un ton hargneux
C *vi* [*animal*] gronder férocement; [*person*] grogner; **the dog ~ed at me** le chien m'a montré les dents
(Phrasal verb)
■ **snarl up**: ▶ **~ up** [*rope*] s'emmêler; ▶ **~ up** [sth] bloquer; **to be ~ed up** être bloqué; [*economy, system*] être paralysé; **I got ~ed up in the traffic** j'ai été pris dans les embouteillages; **the hook got ~ed up in the net** l'hameçon s'est pris dans le filet

snarl-up /ˈsnɑːlʌp/ *n* (in traffic) embouteillage *m*; (in distribution network) blocage *m*

snatch /snætʃ/
A *n* (*pl* **-es**) ①① (fragment) (of conversation) bribe *f*; (of poem, poet) quelques vers *mpl*; (of concerto, composer) quelques mesures *fpl*; (of tune) quelques notes *fpl*; ②② (grab) **to make a ~ at sth** essayer d'attraper qch; ③③ (theft) vol *m*; **bag ~** vol à l'arraché; ④④ Sport (in weightlifting) arraché *m*
B *vtr* ①① (grab) attraper [*book, key*]; saisir [*opportunity*]; arracher [*victory*]; prendre [*lead*]; **to ~ sth from sb** arracher qch à qn; ②② ○(steal) voler [*handbag, jewellery, kiss*] (**from** à); kidnapper [*baby*]; ③③ (take hurriedly) **try to ~ a few hours' sleep** essaie de dormir quelques heures; **have we got time to ~ a meal?** avons-nous le temps de manger quelque chose en vitesse?
C *vi* **to ~ at sth** tendre vivement la main vers [*rope, letter*]
(Phrasal verbs)
■ **snatch away**: ▶ **~** [sth] **away** arracher qch (**from** sb à qn)
■ **snatch up**: ▶ **~ up** [sth] ramasser [qch] en vitesse [*clothes, papers*]; saisir [*child*]; **to ~ up a bargain** faire une affaire

snazzy○ /ˈsnæzɪ/ *adj* tape-à-l'œil○ *inv*

sneak /sniːk/
A ○*n* péj ①① GB (tell-tale) rapporteur/-euse *m/f*; ②② (devious person) sournois/-e *m/f*
B *noun modifier* /sniːk/ *adj* [*raid*] en traître; [*visit*] furtif/-ive
C *vtr* ①① ○(have secretly) manger [qch] en cachette [*chocolate etc*]; fumer [qch] en cachette [*cigarette*]; ②② ○(steal) voler (**out of, from** dans); **they ~ed him out by the back door** ils l'ont fait sortir discrètement par la porte de derrière; **to ~ a look at sth** jeter un coup d'œil furtif à qch
D *vi* ①① (move furtively) **to ~ away** s'éclipser discrètement; **to ~ around** rôder; **to ~ in/out** entrer/sortir furtivement; **to ~ into** se faufiler dans [*room, bed*]; **to ~ up on sb/sth** s'approcher sans bruit de qn/qch; **she ~ed out of the room** elle s'est glissée hors de la pièce; ②② ○GB (tell tales) rapporter; **to ~ on sb** dénoncer qn

sneaker /ˈsniːkə(r)/ *n* US basket *f*, tennis *f*

sneaking /ˈsniːkɪŋ/ *adj* [*suspicion*] vague; **she has a ~ suspicion that he's lying** elle a le vague sentiment qu'il ment; **I have a ~ admiration for her** je ne peux m'empêcher de l'admirer

sneak preview *n* avant-première *f*; **to give sb a ~ of sth** montrer qch à qn en avant-première

sneaky /ˈsniːkɪ/ *adj* ①① péj (cunning) gen sournois; [*method, plan*] rusé○; ②② (furtive) **to have a ~ look at sth** regarder qch en cachette

sneer /snɪə(r)/
A *n* (expression) sourire *m* méprisant
B *vi* (smile) sourire avec mépris; (speak) railler

sneering /ˈsnɪərɪŋ/
A *n* railleries *fpl*
B *adj* [*remark*] railleur/-euse; [*smile*] méprisant

sneeze /sniːz/
A *n* éternuement *m*
B *vi* éternuer
(Idiom) **it is not to be ~d at** ce n'est pas à dédaigner

snide /snaɪd/ *adj* sournois

sniff /snɪf/
A *n* ①① (of person with cold or crying) reniflement *m*; (of disgust, disdain) grimace *f*; ②② (inhalation) inhalation *f*; **to take a ~ of** sentir
B *vtr* [*dog*] flairer; [*person*] humer [*air*]; sentir [*perfume, food*]; inhaler [*glue, cocaine*]
C *vi* lit renifler; fig faire une moue; **to ~ at sth** lit renifler; faire la grimace à [*idea*]; faire la fine bouche devant [*food*]; **a free car is not to be ~ed at** une voiture gratuite, ça ne se refuse pas

S

(Phrasal verb)
■ **sniff out**: ▸ ~ **out [sth]** gen lit, fig flairer

sniffer dog n: chien policier entraîné pour détecter la drogue ou les explosifs

sniffle○ /'snɪfl/
A n (sniff) reniflement m; (slight cold) petit rhume m
B vi renifler

sniffy○ /'snɪfɪ/ adj dédaigneux/-euse; **to be ~ about sth** faire la fine bouche au sujet de qch

snigger /'snɪgə(r)/
A n ricanement m
B vi ricaner; **to ~ at [sb/sth]** se moquer de [person]; ricaner en entendant [remark]; ricaner en voyant [appearance, action]

snip /snɪp/
A n ① (action) petit coup m (de ciseaux etc); ② (onomat) cliquetis m; ③ (piece of fabric) échantillon m; ④ ○(bargain) (bonne) affaire f; ⑤ (horse) gagnant m sûr
B vtr (p prés etc **-pp-**) découper (à petits coups de ciseaux etc) [fabric, paper]; tailler [hedge]

(Phrasal verb)
■ **snip off**: ▸ ~ **[sth] off**, ~ **off [sth]** couper

snipe /snaɪp/
A n Zool bécassine f
B vi **to ~ at** (shoot) tirer sur; (criticize) envoyer des piques à

sniper /'snaɪpə(r)/ n Mil tireur m embusqué

sniping /'snaɪpɪŋ/ n ¢ piques fpl

snippet /'snɪpɪt/ n (gén pl) (of conversation, information) bribes pl; (of text, fabric, music) fragment m

snivel /'snɪvl/ vi (p prés etc **-ll-**) pleurnicher

snob /snɒb/
A n snob mf
B noun modifier [value, appeal] pour les snobs

snobbery /'snɒbərɪ/ n snobisme m

snobbish /'snɒbɪʃ/ adj snob inv

snook /snuːk/ n:
(Idiom) **to cock a ~ at sb** faire la nique à qn

snooker /'snuːkə(r)/ ▸ p. 881
A n ① (game) snooker m (variante du billard); ② (shot) coup m fumant
B vtr Sport, fig coincer [player, person]

snoop○ /snuːp/
A n fouineur/-euse m/f
B vi espionner; **to ~ into** mettre son nez○ dans

(Phrasal verb)
■ **snoop around**○ fouiner, fureter

snoop around○ n **to have a ~** jeter un coup d'œil

snooping○ /'snuːpɪŋ/
A n espionnage m
B adj fouineur/-euse○

snooty○ /'snuːtɪ/ adj [restaurant, club, college] huppé; [tone, person] prétentieux/-ieuse

snooze○ /snuːz/
A n petit somme m
B vi sommeiller

snore /snɔː(r)/
A n ronflement m
B vi ronfler

snoring /'snɔːrɪŋ/ n ¢ ronflements mpl

snorkel /'snɔːkl/
A n (US **schnorkel**) ① (for swimmer) tuba m; ② (on submarine) schnorchel m
B vi (p prés etc **-ll-**) faire de la plongée avec tuba

snorkelling /'snɔːklɪŋ/ ▸ p. 881 n Sport plongée f avec tuba

snort /snɔːt/
A n (of horse, bull) ébrouement m; (of person, pig) grognement m
B vtr argot des drogués sniffer
C vi [person, pig] grogner; [horse, bull] s'ébrouer; **to ~ with laughter** rire comme un cheval

snot○ /snɒt/ n (mucus) morve f

snotty○ /'snɒtɪ/ adj ① [nose] plein de morve; ② [person] prétentieux/-ieuse

snout /snaʊt/ n museau m; (of pig) groin m

snow /snəʊ/
A n (all contexts) neige f

B v impers neiger; **it's ~ing** il neige

(Phrasal verbs)
■ **snow in** (also ~ **up**): **to be ~ed in** être bloqué par la neige

■ **snow under**: **to be ~ed under** lit être couvert de neige; fig être submergé (**with** de)

snowball /'snəʊbɔːl/
A n lit boule f de neige
B vi fig [profits, problem] faire boule de neige
(Idiom) **it hasn't got a ~'s chance in hell**○ c'est perdu d'avance

snow: **~bank** US n congère f; ~ **blindness** n cécité f des neiges

snowboard /'snəʊbɔːd/ Sport
A n surf m des neiges
B vi faire du surf des neiges

snowboarding /'snəʊbɔːdɪŋ/ ▸ p. 881 n surf m (des neiges), snowboard m

snow: **~boot** n après-ski m inv; **~bound** adj gen bloqué par la neige; [region] paralysé par la neige; ~ **chains** npl Aut chaînes fpl; **~drift** n congère f; **~drop** n Bot perce-neige m inv; **~fall** n chute f de neige; **~flake** n flocon m de neige; **~man** n bonhomme m de neige; ~ **mobile** n Aut motoneige f; **~plough** GB, ~ **plow** US n Aut, Sport chasse-neige m inv; ~ **report** n Meteorol bulletin m d'enneigement; ~ **shoe** n raquette f; **~storm** n tempête f de neige; ~ **suit** n combinaison f de ski; ~ **tyre** GB, ~ **tire** US n pneu m clouté

snowy /'snəʊɪ/ adj ① lit (after a snowfall) enneigé; (usually under snow) neigeux/-euse; **it will be ~ tomorrow** il neigera demain; ② fig (white) blanc/blanche (comme neige)

Snr. abrév écrite = **Senior**

snub /snʌb/
A n rebuffade f
B vtr (p prés etc **-bb-**) rembarrer; **to be ~bed** essuyer une rebuffade (**by** de la part de)

snub: ~ **nose** n nez m retroussé; **~-nosed** adj au nez retroussé

snuff /snʌf/
A n tabac m à priser
B vtr (put out) moucher [candle]
(Idiom) **to ~ it**○ casser sa pipe○
(Phrasal verb)
■ **snuff out**: ▸ ~ **out [sth]** ① moucher [candle]; ② fig éteindre [hope, interest]; étouffer [rebellion, enthusiasm]; ③ ○(kill) descendre○ [person]

snuffle /'snʌfl/
A n (of animal, person) reniflement m; **to have the ~s** renifler parce qu'on est enrhumé
B vi renifler
(Phrasal verb)
■ **snuffle around** renifler

snug /snʌg/
A n GB petite arrière-salle d'un bar
B adj [bed, room] douillet; [coat] chaud

snuggle /'snʌgl/ vi se blottir (**into** dans)
(Phrasal verb)
■ **snuggle up** se blottir (**against, beside** contre)

snugly /'snʌglɪ/ adv **the coat fits ~** le manteau est parfaitement ajusté; **the lid should fit ~** le couvercle devrait s'adapter parfaitement; **he's ~ tucked up in bed** il est bien au chaud dans son lit

so /səʊ/
A adv ① (so very) si, tellement; **not ~**○ **thin as** pas aussi maigre que; **I'm not feeling ~ good**○ je ne me sens pas très bien; ② (to limited extent) **we can only work ~ fast and no faster** nous ne pouvons vraiment pas travailler plus vite; **you can only do ~ much (and no more)** tu ne peux rien faire de plus; ③ (in such a way) ~ **arranged that** organisé d'une telle façon que; **walk ~** marchez comme ça; **and ~ on and ~ forth** et ainsi de suite; **just as in the 19th century, ~ today** tout comme au XIXᵉ siècle, aujourd'hui; ~ **be it!** soit!; **she likes everything to be just ~** elle aime que les choses soient parfaitement en ordre; ④ (for that reason) ~ **it was that** c'est ainsi que; **she was young and ~ lacked experience** elle était jeune et donc sans expérience; ⑤ (true) **is that ~?** c'est vrai?; **if (that's) ~** si c'est vrai; ⑥ (also) aussi; ~ **is she** elle aussi; **if they accept**

~ **do I** s'ils acceptent, j'accepte aussi; **7** ○(thereabouts) environ; **20 or** ~ environ 20; **8** (as introductory remark) ~ **there you are** te voilà donc; ~ **that's the reason** voilà donc pourquoi; ~ **you're going are you?** alors tu y vas?; **9** (avoiding repetition) **he's conscientious, perhaps too much** ~ il est consciencieux, peut-être même trop; **he's the owner or** ~ **he claims** c'est le propriétaire du moins c'est ce qu'il prétend; **he dived and as he did** ~... il a plongé et en le faisant...; **perhaps** ~ c'est possible; **I believe** ~ je crois; ~ **I believe** c'est ce que je crois; **I'm afraid** ~ j'ai bien peur que oui *or* si; ~ **it would appear** c'est ce qu'il semble; ~ **to speak** si je puis dire; **I told you** ~ je te l'avais bien dit; ~ **I see** je le vois bien; **who says** ~? qui dit ça?; **only more** ~ mais encore plus; **the question is unsettled and will remain** ~ la question n'est pas résolue et ne le sera pas; **10** sout (referring forward or back) **if you** ~ **wish you may...** si vous le souhaitez, vous pouvez...; **11** (reinforcing a statement) **'I thought you liked it?'**—'~ **I do'** 'je croyais que ça te plaisait'—'mais ça me plaît'; **'it's broken'**—'~ **it is'** 'c'est cassé'—'je le vois bien!'; **'I'm sorry'**—'~ **you should be'** 'je suis désolé'—'j'espère bien'; **it just** ~ **happens that** il se trouve justement que; **12** ○(refuting a statement) **'he didn't hit you'**—'he did ~!' 'il ne t'a pas frappé?'—'si, il m'a frappé'; **I can** ~ **make waffles** si, je sais faire les gaufres; **13** ○(as casual response) et alors; **'I'm leaving'**—'~?' 'je m'en vais'—'et alors?'; ~ **why worry!** et alors il n'y a pas de quoi t'en faire!

B **so (that)** *conj phr* **1** (in such a way that) de façon à ce que; **she wrote the instructions** ~ **that they'd be easily understood** elle a rédigé les instructions de façon à ce qu'elles soient faciles à comprendre; **2** (in order that) pour que

C **so as** *conj phr* pour

D **so much** *adv phr, pron phr* **1** (also ~ **many**) (such large quantity) tant de; ~ **much of her life** une si grande partie de sa vie; ~ **many of her friends** un si grand nombre de ses amis; **2** (also ~ **many**) (limited amount) **I can only make** ~ **much bread** je ne peux pas faire plus de pain; **there's only** ~ **much you can take** il y a des limites à ce qu'on peut supporter; **3** (to such an extent) tellement; ~ **much worse** tellement pire; **thank you** ~ **much** merci beaucoup; **4** (in contrasts) **not** ~ **much X as Y** moins X que Y

E **so much as** *adv phr* (even) même; **he never** ~ **much as apologized** il ne s'est même pas excusé

F **so much for** *prep phr* **1** (having finished with) ~ **much for that problem, now for...** assez parlé de ce problème, parlons maintenant de...; **2** ○(used disparagingly) ~ **much for equality** bonjour l'égalité; ~ **much for saying you'd help** c'était bien la peine de dire que tu aiderais

G **so long as**○ *conj phr* ► **long**

(Idioms) ~ **long**○! à bientôt!; ~ **much the better** tant mieux; ~ **comme ci comme ça**; ~ **there!** d'abord!

soak /səʊk/

A *n* **1** **to give sth a** ~ GB faire tremper qch; **to have a** ~ prendre un long bain; **2** ○(drunk) poivrot/-ote○ *m/f*

B *vtr* **1** (wet) tremper; **to get** ~**ed** se faire tremper; **2** (immerse) faire tremper

C *vi* **1** (be immersed) tremper; **to leave sth to** ~ mettre qch à tremper; **2** (be absorbed) **to** ~ **into** être absorbé par; **to** ~ **through** traverser

D *v refl* **to** ~ **oneself** se tremper

E **soaked** *pp adj* trempé; **to be** ~**ed through** *ou* ~**ed to the skin** être trempé jusqu'aux os

F -**soaked** *combining form* **blood**-~**ed** imbibé de sang; **sweat**-~**ed** trempé de sueur; **sun**-~**ed** ensoleillé

(Phrasal verbs)

■ **soak away** [*water*] être absorbé

■ **soak in** pénétrer

■ **soak off:** ► ~ **off** se décoller; ► ~ [sth] **off,** ~ **off** [sth] décoller [qch] en le mouillant

■ **soak up:** ► ~ [sth] **up,** ~ **up** [sth] absorber; ► ~ **up** [sth] s'imprégner de [*atmosphere*]; **to** ~ **up the sun** faire le plein○ de soleil

soaking /ˈsəʊkɪŋ/

A *n* GB douche○ *f*

B *adj* trempé; **I'm** ~ **wet** je suis trempé jusqu'aux os

soap /səʊp/

A *n* **1** (for washing) savon *m*; **a bar of** ~ un savon; **2** ○(flattery) (also **soft** ~) pommade○ *f*; **3** ○= **soap opera**

B *vtr* savonner

soapbox /ˈsəʊpbɒks/ *n* tribune *f* improvisée; **to get on one's** ~ enfourcher son cheval de bataille; ~ **orator** harangueur/-euse *m/f*

soap: ~**dish** *n* porte-savon *m inv*; ~**flakes** *npl* savon *m* en paillettes; ~ **opera** *n* Radio, TV péj feuilleton *m*; ~ **powder** *n* lessive *f* (en poudre); ~**suds** *npl* (foam) mousse *f* de savon

soapy /ˈsəʊpɪ/ *adj* **1** lit [*water*] savonneux/-euse; [*hands, face*] plein de savon; **2** (cajoling) gen mielleux/-euse; [*manner*] onctueux/-euse

soar /sɔː(r)/ *vi* **1** (rise sharply) gen monter en flèche; [*hopes, spirits*] s'accroître considérablement; **2** gen, Fin (rise) **to** ~ **beyond/above/through** dépasser; **to** ~ **to** atteindre; **3** (rise up) = **soar up**; **4** (glide) planer; **5** littér [*sound*] s'élever; [*tower, cliffs*] se dresser

(Phrasal verb)

■ **soar up** [*bird, plane*] prendre son essor; [*ball*] filer

soaring /ˈsɔːrɪŋ/ *adj* [*inflation, demand, profits*] en forte progression; [*prices, temperatures*] en forte hausse; [*hopes, popularity*] croissant; [*spire*] élancé

sob /sɒb/

A *n* sanglot *m*

B *vtr* (*p prés etc* -**bb**-) **to** ~ **oneself to sleep** s'endormir à force de sangloter

C *vi* (*p prés etc* -**bb**-) sangloter

(Idiom) **to** ~ **one's heart out** pleurer toutes les larmes de son corps

sobbing /ˈsɒbɪŋ/

A *n* **⊄** sanglots *mpl*

B *adj* [*child*] sanglotant

sober /ˈsəʊbə(r)/

A *adj* **1** (not drunk) **I'm** ~ je n'ai pas bu d'alcool; (in protest) je ne suis pas ivre; **2** (no longer drunk) dessoûlé; **3** (serious) [*person*] sérieux/-ieuse; [*mood*] grave; **4** (realistic) gen modéré; [*reminder*] réaliste; **5** (discreet) [*colour, style*] sobre

B *vtr* (make serious) [*news, reprimand*] calmer

(Phrasal verb)

■ **sober up:** ► ~ **up** dessoûler

sobering /ˈsəʊbərɪŋ/ *adj* **it was a** ~ **thought** cette pensée donnait à réfléchir

soberly /ˈsəʊbəlɪ/ *adv* **1** (seriously) [*speak*] avec modération; [*describe*] avec sobriété; **2** (discreetly) [*dressed*] discrètement; [*decorated*] sobrement

sobriety /səˈbraɪətɪ/ *n* **1** (moderation) sobriété *f*; **2** (seriousness) sérieux *m*

sob story *n* mélo○ *m*

soccer /ˈsɒkə(r)/ ► **p. 881**

A *n* football *m*

B *noun modifier* [*player, team, club*] de football; [*star*] du football; ~ **violence** violence *f* dans les tribunes

sociable /ˈsəʊʃəbl/ *adj* [*person*] sociable; [*village*] accueillant

social /ˈsəʊʃl/

A *n* (party) soirée *f*; (gathering) réunion *f*

B *adj* **1** (relating to human society) social; **2** (recreational) [*activity*] de groupes; [*call, visit*] amical; **he's a** ~ **drinker** il boit de l'alcool en société; **he's got no** ~ **skills** il ne sait pas se comporter en société; **3** [*animal*] social

social: ~ **climber** *n* (still rising) arriviste *mf*; (at his/her peak) parvenu/-e *mf*; ~ **club** *n* club *m*; ~ **column** *n* carnet *m* mondain

social conscience *n* **to have a** ~ être conscient des injustices sociales

social: ~ **democrat** *n* social-démocrate *mf*; ~ **engagement** *n* obligation *f* sociale; ~ **evening** *n* soirée *f*; ~ **event** *n* événement *m* mondain; ~ **exclusion** *n* exclusion *f* sociale; ~ **gathering** *n* réunion *f* entre amis; ~ **insurance** *n* US ≈ sécurité *f* sociale

socialism /ˈsəʊʃəlɪzəm/ *n* socialisme *m*

socialist /ˈsəʊʃəlɪst/ *n, adj* (also **Socialist**) socialiste (*mf*)

socialite /ˈsəʊʃəlaɪt/ *n* mondain/-e *m/f*

socialize /ˈsəʊʃəlaɪz/ *vi* (mix socially) rencontrer des gens; **to** ~ **with sb** fréquenter qn

social life *n* (of person) vie *f* sociale; (of town) vie *f* culturelle

socially /ˈsəʊʃəlɪ/ *adv* [*meet, mix*] en société; [*acceptable*] en société; [*inferior, superior*] du point de vue social; [*oriented*]

vers le social; **I know him ~, not professionally** je le connais personnellement, mais pas sur le plan professionnel

socially excluded
A *n* (+ *v pl*) **the ~** les exclus *mpl*
B *adj* exclu

social: **~ misfit** *n* inadapté/-e *m/f*; **~ outcast** *n* paria
m; **~ register** *n* US carnet *m* mondain

social scene *n* **she's well known on the London ~** elle
est très connue dans la société londonienne

social: **~ science** *n* science *f* sociale; **~ secretary**
n (of club) secrétaire *mf* (du club)

social security *n* (benefit) aide *f* sociale; **to be on ~** recevoir l'aide sociale

social: **Social Security Administration, SSA** *n*
US *service de gestion de la retraite et des pensions*; **~ service**
n US ▸ **social work**; **Social Services** *npl* GB services
mpl sociaux; **~ studies** *n* (+ *v sg*) sciences *fpl* humaines;
~ welfare *n* protection *f* sociale; **~ work** *n* travail *m*
social; **~ worker** ▸ p. 1181 *n* travailleur/-euse *m/f*
social/-e

society /səˈsaɪətɪ/
A *n* **1** (community) société *f*; **2** (club) (for social) association *f*; (for
mutual hobbies) club *m*; (for intellectual business, contact) société *f*;
drama ~ société de théâtre; **3** (upper classes) (*also* **high ~**)
haute société *f*; **fashionable ~** le beau monde
B *noun modifier* [*artist, columnist, photographer, wedding*] mondain; [*hostess*] des soirées mondaines; **~ gossip** échos *mpl*
mondains

sociological /ˌsəʊsɪəˈlɒdʒɪkl/ *adj* [*study, research, issue*]
sociologique; [*studies*] de sociologie

sociologist /ˌsəʊsɪˈɒlədʒɪst/ ▸ p. 1181 *n* sociologue *mf*

sociology /ˌsəʊsɪˈɒlədʒɪ/ *n* sociologie *f*

sock /sɒk/ ▸ p. 1191
A *n* (*pl* **~s** *ou* **sox**) **1** (footwear) chaussette *f*; **2** Aviat (*also*
wind ~) manche *f* à air; **3** ○(punch) beigne○ *f*
B ○*vtr* flanquer une beigne○ à

(Idioms) **to put a ~ in it**○ la boucler○; **to ~ it to them**○
donner le maximum; **to pull one's ~s up**○ se remuer

socket /ˈsɒkɪt/ *n* **1** Elec (for plug) prise *f* (de courant); (for
bulb) douille *f*; **2** Anat (of joint) cavité *f* articulaire; (of eye)
orbite *f*; **he nearly pulled my arm out of its ~** il a failli me
déboîter le bras

soda /ˈsəʊdə/
A *n* **1** Chem soude *f*; **2** (*also* **washing ~**) soude *f* ménagère; **3** (*also* **~ water**) eau *f* de seltz; **whisky and ~**
whisky *m* soda; **4** (*also* **~ pop**) US soda *m*
B *noun modifier* [*bottle*] de soda; [*crystals*] de soude

soda: **~ fountain** *n* US distributeur *m* de soda;
~ siphon *n* siphon *m* d'eau de seltz

sodden /ˈsɒdn/ *adj* **1** (wet through) [*towel, clothing*] trempé;
[*ground*] détrempé; **2** fig **~ with drink** abruti d'alcool

Sod's Law○ /ˌsɒdzˈlɔː/ *n* hum loi *f* de l'emmerdement●
maximum

sofa /ˈsəʊfə/ *n* canapé *m*

sofa bed *n* canapé-lit *m*

soft /sɒft, US ˈsɔːft/ *adj* **1** (not rigid or firm) [*ground*] meuble;
Sport lourd; [*rock, metal*] tendre; [*snow*] léger/-ère; [*bed, cush-
ion*] moelleux/-euse; [*fabric, fur, leather*] souple; [*muscle*] flasque; [*dough, butter*]
mou/molle; **to get ~** [*ground, butter, mixture*] s'amollir; **to
make sth ~** amollir [*ground*]; ramollir [*butter, mixture*];
adoucir [*hard water, skin*]; **~ to the touch** doux au toucher;
~ ice cream glace *f* italienne; **2** (muted) [*colour, sound*]
doux/douce; [*step, knock*] feutré; **~ lighting** éclairage *m*
tamisé; **3** (gentle, mild) [*air, climate, rain, water, breeze, look,
words*] doux/douce; [*pressure, touch*] léger/-ère; [*landing*] Aviat
en douceur; [*eyes, heart*] tendre; [*approach*] gen diplomatique; Pol modéré; **the ~ left** la gauche modérée; **to take a
~ line with sb** adopter une ligne modérée avec qn; **4** (not
sharp) [*outline*] flou; [*fold*] souple; **5** Econ [*market*] instable à
la baisse; **6** (lenient) [*parent, teacher*] (trop) indulgent;
7 ○(in love) **to be ~ on sb** en pincer○ pour qn; **8** (idle)
[*life, job*] peinard○; **9** ○(stupid) stupide; **to be ~ in the head**
être ramolli du cerveau

soft: **~back** *n* livre *m* à couverture plastifiée; **~ball** *n*
US *variante du baseball*; **~-boiled** *adj* [*egg*] à la coque;
~-centred *adj* [*chocolate*] fourré; **~ cheese** *n* fromage *m* à pâte molle; **~ copy** *n* Comput visualisation *f*

sur écran; **~ drink** *n* boisson *f* non alcoolisée; **~ drug**
n drogue *f* douce

soften /ˈsɒfn, US ˈsɔːfn/
A *vtr* **1** lit (make less firm or rough) amollir [*ground, metal*]; adoucir [*skin, hard water*]; ramollir [*butter*]; assouplir [*fabric*];
2 fig atténuer [*blow, impact, shock, pain, resistance*]; adoucir
[*refusal*]; assouplir [*attitude, position, rule*]; minimiser [*fact*];
3 (make quieter) adoucir [*sound, voice*]; **4** (make less sharp)
adoucir [*form, outline, light*]
B *vi* **1** lit [*light, outline, music, colour*] s'adoucir; [*skin*] devenir
plus doux; [*substance, ground*] se ramollir; **2** fig [*person,
approach*] s'assouplir (**towards sb** vis-à-vis de qn); **3** Econ
fléchir

(Phrasal verb)
■ **soften up**: ▸ **~ up** amollir; ▸ **~ up [sb]**, **~ [sb] up**
affaiblir [*opponent*]; attendrir [*customer*]

softener /ˈsɒfnə(r), US ˈsɔːf-/ *n* **1** (*also* **fabric ~**) (produit
m) assouplissant *m*; **2** (*also* **water ~**) adoucisseur *m*

softening /ˈsɒfnɪŋ, US ˈsɔːf-/ *n* **1** (becoming soft) lit (of substance, surface) ramollissement *m*; fig (of light, colour, outline, water)
adoucissement *m*; (of character, attitude) assouplissement *m*
(**towards sb/sth** vis-à-vis de qn/qch); (of sound) atténuation
f; **2** Fin fléchissement *m*

soft focus *n* flou *m* artistique

soft: **~ fruit** *n* **C** fruits *mpl* charnus; **~ furnishings**
npl tapis et tissus *mpl* d'ameublement; **~-hearted** *adj*
qui se laisse facilement apitoyer or attendrir

softly /ˈsɒftlɪ, US ˈsɔːft-/ *adv* gen doucement

softly-softly /ˌsɒftlɪˈsɒftlɪ, US ˌsɔːftlɪˈsɔːftlɪ/ *adj* [*approach*]
ultraprudent; **to take a ~ approach** prendre des gants

softness /ˈsɒftnɪs, US ˈsɔːft-/ *n* (of texture, surface, skin, colour,
light, outline, character, sound) douceur *f*; (of substance) consistance
f molle; fig (of attitude, approach, view) modération *f*; (in economy)
fléchissement *m*

soft option *n* **to take the ~** choisir la facilité

soft-pedal /ˌsɒftˈpedl, US ˌsɔːft-/
A **soft pedal** *n* Mus pédale *f* douce
B *vi* (*p prés* **-ll-** GB, **-l-** US) **1** Mus mettre la pédale douce;
2 fig mettre un bémol fig (**on** à)

soft: **~ porn**○ *n* soft○ *m*; **~ sell** *n* (méthode *f* de) vente *f*
persuasive

soft soap
A *n* **1** lit savon *m* semi-liquide; **2** ○fig flagornerie○ *f*
B **soft-soap** *vtr* fig passer de la pommade○ à

soft-spoken /ˌsɒftˈspəʊkn, US ˌsɔːft-/ *adj* à la voix douce;
to be ~ avoir une voix douce

soft spot○ *n* **to have a ~ for sb** avoir un faible○
pour qn

soft: **~ target** *n* Mil, fig cible *f* vulnérable; **~ tissue** *n*
Med parties *fpl* charnues; **~-top** *n* Aut décapotable *f*;
~ touch○ *n* poire○ *f*; **~ toy** *n* peluche *f*

software /ˈsɒftweə(r), US ˈsɔːft-/
A *n* logiciel *m*
B *noun modifier* [*development, engineering, protection*] informatique; [*company, designer*] de logiciels; [*industry, market*] du
logiciel; **~ product** logiciel *m*

software: **~ developer** *n* développeur/-euse *m/f*;
~ house *n* fabricant *m* de logiciels; **~ package** *n*
Comput progiciel *m*

softwood /ˈsɒftwʊd, US ˈsɔːft-/ *n* **1** (timber) bois *m* tendre;
2 (tree) conifère *m*

softy○ /ˈsɒftɪ, US ˈsɔːftɪ/ *n* **1** péj (weak person) mauviette○ *f*;
2 (indulgent person) bonne pâte○ *f*

soggy /ˈsɒgɪ/ *adj* [*ground*] détrempé; [*food*] ramolli

soh /səʊ/ *n* Mus sol *m*

soil /sɔɪl/
A *n* sol *m*, terre *f*; **on British ~** en territoire britannique
B *vtr* lit, fig salir

solace /ˈsɒləs/
A *n* (feeling of comfort) consolation *f*; (source of comfort) récon-
fort *m*
B *vtr* consoler (**for** de)

solar /ˈsəʊlə(r)/ *adj* gen solaire; [*warmth*] du soleil

solar: **~ eclipse** *n* éclipse *f* de soleil; **~ heating** *n*
chauffage *m* solaire; **~ panel** *n* panneau *m* solaire;
~ power *n* énergie *f* solaire

sold /səʊld/ *prét, pp* ▸ **sell**

solder /'səʊldə(r), 'sɒ-, US 'sɒdər/
A *n* soudure *f*
B *vtr, vi* souder (**onto, to** à)
soldering iron *n* fer *m* à souder
soldier /'səʊldʒə(r)/ ▸ p. 1181
A *n* soldat *m*; **old** ~ ancien combattant *m*; **regular** ~ militaire *m* de carrière
B *vi* être militaire *or* dans l'armée
(Phrasal verb)
■ **soldier on** persévérer malgré tout
soldierly /'səʊldʒəlɪ/ *adj* [*person*] à l'allure militaire; [*appearance, bearing*] militaire
sole /səʊl/
A *n* [1] (fish) sole *f*; [2] (of shoe, sock, iron) semelle *f*; (of foot) plante *f*
B *adj* [1] (single) seul, unique; **for the** ~ **purpose of doing** uniquement pour faire; [2] (exclusive) gen exclusif/-ive; [*trader*] indépendant; **to be in** ~ **charge of sth** être seul responsable de qch
C *vtr* ressemeler [*shoe*]
D **-soled** combining form **rubber/leather-**~**d shoes** chaussures à semelle de caoutchouc/cuir
sole beneficiary *n* Jur légataire *m* universel
solecism /'sɒlɪsɪzəm/ *n* [1] Ling solécisme *m*; [2] (social) bévue *f*
solely /'səʊlɪ/ *adv* (wholly) entièrement; (exclusively) uniquement
solemn /'sɒləm/ *adj* [1] (serious) gen solennel/-elle; [*duty, warning*] formel/-elle; [2] (reverent) solennel/-elle
solemnity /sə'lemnətɪ/
A *n* solennité *f*
B **solemnities** *npl* cérémonial *m* **¢**
solemnize /'sɒləmnaɪz/ *vtr* célébrer [*marriage*]; ratifier [*treaty*]
sol-fa /ˌsɒl'fɑː, US ˌsəʊl-/ *n* solfège *m*
solicit /sə'lɪsɪt/
A *vtr* [1] (request) gen solliciter; rechercher [*business, orders*]; [2] [*prostitute*] racoler
B *vi* [1] [*prostitute*] racoler; [2] (request) **to** ~ **for** gen solliciter; rechercher [*orders*]
soliciting /sə'lɪsɪtɪŋ/ *n* Jur racolage *m*
solicitor /sə'lɪsɪtə(r)/ ▸ p. 1181 *n* [1] GB Jur (for documents, oaths) ≈ notaire *m*; (for court and police work) ≈ avocat/-e *m/f*; **a firm of** ~**s** ≈ un cabinet d'avocats; [2] US Comm démarcheur/-euse *m/f*
solicitous /sə'lɪsɪtəs/ *adj* sout [*expression, person*] plein de sollicitude; [*enquiry, letter, response*] attentionné (**about** sur)
solid /'sɒlɪd/
A *n* Chem, Math solide *m*
B **solids** *npl* (food) aliments *mpl* solides
C *adj* [1] (not liquid or gaseous) solide; **to go** *ou* **become** ~ se solidifier; [2] (of one substance) gen massif/-ive; **the gate was made of** ~ **steel** le portail était tout en acier; **a tunnel cut through** ~ **rock** un tunnel taillé dans la masse rocheuse; [3] (dense) compact; [4] (unbroken) [*line, expanse*] continu; **a** ~ **area of red** une surface rouge unie; [5] (uninterrupted) **five** ~ **days, five days** ~ cinq jours entiers; [6] (strong) gen solide; [*building*] massif/-ive; **to be on** ~ **ground** fig être en terrain sûr; [7] (reliable) [*information*] solide; [*advice, worker, work*] sérieux/-ieuse; [*investment*] sûr; [8] (firm) [*grip*] ferme; **the strike has remained** ~ la grève n'a pas fléchi; [9] (respectable) modèle
D *adv* [*freeze*] complètement; fig [*vote*] massivement; **the play is booked** ~ la pièce affiche complet
solidarity /ˌsɒlɪ'dærətɪ/ *n* solidarité *f*; **to feel** ~ **with sb** se sentir solidaire de qn
solid fuel *n* combustible *m* solide
solidify /sə'lɪdɪfaɪ/
A *vtr* solidifier
B *vi* [*liquid*] se solidifier; [*honey, oil*] se figer
solidity /sə'lɪdətɪ/ *n* (of construction, relationship, currency) solidité *f*; (of research, arguments) sérieux *m*
solidly /'sɒlɪdlɪ/ *adv* [1] [*built*] solidement; [2] ~ **packed** [*crowd*] compact; [*earth*] très tassé; [3] (continuously) sans interruption; [4] (staunchly) [*conservative, socialist*] à cent pour cent; **they are** ~ **behind him** ils le soutiennent massivement

solid-state /ˌsɒlɪd'steɪt/ *adj* [*microelectronics*] à semi-conducteur(s); ~ **physics** physique *f* des solides
solitaire /ˌsɒlɪ'teə(r), US 'sɒlɪteər/ *n* [1] (ring, board game) solitaire *m*; [2] US (with cards) réussite *f*
solitary /'sɒlɪtrɪ, US -terɪ/
A *n* (loner) solitaire *mf*
B *adj* [1] (unaccompanied) [*occupation, walker*] solitaire; [2] (lonely) [*person*] très seul; [*farm, village*] isolé; [3] (single) seul; **a** ~ **case of** un cas unique de
solitary confinement *n* Jur, Mil isolement *m* cellulaire
solo /'səʊləʊ/
A *n* gen, Mus solo *m*
B *adj* [1] Mus **for** ~ **piano** pour piano solo; **for** ~ **voice** pour voix seule; [2] [*album, flight, pilot*] en solo
C *adv* [*dance, fly, perform, play*] en solo
soloist /'səʊləʊɪst/ *n* soliste *mf*
solstice /'sɒlstɪs/ *n* solstice *m*
soluble /'sɒljʊbl/ *adj* (all contexts) soluble; **water-**~ soluble dans l'eau
solution /sə'luːʃn/ *n* [1] (answer) solution *f* (**to** de); [2] Chem (dissolving) dissolution *f*; (mixture) solution *f*
solve /sɒlv/ *vtr* résoudre [*equation, problem*]; élucider [*crime*]; trouver la solution de [*mystery*]; trouver la solution à [*clue, crossword*]; trouver une solution à [*crisis, poverty*]
solvency /'sɒlvənsɪ/ *n* Fin solvabilité *f*
solvent /'sɒlvənt/
A *n* Chem solvant *m*
B *adj* [1] Chem dissolvant; [2] Fin solvable
solvent abuse *n* usage *m* de solvants hallucinogènes
sombre GB, **somber** US /'sɒmbə(r)/ *adj* sombre
some /sʌm/

> ⚠ When *some* is used as a quantifier to mean an unspecified amount of something, it is translated by *du, de l'* before vowel or mute h, *de la* or *des* according to the gender and number of the noun that follows: *I'd like some bread* = je voudrais du pain; *have some water* = prenez de l'eau; *we've bought some beer* = nous avons acheté de la bière; *they've bought some peaches* = ils ont acheté des pêches.
> But note that where *some* is followed by an adjective preceding a plural noun, *de* alone is used in all cases: *some pretty dresses* = de jolies robes.
> For particular usages see **A** below.
> When *some* is used as a pronoun it is translated by *en* which is placed before the verb in French: *would you like some?* = est-ce que vous en voulez?; *I've got some* = j'en ai.
> For particular usages see **B** below.

A *det, quantif* [1] (an unspecified amount or number) ~ **cheese** du fromage; ~ **old socks** de vieilles chaussettes; [2] (certain: in contrast to others) certains; ~ **children like it** certains enfants aiment ça; **in** ~ **ways, I agree** d'une certaine façon, je suis d'accord; ~ **people say that** certaines personnes disent que; **in** ~ **parts of Europe** dans certaines parties de l'Europe; [3] (a considerable amount or number) **he has** ~ **cause for complaint** il a des raisons de se plaindre; **it will take** ~ **doing** ça ne va pas être facile à faire; **we stayed there for** ~ **time** nous sommes restés là assez longtemps; **we waited for** ~ **years** nous avons attendu plusieurs années; **he hadn't seen her for** ~ **years** ça faisait plusieurs années qu'il ne l'avait pas vue; [4] (a little, a slight) **the meeting did have** ~ **effect** la réunion a eu un certain effet; **the candidate needs to have** ~ **knowledge of computers** le candidat doit avoir certaines *or* un minimum de connaissances en informatique; **you must have** ~ **idea where the house is** tu dois avoir une idée de l'endroit où la maison se trouve; **this money will go** ~ **way towards compensating her for her injuries** cet argent compensera un peu ses blessures; **to** ~ **extent** dans une certaine mesure; **well that's** ~ **consolation anyway!** c'est toujours ça○!; [5] péj (an unspecified, unknown) ~ **man came to the house** un homme est venu à la maison; **a car of** ~ **sort, sort of car** une sorte de voiture; [6] ○(a remarkable) **that was** ~ **film!** ça c'était un film!; **that's** ~ **woman** *ou* **man!** c'est quelqu'un!; [7] ○(not much) ~ **help you are!** iron c'est ça que tu appelles aider!; ~ **mechanic he is!** tu parles d'un mécanicien!; **'I'd like the work to be finished by Monday'—'**~ **hope!** 'j'aimerais que le travail soit fini avant lundi'—'tu rêves○!'

B *pron* ①▸ (an unspecified amount or number) **I'd like ~ of those** j'en voudrais quelques-uns comme ça; **(do) have ~!** servez-vous!; **(do) have ~ more!** reprenez-en!; ②▸ (certain ones: in contrast to others) **~ (of them) are blue** certains sont bleus; **~ say that** certaines personnes disent que; **I agree with ~ of what you say** je suis d'accord avec une partie de ce que tu dis; **~ (of them) arrived early** certains d'entre eux sont arrivés tôt

C *adv* ①▸ (approximately) environ; **~ 20 people** environ 20 personnes; **~ £50** autour de 50 livres sterling; ②▸ ○US (a lot) un peu; **from here to the town center in 5 minutes, that's going ~**○ aller d'ici au centre ville en 5 minutes, il faut le faire

(Idiom) **~ people!** ah vraiment, il y a des gens!

somebody /'sʌmbədɪ/ *pron* ①▸ (unspecified person) quelqu'un; **~ famous** quelqu'un de célèbre; **Mr Somebody(-or-other)** M. Machin; **ask John or Henry or ~** demande à John, à Henry ou à n'importe qui d'autre; ②▸ (important person) **he (really) thinks he's ~** il ne se prend pas pour n'importe qui; **they think they're ~** ils se prennent pour des gens importants

(Idiom) **~ up there likes me** il y a quelqu'un là-haut qui veille sur moi

somehow /'sʌmhaʊ/ *adv* ①▸ (by some means) (also **~ or other**) (of future action) d'une manière ou d'une autre; (of past action) je ne sais comment; ②▸ (for some reason) **~ it doesn't seem very important** en fait, ça ne semble pas très important; **~ he never seems to get it right** il semble que rien ne lui réussisse jamais

someone /'sʌmwʌn/ *pron* = **somebody**

someplace /'sʌmpleɪs/ *adv* = **somewhere**

somersault /'sʌməsɒlt/
A *n* ①▸ (of gymnast) roulade *f*; (of child) galipette *f*; (of diver) saut *m* périlleux; (accidental) culbute *f*; ②▸ (of vehicle) tonneau *m*
B *vi* [*gymnast*] faire une roulade; [*diver*] faire un saut périlleux; [*vehicle*] faire un tonneau

something /'sʌmθɪŋ/
A *pron* ①▸ (unspecified thing) quelque chose; **~ new/interesting** quelque chose de nouveau/d'intéressant; **he's always trying to get ~ for nothing** il est radin○; **there's ~ wrong** il y a un problème; **~ or other** quelque chose; **she's ~ (or other) in the army** elle est je ne sais quoi dans l'armée; ②▸ (thing of importance, value etc) **it proves ~** ça prouve quelque chose; **to make ~ of oneself** *ou* one's life réussir sa vie; **he got ~ out of it** il en a tiré quelque chose; **he is quite** *ou* **really ~!** c'est vraiment un numéro!; **do you want to make ~ out of it?** tu veux te battre?; **that house is quite** *ou* **really ~!** cette maison c'est quelque chose!; **there's ~ in what he says** il y a du vrai dans ce qu'il dit; **you've got ~ there!** là, tu n'as pas tort!; **he has a certain ~** il a un petit quelque chose; **'I've found the key'—'well that's ~ anyway'** 'j'ai trouvé la clé'—'c'est déjà ça'; **we gave him ~ for his trouble** nous lui avons donné un petit quelque chose pour le dérangement; ③▸ (forgotten, unknown name, amount etc) **his name's Andy ~** il s'appelle Andy quelque chose; **in nineteen-sixty-~** en mille neuf cent soixante et quelques; **she's gone shopping or ~** elle est allée faire les courses ou quelque chose comme ça; **are you stupid or ~?** tu es bête ou quoi○?
B *adv* ①▸ (a bit) un peu; **~ over/under £20** un peu plus de/en dessous de 20 livres sterling; **~ around 100 kilos** environ 100 kilos; ②▸ ○**he was howling ~ awful** *ou* **shocking** il n'arrêtait pas de hurler
C **something of** *adv phr* (rather, quite) **he is (also) ~ of an actor** il est aussi un assez bon acteur; **she is ~ of an expert on...** elle est assez experte en...; **it was ~ of a surprise** c'était assez étonnant; **it was ~ of a disaster** c'était plutôt désastreux

sometime /'sʌmtaɪm/
A *adv* **we'll have to do it ~** il va falloir qu'on le fasse un jour ou l'autre; **all holidays have to end ~** toutes les vacances ont une fin; **I'll tell you about it ~** je te raconterai ça un de ces jours; **I'll phone you ~ tomorrow/next week** je te téléphonerai demain dans la journée/dans le courant de la semaine prochaine
B *adj* ①▸ (former) ancien/-ienne; ②▸ US occasionnel/-elle

sometimes /'sʌmtaɪmz/ *adv* parfois, quelquefois; (in contrast) **~ angry, ~ depressed** tantôt en colère, tantôt déprimé

somewhat /'sʌmwɒt/ *adv* (with adj) plutôt; (with verb, adverb) un peu; **~ differently** un peu différemment; **~ surprisingly** de façon quelque peu surprenante; **~ to her surprise** à sa grande surprise

somewhere /'sʌmweə(r)/ *adv* ①▸ (some place) quelque part; **she's ~ about** *ou* **around** elle est quelque part par là; **~ hot** un endroit chaud; **he needs ~ to sleep** il a besoin d'un endroit pour dormir; **~ or other** je ne sais où; **~ (or other) in Asia** quelque part en Asie; **they live in Manchester or ~**○ ils habitent à Manchester ou quelque chose comme ça; ②▸ (at an unspecified point in range) **~ between 50 and 100 people** entre 50 et 100 personnes; **~ around 10 o'clock** autour de 10 heures

(Idiom) **now we're getting ~!** (in questioning) voilà enfin des informations utiles!; (making progress) on arrive enfin à quelque chose!

son /sʌn/ *n* ①▸ (male child) fils *m* (of de); **an only ~** un fils unique; **my ~ and heir** mon héritier; ②▸ ○(as form of address) (kindly) fiston○ *m*; (patronizingly) mon gars *m*

(Idiom) **every mother's ~ (of them)** tous autant qu'ils sont

sonata /sə'nɑːtə/ *n* sonate *f*; **violin ~** sonate pour violon

song /sɒŋ/ *n* ①▸ Mus chanson *f*; **give us a ~** chante-nous quelque chose; **to burst into ~** se mettre à chanter; ②▸ (of bird) chant *m* (of de)

(Idiom) **for a ~**○ pour rien

song and dance *n* Theat chanson *f* dansée

(Idiom) **to make a ~ about sth**○ GB faire toute une histoire de qch

song: **~bird** *n* oiseau *m* chanteur; **~writer** ▸ p. 1181 *n* (of words) parolier/-ière *m/f*; (of words and music) auteur-compositeur *m* de chansons

sonic /'sɒnɪk/ *adj* [*vibration*] sonore; **~ interference** parasites *mpl*

sonic boom *n* bang *m*

son-in-law /'sɒnɪnlɔː/ *n* gendre *m*

sonnet /'sɒnɪt/ *n* sonnet *m*

sonorous /'sɒnərəs, sə'nɔːrəs/ *adj* gen sonore; [*name*] ronflant

soon /suːn/ *adv* ①▸ (in a short time) bientôt; **it will ~ be three years since we met** voici bientôt trois ans que nous nous sommes rencontrés; **see you ~!** à bientôt!; ②▸ (quickly) vite; **it ~ became clear that** il est vite devenu évident que; ③▸ (early) tôt; **~ enough** assez tôt; **the ~er the better** le plus tôt le mieux; **the ~er we leave, the ~er we'll get there** plus nous partirons tôt et plus nous y serons vite; **as ~ as possible** dès que possible; **I spoke too ~!** j'ai parlé trop vite!; **as ~ as he arrives** dès qu'il arrivera; **~er or later** tôt ou tard; **all too ~ the summer was over** l'été est passé bien trop vite; **tomorrow at the ~est** demain au plus tôt; **and not a moment too ~!** il était temps!; ④▸ (not long) **they left ~ after us** ils sont partis peu après nous; **~ afterwards** peu après; **no ~er had I done sth than...** j'avais à peine fait qch que...; ⑤▸ (rather) **I would just as ~ do X as do Y** j'aime autant faire X que faire Y; **I would ~er not do** j'aime autant ne pas faire; **~er him than me!** plutôt lui que moi!; **he would ~er die than do** il préférerait mourir que de faire

(Idioms) **least said ~est mended** Prov moins on en dit, mieux ça vaut; **no ~er said than done** aussitôt dit aussitôt fait

soot /sʊt/ *n* suie *f*

soothe /suːð/
A *vtr* gen calmer; apaiser [*sunburn*]
B *vi* [*voice*] rassurer; [*lotion, massage*] faire du bien
(Phrasal verb)
■ **soothe away**: ▸ **~ away [sth], ~ [sth] away** calmer

soothing /'suːðɪŋ/ *adj* [*cream, music, person, presence, voice*] apaisant; [*effect*] calmant; [*word*] rassurant

soothingly /'suːðɪŋlɪ/ *adv* [*stroke*] de façon apaisante; [*speak*] de façon rassurante

sooty /'sʊtɪ/ *adj* (covered in soot) [*object*] couvert de suie; [*air*] chargé de suie; (black) tout noir

sop /sɒp/
A *n* ①▸ (of bread) morceau *m* de pain trempé; ②▸ (concession) concession *f* symbolique; **as a ~ to her pride** pour flatter son orgueil; **to offer sth as a ~ to sb** offrir qch pour amadouer qn
B *vtr* (*p prés etc* **-pp-**) tremper [*bread, cake*] (**in** dans)

(Phrasal verb)
■ **sop up** : ▶ ～ **up [sth]**, ～ **[sth] up** éponger

sophisticated /sə'fɪstɪkeɪtɪd/ *adj* ①▸ (smart) [*person*] (cultured) raffiné, sophistiqué pej; (elegant) chic *inv*; [*clothes, fashion*] recherché; [*restaurant, resort*] chic *inv*; [*magazine*] sophistiqué; ②▸ (discriminating) [*mind, taste*] raffiné; [*audience, public*] averti; [*civilization, society*] évolué; ③▸ (elaborate, complex) [*equipment, technology*] sophistiqué; [*argument, joke*] subtil; [*style*] recherché

sophistication /sə,fɪstɪ'keɪʃn/ *n* ①▸ (smartness) (of person) (in lifestyle) raffinement *m*, sophistication *f* pej; (in judgment) finesse *f*; (in appearance) chic *m*; (of restaurant, resort, magazine) chic *m*; (of mind, tastes) raffinement *m*; **lack of ～** simplicité *f*; ②▸ (of audience, public) caractère *m* averti; ③▸ (complexity) (of equipment) sophistication *f*; (of discussion, joke) subtilité *f*

sophomore /'sɒfəmɔː(r)/ *n* US Univ étudiant/-e en deuxième année d'université; Sch étudiant/-e en deuxième année de lycée

soporific /,sɒpə'rɪfɪk/ *adj* (sleep-inducing) soporifique

sopping /'sɒpɪŋ/ *adj* (*also* ～ **wet**) trempé

soppy○ /'sɒpɪ/ *adj* péj sentimental

soprano /sə'prɑːnəʊ, US -'præn-/ ▸ p. 1311
Ⓐ *n* (*pl* ～**s**) ①▸ (person) soprano *mf*; ②▸ (voice, instrument) soprano *m*
Ⓑ *adj* gen de soprano; [*part, aria*] pour soprano

sorcerer /'sɔːsərə(r)/ *n* sorcier *m*

sorcery /'sɔːsərɪ/ *n* (witchcraft) sorcellerie *f*

sordid /'sɔːdɪd/ *adj* sordide; **to go into all the ～ details of sth** hum raconter qch dans tous ses détails

sore /sɔː(r)/
Ⓐ *n* plaie *f*
Ⓑ *adj* ①▸ (sensitive) [*eyes, throat, nose, gums*] irrité; [*muscle, tendon, arm, foot*] endolori; **to have a ～ throat** avoir mal à la gorge; **to be** *ou* **feel ～ (all over)** avoir mal (partout); **my leg is still a bit ～** ma jambe me fait encore un peu mal; **you'll only make it ～ by scratching** tu vas t'irriter encore plus si tu te grattes; ②▸ ○surtout US (peeved) vexé; **to be ～ about** *ou* **over sth** être vexé par qch; **to be ～ at sb** en vouloir à qn; **to get ～** se vexer; ③▸ littér **to be in ～ need of sth** avoir grand besoin de qch; ④▸ (delicate) [*subject, point*] délicat
(Idioms) **to be like a bear with a ～ head** être d'une humeur massacrante○; **it is a sight for ～ eyes** ça réjouit le cœur de voir cela

sorely /'sɔːlɪ/ *adv* [*tempted*] fortement; ～ **tried**, ～ **tested** mis à rude épreuve; **medical aid is ～ needed** on a grandement besoin d'aide médicale

sorority /sə'rɒrɪtɪ, US -'rɔːr-/ *n* US Univ association *f* d'étudiantes; (sisterhood) confrérie *f* féminine

sorrel /'sɒrəl, US 'sɔːrəl/ *n* ①▸ Culin (edible) oseille *f*; ②▸ Bot (*also* **wood ～**) oxalis *m*

sorrow /'sɒrəʊ/ *n* (grief) chagrin *m*; **to my ～** à mon grand chagrin

sorrowful /'sɒrəʊfl/ *adj* gen douloureux/-euse; [*voice*] triste

sorry /'sɒrɪ/
Ⓐ *adj* ①▸ (apologetic) désolé; (for emphasis) navré; **I'm terribly ～** je suis vraiment désolé, je suis navré; **I'm ～ I'm late** je suis désolé d'être en retard; **I'm ～ for the delay** je suis désolé du retard; **I'm ～ to be a nuisance but...** excusez-moi de vous embêter, mais...; **to be ～ about** s'excuser de [*behaviour, mistake, change*]; **～ about that!** (je suis) désolé!; **to say ～** s'excuser; ②▸ (sympathetic) **to be ～ to hear of sth/to hear that** être désolé d'apprendre qch/d'apprendre que; **I'm very ～ about your uncle** je suis désolé à propos de ton oncle; ③▸ (regretful) **to be ～ to do** regretter de faire; **will you be ～ to go back?** est-ce que tu auras des regrets en rentrant?; **no-one will be ～ to see him go!** personne ne regrettera son départ!; **and, I'm ～ to say** et malheureusement; **I felt ～ about it afterwards** j'en ai eu des remords par la suite; **do it now or you'll be ～!** fais-le maintenant ou tu t'en repentiras!; ④▸ (pitying) **to feel ～ for sb** plaindre qn also iron; **to feel ～ for oneself** s'apitoyer sur soi-même; ⑤▸ (pathetic) [*state, sight, business*] triste; [*person*] minable; **this is a ～ state of affairs!** c'est vraiment lamentable!
Ⓑ *excl* ①▸ (apologizing) désolé; ②▸ (failing to hear, understand) ～**?** pardon?; ③▸ (interrupting) ～, **time is running out** je suis désolé, mais nous n'avons plus beaucoup de temps; **so we have two, ～, three options** nous avons donc deux, pardon, trois options; ④▸ (adding a comment) ～, **may I just**

---

say that excusez-moi, je voudrais simplement ajouter que

sort /sɔːt/
Ⓐ *n* ①▸ (kind, type) sorte *f*, genre *m*; **books, records—that ～ of thing** des livres, des disques, ce genre de choses; **that's my ～ of holiday** GB *ou* **vacation** US c'est le genre de vacances que j'aime; **I'm not that ～ of person** ce n'est pas mon genre; **it's some ～ of computer** c'est une sorte d'ordinateur; **this must be some ～ of joke** ça doit être une plaisanterie; **I need a bag of some ～** j'ai besoin d'un sac quelconque; **you must have some ～ of idea** tu dois avoir une idée; **an odd** *ou* **strange ～ of chap** un drôle de type; **radiation of any ～ is harmful** toutes les sortes de radiation sont dangereuses; **any ～ of knife will do** n'importe quel couteau fera l'affaire; **what ～ of person would do such a thing?** qui pourrait faire une chose pareille?; **what ～ of person does she think I am?** pour qui me prend-elle?; **you know the ～ of thing (I mean)** tu vois ce que je veux dire; **the same ～ of thing** la même chose; **something of that** *ou* **the ～** quelque chose comme ça; **I didn't say anything of the ～!** je n'ai jamais dit une chose pareille!; **nothing of the ～** (not in the least) pas du tout; **'I'll pay'—'you'll do nothing of the ～!'** 'je vais payer'–'il n'en est pas question!'; ②▸ (in vague description) espèce *f*, sorte *f*; **some ～ of bird** une sorte *or* espèce d'oiseau; ③▸ (type of person) **I know his ～** je connais les gens de son espèce; **we see all ～s here** on voit toutes sortes de gens ici; **he's a good ～** c'est un brave type; ④▸ Comput tri *m*
Ⓑ **of sorts**, **of a sort** *adv phr* **a duck of ～s** *ou* **of a ～** une sorte de canard; **progress of ～s** un semblant de progrès
Ⓒ **sort of** *adv phr* ①▸ (a bit) **～ of cute** plutôt mignon/-onne; **to ～ of understand** comprendre plus ou moins; **'is it hard?'—'～ of'** 'est-ce que c'est difficile?'—'plutôt, oui'; ②▸ (approximately) **～ of blue-green** dans les bleu-vert; **it just ～ of happened** c'est arrivé comme ça; **he was just ～ of lying there** il était étendu par terre comme ça
Ⓓ *vtr* ①▸ (classify, arrange) classer [*data, files, stamps*]; trier [*letters, apples, potatoes*]; **to ～ books into piles** ranger des livres en piles; ②▸ (separate) séparer
(Idioms) **to be** *ou* **feel out of ～s** (ill) ne pas être dans son assiette; (grumpy) être de mauvais poil○; **it takes all ～s (to make a world)** Prov il faut de tout pour faire un monde Prov

(Phrasal verbs)
■ **sort out** : ▶ ～ **[sth] out**, ～ **out [sth]** ①▸ (resolve) régler [*problem, matter*]; **to ～ out the confusion** dissiper un malentendu; **it will take me hours to ～ this mess out** il va me falloir des heures pour remettre de l'ordre dans tout ça; **I'll ～ it out** je m'en occuperai; **it's time to ～ this thing out** il est temps de tirer cette affaire au clair; ②▸ (organize) s'occuper de [*details, arrangements*]; clarifier [*ideas*]; trouver [*replacement*]; **I'll ～ something out with Tim** j'arrangerai quelque chose avec Tim; ③▸ (tidy up, put in order) ranger [*desk*]; classer [*files*]; mettre de l'ordre dans [*finances, affairs*]; ④▸ (select) trier; ⑤▸ (mend) réparer; ▶ ～ **out [sth]** ①▸ (separate) **to ～ out the clean socks from the dirty** séparer les chaussettes propres des chaussettes sales; ②▸ (establish) **to ～ out who is responsible** établir qui est responsable; **we're still trying to ～ out what happened** nous essayons toujours de comprendre ce qui s'est passé; ▶ ～ **[sb] out** ①▸ (punish) régler son compte à qn○; ②▸ (help) aider; ▶ ～ **[oneself] out** (get organized) s'organiser; (in one's personal life) résoudre ses problèmes; **things will ～ themselves out** les choses vont s'arranger d'elles-mêmes; **the problem ～ed itself out** le problème s'est résolu de lui-même
■ **sort through** : ▶ ～ **through [sth]** regarder

sort code *n* Fin code *m* d'agence

sorter /'sɔːtə(r)/ ▸ p. 1181 *n* ①▸ (person) trieur/-euse *m/f*; ②▸ (machine) gen trieuse *f*; Agric trieur *m*

sorting /'sɔːtɪŋ/ *n* ①▸ gen triage *m*, tri *m*; ②▸ (post) tri *m* postal

sorting office *n* (post) centre *m* de tri

SOS *n* lit SOS *m*; fig appel *m* (au secours)

so-so○ /'səʊ'səʊ/
Ⓐ *adj* moyen/-enne
Ⓑ *adv* comme ci comme ça○

sotto voce /,sɒtəʊ 'vəʊtʃɪ/ *adv* [*say, add*] à mi-voix

sought /sɔːt/ *pp* ▸ **seek**

sought-after /'sɔːtɑːftə(r), US -æf-/ *adj* [*person, skill*] demandé, recherché; [*job, brand, area*] prisé

soul /səʊl/ n **1** (immortal, essential) âme f; **to sell one's ~** fig donner n'importe quoi; **bless my ~!**, **upon my ~!** grand Dieu!; **to be the ~ of discretion** être la discrétion même; **2** (emotional appeal) **to lack ~** [*performance*] être plat; [*city*] ne pas avoir d'âme; **he has no ~!** hum il est trop terre-à-terre!; **3** (person) **a sensitive ~** une âme sensible; **she's a motherly ~** elle est très maternelle; **you mustn't tell a ~!** ne le dis à personne!; **'many people there?'—'not a ~'** il y avait du monde?'—'personne', 'pas un chat°'; **4** ⊄ Mus (*also* **~ music**) soul m

(Idioms) **it's good for the ~** hum ça forme le caractère; **to be the life and ~ of the party** être un *or* une boute-en-train; **to throw oneself into sth heart and ~** se donner corps et âme à qch

soul: **~-destroying** adj abrutissant; **~ food** n US cuisine traditionnelle des Afro-Américains

soulful /'səʊlfl/ adj (all contexts) mélancolique

soulless /'səʊlɪs/ adj [*building, office block*] sans âme; [*job*] abrutissant; [*interpretation*] plat

soul: **~ mate** n âme f sœur; **~-searching** n débat m intérieur; **~-stirring** adj très émouvant

sound /saʊnd/

A n **1** Phys, TV, Radio son m; **2** (noise) gen bruit m; (of bell, instrument, voice) son m; **a grating ~** un grincement; **without a ~** sans bruit; **3** fig (impression from hearsay) **a 24 hour flight? I don't like the ~ of that!** un vol de 24 heures? cela ne me tente pas!; (when situation is threatening) **a reorganization? I don't like the ~ of that** une restructuration? ça m'inquiète; **by the ~ of it** d'après ce qu'on a dit; **he was in a bad temper that day, by the ~ of it** il semble que ce jour-là il ait été de mauvaise humeur; **4** Med sonde f; **5** Geog détroit m; **6** Mus **the Motown ~** le style de Motown

B noun modifier TV, Radio [*engineer*] du son

C adj **1** (in good condition) [*building, heart, constitution*] solide; [*lungs*] sain; [*health*] bon/bonne; **of ~ mind** sain d'esprit; **2** (well-founded) gen solide; [*judgment*] sain; [*sleep*] profond; **some ~ advice** un bon conseil; **he has a ~ grasp of the basic grammar** il a une bonne compréhension des bases grammaticales; **a ~ move** une décision *or* démarche avisée; **3** (of good character) **he's very ~** on peut avoir confiance en lui; **4** Fin, Comm [*investment*] bon/bonne, sûr; [*management*] sain; **5** (correct, acceptable) **that is ~ economics** du point de vue économique, c'est très sensé; **our products are ecologically ~** nos produits ne nuisent pas à l'environnement; **she's politically ~** elle a des idées politiques de bon ton

D vtr **1** faire retentir [*siren*]; **to ~ one's horn** klaxonner; lit, fig **to ~ the alarm** sonner l'alarme; **2** Mus, Mil gen sonner; **3** Ling prononcer [*letter*] (**in** de); **4** (express) donner [*warning*]; **to ~ a note of caution** lancer un appel à la prudence

E vi **1** (seem) sembler; **it ~s as if he's really in trouble** il semble qu'il ait vraiment des ennuis; **it ~s dangerous** ça a l'air dangereux; **it doesn't ~ to me as if she's interested** je ne pense pas qu'elle soit intéressée; **2** (give impression by voice or tone) **to ~ banal/boring** paraître banal/ennuyeux; **you make it ~ interesting** à t'écouter ça a l'air intéressant; **you ~ as if you've got a cold** on dirait que tu es enrhumé; **you ~ like my mother!** on dirait ma mère qui parle!; **I don't want to ~ pessimistic** je ne voudrais pas avoir l'air pessimiste; **spell it as it ~s** écris-le comme ça se prononce; **3** (convey impression) faire; **she calls herself Geraldine—it ~s more sophisticated** elle se fait appeler Géraldine—ça fait plus sophistiqué; **it may ~ silly, but…** ça a peut-être l'air idiot, mais…; **4** (make a noise) gen sonner; [*siren*] hurler

F adv **to be ~ asleep** dormir à poings fermés

(Phrasal verbs)

■ **sound off°** rebattre les oreilles aux gens°

■ **sound out**: ▸ **~ out** [sb], **~** [sb] **out** sonder, interroger

sound: **~ archives** npl archives fpl sonores; **~ barrier** n mur m du son; **~ bite** n: bref extrait d'une interview enregistrée; **~ card** n Comput carte f son, carte f audio; **~ effect** n effet m sonore; **~ head** n Cin lecteur m de son; (on tape recorder) tête f de lecture du son

sounding /'saʊndɪŋ/

A n lit, fig sondage m; **to take ~s** faire des sondages

B -**sounding** combining form **a grand-~/English-~** name un nom qui fait bien/qui fait anglais

sounding-board /'saʊndɪŋbɔːd/ n fig personne f sur qui on peut tester ses idées

sound insulation n isolation f acoustique

soundless /'saʊndlɪs/ adj silencieux/-ieuse

soundlessly /'saʊndlɪslɪ/ adv sans bruit

sound: **~ level** n niveau m sonore; **~ library** n sonothèque f

soundly /'saʊndlɪ/ adv [*sleep*] à poings fermés; **we can sleep ~ in our beds, now that…** nous pouvons dormir tranquilles, maintenant que…; [*beat, defeat*] à plates coutures; [*built, based*] solidement

soundness /'saʊndnɪs/ n (correctness) sûreté f

sound-proof /'saʊndpruːf/

A adj [*wall, room*] insonorisé; [*material*] insonorisant

B vtr insonoriser [*room*]

sound: **~-proofing** n insonorisation f; **~ system** n (hi-fi) stéréo° f; (for disco etc) sono° f; **~-track** n Mus, TV, Cin (of film) bande f sonore; (on record etc) bande f originale

sound wave n onde f sonore

soup /suːp/ n Culin soupe f, potage m

(Idiom) **to be in the ~** être dans le pétrin°

(Phrasal verb)

■ **soup up**: ▸ **~ up** [sth], **~** [sth] **up** gonfler

soup: **~ kitchen** n soupe f populaire; **~ plate** n assiette f creuse; **~spoon** n cuillère f à soupe; **~ tureen** n soupière f

sour /'saʊə(r)/

A adj **1** (bitter) aigre; **to go ~** lit tourner; fig se dégrader; **2** (bad-tempered) revêche

B vtr gâter [*relations, atmosphere*]

C vi [*attitude*] s'aigrir; [*relationship*] se dégrader

source /sɔːs/

A n **1** (origin, informant) source f (**of** de) also Geog, Literat; **energy/food ~s** ressources fpl énergétiques/alimentaires; **at ~** à la source; **2** (cause) **~ of** source f de [*anxiety, resentment, satisfaction*]; cause f de [*problem, error, infection, pollution*]; origine f de [*rumour*]

B noun modifier [*book, code, language, program*] source; **~ material** sources fpl

C vtr se procurer [*products, energy*]

sourdough n US levain m

sour-faced adj [*person*] à la mine revêche

sour grapes npl dépit m; **it's (a touch of) ~!** c'est du dépit!

south /saʊθ/ ▸ p. 1089

A n sud m

B adj gen sud inv; [*wind*] gen du sud; Meteorol de sud

C adv [*move*] vers le sud; [*lie, live*] au sud (**of** de)

south: **South Africa** ▸ p. 774 pr n Afrique f du Sud; **South America** ▸ p. 774 pr n Amérique f du Sud; **~bound** adj en direction du; **~east** ▸ p. 1089 n sud-est m; **~eastern** ▸ p. 1089 adj sud-est inv

southern /'sʌðən/ ▸ p. 1089 adj [*coast, boundary*] sud inv; [*state, region, town, accent*] du sud

Southern Alps pr n Alpes fpl néo-zélandaises

southerner /'sʌðənə(r)/ n **~s** les gens mpl du Sud

southernmost adj à l'extrême sud

south: **~-facing** adj exposé au sud; **South Pole** pr n pôle m Sud; **South Sea Islands** ▸ p. 954 pr npl Océanie f

southward /'saʊθwəd/ ▸ p. 1089

A adj [*side*] sud inv; [*wall, slope*] du côté sud; [*journey*] vers le sud

B adv (also **~s**) vers le sud

southwest /ˌsaʊθ'west/ ▸ p. 1089 n sud-ouest m

southwestern /ˌsaʊθ'westən/ ▸ p. 1089 adj sud-ouest inv

souvenir /ˌsuːvə'nɪə(r), US 'suːvənɪər/ n souvenir m

sovereign /'sɒvrɪn/

A n (monarch) souverain/-e m/f; (coin) souverain m

B adj [*power, state, contempt*] souverain (after n)

sovereignty /'sɒvrəntɪ/ n souveraineté f

Soviet Union /ˌsəʊvɪət 'juːnɪən/ ▸ p. 774 pr n Hist Union f soviétique

sow¹ /saʊ/ n (pig) truie f

sow² /səʊ/ vtr (prét **sowed**, pp **sowed**, **sown**) **1** semer [*seeds, corn*]; **2** ensemencer [*field*]

sowing /'səʊɪŋ/ n **₵** semailles *fpl*

sown /seʊn/ *pp* ▶ sow²

soya /'sɔɪə/
A n soja *m*
B *noun modifier* [*bean, burger, flour, milk*] de soja

soya sauce, **soy sauce** n sauce *f* soja

sozzled○ /'sɒzld/ *adj* pinté○, cuité○

spa /spɑː/ n (town) station *f* thermale; (health club) club *m* de remise en forme

space /speɪs/
A n **1** **₵** (room) place *f*, espace *m*; **to sell (advertising) ~ in a newspaper** vendre des espaces publicitaires dans un journal; **to give sb ~** fig laisser de la liberté à qn; **to invade sb's (personal) ~** empiéter sur l'espace vital de qn; **2** **C** (gap, area of land) gen espace *m*; Mus interligne *m*; **in the ~ provided** (on form etc) dans la case prévue à cet effet; **'watch this ~!'** 'à suivre'; **open ~s** espaces *mpl* libres; **3** (interval of time) intervalle *m*; **in the ~ of five minutes** en l'espace de cinq minutes; **in a short ~ of time** en très peu de temps; **4** **₵** (*also* **outer ~**) espace *m*
B *noun modifier* Aerosp, Phys [*research, programme, lab, vehicle, rocket*] spatial
C *vtr* espacer

(Phrasal verb)
■ **space out**: ▶ **to ~ out** [sth], **~** [sth] **out** gen espacer; échelonner [*payments*]

space: **~ age** n ère *f* spatiale; **~-bar** n barre *f* d'espacement; **~craft** n (*pl* **~**) vaisseau *m* spatial

spaced out○ *adj* **he's completely ~**○ il plane○ complètement

space flight n Aerosp **1** (activity) voyages *mpl* interplanétaires; **2** (single journey) vol *m* spatial

space: **~ helmet** n Aerosp casque *m* de cosmonaute; **Space Invaders**® n (+ v sg) jeu électronique de combats *dans l'espace*; **~man** n cosmonaute *m*; **~ race** n course *f* pour la conquête de l'espace; **~-saving** *adj* qui gagne de la place; **~ship** n vaisseau *m* spatial; **~ station** n station *f* orbitale; **~suit** n combinaison *f* spatiale; **~woman** n cosmonaute *f*

spacing /'speɪsɪŋ/ n gen espacement *m*; (of payments) échelonnement *m*; **in single/double ~** en simple/double interligne

spacious /'speɪʃəs/ *adj* spacieux/-ieuse

spaciousness /'speɪʃəsnɪs/ n **₵** grandeur *f*

spade /speɪd/ ▶ p. 881 n (tool) bêche *f*, pelle *f*; (in cards) pique *m*

(Idiom) **to call a ~ a ~** appeler un chat un chat

spade: **~ful** n pelletée *f*; **~work** n fig travail *m* de base

Spain /speɪn/ ▶ p. 774 *pr* n Espagne *f*

spam /spæm/
A n Comput pourriel *m*, spam *m*
B *vtr* (*p prés etc* **-mm-**) (on the Internet) inonder [qn] de pourriel

spammer /'spæmə(r)/ n expéditeur/-trice *m/f* de pourriel

spamming /'spæmɪŋ/ n envoi *m* de pourriel

span /spæn/
A n **1** (period of time) durée *f*; **time ~** espace *m* de temps; **over a ~ of several years** sur une période de plusieurs années; **2** (width) (across hand, arms, wings) envergure *f*; (of bridge) travée *f*; (of arch) portée *f*; **the bridge crosses the river in a single ~** le pont enjambe la rivière d'une seule travée; **the whole ~ of human history** fig la totalité *or* l'ensemble de l'histoire de l'humanité
B *vtr* (*p prés etc* **-nn-**) **1** [*bridge, arch*] enjamber; **2** fig (encompass) s'étendre sur; **a group ~ning the age range 10 to 14** un groupe comprenant les enfants âgés de 10 à 14 ans

Spaniard /'spænjəd/ ▶ p. 1032 n Espagnol/-e *m/f*

spaniel /'spænjəl/ n épagneul *m*

Spanish /'spænɪʃ/ ▶ p. 1032, p. 969
A n **1** (people) **the ~** les Espagnols *mpl*; **2** (language) espagnol *m*
B *adj* espagnol

Spanish Armada /ˌspænɪʃ ɑːˈmɑːdə/ n **the ~** l'Invincible Armada *f*

spank /spæŋk/
A n fessée *f*

B *vtr* donner une fessée à

spanking /'spæŋkɪŋ/
A n fessée *f*
B ○*adj* **at a ~ pace** à une belle allure
C ○*adv* **a ~ new car** une voiture flambant neuve

spanner /'spænə(r)/ n GB clé *f* (*de serrage*); **adjustable ~** clé à molette

(Idiom) **to put** *ou* **throw a ~ in the works** mettre du sable dans l'engrenage

spar /spɑː(r)/ *vi* (*p prés etc* **-rr-**) [*boxers*] échanger des coups; [*debaters*] se livrer à des joutes oratoires; **to ~ with** s'entraîner à la boxe avec [*partner*]; fig s'affronter à [*opponent*]

spare /speə(r)/
A n Tech, gen (part) pièce *f* de rechange; (wheel) roue *f* de secours; **use my pen, I've got a ~** prends mon stylo, j'en ai un autre
B *adj* **1** (surplus) [*cash, capacity*] restant; [*capital, land, chair, seat*] disponible; [*copy*] en plus; **I've got a ~ ticket** j'ai un ticket en trop; **a ~ moment** un moment de libre; **2** (in reserve) gen de rechange; [*wheel*] de secours; **3** [*person, build*] élancé; [*design, building, style*] simple; **4** ○GB (mad) dingue○
C *vtr* **1** **to have sth to ~** avoir qch de disponible; **have my pen, I've got one to ~** prends mon stylo, j'en ai un autre; **to catch the train with five minutes to ~** prendre le train avec cinq minutes d'avance; **I have no time to ~ for doing** je n'ai pas de temps à perdre à faire; **the project was finished with only days to ~** le projet a été terminé seulement quelques jours avant la date limite; **2** (treat leniently) épargner; **to ~ sb sth** épargner qch à qn; **3** can you ~ a minute/a pound? as-tu un moment/une livre?; **to ~ a thought for** penser à; **4** (manage without) se passer de [*person*]; **to ~ sb for** se passer de qn pour [*task*]
D *v refl* **to ~ oneself sth** s'épargner qch; **to ~ oneself the trouble of doing** s'épargner l'ennui de faire; **to ~ oneself the expense of** faire l'économie de

(Idioms) **to ~ no effort** faire tout son possible; **to ~ no pains** se donner du mal

spare: **~ part** n Aut, Tech pièce *f* de rechange; **~ part surgery** n chirurgie *f* de remplacement; **~ rib** n Culin travers *m* de porc; **~ room** n chambre *f* d'amis; **~ time** n **₵** loisirs *mpl*

spare tyre GB, **spare tire** US n **1** Aut pneu *m* de rechange; **2** ○(fat) bourrelet *m*

spare wheel n Aut roue *f* de secours

sparing /'speərɪŋ/ *adj* [*person, use*] parcimonieux/-ieuse; **to be ~ with** (economical) économiser; (mean) être avare de; (careful) utiliser [qch] avec parsimonie

sparingly /'speərɪŋlɪ/ *adv* [*use, add*] en petite quantité

spark /spɑːk/
A n **1** gen, Elec étincelle *f*; **2** fig (hint) (of originality) éclair *m*; (of enthusiasm) étincelle *f*; (of intelligence) lueur *f*; **the ~ has gone out of their relationship** leur relation a perdu tout son piment
B *vtr* = **spark off**
C *vi* [*fire*] jeter des étincelles; [*wire, switch*] faire des étincelles

(Phrasal verb)
■ **spark off**: ▶ **~ off** [sth] susciter [*interest, anger, fear*]; provoquer [*controversy, speculation, reaction, panic*]; être à l'origine de [*friendship, affair*]; déclencher [*war, riot*]; entraîner [*growth, change*]

sparkle /'spɑːkl/
A n (of light, star, tinsel) scintillement *m*; (in eye) éclair *m*; fig (of performance) éclat *m*; **she's lost her ~** elle a perdu sa joie de vivre; **to add ~ to sth** donner du brillant à [*glasses etc*]
B *vi* **1** (flash) [*flame, light*] étinceler; [*jewel, frost, metal, water*] scintiller; [*eyes*] briller (**with** de); fig [*conversation*] être émaillé de; **2** [*drink*] pétiller

sparkler /'spɑːklə(r)/ n (firework) cierge *m* magique

sparkling /'spɑːklɪŋ/
A *adj* **1** [*light*] étincelant; [*jewel, water*] scintillant; [*eyes*] brillant (**with** de); **2** [*conversation, wit*] plein de brio; **3** [*drink*] pétillant
B *adv* (for emphasis) **~ clean** étincelant de propreté; **~ white** d'un blanc étincelant

spark plug n Elec, Aut bougie *f*

spar: **~ring match** n (in boxing) combat *m* d'entraînement; fig prise *f* de bec○; **~ring partner** n (in boxing) sparring-partner *m*; fig adversaire *m/f*

sparrow /'spærəʊ/ *n* moineau *m*

sparse /spɑːs/ *adj* [*population, vegetation, hair*] clairsemé; [*furnishings*] rare (*before n*); [*resources*] maigre; [*information*] épars; [*use*] modéré; **trading was ~** la Bourse était calme

sparsely /'spɑːslɪ/ *adv* peu; **~ wooded/attended** peu boisé/fréquenté; **~ populated** à faible population

Spartan /'spɑːtən/ *adj* lit, fig spartiate

spasm /'spæzəm/ *n* (of pain) spasme *m* (**of** de); (of anxiety, panic, rage, coughing) accès *m* (**of** de)

spasmodic /spæz'mɒdɪk/ *adj* [*activity*] intermittent; [*coughing, cramp*] spasmodique

spasmodically /spæz'mɒdɪklɪ/ *adv* par à-coups

spastic /'spæstɪk/ *n, adj* Med handicapé/-e (*m/f*) moteur

spat /spæt/

A *prét, pp* ▸ **spit**
B ○*n* (quarrel) prise *f* de bec○ (**with** avec)

spate /speɪt/ *n* ① **in full ~** GB [*river*] en pleine crue; [*person*] en plein discours; ② **a ~ of** une série de [*incidents*]

spatial /'speɪʃl/ *adj* spatial

spatter /'spætə(r)/

A *n* ① (of liquid) éclaboussure *f*; **a ~ of rain** une petite pluie; ② (sound) crépitement *m*
B *vtr* (splash) éclabousser (**with** de)
C *vi* crépiter (**on** sur; **against** contre)

spatula /'spætʃʊlə/ *n* gen spatule *f*; Med abaisse-langue *m inv*

spawn /spɔːn/

A *n* (of frog, fish) frai *m*
B *vtr* engendrer [*product, imitation etc*]
C *vi* ① Zool frayer; ② (multiply) se multiplier

spay /speɪ/ *vtr* enlever les ovaires de [*animal*]

speak /spiːk/

A **-speak** *combining form* jargon *m*; **computer-~** jargon informatique
B *vtr* (*prét* **spoke**; *pp* **spoken**) ① parler [*language*]; **can you ~ English?** parlez-vous (l')anglais?; **'French spoken'** 'on parle français'; **English as it is spoken** l'anglais tel qu'on le parle; ② (tell, utter) dire [*truth, poetry*]; prononcer [*word, name*]; **to ~ one's mind** dire ce qu'on pense
C *vi* (*prét* **spoke**; *pp* **spoken**) ① (talk) parler (**to** à; **about, of** de); **to ~ in a whisper** parler tout bas; **to ~ ill/well of sb** dire du mal/du bien de qn; **to ~ through** parler par l'intermédiaire de [*medium, interpreter*]; **who's ~ing please?** (on phone) qui est à l'appareil s'il vous plaît?; **(this is) Camilla ~ing** c'est Camilla; **'is that Miss Durham?'—'~ing!'** 'Mademoiselle Durham?'—'c'est moi!'; **this is your captain ~ing** Aviat ici le commandant de bord; **~ing of which, have you booked a table?** tiens, à propos, as-tu réservé une table?; **~ing of lunch, Nancy...** à propos du déjeuner, Nancy...; **she is well spoken of in academic circles** elle est bien considérée dans le milieu universitaire; **he spoke very highly of her** il a parlé d'elle en termes très élogieux; **~ing as a layman...** en tant que non-spécialiste...; **generally ~ing** en règle générale; **roughly ~ing** en gros; **strictly ~ing** à proprement parler; **relatively ~ing** relativement parlant; **we've had no trouble to ~ of** nous n'avons pas eu de problème spécial; **they've got no money to ~ of** ils n'ont pour ainsi dire pas d'argent; **not to ~ of the expense** sans parler du coût; **so to ~** pour ainsi dire; **they're not ~ing (to each other)** ils ne se parlent pas; **I know her by sight but not to ~ to** je la connais de vue mais je ne lui ai jamais parlé; ② (make a speech) parler; (more formal) prendre la parole; **to ~ from the floor** Pol parler de sa place; **to ~ about** *ou* **on** parler de; **to ~ for** parler en faveur de; ④ littér **to ~ of** témoigner de [*suffering, emotion*]

Phrasal verbs

■ **speak for:** ▸ **~ for [sth/sb]** ① (on behalf of) parler pour lit; parler de fig; **to ~ for oneself** s'exprimer; **~ for myself...** pour ma part...; **~ for yourself!** parle pour toi!; **the facts ~ for themselves** les faits parlent d'eux-mêmes; ② (reserve) **to be spoken for** [*object*] être réservé *ou* retenu; [*person*] ne pas être libre

■ **speak out** se prononcer; **don't be afraid! ~ out!** n'aie pas peur! exprime-toi!

■ **speak to:** ▸ **~ to [sth]** commenter [*motion*]

■ **speak up** ① (louder) parler plus fort; ② (dare to speak)

intervenir; **to ~ up for sb/sth** intervenir en faveur de qn/qch

speakeasy /'spiːkiːzɪ/ *n* US Hist bar *m* clandestin

speaker /'spiːkə(r)/ *n* ① (person talking) personne *f* qui parle; (orator, public speaker) orateur/-trice *m/f*; (invited lecturer) conférencier/-ière *m/f*; (one of several conference lecturers) intervenant/-e *m/f*; ② (of foreign language) **an Italian/a French ~** un/-e italophone/francophone *mf*; **a Russian ~** quelqu'un qui parle le russe; ③ (*also* **Speaker**) GB Pol président/-e *m/f* des Communes; ④ Elec, Mus haut-parleur *m*

speaking /'spiːkɪŋ/

A *n* (elocution) élocution *f*; (pronunciation) prononciation *f*
B **-speaking** *combining form* **English-/French-~** anglophone/francophone; **Welsh-~** [*person*] qui parle le gallois; [*area*] de langue galloise

speaking engagement *n* **to have a ~** devoir prononcer un discours

speaking part, speaking role *n* rôle *m*

speaking terms *npl* **we're not on ~** nous ne nous adressons pas la parole

speaking tour *n* tournée *f* de conférences

spear /spɪə(r)/

A *n* ① (weapon) lance *f*; ② (of plant) tige *f*; (of asparagus) pointe *f*; (of broccoli) branche *f*
B *vtr* ① harponner [*fish*]; transpercer (d'un coup de lance) [*person*]; ② (with fork etc) piquer

spear carrier *n* figurant/-e *m/f*

spearhead /'spɪəhed/

A *n* lit, fig fer *m* de lance
B *vtr* mener [*campaign, offensive, revolt, reform*]

spearmint *n* menthe *f* verte

spec○ /spek/

A *n* ① (*abrév* = **specification**) spécification *f*; **to ~** selon les spécifications fournies; ② (*abrév* = **speculation**) **on ~** à tout hasard
B **specs**○ *npl* (*abrév* = **spectacles**) binocles○ *mpl*

special /'speʃl/

A *n* ① Culin plat *m* du jour; **the chef's ~** la spécialité du chef; ② (broadcast) émission *f* spéciale; ③ (bus) car *m* spécial; (train) train *m* spécial
B *adj* ① (official, for a specific purpose) spécial; ② (marked) [*affection, interest*] tout/-e particulier/-ière; ③ (particular) [*reason, motive, significance, treatment*] particulier/-ière; **to make a ~ effort** faire un effort; ④ (unique) [*offer, deal, package, skill*] spécial; [*case, quality*] particulier/-ière; **what is so ~ about this computer?** qu'est-ce que cet ordinateur a de particulier?; **I want to make this Christmas really ~** je voudrais que ce Noël sorte de l'ordinaire; ⑤ (out of the ordinary) [*announcement, guest*] spécial; **as a ~ treat** à titre de faveur spéciale; **going anywhere ~?** est-ce que tu sors quelque part?; **you're ~ to me** tu m'es très cher/chère; **the wine is something ~** le vin est exceptionnel; **what's so ~ about him?** qu'est-ce qu'il a de si extraordinaire?; ⑥ (personal) [*chair, recipe*] personnel/-elle; [*friend*] très cher/chère

special: ~ agent *n* agent *m* secret; **Special Branch** *n* GB service *m* de contre-espionnage et de lutte contre la subversion interne; **~ delivery** *n* Post service *m* exprès

special effect

A *n* Cin, TV effet *m* spécial
B **special effects** *noun modifier* [*specialist, team*] des effets spéciaux; [*department*] effets spéciaux

special interest group *n* Pol groupe *m* défendant des intérêts particuliers

specialism /'speʃəlɪzəm/ *n* spécialité *f*

specialist /'speʃəlɪst/

A ▸ **p. 1181** *n* gen, Med spécialiste *mf* (**in** de); **heart ~** cardiologue *m*
B *adj* [*shop, knowledge, care, equipment*] spécialisé; [*help*] d'un spécialiste; [*work*] de spécialiste

speciality GB /ˌspeʃɪ'ælɪtɪ/, **specialty** US /'speʃəltɪ/ *n* spécialité *f*

specialize /'speʃəlaɪz/ *vi* se spécialiser; **to ~ in** se spécialiser en; **we ~ in repairing computers** notre spécialité consiste à réparer les ordinateurs; **a company specializing in machinery** une entreprise spécialisée dans les machines

special licence *n* GB Jur dispense *f* de bans

specially /ˈspeʃəlɪ/ *adv* [1] (specifically) spécialement; **I made it ~ for you** je l'ai fait exprès pour toi; [2] (particularly) gen particulièrement; [*like, enjoy*] surtout

special needs *npl* [1] Sociol problèmes *mpl*; [2] Sch difficultés *fpl* d'apprentissage scolaire

special: **~ relationship** *n* Pol lien *m* privilégié; **~ school** *n* GB établissement *m* médico-éducatif pour enfants handicapés

specialty /ˈspeʃəltɪ/ *n* US = **speciality**

species /ˈspiːʃiːz/ *n* (*pl* **~**) (all contexts) espèce *f*

specific /spəˈsɪfɪk/
A **specifics** *npl* éléments *mpl* spécifiques; **to get down to (the) ~s** entrer dans les détails
B *adj* précis; **~** to spécifique de

specifically /spəˈsɪfɪklɪ/ *adv* [1] (specially) spécialement (**for** pour); [2] (explicitly) explicitement; [3] (in particular) en particulier; **more ~** plus particulièrement

specification /ˌspesɪfɪˈkeɪʃn/
A *n* [1] (*also* **specifications**) (of design, building) spécification *f* (**for, of** de); **built to sb's ~s** fabriqué selon les spécifications de qn; [2] gen, Jur (stipulation) stipulation *f* (**that** que)
B **specifications** *npl* caractéristiques *fpl*

specification sheet *n* fiche *f* technique

specify /ˈspesɪfaɪ/
A *vtr* stipuler; [*person*] préciser (**that** que; **where** où; **who** qui); **as specified above** comme stipulé ci-dessus; **unless otherwise specified** sauf indication contraire
B **specified** *pp adj* [*amount, date, day, value, way*] spécifié

specimen /ˈspesɪmən/
A *n* (of rock, urine, handwriting) échantillon *m* (**of** de); (of blood, tissue) prélèvement (**of** de); (of species, plant) spécimen *m* (**of** de)
B *noun modifier* [*page, copy, signature*] spécimen *inv*

specious /ˈspiːʃəs/ *adj* sout [*argument, reasoning*] spécieux/-ieuse; [*glamour, appearance*] trompeur/-euse

speck /spek/ *n* (small piece) (of dust, soot) grain *m*; (of dirt, mud) petite tache *f* (**of** de); (of blood, ink, light) point *m*; **a ~ on the horizon** un petit point à l'horizon

speckle /ˈspekl/
A *n* (on person's skin, egg) petite tache *f*; (on bird, animal, fabric) moucheture *f*
B *vtr* [*rain*] tacheter; [*sun*] marquer [qch] de petites taches; [*flecks*] moucheter

spec sheet /ˈspekʃiːt/ *n* fiche *f* technique

spectacle /ˈspektəkl/
A *n* spectacle *m*
B *noun modifier* [*case*] à lunettes; [*frame, lens*] de lunettes
C **spectacles** *npl* lunettes *fpl*

spectacular /spekˈtækjʊlə(r)/
A *n* superproduction *f*
B *adj* spectaculaire

spectacularly /spekˈtækjʊləlɪ/ *adv* de façon spectaculaire; **it was ~ successful** cela a été une réussite spectaculaire

spectator /spekˈteɪtə(r)/ *n* spectateur/-trice *m/f*

spectator sport *n* sport *m* qui attire beaucoup de spectateurs

specter *n* US = **spectre**

spectre GB, **specter** US /ˈspektə(r)/ *n* spectre *m*

spectrum /ˈspektrəm/ *n* (*pl* **-tra, -trums**) [1] Phys spectre *m*; [2] (range) gamme *f*; **people across the political ~** des gens de toutes les tendances politiques

speculate /ˈspekjʊleɪt/
A *vtr* **to ~ that** supposer que; **it has been widely ~d that** on a beaucoup spéculé sur le fait que
B *vi* gen, Fin spéculer (**about** à propos de); **to ~ as to why** spéculer sur les raisons pour lesquelles

speculation /ˌspekjʊˈleɪʃn/ *n* [1] ⓒ gen spéculations *fpl*; **~ about** *ou* **over who will win** spéculations sur le gagnant probable; [2] Fin spéculation *f* (**in** sur)

speculative /ˈspekjʊlətɪv, US *also* ˈspekjəleɪtɪv/ *adj* (all contexts) spéculatif/-ive

speculator /ˈspekjʊleɪtə(r)/ *n* spéculateur/-trice *m/f*

sped /sped/ *prét, pp* ▸ **speed B, C**

speech /spiːtʃ/ *n* [1] (oration) discours *m* (**on** sur; **about** à propos de); Theat tirade *f*; **to give/deliver a ~** tenir/prononcer un discours; [2] (faculty) parole *f*; (spoken form) langage *m*; **direct/indirect ~** Ling discours *m* direct/indirect; **in ~** par le langage; [3] (language) langage *m*; [4] US Sch, Univ expression *f* orale

speech: **~ and drama** *n* Sch, Univ art *m* dramatique; **~ clinic** *n* centre *m* d'orthophonie; **~ day** *n* GB Sch (jour *m* de la) distribution *f* des prix; **~ defect** *n* = **speech impediment**

speechifying /ˈspiːtʃɪfaɪɪŋ/ *n* péj belles paroles *fpl*

speech: **~-impaired** *adj* (not having speech) muet/-ette; (having a speech impediment) qui a un défaut d'élocution; **~ impediment** *n* défaut *m* d'élocution

speechless /ˈspiːtʃlɪs/ *adj* muet/-ette; **to be ~ with** rester muet de; **I was ~ de; the news** la nouvelle m'a laissé sans voix; **I'm ~!** je suis soufflé!

speech: **~ recognition** *n* Comput reconnaissance *f* de la parole; **~ synthesis** *n* Comput synthèse *f* de la parole; **~ therapist** ▸ p. 1181 *n* orthophoniste *mf*; **~ training** *n* cours *m* de diction; **~ writer** ▸ p. 1181 *n* personne *f* qui écrit des discours

speed /spiːd/
A *n* [1] (velocity of vehicle, wind, record) vitesse *f*; (rapidity of response, reaction) rapidité *f*; **at (a) great ~** à toute vitesse; **at ~** [*go, run*] à toute vitesse; [*work, read*] en quatrième vitesse; **to pick up ~** prendre de la vitesse; **'full ~ ahead!'** 'en avant toute!'; **what ~ were you doing?** à quelle vitesse est-ce que tu roulais?; [2] (gear) vitesse *f*; [3] Phot (of film) sensibilité *f*; (of shutter) vitesse *f* d'obturation; [4] ○(drug) amphétamines *fpl*
B *vtr* (*prét, pp* **sped** *ou* **speeded**) hâter [*process, recovery*]; rendre [qch] plus fluide [*traffic*]; **to ~ sb on his/her way** souhaiter bon voyage à qn
C *vi* [1] (*prét, pp* **sped**) (move swiftly) **to ~ along** aller à toute allure; **to ~ away** partir à toute vitesse; **the train sped past** le train est passé à toute vitesse; [2] (*prét, pp* **speeded**) (drive too fast) conduire trop vite; **he was caught ~ing** il a eu une contravention (pour excès) de vitesse

(Phrasal verb)
■ **speed up**: ▸ **~ up** [*walker, train*] aller plus vite; [*athlete, car*] accélérer [*worker*] accélérer l'allure; ▸ **~ up [sth]**, **~ [sth] up** gen accélérer

speed: **~boat** *n* hors-bord *m*; **~ camera** *n* ≈ cinémomètre *m*

speed hump *n* ralentisseur *m*

speedily /ˈspiːdɪlɪ/ *adv* rapidement

speeding /ˈspiːdɪŋ/ *n* Aut excès *m* de vitesse

speed limit *n* limitation *f* de vitesse; **to drive within the ~** conduire en respectant la limitation de vitesse

speedometer /spɪˈdɒmɪtə(r)/ *n* compteur *m* (de vitesse)

speed: **~ reading** *n* lecture *f* rapide; **~ restriction** *n* limitation *f* de vitesse; **~ skating** ▸ p. 881 *n* patinage *m* de vitesse; **~ trap** *n* Aut contrôle *m* de vitesse; **~-up** *n* accélération *f*; **~way racing** ▸ p. 881 *n* course *f* de vitesse à moto

speedy /ˈspiːdɪ/ *adj* rapide

speed zone *n* US zone *f* à vitesse limitée

speleology /ˌspiːlɪˈɒlədʒɪ/ ▸ p. 881 *n* spéléologie *f*

spell /spel/
A *n* [1] (period) moment *m*, période *f*; **for a ~** pendant un certain temps; **a ~ in hospital** un séjour à l'hôpital; **a warm ~** une période de beau temps; **rainy ~** ondée *f*; **sunny ~** éclaircie *f*; **to go through a bad ~** traverser une mauvaise passe; [2] (magic words) formule *f* magique; **evil ~** maléfice *m*; **to be under a ~** être envoûté; **to cast** *ou* **put a ~ on sb** lit, fig jeter un sort à qn; **to break a ~** rompre un sortilège; **to break the ~** fig rompre le charme; **to be under sb's ~** fig être sous le charme de qn
B *vtr* (*pp, prét* **spelled** *ou* **spelt**) [1] (aloud) épeler; (on paper) écrire; **she ~s her name with an e** son nom s'écrit avec e; **to ~ sth properly** orthographier qch correctement; **C-A-T ~s cat** les lettres C-A-T forment le mot cat; [2] (imply) signifier [*danger, disaster, ruin*]; sonner [*end*]
C *vi* (*pp, prét* **spelled** *ou* **spelt**) connaître l'orthographe; **he ~s badly/well** il a une mauvaise/bonne orthographe

(Phrasal verb)
■ **spell out**: ▸ **~ out [sth]**, **~ [sth] out** lit épeler [*word*]; fig expliquer [qch] clairement; **do I have to ~ it out?** est-ce qu'il faut que je te fasse un dessin?

spellbinding *adj* envoûtant

spellbound *adj* envoûté (**by** par); **to hold sb ~** tenir qn sous le charme

Speed

Speed of road, rail, air etc. travel

■ *In French, speed is measured in kilometres per hour:*

100 kph = approximately 63 mph
100 mph = approximately 160 kph
50 mph = approximately 80 kph

X miles per hour
= X miles à l'heure

X kilometres per hour
= X kilomètres à l'heure *or* X kilomètres-heure

100 kph
= 100 km/h

what speed was the car going at?
= à quelle vitesse la voiture roulait-elle?

it was going at 150 kph
= elle roulait à 150 km/h (*cent cinquante kilomètres-heure*)

it was going at fifty (mph)
= elle roulait à quatre-vingts à l'heure (*i.e. at 80 kph*)

the speed of the car was 200 kph
= la vitesse de la voiture était de 200 km/h

(*the de must not be omitted here*)

what was the car doing?
= la voiture faisait du combien?

it was doing ninety (mph)
= elle faisait du 150 (*du cent cinquante: i.e. 150 kph*)

it was going at more than 200 kph
= elle roulait à plus de 200 km/h

it was going at less than 40 kph
= elle roulait à moins de 40 km/h

A was going at the same speed as B
= A roulait à la même vitesse que B

A was going faster than B
= A roulait plus vite que B

B was going slower than A
= B roulait moins vite que A
or B roulait plus lentement que A

Speed of light and sound

sound travels at 330 metres per second
= le son se déplace à 330 m/s (*trois cent trente mètres-seconde* or *mètres à la seconde*)

the speed of light is 186,300 miles per second
= la vitesse de la lumière est de 300 000 km/s (*trois cent mille kilomètres-seconde* or *kilomètres à la seconde*) (*note that the de must not be omitted here*)

---

spellcheck(er) *n* Comput correcteur *m* orthographique

speller /'spelə(r)/ *n* **a good/bad** ~ une personne bonne/ mauvaise en orthographe

spelling /'spelɪŋ/
A *n* orthographe *f*
B *noun modifier* [*mistake, test*] d'orthographe

spelt /spelt/ *prét, pp* ▸ **spell B, C**

spend /spend/
A *n* Fin frais *mpl*
B *vtr* (*prét, pp* **spent**) **1** dépenser [*money, salary*] (**on** en); **2** passer [*time*]; **3** épuiser [*ammunition, energy, resources*]
C *vi* (*prét, pp* **spent**) dépenser

spender /'spendə(r)/ *n* **to be a big** ~ être dépensier/ -ière

spending /'spendɪŋ/ *n* dépenses *fpl*; ~ **on education** dépenses d'éducation; **credit-card** ~ achats *mpl* sur carte de crédit; **defence** ~ dépense *f* en matière de défense; **government** ~, **public** ~ dépense *f* publique

spending: ~ **cut** *n* gen réduction *f* des dépenses; Pol restriction *f* budgétaire; ~ **money** *n* argent *m* de poche; ~ **power** *n* Fin pouvoir *m* d'achat; ~ **spree** *n* folie⁰ *f* (de dépense)

spendthrift /'spendθrɪft/
A *n* **to be a** ~ être dépensier/-ière
B *adj* [*person*] dépensier/-ière; [*habit, policy*] dispendieux/ -ieuse

spent /spent/
A *prét, pp* ▸ **spend**
B *adj* **1** (used) [*bullet*] perdu; [*battery*] déchargé; [*match*] utilisé; **2** (exhausted) [*person*] fourbu; [*passion*] éteint; **to be a** ~ **force** fig avoir perdu toute force

sperm /spɜːm/ *n* **1** (cell) spermatozoïde *m*; **2** (semen) sperme *m*

sperm bank *n* banque *f* de sperme

sperm donor *n* donneur *m* de sperme

spermicidal /ˌspɜːmɪˈsaɪdl/ *adj* spermicide

spew /spjuː/
A *vtr* **1** (*also* ~ **out**) vomir [*smoke, lava, propaganda*]; cracher [*insults, coins, paper*]; **2** ⁰(*also* ~ **up**) dégobiller⁰
B *vi* (*also* ~ **out**) [*smoke, insults*] jaillir

sphere /sfɪə(r)/ *n* **1** (shape) sphère *f*; **2** (planet) sphère *f* céleste; **3** (field) domaine *m* (**of** de); ~ **of influence** sphère *f* d'influence; **4** (social circle) milieu *m*

spherical /'sferɪkl/ *adj* sphérique

spice /spaɪs/
A *n* **1** Culin épice *f*; **mixed** ~ épices mélangées; **2** fig piment *m*
B *noun modifier* [*jar, rack*] à épices; [*trade, route*] des épices
C *vtr* **1** Culin épicer [*food*]; **2** (*also* ~ **up**) pimenter [*life, story*]
(Idiom) **variety is the** ~ **of life** la diversité est le sel de la vie

spick-and-span *adj* impeccable

spicy /'spaɪsɪ/ *adj* **1** [*food*] épicé; **2** [*story*] croustillant

spider /'spaɪdə(r)/ *n* **1** Zool araignée *f*; **2** GB (straps) fixe-bagages *m inv*; **3** US poêle *f* (munie de pieds)

spiderweb *n* US toile *f* d'araignée

spidery /'spaɪdərɪ/ *adj* [*writing*] en pattes de mouche

spiel⁰ /ʃpiːl, US spiːl/ *n* baratin⁰ *m*

spike /spaɪk/
A *n* (point) pointe *f* also Sport
B spikes *npl* Sport chaussures *fpl* à pointes
C *vtr* **1** (pierce) embrocher; **2** ⁰corser [*drink*] (**with** de); **3** (reject) mettre [qch] au panier [*story*]; **4** Sport (in volleyball) **to** ~ **the ball** faire un smash; **5** (thwart) contrecarrer [*scheme*]; étouffer [*rumour*]
(Idiom) **to** ~ **sb's guns** déjouer les plans de qn

spiky /'spaɪkɪ/ *adj* **1** (having spikes) [*hair*] en brosse *inv*; [*branch*] piquant; [*object*] acéré; **2** ⁰GB (short-tempered) revêche

spill /spɪl/
A *n* **1** (of oil, etc) déversement *m* accidentel; **2** (fall) accrochage *m*; (from horse) chute *f*; **3** (for lighting candles) allume-feu *m inv*
B *vtr* (*prét, pp* **spilt** *ou* ~**ed**) **1** (pour) (overturn) renverser (**onto, over** sur); (drip) laisser tomber; **2** (disgorge) déverser [*oil, rubbish, chemical*]
C *vi* (*prét, pp* **spilt** *ou* ~**ed**) (empty out) se répandre; **to** ~ **from** *ou* **out of** couler de; **to** ~ (**out**) **into** *ou* **onto the street** [*crowds, people*] se répandre dans la rue
(Idioms) **(it's) no use crying over spilt milk** ça ne sert à rien de pleurer sur ce qui est fait; **to** ~ **the beans**⁰ vendre la mèche⁰; **to** ~ **blood** verser le sang

(Phrasal verbs)
■ **spill out**: ▸ ~ **out** lit se répandre; ▸ ~ **out** [**sth**], ~ [**sth**] **out** lit laisser échapper; fig révéler [*secrets*]; débiter [*story*]

Spelling and punctuation

The alphabet and accents

■ *The names of the letters are given below with their pronunciation in French and, in the right-hand column, a useful way of clarifying difficulties when you are spelling names etc. A comme Anatole means A for Anatole, and so on.*

		When spelling aloud ...	
A	[ɑ]	A	comme Anatole
B	[be]	B	comme Berthe
C	[se]	C	comme Célestin
ç	[sesedij]	c	cédille
D	[de]	D	comme Désiré
E	[ə]	E	comme Eugène
é	[eaksãtegy] *or* [əaksãtegy]	e	accent aigu
è	[eaksãɡʀav] *or* [əaksãɡʀav]	e	accent grave
ê	[eaksãsiʀkɔ̃fleks] *or* [əaksãsiʀkɔ̃fleks]	e	accent circonflexe
ë	[ətʀema]	e	tréma
F	[ɛf]	F	comme François
G*	[ʒe]	G	comme Gaston
H	[aʃ]	H	comme Henri
I	[i]	I	comme Irma
J*	[ʒi]	J	comme Joseph
K	[ka]	K	comme Kléber
L	[ɛl]	L	comme Louis
M	[ɛm]	M	comme Marcel
N	[ɛn]	N	comme Nicolas
O	[o]	O	comme Oscar
P	[pe]	P	comme Pierre
Q	[ky]	Q	comme Quintal
R	[ɛʀ]	R	comme Raoul
S	[ɛs]	S	comme Suzanne
T	[te]	T	comme Thérèse
U	[y]	U	comme Ursule
V	[ve]	V	comme Victor
W	[dubləve]	W	comme William
X	[iks]	X	comme Xavier
Y	[iɡʀɛk]	Y	comme Yvonne
Z	[zɛd]	Z	comme Zoé

Spelling

capital B
= B majuscule

small b
= b minuscule

it has got a capital B
= cela s'écrit avec un B majuscule

in small letters
= en minuscules

double t
= deux t [døte]

double n
= deux n [døzɛn] (*note the liaison which would also be used in deux l, deux r etc.*)

apostrophe
= apostrophe [apɔstʀof]

d apostrophe
= d apostrophe [deapɔstʀof]

hyphen
= trait d'union

rase-mottes has got a hyphen
= rase-mottes s'écrit avec un trait d'union

Dictating punctuation

.	point *or* un point (*full stop*)
,	virgule (*comma*)
:	deux points (*colon*)
;	point-virgule (*semicolon*)
!	point d'exclamation† (*exclamation mark*)
?	point d'interrogation† (*interrogation mark*)
	à la ligne (*new paragraph*)
(	ouvrez la parenthèse (*open brackets*)
)	fermez la parenthèse (*close brackets*)
()	entre parenthèses (*in brackets*)
[]	entre crochets (*in square brackets*)
—	tiret (*dash*)
...	points de suspension (*three dots*)
« ou "	ouvrez les guillemets (*open inverted commas*)
» ou "	fermez les guillemets (*close inverted commas*)
«» ou ""	entre guillemets (*in inverted commas*)

The use of inverted commas in French

■ *In novels and short stories, direct speech is punctuated differently from English:*
The inverted commas lie on the line, e.g.
«Tiens, dit-elle, en ouvrant les rideaux, les voilà!»‡

■ *This example also shows that the inverted commas are not closed after each stretch of direct speech. In modern texts they are often omitted altogether (though this is still sometimes frowned on):*
Il l'interrogea:
– Vous êtes arrivé quand?
– Pourquoi cette question? Je n'ai rien fait de mal.
– C'est ce que nous allons voir.

■ *Note the short dash in this case that introduces each new speaker. Even if inverted commas had been used in the above dialogue, they would have been opened before* vous *and closed after* voir, *and not used at other points.*

■ *English-style inverted commas are used in French to highlight words in a text:*
Le ministre a voulu "tout savoir" sur la question.

* *Note the difference between English and French pronunciation of g and j.*

† *Note that, unlike English, French has a space before* ! *and* ? *and* : *and* ;, *e.g.* Jamais !, Pourquoi ? *etc. This is not usual, however, in dictionaries, where it would take up too much room.*

‡ *Single inverted commas are not much used in French.*

■ **spill over** lit déborder; **to ~ over into** fig gen s'étendre à; dégénérer en [*looting, hostility*]

spillage /'spɪlɪdʒ/ *n* **1** (of oil, chemical, effluent) déversement *m* accidentel; **oil ~** déversement *m* accidentel d'hydrocarbures; **2** (spilling) ¢ déversement *m*

spillover /'spɪləʊvə(r)/ *n* US (overflow) (of traffic) excédent *m*; (of liquid) débordement *m*

spilt /spɪlt/ *prét, pp* ▸ **spill B, C**

spin /spɪn/
A *n* **1** (of wheel) tour *m*; (of dancer, skate) pirouette *f*; **to give sth a ~** faire tourner qch; **2** Sport effet *m*; **to put ~ on a ball** donner de l'effet à une balle; **3** Aviat **to go into a ~** descendre en vrille; **4** (pleasure trip) tour *m*; **to go for a ~** aller faire un tour; **5** US (interpretation) **to put a new ~ on sth** aborder qch sous un nouvel angle

B *vtr* (*p prés* **-nn-**; *prét, pp* **spun**) **1** lancer [*top*]; faire tourner [*globe, wheel*]; **2** (flip) **to ~ a coin** tirer à pile ou face;

③ filer [*wool, thread*]; ④ [*spider*] tisser; ⑤ (wring out) essorer qch à la machine [*clothes*]; ⑥ raconter [*tale*]; **he spun
me some tale about missing his train** il a prétendu qu'il
avait raté son train

C vi (*p prés* **-nn-**; *prét*, *pp* **spun**) ① (rotate) [*wheel*] tourner;
[*weathercock, top*] tournoyer; [*dancer*] pirouetter; **to go
∼ning through the air** [*ball, plate*] aller valser○; **the car
spun off the road** la voiture est allée valser○ dans la
nature; ② fig tourner; **my head is ∼ning** j'ai la tête qui
tourne; **the room was ∼ning** les murs de la pièce tour-
naient; ③ (turn wildly) [*wheels*] patiner; [*plane*] descendre en
vrille

(Idioms) **to be in a ∼** être dans tous ses états; **to ∼ one's
wheels** US fig ne pas avancer fig

(Phrasal verbs)

■ **spin along** [*car*] filer
■ **spin out**: ▶ **∼ [sth] out, ∼ out [sth]** prolonger [*visit*];
faire traîner [*qch*] en longueur [*speech*]; ménager [*money*]
■ **spin round**: ▶ **∼ round** [*person*] se retourner rapidement; [*dancer, skater*] pirouetter; **she spun round in her
chair** elle a pivoté sur sa chaise; [*car*] faire un tête-à-queue;
▶ **∼ [sb/sth] round** faire tourner [*wheel*]; faire tournoyer
[*dancer, top*]

spinach /'spɪnɪdʒ, US -ɪtʃ/ *n* ① (plant) épinard *m*; ② **C**
(vegetable) épinards *mpl*

spinal /'spaɪnl/ *adj* [*injury, damage*] de la colonne vertébrale; [*nerve, muscle*] spinal; [*disc, ligament*] vertébral

spinal: **∼ column** *n* colonne *f* vertébrale; **∼ cord** *n*
moelle *f* épinière

spindle /'spɪndl/ *n* broche *f*

spindly /'spɪndlɪ/ *adj* [*tree, plant*] haut et dégarni; [*legs*]
grêle

spin: **∼-drier, ∼ dryer** *n* essoreuse *f*; **∼-dry** *vtr* essorer [*qch*] (à la machine)

spine /spaɪn/ *n* ① (spinal column) colonne *f* vertébrale; **it
sent shivers up and down my ∼** (of fear) cela m'a donné des
frissons dans le dos; (of pleasure) cela m'a fait frissonner;
② fig (backbone) nerf *m*; ③ (prickle) (of plant) épine *f*; (of animal)
piquant *m*; ④ (of book) dos *m*

spine-chilling *adj* qui donne la chair de poule

spineless /'spaɪnlɪs/ *adj* ① Zool invertébré; ② péj (weak)
mou/molle

spinning /'spɪnɪŋ/
A *n* (for cloth) filage *m*
B *noun modifier* [*thread, wool*] à filer

spinning: **∼ machine** *n* métier *m* à filer; **∼ mill** *n*
filature *f*; **∼ top** *n* toupie *f*; **∼ wheel** *n* rouet *m*

spin-off /'spɪnɒf/
A *n* ① (incidental benefit) retombée *f* favorable; ② (by-product)
sous-produit *m* (of, from de); ③ TV, Cin adaptation *f*; **TV
∼ from the film** adaptation télévisée du film
B *noun modifier* [*effect, profit*] secondaire; [*technology, product*]
dérivé; **∼ series** TV feuilleton télévisé adapté d'un film

spinster /'spɪnstə(r)/ *n* Jur célibataire *f*; péj vieille fille *f*

spiny /'spaɪnɪ/ *adj* [*plant*] épineux; [*animal*] couvert de
piquants

spiral /'spaɪərəl/
A *n* ① (shape) gen, Math, Aviat spirale *f*; **in a ∼** [*object, spring,
curl*] en forme de spirale; ② (trend) spirale *f*; **a ∼ of violence** une escalade de violence; **a downward/upward ∼**
une descente/montée en spirale
B *noun modifier* [*motif, spring, structure*] en spirale
C *vi* (*p prés etc* **-ll-** GB, **-l-** US) ① Econ monter en flèche; **to
∼ downwards** tomber en flèche; ② (of movement) **to
∼ up(wards)/down(wards)** (gently) monter/descendre en
spirale *or* en tournoyant; (rapidly) monter/descendre en
vrille
D **spiralling** GB, **spiraling** US *pres p adj* qui monte en
flèche

spiral: **∼ binding** *n* (reliure *f* à) spirales *fpl*; **∼ notebook** *n* cahier *m* à spirales; **∼ staircase** *n* escalier *m*
en colimaçon

spire /'spaɪə(r)/ *n* Archit flèche *f*

spirit /'spɪrɪt/
A *n* ① (essential nature) (of law, game, era) esprit *m*; **it's not in the
∼ of the agreement** ce n'est pas conforme à l'esprit de
l'accord; ② (mood, attitude) esprit *m* (of de); **in a ∼ of friendship** dans un esprit amical; **a ∼ of forgiveness** une intention d'indulgence; **a ∼ of optimism** une tendance à

l'optimisme; **to do sth in the right/wrong ∼** faire qch de
façon positive/négative; **to take a remark in the right/
wrong ∼** bien/mal prendre une remarque; **to enter into
the ∼ of sth** se conformer à l'esprit de qch; **that's the ∼○!**
c'est ça!; ③ (courage, determination) courage *m*; **to show ∼** se
montrer courageux/-euse; **to break sb's ∼** briser la résistance de qn; **a performance full of ∼** une interprétation
pleine de brio; **with ∼** [*play, defend*] avec détermination;
④ (soul) gen, Mythol, Relig esprit *m*; **the life of the ∼** la vie
spirituelle; **the Holy Spirit** le Saint-Esprit; ⑤ (person) esprit
m; ⑥ (drink) alcool *m* fort; **wines and ∼s** Comm vins et
spiritueux *mpl*; ⑦ Chem alcool *m*
B **spirits** *npl* **to be in good/poor ∼s** être de bonne/
mauvaise humeur; **to be in high ∼s** être d'excellente
humeur; **to keep one's ∼s up** garder le moral; **to raise
sb's ∼s** remonter le moral de qn; **my ∼s rose/sank** j'ai
repris/perdu courage
C *noun modifier* [*lamp, stove*] à alcool
D *vtr* **to ∼ sth/sb away** faire disparaître qch/qn; **to ∼ sth
in/out** introduire/sortir discrètement qch

spirited /'spɪrɪtɪd/ *adj* [*horse, debate, reply*] fougueux/-euse;
[*music, performance*] plein d'entrain; [*attack, defence*] vif/
vive

spiritless /'spɪrɪtləs/ *adj* [*person*] qui manque d'entrain

spirit level *n* niveau *m* à bulle

spiritual /'spɪrɪtʃʊəl/
A *n* Mus spiritual *m*
B *adj* (all contexts) spirituel/-elle; **∼ adviser** *ou* **director** direc-
teur *m* de conscience

spiritualism /'spɪrɪtʃʊəlɪzəm/ *n* (occult) spiritisme *m*

spiritualist /'spɪrɪtʃʊəlɪst/ *n, adj* spiritiste (*mf*)

spirituality /,spɪrɪtʃʊˈælɪtɪ/ *n* spiritualité *f*

spiritually /'spɪrɪtʃʊəlɪ/ *adv* sur le plan spirituel

spit /spɪt/
A *n* ① (saliva) (in mouth) salive *f*; (on ground) crachat *m*; **to give a
∼** cracher; ② Culin broche *f*; **rotating ∼** tournebroche *m*;
③ (of land) pointe *f*
B *vtr* (*p prés* **-tt-**; *prét*, *pp* **spat**) ① lit [*person, volcano*] cracher;
[*pan*] projeter [*oil*]; ② fig proférer [*oath, venom*]
C *vi* (*p prés* **-tt-**; *prét*, *pp* **spat**) ① lit [*cat, person*] cracher (**at,
on** sur; **into** dans; **out of** de); **to ∼ in sb's face** lit, fig cracher
à la figure de qn; ② (be angry) **to ∼ with** écumer de [*rage,
anger*]; ③ (crackle) [*oil, sausage*] grésiller; [*logs, fire*] crépiter
D *v impers* (*p prés* **-tt-**; *prét*, *pp* **spat**) **it's ∼ting (with rain)** il
bruine

(Idioms) **∼ and polish** huile *f* de coude; **to be the (dead)
∼ of sb** être le portrait tout craché de qn

(Phrasal verbs)

■ **spit out**: ▶ **∼ [sth] out, ∼ out [sth]** lit cracher [*blood,
drink*]; fig proférer [*phrase, word*]
■ **spit up**: ▶ **∼ [sth] up, ∼ up [sth]** cracher [*blood*]

spite /spaɪt/
A *n* (malice) méchanceté *f*; (vindictiveness) rancune *f*
B **in spite of** *prep phr* malgré; **in ∼ of the fact that**
bien que
C *vtr* faire du mal à; (less strong) ennuyer

(Idiom) **to cut off one's nose to ∼ one's face** se punir soi-
même

spiteful /'spaɪtfl/ *adj* [*person*] (malicious) méchant; (vindictive)
rancunier/-ière; [*remark*] méchant; [*article*] fielleux/-euse;
∼ gossip commérages *mpl*

spitefully /'spaɪtfəlɪ/ *adv* méchamment

spitting /'spɪtɪŋ/ *n* **∼ is a dirty habit** cracher est une habitude dégoûtante

(Idioms) **to be the ∼ image of sb** être le portrait (tout)
craché de qn; **to be within ∼ distance of** être à deux pas
de

spittle /'spɪtl/ *n* ① (of person) (in mouth) salive *f*; (on surface)
crachat *m*; ② (of animal) bave *f*

splash /splæʃ/
A *n* ① (sound) plouf *m*; **to make a big ∼** lit faire un grand
plouf; fig faire sensation; ② (patch) (of mud) tache *f*; (of water,
oil) éclaboussure *f*; (of colour) touche *f*; (of tonic, soda) goutte *f*
B *vtr* ① (spatter) éclabousser; **to ∼ sth over sb/sth** éclabousser qn/qch de qch; ② (sprinkle) **to ∼ water on to one's face**
s'asperger le visage d'eau; ③ (maliciously) **to ∼ water onto**
envoyer de l'eau sur [*qch*]; ④ (in newspaper) mettre [*qch*] à la
une; **the news was ∼ed across the front page** la nouvelle
s'étalait à la une des journaux

C vi **1** (spatter) faire des éclaboussures (**onto, over** sur); **water was ~ing from the tap** l'eau giclait du robinet; **2** (move) **to ~ through sth** [*person*] traverser qch en pataugeant; [*car*] traverser qch en faisant des éclaboussures; **3** (in sea, pool) faire des éclaboussures (**in** dans)

(Phrasal verbs)

■ **splash around**: ▶ **~ around** barboter (**in** dans); ▶ **~ [sth] around** envoyer [qch] partout
■ **splash down** amerrir
■ **splash out**○ (spend money) faire des folies; **to ~ out on sth** faire la folie de s'offrir qch

splash: **~back** n revêtement m (*autour d'un évier, d'une baignoire*); **~board** n Aut garde-boue m inv; **~down** n amerrissage m; **~guard** n = splashboard

splatter /'splætə(r)/
A n (of rain, bullets) crépitement m
B vtr **to ~ sb/sth with sth, to ~ sth over sb/sth** éclabousser qn/qch de qch; **the car ~ed mud everywhere** la voiture a fait gicler de la boue partout
C vi **1** [*ink, paint, mud*] **to ~ onto** ou **over sth** gicler sur qch; **2** [*body, fruit etc*] s'écraser
D **splattered** pp adj **1** **~ed with** éclaboussé de; **blood-/mud-~ed** éclaboussé de sang/de boue; **2** (squashed) écrasé

splay /spleɪ/
A vtr évaser [*end of pipe etc*]; ébraser [*side of window, door*]; écarter [*legs, feet, fingers*]
B vi (*also* **~ out**) [*end of pipe*] être évasé
C **splayed** pp adj [*feet, fingers, legs*] écarté

spleen /spliːn/ n **1** Anat rate f; **2** fig (bad temper) mauvaise humeur f

splendid /'splendɪd/ adj [*building, scenery, collection, ceremony*] splendide; [*idea, achievement, holiday, performance, victory*] formidable○, merveilleux/-euse; [*opportunity*] fantastique○; **we had a ~ time!** on s'est vraiment bien amusé!; **she did a ~ job** elle a fait un travail remarquable; **~!** (c'est) formidable○!

splendidly /'splendɪdlɪ/ adv magnifiquement, merveilleusement

splendour GB, **splendor** US /'splendə(r)/ n splendeur f; **to live in ~** vivre fastueusement

splice /splaɪs/
A n (in rope) épissure f; (in tape, film) raccord m
B vtr gen coller [*tape, film*]; épisser [*ends of rope*]; fig amalgamer

splint /splɪnt/ n **1** Med attelle f; **to put sb's leg in a ~** éclisser la jambe de qn; **2** (sliver of wood) allume-feu m inv

splinter /'splɪntə(r)/
A n (of glass, metal, wood) éclat m; (of bone) esquille f; **to get a ~ in one's finger** s'enfoncer une écharde dans le doigt
B vtr lit faire voler [qch] en éclats [*glass, windscreen etc*]; fendre [*wood*]; fig scinder [*party, group*]
C vi lit [*glass, windscreen*] se briser; [*wood*] se fendre; fig [*party, alliance etc*] se scinder

splinter group n groupe m dissident

split /splɪt/
A n **1** lit (in fabric, garment) déchirure f; (in rock, wood) fissure f; (in skin) crevasse f; **2** (in party, movement, alliance) scission f (**in** de); (stronger) rupture f (**between** entre; **in, into** dans); **a three-way ~** une scission en trois groupes; **3** (share-out) partage m; **4** US (small bottle) (of soft drink) petite bouteille f; (of wine) demi-bouteille f; **5** Culin (dessert) ≈ coupe f glacée
B **splits** npl grand écart m
C adj [*garment*] déchiré; [*seam*] défait; [*lip*] fendu
D vtr (p prés **-tt-**; prét, pp **split**) **1** (cut, slit) fendre [*wood, log, rock, lip, slate, seam*] (**in, into** en); déchirer [*fabric, garment*]; **2** (cause dissent) diviser [*party, movement, alliance*]; **the committee was (deeply) split on** or **over this issue** la commission était (extrêmement) divisée sur cette question; **3** (divide) ▶ **split up**; **4** (share) partager; **to ~ sth three ways** partager qch en trois
E vi (p prés **-tt-**; prét, pp **split**) **1** [*wood, log, rock, slate*] se fendre (**in, into** en); [*garment*] se déchirer; [*seam*] se défaire; **to ~ in(to) two** [*stream, road*] se diviser en deux; **my head's ~ting** fig j'ai horriblement mal à la tête; **2** gen, Pol [*party, movement, alliance*] se diviser; (stronger) se scinder; **3** (divide) ▶ **split up**; **4** ○GB (tell tales) cafarder○; **5** ○(leave) filer○

(Idioms) **to ~ the difference** couper la poire en deux; **to ~ one's sides**○ (laughing) se tordre de rire

(Phrasal verbs)

■ **split off**: ▶ **~ off** [*branch, piece*] se détacher (**from** de); [*path*] bifurquer; [*political group*] faire scission; [*company*] se séparer (**from** de); ▶ **~ [sth] off** détacher [*piece*]; **to ~ sth off from** détacher qch de [*piece*]; séparer qch de [*company, section*]
■ **split open**: ▶ **~ open** [*bag, fabric*] se déchirer; [*seam*] se défaire; ▶ **~ [sth] open** fendre [*box, coconut*]; **to ~ one's head open** se fendre le crâne
■ **split up**: ▶ **~ up** [*band, couple, members, parents*] se séparer; [*crowd, demonstrators*] se disperser; [*alliance, consortium*] éclater; [*federation*] se scinder (**into** en); **to ~ up with** quitter [*husband etc*]; **to ~ up into groups of five** se mettre en groupes de cinq; ▶ **~ [sb] up** séparer [*friends, partners, group members*] (**from** de); **everyone tried to ~ the couple up** tout le monde a essayé de les écarter l'un de l'autre; **to ~ the children up into groups** répartir les enfants en petits groupes; ▶ **~ [sth] up, ~ up [sth]** partager (**into** en); diviser [*area, group*] (**into** en)

split: **~ decision** n Sport décision f partagée; **~ ends** npl cheveux mpl fourchus; **~ infinitive** n: erreur de grammaire consistant à introduire un adverbe au milieu d'un infinitif, entre 'to' et le verbe

split level
A n **the flat is on ~s** l'appartement a des demi-étages
B **split-level** adj [*cooker*] à plaques de cuisson et four indépendants; [*apartment*] sur deux niveaux

split: **~ peas** npl pois mpl cassés; **~ personality** n double personnalité f; **~ pin** n goupille f fendue; **~ screen** n écran m divisé, split screen m

split second
A n fraction f de seconde
B **split-second** noun modifier [*decision*] éclair inv; **the success of the mission depends on ~ timing** pour réussir il faut que la mission suive un programme fixé à la seconde près

split: **~ shift** n poste m fractionné; **~-site** adj [*factory, school*] dont les locaux sont dispersés; **~ ticket** n US Pol vote m pour une liste panachée

splitting /'splɪtɪŋ/
A n (division) (of wood, stone) fendage m; (of group, profits, proceeds) répartition f
B adj **to have a ~ headache** avoir horriblement mal à la tête

splurge○ /splɜːdʒ/
A n folie○ f
B vtr claquer○ [*money*] (**on** pour)
C vi (*also* **~ out**) claquer○ (**on** pour)

splutter /'splʌtə(r)/
A n (of person) (spitting) crachotement m; (stutter) bafouillement m; (of engine) crachotement m; (of fire, sparks) grésillement m
B vtr (*also* **~ out**) bafouiller [*excuse, apology, words*]
C vi [*person*] (stutter) bafouiller; (spit) crachoter; [*fire, fat, candle, match, sparks*] grésiller; **the engine ~ed to a stop** le moteur s'est arrêté dans un crachotement

spoil /spɔɪl/
A **spoils** npl (of war) butin m; (political, commercial) profits mpl; (sporting) gains mpl
B vtr (prét, pp **~ed** ou **~t** GB) **1** (mar) gen gâcher (**by doing** en faisant); gâter [*place, taste, effect*]; **it will ~ your appetite** ça va te couper l'appétit; **to ~ sth for sb** gâcher qch à qn; **they ~ it** ou **things for other people** ils gâchent le plaisir des autres; **to ~ sb's enjoyment of sth** empêcher qn de profiter de qch; **why did you go and ~ everything?** pourquoi as-tu tout gâché?; **to ~ sb's fun** (thwart) contrarier qn; **2** (ruin) abîmer; **to ~ one's chances of doing** gâcher ses chances de faire (**by doing** en faisant); **3** (pamper) gâter [*person, pet*] (**by doing** en faisant); **to ~ sb rotten**○ pourrir qn; **to ~ sb with** gâter qn en lui offrant [*gift, trip*]; **4** Pol rendre [qch] nul/nulle [*ballot paper*]
C vi (prét, pp **~ed** ou **~t** GB) [*product, foodstuff*] s'abîmer; [*meat*] se gâter; **your dinner will ~!** ça ne va plus être bon!
D v refl (prét, pp **~ed** ou **~t** GB) **to ~ oneself** se faire un petit plaisir; **let's ~ ourselves and eat out!** faisons-nous plaisir en allant au restaurant!

(Idiom) **to be ~ing for a fight** chercher la bagarre○

spoiled, spoilt GB /spɔɪld, spɔɪlt/
A prét, pp ▸ **spoil B, C, D**
B adj **1** péj [*child, dog*] gâté; **a ~ brat** un gamin pourri○;

S

2▶ Pol [*ballot paper*] nul/nulle

(Idiom) **to be ~ for choice** avoir l'embarras du choix

spoiler /'spɔɪlə(r)/ n **1**▶ Aut becquet m; **2**▶ Aviat aéro-frein m

spoilsport○ /'spɔɪlspɔːt/ n **to be a ~** faire son rabat-joie

spoilt /spɔɪlt/ GB prét, pp, adj ▶ **spoiled**

spoke /spəʊk/
A prét ▶ speak B, C
B n (in wheel) rayon m; (on ladder) barreau m

(Idiom) **to put a ~ in sb's wheel** mettre des bâtons dans les roues à qn

spoken /'spəʊkən/
A pp ▶ speak B, C
B adj [*word, dialogue, language*] parlé

spokesman, spokesperson, spokeswoman n porte-parole m inv

sponge /spʌndʒ/
A n **1**▶ (for cleaning) éponge f; **a child's mind is like a ~** le cerveau d'un enfant assimile tout; **2**▶ **Ȼ** (material) éponge f; **3**▶ Zool éponge f; **4**▶ (*also* ~ **cake**) génoise f; **5**▶ Med (pad) compresse f
B vtr frotter [qch] avec une éponge [*material, stain*]; éponger [*wound, excess liquid*]; laver [qch] avec une éponge [*surface*]
C ○vi péj **to ~ off** *ou* **on** vivre sur le dos de [*family, state*]

(Phrasal verb)

■ **sponge down**: ▶ ~ [sth] down, ~ down [sth] laver [qch] avec une éponge [*car, surface*]

sponge: ~ **bag** n GB trousse f de toilette; ~ **finger** n GB biscuit m à la cuiller; ~ **mop** n balai-éponge m; ~ **pudding** n GB gâteau cuit au bain-marie et servi chaud

sponger○ /'spʌndʒə(r)/ n péj parasite m péj

sponge: ~ **roll** n GB biscuit m roulé; ~ **rubber** n caoutchouc m mousse

spongy /'spʌndʒɪ/ adj [*ground, wood*] spongieux/-ieuse; [*texture*] moelleux/-euse; [*flesh*] mou/molle

sponsor /'spɒnsə(r)/
A n **1**▶ Comm, Fin (advertiser, backer) sponsor m; **2**▶ (patron) mécène m; **3**▶ (guarantor) garant/-e m/f; **4**▶ Relig (godparent) parrain/marraine m/f; **5**▶ (for charity) personne qui parraine un participant à une épreuve sportive organisée dans un but caritatif; **6**▶ Pol (of bill, motion, law) initiateur/-trice m/f
B vtr **1**▶ Comm, Fin (fund) sponsoriser [*event, team*]; financer [*student, course, enterprise*]; **2**▶ (support) soutenir [*violence, invasion*]; **3**▶ Pol (advocate) présenter [*bill*]; **4**▶ (for charity) parrainer [*person*]; ~**ed swim** épreuve f de natation parrainée

sponsorship /'spɒnsəʃɪp/ n **1**▶ Comm, Fin (corporate funding) parrainage m, sponsorat m (**from** de); **to seek/raise ~ for sth** chercher/trouver des sponsors pour qch; **2**▶ (backing) (financial) sponsorat m; (cultural) patronage m; (moral, political) parrainage m; **3**▶ **C** (*also* ~ **deal**) contrat m de parrainage; **4**▶ Pol (of bill, motion) soutien m

spontaneity /ˌspɒntə'neɪətɪ/ n spontanéité f

spontaneous /spɒn'teɪnɪəs/ adj spontané

spontaneously /spɒn'teɪnəslɪ/ adv spontanément

spoof○ /spuːf/
A n (parody) parodie f (**on** de)
B noun modifier (parody) **a ~ horror film** une parodie de film d'horreur
C vtr (parody) parodier [*book, film*]

spook○ /spuːk/
A n **1**▶ (ghost) fantôme m; **2**▶ US (spy) espion/-ionne m/f
B vtr (frighten) effrayer [*person*]; (haunt) hanter

spooky○ /'spuːkɪ/ adj [*house, atmosphere*] sinistre; [*story*] qui fait froid dans le dos

spool /spuːl/ n bobine f

spoon /spuːn/
A n cuillère f; (for tea, coffee) petite cuillère f
B vtr (in cooking, serving) **to ~ sth into a dish/bowl** mettre qch dans un plat/bol avec une cuillère

(Idiom) **to be born with a silver ~ in one's mouth** naître dans la soie

spoonerism /'spuːnərɪzəm/ n contrepèterie f (involontaire)

spoon-feed /'spuːnfiːd/ vtr **1**▶ nourrir [qn] à la petite cuillère [*baby, invalid*]; **2**▶ fig péj [*teacher*] mâcher le travail à [*students*]

spoonful /'spuːnfʊl/ n (pl **-fuls** *ou* **-sful**) cuillerée f, cuillère f

sporadic /spə'rædɪk/ adj sporadique

sporadically /spə'rædɪklɪ/ adv sporadiquement

sporran /'spɒrən/ n sporran m (*bourse en cuir ou en fourrure portée sur le devant du kilt*)

sport /spɔːt/ ▶ **p. 881**
A n **1**▶ (physical activity) sport m; **2**▶ Sch (subject) activités fpl sportives; **3**▶ sout (fun) **to have great ~** s'amuser beaucoup; **4**▶ ○(person) **to be a good/bad ~** (in games) être beau/mauvais joueur; (when teased) bien/mal prendre la plaisanterie
B vtr arborer [*hat, rose, moustache*]

sport coat n US = sports jacket

sporting /'spɔːtɪŋ/ adj **1**▶ [*event*] sportif/-ive; **2**▶ (generous) [*offer*] généreux/-euse; **it's very ~ of you** c'est très généreux de votre part; **to have a ~ chance of winning** avoir de bonnes chances de gagner

sportingly /'spɔːtɪŋlɪ/ adv sportivement, généreusement

sport: ~**s car** n voiture f de sport; ~**scast** n US émission f sportive; ~**s centre** GB, ~**s center** US n centre m sportif; ~**s club** n club m sportif; ~**s day** n GB fête f des sports; ~**s ground** n (large) stade m; (in school, club etc) terrain m de sports; ~**s hall** n salle f omnisports; ~**s jacket** n GB veste f en tweed; ~**sman** n sportif m; ~**s shirt** n maillot m de sport; ~**swear** n sportswear m; ~**swoman** n sportive f

sporty○ /'spɔːtɪ/ adj (fond of sport) sportif/-ive

spot /spɒt/
A n **1**▶ (dot) (on animal) tache f; (on fabric) pois m; (on dice, domino) point m; **to see ~s before one's eyes** voir trouble; **2**▶ (stain) tache f; **3**▶ (pimple) bouton m; **to come out in ~s** être couvert de boutons; **4**▶ (place) endroit m; **to be on the ~** gen être sur place; **to decide on the ~** décider sur-le-champ; **this record has been on the top** *ou* **number one ~ for two weeks** ce disque a été numéro un pendant deux semaines; **5**▶ ○(small amount) **a ~ of cream/sightseeing** un peu de crème/du tourisme; **to have** *ou* **be in a ~ of bother (with)** avoir quelques petits ennuis (avec); **6**▶ ○(difficulty) situation f embêtante; **to be in a (tight) ~** être dans une situation embêtante; **7**▶ Comm spot m publicitaire; **8**▶ TV, Radio (regular slot) temps m d'antenne; **9**▶ (moral blemish) tache f; **10**▶ (light) Cin, Theat projecteur m; (in home, display) spot m; **11**▶ Sport (for penalty kick) point m de pénalty; (for snooker ball) mouche f
B vtr (p prés etc **-tt-**) **1**▶ (see) apercevoir [*person*]; voir [*car, roadsign, book*]; **to ~ that...** s'apercevoir que...; **well ~ted!** bien vu!; **2**▶ (recognize) reconnaître [*car, person, symptoms, opportunity*]; repérer [*defect, difference, bargain*]; observer [*birds, trains*]; **3**▶ (stain) tacher
C v impers (p prés etc **-tt-**) (rain) **it's ~ting** il tombe quelques gouttes

(Idioms) **to change one's ~s** changer son caractère; **to knock ~s off sth/sb** être bien meilleur que qch/qn

spot check
A n (unannounced) contrôle m surprise (**on** sur); (random) contrôle m fait au hasard (**on** sur)
B spot-check vtr effectuer un contrôle surprise sur [*passengers*]

spot fine n amende f à régler sur le lieu de l'infraction

spotless /'spɒtlɪs/ adj impeccable

spotlessly /'spɒtlɪslɪ/ adv ~ **clean** d'une propreté impeccable

spotlight /'spɒtlaɪt/
A n **1**▶ (light) Cin, Theat projecteur m; (in home) spot m; **2**▶ fig (focus of attention) **to be in** *ou* **under the ~** [*person*] être sur la sellette; **the ~ is on Aids** le sida fait la une; **to turn** *ou* **put the ~ on sb/sth** attirer l'attention sur qn/qch
B vtr (prét, pp **-lit** *ou* **-lighted**) **1**▶ Cin, Theat diriger les projecteurs sur [*actor, area*]; **2**▶ fig (highlight) mettre [qch] en lumière [*problem*]

spot-on /ˌspɒt'ɒn/ adj GB exact; **he was absolutely ~** il a mis dans le mille

spot price n Fin prix m sur place

spotted /'spɒtɪd/ adj [*fabric*] à pois (*after* n); [*fur, dog*] tacheté

spotted dick n GB Culin pudding m aux raisins secs

spotter /'spɒtə(r)/ n ▶ **train spotter**

spotting /'spɒtɪŋ/ n Med pertes fpl de sang

spotty /'spɒtɪ/ adj **1** (pimply) [adolescent, skin] boutonneux/
-euse; **he's very ~** il est plein de boutons; **2** (patterned)
[dress, fabric] à pois (after n); [dog] tacheté

spot-weld vtr souder [qch] par points

spouse /spaʊz, US spaʊs/ n époux/épouse m/f

spout /spaʊt/
A n (of kettle, teapot) bec m verseur; (of tap) brise-jet m; (of hose)
orifice m; (of fountain) jet m; (of gutter) gargouille f
B vtr **1** (spurt) [pipe, fountain] faire jaillir; **2** péj (recite) débi-
ter [poetry, statistics, theories] (**at** à)
C vi **1** (spurt) jaillir; **2** °GB péj (also ~ **forth**) (talk) discourir
(**about** sur); **3** [whale] souffler
(Idiom) **to be up the ~**° GB être fichu°

sprain /spreɪn/
A n entorse f; (less severe) foulure f
B vtr **to ~ one's ankle/wrist** se faire une entorse à la
cheville/au poignet; (less severely) se fouler la cheville/le
poignet

sprang /spræŋ/ prét ▸ spring C, D

sprat /spræt/ n sprat m

sprawl /sprɔːl/
A n (of suburbs, buildings etc) étendue f; **the ~ of Paris** l'agglomération parisienne
B vi [person] s'étaler; [town, forest] s'étaler; **to lay ~ed across
the sofa** être étalé sur le canapé

sprawling /'sprɔːlɪŋ/ adj [suburb, city] tentaculaire; [hand-
writing] qui s'étale dans tous les sens

spray /spreɪ/
A n **1** **⊄** (seawater) embruns mpl; (other) nuages mpl de (fines)
gouttelettes; **2** (container) (for perfume) vaporisateur m; (for
antifreeze, deodorant, paint etc) bombe f; (for inhalant, throat, nose)
pulvérisateur m; **3** (shower) (of sparks) gerbe f; (of bullets)
pluie f; **4** (of flowers) (bunch) gerbe f; (single branch) rameau m;
(single flowering stem) branche f
B noun modifier [deodorant] en spray; [polish, starch] en atomiseur
C vtr vaporiser [liquid]; asperger [person] (**with** de); arroser
[demonstrator, oilslick] (**with** de); **to ~ sth onto sth** (onto fire)
projeter qch sur qch [foam, water]; **to ~ sth with sth**
asperger qn/qch de qch [water]; fig **to ~ sb/sth with** arroser
qn/qch de [bullets]
D vi gicler; (more violently) jaillir; **to ~ over/out of** gicler
sur/de
spray: ~ **can** n bombe f, aérosol m; ~ **gun** n pistolet m
à peinture; ~**-on** adj [conditioner, glitter] en vaporisateur

spray paint
A n peinture f en aérosol
B **spray-paint** vtr peindre [qch] à l'aérosol [car]; [graffiti
artist] bomber [slogan]

spread /spred/
A n **1** (dissemination) (of disease, drugs) propagation f; (of news,
information) diffusion f; (of democracy, infection, weapons) progression f; **the ~ of sth** l'extension f de qch à [group, area];
2 (extent, range) (of wings, branches) envergure f; (of arch) portée
f; (of products, services) éventail m; **3** (in newspaper) **double-
page ~** page f double; **4** Culin pâte f à tartiner; **5** (assortment of dishes) festin m; **6** US Agric grand ranch m
B vtr (prét, pp **spread**) **1** (unfold) étendre [cloth, map, rug]; (lay
out) étaler [cloth, newspaper, map]; (put) mettre [cloth, news-
paper]; [bird] déployer [wings]; **to ~ a cloth on the table**
mettre une nappe sur la table; ▸ **wing**; **2** (apply in layer)
étaler [butter, jam, glue]; ~ **the butter thinly on the bread**
étaler une mince couche de beurre sur le pain; **3** (distribute over area) disperser [forces, troops]; étaler [cards, docu-
ments]; épandre [fertilizer]; répartir [workload, responsibility];
to ~ grit ou **sand** sabler; **we have to ~ our resources very
thin(ly)** nous devons ménager nos ressources; **4** (also
~ **out**) (space out) étaler, échelonner [payments, meetings,
cost] (**over** sur); **5** (diffuse, cause to proliferate) propager [disease,
fire]; semer [confusion, panic]; faire circuler [rumour, story,
lie]; **to ~ sth to sb** transmettre [qch] à qn [infection, news];
to ~ the word that dire à tout le monde que
C vi (prét, pp **spread**) **1** [butter, glue] s'étaler; **2** (cover area or
time, extend) [forest, drought, network] s'étendre (**over** sur);
[experience, training] s'étendre (**over** sur); **3** (proliferate) [dis-
ease, fear, fire] se propager; [rumour, story] circuler; [stain]
s'étaler; **the rumour was ~ing that** le bruit courait que; **to
~ to** [fire, disease, strike] s'étendre à, gagner [building,
region]; **the disease spread from the liver to the kidney** la
maladie s'est propagée du foie aux reins; **rain will ~ to**

most regions la pluie va s'étendre à la plupart des
régions
(Idiom) **to ~ oneself too thin** fig faire trop de choses à la
fois
(Phrasal verbs)
■ **spread around**, **spread about**: ▸ ~ **[sth] around**
faire circuler [rumour]; **to ~ it around that** faire courir le
bruit que
■ **spread out**: ▸ ~ **out** [group] se disperser (**over** sur);
[wings, tail] se déployer; [landscape, town, woods] s'étendre;
▸ ~ **[sth] out**, ~ **out [sth]** **1** (open out, unfold) étendre [cloth,
map, rug, newspaper] (**on, over** sur); (lay, flatten out) étaler [cloth,
newspaper, map] (**on, over** sur); **2** (distribute over area) étaler
[cards, trinkets]; disperser [forces]

spread-eagled adj bras et jambes écartés

spreadsheet n Comput tableur m

spree /spriː/ n **to go on a ~** (drinking) faire la bringue°; **to
go on a shopping ~** aller faire des folies dans les magasins; **to go on a killing ~** être pris d'une folie meurtrière

sprig /sprɪg/ n (of herb) brin m; (of holly, mistletoe) petite branche f

sprightly /'spraɪtlɪ/ adj alerte, gaillard

spring /sprɪŋ/
A n **1** (season) printemps m; **2** Tech (coil) ressort m;
to be like a coiled ~ fig (tense) être tendu; **3** (leap) bond m;
4 (elasticity) élasticité f; **to have a ~ in one's step** marcher
d'un pas allègre; **5** (water source) source f
B noun modifier [weather, flowers] printanier/-ière; [day, equi-
nox] de printemps
C vtr (prét **sprang**; pp **sprung**) **1** (set off) déclencher [trap,
lock]; **2** (develop) **to ~ a leak** [tank] commencer à fuir;
3 (cause unexpectedly) **to ~ sth on sb** annoncer qch de but
en blanc à qn [news]; **to ~ a surprise** faire une surprise (**on**
à); **4** °(liberate) libérer
D vi (prét **sprang**; pp **sprung**) **1** (jump) bondir (**onto** sur); **to
~ at sb** se jeter sur qn; **to ~ from/over sth** sauter d'un
bond de/par-dessus de qch; **to ~ to one's feet** se lever
d'un bond; **2** (move suddenly) **to ~ open/shut** [door, panel]
s'ouvrir/se fermer brusquement; **to ~ into action** passer à
l'action; **to ~ to sb's defence** se précipiter pour défendre
qn; **tears sprang to his eyes** les larmes lui sont montées
aux yeux; **the first name that sprang to mind was Egbert** le
premier prénom qui m'est venu à l'esprit a été (celui d')
Egbert; **to ~ into** ou **to life** [machine, motor] se mettre en
marche or route; **3** (originate) **to ~ from** naître de [jealousy,
fear]; **where did these people ~ from?** d'où sortent ces
gens?
(Phrasal verbs)
■ **spring back** **1** (step back) reculer d'un bond; **2** (return
to its position) [lever] reprendre sa place
■ **spring up** **1** (get up) [person] se lever d'un bond;
2 (appear) [problem] surgir; [weeds, flowers] sortir de terre;
[building] apparaître; [trend] apparaître

spring: ~ **balance** n balance f à ressort; ~**board** n
Sport, fig tremplin m (**to, for** vers)

spring chicken n Culin jeune poulet m, poulette f
(Idiom) **he's no ~** il n'est plus tout jeune

spring: ~**-clean** vtr nettoyer [qch] de fond en comble
[house]; ~**-cleaning** n grand nettoyage m de printemps;
~ **onion** n GB Culin ciboule f; ~ **roll** n Culin rouleau m de
printemps

springtime /'sprɪŋtaɪm/ n lit, fig printemps m; **in the ~** au
printemps

spring: ~ **vegetable** n légume m de primeur;
~ **water** n eau f de source

springy /'sprɪŋɪ/ adj [mattress, seat] élastique; [floorboards,
ground, curls] souple

sprinkle /'sprɪŋkl/
A n (of salt, flour etc) pincée f
B vtr **1** (scatter) **to ~ sth with sth** saupoudrer qch de [salt,
sugar]; parsemer qch de [herbs]; **to ~ sth with water** humecter qch; **2** (water) arroser [lawn]

sprinkler /'sprɪŋklə(r)/ n (for lawn) arroseur m; (for field)
canon m arroseur; (for fires) diffuseur m

sprinkler system n (of building) système m d'extinction
automatique

sprinkling /'sprɪŋklɪŋ/ n (of salt, sugar) petite pincée f; (of
snow) fine couche f

S

sprint /sprɪnt/
A n (race) sprint m, course f de vitesse; **the final ~** lit, fig la dernière ligne droite (avant l'arrivée)
B vi Sport sprinter; gen courir (à toute vitesse)

sprite /spraɪt/ n lutin m, elfe m

spritzer /'sprɪtsə(r)/ n: vin blanc additionné d'eau gazeuse

sprout /spraʊt/
A n ① (on plant, tree) pousse f; (on potato) germe m; ② Culin (also **Brussels ~**) chou m de Bruxelles
B vtr to make sprout [beard]; **to ~ shoots** germer
C vi ① [bulb, seed, shoot] germer; [grass, weeds] pousser; **buds are ~ing on the trees** les arbres bourgeonnent; ② (develop) [antlers, horns] pousser; fig [child] pousser vite; ③ fig (appear) = **sprout up**
Phrasal verb
■ **sprout up** [plants] surgir de terre; fig [buildings, suburbs] pousser comme des champignons

spruce /spruːs/
A n ① (also **~ tree**) épicéa m; ② (wood) bois m d'épicéa
B adj [person] soigné; [house, garden] bien tenu
Phrasal verb
■ **spruce up:** ▶ **~ up** [sth/sb], **~** [sth/sb] **up** faire beau/belle [person]; astiquer [house]

sprung /sprʌŋ/
A pp ▸ **spring C, D**
B adj [mattress] à ressorts; **well-~** souple

spry /spraɪ/ adj alerte, gaillard

spud /spʌd/ n patate f, pomme f de terre

spun /spʌn/
A prét, pp ▸ **spin B, C**
B adj [glass, gold, sugar] filé; **~ silk** schappe f

spur /spɜː(r)/
A n ① fig (stimulus) motif m; **to be the ~ for** ou **of sth** être la raison de qch; **to act as a ~** être une incitation à [crime, action]; ② (for horse) éperon m; ③ Zool, Anat éperon m; ④ (of rock) contrefort m; ⑤ Rail (also **~ track**) embranchement m
B vtr (p prés etc **-rr-**) ① (stimulate) encourager [growth, increase]; inciter [action, reaction]; **to ~ sb to sth/to do** inciter qn à qch/à faire; ② [rider] éperonner [horse]
Idioms **on the ~ of the moment** sur l'impulsion du moment; **to win one's ~s** faire ses preuves
Phrasal verb
■ **spur on:** ▶ **~** [sth/sb] **on, ~ on** [sth/sb] ① lit lancer [qch] d'un coup d'éperon [horse]; ② fig (encourage) [success, good sign, government] encourager; [fear, threat, example] stimuler; **to ~ sb on to greater efforts** inciter qn à redoubler d'efforts

spurious /'spjʊəriəs/ adj [argument, notion, allegation] fallacieux/-ieuse; [excuse] inventé; [evidence, credentials] faux/fausse; [sentiment] feint

spurn /spɜːn/ vtr refuser [qch] (avec mépris) [advice, offer, help, gift]; éconduire [suitor]

spur road n GB embranchement m

spurt /spɜːt/
A n ① (gush) (of water, oil, blood) giclée f; (of flame) jaillissement m; (of steam) jet m; ② (burst) (of energy) sursaut m; (of activity, enthusiasm) regain m; (in growth) poussée f; **to put on a ~** [runner, cyclist] pousser une pointe de vitesse; **to do sth in ~s** faire qch par à-coups
B vtr **the wound was ~ing blood** le sang giclait de la blessure; **the pipes are ~ing water** l'eau jaillit des tuyaux
C vi (gush) jaillir (**from, out of** de)
Phrasal verb
■ **spurt out:** ▶ **~ out** [flames, liquid] jaillir

sputter /'spʌtə(r)/ n, vtr, vi = **splutter**

sputum /'spjuːtəm/ n **C** crachat m, expectorations fpl

spy /spaɪ/
A n (political, industrial) espion/-ionne m/f; (for police) indicateur/-trice m/f
B noun modifier [film, network] d'espionnage
C vtr remarquer, discerner [figure, object]
D vi **to ~ on sth/sb** espionner qch/qn; **to ~ for sb** faire de l'espionnage pour le compte de qn

spy: ~ glass n longue-vue f; **~hole** n judas m

spying /'spaɪɪŋ/ n espionnage m

spy ring n réseau m d'espionnage

sq. (abrév écrite = square) Math carré m; **10 ~ m** 10 m²

Sq abrév écrite = **Square**

squab /skwɒb/ n Zool pigeonneau m

squabble /'skwɒbl/
A n dispute f, prise f de bec○
B vi se disputer, se chamailler○ (**over** à propos de)

squabbling /'skwɒblɪŋ/ n **C** chamailleries○ fpl, disputes fpl

squad /skwɒd/ n gen, Mil escouade f; Sport sélection f

squad car n voiture f de police

squaddie○ /'skwɒdɪ/ n GB bidasse○ m, soldat m

squadron /'skwɒdrən/ n ① GB Mil escadron m; ② Aviat, Naut escadrille f

squadron leader ▸ p. 1123 n GB Aviat, Mil commandant m (de l'armée de l'air)

squalid /'skwɒlɪd/ adj [house, street] sordide; [furnishings, clothes] crasseux/-euse; [affair, story] sordide

squall /skwɔːl/
A n ① Meteorol bourrasque f, rafale f (**of** de); (at sea) grain m; ② (cry) hurlement m
B vi [baby] hurler, brailler

squalor /'skwɒlə(r)/ n (of house, street, conditions, life) caractère m sordide, misère f (noire)

squander /'skwɒndə(r)/ vtr gaspiller [money, opportunities, talents, resources, time]; gâcher [youth, health]

square /skweə(r)/
A n ① (in town) place f; (in barracks) cour f; **main ~** grand-place f; ② (four-sided shape) carré m; (in board game, crossword) case f; (of glass, linoleum) carreau m; **to divide a page up into ~s** quadriller une feuille; ③ Math (self-multiplied) carré m; ④ Math, Tech (instrument) équerre f; ⑤ ○(old-fashioned person) ringard/-e○ m/f
B adj ① (right-angled) [shape, box, jaw, shoulders] carré; (correctly aligned) bien droit; ② ▸ p. 1240 Math [metre, mile] carré; **four ~ metres** quatre mètres carrés; **an area four metres ~** une surface de quatre mètres sur quatre; ③ fig (level, quits) **to be (all) ~** [accounts] être équilibré; [people] être quitte; [teams] être à égalité; **it's all ~ at two all** il y a égalité à deux partout; ④ (honest) honnête; **to give sb a ~ deal** traiter qn de façon honnête; ⑤ ○(boring) ringard○
C adv (directly) **he hit me ~ on the jaw** il m'a frappé en plein dans la mâchoire; **she looked me ~ in the eye** elle m'a regardé droit dans les yeux
D vtr ① lit équarrir [stone, timber]; couper [qch] au carré or à angle droit [corner, end, section]; **to ~ one's shoulders** redresser les épaules; ② (settle) régler [account, debt]; ③ Sport égaliser [score, series]; ④ (win over) (persuade) s'occuper de; (bribe) graisser la patte à○ [person]; **go home early, I'll ~ it with the boss** pars avant l'heure, j'arrangerai ça avec le patron; **I have problems squaring this with my conscience** j'ai du mal à concilier cela avec ma conscience
E squared pp adj ① [paper] quadrillé; ② Math [number] au carré
Idiom **to go back to ~ one** retourner à la case départ
Phrasal verbs
■ **square up:** ▶ **~ up** ① (prepare to fight) lit se mettre en garde (**to face** à); fig faire face (**to** à); ② (settle accounts) régler ses comptes; ▶ **~ up** [sth], **~** [sth] **up** ① (cut straight) couper [qch] au carré [paper, wood, corner]; ② (align correctly) mettre [qch] bien droit
■ **square with:** ▶ **~ with** [sth] (be consistent with) correspondre à, cadrer avec [evidence, fact]

square bracket n crochet m; **in ~s** entre crochets

square: ~ dance n quadrille m; **~ dancing** n **C** quadrille m américain

squarely /'skweəlɪ/ adv ① (directly) [strike, hit, land] lit en plein milieu; **to look ~ at** regarder [qch] bien en face [problem, situation]; **~ behind sth** directement derrière qch; ② (honestly) honnêtement; ③ (fully) **the blame rests ~ on his shoulders** la responsabilité repose entièrement sur lui

square: ~ meal n vrai repas m; **~ measure** n mesure f de superficie; **~ root** n racine f carrée

squash /skwɒʃ/
A n ① Sport ▸ p. 881 squash m; ② (drink) sirop m; ③ (vegetable) courge f; ④ (crush) **it will be a bit of a ~** on va être un peu serrés
B vtr ① (crush) écraser [fruit, insect]; aplatir [hat]; ② (force) **to ~ sth/sb into sth** caser qch/qn dans qch; ③ (put down)

rabattre le caquet à○ [*person*]; écraser [*revolt*]; stopper [*rumour*]; rejeter [*idea*]
C *vi* ① (become crushed) s'écraser; ② (pack tightly) [*people*] s'entasser (**into** dans)

⌐**Phrasal verbs**¬
■ **squash in**○: ▶ **~ in** se faire de la place; ▶ **~ in [sth/ sb]**, **~ [sth/sb] in** trouver de la place pour
■ **squash up**○: ▶ **~ up** se serrer (**against** contre); **to ~ oneself up against** s'aplatir contre

squashy○ /'skwɒʃɪ/ *adj* mou/molle

squat /skwɒt/
A *n* ① (position) position *f* accroupie; ② ○(home) squat○ *m*
B *adj* [*person, structure, object*] trapu
C *vi* (*p prés etc* **-tt-**) ① (crouch) être accroupi; ② (*also* **~ down**) s'accroupir; ③ (inhabit) **to ~ in** squattériser○, squatter○ [*building*]

squatter /'skwɒtə(r)/ *n* squatter○ *m*

squaw /skwɔː/ *n injur* squaw *f*

squawk /skwɔːk/
A *n* (of hen) gloussement *m*; (of duck, parrot etc) cri *m* rauque; (of person) cri *m* aigu
B *vi* [*hen*] pousser des gloussements; [*duck, parrot, crow etc*] pousser des cris rauques; [*baby*] brailler; [*person*] crier d'une voix hystérique

squeak /skwiːk/
A *n* (noise) (of door, wheel, mechanism, chalk) grincement *m*; (of mouse, soft toy) couinement *m*; (of furniture, shoes) craquement *m*; (of infant) vagissement *m*; **without a ~**○ sans broncher; **there wasn't a ~ from her**○ elle n'a pas émis le moindre mot
B *vi* [*door, wheel, chalk*] grincer; [*mouse, toy*] couiner; [*shoes, furniture*] craquer; [*child*] glapir

squeaky /'skwiːkɪ/ *adj* [*voice*] aigu/-uë; [*gate, hinge, wheel*] grinçant; **~ shoes** des chaussures qui craquent

squeaky-clean○ *adj* ① lit propre et net; ② fig péj [*person*] trop parfait; [*company*] à l'image trop soignée

squeal /skwiːl/
A *n* (of animal, person) cri *m* aigu; (of brakes) grincement *m*; (of tyres) crissement *m*; **~s of laughter** des rires perçants
B *vi* ① (squeak) pousser des cris aigus (**in, with** de); **to ~ with laughter** rire d'une voix aiguë; ② ○(inform) vendre la mèche○; **to ~ on sb** balancer○ qn

squeamish /'skwiːmɪʃ/ *adj* ① (easily sickened) impressionnable, sensible; ② (prudish) prude

squeegee /'skwiːdʒiː/ *n gen*, *Phot* raclette *f*; (for floor) balai-éponge *m*

squeeze /skwiːz/
A *n* ① (application of pressure) **to give sth a ~** presser qch [*hand, tube*]; **to give sb a ~** serrer qn dans ses bras; ② (small amount) **a ~ of glue/lemon** un peu de colle/citron; ③ Econ, Fin resserrement *m* (**on** de); **to feel the ~** se sentir coincé financièrement; **to put the ~ on**○ faire pression sur [*debtors*]; ④ ○(crush) **I can get past, but it will be a tight ~** je peux passer mais ce sera un peu juste
B *vtr* ① (press) presser [*lemon, bottle, tube*]; serrer [*arm, hand*]; appuyer sur [*bag, parcel, trigger*]; percer [*spot*]; **to ~ glue/ toothpaste onto sth** mettre de la colle/du dentifrice sur qch; ② fig (get) **I ~d £10 out of dad** j'ai réussi à obtenir 10 livres sterling de papa; **to ~ the truth/a confession out of sb** arracher la vérité/un aveu à qn; ③ (fit) **we can ~ a few more people into the room** on a encore de la place pour quelques personnes dans la salle; **I can just ~ into that dress** je rentre tout juste dans cette robe; **to ~ behind/ between/under sth** se glisser derrière/entre/sous qch; ④ Econ, Fin resserrer [*profit, margins*]; asphyxier [*small businesses*]

⌐**Phrasal verbs**¬
■ **squeeze in**: ▶ **~ in** [*person*] se glisser; ▶ **~ [sb] in** [*doctor etc*] faire passer [qn] entre deux rendez-vous
■ **squeeze out**: ▶ **~ out** [*person*] arriver à sortir; ▶ **~ [sth] out** extraire [*juice, water*]; **to ~ water out of** essorer [*cloth, sponge*]
■ **squeeze past**: ▶ **~ past** [*car, person*] passer

squelch /skwɛltʃ/
A *n* **the ~ of water in their boots** le flic flac de l'eau dans leurs bottes
B *vi* [*water, mud*] glouglouter; **to ~ along/in/out** avancer/ entrer/sortir en pataugeant

squelchy /'skwɛltʃɪ/ *adj* [*ground, mud*] boueux/-euse

squib /skwɪb/ *n* pétard *m*

⌐**Idiom**¬ **to be a damp ~**○ GB [*event*] être décevant; [*venture, revelation*] être un pétard mouillé○

squid /skwɪd/ *n* calmar *m*, encornet *m*

squidgy○ /'skwɪdʒɪ/ *adj* GB moelleux/-euse

squiggle /'skwɪgl/ *n* gribouillis *m*

squint /skwɪnt/
A *n* Med (strabismus) strabisme *m*; **to have a ~** loucher
B *vi* ① (look) plisser les yeux; ② Med loucher

squire /'skwaɪə(r)/ *n* ① (gentleman) ≈ châtelain *m*; ② (retainer) écuyer *m*; ③ ○GB **cheerio ~**○! salut, chef○ *m*!; ④ US (judge) juge *m* (de paix); (lawyer) avocat *m*

squirm /skwɜːm/ *vi* (wriggle) [*person, snake, worm etc*] se tortiller; [*fish*] frétiller; [*person*] (in pain, agony) se tordre; fig (with embarrassment) être très mal à l'aise

squirrel /'skwɪrəl, US 'skwɜːrəl/ *n* écureuil *m*

squirt /skwɜːt/
A *n* ① (jet) jet *m*; ② (small amount) goutte *f*; ③ ○pej (person) **a little ~** un petit morveux○
B *vtr* faire gicler; **he ~ed some soda water into the glass** il a versé une giclée d'eau de Seltz dans le verre; **to ~ water at sb, to ~ sb with water** asperger qn d'eau
C *vi* [*liquid*] jaillir (**from, out of** de)

⌐**Phrasal verb**¬
■ **squirt out**: ▶ **~ out** [*water, oil*] jaillir (**of, from** de); ▶ **~ [sth] out**, **~ out [sth]** faire gicler [*liquid*]

Sr ① *abrév écrite* = **Senior**; ② *abrév écrite* = **Sister**

SRN *n* GB *abrév* ▸ **State Registered Nurse**

SS ① Naut (*abrév* = **steamship**) **the ~ Titanic** le Titanic; ② Mil Hist **the ~** les SS *mpl*

SSA *n* US *abrév* ▸ **Social Security Administration**

st *n* GB *abrév écrite* = **stone**

St *n* ① *abrév écrite* = **Saint**; ② *abrév écrite* = **Street**

stab /stæb/
A *n* ① (act) coup *m* de couteau; **a ~ in the back** fig un coup en traître; ② fig (of pain) élancement *m*; (of anger, jealousy) accès *m*; **a ~ of fear** une peur soudaine; ③ ○(attempt) essai *m*, tentative *f*; **to make a ~ at sth/at doing** s'essayer à qch/ à faire
B *vtr* (*p prés etc* **-bb-**) ① (pierce) poignarder [*person*]; piquer dans [*meat, food*]; **to ~ sb to death** tuer qn à coups de couteau; **to ~ sb in the back** lit, fig poignarder qn dans le dos; ② (poke) frapper
C *v refl* (*p prés etc* **-bb-**) **to ~ oneself** se blesser avec un couteau

stabbing /'stæbɪŋ/
A *n* agression *f* au couteau
B *adj* [*pain*] lancinant

stability /stə'bɪlətɪ/ *n gen*, Chem stabilité *f*

stabilize /'steɪbəlaɪz/
A *vtr gen* stabiliser; Med rendre [qch] plus stable [*medical condition*]
B *vi* se stabiliser
C **stabilizing** *pres p adj* [*effect, influence*] stabilisateur/-trice

stabilizer /'steɪbəlaɪzə(r)/ *n* ① Aviat, Naut, Tech (device) stabilisateur *m*; ② (substance) stabilisant *m*

stable /'steɪbl/
A *n* ① (building) écurie *f*; ② (string of racehorses) écurie *f* (de courses); ③ fig (of companies, publications) empire *m*; (of people) équipe *f*
B **stables** *npl* écurie *f*; **riding ~s** manège *m*
C *adj* ① (steady) stable; ② (psychologically) équilibré; ③ Chem, Phys stable
D *vtr* mettre [qch] à l'écurie [*horse*]

stable boy ▸ p. 1181 *n* garçon *m* d'écurie

stable door *n* porte *f* d'écurie

⌐**Idiom**¬ **to close the ~ after the horse has bolted** fermer la cage quand les oiseaux se sont envolés

stab wound *n* coup *m* de couteau (blessure)

staccato /stə'kɑːtəʊ/
A *adj* ① Mus [*notes, vocals*] staccato *inv*; ② *gen* [*gasps, shots*] saccadé
B *adv* [*play*] staccato

stack /stæk/
A *n* ① (pile) (of books, chairs, papers, plates, wood) pile *f*; (of hay, straw) meule *f*; ② (chimney) cheminée *f*; ③ Comput pile *f*
B **stacks** *npl* ① (in library) rayons *mpl*; ② ○**~s of** plein de○

[*food, work*]; **we've got ~s**○ **of time** nous avons tout notre temps

C *vtr* [1] Agric mettre [qch] en meule [*hay, straw*]; [2] (*also* **~ up**) (pile) empiler [*boxes, books, plates, chairs*]; [3] (fill) remplir [*shelves*]; [4] Aviat, Telecom mettre [qch] en attente [*planes, calls*]

(Idioms) **to blow one's ~**○ se mettre en boule○; **to have the odds** *ou* **cards ~ed against one** avoir tout contre soi

(Phrasal verb)
■ **stack up**: ▸ **~ up [sth]**, **~ [sth] up** empiler

stadium /'steɪdɪəm/ *n* (*pl* **-iums** *ou* **-ia**) stade *m*

staff /staːf, US stæf/

A *n* [1] (*pl* **staves** /steɪvz/ *ou* **~s**) (stick) (for walking) canne *f*; (crozier) crosse *f*; (as weapon) bâton *m*; [2] (*pl* **~s**) (employees) personnel *m*; **to be on the ~ of a company** faire partie du personnel d'une entreprise; **a small business with a ~ of ten** une petite entreprise de dix employés; [3] **¢** (*also* **teaching ~**) Sch, Univ personnel *m* enseignant; **member of ~** enseignant/-e *m/f*; **a ~ of 50** un effectif de 50 enseignants; [4] **¢** Mil état-major *m*; [5] (*pl* **staves** /steɪvz/ *ou* **~s**) Mus portée *f*

B *vtr* [*owner*] trouver du personnel pour [*company*]; **the restaurant is entirely ~ed by Italians** tout le personnel du restaurant est italien

staff: **~ college** *n* Mil ≈ école *f* supérieure de guerre; **~ discount** *n* rabais *m* accordé au personnel

staffing /'staːfɪŋ, US 'stæf-/ *n* **to have ~ problems** avoir des problèmes de recrutement

staffing levels *npl* nombre *m* d'employés

staff: **~ meeting** *n* Sch réunion *f* du personnel enseignant; **~ nurse** *n* infirmier/-ière *m/f*; **~ officer** ▸ p. 1123 *n* officier *m* d'état-major; **~ of office** *n* bâton *m* de commandement; **~ room** *n* Sch salle *f* des professeurs

Staffs *n* GB Post *abrév écrite* = **Staffordshire**

stag /stæg/ *n* [1] Zool cerf *m*; [2] GB Fin loup *m* de la finance

stage /steɪdʒ/

A *n* [1] (phase) (of illness, career, life, development, match) stade *m* (**of, in** de); (of project, process, plan) phase *f* (**of, in** de); (of journey, negotiations) étape *f* (**of, in** de); **the baby has reached the walking ~** le bébé commence à marcher; **at this ~** (at this point) à ce stade; (yet, for the time being) pour l'instant; **at this ~ in** *ou* **of your career** à ce stade de votre carrière; **at an earlier/later ~** à un stade antérieur/ultérieur; **at every ~** à chaque étape; **she ought to know that by this ~** ça fait longtemps qu'elle devrait le savoir; **by ~s** par étapes; **~ by ~** étape par étape; **in several ~s** en plusieurs étapes; **the project is still in its early ~s** le projet en est encore à ses débuts; **she's going through a difficult ~** elle traverse une période difficile; [2] (raised platform) gen estrade *f*; Theat scène *f*; **to go on ~** monter sur *or* entrer en scène; **to hold the ~** lit, fig être le point de mire; **to set the ~** Theat monter le décor; **to set the ~ for sth** fig préparer qch; [3] Theat the **~** le théâtre; **to go on the ~** faire du théâtre; [4] fig (setting) (actual place) théâtre *m*; (backdrop) scène *f*

B *noun modifier* Theat [*play, equipment*] de théâtre; [*production*] théâtral; [*career, performance*] au théâtre

C *vtr* [1] (organize) organiser [*event, rebellion, strike*]; fomenter [*coup*]; [2] (fake) simuler [*quarrel, scene*]; **the whole thing was ~d** ce n'était qu'une mise en scène; [3] Theat monter [*play, performance*]

stage: **~coach** *n* diligence *f*; **~craft** *n* technique *f* scénique; **~ designer** ▸ p. 1181 *n* décorateur/-trice *m/f* de théâtre; **~ direction** *n* indication *f* scénique; **~ door** *n* entrée *f* des artistes; **~ fright** *n* trac *m*; **~hand** ▸ p. 1181 *n* machiniste *m*; **~ left** *adv* côté *m* cour; **~-manage** *vtr* fig orchestrer; **~-manager** ▸ p. 1181 *n* régisseur/-euse *m/f*; **~ name** *n* nom *m* de théâtre; **~ right** *adv* côté *m* jardin; **~-struck** *adj* passionné de théâtre; **~ whisper** *n* Theat, fig aparté *m*

stagey *adj* = **stagy**

stagger /'stægə(r)/

A *n* (movement) **with a ~** (weakly) d'un pas chancelant; (drunkenly) en titubant

B *vtr* [1] (astonish) stupéfier, abasourdir; [2] (spread out) échelonner [*holidays, journeys, payments*]

C *vi* [*person*] (from weakness, illness) chanceler; (drunkenly) tituber; [*animal*] vaciller; **to ~ in/out/off** entrer/sortir/s'en aller en chancelant

D **staggered** *pp adj* (astonished) abasourdi

staggering /'stægərɪŋ/ *adj* [*amount, increase*] prodigieux/-ieuse; [*news*] renversant; [*event*] bouleversant; [*achievement, contrast*] stupéfiant; [*success*] étourdissant

staggeringly /'stægərɪŋlɪ/ *adv* incroyablement

stag hunting *n* chasse *f* au cerf

staging /'steɪdʒɪŋ/ *n* [1] Theat mise *f* en scène; [2] (for spectators) gradins *mpl* provisoires

staging post *n* Mil poste *m* de ravitaillement; fig point *m* de transition

stagnant /'stægnənt/ *adj* stagnant

stagnate /stæg'neɪt, US 'stægneɪt/ *vi* fig [*person, economy, sales*] stagner; lit [*water*] stagner, croupir

stagnation /stæg'neɪʃn/ *n* stagnation *f*

stag night, **stag party** *n* soirée *f* pour enterrer une vie de garçon

stagy /'steɪdʒɪ/ *adj* péj théâtral

staid /steɪd/ *adj* guindé pej

stain /steɪn/

A *n* [1] (mark) lit, fig tache *f*; **it will leave a ~** ça fera une tache; **without a ~ on one's character** avec une réputation sans tache; [2] (dye) (for wood, fabric etc) teinture *f*

B *vtr* [1] (soil) tacher [*clothes, carpet, table etc*]; [2] Biol, Tech teindre [*wood, fabric, specimen*]

C *vi* [*fabric*] se tacher

D **-stained** *combining form* oil/ink-**~ed** taché d'huile/ d'encre

stain: **~ed glass** *n* (glass) verre *m* coloré; **~ed glass window** *n* vitrail *m*

stainless /'steɪnlɪs/ *adj* [*reputation etc*] sans tache

stainless steel *n* acier *m* inoxydable

stain: **~ remover** *n* détachant *m*; **~-resistant** *adj* antitaches *inv*

stair /steə(r)/

A *n* [1] (step) marche *f* (d'escalier); [2] (staircase) sout escaliers *mpl*

B **stairs** *npl* (staircase) **the ~s** les escaliers *mpl*; **a flight of ~s** un escalier; **to fall down the ~s** tomber dans l'escalier

stair: **~case** *n* escalier *m*; **~ rod** *n* tringle *f* d'escalier; **~way** *n* escalier *m*; **~well** *n* cage *f* d'escalier

stake /steɪk/

A *n* [1] Games, fig (amount risked) enjeu *m*; **to play for high ~s** lit, fig jouer gros; **to raise the ~s** lit augmenter l'enjeu; fig monter la mise; **to be at ~** fig être en jeu; **there is a lot at ~** fig ce n'est pas à prendre à la légère; **to put sth at ~** lit, fig mettre qch en jeu; [2] (investment) participation *f* (**in** dans); [3] (pole) (support) pieu *m*; (thicker) poteau *m*; (marker) piquet *m*; [4] Hist (for execution) bûcher *m*; **to be burnt at the ~** être brûlé sur le bûcher

B *vtr* [1] (gamble) miser [*money, property*]; risquer [*reputation*]; **I would ~ my life on it** j'en mettrais ma tête à couper○; [2] (support) mettre un tuteur à [*plant, tree*]; [3] US (back) financer [*person*]

(Phrasal verb)
■ **stake out**: ▸ **~ out [sth]**, **~ [sth] out** [*police*] surveiller [*place*]

stakeout○ *n* planque○ *f*

stalactite /'stæləktaɪt, US stə'læk-/ *n* stalactite *f*

stalagmite /'stæləgmaɪt, US stə'læg-/ *n* stalagmite *f*

stale /steɪl/

A *adj* [1] (old) [*bread, cake*] rassis; [*beer*] éventé; [*air*] vicié; **to go ~** [*bread*] se rassir; fig [*relationship*] perdre de son charme; **to smell ~** [*room, house*] sentir le renfermé; [2] (hackneyed) [*jokes, ideas*] éculé; [*style, convention*] usé; [3] (tired) [*player*]

B *vi* [*pleasure*] s'affadir; [*pastime*] perdre son charme

stalemate /'steɪlmeɪt/ *n* [1] (in chess) pat *m*; [2] (deadlock) impasse *f*

staleness /'steɪlnɪs/ *n* (of food) manque *m* de fraîcheur; (of air) caractère *m* vicié; (of ideas) banalité *f*

stalk /stɔːk/

A *n* [1] Bot, Culin (of grass, rose, broccoli) tige *f*; (of leaf, apple, pepper) queue *f*; (of mushroom) pied *m*; (of cabbage) trognon *m*; [2] Zool (organ) pédicule *m*

B *vtr* [1] (hunt) [*hunter*] chasser [qch] à l'approche; [*animal*] chasser; [*murderer*] suivre; [2] fig [*fear, danger*] régner sur; [*disease*] sévir; [*killer*] rôder dans [*place*]

C *vi* [1] (walk) **to ~ out of the room** (angry) quitter la pièce d'un air furieux; **2** (prowl) **to ~ through** rôder dans [*countryside, streets*]

(Idiom) **my eyes were out on ~s**° j'avais les yeux qui me sortaient des orbites

stalker /'stɔːkə(r)/ *n* personne malfaisante qui harcèle ses victimes en les suivant et parfois en les menaçant

stalking horse *n* Pol homme *m* de paille

stall /stɔːl/
A *n* **1** (at market, fair) stand *m*; (kiosk) kiosque *m*; **2** (in stable) stalle *f*; **3** (in horse-race) barrière *f* de départ; **4** (in church) stalle *f*; **5** (cubicle) (for shower) compartiment *m*; US (for lavatory) cabinet *m*; **6** US (parking space) place *f* de parking
B **stalls** *npl* GB Theat orchestre *m*; **in the ~s** à l'orchestre
C *vtr* **1** Aut caler [*engine, car*]; **2** (hold up) bloquer [*talks, action, process*]; faire patienter [*person*]
D *vi* **1** Aut caler; Aviat décrocher; **2** (buy time) temporiser; **3** (stagnate) [*market*] stagner; [*talks*] se bloquer

stallholder *n* marchand/-e *m/f*

stallion /'stælɪən/ *n* étalon *m*

stalwart /'stɔːlwət/
A *n* fidèle *mf*
B *adj* (loyal) [*defender, member, supporter*] loyal; [*support*] inconditionnel/-elle; [*defence, resistance*] vaillant

stamina /'stæmɪnə/ *n* résistance *f*, endurance *f*

stammer /'stæmə(r)/
A *n* bégaiement *m*
B *vtr, vi* bégayer

stamp /stæmp/
A *n* **1** Post timbre *m*; **a fifty cent ~** un timbre à cinquante centimes; **'no ~ needed'** 'ne pas affranchir'; **2** (token) (for free gift) timbre *m*; (towards bill) bon *m*; **3** (marking device) (rubber) tampon *m*; (metal) cachet *m*; (for metals) étampe *f*; (for gold) poinçon *m*; **date ~** timbre *m* dateur; **to give sth one's ~ of approval** fig donner son accord à qch; **4** fig (hallmark) marque *f*; **to set one's ~ on sth** imprimer sa marque sur qch; **5** (calibre) trempe *f*; **6** (of feet) piétinement *m*; **with a ~ of her foot** en tapant du pied
B *vtr* **1** (mark) apposer [qch] au tampon [*date, name*] (on sur); tamponner [*ticket, book*]; marquer [*goods, boxes*]; viser [*document, ledger, passport*]; **to ~ one's authority on sth** imprimer son autorité sur qch; **2** (with foot) **to ~ one's foot** (in anger) taper du pied; **to ~ one's feet** (rhythmically) taper des pieds; (for warmth) battre la semelle; **to ~ sth into the ground** enfoncer qch dans le sol du pied; **3** Post affranchir [*envelope*]
C *vi* **1** (thump foot) [*person*] taper du pied; [*horse*] piaffer; **to ~ on** écraser [qch] [*toy, foot*]; (walk heavily) **to ~ into/out of sth** entrer dans/sortir de qch en tapant des pieds; **3** (crush) **to ~ on** lit piétiner [*soil, ground*]; fig écarter [*idea, suggestion*]

(Phrasal verb)
■ **stamp out**: ▸ **~ out** [sth], **~** [sth] **out** **1** (put out) éteindre [qch] en piétinant [*fire*]; **2** (crush) éradiquer [*disease*]; réprimer [*fraud*]; supprimer [*crime*]

stamp: **~-collecting** *n* philatélie *f*; **~-collector** *n* philatéliste *mf*; **~ duty** *n* Jur droit *m* de timbre; **~ed addressed envelope, sae** *n* enveloppe *f* timbrée à votre/son etc adresse

stampede /stæm'piːd/
A *n* **1** (rush) (of animals) débandade *f*; (of humans) ruée *f*; **2** (rodeo) rodéo *m*
B *vtr* **1** lit jeter la panique parmi [*animals, spectators*]; semer la panique dans [*crowd*]; **2** fig (force sb's hand) **to ~ sb into doing** forcer qn à faire
C *vi* [*animals*] courir en troupeau; [*people, crowd*] se précipiter

stamping ground° *n* GB lit, fig domaine *m*

stance /staːns, stæns/ *n* lit, fig position *f*

stanch *vtr* US = **staunch**

stand /stænd/
A *n* **1** (furniture) (for coats) portemanteau *m*; (for hats) porte-chapeau *m*; (for plant, trophy) guéridon *m*; (for music) pupitre *m* à musique; **2** (stall) (on market) éventaire *m*; (kiosk) kiosque *m*; (at exhibition, trade fair) stand *m*; **3** (in stadium) tribunes *fpl*; **4** (witness box) barre *f*; **to take the ~** aller à la barre; **5** (stance) position *f*; **to take** *ou* **make a ~ on sth** prendre position sur qch; **6** (resistance to attack) résistance *f*; **(to make) a last ~** (livrer) une dernière bataille; **7** (standstill) **to come to a ~** s'arrêter
B *vtr* (*prét, pp* **stood**) **1** (place) mettre [*person, object*]; **~ it**

over there mets-le là-bas; **2** (bear) supporter; **he can't ~ to do** *ou* **doing** il ne supporte pas de faire; **she won't ~ any nonsense** elle ne tolère pas qu'on fasse des bêtises; **3** °(pay for) **to ~ sb sth** payer qch à qn; **4** Jur **to ~ trial** passer en jugement; **5** (be liable) **to ~ to lose sth** risquer de perdre qch; **she ~s to gain a million pounds** elle peut gagner un million de livres sterling
C *vi* (*prét, pp* **stood**) **1** (*also* **~ up**) se lever; **2** (be upright) [*person*] se tenir debout; [*object*] tenir debout; **to remain ~ing** rester debout; **there's not much of the cathedral still ~ing** il ne reste que des ruines de la cathédrale; **don't just ~ there, do something!** ne reste pas planté° là! fais quelque chose!; **3** (be positioned) [*building etc*] être; (clearly delineated) se dresser; **the train was ~ing at the platform for half an hour** le train est resté une demi-heure à quai; **4** (step) **to ~ on** marcher sur; **5** (be) **to ~ empty** [*house*] rester vide; **to ~ accused of sth** être accusé de qch; **to ~ ready** être prêt; **as things ~...** étant donné l'état actuel des choses...; **I want to know where I ~** fig je voudrais savoir où j'en suis; **where do you ~ on capital punishment?** quelle est votre position sur la peine de mort?; **nothing ~s between me and the job** rien ne s'oppose à ce que j'obtienne ce poste; **to ~ in sb's way** lit bloquer le passage à qn; fig faire obstacle à qn; **6** (remain valid) [*offer, agreement*] rester valable; **7** (measure) **the hill ~s 500 metres high** la colline fait 500 mètres de haut; **8** (be at certain level) **the total ~s at 300** le total est de 300; **9** (be a candidate) se présenter; **to ~ for parliament** se présenter aux élections législatives; **10** (not move) [*water, mixture*] reposer

(Idioms) **to leave sb ~ing** devancer qn; **to ~ up and be counted** se faire entendre

(Phrasal verbs)
■ **stand about**, **stand around** rester là (**doing** à faire)
■ **stand aside** s'écarter (**to do** pour faire)
■ **stand back**: ▸ **1** (move back) [*person*] reculer (**from** de); fig prendre du recul (**from** par rapport à); **2** (be situated) [*house*] être en retrait (**from** par rapport à)
■ **stand by**: ▸ **~ by 1** [*army, emergency services*] être prêt à intervenir; **to be ~ing to do** [*services*] être prêt à faire; **2** (refuse to act) rester là; **he stood by and did nothing** il est resté là sans intervenir; ▸ **~ by** [sb/sth] (be loyal to) soutenir [*person*]; s'en tenir à [*principles, decision*]; assumer [*actions*]
■ **stand down** (resign) démissionner
■ **stand for**: ▸ **~ for** [sth] **1** (represent) [*party, person*] représenter [*ideal*]; **2** (denote) [*initials*] vouloir dire; [*company, name*] être un gage de [*quality etc*]; **3** (tolerate) [*person*] tolérer [*reduction, insubordination*]
■ **stand in**: **to ~ in for sb** remplacer qn
■ **stand off** (reach a stalemate) aboutir à une impasse
■ **stand out** **1** (be noticeable) [*person*] sortir de l'ordinaire; [*building, design*] se détacher (**against** sur); [*work, ability, person*] être remarquable; **to ~ out from** [*person*] se distinguer de [*group*]; **2** (protrude) [*veins*] saillir
■ **stand over**: ▸ **~ over** [sb] être sur le dos de° [*employee etc*]
■ **stand to** Mil être en état d'alerte
■ **stand up**: ▸ **~ up 1** (rise) se lever (**to do** pour faire); **2** (stay upright) se tenir debout; **3** (withstand investigation) [*theory, story*] tenir debout; **to ~ up to** résister à [*investigation*]; **4** (resist) **to ~ up to** tenir tête à [*person*]; **5** (defend) **to ~ up for** défendre; ▸ **~** [sth] **up** redresser [*object*]; **to ~ sth up against/on** mettre qch contre/sur; ▸ **~** [sb] **up**° (fail to meet) poser un lapin à°

standard /'stændəd/
A *n* **1** (level of quality) niveau *m*; **~s of service** la qualité du service; **this wine is excellent by any ~s** ce vin est incontestablement excellent; **to have high/low ~s** [*worker*] être très/peu consciencieux; [*school, institution*] être d'un bon/mauvais niveau; **to have double ~s** faire deux poids deux mesures; **2** (official specification) norme *f* (**for** de); **3** (requirement) (of student, work) niveau *m* requis; (of hygiene, safety) critères *mpl*; **not to be up to ~** ne pas avoir le niveau requis; **to set the ~ for others to follow** imposer un modèle à suivre; **by today's ~s** selon les critères actuels; **4** (banner) étendard *m*; **5** (song) standard *m*
B *adj* **1** (normal) [*size, equipment, rate*] standard; [*procedure*] habituel/-uelle; [*image*] traditionnel/-elle; **it's ~ practice to do il** est d'usage de faire; **this model includes a car radio as ~** ce modèle est équipé en série d'une autoradio; **2** (authoritative) [*work*] de référence; **3** (*also* **~ class**) GB Rail [*ticket*] de seconde classe

standard: **Standard Assessment Task** n GB Sch test m d'aptitude scolaire (*par tranches d'âge*); **~-bearer** n Mil, fig porte-drapeau m; **~ deviation** n (in statistics) écart-type m; **~-issue** adj réglementaire

standardization /ˌstændədaɪˈzeɪʃn, US -dɪˈz-/ n normalisation f

standardize /ˈstændədaɪz/ vtr normaliser, standardiser

standard: **~ lamp** n GB lampadaire m; **~ of living** n niveau m de vie; **~ time** n heure f légale

standby /ˈstændbaɪ/
A n (person) remplaçant/-e m/f; (food, ingredient) remplacement m; **to be on ~** [*army, emergency services*] être prêt à intervenir; (for airline ticket) être en stand-by
B noun modifier 1 (emergency) [*circuit, battery*] de secours; 2 Tourism [*passenger, ticket*] en stand-by

standee /stænˈdiː/ n (spectator) spectateur/-trice m/f debout; (passenger) voyageur/-euse m/f debout

stand-in /ˈstændɪn/ n gen remplaçant/-e m/f; Cin, Theat doublure f

standing /ˈstændɪŋ/
A n 1 (reputation) réputation f, rang m (with chez); **of high** ou **considerable ~** très réputé; 2 (time) **of long ~** de longue date
B adj 1 (permanent) [*army, committee*] actif/-ive; 2 (continuing) [*rule, invitation*] permanent; **his absent-mindedness is a ~ joke among his friends** sa distraction est un constant sujet de plaisanterie pour ses amis; 3 Sport [*jump*] sans élan

standing: **~ charge** n frais mpl d'abonnement m; **~ order** n Fin virement m automatique; **~ ovation** n ovation f debout; **~ room** n ₵ places fpl debout; **~ stone** n pierre f levée

stand-off /ˈstændɒf/ n 1 (stalemate) impasse f; 2 Sport = **stand-off half**

stand: **~-off half** n Sport demi m d'ouverture; **~-offish**⁰ adj [*person, manner*] distant; **~pipe** n colonne f d'alimentation; **~point** n point m de vue

standstill /ˈstændstɪl/ n 1 (stop) (of traffic) arrêt m; (of economy, growth) point m mort; **to be at a ~** [*traffic*] être à l'arrêt; [*factory, services*] être au point mort; [*talks*] être arrivé à une impasse; **to bring sth to a ~** paralyser qch [*traffic, factory*]; 2 Econ gel m

stand-up /ˈstændʌp/
A n (also **~ comedy**) one man show m comique
B adj 1 Theat, TV **~ comedian** comique mf; 2 [*buffet*] debout inv; 3 (aggressive) [*argument*] en règle

stank /stæŋk/ prét ▸ stink B

Stanley knife® /ˈstænlɪˌnaɪf/ n cutter m

stanza /ˈstænzə/ n strophe f

staple /ˈsteɪpl/
A n 1 (for paper) agrafe f; 2 Constr (U-shaped) clou m cavalier; 3 (basic food) aliment m de base; 4 Econ (crop) culture f principale; (product) principale fabrication f; (industry) industrie f de base; 5 fig (topic, theme) sujet m principal; 6 (fibre) fibre f
B adj (épith) [*product, food, diet*] de base; [*crop, meal*] principal
C vtr (attach) agrafer (**to** à; **onto** sur)

staple gun n agrafeuse f

stapler /ˈsteɪplə(r)/ n agrafeuse f

star /stɑː(r)/
A n 1 (in sky) étoile f; **the ~s are out** les étoiles brillent; 2 (celebrity) vedette f, star f; 3 (asterisk) astérisque m; 4 (award) (to hotel, restaurant) étoile f; (to pupil) bon point m; 5 Mil (mark of rank) étoile f
B stars npl horoscope m; **it's written in the ~s** c'est écrit
C -star combining form Tourism **three-/four-~ hotel** hôtel (à) trois/quatre étoiles
D vtr (p prés etc -rr-) 1 [*film, play*] avoir [qn] pour vedette [*actor*]; **a comedy ~ring Lenny Henry** une comédie avec Lenny Henry en vedette; 2 (mark with star) (gén au passif) marquer [qch] d'un astérisque; 3 (decorate) parsemer (**with** de)
E vi (p prés etc -rr-) [*actor*] jouer le rôle principal (**in** dans); **to ~ as Dracula** jouer (le rôle de) Dracula; **Meryl Streep also ~s** Meryl Streep est également à l'affiche
⟨Idioms⟩ **to reach for the ~s** vouloir décrocher la lune; **to see ~s** voir trente-six chandelles

star anise /ˌstɑːrəˈniːz/ n anis m étoilé

starboard /ˈstɑːbəd/
A n 1 Naut tribord m; **to turn to ~** virer sur la droite; 2 Aviat droite f
B noun modifier tribord m; **on the ~ side** à tribord

starch /stɑːtʃ/
A n 1 ₵ (carbohydrate) féculents mpl; **wheat ~** amidon m de blé; **potato ~** fécule f de pomme de terre; 2 (for clothes) amidon m
B vtr amidonner, empeser

star chart n carte f du ciel

starchy /ˈstɑːtʃɪ/ adj 1 [*food, diet*] riche en féculents; 2 [*substance*] amylacé; 3 ⁰péj [*person, tone*] guindé

stardom /ˈstɑːdəm/ n vedettariat m; **to rise to ~** devenir une vedette

stare /steə(r)/
A n regard m fixe; **she gave me a ~** son regard s'est posé sur moi
B vi regarder fixement; **to ~ at sb/sth** regarder fixement qn/qch; **to ~ at sb in disbelief** regarder qn d'un air incrédule; **to ~ up at sb/sth** lever les yeux pour regarder qn/qch; **to ~ back at sb** rendre son regard à qn
⟨Idioms⟩ **to be staring sb in the face** crever les yeux à qn⁰; **disaster was staring me in the face** j'étais au bord de la catastrophe
⟨Phrasal verbs⟩
■ **stare down** = stare out
■ **stare out**: ▸ **~ [sb] out**, **~ out [sb]** faire baisser les yeux à

star: **~fish** n étoile f de mer; **~ fruit** n carambole f; **~gazer** n (astrologer) astrologue mf; (astronomer) astronome mf

staring /ˈsteərɪŋ/ adj [*eyes*] fixe; [*people, crowd*] curieux/-ieuse

stark /stɑːk/ adj 1 (bare) [*landscape, building, appearance*] désolé; [*room, decor*] nu; [*lighting*] cru; [*beauty*] âpre; 2 (unadorned) [*statement, fact*] brut; [*warning, reminder*] sévère; 3 (total) [*contrast*] saisissant; **in ~ contrast to** en opposition totale avec
⟨Idioms⟩ **to be ~ naked** être complètement nu; **~ raving mad**⁰, **~ staring mad**⁰ GB complètement dingue⁰ or cinglé⁰

starkly /ˈstɑːklɪ/ adv (bluntly) carrément

starless /ˈstɑːlɪs/ adj sans étoiles

starlet /ˈstɑːlɪt/ n starlette f

starlight n lumière f des étoiles

starling /ˈstɑːlɪŋ/ n étourneau m

starry /ˈstɑːrɪ/ adj [*night, sky*] étoilé; [*eyes*] brillant

starry-eyed adj ébloui (**about** par)

star: **Stars and Stripes** n (+ v sg) bannière f étoilée; **~ sign** n signe m astrologique

Star-spangled Banner n bannière f étoilée

> ⓘ The **Star-spangled Banner** L'un des noms du drapeau américain. C'est aussi le titre de l'hymne national américain qui affirme la volonté d'indépendance et de liberté des États-Unis :
> *And the Star-spangled banner in triumph shall wave*
> *O'er the land of the free and the home of the brave.*

star: **~struck** adj impressionné par la célébrité; **~-studded** adj [*cast, line-up*] avec de nombreuses vedettes

star system n 1 (in sky) système m stellaire; 2 Cin star-system m

start /stɑːt/
A n 1 (beginning) début m; **at the ~** au début; **(right) from the start** dès le début; **to make a ~ on doing** se mettre à faire; **to make an early ~** (on journey) partir tôt; **that's a good ~** lit c'est un bon début; iron ça commence bien; **to make a fresh** ou **new ~** prendre un nouveau départ; **from ~ to finish** d'un bout à l'autre; **for a ~** pour commencer; 2 (advantage) avantage m; (in time, distance) avance f; **to give sb a ~ in business** aider qn à démarrer dans les affaires; 3 Sport ligne f de départ; 4 (movement) **with a ~** en sursaut
B vtr 1 (begin) commencer [*day, activity*]; entamer [*bottle, packet*]; **to ~ doing** ou **to do** commencer à faire, se mettre à faire; **don't ~ that again!** ne recommence pas!; 2 (cause, initiate) déclencher [*quarrel, war*]; instaurer [*custom*]; mettre

[*fire*]; être à l'origine de [*trouble, rumour*]; lancer [*fashion, enterprise*]; **to ~ a family** avoir des enfants; [3] (activate) faire démarrer [*car*]; mettre [qch] en marche [*machine*]

C **to start with** *adv phr* [1] (firstly) d'abord, premièrement; [2] (at first) au début; [3] (at all) **I should never have told her to ~ with** pour commencer, je n'aurais jamais dû lui en parler

D *vi* [1] (begin) *gen* commencer (**by doing** par faire); (in job) débuter (**as** comme); **to ~ again** *ou* **afresh** recommencer; **to ~ on** commencer [*memoirs, journey*]; **let's get ~ed on the washing-up** allez! on fait la vaisselle; **don't ~ on me** (in argument) ne recommence pas avec moi; **the day will ~ cloudy** il fera nuageux en début de journée; **~ing Wednesday...** à compter de mercredi...; [2] (depart) partir; [3] (jump nervously) sursauter (**in** de); [4] *Aut, Tech* [*car, engine, machine*] démarrer

(Idioms) **~ as you mean to go on** prenez tout de suite les choses en main; **the ~ of something big** un début prometteur

(Phrasal verbs)
■ **start back** [1] (begin to return) prendre le chemin du retour; [2] (step back) faire un bond en arrière
■ **start off** ▸ **~ off** [1] (set off) [*train, bus*] démarrer; [*person*] partir; [2] (begin) [*person*] commencer (**by doing** par faire; **with** par); [*employee*] débuter; ▸ **~ [sb/sth] off, ~ off [sb/sth]** [1] (begin) commencer [*visit, talk*] (**with** par); mettre [qch] en route [*programme*]; [2] ⁰GB (cause to do) **don't ~ her off laughing** ne la fais pas rire; **don't ~ him off** ne le provoque pas; [3] (put to work) mettre [qch] en marche [*machine*]; [4] *Sport* faire partir [*competitors*]
■ **start out** [1] (set off) (on journey) partir; **he ~ed out with the aim of...** fig il avait d'abord pour but de...; [2] (begin) [*matter, business, employee*] débuter
■ **start over** US recommencer (à zéro)
■ **start up** ▸ **~ up** [*engine*] démarrer; [*noise*] retentir; [*person*] débuter; ▸ **~ [sth] up, ~ up [sth]** faire démarrer [*car*]; ouvrir [*shop*]; créer [*business*]

starter /ˈstɑːtə(r)/ *n* [1] *Sport* (participant) partant/-e *m/f*; **to be a fast ~** être rapide au départ; [2] *Sport* (official) starter *m*; [3] *Aut, Tech* démarreur *m*; [4] *Culin* hors d'œuvre *m inv*

(Idiom) **for ~s**⁰ pour commencer

starter home *n* petite maison *f* (pour acheteurs débutants)

start: **~ing line** *n Sport* ligne *f* de départ; **~ing pistol** *n Sport* pistolet *m* de starter; **~ing point** *n* point *m* de départ; **~ing price** *n* cote *f* au départ; **~ing salary** *n* salaire *m* de départ

startle /ˈstɑːtl/ *vtr* [1] (take aback) surprendre; [2] (alarm) [*sight, sound, person*] effrayer

startled /ˈstɑːtld/ *adj* [1] (taken aback) surpris (**at** de); [2] (alarmed) effrayé; **a ~ cry** un cri d'effroi

startling /ˈstɑːtlɪŋ/ *adj* saisissant

startlingly /ˈstɑːtlɪŋlɪ/ *adv* [*different*] étonnamment; **~ beautiful** d'une beauté saisissante

start-up costs *npl Comm* frais *mpl* de mise en route

star turn *n* [1] (act) clou *m* fig; [2] (person) vedette *f*

starvation /ˌstɑːˈveɪʃn/
A *n* famine *f*; **to die of ~** mourir de faim
B *noun modifier* [*rations*] de survie; [*wages*] de misère

starvation diet *n* **to go on a ~** suivre un régime draconien

starve /stɑːv/
A *vtr* [1] (deliberately) priver [qn] de nourriture, affamer; **to ~ oneself** se sous-alimenter; **to ~ sb to death** laisser qn mourir de faim; [2] (deprive) **to ~ sb/sth of** priver qn/qch de [*cash, oxygen, affection*]; **to be ~d of** être en mal de [*company, conversation*]
B *vi* mourir de faim

(Phrasal verb)
■ **starve out** ▸ **~ [sb] out, ~ out [sb]** affamer

starving /ˈstɑːvɪŋ/ *adj* [1] ⁰(hungry) **to be ~** mourir *or* crever⁰ de faim; [2] (hunger-stricken) affamé

stash⁰ /stæʃ/
A *n* [1] (hiding place) cachette *f*; [2] (hidden supply) provision *f*
B *vtr* cacher [*money, drugs*] (**in** dans; **under** sous)

(Phrasal verb)
■ **stash away**⁰ ▸ **~ [sth] away, ~ away [sth]** mettre [qch] de côté

stasis /ˈsteɪsɪs, ˈstæsɪs/ *n* (stagnation) stagnation *f*

state /steɪt/
A *n* [1] (condition) état *m*; **what ~ is the car in?** dans quel état est la voiture?; **the present ~ of affairs** l'état actuel des choses; **a shocking/an odd ~ of affairs** une situation scandaleuse/très étrange; **to be in a good/bad ~** être en bon/mauvais état; **in a good/bad ~ of repair** bien/mal entretenu; **he's in a confused ~ (of mind)** il ne sait plus où il en est; **to be in no ~ to do** ne pas être en état de faire; **he's not in a fit ~ to drive** il n'est pas en état de conduire; **in a liquid ~** à l'état liquide; **a ~ of emergency/shock** un état d'urgence/de choc; **what's the ~ of play?** *gen* où en êtes-vous?; [2] *Pol* (nation) (*also* **State**) État *m*; **a ~ within a ~** un État dans l'État; [3] (region, area) État *m*; [4] *Pol* (government) État *m*; [5] (ceremonial) pompe *f*; **in ~** en grande pompe; **she will lie in ~** sa dépouille sera exposée; **robes of ~** tenue *f* d'apparat
B **States** *npl* **the States** les États-Unis *mpl*
C *noun modifier* [1] (government) [*school, sector*] public/-ique; [*enterprise, pension, TV, railways, secret*] d'État; [*budget, subsidy*] de l'État; **~ election** (at a national level) élection *f* nationale; US élection *f* au niveau d'un État; [2] (ceremonial) [*coach, occasion*] d'apparat; [*banquet*] de gala; [*funeral*] national; [*visit*] officiel/-ielle
D *vtr* [1] (express, say) exposer [*fact, opinion, truth*]; (provide information) indiquer [*age, income, whereabouts*]; **to ~ that** [*person*] déclarer que; **to ~ one's case** *gen* exposer son cas; *Jur* présenter son dossier; **as ~d above/below** comme mentionné ci-dessus/ci-dessous; [2] (specify) spécifier [*amount, place, terms*]; exprimer [*preference*]; **at ~d times** à dates fixes

(Idiom) **to be in a ~** être dans tous ses états

state: **State capital** *n* US capitale *f* d'État; **State Capitol** *n* US Pol assemblée *f* législative d'État; **~-controlled** *adj* contrôlé par l'État; **State Department** *n* US, Pol ministère *m* américain des affaires étrangères; **~-funded** *adj* subventionné par l'État

State house *n* US (for legislature) siège *m* du Parlement; (for public events) édifice *m* public

stateless /ˈsteɪtlɪs/ *adj* apatride; **~ persons** les apatrides

Stateline *n* US frontière *f* (entre États)

stately /ˈsteɪtlɪ/ *adj* imposant

stately home *n* GB château *m*

statement /ˈsteɪtmənt/ *n* [1] (expression of view) déclaration *f* (**by** de; **on, about** à propos de); (official) communiqué *m*; **~ of belief** profession *f* de foi; **~ of fact** exposé *m* des faits; [2] *Fin* (of bank account) relevé *m* de compte; **a financial ~** un état de la situation financière; [3] *Jur* déclaration *f*

state: **~ of the art** *adj* [*equipment*] ultramoderne; [*technology*] de pointe; **~-owned** *adj* [*company*] étatique; **State Registered Nurse, SRN** ▸ p. 1181 *n* GB Med ≈ infirmier/-ière *m/f* diplômé/-e d'État; **~room** *n* Naut cabine *f* particulière; ⁰(newspaper, radio, television) contrôlé par l'État; [*company*] géré par l'État; **State's attorney** *n* US Jur avocat/-e *m/f* représentant l'État

State's evidence *n* US Jur **to turn ~** dénoncer ses complices

state: **~side** *adj* des États-Unis; **~sman** *n* (*pl* **-men**) homme *m* d'État; **~smanlike** *adj* digne d'un homme d'État; **~ trooper** *n* US policier *m* d'État; **~wide** *adj, adv* US dans tout l'État

static /ˈstætɪk/
A *n* [1] (*also* **~ electricity**) électricité *f* statique; [2] *Radio, TV* (interference) parasites *mpl*
B *adj* [1] (stationary) [*scene, actor, display*] statique; [*image*] fixe; [*traffic*] bloqué; [2] (unchanging) [*society, values*] immuable; [*style, ideas*] statique; [3] (stable) [*population, prices, demand*] stationnaire; [4] *Phys* statique; [5] *Comput* [*memory*] statique; [*data*] fixe

station /ˈsteɪʃn/
A *n* [1] *Rail* gare *f*; [2] *Radio, TV* station *f*; TV chaîne *f*; [3] *Mil, Naut* (base) base *f*; [4] *Mil, Naut, gen* (post) poste *m*; **at one's ~** à son poste; [5] (*also* **police ~**) commissariat *m*; (small) poste *m* de police; [6] *Agric* élevage *m*; [7] †(rank) condition *f*; **to get ideas above one's ~** ne pas avoir les moyens de ses ambitions
B *vtr* poster [*guard*]; stationner [*troops*]; **to be ~ed in Germany** être en garnison en Allemagne
C *v refl* **to ~ oneself** se poster

US states

■ *In some cases, there is a French form of the name, but not always (if in doubt, check in the dictionary). Each state has a gender in French and is used with the definite article, except after the preposition en, e.g.:*

Arkansas
= l'Arkansas *m*

California
= la Californie

Texas
= le Texas

So:

Arkansas is beautiful
= l'Arkansas est beau

I like California
= j'aime la Californie

do you know Texas?
= connaissez-vous le Texas?

In, to and from somewhere

■ *For in and to, use en for feminine states and for masculine ones beginning with a vowel, e.g.:*

in Alaska
= en Alaska

to Alaska
= en Alaska

in California
= en Californie

to California
= en Californie

■ *For in and to, use au for masculine states beginning with a consonant, e.g.:*

in Texas
= au Texas

to Texas
= au Texas

■ *For from use de for feminine states and for masculine ones beginning with a vowel, e.g.:*

from California
= de Californie

from Alaska
= d'Alaska

■ *For from use du for masculine states beginning with a consonant, e.g.:*

from Texas
= du Texas

Coming from somewhere: uses with another noun

■ *There are a few words e.g.* californien, new-yorkais, texan *used as adjectives and as nouns (with a capital letter) referring to the inhabitants. In other cases it is usually safe to use de for feminine states, and to use de l' or du for masculine states, e.g.:*

the Florida countryside
= les paysages de Floride

Illinois representatives
= les représentants de l'Illinois

but

a Louisiana accent
= l'accent de la Louisiane

New-Mexico roads
= les routes du Nouveau-Mexique

---

stationary /ˈsteɪʃənrɪ, US -nerɪ/ *adj* [*queue, vehicle*] à l'arrêt; [*traffic*] bloqué; [*prices*] stable

station break *n* US Radio, TV page *f* de publicité

stationer /ˈsteɪʃnə(r)/ ▸ p. 1181 *n* (*also* ∼'s) (shop) papeterie *f*

stationery /ˈsteɪʃnrɪ, US -nerɪ/
A *n* ⓵ (writing materials) papeterie *f*; (for office) fournitures *fpl* (de bureau); ⓶ (writing paper) papier *m* à lettres
B *noun modifier* [*cupboard*] à fournitures; ∼ **department** papeterie *f*

stationery shop GB ▸ p. 1181 *n* papeterie *f*

station: ∼**master** ▸ p. 1181 *n* chef *m* de gare; ∼ **wagon** *n* US break *m*

statistic /stəˈtɪstɪk/ *n* statistique *f* (**on** de); ∼**s show that...** d'après les statistiques...

statistical /stəˈtɪstɪkl/ *adj* statistique

statistically /stəˈtɪstɪklɪ/ *adv* statistiquement

statistician /ˌstætɪˈstɪʃn/ ▸ p. 1181 *n* statisticien/-ienne *m/f*

statistics /stəˈtɪstɪks/ *n* (subject) (+ *v sg*) statistique *f*

statue /ˈstætʃuː/ *n* statue *f*

statuesque /ˌstætʃʊˈesk/ *adj* sculptural

stature /ˈstætʃə(r)/ *n* ⓵ (height) taille *f*; **small/tall of** ou **∼ de petite/grande taille**; ⓶ (status) envergure *f*; **intellectual ∼** stature *f* intellectuelle

status /ˈsteɪtəs/ *n* (*pl* **-uses**) ⓵ (position) position *f*; ⓶ **¢** (prestige) prestige *m*; ⓷ (official categorization) statut *m* (**as** de); **legal/charitable ∼** statut légal/d'œuvre charitable; **financial ∼** situation *f* financière; **refugee ∼** statut de réfugié

status: ∼ **bar** *n* Comput barre *f* d'état; ∼ **quo** *n* statu quo *m*; ∼ **symbol** *n* signe *m* de prestige

statute /ˈstætʃuːt/ *n* Jur, Pol texte *m* de loi; **by ∼** par la loi

statute book *n* **to be on the ∼** être en vigueur

statutory /ˈstatʃʊtərɪ, US -tɔːrɪ/ *adj* [*powers, requirements, sick pay*] légal; [*body*] officiel/-ielle

staunch /stɔːntʃ/
A *adj* [*supporter, defence*] loyal; [*defender*] ardent
B *vtr* **staunch, stanch** US /stɔːntʃ, stɑːntʃ/ ⓵ lit étancher [*wound*]; ⓶ fig arrêter [*decline*]

staunchly /ˈstɔːntʃlɪ/ *adv* [*defend, oppose*] fermement; [*Catholic, Communist*] résolument

stave /steɪv/ *n* Mus portée *f*
(Phrasal verb)
■ **stave off** (*prét, pp* **staved**): ▸ ∼ **off [sth]** tromper [*hunger, fatigue*]; empêcher [*bankruptcy, crisis*]; écarter [*threat*]

stay /steɪ/
A *n* ⓵ (visit, period) séjour *m*; **to have an overnight ∼ in Athens** passer la nuit à Athènes; **'enjoy your ∼!'** 'bon séjour!'; ⓶ Jur **∼ of execution** sursis *m* (à l'exécution de la peine capitale)
B **stays** *npl* corset *m*
C *vi* ⓵ (remain) rester; **to ∼ for lunch** rester (à) déjeuner; **to ∼ in teaching** rester dans l'enseignement; **to ∼ in nursing** continuer comme infirmier/-ière; **to ∼ in business** (not go under) rester à flot; **to ∼ put** ne pas bouger; **'∼ tuned!'** (on radio) 'restez avec nous!'; **computers are here to ∼** les ordinateurs ne sont pas près de disparaître; ⓶ (have accommodation) loger; **to ∼ in a hotel/at a friend's house** loger à l'hôtel/chez un ami; ⓷ (spend the night) passer la nuit; **why don't you ∼?** tu pourrais passer la nuit ici; **to ∼ overnight** passer la nuit; ⓸ (visit for unspecified time) **to come to ∼** (for a few days) venir passer quelques jours (**with** chez); (for a few weeks) venir passer quelques semaines (**with** chez); **do you often have people to ∼?** tu as souvent des gens chez toi?

(Phrasal verbs)

■ **stay away** ① (not come) ne plus venir; **go away and ~ away!** va-t-en et ne reviens plus!; **to ~ away from** éviter [*town centre*]; ne pas s'approcher de [*window, strangers*]; ② (not attend) **to ~ away from work** s'absenter de son travail

■ **stay in** ① (not go out) rester à la maison; ② [*hook, nail*] tenir

■ **stay out** ① (remain away) **to ~ out late/all night** rentrer tard/ne pas rentrer de la nuit; **to ~ out of trouble** éviter les ennuis; **to ~ out of sb's way** éviter qn; **~ out of this!** ne t'en mêle pas!; ② (continue strike) continuer la grève

■ **stay up** ① (as treat, waiting for sb) veiller; ② (as habit) se coucher tard; ③ (not fall down) tenir

stay-at-home n, adj GB casanier/-ière (m/f)

stayer /'steɪə(r)/ n (person) **to be a ~** être tenace

staying-power n endurance f; Sport **to have ~** avoir du fond

STD n: abrév ▸ **sexually transmitted disease**

STD (area) code n GB indicatif m

stead /sted/ n **in sb's ~** à la place de qn

(Idiom) **to stand sb in good ~** s'avérer utile pour qn

steadfast /'stedfɑːst, US -fæst/ adj [*determination, belief, refusal*] tenace; [*gaze*] franc/franche; **to be ~ in one's belief** être ferme dans sa croyance

steadfastly /'stedfɑːstlɪ, US -fæstlɪ/ adv [*attached, loyal*] indéfectiblement; **to cling ~ to one's beliefs** s'accrocher à ses convictions

steadily /'stedɪlɪ/ adv ① (gradually) progressivement; ② (without interruption) sans interruption; ③ [*gaze*] sans détourner le regard

steady /'stedɪ/
A adj ① (continual) [*stream, increase, decline*] constant; [*rain*] incessant; [*breathing, drip, speed, progress*] régulier/-ière; ② (unwavering) [*hand*] ferme; [*faith*] immuable; ③ (stable) stable; **to keep ou hold sth ~** bien tenir qch; **he isn't very ~ on his feet** (from age) il n'est plus très ferme sur ses jambes; (from drunkenness) il titube; **to hold ~** [*interest rates*] se maintenir; [*gaze*] calme; ④ (calm) [*voice*] ferme; [*gaze*] calme; ⑤ (reliable) [*job*] fixe; [*relationship*] durable; [*worker*] fiable; **do you have a ~ boyfriend?** tu sors avec quelqu'un?
B ○excl GB **~! ou ~ on!** (reprovingly) doucement!
C vtr ① (stop moving) tenir [*camera*]; ② (control) **to ~ one's nerves** se calmer les nerfs
D vi lit, fig se stabiliser
E v refl **to ~ oneself** (physically) rétablir son équilibre; (mentally) se calmer

(Idiom) **to go ~ with sb**○ sortir avec qn

steak /steɪk/ n (of beef) steak m; **~ and chips** steak frites; **salmon/tuna ~** darne f de saumon/thon

steak: **~ and kidney pie**, **~ and kidney pudding** n GB tourte f au bœuf et aux rognons; **~house** n (restaurant m) grill m; **~ sandwich** n sandwich m au biftek

steal /stiːl/
A ○n (bargain) **it's a ~!** c'est donné!
B vtr (prét **stole**; pp **stolen**) (thieve) voler (**from sb** à qn); fig **to ~ a few minutes' sleep** s'offrir en douce quelques minutes de sommeil; **to ~ a glance at** jeter un coup d'œil à; **to ~ a kiss** voler un baiser
C vi (prét **stole**; pp **stolen**) ① (thieve) voler; **to ~ from sb** voler qn; **to ~ from a house** cambrioler une maison; **our luggage was stolen from the car** on nous a volé nos bagages dans la voiture; ② (creep) lit **to ~ out of the room** quitter la pièce subrepticement; **to ~ up on sb** s'approcher de qn subrepticement

(Idioms) **to ~ a march on sb** prendre qn de vitesse; **to ~ the show** éclipser tout le monde

stealing /'stiːlɪŋ/ n vol m

stealth /stelθ/ n **with ~** furtivement

stealthily /'stelθɪlɪ/ adv furtivement

stealthy /'stelθɪ/ adj [*step, glance*] furtif/-ive

steam /stiːm/
A n ① (vapour) vapeur f; (in room, on window) buée f; **powered by ~** à vapeur; ② (from pressure) pression f; **full ~ ahead!** fig en avant toute!
B noun modifier [*bath, cloud*] de vapeur; [*iron, railway*] à vapeur
C vtr faire cuire [qch] à la vapeur [*vegetables*]; **to ~ open a**

letter décacheter une lettre à la vapeur; **~ed pudding** GB pudding cuit à la vapeur
D vi (give off vapour) fumer, dégager de la vapeur; **to ~ through the countryside** traverser la campagne en crachant des nuages de fumée

(Idioms) **to get up ~ ou pick up ~** [*machine*] prendre de la vitesse; [*campaign*] prendre de l'importance; **to run out of ~** s'essouffler; [*worker*] peiner; **to let off ~** se défouler; **under one's own ~** par ses propres moyens

(Phrasal verb)

■ **steam up**: ▸ **~ up** [*window, glasses*] s'embuer; ▸ **~ [sth] up** embuer [*window*]; **to get ~ed up** fig se mettre dans tous ses états (**over** à propos de)

steam: **~boat** n bateau m à vapeur; **~ engine** n locomotive f à vapeur

steamer /'stiːmə(r)/ n (boat) vapeur m

steaming /'stiːmɪŋ/ adj [*bath*] très chaud; [*tea*] brûlant

steam: **~ locomotive** n = steam engine; **~ power** n vapeur f

steamroller /'stiːmrəʊlə(r)/
A n rouleau m compresseur
B vtr briser [*opposition, rival*]; **to ~ a bill through** imposer un projet de loi à [*parliament*]

steamship n gen navire m à vapeur; (for passengers) paquebot m

steamy /'stiːmɪ/ adj ① [*room, window*] embué; [*climate*] chaud et humide; ② ○(erotic) torride

steel /stiːl/
A n ① (metal) acier m; **made of ~** en acier; ② (knife sharpener) aiguisoir m
B noun modifier [*bodywork*] en acier; [*plate, production, manufacturer*] d'acier
C v refl **to ~ oneself** s'armer de courage

steel: **~ band** n steel band m (ensemble musical dont les instruments sont des bidons etc); **~ guitar** ▸ p. 1028 n guitare f hawaïenne; **~ industry** n sidérurgie f; **~worker** ▸ p. 1181 n sidérurgiste mf; **~works**, **~yard** n installations fpl sidérurgiques

steely /'stiːlɪ/ adj ① [*nerves*] inébranlable; **~-eyed** au regard d'acier; ② [*sky*] gris plombé inv

steep /stiːp/
A adj ① (sloping) [*descent, stairs*] raide; [*street*] escarpé; [*roof*] en pente raide; [*ascent*] abrupt; **a ~ drop** un à-pic; ② (sharp) [*rise, fall*] fort (before n); ③ ○(excessive) [*price*] exorbitant; [*bill*] salé○
B vtr (soak) **to ~ sth in** faire tremper qch dans
C vi tremper (**in** dans)

(Idiom) **that's a bit ~**○! c'est un peu fort○!

steeped /stiːpt/ adj **to be ~ in** être imprégné de

steeple /'stiːpl/ n (tower) clocher m; (spire) flèche f

steeple~chase n (for horses) steeple-chase m; (in athletics) 3000m steeple m; **~jack** ▸ p. 1181 n réparateur/-trice m/f de clochers (et de hautes cheminées)

steeply /'stiːplɪ/ adv ① [*rise, drop*] à pic; ② Fin [*rise*] en flèche

steer /stɪə(r)/
A n ① (animal) bouvillon m; ② ○US (tip) **a bum ~** un mauvais tuyau○
B vtr ① (control direction of) piloter; ② (guide) lit diriger, guider [*person*]; fig orienter [*conversation*]; **to ~ a course through** fig manœuvrer délicatement à travers; **to ~ a bill through parliament** faire aboutir un projet de loi
C vi ① gen piloter; **the car ~s well** la direction (de la voiture) répond bien; ② Naut gouverner; **to ~ towards ou for** mettre le cap sur

(Idioms) **to ~ clear of sth/sb** se tenir à l'écart de qch/qn; **to ~ a middle course** adopter une position médiane

steering /'stɪərɪŋ/ n (mechanism) direction f

steering: **~ column** n Aut colonne f de direction; **~ committee** n Admin comité m directeur; **~ lock** n Aut blocage m de direction; **~ wheel** n Aut volant m

stem /stem/
A n ① (of flower, leaf) tige f; (of fruit) queue f; ② (of glass) pied m; (of pipe) tuyau m
B vtr (p prés etc **-mm-**) arrêter [*flow*]; fig enrayer [*advance, tide, increase, inflation*]; contenir [*protest*]
C vi (p prés etc **-mm-**) **to ~ from** provenir de

stem ginger n gingembre m confit

S

stench /stentʃ/ n puanteur f; fig odeur f nauséabonde

stencil /'stensɪl/
A n **1** (card) pochoir m; **2** (pattern) dessin m au pochoir
B vtr décorer [qch] au pochoir [fabric, surface]

stencilling, stenciling US /'stensɪlɪŋ/ n (technique) technique f du pochoir

stenography /ste'nɒgrəfɪ/ n US sténographie f

step /step/
A n **1** (pace) pas m; **to take a ~** faire un pas; **to walk** ou **keep in ~** marcher au pas; **I was a few ~s behind her** je la suivais de près; **to fall into ~ with sb** se mettre au même pas que qn; **one ~ out of line** un pas de travers; **to be out of ~ with the times** ne plus être dans le coup; **to watch one's ~** lit faire attention où l'on met les pieds; **you'd better watch your ~**! fig tu ferais mieux de faire attention!; **to be one ~ ahead of the competition** fig avoir une longueur d'avance sur ses concurrents; **I'm with you every ~ of the way** fig tu peux compter sur moi; **2** (footsteps) pas m; **3** fig (move) pas m; **a ~ forwards/backwards** un pas en avant/en arrière; **it's a ~ up for him** il a gravi un échelon; **it's a ~ in the right direction** c'est un pas dans la bonne voie; **to be one ~ closer to victory** approcher de la victoire; **the first ~ is to…** la première chose à faire est de…; **4** fig (measure) mesure f; (course of action) démarche f; **to take ~s to do** prendre des mesures pour faire; **5** fig (stage) étape f (in dans); **to go one ~ further** aller plus loin; **6** (way of walking) pas m; **7** (dance step) pas m; **8** (stair) marche f; **a flight of ~s** (to upper floor) un escalier m; (outside building) des marches fpl
B **steps** npl **1** (small ladder) escabeau m; **2** (outdoor) marches fpl
C vi (p prés etc **-pp-**) marcher (**in** dans; **on** sur); **to ~ into** entrer dans [lift]; monter dans [dinghy]; **to ~ into sb's office** entrer dans le bureau de qn; **just ~ this way** si vous voulez bien me suivre; **to ~ off** descendre de [pavement]; **to ~ onto** monter sur [scales, pavement]; **to ~ over** enjamber; **to ~ through** passer derrière [curtains]; **to ~ out of line** fig faire un pas de travers; **to ~ up to** s'approcher de [microphone]
⬭ Idioms **to ~ on it**◦ se grouiller◦; **to ~ on the gas**◦ appuyer sur le champignon◦; **one ~ at a time** chaque chose en son temps
⬭ Phrasal verbs
■ **step aside 1** (physically) s'écarter (**in order to** pour); **2** (in job transfer) céder sa place (**in favour of** à)
■ **step back** fig prendre du recul (**from** par rapport à)
■ **step down**: ▶ ~ **down** gen se retirer; (as electoral candidate) se désister
■ **step in** intervenir (**and do** pour faire)
■ **step up**: ▶ ~ **up [sth]** accroître [production]; intensifier [campaign]; renforcer [surveillance]

stepbrother n demi-frère m

step-by-step
A adj [guide] complet/-ète; [reduction] progressif/-ive
B **step by step** adv [analyse] point par point; [explain] étape par étape

step: **~child** n beau-fils/belle-fille m/f; **~ladder** n escabeau m; **~parent** n beau-père/belle-mère m/f; **~ping stone** n lit pierre f de gué; fig tremplin m; **~sister** n demi-sœur f

stereo /'sterɪəʊ/
A n **1** (technique) stéréo f; **2** (also ~ **system**) chaîne f stéréo; **car ~** autoradio m stéréo; **personal ~** baladeur m
B noun modifier [cassette, cassette-player] stéréo inv; [recording, broadcast] en stéréo

stereophonic /ˌsterɪə'fɒnɪk/ adj stéréophonique

stereoscopic /ˌsterɪə'skɒpɪk/ adj stéréoscopique

stereotype /'sterɪətaɪp/
A n (person, idea) stéréotype m
B vtr gen stéréotyper [person]

sterile /'steraɪl, US 'sterəl/ adj (all contexts) stérile

sterilize /'sterəlaɪz/ vtr stériliser

sterling /'stɜːlɪŋ/
A n ▸ p. 782 Fin livre f sterling inv; **~ was up/down** la livre sterling était en hausse/en baisse; **£100 ~** 100 livres sterling
B noun modifier Fin [payment] en livres sterling
C adj (épith) (excellent) remarquable

sterling silver n argent m fin

stern /stɜːn/
A n Naut poupe f
B adj gen sévère; [message] grave

sternly /'stɜːnlɪ/ adv [say, speak] sévèrement; [look] d'un air sévère

steroid /'stɪərɔɪd, 'ste-/ n stéroïde m; **to be on ~s** prendre des stéroïdes; **anabolic ~** anabolisant m

stet /stet/ vtr, vi (mark in proofreading) bon

stetson /'stetsn/ n chapeau m de cow-boy

stew /stjuː, US stuː/
A n ragoût m; (with game) civet m; (with veal, chicken) blanquette f
B vtr cuire [qch] en ragoût; cuire [qch] en civet [game]; faire cuire [fruit, vegetables]; **~ed apples** compote f de pommes
C vi **1** [meat] cuire à l'étouffée; [fruit] cuire (dans son jus); **2** ◦fig [person] (in heat) crever de chaud◦
⬭ Idioms **to be/get in a ~**◦ (worry) être/se mettre dans tous ses états; **to ~ in one's own juice**◦ mijoter dans son jus◦

steward /stjʊəd, US 'stuːərd/ n (on plane, ship) steward m; (of club) intendant/-e m/f; (at races) organisateur m

stewardess /'stjʊədes, US 'stuːərdəs/ n (on plane) hôtesse f (de l'air)

stg n: abrév écrite = **sterling A**

stick /stɪk/
A n **1** (piece of wood) bâton m; (for kindling) bout m de bois; (for lollipop) bâton m; **2** (also **walking ~**) canne f; **3** (rod-shaped piece) **a ~ of chalk/dynamite** un bâton de craie/dynamite; **a ~ of celery** une branche de céleri; **a ~ of rhubarb** une tige de rhubarbe; **a ~ of (French) bread** une baguette; **4** Sport (in hockey) crosse f; **5** (conductor's baton) baguette f; **6** ◦(piece of furniture) **a few ~s of furniture** quelques meubles; **7** ◦GB (person) **a funny old ~** un drôle de bonhomme/une drôle de bonne femme m/f; **he's a dry old ~** il manque d'humour; **8** ◦(criticism) **to get** ou **take (some) ~** se faire critiquer; **to give sb (some) ~** critiquer qn violemment
B ◦**sticks** npl **in the ~s** en pleine cambrousse◦, dans la campagne
C vtr (prét, pp **stuck**) **1** **to ~ sth into sth** planter qch dans qch; **he stuck a knife in her** il l'a poignardée; **2** (put) **he stuck his head round the door** il a passé la tête dans l'entrebâillement de la porte; **she stuck her hands in her pockets** elle a enfoncé ses mains dans ses poches; **~ your coat on the chair**◦ mets ton manteau sur la chaise; **to ~ an advert in the paper**◦ mettre une annonce dans le journal; **to ~ sb in a home**◦ mettre qn dans une maison de retraite; **3** (fix) coller [poster, stamp] (**to** à); '**~ no bills**' 'défense d'afficher'; **4** ◦GB (bear) supporter [person]; **I can't ~ it any longer** je n'en peux plus; **5** ◦(impose) **to ~ an extra £10 on the price** augmenter le prix de 10 livres; **I was stuck with Frank** je me suis retrouvé avec Frank
D vi (prét, pp **stuck**) **1** [stamp, glue] coller; **to ~ to the pan** [sauce, rice] coller au fond de la casserole, attacher◦; **2** (jam) [drawer, door, lift] se coincer; **3** (remain) rester; **to ~ in sb's memory** ou **mind** rester gravé dans la mémoire de qn; **to make the charges ~** prouver la culpabilité de l'accusé; **~ around**◦! reste là!
⬭ Idioms **to have** ou **get hold of the wrong end of the ~** mal comprendre; **to up ~s**◦ plier bagages
⬭ Phrasal verbs
■ **stick at**: ▶ ~ **at [sth]** persévérer dans [task]; ~ **at it!** persévère!
■ **stick by**: ▶ ~ **by [sb]** rester fidèle à [friend]
■ **stick out**: ▶ ~ **out** [nail, sharp object] dépasser (**of** de); **his ears** ~ **out** il a les oreilles décollées; **his stomach ~s out** il a un gros ventre; **her teeth ~ out** elle a les dents qui avancent; ▶ ~ **[sth] out, ~ out [sth] 1** (cause to protrude) **to ~ out one's hand/foot** tendre la main/le pied; **to ~ out one's chest** bomber le torse; **to ~ one's tongue out** tirer la langue; **2** (cope with) **to ~ it out**◦ tenir le coup◦
■ **stick to**: ▶ ~ **to [sth/sb] 1** (keep to) s'en tenir à [facts, point, plan, diet]; maintenir [story, version]; **2** (follow) suivre; **3** (stay faithful to) rester fidèle à
■ **stick together**: ▶ ~ **together 1** (become fixed to each other) [pages] se coller; **2** ◦(be loyal) se serrer les coudes◦, être solidaire; **3** ◦(not separate) rester ensemble; ▶ ~ **[sth] together** coller [pieces]

■ **stick up**: ▶ ~ **up** (project) se dresser; **to ~ up for sb** (defend) défendre qn; (side with) prendre le parti de qn; **to ~ up for oneself** défendre ses intérêts; ▶ ~ **[sth] up**, ~ **up [sth]** (put up) mettre [*poster, notice*]; ~ **'em up**©! haut les mains!

sticker /'stɪkə(r)/ *n* autocollant *m*

sticker price *n* prix *m* affiché

stick: ~**ing plaster** *n* sparadrap *m*; ~**ing point** *n* point *m* de désaccord; ~ **insect** *n* phasme *m*; ~-**in-the-mud**© *n* routinier/-ière© *m/f*

stickler /'stɪklə(r)/ *n* (person) **to be a ~ for sth** être à cheval sur qch

stick: ~-**on** *adj* [*label*] adhésif/-ive; ~-**up**© *n* braquage© *m*, hold-up *m*

sticky /'stɪkɪ/ *n* [1] (tending to adhere) [*hand, floor, substance*] collant; [*label*] adhésif/-ive; [2] (hot and humid) lourd; [3] (sweaty) moite; **to feel** *ou* **be hot and ~** transpirer; [4] (difficult) [*situation, problem*] difficile

(Idiom) **to come to a ~ end** mal finir

sticky: ~ **bun**© *n* GB petit pain enrobé de sucre; ~ **tape**© *n* GB Scotch® *m*, ruban *m* adhésif

stiff /stɪf/

A © *n* [1] (corpse) macchabée❶ *m*; [2] US (humourless person) rabat-joie *mf inv*

B *adj* [1] (restricted in movement) gen raide; (after sport, sleeping badly) courbaturé; **to have a ~ neck** avoir un torticolis; **to have ~ legs** (after sport) avoir des courbatures dans les jambes; [2] (hard to move) [*drawer*] dur à ouvrir; [*lever*] dur à manier; [3] (rigid) [*cardboard*] raide; [4] Culin **beat the egg whites until ~** battre les blancs en une neige ferme; [5] (not relaxed) [*manner, style*] compassé; [6] (harsh) [*warning, sentence*] sévère; [7] (difficult) [*exam, climb*] difficile; [*competition*] rude; [*opposition*] fort; [8] (high) [*charge, fine*] élevé; [9] (strong) [*breeze*] fort; **a ~ drink** un remontant

C *adv*© **to be bored ~** s'ennuyer à mourir; **to be frozen ~** être frigorifié©; **to be scared ~** avoir une peur bleue; **to scare sb ~** faire une peur bleue à qn

(Idiom) **to keep a ~ upper lip** encaisser© sans broncher

stiffen /'stɪfn/

A *vtr* renforcer [*card*]; raidir [*structure*]; empeser [*fabric*]

B *vi* [1] (grow tense) [*person*] se raidir; [2] Culin [*egg whites*] devenir ferme; [*mixture*] prendre de la consistance; [3] [*joint*] s'ankyloser; [*limbs*] se raidir

stiffly /'stɪflɪ/ *adv* [1] [*say*] avec froideur; ~ **polite** d'une politesse rigide; [2] [*move*] avec raideur

stiffness /'stɪfnɪs/ *n* (physical) raideur *f*; (of manner) froideur *f*

stifle /'staɪfl/ *vtr* étouffer; **it's stifling**! on étouffe!

stigma /'stɪgmə/ *n* (*pl* -**mas** *ou* -**mata**) stigmate *m*

stigmatize /'stɪgmətaɪz/ *vtr* stigmatiser

stile /staɪl/ *n* (in wall, hedge) échalier *m*

stiletto /stɪ'letəʊ/ *n* (*pl* -**tos**) [1] (*also* ~ **heel**) (shoe, heel) talon *m* aiguille; [2] (dagger) stylet *m*

still¹ *adv* [1] (up to and including a point in time) encore; (when nothing has changed) toujours; **eat this bread while it's ~ fresh** mange ce pain pendant qu'il est (encore) frais; **you're ~ too young** (not old enough yet) tu es encore trop jeune; (you were and still are too young) tu es toujours trop jeune; **I ~ have some money left** il me reste encore de l'argent; [2] (expressing surprise) toujours, encore; **I ~ can't believe it!** je n'arrive toujours pas à le croire!; [3] (yet to happen) encore; **it has ~ to be decided** c'est encore à décider; **there is ~ a chance that** il est encore possible que (+ *subj*); **if I'm ~ alive** si je suis encore en vie; [4] (nevertheless) quand même; **it ~ doesn't explain why** cela n'explique toujours pas pourquoi; ~, **it's the thought that counts** enfin, c'est l'intention qui compte; [5] (with comparatives: even) encore; **better/worse ~** encore mieux/pire

still² /stɪl/

A *n* [1] (distillery) distillerie *f*; [2] (photo) photographie *f or* photo *f* de plateau; [3] (quiet) **the ~ of the night** littér le silence de la nuit

B *adj* [1] (motionless) calme; [2] (peaceful) tranquille; [3] [*drink*] non gazeux/-euse; [*water*] plat

C *adv* [1] (immobile) [*lie, stay*] immobile; **to hold [sth] ~** bien tenir [*camera, mirror*]; [2] (calmly) **to sit ~** se tenir tranquille; **to keep** *ou* **stand ~** ne pas bouger

D *vtr* faire taire [*critic*]; calmer [*doubt*]

(Idiom) ~ **waters run deep** il faut se méfier de l'eau qui dort

still: ~**birth** *n* mort *f* à la naissance; ~**born** *adj* lit, fig mort-né/-e; ~ **life** *n* (*pl* -**lifes**) nature *f* morte

stillness /'stɪlnɪs/ *n* (of lake, evening) calme *m*

stilt /stɪlt/ *n* (pole) échasse *f*; **on ~s** monté sur des échasses

stilted /'stɪltɪd/ *adj* guindé

stimulant /'stɪmjʊlənt/ *n* stimulant *m* (**to** de)

stimulate /'stɪmjʊleɪt/ *vtr* stimuler [*appetite, creativity, person*]; encourager [*demand*]

stimulating /'stɪmjʊleɪtɪŋ/ *adj* (all contexts) stimulant

stimulation /ˌstɪmjʊ'leɪʃn/ *n* stimulation *f* (**of** de)

stimulus /'stɪmjʊləs/ (*pl* -**li**) *n* [1] (physical) stimulus *m*; [2] (boost) impulsion *f*; [3] (incentive) stimulant *m*

sting /stɪŋ/

A *n* [1] (of insect) aiguillon *m*; [2] (result of being stung) piqûre *f*; **bee ~** piqûre d'abeille; [3] (pain) sensation *f* de brûlure; [4] ©US (rip-off) arnaque *f*

B *vtr* (*prét, pp* **stung**) [1] [*insect*] piquer; [2] [*wind*] cingler; [3] fig [*criticism*] blesser, piquer [qn] au vif

C *vi* (*prét, pp* **stung**) [*eyes, antiseptic*] piquer; [*cut*] cuire; **my knee ~s** mon genou me cuit

(Idioms) **a ~ in the tail** une mauvaise surprise; **to take the ~ out of** rendre [qch] moins blessant [*remark*]; atténuer l'effet de [*action*]

stingily /'stɪndʒɪlɪ/ *adv* chichement

stinginess /'stɪndʒɪnɪs/ *n* radinerie© *f*

stinging /'stɪŋɪŋ/ *adj* [1] [*remark*] blessant; [2] [*sensation*] de brûlure; [*pain*] cuisant

stinging nettle *n* ortie *f*

stingy /'stɪndʒɪ/ *adj* péj [*person*] radin©; [*firm*] près de ses sous©; [*amount*] mesquin

stink /stɪŋk/

A *n* [1] (stench) (mauvaise) odeur *f*; **there's an awful ~!** ça pue!; [2] ©(row) esclandre *m*; **to kick up** *ou* **cause a ~** causer un esclandre

B *vi* (*prét* **stank**, *pp* **stunk**) puer; **to ~ of petrol/death** puer l'essence/la mort; **it ~s** ça pue; **to ~ of corruption** sentir la corruption à plein nez

stink-bomb *n* boule *f* puante

stinker /'stɪŋkə(r)/ *n* casse-tête *m*; **the test was a real ~** l'interrogation était vachement© dure

stinking /'stɪŋkɪŋ/ *adj* [1] (foul-smelling) puant; [2] ©(horrible) (épith) infect; **a ~ cold** un rhume carabiné

(Idiom) **to be ~ rich**© être bourré de fric©

stint /stɪnt/

A *n* **to do a three-year ~ with a company** travailler trois ans pour une entreprise; **I've done my ~ for today** j'en ai assez fait pour aujourd'hui

B *v refl* **to ~ oneself** se priver (**of** de)

stipend /'staɪpend/ *n* traitement *m* (*salaire*)

stipple /'stɪpl/ *vtr* Tech pointiller; **a ~d effect** un effet granité

stipulate /'stɪpjʊleɪt/ *vtr* stipuler (**that** que)

stipulation /ˌstɪpjʊ'leɪʃn/ *n* condition *f*

stir /stɜː(r)/

A *n* [1] **to give the sauce a ~** remuer la sauce; [2] **to cause (quite) a ~** faire sensation

B *vtr* (*p prés* etc -**rr**-) [1] (mix) remuer [*liquid, sauce*]; mélanger [*paint, powder*]; **to ~ sth into sth** incorporer qch à qch; [2] (move slightly) [*breeze*] agiter [*leaves, papers*]; [3] (move, arouse) émouvoir [*person*]; exciter [*curiosity*]; stimuler [*imagination*]; évoquer [*memories*]; **to ~ sb to pity** inspirer de la pitié à qn

C *vi* (*p prés* etc -**rr**-) [1] (move gently) [*leaves, papers*] trembler; [*curtains*] remuer; [*person*] **to ~ in one's sleep** bouger en dormant; [2] (awaken) bouger

D *v refl* (*p prés* etc -**rr**-) **to ~ oneself** se secouer©

(Phrasal verbs)

■ **stir in**: ▶ ~ **[sth] in**, ~ **in [sth]** incorporer [*flour, powder*]; ajouter [*eggs, milk*].

■ **stir up**: ▶ ~ **[sth] up**, ~ **up [sth]** [1] (whip up) [*wind*] faire voler [*dust, leaves*]; [2] fig provoquer [*trouble*]; attiser [*hatred, unrest*]; remuer [*past*]; **to ~ things up** envenimer les choses; ▶ ~ **[sb] up**, ~ **up [sb]** exciter [*crowd*]

stir-crazy© US *adj* rendu fou/folle par la réclusion

S

stir-fry /'stɜːfraɪ/
A *n* Culin sauté *m*
B *vtr* (*prét, pp* **-fried**) faire sauter [*beef, vegetable*]

stirring /'stɜːrɪŋ/
A *n* **to feel a ~ of desire** avoir une bouffée de désir; **the first ~s of nationalism** les premières manifestations du nationalisme
B *adj* [*story*] passionnant; [*music, performance, speech*] enthousiasmant; **to be ~ stuff** être passionnant

stirrup /'stɪrəp/ *n* (all contexts) étrier *m*

stitch /stɪtʃ/
A *n* ① (in sewing, embroidery) point *m*; (single loop in knitting, crochet) maille *f*; (style of knitting, crochet) point *m*; ② Med point *m* de suture; **to have ~es** se faire recoudre; **she had 10 ~es** on lui a fait 10 points de suture (**in, to** à); **to have one's ~es out** se faire retirer les fils; ③ (pain) point *m* de côté; **to have/get (a) ~** avoir/attraper un point de côté
B *vtr* ① coudre (**to, onto** à); ② Med recoudre
〔Idioms〕 **a ~ in time saves nine** un point à temps en épargne cent; **to be in ~es**○ rire aux larmes; **to have sb in ~es**○ faire rire qn aux larmes
〔Phrasal verbs〕
■ **stitch together**: ▸ **~ [sth] together** lit assembler [*garment*]; fig concocter rapidement [*agreement*]
■ **stitch up**: ▸ **~ up [sth], ~ [sth] up** recoudre

stitching /'stɪtʃɪŋ/ *n* couture *f*

St John's Ambulance Brigade *n* GB *organisation bénévole qui assure les premiers soins*

stoat /stəʊt/ *n* hermine *f*

stock /stɒk/
A *n* ① **𝒞** (in shop, warehouse) stock *m*; **to have sth in ~** (in shop) avoir qch en magasin; (in warehouse) avoir qch en stock; **to be out of ~** [*product, model*] être épuisé; **we're out of ~** nous n'en avons plus; **the smaller size is out of ~** il n'y a plus de petites tailles; ② (supply, store) (on large scale) stock *m* (**of** de); (on domestic scale) provisions *fpl*; **~s are running low** les stocks sont presque épuisés; **to get in** ou **lay in ~s of provisions** faire des stocks; **while ~s last** jusqu'à épuisement des stocks; ③ Fin (capital) ensemble *m* du capital or des actions d'une société; ④ (descent) souche *f*, origine *f*; **to be of peasant ~** être de souche paysanne; **to come from farming ~** venir d'une famille d'agriculteurs; ⑤ (standing) cote *f*; **his ~ has risen** sa cote a monté; ⑥ Culin bouillon *m*; **beef ~** bouillon *m* de bœuf; ⑦ (flower) giroflée *f* d'hiver; ⑧ (cravat) lavallière *f*; ⑨ (+ *v pl*) (cattle) bétail *m*, cheptel *m* bovin; (bloodstock) chevaux *mpl* de race
B **stocks** *npl* ① Hist, Jur **the ~s** le pilori; ② GB Fin valeurs *fpl*, titres *mpl*; **government ~** fonds *mpl* d'État; **~s closed higher/lower** la Bourse a clôturé en hausse/en baisse; **~s and shares** valeurs *fpl* mobilières; ③ US actions *fpl*
C *adj* [*size*] courant; [*answer*] classique; [*character*] stéréotypé
D *vtr* ① Comm (sell) avoir, vendre; **we don't ~ it** nous n'en faisons pas; ② (with supplies) remplir [*larder, fridge*]; garnir [*shelves*]; approvisionner [*shop*]; peupler [*lake*]; **well-~ed** [*garden, library*] bien fourni
〔Idiom〕 fig **to take ~** faire le point (**of** sur)
〔Phrasal verb〕
■ **stock up** s'approvisionner (**with, on** en)

stockade /stɒˈkeɪd/ *n* (fence) palissade *f*

stock: **~broker** ▸ p. 1181 *n* agent *m* de change; **~broker belt** *n* GB banlieue *f* cossue

stockbroking /'stɒkbrəʊkɪŋ/
A *n* commerce *m* de titres en Bourse
B *noun modifier* [*firm*] de courtage en Bourse

stock: **~ car** *n* (for racing) stock-car *m*; **~-car racing** ▸ p. 881 *n* course *f* de stock-cars; **~-cube** *n* bouillon-cube® *m*

stock exchange *n* (*also* **Stock Exchange**) **the ~** la Bourse; **to be listed on the ~** être coté en Bourse

stockholder /'stɒkhəʊldə(r)/ *n* actionnaire *mf*

stocking /'stɒkɪŋ/ ▸ p. 1191 *n* bas *m*; **silk ~** bas de soie; **in one's ~(ed) feet** en chaussettes; **Christmas ~** ≈ soulier *m* de Noël

stock-in-trade *n* spécialité *f*; **irony is part of the ~ of any teacher** l'ironie fait partie de la panoplie de tout professeur

stockist /'stɒkɪst/ *n* Comm dépositaire *mf*

stock market
A *n* ① (stock exchange) Bourse *f* des valeurs; ② (prices, trading activity) marché *m* des valeurs
B *noun modifier* [*crash, trading*] boursier/-ière; [*quotation, flotation*] en Bourse; **~ price** ou **value** cote *f*

stockpile /'stɒkpaɪl/
A *n* réserves *fpl*
B *vtr* stocker [*weapons*]; faire des stocks or des réserves de [*food, goods*]

stock: **~piling** *n* stockage *m*; **~pot** *n* marmite *f*; **~ room** *n* magasin *m*

stock-still *adv* **to stand ~** rester cloué sur place

stocktaking /'stɒkteɪkɪŋ/ *n* inventaire *m*

stocky /'stɒkɪ/ *adj* [*person*] trapu; [*animal*] râblé

stodge○ /stɒdʒ/ *n* **𝒞** GB (food) aliments *mpl* bourratifs

stodgy /'stɒdʒɪ/ *adj* [*food*] bourratif/-ive

stoical /'stəʊɪkl/ *adj* stoïque

stoicism /'stəʊɪsɪzəm/ *n* stoïcisme *m*

stoke /stəʊk/ *vtr* (*also* **~ up**) alimenter [*fire, furnace*]; fig entretenir [*fires, flames*]

stole /stəʊl/
A *prét* ▸ **steal** B, C
B *n* étole *f*

stolen /'stəʊlən/ *pp* ▸ **steal** B, C

stolid /'stɒlɪd/ *adj* [*person, character*] flegmatique

stolidly /'stɒlɪdlɪ/ *adv* imperturbablement

stomach /'stʌmək/
A *n* ① estomac *m*; (belly) ventre *m*; **to have a pain in one's ~** avoir mal au ventre or à l'estomac; **to lie on one's ~** être à plat ventre; **to do sth on an empty ~** faire qch à jeun; **to be sick to one's ~** être profondément dégoûté; **to have a strong ~** lit, fig avoir l'estomac bien accroché○; **to turn sb's ~** écœurer qn
B *noun modifier* [*ulcer, operation*] à l'estomac; [*cancer*] de l'estomac; **to have ~ ache** avoir mal au ventre; **to have ~ trouble** souffrir de troubles gastriques
C *vtr* supporter [*person, attitude*]; **I can't ~ that guy**○! je ne peux pas encaisser○ ce type○!
〔Idiom〕 **your eyes are bigger than your ~** tu as les yeux plus grands que le ventre

stomp /stɒmp/ *vi* (walk heavily) **to ~ in/out** entrer/sortir d'un pas lourd; **he ~ed off in a rage** il est parti à grands pas furieux

stomping ground *n* endroit *m* préféré

stone /stəʊn/ ▸ p. 1323
A *n* ① **𝒞** (material) pierre *f*; (**made of**) **~** en pierre; ② pierre *f*; (slightly smaller) caillou *m*; (standing stone) menhir *m*; (engraved headstone) stèle *f*; **to lay a ~** poser une pierre; **not a ~ was left standing** tout était dévasté; ③ (also **precious ~**) (gem) pierre *f*; ④ (in fruit) noyau *m*; ⑤ Med calcul *m*; **kidney ~** calcul *m* rénal; ⑥ GB (weight) = 6,35 kg
B *noun modifier* [*wall, floor*] en pierre; [*jar*] en grès
C *vtr* ① **to ~ sb to death** lapider qn; ② (remove stone from) dénoyauter [*peach, cherry*]
〔Idioms〕 **to leave no ~ unturned** ne négliger aucun détail; **it's a ~'s throw from here** c'est à deux pas d'ici; **to sink like a ~** couler à pic

Stone Age *n* Âge *m* de pierre

stone circle *n* enceinte *f* de monolithes, cromlech *m*

stone-cold
A *adj* glacé
B *adv* **~ sober** parfaitement sobre

stoned○ /stəʊnd/ *adj* défoncé○; **to get ~** se défoncer○ (**on** à)

stone: **~-deaf** *adj* sourd comme un pot○; **~ mason** ▸ p. 1181 *n* tailleur/-euse *m/f* de pierre

stonewall /ˌstəʊnˈwɔːl/ *vi* ① Sport jouer un jeu défensif; ② (filibuster) faire de l'obstruction

stone: **~walling** *n* obstructionnisme *m*; **~ware** *n* poterie *f* en grès; **~washed** *adj* délavé

stonily /'stəʊnɪlɪ/ *adv* d'un air or d'un ton glacial

stony /'stəʊnɪ/ *adj* ① (rocky) pierreux/-euse; ② fig (cold) [*look, silence*] glacial
〔Idiom〕 **to fall on ~ ground** tomber dans le vide

stony-broke○ *adj* GB fauché○, à sec○

stood /stʊd/ *prét, pp* ▸ **stand** B, C

stooge /stuːdʒ/ n **1** ᵒ(dogsbody) larbin m; **2** (partner in comedy act) faire-valoir m inv

stool /stuːl/ n (furniture) tabouret m

(Idiom) **to fall between two ~s** n'être ni chair ni poisson

stool pigeonᵒ n mouchard/-e m/f

stoop /stuːp/

A n **1** (curvature) **to have a ~** avoir le dos voûté; **to walk with a ~** marcher courbé; **2** US (veranda) perron m

B vi **1** (be bent over) être voûté; **2** (lean forward) se pencher; **to ~ down** se baisser; **3** (debase oneself) **to ~ so low as to do sth** s'abaisser jusqu'à faire qch; **to ~ to lying** s'abaisser jusqu'à mentir

stop /stɒp/

A n **1** (halt, pause) arrêt m; (short stay) gen halte f; (stopover) escale f; **the train makes three ~s** le train fait trois arrêts or s'arrête trois fois; **our next ~ will be (in) Paris** (on tour, trip) notre prochaine halte sera Paris; **next ~ Dover** le prochain arrêt à Douvres; **all these ~s and starts!** tous ces arrêts et redémarrages!; **to bring sth to a ~** arrêter qch; **to come to a ~** s'arrêter; **to put a ~ to** mettre fin à; **2** (stopping place) arrêt m; **3** (in telegram) stop m; **4** (on organ) (pipes) jeu m d'orgues; (knob) registre m d'orgues

B noun modifier [button, lever, signal] d'arrêt

C vtr (p prés etc **-pp-**) **1** (cease) [person] arrêter, cesser [work, noise, activity]; **~ it!** arrête!; (that's enough) ça suffit!; **to ~ doing** arrêter or cesser de faire; **to ~ smoking** arrêter or cesser de fumer; (bring to a halt) (completely) gen arrêter, [strike, power cut] entraîner l'arrêt de [activity, production]; (temporarily) gen interrompre; [strike, power cut] provoquer une interruption de [activity, production]; **rain ~ped play** la pluie a interrompu la partie; **to ~ a bullet** recevoir une balle; **3** (prevent) empêcher [war, publication]; empêcher [qch] d'avoir lieu [event]; arrêter [person]; **what's ~ping you?** qu'est-ce qui te retient?, qu'est-ce qui t'en empêche?; **to ~ sb (from) doing** empêcher qn de faire; **there's nothing to ~ you** faites donc!; **4** (refuse to provide) (definitively) supprimer [allowance]; arrêter [payments, deliveries, subscription]; couper [gas, electricity, water]; (suspend) suspendre [grant, payment, leave]; **to ~ a cheque** faire opposition à un chèque; **to ~ £50 out of sb's pay** GB retenir 50 livres sur le salaire de qn; **5** (plug) boucher [gap, hole]; [leak] arrêter

D vi (p prés etc **-pp-**) **1** (halt) s'arrêter; **2** (cease) gen s'arrêter; [pain, worry] cesser; **not to know when to ~** ne pas savoir s'arrêter; **this is going to have to ~** il va falloir que cela cesse; **without ~ping** sans arrêt; **you didn't ~ to think** tu n'as pas pris le temps de réfléchir; **3** ᵒGB (stay) rester; **to ~ for dinner** rester dîner; **I can't ~** je n'ai vraiment pas le temps

E v refl (p prés etc **-pp-**) **I can't ~ myself** je ne peux pas m'en empêcher; **I nearly fell but I ~ped myself** j' ai failli tomber mais je me suis rattrapé

(Idiom) **to pull out all the ~s** frapper un grand coup (**to do** pour faire)

(Phrasal verbs)

■ **stop by**ᵒ: ▸ **~ by** passer; **to ~ by Brad's** passer chez Brad; ▸ **~ by [sth]** passer à [shop, café]

■ **stop off** faire un arrêt; **to ~ off in Bristol** faire un arrêt à Bristol; **to ~ off at Paul's house** passer chez Paul

■ **stop over** (breaking journey) faire escale

■ **stop up**: ▸ **~ [sth] up**, **~ up [sth]** boucher [hole]

stopcock n robinet m d'arrêt

stopgap /stɒpgæp/
A n bouche-trou m
B noun modifier [measure] provisoire

stop: **~-go** adj [policy] d'oscillation; **~-off** n (quick break) arrêt m; (longer) halte f; **~over** n escale f

stoppage /stɒpɪdʒ/ n **1** (strike) interruption f (de travail); **2** GB (deduction from wages) retenue f (sur salaire)

stopper /stɒpə(r)/ n (for bottle, jar) bouchon m

stopping /stɒpɪŋ/
A n 'no ~' 'arrêt m interdit'
B noun modifier Aut [distance, time] d'arrêt

stopping train n omnibus m

stop-press /stɒp'pres/ n dernières nouvelles fpl

stop: **~ sign** n (panneau m de) stop m; **~watch** n chronomètre m

storage /stɔːrɪdʒ/
A n **1** (of food, fuel, goods) stockage m; **to be in ~** [furniture] être au garde-meuble; **2** (space) espace m de rangement;

3 Comput (facility) mémoire f; (process) mise f en mémoire
B noun modifier [compartment, space] de rangement

storage: **~ device** n Comput mémoire f; **~ heater** n Elec radiateur m électrique à accumulation; **~ jar** n (glass) bocal m (de rangement); **~ tank** n réservoir m, tank m; **~ unit** n (cupboard) meuble m de rangement

store /stɔː(r)/
A n **1** ▸ p. 1181 (shop) magasin m; (smaller) boutique f; **the big ~s** les grands magasins; **2** (supply) (of food, fuel, paper) réserve f, provision f; (of information) fonds mpl; **3** (place) (for food, fuel) réserve f; (for furniture) garde-meuble m; (for military supplies) magasin m; **4** (storage) **to put sth in(to) ~** mettre qch au garde-meuble [furniture]; mettre qch en magasin, entreposer [goods]; fig **what's in ~ in 2006?** qu'est-ce que 2006 nous réserve?

B **stores** npl (supplies) provisions fpl

C vtr **1** (keep till needed) conserver [food, information]; ranger [objects, furniture]; stocker [nuclear waste, chemicals]; engranger [crops, grain]; **2** Comput mettre [qch] en mémoire, mémoriser [data]

(Idiom) **to set great ~ by sth** attacher beaucoup d'importance à qch

(Phrasal verb)

■ **store up**: ▸ **~ up [sth]** accumuler; **you're storing up trouble for yourself** tu ne fais qu'accumuler les ennuis

store: **~ cupboard** n armoire f de rangement; **~ detective** ▸ p. 1181 n surveillant/-e m/f (dans un magasin); **~house** n entrepôt m; **~keeper** ▸ p. 1181 n US commerçant/-e m/f; **~room** n (in house, school, office) réserve f; (in factory, shop) magasin m

storey GB, **story** US /stɔːrɪ/ n (pl **-reys** GB, **-ries** US) étage m; **on the third ~** GB au troisième étage; US au quatrième étage; **a three-storeyed building** GB, **a three storied building** US un bâtiment de trois étages

stork /stɔːk/ n cigogne f

storm /stɔːm/
A n **1** (weather) tempête f; (thunderstorm) orage m; **the ~ broke** la tempête a éclaté; **to weather a ~** fig surmonter une mauvaise passe; **2** (attack) **to take a town by ~** Mil prendre une ville d'assaut; **she took Broadway by ~** fig elle a remporté un succès foudroyant à Broadway; **3** (outburst) tempête f; **a ~ of criticism** une tempête de critiques

B vtr **1** (invade) prendre [qch] d'assaut [citadel, prison]; **2** (roar) **'get out!' he ~ed** 'sortez!' cria-t-il dans un accès de colère

C vi **to ~ off** partir avec fracas; **he ~ed off in a temper** il est parti furibond

storm: **~cloud** n lit nuage m orageux; fig nuage m noir; **~ damage** n dégâts mpl causés par la tempête; **~ door** n double porte f; **~ force wind** n vent m de tempête

storming /stɔːmɪŋ/ n prise f

storm: **~ lantern** n lampe-tempête f; **~ trooper** n membre m de section d'assaut; **~ warning** n avis m de tempête; **~ window** n double fenêtre f

stormy /stɔːmɪ/ adj **1** [weather, sky, night] orageux/-euse; [sea] houleux/-euse; **2** (turbulent) [meeting] houleux/-euse; [relationship] orageux/-euse; **~ scenes** éclats mpl

story /stɔːrɪ/ n **1** (account) histoire f (of de); **it's a true ~** c'est une histoire vécue; **to stick to/change one's ~** maintenir/changer sa version des faits; **what is the real ~?** où est la vérité?; **2** (tale) gen histoire f (about, of de); Literat conte m (of de); **read us a (bedtime) ~!** tu nous lis une histoire?; **3** (in newspaper) article m (on, about sur); **exclusive ~** reportage m exclusif; **4** (lie) histoire f; **to make up a ~** inventer une histoire (**about** à propos de); **5** (rumour) rumeur f (**about** sur); **6** (also ~ line) histoire f; **7** US (floor) étage m; **first ~** rez-de-chaussée m; **second ~** premier étage m

(Idioms) **but that's another ~** mais ça c'est une autre histoire; **to cut a long ~ short** bref; **that's not the whole ~** ce n'est pas tout; **that's the ~ of my life!** c'est toujours la même chose, avec moi!; **it's always the same ~**, **it's the same old ~** c'est toujours la même chose; **every picture tells a ~** ça se passe de commentaires; **a likely ~!** elle est bien bonne, celle-là°!; **the ~ goes/has it that** on raconte/dit que; **what's the ~**°? qu'est-ce qui se passe?

storybook /stɔːrɪbʊk/ n livre m de contes

storyteller /stɔːrɪtelə(r)/ n **1** (writer) conteur/-euse m/f; **2** (liar) menteur/-euse m/f

stout /staʊt/
A n (drink) stout f
B adj **1** (fat) [person] corpulent; [animal] gros/grosse; **to grow ~** s'épaissir; **2** (strong) gros/grosse (before n); **3** (valiant) acharné

stoutly /'staʊtlɪ/ adv [deny, resist] avec acharnement

stoutness /'staʊtnɪs/ n (of person) corpulence f

stove /stəʊv/ n **1** (cooker) cuisinière f; **electric/gas ~** cuisinière électrique/à gaz; **2** (heater) poêle m
(Idiom) **to slave over a hot ~** hum trimer devant ses fourneaux

stow /stəʊ/ vtr (pack) ranger [baggage, ropes]
(Phrasal verb)
■ **stow away:** ▸ **~ away** voyager clandestinement; ▸ **~ [sth] away, ~ away [sth]** ranger [baggage]

stowaway /'stəʊəweɪ/ n passager/-ère m/f clandestin/-e

straddle /'strædl/
A n (also **~ jump**) Sport rouleau m (ventral)
B vtr **1** (physically) [person] enfourcher [horse, bike]; s'asseoir à califourchon sur [chair]; **2** (geographically) [village] être traversé par [border]

strafe /strɑːf, streɪf/ vtr mitrailler [qn] en rase-mottes

straggle /'strægl/
A vi **1** (spread untidily) **to ~ along** s'étendre au hasard le long de [road, beach, railtrack]; **2** (dawdle) traîner
B **straggling** pres p adj [village, suburb] s'étendant au hasard

straggler /'stræglə(r)/ n traînard/-e m/f

straggly /'stræglɪ/ adj [hair, beard] en désordre

straight /streɪt/
A n Sport ligne f droite; **back ~** côté m opposé de la piste; **home ~** dernière ligne droite
B adj **1** (not bent or curved) gen droit; [hair] raide; **dead ~** gen tout droit; **in a ~ line** en ligne droite; **2** (level, upright) gen bien droit; [bedclothes, tablecloth] bien mis; **the picture/your tie isn't ~** le tableau/ta cravate est de travers; **3** (tidy, in order) en ordre; **to get** ou **put sth ~** lit, fig mettre qch en ordre; **4** (clear) **to get [sth] ~** comprendre qch; **now let's get one thing ~** que ce soit bien clair; **to put sb ~ about sth** éclairer qn sur qch; **to put** ou **set the record ~** établir la vérité; **5** (honest, direct) [person] honnête, droit; [answer] clair; **to be ~ with sb** jouer franc-jeu avec qn; **6** (unconditional) [majority, profit] net/nette; [choice] simple; **to do a ~ swap** faire simplement l'échange; **~ fight** GB Pol une élection à deux candidats; **7** (undiluted) [drink] sec, sans eau; **8** (consecutive) [wins, defeats] consécutif/-ive; **she got ~ 'A's** Sch elle a eu très bien partout; **in ~ sets** Sport en deux (or trois) sets; **9** Theat [actor, role] sérieux/-ieuse; **10** ○(heterosexual) hétéro○ inv
C adv **1** (not obliquely) gen droit; [shoot] juste; **stand up ~!** tenez-vous droit!; **sit up ~!** asseyez-vous convenablement!; **she held her arm out ~** elle a étendu le bras devant elle; **to go/keep ~ ahead** aller/continuer tout droit; **to look ~ ahead** regarder droit devant soi; **to look sb ~ in the eye** regarder qn droit dans les yeux; **he headed ~ for the bar** il s'est dirigé droit vers le bar; **the car was coming ~ at me** la voiture se dirigeait droit sur moi; **she was looking ~ at me** elle me regardait droit dans ma direction; **~ above our heads** juste au-dessus de nos têtes; **~ up in the air** droit en l'air; **the bullet went ~ through his body** la balle lui a traversé le corps de part en part; **they drove ~ past me** ils sont passés droit devant moi; **she drove ~ into a tree** elle est rentrée droit dans un arbre; **2** (without delay) directement; **to go ~ back to Paris** rentrer directement à Paris; **she wrote ~ back** elle a répondu immédiatement; **to come ~ to the point** aller droit au fait; **~ after tout de suite après; **~ away, ~ off** tout de suite; **he read it ~ off** il l'a lu d'une seule traite; **she told him ~ out that** elle lui a dit carrément or sans ambages que; **it seemed like something ~ out of the Middle Ages** cela semblait sortir tout droit du Moyen Âge; **3** (frankly) tout net; **I'll tell you ~** je vous le dirai tout net; **give it to me ~** dis-moi la vérité; **~ out** carrément; **to play ~ with sb** fig jouer franc-jeu avec qn; **4** Theat [act, produce] de manière classique; **5** (neat) [drink] sec or sans eau
(Idioms) **to keep a ~ face** garder son sérieux; **the ~ and narrow** le droit chemin; **to go ~**○ [criminal] se ranger; **~ up?**○ GB sans blague○?

straightaway /'streɪtəweɪ/ adv tout de suite

straighten /'streɪtn/ vtr **1** tendre [arm, leg]; redresser [picture, teeth]; ajuster [tie, hat]; refaire (en ligne droite) [road]; **to ~ one's back** ou **shoulders** se redresser; **to have one's nose ~ed** se faire refaire le nez; **to have one's teeth ~ed** se faire redresser les dents; **2** (tidy) mettre [qch] en ordre [room]; mettre de l'ordre sur [desk]
(Phrasal verbs)
■ **straighten out:** ▸ **~ out** [road] devenir droit; ▸ **~ out [sth], ~ [sth] out** fig tirer [qch] au clair [problem]; **to ~ things out** arranger les choses
■ **straighten up:** ▸ **~ up** **1** lit [person] se redresser; **2** fig (tidy up) mettre de l'ordre; ▸ **~ up [sb/sth], ~ [sb/sth] up** (tidy) ranger [objects, room]; **to ~ oneself up** s'arranger

straight-faced adj à l'air sérieux

straightforward /ˌstreɪtfɔːˈwəd/ adj **1** (honest) [answer, person] franc/franche; **2** (simple) [account, explanation, case, question] simple

straight: **~-laced** adj collet-monté inv; **~ man** n Theat faire-valoir m inv

straightness /'streɪtnɪs/ n (of hair) raideur f

strain /streɪn/
A n **1** gen, Phys (weight) effort m, contrainte f (**on** sur); (from pulling) tensions fpl (**on** de); **to put a ~ on** fatiguer [heart, lungs]; **to take the ~** [beam, rope] être soumis à des efforts or des sollicitations; **the rope can't take the ~** la corde ne résistera pas; **2** (pressure) (on person) stress m; (in relations) tension f; **mental** ou **nervous ~** tension f nerveuse; **to put a ~ on** avoir un effet néfaste sur [relationship]; créer des tensions au sein de [alliance]; grever [economy, finances]; mettre [qch] à rude épreuve [patience, goodwill]; **to be under ~** [person] être stressé; [relations] être tendu; **he can't take the ~** il supporte mal la situation; **the ~ was beginning to tell** la fatigue commençait à se faire sentir; **it's getting to be a ~** ça commence à devenir pénible; **3** (injury) muscle m froissé; **4** (breed) (of animal) race f; (of plant, seed) variété f; (of virus, bacteria) souche f; **5** (style) veine f, ton m; **in the same ~** dans la même veine
B **strains** npl air m; **to the ~s of** aux accents de
C vtr **1** **to ~ one's eyes** (to see) plisser les yeux; **to ~ one's ears** tendre l'oreille; **to ~ every muscle** tendre tous ses muscles; **2** fig grever [resources, finances]; compromettre [relationship]; mettre [qch] à rude épreuve [patience]; **3** (injure) **to ~ a muscle** se froisser un muscle; **to ~ one's shoulder** se froisser un muscle de l'épaule; **to ~ one's eyes** se fatiguer les yeux; **to ~ one's back** se faire un tour de reins; **4** (sieve) passer [sauce]; égoutter [vegetables, pasta]
D vi **to ~ at** tirer sur [leash, rope]
(Phrasal verb)
■ **strain off:** ▸ **~ [sth] off, ~ off [sth]** faire égoutter [water, liquid, fat]

strained /streɪnd/ adj **1** (tense) tendu; **2** (injured) [muscle] froissé; **3** (sieved) [baby food] en purée

strainer /'streɪnə(r)/ n passoire f

strait /streɪt/
A n Geog détroit m; **the Straits of Gibraltar** le détroit de Gibraltar
B **straits** npl **to be in dire ~s** être aux abois

straitened /'streɪtnd/ adj **in ~ circumstances** dans la gêne

straitjacket /'streɪtdʒækɪt/ n **1** lit camisole f de force; **2** fig carcan m

strait laced /ˌstreɪt 'leɪst/ adj collet monté inv

strand /strænd/
A n **1** (of hair) mèche f; (of fibre, wire) fil m; (of beads) rangée f; **2** fig (element) élément m
B vtr **to be ~ed** être bloqué; **to leave sb ~ed** laisser qn en rade○
C **stranded** pp adj [climber, traveller] bloqué

strange /streɪndʒ/ adj **1** (unfamiliar) inconnu; **a ~ man** un inconnu; **2** (odd) bizarre; **it is ~ (that)** il est bizarre que (+ subj); **it feels ~** cela fait une drôle d'impression; **there's something ~ about her** elle a quelque chose de bizarre; **in a ~ way... curieusement...; **as that might seem** aussi bizarre que cela puisse paraître; **~ but true** incroyable mais vrai; **~ to say** c'est curieux à dire; **3** (unwell) bizarre; **4** (unaccustomed) **to be ~ to** être étranger/-ère à

strangely /'streɪndʒlɪ/ adj [behave, react] d'une façon étrange; [quiet, empty] étrangement; **she looks ~ familiar** c'est curieux, son visage ne m'est pas étranger; **~ enough,...** chose étrange,...

strangeness /'streɪndʒnɪs/ n (of place, routine, thought, feeling) étrangeté f

stranger /'streɪndʒə(r)/ n étranger/-ère m/f; **a complete** ou **total ~** un parfait inconnu; **'hello, ~[○]!'** 'tiens, un revenant[○]!'; **I'm a ~ here myself!** je ne suis pas d'ici!

strangers' gallery n GB tribune f réservée au public

strangle /'stræŋgl/ vtr 1⃝ (throttle) [person] étrangler; **to ~ sb to death** tuer qn par strangulation; **I could cheerfully have ~d him** hum je l'aurais étranglé de bon cœur; 2⃝ (stifle) étouffer [creativity, project]; entraver [development, growth]

stranglehold /'stræŋglhəʊld/ n 1⃝ (physical grip) étranglement m; 2⃝ fig (powerful control) mainmise f

strangler /'stræŋglə(r)/ n étrangleur/-euse m/f

strangulate /'stræŋgjʊleɪt/ vtr étrangler

strangulation /ˌstræŋgjʊ'leɪʃn/ n 1⃝ (of person) strangulation f; 2⃝ fig (of economy) étranglement m

strap /stræp/

A⃝ n 1⃝ (on shoe) bride f; (on bag, case, harness) courroie f; (on watch) bracelet m; (on handbag) bandoulière f; (on bus, train) poignée f; (on dress, bra, overalls) bretelle f; **the ~ has broken** la bretelle a lâché; 2⃝ †(punishment) martinet m

B⃝ vtr (p prés etc -pp-) 1⃝ (secure) attacher (to à); **to ~ sb into** attacher qn dans [pram]; **to ~ sb/sth down** ou **in** ou **on** attacher qn/qch; 2⃝ Sport (bandage) bander

straphanger n voyageur/-euse m/f debout (inv)

strapless /'stræplɪs/ adj [bra, dress] sans bretelles

strapped[○] /stræpt/ adj **to be ~ for** être à court de [cash, staff]

strapping /'stræpɪŋ/ adj costaud

strata /'strɑːtə, US 'streɪtə/ pl ▸ stratum

stratagem /'strætədʒəm/ n stratagème m

strategic /strə'tiːdʒɪk/, **strategical** /strə'tiːdʒɪkl/ adj stratégique

strategically /strə'tiːdʒɪklɪ/ adv [plan, develop] stratégiquement; [important, placed] du point de vue stratégique

strategist /'strætədʒɪst/ n stratège m

strategy /'strætədʒɪ/ n stratégie f; **business ~** stratégie des affaires

stratosphere /'strætəsfɪə(r)/ n stratosphère f

stratum /'strɑːtəm, US 'streɪtəm/ n (pl **-ta**) (social) couche f; (in geology) strate f

straw /strɔː/

A⃝ n paille f; (stem) fétu m or brin m de paille; (for thatch) chaume m; (for drinking) paille f

B⃝ noun modifier [bag, hat] de paille

(Idioms) **to draw the short ~** tirer le mauvais numéro; **to grasp** ou **clutch at ~s** se raccrocher à une chimère; **the last** ou **final ~** la goutte qui fait déborder le vase; **a ~ in the wind** un indice

strawberry /'strɔːbrɪ, US -berɪ/

A⃝ n fraise f; **wild ~** fraise des bois; **strawberries and cream** fraises à la crème; **~ bed** carré m de fraises

B⃝ noun modifier [flan, tart] aux fraises; [ice cream] à la fraise; [jam, field] de fraises

strawberry blonde

A⃝ n femme f aux cheveux blond vénitien

B⃝ adj [hair] blond vénitien inv

straw: ~-coloured adj paille inv; **~ poll** n Pol sondage m non-officiel

stray /streɪ/

A⃝ n (animal) animal m égaré; (dog) chien m errant; (cat) chat m vagabond

B⃝ adj [dog] errant; [cat] vagabond; [sheep] égaré; [bullet] perdu; [car, tourist] isolé

C⃝ vi 1⃝ lit (wander) gen s'égarer; **to ~ from the road** s'écarter de la route; **to ~ from the house** s'éloigner de la maison; **to ~ onto the road** [animal] divaguer sur la route; 2⃝ fig [eyes, mind] errer; [thoughts] vagabonder; **to ~ from the point** s'écarter du sujet; 3⃝ (commit adultery) avoir une aventure

streak /striːk/

A⃝ n 1⃝ (in character) côté m; 2⃝ (period) **to be on a winning/losing ~** être dans une bonne/mauvaise passe; 3⃝ (mark)

(of paint, substance, water) traînée f; (of light) rai m; **~ of lightning** éclair m; 4⃝ (in hair) mèche f; **to have ~s done** se faire faire des mèches

B⃝ vtr 1⃝ (make lines across) strier [sea, sky]; 2⃝ (in hairdressing) **to get one's hair ~ed** se faire faire des mèches

C⃝ vi (move fast) **to ~ past** passer comme une flèche

D⃝ **streaked** pp adj (with tears) sillonné (**with** de); (with dirt) maculé (**with** de); (with colour, light) strié (**with** de)

streaky /'striːkɪ/ adj [surface] couvert de traînées

streaky bacon n GB bacon m entrelardé

stream /striːm/

A⃝ n 1⃝ ruisseau m; 2⃝ fig **a ~ of** un flot de [traffic, customers, questions]; un jet de [light]; une coulée de [lava]; un écoulement de [water]; **a ~ of abuse** un torrent d'insultes; 3⃝ GB, Sch groupe m de niveau; **the top/middle/bottom ~** le groupe des élèves forts/moyens/faibles

B⃝ vtr GB, Sch répartir [qch/qn] en groupes de niveau

C⃝ vi 1⃝ (flow) ruisseler; **sunlight was ~ing into the room** le soleil entrait à flots dans la pièce; **tears were ~ing down his face** les larmes ruisselaient le long de ses joues; 2⃝ (move) **people ~ed out of the theatre** un flot de gens sortait du théâtre; **they ~ed through the gates** ils ont franchi le portail en foule; 3⃝ [banners, hair] **to ~ in the wind** flotter au vent; 4⃝ [eyes, nose] couler; **my eyes were ~ing** j'avais les yeux qui coulaient

streamer /'striːmə(r)/ n (of paper) banderole f

streaming /'striːmɪŋ/

A⃝ n GB, Sch répartition f par groupes de niveau

B⃝ [○]adj **a ~ cold** un très gros rhume

streamline /'striːmlaɪn/ vtr 1⃝ (in design) caréner; 2⃝ (make more efficient) rationaliser [distribution, production]; euph (cut back) dégraisser [company]

streamlined /'striːmlaɪnd/ adj 1⃝ (in design) [cooker, furniture] aux lignes modernes; [hull, body] caréné; 2⃝ (more efficient) [production, system] simplifié

stream of consciousness n courant m de conscience

street /striːt/

A⃝ n rue f; **in** ou **on the ~** dans la rue; **across** ou **over** GB **the ~** de l'autre côté de la rue; **to take to the ~s** [rioters] descendre dans la rue; **the man in the ~** l'homme de la rue

B⃝ noun modifier [plan] des rues; [culture] de la rue

(Idioms) **it's right up your ~[○]** (taste) c'est exactement ce qui te plairait; (ability, dexterity etc) c'est ton rayon; **to be ~s ahead of**[○] GB être bien meilleur que

street: ~car n US tramway m; **~ cleaner** n (person) balayeur m; (machine) balayeuse f; **~ clothes** npl US habits mpl de tous les jours

street cred[○] /ˌstriːt 'kred/ n **to have ~** être dans le coup[○]

street: ~ door n porte f d'entrée; **~ guide** n indicateur m des rues; **~ lamp** n (old gas-lamp) réverbère m; (modern) lampadaire m

street level n rez-de-chaussée m; **at ~** au rez-de-chaussée

street: ~ light n réverbère m; **~ lighting** n éclairage m des rues; **~ market** n marché m en plein air; **~ plan** n ▸ **street guide**; **~ theatre** GB, **~ theater** US n théâtre m de rue; **~ value** n valeur f à la revente; **~ walker** n prostituée f; **~ wise**[○] adj [person] dégourdi[○]

strength /streŋθ/ n 1⃝ (power) (of person, wind, government) force f; (of lens, magnet, voice, army, economy) puissance f; **to build up one's ~** (after illness) reprendre des forces; 2⃝ (dynamism, resources) forces fpl; **to save one's ~** ménager ses forces; 3⃝ (toughness) (of structure, equipment) solidité f; (of material, substance) résistance f; 4⃝ (concentration) (of solution) titre m; (of dose) concentration f; **alcoholic ~** teneur f en alcool; 5⃝ (intensity) (of bond) force f; (of feeling) intensité f; (of bulb) puissance f; 6⃝ Fin fermeté f; **to gain ~** se raffermir; 7⃝ (resolution) force f; **~ of character** force de caractère; **~ of purpose** détermination f; 8⃝ (credibility) (of argument) force f; (of case, claim) solidité f; **convicted on the ~ of the evidence** condamné sur la base des témoignages; **I got the job on the ~ of my research** j'ai obtenu le poste grâce à mes recherches; 9⃝ (asset) qualité f; 10⃝ (total size) **at full ~** au complet; **to bring the team up to ~** compléter l'équipe

(Idioms) **to go from ~ to ~** (person) aller de succès en succès; **give me ~[○]!** hum c'est pas possible[○]!

S

strengthen /'streŋθn/
A vtr renforcer [*building, government, argument, love, position*]; consolider [*bond, links*]; affirmer [*power, role*]; fortifier [*muscles*]; raffermir [*dollar, economy*]; **to ~ sb's hand** fig consolider la position de qn

B vi [*muscles*] se fortifier; [*wind*] augmenter (de force); [*economy, yen*] se raffermir (**against** vis-à-vis de)

strengthening /'streŋθnɪŋ/
A n (of numbers of people) renforcement m; (of bond, ties) **a ~ of the ties between us** une coopération plus étroite

B adj [*current, wind*] qui augmente de forces (*after n*); [*currency, pound*] qui se consolide (*after n*)

strenuous /'strenjʊəs/ adj **1** (demanding) [*exercise*] énergique; [*day, schedule*] chargé; [*work, activity, job*] ardu; **2** (determined) [*protest, disagreement*] vigoureux/-euse; [*effort*] acharné

strenuously /'strenjʊəslɪ/ adv [*deny*] vigoureusement

stress /stres/
A n **1** (nervous) tension f, stress m; **emotional/mental ~** tension émotionnelle/nerveuse; **signs of ~** signes mpl de tension; **to be under ~** ou **suffer from ~** être stressé; **in times of ~** en période de stress; **the ~es and strains of modern life** les agressions fpl de la vie moderne; **2** (emphasis) **to lay** ou **put ~ on** mettre l'accent m sur, insister sur [*fact, problem*]; **3** Phys effort m; **subject to high ~es** soumis à des efforts importants; **4** Ling (in particular case) accent m; **the ~ falls on...** l'accent tombe sur...; **5** (whole system) accentuation f

B vtr **1** (emphasize) mettre l'accent m or insister sur [*issue, difficulty, advantage*]; **to ~ the importance of sth** souligner l'importance f de qch; **to ~ the need for sth/to do** souligner la nécessité de qch/de faire; **to ~ the point that** insister sur le fait que; **to ~ (that)** souligner que; **2** Ling, Mus accentuer [*note, syllable*]

(Phrasal verb)
■ **stress out**○: ▶ **~ [sb] out** stresser [qn]

stressed /strest/ adj **1** gen (also **~ out**) (emotionally) stressé; **to feel ~** se sentir stressé; **2** Phys (épith) [*components, covering, structure*] travaillant; **3** Ling accentué

stress: ~ fracture n fracture f de fatigue; **~-free** adj antistress inv

stressful /'stresfl/ adj stressant

stress mark n accent m

stretch /stretʃ/
A n **1** (in gymnastics) extension f; **to have a ~** s'étirer; **to be at full ~** [*rope, elastic*] être tendu au maximum; [*factory, office*] être à plein régime; **at a ~** fig à la rigueur; **2** (elasticity) élasticité f; **3** (section) (of road, track) tronçon m; (of coastline, river) partie f; **4** (of water, countryside) étendue f; **5** (period) période f; **I did an 18-month ~ in Tokyo** j'ai travaillé 18 mois à Tokyo; **to work for 12 hours at a ~** travailler 12 heures d'affilée; **6** ○(prison sentence) peine f

B adj [*fabric, waist*] extensible; [*limo*] longue

C vtr **1** (extend) tendre [*rope, spring, net*]; **to ~ one's arms** s'étirer les bras; **to ~ one's legs** fig se dégourdir les jambes; **to ~ one's wings** lit, fig déployer ses ailes; **2** (increase the size) lit étirer [*elastic*]; tirer sur [*fabric*]; élargir [*shoe*]; (distort) déformer [*garment, shoe*]; **3** fig déformer [*truth*]; contourner [*rules, regulations*]; **to ~ a point** (make concession) faire une exception; (exaggerate) aller trop loin; **4** (push to the limit) abuser de [*patience*]; utiliser [qch] au maximum [*budget, resources*]; pousser [qn] au maximum de ses possibilités [*person*]; **the system is ~ed to the limit** le système est surchargé; **I need a job that ~es me** j'ai besoin d'un travail qui me stimule; **isn't that ~ing it a bit**○? vous ne poussez pas un peu○?; **5** (eke out) faire durer [*supplies*]

D vi **1** (extend one's limbs) s'étirer; **2** [*road, track, event*] s'étaler (**for, over** sur); [*forest, water, beach, moor*] s'étendre (**for** sur); **to ~ to** ou **as far as sth** [*flex, string*] aller jusqu'à qch; **how far does the queue ~?** jusqu'où va la queue?; **the weeks ~ed into months** les semaines devenaient des mois; **3** (become larger) [*elastic*] s'étendre; [*shoe*] s'élargir; (undesirably) [*fabric, garment*] se déformer; **4** (afford) **I think I can ~ to a bottle of wine** je pense que je peux me permettre une bouteille de vin; **the budget won't ~ to a new computer** le budget ne peut pas supporter l'achat d'un nouvel ordinateur

E v refl **to ~ oneself** s'étirer; fig faire un effort

(Phrasal verb)
■ **stretch out**: ▶ **~ out** s'étendre; ▶ **~ out [sth], ~ [sth] out** tendre [*hand, foot*]; étendre [*arm, leg*]; étaler [*nets, sheet*]; **I ~ed my speech out to an hour** j'ai fait durer mon discours pendant une heure

stretcher /'stretʃə(r)/ n Med brancard m

stretcher: ~-bearer ▸ p. 1181 n brancardier/-ière m/f; **~ case** n blessé/-e m/f grave (incapable de se déplacer)

stretch mark n vergeture f

stretchy /'stretʃɪ/ adj extensible

strew /struː/ vtr (prét **strewed**; pp **strewed** ou **strewn**) éparpiller [*clothes, litter, paper*]; répandre [*sand, straw, wreckage*]; semer [*flowers*]

stricken /'strɪkən/ adj **1** [*face, look, voice*] affligé; [*area*] sinistré; **~ with, ~ by** frappé de [*illness*]; pris de [*fear, guilt*]; atteint de [*chronic illness*]; **2** [*plane, ship*] en détresse

strict /strɪkt/ adj (not lenient) gen strict (**about** sur); [*view*] rigide; [*silence*] absolu; [*Catholic*] de stricte observance; **in ~ confidence** à titre strictement confidentiel; **in ~ secrecy** dans le plus grand secret; **on the ~ understanding that** à la condition expresse que

strictly /'strɪktlɪ/ adv **1** [*treat*] avec sévérité; **2** (absolutely) [*confidential, functional*] strictement; **~ speaking** à proprement parler; **~ between ourselves...** que ceci reste entre nous...; **that is not ~ true** ceci n'est pas tout à fait vrai

strictness /'strɪktnɪs/ n gen sévérité f; (of views, principles) rigueur f

stricture /'strɪktʃə(r)/ n condamnation f (**against** de)

stride /straɪd/
A n **1** (long step) enjambée f; **2** (gait) démarche f; **to lengthen one's ~** allonger le pas

B vi (prét **strode**; pp **stridden**) **to ~ across/out/in** traverser/sortir/entrer à grands pas; **to ~ up and down sth** arpenter qch

(Idioms) **to get into one's ~** trouver son rythme; **to make great ~s** faire de grands progrès; **to put sb off his/her ~** faire perdre le rythme à qn; **to take sth in one's ~** (cope practically) prendre qch calmement; (cope emotionally) accepter qch avec sérénité

strident /'straɪdnt/ adj [*sound, voice*] strident; [*statement, group*] véhément

strife /straɪf/ n (conflict) conflits mpl (**among** au sein de; **in** dans); (dissent) querelles fpl

strife-torn, strife-ridden adj déchiré par les conflits

strike /straɪk/
A n **1** Ind, Comm grève f; **to come out on ~** se mettre en grève; **2** (attack) attaque f (**on, against** contre); **3** (in mining) découverte f (d'un gisement); **lucky ~** fig coup m de chance

B noun modifier Ind, Comm [*committee, notice*] de grève; [*leader*] des grévistes

C vtr (prét, pp **struck**) **1** (hit) gen frapper; heurter [*rock, tree, pedestrian*]; **to ~ sth with** taper qch avec; **he struck his head on the table** il s'est cogné la tête contre la table; **to be struck by lightning** être touché par la foudre; **to ~ sb a blow** lit, fig porter un coup à qn; **to ~ sb dead** [*lightning*] foudroyer qn; **to be struck dumb with amazement** être frappé d'étonnement; **2** (afflict) frapper [*area, people*]; **'earthquake ~s San Francisco'** (headline) 'San Francisco secoué par un tremblement de terre'; **to ~ terror into sb** ou **sb's heart** frapper qn de terreur; **3** (make impression on) [*idea, thought*] venir à l'esprit de; [*resemblance*] frapper; **it ~s me as funny that** je trouve drôle que (+ subj); **to ~ sb as odd** paraître étrange à qn; **how does the idea ~ you?** qu'est-ce que vous pensez de cette idée?; **how did he ~ you?** quelle impression vous a-t-il faite?; **it ~s me (that)** à mon avis; **I was struck**○ **with him** il m'a plu; **4** ○(discover) tomber sur○; **5** (achieve) conclure [*bargain*]; **to ~ a balance** trouver le juste milieu; **6** (ignite) frotter [*match*]; **7** [*clock*] sonner; **it had just struck two** deux heures venaient de sonner; **8** (delete) supprimer; **9** (dismantle) démonter [*tent*]; **to ~ camp** lever le camp; **10** Fin frapper [*coin*]

D vi (prét, pp **struck**) **1** (deliver blow) [*person*] frapper; [*bomb*] tomber; **my head struck against a beam** ma tête a heurté une poutre; **to ~ at** attaquer; **2** (attack) [*killer, disease, storm*] frapper; [*army, animal*] attaquer; **disaster struck** la catastrophe s'est produite; **Henry ~s again**○! hum Henry nous en a fait encore une○; **3** Ind, Comm faire (la) grève;

to ∼ **for/against** faire (la) grève pour obtenir/pour protester contre; ④ [*match*] s'allumer; ⑤ [*clock*] sonner; ⑥ (proceed) to ∼ **north** prendre au nord des terres; **to ∼ across** prendre à travers [*field, country*]

(Phrasal verbs)

■ **strike back** (retaliate) riposter (**at** à)

■ **strike down**: ▶ ∼ **[sb] down**, ∼ **down [sb]** terrasser; **to be struck down by** (by illness) (affected) être frappé par; (incapacitated) être terrassé par; (by bullet) être abattu de

■ **strike off**: ▶ ∼ **off** prendre à travers; ▶ ∼ **[sth] off**, ∼ **off [sth]** (delete) rayer; ▶ ∼ **[sb] off** radier [*doctor*]; ▶ ∼ **[sb/sth] off sth** rayer [qn/qch] de qch [*list*]

■ **strike out**: ▶ ∼ **out** ① (hit out) frapper; s'en prendre à [*critics*]; ② (proceed) **to ∼ out towards** s'élancer vers; fig **to ∼ out in new directions** adopter de nouvelles orientations; **to ∼ out on one's own** gen voler de ses propres ailes; (in business) s'établir à son compte; ▶ ∼ **[sth] out**, ∼ **out [sth]** (delete) rayer

■ **strike up**: ▶ ∼ **up** [*orchestra*] commencer à jouer; ▶ ∼ **up [sth]** (start) [*orchestra*] attaquer; **to ∼ up an acquaintance with** faire connaissance avec; **to ∼ up a conversation with** engager la conversation avec; **to ∼ up a friendship with** se lier d'amitié avec; **to ∼ up a relationship with** établir des rapports avec

strike: ∼**breaker** n briseur/-euse m/f de grève; ∼ **force** n Mil force m d'intervention; ∼ **fund** n caisse f de grève; ∼ **pay** n indemnité f de grève

striker /'straɪkə(r)/ n ① gréviste mf; ② (in football) attaquant/-e m/f

striking /'straɪkɪŋ/
A n ① (of clock) sonnerie f; ② (of coin) frappe f
B adj ① [*person, clothes, pictures*] que l'on remarque; [*design*] qui se remarque; [*similarity, contrast*] frappant; ② Ind, Comm [*worker*] gréviste

striking distance n ① Mil **to be within** ∼ [*army, troops*] être à portée de canon (**of** de); ② fig **to be within** ∼ **of London** être près de Londres

strikingly /'straɪkɪŋlɪ/ adv gen remarquablement; [*stand out, differ*] de manière frappante

string /strɪŋ/
A n ① **₵** (twine) ficelle f; **a piece of** ∼ un bout de ficelle; **tied up with** ∼ ficelé; ② (on garment) cordon m; (on bow, racket) corde f also Mus; (on puppet) fil m; **to pull the** ∼**s** lit, fig tirer les ficelles; ③ (series) **a** ∼ **of** un défilé de [*visitors, boyfriends*]; une série de [*crimes, novels*]; une succession de [*successes, awards*]; une chaîne de [*shops*]; une kyrielle de [*insults*]; ④ (set) ∼ **of onions** chapelet m d'oignons; ∼ **of pearls** collier m de perles; ∼ **of islands** chapelet m d'îles; **a** ∼ **of racehorses** une écurie (de courses); ⑤ Culin (in bean) fil m
B strings npl Mus **the** ∼**s** les cordes fpl
C vtr (prét, pp **strung**) ① Mus, Sport corder [*racket*]; monter [*guitar, violin*]; **to** ∼ **[sth] tightly** faire un cordage tendu à [*racket*]; ② (thread) enfiler (**on** sur); ③ (hang) **to** ∼ **sth (up) above/across** suspendre qch au-dessus de/en travers de; **to** ∼ **sth up on** accrocher qch à; **to** ∼ **sth between** suspendre qch entre

(Idioms) **to have sb on a** ∼ mener qn à la baguette; **to pull** ∼**s** faire jouer le piston°; **without** ∼**s** ou **with no** ∼**s attached** sans conditions

(Phrasal verbs)

■ **string along**° GB: ▶ ∼ **along** suivre; **to** ∼ **along with sb** accompagner qn; ▶ ∼ **[sb] along** péj mener qn en bateau pej

■ **string out**: ▶ ∼ **out** s'échelonner; ▶ ∼ **[sth] out**, ∼ **out [sth]** échelonner; **to be strung out along** [*vehicles*] s'échelonner le long de [*road*]; **to be strung out across** [*people*] se déployer dans [*field*]

■ **string together**: ▶ ∼ **[sth] together**, ∼ **together [sth]** aligner [*sentences, words*]; enchaîner [*songs*]

■ **string up**°: ▶ ∼ **[sb] up** pendre [qn] haut et court

string: ∼ **bag** n filet m à provisions; ∼ **bean** n haricot m à écosser

stringency /'strɪndʒənsɪ/ n ① (of criticism, law, measure) sévérité f; ② (of control, regulation, test) rigueur f

stringent /'strɪndʒənt/ adj [*measure, standard*] rigoureux/-euse; [*ban, order*] formel/-elle

stringently /'strɪndʒəntlɪ/ adv [*observe, respect*] scrupuleusement; [*apply, treat*] avec rigueur; [*examine, test*] rigoureusement

string: ∼ **instrument**, ∼**ed instrument** ▸ p. 1028 n instrument m à cordes; ∼**-pulling**° n piston° m

stringy /'strɪŋɪ/ adj ① péj Culin filandreux/-euse; ② péj [*hair*] plat et sec; ③ (wiry) [*person, build*] filiforme

strip /strɪp/
A n ① (narrow piece) bande f (**of** de); **a** ∼ **of garden/beach** un jardin/une plage tout/-e en longueur; **centre** GB ou **median** US ∼ terre-plein m central; ② (striptease) strip-tease m; ③ Sport tenue f
B vtr (p prés etc **-pp-**) ① (also ∼ **off**) (remove) enlever [*clothes, paint*]; **to** ∼ **sth from** ou **off sth** enlever or arracher qch de qch; ② (remove everything from) déshabiller [*person*]; vider [*house, room*]; dépouiller [*tree, plant*]; défaire [*bed*]; (remove paint from) décaper; (dismantle) démonter; **to** ∼ **sb of** dépouiller qn de [*belongings, rights*]; **to** ∼ **sb of his/her rank** dégrader qn; **he was** ∼**ped of his title** on lui a retiré son titre; ③ (damage) écraser le filet de [*screw*]
C vi (p prés etc **-pp-**) se déshabiller
D stripped pp adj [*pine, wood*] décapé

(Idioms) **to tear sb off a** ∼, **to tear a** ∼ **off sb**° enguirlander° qn

(Phrasal verbs)

■ **strip down**: ▶ ∼ **down** se déshabiller; ▶ ∼ **[sth] down**, ∼ **down [sth]** démonter [*gun, engine*]; défaire [*bed*]; décaper [*woodwork*]

■ **strip off**: ▶ ∼ **off** [*person*] se déshabiller; ▶ ∼ **[sth] off**, ∼ **off [sth]** enlever [*paint, wallpaper, clothes*]; arracher [*leaves*]

strip: ∼ **cartoon** n bande f dessinée; ∼ **club** n boîte° f de strip-tease

stripe /straɪp/ n ① (on fabric, wallpaper) rayure f; (on crockery) filet m; ② (on animal) (isolated) rayure f; (one of many) zébrure f; ③ Mil galon m

striped /straɪpt/ adj rayé; **blue** ∼ rayé de bleu, à rayures bleues

strip: ∼ **light** n lampe f au néon; ∼ **lighting** n éclairage m au néon m

stripper /'strɪpə(r)/ ▸ p. 1181 n strip-teaseur/-euse m/f

strip-search /'strɪpsɜːtʃ/
A n fouille f corporelle
B vtr faire subir une fouille corporelle à [*person*]

strip show n strip-tease m

stripy /'straɪpɪ/ adj rayé, à rayures

strive /straɪv/ vi (prét **strove**; pp **striven**) (try) s'efforcer; **to** ∼ **for sth** rechercher qch

strobe /strəʊb/ n (also ∼ **light**) lumière f stroboscopique; ∼ **lighting** éclairage m stroboscopique

strode /strəʊd/ prét ▸ **stride B**

stroke /strəʊk/
A n ① (blow) gen, Sport coup m; **on the** ∼ **of four** à quatre heures sonnantes; ② fig (touch) coup m; **at one** ou **at a single** ∼ d'un seul coup; **a** ∼ **of luck** un coup de chance; **a** ∼ **of genius** un trait de génie; ③ (single movement in swimming) mouvement m des bras; (particular style) nage f; ④ (of bell) coup m; Art (mark of pen) trait m; (mark of brush) touche f; ⑤ (in punctuation) barre f oblique; ⑥ Med congestion f cérébrale; ⑦ (caress) caresse f; **to give sb/sth a** ∼ caresser qn/qch
B noun modifier Med ∼ **victim**, ∼ **patient** personne f victime d'une congestion cérébrale
C vtr ① (caress) caresser; ② Sport (in rowing) **to** ∼ **an eight** être le chef de nage d'un huit

(Idioms) **not to do a** ∼ **of work** ne rien faire; **to put sb off their** ∼ (upset timing) faire perdre le rythme à qn; (disconcert) faire perdre les pédales° à qn

stroll /strəʊl/
A n promenade f, tour m
B vi (also ∼ **about**, ∼ **around**) (walk) se promener; (aimlessly) flâner; **to** ∼ **in** entrer sans se presser; ② °(also ∼ **home**) (win) gagner facilement

stroller /'strəʊlə(r)/ n ① (walker) promeneur/-euse m/f; (more aimless) flâneur/-euse m/f; ② US (pushchair) poussette f

strong /strɒŋ, US strɔːŋ/ adj ① (powerful) [*arm, person, current, wind*] fort; [*army, swimmer, country, state*] puissant; **the workforce is 500** ∼ la main-d'œuvre est forte de 500 personnes; ② (sturdy) lit solide; fig [*bond*] profond; [*cast, candidate, team, alibi*] bon/bonne; [*currency, market*] ferme; **to have a** ∼ **stomach**° avoir l'estomac bien accroché°; ③ (concentrated) gen fort; [*coffee*] serré; ④ (alcoholic) alcoolisé; ⑤ (noticeable) gen fort; [*colour*] soutenu; [*rhythm*] cadencé;

⑥ (heartfelt) [*conviction*] intime; [*desire, feeling*] profond; [*believer, supporter*] acharné; [*opinion*] arrêté; [*criticism, opposition, reaction*] vif/vive; **I have a ~ feeling that she won't come** je suis pratiquement sûr qu'elle ne viendra pas; **in the ~est possible terms** sans détours; **~ language** mots *mpl* grossiers; ⑦ (resolute) [*ruler, leadership*] à poigne; [*action, measure, sanction*] sévère; ⑧ [*chance, possibility*] fort; ⑨ (good) **to be ~ on physics** être fort en physique; **he finished the race a ~ second** il a fini la course juste derrière le premier; **spelling is not my ~ point** l'orthographe n'est pas mon fort; ⑩ Ling [*verb*] fort; [*syllable*] accentué

⬗Idiom **to be still going ~** se porter toujours très bien

strong-arm /'strɒŋɑːm, US 'strɔːŋ-/
A *adj* brutal; **~ tactics** la manière forte
B *vtr* **to ~ sb into doing** forcer qn à faire

strong: **~box** *n* coffre-fort *m*; **~hold** *n* lit forteresse *f*; fig fief *m*

strongly /'strɒŋlɪ, US 'strɔːŋlɪ/ *adv* ① (with force) lit [*blow*] fort; [*defend oneself*] vigoureusement; fig [*criticize, attack, object, oppose, advise*] vivement; [*protest, deny*] énergiquement; [*suggest, support, defend, suspect*] fortement; [*believe*] fermement; **to feel ~ about sth** avoir des idées arrêtées sur qch; **~ held beliefs** des croyances fortement ancrées; **to be ~ in favour of/against sth** être absolument pour/contre qch; ② (solidly) solidement; ③ **to smell ~** dégager une forte odeur; **~ flavoured** très relevé

strongly-worded *adj* exprimé en termes très vifs

strong: **~-minded** *adj* obstiné; **~room** *n* chambre *f* forte; **~-willed** *adj* obstiné

stroppy○ /'strɒpɪ/ *adj* GB ronchon/-onne○

strove /strəʊv/ *prét* ▸ **strive**

struck /strʌk/ *prét, pp* ▸ **strike C, D**

structural /'strʌktʃərəl/ *adj* ① [*problem, reform*] structurel/-elle; ② Phys, Ling structural; ③ Tech [*defect*] de construction; **~ alterations** transformations *fpl*; **~ damage** dégâts *mpl* matériels

structural: **~ engineer** ▸ p. 1181 *n* ingénieur *m* des ponts et chaussées; **~ engineering** *n* génie *m* civil

structurally /'strʌktʃərəlɪ/ *adv* gen, Bot, Phys structurellement; Tech du point de vue de la construction; **~ sound** de construction solide

structure /'strʌktʃə(r)/
A *n* ① (organization) structure *f*; **wage ~** échelle *f* des salaires; **career ~** plan *m* de carrière; ② (building) construction *f*; (manner of construction) construction *f*
B *vtr* structurer [*ideas, essay*]; organiser [*day*]

struggle /'strʌgl/
A *n* ① (battle, fight) lit, fig lutte *f* (**over** au sujet de; **to do** pour faire); **to put up a (fierce) ~** se défendre (avec acharnement); ② (scuffle) rixe *f*; ③ (difficult task) **it was a ~** cela a été dur; **I find it a real ~ to do** *ou* **doing** il m'est très difficile de faire; **they had a ~ to do** *ou* **doing** ils ont eu du mal à faire
B *vi* ① lit (put up a fight) se débattre; (tussle, scuffle) se battre; **to ~ free** se dégager; ② fig (try hard) lutter; (stronger) se démener; **to ~ with a problem/one's conscience** être aux prises avec un problème/sa conscience; ③ (have difficulty) éprouver des difficultés; **to ~ to keep up** avoir du mal à suivre; ④ (move with difficulty) **he ~d into/out of his jeans** il a enfilé/enlevé son jean avec difficulté; **to ~ to one's feet** se lever avec peine

⬗Phrasal verbs
■ **struggle along, struggle on** lit avancer à grand-peine; fig persévérer
■ **struggle back** revenir à grand-peine *or* avec peine
■ **struggle through**: ▸ **~** s'en sortir tant bien que mal; ▸ **~ through [sth]** se frayer péniblement un chemin dans [*snow, jungle, crowd*]

struggling /'strʌglɪŋ/ *adj* [*writer, artist*] qui essaie de percer

strum /strʌm/ (*p prés etc* **-mm-**)
A *vtr* (carelessly) gratter [*guitar, tune*]; (gently) jouer doucement (de) [*guitar*]; **to ~ a tune** jouer doucement un air
B *vi* gratter (**on** sur); jouer doucement (**on** de)

strung /strʌŋ/ *prét, pp* ▸ **string C**

strung out○ /ˌstrʌŋ 'aʊt/ *adj* (addicted) **to be ~ on** être accro○ à [*drug*]; (from drugs) être en état de manque; gen être au bout du rouleau○

strung up○ /ˌstrʌŋ 'ʌp/ *adj* nerveux/-euse

strut /strʌt/
A *n* (support) montant *m*
B *vi* (also **~ about**) (*p prés etc* **-tt-**) se pavaner

stub /stʌb/
A *n* gen bout *m*; (of cheque, ticket) talon *m*
B *vtr* (*p prés etc* **-bb-**) **to ~ one's toe** se cogner l'orteil

⬗Phrasal verb
■ **stub out**: ▸ **~ [sth] out, ~ out [sth]** écraser

stubble /'stʌbl/ *n* (straw) chaume *m*; (beard) barbe *f* de plusieurs jours

stubbly /'stʌblɪ/ *adj* [*chin*] non rasé

stubborn /'stʌbən/ *adj* [*person, animal, government*] entêté; [*behaviour*] obstiné; [*independence*] tenace; [*resistance, refusal*] opiniâtre; [*stain, illness*] rebelle

stubbornly /'stʌbənlɪ/ *adv* [*refuse, deny, resist*] obstinément; [*behave, act*] de manière têtue

stubby /'stʌbɪ/ *adj* [*finger, tail*] court; [*person*] trapu

stucco /'stʌkəʊ/ *n* (*pl* **~s** *ou* **~es**) (outside plasterwork) enduit *m*; (decorative work) stuc *m*

stuck /stʌk/
A *prét, pp* ▸ **stick C, D**
B *adj* ① (caught) coincé; **to get ~ in mud** s'enliser dans la boue; **to be ~ with**○ se farcir [*task*]; ne pas pouvoir se débarrasser de [*object, person*]; ② ○(stumped) **to be ~ sécher**○; ③ (in a fix) **to be ~** être coincé; **to be ~ for cash** ne pas avoir d'argent; **to be ~ for something to say** ne pas savoir quoi dire

⬗Idiom **to be ~ on sb**○ avoir qn dans la peau○

stud /stʌd/ *n* ① (on jacket, tyre) clou *m*; (on door) clou *m* à grosse tête; (earring) clou *m* d'oreilles; (on shoe) clou *m*; (on boot) crampon *m*; (in road) clou *m* à catadioptre; (wheel bolt) goujon *m* de roue; ② (horse farm) haras *m*; **he's at ~** il est à la reproduction

studded /'stʌdɪd/ *adj* ① lit [*jacket, tyre*] garni de clous; [*door, beam*] clouté; **~ boots, ~ shoes** Sport chaussures *fpl* à crampons; ② **~ with** gen parsemé de; constellé de [*diamonds, jewels*]

student /'stjuːdnt, US 'stuː-/
A *n* élève *mf*; Univ étudiant/-e *m/f*; **a ~ of history** une personne qui s'intéresse à l'histoire
B *noun modifier* Univ [*life, unrest*] étudiant

student: **~ driver** *n* US personne qui apprend à conduire; **~ grant** *n* Univ bourse *f* d'études; **~ ID card** *n* US Univ carte *f* d'étudiant; **~ nurse** *n* élève *mf* infirmier/-ière; **~ teacher** *n* enseignant/-e *m/f* stagiaire; **~ union** *n* (union) syndicat *m* étudiant; (building) maison *f* des étudiants

studhorse *n* étalon *m*

studied /'stʌdɪd/ *adj* étudié

studio /'stjuːdɪəʊ, US 'stuː-/ *n* (*pl* **~s**) ① gen studio *m*; (of painter) atelier *m*; ② Cin société *f* de production

studio: **~ audience** *n* public *m* de studio; **~ portrait** *n* Phot portrait *m* d'art; **~ theatre** GB, **~ theater** US *n* théâtre *m* de poche

studious /'stjuːdɪəs, US 'stuː-/ *adj* (hardworking) studieux/-ieuse; (deliberate) étudié

stud mare *n* (jument *f*) poulinière *f*

study /'stʌdɪ/
A *n* gen, Art, Mus étude *f*; (room) bureau *m*; **a ~ in bigotry** un modèle de bigoterie
B *studies* *npl* études *fpl*; **computer studies** informatique *f*; **social studies** sciences *fpl* humaines
C *noun modifier* [*leave, period, group, visit*] d'étude; **~ tour** *ou* **trip** voyage *m* d'études
D *vtr* (all contexts) étudier; **to ~ to be a teacher** faire des études pour être enseignant
E *vi* (revise) réviser; (be educated) faire ses études (**under sb** avec qn)

⬗Idiom **his face was a ~!** il fallait voir sa tête!

study aid *n* outil *m* pédagogique (destiné à l'élève)

study hall *n* US ① (room) salle *f* d'étude; ② (period) heure *f* d'étude

stuff /stʌf/
A *n* ⊄ ① (unnamed substance) truc○ *m*; **what's that ~ in the bottle?** qu'est-ce que c'est dans la bouteille?; **that cement ~** cette espèce de ciment; **she loves the ~** elle adore ça; **expensive ~, caviar** ça coûte cher, le caviar; **we've sold**

lots of the ~ nous en avons vendu beaucoup; **it's strong** ~ c'est costaud○; **2** ○(unnamed objects) trucs○ mpl; (implying disorder) bazar○ m; (belongings) affaires fpl; **3** ○(content of speech, book, film etc) **who wrote this ~?** gen qui a écrit ça?; pej qui a écrit cette chose?; **there's some good ~ in this art-icle** il y a de bonnes choses dans cet article; **have you read much of her ~?** as-tu lu beaucoup de ce qu'elle a écrit?; **it's romantic ~** c'est romantique; **do you believe all that ~ about his private life?** tu crois à tout ce qu'on dit sur sa vie privée?; **4** (fabric) lit étoffe f; fig essence f; **to be made of somewhat coarser ~** être plus grossier de nature

B vtr **1** (fill, pack) garnir, rembourrer (**with** de); (implying haste) bourrer (**with** de); (block up) boucher (**with** avec); **2** (pack in) fourrer○; **to ~ sth up one's jumper** cacher qch sous son pull; **to ~ food into one's mouth** se bâfrer○; **3** Culin farcir; **4** [taxidermist] empailler

C stuffed pp adj Culin farci; [toy animal] en peluche; [bird, fox] empaillé

(Idioms) **a bit of ~**○ péj une gonzesse○ pej; **to do one's ~**○ faire ce qu'on a à faire; **to know one's ~**○ connaître son affaire○; **that's the ~**○! c'est bon!

(Phrasal verb)

■ **stuff up**: ▸ **~ [sth] up, ~ up [sth]** boucher

stuffed shirt○ n péj **to be a ~** être pompeux et suffi-sant

stuffiness /'stʌfɪnɪs/ n **1** (airlessness) atmosphère f étouf-fante; **2** (staidness) raideur f

stuffing /'stʌfɪŋ/ n **1** Culin farce f; **2** (of furniture, pillow) rembourrage m; (of stuffed animal) paille f

(Idiom) **to knock the ~ out of sb**○ [illness] mettre qn à plat○; [defeat, loss, event] démoraliser qn

stuffy /'stʌfɪ/ adj **1** (airless) étouffant; **2** (staid) guindé; **3** [nose] bouché

stultifying /'stʌltɪfaɪŋ/ adj abrutissant

stumble /'stʌmbl/

A n faux pas m

B vi **1** (trip) trébucher (**on, over** sur); **2** (stagger) **to ~ in/out/off** entrer/sortir/s'en aller en chancelant; **3** (in speech) hésiter; **to ~ over** buter sur

(Phrasal verbs)

■ **stumble across**: ▸ **~ across [sth]** fig tomber par hasard sur

■ **stumble on**: ▸ **~ on [sth], ~ upon [sth]** fig tomber par hasard sur

stumbling block /'stʌmblɪŋ blɒk/ n obstacle m

stump /stʌmp/

A n (of tree) souche f; (of candle, pencil, tooth) bout m; (limb) moi-gnon m; (in cricket) piquet m

B vtr **1** ○(perplex) déconcerter; **to be ~ed by sth** être en peine d'expliquer qch; **to be ~ed for an answer** ne pas trouver de réponse; **I'm ~ed** (in quiz) je sèche○; (nonplussed) aucune idée; **2** US Pol faire une tournée électorale dans [state]

C vi **1** (stamp) **to ~ in/out** entrer/sortir d'un air mécontent; **2** US Pol faire une tournée électorale

(Phrasal verb)

■ **stump up** GB débourser (**for** pour)

stumpy /'stʌmpɪ/ adj [person, legs] courtaud

stun /stʌn/ vtr (p prés etc **-nn-**) lit assommer; fig stupéfier

stung /stʌŋ/ prét, pp ▸ **sting** B, C

stunned /stʌnd/ adj **1** (dazed) assommé; **2** (amazed) [person] stupéfait; [silence] figé

stunning /'stʌnɪŋ/ adj **1** (beautiful) sensationnel/-elle; **2** (amazing) stupéfiant; **3** [blow] étourdissant

stunt /stʌnt/

A n **1** (for attention) coup m organisé, truc○ m; **2** Cin, TV (with risk) cascade f; **aerial ~s** acrobaties fpl aériennes; **3** ○US numéro○ m

B vtr empêcher [development]; Bot étioler [plant]

stunted /'stʌntɪd/ adj lit [tree, plant] rabougri; [body] chétif/ -ive; fig retardé

stunt: **~man** ▸ p. 1181 n cascadeur m; **~ pilot** ▸ p. 1181 n pilote m de voltige

stupefaction /ˌstjuːpɪ'fækʃn/ n (all contexts) stupeur f

stupefy /'stjuːpɪfaɪ/ US /'stuː-/ vtr **1** (astonish) stupéfier; **2** (make torpid) abrutir

stupefying /'stjuːpɪfaɪɪŋ/ US /'stuː-/ adj stupéfiant

stupendous /stjuː'pendəs/ US stu-/ adj [achievement, idea, film, size] prodigieux/-ieuse; [building, view] fantastique; [loss, folly] incroyable

stupid /'stjuːpɪd/ US 'stuː-/ adj **1** (unintelligent) stupide; **it is ~ of you to do** c'est idiot de ta part de faire; **I've done something ~** j'ai fait une bêtise; **the ~ car won't start!** cette idiote de voiture ne veut pas démarrer!; **2** (in a stupor) abruti (**with** de)

stupidity /stjuː'pɪdətɪ, US stu:-/ n (foolishness) bêtise f; (lack of intelligence) stupidité f

stupidly /'stjuːpɪdlɪ, US stu:-/ adv bêtement

stupor /'stjuːpə(r), US 'stu:-/ n stupeur f; **to be in a ~** être à moitié hébété; **in a drunken ~** hébété par l'alcool

sturdy /'stɜːdɪ/ adj robuste

stutter /'stʌtə(r)/

A n bégaiement m; **to have a ~** bégayer

B vtr, vi bégayer

St Valentine's Day n la Saint-Valentin

sty /staɪ/ n **1** (for pigs) porcherie f; **2** (also **stye**) Med orge-let m

style /staɪl/

A n **1** (manner) style m also Literat; **2** (elegance) classe f; **to bring a touch of ~ to** ajouter de la classe à; **to marry in ~** se marier en grande pompe; **to live in ~** mener grand train; **to travel in ~** voyager princièrement; **she likes to do things in ~** elle aime faire les choses en grand; **3** (design) (of car, clothing) modèle m; (of house) type m; **4** (fashion) mode f; (hairstyle) coupe f; **5** (approach) genre m; **I don't like your ~** je n'aime pas ton genre

B **-style** combining form **Californian-~** de style californien; **Italian-~** à l'italienne

C vtr **1** (design) concevoir [car, kitchen, building]; créer [col-lection, dress]; **2** couper [hair]

D v refl **to ~ oneself sth** se donner le titre de qch

styling /'staɪlɪŋ/

A n **1** (design) conception f; **2** (contours) ligne f; **3** (in hair-dressing) coupe f

B noun modifier [gel, mousse, product] fixant; [equipment] de coiffure; **~ brush** brosse f ronde

stylish /'staɪlɪʃ/ adj **1** (smart) [car, coat, flat] beau/belle; [person] élégant; [resort, restaurant] chic inv; **2** (accomplished) [director, performance, player] de grande classe; [thriller, writer] sophistiqué

stylist /'staɪlɪst/ ▸ p. 1181 n **1** (hairdresser) coiffeur/-euse m/f; **2** (writer) styliste mf; **3** (fashion designer) styliste mf; **4** Comm, Ind concepteur/-trice m/f

stylistic /staɪ'lɪstɪk/ adj Comm stylistique; **~ device** Literat procédé m stylistique

stylized /'staɪlaɪzd/ adj (non-realist) stylisé

stylus /'staɪləs/ n (pl **-li** ou **-luses**) Audio pointe f de lec-ture

stymied○ /'staɪmɪd/ adj (thwarted) coincé

suave /swɑːv/ adj gen onctueux/-euse; [person] mielleux/ -euse

sub /sʌb/ n **1** Sport abrév = **substitute**; **2** Naut abrév = **submarine**; **3** abrév = **subscription**; **4** US abrév = **sub-stitute teacher**

subaqua /ˌsʌb'ækwə/ adj [club] de plongée

subcommittee /'sʌbkəmɪtɪ/ n sous-comité m

subconscious /ˌsʌb'kɒnʃəs/

A n **the ~** le subconscient

B adj gen inconscient; Psych subconscient

subconsciously /ˌsʌb'kɒnʃəslɪ/ adv gen inconsciem-ment; Psych de façon subconsciente

subcontinent /ˌsʌb'kɒntɪnənt/ n sous-continent m

subcontract /ˌsʌbkən'trækt/ vtr sous-traiter (**to, out** to à)

subcontracting /ˌsʌbkən'træktɪŋ/ n sous-traitance f

subcontractor /ˌsʌbkən'træktə(r)/ ▸ p. 1181 n sous-traitant m

subdivide /ˌsʌbdɪ'vaɪd/

A vtr subdiviser [house, site]

B vi se subdiviser

subdue /səb'djuː, US -'duː/ vtr soumettre [people, nation]; mater [rebellion]; contenir [emotion]

subdued /səb'djuːd, US -'duːd/ adj [person, mood] silencieux/-ieuse; [voice] terne; [excitement, reaction] conte-nu; [lighting] tamisé; [colour] atténué

S

subedit /ˌsʌb'edɪt/ vtr GB corriger [*text*]

subheading /'sʌbhedɪŋ/ n (in text) sous-titre m

subhuman /ˌsʌb'hjuːmən/ adj [*behaviour*] monstrueux/-euse

subject

A /'sʌbdʒɪkt/ n **1** (topic) sujet m also Art, Phot, Ling; **to change** *ou* **drop the** ~ parler d'autre chose; **to raise a** ~ soulever une question; **while we're on the** ~ **of bonuses...** pendant que nous en sommes aux primes...; **2** (at school, college) matière f; (for research, study) sujet m; **her** ~ **is genetics** elle est spécialisée en génétique; **3** (focus) objet m; **to be the** ~ **of an inquiry** faire l'objet d'une enquête; **4** (citizen) sujet/-ette m/f

B /'sʌbdʒɪkt/ adj **1** (subservient) asservi; **to be** ~ **to** être soumis à [*law, rule*]; **2** (liable) **to be** ~ **to** être sujet/-ette à [*flooding, fits*]; être passible de [*tax*]; **prices are** ~ **to increases** les prix peuvent subir des augmentations; **flights are** ~ **to delay** les vols sont susceptibles d'être en retard; **3** (dependent) **to be** ~ **to** dépendre de [*approval*]; '~ **to alteration**' 'sous réserve de modification'; '~ **to availability**' (of flights, tickets) 'dans la limite des places disponibles'; (of goods) 'dans la limite des stocks disponibles'

C /səb'dʒekt/ vtr (expose) **to** ~ **sb to sth** faire subir qch à qn; **to be** ~**ed to** devoir supporter [*noise*]; faire l'objet de [*attacks*]; être soumis à [*torture*]; **to** ~ **sth to heat** exposer qch à la chaleur

subject: ~ **heading** n sujet m; ~ **index** n (in book) index m des sujets traités; (in library) fichier m par sujets

subjection /səb'dʒekʃn/ n sujétion f (**to** à)

subjective /səb'dʒektɪv/ adj subjectif/-ive

subject matter n sujet m

sub judice /ˌsʌb 'dʒuːdɪsɪ, sʊb 'juːdɪkeɪ/ adj devant les tribunaux

subjugate /'sʌbdʒʊɡeɪt/ vtr subjuguer [*country, people*]; dompter [*desire*]; soumettre [*will*]

subjunctive /səb'dʒʌŋktɪv/

A n subjonctif m

B adj [*form, tense*] du subjonctif; [*mood*] subjonctif/-ive

sublet /'sʌblet, ˌsʌb'let/ vtr, vi (p prés **-tt-**; prét, pp **-let**) sous-louer

sublime /sə'blaɪm/

A n **the** ~ le sublime

B adj **1** (great) sublime; **2** [*indifference*] suprême

sublimely /sə'blaɪmlɪ/ adv **1** [*play, perform, sing*] d'une façon sublime; **2** [*indifferent*] suprêmement

subliminal /səb'lɪmɪnl/ adj subliminal

submachine gun /ˌsʌbmə'ʃiːn/ n mitraillette f

submarine /ˌsʌbmə'riːn, US 'sʌb-/

A n Naut sous-marin m

B adj [*plant, life, cable*] sous-marin

submerge /səb'mɜːdʒ/

A vtr [*sea, flood*] submerger; [*person*] immerger (**in** dans); **to remain** ~**d** [*submarine*] rester en plongée

B submerged pp adj lit, fig submergé

C v refl **to** ~ **oneself in** se plonger dans [*work*]

submission /səb'mɪʃn/ n **1** (obedience, subjection) soumission f (**to** à) also Sport; **to frighten sb into** ~ réduire qn par la peur; **2** (of application etc) soumission f (**to** à); **3** (report) rapport m; **4** Jur conclusions fpl; **to make a** ~ **that** suggérer que

submissive /səb'mɪsɪv/ adj gen soumis; [*behaviour*] docile

submit /səb'mɪt/ (p prés etc **-tt-**)

A vtr **1** soumettre [*report, accounts, plan, script*] (**to** à); présenter [*bill, application, resignation*] (**to** à); déposer [*claim, estimate*] (**to** à); **2** (propose) **to** ~ **that** suggérer que

B vi se soumettre; **to** ~ **to** subir [*indignity, injustice*]; céder à [*will, demand, discipline*]; Jur se soumettre à [*decision*]

subnormal /ˌsʌb'nɔːml/ adj **1** pej [*person*] arriéré; **2** [*temperature*] au-dessous de la normale

subordinate

A /sə'bɔːdɪnət, US -dənət/ n subalterne mf

B /sə'bɔːdɪnət/ adj [*officer, rank, position*] subalterne; [*issue, matter, question*] secondaire (**to** par rapport à)

C /sə'bɔːdɪneɪt/ vtr gen, Ling subordonner (**to** à)

subordinate clause n Ling proposition f subordonnée

subpoena /sə'piːnə/

A n assignation f à comparaître

B vtr assigner [*qn*] à comparaître

subroutine /'sʌbruːtiːn/ n sous-programme m

subscribe /səb'skraɪb/ vi **1** **to** ~ **to** (agree with) partager [*view, values*]; **2** (be subscriber) s'abonner; **to** ~ **to** être abonné à [*magazine etc*]; **3** **to** ~ **to** donner (de l'argent) à [*charity, fund*]

subscriber /səb'skraɪbə(r)/ n **1** Comm (to periodical etc) abonné/-e m/f (**to** de); **2** Telecom abonné/-e m/f (du téléphone); **3** Fin souscripteur m

subscription /səb'skrɪpʃn/ n **1** (magazine) abonnement m (**to** à); **2** GB (to association, scheme) cotisation f (**to** à); **3** (to fund) don m (**to** à)

subscription rate n tarif m d'abonnement

subsection /'sʌbsekʃn/ n Jur alinéa m; gen paragraphe m

subsequent /'sʌbsɪkwənt/ adj (in past) ultérieur; (in future) à venir

subsequently /'sʌbsɪkwəntlɪ/ adv par la suite

subservient /səb'sɜːvɪənt/ adj **1** péj servile pej (**to** envers); **2** (less important) subordonné (**to** à)

subset /'sʌbset/ n Math sous-ensemble m

subside /səb'saɪd/ vi **1** (die down) [*storm, wind, applause, noise*] s'apaiser; [*emotion*] se calmer; [*laughter, fever, excitement*] retomber; [*threat*] diminuer; [*flames*] reculer; **2** (sink) [*water*] se retirer; [*building, land*] s'affaisser; **3** (sink down) [*person*] s'effondrer

subsidence /səb'saɪdns, 'sʌbsɪdns/ n affaissement m

subsidiary /səb'sɪdɪərɪ, US -dɪerɪ/

A n (also ~ **company**) filiale f

B adj (secondary) secondaire (**to** par rapport à)

subsidize /'sʌbsɪdaɪz/ vtr subventionner

subsidy /'sʌbsɪdɪ/ n subvention f (**to, for** à)

subsist /səb'sɪst/ vi subsister

subsistence /səb'sɪstəns/ n subsistance f

subsistence: ~ **farming** n agriculture f de subsistance; ~ **level** n niveau m minimum pour vivre; ~ **wage** n minimum m vital de misère

substance /'sʌbstəns/ n **1** (matter) substance f; **2** (of argument, talks) essentiel m; (of book) substance f; **3** (of argument) poids m; (of claim) fondement m; (of play, book) fond m; **there is no** ~ **to the allegations** les allégations sont dénuées de fondement; **to lend** ~ **to** donner du crédit à [*rumour*]; **something of** ~ quelque chose d'important

substance abuse n abus m de substances toxiques

substandard /ˌsʌb'stændəd/ adj [*goods, housing*] de qualité inférieure; [*essay, performance*] insuffisant; [*workmanship*] défectueux/-euse

substantial /səb'stænʃl/ adj **1** (in amount) [*sum, quantity*] important; [*imports, loss*] considérable; [*majority, number*] appréciable; [*meal*] substantiel/-ielle; **2** (in degree) [*change, difference, fall, impact, risk, damage*] considérable; [*role*] important; **3** (solid) lit, fig solide; **4** (wealthy) [*business*] financièrement solide

substantially /səb'stænʃəlɪ/ adv **1** (considerably) gen considérablement; [*higher, lower, better, less*] nettement; **2** (mainly) en grande partie

substantiate /səb'stænʃɪeɪt/ vtr justifier [*allegation*]; appuyer [*qch*] par des preuves [*statement*]

substitute /'sʌbstɪtjuːt, US -tuːt/

A n **1** (person) gen, Sport remplaçant/-e m/f; **2** (product, substance) produit m de substitution; **coffee** ~ succédané de café; **sugar** ~ édulcorant m de synthèse; **there is no** ~ **for a good education** rien ne remplace une bonne éducation; **there is no** ~ **for real leather** rien ne vaut le cuir véritable

B noun modifier [*machine, device*] de remplacement; [*family, parent*] adoptif/-ive; Sport [*player*] de remplacement

C vtr substituer (**for** à)

D vi **to** ~ **for sb/sth** remplacer qn/qch

substitute: ~**'s bench** n Sport banc m de touche; ~ **teacher** n Sch remplaçant/-e m/f

substitution /ˌsʌbstɪ'tjuːʃn, US -'tuː-/ n substitution f (**for** à)

substratum /ˌsʌb'strɑːtəm, US 'sʌbstreɪtəm/ n (pl **-strata**) gen (basis) fond m; (subsoil) sous-sol m; (bedrock) substratum m; Sociol couche f

subterranean /ˌsʌbtə'reɪnɪən/ adj souterrain

subtext /'sʌbtekst/ n Literat thème m sous-jacent; fig message m sous-jacent

subtitle /'sʌbtaɪtl/
A n sous-titre m
B vtr sous-titrer

subtitling /'sʌbtaɪtlɪŋ/ n sous-titrage m

subtle /'sʌtl/ adj **1** (barely perceptible) gen subtil; [change] imperceptible; **2** (finely tuned) [argument, analysis, allusion] subtil; [humour] très fin; [performance, idea, strategy] habile; [hint] voilé; **3** (perceptive) [analyst] perspicace; [person, mind] subtil; **4** (delicate) gen subtil; [lighting] tamisé

subtlety /'sʌtltɪ/ n **1** gen subtilité f; **2** (of film, book, music, style) complexité f; (of flavour) délicatesse f

subtly /'sʌtlɪ/ adv [change] imperceptiblement; [different] légèrement; [argue] avec subtilité; [analyse, act] avec finesse; [flavoured, coloured] délicatement

subtotal /'sʌbtəʊtl/ n sous-total m

subtract /səb'trækt/
A vtr Math soustraire (**from** de)
B vi faire des soustractions

subtraction /səb'trækʃn/ n soustraction f

suburb /'sʌbɜːb/
A n gen banlieue f; **inner** ∼ faubourg m
B suburbs npl the ∼s la banlieue; **the outer** ∼s la grande banlieue

suburban /sə'bɜːbən/ adj **1** [street, shop, train] de banlieue; [development] suburbain; US [shopping mall] à l'extérieur de la ville; ∼ **sprawl** (phenomenon) développement m des banlieues; **2** péj [outlook] étroit; [values] de petit-bourgeois

suburbanite /sə'bɜːbənaɪt/ n péj banlieusard/-e m/f

suburbia /sə'bɜːbɪə/ n **¢** banlieue f

subvention /səb'venʃn/ n **1** **C** (subsidy) subvention f; **2** **¢** (financing) subventions fpl

subversion /səb'vɜːʃn, US -'vɜːrʒn/ n subversion f

subversive /səb'vɜːsɪv/
A n (person) élément m subversif
B adj (all contexts) subversif/-ive

subvert /səb'vɜːt/ vtr déstabiliser [government]; corrompre [agent]; faire échouer [negotiations]

subway /'sʌbweɪ/
A n **1** GB (for pedestrians) passage m souterrain; **2** US (underground railway) métro m
B noun modifier US [station] de métro; [train] souterrain

sub-zero /ˌsʌb'zɪərəʊ/ adj inférieur à zéro

succeed /sək'siːd/
A vtr succéder à; **she** ∼**ed him as president** elle lui a succédé à la présidence
B vi **1** (achieve success) réussir; **to** ∼ **in doing** réussir à faire; **2** (accede) succéder; **to** ∼ **to** succéder à

succeeding /sək'siːdɪŋ/ adj (in past) suivant; (in future) à venir; **with each** ∼ **year** d'année en année

success /sək'ses/ n **1** succès m, réussite f; **to meet with** ∼ avoir du succès; **to make a** ∼ **of** gen réussir; faire un succès de [business, venture]; **sb's** ∼ **in** le succès de qn à [exam, election]; **his** ∼ **in overcoming his problems** la façon dont il a surmonté ses difficultés; ∼ **with women** succès auprès des femmes; **2** (person, thing that succeeds) succès m; **to be a** ∼ **with** avoir du succès auprès de

successful /sək'sesfl/ adj **1** (effective) [attempt, operation, partnership] réussi; [plan, campaign] couronné de succès; [treatment, policy] efficace; **to be** ∼ **in** ou **at doing** réussir à faire; **2** [film, writer] (profitable) à succès; (well regarded) apprécié; [businessman, company] prospère; [career] brillant; **to be** ∼ réussir; **3** [candidate, outcome] heureux/-euse; [applicant] retenu; [team, contestant] victorieux/-ieuse; **her application was not** ∼ sa candidature n'a pas été retenue

successfully /sək'sesfəlɪ/ adv avec succès

succession /sək'seʃn/ n **1** (sequence) série f; **in** ∼ de suite; **in close** ou **quick** ∼ coup sur coup; **2** (inheriting) succession f (**to** à); (descent) héritiers mpl

successive /sək'sesɪv/ adj gen successif/-ive; [day, week, year] consécutif/-ive; **with each** ∼ **disaster...** à chaque nouvelle catastrophe...

successor /sək'sesə(r)/ n **1** (person) successeur m (**of** ou **to sb** de qn; **to sth** à qch); **to be sb's** ∼ **as** succéder à qn en tant que; **2** (invention, concept) remplaçant/-e m/f

success: ∼ **rate** n taux m de réussite; ∼ **story** n réussite f

succinct /sək'sɪŋkt/ adj gen succinct; [person] concis

succour GB, **succor** US /'sʌkə(r)/ n secours m

succulent /'sʌkjʊlənt/
A n plante f grasse
B adj gen, Bot succulent

succumb /sə'kʌm/ vi (all contexts) succomber (**to** à)

such /sʌtʃ/
A pron (this) ∼ **is life** c'est la vie; **she's a good singer and recognized as** ∼ c'est une bonne chanteuse et elle est reconnue comme telle
B det **1** (of kind previously mentioned) (replicated) tel/telle; (similar) pareil/-eille; (of similar sort) de ce type (after n); ∼ **a situation** une telle situation; **in** ∼ **a situation** dans une situation pareille; **and other** ∼ **arguments** et autres arguments de ce type; **a mouse or some** ∼ **animal** une souris ou un animal semblable; **there was some** ∼ **case last year** il s'est produit la même chose l'année dernière; **there's no** ∼ **person** il/elle n'existe pas; **you'll do no** ∼ **thing!** il n'en est pas question!; **2** (of specific kind) tel/telle que; ∼ **that** être tel/telle que; **his movements were** ∼ **as to arouse suspicion** il se conduisait de telle façon qu'il éveillait les soupçons; **in** ∼ **a way that** d'une telle façon que; **money as I have** le peu d'argent or tout l'argent que j'ai; **until** ∼ **time as** jusqu'à ce que; **4** (so great) tel/telle; ∼ **was his admiration that** son admiration était telle que; **5** iron (of such small worth, quantity) **we picked up the apples,** ∼ **as there were** nous avons ramassé les rares pommes qu'il y avait par terre
C adv **1** (to a great degree) (with adjectives) si, tellement; (with nouns) tel/telle; ∼ **a nice boy!** un garçon si gentil!; ∼ **good quality as this** une telle qualité; ∼ **a lot (of) fun** on s'est tellement amusé; ∼ **a lot of problems** tant de problèmes; **there were (ever**○**)** ∼ **a lot of people** il y avait beaucoup de monde
D such as det phr, conj phr comme, tel/telle que; ∼ **a house as this,** a house ∼ **as this** une maison comme celle-ci; **a person** ∼ **as her** une personne comme elle; ∼ **as?** (as response) gen quoi par exemple?; **there are no** ∼ **things as giants** les géants n'existent pas; **have you** ∼ **a thing as a screwdriver?** auriez-vous un tournevis par hasard?

such and such det tel/telle; **on** ∼ **a topic** sur tel ou tel sujet

suchlike /'sʌtʃlaɪk/
A pron **and** ∼ (of people) et autres; **lions, tigers and** ∼ les lions, les tigres et autres fauves
B adj de ce type

suck /sʌk/
A n **to give sth a** ∼ sucer qch; **to have a** ∼ **of sth** goûter à qch (en suçant)
B vtr **1** (drink in) aspirer [liquid, air] (**through** avec); (extract) sucer (**from** de); **to** ∼ **sb dry** fig (of affection) vampiriser qn; (of money) pomper○ qn jusqu'au dernier sou; **2** (have in mouth) gen sucer; [baby] téter; **3** [current, wind, mud] entraîner; **to be** ∼**ed down** ou **under** être entraîné au fond; **to get** ∼**ed into** fig être entraîné dans
C vi [baby] téter; **to** ∼ **on** tirer sur [pipe]
D sucking pres p adj [noise] de succion

(Phrasal verbs)

■ **suck in**: ▸ ∼ **in [sth]**, ∼ **[sth] in** [machine] aspirer; **to** ∼ **in one's cheeks** creuser les joues; **to** ∼ **in one's stomach** rentrer l'estomac

■ **suck out**: ▸ ∼ **[sth] out**, ∼ **out [sth]** aspirer [air, liquid, dirt] (**from** de); sucer [poison, blood] (**from** de)

■ **suck up**: ▸ ∼ **up**○ faire de la lèche○; **to** ∼ **up to sb** cirer les pompes à qn○; ▸ ∼ **[sth] up**, ∼ **up [sth]** pomper [liquid]; aspirer [dirt]

sucker /'sʌkə(r)/ n **1** (dupe) bonne poire○ f; **he's a** ∼ **for compliments** les compliments le font craquer○; **2** Bot surgeon m; **3** (pad) ventouse f

sucking pig /'sʌkɪŋ/ n cochon m de lait

sucrose /'suːkrəʊz, -rəʊs/ n saccharose f

suction /'sʌkʃn/ n succion f; **by** ∼ par succion

suction: ∼ **pad** n ventouse f; ∼ **pump** n pompe f aspirante

Sudan /suː'dɑːn/ ▸ p. 774 pr n (also **the** ∼) Soudan m

sudden /'sʌdn/ adj [impulse, death] soudain; [movement] brusque; **all of a** ∼ tout à coup; **it was all very** ∼ ça s'est passé très vite

S

sudden: ~ **death play-off** n GB Sport *penalties pour départager deux équipes*; ~ **infant death syndrome**, **SIDS** n Med mort f subite du nourrisson

suddenly /'sʌdnlɪ/ adv [*die, grow pale*] subitement; [*happen*] tout à coup

suddenness /'sʌdnnɪs/ n gen soudaineté f; (of death, illness) caractère m subit

suds /sʌdz/ npl (*also* **soap** ~) (foam) mousse f (de savon); (soapy water) eau f savonneuse

sue /su:, sju:/
A vtr Jur intenter un procès à; **to** ~ **sb for divorce** demander le divorce à qn; **to** ~ **sb for damages** réclamer à qn des dommages-intérêts
B vi Jur intenter un procès

suede /sweɪd/
A n daim m; **imitation** ~ suédine f
B noun modifier [*shoe, glove*] en daim

suet /'su:ɪt, 'sju:ɪt/ n graisse f de rognon de bœuf

suffer /'sʌfə(r)/
A vtr [1] (undergo) gen subir; souffrir de [*hunger*]; **she** ~**ed a great deal of pain** elle a beaucoup souffert; **he** ~**ed a severe neck injury** il a été gravement blessé au cou; **to** ~ **a heart attack** avoir une crise cardiaque; **the region has** ~**ed severe job losses** la région a enregistré d'importantes pertes d'emplois; [2] (tolerate) supporter
B vi [1] (with illness) **to** ~ **from** gen souffrir de; avoir [*headache, cold*]; **to** ~ **from depression** être dépressif/-ive; [2] (experience pain) souffrir; **you'll** ~ **for it later** vous le regretterez plus tard; [3] (do badly) [*company, profits, popularity*] souffrir; [*health, quality, work*] s'en ressentir; **the project** ~**s from a lack of funds** le problème du projet, c'est qu'il est insuffisamment financé

sufferance /'sʌfərəns/ n **I'm only here on** ~ je suis tout juste toléré ici

sufferer /'sʌfərə(r)/ n victime f; **leukemia** ~**s** les leucémiques mpl

suffering /'sʌfərɪŋ/
A n **C** souffrances fpl (**of** de)
B adj souffrant

suffice /sə'faɪs/ sout
A vtr suffire à
B vi suffire

sufficient /sə'fɪʃnt/ adj suffisamment de, assez de; **a** ~ **amount** une quantité suffisante; **to be** ~ suffire; **to be quite** ~ suffire largement; **to be** ~ **for sb to do** suffire à qn pour faire

sufficiently /sə'fɪʃntlɪ/ adv suffisamment, assez

suffix /'sʌfɪks/ n suffixe m

suffocate /'sʌfəkeɪt/
A vtr [*smoke, fumes*] asphyxier; [*person, pillow, rage, anger*] étouffer
B vi [1] lit (by smoke, fumes) [*crowd*] être asphyxié; (by pillow) être étouffé; [2] fig suffoquer (**with** de)

suffocating /'sʌfəkeɪtɪŋ/ adj [*smoke, fumes*] asphyxiant; [*atmosphere*] étouffant; [*heat*] suffocant

suffocation /ˌsʌfə'keɪʃn/ n (by smoke, fumes, enclosed space, crowd) asphyxie f; (by pillow) étouffement m

suffrage /'sʌfrɪdʒ/ n (right) droit m de vote; (system) suffrage m

suffragette /ˌsʌfrə'dʒet/ n suffragette f

suffuse /sə'fju:z/ sout
A vtr se répandre sur
B suffused pp adj ~**d with** [*style*] imprégné de; [*person*] envahi de [*melancholy*]; [*landscape*] inondé de [*light*]

sugar /'ʃʊgə(r)/
A n [1] Culin sucre m; **brown** ~ sucre m roux; [2] ○(endearment) chéri/-e m/f
B noun modifier [*industry, prices*] du sucre; [*production, refinery*] de sucre; [*spoon, canister*] à sucre
C vtr sucrer [*tea, coffee*]
(Idiom) **to** ~ **the pill** dorer la pilule○

sugar: ~ **beet** n betterave f à sucre; ~ **bowl** n sucrier m; ~ **cane** n canne f à sucre; ~ **cube** n morceau m de sucre; ~ **daddy** n vieux protecteur m (d'une jeune fille); ~**ed almond** n dragée f; ~**-free** adj sans sucre; ~ **lump** n morceau m de sucre; ~ **pea** n mange-tout m inv; ~ **plantation** n plantation f de canne à sucre

sugary /'ʃʊgərɪ/ adj lit sucré; fig, gen mielleux/-euse; [*sentimentality*] mièvre

suggest /sə'dʒest, US səg'dʒ-/ vtr [1] (put forward for consideration) suggérer; **can you** ~ **how/where...?** selon vous, comment/où...?; **it would be wrong to** ~ **that...** il serait faux de prétendre que...; **what are you** ~**ing?** qu'est-ce que vous insinuez?; **I venture to** ~ **that...** je me risque à dire que...; [2] (recommend) suggérer; **the committee** ~**s that steps be taken** le comité suggère que des mesures soient prises; **I** ~ **waiting** je suggère d'attendre; **an idea** ~**ed itself (to me)** une idée m'est venue à l'esprit; [3] (indicate) sembler indiquer (**that** que); **it was more difficult than the result might** ~ ce fut plus difficile que le résultat ne semble l'indiquer; [4] (evoke) évoquer

suggestible /sə'dʒestəbl, US səg'dʒ-/ adj influençable

suggestion /sə'dʒestʃn, US səg'dʒ-/ n [1] (proposal) suggestion f (**about** à propos de; **as to** en ce qui concerne); **any** ~**s?** vous avez des idées?; **there is no** ~ **that** on n'a jamais dit que; **there is no** ~ **of fraud** rien ne laisse supposer qu'il y a eu fraude; **at** *ou* **on sb's** ~ sur *or* suivant le conseil de qn; **there was some** ~ **that** il a été suggéré que; [2] (hint) gen soupçon m; (of smile) pointe f; [3] Psych suggestion f; **the power of** ~ la puissance de suggestion

suggestions box n boîte f à idées

suggestive /sə'dʒestɪv, US səg'dʒ-/ adj (all contexts) suggestif/-ive; **to be** ~ **of sth** évoquer qch

suicidal /ˌsu:ɪ'saɪdl, ˌsju:-/ adj lit, fig suicidaire

suicidally /ˌsu:ɪ'saɪdəlɪ, sju:-/ adv [*depressed*] jusqu'au suicide; [*behave, decide, drive*] de manière suicidaire

suicide /'su:ɪsaɪd, 'sju:-/
A n (action) lit, fig suicide m; (person) suicidé/-e m/f; **to commit** ~ se suicider
B noun modifier [*attempt, bid, rate, note*] de suicide

suit /su:t, sju:t/
A n [1] (man's) costume m; (woman's) tailleur m; **to be wearing a** ~ **and tie** être en costume cravate; **a** ~ **of clothes** une tenue; **a** ~ **of armour** une armure (complète); [2] Jur (lawsuit) procès m; [3] (in cards) couleur f; **to be sb's strong** ~ fig être le point fort de qn; **to follow** ~ fig faire de même
B vtr [1] [*colour, outfit*] aller à; **to** ~ **sb down to the ground** aller à qn comme un gant; [2] [*date, climate, arrangement*] convenir à; ~**s me**○! ça me va!; **she's liberal when it** ~**s her** elle est libérale quand ça l'arrange; **it** ~**s him to live alone** ça lui plaît de vivre seul; [3] [*part, job*] convenir à; **a loan that** ~**s your needs** un prêt qui répond parfaitement à vos besoins; [4] (adapt) **to** ~ **sth to** adapter qch à
C vi convenir
D v refl **to** ~ **oneself** faire comme on veut

suitability /ˌsu:tə'bɪlətɪ, ˌsju:t-/ n (of person) aptitude f (**for** pour); (of site, location) commodité f

suitable /'su:təbl, 'sju:-/ adj [*clothing, employment, qualification, venue*] adéquat; [*candidate*] apte; [*treatment, gift*] approprié; **did you see anything** ~? as-tu vu quelque chose qui (te) convienne? **to be** ~ **for** convenir à [*person*]; bien se prêter à [*climate, activity, occasion*]; être fait pour [*role*]; être apte à [*job*]; **to be a** ~ **model for sb** être un exemple convenable pour qn; **to be** ~ **to** convenir à; **now seems a** ~ **time** il semble que ce soit le moment opportun

suitably /'su:təblɪ, 'sju:-/ adv [1] [*dressed, qualified*] convenablement; [2] (to the right degree) [*austere*] suffisamment; [*chastened, impressed*] dûment

suitcase /'su:tkeɪs, 'sju:-/ n valise f; **to be living out of a** ~ passer sa vie à se déplacer

suite /swi:t/ n [1] (furniture) mobilier m; [2] (rooms) suite f; **a** ~ **of rooms** une suite; [3] littér (retinue) suite f; [4] Mus suite f

suited /'su:tɪd, 'sju:-/ adj **to be** ~ **to** [*place, vehicle, clothes*] être commode pour; [*class, game, format, style*] convenir à; [*person*] être fait pour; **they are ideally** ~ **(to each other)** ils sont faits l'un pour l'autre

sulfur n US ▶ **sulphur**

sulk /sʌlk/
A n **to be in a** ~ bouder
B **sulks** npl **to have (a fit of) the** ~**s** bouder
C vi bouder (**about, over** à cause de)

sulkiness /'sʌlkɪnɪs/ n [1] (characteristic) caractère m maussade; [2] (behaviour) bouderies fpl

sulky /'sʌlkɪ/ adj (all contexts) boudeur/-euse; **to look** ~ faire la tête

sullen /'sʌlən/ adj [*person, expression*] renfrogné; [*day, sky, mood*] maussade; [*silence*] obstiné

sulphur GB, **sulfur** US /'sʌlfə(r)/ n soufre m

sulphuric acid n acide m sulfurique

sultana /sʌl'tɑːnə, US -'tænə/ n Culin raisin m de Smyrne

sultry /'sʌltrɪ/ adj ① [day, place] étouffant; [weather] lourd; ② [voice] voluptueux/-euse; [woman, look] sensuel/-elle

sum /sʌm/ n ① (amount of money) somme f; **a large/small ~ of money** une grosse/petite somme; ② (calculation) calcul m; **to be good at ~s** être bon en calcul; **to do one's ~s** fig faire ses comptes; ③ (total) lit somme f; **the ~ of** fig la somme de [experience, happiness]; l'ensemble m de [achievements]

(Phrasal verb)

■ **sum up**: ▶ **~ up** ① gen récapituler; **to ~ up, I'd like to say...** pour récapituler, je voudrais dire...; ② Jur résumer; ▶ **~ up [sth]** ① (summarize) résumer; ② (judge accurately) apprécier [situation]; se faire une idée de [person]

summa cum laude /ˌsʊmə kʊm 'laʊdeɪ/ n US Univ ≈ mention f très bien

summarily /'sʌmərəlɪ, US sə'merəlɪ/ adj sommairement

summarize /'sʌməraɪz/ vtr gen résumer; récapituler [argument, speech]

summary /'sʌmərɪ/

Ⓐ n résumé m

Ⓑ adj gen, Jur sommaire

summer /'sʌmə(r)/

Ⓐ ▶ p. 1166 n été m; **in the ~ of 1991** pendant l'été 1991

Ⓑ noun modifier [weather, evening, resort, clothes, vacation] d'été; **~ tourist** ou **visitor** estivant/-e m/f

summer: **~ camp** n US colonie f de vacances; **~ holiday** GB, **~ vacation** US gen vacances fpl (d'été); Sch, Univ grandes vacances fpl; **~house** n: abri rustique dans un jardin; **~ resort** n station f estivale; **~ school** n université f d'été; **~ term** n Sch, Univ troisième trimestre m

summertime /'sʌmətaɪm/ n ① (period) été m; ② GB **summer time** (by clock) heure f d'été

summery /'sʌmərɪ/ adj estival; **it's quite ~** on se croirait en été

summing-up /ˌsʌmɪŋ'ʌp/ n gen récapitulation f; Jur résumé m

summit /'sʌmɪt/

Ⓐ n sommet m; **Nato ~** sommet de l'OTAN; **peace ~** sommet m pour la paix

Ⓑ noun modifier [meeting, talks] au sommet

summon /'sʌmən/ vtr ① (call for) gen faire venir; convoquer [ambassador]; **to ~ sb to a meeting** convoquer qn à une réunion; **to ~ sb in** faire entrer qn; **to ~ sb to do sth** sommer qn de faire qch; **to ~ help** appeler à l'aide; **to ~ reinforcements/a taxi** appeler des renforts/un taxi; ② Jur citer; ③ (convene) convoquer

(Phrasal verb)

■ **summon up**: ▶ **~ up [sth]** (gather) rassembler [energy]; (evoke) évoquer [image]; **to ~ up spirits** appeler les esprits

summons /'sʌmənz/

Ⓐ n ① Jur citation f (**to do** à faire; **for** pour); **to serve a ~** signifier une citation; **to serve sb with a ~** citer qn à comparaître; ② gen (order) injonction f (**from** de; **to** à)

Ⓑ vtr citer (**to** à; **to do** à faire; **for** pour)

sump /sʌmp/ n ① (for draining water) puisard m; ② Aut carter m; **~ oil** huile f de carter

sumptuous /'sʌmptʃʊəs/ adj somptueux/-euse

sum total n (of money) montant m total; (of achievements) ensemble m; **is that the ~ of your achievements?** iron c'est tout ce que tu as fait?

sun /sʌn/

Ⓐ n soleil m; **in the ~** au soleil; **don't lie right in the ~** ne vous allongez pas en plein soleil; **you should come out of the ~** vous devriez vous mettre à l'ombre; **a place in the ~** (position) un endroit ensoleillé; (house) une maison dans le sud; **it's the most beautiful place under the ~** c'est l'endroit le plus beau du monde; **they sell everything under the ~** ils vendent de tout; **to be up before the ~** être levé avant l'aube

Ⓑ v refl (p prés etc **-nn-**) **to ~ oneself** [person] prendre le soleil; [animal] se chauffer au soleil

Sun abrév écrite = **Sunday**

sunbaked /'sʌnbeɪkt/ adj brûlé par le soleil

sunbathe /'sʌnbeɪð/

Ⓐ GB n bain m de soleil

Ⓑ vi se faire bronzer

sun: **~bather** n personne f qui prend un or des bain(s) de soleil; **~bathing** n bains mpl de soleil; **~beam** n lit, fig rayon m de soleil; **~bed** n (lounger) chaise f longue; (with sunlamp) lit m solaire; **~ blind** n GB store m; **~ block** n crème f écran total; **~burn** n coup m de soleil

sunburned, **sunburnt** /'sʌnbɜːnt/ adj (burnt) brûlé par le soleil; (tanned) GB bronzé; **to get ~** (burn) attraper un coup de soleil; (tan) GB bronzer

Sunday /'sʌndeɪ, -dɪ/ ▶ p. 1322

Ⓐ pr n dimanche m

Ⓑ **Sundays** pr npl **the ~s** les journaux mpl du dimanche

Ⓒ noun modifier [newspaper, lunch] du dimanche

(Idiom) **he'll never do it, not in a month of ~s** il le fera la semaine des quatre jeudis

Sunday best n (**dressed) in one's ~** endimanché

Sunday: **~ observance** n observance f du repos dominical; **~ opening** n ouverture f dominicale (des commerces et des bars); **~ trading** n commerce m dominical

sun: **~deck** n (on ship) pont m supérieur; (in house) terrasse f; **~dial** n cadran m solaire; **~down** n = sunset; **~drenched** adj inondé de soleil; **~dress** n robe f bain de soleil; **~-dried** adj séché au soleil

sundry /'sʌndrɪ/

Ⓐ **sundries** npl articles mpl divers

Ⓑ adj [items, objects, occasions] divers; (**to) all and ~** gen (à) tout le monde; (critical) (à) n'importe qui

sunflower /'sʌnflaʊə(r)/

Ⓐ n tournesol m

Ⓑ noun modifier [oil, seed] de tournesol; [margarine] au tournesol

sung /sʌŋ/ pp ▶ **sing**

sun: **~glasses** npl lunettes fpl de soleil; **~ hat** n chapeau m de soleil

sunk /sʌŋk/ pp ▶ **sink** B, C

sunken /'sʌŋkən/ adj ① (under water) [treasure, wreck] immergé; [vessel] englouti; ② (recessed) [cheek] creux/creuse; [eye] cave; ③ (low) [bath] encastré; [garden, living area] en contrebas

sunlamp /'sʌnlæmp/ n (for tanning) lampe f à bronzer; Med lampe f à rayons ultraviolets

sunlight /'sʌnlaɪt/ n lumière f du soleil; **in the ~** au soleil; **in direct ~** en plein soleil

sun: **~lit** adj ensoleillé; **~ lotion** n = suntan lotion; **~lounger** n chaise f longue

sunny /'sʌnɪ/ adj ① [weather, day] ensoleillé; [room] (facing the sun) exposé au soleil; (sunlit) ensoleillé; **~ interval** période f ensoleillée; **it's going to be ~** il va faire (du) soleil; ② [child, temperament] enjoué; **~ side up** [egg] sur le plat

sun: **~ oil** n = suntan oil; **~ porch** n petite véranda f; **~ protection factor**, **SPF** n indice m de protection, IP m; **~rise** n lever m du soleil; **~rise industry** n US industrie f en pleine expansion; **~roof** n toit m ouvrant; **~screen** n filtre m solaire

sunset /'sʌnset/

Ⓐ n lit coucher m du soleil; fig crépuscule m

Ⓑ adj US Admin, Jur de durée d'application limitée

sunset industry n US industrie f en déclin

sun: **~shade** n (parasol) parasol m; (awning) auvent m; (in car) pare-soleil m inv; **~shield** n pare-soleil m inv

sunshine /'sʌnʃaɪn/

Ⓐ n ① lit soleil m; **12 hours of ~** 12 heures d'ensoleillement; ② ○(term of address) coco/cocotte○ m/f

Ⓑ adj US Admin, Jur [law, bill, clause] sur la transparence

sunshine roof n = sunroof

sunstroke n insolation f

suntan /'sʌntæn/ n bronzage m; **to get a ~** bronzer

sun: **~tan cream** n crème f solaire; **~tan lotion** n lotion f solaire; **~tanned** adj bronzé; **~tan oil** n huile f solaire; **~trap** n coin m ensoleillé; **~ umbrella** n parasol m; **~up**○ n US = sunrise; **~ visor** n (in car) pare-soleil m inv; (for eyes) visière f; **~ worshipper** n gen fanatique mf du soleil

super /'suːpə(r), 'sjuː-/

Ⓐ n ① US (petrol) super (carburant) m; ② ○ abrév = **superintendent**

S

B ° *adj, excl* formidable
C super+ *combining form* super-

superannuated /ˌsuːpərˈænjʊˈeɪtɪd, ˌsjuː-/ *adj* lit mis à la retraite; fig suranné

superannuation /ˌsuːpərˌænjʊˈeɪʃn, ˌsjuː-/
A *n* retraite *f* complémentaire; ~ **scheme** régime *m* de retraite

superb /suːˈpɜːb, sjuː-/ *adj* superbe

Super Bowl *n* US Sport *championnat de football américain*

superbug /ˈsuːpəbʌg, ˈsjuː-/ *n* Med bactérie *f* résistante aux antibiotiques

supercilious /ˌsuːpəˈsɪliəs, ˌsjuː-/ *adj* dédaigneux/-euse

superficial /ˌsuːpəˈfɪʃl, ˌsjuː-/ *adj* superficiel/-ielle

superficiality /ˌsuːpəˌfɪʃɪˈælɪtɪ, ˌsjuː-/ *n* gen caractère *m* superficiel; péj manque *m* de profondeur

superfine /ˈsuːpəfaɪn, ˈsjuː-/ *adj* [*flour, chocolate, needle*] extra-fin; [*quality*] surfin; ~ **sugar** US sucre *m* en poudre

superfluity /ˌsuːpəˈfluːətɪ, ˌsjuː-/ *n* (overabundance) surabondance *f*

superfluous /suːˈpɜːfluəs, sjuː-/ *adj* superflu (**to sth** pour qch); **to feel (rather)** ~ se sentir de trop

superhuman /ˌsuːpəˈhjuːmən, ˌsjuː-/ *adj* surhumain

superimpose /ˌsuːpərɪmˈpəʊz, ˌsjuː-/ *vtr* superposer [*picture, soundtrack*] (**on** à); ~**d images** images en surimpression

superintend /ˌsuːpərɪnˈtend, ˌsjuː-/ *vtr* surveiller [*person, work*]; diriger [*organization, research*]

superintendent /ˌsuːpərɪnˈtendənt, ˌsjuː-/ *n* ⓵ (supervisor) responsable *mf*; ⓶ (in police) *cf* commissaire *m* de police; ⓷ US (for apartments) concierge *mf*; ⓸ US (*also* **school** ~) inspecteur/-trice *m/f*

superior /suːˈpɪərɪə(r), sjuː-, sʊ-/
A *n* gen, Relig supérieur/-e *m/f*
B *adj* ⓵ gen supérieur (**to** à; **in** en); [*product*] de qualité supérieure; (better than another) meilleur; **in** ~ **numbers** en plus grand nombre; ⓶ (condescending) condescendant

superior court *n* US *cour d'appel inférieure à la cour d'appel suprême*

superiority /suːˌpɪərɪˈɒrɪtɪ, sjuː-, -ˈɔːr-/ *n* (all contexts) supériorité *f* (**over, to** sur; **in** en)

superlative /suːˈpɜːlətɪv, sjuː-/
A *n* Ling superlatif *m*
B *adj* ⓵ [*performance, service*] superbe; [*physical condition*] exceptionnel/-elle; [*match, player*] de toute première classe; ⓶ Ling superlatif

superlatively /suːˈpɜːlətɪvlɪ, sjuː-/ *adv* parfaitement

superman /ˈsuːpəmæn, ˈsjuː-/ *n* (*pl* **-men**) surhomme *m*

supermarket /ˈsuːpəmɑːkɪt, ˈsjuː-/ *n* supermarché *m*

supermodel /ˈsuːpəmɒdl, ˈsjuː-/ *n* top model *m*

supernatural /ˌsuːpəˈnætʃrəl, ˌsjuː-/
A *n* surnaturel *m*
B *adj* surnaturel/-elle

supernumerary /ˌsuːpəˈnjuːmərərɪ, ˌsjuː-, US -ˈnuːmrerɪ/
A *n* ⓵ Admin surnuméraire *mf*; ⓶ Cin, Theat (extra) figurant/-e *m/f*
B *adj* (all contexts) surnuméraire

superpower /ˈsuːpəpaʊə(r), ˈsjuː-/ *n* superpuissance *f*; ~ **summit** sommet des superpuissances

superscript /ˈsuːpəskrɪpt, ˈsjuː-/ *adj* [*number, letter*] en exposant

supersede /ˌsuːpəˈsiːd, ˌsjuː-/ *vtr* gen remplacer; supplanter [*belief, theory*]

supersonic /ˌsuːpəˈsɒnɪk, ˌsjuː-/ *adj* supersonique

superstition /ˌsuːpəˈstɪʃn, ˌsjuː-/ *n* superstition *f*

superstitious /ˌsuːpəˈstɪʃəs, ˌsjuː-/ *adj* superstitieux/-ieuse

superstore /ˈsuːpəstɔː(r), ˈsjuː-/ *n* (large supermarket) hypermarché *m*; (specialist shop) grande surface *f*

superstructure /ˈsuːpəstrʌktʃə(r), ˈsjuː-/ *n* superstructure *f*

supertax /ˈsuːpətæks, ˈsjuː-/ *n* Fin *impôt supplémentaire sur les très hauts revenus*

supervise /ˈsuːpəvaɪz, ˈsjuː-/
A *vtr* ⓵ (watch over) superviser [*activity, staff, student, work*];

surveiller [*child, patient*]; diriger [*thesis*]; ⓶ (control) diriger
B *vi* [*supervisor*] superviser; [*doctor, parent*] surveiller; [*manager*] diriger

supervision /ˌsuːpəˈvɪʒn, ˌsjuː-/ *n* ⓵ (of staff, work) supervision *f*; **she is responsible for the** ~ **of two students** Univ elle dirige les recherches de deux étudiants; ⓶ (of child, patient, prisoner) surveillance *f*

supervisor /ˈsuːpəvaɪzə(r), ˈsjuː-/ ► p. 1181 *n* ⓵ Admin, Comm responsable *m*; **factory** ~ ≈ contremaître *m*; **shop** ~ chef *m* de rayon; ⓶ Constr contremaître *m*; **site** ~ chef *m* de chantier; ⓷ GB Univ (for thesis) directeur/-trice *m/f* de thèse; ⓸ US Sch directeur/-trice *m/f* d'études

supervisory /ˈsuːpəvaɪzərɪ, ˈsjuː-, US ˌsuːpəˈvaɪzərɪ/ *adj* de supervision; **she's a** ~ **officer** elle fait partie du personnel d'encadrement; **in a** ~ **capacity** en qualité de superviseur

supine /ˈsuːpaɪn, ˈsjuː-/
A *n* Ling supin *m*
B *adj* ⓵ [*person*] étendu sur le dos; **to be** ~ être allongé sur le dos; ⓶ [*complacency*] mou/molle

supper /ˈsʌpə(r)/ *n* ⓵ (evening meal) dîner *m*; **what's for** ~? qu'est-ce qu'on mange ce soir?; **to have** *ou* **eat** ~ dîner; ⓶ (late snack) collation *f* (*du soir*); ⓷ (after a show) souper *m*; ⓸ Relig **the Last Supper** la Cène

supper: ~ **club** *n* US restaurant *m*; ~ **licence** *n* GB Jur *autorisation de vendre de l'alcool après l'heure légale avec un repas*; ~ **time** *n* heure *f* du dîner

supplant /səˈplɑːnt/ *vtr* gen supplanter; évincer [*lover, rival*]

supple /ˈsʌpl/ *adj* gen souple; [*mind*] délié

supplement
A /ˈsʌplɪmənt/ *n* ⓵ (to diet, income) complément *m* (**to** à); ⓶ Tourism supplément *m* (**of** de); **a single room** ~ un supplément pour chambre à un lit; **flight** ~ supplément *m* de vol; ⓷ (newspaper section) supplément *m*
B *vtr* gen compléter (**with** de); augmenter [*income, staff*] (**with** de)

supplementary /ˌsʌplɪˈmentrɪ, US -terɪ/ *adj* gen supplémentaire; [*heating, income, pension*] d'appoint; [*charge, payment*] additionnel/-elle

supplementary benefit *n* GB autrefois *allocation versée aux personnes n'ayant pas droit au chômage*

suppleness /ˈsʌplnɪs/ *n* (all contexts) souplesse *f*

supplier /səˈplaɪə(r)/ *n* fournisseur *m* (**of, to** de)

supply /səˈplaɪ/
A *n* ⓵ (stock) réserves *fpl*; **a plentiful** ~ **of money** des réserves abondantes d'argent; **in short/plentiful** ~ difficile/facile à obtenir; **to get in a** ~ **of sth** s'approvisionner en qch; ⓶ (of fuel, gas) alimentation *f* (**of** en); (of food) approvisionnement *m*; **the blood** ~ **to the heart** le sang qui alimente le cœur; ⓷ (action of providing) fourniture *f* (**to** à)
B supplies *npl* ⓵ (food, equipment) réserves *fpl*; **food supplies** ravitaillement *m*; **to cut off sb's supplies** couper les vivres à qn; ⓶ (for office, household) (machines, electrical goods) matériel *m*; (stationery, small items) fournitures *fpl*; ⓷ GB Pol, Admin crédits *mpl*
C *noun modifier* [*ship, train*] ravitailleur/-euse; [*route*] (for industry) d'approvisionnement; (for population) de ravitaillement; ~ **company** fournisseur *m*
D *vtr* ⓵ (provide) gen fournir (**to, for** à); apporter [*companionship*] (**to** à); **to** ~ **arms to sb, to** ~ **sb with arms** fournir des armes à qn; **to keep sb supplied with** approvisionner régulièrement qn en; **to keep a machine supplied with fuel** assurer l'alimentation d'un appareil en combustible; **to keep sb supplied with information** tenir qn au courant de ce qui se passe; ⓶ (provide food, fuel for) ravitailler (**with** en); ⓷ (provide raw materials for) approvisionner (**with** en); ⓸ (fulfil) subvenir à [*needs, wants*]; répondre à [*demand, need*]

supply: ~ **and demand** *n* l'offre *f* et la demande; ~ **teacher** *n* GB suppléant/-e *m/f*

support /səˈpɔːt/
A *n* ⓵ (moral, financial, political) soutien *m*, appui *m*; **there is considerable public** ~ **for the strikers** les grévistes bénéficient du soutien d'une grande partie de la population; **there is little public** ~ **for this measure** il y a peu de gens favorables à cette mesure; ~ **for the party is increasing** le parti a de plus en plus de partisans; **air/land/sea** ~ Mil appui *m* aérien/terrestre/maritime; **to give sb/sth (one's)** ~ apporter son soutien à qn/qch; **in** ~ **of sb/sth** en faveur de qn/qch; **in** ~ **of this theory** pour appuyer cette

théorie; **a collection in** ~ **of war victims** une collecte au profit des victimes de guerre; **means of** ~ (financial) moyens *mpl* de subsistance; **2** (physical, for weight) gen support *m*; (for limb) appareil *m* de maintien; **athletic** ~ coquille *f*; **he used his stick as a** ~ il s'appuyait sur sa canne; **3** (person) soutien *m*; **to be a** ~ **to sb** aider qn; **Paul was a great** ~ Paul a été (d')un soutien précieux; **4** (at concert) (band) groupe *m* de la première partie

B *vtr* **1** (provide moral, financial backing) gen soutenir; donner à [*charity*]; **the museum is** ~**ed by public funds** le musée est subventionné par l'État; **2** (physically) supporter [*weight*]; soutenir [*person*]; **3** (validate) confirmer; **4** (maintain) [*breadwinner, land, farm*] faire vivre, subvenir aux besoins de; [*charity*] aider; **he has a wife and children to** ~ il a une femme et des enfants à charge; **she** ~**ed her son through college** elle a payé les études de son fils; **5** (put up with) endurer; **6** Comput prendre en charge

C *v refl* **to** ~ **oneself** subvenir à ses propres besoins

supporter /sə'pɔːtə(r)/ *n* gen partisan *m*; Pol sympathisant/-e *m/f*; Sport supporter *m*

support group *n* groupe *m* de soutien

supporting /sə'pɔːtɪŋ/ *adj* **1** Cin, Theat **'best** ~ **actor/ actress'** 'meilleur second rôle masculin/féminin'; ~ **cast** les seconds rôles; **2** [*wall*] de soutènement; **3** ~ **evidence** preuves *fpl* à l'appui

supportive /sə'pɔːtɪv/ *adj* [*person, organization*] d'un grand secours; [*role, network*] de soutien

support: ~ **services** *n* services *mpl* d'assistance technique; ~ **stockings** *npl* bas *mpl* de maintien; ~ **system** *n* gen réseau *m* de soutien; ~ **tights** *npl* collant *m* anti-fatigue

suppose /sə'pəʊz/

A *vtr* **1** (think) **to** ~ (**that**) penser *or* croire que; **to** ~ **sb to be sth** croire qn qch; **who do you** ~ **I saw yesterday?** devine un peu qui j'ai vu hier; **2** (admit, assume) supposer (**that** que); **it is generally** ~**d that** tout le monde croit que; **I** ~ **so/not** je suppose que oui/non; **even supposing he's there** même en supposant qu'il soit là; ~ (**that**) **it's true, what will you do?** imagine que ça soit vrai, qu'est-ce que tu feras?; ~ (**that**) **he doesn't come?** et s'il ne vient pas?; **3** (making a suggestion) ~ **we go to a restaurant?** et si on allait au restaurant?

B supposed *pp adj* **1** (putative) [*father, owner*] présumé (*before* n), putatif/-ive; (supposed) [*advantage, benefit*] prétendu (*before* n); **2** (expected) **to be** ~**d to do sth** être censé faire; **there was** ~**d to be a room for us** nous étions censés avoir une chambre; **3** (alleged) **it's** ~**d to be a good hotel** il paraît que c'est un bon hôtel

supposedly /sə'pəʊzɪdlɪ/ *adv* **to be** ~ **rich** être censé être riche; **the** ~ **developed nations** les pays soi-disant développés; ~ **she's very shy** il paraît qu'elle est très timide

supposing /sə'pəʊzɪŋ/ *conj* ~ (**that**) **he says no?** et s'il dit non?; ~ **your income is X, you pay Y** supposons que ton revenu soit de X, tu paieras Y

supposition /ˌsʌpə'zɪʃn/ *n* (guess) supposition *f*; (assumption) hypothèse *f*

suppository /sə'pɒzɪtrɪ, US -tɔːrɪ/ *n* suppositoire *m*

suppress /sə'pres/ *vtr* contenir [*anger, excitement*]; refouler [*sexuality*]; supprimer [*evidence, information*]; interdire [*newspaper*]; abolir [*party, group*]; réprimer [*smile, urge, opposition, rebellion*]; étouffer [*criticism, scandal, yawn*]; dissimuler [*truth*]; mettre fin à [*activity*]; retenir [*tears*]; empêcher [*growth*]; affaiblir [*immune system*]; inhiber [*symptom, reaction*]; **to** ~ **a sneeze** se retenir d'éternuer

suppressant /sə'presənt/ *n* (drug etc) inhibiteur *m*

suppression /sə'preʃn/ *n* **1** (of party) abolition *f*; (of truth) dissimulation *f*; (of newspaper) interdiction *f*; (of activity, demonstration, information, report, facts) suppression *f*; (of revolt) répression *f*; (of scandal) étouffement *m*; **2** Psych (of feeling) (deliberate) répression *f*; (involuntary) refoulement *m*; **3** (of growth, development) retard *m*

suppurate /'sʌpjʊreɪt/ *vi* suppurer

supremacy /su:'preməsɪ, sju:-/ *n* **1** (power) suprématie *f*; **2** (greater ability) supériorité *f*

supreme /su:'priːm, sju:-/ *adj* [*ruler, power, achievement, courage*] suprême; [*importance*] capital; [*stupidity, arrogance*] extrême; **to reign** ~ fig régner; **to make the** ~ **sacrifice** mourir pour la patrie

Supreme Commander *n* Mil Commandant *m* en chef

supremely /su:'priːmlɪ, sju:-/ *adv* [*difficult*] extrêmement; [*happy, important*] suprêmement

supremo /su:'priːməʊ, sju:-/ *n* (*pl* **-mos**) leader *m*

surcharge /'sɜːtʃɑːdʒ/

A *n* **1** gen supplément *m*; **2** Elec, Post surcharge *f*

B *vtr* faire payer un supplément à [*person*]

sure /ʃɔː(r), US ʃʊər/

A *adj* **1** (certain) sûr (**about, of** de); **I feel** ~ **that** je suis sûr que; **I'm not** ~ **when he's coming** je ne sais pas trop quand il viendra; **to be** ~ **of one's facts** être sûr de son fait; **one thing you can be** ~ **of…** une chose est sûre…; **I'm** ~ **I don't know, I don't know I'm** ~ je n'en ai pas la moindre idée; **we can never be** ~ on n'est jamais sûr de rien; **I wouldn't be so** ~ **about that!** ce n'est pas si sûr que ça!; **I won't invite them again, and that's for** ~**○**! une chose est sûre, je ne les inviterai plus!; **we'll be there next week for** ~! on y sera la semaine prochaine sans faute!; **nobody knows for** ~ personne ne (le) sait au juste; **there's only one way of finding out for** ~ il n'y a qu'une seule façon de s'en assurer *or* d'en avoir la certitude; **he is, to be** ~**, a very charming man** c'est certes un homme très charmant; **to make** ~ **that** (ascertain) s'assurer que; (ensure) faire en sorte que; **make** ~ **all goes well** fais en sorte que tout se passe bien; **make** ~ **you phone me** n'oublie pas de m'appeler; **she made** ~ **to lock the door behind her** elle a fait bien attention de fermer la porte derrière elle; **he's a** ~ **favourite** c'est le grand favori; **2** (bound) **he's** ~ **to fail** il va sûrement échouer; **3** (confident) sûr; ~ **of oneself** sûr de soi; **4** (reliable) [*friend*] sûr; [*method, remedy*] infaillible; **the** ~**st way to do** le moyen le plus efficace de faire; **she was chain-smoking, a** ~ **sign of agitation** elle fumait sans arrêt, ce qui montrait bien qu'elle était agitée; **5** (steady) [*hand, footing*] sûr; **to have a** ~ **aim** bien viser

B *adv* **1** **○**(yes) bien sûr; **'you're coming?'—'**~**!'** 'tu viens?'—'bien sûr!'; **2** **○**(certainly) **it** ~ **is cold** ça oui, il fait froid; **that** ~ **smells good○**! qu'est-ce que ça sent bon**○**!; **3** ~ **enough** effectivement

Idioms **as** ~ **as eggs is eggs○, as** ~ **as I'm standing here** aussi sûr que deux et deux font quatre; ~ **thing○**! US d'accord!

sure: ~**-fire○** *adj* garanti; ~**-footed** *adj* agile

surely /'ʃɔːlɪ, US 'ʃʊərlɪ/ *adv* **1** (expressing certainty) sûrement, certainement; ~ **we've met before?** nous nous sommes déjà rencontrés, n'est-ce pas?; **you noted his phone number,** ~? tu as noté son numéro de téléphone, j'imagine?; ~ **you can understand that?** c'est quelque chose que tu peux comprendre, n'est-ce pas?; **2** (expressing surprise) tout de même; ~ **you don't think that's true!** tu ne penses quand même pas que c'est vrai!; ~ **not!** pas possible!; ~ **to God** *ou* **goodness you've written that letter by now!** ne me dis pas que tu n'as pas encore écrit cette lettre!; **3** (expressing disagreement) **'it was in 1991'—'1992,** ~**'** 'c'était en 1991'—'1992, tu veux dire'; **4** (yes) bien sûr

sureness /'ʃɔːnɪs, US 'ʃʊərnɪs/ *n* (of technique) précision *f*; (of intent) certitude *f*; ~ **of touch** précision

surety /'ʃɔːrətɪ, US 'ʃʊərtɪ/ *n* Fin Jur (money) dépôt *m* de garantie; (guarantor) garant/-e *m/f*; **to stand** ~ **for sb** se porter garant de qn

surf /sɜːf/

A *n* vagues *fpl* (déferlantes)

B *vtr* Comput **to** ~ **the Web/Net** surfer sur le web/la Toile; **to** ~ **the Internet** surfer sur Internet

C *vi* **1** Sport faire du surf; **2** Comput surfer sur Internet

surface /'sɜːfɪs/

A *n* **1** lit surface *f*; **on the** ~ (of liquid) à la surface; (of solid) sur la surface; **2** fig apparence *f*; **to skim the** ~ effleurer [*problem, issue*]; **beneath the** ~ **he's shy** au fond il est timide; **to come** *ou* **rise to the** ~ se manifester; **3** (of solid, cube) côté *m*; **4** (worktop) plan *m* de travail

B *noun modifier* lit [*transport*] de surface; [*worker*] en surface; [*wound*] superficiel/-ielle; ~ **measurements** superficie *f*; fig superficiel/-ielle

C *vtr* faire le revêtement de; **to** ~ **sth with** revêtir qch de

D *vi* **1** lit [*person, object*] remonter à la surface; [*submarine*] faire surface; **2** fig [*tension, anxiety, racism*] se manifester; [*problem, evidence, scandal*] apparaître; [*person*] (after absence) refaire surface**○**; (from bed) se lever; [*object*] réapparaître

surface: ~ **area** *n* superficie *f*; ~ **mail** *n* courrier *m* par voie de surface; ~ **noise** *n* bruit *m* de surface; ~ **tension** *n* tension *f* superficielle; ~**-to-air** *adj* sol-

Surface area measurements

■ *Note that French has a comma where English has a decimal point.*

1 sq in = 6,45 cm^2 (*centimètres carrés*)*
1 sq ft = 929,03 cm^2
1 sq yd = 0,84 m^2 (*mètres carrés*)
1 acre = 40,47 ares
       = 0,4 ha (*hectares*)
1 sq ml = 2,59 km^2 (*kilomètres carrés*)

* *There are three ways of saying* 6,45 cm^2, *and other measurements like it:*

six virgule quarante-cinq centimètres carrés, *or* (*less formally*) six centimètres carrés virgule quarante-cinq, *or* six centimètres carrés quarante-cinq.

■ *For more details on how to say numbers* ▸ p. 1044.

how big is your garden?
= quelle est la superficie de votre jardin?

what's its area?
= il a quelle superficie?

it's 200 square metres
= il mesure 200 mètres carrés

its surface area is 200 square metres
= il mesure 200 mètres carrés de superficie

it's 20 metres by 10 metres
= il mesure 20 mètres sur 10 mètres
  or il fait 20 mètres sur 10 mètres

sold by the square metre
= vendu au mètre carré

there are 10,000 square centimetres in a square metre
= il y a 10 000 centimètres carrés dans un mètre carré

10,000 square centimetres make one square metre
= 10 000 centimètres carrés font un mètre carré

A is the same area as B
= A a la même superficie que B

A and B are the same area
= A et B ont la même superficie

■ *Note the French construction with* de, *coming after the noun it describes:*

a 200-square-metre plot
= un terrain de 200 mètres carrés

---

air; **~-to-surface** adj sol-sol

surf: **~board** n planche f de surf; **~boarding** ▸ p. 881 n surf m; **~boat** n surf-boat m

surfeit /'sɜːfɪt/ n excès m (**of** de)

surfer /'sɜːfə(r)/ n surfeur/-euse m/f

surfing /'sɜːfɪŋ/ ▸ p. 881 n surf m; **to go ~** aller faire du surf

surge /sɜːdʒ/
A n ⒈ (of water) brusque montée f; (of blood, energy, adrenalin) montée f; (of anger, desire) accès m; (of optimism, enthusiasm) élan m; **he felt a ~ of anger** il sentit la colère monter en lui; ⒉ (rise) (in prices, unemployment, inflation) hausse f (**in** de); (in demand, imports) accroissement m (**in** de); ⒊ (also **power ~**) surtension f; ⒋ (increase in speed) remontée f
B vi ⒈ [water, waves] déferler; [blood, energy, emotion] monter; **the crowd ~d into the stadium** la foule s'est engouffrée dans le stade; **the crowd ~d (out) onto the streets** la foule a déferlé dans les rues; **to ~ forward** [crowd] avancer en masse; [car] démarrer en trombe○; ⒉ [runner] s'élancer
C surging pres p adj [prices] en hausse

surgeon /'sɜːdʒən/ ▸ p. 1181 n chirurgien m

surgery /'sɜːdʒərɪ/ n ⒈ Med (operation) chirurgie f; **to have ~**, **to undergo ~** se faire opérer; **to need ~** avoir besoin d'une opération; ⒉ GB Med (building) cabinet m; **doctor's ~** cabinet médical; ⒊ GB (consultation time) (of doctor) (heures fpl de) consultation f; (of MP) permanence f; **to take ~** assurer la consultation; ⒋ US (operating room) salle f d'opération

surgical /'sɜːdʒɪkl/ adj gen chirurgical; [boot, stocking] orthopédique; [precision] fig scientifique

surgical: **~ appliance** n appareil m orthopédique; **~ dressing** n pansement m

surgically /'sɜːdʒɪklɪ/ adv [treat] par opération; **to remove sth ~** opérer qch

surgical: **~ shock** n choc m opératoire; **~ spirit** n alcool m (à 90 degrés)

surly /'sɜːlɪ/ adj revêche

surmise /sə'maɪz/ vtr conjecturer (**that** que)

surmount /sə'maʊnt/ vtr gen surmonter; résoudre [problem]

surname /'sɜːneɪm/ n nom m de famille

surpass /sə'pɑːs, US -'pæs/
A vtr gen surpasser (**in** en); dépasser [expectations]; **to ~ sth in size/height** être plus grand/haut que qch
B v refl **to ~ oneself** se surpasser

surplus /'sɜːpləs/
A n (pl **~es**) gen surplus m; Econ, Comm excédent m; **to be in ~** être excédentaire; **trade ~** excédent de commercial
B adj (tjrs épith) gen [milk, clothes] en trop; Econ, Comm [money, food, labour] excédentaire

surprise /sə'praɪz/
A n ⒈ (unexpected event, gift) surprise f; **the result came as** ou **was no ~** le résultat n'a surpris personne; **that's a bit of a ~** c'est surprenant; **it comes as** ou **is no ~ that** il n'est pas surprenant que (+ subj); **it comes as** ou **is a ~ to hear that** c'est une surprise d'apprendre que; **it came as no ~ to us to hear that** nous n'avons pas été surpris d'apprendre que; **it came as** ou **was a complete ~ to me** je ne m'y attendais pas du tout; **to spring a ~ on sb** faire une surprise à qn; **~**, **~!** ô surprise!; **is he in for a ~!** ça va être la surprise!; ⒉ (astonishment) surprise f, étonnement m; **to express ~ at sth** se déclarer surpris par qch; **much to my ~** à ma grande surprise; **to take sb by ~** gen prendre qn au dépourvu; Mil surprendre qn
B noun modifier (unexpected) gen surprise; [announcement, closure, result] inattendu; **~ tactics** lit, fig tactique f fondée sur l'effet de la surprise; **to pay sb a ~ visit** aller voir qn sans le prévenir
C vtr ⒈ (astonish) surprendre; **it ~d them that** ils ont été surpris que (+ subj); **it might ~ you to know that...** tu seras peut-être surpris d'apprendre que...; **nothing ~s me any more!** je ne m'étonne plus de rien!; **you (do) ~ me!** iron tu m'étonnes! **go on, ~ me** allez, dis toujours!; ⒉ (come upon) surprendre [intruder]; attaquer [qch] par surprise [garrison]

surprised /sə'praɪzd/ adj étonné; **I'm not ~** ça ne m'étonne pas; **don't look so ~** ne prends pas cet air surpris; **I would be ~ if** cela m'étonnerait que (+ subj); **oh, you'd be ~** détrompe-toi; **I'm ~ at him!** je ne m'attendais pas à cela de sa part!

surprising /sə'praɪzɪŋ/ adj étonnant, surprenant; **what is even more ~ is that he...** plus surprenant encore, il...

surprisingly /sə'praɪzɪŋlɪ/ adv [calm, cheap, strong] incroyablement; [bad] très; [well] étonnamment; **~ frank** d'une franchise étonnante; **they didn't know her, ~ enough** chose étonnante, ils ne la connaissaient pas; **not ~, ...** (ce n'est) pas étonnant que... (+ subj)

surreal /sə'rɪəl/ adj surréaliste

surrealist /sə'rɪəlɪst/ n, adj surréaliste (mf)

surrender /sə'rendə(r)/
A n ⒈ Mil (of army) capitulation f (**to** devant); (of soldier, town) reddition f (**to** à); ⒉ (of territory, power) abandon m (**to** à); (of policy) rachat m; ⒊ (of weapons, ticket, document) remise f (**to** à); ⒋ fig (to joy, despair) abandon m (**to** à)
B vtr ⒈ Mil livrer [town] (**to** à); ⒉ (give up) gen céder (**to** à); racheter [policy]; ⒊ (hand over) gen remettre (**to** à); rendre [passport] (**to** à)
C vi ⒈ Mil gen se rendre (**to** à); [country] capituler (**to** devant); **I ~** je me rends; fig je cède; ⒉ **to ~ to** se livrer à [passion, despair]
D v refl **to ~ oneself to** se livrer à [emotion]

S

surreptitious /ˌsʌrəpˈtɪʃəs/ *adj* [*glance, gesture*] furtif/
-ive; [*search, exit*] discret/-ète

surrogate /ˈsʌrəgeɪt/
A *n* [1] (substitute) substitut *m* (**for** de); [2] (*also* ~ **mother**)
mère *f* porteuse
B *adj* [*sibling, father, religion*] de substitution, de remplacement

surround /səˈraʊnd/
A *n* GB [1] (for fireplace) encadrement *m*; [2] (border) bordure *f*
B *vtr* lit, fig entourer; [*police*] encercler [*building*]; cerner
[*person*]
C *v refl* **to** ~ **oneself with** s'entourer de

surrounding /səˈraʊndɪŋ/ *adj* environnant; **the** ~ **area** *ou*
region les environs *mpl*

surroundings /səˈraʊndɪŋz/ *npl* gen cadre *m*; (of town)
environs *mpl*; **in their natural** ~ dans leur milieu naturel

surtax /ˈsɜːtæks/ *n* (on income) impôt *m* supplémentaire;
(additional tax) surtaxe *f*

surveillance /sɜːˈveɪləns/
A *n* surveillance *f*
B *noun modifier* [*equipment*] de surveillance; [*camera*] de sur-
veillance vidéo

survey
A /ˈsɜːveɪ/ *n* [1] gen enquête *f* (**of** sur); (by questioning people)
sondage *m*; (study, overview of work) étude *f* (**of** de); **a** ~ **of 500**
young people un sondage effectué parmi 500 jeunes
gens; [2] GB (in housebuying) (inspection) expertise *f* (**on** de);
(report) rapport *m* d'expertise; [3] Geog (action) (of land) étude *f*
topographique; [4] Geog (map) (of land) levé *m* topographique; [5] (rapid examination) rapide examen *m*
B /səˈveɪ/ *vtr* [1] (investigate) gen faire une étude de [*market,*
trends]; (by questioning people) faire un sondage parmi [*people*];
faire un sondage sur [*opinions, intentions*]; [2] GB (in housebuying) faire une expertise de; [3] Geog faire l'étude topographique de [*area*]; [4] gen (look at) contempler

surveying /səˈveɪɪŋ/ *n* [1] GB (in housebuying) expertise *f*
(immobilière); [2] Geog topographie *f*

surveyor /səˈveɪə(r)/ ► p. 1181 *n* [1] GB (in housebuying)
expert *m* (en immobilier); [2] (for map-making) topographe
mf; (for industry, oil) ingénieur *m* topographique

survival /səˈvaɪvl/
A *n* gen survie *f* (of de); (of custom, belief) survivance *f* (**of** de); **the**
~ **of the fittest** la survie des plus forts
B *noun modifier* [*kit, equipment, course, bag*] de survie

survive /səˈvaɪv/
A *vtr* [1] (live through) lit survivre à [*winter, operation*]; réchapper
de [*accident*]; fig surmonter [*crisis*]; [2] (live longer than) survivre à [*person*]
B *vi* lit, fig survivre; **to** ~ **on sth** vivre de qch; **I'll** ~ je m'en
tirerai

surviving /səˈvaɪvɪŋ/ *adj* survivant; **the longest** ~ **patient**
le patient qui a vécu le plus longtemps

survivor /səˈvaɪvə(r)/ *n* (of accident, attack) rescapé/-e *m/f*; **to**
be a ~ fig (resilient) avoir de la ressource

susceptibility /səˌseptəˈbɪlətɪ/ *n* [1] gen sensibilité *f* (**to**
à); (to disease) prédisposition *f* (**to** à); [2] (impressionability)
impressionnabilité *f*

susceptible /səˈseptəbl/ *adj* [1] gen sensible (**to** à); (to disease) prédisposé (**to** à); [2] (impressionable) impressionnable

suspect
A /ˈsʌspekt/ *n* suspect/-e *m/f*
B /ˈsʌspekt/ *adj* [*claim, person, vehicle*] suspect; [*item*] d'authenticité douteuse; [*water*] douteux/-euse
C /səˈspekt/ *vtr* [1] (believe) soupçonner [*murder, plot*]; **to**
~ **that** penser que; **we strongly** ~ **that...** nous avons de
bonnes raisons de croire que...; **it isn't, I** ~, **a very difficult**
task ce n'est pas, à mon avis, une tâche très difficile;
[2] (doubt) douter de [*truth, motives*]; [3] (be aware of) **she** ~**s**
nothing elle ne se doute de rien; [4] (have under suspicion)
soupçonner [*person*]
D **suspected** *pp adj* présumé; **a** ~**ed war criminal** une personne soupçonn ée de crimes de guerre

suspend /səˈspend/ *vtr* [1] (hang) suspendre (**from** à);
[2] (float) **to be** ~**ed in** [*balloon, feather*] flotter dans; [3] (call
off) gen suspendre; interrompre [*services, match*]; [4] réserver
[*comment, judgment*]; **to** ~ **disbelief** accepter les invraisem-
blances; [5] suspendre [*employee, official, sportsman*];
exclure [qn] temporairement [*pupil*]; [6] Jur **her sentence**
was ~**ed** elle a été condamnée avec sursis

suspended animation *n* lit engourdissement *m*; **to be**
in a state of ~ fig [*service, business*] végéter

suspended sentence *n* condamnation *f* avec sursis

suspender belt *n* GB porte-jarretelles *m inv*

suspenders /səˈspendəz/ *npl* [1] GB (for stockings) jarretel-
les *fpl*; (for socks) fixe-chaussettes *mpl*; [2] US bretelles *fpl*

suspense /səˈspens/ *n* (tension) suspense *m*; **to keep sb in**
~ laisser qn dans l'expectative; **I'd prefer to keep them in**
~ je préfère ménager mes effets; **the** ~ **is killing me!** je
n'en peux plus d'attendre!

suspension /səˈspenʃn/ *n* [1] (postponement) (of meeting, trial,
services, match) interruption *f*; (of talks, hostilities, payments, quotas)
suspension *f*; [2] (temporary dismissal) gen suspension *f*; (of pupil)
exclusion *f* temporaire

suspension: ~ **bridge** *n* pont *m* suspendu;
~ **points** *npl* points *mpl* de suspension

suspicion /səˈspɪʃn/ *n* [1] (mistrust) méfiance *f* (**of** de); **to**
view sb/sth with ~ se méfier de qn/qch; **to arouse** ~
éveiller des soupçons; [2] (of guilt) **to be arrested on** ~ **of**
murder être arrêté sur présomption de meurtre; **he is**
under ~ il est considéré comme suspect; **to be above** ~
être à l'abri de tout soupçon; [3] (idea, feeling) **to have a**
~ **that** soupçonner que; **I have a strong** ~ **that she is lying**
je suis presque sûr qu'elle ment; **to have** ~**s about sb/sth**
avoir des doutes *mpl* quant à qn/qch; **I have my** ~**s** j'ai ma
petite idée là-dessus

suspicious /səˈspɪʃəs/ *adj* [1] (wary) méfiant; **to be** ~ **of** se
méfier de [*person, motive, scheme*]; **to be** ~ **that** soupçonner
que; **we became** ~ on a commencé à se douter que quelque chose n'allait pas; [2] (suspect) gen suspect; [*behaviour,*
activity] louche

suspiciously /səˈspɪʃəslɪ/ *adv* [1] (warily) d'un air soupçonneux; [2] (oddly) [*behave, act*] de façon suspecte; [*quiet,*
heavy, keen] étrangement; [*clean, tidy*] iron étonnamment; **it**
sounded ~ **like a heart attack to me** cela m'avait tout l'air
d'être une crise cardiaque

suss○ /sʌs/ *vtr* GB résoudre [*problem*]; **to have it** ~**ed** (understand) avoir tout compris; **she's got it** ~**ed** (she's successful)
elle s'est bien débrouillée

⌜Phrasal verb⌝

■ **suss out**○: ► ~ **[sth/sb] out**, ~ **out [sth/sb]** (understand)
comprendre; **to go and** ~ **things** *ou* **the situation out** aller
voir ce qui se passe

sustain /səˈsteɪn/
A *vtr* [1] (maintain) gen maintenir; poursuivre [*war, policy*];
[2] Mus soutenir; [3] (provide strength) (physically) donner des
forces à; (morally) soutenir; [4] (support) soutenir; **to** ~ **life**
rendre la vie possible; [5] (suffer) recevoir [*injury*]; éprouver
[*loss*]; subir, essuyer [*defeat, damage*]; [6] Jur faire droit à
[*claim*]; admettre [*objection*]; **objection** ~**ed!** objection
accordée!
B **sustained** *pp adj* gen soutenu; [*applause, period*] prolongé;
Mus tenu

sustainable /səsˈteɪnəbl/ *adj* [1] Ecol [*development, forestry*]
durable; [*resource*] renouvelable; [2] Econ [*growth*] viable

sustenance /ˈsʌstɪnəns/ *n* (nourishment) valeur *f* nutritive;
(food) nourriture *f*

SW *n* [1] ► p. 1089 Geog (*abrév* = **southwest**) SO *m*; [2] Radio
(*abrév* = **short wave**) OC *fpl*

swab /swɒb/
A *n* Med (for cleaning) tampon *m*; (specimen) prélèvement *m*
B *vtr* (*p prés etc* -**bb**-) Med nettoyer [qch] avec un tampon; gen
(*also* ~ **down**) laver

swagger /ˈswægə(r)/
A *n* démarche *f* arrogante; **with a** ~ en se pavanant
B *vi* [1] (walk) se pavaner; [2] (boast) fanfaronner

swallow /ˈswɒləʊ/
A *n* [1] Zool hirondelle *f*; [2] (gulp) gorgée *f*
B *vtr* [1] (eat) avaler; [2] encaisser○ [*insult, sarcasm*]; ravaler
[*pride, anger*]; [3] ○(believe) avaler○
C *vi* avaler; (nervously) avaler sa salive

⌜Phrasal verbs⌝

■ **swallow back**: ► ~ **back [sth]**, ~ **[sth] back** lit, fig
ravaler

■ **swallow up**: ► ~ **up [sth]**, ~ **[sth] up** lit, fig engloutir
[qch]; **I wanted the ground to** ~ **me up** j'avais envie de
disparaître sous terre

swam /swæm/ *prét* ► swim B, C

swamp /swɒmp/
A *n* marais *m*, marécage *m*
B *vtr* inonder; **to be ~ed with** *ou* **by** être inondé de [*applications, mail*]; être débordé de [*work*]; être envahi par [*tourists*]

swan /swɒn/
A *n* cygne *m*
B ○*vi* (*p prés etc* **-nn-**) **to ~ around** *ou* **about** se pavaner; **to ~ in** arriver comme une fleur○

swanky○ /'swæŋkɪ/ *adj* (posh) rupin○

swan ~sdown *n* (feathers) duvet *m* de cygne; (fabric) molleton *m*; **~song** fig *n* chant *m* du cygne

swap○ /swɒp/
A *n* échange *m*
B *vtr* (*p prés etc* **-pp-**) échanger
(Phrasal verbs)
  ■ **swap around** ▶ **~** [sth] **around**, **~ around** [sth] permuter
  ■ **swap over** GB: ▶ **~ over** échanger; ▶ **~** [sth] **over**, **~ over** [sth] permuter

swarm /swɔːm/
A *n* (of bees) essaim *m*; (of flies, locusts) nuée *f*; **~s of people** une masse de personnes
B *vi* **1** (move in swarm) [*bees*] essaimer; **2** [*people*] **to ~ into/ out of** entrer/sortir en masse; **to ~ around** se presser autour de; [*place*] **to be ~ing with** grouiller de [*people*]

swarthy /'swɔːðɪ/ *adj* basané

swashbuckling /'swɒʃbʌklɪŋ/ *adj* [*adventure, tale*] de cape et d'épée; [*hero, appearance*] bravache

swat /swɒt/
A *n* **1** (object) tapette *f* à mouches; **2** (action) tape *f*
B *vtr* (*p prés etc* **-tt-**) écraser [*fly, wasp*] (**with** avec)

swath(e) /swɒːθ, sweɪð/ *n* **1** (band) (of grass, corn) andain *m*; (of land) bande *f*; **2** (cloth) drapé *m*
(Idiom) **to cut a ~ through** se frayer un chemin au milieu de

swathe /sweɪð/ *vtr* envelopper (**in** dans)

sway /sweɪ/
A *n* **to hold ~** avoir une grande influence; **to hold ~ over** dominer
B *vtr* **1** (influence) influencer; **to ~ sb in favour of doing** déterminer qn à faire; **to ~ the outcome in sb's favour** faire pencher la balance en faveur de qn; **2** (rock) osciller; **to ~ one's hips** se déhancher; **to ~ one's body** se balancer
C *vi* [*tree, building, bridge*] osciller; [*vessel, carriage*] tanguer; [*person, body*] (from weakness, inebriation) chanceler; (to music) se balancer

swear /sweə(r)/ (*prét* **swore**; *pp* **sworn**)
A *vtr* **1** gen, Jur (promise) jurer; **to ~ (an oath of) allegiance to** faire serment d'allégeance à; **to ~ sb to secrecy** faire jurer le secret à qn; **to be sworn into office** prêter serment; **2** (curse) **'damn!' he swore** 'bon Dieu!' jura-t-il; **to ~ at** pester contre; **to be** *ou* **get sworn at** se faire injurier
B *vi* **1** (curse) jurer; **he never ~s** il ne dit jamais de gros mots; **2** (attest) **I wouldn't** *ou* **couldn't ~ to it** je n'en jurerais pas
(Phrasal verbs)
  ■ **swear by**○: ▶ **~ by** [sth/sb] ne jurer que par [*remedy, expert*]
  ■ **swear in** ▶ **~ in** [sb], **~** [sb] **in** faire prêter serment à; **to be sworn in** prêter serment

swearing /'sweərɪŋ/ *n* ¢ jurons *mpl*

swearing-in ceremony *n* cérémonie *f* d'investiture

swearword /'sweəwɜːd/ *n* juron *m*, gros mot *m*

sweat /swet/
A *n* (perspiration) sueur *f*; **to be in a ~** être en sueur; **to be dripping with ~** être en nage; **to break out into a ~** se mettre à suer; **to work up a (good) ~** se prendre une bonne suée; **in a cold ~** lit dans une sueur froide; **to be in a cold ~ about sth** fig avoir des sueurs froides à l'idée de qch
B **sweats** *npl* US survêtement *m*
C *vtr* Culin faire suer [*vegetables*]
D *vi* **1** lit [*person, animal*] suer; [*hands, feet, cheese*] transpirer; **2** ○fig (wait anxiously) **to let** *ou* **make sb ~** laisser mariner○ qn

(Idioms) **no ~**○! pas de problème!; **to be in a ~**○ être dans tous ses états; **to ~ blood over sth** suer sang et eau sur qch
(Phrasal verbs)
  ■ **sweat off**: ▶ **~** [sth] **off**, **~ off** [sth] perdre [qch] à force de transpirer
  ■ **sweat out** to **~ it out**○ s'armer de patience
  ■ **sweat over**○: **to ~ over** [sth] en suer○ pour faire *or* écrire

sweat ~band *n* Sport bandeau *m*; (on hat) cuir *m* intérieur; **~ed labour** *n* main-d'œuvre *f* exploitée

sweater /'swetə(r)/ ▶ p. 1191 *n* pull *m*

sweat ~ pants *npl* US pantalon *m* de survêtement; **~shirt** *n* sweatshirt *m*; **~shop** *n* atelier *m* où on exploite le personnel; **~suit** *n* survêtement *m*

sweaty /'swetɪ/ *adj* **1** [*person*] en sueur; [*palm*] moite; [*foot, cheese*] qui transpire; [*clothing*] couvert de sueur; **2** (hot) [*atmosphere*] étouffant; [*work*] laborieux/-ieuse

swede /swiːd/ *n* GB rutabaga *m*

Swede /swiːd/ ▶ p. 1032 *n* Suédois/-e *m/f*

Sweden /'swiːdn/ ▶ p. 774 *pr n* Suède *f*

Swedish /'swiːdɪʃ/ ▶ p. 969
A *n* (language) suédois *m*
B *adj* suédois

sweep /swiːp/
A *n* **1** (also **~ out**) coup *m* de balai; **to give sth a ~** donner un coup de balai à qch; **2** (movement) **with a ~ of his arm** d'un grand geste du bras; **to make a wide ~ south** faire un grand crochet vers le sud; **3** (of land, woods, hills, cliffs) étendue *f*; (of lawn) surface *f*; (of fabric) drapé *m*; **4** (of events, history, novel, country) ampleur *f*; (of opinion) éventail *m*; (of telescope, gun) champ *m*; **5** (search) (on land) exploration *f*; (by air) survol *m*; (attack) sortie *f*; (to capture) ratissage *m*; **to make a ~ of** (search) (on land) explorer; (by air) survoler; (to capture) ratisser; **6** (also **chimney ~**) ramoneur *m*
B *vtr* (*prét*, *pp* **swept**) **1** (clean) balayer [*floor, path*]; ramoner [*chimney*]; **2** (remove with brush) **to ~ the crumbs off a table** ramasser les miettes d'une table; **3** (push) **to ~ sth off the table** faire tomber qch de la table (d'un grand geste de la main); **to ~ sb off his/her feet** [*sea, wave*] emporter qn; fig (romantically) faire perdre la tête à qn; **to ~ sb overboard** entraîner qn par-dessus bord; **to be swept into power** être porté au pouvoir avec une majorité écrasante; **4** (spread through) [*disease, crime, panic, craze*] déferler sur; [*storm, fire*] ravager; [*rumour*] se répandre dans; **5** (search, survey) [*beam, searchlight*] balayer; [*person*] parcourir [qch] des yeux; Mil [*vessel, submarine*] sillonner; [*police*] ratisser (**for** à la recherche de); **to ~ sth for mines** déminer qch
C *vi* (*prét*, *pp* **swept**) **1** (clean) = **sweep up**; **2** lit, fig (move) **to ~ in/out** (quickly) entrer/sortir rapidement; (majestically) entrer/sortir majestueusement; **the wind swept in from the east** le vent soufflait de l'est; **to ~ into** [*invaders*] envahir; **to ~ (in)to power** être porté au pouvoir (avec une majorité écrasante); **to ~ to victory** remporter une victoire écrasante; **to ~ through** [*disease, crime, panic, craze, change*] balayer; [*fire, storm*] ravager; [*rumour*] se répandre dans; **to ~ over** [*searchlight*] balayer; [*gaze*] parcourir; **3** (extend) **the road ~s north** la route décrit une large courbe vers le nord; **the mountains ~ down to the sea** les montagnes descendent majestueusement jusqu'à la mer
(Idiom) **to ~ sth under the carpet** GB *ou* **rug** US escamoter qch
(Phrasal verbs)
  ■ **sweep along**: ▶ **~** [sb/sth] **along** entraîner; **to be swept along by** être emporté par [*crowd*]; être entraîné par [*public opinion*]
  ■ **sweep aside**: ▶ **~** [sb/sth] **aside**, **~ aside** [sb/sth] écarter [*person, objection*]; repousser [*offer*]
  ■ **sweep away**: ▶ **~** [sth] **away**, **~ away** [sb/sth] **1** lit emporter; **2** fig balayer [*obstacle, difficulty*]; **to be swept away by** se laisser entraîner par [*enthusiasm, optimism*]; être emporté par [*passion*]
  ■ **sweep out** ▶ **~** [sth] **out**, **~ out** [sth] balayer
  ■ **sweep up**: ▶ **~ up** balayer; ▶ **~** [sth] **up**, **~** [sth] **up** **1** (with broom) balayer; **2** (with arms) ramasser [qch] d'un geste large; **3** fig **to be swept up in** être entraîné par [*wave of nationalism, of enthusiasm*]

sweeper /'swiːpə(r)/ *n* **1** (cleaner) (person) balayeur/-euse *m/f*; (machine) balayeuse *f*; **2** Sport libero *m*

sweeping /'swiːpɪŋ/
A **sweepings** *npl* balayures *fpl*
B *adj* **1)** (far-reaching) [*change*] radical; [*legislation, power*] d'une portée considérable; [*cuts, gains, losses*] considérable; **2)** (too general) [*assertion*] péremptoire; [*statement*] trop général; **~ generalization** généralisation *f* à l'emporte-pièce; **3)** [*movement, curve*] large

sweet /swiːt/
A *n* **1)** GB (candy) bonbon *m*; (dessert) dessert *m*; **2)** ○ (term of endearment) ange *m*
B *adj* **1)** lit [*food, tea*] sucré; [*fruit*] (not bitter) doux/douce; (sugary) sucré; [*wine, cider*] (not dry) doux/douce; (sugary) sucré; [*taste*] sucré; [*perfume*] (pleasant) doux/douce; (sickly) écœurant; **to have a ~ tooth** aimer les sucreries; **2)** (kind) [*person*] gentil/-ille; [*face, voice*] doux/douce; **3)** (pure) [*water, smell*] bon/bonne; [*sound*] mélodieux/-ieuse; **4)** (cute) gen mignon/-onne; [*old person*] adorable; **5)** [*certainty, solace*] doux/douce; **6)** iron **to go one's own ~ way** agir comme ça lui/leur etc plaît
C *adv* **to taste ~** avoir un goût sucré; **to smell ~** sentir bon
(Idioms) **to keep sb ~** amadouer qn; **to whisper ~ nothings into sb's ear** susurrer des douceurs à l'oreille de qn

sweet: **~-and-sour** *adj* aigre-doux/-douce; **~bread** *n* (veal) ris *m* de veau; (lamb) ris *m* d'agneau

sweet chestnut *n* **1)** (nut) châtaigne *m*; **2)** (tree) châtaignier *m*

sweetcorn /'swiːtkɔːn/ *n* maïs *m*

sweeten /'swiːtn/ *vtr* **1)** sucrer [*food, drink*]; parfumer [*air*]; **2)** rendre [qch] plus tentant [*offer*]
(Phrasal verb)
■ **sweeten up**: ▸ **~ [sb] up, ~ up [sb]** amadouer

sweetener /'swiːtnə(r)/ *n* **1)** (in food) édulcorant *m*; **2)** ○ (bribe) (legal) incitation *f*; (illegal) pot-de-vin○ *m*

sweetheart /'swiːthɑːt/ *n* (boyfriend) petit ami *m*; (girlfriend) petite amie *f*

sweetly /'swiːtlɪ/ *adv* [*say, smile*] gentiment; [*sing*] d'une voix mélodieuse; [*dressed, decorated*] joliment

sweet: **~meal** *adj* GB ≈ à la farine non blutée; **~-natured** *adj* ▸ **sweet-tempered**

sweetness /'swiːtnɪs/ *n* **1)** (of food, drink) goût *m* sucré; **2)** (of perfume, smile) douceur *f*; (of sound) harmonie *f*; (of music) son *m* mélodieux; (of person) gentillesse *f*
(Idioms) **to be all ~ and light** être tout conciliant

sweet: **~ pea** *n* pois *m* de senteur; **~ potato** *n* patate *f* douce; **~-talk**○ *vtr* baratiner○; **~-tempered** *adj* [*person*] doux/douce; **~ trolley** *n* GB chariot *m* des desserts; **~ william** *n* œillet *m* de poète

swell /swel/
A *n* **1)** (of waves) houle *f*; **2)** Mus crescendo *m* et diminuendo *m*; **3)** (of belly) rondeur *f*
B ○ *adj* US **1)** (smart) [*car, outfit*] classe○ *inv*; [*restaurant*] chic *inv*; **2)** (great) formidable
C *vtr* (*prét* **swelled**; *pp* **swollen** *ou* **swelled**) **1)** (increase) gen gonfler; augmenter [*membership, number*]; **2)** (fill) [*wind*] gonfler; [*floodwater*] grossir
D *vi* (*prét* **swelled**; *pp* **swollen** *ou* **swelled**) **1)** (expand) [*fruit, sail, stomach*] se gonfler; [*dried fruit, wood*] gonfler; [*ankle, gland*] enfler; [*river*] grossir; **2)** (increase) gen s'accroître; **to ~ to 20,000** [*total*] atteindre 20 000; **3)** (grow louder) [*music*] devenir plus fort; [*note, sound*] monter; **4)** (ooze) s'écouler
(Idiom) **to have a swollen head**○ avoir la grosse tête○
(Phrasal verb)
■ **swell up** [*ankle, finger*] enfler

swelling /'swelɪŋ/
A *n* (on limb, skin) enflure *f*; (on head) bosse *f*; (of crowd, population) accroissement *m*
B *adj* croissant; **a ~ tide** fig une poussée

sweltering○ /'sweltərɪŋ/ *adj* [*conditions*] accablant; [*day, heat*] torride; **it's ~ in here** on étouffe ici

swept /swept/ *prét, pp* ▸ **sweep B, C**

swept-back *adj* [*hair*] coiffé en arrière

swerve /swɜːv/
A *n* écart *m*
B *vtr* [*driver*] faire faire un écart à [*vehicle*]
C *vi* **1)** lit [*person, vehicle*] faire un écart; **to ~ into sth** aller

---

s'écraser contre qch; **to ~ off the road** sortir de la route; **2)** fig **to ~ from** s'écarter de

swift /swɪft/
A *n* Zool martinet *m*
B *adj* rapide, prompt; **~ to do** prompt à faire

swiftly /'swɪftlɪ/ *adv* rapidement, vite

swig○ /swɪg/
A *n* gorgée *f* (**of** de)
B *vtr* (*p prés etc* **-gg-**) descendre○, boire à grands traits

swill /swɪl/
A *n* (food) pâtée *f* (des porcs)
B ○*vtr* (drink) écluser○, boire
(Phrasal verbs)
■ **swill around, swill about** se répandre
■ **swill down**: ▸ **~ [sth] down, ~ down [sth]** **1)** ○(drink) descendre○, avaler; **2)** (wash) laver [qch] à grande eau

swim /swɪm/
A *n* baignade *f*; **to go for a ~** (in sea, river) aller se baigner; (in pool) aller à la piscine
B *vtr* (*p prés* **-mm-**; *prét* **swam**; *pp* **swum**) nager [*distance, stroke*]; traverser [qch] à la nage [*river*]; faire [qch] à la nage [*race*]
C *vi* (*p prés* **-mm-**; *prét* **swam**; *pp* **swum**) **1)** [*person, animal*] nager (**in** dans; **out to** vers, jusqu'à); **to ~ across sth** traverser qch à la nage; **2)** (be bathed) **to be ~ming in** baigner dans [*sauce*]; **the kitchen was ~ming in water** la cuisine était inondée; **3)** (wobble) [*scene, room*] tourner
(Idioms) **to be in the ~** être dans le coup○; **sink or ~** marche ou crève○

swimmer /'swɪmə(r)/ *n* nageur/-euse *m/f*

swimming /'swɪmɪŋ/ ▸ p. 881
A *n* natation *f*; **to go ~** (in sea, river) aller se baigner; (in pool) aller à la piscine
B *noun modifier* [*contest, lessons, course*] de natation

swimming: **~ baths** *npl* piscine *f*; **~ cap** *n* GB bonnet *m* de bain; **~ costume** *n* GB maillot *m* de bain; **~ instructor** ▸ p. 1181 *n* maître-nageur *m*; **~ pool** *n* piscine *f*

swimming trunks *npl* slip *m* de bain; **a pair of ~** un slip de bain

swimsuit /'swɪmsuːt, -sjuːt/ *n* maillot *m* de bain

swindle /'swɪndl/
A *n* escroquerie *f*; **a tax ~** une fraude fiscale
B *vtr* escroquer; **to ~ sb out of sth** soutirer *or* escroquer qch à qn

swindler /'swɪndlə(r)/ *n* escroc *m*

swine /swaɪn/ *n* (pig) (*pl* ~) porc *m*
(Idiom) **to cast pearls before ~** jeter des perles aux pourceaux

swing /swɪŋ/
A *n* **1)** (movement) (of pendulum, needle) oscillation *f*; (of body) balancement *m*; Sport swing *m*; **to aim** *ou* **take a ~ at** essayer de donner un coup de poing à; **2)** (in voting, public opinion) revirement *m* (**in** de); (in prices, values, economy) fluctuation *f* (**in** de); (in business activity) variation *f* (**in** de); (in mood) saute *f* (**in** de); **a ~ away from** (in opinions) un mouvement contre; (in behaviour, buying habits) un rejet de; **3)** (in playground) balançoire *f*; **4)** (rhythm) rythme *m*
B *vtr* (*prét, pp* **swung**) **1)** (to and fro) balancer; **2)** (move around, up, away) **to ~ a child round and round** faire tournoyer un enfant; **she swung the telescope through 180°** elle a fait pivoter le télescope de 180°; **3)** (cause to change) **to ~ a trial sb's way** faire basculer un procès en faveur de qn; **to ~ the voters** faire changer les électeurs d'opinion; **4)** ○(cause to succeed) remporter [*election, match*]; **to ~ a deal** emporter une affaire; **can you ~ it for me?** tu peux arranger ça pour moi?
C *vi* (*prét, pp* **swung**) **1)** (to and fro) gen se balancer; [*pendulum*] osciller; **to ~ on the gate** se balancer sur le portillon; **2)** (move along, around) **to ~ onto the ground** s'élancer sur le sol; **to ~ up into the saddle** se mettre en selle d'un geste vif; **to ~ open** s'ouvrir; **the car swung into the drive** la voiture s'est engagée dans l'allée; **to ~ around** [*person*] se retourner (brusquement); **to ~ around in one's chair** pivoter sur sa chaise; **3)** **to ~ at** (with fist) lancer un coup de poing à; **4)** fig (change) **to ~ from optimism to despair** passer de l'optimisme au désespoir; **the party swung towards the left** le parti basculait vers la gauche; **5)** [*music, musician*] avoir du rythme; **6)** ○(be lively) **a club**

S

Swiss cantons

■ *All names of cantons are masculine, and the definite article is normally used:*

Ticino
= le Tessin

Valais
= le Valais

Graubünden
= les Grisons

So:

I like Ticino
= j'aime le Tessin

the Valais is beautiful
= le Valais est beau

do you know Graubünden?
= connaissez-vous les Grisons?

■ *Many cantons have names which are also names of towns. If you are not sure of the name in French,* le canton de X *is usually safe, and in some cases this is the only form available, as, for instance,* le canton de Vaud (*because* le Vaud *sounds like* le veau = *the calf*). *Similarly it is usual to say* le canton de Lucerne, le canton de Berne, le canton de Fribourg *to distinguish them from the towns bearing those names.*

In, to and from somewhere

■ *For* in *and* to, *use* dans le *or* dans les, *and for* from *use* du *or* des:

to live in the Valais
= vivre dans le Valais

to go to the Valais
= aller dans le Valais

to come from the Valais
= venir du Valais

to live in Graubünden
= vivre dans les Grisons

to go to Graubünden
= aller dans les Grisons

to come from Graubünden
= venir des Grisons

to live in the Vaud
= vivre dans le canton de Vaud

to go to the Vaud
= aller dans le canton de Vaud

to come from the Vaud
= venir du canton de Vaud

Uses with other nouns

■ *There are a number of words used as adjectives and as nouns referring to the people of the canton, e.g.:* bernois, valaisan, vaudois. *When nouns, these start with a capital letter.*

■ *However, it is always safe to make a phrase with* du, de l' *or* des:

a Valais accent
= un accent du Valais

the Graubünden area
= la région des Grisons

the Vaud countryside
= les paysages du canton de Vaud

---

which really ~**s** une boîte qui est vraiment branchée○

(Idioms) **to go with a** ~○ [*party*] marcher du tonnerre○; **to get into the** ~ **of things**○ se mettre dans le bain○; **to be in full** ~ battre son plein○

swing: ~**bin** n poubelle f à couvercle basculant; ~**bridge** n pont m tournant; ~ **door** GB, ~**ing door** US n porte f battante

swingeing /'swɪndʒɪŋ/ adj gen drastique; [*attack*] violent

swinging /'swɪŋɪŋ/ adj [*band*] qui swingue (*after* n); [*place, nightlife*] branché○

swingometer /ˌswɪŋ'ɒmɪtə(r)/ n indicateur m de tendances

swipe /swaɪp/
A n **to take a** ~ **at** lit essayer de frapper; fig attaquer
B vtr ① ○(steal) piquer○, voler; ② (validate) passer [qch] dans un lecteur de carte magnétique [*credit card, ID card*]
C vi **to** ~ **at** lit essayer de frapper; fig attaquer

swirl /swɜːl/
A n (shape) tourbillon m (**of** de)
B vi tourbillonner
C swirling pres p adj tourbillonnant

swish /swɪʃ/
A n (of water, skirt) bruissement m
B ○adj chic
C vi [*fabric*] bruire; [*whip*] siffler

Swiss /swɪs/ ▸ p. 1032
A n Suisse mf
B adj suisse

Swiss: ~ **chard** n bette f; ~ **cheese** n gruyère m, emmenthal m

switch /swɪtʃ/
A n ① (change) changement m (**in** de); **the** ~ **(away) from gas to electricity** le passage du gaz à l'électricité; **a** ~ **to the Conservatives** un glissement en faveur des conservateurs; ② (for light) interrupteur m; (on radio, appliance) bouton

m; **on/off** ~ interrupteur m marche-arrêt; **the** ~ **is on/off** c'est allumé/éteint; ③ (whip) badine f
B vtr ① (change) reporter [*support, attention*] (**to** sur); **to** ~ **brands/flights** changer de marque/vol; **she** ~**ed from the violin to the viola** elle est passée du violon à l'alto; **could you** ~ **the TV over?** est-ce que tu pourrais changer de chaîne?; ② (*also* ~ **round**) (change position of) intervertir; **I've** ~**ed the furniture round** j'ai changé la disposition des meubles
C vi ① (change) lit, fig changer; **to** ~ **between two languages** alterner entre deux langues; **we have** ~**ed (over) from oil to gas** nous sommes passés du mazout au gaz; **in the end she** ~**ed back to teaching** finalement elle est revenue à l'enseignement; ② (*also* ~ **over** ou **round**) [*people*] (change positions) changer; (change scheduling) permuter

(Phrasal verbs)
■ **switch off**: ▶ ~ **off** ① (turn off) s'éteindre; ② ○(stop listening) décrocher○; ▶ ~ **off [sth]**, ~ **[sth] off** éteindre [*appliance, light, engine*]; couper [*supply*]
■ **switch on**: ▶ ~ **on** s'allumer; ▶ ~ **on [sth]**, ~ **[sth] on** allumer
■ **switch over** TV, Radio changer de programme

switch: ~**back** n GB (rollercoaster) montagnes fpl russes; (road) route f en lacet; ~**blade** n US (couteau m à) cran m d'arrêt; ~**board** n (installation) standard m; (staff) standardistes mfpl; ~**board operator** ▸ p. 1181 n standardiste mf; ~**over** n passage m (**from** de; **to** à)

Switzerland /'swɪtsələnd/ ▸ p. 774 pr n Suisse f

swivel /'swɪvl/
A adj [*lamp*] pivotant, orientable
B vtr (p prés etc -**ll**- GB, -**l**- US) gen faire pivoter; tourner [*eyes, head, body*]
C vi (p prés etc -**ll**- GB, -**l**- US) pivoter

(Phrasal verb)
■ **swivel round**: ▶ ~ **round** pivoter; ▶ ~ **[sth] round**, ~ **round [sth]** faire pivoter [qch]

swivel chair, swivel seat *n* fauteuil *m* tournant, chaise *f* tournante

swollen /'swəʊlən/
A *pp* ▸ **swell C, D**
B *adj* [*ankle, gland*] enflé; [*eyes*] gonflé; [*river*] en crue
(Idioms) **to have a ~ head**○, **to be ~headed**○ avoir la grosse tête○

swoon /swuːn/
A *n* littér pâmoison *f*
B *vi* lit défaillir (**with** de); fig se pâmer (**with** de)

swoop /swuːp/
A *n* 1 (of bird, plane) descente *f* en piqué; 2 (police raid) rafle *f*
B *vi* 1 [*bird, bat, plane*] plonger; **to ~ down** descendre en piqué; **to ~ down on** fondre sur; 2 [*police, raider*] faire une descente

swoosh /swuʃ/ *vi* onomat [*tall grass, leaves*] bruire

swop /swɒp/ *n, vtr* = **swap**

sword /sɔːd/ *n* épée *f*
(Idioms) **to be a double-edged** *ou* **two-edged ~** être une arme à double tranchant; **to cross ~s with sb** croiser le fer avec qn

swordfish /'sɔːdfɪʃ/ *n* espadon *m*

swore /swɔː(r)/ *prét* ▸ **swear**

sworn /swɔːn/
A *pp* ▸ **swear**
B *adj* 1 Jur [*statement*] fait sous serment; 2 (avowed) [*enemy*] juré; [*ally*] pour la vie

swot○ /swɒt/
A *n* bûcheur/-euse○ *m/f*
B *vi* (*p prés etc* **-tt-**) bûcher○

swum /swʌm/ *pp* ▸ **swim B, C**

swung /swʌŋ/ *prét, pp* ▸ **swing B, C**

swung dash *n* tilde *m*

sycamore /'sɪkəmɔː(r)/ *n* sycomore *m*

sycophant /'sɪkəfænt/ *n* flagorneur/-euse *m/f*

sycophantic /ˌsɪkə'fæntɪk/ *adj* flagorneur/-euse

syllable /'sɪləbl/ *n* syllabe *f*; **in words of one ~** en termes simples; **not one ~** pas un seul mot

syllabus /'sɪləbəs/ *n* (*pl* **-buses** *ou* **-bi**) programme *m*

syllogism /'sɪlədʒɪzəm/ *n* syllogisme *m*

sylph /sɪlf/ *n* (fairy, slender girl) sylphide *f*

symbol /'sɪmbl/ *n* (all contexts) symbole *m* (**of, for** de)

symbolic(al) /sɪm'bɒlɪk(l)/ *adj* symbolique (**of** de)

symbolism /'sɪmbəlɪzəm/ *n* symbolisme *m*

symbolize /'sɪmbəlaɪz/ *vtr* symboliser (**by** par)

symmetric(al) /sɪ'metrɪk(l)/ *adj* symétrique

symmetry /'sɪmətrɪ/ *n* symétrie *f*

sympathetic /ˌsɪmpə'θetɪk/ *adj* 1 (compassionate) compatissant; (understanding) compréhensif/-ive; (kindly) gentil/-ille; (disposed) bien disposé (**to, towards** à l'égard de); **he is ~ to their cause** il est solidaire de leur cause; 2 (friendly) sympathique; 3 [*development*] qui s'harmonise bien avec l'environnement; 4 Med (ortho)sympathique

sympathetically /ˌsɪmpə'θetɪklɪ/ *adv* (compassionately) avec compassion; (kindly) avec bienveillance; (favourably) favorablement

sympathize /'sɪmpəθaɪz/ *vi* 1 (feel compassion) témoigner de la sympathie (**with** à); **I ~ with you in your grief** je compatis à votre douleur; **I ~, I used to be a teacher** je comprends, moi aussi j'ai été professeur; 2 (support) **to ~ with** être solidaire de [*cause, organization*]; souscrire à [*aims, views*]

sympathizer /'sɪmpəθaɪzə(r)/ *n* (supporter) sympathisant/-e *m/f* (**of** de); (at funeral etc) personne *f* qui témoigne de la compassion

sympathy /'sɪmpəθɪ/
A *n* 1 (compassion) compassion *f*; 2 (solidarity) solidarité *f*; **to be in ~ with sb** être d'accord avec qn; **I have little ~ for their cause** j'ai peu de sympathie pour leur cause; 3 (affinity) affinité *f*
B **sympathies** *npl* **what are her political ~s?** quelles sont ses tendances *fpl* politiques?; **to have left-wing ~s** être de

gauche; **my ~s lie with the workers** je suis du côté des ouvriers

symphony /'sɪmfənɪ/ *n* lit, fig symphonie *f*

symphony orchestra *n* orchestre *m* symphonique

symptom /'sɪmptəm/ *n* (all contexts) symptôme *m*

sync(h) /sɪŋk/ *n* (abrév = **synchronization**) synchronisation *f*; **in/out of ~** lit bien/mal synchronisé; **to be in/out of ~ with** fig être en phase/déphasé par rapport à

synchronization /ˌsɪŋkrənaɪ'zeɪʃn/ *n* synchronisation *f*; **in/out of ~** bien/mal synchronisé

synchronize /'sɪŋkrənaɪz/
A *vtr* synchroniser
B *vi* être synchrone

syndicate
A /'sɪndɪkət/ *n* 1 (of people) syndicat *m*; (of companies) consortium *m*; **to be a member of a ~** [*industrialist*] être syndicataire; [*banker*] faire partie d'un consortium; 2 (news agency) syndicat *m* de distribution; 3 (association) (of criminals) association *f* de malfaiteurs; (for lottery) association *f* de joueurs; **drug(s) ~** cartel *m* de la drogue
B /'sɪndɪkeɪt/ *vtr* 1 vendre [qch] par l'intermédiaire d'un syndicat de distribution [*column*]; **~d in over 50 newspapers** publié simultanément dans plus de 50 journaux; 2 US Radio, TV (sell) distribuer [qch] sous licence; 3 (assemble) syndiquer [*workers*]
C **syndicated** *pp adj* [*columnist*] d'agence; [*loan*] participatif; [*shares*] syndiqué

syndrome /'sɪndrəʊm/ *n* (all contexts) syndrome *m*

synonym /'sɪnənɪm/ *n* synonyme *m* (**of, for** de)

synonymous /sɪ'nɒnɪməs/ *adj* synonyme (**with** de)

synopsis /sɪ'nɒpsɪs/ *n* (*pl* **-ses**) gen synopsis *m*; (of book) résumé *m*

syntactic(al) /sɪn'tæktɪk(l)/ *adj* gen syntaxique; **~ errors** erreurs de syntaxe

syntax /'sɪntæks/ *n* syntaxe *f*

synthesis /'sɪnθəsɪs/ *n* (*pl* **-ses**) synthèse *f*

synthesize /'sɪnθəsaɪz/ *vtr* gen synthétiser; Chem, Ind produire [qch] par synthèse

synthesizer /'sɪnθəsaɪzə(r)/ *n* synthétiseur *m*

synthetic /sɪn'θetɪk/
A *n* (textile) (fibre *f*) synthétique *m*; (substance) produit *m* synthétique
B *adj* synthétique

syphon *n* = **siphon**

Syria /'sɪrɪə/ ▸ p. 774 *pr n* Syrie *f*

syringe /sɪ'rɪndʒ/
A *n* seringue *f*
B *vtr* gen, Med seringuer; **to have one's ears ~d** se faire déboucher les oreilles (avec une seringue)

syrup /'sɪrəp/ *n* sirop *m*; **cough ~** sirop contre la toux

system /'sɪstəm/ *n* gen système *m* (**for doing, to do** pour faire); **filing ~** système de classement; **gambling ~** système de probabilités; **public address ~** système de sonorisation; **road/river ~** réseau *m* routier/fluvial; **reproductive ~** appareil *m* reproducteur; **to lack ~** manquer d'organisation; **to store sth in the ~** Comput mettre qch en mémoire; **stereo ~** chaîne *f* stéréo; **braking ~** dispositif *m* de freinage; **to work within the ~** agir de l'intérieur du système; **to beat the ~** contourner le système; **to get sth out of one's ~** lit rendre qch; fig○ oublier qch

systematic /ˌsɪstə'mætɪk/ *adj* [*person, approach*] méthodique; [*method, way*] rationnel/-elle; [*attempts, abuse, destruction*] systématique

systematically /ˌsɪstə'mætɪklɪ/ *adv* [*work, list*] méthodiquement; [*arrange, destroy*] systématiquement

systematize /'sɪstəmətaɪz/ *vtr* systématiser

system: **~s analysis** *n* analyse *f* de systèmes; **~s analyst** ▸ p. 1181 *n* analyste *mf* de systèmes; **~s design** *n* conception *f* de systèmes; **~s disk** *n* disque *m* système; **~s engineer** ▸ p. 1181 *n* ingénieur *m* système; **~s engineering** *n* architecture *f* des systèmes; **~(s) software** *n* logiciel *m* de base; **~s programmer** ▸ p. 1181 *n* programmeur *m* d'étude; **~s theory** *n* théorie *f* des systèmes

S

Tt

t, T /tiː/ n (letter) t, T m

<u>Idioms</u> **that's Robert to a T** c'est signé Robert

tab /tæb/ n ① (on garment) (decorative) patte f; ② (on can) languette f; (on files) onglet m; (for identification) étiquette f; ③ US (bill) note f; **to pick up the ∼** lit, fig payer la note; ④ Comput (tabulator) tabulatrice f; (of word processor, typewriter) (device) tabulateur m; (setting) marque f de tabulation; **to set ∼s** placer des marques de tabulation

<u>Idiom</u> **to keep ∼s on sb**○ tenir qn à l'œil○

tabby(cat) /'tæbɪ/ n chat/chatte m/f tigré/-e

table /'teɪbl/

A n ① (furniture) table f; **to lay** ou **set the ∼** mettre le couvert; **to put sth on the ∼** GB fig (propose) avancer qch; US (postpone) ajourner qch; **the offer is still on the ∼** l'offre tient toujours; ② (list) table f, tableau m; ③ Math table f; **the six-times ∼** la table de six; ④ Sport (also **league ∼**) classement m

B vtr ① GB présenter [bill, amendment]; **to ∼ sth for discussion** soumettre qch au débat; ② US (postpone) ajourner

<u>Idioms</u> **she drank everyone under the ∼** quand tous les autres étaient soûls, elle se tenait toujours debout; **to turn the ∼s on sb** renverser les rôles aux dépens de qn; **to lay** ou **put one's cards on the ∼** jouer cartes sur table

table: **∼cloth** n nappe f; **∼ d'hôte** adj à prix fixe; **∼ football** ▸ p. 881 n baby-foot m

table manners npl **to have good/bad ∼** savoir/ne pas savoir se tenir à table

table: **∼ mat** n (under plate) set m de table; (under serving-dish) dessous-de-plat m inv; **∼ napkin** n serviette f (de table); **∼spoon** n (object) cuillère f de service; Culin (also **∼ful**) cuillerée f à soupe (GB = 18 ml, US = 15 ml)

tablet /'tæblɪt/ n ① (pill) comprimé m (**for** pour); ② (commemorative) plaque f (commémorative); ③ (of chocolate) tablette f; ④ Comput tablette f; ⑤ US (writing pad) bloc-notes m

table: **∼ tennis** n tennis m de table, ping-pong® m; **∼ware** n vaisselle f

tabloid /'tæblɔɪd/

A n (also **∼ newspaper**) tabloïde m pej; **the ∼s** la presse populaire

B noun modifier ① péj [journalism, journalist, press] populaire; ② [format, size] tabloïd(e)

taboo /tə'buː/ n, adj tabou (m)

tabulate /'tæbjʊleɪt/ vtr (set out) présenter [qch] sous forme de tableau; (in typing) tabuler

tabulation /ˌtæbjʊ'leɪʃn/ n (of data, results) disposition f en tableaux; (in typing) tabulation f

tabulator /'tæbjʊleɪtə(r)/ n (on typewriter) tabulateur m; (on computer) tabulatrice f

tachograph /'tækəɡrɑːf, US -ɡræf/ n tachygraphe m

tacit /'tæsɪt/ adj tacite

tack /tæk/

A n ① (nail) clou m; ② US (drawing pin) punaise f; ③ (approach) tactique f; ④ Naut bordée f; ⑤ (for horse) sellerie f; ⑥ (stitch) point m de bâti

B vtr ① (nail) **to ∼ sth to** clouer qch à; ② (in sewing) bâtir

C vi [sailor] faire une bordée; [yacht] louvoyer

<u>Phrasal verbs</u>

■ **tack on:** ▸ **∼ [sth] on, ∼ on [sth]** (stitch) fixer [qch] à points de bâti; fig ajouter [qch] après coup [clause, ending, building] (**to** à)

■ **tack up:** ▸ **∼ [sth] up, ∼ up [sth]** fixer

tacking /'tækɪŋ/ n (stitching) bâti m

tackle /'tækl/

A n ① Sport (in soccer, hockey) tacle m; (in rugby, American football) plaquage m; ② gen (equipment) équipement m; (for fishing) articles mpl de pêche; ③ Naut, Tech (on ship) gréement m; (for lifting) palan m

B vtr ① (handle) gen s'attaquer à; ② (confront) **to ∼ sb** prendre qn de front; **to ∼ sb about** parler à qn de; ③ Sport (intercept) (in soccer, hockey) tacler; (in rugby, American football) plaquer; ④ (take on) maîtriser [intruder]

C vi (in soccer, hockey) tacler; (in rugby, American football) plaquer

tacky /'tækɪ/ adj ① (sticky) collant; **the paint is still ∼** la peinture n'est pas encore tout à fait sèche; ② ○péj [place, garment, object] tocard○ pej

tact /tækt/ n tact m

tactful /'tæktfl/ adj [person, suggestion, reply, letter, intervention] plein de tact; [enquiry] discret/-ète; [attitude, approach] diplomatique; **to be ∼ with sb** user de tact avec qn

tactfully /'tæktfəlɪ/ adv [say, behave, reply, refuse] avec tact; [ask, enquire, phrased] avec diplomatie; [decide, refuse, refrain] par tact

tactic /'tæktɪk/ n ① gen tactique f; **a delaying ∼** une tactique dilatoire; ② (military science) **∼s** (+ v sg) tactique f

tactical /'tæktɪkl/ adj tactique

tactical voting n vote m utile

tactician /tæk'tɪʃn/ n tacticien/-ienne m/f

tactless /'tæktlɪs/ adj gen indélicat; **to be ∼** [person, remark] manquer de tact

tactlessly /'tæktlɪslɪ/ adv indélicatement

tadpole /'tædpəʊl/ n têtard m

taffeta /'tæfɪtə/ n taffetas m

tag /tæɡ/

A n ① (label) gen étiquette f; (on cat, dog) plaque f; (on file) onglet m; (for hanging) bride f; (nickname) étiquette f; ② (game) (jeu m de) chat m; ③ Ling tag m; ④ (quotation) gen citation f; (hackneyed) lieu m commun; ⑤ (for criminal) marqueur m

B vtr (p prés etc **-gg-**) (label) étiqueter [goods]; marquer [clothing, criminal]; apposer un onglet sur [file]

<u>Phrasal verbs</u>

■ **tag along** suivre; **to ∼ along behind** ou **after sb** suivre qn

■ **tag on:** ▸ **∼ [sth] on, ∼ on [sth]** rajouter [paragraph, phrase]; **to ∼ sth onto sth** attacher qch à qch [label, note]

tagging /'tæɡɪŋ/ n (for criminal) marquage m

tag: **∼ question** n Ling queue f de phrase interrogative; **∼ wrestling** ▸ p. 881 n catch m à quatre

tail /teɪl/

A n gen, Zool queue f

B tails npl ① (tailcoat) habit m; **white tie and ∼s** queue-de-pie f; ② (of coin) pile f; **heads or ∼s?** pile ou face?

C ○vtr suivre [suspect, car] (**to** jusqu'à); **we're being ∼ed** on est pris en filature

<u>Idioms</u> **I can't make head (n)or ∼ of this** je ne comprends rien du tout à cela; **to be on sb's ∼** suivre qn de près; **to go off with one's ∼ between one's legs** partir la queue basse; **to turn ∼** tourner les talons

<u>Phrasal verb</u>

■ **tail off** ① (reduce) [figures, demand] diminuer; ② (fade) [remarks] cesser; [voice] s'éteindre

tail: **∼back** n GB bouchon m; **∼board** n hayon m; **∼ end** n (last piece) (of joint) dernier morceau m; (of film, conversation) fin f; **∼gate** n hayon m; **∼light** n feu m arrière; **∼-off** n diminution f

tailor /'teɪlə(r)/ ▸ p. 1181

A n tailleur m

B vtr **1** (adapt) **to ∼ sth to** adapter qch à [needs, person]; **to ∼ sth for** concevoir qch pour [user, market]; **2** (make) confectionner

C tailored pp adj [garment] ajusté

tailor-made /ˌteɪlə'meɪd/ adj fait sur mesure; **to be ∼ for sth/sb** [system, course] être conçu spécialement pour qch/qn

tailspin /'teɪlspɪn/ n **1** Aviat vrille f; **to go into a ∼** descendre en vrille; **2** fig dégringolade° f

taint /teɪnt/

A n **1** (mark) (of crime, corruption, cowardice) souillure f; (of insanity, heresy) tare f; **2** (trace) trace f

B vtr souiller [public figure, reputation]; polluer [air, water]; gâter [meat, food]

tainted /'teɪntɪd/ adj **1** (contaminated) [food] avarié; [water, air] pollué (**with** par); **2** (sullied) [reputation, organization] entaché (**with** de); [money] mal acquis

take /teɪk/ ▸ p. 1191

A n **1** Cin prise f (de vues); Mus enregistrement m; **2** (catch) (of fish) prise f; (of game) tableau m de chasse

B vtr (prét **took**; pp **taken**) **1** (take hold of) prendre [object, money]; **to ∼ sth from** prendre qch sur [shelf, table]; prendre qch dans [drawer, box]; **to ∼ sth out of** sortir qch de [pocket]; **to ∼ sb by the hand/throat** prendre qn par la main/à la gorge; **to ∼ a knife to sb** attaquer qn avec un couteau; **2** (carry with one) emporter, prendre [object]; (carry to a place) emporter, porter [object]; **to ∼ sb sth, to ∼ sth to sb** apporter qch à qn; **did he ∼ an umbrella (with him)?** est-ce qu'il a emporté un parapluie?; **to ∼ a letter to the post office** porter une lettre à la poste; **to ∼ sth upstairs/downstairs** monter/descendre qch; **to ∼ the car to the garage** emmener la voiture au garage; **he took her some flowers** il lui a apporté des fleurs; **3** (accompany, lead) emmener [person]; **to ∼ sb to** [bus, road] conduire qn à [place]; **to ∼ sb to school/work** emmener qn à l'école/au travail; **I'll ∼ you up to your room** je vais vous conduire à votre chambre; **you can't ∼ him anywhere!** hum il n'est pas sortable!; **I'll ∼ you through the procedure** je vous montrerai comment on procède; **his work ∼s him to many different countries** son travail l'appelle à se déplacer dans beaucoup de pays différents; **what took you to Brussels?** qu'est-ce que vous êtes allé faire à Bruxelles?; **4** (go by) prendre [bus, taxi, plane, road, path]; **5** (negotiate) [driver, car] prendre [corner, bend]; [horse] sauter [fence]; **6** (capture, win) [army] prendre [fortress, city, chess piece]; (in cards) faire [trick]; [person] remporter [prize]; **7** (have) prendre [bath, shower, holiday]; prendre [milk, sugar, pills]; **we ∼ the Gazette** nous recevons la Gazette; **I'll ∼ a pound of apples, please** donnez-moi une livre de pommes, s'il vous plaît; **∼ a seat** asseyez-vous; **8** (accept) accepter [job, cheque, credit card, bribe]; prendre [patients, pupils, phone call]; [machine] accepter [coins]; supporter [pain, criticism]; accepter [punishment]; **will you ∼ £10 for the radio?** je vous offre 10 livres sterling en échange de votre radio; **that's my last offer, ∼ it or leave it!** c'est ma dernière proposition, c'est à prendre ou à laisser!; **whisky? I can ∼ it or leave it!** le whisky? je peux très bien m'en passer; **I find their attitude hard to ∼** je trouve leur attitude difficile à accepter; **he can't ∼ being criticized** il ne supporte pas qu'on le critique; **she just sat there and took it** elle est restée là et ne s'est pas défendue; **he can't ∼ a joke** il ne comprend pas la plaisanterie; **I can't ∼ any more!** je n'en peux plus!; **9** (require) [activity, course of action] demander, exiger [patience, skill, courage]; Ling [verb] prendre [object]; [preposition] être suivi de [case]; **it ∼s patience to do** il faut de la patience pour faire; **it ∼s three hours to get there** il faut trois heures pour y aller; **it won't ∼ long** ça ne prendra pas longtemps; **it took her ten minutes to repair it** elle a mis dix minutes pour le réparer; **the wall won't ∼ long to build** le mur sera vite construit; **to have what it ∼s** avoir tout ce qu'il faut (**to do** pour faire); **that'll ∼ some doing!** ce ne sera pas facile!; **she'll ∼ some persuading** ce sera difficile de la convaincre; **10** (react to) prendre [news, matter, comments]; **to ∼ things one step at a time** prendre les choses une par une; **11** (adopt) adopter [view, attitude]; prendre [measures, steps]; **to ∼ the view** ou **attitude that** être d'avis que, considérer que; **12** (assume) **I ∼ it that** je suppose que; **to ∼ sb for** ou **to be sth** prendre qn pour qch; **what do you ∼ me for?** pour qui est-ce que tu me prends?; **what do you ∼ this**

poem to mean? comment est-ce que vous interprétez ce poème?; **13** (consider) prendre [person, example, case]; **∼ Jack (for example), he has brought a family up by himself** prends Jack, il a élevé une famille tout seul; **14** (record) prendre [notes, statement, letter]; prendre [pulse, temperature, blood pressure]; Phot prendre [photograph]; **to ∼ sb's measurements** (for clothes) prendre les mesures de qn; **to ∼ a reading** lire les indications; **15** (hold) [hall, bus] pouvoir contenir [50 people, 50 passengers]; [tank, container] avoir une capacité de [quantity]; **the suitcase won't ∼ any more clothes** il est impossible de mettre plus de vêtements dans cette valise; **16** Sch, Univ (study) prendre, faire [subject]; suivre [course]; (sit) passer [exam, test]; (teach) [teacher, lecturer] faire cours à [students]; **to ∼ sb for Geography** faire cours de géographie à qn; **17** (wear) (in clothes) faire [size]; **what size do you ∼?** (in clothes) quelle taille faîtes-vous?; (in shoes) quelle est votre pointure?, quelle pointure faîtes-vous?; **I ∼ a size 5** (in shoes) je chausse du 38; **18** Math (subtract) soustraire [number, quantity]; **ten ∼ three is seven** dix moins trois égalent sept; **19** (officiate at) [priest] célébrer [service]

C vi (prét **took**; pp **taken**) (have desired effect) [drug] faire effet; [dye] prendre; (grow successfully) [plant] prendre

<u>**Idioms**</u> **to be on the ∼°** toucher des pots-de-vin; **to ∼ it** ou **a lot out of sb** fatiguer beaucoup qn; **to ∼ it upon oneself to do** prendre sur soi de faire; **to ∼ sb out of themselves** changer les idées à qn; **you can ∼ it from me** croyez-moi

<u>**Phrasal verbs**</u>

■ **take aback**: ▸ **∼ [sb] aback** interloquer [person]

■ **take after**: ▸ **∼ after [sb]** tenir de [parent]

■ **take against**: ▸ **∼ against [sb]** prendre [qn] en grippe

■ **take along**: ▸ **∼ [sb/sth] along, ∼ along [sb/sth]** emporter [object]; emmener [person]

■ **take apart**: ▸ **∼ apart** se démonter; ▸ **∼ [sth] apart** **1** (separate into parts) démonter [car, machine]; **2** °(criticize) descendre [qch] en flammes° [essay, film, book]; ▸ **∼ [sb/sth] apart°** (defeat) massacrer°

■ **take aside**: ▸ **∼ [sb] aside** prendre [qn] à part

■ **take away**: ▸ **∼ [sb/sth] away, ∼ away [sb/sth]** **1** (remove) enlever [object]; emmener [person]; supprimer [pain, grief]; **to ∼ away sb's appetite** faire perdre l'appétit à qn; **2** (subtract) soustraire [number]; **ten ∼ away seven is three** dix moins sept égalent trois; **that doesn't ∼ anything away from his achievement** fig ça n'enlève rien à ce qu'il a accompli

■ **take back**: ▸ **∼ [sth] back, ∼ back [sth]** **1** (return to shop) rapporter [goods]; **2** (retract) retirer [statement, words]; ▸ **∼ [sb] back** (cause to remember) rappeler des souvenirs à [person]; ▸ **∼ [sb/sth] back, ∼ back [sb/sth]** (accept again) reprendre

■ **take down**: ▸ **∼ [sth] down, ∼ down [sth]** **1** enlever [picture, curtains]; démonter [tent, scaffolding]; **2** (write down) noter [name, statement, details]

■ **take hold**: ▸ **∼ hold** [disease, epidemic] s'installer; [idea, ideology] se répandre; [influence] s'accroître; **to ∼ hold of** (grasp) prendre [object, hand]; fig (overwhelm) [feeling, anger] envahir; [idea] prendre

■ **take in**: ▸ **∼ [sb] in, ∼ in [sb]** **1** (deceive) tromper; **don't be taken in by appearances** ne te fie pas aux apparences; **I wasn't taken in by him** je ne me suis pas laissé prendre à son jeu; **2** (allow to stay) recueillir [person, refugee]; prendre [lodger]; ▸ **∼ in [sth]** **1** (understand) saisir, comprendre [situation]; **2** (observe) noter [detail]; embrasser [scene]; **3** (encompass) inclure [developments]; **4** (absorb) absorber [nutrients, oxygen]; fig s'imprégner de [atmosphere]; **5** [boat] prendre [water]; **6** (in sewing) reprendre [garment]; **7** (accept for payment) faire [qch] à domicile [washing, mending]; **8** °(visit) aller à [play, exhibition]

■ **take off**: ▸ **∼ off** **1** (leave the ground) [plane] décoller; **2** (be successful) [idea, fashion] prendre; [product] marcher; [sales] décoller; **3** °(leave hurriedly) filer°; ▸ **∼ [sth] off** **1** (deduct) **to ∼ £10 off (the price)** réduire le prix de 10 livres sterling; **2** (have as holiday) **to ∼ two days off** prendre deux jours de congé; **I'm taking next week off** je suis en congé la semaine prochaine; ▸ **∼ [sth] off [sth]** **1** (remove) enlever [clothing, shoes]; enlever [lid, feet, hands] (**from** de); supprimer [dish, train]; amputer [limb]; **to ∼ sth off the market** retirer qch du marché; **2** (withdraw) annuler [show, play]; ▸ **∼ [sb] off, ∼ off [sb]** **1** °(imitate) imiter [person]; **2** (remove) **to ∼ sb off the case** [police] retirer l'affaire à qn; **to ∼ oneself off** partir

t

■ **take on:** ▶ ∼ **on** (get upset) **don't** ∼ **on so** (stay calm) ne t'énerve pas; (don't worry) ne t'en fais pas; ▶ ∼ **[sb/sth] on**, ∼ **on [sb/sth]** ☐ (employ) embaucher [*staff, worker*]; ☐ (compete against) jouer contre [*team, player*]; (fight) se battre contre [*person, opponent*]; **to** ∼ **sb on at chess** jouer aux échecs contre qn; ☐ (accept) prendre [*responsibilities, work, task*]; ☐ (acquire) prendre [*look, colour, meaning*]

■ **take out:** ▶ ∼ **out** s'enlever; ▶ ∼ **[sth] out**, ∼ **out [sth]** ☐ (remove) sortir [*object*] (**from, of** de); extraire [*tooth*]; enlever [*appendix*]; (from bank) retirer [*money*]; ∼ **your hands out of your pockets!** enlève tes mains de tes poches!; ☐ **to** ∼ **sth out on sb** passer qch sur qn [*anger, frustration*]; **to** ∼ **it out on sb** s'en prendre à qn; ▶ ∼ **[sb] out** (go out with) sortir avec [*person*]; **to** ∼ **sb out to dinner** emmener qn dîner

■ **take over:** ▶ ∼ **over** ☐ (take control) [*army, faction*] prendre le pouvoir; ☐ (be successor) [*person*] prendre la suite; **to** ∼ **over from** remplacer [*predecessor*]; ▶ ∼ **over [sth]** (take control of) prendre le contrôle de [*town, country*]; reprendre [*business*]; Fin racheter, prendre le contrôle de [*company*]

■ **take part** prendre part; **to** ∼ **part in** participer à [*production, activity*]

■ **take place** avoir lieu

■ **take to:** ▶ ∼ **to [sb/sth]** ☐ (develop liking for) se prendre de sympathie pour [*person*]; **he has really taken to his new job** son nouvel emploi lui plaît vraiment beaucoup; ☐ (begin) **to** ∼ **to doing** se mettre à faire; **he's taken to smoking** il s'est mis à fumer; ☐ (go) se réfugier dans [*forest, hills*]; **to** ∼ **to one's bed** se mettre au lit; **to** ∼ **to the streets** descendre dans la rue

■ **take up:** ▶ ∼ **up** (continue story etc) reprendre; **to** ∼ **up with** s'attacher à [*person, group*]; ▶ ∼ **up [sth]** ☐ (lift up) enlever [*carpet, pavement, track*]; prendre [*pen*]; ☐ (start) se mettre à [*golf, guitar*]; prendre [*job*]; **to** ∼ **up a career as an actor** se lancer dans le métier d'acteur; **to** ∼ **up one's duties** ou **responsibilities** entrer dans ses fonctions; ☐ (continue) reprendre [*story, discussion, cry, refrain*]; ☐ (accept) accepter [*offer, invitation*]; relever [*challenge*]; **to** ∼ **up sb's case** Jur accepter de défendre qn; ☐ **to** ∼ **sth up with sb** soulever [qch] avec qn [*matter*]; ☐ (occupy) prendre [*space, time, energy*]; ☐ (adopt) prendre [*position, stance*]; ☐ (in sewing) (shorten) raccourcir [*skirt, curtains etc*]; ☐ (absorb) absorber [*liquid*]; ▶ ∼ **[sb] up** ☐ (adopt) adopter; ☐ **to** ∼ **sb up on** (challenge) reprendre qn sur [*point, assertion*]; (accept) **to** ∼ **sb up on an invitation/an offer** accepter l'invitation/l'offre de qn

take-away /ˈteɪkəweɪ/ *n* GB ☐ (meal) repas *m* à emporter; ☐ (restaurant) restaurant *m* qui fait des plats à emporter

take-home pay *n* salaire *m* net

taken /ˈteɪkn/
A *pp* ▶ **take B, C**
B *adj* ☐ (occupied) **to be** ∼ [*seat, room*] être occupé; ☐ (impressed) **to be** ∼ **with** être emballéᵒ par [*idea, person*]; **she's quite/very** ∼ **with him** il lui plaît assez/beaucoup

take-off /ˈteɪkɒf/ *n* ☐ Aviat décollage *m*; ☐ ᵒ(imitation) imitation *f* (**of** de)

take-out /ˈteɪkaʊt/ *adj* US [*food*] à emporter

takeover /ˈteɪkəʊvə(r)/ *n* Fin rachat *m*; Pol prise *f* de pouvoir

takeover bid *n* Fin offre *f* publique d'achat, OPA *f*

taker /ˈteɪkə(r)/ *n* preneur/-euse *m/f*

take-up /ˈteɪkʌp/ *n* (of benefit, rebate, shares) demande *f*

taking /ˈteɪkɪŋ/
A *n* prise *f*; **it was his for the** ∼ il n'avait qu'à se donner la peine de le prendre
B takings *npl* recette *f*

talc /tælk/, **talcum (powder)** /ˈtælkəm (ˌpaʊdə(r))/ *n* talc *m*

tale /teɪl/ *n* (story) histoire *f*; (fantasy story) conte *m*; (narrative, account) récit *m*; (legend) légende *f*; **the figures tell the same/another** ∼ les chiffres disent la même chose/tout autre chose; **the recent events tell their own** ∼ les récents événements parlent d'eux-mêmes; **to spread** ou **tell** ∼**s** raconter des histoires

Idioms **a likely** ∼**!** et puis quoi encore!; **dead men tell no** ∼**s** les morts ne parlent pas; **to live to tell the** ∼ être encore là pour en parler; **to tell** ∼**s out of school** révéler des choses indiscrètes

talent /ˈtælənt/ *n* talent *m*; **to have a** ∼ **for** être doué pour; **there's a lot of** ∼ **in that team** il y a beaucoup de gens de talent dans cette équipe

talent contest *n* concours *m* de jeunes talents *or* d'amateurs (*pour découvrir de futures vedettes*)

talented /ˈtæləntɪd/ *adj* doué, talentueux/-euse

talent ∼ **scout** *n* découvreur/-euse *m/f* de nouveaux talents; ∼ **show** *n* = **talent contest**

talisman /ˈtælɪzmən, ˈtælɪs-/ *n* talisman *m*

talk /tɔːk/
A *n* ☐ (talking, gossip) propos *mpl*; **there is** ∼ **of sth/of doing** il est question de qch/de faire; **there is** ∼ **that** on dit que; **he's all** ∼ il parle beaucoup mais agit peu; **it's just** ∼ ce ne sont que des paroles en l'air; **they are the** ∼ **of the town** on ne parle que d'eux; ☐ (conversation) conversation *f*, discussion *f*; **to have a** ∼ **with sb** parler à qn; ☐ (speech) exposé *m* (**about, on** sur); (more informal) causerie *f*; **to give a** ∼ faire un exposé
B talks *npl* gen négociations *fpl*; Pol pourparlers *mpl*; **arms** ∼**s** conférence sur le désarmement; **pay** ∼**s** négociations salariales
C *vtr* parler; **to** ∼ **business** parler affaires; **to** ∼ **nonsense** raconter n'importe quoi; **we're** ∼**ing three years**ᵒ il faut compter trois ans; **we're** ∼**ing big money**ᵒ here il s'agit ici de sommes importantes; **to** ∼ **sb into/out of doing** persuader/dissuader qn de faire; **you've** ∼**ed me into it!** vous m'avez convaincu!; **he** ∼**ed his way out of it** il s'en est tiré grâce à son bagoutᵒ
D *vi* gen parler; (gossip) bavarder; **to** ∼ **to oneself** parler tout seul; **to** ∼ **at sb** parler à qn sans l'écouter; **to keep sb** ∼**ing** faire parler qn aussi longtemps que possible; ∼**ing of tennis...** à propos de tennis...; **look who's** ∼**ing!**, **you're a fine one to** ∼**!**, **you can** ∼**!** tu peux parler!; **now you're** ∼**ing!** eh bien voilà!; ∼ **about stupid**ᵒ**!** comme idiotie, ça se pose un peu làᵒ!

Phrasal verbs
■ **talk back** répondre (insolemment) (**to** à)
■ **talk down: to** ∼ **down to sb** parler à qn avec condescendance
■ **talk over:** ▶ ∼ **[sth] over** discuter de [*matter, issue*]; ▶ ∼ **[sb] over** faire changer [qn] d'avis
■ **talk round:** ▶ ∼ **round [sth]** tourner autour de [*subject*]; ▶ ∼ **[sb] round** faire changer [qn] d'avis
■ **talk through:** ▶ ∼ **[sth] through** discuter de [qch] tranquillement

talkative /ˈtɔːkətɪv/ *adj* bavard

talked-about /ˈtɔːktəbaʊt/ *adj* **the much** ∼ **group** le groupe dont on a beaucoup parlé

talker /ˈtɔːkə(r)/ *n* **to be a good** ∼ avoir de la conversation; **he's not a great** ∼ il n'est pas bavard; **to be a slow/fluent** ∼ parler lentement/avec aisance

talking /ˈtɔːkɪŋ/
A *n* **there's been enough** ∼ assez de paroles!; **I'll do the** ∼ c'est moi qui parlerai; **'no** ∼**!'** 'silence!'
B *adj* [*bird, doll*] qui parle

talking: ∼ **book** *n* livre *m* enregistré (à l'usage des non-voyants); ∼ **heads** *npl* interlocuteurs/-trices *mpl/fpl*; ∼ **point** *n* sujet *m* de conversation

talking-to /ˈtɔːkɪŋtuː/ *n* réprimande *f*

tall /tɔːl/ ▶ p. 977 *adj* [*person*] grand; [*building, tree, grass, chimney, mast*] haut; **he's six feet** ∼ ≈ il mesure un mètre quatre-vingts; **to get** ou **grow** ∼**er** grandir

Idioms **that's (a bit of) a** ∼ **order!** c'est beaucoup demander!; **a** ∼ **story** ou **tale** une histoire à dormir debout; **to walk** ∼ marcher la tête haute; **to feel (about) ten feet** ∼ se sentir tout fier

tallness /ˈtɔːlnɪs/ *n* (of person) grande taille *f*; (of building, tree, chimney, mast) hauteur *f*

tally /ˈtælɪ/
A *n* compte *m*
B *vi* concorder

talon /ˈtælən/ *n* Zool serre *f*

tambourine /ˌtæmbəˈriːn/ ▶ p. 1028 *n* tambourin *m*

tame /teɪm/
A *adj* ☐ [*animal*] apprivoisé; **to become** ou **grow** ∼ [*animal*] s'apprivoiser; ☐ (unadventurous) [*story, party*] sans relief; [*reform*] timide; [*reply, ending of book, film*] plat
B *vtr* gen apprivoiser; dompter [*lion, tiger*]; fig soumettre [*person*]; contenir [*opposition*]

tamely /'teɪmlɪ/ *adv* (meekly) docilement; (flatly) platement

tamper /'tæmpə(r)/ *vi* **to ~ with** tripoter [*machinery, lock*]; trafiquer [*accounts, evidence, product*]

tan /tæn/
A *n* **1** (*also* **sun~**) bronzage *m*; (weather-beaten) hâle *m*; **to get a ~** bronzer; **2** (colour) fauve *m*
B *adj* fauve
C *vtr* (*p prés etc* **-nn-**) **1** bronzer; **2** tanner [*animal hide*]; **to ~ sb's hide** fig flanquer une raclée à qn○
D *vi* (*p prés etc* **-nn-**) bronzer

tandem /'tændəm/ *n* tandem *m*; **in ~** en tandem

tang /tæŋ/ *n* (taste) goût *m* acidulé; (smell) odeur *f* piquante

tangent /'tændʒənt/ *n* (all contexts) tangente *f*; **to fly off at a ~** [*object, ball*] dévier; **to go off at** *ou* **on a ~** (in speech) partir dans une digression

tangerine /'tændʒəriːn/
A *n* (fruit, colour) mandarine *f*
B *adj* mandarine *inv*

tangible /'tændʒəbl/ *adj* tangible

tangibly /'tændʒəblɪ/ *adv* (clearly) manifestement

tangle /'tæŋgl/
A *n* (of hair, string, wires) enchevêtrement *m*; (of clothes, sheets) fouillis *m*; **in a ~** tout embrouillé; **to get in** *ou* **into a ~** s'embrouiller; **to get in** *ou* **into a ~** fig [*person*] s'empêtrer
B *vtr*= **tangle up**
C *vi* **1** [*hair, string, cable*] s'emmêler; **2** = **tangle up**
(Phrasal verbs)
■ **tangle up:** ▸ **~ up** s'embrouiller; ▸ **~ up [sth]**, **~ [sth] up** embrouiller; **to get ~d up** [*hair, string, wires*] s'emmêler; [*clothes*] s'entortiller; [*person*] fig s'empêtrer
■ **tangle with:** ▸ **~ with [sb/sth]** se frotter à

tangled /'tæŋgld/ *adj* **1** [*hair, wool, wire*] emmêlé; [*brambles, wires, wreckage*] enchevêtré; **2** [*situation*] embrouillé

tango /'tæŋgəʊ/
A *n* tango *m*
B *vi* danser le tango
(Idiom) **it takes two to ~** tous les torts ne peuvent pas être du même côté

tangy /'tæŋɪ/ *adj* acidulé

tank /tæŋk/ *n* **1** (container) (for storage) réservoir *m*; (for heating oil) cuve *f*; (for water) citerne *f*; (for processing) cuve *f*; (small) bac *m*; (for fish) aquarium *m*; Aut réservoir *m*; **2** Mil char *m* (de combat)

tankard /'tæŋkəd/ *n* chope *f* (*souvent en métal*)

tanker /'tæŋkə(r)/ *n* **1** Naut navire-citerne *m*; **oil ~**, **petrol ~** pétrolier *m*; **2** (lorry) camion-citerne *m*

tankful /'tæŋkfʊl/ *n* (of petrol) réservoir *m* plein (**of** de); (of water) citerne *f* pleine (**of** de)

tanned /tænd/ *adj* (*also* **sun~**) bronzé

tannin /'tænɪn/ *n* tanin *m*

tanning /'tænɪŋ/ *n* **1** (by sun) bronzage *m*; **2** (of hides) tannage *m*

Tannoy® /'tænɔɪ/ *n* GB **the ~** le système de haut-parleurs; **over the ~** par les haut-parleurs

tantalize /'tæntəlaɪz/ *vtr* allécher

tantalizing /'tæntəlaɪzɪŋ/ *adj* [*suggestion*] tentant; [*possibility*] séduisant; [*glimpse*] excitant, qui fait envie; [*smell*] alléchant

tantalizingly /'tæntəlaɪzɪŋlɪ/ *adv* **to be ~ close to victory** être à deux doigts de la victoire; **the truth was ~ elusive** la vérité était cruellement insaisissable

tantamount /'tæntəmaʊnt/ *adj* **to be ~ to** équivaloir à, être équivalent à

tantrum /'tæntrəm/ *n* crise *f* (*de colère*); **to throw** *ou* **have a ~** piquer une crise○

tap /tæp/
A *n* **1** (for water, gas) robinet *m*; **the cold/hot ~** le robinet d'eau froide/chaude; **to turn the ~ on/off** ouvrir/fermer le robinet; **on ~** [*beer*] pression *inv*; [*wine*] en fût; fig disponible; **2** (blow) petit coup *m*; **he felt a ~ on his shoulder** il a senti une tape sur son épaule; **she heard a ~ at the door** elle a entendu frapper à la porte; **to give sth a ~** donner un petit coup à qch; **3** (listening device) **to put a ~ on a phone** mettre un téléphone sur écoute
B *vtr* (*p prés etc* **-pp-**) **1** (knock) [*person*] taper (doucement); (repeatedly) tapoter; **to ~ a rhythm** battre la mesure;

2 (install listening device) mettre [qch] sur écoute [*telephone*]; **3** (extract contents) mettre en perce [*barrel*]; inciser [*rubber tree*]; exploiter [*resources, energy*]; **to ~ sb for money**○ taper○ qn
C *vi* (*p prés etc* **-pp-**) [*person, finger, foot*] taper
(Phrasal verb)
■ **tap in:** ▸ **~ [sth] in**, **~ in [sth]** enfoncer [*nail, peg*]; Comput taper [*information, number*]

tap dance *n* (*also* **~ dancing**) claquettes *fpl*

tape /teɪp/
A *n* **1** gen bande *f* (magnétique); (cassette) cassette *f*; (video) cassette *f* vidéo; (recording) enregistrement *m*; **to play a ~** mettre une cassette; **on ~** en cassette; **to make a ~ of** faire un enregistrement de; **2** (strip of fabric) ruban *m*; **3** (*also* **adhesive ~**, **sticky ~**) scotch® *m*; **4** Sport (in race) fil *m* d'arrivée; **5** (for measuring) mètre *m* ruban
B *vtr* **1** (record) enregistrer; **to ~ sth** enregistrer qch transmis à [*radio, TV*]; **2** (stick) **to ~ sb's hands together** attacher les mains de qn avec du scotch®; **to ~ sth to** coller qch à [*surface, door*]
(Idiom) **to have sb ~d**○ savoir ce que vaut qn; **to have sth ~d**○ connaître qch comme sa poche
(Phrasal verb)
■ **tape up:** ▸ **~ [sth] up**, **~ up [sth]** recoller [qch] avec du scotch® [*parcel, box*]

tape: **~ deck** *n* platine *f* cassette; **~ head** *n* tête *f* de lecture; **~ measure** *n* gen mètre *m* ruban; (retractable) mètre *m* enrouleur

taper /'teɪpə(r)/
A *n* (spill) bougie *f* filée; (candle) cierge *m*
B *vtr* tailler [qch] en pointe [*stick, fabric*]
C *vi* [*sleeve, trouser leg*] se resserrer; [*column, spire*] s'effiler; **to ~ to a point** se terminer en pointe
(Phrasal verb)
■ **taper off:** ▸ **~ off** diminuer; ▸ **~ off [sth]**, **~ [sth] off** diminuer [qch] progressivement

tape: **~ recorder** *n* magnétophone *m*; **~ recording** *n* enregistrement *m*

tapered /'teɪpəd/, **tapering** /'teɪpərɪŋ/ *adj* [*trousers*] en forme de fuseau; [*sleeves*] aux poignets étroits; [*column, wing*] fuselé; [*finger, flame*] effilé

tapestry /'tæpəstrɪ/ *n* tapisserie *f*

tapeworm /'teɪpwɜːm/ *n* ver *m* solitaire, ténia *m*

tap water *n* eau *f* du robinet

tar /tɑː(r)/
A *n* gen goudron *m*; (on roads) bitume *m*
B *noun modifier* [*road, paper*] goudronné; **~ content** (of cigarette) taux *m* de goudron
C *vtr* (*p prés etc* **-rr-**) goudronner [*road, roof*]
(Idiom) **to ~ everyone with the same brush** mettre tout le monde dans le même sac

target /'tɑːgɪt/
A *n* **1** gen cible *f*; Mil objectif *m*; **to be right on ~** lit être en plein dans la cible; fig mettre en plein dans le mille; **2** (goal, objective) objectif *m*; **to meet one's ~** atteindre son but; **the figures are way below ~** les chiffres sont très insuffisants; **3** (butt) cible *f*; **to be the ~ of** être objet de [*abuse, ridicule*]
B *noun modifier* [*date, figure*] prévu; [*audience, group*] visé, ciblé
C *vtr* **1** Mil (aim) diriger [*weapon, missile*]; (choose as objective) prendre [qch] pour cible [*city, site, factory*]; **2** fig (in marketing) viser [*group, sector*]; **to be ~ed at** [*product, publication*] viser [*group*]

targeting /'tɑːgɪtɪŋ/ *n* **1** Comm ciblage *m* (**of** de); **2** Mil **the ~ of enemy bases** la prise de bases ennemies comme objectif

target: **~ language** *n* langue *f* cible; **~ practice** *n* ¢ exercices *mpl* de tir sur cible; **~ price** *n* prix *m* indicatif

tariff /'tærɪf/
A *n* (price list) tarif *m*; (customs duty) droit *m* de douane
B *noun modifier* [*agreement, barrier, cut*] tarifaire; [*reform*] des tarifs douaniers

tarmac /'tɑːmæk/
A *n* **1** (*also* **Tarmac**®) macadam *m*; **2** GB (of airfield) piste *f*
B *noun modifier* [*road, footpath*] goudronné
C *vtr* (*p prés etc* **-ck-**) goudronner

tarnish /'tɑːnɪʃ/
A vtr ternir also fig
B vi se ternir also fig

tarpaulin /tɑːˈpɔːlɪn/ n (material) toile f de bâche; (sheet) bâche f

tarragon /'tærəgən/ n estragon m

tart /tɑːt/
A n ① Culin (individual) tartelette f; GB (large) tarte f; ② ○injur pute○ f
B adj [flavour] aigrelet/-ette; [remark] acerbe

(Phrasal verb)
  ■ **tart up**○ GB: ▸ ~ [sth] up, ~ up [sth] retaper○ [house, room]; ▸ ~ oneself up se pomponner○

tartan /'tɑːtn/ n, adj écossais (m)

tartar /'tɑːtə(r)/ n ① (deposit) tartre m; ② (formidable person) (woman) virago f; (man) croque-mitaine m

tartly /'tɑːtlɪ/ adv [say] d'un ton acerbe

task /tɑːsk, US tæsk/ n tâche f; **a hard** ~ une lourde tâche; **to have the** ~ **of doing** avoir pour tâche de faire

(Idiom) **to take sb to** ~ réprimander qn

taskbar /tɑːskbɑː(r), US tæskbɑː(r)/ n barre f des tâches

task force n Mil corps m expéditionnaire; (of police) détachement m spécial; (committee) groupe m de travail

taskmaster /'tɑːskmɑːstə(r), US 'tæsk-/ n tyran m; **to be a hard** ~ être très exigeant

tassel /'tæsl/ n (ornamental) gland m; (on corn etc) barbe f

taste /teɪst/
A n ① (sensation, sense) goût m; **to leave a bad** ou **nasty** ~ **in the mouth** lit, fig laisser un arrière-goût; **have a** ~ **of this** goûtes-en un peu; **add just a** ~ **of brandy** ajoutez une goutte de cognac; ② (brief experience) gen expérience f; (foretaste) avant-goût m; **a** ~ **of life in a big city** un aperçu de la vie dans une grande ville; ③ (liking, preference) goût m; **to acquire** ou **develop a** ~ **for sth** prendre goût à qch; **is this to your** ~? est-ce que ceci vous convient?; **there's no accounting for** ~s chacun ses goûts; **add salt to** ~ saler à volonté; ④ (sense of beauty, appropriateness) goût m; **she has exquisite** ~ **in clothes** elle s'habille avec un goût exquis; **that's a matter of** ~ ça dépend des goûts; **it would be in bad** ou **poor** ~ **to do** ce serait de mauvais goût de faire
B vtr ① (perceive flavour) sentir (le goût de); ② (try) goûter; ③ fig (experience) goûter à [freedom, success, power]; connaître [failure, hardship]
C vi (have flavour) **to** ~ **sweet** avoir un goût sucré; **to** ~ **horrible** avoir mauvais goût; **the milk** ~s **off to me** je crois que ce lait est tourné; **to** ~ **like** sth avoir le goût de qch; **it** ~s **of pineapple** cela a un goût d'ananas

taste bud n papille f gustative

tasteful /'teɪstfl/ adj de bon goût

tastefully /'teɪstfəlɪ/ adv avec goût

tasteless /'teɪstlɪs/ adj ① [remark, joke] de mauvais goût; ② (without flavour) [food, drink] insipide; [medicine, powder] qui n'a aucun goût

taster /'teɪstə(r)/ n ① (person) (to check quality) dégustateur/-trice m/f; (to check for poison) goûteur/-euse m/f; ② (foretaste) avant-goût m (of, for de)

tasting /'teɪstɪŋ/
A n dégustation f
B -**tasting** combining form pleasant-~ (au goût) agréable; sweet-~ (au goût) sucré

tasty /'teɪstɪ/ adj [food] succulent

tattered /'tætəd/ adj [clothing] dépenaillé; [book, document] en lambeaux; [person] déguenillé

tatters /'tætəz/ npl lambeaux mpl; **to be in** ~ [clothing] être en lambeaux; [career, reputation] être en ruines; [hopes] réduit à néant

tattle /'tætl/
A n (also **tittle-tattle**) commérages mpl
B vi jaser (about sur)

tattoo /tə'tuː, US tæ'tuː/
A n ① (on skin) tatouage m; ② Mil (parade) parade f militaire
B vtr tatouer (on sur)

tatty○ /'tætɪ/ adj GB [appearance] négligé; [carpet, garment] miteux/-euse; [book, shoes] en mauvais état; [building, furniture] délabré

taught /tɔːt/ prét, pp ▸ **teach**

taunt /tɔːnt/
A n raillerie f
B vtr railler [person] (about, over à propos de)

taunting /'tɔːntɪŋ/
A n ¢ railleries fpl
B adj railleur/-euse, moqueur/-euse

Taurus /'tɔːrəs/ ▸ p. 1350 n Taureau m

taut /tɔːt/ adj tendu

tauten /'tɔːtn/
A vtr tendre
B vi se tendre

tautology /tɔː'tɒlədʒɪ/ n tautologie f

tawdry /'tɔːdrɪ/ adj [clothes] voyant; [jewellery] clinquant; [furnishings, house] de mauvais goût; fig [motives, methods] bas/basse; [affair] minable

tawny /'tɔːnɪ/ adj ▸ p. 752 fauve

tawny owl n Zool chouette f hulotte

tax /tæks/
A n (on goods, services, property) taxe f; (on income, profits) impôt m; **sales** ~ taxe à l'achat; ~ **is deducted at source** les impôts sont retenus à la source; **to be liable for** ~ être imposable
B vtr ① imposer [earnings, person]; taxer [luxury goods]; ② Aut **to** ~ **a vehicle** payer la vignette; **the car is** ~ed **till November** la vignette est valable jusqu'en novembre; ③ (strain) mettre [qch] à l'épreuve [patience]

taxable /'tæksəbl/ adj imposable

tax: ~ **allowance** n abattement m; ~ **arrears** npl arriérés mpl fiscaux

taxation /tæk'seɪʃn/ n ① (imposition of taxes) imposition f; ② (revenue from taxes) impôts mpl

tax: ~ **bracket** n tranche f d'imposition du revenu; ~ **break** n réduction f d'impôt; ~ **burden** n charge f fiscale; ~ **code** n code m d'imposition; ~ **collector** n percepteur m; ~-**deductible** adj déductible des impôts; ~ **disc** n vignette f (automobile); ~ **evasion** n fraude f fiscale; ~-**exempt** adj exonéré d'impôt; ~ **exile** n: personne qui s'est expatriée pour raisons fiscales; ~ **form** n feuille f d'impôts; ~-**free** adj [income] exempt d'impôt; ~ **haven** n paradis m fiscal

taxi /'tæksɪ/
A n taxi m; **by** ~ en taxi
B vi [plane] rouler doucement

tax incentive n incitation f fiscale

taxing /'tæksɪŋ/ adj épuisant

taxi rank GB, **taxi stand** n station f de taxis

taxman○ /'tæksmæn/ n **the** ~ le fisc

tax office n perception f

taxpayer /'tækspeɪə(r)/ n contribuable mf

tax return n ① (form) feuille f d'impôts; ② (declaration) déclaration f de revenus; **to file a** ~ faire sa déclaration d'impôts

TB n: abrév ▸ **tuberculosis**

tbsp n: abrév écrite = **tablespoon**

te /tiː/ n Mus (also **ti**) si m

tea /tiː/ n ① thé m; ② GB (light afternoon meal) thé m; (for children) goûter m; (evening meal) dîner m

(Idioms) **it's not my cup of** ~ ce n'est pas mon truc○; **to give sb** ~ **and sympathy** réconforter qn

tea: ~ **bag** n sachet m de thé; ~ **break** n GB ≈ pause-café f; ~ **caddy** n boîte f à thé; ~ **cake** n GB brioche f aux raisins

teach /tiːtʃ/ (prét, pp **taught**)
A vtr ① (instruct) enseigner à [children, adults]; (impart) enseigner [foreign language, biology]; **to** ~ **sb about sth** gen enseigner [foreign language, biology]; **to** ~ **sb about sth** gen enseigner qch à qn; (practical skill) apprendre qch à qn; **he taught me (how) to drive** il m'a appris à conduire; **she** ~es **swimming** elle est professeur de natation; **to** ~ **school** US être instituteur/-trice; **to** ~ **sb a lesson** fig [person] donner une bonne leçon à qn; [experience] servir de leçon à qn; ② (advocate) enseigner [creed, virtue]
B vi enseigner
C v refl **to** ~ **oneself to do** s'apprendre à faire; **to** ~ **oneself Spanish** apprendre l'espagnol tout seul

(Idiom) **you can't** ~ **an old dog new tricks** il est difficile de déranger les vieilles habitudes

teacher /'tiːtʃə(r)/ ▸ p. 1181 n (in general) enseignant/-e m/f; (secondary) professeur m; (primary) instituteur/-trice m/f; (special needs) éducateur/-trice m/f

teacher training n formation f pédagogique

teaching /'tiːtʃɪŋ/
A n enseignement m; **to go into** ou **enter ~** entrer dans l'enseignement; **to do some ~ in the evenings** donner quelques cours le soir
B noun modifier [career, post] d'enseignant; [method, qualification] pédagogique; [staff] enseignant

teaching aid n support m pédagogique

teaching assistant, TA ▸ p. 1181 n ⏹ US Univ chargé/-e m/f d'enseignement; ⏹ GB Sch personne sans diplôme d'enseignement qui aide l'instituteur

teaching hospital n centre m hospitalo-universitaire, CHU

teaching practice n GB stage m de formation pédagogique; **to be on** ou **be doing ~** être en stage

tea: **~ cloth** n GB (for drying) torchon m (à vaisselle); **~ cosy** GB, **~ cozy** US n couvre-théière m inv

teacup /'tiːkʌp/ n tasse f à thé
(Idiom) **a storm in a ~** une tempête dans un verre d'eau

teak /tiːk/ n teck m

tea lady ▸ p. 1181 n GB employée qui distribue du thé dans les bureaux

tea leaf n feuille f de thé; **to read the tea-leaves** ≈ lire dans le marc de café

team /tiːm/
A n ⏹ (of people) équipe f; **to work well as a ~** faire un bon travail d'équipe; ⏹ (of animals) attelage m
B vtr (coordinate) associer [garment] (**with** à)
(Phrasal verb)
■ **team up**: ▸ **~ up** [people] faire équipe; [organizations] s'associer; ▸ **~ [sb] up** associer

team: **~ member** n équipier/-ière m/f; **~ spirit** n esprit m d'équipe

teamster /'tiːmstə(r)/ n US routier m

teamwork n collaboration f

tea: **~ party** n thé m; (for children) goûter m; **~ plate** n petite assiette f

teapot /'tiːpɒt/ n théière f

tear¹ /teə(r)/
A n gen accroc m; Med déchirure f
B vtr (prét **tore**; pp **torn**) ⏹ (rip) déchirer [garment, paper]; mettre [qch] en pièces [flesh, prey]; **to ~ sth from** ou **out of** arracher qch de [book, notepad]; **I've torn a hole in my coat** j'ai fait un accroc à mon manteau; **to ~ sth to pieces** ou **bits** ou **shreds** lit mettre qch en morceaux; fig démolir [proposal, book, film]; **to ~ sb to pieces** fig descendre qn en flammes; **to ~ one's hair (out)** lit, fig s'arracher les cheveux; **to ~ a muscle** se déchirer un muscle; **to be torn between** fig être tiraillé entre [options, persons]; ⏹ (remove by force) arracher
C vi (prét **tore**; pp **torn**) ⏹ (rip) se déchirer; ⏹ (rush) **to ~ out/off/past** sortir/partir/passer en trombe; **to ~ up/down the stairs** monter/descendre les escaliers quatre à quatre; ⏹ (pull forcefully) **to ~ at** [animal] déchiqueter [flesh, prey]; [person] s'attaquer à [rubble]; ⏹ ○(criticize) **to ~ into** enguirlander○ [person]; démolir○ [play, film, book]
D tearing pres p adj ⏹ **a ~ing sound** un bruit de déchirement; ⏹ ○**to be in a ~ing hurry** GB être terriblement pressé (**to do** de faire)
(Idiom) **that's torn it**○! GB il ne manquait plus que ça!
(Phrasal verbs)
■ **tear apart**: ▸ **~ [sth] apart, ~ apart [sth]** ⏹ (destroy) lit mettre [qch] en pièces [prey]; démolir [building]; fig déchirer [couple, organization, country]; démolir○ [film, novel, essay]; ⏹ (separate) séparer [connected items]; ▸ **~ [sb] apart** ⏹ ○(criticize) descendre [qn] en flammes; ⏹ (dismember) mettre [qn] en pièces; (separate) séparer [two people]
■ **tear away**: ▸ **~ away** [paper, tape] se déchirer; ▸ **~ away [sth]** arracher [wrapping, bandage]; ▸ **~ [sb] away** arracher [person]; **to ~ one's gaze away** détacher ses yeux
■ **tear down**: ▸ **~ [sth] down, ~ down [sth]** démolir [building, wall]
■ **tear off**: ▸ **~ [sth] off, ~ off [sth]** (remove) (carefully) détacher; (violently) arracher
■ **tear open**: ▸ **~ [sth] open, ~ [sth] open** ouvrir [qch] en le/la déchirant
■ **tear out**: ▸ **~ [sth] out, ~ out [sth]** détacher [coupon, cheque]; arracher [page, picture]

■ **tear up**: ▸ **~ [sth] up, ~ up [sth]** ⏹ (destroy) déchirer [letter, document]; ⏹ (remove) déraciner [tree]; arracher [tracks]; défoncer [pavement]

tear² /tɪə(r)/ n larme f; **close to ~s** au bord des larmes; **to burst into ~s** fondre en larmes; **to shed ~s** pleurer; **it brought ~s to her eyes, it moved her to ~s** elle en avait les larmes aux yeux
(Idiom) **to end in ~s** [game, party] finir par des pleurs; [campaign, experiment] mal se terminer

tearaway /'teərəweɪ/ n casse-cou m inv

tear tɪə(r): **~drop** n larme f; **~ duct** n conduit m lacrymal

tearful /'tɪəfl/ adj [person, face] en larmes; [voice] larmoyant; **to feel ~** avoir envie de pleurer; **a ~ reunion** des retrouvailles émues

tearfully /'tɪəfəlɪ/ adv [say, tell] les larmes aux yeux

tear gas /tɪə(r)/ n gaz m lacrymogène

tear-jerker /'tɪədʒɜːkə(r)/ n hum, péj **this film is a real ~** ce film est un vrai mélo○

tear-off /'teərɒf/ adj [coupon, slip] détachable

tear-stained /'tɪəsteɪnd/ adj [face] barbouillé de larmes; [pillow, letter] mouillé de larmes

tease /tiːz/
A n ⏹ (joker) taquin/-e m/f; ⏹ (woman) péj allumeuse f pej
B vtr ⏹ (provoke) taquiner [person] (**about** à propos de); tourmenter [animal]; ⏹ (backcomb) crêper [hair]
C vi taquiner

teasel /'tiːzl/ n Bot cardère f

teaser /'tiːzə(r)/ n ⏹ ○(puzzle) colle○ f; ⏹ (person) taquin/-e m/f

tea: **~ service, ~ set** n service m à thé; **~ shop** n GB salon m de thé

teasing /'tiːzɪŋ/
A n gen taquineries fpl
B adj taquin, moqueur/-euse

tea: **~spoon** n petite cuillère f, cuillère f à café; **~spoonful** n cuillerée f à café; **~ strainer** n passe-thé m inv, passoire f (à thé)

teat /tiːt/ n ⏹ (of cow, goat, ewe) trayon m; ⏹ GB (on baby's bottle) tétine f

tea: **~time** n (in the afternoon) l'heure f du thé; (in the evening) l'heure f du dîner; **~ towel** n GB torchon m (à vaisselle)

tech /tek/ n ○GB abrév ▸ **technical college**

techie○ /'tekɪ/ n technicien/-ienne m/f pur/-e et dur/-e

technical /'teknɪkl/ adj ⏹ gen, Sport technique; **a ~ hitch** un incident technique; **the ~ staff** les techniciens; ⏹ Jur [point, detail] de procédure; **~ offence** quasi-délit m

technical: **~ college** n institut m d'enseignement technique; **~ drawing** n dessin m industriel

technicality /ˌteknɪ'kælətɪ/ n ⏹ gen (technical detail) détail m technique (**of** de); ⏹ (minor detail) point m de détail; **the case was dismissed on a ~** Jur l'affaire a été renvoyée pour vice de forme; ⏹ (technical nature) technicité f

technically /'teknɪklɪ/ adv ⏹ (strictly speaking) théoriquement; ⏹ (technologically) [advanced, backward, difficult, possible] techniquement; ⏹ (in technique) [good, bad] sur le plan technique

technician /tek'nɪʃn/ ▸ p. 1181 n (all contexts) technicien/-ienne m/f

technique /tek'niːk/ n ⏹ (method) technique f; ⏹ (skill) technique f

technobabble /'teknəʊˌbæbl/ n jargon m technologique

technocrat /'teknəkræt/ n technocrate mf

technological /ˌteknə'lɒdʒɪkl/ adj technologique

technologically /ˌteknə'lɒdʒɪklɪ/ adv sur le plan technologique

technology /tek'nɒlədʒɪ/ n (all contexts) technologie f; **information ~** informatique f

technology park n parc m technologique

teddy /'tedɪ/ n (also **~ bear**) ours m en peluche

tedious /'tiːdɪəs/ adj ennuyeux/-euse

tedium /'tiːdɪəm/ n ⏹ (boredom) ennui m; ⏹ (tediousness) manque m d'intérêt

teem /tiːm/
A vi **to ~ with, to be ~ing with** regorger de [people]; abonder

t

en [*wildlife*]; fourmiller de [*ideas*]
B *v impers* **it was ~ing (with rain)** il pleuvait des cordes
C teeming *pres p adj* [*city, continent, ocean*] grouillant (**with** de); [*masses, crowds*] grouillant

teen○ /tiːn/ *adj* [*fashion*] pour les jeunes; [*idol*] des jeunes

teenage /ˈtiːneɪdʒ/ *adj* [*daughter, son*] qui est adolescent/-e; [*singer, player*] jeune; [*illiteracy, drug-taking*] chez les adolescents; [*pregnancy*] précoce; [*fashion, problem*] des adolescents

teenager /ˈtiːneɪdʒə(r)/ *n* jeune *mf*, adolescent/-e *m/f*

teens /tiːnz/ *npl* adolescence *f*; **to be in one's ~** être adolescent/-e; **to be in one's early/late ~** être au début/à la fin de l'adolescence

tee-shirt /ˈtiːʃɜːt/ *n* tee-shirt, T-shirt *m*

teeter /ˈtiːtə(r)/ *vi* vaciller; **to ~ on the edge** *ou* **brink of sth** fig être au bord de qch

teeter-totter /ˈtiːtətɒtə(r)/ *n* US bascule *f*

teeth /tiːθ/ *npl* ▸ **tooth**

teethe /tiːð/ *vi* faire ses dents

teething /ˈtiːðɪŋ/ *n* poussée *f* des dents

teething troubles *npl* fig difficultés *fpl* initiales

teetotal /tiːˈtəʊtl, US ˈtiːtəʊtl/ *adj* **I'm ~** je ne bois jamais d'alcool

teetotaller GB, **teetotaler** US /tiːˈtəʊtələ(r)/ *n* personne *f* qui ne boit jamais d'alcool

TEFL /ˈtefl/ *n* (*abrév* = **Teaching of English as a Foreign Language**) enseignement *m* de l'anglais langue étrangère

tel *n* (*abrév écrite* = **telephone**) tél

tele+ /ˈtelɪ-/ *combining form* télé+

telebanking /ˈtelɪˌbæŋkɪŋ/ *n* services *mpl* bancaires par téléphone

telecast /ˈtelɪkɑːst, US -kæst/
A *n* émission *f* de télévision
B *vtr* (*prét, pp* **telecast(ed)**) diffuser [qch] à la télévision

telecommunications /ˌtelɪkəˌmjuːnɪˈkeɪʃnz/
A *n* (+ *v sg ou pl*) télécommunications *fpl*
B *noun modifier* [*expert*] en télécommunications; [*firm, satellite*] de télécommunications; [*industry*] des télécommunications

telecommuting /ˌtelɪkəˈmjuːtɪŋ/ *n* télétravail *m*

teleconference /ˈtelɪkɒnfərəns/ *n* téléconférence *f*

telecottage /ˈtelɪkɒtɪdʒ/ *n* cybercentre *m*

telegram /ˈtelɪɡræm/ *n* télégramme *m*

telegraph /ˈtelɪɡrɑːf, US -ɡræf/
A *n* **1** Telecom télégraphe *m*; **2** Naut transmetteur *m* d'ordres
B *noun modifier* [*pole, post, wire*] télégraphique
C *vtr* télégraphier

telegraphy /tɪˈleɡrəfɪ/ *n* télégraphie *f*

telemarketer /ˈtelɪmɑːkɪtə(r)/ *n* téléprospecteur/-trice *m/f*

telemarketing /ˈtelɪmɑːkɪtɪŋ/ *n* télémarketing *m*

telemessage /ˈtelɪmesɪdʒ/ *n* GB télégramme *m*

telepathic /ˌtelɪˈpæθɪk/ *adj* [*communication*] télépathique; [*person*] télépathe

telepathy /tɪˈlepəθɪ/ *n* télépathie *f*

telephone /ˈtelɪfəʊn/
A *n* téléphone *m*; **on** *ou* **over the ~** au téléphone; **to be on the ~** (connected) avoir le téléphone; (talking) être au téléphone
B *noun modifier* [*conversation, equipment, message*] téléphonique; [*engineer*] du téléphone
C *vtr* téléphoner à, appeler [*person, organization*]; téléphoner [*instructions, message*]; **to ~ France** téléphoner en France, appeler la France
D *vi* appeler, téléphoner

telephone: **~ answering machine** *n* répondeur *m* téléphonique; **~ banking** *n* Fin transactions *fpl* bancaires télématiques; **~ book** *n* = telephone directory; **~ booth**, **~ box** GB *n* cabine *f* téléphonique; **~ call** *n* appel *m* téléphonique; **~ directory** *n* annuaire *m* (du téléphone); **~ exchange** *n* centrale *f* téléphonique; **~ number** *n* numéro *m* de téléphone; **~ operator** ▸ p. 1181 *n* standardiste *mf*; **~ subscriber** *n* abonné/-e *m/f* au téléphone

telephonist /tɪˈlefənɪst/ ▸ p. 1181 *n* GB standardiste *mf*

telephoto lens /ˈtelɪfəʊtəʊ lenz/ *n* téléobjectif *m*

Telepoint /ˈtelɪpɔɪnt/ *n* Telecom Pointel *m*

teleprinter /ˈtelɪprɪntə(r)/ *n* téléscripteur *m*

telesales /ˈtelɪseɪlz/ *n* (+ *v sg*) télévente *f*

telescope /ˈtelɪskəʊp/
A *n* télescope *m*, lunette *f* spec
B *vtr* lit replier [*stand, umbrella*]; fig condenser [*content, series*] (**into** en)
C *vi* [*stand, umbrella*] être télescopique; [*car, train*] se télescoper

telescopic /ˌtelɪˈskɒpɪk/ *adj* [*aerial, stand, umbrella*] télescopique; **~ lens** Phot téléobjectif *m*; **~ sight** (on gun) lunette *f* de visée

teleshopping /ˈtelɪʃɒpɪŋ/ *n* téléachat *m*

televise /ˈtelɪvaɪz/
A *vtr* téléviser
B televised *pp adj* télévisé

television /ˈtelɪvɪʒn, -ˈvɪʒn/
A *n* **1** (medium) télévision *f*; **on/for ~** à la/pour la télévision; **live on ~** en direct à la télévision; **it makes good ~** ça marche à la télévision; **2** (set) téléviseur *m*
B *noun modifier* [*broadcast, camera, channel, producer, studio*] de télévision; [*documentary, news, play*] télévisé; [*film, script*] pour la télévision; [*interview*] à la télévision

television: **~ dinner** *n* plateau-télévision *m*; **~ licence** *n* redevance *f* télévision; **~ lounge** *n* salle *f* de télévision; **~ programme** *n* émission *f* de télévision; **~ screen** *n* écran *m* de télévision; **~ set** *n* téléviseur *m*, poste *m* de télévision

televisual /ˌtelɪˈvɪʒʊəl/ *adj* télévisuel/-elle

telex /ˈteleks/ ▸ p. 1181
A *n* télex *m*
B *noun modifier* [*number*] de télex; **~ machine** télex *m*; **~ operator** téléxiste *mf*
C *vtr* télexer

tell /tel/ (*prét, pp* **told**)
A *vtr* **1** gen [*person*] dire [*lie, truth*]; raconter [*joke, story*]; prédire [*future*]; [*manual, gauge*] indiquer; **to ~ sb about** *ou* **of sth** parler de qch à qn; **to ~ sb to do** dire à qn de faire; **to ~ sb not to do** gen dire à qn de ne pas faire; (forbid) défendre à qn de faire; **to ~ sb how to do/what to do** expliquer à qn comment faire/ce qu'il faut faire; **to ~ the time** [*clock*] indiquer *or* marquer l'heure; [*person*] lire l'heure; **can you ~ me the time please?** peux-tu me dire l'heure (qu'il est), s'il te plaît?; **I was told that** on m'a dit que; **his behaviour ~s us a lot about his character** son comportement nous en dit long sur sa personnalité; **I told you so!**, **what did I ~ you!** je te l'avais bien dit!; **you're ~ing me!** à qui le dis-tu!; **it's true, I ~ you!** puisque je te dis que c'est vrai!; **do as you are told!** fais ce qu'on te dit!; **she just won't be told!** elle ne veut pas écouter ce qu'on lui dit; **~ me all about it!** racontez-moi tout!; **I could ~ you a thing or two about her!** je pourrais vous en dire long sur elle!; **stress? ~ me about it!** le stress? j'en sais quelque chose!; **2** (deduce) **you can ~ (that) he's lying** on voit bien qu'il ment; **I can ~ (that) he's disappointed** je sais qu'il est déçu; **you can ~ a lot from the clothes people wear** la façon dont les gens s'habillent est très révélatrice; **3** (distinguish) distinguer; **he can't ~ right from wrong** il ne sait pas distinguer le bien du mal; **can you ~ the difference?** est-ce que vous voyez la différence?; **how can you ~ which is which?, how can you ~ them apart?** comment peut-on les distinguer l'un de l'autre?
B *vi* **1** (reveal secret) **promise me you won't ~!** promets-moi de ne pas le répéter!; **that would be ~ing!** je ne peux pas le dire!; **2** (be evidence of) **to ~ of** témoigner de; **3** (know for certain) **as** *ou* **so far as I can ~** pour autant que je sache; **how can you ~?** comment le sais-tu?; **you never can ~** on ne sait jamais; **4** (produce an effect) **her age is beginning to ~** elle commence à faire son âge; **her inexperience told against her at the interview** son inexpérience a joué contre elle lors de son entretien
C *v refl* **to ~ oneself** se dire (**that** que)

▸ (Idioms) **to ~ all** tout raconter; **~ me another**○! à d'autres○!; **to ~ sb where to get off**○ envoyer promener qn; **you ~ me!** je n'en sais rien!, à ton avis?; **to ~ it like it is** parler net; **time (alone) will ~** (seul) l'avenir le dira

▸ (Phrasal verbs)
■ **tell off**: ▸ **~ [sb] off** (scold) réprimander [*person*]; **she got told off for arriving late** elle s'est fait disputer○ parce

qu'elle était arrivée en retard

■ **tell on:** ▶ ~ **on [sb]** ① (reveal information about) dénoncer [*person*] (**to** à); ② (have visible effect on) **the strain is beginning to** ~ **on him** on commence à voir sur lui les effets de la fatigue; **her age is beginning to** ~ **on her** elle commence à faire son âge

teller /'telə(r)/ ▸ p. 1181 *n* ① (in bank) caissier/-ière *m/f*; ② (in election) scrutateur/-trice *m/f*

telling /'telɪŋ/
A *n* récit *m*; **a funny story that lost nothing in the** ~ une histoire drôle qui ne perdait rien à être racontée; **her adventures grew more and more fantastic in the** ~ ses aventures devenaient de plus en plus fantastiques à mesure qu'elle les racontait
B *adj* ① (effective) [*blow*] bien porté; [*argument*] efficace; ② (revealing) [*remark, omission*] révélateur/-trice
(Idiom) **there's no** ~ **what will happen next** personne ne peut dire ce qui va se passer maintenant

tellingly /'telɪŋlɪ/ *adv* ① (effectively) efficacement; ② (revealingly) ~, **he did not allude to this** fait révélateur, il n'y a pas fait allusion

telling-off /ˌtelɪŋ'ɒf/ *n* réprimande *f*

tell-tale /'telteɪl/
A *n* rapporteur/-euse *m/f*
B *adj* [*sign*] révélateur/-trice

telly○ /'telɪ/ *n* GB télé○ *f*

temerity /tɪ'merətɪ/ *n* audace *f*

temp○ /temp/ GB
A *n* intérimaire *mf*
B *vi* travailler comme intérimaire

temper /'tempə(r)/
A *n* ① (mood) humeur *f*; **to be in a good/bad** ~ être de bonne/mauvaise humeur; **to be in a** ~ être en colère; **to keep** *ou* **control one's** ~ se contrôler; **to lose one's** ~ se mettre en colère (**with** contre); **to fly into a** ~ exploser; ~**s flared** *ou* **frayed** les esprits se sont emportés; ② (nature) caractère *m*; **to have a sweet** ~ être d'un caractère doux; **to have a hot** *ou* **quick** ~ être irascible; **to have a nasty** ~ avoir un sale caractère
B *vtr* ① (moderate) tempérer; ② Ind tremper [*steel*]

temperament /'temprəmənt/ *n* ① (nature) tempérament *m*; ② (excitability) humeur *f*

temperamental /ˌtemprə'mentl/ *adj* ① (volatile) capricieux/-ieuse; ② (natural) [*affinity*] naturel/-elle; [*differences*] de tempérament

temperamentally /ˌtemprə'mentəlɪ/ *adv* ① (by nature) psychologiquement; **they were** ~ **unsuited** il y avait entre eux incompatibilité de caractère; ② (in volatile manner) de façon capricieuse

temperance /'tempərəns/ *n* ① (moderation) modération *f*; ② (being teetotal) sobriété *f*, tempérance *f*

temperate /'tempərət/ *adj* [*climate, zone*] tempéré; [*person, habit*] modéré

temperature /'temprətʃə(r), US 'tempərtʃʊər/ *n* ① Meteorol, Phys température *f*; **at room** ~ à température ambiante; ② Med température *f*; **to be running** *ou* **to have a** ~ avoir de la température *or* de la fièvre; **to have a** ~ **of 39°** avoir 39° de fièvre

temper tantrum *n* caprice *m*

tempest /'tempɪst/ *n* littér lit, fig tempête *f*

tempestuous /tem'pestʃʊəs/ *adj* [*relationship, sea, wind*] tempétueux/-euse; [*music*] impétueux/-euse

temping /'tempɪŋ/ *n* **to do** ~ faire des intérims *mpl*

temping job *n* intérim *m*

template /'templeɪt/ *n* gen gabarit *m*; Comput modèle *m*

temple /'templ/ *n* ① (building) temple *m*; ② (on face) tempe *f*

tempo /'tempəʊ/ *n* (*pl* ~**s** *ou* **tempi**) Mus tempo *m*; fig rythme *m*; **at a fast** ~ sur un tempo rapide

temporal /'tempərəl/ *adj* temporel/-elle

temporarily /'tempərəlɪ, US -pərerɪlɪ/ *adv* (for a limited time) temporairement; (provisionally) provisoirement

temporary /'tempərɪ, US -pererɪ/ *adj* [*job, contract*] temporaire; [*manager, secretary*] intérimaire; [*arrangement, accommodation*] provisoire; **on a** ~ **basis** à titre provisoire

temporize /'tempəraɪz/ *vi* atermoyer

tempt /tempt/ *vtr* tenter; **to be** ~**ed** être tenté; **to** ~ **sb with sth** attirer qn avec qch; **to** ~ **sb into doing sth** inciter

qn à faire qch; **can I** ~ **you to a whisky?** puis-je vous offrir un whisky?

(Idiom) **to** ~ **fate** *ou* **providence** tenter le destin *or* sort

temptation /temp'teɪʃn/ *n* tentation *f*; **to give in to** ~ céder à la tentation; **to put** ~ **in sb's way** exposer qn à la tentation

tempting /'temptɪŋ/ *adj* [*offer, discount, suggestion*] alléchant; [*food, smell*] appétissant; [*idea*] tentant

temptress /'temptrɪs/ *n* tentatrice *f*

ten /ten/ ▸ p. 1044, p. 647, p. 745
A *n* ① (number) dix *m inv*; **in** ~**s** [*sell*] par dizaines; [*count*] de dix en dix; ~**s of thousands** des dizaines de milliers; ② ○US (also ~-**dollar bill**) billet *m* de dix dollars
B *adj* dix *inv*
(Idiom) ~ **to one (it'll rain)** dix contre un○ (qu'il va pleuvoir)

tenable /'tenəbl/ *adj* ① (valid) [*theory, suggestion*] défendable; ② (available) **the job is** ~ **for a year** le poste est accordé pour un an

tenacious /tɪ'neɪʃəs/ *adj* tenace

tenacity /tɪ'næsətɪ/ *n* ténacité *f*

tenancy /'tenənsɪ/ *n* location *f*; **six-month** ~ bail *m* de six mois; **terms of** ~ conditions de bail

tenancy agreement *n* bail *m*

tenant /'tenənt/ *n* locataire *mf*

ten-cent store /ˌtensent 'stɔ:(r)/ *n* US bazar *m*

tend /tend/
A *vtr* soigner [*patient*]; entretenir [*garden*]; s'occuper de [*stall, store*]
B *vi* ① (incline) **to** ~ **to do** avoir tendance à faire; **to** ~ **towards sth** pencher vers qch; **I** ~ **to think that** j'inclinerais à penser que; **it** ~**s to be the case** c'est en général le cas; ② (look after) **to** ~ **to** soigner [*patient*]; s'occuper de [*guests*]; **to** ~ **to sb's needs** veiller aux besoins de qn

tendency /'tendənsɪ/ *n* tendance *f* (**to, towards** à; **to do** à faire); **there is a** ~ **for people to arrive late** les gens ont tendance à arriver en retard

tendentious /ten'denʃəs/ *adj* tendancieux/-ieuse

tender /'tendə(r)/
A *n* ① (offer) soumission *f*; **to put work out to** ~ mettre un ouvrage en adjudication; **to invite** ~**s** faire un appel d'offres; ② (currency) ▸ **legal tender**
B *adj* ① (soft) [*food*] tendre; [*bud, shoot*] fragile; ② (loving) [*kiss, love, smile*] tendre; ~ **care** sollicitude *f*; ③ (sensitive) [*bruise, skin*] sensible; ④ (young) **at the** ~ **age of two** à l'âge tendre de deux ans
C *vtr* offrir [*money*]; présenter [*apology, fare*]; donner [*resignation*]
D *vi* soumissionner, faire une soumission

tenderhearted /ˌtendə'hɑ:tɪd/ *adj* sensible

tenderize /'tendəraɪz/ *vtr* attendrir

tender: ~**loin** *n* Culin milieu *m* de filet de porc; ~**loin district** *n* US quartier *m* malfamé

tenderly /'tendəlɪ/ *adv* tendrement

tenderness /'tendənɪs/ *n* ① (gentleness) tendresse *f*; ② (soreness) sensibilité *f*; ③ (texture) (of shoot) fragilité *f*; (of meat) tendreté *f*

tendon /'tendən/ *n* tendon *m*

tendril /'tendrɪl/ *n* (of plant) vrille *f*; (of hair) mèche *f* folle

tenement /'tenəmənt/ *n* (also ~ **block** *ou* ~ **building** GB, ~ **house** US) immeuble *m* ancien (souvent délabré et insalubre)

tenet /'tenɪt/ *n* gen principe *m*; Philos, Pol, Relig dogme *m*

tenfold /'tenfəʊld/
A *adj* décuple
B *adv* **to increase** *ou* **multiply** ~ décupler

ten four /ˌten 'fɔ:(r)/ US
A *n* that's a ~ c'est exact
B *excl* message reçu!

tenner○ /'tenə(r)/ *n* GB (note) billet *m* de dix livres

tennis /'tenɪs/ ▸ p. 881 *n* tennis *m*; **a game of** ~ une partie de tennis; **men's** ~ tennis masculin

tennis: ~ **court** *n* court *m* de tennis, tennis *m inv*; ~ **whites** *npl* tenue *f* de tennis blanche

tenor /'tenə(r)/ ▸ p. 1311 *n* ① Mus (singer, voice) ténor *m*; ② (of speech, reply) (tone) ton *m*; (drift, meaning) sens *m*; ③ (quality) **the even** ~ **of his life** le cours régulier de sa vie

t

Temperature

■ *Temperatures in French are written as in the tables below. Note the space in French between the figure and the degree sign and letter indicating the scale. When the scale letter is omitted, temperatures are written thus: 20°; 98,4° etc. (French has a comma, where English has a decimal point).*

■ *Note also that there is no capital on centigrade in French; capital C is however used as the abbreviation for Celsius and centigrade as in 60 °C.*

■ *For how to say numbers in French* ▸ **p. 1044.**

Celsius or centigrade (C)	Fahrenheit (F)	
100 °C	212 °F	température d'ébullition de l'eau (boiling point)
90 °C	194 °F	
80 °C	176 °F	
70 °C	158 °F	
60 °C	140 °F	
50 °C	122 °F	
40 °C	104 °F	
37 °C	98,4 °F	
30 °C	86 °F	
20 °C	68 °F	
10 °C	50 °F	
0 °C	32 °F	température de congélation de l'eau (freezing point)
−10 °C	14 °F	
−17,8 °C	0 °F	
−273,15 °C	−459,67 °F	le zéro absolu (absolute zero)

−15°C
= −15 °C (moins quinze degrés Celsius)

the thermometer says 40°
= le thermomètre indique quarante degrés

above 30°C
= plus de trente degrés Celsius

over 30° Celsius
= plus de trente degrés Celsius

below 30°
= en dessous de trente degrés

People

body temperature is 37°C
= la température du corps est de* 37 °C (trente-sept degrés Celsius)

what is his temperature?
= quelle est sa température?

his temperature is 38°
= il a trente-huit (de* température)

* *The de is obligatory here.*

Things

how hot is the milk? or what temperature is the milk?
= à quelle température est le lait?

it's 40°C
= il est à 40 °C

what temperature does water boil at?
= à quelle température l'eau bout-elle?

it boils at 100°C
= elle bout à 100 °C

at a temperature of 200°
= à une température de deux cents degrés

A is hotter than B
= A est plus chaud que B

B is cooler than A
= B est moins chaud que A

B is colder than A
= B est plus froid que A

A is the same temperature as B
= A est à la même température que B

A and B are the same temperature
= A et B sont à la même température

Weather

what's the temperature today?
= quelle température fait-il aujourd'hui? (*this French phrase is also the equivalent of both* how hot is it? *and* how cold is it?)

it's 65°F
= il fait 65 °F (soixante-cinq degrés Fahrenheit)

it's 40 degrees
= il fait 40 degrés

Nice is warmer (or hotter) than London
= il fait plus chaud à Nice qu'à Londres

it's the same temperature in Paris as in London
= il fait la même température à Paris qu'à Londres

---

tenpin bowling /ˌtenpɪn ˈbəʊlɪŋ/ GB, **tenpins** US ▸ p. 881 n bowling m (à dix quilles)

tense /tens/
A n Ling temps m; **the present ~** le présent (**of** de); **in the past ~** au passé
B adj (strained) gen tendu; [moment] de tension; **to make sb ~** rendre qn nerveux
C vtr tendre [muscle]; raidir [body]; **to ~ oneself** se raidir
(Phrasal verb)
 ■ **tense up** ▸ ① (stiffen) [muscle] se tendre; [body] se raidir; ② (become nervous) [person] se crisper

tensely /ˈtenslɪ/ adv (avec) les nerfs tendus; **to smile ~** avoir un sourire crispé

tension /ˈtenʃn/ n gen tension f (**within** au sein de; **over** au sujet de); (suspense) suspense m

tent /tent/ n tente f

tentacle /ˈtentəkl/ n tentacule m

tentative /ˈtentətɪv/ adj [inquiry, smile, suggestion] timide; [movement] hésitant; [conclusion, offer] provisoire

tentatively /ˈtentətɪvlɪ/ adv [agree, conclude] provisoirement; [smile, speak] timidement; [suggest] prudemment

tenterhooks /ˈtentəhʊks/ npl
(idioms) **to be on ~** être sur des charbons ardents; **to keep sb on ~** faire languir qn

tenth /tenθ/ ▸ p. 1044, p. 788
A n ① (in order) dixième mf; ② (of month) dix m inv; ③ (fraction) dixième m
B adj dixième
C adv [come, finish] dixième, en dixième position

tent ~ peg n piquet m de tente; **~ pole** GB, **~ stake** US n mât m de tente

tenuous /ˈtenjʊəs/ adj [link] ténu; [distinction, theory] mince

tenure /ˈtenjʊə(r), US tenjər/ n ① (right of occupancy) **~ of land/property** jouissance f d'un droit à un terrain/une propriété; **tenants do not have security of ~** les locataires n'ont pas de bail assuré; ② Univ (job security) titularisation f d'emploi; **to have ~** être titulaire; ③ (period of office) fonction f

tenured /ˈtenjʊə(r)d, US tenjərd/ adj [professor] titulaire; [job] de titulaire

tepid /ˈtepɪd/ adj tiède

tercentenary /ˌtɜːsenˈtiːnərɪ, tɜːˈsentənərɪ/ n tricentenaire m

term /tɜːm/

A n ① (period of time) gen période f, terme m; Sch, Univ trimestre m; Jur (duration of lease) durée f (de bail); **the president's first ~ of office** le premier mandat du président; **~ of imprisonment** peine f de prison; **to have reached (full) ~** (of pregnancy) être à terme; **autumn/spring/summer ~** Sch, Univ premier/deuxième/troisième trimestre; ② (word, phrase) terme m; **~ of abuse** injure f; **she condemned their action in the strongest possible ~s** elle a condamné leur action très fermement; ③ (limit) terme m also Math

B terms npl ① (conditions) gen termes mpl; (of will) dispositions fpl; Comm conditions fpl de paiement; **name your own ~s** fixez vos conditions; **~s and conditions** Jur modalités fpl; **~s of trade** Comm, Econ termes de l'échange international; **on easy ~s** Comm avec facilités fpl de paiement; **~s of surrender** Pol conditions de la reddition; **~s of reference** attributions fpl; ② **to come to ~s with** assumer [identity, past, condition, disability]; accepter [death, defeat, failure]; affronter [issue]; ③ (relations) termes mpl; **they are on first-name ~s** ils s'appellent par leurs prénoms; ④ (point of view) **in his/their etc ~s** selon ses/leurs etc critères

C **in terms of** prep phr ① gen, Math (as expressed by) en fonction de; ② (from the point of view of) du point de vue de, sur le plan de; **they own very little in ~s of real property** ils ne possèdent pas grand-chose en fait de biens immobiliers; **I was thinking in ~s of how much it would cost** j'essayais de calculer combien cela coûterait

D vtr appeler, nommer

terminal /ˈtɜːmɪnl/

A n ① (at station) terminus m; Aviat aérogare f; **rail ~** terminus m; **oil ~** terminal m pétrolier; **ferry ~** gare f maritime; ② Comput terminal m; ③ Elec borne f

B adj ① [stage, point] terminal; Med [illness, patient] (incurable) incurable; (at final stage) en phase terminale; fig [boredom] mortel/-elle○; ② Comm, Sch trimestriel/-ielle

terminally /ˈtɜːmɪnəlɪ/ adv **the ~ ill** les mourants mpl

terminal: **~ point**, **~ station** n Rail terminus m; **~ ward** n Med ≈ unité f de soins palliatifs

terminate /ˈtɜːmɪneɪt/

A vtr ① mettre fin à [arrangement, discussion, meeting, phase, relationship]; résilier [contract]; interrompre [pregnancy]; annuler [agreement]; arrêter [treatment]; ② US renvoyer [employee]; ③ ○(kill) liquider○

B vi ① (end) [agreement, meeting, commercial contract] se terminer; [employment, offer, work contract] prendre fin; [speaker, programme] terminer; [road] s'arrêter; ② (end route) s'arrêter; **'this train ~s at Oxford'** 'Oxford, terminus du train'

termination /ˌtɜːmɪˈneɪʃn/ n ① (ending) (of contract) résiliation f; (of service) interruption f; (of discussion, relations, scheme) fin f; ② Med interruption f de grossesse; ③ Ling terminaison f

terminology /ˌtɜːmɪˈnɒlədʒɪ/ n terminologie f

terminus /ˈtɜːmɪnəs/ n (pl **-ni** ou **-nuses**) GB terminus m

terrace /ˈterəs/

A n ① (veranda) terrasse f; ② Archit alignement m de maisons (identiques et contiguës)

B terraces npl (in stadium) gradins mpl

C vtr arranger [qch] en terrasses [garden, hillside]

terrace(d) house n maison f (située dans un alignement de maisons identiques et contiguës)

terracotta /ˌterəˈkɒtə/ n ① (earthenware) terre f cuite; ② (colour) ocre brun m

terrain /ˈterem/ n gen, Mil terrain m; **all-~ vehicle** véhicule m tout terrain

terrestrial /təˈrestrɪəl/ adj terrestre

terrible /ˈterəbl/ adj ① [pain, noise, sight, temper] épouvantable; [accident, fight] terrible; [mistake] grave; ② ○[food, weather] affreux/-euse; **to be ~ at** être nul en [rugby, maths]; **he's a ~ liar** c'est un menteur invétéré; **I feel ~** (guilty) je me sens coupable; (ill) je ne me sens pas bien du tout; **you look ~ in that hat** ce chapeau ne te va absolument pas; **it was a ~ shame** c'était vraiment bien dommage

terribly /ˈterəblɪ/ adv ① (very) [flattered, pleased, obvious] très; [clever, easy, hot, polite] extrêmement; **I'm ~ sorry** je suis navré; ② (badly) [limp, suffer, injured] horriblement; [worry] terriblement; [sing, drive, write] affreusement mal

terrific /təˈrɪfɪk/ adj ① (huge) [amount, incentive, pleasure, size] énorme; [pain, heat, noise] épouvantable; [argument] violent; [speed] fou/folle; [accident, problem, shock, worry] terrible; [struggle] acharné; ② ○(wonderful) formidable; **to look ~** (healthy) avoir l'air en pleine forme○; (attractive) être superbe; **we had a ~ time** on s'est vraiment bien amusé

terrifically /təˈrɪfɪklɪ/ adv (extremely) [difficult, gifted, kind, large] extrêmement; [expensive, hot, noisy] épouvantablement

terrified /ˈterɪfaɪd/ adj [animal, face, person] terrifié; [scream] de terreur; **to be ~ of** avoir une terreur folle de

terrify /ˈterɪfaɪ/ vtr terrifier

(Idiom) **to ~ the life out of sb**○ donner une peur bleue à qn○

terrifying /ˈterɪfaɪɪŋ/ adj (frightening) terrifiant; (alarming) effroyable

terrifyingly /ˈterɪfaɪɪŋlɪ/ adv gen terriblement; [fast, normal, real] effroyablement; [shake, tilt] de façon terrifiante

territorial /ˌterəˈtɔːrɪəl/ adj (all contexts) territorial

Territorial Army pr n GB armée f de réservistes volontaires

territory /ˈterətrɪ, US ˈterɪtɔːrɪ/ n ① (land) territoire m also Pol; **her home ~** son territoire; ② (of salesperson) secteur m; ③ (area of influence, knowledge) domaine m; **I'm on familiar ~** je suis sur mon terrain; ④ US Sport camp m

terror /ˈterə(r)/

A n ① (fear) terreur f; **to have a ~ of** être terrifié par; **to strike ~ into (the heart of) sb** semer la terreur chez qn; ② (unruly person) terreur f

B noun modifier [tactic] d'intimidation; **a ~ campaign** une vague terroriste

terrorism /ˈterərɪzəm/ n terrorisme m

terrorist /ˈterərɪst/

A n terroriste mf

B noun modifier [attack, bomb, group, plot] terroriste; **a ~ bombing** un attentat à la bombe

terrorize /ˈterəraɪz/ vtr terroriser; **to ~ sb into doing** terroriser qn jusqu'à ce qu'il/qu'elle fasse

terror-stricken /ˈterəstrɪkən/ adj frappé de terreur

terry /ˈterɪ/ n (also **~ towelling** GB, **~ cloth** US) tissu m éponge

terse /tɜːs/ adj [style] succinct; [person, statement] laconique

tertiary /ˈtɜːʃərɪ, US -ʃɪerɪ/ adj [era, industry, sector] tertiaire; [education, college] supérieur; [burn] au troisième degré; [syphilis] au stade tertiaire

Terylene® /ˈterəliːn/ n tergal® m

TESL /ˈtesl/ n (abrév = **Teaching English as a Second Language**) enseignement m de l'anglais langue étrangère

test /test/

A n ① (of person, ability, resources) gen épreuve f, Psych test m; Sch, Univ (written) contrôle m; (oral) épreuve f orale; **a method that has stood the ~ of time** une méthode éprouvée; **tomorrow's match should be a good ~ of the team's capabilities** le match de demain devrait permettre de savoir de quoi l'équipe est capable; **the best ~ of a good novel is...** le meilleur critère pour juger de la valeur d'un roman est...; ② Comm, Ind, Tech essai m; ③ Med (of blood, urine) analyse f; (of organ) examen m; (to detect virus, cancer) test m de dépistage; Chem analyse f; ④ Aut (also **driving ~**) examen m du permis de conduire

B vtr ① gen évaluer [intelligence, efficiency]; Sch (in classroom) interroger (**on** en); (at exam time) contrôler; Psych tester; ② Comm, Tech essayer; Med, Chem analyser [blood, urine, sample]; expérimenter [new drug]; **to have one's eyes ~ed** se faire faire un examen des yeux; **he was ~ed for Aids** on lui a fait subir un test de dépistage du sida; **all the new equipment has been ~ed for faults** le nouveau matériel a été entièrement testé et essayé; **to ~ the water** [swimmer] prendre la température de l'eau; fig tâter le terrain; ③ (strain) mettre [qch] à l'épreuve [strength, patience]

C vi **to ~ for starch/for alcohol** (in laboratory) faire une recherche d'amidon/d'alcool; **to ~ for an infection/allergy** faire des analyses pour trouver la cause d'une infection/allergie; **his blood ~ed negative** son analyse de sang a été négative

t

testament /ˈtestəmənt/ n [1] Jur the last will and ∼ of les dernières volontés de; [2] (proof) témoignage m; **to be a ∼ to sth** témoigner de qch; [3] **the Old/the New Testament** l'Ancien/le Nouveau Testament

test ∼ ban n interdiction f d'essais nucléaires; **∼ card** n GB TV mire f; **∼ case** n Jur procès m qui fait jurisprudence

test-drive /ˈtestdraɪv/
A n essai m de route
B vtr faire faire un essai de route à, essayer

tester /ˈtestə(r)/ n [1] (person) contrôleur/-euse m/f; (device) testeur m; [2] (sample) (of make-up, perfume) échantillon m

test ∼ flight n vol m d'essai; **∼-fly** vtr essayer

testicle /ˈtestɪkl/ n testicule m

testify /ˈtestɪfaɪ/
A vtr témoigner (**that** que)
B vi témoigner; **to ∼ to** fig attester, témoigner de

testily /ˈtestɪlɪ/ adv [say, reply] avec irritation

testimonial /ˌtestɪˈməʊnɪəl/ n [1] †(reference) lettre f de recommandation; [2] (tribute) témoignage m

testimony /ˈtestɪmənɪ, US -məʊnɪ/ n gen témoignage m; Jur déposition f; **to give ∼** faire une déposition

testing /ˈtestɪŋ/
A n Tech, Ind essai m; (of drug, cosmetic) expérimentation f; (of blood, water etc) analyse f; (of person) gen mise f à l'épreuve; Med examen m; Psych tests mpl; Sch contrôles mpl (des connaissances)
B adj éprouvant

testing ground n Mil site m d'essais (nucléaires); Ind, Tech banc m d'essai; fig terrain m d'essai

test market /test'mɑːkɪt/
A n marché m test
B vtr commercialiser [qch] à titre expérimental

test ∼ marketing n test m de marché; **∼ match** n match m international (de cricket)

test paper n [1] Chem (papier m) réactif m; [2] GB Sch, Univ interrogation f écrite

test ∼ pattern n US TV mire f; **∼ piece** n Mus morceau m de concours; **∼ pilot** n pilote m d'essai; **∼ run** n essai m; **∼ tube** n éprouvette f; **∼-tube baby** n bébé-éprouvette m

testy /ˈtestɪ/ adj [person] irritable; [comment, reply] irrité

tetanus /ˈtetənəs/ ▸ p. 933
A n tétanos m
B noun modifier [injection, vaccine] antitétanique

tetchy /ˈtetʃɪ/ adj gen grincheux/-euse; [behaviour] emporté

tether /ˈteðə(r)/ vtr attacher (**to** à)
(Idiom) **to be at the end of one's ∼** être au bout du rouleau○

Teutonic /tjuːˈtɒnɪk, US tuː-/ adj germanique

text /tekst/
A n [1] texte m (**by** de); [2] (text message) message m texte
B vtr envoyer un message text à [person]; envoyer par message text [news, information]

textbook /ˈtekstbʊk/
A n manuel m (**about, on** sur)
B adj [case, landing, pregnancy] exemplaire; [example] parfait

textile /ˈtekstaɪl/
A n textile m
B textiles npl textile m

text message n (on mobile) message m text

text processing n Comput traitement m de texte

textual /ˈtekstʃʊəl/ adj de texte

texture /ˈtekstʃə(r)/ n lit, fig texture f; (of music) caractère m

textured /ˈtekstʃəd/ adj texturé; **rough-∼** de texture grossière

TGWU n GB (abrév = **Transport and General Workers' Union**) un des principaux syndicats britanniques

Thames /temz/ ▸ p. 1146 pr n **the (river) ∼** la Tamise
(Idiom) **he'll never set the ∼ on fire** GB il ne fera jamais d'étincelles

than /ðæn, ðən/

⚠ When *than* is used as a preposition in expressions of comparison, it is translated by *que* (or *qu'* before a vowel or mute 'h'): *he's taller than me* = il est plus grand que moi; *London is bigger than Oxford* = Londres est plus grand qu'Oxford.
For expressions with numbers, temperatures etc see the entry below.
See also the entries **more, less, hardly, soon, rather, other**.
When *than* is used as a conjunction, it is translated by *que* and the verb following it is preceded by *ne*: *it was farther than I thought* = c'était plus loin que je ne pensais. However, French speakers often try to phrase the comparison differently: *it was more difficult than we expected* = c'était plus difficile que prévu. For other uses see the entry below.
See also the entries **hardly, rather, soon**.

A prep [1] (in comparisons) que; **thinner ∼ him** plus mince que lui; **he has more ∼ me** il en a plus que moi; **I was more surprised ∼ annoyed** j'étais plus étonné qu'ennuyé; [2] (expressing quantity, degree, value) de; **more/less ∼ 100** plus/moins de 100; **more ∼ half** plus de la moitié; **temperatures lower ∼ 30 degrees** des températures de moins de 30 degrés
B conj [1] (in comparisons) que; **he's older ∼ I am** il est plus âgé que moi; **it took us longer ∼ we thought it would** ça nous a pris plus de temps que prévu; **it was further away ∼ I remembered** c'était plus loin que dans mon souvenir; [2] (expressing preferences) **I'd sooner ou rather do X ∼ do Y** je préférerais faire X que (de) faire Y; [3] (when) **hardly ou no sooner had he left ∼ the phone rang** à peine était-il parti que le téléphone a sonné; [4] US (from) **to be different ∼ sth** être différent de qch

thank /θæŋk/ vtr remercier [person]; **we've got Sue to ∼ for that** c'est à Sue que nous devons cela also iron; **you've only got yourself to ∼ for that** tu ne peux t'en prendre qu'à toi-même!; **I'll ∼ you to do** je te serais reconnaissant de faire; **he won't ∼ you for doing** il ne va pas apprécier que tu fasses; **∼ God!, ∼ goodness ou heavens!** Dieu merci!

thankful /ˈθæŋkfl/ adj (grateful) reconnaissant; (relieved) soulagé; **that's something to be ∼ for!** c'est déjà un soulagement!

thankfully /ˈθæŋkfəlɪ/ adv [1] (luckily) heureusement; [2] (with relief) avec soulagement; (with gratitude) avec gratitude

thankless /ˈθæŋklɪs/ adj [task, person] ingrat

thanks /θæŋks/
A npl remerciements mpl; **'received with ∼'** Comm 'avec nos remerciements'
B **thanks to** prep phr grâce à; **we did it, no ∼ to you!**○ on a réussi, mais tu n'y es pour rien○!
C ○ excl merci!; **∼ a lot** merci beaucoup also iron; **no ∼** non merci

Thanksgiving (Day) n US jour m d'Action de Grâces

ⓘ Thanksgiving La moitié de la colonie des Pères Pèlerins fut décimée par la maladie au cours de son premier hiver passé au Nouveau Monde. À l'automne 1621, leur récolte fut bonne et leur permit de survivre. Ils décidèrent de la célébrer en organisant un repas auquel ils convièrent des Indiens, qui leur avaient notamment appris à chasser et à cultiver le maïs. Aujourd'hui, la fête d'Action de Grâces (*Thanksgiving*) est célébrée dans tous les États-Unis le quatrième jeudi de novembre. Les Américains font un repas traditionnel composé de dinde farcie accompagnée de patates douces et d'une sauce à la canneberge (*cranberry sauce*), et d'une tarte au potiron pour le dessert. Cette fête est également célébrée au Canada, le deuxième lundi d'octobre.

thank you /ˈθæŋkjuː/
A n (also **thank-you, thankyou**) merci m; **to say ∼ to sb** dire merci à qn; **to say one's ∼s to sb** dire merci à qn
B noun modifier [letter, gift] de remerciement
C adv merci; **∼ very much** aussi iron merci beaucoup also iron; **no ∼** non merci

that
A /ðæt, ðət/ det (pl **those**) ce/cet/cette/ces; **∼ chair/∼ man over there** cette chaise/cet homme là-bas; **I said ∼ dress!** j'ai dit cette robe-là!; **you can't do it ∼ way** tu ne peux pas le faire comme ça; **he went ∼ way** il est allé par

that

As a determiner

In French, determiners agree in gender and number with the noun they precede; *that* is translated by *ce* + masculine singular noun (*ce monsieur*), *cet* + masculine singular noun beginning with a vowel or mute 'h' (*cet homme*) and *cette* + feminine singular noun (*cette femme*); *those* is translated by *ces*.

Note, however, that the above translations are also used for the English *this* (plural *these*). So when it is necessary to insist on *that* as opposed to another or others of the same sort, the adverbial tag *-là* is added to the noun:

I prefer THAT version
= je préfère cette version-là

For particular usages, see the entry **that**.

As a pronoun meaning *that one, those ones*

In French, pronouns reflect the gender and number of the noun they are referring to. So *that* is translated by *celui-là* for a masculine noun, *celle-là* for a feminine noun and *those* is translated by *ceux-là* for a masculine noun and *celles-là* for a feminine noun:

I think I like that one (dress) best
= je crois que je préfère celle-là

For other uses of *that, those* as pronouns (*e.g. who's that?*) and for adverbial use (*e.g. that much, that many*) there is no straightforward translation, so see the entry **that** for examples of usage.

When used as a relative pronoun, *that* is translated by *qui* when it is the subject of the verb and by *que* when it is the object:

the man that stole the car
= l'homme qui a volé la voiture

the film that I saw
= le film que j'ai vu

Remember that in the present perfect and past perfect tenses, the past participle will agree with the noun to which *que* as object refers:

the apples that I bought
= les pommes que j'ai achetées

When *that* is used as a relative pronoun with a preposition, it is translated by *lequel* when standing for a masculine singular noun, by *laquelle* when standing for a feminine singular noun, by *lesquels* when standing for a masculine plural noun and by *lesquelles* when standing for a feminine plural noun:

the chair that I was sitting on
= la chaise sur laquelle j'étais assise

the children that I bought the books for
= les enfants pour lesquels j'ai acheté les livres

Remember that in cases where the English preposition used would normally be translated by *à* in French (*e.g. to, at*), the translation of the whole (prep + rel pron) will be *auquel, à laquelle, auxquels, auxquelles*:

the girls that I was talking to
= les filles auxquelles je parlais

Similarly, where the English preposition used would normally be translated by *de* in French (*e.g. of, from*), the translation of the whole (prep + rel pron) will be *dont* in all cases:

the Frenchman that I received a letter from
= le Français dont j'ai reçu une lettre

When used as a conjunction, *that* can almost always be translated by *que* (*qu'* before a vowel or mute 'h'):

she said that she would do it
= elle a dit qu'elle le ferait

In certain verbal constructions, *que* is followed by a subjunctive in French. If you are in doubt about the construction to use, consult the appropriate verb entry. For particular usages see the entry **that**.

---

là; **those patients (who are)** able to walk les patients qui sont capables de marcher; ~ **train crash last year** la collision ferroviaire qui a eu lieu l'an dernier; ~ **lazy son of yours** ton paresseux de fils

B /ðæt/ *dem pron* (*pl* **those**) **1** (that one) celui-/celle-/ceux-/celles-là; **we prefer this to** ~ nous préférons celui-ci à celui-là; **2** (the thing or person observed or mentioned) cela, ça, ce; **what's** ~**?** qu'est-ce que c'est que ça?; **who's** ~**?** gen qui est-ce?; (on phone) qui est à l'appareil?; **is** ~ **John?** c'est John?; **who told you** ~**?** qui t'a dit ça?; ~**'s how he did it** c'est comme ça qu'il l'a fait; **what did he mean by** ~**?** qu'est-ce qu'il entendait par là?; ~**'s bureaucrats for you!** c'est ça les bureaucrates!; **before** ~, **he had always lived in London** avant cela, il avait toujours vécu à Londres; **3** (before relative pronoun) **those who...** ceux qui...

C /ðæt/ *rel pron* (subject) qui; (object) que; (with preposition) lequel/laquelle/lesquels/lesquelles; **the woman** ~ **won** la femme qui a gagné; **the book** ~ **I bought** le livre que j'ai acheté; **the house** ~ **they live in** la maison dans laquelle ils vivent; **the man** ~ **I received the letter from** l'homme dont j'ai reçu la lettre; **the day** ~ **she arrived** le jour où elle est arrivée

D /ðæt/ *conj* **1** gen que; **he said** ~ **he had finished** il a dit qu'il avait fini; **it's likely** ~ **they are out** il est probable qu'ils sont sortis; **2** (expressing wish) **oh** ~ **he would come** s'il pouvait venir; (expressing surprise) ~ **she should treat me so badly!** comment peut-elle me traiter comme ça!; ~ **it should come to this!** comment peut-on en arriver là!

E /ðæt/ *adv* (to the extent shown) **it's about** ~ **thick** c'est à peu près épais comme ça; **she's** ~ **much smaller than me** elle est plus petite que moi de ça; **I can't do** ~ **much work in**

one day je ne peux pas faire autant de travail dans une journée; **he can't swim** ~ **far** il ne peut pas nager aussi loin

(Idioms) **...and (all)** ~ ...et tout ça; **...and he's very nice at** ~**!** ...et en plus il est très gentil!; **I might well go at** ~**!** en fait, je pourrais bien y aller!; **at** ~, **he got up and left** en entendant cela, il s'est levé et est parti; **with** ~ **he got up and left** sur ce il s'est levé et est parti; ~ **is (to say)...** c'est-à-dire...; ~**'s it!** (that's right) c'est ça!; (that's enough) ça suffit!; **I don't want to see you again and** ~**'s** ~**!** je ne veux pas te revoir point final!; **well,** ~**'s it then!** il n'y a rien de plus à faire!

thatch /θætʃ/
A *n* (roof) chaume *m*
B *vtr* couvrir [qch] de chaume

thatch: ~**ed cottage** *n* chaumière *f*; ~**ed roof** *n* toit *m* de chaume

thaw /θɔː/
A *n* **1** Meteorol dégel *m*; **2** (political) détente *f*; **a** ~ **in her attitude towards me** (social) une amélioration *f* dans son attitude envers moi
B *vtr* faire fondre [*ice, snow*]; décongeler [*frozen food*]
C *vi* **1** lit [*snow*] fondre; [*ground, frozen food*] dégeler; **2** fig se détendre
D *v impers* dégeler

(Phrasal verb)
■ **thaw out**: ▶ ~ **out** [*frozen food, ground*] dégeler; [*person, fingers*] se réchauffer; ▶ ~ **[sth] out**, ~ **out [sth]** [*person*] décongeler [*frozen food*]; dégeler [*ground*]

t

the

In French, determiners agree in gender and number with the noun they precede; *the* is translated by *le* + masculine singular noun (*le chien*), by *la* + feminine singular noun (*la chaise*), by *l'* + masculine or feminine singular noun beginning with a vowel or mute 'h' (*l'auteur*, *l'homme*, *l'absence*, *l'histoire*) and by *les* + plural noun (*les hommes*, *les femmes*).

When *the* is used after a preposition in English, the two words (prep + *the*) are often translated by one word in French. If the preposition would normally be translated by *de* in French (*of, about, from* etc.) the prep + *the* is translated by *du* + masculine noun (*du chien*), by *de la* + feminine noun (*de la femme*), by *de l'* + singular noun beginning with a vowel or mute 'h' (*de l'auteur*, *de l'histoire*) and by *des* + plural noun (*des hommes*, *des femmes*). If the preposition would usually be translated by *à* (*at, to* etc.) the prep + *the* is translated according to the number and gender of the noun, by *au* (*au chien*), *à la* (*à la femme*), *à l'* (*à l'enfant*), *aux* (*aux hommes*, *aux femmes*).

Other than this, there are few problems in translating *the* into French.

The following cases are, however, worth remembering as not following exactly the pattern of the English:

the good, the poor etc.
= les bons, les pauvres etc.

Charles the First, Elizabeth the Second etc.
= Charles Premier, Elizabeth Deux etc.

she's THE violinist of the century
= c'est LA violoniste du siècle *or* c'est la plus grande violoniste du siècle

the Tudors, the Batemans etc.
= les Tudor, les Bateman etc.

For expressions such as *the more, the better*, see the entry **the**.

This dictionary contains usage notes on such topics as **weight measurement, days of the week, rivers, illnesses, aches and pains, the human body,** and **musical instruments,** many of which use *the*; for the index to these notes ▸ **p. 1354.**

For other particular usages of *the* see the entry **the**.

the /ðɪ, ðə, devant une voyelle ou emphatique ðiː/ *det*
[1] (specifying, identifying etc) le/la/l'/les; **two chapters of** ~ **book** deux chapitres du livre; **I met them at** ~ **supermarket** je les ai rencontrés au supermarché; [2] (best etc) THE **French restaurant** le meilleur restaurant français; THE **way of losing weight** la façon la plus efficace de perdre des kilos; [3] (with era) ~ **fifties** les années cinquante; [4] (with adj) ~ **impossible** l'impossible; **she buys only** ~ **best** elle n'achète que ce qu'il y a de mieux; [5] (with comparative adj) **the news made her all** ~ **sadder** la nouvelle n'a fait que la rendre encore plus triste; [6] (in double comparatives) ~ **more I learn** ~ **less I understand** plus j'apprends moins je comprends; ~ **sooner** ~ **better** le plus tôt sera le mieux; ~ **longer he waits** ~ **harder it will be** plus il attendra plus ce sera difficile; [7] (with superlatives) ~ **fastest train** le train le plus rapide; ~ **prettiest house in the village** la maison la plus jolie du village

theatre, theater US /ˈθɪətə(r)/
A *n* [1] (place, art form) théâtre *m* also Mil; [2] US (cinema) cinéma *m*; [3] (also **lecture** ~) amphithéâtre *m*; [4] GB (also **operating** ~) salle *f* d'opération
B *noun modifier* [1] Theat [*audience, lover, owner, seat, ticket*] de théâtre; [*company, production, programme, stage, workshop*] théâtral; [*manager, staff*] du théâtre; [*visit*] au théâtre; [2] GB Med [*nurse*] au bloc *m* opératoire; [*equipment*] du bloc *m* opératoire; [3] US (cinema) [*owner, seat*] de cinéma; [*manager*] du cinéma

theatre: ~**goer** *n* amateur *mf* de théâtre; ~**land** *n* quartier *m* des théâtres

them

When used as a direct object pronoun, referring to people, animals or things, *them* is translated by *les*:

I know them
= je les connais

Note that the object pronoun normally comes before the verb in French and that in compound tenses like the present perfect and past perfect, the past participle agrees in gender and number with the direct object pronoun:

He's seen them
(*them* being masculine or of mixed gender)
= il les a vus
(*them* being all feminine gender)
= il les a vues

In imperatives, the direct object pronoun is translated by *les* and comes after the verb:

catch them!
= attrape-les! (note the hyphen)

When used as an indirect object pronoun, *them* is translated by *leur*:

I gave them it or *I gave it to them*
= je le leur ai donné

In imperatives, the indirect object pronoun is translated by *leur* and comes after the verb:

phone them!
= téléphone-leur! (note the hyphen)

After prepositions and the verb *to be*, the translation is *eux* for masculine or mixed gender and *elles* for feminine gender:

he did it for them
= il l'a fait pour eux *or* pour elles

it's them
= ce sont eux *or* ce sont elles

For particular usages see the entry **them**.

theatrical /θɪˈætrɪkl/ *adj* [*star*] du théâtre; [*group, photographer*] de théâtre; [*agency, family, gesture, production, technique*] théâtral

theatrically /θɪˈætrɪklɪ/ *adv* [*gifted*] pour le théâtre; [*effective, striking*] du point de vue théâtral; [*behave*] de façon théâtrale

theatricals /θɪˈætrɪklz/ *npl* théâtre *m*

theft /θeft/ *n* vol *m* (**of** de)

their /ðeə(r)/

⚠ In French, determiners agree in gender and number with the noun they precede. So *their* is translated by *leur* + masculine or feminine singular noun (*leur chien*, *leur maison*) and by *leurs* + plural noun (*leurs enfants*).
When *their* is stressed, *à eux* (masculine, mixed) or *à elles* (feminine) is added after the noun: THEIR house = leur maison à eux/à elles.
For *their* used with parts of the body ▸ **p. 698.**

det leur/leurs

theirs /ðeəz/

⚠ In French, possessive pronouns reflect the gender and number of the noun they are standing for; *theirs* is translated by *le leur, la leur, les leurs*, according to what is being referred to.
For examples and particular usages see below.

pron **my car is red but** ~ **is blue** ma voiture est rouge mais la leur est bleue; **the green hats are** ~ les chapeaux verts sont à eux *or* elles; **which house is** ~**?** c'est laquelle leur maison?; **the money wasn't** ~ **to give away** ils *or* elles n'avaient pas à donner cet argent; **I saw them with that dog of** ~ péj je les ai vus avec leur sale chien○

them /ðem, ðəm/ *pron* **both of** ~ tous/toutes les deux; **both of** ~ **work in London** ils/elles travaillent à Londres tous/

toutes les deux; **some of** ~ quelques-uns d'entre eux or quelques-unes d'entre elles; **take** ~ **all** prenez-les tous/toutes; **none of** ~ **wants it** aucun/-e d'entre eux/elles ne le veut; **every single one of** ~ chacun/-e d'entre eux/elles

theme /θiːm/ n [1] (topic, motif) thème m also Mus, Ling; [2] US (essay) rédaction f

theme: ~ **park** n parc m de loisirs (à thème); ~ **song**, ~ **tune** n Cin musique f; Radio, TV indicatif m; fig rengaine f

themselves /ðəmˈselvz/

⚠ When used as a reflexive pronoun, direct and indirect, *themselves* is translated by *se* (or *s'* before a vowel or mute h).
When used as an emphatic the translation is *eux-mêmes* in the masculine and *elles-mêmes* in the feminine: *they did it themselves* = ils l'ont fait eux-mêmes or elles l'ont fait elles-mêmes.
After a preposition the translation is *eux* or *elles* or *eux-mêmes* or *elles-mêmes*: *they bought the painting for themselves* = (masculine or mixed gender) ils ont acheté le tableau pour eux or pour eux-mêmes; (feminine gender) elles ont acheté le tableau pour elles or pour elles-mêmes.

pron [1] (reflexive) se/s'; **they washed** ~ ils se sont lavés; [2] (emphatic) eux-mêmes/elles-mêmes; [3] (after preposition) eux/elles, eux-mêmes/elles-mêmes; **(all) by** ~ tous seuls/toutes seules

then /ðen/

⚠ When *then* is used to mean *at that time*, it is translated by *alors* or *à ce moment-là*: *I was working in Oxford then* = je travaillais alors à Oxford or je travaillais à Oxford à ce moment-là. Note that *alors* always comes immediately after the verb in French.
For particular usages see A 1 in the entry below.
For translations of *since then*, *until then* see the entries **since, until**.
When *then* is used to mean *next* it can be translated by either *puis* or *ensuite*: *a man, a horse and then a dog* = un homme, un cheval puis or et ensuite un chien.
For particular usages see A 2 in the entry below.
When *then* is used to mean *in that case* it is translated by *alors*: *then why worry?* = alors pourquoi s'inquiéter?
For all other uses see the entry below.

A *adv* [1] (at that point in time) alors, à ce moment-là; (implying more distant past) en ce temps-là; **we were living in Dublin** ~ nous habitions alors à Dublin; **just** ~ **she heard a noise** à ce moment-là elle a entendu un bruit; **a large sum of money even** ~ une grosse somme d'argent même à cette époque; **people were idealistic** ~ en ce temps-là les gens étaient idéalistes; **from** ~ **on, life became easier** à partir de ce moment-là la vie est devenue plus facile; **since** ~ **there has been little news** depuis on a eu peu de nouvelles; **by** ~ **the damage had been done** le mal était déjà fait; **they will let us know by** ~ nous aurons la réponse à ce moment-là; **if things haven't changed by** ~ si d'ici là les choses n'ont pas changé; **we won't be in contact until** ~ nous ne serons pas en contact avant (ce moment-là); ▸ **there;** [2] (in sequences: afterwards, next) puis, ensuite; ~ **came the big news** puis or ensuite on nous a annoncé la grande nouvelle; ~ **after that...** ensuite...; **and** ~ **what?** (with bated breath) et ensuite?; [3] (in that case) alors; **I saw them if not yesterday** ~ **the day before** je les ai vus hier ou avant-hier; **if it's a problem for you** ~ **say so** si ça te pose un problème dis-le; **if they're so nice** ~ **why not stay with them?** s'ils sont si agréables pourquoi ne pas rester avec eux?; ~ **why did you tell her?** mais alors pourquoi est-ce que tu le lui as dit?; **how about tomorrow** ~? et demain ça irait?; **well try this** ~ et bien alors essaie ça; ~ **what DO they want?** mais alors qu'est-ce qu'ils veulent?; [4] (summarizing statement: therefore) donc; **these** ~ **are the results of the policy** voici donc les résultats de cette politique; **overall** ~ **it would seem that** en résumé il semble donc que; [5] (in addition, besides) puis...aussi; **and** ~ **there's the fare to consider** et puis il faut aussi tenir compte du prix de billet; [6] (modifying previous statement: on the other hand) d'un autre côté; **she's good but** ~ **so is he** elle est bonne mais lui aussi; **they said it would rain but** ~ **they're often wrong** ils ont prévu de la pluie mais ils se trompent souvent; **he**

looks anxious but ~ **he always does** il a l'air inquiet mais de toute façon il a toujours cet air-là; [7] (rounding off a topic: so) alors; **it's all arranged** ~? tout est arrangé alors?; **that's all right** ~ ça va alors; [8] (focusing on topic) bon; **now** ~ **what's all this?** bon, qu'est-ce qui se passe?; **what's the problem** ~? alors quel est le problème?

B *adj* (épith) **the** ~ **prime minister** le premier ministre de l'époque; **the** ~ **mayor of New York, Mr X** M. X, qui était alors maire de New York

thence /ðens/ *adv* [1] (from there) de là; [2] (therefore) de cela

theologian /ˌθiəˈləʊdʒən/ n théologien/-ienne m/f

theological /ˌθiəˈlɒdʒɪkl/ *adj* [debate, issue, thought, writing] théologique; [book, college, faculty, study] de théologie; [student] en théologie

theology /θiˈɒlədʒi/ n théologie f

theorem /ˈθiərəm/ n théorème m

theoretical /ˌθiəˈretɪkl/ *adj* théorique

theoretically /ˌθiəˈretɪkli/ *adv* théoriquement; ~ **speaking** en théorie

theorize /ˈθiəraɪz/ *vi* théoriser

theory /ˈθiəri/ n théorie f

therapeutic /ˌθerəˈpjuːtɪk/ *adj* thérapeutique

therapist /ˈθerəpɪst/ n thérapeute mf

therapy /ˈθerəpi/
A n Med, Psych thérapie f; **to have** ou **be in** ~ suivre une thérapie
B *noun modifier* [group, session] de thérapie

there /ðeə(r)/

⚠ There is generally translated by *là* after prepositions: *near there* = près de là etc and when emphasizing the location of an object/a point etc visible to the speaker: *put them there* = mettez-les là.
Remember that *voilà* is used to draw attention to a visible place/object/person: *there's my watch* = voilà ma montre, whereas *il y a* is used for generalizations: *there's a village nearby* = il y a un village tout près.
there when unstressed with verbs such as *aller* and *être* is translated by *y*: *we went there last year* = nous y sommes allés l'année dernière, but not where emphasis is made: *it was there that we went last year* = c'est là que nous sommes allés l'année dernière.
For examples of the above and further uses of *there* see the entry below.

A *pron* (as impersonal subject) il; ~ **seems** ou **appears to be** il semble y avoir; ~ **is/are** il y a; ~ **are many reasons** il y a beaucoup de raisons; ~ **is some left** il en reste; **once upon a time** ~ **was** il était une fois; ~'**ll be a singsong later** on va chanter plus tard; ~'**s no denying that** personne ne peut nier que

B *adv* [1] (that place or point) là; **up to** ~, **down to** ~ jusque là; **put it in** ~ mettez-le là-dedans; **in** ~ **please** (ushering sb) par là s'il vous plaît; [2] (at or to that place) là; **stand** ~ mettez-vous là; **go over** ~ va là-bas; **since we were last** ~ depuis la dernière fois que nous y sommes allés; **it's** ~ **that** gen c'est là que; (when indicating) c'est là où; **to go** ~ **and back in an hour** faire l'aller et retour en une heure; **take the offer while it's** ~ fig profite de l'occasion pendant que c'est possible; [3] (to draw attention) (to person, activity etc) voilà; (to place) là; **what have you got** ~? qu'est-ce que tu as là?; ~ **goes the coach** voilà le car qui s'en va; ~ **you again** fig ça y est, c'est reparti; ~ **you are** (seeing somebody arrive) vous voilà; (giving object) tenez, voilà; (that's done) et voilà; ~'**s a bus coming** voilà un bus; **that paragraph** ~ ce paragraphe; **my colleague** ~ **will show you** mon collègue va vous montrer; **which one? this one or that one** ~? lequel? celui-ci ou celui-là?; ~'**s why!** ça explique tout!; [4] (indicating arrival) là; **will she be** ~ **now?** est-ce qu'elle y est maintenant?; **when do they get** ~? quand est-ce qu'ils arrivent là-bas?; ~ **I was at last** j'étais enfin là-bas; **the train won't be** ~ **yet** le train ne sera pas encore là; **we get off** ~ c'est là qu'on descend; [5] (indicating juncture) là; ~ **we must finish** nous devons nous arrêter là; ~ **was our chance** c'était notre chance; **so** ~ **we were in the same cell** et comme ça on s'est retrouvé dans la même cellule; [6] ᴼ(emphatic) **hello** ~! salut!; **hey you** ~! et toi là-bas!

C **there and then** *adv phr* directement

D **there again** *adv phr* (on the other hand) d'un autre côté

E *excl* ~ ~! (soothingly) allez! allez!; ~! (triumphantly) voilà!; ~, **I**

told you! voilà, je te l'avais bien dit! ~, **you've woken the baby!** c'est malin, tu as réveillé le bébé!

thereabouts /ˈðeərəbaʊts/ GB, **thereabout** /ˈðeərəbaʊt/ US adv [1] (in the vicinity) par là; [2] (roughly) **100 dollars or** ~ 100 dollars environ

thereafter /ðeərˈɑːftə(r)/ adv par la suite

thereby /ðeəˈbaɪ, ˈðeə-/ adv ainsi

(Idiom) ~ **hangs a tale** c'est toute une histoire

there'd /ðeəd/ = **there had, there would**

therefore /ˈðeəfɔː(r)/ adv donc, par conséquent

therein /ðeərˈɪn/ adv [1] (in that) ~ **lies...** c'est en cela que réside...; **the aircraft and the persons** ~ l'avion et les personnes qui sont/étaient à l'intérieur; [2] Jur (in contract) **contained** ~ ci-inclus

there'll /ðeəl/ = **there will**

there's /ðeəz/ = **there is, there has**

thereupon /ˌðeərəˈpɒn/ adv sout sur ce

therm /θɜːm/ n thermie f

thermal /ˈθɜːml/
A n courant m ascendant
B adj gen thermique; [spring, treatment] thermal

thermal baths npl thermes mpl

thermal imaging n thermographie f

thermic /ˈθɜːmɪk/ adj thermique

thermometer /θəˈmɒmɪtə(r)/ n thermomètre m

thermos flask n bouteille f thermos®

thermostat /ˈθɜːməstæt/ n thermostat m

thermostatic /ˌθɜːməˈstætɪk/ adj thermostatique

thesaurus /θɪˈsɔːrəs/ n (pl **-ri** ou **-ruses**) [1] (of synonyms etc) dictionnaire m analogique; [2] (of particular field) lexique m

these /ðiːz/ pl ▸ **this**

thesis /ˈθiːsɪs/ n (pl **theses**) [1] Univ (doctoral) thèse f; (master's) mémoire m; [2] (theory) thèse f

they /ðeɪ/

⚠ *They* is translated by *ils* (masculine) or *elles* (feminine). For a group of people or things of mixed gender *ils* is always used. The emphatic form is *eux* (masculine) or *elles* (feminine). For examples and exceptions, see below

pron ~ **have already gone** (masculine or mixed) ils sont déjà partis; (feminine) elles sont déjà parties; **here** ~ **are!** les voici!; **there** ~ **are!** les voilà!; ᴛʜᴇʏ **won't be there** (masculine or mixed) ils ne seront pas là, eux; (feminine) elles ne seront pas là, elles; **she bought one but** ~ **didn't** elle en a acheté un mais eux pas

they'd /ðeɪd/ = **they had, they would**

they'll /ðeɪl/ = **they will**

they're /ðeə(r)/ = **they are**

they've /ðeɪv/ = **they have**

thick /θɪk/
A adj [1] [object, substance, feature] épais/épaisse; [forest, vegetation, fog] dense, épais/épaisse; [accent] fort (before n); **to be 6 cm** ~ faire 6 cm d'épaisseur; **how** ~ **is the wall?** quelle est l'épaisseur du mur?; **to make sth** ~**er** épaissir qch; **to be** ~ **with** être plein de [smoke, noise]; être chargé de [emotion]; **fields** ~ **with poppies** des champs couverts de coquelicots; **the ground was** ~ **with ants** le sol grouillait de fourmis; [2] ᴼ(stupid) bête; **I can't get it into his** ~ **head that** je n'arrive pas à lui enfoncer dans le crâne ᴼ que; [3] ᴼ(friendly) **they're very** ~ **(with each other)** ils sont très liés; [4] ᴼ(unreasonable) **it's a bit** ~ **expecting me to do that!** c'est un peu raide ᴼ d'espérer que je ferai ça!
B adv **don't spread the butter on too** ~ ne mets pas trop de beurre; **the bread was sliced** ~ le pain était coupé en tranches épaisses; **the snow lay** ~ **on the ground** il y avait une épaisse couche de neige sur le sol

(Idioms) **to lay it on** ~ᴼ forcer la dose ᴼ; **offers of help are coming in** ~ **and fast** des propositions d'aide affluent de toutes parts; **through** ~ **and thin** contre vents et marées; **to be in the** ~ **of** être au beau milieu de

thicken /ˈθɪkən/
A vtr épaissir
B vi [sauce, soup, fog, snow, cloud, waistline] s'épaissir; [accent] devenir plus fort; [voice] s'enrouer; [traffic] devenir plus dense

(Idiom) **the plot** ~**s!** l'affaire se corse!

thickening /ˈθɪkənɪŋ/ n gen, Culin épaississant m

thicket /ˈθɪkɪt/ n fourré m

thickly /ˈθɪklɪ/ adv [spread] en une couche épaisse; [cut] en morceaux épais; [say, speak] d'une voix enrouée; **the grass grew** ~ l'herbe poussait dru; **a** ~**-wooded landscape** un paysage très boisé

thickness /ˈθɪknɪs/ n gen épaisseur f

thick: ~**set** adj trapu; [hedge] touffu; ~**-skinned** adj insensible

thief /θiːf/ n (pl **thieves**) voleur/-euse m/f; **stop** ~! au voleur!

(Idioms) **set a** ~ **to catch a** ~ seul un voleur peut en attraper un autre; **to be as thick as thieves** s'entendre comme larrons en foire

thieve /θiːv/ vtr, vi voler

thieves /θiːvz/ pl ▸ **thief**

thieving /ˈθiːvɪŋ/
A n vol m
B adj ~ **children** enfants qui volent

thigh /θaɪ/ n cuisse f

thigh: ~**bone** n fémur m; ~**boot** n cuissarde f

thimble /ˈθɪmbl/ n dé m à coudre

thin /θɪn/
A adj [1] (in width) [nose, lips, stick, wall] mince; [line, stripe, string, wire] fin; [strip] étroit; [2] (in depth) [slice, layer] fin, mince; **the ice is** ~ la couche de glace n'est pas très épaisse; [3] (in consistency) [mud, mixture] liquide; [soup, liquid, sauce] clair; [oil] fluide; [4] (lean) maigre; **to get** ~ maigrir; [5] (fine) [card, paper] fin; [fabric, mist] léger/-ère; [6] (in tone) (high-pitched) aigre; (weak) fluet/fluette; [7] [population, crowd, hair] clairsemé; [8] fig [excuse] peu convaincant; [evidence] insuffisant; [plot] squelettique; **to wear** ~ [joke, excuse] être usé; **my patience is wearing** ~ je commence à perdre patience; [9] [air] raréfié
B ᴼadv [slice] en tranches fpl fines; [spread] en couche mince
C vtr (p prés etc **-nn-**) [1] (also ~ **down**) diluer [paint]; allonger [sauce, soup]; [2] (disperse) = **thin out**
D vi (p prés etc **-nn-**) (also ~ **out**) [fog, mist] se dissiper; [crowd] se disperser; [hair] se raréfier
E **thinning** pres p adj [hair, crowd] clairsemé

(Idioms) **to be** ~ **on the ground** être rare; **to get** ~ **on top** se dégarnir; **to have a** ~ **time of it** traverser une période difficile

(Phrasal verbs)

■ **thin down** US maigrir

■ **thin out**: ▸ ~ [sth] **out**, ~ **out** [sth] éclaircir [seedlings, hedge]; réduire [population]

thing /θɪŋ/
A n [1] (object) chose f, truc ᴼ m; **what's this** ~ **for?** à quoi sert ce truc ᴼ?; **there isn't a** ~ **to eat in the house!** il n'y a rien à manger dans cette maison!; **the one** ~ **he wants for his birthday is a bike** tout ce qu'il veut pour son anniversaire, c'est un vélo; **it was a big box** ~ c'était une espèce de grosse boîte; [2] (action, task, event) chose f; **she'll do great** ~**s in life** elle ira loin dans la vie; **that's the worst** ~ **you could have said** c'était (vraiment) ʟᴀ chose à ne pas dire; **the best** ~ **(to do) would be to go and see her** le mieux serait d'aller la voir; **that was a silly** ~ **to do** c'était stupide de faire cela; **there wasn't a** ~ **I could do** je ne pouvais rien y faire; **it's a good** ~ **you came** heureusement que tu es venu; **the** ~ **to do is to listen carefully to him** ce qu'il faut faire c'est l'écouter attentivement; **I'm sorry, but I haven't done a** ~ **about it yet** je suis désolé, mais je ne m'en suis pas encore occupé; **the heat does funny** ~**s to people** la chaleur a de drôles d'effets sur les gens; **it's all right if you like that sort of** ~ c'est pas mal pour ceux qui aiment ça; [3] (matter, fact) chose f; **the** ~ **to remember is...** ce dont il faut se souvenir c'est...; **I couldn't hear a** ~ **(that) he said** je n'ai rien entendu de ce qu'il a dit; **I said/did no such** ~! je n'ai rien dit/fait de tel!; **the whole** ~ **is crazy!** c'est idiot tout cela!; **the** ~ **is, (that)...** ce qu'il y a, c'est que...; **the only** ~ **is,...** la seule chose, c'est que...; **the funny** ~ **is...** le plus drôle c'est que ...; **the good** ~ **(about it) is...** ce qu'il y a de bien, c'est que...; **the** ~ **about him is that he's very honest** ce qu'il faut lui reconnaître, c'est qu'il est très honnête; **the** ~ **about him is that he can't be trusted** le problème avec lui c'est qu'on ne peut pas lui faire confiance; [4] (person, animal) **she's a**

pretty little ~ c'est une jolie petite fille; **you lucky** ~○! veinard/-e○!; **you stupid** ~○! espèce d'idiot○!; **(the) stupid** ~○ (of object) sale truc○!

B things npl **1** (personal belongings, equipment) affaires fpl; **to wash up the breakfast** ~s faire la vaisselle du petit déjeuner; **2** (situation, circumstances, matters) les choses fpl; **to see** ~s **as they really are** voir les choses en face; ~s **are getting better/worse** cela s'améliore/empire; **how are** ~s **with you?, how are** ~s **going?** comment ça va?; **why do you want to change** ~s? pourquoi est-ce que tu veux tout changer?; **to worry about** ~s se faire du souci; **as** ~s **are** ou **stand** dans l'état actuel des choses; **as** ~s **turned out** en fin de compte; **all** ~s **considered** tout compte fait

(Idioms) **it's not the done** ~ **(to do)** ça ne se fait pas (de faire); **it's the in** ~○ c'est à la mode; **she was wearing the latest** ~ **in hats** elle portait un chapeau dernier cri; **that's just the** ~ ou **the very** ~! c'est tout à fait ce qu'il me/te/lui etc faut!; **it's become quite the** ~ **(to do)** c'est devenu à la mode (de faire); **it was a close** ou **near** ~ c'était juste; **he's on to a good** ~ il a trouvé le bon filon○; **he likes to do his own** ~○ il aime faire ce qui lui plaît; **for one** ~...**(and) for another** ~... premièrement... et deuxièmement...; **to have a** ~ **about** ~ (like) craquer pour○ [blondes, bearded men]; adorer [emeralds, old cars]; (hate) ne pas aimer; **it's a girl/guy** ~○ c'est un truc de filles/de mecs○; **to make a big** ~ **(out) of it**○ en faire toute une histoire; **to know a** ~ **or two about sth**○ s'y connaître en qch; **I could tell you a** ~ **or two about him**○! je pourrais vous en raconter sur son compte!; **and then, of all** ~s, **she...** et alors, allez savoir pourquoi○, elle...; **I must be seeing/hearing** ~s! je dois avoir des visions/entendre des voix!; **it's** ou **it was (just) one of those** ~s c'est la vie; **it's one (damned)** ~ **after another**○! les embêtements○ n'en finissent plus!; **one** ~ **led to another and...** et, de fil en aiguille...; **taking one** ~ **with another** tout bien considéré; **what with one** ~ **and another, I haven't had time to read it** avec tout ce que j'ai eu à faire je n'ai pas eu le temps de le lire; **to (try to) be all** ~s **to all men** (essayer de) faire plaisir à tout le monde

thingumabob /'θɪŋəməbɒb/, **thingumajig**○ /'θɪŋəmədʒɪɡ/ n truc m, machin m

think /θɪŋk/

A n **to have a** ~ **about sth** GB réfléchir à qch

B vtr (prét, pp **thought**) **1** (hold view, believe) croire; **I** ~ **so** je crois; **I don't** ~ **so, I** ~ **not** je ne crois pas; **'is he reliable?'—'I'd like to** ~ **so but...'** 'peut-on lui faire confiance?'—'j'espère bien mais...'; **to** ~ **it best to do/that** penser qu'il serait préférable de faire/que; **I** ~ **it's going to rain** j'ai l'impression qu'il va pleuvoir; **what do you** ~ **it will cost?** combien ça va coûter à ton avis?; **him, a millionaire? I don't** ~! iron lui un millionnaire? sans blague!; **2** (imagine) imaginer, croire; **who'd have thought it!** qui l'aurait cru?; **I never thought you meant it!** je ne t'ai jamais pris au sérieux!; **I can't** ~ **how/why etc** je n'ai aucune idée comment/pourquoi etc; **I can't** ~ **where I've put my keys** je ne sais pas du tout où j'ai mis mes clés; **who do you** ~ **you are?** (indignantly) pour qui vous prenez-vous?; **what on earth do you** ~ **you're doing?** mais qu'est-ce que tu fais?; **I thought as much!** je m'en doutais!; **six weeks' holiday! that's what you** ~! six semaines de vacances! tu te fais des idées!; **and to** ~ **that I believed him!** GB et dire que je le croyais!; **3** (have thought, idea) penser; **I didn't** ~ **to check** je n'ai pas pensé à vérifier; **I was just** ~ing: **suppose we sold the car?** je me posais la question: si nous vendions la voiture?; **we're** ~ing **sex here**○ c'est de sexe qu'il s'agit; **let's** ~ **Green**○! pensons écolo○!; **4** (rate, assess) **to** ~ **a lot/not much of** penser/ne pas penser beaucoup de bien de; **5** (remember) penser; **to** ~ **where/how** se rappeler où/comment

C vi (prét, pp **thought**) **1** gen penser; (before acting or speaking) réfléchir; **I'll have to** ~ **about it** il faudra que j'y réfléchisse; **to** ~ **hard** bien réfléchir; **to** ~ **clearly** ou **straight** avoir les idées claires; **to** ~ **for oneself** avoir des opinions personnelles; **I'm sorry, I wasn't** ~ing je m'excuse, je ne sais pas où j'avais la tête; **we are** ~ing **in terms of economics** nous voyons les choses du point de vue économique; **let's** ~: **three people at £170 each...** voyons: trois personnes à 170 livres sterling chacune...; **come to** ~ **of it...** maintenant que j'y pense...; **he thought better of it** il est revenu sur sa décision; **2** (take into account) **to** ~ **about** ou **of sb/sth** penser à qn/qch; **I can't** ~ **of everything!** je ne peux pas penser à tout!; **3** (consider) **to** ~ **of sb as** considérer qn comme; **he** ~s **of himself as an expert** il se prend

pour un spécialiste; **4** (have in mind) **to** ~ **of doing** envisager de faire; **to** ~ **about doing** penser à faire; **whatever were you** ~ing **of?** qu'est-ce qui t'a pris?; **5** (imagine) **to** ~ **of** penser à; **a million pounds,** ~ **of that!** un million de livres, t'imagines○!; **6** (tolerate idea) (tjrs nég) **not to** ~ **of doing** ne pas penser à faire; **I couldn't** ~ **of letting you pay** il n'est pas question que je te laisse payer; **7** (remember) **to** ~ **of** se rappeler; **if you** ~ **of anything else** si autre chose vous vient à l'esprit

(Idioms) **to have another** ~ **coming**○ GB se tromper lourdement; **to** ~ **on one's feet** réfléchir vite et bien

(Phrasal verbs)

■ **think again** (reflect more) se repencher sur la question; (change mind) changer d'avis; **if that's what you** ~, **you can** ~ **again** si c'est ça que tu penses, tu te trompes

■ **think ahead** bien réfléchir (à l'avance); ~ing **ahead to our retirement,...** quand nous serons à la retraite,...

■ **think back** se reporter en arrière (**to** à)

■ **think out:** ▶ ~ **out [sth],** ~ **[sth] out** bien réfléchir à; **well/badly thought out** bien/mal conçu

■ **think over:** ▶ ~ **over [sth],** ~ **[sth] over** réfléchir à

■ **think through:** ▶ ~ **through [sth],** ~ **[sth] through** bien réfléchir à [proposal, action]; faire le tour de [problem, question]

■ **think up:** ▶ ~ **up [sth]** inventer

thinker /'θɪŋkə(r)/ n penseur/-euse m/f

thinking /'θɪŋkɪŋ/

A n **1** (reflection) réflexion f; **to do some (hard)** ~ (beaucoup) réfléchir; **2** (way one thinks) pensée f; **current** ~ **is that** GB la tendance actuelle de l'opinion est que; **to my way of** ~ à mon avis

B adj [person] réfléchi; **the** ~ **person's pin-up** le sex symbol des intellectuels

think-tank /'θɪŋktæŋk/ n groupe m de réflexion

thin-lipped /,θɪn'lɪpt/ adj [person] aux lèvres minces; [smile] pincé

thinly /'θɪnlɪ/ adv **1** (sparingly) [slice] en tranches fines; [spread] en couche mince; [butter] légèrement; **2** fig ~ **disguised** à peine déguisé

thinner /'θɪnə(r)/

A comparative adj ▸ **thin**

B n (also **thinners** + v sg) diluant m

thin-skinned /,θɪn'skɪnd/ adj susceptible

third /θɜːd/ ▸ p. 1044, p. 788

A n **1** (in order) troisième mf; **2** (of month) trois m inv; **3** (fraction) tiers m; **4** (also ~**-class degree**) GB Univ ≈ licence avec mention passable; **5** Mus tierce f; **6** (also ~ **gear**) Aut troisième f

B adj troisième

C adv [come, finish] troisième; (in list) troisièmement

(Idiom) ~ **time lucky!** la troisième fois sera la bonne!

third-class /,θɜːd'klɑːs/

A adj **1** ~ **mail** US Post ≈ plis mpl non urgents; **2** GB Univ ~ **degree** = **third A 4**

B third class adv **to send sth** ~ envoyer qch en pli non urgent

third degree○ /,θɜːd də'griː/ n **to give sb the** ~ lit soumettre qn à un interrogatoire musclé; fig [parent, teacher] soumettre qn à une interrogation

thirdhand /,θɜːd'hænd/

A adj [vehicle, garment] d'occasion; [report, evidence] indirect

B adv [hear, learn] de manière indirecte

thirdly /'θɜːdlɪ/ adv troisièmement

third party /,θɜːd'pɑːtɪ/

A n (in insurance, law) tiers m

B third-party noun modifier ~ **insurance** assurance f au tiers; ~ **liability** responsabilité f civile

third: ~ **person** n troisième personne f; ~**-rate** adj péj gen de troisième ordre pej; [work] médiocre; **Third World** n tiers-monde m

thirst /θɜːst/ n lit, fig soif f (**for** de)

thirstily /'θɜːstɪlɪ/ adv [drink] à grands traits

thirsty /'θɜːstɪ/ adj lit, fig assoiffé; **to be** ~ lit, fig avoir soif; **to make sb** ~ donner soif à qn

thirteen /,θɜː'tiːn/ ▸ p. 1044, p. 788, p. 647

A n treize m inv

B adj treize inv

this

As a determiner

In French, determiners agree in gender and number with the noun they precede; *this* (plural *these*) is translated by *ce* + masculine singular noun (*ce monsieur*) BUT by *cet* + masculine singular noun beginning with a vowel or mute 'h' (*cet arbre, cet homme*), by *cette* + feminine singular noun (*cette femme*) and by *ces* + plural noun (*ces livres, ces histoires*).

Note, however, that the above translations are also used for the English *that* (plural *those*). So when it is necessary to insist on *this* as opposed to another or others of the same sort, the adverbial tag *-ci*, giving the idea of *this one here*, is added to the noun:

I prefer THIS version
= je préfère cette version-ci

For particular usages see the entry **this**.

This dictionary contains usage notes on such topics as **time units, days of the week** and **months of the year**. For the index to these notes ▸ **p. 1354**.

As a pronoun meaning *this one*

In French, pronouns reflect the gender and number of the noun they are referring to. So *this* is translated by *celui-ci* for a masculine noun, *celle-ci* for a feminine noun; *those* is translated by *ceux-ci* for a masculine plural noun, *celles-ci* for a feminine plural noun:

of all the dresses this is the prettiest one
= de toutes les robes celle-ci est la plus jolie

For other uses of *this* used as a pronoun (*who's this?, this is my brother, this is wrong* etc.) and for *this* used as an adverb (*it was this big* etc.), see the entry **this**.

....

thirteenth /ˌθɜːˈtiːnθ/ ▸ p. 1044, p. 788
A *n* **1** (in order) treizième *mf*; **2** (of month) treize *m inv*; **3** (fraction) treizième *m*
B *adj, adv* treizième

thirtieth /ˈθɜːtɪəθ/ ▸ p. 1044, p. 788
A *n* **1** (in order) trentième *mf*; **2** (of month) trente *m inv*; **3** (fraction) trentième *m*
B *adj, adv* trentième

thirty /ˈθɜːtɪ/ ▸ p. 1044, p. 647, p. 745
A *n* trente *m inv*; **at seven-thirty** à sept heures trente
B *adj* trente *inv*

thirty something *n* jeune cadre de plus de trente ans qui s'installe, fonde une famille, etc

this /ðɪs/
A *det* (*pl* **these**) ce/cet/cette/ces; ~ **paper is too thin** ce papier est trop mince; ~ **man is dangerous** cet homme est dangereux; ~ **lamp doesn't work** cette lampe ne marche pas; **do it** ~ **way not that way** fais-le comme ça et pas comme ça; ~ **woman came up to me**° une femme est venue vers moi°
B *pron* **what's** ~? qu'est-ce que c'est?; **who's** ~? gén qui est-ce?; (on telephone) qui est à l'appareil?; **whose is** ~? à qui appartient ceci?; ~ **is the dining room** voici la salle à manger; **where's** ~? (on photo) où est-ce?; ~ **is my sister Pauline** (introduction) voici ma sœur Pauline; (on photo) c'est ma sœur, Pauline, ~ **is not the right one** ce n'est pas le bon; **what did you mean by** ~? qu'est-ce que tu voulais dire par là?; **who did** ~? qui a fait ça?; **what's all** ~ **about?** qu'est-ce que c'est que cette histoire?; ~ **is what happens when** voilà ce qui se passe quand
C *adv* **it's** ~ **big** c'est grand comme ça; **having got** ~ **far it would be a pity to stop now** lit, fig maintenant qu'on est arrivé jusque-là ce serait dommage de s'arrêter; **I can't eat** ~ **much** je ne peux pas manger tout ça; **I didn't realize it was** ~ **serious** je ne m'étais pas rendu compte que c'était sérieux à ce point-là

(Idioms) **we sat around talking about** ~ **and that** nous avons parlé de tout et de rien; **to run** ~ **way and that** courir dans tous les sens

thistle /ˈθɪsl/ *n* chardon *m*

tho' *abrév écrite* = **though**

thong /θɒŋ/
A *n* **1** (on whip) lanière *f*; **2** (on shoe, garment) lacet *m*; **3** (underwear) string *m* ficelle
B **thongs** *npl* US (sandals) tongs *fpl*

thorn /θɔːn/ *n* **1** (on plant) épine *f*; **2** (bush) buisson *m* épineux
(Idiom) **to be a** ~ **in sb's side** être une source d'irritation pour qn

thorny /ˈθɔːnɪ/ *adj* lit, fig épineux/-euse

thorough /ˈθʌrə, US ˈθʌrəʊ/ *adj* **1** (detailed) gen approfondi; [*preparation, search, work*] minutieux/-ieuse; **to give sth a** ~ **cleaning** nettoyer qch à fond; **he did a** ~ **job on the repair work** il a fait toutes les réparations nécessaires; **to have a** ~ **grasp of sth** maîtriser parfaitement qch; **2** (meticulous) minutieux/-ieuse; **3** **to make a** ~ **nuisance of oneself** se rendre totalement insupportable

thoroughbred /ˈθʌrəbred/
A *n* pur-sang *m*
B *adj* de pure race

thoroughfare /ˈθʌrəfeə(r)/ *n* rue *f*; **'no** ~**'** 'passage interdit'

thoroughgoing /ˈθʌrəgəʊɪŋ/ *adj* [*analysis, education*] en profondeur; [*commitment*] absolu; [*preparation*] minutieux/-ieuse

thoroughly /ˈθʌrəlɪ, US ˈθʌrəʊlɪ/ *adv* **1** (meticulously) gen à fond; [*check, prepare, search, test*] minutieusement; **2** (completely) [*convincing, dangerous, clean, reliable, deserved*] tout à fait; [*depressing, confusing, unpleasant*] profondément; [*beaten*] complètement; **to** ~ **enjoy sth/doing** être tout à fait ravi de qch/de faire; **3** (without reservation) [*agree, approve*] parfaitement; [*recommend*] chaleureusement

thoroughness /ˈθʌrənɪs, US ˈθʌrəʊnɪs/ *n* (all contexts) minutie *f*

those /ðəʊs/ *pl* ▸ **that**

though /ðəʊ/
A *conj* **1** (emphasizing contrast: although) bien que; **strange** ~ **it may seem** si bizarre que ça puisse paraître; **talented** ~ **he is, I don't like him** il a beau être doué, je ne l'aime pas; **2** (modifying information: but) bien que, mais; **a foolish** ~ **courageous act** un acte stupide quoique courageux; **that was delicious** ~ **I say so myself!** sans me vanter, c'était délicieux!
B *adv* quand même, pourtant

thought /θɔːt/
A *prét, pp* ▸ **think B, C**
B *n* **1** (idea) idée *f*, pensée *f*; **that's a** ~! ça c'est une idée!; **it was just a** ~ ce n'était qu'une idée comme ça; **what a kind** ~! comme c'est gentil!; **2** **Ȼ** (reflection) pensée *f*; **deep in** ~ plongé dans ses pensées; **after much** ~ après mûre réflexion; **2** (consideration) considération *f*; **to give** ~ **to sth** considérer qch; **we never gave it much** ~ nous n'y avons pas beaucoup réfléchi; **don't give it another** ~ n'y pense plus; **to put a lot of** ~ **into a gift** choisir un cadeau avec beaucoup de soin; **4** (intention) **to have no** ~ **of doing** n'avoir aucune intention de faire; **I've given up all** ~**s of moving** j'ai abandonné toute idée de déménagement
C **thoughts** *npl* **1** (mind) pensées *fpl* (about au sujet de); **to collect** *ou* **gather one's** ~**s** rassembler ses esprits; **my** ~**s were elsewhere** je pensais à autre chose; **2** (opinions) opinion *f*

thoughtful /ˈθɔːtfl/ *adj* **1** (reflective) gen pensif/-ive; [*silence*] profond; **2** (considerate) [*person, gesture*] prévenant; [*letter, gift*] gentil/-ille; **3** (well thought-out) riche en réflexion

thoughtfully /ˈθɔːtfəlɪ/ *adv* **1** (considerately) [*behave, treat*] avec prévenance; [*chosen, worded*] avec attention; **2** [*stare, smile*] d'un air pensif; **3** [*write, describe*] de façon réfléchie

thoughtfulness /ˈθɔːtflnɪs/ *n* **1** (kindness) prévenance *f*; **2** (of expression, character) sérieux *m*

thoughtless /ˈθɔːtlɪs/ *adj* irréfléchi; **to be** ~ **towards** manquer de considération pour

thoughtlessly /ˈθɔːtlɪslɪ/ *adv* (insensitively) sans considération; (unthinkingly) sans réfléchir

thought-out /ˌθɔːtˈaʊt/ *adj* **well/badly** ~ bien/mal conçu

thought: ~ **process** n mécanismes mpl de la pensée; ~**-provoking** adj qui fait réfléchir

thousand /'θaʊznd/ ▸ p. 1044
A n (figure) mille m inv; **a** ~ **and two** mille deux; **about a** ~ un millier
B **thousands** npl milliers mpl (**of** de); **in their** ~**s** par milliers; **to lose** ~**s** perdre une fortune
C adj mille inv; **four** ~ **pounds** quatre mille livres; **about a** ~ **people** un millier de personnes

thousandth /'θaʊzndθ/ ▸ p. 1044
A n **1** (fraction) millième m; **2** (in order) millième mf
B adj, adv millième

thrash /θræʃ/
A n **1** ⃝GB (party) grande fête f; **2** Mus thrash m
B vtr **1** (whip) rouer [qn] de coups; **2** ⃝Mil, Sport écraser

(Phrasal verbs)
■ **thrash about**, **thrash around**: ▸ ~ **about**, ~ **around** se débattre; ▸ ~ [sth] **around** agiter
■ **thrash out**: ▸ ~ **out** [sth] venir à bout de [difficulties, problem]; réussir à élaborer [plan, compromise]

thrashing /'θræʃɪŋ/ n lit, fig raclée f

thread /θred/
A n **1** lit fil m; **to be hanging by a** ~ lit, fig ne tenir qu'à un fil; **2** fig fil m; **common** ~ **point** m commun; **to pull all the** ~**s together** faire la synthèse; **to pick up the** ~**s of** reprendre le cours de [career, life]; **3** (of screw) filetage m
B vtr **1** lit enfiler [bead, needle]; introduire [film, tape]; **2** fig **to** ~ **one's way through** se faufiler entre
C vi [beads, needle] s'enfiler; [film, tape] passer

(Phrasal verb)
■ **thread up**: ▸ ~ **up** [sth] enfiler le fil de [sewing machine]

threadbare /'θred,beə/ adj lit, fig usé jusqu'à la corde

threat /θret/ n (all contexts) menace f (**to** pour); **to make** ~**s against sb** lancer des menaces contre qn; **to pose a** ~ être une menace pour; **to be under** ~ être menacé (**from** par)

threaten /'θretn/
A vtr menacer; **to be** ~**ed with extinction** risquer de disparaître
B vi [danger, bad weather] menacer; **to** ~ **to do** risquer de faire

threatening /'θretnɪŋ/ adj gen menaçant; [letter] de menaces; **to receive** ~ **phone calls** recevoir des menaces par téléphone

three /θriː/ ▸ p. 1044, p. 647, p. 745
A n trois m inv; **to play the best of** ~ Sport jouer la revanche et la belle
B adj trois inv

three-cornered /,θriː'kɔːnəd/ adj [object] triangulaire; [discussion] tripartite; ~ **hat** tricorne m

three: ~**-day event** n concours m complet; ~**-dimensional** adj en trois dimensions

threefold /'θriːfəʊld/
A adj triple
B adv triplement; **to increase** ~ tripler

three: ~**-legged** adj [object] à trois pieds; ~**-piece suit** n (costume m) trois-pièces m inv; ~**-piece suite** n salon m trois pièces; ~**-ply wool** n laine f triple

three-quarter /,θriː'kwɔːtə(r)/
A n Sport trois-quarts m
B adj [portrait] de trois-quarts; [sleeve] trois-quarts

three-quarters /,θriː'kwɔːtəz/ ▸ p. 1267, p. 745
A n trois-quarts mpl; ~ **of an hour** trois-quarts d'heure
B adv [empty, full, done] aux trois-quarts

three R's n Sch les trois disciplines fpl fondamentales (lecture, écriture, calcul)

> ⓘ The Three R's Il s'agit des disciplines fondamentales dans lesquelles les élèves doivent avoir acquis un niveau minimal à la fin de l'école primaire : *Reading, Writing, Arithmetic*. Quand on prononce ces mots, on a l'impression qu'ils commencent tous par un 'r'.

three: ~**some** n groupe m de trois; ~**-way** adj [junction] à trois voies; [split] en trois; [discussion, battle] tripartite; ~**-wheeler** n (car) voiture f à trois roues

thresh /θreʃ/
A vtr battre

B vi battre le blé

threshold /'θreʃəʊld, -həʊld/ n (all contexts) seuil m; **to cross the** ~ franchir le seuil

threw /θruː/ prét ▸ **throw B, C, D**

thrift /θrɪft/ n **1** (frugality) économie f; **2** Bot armeria f

thrift shop n boutique f d'articles d'occasion

thrifty /'θrɪftɪ/ adj [person] économe (**in** dans); [life, meal] économique

thrill /θrɪl/
A n **1** (sensation) frisson m; **2** (pleasure) plaisir m; **to get a** ~ ou ~**s** se donner des sensations fortes; **what a** ~! quelle émotion!
B vtr (with joy) transporter [qn] de joie; (with admiration) gen transporter [qn] d'admiration; passionner [readers, viewers]
C vi frissonner (**at, to** à)
D thrilled pp adj ravi; ~**ed with** enchanté de

(Idiom) the ~**s and spills of sth** les sensations fortes que procure qch

thriller /'θrɪlə(r)/ n Cin, Literat, TV thriller m

thrilling /'θrɪlɪŋ/ adj gen palpitant; [concert, moment, sensation] exaltant

thrive /θraɪv/ vi (prét **throve** ou **thrived**; pp **thrived**) **1** lit gen se développer; [plant] pousser bien; **2** fig [business, community] prospérer; **she** ~**s on hard work** le travail lui réussit; **children** ~ **on affection** les enfants ont besoin d'affection pour s'épanouir

thriving /'θraɪvɪŋ/ adj [business, community] florissant; [person] prospère; [plant, animal] en pleine santé

throat /θrəʊt/ n gorge f; **sore** ~ mal m de gorge; **to have a lump in one's** ~ avoir la gorge nouée; **to stick in sb's** ~ lit se coincer dans la gorge de qn

(Idioms) **to be at each other's** ~**s**⃝ se disputer; **to cut one's own** ~ travailler à sa propre ruine; **to jump down sb's** ~⃝ s'en prendre à qn

throaty /'θrəʊtɪ/ adj **1** (husky) guttural; **2** ⃝(with sore throat) enroué

throb /θrɒb/
A n **1** (of engine, machine) vibration f; (of music) rythme m; **2** (of heart, pulse) battement m; (of pain) élancement m
B vi (p prés etc **-bb-**) **1** [heart, pulse] battre; **my head is** ~**bing** ça me lance dans la tête; **2** [motor] vibrer; [music, building] résonner; ~**bing with life** fourmillant d'activité

throbbing /'θrɒbɪŋ/
A n **1** (of heart, pulse, blood) battement m; (of pain) élancement m; **2** (of motor) vibration f; (of music, drum) rythme m
B adj [pain, ache, sound, music] lancinant; [head, finger] souffrant de douleurs lancinantes; **2** [engine, motor] qui vibre

throes /θrəʊz/ npl **1** death ~ agonie f also fig; **2** **to be in the** ~ **of sth/of doing** être au beau milieu de qch/de faire

throne /θrəʊn/ n trône m; **on the** ~ sur le trône

(Idiom) **the power behind the** ~ l'éminence grise

throng /θrɒŋ, US θrɔːŋ/
A n foule f (**of** de)
B vtr envahir [street, square, town]
C vi **to** ~ **to** ou **towards** converger vers; **to** ~ **around** se masser autour de

throttle /'θrɒtl/
A n **1** (also ~ **valve**) pointeau m; **2** (accelerator) accélérateur m; **at full** ~ à toute vitesse
B vtr lit étrangler (**with** avec); fig asphyxier [growth, project]

through /θruː/
A prep **1** (from one side to the other) à travers; **the nail went right** ~ **the wall** le clou a traversé le mur; **to stick one's finger** ~ **the slit** passer son doigt dans la fente; **to poke sth** ~ **a hole** enfoncer qch dans un trou; **to drill** ~ **a cable** toucher un fil électrique avec une perceuse; **he was shot** ~ **the head** on lui a tiré une balle dans la tête; **it has a crack running** ~ **it** il est fêlé; **2** (via, by way of) **to go** ~ **the town centre** passer par le centre-ville; **go straight** ~ **that door** passez cette porte; **to look** ~ regarder avec [binoculars, telescope]; regarder par [hole, window]; **3** (past) **to go** ~ brûler [red light]; **to get** ou **go** ~ passer à travers [barricade]; passer [customs]; **4** (among) **to fly** ~ **the clouds** voler au milieu des nuages; **to leap** ~ **the trees** sauter de branche en branche; **5** (expressing source or agency) **it was** ~ **her that I got this job** c'est par son intermédiaire que j'ai eu ce travail; **to book sth** ~ **a travel agent** réserver qch dans une agence

t

de voyage; **I only know her** ∼ **her writings** je ne la connais qu'à travers ses écrits; ⑥ (because of) ∼ **carelessness** par négligence; ∼ **illness** pour cause de maladie; ⑦ (until the end of) **all** ou **right** ∼ **the day** toute la journée; ⑧ (up to and including) jusqu'à; **from Friday** ∼ **to Sunday** de vendredi jusqu'à dimanche; **open April** ∼ **September** US ouvert d'avril à fin septembre

B adj ① ○(finished) fini; **are you** ∼ **with the paper?** as-tu fini de lire le journal?; **we're** ∼ (of a couple) c'est fini entre nous; ② (direct) [train, ticket, route] direct; [freight] à forfait; **'no** ∼ **road'** 'voie sans issue'; **'**∼ **traffic'** (on roadsign) 'autres directions'; ∼ **traffic uses the bypass** pour contourner la ville on prend la rocade; ③ (successful) **to be** ∼ **to the next round** être sélectionné pour le deuxième tour; ④ GB **your trousers are** ∼ **at the knee** ton pantalon est troué au genou

C adv ① (from one side to the other) **the water went right** ∼ l'eau est passée à travers; **to let sb** ∼ laisser passer qn; **cooked right** ∼ bien cuit; ② (from beginning to end) **to read/play sth right** ∼ lire/jouer qch jusqu'au bout; **I'm halfway** ∼ **the article** j'ai lu la moitié de l'article; ③ Telecom **you're** ∼ je vous passe votre correspondant

D **through and through** adv phr **to know sth** ∼ **and** ∼ connaître qch comme sa poche; **English** ∼ **and** ∼ anglais jusqu'au bout des ongles

(Idioms) **to have been** ∼ **a lot** en avoir vu des vertes et des pas mûres○; **you really put her** ∼ **it** tu lui en as vraiment fait voir de toutes les couleurs○

throughout /θru:ˈaʊt/
A prep ① (all over) ∼ **France** dans toute la France; ∼ **the world** dans le monde entier; ② (for the duration of) tout au long de; ∼ **his life** toute sa vie; ∼ **history** à travers l'histoire

B adv ① (in every part) partout; ② (the whole time) tout le temps

through: ∼**put** n Comput, Ind débit m; ∼**way** n US voie f rapide or express

throve /θrəʊv/ prét ▸ thrive

throw /θrəʊ/
A n ① Sport, Games (in football) touche f; (of javelin, discus etc) lancer m; (in judo, wrestling etc) jeté m; (of dice) coup m; ② (each) **CDs £5 a** ∼**!** les compacts à cinq livres (la) pièce!; ③ US (blanket) jeté m (de lit); (rug) carpette f

B vtr (prét **threw**; pp **thrown**) ① gen, Games, Sport (project) (with careful aim) lancer; (downwards) jeter; (with violence) projeter; ∼ **the ball up high** lance la balle en hauteur; **she threw her apron over her head** elle s'est couvert la tête avec son tablier; **she threw her arms around my neck** elle s'est jetée à mon cou; **he was thrown clear and survived** il a été éjecté et a survécu; **two jockeys were thrown** deux jockeys ont été désarçonnés; **to** ∼ **a six** (in dice) faire un six; ② fig (direct) lancer [punch, question]; jeter [glance, look]; envoyer [kiss]; projeter [image, light, shadow] (**on** sur); jeter [shadow] (**on** sur); **we are ready for all the problems that Europe can** ∼ **at us** fig nous somme prêts à affronter tous les problèmes que l'Europe nous pose; **to** ∼ **money at a project** dépenser sans compter pour un projet; **to** ∼ **suspicion on sb/sth** faire naître des soupçons sur qn/qch; ③ fig (disconcert) désarçonner; **to** ∼ **sb/sth] into confusion** ou **disarray** semer la confusion dans [meeting, group]; semer la confusion parmi [people]; ④ Tech actionner [switch, lever]; **the operator threw the machine into gear/reverse** l'opérateur a embrayé l'engin/passé la marche arrière; ⑤ ○(indulge in) **to** ∼ **a fit** fig piquer une crise○; ⑥ ○(organize) **to** ∼ **a party** faire une fête○; ⑦ (in pottery) **to** ∼ **a pot** tourner un pot

C vi (prét **threw**; pp **thrown**) lancer

D v refl (prét **threw**; pp **thrown**) **to** ∼ **oneself** se jeter (**onto** sur); **to** ∼ **oneself to the ground** se jeter par terre; **to** ∼ **oneself into** lit se jeter dans; fig se plonger dans

(Idioms) **it's** ∼**ing it down**○**!** GB ça dégringole○**!**; **to** ∼ **in one's lot with sb** rejoindre qn

(Phrasal verbs)

▪ **throw around, throw about**: ▸ ∼ **[sth] around** ① **to** ∼ **a ball around** s'envoyer un ballon!; ② fig lancer au hasard [ideas etc]; ∼ **money around** jeter l'argent par les fenêtres; ▸ ∼ **oneself around** se débattre

▪ **throw aside**: ▸ ∼ **aside [sth]**, ∼ **[sth] aside** lit lancer [qch] sur le côté; fig rejeter

▪ **throw away**: ▸ Games jeter une carte; ▸ ∼ **[sth] away**, ∼ **away [sth]** ① lit jeter; fig gâcher [chance, life]; gaspiller [money]; **he threw away any advantage he might have had** il

n'a pas su profiter de son avantage; ② (utter casually) lancer [qch] négligemment [remark, information]

▪ **throw back**: ▸ ∼ **back [sth]**, ∼ **[sth] back** rejeter [fish]; relancer [ball]; **she threw it back at him** elle le lui a rendu en le jetant à la figure; **we have been thrown back on our own resources** fig nous avons dû recourir à nos propres ressources

▪ **throw in**: ▸ ∼ **in [sth]**, ∼ **[sth] in** ① Comm (give free) faire cadeau de; ② (add) ajouter [ingredient]; ③ faire [remark]

▪ **throw off**: ▸ ∼ **off [sth]**, ∼ **[sth] off** ① (take off) ôter [qch] en vitesse [clothes]; écarter [bedclothes]; ② fig (cast aside) se débarrasser de [cold, handicap, pursuers]; se soulager de [burden]; se libérer de [tradition]; sortir de [depression]; ③ fig (compose quickly) faire [qch] en cinq minutes [poem, music]; ▸ ∼ **off [sb]**, ∼ **[sb] off** (eject) expulser de [bus, train, plane]

▪ **throw on**: ▸ ∼ **on [sth]**, ∼ **[sth] on** (put on) enfiler [qch] en vitesse

▪ **throw open**: ▸ ∼ **open [sth]**, ∼ **[sth] open** ① ouvrir grand [door, window]; ② fig (to public) ouvrir

▪ **throw out**: ▸ ∼ **out [sb/sth]**, ∼ **[sb/sth] out** jeter [rubbish]; expulser [person] (**of** de); (from membership) renvoyer (**of** de); **to be thrown out of work** être licencié; ▸ ∼ **out [sth]**, ∼ **[sth] out** ① (extend) ∼ **your chest out** sortez la poitrine; ② (reject) Jur rejeter [application, decision]; Pol repousser [bill]; ③ (utter) lancer [comment]; (casually) **he just threw out some comment about wanting...** il a juste dit qu'il voulait...; ▸ ∼ **[sb] out** (mislead) déconcerter; **that's what threw me out** c'est ce qui m'a fait me tromper

▪ **throw over**○ GB: ▸ ∼ **over [sb]**, ∼ **[sb] over** laisser tomber○

▪ **throw together**: ▸ ∼ **[sb] together** réunir [people]; ▸ ∼ **[sth] together** gen improviser; mélanger [ingredients]

▪ **throw up**: ▸ ∼ **up**○ vomir; ▸ ∼ **up [sth]**, ∼ **[sth] up** ① ○(abandon) laisser tomber [job]; ② (reveal) faire apparaître [fact]; créer [idea, problem, obstacle]; engendrer [findings, question, statistic]; ③ cracher [smoke]; émettre [spray]; vomir [lava]; ④ (toss into air) projeter [stone]; lever [arms, hands]; lancer [ball]; ⑤ (open) ouvrir grand [window]; ⑥ (vomit) vomir

throwaway /ˈθrəʊəweɪ/ adj ① (discardable) jetable; ② (wasteful) [society] de consommation; ③ [remark] désinvolte; [entertainment, style] à l'emporte-pièce

throwback /ˈθrəʊbæk/ n lit survivant/-e m/f; fig survivance f (**to** de)

thrower /ˈθrəʊə(r)/ n Sport, gen lanceur/-euse m/f

throw-in /ˈθrəʊɪn/ n Sport touche f

thrown /θrəʊn/ pp ▸ throw B, C, D

thru prep US = **through**

thrush /θrʌʃ/ n ① Zool grive f; ② ▸ p. 933 Med (oral) muguet m (buccal); (vaginal) mycose f vaginale

thrust /θrʌst/
A n ① lit, gen, Mil, Tech, Archit poussée f; **sword** ∼ coup m d'épée; ② (of argument, essay) portée f; ③ fig (attack) **that was a** ∼ **at you** ça c'était une pointe dirigée contre toi

B vtr (prét, pp **thrust**) **to** ∼ **sth towards** ou **at sb** mettre brusquement qch sous le nez de qn; **to** ∼ **sth into sth** enfoncer qch dans qch; **to** ∼ **sb/sth away** ou **out of the way** pousser violemment qn/qch

C v refl (prét, pp **thrust**) **he thrust himself to the front of the crowd** il s'est frayé un passage jusqu'au premier rang de la foule; **to** ∼ **oneself forward** se lancer en avant; fig se mettre en avant; **to** ∼ **oneself on** ou **onto sb** imposer sa présence à qn

(Phrasal verbs)

▪ **thrust aside**: ▸ ∼ **[sth/sb] aside**, ∼ **aside [sth/sb]** lit repousser; fig rejeter

▪ **thrust back**: ▸ ∼ **[sth] back**, ∼ **back [sth]** repousser

▪ **thrust forward**: ▸ ∼ **forward** se précipiter en avant; ▸ ∼ **[sth] forward**, ∼ **forward [sth]** pousser [qch] en avant

▪ **thrust on, thrust onto** = **thrust upon**

▪ **thrust out**: ▸ ∼ **[sth] out**, ∼ **out [sth]** tendre brusquement [hand]; lancer [leg]; projeter [qch] en avant [jaw, chin]; sortir [qch] (d'un geste brusque) [implement]

▪ **thrust upon**: ▸ ∼ **[sth] upon sb** imposer [qch] sur qn; **some have greatness thrust upon them** parfois ce sont les circonstances qui font les grands hommes

thrusting /ˈθrʌstɪŋ/ adj gen agressif/-ive; [ambition] puissant

thud /θʌd/
A n bruit m sourd
B vi (p prés etc **-dd-**) faire un bruit sourd; **they ~ded up the stairs** ils ont monté l'escalier à pas lourds; **her heart was ~ding** son cœur battait à tout rompre

thug /θʌg/ n (hooligan) voyou m; (hired heavy) casseur m

thumb /θʌm/
A n pouce m
B vtr **1** feuilleter [book, magazine]; **a well-~ed book** un livre qui a beaucoup servi; **2** ᴼ(hitchhiking) **to ~ a lift** ou **a ride** faire du stopᴼ

(Idioms) **to be all ~s** être très maladroit; **to be under sb's ~** être sous la domination de qn; **to ~ one's nose at sb** lit faire un pied de nez à qn; fig faire la niqueᴼ à qn; **to stick out like a sore ~** faire tache pej

(Phrasal verb)
■ **thumb through:** ▶ **~ through** [sth] feuilleter [book, magazine]

thumb: **~ index** n répertoire m à onglets; **~nail sketch** n fig (of person) esquisse f (de caractère); (of event) aperçu m

thumbs downᴼ /ˌθʌmz'daʊn/ n (signal) **to give sb/sth the ~** fig rejeter qn/qch; **to get the ~** [candidate, proposal, idea] être rejeté; [new product, experiment] être mal accueilli

thumbs upᴼ /ˌθʌmz'ʌp/ n **to give sb/sth the ~** (approve) approuver qn/qch; **start the car when I give you the ~** démarre quand je te fais signe; **she gave me the ~ as she came out of the interview** elle m'a fait signe que l'entretien s'était bien passé

thumbtack /'θʌmtæk/
A n punaise f
B vtr fixer [qch] avec des punaises

thump /θʌmp/
A n **1** (blow) (grand) coup m; **2** (sound) bruit m sourd
B vtr donner un coup de poing à [person]; donner un coup de poing sur [table]
C vi **1** (pound) [heart] battre violemment; [music, rhythm] résonner; **my head is ~ing** j'ai la tête qui m'élance; **to ~ on** marteler; **2** (clump) **to ~ upstairs** monter l'escalier à pas lourds

thumping /'θʌmpɪŋ/
A n **1** (of drums) battement m; **2** ᴼ(beating) racléeᴼ f
B adj **1** ᴼ(emphatic) **~ big**, **~ great** énorme; **2** (loud) [noise] sourd; [rhythm, sound] lancinant; [headache] lancinant

thunder /'θʌndə(r)/
A n **1** Meteorol tonnerre m; **a clap** ou **peal of ~** un coup de tonnerre; **2** (noise) (of hooves) fracas m; (of traffic) grondement m; (of cannons, applause) tonnerre m
B vtr (shout) (also **~ out**) hurler
C vi **1** (roar) [person, cannon] tonner; [hooves] faire un bruit de tonnerre (**on** sur); **2** (rush) **to ~ along** ou **past** passer dans un vacarme assourdissant
D v impers tonner

(Idioms) **to steal sb's ~** couper l'herbe sous le pied de qn; **with a face like ~** ou **as black as ~** l'air furieux

thunder: **~bolt** n Meteorol foudre f; fig coup m de tonnerre; **~clap** n coup m de tonnerre; **~cloud** n nuage m porteur d'orage

thundering /'θʌndərɪŋ/
A adj **1** (angry) [rage] noir; **2** (huge) [success] énorme; [nuisance] véritable; [music, noise] assourdissant
B ᴼadv GB (intensifier) **a ~ great skyscraper** un gratte-ciel gigantesque

thunderous /'θʌndərəs/ adj **1** (loud) [welcome] tonitruant; [music, noise] assourdissant; **~ applause** un tonnerre d'applaudissements; **2** (angry) [face, expression] orageux/-euse; [look] furieux/-ieuse

thunder: **~storm** n orage m; **~struck** adj abasourdi

thundery /'θʌndərɪ/ adj orageux/-euse

Thur, Thurs abrév écrite = **Thursday**

Thursday /'θɜːzdeɪ, -dɪ/ ▸ p. 1322 pr n jeudi m

thus /θʌs/ adv ainsi; **~ far** jusqu'à présent

thwack /θwæk/
A n (blow) coup m; (with hand) claque f; (sound) coup m sec
B vtr frapper (vigoureusement)

thwart /θwɔːt/
A vtr contrecarrer, contrarier [plan]; contrecarrer les desseins de [person]
B **thwarted** pp adj contrarié (**in** dans)

thy‡ /ðaɪ/ det = **your**

thyme /taɪm/ n thym m

thyroid /'θaɪrɔɪd/ n (also **~ gland**) thyroïde f

ti /tiː/ n Mus si m

tiara /tɪ'ɑːrə/ n (woman's) diadème m; (Pope's) tiare f

Tibet /tɪ'bet/ pr n Tibet m

tick /tɪk/
A n **1** (of clock) tic-tac m; **2** (mark on paper) coche f; **to put a ~ against sth** cocher qch; **3** Zool tique f; **4** ᴼGB (short time) seconde f; **I won't be a ~** j'en ai (juste) pour une seconde; **5** ᴼGB (credit) **on ~** à crédit
B vtr (make mark) cocher [box, name, answer]
C vi [bomb, clock, watch] faire tic-tac; **I know what makes him ~** fig je sais ce qui le motive

(Phrasal verbs)
■ **tick away** [time] passer; [clock, meter] tourner
■ **tick by** [hours, minutes] passer
■ **tick off:** ▶ **~ [sth] off**, **~ off [sth]** (mark) cocher [name, item]; ▶ **~ [sb] off 1** ᴼGB (reprimand) réprimander [person]; **2** ᴼ(annoy) embêter [person]
■ **tick over** GB lit, fig tourner

ticker tape /'tɪkəteɪp/ n bande f de téléscripteur; **to give sb a ~ welcome** ou **reception** accueillir qn par une pluie de serpentins

ticket /'tɪkɪt/
A n **1** gen billet m (**for** pour); (for bus, underground, cloakroom, left-luggage) ticket m; (for library) carte f; (label) étiquette f; **admission by ~ only** entrée sur présentation d'un billet; **2** ᴼAut (for fine) PVᴼ m; **3** US Pol (of political party) liste f (électorale); (platform) programme m; **to run on the Republican ~** se présenter sur la liste des Républicains
B vtr étiqueter [goods, baggage]

(Idiom) **that's (just) the ~**ᴼ! voilà (exactement) ce qu'il nous faut!

ticket: **~ agency** n agence f de spectacles; **~ inspector** ▸ p. 1181 n contrôleur m; **~ office** n (office) bureau m de vente (des billets); (booth) guichet m; **~ tout** n GB revendeur/-euse m/f de billets au marché noir

ticking /'tɪkɪŋ/ n **1** (of clock) tic-tac m; **2** (material) toile f à matelas; (cover) housse f

tickle /'tɪkl/
A n chatouillement m
B vtr **1** [person, feather] chatouiller; [wool, garment] gratter; **2** ᴼfig (gratify) chatouiller [palate, vanity]; exciter [senses]; (amuse) amuser [person]; **to ~ sb's fancy** amuser qn
C vi [blanket, garment] gratter; [feather] chatouiller

(Idiom) **~d pink** ou **to death** ravi

tickling /'tɪklɪŋ/ n chatouillement m

ticklish /'tɪklɪʃ/ adj **1** [person] chatouilleux/-euse; **2** (tricky) [situation, problem] épineux/-euse

tick-tack-toe ▸ p. 881 n US (jeu m de) morpion m

tidal /'taɪdl/ adj [river] à marée; [current, flow, waters] de marée; [energy, power] marémoteur/-trice

tidal wave n lit, fig raz-de-marée m inv

tidbit /'tɪdbɪt/ n US (of food) gâterie f; (of gossip) cancanᴼ m

tiddlyᴼ /'tɪdlɪ/ adj GB (drunk) pompetteᴼ

tiddlywinks /'tɪdlɪwɪŋks/ ▸ p. 881 n jeu m de puce

tide /taɪd/ n **1** marée f; fig (of emotion) vague f; (of events) cours m; **the ~ is in/out** c'est la marée haute/basse; **the ~ is turning** la marée change; **to go/swim against the ~** lit, fig aller/nager à contre-courant; **the ~ has turned** fig la chance a tourné (du bon côté)

(Idiom) **time and ~ wait for no man** on ne peut pas arrêter le temps

(Phrasal verb)
■ **tide over:** ▶ **~ [sb] over** dépanner

tidemark n lit ligne f de marée haute; GB fig (line of dirt) marque f de saleté

tidily /'taɪdɪlɪ/ adv gen soigneusement; [dress] de façon soignée

tidiness /'taɪdɪnɪs/ n (of place) ordre m; (of appearance) aspect m soigné; (of person) sens m de l'ordre

tidings /'taɪdɪŋz/ npl littér nouvelles fpl

tidy /'taɪdɪ/
A n GB = **tidy-out**
B adj **1** [house, room, desk] bien rangé; [garden, work, person,

appearance] soigné; [*habits*] ordonné; [*hair*] bien coiffé; **to make oneself** ~ s'arranger; **2** ○[*amount*] beau/belle

C *vtr* = tidy up

D *vi* = tidy up

(Phrasal verbs)

■ **tidy away:** ▸ ~ **[sth] away,** ~ **away [sth]** ranger

■ **tidy out:** ▸ ~ **[sth] out,** ~ **out [sth]** ranger

■ **tidy up:** ▸ ~ **up** faire du rangement; **to** ~ **up after** ranger derrière [*person*]; ▸ ~ **up [sth],** ~ **[sth] up** ranger [*house, room, objects*]; mettre de l'ordre dans [*garden, town, finances*]; arranger [*appearance, hair*]; ▸ ~ **oneself up** s'arranger

tidy-out /'taɪdɪaʊt/, **tidy-up** /'taɪdɪʌp/ *n* GB rangement *m*; **to have a** ~ faire du rangement

tie /taɪ/

A *n* **1** (piece of clothing) cravate *f*; **2** (fastener) attache *f*; **3** (bond) (*gén pl*) lien *m*; **family** ~**s** liens *mpl* familiaux; **4** (constraint) contrainte *f*; **5** gen, Sport (draw) match *m* nul; **the match ended in a** ~ les deux équipes ont fait match nul; **there was a** ~ **for second place** il y a eu ex-aequo pour la deuxième place; **there was a** ~ **between the candidates** les candidats ont obtenu le même nombre de voix

B *vtr* (*p prés* **tying**) **1** (attach) attacher [*label, animal*] (**to** à); ligoter [*hands*]; ficeler [*parcel, chicken*] (**with** avec); (join in knot) nouer [*scarf, cravate*]; attacher [*laces*]; ~ **a knot in the string** fais un nœud à la ficelle; **2** (link) associer (**to** à); **to be** ~**d to** être lié à [*growth, activity*]; Fin être indexé sur [*inflation, interest*]; **3** **to be** ~**d to** (constrained by) être rivé à [*job*]; être cloué○ à [*house*]

C *vi* (*p prés* **tying**) **1** (fasten) s'attacher; **2** gen, Sport (draw) (in match) faire match nul; (in race) être ex aequo; (in vote) [*candidates*] obtenir le même nombre de voix

(Phrasal verbs)

■ **tie back:** ▸ ~ **[sth] back,** ~ **back [sth]** nouer [qch] derrière [*hair*]; attacher [qch] sur le côté [*curtain*]

■ **tie down:** ▸ ~ **[sb/sth] down,** ~ **down [sb/sth]** (hold fast) attacher [*person*]; **she feels** ~**d down** fig elle se sent coincée○; **he doesn't want to be** ~**d down** il ne veut pas perdre sa liberté; **to** ~ **sb down to** (limit) imposer qch à qn; **to** ~ **sb down to an exact date** arriver à soutirer une date exacte à qn; **to** ~ **oneself down** s'astreindre (**to** à)

■ **tie in with:** ▸ ~ **in with [sth]** **1** (tally) concorder avec [*fact, event*]; **2** (have link) être en rapport avec; ▸ ~ **[sth] in with sth,** ~ **in [sth] with sth** (combine) combiner [qch] avec qch

■ **tie on:** ▸ ~ **[sth] on,** ~ **on [sth]** attacher

■ **tie together:** ▸ ~ **[sth] together,** ~ **together [sth]** attacher [*bundles, objects*]

■ **tie up:** ▸ ~ **[sb/sth] up,** ~ **up [sb/sth]** **1** (secure) ligoter [*prisoner*]; ficeler [*parcel*]; attacher [*animal*]; **2** Fin (freeze) immobiliser [*capital*]; bloquer [*shares*]; **3** (finalize) régler [*details, matters*]; conclure [*deal*]; **to** ~ **up the loose ends** régler les derniers détails; **4** (hinder) bloquer [*procedure*]; US bloquer [*traffic, route*]; US suspendre [*production*]; **5** **to be** ~**d up** (be busy) être pris

tie break(er) *n* (in tennis) tie-break *m*; (in quiz) question *f* subsidiaire

tie-dye /'taɪdaɪ/ *vtr* chiner par teinture

tier /tɪə(r)/

A *n* (of cake, sandwich) étage *m*; (of organization, system) niveau *m*; (of seating) gradin *m*; ▸ **two-tier**

B *vtr* constituer [qch] en niveaux [*organization, system*]; disposer [qch] en gradins [*seating*]

C **tiered** *pp adj* [*seating*] en gradins; [*system*] à plusieurs niveaux; ~**ed cake** pièce *f* montée

tiff /tɪf/ *n* (petite) querelle *f*

tiger /'taɪgə(r)/ *n* tigre *m*

tiger economy *n* Econ économie *f* des tigres asiatiques

tight /taɪt/ ▸ p. 1191

A **tights** *npl* GB collant *m*

B *adj* **1** (firm) [*grip*] ferme; [*knot*] serré; (taut) [*rope, voice*] tendu; **to hold sb in a** ~ **embrace** tenir qn serré dans ses bras; **2** (constrictive) [*space*] étroit; [*clothing*] serré; (closefitting) [*jacket, shirt*] ajusté; **my shoes are too** ~ mes chaussures sont trop étroites; **a pair of** ~ **jeans** un jean moulant; **there were six of us in the car, it was a** ~ **squeeze** on était six dans la voiture, on était très serré; **3** (strict) [*security, deadline*] strict; [*discipline*] rigoureux/-euse; [*budget, credit*] serré; **to exercise** ~ **control over sth/sb** contrôler strictement qch/qn; **to be** ~ **(with one's money)**○ être près de ses sous; **money is a bit** ~ **these days** je suis/on est etc un

peu juste ces temps-ci; **4** (packed, compact) serré; **5** (sharp) [*angle, turn*] aigu/-uë

C *adv* [*hold, grip*] fermement; **to fasten/close sth** ~ bien attacher/fermer qch; **hold** ~! cramponne-toi!; **sit** ~! ne bouge pas!; **I just sat** ~ **and waited for the scandal to pass** fig je suis resté tranquillement dans mon coin en attendant que le scandale passe

(Idioms) **to be in a** ~ **spot** *ou* **situation** *ou* **corner** être dans une situation difficile; **to run a** ~ **ship** tout avoir à l'œil

tighten /'taɪtn/

A *vtr* serrer [*lid, screw*]; resserrer [*grip*]; tendre [*spring, bicycle chain*]; renforcer [*security, restrictions*]; durcir [*legislation, policy*]

B *vi* **1** (contract) [*lips*] se serrer; [*muscle*] se contracter; **2** [*screw, nut*] se resserrer; [*laws, credit controls*] se durcir

(Idiom) **to** ~ **one's belt** se serrer la ceinture

(Phrasal verb)

■ **tighten up:** ▸ ~ **up [sth],** ~ **[sth] up** resserrer [*screw, hinge*]; renforcer [*security*]; durcir [*legislation*]; **to** ~ **up on** durcir la réglementation en matière de [*immigration, fiscal policy*]

tight: ~**-fisted**○ *adj* péj radin○; ~**-fitting** *adj* ajusté; ~**-knit** *adj* fig uni

tight-lipped /ˌtaɪt'lɪpt/ *adj* **they are remaining** ~ **about the events** ils se refusent à tout commentaire sur les événements; **he watched,** ~ il a regardé d'un air pincé *or* d'un air réprobateur

tightly /'taɪtlɪ/ *adv* [*grasp, hold*] fermement; [*embrace*] bien fort; [*tied, fastened*] bien; [*controlled*] strictement; **the** ~ **packed crowd** la foule dense et serrée; **a** ~ **stretched rope** une corde très tendue

tightness /'taɪtnɪs/ *n* (of space, garment) étroitesse *f*; (of restrictions, security) rigueur *f* (**of** de); **to feel a** ~ **in one's chest** se sentir oppressé

tight: ~**rope** *n* corde *f* raide; ~**rope walker** *n* funambule *mf*

tile /taɪl/

A *n* (for roof) tuile *f*; (for floor, wall) carreau *m*

B *vtr* poser des tuiles sur [*roof*]; carreler [*floor, wall*]

(Idiom) **to have a night** *ou* **go out on the** ~**s**○ GB faire la noce○

tiling /'taɪlɪŋ/ *n* ₵ (tiles) (of roof) tuiles *fpl*; (of floor, wall) carrelage *m*

till¹ /tɪl/ ▸ **until**

till² /tɪl/ *n* caisse *f*; **to have one's hand in the** ~ piocher dans la caisse

tiller /'tɪlə(r)/ *n* Naut barre *f*

till receipt *n* ticket *m* (de caisse)

tilt /tɪlt/

A *n* **1** (incline) inclinaison *f*; **to be on** *ou* **at a** ~ être incliné; **2** **to have** *ou* **take a** ~ **at** fig s'en prendre à [*person, organization*]; s'essayer à [*championship*]; **at full** ~ à toute vitesse

B *vtr* (slant) pencher [*table, sunshade*]; incliner [*head*]; rabattre [*hat, cap*]

C *vi* **1** (slant) pencher; **2** **to** ~ **at** fig s'en prendre à [*person, organization*]

timber /'tɪmbə(r)/ *n* (for building) bois *m* (de construction); (trees) arbres *mpl*; (beam) poutre *f*

timbered /'tɪmbə(r)d/ *adj* [*house*] en bois; **half-**~ **house** maison *f* à colombages

timber: ~**land** *n* US terrain *m* forestier exploitable; ~ **yard** *n* scierie *f*

timbre /'tɪmbə(r), 'tæmbrə/ *n* timbre *m*

time /taɪm/ ▸ p. 745

A *n* **1** (continuum) temps *m*; **in** *ou* **with** ~, **in the course of** ~ avec le temps; **as** ~ **goes/went by** avec le temps; **at this point in** ~ à l'heure qu'il est; **for all** ~ à jamais; **2** (specific duration) temps *m*; **flight/journey** ~ durée *f* du vol/voyage; **I was waiting for you here all the** ~ je t'attendais ici et je n'ai pas bougé; **she was lying all the** ~ elle mentait depuis le début; **you've got all the** ~ **in the world,** **you've got plenty of** ~ tu as tout ton temps; **it'll be a long** ~ **before I go back there!** je n'y retournerai pas de sitôt!; **you took a long** ~!, **what a (long)** ~ **you've been!** tu en a mis du temps!; **we had to wait for a long** ~ nous avons dû attendre longtemps; **a long** ~ **ago** il y a longtemps; **we haven't heard from her for some** ~ ça fait un moment qu'on n'a pas eu de ses nouvelles; **in no** ~ **at all, in next to**

Time units

Lengths of time

a second
= une seconde

a week
= une semaine

a minute
= une minute

a month
= un mois

an hour
= une heure

a year
= un an/une année

a day
= un jour

a century
= un siècle

■ *For time by the clock* ► **p. 745**; *for days of the week*
► **p. 1322**; *for months* ► **p. 1020**; *for dates* ► **p. 788**.

How long?

■ *Note the various ways of translating* take *into French.*

how long does it take?
= combien de temps faut-il?

it took me a week
= cela m'a pris une semaine
   or il m'a fallu une semaine

I took an hour to finish it
= j'ai mis une heure pour le terminer

it'll only take a moment
= c'est l'affaire de quelques instants

■ *Translate both* spend *and* have *as* passer:

to have a wonderful evening
= passer une soirée merveilleuse

to spend two days in Paris
= passer deux jours à Paris

■ *Use* dans *for* in *when something is seen as happening in the future:*

I'll be there in an hour
= je serai là dans une heure

in three weeks' time
= dans trois semaines

■ *Use* en *for* in *when expressing the time something took or will take:*

he did it in an hour
= il l'a fait en une heure

■ *The commonest translation of* for *in the 'how long' sense is* pendant:

I worked in the factory for a year
= j'ai travaillé à l'usine pendant un an

■ *But use* pour *for* for *when the length of time is seen as being still to come:*

we're here for a month
= nous sommes là pour un mois

■ *And use* depuis *for* for *when the action began in the past and is or was still going on:*

she has been here for a week
= elle est ici depuis huit jours

she had been there for a year
= elle était là depuis un an

I haven't seen her for years
= je ne l'ai pas vue depuis des années

■ *Note the use of* de *when expressing how long something lasted or will last:*

a two-minute delay
= un retard de deux minutes

an eight-hour day
= une journée de huit heures

five weeks' pay
= cinq semaines de salaire

When?

In the past

when did it happen?
= quand est-ce que c'est arrivé?

two minutes ago
= il y a deux minutes

a month ago
= il y a un mois

years ago
= il y a des années

it'll be a month ago on Tuesday
= ça fera un mois mardi

it's years since he died
= il y a des années qu'il est mort

a month earlier
= un mois plus tôt

a month before
= un mois avant *or* un mois auparavant

the year before
= l'année d'avant *or* l'année précédente

the year after
= l'année d'après *or* l'année suivante

a few years later
= quelques années plus tard

after four days
= au bout de quatre jours

last week
= la semaine dernière

last month
= le mois dernier

last year
= l'année dernière

a week ago yesterday
= il y a eu huit jours hier

a week ago tomorrow
= il y aura huit jours demain

the week before last
= il y a quinze jours

over the past few months
= au cours des derniers mois

In the future

when will you see him?
= quand est-ce que tu le verras?

in a few days
= dans quelques jours (*see also above, the phrases with* in *translated by* dans)

any day now
= d'un jour à l'autre

next week
= la semaine prochaine

next month
= le mois prochain

next year
= l'année prochaine

☛ See next page

t

Time units *continued*

this coming week
= la semaine qui vient
   or (*more formally*) au cours de la semaine à venir

over the coming months
= au cours des mois à venir

a month from tomorrow
= dans un mois demain

....

How often?

how often does it happen?
= cela arrive tous les combien?

every Thursday
= tous les jeudis

every week
= toutes les semaines

every year
= tous les ans

every second day
= tous les deux jours

every third month
= tous les trois mois

day after day
= jour après jour

year after year
= année après année

the last Thursday of the month
= le dernier jeudi du mois

twice a month
= deux fois par mois

once every three months
= une fois tous les trois mois

How much an hour (etc)?

how much do you get an hour?
= combien gagnez-vous de l'heure?

I get $20
= je gagne 20 dollars de l'heure

to be paid $20 an hour
= être payé 20 dollars de l'heure

but note:

to be paid by the hour
= être payé à l'heure

how much do you earn a month?
= combien gagnez-vous par mois?

$3,000 a month
= 3 000 dollars par mois

Forms in -ée: an/année, matin/matinée etc.

■ *The -ée forms are often used to express a rather vague amount of time passing or spent in something, and so tend to give a subjective slant to what is being said, as in:*

a long day/evening/year
= une longue journée/soirée/année

a whole day
= toute une journée *or* une journée entière

we spent a lovely day there
= nous y avons passé une journée merveilleuse

■ *When an exact number is specified, the shorter forms are generally used, as in:*

it lasted six days
= cela a duré six jours

two years' military service
= deux ans de service militaire

■ *However there is no strict rule that applies to all of these words. If in doubt, check in the dictionary.*

---

no ~ en moins de deux; **in five days'/weeks'** ~ dans cinq jours/semaines; **within the agreed** ~ dans les délais convenus; **in your own** ~ (at your own pace) à ton rythme; (outside working hours) en dehors des heures de travail; **on company** ~ pendant les heures de bureau; **my** ~ **is my own** je suis maître de mon temps; ③ (hour of the day, night) heure *f*; **what** ~ **is it?, what's the** ~**?** quelle heure est-il?; **the** ~ **is 11 o'clock** il est 11 heures; **10 am French** ~ 10 heures, heure française; **this** ~ **last week/year** il y a exactement huit jours/un an; **by this** ~ **next year** d'ici un an; **on** ~ à l'heure; **the train** ~s les horaires *mpl* des trains; **it's** ~ **for bed** c'est l'heure d'aller au lit; **it's** ~ **we started** il est temps de commencer; **to lose** ~ [*clock*] retarder; **that clock keeps good** ~ cette horloge est toujours à l'heure; **about** ~ **too!** ce n'est pas trop tôt!; **not before** ~! il était (*or* il est) grand temps!; **to arrive in good** ~ arriver en avance; **in** ~ **for Christmas** à temps pour Noël; **to be behind** ~ avoir du retard; **twenty minutes ahead of** ~ vingt minutes avant l'heure prévue; ④ (era, epoch) époque *f*; **in Dickens'** ~s du temps de Dickens; **at the** ~ à l'époque; ~ **was** *ou* **there was a** ~ **when one could...** à une certaine époque on pouvait...; **to keep up** *ou* **move with the** ~s être à la page; **in** ~s **past, in former** ~s autrefois; **it's just like old** ~s c'est comme au bon vieux temps; **peace in our** ~ la paix de notre vivant; **at my** ~ **of life** à mon âge; **she was a beautiful woman in her** ~ c'était une très belle femme dans son temps; **it was before my** ~ (before my birth) je n'étais pas encore né; (before I came here) je n'étais pas encore ici; **if I had my** ~ **over again** si je pouvais recommencer ma vie; **to die before one's** ~ mourir prématurément; ⑤ (moment) moment *m*; **at** ~s par moments; **at the right** ~ au bon moment; **this is no** ~ **for jokes** ce n'est pas le moment de plaisanter; **at all** ~s à tout moment; **any** ~ **now** d'un

moment à l'autre; **the** ~ **has come for action** l'heure est venue d'agir; **by the** ~ **I finished the letter the post had gone** le temps de finir ma lettre et le courrier était parti; **by the** ~ **she had got downstairs he had gone** avant qu'elle n'arrive en bas il était déjà parti; **by this** ~ **most of them were dead** la plupart d'entre eux étaient déjà morts; **some** ~ **this week** dans la semaine; **some** ~ **next month** dans le courant du mois prochain; **for the** ~ **being** pour l'instant; **from that** *ou* **this** ~ **on** à partir de ce moment; **when the** ~ **comes** le moment venu; **in** ~s **of crisis** dans les périodes de crise; **until such** ~ **as** jusqu'à ce que; **I can't be in two places at the same** ~ je ne peux pas être partout à la fois; ⑥ (occasion) fois *f*; **nine** ~s **out of ten** neuf fois sur dix; **three** ~s **a month** trois fois par mois; ~ **after** ~, ~ **and again** maintes fois; **three at a** ~ trois à la fois; **she passed her driving test first** ~ **round** elle a eu son permis du premier coup; **from** ~ **to** ~ de temps en temps; **for months at a** ~ pendant des mois entiers; (in between) ~s **entre-temps;** ⑦ (experience) **to have a tough** *ou* **hard** ~ **doing** avoir du mal à faire; **he's having a rough** *ou* **hard** *ou* **tough** ~ il traverse une période difficile; **we had a good** ~ on s'est bien amusé; **to have an easy** ~ **(of it)** se la couler douce○; **the good/bad** ~s les moments heureux/difficiles; **she enjoyed her** ~ **in Canada** elle a beaucoup aimé son séjour au Canada; ⑧ Admin (hourly rate) **to work/be paid** ~ travailler/être payé à l'heure; **to be paid** ~ **and a half** être payé une fois et demie le tarif normal; ⑨ Mus mesure *f*; **to beat** *ou* **mark** ~ battre la mesure; **in waltz** ~ sur un rythme de valse; ⑩ Sport temps *m*; **a fast** ~ un bon temps; **to keep** ~ chronométrer; ⑪ Math, fig **three** ~s **four** trois fois quatre; **ten** ~s **longer/stronger** dix fois plus long/plus fort; **eight** ~s **as much** huit fois autant

B *vtr* ① (schedule) gen prévoir; fixer [*appointment, meeting*]; **we**

~ **our trips to fit in with school holidays** nous faisons coïncider nos voyages avec les vacances scolaires; **to be well-/badly-timed** être opportun/inopportun; **the announcement was perfectly** ~**d** la déclaration est tombée à point nommé; **2** (judge) calculer [*blow, shot*]; **to** ~ **a joke** choisir le moment pour faire une plaisanterie; **3** (measure speed, duration) chronométrer [*athlete, cyclist*]; mesurer la durée de [*journey, speech*]

C *v refl* **to** ~ **oneself** se chronométrer

(Idioms) **from** ~ **out of mind** depuis la nuit des temps; **there is a** ~ **and place for everything** il y a un temps pour tout; **there's always a first** ~ il y a un début à tout; **he'll tell you in his own good** ~ il te le dira quand il en aura envie; **all in good** ~ chaque chose en son temps; **only** ~ **will tell** l'avenir nous le dira; **to pass the** ~ **of day with sb** échanger quelques mots avec qn; **I've got no** ~ **for that sort of attitude** je ne supporte pas ce genre d'attitude; **to do** ~○ (prison) faire de la taule○; **give me Lauren Bacall every** ~! rien ne vaut Lauren Bacall!; **long** ~ **no see**○! ça fait un bail○ (qu'on ne s'est pas vu)!

time: ~ **bomb** n lit, fig bombe f à retardement; ~ **check** n annonce f de l'heure; ~**-consuming** adj qui prend du temps (*after n*); ~ **delay** n délai m; ~ **difference** n décalage m horaire; ~**-frame** n (period envisaged) calendrier m; (period allocated) délai m; ~**-honoured** adj consacré par l'usage

timekeeper /ˈtaɪmkiːpə(r)/ n Sport chronométreur m; gen **to be a good** ~ être toujours à l'heure

time-lag n décalage m

timeless /ˈtaɪmlɪs/ adj éternel/-elle

time-limit /ˈtaɪmlɪmɪt/ n **1** (deadline) date f limite; **within the** ~ dans les délais; **2** (maximum duration) durée f maximum; **there's a 20-minute** ~ **on speeches** les discours ne doivent pas dépasser 20 minutes

timely /ˈtaɪmlɪ/ adj opportun

time machine n machine f à explorer le temps

time off /ˌtaɪm ˈɒf/ n (leave) congé m; (free time) temps m libre; **to take** ~ **from work to go to the dentist's** prendre du temps sur son travail pour aller chez le dentiste

time-out n Sport temps m mort; (break) temps m de repos

timer /ˈtaɪmə(r)/ n gen minuterie f; (for cooking) minuteur m

timesaver /ˈtaɪmseɪvə(r)/ n **a dishwasher is a real** ~ un lave-vaisselle fait vraiment gagner du temps

time: ~**-scale** n période f (de temps); ~**share** n (house) maison f en multipropriété; (apartment) appartement m en multipropriété; ~**-sheet** n feuille f de présence; ~**-signal** n signal m horaire; ~**span** n durée f; ~**-switch** n minuterie f

timetable /ˈtaɪmteɪbl/

A n (schedule) gen emploi m du temps; (for plans, negotiations) calendrier m; (for buses, trains etc) horaire m; **a** ~ **for reform** un calendrier de réformes; **to work to a strict** ~ suivre un programme de travail très stricte

B vtr fixer l'heure de [*class, lecture*]; fixer la date de [*meeting, negotiations*]; **the bus is** ~**d to leave at 11.30 am** le bus doit partir à 11 h 30

time: ~ **trial** n (in cycling) épreuve de sélection contre la montre; (in athletics) épreuve f de sélection; ~**-wasting** n perte f de temps; ~**-worn** adj consacré par l'usage; ~ **zone** n fuseau m horaire

timid /ˈtɪmɪd/ adj gen timide; [*animal*] craintif/-ive

timidity /tɪˈmɪdətɪ/ n timidité f

timing /ˈtaɪmɪŋ/ n **1** (scheduling) **the** ~ **of the announcement was unfortunate** le moment choisi pour la déclaration était inopportun; **there is speculation about the** ~ **of the election** la date choisie pour l'élection donne lieu à bien des conjectures; **to get one's** ~ **right/wrong** bien/mal choisir son moment; **2** (coordination) (of operation) minutage m; **3** Aut réglage m de l'allumage; **4** Mus sens m du rythme; Theat **to have a good sense of** ~ savoir rythmer son débit

timorous /ˈtɪmərəs/ adj timoré

timpani /ˈtɪmpənɪ/ ▸ p. 1028 npl timbales fpl

tin /tɪn/

A n **1** (metal) étain m; **2** GB (can) boîte f (de conserve); **to eat**

---

out of ~**s** se nourrir de conserves; **to come out of a** ~ être de la conserve; **3** (container) (for biscuits, cake) boîte f; (for paint) pot m; (for baking) moule m; (for roasting) plat m (à rôtir)

B noun modifier [*mug, bath*] en étain

C vtr GB (*p prés etc* -**nn**-) mettre [qch] en boîte

D tinned pp adj GB [*meat, fruit*] en boîte

tin can n boîte f en fer-blanc

tin foil /ˈtɪnfɔɪl/ n papier m (d')aluminium

tinge /tɪndʒ/

A n (all contexts) nuance f

B vtr teinter (**with** de)

tingle /ˈtɪŋgl/

A n (physical) picotement m; (psychological) frisson m

B vi (physically) picoter; (psychologically) frissonner

tingling /ˈtɪŋglɪŋ/ n picotements mpl

tingly /ˈtɪŋglɪ/ adj **my fingers have gone all** ~ j'ai des picotements dans les doigts

tin: ~ **god** n péj petit chef m; ~ **hat** n casque m

tinker /ˈtɪŋkə(r)/ vi (also **to** ~ **about** ou **around**) bricoler; **to** ~ **with** bricoler [*car, machine*]; faire des retouches à [*wording, document*]

tinkle /ˈtɪŋkl/

A n tintement m; **to give sb a** ~○ GB passer un coup de fil à qn○

B vtr faire tinter

C vi tinter

tinkling /ˈtɪŋklɪŋ/ n tintement m

tinny /ˈtɪnɪ/ adj **1** [*sound, music*] grêle; **2** (badly made) [*radio, car*] de camelote

tin: ~ **opener** n GB ouvre-boîte m; ~**pot**○ adj GB péj [*dictatorship, organization*] de pacotille

tinsel /ˈtɪnsl/ n **C** (decoration) guirlandes fpl; fig, péj clinquant m

tint /tɪnt/

A n (trace) nuance f; (pale colour) teinte f; (hair colour) shampooing m colorant

B vtr teinter; **to get one's hair** ~**ed** se faire faire un shampooing colorant

C tinted pp adj [*colour*] teinté; [*glass, window, spectacles*] fumé; [*hair*] teint

tiny /ˈtaɪnɪ/ adj [*person, object, house*] tout petit; [*improvement*] très faible

tip /tɪp/

A n **1** (end) (of stick, sword, pen, shoe, cue, ski, spire, landmass) pointe f; (of branch, leaf, shoot, tail, feather) extrémité f; (of finger, nose, tongue, wing) bout m; (protective cover) (on umbrella) pointe f; (on shoe heel) bout m ferré; **to stand on the** ~**s of one's toes** être sur la pointe des pieds; **2** GB (waste dump) décharge f; **3** ○GB (mess) fouillis m; **4** (gratuity) pourboire m; **a £5** ~ 5 livres de pourboire; **5** (practical hint) truc○ m, conseil m; (in betting, speculation) tuyau○ m

B -**tipped** combining form **silver-/pink-/spiky-**~**ed** à bout argenté/rose/pointu

C vtr (*p prés etc* -**pp**-) **1** (tilt) incliner; (pour) verser; (dump) déverser [*waste, rubbish*]; **to** ~ **sth to one side** incliner qch sur le côté; **to** ~ **sth on its side** mettre qch sur le côté; **to** ~ **one's chair back** se balancer sur sa chaise; **to** ~ **sth upside down** retourner qch; **to** ~ **sth down the sink** verser qch dans l'évier; **to** ~ **sth away** jeter qch; **to** ~ **the scales at 60 kg** peser 60 kilos; **to** ~ **the balance** ou **scales** fig faire pencher la balance; **to** ~ **sb over the edge** fig faire basculer qn; **2** (predict) **to** ~ **sb/sth to win** prédire que qn/qch va gagner; **to be** ~**ped as a future champion** être donné comme futur champion; **3** (give money to) donner un pourboire à [*waiter, driver*]; **to** ~ **sb £5** donner 5 livres de pourboire à qn; **4** (put something on the end of) recouvrir le bout de [*sword, cane, heel*]; **5** (gently push) **to** ~ **the ball over the net/past the goalkeeper** frapper la balle délicatement pour l'envoyer de l'autre côté du filet/dans le but

D vi (*p prés etc* -**pp**-) **1** (tilt) s'incliner; **to** ~ **forward/back** pencher vers l'avant/vers l'arrière; **2** fig [*balance, scales*] pencher

(Phrasal verbs)

■ **tip down** ○ GB dial: ▸ **it is tipping (it) down** il tombe des cordes○

■ **tip off**: ▸ ~ **off [sb]**, ~ **[sb] off** avertir

■ **tip out**: ▸ ~ **out [sth]**, ~ **[sth] out** vider

■ **tip over**: ▸ ~ **over** [*chair, cupboard*] basculer; [*bucket, pile*] se renverser; ▸ ~ **over [sth]**, ~ **[sth] over** faire basculer [*chair, cupboard*]; renverser [*bucket, pile*]

■ **tip up**: ▶ ~ **up** s'incliner, se pencher; ▶ ~ **up [sth]**, ~ **[sth] up** incliner [*cup, bottle*]; pencher [*chair, wardrobe*]

tip-off *n* dénonciation *f*

tipper lorry GB, **tipper truck** *n* camion *m* à benne basculante

tipple○ /'tɪpl/
A *n* (drink) boisson *f* alcoolisée
B *vi* siroter

tipster /'tɪpstə(r)/ *n* pronostiqueur/-euse *m/f*

tipsy /'tɪpsɪ/ *adj* pompette○

tiptoe /'tɪptəʊ/
A *n* on ~ sur la pointe des pieds
B *vi* marcher sur la pointe des pieds

tip-top○ /ˌtɪp'tɒp/ *adj* excellent

tire /'taɪə(r)/
A *n* US pneu *m*
B *vtr* (make tired) fatiguer
C *vi* ①▸ (get tired) se fatiguer; ②▸ (get bored) **to** ~ **of** se lasser de

⟮Phrasal verb⟯
■ **tire out**: ▶ ~ **[sb] out** épuiser; **to be** ~**d out** être éreinté; **to** ~ **oneself out** se fatiguer (**doing** à faire)

tired /'taɪəd/ *adj* ①▸ (weary) gen fatigué; [*voice*] las/lasse; **it makes me** ~ ça me fatigue; ②▸ (bored) **to be** ~ **of/of doing** en avoir assez de qch/de faire; **to grow** *ou* **get** ~ **of sth/of doing** se lasser de qch/de faire; ③▸ (hackneyed) rebattu; ④▸ (worn out) [*machine*] usé; [*clothes, curtains*] défraîchi; ⑤▸ (wilted) [*lettuce*] fané

tiredness /'taɪədnɪs/ *n* fatigue *f*

tireless /'taɪəlɪs/ *adj* [*person*] inlassable, infatigable; [*efforts*] constant

tirelessly /'taɪəlɪslɪ/ *adv* sans relâche

tiresome /'taɪəsəm/ *adj* [*person, habit*] agaçant; [*problem, duty*] fastidieux/-ieuse

tiring /'taɪərɪŋ/ *adj* fatigant (**to do** de faire)

tissue /'tɪʃuː/ *n* ①▸ Anat, Bot tissu *m*; ②▸ (handkerchief) mouchoir *m* en papier; ③▸ (also ~ **paper**) papier *m* de soie; ④▸ fig tissu *m*; **a** ~ **of lies** un tissu de mensonges

tit /tɪt/ *n* Zool mésange *f*
⟮Idiom⟯ ~ **for tat** un prêté pour un rendu

titbit /'tɪtbɪt/ *n* GB (of food) gâterie *f*; (of gossip) cancan○ *m*

titillating /'tɪtɪleɪtɪŋ/ *adj* émoustillant

titivate /'tɪtɪveɪt/ *vtr* bichonner; **to** ~ **oneself** se pomponner

title /'taɪtl/
A *n* gen, Jur, Sport titre *m*
B **titles** *npl* Cin générique *m*
C *vtr* intituler [*book, play*]

titled /'taɪtld/ *adj* titré

title: ~ **fight** *n* combat *m* pour le titre; ~**holder** *n* tenant/-e *m/f* du titre; ~ **role** *n* rôle *m* titre

titter /'tɪtə(r)/
A *n* ricanement *m*
B *vi* ricaner

tittle-tattle /'tɪtltætl/ *n* potins *mpl* (**about** sur)

titular /'tɪtjʊlə(r)/, US -tʃʊ-/ *adj* [*president, head*] nominal; [*professor, status*] titulaire

tizzy○ /'tɪzɪ/ *n* **to be in/get into a** ~ être dans/se mettre dans tous ses états

T-junction /'tiːdʒʌŋkʃn/ *n* intersection *f* en T

TM *n* (*abrév* = **trademark**) marque *f* de fabrique

TN US Post *abrév écrite* = **Tennessee**

to /tə, devant une voyelle tʊ, tuː, emphatique tuː/ ▸ p. 745
A *infinitive particle* ①▸ (expressing purpose) pour; **to do sth** ~ **impress one's friends** faire qch pour impressionner ses amis; ②▸ (linking consecutive acts) **he looked up** ~ **see...** en levant les yeux, il a vu...; ③▸ (after superlatives) à; **the youngest** ~ **do** le *ou* la plus jeune à faire; ④▸ (avoiding repetition of verb) **'did you go?'—'no I promised not** ~**'** 'tu y es allé?' —'non j'avais promis de ne pas le faire'; **'are you staying? '—'I want** ~ **but...'** 'tu restes?'—'j'aimerais bien mais...'; ⑤▸ (following impersonal verb) **it is difficult** ~ **do sth** il est difficile de faire qch; (expressing wish) **oh** ~ **be able to stay in bed!** hum ô pouvoir rester au lit!

B *prep* ①▸ (in direction of) à [*shops, school*]; (with purpose of visiting) chez [*doctor's, dentist's*]; (towards) vers; **she's gone** ~ **Mary's** elle est partie chez Mary; **to Paris** à Paris; **to Spain** en Espagne; ~ **town** en ville; **the road** ~ **the village** la route qui mène au village; **trains** ~ **and from** les trains à destination et en provenance de [*place*]; **turned** ~ **the wall** tourné vers le mur; **with his back** ~ **them** en leur tournant le dos; **holding the letter** ~ **his chest** tenant la lettre contre sa poitrine; ②▸ (up to) jusqu'à; ~ **the end/this day** jusqu'à la fin/ce jour; **50** ~ **60 people** entre 50 et 60 personnes; **in** ~ **ten minutes** d'ici cinq à dix minutes; ③▸ (in telling time) **ten (minutes)** ~ **three** trois heures moins dix; **it's five** ~ il est moins cinq; ④▸ (introducing direct or indirect object) [*give, offer*] à; **give the book** ~ **Sophie** donne le livre à Sophie; **be nice** ~ **your brother** sois gentil avec ton frère; ~ **me/my daughter it's just a minor problem** pour moi/ma fille ce n'est qu'un problème mineur; ⑤▸ (in toasts, dedications) à; ~ **prosperity** à la prospérité; (on tombstone) ~ **our dear son** à notre cher fils; ⑥▸ (in accordance with) **is it** ~ **your taste?** c'est à ton goût?; **to dance** ~ **the music** danser sur la musique; ⑦▸ (in relationships, comparisons) **to win by three goals** ~ **two** gagner par trois buts à deux; **perpendicular** ~ **the ground** perpendiculaire au sol; **next door** ~ **the school** à côté de l'école; **three weeks** ~ **the day** trois semaines jour pour jour; ~ **scale** à l'échelle; ~ **time** à l'heure; ⑧▸ (showing reason) **to invite sb** ~ **dinner** inviter qn à dîner; ~ **this end** à cette fin; ⑨▸ (belonging to) de; **the key** ~ **the safe** la clé du coffre; **a room** ~ **myself** une chambre pour moi tout seul; **personal assistant** ~ **the director** assistant/-e *m/f* du directeur;

there's no sense ~ it ça n'a aucun sens; [11] (on to) [tied] à; [pinned] à [noticeboard etc]; sur [lapel, dress]; [12] (showing reaction) à; ~ **his surprise/dismay** à sa grande surprise/consternation

C /tu:/ adv [1] ○(closed) fermé; **to push the door** ~ fermer la porte

(Idioms) **that's all there is** ~ **it** (it's easy) c'est aussi simple que ça; (not for further discussion) un point c'est tout; **there's nothing** ~ **it** ce n'est pas compliqué; **what a** ~**-do**○! quelle histoire○!; **what's it** ~ **you**○? qu'est-ce que ça peut te faire?

toad /təʊd/ n crapaud m

toadstool n champignon m vénéneux

toady /ˈtəʊdɪ/
A n flagorneur/-euse m/f
B vi **to** ~ **to** flagorner [patron, boss]

to and fro /tu: ən ˈfrəʊ/ adv [swing] d'avant en arrière; **to go** ~ [person] ne pas arrêter d'aller et venir

toast /təʊst/
A n [1] (grilled bread) toast m; **a piece** ou **slice of** ~ un toast; [2] (tribute) toast m; **to drink a** ~ lever son verre; [3] (popular person) **the** ~ **of** l'idole de [group]; **she's the** ~ **of the town** on ne parle que d'elle
B vtr [1] Culin faire griller; [2] (propose a toast to) porter un toast à
C toasted pp adj grillé

(Idiom) **to be as warm as** ~ [person] être bien au chaud; [bed, room] être bien chaud

toaster /ˈtəʊstə(r)/ n grille-pain m inv

toast rack n porte-toasts m inv

tobacco /təˈbækəʊ/
A n (pl ~**s**) tabac m
B noun modifier [company, leaf] de tabac; [industry] du tabac; ~ **tin** GB, ~ **can** US boîte f à tabac; ~ **plant** tabac m

tobacconist /təˈbækənɪst/ ▸ p. 1181, p. 000 n GB (person) buraliste mf; ~**'s (shop)** bureau m de tabac

toboggan /təˈbɒɡən/
A n luge f, toboggan m
B vi **to** ~ **down a hill** descendre une pente en luge

tobogganning /təˈbɒɡənɪŋ/ ▸ p. 881 n luge f

today /təˈdeɪ/ ▸ p. 788, p. 1322
A n lit, fig aujourd'hui m; **what's** ~**'s date?** on est le combien aujourd'hui?, quel jour sommes-nous aujourd'hui?; ~ **is Monday** (aujourd'hui) nous sommes lundi
B adv gen aujourd'hui; (nowadays) de nos jours; ~ **week, a week from** ~ dans une semaine aujourd'hui; **a month ago** ~ il y a un mois aujourd'hui; **all day** ~ toute la journée d'aujourd'hui; **later** ~ plus tard dans la journée

(Idiom) **he's here** ~**, gone tomorrow** il va et il vient

toddle /ˈtɒdl/ vi [1] (walk) [child] faire ses premiers pas; **to** ~ **to the door** aller d'un pas chancelant vers la porte; [2] ○(go) **to** ~ **into town** faire un tour en ville.

(Phrasal verbs)
■ **toddle about, toddle around** [child] trottiner
■ **toddle off**○ s'en aller, partir

toddler /ˈtɒdlə(r)/ n bébé m (qui fait ses premiers pas)

toddy /ˈtɒdɪ/ n grog m

toe /təʊ/ ▸ p. 698 n [1] Anat orteil m; **big/little** ~ gros/petit orteil; **to stand on one's** ~**s** être sur la pointe des pieds; **to tread** ou **step on sb's** ~**s** lit, fig marcher sur les pieds de qn; [2] (of sock, shoe) bout m

(Idioms) **to keep sb on their** ~**s** obliger qn à ne pas relâcher ses efforts; **to** ~ **the line** marcher droit; **to** ~ **the party line** suivre la ligne du parti; **from top to** ~ de la tête aux pieds

toehold /ˈtəʊhəʊld/ n (in climbing) prise f; fig (access) **to get** ou **gain a** ~ **in** s'introduire dans [market, organization]

toffee /ˈtɒfɪ, US ˈtɔːfɪ/ n caramel m (au beurre)

(Idiom) **he can't sing/write for** ~○ GB il est incapable de chanter/d'écrire

toffee: ~ **apple** n pomme f d'amour (caramélisée); ~**-nosed**○ adj GB péj snobinard○ pej

together /təˈɡeðə(r)/

⚠ *Together* in its main adverbial senses is almost always translated by *ensemble*.

together frequently occurs as the second element in certain verb combinations (*get together, pull together, put together, tie together* etc). For translations for these, see the appropriate verb entry (**get, pull, tie** etc).

For examples and further uses, see the entry below.

A adv [1] gen ensemble; **they're always** ~ ils sont toujours ensemble; **to get back** ~ **again** se remettre ensemble; **to be close** ~ être rapprochés; **she's cleverer than all the rest of them put** ~ elle est plus intelligente que tous les autres réunis; **we're all in this** ~ nous sommes tous impliqués dans cette affaire; **they belong** ~ (objects) ils vont ensemble; (people) ils sont faits l'un pour l'autre; **the talks brought the two sides closer** ~ les négociations ont rapproché les deux parties; [2] (at the same time) à la fois; **they were all talking** ~ ils parlaient tous à la fois; **all my troubles seem to come** ~ tous mes ennuis semblent arriver en même temps; [3] (without interruption) d'affilée; **for four days** ~ pendant quatre jours d'affilée
B ○adj équilibré
C together with prep phr (as well as) ainsi que; (in the company of) avec

(Idioms) **to get one's act** ~**, to get it** ~○ s'organiser

togetherness /təˈɡeðənɪs/ n (in team, friendship) camaraderie f; (in family, couple) intimité f

toggle /ˈtɒɡl/ n (fastening) bouton m de duffel-coat

Togo /ˈtəʊɡəʊ/ ▸ p. 774 pr n Togo m

toil /tɔɪl/
A n labeur m
B vi [1] (also **toil away**) (work) peiner; [2] (struggle) **to** ~ **up the hill** monter péniblement la côte

toilet /ˈtɔɪlɪt/ n toilettes fpl; **public** ~**(s)** toilettes publiques

toilet: ~ **bag** n trousse f de toilette; ~ **paper**, ~ **tissue** n papier m toilette

toiletries /ˈtɔɪlɪtrɪz/ npl articles mpl de toilette

toilet: ~ **roll** n (roll) rouleau m de papier toilette; (tissue) papier m toilette; ~ **seat** n lunette f de WC; ~ **soap** n savon m de toilette

toilet-train /ˈtɔɪlɪttreɪn/ vtr **to** ~ **a child** apprendre à un enfant à être propre

toing and froing /ˌtuːɪŋ ən ˈfrəʊɪŋ/ n **all this** ~ toutes ces allées et venues

token /ˈtəʊkən/
A n [1] (for machine, phone) jeton m; [2] (voucher) bon m; **book/record** ~ chèque-cadeau m pour livre/pour disque; [3] (symbol) témoignage m; **a** ~ **of** un signe de [esteem, gratitude, affection]; **but by the same** ~... mais de la même façon...
B adj gen symbolique; **to make a** ~ **effort/gesture** péj faire un effort/geste pour la forme; **she's the** ~ **woman** péj c'est la femme de service

told /təʊld/ prét, pp ▸ **tell**

tolerable /ˈtɒlərəbl/ adj (bearable) tolérable; (adequate) acceptable

tolerably /ˈtɒlərəblɪ/ adv assez

tolerance /ˈtɒlərəns/ n gen, Med tolérance f

tolerant /ˈtɒlərənt/ adj tolérant

tolerantly /ˈtɒlərəntlɪ/ adv avec tolérance

tolerate /ˈtɒləreɪt/ vtr (permit) tolérer [attitude, difference]; (put up with) supporter [isolation, treatment])

toll /təʊl/
A n [1] (number) **the** ~ **of** le nombre de [victims]; **death** ~ nombre m de victimes (**from** de); [2] (levy) (on road, bridge) péage m; [3] (of bell) gen son m; (for funeral) glas m
B vtr sonner [bell]
C vi sonner

(Idioms) **to take a heavy** ~ (on lives) faire beaucoup de victimes; (on industry, environment) causer beaucoup de dégâts; **to take its** ou **their** ~ faire des ravages

toll: ~**booth** n poste m de péage; ~ **bridge** n pont m à péage; ~ **call** n US communication f interurbaine; ~**-free** adj US [call, number] gratuit

Tom /tɒm/ pr n:

(Idiom) **every** ~**, Dick and Harry** n'importe qui

tomato /təˈmɑːtəʊ, US təˈmeɪtəʊ/

A *n* (*pl* ~**es**) tomate *f*

B *noun modifier* [*puree*] de tomate; [*juice*, *salad*] de tomates; [*soup*] à la tomate; ~ **sauce** sauce *f* tomate

tomb /tuːm/ *n* tombeau *m*

tomboy /ˈtɒmbɔɪ/ *n* garçon *m* manqué

tombstone /ˈtuːmstəʊn/ *n* pierre *f* tombale

tomcat /ˈtɒmkæt/ *n* matou *m*

tome /təʊm/ *n* gros volume *m*

tomfoolery /tɒmˈfuːlərɪ/ *n* pitreries *fpl*, âneries *fpl*

tomorrow /təˈmɒrəʊ/ ▸ p. 788, p. 1322

A *n* lit, fig demain *m*; ~ **will be a difficult day** la journée de demain sera difficile; **who knows what ~ may bring?** de quoi demain sera-t-il fait?; **I'll do it by ~** je le ferai d'ici demain

B *adv* lit, fig demain; **see you ~!** à demain!; ~ **week, a week** ~ demain en huit; **early ~** tôt dans la journée de demain; **as from ~** à partir de demain; **first thing ~** dès demain

(Idioms) ~ **is another day** demain il fera jour; **never put off till ~ what can be done today** Prov il ne faut jamais remettre au lendemain ce qu'on peut faire le jour même Prov; **to live like there was no ~** vivre chaque jour comme si c'était le dernier

tomorrow: ~ **afternoon** *n*, *adv* demain après-midi; ~ **evening** *n*, *adv* demain soir; ~ **morning** *n*, *adv* demain matin

tom-tom /ˈtɒmtɒm/ *n* tam-tam *m*

ton /tʌn/ ▸ p. 1323, p. 723 *n* **1** (in weight) (also **gross** ~ ou **long** ~) ≈ 1016 kg; US (also **net** ~ ou **short** ~) ≈ 907 kg; **metric** ~ tonne *f*; **2** ○(a lot) ~**s of** des tas de○ [*food*, *paper*, *bands*]; **her new car is ~s better than the other one** sa nouvelle voiture est mille fois mieux que l'autre

(Idiom) **they'll come down on us like a ~ of bricks** ils vont nous tomber dessus○

tonal /ˈtəʊnl/ *adj* tonal

tonality /təˈnælətɪ/ *n* tonalité *f*

tone /təʊn/

A *n* **1** gen, Mus (quality of sound) timbre *m*; Telecom tonalité *f*; **2** (character of voice) ton *m*; **his ~ of voice** son ton; **in angry/serious ~s** avec colère/avec sérieux; **3** (character) (of letter, speech, meeting) ton *m*; **to set the ~** donner le ton à (**for** à); **to lower the ~ of** rabaisser le niveau de [*conversation*]; dégrader l'image de [*area*]; **4** (colour) ton *m*; **5** (firmness of muscle) tonus *m*

B *vtr* (*also* ~ **up**) tonifier

C *vi* (*also* ~**in**) (blend) [*colours*] s'harmoniser

(Phrasal verb)

■ **tone down**: ▸ ~ **down [sth]**, ~ **[sth] down** lit atténuer [*colours*, *criticism*]; adoucir le ton de [*letter*, *statement*]

tone-deaf /ˌtəʊnˈdef/ *adj* Mus **to be ~** ne pas avoir l'oreille musicale

toneless /ˈtəʊnlɪs/ *adj* atone

Tonga /ˈtɒŋɡə/ ▸ p. 774, p. 954 *pr n* Tonga *fpl*; **the ~ islands** les îles *fpl* Tonga

tongs /tɒŋz/ *npl* (for coal) pincettes *fpl*; (in laboratory, for sugar) pince *f*

(Idiom) **to go at it hammer and ~** (quarrel) se disputer violemment; (work) travailler avec acharnement

tongue /tʌŋ/

A *n* **1** gen, Anat, Culin langue *f*; (flap on shoe) languette *f*; **to stick one's ~ out at sb** tirer la langue à qn; **to lose/find one's ~** fig avaler/retrouver sa langue; **2** (language) langue *f*; **native ~** langue d'origine

B *vtr* Mus détacher [*note*, *passage*]

(Idioms) **has the cat got your ~?** tu as avalé ta langue?; **to get the rough side ou edge of sb's ~** subir les paroles désobligeantes de qn; **I have his name on the tip of my ~** j'ai son nom sur le bout de la langue; **to loosen sb's ~** délier la langue de qn; **I can't get my ~ round it** je n'arrive pas à le prononcer; **a slip of the ~** un lapsus; **watch your ~!** surveille tes paroles!

tongue: ~**-in-cheek** *adj*, *adv* au deuxième degré; ~**-tied** *adj* muet/-ette; ~**-twister** *n*: phrase amusante *pour exercice de diction*

tonic /ˈtɒnɪk/

A *n* **1** (drink) (*also* ~ **water**) eau *f* tonique; **a gin and ~** un

gin tonic; **2** Med remontant *m*; **to be a ~ for sb** fig remonter le moral de qn; **3** Mus tonique *f*

B *adj* tonique; ~ **wine** vin *m* tonique

tonight /təˈnaɪt/

A *n* ~ **will be overcast** le temps sera couvert ce soir

B *adv* (this evening) ce soir; (after bedtime) cette nuit

toning /ˈtəʊnɪŋ/ *adj* **1** [*colours*] harmonisé; **2** [*gel*, *cream*] tonifiant

tonnage /ˈtʌnɪdʒ/ *n* gen tonnage *m* (**of** de); (total weight) volume *m*

tonne /tʌn/ ▸ p. 1323 *n* tonne *f*

tonsil /ˈtɒnsl/ *n* amygdale *f*; **to have one's ~s out** se faire opérer des amygdales

tonsillitis /ˌtɒnsɪˈlaɪtɪs/ ▸ p. 933 *n* amygdalite *f*

too /tuː/ *adv*

> ⚠ When *too* means *also* it is generally translated by *aussi*: *me too* = moi aussi; *can I have some too?* = est-ce que je peux en avoir aussi?
>
> When *too* means *to an excessive degree* it is translated by *trop*: *too high*, *too dangerous* trop haut, trop dangereux.
>
> For examples of the above and further usages, see the entry below.

1 (also) aussi; **'I love you'—'I love you ~'** 'je t'aime'—'moi aussi, je t'aime'; **have you been to India ~?** (like me) est-ce que toi aussi tu es allé en Inde?; (as well as other countries) est-ce que tu es allé en Inde aussi?; **she's kind but she's strict ~** elle est gentille mais elle est stricte; **she was very annoyed and quite right ~!** elle était vraiment agacée et il y avait de quoi!; **about time ~!** il est bien temps!; **'I'm sorry'—'I should think so ~!'** 'je m'excuse'—'j'espère bien!'; **...and in front of your mother ~!** ...et devant ta mère en plus!; **2** (excessively) trop; **the coat is ~ big for him** le manteau est trop grand pour lui; **it's ~ early to leave** il est trop tôt pour partir; ~ **many/~ few people** trop de/trop peu de gens; **I ate ~ much** j'ai trop mangé; **he was in ~ much of a hurry to talk** il était trop pressé pour parler; ~ **silly for words** d'une bêtise sans nom; **it was ~ little ~ late** c'était trop peu trop tard; **you're ~ kind!** vous êtes trop aimable!; **they'll be only ~ pleased to help** ils seront ravis de rendre service; **he's only ~ ready to criticize** il ne rate pas une occasion de critiquer; **she hasn't been ~ well recently** elle n'est pas vraiment en forme ces temps-ci; **that's ~ bad!** (a pity) c'est tellement dommage!; (hard luck) tant pis!; ~ **right!** et comment!; **we're ~ thrilled** on ne peut pas dire que nous soyons ravis; **I'm not ~ sure about that** je n'en suis pas si sûr; **'they've arrived'—'none ~ soon!'** 'ils sont arrivés' —'ce n'est pas trop tôt!'; ▸ **all, only**

took /tʊk/ *prét* ▸ **take B, C**

tool /tuːl/

A *n* gen, Comput outil *m*; **a set of ~s** un jeu d'outils; **management ~s** instruments *mpl* de gestion; **to down ~s** GB (go on strike) se mettre en grève; (take break from work) arrêter de travailler

B *vtr* travailler, repousser [*leather*]

tool: ~**box** n boîte *f* à outils; ~ **house** *n* US = **tool shed**; ~ **kit** *n* trousse *f* à outils; ~ **shed** *n* cabane *f* à outils

toot /tuːt/

A *n* (sound) (of car-horn) coup *m* de klaxon®; (of train whistle) coup *m* de sifflet

B *vtr* **to ~ one's horn** donner un coup de klaxon®

C *vi* [*car horn*] klaxonner; [*train*] donner un coup de sifflet

tooth /tuːθ/

A *n* (*pl* **teeth**) dent *f*; **set of teeth** (false) dentier *m*; **to cut one's teeth** lit faire ses dents; **to cut one's teeth on** fig se faire les dents sur

B **-toothed** *combining form* **fine-/wide-~ed comb** peigne *m* fin/à dents larges

(Idioms) **to be a bit long in the ~**○ n'être plus tout jeune; **to be fed up to the back teeth** en avoir par-dessus la tête; **to do sth in the teeth of** faire qch malgré or en dépit de; **to get one's teeth into sth** s'investir (à fond) dans qch; **to lie through one's teeth** mentir effrontément; **to set sb's teeth on edge** agacer qn

toothache /ˈtuːθeɪk/ *n* mal *m* de dents; **to have ~** GB ou **a ~** avoir mal aux dents

tooth: **~brush** n brosse f à dents; **~ decay** n carie f dentaire; **~less** adj [grin, person] édenté; fig [law, organization] inefficace; **~paste** n dentifrice m; **~pick** n cure-dents m inv

toothy /'tuːθɪ/ adj **to give a ~ grin** sourire de toutes ses dents

top /tɒp/

A n **1** (highest or furthest part) (of page, ladder, stairs, wall) haut m; (of list) tête f; (of mountain, hill) sommet m; (of garden, field) (autre) bout m; (of vegetable) fane f; (of box, cake) dessus m; (surface) surface f; **at the ~ of** en haut de [page, stairs, street, scale]; au sommet de [hill]; en tête de [list]; **at the ~ of the building** au dernier étage de l'immeuble; **at the ~ of the table** à la place d'honneur; **the ~ of the milk** la crème du lait; **to be at the ~ of one's list** fig venir en tête de sa liste; **to be at the ~ of the agenda** fig être une priorité; Mil **to go over the ~** monter à l'assaut; **2** (highest position) **to aim for the ~** viser haut; **to get to** ou **make it to the ~** réussir; **to be ~ of the class** être le premier/la première de la classe; **to be ~ of the bill** Theat être la tête d'affiche; **3** (cap, lid) (of pen) capuchon m; (of bottle) gen bouchon m; (with serrated edge) capsule f; (of paint-tin, saucepan) couvercle m; **4** (item of clothing) haut m; **a sleeveless summer ~** un haut sans manches pour l'été; **5** (toy) toupie f

B adj **1** (highest) [step, storey] dernier/-ière; [bunk] de haut; [button, shelf, layer, lip] supérieur; [speed] maximum; [concern, priority] fig majeur; **in the ~ left-hand corner** en haut à gauche; **the ~ notes** Mus les notes les plus hautes; **the ~ tax band** la catégorie des plus imposables; **to pay the ~ price for sth** [buyer] acheter qch au prix fort; **to get ~ marks** Sch avoir dix sur dix ou vingt sur vingt; **2** (furthest away) [field, house] du bout; **3** (leading) [adviser, authority, agency] plus grand; [job] élevé; [wine, restaurant] meilleur; **one of their ~ chefs** l'un de leurs plus grands chefs; **to be in the ~ three** être dans les trois premiers

C **on top of** prep phr **1** sur [cupboard, fridge, layer]; **to live on ~ of each other** fig vivre les uns sur les autres; **to be on ~ of a situation** fig contrôler la situation; **things are getting on ~ of her** fig (she's depressed) elle est déprimée; (she can't cope) elle ne s'en sort plus; **2** (in addition to) en plus de [salary, workload]

D vtr (p prés etc **-pp-**) **1** (head) être en tête de [charts, polls]; **2** (exceed) dépasser [sum, figure]; **3** (finish off) gen compléter (**with** par); Culin recouvrir [cake]; **a mosque ~ped with three domes** une mosquée surmontée de trois coupoles

E ᴼv refl (p prés etc **-pp-**) **to ~ oneself** se suicider

(Idioms) **on ~ of all this**, **to ~ it all** par-dessus le marchéᴼ; **from ~ to bottom** de fond en comble; **to be over the ~**, **to be OTT**ᴼ [behaviour, reaction] être exagéré; **to be/stay on ~** avoir/garder le dessus; **to be ~ dog** être le chef; **to come out on ~** (win) l'emporter; (survive) s'en sortir; **to feel on ~ of the world** être aux anges; **to say things off the ~ of one's head** (without thinking) dire n'importe quoi; **I'd say 30, but that's just off the ~ of my head** (without checking) moi, je dirais 30, mais c'est approximatif; **to shout at the ~ of one's voice** crier à tue-tête

(Phrasal verbs)
■ **top off**: ▸ **~ off [sth]**, **~ [sth] off** compléter
■ **top up**: **to ~ up with petrol** faire le plein; ▸ **~ up [sth]**, **~ [sth] up** remplir (à nouveau) [tank, glass]

top-and-tail /ˌtɒpən'teɪl/ vtr équeuter [fruit]; effiler [beans]

topaz /'təʊpæz/ n, adj topaze (f) (inv)

top: **~ banana**ᴼ n US gros bonnet m; **~ brass**ᴼ n huilesᴼ fpl; **~ class** adj de premier ordre; **~-flight** adj de premier ordre; **~ hat** n haut-de-forme m; **~-heavy** adj [structure, object] lourd du haut; fig [firm, bureaucracy] mal équilibré (ayant trop de cadres par rapport aux employés subalternes)

topic /'tɒpɪk/ n (subject) (of conversation, conference) sujet m; (of essay, research) thème m

topical /'tɒpɪkl/ adj d'actualité

topicality /ˌtɒpɪ'kælətɪ/ n actualité f

topless /'tɒplɪs/ adj [model] aux seins nus; [bar] où les serveuses ont les seins nus; **~ swimsuit** monokini m

top: **~-level** adj [talks, negotiations] au plus haut niveau; **~ management** n (haute) direction f; **~-most** adj [branch, fruit] le/la plus haut/-e; **~-notch** adj [business, executive] de premier ordre; **~-of-the-range** adj [model] haut de gamme inv

topping /'tɒpɪŋ/ n (of jam, cream) nappage m; (for pizza) garniture f; **with a ~ of bread crumbs** recouvert d'une couche de chapelure

topple /'tɒpl/

A vtr lit, fig renverser

B vi (sway) [vase, pile of books] vaciller; (fall) (also **~ over**) [vase, person] basculer; [pile of books] s'effondrer; **to ~ over the edge of** tomber de [cliff, table]

top: **~-ranking** adj important; **~ secret** adj ultrasecret; **~ security** adj de haute sécurité; **~soil** n couche f arable; **~ spin** n lift m

topsy-turvyᴼ /ˌtɒpsɪ'tɜːvɪ/ adj, adv sens dessus dessous

torch /tɔːtʃ/

A n (burning) torche f; GB (flashlight) lampe f de poche

B vtr mettre le feu à [building]

(Idiom) **to carry the ~ for democracy** porter le flambeau de la démocratie

torchlight /'tɔːtʃlaɪt/

A n **by ~** (burning torches) à la lueur des flambeaux; GB (electric) à la lueur d'une lampe électrique or de poche

B noun modifier (also **torchlit**) aux flambeaux

tore /tɔː(r)/ prét ▸ **tear¹ B, C**

torment

A /'tɔːment/ n supplice m

B /tɔː'ment/ vtr tourmenter

tormentor /tɔː'mentə(r)/ n persécuteur/-trice m/f

torn /tɔːn/

A pp ▸ **tear¹ B, C**

B adj (all contexts) déchiré

tornado /tɔː'neɪdəʊ/ n (pl **~es** ou **~s**) tornade f

torpedo /tɔː'piːdəʊ/

A n Mil torpille f

B vtr lit, fig torpiller

torpid /'tɔːpɪd/ adj torpide

torrent /'tɒrənt, US 'tɔːr-/ n torrent m; fig flot m

torrential /tə'renʃl/ adj torrentiel/-ielle

torrid /'tɒrɪd, US 'tɔːr-/ adj torride

torso /'tɔːsəʊ/ n (pl **~s**) torse m

tortoise /'tɔːtəs/ n tortue f

tortoiseshell /'tɔːtəʃel/ n **1** (shell) écaille f; **2** Zool (butterfly) vanesse f; (cat) chatte f écaille de tortue

tortuous /'tɔːtʃʊəs/ adj lit, fig tortueux/-euse

torture /'tɔːtʃə(r)/

A n lit torture f; fig supplice m

B vtr lit torturer; fig tourmenter

Tory /'tɔːrɪ/ n GB Tory mf, conservateur/-trice m/f

toss /tɒs/

A n (pl **~es**) **1** (throw) jet m; **a ~ of the head** un mouvement brusque de la tête; **2** (of coin) **to decide sth on the ~ of a coin** décider qch à pile ou face

B vtr **1** (throw) lancer [ball, stick, dice]; faire sauter [pancake]; tourner [salad]; **~ me the newspaper** balance-moiᴼ le journal; **to ~ a coin** tirer à pile ou face; **2** (throw back) [animal] secouer [head, mane]; **to ~ one's head** [person] rejeter la tête en arrière; **3** (unseat) [horse] désarçonner [rider]; **4** (move violently) [wind] agiter [branches, leaves]; [waves] ballotter [boat]

C vi **1** (turn restlessly) [person] se retourner; **I ~ed and turned all night** je me suis tourné et retourné toute la nuit; **2** (flip a coin) tirer à pile ou face; **to ~ for first turn** tirer le premier tour à pile ou face

(Idiom) **I don't** ou **couldn't give a ~**ᴼ je m'en fiche pas malᴼ

(Phrasal verbs)
■ **toss about**, **toss around**: ▸ **~ about** [boat, person] être ballotté; ▸ **~ [sth] around** lit [people] se faire des passes avec [ball]; fig retourner [ideas]
■ **toss away**: ▸ **~ [sth] away**, **~ away [sth]** jeter
■ **toss back**: ▸ **~ [sth] back**, **~ back [sth]** renvoyer
■ **toss off**ᴼ: ▸ **~ [sth] off**, **~ off [sth]** expédier
■ **toss out**: ▸ **~ [sth] out**, **~ out [sth]** jeter [newspaper, empty bottles]; ▸ **~ [sb] out** éjecter (**from** de)
■ **toss up** (flip a coin) tirer à pile ou face

toss-upᴼ /'tɒsʌp/ n **let's have a ~ to decide** décidons à pile ou face; **it's a ~ between a pizza and a sandwich** il faut choisir entre une pizza et un sandwich

tot /tɒt/ n **1** ᴼ(toddler) tout/-e petit/-e enfant m/f; **2** GB (of whisky, rum) petite dose f, doigt m

(Phrasal verb)
■ **tot up** GB: ► ~ **up** [*person*] additionner; ► ~ **up** [**sth**], ~ [**sth**] **up** faire le total de [qch]

total /'təʊtl/
A *n* total *m*; **in** ~ au total; **it comes to a** ~ **of £200** cela fait 200 livres sterling en tout
B *adj* ①(added together) [*cost, amount, profit*] total; ②(complete) [*effect*] global; [*disaster, eclipse*] total; [*ignorance*] complet/-ète
C *vtr* (*p prés etc* **-ll-** GB, **-l-** US) ①(add up) additionner [*figures*]; ②(reach) se monter à [*sum*]

totalitarian /,təʊtælɪ'teərɪən/ *n, adj* totalitaire (*mf*)

totalize /'təʊtəlaɪz/ *vtr* totaliser

totally /'təʊtəlɪ/ *adv* [*blind, deaf*] complètement; [*unacceptable, convinced*] totalement; [*agree, change, new, different*] entièrement

totem /'təʊtəm/ *n* (pole) totem *m*; (symbol) symbole *m*

totter /'tɒtə(r)/ *vi* [*person, regime, government*] chanceler; (drunkenly) tituber; [*baby*] trébucher; [*pile of books, building*] chanceler

tottering /'tɒtərɪŋ/ *adj* gen lit, fig chancelant; [*step*] mal assuré

touch /tʌtʃ/
A *n* ① (physical contact) contact *m* (physique); **the** ~ **of her hand** le contact de sa main; **at the slightest** ~ (of button) à la moindre pression; **I felt a** ~ **on my shoulder** j'ai senti qu'on me touchait l'épaule; ② (sense) toucher *m*; **by** ~ au simple toucher; ③ (style, skill) of artist, writer) touche *f*; (of musician) toucher *m*; **to lose one's** ~ perdre la main; **a fine** ~ **at the net** (in tennis) un toucher délicat au filet; **the Spielberg** ~ le style Spielberg; **this house lacks the feminine** ~ on voit qu'il n'y a pas de femme dans cette maison; **he lacks the human** ~ il manque de chaleur humaine; **a clever** ~ un trait spirituel; **her gift was a nice** ~ son cadeau était un geste délicat; ④ (little) **a** ~ un petit peu; **just a** ~ **(more)** un tout petit peu (plus); **there's a** ~ **of class/of genius about her** elle a quelque chose d'élégant/de génial; **he's got a** ~ **of flu** il est un peu grippé; **with a** ~ **of sadness in her voice** avec une note de tristesse dans sa voix; **a** ~ **of sarcasm/of garlic** une pointe de raillerie/d'ail; ⑤ (communication) contact *m*; **to get/stay in** ~ **with** se mettre/rester en contact avec; **he's out of** ~ **with reality** il est déconnecté de la réalité; ⑥ Sport touche *f*
B *vtr* ① (come into contact with) toucher; (interfere with) toucher à; **to** ~ **sb on the shoulder** toucher l'épaule de qn; **to** ~ **ground** atterrir; **he** ~**ed his hat politely** il a porté poliment la main à son chapeau; **the police can't** ~ **me** la police ne peut rien contre moi; **I never** ~ **alcohol** je ne prends jamais d'alcool; ② (affect) gen toucher; (adversely) affecter; (as matter of concern) concerner; **we were most** ~**ed** nous avons été très touchés; ③ (reach) [*price, temperature*] atteindre [*level*]; **when it comes to cooking, no-one can** ~ **him** pour la cuisine, personne ne peut l'égaler
C *vi* (come together) [*wires, hands*] se toucher; **'do not** ~**'** 'ne pas toucher'

(Idioms) **to be an easy** *ou* **a soft** ~° être un pigeon°; **it's** ~ **and go whether he'll make it through the night** il risque fort de ne pas passer la nuit
(Phrasal verbs)
■ **touch down**: ► ~ **down** ① Aviat atterrir; ② Sport (in rugby) marquer un essai
■ **touch off**: ► ~ [**sth**] **off**, ~ **off** [**sth**] faire partir [*firework*]; déclencher [*riot, debate*]
■ **touch (up)on**: ► ~ **(up)on** [**sth**] effleurer
■ **touch up**: ► ~ [**sth**] **up**, ~ **up** [**sth**] retoucher

touchdown /'tʌtʃdaʊn/ *n* ① Aviat atterrissage *m*; ② Sport essai *m*

touché /tuː'ʃeɪ, 'tuːʃeɪ, US tuː'ʃeɪ/ *excl* fig bien dit!

touched /tʌtʃt/ *adj* ① (emotionally) touché; ② °(mad) dérangé°

touching /'tʌtʃɪŋ/ *adj* touchant

touch: ~ **line** *n* Sport ligne *f* de touche; ~ **pad** *n* Comput touchpad *m*; ~**paper** *n* papier *m* nitraté; ~ **screen** *n* Comput écran *m* tactile; ~**stone** *n* lit, fig pierre *f* de touche; ~**tone** *adj* [*telephone*] à touches; ~**type** *vi* taper au toucher; ~**typing** *n* dactylographie *f* au toucher; ~**wood** *n* amadou *m*

touchy /'tʌtʃɪ/ *adj* [*person*] susceptible (**about** sur la question de); [*subject, issue*] délicat

tough /tʌf/
A *n* (person) dur *m*
B *adj* ① [*businessman*] coriace; [*criminal*] endurci; [*policy, measure, law*] sévère; [*opposition, competition, criticism*] rude; **a** ~ **guy** un dur°; **to get** ~ **with sb** se montrer dur avec qn; ~ **talk** propos *mpl* inflexibles; **that's** ~ manque de pot°!; ~ **luck!** manque de pot°!; (unsympathetically) tant pis pour toi!; ② (difficult) difficile; **to have a** ~ **time** avoir des difficultés; **she's having a** ~ **time** elle traverse une période difficile; ③ (robust) [*person, animal*] robuste; [*plant, material*] résistant; péj [*meat*] coriace pej; ④ (rough) [*area, school*] dur
C °*excl* tant pis pour toi!

(Idiom) **to be as** ~ **as old boots** être coriace
(Phrasal verb)
■ **tough out**°: ► ~ [**sth**] **out** faire face à [*situation*]; **to** ~ **it out** tenir le coup°

toughen /'tʌfn/ *vtr* renforcer [*leather, plastic*]; tremper [*glass, steel*]; durcir [*skin*]; (also ~ **up**) endurcir [*person*]; renforcer [*law*]
(Phrasal verb)
■ **toughen up**: ► ~ **up** [*person*] s'endurcir; ► ~ [**sb**] **up**, ~ **up** [**sb**] endurcir [*person*]

tough love *n* amour *m* qui exclut la permissivité; **to practise** ~ aimer sans tout permettre

tough-minded *adj* ferme et résolu

toughness /'tʌfnɪs/ *n* ① (of businessman, criminal) dureté *f*; (of law, measure) sévérité *f*; (of way of life) dureté *f*; ② (robustness) (of person, plant) résistance *f*; (of material, leather) robustesse *f*; pej (of meat) dureté *f*; ③ (difficulty) (of work, question) difficulté *f*

toupee /'tuːpeɪ, US tuːˈpeɪ/ *n* postiche *m*

tour /tʊə(r), tɔː(r)/
A *n* ① Tourism (of country) circuit *m*; (of city) tour *m*; (of building) visite *f*; (trip in bus) excursion *f*; **cycling/walking** ~ randonnée *f* cycliste/pédestre; **to go on a** ~ visiter [*one thing*]; faire le circuit de [*several things*]; **he took me on a** ~ **of his house** il m'a fait visiter sa maison; **a** ~ **of inspection** une tournée d'inspection; ② Mus, Sport, Theat, Univ tournée *f*; **a** ~ **of duty** Mil une période de service
B *vtr* ① Tourism visiter [*building, country, gallery*]; ② Mus, Sport être en tournée en [*country*]; Theat [*production*] tourner en [*country*]
C *vi* ① Tourism **to go** ~**ing** faire du tourisme; ② [*orchestra, play, team*] être en tournée

tourer /'tʊərə(r), tɔːrə(r)/ *n* (sports car) cabriolet *m* décapotable; GB (caravan) camping-car *m*; (bicycle) vélo *m* de randonnée

touring /'tʊərɪŋ, 'tɔːr-/
A *n* ① Tourism tourisme *m*; ② Mus, Sport, Theat tournée *f*
B *adj* [*exhibition, holiday*] itinérant; [*company, show*] en tournée; [*production*] de tournée

tourism /'tʊərɪzəm, 'tɔːr-/ *n* tourisme *m*

tourist /'tʊərɪst, 'tɔːr-/
A *n* touriste *mf*
B *noun modifier* [*centre, guide, resort, season*] touristique; **the** ~ **trade** le tourisme

tourist: ~ **class** *n* Aviat classe *f* touriste; ~ **(information) office** *n* (in town) syndicat *m* d'initiative; (national organization) office *m* du tourisme; ~ **trap** *n* piège *m* à touristes

touristy° /'tʊərɪstɪ, 'tɔːr-/ *adj* péj envahi par les touristes

tournament /'tɔːnəmənt, US 'tɜːrn-/ *n* tournoi *m*

tousle /'taʊzl/
A *vtr* ébouriffer [*hair*]
B **tousled** *pp adj* [*hair*] ébouriffé; [*person, appearance*] débraillé

tout /taʊt/
A *n* ① GB (selling tickets) revendeur *m* de billets au marché noir; ② Comm (soliciting custom) racoleur/-euse° *m/f* pej; ③ (racing) vendeur *m* de tuyaux
B *vtr* ① [*street seller*] vendre (en faisant du boniment); ② GB (illegally) revendre [qch] au marché noir [*tickets*]; ③ (publicize) vanter les mérites de [*product, invention*]
C *vi* **to** ~ **for business** racoler° la clientèle

tow /təʊ/
A *n* Aut **to be on** ~ être en remorque; **to give sb a** ~ remorquer qn; (following) **a father with two children in** ~ fig un père accompagné de deux enfants
B *vtr* remorquer, tracter [*trailer, caravan*]

(Phrasal verb)

■ **tow away**: ▶ ~ **away [sth]**, ~ **[sth] away** [police] emmener [qch] à la fourrière; [recovery service] remorquer

toward(s) /təˈwɔːd(z), tɔːd(z)/

> ⚠ When *towards* is used to talk about direction or position, it is almost always translated by *vers*: *she ran toward(s) him* = elle a couru vers lui. For particular usages see the entry below.
> When *towards* is used to mean *in relation to*, it is translated by *envers*: *his attitude toward(s) his parents* = son attitude envers ses parents. For particular usages see the entry below.

prep **[1]** (in the direction of) vers; ~ **the east** vers l'est; **he was standing with his back** ~ **me** il était dos à moi; **[2]** (near) vers; ~ **the end of** vers la fin de [day, month, life]; **[3]** (in relation to) envers; **their attitude** ~ **Europe** leur attitude envers l'Europe; **to be friendly/hostile** ~ **sb** se montrer cordial/hostile envers qn; **[4]** (as contribution) **the money will go** ~ **a new car** l'argent servira à payer une nouvelle voiture; **to save** ~ **a holiday** faire des économies pour partir en vacances

towel /ˈtaʊəl/
A *n* gen, serviette *f* (de toilette); ▸ **bath towel**, **tea towel**
B *vtr* (*p prés etc* **-ll-**, US **-l-**) essuyer (avec une serviette)
(Idiom) **to throw** *ou* **chuck**○ **in the** ~ jeter l'éponge

towelling /ˈtaʊəlɪŋ/ *n* (cloth) tissu *m* éponge

towel rail *n* porte-serviettes *m inv*

tower /ˈtaʊə(r)/
A *n* gen, Comput tour *f*
B *vi* **to** ~ **above** *ou* **over** dominer [village, street]
(Idiom) **to be a** ~ **of strength** être solide comme un roc

tower block *n* GB tour *f* (d'habitation)

towering /ˈtaʊərɪŋ/ *adj* (épith) gen imposant; fig [performance] excellent

town /taʊn/ *n* ville *f*; **to go into** ~ aller en ville; **she's out of** ~ **at the moment** elle n'est pas là en ce moment; **look me up next time you're in** ~ viens me voir la prochaine fois que tu passeras par ici
(Idioms) **to go out on the** ~, **to have a night on the** ~ faire la noce; **to go to** ~ **on** ne pas lésiner sur [decor, catering]; exploiter [qch] à fond [story, scandal]; **he's the talk of the** ~ on ne parle que de lui

town: ~**-and-country planning** *n* aménagement *m* du territoire; ~ **centre** *n* centre-ville *m*; ~ **clerk** *n* GB secrétaire *mf* de mairie; ~ **council** *n* GB conseil *m* municipal; ~ **hall** *n* mairie *f*; ~ **house** *n* petite maison *f* en centre ville; (mansion) hôtel *m* particulier; ~ **meeting** *n* US assemblée *f* générale des habitants d'une commune; ~ **planning** *n* GB urbanisme *m*; ~**sfolk** *npl* = townspeople; ~**ship** *n* gen commune *f*; (in South Africa) township *m*; ~**speople** *npl* citadins *mpl*

tow: ~**path** *n* chemin *m* de halage; ~ **truck** *n* dépanneuse *f*

toxic /ˈtɒksɪk/ *adj* toxique

toxic waste *n* déchets *mpl* toxiques

toxin /ˈtɒksɪn/ *n* toxine *f*

toy /tɔɪ/
A *n* jouet *m*
B *noun modifier* [plane, train, railway] miniature; [car, boat] petit; [gun, telephone] d'enfant
C *vi* **to** ~ **with** jouer avec [object, feelings]; caresser [idea]; **to** ~ **with one's food** chipoter

toy: ~ **boy**○ *n* GB péj gigolo *m*; ~ **dog** *n* chien *m* d'appartement; ~ **poodle** *n* caniche *m* nain; ~**shop** *n* magasin *m* de jouets

trace /treɪs/
A *n* **[1]** (evidence) trace *f*; **there is no** ~ **of** il ne reste aucune trace de; **without** ~ [disappear, sink] sans laisser de traces; **[2]** (hint) (of irony, flavour, garlic) soupçon *m*; (of accent) pointe *f*; (of chemical, drug) trace *f*; **[3]** (of harness) trait *m*
B *vtr* **[1]** (locate) retrouver [person, weapon, car]; dépister [fault]; déterminer [cause]; **to** ~ **sb to** retrouver la trace de qn dans [hideout]; **the call was** ~**d to a London number** on a pu établir que le coup de téléphone venait d'un numéro à Londres; **[2]** (trace the history of) retracer [development, growth]; retracer [life, progress]; faire remonter [origins, ancestry]; **[3]** (also ~ **out**) (draw) gen tracer; (copy) décalquer [map, outline]

(Idiom) **to kick over the** ~**s** ruer dans les brancards

(Phrasal verb)

■ **trace back**: ▶ ~ **[sth] back**, ~ **back [sth]** faire remonter (**to** à)

tracer /ˈtreɪsə(r)/ *n* **[1]** Mil (bullet) balle *f* traçante; (shell) obus *m* traçant; **[2]** Chem, Med traceur *m*; **[3]** (instrument) traceur *m*

tracery /ˈtreɪsərɪ/ *n* gen (of pattern, frost) fin réseau *m*; Archit remplage *m*

tracing /ˈtreɪsɪŋ/ *n* **[1]** (of map, motif, diagram) calque *m*; **[2]** (procedure) calquage *m*

tracing paper *n* papier-calque *m*

track /træk/
A *n* **[1]** (print) (of animal, person) empreintes *fpl*, traces *fpl*; (of vehicle) traces *fpl*; **[2]** lit, fig (course, trajectory) (of person) trace *f*; (of missile, aircraft, storm) trajectoire *f*; **to cover one's** ~**s** brouiller les pistes; **to be on** ~ [talks, negotiations] se dérouler comme prévu; **to be on the wrong** ~ faire fausse route; **to keep** ~ **of** [person] se tenir au courant de [developments, events]; suivre le fil de [conversation]; [police] suivre les mouvements de [criminal]; [computer] tenir à jour [bank account, figures]; **to lose** ~ **of** perdre de vue [friend]; perdre la trace de [document, aircraft, suspect]; perdre le fil de [conversation]; **to lose** ~ **of (the) time** perdre la notion du temps; **to make** ~**s for sth** se diriger vers qch; **we'd better be making** ~**s** il est temps de partir; **to stop dead in one's** ~**s** s'arrêter net; **[3]** (path, road) sentier *m*, chemin *m*; Sport piste *f*; **(motor-)racing** ~ (open-air) circuit *m*; (enclosed) autodrome *m*; **cycling** ~ vélodrome *m*; **dog-racing** ~ cynodrome *m*; **[4]** Rail voie *f* ferrée; US (platform) quai *m*; **to leave the** ~**(s)** [train] dérailler; **[5]** (song on record, tape, CD) morceau *m*; (recording channel on tape) piste *f*; **[6]** (of tank, tractor) chenille *f*; **[7]** US Sch (stream) groupe *m* de niveau
B *noun modifier* Sport [event, race] de vitesse
C *vtr* suivre la trace de [person, animal]; suivre la trajectoire de [rocket, plane, comet]
(Idiom) **to come from the wrong side of the** ~**s** venir des quartiers pauvres

(Phrasal verb)

■ **track down**: ▶ ~ **[sb/sth] down**, ~ **down [sb/sth]** retrouver [person, object]

tracked /trækt/ *adj* [vehicle] chenillé, à chenilles

tracker /ˈtrækə(r)/ *n* (of animal) traqueur *m*; (of person) poursuivant/-e *m/f*

tracker dog *n* chien *m* policier

track lighting *n* rampe *f* de spots d'éclairage

trackpad /ˈtrækpæd/ *n* Comput trackpad *m*

track record *n* **to have a good** ~ avoir de bons antécédents; [professional person] avoir de bons antécédents professionnels; **a candidate with a proven** ~ **in sales** un candidat ayant une bonne expérience commerciale

track: ~ **shoe** *n* chaussure *f* de course à pointes; ~**suit** *n* survêtement *m*

tract /trækt/ *n* **[1]** (of land, forest) étendue *f*; **[2]** Anat **digestive/respiratory** ~ appareil *m* digestif/respiratoire; **[3]** (pamphlet) traité *m*; **[4]** US (housing development) lotissement *m*

tractable /ˈtræktəbl/ *adj* [person] docile; [problem] soluble

traction /ˈtrækʃn/ *n* gen traction *f*; (of wheel) adhérence *f*

traction engine *n* locomobile *f*

tractor /ˈtræktə(r)/ *n* tracteur *m*

trade /treɪd/
A *n* **[1]** (activity) commerce *m*; **to do a good** ~ faire de bonnes affaires; **[2]** (sector of industry) industrie *f*; **she's in the furniture** ~ elle travaille dans l'ameublement; **[3]** (profession) (manual) métier *m*; (intellectual) profession *f*; **by** ~ de métier
B *noun modifier* [route, agreement, balance, deficit] commercial; [sanctions, embargo] économique; [association, journal] professionnel/-elle; [barrier] douanier/-ière
C *vtr* échanger
D *vi* Comm faire du commerce; **to** ~ **in sth with sb** vendre qch à qn; **to** ~ **at $10** Fin s'échanger à $10; **to** ~ **on** fig exploiter [name, reputation, image]

(Phrasal verbs)

■ **trade in**: ▶ ~ **[sth] in**, ~ **in [sth]** Comm **he** ~**d in his old car for a new one** on lui a repris sa vieille voiture et il en a acheté une nouvelle

■ **trade off**: ▶ ~ **[sth] off**, ~ **off [sth]** échanger

t

Towns and cities

■ *Occasionally the gender of a town is clear because the name includes the definite article, e.g.* Le Havre *or* La Rochelle. *In most other cases, there is some hesitation, and it is always safer to avoid the problem by using* la ville de:

Toulouse is beautiful
= la ville de Toulouse est belle

In, to and from somewhere

■ *For* in *and* to *with the name of a town, use* à *in French; if the French name includes the definite article,* à *will become* au, à la, à l' *or* aux:

to live in Toulouse
= vivre à Toulouse

to live in La Rochelle
= vivre à La Rochelle

to go to Toulouse
= aller à Toulouse

to go to La Rochelle
= aller à La Rochelle

to live in Le Havre
= vivre au Havre

to live in Les Arcs
= vivre aux Arcs

to go to Le Havre
= aller au Havre

to go to Les Arcs
= aller aux Arcs

■ *Similarly, from is* de, *becoming* du, de la, de l' *or* des *when it combines with the definite article in town names:*

to come from Toulouse
= venir de Toulouse

to come from La Rochelle
= venir de La Rochelle

to come from Le Havre
= venir du Havre

to come from Les Arcs
= venir des Arcs

Belonging to a town or city

■ *English sometimes has specific words for people of a certain city or town, such as* Londoners, New Yorkers *or* Parisians, *but mostly we talk of* the people of Leeds *or the* inhabitants of San Francisco. *On the other hand, most towns in French-speaking countries have a corresponding adjective and noun, and a list of the best-known of these is given at the end of this note.*

■ *The noun forms, spelt with a capital letter, mean a person from X:*

the inhabitants of Bordeaux
= les Bordelais *mpl*

the people of Strasbourg
= les Strasbourgeois *mpl*

■ *The adjective forms, spelt with a small letter, are often used where in English the town name is used as an adjective:*

Paris shops
= les magasins parisiens

■ *However, some of these French words are fairly rare, and it is always safe to say* les habitants de X, *or, for the adjective, simply* de X. *Here are examples of this, using some of the nouns that commonly combine with the names of towns:*

a Bordeaux accent
= un accent de Bordeaux

Toulouse airport
= l'aéroport de Toulouse

the La Rochelle area
= la région de La Rochelle

Limoges buses
= les autobus de Limoges

the Le Havre City Council
= le conseil municipal du Havre

Lille representatives
= les représentants de Lille

Les Arcs restaurants
= les restaurants des Arcs

the Geneva road
= la route de Genève

Brussels streets
= les rues de Bruxelles

the Angers team
= l'équipe d'Angers

the Avignon train
= le train d'Avignon

but note

Orleans traffic
= la circulation à Orléans

Names of cities and towns in French-speaking countries and their adjectives

■ *Remember that when these adjectives are used as nouns, meaning a person from X or the people of X, they are spelt with capital letters.*

Aix-en-Provence	= aixois(e)
Alger	= algérois(e)
Angers	= angevin(e)
Arles	= arlésien(ne)
Auxerre	= auxerrois(e)
Avignon	= avignonnais(e)
Bastia	= bastiais(e)
Bayonne	= bayonnais(e)
Belfort	= belfortain(e)
Berne	= bernois(e)
Besançon	= bisontin(e)
Béziers	= biterrois(e)
Biarritz	= biarrot(e)
Bordeaux	= bordelais(e)
Boulogne-sur-Mer	= boulonnais(e)
Bourges	= berruyer(-ère)
Brest	= brestois(e)
Bruges	= brugeois(e)
Bruxelles	= bruxellois(e)
Calais	= calaisien(ne)
Cannes	= cannais(e)
Carcassonne	= carcassonnais(e)
Chambéry	= chambérien(ne)
Chamonix	= chamoniard(e)
Clermont-Ferrand	= clermontois(e)
Die	= diois(e)
Dieppe	= dieppois(e)
Dijon	= dijonnais(e)
Dunkerque	= dunkerquois(e)
Fontainebleau	= bellifontain(e)
Gap	= gapençais(e)
Genève	= genevois(e)

☞ See next page

t

Towns and cities *continued*

Grenoble	= grenoblois(e)	*Perpignan*	= perpignanais(e)
Havre, Le	= havrais(e)	*Poitiers*	= poitevin(e)
Lens	= lensois(e)	*Pont-à-Mousson*	= mussipontain(e)
Liège	= liégeois(e)	*Québec*	= québécois(e)
Lille	= lillois(e)	*Reims*	= rémois(e)
Lourdes	= lourdais(e)	*Rennes*	= rennais(e)
Luxembourg	= luxembourgeois(e)	*Roanne*	= roannais(e)
Lyon	= lyonnais(e)	*Rouen*	= rouennais(e)
Mâcon	= mâconnais(e)	*Saint-Étienne*	= stéphanois(e)
Marseille	= marseillais(e) *or* phocéen(ne)	*Saint-Malo*	= malouin(e)
Metz	= messin(e)	*Saint-Tropez*	= tropézien(ne)
Modane	= modanais(e)	*Sancerre*	= sancerrois(e)
Montpellier	= montpelliérain(e)	*Sète*	= sétois(e)
Montréal	= montréalais(e)	*Sochaux*	= sochalien(ne)
Moulins	= moulinois(e)	*Strasbourg*	= strasbourgeois(e)
Mulhouse	= mulhousien(ne)	*Tarascon*	= tarasconnais(e)
Nancy	= nancéien(ne)	*Tarbes*	= tarbais(e)
Nantes	= nantais(e)	*Toulon*	= toulonnais(e)
Narbonne	= narbonnais(e)	*Toulouse*	= toulousain(e)
Nevers	= nivernais(e)	*Tours*	= tourangeau(-elle)
Nice	= niçois(e)	*Tunis*	= tunisois(e)
Nîmes	= nîmois(e)	*Valence*	= valentinois(e)
Orléans	= orléanais(e)	*Valenciennes*	= valenciennois(e)
Paris	= parisien(ne)	*Versailles*	= versaillais(e)
Pau	= palois(e)	*Vichy*	= vichyssois(e)
Périgueux	= périgourdin(e)		

■ **trade up** US = **trade in**

trade: **Trade Descriptions Act** n GB Comm Jur *loi qui protège le consommateur des désignations mensongères de marchandise*; **∼ discount** n remise f professionnelle; **∼ fair** n salon m; **∼ figures** npl résultats mpl financiers

trade-in /'treɪdɪn/
A n reprise f (*d'un article usagé à l'achat d'un article neuf*)
B adj [*price*] avec reprise; [*value*] de reprise

trademark /'treɪdmɑːk/ n [1] Comm marque f (de fabrique); [2] (*also* **Trademark, Registered Trademark**) marque f déposée; [3] **the professionalism which is his ∼** fig le professionnalisme qui le caractérise

trade name n nom m (de marque)

trade-off /'treɪdɒf/ n [1] (balance) compromis m; [2] (exchange) échange m

trader /'treɪdə(r)/ n [1] Comm commerçant/-e m/f; [2] Fin (at Stock Exchange) opérateur/-trice m/f (en Bourse)

trade: **∼ secret** n secret m de fabrication; hum secret m d'État; **∼sman** n (delivery man) livreur m; (shopkeeper) commerçant m; **∼sman's entrance** n entrée f de service; **∼s union** n GB ▸ **trade union**; **Trades Union Congress, TUC** n GB Confédération f des syndicats (britanniques)

trade union
A n syndicat m
B noun modifier [*activist, leader, movement*] syndical

trade: **∼ union member** n syndiqué/-e m/f; **∼ war** n guerre f commerciale; **∼ wind** n alizé m

trading /'treɪdɪŋ/
A n [1] Comm commerce m; [2] Fin (at Stock Exchange) transactions fpl (boursières); **at the end of ∼** à la fermeture du marché
B adj [*nation*] commerçant; [*partner*] commercial

trading: **∼ estate** n GB zone f industrielle; **∼ post** n poste m d'approvisionnement (*dans une région isolée*);

Trading Standards Department n: *direction régionale de la protection des consommateurs*

tradition /trə'dɪʃn/ n tradition f

traditional /trə'dɪʃənl/ adj traditionnel/-elle

traditionalist /trə'dɪʃənəlɪst/ n, adj traditionaliste (mf)

traditionally /trə'dɪʃənəli/ adv traditionnellement

traffic /'træfɪk/
A n [1] Aut circulation f; Aviat, Naut, Rail trafic m; **∼ into/out of London** la circulation vers/en sortant de Londres; **to hold up the ∼** provoquer un bouchon; **air/passenger ∼** trafic aérien/de voyageurs; [2] (dealing) (in drugs, arms, slaves, goods) trafic m (in de); (in ideas) mouvement m (in de); [3] Electron, Comput, Telecom trafic m
B noun modifier [*accident, problem, regulations*] de la circulation; **∼ flow** circulation f
C vi (p prés etc **-ck-**) **to ∼ in** faire du trafic de [*drugs, cocaine, arms, stolen goods*]

traffic duty n **to be on ∼** faire la circulation

traffic: **∼ island** n refuge m; **∼ jam** n embouteillage m

trafficker /'træfɪkə(r)/ n trafiquant/-e m/f (in de)

traffic: **∼ lights** npl feux mpl (de signalisation *or* tricolores); **∼ policeman** n agent m de la circulation; **∼ signal** n = **traffic lights**; **∼ warden** ▸ p. 1181 n GB contractuel/-elle m/f

tragedy /'trædʒədɪ/ n gen, Theat tragédie f

tragic /'trædʒɪk/ adj gen, Theat tragique

tragically /'trædʒɪklɪ/ adv tragiquement

trail /treɪl/
A n [1] (path) chemin m, piste f; [2] (of blood, dust, slime) traînée f, trace f; **to leave a ∼ of destruction behind one** tout détruire sur son passage; [3] (trace) trace f, piste f
B vtr [1] (follow) [*animal, person*] suivre la piste de; [*car*] suivre; [2] (drag) traîner; **to ∼ one's hand in the water** laisser traîner sa main dans l'eau
C vi [1] [*skirt, scarf*] traîner; [*plant*] pendre; [2] **to ∼ in/out**

entrer/sortir en traînant les pieds; **3**▸ (lag) traîner; **our team were ~ing by 3 goals to 1** notre équipe avait un retard de 2 buts; **to ~ badly** [*racehorse, team*] être à la traîne

(Phrasal verb)

■ **trail away, trail off** s'arrêter (peu à peu)

trail: ~ bike n moto f tout-terrain; **~ blazer** n pionnier/-ière m/f; **~-blazing** adj innovateur/-trice

trailer /'treɪlə(r)/ n **1**▸ (vehicle, boat) remorque f; **2**▸ US (caravan) caravane f; **3**▸ Cin bande-annonce f

trailing /'treɪlɪŋ/ adj [*plant*] rampant

train /treɪn/

A n **1**▸ Rail train m; (underground) rame f; **on** ou **in the ~** dans le train; **slow ~** omnibus m; **a ~ to Paris** un train pour Paris; **to go to Paris by ~** aller à Paris en train; **2**▸ (succession) (of events) série f; **the bell interrupted my ~ of thought** la sonnette a interrompu le fil de mes pensées; **3**▸ (procession) (of animals, vehicles, people) file f; (of mourners) cortège m; Mil train m; **4**▸ (motion) **to set** ou **put sth in ~** mettre qch en train; **5**▸ †(retinue) suite f; **the war brought famine in its ~** fig la guerre a entraîné la famine dans son sillage; **6**▸ (on dress) traîne f

B noun modifier [*crash, station*] ferroviaire; [*timetable*] des trains; [*driver, ticket*] de train; [*strike*] des chemins de fer

C vtr **1**▸ gen, Mil, Sport former [*staff, worker, musician*] (**to do** à faire); entraîner [*athlete, player*] (**to do** à faire); dresser [*circus animal, dog*]; **to be ~ed on the job** être formé sur le tas; **to ~ sb as a pilot/engineer** donner à qn une formation de pilote/d'ingénieur; **2**▸ (aim) braquer [*gun, binoculars*] (**on** sur); **3**▸ palisser [*plant, tree*]

D vi **1**▸ gen (for profession) être formé, étudier; **he's ~ing to be a doctor** il suit une formation de docteur; **2**▸ Sport s'entraîner

trained /treɪnd/ adj [*staff, worker*] qualifié; [*professional*] diplômé; [*voice, eye, ear*] exercé; [*singer, actor*] professionnel/-elle; [*animal*] dressé; **well ~** bien formé; [*animal*] bien dressé; **when will you be fully ~?** quand est-ce que tu auras fini ta formation?

trainee /treɪ'niː/ n stagiaire mf

trainer /'treɪnə(r)/ n **1**▸ (of athlete, horse) entraîneur/-euse m/f; (of animals, dogs) dresseur/-euse m/f; **2**▸ GB (shoe) (high) basket f; (low) tennis m

training /'treɪnɪŋ/

A n **1**▸ gen formation f; (less specialized) apprentissage m; **~ in medicine** formation à la médecine; **2**▸ Mil, Sport entraînement m; **to be in ~** gen s'entraîner; (following specific programme) suivre un entraînement; **to be out of ~** manquer d'entraînement

B noun modifier gen [*course, period, scheme, agency*] de formation; [*manual*] d'instruction; Mil, Sport d'entraînement

training: ~ college n GB gen école f professionnelle; (for teachers) centre m de formation pédagogique; **~ ship** n navire-école m

train: ~ set n petit train m; **~ spotter** n passionné/-e m/f de trains

traipse /treɪps/ vi traîner; **to ~ around town** traîner partout dans la ville

trait /treɪ, treɪt/ n trait m

traitor /'treɪtə(r)/ n traître/traîtresse m/f (**to** à); **to turn ~** trahir

trajectory /trə'dʒektərɪ/ n trajectoire f

tram /træm/ n GB (also **tramcar** †) tramway m

tramp /træmp/

A n **1**▸ (vagrant) (rural) vagabond m; (urban) clochard/-e m/f; **2**▸ (sound) bruit m; **I heard the ~ of feet** j'ai entendu un bruit de pas; **3**▸ (hike) marche f

B vi **1**▸ (hike) marcher; **2**▸ (walk heavily) marcher à pas lourds

trample /'træmpl/

A vtr piétiner; **to ~ sth underfoot** piétiner qch

B vi **to ~ on** lit piétiner; fig fouler [qn/qch] aux pieds

trampoline /'træmpəliːn/ n trampoline m

trance /trɑːns, US træns/ n transe f; fig état m second; **to go into a ~** lit entrer en transe

tranquil /'træŋkwɪl/ adj tranquille

tranquillity, tranquility US /ˌtræŋ'kwɪlətɪ/ n tranquillité f

tranquillize, tranquilize US /'træŋkwɪlaɪz/ vtr mettre [qn] sous tranquillisants

tranquillizer, tranquilizer US /'træŋkwɪlaɪzə(r)/ n tranquillisant m

transact /træn'zækt/ vtr négocier [*business, rights*]

transaction /træn'zækʃn/

A n **1**▸ gen, Comm, Fin transaction f; (on stock exchange) opération f; **cash/credit card ~** transaction en liquide/effectuée avec une carte de crédit; **2**▸ (negotiating) **the ~ of business** les relations fpl d'affaires

B **transactions** npl (of society etc) actes mpl

transatlantic /ˌtrænzət'læntɪk/ adj [*crossing, flight*] transatlantique; [*attitude, accent*] d'outre-atlantique inv

transcend /træn'send/ vtr gen, Philos transcender; (surpass) surpasser

transcendental /ˌtrænsen'dentl/ adj transcendantal

transcribe /træn'skraɪb/ vtr gen, Mus transcrire

transcript /'trænskrɪpt/ n **1**▸ (copy) transcription f; **2**▸ US Sch duplicata m de livret scolaire

transcription /ˌtræn'skrɪpʃn/ n transcription f

transfer

A /'trænsfɜː(r)/ n **1**▸ gen transfert m; (of property, debt) cession f; (of funds) virement m; **2**▸ (relocation) (of player, patient, prisoner) transfert m; (of employee) mutation f; **3**▸ GB (on skin, china, paper) décalcomanie f; (on T-shirt) transfert m

B /træns'fɜː(r)/ vtr (p prés etc **-rr-**) **1**▸ gen transférer; virer [*money*]; céder [*property, power*]; reporter [*allegiance, support*]; **I'm ~ring you to reception** je vous passe la réception; **2**▸ (relocate) transférer [*office, prisoner, player*]; muter [*employee*]

C /træns'fɜː(r)/ vi (p prés etc **-rr-**) **1**▸ [*player, passenger*] être transféré; [*employee*] être muté; **2**▸ Aviat [*traveller*] changer d'avion; **3**▸ Univ [*student*] (change university) changer d'université; (change course) changer de cours

transferable /træns'fɜːrəbl/ adj gen, Jur transmissible; Fin négociable

transference /'trænsfərəns, US træns'fɜːrəns/ n gen, Psych transfert m

transfer: ~ lounge n salle f de transit; **~ passenger** n passager/-ère m/f en transit; **~red charge call** n appel m en PCV

transfigure /træns'fɪgə(r), US -gjər/ vtr sout transfigurer

transfix /træns'fɪks/ vtr lit transpercer; **~ed** fig (fascinated) fasciné; (horrified) paralysé d'horreur

transform /træns'fɔːm/ vtr transformer

transformation /ˌtrænsfə'meɪʃn/ n transformation f

transformer /træns'fɔːmə(r)/ n transformateur m

transfusion /træns'fjuːʒn/ n transfusion f

transgression /trænz'greʃn/ n **1**▸ Jur transgression f (**against** de); **2**▸ Relig péché m

transient /'trænzɪənt, US 'trænʃnt/ adj [*phase*] transitoire; [*emotion, beauty*] éphémère; [*population*] de passage

transistor /træn'zɪstə(r), -'sɪstə(r)/ n transistor m

transit /'trænzɪt, -sɪt/

A n transit m; **in ~** en transit

B noun modifier [*camp, lounge*] de transit; [*passenger*] en transit

transition /træn'zɪʃn, -'sɪʃn/

A n transition f

B noun modifier [*period, point*] de transition

transitional /træn'zɪʃənl, -'sɪʃənl/ adj [*arrangement, measure*] transitoire; [*period*] de transition

transitive /'trænzətɪv/ adj transitif/-ive

transitory /'trænzɪtrɪ, US -tɔːrɪ/ adj [*stage*] transitoire; [*hope, pain*] passager/-ère

translate /trænz'leɪt/

A vtr traduire; **to ~ theory into practice** traduire la théorie en pratique

B vi [*person*] traduire; [*word, phrase, text*] se traduire; **this word does not ~** ce mot est intraduisible

translation /trænz'leɪʃn/ n traduction f

translator /trænz'leɪtə(r)/ n traducteur/-trice m/f

translucent /trænz'luːsnt/ adj translucide

transmissible /trænz'mɪsəbl/ adj transmissible

transmission /trænz'mɪʃn/ n (all contexts) transmission f

transmit /trænz'mɪt/ (p prés etc **-tt-**)

A vtr transmettre

B vi émettre

transmitter /trænz'mɪtə(r)/ n Radio, TV émetteur m; Telecom capsule f microphonique; **radio** ~ émetteur m radio

transmute /trænz'mjuːt/ vtr Chem, fig transmuer

transparency /træns'pærənsɪ/ n ① gen, fig transparence f; ② Phot gen diapositive f; (for overhead projector) transparent m

transparent /træns'pærənt/ adj lit, fig transparent

transparently /træns'pærəntlɪ/ adv (obviously) manifestement

transpire /træn'spaɪə(r), trɑː-/ vi ① (become known) apparaître; **it ~d that** il est apparu par la suite que; ② (give off) [plant] transpirer

transplant /træns'plɑːnt, US -'plænt/
A n (operation) transplantation f, greffe f; (organ, tissue transplanted) transplant m; **to have a heart** ~ subir une transplantation cardiaque
B vtr transplanter [plant, tree]; repiquer [seedlings]; Med transplanter, greffer

transport /træns'pɔːt/
A n ① transport m; **air/road** ~ transport aérien/par route; **to travel by public** ~ utiliser les transports en commun; **I haven't got any** ~ **at the moment** je n'ai pas de moyen de locomotion en ce moment; ② Mil (ship) (navire m de) transport m de troupes; (aircraft) (avion m de) transport m de troupes; ③ (rapture) **to go into** ~**s of delight** tomber dans les transports de joie
B noun modifier [costs, facilities, ship] de transport; [industry, strike, system] des transports
C vtr transporter [passengers, goods] (**from** de; **to** à)

transportation /ˌtrænspɔː'teɪʃn/ n ① US = **transport A 1, B**; ② (of passengers, goods) transport m; ③ Hist (of criminals) transport m

transport café n GB café m de routiers

transporter /træns'pɔːtə(r)/ n Mil transport m

transpose /træn'spəʊz/ vtr gen, Math, Mus transposer

transposition /ˌtrænspə'zɪʃn/ n gen, Math, Mus transposition f

transsexual /trænz'sekʃʊəl/ n, adj transsexuel/-elle (m/f)

transverse /'trænzvɜːs/
A n partie f transversale
B adj transversal

transvestite /trænz'vestaɪt/ n travesti/-e m/f

trap /træp/
A n ① (snare) piège m; **to set a** ~ **for** poser un piège pour [animal]; tendre un piège à [person]; **to fall into the** ~ **of doing** fig commettre l'erreur de faire; ② (vehicle) cabriolet m; ③ ⓞ(mouth) **shut your** ~! ta gueuleⓞ!
B vtr (p prés etc -**pp**-) ① lit, fig (snare) prendre [qn/qch] au piège [animal, person]; ② (catch, immobilize) coincer [person, finger]; retenir [heat]

trapdoor /'træpdɔː(r)/ n trappe f

trapeze /trə'piːz, US træ-/ n trapèze m

trapper /'træpə(r)/ n trappeur m

trappings /'træpɪŋz/ npl (dress) apparat m; **the** ~ **of** les signes mpl extérieurs de [wealth, success]

trash /træʃ/ n **C** ① US (refuse) (in streets) déchets mpl; (household) ordures fpl; ② ⓞpéj (goods) camelote⁰ f; (nonsense) âneries fpl; **the film is (absolute)** ~ le film est (complètement) nul⁰

trash: ~**can** n US poubelle f; ~ **heap** n tas m d'ordures

trashy⁰ /'træʃɪ/ adj péj [novel, film] nul/nulle⁰; [goods] de pacotille pej

trauma /'trɔːmə, US 'traʊ-/ n (pl -**as**, -**ata**) Med, Psych, fig traumatisme m

traumatic /trɔː'mætɪk, US traʊ-/ adj Psych, fig traumatisant; Med traumatique

traumatize /'trɔːmətaɪz, US 'traʊ-/ vtr traumatiser

travel /'trævl/
A n voyages mpl; **foreign** ~ voyages à l'étranger
B n npl voyages mpl; **he's off on his** ~**s again** il repart en voyage
C noun modifier [plans] de voyage; [brochure, company] de voyages; [expenses] de déplacement; [business] de tourisme; [writer] de récits de voyage
D vtr (p prés etc -**ll**-, US -**l**-) parcourir [country, road, distance]
E vi (p prés etc -**ll**-, US -**l**-) ① (journey) [person] voyager; **he** ~**s**

widely il voyage beaucoup; **to** ~ **abroad/to Brazil** aller à l'étranger/au Brésil; ② (move) [person, object, plane, boat] aller; [car, train] aller, rouler; Phys [light, sound] se propager; **bad news** ~**s fast** les mauvaises nouvelles vont vite; **to** ~ **at 50 km/h** rouler à 50 km/h; **the train was** ~**ling through a tunnel** le train traversait un tunnel; **to** ~ **faster than the speed of sound** dépasser la vitesse du son; **to** ~ **a long way** [person] faire beaucoup de chemin; **to** ~ **back in time** remonter le temps; **his eye** ~**led along the line of men** il a promené son regard sur la rangée d'hommes; ③ Comm (as sales rep) **to** ~ **in** être représentant en [product]; ④ **to** ~ **well** [cheese, wine] supporter le transport

E -**travelled** GB, -**traveled** US combining form **much-** ou **well-**~**led** [road, route] fréquenté; **widely-**~**led** [person] qui a beaucoup voyagé

travel: ~ **agency** n agence f de voyages; ~ **agent** ► p. 1181 n agent m de voyages; ~ **bureau** n = **travel agency**; ~ **card** n GB carte f de transport; ~ **insurance** n assurance f voyage

traveller GB, **traveler** US /'trævlə(r)/ n ① (voyager) voyageur/-euse m/f; ② (commercial) représentant m de commerce; ③ GB (gypsy) nomade mf

traveller's cheque GB, **traveler's check** US n chèque-voyage m

travelling GB, **traveling** US /'trævlɪŋ/
A n en voyages mpl; (on single occasion) voyage m; **to go** ~ partir en voyage; **the job involves** ~ le poste exige des déplacements
B adj ① [actor, company, circus] itinérant; [bank] mobile; **the** ~ **public** les usagers des transports en commun; ② [companion, rug] de voyage; [conditions] (on road) de route; ③ [scholarship] de voyage; [allowance, expenses] de déplacement

travelling: ~ **library** n bibliobus m; ~ **salesman** ► p. 1181 n voyageur m de commerce

travelogue /'trævəlɒg/ GB, **travelog** US /'trævələːg/ n (film) film m de voyage; (talk) conférence f sur son voyage or ses voyages

travel-sick /'trævlsɪk/ adj **to be** ou **get** ~ souffrir du mal des transports

travel-sickness
A n mal m des transports
B noun modifier [pills] contre le mal des transports

traverse /trə'vɜːs/ vtr sout franchir [ocean, desert]; [comet, route] traverser

travesty /'trævəstɪ/ n Art, Literat, fig farce f

trawl /trɔːl/
A n (net) chalet m
B vtr pêcher dans [water, bay]; fig écumer [place]
C vi pêcher au chalut

trawler /'trɔːlə(r)/ n chalutier m

tray /treɪ/ n gen plateau m; **baking** ~ plaque f à pâtisserie; **ice** ~ bac m à glaçons; **in-/out-**~ corbeille f arrivée/départ

treacherous /'tretʃərəs/ adj traître

treacherously /'tretʃərəslɪ/ adv traîtreusement

treachery /'tretʃərɪ/ n traîtrise f

treacle /'triːkl/ n GB (black) mélasse f; (golden syrup) mélasse f raffinée

tread /tred/
A n ① (footstep) pas m; ② (of stair) dessus m (d'une marche); ③ (of tyre) (pattern) sculptures fpl; (outer surface) chape f
B vtr (prét **trod**; pp **trodden**) fouler [street, path, area]; **to** ~ **water** nager sur place; **to** ~ **sth underfoot** piétiner qch; **a well-trodden path** lit, fig une voie très empruntée
C vi (prét **trod**; pp **trodden**) (walk) marcher; **to** ~ **on** (walk) marcher sur; (squash) piétiner; **to** ~ **carefully** ou **warily** fig être prudent

treadmill /'tredmɪl/ n fig (dull routine) train-train m

treason /'triːzn/ n trahison f; **high** ~ haute trahison

treasonable /'triːzənəbl/ adj qui constitue une trahison

treasure /'treʒə(r)/
A n trésor m; fig (prized person) (woman) perle f; (man) homme m en or
B vtr ① (cherish) chérir [person, memory, gift]; ② (prize) tenir beaucoup à [friendship, possession]
C **treasured** pp adj précieux/-ieuse

t

treasure house *n* a ~ **of information** fig une mine d'informations

treasurer /'treʒərə(r)/ *n* ① (on committee) trésorier/-ière *m/f*; ② US (in company) directeur *m* financier

treasure trove *n* (all contexts) trésor *m*

treasury /'treʒərɪ/ *n* ① Fin trésorerie *f*; ② fig (anthology) trésor *m*; ③ (in cathedral) trésor *m*; (in palace) chambre *f* forte

Treasury /'treʒərɪ/ *n* (also ~ **Department**) Fin, Pol ministère *m* des finances

treat /triːt/
A *n* (pleasure) (petit) plaisir *m*; (food) gâterie *f*; **I took them to the museum as a ~** je les ai emmenés au musée pour leur faire plaisir; **oysters! what a ~!** des huîtres! vous nous gâtez!; **as a special ~ I was allowed to stay up late** exceptionnellement on m'a permis de me coucher plus tard; **a ~ in store** une bonne surprise; **it's my ~**○ c'est moi qui paie; **to stand sb a ~**○ offrir qch à qn
B ○**a treat** *adv phr* GB **the plan worked a ~** le projet a marché comme sur des roulettes○; **the show went down a ~ with the children** les enfants ont adoré le spectacle
C *vtr* ① gen traiter [*person, animal, object, topic*]; **to ~ sb well/badly** bien traiter/maltraiter qn; **to ~ sb/sth with care** prendre soin de qn/qch; **to ~ sb with suspicion** se montrer méfiant à l'égard de qn; **to ~ sth as** considérer qch comme [*idol, shrine*]; **they ~ the house like a hotel** ils prennent la maison pour un hôtel; **to ~ the whole thing as a joke** prendre toute l'affaire à la plaisanterie; ② Med traiter [*patient, disease*]; ③ (process) traiter [*chemical, fabric, water*]; ④ (pay for) **to ~ sb to sth** payer *or* offrir qch à qn
D *v refl* **to ~ oneself to** s'offrir [*holiday, hairdo*]

treatise /'triːtɪs, -ɪz/ *n* traité *m* (**on** sur)

treatment /'triːtmənt/ *n* ① gen (of person) traitement *m*; **special ~** (preferential) traitement de faveur; (unusual) traitement spécial; **it won't stand up to rough ~** ça ne résistera pas aux mauvais traitements; ② Med (by specific drug, method) traitement *m*; (general care) soins *mpl*; **a course of ~** un traitement; **to receive ~ for sth** être sous traitement pour qch, recevoir des soins pour qch; **to undergo ~** être en traitement; ③ (processing) traitement *m*

treaty /'triːtɪ/ *n* ① Pol traité *m*; **peace ~** traité de paix; ② Comm Jur contrat *m*; **for sale by private ~** à vendre de gré à gré

treble /'trebl/
A *n* ① Audio aigus *mpl*; ② Mus (voice) soprano *m* (*de garçon avant la mue*); (boy) soprano *m*
B *adj* ① triple; **to reach ~ figures** atteindre la centaine; ② Mus [*voice*] de soprano (*avant la mue*)
C *det* trois fois; **~ the amount** trois fois la quantité
D *vtr, vi* tripler

tree /triː/ *n* arbre *m*; **an apple ~/a cherry ~** un pommier/un cerisier; **the ~ of life** l'arbre de vie
(Idioms) **he can't see the wood** GB *ou* **forest** US **for the ~s** il se perd dans les détails; **money doesn't grow on ~s** l'argent ne se trouve pas sous les sabots d'un cheval; **to be at the top of the ~** être arrivé au sommet

tree: ~-covered *adj* boisé; **~house** *n* cabane *f* dans un arbre

treeless /'triːlɪs/ *adj* dénué d'arbres

tree: ~-lined *adj* bordé d'arbres; **~ ring** *n* cerne *m*; **~ stump** *n* souche *f*; **~top** *n* cime *f* (d'un arbre); **~ trunk** *n* tronc *m* d'arbre

trefoil /'trefɔɪl/ *n* Bot, Archit trèfle *m*

trek /trek/
A *n* (long journey) randonnée *f*; (laborious) randonnée *f* pénible
B *vi* (*p prés etc* **-kk-**) **to ~ across/through** traverser péniblement [*desert, jungle*]; **I had to ~ into town** je me suis tapé○ le trajet à pied jusqu'à la ville

trekking /'trekɪŋ/ ▸ p. 881 *n* **to go ~** faire de la randonnée pédestre

trellis /'trelɪs/ *n* gen treillis *m*; (sturdier) treillage *m*

tremble /'trembl/ *vi* trembler

trembling /'tremblɪŋ/
A *n* tremblement *m*
B *adj* tremblant

tremendous /trɪ'mendəs/ *adj* ① (great) [*effort, improvement, amount*] énorme; [*pleasure*] immense; [*storm, explosion*] violent; [*success*] fou/folle○ *f*; ② ○(marvellous) formidable○

tremendously /trɪ'mendəslɪ/ *adv* extrêmement

tremor /'tremə(r)/ *n* gen tremblement *m*; (of delight, fear) frisson *m*; (in earthquake) secousse *f*

tremulous /'tremjʊləs/ *adj* [*voice*] (with emotion) tremblant; (from weakness) tremblotant; (with excitement) frémissant; [*smile*] timide

trench /trentʃ/ *n* gen, Mil tranchée *f*

trenchant /'trentʃənt/ *adj* incisif/-ive

trench coat *n* imperméable *m*, trench-coat *m*

trend /trend/ *n* ① (tendency) tendance *f*; **a ~ in** une tendance dans le domaine de [*medicine, education*]; **a ~ away from** un désintérêt pour [*arts, studies*]; ② (fashion) mode *f*; **to set a new ~** lancer une nouvelle mode

trendsetter /'trendsetə(r)/ *n* innovateur/-trice *m/f*; **to be a ~** lancer des modes

trendy○ /'trendɪ/
A *n* branché/-e○ *m/f*
B *adj* branché○

trepidation /ˌtrepɪ'deɪʃn/ *n* appréhension *f*

trespass /'trespəs/ *vi* (enter unlawfully) gen s'introduire illégalement; **to ~ on** gen pénétrer illégalement dans; Jur violer [*property*]; **'no ~ing'** 'défense d'entrer'; **to ~ on** fig abuser de [*time, generosity*]

trespasser /'trespəsə(r)/ *n* intrus/-e *m/f*; **'~s will be prosecuted'** 'défense d'entrer sous peine de poursuites'

trestle /'tresl/ *n* tréteau *m*

trial /'traɪəl/
A *n* ① Jur procès *m*; **to be on ~** être jugé; **to go to ~** [*case*] être jugé; **to go on ~**, **to stand ~** passer en jugement; **to come up for ~** [*person*] comparaître en justice; [*case*] être jugé; **to put sb on ~** lit juger qn; fig [*press, public*] condamner qn; ② (test) (of machine, recruit, vehicle) essai *m*; (of drug, new product) test *m*; **to put sth through ~s** soumettre qch à des essais *or* tests; **take it on ~** prenez-le à l'essai; **by ~ and error** par expérience; ③ Mus, Sport épreuve *f*; ④ (trouble) épreuve *f*; (less strong) difficulté *f*; **the ~s of being a mother** les épreuves de la maternité; **to be a ~** [*person*] être pénible à supporter
B *noun modifier* [*period, separation*] d'essai; **on a ~ basis** à titre expérimental

trial run *n* essai *m*; **to take a car for a ~** essayer une voiture

triangle /'traɪæŋgl/ *n* triangle *m*

tribal /'traɪbl/ *adj* tribal

tribe /traɪb/ *n* tribu *f*

tribulation /ˌtrɪbjʊ'leɪʃn/ *n* **trials and ~s** tribulations *fpl*

tribunal /traɪ'bjuːnl/ *n* tribunal *m*

tribune /'trɪbjuːn/ *n* (platform) tribune *f*

tributary /'trɪbjʊtərɪ, US -terɪ/ *n* affluent *m*

tribute /'trɪbjuːt/ *n* hommage *m*; **to pay ~ to** rendre hommage à; **as a ~ to** en hommage à; **floral ~** gen fleurs *fpl*; (spray) gerbe *f*; (wreath) couronne *f*; **this is a ~ to her genius** fig cela témoigne de son génie

trice /traɪs/ *n* **in a ~** en un rien de temps

tricentenary /ˌtraɪsen'tiːnərɪ/ *n, adj* tricentenaire (*m*)

trick /trɪk/
A *n* ① gen tour *m*; (dishonest) combine *f*, truc○ *m*; **a clever ~** un tour habile; **a ~ of the light** un effet de lumière; ② (by magician, conjurer, dog) tour *m*; **he is up to his ~s again** il continue à faire des siennes; ③ (knack, secret) astuce *f*; **to have a ~ of doing sth** avoir le chic pour faire qch; **to know a ~ or two** *ou* **a few ~s** s'y connaître (**about** en); ④ (habit, mannerism) manie *f*; **to have a ~ of doing** avoir la manie de faire; ⑤ (in cards) pli *m*; **to take** *ou* **win a ~** faire un pli
B *noun modifier* [*photo, shot*] truqué
C *vtr* duper, rouler○; **to ~ sb into doing sth** amener qn à faire qch par la ruse; **to ~ sb out of their inheritance** escroquer qn de son héritage
(Idioms) **the ~s of the trade** les ficelles du métier; **that will do the ~** ça fera l'affaire; **he never misses a ~** il ne rate jamais un détail

trickery /'trɪkərɪ/ *n* tromperie *f*

trickle /'trɪkl/
A *n* (of liquid) filet *m*; (of powder, sand) écoulement *m*; (of investment, orders) petite quantité *f*; (of people) petit nombre *m*
B *vi* **to ~ down** dégouliner le long de [*pane, wall*]; **to ~ from** couler de [*tap, spout*]; **to ~ into** [*liquid*] s'écouler dans [*container*]; [*people*] s'infiltrer dans [*country, organization*]; [*ball*]

rouler dans [*net*]; **to ~ out of** [*liquid*] suinter de [*crack, wound*]

Phrasal verbs

■ **trickle away** [*water*] s'écouler lentement; [*people*] s'éloigner lentement

■ **trickle in** arriver au compte-gouttes

trick or treat /ˌtrɪkɔːˈtriːt/ *n* collecte de bonbons et d'argent faite par les enfants le soir du 31 octobre; '**~!**' 'des bonbons ou des sous, sinon gare à vous!'

trick question *n* question *f* piège

trickster /ˈtrɪkstə(r)/ *n* escroc *m*

tricky /ˈtrɪkɪ/ *adj* ① [*decision, business, task*] difficile; [*problem, question*] épineux/-euse; [*situation*] délicat; ② (sly, wily) malin/-igne

tricolour GB, **tricolor** US /ˈtrɪkələ(r)/, US ˈtraɪkʌlə(r)/ *n* drapeau *m* tricolore

tricycle /ˈtraɪsɪkl/ *n* (cycle) tricycle *m*

tried /traɪd/
A *prét, pp* ▸ **try B, C**
B *pp adj* **a ~ and tested remedy** un médicament infaillible

trifle /ˈtraɪfl/
A *n* ① **a ~** (slightly) un peu; ② (triviality) (gift, money) bagatelle *f*; (matter, problem) détail *m*; **to waste time on ~s** perdre son temps à des broutilles; ③ GB Culin ≈ diplomate *m*
B *vi* **to ~ with** jouer avec [*feelings, affections*]; **to ~ with sb** traiter qn à la légère

trifling /ˈtraɪflɪŋ/ *adj* [*sum, cost, detail*] insignifiant

trigger /ˈtrɪɡə(r)/
A *n* ① (on gun) gâchette *f*; **to pull the ~** appuyer sur la gâchette; ② (on machine) manette *f*; ③ fig **to be the ~ for sth** déclencher qch
B *vtr* = **trigger off**

Phrasal verb

■ **trigger off**: ▸ **~ off [sth]** déclencher

trigger-happy° /ˈtrɪɡəhæpɪ/ *adj* ① lit à la gâchette facile; ② fig impulsif/-ive

trigonometry /ˌtrɪɡəˈnɒmətrɪ/ *n* trigonométrie *f*

trilby /ˈtrɪlbɪ/ *n* GB chapeau *m* en feutre, feutre *m*

trill /trɪl/
A *n* ① Mus trille *m*; ② Ling r roulé *m*
B *vtr* ① Mus triller; ② Ling rouler
C *vi* triller

trilogy /ˈtrɪlədʒɪ/ *n* trilogie *f*

trim /trɪm/
A *n* ① (cut) (of hair) coupe *f* d'entretien; (of hedge) taille *f*; ② (good condition) **to keep oneself in ~** se maintenir en bonne forme physique; ③ (border) (on clothing) bordure *f*; (of braid) galon *m*; (on woodwork) moulure *f*; ④ Aut **exterior ~** finition *f* extérieure; **interior ~** garniture *f* intérieure
B *adj* [*garden, person*] soigné; [*boat, house*] bien tenu; [*figure*] svelte; [*waist*] fin
C *vtr* (*p prés etc* **-mm-**) ① (cut) couper [*hair, grass, material*]; tailler [*beard, hedge*]; ébouter [*wood*]; ② (reduce) réduire [*budget, expenditure, workforce*] (**by** de); raccourcir [*article, speech*] (**by** de); ③ Culin dégraisser [*meat*]; ④ (decorate) décorer [*tree, furniture*]; border [*dress, handkerchief*]

trimming /ˈtrɪmɪŋ/ *n* (on clothing) garniture *f*; (on soft furnishings) passementerie *f*; **~s** Culin (with dish) accompagnements *mpl* traditionnels; (of pastry) rognures *fpl*; **with all the ~s** fig avec tout le tralala°

Trinidad /ˈtrɪnɪdæd/ ▸ **p. 954** *pr n* (l'île *f* de) la Trinité *f*

Trinity /ˈtrɪnətɪ/ *n* **the ~** la Trinité *f*

Trinity term *n* GB Univ troisième trimestre *m*

trinket /ˈtrɪŋkɪt/ *n* babiole *f*

trio /ˈtriːəʊ/ *n* trio *m* (**of** de)

trip /trɪp/
A *n* ① (journey) (abroad) voyage *m*; (excursion) excursion *f*; **business ~** voyage d'affaires; **to be away on a ~** être en voyage; **we did the ~ in five hours** nous avons fait le trajet en cinq heures; **it's only a short ~ into London** c'est juste un petit tour à Londres; ② °argot des drogués **trip**° *m*
B *vtr* (*p prés etc* **-pp-**) gen faire trébucher; (with foot) faire un croche-pied à [*person*]
C *vi* (*p prés etc* **-pp-**) ① (also **~ over**, **~ up**) (stumble) trébucher, faire un faux pas; **to ~ on** *ou* **over** trébucher sur [*step, rock*]; se prendre les pieds dans [*scarf, rope*]; ② **to ~ along** [*child*] gambader; [*adult*] marcher d'un pas léger

---

Phrasal verb

■ **trip up**: ▸ **~ up** trébucher; fig (make an error) se tromper; ▸ **~ [sb] up**, **~ up [sb]** gen faire trébucher; (with foot) faire un croche-pied à

tripe /traɪp/ *n* **Ȼ** Culin tripes *fpl*; fig °(nonsense) foutaises° *fpl*

triple /ˈtrɪpl/ *adj* gen triple; Mus **in ~ time** à trois temps

triplet /ˈtrɪplɪt/ *n* (child) triplé/-e *m/f*

triplicate /ˈtrɪplɪkət/: **in ~** *adv phr* en trois exemplaires

tripod /ˈtraɪpɒd/ *n* trépied *m*

tripper /ˈtrɪpə(r)/ *n* excursionniste *mf*, touriste *mf*

trite /traɪt/ *adj* banal; **~ comments** banalités *fpl*

triumph /ˈtraɪʌmf/
A *n* triomphe *m*
B *vi* triompher (**over** de)

triumphant /traɪˈʌmfnt/ *adj* [*person, team*] triomphant; [*return, success*] triomphal

triumphantly /traɪˈʌmfntlɪ/ *adv* [*march, return*] triomphalement; [*say*] d'une voix triomphante

triumvirate /traɪˈʌmvɪrət/ *n* triumvirat *m*

trivia /ˈtrɪvɪə/ *npl* (+ *v sg ou pl*) futilités *fpl*

trivial /ˈtrɪvɪəl/ *adj* [*matter, scale, film*] insignifiant; [*error, offence*] léger/-ère; [*conversation, argument, person*] futile

triviality /ˌtrɪvɪˈælətɪ/ *n* banalité *f*

trivialize /ˈtrɪvɪəlaɪz/ *vtr* gen banaliser; minimiser [*rôle, art*]

trod /trɒd/ *prét* ▸ **tread B, C**

trodden /ˈtrɒdn/ *pp* ▸ **tread B, C**

Trojan /ˈtrəʊdʒən/
A *n* Hist Troyen/-enne *m/f*
B *adj* troyen/-enne; **the ~ War** la guerre de Troie

Idiom **to work like a ~** GB travailler comme un forçat

troll /trəʊl/ *n* troll *m*

trolley /ˈtrɒlɪ/ *n* ① GB (on wheels) chariot *m*; **drinks ~** chariot à boissons; ② US tramway *m*

trolley: **~ bus** *n* trolleybus *m*; **~ car** *n* tramway *m*, tram *m*

troop /truːp/
A *n* troupe *f*
B *noun modifier* [*movements, carrier*] de troupes; [*train, plane*] de transport de troupes
C *vi* **to ~ in/out** entrer/sortir en masse

trooper /ˈtruːpə(r)/ *n* ① Mil homme *m* de troupe; ② US (policeman) policier *m*

Idiom **to swear like a ~** jurer comme un charretier *or* troupier

trooping /ˈtruːpɪŋ/ *n* **the Trooping of the Colour** GB parade *f* militaire

trophy /ˈtrəʊfɪ/ *n* trophée *m*

tropic /ˈtrɒpɪk/ *n* tropique *m*; **the ~ of Cancer** le tropique du Cancer; **in the ~s** sous les tropiques

tropical /ˈtrɒpɪkl/ *adj* tropical

trot /trɒt/
A *n* trot *m*; **at a ~** au trot; **to break into a ~** [*animal*] se mettre au trot; [*person*] se mettre à trotter
B *vi* (*p prés etc* **-tt-**) [*animal, rider*] trotter; [*person*] courir, trotter°; [*child*] trottiner

Idiom **on the ~**° ① (one after the other) coup sur coup; ② (continuously) d'affilée

Phrasal verb

■ **trot out**°: ▸ **~ out [sth]** débiter [*excuse, explanation, argument*]

trotter /ˈtrɒtə(r)/ *n* pigs' **~s** Culin pieds *mpl* de cochon

trouble /ˈtrʌbl/
A *n* **Ȼ** ① (problems) gen problèmes *mpl*; (personal) ennuis *mpl*; **engine ~** problèmes de moteur; **this car has been nothing but ~** cette voiture ne m'a apporté que des ennuis; **to get sb into ~** créer des ennuis à qn; **to make ~ for oneself** s'attirer des ennuis; **to be asking for ~** chercher des ennuis; **the ~ with you is that** l'ennui avec toi c'est que; **back ~** mal *m* de dos; **what's the ~?** qu'est-ce qui ne va pas?; ② (difficulties) gen difficultés *fpl*; **to be in** *ou* **get into ~** gen [*person*] avoir des ennuis; [*company*] avoir des difficultés; **to have ~ doing** avoir du mal à faire; **to get sb out of ~** tirer qn d'affaire; **to stay out of ~** éviter des ennuis; ③ (effort, inconvenience) peine *f*; **it's not worth the ~** cela n'en

vaut pas la peine; **to take the ∼ to do, to go to the ∼ of doing** se donner la peine de faire; **to save sb the ∼ of doing** épargner à qn la peine de faire; **to go to a lot of ∼** se donner beaucoup de mal; **I don't want to put you to any ∼** je ne veux pas te déranger; **it's no ∼** cela ne me dérange pas; **to be more ∼ than it's worth** donner plus de mal qu'il n'en vaut la peine; **not to be any ∼** [child] être sage; [task] ne poser aucun problème; **all that ∼ for nothing** tout ce mal pour rien; **nothing is too much ∼ for him** il est très serviable; **if it's too much ∼, say so** si ça t'ennuie, dis-le-moi; **all the ∼ and expense** tous les dérangements et toutes les dépenses; ④ (discord) gen problèmes mpl; (with personal involvement) ennuis mpl; **I don't want any ∼** je ne veux pas d'ennuis; **there'll be ∼** il y aura du remous; **to expect ∼** [police] s'attendre à des incidents; **to be looking for ∼** chercher les ennuis; **to get into ∼** s'attirer des ennuis; **to make ∼** faire des histoires○; **it will lead to ∼** ça va mal finir; **at the first sign of ∼** au moindre signe d'agitation; **there's ∼ brewing** il y a de l'orage dans l'air fig

B troubles npl soucis mpl; **money ∼s** problèmes mpl d'argent

C vtr ① (disturb, inconvenience) [person] déranger [person]; **to ∼ sb for sth** déranger qn pour lui demander qch; **may ou could I ∼ you to do?** puis-je vous demander de faire?; **I won't ∼ you with the details** je te fais grâce des détails; ② (bother) **to be ∼d by** être incommodé par [cough, pain]; ③ (worry) tracasser [person]; tourmenter [mind]; **don't let that ∼ you** ne te tracasse pas pour cela

D vi **to ∼ to do** se donner la peine de faire

E v refl **to ∼ oneself to do** se donner la peine de faire

troubled /'trʌbld/ adj [person, expression] soucieux/-ieuse; [mind] inquiet/-iète; [sleep, times, area] agité; littér [waters] troublé

trouble: **∼free** adj [period, operation] sans problèmes; **∼maker** n fauteur/-trice m/f de troubles; **∼shooter** n gen conciliateur/-trice m/f; Tech expert m; Ind consultant/-e m/f en gestion des entreprises; **∼some** adj [person] ennuyeux/-euse; [problem] gênant; [cough, pain] désagréable; **∼ spot** n point m chaud

trough /trɒf, US trɔːf/ n ① (for drinking) abreuvoir m; (for animal feed) auge f; ② (depression) (between waves, hills, on graph) also Econ creux m; **to have peaks and ∼s** avoir des hauts et des bas; ③ Meteorol zone f dépressionnaire

trouser /'traʊzə(r)/ ▸ p. 1191
A noun modifier [belt, leg] de pantalon
B trousers npl pantalon m; **short ∼s** short m
(Idiom) **to wear the ∼s** GB porter la culotte○

trouser suit n GB ensemble-pantalon m

trousseau /'truːsəʊ/ n trousseau m (de mariage)

trout /traʊt/
A n truite f
B noun modifier [fishing] à la truite; [stream] à truites

trowel /'traʊəl/ n ① (for cement) truelle f; ② (for gardening) déplantoir m
(Idiom) **to lay it on with a ∼**○ mettre le paquet○

truancy /'truːənsɪ/ n absentéisme m

truant /'truːənt/ n **to play ∼** faire l'école buissonnière

truce /truːs/ n trêve f

truck /trʌk/
A n ① (lorry) camion m; ② (rail wagon) wagon m de marchandises
B vtr camionner
C vi US conduire un camion
(Idiom) **to have no ∼ with sb/sth** GB ne rien avoir à faire avec qn/qch

truck driver ▸ p. 1181 n routier m

trucker○ /'trʌkə(r)/ ▸ p. 1181 n (lorry driver) routier m

trucking /'trʌkɪŋ/ n (transporting) transport m routier

truckload /'trʌkləʊd/ n (of goods, produce) chargement m (of de); (of soldiers, refugees) camion m (of de)

truck stop n (restaurant m) routier m

truculent /'trʌkjʊlənt/ adj agressif/-ive

trudge /trʌdʒ/ vi (also ∼ along) marcher d'un pas lourd; **to ∼ through the snow** marcher péniblement dans la neige; **to ∼ round the shops** se traîner de magasin en magasin

true /truː/
A adj ① (based on fact) [news, fact, story] vrai; (from real life) [story]

vécu; **it is ∼ to say that** on peut dire que; **the same is ou holds ∼ of the new party** il en va de même pour le nouveau parti; **to prove ∼** se révéler exact; **it can't be ∼!** ce n'est pas possible!; **that's ∼** (when agreeing) c'est juste; **too ∼**○! je ne vous/te le fais pas dire!; ② (real, genuine) [god, cost, meaning, democracy, American] vrai; [identity, age] véritable; **to come ∼** se réaliser; **it is hard to get the ∼ picture** il est difficile de savoir ce qui se passe vraiment or en réalité; **an artist in the ∼ sense of the word** un artiste dans toute l'acception du terme; ③ (heartfelt, sincere) [feeling, repentance, understanding] sincère; **∼ love** le véritable amour; ④ (accurate) [copy] conforme; [assessment] juste; **to be ∼ to life** [film, book] être vrai; ⑤ (faithful, loyal) [servant, knight] fidèle; **to be ∼ to sth** être fidèle à qch; ⑥ Constr **to be out of ∼** [window, post, frame] ne pas être d'aplomb; ⑦ Mus [note, instrument] juste
B adv (straight) [aim, fire] juste

(Idioms) **to be too good to be ∼** être trop beau pour être vrai; **∼ to form, he...** égal à lui-même, il...; **to be/remain ∼ to type** [person] être/rester semblable à lui-même/elle-même etc

true: **∼-blue** adj [conservative, loyalist] bon teint inv; **∼-life** adj [adventure, story] vécu; **∼love** n littér bien-aimé/-e m/f

truffle /'trʌfl/ n truffe f

truism /'truːɪzəm/ n truisme m

truly /'truːlɪ/ adv ① (extremely) [amazing, delighted, sorry, horrendous] vraiment; ② (really, in truth) [be, belong, think] vraiment; **really and ∼?** vraiment?; **well and ∼** carrément; ③ (in letter) **yours ∼** je vous prie d'agréer l'expression de mes sentiments distingués fml; **...and who got it all wrong? yours ∼!** (referring to oneself) ...et qui s'est trompé? mézigue○!

trump /trʌmp/
A n Games atout m
B trumps npl Games atout m; **spades are ∼s** atout pique
C vtr ① Games couper; ② (beat) battre [person, rival]
(Idiom) **to come up** ou **turn up ∼s** sauver la situation

trump card n atout m

trumped-up /ˌtrʌmpt'ʌp/ adj [charge] forgé de toutes pièces

trumpet /'trʌmpɪt/ ▸ p. 1028
A n ① Mus (instrument, player) trompette f; ② (elephant call) barrissement m
B noun modifier [solo] de trompette; **∼ call** fig vibrant appel m
C vtr [group, party] vanter les mérites de [lifestyle, success]; [newspaper] claironner
D vi [elephant] barrir
(Idiom) **to blow one's own ∼** vanter ses propres mérites

trumpeter /'trʌmpɪtə(r)/ ▸ p. 1181, p. 1028 n trompettiste mf

truncate /trʌn'keɪt, US 'trʌŋ-/ vtr ① tronquer [text]; écourter [process, journey, event]; ② Comput, Math tronquer

truncheon /'trʌntʃən/ n matraque f

trundle /'trʌndl/
A vtr **to ∼ sth out** sortir qch; **to ∼ sth in** entrer en poussant qch
B vi [vehicle] avancer lourdement; **the lorries were trundling up and down the street** les camions montaient et descendaient lourdement la rue

trunk /trʌŋk/
A n ① (of tree, body) tronc m; ② (of elephant) trompe f; ③ (for travel) malle f; ④ US (car boot) coffre m; ⑤ (duct) conduite f
B trunks npl maillot m de bain (pour hommes)

truss /trʌs/
A n ① (of hay) botte f; ② Med bandage m herniaire; ③ Constr armature f, ferme f
B vtr ① (bind) = **truss up**; ② Constr armer
(Phrasal verb)
■ **truss up**: ▸ **∼ up** [sth], **∼** [sth] **up** brider, trousser [chicken]; ligoter [person]; botteler [hay]

trust /trʌst/
A n ① (faith) confiance f; **to put one's ∼ in** se fier à; **to take sth on ∼** croire qch sur parole; ② Jur (arrangement) fidéicommis m; (property involved) propriété f fiduciaire; ③ Fin (large group of companies) trust m; ④ Fin ▸ **investment trust**
B vtr ① (believe) se fier à [person, judgment]; ② (rely on) faire

confiance à; **~ her!** (amused or annoyed) tu peux compter sur elle pour ça!; **3** (entrust) **to ~ sb with sth** confier qch à qn; **4** (hope) espérer

C *vi* **to ~ in** faire confiance à [*person*]; croire en [*God, fortune*]; **to ~ to luck** se fier au hasard

D **trusted** *pp adj* [*friend*] fidèle

E *v refl* **to ~ oneself to do** être sûr de pouvoir faire; **I couldn't ~ myself to speak** j'ai préféré me taire

trust company *n* société *f* fiduciaire

trustee /trʌs'tiː/ *n* **1** (who administers property in trust) fiduciaire *m*; **2** (who administers a company) administrateur/-trice *m*/*f* (**of** de)

trust fund *n* fonds *m* en fidéicommis

trusting /'trʌstɪŋ/ *adj* [*person*] qui fait facilement confiance aux gens; **you're too ~** tu es trop naïf/naïve

trustworthy /'trʌstwɜːði/ *adj* [*staff, firm*] sérieux/-ieuse; [*source*] fiable; [*confidante, lover*] digne de confiance

trusty /'trʌsti/ *adj* †hum fidèle

truth /truːθ/ *n* **1** (real facts) **the ~** la vérité; **the whole ~** toute la vérité; **the ~ (of the matter) is that** la vérité, c'est que; **whatever the ~ of the matter** quoi qu'il en soit; **to tell you the ~** à vrai dire; **nothing could be further from the ~** c'est absolument faux; **2** (accuracy) **to confirm/deny the ~ of sth** confirmer/nier l'exactitude de qch; **3** Philos, Relig vérité *f*; **4** (foundation) **there is no ~ in that** c'est absolument faux; **there is some ~ in it** il y a du vrai dans cela

Idioms **~ will out** la vérité se fera jour; **~ is stranger than fiction** la réalité dépasse la fiction; **to tell sb a few home ~s** dire à qn ses quatre vérités

truth drug *n* sérum *m* de vérité

truthful /'truːθfl/ *adj* [*person*] honnête; [*account, version*] vrai; **to be absolutely** ou **perfectly ~** en toute franchise

truthfully /'truːθfəli/ *adv* sans mentir

truthfulness /'truːθflnɪs/ *n* véracité *f*

try /traɪ/ (*pl* **tries**)

A *n* **1** (attempt) essai *m*; **to have a ~ at doing** essayer de faire; **nice ~!** bel essai!; iron bel effort!; **to have a good ~** faire tout ce qu'on peut; **2** Sport (in rugby) essai *m*

B *vtr* (*prét, pp* **tried**) **1** (attempt) essayer de répondre à [*exam question*]; **to ~ doing** ou **to do** essayer de faire; **to ~ hard to do** faire de gros efforts pour faire; **let's ~ and phone them** essayons de leur téléphoner; **it's ~ing to rain/snow** il a l'air de vouloir pleuvoir/neiger; **2** (test out) essayer [*tool, product, method, activity*]; prendre [qn] à l'essai [*person*]; [*thief*] essayer d'ouvrir [*door, window*]; tourner [*door knob*]; **to ~ one's hand at pottery/weaving** s'essayer à la poterie/au tissage; **~ that for size** ou **length** essaie pour voir si ça te va; **I'll ~ anything once** je suis toujours prêt à faire de nouvelles expériences; **3** (taste) goûter [*food*]; **4** (consult) demander à [*person*]; consulter [*book*]; **~ the library** demandez à la bibliothèque; **5** (subject to stress) mettre [qch] à rude épreuve [*tolerance, faith*]; **to ~ sb's patience** pousser qn à bout; **6** Jur juger [*case, criminal*]

C *vi* (*prét, pp* **tried**) (make attempt) essayer; **to ~ again** (to perform task) recommencer; (to see somebody) repasser; (to phone) rappeler; **~ and relax** essaie de rester calme; **to ~ for** essayer d'obtenir [*loan, university place*]; essayer de battre [*world record*]; essayer d'avoir [*baby*]; **just you ~!** (as threat) essaie un peu○!; **keep ~ing!** essaie encore!; **I'd like to see you ~!** j'aimerais bien t'y voir!; **she did it without even ~ing** elle l'a fait sans le moindre effort; **at least you tried** au moins tu as fait tout ce que tu as pu

Idiom **these things are sent to ~ us** hum tout ça c'est pour notre bien

Phrasal verbs

■ **try on**: ▸ **~ [sth] on, ~ on [sth]** essayer [*hat, dress*]; **to ~ it on**○ fig bluffer

■ **try out**: ▸ **~ out** [*sportsman*] faire un essai; [*actor*] auditionner; ▸ **~ [sth] out, ~ out [sth]** essayer [*machine, theory, language, recipe*]; ▸ **~ [sb] out, ~ out [sb]** prendre [qn] à l'essai

trying /'traɪɪŋ/ *adj* [*person*] pénible; [*experience*] éprouvant

tsar /zɑː(r)/ *n* **1** (ruler) tsar *m*; **2** (government supremo) **drugs ~** Monsieur drogue; **homelessness ~** Monsieur sans-abri

T-shaped *adj* en (forme de) T

T-shirt *n* T-shirt *m*

tsp *abrév écrite* = **teaspoonful**

tub /tʌb/ *n* **1** (large) (for flowers, water) bac *m*; (small) (for ice cream, pâté) pot *m*; **2** (contents) pot *m*; **3** US (bath) baignoire *f*

tubby○ /'tʌbi/ *adj* grassouillet/-ette○

tube /tjuːb, US 'tuːb/ *n* **1** (cylinder, container) tube *m*; **2** ○GB **the ~** le métro (londonien); **3** ○US (TV) télé○ *f*; **4** (in TV set) tube *m* cathodique

Idiom **to go down the ~s** [*plans*] tomber à l'eau; [*economy*] tomber en ruines

tuberculosis /tjuːˌbɜːkjʊ'ləʊsɪs, US 'tuː-/ ▸ p. 933 *n* tuberculose *f*

tubing /'tjuːbɪŋ, US 'tuː-/ *n* tuyauterie *f*

tub-thumping /'tʌbθʌmpɪŋ/ *n* éloquence *f* de bas étage

tubular /'tjuːbjʊlə(r), US 'tuː-/ *adj* tubulaire

TUC *n*: *abrév* ▸ **Trades Union Congress**

tuck /tʌk/

A *n* gen pli *m*; (to shorten) pli *m* horizontal

B *vtr* glisser; **to ~ one's shirt into one's trousers** rentrer sa chemise dans son pantalon; **to ~ one's trousers into one's boots** enfiler son pantalon dans ses bottes; **to ~ a blanket under sb** plier une couverture sous qn; **she ~ed her feet up under her** elle a ramené ses pieds sous elle; **it ~ed its head under its wing** il a enfoui la tête sous son aile

Phrasal verbs

■ **tuck away**: ▸ **~ [sth] away, ~ away [sth]** **1** (safely, in reserve) enfouir [*object*]; mettre en sécurité [*money, valuable*]; **2** (hard to find) **to be ~ed away** [*village, document, object*] se nicher (**in** dans; **behind** derrière)

■ **tuck in**: ▸ **~ in** (start eating) attaquer; ▸ **~ in [sth], ~ [sth] in** rentrer [*garment, shirt*]; border [*bedclothes*]; ▸ **~ [sb] in, ~ in [sb]** border

■ **tuck up**: ▸ **~ up [sb], ~ [sb] up** border

Tue(s) *abrév écrite* = **Tuesday**

Tuesday /'tjuːzdeɪ, -dɪ, US 'tuː-/ ▸ p. 1322 *pr n* mardi *m*

tuft /tʌft/ *n* touffe *f*

tufted /'tʌftɪd/ *adj* [*grass*] en touffes; [*bird*] huppé; [*carpet*] tufté

tug /tʌg/

A *n* **1** (pull) (on rope, in sails) résistance *f*; (on fishing line) secousse *f*; **to give sth a ~** tirer sur qch; **to feel a ~ of loyalties** se sentir partagé; **2** Naut (also **tug boat**) remorqueur *m*

B *vtr* (*p prés etc* **-gg-**) (pull) tirer

C *vi* (*p prés etc* **-gg-**) **to ~ at** ou **on** tirer sur [*rope, hair*]

tug-of-love /ˌtʌgəv'lʌv/ *n* GB lutte entre les parents pour la garde de l'enfant

tug-of-war /ˌtʌgəv'wɔː(r)/ *n* Sport gagne-terrain *m*; fig lutte *f*

tuition /tjuː'ɪʃn, US tuː-/ *n* cours *mpl*

tuition fees *npl* frais *mpl* pédagogiques

tulip /'tjuːlɪp, US 'tuː-/ *n* tulipe *f*

tumble /'tʌmbl/

A *n* **1** (fall) chute *f*; **to take a ~** [*person*] faire une chute; [*price, share*] chuter; **2** (of clown, acrobat) culbute *f*; **3** (jumble) tas *m*

B *vi* **1** (fall) [*person, object*] tomber (**off, out of** de); **to ~ down sth** [*water*] dévaler qch en cascade; **2** [*price, share, currency*] chuter; **3** Sport [*clown, acrobat, child*] faire des culbutes; **4** ○**to ~ to sth** (understand) comprendre [*fact, plan*]

Phrasal verbs

■ **tumble down** [*wall, building*] s'écrouler

■ **tumble out** [*contents*] se renverser; [*words, feelings*] jaillir en désordre

tumble: **~down** *adj* délabré; **~-drier**, **~-dryer** *n* sèche-linge *m inv*; **~-dry** *vtr* sécher (en machine)

tumbler /'tʌmblə(r)/ *n* (glass) verre *m* droit

tummy○ /'tʌmi/ *n* lang enfantin ventre *m*

tumour GB, **tumor** US /'tjuːmə(r), US 'tuː-/ *n* tumeur *f*

tumult /'tjuːmʌlt, US 'tuː-/ *n* **1** (noise) tumulte *m*; **to be in ~** [*feelings*] être en émoi; **2** (disorder) agitation *f*

tumultuous /tjuː'mʌltjʊəs, US 'tuː-/ *adj* tumultueux/-euse

tuna /'tjuːnə, US 'tuː-/ *n* (also **~ fish**) thon *m*

tune /tjuːn, US tuːn/

A *n* **1** Mus air *m*; **2** (accurate pitch) **to be in/out of ~** lit, fig être/ne pas être en accord; **to sing in/out of ~** chanter juste/faux; **3** ○(amount) **to the ~ of** pour un montant de

B vtr accorder [musical instrument]; régler [engine, radio, TV]; **stay ~d!** restez à l'écoute!

(Idioms) **to call the ~** mener la danse; **to change one's ~, to sing a different ~** changer d'avis; **to dance to sb's ~** se plier aux exigences de qn

(Phrasal verbs)

■ **tune in** mettre la radio; **to ~ in to** se mettre à l'écoute de [programme]; régler sur [channel]; ▸ **~ [sth] in** régler (**to** sur)

■ **tune up** [musician] s'accorder; ▸ **~ up [sth], ~ [sth] up** accorder [musical instrument]

tuneful /'tjuːnfl, US 'tuː-/ adj mélodieux/-ieuse

tuner /'tjuːnə(r), US 'tuː-/ n **1** ▸ p. 1181 Mus (person) accordeur m; **organ/piano ~** accordeur m d'orgues/de piano; **2** Audio (unit) tuner m; (knob) (bouton m de) réglage

tunic /'tjuːnɪk, US 'tuː-/ n gen tunique f; (uniform) (for nurse, schoolgirl) blouse f; (for soldier) vareuse f

tuning /'tjuːnɪŋ, US 'tuː-/ n (of musical instrument, choir) accord m; (of radio, TV, engine) réglage m

tuning fork n Mus diapason m

Tunisia /tjuː'nɪzɪə, US tuː-/ ▸ p. 774 pr n Tunisie f

tunnel /'tʌnl/
A n tunnel m; **to use a ~** emprunter un tunnel
B vtr, vi (p prés etc **-ll-** GB, **-l-** US) creuser

(Idiom) **to see (the) light at the end of the ~** voir le bout du tunnel

tunnel vision n Med rétrécissement m (tubulaire) du champ visuel; fig **to have ~** avoir des œillères

tuppence /'tʌpəns/ n deux pence

turbine /'tɜːbaɪn/ n turbine f

turbo /'tɜːbəʊ/ n (engine) turbo m; (car) turbo f

turbocharged /ˌtɜːbəʊ'tʃɑːdʒd/ adj turbo inv

turbot /'tɜːbət/ n turbot m

turbulence /'tɜːbjʊləns/ n ¢ **1** (of air) turbulences fpl; (of waves) turbulence f; **2** (turmoil) agitation f; (unrest) perturbations fpl

turbulent /'tɜːbjʊlənt/ adj **1** [water] agité; **2** [times, situation] agité; [career, history] mouvementé; [passions, character, faction] turbulent

tureen /tə'riːn/ n soupière f

turf /tɜːf/
A n (pl **~s, turves**) **1** (grass) gazon m; (peat) tourbe f; **2** (horse racing) **the ~** le turf m
B vtr **1** gazonner [lawn, patch, pitch]; **2** ᴼ(throw) balancerᴼ
(Phrasal verb)
■ **turf out** ▸ **~ out [sb/sth], ~ [sb/sth] out** virerᴼ

turf accountant ▸ p. 1181 n bookmaker m

turgid /'tɜːdʒɪd/ adj [style] boursouflé; [water] gonflé

Turk /tɜːk/ ▸ p. 1032 n (person) Turc/Turque m/f

turkey /'tɜːkɪ/ n **1** (bird) dinde f; **2** ᴼUS péj Theat, Cin (flop) bideᴼ m; (bad film) navetᴼ m; **3** ᴼUS (person) clocheᴼ f
(Idiom) **to talk ~**ᴼ dire les choses toutes cruesᴼ

Turkey /'tɜːkɪ/ ▸ p. 774 pr n Turquie f

Turkish /'tɜːkɪʃ/ ▸ p. 1032, p. 969
A n (language) turc m
B adj turc/turque

Turkish: ~ bath n bain m turc; **~ coffee** n café m turc; **~ delight** n loukoum m; **~ towel** n serviette f éponge

turmeric /'tɜːmərɪk/ n (plant) curcuma m; (spice) safran m des Indes

turmoil /'tɜːmɔɪl/ n (political, emotional) désarroi m

turn /tɜːn/ ▸ p. 803
A n **1** (in games, sequence) tour m; **whose ~ is it?** c'est à qui le tour?; **'miss a ~'** 'passez votre tour'; **to be sb's ~ to do** être au tour de qn de faire; **it was his ~ to feel rejected** il se sentait rejeté à son tour; **to have a ~ on** ou **at** ou **with the computer** utiliser l'ordinateur à son tour; **to take ~s at** doing, **to take it in ~s to do** faire qch à tour de rôle; **take it in ~s!** chacun son tour!; **by ~s** tour à tour; **to speak out of ~** fig commettre un impair; **to give sth a ~** tourner qch; **to do a ~** [dancer] faire un tour; **to take a ~ in the park** faire un tour dans le parc; **3** (in vehicle) virage m; **to make** ou **do a left/right ~** tourner à gauche/à droite; **to do a ~ in the road** faire un demi-tour; **'no left ~'** 'défense de tourner à gauche'; **4** (bend,

side road) tournant m, virage m; **take the next right ~, take the next ~ on the right** prenez la prochaine (rue) à droite; **5** (change, development) tournure f; **to take a ~ for the better** [person, situation] s'améliorer; [things, events] prendre une meilleure tournure; **to take a ~ for the worse** [situation] se dégrader; [health] s'aggraver; **to be on the ~** [luck, milk] commencer à tourner; [tide] commencer à tourner; ▸ **century**; **6** ᴼGB (attack) crise f; **a giddy** ou **dizzy ~** un vertige; **to have a funny ~** se sentir tout/-e choseᴼ; **it gave me quite a ~, it gave me a nasty ~** ça m'a fait un coupᴼ; **7** (act) numéro m

B **in turn** adv phr **1** (in rotation) [answer, speak] à tour de rôle; **she spoke to each of us in ~** elle nous a parlé chacun à notre tour; **2** (linking sequence) à son tour

C vtr **1** (rotate) [person] tourner [wheel, handle]; serrer [screw]; [mechanism] faire tourner [cog, wheel]; **to ~ the key in the door** ou **lock** (lock up) fermer la porte à clé; (unlock) tourner la clé dans la serrure; **2** (turn over, reverse) retourner [mattress, soil, steak, collar]; tourner [page]; **to ~ one's ankle** se tordre la cheville; **it ~s my stomach** cela me soulève le cœur; **3** (change direction of) tourner [chair, head, face, car]; **to ~ one's back on** lit tourner le dos à [group, place]; fig laisser tomber [friend, ally]; abandonner [homeless, needy]; **4** (focus direction of) **to ~ sth on sb** braquer qch sur qn [gun, hose, torch]; fig diriger qch sur qn [anger, scorn]; **5** (transform) **to ~ sth white/black** blanchir/noircir qch; **to ~ sth milky/opaque** rendre qch laiteux/opaque; **to ~ sth into** transformer qch en [office, car park, desert]; **to ~ water into ice/wine** changer de l'eau en glace/vin; **to ~ a book into a film** adapter un livre pour l'écran; **to ~ sb into** [magician] changer qn en [frog]; [experience] faire de qn [extrovert, maniac]; **6** (deflect) détourner [person, conversation] (**towards** vers; **from** de); **7** ᴼ(pass the age of) **he has ~ed 50** il a 50 ans passés; **she has just ~ed 20/30** elle vient d'avoir 20/30 ans; **8** (on lathe) tourner [wood, piece, spindle]

D vi **1** (change direction) [person, car, plane, road] tourner; [ship] virer; **to ~ down** ou **into** tourner dans [street, alley]; **to ~ towards** tourner en direction de [village, mountains]; **the conversation ~ed to Ellie** on en est venu/ils en sont venus à parler d'Ellie; **2** (reverse direction) [person, vehicle] faire demi-tour; [tide] changer; [luck] tourner; ▸ **turn around**; **3** (revolve) [key, wheel, planet] tourner; [person] se tourner; **to ~ in one's chair** se retourner dans son fauteuil; **to ~ and walk out of the room** faire demi-tour et sortir de la pièce; **I ~ed once again to my book** j'ai repris encore une fois ma lecture; **4** fig (hinge) **to ~ on** [argument] tourner autour de [point, issue]; [outcome] dépendre de [factor]; **5** (spin round angrily) **to ~ on sb** [dog] attaquer qn; [person] se retourner contre qn; **6** fig (resort to) **to ~ to** se tourner vers [person, religion]; **to ~ to drink/drugs** se mettre à boire/se droguer; **I don't know where** ou **which way to ~** je ne sais plus où donner de la têteᴼ; **7** (change) **to ~ into** [person, tadpole] se transformer en [frog]; [sofa] se transformer en [bed]; [situation, evening] tourner à [farce, disaster]; **to ~ to** [substance] se changer en [ice, gold]; [fear, surprise] faire place à [horror, relief]; **8** (become by transformation) devenir [pale, cloudy, green]; **to ~ white/black/red** blanchir/noircir/rougir; **the weather is ~ing cold/warm** le temps se rafraîchit/se réchauffe; **9** ᴼ(become) devenir [Conservative, Communist]; **businesswoman ~ed politician** ancienne femme d'affaires devenue politicienne; **10** (go sour) [milk] tourner; **11** [trees, leaves] jaunir

(Idioms) **at every ~** (all the time) à tout moment; (everywhere) partout; **one good ~ deserves another** Prov c'est un prêté pour un rendu; **to be done to a ~** être cuit à point; **to do sb a good ~** rendre un service à qn

(Phrasal verbs)

■ **turn about** faire demi-tour
■ **turn against** ▸ **~ against [sb/sth]** se retourner contre; ▸ **~ [sb] against** retourner [qn] contre
■ **turn around** ▸ **~ around** **1** (to face other way) [person] se retourner; [bus, vehicle] faire demi-tour; **you can't just ~ around and say you've changed your mind** fig tu ne peux pas tout simplement dire que tu as changé d'avis; **2** (revolve, rotate) [object, windmill, dancer] tourner; **3** (change trend) **the market has ~ed around** il y a eu un renversement de situation sur le marché; ▸ **~ [sth] around, ~ around [sth]** **1** (to face other way) tourner [qch] dans l'autre sens [object]; **2** (reverse decline in) redresser [situation, economy, company]; **3** (rephrase) reformuler [question, sentence]
■ **turn aside** se détourner (**from** de)

■ **turn away**: ▸ ~ **away** se détourner; ▸ ~ **[sth] away**, ~ **away [sth]** détourner [*head, torch*]; ▸ ~ **[sb] away**, ~ **away [sb]** refuser [*spectator, applicant*]; ne pas laisser entrer [*salesman, caller*]

■ **turn back**: ▸ ~ **back** [1] (turn around) (on foot) rebrousser chemin; (in vehicle) faire demi-tour; **there's no ~ing back** fig il n'est pas question de revenir en arrière; [2] (in book) revenir; ▸ ~ **[sth] back**, ~ **back [sth]** [1] (rotate backwards) reculer [*dial, clock*]; [2] (fold back) rabattre [*sheet, lapel*]; replier [*corner, page*]; ▸ ~ **[sb] back**, ~ **back [sb]** refouler [*people, vehicles*]

■ **turn down**: ▸ ~ **down**: **his mouth ~s down at the corners** il a une bouche aux commissures tombantes; ▸ ~ **[sth] down**, ~ **down [sth]** [1] (reduce) baisser [*volume, radio, gas*]; [2] (fold over) rabattre [*sheet, collar*]; retourner [*corner of page*]; ▸ ~ **[sb/sth] down**, ~ **down [sb/sth]** refuser [*person, request*]; rejeter [*offer, suggestion*]

■ **turn in**: ▸ ~ **in** [1] ○(go to bed) aller se coucher; [2] (point inwards) **to ~ in on itself** [*leaf, page*] se recroqueviller; **to ~ in on oneself** fig se replier sur soi-même; ▸ ~ **in [sth]**, ~ **[sth] in**○ [1] (hand in) rendre [*badge, homework*]; [2] (produce) **to ~ in a profit** rapporter un bénéfice; **to ~ in a good performance** [*player*] bien jouer; [*company*] avoir de bons résultats; [3] (give up) laisser tomber○ [*job, activity*]; ▸ ~ **[sb] in**, ~ **in [sb]** livrer [*suspect*]; ▸ ~ **oneself in** se livrer

■ **turn off**: ▸ ~ **off** [1] (leave road) tourner; ~ **off at the next exit** prends la prochaine sortie; [2] [*motor, fan*] s'arrêter; ▸ ~ **off [sth]**, ~ **[sth] off** [1] (stop) éteindre [*light, oven, TV, radio*]; fermer [*tap*]; couper [*water, gas, engine*]; [2] (leave) quitter [*road*]; ▸ ~ **[sb] off**○ rebuter

■ **turn on**: ▸ ~ **on [sth]**, ~ **[sth] on** allumer [*light, oven, TV, radio, gas*]; ouvrir [*tap*]; ▸ **charm**; ▸ ~ **[sb] on**, ~ **on [sb]**○ exciter

■ **turn out**: ▸ ~ **out** [1] (be eventually) **to ~ out well/badly** bien/mal se terminer; **to ~ out differently** prendre une tournure différente; **to ~ out all right** s'arranger; **it depends how things ~ out** cela dépend de la façon dont les choses vont tourner; **to ~ out to be wrong/easy** (prove to be) se révéler faux/facile; **it ~s out that** il se trouve que; **as it ~ed out** en fin de compte; [2] (come out) [*crowd, people*] venir; [3] (point outwards) **his toes** *ou* **feet ~ out** il a les pieds tournés en dehors; ▸ ~ **[sth] out**, ~ **out [sth]** [1] (turn off) éteindre [*light*]; [2] (empty) vider [*pocket, bag*]; Culin démouler [*mousse*]; [3] (produce) fabriquer [*goods*]; former [*scientists, graduates*]; ▸ ~ **[sb] out**, ~ **out [sb]** (evict) mettre [qn] à la porte

■ **turn over**: ▸ ~ **over** [1] (roll over) [*person, vehicle*] se retourner; [2] (turn page) tourner la page; [3] [*engine*] se mettre en marche; ▸ ~ **[sth/sb] over**, ~ **over [sth/sb]** [1] (turn) tourner [*page, paper*]; retourner [*card, object, mattress, soil, patient*]; [2] (hand over) remettre [*object, money, find, papers*]; livrer [*person*] (**to** à); remettre la succession de [*company*]; transmettre [*control, power*]; [3] (reflect) **I've been ~ing it over in my mind** j'y ai bien réfléchi; [4] ○GB (rob) cambrioler [*shop, place*]; [5] Fin (have turnover of) faire un chiffre d'affaires de [*amount*]

■ **turn round** GB = **turn around**

■ **turn up**: ▸ ~ **up** [1] (arrive, show up) arriver, se pointer○; **don't worry—it will ~ up** ne t'inquiète pas—tu finiras par le retrouver; [2] (present itself) [*opportunity, job*] se présenter; [3] (point up) [*corner, edge*] être relevé; ▸ ~ **up [sth]**, ~ **[sth] up** [1] (increase, intensify) augmenter [*heating, volume, gas*]; mettre [qch] plus fort [*TV, radio, music*]; [2] (dig up) relever [*collar*]; [3] (discover) déterrer [*buried object*]; [*person*] découvrir [*information*]

turnaround /'tɜːnəraʊnd/ n [1] (in attitude) revirement m; [2] (of fortune) revirement m (**in** de); (for the better) redressement m (**in** de)

turn: ~**coat** n traître/traîtresse m/f, personne f qui retourne sa veste○; ~**down** n baisse f

turned-out /ˌtɜːnd'aʊt/ adj **to be well** ~ être élégant

turned-up /ˌtɜːnd'ʌp/ adj [*nose*] retroussé

turning /'tɜːnɪŋ/ ▸ p. 803 n [1] GB (in road) virage m; **to take a wrong** ~ tourner au mauvais endroit; **the next** ~ **on the right** la prochaine (rue) à droite; **I've missed my** ~ j'aurais dû tourner plus tôt; [2] (work on lathe) tournage m

turning: ~ **circle** n rayon m de braquage; ~ **point** n tournant m (**in, of** de)

turnip /'tɜːnɪp/ n navet m

turnoff /'tɜːnɒf/ n [1] (in road) embranchement m; [2] ○(person) **to be a real** ~ être vraiment repoussant

turn: ~ **of mind** n tournure f d'esprit; ~ **of phrase** n (expression) expression f; (way of expressing oneself) façon f de parler

turn-on○ /'tɜːnɒn/ n **to be a real** ~ être vachement○ excitant

turnout /'tɜːnaʊt/ n [1] (to vote, strike, demonstrate) taux m de participation; **there was a magnificent** ~ **for the parade** beaucoup de gens sont venus voir le défilé; [2] (clearout) nettoyage m; [3] ○(appearance) tenue f

turnover /'tɜːnəʊvə(r)/ n [1] (of company) chiffre m d'affaires; [2] (rate of replacement) (of stock) rotation f; (of staff) taux m de renouvellement; [3] Culin chausson m

turn: ~**pike** n (tollgate) barrière f de péage; US (toll expressway) autoroute f à péage; ~**stile** n gen tourniquet m; (to count number of visitors) compteur m pour entrées

turntable /'tɜːnteɪbl/ n [1] (on record player) platine f; [2] Rail, Aut plaque f tournante

turnup /'tɜːnʌp/ n GB (of trousers) revers m

(idiom) **a** ~ **for the books** GB une grande surprise

turpentine /'tɜːpəntaɪn/ n térébenthine f

turret /'tʌrɪt/ n (all contexts) tourelle f

turtle /'tɜːtl/ n GB tortue f marine; US tortue f

(idiom) **to turn** ~ se retourner

turtle: ~ **dove** n tourterelle f; ~**neck** n (neckline) col m montant

Tuscany /'tʌskənɪ/ pr n Toscane f

tusk /tʌsk/ n (of elephant, walrus) défense f

tussle /'tʌsl/
A n empoignade f (**for** pour)
B vi être aux prises

tussock /'tʌsək/ n touffe f d'herbe

tut /tʌt/
A excl tss-tss!
B vi (*p prés etc* **-tt-**) produire un tss-tss de désapprobation

tutee /tjuː'tiː, US tuː-/ n gen étudiant/-e m/f; (individual) élève mf particulier/-ière

tutor /'tjuːtə(r), US tuː-/ ▸ p. 1181
A n [1] (private teacher) professeur m particulier; [2] GB Univ (teacher) chargé/-e m/f de travaux dirigés; (for general welfare) conseiller/-ère m/f d'éducation; [3] US Univ assistant/-e m/f; [4] GB Sch (of class) professeur m principal; (of year group) responsable mf pédagogique d'année; [5] Mus (instruction book) méthode f
B vtr donner des leçons particulières à (**in** de)
C vi donner des cours (**in** de)

tutorial /tjuː'tɔːrɪəl, US tuː-/ n Univ (group) classe f de travaux dirigés; (private) cours m privé

tuxedo /tʌk'siːdəʊ/ n US smoking m

TV○ n (abrév = **television**) télé○ f

TV: ~ **dinner** n plateau m télé; ~ **screen** n écran m télé

twaddle○ /'twɒdl/ n balivernes fpl

twain /tweɪn/ npl **the** ~ les deux; **never the** ~ **shall meet** les deux sont inconciliables

twang /twæŋ/
A n (of string, wire) vibration f; (of tone) ton m nasillard
B vtr pincer [*instrument*]
C vi [*string, wire*] produire une vibration; [*instrument*] vibrer

tweak /twiːk/
A n [1] (tug) coup m sec; [2] Comput amélioration f
B vtr tordre [*ear, nose*]; tirer [*hair, moustache*]

twee /twiː/ adj GB péj [*house, décor*] mièvre; [*manner*] emprunté

tweezers /'twiːzəz/ npl gen pincettes fpl; (for eyebrows) pince f à épiler

twelfth /twelfθ/ ▸ p. 1044, p. 788
A n [1] (in order) douzième mf; [2] (of month) douze m inv; [3] (fraction) douzième m; [4] Mus douzième f
B adj, adv douzième

twelve /twelv/ ▸ p. 1044, p. 647, p. 745
A n douze m inv
B adj douze inv; **the Twelve** Bible les douze apôtres

twentieth /'twentɪəθ/ ▸ p. 1044, p. 788
A n [1] (in order) vingtième mf; [2] (of month) vingt m; [3] (fraction) vingtième m

B *adj*, *adv* vingtième

twenty /'twentɪ/ ▸ p. 1044, p. 647, p. 745 *n*, *adj* vingt *(m) inv*

twenty: **~-one** ▸ p. 881 *n* Games vingt-et-un *m*; **~-twenty** *adj* [*vision*] de dix à chaque œil

twerp○ /twɜːp/ *n* péj crétin/-e○ *m/f*

twice /twaɪs/ *adv* deux fois; **~ a day** *ou* **daily** deux fois par jour; **she's ~ his age** elle a le double de son âge; **~ as much, ~ as many** deux fois plus; **~ over** deux fois; **you need to be ~ as careful** il faut redoubler de prudence

(Idiom) **once bitten ~ shy** Prov chat échaudé craint l'eau froide Prov

twiddle /'twɪdl/ *vtr* tripoter; **to ~ one's thumbs** lit, fig se tourner les pouces

twig /twɪg/
A *n* brindille *f*
B ○*vtr*, *vi* (*p prés etc* **-gg-**) piger○

twilight /'twaɪlaɪt/
A *n* lit, fig crépuscule *m*
B *noun modifier* [*hours*] du crépuscule; [*world*] énigmatique; **~ years** dernières années

twilight zone *n* zone *f* d'ombre

twill /twɪl/ *n* sergé *m*

twin /twɪn/
A *n* ① (one of two children) jumeau/-elle *m/f*; ② (one of two objects) **this vase is the ~ to yours** ce vase est celui qui va avec le tien
B *noun modifier* ① [*brother, sister*] jumeau/-elle; ② (two) [*masts, propellers*] jumeaux/-elles (*after n*); [*speakers*] jumelés; **the ~ aims of** le double but de
C *vtr* (*p prés etc* **-nn-**) jumeler [*town*] (**with** avec)

twine /twaɪn/
A *n* ficelle *f*
B *vtr* enrouler [*rope*] (**around** autour de)
C *v refl* **to ~ itself** [*snake, vine*] s'enrouler

twinge /twɪndʒ/ *n* (of pain) élancement *m*; (of conscience, doubt) accès *m*; (of jealousy) pointe *f*

twinkle /'twɪŋkl/
A *n* (of light, jewel) scintillement *m*; (of eyes) pétillement *m*
B *vi* [*light, star, jewel*] scintiller; [*eyes*] pétiller

twinkling /'twɪŋklɪŋ/
A *n* scintillement *m*
B *adj* [*light, star, eyes*] scintillant

(Idiom) **in the ~ of an eye** en un clin d'œil

twinning /'twɪnɪŋ/ *n* jumelage *m*

twin town *n* ville *f* jumelle

twirl /twɜːl/
A *n* ① (spin) tournoiement *m*; **to do a ~** [*person*] tournoyer; ② (spiral) volute *f*
B *vtr* faire tournoyer [*baton, lasso, partner*]; tortiller [*hair, moustache*]; entortiller [*ribbon, vine*]
C *vi* [*dancer*] tournoyer; **to ~ round** (turn round) se retourner brusquement

twist /twɪst/
A *n* ① (action) **he gave the cap a ~** (to open) il a dévissé le bouchon; (to close) il a vissé le bouchon; **with a couple of ~s she unscrewed the lid** en deux tours de poignet elle a dévissé le couvercle; ② (in rope, cord, wool) tortillon *m*; (in road) zigzag *m*; (in river) coude *m*; ③ (in play, story) coup *m* de théâtre; (episode in crisis, events) rebondissement *m*; **the ~s and turns of the plot** le fil tortueux de l'intrigue; ④ (small amount) (of yarn, thread, hair) torsade *f*; **a ~ of lemon** une tranche de citron; ⑤ (dance) **the ~** le twist
B *vtr* ① (turn) tourner [*knob, handle*]; (open) dévisser [*cap, lid*]; (close) visser [*cap, lid*]; **to ~ sth off** dévisser qch [*cap, lid*]; **to ~ sb's arm** lit tordre le bras à qn; fig forcer la main à qn; ② (wind, twine) **to ~ threads together** torsader des fils; **to ~ X round Y** enrouler X autour de Y; **she ~ed the scarf (round) in her hands** elle tortillait l'écharpe entre ses doigts; ③ (bend, distort) tordre [*metal, rod, branch*]; fig déformer [*words, facts, meaning*]; **his face was ~ed with pain** son visage était tordu de douleur; ④ (injure) **to ~ one's ankle/wrist** se tordre la cheville/le poignet; **to ~ one's neck** attraper un torticolis
C *vi* ① [*person*] **he lay ~ing and writhing on the ground** il se tordait et se contorsionnait sur le sol; **to ~ round** (turn round) se retourner; **he ~ed around in his chair** il s'est retourné dans son fauteuil; ② [*rope, flex, coil*] s'entortiller; [*river, road*] serpenter; **to ~ and turn** [*road, path*] serpenter

(Idiom) **(to have a) ~ in the tail** (avoir un) dénouement inattendu; **to go round the ~**○ devenir fou/folle; **to drive sb round the ~**○ rendre qn fou/folle

twisted /'twɪstɪd/ *adj* [*wire, metal, rod*] tordu; [*rope, cord*] entortillé; [*ankle, wrist*] tordu; pej [*logic*] faux/fausse; [*sense of humour*] malsain

twisting /'twɪstɪŋ/ *adj* sinueux/-euse

twit○ /twɪt/ *n* idiot/-e *m/f*

twitch /twɪtʃ/
A *n* ① (tic) tic *m*; **to have a ~ in one's eye** avoir un tic à l'œil; ② (spasm) soubresaut *m*; **to give a ~** avoir un soubresaut; ③ (jerk) **to give the curtain a ~** réajuster le rideau d'un coup sec
B *vtr* tirer sur [qch] d'un coup sec [*fabric, curtain*]; **the dog ~ed its ears** le chien remuait les oreilles
C *vi* ① (quiver) [*person, animal*] trembloter; [*mouth*] trembler; [*eye*] cligner nerveusement; [*limb, muscle*] tressauter; [*fishing line*] vibrer; ② (tug) **to ~ at** [*person*] tirer d'un coup sec sur [*curtain*]

twitchy /'twɪtʃɪ/ *adj* agité

twitter /'twɪtə(r)/
A *n* gazouillement *m*; **to be all of a ~** hum être tout excité/tout excitée
B *vi* [*bird*] gazouiller; [*person*] babiller

two /tuː/ ▸ p. 1044, p. 745, p. 647
A *n* deux *m inv*; **in ~s** par deux; **in ~s and threes** par deux ou trois, deux ou trois à la fois
B *det* deux *inv*
C *pron* deux *inv*; **I bought ~ of them** j'en ai acheté deux; **to break sth in ~** casser qch en deux

(Idioms) **that makes ~ of us** nous sommes tous les deux dans le même cas; **to be in ~ minds about doing** hésiter à faire; **to put ~ and ~ together** faire le rapprochement; **there are ~ sides to every story** ≈ autant d'hommes, autant d'avis

two: **~-bit**○ *adj* péj US [*show, comedian*] médiocre, à la gomme○; **~-edged** *adj* fig à double tranchant; **~-faced** *adj* péj hypocrite, fourbe

twofold /'tuːfəʊld/
A *adj* double
B *adv* doublement

two: **~-party system** *n* Pol système *m* bipartite; **~-penny-halfpenny**○ *adj* GB péj de rien du tout; **~-phase** *adj* Elec diphasé; **~-piece** *n* (also **~-piece suit**) (woman's) tailleur *m*; (man's) costume *m* (deux-pièces); **~-pin** *adj* [*plug, socket*] à deux fiches; **~-ply** *adj* [*wool*] à deux fils; [*wood*] contreplaqué à double épaisseur; **~-seater** *n* Aut voiture *f* à deux places; Aviat avion *m* à deux places; **~-some** *n* (two people) couple *m*; **~-storey** *adj* à deux étages; **~-tier** *adj* [*bureaucracy*] à deux niveaux or étages; [*society, health service etc*] à deux vitesses

two-time○ /'tuːtaɪm/
A *vtr* être infidèle envers, tromper [*partner*]
B *vi* être infidèle

two-tone /'tuːtəʊn/ *adj* (in hue) de deux tons; (in sound) à deux tons *or* timbres

two-way /ˌtuː'weɪ/ *adj* ① [*street*] à double sens; [*traffic*] dans les deux sens; fig [*communication, exchange*] bilatéral; ② Elec [*switch*] va-et-vient *inv*

two: **~-way mirror** *n* glace *f* sans tain; **~-way radio** *n* émetteur-récepteur *m*; **~-wheeler**○ *n* (vehicle, bicycle) deux-roues *m inv*

TX US Post *abrév écrite* = **Texas**

tycoon /taɪ'kuːn/ *n* magnat *m*; **publishing ~** magnat de l'édition

type /taɪp/
A *n* ① (variety, kind) type *m*, genre *m*; **he's an army ~** il a le genre militaire; **you're not my ~** tu n'es pas mon genre; **they're our ~ of people** c'est le genre de personnes que nous aimons bien; **I'm not that ~, I don't go in for that ~ of thing** ce n'est pas mon genre; **he's one of those pretentious university ~s** c'est un de ces individus prétentieux de l'université; **I know his ~** péj je connais les gens de son espèce; **you know the ~ of thing I mean** vous voyez à peu près ce que je veux dire; **he's reverted to ~** le naturel a repris le dessus; **to play** *ou* **be cast against ~** Cin, Theat jouer à contre-emploi; ② (in printing) caractères *mpl*; **printed in small/large ~** imprimé en petits/gros caractères
B *vtr* ① taper (à la machine) [*word, letter*]; **a ~d letter** une lettre dactylographiée; ② (classify) classifier [*blood sample*];

cataloguer [*person*] (**as** comme)
C *vi* taper (à la machine)

(Phrasal verbs)

■ **type in**: ▶ ~ **in [sth]**, ~ **[sth] in** taper [*word, character*]
■ **type out**: ▶ ~ **out [sth]**, ~ **[sth] out** taper (à la machine) [*letter*]
■ **type over**: ▶ ~ **over [sth]** (erase) effacer
■ **type up** taper, dactylographier *fml*

type: ~**cast** *vtr* (*prét, pp* **-cast**) Theat, fig cataloguer [*person*]; ~**face** *n* police *f* (de caractères); ~**script** *n* texte *m* dactylographié; ~**set** *vtr* composer; ~**setter** *n* typographe *mf*; ~**setting** *n* composition *f*; ~**writer** *n* machine *f* à écrire; ~**written** *adj* tapé (à la machine), dactylographié *fml*

typhoid /'taɪfɔɪd/ ▸ p. 933 *n* (*also* ~ **fever**) (fièvre *f*) typhoïde *f*

typhoon /taɪ'fuːn/ *n* typhon *m*

typical /'tɪpɪkl/ *adj* [*case, example, day, village*] typique; [*generosity, compassion*] caractéristique; ~ **feature** caractéristique *f*; **it's** ~ **of him to be late** cela ne m'étonne pas de lui qu'il soit en retard; ~! ça ne m'étonne pas!

typically /'tɪpɪklɪ/ *adv* [*behave*] (of person) comme à mon/ton etc habitude; ~ **English** [*place, behaviour*] typiquement anglais; **she's** ~ **English** c'est l'Anglaise type

typify /'tɪpɪfaɪ/ *vtr* [*feature, behaviour*] caractériser; [*person, institution*] être le type même de; **as typified by the EU** comme le représente la UE

typing /'taɪpɪŋ/
A *n* **1** (skill) dactylographie *f*; **my** ~ **is slow** ma frappe est lente; **2** (typed material) **two pages of** ~ deux pages dactylographiées
B *noun modifier* [*course*] de dactylo; [*error*] de frappe; [*paper*] pour machine à écrire

typing pool *n* **to work in the** ~ travailler au service dactylo○

typing speed *n* vitesse *f* de frappe

typist /'taɪpɪst/ *n* dactylo *mf*

typographic(al) /ˌtaɪpə'græfɪk(l)/ *adj* typographique

typography /taɪ'pɒgrəfɪ/ *n* typographie *f*

tyrannic(al) /tɪ'rænɪk(l)/ *adj* tyrannique

tyrannize /'tɪrənaɪz/
A *vtr* tyranniser
B *vi* tyranniser; **to** ~ **over sb** tyranniser qn

tyranny /'tɪrənɪ/ *n* tyrannie *f* (**over** sur)

tyrant /'taɪərənt/ *n* tyran *m*

tyre GB, **tire** US /'taɪə(r)/ *n* pneu *m*; **spare** ~ lit pneu *m* de rechange; fig (fat) bourrelet *m*

tyre: ~ **lever** *n* démonte-pneu *m*; ~ **pressure** *n* pression *f* des pneus; ~ **pressure gauge** *n* manomètre *m* (pour pneus)

tzar *n* = **tsar**

t

Uu

u, U /juː/ n 1 (letter) u, U m; 2 GB Cin (*abrév* = **universal**) ≈ tous publics

U-bend n (in pipe) courbure f en U; (in road) virage m en épingle à cheveux

ubiquitous /juːˈbɪkwɪtəs/ adj omniprésent

udder /ˈʌdə(r)/ n pis m

UFO n (*abrév* = **unidentified flying object**) ovni m inv

Uganda /juːˈgændə/ ▸ p. 774 pr n Ouganda m

Ugandan /juːˈgændən/ ▸ p. 1032
A n Ougandais/-e m/f
B adj ougandais/-e

ugliness /ˈʌglɪnɪs/ n laideur f

ugly /ˈʌglɪ/ adj 1 (hideous) [*person, appearance, furniture, building*] laid; [*sound*] désagréable; [*wound*] vilain (*before* n); **to be an ~ sight** être hideux/-euse à voir; 2 (vicious) [*situation, conflict*] dangereux/-euse; [*tactics, campaign*] bas/basse; **to be in an ~ mood** [*group, mob*] gronder; [*individual*] être d'une humeur massacrante○

(Idioms) **an ~ customer**○ un sale type○; **as ~ as sin** laid comme un pou; **racism rears its ~ head** on voit surgir le spectre du racisme

UK ▸ p. 774
A pr n (*abrév* = **United Kingdom**) Royaume-Uni m
B noun modifier [*citizen, passport*] britannique

Ukraine /juːˈkreɪn/ ▸ p. 774 pr n **the ~** l'Ukraine f

Ukrainian /juːˈkreɪnɪən/ ▸ p. 1032, p. 969
A n 1 (person) Ukrainien/-ienne m/f; 2 (language) ukrainien m
B adj ukrainien/-ienne

ulcer /ˈʌlsə(r)/ n ulcère m

Ulster /ˈʌlstə(r)/
A pr n Ulster m, Irlande f du Nord
B noun modifier [*people, accent*] d'Irlande du Nord

ulterior /ʌlˈtɪərɪə(r)/ adj 1 (hidden) [*motive, purpose*] inavoué; **with any ~ motive** sans arrière-pensée; 2 (subsequent) ultérieur

ultimate /ˈʌltɪmət/
A n **the ~ in** le nec plus ultra de [*comfort, luxury*]
B adj 1 [*result, destination*] final; [*sacrifice*] ultime (*before* n); **~ power lies with the president** en dernier ressort c'est le président qui a le pouvoir de décision; **the ~ weapon** l'arme absolue; 2 (fundamental) [*question, truth*] fondamental

ultimately /ˈʌltɪmətlɪ/ adv en fin de compte, au bout du compte

ultimatum /ˌʌltɪˈmeɪtəm/ n (pl **~s** ou **-mata**) ultimatum m; **to issue an ~** adresser un ultimatum (**to** à); **cease-fire ~** ultimatum de cessez-le-feu

ultraconservative /ˌʌltrəkənˈsɜːvətɪv/ adj ultraconservateur/-trice

ultramarine /ˌʌltrəməˈriːn/ n, adj outremer (m) (inv)

ultrasound /ˈʌltrəsaʊnd/ n ultrasons mpl

ultrasound: **~ scan** n échographie f; **~ scanner** n échographe m

ultraviolet /ˌʌltrəˈvaɪələt/ adj ultraviolet/-ette

umber /ˈʌmbə(r)/ n Art terre f d'ombre

umbilical /ʌmˈbɪlɪkl, ˌʌmbɪˈlaɪkl/ adj ombilical; **~ cord** cordon m ombilical

umbrage /ˈʌmbrɪdʒ/ n **to take ~** prendre ombrage (**at** de)

umbrella /ʌmˈbrelə/ n parapluie m; **under the ~ of** fig (protection) sous la protection de; (authority) sous l'égide f de

umbrella: **~ stand** n porte-parapluies m inv; **~ term** n terme m générique; **~ tree** n magnolia m parasol

umpire /ˈʌmpaɪə(r)/
A n Sport, fig arbitre m
B vtr Sport arbitrer
C vi Sport être l'arbitre; **to ~ at a match** arbitrer un match

umpteen○ /ˈʌmpˈtiːn/ adj des tas de○; **~ times** trente-six fois

umpteenth○ /ˈʌmpˈtiːnθ/ adj énième

UN pr n (*abrév* = **United Nations**) **the ~** l'ONU f

unabashed /ˌʌnəˈbæʃt/ adj **he seemed quite ~** il ne semblait aucunement décontenancé

unabated /ˌʌnəˈbeɪtɪd/ adj **to continue ~** [*fighting, storm*] continuer avec la même violence

unable /ʌnˈeɪbl/ adj **to be ~ to do** (lacking means or opportunity) ne pas pouvoir faire; (lacking knowledge or skill) ne pas savoir faire; (incapable, not qualified) être incapable de faire

unabridged /ˌʌnəˈbrɪdʒd/ adj intégral

unacceptable /ˌʌnəkˈseptəbl/ adj [*proposal, suggestion*] inacceptable; [*behaviour, situation*] inadmissible

unaccompanied /ˌʌnəˈkʌmpənɪd/ adj [*child, baggage*] non accompagné; [*man, woman*] seul; Mus sans accompagnement

unaccountable /ˌʌnəˈkaʊntəbl/ adj [*phenomenon, feeling*] inexplicable

unaccounted /ˌʌnəˈkaʊntɪd/ adj **to be ~ for** gen être introuvable; **two of the crew are still ~ for** deux membres de l'équipage sont toujours portés disparus

unaccustomed /ˌʌnəˈkʌstəmd/ adj [*luxury, speed, position*] inhabituel/-elle; **to be ~ to sth/to doing** ne pas avoir l'habitude de qch/de faire

unacknowledged /ˌʌnəkˈnɒlɪdʒd/ adj [*genius, contribution*] non reconnu; **her letter remained ~** on n'a pas accusé réception de sa lettre

unacquainted /ˌʌnəˈkweɪntɪd/ adj **to be ~ with sth/sb** ne pas connaître qch/qn; **to be ~ with the facts** ne pas être au courant des faits

unadorned /ˌʌnəˈdɔːnd/ adj [*walls*] sans ornement; **the plain ~ facts** les faits tout simples

unadulterated /ˌʌnəˈdʌltəreɪtɪd/ adj [*water*] pur; [*wine*] non frelaté; fig [*pleasure, misery*] pur (*before* n); **~ nonsense** des bêtises pures et simples

unadventurous /ˌʌnədˈventʃərəs/ adj [*meal*] pas très original; [*person, production, style*] qui manque d'audace

unaffected /ˌʌnəˈfektɪd/ adj 1 (untouched) **to be ~** ne pas être affecté (**by** par); 2 (natural, spontaneous) tout simple

unaffectedly /ˌʌnəˈfektɪdlɪ/ adv sans affectation

unafraid /ˌʌnəˈfreɪd/ adj [*person*] sans peur

unaided /ʌnˈeɪdɪd/
A adj **~ by sth** sans l'aide de qch
B adv [*stand, sit, walk*] sans aide extérieure

unaltered /ʌnˈɔːltəd/ adj inchangé

unambiguous /ˌʌnæmˈbɪgjʊəs/ adj sans équivoque

unambiguously /ˌʌnæmˈbɪgjʊəslɪ/ adv [*define, deny*] sans équivoque; [*interpret*] sans ambiguïté

unambitious /ˌʌnæmˈbɪʃəs/ adj [*person*] sans ambition; [*reform*] modeste; [*novel*] sans prétention

unanimity /ˌjuːnəˈnɪmətɪ/ n unanimité f (**between, among** entre)

u

unanimous /juːˈnænɪməs/ *adj* unanime

unanimously /juːˈnænɪməslɪ/ *adv* [*agree, condemn, approve*] unanimement; [*vote, acquit*] à l'unanimité

unannounced /ˌʌnəˈnaʊnst/ *adv* [*arrive, call*] sans prévenir

unanswerable /ʌnˈɑːnsərəbl, US ʌnˈæn-/ *adj* [*question*] à laquelle il n'y a pas de réponse possible; [*remark, case*] irréfutable

unanswered /ʌnˈɑːnsəd, US ʌnˈæn-/ *adj* [*letter, question*] resté sans réponse

unappealing /ˌʌnəˈpiːlɪŋ/ *adj* peu attrayant

unappetizing /ʌnˈæpɪtaɪzɪŋ/ *adj* peu appétissant

unappreciated /ˌʌnəˈpriːʃɪeɪtɪd/ *adj* [*work of art*] non reconnu; **to feel ∼** se sentir sous-estimé

unappreciative /ˌʌnəˈpriːʃətɪv/ *adj* [*person, audience*] ingrat

unapproachable /ˌʌnəˈprəʊtʃəbl/ *adj* inaccessible

unarmed /ʌnˈɑːmd/ *adj* [*person*] non armé; [*combat*] sans armes

unashamedly /ˌʌnəˈʃeɪmɪdlɪ/ *adv* ouvertement

unasked /ʌnˈɑːskt, US ʌnˈæskt/ *adv* [*come, attend*] sans être invité; **to do sth ∼** faire qch spontanément

unassailable /ˌʌnəˈseɪləbl/ *adj* gen inattaquable; [*optimism, case*] à toute épreuve

unassisted /ˌʌnəˈsɪstɪd/ *adv* sans assistance

unassuming /ˌʌnəˈsjuːmɪŋ, US ˌʌnəˈsuː-/ *adj* modeste

unattached /ˌʌnəˈtætʃt/ *adj* [1] [*part, element*] détaché; fig [*organization*] indépendant; [2] (single) [*person*] célibataire

unattainable /ˌʌnəˈteɪnəbl/ *adj* inaccessible

unattended /ˌʌnəˈtendɪd/ *adj* [*vehicle, dog, child*] laissé sans surveillance

unattractive /ˌʌnəˈtræktɪv/ *adj* [*furniture, characteristic, idea*] peu attrayant; [*person*] peu attirant; [*proposition*] peu intéressant (**to** pour)

unauthorized /ʌnˈɔːθəraɪzd/ *adj* gen fait sans autorisation; [*visit*] interdit

unavailable /ˌʌnəˈveɪləbl/ *adj* [*person*] qui n'est pas disponible; [*information*] qu'on ne peut pas obtenir; **to be ∼ for comment** se refuser à tout commentaire

unavailing /ˌʌnəˈveɪlɪŋ/ *adj* sout [*efforts*] vain

unavoidable /ˌʌnəˈvɔɪdəbl/ *adj* inévitable

unavoidably /ˌʌnəˈvɔɪdəblɪ/ *adv* **he was ∼ detained** il n'a absolument pas pu se libérer

unaware /ˌʌnəˈweə(r)/ *adj* [1] (not informed) **to be ∼ of sth/ that** ignorer qch/que; [2] (not conscious) **to be ∼ of sth** ne pas être conscient de qch; **she was ∼ of his presence** elle ne savait pas qu'il était là; **to be politically ∼** ne pas être politisé

unawares /ˌʌnəˈweəz/ *adv* **to catch** ou **take sb ∼** prendre qn au dépourvu

unbalanced /ʌnˈbælənst/ *adj* [1] [*person, mind*] instable; [2] (biased) [*reporting*] partial; [3] (uneven) [*diet, economy, load*] pas équilibré

unbearable /ʌnˈbeərəbl/ *adj* insupportable

unbearably /ʌnˈbeərəblɪ/ *adv* [1] [*hurt, tingle*] de manière insupportable; [2] (emphatic) [*hot, cynical, tedious*] incroyablement

unbeatable /ʌnˈbiːtəbl/ *adj* imbattable; **it's ∼ value** c'est un prix imbattable

unbeaten /ʌnˈbiːtn/ *adj* [*player, team*] invaincu; [*score, record*] qui n'a pas été battu

unbecoming /ˌʌnbɪˈkʌmɪŋ/ *adj* sout [*garment*] peu seyant; [*behaviour*] inconvenant

unbeknown /ˌʌnbɪˈnəʊn/, **unbeknownst** /ˌʌnbɪˈnəʊnst/ *adv* **∼ to sb** à l'insu de qn

unbelievable /ˌʌnbɪˈliːvəbl/ *adj* incroyable

unbeliever /ˌʌnbɪˈliːvə(r)/ *n* incroyant/-e *m/f*

unbend /ʌnˈbend/ (*prét, pp* **-bent**)
A *vtr* (straighten) détordre
B *vi* devenir moins inflexible

unbending /ʌnˈbendɪŋ/ *adj* inflexible

unbias(s)ed /ʌnˈbaɪəst/ *adj* impartial

unbidden /ʌnˈbɪdn/ *adv* littér **to do sth ∼** faire qch sans en être prié

unbind /ʌnˈbaɪnd/ *vtr* (*prét, pp* **-bound**) délier

unbleached /ʌnˈbliːtʃt/ *adj* [*cloth*] écru; [*flour*] non blanchi

unblock /ʌnˈblɒk/ *vtr* déboucher [*pipe, sink*]

unbolt /ʌnˈbəʊlt/
A *vtr* déverrouiller [*door*]
B **unbolted** *pp adj* **to be ∼ed** ne pas être verrouillé

unborn /ʌnˈbɔːn/ *adj* [*child*] à naître; fig [*generation*] à venir; **her ∼ child** l'enfant qu'elle porte/portait etc

unbounded /ʌnˈbaʊndɪd/ *adj* [*joy*] sans bornes; [*love*] démesuré

unbowed /ʌnˈbaʊd/ *adj* littér invaincu

unbreakable /ʌnˈbreɪkəbl/ *adj* incassable

unbridled /ʌnˈbraɪdld/ *adj* [*imagination*] débridé; [*optimism*] effréné

unbroken /ʌnˈbrəʊkən/ *adj* [1] (uninterrupted) [*sequence, silence, view*] ininterrompu; [*curve*] parfait; **to descend in an ∼ line from** descendre en ligne directe de; [2] (intact) [*pottery*] intact; **it's an ∼ record** le record n'a pas été battu

unbuckle /ʌnˈbʌkl/ *vtr* déboucler [*belt*]; défaire la boucle de [*shoe*]

unburden /ʌnˈbɜːdn/ *v refl* sout **to ∼ oneself** se confier (**to sb** à qn)

unbusinesslike /ʌnˈbɪznɪslaɪk/ *adj* [*person*] qui n'a pas le sens des affaires; [*method, conduct*] peu professionnel/ -elle

unbutton /ʌnˈbʌtn/ *vtr* déboutonner

uncalled-for /ʌnˈkɔːldfɔː(r)/ *adj* [*remark*] déplacé

uncannily /ʌnˈkænɪlɪ/ *adv* (very much) incroyablement; (surprisingly) étrangement

uncanny /ʌnˈkænɪ/ *adj* [1] (strange) [*resemblance*] étrange; [*accuracy*] étonnant; [2] (frightening) troublant

uncared-for /ʌnˈkeədfɔː(r)/ *adj* [*house*] mal entretenu; [*pet*] mal soigné; **an ∼ child** un enfant dont on s'occupe mal

uncaring /ʌnˈkeərɪŋ/ *adj* [*world*] indifférent

unceasingly /ʌnˈsiːsɪŋlɪ/ *adv* sans cesse

uncensored /ʌnˈsensəd/ *adj* [*film, book*] non censuré; fig [*version*] intégral

unceremonious /ˌʌnˌserɪˈməʊnɪəs/ *adj* [*departure, end*] précipité

unceremoniously /ˌʌnˌserɪˈməʊnɪəslɪ/ *adv* [*dismiss*] sans cérémonie

uncertain /ʌnˈsɜːtn/
A *adj* [1] (unsure) incertain; **to be ∼ about** ne pas être certain de; **to be ∼ whether to stay** ne pas savoir si l'on doit rester; **it is ∼ whether** il n'est pas certain que (+ *subj*); [2] (changeable) [*temper*] instable; [*weather*] variable
B **in no ∼ terms** *adv phr* [*state*] en termes on ne peut plus clairs

uncertainty /ʌnˈsɜːtntɪ/ *n* incertitude *f* (**about** en ce qui concerne)

uncertified /ʌnˈsɜːtɪfaɪd/ *adj* Admin [*document*] non certifié

unchallenged /ˌʌnˈtʃælɪndʒd/ *adj* incontesté; **to go ∼** [*statement, decision*] ne pas être récusé

unchangeable /ʌnˈtʃeɪndʒəbl/ *adj* immuable

unchanged /ʌnˈtʃeɪndʒd/ *adj* inchangé

unchanging /ʌnˈtʃeɪndʒɪŋ/ *adj* immuable

uncharacteristic /ˌʌnkærɪktəˈrɪstɪk/ *adj* [*generosity*] peu habituel/-elle; **it was ∼ of him to...** ce n'est pas son genre de...

uncharitable /ʌnˈtʃærɪtəbl/ *adj* peu charitable (**to do** de faire)

unchecked /ʌnˈtʃekt/
A *adj* [1] (uncontrolled) [*development, proliferation*] incontrôlé; [2] (unverified) non vérifié
B *adv* [*develop, grow, spread*] de manière incontrôlée

uncivil /ʌnˈsɪvɪl/ *adj* discourtois (**to** envers)

uncivilized /ʌnˈsɪvɪlaɪzd/ *adj* [1] (inhumane) [*treatment, conditions*] inhumain; [2] (uncouth, rude) grossier/-ière; [3] (barbarous) [*people, nation*] non civilisé

unclaimed /ʌnˈkleɪmd/ *adj* [*lost property, reward*] non réclamé

unclassified /ʌnˈklæsɪfaɪd/ *adj* [*document, information*] non classifié; [*road*] non classé

uncle /'ʌŋkl/ n oncle m

(Idioms) **Bob's your ~!** GB c'est simple comme bonjour!; **to cry ~** US demander grâce

unclean /ʌn'kli:n/ adj **1** [water, beaches] sale; **2** Relig impur

unclear /ʌn'klɪə(r)/ adj **1** (après v) [motive, reason, circumstances] peu clair; [future] incertain; **it is ~ how/whether...** on ne sait pas très bien comment/si...; **to be ~ about sth** [person] ne pas être sûr de qch; **2** (not comprehensible) [instructions, voice] pas clair; [answer] peu clair; [handwriting] difficile à lire

uncleared /ʌn'klɪəd/ adj [cheque] non compensé; [goods] non dédouané

unclench /ʌn'klentʃ/ vtr desserrer [fist, jaw]

unclog /ʌn'klɒg/ vtr (p prés etc **-gg-**) déboucher [pipe]

uncoil /ʌn'kɔɪl/
A vtr dérouler
B vi [spring] se détendre; [rope, snake] se dérouler

uncollected /ʌnkə'lektɪd/ adj [mail, luggage] non réclamé; [taxes] non perçu; [refuse] non ramassé

uncomfortable /ʌn'kʌmftəbl, US -fərt-/ adj **1** [shoes, seat] inconfortable; [journey, heat] pénible; **you look ~ in that chair** tu n'as pas l'air à l'aise dans ce fauteuil; **the jacket feels ~** la veste n'est pas confortable; **2** (emotionally) [feeling, silence, situation, reminder] pénible; **to be/to feel ~** être/se sentir gêné; **to make sb (feel) ~** mettre qn mal à l'aise; **to be ~ about** se sentir gêné par [rôle, decision, fact]; **I feel ~ talking about it** ça me gêne d'en parler; **to make life** ou **things ~ for sb** rendre la vie difficile à qn

uncomfortably /ʌn'kʌmftəblɪ, US -fərt-/ adv **1** [seated] inconfortablement; [loud, bright] désagréablement; **it's ~ hot** il fait une chaleur pénible; **2** (awkwardly) [say, laugh] d'un air gêné; **to be ~ aware of sth** se rendre compte avec gêne de qch

uncommon /ʌn'kɒmən/ adj rare; **it is not ~ to do it** il n'est pas rare de faire

uncommonly /ʌn'kɒmənlɪ/ adv (very) exceptionnellement; **not ~** (often) assez souvent

uncommunicative /ʌnkə'mju:nɪkətɪv/ adj peu communicatif/-ive; **to be ~ about sth** se montrer réservé sur qch

uncomplaining /ʌnkəm'pleɪnɪŋ/ adj [patience, acceptance] résigné; [person] qui ne se plaint pas

uncomplainingly /ʌnkəm'pleɪnɪŋlɪ/ adv sans se plaindre

uncomplicated /ʌn'kɒmplɪkeɪtɪd/ adj [plot] pas compliqué; [meal] simple

uncomplimentary /ʌnkɒmplɪ'mentrɪ, US -terɪ/ adj peu flatteur/-euse

uncompromising /ʌn'kɒmprəmaɪzɪŋ/ adj [person, attitude] intransigeant; [standards] sans concession

uncompromisingly /ʌn'kɒmprəmaɪzɪŋlɪ/ adv [reply, state] catégoriquement; [harsh] implacablement

unconcealed /ʌnkən'si:ld/ adj non déguisé

unconcerned /ʌnkən'sɜ:nd/ adj (uninterested) indifférent (**with** à); (not caring) insouciant; (untroubled) imperturbable

unconditional /ʌnkən'dɪʃənl/ adj [obedience] inconditionnel/-elle; [offer, surrender] sans condition

unconditionally /ʌnkən'dɪʃənəlɪ/ adv [support, surrender] inconditionnellement; [promise, lend] sans condition

unconfirmed /ʌnkən'fɜ:md/ adj non confirmé

uncongenial /ʌnkən'dʒi:nɪəl/ adj [atmosphere, job] peu agréable; [person] peu sympathique

unconnected /ʌnkə'nektɪd/ adj **1** gen [incidents, facts] sans lien entre eux/elles; **to be ~ with** [event, fact] n'avoir aucun rapport avec; [person] n'avoir aucun lien avec; **2** Elec, Telecom pas branché

unconscious /ʌn'kɒnʃəs/
A n **the ~** l'inconscient m
B adj **1** (insensible) sans connaissance; **to knock sb ~** faire perdre connaissance à qn; **to fall ~** perdre connaissance; **2** (unaware) **to be ~ of sth/of doing** ne pas être conscient de qch/de faire; **3** (unintentional) [bias, impulse, hostility] inconscient

unconsciously /ʌn'kɒnʃəslɪ/ adv inconsciemment

unconsciousness /ʌn'kɒnʃəsnɪs/ n **1** (comatose state) inconscience f; **2** (unawareness) inconscience f

unconstitutional /ˌʌnkɒnstɪ'tju:ʃənl/ adj inconstitutionnel/-elle

uncontested /ˌʌnkən'testɪd/ adj gen incontesté; Pol [seat] non disputé

uncontrollable /ˌʌnkən'trəʊləbl/ adj gen incontrôlable; [tears] qu'on ne peut retenir

uncontrollably /ˌʌnkən'trəʊləblɪ/ adv [laugh, sob] sans pouvoir se contrôler; [increase, decline] irrésistiblement; **his hand shook ~** sa main tremblait de manière incontrôlable

uncontroversial /ˌʌnkɒntrə'vɜ:ʃl/ adj anodin

unconventional /ˌʌnkən'venʃənl/ adj peu conventionnel/-elle

unconvinced /ˌʌnkən'vɪnst/ adj pas convaincu; **to be ~ of sth** ne pas être convaincu de qch; **to be ~ that** ne pas être convaincu que

unconvincing /ˌʌnkən'vɪnsɪŋ/ adj peu convaincant

uncooked /ʌn'kʊkt/ adj non cuit

uncooperative /ˌʌnkəʊ'ɒpərətɪv/ adj peu coopératif/-ive

uncoordinated /ˌʌnkəʊ'ɔ:dɪneɪtɪd/ adj [effort, performance, service] désordonné; **to be ~** [person] manquer de coordination

uncork /ʌn'kɔ:k/ vtr déboucher [bottle, wine]

uncorroborated /ˌʌnkə'rɒbəreɪtɪd/ adj non corroboré; **~ evidence** Jur preuve f par présomption

uncountable /ʌn'kaʊntəbl/ adj Ling indénombrable

uncouple /ʌn'kʌpl/ vtr détacher [wagon]; découpler [locomotive]

uncouth /ʌn'ku:θ/ adj [person] grossier/-ière; [accent] peu raffiné

uncover /ʌn'kʌvə(r)/ vtr **1** (expose) dévoiler [scandal]; **2** (discover) découvrir [evidence, treasure]; **3** (remove covering from) découvrir [body]

uncritical /ʌn'krɪtɪkl/ adj peu critique; **to be ~ of sb/sth** ne pas être critique envers qn/qch

uncritically /ʌn'krɪtɪklɪ/ adv [accept, endorse] sans se poser de questions; [regard] sans faire preuve d'esprit critique

uncross /ʌn'krɒs, US -'krɔ:s/ vtr décroiser [legs, arms]

unctuous /'ʌŋktjʊəs/ adj onctueux/-euse, mielleux/-euse

uncultivated /ʌn'kʌltɪveɪtɪd/ adj (all contexts) inculte

uncut /ʌn'kʌt/ adj **1** [branch, crops] non coupé; **2** [film, version] intégral; **3** [book] aux pages non coupées; [page] non coupé; **4** [gem] non taillé

undamaged /ʌn'dæmɪdʒd/ adj [crops] non endommagé; [building, reputation] intact; **psychologically ~** psychologiquement indemne

undated /ʌn'deɪtɪd/ adj [letter, painting] non daté

undaunted /ʌn'dɔ:ntɪd/ adj imperturbable; **~ by criticism** nullement ébranlé par les critiques

undecided /ʌndɪ'saɪdɪd/ adj [person] indécis; [outcome] incertain; **the jury is ~** le jury n'a pas encore décidé

undeclared /ʌndɪ'kleəd/ adj **1** (illegal) non déclaré; **2** (unspoken) inavoué

undefended /ʌndɪ'fendɪd/ adj **1** [frontier, citizens] non défendu; [chess piece] non protégé; **2** Jur [case] non contesté

undefined /ʌndɪ'faɪnd/ adj **1** [objective] non défini; [nature] indéterminé; [space] vague; **2** Comput indéfini

undelete /ʌndɪ'li:t/ vtr Comput annuler

undelivered /ʌndɪ'lɪvəd/ adj [mail] non distribué

undemanding /ʌndɪ'mɑ:ndɪŋ, US -'mænd-/ adj [task] peu fatigant; [person] peu exigeant

undemocratic /ˌʌndemə'krætɪk/ adj antidémocratique

undemonstrative /ˌʌndɪ'mɒnstrətɪv/ adj peu démonstratif/-ive

undeniable /ˌʌndɪ'naɪəbl/ adj (irrefutable) indéniable; (clear) incontestable

undeniably /ˌʌndɪ'naɪəblɪ/ adv gen incontestablement; [superb, powerful, beautiful] indiscutablement

under /'ʌndə(r)/

When *under* is used as a straightforward preposition in English it can almost always be translated by *sous* in French: *under the table* = sous la table; *under a sheet* = sous un drap; *under a heading* = sous un titre.
   under is often used before a noun in English to mean *subject to* or *affected by* (*under control*, *under fire*, *under oath*, *under review* etc). For translations, consult the appropriate noun entry (**control, fire, oath, review** etc).
   under is also often used as a prefix in combinations such as *undercook*, *underfunded*, *underprivileged* and *undergrowth*, *underpass*. These combinations are treated as headwords in the dictionary.
   For particular usages, see the entry below.

A *prep* **1** (physically beneath or below) sous; ∼ **the bed** sous le lit; ∼ **it** en dessous; **it's ∼ there** c'est là-dessous; **to come out from ∼ sth** sortir de dessous qch; **2** (less than) ∼ **£10** moins de 10 livres sterling; **children ∼ five** les enfants de moins de cinq ans *or* en dessous de cinq ans; **a number ∼ ten** un nombre inférieur à dix; **temperatures ∼ 10°C** des températures inférieures à 10°C; **3** (according to) ∼ **the law** selon la loi; **fined ∼ a rule** condamné à une amende en vertu d'une règle; **4** (subordinate to) sous; **I have 50 people ∼ me** j'ai 50 employés sous mes ordres; **5** (in classification) sous; **do I look for Le Corbusier ∼ 'le' or 'Corbusier'?** est-ce que je dois chercher Le Corbusier sous 'le' ou 'Corbusier'?

B *adv* **1** (physically beneath or below something) [*crawl, sit, hide*] en dessous; **to go ∼** [*diver, swimmer*] disparaître sous l'eau; **2** (less) moins; **£10 and ∼** 10 livres sterling et moins; **children of six and ∼** des enfants de six ans et moins; **to run five minutes ∼** [*event, programme*] durer cinq minutes de moins que prévu; **3** (anaesthetized) **to put sb ∼** endormir qn; **4** (subjugated) **to keep sb ∼** opprimer qn; **5** (below, later in text) **see ∼** voir ci-dessous

underachieve /ˌʌndərəˈtʃiːv/ *vi* Sch ne pas obtenir les résultats dont on est capable

underage /ˌʌndərˈeɪdʒ/ *adj* ∼ **drinker** personne qui consomme de l'alcool sans avoir atteint l'âge légal; **to be ∼** être mineur/-e

underarm /ˈʌndərɑːm/ *adj* [*deodorant*] pour les aisselles; [*hair*] des aisselles; [*service, throw*] à la cuillère

undercarriage /ˈʌndəkærɪdʒ/ *n* Aviat train *m* d'atterrissage

undercharge /ˌʌndəˈtʃɑːdʒ/
A *vtr* faire porter un débit moindre à [*account*]; **he ∼d me for the wine** il m'a fait payer le vin moins cher qu'il n'aurait dû
B *vi* **he ∼d for the wine** il a fait payer le vin moins cher qu'il n'aurait dû

underclassman /ˌʌndəˈklæsmən/ *n* US Sch, Univ étudiant *m* de première année

underclothes /ˈʌndəkləʊðz/ *npl* sous-vêtements *mpl*

undercoat /ˈʌndəkəʊt/ *n* **1** (of paint, varnish) couche *f* de fond; **2** US Aut peinture *f* antirouille pour châssis

undercook /ˌʌndəˈkʊk/ *vtr* ne pas faire assez cuire; **the meat is ∼ed** la viande n'est pas assez cuite

undercover /ˌʌndəˈkʌvə(r)/ *adj* gen clandestin; ∼ **agent** agent *m* secret

undercurrent /ˈʌndəkʌrənt/ *n* **1** (in water) gen courant *m* profond; (in sea) courant *m* sous-marin; **2** fig courant *m* sous-jacent

undercut
A /ˈʌndəkʌt/ *n* **1** GB Culin filet *m*; **2** Sport balle *f* coupée
B /ˌʌndəˈkʌt/ *vtr* (*p prés* **-tt-**; *prét, pp* **-cut**) **1** Comm concurrencer [qn] en offrant des prix plus intéressants; concurrencer [*prices*]; **2** (cut away) miner [*cliff, bank*]; **3** fig saper [*position, efforts*]; couler° [*person*]; **4** Econ réduire [*inflation*]; **5** Sport couper

underdeveloped /ˌʌndədɪˈveləpt/ *adj* [*country*] sous-développé; [*person, physique*] peu développé; Phot pas assez développé

underdog /ˈʌndədɒg, US -dɔːg/ *n* **1** (in society) opprimé/-e *m/f*; **2** (in game, contest) perdant/-e *m/f*

underdone /ˌʌndəˈdʌn/ *adj* [*food*] pas assez cuit; [*steak*] GB saignant

underemployed /ˌʌndərɪmˈplɔɪd/ *adj* [*person*] sous-employé; [*resources, equipment etc*] sous-exploité

underequipped /ˌʌndərɪˈkwɪpt/ *adj* sous-équipé

underestimate /ˌʌndərˈestɪmeɪt/ *vtr* sous-estimer

underexpose /ˌʌndərɪkˈspəʊz/ *vtr* Phot sous-exposer

underfed /ˌʌndəˈfed/ *adj* sous-alimenté

underfeed /ˌʌndəˈfiːd/ *vtr* (*prét, pp* **-fed**) sous-alimenter

underfeeding /ˌʌndəˈfiːdɪŋ/ *n* sous-alimentation *f*

underfloor /ˈʌndəflɔː(r)/ *adj* [*pipes, wiring*] (wooden floor) situé sous le plancher; (concrete floor) situé sous le sol; ∼ **heating** chauffage par le sol

underfoot /ˌʌndəˈfʊt/ *adv* sous les pieds; **the ground was wet ∼** le sol était humide; **to trample sb/sth ∼** lit, fig fouler qn/qch aux pieds

underfunded /ˌʌndəˈfʌndɪd/ *adj* insuffisamment financé

underfunding /ˌʌndəˈfʌndɪŋ/ *n* manque *m* de fonds

undergo /ˌʌndəˈgəʊ/ *vtr* (*prét* **-went**; *pp* **-gone**) subir [*change, test, operation*]; suivre [*treatment, training*]; endurer [*hardship*]; **to ∼ surgery** subir une intervention chirurgicale; **to be ∼ing renovations** être en rénovation

undergraduate /ˌʌndəˈgrædʒʊət/ *n* ≈ étudiant/-e *m/f* (*de première, deuxième ou troisième année*)

underground
A /ˈʌndəgraʊnd/ *n* **1** GB (subway) métro *m*; **on the ∼** dans le métro; **2** (secret movement) mouvement *m* clandestin; **3** Art, Mus, Theat underground *m*
B /ˈʌndəgraʊnd/ *noun modifier* GB [*network*] de métro; [*map, strike*] du métro
C /ˈʌndəgraʊnd/ *adj* **1** (below ground) souterrain; **2** (secret) clandestin; **3** Art, Mus, Theat [*art, film, movement*] underground *inv*
D /ˌʌndəˈgraʊnd/ *adv* **1** (below ground) sous terre; **2** (secretly) **to go ∼** passer dans la clandestinité

undergrowth /ˈʌndəgrəʊθ/ *n* sous-bois *m*

underhand /ˌʌndəˈhænd/ *adj* **1** (*also* US **underhanded**) péj [*person, method*] sournois; **an ∼ trick** un sale coup°; ∼ **dealings** magouilles° *fpl*; **2** Sport **to have an ∼ serve** servir à la cuillère

underlay /ˌʌndəˈleɪ/
A *prét* ▸ **underlie**
B *vtr* (*prét, pp* **-laid**) **to be underlaid by** avoir une sous-couche de [*gravel, rock*]

underlie /ˌʌndəˈlaɪ/ *vtr* (*p prés* **-lying**; *prét* **-lay**; *pp* **-lain**) **1** [*rock*] être sous [*topsoil*]; **2** [*theory*] sous-tendre [*principle, work*]

underline /ˌʌndəˈlaɪn/ *vtr* lit, fig souligner

underling /ˈʌndəlɪŋ/ *n* péj subordonné/-e *m/f*

underlying /ˌʌndəˈlaɪɪŋ/
A *p prés* ▸ **underlie**
B *adj* [*claim*] prioritaire; [*problem*] sous-jacent

undermanned /ˌʌndəˈmænd/ *adj* [*factory*] en sous-effectif *inv*

undermentioned /ˌʌndəˈmenʃnd/ *adj* [*item, list*] ci-dessous; [*person*] nommé ci-dessous; [*name*] cité ci-dessous

undermine /ˌʌndəˈmaɪn/ *vtr* **1** lit saper [*cliff, foundations, road*]; **2** fig (shake, subvert) saper [*authority, efforts*]; ébranler [*confidence, position, value*]

underneath /ˌʌndəˈniːθ/
A *n* dessous *m*
B *adj* d'en dessous
C *adv* lit, fig dessous, en dessous
D *prep* lit, fig sous, au-dessous de; **from ∼ a pile of books** de dessous une pile de livres

undernourished /ˌʌndəˈnʌrɪʃt/ *adj* sous-alimenté

underpaid /ˌʌndəˈpeɪd/ *prét, pp* ▸ **underpay**

underpants /ˈʌndəpænts/ *npl* slip *m*; **a pair of ∼** un slip

underpass /ˈʌndəpɑːs, US -pæs/ *n* **1** (for traffic) voie *f* inférieure (*dans un échangeur*); **2** (for pedestrians) passage *m* souterrain

underpay /ˌʌndəˈpeɪ/ *vtr* (*prét, pp* **-paid**) **1** (pay badly) sous-payer [*employee*]; **2** (pay too little) **I was underpaid this month** je n'ai pas eu mon salaire intégral ce mois-ci

underpin /ˌʌndəˈpɪn/ *vtr* (*p prés etc* **-nn-**) **1** Constr étayer [*wall*]; reprendre [qch] en sous-œuvre, étayer [*building*]; **2** fig (strengthen) être à la base de [*religion, society*]; étayer [*currency, power, theory*]

u

underplay /ˌʌndəˈpleɪ/ vtr **1** gen minimiser [aspect, impact]; **2** Theat jouer [qch] de façon plate [role]

underpopulated /ˌʌndəˈpɒpjʊleɪtɪd/ adj sous-peuplé

underprivileged /ˌʌndəˈprɪvəlɪdʒd/ adj [area, background, person] défavorisé

underproduction /ˌʌndəprəˈdʌkʃn/ n sous-production f

underrate /ˌʌndəˈreɪt/ vtr sous-estimer

underripe /ˌʌndəˈraɪp/ adj (fruit) pas mûr; (cheese) pas fait

underscore /ˈʌndəskɔː(r)/ n Comput caractère m de soulignement

undersea /ˈʌndəsiː/ adj sous-marin

underseal /ˈʌndəsiːl/ n Aut (peinture f) antirouille m

under-secretary /ˌʌndəˈsekrətrɪ, US -terɪ/ n (also ~ **of state**) GB Pol sous-secrétaire mf d'État

undersell /ˌʌndəˈsel/ (prét, pp **-sold**)
A vtr **1** (undercut) vendre moins cher que [competitor]; **2** (sell discreetly) pratiquer une publicité trop discrète pour [product]
B vi vendre à bas prix
C v refl to ~ **oneself** se dévaloriser

undersexed /ˌʌndəˈsekst/ adj to be ~ avoir un faible appétit sexuel

undershirt /ˈʌndəʃɜːt/ n US maillot m de corps

undershoot /ˌʌndəˈʃuːt/ (prét, pp **-shot**)
A vtr se poser avant [runway]
B vi [aircraft] atterrir trop court; [pilot] se présenter trop court

undersigned /ˌʌndəˈsaɪnd/ n soussigné/-e m/f; **we, the ~** nous, soussignés

undersized /ˌʌndəˈsaɪzd/ adj [person] chétif/-ive; [portion, ration] maigre (before n); [animal, plant] rachitique

understaffed /ˌʌndəˈstɑːft, US -ˈstæft/ adj to be ~ manquer de personnel

understand /ˌʌndəˈstænd/ (prét, pp **-stood**)
A vtr **1** (intellectually) comprendre; **is that understood?** c'est compris?; **to ~ that/how** comprendre que/comment; **I can't ~ why** je n'arrive pas à comprendre pourquoi; **to make oneself understood** se faire comprendre; **2** (emotionally) comprendre; **I don't ~ you** je ne te comprends pas; **to ~ sb doing** comprendre que qn fasse; **3** (interpret) comprendre; **as I ~ it** si je comprends bien; **I understood him to say** ou **as saying** que... j'ai compris qu'il disait que...; **4** (believe) **to ~ that** croire que; **it was understood that on** pensait que; **he was given to ~ that** on lui a donné à entendre que; **you won I ~** vous avez gagné si je comprends bien; **5** (accept mutually) **to be understood** être entendu; **I thought that was understood** je pensais que c'était entendu; **6** Ling (imply) **to be understood** [subject] être sous-entendu
B vi **1** (comprehend) comprendre (about à propos de); **2** (sympathize) comprendre; **I quite ~** je comprends tout à fait

understandable /ˌʌndəˈstændəbl/ adj compréhensible; **it's ~** ça se comprend, c'est compréhensible

understandably /ˌʌndəˈstændəblɪ/ adv naturellement

understanding /ˌʌndəˈstændɪŋ/
A n **1** (grasp of subject, issue) compréhension f; **to show an ~ of** faire preuve d'une bonne compréhension de; **2** (perception, interpretation) interprétation f; **our ~ was that** nous avions compris que; **3** (arrangement) entente f (about sur; between entre); **there is an ~ that** il est entendu que; **on that ~** sur cette base; **4** (sympathy) compréhension f; **5** (powers of reason) entendement m
B adj [tone] bienveillant; [person] compréhensif/-ive

understandingly /ˌʌndəˈstændɪŋlɪ/ adv avec bienveillance

understatement /ˈʌndəsteɪtmənt/ n **1** (remark) litote f, euphémisme m; **that's an ~!** c'est le moins qu'on puisse dire!; **2** ȼ (style) (of person) réserve f, sens m de la litote; **3** (subtlety) (of dress, decor) discrétion f

understood /ˌʌndəˈstʊd/ prét, pp ▸ **understand**

understudy /ˈʌndəstʌdɪ/ n Theat doublure f (to de)

undertake /ˌʌndəˈteɪk/ vtr (prét **-took**; pp **-taken**) **1** (carry out) entreprendre [search, study, trip]; occuper [function]; se charger de [mission, offensive]; **2** (guarantee) **to ~ to do** s'engager à faire

undertaker /ˈʌndəteɪkə(r)/ n **1** (person) entrepreneur m de pompes funèbres; **2** (company) entreprise f de pompes

funèbres; **at the ~'s** aux pompes funèbres

undertaking /ˌʌndəˈteɪkɪŋ/ n **1** (venture) entreprise f; **2** (promise) garantie f; **to give sb an ~ that** promettre à qn que; **to give a written ~ to do** s'engager par écrit à faire; **3** (company) entreprise f; **4** ȼ (funeral business) pompes fpl funèbres

under-the-counter adj [goods, supply, trade] illicite; [payment] sous le manteau

undertone /ˈʌndətəʊn/ n **1** (low voice) voix f basse; **in an ~** à voix basse; **2** (undercurrent) un relent de jalousie; **comic ~s** un côté comique; **3** (hint) nuance f

undertow /ˈʌndətəʊ/ n **1** (of wave) reflux m; **2** (at sea) contre-courant m; **3** (influence) influence f sous-jacente

undervalue /ˌʌndəˈvæljuː/ vtr **1** Fin sous-évaluer; **2** (not appreciate) sous-estimer [person, quality]; ne pas apprécier [qch] à sa juste valeur [opinion, theory]

undervoltage /ˈʌndəvəʊltɪdʒ/ n Elec sous-tension f

underwater /ˌʌndəˈwɔːtə(r)/
A adj [cable, exploration, test, world] sous-marin; [lighting] sous l'eau; [birth] dans l'eau
B adv sous l'eau

underway /ˌʌndəˈweɪ/ adj to be ~ [vehicle] être en route; [filming, talks] être en cours; **to get ~** [vehicle] se mettre en route; [preparation, season] commencer; **to get sth ~** mettre qch en route

underwear /ˈʌndəweə(r)/ n ȼ sous-vêtements mpl

underweight /ˌʌndəˈweɪt/ adj maigre; **this child is four kilos ~** il manque quatre kilos à cet enfant

underwent /ˌʌndəˈwent/ prét ▸ **undergo**

underwired /ˌʌndəˈwaɪəd/ adj [bodice, bra] à armature

underworld /ˈʌndəwɜːld/ n **1** (criminal world) milieu m, pègre f; **the criminal ~** le milieu; **2** Mythol **the ~** les enfers mpl

underwrite /ˌʌndəˈraɪt/ vtr (prét **-wrote**; pp **-written**) **1** (in insurance) garantir, souscrire [policy]; souscrire [risk]; assurer [property]; **2** Fin financer [project]; prendre en charge [expense, loss]; **3** (approve) donner son accord à [decision]; soutenir [proposal, theory]

underwriter /ˈʌndəraɪtə(r)/ n **1** Fin (of share issue) soumissionnaire m; **2** (in insurance) assureur m, souscripteur m

undeservedly /ˌʌndɪˈzɜːvɪdlɪ/ adv [blame, punish] injustement; [praise, reward, win] de façon imméritée

undeserving /ˌʌndɪˈzɜːvɪŋ/ adj ~ **of praise** indigne de louanges

undesirable /ˌʌndɪˈzaɪərəbl/
A n indésirable mf
B adj [aspect, habit, result] indésirable; [influence] néfaste; [friend] peu recommandable; **it is ~ to do** il n'est pas souhaitable de faire; ~ **alien** Jur étranger/-ère m/f indésirable

undetected /ˌʌndɪˈtektɪd/
A adj [intruder] inaperçu; [cancer] non décélé; [flaw, movement] non détecté; [crime] non découvert
B adv [break in, listen] sans être aperçu; **to go ~** [person] rester inaperçu; [cancer] rester non décélé; [crime] rester non découvert

undetermined /ˌʌndɪˈtɜːmɪnd/ adj **1** (unknown) indéterminé; **2** (unresolved) [problem] indéterminé; [outcome] inconnu

undeterred /ˌʌndɪˈtɜːd/ adj to be ~ **by sth/sb** ne pas se laisser démonter par qch/qn

undeveloped /ˌʌndɪˈveləpt/ adj [person, fruit] chétif/-ive; [limb, organ] atrophié; [land] inexploité; [idea, theory] en état de germe; [country] sous-développé

undid /ʌnˈdɪd/ prét ▸ **undo**

undignified /ʌnˈdɪɡnɪfaɪd/ adj [behaviour, fate, person] indigne; [haste, language] choquant; [position] inélégant

undiluted /ˌʌndaɪˈljuːtɪd/ adj [liquid, version] non dilué; [admiration] sans retenue; [hostility, passion] sans mélange; [Christianity, Marxism] à l'état pur

undiminished /ˌʌndɪˈmɪnɪʃt/ adj gen intact; [appeal] toujours aussi fort

undimmed /ʌnˈdɪmd/ adj [beauty, memory] intact; [eyesight] parfait

undiplomatic /ˌʌndɪpləˈmætɪk/ adj he is ~ il manque de diplomatie; **it was ~ of you to say that** ce n'était pas diplomatique de votre part de dire cela

undipped /ʌn'dɪpt/ adj Aut **with ~ headlights** en pleins phares

undisciplined /ʌn'dɪsɪplɪnd/ adj indiscipliné

undiscovered /ˌʌndɪs'kʌvəd/ adj [secret] non révélé; [land] inexploré; [species] inconnu; [crime, document] non découvert; [talent] méconnu

undiscriminating /ˌʌndɪ'skrɪmɪneɪtɪŋ/ adj sans discernement

undisguised /ˌʌndɪs'gaɪzd/ adj [anger, curiosity] non déguisé (after n)

undisputed /ˌʌndɪ'spju:tɪd/ adj [capital, champion, leader] incontesté; [fact, right] incontestable

undistinguished /ˌʌndɪ'stɪŋgwɪʃt/ adj [career, building] médiocre; [appearance, person] insignifiant

undisturbed /ˌʌndɪ'stɜːbd/ adj (peaceful) [sleep, night] paisible, tranquille; **to work ~ by the noise** travailler sans être dérangé par le bruit

undivided /ˌʌndɪ'vaɪdɪd/ adj [loyalty] entier/-ière; **to give sb one's ~ attention** accorder à qn toute son attention

undo /ʌn'duː/ vtr (3ᵉ pers sg prés **-does**; prét **-did**; pp **-done**) **1** (unfasten) défaire [fastening, lock]; ouvrir [zip, parcel]; **2** (cancel out) détruire [good, effort]; réparer [harm]; **3** Comput annuler

(Idiom) **what's done cannot be undone** ce qui est fait est fait

undone /ʌn'dʌn/
A pp ▸ undo
B adj **1** (not fastened) [parcel, button] défait; **to come ~** se défaire; **2** (not done) **to leave sth ~** ne pas faire qch

undoubtedly /ʌn'daʊtɪdlɪ/ adv indubitablement

undress /ˌʌn'dres/
A vtr déshabiller; **to ~ oneself** se déshabiller
B vi se déshabiller

undressed /ʌn'drest/ adj **1** gen déshabillé; **to get ~** se déshabiller; **2** Culin sans assaisonnement; **3** Constr [metal, stone] à nu

undrinkable /ʌn'drɪŋkəbl/ adj **1** (unpleasant) imbuvable; **2** (dangerous) non potable

undue /ʌn'djuː, US -'duː/ adj excessif/-ive

undulate /'ʌndjʊleɪt, US -dʒʊ-/
A vi onduler
B **undulating** pres p adj [movement] sinueux/-euse; [surface, landscape] onduleux/-euse; [plants] ondoyant

unduly /ˌʌn'djuːlɪ, US -'duːlɪ/ adv [concerned, optimistic, surprised] excessivement; [flatter, worry] outre mesure

undying /ʌn'daɪɪŋ/ adj [love] éternel/-elle

unearned /ʌn'ɜːnd/ adj **1** gen immérité; **2** Fin **~ income** rentes fpl

unearthly /ʌn'ɜːθlɪ/ adj **1** [apparition, light, sight] surnaturel/-elle; [cry, silence] étrange; [beauty] immatériel/-ielle; **2** (unreasonable) **at an ~ hour** à une heure indue

uneasily /ʌn'iːzɪlɪ/ adv **1** (anxiously) avec inquiétude; **2** (uncomfortably) avec gêne; **3** (with difficulty) avec difficulté

uneasiness /ʌn'iːzɪnɪs/ n **1** (worry) appréhension f (about au sujet de); **2** (dissatisfaction) malaise m

uneasy /ʌn'iːzɪ/ adj **1** (worried) [person] inquiet/-iète (about, at au sujet de); [conscience] pas tranquille; **I had an ~ feeling that** j'avais le sentiment désagréable que; **2** (precarious) [compromise] difficile; [alliance, peace] boiteux/-euse; [silence] gêné; **3** (agitated) [sleep] agité; **4** (ill at ease) mal à l'aise

uneconomical /ˌʌnˌiːkə'nɒmɪkl, -ˌekə-/ adj **1** (wasteful) pas économique; **2** (not profitable) pas rentable

uneducated /ʌn'edʒʊkeɪtɪd/ adj **1** [person] sans instruction; **2** péj [person, speech] inculte; [accent, tastes] commun

unemotional /ˌʌnɪ'məʊʃənl/ adj [person, approach] impassible; [reunion] froid; [account] qui n'appelle pas aux sentiments

unemployed /ˌʌnɪm'plɔɪd/
A n **the ~** (+ v pl) les chômeurs mpl
B adj **1** (out of work) au chômage, sans emploi; **~ people** chômeurs mpl; **2** Fin [capital] inutilisé

unemployment /ˌʌnɪm'plɔɪmənt/ n chômage m; **with ~ at 20%** avec un chômage de 20%

unemployment: **~ benefit** GB, **~ compensation** US allocations fpl de chômage; **~ figures** npl chiffres mpl du chômage

unending /ʌn'endɪŋ/ adj sans fin

unenterprising /ʌn'entəpraɪzɪŋ/ adj [person, organization, behaviour] sans initiative; [decision, policy] timide

unenthusiastic /ˌʌnɪnˌθjuːzɪ'æstɪk, US -ˌθuːz-/ adj peu enthousiaste (**about** au sujet de)

unenviable /ʌn'envɪəbl/ adj peu enviable

unequal /ʌn'iːkwəl/ adj **1** (not equal) [amounts, contest, pay] inégal; **2** (inadequate) **to be ~ to** ne pas être à la hauteur de [task]

unequalled, unequaled US /ʌn'iːkwəld/ adj [achievement, quality, record] inégalé; [person] incomparable (**as** en tant que)

unequivocal /ˌʌnɪ'kwɪvəkl/ adj [person, declaration] explicite; [attitude, answer, pleasure, support] sans équivoque

unerring /ʌn'ɜːrɪŋ/ adj infaillible

Unesco, UNESCO /juː'neskəʊ/ pr n (abrév = **United Nations Educational, Scientific and Cultural Organization**) UNESCO f

unethical /ʌn'eθɪkl/ adj **1** gen, Comm contraire à la morale (**to do** de faire); **2** Med contraire à la déontologie (**to do** de faire)

uneven /ʌn'iːvn/ adj **1** (variable) [colouring, hem, results, rhythm, teeth] irrégulier/-ière; [contest, performance, surface] inégal; [voice] tremblant; **2** Sport **~ bars** barres fpl asymétriques

uneventful /ˌʌnɪ'ventfl/ adj [day, occasion, life, career] ordinaire; [journey, period] sans histoires; [place] où il ne se passe rien

unexciting /ˌʌnɪk'saɪtɪŋ/ adj sans intérêt

unexpected /ˌʌnɪk'spektɪd/
A n **the ~** l'imprévu m
B adj [arrival, danger, event, success] imprévu; [ally, gift, outcome, announcement] inattendu; [death, illness] inopiné

unexpectedly /ˌʌnɪk'spektɪdlɪ/ adv [happen] à l'improviste; [large, small, fast] étonnamment

unexplored /ˌʌnɪk'splɔːd/ adj inexploré

unexposed /ˌʌnɪk'spəʊzd/ adj Phot vierge

unfailing /ʌn'feɪlɪŋ/ adj [support] fidèle; [kindness, optimism] à toute épreuve; [efforts] constant; [source] intarissable

unfair /ʌn'feə(r)/ adj [person, action, decision, advantage] injuste (**to, on** envers; **to do** de faire); [play, tactics] irrégulier/-ière; [trading] frauduleux/-euse; [competition] déloyal

unfair dismissal n Jur licenciement m abusif

unfairly /ʌn'feəlɪ/ adv [treat] injustement; [play] irrégulièrement; [critical] injustement; **to be ~ dismissed** Jur faire l'objet d'un licenciement abusif

unfairness /ʌn'feənɪs/ n injustice f

unfaithful /ʌn'feɪθfl/ adj [partner] infidèle (**to** à)

unfaithfulness /ʌn'feɪθflnɪs/ n infidélité f

unfaltering /ʌn'fɔːltərɪŋ/ adj [step, voice] assuré; [devotion, loyalty] à toute épreuve

unfamiliar /ˌʌnfə'mɪlɪə(r)/ adj **1** (strange) [face, name, place] peu familier/-ière (**to** à); [appearance, concept, feeling, situation] inhabituel/-elle (**to** à); [artist, subject] mal connu; **2** **to be ~ with sth** mal connaître qch

unfamiliarity /ˌʌnfəmɪlɪ'ærətɪ/ n **1** (strangeness) caractère m insolite; **2** **his ~ with sth** sa mauvaise connaissance de qch

unfashionable /ʌn'fæʃənəbl/ adj qui n'est pas à la mode

unfasten /ʌn'fɑːsn/ vtr défaire [clothing, button]; ouvrir [bag, zip]

unfathomable /ʌn'fæðəməbl/ adj littér insondable liter

unfavourable /ʌn'feɪvərəbl/ adj défavorable (**for sth** à qch; **to** à)

unfeeling /ʌn'fiːlɪŋ/ adj [person] insensible (**towards** envers); [remark] dépourvu de tact; [attitude, behaviour] froid

unfettered /ʌn'fetəd/ adj [liberty, right, competition, market] sans entraves; [emotion, expression, power] sans retenue

unfinished /ʌn'fɪnɪʃt/ adj [work, product] inachevé; [matter] en cours; **we have some ~ business** nous avons des choses à régler

unfit /ʌn'fɪt/ adj **1** (unhealthy) (ill) malade; (out of condition) **I'm ~** physiquement, je ne suis pas en forme; **2** (sub-standard)

u

[housing] inadéquat; [pitch, road] impraticable (for à); ~ for human habitation/consumption impropre à l'habitation/la consommation humaine; ③ (unsuitable) [parent] inapte; ~ for work inapte au travail; ~ to run the country inapte à gouverner le pays; ④ Jur incapable; to be ~ to give evidence être inapte à témoigner

unflagging /ʌnˈflæɡɪŋ/ adj [energy] infatigable; [interest] inlassable

unflappable○ /ʌnˈflæpəbl/ adj imperturbable

unflattering /ʌnˈflætərɪŋ/ adj [clothes, portrait] peu flatteur/-euse; to be ~ to sb [clothes, hairstyle] ne pas avantager qn; [portrait, description] ne pas flatter qn

unflatteringly /ʌnˈflætərɪŋlɪ/ adv d'une manière peu flatteuse

unflinching /ʌnˈflɪntʃɪŋ/ adj ① [stare] impassible; [courage] à toute épreuve; [commitment] inébranlable; ② [account] impitoyable

unflinchingly /ʌnˈflɪntʃɪŋlɪ/ adv inébranlablement

unfold /ʌnˈfəʊld/
A vtr ① (open) déplier [paper]; déployer [wings]; décroiser [arms]; ② fig dévoiler [plan]
B vi ① [deckchair, map] se déplier; [flower, leaf] s'ouvrir; ② fig [scene] se dérouler; [mystery] se dévoiler

unforeseeable /ˌʌnfɔːˈsiːəbl/ adj imprévisible

unforeseen /ˌʌnfɔːˈsiːn/ adj imprévu

unforgettable /ˌʌnfəˈɡetəbl/ adj inoubliable

unforgivable /ˌʌnfəˈɡɪvəbl/ adj impardonnable

unforgivably /ˌʌnfəˈɡɪvəblɪ/ adv ~ rude/biased d'une grossièreté/d'un parti pris impardonnable

unforgiving /ˌʌnfəˈɡɪvɪŋ/ adj impitoyable

unformed /ʌnˈfɔːmd/ adj [idea, belief] informe; [personality] pas encore formé

unforthcoming /ˌʌnfɔːθˈkʌmɪŋ/ adj réservé (about au sujet de)

unfortunate /ʌnˈfɔːtʃənət/ adj ① (pitiable) malheureux/-euse; ② (regrettable) [incident, choice] malencontreux/-euse; [remark] fâcheux/-euse; ③ (unlucky) malchanceux/-euse; to be ~ enough to do avoir la malchance de faire

unfortunately /ʌnˈfɔːtʃənətlɪ/ adv [end] fâcheusement; [worded] malencontreusement; ~, she... malheureusement, elle...

unfounded /ʌnˈfaʊndɪd/ adj sans fondement

unfreeze /ʌnˈfriːz/ (prét **-froze**; pp **-frozen**) vtr ① faire dégeler [pipe]; ② Fin libérer [prices]; débloquer [assets]; ③ Comput libérer

unfriendly /ʌnˈfrendlɪ/ adj [person, attitude] peu amical, inamical; [reception] hostile; [place, climate] inhospitalier/-ière; [remark] malveillant; [product] nocif/-ive

unfroze /ʌnˈfrəʊz/ prét ▸ unfreeze

unfrozen /ʌnˈfrəʊzn/ pp ▸ unfreeze

unfulfilled /ˌʌnfʊlˈfɪld/ adj [ambition] non réalisé; [desire, need] inassouvi; [promise] non tenu; [condition] non rempli; [prophecy] inaccompli; to feel ~ se sentir insatisfait

unfurnished /ʌnˈfɜːnɪʃt/ adj [accommodation] non meublé

ungainly /ʌnˈɡeɪnlɪ/ adj gauche, maladroit

ungenerous /ʌnˈdʒenərəs/ adj ① (mean) peu généreux/-euse (to envers); ② (unsympathetic) dur (towards envers); that was ~ of you ce n'était pas très charitable de ta part

ungentlemanly /ʌnˈdʒentlmənlɪ/ adj discourtois (of de la part de)

ungodly /ʌnˈɡɒdlɪ/ adj gen impie; at some ~ hour à une heure indue

ungovernable /ʌnˈɡʌvənəbl/ adj ① [country, people] ingouvernable; ② [desire, anger] indomptable

ungracious /ʌnˈɡreɪʃəs/ adj désobligeant (of de la part de)

ungrammatical /ˌʌnɡrəˈmætɪkl/ adj incorrect

ungrateful /ʌnˈɡreɪtfl/ adj ingrat (of de la part de; towards envers)

ungrudging /ʌnˈɡrʌdʒɪŋ/ adj [support] inconditionnel/-elle; [praise] sincère

unguarded /ʌnˈɡɑːdɪd/ adj ① (unprotected) sans surveillance; ② (careless) [remark, criticism] irréfléchi

unhampered /ʌnˈhæmpəd/ adj ~ by sans être encombré par [luggage]; sans être entravé par [red tape]

unhappily /ʌnˈhæpɪlɪ/ adv ① (miserably) d'un air malheureux; ~ married malheureux en mariage; ② (unfortunately) malheureusement; ③ (inappropriately) malencontreusement

unhappiness /ʌnˈhæpɪnɪs/ n ① (misery) tristesse f; ② (dissatisfaction) mécontentement m (about, with au sujet de)

unhappy /ʌnˈhæpɪ/ adj ① (miserable) [person, childhood] malheureux/-euse; [face, occasion] triste; ② (dissatisfied) mécontent; to be ~ about ou with sth ne pas être satisfait de qch; ③ (concerned) inquiet/-iète (about à propos de); to be ~ about doing ne pas aimer faire; to be ~ at the idea that être contrarié par l'idée que; ④ (unfortunate) [situation, choice] malheureux/-euse

unharmed /ʌnˈhɑːmd/ adj [person] indemne; [object] intact

unhealthy /ʌnˈhelθɪ/ adj ① Med, fig [person, cough] maladif/-ive; [economy, diet] malsain; [conditions] insalubre; ② (unwholesome) malsain

unheard-of /ʌnˈhɜːdɒv/ adj ① (shocking) inouï; ② (previously unknown) [levels, price] record inv; [actor, brand] inconnu; previously ~ inconnu jusqu'alors

unheated /ʌnˈhiːtɪd/ adj non chauffé

unheeded /ʌnˈhiːdɪd/ adj to go ~ [warning, plea] rester vain

unhelpful /ʌnˈhelpfl/ adj [employee] peu serviable; [witness] peu coopératif/-ive; [remark] qui n'apporte rien d'utile; [attitude] peu obligeante

unhesitating /ʌnˈhezɪteɪtɪŋ/ adj spontané

unhide /ʌnˈhaɪd/ vtr (prét **-hid**; pp **-hidden**) Comput afficher

unhindered /ʌnˈhɪndəd/ adj [access] libre; [freedom] total; ~ by sans être entravé par [rules]; sans être encombré par [luggage]

unhinge /ʌnˈhɪndʒ/ vtr (p prés **-hingeing**) ① lit enlever [qch] de ses gonds [door]; ② ○fig déstabiliser [person, mind]

unholy /ʌnˈhəʊlɪ/ adj ① (shocking) [alliance, pact] contre nature; ② (horrendous) épouvantable; ③ (profane) impie

unhook /ʌnˈhʊk/ vtr dégrafer [skirt]; décrocher [picture] (from de)

unhopeful /ʌnˈhəʊpfl/ adj [person] pessimiste; [situation] guère encourageant; [outlook, start] guère prometteur/-euse

unhurried /ʌnˈhʌrɪd/ adj [person] posé; [pace, meal] tranquille

unhurt /ʌnˈhɜːt/ adj indemne

unhygienic /ˌʌnhaɪˈdʒiːnɪk/ adj [conditions] insalubre; [way, method] peu hygiénique

UNICEF /ˈjuːnɪsef/ n (abrév = **United Nations Children's Fund**) UNICEF m, FISE m

unicorn /ˈjuːnɪkɔːn/ n licorne f

unidentified /ˌʌnaɪˈdentɪfaɪd/ adj non identifié

unification /ˌjuːnɪfɪˈkeɪʃn/ n unification f (of de)

uniform /ˈjuːnɪfɔːm/
A n uniforme m; out of ~ Mil en civil
B adj [temperature] constant; [shape, size, colour] identique

uniformity /ˌjuːnɪˈfɔːmətɪ/ n uniformité f

unify /ˈjuːnɪfaɪ/ vtr unifier

unilateral /ˌjuːnɪˈlætrəl/ adj unilatéral

unimaginable /ˌʌnɪˈmædʒɪnəbl/ adj inimaginable

unimaginably /ˌʌnɪˈmædʒɪnəblɪ/ adv incroyablement

unimaginative /ˌʌnɪˈmædʒɪnətɪv/ adj [person] sans imagination; [style, production] sans originalité; to be ~ manquer d'imagination

unimaginatively /ˌʌnɪˈmædʒɪnətɪvlɪ/ adv [talk, write, describe] platement; [captain, manage] sans brio

unimpaired /ˌʌnɪmˈpeəd/ adj intact

unimpeachable /ˌʌnɪmˈpiːtʃəbl/ adj irréprochable; Jur non récusable

unimpeded /ˌʌnɪmˈpiːdɪd/ adj [access, influx] libre; to be ~ by sth ne pas être entravé par qch

unimportant /ˌʌnɪmˈpɔːtnt/ adj sans importance (for, to pour)

unimpressed /ˌʌnɪmˈprest/ adj (by person, performance) peu enthousiaste; to be ~ by être peu impressionné par [*person, performance*]; n'être guère convaincu par [*argument*]

uninformative /ˌʌnɪnˈfɔːmətɪv/ *adj* **to be ~** ne rien apporter

uninformed /ˌʌnɪnˈfɔːmd/ *adj* [*person*] sous-informé (**about** quant à); **the ~ reader** le non-spécialiste

uninhabitable /ˌʌnɪnˈhæbɪtəbl/ *adj* inhabitable

uninhibited /ˌʌnɪnˈhɪbɪtɪd/ *adj* [*attitude, person*] sans complexes (**about** en ce qui concerne); [*performance, remarks*] sans retenue; **to be ~ about doing** n'avoir aucun complexe à faire

uninitiated /ˌʌnɪˈnɪʃɪeɪtɪd/
A *n* **the ~** (+ *v pl*) le profane (+ *v sg*)
B *adj* [*person*] non initié (**into** dans)

uninjured /ʌnˈɪndʒəd/ *adj* indemne; **to escape ~** sortir indemne

uninspired /ˌʌnɪnˈspaɪəd/ *adj* [*approach, team, times*] terne; [*performance*] honnête; [*budget, syllabus*] sans imagination; **to be ~** [*person*] manquer d'inspiration; [*strategy*] manquer d'imagination

uninstal(l) /ˌʌnɪnˈstɔːl/ *vtr* Comput désinstaller [*software*]

uninsured /ˌʌnɪnˈʃɔːd, US ˌʌnɪnˈʃʊəd/ *adj* non assuré

unintelligible /ˌʌnɪnˈtelɪdʒəbl/ *adj* incompréhensible (**to** pour)

unintended /ˌʌnɪnˈtendɪd/ *adj* [*slur, irony*] involontaire; [*consequence*] non voulu; **to be ~** ne pas être voulu

unintentional /ˌʌnɪnˈtenʃənl/ *adj* involontaire

uninterested /ʌnˈɪntrəstɪd/ *adj* indifférent (**in** à)

uninteresting /ʌnˈɪntrəstɪŋ/ *adj* sans intérêt

uninvited /ˌʌnɪnˈvaɪtɪd/ *adj* **1** (unsolicited) [*attentions*] non sollicité; [*remark*] gratuit; **2** (without invitation) **~ guest** intrus/-e *m/f*

uninviting /ˌʌnɪnˈvaɪtɪŋ/ *adj* [*place, prospect*] rébarbatif/ -ive; [*food*] peu appétissant

union /ˈjuːnɪən/
A *n* **1** (*also* **trade ~**) Ind syndicat *m*; **to join a ~** se syndiquer; **2** Pol union *f*; **3** (uniting) union *f*; (marriage) union *f*, mariage *m*; **4** (*also* **student ~**) GB Univ (building) maison *f* des étudiants; (organization) syndicat *m* d'étudiants
B **Union** *pr n* US Pol États-Unis *mpl*; US Hist Union *f*
C *noun modifier* Ind [*card, movement*] syndical

union: **~ bashing** *n* Ind attaques *fpl* contre le pouvoir des syndicats; **~ dues** *npl* cotisation *f* syndicale

Unionist /ˈjuːnɪənɪst/ *n, adj* Pol unioniste (*mf*)

unionize /ˈjuːnɪənaɪz/ *vtr* Ind syndicaliser

union: **Union Jack** *n* drapeau *m* du Royaume-Uni; **~ member** *n* Ind syndiqué/-e *m/f*; **Union of Soviet Socialist Republics**, **USSR** *pr n* Hist Union *f* des Républiques Socialistes Soviétiques, URSS *f*; **~ shop** *n* US Ind *établissement dont tous les employés doivent être ou devenir membres d'un même syndicat*

unique /juːˈniːk/ *adj* **1** (sole) unique (**in that** en ce que); **to be ~ in doing** être seul à faire; **to be ~ to** être particulier à; **2** (remarkable) [*individual, skill*] unique, exceptionnel/ -elle

unisex /ˈjuːnɪseks/ *adj* unisexe

unison /ˈjuːnɪsn, ˈjuːnɪzn/ *n* **in ~** [*say, recite, sing*] à l'unisson

unit /ˈjuːnɪt/ *n* **1** (whole) unité *f*; **2** (group with specific function) gen groupe *m*; (in army, police) unité *f*; **3** (building, department) gen, Med service *m*; Ind unité *f*; **casualty ~** service des urgences; **production ~** unité de production; **4** (in measurements) also Math unité *f*; **monetary ~** unité monétaire; **5** (part of machine) unité *f*; **6** (piece of furniture) élément *m*; **7** Univ unité *f* de valeur; **8** Sch (in textbook) unité *f*; **9** US (apartment) appartement *m*

unitary /ˈjuːnɪtrɪ, US -terɪ/ *adj* unitaire

unite /juːˈnaɪt/
A *vtr* unir (**with** à)
B *vi* s'unir (**with** à)

united /juːˈnaɪtɪd/ *adj* [*group, front*] uni (**in** dans); [*effort*] conjoint

Idiom **~ we stand, divided we fall** Prov l'union fait la force Prov

United Arab Emirates ▸ p. 774 *pr npl* Émirats *mpl* arabes unis

United Kingdom (of Great Britain and Northern Ireland) ▸ p. 774 *pr n* Royaume-Uni *m* (de Grande-Bretagne et d'Irlande du Nord)

> **ⓘ United Kingdom** Monarchie constitutionnelle constituée d'une grande île, la Grande-Bretagne, divisée en trois pays : l'Angleterre, l'Écosse et le pays de Galles, à laquelle s'ajoute l'Irlande du Nord.

united: **United Nations (Organization)** *n* (Organisation *f* des) Nations *fpl* unies; **United States (of America)** ▸ p. 774 *pr n* États-Unis *mpl* (d'Amérique)

unit: **~ furniture** *n* mobilier *m* en éléments; **~ trust** *n* GB Fin ≈ société *f* d'investissement à capital variable, SICAV *f*

unity /ˈjuːnətɪ/ *n* unité *f*

Univ *abrév écrite* = **University**

universal /ˌjuːnɪˈvɜːsl/
A *n* Philos universel *m*
B **universals** *npl* Philos universaux *mpl*
C *adj* **1** (general) [*acclaim, reaction*] général; [*education, health care*] pour tous; [*principle, truth, message*] universel/-elle; [*use*] généralisé; **the suggestion gained ~ acceptance** la suggestion a été acceptée par tout le monde; **2** Ling universel/-elle

universally /ˌjuːnɪˈvɜːsəlɪ/ *adv* [*believed, criticized*] par tous, universellement; [*known, loved*] de tous

universal time *n* temps *m* universel

universe /ˈjuːnɪvɜːs/ *n* univers *m*

university /ˌjuːnɪˈvɜːsətɪ/
A *n* université *f*
B *noun modifier* [*degree, town*] universitaire; [*place*] à l'université; **~ entrance** entrée *f* à l'université

unjust /ʌnˈdʒʌst/ *adj* injuste (**to** envers)

unjustifiably /ʌnˈdʒʌstɪfaɪəblɪ/ *adv* [*claim, condemn*] sans justification; [*act*] d'une manière injustifiable

unjustified /ʌnˈdʒʌstɪfaɪd/ *adj* injustifié

unkempt /ʌnˈkempt/ *adj* [*person, appearance*] négligé; [*hair*] ébouriffé; [*beard*] peu soigné

unkind /ʌnˈkaɪnd/ *adj* [*person, thought, act*] pas très gentil/ -ille; [*remark*] hostile; [*climate, environment*] rude; [*fate*] littér cruel/-elle; **it was a bit ~** ce n'était pas très gentil; **it was ~ of her to do** ce n'était pas très gentil de sa part de faire; **to be ~ to sb** (by deed) ne pas être gentil avec qn; (verbally) être méchant avec qn

unkindness /ʌnˈkaɪndnɪs/ *n* (of person) dureté *f*; littér (of fate) cruauté *f*

unknown /ʌnˈnəʊn/
A *n* **1** (unfamiliar place or thing) inconnu *m*; **2** (person not famous) inconnu/-e *m/f*; **3** Math inconnue *f*
B *adj* inconnu; **the place was ~ to me** l'endroit m'était inconnu; **~ to me, they had already left** à mon insu, ils étaient déjà partis; **it is not ~ for sb to do** il arrive à qn de faire; **~ quantity** Math inconnue *f*; **she is an ~ quantity** fig (her abilities are untested) on ne sait pas ce qu'elle vaut; (not much is known about her) on sait peu de choses sur elle; **Mr X, address ~** M. X, adresse inconnue

Unknown Soldier, **Unknown Warrior** *n* Soldat *m* inconnu

unladylike /ʌnˈleɪdɪlaɪk/ *adj* inélégant

unlatch /ʌnˈlætʃ/ *vtr* soulever le loquet de; **to leave the door ~ed** laisser la porte sans (mettre le) loquet

unlawful /ʌnˈlɔːfl/ *adj* [*activity, possession*] illégal; [*killing*] indiscriminé; [*detention*] arbitraire; [*arrest*] (without cause) arbitraire; (with incorrect procedure) sommaire; **~ assembly** Jur rassemblement *m* de nature à troubler l'ordre public

unlawfully /ʌnˈlɔːfəlɪ/ *adv* **1** Jur de façon criminelle; **~ detained** détenu arbitrairement; **2** gen illégalement

unleaded /ʌnˈledɪd/ *adj* [*petrol*] sans plomb

unleash /ʌnˈliːʃ/ *vtr* **1** (release) lâcher [*animal*]; libérer [*aggression*]; déchaîner [*violence, passion*]; déverser [*torrent*]; **2** (trigger) déclencher [*wave, war*]; **3** (launch) lancer [*force, attack*] (**against** contre)

unless /ənˈles/ *conj* **1** (except if) à moins que (+ *subj*), à moins de (+ *infinitive*), sauf si (+ *indic*); **he won't come ~ you invite him** il ne viendra pas à moins que tu (ne) l'invites *or* sauf si tu l'invites; **she can't take the job ~ she finds a nanny** elle ne peut pas accepter le poste à moins de trouver une nourrice; **~ I get my passport back, I can't**

leave the country si je ne récupère pas mon passeport je ne pourrai pas quitter le pays; **it won't work ~ you plug it in!** ça ne marchera pas si tu ne le branches pas!; **~ I'm very much mistaken** si je ne m'abuse *fml or* à moins que je (ne) me trompe; **~ otherwise agreed** sauf accord contraire; **~** (except when) sauf quand

unlicensed /ʌnˈlaɪsnst/ *adj* [*activity*] non autorisé; [*vehicle*] non immatriculé; [*transmitter*] sans licence

unlike /ʌnˈlaɪk/
A *prep* **1** (in contrast to) contrairement à, à la différence de; **2** (different from) différent de; **they are quite ~ each other** ils ne se ressemblent pas du tout; **3** (uncharacteristic of) **it's ~ her (to be so rude)** ça ne lui ressemble pas *or* ce n'est pas du tout son genre (d'être aussi impolie)
B *adj* (*jamais épith*) **the two brothers are ~ in every way** les deux frères ne se ressemblent pas du tout

unlikely /ʌnˈlaɪklɪ/ *adj* **1** (unexpected) improbable, peu probable; **it is ~ that** il est peu probable que (+ *subj*); **they are ~ to succeed** il est peu probable qu'ils réussissent; **2** (strange) [*partner, choice, situation*] inattendu; **3** (probably untrue) [*story*] invraisemblable; [*excuse*] peu probable

unlimited /ʌnˈlɪmɪtɪd/ *adj* illimité

unlined /ʌnˈlaɪnd/ *adj* **1** [*garment, curtain*] sans doublure; **2** [*paper*] non réglé; [*face*] sans rides

unlisted /ʌnˈlɪstɪd/ *adj* **1** gen [*campsite, hotel*] non homologué; **2** Fin [*account*] ne figurant pas sur les registres; [*company, share*] non coté; **3** Telecom **her number is ~** elle n'est pas dans l'annuaire; **4** Constr, Jur [*building*] non classé

unlit /ʌnˈlɪt/ *adj* **1** [*room, street*] non éclairé; **to be ~** ne pas être éclairé; **2** [*cigarette, fire*] non allumé

unload /ʌnˈləʊd/
A *vtr* **1** décharger [*goods, vessel*]; **2** Tech décharger [*gun, camera*]; **3** Comm déverser [*stockpile, goods*] (**on(to)** sur); **4** fig **to ~ one's problems** s'épancher (**on(to)** auprès de)
B *vi* [*truck, ship*] décharger

unloading /ʌnˈləʊdɪŋ/ *n* déchargement *m*

unlock /ʌnˈlɒk/ *vtr* (with key) ouvrir; **to be ~ed** ne pas être fermé à clé

unlovable /ʌnˈlʌvəbl/ *adj* rebutant

unloved /ʌnˈlʌvd/ *adj* **to feel ~** [*person*] se sentir délaissé

unloving /ʌnˈlʌvɪŋ/ *adj* [*person, behaviour*] peu affectueux/-euse

unluckily /ʌnˈlʌkɪlɪ/ *adv* malheureusement (**for** pour)

unlucky /ʌnˈlʌkɪ/ *adj* **1** (unfortunate) [*person*] malchanceux/-euse; [*coincidence, event*] malencontreux/-euse; [*day*] de malchance; **to be ~ enough to do** avoir la malchance de faire; **you were ~ not to get the job** c'est pure malchance que tu n'aies pas obtenu le poste; **he is ~ in love** il n'a jamais de chance en amour; **2** (causing bad luck) néfaste, maléfique; **it's ~ to walk under a ladder** ça porte malheur de marcher sous une échelle

unmade /ʌnˈmeɪd/ *adj* [*bed*] défait; [*road*] non goudronné

unmanageable /ʌnˈmænɪdʒəbl/ *adj* [*child, animal*] farouche; [*prison, system*] ingérable; [*hair*] rebelle; [*size, number*] démesuré

unmanly /ʌnˈmænlɪ/ *adj* pusillanime

unmanned /ʌnˈmænd/ *adj* [*flight, rocket*] non habité; [*train*] automatique; **to leave the desk ~** laisser le bureau sans personne

unmarked /ʌnˈmɑːkt/ *adj* **1** (not labelled) [*container*] sans étiquette; [*police car*] banalisé; **2** (unblemished) [*skin*] sans marques; **3** Ling non marqué; **4** Sport démarqué

unmarketable /ʌnˈmɑːkɪtəbl/ *adj* non commercialisable

unmarried /ʌnˈmærɪd/ *adj* célibataire

unmask /ʌnˈmɑːsk, US -ˈmæsk/ *vtr* lit, fig démasquer

unmentionable /ʌnˈmenʃənəbl/ *adj* **1** (improper to mention) [*activity*] inracontable; [*subject*] tabou; **2** (unspeakable) [*suffering*] indescriptible

unmistakable /ˌʌnmɪˈsteɪkəbl/ *adj* **1** (recognizable) caractéristique (**of** de); **2** (unambiguous) sans ambiguïté; **3** (marked) net/nette

unmistakably /ˌʌnmɪˈsteɪkəblɪ/ *adv* [*smell, hear*] distinctement; [*his, hers*] indubitablement

unmitigated /ʌnˈmɪtɪgeɪtɪd/ *adj* [*disaster*] complet/-ète; [*cruelty*] non tempéré; [*terror, nonsense*] absolu; [*liar*] fini

unmotivated /ʌnˈməʊtɪveɪtɪd/ *adj* **1** (lacking motive) [*crime, act*] gratuit; **2** (lacking motivation) [*person*] non motivé

unmoved /ʌnˈmuːvd/ *adj* **1** (unperturbed) indifférent (**by** à); **2** (not moved emotionally) insensible (**by** à)

unmusical /ʌnˈmjuːzɪkl/ *adj* [*sound*] discordant; [*person*] peu musicien/-ienne

unnamed /ʌnˈneɪmd/ *adj* **1** (name not divulged) [*company, source*] dont le nom n'a pas été divulgué; **2** (without name) [*club, virus*] **as yet ~** encore à la recherche d'un nom

unnatural /ʌnˈnætʃrəl/ *adj* **1** (odd) anormal; **it is ~ that** ce n'est pas normal que (+ *subj*); **2** (affected) [*style, laugh*] affecté; **3** (unusual) [*silence, colour*] insolite; **4** (unhealthy) [*interest*] malsain

unnecessary /ʌnˈnesəsrɪ, US -serɪ/ *adj* **1** (not needed) inutile; **it is ~ to do** il est inutile de faire; **it is ~ for you to do** il est inutile que tu fasses; **2** (uncalled for) déplacé

unnerving /ʌnˈnɜːvɪŋ/ *adj* déroutant

unnoticed /ʌnˈnəʊtɪst/ *adj* inaperçu

UNO /ˈjuːnəʊ/ *n* (*abrév* = **United Nations Organization**) ONU *f*

unobjectionable /ˌʌnəbˈdʒekʃənəbl/ *adj* inoffensif/-ive

unobservant /ˌʌnəbˈzɜːvənt/ *adj* peu perspicace

unobserved /ˌʌnəbˈzɜːvd/ *adj* inaperçu

unobstructed /ˌʌnəbˈstrʌktɪd/ *adj* [*view, exit*] dégagé

unobtainable /ˌʌnəbˈteɪnəbl/ *adj* **1** Comm [*supplies*] impossible à se procurer; **2** Telecom [*number*] impossible à obtenir

unobtrusive /ˌʌnəbˈtruːsɪv/ *adj* [*person*] effacé; [*site, object, noise*] discret/-ète

unoccupied /ʌnˈɒkjʊpaɪd/ *adj* **1** [*house, block, shop*] inoccupé; [*seat*] libre; **2** Mil [*territory*] libre

unofficial /ˌʌnəˈfɪʃl/ *adj* [*figure*] officieux/-ieuse; [*candidate*] indépendant; [*biography*] non autorisé; [*strike*] sauvage

unofficially /ˌʌnəˈfɪʃəlɪ/ *adv* [*tell, estimate*] officieusement

unopened /ʌnˈəʊpənd/ *adj* [*bottle, packet*] non entamé; [*package*] non ouvert

unorganized /ʌnˈɔːgənaɪzd/ *adj* **1** [*labour, worker*] non syndiqué; **2** [*event*] mal organisé; [*group*] qui ne sait pas s'organiser

unoriginal /ˌʌnəˈrɪdʒənl/ *adj* [*idea, plot, style*] sans originalité; **to be ~** manquer d'originalité

unorthodox /ʌnˈɔːθədɒks/ *adj* (unconventional) peu orthodoxe

unpack /ʌnˈpæk/ *vtr* défaire [*suitcase*]; déballer [*belongings*]

unpacking /ʌnˈpækɪŋ/ *n* déballage *m*

unpaid /ʌnˈpeɪd/ *adj* [*bill, tax*] impayé; [*debt*] non acquitté; [*work, volunteer*] non rémunéré; **~ leave** congé *m* sans solde

unpalatable /ʌnˈpælətəbl/ *adj* **1** fig [*truth, statistic*] inconfortable; [*advice*] dur à avaler; **2** [*food*] qui n'a pas bon goût

unparalleled /ʌnˈpærəleld/ *adj* **1** (unequalled) [*strength, luxury*] sans égal; [*success*] hors pair; **2** (unprecedented) sans précédent

unpardonable /ʌnˈpɑːdənəbl/ *adj* impardonnable

unpasteurized /ʌnˈpɑːstʃəraɪzd/ *adj* [*milk*] cru; [*cheese*] au lait cru

unperturbed /ˌʌnpəˈtɜːbd/ *adj* imperturbable

unpick /ʌnˈpɪk/ *vtr* **1** lit (undo) défaire; **2** démêler [*truth*] (**from** de)

unplaced /ʌnˈpleɪst/ *adj* [*competitor*] non classé; [*horse*] non placé

unplanned /ʌnˈplænd/ *adj* [*stoppage, increase*] imprévu; [*pregnancy, baby*] non prévu

unpleasant /ʌnˈpleznt/ *adj* désagréable

unpleasantness /ʌnˈplezntnɪs/ *n* **1** (of odour, experience, remark) caractère *m* désagréable; **2** (bad feeling) dissensions *fpl* (**between** entre)

unplug /ʌnˈplʌg/ *vtr* (*p prés etc* **-gg-**) débrancher [*appliance*]; déboucher [*sink*]

unpolished /ʌnˈpɒlɪʃt/ *adj* **1** lit [*floor*] non ciré; [*silver*] non astiqué; [*gem*] non poli; **2** fig [*person*] gauche; [*manners*] fruste; [*form*] ébauché

unpolluted /ˌʌnpəˈluːtɪd/ adj [water] non pollué; [mind] non contaminé

unpopular /ʌnˈpɒpjʊlə(r)/ adj impopulaire (**with** auprès de); **to be ~ with sb** être mal en cours auprès de qn

unprecedented /ʌnˈpresɪdentɪd/ adj sans précédent

unpredictable /ˌʌnprɪˈdɪktəbl/ adj [event] imprévisible; [weather] incertain; **he's ~** on ne sait jamais à quoi s'attendre avec lui

unprejudiced /ʌnˈpredʒʊdɪst/ adj [person] sans préjugés; [opinion, judgment] impartial

unpremeditated /ˌʌnpriːˈmedɪteɪtɪd/ adj non prémédité

unprepared /ˌʌnprɪˈpeəd/ adj **1** (not ready) [person] pas préparé (**for** pour); **to be ~ to do** ne pas être disposé à faire; **to catch sb ~** prendre qn au dépourvu; **2** [speech] improvisé; [translation] non préparé

unprepossessing /ˌʌnˌpriːpəˈzesɪŋ/ adj peu avenant

unpretentious /ˌʌnprɪˈtenʃəs/ adj sans prétention

unprincipled /ʌnˈprɪnsəpld/ adj peu scrupuleux/-euse

unprivileged /ʌnˈprɪvɪlɪdʒd/ adj défavorisé

unprofessional /ˌʌnprəˈfeʃənəl/ adj peu professionnel/-elle

unprofitable /ʌnˈprɒfɪtəbl/ adj **1** Fin [company, venture] non rentable; **2** fig [investigation, discussion] improductif/-ive

unprompted /ʌnˈprɒmptɪd/ adj non sollicité

unpronounceable /ˌʌnprəˈnaʊnsəbl/ adj imprononçable

unprotected /ˌʌnprəˈtektɪd/ adj **1** (unsafe) [person, area] sans protection (**from** contre); **2** (bare) [wood, metal] sans revêtement

unprovoked /ˌʌnprəˈvəʊkt/ adj [attack, aggression] délibéré; **the attack was ~** l'attaque n'avait pas été provoquée

unpublished /ʌnˈpʌblɪʃt/ adj non publié

unpunished /ʌnˈpʌnɪʃt/ adj [crime, person] impuni; **to go ~** [crime] rester impuni

unqualified /ʌnˈkwɒlɪfaɪd/ adj **1** (without qualifications) non qualifié; **to be ~ to do** ne pas être qualifié (**for** pour; **to do** faire); **2** (total) [support, respect] inconditionnel/-elle; [ceasefire] sans condition; [success] grand

unquenchable /ʌnˈkwentʃəbl/ adj [thirst, fire] inextinguible

unquestionable /ʌnˈkwestʃənəbl/ adj incontestable

unquestioning /ʌnˈkwestʃənɪŋ/ adj inconditionnel/-elle

unquote /ʌnˈkwəʊt/ adv fin de citation

unravel /ʌnˈrævl/
A vtr (p prés etc **-ll-** GB, **-l-** US) défaire [knitting]; démêler [thread, mystery]; dénouer [intrigue]
B vi (p prés etc **-ll-** GB, **-l-** US) [knitting] se défaire; [mystery, thread] se démêler; [plot] se dénouer

unreadable /ʌnˈriːdəbl/ adj [book, writing] illisible

unreal /ʌnˈrɪəl/ adj **1** (not real) [situation, conversation] irréel/-éelle; **it seemed a bit ~ to me** j'avais un peu l'impression de rêver; **2** ○péj (unbelievable) incroyable; **3** ○(amazingly good) incroyable

unrealistic /ˌʌnrɪəˈlɪstɪk/ adj [expectation, aim] irréaliste; [character, presentation] peu réaliste; [person] qui manque de réalisme

unrealizable /ʌnˈrɪəlaɪzəbl/ adj irréalisable

unrealized /ʌnˈrɪəlaɪzd/ adj [ambition, potential] non réalisé; **to be** ou **remain ~** ne pas être réalisé

unreasonable /ʌnˈriːznəbl/ adj **1** (not rational) [views, behaviour, expectation] irréaliste; **it's not ~ to** ce n'est pas déraisonnable; **2** (excessive) [price] excessif/-ive; [demand] irréaliste; **at an ~ hour** à une heure indue

unreasonably /ʌnˈriːznəblɪ/ adv [behave] de façon peu raisonnable; **~ high rents** des loyers excessifs; **not ~** à juste titre

unreasoning /ʌnˈriːzənɪŋ/ adj [person, response] irrationnel/-elle

unreceptive /ˌʌnrɪˈseptɪv/ adj peu réceptif/-ive (**to** à)

unrecognizable /ʌnˈrekəɡnaɪzəbl/ adj méconnaissable

unrecognized /ʌnˈrekəɡnaɪzd/ adj **1** (unacknowledged) méconnu (**by** de); **to go ~** rester méconnu; **2** Pol [regime,

government] non reconnu; **3** **he crossed the city ~** il a traversé la ville sans être reconnu

unreconstructed /ˌʌnriːkənˈstrʌktɪd/ adj (all contexts) irréductible

unrecorded /ˌʌnrɪˈkɔːdɪd/ adj **to go ~** ne pas être répertorié

unrefined /ˌʌnrɪˈfaɪnd/ adj **1** [flour, sugar] non raffiné; [oil] brut, non raffiné; **2** [person, manners, style] peu raffiné

unreflecting /ˌʌnrɪˈflektɪŋ/ adj irréfléchi

unregistered /ʌnˈredʒɪstəd/ adj [claim, firm, animal] non enregistré; [birth] non déclaré; [letter] non recommandé; [vehicle] non immatriculé; **to go ~** passer inaperçu

unrehearsed /ˌʌnrɪˈhɜːst/ adj [response, action, speech] impromptu; [play] sans répétitions

unrelated /ˌʌnrɪˈleɪtɪd/ adj **1** (not logically connected) sans rapport (**to** avec); **his success is not ~ to the fact that he has money** son succès n'est pas sans rapport avec sa fortune; **2** (as family) **to be ~** ne pas avoir de lien de parenté

unrelenting /ˌʌnrɪˈlentɪŋ/ adj [heat, stare, person] implacable; [pursuit, zeal, position] acharné

unreliability /ˌʌnrɪˌlaɪəˈbɪlətɪ/ n (of person) manque m de sérieux; (of machine, method, technique) manque m de fiabilité

unreliable /ˌʌnrɪˈlaɪəbl/ adj [evidence] douteux/-euse; [method, employee] peu sûr; [equipment] peu fiable; **she's very ~** on ne peut pas compter sur elle

unrelieved /ˌʌnrɪˈliːvd/ adj [substance, colour] uniforme; [darkness, gloom, anxiety] permanent; [boredom] mortel/-elle

unremarkable /ˌʌnrɪˈmɑːkəbl/ adj quelconque

unremarked /ˌʌnrɪˈmɑːkt/ adj **to go** ou **pass ~** passer inaperçu

unremitting /ˌʌnrɪˈmɪtɪŋ/ adj [boredom, flow] incessant; [hostility] implacable; [pressure, effort] continu; [struggle] sans relâche

unremittingly /ˌʌnrɪˈmɪtɪŋlɪ/ adv inlassablement

unrepeatable /ˌʌnrɪˈpiːtəbl/ adj **1** (unique) [bargain, sight] unique en son genre; [offer] exceptionnel/-elle; **2** (vulgar) **his comment was ~** son commentaire était du genre à ne pas répéter

unrepentant /ˌʌnrɪˈpentənt/ adj impénitent

unreported /ˌʌnrɪˈpɔːtɪd/ adj [incident, attack] non déclaré

unrepresentative /ˌʌnreprɪˈzentətɪv/ adj non représentatif/-ive

unrequited /ˌʌnrɪˈkwaɪtɪd/ adj [love] sans retour

unreserved /ˌʌnrɪˈzɜːvd/ adj **1** (free) [seat] non réservé; **2** (wholehearted) [support, welcome] sans réserve

unresisting /ˌʌnrɪˈzɪstɪŋ/ adj sans résistance

unresolved /ˌʌnrɪˈzɒlvd/ adj irrésolu

unresponsive /ˌʌnrɪˈspɒnsɪv/ adj peu réceptif/-ive

unrest /ʌnˈrest/ n ₵ **1** (dissatisfaction) malaise m; **2** (agitation) troubles mpl

unrestrained /ˌʌnrɪˈstreɪnd/ adj [growth] effréné; [emotion] non contenu; [freedom] sans limites

unrestricted /ˌʌnrɪˈstrɪktɪd/ adj [access] libre (**before** n); [power] illimité; [testing, disposal] incontrôlé; [warfare] à outrance; [roadway] dégagé

unrewarding /ˌʌnrɪˈwɔːdɪŋ/ adj (unfulfilling) peu gratifiant; (thankless) ingrat

unripe /ʌnˈraɪp/ adj [fruit] pas mûr; [wheat] en herbe

unrivalled /ʌnˈraɪvld/ adj sans égal

unroll /ʌnˈrəʊl/ vtr dérouler

unromantic /ˌʌnrəˈmæntɪk/ adj peu romantique; **to be ~** manquer de romantisme

unruffled /ʌnˈrʌfld/ adj **1** (calm) imperturbable; **to be ~** ne pas être perturbé (**by** par); **2** (smooth) [water, hair] lisse

unruly /ʌnˈruːlɪ/ adj [behaviour, hair] indiscipliné

unsafe /ʌnˈseɪf/ adj **1** [environment] malsain; [drinking water] non potable; [goods] dangereux/-euse; [working conditions] risqué; **the car is ~ to drive** il est dangereux de conduire cette voiture; **the building was declared ~** l'édifice a été déclaré dangereux; **2** (threatened) **to feel ~** ne

u

pas se sentir en sécurité; ③ Jur [*conviction, verdict*] douteux/-euse

unsaid /ʌnˈsed/ *adj* **to leave sth** ∼ passer qch sous silence

unsalaried /ʌnˈsælərɪd/ *adj* non rémunéré

unsalted /ʌnˈsɔːltɪd/ *adj* non salé

unsatisfactory /ˌʌnsætɪsˈfæktərɪ/ *adj* insatisfaisant

unsatisfied /ʌnˈsætɪsfaɪd/ *adj* [*person*] insatisfait; [*need*] inassouvi; **she remains** ∼ elle n'est toujours pas satisfaite (**with** de)

unsatisfying /ʌnˈsætɪsfaɪɪŋ/ *adj* peu satisfaisant

unsavoury GB, **unsavory** US /ʌnˈseɪvərɪ/ *adj* [*business, individual*] louche, répugnant; [*object, smell*] peu appétissant

unscathed /ʌnˈskeɪðd/ *adj* (all contexts) indemne

unscented /ʌnˈsentɪd/ *adj* non parfumé

unscheduled /ʌnˈʃedjuːld, US ʌnˈskedʒʊld/ *adj* [*appearance, speech*] surprise (*after n*); [*flight*] supplémentaire; [*stop*] qui n'a pas été prévu

unscientific /ˌʌnsaɪənˈtɪfɪk/ *adj* [*approach*] non scientifique; **to be** ∼ [*method, theory*] ne pas être scientifique; [*person*] ne pas avoir l'esprit scientifique

unscramble /ʌnˈskræmbl/ *vtr* déchiffrer [*code, words*]; remettre de l'ordre dans [*ideas, thoughts*]

unscrew /ʌnˈskruː/ *vtr* dévisser

unscrupulous /ʌnˈskruːpjʊləs/ *adj* [*person*] sans scrupules; [*tactic*] peu scrupuleux/-euse; **she is completely** ∼ elle n'a aucun scrupule

unsealed /ʌnˈsiːld/ *adj* [*envelope*] décacheté

unseasonable /ʌnˈsiːznəbl/ *adj* [*food, clothing*] hors de saison

unseasoned /ʌnˈsiːznd/ *adj* ① [*food*] non assaisonné; ② [*wood*] vert

unseat /ʌnˈsiːt/ *vtr* ① (unsaddle) désarçonner [*rider*]; ② Pol **the MP was** ∼**ed** le député a perdu son siège

unseeded /ʌnˈsiːdɪd/ *adj* Sport non classé

unseemly /ʌnˈsiːmlɪ/ *adj* sout inconvenant fml

unseen /ʌnˈsiːn/
A *n* GB Sch **a French** ∼ une version française non préparée
B *adj* ① (invisible) [*figure, hands*] invisible; ② Sch non préparé
C *adv* [*escape, slip away*] sans être vu

unselfconscious /ˌʌnselfˈkɒnʃəs/ *adj* (natural, spontaneous) naturel/-elle; (uninhibited) sans complexes

unselfish /ʌnˈselfɪʃ/ *adj* [*person*] qui pense aux autres; [*act*] désintéressé

unselfishness /ʌnˈselfɪʃnɪs/ *n* désintéressement *m*

unsentimental /ˌʌnsentɪˈmentl/ *adj* [*speech, account, film, novel*] qui ne donne pas dans la sensiblerie; [*person*] qui ne fait pas de sentiment

unsettled /ʌnˈsetld/ *adj* ① [*weather, economic climate*] instable; ② (not paid) [*account*] impayé; ③ (disrupted) [*schedule*] perturbé

unsettling /ʌnˈsetlɪŋ/ *adj* [*question, experience*] troublant; [*work of art*] dérangeant; **psychologically** ∼ traumatisant

unshak(e)able /ʌnˈʃeɪkəbl/ *adj* inébranlable

unshaken /ʌnˈʃeɪkən/ *adj* [*person*] imperturbable (**by** devant); [*belief, spirit*] inébranlable

unshaven /ʌnˈʃeɪvn/ *adj* pas rasé

unshockable /ʌnˈʃɒkəbl/ *adj* **she's** ∼ rien ne peut la choquer

unshrinkable /ʌnˈʃrɪŋkəbl/ *adj* irrétrécissable

unsightliness /ʌnˈsaɪtlɪnɪs/ *n* laideur *f*

unsightly /ʌnˈsaɪtlɪ/ *adj* [*blemish*] disgracieux/-ieuse; [*building*] laid

unsigned /ʌnˈsaɪnd/ *adj* [*document, letter*] non signé

unsinkable /ʌnˈsɪŋkəbl/ *adj* ① [*ship, object*] insubmersible; ② fig, hum [*personality*] que rien ne peut atteindre

unskilled /ʌnˈskɪld/ *adj* [*worker, labour*] non qualifié; [*job, work*] qui n'exige pas de qualification professionnelle

unskimmed /ʌnˈskɪmd/ *adj* [*milk*] non écrémé

unsmiling /ʌnˈsmaɪlɪŋ/ *adj* [*person*] qui ne sourit pas; [*face*] grave

unsociable /ʌnˈsəʊʃəbl/ *adj* peu sociable

unsocial /ʌnˈsəʊʃl/ *adj* ∼ **hours** heures *fpl* indues

unsold /ʌnˈsəʊld/ *adj* invendu

unsolicited /ˌʌnsəˈlɪsɪtɪd/ *adj* non sollicité

unsolved /ʌnˈsɒlvd/ *adj* [*problem*] non résolu; [*murder*] non éclairci

unsophisticated /ˌʌnsəˈfɪstɪkeɪtɪd/ *adj* [*person*] sans façons; [*mind*] simple; [*analysis*] simpliste

unsound /ʌnˈsaʊnd/ *adj* [*roof, ship*] en mauvais état; [*argument*] peu valable; [*credits, investment*] Fin douteux/-euse; **he is politically** ∼, **his views are politically** ∼ il a des idées politiques suspectes; **to be of** ∼ **mind** Jur ne pas jouir de toutes ses facultés mentales

unsparing /ʌnˈspeərɪŋ/ *adj* ① **to be** ∼ **in one's efforts to do** ne pas ménager ses efforts pour faire; ② (merciless) impitoyable

unsparingly /ʌnˈspeərɪŋlɪ/ *adv* ① [*give*] sans compter; [*strive*] de tout son être; ② [*critical*] implacablement

unspeakable /ʌnˈspiːkəbl/ *adj* ① (dreadful) [*pain, sorrow*] inexprimable; [*noise*] épouvantable; [*act*] innommable; ② (inexpressible) indescriptible

unspeakably /ʌnˈspiːkəblɪ/ *adv* ① (dreadfully) épouvantablement; ② (inexpressibly) ∼ **beautiful** d'une beauté indescriptible

unspent /ʌnˈspent/ *adj* ① lit [*money*] non dépensé; ② fig [*rage*] toujours vivace

unspoiled /ʌnˈspɔɪld/ *adj* [*landscape, town*] préservé intact; **she was** ∼ **by fame** la célébrité ne l'avait pas changée

unspoilt /ʌnˈspɔɪlt/ *adj* [*island, area*] préservé

unspoken /ʌnˈspəʊkən/ *adj* ① (secret) inexprimé; ② (implicit) tacite

unsportsmanlike /ˌʌnˈspɔːtsmənlaɪk/ *adj* Sport ∼ **conduct** conduite indigne d'un sportif

unstable /ʌnˈsteɪbl/ *adj* (all contexts) instable

unstated /ʌnˈsteɪtɪd/ *adj* [*violence, assumption*] tacite; [*policy, conviction*] inexprimé

unstatesmanlike /ʌnˈsteɪtsmənlaɪk/ *adj* indigne d'un homme d'État

unsteadily /ʌnˈstedɪlɪ/ *adv* [*walk, rise*] en chancelant

unsteady /ʌnˈstedɪ/ *adj* ① (wobbly) [*steps, legs, voice*] chancelant; [*ladder*] instable; [*hand*] tremblant; **to be** ∼ **on one's feet** marcher de façon mal assurée; ② (irregular) [*rhythm, speed*] irrégulier/-ière

unstinting /ʌnˈstɪntɪŋ/ *adj* [*effort*] soutenu; [*support*] généreux/-euse; **to be** ∼ **in one's praise of sb** se répandre en louanges sur qn

unstitch /ʌnˈstɪtʃ/ *vtr* **to come** ∼**ed** se découdre

unstoppable /ʌnˈstɒpəbl/ *adj* [*force, momentum*] irrésistible; [*athlete, leader*] imbattable

unstrap /ʌnˈstræp/ (*p prés etc* **-pp-**) *vtr* ① (undo) défaire les sangles de [*suitcase*]; ② (detach) détacher [*case, bike*] (**from** de)

unstressed /ʌnˈstrest/ *adj* Ling [*vowel, word*] non accentué

unstrung /ʌnˈstrʌŋ/ *adj* **to come** ∼ [*racket, instrument*] se détendre; [*beads*] se désenfiler

unstuck /ʌnˈstʌk/ *adj* ① lit **to come** ∼ se décoller; ② ᴼfig [*person, organization*] connaître un échec, aller à vau l'eau; [*plans*] tomber à l'eau; **to come** ∼ **in one's exams** échouer à ses examens

unsubsidized /ʌnˈsʌbsɪdaɪzd/ *adj* non subventionné

unsubstantiated /ˌʌnsəbˈstænʃɪeɪtɪd/ *adj* non corroboré

unsuccessful /ˌʌnsəkˈsesfl/ *adj* ① [*campaign*] infructueux/-euse; [*production, film*] sans succès; [*lawsuit*] perdu; [*love affair*] malheureux/-euse; [*search*] vain; **to be** ∼ [*attempt*] échouer; ② [*candidate*] (for job) malchanceux/-euse; (in election) malheureux/-euse; [*businessperson*] malchanceux/-euse; [*artist*] inconnu; **to be ~ in doing** ne pas réussir à faire

unsuccessfully /ˌʌnsək'sesfəlɪ/ *adv* [*try*] en vain; [*challenge, bid*] sans succès

unsuitable /ʌn'suːtəbl/ *adj* [*location, clothing, accommodation, time*] inapproprié; [*moment*] inopportun; [*friend*] peu convenable; **to be ~** ne pas convenir (**for sb** à qn); **to be ~ for a job** ne pas être fait pour un travail

unsuitably /'ʌn'suːtəblɪ/ *adv* **he was ~ dressed** sa tenue était inappropriée; **to be ~ matched** ne pas être faits l'un pour l'autre

unsuited /ʌn'suːtɪd/ *adj* [*place, person*] inadapté (**to** à); **posts ~ to their talents** des postes qui ne conviennent pas à leurs aptitudes; **she was ~ to country life** elle n'était pas faite pour la vie à la campagne; **they're ~ (as a couple)** ils sont mal assortis

unsupervised /ʌn'suːpəvaɪzd/ *adj* [*activity*] non encadré; [*child*] laissé sans surveillance

unsupported /ˌʌnsə'pɔːtɪd/ *adj* **1** [*allegation, hypothesis*] non confirmé; **2** Mil [*troops*] sans renfort; **3** [*family, mother*] sans soutien de famille

unsure /ʌn'ʃɔː(r), US -'ʃʊər/ *adj* peu sûr (**of** de); **to be ~ about how/about going** ne pas savoir très bien comment/si on doit partir; **to be ~ of oneself** manquer de confiance en soi

unsurpassed /ˌʌnsə'pɑːst, US -'pæs-/ *adj* [*beauty*] sans égal; **to be ~** être inégalé (**in** dans; **as** comme)

unsuspected /ˌʌnsə'spektɪd/ *adj* insoupçonné

unsuspecting /ˌʌnsə'spektɪŋ/ *adj* [*person*] naïf/-ïve, sans méfiance; [*public*] non averti; **completely ~** sans aucune méfiance

unsweetened /ʌn'swiːtnd/ *adj* sans sucre, non sucré

unswerving /ʌn'swɜːvɪŋ/ *adj* inébranlable

unsympathetic /ˌʌnsɪmpə'θetɪk/ *adj* **1** (*uncaring*) [*person, attitude, manner, tone*] peu compatissant; **to be ~ to sb** se montrer peu compatissant envers qn; **2** (*unattractive*) [*person, character*] antipathique; [*environment, building*] peu attirant; **3** (*unsupportive*) **to be ~ to** ne pas soutenir [*cause, movement, policy*]; **she is ~ to the cause** elle ne sympathise pas avec la cause

unsystematic /ˌʌnsɪstə'mætɪk/ *adj* peu méthodique

untainted /ʌn'teɪntɪd/ *adj* [*food*] non avarié; [*reputation*] non entaché; [*mind*] non corrompu

untamed /ʌn'teɪmd/ *adj* [*passion, person, lion*] indompté; [*garden, beauty*] (à l'état) sauvage; [*bird, fox*] non dressé

untangle /ʌn'tæŋgl/ *vtr* démêler [*threads*], also fig; élucider [*difficulties, mystery*]; **to ~ oneself** (from net, situation) se dégager (**from** de)

untapped /ʌn'tæpt/ *adj* inexploité

untaxed /ʌn'tækst/ *adj* **1** [*income*] non imposable; [*goods*] non taxé; **2** GB Aut [*car*] sans vignette

untenable /ʌn'tenəbl/ *adj* [*position, standpoint*] intenable; [*claim, argument*] indéfendable

untested /ʌn'testɪd/ *adj* **1** [*theory*] non vérifié; [*method, drug*] non testé; **2** Psych [*person*] non testé

unthinkable /ʌn'θɪŋkəbl/ *adj* [*prospect, action*] impensable

unthinking /ʌn'θɪŋkɪŋ/ *adj* [*person*] irréfléchi; [*remark, criticism*] inconsidéré

unthinkingly /ʌn'θɪŋkɪŋlɪ/ *adv* [*behave, react*] sans réfléchir

unthought-of /ʌn'θɔːtɒv/ *adj* original, inédit; **hitherto ~** encore inédit

untidily /ʌn'taɪdɪlɪ/ *adv* [*kept, scattered, strewn*] en désordre; **~ dressed** habillé de façon débraillée

untidiness /ʌn'taɪdɪnɪs/ *n* désordre *m*

untidy /ʌn'taɪdɪ/ *adj* [*person*] (in habits) désordonné; (in appearance) peu soigné; [*habits, clothes*] négligé; [*room*] en désordre

untie /ʌn'taɪ/ *vtr* (*p prés* **-tying**) défaire, dénouer [*knot, rope, laces*]; défaire [*parcel*]; délier [*hands, hostage*]; **to come ~d** [*laces, parcel*] se défaire; [*hands*] se délier

until /ən'tɪl/

When used as a preposition in positive sentences *until* is translated by *jusqu'à*: *they're staying until Monday* = ils restent jusqu'à lundi.

Remember that *jusqu'à + le* becomes *jusqu'au* and *jusqu'à + les* becomes *jusqu'aux*: *until the right moment* = jusqu'au bon moment; *until the exams* = jusqu'aux examens.

In negative sentences *not until* is translated by *ne...pas avant*: *I can't see you until Friday* = je ne peux pas vous voir avant vendredi.

When used as a conjunction in positive sentences *until* is translated by *jusqu'à ce que + subjunctive*: *we'll stay here until Maya comes back* = nous resterons ici jusqu'à ce que Maya revienne.

In negative sentences where the two verbs have different subjects *not until* is translated by *ne...pas avant que + subjunctive*: *we won't leave until Maya comes back* = nous ne partirons pas avant que Maya revienne.

In negative sentences where the two verbs have the same subject *not until* is translated by *ne...pas avant de + infinitive*: *we won't leave until we've seen Claire* = nous ne partirons pas avant d'avoir vu Claire.

For more examples and particular usages see the entry below.

A *prep* **1** (*also* **till**) (up to a specific time) jusqu'à; (after negative verb) avant; **~ Tuesday** jusqu'à mardi; **~ the sixties** jusqu'aux années soixante; **~ very recently** il n'y a encore pas si longtemps; **~ a year ago** jusqu'à il y a un an; **~ now** jusqu'à présent; **~ then** jusqu'à ce moment-là, jusque-là; **(up) ~ 1901** jusqu'en *or* jusqu'à 1901; **valid (up) ~ April 1993** valable jusqu'en avril 1993 ; **~ the day he died** jusqu'à sa mort; **~ well after midnight** bien au-delà de minuit; **to wait ~ after Easter** attendre après Pâques; **from Monday ~ Saturday** du lundi au samedi; **put it off ~ tomorrow** remets-le à demain; **~ such time as you find work** jusqu'à ce que tu trouves (*subj*) du travail, en attendant que tu trouves (*subj*) du travail; **I won't know ~ Tuesday** je n'aurai pas la réponse avant mardi; **they didn't ring ~ the following day** ils n'ont pas appelé avant le lendemain; **it wasn't ~ the 50's that...** ce n'est qu'à partir des années cinquante que...; **2** (as far as) jusqu'à

B *conj* (*also* **till**) jusqu'à ce que (+ *subj*); (in negative constructions) avant que (+ *subj*), avant de (+ *infinitive*); **we'll stay ~ a solution is reached** nous resterons jusqu'à ce que nous trouvions une solution; **let's watch TV ~ they arrive** regardons la télévision en attendant qu'ils arrivent (*subj*); **things won't improve ~ we have democracy** la situation ne s'améliorera pas tant que nous ne serons pas en démocratie; **stir mixture ~ (it is) smooth** Culin mélangez bien jusqu'à obtenir une pâte lisse; **~ you are dead** jusqu'à ce que mort s'ensuive; **wait ~ I get back** attends que je rentre (*subj*); **I'll wait ~ I get back** j'attendrai d'être rentré (before doing pour faire); **she waited ~ she was alone/they were alone** elle a attendu d'être seule/qu'ils soient seuls; **don't look ~ I tell you to** ne regarde pas avant que je te le dise; **you can't leave ~ you've completed the course** tu ne peux pas partir avant d'avoir fini le stage

untimely /ʌn'taɪmlɪ/ *adj* littér [*arrival, intervention*] inopportun; [*death*] prématuré; **to come to an ~ end** [*person, project*] connaître une fin prématurée

untiring /ʌn'taɪərɪŋ/ *adj* [*person, enthusiasm*] infatigable (**in** dans)

untold /ʌn'təʊld/ *adj* **1** (not quantifiable) **~ millions** des millions et des millions; **~ damage** d'énormes dégâts; **2** (endless) [*misery, damage, joy*] indicible

untouched /ʌn'tʌtʃt/ *adj* **1** (unchanged, undisturbed) intact; **2** (unscathed) indemne; **3** (unaffected) non affecté (**by** par); **4** (uneaten) intact; **to leave a meal ~** laisser un repas sans y toucher

untoward /ˌʌntə'wɔːd, US ʌn'tɔːrd/ *adj* fâcheux/-euse

untraceable /ʌn'treɪsəbl/ *adj* introuvable

untrained /ʌn'treɪnd/ *adj* **1** [*worker*] sans formation; **2** [*voice*] non travaillé; [*eye*] inexercé; [*artist, actor*] non formé; **to be ~** n'avoir aucune formation (**in** en); **3** [*animal*] non dressé

untranslatable /ˌʌntrænz'leɪtəbl/ *adj* intraduisible (**into** en)

untreated /ʌn'triːtɪd/ *adj* [*sewage, water*] non traité; [*illness*] non soigné; [*road*] non sablé

untried /ʌnˈtraɪd/ adj ① [recruit] inexpérimenté; [method] non essayé; [product] non testé; ② Jur [prisoner] non jugé

untroubled /ʌnˈtrʌbld/ adj [face, life] paisible; [person] serein; **to be ~** (by news) ne pas être troublé (**by** par)

untrue /ʌnˈtruː/ adj ① (false) faux/fausse; ② **it is ~ to say that** il est faux or inexact de dire que

untrustworthy /ʌnˈtrʌstwɜːðɪ/ adj [source, information] douteux/-euse; [person] indigne de confiance; [witness] non digne de foi

untruthful /ʌnˈtruːθfl/ adj [person] menteur/-euse; [account] mensonger/-ère

untypical /ʌnˈtɪpɪkl/ adj [person, behaviour] hors du commun; **to be ~ of sb** ne pas ressembler à qn (**to do** de faire)

unused[1] /ʌnˈjuːst/ adj (unaccustomed) **to be ~ to sth/to doing** ne pas être habitué à qch/à faire

unused[2] /ʌnˈjuːzd/ adj (not used) [machine, building] inutilisé; [stamp] neuf/neuve; **'computer, ~'** (in ad) 'ordinateur, état neuf'

unusual /ʌnˈjuːʒl/ adj [colour, flower] peu commun; [feature, occurrence] peu commun, inhabituel/-elle; [dish, person] original; **of ~ intelligence** d'une intelligence hors du commun; **to have an ~ way of doing** avoir une manière originale de faire; **it is ~ to find/see** il est rare de trouver/voir; **it's ~ for sb to do** il est rare que qn fasse; **there's nothing ~ about it** cela n'a rien d'extraordinaire

unusually /ʌnˈjuːʒəlɪ/ adv ① (exceptionally) [large, difficult, talented] exceptionnellement; ② (surprisingly) exceptionnellement; **~ for her, she...** chose rare, elle...

unutterable /ʌnˈʌtərəbl/ adj indicible

unvarying /ʌnˈveərɪŋ/ adj [routine] invariable

unveil /ʌnˈveɪl/ vtr dévoiler [statue, details]

unveiling /ʌnˈveɪlɪŋ/ n ① (of statue) dévoilement m; ② (official ceremony) inauguration f; ③ (of latest model, details) annonce f

unvoiced /ʌnˈvɔɪst/ adj ① (private) inexprimé; ② Ling non voisé

unwaged /ʌnˈweɪdʒd/ adj [work, worker] non salarié

unwanted /ʌnˈwɒntɪd/ adj [goods, produce] superflu; [pet] abandonné; [visitor] indésirable; [child] non souhaité; **to feel ~** se sentir de trop

unwarranted /ʌnˈwɒrəntɪd, US -ˈwɔːr-/ adj injustifié

unwary /ʌnˈweərɪ/
A n **the ~** (+ v pl) les imprudents
B adj [person] sans méfiance

unwashed /ʌnˈwɒʃt/ adj [clothes, dishes] sale, pas lavé

unwavering /ʌnˈweɪvərɪŋ/ adj [devotion] inébranlable; [gaze] résolu

unwearable /ʌnˈweərəbl/ adj immettable

unwearying /ʌnˈwɪərɪŋ/ adj [patience] inlassable

unwelcome /ʌnˈwelkəm/ adj ① [visitor, interruption] importun; **he felt most ~** elle ne se sentait pas la bienvenue; **to make sb feel ~** faire sentir à qn qu'il n'est pas le bienvenu; ② [news] fâcheux/-euse; [truth] gênant; [proposition] inopportun

unwelcoming /ˌʌnˈwelkəmɪŋ/ adj [atmosphere] peu accueillant

unwell /ʌnˈwel/ adj souffrant; **he is feeling ~** il ne se sent pas très bien; **are you ~?** vous êtes souffrant?

unwholesome /ʌnˈhəʊlsəm/ adj malsain

unwieldy /ʌnˈwiːldɪ/ adj [tool] peu maniable; [parcel] encombrant; [bureaucracy, organization] lourd

unwilling /ʌnˈwɪlɪŋ/ adj [attention, departure] forcé; **he is ~ to do it** il n'est pas disposé à le faire; (stronger) il ne veut pas le faire; **~ accomplice** complice malgré moi/lui etc

unwillingly /ʌnˈwɪlɪŋlɪ/ adv à contrecœur

unwillingness /ʌnˈwɪlɪŋnɪs/ n réticence f (**to do** à faire)

unwind /ʌnˈwaɪnd/ (prét, pp **-wound**)
A vtr dérouler
B vi ① [tape, cable, scarf] se dérouler; ② (relax) se relaxer

unwise /ʌnˈwaɪz/ adj [choice, loan, decision] peu judicieux/-ieuse; [person] imprudent; **it is ~ to do** il est imprudent de faire

unwittingly /ʌnˈwɪtɪŋlɪ/ adv ① (innocently) innocemment; ② (without wanting to) involontairement; ③ (accidentally) accidentellement

unworldly /ʌnˈwɜːldlɪ/ adj ① (not materialistic) détaché de ce monde; ② (naive) naïf/naïve; ③ (spiritual) surnaturel/-elle

unworthy /ʌnˈwɜːðɪ/ adj indigne (**of** de)

unwrap /ʌnˈræp/ (p prés etc **-pp-**) vtr déballer

unwritten /ʌnˈrɪtn/ adj ① (tacit) [rule, agreement] tacite; ② (not written) [story, song] non écrit; [tradition] oral

unyielding /ʌnˈjiːldɪŋ/ adj ① lit rigide; ② fig inflexible

unzip /ʌnˈzɪp/ (p prés etc **-pp-**)
A vtr ① défaire la fermeture à glissière de [garment, bag]; ② Comput dézipper, décompresser [file]
B vi s'ouvrir

up /ʌp/

> ⚠ *Up* appears frequently in English as the second element of phrasal verbs (*get up*, *pick up* etc). For translations, consult the appropriate verb entry (**get, pick** etc)

A adj ① (out of bed) **she's ~** elle est levée; **they're often ~ early** ils se lèvent souvent tôt; **we were ~ very late last night** nous nous sommes couchés très tard hier soir; **they were ~ all night** ils ont veillé toute la nuit; **I was still ~ at 2 am** j'étais toujours debout à 2 heures du matin; ② (higher in amount, level) **sales/prices are ~ (by 10%)** les ventes/les prix ont augmenté (de 10%); **shares/numbers are ~** les actions sont/le nombre est en hausse; **production is ~ (by) 5%** la production a augmenté de 5%; **his temperature is ~ 2 degrees** sa température a augmenté de 2°; **sales are 10% ~ on last year** les ventes ont augmenté de 10% par rapport à l'an dernier; ③ ○(wrong) **what's ~?** qu'est-ce qui se passe?; **what's ~ with him?** qu'est-ce qu'il lui arrive?; **there's something ~** il y a quelque chose qui ne va pas; **what's ~ with the TV?** qu'est-ce qu'elle a à la télé?; **there's something ~ with the brakes** il y a un problème avec les freins; ④ (erected, affixed) **the notice is ~ on the board** l'annonce est affichée sur le panneau; **is the tent ~?** est-ce que la tente est déjà montée?; **the building will soon be ~** le bâtiment sera bientôt terminé; **he had his hand ~ for five minutes** il a gardé la main levée pendant cinq minutes; ⑤ (open) **she had her umbrella ~** elle avait son parapluie ouvert; **the hood of the car was ~** la capote de la voiture était fermée; **the blinds were ~** les stores étaient levés; **when the lever is ~ the machine is off** si le levier est vers le haut la machine est arrêtée; **when the barrier is ~ you can go through** quand la barrière est levée vous pouvez passer; ⑥ (finished) **'time's ~!'** 'le temps est épuisé!'; **his leave is almost ~** son congé est presque terminé; **it's all ~○ with him** il est fini○; ⑦ (facing upwards) **'this side ~'** (on parcel, box) 'haut'; **she was floating face ~** elle flottait sur le dos; **the bread landed with the buttered side ~** la tartine est tombée côté beurré vers le haut; ⑧ (rising) **the river is ~** la rivière est en crue; **the wind is ~** le vent est fort; **his colour's ~** il est tout rouge; **her blood's ~** fig la moutarde lui monte au nez; ⑨ (pinned up) **her hair was ~** elle avait les cheveux relevés; ⑩ (cheerful) **to be ~** être en forme; ⑪ (being repaired) **the road is ~** la route est en travaux; ⑫ (in upward direction) **the ~ escalator** l'escalier mécanique qui monte; ⑬ (on trial) **to be ~ before a judge** passer devant le tribunal; **he's ~ for murder** il est accusé de meurtre

B adv ① (high) **~ here/there** là-haut; **~ on the wardrobe** sur l'armoire; **~ in the tree/the clouds** dans l'arbre/les nuages; **~ on top of the mountain** au sommet de la montagne; **~ to/in London** à Londres; **~ to/in Scotland** en Écosse; **~ North** au Nord; **four floors ~ from here** quatre étages au-dessus; **I live two floors ~** j'habite au deuxième étage; **the second shelf ~** la deuxième étagère en partant du bas; **I'm on my way ~** je monte; **I'll be right ~** je monte tout de suite; **all the way ~** jusqu'en haut, jusqu'au sommet; ② (ahead) d'avance; **to be four points ~ (on sb)** avoir quatre points d'avance (sur qn); **they were two goals ~** ils menaient avec deux buts d'avance; **she's 40–15 ~** (in tennis) elle mène 40-15; ③ (upwards) **t-shirts from £2 ~** des t-shirts à partir de deux livres; **from (the age of) 14 ~** à partir de 14 ans; ④ (to high status) **~ the workers!** vive les travailleurs!

C prep ① (at, to higher level) **~ the tree** dans l'arbre; **a ladder ~ the wall** sur une échelle; **the library is ~ the stairs** la bibliothèque se trouve en haut de l'escalier; **he ran ~ the stairs** il a monté l'escalier en courant; **the road ~ the mountain** la route qui gravit la montagne; **2** (in direction) **it's ~ the road** c'est plus loin dans la rue; **she lives ~ that road there** elle habite dans cette rue; **he lives just ~ the road** il habite juste à côté; **his office is ~ the corridor from mine** son bureau est dans le même couloir que le mien; **he walked ~ the road** il a remonté la rue; **she's got water ~ her nose** elle a de l'eau dans le nez; **he put it ~ his sleeve** il l'a mis dans sa manche

D **up above** adv phr, prep phr gen au-dessus; Relig au ciel; **~ above sth** au-dessus de qch

E **up against** prep phr **~ against the wall** contre le mur; **to be** ou **come ~ against opposition** rencontrer de l'opposition; **they're ~ against a very strong team** ils sont confrontés à une équipe très forte; **it helps to know what you are ~ against** il faut savoir ce contre quoi on se bat; **we're really ~ against it** on a vraiment des problèmes

F **up and about** adv phr (out of bed) debout, réveillé; (after illness) **to be ~ and about again** être de nouveau sur pied

G **up and down** adv phr, prep phr **1** (to and fro) **to walk** ou **pace ~ and down** aller et venir, faire les cent pas; **he was walking ~ and down the garden** il faisait les cent pas dans le jardin; **2** (throughout) **~ and down the country** dans tout le pays

H **up and running** adj phr, adv phr **to be ~ and running** [company, project] bien marcher; [system] bien fonctionner; **to get sth ~ and running** faire marcher or fonctionner qch

I **up for** prep phr **he's ~ for election** il se présente aux élections; **the subject ~ for discussion is...** le sujet qu'on aborde est...

J **up to** prep phr **1** (to particular level) jusqu'à; **~ to here** jusqu'ici; **~ to there** jusque là; **I was ~ to my knees in water** j'étais dans l'eau jusqu'aux genoux; **2** (as many as) jusqu'à, près de; **~ to 50 dollars** jusqu'à 50 dollars; **~ to 500 people** près de 500 personnes; **reductions of ~ to 50%** des réductions qui peuvent atteindre 50%; **tax on profits of ~ to £150,000** les impôts sur les bénéfices de moins de 150 000 livres sterling; **to work for ~ to 12 hours a day** travailler jusqu'à 12 heures par jour; **3** (until) jusqu'à; **~ to 1964** jusqu'en 1964; **~ to 10.30 pm** jusqu'à 22 h 30; **~ to now** jusqu'à maintenant; **4** (good enough for) **I'm not ~ to it** (not capable) je n'en suis pas capable; (not well enough) je n'en ai pas la force; **I'm not ~ to going to London** je n'ai pas le courage d'aller à Londres; **I'm not ~ to writing a book** je ne suis pas capable d'écrire un livre; **the play wasn't ~ to much** la pièce n'était pas formidable; **this work wasn't ~ to your usual standard** ce travail n'est pas au niveau de ce que vous faites d'habitude; **5** (expressing responsibility) **it's ~ to him to do** c'est à lui de faire; **it's ~ to you!** c'est à toi de décider!; **if it were ~ to me** si ça dépendait de moi; **6** (doing) **what is he ~ to?** qu'est-ce qu'il fait?; **what are those children ~ to?** qu'est-ce qu'ils fabriquent○ ces enfants?; **they're ~ to something** ils mijotent○ quelque chose

K vtr (p prés etc **-pp-**) (increase) augmenter

L vi (p prés etc **-pp-**) **he ~ped and left** tout d'un coup il s'est levé et est parti

Idioms **the company is on the ~ and ~** ça marche très bien pour l'entreprise; **to be one ~ on sb** faire mieux que qn; **to be (well) ~ on sb** s'y connaître en [art, history etc]; être au courant de [news, developments]; **the ~s and downs** les hauts et les bas (**of** de)

up and coming adj prometteur/-euse

upbeat /'ʌpbiːt/ adj fig optimiste

upbringing /'ʌpbrɪŋɪŋ/ n éducation f

update

A /'ʌpdeɪt/ n mise f à jour (**on** de); **news ~** dernières nouvelles fpl

B /ˌʌp'deɪt/ vtr **1** (revise) mettre [qch] à jour [database, figure]; actualiser [price]; **2** (modernize) moderniser [machinery]; remettre [qch] au goût du jour [image]; **3** mettre [qn] au courant [person]

upfront○ /ˌʌp'frʌnt/

A adj **1** (frank) franc/franche; **2** (conspicuous) en vue; **3** [money] payé d'avance

B adv [pay] d'avance

upgrade

A /'ʌpɡreɪd/ n Comput (of software) mise f à jour; (of hardware) version f plus puissante

B /ˌʌp'ɡreɪd/ vtr **1** (modernize) moderniser; (improve) améliorer; **2** Comput augmenter [memory]; améliorer [system];

passer à une version plus puissante de [hardware]; passer à une version plus récente de [software]; **3** (raise) promouvoir [person]; revaloriser [job]

upheaval /ˌʌp'hiːvl/ n **1** **C** (disturbance) (political, emotional) bouleversement m; (physical) (in house etc) remue-ménage m inv; **2** **Ȼ** (instability) (political, emotional) bouleversements mpl; (physical) remue-ménage m inv; **emotional ~** un bouleversement affectif

uphill /ˌʌp'hɪl/

A adj **1** lit [road, slope] qui monte; **2** fig (difficult) [task] difficile; **it will be an ~ struggle** ou **battle** cela va être difficile

B adv [go, walk] en montée; **the path led ~** le sentier montait; **it's ~ all the way** lit ça monte tout le temps; fig ce n'est pas une tâche facile

uphold /ˌʌp'həʊld/ vtr (prét, pp **-held**) soutenir [principle]; faire respecter [law]; confirmer [decision]

upholster /ˌʌp'həʊlstə(r)/ vtr rembourrer [chair, sofa]

upholsterer /ˌʌp'həʊlstərə(r)/ ▸ p. 1181 n tapissier/-ière m/f

upholstery /ˌʌp'həʊlstərɪ/ n **1** (covering) revêtement m; **2** (stuffing) rembourrage m; **3** (technique) tapisserie f

upkeep /'ʌpkiːp/ n **1** (care) (of house, garden) entretien m (**of** de); (of animal) garde f (**of** de); **2** (cost of care) frais mpl d'entretien

uplifting /ˌʌp'lɪftɪŋ/ adj tonique

uplighter /'ʌplaɪtə(r)/ n (lamp) luminaire m à éclairage indirect; (shade) abat-jour m pour luminaire à éclairage indirect

upload /'ʌpləʊd/ vtr Comput télécharger, télétransmettre [data]

upmarket /ˌʌp'mɑːkɪt/ adj [car, hotel] haut de gamme; [area] riche

upmost /'ʌpməʊst/ adj ▸ **uppermost**

upon /ə'pɒn/ prep **1** fml ▸ **on A** 1, 3, 7, 10; **2** (linking two nouns) **thousands ~ thousands of people** des milliers et des milliers de personnes; **disaster ~ disaster** un désastre après l'autre; **3** (imminent) **spring is almost ~ us** le printemps approche

upper /'ʌpə(r)/

A n **1** (of shoe) empeigne f; **'leather ~'** 'dessus en cuir'; **2** argot des drogués stimulant m

B adj **1** (in location) [shelf] du haut; [deck] supérieur; [jaw, lip] supérieur; [teeth] du haut; **the ~ body** la partie supérieure du corps; **2** (in rank) supérieur; **3** (on scale) [register, scale] supérieur; **the ~ limit** la limite maximale (**on** de); **temperatures are in the ~ twenties** les températures dépassent 25°

Idioms **to be on one's ~s**○ être dans la dèche○; **to have/ get the ~ hand** avoir/prendre le dessus. ▸ **stiff**

upper case adj **~ letters** (lettres fpl) majuscules fpl

upper circle n Theat deuxième balcon m

upper class

A n (pl **~es**) **the ~, the ~es** l'aristocratie f et la haute bourgeoisie

B **upper-class** adj [accent, background, person] distingué; **in ~ circles** dans la haute société

upper crust○ hum

A n **the ~** le gratin○ m

B **upper-crust** adj [accent, family] de la haute○

upper: Upper House n Chambre f haute; **~-income bracket** n tranche f des revenus élevés

upper middle class n **the ~, the ~es** la haute bourgeoisie f

uppermost /'ʌpəməʊst/ adj **1** (highest) [deck, branch] le plus haut; (in rank) [echelon] le plus élevé; **2** (to the fore) prédominant; **to be ~ in sb's mind** être au premier plan des pensées de qn

upper sixth n GB Sch cf (classe f) terminale f

upright /'ʌpraɪt/

A n **1** Constr montant m; **2** (in football) montant m de but

B adj lit, fig droit; **to stay ~** [person] rester debout

C adv **to stand ~** se tenir droit; **to sit ~** (action) se redresser

upright: ~ freezer n congélateur m armoire; **~ piano** ▸ p. 1028 n piano m droit

uprising /'ʌpraɪzɪŋ/ n soulèvement m

upriver /ˌʌp'rɪvə(r)/ adv vers l'amont

uproar /'ʌprɔː(r)/ n **1** (violent indignation) indignation f; **to cause an international** ~ soulever une indignation internationale; **2** (noisy reaction) tumulte m; **to cause (an)** ~ déclencher un tumulte de protestations; **3** (chaos) **to be in** ~ être dans la plus vive agitation

uproarious /ʌp'rɔːrɪəs/ adj **1** (funny) désopilant; **2** (rowdy) [behaviour] tapageur/-euse; [laughter] tonitruant

uproot /ʌp'ruːt/ vtr lit, fig déraciner

upset
A /'ʌpset/ n **1** (surprise, setback) Pol, Sport revers m; **to suffer an** ~ subir un revers; **to cause an** ~ causer la surprise; **2** (upheaval) bouleversement m; **3** (distress) peine f; **4** Med **to have a stomach** ~ avoir un problème d'estomac
B /ʌp'set/ vtr (p prés **-tt-**; prét, pp **-set**) **1** (distress) [sight, news] retourner, bouleverser; [person] faire de la peine à; **2** (annoy) contrarier; **3** fig (throw into disarray) bouleverser [plan]; déjouer [calculations]; affecter [pattern, situation]; **4** (destabilize) rompre [balance]; (knock over) renverser; **5** Pol, Sport (topple) déloger [leader, party]; **6** Med rendre [qn] malade [person]; perturber [digestion]
C /ʌp'set/ pp adj **to be** ou **feel** ~ (distressed) être très affecté (**at, about** par); (annoyed) être contrarié (**at, about** par); **to get** ~ (angry) se fâcher (**about** pour); (distressed) se tracasser (**about** pour)

upsetting /ʌp'setɪŋ/ adj (distressing) navrant, affligeant; (annoying) contrariant

upshot /'ʌpʃɒt/ n résultat m

upside down /ʌpsaɪd 'daʊn/
A adj lit à l'envers; fig sens dessus dessous; ~ **cake** Culin gâteau m renversé
B adv **1** lit à l'envers; **2** fig **to turn the house** ~ mettre la maison sens dessus dessous; **to turn sb's life** ~ bouleverser la vie de qn

upstage /ʌp'steɪdʒ/
A adv Theat [stand] au fond de la scène; [move] vers le fond de la scène
B vtr Theat, fig éclipser

upstairs /ʌp'steəz/
A n haut m; **the** ~ **is much nicer** le haut est beaucoup plus joli; **there is no** ~ il n'y a pas d'étage
B noun modifier [room] du haut; [neighbours] du dessus; **an** ~ **bedroom** une chambre à l'étage; **the** ~ **bedroom** la chambre du haut; **the** ~ **flat** GB l'appartement du haut or d'en haut; **with** ~ **bathroom** avec salle de bains à l'étage
C adv en haut; **to go** ~ monter (l'escalier)
⟨Idioms⟩ **he hasn't got much** ~° il n'a pas grand-chose dans le ciboulot° or dans la tête; **to be kicked** ~° recevoir une promotion placard

upstart /'ʌpstɑːt/ n, adj arriviste (mf)

upstate /'ʌpsteɪt/
A adj ~ **New York** la partie nord de l'État de New York
B adv **to go/come from** ~ aller vers le/venir du nord (d'un État)

upstream /ʌp'striːm/ adv [travel] vers l'amont; ~ **from here** en amont d'ici

upsurge /'ʌpsɜːdʒ/ n (of violence) montée f (**of** de); (in debt, demand, industrial activity) augmentation f (**in** de)

uptake /'ʌpteɪk/ n:
⟨Idiom⟩ **to be quick/slow on the** ~° comprendre/ne pas comprendre vite

uptight° /ʌp'taɪt/ adj (tense) tendu; péj (reserved) coincé°

up-to-date /ʌptə'deɪt/ adj **1** (modern, fashionable) [music, clothes] à la mode; [equipment] moderne; **2** (containing latest information) [records, timetable] à jour; [information] récent; **to keep sth up to date** tenir qch à jour; **3** (informed) [person] au courant; **to keep up to date with** se tenir au courant de [developments]; être au courant de [gossip]; **to bring/to keep sb up to date** mettre/tenir qn au courant (**about** de)

up-to-the-minute adj [information] dernier/-ière

uptown /ʌp'taʊn/ US
A adj (smart) chic
B adv **1** (upmarket) **to move** ~ aller habiter dans un quartier résidentiel chic; fig réussir socialement; **2** (central) **to go** ~ aller dans le centre

upturned /ʌp'tɜːnd/ adj [box] posé à l'envers; [brim] remonté; [soil] retourné; [nose] retroussé

upward /'ʌpwəd/
A adj [push, movement] vers le haut; [path, road] qui monte; [trend] à la hausse; **an** ~ **slope** une montée

B adv ▸ **upwards**

upwardly mobile adj en pleine ascension sociale

upwards /'ʌpwədz/
A adv **1** lit [look, point] vers le haut; **to go** ou **move** ~ monter; **2** fig **to push prices** ~ faire monter les prix; **from five years/£10** ~ à partir de cinq ans/10 livres sterling
B **upwards of** prep phr plus de

uranium /jʊ'reɪnɪəm/ n uranium m

urban /'ɜːbən/ adj [environment, life, transport] urbain; [school] en ville; ~ **dweller** citadin/-e m/f

urban blight, urban decay n dégradation f urbaine

urbane /ɜː'beɪn/ adj [person] plein de savoir-faire; [grace, style] raffiné

urbanization /ˌɜːbənaɪ'zeɪʃn, US -nɪ'z-/ n urbanisation f

urbanize /'ɜːbənaɪz/ vtr **to become** ~**d** s'urbaniser

urban: ~ **planner** ▸ p. 1181 n urbaniste mf; ~ **planning** n urbanisme m

urchin /'ɜːtʃɪn/ n gamin m; **street** ~ gamin des rues

urge /ɜːdʒ/
A n forte envie f, désir m (**to do** de faire)
B vtr (encourage) préconiser [caution, restraint, resistance]; **to** ~ **sb to do** conseiller vivement à qn de faire; (stronger) pousser or exhorter qn à faire; **I** ~**d them not to go** je leur ai vivement déconseillé d'y aller; **to** ~ **patience on sb** exhorter qn à la patience
⟨Phrasal verb⟩
■ **urge on:** ▸ ~ **on [sb],** ~ **[sb] on 1** (encourage) encourager; **to** ~ **sb on to do** inciter or pousser qn à faire; **2** (make go faster) talonner [horse]

urgency /'ɜːdʒənsɪ/ n (of situation, appeal, request) urgence f; (of voice, tone) insistance f; **a matter of** ~ une affaire urgente; **to do sth as a matter of** ~ faire qch d'urgence; **there's no** ~ ce n'est pas urgent

urgent /'ɜːdʒənt/ adj **1** (pressing) [case, need] urgent, pressant; [message, demand] urgent; [investigation, measures] d'urgence; **to be in** ~ **need of** avoir un besoin urgent de; **it is** ~ **that we (should) find a solution** il est urgent que nous trouvions une solution; **it's** ~**!** c'est urgent!; **it requires your** ~ **attention** il faut que vous vous en occupiez d'urgence; **2** (desperate) [plea, tone] insistant, pressant

urgently /'ɜːdʒəntlɪ/ adv [request] d'urgence; [plead] instamment; **books are** ~ **needed** il y a un besoin urgent de livres

urinal /jʊə'raɪnl, 'jʊərɪnl/ n (place) urinoir m; (fixture) urinal m

urinary /'jʊərɪnərɪ, US -nerɪ/ adj urinaire

urinate /'jʊərɪneɪt/ vi uriner

urine /'jʊərɪn/ n urine f

URL n (abrév = **uniform resource locator**) URL f

urn /ɜːn/ n urne f

urologist /jʊə'rɒlədʒɪst/ ▸ p. 1181 n urologue mf

Uruguay /'jʊərəgwaɪ/ ▸ p. 774 pr n Uruguay m

us /ʌs, əs/

> ⚠ The direct or indirect object pronoun us is always translated by nous: she knows us = elle nous connaît. Note that both the direct and the indirect object pronouns come before the verb in French and that in compound tenses like the present perfect and past perfect, the past participle agrees in gender and number with the direct object pronoun: he's seen us (masculine or mixed gender object) il nous a vus; (feminine object) il nous a vues.
> In imperatives nous comes after the verb: tell us! = dis-nous!; give it to us or give us it = donne-le-nous (note the hyphens).
> After the verb to be and after prepositions the translation is also nous: it's us = c'est nous.
> For expressions with let us or let's see the entry let.
> For particular usages see the entry below.

pron nous; **both of** ~ tous/toutes les deux; **every single one of** ~ chacun/-e d'entre nous; **people like** ~ des gens comme nous; **some of** ~ quelques uns/unes d'entre nous; **she's one of** ~ elle est des nôtres; **give** ~ **a hand, will you**°? tu peux me donner un coup de main s'il te plaît?; **give** ~ **a look**°! fais voir!

US
A n (abrév = **United States**) USA mpl

u

B *adj* américain

USA *n* (*abrév* = **United States of America**) USA *mpl*

USAF (*abrév* = **United States Air Force**) *n* armée *f* de l'air des États-Unis

usage /'juːsɪdʒ, 'juːzɪdʒ/ *n* **1** (custom) usage *m*, coutume *f*; **2** Ling usage *m*; **in** ~ en usage; **3** (way sth is used) utilisation *f*; **4** (amount used) consommation *f*

USB *n* (*abrév* = **universal serial bus**) USB *m*

use

A /juːs/ *n* **1** ₵ (act of using) (of substance, object, machine) emploi *m*, utilisation *f* (**of** de); (of word, expression, language) emploi *m*, usage *m* (**of** de); **the** ~ **of force** le recours à la force, l'usage de la force; **the** ~ **of sth as/for sth** l'emploi ou l'utilisation de qch comme/pour qch; **for the** ~ **of sb**, **for** ~ **by sb** (customer, staff) à l'usage de qn; **for my own** ~ pour mon usage personnel; **to make** ~ **of sth** utiliser qch; **to put sth to good** ~, **to make good** ~ **of sth** tirer bon parti de qch; **while the machine is in** ~ lorsque la machine est en service *or* en fonctionnement; **external** ~ **only** usage externe; **a word in common** *ou* **general** ~ un mot d'usage courant; **out of** *ou* **no longer in** ~ [*machine*] (broken) hors service; (because obsolete) plus utilisé; [*word, expression*] plus en usage; **worn with** ~ râpé par l'usage; **this machine came into** ~ **in the 1950s** cette machine a fait son apparition pendant les années cinquante; **the new system comes into** ~ **next year** le nouveau système entrera en service l'année prochaine; **2** ₵ (way of using) (of resource, object, material) utilisation *f*; (of term) emploi *m*; **she has her** ~**s** elle a son utilité; **to have no further** ~ **for sth/sb** ne plus avoir besoin de qch/qn; **3** (right to use) **to have the** ~ **of** avoir l'usage de [*house, car, kitchen*]; avoir la jouissance de [*garden*]; **to let sb have the** ~ **of sth** permettre à qn de se servir de qch; **to lose/still have the** ~ **of one's legs** perdre/conserver l'usage de ses jambes; **with** ~ **of** avec usage de [*kitchen*]; **4** (usefulness) **to be of** ~ être utile (**to** à); **to be (of) no** ~ [*object*] ne servir à rien; [*person*] n'être bon à rien; **to be (of) no** ~ **to sb** [*object*] ne pas servir à qn; [*person*] n'être d'aucune utilité à qn; **what** ~ **is a wheel without a tyre?** à quoi sert une roue sans pneu?; **what's the** ~ **of crying?** à quoi bon pleurer?; **oh, what's the** ~**?** oh, et puis à quoi bon?; **it's no** ~ **asking me** inutile de me demander

B /juːz/ *vtr* **1** (employ) se servir de, utiliser [*object, car, room, money, tool*]; employer, utiliser [*method*]; employer [*word, expression*]; profiter de, saisir [*opportunity*]; faire jouer [*influence*]; avoir recours à [*blackmail, force, power*]; utiliser [*knowledge, talent*]; **to** ~ **sth/sb as sth** se servir de qch/qn comme qch; **to** ~ **sth for sth/to do** se servir de *or* utiliser qch pour qch/pour faire; **to be** ~**d for sth/to do** servir à qch/à faire, être utilisé pour qch/pour faire; ~ **your head** *ou* **loaf**°! fais marcher un peu ta cervelle°; **I could** ~°**a drink!** j'aurais bien besoin d'un verre!; **2** (*also* ~ **up**) (consume) consommer [*fuel, food*]; utiliser [*water, leftovers*]; **3** (exploit) *péj* se servir de [*person*]; **4** (take habitually) prendre [*drugs*]

C **used** *pp adj* [*car*] d'occasion; [*crockery*] sale

(Phrasal verb)

■ **use up**: ▸ ~ [sth] **up**, ~ **up** [sth] finir, utiliser [*remainder, food*]; dépenser [*money, savings*]; épuiser [*supplies, fuel, energy*]

use-by date /'juːzbaɪ deɪt/ *n* (on food, medicine) date *f* limite de consommation; (on film, pharmacy goods) date *f* limite d'utilisation

used¹

⚠️ To translate *used to do*, use the imperfect tense in French: *he used to live in York* = il habitait York. To stress that something was done repeatedly, you can use *avoir l'habitude de faire*: *she used to go out for a walk in the afternoon* = elle avait l'habitude de sortir le soir se promener l'après-midi.
   To emphasize a contrast between past and present, you can use *avant*: *I used to love sport* = j'adorais le sport avant.
   For more examples and particular usages, see the entry below.

A /juːst/ *modal aux* **I** ~ **to do** je faisais; **he didn't** ~ **to** *ou* **he** ~ **not to smoke** il ne fumait pas avant; **didn't she** ~ **to smoke?** est-ce qu'elle ne fumait pas, avant?; **she** ~ **to smoke, didn't she?** elle fumait avant, non?; **it** ~ **to be thought that** avant on pensait que; **there** ~ **to be a pub**

here il y avait un pub ici (dans le temps)

B /juːzt/ *adj* (accustomed) **to be** ~ **to sth** avoir l'habitude de qch, être habitué à qch; **I'm not** ~ **to this sort of treatment** je n'ai pas l'habitude qu'on me traite (*subj*) ainsi; **to be** ~ **to sb** être habitué à qn; **to get** ~ **to** s'habituer à; **to be** ~ **to doing** avoir l'habitude de faire; **to get** ~ **to doing** s'habituer à faire; **to be** ~ **to sb doing** être habitué à ce que qn fasse; **I'm not** ~ **to it** je n'ai pas l'habitude; **it takes a bit of getting** ~ **to** ça prend du temps pour s'y habituer

used² /juːzd/ *prét, pp, pp adj* ▸ **use**

useful /'juːsfl/ *adj* **1** (helpful) utile; ~ **for doing** utile pour faire; **to be** ~ **to sb** être utile à qn; **it is** ~ **to do** il est utile de faire; **to make oneself** ~ se rendre utile; **2** °(competent) [*footballer, cook etc*] bon/bonne (*before n*); **to be** ~ **with a gun** savoir se servir d'un fusil, savoir manier un fusil; **to be** ~ **at cooking** savoir cuisiner

usefulness /'juːsflnɪs/ *n* utilité *f*

useless /'juːslɪs/ *adj* **1** (not helpful) inutile; **it's** ~ **to do** *ou* **doing** il est inutile de faire; **2** (not able to be used) inutilisable; **3** °(incompetent) incapable, nul/nulle°; **to be** ~ **at sth/doing** être nul en qch/pour (ce qui est de) faire

uselessly /'juːslɪslɪ/ *adv* inutilement

uselessness /'juːslɪsnɪs/ *n* (of object, machine, effort, information) inutilité *f*; (of person) incompétence *f*

user /'juːzə(r)/ *n* **1** (of road, public transport, service) usager *m*; (of product, machine, credit card) utilisateur/-trice *m/f*; **2** (*also* **drug** ~) toxicomane *mf*; **cocaine** ~ cocaïnomane *mf*; **heroin** ~ héroïnomane *mf*; **3** *péj* (exploiter) homme/femme *m/f* intéressé/-e

user-: ~ **friendliness** *n* Comput convivialité *f*; gen facilité *f* d'emploi; ~**-friendly** *adj* Comput convivial; gen facile à utiliser; ~ **interface** *n* Comput interface *f* utilisateur

usher /'ʌʃə(r)/ ▸ p. 1181

A *n* (at function, lawcourt) huissier *m*; (in theatre, church) placeur *m*

B *vtr* conduire, escorter; **to** ~ **sb in/out** faire entrer/sortir qn; **to** ~ **sb to the door** conduire qn à la porte

(Phrasal verb)

■ **usher in**: ▸ ~ **in [sth]** ouvrir la voie à [*era, negotiations*]; introduire [*scheme, reforms*]

usherette /ˌʌʃə'ret/ ▸ p. 1181 *n* ouvreuse *f*

USMC *n* US (*abrév* = **United States Marine Corps**) corps *m* des marines américains

USN *n* US (*abrév* = **United States Navy**) marine *f* des États-Unis

USSR ▸ p. 774 *n* Hist (*abrév* = **Union of Soviet Socialist Republics**) URSS *f*

usual /'juːʒl/

A °*n* **the** ~ la même chose que d'habitude; **'what did he say?'—'oh, the** ~**'** 'qu'est-ce qu'il a dit?'—'oh, toujours la même chose'; **your** ~, **sir?** (in bar) comme d'habitude, monsieur?

B *adj* [*behaviour, form, procedure, problem, route, place, time*] habituel/-elle; [*word, term*] usuel/-elle; **earlier than** ~ plus tôt que d'habitude; **it is** ~ **to do, the** ~ **practice is to do** il est d'usage de faire; **they did all the** ~ **things** ils ont fait tout ce qu'il est d'usage de faire; **she was her** ~ **cheerful self** elle était gaie, comme d'habitude; **as** ~ comme d'habitude; **'business as** ~**'** 'la vente continue'; **as is** ~ **at this time of year** comme il est d'usage à cette époque de l'année; **more/less than** ~ plus/moins que d'habitude

usually /'juːʒəlɪ/ *adv* d'habitude, normalement; **more than** ~ **friendly** plus aimable que d'habitude

usurp /juː'zɜːp/ *vtr* usurper

usurper /juː'zɜːpə(r)/ *n* usurpateur/-trice *m/f*

UT US Post *abrév écrite* = **Utah**

utensil /juː'tensl/ *n* ustensile *m*

uterus /'juːtərəs/ *n* utérus *m*

utilitarian /ˌjuːtɪlɪ'teərɪən/

A *n* Philos utilitariste *mf*

B *adj* **1** [*doctrine, ideal*] utilitariste; **2** (practical) [*object, vehicle*] utilitaire; [*building*] fonctionnel/-elle; [*clothing*] pratique

utility /juː'tɪlətɪ/

A *n* **1** (usefulness) utilité *f*; **2** (*also* **public** ~) (service) service *m* public, commodité *f*; **3** Comput utilitaire *m*

B **utilities** *npl* US factures *fpl*

C *noun modifier* (functional) [*vehicle*] tous usages *inv*; [*object*] utilitaire

utility: ~ **company** n société f chargée d'assurer un service public; ~ **room** n buanderie f

utilization /ˌjuːtəlaɪˈzeɪʃn/ n utilisation f

utilize /ˈjuːtəlaɪz/ vtr utiliser [object, idea]; exploiter [resource]

utmost /ˈʌtməʊst/

A n to do ou try one's ~ to come faire tout son possible pour venir; **to do sth to the** ~ **of one's abilities** faire qch au maximum de ses capacités; **at the** ~ au maximum, au plus

B adj **1** (greatest) [caution, ease, secrecy] le plus grand/la plus grande (before n); [limit] extrême; **of the** ~ **importance** extrêmement important; **with the** ~ **haste** aussi vite que possible; **2** (furthest) **the** ~ **ends of the earth** les confins mpl de la terre

Utopia /juːˈtəʊpɪə/ n utopie f

Utopian /juːˈtəʊpɪən/

A n utopiste mf

B adj utopique

utter /ˈʌtə(r)/

A adj [disaster, amazement, despair] total; [sincerity] absolu; [fool, scoundrel] fieffé (before n); [stranger] parfait (before n); ~ **rubbish!** pure sottise!

B vtr **1** prononcer [word, curse]; pousser [cry]; émettre [sound]; **2** Jur répandre [libel]; mettre en circulation [forged banknotes]

utterance /ˈʌtərəns/ n **1** (statement) parole f; **to give** ~ **to** exprimer, formuler; **2** Ling énoncé m

utterly /ˈʌtəlɪ/ adv complètement; **we** ~ **condemn this action** nous condamnons cette action jusqu'au bout

U-turn n demi-tour m; fig volte-face f inv; **to do a** ~ fig faire volte-face

UV adj (abrév = **ultraviolet**) ultraviolet/-ette

Uzbekistan /ˌʌzbekɪˈstɑːn, ˌʊz-/ ▸ p. 774 pr n Ouzbékistan m

u

v, V /viː/ n ⓵ (letter) v, V m; ⓶ v (abrév écrite = **versus**) contre; ⓷ v (abrév écrite = **vide**) voir; ⓸ V Elec (abrév écrite = **volt**) V, volt m

vac⁰ /væk/ n GB (abrév = **vacation**) vacances fpl

vacancy /ˈveɪkənsɪ/ n ⓵ (free room) chambre f libre; **'vacancies'** 'chambres libres'; **'no vacancies'** 'complet'; ⓶ (unfilled job) poste m à pourvoir, poste m vacant; **a ~ for an accountant** un poste de comptable à pourvoir; **to fill a ~** pourvoir un poste (**for** de); **to advertise a ~** faire paraître une offre d'emploi; **'no vacancies'** 'pas d'embauche'

vacant /ˈveɪkənt/ adj ⓵ (unoccupied) [flat, room, seat] libre, disponible; [office, land] inoccupé; ⓶ (available) [job, post] vacant, à pourvoir; **to become** ou **fall ~** se libérer; **'Situations ~'** 'offres d'emploi'; ⓷ (dreamy) [look, stare] absent; [expression] vide

vacant lot n US terrain m vague

vacantly /ˈveɪkəntlɪ/ adv [answer, stare] d'un air absent

vacant possession n GB Jur jouissance f immédiate

vacate /vəˈkeɪt, US ˈveɪkeɪt/ vtr quitter [house, premises, job]; libérer [room, seat]

vacation /vəˈkeɪʃn, US veɪ-/
A n gen, Univ vacances fpl; Jur vacances fpl judiciaires; **on ~** en vacances; **to take a ~** prendre des vacances
B vi US **he's ~ing in Miami** il est en vacances à Miami

vacationer /vəˈkeɪʃənə(r), US veɪ-/ n US vacancier/-ière m/f

vaccinate /ˈvæksɪneɪt/ vtr vacciner (**against** contre)

vaccination /ˌvæksɪˈneɪʃn/ n vaccination f (**against** contre); **to have a ~** se faire vacciner

vaccine /ˈvæksiːn, US vækˈsiːn/ n vaccin m (**against** contre); **tetanus ~** vaccin contre le tétanos

vacillate /ˈvæsəleɪt/ vi hésiter (**over** au sujet de)

vacuous /ˈvækjʊəs/ adj sout [person, look, expression] niais; [optimism, escapism] béat pej

vacuum /ˈvækjʊəm/
A n ⓵ Phys vide m; **to create a ~** faire le vide; ⓶ (lonely space) vide m; **emotional ~** vide affectif; **it left a ~ in our lives** ça a fait un grand vide dans notre vie; ⓷ (also **~ cleaner**) aspirateur m; ⓸ (also **~ clean**) **to give [sth] a ~** passer un coup d'aspirateur sur [carpet]; passer l'aspirateur dans [room]
B vtr passer [qch] à l'aspirateur [carpet]; passer l'aspirateur dans [room]

vacuum: ~ bottle n US = **vacuum flask; ~ cleaner** n aspirateur m; **~ flask** n bouteille f thermos®; **~ pack** vtr emballer [qch] sous vide

vagabond /ˈvægəbɒnd/ n, adj vagabond/-e (m/f)

vagary /ˈveɪgərɪ/ n sout caprice m

vagina /vəˈdʒaɪnə/ n (pl **-nas** ou **-nae**) vagin m

vagrancy /ˈveɪgrənsɪ/ n gen, Jur vagabondage m

vagrant /ˈveɪgrənt/ n, adj gen, Jur vagabond/-e (m/f)

vague /veɪg/ adj ⓵ (imprecise) [person, account, idea, memory, rumour, term] vague; ⓶ (evasive) **to be ~** rester vague sur or évasif/-ive au sujet de [plans, past]; ⓷ (distracted) [person, expression] distrait; [gesture] vague; **to look ~** avoir l'air distrait; ⓸ (faint, slight) [sound, smell, taste] vague, imprécis; [fear, embarrassment] vague (before n); [doubt] léger/-ère (before n); ⓹ (unsure) **I am (still) a bit ~ about events** je ne sais (toujours) pas très bien ce qui s'est passé

vaguely /ˈveɪglɪ/ adv ⓵ (faintly, slightly) vaguement; **it seems ~ familiar** cela me dit vaguement quelque chose; **it feels**

~ like a bee sting cela fait un peu comme une piqûre d'abeille; ⓶ (distractedly) [smile, gaze, say] d'un air distrait or vague; [wander, move about] distraitement; ⓷ (imprecisely) [remember, understand, reply] vaguement; [describe] de manière vague or imprécise; [defined, formulated] vaguement

vagueness /ˈveɪgnɪs/ n ⓵ (imprecision) (of wording, proposals) flou m; (of thinking) imprécision f; (of image) manque m de netteté; ⓶ (absent-mindedness) distraction f

vain /veɪn/
A adj ⓵ (conceited) vaniteux/-euse, vain (after n); **to be ~ about sth** tirer vanité de qch; ⓶ (futile) [attempt, hope] vain (before n); [show] futile
B **in vain** adv phr en vain

ⓘ **to take sb's name in ~** hum parler de qn (derrière son dos)

vainly /ˈveɪnlɪ/ adv ⓵ (futilely) [try, wait, struggle] vainement, en vain; ⓶ (conceitedly) [look, stare] avec vanité

valance /ˈvæləns/ n (on bed base) tour m de lit; (round canopy) lambrequin m; (above curtains) cantonnière f

valency /ˈveɪlənsɪ/ n Chem, Ling valence f

valentine /ˈvæləntaɪn/ n (also **~ card**) carte f de la Saint-Valentin

Valentine('s) Day n la Saint-Valentin

valet /ˈvælɪt, -leɪ/ ▸ p. 1181
A n ⓵ (employee) valet m de chambre; ⓶ US (rack) valet m de nuit
B vtr nettoyer [clothes, car interior]

valiant /ˈvælɪənt/ adj [soldier] vaillant; [attempt] courageux/-euse; **to make a ~ attempt to do** tenter courageusement de faire; **to make a ~ effort to smile** s'efforcer bravement de sourire

valiantly /ˈvælɪəntlɪ/ adv [fight] vaillamment; [try] courageusement

valid /ˈvælɪd/ adj ⓵ (still usable) [passport, licence] valide; [ticket, offer] valable; ⓶ (well-founded) [argument, excuse] valable; [complaint] fondé; [point, comment] pertinent; [comparison] légitime; ⓷ (in law) valable, valide

validate /ˈvælɪdeɪt/ vtr ⓵ prouver le bien-fondé de [claim, theory]; ⓶ valider [document, passport]

validity /vəˈlɪdətɪ/ n ⓵ Jur (of ticket, document, consent) validité f; (of argument, excuse, method) validité f; (of complaint, objection) bien-fondé m

valley /ˈvælɪ/ n (pl **~s**) vallée f; (small) vallon m

valour GB, **valor** US /ˈvælə(r)/ n littér valeur f liter, bravoure f

ⓘ **discretion is the better part of ~** Prov prudence est mère de sûreté Prov

valuable /ˈvæljʊəbl/ adj ⓵ [commodity, asset] de valeur; **to be ~** avoir de la valeur; **very ~** de grande valeur; ⓶ [advice, information, lesson] précieux/-ieuse

valuables /ˈvæljʊəblz/ npl objets mpl de valeur

valuation /ˌvæljʊˈeɪʃn/ n (of house, land, company) évaluation f; (of antique, art) expertise f; **to have a ~ done on sth** faire évaluer qch; **a ~ of £50** une valeur estimée de 50 livres sterling

value /ˈvæljuː/
A n ⓵ (monetary worth) valeur f; **of little ~** de peu de valeur; **of no ~** sans valeur; **to have a ~ of £5** valoir 5 livres sterling; **to the ~ of** d'une valeur de; ⓶ (usefulness, general worth) valeur f; **to have** ou **be of educational ~** avoir une valeur éducative; **the ~ of sb as** la valeur de qn en tant

que; **the** ~ **of doing** l'importance de faire; **novelty** ~ caractère nouveau; ③ (worth relative to cost) **to be good** ~ avoir un bon rapport qualité-prix; **to be good** ~ **at £5** ne pas être cher/chère à 5 livres sterling; **you get good** ~ **at Buymore** on en a pour son argent à Buymore; **to get** ~ **for money** en avoir pour son argent; **a** ~**-for-money product** un produit qui vous en donne pour votre argent; ④ (standards, ideals) valeur *f*; **family** ~**s** valeurs familiales
🇧 *vtr* ① (assess worth of) évaluer [*house, asset, company*] (**at** à); expertiser [*antique, jewel, painting*]; **to have sth** ~**d** faire évaluer *or* expertiser qch; ② (appreciate) apprécier [*person, friendship, opinion, help*]; tenir à [*reputation, independence, life*]; **to** ~ **sb as a friend** apprécier qn en tant qu'ami

value-added tax, VAT *n* taxe *f* à la valeur ajoutée, TVA *f*

valued /'vælju:d/ *adj* [*person*] apprécié; [*contribution, opinion*] précieux/-ieuse

valueless /'vælju:lɪs/ *adj* sans valeur (*after n*)

valuer /'vælju:ə(r)/ ▶ p. 1181 *n* expert *m*

valve /vælv/ *n* ① (in machine, engine) soupape *f*; (on tyre, football) valve *f*; ② Anat (of organ) valvule *f*; ③ (of mollusc, fruit) valve *f*; ④ (on brass instrument) piston *m*; ⑤ GB lampe *f*

vamp /væmp/ *n* ① †péj (woman) vamp *f*; ② (on shoe) empeigne *f*

vampire /'væmpaɪə(r)/ *n* vampire *m*; ~ **bat** vampire *m*

van /væn/ *n* ① Aut (small, for deliveries etc) fourgonnette *f*, camionnette *f*; (larger, for removals etc) fourgon *m*; ② US (camper) auto-caravane *f*, camping-car *m*; ③ (vanguard) avant-garde *f*

vandal /'vændl/ *n* vandale *mf*

vandalism /'vændəlɪzəm/ *n* vandalisme *m*

vandalize /'vændəlaɪz/ *vtr* vandaliser

van driver ▶ p. 1181 *n* chauffeur *m* de camionnette

vane /veɪn/ *n* ① (also **weather** ~) girouette *f*; ② (of windmill) aile *f*

vanguard /'vænɡɑ:d/ *n* Mil, fig avant-garde *f*; **in the** ~ à l'avant-garde

vanilla /və'nɪlə/
🇦 *n* Culin, Bot vanille *f*
🇧 *noun modifier* [*sauce, icecream*] à la vanille; [*pod, plant*] de vanille; ~ **essence** extrait *m* de vanille

vanish /'vænɪʃ/ *vi* disparaître (**from** de); **to** ~ **into the distance** disparaître au loin; **to** ~ **into thin air** fig se volatiliser

vanishing /'vænɪʃɪŋ/
🇦 *n* disparition *f*
🇧 *adj* [*species, environment*] en voie de disparition
(Idiom) **to do a** ~ **act** se volatiliser

vanishing: ~ **cream** *n* crème *f* de jour; ~ **point** *n* point *m* de fuite; ~ **trick** *n* tour *m* de passe-passe

vanity /'vænɪtɪ/ *n* vanité *f*

vanity: ~ **case** *n* vanity-case *m*; ~ **mirror** *n* Aut miroir *m* de courtoisie; ~ **unit** *n* meuble *m* sous-vasque

vanquish /'væŋkwɪʃ/ *vtr* littér défaire liter, vaincre [*enemy*]

vantage point *n* ① gen, Mil point *m* de vue, position *f* élevée; **from the** ~ **of** du haut de; ② fig (point of view) perspective *f*

vapid /'væpɪd/ *adj* [*person, expression, remark, debate*] mièvre, fade; [*style, novel*] insipide, fade

vaporize /'veɪpəraɪz/
🇦 *vtr* vaporiser [*liquid*]
🇧 *vi* se vaporiser

vaporizer /'veɪpəraɪzə(r)/ *n* vaporisateur *m*

vapour GB, **vapor** US /'veɪpə(r)/ *n* vapeur *f*

vapour trail *n* traînée *f* de condensation, traînée *f* d'un avion

variable /'veərɪəbl/
🇦 *n* gen, Comput, Math variable *f*
🇧 *adj* gen, Comput variable

variance /'veərɪəns/ *n* ① gen désaccord *m* (**between** entre); **to be at** ~ **with** être en désaccord avec [*evidence, facts*]; **my views are at** ~ **with his** mes opinions divergent des siennes; **that is at** ~ **with what you said yesterday** cela ne concorde pas avec ce que vous avez dit hier; ② Math variance *f*

variant /'veərɪənt/
🇦 *n* variante *f* (**of** de; **on** par rapport à)

🇧 *adj* [*colour, species, strain*] différent; ~ **reading** *ou* **text** *ou* **version** variante *f*; ~ **form** Bot variante *f*

variation /ˌveərɪ'eɪʃn/ *n* ① (change) variation *f*, différence *f* (**in, of** de); **regional** ~ variations régionales; ~ **between A and B** différence entre A et B; **subject to considerable** ~ sujet à des variations importantes; ② (version) version *f* (**of** de); (new version) variante *f* (**of** de); Mus variation *f* (**on** sur)

varicose /'værɪkəʊs/ *adj* variqueux/-euse; ~ **veins** varices *fpl*

varied /'veərɪd/ *adj* varié

variegated /'veərɪɡeɪtɪd/ *adj* ① gen varié; ② Bot, Zool panaché

variety /və'raɪətɪ/
🇦 *n* ① (diversity, range) variété *f* (**in, of** de); **wide** ~ grande variété; **for a** ~ **of reasons** pour diverses raisons; **the dresses come in a** ~ **of sizes** ces robes existent dans un grand choix de tailles; ② (type) gen type *m*; Bot variété *f*; ③ ℂ Theat, TV variétés *fpl*
🇧 *noun modifier* [*artist, act*] de variétés

various /'veərɪəs/ *adj* ① (different) différents (*before n*); **at their** ~ **addresses** à leurs différentes adresses; ② (several) divers; **at** ~ **times** à diverses reprises; **in** ~ **ways** de diverses manières

variously /'veərɪəslɪ/ *adv* (in different ways) [*arranged, decorated*] de différentes manières; (by different people) [*called, described, estimated*] à tour de rôle

varnish /'vɑ:nɪʃ/
🇦 *n* vernis *m*
🇧 *vtr* vernir [*woodwork*]; **to** ~ **one's nails** se vernir les ongles

varnishing /'vɑ:nɪʃɪŋ/ *n* vernissage *m*

vary /'veərɪ/
🇦 *vtr* varier [*menu, programme*]; faire varier [*flow, temperature*]; changer de [*pace, route*]
🇧 *vi* [*objects, people, tastes*] varier (**with, according to** selon); **to** ~ **from sth** différer de qch; **to** ~ **from X to Y** varier de X à Y; **they** ~ **in cost/in size** ils varient quant au coût/à la taille

varying /'veərɪɪŋ/ *adj* [*amounts, degrees, opinions*] variable; [*circumstances*] varié; **with** ~ **(degrees of) success** avec plus ou moins de succès

vascular /'væskjʊlə(r)/ *adj* Anat, Bot vasculaire

vase /vɑ:z, US veɪs, veɪz/ *n* vase *m*

vasectomy /və'sektəmɪ/ *n* vasectomie *f*

vast /vɑ:st, US væst/ *adj* ① (quantitatively) [*amount, sum, improvement, difference*] énorme; [*number*] très grand; [*knowledge*] extrêmement étendu; **the** ~ **majority** la très grande majorité; ② (spatially) [*room, area, plain*] vaste (*before n*), immense

vastly /'vɑ:stlɪ, US væstlɪ/ *adv* [*improved, overrated, superior*] considérablement, infiniment; [*complex, popular*] terriblement; [*different*] complètement

vastness /'vɑ:stnɪs, US væstnɪs/ *n* immensité *f*

vat /væt/ *n* cuve *f*; **beer/wine** ~ cuve à bière/vin

VAT /ˌvi:eɪ'ti:/ *n* (*abrév* = **value-added tax**) GB TVA *f*

vaudeville /'vɔ:dəvɪl/ *n* Theat variétés *fpl*

vault /vɔ:lt/
🇦 *n* ① (roof) voûte *f*; **the** ~ **of heaven** la voûte céleste; ② (cellar) (of house, for wine) cave *f*; (tomb) caveau *m*; (of bank) chambre *f* forte; (for safe-deposit boxes) salle *f* des coffres; ③ (jump) saut *m*
🇧 *vtr* gen, Sport sauter par-dessus [*fence, bar*]
🇨 *vi* gen, Sport sauter (**over** par-dessus)

vaulted /'vɔ:ltɪd/ *adj* Archit voûté

vaulting /'vɔ:ltɪŋ/
🇦 *n* ① Archit voûtes *fpl*; ② ▶ p. 881 (in gym) saut *m*
🇧 *adj* [*ambition, arrogance*] démesuré

VC *n* ① (*abrév* = **vice chairman**) vice-président/-e *m/f*; ② GB Univ (*abrév* = **vice chancellor**) ≈ président/-e *m/f* d'université

VCR *n* (*abrév* = **video cassette recorder**) magnétoscope *m*

VD ▶ p. 933 (*abrév* = **venereal disease**)
🇦 *n* MST *f*
🇧 *noun modifier* [*clinic*] de vénérologie

VDU *n* (*abrév* = **visual display unit**) écran *m* de visualisation; ~ **operator** opérateur/-trice *m/f* de terminal de visualisation

veal /viːl/
A n veau m
B noun modifier [stew, cutlet] de veau

vector /'vektə(r)/ n **1** Biol, Math vecteur m; **2** Aviat trajectoire f

veer /vɪə(r)/ vi **1** lit (change direction) [ship] virer; [person, road] tourner; **to ~ away from/towards sth** se détourner de/vers qch; **to ~ away** ou **off** s'éloigner; **to ~ off course** dévier de sa route; **to ~ across the road** traverser la route; **2** fig [person, opinion] changer; **to ~ (away) from sth** se détourner de qch; **to ~ towards sth** se tourner vers qch

vegan /'viːgən/ n, adj végétalien/-ienne (m/f)

veganism /'viːgənɪzəm/ n végétalisme m

vegetable /'vedʒtəbl/
A n **1** (edible plant) légume m; **2** (as opposed to mineral, animal) végétal m; **3** °fig **to become a ~** être réduit à l'état de légume
B noun modifier [knife, dish] à légumes; [soup, patch] de légumes; [fat, oil, matter] végétal; **~ garden** potager m; **~ peeler** épluche-légumes m

vegetarian /ˌvedʒɪ'teərɪən/ n, adj végétarien/-ienne (m/f)

vegetarianism /ˌvedʒɪ'teərɪənɪzəm/ n végétarisme m

vegetate /'vedʒɪteɪt/ vi végéter

vegetation /ˌvedʒɪ'teɪʃn/ n végétation f

vehemence /'viːəməns/ n (of speech, action) véhémence f; (of feelings) intensité f

vehement /'viːəmənt/ adj [tirade, gesture, attack] véhément; [dislike, disapproval] violent

vehemently /'viːəməntlɪ/ adv [speak, react] avec véhémence

vehicle /'vɪəkl, US 'viːhɪkl/ n **1** Aut véhicule m; **'closed to ~s'** 'interdit à la circulation'; **2** (medium) véhicule m (**for** de)

vehicular /vɪ'hɪkjʊlə(r), US viː-/ adj **'no ~ access'**, **'no ~ traffic'** 'circulation interdite'

veil /veɪl/
A n **1** voile m also Relig; (on hat) voilette f; **to take the ~** prendre le voile; **2** fig voile m; **a ~ of secrecy** le voile du secret; **let's draw a ~ over that episode** oublions cet épisode
B vtr **1** [mist, cloud] voiler; **2** fig (hide) dissimuler [emotion]
C veiled pp adj **1** [person] voilé; **2** (indirect) [hint, threat] voilé; **thinly ~ed** [allusion] à peine voilé

vein /veɪn/ n **1** (blood vessel) veine f; **2** (on insect wing, leaf) nervure f; **3** (thread of colour) (in marble) veine f; (in cheese) veinure f; **4** (of ore) veine f; **5** (theme) veine f; **to continue in a similar ~** continuer dans la même veine; **a ~ of nostalgia** un élément de nostalgie; **in the same ~** dans la même esprit

veined /veɪnd/ adj [hand, rock, cheese] veiné; [leaf] nervuré

Velcro® /'velkrəʊ/ n velcro® m

vellum /'veləm/ n vélin m; **in/on ~** en/sur vélin

velocity /vɪ'lɒsətɪ/ n **1** Tech vitesse f; **2** fml vélocité f

velvet /'velvɪt/
A n velours m; **crushed ~** velours frappé
B noun modifier [garment, curtain] en velours
C adj [skin, eyes] de velours; [tones, softness] velouté; fig [glove, revolution] de velours

velvety /'velvətɪ/ adj velouté

venal /'viːnl/ adj vénal

vending machine n distributeur m automatique

vendor /'vendə(r)/ n **1** (in street, kiosk) marchand/-e m/f; **2** (as opposed to buyer) vendeur/-euse m/f; **3** US (machine) distributeur m automatique

veneer /vɪ'nɪə(r)/ n **1** (on wood) placage m; **2** fig (surface show) vernis m

venerable /'venərəbl/ adj vénérable

venerate /'venəreɪt/ vtr vénérer

veneration /ˌvenə'reɪʃn/ n vénération f (**for** pour)

venereal /və'nɪərɪəl/ ▸ p. 933 adj vénérien/-ienne; **~ disease** maladie f vénérienne

Venetian blind n store m vénitien

Venezuela /ˌvenɪ'zweɪlə/ ▸ p. 774 pr n Venezuela m

vengeance /'vendʒəns/ n vengeance f; **to take ~ (up)on sb** se venger de qn; **with a ~** de plus belle

venial /'viːnɪəl/ adj sout véniel/-ielle

Venice /'venɪs/ ▸ p. 1276 pr n Venise

venison /'venɪsn, -zn/ n (viande f de) chevreuil m

venom /'venəm/ n Zool, fig venin m

venomous /'venəməs/ adj Zool, fig venimeux/-euse

venous /'viːnəs/ adj veineux/-euse

vent /vent/
A n **1** (outlet for gas, pressure) bouche f, conduit m; **air ~** bouche d'aération; **to give ~ to** fig décharger [anger, feelings]; **2** (of volcano) cheminée f; **3** (slit) fente f; **4** US (window) déflecteur m
B vtr **1** fig (release) décharger [anger, spite, frustration] (**on** sur); **2** (let out) évacuer [gas, smoke]
C vi [gas, chimney, volcano] s'évacuer

ventilate /'ventɪleɪt/ vtr **1** (provide with air) aérer [room]; **2** Med ventiler

ventilation /ˌventɪ'leɪʃn/ n **1** aération f, ventilation f; **~ shaft** puits m d'aérage; **2** Med (of patient) ventilation f artificielle

ventilator /'ventɪleɪtə(r)/ n **1** Med respirateur m artificiel; **2** Constr (opening) aérateur m; (fan) ventilateur m

ventriloquist /ven'trɪləkwɪst/ ▸ p. 1181 n ventriloque mf; **~'s dummy** pantin m de ventriloque

venture /'ventʃə(r)/
A n **1** Comm, Fin (undertaking) aventure f, entreprise f; **a publishing/media ~** une aventure éditoriale/médiatique; **her first ~ into marketing** sa première expérience dans le marketing; **2** (experiment) essai m; **his first ~ into fiction** sa première tentative dans le domaine de la fiction
B vtr **1** (offer) hasarder [opinion, suggestion]; **to ~ the opinion that** hasarder l'opinion selon laquelle; **might I ~ a suggestion?** puis-je me permettre une suggestion?; **to ~ to do** se risquer à faire; **2** (gamble) risquer [bet, money] (**on** sur)
C vi **1** (go) **to ~ into** s'aventurer dans [place, street, city]; **to ~ out(doors)** s'aventurer dehors; **to ~ forth** littér se risquer à sortir; **2** Comm (make foray) **to ~ into** se lancer dans [retail market, publishing]
(Idiom) **nothing ~d nothing gained** qui ne risque rien n'a rien

venture: **~ capital** n capital-risque m; **~ capitalist** n capital-risqueur m

venue /'venjuː/ n lieu m; **the ~ for the match will be** le match aura lieu à

veracity /və'ræsətɪ/ n sout véracité f

veranda(h) /və'rændə/ n véranda f; **on the ~** sous la véranda

verb /vɜːb/ n verbe m

verbal /'vɜːbl/ adj gen, Ling verbal

verbally /'vɜːbəlɪ/ adv verbalement

verbatim /vɜː'beɪtɪm/
A adj [report, account] textuel/-elle
B adv [describe, record] mot pour mot

verbena /vɜː'biːnə/ n verveine f

verbose /vɜː'bəʊs/ adj verbeux/-euse

verdict /'vɜːdɪkt/ n **1** Jur verdict m; **to return a ~** rendre un verdict; **to reach a ~** arriver au verdict; **a ~ of guilty** un verdict positif; **the ~ was suicide** l'enquête a conclu au suicide; **2** fig (opinion) verdict m; **well, what's the ~○?** eh bien, qu'est-ce que tu en penses?; **to give one's ~ on sth** se prononcer sur qch

verdigris /'vɜːdɪgrɪs, -griːs/ n vert-de-gris m inv

verge /vɜːdʒ/ n **1** GB (by road) accotement m, bas-côté m; **soft ~** accotement non stabilisé; **2** (brink) **on the ~ of au** bord de [tears]; au seuil de [adolescence, death]; **on the ~ of success** sur le point de réussir; **on the ~ of doing** sur le point de faire; **to bring** ou **drive sb to the ~ of** amener qn au bord de [bankruptcy, despair, suicide]; **to bring** ou **drive sb to the ~ of doing** amener qn au point de faire
(Phrasal verb)
■ **verge on**: ▸ **~ on [sth]** friser [panic, stupidity]

verger /'vɜːdʒə(r)/ ▸ p. 1181 n Relig bedeau m

verifiable /'verɪfaɪəbl/ adj vérifiable

verification /ˌverɪfɪ'keɪʃn/ n vérification f

verify /'verɪfaɪ/ vtr vérifier

veritable /'verɪtəbl/ adj sout véritable

vermicelli /ˌvɜːmɪ'selɪ, -'tʃelɪ/ n **C** (pasta, chocolate) vermicelle m

vermilion /vəˈmɪlɪən/ ▸ p. 752 *n, adj* vermillon (*m*) *inv*

vermin /ˈvɜːmɪn/ *n* ① ₵ (rats etc) animaux *mpl* nuisibles; ② (lice, insects) vermine *f*; ③ péj (person) canaille *f*

vermouth /ˈvɜːməθ, US vərˈmuːθ/ *n* vermouth *m*

vernacular /vəˈnækjʊlə(r)/
A *n* ① (language) **the ~** la langue vulgaire; **in the ~** (in local dialect) en dialecte; ② (jargon) jargon *m*
B *adj* [*architecture*] en style local; [*writing*] dans la langue vulgaire

verruca /vəˈruːkə/ *n* (*pl* **-cae** *ou* **-cas**) verrue *f* plantaire

versatile /ˈvɜːsətaɪl/ *adj* ① (flexible) [*person*] plein de ressources, aux talents divers (*after n*); [*mind*] souple; ② (with many uses) [*vehicle*] polyvalent; [*equipment*] à usages multiples

versatility /ˌvɜːsəˈtɪlətɪ/ *n* ① (flexibility) (of person) adaptabilité *f*; (of mind) souplesse *f*; ② (of equipment) polyvalence *f*

verse /vɜːs/ *n* ① (poems) poésie *f*; **to write ~** écrire des poèmes; ② (form) vers *mpl*; **in ~** en vers; ③ (part of poem) strophe *f*; (of song) couplet *m*; ④ Bible verset *m*; ⑤ (single line) vers *m*

versed /vɜːst/ *adj* (*also* **well-versed**) versé (**in** dans)

versifier /ˈvɜːsɪfaɪə(r)/ *n* rimailleur/-euse *m/f*

version /ˈvɜːʃn, US -ʒn/ *n* version *f* (**of** de)

versus /ˈvɜːsəs/ *prep* (all contexts) contre

vertebra /ˈvɜːtɪbrə/ *n* (*pl* **-brae**) vertèbre *f*

vertebral /ˈvɜːtɪbrəl/ *adj* vertébral

vertebrate /ˈvɜːtɪbreɪt/ *n, adj* vertébré (*m*)

vertex /ˈvɜːteks/ *n* (*pl* **-tices**) ① Math sommet *m*; ② Anat vertex *m*

vertical /ˈvɜːtɪkl/
A *n* verticale *f*; **out of the ~** pas d'aplomb
B *adj* [*line, take-off*] vertical; [*cliff*] à pic

vertically /ˈvɜːtɪklɪ/ *adv* verticalement

vertigo /ˈvɜːtɪɡəʊ/ *n* vertige *m*; **to get ~** avoir le vertige

verve /vɜːv/ *n* brio *m*, verve *f*

very /ˈverɪ/
A *adj* ① (actual) même (*after n*); **this ~ second** à la seconde même; ② (ideal) **the ~ person I need** exactement la personne qu'il me faut; **the ~ thing I need** exactement ce qu'il me faut; ③ (ultimate) tout; **from the ~ beginning** depuis le tout début; **at the ~ front** tout devant; **to the ~ end** jusqu'au bout; **on the ~ edge** à l'extrême bord; ④ (mere) [*mention, thought*] seul (*before n*); **the ~ idea!** quelle idée!
B *adv* ① (extremely) très; **I'm ~ sorry** je suis vraiment désolé; **~ well** très bien; **she couldn't ~ well do that** elle ne pouvait pas vraiment faire cela; **that's all ~ well but** c'est fort bien mais; **~ much** beaucoup; **I didn't eat/find ~ much** je n'ai pas mangé/trouvé grand-chose; **to be ~ much a city dweller** être un vrai citadin; ② (absolutely) **the ~ best thing** de loin la meilleure chose; **in the ~ best of health** en pleine santé; **at the ~ latest** au plus tard; **at the ~ least** tout au moins; **the ~ first** le tout premier; **the ~ same words** exactement les mêmes mots; **the ~ next day** le lendemain même; **the ~ next person I met** la toute première personne que j'ai rencontrée ensuite; **a car of your ~ own** ta propre voiture

vespers /ˈvespəz/ *n* (+ *v sg ou pl*) vêpres *fpl*

vessel /ˈvesl/ *n* ① Naut vaisseau *m*; ② Anat vaisseau *m*; ③ (container) vase *m*; (for liquids only) coupe *f*; ④ fig (person) instrument *m* (**for** de)

vest /vest/ ▸ p. 1191
A *n* ① (underwear) maillot *m* de corps; ② (for sport) débardeur *m*; ③ US (waistcoat) gilet *m*
B *vtr* conférer [*authority, power*] (**in** à)

vested interest *n* ① gen intérêt *m* personnel; **to have a ~** être personnellement intéressé (**in** dans); ② Jur droit *m* acquis

vestige /ˈvestɪdʒ/ *n* ① (trace) (*gén pl*) (of civilization, faith, system) vestige *m*; (of emotion, truth, stammer) trace *f*; ② Anat, Zool vestige *m*

vestment /ˈvestmənt/ *n* habit *m* sacerdotal

vest pocket US
A *n* poche *f* de gilet
B **vest-pocket** *adj* [*dictionary, calculator*] de poche

vestry /ˈvestrɪ/ *n* Relig sacristie *f*

vet /vet/
A *n* ▸ p. 1181 ① (abrév = **veterinary surgeon**) vétérinaire *mf*; ② ○US Mil ancien combattant *m*, vétéran *m*
B *vtr* (*p prés etc* **-tt-**) mener une enquête approfondie sur [*person*]; passer [qch] en revue [*plan*]; approuver [*publication*]

veteran /ˈvetərən/
A *n* gen vétéran *m*; Mil ancien combattant *m*, vétéran *m*
B *noun modifier* [*sportsman, politician*] chevronné; [*marathon*] vétéran; **a ~ campaigner** un vieux routier

veteran: **~ car** *n* GB voiture *f* ancienne (construite avant 1905); **Veterans Day** *n* US jour *m* des anciens combattants

veterinary /ˈvetrɪnrɪ, US ˈvetərɪnərɪ/ ▸ p. 1181 *n, adj* vétérinaire (*mf*)

veterinary: **~ surgeon** ▸ p. 1181 *n* vétérinaire *mf*; **~ surgery** *n* clinique *f* vétérinaire

veto /ˈviːtəʊ/
A *n* (*pl* **-toes**) ① (practice) veto *m*; ② (right) droit *m* de veto (**over, on** sur)
B *vtr* (3ᵉ *pers sg prés* **-toes**; *prét, pp* **-toed**) mettre *or* opposer son veto à

vetting /ˈvetɪŋ/ *n* contrôle *m*; **security ~** enquête *f* de sécurité

vex /veks/ *vtr* (annoy) contrarier; (worry) tracasser

vexation /vekˈseɪʃn/ *n* (annoyance) contrariété *f*; (worry) tracas *m*

vexatious /vekˈseɪʃəs/ *adj* [*situation*] contrariant; [*person*] agaçant

vexed /vekst/ *adj* ① (annoyed) mécontent (**with** de); ② (problematic) [*question, issue, situation*] épineux/-euse

vexing /ˈveksɪŋ/ *adj* = **vexatious**

VHF *n* (abrév = **very high frequency**) VHF

via /ˈvaɪə/ *prep* ① (by way of) (on ticket, timetable) via; gen en passant par; ② (by means of) par

viability /ˌvaɪəˈbɪlətɪ/ *n* ① (feasibility) (of company, government, farm) viabilité *f*; (of project, idea, plan) validité *f*; ② Biol, Zool, Med viabilité *f*

viable /ˈvaɪəbl/ *adj* ① (feasible) [*company, government, farm*] viable; [*project, idea, plan*] réalisable, valable; ② Biol, Zool, Med viable

viaduct /ˈvaɪədʌkt/ *n* viaduc *m*

Viagra® /vaɪˈæɡrə/ *n* Pharm Viagra® *m*

vibes○ /vaɪbz/ *npl* **to have good/bad ~** dégager de bonnes/mauvaises vibrations○

vibrant /ˈvaɪbrənt/ *adj* ① (lively) [*person, place, personality*] plein de vie; [*colour*] éclatant; ② (resonant) sonore; **a voice ~ with emotion** une voix vibrante d'émotions

vibrate /vaɪˈbreɪt, US ˈvaɪbreɪt/
A *vtr* faire vibrer
B *vi* vibrer (**with** de)

vibration /vaɪˈbreɪʃn/ *n* vibration *f*

vicar /ˈvɪkə(r)/ *n* pasteur *m* (anglican ou de l'Église épiscopale)

vicarage /ˈvɪkərɪdʒ/ *n* presbytère *m*

vicarious /vɪˈkeərɪəs, US vaɪˈk-/ *adj* (indirect) indirect; (delegated) [*power*] délégué

vice /vaɪs/
A *n* ① vice *m*; hum faiblesse *f*; ② (*also* **vise** US) Tech étau *m*
B *noun modifier* [*laws*] sur les mœurs; [*scandal*] des mœurs

vice: **~-captain** *n* Sport capitaine *m* en second; **~-chair** *n* vice-président/-e *m/f*; **~-chancellor** ▸ p. 1181 *n* GB Univ président/-e *m/f* d'Université; US Jur *juge assistant*/-e; **~-president, VP** *n* vice-président/-e *m/f*; **~-presidential** *adj* [*candidate, race*] à la vice-présidence; [*residence*] vice-présidentiel/-ielle; **~-principal** *n* Sch (of senior school) proviseur *m* adjoint; (of junior school, college) directeur/-trice *m/f* adjoint/-e; **~ squad** *n* brigade *f* des mœurs

vicinity /vɪˈsɪnətɪ/ *n* voisinage *m*; **in the (immediate) ~ of Oxford** à proximité (immédiate) d'Oxford

vicious /ˈvɪʃəs/ *adj* [*person, animal, power*] malfaisant; [*speech, attack, price cut, revenge*] brutal; [*rumour, sarcasm, lie*] malveillant

vicious circle *n* cercle *m* vicieux

viciously /ˈvɪʃəslɪ/ *adv* ① (savagely) brutalement; ② (perversely) méchamment

victim /'vɪktɪm/ n lit, fig victime f; **to fall ∼ to** être victime de [disease, disaster]; succomber à [charm]

victimization /ˌvɪktɪmaɪˈzeɪʃn/ n persécution f

victimize /'vɪktɪmaɪz/ vtr persécuter

victor /'vɪktə(r)/ n vainqueur m

Victorian /vɪk'tɔːrɪən/
A n homme/femme m/f de l'époque victorienne
B adj gen victorien/-ienne; [writer, poverty] de l'époque victorienne

victorious /vɪk'tɔːrɪəs/ adj victorieux/-ieuse

victory /'vɪktərɪ/ n victoire f; **to win a ∼** remporter une victoire

video
A n (pl ∼s) **①** (also ∼ **recorder**) magnétoscope m; **②** (also ∼ **cassette**) cassette f vidéo; **on ∼** en vidéo; **③** (also ∼ **film**) vidéo f; **④** US (television) télévision f
B noun modifier [company, footage] de vidéo; [market] de la vidéo; [channel, evidence, link, game, recording] vidéo; [interview] en vidéo; [distributor] de vidéos
C vtr (3ᵉ pers sg prés ∼s; prét, pp ∼ed) **①** (from TV) enregistrer [qch]; **②** (on camcorder) filmer [qch] en vidéo

video: ∼ **camera** n caméra f vidéo; ∼ **card** n carte f vidéo; ∼ **clip** n Cin, TV extrait m; ∼ **diary** n vidéojournal m; ∼ **library** n vidéothèque f; ∼ **RAM** n mémoire f vidéo; ∼ **shop** GB, ∼ **store** US ▸ p. 1181 n magasin m (de) vidéo

videotape /'vɪdɪəʊteɪp/
A n bande f vidéo
B vtr enregistrer [qch] en vidéo

videotaping /'vɪdɪəʊteɪpɪŋ/ n enregistrement m en vidéo

vie /vaɪ/ vi (p prés **vying**) rivaliser (**with** avec)

Vietnam /ˌvjet'næm/ ▸ p. 774 pr n Việt Nam m

view /vju:/
A n **①** lit, fig vue f; **the trees cut off the ∼** la vue est cachée par les arbres; **you're blocking my ∼!** tu me bouches la vue!; **we moved forward to get a better ∼** nous nous sommes avancés pour mieux voir; **to have a front ∼ of sth** voir qch de face; **an overall ∼ of** une vue d'ensemble de; **an inside ∼ of the situation** une idée de la situation vue de l'intérieur; **to take the long(-term) ∼ of sth** avoir une vision à long terme de qch; **the lake was within ∼ of the house** on pouvait voir le lac de la maison; **to do sth in (full) ∼ of sb** faire qch devant qn ou sous les yeux de qn; **to have sth in ∼** fig penser faire qch; **to keep sth in ∼** lit, fig ne pas perdre qch de vue; **to disappear from ∼** lit disparaître; **to hide sth from ∼** cacher qch; **to be on ∼** [exhibition] être présenté; [new range] être exposé; **②** (personal opinion, attitude) avis m, opinion f; **point of ∼** point m de vue; **in his ∼** à son avis; **in the ∼ of Mr Jones** selon M. Jones; **③** (of exhibition, house) visite f; (of film) projection f; (of new range) présentation f
B in view of prep phr (considering) vu, étant donné
C with a view to prep phr **with a ∼ to** en vue de qch; **with a ∼ to sb** ou **sb's doing** afin que qn fasse
D vtr **①** (consider) considérer; (envisage) envisager; **to ∼ sb with suspicion** être méfiant à l'égard de qn; **②** (look at) gen voir [scene, building, exhibition]; visiter [house, castle]; visionner [slide, microfiche]; examiner [documents]; regarder [television, programme]
E vi TV regarder la télévision

viewer /'vju:ə(r)/ n **①** (of TV) téléspectateur/-trice m/f; **②** (of exhibition, property) visiteur/-euse m/f; **③** Phot visionneuse f

viewfinder /'vju:ˌfaɪndə(r)/ n viseur m

viewing /'vju:ɪŋ/
A n **①** TV **we plan our ∼ ahead** nous choisissons à l'avance ce que nous allons regarder (à la télévision); **'and that concludes Saturday night's ∼'** 'et avec ceci se termine votre programme du samedi soir'; **essential ∼ for teachers** à voir impérativement pas les enseignants; **the film makes compulsive ∼** le film est captivant; **②** (of exhibition, house) visite f; (of film) projection f; (of new range) présentation f; **'∼ by appointment only'** 'visite sur rendez-vous uniquement'
B noun modifier TV [trends, patterns] d'écoute; [habits, preferences] des téléspectateurs; ∼ **figures** taux m d'écoute; **the ∼ public** les téléspectateurs mpl

view: ∼**phone** n vidéophone m; ∼**point** n (all contexts) point m de vue

vigil /'vɪdʒɪl/ n gen veille f; (by sickbed) veillée f; Relig vigile f; Pol manifestation f silencieuse

vigilance /'vɪdʒɪləns/ n vigilance f

vigilant /'vɪdʒɪlənt/ adj vigilant

vigilante /ˌvɪdʒɪ'læntɪ/
A n membre m d'un groupe d'autodéfense
B noun modifier [group, attack, role] d'autodéfense

vigor n US = **vigour**

vigorous /'vɪgərəs/ adj [person, plant, attempt, exercise] vigoureux/-euse; [campaign] énergique; [denial] catégorique; [defender, supporter] ardent

vigorously /'vɪgərəslɪ/ adv gen vigoureusement; [defend, campaign, deny] énergiquement

vigour GB, **vigor** US /'vɪgə(r)/ n gen vigueur f; (of campaign, efforts) énergie f

vile /vaɪl/ adj **①** (unpleasant) [smell, taste] infect; [weather] abominable; [place, experience, colour] horrible; [mood, behaviour] exécrable; **②** (wicked) vil, ignoble

vilification /ˌvɪlɪfɪ'keɪʃn/ n diffamation f (**of** de)

villa /'vɪlə/ n (in town) pavillon m; (for holiday) villa f

village /'vɪlɪdʒ/
A n (place, community) village m
B noun modifier [shop, fête, school] du village

village: ∼ **green** n terrain m communal; ∼ **hall** n salle f des fêtes

villager /'vɪlɪdʒə(r)/ n villageois/-e m/f

villain /'vɪlən/ n (scoundrel) canaille f; (criminal) bandit m; (in book, film) méchant m; (child) coquin/-e m/f

villainous /'vɪlənəs/ adj gen infâme; [plot, expression] diabolique

vindicate /'vɪndɪkeɪt/ vtr gen donner raison à; Jur innocenter [person]; justifier [action, claim, judgment]

vindication /ˌvɪndɪ'keɪʃn/ n gen justification f; Jur (of person) disculpation f

vindictive /vɪn'dɪktɪv/ adj [person, behaviour] vindicatif/-ive; [decision, action] revanchard

vine /vaɪn/ n **①** (producing grapes) vigne f; **②** (climbing plant) plante f grimpante

vinegar /'vɪnɪgə(r)/ n vinaigre m

vinegary /'vɪnɪgərɪ/ adj lit de vinaigre; fig acide

vineyard /'vɪnjəd/ n vignoble m

vintage /'vɪntɪdʒ/
A n **①** (wine) millésime m; **②** (era) époque f
B adj **①** [wine, champagne] millésimé; [port] vieux/vieille; **②** [performance, comedy] classique; **it's ∼ Armstrong** c'est du Armstrong du meilleur cru

vintage: ∼ **car** n voiture f d'époque; ∼ **year** n lit, fig grande année f

vinyl /'vaɪnl/
A n **①** vinyle m; **②** (record) disque m noir
B noun modifier gen en vinyle; [paint] vinylique

viola¹ /vɪ'əʊlə/ ▸ p. 1028 n (violon m) alto m

viola² /'vaɪələ/ n Bot (genus) violacée f; (flower) pensée f

violate /'vaɪəleɪt/ vtr **①** (infringe) gen violer; transgresser [criteria, duty, taboo]; Jur enfreindre [rule, regulation]; **②** profaner [sacred place]; troubler [peace]

violation /ˌvaɪə'leɪʃn/ n **①** gen violation f; (of criteria, duty, taboo) transgression f; **②** (of sacred place) profanation f; **③** Jur infraction f

violence /'vaɪələns/ n lit, fig violence f; **two days of ∼** deux jours d'incidents violents

violent /'vaɪələnt/ adj **①** violent; **a ∼ attack** (physical) une attaque violente; (verbal) une attaque virulente; **②** (sudden) [acceleration, braking] soudain; [change, contrast] brutal; **③** [colour] criard

violently /'vaɪələntlɪ/ adv **①** [push, attack, blush, cough, shake] violemment; [struggle] furieusement; [assault] sauvagement; **to die ∼** mourir de mort violente; **to be ∼ ill** ou **sick** GB avoir de violentes nausées; **②** [brake, swerve, alter, swing] brusquement; **③** [react, object] violemment

violet /'vaɪələt/ ▸ p. 752
A n **①** Bot violette f; **②** (colour) violet m
B adj violet/-ette

violin /ˌvaɪə'lɪn/ ▸ p. 1028 n violon m

VIP (abrév = **very important person**)
A n personnalité f (en vue)

B *adj* réservé aux personnalités; **to give sb (the) ~ treatment** recevoir qn en hôte de marque

viper /'vaɪpə(r)/ *n* Zool, fig vipère *f*

virgin /'vɜːdʒɪn/
A *n* (woman) (femme) vierge *f*; (man) homme *m* vierge
B *adj* (all contexts) vierge

virginal /'vɜːdʒɪnl/
A *n* Mus virginal *m*
B *adj* gen innocent; [*white, innocence*] virginal

Virginia creeper /vɜː'dʒɪnjə,kriː.pə(r)/ *n* vigne *f* vierge

virginity /və'dʒɪnəti/ *n* virginité *f*

Virgo /'vɜːgəʊ/ ▸ p. 1350 *n* Vierge *f*

virile /'vɪraɪl, US 'vɪrəl/ *adj* lit, fig viril

virologist /vaɪə'rɒlədʒɪst/ ▸ p. 1181 *n* virologue *mf*, virologiste *mf*

virtual /'vɜːtʃʊəl/ *adj* **1** (almost complete) quasi-total; **to be a ~ prisoner** être pratiquement prisonnier/ière; **she is the ~ ruler of the country** de fait c'est elle qui dirige le pays; **2** Comput, Phys virtuel/-elle

virtually /'vɜːtʃʊəlɪ/ *adv* pratiquement, presque; **it's ~ impossible** c'est quasiment○ impossible; **~ every household** chaque ménage ou presque

virtual: **~ pet** *n* Games animal *m* virtuel; **~ reality** *n* réalité *f* virtuelle

virtue /'vɜːtʃuː/
A *n* **1** (goodness) vertu *f*; **a woman of easy ~** une femme de petite vertu; **2** (advantage) avantage *m*; **to extol the ~s of sth** vanter les mérites de qch
B **by virtue of** *prep phr* en raison de

virtuoso /,vɜːtjʊ'əʊsəʊ, -zəʊ/
A *n* (*pl* **-sos** *ou* **-si**) virtuose *mf* (**of** de)
B *adj* de virtuose

virtuous /'vɜːtʃʊəs/ *adj* vertueux/-euse

virtuously /'vɜːtʃʊəslɪ/ *adv* **1** (morally) [*behave, live*] de façon vertueuse; [*help, act*] vertueusement; **2** (self-righteously) avec satisfaction

virulent /'vɪrʊlənt/ *adj* Med, fig virulent

virus /'vaɪərəs/ ▸ p. 933 *n* Med, Comput virus *m*

virus checker *n* Comput logiciel *m* antivirus

visa /'viːzə/ *n* visa *m*

vis-à-vis /,viː.zɑː'viː/
A *n* (person) homologue *m*
B *prep* (in relation to) par rapport à; (concerning) en ce qui concerne

visceral /'vɪsərəl/ *adj* lit, fig viscéral; [*power, performance*] qui vous prend aux tripes○

viscose /'vɪskəʊz, -kəʊs/ *n* viscose *f*

viscount /'vaɪkaʊnt/ ▸ p. 869 *n* vicomte *m*

viscous /'vɪskəs/ *adj* visqueux/-euse, gluant

vise /vaɪs/ *n* US étau *m*

visibility /,vɪzə'bɪlətɪ/ *n* **1** (ability to see) visibilité *f*; **to have restricted ~** avoir une visibilité limitée; **2** (ability to be seen) visibilité *f*

visible /'vɪzəbl/ *adj* **1** (able to be seen) visible; **clearly ~** bien visible; **2** (concrete) [*improvement, sign*] évident; [*evidence*] flagrant; **with no ~ means of support** sans ressources apparentes

visibly /'vɪzəblɪ/ *adv* (to the eye) visiblement; (clearly) manifestement

vision /'vɪʒn/
A *n* **1** (idea, mental picture, hallucination) vision *f*; **to appear to sb in a ~** apparaître à qn; **Rousseau's ~ of the ideal society** l'idée de la société idéale selon Rousseau; **2** (imaginative foresight) sagacité *f*; **a man of ~** un visionnaire; **3** (ability to see) vue *f*; **to have blurred ~** voir trouble; **to come into ~** devenir visible; **4** (visual image) image *f*
B *vtr* US imaginer

visionary /'vɪʒnrɪ, US 'vɪʒənerɪ/ *n, adj* visionnaire (*mf*)

vision mixer *n* (person) réalisateur *m* de direct; (equipment) mélangeur *m* d'images

visit /'vɪzɪt/
A *n* **1** (call) visite *f*; **a state ~** une visite officielle; **a flying ~** une visite éclair; **on her first/last ~ to China, she...** la première/dernière fois qu'elle est allée en Chine, elle...; **to pay a ~ to sb, to pay sb a ~** aller voir qn; **to have a ~ from** recevoir la visite de; **to make a ~ to** visiter; **2** (stay) séjour *m*; **to go on a ~** faire un séjour

B *vtr* **1** (call on, see) aller voir; **2** (inspect) inspecter; **3** (on holiday etc) venir chez qn; **to ~ a country** faire un séjour dans un pays; **come and ~ us for a few days** venez passer quelques jours avec nous; **4** US (socially) **to ~ with** aller voir; **5** †**to ~ sth (up)on sb** infliger qch à qn

visiting /'vɪzɪtɪŋ/ *adj* [*statesman*] en visite; [*athlete*] visiteur/-euse; [*orchestra*] invité

visiting: **~ card** *n* US carte *f* de visite; **~ hours** *npl* heures *fpl* de visite; **~ lecturer** *n* (short term) maître *m* de conférence invité; (long term) maître *m* de conférence associé; **~ nurse** ▸ p. 1181 *n* US infirmier/-ière *m/f* à domicile; **~ team** *n* visiteurs/-euses *mpl/fpl*; **~ time** *n* heures *fpl* de visite

visitor /'vɪzɪtə(r)/ *n* **1** (caller) invité/-e *m/f*; **we have ~s** nous avons de la visite; **2** (tourist) visiteur/-euse *m/f*; **I've been a regular ~ to France** je vais souvent en France; **3** (animal, bird) migrateur *m*

visitor: **~ centre** *n* centre *m* d'accueil et d'information des visiteurs; **~s' book** *n* (in exhibition) livre *m* d'or; (in hotel) registre *m*

visor /'vaɪzə(r)/ *n* (eyeshade) visière *f*; Aut pare-soleil *m* *inv*

vista /'vɪstə/ *n* lit panorama *m*; fig perspective *f*

visual /'vɪʒʊəl/
A visuals *npl* (photographs, pictures) images *fpl*; Cin effets *mpl* visuels
B *adj* (all contexts) visuel/-elle

visual: **~ aid** *n* support *m* visuel; **~ arts** *npl* arts *mpl* plastiques; **~ display terminal, VDT, ~ display unit, VDU** *n* Comput écran *m* de visualisation

visualize /'vɪʒʊəlaɪz/ *vtr* **1** (picture) s'imaginer; **2** (envisage) envisager

visually /'vɪʒʊəlɪ/ *adv* visuellement

visually handicapped *adj* (partially-sighted) malvoyant; (non-sighted) nonvoyant

visually impaired *n* the **~** (+ *v pl*) les malvoyants *mpl*

vital /'vaɪtl/ *adj* **1** (essential) [*asset, document, information, research, supplies, interest*] primordial; [*match, support, factor*] décisif/-ive; [*service, help*] indispensable; [*treatment, organ*] vital; **of ~ importance** d'une importance capitale; **2** (lively) [*person*] plein de vie *or* de vitalité; [*culture, music*] vivant

vitality /vaɪ'tælətɪ/ *n* vitalité *f*

vitally /'vaɪtlɪ/ *adv* [*important*] extrêmement; [*needed*] absolument

vital statistics *n* Comm, Admin données *fpl* démographiques; hum gen informations *fpl* essentielles; (of woman) mensurations *fpl*

vitamin /'vɪtəmɪn, US 'vaɪt-/
A *n* vitamine *f*; **with added ~s, ~ enriched** vitaminé
B *noun modifier* [*requirements*] en vitamines; **to have a high ~ content** être riche en vitamines

vitreous /'vɪtrɪəs/ *adj* [*enamel*] vitrifié; [*rock, china*] vitreux/-euse

vitriolic /,vɪtrɪ'ɒlɪk/ *adj* Chem de vitriol; fig au vitriol

vituperative /vɪ'tjuːpərətɪv, US vaɪ'tuːpəreɪtɪv/ *adj* injurieux/-ieuse

viva
A /'vaɪvə/ *n* GB Univ oral *m*
B /'viːvə/ *excl* vive!; **~ freedom!** vive la liberté!

vivacious /vɪ'veɪʃəs/ *adj* plein de vivacité

vivacity /vɪ'væsətɪ/ *n* vivacité *f*

vivid /'vɪvɪd/ *adj* **1** (bright) [*colour, light*] vif/vive; [*garment*] aux couleurs vives; **2** (graphic) [*imagination*] vif/vive; [*memory, picture*] (très) net/nette; [*dream, impression, description, example, language, imagery*] frappant

vividly /'vɪvɪdlɪ/ *adv* [*shine*] d'une lumière éclatante; [*picture, dream*] de façon très nette; [*describe*] de façon très vivante; **~ coloured** aux couleurs vives; **I remember it ~!** je m'en souviens très bien!

vividness /'vɪvɪdnɪs/ *n* (of colour, light, sunset, garment) éclat *m*; (of memory, dream, description) netteté *f*; (of language, imagery) richesse *f*; (of style) vigueur *f*

vivisect /'vɪvɪsekt/ *vtr* pratiquer une vivisection sur

vivisection /,vɪvɪ'sekʃn/ *n* vivisection *f*

vixen /'vɪksn/ *n* **1** Zool renarde *f*; **2** péj (woman) mégère *f*

viz /vɪz/ *adv* sout (*abrév* = **videlicet**) à savoir

vocabulary /və'kæbjʊlərɪ, US -lerɪ/ *n* gen vocabulaire *m*; (glossary) lexique *m*

The human voice

Voices and singers

	voice	singer
soprano	= soprano *m*	soprano *m* or *f* (*depending on whether a boy soprano or a woman*)
mezzo-soprano	= mezzo-soprano *m*	mezzo-soprano *f*
contralto	= contralto *m*	contralto *f*
alto	= alto *m*	alto *m*
counter-tenor	= haute-contre *f*	haute-contre *m*
tenor	= ténor *m*	ténor *m*
baritone	= baryton *m*	baryton *m*
bass-baritone	= baryton-basse *m*	baryton-basse *m*
bass	= basse *f*	basse *f*

■ *In the following examples* tenor *and* ténor *stand for any of the above voices:*

he's a tenor
= il est ténor
or c'est un ténor

he sings tenor
= il chante ténor

a tenor voice
= une voix de ténor

the tenor part
= la partie ténor

a tenor solo
= un solo de ténor

---

vocal /'vəʊkl/
A vocals *npl* chant *m*; **who did the ~s?** qui a assuré la partie vocale?; **to do the backing ~s** faire les chœurs
B *adj* ⚊ lit vocal; ⚋ (vociferous) qui se fait entendre

vocalist /'vəʊkəlɪst/ *n* chanteur/-euse *m*/*f* (*dans un groupe pop*)

vocalize /'vəʊkəlaɪz/
A *vtr* ⚊ lit vocaliser; ⚋ fig exprimer
B *vi* Mus vocaliser, faire des vocalises

vocally /'vəʊkəlɪ/ *adj* ⚊ Mus vocalement; ⚋ (vociferously) haut et fort

vocation /vəʊ'keɪʃn/ *n* vocation *f*

vocational /vəʊ'keɪʃənl/ *adj* gen professionnel/-elle; [*syllabus, approach*] à orientation professionnelle; **~ course** stage *m* de formation professionnelle

vociferous /və'sɪfərəs, US vəʊ-/ *adj* [*person, protest*] véhément

vogue /vəʊg/
A *n* vogue *f* (**for** de); **to go out of ~** se démoder; **to be out of ~** être démodé
B *noun modifier* [*word*] en vogue, à la mode

voice /vɔɪs/
A *n* ⚊ (speaking) voix *f*; **in a loud ~** à haute voix; **in a low ~** à voix basse; **in a cross ~** d'une voix irritée; **keep your ~ down!** baisse la voix!; **his ~ is breaking** sa voix mue; **to lose one's ~** (when ill) perdre la voix; **to give ~ to sth** exprimer qch; **at the top of one's ~** à tue-tête; ⚋ (for singing) voix *f*; **to have a good ~** avoir une belle voix; **to be in fine ~** être en voix; ⚌ (opinion, expression) voix *f*; **to have a ~** avoir voix au chapitre (**in sth** en matière de qch; **in doing** pour ce qui est de faire); **to add one's ~ to sth** unir sa voix à qch; **to demand sth with one ~** exiger unanimement qch; ④ (representative organization) porte-parole *m*; ⑤ Literat (of writer) style *m*; **narrative ~** voix *f* du narrateur; ⑥ Ling voix *f*
B -voiced *combining form* **hoarse-/deep-~d** à la voix rauque/grave
C *vtr* exprimer [*concern, grievance*]; sonoriser [*consonant*]
(Idiom) **to like the sound of one's own ~** s'écouter parler

voice: **~ box** *n* larynx *m*; **~d consonant** *n* consonne *f* sonore

voiceless /'vɔɪslɪs/ *adj* [*minority, group*] privé de la parole

voice: **~-over** *n* voix-off *f*; **~ print** *n* empreinte *f* vocale; **~ vote** *n* US vote *m* par acclamation

void /vɔɪd/
A *n* lit, fig vide *m*; **to fill the ~** combler le vide
B *adj* ⚊ Jur [*contract, agreement*] nul/nulle; [*cheque*] annulé; **to**

Volume measurement

■ *For pints, gallons, litres etc.* ▸ **p. 723**.

■ *Note that French has a comma where English has a decimal point.*

1 cu in
= 16,38 cm³

1 cu ft
= 0,03 m³

1 cu yd
= 0,76 m³

■ *There are three ways of saying* 16,38 cm³, *and other measurements like it:* seize virgule trente-huit centimètres cubes *or* (*less formally*) seize centimètres cubes virgule trente-huit *or* seize centimètres cubes trente-huit. *For more details on how to say numbers* ▸ **p. 1044**.

what is its volume?
= quel est son volume?

its volume is 200 cubic metres
= ça fait 200 mètres cubes

it's 200 cubic metres
= ça fait 200 mètres cubes

it's one metre by two metres by three metres
= ça mesure un mètre sur deux mètres sur trois mètres

sold by the cubic metre
= vendu au mètre cube

A has a greater volume than B
= le volume de A est supérieur à celui de B

B has a smaller volume than A
= le volume de B est inférieur à celui de A

■ *Note the use of* de *in this construction.*

there are a million cubic centimetres in a cubic metre
= il y a un million de centimètres cubes dans un mètre cube

a million cubic centimetres make one cubic metre
= un million de centimètres cubes font un mètre cube

■ *Note the French construction with* de, *coming after the noun it describes:*

a 200-cubic-metre tank
= un réservoir de 200 mètres cubes

---

make *ou* **render ~** annuler; ⚋ (empty) vide; **~ of** dépourvu de
C *vtr* Jur annuler

vol /vɒl/ *n* (*pl* **-s**) *abrév* = **volume**

volatile /'vɒlətaɪl, US -tl/ *adj* ⚊ Chem volatil; ⚋ fig [*situation*] explosif/-ive; [*person*] lunatique; [*mood*] changeant; ⚌ Econ instable

volcanic /vɒl'kænɪk/ *adj* volcanique

volcano /vɒl'keɪnəʊ/ *n* (*pl* **-noes** *ou* **-nos**) volcan *m*

volition /və'lɪʃn, US vəʊ-/ *n* volonté *f*; **of one's own ~** de son propre gré

volley /'vɒlɪ/
A *n* ⚊ Sport (in tennis) volée *f*; (in soccer) reprise *f* de volée; ⚋ (of gunfire) salve *f*; (of missiles) volée *f*; ⚌ fig (series) **a ~ of** un feu roulant de [*questions, words*]; une bordée de [*insults, oaths*]
B *vtr* (in tennis) prendre [qch] de volée; (in soccer) reprendre [qch] de volée
C *vi* (in tennis) jouer à la volée

volleyball /'vɒlɪˌbɔːl/ ▸ **p. 881**
A *n* volley(-ball) *m*
B *noun modifier* [*match, court*] de volley(-ball)

volt /vəʊlt/ *n* volt *m*; **nine-~ battery** pile *f* de neuf volts

voltage /'vəʊltɪdʒ/ *n* tension *f*

volume /'vɒljuːm, US -jəm/
A *n* ⚊ gen, Audio, Phys volume *m*; (of container) capacité *f*; **by ~** au volume; ⚋ (book) volume *m*; (part of set) tome *m*

B *noun modifier* Comm (bulk) [*production, purchasing, sales*] en nombre

(Idiom) **to speak** ~s **(about)** en dire long (sur)

volume: ~ **control** *n* Audio (bouton *m* de) réglage *m* du volume; ~ **discount** *n* Comm remise *f*, ristourne *f* (sur quantité)

voluntarily /'vɒləntrəlɪ, US ˌvɒlən'terɪlɪ/ *adv* de plein gré, volontairement

voluntary /'vɒləntrɪ, US -terɪ/
A *n* Mus voluntary *m*
B *adj* **1** (not imposed) [*consent, euthanasia*] volontaire; [*statement*] spontané; [*agreement, ban*] librement consenti; [*participation*] facultatif/-ive; [*sanction*] non obligatoire; **on a** ~ **basis** sur une base volontaire; **2** (unpaid) bénévole; **to work on a** ~ **basis** travailler bénévolement; **3** [*movement*] volontaire

voluntary: ~ **hospital** *n* US ≈ hôpital *m* privé; ~ **redundancy** *n* GB départ *m* volontaire

volunteer /ˌvɒlən'tɪə(r)/
A *n* **1** gen, Mil volontaire *mf*; **2** (unpaid worker) bénévole *mf*
B *noun modifier* **1** (unpaid) [*driver, fire brigade, helper, work*] bénévole; **2** Mil [*force, division*] de volontaires
C *vtr* **1** (offer) offrir; **to** ~ **to do** offrir de faire, se porter volontaire pour faire; **2** (divulge) fournir [qch] spontanément; **'it was me,' he** ~**ed** 'c'était moi,' dit-il de lui-même
D *vi* **1** gen se porter volontaire (**for** pour); **2** Mil s'engager comme volontaire

voluptuous /və'lʌptʃʊəs/ *adj* voluptueux/-euse

vomit /'vɒmɪt/
A *n* vomi *m*
B *vtr, vi* vomir

vomiting /'vɒmɪtɪŋ/ *n* vomissement *m*

voodoo /'vuːduː/ *n, noun modifier* vaudou (*m*)

voracious /və'reɪʃəs/ *adj* vorace

vortex /'vɔːteks/ *n* (*pl* ~**es** *ou* **-tices**) lit, fig tourbillon *m*

vote /vəʊt/
A *n* **1** (choice) vote *m*; **to cast one's** ~ voter; **one man one** ~ ≈ suffrage universel; **that gets my** ~! fig moi je suis pour!; **2** (franchise) **the** ~ le droit de vote; **3** (ballot) vote *m*; **to have a** ~ voter; **to take a** ~ **on** voter sur; **to put sth to the** ~ mettre qch aux voix; **4** (body of voters) voix *fpl*; **by a majority** ~ à la majorité des voix; **to increase one's** ~ **by 10%** recevoir 10% de voix en plus
B *vtr* **1** (affirm choice of) voter; **what** *ou* **how do you** ~? pour qui votes-tu?; **to** ~ **sb into/out of office** élire/ne pas réélire qn; **2** (authorize) **to** ~ **sb sth** accorder qch à qn; **3** ○(propose) proposer
C *vi* voter; **to** ~ **for reform** voter en faveur de la réforme; **to** ~ **on whether** voter pour décider si; **let's** ~ **on it** mettons-le aux voix

(Idiom) **to** ~ **with one's feet** (by leaving) quitter le navire○

(Phrasal verbs)

■ **vote down:** ▸ ~ **[sb/sth] down**, ~ **down [sb/sth]** battre [qn] aux voix [*person*]; rejeter [*motion*]
■ **vote in:** ▸ ~ **[sb] in**, ~ **in [sb]** élire
■ **vote out:** ▸ ~ **[sb/sth] out**, ~ **out [sb/sth]** ne pas réélire [*person*]; rejeter [*motion*]

■ **vote through:** ▸ ~ **[sth] through**, ~ **through [sth]** faire adopter

vote: ~ **of censure** *n* Pol vote *m* sur une motion de censure; ~ **of confidence** *n* Pol, fig vote *m* de confiance (**in** en); ~ **of thanks** *n* discours *m* de remerciement

voter /'vəʊtə(r)/ *n* Pol électeur/-trice *m/f*

voter: ~ **registration** *n* US inscription *f* sur les listes électorales; ~ **registration card** *n* US carte *f* d'électeur

voting /'vəʊtɪŋ/
A *n* scrutin *m*
B *noun modifier* [*patterns, intentions, rights*] de vote

voting: ~ **age** *n* majorité *f* électorale; ~ **booth** *n* isoloir *m*

vouch /vaʊtʃ/ *vtr* **to** ~ **that** garantir que

(Phrasal verb)

■ **vouch for:** ▸ ~ **for [sb/sth]** **1** (informally) répondre de [*person*]; témoigner de [*fact*]; **2** (officially) se porter garant de

voucher /'vaʊtʃə(r)/ *n* **1** (for gift, concession) bon *m*; **2** (receipt) reçu *m*

vow /vaʊ/
A *n* (religious) vœu *m*; (of honour) serment *m*; **to be under a** ~ **of silence** avoir fait le serment de garder le secret
B **vows** *npl* **1** Relig vœux *mpl*; **2** **marriage** *ou* **wedding** ~**s** serments *mpl* du mariage
C *vtr* faire vœu de; **to** ~ **to do** jurer de faire; (privately) se jurer de faire

vowel /'vaʊəl/
A *n* voyelle *f*
B *noun modifier* [*sound*] vocalique; ~ **shift** mutation *f* vocalique

vox pop○ /ˌvɒks 'pɒp/ *n* **1** (*also* **vox populi**) opinion *f* publique; **2** TV, Radio interviews *mpl* pris dans la rue

voyage /'vɔɪɪdʒ/
A *n* lit, fig voyage *m*; **on the** ~ pendant le voyage; **to go on a** ~ partir en voyage; **the outward** ~ le voyage aller
B *vi* littér voyager; **to** ~ **across** traverser

V-sign /'viːsaɪn/ *n* (victory sign) V *m* de la victoire; (offensive gesture) GB geste *m* obscène

VSO *n* GB (*abrév* = **Voluntary Service Overseas**) coopération *f* civile

vulgar /'vʌlgə(r)/ *adj* **1** [*furniture, clothes*] de mauvais goût; [*behaviour, curiosity*] déplacé; [*taste*] douteux/-euse; [*person*] vulgaire; **2** (rude) grossier/-ière

vulgar fraction *n* Math fraction *f* ordinaire

vulgarity /vʌl'gærətɪ/ *n* **1** (of furniture, clothes) mauvais goût *m*; (of person, behaviour) vulgarité *f*; **2** (rudeness) grossièreté *f*

vulgarize /'vʌlgəraɪz/ *vtr* **1** populariser [*place, activity*]; vulgariser [*study, theory, art*]; **2** (make rude) rendre [qch] vulgaire

vulgarly /'vʌlgəlɪ/ *adv* **1** [*dressed, furnished*] avec mauvais goût; [*behave*] avec vulgarité; **2** (rudely) avec grossièreté

vulnerable /'vʌlnərəbl/ *adj* vulnérable (**to** à)

vulture /'vʌltʃə(r)/ *n* lit, fig vautour *m*

vying /'vaɪɪŋ/ *p prés* ▸ **vie**

w, W /ˈdʌblju:/ n ① (letter) w, W m; ② W Elec *abrév écrite* = **watt**; ③ W Geog *abrév écrite* = **West**

WA n: *abrév écrite* = **Washington**

wad /wɒd/
A n ① (bundle) liasse f; ② (lump) balle f
B wads npl US ~**s of**○ des tas○ de

wadding /ˈwɒdɪŋ/ n ① (padding) ouatage m; ② (for gun) bourre f

waddle /ˈwɒdl/
A n dandinement m
B vi [*duck, person*] se dandiner

wade /weɪd/ vi ① (in water) **to ~ into the water** entrer dans l'eau; **to ~ ashore** regagner la rive à pied; **to ~ across** traverser à gué; ② (proceed with difficulty) **to ~ through sth** lit se frayer un chemin pour traverser qch; **I managed to ~ through the work** j'ai réussi péniblement à terminer le travail
(Phrasal verbs)
■ **wade in**○ ① (start with determination) se mettre au travail; ② (attack) passer à l'attaque
■ **wade into**○: ▸ ~ **into [sth]** se mettre à [*task*]; ▸ ~ **into [sb]** (attack) se jeter sur

wader /ˈweɪdə(r)/ n ① Zool échassier m; ② US personne f en train de barboter

waders /ˈweɪdəz/ npl cuissardes fpl

wafer /ˈweɪfə(r)/ n Culin gaufrette f; Relig hostie f; (of silicon) tranche f (de silicium); (on letter) cachet m

wafer-thin /ˌweɪfəˈθɪn/ adj ultrafin

waffle /ˈwɒfl/
A n ① Culin gaufre f; ② ○péj (empty words) verbiage m; (in essay) remplissage m
B ○vi (also ~ **on**) (speaking) bavasser○; (writing) faire du remplissage

waffle iron n Culin gaufrier m

waft /wɒft, US wæft/
A vtr **to ~ sth through/towards** [*wind*] apporter qch dans/vers
B vi **to ~ towards** flotter dans la direction de; **to ~ up** monter

wag /wæg/
A vtr (p prés etc -**gg**-) remuer [*tail*]; hocher [*head*]; **to ~ one's finger at sb** agiter son doigt dans la direction de qn
B vi (p prés etc -**gg**-) [*tail*] remuer, frétiller; [*head*] s'agiter; **tongues will ~** fig ça va faire jaser
(Idiom) **it's the tail ~ging the dog** c'est le monde à l'envers

wage /weɪdʒ/
A n (also ~**s**) salaire m
B noun modifier [*agreement, claim, inflation, negotiations, rate, settlement, talks*] salarial; [*increase, rise*] de salaire; [*policy, restraint, freeze*] des salaires
C vtr mener [*campaign*]; **to ~ (a) war against sth/sb** lit, fig faire la guerre contre qch/qn

waged /weɪdʒd/ adj salarié

wage earner n ① (person earning a wage) salarié/-e m/f (hebdomadaire); ② (breadwinner) soutien m de famille

wage packet n ① lit (envelope) enveloppe f de paie; ② (money) paie f

wager /ˈweɪdʒə(r)/
A n pari m; **to make** ou **lay a ~** parier
B vtr parier (**on** sur; **that** que)

wage: ~ **round** n réajustement m des salaires; ~**s council** n ≈ commission f des salaires; ~ **sheet**, ~ **slip** n feuille f de paie

waggle /ˈwægl/
A vtr remuer [*tail*]; faire bouger [*tooth, ear, object*]; (shake) agiter [*object*]; **to ~ one's hips** rouler des hanches
B vi (also ~ **around**, ~ **about**) remuer

waggon GB, **wagon** /ˈwægən/ n ① (horse-drawn) chariot m; ② GB Rail wagon m (de marchandises); ③ US = **station wagon**; ④ US (petit) chariot m (*jouet*)
(Idiom) **to be on the ~**○ être au régime sec hum

wagon train n US Hist convoi m de chariots

waif /weɪf/ n enfant m abandonné

wail /weɪl/
A n (of person, wind) gémissement m; (of siren) hurlement m; (of musical instrument) son m plaintif
B vtr **'oh no!'** he ~**ed** 'oh non!' gémit-il
C vi [*person, wind*] gémir; [*siren*] hurler; [*music*] pleurer

wailing /ˈweɪlɪŋ/
A n (of person) gémissements mpl; (of wind) gémissement m; (of siren) hurlement m; (of music) son m plaintif
B adj gén plaintif/-ive; [*siren*] strident

Wailing Wall pr n Mur m des Lamentations

waist /weɪst/ ▸ p. 1191 n taille f; **to have a 70 cm ~** avoir un tour de taille de 70 cm

waist: ~**band** n ceinture f; ~**coat** n GB gilet m

waisted /ˈweɪstɪd/ adj cintré; **a high-~ dress** une robe à taille haute

waist: ~**line** n ligne f; ~ **measurement** ▸ p. 1191 n tour m de taille

wait /weɪt/
A n attente f; **an hour's ~** une heure d'attente; **to have a long ~** devoir attendre longtemps; **it will only be a short ~** ce ne sera pas long
B vtr ① (await) attendre; **don't ~ dinner for me**○ US ne m'attendez pas pour dîner; ② US **to ~ table** servir à table
C vi ① (remain patiently) attendre; **to keep sb ~ing** faire attendre qn; **to ~ for sb/sth** attendre qn/qch; **to ~ for sb/sth to do** attendre que qn/qch fasse; **she can't ~ to start** elle a hâte de commencer; **I can hardly ~ to do** je meurs d'impatience de faire; **you'll just have to ~ and see** attends et tu verras; **(just you) ~ and see** tu verras bien○; **just you ~!** (as threat) tu vas voir○!; **~ for it!** tiens-toi bien○!; Mil pas encore!; ② (be left until later) attendre; ③ (serve) **to ~ at** ou **on table** être serveur/-euse m/f
(Idioms) **to lie in ~** être à l'affût; **to lie in ~ for sb** [*ambushers*] guetter qn; [*reporter, attacker*] tendre une embuscade à qn
(Phrasal verbs)
■ **wait around**, **wait about** GB attendre
■ **wait behind** attendre un peu; **to ~ behind for sb** attendre qn
■ **wait on**: ▸ ~ **on [sb]** (serve) servir; **to be ~ed on** être servi; **to ~ on sb hand and foot** être aux petits soins pour qn
■ **wait up** ① (stay awake) veiller; **to ~ up for sb** veiller jusqu'au retour de qn; ② US (stay patiently) ~ **up!** attends!

waiter /ˈweɪtə(r)/ ▸ p. 1181 n serveur m; '~**!**' 'monsieur!'; ~ **service** service m à table

waiter service n service m à table

waiting /'weɪtɪŋ/
A n attente f; **'no ~'** 'arrêt et stationnement interdits'
B adj (épith) [taxi, crowd] qui attend/attendait etc; [reporter] à l'affût; **sb's ~ arms** les bras ouverts de qn

waiting game n attentisme m; **to play a ~** faire de l'attentisme

waiting: **~ list** n liste f d'attente; **~ room** n salle f d'attente

waitress /'weɪtrɪs/ ▸ p. 1181 n serveuse f; **'~!'** 'madame!', 'mademoiselle!'

waive /weɪv/ vtr déroger à [rule]; renoncer à [claim, demand, right]; supprimer [fee, condition]

waiver /'weɪvə(r)/ n Jur renonciation f

wake /weɪk/
A n ① lit, fig sillage m; ② (over dead person) veillée f funèbre (accompagnée de célébrations)
B vtr (also ~ **up**) (prét **woke, waked†**; pp **woken, waked†**) lit, fig réveiller (**from** de); **to ~ sb from a dream** tirer qn d'un rêve
C vi (also ~ **up**) (prét **woke, waked†**; pp **woken, waked†**) se réveiller; **I woke (up) to find him gone** à mon réveil, il était parti; **to ~ (up) from a deep sleep** sortir d'un profond sommeil; **she finally woke (up) to her responsibilities** elle est finalement revenue à ses responsabilités

(Phrasal verb)
■ **wake up**: ▸ ~ **up** se réveiller; ~ **up!** lit réveille-toi!; fig ouvre les yeux!; ~ **up to sth** fig prendre conscience de qch; ▸ ~ **up** [sb], ~ [sb] **up** = wake B

wakeful /'weɪkfl/ adj éveillé; **to have a ~ night** passer une nuit blanche

waken /'weɪkən/ vtr, vi = wake B, C

waker /'weɪkə(r)/ n **to be an early/late ~** se réveiller tôt/tard

wake-up call n réveil m téléphoné

waking /'weɪkɪŋ/
A n (état m de) veille f; **between sleeping and ~** dans un demi-sommeil
B adj **in** ou **during one's ~ hours** pendant la journée

Wales /weɪlz/ ▸ p. 774 pr n pays m de Galles

walk /wɔːk/
A n ① promenade f; (shorter) tour m; (hike) randonnée f; **it's about ten minutes' ~** c'est environ à dix minutes à pied; **on the ~ home** en rentrant à pied à la maison; **to go for** ou **on a ~** (aller) faire une promenade; **to have** ou **take a ~** faire une promenade; (shorter) faire un tour○; **to take sb for a ~** emmener qn faire une promenade or (shorter) un tour○; **to take the dog for a ~** promener le chien; **it's a long ~ back to the hotel** il y a une longue marche d'ici à l'hôtel; ② (gait) démarche f; ③ (pace) pas m; **to slow down to a ~** se mettre à marcher (après avoir couru); ④ (path) allée f; **people from all ~s of life** des gens de tous les milieux; ⑤ Sport épreuve f de marche
B vtr ① (cover on foot) faire [qch] à pied [path, road]; parcourir [qch] à pied [countryside]; (patrol) parcourir; **I can't ~ another step** je ne peux pas faire un pas de plus; **to ~ it**○ Sport gagner haut la main; ② (lead, escort) conduire [horse etc]; promener [dog]; **to ~ sb home** raccompagner qn chez lui/elle
C vi ① (in general) marcher; (for pleasure) se promener; (not run) aller au pas; (not ride or drive) aller à pied; **to ~ with a limp** boiter; ~○ US (at traffic lights) ≈ traversez; **it's not very far, let's ~** ce n'est pas très loin, allons-y à pied; **to ~ across** ou **through sth** traverser qch (à pied) (see note); **a policeman ~ed by** un policier est passé; **he ~ed up/down the road** il a remonté/descendu la rue (à pied) (see note); **we've been ~ing round in circles for hours** nous tournons en rond depuis des heures; **someone was ~ing around** ou **about upstairs** quelqu'un allait et venait à l'étage supérieur; **I'd just ~ed in at the door when…** je venais à peine de passer la porte, quand…; **suddenly in ~ed my father** soudain voilà que mon père est entré; **to ~ in one's sleep** être somnambule; **to ~ up and down** faire les cent pas; **to ~ up and down a room** arpenter une pièce; **shall I ~ with you to the bus?** veux-tu que je t'accompagne au bus?; ② ○hum (disappear) se faire la malle○

(Idioms) **take a ~**○! US dégage○!; **you must ~ before you can run** il ne faut pas brûler les étapes.

⚠ à pied is often omitted with movement verbs if we already know that the person is on foot. If it is surprising or ambiguous, à pied should be included

(Phrasal verbs)
■ **walk across** traverser; **to ~ across to sth/sb** s'approcher de qch/qn; ▸ ~ **across** [sth] traverser
■ **walk around**: ▸ ~ **around** lit se promener; (aimlessly) traîner; ▸ ~ **around** [sth] (to and fro) faire un tour dans; (make circuit of) faire le tour de; **we ~ed around Paris for hours** nous nous sommes promenés dans Paris pendant des heures
■ **walk away** ① lit s'éloigner (**from** de); ② fig **to ~ away from a problem** fuir un problème; ③ fig (survive unscathed) sortir indemne (**from** de); ④ **to ~ away with** gagner [qch] haut la main [game, tournament]; remporter [qch] haut la main [election]; décrocher [prize, honour]; ⑤ Sport **to ~ away from sb/sth** laisser qn/qch loin derrière
■ **walk back** revenir sur ses pas (**to** jusqu'à); **we ~ed back (home)** nous sommes rentrés à pied
■ **walk in** entrer; **who should ~ in but my husband!** devine qui est arrivé?—mon mari!; **'please ~ in'** (sign) 'entrez sans frapper'
■ **walk into**: ▸ ~ **into** [sth] ① (enter) entrer dans; **she ~ed into that job** fig elle a eu ce poste sans lever le petit doigt; ② tomber dans [trap, ambush]; **you ~ed right into that one**○! tu es tombé dans le panneau○!; ③ (bump into) rentrer dans
■ **walk off**: ▸ ~ **off** ① lit partir brusquement; ② ○fig **to ~ off with sth** (innocently) partir avec qch; (as theft) filer○ avec qch; ▸ ~ **off** [sth], ~ [sth] **off** se promener pour faire passer [hangover, large meal]
■ **walk on** ① (continue) continuer à marcher; ② Theat être figurant
■ **walk out** ① lit sortir (**of** de); ② fig (desert) partir; **to ~ out on** laisser tomber○ [lover]; rompre [contract, undertaking]; ③ (as protest) partir en signe de protestation; (on strike) se mettre en grève
■ **walk over** ① (a few steps) s'approcher (**to** de); (a short walk) faire un saut○ (**to** à); ▸ ~ **over** [sb]○ (humiliate) marcher sur les pieds de; **he lets her ~ all over him** elle le mène par le bout du nez
■ **walk round**: ▸ ~ **round** faire le tour; ▸ ~ **round** [sth] (round edge of) faire le tour de; (visit) visiter
■ **walk through**: ▸ ~ **through** lit traverser; ▸ ~ **through** [sth] ① traverser [house, forest]; passer [door]; par courir [streets]; marcher dans [snow, mud, grass]; ② Theat répéter les déplacements de
■ **walk up to** ~ **up to** s'approcher de

walkabout /'wɔːkəbaʊt/ n bain m de foule

walker /'wɔːkə(r)/ n ① (for pleasure) promeneur/-euse m/f; (for exercise) marcheur/-euse m/f; **she's a fast ~!** elle marche vite!; ② (for baby) trotteur m

walkie-talkie /ˌwɔːkɪ'tɔːkɪ/ n talkie-walkie m

walk-in /'wɔːkɪn/ adj ① [closet] où l'on peut tenir debout; ② US [apartment] de plain-pied sur la rue; [clinic] qui reçoit les clients sans rendez-vous

walking /'wɔːkɪŋ/
A n (for pleasure) promenades fpl à pied; (for exercise, sport) marche f à pied
B adj hum **she's a ~ dictionary** c'est un dictionnaire ambulant

walking boots npl chaussures fpl de marche

walking distance n **to be within ~** être à quelques minutes de marche (**of** de)

walking: **~ frame** n Med déambulateur m; **~ holiday** n vacances fpl de randonnée

walking pace n pas m; **at a ~** au pas

walking: **~ race** n épreuve f de marche; **~ shoes** npl chaussures fpl de marche; **~ stick** n canne f; **~ tour** n randonnée f à pied; **~ wounded** npl blessés mpl capables de marcher

walkman® /'wɔːkmən/ n (pl **-mans**) walkman® m, baladeur m

walk-on /ˌwɔːk'ɒn/
A n Theat figurant/-e m/f
B adj [role] de figurant

walk: **~out** n (from conference) départ m en signe de protestation; (strike) grève f surprise; **~over** n victoire f facile (for pour); **∼-up** n US immeuble m sans ascenseur; **∼way** n allée f

wall /wɔːl/ n ⟦1⟧ gen, lit, fig mur m; ⟦2⟧ (of cave, tunnel) paroi f; ⟦3⟧ Anat paroi f; **the stomach ∼** la paroi stomacale; ⟦4⟧ (of tyre) flanc m

(Idioms) **to be a fly on the ∼** être une mouche; **to be off the ∼**○ [person] être dingue○; [comments] être incohérent; **to drive sb up the ∼**○ exaspérer qn; **to go to the ∼** faire faillite; **to have sb up against the ∼** mettre qn au pied du mur

(Phrasal verbs)
- **wall in:** ▸ **∼ in [sth], ∼ [sth] in** entourer
- **wall off:** ▸ **∼ off [sth], ∼ [sth] off** (block off) condamner; (separate by wall) séparer [qch] par un mur
- **wall up:** ▸ **∼ up [sb/sth], ∼ [sb/sth] up** emmurer

wall: **∼bars** npl espalier m; **∼ chart** n affiche f; **∼ covering** n revêtement m mural; **∼ cupboard** n élément m (mural)

walled /wɔːld/ adj [city] fortifié; [garden] clos

wallet /'wɒlɪt/ n (for notes) portefeuille m; (for documents) porte-documents m inv; **kind to your ∼** bon marché

walleyed○ /'wɔːlaɪd/ adj **to be ∼** loucher

wallflower /'wɔːlflaʊə(r)/ n Bot giroflée f jaune

(Idiom) **to be a ∼** faire tapisserie

wall: **∼ hanging** n tapisserie f; **∼ heater** n radiateur m mural; **∼ light** n applique f murale; **∼-mounted** adj fixé au mur

wallop○ /'wɒləp/
A n ⟦1⟧ (punch) beigne○ f; ⟦2⟧ (loud noise) vlan!
B vtr ⟦1⟧ (hit) flanquer une raclée à○ [person]; taper dans [ball]; ⟦2⟧ (defeat) battre [qn] à plates coutures

walloping○ /'wɒləpɪŋ/
A n raclée f
B adj, adv super

wallow /'wɒləʊ/
A n **to have a ∼** se vautrer
B vi ⟦1⟧ **to ∼ in** se vautrer dans [mud, luxury]; se complaire dans [self-pity, nostalgia]; ⟦2⟧ [ship] ballotter

wallpaper /'wɔːlpeɪpə(r)/
A n ⟦1⟧ papier m peint; ⟦2⟧ Comput fond m d'écran
B vtr tapisser [room]

Wall Street /'wɔːl striːt/ pr n US Fin Wall Street; **on ∼** à Wall Street

> ⓘ **Wall Street** Cette petite rue new yorkaise est le centre de la finance et des affaires aux États-Unis. *Wall Street* est souvent employé pour désigner la Bourse de New York, également située dans cette rue.

wall-to-wall /ˌwɔːltə'wɔːl/ adj ⟦1⟧ **∼ carpet** moquette f; ⟦2⟧ fig **the ∼ silence of large art galleries** le silence complet des grandes galeries d'art

walnut /'wɔːlnʌt/
A n ⟦1⟧ (nut) noix f; ⟦2⟧ (tree, wood) noyer m
B noun modifier [cake, yoghurt] aux noix; [oil, shell] de noix; [furniture] en noyer

walrus /'wɔːlrəs/ n morse m; **∼ moustache** moustache f à la gauloise

waltz /wɔːls, US wɔːlts/
A n valse f
B vi ⟦1⟧ (dance) danser la valse; ⟦2⟧ **to ∼ out of sth** sortir de qch d'un pas désinvolte; ⟦3⟧ **to ∼ off with sth** gagner qch haut la main○; **to ∼ through an exam** réussir un examen facilement

wan /wɒn/ adj blême

wand /wɒnd/ n (all contexts) baguette f

wander /'wɒndə(r)/
A n promenade f; **to have** ou **take a ∼** faire une balade○; **to have a ∼ round the shops** faire un tour dans les magasins
B vtr parcourir; **to ∼ the streets** traîner dans la rue
C vi ⟦1⟧ (walk, stroll) se promener; **the chickens are free to ∼** les poulets sont libres d'aller et de venir; **to ∼ around town** se balader en ville; **to ∼ in and out of the shops** flâner dans les magasins; ⟦2⟧ (stray) errer; **to ∼ into the next field** s'égarer dans le champ voisin; **to ∼ away** s'éloigner (from de); ⟦3⟧ **to ∼ in** arriver tranquillement; **to ∼ over to** ou **up to sb** s'approcher tranquillement de qn; ⟦4⟧ [mind, attention] (through boredom, inattention) s'égarer; (through age, illness) divaguer; [eyes, hands] errer (over sur); **her**

mind ∼ed back to son esprit revenait sur; **to ∼ off the point** ou **subject** s'éloigner du sujet

(Phrasal verbs)
- **wander about, wander around** (stroll) se balader; (when lost) errer
- **wander off** [child, animal] s'éloigner

wanderer /'wɒndərə(r)/ n voyageur/-euse m/f

wandering /'wɒndərɪŋ/ adj [person] itinérant; [animal] voyageur/-euse; [gaze, eye] qui s'égare; [attention, mind] vagabond

wanderings /'wɒndərɪŋz/ npl ⟦1⟧ (journeys) vagabondages mpl; ⟦2⟧ (confusion) divagations fpl

wanderlust /'wɒndəlʌst/ n envie f de voyager

wane /weɪn/
A n **to be on the ∼** être sur le déclin
B vi [moon] décroître; fig diminuer

wangle○ /'wæŋgl/
A n (trick) combine○ f
B vtr carotter○ [gift]; réussir à obtenir [leave, meeting]; **to ∼ sth out of sb** soutirer qch à qn [job, money, promise]; **to ∼ sth for sb** arranger qch à qn○; **to ∼ one's way into** réussir à s'introduire dans

waning /'weɪnɪŋ/
A n (of moon) déclin m; fig (lowering) baisse f (of de); (weakening) déclin m (of de)
B adj [moon] décroissant; [popularity] en baisse

wanly /'wɒnlɪ/ adv [smile] d'un air las; [shine] d'une lueur blême

wanna○ /'wɒnə/ = **want to, want a**

wannabe(e)○ /'wɒnəbiː/ n: personne qui rêve d'être célèbre

want /wɒnt/
A n ⟦1⟧ (need) besoin m; **to be in ∼ of** avoir besoin de; ⟦2⟧ (deprivation) indigence f; ⟦3⟧ (lack) défaut m; **for ∼ of** à défaut ou faute de; **it's not for ∼ of trying** ce n'est pas faute d'avoir essayé
B vtr ⟦1⟧ (desire) vouloir; **I ∼** (as general statement) je veux; (would like) je voudrais; (am seeking) je souhaite; **what** ou **how much do you ∼ for this chair?** combien voulez-vous pour ce fauteuil?; **I ∼ the job finished** je voudrais que ce travail soit fini; **I don't ∼ to** je n'ai pas envie; **to ∼ sb to do** vouloir que qn fasse; **where do you ∼ me?** où voulez-vous que je me mette?; **he doesn't ∼ much does he?** iron il est toujours aussi peu exigeant! iron; **they just don't ∼ to know** ils préfèrent ne rien savoir; ⟦2⟧ ○(need) avoir besoin de; **you're ∼ed at the meeting** on n'aura pas besoin de vous à la réunion; **to ∼ to do**○ devoir faire; **you ∼ to watch out** tu devrais faire attention; **what do they ∼ with all those machines?** pourquoi est-ce qu'ils ont besoin de toutes ces machines?; **what do you ∼ with me?** qu'est-ce que vous me voulez?; **all that's ∼ed is your signature** il ne manque plus que votre signature; **several jobs ∼ doing** GB il y a plusieurs tâches à faire; ⟦3⟧ (require presence of) demander; **you're ∼ed on the phone** on vous demande au téléphone; **the boss ∼s you** le patron veut te voir; **to be ∼ed by the police** être recherché par la police; **I know when I'm not ∼ed** je sens bien que je suis de trop
C vi **to ∼ for** manquer de

(Phrasal verbs)
- **want in**○ ⟦1⟧ (asking to enter) vouloir entrer; ⟦2⟧ (asking to participate) vouloir participer; **I ∼ in on the deal** je veux être dans le coup○
- **want out**○ ⟦1⟧ (asking to exit) vouloir sortir; ⟦2⟧ (discontinuing participation) vouloir laisser tomber○; **to ∼ out of** vouloir se retirer de

want ad n US petite annonce f

wanted /'wɒntɪd/ adj ⟦1⟧ (by police) recherché par la police; ⟦2⟧ (loved) **to be (very much) ∼** (before birth) être (très) désiré; (after birth) être (très) aimé

wanted list n liste f des suspects

wanting /'wɒntɪŋ/ adj **to be ∼** faire défaut; **to be ∼ in** manquer de; **to be found ∼** être réprouvé

wanton /'wɒntən, US 'wɔːn-/ adj ⟦1⟧ [cruelty, damage, waste] gratuit; [disregard] délibéré; ⟦2⟧ littér [mood] joueur/-euse; ⟦3⟧ †(immoral) dévergondé

wantonly /'wɒntənlɪ, US 'wɔːn-/ adv ⟦1⟧ (gratuitously) sans raison; ⟦2⟧ littér (playfully) de façon capricieuse; ⟦3⟧ †(provocatively) de façon dévergondée

WAP /wæp/ n (abrév = **wireless application protocol**) WAP m; ~ **technology** technologie WAP; ~ **phone** téléphone WAP

war /wɔː(r)/
A n **1** (armed conflict) guerre f; ~ **broke out** la guerre a éclaté; **in the** ~ à la guerre; **to go off to the** ~ partir à la guerre; **to go to** ~ **against** entrer en guerre contre; **to wage** ~ **on** faire la guerre contre; **to be at** ~ **with a country** être en guerre avec un pays; **a** ~ **over** ou **about** une guerre pour [land, independence]; une guerre sur [issue]; **2** fig (competition) guerre f; **price/trade** ~ guerre des prix/commerciale; **a** ~ **of words** un conflit verbal; **3** fig (to eradicate sth) lutte f; **to wage** ~ **on** ou **against** mener une lutte contre
B noun modifier [correspondent, crime, dance, effort, film, historian, medal, widow, wound] de guerre; [cemetery, leader, grave, zone] militaire; [hero] de la guerre; ~ **deaths** victimes fpl de la guerre; **he has a good** ~ **record** il a de bons états de service
C vi (p prés etc **-rr-**) **to** ~ **with a country** être en guerre contre un pays (**over** à cause de)

warble /'wɔːbl/ vi **1** [bird] gazouiller; **2** péj [singer] roucouler

war: ~ **cabinet** n conseil m de guerre; ~ **cry** n cri m de guerre also fig

ward /wɔːd/ n **1** (in hospital) (unit) service m; (room) unité f; (building) pavillon m; **he's in** ~ **3** il est à l'unité 3; **maternity** ~ service de maternité; **hospital** ~ salle f d'hôpital; **2** Pol circonscription f électorale; **3** (also ~ **of court**) pupille m; **to be made a** ~ **of court** être placé sous tutelle judiciaire.
(Phrasal verb)
■ **ward off**: ▶ ~ **off** [sth] chasser [evil, predator]; faire taire [criticism]; écarter [threat]; éviter [bankruptcy, disaster]

warden /'wɔːdn/ ▶ p. 1181 n gen directeur/-trice m/f; (of park, estate) gardien/-ienne m/f

warder /'wɔːdə(r)/ n GB gardien/-ienne m/f

wardrobe /'wɔːdrəʊb/ n (furniture) armoire f; (set of clothes) garde-robe f; Theat costumes mpl

wardrobe: ~ **assistant** ▶ p. 1181 n assistant/-e m/f costumier/-ière; ~ **director** n costumier/-ière m/f

ward: ~ **room** n Mil Naut carré m (des officiers); ~ **round** n Med visite f (du médecin hospitalier); ~ **sister** n GB Med infirmière f en chef

ware /weə(r)/
A n **C** articles mpl
B **wares** npl marchandises fpl

warehouse /'weəhaʊs/
A n entrepôt m
B vtr entreposer

warfare /'wɔːfeə(r)/ n **modern** ~ conflits mpl modernes; **chemical** ~ guerre f chimique

war: ~ **game** n Mil manœuvre f militaire; Games jeu m de stratégie (militaire); ~ **games** npl Games (with nonmilitary participants) guerre f simulée; ~**head** n ogive f; ~ **horse** n lit cheval m de bataille; fig (campaigner) vétéran m

warily /'weərɪlɪ/ adv **1** (cautiously) avec prudence; **2** (mistrustfully) avec méfiance

warlike /'wɔːlaɪk/ adj [people] guerrier/-ière; [mood, words] belliqueux/-euse

warm /wɔːm/
A ○n **1** GB **the** ~ le chaud; **2** **to give sth a** ~ gen chauffer; réchauffer [part of body]
B adj **1** (not cold) gen chaud; [trail] (encore) frais/fraîche; **in** ~ **weather** quand il fait chaud; **to be** ~ [person] avoir chaud; [weather] faire chaud; **it's nice and** ~ **in here** on est bien au chaud ici; **in a** ~ **oven** Culin à four très doux; **'serve** ~**'** Culin 'servir tiède'; **to get (oneself)** ~ se réchauffer; **you're getting** ~**er!** (in guessing game) tu chauffes!; **to get sb/sth** ~ réchauffer qn/qch; **to keep (oneself)** ~ (wrap up) ne pas prendre froid; (take exercise) se réchauffer; (stay indoors) rester au chaud; **to keep sb** ~ tenir chaud à qn; **to keep sth** ~ tenir [qch] au chaud [food]; chauffer [qch] (en permanence) [room]; **2** (enthusiastic) gen chaleureux/-euse; [admiration, support] enthousiaste; **to have a** ~ **heart** être chaleureux/-euse; ~**(est) regards** meilleures amitiés; **3** (mellow) [colour] chaud; [sound] chaleureux/-euse
C vtr chauffer [plate, food, water]; réchauffer [implement, bed]; se réchauffer [part of body]
D vi [food, liquid, object] chauffer
E v refl **to** ~ **oneself** se réchauffer

(Phrasal verbs)
■ **warm to**, **warm towards**: ▶ ~ **to [sb/sth]** se prendre de sympathie pour [acquaintance]; s'enthousiasmer pour [artist, idea]; s'attaquer avec enthousiasme à [task]; **'and then,' he said,** ~**ing to his theme** 'ensuite,' dit-il, de plus en plus enthousiaste
■ **warm up**: ▶ ~ **up 1** [person, room, house] se réchauffer; [food, liquid, car, engine, radio] chauffer; **2** fig (become lively) s'animer; **3** [athlete] s'échauffer; [singer] s'échauffer la voix; [orchestra, musician] se préparer; ▶ ~ **up [sth]**, ~ **[sth] up 1** (heat) réchauffer [room, bed, person]; faire réchauffer [food]; **2** (prepare) chauffer○ [audience]; échauffer [player, athlete]; [singer] s'échauffer [voice]; [musician] chauffer [instrument]

warm-blooded /ˌwɔːm'blʌdɪd/ adj Zool à sang chaud; fig ardent

war memorial n monument m aux morts

warm-hearted adj chaleureux/-euse

warming /'wɔːmɪŋ/
A n réchauffement m
B adj lit qui réchauffe; fig de plus en plus chaleureux/-euse

warmly /'wɔːmlɪ/ adv **1** lit chaudement; **the sun shone** ~ le soleil était chaud; **2** fig, gen chaleureusement; [speak, praise] avec enthousiasme

warmongering /'wɔːmʌŋɡərɪŋ/
A n propagande f belliciste
B adj [person, article] belliciste

warmth /wɔːmθ/ n lit, fig chaleur f; **he replied with some** ~ **that** il a répondu vivement que

warm-up /'wɔːmʌp/ n Mus, Sport, Theat échauffement m

warn /wɔːn/
A vtr avertir (**that** que); **to** ~ **that** dire or annoncer que; **to** ~ **sb about** ou **against sth** mettre qn en garde contre qch; **to** ~ **sb about** ou **against doing** déconseiller à qn de faire; **to** ~ **sb to do** conseiller or dire à qn de faire; **you have been** ~**ed!** tu es prévenu!; **I shan't** ~ **you again** c'est la dernière fois que je te le dis
B vi **to** ~ **of sth** annoncer qch
(Phrasal verb)
■ **warn off**: ▶ ~ **[sb] off**, ~ **off [sb]** décourager; **to** ~ **sb off doing** déconseiller à qn de faire; **to** ~ **sb off one's land** demander à qn de quitter ses terres

warning /'wɔːnɪŋ/
A n gen avertissement m; (by an authority) avis m; (by light, siren) signal m; **a** ~ **against sth** une mise en garde contre qch; **a** ~ **about** ou **on sth** une mise en garde à propos de qch; **to give sb a** ~ **not to do** déconseiller à qn de faire; **to give sb a** ~ avertir qn (**of** de); **advance** ~ préavis m; **health** ~ mise en garde; **flood** ~ avis de crue; **an official** ~ un avis officiel
B noun modifier **1** (giving notice of danger) [siren, bell, light] d'alarme; [notice] d'avertissement; ~ **shot** lit, fig coup m de semonce; ~ **sign** lit panneau m d'avertissement; fig signe m annonciateur; **2** (threatening) [gesture, tone] de mise en garde; (stronger) menaçant

warp /wɔːp/
A n **1** (deformity) déformation f (**in** de); **2** (in weave) chaîne f; **3** fig **the** ~ **(and woof) of sth** l'étoffe f dont qch est fait
B vtr lit déformer; fig pervertir [mind, personality]; fausser [judgment, thinking]
C vi se déformer

warpaint /'wɔːpeɪnt/ n Mil peinture f de guerre

warpath /'wɔːpɑːθ/ n:
(Idiom) **to be on the** ~ être sur le sentier de la guerre

warped /wɔːpt/ adj **1** lit déformé; **to become** ~ se déformer; **2** fig [mind, humour] tordu; [personality, sexuality] perverti; [account, judgment, view] faussé

warplane /'wɔːpleɪn/ n avion m militaire

warrant /'wɒrənt, US 'wɔːr-/
A n **1** Jur mandat m; **to issue a** ~ établir un mandat; **a** ~ **for sb's arrest** un mandat d'arrêt contre qn; **a** ~ **is out for his arrest** un mandat a été lancé contre lui; **2** Fin bon m de souscription; **dividend** ~ coupon m de dividende
B vtr (justify) justifier; (guarantee) garantir; (bet) parier
C vi parier
D **warranted** pp adj (justified) justifié; (guaranteed) garanti

warrant card n plaque f (de police)

warranty /'wɒrəntɪ, US 'wɔːr-/ n Comm garantie f; (insurance) condition f d'application

warren /'wɒrən, US 'wɔːrən/ n [1] (rabbits') garenne f; [2] (building, maze of streets) labyrinthe m

warring /'wɔːrɪŋ/ adj [parties, nations] en conflit

warrior /'wɒrɪə(r), US 'wɔːr-/ n, adj guerrier/-ière (m/f)

Warsaw /'wɔːsɔːw/ ▸ p. 1276 pr n Varsovie

warship /'wɔːʃɪp/ n navire m de guerre

wart /wɔːt/ n (on skin) verrue f

(Idiom) **to describe sb** ~**s and all** décrire qn avec tous ses défauts

wartime /'wɔːtaɪm/

A n **in** ~ en temps de guerre

B noun modifier [economy, memories, rationing] de guerre; **a story set in** ~ **Berlin** une histoire qui se passe à Berlin pendant la guerre

war-torn adj déchiré par la guerre

wary /'weərɪ/ adj [1] (cautious) prudent; **to be** ~ montrer de la circonspection (**of** vis-à-vis de); [2] (distrustful) méfiant; **to be** ~ se méfier (**of** de)

was /wɒz, wəz/ prét ▸ **be**

wash /wɒʃ/

A n [1] ¢ (by person) **to give [sth] a** ~ laver [window, floor]; nettoyer [object]; lessiver [paintwork]; se laver [hands, face]; **to give sb a** ~ débarbouiller [child]; **to have a quick** ~ faire un brin de toilette○; [2] (laundry process) lavage m; **weekly** ~ lessive f hebdomadaire; **in the** ~ (about to be cleaned) au sale; (being cleaned) au lavage; [3] (from boat) remous m; [4] (coating) gen couche f (de peinture); Art lavis m; [5] (for face) lotion f

B noun modifier **frequent** ~ **shampoo** shampooing m pour lavages fréquents; **pen and** ~ **drawing** dessin m à la plume et au lavis

C /wɒʃ, US wɔːʃ/ vtr [1] (clean) laver [person, clothes, floor]; nettoyer [object, wound]; lessiver [surface]; **to get** ~**ed** se laver; **to** ~ **one's hands/face** se laver les mains/le visage; **to** ~ **the dishes** faire la vaisselle; [2] (carry along) entraîner [silt, debris]; **to** ~ **sb/sth overboard** emporter qn/qch par-dessus bord; [3] littér (lap against) lécher; [4] (coat) Art laver; gen, Tech passer une légère couche de peinture sur [wall]

D vi (clean oneself) [person] se laver, faire sa toilette; [animal] faire sa toilette; (clean clothes) faire la lessive; (become clean) se laver; **that excuse won't** ~ **with me**○ fig cette excuse ne me satisfait pas

E v réfl **to** ~ **oneself** [person] se laver; [animal] faire sa toilette

(Idioms) **it will all come out in the** ~ (be revealed) tout finira bien par se savoir; (be resolved) tout finira par s'arranger; **to** ~ **one's hands of** se laver les mains de [matter]; se désintéresser de [person]

(Phrasal verbs)

■ **wash away:** ▸ ~ **[sth] away,** ~ **away [sth]** [1] (clean) faire partir; [2] (carry off) emporter [structure, debris]; (by erosion) éroder; ▸ ~ **[sb] away** emporter

■ **wash down:** ▸ ~ **[sth] down,** ~ **down [sth]** [1] (clean) laver [qch] à grande eau [surface, vehicle]; lessiver [paintwork]; [2] ○faire descendre [pill]; faire passer [unpleasant food]; arroser [food]

■ **wash off:** ▸ ~ **off** partir au lavage; ▸ ~ **[sth] off,** ~ **off [sth]** faire partir [qch] à l'eau; **to** ~ **the mud off the car** laver la voiture pour faire partir la boue

■ **wash out:** ▸ ~ **out** [1] (disappear by cleaning) [stain] partir au lavage; [colour] passer; [2] ○US **she** ~**ed out of college** elle s'est fait recaler aux examens d'entrée en fac○; ▸ ~ **[sth] out,** ~ **out [sth]** [1] (remove by cleaning) faire partir [qch] au lavage [stain]; faire passer [colour]; [2] (rinse inside) rincer; [3] (clean quickly) passer [qch] à l'eau

■ **wash over:** lit balayer; **everything I say just** ~**es over him** tout ce que je dis glisse sur lui; **a great feeling of relief** ~**ed over me** un immense soulagement m'a envahi

■ **wash through:** ▸ ~ **[sth] through** passer [qch] à l'eau

■ **wash up:** ▸ ~ **up** [1] GB (do dishes) faire la vaisselle; [2] US (clean oneself) faire un brin de toilette○; ▸ ~ **[sth] up,** ~ **up [sth]** [1] (clean) laver [plate]; nettoyer [pan]; [2] (bring to shore) rejeter

washable /'wɒʃəbl, US 'wɔːʃ-/ adj lavable

wash: ~**-and-wear** adj d'entretien facile; ~**basin** n lavabo m; ~**bowl** n US lavabo m; ~**cloth** n US lavette f

washed-out /ˌwɒʃt'aʊt, US ˌwɔːʃ-/ adj [1] (faded) délavé; [2] (tired) épuisé

washed-up○ /ˌwɒʃt'ʌp, US ˌwɔːʃ-/ adj (finished) fichu○; US (tired) épuisé

washer /'wɒʃə(r), US 'wɔːʃər/ n [1] Tech rondelle f; (as seal) joint m; [2] ○machine f à laver

washer-dryer /ˌwɒʃə'draɪə(r), US ˌwɔːʃ-/ n lave-linge/ sèche-linge m inv

wash: ~**-hand basin** n lavabo m; ~**house** n buanderie f

washing /'wɒʃɪŋ, US 'wɔːʃɪŋ/ n [1] (act) (of oneself) toilette f; (of clothes) lessive f; [2] (laundry) (to be cleaned) linge m sale; (when clean) linge m; **to do the** ~ faire la lessive

washing: ~ **facilities** npl douches-lavabos fpl; ~ **line** n corde f à linge; ~ **machine** n machine f à laver; ~ **powder** n GB lessive f (en poudre); ~ **soda** n soude f ménagère; ~**-up** n GB vaisselle f; ~**-up bowl** n GB cuvette f (pour la vaisselle); ~**-up liquid** n GB liquide m à vaisselle; ~**-up water** n GB eau f de vaisselle

Washington /'wɒʃɪŋtən, US 'wɔːʃ-/ ▸ p. 1276, p. 1222 pr n (city, state) Washington m

ⓘ **Washington DC** Capitale fédérale des États-Unis située sur un territoire indépendant, le district de Columbia. Les fonctions administratives et culturelles y sont prédominantes : Washington rassemble les trois branches du gouvernement américain (*White House, Congress, Supreme Court*), et de grands musées nationaux (*Smithsonian Institution, National Gallery of Art*).
▸ **Congress**

wash: ~ **leather** n peau f de chamois; ~ **load** n capacité f de lavage

washout /'wɒʃˌaʊt/ n [1] ○(project, system) fiasco m; [2] ○(person) nullité f; [3] (game, camp) fiasco m dû à la pluie

wash: ~**room** n toilettes fpl; ~**-stand** n US lavabo m

wasn't /'wɒznt/ = **was not**

wasp /wɒsp/ n guêpe f

WASP /wɒsp/ n US (abrév = **White Anglo-Saxon Protestant**) membre de l'élite des blancs protestants d'origine anglo-saxonne

waspish /'wɒspɪʃ/ adj acerbe

wastage /'weɪstɪdʒ/ n [1] (of money, resources, talent) gaspillage m; (of heat, energy) déperdition f; **through** ~ par gaspillage; [2] (also **natural** ~) Econ élimination f naturelle

waste /weɪst/

A n [1] (squandering) gen gaspillage m (**of** de); (of time) perte f (**of** de); **that was a complete** ~ **of an afternoon** l'après-midi a été perdu pour rien; **a** ~ **of effort** un effort inutile; **taking taxis is a** ~ **of money** prendre des taxis c'est jeter l'argent par les fenêtres; **it's a** ~ **of time trying to explain it** on perd son temps à essayer de l'expliquer; **to go to** ~ être gaspillé; **that's another good opportunity gone to** ~ et voilà encore une bonne occasion de perdue; **to let sth go to** ~ gaspiller qch; **there is no** ~, **every part is used** il n'y a pas de déchets, chaque élément est utilisé; [2] ¢ (detritus) gen, Ind déchets mpl (**from** de); [3] (wasteland) désert m

B **wastes** npl [1] (wilderness) étendues fpl sauvages; [2] US = **waste A 2**

C adj [1] [food] inutilisé; [heat, energy] gaspillé; [water] usé; ~ **materials** ou **matter** déchets mpl; ~ **products** Ind déchets mpl de fabrication; Biol, Med déchets mpl; ~ **plastics** plastiques mpl de rebut; [2] [land] inculte; [3] **to lay** ~ (**to**) dévaster

D vtr [1] (squander) gaspiller [food, energy, money, talents]; perdre [time, opportunity]; user [strength]; gâcher [youth]; **all our efforts were** ~**d** tous nos efforts ont été vains; **he didn't** ~ **words** il a été franc et direct; **she** ~ **d no time in contacting the police** elle a appelé la police sans perdre un instant; **subtlety is** ~**d on her** la subtilité lui passe au-dessus de la tête; **good wine is** ~**d on him** il n'est pas capable d'apprécier un bon vin; [2] (make weaker) atrophier; [3] ○US (kill) supprimer○

E vi se perdre

(Idiom) ~ **not want not** Prov l'économie protège du besoin

(Phrasal verb)

■ **waste away** dépérir

waste: ~**basket** n corbeille f à papier; ~**bin** n GB (for paper) corbeille f à papier; (for rubbish) poubelle f

wasted /'weɪstɪd/ adj ① [care, effort, expense, life, vote] inutile; [commodity, energy, years] gaspillé; **another ~ opportunity** encore une occasion de perdue; ② (fleshless) [body, limb] décharné; [face] émacié; (weak) [body, limb] atrophié

waste disposal
A n traitement m des déchets
B noun modifier [company, industry, system] de traitement des déchets

waste: **~ disposal unit** n GB broyeur m d'ordures; **~ dump** n dépotoir m

wasteful /'weɪstfl/ adj [product, machine] qui consomme beaucoup; [method, process] peu économique; [person] gaspilleur/-euse; **to be ~ of** gaspiller [resources, energy]; perdre beaucoup de [space, time]

wastefully /'weɪstfəlɪ/ adv inutilement

wastefulness /'weɪstflnɪs/ n (extravagance) gaspillage m; (inefficiency) manque m de rentabilité

waste: **~land** n (urban) terrain m vague; (rural) terre f à l'abandon; fig désert m; **~paper** n ₵ vieux papiers mpl; **~paper basket**, **~paper bin** GB n corbeille f à papier; **~ pipe** n tuyau m de vidange; **~ service** n service m de voirie

wasting /'weɪstɪŋ/ adj [disease] débilitant

watch /wɒtʃ/
A n ① (timepiece) montre f; **my ~ is slow/fast** ma montre retarde/avance; **to set one's ~** mettre sa montre à l'heure; **you can set your ~ by him** vous pouvez vous régler sur lui; ② (surveillance) gen, Mil surveillance f (on sur); **to keep ~** monter la garde; **to keep (a) ~ on sb/sth** lit, fig surveiller qn/qch; **to be on the ~** être sur ses gardes; **to be on the ~ for sb/sth** lit guetter qn/qch; fig être à l'affût de qn/qch; **to set a ~ on sb/sth** tenir qn/qch à l'œil; **tornado ~** Meteorol surveillance f des cyclones; ③ Naut (time on duty) quart m
B noun modifier [chain, spring, strap] de montre
C vtr ① (look at) regarder; (observe) observer; **is there anything worth ~ing on television?** y a-t-il quelque chose à voir à la télévision?; **the match, ~ed by a huge crowd...** le match, suivi par une foule immense...; ② fig suivre [career, development]; surveiller [situation]; **we had to sit by and ~ the collapse of all our hopes** nous avons dû assister impuissants à l'effondrement de tous nos espoirs; ③ lit (keep under surveillance) surveiller; **~ this noticeboard for further details** lire ce panneau d'affichage pour plus de détails; ④ (pay attention to) faire attention à [obstacle, dangerous object etc]; surveiller [language, manners, time, money, weight]; **you don't spill it** fais attention à ne pas le renverser; **~ that she doesn't go out alone** veille à ce qu'elle ne sorte pas seule; **~ where you put that paint-brush!** ne mets pas ce pinceau n'importe où!; **~ it**⁰! fais gaffe⁰!; **to ~ one's step** lit, fig regarder où on met les pieds; **~ your back**⁰! lit attention devant!; fig surveille tes arrières!; ⑤ (look after) garder
D vi ① (look) regarder; **they are ~ing to see what will happen next** ils attendent pour voir ce qui va se passer maintenant; ② †(keep vigil) veiller
E v refl **to ~ oneself** lit se regarder; fig faire attention

(Phrasal verbs)
■ **watch for**: ▸ **~ for [sb/sth]** guetter [person, event]; surveiller l'apparition de [symptom, phenomenon]
■ **watch out** (be careful) faire attention (**for** à); (keep watch) guetter; **~ out!** attention!; **I'll ~ out for her when I'm in town** je guetterai si je la vois quand je serai en ville; **~ out for trouble!** gare aux ennuis!
■ **watch over**: ▸ **~ over [sb/sth]** veiller sur [person]; veiller à [interests, rights, welfare]

watchable /'wɒtʃəbl/ adj qui se laisse regarder

watchband /'wɒtʃbænd/ n US bracelet m de montre

watchdog /'wɒtʃdɒg/ n ① (dog) chien m de garde; ② Admin, Econ (person) observateur m; (organization) organisme m de surveillance; **consumer ~** service m de protection du consommateur

watcher /'wɒtʃə(r)/ n (at event) spectateur/-trice m/f; (hidden) guetteur/-euse m/f; (monitoring) observateur/-trice m/f; **television ~** téléspectateur/-trice m/f

watchful /'wɒtʃfl/ adj vigilant

watchmaker /'wɒtʃˌmeɪkə(r)/ ▸ p. 1181 n horloger/-ère m/f

watchman /'wɒtʃmən/ ▸ p. 1181 n ① Hist **(night) ~** veilleur m (de nuit); ② (guard) gardien m

watchword /'wɒtʃwɜːd/ n gen (slogan) slogan m

water /'wɔːtə(r)/
A n eau f; **drinking ~** eau potable; **by ~** par bateau; **under ~** (submerged) sous l'eau; (flooded) inondé; **at high/low ~** à marée haute/basse; **to let in ~** prendre l'eau; **to pass ~** uriner; **to turn the ~ on/off** ouvrir/fermer le robinet; **he lives across the ~** il habite sur le continent; **the wine was flowing like ~** le vin coulait à flots; **to keep one's head above ~** lit garder la tête hors de l'eau; fig (financially) faire face à ses engagements
B **waters** npl ① Med, Naut eaux fpl; ② (spa water) **to take the ~s** faire une cure thermale
C noun modifier [glass, jug, tank] à eau; [filter, pump] à eau; [pipe, shortage] d'eau; [industry] de l'eau
D vtr arroser [lawn, plant]; irriguer [crop, field]; abreuver [livestock]
E vi **the smell of cooking makes my mouth ~** l'odeur de cuisine me fait venir l'eau à la bouche; **the smoke made her eyes ~** la fumée l'a fait pleurer

(Idioms) **to spend money like ~** jeter l'argent par les fenêtres; **not to hold ~** [theory] ne pas tenir debout

(Phrasal verb)
■ **water down**: ▸ **~ down [sth]** lit couper [qch] d'eau; fig gen atténuer; édulcorer [description]

water: **~ authority** n compagnie f des eaux; **~ bird** n oiseau m aquatique; **~ board** n compagnie f des eaux; **~ bottle** n (for cyclist) bidon m; **~ butt** n citerne f; **~colour** GB, **~color** US n (paint) peinture f pour aquarelle; (painting) aquarelle f; **~-cooled** adj à refroidissement à eau; **~cress** n cresson m (de fontaine); **~ divining** n radiesthésie f

watered-down /ˌwɔːtəd'daʊn/ adj ① lit coupé d'eau; ② fig gen atténué; [version] édulcoré

water: **~ed silk** n soie f moirée; **~fall** n cascade f; **~ filter** n filtre m à eau; **~front** n (on harbour) front m de mer; (by lakeside, riverside) bord m de l'eau; **~-heater** n chauffe-eau m (inv); **~ hole** n point m d'eau; **~ ice** n sorbet m

watering /'wɔːtərɪŋ/ n arrosage m; Agric irrigation f

watering can n arrosoir m

water: **~ lily** n nénuphar m; **~ line** n ligne f de flottaison; **~logged** adj [pitch] détrempé; [carpet] plein d'eau; **~ main** n canalisation f d'eau

watermark /'wɔːtəmɑːk/ n ① (of sea) laisse f; (of river) ligne f des hautes eaux; ② (on paper) filigrane m

water: **~ meadow** n prairie f inondable; **~melon** n pastèque f; **~ mill** n moulin m à eau; **~ power** n énergie f hydraulique

waterproof /'wɔːtəpruːf/
A n (coat) imperméable m
B **waterproofs** npl vêtements mpl imperméables
C adj [coat] imperméable; [make-up] résistant à l'eau

water: **~ rates** npl GB taxe f sur l'eau; **~-resistant** adj qui resiste à l'eau; **~shed** n Geog ligne f de partage des eaux; fig tournant m

waterside /'wɔːtəsaɪd/
A n bord m de l'eau
B noun modifier [cafe, hotel, house] au bord de l'eau; [plant, wildlife] du bord de l'eau

water-ski /'wɔːtəskiː/ Sport
A n ski m nautique
B vi faire du ski nautique

water: **~-skiing** ▸ p. 881 n ski m nautique; **~ slide** n toboggan m de piscine; **~ softener** n (equipment) adoucisseur m (d'eau); (substance) adoucissant m; **~-soluble** adj soluble dans l'eau; **~ sport** n sport m nautique; **~ supply** n (in an area) approvisionnement m en eau; (to a building) alimentation f en eau

water system n (network) (for town) système m d'approvisionnement en eau; (for building) système m d'alimentation en eau

water table n Geog niveau m hydrostatique

watertight /'wɔːtətaɪt/ adj ① lit étanche; ② fig (perfect) infaillible; ③ fig (irrefutable) [argument, case] incontestable; [alibi] irréfutable

water: **~ tower** n château m d'eau; **~ trough** n abreuvoir m; **~ way** n voie f navigable; **~ wheel** n roue f hydraulique; **~ wings** npl bracelets mpl de natation; **~works** n Tech station f de pompage

watery /'wɔːtərɪ/ *adj* **1** lit gen trop liquide; [*coffee*] trop léger/-ère; **2** fig pâle; **3** (secreting liquid) [*eye*] qui pleure; [*vegetables*] mal égoutté

watt /wɒt/ *n* watt *m*; **100-~ bulb** ampoule de 100 watts

wattage /'wɒtɪdʒ/ *n* puissance *f* en watts

wave /weɪv/

A *n* **1** (hand gesture) signe *m* (de la main); **she gave him a ~ from the bus** elle lui a fait signe du bus; **with a ~ of his wand** d'un coup de baguette magique; **2** (of water) vague *f*; **to make ~s** [*wind*] faire des vagues; fig (cause a stir) faire du bruit; (cause trouble) créer des histoires; **3** (outbreak, surge) vague *f*; **4** (in hair) cran *m*; **5** Phys onde *f*

B *vtr* **1** (move from side to side) gen agiter; brandir [*stick, gun*]; **2** to ~ goodbye to lit faire au revoir de la main à; fig **you can ~ goodbye to your chances of winning** tu peux dire adieu à tes chances de gagner; **3** (direct) **they ~d us on/away** ils nous ont fait signe d'avancer/de nous éloigner; **4** **to have one's hair ~d** se faire faire une mise en plis

C *vi* **1** (with hand) **to ~ to** *ou* **at sb** saluer qn de la main; **to ~ to sb to do** faire signe à qn de faire; **2** [*branches*] onduler; [*corn*] ondoyer; [*flag*] flotter au vent

⬭ Phrasal verbs

■ **wave around, wave about**: ▸ **~ around** [*flag, washing*] flotter; ▸ **~ [sth] around** brandir; **to ~ one's arms around** agiter les bras dans tous les sens

■ **wave aside**: ▸ **~ [sth] aside**, **~ aside [sth]** repousser [*qch*] d'un geste; ▸ **~ [sb] aside** écarter qn

■ **wave off**: ▸ **~ [sb] off**, **~ off [sb]** faire au revoir de la main à qn

wave: **~ band** *n* bande *f* de fréquence; **~ energy** *n* = **wave power**; **~length** *n* Phys, Radio longueur *f* d'onde; **~ power** *n* énergie *f* des vagues

waver /'weɪvə(r)/ *vi* **1** (weaken) [*person, look*] vaciller; [*courage, faith, love*] faiblir; [*voice*] trembler; **2** (flicker) [*flame, light*] vaciller; [*needle*] osciller; **3** (hesitate) hésiter (**between** entre; **over** sur)

wavering /'weɪvərɪŋ/

A *n* **1** (hesitation) hésitation *f*; **2** (of flame) vacillement *m*

B *adj* [*person, politician, voice*] hésitant; [*voter*] indécis; [*confidence, courage, faith, flame*] vacillant

wavy /'weɪvɪ/ *adj* [*hair, line*] ondulé

wax /wæks/

A *n* gen cire *f*; (for skis) fart *m*; (mineral wax) paraffine *f*; (in ear) cérumen *m*

B *noun modifier* [*candle, figure, polish, seal*] en cire

C *vtr* **1** cirer [*floor, table*]; lustrer [*car*]; farter [*ski*]; **2** (depilate) épiler [*qch*] à la cire

D *vi* **1** [*moon*] croître; **2** **to ~ lyrical** disserter avec lyrisme

E **waxed** *pp adj* [*fabric, wood*] ciré; [*paper*] paraffiné; [*thread*] poissé; **~ed jacket** GB ciré *m*

waxy /'wæksɪ/ *adj* [*skin, texture*] cireux/-euse; [*potato*] ferme

way /weɪ/

A *n* **1** (route, road) chemin *m* (**from** de; **to** à); **to live over the ~** habiter en face; **the quickest ~ to town** le chemin le plus court pour aller en ville; **if we go this ~** si nous prenons cette route; **to ask the ~ to** demander le chemin pour aller à; **how did that find its ~ in here?** comment est-ce que c'est arrivé ici?; **the ~ ahead** lit le chemin devant moi/eux etc; **the ~ ahead looks difficult** fig l'avenir s'annonce difficile; **there is no ~ around the problem** il n'y a pas moyen de contourner le problème; **on the ~ back** sur le chemin du retour; **on the ~ back from the meeting** en revenant de la réunion; **the ~ forward** fig la clé de l'avenir; **the ~ in** l'entrée (**to** de); **'~ in'** 'entrée'; **the ~ out** la sortie (**of** de); **the quickest ~ out is through here** c'est par ici que l'on sort le plus vite; **there's no ~ out** fig il n'y a pas d'échappatoire; **a ~ out of our difficulties** un moyen de nous sortir de nos difficultés; **the ~ up** la montée; **on the ~** en route; **we're on the ~ to Mary's** nous allons chez Mary; **on the ~ past** en passant; **I'm on my ~** j'arrive; **on your ~ through town** en traversant la ville; **his house is on your ~ to town** tu passes devant chez lui en allant au centre-ville; **I must be on my ~** il faut que je parte; **to go on one's ~** se remettre en route; **to send sb on his ~** (tell to go away) envoyer promener qn○; **to be well on the** *ou* **one's ~ to doing** être bien parti pour faire; **to be on the ~ out** fig passer de mode; **she's got four kids and another one on the ~**○ elle a quatre gosses et un autre en route○;

to be out of sb's ~ ne pas être sur le chemin de qn; **don't go out of your ~ to do** ne t'embête pas à faire; **to go out of one's ~ to make sb feel uncomfortable** tout faire pour que qn se sente mal à l'aise; **out of the ~** (isolated) isolé; (unusual) extraordinaire; **along the ~** lit en chemin; fig en cours de route; **by ~ of** (via) en passant par; **to go the ~ of sb/sth** finir comme qn/qch; **to make one's ~ towards** se diriger vers; **to make one's ~ along** avancer le long de; **to make one's own ~ there** se débrouiller seul pour y arriver; **to lie one's ~ out of trouble** se sortir d'affaire en mentant; **2** (direction) direction *f*, sens *m*; **which ~ did he go?** dans quelle direction est-il parti?; **he went that ~** il est parti par là; **come** *ou* **step this ~** suivez-moi, venez par ici; **'this ~ for the zoo'** 'vers le zoo'; **'this ~ up'** 'haut'; **to look this ~ and that** regarder dans toutes les directions; **to look the other ~** (to see) regarder de l'autre côté; (to avoid unpleasant thing) détourner les yeux; fig (to ignore) fermer les yeux; **to go every which ~** partir dans tous les sens; **the other ~ up** dans l'autre sens; **the right ~ up** le bon sens; **the wrong ~ up** à l'envers; **to turn sth the other ~ around** retourner qch; **I didn't ask her, it was the other ~ around** ce n'est pas moi qui lui ai demandé, c'est l'inverse; **the wrong/right ~ around** dans le mauvais/bon sens; **you're Ben and you're Tom, is that the right ~ around?** tu es Ben, et toi tu es Tom, c'est bien ça?; **if you're ever down our ~** si jamais tu passes près de chez nous; **she's coming our ~** elle vient vers nous; **an opportunity came my ~** une occasion s'est présentée; **to put sth sb's ~**○ filer qch à qn○; **everything's going my ~** tout me sourit; **3** (space in front, projected route) passage *m*; **to be in sb's ~** empêcher qn de passer; **to be in the ~** gêner le passage; **she won't let anything get in the ~ of her ambition** elle ne laissera rien entraver son ambition; **to get out of the ~** s'écarter (du chemin); **to get out of sb's ~** laisser passer qn; **put that somewhere out of the ~** mets ça quelque part où ça ne gêne pas; **out of my ~!** pousse-toi!; **get him out of the ~ before the boss gets here!** fais-le disparaître d'ici avant que le patron arrive!; **once the election is out of the ~** une fois les élections passées; **to keep out of the ~** rester à l'écart; **to keep out of sb's ~** éviter qn; **to keep sb out of sb's ~** (to avoid annoyance) tenir qn à l'écart de qn; **to keep sth out of sb's ~** (to avoid injury, harm) garder qch hors de portée de qn; **to make ~** s'écarter; **to make ~ for sb/sth** faire place à qn/qch; **4** (distance) distance *f*; **it's a long ~** c'est loin (**to** jusqu'à); **to be a short ~ off** lit être près; **my birthday is still some ~ off** mon anniversaire est encore loin; **we still have some ~ to go before doing** lit, fig avons encore du chemin à faire avant de faire; **to go all the ~ to China** faire tout le voyage jusqu'en Chine; **I'm with you** *ou* **behind you all the ~** je suis de tout cœur avec toi; **5** (manner) façon *f*, manière *f*; (means) un moyen de faire; **to my ~ of thinking** à mon avis; **that's the ~ to do it!** voilà comment il faut s'y prendre!; **that's the ~!** voilà, c'est bien!; **what a ~ to run a company!** en voilà une façon de gérer une entreprise!; **I like the ~ he dresses** j'aime la façon dont il s'habille; **whichever ~ you look at it** de quelque façon que tu envisages les choses; **either ~, she's wrong** de toute façon, elle a tort; **one ~ or another** d'une façon ou d'une autre; **one ~ and another it's been rather eventful** tout compte fait ça a été assez mouvementé; **I don't care one ~ or the other** ça m'est égal; **no two ~s about it** cela ne fait aucun doute; **you can't have it both ~s** on ne peut pas avoir le beurre et l'argent du beurre; **no ~!**○ pas question○!; **6** (respect, aspect) sens *m*; **in a ~ it's sad** en un sens c'est triste; **in a ~ that's true** dans une certaine mesure c'est vrai; **can I help in any ~?** puis-je faire quoi que ce soit?; **in every ~ possible** dans la mesure du possible; **in many ~s** à bien des égards; **in some ~s** à certains égards; **in no ~, not in any ~** aucunement; **this is in no ~ a criticism** cela n'est en aucune façon une critique; **not much in the ~ of news** il n'y a pas beaucoup de nouvelles; **what have you**

got in the ~ of drinks? qu'est-ce que vous avez comme boissons?; by ~ of light relief en guise de divertissement; **7** (custom, manner) coutume f, manière f; **that's the modern ~** c'est la coutume d'aujourd'hui; **I know all her little ~s** je connais toutes ses petites habitudes; **that's just his ~** il est comme ça; **it's the ~ of the world** c'est la vie; **8** (will, desire) **to get one's ~, to have one's own ~** faire à son idée; **she likes (to have) her own ~** elle aime n'en faire qu'à sa tête; **if I had my ~...** si cela ne tenait qu'à moi...; **have it your (own) ~** comme tu voudras

B adv **we went ~ over budget** le budget a été largement dépassé; **to be ~ out** (in guess, estimate) être loin du compte; **to go ~ beyond what is necessary** aller bien au-delà de ce qui est nécessaire; **that's ~ out of order** je trouve ça un peu fort

C by the way adv phr en passant; **by the ~,...** à propos,...; **what time is it, by the ~?** quelle heure est-il, au fait?; **but that's just by the ~** mais ce n'est qu'une parenthèse

waylay /ˌweɪˈleɪ/ vtr (prét, pp **-laid**) [bandit, attacker] attaquer; [beggar, friend] arrêter, harponner○ hum

way-out○ /ˌweɪˈaʊt/ adj **1** (unconventional) excentrique; **2** †(great) super○, formidable

way; ~s and means npl moyens mpl; **Ways and Means (Committee)** n Pol Commission f des Finances

wayside /ˈweɪsaɪd/ n littér bord m de la route

(Idiom) **to fall by the ~** (morally) quitter le droit chemin; (fail) être éliminé; (fall through) tomber à l'eau

wayward /ˈweɪwəd/ adj [person, nature] difficile; [horse] incontrôlable; [husband, wife] volage

we /wiː, wɪ/

⚠️ In standard French, we is translated by nous but in informal French on is frequently used: we're going to the cinema = nous allons au cinéma or (more informally) on va au cinéma.

on is also used in correct French to refer to a large, vaguely defined group: we shouldn't lie to our children = on ne devrait pas mentir à ses enfants. For particular usages see the entry below.

pron nous; **~ left at six** gen nous sommes partis à six heures; (informal) on est parti○ à six heures; **~ Scots like the sun** nous autres Écossais, nous aimons le soleil; **WE didn't say that** gen nous, nous n'avons pas dit cela; (informal) nous, on n'a pas dit ça○; **~ four are agreed that** nous quatre sommes convenus que; **~ all make mistakes** tout le monde peut se tromper

weak /wiːk/ adj **1** (in bodily functions) [person, animal, muscle, limb] faible; [health, ankle, heart, eyes, chest, nerves] fragile; [digestion] difficile; [stomach] délicat; [intellect] médiocre; [memory] défaillant; [chin] fuyant; [mouth] tombant; **to be ~ with** ou **from** être affaibli par; **to grow** ou **become ~(er)** [person] s'affaiblir; [pulse, heartbeat] faiblir; **2** Tech gen peu solide; [structure] fragile; **3** (lacking authority, strength) [government, team, pupil, performance] faible; [parent, teacher] qui manque de fermeté; [script, novel] inconsistant; [plot] mince; [actor, protest, excuse, argument] peu convaincant; [evidence] peu concluant; **~ link** ou **point** ou **spot** lit, fig point m faible; **to grow** ou **become ~er** [government, team] s'affaiblir; [position] devenir de plus en plus précaire; **in a ~ moment** dans un moment de faiblesse; **4** (faint) [light, current, sound, laugh] faible; [tea, coffee] léger/-ère; [solution] dilué; **5** Econ, Fin gen faible (against par rapport à); [share] à bas prix; **6** Ling (regular) faible; (unaccented) inaccentué

weaken /ˈwiːkən/

A vtr **1** lit affaiblir [person, heart, structure]; diminuer [resistance]; rendre [qch] moins solide [joint, wall]; **2** fig nuire à l'autorité de [government]; affaiblir [company, authority, resolve, cause, defence]; diminuer [support, influence]; amoindrir [argument, power]; nuire à [morale]; ébranler [will]; **3** (dilute) diluer; **4** Econ, Fin affaiblir [economy, currency]; faire baisser [prices, demand, shares]

B vi **1** (physically) gen s'affaiblir; [grip] se relâcher; **2** (lose power) [government, country, resistance] fléchir; [support, alliance] se relâcher; **3** Econ être en baisse

weakening /ˈwiːkənɪŋ/ n **1** (physical) gen affaiblissement m; (of structure) dégradation f; **2** (loss of power) gen, Fin affaiblissement m; (of ties, alliance, friendship) relâchement m

weak-kneed /ˌwiːkˈniːd/ adj faible

weakling /ˈwiːklɪŋ/ n (physically) gringalet m

weakly /ˈwiːklɪ/ adv [move, struggle] faiblement; (ineffectually) mollement

weak-minded /ˌwiːkˈmaɪndɪd/ adj **1** (indecisive) irrésolu; **2** euph (simple) faible d'esprit

weakness /ˈwiːknɪs/ n **1** (weak point) point m faible; **2** (liking) faible m; **3** (physical) (of person, limb, eyesight, heart, memory) faiblesse f; (of digestion) délicatesse f; (of structure) fragilité f; **4** (lack of authority) gen faiblesse f; (of evidence, position) fragilité f; **5** (faintness) gen faiblesse f; (of tea, solution) légèreté f; **6** Fin faiblesse f

weak-willed /ˌwiːkˈwɪld/ adj **to be ~** manquer de fermeté

weal /wiːl/ n (mark) marque f (de coup)

wealth /welθ/ n **1** (possessions) fortune f; **2** (state) richesse f; **3** (resources) richesses fpl; **4** (large amount) **a ~ of** une mine de [information, opportunity]; une profusion de [detail, ideas]; énormément de [experience, talent]; un grand nombre de [books, documents]

wealthy /ˈwelθɪ/ adj riche

wean /wiːn/ vtr lit sevrer [baby]; fig **to ~ sb away from** ou **off sth** détourner qn de qch; **to ~ sb from/onto sth** faire passer qn de/à qch

weapon /ˈwepən/

A n lit, fig arme f

B noun modifier (also **weapons**) [capability, factory, manufacturer, system] d'armes; **~ of mass destruction** ADM f

wear /weə(r)/

A n ¢ **1** (clothing) vêtements mpl; **sports ~** tenue f de sport; **2** (use) **for everyday ~** de tous les jours; **for summer ~** pour l'été; **to stretch with ~** s'assouplir à l'usage; **I've had three years' ~ out of these boots** ces bottes m'ont duré trois ans; **there's some ~ left in these tyres** ces pneus ne sont pas encore usés; **3** (damage) usure f (on de); **~ and tear** usure f; **normal ~ and tear** usure normale; **to get heavy ~** servir beaucoup; **to look the worse for ~** (damaged) être abîmé; **to be somewhat the worse for ~** (drunk) être ivre; (tired) être épuisé

B vtr (prét **wore**, pp **worn**) **1** (be dressed in) porter; **to ~ blue** s'habiller en bleu; **to ~ one's hair short** avoir les cheveux courts; **to ~ one's skirts long** s'habiller long; **to ~ one's clothes loose** aimer les vêtements lâches; **2** (put on, use) mettre; **I haven't got a thing to ~** je n'ai rien à me mettre; **to ~ make-up** se maquiller; **3** (display) **his face** ou **he wore a puzzled frown** il fronçait les sourcils d'un air perplexe; **4** (damage by use) user; **to ~ a hole in** trouer; **to ~ a track in** creuser un sentier dans; **5** ○(accept) tolérer [behaviour]; accepter [excuse]

C vi (prét **wore**, pp **worn**) **1** (become damaged) s'user; **my patience is ~ing thin** je commence à être à bout de patience; **2** (withstand use) **a fabric that will ~ well** un tissu solide; **he's worn very well** fig il est encore bien pour son âge

(Phrasal verbs)

■ **wear away**: ▸ **~ away** [inscription] s'effacer; [tread, cliff, façade] s'user; ▸ **~ away [sth], ~ [sth] away** [rubbing, footsteps] user; [water] ronger

■ **wear down**: ▸ **~ down** s'user; **to be worn down** être usé; ▸ **~ down [sth], ~ [sth] down** lit user; fig saper; ▸ **~ [sb] down** épuiser

■ **wear off**: ▸ **~ off** [drug, effect] se dissiper; [sensation] passer; **2** (come off) s'effacer; ▸ **~ [sth] off, ~ off [sth]** effacer [inscription]

■ **wear on** [day, evening] s'avancer

■ **wear out**: ▸ **~ out** s'user; **my patience is beginning to ~ out** je commence à perdre patience; ▸ **~ out [sth], ~ [sth] out** user; **to ~ out one's welcome** lasser l'amabilité de ses hôtes; ▸ **~ [sb] out** épuiser

■ **wear through** [elbow, trousers] se trouer; [sole, metal, fabric] se percer

wearable /ˈweərəbl/ adj mettable

wearily /ˈwɪərɪlɪ/ adv [sigh, smile, gesture] d'un air las; [say, ask] d'un ton las; [get up] péniblement

weariness /ˈwɪərɪnɪs/ n lassitude f

wearing /ˈweərɪŋ/ adj (exhausting) fatigant; (irritating) pénible

weary /ˈwɪərɪ/

A adj [person, smile, sigh, voice, gesture] las/lasse; [eyes, limbs, mind] fatigué; [journey, task, day] fatigant; [routine] lassant; **to grow ~** se lasser

B vtr lasser, fatiguer

C vi se lasser (**of** de; **of doing** de faire)

weasel /'wiːzl/ n ① Zool belette f; ② péj (sly person) sournois/-e m/f; ~ **words** mots mpl équivoques

weather /'weðə(r)/

A n temps m; **what's the ~ like?** quel temps fait-il?; **the ~ here is hot** il fait chaud ici; **in hot/cold ~** quand il fait chaud/froid; **you can't go out in this ~!** tu ne peux pas sortir par un temps pareil!; **when the good ~ comes** quand il fera beau; **if the ~ breaks** si le temps change; **if the ~ clears up** si le temps s'arrange; **~ permitting** si le temps le permet; **in all ~s** par tous les temps; **whatever the ~** lit par tous les temps; fig qu'il pleuve ou qu'il vente

B noun modifier [chart, check, conditions, map, satellite, station] météorologique; [centre] de météorologie

C vtr ① (withstand) lit essuyer; fig se tirer de; **to ~ the storm** fig surmonter la crise; ② éroder [rocks, stone]; battre [landscape, hills]; hâler [face]

D vi [rocks, landscape] s'éroder; **he has not ~ed well** fig il n'a pas bien vieilli

E **weathered** pp adj [stone] patiné; [face] hâlé

(Idioms) **to be under the ~** ne pas se sentir bien; **to keep a ~ eye on sb/sth** avoir qn/qch à l'œil; **to make heavy ~ of sth** avoir du mal à faire qch; **he made heavy ~ of it** il en a fait tout un plat○

weather: ~ **balloon** n ballon-sonde m météorologique; ~**beaten** adj [face] hâlé; [stone, brick] érodé; ~**cock** n girouette f; ~ **forecast** n bulletin m météorologique; ~ **forecaster** ▸ p. 1181 n (on TV) présentateur/-trice m/f de la météo; (in weather centre) météorologue mf, météorologiste mf; ~**man**○ n (on TV) = weather forecaster

weatherproof /'weðəpruːf/

A adj [garment, shoe] imperméable; [shelter, door] étanche

B vtr imperméabiliser [fabric, garment]

weather: ~ **report** n = weather forecast; ~ **vane** n girouette f

weave /wiːv/

A n tissage m

B vtr (prét **wove** ou **weaved**; pp **woven** ou **weaved**) ① tisser; ② (interlace) gen tresser; [spider] tisser; ③ fig inventer [story]; ④ (move) **to ~ one's way through sth** se faufiler entre qch

C vi (prét **wove** ou **weaved**; pp **woven** ou **weaved**) **to ~ in and out** se faufiler (**of** entre); **to ~ towards sth** (drunk) s'approcher en titubant de qch; (avoiding obstacles) se frayer un chemin vers qch

D **woven** pp adj [fabric, cloth, jacket] tissé

weaving /'wiːvɪŋ/

A n tissage m

B noun modifier [frame, machine, machinery] à tisser; [factory, mill] de tissage; [industry] du tissage

web /web/ n ① (also **spider's** ~) toile f (d'araignée); ② fig **a ~ of** un réseau de [ropes, lines]; **a ~ of lies** ou **deceit** un tissu de mensonges; ③ Zool palmure f

Web n /web/ Comput (also **web**) web m, Toile f

webbing /'webɪŋ/ n ¢ (material) sangles fpl

web: ~ **browser** n Comput navigateur m, fureteur m Can; ~**cam** n Comput webcam f; ~**cast** n Comput diffusion f de scènes filmées sur des webcams; ~ **foot** n (pl web feet) patte f palmée; ~**master** n Comput webmestre m, administrateur/-trice m/f de site Internet; ~ **page** n Comput page f web; ~ **search** n Comput recherche f sur le web; ~**site** n Comput site m web; ~**space** n Comput espace m web

wed /wed/

A n **the newly ~s** les jeunes mariés mpl

B vtr (p prés etc **-dd-**; prét, pp **wedded** ou **wed**) ① lit épouser; **to get wed** se marier; ② fig allier; **to be ~ded to** être attaché à

C vi (p prés etc **-dd-**; prét, pp **wedded** ou **wed**) se marier

D **wedded** pp adj marié; ~**ded bliss** hum bonheur m conjugal; **my lawful ~ded wife** mon épouse légitime

we'd /wiːd/ = we had, we would

Wed abrév écrite = Wednesday

wedding /'wedɪŋ/

A n ① mariage m; **a church ~** un mariage religieux; ② (also ~ **anniversary**) noces fpl

B noun modifier [cake, ceremony, present] de mariage

wedding bells npl lit cloches fpl; **I can hear ~** fig je crois qu'il y a un mariage dans l'air

wedding: ~ **breakfast** n repas m de mariage; ~ **day** n jour m des noces; ~ **dress**, ~ **gown** n robe f de mariée; ~ **march** n marche f nuptiale; ~ **night** n nuit f de noces; ~ **reception** n repas m de mariage; ~ **ring** n alliance f; ~ **vows** n vœux mpl

wedge /wedʒ/

A n ① (to insert in rock, wood etc) coin m; (to hold sth in position) cale f; (of cake, pie, cheese) morceau m; **a ~ of lemon** une tranche de citron; ② (in golf) cocheur m de sable; ③ (heel) semelle f compensée; (shoe) chaussure f à semelle compensée

B noun modifier ~**-shaped** en forme de coin

C vtr ① (make firm) **to ~ sth in** ou **into place** caler qch; **to ~ a door open** caler une porte pour la tenir ouverte; **the door is ~d shut** (stuck) la porte est coincée; ② (jam) **to ~ sth into** enfoncer qch dans; **to be ~d against/between** être coincé contre/entre

D v refl **to ~ oneself** se coincer

(Idioms) **to drive a ~ between X and Y** monter X contre Y; **it's (only) the thin end of the ~** ce n'est qu'un début

(Phrasal verb)

■ **wedge in:** ▸ ~ [sb/sth] **in**, ~ **in** [sb/sth] coincer

Wednesday /'wenzdeɪ, -dɪ/ ▸ p. 1322 n mercredi m

wee /wiː/

A n○ GB pipi○ m

B adj (tout) petit

C vi○ GB faire pipi

weed /wiːd/

A n ① (wild plant) mauvaise herbe f; (in water) herbes fpl aquatiques; ② ○GB péj mauviette○ f péj; ③ ○marijuana f

B vtr, vi désherber

(Phrasal verb)

■ **weed out:** ▸ ~ [sb] **out**, ~ **out** [sb] gen éliminer; se débarrasser de [employee]; ▸ ~ [sth] **out**, ~ **out** [sth] se débarrasser de [stock, items]; arracher [dead plants]

weeding /'wiːdɪŋ/ n désherbage m; **to do some ~** désherber

weedkiller /'wiːdkɪlə(r)/ n désherbant m, herbicide m

weedy /'wiːdɪ/ adj ① ○péj [person, build] malingre; [character, personality] faible; ② (full of weeds) [garden] envahi de mauvaises herbes; [pond] envahi d'herbes aquatiques

week /wiːk/ ▸ p. 1267 n semaine f; **what day of the ~ is it?** quel jour de la semaine sommes-nous?; **the ~ before last** il y a deux semaines; **the ~ after next** dans deux semaines; **every other ~** tous les quinze jours; **I'll do it some time this ~** je le ferai dans le courant de la semaine; ~ **in ~ out** toutes les semaines; **a ~ today** GB, **today ~** aujourd'hui en huit; **a ~ yesterday** GB, **a ~ from yesterday** US il y a eu huit jours or une semaine hier; **a ~'s wages** une semaine de salaire; **to pay by the ~** payer à la semaine; **during the ~** gen pendant la semaine; (Monday to Friday) en semaine; **the working** ou **work** US ~ la semaine de travail; **the ~ ending June 10** la semaine du 3 au 10 juin

weekday /'wiːkdeɪ/

A n jour m de (la) semaine; **on ~s** en semaine

B noun modifier [evening, morning, programme] de la semaine; [train] circulant du lundi au vendredi; [flight] assuré du lundi au vendredi

weekend /ˌwiːk'end, US 'wiːk-/

A n week-end m; **the ~ after (that)** le week-end suivant; **at the ~** GB, **on the ~** US pendant le week-end; **at ~s** GB, **on ~s** US le week-end

B noun modifier [break] de week-end; [performance] du samedi et du dimanche; ~ **bag** petit sac m de voyage; ~ **cottage** résidence f secondaire; ~ **ticket** ticket m valable (uniquement) le week-end

C vi passer le week-end

weekly /'wiːklɪ/

A n (newspaper) journal m hebdomadaire; (magazine) (revue f) hebdomadaire m

B adj hebdomadaire; **on a ~ basis** à la semaine

C adv [pay] à la semaine; [check] chaque semaine; [meet, leave] une fois par semaine

weep /wiːp/

A n **to have a little ~** verser quelques larmes

B vtr (prét, pp **wept**) **to ~ tears of joy** verser des larmes de joie

C vi (prét, pp **wept**) ① (cry) pleurer (**over** sur); **to ~ for sb** pleurer sur le sort de qn; ② (ooze) suinter

weeping /'wiːpɪŋ/ n ¢ pleurs mpl

The days of the week

■ *Note that the French uses lower-case letters for the names of days; also, French speakers normally count the week as starting on Monday.*

■ *Write the names of days in full; do not abbreviate as in English (Tues, Sat and so on). The French only abbreviate in printed calendars, diaries etc.*

Monday
= lundi

Tuesday
= mardi

Wednesday
= mercredi

Thursday
= jeudi

Friday
= vendredi

Saturday
= samedi

Sunday
= dimanche

What day is it?

(Lundi in this note stands for any day; they all work the same way; for more information on dates in French ▸ **p. 788**.)

what day is it?
= quel jour sommes-nous?
or (very informally) on est quel jour?

it is Monday
= nous sommes lundi

today is Monday
= c'est lundi aujourd'hui

■ *Note the use of French* le *for regular occurrences, and no article for single ones. (Remember: do not translate* on.)

on Monday
= lundi

on Monday, we're going to the zoo
= lundi, on va au zoo

I'll see you on Monday morning
= je te verrai lundi matin

but

on Mondays
= le lundi

on Mondays, we go to the zoo
= le lundi, on va au zoo

I see her on Monday mornings
= je la vois le lundi matin

Specific days

Monday afternoon
= lundi après-midi

one Monday evening
= un lundi soir

that Monday morning
= ce lundi matin-là

last Monday night
= la nuit de lundi dernier
or (if evening) lundi dernier dans la soirée

early on Monday
= lundi matin de bonne heure

late on Monday
= lundi soir tard

this Monday
= ce lundi

that Monday
= ce lundi-là

that very Monday
= précisément ce lundi-là

last Monday
= lundi dernier

next Monday
= lundi prochain

the Monday before last
= l'autre lundi

a month from Monday
= dans un mois lundi

in a month from last Monday
= dans un mois à dater de lundi dernier

finish it by Monday
= termine-le avant lundi

from Monday on
= à partir de lundi

Regular events

every Monday
= tous les lundis

each Monday
= chaque lundi

every other Monday
= un lundi sur deux

every third Monday
= un lundi sur trois

Sometimes

most Mondays
= presque tous les lundis

some Mondays
= certains lundis

on the second Monday in the month
= le deuxième lundi de chaque mois

the odd Monday *or* **the occasional Monday**
= le lundi de temps en temps

Happening etc. on that day

Monday's paper
= le journal de lundi *or* de ce lundi

the Monday papers
= les journaux du lundi

Monday flights
= les vols du lundi

the Monday flight
= le vol du lundi

Monday closing (of shops)
= la fermeture du lundi

Monday's classes
= les cours de lundi *or* de ce lundi

Monday classes
= les cours du lundi

Monday trains
= les trains du lundi

W

Weight measurement

■ *Note that French has a comma where English has a decimal point.*

1 oz
= 28,35 g* (grammes)

1 cwt
= 50,73 kg

1 lb†
= 453,60 g

1 ton
= 1014,60 kg

1 st
= 6,35 kg (kilos)

* *There are three ways of saying* 28,35 g, *and other measurements like it:* vingt-huit virgule trente-cinq grammes, *or* (*less formally*) vingt-huit grammes virgule trente-cinq, *or* vingt-huit grammes trente-cinq.

■ *For more details on how to say numbers* ▸ **p. 1044**.

† *English* a pound *is translated by* une livre *in French, but note that the French* livre *is actually 500 grams (half a kilo).*

People

what's his weight?
= combien pèse-t-il?

how much does he weigh?
= combien pèse-t-il?

he weighs 10 st (or 140 lbs)
= il pèse 63 kg 500 (soixante-trois kilos et demi)

he weighs more than 20 st
= il pèse plus de 127 kilos

Things

what does the parcel weigh?
= combien pèse le colis?

how heavy is it?
= quel poids fait-il?

it weighs ten kilos
= il pèse dix kilos

about ten kilos
= environ dix kilos

it was 2 kilos overweight
= il pesait deux kilos de trop

A weighs more than B
= A pèse plus lourd que B

A is heavier than B
= A est plus lourd que B

B is lighter than A
= B est plus léger que A

A is as heavy as B
= A est aussi lourd que B

A is the same weight as B
= A a le même poids que B

A and B are the same weight
= A et B ont le même poids

6 lbs of carrots
= six livres de carottes

2 kilos of butter
= deux kilos de beurre

1½ kilos of tomatoes
= un kilo cinq cents de tomates

sold by the kilo
= vendu au kilo

there are about two pounds to a kilo
= il y a à peu près deux livres anglaises dans un kilo

■ *Note the French construction with* de, *coming after the noun it describes:*

a 3-lb potato
= une pomme de terre de trois livres

a parcel 3 kilos in weight
= un colis de trois kilos

---

weeping willow *n* saule *m* pleureur

weepy /'wiːpɪ/ *adj* [*film*] larmoyant; **to feel** ~ avoir envie de pleurer

weigh /weɪ/
A *vtr* ⓵ lit peser; **to** ~ **sth in one's hand** soupeser qch; ⓶ fig gen évaluer; peser [*consequences, risk, words*]; **to** ~ **sth against sth** mettre en balance qch et qch; **to** ~ **sth in the balance** évaluer soigneusement qch; ⓷ Naut **to** ~ **anchor** lever l'ancre
B *vi* ⓵ (have influence) **to** ~ **with sb** compter pour qn; **to** ~ **against sb** faire du tort à qn; **to** ~ **in sb's favour** jouer en faveur de qn; ⓶ (be a burden) **to** ~ **on sb** peser sur qn; **to** ~ **on sb's mind** préoccuper qn
C *v refl* **to** ~ **oneself** se peser
⟨Phrasal verbs⟩
■ **weigh down:** ▸ ~ **down on** [*sb/sth*] peser sur; ▸ ~ **down** [*sth/sb*], ~ [*sth/sb*] **down** lit surcharger [*vehicle*]; bloquer [*papers*]; fig accabler; **to be** ~**ed down with** crouler sous le poids de [*luggage*]; être comblé de [*gifts, prizes*]; être accablé de [*worry*]
■ **weigh in** ⓵ [*boxer, wrestler*] se faire peser; [*jockey*] aller au pesage; ⓶ (contribute) contribuer; **to** ~ **in with sth** donner qch; ⓷ (intervene in debate) intervenir
■ **weigh out** peser [*ingredients, quantity*]
■ **weigh up:** ▸ ~ **up** [*sth/sb*], ~ [*sth/sb*] **up** ⓵ fig évaluer [*situation*]; juger [*person*]; mettre [qch] en balance [*options, risks*]; **after** ~**ing things up, I decided...** tout bien pesé, j'ai décidé...; ⓶ lit peser [*goods*]

weighing machine /'weɪɪŋ məʃiːn/ *n* ⓵ (for people) balance *f*; ⓶ (for luggage, freight) bascule *f*

weight /weɪt/
A *n* lit, fig poids *m*; **to put on** ~ prendre du poids; **to be**

under/over 1 kilo in ~ avoir un poids inférieur/supérieur à 1 kilo; **by** ~ au poids; **what is your** ~? combien pesez-vous?; **not to carry much** ~ fig ne pas peser lourd (**with** pour); **to add one's** ~ **to sth** faire jouer son influence en faveur de qch; **to throw one's** ~ **behind sth** soutenir qch à fond; **to give due** ~ **to a proposal** accorder à une proposition l'importance qu'elle mérite
B *vtr* ⓵ lit lester; ⓶ (bias) **to** ~ **sth against sb/sth** faire jouer qch contre qn/qch; **to** ~ **sth in favour of sb/sth** faire jouer qch en faveur de qn/qch; ⓷ (in statistics) pondérer
⟨Idioms⟩ **by (sheer)** ~ **of numbers** par la force du nombre; **to be a** ~ **off one's mind** être un grand soulagement; **to pull one's** ~ faire sa part de travail; **to take the** ~ **off one's feet** s'asseoir; **to throw one's** ~ **about** *ou* **around** faire l'important/-e *m/f*
⟨Phrasal verb⟩
■ **weight down:** ▸ ~ **down** [*sth*], ~ [*sth*] **down** retenir [qch] avec un poids [*paper*]; lester [*body*]

weighting /'weɪtɪŋ/ *n* (of index, variable) pondération *f*; **London** ~ indemnité *f* pour résidence à Londres

weightlessness /'weɪtlɪsnɪs/ *n* ⓵ (in space) apesanteur *f*; ⓶ (of dancer) légèreté *f* aérienne

weight: ~**lifter** *n* haltérophile *m*; ~ **training** ▸ p. 881 *n* musculation *f* (en salle); ~**watcher** *n* (in group) personne *f* qui suit un régime amaigrissant

weighty /'weɪtɪ/ *adj* ⓵ (serious) de grand poids; ⓶ [*book*] monumental; [*object, responsibility*] lourd

weir /wɪə(r)/ *n* (dam) barrage *m*

weird /wɪəd/ *adj* (odd) bizarre; (eerie) mystérieux/-ieuse

welcome /'welkəm/
A *n* accueil *m*
B *noun modifier* [*speech*] de bienvenue

w

C adj **1** (gratefully received) bienvenu; **that's a ~ sight!** ça fait plaisir à voir!; **nothing could be more ~** I rien ne pourrait tomber plus à propos!; **2** (warmly greeted) **to be ~** être le bienvenu/la bienvenue m/f; **to make sb ~** (on arrival) réserver un bon accueil à qn; (over period of time) accueillir qn à bras ouverts; **3** (warmly invited) **if you want to finish my fries you're ~ to them** (politely) si tu veux finir mes frites, ne te gêne pas; **if you want to watch such rubbish you're ~ to it!** (rudely) si tu veux regarder ces idioties, libre à toi!; **you're ~** (acknowledging thanks) de rien

D excl (to respected guest) soyez le bienvenu/la bienvenue m/f chez nous!; (greeting friend) entre donc!; **~ back**, **~ home!** je suis content que tu sois de retour!

E vtr accueillir [person]; se réjouir de [news, decision, change]; être heureux/-euse de recevoir [contribution]; accueillir favorablement [initiative, move]; **we would ~ your view on this matter** nous aimerions savoir ce que vous pensez de cette affaire; **'please ~ our guest tonight, Willie Mays'** 'applaudissons notre invité d'honneur, Willie Mays'

(Idiom) **to wear out one's ~** abuser de l'hospitalité de qn

(Phrasal verbs)

■ **welcome back**: ▸ **~ back [sb]**, **~ [sb] back** accueillir [qn] à son retour; (more demonstratively) faire fête à [qn] à son retour

■ **welcome in**: ▸ **~ in [sb]**, **~ [sb] in** faire entrer [qn] chez soi

welcoming /'welkəmɪŋ/ adj gen accueillant; [ceremony, committee] d'accueil

weld /weld/
A vtr lit, fig souder (**on, to** à)
B vi [metal, joint] être soudé ensemble

welding /'weldɪŋ/ n **1** lit soudage m; **2** fig union f

welfare /'welfeə(r)/
A n **1** gen (well-being) bien-être m inv; (interest) intérêt m; **to be concerned about sb's ~** se faire du souci pour le sort de qn; **to be responsible for sb's ~** avoir la responsabilité de qn; **2** (state assistance) assistance f sociale; (money) aide f sociale; **to go on ~** US demander l'aide sociale
B noun modifier [system] de protection sociale; **~ cuts** réductions fpl dans les dépenses sociales

> ⓘ **Welfare** Aux États-Unis, les programmes de protection sociale du *Welfare* offrent une assistance minimale aux personnes sans ressources. *Medicaid*, créé en 1965, leur assure la gratuité des soins, tandis que des coupons d'alimentation (*food stamps*) leur permettent de se nourrir. Il existe également des aides financières et un programme d'aide à la scolarisation (*Head Start*) pour les enfants des familles démunies.

welfare: **~ benefit** n prestation f sociale; **~ department** n service m d'aide sociale; **~ services** n services mpl sociaux

welfare state n (as concept) État-providence m; (stressing state assistance) protection f sociale

> ⓘ **Welfare state** Au Royaume-Uni, on désigne ainsi le système dans lequel l'État prend en charge les citoyens et leur assure les soins médicaux ainsi que des allocations familiales et des aides financières. Cette expression recouvre essentiellement les organismes du *National Health Service* (NHS), *National Insurance* et *Social Security*.

welfare work n assistance f sociale

well¹ /wel/
A adj (comparative **better**, superlative **best**) **1** (in good health) **to feel ~** se sentir bien; **are you ~?** vous allez bien?, tu vas bien?; **she's not ~ enough to travel** elle n'est pas en état de voyager; **he's not a ~ man** il a des problèmes de santé; **she doesn't look at all ~** elle n'a pas l'air en forme du tout; **to get ~** se rétablir; **'how is he?'—'as ~ as can be expected'** 'comment va-t-il?'—'pas trop mal étant donné les circonstances'; **2** (in satisfactory state) bien; **all is not ~ in their marriage** il y a des problèmes dans leur mariage; **that's all very ~,** but tout ça c'est bien beau, mais; **it's all very ~ for you to laugh,** but tu peux rire, mais; **~ and good** c'est très bien; **3** (prudent) **it would be just as ~ to check** il vaudrait mieux vérifier; **it would be as ~ for you not to get involved** tu ferais mieux de ne pas t'en mêler; **4** (fortunate) **it was just as ~ for him that the shops were still open** il a eu de la chance que les magasins aient été encore ouverts; **the flight was delayed, which was just as**

~ le vol a été retardé, ce qui n'était pas plus mal

B adv (comparative **better**, superlative **best**) **1** (satisfactorily) bien; **he isn't eating very ~** il ne mange pas beaucoup; **that boy will do ~** ce garçon ira loin; **he hasn't done as ~ as he might** il n'a pas réussi aussi bien qu'il aurait pu; **I did ~ in the general knowledge questions** je me suis bien débrouillé pour les questions de culture générale; **to do ~ at school** être bon/bonne élève; **mother and baby are both doing ~** la mère et l'enfant se portent bien; **the operation went ~** l'opération s'est bien passée; **you did ~ to tell me** tu as bien fait de me le dire; **we'll be doing ~ if we get there on time** on aura de la chance si on arrive à l'heure; **~ done!** bravo!; **he has done very ~ for himself** il s'en tire très bien; **to do oneself ~** bien se soigner; **to do ~ by sb** se montrer généreux/-euse avec qn; **some businessmen did ~ out of the war** certains hommes d'affaires se sont enrichis pendant la guerre; **she didn't come out of it very ~** (of situation) elle ne s'en est pas très bien sortie; (of article, programme etc) ce n'était pas très flatteur pour elle; **2** (used with modal verbs) **you may ~ be right** il se pourrait bien que tu aies raison; **I can ~ believe it** je veux bien le croire, je n'ai pas de mal à le croire; **it may ~ be that** il se pourrait bien que; **I couldn't very ~ say no** je pouvais difficilement dire non; **you may ~ ask!** je me le demande bien!; **we may as ~ go home** on ferait aussi bien de rentrer; **'shall I shut the door?'—'you might as ~'** 'est-ce que je ferme la porte?'—'pourquoi pas'; **she looked shocked, as ~ she might** elle a eu l'air choquée, ce qui n'avait rien d'étonnant; **3** (intensifier) bien, largement; **it was ~ worth waiting for** ça valait vraiment la peine d'attendre; **the weather remained fine ~ into September** le temps est resté au beau fixe pendant une bonne partie du mois de septembre; **she was active ~ into her eighties** elle était toujours active même au-delà de ses quatre-vingts ans; **profits are ~ above average** les bénéfices sont nettement supérieurs à la moyenne; **4** (approvingly) **to speak ~ of sb** dire du bien de qn; **5** **to wish sb ~** souhaiter beaucoup de chance à qn

C excl **1** (expressing astonishment) eh bien!; (expressing indignation, disgust) ça alors!; (expressing disappointment) tant pis!; (after pause in conversation, account) bon; (qualifying statement) enfin; **~, you may be right** après tout, tu as peut-être raison; **~, that's too bad** c'est vraiment dommage; **~ then, what's the problem?** alors, quel est le problème?; **oh ~, there's nothing I can do about it** ma foi, je n'y peux rien; **~, ~, ~, so you're off to America?** alors comme ça, tu pars aux États-Unis!; **very ~ then** très bien

D **as well** adv phr aussi

E **as well as** prep phr aussi bien que; **they have a house in the country as ~ as an apartment in Paris** ils ont à la fois une maison à la campagne et un appartement à Paris; **by day as ~ as by night** de jour comme de nuit

(Idioms) **to be ~ in with sb**○ être bien avec qn○; **to be ~ up in sth** s'y connaître en qch; **to leave ~ alone** GB ou **~ enough alone** US ne pas s'en mêler; **you're ~, ~, ~, so out of it**○! heureusement que tu n'as plus rien à voir avec ça!; **~ and truly** bel et bien

well² /wel/
A n (in ground) puits m; (pool) source f
B vi = **well up**

(Phrasal verb)

■ **well up** monter

we'll /wiːl/ = we shall; we will

well-attended adj **the meeting was ~** il y avait beaucoup de monde à la réunion

well wel: **~-behaved** adj [child] sage; [animal] bien dressé; **~-being** n bien-être m inv

well-bred /ˌwel'bred/ adj **1** [person] (of good birth) bien né; (having good manners) bien élevé; **2** [animal] gen de pure race; [horse] pur sang

well-defined adj [outline] net/nette; [role, boundary] bien défini

well-disposed /ˌweldr'spəʊzd/ adj **to be ~ towards** être bien disposé envers [person]; être favorable à [regime, idea, policy]

well wel: **~ done** adj Culin bien cuit; [task] bien fait; **~-educated** adj (having a good education) instruit; (cultured) cultivé; **~-founded** adj fondé; **~-heeled**○ adj riche

well-informed /ˌwelɪnˈfɔːmd/ adj bien informé (**about** sur); **he's very** ∼ il est très au courant de l'actualité; ∼ **source** Journ source f sérieuse

wellington (boot) /ˈwelɪŋtən/ n GB botte f de caoutchouc

well wel: ∼**-judged** adj [statement, phrase] bien senti; [performance] intelligent; ∼**-kept** adj bien entretenu

well-known /ˌwelˈnəʊn/ adj ① (famous) célèbre; **to be** ∼ **to sb** être connu de qn; ② **it is** ∼ **that, it is a** ∼ **fact that** il est bien connu que

well wel: ∼**-liked** adj très apprécié; ∼**-made** adj bien fait; ∼**-mannered** adj bien élevé; ∼**-meaning** adj bien intentionné; [advice, suggestion, gesture] qui part d'une bonne intention

well-meant /ˌwelˈment/ adj **his offer was** ∼, **but** sa proposition partait d'une bonne intention, mais; **my remarks were** ∼ je ne voulais pas être désagréable dans ce que je disais

well-nigh /ˌwelˈnaɪ/ adv sout pratiquement, presque

well-off /ˌwelˈɒf/
Ⓐ n (+ v pl) **the** ∼ les gens mpl aisés; **the less** ∼ les plus défavorisés mpl
Ⓑ adj (wealthy) aisé; **you don't know when you're** ∼ tu ne connais pas ton bonheur; **to be** ∼ **for** avoir beaucoup de [space, provisions etc]

well wel: ∼**-read** adj cultivé; ∼**-respected** adj très respecté; ∼**-spoken** adj [person] qui parle bien

well-spoken-of adj **he's very** ∼ on dit beaucoup de bien de lui

well wel: ∼**-thought-of** adj apprécié; ∼**-thought-out** adj bien élaboré

well-timed adj qui tombe/tombait à point; **that was well timed!** (of entrance, phonecall etc) c'est bien tombé!

well-to-do
Ⓐ n **the** ∼ (+ v pl) les gens mpl aisés
Ⓑ adj aisé

well-trodden /ˌwelˈtrɒdn/ adj **a** ∼ **path** lit, fig une voie très empruntée

well wel: ∼**-wisher** n gen personne f qui veut témoigner sa sympathie; Pol sympathisant/-e m/f; ∼**-worn** adj [carpet, garment] élimé; [steps, floorboards] usé; fig rebattu

welsh /welʃ/ vi **to** ∼ **on** manquer à [promise, deal]

Welsh /welʃ/ ▸ p. 1032, p. 969
Ⓐ n ① (language) gallois m; ② (people) **the** ∼ les Gallois mpl
Ⓑ adj gallois

ⓘ **Welsh** D'origine celtique, comme le breton ou le gaélique, le gallois est avec l'anglais la langue officielle du pays de Galles. C'est la langue maternelle de plus de 20% de la population galloise et son enseignement est obligatoire à l'école. À l'image d'autres langues régionales, le gallois connaît aujourd'hui un regain de vitalité qui se manifeste dans la vie de tous les jours : les panneaux de signalisation routière et publicitaires sont bilingues et des programmes en gallois sont diffusés à la radio et à la télévision.

Welsh rarebit, **Welsh rabbit** n toast m au fromage

welt /welt/ n (on shoe) trépointe f; (on garment) bordure f en côtes; (on skin) marque f (de coup)

wend /wend/ vtr **to** ∼ **one's way** cheminer (**to, towards** vers)

went /went/ prét ▸ **go**

wept /wept/ prét, pp ▸ **weep**

were /wɜː(r), wə(r)/ prét ▸ **be**

we're /wɪə(r)/ = we are

weren't /wɜːnt/ = were not

west /west/ ▸ p. 1089
Ⓐ n ouest m
Ⓑ **West** n Pol, Geog **the West** l'Ouest m, l'Occident m
Ⓒ adj gen ouest inv; [wind] d'ouest
Ⓓ adv [move] vers l'ouest; [lie, live] à l'ouest (**of** de)
(Idiom) **to go** ∼ (die) euph passer l'arme à gauche

west: **West Bank** pr n Cisjordanie f; **West Bengal** pr n Bengale-Occidental m; ∼**bound** adj en direction de l'ouest

West Country pr n GB **the** ∼ le Sud-Ouest (de l'Angleterre)

West End pr n GB **the** ∼ le West End m (quartier de théâtres et de boutiques chic au centre ouest de Londres)

westerly /ˈwestəlɪ/
Ⓐ n vent m d'ouest
Ⓑ adj [wind] d'ouest; [point] à l'ouest; [area] de l'ouest; [breeze] venant de l'ouest

western /ˈwestən/ ▸ p. 1089
Ⓐ n Cin western m
Ⓑ adj (épith) ① Geog [coast, boundary] ouest inv; [town, region, custom, accent] de l'ouest; ② Pol occidental

westerner /ˈwestənə(r)/ n Occidental/-e m/f

Western Isles ▸ p. 954 pr npl îles fpl Hébrides occidentales

westernize /ˈwestənaɪz/ vtr occidentaliser

west-facing /ˈwestfeɪsɪŋ/ adj exposé à l'ouest

West Indian /ˌwest ˈɪndɪən/ ▸ p. 1032
Ⓐ n Antillais/-e m/f
Ⓑ adj antillais

West Indies /ˌwest ˈɪndiːz/ ▸ p. 774, p. 954 pr npl Antilles fpl

Westminster /ˈwestmɪnstə(r)/ n Westminster (siège du parlement de Grande-Bretagne); **to be elected to** ∼ être élu au Parlement (de Grande-Bretagne)

ⓘ **Westminster** Quartier de Londres où se trouvent tous les centres nerveux du gouvernement et de l'administration (Houses of Parliament, Downing Street, administrations de Whitehall), les résidences de la famille royale (Buckingham Palace et St James's Palace) et l'abbaye de Westminster. Toutefois, quand on emploie le mot Westminster seul, c'est généralement au Parlement britannique que l'on fait allusion. ▸ **Parliament**

West Point n US West Point m (académie militaire américaine)

westward /ˈwestwəd/ ▸ p. 1089
Ⓐ adj [side] ouest; [wall, slope] du côté ouest; [journey, route] vers l'ouest
Ⓑ adv (also ∼s) vers l'ouest

wet /wet/
Ⓐ n ① (dampness) humidité f; **the car won't start in the** ∼ la voiture ne veut pas démarrer par temps humide; **the tyre performs well in the** ∼ le pneu a de bons résultats sur terrain mouillé; ② ᴼGB péj chiffe f molleᴼ pej; ③ GB Pol conservateur/-trice m/f modéré/-e
Ⓑ adj ① (damp) mouillé; ∼ **with rain** mouillé par la pluie; ∼ **with blood** mouillé de sang; **her face was** ∼ **with tears** son visage était baigné de larmes; **to get** ∼ se faire mouiller; **to get one's feet** ∼ se mouiller les pieds; **to get the floor** ∼ tremper le sol; ∼ **through** trempé; ② (freshly applied) pas humide; '∼ **paint**' 'peinture fraîche'; **the ink is still** ∼ l'encre n'est pas encore sèche; **to keep sth** ∼ empêcher qch de sécher; ③ (rainy) [weather, season, day] humide; [conditions] d'humidité; [spell] de pluie; **tomorrow, the North will be** ∼ demain, il pleuvra dans le nord; **when it's** ∼ quand il pleut; ④ GB péj [person] qui manque de caractère; [remark] sans intérêt; **don't be so** ∼! du nerf! ⑤ GB Pol modéré
Ⓒ vtr ① (p prés -tt-; prét, pp wet) mouiller [floor, object, clothes]; ② (urinate in or on) **to** ∼ **one's pants/the bed** [child] faire pipi dans sa culotte/dans son lit
Ⓓ v refl **to** ∼ **oneself** gen mouiller sa culotte; [child] faire pipi dans sa culotte

wet: ∼ **blanket**ᴼ n rabat-joie mf inv; ∼ **fish** n GB poisson m frais; ∼**land** n terres fpl marécageuses; ∼**-look** adj [plastic, leather] luisant

wetness /ˈwetnɪs/ n humidité f

wetnurse /ˈwetnɜːs/
Ⓐ n nourrice f
Ⓑ **wet-nurse** vtr lit allaiter [baby]

wet suit n combinaison f de plongée

we've /wiːv/ abrév = we have

W Glam n: abrév écrite = West Glamorgan

whack /wæk, US hwæk/
Ⓐ n ① (blow) (grand) coup m; ② ᴼ(share) part f; **to do one's** ∼ faire ce qu'on doit; ③ GBᴼ (wage) **to pay/earn top** ∼ payer/recevoir un très gros salaire; ④ ᴼ(try) essai m; **to**

get first ~ at sth avoir la primeur de qch

B *excl* paf!

C *vtr* **1** (hit) battre [*person, animal*]; frapper [*ball*]; **2** ○GB (defeat) piler○; **3** fig to ~ **£10 off the price** réduire le prix de dix livres

whacked○ /wækt, US hwækt/ *adj* (tired) vanné○; US défoncé●

whacking○ /'wækɪŋ, US 'hwæk-/
A *n* raclée○ *f*
B *adj* GB énorme

whacky○ /'wækɪ, US 'hwækɪ/ *adj* [*person*] dingue○; [*joke*] farfelu○; [*party, clothes*] délirant○

whale /weɪl, US hweɪl/
A *n* **1** Zool baleine *f*; **2** ○a ~ **of a difference/story** une super○ différence/histoire; **to have a ~ of a time** s'amuser comme un fou
B ○*vtr* US (thrash) lit, fig donner une raclée○ à

whaler /'weɪlə(r), US 'hweɪlər/ ▸ p. 1181 *n* **1** (ship) baleinier *m*; **2** (person) pêcheur *m* de baleines

whaling /'weɪlɪŋ, US 'hweɪlɪŋ/ *n* **1** (whale fishing) pêche *f* à la baleine; **to go** ~ aller pêcher la baleine; **2** ○US (thrashing) lit, fig raclée○ *f*

wham /wæm, US hwæm/
A *n* grand coup *m*
B *excl* vlan!

whammy○ /'wæmɪ, US 'hwæmɪ/ *n* US poisse *f*

wharf /wɔːf, US hwɔːf/
A *n* (*pl* **wharves**) quai *m*
B *vi* [*boat*] se mettre à quai

what /wɒt, US hwɒt/
A *pron* **1** (what exactly) (as subject) qu'est-ce qui; (as object) que, qu'est-ce que; (with prepositions) quoi; ~ **is happening?** qu'est-ce qui se passe?; ~ **are you doing?** qu'est-ce que tu fais?; **with** ~? avec quoi?; **and** ~ **else?** et quoi d'autre?; ~ **is to be done?** que faire?; ~ **does it matter?** qu'est-ce que ça peut faire?; ~'s **her telephone number?** quel est son numéro de téléphone?; ~'s **that button for?** à quoi sert ce bouton?; ~ **for?** (why) pourquoi?; (concerning what) à propos de quoi?; ~'s **it like?** comment c'est?; ~'s **this called in Flemish?**, ~'s **the Flemish for this?** comment dit-on cela en flamand?; ~ **did it cost?** combien est-ce que ça a coûté?; **2** (in rhetorical questions) ~'s **life without love?** que serait la vie sans l'amour?; ~'s **the use?** (enquiringly) à quoi bon?; (exasperatedly) à quoi ça sert?; ~ **does he care?** qu'est-ce que ça peut bien lui faire?; **3** (whatever) **do** ~ **you want** fais ce que tu veux; **4** (in clauses) (as subject) ce qui; (as object) ce que, (before vowel) ce qu'; **this is** ~ **is called a 'monocle'** c'est ce qu'on appelle un 'monocle'; **do you know** ~ **that device is?** sais-tu ce que c'est que cet appareil?; ~ **I need is** ce dont j'ai besoin c'est; **drinking** ~ **looked like whisky** buvant quelque chose qui ressemblait à du whisky; **and** ~'s **more** et en plus; **and** ~'s **worse** *ou* **better** et en plus; **5** ○(when guessing) **it'll cost,** ~, **£50** ça coutera, quoi, dans les 50 livres?; **6** (inviting repetition) ~'s **that?**, ~ **did you say?** quoi? qu'est-ce que tu as dit?; **he earns** ~? il gagne combien?; **he did** ~? il a fait quoi?; **George** ~? George comment?
B *det* **1** (which) quel/quelle/quels/quelles; ~ **time is it?** quelle heure est-il?; **2** (in exclamations) quel/quelle; ~ **a nice car!** quelle belle voiture!; ~ **a strange thing to do!** quelle drôle d'idée!; ~ **use is that?** lit, fig à quoi ça sert?; **3** (the amount of) ~ **money he earns he spends** tout ce qu'il gagne, il le dépense; ~ **little she has** le peu qu'elle a, tout ce qu'elle a; ~ **few friends she had** les quelques amis qu'elle avait
C **what about** *prep phr* **1** (when drawing attention) ~ **about the letter they sent?** et la lettre qu'ils ont envoyée, alors?; ~ **about the children?** et les enfants (alors)?; **2** (when making suggestion) ~ **about a meal out?** et si on dînait au restaurant?; ~ **about Tuesday?** qu'est-ce que tu dirais de mardi?; **3** (in reply) '~ **about your sister?'**—'~ **about her?'** 'et ta sœur?'—'quoi ma sœur?'
D **what if** *prep phr* et si
E **what with** *prep phr* ~ **with her shopping bags and her bike** avec ses sacs à provisions et son vélo en plus; ~ **with the depression and unemployment** entre la dépression et le chômage; ~ **with one thing and another** avec ceci et cela

what

As a pronoun

In questions

When used in questions as an object pronoun, *what* is translated by *que* or *qu'est-ce que*.

After *que* the verb and subject are inverted and a hyphen is placed between them:

what is he doing?
= que fait-il? *or* qu'est-ce qu'il fait?

When used in questions as a subject pronoun, *what* is translated by *qu'est-ce qui*:

what happened?
= qu'est-ce qui s'est passé?

Used with a preposition

After a preposition the translation is *quoi*.

Unlike in English, the preposition must always be placed immediately before *quoi*:

with what did she cut it? or what did she cut it with?
= avec quoi l'a-t-elle coupé?

To introduce a clause

When used to introduce a clause as the object of the verb, *what* is translated by *ce que* (*ce qu'* before a vowel):

I don't know what he wants
= je ne sais pas ce qu'il veut

When *what* is the subject of the verb it is translated by *ce qui*:

tell me what happened
= raconte-moi ce qui s'est passé

For particular usages see **A** in the entry **what**.

....

As a determiner

what used as a determiner is translated by *quel, quelle, quels* or *quelles* according to the gender and number of the noun that follows:

what train did you catch?
= quel train as-tu pris?

what books do you like?
= quels livres aimes-tu?

what colours do you like?
= quelles couleurs aimes-tu?

For particular usages see **B** in the entry **what**.

F *excl* quoi!, comment!

(Idioms) **I'll tell you** ~ tu sais quoi; **to give sb** ~ **for**○ GB passer un savon○ à qn; **to know** ~'s ~ s'y connaître; **well,** ~ **do you know** iron tout arrive; ~ **do you think I am**○! tu me prends pour quoi!; ~'s **it to you**○? en quoi ça vous regarde?

what: ~-**d'yer-call-him**○, ~'s-**his-name**○ *n* Machin○ *m*; ~-**d'yer-call-it**○, ~'s-**its-name**○ *n* machin○ *m*

whatever /wɒt'evə(r), US hwɒt-/
A *pron* **1** (that which) (as subject) ce qui; (as object) ce que; **to do** ~ **is required** faire ce qui est exigé; **2** (anything that) (as subject) tout ce qui; (as object) tout ce que; **do** ~ **you like** fais tout ce que tu veux; ~ **he says goes** c'est lui qui décide; ~ **you say** (as you like) tout ce qui vous plaira; **3** (no matter what) quoi que (+ *subj*); ~ **happens** quoi qu'il arrive; ~ **it costs it doesn't matter** quel que soit le prix, ça n'a pas d'importance; **4** (what on earth) (as subject) qu'est-ce qui; (as object) qu'est-ce que; ~'s **the matter?** qu'est-ce qui ne va

pas?; ∼ **do you mean?** qu'est-ce que tu veux dire par là?; **'let's go'—'∼ for?'** 'allons-y'–'pour quoi faire?'; ∼ **next!** qu'est-ce que ça sera la prochaine fois?; [5] ○(the like) curtains, cushions and ∼ des rideaux, des coussins et toutes sortes de choses

B *det* [1] (any) ∼ **hope he once had** tous les espoirs qu'il avait; **they eat** ∼ **food they can get** ils mangent tout ce qu'ils trouvent à manger; [2] (no matter what) ∼ **the reason** quelle que soit la raison; **for** ∼ **reason** pour je ne sais quelle raison; **any race of** ∼ **creed** toutes les races quelles que soient leurs croyances; [3] (expressing surprise) ∼ **idiot forgot the key?** quel est l'imbécile qui a oublié la clé?

C *adv* (at all) **to have no idea** ∼ ne pas avoir la moindre idée; **'any chance?'—'none** ∼' 'il y a une chance?'–'pas la moindre'; **'any petrol?'—'none** ∼' 'il y a de l'essence?' –'pas du tout'; **anything** ∼ n'importe quoi

whatnot /'wɒtnɒt, US 'hwɒt-/ *n* [1] (furniture) étagère *f*; [2] ○(unspecified person or thing) machin○ *m*; [3] ○(and so on) ...and ∼.... et ainsi de suite

whatsit○ /'wɒtsɪt, US 'hwɒt-/ *n* machin○ *m*, truc○ *m*

whatsoever /ˌwɒtsəʊ'evə(r), US 'hwɒt-/ *adv* = whatever C

wheat /wiːt, US hwiːt/ *n* blé *m*

wheat: ∼ **germ** *n* germe *m* de blé; ∼**meal** *n* farine *f* complète

wheedle /'wiːdl, US 'hwiːdl/ *vtr* to ∼ **sth out of sb** soutirer qch à qn par la cajolerie

wheel /wiːl, US hwiːl/

A *n* [1] (on vehicle) roue *f*; (on furniture) roulette *f*; [2] (for steering) volant *m*; Naut roue *f* (de gouvernail); **to be at** *ou* **behind the** ∼ être au volant; [3] (in mechanism) rouage *m* also *fig*

B ○**wheels** *npl* bagnole○ *f*; **have you got** ∼**s?** tu es motorisé○?

C *vtr* pousser; **they** ∼**ed me into the operating theatre** ils m'ont emmené dans la salle d'opération sur un chariot

D *vi* [1] (also ∼ **round**) (circle) [*bird*] tournoyer; [2] (turn sharply) [*person, regiment*] faire demi-tour; [*car, motorbike*] braquer fortement; [*ship*] virer de bord

E -**wheeled** *combining form* **a three-/four-**∼**ed vehicle** un véhicule à trois/quatre roues

(Idioms) **to** ∼ **and deal** magouiller; **it's** ∼**s within** ∼**s** l'affaire est plus compliquée qu'elle n'en a l'air

(Phrasal verbs)

■ wheel in = wheel out

■ **wheel out**: ▸ ∼ **[sth] out**, ∼ **out [sth]** remettre [qch] sur le tapis [*argument, story*]; ressortir [*excuse, statistics*]

wheel: ∼**barrow** *n* brouette *f*; ∼**chair** *n* fauteuil *m* roulant

wheelclamp /'wiːlklæmp, US 'hwiːl-/
A *n* Aut sabot *m* de Denver
B *vtr* mettre un sabot de Denver à [*car*]

-**wheeler** /'wiːlə(r), US 'hwiːlər/ *combining form* **it's a two/ three-**∼ (vehicle) il/elle a deux/trois roues

wheeler dealer○ *n* péj magouilleur/-euse○ *m/f*

wheeling and dealing *n* (+ *v sg*) péj *gen* manigances *fpl*; (during negotiations) tractations *fpl*

wheeze /wiːz, US hwiːz/
A *vtr* dire d'une voix rauque
B *vi* [*person, animal*] ahaner; [*engine*] crachoter

wheezy /'wiːzɪ, US 'hwiːzɪ/ *adj* [*voice, cough*] rauque; **to have a** ∼ **chest** avoir la respiration sifflante

when /wen, US hwen/
A *pron* [1] (with prepositions) quand; **since** ∼? depuis quand? also *iron*; [2] (the time when) **that was** ∼ **it all started to go wrong** c'est à ce moment-là que tout a commencé à mal aller; **that's** ∼ **I was born** (day) c'est le jour où je suis né; (year) c'est l'année où je suis né; **he spoke of** ∼ **he was a child** il a parlé de l'époque où il était enfant

B *adv* [1] (as interrogative) quand (est-ce que); ∼ **are we leaving?** quand est-ce qu'on part?; **I wonder** ∼ **the film starts** je me demande à quelle heure commence le film; **I forget exactly** ∼ (time) j'ai oublié l'heure exacte; (date) j'ai oublié la date exacte; **tell me** *ou* **say** ∼ (pouring drink) dis-moi stop; [2] (as relative) **in 1993** ∼ en 1993 quand; **at the time** ∼

---

when

when can very often be translated by *quand* in time expressions:

when did she leave?
= quand est-ce qu'elle est partie?
  or elle est partie quand?
  or quand est-elle partie?

Note that in questions *quand* on its own requires inversion of the verb and subject:

when are they arriving?
= quand arrivent-ils?

but *when* followed by *est-ce que* needs no inversion: *quand est-ce qu'ils arrivent?*

Occasionally a more precise time expression is used in French:

when's your birthday?
= quelle est la date de ton anniversaire?

when did he set off?
= à quelle heure est-il parti?

Remember that the future tense is used after *quand* if future time is implied:

tell him when you see him
= dis-le-lui quand tu le verras

It is often possible to give a short neat translation for a *when* clause if there is no change of subject in the sentence:

when I was very young, I lived in Normandy
= tout jeune, j'habitais en Normandie

when he was leaving, he asked for my address
= en partant, il m'a demandé mon adresse

In expressions such as *the day when*, *the year when*, *où* is used:

the day when we got married
= le jour où nous nous sommes mariés

For examples of the above and further uses of *when*, see the entry **when.**

(precise moment) au moment où; (during same period) à l'époque où; **the week** ∼ **it all happened** la semaine où tout s'est passé; **on those rare occasions** ∼ les rares fois où; **it's times like that** ∼ c'est dans ces moments-là que; **one morning** ∼ **he was getting up, he...** un matin en se levant, il...; [3] (then) **she resigned in May, since** ∼ **we've had no applicants** elle a démissionné en mai, et depuis (lors) nous n'avons reçu aucune candidature; **until** ∼ **we must stay calm** d'ici là nous devons rester calmes; **by** ∼ **we will have received the information** d'ici là nous aurons reçu toutes les informations; [4] (whenever) quand; **he's only happy** ∼ **he's moaning** il n'est content que quand il rouspète; ∼ **I sunbathe, I get freckles** chaque fois que je prends un bain de soleil, j'ai des taches de rousseur; ∼ **possible** dans la mesure du possible

C *conj* [1] (at the precise time when) quand, lorsque; ∼ **she reaches 18** quand elle aura 18 ans; [2] (during the period when) quand, lorsque; ∼ **he was at school** quand il était à l'école; [3] (as soon as) quand, dès que; **I was strolling along** ∼ **all of a sudden...** je marchais tranquillement quand tout d'un coup...; [4] (when it is the case that) alors que; **why buy their products** ∼ **ours are cheaper?** pourquoi acheter leurs produits alors que les nôtres sont moins chers?; [5] (whereas) alors que; **he refused** ∼ **I would have gladly accepted** il a refusé alors que j'aurais été ravi d'accepter

whenever /wen'evə(r), US hwen-/ *adv* [1] (as interrogative) ∼ **will he arrive?** quand est-ce qu'il va finir par arriver?; ∼ **did she find the time?** comment est-ce qu'elle a bien pu trouver le temps?; [2] (no matter when) ∼ **you want** quand tu veux; **till** ∼ **you like** aussi longtemps que tu veux; ∼ **he does it, it won't matter** il peut le faire quand il veut, ça n'a pas d'importance; **I'll come** ∼ **it is convenient** je viendrai

W

quand cela vous arrangera; ③ ○(some time) **or** ~ ou n'importe quand; ④ (every time that) chaque fois que; ~ **I see a black cat, I make a wish** chaque fois que je vois un chat noir, je fais un vœu; ⑤ (expressing doubt) **she promised to return them soon,** ~ **that might be!** elle a promis de les rendre bientôt, mais je ne sais pas quand

where /weə(r), US hweər/

> ⚠️ *Where* is generally translated by *où*: *where are the plates?* = où sont les assiettes?; *do you know where he's going?* = est-ce que tu sais où il va?; *I don't know where the knives are* = je ne sais pas où sont les couteaux.
> Note that in questions *où* on its own requires inversion of the verb: *where are you going?* = où allez-vous? but *où* followed by *est-ce que* needs no inversion: où est-ce que vous allez?

A *pron* ① (with prepositions) où; **from** ~? d'où?; **near** ~? près d'où?; **to go up to** ~ **sb is standing** s'approcher de qn; **not from** ~ **I'm standing** lit pas de là où je suis; fig ce n'est pas mon avis; ② (the place or point where) là que; **this is** ~ **it happened** c'est là que c'est arrivé; **that is** ~ **he's mistaken** c'est là qu'il se trompe; **France is** ~ **you'll find good wine** c'est en France que vous trouverez du bon vin

B *adv* ① (as interrogative) où (est-ce que); ~ **is my coat?** où est mon manteau?; ~ **does Martin figure in all this?** qu'est-ce que Martin vient faire dans tout ça?; ~'**s the harm?** quel mal y a-t-il à ça?; ~'**s the problem?** je ne vois pas le problème; ~ **have you got to in your book?** où est-ce que vous en êtes dans votre lecture?; ② (as indirect interrogative) où; **I wonder** ~ **he's going** je me demande où il va; **to know** ~ **one is going** savoir où on va; fig savoir ce qu'on veut; **you don't know** ~ **it's been!** tu ne sais pas où ça a traîné!; ③ (as relative) où; **the village** ~ **we live** le village où nous habitons; **in several cases** ~ dans plusieurs cas où; ④ (here where, there where) **stay** ~ **it's dry** reste à l'abri; **it's cold** ~ **we live** il fait froid là où nous habitons; **it's not** ~ **you said** (not there) ça n'y est pas; (found elsewhere) ce n'est pas là où tu crois; ⑤ (wherever) où; **put them/go** ~ **you want** mets-les/va où tu veux; ⑥ (whenever) quand; ~ **necessary** si nécessaire; **she's stupid** ~ **he's concerned** elle se conduit toujours de façon stupide quand il s'agit de lui; ~ **possible** dans la mesure du possible

C *conj* = **whereas**

whereabouts

A /ˈweərəbaʊts, US ˈhweər-/ *n* **do you know his** ~? savez-vous où il est?

B /ˌweərəˈbaʊts/ *adv* gen où; '**I've put them in the living room'**—'~?' 'je les ai mis dans le salon'—'où ça?'

whereas /ˌweərˈæz, US ˌhweər-/ *conj* **she likes dogs** ~ **I prefer cats** elle aime les chiens mais moi je préfère les chats; **he chose to stay quiet** ~ **I would have complained** il a choisi de ne rien dire alors que moi je me serais sûrement plaint

whereby /weəˈbaɪ, US hweər-/ *conj* **a system** ~ **all staff will carry identification** un système qui prévoit que tous les membres du personnel auront une carte; **the criteria** ~ **allowances are allocated** les critères selon lesquels les allocations sont attribuées

whereupon /ˌweərəˈpɒn, US ˌhweər-/ *conj* sout sur quoi

wherever /weərˈevə(r), US hweər-/ *adv* ① (as interrogative) ~ **did you put them?** où est-ce que tu as bien pu les mettre?; ~ **has he got to?** où est-ce qu'il a bien pu passer?; ② (anywhere) ~ **she goes I'll go** où qu'elle aille, j'irai; ~ **you want** où tu veux; **we'll meet** ~'**s convenient for you** nous nous retrouverons là où ça t'arrange; ③ ○(somewhere) **or** ~ ou n'importe où ailleurs; ④ (whenever) ~ **there's an oasis, there's a settlement** dès qu'il y a une oasis, il y a une implantation; ~ **necessary** quand c'est nécessaire; ~ **possible** dans la mesure du possible; ⑤ (expressing doubt) **she's from Vernoux** ~ **that is!** elle vient de Vernoux mais ne me demande pas où c'est!

wherewithal /ˈweəwɪˌðɔːl/ *n* **the** ~ les moyens *mpl*

whet /wet, US hwet/ *vtr* (*p prés etc* **-tt-**) ① (stimulate) **to** ~ **the appetite** stimuler l'appétit; **the book** ~**ted his appetite for travel** les livres lui donnèrent envie de voyager; ② ‡ aiguiser

whether /ˈweðə(r), US ˈhweðər/

> ⚠️ When *whether* is used to mean *if*, it is translated by *si*: *I wonder whether she got my letter* = je me demande si elle a reçu ma lettre. See 1 in the entry below.
> *whether* often occurs after verbs such as *ask*, *doubt, decide, know, say, see* and *wonder*, with adjectives such as *doubtful, sure*, and with nouns like *doubt, question*. You can find further examples at these entries.
> In *whether…or not* sentences *whether* is translated by *que* and the verb that follows is in the subjunctive: *whether you agree or not* = que vous soyez d'accord ou non. See 2 in the entry below.

conj ① (when outcome is uncertain: if) si; **I wasn't sure** ~ **to answer or not** ou ~ **or not to answer** je ne savais pas s'il fallait répondre, je n'étais pas sûr qu'il faille répondre; **I wonder** ~ **it's true** je me demande si c'est vrai; **the question is** ~ **anyone is interested** le problème est de savoir si quelqu'un est intéressé; **she was worried about** ~ **to invite them** elle se demandait si elle devait les inviter; ② (when outcome is fixed: no matter if) **you're going to school** ~ **you like it or not!** tu iras à l'école que cela te plaise ou non!; ~ **you have children or not, this book should interest you** que vous ayez des enfants ou non, ce livre devrait vous intéresser; ~ **or not people are happy is of little importance** que les gens soient heureux ou non ce n'est pas très important; **everyone,** ~ **students or townspeople, celebrates** tout le monde, que ce soient les étudiants ou les habitants de la ville, fait la fête

which /wɪtʃ, US hwɪtʃ/

A *pron* ① (also ~ **one**) lequel *m*, laquelle *f*; ~ **do you want, the red skirt or the blue one?** laquelle est-ce que tu veux, la jupe rouge ou la bleue?; ~ **of the groups…?** (referring to one) lequel des groupes…?; (referring to several) lesquels des groupes…?; **show her** ~ **you mean** montre-lui celui/celle etc que tu veux dire; **do you mind** ~ **you have?** est-ce que tu as une préférence?; **I don't mind** ~ ça m'est égal; **can you tell** ~ **is** ~? peux-tu les distinguer?; ② (relative to preceding noun) (as subject) qui; (as object) que; (after prepositions) lequel/laquelle/lesquels/lesquelles; **the contract** ~ **he's spoken about** *ou* **about** ~ **he's spoken** le contrat dont il a parlé; ③ (relative to preceding clause or concept) (as subject) ce qui; (as object) ce que; ~ **reminds me…** ce qui me fait penser que…; **we'll be moving, before** ~ **we need to…** nous allons déménager mais avant il faut que nous…; **he's resigned, from** ~ **we must assume that** il a démissionné, d'où on peut déduire que

B *det* ① (interrogative) quel/quelle/quels/quelles (before *n*); ~ **books?** quels livres?; ~ **one of the children?** lequel *or* laquelle des enfants?; ② (relative) **he left the room, during** ~ **time…** il a quitté la pièce et pendant ce temps-là…; **you may wish to join, in** ~ **case…** vous voulez peut-être vous inscrire, auquel cas…

whichever /wɪtʃˈevə(r), US hwɪtʃ-/

A *pron* ① (the one that) (as subject) celui *m* qui, celle *f* qui; (as object) celui *m* que, celle *f* que; '**which restaurant?'**—'~ **is nearest'** 'quel restaurant?'—'celui qui est le plus proche'; **come at 2 or 2.30,** ~ **suits you best** viens à 14 h ou 14 h 30, comme cela te convient le mieux; **choose either alternative,** ~ **is the cheaper** choisis la moins chère des deux solutions; ② (no matter which one) (as subject) quel *m* que soit celui qui, quelle *f* que soit celle qui; (as object) quel *m* que soit celui que, quelle *f* que soit celle que; '**do you want the big piece or the small piece?'**—'~' 'est-ce que tu veux le gros ou le petit morceau?'—'n'importe'

B *det* ① (the one that) **let's go to** ~ **station is nearest** allons à la gare la plus proche; **you may have** ~ **dress you prefer** tu peux choisir la robe que tu préfères; ② (no matter which) **it won't matter** ~ **hotel we go to** peu importe l'hôtel où nous irons; **I'll be happy** ~ **horse wins** quel que soit le cheval qui gagne je serai content; ③ (which on earth) ~ **one do you mean?** mais duquel/de laquelle est-ce que tu peux bien parler?

whiff /wɪf, US hwɪf/ *n* (of perfume, food, dung) odeur *f* (**of** de); (of smoke, garlic) bouffée *f* (**of** de); fig relent *m* (**of** de)

while /waɪl, US hwaɪl/

A *conj* ① (although) bien que, quoique; ② (as long as) tant que; ③ (during the time that) pendant que; **he made a sandwich** ~ **I phoned** il s'est fait un sandwich pendant que je téléphonais; **he collapsed** ~ **mowing the lawn** il a eu un malaise alors qu'il tondait le gazon; ④ (at the same time as) en (+

which

As a pronoun

In questions

When *which* is used as a pronoun in questions it is translated by *lequel*, *laquelle*, *lesquels* or *lesquelles* according to the gender and number of the noun it is referring to:

there are three peaches, which do you want?
= il y a trois pêches, laquelle veux-tu?

'Lucy's borrowed three of your books' 'which did she take?'
= 'Lucy t'a emprunté trois livres' 'lesquels a-t-elle pris?'

The exception to this is when *which* is followed by a superlative adjective, when the translation is *quel*, *quelle*, *quels* or *quelles*:

which is the biggest (apple)?
= quelle est la plus grande?

which are the least expensive (books)?
= quels sont les moins chers?

In relative clauses as subject or object

When *which* is used as a relative pronoun as the subject of a verb, it is translated by *qui*:

the book which is on the table
= le livre qui est sur la table

the books which are on the table
= les livres qui sont sur la table

When *which* is the object of a verb it is translated by *que* (*qu'* before a vowel or mute 'h'):

the book which Tina is reading
= le livre que lit Tina

Note the inversion of subject and verb; this is the case where the subject is a noun but not where the subject is a pronoun:

the book which I am reading
= le livre que je lis

In compound tenses such as the present perfect and past perfect, the past participle agrees in gender and number with the noun *que* is referring to:

the books which I gave you
= les livres que je t'ai donnés

the dresses which she bought yesterday
= les robes qu'elle a achetées hier

In relative clauses after a preposition

Here the translation is *lequel*, *laquelle*, *lesquels* or *lesquelles* according to the gender and number of the noun referred to:

the road by which we came or **the road which we came by**
= la route par laquelle nous sommes venus

the expressions for which we have translations
= les expressions pour lesquelles nous avons une traduction

Remember that if the preposition would normally be translated by *à* in French (*to*, *at* etc.), the preposition + *which* is translated by *auquel*, *à laquelle*, *auxquels* or *auxquelles*:

the addresses to which we sent letters
= les adresses auxquelles nous avons envoyé des lettres

With prepositions normally translated by *de* (*of*, *from* etc.) the translation of the preposition *which* becomes *dont*:

a blue book, the title of which I've forgotten
= un livre bleu dont j'ai oublié le titre

However, if *de* is part of a prepositional group, as for example in the case of *près de* meaning *near*, the translation becomes *duquel*, *de laquelle*, *desquels* or *desquelles*:

the village near which they live
= le village près duquel ils habitent

the houses near which she was waiting
= les maisons près desquelles elle attendait

The translation *duquel* etc. is also used where a preposition + noun precedes *of which*:

a hill at the top of which there is a house
= une colline au sommet de laquelle il y a une maison

....

As a determiner

In questions

When *which* is used as a determiner in questions it is translated by *quel*, *quelle*, *quels* or *quelles* according to the gender and number of the noun that follows:

which car is yours?
= quelle voiture est la vôtre?

which books did he borrow?
= quels livres a-t-il empruntés?

Note that in the second example the object precedes the verb so that the past participle agrees in gender and number with the object.

For translations of *which* as a determiner in relative clauses see **B2** in the entry **which**.

---

gerund); **I fell asleep ~ watching TV** je me suis endormi en regardant la télé; **close the door ~ you're about** *ou* **at it** ferme la porte pendant que tu y es; **'MOT ~ you wait'** 'contrôle technique express'; **5** (whereas) tandis que

B *n* **a ~ ago** *ou* **back** il y a quelque temps; **a ~ later** quelque temps plus tard; **for a good ~** pendant longtemps; **a short** *ou* **little ~ ago** il y a peu de temps; **it will be** *ou* **take a ~** cela va prendre un certain temps; **to stop for a ~** s'arrêter un peu; **after a ~ he fell asleep** au bout d'un moment il s'est endormi; **he worked, humming all the ~** il travaillait tout en chantonnant; **and all the ~** *ou* **the whole ~, he was cheating on her** et depuis le début, il la trompait; **once in a ~** de temps en temps; **in between ~s** entre-temps

(Phrasal verb)

■ **while away**: ▸ **~ away [sth]** tuer [*time*]

whilst /waɪlst, US hwaɪlst/ *conj* = **while A**

whim /wɪm, US hwɪm/ *n* caprice *m*; **on a ~** sur un coup de tête

whimper /ˈwɪmpə(r), US ˈhwɪm-/
A *n* gémissement *m*
B *vtr* **'I'm cold,' she ~ed** 'j'ai froid,' dit-elle en gémissant
C *vi* **1** [*person, animal*] gémir; **2** péj (whinge) [*person*] pleurnicher

whimsical /ˈwɪmzɪkl, US ˈhwɪm-/ *adj* [*person*] fantasque; [*play, tale, manner, idea*] saugrenu

whine /waɪn, US hwaɪn/
A *n* (of person, animal) geignement *m*; (of engine) plainte *f*; (of bullet) sifflement *m*
B *vtr* **'I'm hungry,' he ~d** 'j'ai faim,' dit-il d'une voix geignarde
C *vi* (complain) se plaindre (**about** de); (snivel) pleurnicher; [*dog*] gémir

W

whining /'waɪnɪŋ, US 'hwaɪn-/
A n (complaints) jérémiades fpl; (of engine) gémissements mpl aigus; (of dog) gémissements mpl
B adj [voice] (complaining, high-pitched) geignard; [child] pleurnicheur/-euse; [letter] de réclamation

whinny /'wɪnɪ, US 'hwɪnɪ/
A n faible hennissement m
B vi [horse] hennir doucement

whip /wɪp, US hwɪp/
A n ① (for punishment) fouet m; (for horse) cravache f; ② GB Pol (official) député chargé d'assurer la discipline de vote des membres de son parti; (summons) convocation f (envoyée aux membres d'un parti lors d'une séance de Parlement importante); **three-line** ~ convocation f urgente; ③ Culin mousse f
B vtr (p prés etc **-pp-**) ① (beat) fouetter; ② Culin fouetter [cream]; battre [qch] en neige [egg whites]; ③ ○(remove quickly) **I** ~**ped the key out of his hand** je lui ai arraché la clé des mains; ④ GB (steal) piquer○ (**from sb** à qn)
C ○vi (p prés etc **-pp-**) **to** ~ **round** se retourner brusquement

(Phrasal verbs)
■ **whip away**: ▸ ~ **away** [sth], ~ [sth] **away** [person] retirer prestement; [wind] faire voler
■ **whip back**: ▸ ~ **back** revenir brusquement en arrière; ▸ ~ **back** [sth], ~ [sth] **back** récupérer [qch] brusquement
■ **whip in**: ▸ ~ **in** [sth], ~ [sth] **in** ① rassembler [hounds]; ② Culin incorporer [qch] (avec un fouet); ▸ ~ **in** [sb], ~ [sb] **in** US Pol rallier
■ **whip off**: ▸ ~ **off** [sth], ~ [sth] **off** enlever [qch] à toute vitesse
■ **whip on**: ▸ ~ **on** [sth], ~ [sth] **on** ① enfiler [qch] à toute vitesse; ② cravacher [horse]
■ **whip out**: ▸ ~ **out** [sth] sortir [qch] brusquement
■ **whip through** expédier [task, book]
■ **whip up**: ▸ ~ **up** [sth] ① (incite) attiser [hatred]; ranimer [indignation, hostility]; éveiller [interest]; rallier [support]; inciter [unrest]; ② Culin battre [qch] au fouet; ③ (produce) préparer [qch] en vitesse

whip hand n to have the ~ avoir le dessus; **to have the** ~ **over sb** l'emporter sur qn

whiplash injury n Med coup m du lapin

whipping /'wɪpɪŋ, US 'hwɪp-/ n correction f (au fouet)

whipping boy n souffre-douleur m inv

whip-round○ n GB collecte f

whirl /wɜːl, US hwɜːl/
A n lit, fig gen tourbillon m (**of** de); (spiral motif) spirale f
B vtr (swirl) faire tournoyer; **to** ~ **sb along/away** entraîner/emmener qn à toute vitesse
C vi ① [dancer] tournoyer; [blade, propeller] tourner; [snowflakes, dust, mind, thoughts] tourbillonner; ② [person, vehicle] **to** ~ **past** filer à toute vitesse

(Idiom) **to give sth a** ~○ essayer qch

(Phrasal verb)
■ **whirl round**: ▸ ~ **round** [person] se retourner brusquement; ▸ ~ [sth] **round** faire tournoyer

whirl: ~**pool** n tourbillon m; ~**pool bath** n bain m bouillonnant; ~**wind** n tourbillon m

whirr /wɜː(r), US hwɜːr/
A n (of motor) vrombissement m; (of toy, camera, insect) bourdonnement m; (of wings) bruissement m
B vi [motor] vrombir; [camera, fan] tourner; [insect] bourdonner; [wings] bruire

whisk /wɪsk, US hwɪsk/
A n Culin (also **egg** ~) (manual) fouet m; (electric) batteur m
B vtr ① Culin battre; ② (transport quickly) **he was** ~**ed off to meet the president** on l'a emmené voir le champ rencontrer le président; **she was** ~**ed off to hospital** elle a été emmenée d'urgence à l'hôpital; ③ (flick) **she** ~**ed the fly away** elle a chassé la mouche d'un geste
C vi **he** ~**ed off** il est parti rapidement; **he** ~**ed around the room with a duster** il a donné un rapide coup de chiffon dans la pièce

whisker /'wɪskə(r), US 'hwɪsk-/
A n ① lit poil m de moustache; ② fig **to lose/win by a** ~ perdre/gagner d'un poil○
B **whiskers** npl (of animal) moustaches fpl; (of man) (side-whiskers) favoris mpl; (beard) barbe f; (moustache) moustache f

whisper /'wɪspə(r), US 'hwɪs-/
A n lit gen chuchotement m; fig rumeur f; **to speak in a** ~ ou in

~**s** parler à voix basse; **his voice dropped to a** ~ il a baissé la voix et s'est mis à chuchoter
B vtr chuchoter (**to** à); **to** ~ **sth to sb** chuchoter qch à qn; **it is** ~**ed that** fig on dit que
C vi gen chuchoter; [water] murmurer; **to** ~ **to sb** parler à voix basse à qn

whispering /'wɪspərɪŋ, US 'hwɪ-/
A n gen chuchotement m; fig rumeurs fpl insidieuses
B adj [person] qui chuchote; [leaves, trees, wind, water] murmurant

whispering: ~ **campaign** n campagne f de diffamation; ~ **gallery** n galerie f à écho

whistle /'wɪsl, US 'hwɪ-/
A n ① (small pipe) sifflet m; (siren) sirène f; **to blow the** ou **one's** ~ donner un coup de sifflet; ② (sound) gen sifflement m; (with small pipe) coup m de sifflet
B vtr gen siffler; (casually) siffloter [melody]
C vi ① (make noise) siffler; **to** ~ **at sb/sth** siffler qn/qch; **to** ~ **for** siffler [dog]; ② (move fast) **to** ~ **past** ou **by** [bullet] passer en sifflant; [train] passer à toute vitesse

(Idioms) **to blow the** ~ **on sb** dénoncer qn; **to blow the** ~ **on sth** révéler qch; **you can** ~ **for it**○! tu peux toujours courir○!; **to** ~ **in the dark** essayer de se donner du courage

(Phrasal verb)
■ **whistle up**: ▸ ~ **up** [sth] dégoter○

whistle-stop tour n (by diplomat, president) tournée f éclair inv (**of** de); (by candidate on campaign) tournée f électorale (**of** de)

Whit /wɪt, US hwɪt/ n: abrév ▸ **Whitsun**

white /waɪt, US hwaɪt/ ▸ p. 752
A n ① (colour, part of egg, eye) blanc m; ② (also **White**) (Caucasian) Blanc/Blanche m/f; ③ (wine) blanc m; ④ (in chess, draughts) blancs mpl
B **whites** npl **tennis/chef's** ~**s** tenue f de tennis/de chef-cuisinier
C adj ① blanc/blanche; ② [race, child, skin] blanc/blanche; [area] habité par des Blancs; [culture, prejudice, fears] des Blancs; **a** ~ **man/woman** un Blanc/une Blanche; ③ (pale) pâle (**with** de); **to go** ou **turn** ~ pâlir (**with** de)

(Idioms) **he would swear black was** ~ il a l'esprit de contradiction; **the men in** ~ **coats** hum les infirmiers psychiatriques; **whiter than** ~ plus blanc/blanche que neige

whitebait /'waɪtbeɪt, US 'hwaɪt-/ n (raw) blanchaille f; (fried) petite friture f

white: ~**board** n tableau m blanc; ~ **coffee** n (at home) café m au lait; (in café) café m crème; ~**-collar** adj [job, work] d'employé de bureau; [staff] de bureau; [vote] des cols blancs; [neighbourhood] US résidentiel/-ielle

white elephant n péj ① (item, knickknack) bibelot m; ② (public project) réalisation f coûteuse et peu rentable

white goods n ① (appliances) gros électro-ménager m; ② (linens) blanc m ©

white-haired /,waɪt'heəd, US ,hwaɪt-/ adj aux cheveux blancs

Whitehall /'waɪthɔːl, US 'hwaɪt-/ pr n GB Pol avenue à Londres où sont concentrés les principaux ministères et administrations publiques

white: ~ **hope** n espoir m; ~ **horses** n (waves) moutons mpl; ~ **hot** adj lit, fig incandescent

White House n Maison f Blanche; **a** ~~ **spokesman** un porte-parole de la Maison Blanche

white: ~ **lead** n blanc m de céruse; ~ **lie** n pieux mensonge m

whiten /'waɪtn, US 'hwaɪtn/
A vtr blanchir
B vi [sky, face, cheeks] pâlir; [knuckles] blanchir

whitener /'waɪtnə(r), US 'hwaɪt-/ n ① (for clothes) agent m blanchissant; ② (for shoes) produit m pour blanchir; ③ (for coffee, tea) succédané m de lait en poudre

whiteness /'waɪtnɪs, US 'hwaɪt-/ n blancheur f

whiteout /'waɪtaʊt, US 'hwaɪt-/ n Meteorol voile m blanc

White Russian n ① (Tsarist) Russe mf blanc/blanche; ② (Byelorussian) Biélorusse mf

white spirit n white-spirit m

white tie
A n ① (tie) nœud m papillon blanc; ② (formal dress) habit m; ~ **and tails** queue f de pie

B **white-tie** *noun modifier* [*dinner, occasion*] habillé

white: ∼ **trash** *n* **⊄** US péj pauvre Blanc/Blanche;
∼**wall (tyre)** GB, ∼**wall (tire)** US *n* pneu *m* à flanc
blanc

whitewash /'waɪtwɒʃ, US 'hwaɪt-/
A *n* 1 (for walls) lait *m* de chaux; 2 fig (cover-up) mise *f* en
scène; 3 ○Sport déculottée○ *f*
B *vtr* 1 lit blanchir [qch] à la chaux; 2 (*also* ∼ **over**) fig
blanchir; 3 ○Sport flanquer une déculottée à○; 4 Fin
réhabiliter

white: ∼ **water** *n* eau *f* vive; ∼ **wedding** *n* mariage *m*
en blanc

whitey /'waɪtɪ, US 'hwaɪtɪ/ *adj* [*blue*] laiteux/-euse

whither /'wɪðə(r), US 'hwɪðər/ *adv* littér où

whiting /'waɪtɪŋ, US 'hwaɪt-/ *n* (*pl* ∼) Zool merlan *m*

whitish /'waɪtɪʃ, US 'hwaɪt-/ ▸ p. 752 *adj* tirant sur le
blanc, blanchâtre pej

Whit Monday *n* lundi *m* de Pentecôte

Whitsun /'wɪtsn, US hwɪ-/ *n* (*also* **Whitsuntide**) Pentecôte *f*

Whit Sunday *n* Pentecôte *f*

whittle /'wɪtl, US 'hwɪt-/ *vtr* tailler [qch] au couteau

(Phrasal verbs)

■ **whittle away**: ▸ ∼ **away [sth]** fig réduire [*advantage,
lead*]; ▸ ∼ **away at [sth]** lit tailler [*stick*]; fig réduire [*advantage, lead, profits*]
■ **whittle down**: ▸ ∼ **down [sth]**, ∼ **[sth] down** réduire
(**to** à)

whizz /wɪz, US hwɪz/
A *n* 1 ○(expert) as○ *m* (**at** en); 2 (whirr) sifflement *m*;
3 ○(quick trip) tour *m* rapide (**around** de); 4 ○Culin **give the
mixture a** ∼ **in the blender** faites passer rapidement le
mélange au mixer
B ○*vtr* (deliver quickly) filer○
C *vi* **to** ∼ **by** *ou* **past** [*arrow, bullet*] passer en sifflant; [*car*]
passer à toute allure; [*person*] passer rapidement; **to** ∼ **up
sth** réduire qch en purée

whizz-kid○ /'wɪzkɪd, US 'hwɪz-/ *n* jeune prodige *m*

who /huː/

⚠ *Who* is translated by *qui*.
In questions *qui* on its own as the object of a
verb requires inversion of the verb: *who did he call?* =
qui a-t-il appelé? but *qui* followed by *est-ce que* or *est-
ce qui* needs no inversion: qui est-ce qu'il a appelé?
Note, however, that the form *il a appelé qui?* is also
used in spoken French.
For particular usages see the entry below.

pron 1 (interrogative) (as subject) qui (est-ce qui); (as object) qui
(est-ce que); (after prepositions) qui; ∼ **knows the answer?** qui
connaît la réponse?; ∼ **did you invite?** qui est-ce que tu as
invité?, qui as-tu invité?; ∼**'s going to be there?** qui sera
là?; ∼ **was she with?** avec qui était-elle?; ∼ **did you get it
from?** qui te l'a donné?; **do you know** ∼**'s** ∼**?** est-ce que
tu sais qui est qui?; **I was strolling along when** ∼ **should I
see but Diane** je me promenais et devine qui j'ai rencontré...Diane; ∼ **shall I say is calling?** (on phone) c'est de la
part de qui?; 2 (relative) (as subject) qui; (as object) que; (after
prepositions) qui; **his friend,** ∼ **lives in Paris** son ami qui
habite Paris; **his friend** ∼ **he sees once a week** l'ami qu'il
voit une fois par semaine; **he/she** ∼ celui/celle qui; **they**
ou **those** ∼ ceux/celles qui; **those** ∼ **have something to
say should speak up now** quiconque a quelque chose à
dire doit le dire *ou* ceux qui ont quelque chose à dire
doivent le dire maintenant; 3 (whoever) **bring** ∼ **you like**
tu peux amener qui tu veux; ∼ **do you think you are?** tu
te prends pour qui?; ∼**'s he to tell you what to do?** de quel
droit est-ce qu'il te donne des ordres?

WHO *n* (*abrév* = **World Health Organization**) OMS *f*

who'd /huːd/ = **who had**, **who would**

whodun(n)it /ˌhuːˈdʌnɪt/ *n* polar○ *m*, roman *m* policier

whoever /huːˈevə(r)/ *pron* 1 (the one that) ∼ **wins the election will have to deal with the problem** celui ou celle qui
gagnera les élections devra faire face au problème;
2 (anyone that) qui; **invite** ∼ **you like** invite qui tu veux;
∼ **saw the accident should contact the police** quiconque a
assisté à l'accident devrait contacter la police; 3 (all who)
tous ceux qui; 4 (no matter who) **come out** ∼ **you are** qui
que vous soyez, sortez de là; **write to the minister or** ∼
écris au ministre ou à n'importe qui d'autre; 5 (who on

earth) qui; ∼ **did that to you?** (mais) qui a bien pu te
faire ça?

whole /həʊl/
A *n* 1 (total unit) tout *m*; **as a** ∼ (not in separate parts) en entier;
(overall) dans l'ensemble; **taken as a** ∼ pris dans l'ensemble; 2 (all) **the** ∼ **of** tout/-e; **the** ∼ **of London is talking
about it** tout Londres en parle; **nearly the** ∼ **of Berlin was
destroyed** Berlin a été presque entièrement détruit
B *adj* 1 (entire) tout, entier/-ière; (more emphatic) tout entier/
-ière; **the most beautiful city in the** ∼ **world** la plus belle
ville du monde; **a** ∼ **hour** une heure entière; **a** ∼ **day**
toute une journée; **the** ∼ **truth** toute la vérité; **this doesn't
give the** ∼ **picture** ceci ne dit pas tout; **let's forget the**
∼ **thing!** oublions tout ça!; **she made the** ∼ **thing up** elle a
tout inventé; 2 (emphatic use) **he looks a** ∼ **lot better** il a
vraiment bien meilleure mine; **there were a** ∼ **lot of them**
[*objects*] il y en avait tout un tas○; [*people*] il y en avait
toute une bande○; **a** ∼ **lot of money** un tas○ d'argent;
that goes for the ∼ **lot of you!** ça s'applique à vous tous!; **a**
∼ **new way of life** un mode de vie complètement différent; **that's the** ∼ **point of the exercise** c'est tout l'intérêt
de l'exercice; 3 (intact) intact; **to make sb** ∼ guérir qn
C *adv* [*swallow, cook*] tout entier
D **on the whole** *adv phr* dans l'ensemble

whole: ∼**food** *n* GB produits *mpl* biologiques; ∼**food
shop** ▸ p. 1181 *n* GB magasin *m* de produits diététiques;
∼**grain** *adj* complet/-ète

wholehearted /ˌhəʊl'hɑːtɪd/ *adj* sans réserve; **to be in**
∼ **agreement** with être en accord total avec

whole: ∼**heartedly** *adv* sans réserve; ∼**meal** *adj*
complet/-ète; ∼ **milk** *n* lait *m* entier; ∼ **number** *n*
(nombre *m*) entier *m*

wholesale /'həʊlseɪl/
A *n* vente *f* en gros
B *adj* 1 Comm de gros; 2 (large-scale) [*destruction, alteration,
commitment*] total; [*acceptance, rejection*] en bloc; [*attack*] sur
tous les fronts
C *adv* 1 Comm en gros; **I can get it for you** ∼ je peux vous
l'avoir au prix de gros; 2 fig en bloc

wholesaler /'həʊlseɪlə(r)/ *n* grossiste *mf*, marchand/-e
m/f en gros; **wine** ∼ marchand de vin en gros

wholesome /'həʊlsəm/ *adj* 1 (healthy) sain; 2 (decent)
[*person*] bien propre; [*entertainment*] innocent

wholewheat *adj* = **wholemeal**

who'll /huːl/ = **who will**, **who shall**

wholly /'həʊllɪ/ *adv* entièrement, tout à fait

whom /huːm/

⚠ In questions, *qui* on its own requires inversion of
the verb: *whom do you wish to see?* = qui voulez-
vous voir? but *qui* followed by *est-ce que* needs no
inversion: qui est-ce que vous voulez voir?

pron 1 (interrogative) qui (est-ce que); (after prepositions) qui;
∼ **did she meet?** qui a-t-elle rencontré?, qui est-ce qu'elle
a rencontré?; **to** ∼ **are you referring?** à qui est-ce que vous
faites allusion?; **the article is by** ∼**?** de qui est l'article?;
2 (relative) que; (after prepositions) qui; **the minister** ∼ **he'd
seen** le ministre qu'il avait vu; **the person to** ∼**/of** ∼ **I
spoke** la personne à qui/de qui *ou* dont j'ai parlé; **those**
∼ **he baptized** ceux qu'il a baptisés; **...four of** ∼ **are young
and all of** ∼ **are single** ...dont quatre sont jeunes et qui
sont tous célibataires; **Kirsten and Matthew, both of** ∼ **had
ridden before** Kirsten et Matthew, qui avaient déjà fait du
cheval tous les deux; **she pointed to the boys, one of**
∼ **was laughing** elle a indiqué le groupe de garçons dont
un riait; **he was particular about** ∼ **he chose** il était exigeant quant à ceux qu'il choisissait; 3 (whoever) qui

whoop /huːp, wuːp, US hwuːp/
A *n* (shout) cri *m*
B *vi* 1 (shout) pousser des cris (**with** de); 2 Med avoir une
quinte de toux (*due à la coqueluche*)

(Phrasal verb)

■ **whoop it up**○ s'éclater○

whoopee○ /'wʊpiː, US 'hwʊ-/
A *n* **to make** ∼ hum (make love) faire l'amour; (have fun) faire la
foire○
B *excl* youpi!

whooping cough ▸ p. 933 *n* coqueluche *f*

whoosh○ /wʊʃ, US hwʊʃ/
A *excl* zoum!

B *vi* **to ~ in/past** entrer/passer à toute allure

whopper° /'wɒpə(r), US 'hwɒpər/ *n* (large thing) monstre *m*; (lie) bobard° *m*

whopping° /'wɒpɪŋ, US 'hwɒpɪŋ/ *adj* (*also* **~ great**) monstre°

whore /hɔ:(r)/ *n* injur prostituée *f*

who're /'hu:ə(r)/ = **who are**

whorl /wɜ:l, US hwɜ:l/ *n* (of cream, chocolate etc) spirale *f*; (on fingerprint) volute *f*; (shell pattern) spire *f*

who's /hu:z/ = **who is, who has**

whose /hu:z/

A *pron* à qui; **~ is this?** à qui est ceci?; **~ did you take?** tu as pris celui/celle etc de qui?

B *adj* **1** (interrogative) **~ pen is that?** à qui est ce stylo?; **do you know ~ car was stolen?** est-ce que tu sais à qui appartenait la voiture volée?; **~ coat did you take?** tu as pris le manteau de qui?; **with ~ permission?** avec la permission de qui?; **2** (relative) **the boy ~ dog was killed** le garçon dont le chien a été tué

Who's Who *pr n* ≈ bottin® *m* mondain

who've /hu:v/ = **who have**

why /waɪ, US hwaɪ/

> ⚠ *Why* translates as *pourquoi* in French, but see B, C below for exceptions.
>
> As with other words such as *où, quand, comment* etc, questions are formed by inserting *est-ce que* after the question word: *why did you go?* = pourquoi est-ce que tu y es allé? or by inverting the subject and verb after the question word, which is slightly more formal: pourquoi y es-tu allé? In spoken French the question word can be put at the end: *tu y es allé pourquoi?*
>
> *why* occurs with certain reporting verbs such as *ask, explain, know, think* and *wonder*. For translations, see these entries.

A *adv* **1** (in questions) pourquoi; **~ do you ask?** pourquoi est-ce que tu me poses la question?, pourquoi me poses-tu la question?; **'I'm annoyed'—'~ is that?'** 'je suis vexé'—'pourquoi?'; **oh no, ~ me?** oh non, pourquoi est-ce que ça me tombe dessus°?; **'it's not possible'—'~ not?'** 'ce n'est pas possible'—'pourquoi pas?'; **'can I apply?'—'I don't see ~ not'** 'est-ce que je peux m'inscrire?'—'je ne vois pas pourquoi tu ne pourrais pas'; **2** (when making suggestions) pourquoi; **~ don't we go away for the weekend?** pourquoi ne pas partir quelque part pour le week-end?; **~ don't I invite them for dinner?** et si je les invitais à manger?; **~ not send off now for our brochure?** pourquoi ne pas demander dès maintenant notre brochure?; **3** (expressing irritation, defiance) pourquoi; **~ can't you be quiet?** tu ne peux pas te taire?; **~ do I bother?** à quoi ça sert que je me donne du mal?; **~ should they get all the praise?** pourquoi est-ce que c'est eux qui auraient tous les compliments?; **'tell them'—'~ should I?'** 'dis-leur'—'et pourquoi (est-ce que je devrais le faire)?'; **4** (*also* **~ever**) (expressing surprise) **~ever not?** GB pourquoi pas?

B *conj* pour ça; **that is ~ they came** c'est pour ça qu'ils sont venus; **that's not ~ I asked** ce n'est pas pour ça que j'avais posé la question; **so that's ~!** (finally understanding) ah, c'est pour ça!; **'~?'—'because you're stubborn, that's ~!'** 'pourquoi?'—'parce que tu es têtu, c'est tout!'; **the reason ~** la raison pour laquelle; **I need to know the reason ~** j'ai besoin de savoir pourquoi; ▸ **reason A 1**

C †*excl* mais

WI *n* **1** GB *abrév* ▸ **Women's Institute**; **2** US Post *abrév écrite* = **Wisconsin**; **3** *abrév écrite* = **West Indies**

wick /wɪk/ *n* (of candle, lamp etc) mèche *f*

wicked /'wɪkɪd/ *adj* **1** (evil) [*person*] méchant; [*heart, deed*] cruel-elle; [*plot*] pernicieux/-ieuse; [*intention*] mauvais; **2** (mischievous) malicieux/-ieuse; **3** (naughty) pervers; **4** (vicious) [*wind*] méchant; [*weapon*] redoutable; [*sarcasm*] cinglant; **a ~ tongue** une mauvaise langue; **5** °(terrible) **a ~ waste** un vrai gâchis; **it was a ~ shame** c'était vraiment une honte

> (Idiom) **no peace** *ou* **rest for the ~** pas de repos pour les braves°

wickedly /'wɪkɪdlɪ/ *adv* **1** (maliciously) avec malice; **2** (evilly) avec méchanceté

wickedness /'wɪkɪdnɪs/ *n* **1** (evil) (of person, deed, regime, heart) cruauté *f*; **the ~ of all that waste** le scandale de tout ce gâchis; **2** (of grin, joke) malice *f*

wicker /'wɪkə(r)/

A *n* (*also* **wickerwork**) osier *m*

B *noun modifier* [*basket, furniture*] en osier

wicket /'wɪkɪt/ *n* **1** (field gate) portillon *m*; (sluice gate) petite porte *f* d'écluse; **2** US (transaction window) guichet *m*; **3** Sport guichet *m*

> (Idiom) **to be on a sticky ~**° être dans le pétrin°

wide /waɪd/

A *adj* **1** (broad) gen large; [*margin*] grand; **how ~ is your garden?** quelle est la largeur de votre jardin?; **it's 30 cm ~** il a 30 cm de large; **they're making the street ~r** ils élargissent la rue; **her eyes were ~ with fear** ses yeux étaient agrandis par la peur; **2** (immense) vaste; **3** (extensive) [*variety, choice*] grand; **a woman of ~ interests** une femme qui s'intéresse à beaucoup de choses; **a ~ range of products** une vaste gamme de produits; **a ~ range of opinions** une grande variété d'opinions; **in the ~st sense of the word** au sens le plus large du mot; **4** Sport [*ball, shot*] perdu

B *adv* **to open one's eyes ~** ouvrir grand les yeux; **his eyes are ~ apart** il a les yeux très écartés; **open ~!** ouvrez grand (la bouche)!; **to be ~ of the mark** [*ball*] être à côté; fig [*guess*] être loin de la vérité

wide: **~-angle lens** *n* objectif *m* à grand angle; **~ awake** *adj* complètement éveillé

wide-eyed /,waɪd'aɪd/ *adj* **1** (with fear, surprise) **he was ~** il ouvrait de grands yeux; **~ with fear** les yeux écarquillés de peur; **2** (naïve) [*person, innocence*] ingénu

widely /'waɪdlɪ/ *adv* **1** (commonly) largement; **it is ~ believed that** beaucoup de gens pensent que; **a country ~ admired for its technology** un pays qui fait l'admiration générale pour sa technologie; **to be ~ available** [*product*] être en vente libre; **to be ~ known** être bien connu (**for** pour); **these are not ~ held views** ce ne sont pas des opinions très répandues; **2** (spaced) à de grands intervalles; [*travel, differ*] beaucoup

widely-read /,waɪdlɪ'red/ *adj* [*student*] qui lit beaucoup; [*author*] beaucoup lu

widen /'waɪdn/

A *vtr* gen élargir; étendre [*powers*]; **this has ~ed their lead in the opinion polls** ceci a renforcé leur position dominante dans les sondages

B *vi* **1** [*river, road*] s'élargir; **his eyes ~ed** il a ouvert grand les yeux; **2** (increase) **the gap is ~ing between rich and poor** le fossé entre riches et pauvres s'élargit

C widening *pres p adj* [*division*] de plus en plus grand; [*gap*] qui s'élargit de plus en plus

wide open *adj* **1** [*door, window, eyes*] grand ouvert; **2** **the race is ~** l'issue de la course est indécise; **3** **to lay oneself ~ to criticism** prêter le flanc à la critique

wide-ranging /,waɪd'reɪndʒɪŋ/ *adj* gen de grande envergure; **a ~ discussion** une discussion couvrant un grand nombre de sujets

wide screen *n* Cin grand écran *m*

widespread /'waɪdspred/ *adj* [*epidemic*] généralisé; [*devastation*] étendu; [*belief*] très répandu

widget /'wɪdʒɪt/ *n* Comput (program) composant *m* logiciel réutilisable; (in graphical user interface) widget *m*, élément *m* d'interface graphique

widow /'wɪdəʊ/

A *n* gen veuve *f*; **golf ~** hum femme *f* délaissée par son mari golfeur; **war ~** veuve de guerre

B *vtr* **to be ~ed** devenir veuf/veuve *m/f*; **she has been ~ed for two years** elle est veuve depuis deux ans

widower /'wɪdəʊə(r)/ *n* veuf *m*

width /wɪdθ, wɪtθ/ *n* ▸ p. 977 *n* **1** largeur *f*; **it is 30 metres in ~** il fait *or* mesure 30 mètres de large; **2** (of fabric) lé *m*

widthways, widthwise /'wɪdθweɪz, 'wɪtθ-, 'wɪdθwaɪz, 'wɪtθ-/ *adv* dans la largeur

wield /wi:ld/ *vtr* lit brandir; fig exercer (**over** sur)

wife /waɪf/ *n* (*pl* **wives**) (spouse) gen femme *f*; Admin, Jur épouse *f*; **the baker's/farmer's ~** la boulangère/la fermière

wife battering *n* violence *f* corporelle contre les femmes

wig /wɪg/ *n* (whole head) perruque *f*; (partial) postiche *m*

will¹

The future tense

When *will* is used to express the future in French, the future tense of the French verb is generally used:

he'll come
= il viendra

In spoken and more informal French or when the very near future is implied, the present tense of *aller* + infinitive can be used:

I'll do it now
= je vais le faire tout de suite

If the subject of the modal auxiliary *will* is *I* or *we*, *shall* is sometimes used instead of *will* to talk about the future. For further information, consult the entry **shall** in the dictionary.

Note that **would** and **should** are treated as separate entries in the dictionary.

Tag questions

French has no direct equivalent of tag questions like *won't he?* or *will they?* There is a general tag question *n'est-ce pas?* which will work in many cases:

you'll do it tomorrow, won't you?
= tu le feras demain, n'est-ce pas?

In cases where an opinion is being sought, *non?* meaning *is that not so?* can be useful:

that will be easier, won't it?
= ce sera plus facile, non?

In many other cases the tag question is simply not translated at all and the speaker's intonation will convey the implied question.

Short answers

Again, there is no direct equivalent for short answers like *no she won't*, *yes they will* etc. Where the answer *yes* is given to contradict a negative question or statement, the most useful translation is *si*:

'they won't forget' 'yes they will'
= 'ils n'oublieront pas' 'si'
or (*for more emphasis*) bien sûr que si

Where the answer *no* is given to contradict a positive question or statement, the most useful translation is *bien sûr que non*:

'she'll post the letter, won't she?' 'no she won't'
= 'elle va poster la lettre?' 'bien sûr que non'

In reply to a standard enquiry the tag will not be translated:

'you'll be ready at midday then?' 'yes I will'
= 'tu seras prêt à midi?' 'oui'

For more examples and other uses, see the entry **will¹**.

---

wiggle○ /'wɪgl/
A n a ~ **of the hips** un roulement des hanches; **to give sth a** ~ faire bouger qch
B vtr faire bouger [*tooth, object*]; **to** ~ **one's hips** rouler des hanches; **to** ~ **one's toes** agiter les orteils
C vi [*snake, worm*] se tortiller

wild /waɪld/
A n **in the** ~ [*conditions, life*] en liberté; **to grow in the** ~ pousser à l'état sauvage; **the call of the** ~ l'appel de la nature
B wilds npl **to live in the** ~s **of Arizona** habiter au fin fond de l'Arizona
C adj ① (in natural state, desolate) sauvage; ~ **beast** bête fauve; **the pony is still quite** ~ le poney est encore assez farouche; ② (turbulent) [*wind*] violent; [*sea*] agité; **it was a** ~ **night** c'était une nuit de tempête; ③ (unrestrained) [*party, laughter, person*] fou/folle; [*imagination*] délirant; [*applause*] déchaîné; **to go** ~ se déchaîner; **she led a** ~ **life in her youth** elle a fait les quatre cents coups dans sa jeunesse; **his hair was** ~ **and unkempt** il avait les cheveux en bataille; ~ **mood swings** changements d'humeur brutaux; ④ ○(furious) furieux/-ieuse; **he'll go** ~ ou **be** ~! ça va le mettre hors de lui!; ⑤ ○(enthusiastic) **to be** ~ **about** être un fana○ de; **I'm not** ~ **about him/it** il/ça ne m'emballe○ pas; ⑥ (outlandish) [*idea*] fou/folle; [*claim, accusation*] extravagant; [*story*] farfelu○
D adv ① [*grow*] à l'état sauvage; **those children are allowed to run** ~! on permet à ces enfants de faire n'importe quoi; **to let one's imagination run** ~ laisser libre cours à son imagination

wild boar n sanglier m

wild card n ① Games, Comput joker m; ② fig (unpredictable element) élément m imprévisible; ③ Sport wild-card f

wildcat /'waɪldkæt/
A n Zool chat m sauvage
B adj US [*scheme, venture*] risqué

wildcat strike n grève f sauvage

wild dog n dingo m

wilderness /'wɪldənɪs/ n ① (wasteland) étendue f sauvage et désolée; ② (uncultivated area) étendue f sauvage; **the garden has become a** ~ le jardin est devenu une vraie jungle

(Idiom) **to be a voice crying in the** ~ prêcher dans le désert

wild-eyed /,waɪld'aɪd/ adj au regard égaré

wildfire /'waɪldfaɪə(r)/ n **to spread like** ~ se répandre comme une traînée de poudre

wild: ~ **flower** n fleur f des champs, fleur f sauvage; ~**fowl** n (wild bird) oiseau m sauvage; (birds collectively) oiseaux mpl sauvages; (game) gibier m à plume

wild-goose chase /,waɪld'guːs tʃeɪs/ n **it turned out to be a** ~ ça n'a abouti à rien; **to lead sb on a** ~ mettre qn sur une mauvaise piste

wild: ~**life** n (animals) faune f; (animals and plants) faune f et flore f; ~**life park**, ~**life reserve**, ~**life sanctuary** n réserve f naturelle

wildly /'waɪldlɪ/ adv ① (recklessly) [*spend, talk*] de façon insensée; [*fire*] au hasard; **to hit out/run** ~ envoyer des coups/courir dans tous les sens; ② [*wave, gesture*] de manière très agitée; [*applaud*] à tout rompre; **to fluctuate** ~ subir des fluctuations violentes; **his heart was beating** ~ son cœur battait à tout rompre; ③ [*enthusiastic, optimistic*] extrêmement

wildness /'waɪldnɪs/ n ① (of landscape) aspect m sauvage; (of weather) violence f; ② (disorderliness) (of person) caractère m débridé; (of appearance) désordre m; (of party) folie f; ③ (extravagance) (of idea) extravagance f

wild: ~ **rose** n rosier m sauvage; ~ **water rafting** ▸ p. 881 n rafting m; **Wild West** n Far West m

wiles /waɪlz/ npl ruses fpl

wilful GB, **willful** US /'wɪlfl/ adj [*person, behaviour*] volontaire also Jur; [*damage, disobedience*] délibéré

wilfully GB, **willfully** US /'wɪlfəlɪ/ adv ① (in headstrong way) obstinément; ② (deliberately) délibérément

will¹ /wɪl, əl/
A modal aux ① (to express the future) **she'll help you** elle t'aidera; (in the near future) elle va t'aider; **must I phone him or** ~ **you?** est-ce que je dois lui téléphoner ou est-ce que tu vas le faire?; **I've said I'll repay you and I** ~ j'ai dit que je te rembourserai et je le ferai; ② (expressing consent, willingness) '~ **you help me?'**—'yes, I ~' 'est-ce que tu m'aideras?'—'oui, bien sûr'; **he won't cooperate** il ne veut pas coopérer; **'have a chocolate'**—**'thank you, I** ~' 'prends un

chocolat'—'volontiers, merci'; **I ∼ not be talked to like that** je n'accepte pas qu'on me parle sur ce ton; **I won't have it said of me that I'm mean** il ne sera pas dit que je suis mesquin; **∼ you or won't you?** c'est oui ou c'est non?; **do what** *ou* **as you ∼** fais ce que tu veux; **∼ do**°! d'accord!; ③ (in commands, requests) **∼ you pass the salt, please?** est-ce que tu peux me passer le sel, s'il te plaît?; **'I can give the speech'**—**'you ∼ not!'** 'je peux faire le discours'—'pas question!'; **'I'll do it'**—**'no you won't'** 'je vais le faire'—'il n'en est pas question'; **∼ you please listen to me!** est-ce que tu vas m'écouter!; **wait a minute ∼ you!** attends un peu!; ④ (in offers, invitations) **∼ you marry me?** est-ce que tu veux m'épouser?; **you'll have another cake, won't you?** vous prendrez bien un autre gâteau?; ⑤ (expressing custom or habit) **they ∼ usually ask for a deposit** ils demandent généralement une caution; **any teacher ∼ tell you that...** n'importe quel professeur te dira que...; **these things ∼ happen** ce sont des choses qui arrivent; (in exasperation) **she ∼ keep repeating the same old jokes** elle n'arrête pas de répéter les mêmes blagues; ⑥ (expressing conjecture or assumption) **that ∼ be my sister** ça doit être ma sœur; **they won't be aware of what has happened** ils ne doivent pas savoir ce qui s'est passé; **that ∼ have been last month** ça devait être le mois dernier; **you'll have gathered that** vous aurez compris que; ⑦ (expressing ability or capacity to do) **the lift ∼ hold 12** l'ascenseur peut transporter 12 personnes; **that jug won't hold a litre** ce pichet ne contient pas un litre; **this chicken won't feed six** ce poulet n'est pas assez gros pour six personnes; **the car won't start** la voiture ne veut pas démarrer

B *vtr* ① (urge) **to ∼ sb's death** souhaiter ardemment la mort de qn; **to ∼ sb to do** supplier mentalement qn de faire; **to ∼ sb to live** prier pour que qn vive; ② (wish, desire) vouloir; ③ Jur léguer

C *v refl* **he ∼ed himself to stand up** au prix d'un effort surhumain il a réussi à se lever

will² /wɪl/

A *n* ① volonté *f* (**to do** de faire); **to have a strong/weak ∼** avoir beaucoup/peu de volonté; **to have a ∼ of one's own** faire ce qu'on a envie de faire; **strength of ∼** force de caractère; **against my ∼** contre mon gré; **to do sth with a ∼** faire qch de bon cœur; **to lose the ∼ to live** ne plus avoir envie de vivre; ② Jur testament *m*; **the last ∼ and testament of** les dernières volontés de; **to leave sb sth in one's ∼** léguer qch à qn

B at will *adv phr* [*select, take*] à volonté; **you can change it at ∼** tu peux le changer quand tu veux

(Idiom) **where there's a ∼ there's a way** Prov quand on veut on peut Prov

willful *adj* US = **wilful**

William /'wɪlɪəm/ *pr n* Guillaume; **∼ the Conqueror** Guillaume le Conquérant

willing /'wɪlɪŋ/ *adj* ① (prepared) **to be ∼ to do** être prêt à faire; **I'm quite ∼** je veux bien; **I'm more than ∼ to help you** j'accepte volontiers de vous aider; ② (eager) [*pupil, helper*] de bonne volonté; [*slave*] consentant; [*recruit, victim*] volontaire; **to show ∼** faire preuve de bonne volonté; **we need some ∼ hands to clean up** nous avons besoin de volontaires pour nettoyer; ③ [*sacrifice*] volontaire

(Idiom) **the spirit is ∼ but the flesh is weak** l'esprit est ardent mais la chair est faible

willingly /'wɪlɪŋlɪ/ *adv* [*accept, help*] volontiers; [*work*] avec bonne volonté; **did she go ∼?** est-elle partie de son propre gré?

willingness /'wɪlɪŋnɪs/ *n* ① (readiness) volonté *f* (**to do** de faire); ② (helpfulness) bonne volonté *f*

willow /'wɪləʊ/ *n* ① (*also* **∼ tree**) saule *m*; ② (wood) bois *m* de) saule *m*; ③ (for weaving) osier *m*

willow pattern *n* motif *m* chinois (bleu sur fond blanc)

willowy /'wɪləʊɪ/ *adj* [*person, figure*] élancé

will power *n* volonté *f* (**to do** de faire)

willy-nilly /ˌwɪlɪ'nɪlɪ/ *adv* (regardless of choice) bon gré mal gré

wilt /wɪlt/

A *vtr* faire dépérir [*plant*]

B *vi* lit [*plant, flower*] se faner; fig [*person*] (from heat, fatigue) se sentir faible; (at daunting prospect) perdre courage

C wilted *pp adj* fané

Wilts *n* GB Post *abrév écrite* = **Wiltshire**

wily /'waɪlɪ/ *adj* rusé

wimp° /wɪmp/ *n* péj (ineffectual) lavette° *f*; (fearful) poule *f* mouillée

(Phrasal verb)
▪ **wimp out** se défiler°

wimpish° /'wɪmpɪʃ/, **wimpy**° /'wɪmpɪ/ *adj* péj [*person*] mollasson/-onne°; [*behaviour*] mou/molle°

win /wɪn/

A *n* ① (victory) victoire *f* (**over** sur); **to have a ∼ over sb in sth** remporter une victoire sur qn dans qch; ② (successful bet) pari *m* gagnant

B *vtr* (*p prés* **-nn-**; *prét, pp* **won**) ①▸ Games, Mil, Sport gagner; Pol gagner [*election, votes*] (**from sb** aux dépens de qn); gagner les élections dans [*region, city*] (**from sb** aux dépens de qn); **to ∼ a (parliamentary) seat** être élu député (**from sb** aux dépens de qn); ② (acquire) obtenir [*reprieve*] (**from** de); gagner [*friendship, heart*]; s'attirer [*sympathy*]; s'acquérir [*support*] (**of** de); **it won him the admiration of his colleagues** cela lui a valu l'admiration de ses collègues; **to ∼ sb's love/respect** se faire aimer/respecter de qn

C *vi* (*p prés* **-nn-**; *prét, pp* **won**) gagner; **to ∼ against sb** l'emporter sur qn; **to ∼ by two goals** gagner de deux buts; **you ∼!** (in argument) je m'incline!; **I've done my best to please her, but you just can't ∼** j'ai tout fait pour lui plaire, mais rien à faire; **∼ or lose, the discussions have been valuable** quoi qu'il arrive, les discussions ont été profitables; **it's a ∼ or lose situation** tout se joue là-dessus

(Idiom) **∼ some, lose some** on ne peut pas gagner à tous les coups

(Phrasal verbs)
▪ **win back:** ▸ **∼ [sth] back**, **∼ back [sth]** récupérer [*support, votes*] (**from sb** sur qn); regagner [*affection, respect*]; reprendre [*prize, territory*] (**from** à)
▪ **win out** l'emporter; **to ∼ out over sth** vaincre qch
▪ **win over, win round:** ▸ **∼ over [sb]**, **∼ [sb] over** convaincre
▪ **win through** finir par gagner; **to ∼ through to** Sport se qualifier pour [*semifinal etc*]

wince /wɪns/

A *n* grimace *f*

B *vi* grimacer, faire une grimace

winch /wɪntʃ/

A *n* treuil *m*

B *vtr* **to ∼ sth down/up** descendre/hisser qch au treuil

wind¹ /wɪnd/

A *n* ① Meteorol vent *m*; **North ∼** vent du nord; **the ∼ is blowing** il y a du vent; **which way is the ∼ blowing?** d'où vient le vent?; **a high ∼** un vent fort; ② (breath) souffle *m*; **to knock the ∼ out of** couper le souffle à; **to get one's ∼** reprendre souffle; **to get one's second ∼** fig reprendre ses forces; ③ fig vent *m*; **the ∼ of change** le vent du changement; **there is something in the ∼** il y a quelque chose dans l'air; ④ (flatulence) vents *mpl*; **to break ∼** lâcher un vent; **to bring up ∼** avoir des renvois; ⑤ Mus **the ∼** les instruments *mpl* à vent

B *vtr* ① (make breathless) [*blow*] couper la respiration à; [*exertion*] essouffler; ② faire son rot à [*baby*]

(Idioms) **to get ∼ of** avoir vent de; **to get the ∼ up**° avoir la trouille°; **to put the ∼ up sb**° flanquer la trouille° à qn; **to see which way the ∼ blows** voir de quel côté souffle le vent

wind² /waɪnd/

A *n* ① (of road) tournant *m*; ② (movement) (of handle) tour *m*

B *vtr* (*prét, pp* **wound**) ① (coil up) enrouler; **she wound her arms around him** elle l'a enlacé; ② (*also* **∼ up**) remonter [*clock, toy*]; ③ donner un tour de [*handle*]; ④ **to ∼ one's** *ou* **its way** serpenter

C *vi* (*prét, pp* **wound**) gen serpenter (**along** le long de); [*stairs*] tourner

(Phrasal verbs)
▪ **wind down:** ▸ **∼ down** ① [*organization*] réduire ses activités; [*activity, production*] toucher à sa fin; [*person*] se détendre; [*clockwork*] être sur le point de s'arrêter; ▸ **∼ down [sth]**, **∼ [sth] down** ① baisser [*car window*]; ② mettre fin à [*activity, organization*]
▪ **wind in:** ▸ **∼ in [sth]**, **∼ [sth] in** remonter [*cable, line, fish*]
▪ **wind on:** ▸ **∼ on** [*film*] s'enrouler; ▸ **∼ on [sth]**, **∼ [sth] on** enrouler
▪ **wind up:** ▸ **∼ up** ① (finish) [*event*] se terminer (**with** par); [*speaker*] conclure; ② °(end up) finir, se retrouver;

▸ ~ **up** [sth], ~ [sth] **up** ⬛1⬛ liquider [*business*]; fermer [*account*]; mettre fin à [*campaign, meeting, project*]; Jur régler [*estate*]; ⬛2⬛ remonter [*clock, car window*]; ▸ ~ [sb] **up**, ~ **up** [sb] ⬛1⬛ (*tease*) faire marcher [*person*]; ⬛2⬛ (*make tense*) énerver

wind wind: ~**blown** *adj* ébouriffé par le vent; ~**borne** *adj* apporté par le vent; ~**break** *n* (natural) brise-vent *m inv*; (on beach) pare-vent *m inv*; ~**cheater** *n* GB coupe-vent *m inv*; ~**chill factor** *n* facteur *m* de refroidissement de la température dû au vent; ~ **chimes** *npl* carillon *m* éolien; ~ **energy** *n* énergie *f* éolienne

winder /'waɪndə(r)/ *n* (for watch) remontoir *m*; (for wool, thread) dévidoir *m*; (for window) lève-glace *m inv*

windfall /'wɪndfɔːl/ *n* lit fruit *m* tombé par terre; fig aubaine *f*

wind wind: ~**fall profit** *n* profit *m* inattendu; ~ **farm** *n* ferme *f* d'aérogénérateurs, ferme *f* d'éoliennes; ~ **gauge** *n* anémomètre *m*

winding /'waɪndɪŋ/ *adj* gen sinueux/-euse; [*stairs*] en spirale

winding-up *n* (of business, affairs) clôture *f*

wind instrument ▸ p. 1028 *n* instrument *m* à vent

windless /'wɪndləs/ *adj* sans vent

windmill /'wɪndmɪl/ *n* ⬛1⬛ moulin *m* à vent; ⬛2⬛ (toy) moulinet *m*

window /'wɪndəʊ/ *n* ⬛1⬛ (of house, room, vehicle, envelope) fenêtre *f* also Comput; (of shop, public building) vitrine *f*; (of plane) hublot *m*; (stained glass) vitrail *m*; **I'd like a seat by a ~** Aviat j'aimerais une place côté fenêtre; **to look out of** *ou* **through the ~** regarder par la fenêtre; ⬛2⬛ (for service at bank or post office) guichet *m*; ⬛3⬛ (space in diary, time) créneau *m*

(Idiom) **to go** *ou* **fly out the ~**○ [*plans*] tomber à l'eau; [*hopes*] s'écrouler

window: ~ **blind** *n* store *m*; ~ **box** *n* jardinière *f*; ~ **cleaner** *n* (person) laveur/-euse *m/f* de carreaux; (product) produit *m* pour nettoyer les vitres; ~ **display** *n* Comm vitrine *f*; ~ **dresser** ▸ p. 1181 *n* étalagiste *mf*

window dressing *n* ⬛1⬛ lit composition *f* de vitrines; ⬛2⬛ fig **it's all** ~ péj c'est de la poudre aux yeux○; ⬛3⬛ Fin habillage *m* de bilan

window: ~ **frame** *n* châssis *m* de fenêtre; ~ **ledge** *n* appui *m* de fenêtre; ~**pane** *n* carreau *m*

window-shopping *n* **to go** ~ faire du lèche-vitrines○ *m inv*

windowsill *n* rebord *m* de fenêtre

wind wind: ~**pipe** *n* trachée-artère *f*; ~**power** *n* énergie *f* éolienne; ~**screen** *n* GB Aut pare-brise *m inv*; ~**screen washer** *n* GB Aut lave-glace *m*; ~**screen wiper** *n* GB Aut essuie-glace *m inv*; ~ **section** *n* instruments *mpl* à vent; ~**shield** *n* US Aut = **windscreen**; ~**sleeve**, ~**sock** *n* manche *f* à air; ~**surf** *vi* faire de la planche à voile; ~**surfer** *n* (person) véliplanchiste *mf*; (board) planche *f* à voile; ~**swept** *adj* venteux/-euse

windward /'wɪndwəd/
Ⓐ *n* côté *m* du vent
Ⓑ *adj, adv* contre le vent

windy /'wɪndɪ/ *adj* ⬛1⬛ [*place*] venteux/-euse; [*day*] de vent; **it** *ou* **the weather was very** ~ il faisait beaucoup de vent; ⬛2⬛ péj (verbose) verbeux/-euse

wine /waɪn/ ▸ p. 752
Ⓐ *n* ⬛1⬛ (drink) vin *m*; ⬛2⬛ (colour) lie-de-vin *m*
Ⓑ *noun modifier* [*production*] de vin; [*cellar, glass, cask*] à vin
Ⓒ *adj* (also ~**-coloured**) lie-de-vin *inv*

(Idiom) **to** ~ **and dine** manger dans les bons restaurants

wine: ~ **bar** *n* bar *m* à vin; ~ **box** *n* ≈ cubitainer® *m*; ~ **cellar** *n* cave *f*

wine cooler *n* ⬛1⬛ (ice bucket) seau *m* à rafraîchir; ⬛2⬛ US (drink) boisson légèrement alcoolisée

wine growing
Ⓐ *n* viticulture *f*
Ⓑ *noun modifier* [*region*] vinicole

wine: ~ **list** *n* carte *f* des vins; ~ **merchant** ▸ p. 1181 *n* négociant *m* en vins; ~ **producer** ▸ p. 1181 *n* viticulteur/-trice *m/f*; ~ **rack** *n* cellier *m*; ~ **shop** ▸ p. 1181 *n* marchand *m* de vin; ~ **taster** ▸ p. 1181 *n* dégustateur/-trice *m/f*; ~ **tasting** *n* dégustation *f* de vins; ~ **vinegar** *n* vinaigre *m* de vin; ~ **waiter** ▸ p. 1181 *n* sommelier/-ière *m/f*

wing /wɪŋ/
Ⓐ *n* ⬛1⬛ (of bird, insect) aile *f*; **to be on the** ~ être en vol; ⬛2⬛ (of building, plane, car) aile *f*; (of armchair) oreille *f*; ⬛3⬛ Mil, Pol aile *f*; (unit in air force) escadre *f*; ⬛4⬛ Sport (player) ailier *m*; (side of pitch) aile *f*; **to play on the right** ~ être ailier droit
Ⓑ **wings** *npl* ⬛1⬛ Theat **the** ~**s** les coulisses *fpl*; **to be waiting in the** ~**s** fig attendre son heure; ⬛2⬛ Aviat **to get one's** ~**s** obtenir l'insigne de pilote
Ⓒ *vtr* ⬛1⬛ **to** ~ **one's way to** voler vers; ⬛2⬛ [*bullet*] érafler

(Idioms) **to clip sb's** ~**s** rogner les ailes à qn; **to spread one's** ~**s** (entering adult life) voler de ses propres ailes; (entering wider career) voir autre chose

wing: ~ **chair** *n* fauteuil *m* à oreilles; ~ **collar** *n* col *m* cassé; ~ **commander** ▸ p. 1123 *n* lieutenant-colonel *m* de l'armée de l'air

winged /wɪŋd/ *adj* gen ailé; [*insect*] volant

winger○ /'wɪŋə(r)/ *n* GB ailier *m*

wing: ~ **forward** *n* (in rugby) avant *m* troisième ligne; ~ **half** *n* (in soccer) demi-droit *m*; ~ **mirror** *n* GB rétroviseur *m* extérieur; ~ **nut** *n* écrou *m* à oreilles; ~**span** *n* envergure *f*; ~ **three-quarter** *n* (in rugby) trois-quarts aile *m*

wink /wɪŋk/
Ⓐ *n* clin d'œil; **to give sb a** ~ faire un clin d'œil à qn; **we didn't get a** ~ **of sleep all night** nous n'avons pas fermé l'œil de la nuit
Ⓑ *vtr* **to** ~ **one's eye** cligner de l'œil
Ⓒ *vi* ⬛1⬛ cligner de l'œil; **to** ~ **at sb** faire un clin d'œil à qn; ⬛2⬛ [*light*] clignoter; [*jewellery*] briller

(Idioms) **a nod is as good as a** ~ **to a blind horse** *ou* **man** c'est bien, on a compris; **to tip sb the** ~○ avertir qn

winner /'wɪnə(r)/ *n* ⬛1⬛ (victor) gagnant/-e *m/f*; **to be the** ~**(s)** Sport finir gagnant; **to be on to a** ~ jouer gagnant; **to back the** ~ parier sur le gagnant; ~ **takes all** Games le gagnant rafle tout; ⬛2⬛ (success) **to be a** ~ avoir un gros succès

winning /'wɪnɪŋ/
Ⓐ *n* réussite *f*
Ⓑ **winnings** *npl* gains *mpl*
Ⓒ *adj* ⬛1⬛ (victorious) gagnant; ⬛2⬛ [*smile*] engageant; **to have** ~ **ways** avoir du charme

winning post *n* poteau *m* d'arrivée

winning streak *n* **to be on a** ~ être dans une bonne période

winsome /'wɪnsəm/ *adj* [*person*] charmant

winter /'wɪntə(r)/ ▸ p. 1166
Ⓐ *n* hiver *m*
Ⓑ *noun modifier* [*activity, clothes, weather*] d'hiver
Ⓒ *vi* passer l'hiver

winter: ~ **sleep** *n* hibernation *f*; ~ **sports** *npl* sports *mpl* d'hiver; ~**time** *n* hiver *m*

wintry /'wɪntrɪ/ *adj* lit hivernal; fig glacé

wipe /waɪp/
Ⓐ *n* ⬛1⬛ (act of wiping) **to give sth a** ~ (with dry cloth) donner un coup de torchon sur qch; (with wet cloth) donner un coup d'éponge sur qch; ⬛2⬛ (for face, baby) lingette *f*; Med tampon *m*; ⬛3⬛ Cin effaçage *m*
Ⓑ *vtr* ⬛1⬛ (mop) essuyer (**on** sur; **with** avec); **to** ~ **one's nose** se moucher; **to** ~ **one's bottom** se torcher; **to** ~ **sth clean** essuyer qch; ~ **that smile off your face!** arrête de sourire!; ⬛2⬛ Cin, Comput, Radio, TV effacer

(Phrasal verbs)

■ **wipe away**: ▸ ~ **away** [sth], ~ [sth] **away** essuyer [*tears, sweat*]; faire partir [*dirt, mark*]

■ **wipe down**: ▸ ~ **down** [sth], ~ [sth] **down** nettoyer [*wall, floor*]

■ **wipe off**: ▸ ~ **off** [sth], ~ [sth] **off** ⬛1⬛ faire partir [*dirt, mark*]; ⬛2⬛ Audio, Cin, Comput, Video effacer

■ **wipe out**: ▸ ~ **out** [sth], ~ [sth] **out** ⬛1⬛ (clean) nettoyer; ⬛2⬛ (erase) effacer; ⬛3⬛ fig effacer [*memory, past*]; liquider [*debt*]; annuler [*chances, gains, losses*]; anéantir [*enemy, population*]; ⬛4⬛ (defeat) lessiver○

■ **wipe up**: ▸ ~ **up** essuyer la vaisselle; ▸ ~ **up** [sth], ~ [sth] **up** essuyer

wipe-clean *adj* facile à nettoyer

wiper /'waɪpə(r)/ *n* ⬛1⬛ Aut (also **windscreen** ~ GB, **windshield** ~ US) essuie-glace *m inv*; ⬛2⬛ (cloth) torchon *m*

wiper: ~ **arm** *n* Aut bras *m* d'essuie-glace; ~ **blade** *n* Aut balai *m* d'essuie-glace

W

wire /ˈwaɪə(r)/
A n ① (length of metal) fil m; ② US (telegram) télégramme m
B vtr ① Elec **to ~ a house** installer l'électricité dans une maison; **to ~ a plug/a lamp** connecter une prise/une lampe; ② (send telegram to) télégraphier à

(Idioms) **down to the ~** US jusqu'au tout dernier moment; **to pull ~s** US se faire pistonner○; **to get one's ~s** *ou* **lines crossed** se comprendre de travers

(Phrasal verb)

■ **wire up:** ▸ **~ [sth] up to sth** relier [qch] à qch

wire: **~ brush** n brosse f métallique; **~ cutters** npl cisailles fpl; **~ glass** n verre m armé

wireless /ˈwaɪəlɪs/ n (transmitter, receiver) radio f

wireless: **~ message** n message m radio(phonique); **~ operator** ▸ p. 1181 n radiotélégraphiste mf; **~ room** n cabine f radio; **~ set†** n poste m de radio; **~ telegraphy** n télégraphie f sans fil

wire: **~ mesh** n treillis m métallique; **~ netting** n grillage m; **~ service** n (agency) agence f de presse; (facility) lignes fpl d'une agence de presse; **~ tapping** n espionnage m électronique; **~ wool** n paille f de fer

wiring /ˈwaɪərɪŋ/ n (in house) installation f électrique; (in appliance) circuit m (électrique); **the ~ in the oven is faulty** le four est mal connecté

wiry /ˈwaɪərɪ/ adj ① [person] maigre; ② [hair] raide; **to have a ~ coat** [animal] avoir le poil raide

wisdom /ˈwɪzdəm/ n sagesse f; **to doubt** *ou* **question the ~ of doing** douter qu'il soit sage de faire; **in his ~** iron dans son infinie sagesse

wisdom tooth n dent f de sagesse

wise /waɪz/
A sout † n façon f
B adj ① (prudent) gen sage; [choice] judicieux/-ieuse; **it is ~ of sb to do** il est prudent de la part de qn de faire; **you would be ~ to do** tu ferais bien de faire; **to be ~ enough to do** avoir le bon sens de faire; **was that ~?** était-ce bien raisonnable?; **to be ~ after the event** être sage après coup; ② (learned) pertinent; **to be none the ~r** (understand no better) ne pas être plus avancé; (not realize) ne s'apercevoir de rien; **to be sadder and ~r** tirer une leçon d'une triste expérience; ③ (aware) **to be ~ to** être au courant de; **to get ~ to** prendre le coup de [situation]; **to get ~ to sb** saisir○ à qui on a affaire
C **-wise** combining form ① (direction) dans le sens de; **length-~** dans le sens de la longueur; ② (with regard to) **work-~** pour ce qui est du travail

(Idiom) **a word to the ~:...** en tout cas un conseil:...

wise: **~crack** n vanne○ f; **~ guy**○ n gros malin○ m

wisely /ˈwaɪzlɪ/ adv judicieusement

Wise Men npl **the three ~** les Rois mpl Mages

wish /wɪʃ/
A n ① (desire) désir m (**for** de; **to do** de faire); (in story) souhait m (**for** de); **to make a ~** faire un vœu; **to grant sb's ~** gen accéder au désir de qn; [fairy] exaucer le souhait de qn; **I have no ~ to disturb you** je n'ai pas l'intention de vous déranger
B **wishes** npl vœux mpl; **good** *ou* **best ~es** meilleurs vœux; (ending letter) bien amicalement; **please give him my best ~es** je vous prie de lui faire toutes mes amitiés;
C vtr ① (expressing longing) **I ~ he were here** si seulement il était ici; **I just ~ we lived closer** si seulement nous habitions plus près; **he ~ed he had written** il regrettait de ne pas avoir écrit; **he wishes his mother would write** il voudrait que sa mère écrive; **he bought it and then ~ed he hadn't** il l'a acheté et puis a regretté de l'avoir fait; **I ~ed myself single again** j'aurais voulu être à nouveau célibataire; ② (express congratulations, greetings) **to ~ sb joy** *ou* **happiness** souhaiter à qn d'être heureux; **to ~ sb joy of sth/sb** iron souhaiter bien du plaisir à qn avec qch/qn; **we ~ed each other goodbye and good luck** nous nous sommes dit au revoir et bonne chance; **I ~ed him well** j'espérais que tout irait bien pour lui; ③ (want) souhaiter; (weaker) désirer
D vi ① (desire, want) vouloir; **just as you ~** comme vous voudrez; **to ~ for** souhaiter, espérer; **what more could one ~ for?** qu'est-ce qu'on pourrait espérer *or* souhaiter de plus?; ② (in fairy story) faire un vœu

(Phrasal verb)

■ **wish on:** ▸ **~ [sth] on sb** fourguer○ [qch] à qn

wish: **~bone** n bréchet m; **~ fulfilment** n Psych accomplissement m du désir

wishful thinking /ˌwɪʃfl ˈθɪŋkɪŋ/ n **that's ~** c'est prendre ses désirs pour des réalités

wishy-washy○ /ˈwɪʃɪwɒʃɪ/ adj ① [colour] délavé; ② péj [person, approach] incolore et inodore○

wisp /wɪsp/ n (of hair) mèche f; (of straw) brin m; (of smoke, cloud) volute f; **a ~ of a girl** un petit bout de fille

wispy /ˈwɪspɪ/ adj [hair, beard] fin; [cloud, smoke] léger/-ère; [piece, straw] menu

wistful /ˈwɪstfl/ adj (sad) mélancolique; (nostalgic) nostalgique

wit /wɪt/
A n ① (sense of humour) esprit m; **to have a quick/ready ~** avoir la repartie facile/l'esprit d'à-propos; **to have a dry ~** être pince-sans-rire; ② (witty person) personne f spirituelle
B **wits** npl (intelligence) intelligence f; (presence of mind) présence f d'esprit; **to have** *ou* **keep (all) one's ~s about one** (vigilant) rester attentif/-ive; (level-headed) conserver sa présence d'esprit; **to collect** *ou* **gather one's ~s** rassembler ses esprits; **to sharpen one's ~s** se dégourdir l'esprit; **to frighten sb out of their ~s** faire une peur épouvantable à qn; **to pit one's ~s against sb** se mesurer (intellectuellement) à qn; **to live by one's ~s** vivre d'expédients; **to lose one's ~s** ne plus savoir où on est; **a battle of ~s** une joute verbale
C **to wit** adv phr sout à savoir

(Idiom) **to be at one's ~s' end** ne plus savoir quoi faire

witch /wɪtʃ/ n sorcière f

witch: **~craft** n sorcellerie f; **~ doctor** n shaman m; **~-hunt** n lit, fig chasse f aux sorcières

with /wɪð, wɪθ/

> ⚠ If you have any doubts about how to translate a phrase or expression beginning with *with* (*with a vengeance, with all my heart, with a bit of luck, with my blessing etc*) you should consult the appropriate noun entry (**vengeance, heart, luck, blessing** etc).
> *with* is often used after verbs in English (*dispense with, part with, get on with etc*). For translations, consult the appropriate verb entry (**dispense, part, get** etc).
> This dictionary contains usage notes on such topics as the human body and illnesses, aches and pains which use the preposition *with*. For the index to these Notes ▸ p. 1354.
> For further uses of *with*, see the entry below.

① (in descriptions) **a girl ~ black hair** une fille aux cheveux noirs; **the boy ~ the broken leg** le garçon à la jambe cassée; **a boy ~ a broken leg** un garçon avec une jambe cassée; **a dress ~ a large collar** une robe avec un large col; **a TV ~ remote control** une télévision avec télécommande; **furnished ~ antiques** décoré avec des meubles anciens; **covered ~ mud** couvert de boue; **wet ~ dew** couvert de rosée; **to lie ~ one's eyes closed** être allongé les yeux fermés; **filled ~** rempli de; ② (involving, concerning) avec; **a treaty/a discussion ~ sb** un traité/une discussion avec qn; ③ (indicating an agent) avec; **to hit sb ~ sth** frapper qn avec qch; **to walk ~ a stick** marcher avec une canne; **to cut sth ~ a penknife** couper qch avec un canif; ④ (indicating manner, attitude) **~ difficulty/pleasure** avec difficulté/plaisir; **to be patient ~ sb** être patient avec qn; **'OK,' he said ~ a smile/sigh** 'd'accord,' a-t-il dit en souriant/soupirant; **delighted ~ sth** ravi de qch; ⑤ (according to) **to increase ~ time** augmenter avec le temps; **to expand ~ heat** se dilater sous l'action de la chaleur; **to vary ~ the temperature** varier selon la température; ⑥ (accompanied by, in the presence of) avec; **to travel ~ sb** voyager avec qn; **bring a friend ~ you** viens avec un ami; **she's got her brother ~ her** (on one occasion) elle est avec *or* accompagnée de son frère; (staying with her) son frère est chez elle; **to live ~ sb** (in one's own house) vivre avec qn; (in their house) vivre chez qn; **I'll be ~ you in a second** je suis à vous dans un instant; **take your umbrella ~ you** emporte ton parapluie; ⑦ (owning, bringing) **passengers ~ tickets** les passagers munis de billets; **people ~ qualifications** les gens qualifiés; **somebody ~ your experience** quelqu'un qui a ton expérience; **have you got the report ~ you?** est-ce que tu as (amené) le rapport?; ⑧ (in relation to, as regards) **the frontier ~ Belgium** la frontière avec la Belgique; **how are things ~ you?** comment ça va?; **what's up ~ Amy?**,

W

what's ~ Amy? US qu'est-ce qui ne va pas avec Amy?; **what do you want ~ another car?** qu'est-ce que tu veux faire d'une deuxième voiture?; **it's a habit ~ her** c'est une habitude chez elle; 9 (showing consent, support) **I'm ~ you on this matter** je suis tout à fait d'accord avec toi là-dessus; **I'm ~ you 100%** ou **all the way** je suis tout à fait d'accord avec toi; 10 (because of) **sick ~ worry** malade ou mort d'inquiétude; **to blush ~ embarrassment** rougir d'embarras; **I can't do it ~ you watching** je ne peux pas le faire si tu me regardes; ~ **summer coming** avec l'été qui approche; 11 (remaining) ~ **only two days to go before the election** alors qu'il ne reste plus que deux jours avant les élections; 12 (suffering from) **people ~ Aids/leukemia** les personnes atteintes du sida/de la leucémie; **to be ill ~ flu** avoir la grippe; **to be in bed ~ chickenpox** être au lit avec la varicelle; 13 (in the care or charge of) **you're safe ~ us** tu es en sécurité avec nous; **the blame lies ~ him** c'est de sa faute; 14 (against) avec; **the war ~ Germany** la guerre avec l'Allemagne; **to be in competition ~ sb** être en concurrence avec qn; 15 (showing simultaneity) ~ **the approach of spring** à l'approche du printemps; ~ **the introduction of the reforms** avec l'introduction des nouvelles réformes; ~ **that, he left** sur ce, il est parti; 16 (employed by, customer of) **a reporter ~ the Gazette** un journaliste de la Gazette; **he's ~ the UN** il travaille pour l'ONU; **we're ~ the National Bank** nous sommes à la National Bank; 17 (in the same direction as) **to sail ~ the wind** naviguer dans le sens du vent; **to drift ~ the tide** dériver avec le courant

(Idioms) **to be ~ it**○ (on the ball) être dégourdi; (trendy) être dans le vent; **I'm not really ~ it today**○ j'ai l'esprit ailleurs aujourd'hui; **get ~ it**○! (wake up) réveille-toi!; (face the facts) redescends sur terre!; **I'm not ~ you, can you repeat?** je ne te suis pas, tu peux répéter?

withdraw /wɪð'drɔː, wɪθ'd-/ (prét **-drew**, pp **-drawn**)
A vtr retirer [hand, money, support, application, offer] (**from** de); retirer [aid, permission] (**from** à); renoncer à, retirer [claim]; rétracter [accusation, statement]; Mil retirer [troops] (**from** de); Pol rappeler [diplomat]; **to ~ a product from sale** Comm retirer un produit de la vente; **to ~ one's labour** GB Ind faire un arrêt de travail

B vi 1 [person, troops] se retirer (**from** de); [applicant, candidate] se retirer; **to ~ from a game** se retirer d'un jeu; **to ~ to one's room** se retirer dans sa chambre; **to ~ from one's position** Mil abandonner sa position; 2 Psych se replier

withdrawal /wɪð'drɔːəl, wɪθ'd-/ n 1 gen, Fin, Mil retrait m (**of, from** de); Pol (of ambassador) rappel m; **he has made several ~s from his account** il a effectué plusieurs retraits de son compte; ~ **of labour** GB arrêt m de travail; 2 Psych repli m sur soi; 3 (of drug addict) état m de manque

withdrawal slip n bordereau m de retrait

withdrawal symptoms npl symptômes mpl de manque; **to be suffering from ~** être en état de manque

withdrawn /wɪð'drɔːn, wɪθ'd-/
A pp ▸ **withdraw**
B adj [person] renfermé, replié sur soi-même

wither /'wɪðə(r)/
A vtr flétrir
B vi se flétrir
(Phrasal verb)
■ **wither away** [hope, interest] s'évanouir

withered /'wɪðəd/ adj [plant, skin, cheek] flétri; [arm] atrophié

withering /'wɪðərɪŋ/ adj [look] plein de mépris; [contempt, comment] cinglant

withhold /wɪð'həʊld/ vtr (prét, pp **-held**) différer [payment]; retenir [tax, grant, rent]; refuser [consent, permission]; ne pas divulguer [information]

within /wɪ'ðɪn/
A prep 1 (enclosed in) ~ **the city walls** dans l'enceinte de la ville; ~ **the boundaries of the estate** dans l'enceinte de la propriété; **to lie ~ Italy's borders** être en Italie; 2 (inside) ~ **the party** au sein du parti; **conditions ~ the camp** les conditions de vie dans le camp; **candidates from ~ the company** les candidats internes; **it appeals to something deep ~ us all** cela touche quelque chose de profond en nous; **it's a play ~ a play** c'est une pièce dans la pièce; 3 (in expressions of time) **I'll do it ~ the hour** je le ferai en moins d'une heure; **15 burglaries ~ a month** 15 cambriolages en moins d'un mois; **'please reply ~ the week'**

'prière de répondre dans la semaine'; **'use ~ 24 hours of purchase'** 'à consommer dans les 24 heures'; ~ **minutes he was back** quelques minutes plus tard il était de retour; **they died ~ a week of each other** ils sont morts à une semaine d'intervalle; 4 (not more than) **to be ~ several metres of sth** être à quelques mètres seulement de qch; **it's accurate to ~ a millimetre** c'est exact au millimètre près; ▸ **inch**; 5 (not beyond the range of) **to be ~ sight** lit [coast, town] être en vue; fig [end] être proche; **stay ~ sight of the car** ne vous éloignez pas de la voiture; **to be ~ range of** être à portée de [enemy guns]; 6 (not beyond a permitted limit) **to stay ~ budget** ne pas dépasser le budget; **to live ~ one's income** vivre selon ses moyens

B adv à l'intérieur; **seen from ~** vu de l'intérieur

without /wɪ'ðaʊt/
A prep 1 (lacking, not having) sans; ~ **a key** sans clé; **to be ~ friends** ne pas avoir d'amis; **to be ~ shame** n'avoir aucune honte; **she left ~ it** elle est partie sans; 2 (not) sans; ~ **doing** sans faire; **do it ~ him noticing** fais-le sans qu'il s'en aperçoive; ~ **saying a word** sans mot dire

B adv à l'extérieur; **from ~** de l'extérieur

withstand /wɪð'stænd/ vtr (prét, pp **-stood**) résister à

witness /'wɪtnɪs/
A n 1 gen, Jur (person) témoin m; **she was a ~ to the accident** elle a été témoin de l'accident; ~ **for the prosecution/the defence** témoin à charge/à décharge; **to call sb as a ~** citer qn comme témoin; 2 (testimony) témoignage m; **to be ~ ou bear ~ to sth** témoigner de qch

B vtr 1 (see) être témoin de, assister à; 2 (at official occasion) servir de témoin lors de la signature de [document, treaty]; être témoin à [marriage]; 3 fig **we are about to ~ a transformation of the economy** nous sommes sur le point d'assister à une transformation de l'économie; **his hard work has paid off, (as) ~ his exam results** son travail acharné a payé, comme en témoignent ses résultats d'examen

witness box GB, **witness stand** US n barre f des témoins

witticism /'wɪtɪsɪzəm/ n bon mot m

wittily /'wɪtɪlɪ/ adv avec esprit

witty /'wɪtɪ/ adj spirituel/-elle

wives /waɪvz/ pl ▸ **wife**

wizard /'wɪzəd/ n 1 (magician) magicien m; 2 fig (expert) **to be a ~ at** avoir le génie de [chess, computing etc]; **to be a ~ at doing** être très fort pour faire

wizened /'wɪznd/ adj ratatiné

wk abrév écrite = **week**

WMD n (abrév = **weapon of mass destruction**) ADM f

wobble /'wɒbl/
A n (in voice) tremblement m; (in movement) oscillation f; fig vacillation f
B vtr faire bouger [table, tooth]
C vi [table, chair] branler; [pile of books, plates etc] osciller; [voice] trembler; [person] (on bicycle) osciller; (on ladder, tightrope) chanceler; **his legs were wobbling under him** ses jambes flageolaient

wobbly /'wɒblɪ/ adj [table, chair] bancal; [tooth] branlant; [chin, voice, jelly] tremblotant; [handwriting, line] tremblant; fig [theory, plot] boiteux/-euse; **he is still a bit ~ on his legs** il est encore un peu faible sur ses jambes
(Idiom) **to throw a ~**○ GB piquer une crise○

woe /wəʊ/
A n malheur m
B excl ou hum ~ **betide him if he's late** gare à lui s'il est en retard

woeful /'wəʊfl/ adj 1 (mournful) [look] affligé; [story, sight] affligeant; 2 (deplorable) [lack] déplorable

woke /wəʊk/ prét ▸ **wake B, C**

woken /'wəʊkən/ pp ▸ **wake B, C**

wolf /wʊlf/
A n (pl **wolves**) loup m; **she-~** louve f
B vtr (also ~ **down**) engloutir
(Idioms) **to cry ~** crier au loup; **to keep the ~ from the door** mettre qn à l'abri du besoin; **a lone ~** un/une solitaire m/f

wolf: ~ cub n louveteau m; ~ **dog** US, ~**hound** GB n chien-loup m

wolfish /'wʊlfɪʃ/ adj féroce

W

wolf-whistle /'wʊlfwɪsl, US -hwɪ-/
A n sifflement m (au passage d'une femme)
B vi siffler (au passage d'une femme)

wolves /wʊlvz/ pl ▸ **wolf**

woman /'wʊmən/
A n (pl **women**) femme f; **the working** ~ la femme active; **a ~ comes in to clean twice a week** une femme de ménage vient deux fois par semaine; **she's her own** ~ elle est maîtresse de sa vie; **to talk about sth ~ to** ~ parler de qch entre femmes; **for heaven's sake,** ~**!** mais enfin tu es idiote ou quoi?; **the other** ~ péj l'autre
B noun modifier **a** ~ **Prime Minister** une femme premier ministre; **women drivers** les femmes au volant; **he has lots of women friends** il a beaucoup d'amies; **women voters** électrices fpl; **women writers** femmes fpl écrivains
(Idiom) **a** ~**'s place is in the home** la place d'une femme est au foyer

womanizer /'wʊmənaɪzə(r)/ n coureur m (de jupons○)

womanly /'wʊmənlɪ/ adj féminin

woman police constable, WPC n GB femme f agent de police

womb /wu:m/ n ventre m, utérus m

women /'wɪmɪn/ pl ▸ **woman**

women: ~**'s group** n groupe m féministe; **Women's Institute, WI** n GB association de femmes qui s'intéresse aux problèmes du foyer et qui organise des œuvres de bienfaisance; **Women's Liberation Movement, Women's Lib**○**, WLM** n mouvement m de libération de la femme, MLF m; ~**'s magazine** n magazine m féminin; ~**'s movement** n mouvement m des femmes; ~**'s page** n Journ page f des lectrices; ~**'s refuge** n foyer m pour femmes battues; ~**'s studies** npl études fpl féministes; ~**'s suffrage** n droit m de vote pour les femmes

won /wʌn/ prét, pp ▸ **win B, C**

wonder /'wʌndə(r)/
A n ① (miracle) merveille f; **it's a** ~ **that** c'est extraordinaire que; **(it's) no** ~ **that** (ce n'est) pas étonnant que; **small ou little** ~ **that** ce n'est guère étonnant que; **she's a** ~ elle est merveilleuse!; **the** ~**s of modern medicine** les prodiges de la médecine moderne; ② (amazement) émerveillement m; **in** ~ avec émerveillement; **lost in** ~ émerveillé
B noun modifier [cure, drug] miracle (after n)
C vtr ① (ask oneself) se demander; **I** ~ **how/why** je me demande comment/pourquoi; **I** ~ **if you could help me?** peut-être pourriez-vous m'aider?; **it makes you** ~ on peut se poser des questions; **it makes you** ~ **why/if/how** c'est à se demander pourquoi/si/comment; ② (be surprised) **I** ~ **that** cela m'étonne que (+ subj)
D vi ① (think) **to** ~ **about sth** penser à qch; ② (be surprised) **to** ~ **at sth** s'étonner de qch; (admiringly) s'émerveiller de qch; **they'll be late again, I shouldn't** ~ cela ne m'étonnerait pas qu'ils soient encore en retard

wonderful /'wʌndəfl/ adj [book, film, meal, experience, holiday] merveilleux/-euse; [musician, teacher] excellent; [achievement] beau/belle (before n); **to be** ~ **with** [children, animals] s'y prendre avec; **to be** ~ **with computers** s'y connaître en informatique; **I feel** ~ je suis en pleine forme; **you look** ~**!** (healthy) tu as l'air en pleine forme!; (attractive) tu es superbe!

wonderfully /'wʌndəfəlɪ/ adv (very) très; (splendidly) admirablement

wondering /'wʌndərɪŋ/ adj (full of wonder) émerveillé; (puzzled) étonné

wonderland /'wʌndələænd/ n pays m enchanté

wonky /'wɒŋkɪ/ adj GB ① (crooked) de traviole○; ② (wobbly) [furniture] bancal; [legs] flageolant; ③ (faulty) **the television is** ~ la télé est détraquée○

wont /wəʊnt, US wɔ:nt/ adj **to be** ~ **to do** avoir coutume de faire; **as is his/their** ~ comme à son/leur habitude

won't /wəʊnt/ = **will not**

woo /wu:/ vtr courtiser

wood /wʊd/
A n ① (fuel, timber) bois m; ② (barrel) fût m; ③ (forest) bois m; ④ Sport (in bowls) boule f (en bois); (in golf) bois m
B **woods** npl bois mpl
C noun modifier [fire, smoke] de bois
(Idioms) **touch** ~**!** GB, **knock on** ~**!** US touchons du bois!; **we are not out of the** ~ **yet** on n'est pas encore sorti de l'auberge

wood: ~**block** n (for flooring) latte f; US Art planche f; ~**-block floor** n parquet m; ~**-burning stove** n = wood stove; ~**carving** n sculpture f sur bois; ~**craft** n connaissance f des bois; ~**cut** n (block) planche f; (print) xylographie f; ~**cutting** n abattage m des arbres

wooded /'wʊdɪd/ adj boisé; **thickly** ~ très boisé

wooden /'wʊdn/ adj ① gen en bois; [leg] de bois; ② fig figé

wooden: ~ **horse** n cheval m de Troie also fig; ~ **nickel** n US objet m sans valeur; ~ **spoon** n cuillère f de bois; fig prix m de consolation

woodland /'wʊdlənd/
A n bois m
B noun modifier [animal, plant] des bois; [scenery] boisé; [walk] dans les bois; ~ **management** exploitation f forestière

wood: ~**louse** n cloporte m; ~**pecker** n pic m; ~ **pigeon** n pigeon m ramier; ~**pile** n tas m de bois; ~ **shavings** npl copeaux mpl; ~**shed** n remise f à bois; ~ **stove** n poêle m à bois

woodwind /'wʊdwɪnd/
A npl bois mpl
B noun modifier [instrument] à bois; [player] d'instrument à bois; [section] des bois

woodwork /'wʊdwɜ:k/
A n (carpentry) menuiserie f; (doors, windows etc) boiseries fpl
B noun modifier [teacher, class] de menuiserie; [student] en menuiserie
(Idiom) **to come out of the** ~○ hum surgir d'un peu partout○

woodworm /'wʊdwɜ:m/ n (disease) maladie f du ver à bois; **to have** ~ être vermoulu

woody /'wʊdɪ/ adj [hill, landscape] boisé; [plant, stem] ligneux/-euse; [smell] de bois

wool /wʊl/
A n laine f; **pure (new)** ~ pure laine (vierge)
B noun modifier [carpet, coat, shop] de laine; [trade] lainier/-ière
(Idiom) **to pull the** ~ **over sb's eyes** duper qn

woollen GB, **woolen** US /'wʊlən/
A n ① (garment) lainage m; ② (piece of cloth) tissu m en laine
B adj [garment] de laine; ~ **mill** lainerie f

woolly GB, **wooly** US /'wʊlɪ/
A n○ lainage m
B adj [garment] de laine; [animal coat] laineux/-euse; [cloud] cotonneux/-euse; fig [thinking] flou

woozy○ /'wu:zɪ/ adj **to feel** ~ avoir la tête qui tourne

Worcs n GB Post abrév écrite = **Worcestershire**

word /wɜ:d/
A n ① (verbal expression) mot m; **those were his very** ~**s** ce sont ses propres mots; **to have no** ~**s to express sth** ne pas trouver les mots pour exprimer qch; **long** ~**s** mots savants; **with these** ~**s he left** sur ces mots il est parti; **in your own** ~**s** avec tes propres mots; **I don't think 'aunt' is quite the right** ~ je ne suis pas sûr que 'tante' soit le mot qui convienne; **the last** ~ fig le dernier cri (**in** en); **to get a** ~ **in** placer un mot; **not in so many** ~**s** pas exactement; **in other** ~**s** en d'autres termes; **the spoken** ~ la langue parlée; **to put one's feelings ou thoughts into** ~**s** exprimer ce qu'on ressent; **there's no such** ~ **as 'can't'** 'impossible' n'est pas français; **what's the Greek** ~ **for 'table'?** comment dit-on 'table' en grec?; **a** ~ **of warning** un avertissement; **a** ~ **of advice** un conseil; **I've said my last** ~ **on the subject** j'ai dit tout ce que j'avais à dire sur le sujet; **too sad for** ~**s** trop triste; **in the** ~**s of Washington** pour reprendre l'expression de Washington; **I believed every** ~ **he said** je croyais tout ce qu'il me disait; **I mean every** ~ **of it** je pense ce que je dis; **a** ~ **to all those who...** quelques conseils pour tous ceux qui...; **a man of few** ~**s** un homme peu loquace; ② (anything, something) mot m; **not a** ~ **to anybody** pas un mot à qui que ce soit; **I don't believe a** ~ **of it** je n'en crois pas un mot; **not to have a good** ~ **to say about sb** n'avoir rien de bon à dire de qn; **I want to say a** ~ **about honesty** je voudrais dire quelque chose au sujet de l'honnêteté; **I didn't say a** ~**!** je n'ai pas ouvert la bouche!; **he won't hear a** ~ **against her** il ne supporte pas qu'on dise quoi que ce soit contre elle; ③ **C** (information) nouvelles fpl (about concernant); **there is no** ~ **of the missing climbers** on est sans nouvelles des alpinistes disparus; **we are hoping for** ~ **that all is well** nous

espérons de bonnes nouvelles; ∼ **got out that...** la nouvelle a transpiré que...; **to bring/send** ∼ **that** annoncer/faire savoir que; **he left** ∼ **at the desk that...** il a laissé un message à la réception disant que...; **4** (promise, affirmation) parole f; **he gave me his** ∼ il m'a donné sa parole; **to break one's** ∼ ne pas tenir parole; **to hold sb to his/her** ∼ obliger qn à tenir parole; **a woman of her** ∼ une femme de parole; **to take sb's** ∼ **for it** croire qn sur parole; **to doubt sb's** ∼ douter des paroles de qn; **take my** ∼ **for it!** crois-moi!; **to go back on one's** ∼ revenir sur sa promesse; **to be as good as one's** ∼ tenir parole; **5** (rumour) ∼ **has it that he's a millionaire** on dit qu'il est millionnaire; ∼ **got round** ou **around that...** le bruit a couru que...; **6** (command) ordre m; **if you need anything just say the** ∼ si tu as besoin de quoi que ce soit, dis-le; **just say the** ∼ **and I'll come** tu n'as qu'un mot à dire et je viendrai; **their** ∼ **is law** ils font la loi

B **words** npl **1** (oratory) paroles fpl; **empty** ∼**s** paroles vides de sens; **2** Theat, Mus (of play) texte m; (of song) paroles fpl

C -**worded** combining form **a carefully-**∼**ed letter** une lettre soigneusement formulée; **a strongly-**∼**ed statement** un communiqué ferme

D vtr formuler [reply, letter, statement]

(Idioms) **my** ∼**!** (in surprise) ma parole!; (in reproof) tu vas voir!; **right from the** ∼ **go** dès le départ; **to have a** ∼ **with sb about sth** parler (un peu) à qn à propos de qch; **to have** ∼**s with sb** s'accrocher avec qn; **to put in a good** ∼ **for sb** glisser un mot en faveur de qn

word: ∼ **blindness** n dyslexie f; ∼**break** n coupure f (du mot); ∼**count** n Comput nombre m de mots; ∼-**for-word** adj, adv mot à mot inv; ∼ **game** n jeu m de lettres

wording /'wɜːdɪŋ/ n formulation f

wordlist /'wɜːdlɪst/ n gen liste f de mots; (in dictionary) nomenclature f

word-of-mouth
A adj [promise] verbal
B **by word of mouth** adv phr verbalement

word-perfect /ˌwɜːd'pɜːfɪkt/ adj parfait; **to be** ∼ [person] connaître son texte sur le bout des doigts

word: ∼ **processing, WP** n Comput traitement m de texte; ∼ **processor** n Comput machine f à traitement de texte

wordy /'wɜːdɪ/ adj verbeux/-euse

wore /wɔː(r)/ prét ▸ wear B, C

work /wɜːk/
A n **1** (physical or mental activity) travail m (on sur); **to be at** ∼ **on sth** être en train de travailler à qch; **to go** ou **set** ou **get to** ∼ se mettre au travail; **to set to** ∼ **doing** se mettre à faire; **to put a lot of** ∼ **into** travailler [essay, speech]; passer beaucoup de temps sur [meal, preparations]; **to put** ou **set sb to** ∼ faire travailler qn; **we put him to** ∼ **doing** nous lui avons donné pour tâche de faire; **it was hard** ∼ **doing** ça a été dur de faire; **to be hard at** ∼ travailler consciencieusement; **your essay needs more** ∼ tu dois travailler davantage ta rédaction; **to make short** ou **light** ∼ **of sth** expédier qch; **to make short** ∼ **of sb** envoyer promener qn; **it's all in a day's** ∼ c'est une question d'habitude; **it's hot/thirsty** ∼ ça donne chaud/soif; **2** (occupation) travail m; **to be in** ∼ avoir du travail ou un emploi; **place of** ∼ lieu m de travail; **to be off** ∼ (on vacation) être en congé; **to be off** ∼ **with flu** être en arrêt de travail parce qu'on a la grippe; **to be out of** ∼ être au chômage; **3** (place of employment) (office) bureau m; (factory) usine f; **to go to** ∼ aller au travail; **don't phone me at** ∼ ne me téléphone pas à mon travail; **4** (building, construction) travaux mpl (on sur); **5** (papers) **to take one's** ∼ **home** lit emporter du travail chez soi; fig ramener ses soucis professionnels à la maison; **6** (achievement, product) (essay, report) travail m; (artwork, novel, sculpture) œuvre f (by de); (study) ouvrage m (by de; on sur); **is this all your own** ∼? est-ce que vous l'avez fait tout seul?; **to mark students'** ∼ noter les devoirs des étudiants; **a** ∼ **of genius** une œuvre de génie; **a** ∼ **of reference** un ouvrage de référence; **this attack is the** ∼ **of professionals** l'attaque est l'œuvre de professionnels; **7** (research) recherches fpl (on sur); **8** (effect) **to go to** ∼ [drug, detergent] agir
B **works** npl **1** (factory) usine f; ∼**s canteen** cantine f de l'usine; **2** (building work) travaux mpl; **3** ○(everything) **the (full** ou **whole)** ∼**s** toute la panoplie○
C noun modifier [clothes, shoes] de travail; [phone number] au travail

D vtr **1** (drive) **to** ∼ **sb hard** surmener qn; **2** (labour) **to** ∼ **shifts** travailler en équipes (de travail posté); **to** ∼ **days/nights** travailler de jour/de nuit; **to** ∼ **one's way through university** travailler pour payer ses études; **to** ∼ **one's way through a book** lire péniblement un livre, venir à bout○ d'un livre; **to** ∼ **a 40 hour week** faire la semaine de 40 heures; **3** (operate) se servir de; **4** (exploit commercially) exploiter; **5** (have as one's territory) couvrir [region]; **6** (consume) **to** ∼ **one's way through** (use) utiliser [amount, quantity]; **7** (bring about) **to** ∼ **wonders** lit, fig faire des merveilles; **8** (use to one's advantage) **to** ∼ **the system** profiter du système; **how did you manage to** ∼ **it?** comment as-tu pu arranger ça?; **I've** ∼**ed things so that...** j'ai arrangé les choses de sorte que...; **9** (fashion) travailler [clay, metal]; **10** (embroider) broder; **11** (manoeuvre) **to** ∼ **sth into** introduire qch dans [slot, hole]; **to** ∼ **a lever up and down** actionner un levier; **12** (exercise) faire travailler [muscles]; **13** (move) **to** ∼ **one's way through** se frayer un passage à travers [crowd]; **to** ∼ **one's hands free** se libérer les mains; **it** ∼**ed its way** ou **itself loose** cela s'est desserré peu à peu; **to** ∼ **its way into** passer dans; **start at the top and** ∼ **your way down** commencez par le haut et continuez jusqu'en bas

E vi **1** (engage in activity) travailler (doing à faire); **to** ∼ **at home** travailler à domicile; **to** ∼ **for a living** gagner sa vie; **to** ∼ **in oils** [painter] travailler à l'huile; **2** (strive) lutter (against contre; for pour; to do pour faire); **to** ∼ **towards** se diriger vers [solution]; s'acheminer vers [compromise]; négocier [agreement]; **3** (function) fonctionner; **to** ∼ **on electricity** marcher or fonctionner à l'électricité; **to** ∼ **off the mains** marcher sur secteur; **the washing machine isn't** ∼**ing** la machine à laver est en panne; **4** (act, operate) **it doesn't** ou **things don't** ∼ **like that** ça ne marche pas comme ça; **to** ∼ **on the assumption that** présumer que; **to** ∼ **in sb's favour, to** ∼ **to sb's advantage** tourner à l'avantage de qn; **to** ∼ **against sb, to** ∼ **to sb's disadvantage** jouer en la défaveur de qn; **5** (be successful) [treatment] avoir de l'effet; [detergent, drug] agir; [plan] réussir; [argument] tenir debout; **flattery won't** ∼ **with me** la flatterie ne marche pas avec moi; **the adaptation really** ∼**s** l'adaptation est vraiment réussie; **6** [face, features] se contracter

F v refl **1** (labour) **to** ∼ **oneself too hard** se surmener; **to** ∼ **oneself to death** se tuer à la tâche; **2** **to** ∼ **oneself into a rage** se mettre en colère

(Idioms) **to** ∼ **one's way up** gravir tous les échelons; **to** ∼ **one's way up the company** faire son chemin dans l'entreprise

(Phrasal verbs)

■ **work around**: ▸ ∼ **around to [sth]** aborder; **it took him ages to** ∼ **around to what he wanted to say** il lui a fallu un temps fou pour exprimer ce qu'il avait à dire; **to** ∼ **the conversation around to sth** faire tourner la conversation autour de qch

■ **work in**: ▸ ∼ **in [sth],** ∼ **[sth] in** **1** glisser [joke]; mentionner [fact, name]; **2** Culin incorporer

■ **work off**: ▸ ∼ **[sth] off,** ∼ **off [sth]** **1** (remove) retirer [lid]; **2** (repay) travailler pour rembourser [loan, debt]; **3** (get rid of) se débarrasser de [excess weight]; dépenser [excess energy]; passer [anger, frustration]

■ **work on**: ▸ ∼ **on** continuer à travailler; ▸ ∼ **on [sb]** travailler○ [person]; ▸ ∼ **on [sth]** travailler à [book, report]; travailler sur [project]; s'occuper de [case, problem]; chercher [cure, solution]; examiner [idea]; **'have you found a solution?'—'I'm** ∼**ing on it'** 'as-tu trouvé une solution?' —'j'y réfléchis'

■ **work out**: ▸ ∼ **out** **1** (exercise) s'entraîner; **2** (go according to plan) marcher; **3** (add up) **to** ∼ **out at** GB ou **to** US s'élever à; ▸ ∼ **out [sth],** ∼ **[sth] out** **1** (calculate) calculer [amount]; **2** (solve) trouver [answer, reason, culprit]; résoudre [problem]; comprendre [clue]; **3** (devise) concevoir [plan, scheme]; trouver [route]; ▸ ∼ **[sb] out** comprendre [person]; **I can't** ∼ **her out** je n'arrive pas à la comprendre

■ **work over**○: ▸ ∼ **[sb] over** passer [qn] à tabac○

■ **work to**: ▸ ∼ **to [sth]** s'astreindre à [budget]; **to** ∼ **to deadlines** travailler en respectant des délais

■ **work up**: ▸ ∼ **up [sth]** développer [interest]; accroître [support]; **to** ∼ **up the courage to do** trouver le courage de faire; **to** ∼ **up some enthusiasm for** s'enthousiasmer pour; **to** ∼ **up an appetite** s'ouvrir l'appétit; ▸ ∼ **to [sth]** se préparer à; ▸ ∼ **up [sb],** ∼ **[sb] up** **1** (excite) exciter [child, crowd]; **he** ∼**ed the crowd up into a frenzy** il a

W

mis la foule en délire; **2** (annoy) énerver; **to get ~ed up,
to ~ oneself up** s'énerver; **to ~ oneself up into a state** ou
frenzy se mettre dans tous ses états

workable /'wɜːkəbl/ adj **1** (feasible) [idea, plan] réalisable;
[system] pratique; [arrangement] possible; **2** Agric, Ind
exploitable; [cement] maniable

workaday /'wɜːkədeɪ/ adj [clothes, life] ordinaire

workaholic○ /ˌwɜːkə'hɒlɪk/ n bourreau m de travail

work: **~ basket** n corbeille f à ouvrage; **~bench** n
établi m; **~book** n (blank) cahier m; (with exercises) livre m
d'exercices; **~day** n gen jour m de travail; Comm jour m
ouvrable

worker /'wɜːkə(r)/
A n **1** (employee) (in manual job) ouvrier/-ière m/f; (in white-collar
job) employé/-e m/f; **she's a good/slow ~** elle travaille
bien/lentement; **2** (proletarian) prolétaire mf
B noun modifier [ant, bee] ouvrier/-ière

worker: **~ participation** n participation f des travailleurs à la gestion; **~s' control** n autogestion f

work: **~ ethic** n culte m puritain du travail; **~ experience** n stage m; **~force** n (+ v sg ou pl) (in industry) main-
d'œuvre f; (in service sector) effectifs mpl; **~horse** n fig bête
f de travail; **~-in** n occupation f du lieu de travail (sans
arrêt de la production)

working /'wɜːkɪŋ/
A n **1** (functioning) fonctionnement m; **2** (shaping, preparation)
travail m **(of** de); **3** (draft solution) calculs mpl; **4** Ind (mine)
chantier m de mine; (quarry) chantier m de carrière
B workings npl lit, fig rouages mpl
C adj **1** [parent, woman] qui travaille; [conditions, environment, methods] de travail; [population, life] actif/-ive; [lunch,
day, week] de travail; **during ~ hours** (in office) pendant les
heures de bureau; (in shop) pendant les heures de travail;
we have a good ~ relationship nous avons de bons rapports professionnels; **2** (provisional) [document, hypothesis] de
travail; [definition, title] provisoire; **3** (functional) [model] qui
fonctionne; [mine] en exploitation; **in full ~ order** en
parfait état de marche; **4** Econ [expenses, stock] d'exploitation

working class
A n classe f ouvrière; **the ~es** les classes fpl laborieuses
B working-class adj [area, background, childhood, family, life]
ouvrier/-ière; [culture, London] prolétarien/-ienne; [person]
de la classe ouvrière

working: **~ dog** n chien m d'utilité; **~ majority** n
majorité f suffisante; **~-over**○ n passage m à tabac○;
~ party n Admin groupe m de travail; Mil escouade f;
~ week n semaine f (de travail)

workload /'wɜːkləʊd/ n charge f de travail; **to have a
light/heavy ~** avoir peu/beaucoup de travail

work: **~man** n ouvrier m; **~manlike** adj (effective)
soigné; péj (uninspired) honnête

workmanship /'wɜːkmənʃɪp/ n **a carpenter famous for
sound ~** un menuisier connu pour la qualité de son travail; **furniture of the finest ~** des meubles d'une belle facture; **a piece of poor** ou **shoddy ~** du travail mal fait or
bâclé

work: **~mate** n collègue mf de travail; **~ of art** n
œuvre f d'art; **~out** n séance f de mise en forme;
~pack n fiches fpl de travail; **~ permit** n permis m
de travail

workplace /'wɜːkpleɪs/
A n lieu m de travail
B noun modifier [creche, nursery] d'entreprise

work: **~room** n atelier m; **~s committee,
~ council** n GB Ind comité m d'entreprise; **~-sharing**
n partage m du travail; **~sheet** n feuille f d'opérations; Sch feuille f de questions; **~shop** n atelier m;
~shy adj péj paresseux/-euse; **~s manager** ▸ p. 1181
n directeur m d'usine; **~space** n Comput espace m de
travail; **~ station** n poste m de travail; **~ study** n
étude f ergonomique; **~ surface** n plan m de travail;
~table n table f de travail; **~top** n plan m de travail;
~-to-rule n grève f du zèle

world /wɜːld/
A n **1** (planet) monde m; **throughout the ~** dans le monde
entier; **to go round the ~** faire le tour du monde; **this
~ and the next** le monde d'ici-bas et l'au-delà; **the next ~**
l'autre monde; **to lead the ~ in electronics** être à la

pointe de l'électronique; **to come into the ~** voir le jour;
2 (group of people) monde m; **the ~ of politics** le monde de
la politique; **to go up in the ~** faire son chemin; **to go
down in the ~** déchoir; **for all the ~ to see** devant le
monde; **the outside ~** le reste du monde; **3** (section of the
earth) pays mpl; **the Eastern/Western ~** les pays de l'Est/
occidentaux; **4** (environment) monde m, univers m; **he lives
in a ~ of his own** ou **a private ~** il vit dans un monde à
part
B noun modifier [events, leader, politics] mondial; [record, tour,
championship] du monde; [cruise] autour du monde

Idioms **(all) the ~ and his wife** hum tout le monde; **a
~ away from sth** très éloigné de qch; **to be on top of the ~**
être aux anges; **for all the ~ like/as if** exactement comme/
comme si; **he's one of the Don Juans of this ~** c'est un
véritable Don Juan; **how in the ~ did you know?** comment diable l'as-tu su?; **to get the best of both ~s** gagner
sur les deux tableaux; **I'd give the ~ to do** je donnerais
n'importe quoi pour faire; **a man of the ~** un homme
d'expérience; **not for (all) the ~** pas pour tout l'or du
monde; **out of this ~** extraordinaire; **that's the way of the
~** c'est la vie; **there's a ~ of difference** il y a une différence énorme; **it did him the** ou **a ~ of good** ça lui a fait
énormément de bien; **he'll never set the ~ on fire** il ne
fera jamais d'étincelles; **to think the ~ of sb** penser le
plus grand bien de qn; **to watch the ~ go by** regarder le
monde s'agiter; **what/where/who etc in the ~?** que/
où/qui etc diable?; **~s apart** diamétralement opposé

world: **~-beater** n (person) personne f qui surpasse les
autres; (product) produit m qui se vend le mieux;
~-beating adj qui surpasse les autres; **~-class** adj
de niveau mondial; **World Cup** n (in football) Coupe f du
Monde; **World Fair** n Exposition f universelle;
~-famous adj mondialement connu; **World
Health Organization, WHO** n Organisation f mondiale de la santé

world leader n **1** Pol chef m d'État; **2** (best in the world)
Sport meilleur/-e m/f du monde; Comm (company) leader m
mondial

worldly /'wɜːldlɪ/ adj **1** (not spiritual) matériel/-ielle;
~ goods les biens matériels; **~ wisdom** la sagesse des
nations; **2** (materialistic) péj matérialiste

worldly-wise /ˌwɜːldlɪ'waɪz/ adj avisé, qui a de l'expérience

world: **~ power** n puissance f mondiale; **World Service** n GB service m international de la BBC; **~view** n
vision f du monde

world war n guerre f mondiale; **World War One/Two** la
Première/Seconde Guerre mondiale

world-weary adj fatigué de la vie

world(-)wide /ˌwɜːld'waɪd/
A adj mondial
B adv dans le monde entier

worm /wɜːm/
A n **1** ver m; **a dog with ~s** un chien infesté de vers;
2 ○(wretch) vermine○ f; **3** Comput (disk) (abrév = write-
once read many times) disque m inscriptible une seule
fois; (virus) virus m
B vtr **1** [vet] vermifuger; **2** (wriggle) **to ~ one's way** lit se
faufiler (**along** le long de); fig s'insinuer (**into** dans); **to
~ one's way into sb's affections** gagner les bonnes grâces
de qn

Idioms **the ~ has turned** la situation s'est renversée; **a can
of ~s** un sac de nœuds

Phrasal verb
■ worm out: ▸ ~ [sth] out arracher (**of** sb à qn)

worm: **~-eaten** adj [fruit] véreux/-euse; [wood] vermoulu; **~hole** n (in fruit, plant) trou m de ver; (in wood) vermou-
lure f

wormy /'wɜːmɪ/ adj **1** [wood] vermoulu; [fruit] véreux/
-euse; **2** US (grovelling) [person] servile

worn /wɔːn/
A pp ▸ wear B, C
B adj [carpet, clothing, shoe, tyre] usé; [façade, stone] abîmé;
[tread] lisse

worn-out /ˌwɔːn'aʊt/ adj **1** [carpet, brake] complètement
usé; **2** (exhausted) [person] épuisé

worried /'wʌrɪd/ adj soucieux/-ieuse; **to be ~ about
sb/sth** se faire du souci or s'inquiéter pour qn/qch; **to be**

~ **about doing** avoir peur de faire; **to be ~ that** avoir peur que; **there's no need to be ~** il n'y a pas de souci à se faire

worrier /'wʌrɪə(r)/ n anxieux/-ieuse m/f

worry /'wʌrɪ/
A n **1** **C** (anxiety) soucis mpl (**about, over** à propos de); **2** (problem) souci m (**about, over** au sujet de); **that's the least of my worries** c'est le dernier de mes soucis; **he's a ~ to his parents** il cause des soucis à ses parents
B vtr **1** (concern) inquiéter; **I ~ that** j'ai peur que; **it worried him that he couldn't find the keys** ça l'a inquiété de ne pas trouver les clés; **2** (alarm) tracasser; **3** (bother) ennuyer; **would it ~ you if I opened the window?** est-ce que ça vous ennuierait que j'ouvre la fenêtre?; **4** (chase) harceler [sheep]; (toss about) secouer [qch] entre les dents
C vi (be anxious) s'inquiéter; **to ~ about** ou **over sth/sb** s'inquiéter pour qch/qn; **to ~ about doing** avoir peur de faire; **I ~ for his sanity sometimes** je me fais parfois du souci pour sa santé mentale; **there's nothing to ~ about** il n'y a pas lieu de s'inquiéter; **not to ~** ne t'inquiète pas; **he'll be punished, don't you ~!** il sera puni, tu peux en être sûr!; **he said it's nothing to ~ about** il a dit qu'il n'y avait là rien d'inquiétant
D v refl **to ~ oneself** s'inquiéter, se faire de souci (**about sb** au sujet de qn; **about sth** à propos de qch); **to ~ oneself sick over sth** se ronger les sangs au sujet de qch

(Phrasal verb)

■ **worry at:** ▸ **~ at [sth]** lit secouer [qch] entre les dents; fig retourner [qch] dans tous les sens [problem]

worry beads npl chapelet m antistress

worrying /'wʌrɪɪŋ/
A n **all this ~ is making you ill** tout ce souci que tu te fais te rend malade
B adj inquiétant; **the ~ thing is that** ce qu'il y a d'inquiétant c'est que

worse /wɜːs/
A adj (comparative of **bad**) **1** (more unsatisfactory, unpleasant) pire; **there's only one thing ~ than** il n'y a qu'une chose qui soit pire que; **the noise is ~** il y a plus de bruit; **to get ~** [pressure, noise] augmenter; [conditions, weather] empirer; **'you missed the bus'—'yes ~ luck!'** 'tu as raté le bus'—'oui pas de veine○!'; **2** (more serious, severe) pire (**than** que); **it looks ~ than it is!** ça a l'air pire que ça ne l'est en vérité!; **it couldn't be ~!** ça ne pourrait pas être pire!; **and what is ~, she doesn't care** et le pire, c'est que ça lui est égal; **to go from bad to ~** aller de pire en pire; **to get ~ (and ~)** [illness, conflict] s'aggraver; [patient] aller de pire en plus mal; **to be made ~ (by** par); **you'll only make things** ou **it ~!** tu ne feras qu'empirer les choses!; **and to make matters ~,** he lied et pour ne rien arranger, il a menti; **3** (of lower standard) pire (**than** que); **to be even ~ at languages** être encore plus mauvais en langues; **4** (more unwell, unhappy) **he's getting ~** il va plus mal; **the cough is getting ~** la toux empire; **to feel ~** (more ill) se sentir plus malade; (more unhappy) aller moins bien; **his death made me feel ~** sa mort m'a démoralisé encore plus; **he is none the ~ for the experience** il ne se porte pas plus mal après cette expérience; **so much the ~ for them!** tant pis pour eux!; **5** (more inappropriate) **he couldn't have chosen a ~ place to meet** il n'aurait pas pu choisir un lieu de rendez-vous moins approprié; **the decision couldn't have come at a ~ time** la décision n'aurait pas pu arriver à un moment plus inopportun
B n **there is ~ to come** ce n'est pas encore le pire; **to change for the ~** empirer; **things took a turn for the ~** les choses ont empiré
C adv (compar de **badly**) **1** (more unsatisfactorily, incompetently) moins bien (**than** que); **to behave ~** se conduire plus mal; **she could do ~ than follow his example** ce ne serait pas si mal si elle suivait son exemple; **2** (more seriously, severely) [cough, bleed, vomit] plus; **~ still** pire encore

worsen /'wɜːsn/
A vtr aggraver [situation, problem]
B vi [condition, health, weather, situation] se détériorer; [problem, crisis, shortage, flooding] s'aggraver

worsening /'wɜːsnɪŋ/
A n aggravation f (**of** de)
B adj [situation] en voie de détérioration; [problem, shortage] en voie d'aggravation

worse off adj **1** (less wealthy) **to be ~** avoir moins d'argent (**than** que); **to end up ~** finir avec moins d'argent; **I'm £10** a week **~** j'ai dix livres de moins par semaine; **2** (in a worse situation) **to be ~** être dans une situation pire; **to be no ~ without sth** pouvoir parfaitement se passer de qch

worship /'wɜːʃɪp/
A n **1** (veneration) gen vénération f; Relig culte m; **2** (religious practice) pratique f religieuse; **freedom of ~** liberté f de culte; **place of ~** lieu m de culte; **an act of ~** un acte de dévotion
B **Worship** pr n GB ▸ **p. 869** (for man) monsieur m; (for woman) madame f; **his Worship the mayor** Monsieur le maire
C vtr (p prés etc **-pp-**) **1** Relig (venerate) adorer; (give praise) rendre hommage à; **2** (idolize) lit vénérer; fig être en adoration devant
D vi (p prés etc **-pp-**) pratiquer sa religion

worshipper /'wɜːʃɪpə(r)/ n (in established religion) fidèle mf; (in nonestablished religion) adorateur/-trice m/f

worst /wɜːst/
A n **1** (most difficult, unpleasant) **the ~** le/la pire m/f; **the storm was one of the ~ in recent years** la tempête était parmi les pires qu'il y ait eu ces dernières années; **last year was the ~ for strikes** du point de vue des grèves l'année dernière a été la pire; **they're the ~ of all** (people) ce sont eux les pires; (things, problems, ideas) c'est ce qu'il y a de pire; **he's not the ~** il y a pire que lui; **we're over the ~ now** nous avons passé le pire; **the ~ was yet to come** le plus dur était encore à venir; **the ~ of it is there's no solution** le pire c'est qu'il n'y a pas de solution; **during the ~ of the recession** au plus fort de la crise; **the ~ of the heat is over** les plus fortes chaleurs sont passées; **do your ~!** essaie un peu pour voir!; **2** (expressing the most pessimistic outlook) **the ~** le pire m; **to think the ~ of sb** avoir une mauvaise opinion de qn; **if the ~ were to happen, if the ~ came to the ~** (in serious circumstances) dans le pire des cas; (involving fatality, death) si le pire devait arriver; **3** (most unbearable) **to be at its ~** aller au plus mal; **at its ~, the noise could be heard everywhere** quand le bruit était à sa puissance maximum, on l'entendait partout; **when the heat is at its ~** au plus fort de la chaleur; **these are fanatics at their ~** ce sont des fanatiques dans ce qu'ils ont de pire; **when you see people at their ~** quand on voit les gens sous leur plus mauvais jour; **I'm at my ~ in the morning** (in temper) c'est le matin que je suis de plus mauvaise humeur; **4** (most negative trait) **to bring out the ~ in sb** mettre à jour ce qu'il y a de plus mauvais chez qn; **5** (of the lowest standard, quality) **the ~** le plus mauvais/la plus mauvaise m/f; **to be the ~ at French** être le plus mauvais en français
B adj (superl of **bad**) **1** (most unsatisfactory, unpleasant) plus mauvais; **the ~ book I've ever read** le plus mauvais livre que j'aie jamais lu; **hypocrites of the ~ kind** des hypocrites de la pire espèce; **the ~ thing about the film is** ce qu'il y a de pire dans le film c'est; **and the ~ thing about it is (that)** et le pire c'est que; **2** (most serious) plus grave; **one of the ~ recessions** une des crises les plus graves; **the ~ mistake you could have made** la pire erreur possible; **3** (most inappropriate) pire; **the ~ possible place to do** le pire endroit pour faire; **she rang at the ~ possible time** elle a téléphoné au plus mauvais moment; **it's the ~ thing you could have said!** c'était vraiment la chose à ne pas dire!; **4** (of the poorest standard) pire, plus mauvais
C adv (the children suffer (the) **~** ce sont les enfants qui souffrent le plus; **they were (the) ~ affected** ou **hit by the strike** ce sont eux qui ont été les plus touchés par la grève; **to smell the ~** sentir le plus mauvais; **to come off ~** perdre le plus; **the ~-off groups in society** les groupes les plus démunis de la société; **the ~-behaved child he'd ever met** l'enfant le plus mal élevé qu'il ait jamais rencontré; **~ of all,...** le pire de tout, c'est que...; **they did (the) ~ of all the group in the exam** ce sont eux qui ont le moins bien réussi l'examen

worsted /'wʊstɪd/ n tissu m en laine peignée

worth /wɜːθ/
A n **C** **1** Fin (measure, quantity) **five pounds' ~ of sth** pour cinq livres de qch; **thousands of pounds' ~ of damage** des milliers de livres de dégâts; **a day's ~ of fuel** un jour de combustible; **a week's ~ of supplies** une semaine de provisions; **to get one's money's ~** en avoir pour son argent; **2** (value, usefulness) valeur f; **of no ~** sans valeur; **what is its ~ in pounds?** combien cela fait-il en livres sterling?
B adj **1** (of financial value) **to be ~ sth** valoir qch; **the pound is ~ 10 francs** la livre vaut 10 francs; **it's not ~ much** ça ne vaut pas grand-chose; **he is ~ £50,000** sa fortune s'élève à 50 000 livres; **2** (of abstract value) **to be ~ sth** valoir qch; **an**

w

experienced worker is ~ three novices un travailleur expérimenté vaut trois débutants; **unsubstantiated reports are not ~ much** les rapports sans fondement concret ne valent pas grand-chose; **it's as much as my job's ~ to give you the keys** je risque mon emploi si je te donne les clés; **the house is only ~ what you can get for it** la maison ne vaut que ce qu'elle vaut; **to be ~ a mention** mériter une mention; **to be ~ a try** valoir la peine d'essayer; **to be ~ it** valoir la peine; **don't get upset, he's not ~ it** ne te fâche pas, il n'en vaut pas la peine; **the book isn't ~ reading** le livre ne vaut pas la peine d'être lu; **that suggestion is ~ considering** la suggestion mérite réflexion; **that's ~ knowing** cela est utile à savoir; **everyone ~ knowing had left town** tous ceux qui comptaient avaient quitté la ville; **what he doesn't know about farming isn't ~ knowing** il sait tout ce qu'on peut savoir sur le travail à la ferme; **those little pleasures that make life ~ living** ces petits plaisirs qui rendent la vie agréable

(Idioms) **for all one is ~** de toutes ses forces; **for what it's ~** pour ce que cela vaut; **to be ~ sb's while** valoir le coup; **if you come I'll make it ~ your while** si tu viens, tu ne le regretteras pas

worthily /'wɜːðɪlɪ/ *adv* dignement

worthless /'wɜːθlɪs/ *adj* sans valeur; **he's ~** c'est un bon à rien

worthwhile /wɜːθ.θ'waɪl/ *adj* [*discussion, undertaking, visit*] qui en vaut la peine; [*career, project*] intéressant; **to be ~ doing** valoir la peine de faire; **it's been well ~** cela en valait vraiment la peine

worthy /'wɜːðɪ/
A *n* notable *m*
B *adj* **1** (deserving) **to be ~ of sth** mériter qch, être digne de qch; **~ of note** digne d'intérêt; **to be ~ of doing** mériter d'être fait; **2** (admirable) [*cause*] noble; [*citizen, friend*] digne; **3** (appropriate) **~ of sth/sb** digne de qn/qch; **a speech ~ of the occasion** un discours digne des circonstances

would /wʊd, wəd/

> ⚠️ When *would* is used with a verb in English to form the conditional tense, *would* + *verb* is translated by the present conditional of the appropriate verb in French and *would have* + *verb* by the past conditional of the appropriate verb: *I would do it if I had time* = je le ferais si j'avais le temps; *I would have done it if I had had time* = je l'aurais fait si j'avais eu le temps; *he said he would fetch the car* = il a dit qu'il irait chercher la voiture.
> For more examples, particular usages and all other uses of *would* see the entry below.

modal aux (*aussi* **'d**; *nég* **wouldn't**) **1** (in sequence of past tenses, in reported speech) **she said she wouldn't come** elle a dit qu'elle ne viendrait pas; **we thought we ~ be late** nous avons pensé que nous serions en retard; **I was sure you'd like it** j'étais sûr que ça te plairait; **they promised that they'd come back** ils ont promis de revenir; **he thought she ~ have forgotten** il pensait qu'elle aurait oublié; **I wish he ~ shut the door!** il pourrait fermer la porte!; **I wish you'd be quiet!** tu ne pourrais pas te taire!; **2** (in conditional statements) **it ~ be wonderful if they came** ce serait merveilleux s'ils venaient; **if we'd left later we ~ have missed the train** si nous étions partis plus tard nous aurions raté le train; **we wouldn't be happy anywhere else** nous ne serions heureux nulle part ailleurs; **who ~ ever have believed it?** qui l'aurait cru?; **you wouldn't have thought it possible!** on n'aurait jamais cru que c'était possible!; **wouldn't it be nice if...** ce serait bien si...; **it cost far less than I ~ have expected** ça a coûté beaucoup moins cher que je n'aurais pensé; **3** (expressing willingness to act) **do you know anyone who ~ do it?** est-ce que tu connais quelqu'un qui le ferait?; **they couldn't find anyone who ~ take the job** ils n'arrivaient pas à trouver quelqu'un qui accepte le poste; **she just wouldn't listen** elle ne voulait rien entendre; **after that I wouldn't eat any canned food** après cela je ne voulais plus manger de conserves; **he wouldn't do a thing to help** il n'a rien voulu faire pour aider; **the police wouldn't give any further details** la police a refusé de donner plus de détails; **they asked me to leave but I wouldn't** ils m'ont demandé de partir mais j'ai refusé; **4** (expressing inability to function) **the door wouldn't close** la porte ne voulait pas se fermer; **5** (expressing desire, preference) **we ~ like to stay another night** nous aimerions rester une nuit de plus; **we'd really love to see you** nous

aimerions vraiment te voir; **I ~ much rather travel alone** je préférerais nettement voyager seul; **she ~ have preferred a puppy** elle aurait préféré un chiot; **I wouldn't mind another slice of cake** je prendrais bien un autre morceau de gâteau; **it's what he ~ have wanted** c'est ce qu'il aurait voulu; **6** (in polite requests or proposals) **~ you like something to eat?** voudriez-vous quelque chose à manger?; **~ you like some more tea?** voulez-vous encore du thé?; **~ you help me set the table?** est-ce que tu pourrais m'aider à mettre la table?; **switch off the radio, ~ you?** éteins la radio, tu veux bien?; **~ you like to go to a concert?** est-ce que tu aimerais aller à un concert?; **~ you give her the message?** est-ce que vous voulez bien lui transmettre le message?; **~ you mind not smoking please?** est-ce que ça vous ennuierait de ne pas fumer s'il vous plaît?; **7** (used to attenuate statements) **it ~ seem that he was right** il semblerait qu'il avait raison; **so it ~ seem** c'est ce qu'il semble; **you ~ think they'd be satisfied!** on aurait pu penser qu'ils seraient satisfaits!; **I wouldn't say that** je ne dirais pas ça; **I ~ have thought it was obvious** j'aurais pensé que c'était évident; **I wouldn't know** je ne pourrais pas vous le dire; **8** (when giving advice) **I wouldn't do that if I were you** je ne ferais pas ça à ta place; **I ~ check the timetable first** tu ferais bien de vérifier l'horaire d'abord; **I'd give her a ring now** tu devrais lui téléphoner maintenant; **wouldn't it be better to write?** est-ce que ce ne serait pas mieux d'écrire?; **9** (expressing exasperation) **'he denies it'—'well he ~, wouldn't he?'** 'il le nie'—'évidemment!'; **of course you ~ contradict him!** bien sûr il a fallu que tu le contredises!; **'she put her foot in it°'—'she ~!'** 'elle a mis les pieds dans le plat°'—'tu m'étonnes!'; **10** (expressing an assumption) **what time ~ that be?** c'était vers quelle heure?; **I suppose it ~ have been about 3 pm** je pense qu'il était à peu près 15 h 00; **let's see, that ~ be his youngest son** voyons, ça doit être son plus jeune fils; **it ~ have been about five years ago** ça devait être il y a environ cinq ans; **you'd never have guessed she was German** on n'aurait jamais cru qu'elle était allemande; **11** (indicating habitual event or behaviour in past: used to) **she ~ sit for hours at the window** elle passait des heures assise à la fenêtre

would-be /'wʊdbiː/ *adj* (desirous of being) **~ investors** des investisseurs en puissance; **~ intellectuals** *péj* des soi-disant intellectuels *pej*; (having intended to be) **the ~ thieves were arrested** les voleurs ont été arrêtés avant qu'ils aient pu passer à l'acte

wouldn't /'wʊd(ə)nt/ = would not

would've /'wʊdəv/ = would have

wound¹ /wuːnd/
A *n* **1** (injury) blessure *f*; **a ~ to** *ou* **in the head** une blessure à la tête; **to die from** *ou* **of one's ~s** succomber à ses blessures; **2** (cut, sore) plaie *f*; **3** *fig* blessure *f*; **it takes time for the ~s to heal** il faut longtemps pour que les plaies se cicatrisent
B *vtr* (all contexts) blesser

(Idioms) *fig* **to lick one's ~s** panser ses blessures; **to rub salt into the ~** remuer le couteau dans la plaie

wound² /waʊnd/ *prét, pp* ▸ **wind²** B, C

wounded /'wuːndɪd/
A *n* **the ~** (+ *v pl*) les blessés/-es *m/f*
B *adj* blessé; **~ in the arm** blessé au bras

wounding /'wuːndɪŋ/ *adj* blessant

wove /wəʊv/ *prét* ▸ **weave** B, C

woven /'wəʊvn/ *pp, pp adj* ▸ **weave** B, C

wow° /waʊ/
A *n* **1** (success) succès *m*; **2** Audio (distortion) pleurage *m*
B *excl* hou là!
C *vtr* (enthuse) emballer° [*person*]

WP *abrév* = **word processing**

WPC *n*: *abrév* = **woman police constable**

wpm (*abrév* = **words per minute**) mots/min

WRAC *n* Mil (*abrév* = **Women's Royal Army Corps**) *services féminins de l'armée britannique*

WRAF *n* (*abrév* = **Women's Royal Air Force**) *services féminins de l'armée de l'air britannique*

wrangle /'ræŋgl/
A *n* querelle *f*
B *vi* se quereller (**over, about** sur, à propos de)

wrangling /'ræŋglɪŋ/ *n* tractations *fpl* (**over** à propos de)

W

wrap /ræp/
A n **1** (shawl) châle m; (stole) étole f; (dressing-gown) peignoir m; **2** (packaging) emballage m; **3** Cin **it's a ~** c'est dans la boîte
B vtr (p prés etc **-pp-**) lit (in paper) emballer (**in** dans); (in blanket, garment) envelopper (**in** dans); **to ~ a book in paper** envelopper un livre dans du papier; **I ~ped a handkerchief around my finger** je me suis noué un mouchoir autour du doigt; **to ~ tape around a join** enrouler du ruban adhésif autour d'une jointure; **to be ~ped in** lit (for warmth, protection) être emmitouflé dans; (for disposal) être enveloppé dans; fig être enveloppé de [mystery]; **would you like it ~ped?** je vous fais un paquet?
C v refl (p prés etc **-pp-**) **to ~ oneself in sth** s'envelopper dans qch
D **-wrapped** combining form foil-/plastic-~ped emballé dans du papier d'aluminium/du plastique
(Idioms) **to keep sth/to be under ~s** garder qch/être secret; **to take the ~s off sth** dévoiler qch
(Phrasal verb)
■ **wrap up:** ▸ **~ up 1** (dress warmly) s'emmitoufler; **~ up well** ou **warm!** couvre-toi bien!; **2** ᵒGB (shut up) la fermer◌; **~ up!** ferme-la!◌; ▸ **~ up [sth], ~ [sth] up 1** lit faire [parcel]; envelopper [gift, purchase]; emballer [rubbish]; **it's cold, ~ the children up warm!** il fait froid, couvre bien les enfants!; **2** fig (terminate) conclure; **3** (settle) régler [project, event]; conclure [deal, negotiations]; s'assurer [title, victory]; **4** (involve) **to be ~ped up in** ne s'occuper que de [person, child]; être absorbé dans [activity, work]; être absorbé par [problem]; **they are completely ~ped up in each other** ils ne vivent que l'un pour l'autre; **he is ~ped up in himself** il est replié sur lui-même; **there is £50,000 ~ped up in the project** il y a 50 000 livres sterling d'investies dans le projet; **5** fig dissimuler [ideas] (**in** derrière)
wrap: **~-around** adj [window, windscreen] panoramique; [skirt] portefeuille; **~-around sunglasses** npl lunettes fpl de soleil enveloppantes
wrapper /'ræpə(r)/ n (of sweet, chocolate etc) papier m; (of package) emballage m; (of newspaper) bande f; **sweet ~** papier m de bonbon
wrapping /'ræpɪŋ/ n emballage m
wrapping paper n (brown) papier m d'emballage; (decorative) papier m cadeau
wreak /riːk/ vtr assouvir [revenge] (**on** sur); **to ~ havoc** ou **damage** infliger des dégâts; **to ~ havoc** ou **damage on sth** dévaster qch
wreath /riːθ/ n **1** (of flowers, leaves) couronne f; **to lay a ~** déposer une gerbe; **2** (of smoke) ruban m
wreathe /riːð/
A vtr (weave, fashion) lisser
B **wreathed** pp adj ~d in enveloppé de [mist, smoke]; **to be ~d in smiles** être tout sourire
wreck /rek/
A n **1** (car, plane) (crashed) épave f; (burnt out) carcasse f; **2** ᵒ(old car) tas m de ferraille◌; **3** (sunken ship) épave f; **4** (sinking, destruction) (of ship) naufrage m; fig **the ~ of sb's hopes/ dreams** le naufrage des espoirs/rêves de qn; **5** (person) épave f
B vtr **1** lit [explosion, fire, vandals, looters] dévaster; [person, driver, crash, impact] détruire; **2** fig ruiner [career, chances, future, health, life, marriage]; gâcher [holiday, weekend]; faire échouer [negotiations]
wreckage /'rekɪdʒ/ n **1** lit (of plane, car) épave f; (of building) décombres mpl; **2** fig naufrage m
wrecked /rekt/ adj **1** lit [car, plane] accidenté; [ship] naufragé; [building] démoli; **2** fig ruiné; **3** ᵒ(exhausted) claqué◌
wren /ren/ n Zool roitelet m
wrench /rentʃ/
A n **1** (tool) tourne-à-gauche m inv; **2** (movement) (of handle, lid) mouvement m brusque (tournant); **3** fig déchirement m
B vtr tourner [qch] brusquement [handle]; **to ~ one's ankle/ knee** se tordre la cheville/le genou; **to ~ sth from sb** arracher qch à qn; **to ~ sth away from** ou **off sth** arracher qch de qch; **to ~ a door open** ouvrir une porte d'un mouvement brusque
C vi **to ~ at sth** tirer sur qch
D v refl **to ~ oneself free** se dégager d'un mouvement brusque
(Idiom) **to throw a ~ in the works** US créer des difficultés

wrest /rest/ vtr (all contexts) arracher (**from sb** à qn)
wrestle /'resl/
A vtr **to ~ sb for sth** lutter contre qn pour qch; **to ~ sb to the ground** terrasser qn
B vi **1** Sport faire du catch; **2** (struggle) **to ~ with** se débattre avec [person, problem, homework, conscience]; se battre avec [controls, zip, suitcase]; lutter contre [temptation]
wrestler /'reslə(r)/ n **1** Sport catcheur/-euse m/f; **2** Hist lutteur m
wrestling /'reslɪŋ/ ▸ p. 881 n **1** Sport catch m; **2** Hist lutte f
wretch /retʃ/ n **1** (unlucky) miséreux/-euse m/f; **2** (evil) misérable mf also hum; (child) hum coquin/-e m/f
wretched /'retʃɪd/ adj **1** (miserable) [person] infortuné; [appearance, conditions] misérable; [weather] affreux/-euse; [accommodation] minable; **to feel ~** (ill) être à plat; (due to hangover) se sentir abruti; **to feel ~ about** être honteux/ -euse de; **what ~ luck!** quelle malchance!; **2** ᵒ(damned) fichu◌
wretchedly /'retʃɪdlɪ/ adv **1** (badly, pitifully) [treat] très mal; [clothed, furnished] misérablement; [paid, small] dérisoirement; **2** (unhappily) piteusement
wretchedness /'retʃɪdnɪs/ n **1** (unhappiness) détresse f; **2** (poverty) misère f
wriggle /'rɪgl/
A vtr **to ~ one's toes/fingers** remuer les orteils/doigts; **to ~ one's way out of sth** lit, fig se sortir de qch
B vi [person] s'agiter, gigoter; [snake, worm] se tortiller; **to ~ along the ground** ramper ou se tortillant; **to ~ under sth** se glisser sous qch; **to ~ free** arriver à se dégager
(Phrasal verbs)
■ **wriggle about, wriggle around** gen se tortiller; [fish] frétiller
■ **wriggle out** se dégager or se sortir en se tortillant; **to ~ out of sth** fig se défiler devant [task, duty]
wriggly /'rɪglɪ/ adj [snake, worm] frétillant; [person] remuant
wring /rɪŋ/
A n **to give sth a ~** essorer qch
B vtr (prét, pp **wrung**) **1** (also ~ **out**) (squeeze) (by twisting) tordre; (by pressure, centrifugal force) essorer; **2** fig (extract) arracher (**from, out of** à); **3** (twist) **to ~ sb's/sth's neck** lit, fig tordre le cou à qn/qch; **to ~ one's hands** se tordre les mains; fig se lamenter
C **wringing** adv ~**ing wet** trempé
(Phrasal verb)
■ **wring out:** ▸ **~ [sth] out, ~ out [sth]** tordre [cloth, clothes]; **to ~ the water out from one's clothes** essorer ses vêtements
wrinkle /'rɪŋkl/
A n (on skin) ride f; (in fabric) pli m; **to iron out the ~s** lit enlever les plis au fer à repasser; fig aplanir les difficultés
(Idiom) **he knows a ~ or two** il est loin d'être bête
B vtr **1** rider [skin]; **to ~ one's nose** faire la grimace (**at** à); **to ~ one's forehead** plisser le front; **2** froisser [fabric]
C vi [skin] se rider; [fabric] se froisser; [wallpaper] se gondoler; [rug, mat] faire des plis
wrinkled /'rɪŋkld/ adj **1** [face, skin] ridé; [brow] froncé; [apple] fripé; **2** [fabric, clothing] froissé; [stockings] qui font des plis
wrinkly◌ /'rɪŋklɪ/ adj = **wrinkled**
wrist /rɪst/ ▸ p. 698 n poignet m
(Idiom) **to get a slap on the ~** se faire taper sur les doigts
wrist: **~band** n (for tennis, on sleeve) poignet m; (on watch) bracelet m (de montre); **~ rest** n Comput repose-poignets m inv; **~watch** n montre-bracelet f
writ /rɪt/
A n Jur assignation f (**for** pour); **to issue** ou **serve a ~ against sb** assigner qn en justice
B vtr (prét, pp désuets du verbe **write**) fig **disappointment was ~ large across his face** la déception se lisait sur son visage
writable /'raɪtəbl/ adj Comput inscriptible
write /raɪt/ (prét **wrote**; pp **written**)
A vtr **1** (put down on paper) écrire [letter, novel]; composer [song, symphony]; rédiger [business letter, article, essay]; faire [cheque, prescription]; écrire [software, program]; **I wrote home** j'ai écrit à ma famille; **to ~ sth into a contract** inclure qch dans un contrat; **guilt was written all over her face** fig la

culpabilité se lisait sur son visage; **he had 'policeman' written all over him** fig ça crevait les yeux qu'il était policier; [2] US (compose a letter to) écrire à [*person*]

B vi [1] (form words, correspond) écrire; **to ~ in pencil** écrire au crayon; **this pen doesn't ~** ce stylo n'écrit pas; **I have nothing to ~ with** je n'ai rien pour écrire; [2] (compose professionally) écrire (**for** pour); **I ~ for a living** je suis écrivain de métier; **to ~ about** *ou* **on** traiter de

(Phrasal verbs)

■ **write away** écrire (**to** à); **to ~ away for sth** demander qch par écrit [*catalogue, details*]

■ **write back**: ▸ **~ back** répondre (**to** à); ▸ **~ back [sth]** écrire [*letter*]

■ **write down**: ▸ **~ [sth] down**, **~ down [sth]** [1] (note) noter [*details, name*]; mettre [qch] par écrit [*ideas, suggestions*]; [2] (record) consigner [qch] par écrit [*information*]; [3] Fin dévaluer [*stocks*]

■ **write in**: ▸ **~ in** écrire (**to sb** à qn; **to do** pour faire); **please ~ in with your suggestions** vous êtes invités à nous envoyer vos suggestions; **to ~ in to** écrire une lettre à; ▸ **~ [sb] in** US Pol inscrire le nom de [*candidate*]

■ **write off**: ▸ **~ off** écrire une lettre (**to** à); **to ~ off for** écrire pour demander; ▸ **~ [sth/sb] off** [1] (wreck) gen bousiller⊖ complètement [*car*]; [2] (in bookkeeping) passer [qch] par pertes et profits [*bad debt, loss*]; amortir [*capital*]; [3] (end) annuler [*debt, project*]; [4] (dismiss) enterrer⊖

■ **write out**: ▸ **~ [sth] out**, **~ out [sth]** [1] (put down on paper) écrire; [2] (copy) copier; ▸ **~ [sb] out** supprimer [*character*] (**of** de)

■ **write up**: ▸ **~ [sth] up**, **~ up [sth]** [1] (produce in report form) rédiger; [2] Fin réévaluer [*asset*]

write-in *n* US Pol vote *m* par correspondance

write-off /'raɪtɒf/ *n* [1] US (in taxation) somme *f* déductible de la déclaration des revenus; [2] (wreck) épave *f*

write once read many disk *n* Comput disque *m* inscriptible une seule fois

writer /'raɪtə(r)/ ▸ p. 1181 *n* (professional) écrivain *m*; (amateur) auteur *m*; **sports ~** journaliste *mf* spécialisé/-e en sport; **he's a neat ~** il écrit avec soin

writer's block *n* angoisse *f* de la page blanche

write-up /'raɪtʌp/ *n* [1] (review) critique *f*; [2] (account) rapport *m* (**of** sur); [3] US (in bookkeeping) fausse déclaration *f* (dans un bilan)

(Idiom) **the ~ is on the wall** la catastrophe est imminente

writing /'raɪtɪŋ/ *n* [1] ¢ (activity) **~ is her life** écrire, c'est sa vie; [2] (handwriting) écriture *f*; **his ~ is poor/good** il écrit mal/bien; [3] (words and letters) écriture *f*; **to put sth in ~** mettre qch par écrit; [4] (literature) littérature *f*; **American ~** littérature américaine; **the ~s of Colette** l'œuvre *m* de Colette; **it was an excellent piece of ~** c'était très bien écrit

(Idiom) **the ~ case** *n* nécessaire *m* de correspondance; **~ desk** *n* secrétaire *m*; **~ pad** *n* bloc *m* de papier à lettres; **~ paper** *n* papier *m* à lettres

written /'rɪtn/

A *pp* ▸ **write**

B *adj* écrit; **he failed the ~ paper** il a échoué à l'écrit; **~ evidence/proof** Admin pièces *fpl* justificatives; Jur preuves *fpl* écrites; **the ~ word** l'écriture *f*

wrong /rɒŋ, US rɔːŋ/

A *n* [1] ¢ (evil) mal *m*; **in their eyes, she could do no ~** pour eux, tout ce qu'elle faisait était parfait; [2] (injustice) tort *m*; **to right a ~** réparer un tort; **the rights and ~s of the matter** les aspects moraux de la question; [3] Jur délit *m*

B *adj* [1] (incorrect) (ill-chosen) mauvais; (containing errors) erroné; **it's the ~ glue for the purpose** ce n'est pas la colle qu'il faut; **to prove to be ~** se révéler faux; **to go the ~ way** se tromper de chemin; **to take the ~ road** se tromper de route; **to take the ~ turning** GB *ou* **turn** ne pas tourner au

bon endroit; **to give the ~ answer** ne pas donner la bonne réponse; **everything I do is ~** je ne fais jamais rien de bien; **it was the ~ thing to say** c'était la chose à ne pas dire; **to say the ~ thing** faire une gaffe; **don't get the ~ idea** ne te méprends pas; **don't get me ~, I'm not saying that he's stupid but…** ne te méprends pas, je ne dis pas qu'il est idiot mais…; **don't get me ~, I'm not criticizing you** ne le prends pas mal, je ne te critique pas; **you've got the ~ number** vous faites erreur; [2] (reprehensible) **it is ~ to do** c'est mal de faire; **she hasn't done anything ~** elle n'a rien fait de mal; **it was ~ of me to do** je n'aurais pas dû faire; **it is ~ for sb to do** ce n'est pas juste que qn fasse; **it is ~ that** c'est injuste que; **there's nothing ~ with** il n'y a pas de mal à qch; **what's ~ with trying?** quel mal y a-t-il à essayer?; **(so) what's ~ with that?** où est le mal?; [3] (mistaken) **to be ~** [*person*] avoir tort, se tromper; **that's where you're ~** c'est là que tu te trompes; **how ~ can you be!** comme on peut se tromper!; **I might be ~** il se peut que je me trompe; **to be ~ about** se tromper sur; **she was ~ about him** elle s'est trompée sur son compte; **am I ~ in thinking that…?** ai-je tort de penser que…?; **to prove sb ~** donner tort à qn; [4] (not as it should be) **there is something (badly) ~** il y a quelque chose qui ne va pas (du tout); **there's something ~ with this computer** il y a un problème avec cet ordinateur; **what's ~ with your arm?** qu'est-ce que tu as au bras?; **what's ~ with you?** (to person suffering) qu'est-ce que tu as?; (to person behaving oddly) qu'est-ce qui t'arrive? **nothing ~ is there?** tout va bien?

C *adv* **to get sth ~** se tromper de qch [*date, time, details*]; se tromper dans qch [*calculations*]; **I think you've got it ~** je pense que tu te trompes; **to go ~** [*person*] se tromper; [*machine*] ne plus marcher; [*plan*] ne pas marcher; **you won't go far ~** vous ne risquez pas de faire fausse route si…; **you can't go ~** (in choice of route) tu ne peux pas te tromper; (are bound to succeed) tu peux être tranquille

D *vtr* (treat unjustly) faire du tort à [*person, family*]

(Idioms) **to be in the ~** être dans mon/ton etc tort; **to be ~ in the head**⊖ être dérangé⊖; **to get into the ~ hands** tomber dans de mauvaises mains; **to get on the ~ side of sb** se faire mal voir de qn; **to go down the ~ way** [*food, drink*] passer de travers; **two ~s don't make a right** on ne répare pas une injustice avec une autre; **you've got me all ~** vous ne m'avez pas du tout compris

wrong: **~doer** *n* malfaiteur *m*; **~doing** *n* méfait *m*; **~foot** *vtr* Sport prendre [qn] à contre-pied; fig prendre [qn] au dépourvu

wrongful /'rɒŋfl, US 'rɔːŋ-/ *adj* Jur arbitraire

wrongfully /'rɒŋfəlɪ, US 'rɔːŋ-/ *adv* Jur injustement

wrong-headed /ˌrɒŋ'hedɪd, US ˌrɔːŋ-/ *adj* [1] (stubborn) buté; [2] (perverse) [*policy, decision*] aveugle

wrongly /'rɒŋlɪ, US 'rɔː-/ *adv* mal; **he concluded, ~, that…** il a conclu, à tort, que…; **rightly or ~** à tort ou à raison

wrote /rəʊt/ *prét* ▸ **write**

wrought /rɔːt/

A *prét, pp* **it ~ havoc** *ou* **destruction** cela a fait des ravages; **the changes ~ by sth** les changements apportés par qch

B *adj* [1] [*silver, gold*] travaillé; [2] **finely/carefully ~** [*plot, essay*] finement/soigneusement travaillé

wrought: **~ iron** *n* fer *m* forgé; **~ iron work** *n* ferronnerie *f*

wrung /rʌŋ/ *prét, pp* ▸ **wring B**

wry /raɪ/ *adj* [1] (ironic) narquois; **to have a ~ sense of humour** être pince-sans-rire; [2] (disgusted) **to make a ~ face** faire une drôle de tête

wt *n*: *abrév écrite* = **weight**

WV US Post *abrév écrite* = **West Virginia**

WWI *n*: *abrév écrite* = **World War One**

WWII *n*: *abrév écrite* = **World War Two**

WY US Post *abrév écrite* = **Wyoming**

WYSIWYG /'wɪzɪwɪg/ Comput (*abrév* = **what you see is what you get**) tel écran-tel écrit, tel-tel *inv*

x, **X** /eks/ n ① (letter) x, X m; ② x Math x m; **for x people** pour x personnes; ③ **X** (anonymous person, place) X m; **Ms X** Mme X; **X marks the spot** l'endroit est marqué d'une croix; ④ x (at end of letter) **x x x** grosses bises; ⑤ **X** (as signature) croix f

X certificate n GB **the film was given an** ~ le film a été interdit aux moins de 18 ans

xenophobia /ˌzenəˈfəʊbɪə/ n xénophobie f

xerox, **Xerox**® /ˈzɪərɒks/

A n ① (machine) photocopieuse f; ② (process) (procédé de) photocopie f; ③ (copy) (photo)copie f

B vtr photocopier

Xmas n: abrév écrite = **Christmas**

X rated adj [film, video] interdit aux moins de 18 ans

X-ray /ˈeksreɪ/

A n ① (ray) rayon m X; ② (photo) radiographie f, radio° f; ③ (process) radiographie f, radioscopie f; **to have an** ~ se faire radiographier; **to give sb an** ~ faire une radiographie à qn

B vtr radiographier

X-ray: ~ **machine** n générateur m à rayons X; ~ **unit** n service m de radiologie

x

Yy

y, Y /waɪ/ n ⒈ (lettre) y, Y m; ⒉ **y** Math y m
yacht /jɒt/
A n yacht m
B noun modifier [crew] de yacht; [race] de yachts; **~ club** yacht-club m
C vi faire du yachting
yachting /'jɒtɪŋ/ ▸ p. 881
A n yachting m
B noun modifier [clothes] de yachtman; [enthusiast] du yachting; [course] de yachting; [holiday] en yacht
yahoo /jə'huː/
A n abruti/-e○ m/f
B excl hourra!
yak /jæk/ n Zool yack m
Yale® /jeɪl/ n (also **Yale lock**) serrure f de sûreté
yam /jæm/ n ⒈ (tropical) igname f; ⒉ US (sweet potato) patate f douce
yank /jæŋk/
A n coup m sec
B vtr tirer [person, rope]
⟨Phrasal verb⟩
■ **yank off:** ▸ **~ [sth] off, ~ off [sth]** arracher
Yank○ /jæŋk/ n injur yankee mf offensive
Yankee /'jæŋkɪ/ n ⒈ US (inhabitant of New England) habitant/-e m/f de la Nouvelle Angleterre; (of North) habitant/-e m/f du Nord (des États-Unis); ⒉ (soldier) Nordiste m; ⒊ (American) injur yankee m offensive
yap /jæp/ vi [dog] japper (**at** après)
yapping /'jæpɪŋ/
A n **C** jappements mpl
B adj [dog] jappeur/-euse
yard /jɑːd/
A n ⒈ ▸ p. 977 yard m (= 0.9144 m); ⒉ fig **she writes poetry by the ~** elle écrit des pages et des pages de poésie; ⒊ (of house, farm, prison, hospital) cour f; ⒋ US (garden) jardin m; ⒌ (for storage) dépôt m; (for construction) chantier m
B Yard pr n GB **the ~** police judiciaire britannique
yardstick /'jɑːdstɪk/ n fig point m de référence
yarn /jɑːn/ n ⒈ (wool) fil m (à tricoter); ⒉ (tale) histoire f
yashmak /'jæʃmæk/ n voile m islamique
yawn /jɔːn/
A n lit bâillement m; **to give a ~** bâiller; fig (bore) **what a ~**○! que c'est barbant○!
B vi ⒈ [person] bâiller; ⒉ fig [abyss, chasm] béer
yawning /'jɔːnɪŋ/
A n bâillements mpl
B adj [abyss] béant; fig **the ~ gap between the two countries** l'abîme qui sépare les deux pays
yd abrév écrite = **yard A 1**
yea /jeɪ/
A ‡particle oui m
B n Pol **the ~s and the nays** les oui et les non
yeah○ /jeə/ particle ouais○, oui; **oh ~?** vraiment?
year /jɪə(r), jɜː(r)/ ▸ p. 1267
A n ⒈ (period of time) an m, année f; **two ~s ago** il y a deux ans; **all (the) ~ round** toute l'année; **over the ~s** au cours des ans ou années; **the ~ before last** il y a deux ans; **~ by ~** d'année en année; **~ in ~ out** tous les ans; **for the first time in ~s** pour la première fois depuis des années; **it was a ~ ago last October that I heard the news** il y a eu un an en octobre que j'ai appris la nouvelle; **it will be four ~s in July since he died** cela fera quatre ans en juillet

qu'il est mort; **it's a ~ since I heard from him** je n'ai plus de ses nouvelles depuis un an; **in all my ~s as a journalist** dans toute ma carrière de journaliste; **to earn £30,000 a ~** gagner 30 000 livres sterling par an; ⒉ (indicating age) **to be 19 ~s old** ou **19 ~s of age** avoir 19 ans; **a two-~-old child** un enfant de deux ans; ⒊ Sch, Univ année f; ⒋ GB Sch (pupil) **first/second-~** ≈ élève mf de sixième/cinquième
B years npl ⒈ (age) âge m; **from her earliest ~s** dès son plus jeune âge; ⒉ ○(a long time) **but that would take ~s!** ça prendrait une éternité!; **it's ~s since we last met!** ça fait un siècle qu'on ne s'est pas vus!; **this job has put ~s on me!** ce travail m'a vieilli de dix ans!
yearbook /'jɪəbʊk, 'jɜː-/ n ⒈ (directory) annuaire m; ⒉ US Sch, Univ album m de promotion
yearly /'jɪəlɪ, 'jɜː-/
A adj [visit, income] annuel/-elle
B adv annuellement
yearn /jɜːn/ vi ⒈ (desire) **to ~ for** désirer (avoir) [child, food]; aspirer à [freedom]; attendre [era, event]; **to ~ to do** avoir très envie de faire; ⒉ (miss) **she ~s for her son** son fils lui manque terriblement
yearning /'jɜːnɪŋ/
A n désir m ardent (**for** de)
B yearnings npl aspirations fpl
year out n année f de coupure (avant d'entrer à l'université)
year-round adj [supply, source] permanent; **for ~ use** pour être utilisé toute l'année
yeast /jiːst/ n levure f
yell /jel/
A n (shout) cri m; (of rage, pain) hurlement m
B vtr crier [warning]; (louder) hurler [insults]
C vi (shout) crier; **to ~ at sb** crier après qn
yelling /'jelɪŋ/
A n cris mpl
B adj [mob, crowd] vociférant
yellow /'jeləʊ/ ▸ p. 752
A n jaune m
B adj ⒈ (in colour) jaune; **to go** ou **turn ~** jaunir; **the lights are on ~** les feux sont à l'orange; ⒉ ○(cowardly) trouillard○
C vtr, vi jaunir
yellow: ~-belly○ n trouillard/-e○ m/f; **~ card** n Sport carton m jaune
yellowish /'jeləʊɪʃ/ ▸ p. 752 adj tirant sur le jaune, jaunâtre pej
yellow: ~ metal n (brass) cuivre m jaune; (gold) métal m jaune; **~ pages** npl pages fpl jaunes
yellowy /'jeləʊɪ/ ▸ p. 752 adj tirant sur le jaune, jaunâtre pej
yelp /jelp/
A n (of person) glapissement m; (of animal) (of pain, fear) glapissement m; (of happiness) jappement m
B vi [person] glapir (**with** de); [animal] (with pain, fear) glapir; (with happiness) japper
Yemen /'jemən/ ▸ p. 774 pr n Yémen m; **North/South ~** Hist Yémen m du Nord/du Sud
yen /jen/ ▸ p. 782 n ⒈ Fin yen m; ⒉ ○(craving) **to have a ~ for sth/to do** avoir grande envie de qch/de faire
yeoman /'jəʊmən/ n (pl **-men**) ⒈ (also **~ farmer**) GB Hist franc tenancier m; ⒉ GB Mil Hist cavalier m (volontaire); **~ of the guard** membre m de la garde royale

y

yep○ /jep/, **yup**○ /jʌp/ *particle* US ouais○, oui
yes /jes/

> ⚠ *Yes* is translated by *oui*, except when used in
> reply to a negative question when the translation
> is *si* or, more emphatically, *si, si* or *mais si*: *'did you*
> *see him?'–'yes (I did)'* = 'est-ce que tu l'as vu?'–'oui
> (je l'ai vu)'; *'you're not hungry, are you?'–'yes I am'* =
> 'tu n'as pas faim?'–'si (j'ai faim)'
> Note that there are no direct equivalents in
> French for tag questions and short replies such as *yes I*
> *did, yes I am.*
> For some suggestions on how to translate these,
> see the notes at **do** and **be**.

particle, n oui; (in reply to negative question) si; **to say** ~ dire oui;
the ~**es and the nos** les oui et les non

yes-man○ *n* (*pl* **-men**) *péj* lèche-bottes *m inv*

yesterday /'jestədeɪ, -dɪ/ ▸ **p. 788, p. 1322**

Ⓐ *n* ① lit hier *m*; ~ **was a sad day for all of us** la journée
d'hier a été triste pour nous tous; ~ **was the fifth of April**
hier nous étions le cinq avril; **the day before** ~ avant-
hier; ② *fig* (the past) ~**'s fashions** la mode d'hier; ~**'s men**
péj hommes *mpl* du passé; **all our** ~**s** tout notre passé

Ⓑ *adv* ① lit hier; **I saw her only** ~ je l'ai vue pas plus tard
qu'hier; **all day** ~ toute la journée d'hier; **it was** ~ **week**
ou **a week** ~ cela fait une semaine hier; **early/late** ~ tôt/
tard dans la journée d'hier; **only** ~ **he was saying to me**...
hier encore il me disait...; ② *fig* (in the past) hier, autrefois

yesterday: ~ **afternoon** *n, adv* hier après-midi;
~ **evening** *n, adv* hier soir; ~ **morning** *n, adv* hier
matin

yet /jet/

Ⓐ *conj* (nevertheless) pourtant

Ⓑ *adv* ① (up till now, so far: with negatives) encore, jusqu'à présent;
(in questions) déjà; (with superlatives) jusqu'ici; **it's not ready** ~,
it's not ~ **ready** ce n'est pas encore prêt; **has he arrived**
~? est-il (déjà) arrivé?; **not** ~ pas encore, pas pour l'instant; **this is his best/worst** ~ c'est ce qu'il a fait de
mieux/de pire jusqu'ici; **it's the best** ~ jusqu'ici, c'est le
mieux; ② (*also* **just** ~) (now) tout de suite, encore; **don't**
start (just) ~ ne commence pas tout de suite; ③ (still)
encore; **they may** ~ **come** ils pourraient encore arriver;
he'll finish it ~ il va le finir; **the news has** ~ **to reach them**
il faut encore que la nouvelle leur parvienne; **the as**
~ **unfinished building** le bâtiment encore inachevé; **there**
is a year to go ~ **before he retires** il reste encore un an
avant qu'il parte en retraite; **he won't come for hours** ~ il
ne viendra pas avant quelques heures; ④ (even, still: with
comparatives etc) encore; ~ **more cars** encore plus de voitures; ~ **louder** encore plus fort; ~ **another attack** encore
une autre attaque; ~ **again** encore une fois

yew /ju:/ *n* ① (*also* ~ **tree**) if *m*; ② (wood) bois *m* d'if

Y-fronts *npl* GB slip *m* ouvert

YHA GB (*abrév* = **Youth Hostels Association**) association
f des auberges de jeunesse

yield /ji:ld/

Ⓐ *n* gen, Fin rendement *m*; **the annual milk** ~ la production
laitière annuelle

Ⓑ *vtr* ① gen, Agric produire; ② Fin rapporter; ③ (provide)
donner, fournir [*information, result, meaning*]; produire
[*clue*]; livrer [*secret*]; ④ (surrender) céder (**to** à); **to** ~ **ground**
to Mil, fig céder du terrain à

you

In English *you* is used to address everybody, whereas
French has two forms: *tu* and *vous*. The usual word to use
when you are speaking to anyone you do not know very
well is *vous*. This is sometimes called the *polite form* and
is used for the subject, object, indirect object and
emphatic pronoun:

would you like some coffee?
= voulez-vous du café?

can I help you?
= est-ce que je peux vous aider?

what can I do for you?
= qu'est-ce que je peux faire pour vous?

The more informal pronoun *tu* is used between close
friends and family members, within groups of children
and young people, by adults when talking to children and
always when talking to animals; *tu* is the subject form,
the direct and indirect object form is *te* (*t'* before a vowel)
and the form for emphatic use or use after a preposition
is *toi*:

would you like some coffee?
= veux-tu du café?

can I help you?
= est-ce que je peux t'aider?

there's a letter for you
= il y a une lettre pour toi

As a general rule, when talking to a French person use
vous, wait to see how they address you and follow suit.
It is safer to wait for the French person to suggest using
tu. The suggestion will usually be phrased as *on se*
tutoie? or *on peut se tutoyer?*

Note that *tu* is only a singular pronoun and *vous* is the
plural form of *tu*.

Remember that in French the object and indirect object
pronouns are always placed before the verb:

she knows you
= elle vous connaît *or* elle te connaît

In compound tenses like the present perfect and the past
perfect, the past participle agrees in number and gender
with the direct object:

I saw you on Saturday
(to one male: polite form)
= je vous ai vu samedi
(to one female: polite form)
= je vous ai vue samedi
(to one male: informal form)
= je t'ai vu samedi
(to one female: informal form)
= je t'ai vue samedi
(to two or more people, male or mixed)
= je vous ai vus samedi
(to two or more females)
= je vous ai vues samedi

When *you* is used impersonally as the more informal form
of *one*, it is translated by *on* for the subject form and by
vous or *te* for the object form, depending on whether the
comment is being made amongst friends or in a more
formal context:

you can do as you like here
= on peut faire ce qu'on veut ici

these mushrooms can make you ill
= ces champignons peuvent vous rendre malade
or ces champignons peuvent te rendre malade

you could easily lose your bag here
= on pourrait facilement perdre son sac ici

Note that *your* used with *on* is translated by *son/sa/ses*
according to the gender and number of the noun that
follows.

For verb forms with *vous*, *tu* and *on* see the French verb
tables.

For particular usages see the entry **you.**

y

C vi ①︎ *f* (give in) (to person, temptation, pressure, threats) céder (**to** à); (to army, arguments) se rendre (**to** à); **to ~ to force** céder devant la force; **to ~ to persuasion** se laisser persuader; ②︎ (under weight, pressure) céder; ③︎ (be superseded) **to ~ to** [*technology*] céder le pas à; [*land, countryside*] céder la place à; ④︎ (be productive) **to ~ well/poorly** avoir un bon/mauvais rendement; ⑤︎ US Aut céder le passage (**to** à)

⌜Phrasal verb⌝

■ **yield up** livrer [*secret, treasure*]

yielding /ˈjiːldɪŋ/ *adj* [*person*] (accommodating) accommodant; (submissive) soumis

YMCA (*abrév* = **Young Men's Christian Association**) ≈ Union *f* Chrétienne des Jeunes Gens

yodel /ˈjəʊdl/ *vi* (*p prés etc* **-ll-**) jodler, iodler

yoghurt /ˈjɒɡət, US ˈjəʊɡərt/ *n* yaourt *m*, yoghourt *m*

yoke /jəʊk/
A *n* ①︎ lit (for oxen) joug *m*; (for person) palanche *f*; fig joug *m*; **to throw off the ~** briser le joug; ②︎ (of garment) empiècement *m*
B *vtr* lit (*also* **~ up**) atteler; fig joindre

yokel /ˈjəʊkl/ *n* pej péquenaud/-e○ *m/f*, plouc○ *mf*

yolk /jəʊk/ *n* jaune *m* (d'œuf)

yonks○ /jɒŋks/ *npl* GB **I haven't seen him for ~** ça fait une éternité que je ne l'ai pas vu

yore /jɔː(r)/ *n* littér **in days of ~** jadis

you /juː, jʊ/ *pron* ①︎ (addressing sb) **I saw ~ on Saturday** (one person) (polite) je vous ai vu samedi; (informal) je t'ai vu samedi; (more than one person) je vous ai vus samedi; **you would never do that** (polite) vous, vous ne feriez jamais cela; (informal) toi, tu ne ferais jamais ça; **there's a manager for ~**○! iron ça c'est un patron!; **~ English** vous autres Anglais; **~ idiot**○! espèce d'imbécile○!; **~ two can stay** vous deux vous pouvez rester; **do ~ people smoke?** vous fumez?; ②︎ (as indefinite pronoun) (subject) on; (object, indirect object) vous, te; **~ never know!** on ne sait jamais!; **they say sweets give ~ spots** on dit que les bonbons donnent des boutons

you'd /juːd/ = **you had**, **you would**

you: **~-know-what**○ *pron* vous-savez-quoi, tu-sais-quoi; **~-know-who**○ *pron* qui-vous-savez, qui-tu-sais

you'll /juːl/ = **you will**

young /jʌŋ/
A *n* ①︎ (young people) **the ~** les jeunes *mpl*, la jeunesse *f*; **for ~ and old** (alike) pour les jeunes comme pour les vieux; ②︎ (animal's offspring) petits *mpl*
B *adj* jeune; **to be ~ at heart** avoir l'esprit jeune; **she is ten years ~er than him** elle a dix ans de moins que lui; **I feel ten years ~er** j'ai l'impression d'avoir rajeuni de dix ans; **in my ~ days** quand j'étais jeune; **you're only ~ once!** on n'est jeune qu'une fois; **children as ~ as five years old worked** des enfants dont certains n'avaient que cinq ans travaillaient; **the night is ~** la nuit ne fait que commencer; **Mr Brown the ~er** M. Brown le jeune; (Mr Brown's son) M. Brown fils; **~ lady** jeune femme *f*; **~ people** jeunes gens *mpl*; **~ person** jeune *m*; **the ~er generation** la jeune génération; **her ~er brother** son frère cadet; **the two ~er children** les deux cadets; **I'm not as ~ as I used to be** je n'ai plus 20 ans; **we're not getting any ~er** nous ne rajeunissons pas

young blood *n* sang *m* neuf

youngish /ˈjʌnɪʃ/ *adj* assez jeune

young-looking *adj* **to be ~** faire (très) jeune

young offender *n* délinquant/-e *m/f*

youngster /ˈjʌnstə(r)/ *n* ①︎ (young person) jeune *m*; ②︎ (child) enfant *mf*

your /jɔː(r), jʊə(r)/ *det* votre/vos; (more informally) ton/ta/tes; **you should always look after ~ skin** il faut prendre soin de sa peau

you're /jʊə(r), jɔː(r)/ = **you are**

yours /jɔːz, US jʊərz/

---

your

For a full note on the use of the *vous* and *tu* forms in French, see the entry **you**.

In French, determiners agree in gender and number with the noun they qualify. So *your*, when addressing one person, is translated by *votre*, or more familiarly *ton*, + masculine singular noun (*votre chien* or *ton chien*), by *votre* or *ta* + feminine singular noun (*votre maison* or *ta maison*) and by *vos* or *tes* + plural noun (*vos enfants* or *tes enfants*). Note that *ton* is used with a feminine noun beginning with a vowel or mute 'h' (*ton adresse*).

When addressing more than one person, the translation is *votre* + singular noun and *vos* + plural noun. When *your* is stressed, *à vous* or *à toi* is added after the noun:

your house
= votre maison à vous

When used impersonally to mean *one's*, *your* is translated by *son*, *sa* or *ses* when *you* is translated by *on*:

you buy your tickets at the door
= on prend ses billets à l'entrée

The translation after an impersonal verb in French is *son*, *sa*, *ses*:

you have to buy your tickets at the door
= il faut prendre ses billets à l'entrée

Note, however, the following:

sweets are bad for your teeth
= les bonbons sont mauvais pour les dents

your average student
= l'étudiant moyen

For *your* used with parts of the body ▸ **p. 698**.

⚠️ For a full note on the use of the *vous* and *tu* forms in French, see the entry **you**.
In French, possessive pronouns reflect the gender and number of the noun they are standing for. When *yours* is referring to only one person it is translated by *le vôtre*, *la vôtre*, *les vôtres* or, more familiarly, *le tien*, *la tienne*, *les tiens*, *les tiennes*. When *yours* is referring to more than one person it is translated by *le vôtre*, *la vôtre*, *les vôtres*.
For examples and particular usages see the entry below.

pron **my car is red but ~ is blue** ma voiture est rouge mais la vôtre *or* la tienne est bleue; **which house is ~?** votre *or* ta maison c'est laquelle?; **he's a colleague of ~** c'est un de vos *or* tes collègues; **it's not ~ to give away** vous n'aviez pas à vous *or* à toi; **the money wasn't ~ to give away** vous n'aviez pas à donner cet argent; **~ was not an easy task** votre tâche n'était pas facile; **I'm fed up**○ **with that dog of ~!** j'en ai marre de ton sale chien○!

yourself /jɔːˈself, US jʊərˈself/

⚠️ For a full note on the use of the *vous* and *tu* forms in French, see the entry **you**.
When used as a reflexive pronoun, direct and indirect, *yourself* is translated by *vous* or familiarly *te* or *t'* before a vowel: **you've hurt yourself** = vous vous êtes fait mal *or* tu t'es fait mal.
In imperatives, the translation is *vous* or *toi*: **help yourself** = servez-vous *or* sers-toi.
When used in emphasis the translation is *vous-même* or *toi-même*: **you yourself don't know** = vous ne savez pas vous-même *or* tu ne sais pas toi-même.
After a preposition the translation is *vous* or *vous-même* or *toi* or *toi-même*: **you can be proud of yourself** = vous pouvez être fier de vous *or* vous-même, tu peux être fier de toi *or* toi-même.

pron ①︎ (reflexive) vous, te, (*before vowel*) t'; **have you hurt ~?** est-ce que tu t'es fait mal?; ②︎ (in imperatives) vous, toi; ③︎ (emphatic) vous-même, toi-même; ④︎ (after prep) vous,

y

vous-même, toi, toi-même; ⑤ (expressions) **(all) by** ∼ tout seul/toute seule; **you're not** ∼ **today** tu n'as pas l'air dans ton assiette aujourd'hui

yourselves /jə'selvz/

> ⚠️ When used as a reflexive pronoun, direct and indirect, *yourselves* is translated by *vous*: *help yourselves* = servez-vous.
> When used as an emphatic, the translation is *vous-mêmes*: *do it yourselves* = faites-le vous-mêmes.
> After a preposition the translation is *vous* or *vous-mêmes*: *did you buy it for yourselves?* = est-ce que vous l'avez acheté pour vous *or* pour vous-mêmes?

pron ① (reflexive) vous; ② (emphatic) vous-mêmes; ③ (after prep) vous, vous-mêmes; **all by** ∼ tous seuls/toutes seules

youth /ju:θ/

A *n* (*pl* ∼**s** /ju:ðz/) ① (young man) jeune homme *m*; **a gang of** ∼**s** péj une bande de jeunes gens; ② (being young) jeunesse *f*; **despite his** ∼ malgré son jeune âge; ③ (young people) jeunes *mpl*

B *noun modifier* [*club*] de jeunes; [*TV, magazine*] pour les jeunes *or* la jeunesse; [*culture*] des jeunes

youthful /'ju:θfl/ *adj* ① (young) jeune; ② (typical of youth) de la jeunesse; **his** ∼ **looks** *ou* **appearance** son air jeune;

she's very ∼ **for 65**, **she's a very** ∼ **65** elle fait très jeune pour ses 65 ans

youth: ∼ **hostel** *n* auberge *f* de jeunesse; ∼ **hostelling** *n* randonnée *f* avec logement en auberges de jeunesse; ∼ **leader** ▸ p. 1181 *n* animateur/-trice *m/f* de groupe de jeunes; ∼ **work** *n* travail *m* social auprès des jeunes; ∼ **worker** ▸ p. 1181 *n* éducateur/-trice *m/f*

you've /ju:v/ = **you have**

yo-yo ® /'jəʊjəʊ/

A *n* ① gen yo-yo® *m*; ② °US péj (fool) abruti/-e° *m/f*

B °*vi* [*prices, inflation*] fluctuer

yr *abrév écrite* = **year**

Yugoslavia /ˌju:gəʊ'slɑːvɪə/ ▸ p. 774 *pr n* Yougoslavie *f*

Yule log /'ju:l lɒg/ *n* bûche *f* de Noël

yuppie /'jʌpɪ/ *n* péj jeune cadre *m* dynamique, yuppie *m* péj

yuppie flu ▸ p. 933 *n* péj syndrome *m* de la fatigue chronique

YWCA (*abrév* = **Young Women's Christian Association**) ≈ Union *f* Chrétienne des Jeunes Femmes

y

Zz

z, Z /zed, US zi:/ n z, Z m

zany /'zeɪnɪ/ adj loufoque○

zap○ /zæp/
A n (energy) tonus m
B vtr (p prés etc **-pp-**) ⓵ (destroy) détruire [town]; tuer [person, animal]; ⓶ (fire at) tirer sur [person]; ⓷ Comput (delete) supprimer
C vi (p prés etc **-pp-**) **to ~ into town** faire un saut○ en ville; **to ~ from channel to channel** zapper○

zapper /'zæpə(r)/ n télécommande f

zeal /zi:l/ n ⓵ (fanaticism) gen zèle m; (religious) ferveur f; ⓶ (enthusiasm) ardeur f, zèle m

zealot /'zelət/ n gen, pej fanatique mf

zealous /'zeləs/ adj [supporter] zélé; [determination] acharné; **to be ~ to do** avoir très envie de faire

zebra /'zebrə, 'zi:-/ n zèbre m

zebra crossing n GB passage m pour piétons

zero /'zɪərəʊ/ ▸ p. 1044
A n gen, Math, Meteorol zéro m
B noun modifier [altitude, growth, inflation] zéro inv; [confidence, interest, development] nul/nulle
(Phrasal verb)
 ■ **zero in** Mil viser; **to ~ in on sth** Mil viser [target]; fig (pinpoint) cerner [problem]; se rabattre sur [option]; foncer droit sur [person]; repérer [place]
zero: **~ gravity** n apesanteur f; **~ hour** n Mil, fig heure f H; **~-rated** adj GB exempté de TVA; **~ tolerance** n tolérance f zéro

zest /zest/ n ⓵ (enthusiasm) entrain m; ⓶ (piquancy) piquant m; ⓷ (of fruit) zeste m

zigzag /'zɪgzæg/
A n zigzag m
B vi (p prés etc **-gg-**) [person, road] zigzaguer; [river] serpenter; **to ~ up** monter en zigzag

zilch○ /zɪltʃ/ n que dalle❶

Zimbabwe /zɪm'bɑ:bwɪ, -weɪ/ ▸ p. 774 pr n Zimbabwe m

zimmer® /'zɪmə(r)/ n GB déambulateur m

zinc /zɪŋk/ n zinc m

zinc: **~ ointment** n pommade f à l'oxyde de zinc; **~ oxide** n oxyde m de zinc

zing○ /zɪŋ/
A n ⓵ (sound) sifflement m; ⓶ (energy) entrain m
B vtr US fig (criticize) démolir○ [person]
C vi siffler
(Phrasal verb)
 ■ **zing along**○ US [car] filer○ à toute allure

Zionism /'zaɪənɪzəm/ n sionisme m

zip /zɪp/
A n ⓵ fermeture f à glissière, fermeture f éclair®; **to do up/undo a ~** fermer/ouvrir une fermeture à glissière; ⓶ ○(energy) tonus m; ⓷ (sound) sifflement m; ⓸ US Post = **zip code**; ⓹ ○US (zero) zéro m
B vtr (p prés etc **-pp-**) ⓵ **to ~ sth open/shut** ouvrir/fermer la fermeture à glissière de qch; ⓶ Comput zipper, compresser [qch] au format zip
C ○vi (p prés etc **-pp-**) **to ~ along, to ~ past** filer à toute allure

---

The signs of the Zodiac

Aries		
= le Bélier	[belje]	21 mars–20 avril
Taurus		
= le Taureau	[tɔʀo]	21 avril–20 mai
Gemini		
= les Gémeaux	[ʒemo]	21 mai–21 juin
Cancer		
= le Cancer	[kɑ̃sɛʀ]	22 juin–22 juillet
Leo		
= le Lion	[ljɔ̃]	23 juillet–22 août
Virgo		
= la Vierge	[vjɛʀʒ]	23 août–22 septembre
Libra		
= la Balance	[balɑ̃s]	23 septembre–23 octobre
Scorpio		
= le Scorpion	[skɔʀpjɔ̃]	24 octobre–21 novembre
Sagittarius		
= le Sagittaire	[saʒitɛʀ]	22 novembre–21 décembre
Capricorn		
= le Capricorne	[kapʀikɔʀn]	22 décembre–19 janvier
Aquarius		
= le Verseau	[vɛʀso]	20 janvier–18 février
Pisces		
= les Poissons	[pwasɔ̃]	19 février–20 mars

I'm Leo
= je suis Lion

I'm Gemini
= je suis Gémeaux

born in Leo or ***under the sign of Leo***
= né sous le signe du Lion

born in Gemini
= né sous le signe des Gémeaux

Leos/Aries are very generous
= les Lions/les Béliers sont très généreux

what's the horoscope for Leos?
= que dit l'horoscope pour les Lions?

the sun is in Leo
= le soleil est au Lion

■ *All the signs work in the same way in French.*

(Phrasal verbs)
 ■ **zip on** s'attacher par une fermeture à glissière; ▸ ~ [sth] on, ~ on [sth] remonter la fermeture à glissière de qch
 ■ **zip through**○: **to ~ through a book** lire un livre en diagonale○
 ■ **zip up** [garment, bag] se fermer par une fermeture à glissière; ▸ ~ [sb/sth] up, ~ up [sb/sth] remonter la fermeture à glissière de qn/qch
zip: **~ code** n US Post code m postal; **Zip**® **disk** n disquette f Zip®; **Zip**® **drive** n lecteur m Zip®; **~ fastener** n = **zip A 1**

zipper /'zɪpə(r)/ n US = **zip A 1**

zippy○ /'zɪpɪ/ adj [vehicle] qui pète le feu○

zither /ˈzɪðə(r)/ ▸ p. 1028 *n* cithare *f*

zodiac /ˈzəʊdɪæk/ *n* zodiaque *m*

zombie /ˈzɒmbɪ/ *n* Relig zombi(e) *m*; fig abruti/-e° *m/f*

zonal /ˈzəʊnl/ *adj* [*administration*] par zone; [*boundary, organizer*] de zone; [*soil, climate*] zonal

zone /zəʊn/
A *n* (all contexts) zone *f*
B *vtr* ① (divide) diviser [qch] en zones; ② (assign) réserver; **~d for housing** réservé au logement

zoning /ˈzəʊnɪŋ/ *n* découpage *m* par zones

zonked° /zɒŋkt/ *adj* (*also* **zonked out**) (tired) crevé°; (drunk) bourré°; (on drugs) défoncé°

zoo /zuː/ *n* zoo *m*

zoological /ˌzəʊəˈlɒdʒɪkl/ *adj* zoologique

zoologist /zəʊˈɒlədʒɪst/ ▸ p. 1181 *n* zoologue *mf*, zoologiste *mf*

zoology /zəʊˈɒlədʒɪ/ *n* zoologie *f*

zoom /zuːm/
A *n* ① (of traffic, aircraft) vrombissement *m*, vacarme *m*; ② Phot (*also* **~ lens**) zoom *m*
B *vi* ① °(move quickly) **to ~ past** passer en trombe; **to ~ around** passer à toute vitesse dans; **he's ~ed off to Paris** il a foncé° à Paris; ② °[*prices*] monter en flèche; ③ Aviat monter en chandelle

(Phrasal verbs)
■ **zoom in** Cin, Phot faire un zoom (**on** sur)
■ **zoom out** Cin, Phot faire un zoom arrière

zucchini /zuːˈkiːnɪ/ *n* (*pl* **~** *ou* **~s**) US courgette *f*

zwieback /ˈzwiːbæk, ˈtsviːbɑːk/ *n* US ≈ biscotte *f*

z

Appendices

Index to English lexical notes

Notes d'usage lexicales françaises

Notes culturelles anglo-saxonnes

French cultural notes

Verbes irréguliers anglais

Vous trouverez ci-après la liste des formes irrégulières des verbes qui figurent dans le dictionnaire, à l'exception:

- des verbes composés s'écrivant avec un trait d'union et dont l'un des éléments est un verbe irrégulier (ex. *baby-sit*);
- des verbes dont on double la dernière consonne au prétérit et au participe passé (ex. *spot*)

(la conjugaison est indiquée dans le dictionnaire pour cette catégorie);

- des verbes dont le *y* final devient *-ie* dès que l'on ajoute la désinence *-d* ou *-s* (ex. *try*).

Les verbes dont les formes irrégulières ne s'appliquent qu'à certains sens sont signalés par un astérisque (*) (ex. *costed*).

Infinitif	Prétérit	Participe Passé
abide	abided, *abode	abided, *abode
arise	arose	arisen
awake	awoke	awoken
be	was/were	been
bear	bore	borne
beat	beat	beaten
become	became	become
befall	befell	befallen
beget	begot, ‡begat	begotten
begin	began	begun
behold	beheld	beheld
bend	bent	bent
beseech	beseeched, besought	beseeched, besought
beset	beset	beset
bespeak	bespoke	bespoken, bespoke
bestride	bestrode	bestridden
bet	bet	bet
bid	*bade, bid	*bidden, bid
bind	bound	bound
bite	bit	bitten
bleed	bled	bled
bless	blessed	blessed, ‡blest
blow	blew	blown, *blowed
break	broke	broken
breed	bred	bred
bring	brought	brought
broadcast	broadcast	broadcast
browbeat	browbeat	browbeaten
build	built	built
burn	burned, burnt	burned, burnt
bust	busted, bust *GB*	busted, bust *GB*
buy	bought	bought
cast	cast	cast
catch	caught	caught
chide	chided, chid	chided, chid, chidden
choose	chose	chosen
cleave	cleaved, *cleft, *‡clove	cleaved, *cleft, *‡cloven
cling	clung	clung
come	came	come
cost	*cost, *costed	*cost, *costed

Infinitif	Prétérit	Participe Passé
countersink	countersank	countersunk
creep	crept	crept
crow	crowed, ‡crew	crowed
cut	cut	cut
deal	dealt	dealt
dig	dug	dug
dive	dived, dove *US*	dived
do	did	done
draw	drew	drawn
dream	dreamed, dreamt *GB*	dreamed, dreamt *GB*
drink	drank	drunk
drive	drove	driven
dwell	dwelt, dwelled	dwelt, dwelled
eat	ate	eaten
fall	fell	fallen
feed	fed	fed
feel	felt	felt
fight	fought	fought
find	found	found
flee	fled	fled
fling	flung	flung
floodlight	floodlit	floodlit
fly	flew	flown
forbear	forbore	forborne
forbid	forbade, forbad	forbidden
forecast	forecast, forecasted	forecast, forecasted
foresee	foresaw	foreseen
foretell	foretold	foretold
forget	forgot	forgotten
forgive	forgave	forgiven
forsake	forsook	forsaken
forswear	forswore	forsworn
freeze	froze	frozen
gainsay	gainsaid	gainsaid
get	got	got, gotten *US*
gird	girded, girt	girded, girt
give	gave	given
go	went	gone

Verbes irréguliers anglais

Infinitif	Prétérit	Participe Passé	Infinitif	Prétérit	Participe Passé
grind	ground	ground	outsell	outsold	outsold
grow	grew	grown	outshine	outshone	outshone
			overbid	overbid	overbid
hamstring	hamstrung	hamstrung	overcome	overcame	overcome
hang	*hung, *hanged	*hung, *hanged	overdo	overdid	overdone
have	had	had	overdraw	overdrew	overdrawn
hear	heard	heard	overeat	overate	overeaten
heave	*heaved, *hove	*heaved, *hove	overfly	overflew	overflown
hew	hewed	hewn, hewed	overhang	overhung	overhung
hide	hid	hidden, ‡hid	overhear	overheard	overheard
hit	hit	hit	overlay	overlaid	overlaid
hold	held	held	overlie	overlay	overlain
hurt	hurt	hurt	overpay	overpaid	overpaid
inlay	inlaid	inlaid	override	overrode	overridden
input	input, inputted	input, inputted	overrun	overran	overrun
inset	inset, insetted US	inset, insetted US	oversee	oversaw	overseen
interweave	interwove,	interwoven,	overshoot	overshot	overshot
	interweaved	interweaved	oversleep	overslept	overslept
			overtake	overtook	overtaken
keep	kept	kept	overthrow	overthrew	overthrown
kneel	kneeled, knelt	kneeled, knelt			
knit	knitted, *knit	knitted, *knit	partake	partook	partaken
know	knew	known	pay	paid	paid
			plead	pleaded, pled US	pleaded, pled US
lay	laid	laid	prove	proved	proved, proven
lead	led	led	put	put	put
lean	leaned, leant GB	leaned, leant GB			
leap	leaped, leapt GB	leaped, leapt GB	quit	quit, quitted	quit, quitted
learn	learned, learnt GB	learned, learnt GB			
leave	left	left	read /riːd/	read /red/	read /red/
lend	lent	lent	rebuild	rebuilt	rebuilt
let	let	let	recast	recast	recast
lie	lay	lain	redo	redid	redone
light	lighted, lit	lighted, lit	remake	remade	remade
lose	lost	lost	rend	rent	rent
			repay	repaid	repaid
make	made	made	reread	reread	reread
mean	meant	meant	/ˈriːˈriːd/	/ˈriːˈred/	/ˈriːˈred/
meet	met	met	rerun	reran	rerun
miscast	miscast	miscast	resell	resold	resold
misdeal	misdealt	misdealt	reset	reset	reset
mishear	misheard	misheard	resit	resat	resat
mishit	mishit	mishit	retake	retook	retaken
mislay	mislaid	mislaid	retell	retold	retold
mislead	misled	misled	rethink	rethought	rethought
misread	misread	misread	rewrite	rewrote	rewritten
/ˈmɪsˈriːd/	/ˈmɪsˈred/	/ˈmɪsˈred/	rid	rid	rid
misspell	misspelled,	misspelled,	ride	rode	ridden
	misspelt GB	misspelt GB	ring	rang	rung
misspend	misspent	misspent	rise	rose	risen
mistake	mistook	mistaken	run	ran	runx
misunder -stand	misunderstood	misunderstood	saw	sawed	sawed, sawn GB
mow	mowed	mown, mowed	say	said	said
			see	saw	seen
outbid	outbid	outbid, outbidden US	seek	sought	sought
outdo	outdid	outdone	sell	sold	sold
outfight	outfought	outfought	send	sent	sent
outgrow	outgrew	outgrown	set	set	set
outlay	outlaid	outlaid	sew	sewed	sewn, sewed
output	output, outputted	output, outputted	shake	shook	shaken
outrun	outran	outrun	shear	sheared	*shorn, *sheared

Infinitif	Prétérit	Participe Passé	Infinitif	Prétérit	Participe Passé
shed	shed	shed	swim	swam	swum
shine	*shone, *shined	*shone, *shined	swing	swung	swung
shit	shit, shat	shit, shat			
shoe	shod	shod	take	took	taken
shoot	shot	shot	teach	taught	taught
show	showed	shown, showed	tear	tore	torn
shrink	shrank, shrunk	shrunk, shrunken	tell	told	told
shrive	shrove, shrived	shriven, shrived	think	thought	thought
shut	shut	shut	thrive	thrived, (liter) throve	thrived, ‡thriven
sing	sang	sung	throw	threw	thrown
sink	sank	sunk	thrust	thrust	thrust
sit	sat	sat	tread	trod	trodden, trod
slay	slew	slain	typecast	typecast	typecast
sleep	slept	slept	typeset	typeset	typeset
slide	slid	slid	typewrite	typewrote	typewritten
sling	slung	slung	unbend	unbent	unbent
slink	slunk	slunk	underbid	underbid	underbid
slit	slit	slit	undercut	undercut	undercut
smell	smelled, smelt GB	smelled, smelt GB	undergo	underwent	undergone
smite	smote	smitten	underlie	underlay	underlain
sow	sowed	sowed, sown	underpay	underpaid	underpaid
speak	spoke	spoken	undersell	undersold	undersold
speed	*sped, *speeded	*sped, *speeded	understand	understood	understood
spell	spelled, spelt GB	spelled, spelt GB	undertake	undertook	undertaken
spend	spent	spent	underwrite	underwrote	underwritten
spill	spilled, spilt	spilled, spilt	undo	undid	undone
spin	spun, ‡span	spun	unfreeze	unfroze	unfrozen
spit	spat, spit US	spat, spit US	unlearn	unlearned, unlearnt GB	unlearned, unlearnt GB
split	split	split	unstick	unstuck	unstuck
spoil	spoiled, spoilt GB	spoiled, spoilt GB	unwind	unwound	unwound
spotlight	*spotlit, *spotlighted	*spotlit, *spotlighted	uphold	upheld	upheld
spread	spread	spread	upset	upset	upset
spring	sprang, sprung US	sprung			
stand	stood	stood	wake	woke	woken
stave	staved, *stove	staved, *stove	waylay	waylaid	waylaid
steal	stole	stolen	wear	wore	worn
stick	stuck	stuck	weave	wove, *weaved	woven, *weaved
sting	stung	stung	wed	wedded, wed	wedded, wed
stink	stank, stunk	stunk	weep	wept	wept
strew	strewed	strewn, strewed	wet	wet, wetted	wet, wetted
stride	strode	stridden	win	won	won
strike	struck	struck	wind	wound	wound
string	strung	strung		/waɪnd/	/waʊnd/	/waʊnd/
strive	strove	striven	withdraw	withdrew	withdrawn
sublet	sublet	sublet	withhold	withheld	withheld
swear	swore	sworn	withstand	withstood	withstood
sweat	sweated, sweat US	sweated, sweat US	work	worked, *wrought	worked, *wrought
sweep	swept	swept	wring	wrung	wrung
swell	swelled	swollen, swelled US	write	wrote	written

French verbs

Standard verb endings

	-er	**-ir**	**-r, -re**		**-er**	**-ir**	**-r, -re**
	Indicative Present				**Subjunctive** Present		
Singular 1	-e	-is	-s *or* -e	**Singular 1**	-e	-(iss)e	-e
2	-es	-is	-s *or* -es	**2**	-es	-(iss)es	-es
3	-e	-it	-t *or* -e	**3**	-e	-(iss)e	-e
Plural 1	-ons	-(iss)ons	-ons	**Plural 1**	-ions	-(iss)ions	-ions
2	-ez	-(iss)ez	-ez	**2**	-iez	-(iss)iez	-iez
3	-ent	-(iss)ent	-ent	**3**	-ent	-(iss)ent	-ent
	Indicative Imperfect				**Subjunctive** Imperfect		
Singular 1	-ais	-(iss)ais	-ais	**Singular 1**	-asse	-sse	-sse
2	-ais	-(iss)ais	-ais	**2**	-asses	-sses	-sses
3	-ait	-(iss)ait	-ait	**3**	-ât	-ît	-ît *or* -ût
Plural 1	-ions	-(iss)ions	-ions	**Plural 1**	-assions	-ssions	-ssions
2	-iez	-(iss)iez	-iez	**2**	-assiez	-ssiez	-ssiez
3	-aient	-(iss)aient	-aient	**3**	-assent	-issent	-ssent
	Indicative Past historic				**Imperative** Present		
Singular 1	-ai	-is	-s	**Singular**			
2	-as	-is	-s				
3	-a	-it	-t	**3**	-e	-s	-s
Plural 1	-âmes	-îmes	-mes	**Plural 1**	-ons	-(iss)ons	-ons
2	-âtes	-îtes	-tes	**2**	-ez	-(iss)ez	-ez
3	-èrent	-irent	-rent				
	Indicative Future				**Conditional** Present		
Singular 1	-erai	-rai	-rai	**Singular 1**	-erais	-rais	-rais
2	-eras	-ras	-ras	**2**	-erais	-rais	-rais
3	-era	-ra	-ra	**3**	-erait	-rait	-rait
Plural 1	-erons	-rons	-rons	**Plural 1**	-erions	-rions	-rions
2	-erez	-rez	-rez	**2**	-eriez	-riez	-riez
3	-eront	-ront	-ront	**3**	-eraient	-raient	-raient
	Infinitive				**Participle**		
Present	-er	-ir	-r *or* -re	**Present**	-ant	-(iss)ant	-ant
				Past	-é	-i	-i *or* -u

French verbs

1 aimer

Indicative

Present

j'	aime
tu	aimes
il	aime
nous	aimons
vous	aimez
ils	aiment

Imperfect

j'	aimais
tu	aimais
il	aimait
nous	aimions
vous	aimiez
ils	aimaient

Past historic

j'	aimai
tu	aimas
il	aima
nous	aimâmes
vous	aimâtes
ils	aimèrent

Future

j'	aimerai
tu	aimeras
il	aimera
nous	aimerons
vous	aimerez
ils	aimeront

Perfect

j'	ai	aimé
tu	as	aimé
il	a	aimé
nous	avons	aimé
vous	avez	aimé
ils	ont	aimé

Pluperfect

j'	avais	aimé
tu	avais	aimé
il	avait	aimé
nous	avions	aimé
vous	aviez	aimé
ils	avaient	aimé

Past anterior

j'	eus	aimé
tu	eus	aimé
il	eut	aimé
nous	eûmes	aimé
vous	eûtes	aimé
ils	eurent	aimé

Future perfect

j'	aurai	aimé
tu	auras	aimé
il	aura	aimé
nous	aurons	aimé
vous	aurez	aimé
ils	auront	aimé

Imperative

Present

	aime
	aimons
	aimez

Past

	aie	aimé
	ayons	aimé
	ayez	aimé

Subjunctive

Present

(que) j'	aime
(que) tu	aimes
(qu') il	aime
(que) nous	aimions
(que) vous	aimiez
(qu') ils	aiment

Imperfect

(que) j'	aimasse
(que) tu	aimasses
(qu') il	aimât
(que) nous	aimassions
(que) vous	aimassiez
(qu') ils	aimassent

Perfect

(que) j'	aie	aimé
(que) tu	aies	aimé
(qu') il	ait	aimé
(que) nous	ayons	aimé
(que) vous	ayez	aimé
(qu') ils	aient	aimé

Pluperfect

(que) j'	eusse	aimé
(que) tu	eusses	aimé
(qu') il	eût	aimé
(que) nous	eussions	aimé
(que) vous	eussiez	aimé
(qu') ils	eussent	aimé

Conditional

Present

j'	aimerais
tu	aimerais
il	aimerait
nous	aimerions
vous	aimeriez
ils	aimeraient

Past I

j'	aurais	aimé
tu	aurais	aimé
il	aurait	aimé
nous	aurions	aimé
vous	auriez	aimé
ils	auraient	aimé

Past II

j'	eusse	aimé
tu	eusses	aimé
il	eût	aimé
nous	eussions	aimé
vous	eussiez	aimé
ils	eussent	aimé

Participle

Present aimant

Past aimé, -e
ayant aimé

Infinitive

Present aimer

Past avoir aimé

2 plier

Indicative

Present

je	plie
tu	plies
il	plie
nous	plions
vous	pliez
ils	plient

Imperfect

je	pliais
tu	pliais
il	pliait
nous	pliions
vous	pliiez
ils	pliaient

Past historic

je	pliai
tu	plias
il	plia
nous	pliâmes
vous	pliâtes
ils	plièrent

Future

je	plierai
tu	plieras
il	pliera
nous	plierons
vous	plierez
ils	plieront

Perfect

j'	ai	plié
tu	as	plié
il	a	plié
nous	avons	plié
vous	avez	plié
ils	ont	plié

Pluperfect

j'	avais	plié
tu	avais	plié
il	avait	plié
nous	avions	plié
vous	aviez	plié
ils	avaient	plié

Past anterior

j'	eus	plié
tu	eus	plié
il	eut	plié
nous	eûmes	plié
vous	eûtes	plié
ils	eurent	plié

Future perfect

j'	aurai	plié
tu	auras	plié
il	aura	plié
nous	aurons	plié
vous	aurez	plié
ils	auront	plié

Imperative

Present

	plie
	plions
	pliez

Past

	aie	plié
	ayons	plié
	ayez	plié

Subjunctive

Present

(que) je	plie
(que) tu	plies
(qu') il	plie
(que) nous	pliions
(que) vous	pliiez
(qu') ils	plient

Imperfect

(que) je	pliasse
(que) tu	pliasses
(qu') il	pliât
(que) nous	pliassions
(que) vous	pliassiez
(qu') ils	pliassent

Perfect

(que) j'	aie	plié
(que) tu	aies	plié
(qu') il	ait	plié
(que) nous	ayons	plié
(que) vous	ayez	plié
(qu') ils	aient	plié

Pluperfect

(que) j'	eusse	plié
(que) tu	eusses	plié
(qu') il	eût	plié
(que) nous	eussions	plié
(que) vous	eussiez	plié
(qu') ils	eussent	plié

Conditional

Present

je	plierais
tu	plierais
il	plierait
nous	plierions
vous	plieriez
ils	plieraient

Past I

j'	aurais	plié
tu	aurais	plié
il	aurait	plié
nous	aurions	plié
vous	auriez	plié
ils	auraient	plié

Past II

j'	eusse	plié
tu	eusses	plié
il	eût	plié
nous	eussions	plié
vous	eussiez	plié
ils	eussent	plié

Participle

Present pliant

Past plié, -e
ayant plié

Infinitive

Present plier

Past avoir plié

3 finir

Indicative

Present
je	fin**is**
tu	fin**is**
il	fin**it**
nous	fin**issons**
vous	fin**issez**
ils	fin**issent**

Imperfect
je	fin**issais**
tu	fin**issais**
il	fin**issait**
nous	fin**issions**
vous	fin**issiez**
ils	fin**issaient**

Past historic
je	fin**is**
tu	fin**is**
il	fin**it**
nous	fin**îmes**
vous	fin**îtes**
ils	fin**irent**

Future
je	fin**irai**
tu	fin**iras**
il	fin**ira**
nous	fin**irons**
vous	fin**irez**
ils	fin**iront**

Perfect
j'	ai	fini
tu	as	fini
il	a	fini
nous	avons	fini
vous	avez	fini
ils	ont	fini

Pluperfect
j'	avais	fini
tu	avais	fini
il	avait	fini
nous	avions	fini
vous	aviez	fini
ils	avaient	fini

Past anterior
j'	eus	fini
tu	eus	fini
il	eut	fini
nous	eûmes	fini
vous	eûtes	fini
ils	eurent	fini

Future perfect
j'	aurai	fini
tu	auras	fini
il	aura	fini
nous	aurons	fini
vous	aurez	fini
ils	auront	fini

Imperative

Present
| fin**is** |
| fin**issons** |
| fin**issez** |

Past
aie	fini
ayons	fini
ayez	fini

Subjunctive

Present
(que) je	fin**isse**
(que) tu	fin**isses**
(qu') il	fin**isse**
(que) nous	fin**issions**
(que) vous	fin**issiez**
(qu') ils	fin**issent**

Imperfect
(que) je	fin**isse**
(que) tu	fin**isses**
(qu') il	fin**ît**
(que) nous	fin**issions**
(que) vous	fin**issiez**
(qu') ils	fin**issent**

Perfect
(que) j'	aie	fini
(que) tu	aies	fini
(qu') il	ait	fini
(que) nous	ayons	fini
(que) vous	ayez	fini
(qu') ils	aient	fini

Pluperfect
(que) j'	eusse	fini
(que) tu	eusses	fini
(qu') il	eût	fini
(que) nous	eussions	fini
(que) vous	eussiez	fini
(qu') ils	eussent	fini

Conditional

Present
je	fin**irais**
tu	fin**irais**
il	fin**irait**
nous	fin**irions**
vous	fin**iriez**
ils	fin**iraient**

Past I
j'	aurais	fini
tu	aurais	fini
il	aurait	fini
nous	aurions	fini
vous	auriez	fini
ils	auraient	fini

Past II
j'	eusse	fini
tu	eusses	fini
il	eût	fini
nous	eussions	fini
vous	eussiez	fini
ils	eussent	fini

Participle

Present	fin**issant**
Past	fini, -e
	ayant fini

Infinitive

| Present | fin**ir** |
| Past | avoir fini |

4 offrir

Indicative

Present
j'	offre
tu	offr**es**
il	offre
nous	offr**ons**
vous	offr**ez**
ils	offr**ent**

Imperfect
j'	offr**ais**
tu	offr**ais**
il	offr**ait**
nous	offr**ions**
vous	offr**iez**
ils	offr**aient**

Past historic
j'	offr**is**
tu	offr**is**
il	offr**it**
nous	offr**îmes**
vous	offr**îtes**
ils	offr**irent**

Future
j'	offr**irai**
tu	offr**iras**
il	offr**ira**
nous	offr**irons**
vous	offr**irez**
ils	offr**iront**

Perfect
j'	ai	offert
tu	as	offert
il	a	offert
nous	avons	offert
vous	avez	offert
ils	ont	offert

Pluperfect
j'	avais	offert
tu	avais	offert
il	avait	offert
nous	avions	offert
vous	aviez	offert
ils	avaient	offert

Past anterior
j'	eus	offert
tu	eus	offert
il	eut	offert
nous	eûmes	offert
vous	eûtes	offert
ils	eurent	offert

Future perfect
j'	aurai	offert
tu	auras	offert
il	aura	offert
nous	aurons	offert
vous	aurez	offert
ils	auront	offert

Imperative

Present
| offr**e** |
| offr**ons** |
| offr**ez** |

Past
aie	offert
ayons	offert
ayez	offert

Subjunctive

Present
(que) j'	offre
(que) tu	offr**es**
(qu') il	offr**e**
(que) nous	offr**ions**
(que) vous	offr**iez**
(qu') ils	offr**ent**

Imperfect
(que) j'	offr**isse**
(que) tu	offr**isses**
(qu') il	offr**ît**
(que) nous	offr**issions**
(que) vous	offr**issiez**
(qu') ils	offr**issent**

Perfect
(que) j'	aie	offert
(que) tu	aies	offert
(qu') il	ait	offert
(que) nous	ayons	offert
(que) vous	ayez	offert
(qu') ils	aient	offert

Pluperfect
(que) j'	eusse	offert
(que) tu	eusses	offert
(qu') il	eût	offert
(que) nous	eussions	offert
(que) vous	eussiez	offert
(qu') ils	eussent	offert

Conditional

Present
j'	offr**irais**
tu	offr**irais**
il	offr**irait**
nous	offr**irions**
vous	offr**iriez**
ils	offr**iraient**

Past I
j'	aurais	offert
tu	aurais	offert
il	aurait	offert
nous	aurions	offert
vous	auriez	offert
ils	auraient	offert

Past II
j'	eusse	offert
tu	eusses	offert
il	eût	offert
nous	eussions	offert
vous	eussiez	offert
ils	eussent	offert

Participle

Present	offr**ant**
Past	offert, -e
	ayant offert

Infinitive

| Present | offr**ir** |
| Past | avoir offert |

5 recevoir

Indicative

Present
je	reçois
tu	reçois
il	reçoit
nous	recevons
vous	recevez
ils	reçoivent

Imperfect
je	recevais
tu	recevais
il	recevait
nous	recevions
vous	receviez
ils	recevaient

Past historic
je	reçus
tu	reçus
il	reçut
nous	reçûmes
vous	reçûtes
ils	reçurent

Future
je	recevrai
tu	recevras
il	recevra
nous	recevrons
vous	recevrez
ils	recevront

Perfect
j'	ai	reçu
tu	as	reçu
il	a	reçu
nous	avons	reçu
vous	avez	reçu
ils	ont	reçu

Pluperfect
j'	avais	reçu
tu	avais	reçu
il	avait	reçu
nous	avions	reçu
vous	aviez	reçu
ils	avaient	reçu

Past anterior
j'	eus	reçu
tu	eus	reçu
il	eut	reçu
nous	eûmes	reçu
vous	eûtes	reçu
ils	eurent	reçu

Future perfect
j'	aurai	reçu
tu	auras	reçu
il	aura	reçu
nous	aurons	reçu
vous	aurez	reçu
ils	auront	reçu

Imperative

Present
	reçois
	recevons
	recevez

Past
aie	reçu
ayons	reçu
ayez	reçu

Subjunctive

Present
(que) je	reçoive
(que) tu	reçoives
(qu') il	reçoive
(que) nous	recevions
(que) vous	receviez
(qu') ils	reçoivent

Imperfect
(que) je	reçusse
(que) tu	reçusses
(qu') il	reçût
(que) nous	reçussions
(que) vous	reçussiez
(qu') ils	reçussent

Perfect
(que) j'	aie	reçu
(que) tu	aies	reçu
(qu') il	ait	reçu
(que) nous	ayons	reçu
(que) vous	ayez	reçu
(qu') ils	aient	reçu

Pluperfect
(que) j'	eusse	reçu
(que) tu	eusses	reçu
(qu') il	eût	reçu
(que) nous	eussions	reçu
(que) vous	eussiez	reçu
(qu') ils	eussent	reçu

Conditional

Present
je	recevrais
tu	recevrais
il	recevrait
nous	recevrions
vous	recevriez
ils	recevraient

Past I
j'	aurais	reçu
tu	aurais	reçu
il	aurait	reçu
nous	aurions	reçu
vous	auriez	reçu
ils	auraient	reçu

Past II
j'	eusse	reçu
tu	eusses	reçu
il	eût	reçu
nous	eussions	reçu
vous	eussiez	reçu
ils	eussent	reçu

Participle

Present recevant

Past reçu, -e
ayant reçu

Infinitive

Present recevoir

Past avoir reçu

6 rendre

Indicative

Present
je	rends
tu	rends
il	rend
nous	rendons
vous	rendez
ils	rendent

Imperfect
je	rendais
tu	rendais
il	rendait
nous	rendions
vous	rendiez
ils	rendaient

Past historic
je	rendis
tu	rendis
il	rendit
nous	rendîmes
vous	rendîtes
ils	rendirent

Future
je	rendrai
tu	rendras
il	rendra
nous	rendrons
vous	rendrez
ils	rendront

Perfect
j'	ai	rendu
tu	as	rendu
il	a	rendu
nous	avons	rendu
vous	avez	rendu
ils	ont	rendu

Pluperfect
j'	avais	rendu
tu	avais	rendu
il	avait	rendu
nous	avions	rendu
vous	aviez	rendu
ils	avaient	rendu

Past anterior
j'	eus	rendu
tu	eus	rendu
il	eut	rendu
nous	eûmes	rendu
vous	eûtes	rendu
ils	eurent	rendu

Future perfect
j'	aurai	rendu
tu	auras	rendu
il	aura	rendu
nous	aurons	rendu
vous	aurez	rendu
ils	auront	rendu

Imperative

Present
	rends
	rendons
	rendez

Past
aie	rendu
ayons	rendu
ayez	rendu

Subjunctive

Present
(que) je	rende
(que) tu	rendes
(qu') il	rende
(que) nous	rendions
(que) vous	rendiez
(qu') ils	rendent

Imperfect
(que) je	rendisse
(que) tu	rendisses
(qu') il	rendît
(que) nous	rendissions
(que) vous	rendissiez
(qu') ils	rendissent

Perfect
(que) j'	aie	rendu
(que) tu	aies	rendu
(qu') il	ait	rendu
(que) nous	ayons	rendu
(que) vous	ayez	rendu
(qu') ils	aient	rendu

Pluperfect
(que) j'	eusse	rendu
(que) tu	eusses	rendu
(qu') il	eût	rendu
(que) nous	eussions	rendu
(que) vous	eussiez	rendu
(qu') ils	eussent	rendu

Conditional

Present
je	rendrais
tu	rendrais
il	rendrait
nous	rendrions
vous	rendriez
ils	rendraient

Past I
j'	aurais	rendu
tu	aurais	rendu
il	aurait	rendu
nous	aurions	rendu
vous	auriez	rendu
ils	auraient	rendu

Past II
j'	eusse	rendu
tu	eusses	rendu
il	eût	rendu
nous	eussions	rendu
vous	eussiez	rendu
ils	eussent	rendu

Participle

Present rendant

Past rendu, -e
ayant rendu

Infinitive

Present rendre

Past avoir rendu

7 être

Indicative

Present
je	suis
tu	es
il	est
nous	sommes
vous	êtes
ils	sont

Imperfect
j'	étais
tu	étais
il	était
nous	étions
vous	étiez
ils	étaient

Past historic
je	fus
tu	fus
il	fut
nous	fûmes
vous	fûtes
ils	furent

Future
je	serai
tu	seras
il	sera
nous	serons
vous	serez
ils	seront

Perfect
j'	ai	été
tu	as	été
il	a	été
nous	avons	été
vous	avez	été
ils	ont	été

Pluperfect
j'	avais	été
tu	avais	été
il	avait	été
nous	avions	été
vous	aviez	été
ils	avaient	été

Past anterior
j'	eus	été
tu	eus	été
il	eut	été
nous	eûmes	été
vous	eûtes	été
ils	eurent	été

Future perfect
j'	aurai	été
tu	auras	été
il	aura	été
nous	aurons	été
vous	aurez	été
ils	auront	été

Imperative

Present
	sois
	soyons
	soyez

Past
	aie	été
	ayons	été
	ayez	été

Subjunctive

Present
(que)	je	sois
(que)	tu	sois
(qu')	il	soit
(que)	nous	soyons
(que)	vous	soyez
(qu')	ils	soient

Imperfect
(que)	je	fusse
(que)	tu	fusses
(qu')	il	fût
(que)	nous	fussions
(que)	vous	fussiez
(qu')	ils	fussent

Perfect
(que)	j'	aie	été
(que)	tu	aies	été
(qu')	il	ait	été
(que)	nous	ayons	été
(que)	vous	ayez	été
(qu')	ils	aient	été

Pluperfect
(que)	j'	eusse	été
(que)	tu	eusses	été
(qu')	il	eût	été
(que)	nous	eussions	été
(que)	vous	eussiez	été
(qu')	ils	eussent	été

Conditional

Present
je	serais
tu	serais
il	serait
nous	serions
vous	seriez
ils	seraient

Past I
j'	aurais	été
tu	aurais	été
il	aurait	été
nous	aurions	été
vous	auriez	été
ils	auraient	été

Past II
j'	eusse	été
tu	eusses	été
il	eût	été
nous	eussions	été
vous	eussiez	été
ils	eussent	été

Participle

Present étant

Past été (invariable)
ayant été

Infinitive

Present être

Past avoir été

8 avoir

Indicative

Present
j'	ai
tu	as
il	a
nous	avons
vous	avez
ils	ont

Imperfect
j'	avais
tu	avais
il	avait
nous	avions
vous	aviez
ils	avaient

Past historic
j'	eus
tu	eus
il	eut
nous	eûmes
vous	eûtes
ils	eurent

Future
j'	aurai
tu	auras
il	aura
nous	aurons
vous	aurez
ils	auront

Perfect
j'	ai	eu
tu	as	eu
il	a	eu
nous	avons	eu
vous	avez	eu
ils	ont	eu

Pluperfect
j'	avais	eu
tu	avais	eu
il	avait	eu
nous	avions	eu
vous	aviez	eu
ils	avaient	eu

Past anterior
j'	eus	eu
tu	eus	eu
il	eut	eu
nous	eûmes	eu
vous	eûtes	eu
ils	eurent	eu

Future perfect
j'	aurai	eu
tu	auras	eu
il	aura	eu
nous	aurons	eu
vous	aurez	eu
ils	auront	eu

Imperative

Present
	aie
	ayons
	ayez

Past
	aie	eu
	ayons	eu
	ayez	eu

Subjunctive

Present
(que)	j'	aie
(que)	tu	aies
(qu')	il	ait
(que)	nous	ayons
(que)	vous	ayez
(qu')	ils	aient

Imperfect
(que)	j'	eusse
(que)	tu	eusses
(qu')	il	eût
(que)	nous	eussions
(que)	vous	eussiez
(qu')	ils	eussent

Perfect
(que)	j'	aie	eu
(que)	tu	aies	eu
(qu')	il	ait	eu
(que)	nous	ayons	eu
(que)	vous	ayez	eu
(qu')	ils	aient	eu

Pluperfect
(que)	j'	eusse	eu
(que)	tu	eusses	eu
(qu')	il	eût	eu
(que)	nous	eussions	eu
(que)	vous	eussiez	eu
(qu')	ils	eussent	eu

Conditional

Present
j'	aurais
tu	aurais
il	aurait
nous	aurions
vous	auriez
ils	auraient

Past I
j'	aurais	eu
tu	aurais	eu
il	aurait	eu
nous	aurions	eu
vous	auriez	eu
ils	auraient	eu

Past II
j'	eusse	eu
tu	eusses	eu
il	eût	eu
nous	eussions	eu
vous	eussiez	eu
ils	eussent	eu

Participle

Present ayant

Past eu, -e
ayant eu

Infinitive

Present avoir

Past avoir eu

9 aller

Indicative

Present
je	vais
tu	vas
il	va
nous	allons
vous	allez
ils	vont

Imperfect
j'	allais
tu	allais
il	allait
nous	allions
vous	alliez
ils	allaient

Past historic
j'	allai
tu	allas
il	alla
nous	allâmes
vous	allâtes
ils	allèrent

Future
j'	irai
tu	iras
il	ira
nous	irons
vous	irez
ils	iront

Perfect
je	suis	allé
tu	es	allé
il	est	allé
nous	sommes	allés
vous	êtes	allés
ils	sont	allés

Pluperfect
j'	étais	allé
tu	étais	allé
il	était	allé
nous	étions	allés
vous	étiez	allés
ils	étaient	allés

Past anterior
je	fus	allé
tu	fus	allé
il	fut	allé
nous	fûmes	allés
vous	fûtes	allés
ils	furent	allés

Future perfect
je	serai	allé
tu	seras	allé
il	sera	allé
nous	serons	allés
vous	serez	allés
ils	seront	allés

Imperative

Present
	va	
	allons	
	allez	

Past
	sois	allé
	soyons	allés
	soyez	allés

Subjunctive

Present
(que) j'	aille	
(que) tu	ailles	
(qu') il	aille	
(que) nous	allions	
(que) vous	alliez	
(qu') ils	aillent	

Imperfect
(que) j'	allasse	
(que) tu	allasses	
(qu') il	allât	
(que) nous	allassions	
(que) vous	allassiez	
(qu') ils	allassent	

Perfect
(que) je	sois	allé
(que) tu	sois	allé
(qu') il	soit	allé
(que) nous	soyons	allés
(que) vous	soyez	allés
(qu') ils	soient	allés

Pluperfect
(que) je	fusse	allé
(que) tu	fusses	allé
(qu') il	fût	allé
(que) nous	fussions	allés
(que) vous	fussiez	allés
(qu') ils	fussent	allés

Conditional

Present
j'	irais
tu	irais
il	irait
nous	irions
vous	iriez
ils	iraient

Past I
je	serais	allé
tu	serais	allé
il	serait	allé
nous	serions	allés
vous	seriez	allés
ils	seraient	allés

Past II
je	fusse	allé
tu	fusses	allé
il	fût	allé
nous	fussions	allés
vous	fussiez	allés
ils	fussent	allés

Participle

Present allant

Past allé, -e
étant allé

Infinitive

Present aller

Past être allé

10 faire

Indicative

Present
je	fais
tu	fais
il	fait
nous	faisons
vous	faites
ils	font

Imperfect
je	faisais
tu	faisais
il	faisait
nous	faisions
vous	faisiez
ils	faisaient

Past historic
je	fis
tu	fis
il	fit
nous	fîmes
vous	fîtes
ils	firent

Future
je	ferai
tu	feras
il	fera
nous	ferons
vous	ferez
ils	feront

Perfect
j'	ai	fait
tu	as	fait
il	a	fait
nous	avons	fait
vous	avez	fait
ils	ont	fait

Pluperfect
j'	avais	fait
tu	avais	fait
il	avait	fait
nous	avions	fait
vous	aviez	fait
ils	avaient	fait

Past anterior
j'	eus	fait
tu	eus	fait
il	eut	fait
nous	eûmes	fait
vous	eûtes	fait
ils	eurent	fait

Future perfect
j'	aurai	fait
tu	auras	fait
il	aura	fait
nous	aurons	fait
vous	aurez	fait
ils	auront	fait

Imperative

Present
	fais
	faisons
	faites

Past
	aie	fait
	ayons	fait
	ayez	fait

Subjunctive

Present
(que) je	fasse	
(que) tu	fasses	
(qu') il	fasse	
(que) nous	fassions	
(que) vous	fassiez	
(qu') ils	fassent	

Imperfect
(que) je	fisse	
(que) tu	fisses	
(qu') il	fît	
(que) nous	fissions	
(que) vous	fissiez	
(qu') ils	fissent	

Perfect
(que) j'	aie	fait
(que) tu	aies	fait
(qu') il	ait	fait
(que) nous	ayons	fait
(que) vous	ayez	fait
(qu') ils	aient	fait

Pluperfect
(que) j'	eusse	fait
(que) tu	eusses	fait
(qu') il	eût	fait
(que) nous	eussions	fait
(que) vous	eussiez	fait
(qu') ils	eussent	fait

Conditional

Present
je	ferais
tu	ferais
il	ferait
nous	ferions
vous	feriez
ils	feraient

Past II
j'	aurais	fait
tu	aurais	fait
il	aurait	fait
nous	aurions	fait
vous	auriez	fait
ils	auraient	fait

Past II
j'	eusse	fait
tu	eusses	fait
il	eût	fait
nous	eussions	fait
vous	eussiez	fait
ils	eussent	fait

Participle

Present faisant

Past fait, -e
ayant fait

Infinitive

Present faire

Past avoir fait

PASSIVE être aimé

Indicative

Present

je	suis	aimé
tu	es	aimé
il	est	aimé
nous	sommes	aimés
vous	êtes	aimés
ils	sont	aimés

Imperfect

j'	étais	aimé
tu	étais	aimé
il	était	aimé
nous	étions	aimés
vous	étiez	aimés
ils	étaient	aimés

Past historic

je	fus	aimé
tu	fus	aimé
il	fut	aimé
nous	fûmes	aimés
vous	fûtes	aimés
ils	furent	aimés

Future

je	serai	aimé
tu	seras	aimé
il	sera	aimé
nous	serons	aimés
vous	serez	aimés
ils	seront	aimés

Perfect

j'	ai	été	aimé
tu	as	été	aimé
il	a	été	aimé
nous	avons	été	aimés
vous	avez	été	aimés
ils	ont	été	aimés

Pluperfect

j'	avais	été	aimé
tu	avais	été	aimé
il	avait	été	aimé
nous	avions	été	aimés
vous	aviez	été	aimés
ils	avaient	été	aimés

Past anterior

j'	eus	été	aimé
tu	eus	été	aimé
il	eut	été	aimé
nous	eûmes	été	aimés
vous	eûtes	été	aimés
ils	eurent	été	aimés

Future perfect

j'	aurai	été	aimé
tu	auras	été	aimé
il	aura	été	aimé
nous	aurons	été	aimés
vous	aurez	été	aimés
ils	auront	été	aimés

Imperative

Present

	sois	aimé
	soyons	aimés
	soyez	aimés

Past *(obsolete)*

Subjunctive

Present

(que) je	sois	aimé
(que) tu	sois	aimé
(qu') il	soit	aimé
(que) nous	soyons	aimés
(que) vous	soyez	aimés
(qu') ils	soient	aimés

Imperfect

(que) je	fusse	aimé
(que) tu	fusses	aimé
(qu') il	fut	aimé
(que) nous	fussions	aimés
(que) vous	fussiez	aimés
(qu') ils	fussent	aimés

Perfect

(que) j'	aie	été aimé
(que) tu	aies	été aimé
(qu') il	ait	été aimé
(que) nous	ayons	été aimés
(que) vous	ayez	été aimés
(qu') ils	aient	été aimés

Pluperfect

(que) j'	eusse	été aimé
(que) tu	eusses	été aimé
(qu') il	eût	été aimé
(que) nous	eussions	été aimés
(que) vous	eussiez	été aimés
(qu') ils	eussent	été aimés

Conditional

Present

je	serais	aimé
tu	serais	aimé
il	serait	aimé
nous	serions	aimés
vous	seriez	aimés
ils	seraient	aimés

Past I

j'	aurais	été aimé
tu	aurais	été aimé
il	aurait	été aimé
nous	aurions	été aimés
vous	auriez	été aimés
ils	auraient	été aimés

Past II

j'	eusse	été aimé
tu	eusses	été aimé
il	eût	été aimé
nous	eussions	été aimés
vous	eussiez	été aimés
ils	eussent	été aimés

Participle

Present étant aimé

Past été aimé
ayant été aimé

Infinitive

Present être aimé

Past avoir été aimé

REFLEXIVE s'adonner

Indicative

Present

je	m'	adonne
tu	t'	adonnes
il	s'	adonne
nous	nous	adonnons
vous	vous	adonnez
ils	s'	adonnent

Imperfect

je	m'	adonnais
tu	t'	adonnais
il	s'	adonnait
nous	nous	adonnons
vous	vous	adonniez
ils	s'	adonnaient

Past historic

je	m'	adonnai
tu	t'	adonnas
il	s'	adonna
nous	nous	adonnâmes
vous	vous	adonnâtes
ils	s'	adonnèrent

Future

je	m'	adonnerai
tu	t'	adonneras
il	s'	adonnera
nous	nous	adonnerons
vous	vous	adonnerez
ils	s'	adonneront

Perfect

je	me suis	adonné
tu	t' es	adonné
il	s' est	adonné
nous ns	sommes	adonnés
vous vs	êtes	adonnés
ils se	sont	adonnés

Pluperfect

je	m' étais	adonné
tu	t' étais	adonné
il	s' était	adonné
nous ns	étions	adonnés
vous vs	étiez	adonnés
ils s'	étaient	adonnés

Past anterior

je	me fus	adonné
tu	te fus	adonné
il	se fut	adonné
nous ns	fûmes	adonnés
vous vs	fûtes	adonnés
ils se	furent	adonnés

Future perfect

je	me serai	adonné
tu	te seras	adonné
il	se sera	adonné
nous ns	serons	adonnés
vous vs	serez	adonnés
ils se	seront	adonnés

Imperative

Present adonne - toi
adonnons - nous
adonnez - vous

Past *(obsolete)*

Subjunctive

Present

(que) je	m'	adonne
(que) tu	t'	adonnes
(qu') il	s'	adonne
(que) nous ns		adonnions
(que) vous vs		adonniez
(qu') ils	s'	adonnent

Imperfect

(que) je	m'	adonnasse
(que) tu	t'	adonnasses
(qu') il	s'	adonnât
(que) nous ns		adonnassions
(que) vous vs		adonnassiez
(qu') ils	s'	adonnassent

Perfect

(que) je	me sois	adonné
(que) tu	te sois	adonné
(qu') il	se soit	adonné
(que) ns ns	soyons	adonnés
(que) vs vs	soyez	adonnés
(qu') ils	se soient	adonnés

Pluperfect

(que) je	me fusse	adonné
(que) tu	te fusses	adonné
(qu') il	se fût	adonné
(que) ns ns	fussions	adonnés
(que) vs vs	fussiez	adonnés
(qu') ils	se fussent	adonnés

Conditional

Present

je	m'	adonnerais
tu	t'	adonnerais
il	s'	adonnerait
nous	nous	adonnerions
vous	vous	adonneriez
ils	s'	adonneraient

Past I

je	me serais	adonné
tu	te serais	adonné
il	se serait	adonné
nous ns	serions	adonnés
vous vs	seriez	adonnés
ils se	seraient	adonnés

Past II

je	me fusse	adonné
tu	te fusses	adonné
il	se fût	adonné
nous ns	fussions	adonnés
vous vs	fussiez	adonnés
ils se	fussent	adonnés

Participle

Present s'adonnant

Past s'étant adonné

Infinitive

Present s'adonner

Past s'être adonné

Infinitive		Indicative			
	Rules	Present	Imperfect	Past Historic	Future
11 créer	*always* é	je crée, -es, -e, -ent nous créons, -ez	je créais …	je créai …	je créerai …
12 placer	c	je place, -es, -e, -ez, -ent	nous placions, -iez	ils placèrent	je placerai …
	ç *before* a *and* o	nous plaçons	je plaçais, -ais, -ait, -aient	je plaçai, -as, -a, -âmes, -âtes	
13 manger	g	je mange, -es, -e, -ez, -ent	nous mangions, -iez	ils mangèrent	je mangerai …
	ge *before* a *and* o	nous mangeons	je mangeais, -eais, -eait, -eaient	je mangeai, -as, -a, -âmes, -âtes	
14 céder	è *before silent final syllable*	je cède, -es, -e, -ent			
	é	nous cédons, -ez	je cédais …	je cédai …	je céderai …
15 assiéger	è *before silent final syllable*	j'assiège, -es, -e, -ent			
	ge *before* a *and* o	nous assiégeons	j'assiégeais, -eais, -eait, -eaient	j'assiégeai	
	é *before silent syllable*				j'assiégerai …
16 lever	è *before silent syllable*	je lève, -es, -e, -ent			je lèverai …
	e	nous levons, -ez	je levais …	je levai …	
17 geler	è *before silent syllable*	je gèle, -es, -e, -ent			je gèlerai …
	e	nous gelons, -ez	je gelais …	je gelai …	
18 acheter	è *before silent syllable*	j'achète, -es, -e, -ent			j'achèterai …
	e	nous achetons, -ez	j'achetais …	j'achetai …	
19 appeler	ll *before mute* e	j'appelle, -es, -e, -ent			j'appellerai …
	l	nous appelons, -ez	j'appelais …	j'appelai …	
20 jeter	tt *before mute* e	je jette, -es, -e, -ent			je jetterai …
	t	nous jetons, -ez	je jetais …	je jetai …	
21 payer	i *before mute* e	je paie, -es, -e, -ent			je paierai …
	or y	je paye, -es, -e, -ent nous payons, -ez	je payais …	je payai …	je payerai …

Conditional	Subjunctive		Imperative	Participle		
Present	Present	Imperfect		Present	Past	
je créerais …	que je crée …	que je créasse …	crée	créant	créé, -e	**11**
			créons, -ez			
je placerais …	que je place …		place, -ez		placé, -e	**12**
		que je plaçasse …	plaçons	plaçant		
je mangerais …	que je mange …		mange, -ez		mangé, -e	**13**
		que je mangeasse …	mangeons	mangeant		
	que je cède, -es, -e, -ent		cède			**14**
je céderais …	que nous cédions, -iez	que je cédasse …	cédons, -ez	cédant	cédé, -e	
	que j'assiège …		assiège			**15**
j'assiégerais …	que nous assiégions, -iez	que j'assiégeasse …	assiégeons	assiégeant	assiégé, -e	
je lèverais …	que je lève, -es, -e, -ent		lève			**16**
	que nous levions, -iez	que je levasse …	levons, -ez	levant	levé, -e	
je gèlerais …	que je gèle, -es, -e, -ent		gèle			**17**
	que nous gelions, -iez	que je gelasse …	gelons, -ez	gelant	gelé, -e	
j'achèterais …	que j'achète, -es, -e, -ent		achète			**18**
	que nous achetions, -iez	que j'achetasse …	achetons, -ez	achetant	acheté, -e	
j'appellerais …	que j'appelle, -es, -e, -ent		appelle			**19**
	que nous appelions, -iez	que j'appelasse …	appelons, -ez	appelant	appelé, -e	
je jetterais …	que je jette, -es, -e, -ent		jette			**20**
	que nous jetions, -iez	que je jetasse …	jetons, -ez	jetant	jeté, -e	
je paierais …	que je paie, -es, -e, -ent		paie			**21**
je payerais …	que je paye, -es, -e, -ent	que je payasse …	paye			
	que nous payions, -iez		payons, -ez	payant	payé, -e	

Infinitive	Indicative				
	Rules	Present	Imperfect	Past Historic	Future
22 essuyer	i *before mute* e	j'essuie, -es, -e, -ent			j'essuierai ...
	y	nous essuyons, -ez	j'essuyais ...	j'essuyai ...	
23 employer	i *before mute* e	j'emploie, -es, -e, -ent			j'emploierai ..
	y	nous employons, -ez	j'employais ...	j'employai ...	
24 envoyer	i *before mute* e	j'envoie, -es, -e, -ent			
	y	nous envoyons, -ez	j'envoyais ...	j'envoyai ...	
	err				j'enverrai ...
25 haïr	i	je hais, -s, -t			
	ï	ns haïssons, -ez, -ent	je haïssais ...	je haïs ... (haïmes, haïtes)	je haïrai ...
26 courir		je cours ...	je courais ...	je courus ...	je courrai ...
27 cueillir		je cueille, -es, -e, nous cueillons ...	je cueillais ...	je cueillis ...	je cueillerai ...
28 assaillir		j'assaille, -es, -e, nous assaillons, -ez, -ent	j'assaillais ...	j'assaillis ...	j'assaillirai ...
29 fuir	i *before consonants and* e	je fuis, -s, -t, -ent		je fuis ...	je fuirai ...
	y *before* a, ez, i, o	nous fuyons, -ez	je fuyais ...		
30 partir	*without* t	je pars ...			
	with t	il part ...	je partais ...	je partis ...	je partirai ...
31 bouillir	ou	je bous, -s, -t			
	ouill	nous bouillons ...	je bouillais ...	je bouillis ...	je bouillirai ...
32 couvrir		je couvre, -es, -e, nous couvrons ...	je couvrais ...	je couvris ...	je couvrirai ...
33 vêtir		je vêts ...	je vêtais ...	je vêtis ...	je vêtirai ...
34 mourir	eur	je meurs, -s, -t, -ent			
	our	nous mourons, -ez	je mourais ...	je mourus ...	je mourrai ...
35 acquérir	quier	j'acquiers, -s, -t, -ièrent			
	quer	nous acquérons -ez	j'acquérais ...		j'acquerrai ...
	qu		j'acquis ...		

Conditional	Subjunctive		Imperative	Participle		
Present	Present	Imperfect		Present	Past	
j'essuierais ...	que j'essuie, -es, -e, -ent		essuie			**22**
	que nous essuyions, -iez	que j'essuyasse...	essuyons, -ez	essuyant	essuyé, e	
j'emploierais ...	que j'emploie, -es, -e, -ent		emploie			**23**
	que nous employions, -iez	que j'employasse ...	employons, -ez	employant	employé, -e	
	que j'envoie, -es, -e, -ent		envoie			**24**
	que nous envoyions, -iez	que j'envoyasse ...	envoyons, -ez	envoyant	envoyé, -e	
j'enverrais ...						
			hais			**25**
je haïrais ...	que je haïsse, qu'il haïsse	que je haïsse, qu'il haït	haïssons, haïssez	haïssant	haï, -e	
je courrais ...	que je coure ...	que je courusse ...	cours, courons, -ez	courant	couru, -e	**26**
je cueillerais ...			cueille			**27**
	que je cueille ...	que je cueillisse ...	cuillons, -ez	cueillant	cueilli, -e	
j'assaillirais ...	que j'assaille ...	que j'assaillisse	assaille assaillons, -ez	assaillant	assailli, -e	**28**
je fuirais ...	que je fuie, -es, -e, -ent	que je fuisse ...	fuis		fui, -e	**29**
	que nous fuyions, -iez		fuyons, -ez	fuyant		
			pars			**30**
je partirais ...	que je parte ...	que je partisse ...	partons, -ez	partant	parti, -e	
			bous			**31**
je bouillirais ...	que je bouille ...	que je bouillisse ...	bouillons, -ez	bouillant	bouilli, -e	
	que je couvre, -es, -e, que nous couvrions ...	que je couvrisse ...	couvre couvrons, -ez	couvrant	couvert, -e	**32**
je couvrirais ...						
je vêtirais ...	que je vête ...	que je vêtisse ...	vêts vêtons, vêtez	vêtant	vêtu, -e	**33**
	que je meure ...		meurs		mort, -e	**34**
je mourrais ...		que je mourusse ...	mourons, -ez	mourant		
	que j'acquière, -es, -e, -ent		acquiers			**35**
j'acquerrais ...	que nous acquérions, -iez		acquérons, -ez	acquérant		
		que j'acquisse ...			acquis, -e	

French verbs

▸ 1372

Infinitive		Indicative			
	Rules	Present	Imperfect	Past Historic	Future
36 venir	i	je viens, -s, -t, -nent		je vins … ils vinrent	je viendrai …
	e	nous venons, -ez	je venais …		
37 gésir	*Defective*	je gis, tu gis, il gît, nous gisons, -ez, -ent	je gisais …		
38 ouïr	*Archaic*	j'ois … nous oyons …	j'oyais …	j'ouïs …	j'ouïrai …
39 pleuvoir		il pleut	il pleuvait	il plut	il pleuvra
		ils pleuvent	ils pleuvaient	ils plurent	ils pleuvront
40 pourvoir	i	je pourvois, -s, -t, -ent			je pourvoirai …
	y	nous pourvoyons, -ez	je pourvoyais …		
	u			je pourvus …	
41 asseoir	ie	j'assieds, -ds, -d			j'assiérai …
	ey	nous asseyons, -ez, -ent	j'asseyais …		
	i			j'assis …	
asseoir (oi/oy replace ie/ey)	oi	j'assois, -s, -t, -ent			j'assoirai …
	oy	nous assoyons, -ez	j'assoyais …		
42 prévoir	oi	je prévois, -s, -t, -ent			je prévoirai …
	oy	nous prévoyons, -ez	je prévoyais …		
	i/u			je prévis …	
43 mouvoir	eu	je meus, -s, -t, -vent			
	ou	nous mouvons, -ez	je mouvais …		je mouvrai …
	u			je mus, -s, -t, -(û)mes, -(û)tes, -rent	
44 devoir	û *in the past participle masc. sing.*	je dois, -s, -t -vent nous devons, -ez	je devais …	je dus …	je devrai …
45 valoir	au, aille	je vaux, -x, -t			je vaudrai …
	al	nous valons, -ez, -ent	je valais …	je valus …	
prévaloir					

Conditional	Subjunctive		Imperative	Participle		
Present	Present	Imperfect		Present	Past	
je viendrais ...	que je vienne, -es, -e, -ent	que je vinsse ...	viens			**36**
	que nous venions, -iez		venons, -ez	venant	venu, -e	
				gisant		**37**
j'ouïrais ...	que j'oie ...	que j'ouïsse ...	ois		ouï, -e	**38**
	que nous oyions ...		oyons, -ez	oyant		
il pleuvrait	qu'il pleuve	qu'il plût		pleuvant	plu	**39**
ils pleuvraient	qu'ils pleuvent	qu'ils plussent				
je pourvoirais ...	que je pourvoie, -es, -e, -ent		pourvois			**40**
	que nous pourvoyions, -iez		pourvoyons, -ez	pourvoyant		
		que je pourvusse ...			pourvu, -e	
j'assiérais ...			assieds			**41**
	que j' asseye ...		asseyons, -ez	asséyant		
	que nous asseyions ...					
		que j'assisse ...			assis, -e	
j'assoirais ...	que j'assoie, -es, -e, -ent		assois			
	que nous assoyions, -iez		assoyons, -ez	assoyant		
je prévoirais ...	que je prévoie, -es, -e, -ent		prévois			**42**
	que ns prévoyions, -iez		prévoyons, -ez	prévoyant		
		que je prévisse ...			prévu, -e	
	que je meuve, -es, -e, -ent		meus		mû, mue	**43**
je mouvrais ...	que nous mouvions, -iez		mouvons, -ez	mouvant		
		que je musse ...			mû, mue	
	que je doive, -es, -e, -ent	que je dusse ...	dois		dû, due	**44**
je devrais ...	que nous devions, -iez		devons, -ez	devant		
je vaudrais ...	que je vaille, -es, -e, -ent		vaux			**45**
	que nous valions, -iez	que je valusse ...	valons, -ez	valant	valu, -e	
	que je prévale, -es, -e					

Infinitive		Indicative			
	Rules	Present	Imperfect	Past Historic	Future
46 voir	oi	je vois, -s, -t, -ent			
	oy	nous voyons, -ez	je voyais …		
	i/e/u			je vis …	je verrai …
47 savoir	5 forms	je sais, -s, -t, nous savons, -ez, -ent	je savais …	je sus …	je saurai …
48 vouloir	veu/veuil	je veux, -x, -t, veulent			
	voul/voudr	nous voulons, -ez	je voulais …	je voulus …	je voudrai …
49 pouvoir	eu/u(i)	je peux, -x, -t, peuvent		je pus …	
	ouv/our	nous pouvons, -ez	je pouvais …		je pourrai …
50 falloir	*Impersonal*	il faut	il fallait	il fallut	il faudra
51 déchoir	choir *and* échoir *are defective*	je déchois, -s, -t, -ent nous déchoyons, -ez	je déchoyais …	je déchus …	je décherrai …
52 prendre	prend	je prends, -ds, -d			je prendrai …
	pren	nous prenons, -ez ils prennent	je prenais …		
	pri(s)			je pris …	
53 rompre		je romps, -ps, -pt, nous rompons …	je rompais …	je rompis …	je romprai …
54 craindre	ain/aind	je crains, -s, -t			je craindrai …
	aign	nous craignons, -ez, -ent	je craignais …	je craignis …	
55 peindre	ein	je peins, -s, -t			je peindrai …
	eign	nous peignons, -ez, -ent	je peignais …	je peignis …	
56 joindre	oin/oind	je joins, -s, -t			je joindrai …
	oign	nous joignons, -ez, -ent	je joignais …	je joignis …	
57 vaincre	ainc	je vaincs, -cs, -c			je vaincrai …
	ainqu	nous vainquons, -ez, -ent	je vainquais …	je vainquis …	
58 traire	i	je trais, -s, -t, -ent		*(obsolete)*	je trairai …
	y	nous trayons, -ez	je trayais …		

| Conditional | Subjunctive | | Imperative | Participle | | |
Present	Present	Imperfect		Present	Past	
	que je voie, -es, -e, -ent		vois			**46**
	que nous voyions, -iez		voyons, -ez	voyant		
je verrais …		que je visse …			vu, -e	
je saurais …	que je sache …	que je susse …	sache, -ons, -ez	sachant	su, -e	**47**
	que je veuille, -es, -e, -ent		veux (veuille)			**48**
je voudrais …	que nous voulions, -iez	que je voulusse …	voulons, -ez (veuillez)	voulant	voulu, -e	
	que je puisse …	que je pusse …	(*obsolete*)		pu	**49**
je pourrais …				pouvant		
il faudrait	qu'il faille	qu'il fallût	(*no form*)	(*obsolete*)	fallu	**50**
	que je déchoie, -es, -e, -ent		déchois	(*no form but* échéant)		**51**
je décherrais …	que nous déchoyions, -iez	que je déchusse …	déchoyons, -ez		déchu, -e	
je prendrais …			prends			**52**
	que je prenne …		prenons, -ez	prenant		
		que je prisse …			pris, -e	
je romprais …	que je rompe …	que je rompisse …	romps -pons, -pez	rompant	rompu, -e	**53**
je craindrais …			crains		craint, -e	**54**
	que je craigne …	que je craignisse …	craignons, -ez	craignant		
je peindrais …			peins		peint, -e	**55**
	que je peigne …	que je peignisse …	peignons, -ez	peignant		
je joindrais …			joins		joint, -e	**56**
	que je joigne …	que je joignisse …	joignons, -ez	joignant		
je vaincrais …			vaincs		vaincu, -e	**57**
	que je vainque …	que je vainquisse …	vainquons, -ez	vainquant		
je trairais …	que je traie, -es, -e, -ent	(*obsolete*)	trais		trait, -e	**58**
	que nous trayions, -yiez		trayons, -ez	trayant		

. . . .

Infinitive		Indicative			
	Rules	Present	Imperfect	Past Historic	Future
59 plaire	ai	je plais, tu plais, il plaît (*but* il tait) nous plaisons …	je plaisais …		je plairai …
	u			je plus …	
60 mettre	met	je mets, nous mettons	je mettais …		je mettrai …
	mis			je mis …	
61 battre	t	je bats, -ts, -t			
	tt	nous battons …	je battais …	je battis …	je battrai …
62 suivre	ui	je suis, -s, -t			
	uiv	nous suivons …	je suivais …	je suivis …	je suivrai …
63 vivre	vi/viv	je vis, -s, -t, nous vivons …	je vivais …		je vivrai …
	véc			je vécus …	
64 suffire		je suffis, -s, -t, nous suffisons …	je suffisais …	je suffis …	je suffirai …
65 médire		je médis, -s, -t, nous médisons, vous médisez (*but* vous dites, redites)	je médisais …	je médis …	je médirai …
66 lire	i	je lis, -s, -t			je lirai …
	is	nous lisons, -ez, -ent	je lisais …		
	u			je lus …	
67 écrire	i	j'écris, -s, -t			j'écrirai …
	iv	nous écrivons, -ez, -ent	j'écrivais …	j'écrivis …	
68 rire		je ris, -s, -t, nous rions …	je riais … nous riions, -iez	je ris … nous rîmes …	je rirai …
69 conduire		je conduis …	je conduisais …	je conduisis…	je conduirai ..
70 boire	oi	je bois, -s, -t, -vent			je boirai …
	u(v)	nous buvons, -ez	je buvais …	je bus …	
71 croire	oi	je crois, -s, -t, ils croient			je croirai …
	oy	nous croyons, -ez	je croyais …		
	u			je crus …	

French verbs

Conditional	Subjunctive			Imperative	Participle		
Present	**Present**	**Imperfect**			**Present**	**Past**	
je plairais …	que je plaise …			plais plaisons, -ez	plaisant		**59**
		que je plusse …				plu	
je mettrais …	que je mette …			mets mettons, -ez	mettant		**60**
		que je misse …				mis, -e	
				bats			**61**
je battrais …	que je batte …	que je battisse …		battons, -ez	battant	battu, -e	
				suis			**62**
je suivrais …	que je suive …	que je suivisse …		suivons, -ez	suivant	suivi, -e	
je vivrais …	que je vive …			vis vivons, -ez	vivant		**63**
		que je vécusse …				vécu, -e	
je suffirais …	que je suffise …	que je suffisse …		suffis suffisons, -ez	suffisant	suffi (*but* confit, déconfit, frit, circoncis)	**64**
je médirais …	que je médise … que nous médisions, -iez	que je médisse …		médis médisons médisez (*but* dites, redites)	médisant	médit	**65**
je lirais …				lis			**66**
	que je lise …			lisons, -ez	lisant		
		que je lusse …				lu, -e	
j'écrirais …				écris		écrit, -e	**67**
	que j'écrive …	que j'écrivisse …		écrivons, -ez	écrivant		
je rirais …	que je rie …	que je risse …		ris, rions, riez	riant	ri	**68**
	que nous riions, -iez	que nous rissions …					
je conduirais …	que je conduise …	que je conduisisse …		conduis conduisons, -ez	conduisant	conduit, -e (*but* lui, nui)	**69**
je boirais …	que je boive, -es, -e, -ent			bois			**70**
	que nous buvions, -iez	que je busse …		buvons, -ez	buvant	bu, -e	
je croirais …	que je croie …			crois			**71**
				croyons, -ez	croyant		
		que je crusse …				cru, -e	

Infinitive		Indicative			
	Rules	**Present**	**Imperfect**	**Past Historic**	**Future**
72 croître	oî	je croîs, -s, -t oiss -ez, -ent	nous croissons,	je croissais …	je croîtrai …
	û			je crûs …	
73 connaître		je connais, -s, -ssons, -ssez, -ssent	je connaissais …	je connus …	
	î *before* t	il connaît			je connaîtrai …
74 naître	î *before* t	je nais, nais, naît			je naîtrai …
	naisse	nous naissons, -ez, -ent	je naissais …		
	naqu			je naquis …	
75 résoudre	ou/oudr	je résous, -s, -t		(absoudre	je résoudrai…
	ol/olv	nous résolvons, -ez, -ent	je résolvais …	*and* dissoudre *have no past historic*)	
	olu			je résolus …	
76 coudre	oud	je couds, -ds, -d			je coudrai …
	ous	nous cousons, -ez, -ent	je cousais …	je cousis …	
77 moudre	moud	je mouds, -ds, -d			je moudrai …
	moul	nous moulons, -ez, -ent	je moulais …	je moulus …	
78 conclure		je conclus, -s, -t, nous concluons, -ez, -ent	je concluais …	je conclus …	je conclurai …
79 clore	*Defective*	je clos, -os, -ôt ils closent	(*obsolete*)	(*obsolete*)	je clorai …
80 maudire		je maudis, -s, -t nous maudissons, -ez, -ent	je maudissais …	je maudis …	je maudirai …

Conditional	Subjunctive		Imperative	Participle		
Present	Present	Imperfect		Present	Past	
je croîtrais...	que je croisse ...	que je crûsse ...	croîs / croissons, -ez	croissant	croissant crû, crue (*but* accru, -e)	**72**
je connaîtrais ...	que je connaisse ...	que je connusse ...	connais, -ssons, -ssez	connaissant	connu, -e	**73**
je naîtrais ...	que je naisse ...	que je naquisse ...	nais / naissons, -ez	naissant	né, -e	**74**
je résoudrais ...	que je résolve ...	que je résolusse ...	résous / résolvons, -ez	résolvant	(absous, -oute; dissous, -oute) résolu, -e	**75**
je coudrais ...	que je couse ...	que je cousisse ...	couds / cousons, -ez	cousant	cousu, -e	**76**
je moudrais ...	que je moule ...	que je moulusse ...	mouds / moulons, -ez	moulant	moulu, -e	**77**
je conclurais ...	que je conclue ...	que je conclusse ...	conclus / concluons, -ez	concluant	conclu, -e (*but* inclus, -e)	**78**
je clorais ...	que je close ...	(*obsolete*)	clos	closant	clos, -e	**79**
je maudirais ...	que je maudisse qu'il maudisse	que je maudisse qu'il maudît	maudis -ssons, -ssez	maudissant	maudit, -e	**80**

Also available from Oxford University Press

Oxford-Hachette French Dictionary

■ Over 900,000 words, phrases, and translations

978-0-19-860363-4

Pocket Oxford-Hachette French Dictionary

■ Over 200,000 words, phrases, and translations

978-0-19-861071-7

Oxford Business French Dictionary

■ 50,000 words and phrases

978-0-19-860483-9

Oxford Colour French Dictionary Plus

■ Over 100,000 words, phrases, and translations, with colour headwords throughout

978-0-19-860900-1
978-0-19-860898-1
(US edition)

Oxford French Minidictionary

■ Ultra compact– ideal for business and travel

978-0-19-861045-8

Oxford Take Off in French

■ Language-learning course with 5 hours of audio, a clear, user-friendly coursebook, and a free travel dictionary and phrasebook.

978-0-19-860907-0
(Book and 5 CDs)

Oxford Beginner's French Dictionary

■ A brand new easy-to-use French dictionary for first-time learners.

978-0-19-929858-7

OXFORD
UNIVERSITY PRESS

abbreviation	**abbr, abrév**	abréviation
adjective	**adj**	adjectif
demonstrative adjective	**adj dém**	adjectif démonstratif
exclamatory adjective	**adj excl**	adjectif exclamatif
indefinite adjective	**adj indéf**	adjectif indéfini
interrogative adjective	**adj inter**	adjectif interrogatif
adjectival phrase	**adj phr**	locution adjective
possessive adjective	**adj poss**	adjectif possessif
relative adjective	**adj rel**	adjectif relatif
administration	**Admin**	administration
adverb	**adv**	adverbe
adverbial phrase	**adv phr**	locution adverbiale
aerospace	**Aerosp**	astronautique
agriculture	**Agric**	agriculture
anatomy	**Anat**	anatomie
architecture	**Archit**	architecture
definite article	**art déf**	article défini
indefinite article	**art indéf**	article indéfini
aerospace	**Astronaut**	astronautique
Australian	**Austral**	anglais d'Australie
automobile	**Aut**	automobile
auxiliary	**aux**	auxiliaire
aviation	**Aviat**	aviation
Belgian French	**B**	belgicisme
biology	**Biol**	biologie
botany	**Bot**	botanique
Canadian French	**C**	canadianisme
chemistry	**Chem**	chimie
cinema	**Cin**	cinéma
commerce	**Comm**	commerce
computing	**Comput**	informatique
conjunction	**conj**	conjonction
conjunctional phrase	**conj phr**	locution conjonctive
construction	**Constr**	construction, bâtiment
controversial	**controv**	usage critiqué
culinary	**Culin**	culinaire
demonstrative	**dém**	démonstratif
determiner	**det, dét**	déterminant
demonstrative determiner	**dét dém**	déterminant démonstratif
indefinite determiner	**dét indéf**	déterminant indéfini
interrogative determiner	**dét inter**	déterminant interrogatif
dialect	**dial**	dialecte
ecology	**Ecol, Écol**	écologie
economy	**Econ, Écon**	économie
electricity	**Elec**	électrotechnique
electricity	**Électrotech**	électrotechnique
attributive	**épith**	épithète
euphemistic	**euph**	euphémique
exclamation	**excl**	exclamation
feminine	**f**	féminin
figurative	**fig**	figuré
finance	**Fin**	finance
formal	**fml**	soutenu
British English	**GB**	anglais britannique
generally	**gen, gén**	généralement
geography	**Geog, Géog**	géographie
Swiss French	**H**	helvétisme
history	**Hist**	histoire
humorous	**hum**	humoristique
industry	**Ind**	industrie
indicative	**indic**	indicatif
offensive	**injur**	injurieux
invariable	**inv**	invariable
ironic	**iron**	ironique
journalism	**Journ**	presse
law	**Jur**	droit
baby talk	**lang**	langage enfantin enfantin
linguistics	**Ling**	linguistique
literal	**lit**	littéral
literary	**liter, littér**	littéraire
literature	**Literat**	littérature
literature	**Littérat**	littérature
phrase	**loc**	locution
adjectival phrase	**loc adj**	locution adjective
adverbial phrase	**loc adv**	locution adverbiale
conjunctional phrase	**loc conj**	locution conjonctive
exclamatory phrase	**loc excl**	locution exclamative
noun phrase	**loc nom**	locution nominale
prepositional phrase	**loc prép**	locution prépositive
masculine	**m**	masculin
mathematics	**Math**	mathématique
medicine	**Med, Méd**	médecine
meteorology	**Meteorol**	météorologie
meteorology	**Météo**	météorologie
military	**Mil**	armée
music	**Mus**	musique
mythology	**Mythol**	mythologie
noun	**n**	nom
nautical	**Naut**	nautisme
negative	**nég**	négatif
feminine noun	**nf**	nom féminin
masculine noun	**nm**	nom masculin
masculine and feminine noun	**nm,f**	nom masculin et féminin
masculine and feminine noun	**nmf**	nom masculin et féminin
plural noun	**npl**	nom pluriel
proper noun	**npr**	nom propre
onomatopoeia	**onomat**	onomatopée